The National Hockey League

Official Guide & Record Book

2007

THE NATIONAL HOCKEY LEAGUE
Official Guide & Record Book/2007

TERMS & CONDITIONS FOR USING THIS BOOK

ATTENTION: PLEASE READ THIS DOCUMENT CAREFULLY BEFORE USING THIS BOOK (THE "BOOK") AND/OR THE DATA IT CONTAINS (THE "DATA"). INDIVIDUALS OR ENTITIES USING THE BOOK AND/OR THE DATA ("END USERS") AGREE TO BE BOUND BY THE TERMS OF THIS LICENSE. IF YOU DO NOT AGREE TO THE TERMS OF THIS LICENSE, DO NOT USE THE BOOK OR THE DATA AND PROMPTLY RETURN THE UNUSED BOOK AND PROOF OF PAYMENT TO THE FOLLOWING ADDRESS FOR A REFUND:

> Dan Diamond & Associates, Inc.
> 194 Dovercourt Road, Toronto, Ontario, Canada M6J 3C8
> dda.nhl@sympatico.ca.

Dan Diamond & Associates, Inc. (the "Publisher") owns, and retains ownership of, the Data. The Publisher reserves any right not expressly granted to End Users below.

1. License. End-Users are granted a limited, non-exclusive license to do only the following, subject to the restrictions set out in Section 2 below:
   (a) End-Users may use the Book and the Data for personal, non-commercial purposes.
   (b) End-Users may reproduce individual player records, tables and data panels in connection with bona fide private study and research.
   (c) End-Users who are journalists may reproduce individual player records, tables and data panels for use by the broadcast and print media.

2. Restrictions. End-Users may NOT reproduce the Book or the Data, in whole or in part, in any form or by any means, electronic or mechanical, including photocopying, recording, or by any information storage and retrieval system now known or hereafter invented, without written permission from the Publisher. End-Users may NOT sublicense, assign, or distribute (via the World Wide Web or otherwise) copies of the Book or the Data, in whole or in part, to others. END-USERS MAY NOT MODIFY, ADAPT, TRANSLATE, RENT, LEASE, LOAN, RESELL FOR PROFIT, DISTRIBUTE, OR OTHERWISE ASSIGN OR TRANSFER THE BOOK OR THE DATA, OR CREATE DERIVATIVE WORKS BASED UPON THE BOOK OR THE DATA OR ANY PART THEREOF, EXCEPT AS PROVIDED ABOVE.

3. Commercial Users. Commercial users (such as sports reference and sports gaming websites) may obtain a license to use customized Data upon payment of a reasonable fee. Please contact the Publisher at the address provided above.

4. Termination. This License is effective until terminated. This License will terminate immediately without notice from the Publisher if the End User fails to comply with any of its provisions. Upon termination End Users must destroy the Book, the Data and all copies thereof.

5. General. This License will be governed by and construed in accordance with the laws of the province of Ontario and the laws of Canada applicable therein, and shall inure to the benefit of the Publisher and End-Users and their successors, assigns and legal representatives. If any provision of this License is held by a court of competent jurisdiction to be invalid or unenforceable to any extent under applicable law, that provision will be enforced to the maximum extent permissible and the remaining provisions of this License will remain in full force and effect. Any notices or other communications to be sent to the Publisher must be mailed first class, postage prepaid, to the address provided above. This Agreement constitutes the entire agreement between the parties with respect to the subject matter hereof, and all prior proposals, agreements, representations, statements and undertakings are hereby expressly cancelled and superseded. This Agreement may not be changed or amended except by a written instrument executed by a duly authorized officer of the Publisher.

6. Acknowledgment. BY USING THE BOOK OR THE DATA, THE END-USER ACKNOWLEDGES THAT IT HAS READ THIS LICENSE, UNDERSTANDS IT, AND AGREES TO BE BOUND BY ITS TERMS AND CONDITIONS. Should you have any questions concerning this License, contact the Publisher at the address provided above.

Copyright © 2006 by the National Hockey League.
Compiled by the NHL Public Relations Department and the 30 NHL Club Public Relations Directors.
Printed in Canada. All rights reserved under the Pan-American and International Copyright Conventions.
Published in Canada by: Dan Diamond and Associates, Inc., 194 Dovercourt Road, Toronto, Ontario M6J 3C8 Canada
ISBN in Canada 1-894801-02-4; ISBN-13 in Canada 978-1-894801-02-7
Published in the United States by: Triumph Books, 542 South Dearborn Street, Chicago, Illinois 60605
ISBN in USA 1-57243-917-3; ISBN-13 in USA 978-1-57243-917-7

Staff

For the NHL: Dave McCarthy; Supervising Editor: Greg Inglis; Statistician: Benny Ercolani;
Editorial Staff: John Halligan, David Keon, Dave Baker, Jackie Rinaldi, Kelley Rosset, Julie Young.

Senior Managing Editor: Ralph Dinger
International Editor: Igor Kuperman
Publisher: Dan Diamond

Associate Managing Editor: Paul Bontje
Production Editors: John Pasternak, Alex Dubiel

Photo Editor: Eric Zweig
Assistant Editor: Rachel Carr

Data Management and Typesetting: Caledon Data Management, Orangeville, Ontario
Film Output and Scanning: Embassy Graphics, Toronto, Ontario
Printing: Sunrise Consulting Inc., Port Perry, Ontario; Webcom, Toronto, Ontario
Production Management: Dan Diamond and Associates, Inc., Toronto, Ontario
Contributors and Photo Credits: see page 653

Distribution

Trade sales and distribution in Canada by:
North 49 Books, 35 Prince Andrew Drive, Toronto, Ontario M3C 2H2   416/449-4000; Fax 416/449-9924
Dan Diamond and Associates, Inc., Toronto   416/531-6535; Fax 416/531-3939   dda.nhl@sympatico.ca   www.nhlofficialguide.com
Trade sales and distribution in the United States by:
Triumph Books, 542 South Dearborn Street, Chicago, Illinois 60605   312/939-3330; Fax 312/663-3557
International representatives:
Barkers Worldwide Publications, Unit 6/7 The Elms Centre, Glaziers Lane, Normandy, Guildford, Surrey GU3 2DF England
Tel 011/441/483/811-971; Fax 011/441/483/811-972   sales@bwpu.demon.co.uk   www.bwpu.demon.co.uk

Licensed by the National Hockey League.®

NHL and the NHL Shield are registered trademarks of the National Hockey League.
All NHL logos and marks and team logos and marks depicted herein are the property of the NHL and the respective teams and may not be reproduced without the prior written consent of Enterprises, L.P. © NHL 2006. All Rights Reserved.

The National Hockey League
1251 Avenue of the Americas, 47th Floor, New York, New York 10020-1198
1800 McGill College Ave., Suite 2600, Montreal, Quebec H3A 3J6
50 Bay Street, 11th Floor, Toronto, Ontario M5J 2X8

Table of Contents

Table of Contents *continued*

WELCOME TO THE **75**TH EDITION OF *THE* N*ATIONAL* H*OCKEY* L*EAGUE* O*FFICIAL* G*UIDE* & R*ECORD* B*OOK*. The 2006-07 season also is the NHL's 90th, so the *Guide* and the League again celebrate a double anniversary. Originally published as a vest-pocket sized 140-pager in 1932, the *NHL Guide* has seen it all, from the "temporary" addition of the center ice red line in 1942-43 to its "removal" (in most playing situations) in 2005-06. The Guide has seen hockey's greatest players arrive and leave their mark on the game, from Howie Morenz to Rocket Richard, Gordie Howe, Bobby Orr, Wayne Gretzky, Mario Lemieux and now, in 2005-06, Alex Ovechkin and Sidney Crosby. All of these great players, and approximately 5,800 others, can be found in this 75th edition, either in the regular-season or playoff Record Books (pages 164 and 240), Hall of Fame section (233), All-Star Teams (226), Award Winners (210), Active Player Register (347) or Retired Players Index (612). A special tribute to Steve Yzerman, the talented captain of the Detroit Red Wings, is found on page 585.

The 2005-06 season was the National Hockey League's first played under modified rules. The intent of this rules package was to emphasize entertainment, skill and competition on the ice, and by both objective and subjective measure, this goal was met. Scoring increased and, perhaps more importantly, exciting play did as well. The statistics in the *NHL Guide* bear this out: in 2005-06, five players scored 50-or-more goals and seven recorded 100-point seasons. In 2003-04, no player in the NHL reached either milestone. (An all-time list of 50-goal and 100-point seasons begins on page 196. Detailed statistics for 2005-06 begin on page 135.)

Of the 1,230 games played in the NHL this past season, not one ended in a tie as the League added a shootout that would take place if sixty minutes of regulation time and five minutes of sudden-death overtime failed to determine a winner. The shootout proved to be immensely popular and created some unlikely heroes. Jussi Jokinen of the Dallas Stars scored on his first nine shootout attempts and finished the season with a league-leading 10 shootout goals on 13 attempts. Marek Malik of the New York Rangers ended the longest shootout game of the season by scoring on a between-the-legs trick shot after 29 previous shooters had failed to determine a winner. Complete team and individual shootout statistics are found on page 143. Thanks to MSG Photo for the excellent image of Malik's goal.

Eliminating tie games has created some challenges in presenting team and individual statistics. On the first page of each club's section (e.g. Anaheim Ducks, page 15), the club's previous season's results are listed with separate numbers for overtime losses (OTL) and shootout losses (SOL). In the year-by-year club results on that same page, overtime and shootout losses are combined into one "OL" column that includes all games in which the club earned one point. Because an NHL game can no longer end in with a tie score, the Ties column is left blank ("....") beginning with 2005-06.

Because space is at a premium in the Goaltenders Register (beginning on page 587), the tie game column has been renamed "O/T". Recorded in this column are combined overtime losses and shootout losses beginning with the 2005-06 season. In previous seasons, this column lists tie games. This combined O/T column serves a similar function in coach's data panels that appear in each club's section and in the All-Time Regular-Season NHL Coaching Register that begins on page 188.

In addition to Ovechkin and Crosby, hockey fans enjoyed watching other talented rookies in 2005-06. Because no games were played in 2004-05, this past season brought a double cohort of young talent to the NHL. Colorado's Marek Svatos and Petr Prucha of the Rangers reached the 30-goal plateau. Jeff Carter of Philadelphia and Calgary's Dion Phaneuf each scored seven game-winning goals while Andrej Meszaros of the Ottawa Senators finished the season with a plus/minus rating of +34. In goal, Henrik Lundqvist of the Rangers finished fifth overall in the NHL with a goals-against average of 2.29. In the playoffs, rookie Carolina goaltender Cam Ward won 15 games for the Cup-champion Hurricanes, finished with a goals-against average of 2.14 and was awarded the Conn Smythe Trophy as playoff MVP. Rookie leaders are found on page 137. Goaltending leaders are on page 139. Playoff goaltending leaders are on page 238.

In addition to NHL rookies, the Guide & Record Book contains a comprehensive Prospect Register made up of data panels for more than 1,000 players who have yet to appear in an NHL game. These players are draft choices or free agent signings. Approximately 120 of them will make their NHL debut in 2006-07. Included in this register are data panels for the 213 players selected in the 2006 NHL Entry Draft. Every one from first overall selection Erik Johnson to the last player selected in the seventh round is included. Each newly drafted player's data panel contains several years of statistics, including, in many cases, high school, U.S. or Canadian provincial junior clubs and/or youth hockey. The Prospect Register begins on page 273. The NHL Entry Draft begins on page 212, providing full coverage of the most recent Draft, the first two rounds from 2003 to 2005 and the first round plus notable selections for every Entry and Amateur Draft from 1969 to 2002.

NHL players participated in the Winter Olympics for the third time in 2006, representing their countries in Torino, Italy. Sweden defeated Finland in a gold-medal game that featured five NHL team captains, the NHL's all-time top goal-scoring rookie, a former Art Ross Trophy winner and players who would go on to win the Masterton and Norris trophies at the NHL Awards ceremony in Vancouver in June of 2006. The Olympic Review is on page 13. NHL Awards coverage begins on page 204.

A key to the abbreviations and symbols used in individual player and goaltender data panels, along with useful information on how to use the Registers, is found on page 272. A list of abbreviations used for league names is found on page 346. Late additions are found on page 611 and each NHL club's minor-pro affiliates are found on page 14. Referees and linesmen are listed on page 8.

As always, our thanks to readers, correspondents and members of the media who take the time to comment on the *Guide & Record Book*. Thanks as well to the people working in the communications departments of the NHL's member clubs and to their counterparts in minor pro, junior, college and European hockey. Your help has been appreciated for 75 years.

Best wishes for an enjoyable 2006-07 season.

A*CCURACY* REMAINS THE *GUIDE* & R*ECORD* B*OOK*'S TOP PRIORITY.

We appreciate comments and clarification from our readers. Please direct these to:

- Ralph Dinger   Senior Managing Editor, 194 Dovercourt Road, Toronto, Ontario M6J 3C8. e-mail: ralph.dda@sympatico.ca.
- Greg Inglis   47th floor, 1251 Avenue of the Americas, New York, New York 10020-1198 . . . or . . .
- David Keon   50 Bay Street, 11ᵗʰ Floor, Toronto, Ontario, M5J 2X8

Your involvement makes a better book.

NATIONAL HOCKEY LEAGUE

New York, 1251 Avenue of the Americas, 47th Floor, New York, NY 10020-1198, 212/789-2000, Fax: 212/789-2020, PR Fax: 212/789-2080
Montréal, 1800 McGill College Avenue, Suite 2600, Montréal, Québec, H3A 3J6, 514/841-9220, Fax: 514/841-1070
Toronto, 50 Bay Street, 11th Floor, Toronto, Ontario, M5J 2X8, 416/981-2777, Fax: 416/981-2779
NHL Enterprises, L.P. — 1251 Avenue of the Americas, 47th Floor, New York, NY 10020-1198, 212/789-2000, Fax: 212/789-2020
NHL Enterprises Canada, L.P. — 50 Bay Street, 11th Floor, Toronto, Ontario, M5J 2X8, 416/981-2777, Fax: 416/981-2779
NHL Productions/NHL Images — 240 Pegasus Avenue, Northvale, NJ 07647, 201/750-5800, Fax: 201/750-5850

Executive

Commissioner....Gary B. Bettman
Deputy Commissioner....William Daly
Senior Executive Vice President & Director of Hockey Operations....Colin Campbell
Senior Executive Vice President & Chief Financial Officer....Craig Harnett
V.P., Administration, Human Resources & Executive Assistant to the Commissioner....Debbie Jordan

Administration

Vice President, Administration & Human Resources....Debbie Jordan
Director, Offices & Facilities....Andrew Crawford
Director, Human Resources....Patrice Distler
Manager, Employee Benefits....Josie Russell

Communications

Executive Vice President, Communications and Brand Strategy....Karen Durkin
Senior Vice President, Communications....Bernadette Mansur
Group Vice President, Media Relations....Frank Brown
Group Vice President, Public Relations & Media Services (Toronto)....Gary Meagher
Vice President, Public Relations....Jamey Horan
Statistician and Information Officer (Toronto)....Benny Ercolani
Senior Director, Community and Diversity Programming....Ken Martin
Director, News Services....Greg Inglis
Director, Youth Development, NHL Diversity....Willie O'Ree
Senior Manager, Corporate Communications....Nirva Milord
Senior Manager, Public Relations (Toronto)....Julie Young
Manager, Public Relations (Toronto)....David Keon
Manager, Community Relations....Ann Marie Lynch

Events and Entertainment

Senior Vice President....Ken Yaffe
Vice President....Bill Miller
Director....Dean Matsuzaki

Finance

Senior Executive Vice President & Chief Financial Officer....Craig Harnett
Executive Vice President, Finance....Joseph DeSousa
Senior Director of Financial Reporting....Robert Dixon
Director, Finance....Marie-Josee Ashby

Hockey Operations

Senior Executive Vice President of Hockey Operations....Colin Campbell
Senior Vice President, Hockey Operations (Toronto)....Jim Gregory
Senior Vice President & Director of Officiating (Toronto)....Stephen Walkom
Senior Vice President, Hockey Operations (Toronto)....Mike Murphy
Director, Hockey Operations (Toronto)....Kris King
Vice President & Managing Director, Central Registry (Toronto)....Sean MacLeod
Director of Systems, Central Registry (Montreal)....Madeleine Supino
Director, Central Scouting (Toronto)....E.J. McGuire
Director of Alumni Relations (Toronto)....Patrick Flatley
Managers, Officiating (Toronto)....Dave Baker, Randy Hall
Manager, Central Scouting....Brandon Pridham
Consultant (Toronto)....Frank Bonello
Consultant, Goaltender Equipment....Kay Whitmore
Facilities Operations Manager....Dan Craig
Video Director....Damian Echevarrieta
Video Coordinator (Toronto)....Paul Brighty
Video Technologies Consultant....Jed Dole

Information Technology

Senior Vice President, Information Technology....Peter DelGiacco
Assistant Director (Montreal)....Luc Coulombe
Director, Network Services....Patrick Powers
Sr. Manager, Technical Support....Dan O'Neill
Manager, Statistical Information Systems....Neil Pierson

Legal

Executive Vice President, General Counsel....David Zimmerman
Sr. Vice President, Deputy General Counsel....Julie Grand
Associate Counsel....Daniel Ages

Pension

Vice President and Managing Director, Pension (Montreal)....Yvon Chamberland
Sr. Director, Pension (Montreal)....Mary Skiadopoulos
Manager, Pension (Montreal)....Lise de Jocas

Security

Senior Vice President, Security....Dennis Cunningham
Senior Director, Security....Joseph Caporicci
Manager, Security....Al Young

NHL Media

Executive Vice President, Media....Doug Perlman
Group Vice President, Center Ice & NHL Network....Jody Shapiro
Vice President, NHL Media....John Tortora
Manager, Center Ice Operations....Jennifer Wisniewski

NHL Media – Legal
Group Vice President & General Counsel....Robert Hawkins

NHL Interactive CyberEnterprises (NHL ICE)
President, NHL ICE & Senior Vice President, New Business Development....Keith Ritter
Vice President, Editorial & Production....Richard Libero
Senior Director, Web Operations....Grant Nodine
Director, New Media Business Development....Troy Ewanchyna

NHL Productions

Group Vice President, Video Production and Programming....Ken Rosen
Group Vice President, Media Operations/Planning....Patti Fallick
Senior Producer....Darryl Lepik
Senior Director, Operations/Footage....Peg Walsh
Manager, Video Services....Chris Cesa

NHL Images

Group Vice President....Patti Fallick
Manager....Jessica Tomao

Broadcasting

Senior Vice President, Broadcasting....John Shannon
Vice President, Broadcasting & Programming....Adam Acone
Director, Broadcast Operations....Jim Wilkes
Director, NHL Radio....Gregg Baldinger
Senior Manager....Phyllis DeCongilio

Scheduling

Group Vice President, Scheduling, Operations & Research (Montreal)....Steve Hatze Petros
Director, Research & Scheduling....Mark Erlichson

NHL Enterprises

President, NHL Enterprises....Ed Horne

Consumer Products Marketing

Group Vice President, Consumer Products Marketing....Brian Jennings
Vice President, Consumer Products Marketing....James Haskins
Senior Director, Retail Sales & Marketing, Canada (Toronto)....Barry Monaghan
Senior Director, Entertainment Products....Dave McCarthy
Senior Manager, Center Ice & Sporting Goods....Richard Villani
Senior Manager, Consumer Products Marketing, Canada (Toronto)....Angie Andreou
Manager, Retail Sales & Marketing....Dan Near
Manager, Entertainment Products....Bobbi Wilson

Corporate Marketing

Managing Director, Corporate Marketing (Toronto)....Doug Brooks
Senior Director, Canada (Toronto)....Laurie Kepron
Senior Director....David Lehanski
Senior Manager, Canada (Toronto)....Kyle McMann

Creative Services

Creative Director, Creative Services....Kathy Drew

Marketing / Fan Development

Vice President, Fan Development....Alysse Soll
Senior Manager....Suzanne Sherman

Finance

Group Vice President, Finance – NHL Enterprises....Mary McCarthy
Senior Director, Finance....Frank Dowling
Director, Finance....Mona Doshi

International

Senior Vice President, NHL International....Ken Yaffe
Sr. Director, International Licensing & Special Projects....Lynn White

NHLE Legal and Business Affairs

Executive Vice President & General Counsel....Richard Zahnd
Vice President, Legal & Business Affairs....Matthew Kline
Vice President, Legal & Business Affairs....Tom Prochnow
Associate Counsel....Michael Gold
Staff Attorney....Benjamin Faulkner
Senior Manager, Intellectual Property....Alison Nunez
Manager, Contracts Administration....Sara Cox
Manager, Contracts Administration....Linda Tomm

Quality Control

Vice President, Licensing and Trademark Compliance....Ruth Gruhin
Manager, Quality Control....Erin Versaggi

Club Services

Group Vice President, Club Services....Susan Cohig
Senior Manager, Club Services....Nicole Allison

BOARD OF GOVERNORS

Chairman of the Board – Harley N. Hotchkiss

Anaheim Ducks

Henry Samueli ....Governor
Michael Schulman ....Alternate Governor
Brian Burke ....Alternate Governor
Tim Ryan ....Alternate Governor
Susan Samueli ....Alternate Governor

Atlanta Thrashers

Bruce Levenson ....Governor
Don Waddell ....Alternate Governor
Bernie Mullin ....Alternate Governor
J. Rutherford Seydel, II ....Alternate Governor

Boston Bruins

Jeremy M. Jacobs ....Governor
Louis Jacobs ....Alternate Governor
Jeremy Jacobs, Jr. ....Alternate Governor
Charles Jacobs ....Alternate Governor
Harry J. Sinden ....Alternate Governor

Buffalo Sabres

B. Thomas Golisano ....Governor
Lawrence Quinn ....Alternate Governor
Daniel J. DiPofi ....Alternate Governor
Darcy Regier ....Alternate Governor

Calgary Flames

Harley N. Hotchkiss...................................Governor
N. Murray Edwards ....Alternate Governor
Alvin Libin ....Alternate Governor
Ken King ....Alternate Governor
Darryl Sutter ....Alternate Governor

Carolina Hurricanes

Peter Karmanos, Jr. ....Governor
Jason Karmanos ....Alternate Governor
Jim Rutherford ....Alternate Governor
Michael Amendola ....Alternate Governor

Chicago Blackhawks

William W. Wirtz ....Governor
Robert J. Pulford ....Alternate Governor
Peter R. Wirtz...............................Alternate Governor
John A. Ziegler, Jr. ....Alternate Governor

Colorado Avalanche

Stan Kroenke ....Governor
Pierre Lacroix ....Alternate Governor
Paul Andrews ....Alternate Governor
Francois Giguere ....Alternate Governor

Columbus Blue Jackets

John H. McConnell....................................Governor
Doug MacLean ....Alternate Governor
John P. McConnell..........................Alternate Governor
Mike Priest ....Alternate Governor

Dallas Stars

Tom Hicks..Governor
Doug Armstrong ....Alternate Governor
Jim Lites.......................................Alternate Governor

Detroit Red Wings

Michael Ilitch ....Governor
Jim Devellano ....Alternate Governor
Ken Holland ....Alternate Governor
Christopher Ilitch..........................Alternate Governor

Edmonton Oilers

Cal Nichols ....Governor
William K. Butler ....Alternate Governor
Patrick LaForge.............................Alternate Governor
Kevin Lowe ....Alternate Governor

Florida Panthers

Alan Cohen ....Governor
Jordan Zimmerman ....Alternate Governor
Steven Cohen ....Alternate Governor
William A. Torrey...........................Alternate Governor
Richard Lehman ....Alternate Governor
Mike Keenan ....Alternate Governor
Michael Yormark ....Alternate Governor

Los Angeles Kings

Timothy J. Leiweke ....Governor
Philip F. Anschutz ....Alternate Governor
Christian Anschutz ....Alternate Governor
Shawn Hunter ....Alternate Governor

Minnesota Wild

Robert O. Naegele, Jr. ....Governor
Doug Risebrough ....Alternate Governor
Jac Sperling..................................Alternate Governor

Montréal Canadiens

George Gillett, Jr. ....Governor
Pierre Boivin ....Alternate Governor
Jeff Joyce ....Alternate Governor
Fred Steer ....Alternate Governor
Foster Gillett.................................Alternate Governor
Bob Gainey ....Alternate Governor

Nashville Predators

Craig Leipold ....Governor
Steve Violetta ....Alternate Governor
Ed Lang..Alternate Governor
David Poile ....Alternate Governor

New Jersey Devils

Lou Lamoriello..Governor
Jeff Vanderbeek ....Alternate Governor
Michael Gilfillan ....Alternate Governor

New York Islanders

Charles Wang ....Governor
Garth Snow ....Alternate Governor
Roy Reichbach...............................Alternate Governor
Arthur J. McCarthy........................Alternate Governor
Ted Nolan ....Alternate Governor
Mike Milbury..................................Alternate Governor
Michael J. Picker...........................Alternate Governor

New York Rangers

James L. Dolan ....Governor
Steve Mills ....Alternate Governor
Glen Sather...................................Alternate Governor
Hank Ratner..................................Alternate Governor

Ottawa Senators

Eugene Melnyk..Governor
Roy Mlakar....................................Alternate Governor
Sheldon Plener ....Alternate Governor

Philadelphia Flyers

Edward M. Snider....................................Governor
Bob Clarke ....Alternate Governor
Philip I. Weinberg ....Alternate Governor
Peter Luukko ....Alternate Governor

Phoenix Coyotes

Steve Ellman..Governor
Wayne Gretzky...............................Alternate Governor
Mike Barnett ....Alternate Governor
Doug Moss ....Alternate Governor

Pittsburgh Penguins

Ken Sawyer ....Governor
Ronald Burkle................................Alternate Governor
Anthony Liberati ....Alternate Governor

St. Louis Blues

Dave Checketts ....Governor
Kenneth Munoz..............................Alternate Governor
John Davidson................................Alternate Governor
Larry Pleau ....Alternate Governor

San Jose Sharks

Greg Jamison...Governor
Kevin Compton...............................Alternate Governor
Doug Wilson ....Alternate Governor

Tampa Bay Lightning

Thomas S. Wilson....................................Governor
Ronald J. Campbell ....Alternate Governor
Jay H. Feaster...............................Alternate Governor

Toronto Maple Leafs

Larry Tanenbaum ....Governor
Richard A. Peddie...........................Alternate Governor
Dale Lastman ....Alternate Governor
Dean Metcalf ....Alternate Governor
John Ferguson................................Alternate Governor

Vancouver Canucks

John E. McCaw, Jr. ....Governor
Francesco Aquilini ....Alternate Governor
David M. Nonis ....Alternate Governor
Melvin E. Wheaton.........................Alternate Governor

Washington Capitals

Richard M. Patrick ....Governor
Ted Leonsis...................................Alternate Governor
George McPhee ....Alternate Governor

Commissioner and League Presidents

Gary B. Bettman

Gary B. Bettman took office as the NHL's first Commissioner on February 1, 1993. Since the League was formed in 1917, there have been five League Presidents.

NHL President	Years in Office
Frank Calder	1917-1943
Mervyn "Red" Dutton	1943-1946
Clarence Campbell	1946-1977
John A. Ziegler, Jr.	1977-1992
Gil Stein	1992-1993

Hockey Hall of Fame

BCE Place
30 Yonge Street
Toronto, Ontario M5E 1X8
Phone: 416/360-7735
Executive Fax: 416/360-1501
Resource Centre Fax: 416/360-1316
www.hhof.com

William C. Hay – Chairman and Chief Executive Officer
Jeff Denomme – President, C.O.O. and Treasurer
Craig Baines – Vice President, Operations
Ron Ellis – Director, Public Affairs
and Assistant to the President
Peter Jagla – Vice President, Marketing
Phil Pritchard – Vice President, Resource Centre
and Curator
Steve Ozimec – Manager, Special Events
and Hospitality
Craig Campbell – Manager, Photography, Archives
and Sales
Kelly Massé – Manager, Corporate Development
and Media Relations
Matt Manor and Dave Sanford – Photographers

National Hockey League Players' Association

20 Bay Street, Suite 1700
Toronto, Ontario M5J 2R8
Phone: 416/313-2300
Fax: 416/313-2301
www.nhlpa.com

Ted Saskin – Executive Director and General Counsel
Kenneth Kim – Director, Marketing
Ian Penny – Associate Counsel, Labour
Roland Lee – Associate Counsel, Labour
Stu Grimson – Associate Counsel, Labour
Adam Larry – Associate Counsel, Licensing
Mike Gartner – Director, Hockey Affairs
Vincent Damphousse – Director, Business Relations
Kim Murdoch – Manager, Pensions and Benefits
Devin Smith – Director, Club Marketing
and Community Relations
Jonathan Weatherdon – Director, Communications

NHL On-Ice Officials

Total NHL Games and 2005-06 Games columns count regular-season games only.

Referees

#	Name	Birthplace	Birthdate	First NHL Game	Total NHL Games	2005-06 Games
15	Stephane Auger	Montreal, Que.	12/9/70	4/1/00	310	70
41	Chris Ciamaga	Cheektowaga, NY	9/13/77	…	…	…
10	Paul Devorski	Guelph, Ont.	8/18/58	10/14/89	966	71
39	Gord Dwyer	Halifax, N.S.	5/18/77	11/19/05	21	21
2	Kerry Fraser	Sarnia, Ont.	5/30/52	4/6/75	1623	72
27	Eric Furlatt	Cap de la Madelaine, Que.	12/2/71	10/8/01	239	72
30	Mike Hasenfratz	Regina, Sask.	7/19/66	10/21/00	321	72
8	Dave Jackson	Montreal, Que.	11/28/64	12/23/90	826	72
25	Marc Joannette	Verdun, Que.	11/3/68	10/27/99	361	72
18	Greg Kimmerly	Toronto, Ont.	12/8/64	11/30/96	448	72
12	Don Koharski	Halifax, N.S.	12/2/55	10/14/77	[1]1506	72
32	Tom Kowal	Vernon, B.C.	11/2/67	10/29/99	247	72
40	Steve Kozari	Penticton, B.C.	6/20/73	10/15/05	21	21
14	Dennis LaRue	Savannah, GA	7/14/59	3/26/91	647	71
48	Frederick L'Ecuyer	Trois-Rivieres, Que.	7/28/77	…	…	…
28	Chris Lee	Saint John, N.B.	7/7/70	4/2/00	219	72
3	Mike Leggo	North Bay, Ont.	10/7/64	3/3/98	440	72
6	Dan Marouelli	Edmonton, Alta.	7/16/55	11/2/84	1337	71
26	Rob Martell	Winnipeg, Man.	10/21/63	3/14/84	[2]361	72
4	Wes McCauley	Georgetown, Ont.	1/11/72	1/20/03	94	71
7	Bill McCreary	Guelph, Ont.	11/17/55	11/3/84	1377	72
19	Mick McGeough	Regina, Sask.	6/20/57	1/19/89	949	72
34	Brad Meier	Dayton, OH	4/11/67	10/23/99	363	72
36	Dean Morton	Peterborough, Ont.	2/27/68	11/11/00	38	7
13	Dan O'Halloran	Essex, Ont.	3/25/64	10/14/95	518	71
42	Dan O'Rourke	Calgary, Alta.	8/31/72	10/2/99	[3]97	72
20	Tim Peel	Toronto, Ont.	4/27/66	10/21/99	371	72
43	Brian Pochmara	Detroit, MI	11/27/76	12/23/05	11	11
33	Kevin Pollock	Kincardine, Ont.	2/7/70	3/28/00	367	71
5	Chris Rooney	Boston, MA	5/26/74	11/22/00	264	72
38	Francois St. Laurent	Greenfield Park, Que.	6/26/77	11/10/05	12	12
45	Justin St. Pierre	Dolbeau, Que.	2/17/72	11/9/05	26	26
16	Rob Shick	Port Alberni, B.C.	12/4/57	4/6/86	1144	70
22	Craig Spada	Welland, Ont.	9/7/71	3/28/02	162	72
11	Kelly Sutherland	Victoria, B.C.	4/18/71	12/19/00	304	72
21	Don Van Massenhoven	Parkhill, Ont.	7/17/60	11/11/93	752	60
29	Ian Walsh	Philadelphia, PA	5/9/72	10/14/00	206	72
35	Dean Warren	Toronto, Ont.	7/22/63	10/8/99	365	72
23	Brad Watson	Regina, Sask.	10/4/61	2/5/94	468	72

[1] plus 163 games as a linesman. [2] plus 1 game as a linesman. [3] plus 120 games as a linesman.

Linesmen

#	Name	Birthplace	Birthdate	First NHL Game	Total NHL Games	2005-06 Games
75	Derek Amell	Port Colborne, Ont.	9/16/68	10/13/97	506	73
59	Steve Barton	Ottawa, Ont.	12/27/71	11/1/00	283	73
96	David Brisebois	Sudbury, Ont.	4/14/76	10/11/99	239	74
74	Lonnie Cameron	Victoria, B.C.	7/15/64	10/5/96	624	74
67	Pierre Champoux	Ville St-Pierre, Que.	4/18/63	10/8/88	1078	73
76	Michel Cormier	Trois-Rivieres, Que.	5/28/74	10/10/03	144	73
88	Mike Cvik	Calgary, Alta.	7/6/62	10/8/87	1206	72
60	Pat Dapuzzo	Hoboken, NJ	12/29/58	12/5/84	1442	74
54	Greg Devorski	Guelph, Ont.	8/3/69	10/9/93	785	71
68	Scott Driscoll	Seaforth, Ont.	5/2/68	10/10/92	856	74
66	Darren Gibbs	Edmonton, Alta.	9/30/66	10/1/97	475	74
82	Ryan Galloway	Winnipeg, Man.	7/12/72	10/17/02	171	73
91	Don Henderson	Calgary, Alta.	9/23/68	3/10/95	610	73
55	Shane Heyer	Summerland, B.C.	2/7/64	10/5/88	[4]785	72
71	Brad Kovachik	Woodstock, Ont.	3/7/71	10/10/96	595	74
86	Brad Lazarowich	Vancouver, B.C.	8/4/62	10/9/86	1302	74
78	Brian Mach	Little Falls, MN	4/15/74	10/7/00	[5]348	74
90	Andy McElman	Chicago Heights, IL	8/4/61	10/7/93	791	74
89	Steve Miller	Stratford, Ont.	6/22/72	10/11/00	335	71
97	Jean Morin	Sorel, Que.	8/10/63	10/5/91	900	73
93	Brian Murphy	Dover, NH	12/13/64	10/7/88	[5]1000	72
95	Jonny Murray	Beauport, Que.	8/10/74	10/7/00	350	73
70	Derek Nansen	Ottawa, Ont.	12/6/71	10/11/02	209	73
80	Thor Nelson	Westminister, CA	1/6/68	2/16/95	509	70
77	Tim Nowak	Buffalo, NY	9/6/67	10/8/93	98	70
79	Mark Paré	Windsor, Ont.	7/26/57	10/11/79	1886	72
65	Pierre Racicot	Verdun, Que.	2/15/67	10/12/93	820	73
73	Vaughan Rody	Winnipeg, Man.	12/13/68	10/8/00	339	72
52	Dan Schachte	Madison, WI	7/13/58	10/6/82	1610	72
61	Lyle Seitz	Brooks, Alta.	1/22/69	10/6/92	[6]455	59
84	Anthony Sericolo	Troy, NY	7/17/68	10/21/98	443	73
57	Jay Sharrers	Jamaica, West Indies	7/3/67	10/6/90	[7]715	73
92	Mark Shewchuk	Hamilton, Ont.	6/1/75	10/9/03	142	71
56	Mark Wheler	North Battleford, Sask.	9/20/65	10/10/92	887	73

[4] plus 386 games as a referee. [5] plus 88 games as a referee. [6] plus 10 games as a referee. [7] plus 136 games as a referee.

NHL History

1917 — National Hockey League organized November 26 in Montreal following suspension of operations by the National Hockey Association of Canada Limited (NHA). Montreal Canadiens, Montreal Wanderers, Ottawa Senators and Quebec Bulldogs attended founding meeting. Delegates decided to use NHA rules.

Toronto Arenas were later admitted as fifth team; Quebec decided not to operate during the first season. Quebec players allocated to remaining four teams.

Frank Calder elected president and secretary-treasurer.

First NHL games played December 19, with Toronto only arena with artificial ice. Clubs played 22-game split schedule.

1918 — Emergency meeting held January 3 due to destruction by fire of Montreal Arena which was home ice for both Canadiens and Wanderers.

Wanderers withdrew, reducing the NHL to three teams; Canadiens played remaining home games at 3,250-seat Jubilee rink.

Quebec franchise sold to P.J. Quinn of Toronto on October 18 on the condition that the team operate in Quebec City for 1918-19 season. Quinn did not attend the November League meeting and Quebec did not play in 1918-19.

1919-20 — NHL reactivated Quebec Bulldogs franchise. Former Quebec players returned to the club. New Mount Royal Arena became home of Canadiens. Toronto Arenas changed name to St. Patricks. Clubs played 24-game split schedule.

1920-21 — H.P. Thompson of Hamilton, Ontario made application for the purchase of an NHL franchise. Quebec franchise shifted to Hamilton with other NHL teams providing players to strengthen the club.

1921-22 — Split schedule abandoned. First and second place teams at the end of full schedule to play for championship.

1922-23 — Clubs agreed that players could not be sold or traded to clubs in any other league without first being offered to all other clubs in the NHL. In March, Foster Hewitt broadcasts radio's first hockey game.

1923-24 — Ottawa's new 10,000-seat arena opened. First U.S. franchise granted to Boston for following season.

Dr. Cecil Hart Trophy donated to NHL to be awarded to the player judged most useful to his team.

1924-25 — Canadian Arena Company of Montreal granted a franchise to operate Montreal Maroons. NHL now six team league with two clubs in Montreal. Inaugural game in new Montreal Forum played November 29, 1924 as Canadiens defeated Toronto 7-1. Forum was home rink for the Maroons, but no ice was available in the Canadiens arena November 29, resulting in a shift to the Forum.

Hamilton finished first in the standings, receiving a bye into the finals. But Hamilton players, demanding $200 each for additional games in the playoffs, went on strike. The NHL suspended all players, fining them $200 each. Stanley Cup finalist to be the winner of NHL semi-final between Toronto and Canadiens.

Prince of Wales and Lady Byng trophies donated to NHL.

Clubs played 30-game schedule.

1925-26 — Hamilton club dropped from NHL. Players signed by new New York Americans franchise. Pittsburgh Pirates granted franchise.

Clubs played 36-game schedule.

1926-27 — New York Rangers granted franchise May 15, 1926. Chicago Black Hawks and Detroit Cougars granted franchises September 25, 1926. NHL now ten-team league with an American and a Canadian Division.

Stanley Cup came under the control of NHL. In previous seasons, winners of the now-defunct Western or Pacific Coast leagues would play NHL champion in Cup finals.

Toronto franchise sold to a new company controlled by Hugh Aird and Conn Smythe. Name changed from St. Patricks to Maple Leafs.

Clubs played 44-game schedule.

The Montreal Canadiens donated the Vezina Trophy to be awarded to the team allowing the fewest goals-against in regular season play. The winning team would, in turn, present the trophy to the goaltender playing in the greatest number of games during the season.

1930-31 — Detroit franchise changed name from Cougars to Falcons. Pittsburgh transferred to Philadelphia for one season. Pirates changed name to Philadelphia Quakers. Trading deadline for teams set at February 15 of each year. NHL approved operation of farm teams by Rangers, Americans, Falcons and Bruins. Four-sided electric arena clock first demonstrated.

1931-32 — Philadelphia dropped out. Ottawa withdrew for one season. New Maple Leaf Gardens completed.

Clubs played 48-game schedule

1932-33 — Detroit franchise changed name from Falcons to Red Wings. Franchise application received from St. Louis but refused because of additional travel costs. Ottawa team resumed play.

1933-34 — First All-Star Game played as a benefit for injured player Ace Bailey. Leafs defeated All-Stars 7-3 in Toronto.

1934-35 — Ottawa franchise transferred to St. Louis. Team called St. Louis Eagles and consisted largely of Ottawa's players.

1935-36 — Ottawa-St. Louis franchise terminated. Montreal Canadiens finished season with very poor record. To strengthen the club, NHL gave Canadiens first call on the services of all French-Canadian players for three seasons.

1937-38 — Second benefit All-Star game staged November 2 in Montreal in aid of the family of the late Canadiens star Howie Morenz.

Montreal Maroons withdrew from the NHL on June 22, 1938, leaving seven clubs in the League.

1938-39 — Expenses for each club regulated at $5 per man per day for meals and $2.50 per man per day for accommodation.

1939-40 — Benefit All-Star Game played October 29, 1939 in Montreal for the children of the late Albert (Babe) Siebert.

1940-41 — Ross-Tyer puck adopted as the official puck of the NHL. Early in the season it was apparent that this puck was too soft. The Spalding puck was adopted in its place.

On May 16, 1941, Arthur Ross, NHL governor from Boston, donated a perpetual trophy to be awarded annually to the player voted outstanding in the league. Due to wartime restrictions, the trophy was never awarded.

1941-42 — New York Americans changed name to Brooklyn Americans.

1942-43 — Brooklyn Americans withdrew from NHL, leaving six teams: Boston, Chicago, Detroit, Montreal, New York and Toronto. Playoff format saw first-place team play third-place team and second play fourth.

Clubs played 50-game schedule.

Frank Calder, president of the NHL since its inception, died in Montreal. Meryn "Red" Dutton, former manager of the New York Americans, became president. The NHL commissioned the Calder Memorial Trophy to be awarded to the League's outstanding rookie each year.

1945-46 — Philadelphia, Los Angeles and San Francisco applied for NHL franchises.

The Philadelphia Arena Company of the American Hockey League applied for an injunction to prevent the possible operation of an NHL franchise in that city.

1946-47 — Mervyn Dutton retired as president of the NHL prior to the start of the season. He was succeeded by Clarence S. Campbell.

Individual trophy winners and all-star team members to receive $1,000 awards.

Playoff guarantees for players introduced.

Clubs played 60-game schedule.

1947-48 — The first annual All-Star Game for the benefit of the players' pension fund was played when the All-Stars defeated the Stanley Cup Champion Toronto Maple Leafs 4-3 in Toronto on October 13, 1947.

Criteria for awarding Art Ross Trophy changed. Now awarded to top scorer. Elmer Lach was its first winner.

Philadelphia and Los Angeles franchise applications refused.

National Hockey League Pension Society formed.

1949-50 — Clubs played 70-game schedule.

First intra-league draft held April 30, 1950. Clubs allowed to protect 30 players. Remaining players available for $25,000 each.

1951-52 — Referees included in the League's pension plan.

1952-53 — In May of 1952, City of Cleveland applied for NHL franchise. Application denied. In March of 1953, the Cleveland Barons of the AHL challenged the NHL champions for the Stanley Cup. The NHL governors did not accept this challenge.

1953-54 — The James Norris Memorial Trophy presented to the NHL for annual presentation to the League's best defenseman.

Intra-league draft rules amended to allow teams to protect 18 skaters and two goaltenders, claiming price reduced to $15,000.

1954-55 — Each arena to operate an "out-of-town" scoreboard.

1956-57 — Referees and linesmen to wear shirts of black and white vertical stripes. Standardized signals for referees and linesmen introduced.

1960-61 — Canadian National Exhibition, City of Toronto and NHL reach agreement for the construction of a Hockey Hall of Fame on the CNE grounds. Hall opens on August 26, 1961.

1963-64 — Player development league established with clubs operated by NHL franchises located in Minneapolis, St. Paul, Indianapolis, Omaha and, beginning in 1964-65, Tulsa. First universal amateur draft took place. All players of qualifying age (17) unaffected by sponsorship of junior teams available to be drafted.

1964-65 — Conn Smythe Trophy presented to the NHL to be awarded annually to the outstanding player in the Stanley Cup playoffs.

Minimum age of players subject to amateur draft changed to 18.

1965-66 — NHL announced expansion plans for a second six-team division to begin play in 1967-68.

1966-67 — Fourteen applications for NHL franchises received.

Lester Patrick Trophy presented to the NHL to be awarded annually for outstanding service to hockey in the United States.

NHL sponsorship of junior teams ceased, making all players of qualifying age not already on NHL-sponsored lists eligible for the amateur draft.

1967-68 — Six new teams added: California Seals, Los Angeles Kings, Minnesota North Stars, Philadelphia Flyers, Pittsburgh Penguins, St. Louis Blues. New teams to play in West Division. Remaining six teams to play in East Division.

Minimum age of players subject to amateur draft changed to 20.

Clubs played 74-game schedule.

Clarence S. Campbell Trophy awarded to team finishing the regular season in first place in West Division.

California Seals change name to Oakland Seals on December 8, 1967.

1968-69 — Clubs played 76-game schedule.

Amateur draft expanded to cover any amateur player of qualifying age throughout the world.

1970-71 — Two new teams added: Buffalo Sabres and Vancouver Canucks. These teams joined East Division: Chicago switched to West Division. Oakland Seals change name to California Golden Seals prior to season.

Clubs played 78-game schedule.

1971-72 — Playoff format amended. In each division, first to play fourth; second to play third.

1972-73 — Soviet Nationals and Canadian NHL stars play eight-game pre-season series. Canadians win 4-3-1.

Two new teams added. Atlanta Flames join West Division; New York Islanders join East Division.

1974-75 — Two new teams added: Kansas City Scouts and Washington Capitals. Teams realigned into two nine-team conferences, the Prince of Wales made up of the Norris and Adams Divisions, and the Clarence Campbell made up of the Smythe and Patrick Divisions.

Clubs played 80-game schedule.

1976-77 — California franchise transferred to Cleveland. Team named Cleveland Barons. Kansas City franchise transferred to Denver. Team named Colorado Rockies.

1977-78 — Clarence S. Campbell retires as NHL president. Succeeded by John A. Ziegler, Jr.

1978-79 — Cleveland and Minnesota franchises merge, leaving NHL with 17 teams. Merged team placed in Adams Division, playing home games in Minnesota.

Minimum age of players subject to amateur draft changed to 19.

1979-80 — Four new teams added: Edmonton Oilers, Hartford Whalers, Quebec Nordiques and Winnipeg Jets.

Minimum age of players subject to entry draft changed to 18.

1980-81 — Atlanta franchise shifted to Calgary, retaining "Flames" name.

1981-82 — Teams realigned within existing divisions. New groupings based on geographical areas. Unbalanced schedule adopted.

1982-83 — Colorado Rockies franchise shifted to East Rutherford, New Jersey. Team named New Jersey Devils. Franchise moved to Patrick Division from Smythe; Winnipeg moved to Smythe Division from Norris.

NHL History — continued

1991-92 — San Jose Sharks added, making the NHL a 22-team league. NHL celebrates 75th Anniversary Season. The 1991-92 regular season suspended due to a players' strike on April 1, 1992. Play resumed April 12, 1992.

1992-93 — Gil Stein named NHL president (October, 1992). Gary Bettman named first NHL Commissioner (February, 1993). Ottawa Senators and Tampa Bay Lightning added, making the NHL a 24-team league. NHL celebrates Stanley Cup Centennial. Clubs played 84-game schedule.

1993-94 — Mighty Ducks of Anaheim and Florida Panthers added, making the NHL a 26-team league. Minnesota franchise shifted to Dallas, team named Dallas Stars. Prince of Wales and Clarence Campbell Conferences renamed Eastern and Western. Adams, Patrick, Norris and Smythe Divisions renamed Northeast, Atlantic, Central and Pacific. Winnipeg moved to Central Division from Pacific; Tampa Bay moved to Atlantic Division from Central; Pittsburgh moved to Northeast Division from Atlantic.

1994-95 — A lockout resulted in the cancellation of 468 games from October 1, 1994 to January 19, 1995. Clubs played a 48-game schedule that began January 20, 1995 and ended May 3, 1995. No inter-conference games were played.

1995-96 — Quebec franchise transferred to Denver. Team named Colorado Avalanche and placed in Pacific Division of Western Conference. Clubs to play 82-game schedule.

1996-97 — Winnipeg franchise transferred to Phoenix.

Team named Phoenix Coyotes and placed in Central Division of Western Conference.

1997-98 — Hartford franchise transferred to Raleigh. Team named Carolina Hurricanes and remains in Northeast Division of Eastern Conference.

1998-99 — The addition of the Nashville Predators made the NHL a 27-team league and brought about the creation of two new divisions and a League-wide realignment in preparation for further expansion to 30 teams by 2000-2001. Nashville was added to the Central Division of the Western Conference, while Toronto moved into the Northeast Division of the Eastern Conference. Pittsburgh was shifted from the Northeast to the Atlantic, while Carolina left the Northeast for the newly created Southeast Division of the Eastern Conference. Florida, Tampa Bay and Washington also joined the Southeast. In the Western Conference, Calgary, Colorado, Edmonton and Vancouver make up the new Northwest Division. Dallas and Phoenix moved from the Central to the Pacific Division.

The NHL retired uniform number 99 in honor of all-time scoring leader Wayne Gretzky who retired at the end of the season.

1999-2000 — Atlanta Thrashers added, making the NHL a 28-team league.

2000-01 — Columbus Blue Jackets and Minnesota Wild added, making the NHL a 30-team league.

2003-04 — First outdoor NHL game and largest crowd in League history as 57,167 attend Heritage Classic at Edmonton's Commonwealth Stadium. Montreal defeated Edmonton 4-3, November 22, 2003.

2004-05 — A lockout resulted in the cancellation of the season.

Major Rule Changes

1910-11 — Game changed from two 30-minute periods to three 20-minute periods.

1911-12 — National Hockey Association (forerunner of the NHL) originated six-man hockey, replacing seven-man game.

1917-18 — Goalies permitted to fall to the ice to make saves. Previously a goaltender was penalized for dropping to the ice.

1918-19 — Penalty rules amended. For minor fouls, substitutes not allowed until penalized player had served three minutes. For major fouls, no substitutes for five minutes. For match fouls, no substitutes allowed for the remainder of the game.

With the addition of two lines painted on the ice twenty feet from center, three playing zones were created, producing a forty-foot neutral center ice area in which forward passing was permitted. Kicking the puck was permitted in this neutral zone.

Tabulation of assists began.

1921-22 — Goaltenders allowed to pass the puck forward up to their own blue line.

Overtime limited to twenty minutes.

Minor penalties changed from three minutes to two minutes.

1923-24 — Match foul defined as actions deliberately injuring or disabling an opponent. For such actions, a player was fined not less than $50 and ruled off the ice for the balance of the game. A player assessed a match penalty may be replaced by a substitute at the end of 20 minutes. Match penalty recipients must meet with the League president who can assess additional punishment.

1925-26 — Delayed penalty rules introduced. Each team must have a minimum of four players on the ice at all times.

Two rules were amended to encourage offense: No more than two defensemen permitted to remain inside a team's own blue line when the puck has left the defensive zone. A faceoff to be called for ragging the puck unless short-handed.

Team captains only players allowed to talk to referees.

Goaltender's leg pads limited to 12-inch width.

Timekeeper's gong to mark end of periods rather than referee's whistle. Teams to dress a maximum of 12 players for each game from a roster of no more than 14 players.

1926-27 — Blue lines repositioned to sixty feet from each goal-line, thereby enlarging the neutral zone and standardizing distance from blue line to goal.

Uniform goal nets adopted throughout NHL with goal posts securely fastened to the ice.

1927-28 — To further encourage offense, forward passes allowed in defending and neutral zones and goaltender's pads reduced in width from 12 to 10 inches.

Game standardized at three twenty-minute periods of stop-time separated by ten-minute intermissions.

Teams to change ends after each period.

Ten minutes of sudden-death overtime to be played if the score is tied after regulation time.

Minor penalty to be assessed to any player other than a goaltender for deliberately picking up the puck while it is in play. Minor penalty to be assessed for deliberately shooting the puck out of play.

The Art Ross goal net adopted as the official net of the NHL.

Maximum length of hockey sticks limited to 53 inches measured from heel of blade to end of handle. No minimum length stipulated.

Home teams given choice of end to defend at start of game.

1928-29 — Forward passing permitted in defensive and neutral zones and into attacking zone if pass receiver is in neutral zone when pass is made. No forward passing allowed inside attacking zone.

Minor penalty to be assessed to any player who delays the game by passing the puck back into his defensive zone.

Ten-minute overtime without sudden-death provision to be played in games tied after regulation time. Games tied after this overtime period declared a draw.

Exclusive of goaltenders, team to dress at least 8 and no more than 12 skaters.

NHL Attendance

Season	Games	Regular Season Attendance	Games	Playoffs Attendance	Total Attendance
1960-61	210	2,317,142	17	242,000	2,559,142
1961-62	210	2,435,424	18	277,000	2,712,424
1962-63	210	2,590,574	16	220,906	2,811,480
1963-64	210	2,732,642	21	309,149	3,041,791
1964-65	210	2,822,635	20	303,859	3,126,494
1965-66	210	2,941,164	16	249,000	3,190,184
1966-67	210	3,084,759	16	248,336	3,333,095
1967-68	444	4,938,043	40	495,089	5,433,132
1968-69	456	5,550,613	33	431,739	5,982,352
1969-70	456	5,992,065	34	461,694	6,453,759
1970-71	546	7,257,677	43	707,633	7,965,310
1971-72	546	7,609,368	36	582,666	8,192,034
1972-73	624	8,575,651	38	624,637	9,200,288
1973-74	624	8,640,978	38	600,442	9,241,420
1974-75	720	9,521,536	51	784,181	10,305,717
1975-76	720	9,103,761	48	726,279	9,830,040
1976-77	720	8,563,890	44	646,279	9,210,169
1977-78	720	8,526,564	45	686,634	9,213,198
1978-79	680	7,758,053	45	694,521	8,452,574
1979-80	840	10,533,623	63	976,699	11,510,322
1980-81	840	10,726,198	68	966,390	11,692,588
1981-82	840	10,710,894	71	1,058,948	11,769,842
1982-83	840	11,020,610	66	1,088,222	12,028,832
1983-84	840	11,359,386	70	1,107,400	12,466,786
1984-85	840	11,633,730	70	1,107,500	12,741,230
1985-86	840	11,621,000	72	1,152,503	12,773,503
1986-87	840	11,855,880	87	1,383,967	13,239,847
1987-88	840	12,117,512	83	1,336,901	13,454,413
1988-89	840	12,417,969	83	1,327,214	13,745,183
1989-90	840	12,579,651	85	1,355,593	13,935,244
1990-91	840	12,343,897	92	1,442,203	13,786,100
1991-92	880	12,769,676	86	1,327,920	14,097,596
1992-93	1,008	14,158,177[1]	83	1,346,034	15,504,211
1993-94	1,092	16,105,604[2]	90	1,440,095	17,545,699
1994-95	624[3]	9,233,884	81	1,329,130	10,563,014
1995-96	1,066	17,041,614	86	1,540,140	18,581,754
1996-97	1,066	17,640,529	82	1,494,878	19,135,407
1997-98	1,066	17,264,678	82	1,507,416	18,772,094
1998-99	1,107	18,001,741	86	1,509,411	19,511,152
1999-2000	1,148	18,800,139	83	1,524,629	20,324,768
2000-01	1,230	20,373,379	86	1,584,011	21,957,390
2001-02	1,230	20,614,613	90	1,691,174	22,305,787
2002-03	1,230	20,408,704	89	1,636,120	22,044,824
2003-04	1,230	20,356,199	89	1,708,691	22,064,890
2004-05	....	....	....	....	....
2005-06	1,230	20,854,169	83	1,530,405	22,384,574

NHL Expansion: the NHL operated as a six-team league from 1942-43 to 1966-67. Six teams were added in 1967-68: California (later to move to Cleveland), Los Angeles, Minnesota (later to move to Dallas), Philadelphia, Pittsburgh and St. Louis. In 1970-71: Buffalo and Vancouver. In 1972-73: Atlanta (later to move to Calgary) and NY Islanders. In 1974-75: Kansas City (later to move to Colorado and then to New Jersey) and Washington. In 1979-80, Hartford (later to move to Carolina), Edmonton, Quebec (later to move to Colorado) and Winnipeg (later to move to Phoenix). In 1991-92, San Jose. In 1992-93, Ottawa and Tampa Bay. In 1993-94, Anaheim and Florida. In 1998-99, Nashville. In 1999-2000, Atlanta. In 2000-01, Columbus and Minnesota.

[1] Includes 24 neutral site games • [2] Includes 26 neutral site games
[3] Lockout resulted in the cancellation of 468 regular-season games.

Major Rule Changes — *continued*

1929-30 — Forward passing permitted inside all three zones but not permitted across either blue line.

Kicking the puck allowed, but a goal cannot be scored by kicking the puck in.

No more than three players including the goaltender may remain in their defensive zone when the puck has gone up ice. Minor penalties to be assessed for the first two violations of this rule in a game; major penalties thereafter.

Goaltenders forbidden to hold the puck. Pucks caught must be cleared immediately. For infringement of this rule, a faceoff to be taken ten feet in front of the goal with no player except the goaltender standing between the faceoff spot and the goal-line.

Highsticking penalties introduced.

Maximum number of players in uniform increased from 12 to 15.

December 21, 1929 — Forward passing rules instituted at the beginning of the 1929-30 season more than doubled number of goals scored. Partway through the season, these rules were further amended to read, ''No attacking player allowed to precede the play when entering the opposing defensive zone.'' This is similar to modern offside rule.

1930-31 — A player without a complete stick ruled out of play and forbidden from taking part in further action until a new stick is obtained. A player who has broken his stick must obtain a replacement at his bench.

A further refinement of the offside rule stated that the puck must first be propelled into the attacking zone before any player of the attacking side can enter that zone; for infringement of this rule a faceoff to take place at the spot where the infraction took place.

1931-32 — Though there is no record of a team attempting to play with two goaltenders on the ice, a rule was instituted which stated that each team was allowed only one goaltender on the ice at one time.

Attacking players forbidden to impede the movement or obstruct the vision of opposing goaltenders.

Defending players with the exception of the goaltender forbidden from falling on the puck within 10 feet of the net.

1932-33 — Each team to have captain on the ice at all times.

If the goaltender is removed from the ice to serve a penalty, the manager of the club to appoint a substitute.

Match penalty with substitution after five minutes instituted for kicking another player.

1933-34 — Number of players permitted to stand in defensive zone restricted to three including goaltender.

Visible time clocks required in each rink.

Two referees replace one referee and one linesman.

1934-35 — Penalty shot awarded when a player is tripped and thus prevented from having a clear shot on goal, having no player to pass to other than the offending player. Shot taken from inside a 10-foot circle located 38 feet from the goal. The goaltender must not advance more than one foot from his goal-line when the shot is taken.

1937-38 — Rules introduced governing icing the puck.

Penalty shot awarded when a player other than a goaltender falls on the puck within 10 feet of the goal.

1938-39 — Penalty shot modified to allow puck carrier to skate in before shooting.

One referee and one linesman replace two referee system.

Blue line widened to 12 inches.

Maximum number of players in uniform increased from 14 to 15.

1939-40 — A substitute replacing a goaltender removed from ice to serve a penalty may use a goaltender's stick and gloves but no other goaltending equipment.

1940-41 — Flooding ice surface between periods made obligatory.

1941-42 — Penalty shots classified as minor and major. Minor shot to be taken from a line 28 feet from the goal. Major shot, awarded when a player is tripped with only the goaltender to beat, permits the player taking the penalty shot to skate right into the goalkeeper and shoot from point-blank range.

One referee and two linesmen employed to officiate games.

For playoffs, standby minor league goaltenders employed by NHL as emergency substitutes.

1942-43 — Because of wartime restrictions on train scheduling, regular-season overtime was discontinued on November 21, 1942.

Player limit reduced from 15 to 14. Minimum of 12 men in uniform abolished.

1943-44 — Red line at center ice introduced to speed up the game and reduce offside calls. This rule is considered to mark the beginning of the modern era in the NHL.

1945-46 — Goal indicator lights synchronized with official time clock required at all rinks.

1946-47 — System of signals by officials to indicate infractions introduced.

Linesmen from neutral cities employed for all games.

1947-48 — Goal awarded when a player with the puck has an open net to shoot at and a thrown stick prevents the shot on goal. Major penalty to any player who throws his stick in any zone other than defending zone. If a stick is thrown by a player in his defending zone but the thrown stick is not considered to have prevented a goal, a penalty shot is awarded.

All playoff games played until a winner determined, with 20-minute sudden-death overtime periods separated by 10-minute intermissions.

1949-50 — Ice surface painted white.

Clubs allowed to dress 17 players exclusive of goaltenders.

Major penalties incurred by goaltenders served by a member of the goaltender's team instead of resulting in a penalty shot.

1950-51 — Each team required to provide an emergency goaltender in attendance with full equipment at each game for use by either team in the event of illness or injury to a regular goaltender.

1951-52 — Home teams to wear basic white uniforms; visiting teams basic colored uniforms.

Goal crease enlarged from 3 × 7 feet to 4 × 8 feet.

Number of players in uniform reduced to 15 plus goaltenders.

Faceoff circles enlarged from 10-foot to 15-foot radius.

1952-53 — Teams permitted to dress 15 skaters on the road and 16 at home.

1953-54 — Number of players in uniform set at 16 plus goaltenders.

1954-55 — Number of players in uniform set at 18 plus goaltenders up to December 1 and 16 plus goaltenders thereafter. Teams agree to wear colored uniforms at home and white uniforms on the road.

1956-57 — Player serving a minor penalty allowed to return to ice when a goal is scored by opposing team.

1959-60 — Players prevented from leaving their benches to enter into an altercation. Substitutions permitted providing substitutes do not enter into altercation.

1960-61 — Number of players in uniform set at 16 plus goaltenders.

1961-62 — Penalty shots to be taken by the player against whom the foul was committed. In the event of a penalty shot called in a situation where a particular player hasn't been fouled, the penalty shot to be taken by any player on the ice when the foul was committed.

1964-65 — No body contact on faceoffs.

In playoff games, each team to have its substitute goaltender dressed in his regular uniform except for leg pads and body protector. All previous rules governing standby goaltenders terminated.

1965-66 — Teams required to dress two goaltenders for each regular-season game. Maximum stick length increased to 55 inches.

1966-67 — Substitution allowed on coincidental major penalties.

Between-periods intermissions fixed at 15 minutes.

1967-68 — If a penalty incurred by a goaltender is a co-incident major, the penalty to be served by a player of the goaltender's team on the ice at the time the penalty was called. Limit of curvature of hockey stick blade set at 1½ inches.

1969-70 — Limit of curvature of hockey stick blade set at 1 inch.

1970-71 — Home teams to wear basic white uniforms; visiting teams basic colored uniforms.

Limit of curvature of hockey stick blade set at ½ inch.

Minor penalty for deliberately shooting the puck out of the playing area.

1971-72 — Number of players in uniform set at 17 plus 2 goaltenders.

Third man to enter an altercation assessed an automatic game misconduct penalty.

1972-73 — Minimum width of stick blade reduced to 2 inches from 2½ inches.

1974-75 — Bench minor penalty imposed if a penalized player does not proceed directly and immediately to the penalty box.

1976-77 — Rule dealing with fighting amended to provide a major and game misconduct penalty for any player who is clearly the instigator of a fight.

1977-78 — Teams requesting a stick measurement to be assessed a minor penalty in the event that the measured stick does not violate the rules.

1979-80 — Wearing of helmets made mandatory for players entering the NHL.

1980-81 — Maximum stick length increased to 58 inches.

1981-82 — If both of a team's listed goaltenders are incapacitated, the team can dress and play any eligible goaltender who is available.

1982-83 — Number of players in uniform set at 18 plus 2 goaltenders.

1983-84 — Five-minute sudden-death overtime to be played in regular-season games that are tied at the end of regulation time.

1985-86 — Substitutions allowed in the event of co-incidental minor penalties. Maximum stick length increased to 60 inches.

1986-87 — Delayed off-side is no longer in effect once the players of the offending team have cleared the opponents' defensive zone.

1990-91 — The goal lines, blue lines, defensive zone face-off circles and markings all moved one foot out from the end boards, creating 11 feet of room behind the nets and shrinking the neutral zone from 60 to 58 feet.

1991-92 — Video replays employed to assist referees in goal/no goal situations. Size of goal crease increased. Crease changed to semi-circular configuration. Time clock to record tenths of a second in last minute of each period and overtime. Major and game misconduct penalty for checking from behind into boards. Penalties added for crease infringement and unnecessary contact with goaltender. Goal disallowed if puck enters net while a player of the attacking team is standing on the goal crease line, is in the goal crease or places his stick in the goal crease.

1992-93 — No substitutions allowed in the event of coincidental minor penalties called when both teams are at full strength. Minor penalty for attempting to draw a penalty ("diving"). Major and game misconduct penalty for checking from behind into goal frame. Game misconduct penalty for instigating a fight. High sticking redefined to include any use of the stick above waist-height. Previous rule stipulated shoulder-height.

1993-94 — High sticking redefined to allow goals scored with a high stick below the height of the crossbar of the goal frame.

1996-97 — Maximum stick length increased to 63 inches. All players must be clear of the attacking zone prior to the puck being shot into that zone. The opportunity to "tag-up" and return into the zone has been removed.

1998-99 — The league instituted a two-referee system with each team to play 20 regular-season games with two referees and a pair of linesmen. Goal line moved to 13 feet from end boards. Goal crease altered to extend one foot beyond each goal post (eight feet across in total). Sides of crease squared off, extending 4'6". Only the top of the crease remains rounded. Only the top of the crease remains rounded.

1999-2000 — Each team to play 25 home and 25 road games using the two-referee system. Crease rule revised to implement a "no harm, no foul, no video review" standard. Teams to play with four skaters and a goaltender in regular-season overtime. If a goal is scored in regular-season overtime, the winner is awarded two points and the loser one point. In no goal is scored in overtime, both teams are awarded one point.

2000-01 — All games to be played using the two-referee system.

2002-03 — "Hurry-up" faceoff and line-change rules implemented.

2003-04 — Home teams to wear basic colored uniforms; visiting teams basic white uniforms. Maximum length of goaltender's pads set at 38 inches.

2005-06 — The NHL adopted a comprehensive package of rule changes that included the following:

Goal line moved to 11 feet from end boards; blue lines moved to 75 feet from end boards, reducing neutral zone from 54 feet to 50 feet. Center red line eliminated for two-line passes. "Tag-up" off-side rule reinstituted. This rule was previously used from 1986-87 through 1995-96. Goaltender not permitted to play the puck outside a designated trapezoid-shaped area behind the net. A team that ices the puck will not be permitted to make any player substitutions prior to the ensuing faceoff. A player who instigates a fight in the final five minutes of regulation time or at any time of overtime will receive a minor, a major, a misconduct and an automatic one-game suspension. The size of goaltender equipment has been reduced by approximately 11 percent. If a game remains tied after five minutes of overtime, a shootout will be conducted to determine a winner.

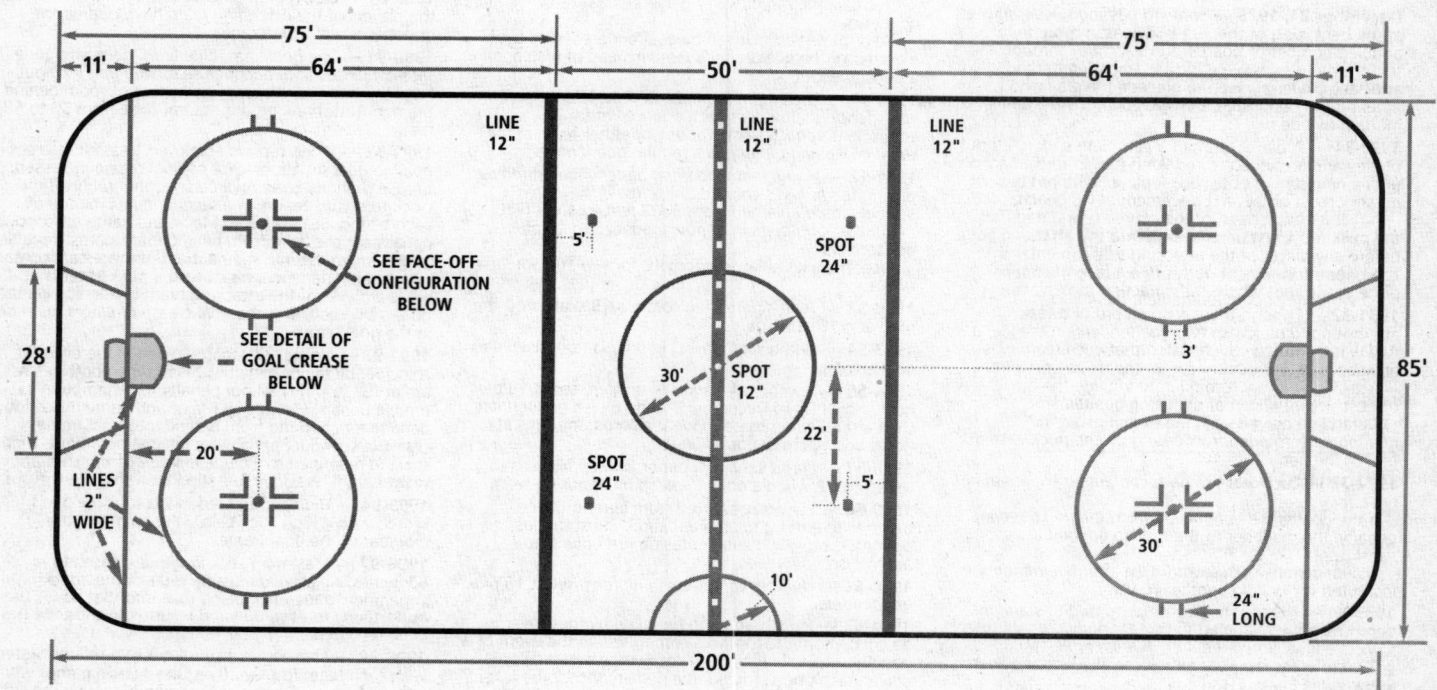

NHL RINK DIMENSIONS

FACEOFF CONFIGURATION

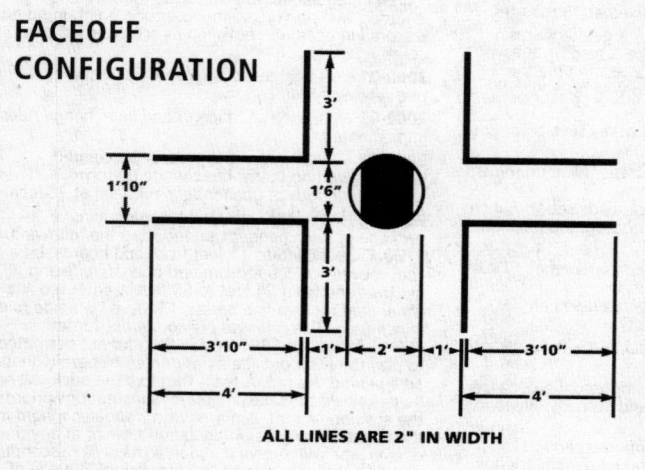

ALL LINES ARE 2" IN WIDTH

CREASE DIMENSIONS

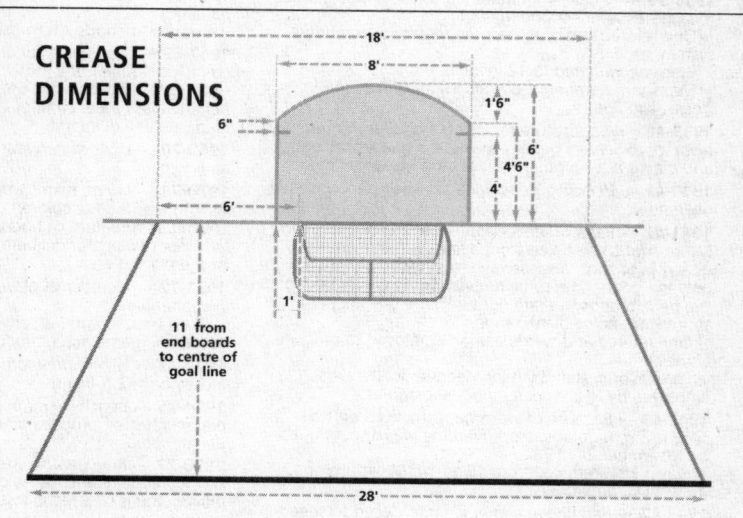

Success is Swede at the 2006 Olympic Winter Games

LIKE THE TOURNAMENT AT SALT LAKE CITY FOUR YEARS EARLIER, several teams displayed gold medal form during the 2006 Torino Games, most notably Finland, which was undefeated before facing their archrivals from Sweden in the tournament final. The Finns were seeking their first Olympic gold medal, but in the end it was the Swedes who went home with the top prize. The win represented a redemption of sorts for the Swedes who had suffered a stunning quarterfinal loss to Belarus in 2002.

After losing to undefeated Slovakia in their final game of the preliminary round, Sweden fell to third place in Group B, but then defeated a surprising Swiss team 6-2 in the quarterfinals. Next up was the Czech Republic. The Czechs had defeated Slovakia in the quarterfinals, but fell 7-3 to Sweden in the semis to set up an all-Scandinavian gold medal game. Kimmo Timonen (an all-star on defense, along with Sweden's Nicklas Lidstrom) got Finland on the scoreboard late in the first period, but Sweden took a 2-1 lead midway through the second on goals by Henrik Zetterberg and Niklas Kronwall. Ville Peltonen (who had scored the winning goal for Finland versus Sweden in the gold medal game at the 1995 World Championship) evened matters late in the period. Then, just ten seconds into the third period, Lidstrom, on a set up from Mats Sundin and Peter Forsberg, scored the winning goal. Henrik Lundqvist withstood a late Finnish rally, and Sweden held on for a 3-2 gold medal victory.

Sweden was also the big story in women's hockey at Torino, where Canada's one-sided wins early in the tournament had critics wondering about the state of the women's game. Though Canada did, indeed, cruise to a second straight Olympic gold medal, the tournament featured the biggest upset in women's hockey history as Sweden shocked the United States with a 3-2 shootout victory in the semifinals. The Swedes' silver medal represented the first time a non-North American women's team had finished ahead of Canada or the United States in World or Olympic competition.

Men's Standings • 2006
Preliminary Round
Group A

Team	GP	W	L	T	GF	GA	Pts
Finland	5	5	0	0	19	2	10
Switzerland	5	2	1	2	10	12	6
Canada	5	3	2	0	15	9	6
Czech Rep.	5	2	3	0	14	12	4
Germany	5	0	3	2	7	16	2
Italy	5	0	3	2	9	23	2

Group B

Team	GP	W	L	T	GF	GA	Pts
Slovakia	5	5	0	0	18	8	10
Russia	5	4	1	0	23	11	8
Sweden	5	3	2	0	15	12	6
USA	5	1	3	1	13	13	3
Kazakhstan	5	1	4	0	9	16	2
Latvia	5	0	4	1	11	29	1

2006 Final Rankings

1. Sweden
2. Finland
3. Czech Republic
4. Russia
5. Slovakia
6. Switzerland
7. Canada
8. United States
9. Kazakhstan
10. Germany
11. Italy
12. Latvia

2006 Scoring Leaders

Player	Team	GP	G	A	PTS	PIM
Teemu Selanne	Finland	8	6	5	11	4
Saku Koivu	Finland	8	3	8	11	12
Marian Hossa	Slovakia	6	5	5	10	4
Daniel Alfredsson	Sweden	8	5	5	10	4
Ville Peltonen	Finland	8	4	5	9	6
Olli Jokinen	Finland	8	6	2	8	2
Mats Sundin	Sweden	8	3	5	8	4
Jere Lehtinen	Finland	8	3	5	8	0
Martin Straka	Czech Rep.	8	2	6	8	6
Pavel Datsyuk	Russia	8	1	7	8	10
Y. Koreshkov	Kazak.	5	5	2	7	6
Martin Gaborik	Slovakia	6	3	4	7	4
Pavol Demitra	Slovakia	6	2	5	7	2
Jaromir Jagr	Czech Rep.	8	2	5	7	6
Vacláv Prospal	Czech Rep.	8	4	2	6	2
Alex Kovalev	Russia	8	4	2	6	4
P.J. Axelsson	Sweden	8	3	3	6	0
H. Zetterberg	Sweden	8	3	3	6	0
Evgeni Malkin	Russia	7	2	4	6	31
Nicklas Lidstrom	Sweden	8	1	5	6	0
Peter Forsberg	Sweden	6	0	6	6	0

2006 Goaltending Leaders
(Minimum 150 Mins)

Player	Team	GP	Min	GA	SO	GAA
E. Nabokov	Russia	7	359	8	3	1.34
A. Niittymaki	Finland	6	359	8	3	1.34
Martin Brodeur	Canada	4	239	8	0	2.01
Peter Budaj	Slovakia	3	179	6	0	2.01
David Aebischer	Switzerland	4	200	7	0	2.10
Rick DiPietro	USA	4	237	9	0	2.28
Henrik Lundqvist	Sweden	6	360	14	0	2.33
Tomas Vokoun	Czech Rep.	7	342	14	1	2.46
Olaf Kolzig	Germany	3	179	8	0	2.68

Women's Standings • 2006
Preliminary Round
Group A

Team	GP	W	L	T	GF	GA	Pts
Canada	3	3	0	0	36	1	6
Sweden	3	2	1	0	15	9	4
Russia	3	1	2	0	6	16	2
Italy	3	0	3	0	1	32	2

Group B

Team	GP	W	L	T	GF	GA	Pts
USA	3	3	0	0	18	3	6
Finland	3	2	1	0	10	7	4
Germany	3	1	2	0	2	9	2
Switzerland	3	0	3	0	1	12	0

2006 Final Rankings

1. Canada
2. Sweden
3. United States
4. Finland
5. Germany
6. Russia
7. Switzerland
8. Italy

2006 Scoring Leaders

Player	Team	GP	G	A	PTS	PIM
H. Wickenheiser	Canada	5	5	12	17	6
Cherie Piper	Canada	5	7	8	15	0
Gillian Apps	Canada	5	7	7	14	14
Caroline Oulette	Canada	5	5	4	9	4
Maria Rooth	Sweden	5	5	4	9	2
Jenny Potter	USA	5	2	7	9	4
Katie King	USA	5	6	2	8	2
Sarah Parsons	USA	5	4	3	7	0
Jayna Hefford	Canada	5	3	4	7	4
Jennifer Botterill	Canada	5	1	6	7	4
Danielle Goyette	Canada	5	4	2	6	6
G. Andersson	Sweden	5	3	3	6	4
Natalie Darwitz	USA	5	3	3	6	8
Angela Ruggiero	USA	5	2	4	6	6
S. Vaillancourt	Canada	5	2	4	6	2
K. Weatherston	Canada	5	4	1	5	2
Maritta Becker	Germany	5	3	2	5	10
Kathrin Lehmann	Switzerland	5	3	2	5	29
Erika Holst	Sweden	5	1	4	5	2
Julie Chu	USA	5	0	5	5	2
Cassie Campbell	Canada	5	0	5	5	2

2006 Goaltending Leaders

Player	Team	GP	Min	GA	SO	GAA
Pam Dwyer	USA	1	60	0	1	0.00
Charline Labonte	Canada	3	180	1	2	0.33
Kim St. Pierre	Canada	2	120	1	1	0.50
Chanda Gunn	USA	4	250	6	1	1.44
Jennifer Harss	Germany	3	190	6	1	1.89
Kim Martin	Sweden	3	190	7	0	2.21
F. Schelling	Switzerland	3	150	6	1	2.40
S. Wartosch-Kuerten	Germany	2	120	5	0	2.50
I. Gashennikova	Russia	5	266	12	0	2.70
Maija Hassinen	Finland	4	195	11	0	3.38

2006 Men's Olympic Hockey Results

Preliminary Round (round robin)

Feb. 15				
	Kazakhstan	2	Sweden	7
	Italy	2	Canada	7
	Switzerland	0	Finland	5
	Germany	1	Czech Republic	4
	Russia	3	Slovakia	5
	Latvia	3	USA	3
Feb. 16				
	Finland	6	Italy	0
	Czech Republic	2	Switzerland	3
	Sweden	0	Russia	5
	Slovakia	6	Latvia	3
	Canada	5	Germany	1
	USA	4	Kazakhstan	1
Feb. 18				
	Kazakhstan	2	Russia	1
	Italy	3	Germany	3
	Canada	0	Switzerland	2
	Sweden	6	Latvia	1
	Slovakia	2	USA	1
	Czech Republic	2	Finland	4
Feb. 19				
	Germany	2	Switzerland	2
	Russia	9	Latvia	2
	Slovakia	2	Kazakhstan	1
	USA	1	Sweden	2
	Czech Republic	4	Italy	1
	Finland	2	Canada	0
Feb. 21				
	Latvia	2	Kazakhstan	5
	Switzerland	3	Italy	3
	Canada	3	Czech Republic	2
	Finland	2	Germany	0
	Sweden	0	Slovakia	3
	USA	4	Russia	4

Playoff Round (single elimination)

Feb. 22				
	Finland	4	USA	3
	Switzerland	2	Sweden	6
	Canada	0	Russia	2
	Slovakia	1	Czech Republic	3
Feb. 24 Semifinals				
	Sweden	7	Czech Republic	3
	Finland	4	Russia	0
Feb. 25 Bronze Medal Game				
	Czech Republic	3	Russia	0
Feb. 26 Gold Medal Game				
	Sweden	3	Finland	2

2006 Women's Olympic Hockey Results

Preliminary Round (round robin)

Feb. 11				
	Finland	3	Germany	0
	Sweden	3	Russia	1
	United States	6	Switzerland	0
	Canada	16	Italy	0
Feb. 12				
	Russia	0	Canada	12
	Germany	0	United States	5
Feb. 13				
	Sweden	11	Italy	0
	Finland	4	Switzerland	0
Feb. 14				
	Italy	1	Russia	5
	Canada	8	Sweden	1
	Switzerland	1	Germany	2
	United States	7	Finland	3

Playoff Round (single elimination)

Feb. 17 Classification Games				
	Russia	6	Switzerland	2
	Germany	5	Italy	2
Semifinals				
	Canada	6	Finland	0
	United States	2	Sweden	3 (SO)
Feb. 20 7th place game				
	Switzerland	11	Italy	0
5th place game				
	Germany	1	Italy	0 (SO)
Bronze Medal Game				
	United States	4	Finland	0
Gold Medal Game				
	Canada	4	Sweden	1

Cumulative Medal Standings, Women's Olympic Hockey, 1998-2006

		G	S	B	TOTAL	LAST MEDAL
1.	Canada	2	1	0	3	Gold 06
2.	USA	1	1	1	3	Bronze 06
3.	Sweden	0	1	1	2	Silver 06
4.	Finland	0	0	1	1	Bronze 98

Cumulative Medal Standings, Men's Olympic Hockey, 1924-2002

		G	S	B	TOTAL	LAST MEDAL
1.	USSR/Russia*	8	2	2	12	Bronze 02
2.	Canada	6	4	2	12	Gold 02
3.	USA	2	6	1	9	Silver 02
4.	Sweden	2	2	4	8	Gold 06
5.	Czechoslovakia/Czech Rep.	1	4	4	9	Bronze 06
6.	Great Britain	1	0	1	2	Gold 36
7.	Finland	0	2	2	4	Silver 06
8.	W. Germany	0	0	2	2	Bronze 76
9.	Switzerland	0	0	2	2	Bronze 48

Soviet Union/Russia played as the Unified Team in 1992.

NHL Clubs' Minor-League Affiliations, 2006-07

NHL Club	Minor-League Affiliates
Anaheim	Portland Pirates (AHL)
	Augusta Lynx (ECHL)
Atlanta	Chicago Wolves (AHL)
	Gwinnett Gladiators (ECHL)
Boston	Providence Bruins (AHL)
Buffalo	Rochester Americans (AHL)
Calgary	Omaha Ak-Sar-Ben Knights (AHL)
	Las Vegas Wranglers (ECHL)
Carolina	Albany River Rats (AHL)
	Florida Everblades (ECHL)
Chicago	Norfolk Admirals (AHL)
	Greenville Grrrowl (ECHL)
Colorado	Albany River Rats (AHL)
	Arizona Sun Dogs (CHL)
Columbus	Syracuse Crunch (AHL)
	Dayton Bombers (ECHL)
Dallas	Iowa Stars (AHL)
	Idaho Steelheads (ECHL)
Detroit	Grand Rapids Griffins (AHL)
	Toledo Storm (ECHL)
Edmonton	Stockton Thunder (ECHL)
Florida	Rochester Americans (AHL)
	Florida Everblades (ECHL)
Los Angeles	Manchester Monarchs (AHL)
	Reading Royals (ECHL)
Minnesota	Houston Aeros (AHL)
	Texas Wildcatters (ECHL)
	Austin Ice Bats (CHL)

NHL Club	Minor-League Affiliates
Montreal	Hamilton Bulldogs (AHL)
	Cincinnati Cyclones (ECHL)
Nashville	Milwaukee Admirals (AHL)
New Jersey	Lowell Devils (AHL)
NY Islanders	Bridgeport Sound Tigers (AHL)
NY Rangers	Hartford Wolf Pack (AHL)
	Charlotte Checkers (ECHL)
Ottawa	Binghamton Senators (AHL)
	Charlotte Checkers (ECHL)
Philadelphia	Philadelphia Phantoms (AHL)
	Trenton Titans (ECHL)
Phoenix	San Antonio Rampage (AHL)
	Phoenix RoadRunners (ECHL)
	Laredo Bucks (CHL)
Pittsburgh	Wilkes-Barre/Scranton Penguins (AHL)
	Wheeling Nailers (ECHL)
St. Louis	Peoria Rivermen (AHL)
	Alaska Aces (ECHL)
San Jose	Worcester Sharks (AHL)
	Fresno Falcons (ECHL)
	Toledo Storm (ECHL)
Tampa Bay	Springfield Falcons (AHL)
	Johnstown Chiefs (ECHL)
Toronto	Toronto Marlies (AHL)
	Columbia Inferno (ECHL)
Vancouver	Manitoba Moose (AHL)
	Victoria Salmon Kings (ECHL)
Washington	Hershey Bears (AHL)
	South Carolina Stingrays (ECHL)

Anaheim Ducks

2005-06 Results: 43W-27L-5OTL-7SOL 98PTS.
Third, Pacific Division

Year-by-Year Record

Season	GP	Home				Road				Overall				GF	GA	Pts.	Finished	Playoff Result
		W	L	T	OL	W	L	T	OL	W	L	T	OL					
2005-06	82	26	10	....	5	17	17	....	7	43	27	....	12	254	229	98	3rd, Pacific Div.	Lost Conf. Final
2004-05	....	....	....	....	....	....	....	....	....	....	....	....	....	....	....			
2003-04	82	19	11	7	4	10	24	3	4	29	35	10	8	184	213	76	4th, Pacific Div.	Out of Playoffs
2002-03	82	22	10	7	2	18	17	2	4	40	27	9	6	203	193	95	2nd, Pacific Div.	Lost Final
2001-02	82	15	19	5	2	14	23	3	1	29	42	8	3	175	198	69	5th, Pacific Div.	Out of Playoffs
2000-01	82	15	20	4	2	10	21	7	3	25	41	11	5	188	245	66	5th, Pacific Div.	Out of Playoffs
1999-2000	82	19	13	7	2	15	20	5	1	34	33	12	3	217	227	83	3rd, Pacific Div.	Lost Conf. Quarter-Final
1998-99	82	21	14	6	....	14	20	7	....	35	34	13	....	215	206	83	3rd, Pacific Div.	Out of Playoffs
1997-98	82	12	23	6	....	14	20	7	....	26	43	13	....	205	261	65	6th, Pacific Div.	Lost Conf. Semi-Final
1996-97	82	23	12	6	....	13	21	7	....	36	33	13	....	245	233	85	2nd, Pacific Div.	Lost Conf. Semi-Final
1995-96	82	22	15	4	....	13	24	4	....	35	39	8	....	234	247	78	4th, Pacific Div.	Out of Playoffs
1994-95	48	11	9	4	....	5	18	1	....	16	27	5	....	125	164	37	6th, Pacific Div.	Out of Playoffs
1993-94	84	14	26	2	....	19	20	3	....	33	46	5	....	229	251	71	4th, Pacific Div.	Out of Playoffs

2006-07 Schedule

Oct.
Fri. 6 Los Angeles
Sat. 7 at Phoenix
Mon. 9 St. Louis
Wed. 11 NY Islanders
Sun. 15 Dallas*
Wed. 18 Detroit
Fri. 20 Minnesota
Sun. 22 at Los Angeles*
Wed. 25 Edmonton
Fri. 27 at Minnesota
Sat. 28 at Chicago
Mon. 30 at St. Louis

Nov.
Wed. 1 NY Rangers
Fri. 3 Phoenix
Mon. 6 Pittsburgh
Thu. 9 at Vancouver
Fri. 10 at Calgary
Sun. 12 Minnesota*
Wed. 15 Philadelphia
Fri. 17 Chicago
Sun. 19 Phoenix*
Tue. 21 San Jose
Wed. 22 at Colorado
Fri. 24 New Jersey*
Sun. 26 Calgary*
Tue. 28 at Edmonton
Thu. 30 at Vancouver

Dec.
Sat. 2 at Los Angeles*
Sun. 3 Los Angeles*
Wed. 6 Nashville
Fri. 8 at Washington
Sat. 9 at Tampa Bay
Tue. 12 at Florida
Wed. 13 at Atlanta
Sat. 16 at San Jose
Mon. 18 Calgary
Wed. 20 Dallas
Sat. 23 at Phoenix
Tue. 26 at San Jose
Fri. 29 at Carolina
Sun. 31 at Minnesota*

Jan.
Tue. 2 at Detroit
Fri. 5 Columbus
Sun. 7 Detroit*
Tue. 9 at Nashville
Thu. 11 at Dallas
Sat. 13 Colorado
Tue. 16 St. Louis
Thu. 18 at Edmonton
Fri. 19 at Calgary
Sun. 28 Dallas*
Wed. 31 Phoenix

Feb.
Sat. 3 at Nashville
Tue. 6 at San Jose
Wed. 7 San Jose
Sat. 10 at Dallas*
Tue. 13 at Colorado
Thu. 15 at Phoenix
Sat. 17 at Los Angeles
Sun. 18 Los Angeles*
Tue. 20 Vancouver
Fri. 23 at Dallas
Sun. 25 Colorado*
Mon. 26 at San Jose

Mar.
Thu. 1 at Los Angeles
Fri. 2 San Jose
Sun. 4 Nashville*
Wed. 7 Phoenix
Fri. 9 Edmonton
Sun. 11 Vancouver*
Wed. 14 Columbus
Fri. 16 Chicago
Sun. 18 Los Angeles*
Thu. 22 at Phoenix
Fri. 23 Dallas
Mon. 26 at Detroit
Wed. 28 at Chicago
Thu. 29 at Columbus
Sat. 31 at St. Louis

Apr.
Wed. 4 San Jose
Fri. 6 at Dallas
Sat. 7 at Columbus

* Denotes afternoon game.

Franchise date: June 15, 1993

WESTERN CONFERENCE
PACIFIC DIVISION

14th NHL Season

Andy McDonald and Teemu Selanne celebrate a Ducks goal. Selanne led the team (and tied for tenth in the NHL) with 40 goals. McDonald's team-leading 51 assists almost equaled his previous career total of 53 for his first four seasons.

2006-07 Player Personnel

FORWARDS	HT	WT	S	Place of Birth	Date	2005-06 Club
BRENT, Tim	6-0	196	R	Cambridge, Ont.	3/10/84	Portland (AHL)
CARTER, Ryan	6-1	200	L	White Bear Lake, MN	8/3/83	Minnesota State
CHISTOV, Stanislav	5-10	193	R	Chelyabinsk, USSR	4/17/83	Magnitogorsk
FEDORUK, Todd	6-2	235	L	Redwater, Alta.	2/13/79	Anaheim
GENOWAY, Colby	6-1	201	R	Morden, Man.	12/12/83	Hartford
GETZLAF, Ryan	6-3	210	R	Regina, Sask.	5/10/85	Anaheim-Portland (AHL)
GILLIES, Trevor	6-3	210	L	Cambridge, Ont.	1/30/79	Anaheim-Portland (AHL)
GLENCROSS, Curtis	6-1	186	L	Kindersley, Sask.	12/28/82	Portland (AHL)
GREEN, Travis	6-2	200	R	Castlegar, B.C.	12/20/70	Boston
HYNES, Shane	6-3	224	R	Montreal, Que.	11/7/83	Portland (AHL)
KUNITZ, Chris	6-0	194	L	Regina, Sask.	9/26/79	Atl-Ana-Port (AHL)
MARCHANT, Todd	5-10	180	L	Buffalo, NY	8/12/73	Columbus-Anaheim
McDONALD, Andy	5-10	186	L	Strathroy, Ont.	8/25/77	Anaheim
MELIN, Bjorn	6-1	205	R	Jonkoping, Sweden	7/4/81	HV 71
MILLER, Drew	6-2	170	L	Dover, NJ	2/17/84	Michigan State
MOEN, Travis	6-2	210	L	Stewart Valley, Sask.	4/6/82	Anaheim
NIEDERMAYER, Rob	6-2	204	L	Cassiar, B.C.	12/28/74	Anaheim
PAHLSSON, Samuel	5-11	212	L	Ornskoldsvik, Sweden	12/17/77	Anaheim
PARENTEAU, Pierre	5-11	195	R	Hull, Que.	3/24/83	Portland (AHL)-Augusta
PENNER, Dustin	6-4	245	L	Winkler, Man.	9/28/82	Anaheim-Portland (AHL)
PERRY, Corey	6-2	202	R	Peterborough, Ont.	5/16/85	Anaheim-Portland (AHL)
PETERS, Geoff	6-1	205	L	Hamilton, Ont.	4/30/78	Portland (AHL)
SELANNE, Teemu	6-0	205	R	Helsinki, Finland	7/3/70	Anaheim
SHANNON, Ryan	5-9	178	R	Darien, CT	3/2/83	Portland (AHL)
THORNTON, Shawn	6-1	209	R	Oshawa, Ont.	7/23/77	Chicago-Norfolk
WIRTANEN, Petteri	6-1	202	L	Hyvinkaa, Finland	5/28/86	Suomi U20-HPK Jr.-HPK
DEFENSEMEN						
BEAUCHEMIN, Francois	6-0	214	L	Sorel, Que.	6/4/80	Columbus-Anaheim
DiPENTA, Joe	6-2	205	L	Barrie, Ont.	2/25/79	Anaheim
FESTERLING, Brett	6-1	180	L	Quesnel, B.C.	3/3/86	Vancouver (WHL)
HUSKINS, Kent	6-3	215	L	Ottawa, Ont.	5/4/79	Portland (AHL)
KONDRATIEV, Maxim	6-1	192	L	Togliatti, USSR	1/20/83	NYR-Hart-Port (AHL)
MORAN, Ian	6-0	200	R	Cleveland, OH	8/24/72	Boston
NIEDERMAYER, Scott	6-1	200	L	Edmonton, Alta.	8/31/73	Anaheim
O'BRIEN, Shane	6-2	237	L	Port Hope, Ont.	8/9/83	Portland (AHL)
O'DONNELL, Sean	6-3	227	L	Ottawa, Ont.	10/13/71	Phoenix-Anaheim
PRONGER, Chris	6-6	220	L	Dryden, Ont.	10/10/74	Edmonton
ROME, Aaron	6-1	230	L	Nesbitt, Man.	9/27/83	Portland (AHL)
ST. JACQUES, Bruno	6-2	210	L	Montreal, Que.	8/22/80	Anaheim-Portland (AHL)
SALCIDO, Brian	6-2	195	L	Los Angeles, CA	4/14/85	Colorado College
SAUNDERS, Nathan	6-4	216	R	Charlottetown, P.E.I.	4/25/85	Portland (AHL)
SKINNER, Brett	6-1	195	L	Brandon, Man.	6/28/83	Manitoba
VISHNEVSKI, Vitaly	6-2	203	L	Kharkov, USSR	3/18/80	Anaheim
WILSON, Clay	6-0	195	L	Sturgeon Lake, MN	4/5/83	Muskegon-Grand Rapids

GOALTENDERS	HT	WT	C	Place of Birth	Date	2005-06 Club
BRYZGALOV, Ilya	6-3	198	L	Togliatti, USSR	6/22/80	Anaheim
GIGUERE, Jean-Sebastien	6-1	199	L	Montreal, Que.	5/16/77	Anaheim
LEIGHTON, Michael	6-3	186	L	Petrolia, Ont.	5/19/81	Rochester
MARSTERS, Nathan	6-4	190	L	Burlington, Ont.	1/28/80	Portland (AHL)-Augusta
MCKEE, David	6-1	180	L	Irving, TX	12/5/83	Cornell
WALL, Michael	6-1	209	L	Telkwa, B.C.	7/25/85	Augusta-Portland (AHL)

Coach

CARLYLE, RANDY
Coach, Anaheim Ducks. Born in Sudbury, Ont., April 19, 1956.

Randy Carlyle was hired as the head coach in Anaheim on August 1, 2005. In his first season behind the bench in 2005-06, he led the Ducks to the Western Conference Final.

Carlyle spent the 2004-05 season as head coach of the Manitoba Moose, the Vancouver Canucks' primary development affiliate in the American Hockey League. That year, he led Manitoba to a 44-26-3-7 record and an appearance in the Calder Cup semifinals. In all, Carlyle spent six seasons between 1996 and 2005 as head coach in Manitoba (both in the International and American Hockey Leagues) with his team posting an overall record of 222-159-52-7. He had the additional duties of general manager of the Moose from 1996 to 2000, and served as club president for the 2001-02 season. The Sudbury, Ontario, native helped the Moose to a 47-21-14 record for 108 points in 1998-99, for which he was named the IHL's general manager of the year.

Following the 2001-02 season, Carlyle joined the coaching staff of the Washington Capitals. He served as an assistant coach with Washington for two seasons (2002 to 2004), before rejoining Manitoba in 2004–05.

Carlyle played 17 seasons in the NHL with Toronto, Pittsburgh and Winnipeg. He appeared in 1,055 games and had 148 goals and 499 assists for 647 points. Known as a fiery, tough-nosed defenseman, he was selected to play in four NHL All-Star Games, winning the Norris Trophy as the league's top defenseman in 1981. At the conclusion of his playing career in 1993, Carlyle remained with the Winnipeg organization's hockey operations staff, eventually becoming an assistant coach for the 1995-96 season.

Coaching Record

		Regular Season				Playoffs		
Season	Team	Games	W	L	O/T	Games	W	L
1996-97	Manitoba (IHL)	32	16	14	2	....	....	....
1997-98	Manitoba (IHL	82	39	36	7	3	0	3
1998-99	Manitoba (IHL)	82	47	21	14	5	2	3
99-2000	Manitoba (IHL)	82	37	31	14	2	0	2
2000-01	Manitoba (IHL)	82	39	31	12	13	6	7
2004-05	Manitoba (AHL)	80	44	33	3	14	6	8
2005-06	**Anaheim (NHL)**	**82**	**43**	**27**	**12**	**16**	**9**	**7**
	NHL Totals	**82**	**43**	**27**	**12**	**16**	**9**	**7**

2005-06 Scoring

* – rookie

Regular Season

Pos	#	Player	Team	GP	G	A	Pts	+/–	PIM	PP	SH	GW	S	%
R	13	Teemu Selanne	ANA	80	40	50	90	28	44	18	0	5	267	15.0
C	19	Andy McDonald	ANA	82	34	51	85	24	32	13	0	7	229	14.8
D	27	Scott Niedermayer	ANA	82	13	50	63	8	96	9	0	3	181	7.2
R	15	Joffrey Lupul	ANA	81	28	25	53	–13	48	12	2	2	296	9.5
L	38 *	Chris Kunitz	ATL	2	0	0	0	–3	2	0	0	0	0	0.0
			ANA	67	19	22	41	19	69	5	1	2	149	12.8
			TOTAL	69	19	22	41	16	71	5	1	2	149	12.8
C	44	Rob Niedermayer	ANA	76	15	24	39	–5	89	4	1	2	140	10.7
C	51 *	Ryan Getzlaf	ANA	57	14	25	39	6	22	10	0	1	116	12.1
D	23 *	Francois Beauchemin	CBJ	11	0	2	2	–6	11	0	0	0	16	0.0
			ANA	61	8	26	34	8	41	4	0	3	121	6.6
			TOTAL	72	8	28	36	2	52	4	0	3	137	5.8
C	22	Todd Marchant	CBJ	18	3	6	9	–1	20	0	0	0	42	7.1
			ANA	61	6	19	25	3	46	0	0	0	90	6.7
			TOTAL	79	9	25	34	2	66	0	0	0	132	6.8
R	17	Jonathan Hedstrom	ANA	79	13	14	27	2	48	2	2	5	99	13.1
R	61 *	Corey Perry	ANA	56	13	12	25	1	50	4	0	2	98	13.3
L	29	Todd Fedoruk	ANA	76	4	19	23	6	174	0	0	1	69	5.8
C	26	Samuel Pahlsson	ANA	82	11	10	21	–1	34	0	3	1	116	9.5
D	24	Ruslan Salei	ANA	78	1	18	19	17	114	0	0	0	108	0.9
L	12	Jeff Friesen	WSH	33	3	4	7	–11	24	0	0	0	64	4.7
			ANA	18	1	3	4	–4	8	0	0	1	11	9.1
			TOTAL	51	4	7	11	–15	32	0	0	1	75	5.3
D	21	Sean O'Donnell	PHX	57	1	7	8	3	121	0	0	0	23	4.3
			ANA	21	1	2	3	3	26	0	0	0	10	10.0
			TOTAL	78	2	9	11	6	147	0	0	0	33	6.1
R	28	Tyler Wright	CBJ	18	0	4	4	–3	20	0	0	0	26	0.0
			ANA	25	2	2	4	2	31	0	0	1	17	11.8
			TOTAL	43	2	6	8	–1	51	0	0	1	43	4.7
D	33	Joe Dipenta	ANA	72	2	6	8	8	46	0	0	0	27	7.4
D	5	Vitaly Vishnevski	ANA	82	1	7	8	8	91	0	0	0	90	1.1
C	76 *	Dustin Penner	ANA	19	4	3	7	3	14	2	0	1	46	8.7
C	25 *	Zenon Konopka	ANA	23	4	3	7	–4	48	2	0	0	18	22.2
L	32	Travis Moen	ANA	39	4	1	5	–3	72	0	0	0	28	14.3
D	6	Jason Marshall	ANA	23	0	4	4	2	34	0	0	0	25	0.0
D	7	Bruno St. Jacques	ANA	1	1	0	1	1	0	0	0	0	2	50.0
L	37	Kip Brennan	ANA	12	0	1	1	–2	35	0	0	0	5	0.0
L	42	Trevor Gillies	ANA	1	0	0	0	0	21	0	0	0	1	0.0
C	40	Aaron Gavey	ANA	5	0	0	0	0	2	0	0	0	2	0.0

Goaltending

No.	Goaltender	GPI	Mins	Avg	W	L	OT	EN	SO	GA	SA	S%	G	A	PIM
30	* Ilja Bryzgalov	31	1575	2.51	13	12	1	2	1	66	733	.910	0	2	4
35	J-S Giguere	60	3381	2.66	30	15	11	4	2	150	1692	.911	0	0	20
	Totals	**82**	**4987**	**2.67**	**43**	**27**	**12**	**6**	**3**	**222**	**2431**	**.909**			

Playoffs

Pos	#	Player	Team	GP	G	A	Pts	+/–	PIM	PP	SH	GW	OT	S	%
R	13	Teemu Selanne	ANA	16	6	8	14	0	6	1	0	2	0	53	11.3
C	22	Todd Marchant	ANA	16	3	10	13	14	14	0	0	0	0	26	11.5
R	15	Joffrey Lupul	ANA	16	9	2	11	9	31	1	0	1	1	62	14.5
D	27	Scott Niedermayer	ANA	16	2	9	11	1	14	1	1	1	0	48	4.2
R	76 *	Dustin Penner	ANA	13	3	6	9	10	12	0	0	0	0	41	7.3
D	23 *	Francois Beauchemin	ANA	16	3	6	9	0	11	3	0	0	0	35	8.6
C	19	Andy McDonald	ANA	16	2	7	9	0	10	2	0	0	0	48	4.2
L	38 *	Chris Kunitz	ANA	16	3	5	8	–1	8	0	0	0	0	34	8.8
C	51 *	Ryan Getzlaf	ANA	16	3	4	7	–3	13	2	0	1	0	38	7.9
D	24	Ruslan Salei	ANA	16	3	2	5	10	18	0	0	1	0	27	11.1
D	21	Sean O'Donnell	ANA	16	2	3	5	8	23	0	0	1	1	10	20.0
C	26	Samuel Pahlsson	ANA	16	2	3	5	2	18	0	0	2	0	22	9.1
L	12	Jeff Friesen	ANA	16	3	1	4	–1	6	0	0	0	0	15	20.0
C	44	Rob Niedermayer	ANA	16	1	3	4	–1	10	1	0	0	0	24	4.2
D	5	Vitaly Vishnevski	ANA	16	0	4	4	2	10	0	0	0	0	8	0.0
R	61 *	Corey Perry	ANA	11	0	3	3	–4	16	0	0	0	0	14	0.0
L	32	Travis Moen	ANA	9	1	0	1	1	10	0	0	0	0	5	20.0
R	17	Jonathan Hedstrom	ANA	3	0	1	1	0	2	0	0	0	0	1	0.0
L	29	Todd Fedoruk	ANA	12	0	0	0	–1	16	0	0	0	0	12	0.0
D	33	Joe Dipenta	ANA	16	0	0	0	1	13	0	0	0	0	5	0.0

Goaltending

No.	Goaltender	GPI	Mins	Avg	W	L	EN	SO	GA	SA	S%	G	A	PIM
30	* Ilja Bryzgalov	11	659	1.46	6	4	2	3	16	285	.944	0	0	2
35	J-S Giguere	6	318	3.40	3	3	0	0	18	132	.864	0	0	0
	Totals	**16**	**988**	**2.19**	**9**	**7**	**2**	**3**	**36**	**419**	**.914**			

Club Records

Team

(Figures in brackets for season records are games played; records for fewest points, wins, ties, losses, goals, goals against are for 70 or more games)

Most Points	98	2005-06 (82)
Most Wins	43	2005-06 (82)
Most Ties	13	1996-97 (82), 1997-98 (82), 1998-99 (82)
Most Losses	46	1993-94 (84)
Most Goals	254	2005-06 (82)
Most Goals Against	261	1997-98 (82)
Fewest Points	65	1997-98 (82)
Fewest Wins	25	2000-01 (82)
Fewest Ties	5	1993-94 (84)
Fewest Losses	27	2002-03 (82), 2005-06 (82)
Fewest Goals	175	2001-02 (82)
Fewest Goals Against	193	2002-03 (82)

Longest Winning Streak

Overall	7	Feb. 20-Mar. 7/99
Home	7	Mar. 7-Apr. 4/06
Away	5	Nov. 26-Dec. 26/99

Longest Undefeated Streak

Overall	12	Feb. 22-Mar. 19/97 (7 wins, 5 ties)
Home	14	Feb. 12-Apr. 9/97 (10 wins, 4 ties)
Away	5	Five times

Longest Losing Streak

Overall	8	Oct. 12-30/96, Nov. 3-20/05
Home	8	Jan. 10-Feb. 9/01
Away	7	Oct. 8-Nov. 12/05

Longest Winless Streak

Overall	9	Three times
Home	11	Jan. 5-Feb. 14/01 (8 losses, 3 ties)
Away	13	Nov. 1-Dec. 27/03 (11 losses, 2 ties)

Most Shutouts, Season	9	2002-03 (82)
Most PIM, Season	1,843	1997-98 (82)
Most Goals, Game	8	Three times

Individual

Most Seasons	10	Steve Rucchin
Most Games	616	Steve Rucchin
Most Goals, Career	300	Paul Kariya
Most Assists, Career	369	Paul Kariya
Most Points, Career	669	Paul Kariya (300G, 369A)
Most PIM, Career	788	Dave Karpa
Most Shutouts, Career	27	Guy Hebert
Longest Consecutive Games Streak	237	Oleg Tverdovsky (Oct. 2/99-Mar. 24/02)
Most Goals, Season	52	Teemu Selanne (1997-98)
Most Assists, Season	62	Paul Kariya (1998-99)

Most Points, Season	109	Teemu Selanne (1996-97; 51G, 58A)
Most PIM, Season	285	Todd Ewen (1995-96)
Most Points, Defenseman, Season	63	Scott Niedermayer (2005-06; 13G, 50A)
Most Points, Center, Season	85	Andy McDonald (2005-06; 34G, 51A)
Most Points, Right Wing, Season	109	Teemu Selanne (1996-97; 51G, 58A)
Most Points, Left Wing, Season	108	Paul Kariya (1995-96; 50G, 58A)
Most Points, Rookie, Season	41	Chris Kunitz (2005-06; 19G, 22A)
Most Shutouts, Season	8	Jean-Sebastien Giguere (2002-03)
Most Goals, Game	3	Twenty-two times
Most Assists, Game	5	Dmitri Mironov (Dec. 12/97)
Most Points, Game	5	Six times

General Managers' History

Jack Ferreira, 1993-94 to 1997-98; Pierre Gauthier, 1998-99 to 2001-02; Bryan Murray, 2002-03, 2003-04; Al Coates, 2004-05; Brian Burke, 2005-06 to date.

Coaching History

Ron Wilson, 1993-94 to 1996-97; Pierre Page, 1997-98; Craig Hartsburg, 1998-99, 1999-2000; Craig Hartsburg and Guy Charron, 2000-01; Bryan Murray, 2001-02; Mike Babcock, 2002-03 to 2004-05; Randy Carlyle, 2005-06 to date.

Captains' History

Troy Loney, 1993-94; Randy Ladouceur, 1994-95, 1995-96; Paul Kariya, 1996-97; Paul Kariya and Teemu Selanne, 1997-98; Paul Kariya, 1998-99 to 2002-03; Steve Rucchin, 2003-04; Scott Niedermayer, 2005-06 to date.

All-time Record vs. Other Clubs

Regular Season

	At Home								On Road								Total							
	GP	W	L	T	OL	GF	GA	PTS	GP	W	L	T	OL	GF	GA	PTS	GP	W	L	T	OL	GF	GA	PTS
Atlanta	5	3	2	0	0	14	14	6	4	3	1	0	0	16	10	6	9	6	3	0	0	30	20	12
Boston	9	2	3	2	2	18	24	8	9	4	4	0	1	27	27	9	18	6	7	2	3	45	51	17
Buffalo	9	2	7	0	0	15	30	4	10	2	4	3	1	22	28	8	19	4	11	3	1	37	58	12
Calgary	28	14	8	6	0	88	73	34	27	9	17	1	0	62	78	19	55	23	25	7	0	150	151	53
Carolina	10	5	4	1	0	31	32	11	9	3	5	1	0	19	23	7	19	8	9	2	0	50	55	18
Chicago	24	14	7	3	0	65	49	31	26	12	12	2	0	65	71	26	50	26	19	5	0	130	120	57
Colorado	23	8	11	3	1	55	60	20	23	6	12	4	1	59	73	17	46	14	23	7	2	114	133	37
Columbus	10	6	2	1	1	30	22	14	10	3	7	0	0	19	27	6	20	9	9	1	1	49	49	20
Dallas	31	12	16	3	0	72	82	27	31	6	21	2	2	59	111	16	62	18	37	5	2	131	193	43
Detroit	24	8	12	4	0	55	68	20	24	2	17	3	2	52	89	9	48	10	29	7	2	107	157	29
Edmonton	28	15	11	2	0	76	74	32	27	8	16	0	3	56	65	19	55	23	27	2	3	132	139	51
Florida	10	4	5	1	0	28	30	9	8	2	3	2	1	17	23	7	18	6	8	3	1	45	53	16
Los Angeles	34	16	6	7	5	119	91	44	34	11	18	4	1	85	99	27	68	27	24	11	6	204	190	71
Minnesota	10	6	2	0	2	26	23	14	10	3	5	4	2	0	24	27	8	17	6	9	2	0	49	54	14
Montreal	8	3	5	0	0	25	27	6	9	3	4	2	0	24	29	15	28	17	6	2	3	77	53	39
Nashville	14	11	1	0	2	43	24	24	14	6	5	2	1	34	29	15	18	5	11	1	1	40	57	12
New Jersey	10	4	5	1	0	26	26	9	8	1	6	0	1	14	31	3	17	5	11	1	1	40	57	12
NY Islanders	9	2	4	3	0	18	24	7	8	3	4	1	0	23	24	7	17	5	8	4	0	41	48	14
NY Rangers	8	5	1	1	1	32	25	13	9	5	1	1	1	26	23	12	17	11	3	1	2	58	48	25
Ottawa	9	4	3	2	0	21	18	10	9	4	4	1	0	23	27	9	17	6	6	3	0	44	44	15
Philadelphia	9	4	3	2	0	30	28	10	8	2	3	3	0	17	22	7	17	6	6	5	0	47	50	17
Phoenix	31	19	9	3	0	93	75	41	30	16	10	2	2	90	83	36	61	35	19	5	2	183	158	77
Pittsburgh	8	5	3	0	0	29	24	10	9	2	5	2	0	27	29	6	17	7	8	2	0	56	53	16
St. Louis	24	9	13	2	0	66	72	20	24	8	11	4	1	63	74	21	48	17	24	5	2	129	146	41
San Jose	34	13	18	2	1	92	114	29	34	16	15	2	1	89	94	35	68	29	33	4	2	181	208	64
Tampa Bay	9	5	3	1	0	28	22	11	9	5	4	0	0	23	31	10	18	10	7	1	0	51	39	21
Toronto	11	5	5	1	0	34	28	11	16	2	10	4	0	32	53	8	27	7	15	5	0	66	81	19
Vancouver	27	8	11	7	1	67	79	24	28	10	16	2	0	66	94	22	55	18	27	9	1	133	173	46
Washington	10	6	2	1	1	31	25	14	9	4	5	0	0	22	16	10	19	11	6	1	1	53	41	24
Totals	**476**	**219**	**182**	**58**	**17**	**1327**	**1279**	**513**	**476**	**162**	**245**	**49**	**20**	**1147**	**1388**	**393**	**952**	**381**	**427**	**107**	**37**	**2474**	**2667**	**906**

Playoffs

	Series	W	L	GP	W	L	T	GF	GA	Last Mtg.	Rnd.	Result
Calgary	1	1	0	7	4	3	0	17	16	2006	CQF	W 4-3
Colorado	1	1	0	4	4	0	0	16	4	2006	CSF	W 4-0
Dallas	1	1	0	6	4	2	0	14	14	2003	CSF	W 4-2
Detroit	3	1	2	12	4	8	0	24	36	2003	CQF	W 4-0
Edmonton	1	0	1	5	1	4	0	13	16	2006	CF	L 1-4
Minnesota	1	1	0	4	4	0	0	9	1	2003	CF	W 4-0
New Jersey	1	0	1	7	3	4	0	19	19	2003	F	L 3-4
Phoenix	1	1	0	7	4	3	0	17	17	1997	CQF	W 4-3
Totals	**10**	**6**	**4**	**52**	**28**	**24**	**0**	**122**	**123**			

Carolina totals include Hartford, 1993-94 to 1996-97.
Colorado totals include Quebec, 1993-94 to 1994-95.
Phoenix totals include Winnipeg, 1993-94 to 1995-96.

Playoff Results 2006-2001

Year	Round	Opponent	Result	GF	GA
2006	CF	Edmonton	L 1-4	13	16
	CSF	Colorado	W 4-0	16	4
	CQF	Calgary	W 4-3	17	16
2003	F	New Jersey	L 3-4	.12	19
	CF	Minnesota	W 4-0	9	1
	CSF	Dallas	W 4-2	14	14
	CQF	Detroit	W 4-0	10	6

Abbreviations: Round: F – Final; CF – conference final; **CSF** – conference quarter-final; **CQF** – conference quarter-final

2005-06 Results

Oct.	5	at Chicago	5-3		9	Los Angeles	6-2
	8	at Nashville	2-3†		13	Washington	2-3*
	10	Edmonton	2-4		16	at Boston	3-4*
	14	Columbus	4-3		19	at Ottawa	4-3†
	16	at Minnesota	1-4		21	Florida	1-0
	19	at St. Louis	2-3		23	at Los Angeles	2-3†
	21	at Detroit	2-3		25	Edmonton	3-6
	23	Phoenix	5-3		26	at San Jose	2-0
	25	at Los Angeles	1-3		28	at Los Angeles	6-2
	26	Calgary	4-1		30	Los Angeles	4-3*
	28	St. Louis	6-4	Feb.	1	San Jose	4-6
	30	Phoenix	3-2		4	at San Jose	2-0
Nov.	1	Nashville	4-1		6	at Edmonton	5-6†
	3	at Colorado	3-4		8	at Calgary	1-3
	4	San Jose	0-1*		10	at Vancouver	3-1
	6	Minnesota	3-4†		12	Chicago	4-1
	12	at Phoenix	1-2*	Mar.	1	Detroit	0-2
	13	Dallas	1-3		3	Minnesota	4-2
	16	Dallas	2-4		5	Columbus	2-3†
	18	Colorado	2-3		7	San Jose	5-4*
	20	Vancouver	2-3		11	at Phoenix	5-3
	22	at Phoenix	2-1		12	Phoenix	5-2
	23	at Dallas	1-3		15	at Detroit	1-3
	25	Detroit	3-1		17	at Chicago	2-1
	27	Chicago	3-1		19	at Columbus	4-3
	30	Phoenix	6-1		20	at Dallas	2-1
Dec.	3	Atlanta	2-1		22	Colorado	5-4*
	6	Carolina	2-6		24	Nashville	6-3
	8	at Buffalo	2-3*		25	at Phoenix	5-2
	10	at Montreal	5-3		28	at Colorado	3-4
	12	at Toronto	2-3		29	at Dallas	1-2
	14	Tampa Bay	4-2		31	Dallas	5-4†
	16	Los Angeles	3-4†	Apr.	2	Vancouver	6-2
	18	San Jose	5-4		4	Los Angeles	6-2
	20	at San Jose	2-4		6	Dallas	3-5
	21	St. Louis	6-3		8	at Los Angeles	4-2
	28	at Columbus	0-1		10	at Vancouver	4-2
	31	at St. Louis	5-4†		11	at Calgary	0-3
Jan.	1	at Nashville	4-2		13	at Edmonton	1-2
	6	at Dallas	3-4†		15	at San Jose	3-6
	7	at Minnesota	1-4		17	Calgary	4-3

* – Overtime   † – Shootout

Entry Draft
Selections 2006-1993

2006 Pick		2002 Pick		1999 Pick		1995 Pick	
19	Mark Mitera	7	Joffrey Lupul	44	Jordan Leopold	4	Chad Kilger
38	Bryce Swan	37	Tim Brent	83	Niclas Havelid	29	Brian Wesenberg
83	John Degray	71	Brian Lee	105	Alexandr Chagodayev	55	Mike Leclerc
112	Matt Beleskey	103	Joonas Vihko	141	Maxim Rybin	107	Igor Nikulin
172	Petteri Wirtanen	140	George Davis	173	Jan Sandstrom	133	Peter LeBoutillier
		173	Luke Fritshaw	230	Petr Tenkrat	159	Mike LaPlante
2005 Pick		261	Francois Caron	258	Brian Gornick	185	Igor Karpenko
2	Bobby Ryan	267	Chris Petrow				
31	Brendan Mikkelson			**1998 Pick**		**1994 Pick**	
63	Jason Bailey	**2001 Pick**		5	Vitaly Vishnevski	2	Oleg Tverdovsky
127	Bobby Bolt	5	Stanislav Chistov	32	Stephen Peat	28	Johan Davidsson
141	Brian Salcido	35	Mark Popovic	112	Viktor Wallin	67	Craig Reichert
197	Jean-Philippe Levasseur	69	Joel Stepp	150	Trent Hunter	80	Byron Briske
		102	Timo Parssinen	178	Jesse Fibiger	106	Pavel Trnka
2004 Pick		105	Vladimir Korsunov	205	David Bernier	132	Bates Battaglia
9	Ladislav Smid	118	Brandon Rogers	233	Pelle Prestberg	158	Rocky Welsing
39	Jordan Smith	137	Joel Perreault	245	Andreas Andersson	184	Brad Englehart
74	Kyle Klubertanz	170	Jan Tabacek			236	Tommi Miettinen
75	Tim Brent	224	Tony Martensson	**1997 Pick**		262	Jeremy Stevenson
172	Matt Auffrey	232	Martin Gerber	18	Michael Holmqvist		
203	Gabriel Bouthillette	264	Pierre Parenteau	45	Maxim Balmochnykh	**1993 Pick**	
236	Matt Christie			72	Jay Legault	4	Paul Kariya
269	Janne Pesonen	**2000 Pick**		125	Luc Vaillancourt	30	Nikolai Tsulygin
		12	Alexei Smirnov	178	Tony Mohagen	56	Valeri Karpov
2003 Pick		44	Ilya Bryzgalov	181	Mat Snesrud	82	Joel Gagnon
19	Ryan Getzlaf	98	Jonas Ronnqvist	209	Rene Stussi	108	Mikhail Shtalenkov
28	Corey Perry	134	Peter Podhradsky	235	Tommi Degerman	134	Antti Aalto
86	Shane Hynes	153	Bill Cass			160	Matt Peterson
90	Juha Alen			**1996 Pick**		186	Tom Askey
119	Nathan Saunders			9	Ruslan Salei	212	Vitali Kozel
186	Drew Miller			35	Matt Cullen	238	Anatoli Fedotov
218	Dirk Southern			117	Brendan Buckley	264	David Penney
250	Shane O'Brien			149	Blaine Russell		
280	Ville Mantymaa			172	Timo Ahmaoja		
				198	Kevin Kellett		
				224	Tobias Johwelin		

Club Directory

Honda Center

Anaheim Ducks
Honda Center
2695 Katella Ave.
Anaheim, CA 92806
Phone **714/940-2900**
FAX 714/940-2953
Ticket Information 877/WILDWING
www.anaheimducks.com
Capacity: 17,174

Executive Management
Owners . . . . Susan and Henry Samueli
Chief Executive Officer . . . . Michael Schulman
Executive Vice President/General Manager . . . . . . Brian P. Burke
Executive Vice President/COO . . . . Tim Ryan
Senior Vice President/G.M., Arrowhead Pond . . . . Mike O'Donnell
Senior Vice President, Hockey Operations . . . . . . Bob Murray
Senior Vice President/Chief Marketing Officer . . . . Bob Wagner
Vice President of Sales & Marketing . . . . Steve Obert
Assistant General Manager . . . . David McNab
Senior Advisor to the General Manager . . . . Al Coates
Executive Assistant to the Exec. V.P./G.M. . . . . . . Maureen Nyeholt
Executive Assistant to the Exec. V.P./COO . . . . . . Cheryl Gorman
Executive Assistant/Booking & Contracts . . . . Jo-Ann Armstrong
Executive Assistants . . . . Janet Conley, Robin Schuette
Administrative Assistant, Hockey Operations . . . . . Christina Morrow

Coaching Staff
Head Coach . . . . Randy Carlyle
Assistant Coach . . . . Dave Farrish
Assistant Coach . . . . Newell Brown
Goaltending Consultant . . . . Francois Allaire
Video Coordinator . . . . Joe Trotta

Hockey Club Operations
Director of Professional Scouting . . . . Rick Paterson
Director of Amateur Scouting . . . . Alain Chainey
Scouting Staff . . . . Jeff Crisp, Jan-Åke Danielson, Brent Flahr, Todd Hearty, Pavel Routa, John McMorrow, Casey Hankinson, Konstantin Krylov
Head Trainer . . . . Tim Clark
Strength & Conditioning Coach . . . . Sean Skahan
Massage Therapist . . . . James Partida
Equipment Manager . . . . Mark O'Neill
Assistant Equipment Manager . . . . John Allaway
Portland Pirates (AHL) Head Coach . . . . Kevin Dineen
Portland Assistant Coaches . . . . Bruce Crowder, Eric Weinrich
Portland Athletic Trainer . . . . Angel Soutuyo
Portland Equipment Manager . . . . Brock Myles
Team Physicians . . . . Dr. Ronald Glousman, Dr. Craig Milhouse
Oral Surgeon . . . . Dr. Jeff Pulver
Visiting Team Equipment Attendant . . . . Chris Kincaid

Broadcasting
Director of Broadcasting . . . . Aaron Teats
Telecast Director . . . . Mike Levy
Associate Producer . . . . Bob Sipowich
TV, Fox Sports Prime Ticket (Cable), KDOC-TV . . . John Ahlers, Brian Hayward
Radio, KLAA AM 830 & Ducks Radio Network . . . . Steve Carroll, Brent Severyn

Communications
Director of Media & Communications . . . . Alex Gilchrist
Media & Communications Manager . . . . Merit Tully
Publications Manager . . . . Adam Brady
Communications & Team Travel Coordinator . . . . . Ryan Lichtenfels
Communications/Publicity Coordinator . . . . Lauren O'Gorman
Game Night Communications Staff . . Lisa Parris, Courtney Strayer, Larry Woodard, Lindsay McHolm

Community Relations
Director of Community Relations & Public Affairs . . Wendy Yamagishi
Community Relations Associates . . . . Jesse Tyler, Jennifer Walker

Entertainment
Director of Entertainment/Multi-Media . . . . Rod Murray
Production Manager . . . . Kent French
Entertainment Manager . . . . Chris Brown
Editor/Producer . . . . Rich Cooley

Fan Development
Director of Fan Development . . . . Matt Savant
Manager, School & Education Programs . . . . Joseph Hwang
Manager, Youth Hockey Programs . . . . Lynsie Estes

Finance and Administration
Vice President of Human Resources . . . . Kim Kutcher
Vice President of Finance . . . . Doug Heller
IT Manager . . . . Mike Wing

Sponsorship Sales
Director of Corporate Sales . . . . Wendy Grover
Senior Sales Manager . . . . Bonner Paddock
Sales Managers . . . . Matt Wiech, Bret Gerber
Sponsorship Manager . . . . Alex Evezich

Web Development
Director of Web Development . . . . Gloria Steinert

Marketing
Director of Marketing . . . . Tracie Jones
Premium Marketing Manager . . . . Melissa Goldstein
Marketing Manager . . . . Chris DiPierro
Promotions Manager . . . . Allison Wright
Signature Programs & Events Manager . . . . Kris Loomis
Manager of Graphic Design . . . . Seth Cable
Media Buying Manager . . . . Adam Mendelsohn

Premium Sales and Service
Director of Premium Sales & Service . . . . Jim Panetta
Premium Account Executive . . . . Geoff Matthews
Premium Manager . . . . Jana Cannavo

Ticketing
Manager of Ticket Operations . . . . James Bakken
Assistant Ticketing Manager . . . . Jonas Calicdan
Assistant Manager, Premium Ticketing . . . . Gina Bulgheroni

Ticket Sales and Customer Service
Director of Ticket Sales & Service . . . . Lisa Johnson
Manager of Group Sales . . . . Ken Bamberg
Manager of Season Sales . . . . Mike Morrow
Manager of Inside Sales & Telemarketing . . . . Damon Roschke

Vice President and General Manager

BURKE, BRIAN
Executive Vice President/General Manager, Anaheim Ducks.
Born in Providence, RI, June 30, 1955.

Brian Burke, former president and general manager of the Vancouver Canucks, was named Anaheim's new executive vice president and general manager on June 20, 2005. In his first year on the job in 2005-06, the Ducks reached the Western Conference Final.

Burke had served as the president and general manager of the Vancouver Canucks from 1998 to 2004. Under his leadership, the team increased its point total four consecutive years from 1999 to 2003. With 104 and 101 points respectively the last two NHL seasons (2002 to 2004), the Canucks joined only Detroit, Ottawa and Philadelphia to record consecutive seasons with at least 100 points. The 2003–04 Canucks finished with a record of 43-24-10-5 for 101 points, winning the Northwest Division. Over his last four seasons with the team, Burke engineered four consecutive seasons of at least 90 points.

Named by The Sporting News as NHL executive of the year in 2001, Burke acquired the majority of the current Canucks roster. Vancouver ranked third in the NHL in goals scored over his last three years with the team (753, behind only Detroit and Ottawa), including a league-leading 254 goals in 2001–02.

One of the most respected and experienced executives in the NHL, Burke originally joined the Canucks in June, 1987 as vice president and director of hockey operations. He left the Canucks in 1992 to become general manager of the Hartford Whalers, before being named NHL senior vice president and director of hockey operations (1993 to 1998). While working at the NHL league office, Burke worked closely with commissioner Gary Bettman on a wide variety of league issues and policies and was the NHL's chief disciplinarian.

Burke was born in New England and raised in Minnesota. He signed with the Philadelphia Flyers in 1977 as a player and was a member of the 1978 Calder Cup champion Maine Mariners. Burke then returned to Harvard Law School, where he graduated in 1981 before practicing law for six years in Boston. During his two stints in Vancouver, Burke was a valued and active member of the community, including his serving on the board of directors for Canuck Place.

Atlanta Thrashers

2005-06 Results: 41w-33l-3otl-5sol 90pts.
Third, Southeast Division

2006-07 Schedule

Oct.	Thu.	5	Tampa Bay	Tue.	2	at Minnesota
	Sat.	7	Florida	Fri.	5	Phoenix
	Mon.	9	at Tampa Bay	Sat.	6	at Washington
	Wed.	11	Boston	Tue.	9	at Montreal
	Fri.	13	Carolina	Fri.	12	at New Jersey
	Sat.	14	at Washington	Sat.	13	at Carolina
	Thu.	19	Washington	Tue.	16	Los Angeles
	Sat.	21	Florida	Thu.	18	Montreal
	Mon.	23	at Florida	Sat.	20	at NY Rangers*
	Wed.	25	at Carolina	Fri.	26	NY Islanders
	Thu.	26	at Philadelphia	Sun.	28	Philadelphia*
	Sat.	28	at Buffalo	Tue.	30	New Jersey
	Mon.	30	at Toronto	**Feb.** Thu.	1	NY Islanders
Nov.	Wed.	1	Carolina	Sat.	3	Philadelphia
	Fri.	3	at Washington	Tue.	6	Buffalo
	Sat.	4	at NY Islanders	Thu.	8	at Colorado
	Mon.	6	Boston	Sat.	10	at Vancouver
	Wed.	8	Ottawa	Sun.	11	at Edmonton
	Fri.	10	NY Rangers	Tue.	13	at Calgary
	Sat.	11	at Tampa Bay	Sat.	17	at Ottawa*
	Fri.	17	Dallas	Tue.	20	at Carolina
	Sat.	18	at Montreal	Thu.	22	Tampa Bay
	Wed.	22	at Washington	Sat.	24	Carolina
	Fri.	24	at Tampa Bay	Mon.	26	at Boston
	Sat.	25	Florida	**Mar.** Fri.	2	Ottawa
	Tue.	28	at NY Rangers	Sun.	4	Carolina*
	Thu.	30	Toronto	Tue.	6	Florida
Dec.	Sat.	2	at Florida	Thu.	8	Montreal
	Tue.	5	at Toronto	Sat.	10	at Florida
	Thu.	7	at Tampa Bay	Mon.	12	Washington
	Sat.	9	Pittsburgh	Thu.	15	at Philadelphia
	Wed.	13	Anaheim	Fri.	16	NY Rangers
	Fri.	15	Washington	Sun.	18	Buffalo*
	Sat.	16	at NY Islanders	Thu.	22	San Jose
	Tue.	19	at New Jersey	Sat.	24	at Pittsburgh*
	Thu.	21	Pittsburgh	Wed.	28	at Florida
	Sat.	23	New Jersey	Thu.	29	Toronto
	Tue.	26	Tampa Bay	Sat.	31	at Boston*
	Wed.	27	at Pittsburgh	**Apr.** Wed.	4	Washington
	Sat.	30	at Buffalo	Fri.	6	at Carolina
Jan.	Mon.	1	at Ottawa*	Sat.	7	Tampa Bay

* Denotes afternoon game.

Year-by-Year Record

Season	GP	Home				Road				Overall						Pts.	Finished	Playoff Result
		W	L	T	OL	W	L	T	OL	W	L	T	OL	GF	GA			
2005-06	82	24	13	....	4	17	20	....	4	41	33	....	8	281	275	90	3rd, Southeast Div.	Out of Playoffs
2004-05	....																	
2003-04	82	18	17	..	2	15	20	..	4	33	37	..	8	214	243	78	2nd, Southeast Div.	Out of Playoffs
2002-03	82	15	19	4	3	16	20	3	2	31	39	7	5	226	284	74	3rd, Southeast Div.	Out of Playoffs
2001-02	82	11	21	9	0	8	26	2	5	19	47	11	5	187	288	54	5th, Southeast Div.	Out of Playoffs
2000-01	82	10	23	6	2	13	22	6	0	23	45	12	2	211	289	60	4th, Southeast Div.	Out of Playoffs
1999-2000	82	9	26	3	3	5	31	4	1	14	57	7	4	170	313	39	5th, Southeast Div.	Out of Playoffs

Franchise date: June 25, 1997

EASTERN NHL CONFERENCE

SOUTHEAST DIVISION

8th NHL Season

Ilya Kovalchuk's scoring numbers rose for the fourth straight season in 2005-06, as he established career highs with 52 goals and 98 points. His 27 power-play goals were tops in the NHL.

2006-07 Player Personnel

FORWARDS	HT	WT	S	Place of Birth	Date	2005-06 Club
BABY, Stephen	6-5	235	R	Chicago, IL	1/31/80	Chicago (AHL)
BOULTON, Eric	6-1	225	L	Halifax, N.S.	8/17/76	Atlanta
BOURRET, Alex	5-10	210	L	Drummondville, Que.	10/5/86	Shawinigan
DESBIENS, Guillaume	6-2	210	L	Alma, Que.	4/20/85	Chicago (AHL)-Gwinnett
DOELL, Kevin	5-11	190	L	Saskatoon, Sask.	7/15/79	Chicago (AHL)
HAYDAR, Darren	5-9	166	L	Toronto, Ont.	10/22/79	Milwaukee
HOLIK, Bobby	6-4	240	R	Jihlava, Czech.	1/1/71	Atlanta
HOSSA, Marian	6-1	210	L	Stara Lubovna, Czech.	1/12/79	Atlanta
KAPANEN, Niko	5-9	180	L	Hameenlinna, Finland	4/29/78	Dallas
KOVALCHUK, Ilya	6-1	225	R	Tver, USSR	4/15/83	Atlanta
KOZLOV, Vyacheslav	5-10	190	L	Voskresensk, USSR	5/3/72	Atlanta
KROG, Jason	5-11	191	L	Fernie, B.C.	10/9/75	Geneve-Frolunda
LAROSE, Cory	5-0	191	L	Campbellton, N.B.	5/14/75	Langnau
LARSEN, Brad	6-0	210	L	Nakusp, B.C.	6/28/77	Atlanta-Chicago (AHL)
LaVALLEE, Jordan	6-3	215	L	Corvallis, OR	5/11/86	Quebec (QMJHL)
MacKENZIE, Derek	5-11	180	L	Sudbury, Ont.	6/11/81	Atlanta-Chicago (AHL)
MELLANBY, Scott	6-1	210	R	Montreal, Que.	6/11/66	Atlanta
METROPOLIT, Glen	5-10	195	R	Toronto, Ont.	6/25/74	Lugano
PAINCHAUD, Chad	5-11	195.	L	Mississauga, Ont.	5/27/86	Sarnia
RUCCHIN, Steve	6-2	211	L	Thunder Bay, Ont.	7/4/71	NY Rangers
SCHELL, Brad	6-1	190	L	Scott, Sask.	8/5/84	Chicago (AHL)-Gwinnett
SIM, Jon	5-10	190	L	New Glasgow, N.S.	9/29/77	Philadelphia-Florida
SLATER, Jim	6-0	190	L	Petoskey, MI	12/9/82	Atlanta-Chicago (AHL)
SMYTH, Adam	6-1	225	R	Wiarton, Ont.	9/8/83	Chicago (AHL)-Gwinnett
STERLING, Brett	5-7	185	L	Los Angeles, CA	4/24/84	Colorado College
STEWART, Karl	5-10	180	L	Aurora, Ont.	6/30/83	Atlanta-Chicago (AHL)
STUART, Colin	6-2	205	L	Rochester, MN	7/8/82	Chicago (AHL)
VIGIER, J.P.	6-0	200	R	Notre Dame de Lourdes, Man.	9/11/76	Atlanta
WANVIG, Kyle	6-2	219	R	Calgary, Alta.	1/29/81	Minnesota

DEFENSEMEN						
COBURN, Braydon	6-5	220	L	Calgary, Alta.	2/27/85	Atlanta-Chicago (AHL)
de VRIES, Greg	6-2	210	L	Sundridge, Ont.	1/4/73	Atlanta
EXELBY, Garnet	6-1	215	L	Ste. Anne, Man.	8/16/81	Atlanta
HAVELID, Niclas	6-0	200	L	Stockholm, Sweden	4/12/73	Atlanta
HNIDY, Shane	6-2	205	R	Neepawa, Man.	11/8/75	Atlanta
LEHMAN, Scott	6-1	205	L	Fort McMurray, Alta.	1/6/86	St. Michael's
MANSON, Lane	6-9	245	L	Watrous, Sask.	2/14/84	Gwinnett
McCARTHY, Steve	6-1	198	L	Trail, B.C.	2/3/81	Vancouver-Atlanta
OYSTRICK, Nathan	6-0	200	L	Regina, Sask.	12/17/82	Northern Mich.-Chi (AHL)
POPOVIC, Mark	6-1	210	L	Stoney Creek, Ont.	10/11/82	Atlanta-Chicago (AHL)
SHARROW, Jim	6-2	195	R	Framingham, MA	1/31/85	Chicago (AHL)-Gwinnett
SUTTON, Andy	6-6	245	L	Kingston, Ont.	3/10/75	Atlanta
VALABIK, Boris	6-7	230	L	Nitra, Czech.	2/14/86	Kitchener

GOALTENDERS	HT	WT	C	Place of Birth	Date	2005-06 Club
BRATHWAITE, Fred	5-7	175	L	Ottawa, Ont.	11/24/72	Kazan
CARUSO, David	6-1	210	L	Roswell, GA	6/18/82	Ohio State
GARNETT, Michael	6-1	205	L	Saskatoon, Sask.	11/25/82	Atlanta-Chicago (AHL)
HEDBERG, Johan	6-0	184	L	Leksand, Sweden	5/5/73	Dallas
LEHTONEN, Kari	6-4	195	L	Helsinki, Finland	11/16/83	Atlanta
TURPLE, Dan	6-5	220	L	Oakville, Ont.	1/1/85	Kitchener

2005-06 Scoring

*– rookie

Regular Season

Pos	#	Player	Team	GP	G	A	Pts	+/-	PIM	PP	SH	GW	S	%
L	17	Ilya Kovalchuk	ATL	78	52	46	98	-6	68	27	0	7	323	16.1
C	9	Marc Savard	ATL	82	28	69	97	7	100	14	1	4	212	13.2
R	18	Marian Hossa	ATL	80	39	53	92	17	67	14	7	7	341	11.4
L	13	Vyacheslav Kozlov	ATL.	82	25	46	71	14	33	8	0	1	206	12.1
R	12	Peter Bondra	ATL	60	21	18	39	-3	40	8	0	1	143	14.7
D	44	Jaroslav Modry	ATL	79	7	31	38	-9	76	5	0	2	143	4.9
D	7	Greg de Vries	ATL	82	7	28	35	1	76	3	0	2	111	6.3
R	19	Scott Mellanby	ATL	71	12	22	34	5	55	3	0	3	100	12.0
C	16	Bobby Holik	ATL	64	15	18	33	-6	79	5	0	0	151	9.9
D	28	Niclas Havelid	ATL	82	4	28	32	9	48	2	0	0	84	4.8
D	25	Andy Sutton	ATL	76	8	17	25	13	144	2	1	3	86	9.3
C	27	Patrik Stefan	ATL	64	10	14	24	3	36	2	0	3	81	12.3
C	10	Serge Aubin	ATL	74	7	17	24	-4	79	1	0	0	82	8.5
C	23 *	Jim Slater	ATL	71	10	10	20	1	46	1	0	0	108	9.3
R	26	Ronald Petrovicky	ATL	60	8	12	20	-8	62	2	0	2	70	11.4
D	5	Steve McCarthy	VAN	51	2	4	6	3	43	0	0	0	46	4.3
			ATL	16	7	3	10	0	8	2	0	0	20	35.0
			TOTAL	67	9	7	16	3	51	2	0	0	66	13.6
L	29	Brad Larsen	ATL	62	7	8	15	-3	21	0	3	1	48	14.6
R	11	Jean-Pierre Vigier	ATL	41	4	6	10	-4	40	1	1	0	53	7.5
D	2	Garnet Exelby	ATL	75	1	9	10	11	75	0	0	0	44	2.3
D	36	Eric Boulton	ATL	51	4	5	9	-4	87	0	0	0	28	14.3
D	34	Shane Hnidy	ATL	66	0	3	3	1	33	0	0	0	50	0.0
D	24	Ramzi Abid	ATL	6	0	2	2	1	6	0	0	0	6	0.0
D	4 *	Braydon Coburn	ATL	9	0	1	1	-2	4	0	0	0	4	0.0
C	21 *	Derek MacKenzie	ATL	11	0	1	1	0	8	0	0	0	11	0.0
D	5	Tomas Kloucek	ATL	1	0	0	0	0	0	0	0	0	0	0.0
C	47	Scott Barney	ATL	3	0	0	0	0	0	0	0	0	4	0.0
R	22	Francis Lessard	ATL	6	0	0	0	-2	0	0	0	0	0	0.0
D	39 *	Mark Popovic	ATL	7	0	0	0	-5	0	0	0	0	6	0.0
L	42 *	Karl Stewart	ATL	8	0	0	0	-3	15	0	0	0	6	0.0

Goaltending

No.	Goaltender	GPI	Mins	Avg	W	L	OT	EN	SO	GA	SA	S%	G	A	PIM
1	Mike Dunham	17	779	2.77	8	5	2	1	1	36	336	.893	0	0	0
32	* Kari Lehtonen	38	2166	2.94	20	15	0	3	2	106	1123	.906	0	1	4
35	* Michael Garnett	24	1271	3.45	10	7	4	2	2	73	634	.885	0	2	0
33	* Adam Berkhoel	9	473	3.81	2	4	1	0	0	30	255	.882	0	0	0
31	Steve Shields	5	266	4.29	1	2	1	0	0	19	129	.853	0	0	0
	Totals	82	4986	3.25	41	33	8	6	6	270	2483	.891			

Mike Dunham and Adam Berkhoel shared a shutout vs. Carolina on November 12, 2005.

Vice President and General Manager

WADDELL, DON
Vice President/General Manager, Atlanta Thrashers.
Born in Detroit, MI, August 19, 1958.

As the only general manager in the history of the Atlanta Thrashers, Don Waddell has established a foundation for long-term success in Atlanta by infusing the club with solid veterans to support a talented young line-up.

Waddell has built a team that set club records in wins (41) and points (90) in 2005-06, narrowly missing the playoffs. The team's first step toward achieving this success came during the 2002-03 season when it made a very dramatic second-half turnaround which was keyed by Waddell's decision to hire proven Stanley Cup winner Bob Hartley as coach. Prior to hiring Hartley, Waddell made his own successful NHL coaching debut with a win at Carolina on December 27, 2002. (He served as interim head coach until January 13, 2003.)

Waddell came to the franchise on June 23, 1998 – almost a year to the day after the NHL granted Atlanta a team. He has built the core of the franchise through the NHL Entry Draft and by stockpiling impressive prospects. He made Ilya Kovalchuk the first Russian player selected first overall in the history of the Entry Draft. In the 2002 Entry Draft, Waddell made Kari Lehtonen of Finland the highest-selected European goaltender in NHL draft history.

Waddell has a long-standing relationship with USA Hockey as a player and in management, and served as assistant general manager for the 2004 World Championship and World Cup teams. He was general manager of the 2005 World Championship team and the 2006 Olympic team. His extensive organizational experience also includes having previously built two professional hockey franchises: the San Diego Gulls and the Orlando Solar Bears of the now-defunct International Hockey League. He's also no stranger to winning through his role as assistant general manager for the Stanley Cup champion Detroit Red Wings during the 1997-98 season.

Waddell's playing experience includes more than nine seasons of professional hockey, mostly in the IHL. He was drafted by the NHL's Los Angeles Kings in 1978 and spent three years with the organization from 1980 to 1983. During a successful amateur career, Waddell helped the U.S. national team win the gold medal at the 1983 B-Pool World Championships. He played Division I hockey at Northern Michigan University from 1976 to 1980, where he majored in business management.

General Managers' History
Don Waddell, 1999-2000 to date.

Captains' History
Kelly Buchberger, 1999-2000; Steve Staios, 2000-01; Ray Ferraro, 2001-02; no captain, 2002-03; Shawn McEachern, 2003-04; Scott Mellanby, 2005-06.

Coaching History
Curt Fraser, 1999-2000 to 2001-02; Curt Fraser, Don Waddell and Bob Hartley, 2002-03; Bob Hartley, 2003-04 to date.

NHL Coaching Record

Season	Team		Regular Season				Playoffs		
		Games	W	L	T		Games	W	L
2002-03	Atlanta	10	4	5	1		....	....	....
	NHL Totals	10	4	5	1		....	....	....

Club Records

Team

(Figures in brackets for season records are games played.)

Most Points 90 2005-06 (82)
Most Wins 41 2005-06 (82)
Most Ties 12 2000-01 (82)
Most Losses 57 1999-2000 (82)
Most Goals 281 2005-06 (82)
Most Goals Against 313 1999-2000 (82)
Fewest Points 39 1999-2000 (82)
Fewest Wins 14 1999-2000 (82)
Fewest Ties 7 1999-2000 (82), 2002-03 (82)
Fewest Losses 33 2005-06 (82)
Fewest Goals 170 1999-2000 (82)
Fewest Goals Against 243 2003-04 (82)

Longest Winning Streak
Overall .... 5 Jan. 6-18/06
Home .... 6 Mar. 20-Apr. 15/06
Away .... 4 Jan. 13-Feb. 7/03

Longest Undefeated Streak
Overall .... 5 Oct. 9-18/03
(3 wins, 2 ties)
Home .... 6 Mar. 20-Apr. 15/06
(6 wins)
Away .... 7 Oct. 21-Nov. 13/00
(3 wins, 4 ties)

Longest Losing Streak
Overall .... 12 Jan. 24-Feb. 20/00
Home .... *11 Jan. 24-Mar. 16/00
Away .... 10 Oct. 6-Nov. 18/01

Longest Winless Streak
Overall .... 16 Jan. 16-Feb. 20/00
(2 ties, 14 losses)
Home .... *17 Jan. 19-Mar. 29/00
(2 ties, 15 losses)
Away .... 10 Oct. 6-Nov. 18/01
(10 losses)

Most Shutouts, Season 5 2005-06 (82)
Most PIM, Season 1,505 2003-04 (82)
Most Goals, Game .... 9 Nov. 12/05
(Atl. 9 at Car. 0)

Individual

Most Seasons .... 6 Patrik Stefan
Most Games .... 414 Patrik Stefan
Most Goals, Career .... 160 Ilya Kovalchuk
Most Assists, Career ...... 143 Ilya Kovalchuk
Most Points, Career ...... 303 Ilya Kovalchuk
(160G, 143A)
Most PIM, Career .... 532 Jeff Odgers
Most Shutouts, Career .... 5 Milan Hnilicka,
Pasi Nurminen
Longest Consecutive
Games Streak .... 136 Ilya Kovalchuk
(Nov. 2/02-Feb. 25/04)
Most Goals, Season .... 52 Ilya Kovalchuk
(2005-06)
Most Assists, Season .... 69 Marc Savard
(2005-06)
Most Points, Season .... 98 Ilya Kovalchuk
(2005-06; 52G, 46A)
Most PIM, Season .... 226 Jeff Odgers
(2000-01)

Most Points, Defenseman,
Season .... 38 Jaroslav Modry
(2005-06; 7G, 31A)
Most Points, Center,
Season .... 97 Marc Savard
(2005-06; 28G, 69A)
Most Points, Right Wing,
Season .... 92 Marian Hossa
(2005-06; 39G, 53A)
Most Points, Left Wing,
Season .... 98 Ilya Kovalchuk
(2005-06; 52G, 46A)
Most Points, Rookie,
Season .... 67 Dany Heatley
(2001-02; 26G, 41A)
Most Shutouts, Season .... 3 Milan Hnilicka
(2001-02),
Pasi Nurminen
(2003-04)
Most Goals, Game .... 4 Pascal Rheaume
(Jan. 19/02),
Ilya Kovalchuk
(Nov. 11/05)
Most Assists, Game .... 4 Five times
Most Points, Game .... 5 Six times
* NHL Record.

Out with injuries early in the year, Kari Lehtonen returned to win 20 games for the Thrashers.

All-time Record vs. Other Clubs

Regular Season

	At Home							On Road							Total						
	GP	W	L	T	OL	GF	GA	PTS	GP	W	L	T	OL	GF	GA	PTS	GP	W	L	T	OL	GF	GA	PTS
Anaheim	4	1	3	0	0	.10	16	2	5	2	3	0	0	10	14	4	9	3	6	0	0	20	30	6
Boston	12	5	7	0	0	34	36	10	12	4	4	2	2	45	43	12	24	9	11	2	2	79	79	22
Buffalo	12	7	3	1	1	38	36	16	12	5	7	0	0	34	49	10	24	12	10	1	1	72	85	26
Calgary	4	3	0	1	0	8	5	7	3	0	3	0	0	6	14	0	7	3	3	1	0	14	19	7
Carolina	17	4	7	3	3	44	51	14	17	4	10	1	2	49	57	11	34	8	17	4	5	93	108	25
Chicago	5	2	3	0	0	18	15	5	2	0	2	0	0	10	17	4	7	2	5	0	0	17	25	8
Colorado	4	1	1	1	1	7	8	4	4	2	1	0	1	11	12	5	8	3	2	1	2	18	20	11
Columbus	4	3	1	0	0	10	8	6	4	2	1	0	1	8	19	5	8	5	2	0	1	18	27	3
Dallas	4	0	3	0	1	9	16	1	5	1	4	0	0	13	26	2	9	1	7	0	1	22	42	4
Detroit	4	1	3	0	0	14	25	2	4	0	2	0	2	8	17	2	8	1	5	0	2	22	42	5
Edmonton	3	1	2	0	0	3	8	2	4	1	2	1	0	11	14	3	7	2	4	1	0	14	22	5
Florida	17	9	3	4	1	59	52	23	17	9	6	1	1	52	42	20	34	18	9	5	2	111	94	43
Los Angeles	4	1	3	0	0	7	16	2	5	1	4	0	0	15	26	2	9	2	7	0	0	22	42	4
Minnesota	2	0	2	0	0	6	10	0	3	0	2	1	0	5	8	1	5	0	4	1	0	11	18	1
Montreal	12	2	8	2	0	16	33	6	12	4	7	0	1	28	38	9	24	6	15	2	1	44	71	15
Nashville	5	3	0	1	1	16	13	8	12	5	6	0	1	24	35	11	24	8	13	3	0	47	79	19
New Jersey	12	3	7	2	0	23	44	8	12	5	5	0	0	29	45	10	24	8	14	2	0	63	91	18
NY Islanders	12	3	7	2	0	34	46	8	12	7	4	0	0	38	45	15	24	11	12	1	0	72	77	23
NY Rangers	12	4	8	0	0	34	42	8	12	4	5	0	2	38	35	15	24	5	13	1	2	72	105	16
Ottawa	12	3	8	1	0	40	51	7	12	4	7	0	0	32	54	9	24	7	16	1	0	66	97	13
Philadelphia	12	2	7	1	2	29	42	7	12	2	8	2	0	37	55	6	24	4	16	3	0	66	97	13
Phoenix	4	1	3	0	0	11	11	2	6	0	5	1	0	8	21	1	10	1	8	1	0	15	33	3
Pittsburgh	12	3	8	0	1	35	43	7	12	3	8	0	1	34	49	7	24	6	16	0	2	69	92	14
St. Louis	5	2	2	1	0	16	16	5	5	0	3	0	0	1	16	0	10	2	5	1	0	17	32	4
San Jose	4	1	2	1	0	7	11	3	5	1	4	0	0	10	21	1	9	2	6	1	0	17	32	4
Tampa Bay	17	9	5	3	0	55	47	21	17	5	9	1	1	46	62	13	34	14	14	4	2	101	109	34
Toronto	11	3	7	0	1	17	44	7	12	3	8	0	0	23	42	7	23	6	15	0	1	40	86	14
Vancouver	3	1	1	0	1	11	12	3	3	1	1	0	1	5	1	3	6	2	2	0	2	16	13	6
Washington	17	5	6	5	1	49	50	21	17	7	8	0	2	47	64	16	34	12	14	5	3	96	114	32
Totals	246	87	119	26	14	655	808	214	246	74	139	19	14	634	884	181	492	161	258	45	28	1289	1692	395

2005-06 Results

	Oct.							
Oct.	5	at Florida	0-2		4	at Carolina	3-4
	7	at Washington	7-3		6	Pittsburgh	6-4
	8	Washington	8-1		7	at Pittsburgh	4-3
	12	Montreal	0-2		11	Nashville	4-3†
	14	Toronto	1-9		13	St. Louis	2-0
	15	at NY Rangers	1-5		18	at Dallas	5-2
	20	Tampa Bay	0-6		19	at Los Angeles	6-8
	22	New Jersey	4-3		21	Tampa Bay	0-2
	25	at NY Islanders	3-4		24	Boston	2-3
	27	at Pittsburgh	5-7		26	Carolina	1-5
	29	Tampa Bay	2-3		28	at Carolina	1-4
Nov.	1	at Tampa Bay	6-4		31	Buffalo	2-5
	4	at Washington	2-3†	Feb.	3	at Florida	2-5
	5	at Philadelphia	3-4		4	Florida	6-4
	9	Pittsburgh	5-0		7	at Toronto	1-4
	11	Tampa Bay	5-2		9	at Ottawa	2-1
	12	at Carolina	9-0		11	at Montreal	2-1†
	16	NY Islanders	3-7	Mar.	1	at Buffalo	4-2
	18	at Philadelphia	6-5*		2	at Boston	2-3
	19	at Toronto	1-5		4	Washington	3-2*
	22	at Montreal	2-3†		6	Florida	4-3†
	24	NY Rangers	3-6		8	NY Rangers	3-2†
	26	Florida	7-4		10	Ottawa	1-3
	27	at Carolina	5-2		12	at NY Rangers	3-2*
	29	Carolina	3-4*		16	NY Islanders	4-2
Dec.	1	Toronto	0-4		18	Philadelphia	2-4
	3	at Anaheim	1-2		20	Buffalo	5-0
	5	at Phoenix	2-5		21	at Boston	5-4†
	6	at San Jose	3-5		23	New Jersey	6-5*
	9	Columbus	3-2		25	at NY Islanders	1-5
	11	Chicago	4-5†		30	at Tampa Bay	3-4
	13	Detroit	7-6	Apr.	1	Carolina	5-2
	15	at New Jersey	3-2*		3	at Ottawa	4-6
	17	Florida	2-1		5	at Florida	5-2
	22	Washington	5-6†		6	at Tampa Bay	2-3†
	23	at New Jersey	1-0		8	Carolina	5-2
	26	Montreal	4-0		11	at Tampa Bay	4-0
	28	Philadelphia	3-4*		13	Washington	5-3
	30	at Buffalo	1-4		15	Boston	4-3
Jan.	1	at Washington	5-2		17	at Washington	4-6
	2	Ottawa	8-3		18	at Florida	1-2*

* – Overtime   † – Shootout

Entry Draft
Selections 2006-1999

2006
Pick
12	Bryan Little
43	Riley Holzapfel
80	Michael Forney
135	Alex Kangas
165	Jonas Enlund
195	Jesse Martin
200	Arturs Kulda
210	Will O'Neill

2005
Pick
16	Alex Bourret
41	Ondrej Pavelec
49	Chad Denny
53	Andrew Kozek
116	Jordan Lavallee
135	Tomas Pospisil
187	Andrei Zubarev
207	Myles Stoesz

2004
Pick
10	Boris Valabik
40	Grant Lewis
76	Scott Lehman
106	Chad Painchaud
142	Juraj Gracik
186	Dan Turple
204	Miikka Tuomainen
237	Mitch Carefoot
270	Matt Siddall

2003
Pick
8	Braydon Coburn
110	Jim Sharrow
116	Guillaume Desbiens
136	Michael Vannelli
145	Brett Sterling
175	Mike Hamilton
203	Denis Loginov
239	Tobias Enstrom
269	Rylan Kaip

2002
Pick
2	Kari Lehtonen
30	Jim Slater
116	Patrick Dwyer
124	Lane Manson
144	Paul Flache
167	Brad Schell
198	Nathan Oystrick
230	Colton Fretter
236	Tyler Boldt
257	Pauli Levokari

2001
Pick
1	Ilya Kovalchuk
80	Michael Garnett
100	Brian Sipotz
112	Milan Gajic
135	Colin Stuart
189	Pasi Nurminen
199	Matt Suderman
201	Colin FitzRandolph
262	Mario Cartelli

2000
Pick
2	Dany Heatley
31	Ilja Nikulin
42	Libor Ustrnul
107	Carl Mallette
108	Blake Robson
147	Matt McRae
168	Zdenek Smid
178	Jeff Dwyer
180	Darcy Hordichuk
230	Samu Isosalo
242	Evan Nielsen
244	Eric Bowen
288	Mark McRae
290	Simon Gamache

1999
Pick
1	Patrik Stefan
30	Luke Sellars
68	Zdenek Blatny
98	David Kaczowka
99	Rob Zepp
128	Derek MacKenzie
159	Yuri Dobryshkin
188	Stephen Baby
217	Garnet Exelby
245	Tommi Santala
246	Raymond DiLauro

Coach

HARTLEY, BOB
Coach, Atlanta Thrashers. Born in Hawkesbury, Ont., September 7, 1960.

Bob Hartley, the second head coach in Thrashers history, has used his experience as a Stanley Cup champion in Colorado to develop the young talent in the organization. In 2005-06, Hartley's team set club records with 41 wins and 90 points. Hartley joined the Thrashers on January 14, 2003 and became the seventh-fastest coach in NHL history to reach 200 wins with a 4-2 Atlanta victory at New Jersey on February 7, 2003, in his 369th game.

Prior to joining the Thrashers, Hartley guided the Colorado Avalanche to the 2001 Stanley Cup championship. In the 2002 playoffs, he became the first NHL coach to lead his team to the Conference Final in each of his first four seasons with the same club. His Avalanche teams won at least 42 games in four consecutive seasons from 1998 to 2002.

Hartley became the second head coach of the Avalanche, and the 11th in franchise history, when he was named to the position on June 30, 1998. He served there until December 18, 2002 and is Colorado's all-time coaching victory leader (193), having guided the Avalanche to four consecutive Northwest Division titles and four straight trips to the Western Conference Final. Hartley guided the 2000-01 Avalanche to its most successful season in franchise history. Colorado established team records for points (118), wins (52) and goals against (192).

Hartley has been a proven winner at every level he has coached. Prior to joining Colorado, Hartley coached four seasons in the American Hockey League from 1994 to 1998, posting a 151-136-33 regular-season record and making four consecutive trips to the playoffs with Cornwall (1994 to 1996) and Hershey (1996 to 1998). He guided Hershey to the 1997 Calder Cup championship. After serving as an assistant coach for Cornwall in 1993-94, Hartley guided the Aces to the Southern Division title in 1994-95, and a trip to the Southern Division Final again in 1995-96. He led Laval to the Quebec Major Junior Hockey League championship and the Memorial Cup in 1993, and compiled an 81-52-7 record in two seasons with Laval from 1991 to 1993.

From 1987 to 1991, Hartley served as head coach for Hawkesbury of the Canadian Junior Hockey League. After enduring an 18-point season in his rookie term behind the Hawks' bench, he guided the club to an impressive 117-45-5 mark during the next three seasons, including CJHL championships in 1990 and 1991. His teams dropped just three postseason games in 1990 and 1991, going 24-3 in that span. Overall, his teams in Hawkesbury advanced to the playoffs four consecutive seasons and finished 31-13 in the postseason during that span.

Throughout his coaching career, Hartley has shared a strong sense of dedication with his community. He was honored in his hometown of Hawkesbury, where the local ice arena was renamed Complex Bob Hartley in August 1998 in recognition of his service to the community where he grew up and coached. He has been involved in hockey camps and charitable endeavors throughout his career.

Club Directory

Philips Arena

Atlanta Thrashers
Centennial Tower
101 Marietta St.
Suite 1900
Atlanta, GA 30303
Phone 404/878-3800
FAX 404/878-3712
www.atlantathrashers.com
Capacity: 18,545

Ownership – Atlanta Spirit, LLC
Owners . . . . Bruce Levenson, Michael Gearon, Steve Belkin, Ed Peskowitz, Rutherford Seydel, Todd Foreman, Felix Riccio

Executive Management – Atlanta Spirit, LLC
President and CEO/Alternate Governor . . . . Bernard J. Mullin
Executive V.P. and G.M./Alternate Governor . . . . . . Don Waddell
President of Philips Arena . . . . Bob Williams
Executive V.P. and Chief Financial Officer . . . . Bill Duffy
Executive V.P./Chief Marketing Officer . . . . Lou DePaoli
Sr. V.P. of Broadcast and Corporate Partnerships . . Tracy White
Sr. V.P. of Communications . . . . Tom Hughes
Sr. V.P and Chief Legal Officer . . . . T. Scott Wilkinson
Vice President of Business Development . . . . David Lee
Vice President of Strategic Planning . . . . Ailey Penningroth
Vice President of Community Development. . . . . . . LaVerne Henderson
Vice President of Marketing,
 Advertising and Branding . . . . Jim Pfeifer
Vice President of Sales of Service. . . . . Brendan Donahue
Vice President of Human Resources. . . . . Ginni Siler

Hockey Operations
Vice President and Assistant General Manager . . . . Larry Simmons
Director of Amateur Scouting and
 Player Development. Dan Marr
Director of Player Personnel . . . . Mark Dobson
Senior Director of Team Services . . . . Michele Zarzaca
Assistant to Don Waddell/Practice Facility
 Office Manager . . . . Leisa Ludwin

Coaching Staff
Head Coach. . . . . Bob Hartley
Assistant Coaches. . . . . Brad McCrimmon, Steve Weeks
Video Coach . . . . Tony Borgford

Scouting Staff
Head Scout. . . . . Marcel Comeau
Full-Time Scouts . . . . Evgeny Bogdanovich, Bernd Freimuller, Mark Hillier, Peter Mahovlich, Bob Owen, John Perpich, Normand Poisson
Part-Time Scouts . . . . Terry Brennan, Pat Carmichael, Kevin Sullivan

Training Staff
Strength and Conditioning Coach. . . . . Ray Bear
Head Athletic Trainer . . . . Craig Brewer
Assistant Athletic Trainer. . . . . Stephen Roberts
Massage Therapist . . . . Inar Treiguts

Equipment Staff
Head Equipment Manager . . . . Bobby Stewart
Assistant Equipment Managers . . . . Joe Guilmet, Jim Guilmet

Medical Staff
Team Physician . . . . Dr. Scott Gillogly
Team Internist . . . . Dr. William Whaley
Team Dentists . . . . Dr. Gary Saban, Dr. Lawrence Saltzman, Dr. Brett Silverman

Public Relations
Senior Director of Public Relations . . . . Rob Koch
Assistant Director of Media Relations . . . . Brian Potter
Manager of Media Relations . . . . John Heid

Miscellaneous
Television . . . . Turner South
Television Announcers . . . . J.P. Dellacamera, Darren Eliot
Flagship Radio Station. WCNN-AM 680 The Fan
Radio Announcers . . . . Dan Kamal, Billy Jaffe

Coaching Record

Season	Team	Games	W	L	O/T	Games	W	L
			Regular Season				**Playoffs**	
1991-92	Laval (QMJHL)	70	38	27	5	10	4	6
1992-93	Laval (QMJHL)	70	43	25	2	13	12	1
1994-95	Cornwall (AHL)	80	38	33	9	15	8	7
1995-96	Cornwall (AHL)	80	34	39	7	8	3	5
1996-97	Hershey (AHL)	80	43	27	10	23	15	8
1997-98	Hershey (AHL)	80	36	37	7	7	3	4
1998-99	**Colorado (NHL)**	82	44	28	10	19	11	8
1999-2000	**Colorado (NHL)**	82	42	29	11	17	11	6
2000-01*	**Colorado (NHL)**	82	52	20	10	23	16	7
2001-02	**Colorado (NHL)**	82	45	29	8	21	11	10
2002-03	**Colorado (NHL)**	31	10	12	9	....	....	....
	Atlanta (NHL)	39	19	15	5	....	....	....
2003-04	**Atlanta (NHL)**	82	33	41	8	....	....	....
2004-05	**Atlanta (NHL)**			Season Cancelled				
2005-06	**Atlanta (NHL)**	82	41	33	8	....	....	....
	NHL Totals	562	286	207	69	80	49	31

*Stanley Cup win.

Patrice Bergeron led the Bruins with 31 goals and 73 points in 2005-06.

Boston Bruins

2005-06 Results: 29W-37L-8OTL-8SOL 74PTS.
Fifth, Northeast Division

2006-07 Schedule

Month	Day	Date	Opponent
Oct.	Fri.	6	at Florida
	Sat.	7	at Tampa Bay
	Wed.	11	at Atlanta
	Thu.	12	at St. Louis
	Sat.	14	at NY Islanders
	Thu.	19	Calgary
	Sat.	21	Buffalo
	Thu.	26	Montreal
	Sat.	28	Ottawa
Nov.	Thu.	2	Buffalo
	Sat.	4	Tampa Bay
	Mon.	6	at Atlanta
	Thu.	9	Toronto
	Sat.	11	Ottawa
	Wed.	15	at Washington
	Thu.	16	Toronto
	Sat.	18	Washington
	Mon.	20	Florida
	Wed.	22	at Pittsburgh
	Fri.	24	Carolina*
	Sat.	25	at Toronto
	Tue.	28	at Toronto
	Thu.	30	Tampa Bay
Dec.	Sat.	2	at Carolina
	Mon.	4	at Montreal
	Thu.	7	Toronto
	Sat.	9	New Jersey
	Tue.	12	at Montreal
	Thu.	14	New Jersey
	Sat.	16	Florida
	Tue.	19	at Ottawa
	Thu.	21	Vancouver
	Sat.	23	Montreal
	Tue.	26	at Columbus
	Fri.	29	at Chicago
	Sat.	30	at Nashville
Jan.	Mon.	1	at Toronto
	Thu.	4	Toronto
	Sat.	6	Philadelphia*
	Tue.	9	at Ottawa
	Thu.	11	NY Islanders
	Sat.	13	at NY Rangers*
	Mon.	15	Buffalo*
	Wed.	17	at Buffalo
	Thu.	18	Pittsburgh
	Sat.	20	Ottawa
	Sat.	27	at Ottawa*
	Mon.	29	NY Rangers
	Tue.	30	at Buffalo
Feb.	Thu.	1	Buffalo
	Sat.	3	at Carolina
	Tue.	6	at Washington
	Thu.	8	Carolina
	Sat.	10	NY Islanders
	Tue.	13	Edmonton
	Thu.	15	at NY Islanders
	Sat.	17	at Buffalo
	Mon.	19	at Philadelphia
	Tue.	20	at Toronto
	Fri.	23	at Tampa Bay
	Sat.	24	at Florida
	Mon.	26	Atlanta
Mar.	Thu.	1	Philadelphia
	Sat.	3	Montreal
	Sun.	4	at New Jersey
	Tue.	6	Colorado
	Thu.	8	Minnesota
	Sat.	10	at Philadelphia*
	Sun.	11	at Detroit*
	Thu.	15	Washington
	Sat.	17	at NY Rangers
	Tue.	20	at Montreal
	Thu.	22	Montreal
	Sat.	24	NY Rangers*
	Sun.	25	at Pittsburgh*
	Tue.	27	at Ottawa
	Thu.	29	Pittsburgh
	Sat.	31	Atlanta*
Apr.	Sun.	1	at New Jersey*
	Tue.	3	at Montreal
	Thu.	5	at Buffalo
	Sat.	7	Ottawa

* Denotes afternoon game.

Franchise date: November 1, 1924

EASTERN CONFERENCE

NORTHEAST DIVISION

83rd NHL Season

Year-by-Year Record

		Home				Road				Overall								
Season	GP	W	L	T	OL	W	L	T	OL	W	L	T	OL	GF	GA	Pts.	Finished	Playoff Result
2005-06	82	16	15	....	10	13	22	....	6	29	37	....	16	230	266	74	5th, Northeast Div.	Out of Playoffs
2004-05	....	....	....	....	....	....	....	....	....	....	....	....	....	....	....	....		
2003-04	82	18	12	9	2	23	7	6	5	41	19	15	7	209	188	104	1st, Northeast Div.	Lost Conf. Quarter-Final
2002-03	82	23	11	5	2	13	20	6	2	36	31	11	4	245	237	87	3rd, Northeast Div.	Lost Conf. Quarter-Final
2001-02	82	23	11	2	5	20	13	4	4	43	24	6	9	236	201	101	1st, Northeast Div.	Lost Conf. Quarter-Final
2000-01	82	21	12	5	3	15	18	3	5	36	30	8	8	227	249	88	4th, Northeast Div.	Out of Playoffs
1999-2000	82	12	17	11	1	12	16	8	5	24	33	19	6	210	248	73	5th, Northeast Div.	Out of Playoffs
1998-99	82	22	10	9	....	17	20	4	....	39	30	13	....	214	181	91	3rd, Northeast Div.	Lost Conf. Semi-Final
1997-98	82	19	16	6	....	20	14	7	....	39	30	13	....	221	194	91	2nd, Northeast Div.	Lost Conf. Quarter-Final
1996-97	82	14	20	7	....	12	27	2	....	26	47	9	....	234	300	61	6th, Northeast Div.	Out of Playoffs
1995-96	82	22	14	5	....	18	17	6	....	40	31	11	....	282	269	91	2nd, Northeast Div.	Lost Conf. Quarter-Final
1994-95	48	15	7	2	....	12	11	1	....	27	18	3	....	150	127	57	3rd, Northeast Div.	Lost Conf. Quarter-Final
1993-94	84	20	14	8	....	22	15	5	....	42	29	13	....	289	252	97	2nd, Northeast Div.	Lost Conf. Semi-Final
1992-93	84	29	10	3	....	22	16	4	....	51	26	7	....	332	268	109	1st, Adams Div.	Lost Div. Semi-Final
1991-92	80	23	11	6	....	13	21	6	....	36	32	12	....	270	275	84	2nd, Adams Div.	Lost Conf. Championship
1990-91	80	26	9	5	....	18	15	7	....	44	24	12	....	299	264	100	1st, Adams Div.	Lost Conf. Championship
1989-90	80	23	13	4	....	23	12	5	....	46	25	9	....	289	232	101	1st, Adams Div.	Lost Final
1988-89	80	17	15	8	....	20	14	6	....	37	29	14	....	289	256	88	2nd, Adams Div.	Lost Div. Final
1987-88	80	24	13	3	....	20	17	3	....	44	30	6	....	300	251	94	2nd, Adams Div.	Lost Final
1986-87	80	25	11	4	....	14	23	3	....	39	34	7	....	301	276	85	3rd, Adams Div.	Lost Div. Semi-Final
1985-86	80	24	9	7	....	13	22	5	....	37	31	12	....	311	288	86	3rd, Adams Div.	Lost Div. Semi-Final
1984-85	80	21	15	4	....	15	19	6	....	36	34	10	....	303	287	82	4th, Adams Div.	Lost Div. Semi-Final
1983-84	80	25	12	3	....	24	13	3	....	49	25	6	....	336	261	104	1st, Adams Div.	Lost Div. Semi-Final
1982-83	80	28	6	6	....	22	14	4	....	50	20	10	....	327	228	110	1st, Adams Div.	Lost Conf. Championship
1981-82	80	24	12	4	....	19	15	6	....	43	27	10	....	323	285	96	2nd, Adams Div.	Lost Div. Final
1980-81	80	26	10	4	....	11	20	9	....	37	30	13	....	316	272	87	2nd, Adams Div.	Lost Prelim. Round
1979-80	80	27	9	4	....	19	12	9	....	46	21	13	....	310	234	105	2nd, Adams Div.	Lost Quarter-Final
1978-79	80	25	10	5	....	18	13	9	....	43	23	14	....	316	270	100	1st, Adams Div.	Lost Semi-Final
1977-78	80	29	6	5	....	22	12	6	....	51	18	11	....	333	218	113	1st, Adams Div.	Lost Final
1976-77	80	27	7	6	....	22	16	2	....	49	23	8	....	312	240	106	1st, Adams Div.	Lost Final
1975-76	80	27	5	8	....	21	10	9	....	48	15	17	....	313	237	113	1st, Adams Div.	Lost Semi-Final
1974-75	80	29	5	6	....	11	21	8	....	40	26	14	....	345	245	94	2nd, Adams Div.	Lost Prelim. Round
1973-74	78	33	4	2	....	19	13	7	....	52	17	9	....	349	221	113	1st, East Div.	Lost Final
1972-73	78	27	10	2	....	24	12	3	....	51	22	5	....	330	235	107	2nd, East Div.	Lost Quarter-Final
1971-72	**78**	**28**	**4**	**7**	....	**26**	**9**	**4**	....	**54**	**13**	**11**	....	**330**	**204**	**119**	**1st, East Div.**	**Won Stanley Cup**
1970-71	78	33	4	2	....	24	10	5	....	57	14	7	....	399	207	121	1st, East Div.	Lost Quarter-Final
1969-70	**76**	**27**	**3**	**8**	....	**13**	**14**	**11**	....	**40**	**17**	**19**	....	**277**	**216**	**99**	**2nd, East Div.**	**Won Stanley Cup**
1968-69	76	29	3	6	....	13	15	10	....	42	18	16	....	303	221	100	2nd, East Div.	Lost Semi-Final
1967-68	74	22	9	6	....	15	18	4	....	37	27	10	....	259	216	84	3rd, East Div.	Lost Quarter-Final
1966-67	70	10	21	4	....	7	22	6	....	17	43	10	....	182	253	44	6th,	Out of Playoffs
1965-66	70	15	17	3	....	6	26	3	....	21	43	6	....	174	275	48	5th,	Out of Playoffs
1964-65	70	12	17	6	....	9	26	0	....	21	43	6	....	166	253	48	6th,	Out of Playoffs
1963-64	70	13	15	7	....	5	25	5	....	18	40	12	....	170	212	48	6th,	Out of Playoffs
1962-63	70	7	18	10	....	7	21	7	....	14	39	17	....	198	281	45	6th,	Out of Playoffs
1961-62	70	9	22	4	....	6	25	4	....	15	47	8	....	177	306	38	6th,	Out of Playoffs
1960-61	70	13	17	5	....	2	25	8	....	15	42	13	....	176	254	43	6th,	Out of Playoffs
1959-60	70	21	11	3	....	7	23	5	....	28	34	8	....	220	241	64	5th,	Out of Playoffs
1958-59	70	21	11	3	....	11	18	6	....	32	29	9	....	205	215	73	2nd,	Lost Semi-Final
1957-58	70	15	14	6	....	12	14	9	....	27	28	15	....	199	194	69	4th,	Lost Final
1956-57	70	20	9	6	....	14	15	6	....	34	24	12	....	195	174	80	3rd,	Lost Final
1955-56	70	14	14	7	....	9	20	6	....	23	34	13	....	147	185	59	5th,	Out of Playoffs
1954-55	70	16	10	9	....	7	16	12	....	23	26	21	....	169	188	67	4th,	Lost Semi-Final
1953-54	70	22	8	5	....	10	20	5	....	32	28	10	....	177	181	74	4th,	Lost Semi-Final
1952-53	70	19	10	6	....	9	19	7	....	28	29	13	....	152	172	69	3rd,	Lost Final
1951-52	70	15	12	8	....	10	17	8	....	25	29	16	....	162	176	66	4th,	Lost Semi-Final
1950-51	70	13	12	10	....	9	18	8	....	22	30	18	....	178	197	62	4th,	Lost Semi-Final
1949-50	70	15	12	8	....	7	20	8	....	22	32	16	....	198	228	60	5th,	Out of Playoffs
1948-49	60	18	10	2	....	11	13	6	....	29	23	8	....	178	163	66	2nd,	Lost Semi-Final
1947-48	60	12	8	10	....	11	16	3	....	23	24	13	....	167	168	59	3rd,	Lost Semi-Final
1946-47	60	18	7	5	....	8	16	6	....	26	23	11	....	190	175	63	3rd,	Lost Semi-Final
1945-46	50	11	5	4	....	13	13	4	....	24	18	8	....	167	156	56	2nd,	Lost Final
1944-45	50	11	12	2	....	5	18	2	....	16	30	4	....	179	219	36	4th,	Lost Semi-Final
1943-44	50	15	8	2	....	4	18	3	....	19	26	5	....	223	268	43	5th,	Out of Playoffs
1942-43	50	17	3	5	....	7	14	4	....	24	17	9	....	195	176	57	2nd,	Lost Final
1941-42	48	17	4	3	....	8	13	3	....	25	17	6	....	160	118	56	3rd,	Lost Semi-Final
1940-41	**48**	**15**	**4**	**5**	....	**12**	**4**	**8**	....	**27**	**8**	**13**	....	**168**	**102**	**67**	**1st,**	**Won Stanley Cup**
1939-40	48	20	3	1	....	11	9	4	....	31	12	5	....	170	98	67	1st,	Lost Semi-Final
1938-39	**48**	**20**	**2**	**2**	....	**16**	**8**	**0**	....	**36**	**10**	**2**	....	**156**	**76**	**74**	**1st,**	**Won Stanley Cup**
1937-38	48	18	3	3	....	12	8	4	....	30	11	7	....	142	89	67	1st, Amn. Div.	Lost Semi-Final
1936-37	48	9	11	4	....	14	7	3	....	23	18	7	....	120	110	53	2nd, Amn. Div.	Lost Quarter-Final
1935-36	48	15	8	1	....	7	12	5	....	22	20	6	....	92	83	50	2nd, Amn. Div.	Lost Quarter-Final
1934-35	48	17	7	0	....	9	9	6	....	26	16	6	....	129	112	58	1st, Amn. Div.	Lost Semi-Final
1933-34	48	11	11	2	....	7	14	3	....	18	25	5	....	111	130	41	4th, Amn. Div.	Out of Playoffs
1932-33	48	19	2	3	....	6	13	5	....	25	15	8	....	124	88	58	1st, Amn. Div.	Lost Semi-Final
1931-32	48	11	10	3	....	4	11	9	....	15	21	12	....	122	117	42	4th, Amn. Div.	Out of Playoffs
1930-31	44	16	1	5	....	12	9	1	....	28	10	6	....	143	90	62	1st, Amn. Div.	Lost Semi-Final
1929-30	44	21	1	0	....	17	4	1	....	38	5	1	....	179	98	77	1st, Amn. Div.	Lost Final
1928-29	**44**	**15**	**6**	**1**	....	**11**	**7**	**4**	....	**26**	**13**	**5**	....	**89**	**52**	**57**	**1st, Amn. Div.**	**Won Stanley Cup**
1927-28	44	13	4	5	....	7	9	6	....	20	13	11	....	77	70	51	1st, Amn. Div.	Lost Semi-Final
1926-27	44	15	7	0	....	6	13	3	....	21	20	3	....	97	89	45	2nd, Amn. Div.	Lost Final
1925-26	36	10	7	1	....	7	8	3	....	17	15	4	....	92	85	38	4th,	Out of Playoffs
1924-25	30	3	12	0	....	3	12	0	....	6	24	0	....	49	119	12	6th,	Out of Playoffs

2006-07 Player Personnel

FORWARDS	HT	WT	S	Place of Birth	Date	2005-06 Club
AXELSSON, P.J.	6-1	184	L	Kungalv, Sweden	2/26/75	Boston
BERGERON, Patrice	6-0	197	R	Ancienne-Lorette, Que.	7/24/85	Boston
BOYES, Brad	6-1	195	R	Mississauga, Ont.	4/17/82	Boston
COLLINS, Chris	5-10	190	R	Fairport, NY	6/8/84	Boston College
DiCASMIRRO, Nate	5-11	205	L	Atikokan, Ont	9/27/78	Grand Rapids
DONOVAN, Shean	6-2	209	R	Timmins, Ont.	1/22/75	Calgary
HOGGAN, Jeff	6-1	195	L	Hope, B.C.	2/1/78	St. Louis
KALUS, Petr	6-1	186	L	Ostrava, Czech.	6/29/87	Regina
KARSUMS, Martins	5-10	180	R	Riga, Latvia	2/26/86	Moncton
KESSEL, Phil	6-0	189	R	Madison, WI	10/2/87	U. of Minnesota
KREJCI, Dave	5-11	176	R	Sternberk, Czech.	4/28/86	Gatineau
MOWERS, Mark	5-11	185	R	Decatur, GA	2/16/74	Detroit
MURRAY, Glen	6-3	225	R	Halifax, N.S.	11/1/72	Boston
PACKARD, Dennis	6-4	235	L	St. Catherines, Ont.	2/9/82	Springfield-Johnstown
PELLETIER, Pascal	5-11	197	R	Labrador City, Nfld.	6/16/83	Gwinnett-Providence (AHL)
PRIMEAU, Wayne	6-4	230	L	Scarborough, Ont.	6/4/76	San Jose-Boston
REDENBACH, Tyler	6-0	195	L	Melville, Sask.	9/25/84	Providence (AHL)
REICH, Jeremy	6-1	204	L	Craik, Sask.	2/11/79	Providence (AHL)
SAVARD, Marc	5-10	195	L	Ottawa, Ont.	7/17/77	Atlanta
STASTNY, Yan	5-11	175	L	Quebec City, Que.	9/30/82	Edm-Iowa-Bos-Prov (AHL)
STURM, Marco	6-0	195	L	Dingolfing, West Germany	9/8/78	San Jose-Boston
TENKRAT, Petr	6-0	183	R	Kladno, Czech.	5/31/77	Karpat
THOMPSON, Nate	6-0	206	L	Anchorage, AK	10/5/84	Providence (AHL)
VERSTEEG, Kris	5-9	160	R	Lethbridge, Alta.	5/13/86	Kamlps-R.Deer-Prov (AHL)
WALTER, Ben	6-1	195	L	Beaconsfield, Que.	5/11/84	Boston-Providence (AHL)
ZHAMNOV, Alex	6-1	204	L	Moscow, USSR	10/1/70	Boston
DEFENSEMEN						
ALBERTS, Andrew	6-4	218	L	Minneapolis, MN	6/30/81	Boston-Providence (AHL)
ALLEN, Bobby	6-0	200	L	Braintree, MA	11/14/78	Albany
BROOKBANK, Wade	6-4	225	L	Lanigan, Sask.	9/29/77	Vancouver
CHARA, Zdeno	6-9	260	L	Trencin, Czech.	3/18/77	Ottawa
DEMPSEY, Nathan	6-0	190	R	Spruce Grove, Alta.	7/14/74	Los Angeles
JURCINA, Milan	6-4	233	R	Liptovsky Mikulas, Czech.	6/7/83	Boston-Providence (AHL)
LASHOFF, Matt	6-1	201	L	East Greenbush, NY	9/29/86	Kitchener-Providence (AHL)
LEACH, Jay	6-4	220	L	Syracuse, NY	9/2/79	Boston-Providence (AHL)
MARA, Paul	6-4	219	L	Ridgewood, NJ	9/7/79	Phoenix
SIGALET, Jonathan	6-1	185	L	Vancouver, B.C.	2/12/86	Providence (AHL)
STUART, Brad	6-2	220	L	Rocky Mountain House, Alta.	11/6/79	San Jose-Boston
STUART, Mark	6-1	216	L	Rochester, MN	4/27/84	Boston-Providence (AHL)
YORK, Jason	6-1	208	R	Nepean, Ont.	5/20/70	Lugano

GOALTENDERS	HT	WT	C	Place of Birth	Date	2005-06 Club
BROWN, Mike	6-0	203	L	Syracuse, NY	3/4/85	Prov (AHL)-S.Carolina-Day
FINLEY, Brian	6-3	205	R	Sault Ste. Marie, Ont.	7/13/81	Nashville-Milwaukee
SIGALET, Jordan	6-1	170	L	New Westminster, B.C.	2/19/81	Boston-Providence (AHL)
THOMAS, Tim	5-11	181	L	Flint, MI	4/15/74	Boston-Providence (AHL)
TOIVONEN, Hannu	6-2	200	L	Kalvola, Finland	5/18/84	Boston

Coach

LEWIS, DAVE
Coach, Boston Bruins. Born in Kindersley, Sask., July 3, 1953.

The Boston Bruins announced the signing of Dave Lewis as the 27th head coach in team history on June 29, 2006. Lewis came to Boston after 20 years with the Detroit Red Wings as a player, assistant coach, associate coach, head coach and professional scout. He joined the Red Wings coaching staff immediately upon his retirement as a player in November of 1987 and served as an assistant coach of the team through the 1994-95 season. He was named an associate coach at the start of the 1995-96 campaign and remained in that position for six years. He worked under three head coaches during those 15-years – Jacques Demers, Bryan Murray and a nine-year span under legendary coach Scotty Bowman – and won Stanley Cup championships with the team, in 1996-97, 1997-98 and 2001-02.

Lewis was named as the Red Wings head coach on July 17, 2002 upon Bowman's retirement and remained behind the Red Wings bench for two seasons. He led the Red Wings to two 48-win and 100+ point seasons and two Central Division titles. The Red Wings took the President's Trophy with the league's top record in 2002-03. He was replaced behind the bench following the 2004-05 lockout year and worked for the team as a professional leagues scout in 2005-06.

The native of Kindersley, Saskatchewan played two seasons of junior hockey with the Saskatoon Blades and was drafted by the New York Islanders as their second pick, 33rd overall, in the 1973 NHL Amateur Draft. The 6'2" defenseman never played a game in the minor leagues, making the jump directly from juniors to the NHL with the Islanders in 1973-74. He played seven seasons in New York before going to the Los Angeles Kings in a trade on March 10, 1980 and played three seasons with the Kings before moving again in a trade to New Jersey, where he also remained for three seasons. He signed with the Red Wings as a free agent on July 27, 1986 and completed his playing career in Detroit. He played his 1,000th NHL game on April 1, 1987 versus Philadelphia and retired as a player on November 6, 1987 to join the Red Wings' coaching staff. His 15-year career totals as a player were 36 goals and 187 assists for 223 points and 953 penalty minutes in 1,008 career NHL games.

Coaching Record

		Regular Season				Playoffs		
Season	**Team**	**Games**	**W**	**L**	**T**	**Games**	**W**	**L**
1998-99	**Detroit (NHL)**	**5**	**4**	**1**	**0**	....	....	....
2002-03	**Detroit (NHL)**	**82**	**48**	**24**	**10**	**4**	**0**	**4**
2003-04	**Detroit (NHL)**	**82**	**48**	**23**	**11**	**12**	**6**	**6**
2004-05	**Detroit (NHL)**				Season Cancelled			
	NHL Totals	**169**	**100**	**48**	**21**	**16**	**6**	**10**

Shared a 4-1-0 record with associate coach Barry Smith while serving as co-head coaches until Scotty Bowman received medical clearance and returned to coaching on October 23, 1998.

2005-06 Scoring

* – rookie

Regular Season

Pos	#	Player	Team	GP	G	A	Pts	+/–	PIM	PP	SH	GW	S	%
C	37	Patrice Bergeron	BOS	81	31	42	73	3	22	12	1	6	310	10.0
C	26 *	Brad Boyes	BOS	82	26	43	69	11	30	8	0	3	203	12.8
L	16	Marco Sturm	S.J.	23	6	10	16	–8	16	3	0	0	48	12.5
			BOS	51	23	20	43	14	32	5	0	6	132	17.4
			TOTAL	74	29	30	59	6	48	8	0	6	180	16.1
R	27	Glen Murray	BOS	64	24	29	53	–8	52	6	1	3	195	12.3
D	6	Brad Stuart	S.J.	23	2	10	12	–2	14	1	0	0	41	4.9
			BOS	55	10	21	31	–6	38	6	0	2	122	8.2
			TOTAL	78	12	31	43	–8	52	7	0	2	163	7.4
C	36	Marty Reasoner	EDM	58	9	17	26	–12	20	5	0	1	63	14.3
			BOS	19	2	6	8	–2	8	1	0	0	39	5.1
			TOTAL	77	11	23	34	–14	28	6	0	1	102	10.8
D	22	Brian Leetch	BOS	61	5	27	32	–10	36	4	0	0	130	3.8
L	11	P.J. Axelsson	BOS	59	10	18	28	–3	4	1	2	1	113	8.8
L	21	Brad Isbister	BOS	58	6	17	23	–2	46	1	0	0	112	5.4
C	20	Wayne Primeau	S.J.	21	5	3	8	–6	17	1	1	1	35	14.3
			BOS	50	6	8	14	–10	40	0	0	0	66	9.1
			TOTAL	71	11	11	22	–16	57	1	1	1	101	10.9
C	39	Travis Green	BOS	82	10	12	22	–2	79	0	2	1	118	8.5
D	55	David Tanabe	PHX	21	0	4	4	–5	8	0	0	0	21	0.0
			BOS	54	4	12	16	0	48	0	0	1	82	4.9
			TOTAL	75	4	16	20	–5	56	0	0	1	103	3.9
D	71	Jiri Slegr	BOS	32	5	11	16	–2	56	4	0	0	59	8.5
D	44	Nick Boynton	BOS	54	5	7	12	–7	93	1	1	0	89	5.6
L	23	Josh Langfeld	S.J.	39	2	9	11	4	16	0	1	0	53	3.8
			BOS	18	0	1	1	–6	10	0	0	0	32	0.0
			TOTAL	57	2	10	12	–2	26	0	1	0	85	2.4
D	68 *	Milan Jurcina	BOS	51	6	5	11	3	54	2	0	0	64	9.4
R	29	Mariusz Czerkawski	TOR	19	4	1	5	–2	6	1	0	0	41	9.8
			BOS	16	4	1	5	–4	4	0	0	0	31	12.9
			TOTAL	35	8	2	10	–6	10	1	0	0	72	11.1
R	12	Tom Fitzgerald	BOS	71	4	6	10	–10	40	0	0	0	50	8.0
C	10	Alex Zhamnov	BOS	24	1	9	10	–4	30	0	0	1	37	2.7
D	25	Hal Gill	BOS	80	1	9	10	–4	124	0	0	0	68	1.5
R	83	Patrick Leahy	BOS	43	4	4	8	–2	19	0	0	0	46	8.7
L	17	Shawn McEachern	BOS	28	2	6	8	–12	22	1	0	0	40	5.0
D	41 *	Andrew Alberts	BOS	73	1	6	7	3	68	0	1	0	30	3.3
R	47	Eric Nickulas	BOS	16	2	4	6	2	8	0	0	0	14	14.3
L	28	Dan Lacouture	BOS	55	2	2	4	–6	53	0	1	0	37	5.4
C	43 *	Yan Stastny	EDM	3	0	0	0	–2	0	0	0	0	1	0.0
			BOS	17	1	3	4	–2	10	0	0	0	13	7.7
			TOTAL	20	1	3	4	–4	10	0	0	0	14	7.1
D	18	Ian Moran	BOS	12	1	1	2	0	10	0	0	0	7	14.3
D	45 *	Mark Stuart	BOS	17	1	1	2	–1	10	0	0	0	9	11.1
R	50	Ben Guite	BOS	1	0	0	0	0	0	0	0	0	2	0.0
D	48	Jay Leach	BOS	2	0	0	0	1	7	0	0	0	0	0.0
C	40	Eric Healey	BOS	2	0	0	0	0	2	0	0	0	1	0.0
L	51 *	Nathan Robinson	BOS	2	0	0	0	0	0	0	0	0	1	0.0
L	89 *	Zdenek Blatny	BOS	5	0	0	0	–2	2	0	0	0	3	0.0
C	72	Ben Walter	BOS	6	0	0	0	2	4	0	0	0	6	0.0

Goaltending

No.	Goaltender	GPI	Mins	Avg	W	L	OT	EN	SO	GA	SA	S%	G	A	PIM
57	* Jordan Sigalet	1	1	0.00	0	0	0	0	0	0	0	.000	0	0	0
33	* Hannu Toivonen	20	1163	2.63	9	5	4	0	1	51	590	.914	0	0	6
30	Tim Thomas	38	2187	2.77	12	13	10	3	1	101	1213	.917	0	1	4
1	Andrew Raycroft	30	1619	3.71	8	19	2	3	0	100	824	.879	0	0	0
	Totals	**82**	**4997**	**3.10**	**29**	**37**	**16**	**6**	**2**	**258**	**2633**	**.902**			

Captains' History

No captain, 1924-25 to 1926-27; Lionel Hitchman, 1927-28 to 1930-31; George Owen, 1931-32; Dit Clapper, 1932-33 to 1937-38; Cooney Weiland, 1938-39; Dit Clapper, 1939-40 to 1945-46; Dit Clapper and John Crawford, 1946-47; John Crawford 1947-48 to 1949-50; Milt Schmidt, 1950-51 to 1953-54; Milt Schmidt, Ed Sanford, 1954-55; Fern Flaman, 1955-56 to 1960-61; Don McKenney, 1961-62, 1962-63; Leo Boivin, 1963-64 to 1965-66; John Bucyk, 1966-67; no captain, 1967-68 to 1972-73; John Bucyk, 1973-74 to 1976-77; Wayne Cashman, 1977-78 to 1982-83; Terry O'Reilly, 1983-84, 1984-85; Raymond Bourque, Rick Middleton (co-captains) 1985-86 to 1987-88; Raymond Bourque, 1988-89 to 1999-2000; Jason Allison, 2000-01; no captain, 2001-02; Joe Thornton, 2002-03, 2003-04; Joe Thornton and no captain, 2005-06.

Coaching History

Art Ross, 1924-25 to 1927-28; Cy Denneny, 1928-29; Art Ross, 1929-30 to 1933-34; Frank Patrick, 1934-35, 1935-36; Art Ross, 1936-37 to 1938-39; Cooney Weiland, 1939-40, 1940-41; Art Ross, 1941-42 to 1944-45; Dit Clapper, 1945-46 to 1948-49; Georges Boucher, 1949-50; Lynn Patrick, 1950-51 to 1953-54; Lynn Patrick and Milt Schmidt, 1954-55; Milt Schmidt, 1955-56 to 1960-61; Phil Watson, 1961-62; Phil Watson and Milt Schmidt, 1962-63; Milt Schmidt, 1963-64 to 1965-66; Harry Sinden, 1966-67 to 1969-70; Tom Johnson, 1970-71, 1971-72; Tom Johnson and Bep Guidolin, 1972-73; Bep Guidolin, 1973-74; Don Cherry, 1974-75 to 1978-79; Fred Creighton and Harry Sinden, 1979-80; Gerry Cheevers, 1980-81 to 1983-84; Gerry Cheevers and Harry Sinden, 1984-85; Butch Goring, 1985-86; Butch Goring and Terry O'Reilly, 1986-87; Terry O'Reilly, 1987-88, 1988-89; Mike Milbury, 1989-90, 1990-91; Rick Bowness, 1991-92; Brian Sutter, 1992-93 to 1994-95; Steve Kasper, 1995-96, 1996-97; Pat Burns, 1997-98 to 1999-2000; Pat Burns and Mike Keenan, 2000-01; Robbie Ftorek, 2001-02; Robbie Ftorek and Mike O'Connell, 2002-03; Mike Sullivan, 2003-04 to 2005-06; Dave Lewis, 2006-07.

Club Records

Team

(Figures in brackets for season records are games played; records for fewest points, wins, ties, losses, goals, goals against are for 70 or more games)

Most Points **121** 1970-71 (78)
Most Wins **57** 1970-71 (78)
Most Ties **21** 1954-55 (70)
Most Losses **47** 1961-62 (70), 1996-97 (82)
Most Goals **399** 1970-71 (78)
Most Goals Against **306** 1961-62 (70)
Fewest Points **38** 1961-62 (70)
Fewest Wins **14** 1962-63 (70)
Fewest Ties **5** 1972-73 (78)
Fewest Losses **13** 1971-72 (78)
Fewest Goals **147** 1955-56 (70)
Fewest Goals Against **172** 1952-53 (70)

Longest Winning Streak
Overall .... **14** Dec. 3/29-Jan. 9/30
Home .... ***20** Dec. 3/29-Mar. 18/30
Away .... **8** Feb. 17-Mar. 8/72, Mar. 15-Apr. 14/93

Longest Undefeated Streak
Overall .... **23** Dec. 22/40-Feb. 23/41 (15 wins, 8 ties)
Home .... **27** Nov. 22/70-Mar. 20/71 (26 wins, 1 tie)
Away .... **15** Dec. 22/40-Mar. 16/41 (9 wins, 6 ties)

Longest Losing Streak
Overall .... **11** Dec. 3/24-Jan. 5/25
Home .... ***11** Dec. 8/24-Feb. 17/25
Away .... **14** Dec. 27/64-Feb. 21/65

Longest Winless Streak
Overall .... **20** Jan. 28-Mar. 11/62 (16 losses, 4 ties)
Home .... **11** Dec. 8/24-Feb. 17/25 (11 losses)
Away .... **14** Three times

Most Shutouts, Season **15** 1927-28 (44)
Most PIM, Season **2,443** 1987-88 (80)
Most Goals, Game .... **14** Jan. 21/45 (NYR 3 at Bos. 14)

Individual

Most Seasons .... **21** John Bucyk, Raymond Bourque
Most Games .... **1,518** Raymond Bourque
Most Goals, Career .... **545** John Bucyk
Most Assists, Career ...... **1,111** Raymond Bourque
Most Points, Career .... **1,506** Raymond Bourque (395G, 1,111A)
Most PIM, Career .... **2,095** Terry O'Reilly
Most Shutouts, Career .... **74** Tiny Thompson
Longest Consecutive Games Streak .... **418** John Bucyk (Jan. 23/69-Mar. 2/75)
Most Goals, Season .... **76** Phil Esposito (1970-71)
Most Assists, Season .... **102** Bobby Orr (1970-71)
Most Points, Season .... **152** Phil Esposito (1970-71; 76G, 76A)
Most PIM, Season .... **302** Jay Miller (1987-88)
Most Points, Defenseman, Season .... ***139** Bobby Orr (1970-71; 37G, 102A)
Most Points, Center, Season .... **152** Phil Esposito (1970-71; 76G, 76A)
Most Points, Right Wing, Season .... **105** Ken Hodge (1970-71; 43G, 62A), (1973-74; 50G, 55A), Rick Middleton (1983-84; 47G, 58A)
Most Points, Left Wing, Season .... **116** John Bucyk (1970-71; 51G, 65A)
Most Points, Rookie, Season .... **102** Joe Juneau (1992-93; 32G, 70A)
Most Shutouts, Season .... **15** Hal Winkler (1927-28)
Most Goals, Game .... **4** Twenty times
Most Assists, Game .... **6** Ken Hodge (Feb. 9/71), Bobby Orr (Jan. 1/73)
Most Points, Game .... **7** Bobby Orr (Nov. 15/73; 3G, 4A), Phil Esposito (Dec. 19/74; 3G, 4A), Barry Pederson (Apr. 4/82; 3G, 4A), Cam Neely (Oct. 16/88; 3G, 4A)

* NHL Record.

Retired Numbers

2	Eddie Shore	1926-1940
3	Lionel Hitchman	1925-1934
4	Bobby Orr	1966-1976
5	Dit Clapper	1927-1947
7	Phil Esposito	1967-1975
8	Cam Neely	1986-1996
9	John Bucyk	1957-1978
15	Milt Schmidt	1936-1955
24	Terry O'Reilly	1971-1985
77	Raymond Bourque	1979-2000

All-time Record vs. Other Clubs

Regular Season

	At Home								On Road								Total							
	GP	W	L	T	OL	GF	GA	PTS	GP	W	L	T	OL	GF	GA	PTS	GP	W	L	T	OL	GF	GA	PTS
Anaheim	9	5	4	0	0	27	27	10	9	5	2	2	0	24	18	12	18	10	6	2	0	51	45	22
Atlanta	12	6	2	2	2	43	45	16	12	7	4	0	1	36	34	15	24	13	6	2	3	79	79	31
Buffalo	111	62	35	14	0	412	325	138	112	40	56	15	1	330	403	96	223	102	91	29	1	742	728	234
Calgary	47	28	12	6	1	165	130	63	45	22	19	4	0	154	163	48	92	50	31	10	1	319	293	111
Carolina	80	47	25	7	1	281	213	102	78	36	32	9	1	269	260	82	158	83	57	16	2	550	473	184
Chicago	284	161	89	34	0	1023	808	356	286	94	145	45	2	767	926	235	570	255	234	79	2	1790	1734	591
Colorado	62	31	21	9	1	240	192	72	67	36	25	6	0	272	238	78	129	67	46	15	1	512	430	150
Columbus	2	1	1	0	0	8	7	2	3	2	0	0	1	14	3	5	5	3	1	0	1	22	10	7
Dallas	61	41	9	10	1	259	148	93	61	30	17	13	1	220	175	74	122	71	26	23	2	479	323	167
Detroit	287	154	89	43	1	1007	761	352	285	79	153	52	1	720	952	211	572	233	242	95	2	1727	1713	563
Edmonton	30	21	6	3	0	126	80	45	30	16	11	3	0	102	102	35	60	37	17	6	0	228	182	80
Florida	24	9	10	4	1	63	62	23	23	11	9	2	1	67	65	25	47	20	19	6	2	130	127	48
Los Angeles	62	44	12	6	0	287	175	94	61	33	21	7	0	224	210	73	123	77	33	13	0	511	385	167
Minnesota	3	0	3	0	0	4	13	0	3	1	2	0	0	5	9	2	6	1	5	0	0	9	22	2
Montreal	339	156	125	56	2	997	914	370	338	98	193	47	0	796	1133	243	677	254	318	103	2	1793	2047	613
Nashville	5	2	2	1	0	14	9	5	6	4	1	0	1	16	13	9	11	6	3	1	1	30	22	14
New Jersey	58	31	15	8	4	224	179	74	55	27	15	11	2	176	146	67	113	58	30	19	6	400	325	141
NY Islanders	61	32	17	11	1	224	171	76	63	27	25	10	1	204	211	65	124	59	42	21	2	428	382	141
NY Rangers	300	160	95	42	3	1081	841	365	304	116	133	55	0	857	929	287	604	276	228	97	3	1938	1770	652
Ottawa	37	22	10	5	0	135	101	49	35	16	10	3	6	104	91	41	72	38	20	8	6	239	192	90
Philadelphia	78	46	20	11	1	286	217	104	75	32	32	10	1	219	247	75	153	78	52	21	2	505	464	179
Phoenix	31	22	4	4	1	137	94	49	30	14	13	3	0	102	101	31	61	36	17	7	1	239	195	80
Pittsburgh	80	58	16	6	0	355	224	122	82	35	31	15	1	296	280	86	162	93	47	21	1	651	504	208
St. Louis	59	35	14	9	1	247	161	80	59	23	24	9	3	198	188	58	118	58	38	18	4	445	349	138
San Jose	11	7	1	3	0	41	32	17	11	5	4	2	0	38	30	12	22	12	5	5	0	79	62	29
Tampa Bay	25	17	2	6	0	95	58	40	25	12	10	3	0	72	73	27	50	29	12	9	0	167	131	67
Toronto	302	164	90	47	1	977	794	376	303	93	157	51	2	783	1018	239	605	257	247	98	3	1760	1812	615
Vancouver	52	38	7	7	0	217	124	83	52	27	17	8	0	211	171	62	104	65	24	15	0	428	295	145
Washington	58	33	15	9	1	213	155	76	57	28	16	12	1	198	160	69	115	61	31	21	2	411	315	145
Defunct Clubs	164	112	39	13	0	525	306	237	164	79	67	18	0	496	440	176	328	191	106	31	0	1021	746	413
Totals	**2734**	**1545**	**790**	**376**	**23**	**9713**	**7366**	**3489**	**2734**	**1048**	**1244**	**415**	**27**	**7970**	**8789**	**2538**	**5468**	**2593**	**2034**	**791**	**50**	**17683**	**16155**	**6027**

Playoffs

	Series	W	L	GP	W	L	T	GF	GA	Last Mtg.	Rnd.	Result
Buffalo	7	5	2	39	21	18	0	139	130	1999	CSF	L 2-4
Carolina	3	3	0	19	12	7	0	63	48	1999	CQF	W 4-2
Chicago	6	5	1	22	16	5	1	97	63	1978	QF	W 4-0
Colorado	2	1	1	11	6	5	0	37	36	1983	DSF	W 3-1
Dallas	1	0	1	3	0	3	0	13	20	1981	PRE	L 0-3
Detroit	7	4	3	33	19	14	0	96	98	1957	SF	W 4-1
Edmonton	2	0	2	9	1	8	0	20	41	1990	F	L 1-4
Florida	1	0	1	5	1	4	0	16	22	1996	CQF	L 1-4
Los Angeles	2	2	0	13	8	5	0	56	38	1977	QF	W 4-2
Montreal	30	7	23	152	57	95	0	371	469	2004	CQF	L 3-4
New Jersey	4	1	3	23	8	15	0	60	68	2003	CQF	L 1-4
NY Islanders	2	0	2	11	3	8	0	35	49	1983	CF	L 2-4
NY Rangers	9	6	3	42	22	18	2	114	104	1973	QF	L 1-4
Philadelphia	4	2	2	20	11	9	0	60	57	1978	SF	W 4-1
Pittsburgh	4	2	2	19	9	10	0	62	67	1992	CF	L 0-4
St. Louis	2	2	0	8	8	0	0	48	15	1972	SF	W 4-0
Toronto	13	5	8	62	30	31	1	153	150	1974	QF	W 4-0
Washington	2	1	1	10	6	4	0	28	21	1998	CQF	L 2-4
Defunct Clubs	3	1	2	11	4	5	2	20	20			
Totals	**104**	**47**	**57**	**512**	**242**	**264**	**6**	**1488**	**1516**			

Calgary totals include Atlanta Flames, 1972-73 to 1979-80. Carolina totals include Hartford, 1979-80 to 1996-97.
Colorado totals include Quebec, 1979-80 to 1994-95. Dallas totals include Minnesota North Stars, 1967-68 to 1992-93.
New Jersey totals include Kansas City, 1974-75 to 1975-76, and Colorado Rockies, 1976-77 to 1981-82.
Phoenix totals include Winnipeg, 1979-80 to 1995-96.

Playoff Results 2006-2001

Year	Round	Opponent	Result	GF	GA
2004	CQF	Montreal	L 3-4	14	19
2003	CQF	New Jersey	L 1-4	8	13
2002	CQF	Montreal	L 2-4	18	20

Abbreviations: Round: F - Final; **CF** - conference final; **CSF** - conference semi-final; **CQF** - conference quarter-final; **DSF** - division semi-final; **SF** - semi-final; **QF** - quarter-final; **PRE** - preliminary round.

2005-06 Results

Oct.	5	Montreal	1-2
	7	at Buffalo	1-4
	8	at Pittsburgh	7-6*
	10	at Tampa Bay	4-2
	13	at Florida	5-2
	15	at Ottawa	1-5
	18	at Montreal	3-4
	20	Buffalo	3-4
	22	Pittsburgh	6-3
	24	at Toronto	4-5†
	26	at Carolina	3-4*
	27	Toronto	2-1
	29	New Jersey	4-5†
Nov.	1	at NY Islanders	3-4*
	3	Florida	4-1
	5	Pittsburgh	6-3
	8	at Philadelphia	3-4*
	10	Ottawa	2-5
	12	at NY Islanders	2-5
	17	Toronto	1-4
	19	Buffalo	2-3
	20	at NY Rangers	2-3
	23	at Toronto	5-1
	25	Philadelphia	3-5
	26	at Ottawa	2-4
	29	at New Jersey	2-3
Dec.	1	Ottawa	3-0
	3	at Edmonton	5-4*
	4	at Vancouver	2-5
	7	at Colorado	1-4
	11	Phoenix	1-2*
	15	at Minnesota	3-2
	17	at Calgary	0-3
	22	Toronto	4-1
	23	at Toronto	1-2
	27	at Washington	4-3*
	28	at Florida	4-6
	30	at Tampa Bay	2-1
Jan.	2	Philadelphia	0-1
	5	Ottawa	4-2
	7	Tampa Bay	6-3
	10	San Jose	2-6
	12	Los Angeles	0-6
	14	Dallas	1-2†
	16	Anaheim	4-3*
	19	at Philadelphia	5-2
	21	NY Rangers	2-3†
	23	at Washington	3-2
	24	at Atlanta	3-2
	26	Washington	3-2
	28	NY Islanders	3-4
	30	at Ottawa	5-0
Feb.	2	Montreal	3-1
	4	at Montreal	0-2
	5	Carolina	3-4†
	8	at Pittsburgh	3-1
	9	New Jersey	2-3*
	11	Tampa Bay	5-6
Mar.	1	at Carolina	3-4
	2	Atlanta	3-2
	4	Buffalo	2-3
	7	at Buffalo	2-3
	9	Montreal	0-3
	11	NY Islanders	1-3
	12	at Buffalo	2-6
	14	at Toronto	4-5†
	16	Ottawa	3-2†
	18	Carolina	4-2
	20	at NY Rangers	2-5
	21	Atlanta	4-5†
	24	at New Jersey	2-4
	25	Buffalo	5-4
	27	Florida	3-4†
	29	at Buffalo	3-4
Apr.	1	at Montreal	0-2
	4	at Montreal	3-5
	6	Toronto	3-2†
	8	NY Rangers	3-4*
	10	Washington	1-2*
	11	at Ottawa	3-4*
	13	Montreal	3-4
	15	at Atlanta	3-4

* – Overtime † – Shootout

Entry Draft
Selections 2006-1992

2006
Pick
5	Phil Kessel
37	Yuri Alexandrov
50	Milan Lucic
71	Brad Marchand
128	Andrew Bodnarchuk
158	Levi Nelson

2005
Pick
22	Matt Lashoff
39	Petr Kalus
83	Mikko Lehtonen
100	Jonathan Sigalet
106	Vladimir Sobotka
154	Wacey Rabbit
172	Lukas Vantuch
217	Brock Bradford

2004
Pick
63	Dave Krejci
64	Martins Karsums
108	Ashton Rome
134	Kris Versteeg
160	Ben Walter
224	Matt Hunwick
255	Anton Hedman

2003
Pick
21	Mark Stuart
45	Patrice Bergeron
66	Masi Marjamaki
107	Byron Bitz
118	Frank Rediker
129	Patrik Valcak
153	Mike Brown
183	Nate Thompson
247	Benoit Mondou
277	Kevin Regan

2002
Pick
29	Hannu Toivonen
56	Vladislav Evseev
130	Jan Kubista
153	Peter Hamerlik
228	Dmitri Utkin
259	Yan Stastny
290	Pavel Frolov

2001
Pick
19	Shaone Morrisonn
77	Darren McLachlan
111	Matti Kaltiainen
147	Jiri Jakes
179	Andrew Alberts
209	Jordan Sigalet
241	Milan Jurcina
282	Marcel Rodman

2000
Pick
7	Lars Jonsson
27	Martin Samuelsson
37	Andy Hilbert
59	Ivan Huml
66	Tuukka Makela
73	Sergei Zinovjev
102	Brett Nowak
174	Jarno Kultanen
204	Chris Berti
237	Zdenek Kutlak
268	Pavel Kolarik
279	Andreas Lindstrom

1999
Pick
21	Nick Boynton
56	Matt Zultek
89	Kyle Wanvig
118	Jaakko Harikkala
147	Seamus Kotyk
179	Donald Choukalos
207	Greg Barber
236	John Cronin
247	Mikko Eloranta
264	Georgy Pujacs

1998
Pick
48	Jonathan Girard
52	Bobby Allen
78	Peter Nordstrom
135	Andrew Raycroft
165	Ryan Milanovic

1997
Pick
1	Joe Thornton
8	Sergei Samsonov
27	Ben Clymer
54	Mattias Karlin
63	Lee Goren
81	Karol Bartanus
135	Denis Timofeev
162	Joel Trottier
180	Jim Baxter
191	Antti Laaksonen
218	Eric Van Acker
246	Jay Henderson

1996
Pick
8	Johnathan Aitken
45	Henry Kuster
53	Eric Naud
80	Jason Doyle
100	Trent Whitfield
132	Elias Abrahamsson
155	Chris Lane
182	Thomas Brown
208	Bob Prier
234	Anders Soderberg

1995
Pick
9	Kyle McLaren
21	Sean Brown
47	Paxton Schafer
73	Bill McCauley
99	Cameron Mann
151	Yevgeny Shaldybin
177	P.J. Axelsson
203	Sergei Zhukov
229	Jonathon Murphy

1994
Pick
21	Evgeni Ryabchikov
47	Daniel Goneau
99	Eric Nickulas
125	Darren Wright
151	Andre Roy
177	Jeremy Schaefer
229	John Grahame
255	Neil Savary
281	Andrei Yakhanov

1993
Pick
25	Kevyn Adams
51	Matt Alvey
88	Charles Paquette
103	Shawn Bates
129	Andrei Sapozhnikov
155	Milt Mastad
181	Ryan Golden
207	Hal Gill
233	Joel Prpic
259	Joakim Persson

1992
Pick
16	Dmitri Kvartalnov
55	Sergei Zholtok
112	Scott Bailey
133	Jiri Dopita
136	Grigori Panteleev
184	Kurt Seher
208	Mattias Timander
232	Chris Crombie
256	Denis Chervyakov
257	Evgeny Pavlov

Club Directory

TD Banknorth Garden

Boston Bruins
TD Banknorth Garden
100 Legends Way
Boston, MA 02114
Phone 617/624-2327
FAX 617/523-7184
www.bostonbruins.com
Capacity: 17,565

Executive
Owner and Governor	Jeremy M. Jacobs
Alternate Governors	Charles Jacobs, Jeremy Jacobs Jr., Louis Jacobs, Harry Sinden
Senior Advisor to the Owner	Harry Sinden
Executive Vice President	Charles Jacobs
Senior Assistant to the Senior Advisor	Nate Greenberg
Director of Administration	Dale Hamilton-Powers
Assistant to the Senior Advisor	Joe Curnane
Executive Secretary	Rita Brandano
Administrative Assistant	Karen Ondo

Hockey Operations
General Manager	Peter Chiarelli
Assistant General Manager	Jeff Gorton
Director of Player Personnel	Jim Benning
Director of Player Development	Don Sweeney
Director of Amateur Scouting	Scott Bradley
Scouting Staff	Adam Creighton, Daniel Dore, Scott Fitzgerald, Bill Lesuk, Don Matheson, Mike McGraw, Tom McVie, Wayne Smith, Tom Songin, Svenake Svensson, John Weisbrod
Asst. Director of Administration/Travel Coordinator	Carol Gould
Team Road Services Coordinator	John Bucyk

Coaching
Head Coach	Dave Lewis
Associate Coach	Marc Habscheid
Assistant Coach	Doug Houda
Goaltending Coach	Bob Essensa
Video Coordinator	Brant Berglund

Medical & Training
Strength & Conditioning Coach	John Whitesides
Athletic Trainer	Don DelNegro
Physical Therapist	Scott Waugh
Equipment Manager	Mark Dumas
Assistant Equipment Managers	Chris "Muggsy" Aldrich, Keith Robinson

Media Relations & Community Relations
Director of Media Relations	Heidi Holland
Media Relations Manager	Ryan Nadeau
Director of Community Relations and Promotions	Kerry Collins
Community Relations Coordinator	Eryn Gallagher
Director of Development, Boston Bruins Foundation	Paul Stewart
Boston Bruins Foundation Coordinator	Jay Southwood
Administrative Assistant, Alumni Office	Mal Viola

Sales & Marketing
Senior Vice President of Sales and Marketing	Amy Latimer
Vice President of Advertising and Promotions	Sue Byrne
Promotions Manager	Brian Hayes
Advertising Coordinator	Liz d'Entremont
Promotions Coordinator	Dave Mello

Finance, Legal & Box Office
Vice President of Business Operations	Daniel J. Zimmer
Chief Financial Officer	Jessica Rahuba
Chief Legal Officer	Michael Wall
Controller	Rick McGlinchey
Accounts Payable	Linda Bartlett
Payroll and Benefits	Botin Bou
Director of Ticket Operations	Matt Brennan
Assistant Director of Ticket Operations	Jim Foley
Ticket Office Receptionist	Jo-Ann Connolly-White

Miscellaneous
Television	New England Sports Network (NESN)
Radio	WBZ (1030 AM) and Bruins Radio Network
Television Broadcasters	Play-by-Play, Dale Arnold (home) & Jack Edwards (road); Color, Andy Brickley
Radio Broadcasters	Play-by-Play, Dave Goucher; Color, Bob Beers

General Manager

CHIARELLI, PETER
General Manager, Boston Bruins. Born in Nepean, Ont., August 5, 1964.

Peter Chiarelli became just the seventh man in club history to hold the position of general manager when he was named to the post on May 26, 2006. He is in charge of every aspect of the team's hockey operations. He officially began his position in Boston on July 10, 2006 as a result of a league-arbitrated compensation agreement that saw the Bruins surrender a third-round draft pick in the 2006 NHL Entry Draft (Eric Gryba, 68th overall) to the Ottawa Senators.

Chiarelli came to the Bruins after seven seasons with the Ottawa Senators, five as the director of legal relations and the last two as assistant general manager. He was involved in all aspects of that team's hockey operations, including contract research and negotiations, salary arbitration and all player personnel matters. He was also involved in overseeing Ottawa's top developmental affiliate, the Binghamtom Senators of the American Hockey League. The Senators had four 100+ point seasons during his tenure and never finished below 94 points, finished with the NHL's top record in 2002-03 (113 points) and the best record in the Eastern Conference in 2005-06 (113 points).

A native of the Ottawa area, Chiarelli played four seasons of college hockey at Harvard University where he served the team as captain and was a teammate of former Bruin Don Sweeney. He had 21 goals and 28 assists for 49 points with 70 penalty minutes in 109 career college games and earned his degree in Economics in 1987. He played professionally in Europe for one year before returning to school and obtaining his law degree from the University of Ottawa. He was admitted to the Ontario bar in 1993 and spent six years as a lawyer and player agent prior to joining the Senators front office in 1999.

General Managers' History

Art Ross, 1924-25 to 1953-54; Lynn Patrick, 1954-55 to 1964-65; Hap Emms, 1965-66, 1966-67; Milt Schmidt, 1967-68 to 1971-72; Harry Sinden, 1972-73 to 1999-2000; Harry Sinden and Mike O'Connell, 2000-01; Mike O'Connell, 2001-02 to 2005-06; Peter Chiarelli, 2006-07.

Buffalo Sabres

2005-06 Results: 52w-24L-1oTL-5SOL 110PTS.
Second, Northeast Division

2006-07 Schedule

Oct.	Wed.	4	at Carolina	Sat.	6	at Toronto
	Fri.	6	Montreal	Wed.	10	at Chicago
	Sat.	7	at Ottawa	Thu.	11	Toronto
	Fri.	13	at Detroit	Sat.	13	Tampa Bay
	Sat.	14	NY Rangers	Mon.	15	at Boston*
	Tue.	17	Philadelphia	Wed.	17	Boston
	Fri.	20	Carolina	Fri.	19	Vancouver
	Sat.	21	at Boston	Sat.	20	at Montreal
	Mon.	23	at Montreal	Fri.	26	at Columbus
	Thu.	26	at NY Islanders	Sat.	27	at NY Islanders
	Sat.	28	Atlanta	Tue.	30	Boston
Nov.	Thu.	2	at Boston	**Feb.** Thu.	1	at Boston
	Sat.	4	Toronto	Sat.	3	at New Jersey
	Sun.	5	at NY Rangers*	Tue.	6	at Atlanta
	Fri.	10	Florida	Wed.	7	Ottawa
	Sat.	11	at Philadelphia	Sat.	10	Calgary
	Mon.	13	at Carolina	Thu.	15	Edmonton
	Wed.	15	Ottawa	Sat.	17	Boston
	Fri.	17	Pittsburgh	Tue.	20	Philadelphia
	Sat.	18	at Ottawa	Thu.	22	Ottawa
	Mon.	20	Tampa Bay	Sat.	24	at Ottawa
	Wed.	22	Toronto	Tue.	27	at Toronto
	Fri.	24	Montreal	**Mar.** Fri.	2	Montreal
	Sun.	26	at NY Rangers	Sat.	3	at Toronto
Dec.	Fri.	1	NY Rangers	Wed.	7	Colorado
	Sat.	2	at Washington	Fri.	9	Minnesota
	Tue.	5	at Tampa Bay	Sat.	10	New Jersey
	Thu.	7	at Florida	Tue.	13	at Pittsburgh
	Sat.	9	at Montreal	Thu.	15	at Florida
	Tue.	12	at New Jersey	Fri.	16	at Tampa Bay
	Thu.	14	Florida	Sun.	18	at Atlanta*
	Sat.	16	Ottawa	Wed.	21	Washington
	Tue.	19	Montreal	Fri.	23	Toronto
	Thu.	21	at Nashville	Sat.	24	at Toronto
	Sat.	23	at St. Louis	Wed.	28	New Jersey
	Tue.	26	Washington	Fri.	30	NY Islanders
	Thu.	28	Carolina	Sat.	31	at Montreal
	Sat.	30	Atlanta	**Apr.** Tue.	3	at Pittsburgh
Jan.	Mon.	1	NY Islanders*	Thu.	5	Boston
	Wed.	3	at Ottawa	Sat.	7	at Washington*
	Fri.	5	Pittsburgh	Sun.	8	at Philadelphia*

* Denotes afternoon game.

Maxim Afinogenov established new career highs with 22 goals, 51 assists, and 73 points in 2005-06. His assists and points were tops on the team.

Franchise date: May 22, 1970

NORTHEAST DIVISION

37th NHL Season

Year-by-Year Record

		Home				Road				Overall								
Season	GP	W	L	T	OL	W	L	T	OL	W	L	T	OL	GF	GA	Pts.	Finished	Playoff Result
2005-06	82	27	11	....	3	25	13	....	3	52	24	....	6	281	239	110	2nd, Northeast Div.	Lost Conf. Final
2004-05	....	....	....	....	....	....	....	....	....	....	....	....	....	....	....	....		
2003-04	82	21	13	4	3	16	21	3	1	37	34	7	4	220	221	85	5th, Northeast Div.	Out of Playoffs
2002-03	82	18	16	5	2	9	21	5	6	27	37	10	8	190	219	72	5th, Northeast Div.	Out of Playoffs
2001-02	82	20	16	5	0	15	19	6	1	35	35	11	1	213	200	82	5th, Northeast Div.	Out of Playoffs
2000-01	82	26	12	3	0	20	18	2	1	46	30	5	1	218	184	98	2nd, Northeast Div.	Lost Conf. Semi-Final
1999-2000	82	21	14	5	1	14	18	6	3	35	32	11	4	213	204	85	3rd, Northeast Div.	Lost Conf. Quarter-Final
1998-99	82	23	12	6	....	14	16	11	....	37	28	17	....	207	175	91	4th, Northeast Div.	Lost Final
1997-98	82	20	13	8	....	16	16	9	....	36	29	17	....	211	187	89	3rd, Northeast Div.	Lost Conf. Final
1996-97	82	24	11	6	....	16	19	6	....	40	30	12	....	237	208	92	1st, Northeast Div.	Lost Conf. Semi-Final
1995-96	82	19	17	5	....	14	25	2	....	33	42	7	....	247	262	73	5th, Northeast Div.	Out of Playoffs
1994-95	48	15	8	1	....	7	11	6	....	22	19	7	....	130	119	51	4th, Northeast Div.	Lost Conf. Quarter-Final
1993-94	84	22	17	3	....	21	15	6	....	43	32	9	....	282	218	95	4th, Northeast Div.	Lost Conf. Quarter-Final
1992-93	84	25	15	2	....	13	21	8	....	38	36	10	....	335	297	86	4th, Adams Div.	Lost Div. Final
1991-92	80	22	13	5	....	9	24	7	....	31	37	12	....	289	299	74	3rd, Adams Div.	Lost Div. Semi-Final
1990-91	80	15	13	12	....	16	17	7	....	31	30	19	....	292	278	81	3rd, Adams Div.	Lost Div. Semi-Final
1989-90	80	27	11	2	....	18	16	6	....	45	27	8	....	286	248	98	2nd, Adams Div.	Lost Div. Semi-Final
1988-89	80	25	12	3	....	13	23	4	....	38	35	7	....	291	299	83	3rd, Adams Div.	Lost Div. Semi-Final
1987-88	80	19	14	7	....	18	18	4	....	37	32	11	....	283	305	85	3rd, Adams Div.	Lost Div. Semi-Final
1986-87	80	18	18	4	....	10	26	4	....	28	44	8	....	280	308	64	5th, Adams Div.	Out of Playoffs
1985-86	80	23	16	1	....	14	21	5	....	37	37	6	....	296	291	80	5th, Adams Div.	Out of Playoffs
1984-85	80	23	10	7	....	15	18	7	....	38	28	14	....	290	237	90	3rd, Adams Div.	Lost Div. Semi-Final
1983-84	80	25	9	6	....	23	16	1	....	48	25	7	....	315	257	103	2nd, Adams Div.	Lost Div. Semi-Final
1982-83	80	25	7	8	....	13	22	5	....	38	29	13	....	318	285	89	3rd, Adams Div.	Lost Div. Final
1981-82	80	23	8	9	....	16	19	5	....	39	26	15	....	307	273	93	3rd, Adams Div.	Lost Div. Semi-Final
1980-81	80	21	7	12	....	18	13	9	....	39	20	21	....	327	250	99	1st, Adams Div.	Lost Quarter-Final
1979-80	80	27	5	8	....	20	12	8	....	47	17	16	....	318	201	110	1st, Adams Div.	Lost Semi-Final
1978-79	80	19	13	8	....	17	15	8	....	36	28	16	....	280	263	88	2nd, Adams Div.	Lost Prelim. Round
1977-78	80	25	7	8	....	19	12	9	....	44	19	17	....	288	215	105	2nd, Adams Div.	Lost Quarter-Final
1976-77	80	27	8	5	....	21	16	3	....	48	24	8	....	301	220	104	2nd, Adams Div.	Lost Quarter-Final
1975-76	80	28	7	5	....	18	14	8	....	46	21	13	....	339	240	105	2nd, Adams Div.	Lost Quarter-Final
1974-75	80	28	6	6	....	21	10	9	....	49	16	15	....	354	240	113	1st, Adams Div.	Lost Final
1973-74	78	23	10	6	....	9	24	6	....	32	34	12	....	242	250	76	5th, East Div.	Out of Playoffs
1972-73	78	30	6	3	....	7	21	11	....	37	27	14	....	257	219	88	4th, East Div.	Lost Quarter-Final
1971-72	78	11	19	9	....	5	24	10	....	16	43	19	....	203	289	51	6th, East Div.	Out of Playoffs
1970-71	78	16	13	10	....	8	26	5	....	24	39	15	....	217	291	63	5th, East Div.	Out of Playoffs

2006-07 Player Personnel

FORWARDS

	HT	WT	S	Place of Birth	Date	2005-06 Club
AFINOGENOV, Maxim	6-0	190	L	Moscow, USSR	9/4/79	Buffalo
BRIERE, Daniel	5-10	178	R	Gatineau, Que.	10/6/77	Buffalo
CONNOLLY, Tim	6-1	190	R	Syracuse, NY	5/7/81	Buffalo
DRURY, Chris	5-10	200	R	Trumbull, CT	8/20/76	Buffalo
GAUSTAD, Paul	6-4	220	L	Fargo, ND	2/3/82	Buffalo
HECHT, Jochen	6-1	200	L	Mannheim, W. Germany	6/21/77	Buffalo
KOTALIK, Ales	6-1	227	R	Jindrichuv Hradec, Czech.	12/23/78	Buffalo
MacARTHUR, Clarke	6-0	180	L	Lloydminster, Alta.	4/6/85	Rochester
MAIR, Adam	6-2	208	R	Hamilton, Ont.	2/15/79	Buffalo
NOVOTNY, Jiri	6-2	204	R	Pelhrimov, Czech.	8/12/83	Buffalo-Rochester
PAILLE, Dan	6-0	200	L	Welland, Ont.	4/15/84	Buffalo-Rochester
PETERS, Andrew	6-4	240	L	St. Catharines, Ont.	5/5/80	Buffalo
POMINVILLE, Jason	6-0	186	R	Repentigny, Que.	11/30/82	Buffalo-Rochester
ROY, Derek	5-9	186	L	Ottawa, Ont.	5/4/83	Buffalo
RYAN, Michael	6-1	180	L	Boston, MA	5/16/80	Rochester
THORBURN, Chris	6-3	220	R	Sault Ste. Marie, Ont.	6/3/83	Buffalo-Rochester
VANEK, Thomas	6-2	210	R	Vienna, Austria	1/19/84	Buffalo

DEFENSEMEN

	HT	WT	S	Place of Birth	Date	2005-06 Club
CAMPBELL, Brian	6-0	190	L	Strathroy, Ont.	5/23/79	Buffalo
JILLSON, Jeff	6-3	215	R	North Smithfield, RI	7/24/80	Buffalo-Rochester
KALININ, Dmitri	6-3	206	L	Chelyabinsk, USSR	7/22/80	Buffalo
LYDMAN, Toni	6-1	202	L	Lahti, Finland	9/25/77	Buffalo
NUMMINEN, Teppo	6-1	198	R	Tampere, Finland	7/3/68	Buffalo
PAETSCH, Nathan	6-0	198	L	Humboldt, Sask.	3/30/83	Buffalo-Rochester
SPACEK, Jaroslav	5-11	206	L	Rokycany, Czech.	2/11/74	Chicago-Edmonton
TALLINDER, Henrik	6-3	215	L	Stockholm, Sweden	1/10/79	Buffalo

GOALTENDERS

	HT	WT	C	Place of Birth	Date	2005-06 Club
BIRON, Martin	6-2	170	L	Lac-St-Charles, Que.	8/15/77	Buffalo
MILLER, Ryan	6-2	170	L	East Lansing, MI	7/17/80	Buffalo-Rochester

Coaching History

Punch Imlach, 1970-71; Punch Imlach, Floyd Smith and Joe Crozier, 1971-72; Joe Crozier, 1972-73, 1973-74; Floyd Smith, 1974-75 to 1976-77; Marcel Pronovost, 1977-78; Marcel Pronovost and Billy Inglis, 1978-79; Scotty Bowman, 1979-80; Roger Neilson, 1980-81; Jim Roberts and Scotty Bowman, 1981-82; Scotty Bowman 1982-83 to 1984-85; Jim Schoenfeld and Scotty Bowman, 1985-86; Scotty Bowman, Craig Ramsay and Ted Sator, 1986-87; Ted Sator, 1987-88, 1988-89; Rick Dudley, 1989-90, 1990-91; Rick Dudley and John Muckler, 1991-92; John Muckler, 1992-93 to 1994-95; Ted Nolan, 1995-96, 1996-97; Lindy Ruff, 1997-98 to date.

Head Coach

RUFF, LINDY
Head Coach, Buffalo Sabres. Born in Warburg, Alta., February, 17, 1960.

A former captain of the Sabres, Lindy Ruff was appointed as the club's 15th head coach on July 21, 1997. In 1999, he led the Sabres to the Stanley Cup Finals for just the second time in club history and in 2006 he guided the Sabres to the Eastern Conference Final and was rewarded with the Jack Adams Award as coach of the year. With 305 victories behind the bench, Ruff has surpassed Scotty Bowman (210) as the winningest coach in Sabres history. As a player, Ruff was drafted 32nd overall by the Sabres in the 1979 Entry Draft. He played both defense and left wing in an NHL career that spanned 12 seasons including 608 regular-season games with Buffalo. He became a playing assistant coach with Rochester of the AHL in 1991-92 and San Diego of the IHL in 1992-93. Ruff's San Diego club set a pro hockey record with 62 wins. In 1993-94 he became an NHL assistant coach with the Florida Panthers.

Coaching Record

Season	Team	Games	Regular Season W	L	O/T	Playoffs Games	W	L
1997-98	Buffalo (NHL)	82	36	29	17	15	10	5
1998-99	Buffalo (NHL)	82	37	28	17	21	14	7
1999-2000	Buffalo (NHL)	82	35	36	11	5	1	4
2000-01	Buffalo (NHL)	82	46	31	5	13	7	6
2001-02	Buffalo (NHL)	82	35	36	11	....	....	....
2002-03	Buffalo (NHL)	82	27	45	10	....	....	....
2003-04	Buffalo (NHL)	82	37	38	7	....	....	....
2004-05				Season Cancelled				
2005-06	Buffalo (NHL)	82	52	24	6	18	11	7
NHL Totals		**656**	**305**	**267**	**84**	**72**	**43**	**29**

Assistant coaches Brian McCutheon and Scott Arniel shared an 0-1 record as replacement coach when Ruff was sidelined due to a family illness, March 20, 2006. Loss is credited to Ruff's coaching record.

2005-06 Scoring
*– rookie

Regular Season

Pos	#	Player	Team	GP	G	A	Pts	+/-	PIM	PP	SH	GW	S	%
R	61	Maxim Afinogenov	BUF	77	22	51	73	6	84	11	0	3	241	9.1
C	23	Chris Drury	BUF	81	30	37	67	-11	32	16	2	5	172	17.4
R	12	Ales Kotalik	BUF	82	25	37	62	-3	62	10	0	5	261	9.6
C	48	Daniel Briere	BUF	48	25	33	58	3	48	11	0	4	147	17.0
C	19	Tim Connolly	BUF	63	16	39	55	5	28	7	0	3	99	16.2
L	26	* Thomas Vanek	BUF	81	25	23	48	-11	72	11	0	4	204	12.3
C	9	Derek Roy	BUF	70	18	28	46	1	57	5	1	1	151	11.9
D	51	Brian Campbell	BUF	79	12	32	44	-14	16	5	0	5	105	11.4
C	55	Jochen Hecht	BUF	64	18	24	42	10	34	4	2	4	179	10.1
R	17	J.P. Dumont	BUF	54	20	20	40	-1	38	9	0	4	116	17.2
C	27	Teppo Numminen	BUF	75	2	38	40	6	36	0	0	0	60	3.3
R	29	* Jason Pominville	BUF	57	18	12	30	-4	22	10	2	2	124	14.5
C	28	* Paul Gaustad	BUF	78	9	15	24	4	65	0	0	0	113	8.0
R	25	Mike Grier	BUF	81	7	16	23	-7	28	0	4	4	109	6.4
D	10	Henrik Tallinder	BUF	82	6	15	21	10	74	0	1	1	79	7.6
D	45	Dmitri Kalinin	BUF	55	2	16	18	14	54	0	0	0	47	4.3
D	5	Toni Lydman	BUF	75	1	16	17	9	82	0	0	0	68	1.5
D	74	Jay McKee	BUF	75	5	11	16	0	57	0	1	0	50	10.0
L	24	Taylor Pyatt	BUF	41	6	6	12	-1	33	0	0	1	62	9.7
D	8	Rory Fitzpatrick	BUF	56	4	5	9	-18	50	2	0	1	45	8.9
C	22	Adam Mair	BUF	40	2	5	7	-2	47	0	0	0	40	5.0
C	13	* Jiri Novotny	BUF	14	2	3	5	-5	0	1	0	0	15	13.3
L	20	* Dan Paille	BUF	14	2	3	5	1	2	0	0	0	15	6.7
D	38	* Nathan Paetsch	BUF	1	0	1	1	1	0	0	0	0	6	0.0
D	47	* Chris Thorburn	BUF	2	0	1	1	-1	7	0	0	0	1	0.0
D	34	Jeff Jillson	BUF	2	0	0	0	0	4	0	0	0	1	0.0
L	76	Andrew Peters	BUF	28	0	0	0	-2	100	0	0	0	6	0.0

Goaltending

No.	Goaltender	GPI	Mins	Avg	W	L	OT	EN	SO	GA	SA	S%	G	A	PIM
30	* Ryan Miller	48	2862	2.60	30	14	3	1	1	124	1440	.914	0	2	0
43	Martin Biron	35	1934	2.89	21	8	3	2	1	93	980	.905	0	1	10
31	Mika Noronen	4	169	4.26	1	2	0	0	0	12	77	.844	0	0	2
	Totals	82	4986	2.82	52	24	6	5	2	234	2502	.906			

Playoffs

Pos	#	Player	Team	GP	G	A	Pts	+/-	PIM	PP	SH	GW	OT	S	%
C	48	Daniel Briere	BUF	18	8	11	19	0	12	3	0	2	2	47	17.0
C	23	Chris Drury	BUF	18	9	9	18	5	10	5	1	1	1	42	21.4
C	9	Derek Roy	BUF	18	5	10	15	7	16	1	0	0	0	33	15.2
R	17	J.P. Dumont	BUF	18	7	7	14	1	14	3	0	1	1	25	28.0
C	19	Tim Connolly	BUF	18	5	6	11	3	0	1	1	1	0	11	45.5
R	12	Ales Kotalik	BUF	18	4	7	11	4	8	0	0	3	0	51	7.8
R	29	* Jason Pominville	BUF	18	5	5	10	0	8	1	1	1	1	22	22.7
R	25	Mike Grier	BUF	18	3	5	8	3	10	0	0	1	0	32	9.4
R	61	Maxim Afinogenov	BUF	18	3	5	8	3	10	0	0	0	0	43	7.0
D	10	Henrik Tallinder	BUF	14	2	6	8	14	16	0	0	0	0	12	16.7
L	55	Jochen Hecht	BUF	15	2	4	6	-5	2	0	0	0	0	36	5.6
D	51	Brian Campbell	BUF	18	2	4	6	-5	12	0	0	0	0	29	0.0
D	74	Jay McKee	BUF	17	2	3	5	7	16	0	0	0	0	21	9.5
D	5	Toni Lydman	BUF	18	1	4	5	14	18	0	0	0	0	14	7.1
L	24	Taylor Pyatt	BUF	14	0	5	5	-2	10	0	0	0	0	17	0.0
D	8	Rory Fitzpatrick	BUF	11	0	4	4	-1	16	0	0	0	0	10	0.0
C	28	* Paul Gaustad	BUF	18	0	4	4	1	14	0	0	0	0	13	0.0
L	26	* Thomas Vanek	BUF	10	2	0	2	-1	6	2	0	0	0	16	12.5
D	27	Teppo Numminen	BUF	12	1	1	2	3	4	1	0	0	0	7	14.3
D	45	Dmitri Kalinin	BUF	8	0	2	2	3	4	0	0	0	0	11	0.0
D	33	* Doug Janik	BUF	4	1	0	1	-2	2	0	0	0	0	4	25.0
D	38	* Nathan Paetsch	BUF	1	0	0	0	0	0	0	0	0	0	0	0.0
C	22	Adam Mair	BUF	3	0	0	0	-2	0	0	0	0	0	4	0.0
D	34	Jeff Jillson	BUF	4	0	0	0	-4	0	0	0	0	0	5	0.0
C	13	* Jiri Novotny	BUF	4	0	0	0	-1	0	0	0	0	0	3	0.0

Goaltending

No.	Goaltender	GPI	Mins	Avg	W	L	EN	SO	GA	SA	S%	G	A	PIM
30	* Ryan Miller	18	1123	2.56	11	7	1	1	48	522	.908	0	0	2
	Totals	18	1128	2.61	11	7	1	1	49	523	.906			

Captains' History

Floyd Smith, 1970-71; Gerry Meehan, 1971-72 to 1973-74; Gerry Meehan and Jim Schoenfeld, 1974-75; Jim Schoenfeld, 1975-76, 1976-77; Danny Gare, 1977-78 to 1980-81; Danny Gare and Gilbert Perreault, 1981-82; Gilbert Perreault, 1982-83 to 1985-86; Gilbert Perreault and Lindy Ruff, 1986-87; Lindy Ruff, 1987-88; Lindy Ruff and Mike Foligno, 1988-89; Mike Foligno, 1989-90; Mike Foligno and Mike Ramsey, 1990-91; Mike Ramsey, 1991-92; Mike Ramsey and Pat LaFontaine, 1992-93; Pat LaFontaine and Alexander Mogilny, 1993-94; Pat LaFontaine, 1994-95 to 1996-97; Donald Audette and Michael Peca, 1997-98; Michael Peca, 1998-99, 1999-2000; no captain, 2000-01; Stu Barnes. 2001-02, 2002-03; Miroslav Satan, Chris Drury, James Patrick, J.P. Dumont, Daniel Briere, 2003-04; Daniel Briere and Chris Drury, 2005-06.

Club Records

Team

(Figures in brackets for season records are games played; records for fewest points, wins, ties, losses, goals, goals against are for 70 or more games)

Most Points **113** 1974-75 (80)
Most Wins **52** 2005-06 (82)
Most Ties **21** 1980-81 (80)
Most Losses **44** 1986-87 (80)
Most Goals **354** 1974-75 (80)
Most Goals Against **308** 1986-87 (80)
Fewest Points **51** 1971-72 (78)
Fewest Wins **16** 1971-72 (78)
Fewest Ties **5** 2000-01 (82)
Fewest Losses **16** 1974-75 (80)
Fewest Goals **190** 2002-03 (82)
Fewest Goals Against **175** 1998-99 (82)
Longest Winning Streak
Overall .... **10** Jan. 4-23/84
Home .... **12** Nov. 12/72-Jan. 7/73, Oct. 13-Dec. 10/89
Away .... ***10** Dec. 10/83-Jan. 23/84
Longest Undefeated Streak
Overall .... **14** Mar. 6-Apr. 6/80 (8 wins, 6 ties)
Home .... **21** Oct. 8/72-Jan. 7/73 (18 wins, 3 ties)
Away .... **10** Dec. 10/83-Jan. 23/84 (10 wins)
Longest Losing Streak
Overall .... **7** Four times
Home .... **6** Oct. 10-Nov. 10/93, Mar. 3-Apr. 3/96
Away .... **7** Oct. 14-Nov. 7/70, Feb. 6-27/71, Jan. 10-Feb. 3/96
Longest Winless Streak
Overall .... **12** Nov. 23-Dec. 20/91 (8 losses, 4 ties)
Home .... **12** Jan. 27-Mar. 10/91 (7 losses, 5 ties)
Away .... **23** Oct. 30/71-Feb. 19/72 (15 losses, 8 ties)
Most Shutouts, Season **13** 1997-98 (82)
Most PIM, Season ***2,713** 1991-92 (80)
Most Goals, Game .... **14** Jan. 21/75 (Wsh. 2 at Buf. 14), Mar. 19/81 (Tor. 4 at Buf. 14)

Individual

Most Seasons .... **17** Gilbert Perreault
Most Games .... **1,191** Gilbert Perreault
Most Goals, Career .... **512** Gilbert Perreault
Most Assists, Career .... **814** Gilbert Perreault
Most Points, Career .... **1,326** Gilbert Perreault (512G, 814A)
Most PIM, Career .... **3,189** Rob Ray
Most Shutouts, Career .... **55** Dominik Hasek
Longest Consecutive Games Streak .... **776** Craig Ramsay (Mar. 27/73-Feb. 10/83)
Most Goals, Season .... **76** Alexander Mogilny (1992-93)
Most Assists, Season .... **95** Pat LaFontaine (1992-93)
Most Points, Season .... **148** Pat LaFontaine (1992-93; 53G, 95A)
Most PIM, Season .... **354** Rob Ray (1991-92)
Most Points, Defenseman, Season .... **81** Phil Housley (1989-90; 21G, 60A)
Most Points, Center, Season .... **148** Pat LaFontaine (1992-93; 53G, 95A)
Most Points, Right Wing, Season .... **127** Alexander Mogilny (1992-93; 76G, 51A)
Most Points, Left Wing, Season .... **95** Rick Martin (1974-75; 52G, 43A)
Most Points, Rookie, Season .... **74** Rick Martin (1971-72; 44G, 30A)
Most Shutouts, Season .... **13** Dominik Hasek (1997-98)
Most Goals, Game .... **5** Dave Andreychuk (Feb. 6/86)
Most Assists, Game .... **5** Gilbert Perreault (Feb. 1/76, Mar. 9/80, Jan. 4/84), Dale Hawerchuk (Jan. 15/92), Pat LaFontaine (Dec. 31/92, Feb. 10/93)
Most Points, Game .... **7** Gilbert Perreault (Feb. 1/76; 2G, 5A)

* NHL Record.

Retired Numbers

2	Tim Horton	1972-1974
7	Rick Martin	1971-1981
11	Gilbert Perreault	1970-1987
14	Rene Robert	1971-1979
16	Pat Lafontaine	1991-1996
18	Danny Gare	1974-1981

All-time Record vs. Other Clubs

Regular Season

	At Home								On Road								Total							
	GP	W	L	T	OL	GF	GA	PTS	GP	W	L	T	OL	GF	GA	PTS	GP	W	L	T	OL	GF	GA	PTS
Anaheim	10	5	2	3	0	28	22	13	9	7	2	0	0	30	15	14	19	12	4	3	0	58	37	27
Atlanta	12	7	5	0	0	49	34	14	12	4	6	1	1	36	38	10	24	11	11	1	1	85	72	24
Boston	112	57	39	15	1	403	330	130	111	35	61	14	1	325	412	85	223	92	100	29	2	728	742	215
Calgary	45	27	13	5	0	189	131	59	47	18	18	11	0	147	156	47	92	45	31	16	0	336	287	106
Carolina	79	46	25	7	1	315	235	100	80	36	32	11	1	237	231	84	159	82	57	18	2	552	466	184
Chicago	53	32	14	7	0	199	138	71	51	18	27	6	0	139	164	42	104	50	41	13	0	338	302	113
Colorado	63	36	18	9	0	247	204	81	65	23	31	11	0	203	231	57	128	59	49	20	0	450	435	138
Columbus	4	2	2	0	0	13	9	4	2	0	1	1	0	4	5	1	6	2	3	1	0	17	14	5
Dallas	53	29	13	11	0	192	142	69	54	21	27	6	0	156	173	48	107	50	40	17	0	348	315	117
Detroit	52	33	11	8	0	226	153	74	55	18	31	5	1	159	203	42	107	51	42	13	1	385	356	116
Edmonton	30	10	13	7	0	109	112	27	30	6	21	3	0	77	121	15	60	16	34	10	0	186	233	42
Florida	25	16	6	3	0	70	42	35	23	10	12	1	0	66	66	21	48	26	18	4	0	136	108	56
Los Angeles	54	29	16	9	0	227	158	67	54	23	22	9	0	187	185	55	108	52	38	18	0	414	343	122
Minnesota	3	1	2	0	0	7	8	2	4	3	1	0	0	10	6	6	7	4	3	0	0	17	14	8
Montreal	106	56	30	19	1	327	276	132	107	37	58	12	0	318	401	86	213	93	88	31	1	645	677	218
Nashville	4	0	3	1	0	9	16	1	5	3	2	0	0	9	10	6	9	3	5	1	0	18	26	7
New Jersey	56	32	16	8	0	219	169	72	56	26	20	9	1	180	168	62	112	58	36	17	1	399	337	134
NY Islanders	63	34	19	9	1	209	171	78	63	27	26	9	1	176	179	64	126	61	45	18	2	385	350	142
NY Rangers	70	40	19	10	1	284	216	91	68	24	27	15	2	186	220	65	138	64	46	25	3	470	436	156
Ottawa	35	23	9	3	0	111	66	49	37	17	12	7	1	95	93	42	72	40	21	10	1	206	159	91
Philadelphia	65	33	24	8	0	215	182	74	69	17	39	12	1	170	234	47	134	50	63	20	1	385	416	121
Phoenix	32	20	6	5	1	128	82	46	29	14	13	2	0	92	87	30	61	34	19	7	1	220	169	76
Pittsburgh	73	36	18	17	2	281	195	91	73	19	36	18	0	224	271	56	146	55	54	35	2	505	466	147
St. Louis	52	29	17	6	0	200	164	64	50	14	28	7	1	125	180	36	102	43	45	13	1	325	344	100
San Jose	12	11	1	0	0	52	32	22	10	1	4	4	1	33	36	7	22	12	5	4	1	85	68	29
Tampa Bay	25	15	8	2	0	74	69	32	25	16	6	3	0	78	53	35	50	31	14	5	0	152	122	67
Toronto	73	47	19	6	1	299	189	101	71	29	27	12	3	242	220	73	144	76	46	18	4	541	409	174
Vancouver	52	26	18	8	0	186	152	60	53	16	26	11	0	163	197	43	105	42	44	19	0	349	349	103
Washington	58	36	16	6	0	226	154	78	58	34	15	9	0	205	146	77	116	70	31	15	0	431	300	155
Defunct Clubs	23	13	5	5	0	94	63	31	23	12	8	3	0	97	76	27	46	25	13	8	0	191	139	58
Totals	**1394**	**781**	**407**	**197**	**9**	**5188**	**3914**	**1768**	**1394**	**528**	**639**	**212**	**15**	**4169**	**4577**	**1283**	**2788**	**1309**	**1046**	**409**	**24**	**9357**	**8491**	**3051**

Playoffs

	Series	W	L	GP	W	L	T	GF	GA	Last Mtg.	Rnd.	Result
Boston	7	2	5	39	18	21	0	130	139	1999	CSF	W 4-2
Carolina	1	0	1	7	3	4	0	17	22	2006	CF	L 3-4
Chicago	2	2	0	9	8	1	0	36	17	1980	QF	W 4-0
Colorado	2	0	2	8	2	6	0	27	35	1985	DSF	L 2-3
Dallas	3	1	2	13	5	8	0	37	39	1999	F	L 2-4
Montreal	7	3	4	35	17	18	0	111	124	1998	CSF	W 4-0
New Jersey	1	0	1	7	3	4	0	14	14	1994	CQF	L 3-4
NY Islanders	3	0	3	16	4	12	0	45	59	1980	SF	L 2-4
NY Rangers	1	1	0	3	2	1	0	11	6	1978	PRE	W 2-1
Ottawa	3	3	0	16	12	4	0	42	32	2006	CSF	W 4-1
Philadelphia	8	3	5	43	18	25	0	123	124	2006	CQF	W 4-2
Pittsburgh	2	0	2	10	4	6	0	26	26	2001	CSF	L 3-4
St. Louis	1	1	0	3	2	1	0	7	8	1976	PRE	W 2-1
Toronto	1	1	0	5	4	1	0	21	16	1999	CF	W 4-1
Vancouver	2	2	0	7	6	1	0	28	14	1981	PRE	W 3-0
Washington	1	0	1	6	2	4	0	11	13	1998	CF	L 2-4
Totals	**45**	**19**	**26**	**227**	**110**	**117**	**0**	**686**	**688**			

Playoff Results 2006-2001

Year	Round	Opponent	Result	GF	GA
2006	CF	Carolina	L 3-4	17	22
	CSF	Ottawa	W 4-1	16	13
	CQF	Philadelphia	W 4-2	27	14
2001	CSF	Pittsburgh	L 3-4	17	17
	CQF	Philadelphia	W 4-2	21	13

Abbreviations: Round: F - Final; **CF** - conference final; **CSF** - conference semi-final; **CQF** - conference quarter-final; **DSF** - division semi-final; **SF** - semi-final; **QF** - quarter-final; **PRE** - preliminary round.

Calgary totals include Atlanta Flames, 1972-73 to 1979-80.
Carolina totals include Hartford, 1979-80 to 1996-97.
Colorado totals include Quebec, 1979-80 to 1994-95.
Dallas totals include Minnesota North Stars, 1970-71 to 1992-93.
New Jersey totals include Kansas City, 1974-75 to 1975-76, and Colorado Rockies, 1976-77 to 1981-82.
Phoenix totals include Winnipeg, 1979-80 to 1995-96.

2005-06 Results

Oct.	5	NY Islanders	6-4
	7	Boston	4-1
	8	at Ottawa	0-5
	10	Pittsburgh	3-2*
	13	at Tampa Bay	4-3†
	15	at Florida	2-3
	20	at Boston	4-3
	22	NY Rangers	3-1
	26	Washington	2-3
	28	at New Jersey	2-3
	29	at NY Islanders	6-4
Nov.	2	Ottawa	4-10
	4	Montreal	2-3
	5	at Montreal	2-3
	9	Carolina	3-5
	11	Toronto	5-2
	12	at Ottawa	1-6
	15	New Jersey	4-1
	17	Washington	8-5
	19	at Boston	3-2
	22	NY Rangers	2-3†
	23	at NY Islanders	4-3†
	25	Montreal	3-1
	27	at Washington	3-2
	29	at Pittsburgh	3-2
Dec.	1	at Montreal	3-2*
	2	San Jose	0-5
	4	at Colorado	6-4
	8	Anaheim	3-2*
	11	at Minnesota	3-2
	14	Dallas	4-3
	16	at Pittsburgh	4-3*
	17	Pittsburgh	4-3
	19	at Philadelphia	2-1†
	22	at Florida	1-4
	23	at Tampa Bay	4-1
	26	NY Islanders	6-3
	29	at Toronto	3-4†
	30	Atlanta	4-1
Jan.	1	Florida	1-2
	5	Tampa Bay	3-1
	7	New Jersey	2-3
	12	Phoenix	1-2†
	14	Los Angeles	10-1
	16	at Edmonton	3-1
	19	at Vancouver	1-4
	21	at Calgary	1-4
	24	at NY Rangers	2-1
	26	at Toronto	8-4
	31	at Atlanta	5-2
Feb.	2	Philadelphia	4-2
	4	Ottawa	2-1†
	7	at Montreal	3-2*
	9	Montreal	2-3*
	11	Florida	5-3
	12	at Carolina	3-4†
Mar.	1	Atlanta	2-4
	3	Toronto	6-2
	4	at Boston	3-2
	7	Boston	3-2
	9	Tampa Bay	8-5
	11	at Philadelphia	6-5
	12	Boston	6-2
	14	at Washington	6-4
	16	Toronto	3-1
	18	at Ottawa	2-4
	20	at Atlanta	0-5
	22	Carolina	3-4
	24	Ottawa	1-3
	25	at Boston	4-5
	27	at NY Rangers	4-5†
	29	Boston	4-3
	30	at New Jersey	1-3
Apr.	1	at Toronto	0-7
	3	at Toronto	3-2†
	5	Ottawa	5-4*
	7	Philadelphia	2-4
	8	at Ottawa	6-2
	12	Montreal	3-1
	15	at Montreal	4-2
	16	Toronto	6-0
	18	at Carolina	4-0

* – Overtime † – Shootout

Entry Draft
Selections 2006-1992

2006		2002		1998		1994	
Pick		**Pick**		**Pick**		**Pick**	
24	Dennis Persson	11	Keith Ballard	18	Dmitri Kalinin	17	Wayne Primeau
46	Jhonas Enroth	20	Dan Paille	34	Andrew Peters	43	Curtis Brown
57	Mike Weber	76	Michael Tessier	47	Norm Milley	69	Rumun Ndur
117	Felix Schutz	82	John Adams	50	Jaroslav Kristek	121	Sergei Klimentiev
147	Alex Biega	108	Jakub Hulva	77	Mike Pandolfo	147	Cal Benazic
207	Benjamin Breault	121	Marty Magers	137	Aaron Goldade	168	Steve Plouffe
		178	Maxim Schevjev	164	Ales Kotalik	173	Shane Hnidy
2005		208	Radoslav Hecl	191	Brad Moran	176	Steve Webb
Pick		241	Dennis Wideman	218	David Moravec	199	Bob Westerby
13	Marek Zagrapan	271	Martin Cizek	249	Edo Terglav	225	Craig Millar
48	Philip Gogulla					251	Mark Polak
87	Marc-Andre Gragnani	**2001**		**1997**		277	Shayne Wright
96	Chris Butler	**Pick**		**Pick**			
142	Nathan Gerbe	22	Jiri Novotny	21	Mika Noronen	**1993**	
182	Adam Dennis	32	Derek Roy	48	Henrik Tallinder	**Pick**	
191	Vyacheslav Buravchikov	50	Chris Thorburn	69	Maxim Afinogenov	38	Denis Tsygurov
208	Matt Generous	55	Jason Pominville	75	Jeff Martin	64	Ethan Philpott
227	Andrew Orpik	155	Michal Vondrka	101	Luc Theoret	116	Richard Safarik
		234	Calle Aslund	128	Torrey DiRoberto	142	Kevin Pozzo
2004		247	Marek Dubec	156	Brian Campbell	168	Sergei Petrenko
Pick		279	Ryan Jorde	184	Jeremy Adduono	194	Mike Barrie
13	Drew Stafford			212	Kamil Piros	220	Barrie Moore
43	Michael Funk	**2000**		238	Dylan Kemp	246	Chris Davis
71	Andrej Sekera	**Pick**				272	Scott Nichol
145	Michal Valent	15	Artem Kryukov	**1996**			
176	Patrick Kaleta	48	Gerard Dicaire	**Pick**		**1992**	
207	Mark Mancari	111	Ghyslain Rousseau	7	Erik Rasmussen	**Pick**	
241	Mike Card	149	Denis Denisov	27	Cory Sarich	11	David Cooper
273	Dylan Hunter	213	Vasili Bizyayev	33	Darren Van Oene	35	Jozef Cierny
		220	Paul Gaustad	54	Francois Methot	59	Ondrej Steiner
2003		258	Sean McMorrow	87	Kurt Walsh	80	Dean Melanson
Pick		277	Ryan Courtney	106	Mike Martone	83	Matthew Barnaby
5	Thomas Vanek			115	Alexei Tezikov	107	Markus Ketterer
65	Branislav Fabry	**1999**		142	Ryan Davis	108	Yuri Khmylev
74	Clarke MacArthur	**Pick**		161	Darren Mortier	131	Paul Rushforth
106	Jan Hejda	20	Barrett Heisten	222	Scott Buhler	179	Dean Tiltgen
114	Denis Ezhov	35	Milan Bartovic			203	Todd Simon
150	Thomas Morrow	55	Doug Janik	**1995**		227	Rick Kowalsky
172	Pavel Voroshnin	64	Mike Zigomanis	**Pick**		251	Chris Clancy
202	Nathan Paetsch	73	Tim Preston	14	Jay McKee		
235	Jeff Weber	117	Karel Mosovsky	16	Martin Biron		
266	Louis-Philippe Martin	138	Ryan Miller	42	Mark Dutiaume		
		146	Matt Kinch	68	Mathieu Sunderland		
		178	Seneque Hyacinthe	94	Matt Davidson		
		206	Bret DeCecco	111	Marian Menhart		
		235	Brad Self	119	Kevin Popp		
		263	Craig Brunel	123	Daniel Bienvenue		
				172	Brian Scott		
				198	Mike Zanutto		
				224	Rob Skrlac		

General Managers' History

Punch Imlach, 1970-71 to 1977-78; John Anderson, 1978-79; Scotty Bowman, 1979-80 to 1985-86; Scotty Bowman and Gerry Meehan, 1986-87; Gerry Meehan, 1987-88 to 1992-93; John Muckler, 1993-94 to 1996-97; Darcy Regier, 1997-98 to date.

General Manager

REGIER, DARCY
General Manager, Buffalo Sabres. Born in Swift Current, Sask., Nov. 27, 1957.

Darcy Regier became the sixth general manager of the Buffalo Sabres on June 11, 1997 after a lengthy management apprenticeship in the New York Islanders organization. As a player, Regier played eight pro seasons, including part of the 1977-78 season with the Cleveland Barons and parts of the 1982-83 and 1983-84 campaigns with the New York Islanders.

He began his career as an administrator with the Islanders in 1984-85 and went on to serve in a variety of capacities including director of administration, assistant director of hockey operations, assistant coach and assistant general manager. He also served as an assistant coach with Hartford in 1991-92.

While with the Islanders, Regier benefitted from working with talented managers and coaches including Bill Torrey and Al Arbour. As a minor pro player with Indianapolis of the CHL he became associated with another important influence on his hockey career, current Detroit Red Wing executive Jim Devellano.

Club Directory

HSBC Arena

Buffalo Sabres
HSBC Arena
One Seymour H. Knox III Plaza
Buffalo, NY 14203
Phone **716/855-4100**
Fax 716/855-4110
Tickets, U.S.: 888/GO-SABRES
Canada: 888/669-GOAL
www.sabres.com
Capacity: 18,690

Executive
Owner . . . . B. Thomas Golisano
Managing Partner . . . . Lawrence Quinn
Chief Operating Officer . . . . Daniel DiPofi

Hockey Department
General Manager . . . . Darcy Regier
Professional Scout . . . . Jon Christiano
Amateur Scouts . . . . Bo Berglund, Kevin Devine, Iouri Khmylev, Paul Merritt, Darryl Plandowski
Coordinator of Amateur Scouting & Operations . . . Scott Schranz
Hockey Department Analyst . . . . Mark Jakubowski
Hockey Video Analyst . . . . Corey Smith
Coordinator of Hockey Operations . . . . Michael Bermingham

Coaching Staff
Head Coach . . . . Lindy Ruff
Associate Coach . . . . Brian McCutcheon
Assistant Coach . . . . James Patrick
Strength and Conditioning Coach . . . . Doug McKenney
Asst. Strength and Conditioning Coach . . . . . Kevin Collins
Goaltender Coach . . . . Jim Corsi
Administrative Assistant Coach . . . . Corey Smith
Athletic Trainer . . . . Tim Macre
Head Equipment Manager . . . . Dave Williams
Equipment Manager . . . . Rip Simonick
Assistant Equipment Managers . . . . George Babcock, Dave Williams
Massage Therapist . . . . Chuck Garlow

Medical
Team Doctor . . . . Les Bisson, M.D.
Doctors . . . . Nicholas Aquino, M.D., William Hartrich, M.D.
Oral Surgeon . . . . Steven Jenson, DDS
Team Dentist . . . . Daniel Yustin, DDS, M.S.
Team Doctor Emeritus . . . . John L. Butsch, M.D.

Legal
Director of Legal Affairs and Human Resources . . . . Richard Mugel

Finance and Administration
Director of Finance and Administration . . . . Chuck LaMattina
Accounting Manager . . . . Christine Ivansitz
Payroll & Human Resource Manager . . . . Birgid Haensel
Accounts Payable Clerk . . . . Kim Binkley
Manager of IT Services . . . . Jon Lamont

Broadcast Production
Staff Producer . . . . Joe Pinter
Staff Director . . . . Eric Grossman
Manager of Production Services . . . . Chrisanne Bellas
Feature Producer/Editor . . . . Jeff Hill
Assistant Producer . . . . Matt Gould
Broadcast Team . . . . Rick Jeanneret (Play-by-Play), Jim Lorentz (Commentator)

Merchandise
Director of Merchandise . . . . Mike Kaminska
Merchandise Manager – Inventory Control . . . . . Glenn Barker
Merchandise Manager – Event Sales . . . . Jeff Smith

Marketing
Director of Marketing . . . . Rob Kopacz
Director of Game Presentation . . . . Martin McCreary
Asst. Director of Game Presentation . . . . Rich Wall
Database Marketing Manager . . . . Tom Matheny
Director of Creative Services . . . . Frank Cravotta

Public and Community Relations
Director of Public Relations . . . . Michael Gilbert
Manager of Publications & Hockey Information . . . . Kevin Snow
Coordinator of Media Relations . . . . Chris Bandura
Community Relations Assistant . . . . Teresa Belbas
Mascot Coordinator . . . . Ed Grudzinski
Graduate Assistant . . . . Rob Crean
Team Photographer . . . . Bill Wippert
Director of Alumni Relations . . . . Larry Playfair
Corporate & Community Relations Liaison . . . . Gilbert Perreault

Sales and Business Development
V.P. Sales & Business Development . . . . John Livsey
Senior Account Managers . . . . Joe Foy, Chris Luterek
Account Manager . . . . Joe Shaw
Director of Sales/Marketing – Rochester . . . . Gary Muxworthy

Ticket Sales & Sales Operations
Director of Ticket Operations & Services . . . . John Sinclair
Account Services Representatives . . . . Roxanne Anderson, Gretchen Huzinec, Andrea Keane, Lisa Wells, Melissa Rugg
Account Services Manager . . . . Michael Tout
Box Office Manager . . . . Christopher Makowski
Assistant Box Office Manager . . . . Marty Maloney

HSBC Arena
Director of Arena Operations . . . . Stan Makowski, Jr.
Director of Event Booking . . . . Jennifer Van Rysdam
Arena Marketing Manager . . . . Christine Adamczyk
Director of Amateur Athletics . . . . Kevin Sylvester
Event Managers . . . . Matt Rabinowitz, Beth Guiliani Gatto
Communications Technician . . . . Mike Queeno
Chief Engineer . . . . Barry Becker

Calgary Flames

2005-06 Results: 46w-25L-4OTL-7SOL 103PTS.
First, Northwest Division

Flames team leader Jarome Iginla celebrates one of his 35 goals. The 2005-06 season marked the fifth straight year he has scored more than 30 goals.

2006-07 Schedule

Oct.	Thu.	5	at Edmonton	Tue.	9	Minnesota
	Sat.	7	Edmonton	Thu.	11	at Colorado
	Mon.	9	San Jose	Sat.	13	Edmonton
	Thu.	12	at Ottawa	Mon.	15	at Nashville*
	Sat.	14	at Toronto	Wed.	17	at Dallas
	Tue.	17	at Montreal	Fri.	19	Anaheim
	Thu.	19	at Boston	Sat.	20	at Edmonton
	Tue.	24	Phoenix	Fri.	26	at Minnesota
	Sat.	28	Nashville	Sun.	28	at Chicago*
	Mon.	30	Washington	Tue.	30	Los Angeles
Nov.	Wed.	1	at Detroit	**Feb.** Fri.	2	Columbus
	Fri.	3	at Columbus	Sat.	3	Vancouver
	Sat.	4	at St. Louis	Tue.	6	Chicago
	Tue.	7	Dallas	Thu.	8	at Columbus
	Fri.	10	Anaheim	Sat.	10	at Buffalo
	Sat.	11	at Vancouver	Sun.	11	at Detroit
	Tue.	14	St. Louis	Tue.	13	Atlanta
	Fri.	17	Detroit	Thu.	15	Colorado
	Tue.	21	at Edmonton	Sat.	17	Colorado
	Wed.	22	Chicago	Tue.	20	at Colorado
	Sat.	25	at Los Angeles	Thu.	22	at Phoenix
	Sun.	26	at Anaheim*	Sat.	24	San Jose
	Tue.	28	Colorado	Mon.	26	Phoenix
Dec.	Fri.	1	Columbus	Wed.	28	Minnesota
	Tue.	5	Carolina	**Mar.** Sat.	3	at Edmonton
	Thu.	7	at Minnesota	Tue.	6	at St. Louis
	Sat.	9	Vancouver	Thu.	8	at Nashville
	Tue.	12	Minnesota	Sat.	10	Tampa Bay
	Thu.	14	at Vancouver	Mon.	12	St. Louis
	Sat.	16	at Phoenix	Wed.	14	at Colorado
	Mon.	18	at Anaheim	Thu.	15	at Dallas
	Tue.	19	at Los Angeles	Sat.	17	Minnesota
	Thu.	21	at Colorado	Tue.	20	Detroit
	Sat.	23	at San Jose	Thu.	22	Nashville
	Tue.	26	Vancouver	Sun.	25	at Chicago*
	Wed.	27	at Minnesota	Tue.	27	at Minnesota
	Fri.	29	Los Angeles	Thu.	29	at Minnesota
	Sun.	31	Edmonton	Sat.	31	at Vancouver
Jan.	Tue.	2	Vancouver	**Apr.** Tue.	3	Colorado
	Thu.	4	Florida	Thu.	5	at San Jose
	Sat.	6	Dallas	Sat.	7	Edmonton

* Denotes afternoon game.

Franchise date: June 6, 1972
Transferred from Atlanta to Calgary, June 24, 1980.

NORTHWEST DIVISION

35th NHL Season

Year-by-Year Record

Season	GP	Home W	L	T	OL	Road W	L	T	OL	Overall W	L	T	OL	GF	GA	Pts.	Finished	Playoff Result
2005-06	82	30	7	....	4	16	18	....	7	46	25	....	11	218	200	103	1st, Northwest Div.	Lost Conf. Quarter-Final
2004-05	....	...	...	....	...	...	...	....	...	...	...	....	...	....	....	....		
2003-04	82	21	14	5	1	21	16	2	2	42	30	7	3	200	176	94	3rd, Northwest Div.	Lost Final
2002-03	82	14	16	10	1	15	20	3	3	29	36	13	4	186	228	75	5th, Northwest Div.	Out of Playoffs
2001-02	82	20	14	5	2	12	21	7	1	32	35	12	3	201	220	79	4th, Northwest Div.	Out of Playoffs
2000-01	82	12	18	9	2	15	18	6	2	27	36	15	4	197	236	73	4th, Northwest Div.	Out of Playoffs
1999-2000	82	20	14	6	1	11	22	4	4	31	36	10	5	211	256	77	4th, Northwest Div.	Out of Playoffs
1998-99	82	15	20	6	....	15	20	6	....	30	40	12	....	211	234	72	3rd, Northwest Div.	Out of Playoffs
1997-98	82	18	17	6	....	8	24	9	....	26	41	15	....	217	252	67	5th, Pacific Div.	Out of Playoffs
1996-97	82	21	18	2	....	11	23	7	....	32	41	9	....	214	239	73	5th, Pacific Div.	Out of Playoffs
1995-96	82	18	18	5	....	16	19	6	....	34	37	11	....	241	240	79	2nd, Pacific Div.	Lost Conf. Quarter-Final
1994-95	48	15	7	2	....	9	10	5	....	24	17	7	....	163	135	55	1st, Pacific Div.	Lost Conf. Quarter-Final
1993-94	84	25	12	5	....	17	17	8	....	42	29	13	....	302	256	97	1st, Pacific Div.	Lost Conf. Quarter-Final
1992-93	84	23	14	5	....	20	16	6	....	43	30	11	....	322	282	97	2nd, Smythe Div.	Lost Div. Semi-Final
1991-92	80	19	14	7	....	12	23	5	....	31	37	12	....	296	305	74	5th, Smythe Div.	Out of Playoffs
1990-91	80	29	8	3	....	17	18	5	....	46	26	8	....	344	263	100	2nd, Smythe Div.	Lost Div. Semi-Final
1989-90	80	28	7	5	....	14	16	10	....	42	23	15	....	348	265	99	1st, Smythe Div.	Lost Div. Semi-Final
1988-89	**80**	**32**	**4**	**4**	....	**22**	**13**	**5**	....	**54**	**17**	**9**	....	**354**	**226**	**117**	**1st, Smythe Div.**	**Won Stanley Cup**
1987-88	80	26	11	3	....	22	12	6	....	48	23	9	....	397	305	105	1st, Smythe Div.	Lost Div. Final
1986-87	80	25	13	2	....	21	18	1	....	46	31	3	....	318	289	95	2nd, Smythe Div.	Lost Div. Semi-Final
1985-86	80	23	11	6	....	17	20	3	....	40	31	9	....	354	315	89	2nd, Smythe Div.	Lost Final
1984-85	80	23	11	6	....	18	16	6	....	41	27	12	....	363	302	94	3rd, Smythe Div.	Lost Div. Semi-Final
1983-84	80	22	11	7	....	12	21	7	....	34	32	14	....	311	314	82	2nd, Smythe Div.	Lost Div. Final
1982-83	80	21	12	7	....	11	22	7	....	32	34	14	....	321	317	78	2nd, Smythe Div.	Lost Div. Final
1981-82	80	20	11	9	....	9	23	8	....	29	34	17	....	334	345	75	3rd, Smythe Div.	Lost Div. Semi-Final
1980-81	80	25	5	10	....	14	22	4	....	39	27	14	....	329	298	92	3rd, Patrick Div.	Lost Semi-Final
1979-80*	80	18	15	7	....	17	17	6	....	35	32	13	....	282	269	83	4th, Patrick Div.	Lost Prelim. Round
1978-79*	80	25	11	4	....	16	20	4	....	41	31	8	....	327	280	90	4th, Patrick Div.	Lost Prelim. Round
1977-78*	80	20	13	7	....	14	14	12	....	34	27	19	....	274	252	87	3rd, Patrick Div.	Lost Prelim. Round
1976-77*	80	22	11	7	....	12	23	5	....	34	34	12	....	264	265	80	3rd, Patrick Div.	Lost Prelim. Round
1975-76*	80	19	14	7	....	16	24	0	....	35	33	12	....	262	237	82	3rd, Patrick Div.	Lost Prelim. Round
1974-75*	80	24	9	7	....	10	22	8	....	34	31	15	....	243	233	83	4th, Patrick Div.	Out of Playoffs
1973-74*	78	17	15	7	....	13	19	7	....	30	34	14	....	214	238	74	4th, West Div.	Lost Quarter-Final
1972-73*	78	16	16	7	....	9	22	8	....	25	38	15	....	191	239	65	7th, West Div.	Out of Playoffs

* Atlanta Flames

2006-07 Player Personnel

FORWARDS

Player	HT	WT	S	Place of Birth	Date	2005-06 Club
AMONTE, Tony	6-0	200	L	Hingham, MA	8/2/70	Calgary
FRIESEN, Jeff	6-1	205	L	Meadow Lake, Sask.	8/5/76	Washington-Anaheim
GERMYN, Carsen	5-10	185	R	Campbell River, B.C.	2/22/82	Calgary-Omaha
GODARD, Eric	6-4	220	R	Vernon, B.C.	3/7/80	NY Islanders
HUSELIUS, Kristian	6-1	190	L	Osterhaninge, Sweden	11/10/78	Florida-Calgary
IGINLA, Jarome	6-1	208	R	Edmonton, Alta.	7/1/77	Calgary
KOBASEW, Chuck	6-1	195	R	Osoyoos, B.C.	4/17/82	Calgary
LANGKOW, Daymond	5-11	192	L	Edmonton, Alta.	9/27/76	Calgary
LOMBARDI, Matthew	6-0	195	L	Montreal, Que.	3/18/82	Calgary-Omaha
LUNDMARK, Jamie	6-0	200	R	Edmonton, Alta.	1/16/81	NYR-Phx-San Antonio-Cgy
McCARTY, Darren	6-1	210	R	Burnaby, B.C.	4/1/72	Calgary
NILSON, Marcus	6-2	195	R	Balsta, Sweden	3/1/78	Calgary
NYSTROM, Eric	6-1	205	L	Syosset, NY	2/14/83	Calgary-Omaha
RITCHIE, Byron	5-10	195	L	Burnaby, B.C.	4/24/77	Calgary
TANGUAY, Alex	6-0	190	L	Ste-Justine, Que.	11/21/79	Colorado
YELLE, Stephane	6-1	190	L	Ottawa, Ont.	5/9/74	Calgary

DEFENSEMEN

Player	HT	WT	S	Place of Birth	Date	2005-06 Club
FERENCE, Andrew	5-10	196	L	Edmonton, Alta.	3/17/79	Calgary
FERENCE, Brad	6-3	218	R	Calgary, Alta.	4/2/79	San Antonio-Albany
GIORDANO, Mark	6-0	203	L	Toronto, Ont.	5/10/83	Calgary-Omaha
HAMRLIK, Roman	6-2	210	L	Gottwaldov/Zlin, Czech.	4/12/74	Calgary
PHANEUF, Dion	6-3	213	L	Edmonton, Alta.	4/10/85	Calgary
REGEHR, Richie	6-0	190	R	Bundung, Indonesia	1/17/83	Calgary-Omaha
REGEHR, Robyn	6-2	226	L	Recife, Brazil	4/19/80	Calgary
WARRENER, Rhett	6-2	217	R	Shaunavon, Sask.	1/27/76	Calgary
ZYUZIN, Andrei	6-1	215	L	Ufa, USSR	1/21/78	Minnesota

GOALTENDERS

Player	HT	WT	C	Place of Birth	Date	2005-06 Club
KIPRUSOFF, Miikka	6-2	190	L	Turku, Finland	10/26/76	Calgary
McLENNAN, Jamie	6-0	190	L	Edmonton, Alta.	6/30/71	Florida

Coaching History

Bernie Geoffrion, 1972-73, 1973-74; Bernie Geoffrion and Fred Creighton, 1974-75; Fred Creighton, 1975-76 to 1978-79; Al MacNeil, 1979-80 to 1981-82; Bob Johnson, 1982-83 to 1986-87; Terry Crisp, 1987-88 to 1989-90; Doug Risebrough, 1990-91; Doug Risebrough and Guy Charron, 1991-92; Dave King, 1992-93 to 1994-95; Pierre Page, 1995-96, 1996-97; Brian Sutter, 1997-98 to 1999-2000; Don Hay and Greg Gilbert, 2000-01; Greg Gilbert, 2001-02; Greg Gilbert, Al MacNeil and Darryl Sutter, 2002-03; Darryl Sutter, 2003-04 to 2005-06; Jim Playfair, 2006-07.

Coach

PLAYFAIR, JIM
Coach, Calgary Flames. Born in Fort St. James, B.C., May 22, 1964.

Jim Playfair was named head coach of the Calgary Flames on July 12, 2006 after spending three seasons as an assistant coach, beginning on January 3, 2003. Before joining the parent club, Playfair spent three seasons with Calgary's primary development club of the American Hockey League as head coach. During the 2000-01 season he led the Saint John Flames to their first AHL Calder Cup championship and was named minor professional coach of the year by The Hockey News.

Prior to joining the Flames organization, Playfair was the head coach of the Michigan K-Wings of the International Hockey League. He served as an assistant coach with the K-Wings for three seasons before being named head coach on January 25, 2000. His other head coaching experience includes three seasons as bench boss of the Dayton Bombers of the East Coast Hockey League.

Playfair played nine seasons of professional hockey including 21 games in the NHL with Edmonton and Chicago. He was Edmonton's first choice, 20th overall, in the 1982 NHL Entry Draft. Playfair captained the Indianapolis Ice to the 1990 Turner Cup championship but was forced to retire from playing due to a retina injury suffered during the 1991-92 campaign. As a junior, Playfair performed with the Portland Winter Hawks for two seasons before concluding his junior career as a member of the Calgary Wranglers in 1984. He was a member of Portland's 1983 Memorial Cup championship team.

Coaching Record

Season	Team	Games	W	L	T	Games	W	L
			Regular Season			Playoffs		
1993-94	Dayton (ECHL)	68	29	31	8	3	1	2
1994-95	Dayton (ECHL)	68	42	17	9	8	5	3
1995-96	Dayton (ECHL)	70	35	28	7	....		
1999-2000	Michigan (IHL)	41	18	14	9	....		
2000-01	Saint John (AHL)	80	44	29	7	19	15	4
2001-02	Saint John (AHL)	80	29	38	13	....		
2002-03	Saint John (AHL)	32	10	20	2	....		

2005-06 Scoring

* – rookie

Regular Season

Pos	#	Player	Team	GP	G	A	Pts	+/-	PIM	PP	SH	GW	S	%
R	12	Jarome Iginla	CGY	82	35	32	67	5	86	17	1	6	293	11.9
C	22	Daymond Langkow	CGY	82	25	34	59	2	46	11	0	7	171	14.6
D	3 *	Dion Phaneuf	CGY	82	20	29	49	5	93	16	0	7	242	8.3
R	20	Kristian Huselius	FLA	24	5	3	8	-11	4	2	0	0	57	8.8
			CGY	54	15	24	39	2	36	6	0	4	107	14.0
			TOTAL	78	20	27	47	-9	40	8	0	4	164	12.2
R	10	Tony Amonte	CGY	80	14	28	42	3	43	3	1	3	155	9.0
R	19	Chuck Kobasew	CGY	77	20	11	31	-10	64	10	0	4	143	14.0
D	21	Andrew Ference	CGY	82	4	27	31	-12	85	2	0	0	111	3.6
C	24	Jamie Lundmark	NYR	3	1	0	1	-2	6	0	0	0	1	100.0
			PHX	38	5	13	18	-1	36	1	0	0	61	8.2
			CGY	12	4	6	10	2	20	1	0	1	16	25.0
			TOTAL	53	10	19	29	-1	62	2	0	1	78	12.8
L	27	Mike Leclerc	PHX	35	9	12	21	0	29	4	0	0	44	20.5
			CGY	15	1	4	5	0	8	0	0	1	21	4.8
			TOTAL	50	10	16	26	0	37	4	0	1	65	15.4
D	4	Roman Hamrlik	CGY	51	7	19	26	8	56	1	1	0	89	7.9
C	18	Matthew Lombardi	CGY	55	6	20	26	-1	48	1	2	2	72	8.3
C	28	Robyn Regehr	CGY	68	6	20	26	6	67	5	0	2	89	6.7
L	17	Chris Simon	CGY	72	8	14	22	0	94	2	0	3	76	10.5
R	16	Shean Donovan	CGY	80	9	11	20	9	82	0	1	0	132	6.8
D	6	Jordan Leopold	CGY	74	2	18	20	6	68	2	0	1	87	2.3
C	11	Stephane Yelle	CGY	74	6	14	18	10	48	1	0	1	93	4.3
L	26	Marcus Nilson	CGY	70	6	11	17	13	32	2	0	2	83	7.2
R	25	Darren McCarty	CGY	67	7	6	13	-1	117	1	0	0	67	10.4
C	15	Byron Ritchie	CGY	45	4	2	6	-2	69	0	0	0	34	11.8
D	44	Rhett Warrener	CGY	61	3	3	6	7	54	0	1	0	40	7.5
C	29	Craig MacDonald	CGY	25	3	2	5	5	8	1	0	0	27	11.1
D	32	Cale Hulse	CBJ	27	0	3	3	-9	43	0	0	0	27	0.0
			CGY	12	0	1	1	1	20	0	0	0	7	0.0
			TOTAL	39	0	4	4	-8	63	0	0	0	34	0.0
D	7	Bryan Marchment	CGY	37	1	2	3	8	75	0	0	0	16	6.3
D	49 *	Richie Regehr	CGY	14	0	2	2	0	6	0	0	0	12	0.0
D	46 *	Mark Giordano	CGY	7	0	1	1	2	8	0	0	0	5	0.0
C	37	Lynn Loyns	CGY	1	0	0	0	0	0	0	0	0	0	0.0
L	23 *	Eric Nystrom	CGY	2	0	0	0	-1	0	0	0	0	0	0.0
C	39 *	Carsen Germyn	CGY	2	0	0	0	0	0	0	0	0	0	0.0

Goaltending

No.	Goaltender	GPI	Mins	Avg	W	L	OT	EN	SO	GA	SA	S%	G	A	PIM
34	Miikka Kiprusoff	74	4380	2.07	42	20	11	5	10	151	1951	.923	0	2	10
35	* Philippe Sauve	8	402	3.28	3	3	0	0	0	22	202	.891	0	0	21
33	Brian Boucher	3	182	4.95	1	2	0	0	0	15	103	.854	0	0	0
	Totals	82	4984	2.32	46	25	11	5	10	193	2261	.915			

Playoffs

Pos	#	Player	Team	GP	G	A	Pts	+/-	PIM	PP	SH	GW	OT	S	%
R	12	Jarome Iginla	CGY	7	5	3	8	3	11	1	0	0	0	24	20.8
R	20	Kristian Huselius	CGY	7	2	4	6	1	4	2	0	0	0	14	14.3
C	22	Daymond Langkow	CGY	7	1	5	6	4	6	1	0	0	0	18	5.6
D	28	Robyn Regehr	CGY	7	1	3	4	5	6	1	0	0	0	9	11.1
D	21	Andrew Ference	CGY	7	0	4	4	3	12	0	0	0	0	10	0.0
R	10	Tony Amonte	CGY	7	2	1	3	2	10	0	1	0	0	13	15.4
R	25	Darren McCarty	CGY	7	2	1	3	1	15	0	0	1	1	7	28.6
D	4	Roman Hamrlik	CGY	7	0	3	3	-7	2	0	0	0	0	10	0.0
C	18	Matthew Lombardi	CGY	7	0	3	3	1	6	0	0	0	0	9	0.0
C	11	Stephane Yelle	CGY	7	1	0	1	-1	8	0	0	0	0	7	14.3
R	19	Chuck Kobasew	CGY	7	1	0	1	-3	0	0	0	0	0	13	7.7
D	3 *	Dion Phaneuf	CGY	7	1	0	1	-8	7	1	0	0	0	13	7.7
C	24	Jamie Lundmark	CGY	4	0	1	1	-1	9	0	0	0	0	4	0.0
L	17	Chris Simon	CGY	6	0	1	1	2	6	0	0	0	0	8	0.0
D	6	Jordan Leopold	CGY	7	0	1	1	3	2	0	0	0	0	14	0.0
C	29	Craig MacDonald	CGY	1	0	0	0	-1	0	0	0	0	0	2	0.0
L	27	Mike Leclerc	CGY	1	0	0	0	0	0	0	0	0	0	0	0.0
R	16	Shean Donovan	CGY	7	0	0	0	-2	6	0	0	0	0	8	0.0
D	44	Rhett Warrener	CGY	7	0	0	0	4	14	0	0	0	0	5	0.0
C	15	Byron Ritchie	CGY	7	0	0	0	-2	0	0	0	0	0	4	0.0

Goaltending

No.	Goaltender	GPI	Mins	Avg	W	L	EN	SO	GA	SA	S%	G	A	PIM
34	Miikka Kiprusoff	7	428	2.24	3	4	1	0	16	202	.921	0	0	2
	Totals	7	431	2.37	3	4	1	0	17	203	.916			

Captains' History

Keith McCreary, 1972-73 to 1974-75; Pat Quinn, 1975-76, 1976-77; Tom Lysiak, 1977-78, 1978-79; Jean Pronovost, 1979-80; Brad Marsh, 1980-81; Phil Russell, 1981-82, 1982-83; Lanny McDonald, Doug Risebrough (co-captains), 1983-84; Lanny McDonald, Doug Risebrough, Jim Peplinski (tri-captains), 1984-85 to 1986-87; Lanny McDonald, Jim Peplinski (co-captains), 1987-88; Lanny McDonald, Jim Peplinski, Tim Hunter (tri-captains), 1988-89; Brad McCrimmon, 1989-90; alternating captains, 1990-91; Joe Nieuwendyk, 1991-92 to 1994-95; Theoren Fleury, 1995-96, 1996-97; Todd Simpson, 1997-98, 1998-99; Steve Smith, 1999-2000; Steve Smith and Dave Lowry, 2000-01; Dave Lowry, Bob Boughner and Craig Conroy (co-captains), 2001-02; Bob Boughner and Craig Conroy (co-captains), 2002-03; Jarome Iginla, 2003-04 to date.

Club Records

Team

(Figures in brackets for season records are games played; records for fewest points, wins, ties, losses, goals, goals against are for 70 or more games)

Most Points **117** 1988-89 (80)
Most Wins **54** 1988-89 (80)
Most Ties **19** 1977-78 (80)
Most Losses **41** 1996-97 (82), 1997-98 (82), 1999-2000 (82)
Most Goals **397** 1987-88 (80)
Most Goals Against **345** 1981-82 (80)
Fewest Points **65** 1972-73 (78)
Fewest Wins **25** 1972-73 (78)
Fewest Ties **3** 1986-87 (80)
Fewest Losses **17** 1988-89 (80)
Fewest Goals **186** 2002-03 (82)
Fewest Goals Against **176** 2003-04 (82)

Longest Winning Streak
Overall .... **10** Oct. 14-Nov. 3/78
Home .... **9** Oct. 17-Nov. 15/78, Jan. 3-Feb. 5/89, Mar. 3-Apr. 1/90, Feb. 21-Mar. 14/91
Away .... **7** Nov. 10-Dec. 4/88

Longest Undefeated Streak
Overall .... **13** Nov. 10-Dec. 8/88 (12 wins, 1 tie)
Home .... **18** Dec. 29/90-Mar. 14/91 (17 wins, 1 tie)
Away .... **9** Feb. 20-Mar. 21/88 (6 wins, 3 ties), Nov. 11-Dec. 16/90 (6 wins, 3 ties)

Longest Losing Streak
Overall .... **11** Dec. 14/85-Jan. 7/86
Home .... **6** Dec. 5-31/98
Away .... **9** Dec. 1/85-Jan. 12/86

Longest Winless Streak
Overall .... **11** Dec. 14/85-Jan. 7/86 (11 losses), Jan. 5-26/93 (9 losses, 2 ties)
Home .... **10** Oct. 21-Dec. 4/00 (6 losses, 4 ties)
Away .... **13** Feb. 3-Mar. 29/73 (10 losses, 3 ties)

Most Shutouts, Season **11** 2003-04 (82)
Most PIM, Season **2,643** 1991-92 (80)
Most Goals, Game .... **13** Feb. 10/93 (S.J. 1 at Cgy. 13)

Individual

Most Seasons .... **13** Al MacInnis
Most Games .... **803** Al MacInnis
Most Goals, Career .... **364** Theoren Fleury
Most Assists, Career .... **609** Al MacInnis
Most Points, Career .... **830** Theoren Fleury (364G, 466A)
Most PIM, Career .... **2,405** Tim Hunter
Most Shutouts, Career .... **20** Dan Bouchard
Longest Consecutive Games Streak .... **257** Brad Marsh (Oct. 11/78-Nov. 10/81)
Most Goals, Season .... **66** Lanny McDonald (1982-83)
Most Assists, Season .... **82** Kent Nilsson (1980-81)
Most Points, Season .... **131** Kent Nilsson (1980-81; 49G, 82A)
Most PIM, Season .... **375** Tim Hunter (1988-89)
Most Points, Defenseman, Season .... **103** Al MacInnis (1990-91; 28G, 75A)
Most Points, Center, Season .... **131** Kent Nilsson (1980-81; 49G, 82A)
Most Points, Right Wing, Season .... **110** Joe Mullen (1988-89; 51G, 59A)
Most Points, Left Wing, Season .... **90** Gary Roberts (1991-92; 53G, 37A)
Most Points, Rookie, Season .... **92** Joe Nieuwendyk (1987-88; 51G, 41A)
Most Shutouts, Season .... **10** Miikka Kiprusoff (2005-06)
Most Goals, Game .... **5** Joe Nieuwendyk (Jan. 11/89)
Most Assists, Game .... **6** Guy Chouinard (Feb. 25/81), Gary Suter (Apr. 4/86)
Most Points, Game .... **7** Sergei Makarov (Feb. 25/90; 2G, 5A)

Records include Atlanta Flames, 1972-73 through 1979-80.

Retired Numbers

9	Lanny McDonald	1981-1989

All-time Record vs. Other Clubs

Regular Season

	At Home								On Road								Total							
	GP	W	L	T	OL	GF	GA	PTS	GP	W	L	T	OL	GF	GA	PTS	GP	W	L	T	OL	GF	GA	PTS
Anaheim	27	17	9	1	0	78	62	35	28	8	12	6	2	73	88	24	55	25	21	7	2	151	150	59
Atlanta	3	3	0	0	0	14	6	6	4	0	3	1	0	5	8	1	7	3	3	1	0	19	14	7
Boston	45	19	22	4	0	163	154	42	47	13	28	6	0	130	165	32	92	32	50	10	0	293	319	74
Buffalo	47	18	18	11	0	156	147	47	45	13	26	5	1	131	189	32	92	31	44	16	1	287	336	79
Carolina	29	21	6	2	0	140	92	44	28	13	10	5	0	103	91	31	57	34	16	7	0	243	183	75
Chicago	65	30	22	13	0	206	195	73	63	23	27	13	0	184	201	59	128	53	49	26	0	390	396	132
Colorado	51	24	17	9	1	177	150	58	51	19	20	11	1	164	184	50	102	43	37	20	2	341	334	108
Columbus	10	6	3	0	1	27	21	13	10	3	7	0	0	21	30	6	20	9	10	0	1	48	51	19
Dallas	64	34	15	14	1	211	158	83	64	21	31	11	1	199	233	54	128	55	46	25	2	410	391	137
Detroit	62	35	20	6	1	232	182	77	61	19	32	10	0	180	223	48	123	54	52	16	1	412	405	125
Edmonton	85	46	29	9	1	337	283	102	85	31	42	10	2	278	316	74	170	77	71	19	3	615	599	176
Florida	8	4	3	1	0	21	20	9	9	4	3	2	0	22	21	10	17	8	6	3	0	43	41	19
Los Angeles	96	56	28	12	0	417	316	124	93	37	45	9	2	320	342	85	189	93	73	21	2	737	658	209
Minnesota	14	9	1	3	1	35	26	22	15	7	6	1	1	31	36	16	29	16	7	4	2	66	62	38
Montreal	50	17	26	7	0	149	166	41	46	12	26	8	0	112	163	32	96	29	52	15	0	261	329	73
Nashville	14	6	4	3	1	40	33	16	15	4	10	1	0	29	50	9	29	10	14	4	1	69	83	25
New Jersey	42	28	6	8	0	184	111	64	46	28	15	3	0	166	129	59	88	56	21	11	0	350	240	123
NY Islanders	49	24	14	11	0	172	145	59	52	17	26	9	0	145	194	43	101	41	40	20	0	317	339	102
NY Rangers	49	27	11	10	1	216	148	65	53	23	23	5	2	186	182	53	102	50	34	15	3	402	330	118
Ottawa	12	7	4	1	0	40	26	15	10	2	5	3	0	24	27	7	22	9	9	4	0	64	53	22
Philadelphia	52	25	18	9	0	208	172	59	52	15	33	3	1	137	200	34	104	40	51	12	1	345	372	93
Phoenix	73	40	23	9	1	300	231	90	72	26	34	11	1	244	270	64	145	66	57	20	2	544	501	154
Pittsburgh	46	27	11	8	0	204	140	62	45	11	24	10	0	136	169	32	91	38	35	18	0	340	309	94
St. Louis	64	31	26	5	2	207	183	69	66	25	31	9	1	204	234	60	130	56	57	14	3	411	417	129
San Jose	34	20	10	4	0	121	89	44	36	18	13	4	1	108	106	41	70	38	23	8	1	229	195	85
Tampa Bay	10	6	4	0	0	32	24	12	10	4	5	1	0	32	31	9	20	10	9	1	0	64	55	21
Toronto	62	35	22	5	0	240	195	75	53	18	28	7	0	189	202	43	115	53	50	12	0	429	397	118
Vancouver	102	59	28	15	0	399	291	133	103	47	35	18	3	340	348	115	205	106	63	33	3	739	639	248
Washington	38	24	7	7	0	157	93	55	41	14	21	6	0	139	153	34	79	38	28	13	0	296	246	89
Defunct Clubs	13	8	4	1	0	51	34	17	13	7	3	3	0	43	33	17	26	15	7	4	0	94	67	34
Totals	**1316**	**706**	**411**	**188**	**11**	**4934**	**3893**	**1611**	**1316**	**482**	**624**	**191**	**19**	**4075**	**4618**	**1174**	**2632**	**1188**	**1035**	**379**	**30**	**9009**	**8511**	**2785**

Playoffs

	Series	W	L	GP	W	L	T	GF	GA	Last Mtg.	Rnd.	Result
Anaheim	1	0	1	7	3	4	0	16	17	2006	CQF	L 3-4
Chicago	3	2	1	12	7	5	0	37	33	1996	CQF	L 0-4
Dallas	1	0	1	6	2	4	0	18	25	1981	SF	L 2-4
Detroit	2	1	1	8	4	4	0	16	20	2004	CSF	W 4-2
Edmonton	5	1	4	30	11	19	0	96	132	1991	DSF	L 3-4
Los Angeles	6	2	4	26	13	13	0	102	105	1993	DSF	L 2-4
Montreal	2	1	1	11	5	6	0	32	31	1989	F	W 4-2
NY Rangers	1	0	1	4	1	3	0	8	14	1980	PRE	L 1-3
Philadelphia	2	1	1	11	4	7	0	28	43	1981	QF	W 4-3
Phoenix	3	1	2	13	6	7	0	43	45	1987	DSF	L 2-4
St. Louis	1	1	0	7	4	3	0	28	22	1986	CF	W 4-3
San Jose	2	1	1	13	7	6	0	51	38	2004	CF	W 4-2
Tampa Bay	1	0	1	7	3	4	0	14	13	2004	F	L 3-4
Toronto	1	0	1	2	0	2	0	5	9	1979	PRE	L 0-2
Vancouver	6	4	2	32	17	15	0	101	96	2004	CQF	W 4-3
Totals	**37**	**15**	**22**	**189**	**87**	**102**	**0**	**595**	**643**			

Playoff Results 2006-2001

Year	Round	Opponent	Result	GF	GA
2006	CQF	Anaheim	L 3-4	16	17
2004	F	Tampa Bay	L 3-4	14	13
	CF	San Jose	W 4-2	16	12
	CSF	Detroit	W 4-2	11	12
	CQF	Vancouver	W 4-3	19	16

Abbreviations: Round: F - Final; **CF** - conference final; **CSF** - conference semi-final; **CQF** - conference quarter-final; **DSF** - division semi-final; **SF** - semi-final; **QF** - quarter-final; **PRE** - preliminary round.

Carolina totals include Hartford, 1979-80 to 1996-97.
Colorado totals include Quebec, 1979-80 to 1994-95.
Dallas totals include Minnesota North Stars, 1972-73 to 1992-93.
New Jersey totals include Kansas City, 1974-75 to 1975-76, and Colorado Rockies, 1976-77 to 1981-82.
Phoenix totals include Winnipeg, 1979-80 to 1995-96.

2005-06 Results

Month	Day	Opponent	Score
Oct.	5	at Minnesota	3-6
	7	at Columbus	3-1
	9	at Detroit	3-6
	10	at Colorado	3-7
	13	Dallas	2-3*
	15	Edmonton	3-0
	17	Phoenix	0-2
	20	Edmonton	3-1
	22	at Dallas	1-2
	23	at Los Angeles	3-2
	26	at Anaheim	1-4
	27	at Phoenix	2-3
	29	at San Jose	2-3†
Nov.	1	Minnesota	3-0
	3	Columbus	2-1
	5	Vancouver	1-0
	7	Vancouver	4-3
	10	at Phoenix	4-3
	12	Colorado	5-3
	14	Minnesota	3-2
	16	Detroit	3-1
	18	Chicago	2-5
	21	at Colorado	3-2†
	23	San Jose	3-2
	25	Edmonton	1-2†
	29	at Nashville	0-2
Dec.	1	at Detroit	3-2
	3	at Pittsburgh	3-2
	6	at Philadelphia	0-1†
	7	at New Jersey	4-1
	10	Ottawa	2-1*
	17	Boston	3-0
	19	at Edmonton	4-5
	21	Los Angeles	2-5
	23	at Vancouver	6-5†
	26	at Vancouver	2-1
	27	Nashville	3-4
	29	Minnesota	4-2
	31	Edmonton	6-5
Jan.	2	Chicago	3-2
	6	Toronto	1-0
	7	at Vancouver	3-4*
	10	at NY Rangers	2-4
	12	at NY Islanders	2-3
	14	at Minnesota	4-1
	19	Montreal	3-2
	21	Buffalo	4-1
	23	at Edmonton	3-1
	24	at Colorado	4-7
	26	at Chicago	0-2
	29	at Chicago	5-3
	30	at St. Louis	2-3†
Feb.	1	Columbus	1-2†
	3	Vancouver	1-3
	6	at San Jose	4-3
	8	Anaheim	3-1
	10	St. Louis	3-2*
	28	Vancouver	1-2
Mar.	2	St. Louis	3-1
	4	San Jose	2-0
	7	Nashville	2-3
	9	Dallas	1-0
	12	at Colorado	0-3
	13	Colorado	4-3
	16	at Edmonton	2-3*
	18	at Nashville	4-9
	19	at Minnesota	3-2
	21	at Minnesota	1-3
	23	at St. Louis	7-2
	24	at Columbus	2-3
	26	at Dallas	2-3
	29	Los Angeles	2-1
	31	Colorado	6-3
Apr.	1	at Edmonton	4-1
	3	Detroit	1-2†
	5	Phoenix	5-2
	7	Minnesota	2-1
	8	at Vancouver	2-3*
	11	Anaheim	3-0
	13	Colorado	2-0
	15	at Los Angeles	1-2†
	17	at Anaheim	3-4

* – Overtime † – Shootout

Entry Draft
Selections 2006-1992

2006
Pick
26 Leland Irving
87 John Armstrong
89 Aaron Marvin
118 Hugo Carpentier
149 Juuso Puustinen
179 Jordan Fulton
187 Devin Didiomete
209 Per Jonsson

2005
Pick
26 Matt Pelech
69 Gord Baldwin
74 Dan Ryder
111 J.D. Watt
128 Kevin Lalande
158 Matt Keetley
179 Brett Sutter
221 Myles Rumsey

2004
Pick
24 Kris Chucko
70 Brandon Prust
98 Dustin Boyd
118 Aki Seitsonen
121 Kris Hogg
173 Adam Pardy
182 Fred Wikner
200 Matt Schneider
213 James Spratt
279 Adam Cracknell

2003
Pick
9 Dion Phaneuf
39 Tim Ramholt
97 Ryan Donally
112 Jamie Tardif
143 Greg Moore
173 Tyler Johnson
206 Thomas Bellemare
240 Cam Cunning
270 Kevin Harvey

2002
Pick
10 Eric Nystrom
39 Brian McConnell
90 Matthew Lombardi
112 Yuri Artemenkov
141 Jiri Cetkovsky
142 Emanuel Peter
146 Viktor Bobrov
159 Kristofer Persson
176 Curtis McElhinney
206 David Van Der Gulik
207 Pierre Johnsson
238 Jyri Marttinen

2001
Pick
14 Chuck Kobasew
41 Andrei Taratukhin
56 Andrei Medvedev
108 Tomi Maki
124 Yegor Shastin
145 James Hakewill
164 Yuri Trubachev
207 Garrett Bembridge
220 Dave Moss
233 Joe Campbell
251 Ville Hamalainen

2000
Pick
9 Brent Krahn
40 Kurtis Foster
46 Jarret Stoll
116 Levente Szuper
141 Wade Davis
155 Travis Moen
176 Jukka Hentunen
239 David Hajek
270 Micki DuPont

1999
Pick
11 Oleg Saprykin
38 Dan Cavanaugh
77 Craig Anderson
106 Roman Rozakov
135 Matt Doman
153 Jesse Cook
166 Cory Pecker
170 Matt Underhill
190 Blair Stayzer
252 Dmitri Kirilenko

1998
Pick
6 Rico Fata
33 Blair Betts
62 Paul Manning
102 Shaun Sutter
108 Dany Sabourin
120 Brent Gauvreau
192 Radek Duda
206 Jonas Frogren
234 Kevin Mitchell

1997
Pick
6 Daniel Tkaczuk
32 Evan Lindsay
42 John Tripp
51 Dmitri Kokorev
60 Derek Schutz
70 Erik Andersson
92 Chris St. Croix
100 Ryan Ready
113 Martin Moise
140 Ilja Demidov
167 Jeremy Rondeau
223 Dustin Paul

1996
Pick
13 Derek Morris
39 Travis Brigley
40 Steve Begin
73 Dmitri Vlasenkov
89 Toni Lydman
94 Christian Lefebvre
122 Josef Straka
202 Ryan Wade
228 Ronald Petrovicky

1995
Pick
20 Denis Gauthier
46 Pavel Smirnov
72 Rocky Thompson
98 Jan Labraaten
150 Clarke Wilm
176 Ryan Gillis
233 Steve Shirreffs

1994
Pick
19 Chris Dingman
45 Dmitri Ryabykin
77 Chris Clark
91 Ryan Duthie
97 Johan Finnstrom
107 Nils Ekman
123 Frank Appel
149 Patrick Haltia
175 Ladislav Kohn
201 Keith McCambridge
227 Jorgen Jonsson
253 Mike Peluso
279 Pavel Torgaev

1993
Pick
18 Jesper Mattsson
44 Jamie Allison
70 Dan Tompkins
95 Jason Smith
96 Marty Murray
121 Darryl Lafrance
122 John Emmons
148 Andreas Karlsson
200 Derek Sylvester
252 German Titov
278 Burke Murphy

1992
Pick
6 Cory Stillman
30 Chris O'Sullivan
54 Mathias Johansson
78 Robert Svehla
102 Sami Helenius
126 Ravil Yakubov
129 Joel Bouchard
150 Pavel Rajnoha
174 Ryan Mulhern
198 Brandon Carper
222 Jonas Hoglund
246 Andrei Potaichuk

General Managers' History

Cliff Fletcher, 1972-73 to 1990-91; Doug Risebrough, 1991-92 to 1994-95; Doug Risebrough and Al Coates, 1995-96; Al Coates, 1996-97 to 1999-2000; Craig Button, 2000-01 to 2002-03; Darryl Sutter, 2003-04 to date.

General Manager

SUTTER, DARRYL
General Manager, Calgary Flames. Born in Viking, Alta., August 19, 1958.

Darryl Sutter was named general manager of the Calgary Flames on April 11, 2003 adding the portfolio to his head coaching position. On July 12, 2006, he stepped down as coach to concentrate solely on his duties as general manager. Sutter had joined the Flames as coach on December 28, 2002. In his first full season with the Flames in 2003-04, he led the team back to the playoffs after a seven-year absence and guided the club on a thrilling run to the seventh game of the Stanley Cup Finals.

Before joining the Flames, Sutter was the San Jose Sharks franchise leader in regular-season games coached (434) and wins (192). Through the 2001-02 season, Sutter became only the second coach in NHL history (Al Arbour, New York Islanders) to improve his team's point total for five consecutive years.

Prior to San Jose, Sutter coached Chicago for three years (1992 to 1995) and spent two seasons (1995 to 1997) with the Blackhawks as a consultant for special assignments. He spent the 1987-88 campaign as a Blackhawks assistant coach to Bob Murdoch and served as an associate coach for Mike Keenan during the 1990-91 and 1991-92 seasons. During his final season as associate coach, the Blackhawks advanced to the Stanley Cup Finals. Sutter spent two seasons coaching the Blackhawks top development affiliate in the IHL, which played in Saginaw (1988-89) and in Indianapolis (1989-90). Under his leadership, the Indianapolis Ice stormed through the regular season with 114 points and won the Turner Cup championship. He was named IHL coach of the year.

As a player, Sutter was selected by Chicago in the ninth round, 179th overall, in the 1978 NHL Entry Draft. During his eight-year career with the Blackhawks from 1979 to 1987, he scored 279 points (161 goals, 118 assists) with 288 penalty minutes in 406 NHL career games. Sutter served as team captain with the Blackhawks for five seasons, beginning in the 1982-83 season through 1986-87 when he was forced to retire prematurely due to a series of injuries.

Darryl is a member of the famous Sutter hockey family, who had six brothers that played in the NHL. They were all inducted into the Alberta Sports Hall of Fame in May 2000 under the Lifetime Achievement category. Along with his brothers, Darryl is very involved in the Sutter Foundation, started by he and his family in Alberta, which raises money for non-profit organizations.

Club Directory

Pengrowth Saddledome

Calgary Flames
Pengrowth Saddledome
P.O. Box 1540 Station M
Calgary, Alberta T2P 3B9
Phone **403/777-4646**
FAX 403/777-2171
www.calgaryflames.com
Capacity: 19,289

Owners: N. Murray Edwards (Chairman), Harley N. Hotchkiss, Alvin G. Libin, Allan P. Markin, Jeffrey J. McCaig, Clayton H. Riddell, Byron J. Seaman, Daryl K. Seaman

Executive
President & Chief Executive Officer . . . . Ken King
General Manager . . . . Darryl Sutter
V.P., Hockey Administration/CFO . . . . Michael Holditch
V.P., Building Operations . . . . Libby Raines
V.P., Advertising, Sponsorship & Marketing . . . . Jim Bagshaw
V.P., Sales . . . . Rollie Cyr
V.P., Communications . . . . Peter Hanlon
V.P., Business Development . . . . Jim Peplinski
V.P., Food and Beverage . . . . Mark Valliant

Hockey Club Personnel
General Manager . . . . Darryl Sutter
V.P., Hockey Administration/CFO . . . . Michael Holditch
President, Omaha/Assistant GM Calgary . . . . . . Doug Soetaert
Director, Hockey Administration . . . . Mike Burke
Head Coach . . . . Jim Playfair
Assistant Coaches . . . . Rich Preston, Rob Cookson, Wayne Fleming
Goaltending Coach . . . . David Marcoux
Team Services Manager . . . . Sean O'Brien
Exec. Asst. to GM and Hockey Operations . . . . . . Brenda Koyich
Director of Scouting . . . . Tod Button
Director of Amateur Scouting . . . . Mike Sands
Pro Scouts . . . . Ron Sutter (West), Tom Webster (East)
Scouts . . . . Tomas Jelinek, Sergei Samoilov, Al Tuer, Craig Demetrick, Fred Devereaux, Randy Hansch, Greg Rajanen, Ralph Schmidt, Anders Steen, Rich Thibeau

Medical/Training Staff
Athletic Therapist . . . . Morris Boyer
Assistant Athletic Therapist . . . . Gerry Kurylowich
Strength & Conditioning Coach . . . . Rich Hesketh
Equipment Manager . . . . Gus Thorson
Assistant Equipment Manager . . . . Mark DePasquale
Team Physicians . . . . Dr. Kelly Brett, Dr. Jim Thorne
Team Dentist . . . . Dr. Bill Blair
Dressing Room Attendant . . . . Jules Carriere

Omaha Ak-Sar-Ben Knights
Head Coach, Omaha . . . . Ryan McGill
Assistant Coach, Omaha . . . . Scott Allen
Athletic Trainer . . . . DJ Amadio
Equipment Manager . . . . Greg Sieg
Director of Communications & Broadcasting . . . . . Dave Ahlers

Communications
V.P., Communications . . . . Peter Hanlon
Media Relations Coordinator . . . . TBA
Administrative Assistant, Communications . . . . . . Bernie Hargrave

Administration
Director of Financial Reporting . . . . Lisa Gutierrez
Controllers . . . . Karen Kingham, Scott Budau
Exec. Asst. to President/CEO . . . . Judy O'Brien
Exec. Asst. to VP Hockey Admin./CFO . . . . Jill Stang

Marketing/Ticketing
Senior Director, Advertising . . . . Pat Halls
Director, Corporate Sponsorship . . . . Kevin Gross
Corporate, Key Account Manager . . . . Mark Stiles
Advertising/Promotions Manager . . . . Cheryl Sundell
Executive Assistant Marketing . . . . Yvette Mutcheson
Director, Executive Suites . . . . Bob White
Sales Manager . . . . Mike Franco
Customer Service Manager . . . . Marc Leost
Director/Producer, Jumbotron . . . . Carlo Petrini
Entertainment Coordinator . . . . Steve Johnston
Director, Retail/FanAttic . . . . Kevin Lawton
Publishing . . . . Laurie Wheeler

Pengrowth Saddledome
Operations Manager . . . . George Greenwood
Director, Food Services . . . . Art Hernandez
Concessions Manager . . . . Sheila Parisien
Security/Parking Manager . . . . Bob Godun

Miscellaneous
Radio Affiliate . . . . The FAN 960 (960 AM)
TV Affiliate . . . . Rogers Sportsnet, CBC-TV, Flames PPV, TSN
Mascot . . . . Harvey the Hound

NHL Coaching Record

| Season | Team | Games | Regular Season | | | Games | Playoffs | |
			W	L	O/T		W	L
1992-93	Chicago	84	47	25	12	4	0	4
1993-94	Chicago	84	39	36	9	6	2	4
1994-95	Chicago	48	24	19	5	16	9	7
1997-98	San Jose	82	34	38	10	6	2	4
1998-99	San Jose	82	31	33	18	6	2	4
1999-2000	San Jose	82	35	37	10	12	5	7
2000-01	San Jose	82	40	30	12	6	2	4
2001-02	San Jose	82	44	30	8	12	7	5
2002-03	San Jose	24	8	14	2	....	....	....
	Calgary	46	19	19	8	....	....	....
2003-04	Calgary	82	42	33	7	26	15	11
2005-06	Calgary	82	46	25	11	7	3	4
NHL Totals		**860**	**409**	**339**	**112**	**101**	**47**	**54**

Carolina Hurricanes

2005-06 Results: 52w-22L-6OTL-2SOL 112PTS.
First, Southeast Division

2006-07 Schedule

Oct.	Wed.	4	Buffalo
	Fri.	6	New Jersey
	Sat.	7	at Washington
	Wed.	11	at Florida
	Fri.	13	at Atlanta
	Sat.	14	at Pittsburgh
	Mon.	16	at Tampa Bay
	Fri.	20	at Buffalo
	Sat.	21	at NY Islanders
	Wed.	25	Atlanta
	Thu.	26	at Tampa Bay
	Sat.	28	Tampa Bay
Nov.	Wed.	1	at Atlanta
	Thu.	2	Montreal
	Sat.	4	at Ottawa
	Tue.	7	at New Jersey
	Thu.	9	Washington
	Sat.	11	Pittsburgh
	Mon.	13	Buffalo
	Wed.	15	NY Rangers
	Fri.	17	at Washington
	Sat.	18	Dallas
	Tue.	21	at NY Rangers
	Wed.	22	at NY Islanders
	Fri.	24	at Boston*
	Tue.	28	Ottawa
	Thu.	30	Montreal
Dec.	Sat.	2	Boston
	Tue.	5	at Calgary
	Wed.	6	at Edmonton
	Fri.	8	at Vancouver
	Mon.	11	at Colorado
	Fri.	15	Toronto
	Sat.	16	at Tampa Bay
	Tue.	19	at Philadelphia
	Fri.	22	NY Islanders
	Sat.	23	at Florida
	Tue.	26	Florida
	Thu.	28	at Buffalo
	Fri.	29	Anaheim
	Sun.	31	Philadelphia
Jan.	Tue.	2	at Pittsburgh
	Thu.	4	Phoenix
	Sat.	6	NY Islanders
	Tue.	9	at Toronto
	Thu.	11	Florida
	Sat.	13	Atlanta
	Tue.	16	at Florida
	Thu.	18	Washington
	Sat.	20	Tampa Bay
	Fri.	26	Washington
	Sat.	27	at Washington
	Tue.	30	Toronto
Feb.	Thu.	1	Tampa Bay
	Sat.	3	Boston
	Tue.	6	at Montreal
	Thu.	8	at Boston
	Sat.	10	at Minnesota
	Tue.	13	Los Angeles
	Thu.	15	NY Rangers
	Sat.	17	at Montreal
	Tue.	20	Atlanta
	Thu.	22	Philadelphia
	Sat.	24	at Atlanta
	Tue.	27	Ottawa
	Wed.	28	at Ottawa
Mar.	Fri.	2	Pittsburgh
	Sun.	4	at Atlanta*
	Fri.	9	at Washington
	Sun.	11	at NY Rangers*
	Tue.	13	Florida
	Thu.	15	New Jersey
	Sat.	17	at New Jersey*
	Thu.	22	Washington
	Sat.	24	San Jose
	Tue.	27	at Toronto
	Wed.	28	at Philadelphia
	Fri.	30	Tampa Bay
Apr.	Sun.	1	at Florida*
	Tue.	3	at Tampa Bay
	Fri.	6	Atlanta
	Sat.	7	Florida

* Denotes afternoon game.

Franchise date: June 22, 1979
Transferred from Hartford to Carolina, June 25, 1997.

SOUTHEAST DIVISION

28th NHL Season

21-year-old Eric Staal (holding off New Jersey's John Madden) joined the league's elite with 100 points in 2005-06. He led all playoff performers with 28 points in 26 games as Carolina won the Stanley Cup.

Year-by-Year Record

Season	GP	Home W	L	T	OL	Road W	L	T	OL	Overall W	L	T	OL	GF	GA	Pts.	Finished	Playoff Result
2005-06	82	31	8	....	2	21	14	....	6	52	22	....	8	294	260	112	1st, Southeast Div.	Won Stanley Cup
2004-05																		
2003-04	82	13	18	8	2	15	16	6	4	28	34	14	6	172	209	76	3rd, Southeast Div.	Out of Playoffs
2002-03	82	12	17	9	3	10	26	2	3	22	43	11	6	171	240	61	5th, Southeast Div.	Out of Playoffs
2001-02	82	15	13	11	2	20	13	5	3	35	26	16	5	217	217	91	1st, Southeast Div.	Lost Final
2000-01	82	23	15	3	0	15	17	6	3	38	32	9	3	212	225	88	2nd, Southeast Div.	Lost Conf. Quarter-Final
1999-2000	82	20	16	5	0	17	19	5	0	37	35	10	0	217	216	84	3rd, Southeast Div.	Out of Playoffs
1998-99	82	20	12	9	....	14	18	9	....	34	30	18	....	210	202	86	1st, Southeast Div.	Lost Conf. Quarter-Final
1997-98	82	16	18	7	....	17	23	1	....	33	41	8	....	200	219	74	6th, Northeast Div.	Out of Playoffs
1996-97*	82	23	15	3	....	9	24	8	....	32	39	11	....	226	256	75	5th, Northeast Div.	Out of Playoffs
1995-96*	82	22	15	4	....	12	24	5	....	34	39	9	....	237	259	77	4th, Northeast Div.	Out of Playoffs
1994-95*	48	12	10	2	....	7	14	3	....	19	24	5	....	127	141	43	5th, Northeast Div.	Out of Playoffs
1993-94*	84	14	22	6	....	13	26	3	....	27	48	9	....	227	288	63	6th, Northeast Div.	Out of Playoffs
1992-93*	84	12	25	5	....	14	27	1	....	26	52	6	....	284	369	58	5th, Adams Div.	Out of Playoffs
1991-92*	80	13	17	10	....	13	24	3	....	26	41	13	....	247	283	65	4th, Adams Div.	Lost Div. Semi-Final
1990-91*	80	18	16	6	....	13	22	5	....	31	38	11	....	238	276	73	4th, Adams Div.	Lost Div. Semi-Final
1989-90*	80	17	18	5	....	21	15	4	....	38	33	9	....	275	268	85	4th, Adams Div.	Lost Div. Semi-Final
1988-89*	80	21	17	2	....	16	21	3	....	37	38	5	....	299	290	79	4th, Adams Div.	Lost Div. Semi-Final
1987-88*	80	21	14	5	....	14	24	2	....	35	38	7	....	249	267	77	4th, Adams Div.	Lost Div. Semi-Final
1986-87*	80	26	9	5	....	17	21	2	....	43	30	7	....	287	270	93	1st, Adams Div.	Lost Div. Semi-Final
1985-86*	80	21	17	2	....	19	19	2	....	40	36	4	....	332	302	84	4th, Adams Div.	Lost Div. Final
1984-85*	80	17	18	5	....	13	23	4	....	30	41	9	....	268	318	69	5th, Adams Div.	Out of Playoffs
1983-84*	80	19	16	5	....	9	26	5	....	28	42	10	....	288	320	66	5th, Adams Div.	Out of Playoffs
1982-83*	80	13	22	5	....	6	32	2	....	19	54	7	....	261	403	45	5th, Adams Div.	Out of Playoffs
1981-82*	80	13	17	10	....	8	24	8	....	21	41	18	....	264	351	60	5th, Adams Div.	Out of Playoffs
1980-81*	80	14	17	9	....	7	24	9	....	21	41	18	....	292	372	60	4th, Norris Div.	Out of Playoffs
1979-80*	80	22	12	6	....	5	22	13	....	27	34	19	....	303	312	73	4th, Norris Div.	Lost Prelim. Round

* Hartford Whalers

2006-07 Player Personnel

FORWARDS	HT	WT	S	Place of Birth	Date	2005-06 Club
ADAMS, Craig	6-0	200	R	Seria, Brunei	4/26/77	Carolina-Lowell
ADAMS, Kevyn	6-1	195	R	Washington, DC	10/8/74	Carolina
ANGELIDIS, Mike	6-1	220	L	Woodbridge, Ont.	6/27/85	Owen Sound
AUCOIN, Keith	5-9	185	R	Waltham, MA	11/6/78	Carolina-Lowell
BAYDA, Ryan	5-11	185	L	Saskatoon, Sask.	12/9/80	Manitoba
BELLISSIMO, Vince	6-0	199	R	Toronto, Ont.	12/14/82	Lowell-Florida (ECHL)
BOULERICE, Jesse	6-2	215	R	Plattsburgh, NY	8/10/78	Carolina-St. Louis
BRIND'AMOUR, Rod	6-1	200	L	Ottawa, Ont.	8/9/70	Carolina
COLE, Erik	6-2	200	L	Oswego, NY	11/6/78	Carolina
DWYER, Patrick	5-11	185	R	Great Falls, MT	6/22/83	Chicago (AHL)
ESTRADA, Kevin	5-11	185	L	Surrey, B.C.	5/28/82	Lowell-Florida (ECHL)
GOVE, David	5-9	190	L	Centerville, MA	5/4/78	Carolina-Lowell
KELMAN, Scott	6-3	215	L	Winnipeg, Man.	5/7/81	Man-Her-Lowell (AHL)-Gwinnett-Fresno
LADD, Andrew	6-2	200	L	Maple Ridge, B.C.	12/12/85	Carolina-Lowell
LaROSE, Chad	5-10	173	R	Fraser, MI	3/27/82	Carolina-Lowell
LETOWSKI, Trevor	5-10	180	R	Thunder Bay, Ont.	4/5/77	Columbus
PEAT, Stephen	6-3	230	R	Princeton, B.C.	3/10/80	Wsh-Her-Lowell (AHL)
STAAL, Eric	6-3	200	L	Thunder Bay, Ont.	10/29/84	Carolina
STILLMAN, Cory	6-0	194	L	Peterborough, Ont.	12/20/73	Carolina
WALKER, Scott	5-10	196	R	Cambridge, Ont.	7/19/73	Nashville
WHITNEY, Ray	5-10	178	R	Fort Saskatchewan, Alta.	5/8/72	Carolina
WILLIAMS, Justin	6-1	190	R	Cobourg, Ont.	10/4/81	Carolina
WILLIS, Shane	6-1	195	R	Edmonton, Alta.	6/13/77	Davos-Linkoping
DEFENSEMEN						
BABCHUK, Anton	6-5	202	R	Kiev, USSR	5/6/84	Chicago-Norfolk-Carolina-Lowell (AHL)
CARSON, Brett	6-4	220	R	Regina, Sask.	11/29/85	Calgary (WHL)
COMMODORE, Mike	6-4	230	R	Fort Saskatchewan, Alta.	11/7/79	Carolina
CONBOY, Tim	6-1	205	R	Farmington, MN	3/22/82	Cleveland
FORREST, J.D.	5-9	185	L	Auburn, NY	4/15/81	Assat
HEDICAN, Bret	6-2	205	L	St. Paul, MN	8/10/70	Carolina
HUTCHINSON, Andrew	6-2	204	R	Evanston, IL	3/24/80	Carolina
KABERLE, Frantisek	6-1	190	L	Kladno, Czech.	11/8/73	Carolina
TVERDOVSKY, Oleg	6-1	205	L	Donetsk, USSR	5/18/76	Carolina
WALLIN, Niclas	6-3	220	L	Boden, Sweden	2/20/75	Carolina
WALSER, Derrick	5-10	196	L	New Glasgow, N.S.	5/12/78	Eisbaren Berlin
WESLEY, Glen	6-1	205	L	Red Deer, Alta.	10/2/68	Carolina

GOALTENDERS	HT	WT	C	Place of Birth	Date	2005-06 Club
GRAHAME, John	6-2	220	L	Denver, CO	8/31/75	Tampa Bay
KOWALSKI, Craig	5-10	190	L	Warren, MI	1/15/81	Lowell-Florida (ECHL)
MANZATO, Daniel	6-0	178	L	Fribourg, Switz.	1/17/84	Basel
NASTIUK, Kevin	6-2	176	L	Edmonton, Alta.	7/20/85	Florida (ECHL)-Lowell
PETERS, Justin	6-0	209	L	Blyth, Ont.	8/30/86	St. Michael's-Plymouth
WARD, Cam	6-0	176	L	Saskatoon, Sask.	2/29/84	Carolina-Lowell

Coach

LAVIOLETTE, PETER
Coach, Carolina Hurricanes. Born in Norwood, MA, December 7, 1964

On December 15, 2003 the Carolina Hurricanes made Peter Laviolette the 11th head coach in team history. Laviolette most recently coached the New York Islanders during the 2001-02 and 2002-03 seasons, and led the Islanders to the playoffs both seasons after the team missed the postseason seven straight times between 1994 and 2001. In 2006, he led Carolina to the first Stanley Cup victory in franchise history.

Prior to joining the Islanders, Laviolette served as an assistant coach with the Boston Bruins after two years of guiding Boston's AHL affiliate, Providence. In 1998-99, Laviolette led the Providence Bruins to a 56-16-8 regular-season record, and a 15-4 playoff record that culminated with Providence hoisting the Calder Cup and Laviolette being named AHL coach of the year.

Laviolette played 11 seasons of professional hockey, mostly in the AHL and IHL, but did play 12 games with the New York Rangers during the 1988-89 season. He was a member of the 1988 and 1994 U.S. Olympic hockey teams, and captained the 1994 Olympic squad.

In the spring of 2004, Laviolette helped assure the United States a spot in the 2006 Olympic Games in Torino, Italy, when he guided Team USA to a bronze medal at the 2004 World Championship in the Czech Republic. He also served as an assistant to San Jose Sharks head coach Ron Wilson behind the bench for Team USA in the 2004 World Cup of Hockey and was head coach again at the 2005 World Championship and 2006 Olympics.

Coaching Record

		Regular Season				Playoffs		
Season	Team	Games	W	L	O/T	Games	W	L
1997-98	Wheeling (ECHL)	70	37	24	9	15	8	7
1998-99	Providence (AHL)	80	56	16	8	19	15	4
1999-00	Providence (AHL)	80	33	38	9	14	10	4
2001-02	**NY Islanders (NHL)**	**82**	**42**	**32**	**8**	**7**	**3**	**4**
2002-03	**NY Islanders (NHL)**	**82**	**35**	**36**	**11**	**5**	**1**	**4**
2003-04	**Carolina (NHL)**	**52**	**20**	**26**	**6**	....	....	....
2004-05	**Carolina (NHL)**			Season Cancelled				
2005-06	**Carolina (NHL)**	**82**	**52**	**22**	**8**	**25**	**16**	**9**
	NHL Totals	**298**	**149**	**116**	**33**	**37**	**20**	**17**

2005-06 Scoring

* – rookie

Regular Season

Pos	#	Player	Team	GP	G	A	Pts	+/–	PIM	PP	SH	GW	S	%
C	12	Eric Staal	CAR	82	45	55	100	–8	81	19	4	4	279	16.1
R	11	Justin Williams	CAR	82	31	45	76	1	60	8	4	4	255	12.2
L	61	Cory Stillman	CAR	72	21	55	76	–9	32	10	0	3	177	11.9
C	17	Rod Brind'Amour	CAR	78	31	39	70	8	68	19	2	5	198	15.7
R	18	Mark Recchi	PIT	63	24	33	57	–28	56	11	0	2	164	14.6
			CAR	20	4	3	7	–8	12	2	0	1	35	11.4
			TOTAL	83	28	36	64	–36	68	13	0	3	199	14.1
L	26	Erik Cole	CAR	60	30	29	59	19	54	3	3	8	164	18.3
C	39	Doug Weight	STL	47	11	33	44	–11	50	7	0	1	123	8.9
			CAR	23	4	9	13	–6	25	2	0	0	52	7.7
			TOTAL	70	15	42	57	–17	75	9	0	1	175	8.6
L	13	Ray Whitney	CAR	63	17	38	55	0	42	12	0	2	147	11.6
C	8	Matt Cullen	CAR	78	25	24	49	4	40	8	0	5	214	11.7
D	5	Frantisek Kaberle	CAR	77	6	38	44	8	46	1	0	3	126	4.8
D	6	Bret Hedican	CAR	74	5	22	27	11	58	2	1	1	73	6.8
D	4	Aaron Ward	CAR	71	6	19	25	2	62	0	0	1	60	10.0
C	14	Kevyn Adams	CAR	82	15	8	23	0	36	0	2	2	160	9.4
D	70	Oleg Tverdovsky	CAR	72	3	20	23	–1	37	0	0	0	91	3.3
R	27	Craig Adams	CAR	67	10	11	21	1	51	1	1	2	68	14.7
D	22	Mike Commodore	CAR	72	3	10	13	12	138	0	0	2	72	4.2
R	59 *	Chad Larose	CAR	49	1	12	13	7	35	0	0	1	62	1.6
L	16 *	Andrew Ladd	CAR	29	6	5	11	0	4	3	0	0	43	14.0
D	24 *	Andrew Hutchinson	CAR	36	3	8	11	–2	18	2	0	0	33	9.1
D	48 *	Anton Babchuk	CHI	17	2	3	5	–5	16	1	0	0	24	8.3
			CAR	22	3	2	5	–2	6	2	0	0	32	9.4
			TOTAL	39	5	5	10	–7	22	3	0	0	56	8.9
D	2	Glen Wesley	CAR	64	2	8	10	10	46	0	0	0	28	7.1
C	63	Josef Vasicek	CAR	23	4	5	9	3	8	0	0	0	41	9.8
D	7	Niclas Wallin	CAR	50	4	4	8	2	42	0	0	0	44	9.1
L	34	David Gove	CAR	1	0	1	1	2	0	0	0	0	0	0.0
R	37	Keith Aucoin	CAR	7	0	1	1	–4	4	0	0	0	3	0.0

Goaltending

No.	Goaltender	GPI	Mins	Avg	W	L	OT	EN	SO	GA	SA	S%	G	A	PIM
29	Martin Gerber	60	3493	2.78	38	14	6	5	3	162	1719	.906	0	2	4
30	* Cam Ward	28	1484	3.68	14	8	2	0	0	91	773	.882	0	2	0
	Totals	**82**	**4997**	**3.10**	**52**	**22**	**8**	**5**	**4**	**258**	**2497**	**.897**			

Martin Gerber and Cam Ward shared a shutout vs. Washington on October 22, 2005.

Playoffs

Pos	#	Player	Team	GP	G	A	Pts	+/–	PIM	PP	SH	GW	OT	S	%
C	12	Eric Staal	CAR	25	9	19	28	0	8	7	0	1	1	87	10.3
L	61	Cory Stillman	CAR	25	9	17	26	12	14	4	0	3	2	75	12.0
C	17	Rod Brind'Amour	CAR	25	12	6	18	9	16	6	0	4	0	75	16.0
R	11	Justin Williams	CAR	25	7	11	18	12	34	0	1	1	0	71	9.9
C	8	Matt Cullen	CAR	25	4	14	18	2	12	2	0	1	0	56	7.1
R	18	Mark Recchi	CAR	25	7	9	16	–5	18	2	0	2	0	45	15.6
C	39	Doug Weight	CAR	23	3	13	16	–3	20	2	0	0	0	35	8.6
L	13	Ray Whitney	CAR	24	9	6	15	–1	14	5	0	1	0	40	22.5
D	5	Frantisek Kaberle	CAR	25	4	9	13	–7	8	3	0	1	0	35	11.4
D	6	Bret Hedican	CAR	25	2	9	11	6	42	0	0	0	0	23	8.7
L	16 *	Andrew Ladd	CAR	17	2	3	5	0	4	0	0	1	0	13	15.4
D	4	Aaron Ward	CAR	25	2	3	5	0	18	0	0	0	0	18	11.1
D	7	Niclas Wallin	CAR	25	1	4	5	3	14	0	0	1	1	19	5.3
D	22	Mike Commodore	CAR	25	2	2	4	1	33	0	1	0	0	27	7.4
D	2	Glen Wesley	CAR	25	0	2	2	1	16	0	0	0	0	15	0.0
R	59 *	Chad Larose	CAR	21	0	1	1	–2	10	0	0	0	0	15	0.0
L	26	Erik Cole	CAR	2	0	0	0	–1	0	0	0	0	0	3	0.0
D	70	Oleg Tverdovsky	CAR	5	0	0	0	–1	0	0	0	0	0	2	0.0
C	63	Josef Vasicek	CAR	8	0	0	0	–2	2	0	0	0	0	13	0.0
C	14	Kevyn Adams	CAR	25	0	0	0	–4	14	0	0	0	0	36	0.0
R	27	Craig Adams	CAR	25	0	0	0	–4	10	0	0	0	0	18	0.0

Goaltending

No.	Goaltender	GPI	Mins	Avg	W	L	EN	SO	GA	SA	S%	G	A	PIM
30	* Cam Ward	23	1320	2.14	15	8	0	2	47	584	.920	0	1	0
29	Martin Gerber	6	221	3.53	1	1	0	1	13	90	.856	0	0	4
	Totals	**25**	**1547**	**2.33**	**16**	**9**	**0**	**3**	**60**	**674**	**.911**			

Coaching History

Don Blackburn, 1979-80; Don Blackburn and Larry Pleau, 1980-81; Larry Pleau, 1981-82; Larry Kish, Larry Pleau and John Cuniff, 1982- 83; Jack Evans, 1983-84 to 1986-87; Jack Evans and Larry Pleau, 1987-88; Larry Pleau, 1988-89; Rick Ley, 1989-90, 1990-91; Jim Roberts, 1991-92; Paul Holmgren, 1992-93; Paul Holmgren and Pierre Maguire, 1993-94; Paul Holmgren, 1994-95; Paul Holmgren and Paul Maurice, 1995-96; Paul Maurice, 1996-97 to 2002-03; Paul Maurice and Peter Laviolette, 2003-04; Peter Laviolette, 2004-05 to date.

Captains' History

Rick Ley, 1979-80; Rick Ley and Mike Rogers, 1980-81; Dave Keon, 1981-82; Russ Anderson, 1982-83; Mark Johnson, 1983-84; Mark Johnson and Ron Francis, 1984-85; Ron Francis, 1985-86 to 1990-91; Randy Ladouceur, 1991-92; Pat Verbeek, 1992-93 to 1994-95; Brendan Shanahan, 1995-96; Kevin Dineen, 1996-97, 1997-98; Keith Primeau, 1998-99; Keith Primeau and Ron Francis, 1999-2000; Ron Francis, 2000-01 to 2003-04; Rod Brind'Amour, 2005-06 to date.

Club Records

Team

(Figures in brackets for season records are games played; records for fewest points, wins, ties, losses, goals, goals against are for 70 or more games)

Most Points	112	2005-06 (82)
Most Wins	52	2005-06 (82)
Most Ties	19	1979-80 (80)
Most Losses	54	1982-83 (80)
Most Goals	332	1985-86 (80)
Most Goals Against	403	1982-83 (80)
Fewest Points	45	1982-83 (80)
Fewest Wins	19	1982-83 (80)
Fewest Ties	4	1985-86 (80)
Fewest Losses	22	2005-06 (82)
Fewest Goals	171	2002-03 (82)
Fewest Goals Against	202	1998-99 (82)

Longest Winning Streak
Overall...................9 Oct. 22-Nov. 11/05,
Dec. 31/05-Jan. 19/06
Home....................9 Dec. 31/05-Jan. 28/06
Away....................6 Nov. 10-Dec. 7/90

Longest Undefeated Streak
Overall..................10 Jan. 20-Feb. 10/82
(6 wins, 4 ties)
Home....................9 Dec. 15/00-Jan. 18/01
(8 wins, 1 tie),
Dec. 31/05-Jan. 28/06
(9 wins)
Away....................8 Nov. 11-Dec. 5/96
(4 wins, 4 ties)

Longest Losing Streak
Overall...................9 Feb. 19-Mar. 8/83
Home....................7 Dec. 27/02-Jan. 20/03
Away....................13 Dec. 18/82-Feb. 5/83

Longest Winless Streak
Overall..................14 Jan. 4-Feb. 9/92
(8 losses, 6 ties)
Home....................13 Jan. 15-Mar. 10/85
(11 losses, 2 ties)
Away....................15 Nov. 11/79-Jan. 9/80
(11 losses, 4 ties),
Jan. 7-Mar. 2/03
(13 losses, 2 ties)

Most Shutouts, Season.........8 1998-99 (82)
Most PIM, Season..........2,354 1992-93 (84)
Most Goals, Game...........11 Feb. 12/84
(Edm. 0 at Hfd. 11),
Oct. 19/85
(Mtl. 6 at Hfd. 11),
Jan. 17/86
(Que. 6 at Hfd. 11),
Mar. 15/86
(Chi. 4 at Hfd. 11)

Individual

Most Seasons	16	Ron Francis
Most Games	1,186	Ron Francis
Most Goals, Career	382	Ron Francis
Most Assists, Career	793	Ron Francis
Most Points, Career	1,175	Ron Francis
		(382G, 793A)
Most PIM, Career	1,439	Kevin Dineen
Most Shutouts, Career	20	Arturs Irbe

Longest Consecutive
Games Streak............419 Dave Tippett
(Mar. 3/84-Oct. 7/89)
Most Goals, Season...........56 Blaine Stoughton
(1979-80)
Most Assists, Season..........69 Ron Francis
(1989-90)
Most Points, Season..........105 Mike Rogers
(1979-80; 44G, 61A),
(1980-81; 40G, 65A)
Most PIM, Season..........358 Torrie Robertson
(1985-86)

Most Points, Defenseman,
Season...................69 Dave Babych
(1985-86; 14G, 55A)
Most Points, Center,
Season...................105 Mike Rogers
(1979-80; 44G, 61A),
(1980-81; 40G, 65A)
Most Points, Right Wing,
Season...................100 Blaine Stoughton
(1979-80; 56G, 44A)
Most Points, Left Wing,
Season...................89 Geoff Sanderson
(1992-93; 46G, 43A)
Most Points, Rookie,
Season...................72 Sylvain Turgeon
(1983-84; 40G, 32A)
Most Shutouts, Season........6 Arturs Irbe
(1998-99, 2000-01),
Kevin Weekes
(2003-04)
Most Goals, Game............4 Jordy Douglas
(Feb. 3/80),
Ron Francis
(Feb. 12/84)
Most Assists, Game..........6 Ron Francis
(Mar. 5/87)
Most Points, Game...........6 Paul Lawless
(Jan. 4/87; 2G, 4A),
Ron Francis
(Mar. 5/87; 6A),
(Oct. 8/89; 3G, 3A)

Records include Hartford Whalers, 1979-80 through 1996-97.

All-time Record vs. Other Clubs
Regular Season

	At Home								On Road								Total							
	GP	W	L	T	OL	GF	GA	PTS	GP	W	L	T	OL	GF	GA	PTS	GP	W	L	T	OL	GF	GA	PTS
Anaheim	9	5	3	1	0	23	19	11	10	4	5	1	0	32	31	9	19	9	8	2	0	55	50	20
Atlanta	17	12	4	1	0	57	49	25	17	10	3	3	1	51	44	24	34	22	7	4	1	108	93	49
Boston	78	33	36	9	0	260	269	75	80	26	47	7	0	213	281	59	158	59	83	16	0	473	550	134
Buffalo	80	33	36	11	0	231	237	77	79	26	45	7	1	235	315	60	159	59	81	18	1	466	552	137
Calgary	28	10	13	5	0	91	103	25	29	6	21	2	0	92	140	14	57	16	34	7	0	183	243	39
Chicago	31	15	12	4	0	102	96	34	29	10	16	3	0	83	117	23	60	25	28	7	0	185	213	57
Colorado	62	24	25	12	1	203	214	61	65	17	39	9	0	191	274	43	127	41	64	21	1	394	488	104
Columbus	5	4	1	0	0	15	12	8	3	2	1	0	0	9	6	4	8	6	2	0	0	24	18	12
Dallas	32	13	15	4	0	101	110	30	30	10	16	2	2	90	120	24	62	23	31	6	2	191	230	54
Detroit	31	18	12	1	0	107	88	37	31	7	16	7	1	86	119	22	62	25	28	8	1	193	207	59
Edmonton	29	11	11	7	0	112	98	29	31	7	19	5	0	92	121	19	60	18	30	12	0	204	219	48
Florida	29	17	9	3	0	87	70	37	30	9	11	8	2	66	86	28	59	26	20	11	2	153	156	65
Los Angeles	31	15	11	5	0	114	115	35	31	11	17	3	0	116	131	25	62	26	28	8	0	230	246	60
Minnesota	2	2	0	0	0	3	0	4	4	1	1	2	0	12	9	4	6	3	1	2	0	15	9	8
Montreal	80	31	36	13	0	236	274	75	77	20	49	7	1	226	312	48	157	51	85	20	1	462	586	123
Nashville	6	3	1	1	1	19	17	8	4	1	3	0	0	7	9	2	10	4	4	1	1	26	26	10
New Jersey	46	19	18	8	1	144	137	47	47	17	25	4	1	146	162	39	93	36	43	12	2	290	299	86
NY Islanders	47	23	18	5	1	160	152	52	46	21	20	4	1	126	135	47	93	44	38	9	2	286	287	99
NY Rangers	45	26	16	3	0	155	141	55	47	15	28	4	0	120	177	34	92	41	44	7	0	275	318	89
Ottawa	29	17	8	4	0	87	72	38	31	14	13	4	0	82	88	32	60	31	21	8	0	169	160	70
Philadelphia	46	14	21	9	2	151	168	39	45	10	27	5	3	113	168	28	91	24	48	14	5	264	336	67
Phoenix	30	14	10	6	0	103	89	34	32	15	15	2	0	116	118	32	62	29	25	8	0	219	207	66
Pittsburgh	50	23	22	5	0	184	183	51	48	19	22	6	1	182	193	45	98	42	44	11	1	366	376	96
St. Louis	32	13	17	2	0	96	99	28	31	9	18	3	1	94	119	22	63	22	35	5	1	190	218	50
San Jose	11	6	5	0	0	34	23	12	12	4	8	0	0	34	54	8	23	10	13	0	0	68	77	20
Tampa Bay	31	18	5	7	1	96	79	44	30	9	16	3	2	78	91	23	61	27	21	10	3	174	170	67
Toronto	39	20	12	6	1	152	125	47	38	18	14	5	1	132	128	42	77	38	26	11	2	284	253	89
Vancouver	29	12	12	5	0	94	100	29	30	10	13	6	1	81	105	27	59	22	25	11	1	175	205	56
Washington	53	17	25	10	1	143	167	45	51	17	30	4	0	132	174	38	104	34	55	14	1	275	341	83
Totals	**1038**	**468**	**414**	**147**	**9**	**3360**	**3306**	**1092**	**1038**	**345**	**558**	**116**	**19**	**3037**	**3827**	**825**	**2076**	**813**	**972**	**263**	**28**	**6397**	**7133**	**1917**

Playoffs

	Series	W	L	GP	W	L	T	GF	GA	Last
Boston	3	0	3	19	7	12	0	48	63	1999
Buffalo	1	1	0	7	4	3	0	22	17	2006
Colorado	2	1	1	9	5	4	0	35	34	1987
Detroit	1	0	1	5	1	4	0	7	14	2002
Edmonton	1	1	0	7	4	3	0	19	16	2006
Montreal	7	2	5	39	16	23	0	106	125	2006
New Jersey	3	2	1	17	10	7	0	34	41	2006
Toronto	1	1	0	6	4	2	0	10	6	2002
Totals	**19**	**8**	**11**	**109**	**51**	**58**	**0**	**281**	**316**	

Playoff Results 2006-2001

Year	Round	Opponent	Result	GF	GA
2006	F	**Edmonton**	**W 4-3**	**19**	**16**
	CF	Buffalo	W 4-3	22	17
	CSF	New Jersey	W 4-1	17	10
	CQF	Montreal	W 4-2	15	17
2002	F	Detroit	L 1-4	7	14
	CF	Toronto	W 4-2	10	6
	CSF	Montreal	W 4-2	21	12
	CQF	New Jersey	W 4-2	9	11
2001	CQF	New Jersey	L 2-4	8	20

Abbreviations: Round: F - Final; **CF** - conference final; **CSF** - conference semi-final; **CQF** - conference quarter-final; **DSF** - division semi-final.

Calgary totals include Atlanta Flames, 1979-80.
Dallas totals include Minnesota North Stars, 1979-80 to 1992-93.
Phoenix totals include Winnipeg, 1979-80 to 1995-96.

Colorado totals include Quebec, 1979-80 to 1994-95.
New Jersey totals include Colorado Rockies, 1979-80 to 1981-82.

2005-06 Results

Oct.	5	at Tampa Bay	2-5		10	Detroit	3-2
	7	Pittsburgh	3-2†		13	Nashville	5-4*
	8	at NY Islanders	2-3		15	St. Louis	4-2
	12	Washington	7-2		17	at Philadelphia	4-3†
	15	at New Jersey	6-1		19	NY Islanders	4-3
	20	at Toronto	4-5*		21	at Washington	2-5
	22	at Washington	4-0		23	Montreal	7-3
	24	Ottawa	3-2		25	at Florida	4-3†
	26	Boston	4-3*		26	at Atlanta	5-1
	28	Philadelphia	8-6		28	Atlanta	4-1
	31	at Pittsburgh	5-3		31	at Montreal	8-2
Nov.	3	Toronto	4-3	**Feb.**	3	at New Jersey	0-3
	5	Florida	2-0		5	at Boston	4-3†
	9	at Buffalo	5-3		9	at Tampa Bay	3-5
	11	at Florida	1-0		10	Pittsburgh	3-4
	12	Atlanta	0-9		12	Buffalo	4-3†
	15	at Ottawa	2-1	**Mar.**	1	Boston	4-3
	17	NY Rangers	5-1		3	Florida	5-2
	19	at NY Rangers	3-4		4	at Pittsburgh	7-5
	20	Tampa Bay	2-5		6	at NY Rangers	2-1
	22	Ottawa	3-5		8	at Philadelphia	2-3†
	25	Toronto	4-3†		10	at Florida	3-5
	27	Atlanta	2-5		11	at Florida	3-4*
	29	at Atlanta	4-3*		14	NY Rangers	5-3
Dec.	2	at Dallas	4-5†		16	at Montreal	5-1
	3	at Phoenix	4-8		18	at Boston	2-4
	6	at Anaheim	6-2		21	at Toronto	2-3
	8	at Los Angeles	3-2		22	at Buffalo	4-3
	10	at San Jose	3-4		25	Washington	1-3
	13	Chicago	5-3		27	at Tampa Bay	2-1
	15	Columbus	2-1		29	Washington	1-5
	17	New Jersey	4-1		31	Florida	3-2
	20	Tampa Bay	6-4	**Apr.**	1	at Atlanta	2-5
	23	Florida	4-3		3	Washington	6-5†
	26	at Tampa Bay	4-5*		5	at Washington	4-3†
	28	at Ottawa	2-6		7	at Washington	4-3
	29	Philadelphia	3-4*		8	at Atlanta	2-5
	31	Montreal	5-3		11	New Jersey	3-4*
Jan.	4	Atlanta	4-3		14	Tampa Bay	5-4†
	6	NY Islanders	4-1		15	at Tampa Bay	2-3†
	7	at NY Islanders	3-0		18	Buffalo	0-4

* – Overtime † – Shootout

Entry Draft
Selections 2006-1992

2006 Pick		2002 Pick		1998 Pick		1995 Pick	
63	Jamie McBain	25	Cam Ward	11	Jeff Heerema	13	Jean-Sebastien Giguere
93	Harrison Reed	91	Jesse Lane	70	Kevin Holdridge	35	Sergei Fedotov
123	Bobby Hughes	160	Daniel Manzato	71	Erik Cole	85	Ian MacNeil
153	Stefan Chaput	224	Adam Taylor	91	Josef Vasicek	87	Sami Kapanen
183	Nick Dodge			93	Tommy Westlund	113	Hugh Hamilton
213	Justin Krueger	**2001 Pick**		97	Chris Madden	165	Byron Ritchie
		15	Igor Knyazev	184	Don Smith	191	Milan Kostolny
2005 Pick		46	Mike Zigomanis	208	Jaroslav Svoboda	217	Mike Rucinski
3	Jack Johnson	91	Kevin Estrada	211	Mark Kosick		
58	Nate Hagemo	110	Rob Zepp	239	Brent McDonald	**1994 Pick**	
64	Joe Barnes	181	Daniel Boisclair			5	Jeff O'Neill
94	Jakub Vojta	211	Sean Curry	**1997 Pick**		83	Hnat Domenichelli
123	Ondrej Otcenas	244	Carter Trevisani	22	Nikos Tselios	109	Ryan Risidore
145	Tim Kunes	274	Peter Reynolds	28	Brad DeFauw	187	Tom Buckley
159	Risto Korhonen			80	Francis Lessard	213	Ashlin Halfnight
192	Nicolas Blanchard	**2000 Pick**		88	Shane Willis	230	Matt Ball
198	Kyle Lawson	32	Tomas Kurka	142	Kyle Dafoe	239	Brian Regan
		80	Ryan Bayda	169	Andrew Merrick	265	Steve Nimigon
2004 Pick		97	Niclas Wallin	195	Niklas Nordgren		
4	Andrew Ladd	110	Jared Newman	199	Randy Fitzgerald	**1993 Pick**	
38	Justin Peters	181	J.D. Forrest	225	Kent McDonell	2	Chris Pronger
69	Casey Borer	212	Magnus Kahnberg			72	Marek Malik
109	Brett Carson	235	Craig Kowalski	**1996 Pick**		84	Trevor Roenick
137	Magnus Akerlund	276	Troy Ferguson	34	Trevor Wasyluk	115	Nolan Pratt
202	Ryan Pottruff			61	Andrei Petrunin	188	Manny Legace
235	Jonas Fiedler	**1999 Pick**		88	Craig MacDonald	214	Dmitri Gorenko
268	Martin Vagner	16	Dave Tanabe	104	Steve Wasylko	240	Wes Swinson
		49	Brett Lysak	116	Mark McMahon	266	Igor Chibirev
2003 Pick		84	Brad Fast	143	Aaron Baker		
2	Eric Staal	113	Ryan Murphy	171	Greg Kuznik	**1992 Pick**	
31	Danny Richmond	174	Damian Surma	197	Kevin Marsh	9	Robert Petrovicky
102	Aaron Dawson	202	Jim Baxter	223	Craig Adams	47	Andrei Nikolishin
126	Kevin Nastiuk	231	David Evans	231	Ashkat Rakhmatullin	57	Jan Vopat
130	Matej Trojovsky	237	Antti Jokela			79	Kevin Smyth
137	Tyson Strachan	259	Yevgeny Kurilin			81	Jason McBain
198	Shay Stephenson					143	Jarrett Reid
230	Jamie Hoffmann					153	Ken Belanger
262	Ryan Rorabeck					177	Konstantin Korotkov
						201	Greg Zwakman
						225	Steven Halko
						249	Joacim Esbjors

General Managers' History

Jack Kelley, 1979-80, 1980-81; Larry Pleau, 1981-82, 1982-83; Emile Francis, 1983-84 to 1988-89; Eddie Johnston, 1989-90 to 1991-92; Brian Burke, 1992-93; Paul Holmgren, 1993-94; Jim Rutherford, 1994-95 to date.

President and General Manager

RUTHERFORD, JIM
President/General Manager, Carolina Hurricanes.
Born in Beeton, Ont., February 17, 1949.

Jim Rutherford, a former NHL goaltender, is the franchise's seventh general manager and the only general manager of the Carolina Hurricanes. Named to his position on June 28, 1994, Rutherford has always taken an aggressive approach towards improving the fortunes of the franchise through trades and the NHL entry draft. In 2002, the team reached the Stanley Cup Finals for the first time in history. The Hurricanes won the Cup in 2006.

A veteran of 13 NHL seasons, Rutherford began his professional goaltending career in 1969 as a first-round selection of the Detroit Red Wings. While playing for Detroit, Pittsburgh, Toronto and Los Angeles, Rutherford collected 14 career shutouts. For five seasons he also served as the Red Wings' player representative. Rutherford also played for Team Canada at the World Championships in Vienna in 1977 and Moscow in 1979.

After his playing days with the Red Wings, Rutherford joined Compuware to serve as the director of hockey operations for Compuware Sports Corporation. Rutherford gained a wealth of experience in youth hockey and junior programs. As a former player, coach, and general manager, his ability to develop players and produce winning programs is widely respected throughout the hockey community.

He started his management career by guiding Compuware Sports Corporation's purchase of the Windsor Spitfires of the Ontario Hockey League in April of 1984. During the next four years, Rutherford acted as general manager of the Spitfires. After the Spitfires advanced to the 1988 Memorial Cup finals, Rutherford led Compuware's efforts to bring the first American-based OHL franchise to Detroit on December 11, 1989. Rutherford was voted the 1987 executive of the year in both the OHL and the Canadian Hockey League and won the OHL executive of the year award again in 1988.

Club Directory

RBC Center

Carolina Hurricanes
1400 Edwards Mill Rd.
Raleigh, NC 27607
Phone **919/467-7825**
FAX 919/462-0123
Tickets 1.866.NHL.CANES
www.carolinahurricanes.com
Capacity: 18,730

Executive Management
Chief Executive Officer/Owner/Governor	Peter Karmanos, Jr.
President/General Manager	Jim Rutherford
General Partner	Thomas Thewes
Vice President/Assistant General Manager	Jason Karmanos
Chief Financial Officer	Mike Amendola
Vice President and G.M., RBC Center	Davin Olsen

Hockey Operations
Head Coach	Peter Laviolette
Associated Head Coach	Kevin McCarthy
Assistant Coach	Jeff Daniels
Goaltending Coach/Pro Scout	Greg Stefan
Director of Amateur Scouting	Sheldon Ferguson
Amateur Scouts	Tony MacDonald, Martin Madden, Bert Marshall
Director of Pro Scouting	Marshall Johnston
Pro Scouts	Claude Larose, Ron Smith
Video Coordinator	Chris Huffine
Head Athletic Therapist/Strength Conditioning Coach	Peter Friesen
Associate Athletic Therapist	TBD
Equipment Managers	Wally Tatomir, Skip Cunningham, Bob Gorman
Lowell Lock Monsters Head Coach/G.M.	Tom Rowe
Director of Team Operations	Brian Tatum
Hockey Event Coordinator	Kelly Kirwin
Motivational Consultant/Community Programs	Doris E. Barksdale

Administration
Receptionists	Mary Lou Ruetz, Janet Davis
General Office Assistant	Angela Dennis

Arena Operations
Assistant General Manager, RBC Center	Larry Perkins
Marketing Coordinator	Crystal Pace
Guest Services Coordinator/Executive Assistant	April Keeley
Security Manager	Clinton Peterson
Parking Manager	Mike Alexander
Event Services Manager	Jeff Dow
Premium Services Manager	Mary Pat Mooney
Premium Services Coordinator/Guest Services Rep.	Katrina Ryan
Premium Services Coordinator	Jacqueline Barry
Senior Event Coordinator	Rob Douglas
Event Coordinator	Allee Byrd
Building Superintendent	Donnie MacMillian
Production Supervisor	Barry Steiman
Operations Manager	Dan McGowan
Assistant Operations Manager	Brett Shaw
Operations Supervisor	Rusty Davis, Melvin Terrell
Facility Systems Manager	Rick Dunning
Facility Systems Assistant Manager	Donald Sykes
Director of Ticket Operations	Bill Nowicki
Box Office Manager	Joe Sousa
Ticket Operations Supervisor	Chris Jovino
Ticket Operations Representative	Tansley Cooke
Arena Office Manager	Hilman Huskey

Broadcasters
Television Play-by-Play	John Forslund
Television Analyst	Tripp Tracy
Radio Play-by-Play	Chuck Kaiton

Communications
Director of Media Relations	Mike Sundheim
Manager of Media Relations/Broadcast Coordinator	Kyle Hanlin
Community Relations Manager	Chris Diamond
Community Relations Coordinator	Anne Nelson
Community Relations Assistant	Mike King
Team Photographer	Gregg Forwerk

Finance/Information Technology
Director of Arena Finance	William Traurig
Accounts Payable	Michael Arrington
Accounts Receivable	Patty Hilliard, Temika Smith-Harris
Payroll/Human Resources Coordinators	Carrie Hubinek, Irene Cantelli
Director of Information Technology	Glenn Johnson
Client/Server Technologists	Alex Byrd, Dwight Baptist, Myatt Williams

Food and Beverage
Director of Food and Beverage	Michael Bekolay
Concessions Manager	Rick Rhodes
Chefs	Dennis Atkinson, Michael Flood, Andrew Booger, Lecan Huynh
Restaurant/Club Manager	Keith Register
Commissary Manager	Gary Berry
Suites Food and Beverage Manager	Lori Holtz
Assistant Suites Manager	Beth Nooe
Senior Assistant Manager of Concessions	Jim O'Brien

Marketing
Director of Marketing/Creative Services	Howard Sadel
Manager of Creative Services	Ben Aycock
Website Producer	David Pond
Graphic Designer	Kara Kelly
Junior Graphic Designer	Nick Kelley
Manager of Promotions and Fan Development	Doug Warf
Youth and Amateur Hockey Coordinator	Paul Strand
Promotions Assistant	Jon Chase

Gale Force Media, CanesVision and Wolfpack TV
Director	Pete Soto
Producer	Chris Hooks, Don Sill
Graphics Producer	Stephen Rutherford
Mascot Coordinator	George Brown

Merchandise
Retail Operations Manager	James Blitch

Sales
Director of Corporate, Advertising & Broadcast Sales	Mike Hurley
Senior Sales Executive Corporate Suites	Kristina Ryan
Senior Account Executives	Timothy Kuhl, Julia Zeigler
Sponsorship Sales Executive	Derrick Pyke
Corporate Sales Account Executive	Marsha Moore
Director of Ticket Sales	Kyle Prairie
Account Executives, Ticket Sales	Peterson J. Avetta, Brian Kapusta, Michael Miller
Client Relations Executive	D.J. Ketchabaw
Client Relations Representatives	Megan Aukland, Matthew Horton
RBC Center Group Sales Manager	Brian Slais
Group Sales Representative	Dustin Kilpatrick
Ticket Sales Coordinator	Karen Price
Corporate Sales Service Assistant	Jenny Blackwelder
Corporate Sales Service Coordinator	Elizabeth Layton

Brent Seabrook topped Blackhawks blueliners with 32 points in 69 games in 2005-06.

Chicago Blackhawks

2005-06 Results: 26w-43L-7OTL-6SOL 65PTS.
Fourth, Central Division

2006-07 Schedule

Oct.	Thu.	5	at Nashville		Sun.	7	Phoenix*
	Sat.	7	Columbus		Wed.	10	Buffalo
	Thu.	12	Nashville		Sat.	13	at Detroit
	Sat.	14	at St. Louis		Sun.	14	Minnesota
	Mon.	16	at Colorado		Tue.	16	Columbus
	Wed.	18	Montreal		Fri.	19	Minnesota
	Fri.	20	at Dallas		Sat.	20	at Nashville
	Sat.	21	St. Louis		Fri.	26	Nashville
	Wed.	25	Vancouver		Sun.	28	Calgary*
	Sat.	28	Anaheim	Feb.	Thu.	1	at Los Angeles
	Mon.	30	at Philadelphia		Sat.	3	at San Jose*
	Tue.	31	at NY Islanders		Tue.	6	at Calgary
Nov.	Thu.	2	Detroit		Wed.	7	at Vancouver
	Thu.	9	at New Jersey		Fri.	9	at Edmonton
	Fri.	10	St. Louis		Sun.	11	at Columbus*
	Sun.	12	Columbus		Wed.	14	at Pittsburgh
	Thu.	16	at Phoenix		Fri.	16	Vancouver
	Fri.	17	at Anaheim		Sun.	18	at NY Rangers*
	Sun.	19	at Vancouver		Wed.	21	at Detroit
	Wed.	22	at Calgary		Thu.	22	San Jose
	Fri.	24	at Edmonton		Sun.	25	St. Louis*
	Wed.	29	Dallas		Tue.	27	Detroit
Dec.	Fri.	1	St. Louis	Mar.	Thu.	1	Colorado
	Sat.	2	at Nashville		Fri.	2	at Detroit
	Tue.	5	at Minnesota		Sun.	4	Ottawa*
	Thu.	7	Phoenix		Tue.	6	Los Angeles
	Sat.	9	at Minnesota		Sat.	10	at Phoenix
	Sun.	10	Edmonton		Tue.	13	at San Jose
	Tue.	12	at St. Louis		Thu.	15	at Los Angeles
	Thu.	14	Detroit		Fri.	16	at Anaheim
	Sat.	16	at Columbus		Tue.	20	at Columbus
	Sun.	17	Colorado		Wed.	21	San Jose
	Wed.	20	Nashville		Fri.	23	Los Angeles
	Fri.	22	Toronto		Sun.	25	Calgary*
	Sat.	23	at Colorado		Wed.	28	Anaheim
	Tue.	26	Dallas		Fri.	30	Columbus
	Fri.	29	Boston	Apr.	Sun.	1	Edmonton*
	Sun.	31	at Columbus		Tue.	3	at Nashville
Jan.	Tue.	2	at St. Louis		Thu.	5	Detroit
	Thu.	4	at St. Louis		Sat.	7	at Detroit*
	Fri.	5	Nashville		Sun.	8	at Dallas*

* Denotes afternoon game.

Franchise date: September 25, 1926

81st NHL Season

CENTRAL DIVISION

Year-by-Year Record

Season	GP	Home W	L	T	OL	Road W	L	T	OL	Overall W	L	T	OL	GF	GA	Pts.	Finished	Playoff Result
2005-06	82	16	19	....	6	10	24	....	7	26	43	....	13	211	285	65	4th, Central Div.	Out of Playoffs
2004-05	....																	
2003-04	82	13	17	6	5	7	26	5	3	20	43	11	8	188	259	59	5th, Central Div.	Out of Playoffs
2002-03	82	17	15	7	2	13	18	6	4	30	33	13	6	207	226	79	3rd, Central Div.	Out of Playoffs
2001-02	82	28	7	5	1	13	20	8	0	41	27	13	1	216	207	96	3rd, Central Div.	Lost Conf. Quarter-Final
2000-01	82	14	21	4	2	15	19	4	3	29	40	8	5	210	246	71	4th, Central Div.	Out of Playoffs
1999-2000	82	16	19	5	1	17	18	5	1	33	37	10	2	242	245	78	3rd, Central Div.	Out of Playoffs
1998-99	82	20	17	4	....	9	24	8	....	29	41	12	....	202	248	70	3rd, Central Div.	Out of Playoffs
1997-98	82	14	19	8	....	16	20	5	....	30	39	13	....	192	199	73	5th, Central Div.	Out of Playoffs
1996-97	82	16	21	4	....	18	14	9	....	34	35	13	....	223	210	81	5th, Central Div.	Lost Conf. Quarter-Final
1995-96	82	22	13	6	....	18	15	8	....	40	28	14	....	273	220	94	2nd, Central Div.	Lost Conf. Semi-Final
1994-95	48	11	10	3	....	13	9	2	....	24	19	5	....	156	115	53	3rd, Central Div.	Lost Conf. Championship
1993-94	84	21	16	5	....	18	20	4	....	39	36	9	....	254	240	87	5th, Central Div.	Lost Conf. Quarter-Final
1992-93	84	25	11	6	....	22	14	6	....	47	25	12	....	279	230	106	1st, Norris Div.	Lost Div. Semi-Final
1991-92	80	23	9	8	....	13	20	7	....	36	29	15	....	257	236	87	2nd, Norris Div.	Lost Final
1990-91	80	28	8	4	....	21	15	4	....	49	23	8	....	284	211	106	1st, Norris Div.	Lost Div. Semi-Final
1989-90	80	25	13	2	....	16	20	4	....	41	33	6	....	316	294	88	1st, Norris Div.	Lost Conf. Championship
1988-89	80	16	14	10	....	11	27	2	....	27	41	12	....	297	335	66	4th, Norris Div.	Lost Conf. Championship
1987-88	80	21	17	2	....	9	24	7	....	30	41	9	....	284	328	69	3rd, Norris Div.	Lost Div. Semi-Final
1986-87	80	18	13	9	....	11	24	5	....	29	37	14	....	290	310	72	3rd, Norris Div.	Lost Div. Semi-Final
1985-86	80	23	12	5	....	16	21	3	....	39	33	8	....	351	349	86	1st, Norris Div.	Lost Div. Semi-Final
1984-85	80	22	16	2	....	16	19	5	....	38	35	7	....	309	299	83	2nd, Norris Div.	Lost Conf. Championship
1983-84	80	25	13	2	....	5	29	6	....	30	42	8	....	277	311	68	4th, Norris Div.	Lost Div. Semi-Final
1982-83	80	29	8	3	....	18	15	7	....	47	23	10	....	338	268	104	1st, Norris Div.	Lost Conf. Championship
1981-82	80	20	13	7	....	10	25	5	....	30	38	12	....	332	363	72	4th, Norris Div.	Lost Conf. Championship
1980-81	80	21	11	8	....	10	22	8	....	31	33	16	....	304	315	78	2nd, Smythe Div.	Lost Prelim. Round
1979-80	80	21	12	7	....	13	15	12	....	34	27	19	....	241	250	87	1st, Smythe Div.	Lost Quarter-Final
1978-79	80	18	12	10	....	11	24	5	....	29	36	15	....	244	277	73	1st, Smythe Div.	Lost Quarter-Final
1977-78	80	20	9	11	....	12	20	8	....	32	29	19	....	230	220	83	1st, Smythe Div.	Lost Quarter-Final
1976-77	80	19	16	5	....	7	27	6	....	26	43	11	....	240	298	63	3rd, Smythe Div.	Lost Prelim. Round
1975-76	80	17	15	8	....	15	15	10	....	32	30	18	....	254	261	82	1st, Smythe Div.	Lost Quarter-Final
1974-75	80	24	12	4	....	13	23	4	....	37	35	8	....	268	241	82	3rd, Smythe Div.	Lost Quarter-Final
1973-74	78	20	6	13	....	21	8	10	....	41	14	23	....	272	164	105	2nd, West Div.	Lost Semi-Final
1972-73	78	26	9	4	....	16	18	5	....	42	27	9	....	284	225	93	1st, West Div.	Lost Final
1971-72	78	28	3	8	....	18	14	7	....	46	17	15	....	256	166	107	1st, West Div.	Lost Semi-Final
1970-71	78	30	6	3	....	19	14	6	....	49	20	9	....	277	184	107	1st, West Div.	Lost Final
1969-70	76	26	7	5	....	19	15	4	....	45	22	9	....	250	170	99	1st, East Div.	Lost Semi-Final
1968-69	76	20	14	4	....	14	19	5	....	34	33	9	....	280	246	77	6th, East Div.	Out of Playoffs
1967-68	74	20	13	4	....	12	13	12	....	32	26	16	....	212	222	80	4th, East Div.	Lost Semi-Final
1966-67	70	24	5	6	....	17	12	6	....	41	17	12	....	264	170	94	1st,	Lost Semi-Final
1965-66	70	21	8	6	....	16	17	2	....	37	25	8	....	240	187	82	2nd,	Lost Semi-Final
1964-65	70	20	13	2	....	14	15	6	....	34	28	8	....	224	176	76	3rd,	Lost Final
1963-64	70	26	4	5	....	10	18	7	....	36	22	12	....	218	169	84	2nd,	Lost Semi-Final
1962-63	70	17	9	9	....	15	12	8	....	32	21	17	....	194	178	81	2nd,	Lost Final
1961-62	70	20	10	5	....	11	16	8	....	31	26	13	....	217	186	75	3rd,	Lost Final
1960-61	**70**	**20**	**6**	**9**		**9**	**18**	**8**		**29**	**24**	**17**		**198**	**180**	**75**	**3rd,**	**Won Stanley Cup**
1959-60	70	18	11	6	....	10	18	7	....	28	29	13	....	191	180	69	3rd,	Lost Semi-Final
1958-59	70	14	12	9	....	14	17	4	....	28	29	13	....	197	208	69	3rd,	Lost Semi-Final
1957-58	70	15	17	3	....	9	22	4	....	24	39	7	....	163	202	55	5th,	Out of Playoffs
1956-57	70	12	15	8	....	4	24	7	....	16	39	15	....	169	225	47	6th,	Out of Playoffs
1955-56	70	9	19	7	....	10	20	5	....	19	39	12	....	155	216	50	6th,	Out of Playoffs
1954-55	70	6	21	8	....	7	19	9	....	13	40	17	....	161	235	43	6th,	Out of Playoffs
1953-54	70	8	21	6	....	4	30	1	....	12	51	7	....	133	242	31	6th,	Out of Playoffs
1952-53	70	14	11	10	....	13	17	5	....	27	28	15	....	169	175	69	4th,	Lost Semi-Final
1951-52	70	9	19	7	....	8	25	2	....	17	44	9	....	158	241	43	6th,	Out of Playoffs
1950-51	70	9	22	5	....	5	25	5	....	13	47	10	....	171	280	36	6th,	Out of Playoffs
1949-50	70	13	18	4	....	9	20	6	....	22	38	10	....	203	244	54	6th,	Out of Playoffs
1948-49	60	13	12	5	....	8	19	3	....	21	31	8	....	173	211	50	5th,	Out of Playoffs
1947-48	60	10	17	3	....	10	17	3	....	20	34	6	....	195	225	46	6th,	Out of Playoffs
1946-47	60	10	17	3	....	9	20	1	....	19	37	4	....	193	274	42	6th,	Out of Playoffs
1945-46	50	15	5	5	....	8	15	2	....	23	20	7	....	200	178	53	3rd,	Lost Semi-Final
1944-45	50	9	14	2	....	4	16	5	....	13	30	7	....	141	194	33	5th,	Out of Playoffs
1943-44	50	15	6	4	....	7	17	1	....	22	23	5	....	178	187	49	4th,	Lost Final
1942-43	50	14	3	8	....	3	15	7	....	17	18	15	....	179	180	49	5th,	Out of Playoffs
1941-42	48	15	8	1	....	7	15	2	....	22	23	3	....	145	155	47	4th,	Lost Semi-Final
1940-41	48	11	10	3	....	5	15	4	....	16	25	7	....	112	139	39	5th,	Lost Quarter-Final
1939-40	48	15	7	2	....	8	12	4	....	23	19	6	....	112	120	52	4th,	Lost Quarter-Final
1938-39	48	5	13	6	....	7	15	2	....	12	28	8	....	91	132	32	7th,	Out of Playoffs
1937-38	**48**	**10**	**10**	**4**		**4**	**15**	**5**		**14**	**25**	**9**		**97**	**139**	**37**	**3rd, Amn. Div.**	**Won Stanley Cup**
1936-37	48	8	13	3	....	6	14	4	....	14	27	7	....	99	131	35	4th, Amn. Div.	Out of Playoffs
1935-36	48	15	7	2	....	6	12	6	....	21	19	8	....	93	92	50	3rd, Amn. Div.	Lost Quarter-Final
1934-35	48	12	8	3	....	14	8	2	....	26	17	5	....	118	88	57	2nd, Amn. Div.	Lost Quarter-Final
1933-34	**48**	**13**	**4**	**7**		**7**	**13**	**4**		**20**	**17**	**11**		**88**	**83**	**51**	**2nd, Amn. Div.**	**Won Stanley Cup**
1932-33	48	12	7	5	....	4	13	7	....	16	20	12	....	88	101	44	4th, Amn. Div.	Out of Playoffs
1931-32	48	13	5	6	....	5	14	5	....	18	19	11	....	86	101	47	2nd, Amn. Div.	Lost Quarter-Final
1930-31	44	13	8	1	....	11	9	2	....	24	17	3	....	108	78	51	2nd, Amn. Div.	Lost Final
1929-30	44	12	9	1	....	9	9	4	....	21	18	5	....	117	111	47	2nd, Amn. Div.	Lost Quarter-Final
1928-29	44	3	13	6	....	4	16	2	....	7	29	8	....	33	85	22	5th, Amn. Div.	Out of Playoffs
1927-28	44	2	18	2	....	5	16	1	....	7	34	3	....	68	134	17	5th, Amn. Div.	Out of Playoffs
1926-27	44	12	8	2	....	7	14	1	....	19	22	3	....	115	116	41	3rd, Amn. Div.	Lost Quarter-Final

2006-07 Player Personnel

FORWARDS	HT	WT	S	Place of Birth	Date	2005-06 Club
ARKHIPOV, Denis	6-3	214	L	Kazan, USSR	5/19/79	Mytischi
BERTI, Adam	6-3	207	L	Scarborough, Ont.	7/1/86	Oshawa-Erie (OHL)
BICKELL, Bryan	6-4	226	L	Bowmanville, Ont.	3/9/86	Ottawa (OHL)-Windsor
BLUNDEN, Michael	6-3	207	R	Toronto, Ont.	12/15/86	Erie (OHL)-Norfolk
BOCHENSKI, Brandon	6-0	196	R	Blaine, MN	4/4/82	Ottawa-Binghamton-Chicago-Norfolk
BOLLAND, Dave	6-0	170	R	Toronto, Ont.	6/5/86	London
BOURQUE, Rene	6-2	205	L	Lac La Biche, Alta.	12/10/81	Chicago
BROUWER, Troy	6-3	220	R	Vancouver, B.C.	8/17/85	Moose Jaw
BURISH, Adam	6-1	189	R	Madison, WI	1/6/83	U. of Wisconsin
FRASER, Colin	6-1	182	L	Sicamous, B.C.	1/28/85	Norfolk
HANDZUS, Michal	6-5	217	L	Banska Bystrica, Czech.	3/11/77	Philadelphia
HAVLAT, Martin	6-1	190	L	Mlada Boleslav, Czech.	4/19/81	Ottawa
HOLMQVIST, Michael	6-3	205	L	Stockholm, Sweden	6/8/79	Chicago
KEITH, Matt	6-2	200	R	Edmonton, Alta.	4/11/83	Chicago-Norfolk
LAPOINTE, Martin	5-11	215	R	Ville St-Pierre, Que.	9/12/73	Chicago
LOW, Reed	6-4	220	R	Moose Jaw, Sask.	6/21/76	Peoria-Missouri
MacDONALD, Craig	6-1	195	L	Antigonish, N.S.	4/7/77	Calgary-Omaha
NORDQVIST, Jonas	6-3	202	L	Leksand, Sweden	4/26/82	Lulea
RUUTU, Tuomo	6-1	208	L	Vantaa, Finland	2/16/83	Chicago
ST. PIERRE, Martin	5-9	185	L	Ottawa, Ont.	8/11/83	Chicago-Norfolk
SALMELAINEN, Tony	5-9	185	R	Espoo, Finland	8/8/81	HIFK
SHARP, Patrick	6-0	197	R	Thunder Bay, Ont.	12/27/81	Philadelphia-Chicago
SMOLINSKI, Bryan	6-1	208	R	Toledo, OH	12/27/71	Ottawa
VOROBIEV, Pavel	6-0	194	L	Karaganda, USSR	5/5/82	Chicago-Norfolk
VRBATA, Radim	6-1	190	R	Mlada Boleslav, Czech.	6/13/81	Carolina-Chicago
DEFENSEMEN						
AUCOIN, Adrian	6-2	214	R	Ottawa, Ont.	7/3/73	Chicago
BARKER, Cam	6-3	222	L	Winnipeg, Man.	4/4/86	Medicine Hat-Chicago
BYFUGLIEN, Dustin	6-3	246	R	Minneapolis, MN	3/27/85	Chicago-Norfolk
CULLIMORE, Jassen	6-5	244	L	Simcoe, Ont.	12/4/72	Chicago
KEITH, Duncan	6-0	182	L	Winnipeg, Man.	7/16/83	Chicago
RICHMOND, Danny	6-0	190	L	Chicago, IL	8/1/84	Carolina-Lowell (AHL)-Chicago-Norfolk
SEABROOK, Brent	6-3	215	R	Richmond, B.C.	4/20/85	Chicago
VANDERMEER, Jim	6-1	218	L	Caroline, Alta.	2/21/80	Chicago
WISNIEWSKI, James	6-0	206	R	Canton, MI	2/21/84	Chicago-Norfolk

GOALTENDERS	HT	WT	C	Place of Birth	Date	2005-06 Club
BRODEUR, Mike	6-2	170	L	Calgary, Alta.	3/30/83	Greenville
CARON, Sebastian	6-1	170	L	Amqui, Que.	6/25/80	Pittsburgh-Wilkes-Barre
CRAWFORD, Corey	6-2	190	L	Montreal, Que.	12/31/84	Chicago-Norfolk
KHABIBULIN, Nikolai	6-1	203	L	Sverdlovsk, USSR	1/13/73	Chicago
LALIME, Patrick	6-3	189	L	St-Bonaventure, Que.	7/7/74	St. Louis-Peoria

2005-06 Scoring

* – rookie

Regular Season

Pos	#	Player	Team	GP	G	A	Pts	+/–	PIM	PP	SH	GW	S	%
L	19	Kyle Calder	CHI	79	26	33	59	–4	52	6	2	6	183	14.2
L	28	Mark Bell	CHI	82	25	23	48	–14	107	11	1	1	227	11.0
R	16	Radim Vrbata	CAR	16	2	3	5	0	6	1	0	0	38	5.3
			CHI	45	13	21	34	4	16	5	0	0	147	8.8
			TOTAL	61	15	24	39	4	22	6	0	0	185	8.1
L	14 *	Rene Bourque	CHI	77	16	18	34	3	56	4	0	2	180	8.9
D	7 *	Brent Seabrook	CHI	69	5	27	32	5	60	1	0	2	114	4.4
R	10	Patrick Sharp	PHI	22	5	3	8	4	10	1	0	3	33	15.2
			CHI	50	9	14	23	1	36	0	1	2	111	8.1
			TOTAL	72	14	17	31	5	46	1	1	5	144	9.7
R	22	Martin Lapointe	CHI	82	14	17	31	–30	106	6	0	3	135	10.4
R	36	Matthew Barnaby	CHI	82	8	20	28	–11	178	0	0	1	85	9.4
D	23	Jim Vandermeer	CHI	76	6	18	24	–2	116	2	0	1	93	6.5
R	32 *	Pavel Vorobiev	CHI	39	9	12	21	–2	34	2	0	0	87	10.3
D	2 *	Duncan Keith	CHI	81	9	12	21	–11	79	1	1	0	134	6.7
C	17	Mikael Holmqvist	CHI	72	10	10	20	–14	16	2	0	1	106	9.4
R	20 *	Brandon Bochenski	OTT	20	6	7	13	7	14	2	0	0	39	15.4
			CHI	20	2	2	4	–9	8	0	0	0	23	8.7
			TOTAL	40	8	9	17	–2	22	2	0	0	62	12.9
C	48	Mark Cullen	CHI	29	7	9	16	7	2	0	0	0	45	15.6
C	37	Curtis Brown	CHI	71	5	10	15	–9	38	0	1	0	84	6.0
D	43 *	James Wisniewski	CHI	19	2	5	7	0	36	0	0	0	25	8.0
R	26 *	Milan Bartovic	CHI	24	1	6	7	0	8	0	0	0	35	2.9
D	5	Jassen Cullimore	CHI	54	1	6	7	–24	53	1	0	1	23	4.3
D	33	Adrian Aucoin	CHI	33	1	5	6	–13	38	1	0	0	59	1.7
D	52 *	Dustin Byfuglien	CHI	25	3	2	5	–6	24	0	0	1	45	6.7
C	15	Tuomo Ruutu	CHI	15	2	3	5	–7	31	1	0	0	30	6.7
C	38	Jason Morgan	CHI	7	1	1	2	1	6	0	0	0	6	16.7
L	56	Mike Brown	CHI	2	0	1	1	0	9	0	0	0	1	0.0
D	44 *	Danny Richmond	CAR	10	0	1	1	–3	7	0	0	0	7	0.0
			CHI	10	0	0	0	–3	18	0	0	0	6	0.0
			TOTAL	20	0	1	1	–6	25	0	0	0	13	0.0
D	42 *	Michal Barinka	CHI	25	0	1	1	–7	20	0	0	0	19	0.0
L	55	Eric Daze	CHI	1	0	0	0	–2	2	0	0	0	0	0.0
D	25 *	Cam Barker	CHI	1	0	0	0	0	0	0	0	0	1	0.0
R	11 *	Matt Keith	CHI	2	0	0	0	0	0	0	0	0	6	0.0
C	47 *	Martin St. Pierre	CHI	2	0	0	0	–1	0	0	0	0	1	0.0
L	29	Shawn Thornton	CHI	10	0	0	0	–5	16	0	0	0	16	0.0

Goaltending

No.	Goaltender	GPI	Mins	Avg	W	L	OT	EN	SO	GA	SA	S%	G	A	PIM
30	* Adam Munro	10	501	2.99	3	5	2	1	1	25	234	.893	0	1	0
31	Craig Anderson	29	1553	3.32	6	12	4	2	1	86	757	.886	0	1	14
53	Nikolai Khabibulin	50	2815	3.35	17	26	6	3	0	157	1379	.886	0	1	10
50	* Corey Crawford	2	86	3.49	0	0	1	0	0	5	41	.878	0	0	0
	Totals	**82**	**4997**	**3.35**	**26**	**43**	**13**	**6**	**2**	**279**	**2417**	**.885**			

Coach

YAWNEY, TRENT
Coach, Chicago Blackhawks. Born in Hudson Bay, Sask., September 29, 1965.

The Chicago Blackhawks named Trent Yawney the 35th head coach in the team's history on July 7, 2005. Yawney served as the head coach of the Blackhawks' American Hockey League affiliate in Norfolk for five seasons, taking over the coaching reigns of the Admirals on June 23, 2000, for their inaugural season in the AHL.

Under Yawney's guidance, Norfolk won back-to-back South Division titles in 2001–02 and 2002–03. The Admirals made five consecutive playoff appearances and advanced to the conference semifinals twice while seeing over 50 players advance to the Blackhawks during that span. Such players as Tyler Arnason, Mark Bell, Kyle Calder, Craig Anderson, Michael Leighton, Steve McCarthy, Matt Ellison, Matt Keith, Travis Moen, Quintin Laing, Pavel Vorobiev, Mikhail Yakubov, Anton Babchuk and Michal Barinka were developed under Yawney's leadership.

Yawney was honored by The Hockey News as their minor pro coach of the year for the 2003–04 season. The only coach in the AHL to work without an assistant coach, he guided a squad full of rookies which was also depleted by injuries and NHL call-ups to a postseason appearance. The 2004-05 season saw the Admirals establish a new franchise record for wins (43) as well as points (93) during one of the most competitive years in AHL history on the ice.

Yawney was originally drafted by the Blackhawks in the third round, 45th overall, in the 1984 NHL Entry Draft out of Saskatoon in the Western Hockey League. After playing three seasons with the Blades, he joined the Canadian national team in 1985 for three seasons, culminating in the 1988 Winter Olympics in Calgary, Alberta, where he served as captain for Team Canada. Following the Olympics, Yawney joined the Blackhawks making his National Hockey League debut on March 5, 1988. In his 12-year NHL career, Yawney played in 593 regular-season games with the Blackhawks, Calgary Flames and St. Louis Blues recording 27 goals and 102 assists for 129 points with 783 penalty minutes. He also played in 60 career playoff games recording nine goals and 17 assists for 26 points and 81 penalty minutes.

Coaching Record

		Regular Season				Playoffs		
Season	Team	Games	W	L	O/T	Games	W	L
2000-01	Norfolk (AHL)	80	36	31	13	9	4	5
2001-02	Norfolk (AHL)	80	38	30	12	4	1	3
2002-03	Norfolk (AHL)	80	37	31	12	9	5	4
2003-04	Norfolk (AHL)	80	35	41	4	8	4	4
2004-05	Norfolk (AHL)	80	43	31	6	6	2	4
2005-06	**Chicago (NHL)**	**82**	**26**	**43**	**13**	....	....	....
	NHL Totals	**82**	**26**	**43**	**13**	....	....	....

General Managers' History

Major Frederic McLaughlin, 1926-27 to 1941-42; Bill Tobin, 1942-43 to 1953-54; Tommy Ivan, 1954-55 to 1976-77; Bob Pulford, 1977-78 to 1989-90; Mike Keenan, 1990-91, 1991-92; Mike Keenan and Bob Pulford, 1992-93; Bob Pulford, 1993-94 to 1996-97; Bob Murray, 1997-98, 1998-99; Bob Murray and Bob Pulford, 1999-2000; Mike Smith, 2000-01 to 2002-03; Mike Smith and Bob Pulford, 2003-04; Bob Pulford, 2004-05; Dale Tallon, 2005-06 to date.

Vice President and General Manager

TALLON, DALE
General Manager, Chicago Blackhawks.
Born in Noranda, Que., October 19, 1950.

The Chicago Blackhawks announced on June 21, 2005 that Dale Tallon had been named the eighth general manager in the team's storied history. Tallon, in his second stint with the Blackhawks front office, was named assistant general manager on November 5, 2003. He served four years (1998 to 2002) as the Blackhawks' director of player personnel before he returned to the radio and television booth prior to the 2002-03 season as color analyst for Blackhawk hockey.

Tallon was the Vancouver Canucks' first-round selection and the second player chosen overall (behind Gilbert Perreault, Buffalo) in the 1970 NHL Entry Draft. A defenseman, he immediately jumped into the NHL with the Canucks in the 1970–71 season. Tallon recorded a career-high 17 goals in 69 games with Vancouver during the 1971–72 season and appeared in the 1971 and 1972 NHL All-Star Games.

Tallon was traded to the Blackhawks for Jerry Korab and Gary Smith on May 14,1973. He had his best season as a professional with Chicago in 1975–76 with a career-high 47 assists and 62 points in 80 games. During his five-year Blackhawk career (1973 to 1978), Tallon scored 44 goals and added 112 assists for 156 points with 296 penalty minutes. He was dealt to Pittsburgh on October 9, 1978 and finished his playing career by playing two seasons with the Penguins. During his 10-year NHL career, Tallon scored 98 goals and added 238 assists for 336 points in 642 games. After retiring from the NHL following the 1979–80 season, he served as the Blackhawks color analyst for radio and television broadcasts for 16 seasons.

At the start of the 1998-99 season, Tallon joined the Blackhawk front office as director of player personnel. As he traveled the world scouting hockey, Tallon's knowledge and expertise of the game were honed while aiding in selecting and developing the Blackhawks' young prospects.

Club Records

Team

(Figures in brackets for season records are games played; records for fewest points, wins, ties, losses, goals, goals against are for 70 or more games)

Most Points	107	1970-71 (78), 1971-72 (78)
Most Wins	49	1970-71 (78), 1990-91 (80)
Most Ties	23	1973-74 (78)
Most Losses	56	2005-06 (82)
Most Goals	351	1985-86 (80)
Most Goals Against	363	1981-82 (80)
Fewest Points	31	1953-54 (70)
Fewest Wins	12	1953-54 (70)
Fewest Ties	6	1989-90 (70)
Fewest Losses	14	1973-74 (78)
Fewest Goals	*133	1953-54 (70)
Fewest Goals Against	164	1973-74 (78)

Longest Winning Streak
- Overall ... 8 — Dec. 9-26/71, Jan. 4-21/81
- Home ... 13 — Nov. 11-Dec. 20/70
- Away ... 7 — Dec. 9-29/64

Longest Undefeated Streak
- Overall ... 15 — Jan. 14-Feb. 16/67 (12 wins, 3 ties), Oct. 29-Dec. 3/75 (6 wins, 9 ties)
- Home ... 18 — Oct. 11-Dec. 20/70 (16 wins, 2 ties)
- Away ... 12 — Nov. 2-Dec. 16/67 (6 wins, 6 ties)

Longest Losing Streak
- Overall ... 12 — Feb. 25-Mar. 25/51
- Home ... 10 — Jan. 29-Mar. 21/28
- Away ... 19 — Nov. 10/03-Jan. 29/04

Longest Winless Streak
- Overall ... 21 — Dec. 17/50-Jan. 28/51 (18 losses, 3 ties)
- Home ... 15 — Dec. 16/28-Feb. 28/29 (11 losses, 4 ties)
- Away ... 22 — Dec. 19/50-Mar. 25/51 (20 losses, 2 ties)

Most Shutouts, Season ... 15 — 1969-70 (76)
Most PIM, Season ... 2,663 — 1991-92 (80)
Most Goals, Game ... 12 — Jan. 30/69 (Chi. 12 at Phi. 0)

Individual

Most Seasons	22	Stan Mikita
Most Games	1,394	Stan Mikita
Most Goals, Career	604	Bobby Hull
Most Assists, Career	926	Stan Mikita
Most Points, Career	1,467	Stan Mikita (541G, 926A)
Most PIM, Career	1,495	Chris Chelios
Most Shutouts, Career	74	Tony Esposito

Longest Consecutive Games Streak ... 884 — Steve Larmer (Oct. 6/82-Apr. 15/93)
Most Goals, Season ... 58 — Bobby Hull (1968-69)
Most Assists, Season ... 87 — Denis Savard (1981-82, 1987-88)
Most Points, Season ... 131 — Denis Savard (1987-88; 44G, 87A)

Most PIM, Season ... 408 — Mike Peluso (1991-92)
Most Points, Defenseman, Season ... 85 — Doug Wilson (1981-82; 39G, 46A)
Most Points, Center, Season ... 131 — Denis Savard (1987-88; 44G, 87A)
Most Points, Right Wing, Season ... 101 — Steve Larmer (1990-91; 44G, 57A)
Most Points, Left Wing, Season ... 107 — Bobby Hull (1968-69; 58G, 49A)
Most Points, Rookie, Season ... 90 — Steve Larmer (1982-83; 43G, 47A)
Most Shutouts, Season ... 15 — Tony Esposito (1969-70)
Most Goals, Game ... 5 — Grant Mulvey (Feb. 3/82)
Most Assists, Game ... 6 — Pat Stapleton (Mar. 30/69)
Most Points, Game ... 7 — Max Bentley (Jan. 28/43; 4G, 3A), Grant Mulvey (Feb. 3/82; 5G, 2A)

* NHL Record.

Retired Numbers

1	Glenn Hall	1957-1967
9	Bobby Hull	1957-1972
18	Denis Savard	1980-1990, 1995-1997
21	Stan Mikita	1958-1980
35	Tony Esposito	1969-1984

All-time Record vs. Other Clubs

Regular Season

	At Home GP	W	L	T	OL	GF	GA	PTS	On Road GP	W	L	T	OL	GF	GA	PTS	Total GP	W	L	T	OL	GF	GA	PTS
Anaheim	26	12	12	2	0	71	65	26	24	7	14	3	0	49	65	17	50	19	26	5	0	120	130	43
Atlanta	2	2	0	0	0	6	4	4	5	3	2	0	0	15	18	6	7	5	2	0	0	21	18	10
Boston	286	147	94	45	0	926	767	339	284	89	161	34	0	808	1023	212	570	236	255	79	0	1734	1790	551
Buffalo	51	27	17	6	1	164	139	61	53	14	32	7	0	138	199	35	104	41	49	13	1	302	338	96
Calgary	63	27	23	13	0	201	184	67	65	22	29	13	1	195	206	58	128	49	52	26	1	396	390	125
Carolina	29	16	9	3	1	117	83	36	31	12	15	4	0	96	102	28	60	28	24	7	1	213	185	64
Colorado	43	22	15	3	3	149	134	50	41	13	22	6	0	130	164	32	84	35	37	9	3	279	298	82
Columbus	14	9	4	1	0	41	26	19	15	5	7	1	2	44	47	13	29	14	11	2	2	85	73	32
Dallas	112	64	33	15	0	417	301	143	114	44	52	16	2	343	389	106	226	108	85	31	2	760	690	249
Detroit	342	155	133	51	3	1025	970	364	339	100	205	33	1	843	1161	234	681	255	338	84	4	1868	2131	598
Edmonton	46	22	15	7	2	173	157	53	47	19	23	5	0	151	173	43	93	41	38	12	2	324	330	96
Florida	10	5	3	2	0	34	30	12	9	5	2	1	1	33	22	12	19	10	5	3	1	67	52	24
Los Angeles	77	36	32	9	0	266	227	81	76	33	34	8	1	252	253	75	153	69	66	17	1	518	480	156
Minnesota	10	4	5	1	0	23	30	9	10	2	7	0	1	21	34	5	20	6	12	1	1	44	64	14
Montreal	273	93	125	55	0	731	761	241	276	54	173	48	1	653	1067	157	549	147	298	103	1	1384	1828	398
Nashville	21	12	7	1	1	58	53	26	20	6	9	3	2	50	66	17	41	18	16	4	3	108	119	43
New Jersey	47	24	12	10	1	178	130	59	47	16	20	11	0	142	147	43	94	40	32	21	1	320	277	102
NY Islanders	49	26	17	5	1	163	164	58	47	14	18	15	0	141	163	43	96	40	35	20	1	304	327	101
NY Rangers	287	129	115	43	0	872	793	301	285	113	117	55	0	807	841	281	572	242	232	98	0	1679	1634	582
Ottawa	8	4	2	2	0	18	18	10	10	6	4	0	0	30	31	12	18	10	6	2	0	48	49	22
Philadelphia	61	26	16	19	0	207	175	71	62	16	35	11	0	162	204	43	123	42	51	30	0	369	379	114
Phoenix	50	27	13	10	0	188	132	64	52	19	27	5	1	160	169	44	102	46	40	15	1	348	301	108
Pittsburgh	61	40	11	10	0	240	158	90	59	23	29	7	0	190	210	53	120	63	40	17	0	430	368	143
St. Louis	122	68	36	18	0	445	355	154	119	43	57	17	2	372	405	105	241	111	93	35	2	817	760	259
San Jose	27	14	9	2	2	86	85	32	28	10	14	3	1	74	78	24	55	24	23	5	3	160	163	56
Tampa Bay	14	8	4	2	0	45	35	18	12	4	4	3	1	30	29	12	26	12	8	5	1	75	64	30
Toronto	318	156	120	42	0	968	831	354	315	97	164	54	0	821	1071	248	633	253	284	96	0	1789	1902	602
Vancouver	73	47	17	7	2	273	172	103	74	22	36	15	1	213	227	60	147	69	53	22	3	486	399	163
Washington	40	22	12	6	0	151	120	50	42	16	21	5	0	131	148	37	82	38	33	11	0	282	268	87
Defunct Clubs	139	79	40	20	0	408	268	178	140	52	67	21	0	316	346	125	279	131	107	41	0	724	614	303
Totals	2701	1323	951	410	17	8644	7363	3073	2701	879	1400	404	18	7410	9058	2180	5402	2202	2351	814	35	16054	16421	5253

Playoffs

	Series	W	L	GP	W	L	T	GF	GA	Last Mtg.	Rnd.	Result
Boston	6	1	5	22	5	16	1	63	97	1978	QF	L 0-4
Buffalo	2	0	2	9	1	8	0	17	36	1980	QF	L 0-4
Calgary	3	1	2	12	5	7	0	33	37	1996	CQF	W 4-0
Colorado	2	0	2	12	4	8	0	28	49	1997	CQF	L 2-4
Dallas	6	4	2	33	19	14	0	120	118	1991	DSF	L 2-4
Detroit	14	8	6	69	38	31	0	210	190	1995	CF	L 1-4
Edmonton	4	1	3	20	8	12	0	77	102	1992	CF	W 4-0
Los Angeles	1	1	0	5	4	1	0	10	7	1974	QF	W 4-1
Montreal	17	5	12	81	29	50	2	185	261	1976	QF	L 0-4
NY Islanders	2	0	2	6	0	6	0	6	21	1979	QF	L 0-4
NY Rangers	5	4	1	24	14	10	0	66	54	1973	SF	W 4-1
Philadelphia	1	1	0	4	4	0	0	20	8	1971	QF	W 4-0
Pittsburgh	2	1	1	8	4	4	0	24	23	1992	F	L 0-4
St. Louis	10	7	3	50	28	22	0	171	142	2002	CQF	L 1-4
Toronto	9	3	6	38	15	22	1	89	111	1995	CQF	W 4-3
Vancouver	1	0	1	4	0	4	0	14	24	1995	CSF	W 4-0
Defunct Clubs	4	2	2	9	5	3	1	16	15			
Totals	90	40	50	411	188	218	5	1159	1295			

Playoff Results 2006-2001

Year	Round	Opponent	Result	GF	GA
2002	CQF	St. Louis	L 1-4	5	13

Abbreviations: Round: F - Final;
CF - conference final; **CSF** - conference semi-final;
CQF - conference quarter-final; **DSF** - division semi-final; **SF** - semi-final; **QF** - quarter-final.

Calgary totals include Atlanta Flames, 1972-73 to 1979-80.
Colorado totals include Quebec, 1979-80 to 1994-95.
New Jersey totals include Kansas City, 1974-75 to 1975-76.
Phoenix totals include Winnipeg, 1979-80 to 1995-96.
Carolina totals include Hartford, 1979-80 to 1996-97.
Dallas totals include Minnesota North Stars, 1967-68 to 1992-93, and Colorado Rockies, 1976-77 to 1981-82.

2005-06 Results

Oct.	5	Anaheim	3-5	10	at Washington	4-3*
	7	San Jose	6-3	11	Philadelphia	2-5
	9	Columbus	2-3	13	Pittsburgh	4-1
	11	at St. Louis	1-4	15	New Jersey	2-3†
	14	at Colorado	3-2†	17	NY Islanders	1-2*
	15	at San Jose	3-4	19	Colorado	4-2
	18	at Vancouver	2-6	20	at Minnesota	1-4
	23	Minnesota	4-2	22	Minnesota	2-3
	25	at Nashville	3-5	26	Calgary	2-0
	27	at Detroit	2-5	29	Calgary	3-5
	29	Detroit	2-4	Feb. 2	at St. Louis	5-6†
Nov.	1	at Detroit	1-4	4	at Nashville	0-6
	2	at St. Louis	6-5*	7	at Phoenix	3-1
	4	at Dallas	1-9	8	at San Jose	1-2
	6	Phoenix	2-1*	11	at Los Angeles	4-5*
	10	at St. Louis	4-2	12	at Anaheim	1-4
	11	Los Angeles	2-4	Mar. 1	Nashville	3-0
	13	Edmonton	3-1	3	Vancouver	4-5†
	18	at Calgary	5-2	5	Dallas	2-7
	19	at Edmonton	4-3	7	at Columbus	3-1
	22	at Vancouver	1-3	9	Colorado	1-2
	26	at Los Angeles	2-3	11	at Detroit	4-6
	27	at Anaheim	1-3	12	Detroit	3-5
	30	Los Angeles	3-2	15	Columbus	3-2
Dec.	2	at Tampa Bay	2-3†	17	Anaheim	1-2
	3	at Florida	3-4*	19	Phoenix	2-3
	7	NY Rangers	2-1*	23	at Phoenix	3-4
	11	at Atlanta	5-4†	24	at Dallas	2-3†
	13	at Carolina	3-5	26	San Jose	4-5*
	15	at Nashville	3-5	29	St. Louis	3-2*
	16	St. Louis	5-1	31	at Detroit	3-2*
	18	Dallas	3-5	Apr. 1	at Columbus	2-5
	21	Nashville	1-6	3	at Colorado	3-4
	23	Detroit	2-3*	5	Nashville	4-3
	26	at Columbus	3-4*	7	Edmonton	3-4*
	28	St. Louis	1-2	8	at Nashville	1-2†
	30	Columbus	2-3	11	at Minnesota	0-2
Jan.	2	at Calgary	2-3	13	Detroit	3-7
	3	at Edmonton	0-5	15	at Columbus	2-5
	5	Vancouver	2-3	16	Columbus	4-3
	8	Nashville	1-5	18	St. Louis	3-2*

* – Overtime   † – Shootout

Entry Draft
Selections 2006-1992

2006
Pick
3 Jonathan Toews
33 Igor Makarov
61 Simon Danis-Pepin
76 Tony Lagerstrom
95 Ben Shutron
96 Joe Palmer
156 Jan-Mikael Juutilainen
169 Chris Auger
186 Peter Leblanc

2005
Pick
7 Jack Skille
43 Michael Blunden
54 Dan Bertram
68 Evan Brophey
108 Niklas Hjalmarsson
113 Nathan Davis
117 Denis Istomin
134 Brennan Turner
167 Joseph Fallon
188 Joe Charlebois
202 David Kuchejda
203 Adam Hobson

2004
Pick
3 Cam Barker
32 Dave Bolland
41 Bryan Bickell
45 Ryan Garlock
54 Jakub Sindel
68 Adam Berti
120 Mitch Maunu
123 Karel Hromas
131 Trevor Kell
140 Jake Dowell
165 Scott McCulloch
196 Petri Kontiola
214 Troy Brouwer
223 Jared Walker
229 Eric Hunter
256 Matthew Ford
260 Marko Anttila

2003
Pick
14 Brent Seabrook
52 Corey Crawford
59 Michal Barinka
151 Lasse Kukkonen
156 Alexei Ivanov
181 Johan Andersson
211 Mike Brodeur
245 Dustin Byfuglien
275 Michael Grenzy
282 Chris Porter

2002
Pick
21 Anton Babchuk
54 Duncan Keith
93 Alexander Kojevnikov
128 Matt Ellison
156 James Wisniewski
188 Kevin Kantee
219 Tyson Kellerman
251 Jason Kostadine
282 Adam Burish

2001
Pick
9 Tuomo Ruutu
29 Adam Munro
59 Matt Keith
73 Craig Anderson
104 Brent MacLellan
115 Vladimir Gusev
119 Alexei Zotkin
142 Tommi Jaminki
174 Alexander Golovin
186 Petr Puncochar
205 Teemu Jaaskelainen
216 Oleg Minakov
268 Jeff Miles

2000
Pick
10 Mikhail Yakubov
11 Pavel Vorobiev
49 Jonas Nordqvist
74 Igor Radulov
106 Scott Balan
117 Olli Malmivaara
151 Alexander Barkunov
177 Michael Ayers
193 Joey Martin
207 Cliff Loya
225 Vladislav Luchkin
240 Adam Berkhoel
262 Peter Flache
271 Reto Von Arx
291 Arne Ramholt

1999
Pick
23 Steve McCarthy
46 Dimitri Levinski
63 Stepan Mokhov
134 Michael Jacobsen
165 Michael Leighton
194 Mattias Wennerberg
195 Yorick Treille
223 Andrew Carver

1998
Pick
8 Mark Bell
94 Matthias Trattnig
156 Kent Huskins
158 Jari Viuhkola
166 Jonathan Pelletier
183 Tyler Arnason
210 Sean Griffin
238 Alexandre Couture
240 Andrei Yershov

1997
Pick
13 Daniel Cleary
16 Ty Jones
39 Jeremy Reich
67 Mike Souza
110 Ben Simon
120 Peter Gardiner
130 Kyle Calder
147 Heath Gordon
174 Jerad Smith
204 Sergei Shikhanov
230 Chris Feil

1996
Pick
31 Remi Royer
42 Jeff Paul
46 Geoff Peters
130 Andy Johnson
184 Mike Vellinga
210 Chris Twerdun
236 Andrei Kozyrev

1995
Pick
19 Dmitri Nabokov
45 Christian Laflamme
71 Kevin McKay
82 Chris Van Dyk
97 Pavel Kriz
146 Marc Magliarditi
149 Marty Wilford
175 Steve Tardif
201 Casey Hankinson
227 Mike Pittman

1994
Pick
14 Ethan Moreau
40 Jean-Yves Leroux
85 Steve McLaren
118 Marc Dupuis
144 Jim Enson
170 Tyler Prosofsky
196 Mike Josephson
222 Lubomir Jandera
248 Lars Weibel
263 Rob Mara

1993
Pick
24 Eric Lecompte
50 Eric Manlow
54 Bogdan Savenko
76 Ryan Huska
90 Eric Daze
102 Patrik Pysz
128 Jonni Vauhkonen
180 Tom White
206 Sergei Petrov
232 Mike Rusk
258 Mike McGhan
284 Tom Noble

1992
Pick
12 Sergei Krivokrasov
36 Jeff Shantz
41 Sergei Klimovich
89 Andy MacIntyre
113 Tim Hogan
137 Gerry Skrypec
161 Mike Prokopec
185 Layne Roland
209 David Hymovitz
233 Richard Raymond

Club Directory

United Center

Chicago Blackhawks
United Center
1901 W. Madison Street
Chicago, IL 60612
Phone **312/455-7000**
FAX 312/455-7041
www.chicagoblackhawks.com
Capacity: 20,500

President . . . . William W. Wirtz
Senior Vice President. . . . . Robert J. Pulford
Vice President. . . . . Jack Davison
Vice President. . . . . Peter R. Wirtz
General Manager . . . . Dale Tallon
Assistant General Manager . . . . Rick Dudley
Director of Hockey Operations . . . . Stan Bowman
Norfolk G.M. & Pro Scout . . . . Al MacIsssac
Head Coach . . . . Trent Yawney
Assistant Coach . . . . Denis Savard
Assistant Coach . . . . Mark Hardy
Skating Coach . . . . Dan Jansen
Strength & Conditioning Coach . . . . Phil Walker
Goaltending Consultant . . . . Vladislav Tretiak
Goaltending Coach. Stephane Waite
Chief Amateur Scout . . . . Michel Dumas
Amateur Scouts. . . . . Ron Anderson, Bruce Franklin, Mark Kelley, Tim Keon, Rob Pulford
European Scouting Coordinator . . . . Sakari Pietila
European Amateur Scouts. . . . . Karl Pavlik, Ruslan Shabanov
Pro Scout . . . . Marc Bergevin
European Pro Scout . . . . Mats Hallin
Executive Assistant . . . . Cindy Brueck
Video Coordinator . . . . Ryan Stewart

Training/Equipment Staff
Head Athletic Trainer . . . . Michael Gapski
Assistant Athletic Trainer. . . . . Jeff Thomas
Massage Therapist . . . . Pawel Prylinski
Equipment Manager. . . . . Troy Parchman

Medical Staff
Head Team Physicians, Orthopedics . . . . Michael Terry, Sherwin Ho, Bruce Reider
Team Physicians, Internal Medicine . . . . William Harper, Carl Meyer, Todd Stern
Team Dentists. . . . . Russ Baer, Anthony LaVacca, Martin Marcus
Oral Surgeon . . . . Eric Pulver
Eye Doctor . . . . William Mieler

Public Relations & Marketing
Exec. Dir. of Communications, Broadcasting
& Community Outreach . . . . Jim De Maria
Mgr. of Public Relations & Team Services. . . . . Tony Ommen
Director of Community Outreach . . . . Jim Blaney
Manager of Community Outreach . . . . Angela Armbruster
Communications Manager . . . . Pete Hassen
Website Producer . . . . Adam Kempenaar
Exec. Dir. of Sales & Marketing . . . . Jim Sofranko
Director of Corporate Sponsorships. . . . . . . Steve Waight
Manager, Client Services. . . . . Kelly Bodnarchuk
Account Exec., Corporate Sponsorships . . . . Sara Bailey
Manager, Game Operations . . . . Ben Broder
Executive Assistant . . . . Alison Finley

Finance
Controller. . . . . John Kerr

Ticketing
Exec. Dir., Ticket Operations . . . . James K. Bare
Director, Ticket Sales & Customer Services. . . . . . Doug Ryan
Senior Account Executives. . . . . Brad Bober, Ildegardo Esparza, Julianna Ilg, Steve McNelley, Rich Sommers
Senior Ticket Services Specialist . . . . Kathie Raimondi

Miscellaneous
Team Photographer . . . . Bill Smith
Assistant Photographer . . . . Rudy Ayasse
Organist . . . . Frank Pellico
Public Address Announcer . . . . Gene Honda
Website Contributor . . . . Harvey Wittenberg
Radio Station . . . . WSCR (AM 670)
Television Station . . . . Comcast Sports Net Chicago
TV Play-By-Play . . . . Dan Kelly
TV Analyst . . . . Ed Olczyk
Radio Play-by-Play . . . . John Wiedeman
Radio Analyst . . . . Troy Murray
Radio Studio Host . . . . Jesse Rogers

Coaching History

Pete Muldoon, 1926-27; Barney Stanley and Hugh Lehman, 1927-28; Herb Gardiner and Dick Irvin, 1928-29; Tom Shaughnessy and Bill Tobin, 1929-30; Dick Irvin, 1930-31; Bill Tobin, 1931-32; Emil Iverson, Godfrey Matheson and Tommy Gorman, 1932-33; Tommy Gorman, 1933-34; Clem Loughlin, 1934-35 to 1936-37; Bill Stewart, 1937-38; Bill Stewart and Paul Thompson, 1938-39; Paul Thompson, 1939-40 to 1943-44; Paul Thompson and Johnny Gottselig, 1944-45; Johnny Gottselig, 1945-46, 1946-47; Johnny Gottselig and Charlie Conacher, 1947-48; Charlie Conacher, 1948-49, 1949-50; Ebbie Goodfellow, 1950-51, 1951-52; Sid Abel, 1952-53, 1953-54; Frank Eddolls, 1954-55; Dick Irvin, 1955-56; Tommy Ivan, 1956-57; Tommy Ivan and Rudy Pilous; 1957-58; Rudy Pilous, 1958-59 to 1962-63; Billy Reay, 1963-64 to 1975-76; Billy Reay and Bill White, 1976-77; Bob Pulford, 1977-78, 1978-79; Eddie Johnston, 1979-80; Keith Magnuson, 1980-81; Keith Magnuson and Bob Pulford, 1981-82; Orval Tessier, 1982-83, 1983-84; Orval Tessier and Bob Pulford, 1984-85; Bob Pulford, 1985-86, 1986-87; Bob Murdoch, 1987-88; Mike Keenan, 1988-89 to 1991-92; Darryl Sutter, 1992-93 to 1994-95; Craig Hartsburg, 1995-96 to 1997-98; Dirk Graham and Lorne Molleken, 1998-99; Lorne Molleken and Bob Pulford, 1999-2000; Alpo Suhonen, 2000-01; Brian Sutter, 2001-02 to 2003-04; Trent Yawney, 2005-06 to date.

Captains' History

Dick Irvin, 1926-27 to 1928-29; Duke Dukowski, 1929-30; Ty Arbour, 1930-31; Cy Wentworth, 1931-32; Helge Bostrom, 1932-33; Charlie Gardiner, 1933-34; no captain, 1934-35; Johnny Gottselig, 1935-36 to 1939-40; Earl Seibert, 1940-41, 1941-42; Doug Bentley, 1942-43, 1943-44; Clint Smith 1944-45; John Mariucci, 1945-46; Red Hamill, 1946-47; John Mariucci, 1947-48; Gaye Stewart, 1948-49; Doug Bentley, 1949-50; Jack Stewart, 1950-51, 1951-52; Bill Gadsby, 1952-53, 1953-54; Gus Mortson, 1954-55 to 1956-57; no captain, 1957-58; Ed Litzenberger, 1958-59 to 1960-61; Pierre Pilote, 1961-62 to 1967-68, no captain, 1968-69; Pat Stapleton, 1969-70; no captain, 1970-71 to 1974-75; Stan Mikita and Pit Martin, 1975-76; Stan Mikita, Pit Martin and Keith Magnuson, 1976-77; Keith Magnuson, 1977-78, 1978-79; Keith Magnuson and Terry Ruskowski, 1979-80; Terry Ruskowski, 1980-81, 1981-82; Darryl Sutter, 1982-83 to 1984-85; Darryl Sutter and Bob Murray, 1985-86; Darryl Sutter, 1986-87; no captain, 1987-88; Denis Savard and Dirk Graham, 1988-89; Dirk Graham, 1989-90 to 1994-95; Chris Chelios, 1995-96 to 1998-99; Doug Gilmour, 1999-2000; Tony Amonte, 2000-01, 2001-02; Alex Zhamnov, 2002-03, 2003-04; Adrian Aucoin and Martin Lapointe, 2005-06.

Colorado Avalanche

2005-06 Results: 43w-30L-3otl-6sol 95pts.
Second, Northwest Division

2006-07 Schedule

Oct.	Wed.	4	Dallas
	Thu.	5	at Minnesota
	Sun.	8	Vancouver
	Sat.	14	Edmonton
	Mon.	16	Chicago
	Wed.	18	at Toronto
	Thu.	19	at Ottawa
	Sat.	21	at Montreal
	Mon.	23	Los Angeles
	Wed.	25	Washington
	Sun.	29	Minnesota
Nov.	Wed.	1	at Columbus
	Thu.	2	at St. Louis
	Sat.	4	Vancouver
	Tue.	7	Los Angeles
	Sat.	11	at Nashville
	Mon.	13	Edmonton
	Wed.	15	San Jose
	Fri.	17	at Columbus
	Sat.	18	at Minnesota
	Mon.	20	at Dallas
	Wed.	22	Anaheim
	Sat.	25	Vancouver
	Tue.	28	at Calgary
	Thu.	30	at Edmonton
Dec.	Sat.	2	at Vancouver
	Tue.	5	Columbus
	Thu.	7	at San Jose
	Sat.	9	at Los Angeles
	Mon.	11	Carolina
	Wed.	13	St. Louis
	Fri.	15	Edmonton
	Sun.	17	at Chicago
	Tue.	19	at Edmonton
	Thu.	21	Calgary
	Sat.	23	Chicago
	Wed.	27	Dallas
	Fri.	29	St. Louis
	Sat.	30	at St. Louis
Jan.	Mon.	1	at Nashville*
	Fri.	5	Tampa Bay

	Sat.	6	at Minnesota
	Tue.	9	Detroit
	Thu.	11	Calgary
	Sat.	13	at Anaheim
	Mon.	15	at San Jose
	Wed.	17	Phoenix
	Sat.	20	Detroit
	Fri.	26	Phoenix
	Sun.	28	at Detroit*
	Tue.	30	Nashville
Feb.	Thu.	1	Minnesota
	Sat.	3	Edmonton*
	Tue.	6	Florida
	Thu.	8	Atlanta
	Sun.	11	at Dallas*
	Tue.	13	Anaheim
	Thu.	15	at Calgary
	Sat.	17	at Calgary
	Sun.	18	at Vancouver
	Tue.	20	Calgary
	Thu.	22	Minnesota
	Sat.	24	at Los Angeles
	Sun.	25	at Anaheim*
	Tue.	27	Columbus
Mar.	Thu.	1	at Chicago
	Sun.	4	at Detroit*
	Tue.	6	at Boston
	Wed.	7	at Buffalo
	Sun.	11	at Minnesota*
	Wed.	14	Calgary
	Sat.	17	at Phoenix
	Sun.	18	San Jose
	Wed.	21	at Edmonton
	Fri.	23	at Edmonton
	Sun.	25	at Vancouver
	Tue.	27	Vancouver
	Thu.	29	at Phoenix
	Sat.	31	Minnesota*
Apr.	Tue.	3	at Calgary
	Thu.	5	at Vancouver
	Sat.	7	Nashville

* Denotes afternoon game.

Though injuries limited him to just 61 games, Marek Svatos tied Joe Sakic for the team lead with 32 goals in 2005-06. Among NHL rookies, only Alex Ovechkin (52) and Sidney Crosby (39) scored more goals that Svatos.

Franchise date: June 22, 1979
Transferred from Quebec to Denver, June 21, 1995

WESTERN CONFERENCE
NORTHWEST DIVISION

28th NHL Season

Year-by-Year Record

| | | Home | | | | Road | | | | Overall | | | | | | | |
Season	GP	W	L	T	OL	W	L	T	OL	W	L	T	OL	GF	GA	Pts.	Finished	Playoff Result
2005-06	82	25	10	....	6	18	20	....	3	43	30	....	9	283	257	95	2nd, Northwest Div.	Lost Conf. Semi-Final
2004-05	....	....		....		....		....		....		....		....				
2003-04	82	19	14	6	2	21	8	7	5	40	22	13	7	236	198	100	2nd, Northwest Div.	Lost Conf. Semi-Final
2002-03	82	21	9	8	3	21	10	5	5	42	19	13	8	251	194	105	1st, Northwest Div.	Lost Conf. Quarter-Final
2001-02	82	24	12	4	1	21	16	4	0	45	28	8	1	212	169	99	1st, Northwest Div.	Lost Conf. Championship
2000-01	**82**	**28**	**6**	**5**	**2**	**24**	**10**	**5**	**2**	**52**	**16**	**10**	**4**	**270**	**192**	**118**	**1st, Northwest Div.**	**Won Stanley Cup**
1999-2000	82	25	12	4	0	17	16	7	1	42	28	11	1	233	201	96	1st, Northwest Div.	Lost Conf. Championship
1998-99	82	21	14	6	....	23	14	4	....	44	28	10	....	239	205	98	1st, Northwest Div.	Lost Conf. Championship
1997-98	82	21	10	10	....	18	16	7	....	39	26	17	....	231	205	95	1st, Pacific Div.	Lost Conf. Quarter-Final
1996-97	82	26	10	5	....	23	14	4	....	49	24	9	....	277	205	107	1st, Pacific Div.	Lost Conf. Championship
1995-96	**82**	**24**	**10**	**7**	....	**23**	**15**	**3**	....	**47**	**25**	**10**	....	**326**	**240**	**104**	**1st, Pacific Div.**	**Won Stanley Cup**
1994-95*	48	19	1	4	....	11	12	1	....	30	13	5	....	185	134	65	1st, Northeast Div.	Lost Conf. Quarter-Final
1993-94*	84	19	17	6	....	15	25	2	....	34	42	8	....	277	292	76	5th, Northeast Div.	Out of Playoffs
1992-93*	84	23	17	2	....	24	10	8	....	47	27	10	....	351	300	104	2nd, Adams Div.	Lost Div. Semi-Final
1991-92*	80	18	19	3	....	2	29	9	....	20	48	12	....	255	318	52	5th, Adams Div.	Out of Playoffs
1990-91*	80	9	23	8	....	7	27	6	....	16	50	14	....	236	354	46	5th, Adams Div.	Out of Playoffs
1989-90*	80	8	26	6	....	4	35	1	....	12	61	7	....	240	407	31	5th, Adams Div.	Out of Playoffs
1988-89*	80	16	20	4	....	11	26	3	....	27	46	7	....	269	342	61	5th, Adams Div.	Out of Playoffs
1987-88*	80	15	23	2	....	17	20	3	....	32	43	5	....	271	306	69	5th, Adams Div.	Out of Playoffs
1986-87*	80	20	13	7	....	11	26	3	....	31	39	10	....	267	276	72	4th, Adams Div.	Lost Div. Final
1985-86*	80	23	13	4	....	20	18	2	....	43	31	6	....	330	289	92	1st, Adams Div.	Lost Div. Semi-Final
1984-85*	80	24	12	4	....	17	18	5	....	41	30	9	....	323	275	91	2nd, Adams Div.	Lost Conf. Championship
1983-84*	80	24	11	5	....	18	17	5	....	42	28	10	....	360	278	94	3rd, Adams Div.	Lost Div. Final
1982-83*	80	23	10	7	....	11	24	5	....	34	34	12	....	343	336	80	4th, Adams Div.	Lost Div. Semi-Final
1981-82*	80	24	13	3	....	9	18	13	....	33	31	16	....	356	345	82	4th, Adams Div.	Lost Conf. Championship
1980-81*	80	18	11	11	....	12	21	7	....	30	32	18	....	314	318	78	4th, Adams Div.	Lost Prelim. Round
1979-80*	80	17	16	7	....	8	28	4	....	25	44	11	....	248	313	61	5th, Adams Div.	Out of Playoffs

* Quebec Nordiques

2006-07 Player Personnel

FORWARDS	HT	WT	S	Place of Birth	Date	2005-06 Club
ARNASON, Tyler	5-11	204	L	Oklahoma City, OK	3/16/79	Chicago-Ottawa
BRUNETTE, Andrew	6-1	210	L	Sudbury, Ont.	8/24/73	Colorado
DASILVA, Daniel	6-1	195	R	Saskatoon, Sask.	4/30/85	Lowell-San Diego
GUITE, Ben	6-1	211	R	Montreal, Que.	7/17/78	Boston-Providence (AHL)
HEJDUK, Milan	6-0	190	R	Usti nad Labem, Czech.	2/14/76	Colorado
KONOWALCHUK, Steve	6-1	207	L	Salt Lake City, UT	11/11/72	Colorado
LAAKSONEN, Antti	6-0	187	L	Tammela, Finland	10/3/73	Colorado
LAPERRIERE, Ian	6-1	201	R	Montreal, Que.	1/19/74	Colorado
MAY, Brad	6-1	217	L	Toronto, Ont.	11/29/71	Colorado
McCORMICK, Cody	6-3	215	R	London, Ont.	4/18/83	Colorado-Lowell
McLEAN, Brett	5-11	194	L	Comox, B.C.	8/14/78	Colorado
McLEOD, Cody	6-2	210	L	Binscarth, Man.	6/26/84	Lowell-San Diego
MURLEY, Matt	6-1	206	L	Troy, NY	12/17/79	Pittsburgh
RICHARDSON, Brad	5-11	178	L	Belleville, Ont.	2/4/85	Colorado-Lowell
RYCROFT, Mark	6-0	192	R	Penticton, B.C.	7/12/78	St. Louis
SAKIC, Joe	5-11	195	L	Burnaby, B.C.	7/7/69	Colorado
STASTNY, Paul	6-0	201	L	Quebec City, Que.	12/27/85	U. of Denver
STEEVES, Ryan	6-0	195	L	Ottawa, Ont.	12/31/82	Lowell
SVAGROVSKY, David	6-3	205	R	Prague, Czech.	12/21/84	Lowell-San Diego
SVATOS, Marek	5-10	170	R	Kosice, Czech.	6/17/82	Colorado
TURGEON, Pierre	6-1	199	L	Rouyn, Que.	8/28/69	Colorado
WOLSKI, Wojtek	6-3	200	L	Zabrze, Poland	2/24/86	Colorado-Brampton

DEFENSEMEN	HT	WT	S	Place of Birth	Date	2005-06 Club
BOYCHUK, Johnny	6-3	225	R	Edmonton, Alta.	1/19/84	Lowell
BRISEBOIS, Patrice	6-2	203	R	Montreal, Que.	1/27/71	Colorado
CLARK, Brett	6-1	195	L	Wapella, Sask.	12/23/76	Colorado
FINGER, Jeff	6-2	195	R	Hancock, MI	12/18/79	Lowell
KLEE, Ken	6-0	210	R	Indianapolis, IN	4/24/71	Toronto-New Jersey
LEOPOLD, Jordan	6-1	200	L	Golden Valley, MN	8/3/80	Calgary
LILES, John-Michael	5-10	185	L	Zionsville, IN	11/25/80	Colorado
LOVE, Mitchell	6-0	200	L	Quesnel, B.C.	6/15/84	Lowell
SAUER, Kurt	6-4	225	L	St. Cloud, MN	1/16/81	Colorado-Lowell
SKRASTINS, Karlis	6-1	212	L	Riga, Latvia	7/9/74	Colorado
VAANANEN, Ossi	6-4	215	L	Vantaa, Finland	8/18/80	Colorado
VERNACE, Michael	6-2	200	L	Toronto, Ont.	5/26/86	Brampton

GOALTENDERS	HT	WT	C	Place of Birth	Date	2005-06 Club
BUDAJ, Peter	6-1	200	L	Banska Bystrica, Czech.	9/18/82	Colorado
THEODORE, Jose	5-11	182	R	Laval, Que.	9/13/76	Montreal-Colorado
WEIMAN, Tyler	5-11	180	L	Saskatoon, Sask.	6/5/84	San Diego-Lowell

Coach

QUENNEVILLE, JOEL
Coach, Colorado Avalanche. Born in Windsor, Ont., September 15, 1958.

Joel Quenneville returned to the franchise where he began his NHL coaching career in 1994-95 when he was named the fourth head coach in Colorado Avalanche, and the 12th in franchise history on July 7, 2004.

The former Colorado Rockies defenseman was the winningest coach in St. Louis Blues history, compiling a 307-209-77 record while spending 593 regular-season games behind the St. Louis bench, the most of any Blues coach. He reached the personal milestone of 500 career games coached on January 23, 2003 versus Chicago.

Under his guidance, the Blues reached the Western Conference Finals in 2001, the first time the team had done so since 1986, and won the Presidents' Trophy in 1999-2000 with a league-leading and franchise-high 114 points. He served as head coach of the North American All-Stars at the 2001 All-Star Game in Denver, and was named the NHL's coach of the year for 1999-00, capturing the Jack Adams Award.

The former NHL defenseman spent two-and-a-half seasons with the Colorado Avalanche/Quebec Nordiques as an assistant coach prior to being named the Blues' head coach on January 6, 1997. He was instrumental in the Avs' drive for their first Stanley Cup in 1996. He retired as an active player after the 1991-92 season, when he served as a player-coach for the St. John's Maple Leafs (AHL). Quenneville played 13 seasons in the NHL, closing out his career with 54 goals and 136 assists for 190 points adding 705 penalty minutes in 803 games played with Hartford, Washington, New Jersey, Toronto, and the Colorado Rockies. A short time later, he received his first coaching opportunity with the Springfield Indians (AHL) in 1993-94.

Coaching Record

		Regular Season				Playoffs		
Season	Team	Games	W	L	O/T	Games	W	L
1993-94	Springfield (AHL)	80	29	38	13	6	2	4
1996-97	**St. Louis (NHL)**	**40**	**18**	**15**	**7**	**6**	**2**	**4**
1997-98	**St. Louis (NHL)**	**82**	**45**	**29**	**8**	**10**	**6**	**4**
1998-99	**St. Louis (NHL)**	**82**	**37**	**32**	**13**	**13**	**6**	**7**
1999-2000	**St. Louis (NHL)**	**82**	**51**	**20**	**11**	**7**	**3**	**4**
2000-01	**St. Louis (NHL)**	**82**	**43**	**27**	**12**	**15**	**9**	**6**
2001-02	**St. Louis (NHL)**	**82**	**43**	**31**	**8**	**10**	**5**	**5**
2002-03	**St. Louis (NHL)**	**82**	**41**	**30**	**11**	**7**	**3**	**4**
2003-04	**St. Louis (NHL)**	**61**	**29**	**25**	**7**	....	....	....
2004-05	**Colorado (NHL)**			Season Cancelled				
2005-06	**Colorado (NHL)**	**82**	**43**	**30**	**9**	**9**	**4**	**5**
	NHL Totals	**675**	**350**	**239**	**86**	**77**	**38**	**39**

2005-06 Scoring

* – rookie

Regular Season

Pos	#	Player	Team	GP	G	A	Pts	+/–	PIM	PP	SH	GW	S	%
C	19	Joe Sakic	COL	82	32	55	87	10	60	10	0	6	263	12.2
L	18	Alex Tanguay	COL	71	29	49	78	8	46	8	0	4	125	23.2
L	15	Andrew Brunette	COL	82	24	39	63	9	48	11	0	2	129	18.6
R	23	Milan Hejduk	COL	74	24	34	58	13	24	14	1	2	221	10.9
D	4	Rob Blake	COL	81	14	37	51	2	94	7	1	1	264	5.3
R	40 *	Marek Svatos	COL	61	32	18	50	0	60	12	0	9	165	19.4
D	26	John-Michael Liles	COL	82	14	35	49	5	44	6	0	1	154	9.1
C	87	Pierre Turgeon	COL	62	16	30	46	1	32	7	0	1	94	17.0
R	14	Ian Laperriere	COL	82	21	24	45	3	116	1	1	3	133	15.8
C	53	Brett McLean	COL	82	9	31	40	–7	51	1	0	0	115	7.8
D	71	Patrice Brisebois	COL	80	10	28	38	1	55	4	0	2	107	9.3
D	5	Brett Clark	COL	80	9	27	36	3	56	4	0	1	148	6.1
L	24	Antti Laaksonen	COL	81	16	18	34	–2	40	0	2	4	141	11.3
C	38	Jim Dowd	CHI	60	3	12	15	–5	38	0	0	0	55	5.5
			COL	18	2	1	3	–6	2	0	1	0	12	16.7
			TOTAL	78	5	13	18	–11	40	0	1	0	67	7.5
L	22	Steve Konowalchuk	COL	21	6	9	15	5	14	1	2	0	39	15.4
D	3	Karlis Skrastins	COL	82	3	11	14	–7	65	0	2	0	58	5.2
R	13	Dan Hinote	COL	73	5	8	13	–5	48	0	1	2	70	7.1
C	12 *	Brad Richardson	COL	41	3	10	13	0	12	1	0	0	51	5.9
C	11	Cody McCormick	COL	45	4	4	8	1	29	0	0	1	43	9.3
D	6	Bob Boughner	COL	41	1	6	7	2	54	0	0	1	15	6.7
L	10	Brad May	COL	54	3	3	6	–14	82	0	0	0	55	5.5
L	8 *	Wojtek Wolski	COL	9	2	4	6	–5	4	2	0	0	9	22.2
D	34	Kurt Sauer	COL	37	1	4	5	5	24	0	0	0	19	5.3
D	27	Ossi Vaananen	COL	53	0	4	4	10	56	0	0	0	34	0.0
R	37	Paul Healey	COL	2	0	0	0	0	14	0	0	0	0	0.0

Goaltending

No.	Goaltender	GPI	Mins	Avg	W	L	OT	EN	SO	GA	SA	S%	G	A	PIM
31	* Peter Budaj	34	1803	2.86	14	10	6	3	2	86	864	.900	0	1	4
30	David Aebischer	43	2477	2.98	25	14	2	2	3	123	1233	.900	0	3	16
60	Jose Theodore	5	296	3.04	1	3	1	2	0	15	133	.887	0	0	0
20	Vitaliy Kolesnik	8	370	3.24	3	3	0	0	0	20	178	.888	0	1	2
	Totals	**82**	**4982**	**3.02**	**43**	**30**	**9**	**7**	**5**	**251**	**2415**	**.896**			

Playoffs

Pos	#	Player	Team	GP	G	A	Pts	+/–	PIM	PP	SH	GW	OT	S	%
C	19	Joe Sakic	COL	9	4	5	9	–1	6	1	0	1	1	21	19.0
L	15	Andrew Brunette	COL	9	3	6	9	–2	8	1	0	1	1	15	20.0
R	23	Milan Hejduk	COL	9	2	6	8	3	2	0	0	0	0	24	8.3
L	18	Alex Tanguay	COL	9	2	4	6	1	12	0	0	1	1	20	10.0
C	38	Jim Dowd	COL	9	2	3	5	3	20	0	1	0	0	6	33.3
D	4	Rob Blake	COL	9	3	1	4	1	8	2	0	1	0	42	7.1
D	5	Brett Clark	COL	9	2	2	4	–2	2	0	1	0	0	19	10.5
L	8 *	Wojtek Wolski	COL	8	1	3	4	–3	2	0	0	0	0	9	11.1
D	26	John-Michael Liles	COL	9	1	2	3	–1	6	1	0	0	0	15	6.7
R	13	Dan Hinote	COL	9	1	1	2	–2	31	0	0	0	0	10	10.0
C	87	Pierre Turgeon	COL	5	0	2	2	–3	6	0	0	0	0	9	0.0
L	24	Antti Laaksonen	COL	9	0	2	2	–3	2	0	0	0	0	16	0.0
C	12 *	Brad Richardson	COL	9	1	0	1	–3	6	0	0	0	0	7	14.3
C	53	Brett McLean	COL	8	0	1	1	–5	4	0	0	0	0	8	0.0
D	71	Patrice Brisebois	COL	9	0	1	1	–7	4	0	0	0	0	10	0.0
R	14	Ian Laperriere	COL	9	0	1	1	–6	27	0	0	0	0	9	0.0
D	3	Karlis Skrastins	COL	9	0	1	1	–3	10	0	0	0	0	9	0.0
D	27	Ossi Vaananen	COL	1	0	0	0	0	0	0	0	0	0	1	0.0
L	22	Steve Konowalchuk	COL	2	0	0	0	–1	4	0	0	0	0	1	0.0
L	10	Brad May	COL	3	0	0	0	–3	0	0	0	0	0	5	0.0
D	34	Kurt Sauer	COL	9	0	0	0	–3	4	0	0	0	0	1	0.0

Goaltending

No.	Goaltender	GPI	Mins	Avg	W	L	EN	SO	GA	SA	S%	G	A	PIM
60	Jose Theodore	9	573	3.04	4	5	2	0	29	296	.902	0	0	0
	Totals	**9**	**576**	**3.23**	**4**	**5**	**2**	**0**	**31**	**298**	**.896**			

Coaching History

Jacques Demers, 1979-80; Maurice Filion and Michel Bergeron, 1980-81; Michel Bergeron, 1981-82 to 1986-87; Andre Savard and Ron Lapointe, 1987-88; Ron Lapointe and Jean Perron, 1988-89; Michel Bergeron, 1989-90; Dave Chambers, 1990-91; Dave Chambers and Pierre Page, 1991-92; Pierre Page, 1992-93, 1993-94; Marc Crawford, 1994-95 to 1997-98; Bob Hartley, 1998-99 to 2001-02; Bob Hartley and Tony Granato, 2002-03; Tony Granato, 2003-04; Joel Quenneville, 2004-05 to date.

Captains' History

Marc Tardif, 1979-80, 1980-81; Robbie Ftorek and Andre Dupont, 1981-82; Mario Marois, 1982-83 to 1984-85; Mario Marois and Peter Stastny, 1985-86; Peter Stastny, 1986-87 to 1989-90; Joe Sakic and Steven Finn, 1990-91; Mike Hough, 1991-92; Joe Sakic, 1992-93 to date.

Club Records

Team

(Figures in brackets for season records are games played; records for fewest points, wins, ties, losses, goals, goals against are for 70 or more games)

Most Points	**118**	2000-01 (82)
Most Wins	**52**	2000-01 (82)
Most Ties	**18**	1980-81 (80)
Most Losses	**61**	1989-90 (80)
Most Goals	**360**	1983-84 (80)
Most Goals Against	**407**	1989-90 (80)
Fewest Points	**31**	1989-90 (80)
Fewest Wins	**12**	1989-90 (80)
Fewest Ties	**5**	1987-88 (80)
Fewest Losses	**16**	2000-01 (82)
Fewest Goals	**212**	2001-02 (82)
Fewest Goals Against	**169**	2001-02 (82)
Longest Winning Streak		
Overall	**12**	Jan. 10-Feb. 7/99
Home	**10**	Nov. 26/83-Jan. 10/84, Mar. 6-Apr. 16/95
Away	**7**	Jan. 10-Feb. 7/99
Longest Undefeated Streak		
Overall	**12**	Dec. 23/96-Jan. 20/97 (9 wins, 3 ties), Jan. 10-Feb. 7/99 (12 wins)
Home	**14**	Nov. 19/83-Jan. 21/84 (11 wins, 3 ties)
Away	**10**	Jan. 10-Mar. 3/99 (8 wins, 2 ties)
Longest Losing Streak		
Overall	**14**	Oct. 21-Nov. 19/90
Home	**8**	Oct. 21-Nov. 24/90
Away	**18**	Jan. 18-Apr. 1/90
Longest Winless Streak		
Overall	**17**	Oct. 21-Nov. 25/90 (15 losses, 2 ties)
Home	**11**	Nov. 14-Dec. 26/89 (7 losses, 4 ties)
Away	**33**	Oct. 8/91-Feb. 27/92 (25 losses, 8 ties)
Most Shutouts, Season	**11**	2001-02 (82)
Most PIM, Season	**2,104**	1989-90 (80)
Most Goals, Game	**12**	Three times

Individual

Most Seasons	**17**	Joe Sakic
Most Games	**1,237**	Joe Sakic
Most Goals, Career	**574**	Joe Sakic
Most Assists, Career	**915**	Joe Sakic
Most Points, Career	**1,489**	Joe Sakic (574G, 915A)
Most PIM, Career	**1,562**	Dale Hunter
Most Shutouts, Career	**37**	Patrick Roy
Longest Consecutive Games Streak	**312**	Dale Hunter (Oct. 9/80-Mar. 13/84)
Most Goals, Season	**57**	Michel Goulet (1982-83)
Most Assists, Season	**93**	Peter Stastny (1981-82)
Most Points, Season	**139**	Peter Stastny (1981-82; 46G, 93A)
Most PIM, Season	**301**	Gord Donnelly (1987-88)
Most Points, Defenseman, Season	**82**	Steve Duchesne (1992-93; 20G, 62A)
Most Points, Center, Season	**139**	Peter Stastny (1981-82; 46G, 93A)
Most Points, Right Wing, Season	**103**	Jacques Richard (1980-81; 52G, 51A)
Most Points, Left Wing, Season	**121**	Michel Goulet (1983-84; 56G, 65A)
Most Points, Rookie, Season	**109**	Peter Stastny (1980-81; 39G, 70A)
Most Shutouts, Season	**9**	Patrick Roy (2001-02)
Most Goals, Game	**5**	Mats Sundin (Mar. 5/92), Mike Ricci (Feb. 17/94)
Most Assists, Game	**5**	Six times
Most Points, Game	**8**	Peter Stastny (Feb. 22/81; 4G, 4A), Anton Stastny (Feb. 22/81; 3G, 5A)

Records include Quebec Nordiques, 1979-80 through 1994-95.

Retired Numbers

3	J.C. Tremblay*	1972-1979
8	Marc Tardif*	1979-1983
16	Michel Goulet*	1979-1990
26	Peter Stastny*	1980-1990
33	Patrick Roy	1995-2003
77	Raymond Bourque	2000-2001

* Quebec Nordiques

All-time Record vs. Other Clubs

Regular Season

	At Home								On Road								Total							
	GP	W	L	T	OL	GF	GA	PTS	GP	W	L	T	OL	GF	GA	PTS	GP	W	L	T	OL	GF	GA	PTS
Anaheim	23	13	5	4	1	73	59	31	23	12	5	3	3	60	55	30	46	25	10	7	4	133	114	61
Atlanta	4	2	1	0	1	17	10	5	4	2	1	1	0	8	7	5	8	4	2	1	1	25	17	10
Boston	67	25	36	6	0	238	272	56	62	22	31	9	0	192	240	53	129	47	67	15	0	430	512	109
Buffalo	65	31	22	11	1	231	203	74	63	18	35	9	1	204	247	46	128	49	57	20	2	435	450	120
Calgary	51	21	18	11	1	184	164	54	51	18	24	9	0	150	177	45	102	39	42	20	1	334	341	99
Carolina	65	39	17	9	0	274	191	87	62	26	24	12	0	214	203	64	127	65	41	21	0	488	394	151
Chicago	41	22	12	6	1	164	130	51	43	18	22	3	0	134	149	39	84	40	34	9	1	298	279	90
Columbus	10	10	0	0	0	42	12	20	10	8	0	1	1	40	14	18	20	18	0	1	1	82	26	38
Dallas	43	23	11	7	2	154	109	55	43	16	21	5	1	121	138	38	86	39	32	12	3	275	247	93
Detroit	44	20	19	4	1	151	149	45	42	15	25	1	1	126	155	32	86	35	44	5	2	277	304	77
Edmonton	51	26	20	4	1	194	183	57	50	19	26	4	1	152	197	43	101	45	46	8	2	346	380	100
Florida	11	4	4	3	0	30	27	11	11	10	1	0	0	48	30	20	22	14	5	3	0	78	57	31
Los Angeles	44	23	18	3	0	176	150	49	45	14	26	5	0	145	180	33	89	37	44	8	0	321	330	82
Minnesota	15	11	2	2	0	49	34	24	14	8	3	1	2	48	34	19	29	19	5	3	2	97	68	43
Montreal	64	33	26	5	0	218	223	71	64	16	38	10	0	198	261	42	128	49	64	15	0	416	484	113
Nashville	14	7	4	2	1	39	29	17	14	6	3	3	2	50	43	17	28	13	7	5	3	89	72	34
New Jersey	35	18	13	4	0	124	98	40	37	14	19	4	0	125	150	32	72	32	32	8	0	249	248	72
NY Islanders	34	20	11	3	0	123	97	43	33	13	19	1	0	113	134	27	67	33	30	4	0	236	231	70
NY Rangers	35	19	13	3	0	143	130	41	35	12	19	4	0	101	135	28	70	31	32	7	0	244	265	69
Ottawa	16	12	3	1	0	72	47	25	18	7	8	3	0	64	53	17	34	19	11	4	0	136	100	42
Philadelphia	35	12	10	12	1	124	122	37	35	11	21	2	1	95	125	25	70	23	31	14	2	219	247	62
Phoenix	43	23	15	5	0	155	141	51	42	19	15	7	1	150	147	46	85	42	30	12	1	305	288	97
Pittsburgh	32	17	13	2	0	142	122	36	38	17	16	5	0	155	149	39	70	34	29	7	0	297	271	75
St. Louis	43	22	13	7	1	148	114	52	42	16	22	4	0	129	151	36	85	38	35	11	1	277	265	88
San Jose	25	15	5	4	1	88	46	35	26	16	9	1	0	96	76	33	51	31	14	5	1	184	122	68
Tampa Bay	13	8	3	2	0	50	28	18	12	3	8	1	0	32	39	7	25	11	11	3	0	82	67	25
Toronto	30	18	7	5	0	116	90	41	35	15	16	4	0	133	118	34	65	33	23	9	0	249	208	75
Vancouver	51	25	17	8	1	176	144	59	51	24	18	7	2	195	171	57	102	49	35	15	3	371	315	116
Washington	34	15	14	5	0	105	116	35	33	11	18	4	0	105	131	26	67	26	32	9	0	210	247	61
Totals	**1038**	**534**	**352**	**138**	**14**	**3800**	**3240**	**1220**	**1038**	**406**	**493**	**123**	**16**	**3383**	**3709**	**951**	**2076**	**940**	**845**	**261**	**30**	**7183**	**6949**	**2171**

Playoffs

	Series	W	L	GP	W	L	T	GF	GA	Last Mtg.	Rnd.	Result
Anaheim	1	0	1	4	0	4	0	4	16	2006	CSF	L 0-4
Boston	2	1	1	11	5	6	0	36	37	1983	DSF	L 1-3
Buffalo	2	2	0	8	6	2	0	35	27	1985	DSF	W 3-2
Carolina	2	1	1	9	4	5	0	34	35	1987	DSF	W 4-2
Chicago	2	2	0	12	8	4	0	49	28	1997	CQF	W 4-2
Dallas	4	2	2	24	14	10	0	66	62	2006	CQF	W 4-1
Detroit	5	3	2	30	17	13	0	79	76	2002	CF	L 3-4
Edmonton	2	1	1	12	7	5	0	35	30	1998	CQF	L 3-4
Florida	1	1	0	4	4	0	0	15	4	1996	F	W 4-0
Los Angeles	2	2	0	14	8	6	0	33	23	2002	CQF	W 4-3
Minnesota	1	0	1	7	3	4	0	17	16	2003	CQF	L 3-4
Montreal	5	2	3	31	14	17	0	85	105	1993	DSF	L 2-4
New Jersey	1	1	0	7	4	3	0	19	11	2001	F	W 4-3
NY Islanders	1	0	1	4	0	4	0	9	18	1982	CF	L 0-4
NY Rangers	1	0	1	6	2	4	0	19	25	1995	CQF	L 2-4
Philadelphia	2	0	2	11	4	7	0	29	39	1985	CF	L 2-4
Phoenix	1	1	0	5	4	1	0	17	10	2000	CQF	W 4-1
St. Louis	1	1	0	5	4	1	0	17	11	2001	CF	W 4-1
San Jose	3	2	1	19	10	9	0	51	52	2004	CSF	L 2-4
Vancouver	2	2	0	10	8	2	0	40	26	2001	CQF	W 4-0
Totals	**41**	**24**	**17**	**233**	**126**	**107**	**0**	**689**	**651**			

Playoff Results 2006-2001

Year	Round	Opponent	Result	GF	GA
2006	CSF	Anaheim	L 0-4	4	16
	CQF	Dallas	W 4-1	18	15
2004	CSF	San Jose	L 2-4	7	14
	CQF	Dallas	W 4-1	19	10
2003	CQF	Minnesota	L 3-4	17	16
2002	CF	Detroit	L 3-4	13	22
	CSF	San Jose	W 4-3	25	21
	CQF	Los Angeles	W 4-3	16	13
2001	**F**	**New Jersey**	**W 4-3**	**19**	**11**
	CF	St. Louis	W 4-1	17	11
	CSF	Los Angeles	W 4-3	17	10
	CQF	Vancouver	W 4-0	16	9

Abbreviations: Round: F - Final; **CF** - conference final; **CSF** - conference semi-final; **CQF** - conference quarter-final; **DSF** - division semi-final.

Calgary totals include Atlanta Flames, 1979-80.
Dallas totals include Minnesota North Stars, 1979-80 to 1992-93.
Phoenix totals include Winnipeg, 1979-80 to 1995-96.

Carolina totals include Hartford, 1979-80 to 1996-97.
New Jersey totals include Colorado Rockies, 1979-80 to 1981-82.

2005-06 Results

Oct.	5	at Edmonton	3-4
	8	at Dallas	3-2
	10	Calgary	7-3
	12	Nashville	4-5
	14	Chicago	2-3†
	19	Los Angeles	4-5
	21	at Edmonton	7-1
	22	at Vancouver	4-6
	25	Edmonton	5-3
	27	Vancouver	6-2
	29	Vancouver	4-3*
Nov.	3	Anaheim	4-3
	5	Dallas	2-3†
	8	San Jose	5-2
	10	at Vancouver	5-3
	12	at Calgary	3-5
	14	Edmonton	2-5
	16	at Phoenix	3-1
	18	at Anaheim	3-2
	19	at Los Angeles	3-4
	21	Calgary	2-3†
	23	at Detroit	3-7
	25	at Columbus	5-0
	27	Vancouver	6-2
	29	at Edmonton	3-2
	30	at Vancouver	2-5
Dec.	4	Buffalo	4-6
	7	Boston	4-1
	9	at New Jersey	4-3†
	10	at Pittsburgh	3-4
	12	Ottawa	2-6
	17	at NY Islanders	4-5
	18	at NY Rangers	2-1
	20	at Nashville	2-3
	22	Minnesota	4-3
	23	at Minnesota	3-5
	26	Phoenix	7-4
	28	Los Angeles	3-5
	30	at San Jose	2-5
	31	at Phoenix	5-2
Jan.	3	Nashville	3-0
	5	at Minnesota	4-2
	7	Columbus	3-2†
	9	St. Louis	6-1
	11	Montreal	2-1
	14	at Philadelphia	4-3*
	17	Toronto	5-3
	19	at Chicago	2-4
	21	Detroit	3-4
	24	Calgary	7-4
	26	Dallas	2-3†
	28	Vancouver	3-4†
	31	Minnesota	3-2
Feb.	2	at Nashville	3-4*
	4	Detroit	0-3
	7	Edmonton	5-2
	9	at Minnesota	2-1
	10	at Columbus	4-1
	12	at Detroit	3-6
	28	Minnesota	4-2
Mar.	2	Columbus	1-0
	4	at Dallas	3-5
	5	at Minnesota	3-5
	7	at St. Louis	2-1†
	9	at Chicago	2-1
	12	Calgary	3-0
	13	at Calgary	3-4
	19	at San Jose	5-6
	20	at Los Angeles	5-0
	22	at Anaheim	4-5*
	25	at St. Louis	3-2*
	26	Edmonton	3-4†
	28	Anaheim	4-3
	31	at Calgary	3-6
Apr.	3	Chicago	4-3
	5	San Jose	1-2
	8	St. Louis	4-2
	9	Minnesota	2-5
	11	Phoenix	6-4
	13	at Calgary	0-2
	15	at Vancouver	3-4*
	17	at Edmonton	2-4

* – Overtime † – Shootout

Entry Draft
Selections 2006-1992

2006 Pick		2002 Pick		1998 Pick		1994 Pick	
18	Chris Stewart	28	Jonas Johansson	12	Alex Tanguay	12	Wade Belak
51	Nigel Williams	61	Johnny Boychuk	17	Martin Skoula	22	Jeffrey Kealty
59	Codey Burki	94	Eric Lundberg	19	Robyn Regehr	35	Josef Marha
81	Michael Carman	107	Mikko Kalteva	20	Scott Parker	61	Sebastien Bety
110	Kevin Montgomery	129	Tom Gilbert	28	Ramzi Abid	72	Chris Drury
201	Billy Sauer	164	Tyler Weiman	38	Philippe Sauve	87	Milan Hejduk
		195	Taylor Christie	53	Steve Moore	113	Tony Tuzzolino
2005 Pick		227	Ryan Steeves	79	Evgeny Lazarev	139	Nicholas Windsor
34	Ryan Stoa	258	Sergei Shemetov	141	K.C. Timmons	465	Calvin Elfring
44	Paul Stastny	289	Sean Collins	167	Alexander Riazantsev	191	Jay Bertsch
47	Tom Fritsche					217	Tim Thomas
52	Chris Durand	**2001 Pick**		**1997 Pick**		243	Chris Pittman
88	T.J. Hensick	63	Peter Budaj	26	Kevin Grimes	285	Steven Low
124	Raymond Macias	97	Danny Bois	53	Graham Belak		
166	Jason Lynch	130	Colt King	55	Rick Berry	**1993 Pick**	
168	Justin Mercier	143	Frantisek Skladany	78	Ville Nieminen	10	Jocelyn Thibault
222	Kyle Cumiskey	144	Cody McCormick	87	Brad Larsen	14	Adam Deadmarsh
		149	Mikko Viitanen	133	Aaron Miskovich	49	Ashley Buckberger
2004 Pick		165	Pierre-Luc Emond	161	David Aebischer	75	Bill Pierce
21	Wojtek Wolski	184	Scott Horvath	217	Doug Schmidt	101	Ryan Tocher
55	Victor Oreskovich	196	Charlie Stephens	243	Kyle Kidney	127	Anders Myrvold
72	Denis Parshin	227	Marek Svatos	245	Stephen Lafleur	137	Nicholas Checco
154	Richard					153	Christian Matte
	Demen-Willaume	**2000 Pick**		**1996 Pick**		179	David Ling
184	Derek Peltier	14	Vaclav Nedorost	25	Peter Ratchuk	205	Petr Franek
215	Ian Keserich	47	Jared Aulin	51	Yuri Babenko	231	Vincent Auger
239	Brandon Yip	50	Sergei Soin	79	Mark Parrish	257	Mark Pivetz
249	J.D. Corbin	63	Agris Saviels	98	Ben Storey	283	John Hillman
281	Steve McClellan	88	Kurt Sauer	107	Randy Petruk		
		92	Sergei Klyazmin	134	Luke Curtin	**1992 Pick**	
2003 Pick		119	Brian Fahey	146	Brian Willsie	4	Todd Warriner
63	David Liffiton	159	John-Michael Liles	160	Kai Fischer	28	Paul Brousseau
131	David Svagrovsky	189	Chris Bahen	167	Dan Hinote	29	Tuomas Gronman
146	Mark McCutcheon	221	Aaron Molnar	176	Samuel Pahlsson	52	Manny Fernandez
163	Brad Richardson	252	Darryl Bootland	188	Roman Pylner	76	Ian McIntyre
204	Linus Videll	266	Sean Kotary	214	Matt Scorsune	100	Charlie Wasley
225	Brett Hemingway	285	Blake Ward	240	Justin Clark	124	Paxton Schulte
257	Darryl Yacboski					148	Martin Lepage
288	David Jones	**1999 Pick**		**1995 Pick**		172	Mike Jickling
		25	Mikhail Kuleshov	25	Marc Denis	196	Steve Passmore
		45	Martin Grenier	51	Nic Beaudoin	220	Anson Carter
		93	Branko Radivojevic	77	John Tripp	244	Aaron Ellis
		112	Sanny Lindstrom	81	Tomi Kallio		
		122	Kristian Kovac	129	Brent Johnson		
		142	Will Magnuson	155	John Cirjak		
		152	Jordan Krestanovich	181	Dan Smith		
		158	Anders Lovdahl	207	Tomi Hirvonen		
		183	Riku Hahl	228	Chris George		
		212	Radim Vrbata				
		240	Jeff Finger				

General Managers' History

Maurice Filion, 1979-80 to 1987-88; Martin Madden, 1988-89; Martin Madden and Maurice Filion, 1989-90; Pierre Page, 1990-91 to 1993-94; Pierre Lacroix, 1994-95 to 2005-06; Francois Giguere, 2006-07.

Executive Vice President/ General Manager

GIGUERE, FRANCOIS
Executive Vice President/General Manager, Colorado Avalanche.
Born in Ste-Foy, Que., June 24, 1963.
On May 24, 2006, the Colorado Avalanche announced the appointment of Francois Giguere as the club's executive vice president and general manager to lead the day-to-day operations of the club. Giguere returned to the franchise where he began his hockey tutelage over 16 years before. During that time, Giguere was involved with nearly every facet of an NHL hockey operation. Before spending five years with the Dallas Stars as assistant general manager, Giguere served as vice president of hockey operations for the Colorado Avalanche during the 2000-01 season. His roots with the organization date back to 1990 when he served as controller in the finance department with the Quebec Nordiques. In addition, he's held hockey administration (1992 to 1995), assistant GM (1995 to 2000) and VP hockey operations (2000-01) posts within the organization.

During his tenure with the Avalanche, Giguere was instrumental in developing and managing the hockey operations budget, and worked closely with Pierre Lacroix on contract negotiations, arbitration cases, player transactions and matters involving player personnel. He was also responsible for overseeing player development and player personnel staff and was the club's central liaison with its minor league hockey affiliates.

A 1985 graduate of Laval University where he obtained a degree in Administration, a license in accounting and a law certificate, Giguere worked for three years with a prominent Quebec accounting firm Caron Belanger Ernst and Young before being hired by the Nordiques as controller in 1990. His role with the Nordiques was expanded in 1992 to include hockey administration responsibilities by then general manager Pierre Page who needed additional support after Page assumed the head coaching role with the Nordiques in 1991. Pierre Lacroix named Giguere as assistant GM before the shortened 1994-95 season and he accompanied the franchise in its move to Colorado in May 1995.

Club Directory

Pepsi Center

Colorado Avalanche
Pepsi Center
1000 Chopper Circle
Denver, CO 80204
Phone **303/405-1100**
FAX 303/893-0614
Press Box 303/575-1926
www.coloradoavalanche.com
Capacity: 18,007

Owner & Governor	E. Stanley Kroenke
President	Pierre Lacroix
Executive Vice President & General Manager	Francois Giguere
Head Coach	Joel Quenneville
Assistant Coach	Jacques Cloutier
Assistant Coach	Tony Granato
Goaltending Coach	Jeff Hackett
Assistant General Manager	Greg Sherman
Assistant to the Executive Vice President/ General Manager	Michel Goulet
Director of Player Personnel	Brad Smith
Director of Player Development	Craig Billington
Executive Director of Hockey Administration	Charlotte Grahame
Video Coordinator	Bryan Vines
Team Services Coordinator	Ronnie Jameson
Hockey Administration Assistant	Elizabeth Severy
Chief Scout	Ted Hampson
Pro Scouts	Garth Joy, Terry Martin
Scouts	Glen Cochrane, Luc Gauthier, Alan Hepple, Kiril Ladygin, Joni Lehto, Don Paarup, Richard Pracey
Strength and Conditioning Coach	Paul Goldberg
Head Athletic Trainer	Matthew Sokolowski
Assistant Athletic Trainer	Scott Woodward
Massage Therapist	Gregorio Pradera
Head Equipment Manager	Mark Miller
Inventory Manager	Wayne Flemming
Assistant Equipment Managers	Terry Geer, Cliff Halstead

Communications Department

Senior Vice President, Communications & Business Operations	Jean Martineau
Director of Communications	Damen Zier
Director of Media Services/Internet	Brendan McNicholas

After three seasons with the Calgary Flames, Colorado picked up defenseman Jordan Leopold in a deal for Alex Tanguay.

Columbus Blue Jackets

2005-06 Results: 35W-43L-1OTL-3SOL 74PTS.
Third, Central Division

Year-by-Year Record

Season	GP	Home				Road				Overall				GF	GA	Pts	Finished	Playoff Result
		W	L	T	OL	W	L	T	OL	W	L	T	OL					
2005-06	82	23	18	....	0	12	25	....	4	35	43	....	4	223	279	74	3rd, Central Div.	Out of Playoffs
2004-05	....																	
2003-04	82	17	18	4	2	8	27	4	2	25	45	8	4	177	238	62	4th, Central Div.	Out of Playoffs
2002-03	82	20	14	5	2	9	28	3	1	29	42	8	3	213	263	69	5th, Central Div.	Out of Playoffs
2001-02	82	14	18	5	4	8	29	3	1	22	47	8	5	164	255	57	5th, Central Div.	Out of Playoffs
2000-01	82	19	15	4	3	9	24	5	3	28	39	9	6	190	233	71	5th, Central Div.	Out of Playoffs

2006-07 Schedule

Oct.	Fri.	6	Vancouver
	Sat.	7	at Chicago
	Mon.	9	Phoenix
	Sat.	14	at Minnesota
	Fri.	20	Toronto
	Sat.	21	at Pittsburgh
	Mon.	23	San Jose
	Fri.	27	Los Angeles
	Sat.	28	at New Jersey
Nov.	Wed.	1	Colorado
	Fri.	3	Calgary
	Sat.	4	at Detroit
	Thu.	9	at St. Louis
	Fri.	10	Edmonton
	Sun.	12	at Chicago
	Wed.	15	Nashville
	Fri.	17	Colorado
	Sat.	18	at Nashville
	Mon.	20	Nashville
	Wed.	22	St. Louis
	Fri.	24	at Philadelphia*
	Sat.	25	Minnesota
	Tue.	28	at Vancouver
Dec.	Fri.	1	at Calgary
	Sat.	2	at Edmonton
	Tue.	5	at Colorado
	Sat.	9	at St. Louis
	Sun.	10	Ottawa
	Tue.	12	at Dallas
	Thu.	14	at Phoenix
	Sat.	16	Chicago
	Mon.	18	Detroit
	Wed.	20	at Detroit
	Fri.	22	Vancouver
	Sat.	23	at NY Islanders
	Tue.	26	Boston
	Thu.	28	Detroit
	Fri.	29	at Minnesota
	Sun.	31	Chicago
Jan.	Wed.	3	at Los Angeles
	Fri.	5	at Anaheim
	Sat.	6	at San Jose
	Tue.	9	St. Louis
	Fri.	12	at Nashville
	Sat.	13	Nashville
	Tue.	16	at Chicago
	Thu.	18	at Nashville
	Fri.	19	Detroit
	Fri.	26	Buffalo
	Sat.	27	Minnesota
	Tue.	30	at Vancouver
	Wed.	31	at Edmonton
Feb.	Fri.	2	at Calgary
	Tue.	6	Phoenix
	Thu.	8	Calgary
	Sun.	11	Chicago*
	Wed.	14	St. Louis
	Fri.	16	San Jose
	Sun.	18	Montreal
	Tue.	20	at St. Louis
	Thu.	22	Edmonton
	Sat.	24	at NY Rangers
	Sun.	25	Nashville
	Tue.	27	at Colorado
Mar.	Fri.	2	at Dallas
	Sat.	3	at Phoenix
	Wed.	7	Los Angeles
	Fri.	9	Dallas
	Sat.	10	at Nashville
	Wed.	14	at Anaheim
	Fri.	16	at San Jose
	Sat.	17	at Los Angeles
	Tue.	20	Chicago
	Thu.	22	at Detroit
	Sun.	25	St. Louis*
	Tue.	27	at St. Louis
	Thu.	29	Anaheim
	Fri.	30	at Chicago
Apr.	Sun.	1	Detroit*
	Tue.	3	at Detroit
	Thu.	5	Dallas
	Sat.	7	Anaheim

* Denotes afternoon game.

Franchise date: June 25, 1997

CENTRAL DIVISION

7th NHL Season

David Vyborny (left) heads up ice with Sergei Fedorov. Vyborny led the Blue Jackets with 43 assists and 65 points in 2005-06. Fedorov was second on the team with 31 assists in 62 games after joining Columbus from Anaheim.

2006-07 Player Personnel

FORWARDS

	HT	WT	S	Place of Birth	Date	2005-06 Club
BALASTIK, Jaroslav	6-2	205	L	Gottwaldov, Czech.	11/28/79	Columbus-Syracuse
BRULE, Gilbert	5-10	180	R	Edmonton, Alta.	1/1/87	Columbus-Van (WHL)
CHIMERA, Jason	6-2	206	L	Edmonton, Alta.	5/2/79	Columbus
FEDOROV, Sergei	6-2	205	L	Pskov, USSR	12/13/69	Anaheim-Columbus
FRITSCHE, Dan	6-1	202	R	Parma, OH	7/13/85	Columbus-Syracuse
GOERTZEN, Steven	6-1	216	R	Stony Plain, Alta.	5/26/84	Columbus-Syracuse
HARTIGAN, Mark	6-0	200	L	Fort St. John, B.C.	10/15/77	Columbus-Syracuse
HAUHTONEN, Janne	6-3	205	R	Pori, Finland	7/5/79	HIFK
LINDSTROM, Joakim	6-0	187	L	Skelleftea, Sweden	12/5/83	Columbus-Syracuse
MALHOTRA, Manny	6-2	215	L	Mississauga, Ont.	5/18/80	Columbus
MODIN, Fredrik	6-4	220	L	Sundsvall, Sweden	10/8/74	Tampa Bay
MOTZKO, Joe	6-0	196	R	Bemidji, MN	3/14/80	Columbus-Syracuse
NASH, Rick	6-4	215	L	Brampton, Ont.	6/16/84	Columbus
PICARD, Alexandre	6-2	190	L	Les Saules, Que.	10/9/85	Columbus-Syracuse
PLATT, Geoff	5-9	175	L	Toronto, Ont.	7/10/85	Columbus-Syracuse
SHELLEY, Jody	6-4	230	L	Thompson, Man.	2/7/76	Columbus
SVITOV, Alexander	6-3	228	L	Omsk, USSR	11/3/82	Omsk
VYBORNY, David	5-10	189	L	Jihlava, Czech.	1/22/75	Columbus
ZHERDEV, Nikolai	6-2	197	R	Kiev, USSR	11/5/84	Columbus-Syracuse

DEFENSEMEN

	HT	WT	S	Place of Birth	Date	2005-06 Club
BERARD, Bryan	6-2	220	L	Woonsocket, RI	3/5/77	Columbus
ERIKSSON, Anders	6-2	220	L	Bollnas, Sweden	1/9/75	Magnitogorsk-Springfield
FOOTE, Adam	6-2	224	R	Toronto, Ont.	7/10/71	Columbus
HAINSEY, Ron	6-3	211	L	Bolton, CT	3/24/81	Hamilton-Columbus
JOHNSON, Aaron	6-2	211	L	Port Hawkesbury, N.S.	4/30/83	Columbus-Syracuse
KLESLA, Rostislav	6-3	216	L	Novy Jicin, Czech.	3/21/82	Columbus
KLOUCEK, Tomas	6-3	235	L	Prague, Czech.	3/7/80	Atlanta-Chicago (AHL)
METHOT, Marc	6-3	224	L	Ottawa, Ont.	6/21/85	Syracuse
NOVAK, Filip	6-1	198	L	Ceske Budejovice, Czech.	5/7/82	Ottawa-Binghamton
PUSHOR, Jamie	6-3	218	R	Lethbridge, Alta.	2/11/73	Columbus-Syracuse
TOLLEFSEN, Ole-Kristian	6-2	211	L	Oslo, Norway	3/29/84	Columbus-Syracuse
WESTCOTT, Duvie	5-11	197	L	Winnipeg, Man.	10/30/77	Columbus

GOALTENDERS

	HT	WT	C	Place of Birth	Date	2005-06 Club
CONKLIN, Ty	6-0	184	L	Anchorage, AK	3/30/76	Edmonton-Hamilton-Hartford
LECLAIRE, Pascal	6-2	200	L	Repentigny, Que.	11/7/82	Columbus-Syracuse
NORRENA, Fredrik	6-0	189	L	Pietarsaari, Finland	11/29/73	Linkoping
POPPERLE, Tomas	6-1	187	L	Broumov, Czech.	10/10/84	Eisbaren Berlin

General Managers' History

Doug MacLean, 2000-01 to date.

2005-06 Scoring

* – rookie

Regular Season

Pos	#	Player	Team	GP	G	A	Pts	+/-	PIM	PP	SH	GW	S	%
R	9	David Vyborny	CBJ	80	22	43	65	-9	50	5	2	6	145	15.2
L	61	Rick Nash	CBJ	54	31	23	54	5	51	11	0	4	170	18.2
R	13	Nikolai Zherdev	CBJ	73	27	27	54	-13	50	10	0	0	194	13.9
C	91	Sergei Fedorov	ANA	5	0	1	1	-1	2	0	0	0	18	0.0
			CBJ	62	12	31	43	-1	64	3	1	2	142	8.5
			TOTAL	67	12	32	44	-2	66	3	1	2	160	7.5
C	38	Jan Hrdina	CBJ	75	10	23	33	-8	78	4	1	0	78	12.8
D	4	Bryan Berard	CBJ	44	12	20	32	-29	32	11	0	2	126	9.5
C	27	Manny Malhotra	CBJ	58	10	21	31	1	41	1	1	0	102	9.8
L	25	Jason Chimera	CBJ	80	17	13	30	-10	95	1	1	5	127	13.4
R	10	Trevor Letowski	CBJ	81	10	18	28	-2	36	1	1	1	135	7.4
D	15	Duvie Westcott	CBJ	78	6	22	28	1	133	1	1	0	113	5.3
L	40 *	Jaroslav Balastik	CBJ	66	12	10	22	-1	26	7	0	2	158	7.6
D	52	Adam Foote	CBJ	65	6	16	22	-16	89	2	2	1	67	9.0
D	97	Rostislav Klesla	CBJ	51	6	13	19	-4	75	2	0	1	84	7.1
D	6	Ron Hainsey	CBJ	55	2	15	17	13	43	1	0	0	81	2.5
C	49 *	Dan Fritsche	CBJ	59	6	7	13	-14	22	0	0	0	93	6.5
C	42	Mark Hartigan	CBJ	33	9	3	12	-1	22	3	0	1	54	16.7
L	45	Jody Shelley	CBJ	80	3	7	10	-4	163	0	0	1	39	7.7
D	47	Aaron Johnson	CBJ	26	2	6	8	9	23	1	0	1	28	7.1
D	21	Radoslav Suchy	CBJ	79	1	7	8	-8	30	0	0	0	33	3.0
R	20	Mike Rupp	PHX	1	0	0	0	0	0	0	0	0	1	0.0
			CBJ	39	4	2	6	-3	58	0	0	0	38	10.5
			TOTAL	40	4	2	6	-3	58	0	0	0	39	10.3
C	18 *	Geoff Platt	CBJ	15	0	5	5	-4	16	0	0	0	29	0.0
C	17 *	Gilbert Brule	CBJ	7	2	2	4	-2	0	0	0	0	11	18.2
D	5	Jamie Pushor	CBJ	4	1	2	3	1	0	0	0	0	2	50.0
C	44	Peter Sarno	CBJ	1	0	0	0	0	0	0	0	0	0	0.0
R	37 *	Joe Motzko	CBJ	2	0	0	0	-2	0	0	0	0	3	0.0
C	50 *	Joakim Lindstrom	CBJ	3	0	0	0	0	0	0	0	0	4	0.0
L	24	Cam Severson	CBJ	2	0	0	0	0	0	0	0	0	2	0.0
D	55 *	Ole-Kristian Tollefsen	CBJ	5	0	0	0	-2	2	0	0	0	3	0.0
D	51	Andy Delmore	CBJ	7	0	0	0	-1	2	0	0	0	7	0.0
C	41	Ben Simon	CBJ	13	0	0	0	-4	4	0	0	0	7	0.0
L	19 *	Alexandre Picard	CBJ	17	0	0	0	-2	14	0	0	0	10	0.0
R	39 *	Steven Goertzen	CBJ	39	0	0	0	-17	44	0	0	0	23	0.0

Goaltending

No.	Goaltender	GPI	Mins	Avg	W	L	OT	EN	SO	GA	SA	S%	G	A	PIM
35	Martin Prusek	9	373	3.22	3	3	0	0	0	20	165	.879	0	0	0
31	* Pascal Leclaire	33	1804	3.23	11	15	3	2	0	97	1084	.911	0	1	2
30	Marc Denis	49	2786	3.25	21	25	1	6	1	151	1505	.900	0	1	2
	Totals	82	4996	3.31	35	43	4	8	1	276	2762	.900			

President and General Manager

MacLEAN, DOUG
President/General Manager, Columbus Blue Jackets.
Born in Summerside, P.E.I., April 12, 1954.

Doug MacLean was named the first general manager of the Blue Jackets on February 11, 1998. A month later he was named president of the organization and as its top executive, he holds the dual role of overseeing both the business and hockey operations of the franchise as well as the management of Nationwide Arena. MacLean also coached the team for parts of the 2002-03 and 2003-04 seasons.

Under MacLean's guidance, the Blue Jackets have established themselves as one of the most successful business franchises in the NHL. The Blue Jackets have made a significant impact in the Columbus community through its business operations and community service programs.

Prior to joining the Blue Jackets, MacLean served as head coach of the Florida Panthers, where he led his teams into the playoffs in both of his full seasons behind the bench (1995-96, 1996-97). In his first season as an NHL head coach, MacLean led Florida to the Stanley Cup Finals.

MacLean began his NHL coaching career in 1986 as an assistant to Jacques Martin in St. Louis. He spent two seasons with the Blues before joining the Washington Capitals in 1988, assisting Bryan Murray behind the bench. He was named coach of the Capitals' American Hockey League affiliate in Baltimore for the final 35 games of the 1989-90 season.

The following season, MacLean joined Murray on the Detroit Red Wings, serving as an assistant coach for two years. In 1992, MacLean was named assistant general manager of the Red Wings and also served as general manager of the team's AHL affiliate in Adirondack for two years. MacLean followed Murray to the Panthers in 1994, becoming the expansion club's director of player development. He was named head coach on July 24, 1995.

A collegiate hockey player at the University of Prince Edward Island, MacLean graduated with a bachelor's degree in education. He also played for the Montreal Jr. Canadiens and was invited to training camp with the St. Louis Blues in 1974. Following his playing career, MacLean enrolled at the University of Western Ontario, where he received a master's degree in educational psychology. While attending Western, MacLean began his coaching career as an assistant with London of the Ontario Hockey League.

NHL Coaching Record

Season	Team	Games	Regular Season W	L	T	Playoffs Games	W	L
1995-96	Florida	82	41	31	10	22	12	10
1996-97	Florida	82	35	28	19	5	1	4
1997-98	Florida	23	7	12	4	....	....	....
2002-03	Columbus	42	15	23	4	....	....	....
2003-04	Columbus	37	9	24	4	....	....	....
	NHL Totals	266	107	118	41	27	13	14

Fredrik Modin joins the Blue Jackets from Tampa Bay, where he scored 31 goals in 2005-06. Modin picked up an Olympic gold medal with Sweden in 2006 to add to his 2004 Stanley Cup ring.

Club Records

Team
(Figures in brackets for season records are games played.)

Most Points 74 2005-06 (82)
Most Wins 35 2005-06 (82)
Most Ties 9 2000-01 (82)
Most Losses 47 2001-02 (82)
Most Goals 223 2005-06 (82)
Most Goals Against 279 2005-06 (82)
Fewest Points 57 2001-02 (82)
Fewest Wins 22 2001-02 (82)
Fewest Ties 8 2001-02 (82), 2002-03 (82), 2003-04 (82)
Fewest Losses 39 2000-01 (82)
Fewest Goals 164 2001-02 (82)
Fewest Goals Against 233 2000-01 (82)

Longest Winning Streak
Overall . . . . 6 Mar. 24-Apr. 3/06
Home . . . . 5 Jan. 20-Feb. 6/06
Away . . . . 3 Jan. 8-11/03, Mar. 25-Apr. 3/06

Longest Undefeated Streak
Overall . . . . 4 Nov. 9-Nov. 16/00 (4 wins), Mar. 21-27/04 (4 wins)
Home . . . . 6 Jan. 20-Feb. 12/03 (4 wins, 2 ties)
Away . . . . 4 Jan. 3-11/03 (3 wins, 1 tie)

Longest Losing Streak
Overall . . . . 8 Nov. 17-Dec. 3/00, Mar. 3-18/04
Home . . . . 6 Oct. 12-Nov. 9/01
Away . . . . 11 Mar. 25-Oct. 29/02

Longest Winless Streak
Overall . . . . 9 Dec. 4-23/03 (8 losses, 1 tie)
Home . . . . 8 Oct. 4-Nov. 9/01 (6 losses, 2 ties), Dec. 4-31/03 (7 losses, 1 tie)
Away . . . . 14 Oct. 9-Dec. 23/03 (13 losses, 1 tie)

Most Shutouts, Season 5 2002-03 (82), 2003-04 (82)
Most PIM, Season 1,505 2002-03 (82)
Most Goals, Game . . . . 7 Three times

Individual

Most Seasons . . . . 5 Marc Denis, Jody Shelley, David Vyborny, Tyler Wright
Most Games . . . . 395 David Vyborny
Most Goals, Career . . . . 90 David Vyborny
Most Assists, Career . . . . . 137 David Vyborny
Most Points, Career . . . . . . 227 David Vyborny (90G, 137A)
Most PIM, Career . . . . 856 Jody Shelley
Most Shutouts, Career . . . . . 12 Marc Denis
Longest Consecutive
Games Streak . . . . 194 David Vyborny (Oct. 17/02 to Dec. 20/05)
Most Goals, Season . . . . 41 Rick Nash (2003-04)

Most Assists, Season . . . . . . 52 Ray Whitney (2002-03)
Most Points, Season . . . . . . 76 Ray Whitney (2002-03; 24G, 52A)
Most PIM, Season . . . . 249 Jody Shelley (2002-03)
Most Points, Defenseman, Season . . . . 45 Jaroslav Spacek (2002-03; 9G, 36A)
Most Points, Center, Season . . . . 68 Andrew Cassels (2002-03; 20G, 48A)
Most Points, Right Wing, Season . . . . 65 David Vyborny (2005-06; 22G, 43A)
Most Points, Left Wing, Season . . . . 76 Ray Whitney (2002-03; 24G, 52A)
Most Points, Rookie, Season . . . . 39 Rick Nash (2002-03; 17G, 22A)
Most Shutouts, Season . . . . . 5 Marc Denis (2002-03, 2003-04)
Most Goals, Game . . . . 4 Geoff Sanderson (Jan. 11/03)
Most Assists, Game . . . . 5 Espen Knutsen (Mar. 24/01)
Most Points, Game . . . . 5 Espen Knutsen (Mar. 24/01; 5A), Geoff Sanderson (Jan. 11/03; 4G, 1A), Andrew Cassels (Jan. 11/03; 1G, 4A), David Vyborny (Feb. 28/04; 1G, 4A)

Rick Nash (left) and Adam Foote both lost time to injuries last season, but Nash still led the team with 31 goals in just 54 games.

Captains' History
Lyle Odelein, 2000-01, 2001-02; Ray Whitney, 2002-03; Luke Richardson, 2003-04; Luke Richardson and Adam Foote, 2005-06.

2005-06 Results

Oct.	5	at Washington	2-3		8	at Phoenix	5-2
	7	Calgary	1-3		11	Pittsburgh	6-1
	9	at Chicago	3-2		13	at Tampa Bay	2-4
	12	at San Jose	1-4		14	at Florida	5-4*
	14	at Anaheim	3-4		16	NY Rangers	4-3
	16	at Los Angeles	1-3		18	Detroit	0-4
	21	San Jose	4-1		20	St. Louis	4-3†
	22	Detroit	0-6		21	at Nashville	2-7
	24	Detroit	2-6		24	Vancouver	6-5
	26	Nashville	3-2*		27	Minnesota	4-3
	28	Minnesota	2-1†		28	Nashville	4-3
	29	at Minnesota	1-3	Feb.	1	at Calgary	2-1†
Nov.	1	at Edmonton	1-5		2	at Edmonton	2-1†
	3	at Calgary	1-2		6	at Vancouver	4-7
	4	at Vancouver	3-5		8	Los Angeles	7-4
	9	St. Louis	3-1		10	Colorado	1-4
	11	Edmonton	1-3		11	at Nashville	2-5
	13	Los Angeles	2-8	Mar.	2	at Colorado	0-1
	16	St. Louis	0-2		4	at Los Angeles	2-3
	18	at Dallas	3-6		5	at Anaheim	3-2†
	20	at Phoenix	1-5		7	Chicago	1-3
	23	Nashville	2-4		9	Phoenix	5-4
	25	Colorado	0-5		11	Edmonton	4-3*
	26	at St. Louis	4-3		13	at St. Louis	2-3*
	30	at Minnesota	3-2†		15	at Chicago	2-3
Dec.	1	at St. Louis	1-4		17	Vancouver	2-3
	8	NY Islanders	4-3†		19	Anaheim	3-4
	9	at Atlanta	2-5		21	Phoenix	2-5
	11	New Jersey	3-2*		24	Calgary	3-2
	13	Philadelphia	1-3		25	at Detroit	5-4†
	15	at Carolina	1-2		28	San Jose	4-1
	17	at Nashville	3-7		31	at St. Louis	4-2
	20	at Detroit	3-4†	Apr.	1	Chicago	5-2
	21	Dallas	3-5		3	at Nashville	3-1
	23	Nashville	4-5		7	at Detroit	5-6†
	26	Chicago	4-3*		8	Detroit	2-4
	28	Anaheim	1-0		11	at Dallas	2-3
	30	at Colorado	3-2		13	St. Louis	4-1
	31	at Detroit	2-5		15	Chicago	5-2
Jan.	5	at San Jose	3-6		16	at Chicago	3-4
	7	at Colorado	2-3†		18	Dallas	5-4*

* – Overtime   † – Shootout

All-time Record vs. Other Clubs

Regular Season

	At Home								On Road								Total							
	GP	W	L	T	OL	GF	GA	PTS	GP	W	L	T	OL	GF	GA	PTS	GP	W	L	T	OL	GF	GA	PTS
Anaheim	10	7	3	0	0	27	19	14	10	3	5	1	1	22	30	8	20	10	8	1	1	49	49	22
Atlanta	4	2	2	0	0	12	11	4	4	1	3	0	0	8	10	2	8	3	5	0	0	20	21	6
Boston	3	1	0	0	0	3	14	2	2	1	1	0	0	7	8	2	5	2	3	0	0	10	22	4
Buffalo	2	1	0	1	0	5	4	3	4	2	2	0	0	9	13	4	6	3	2	1	0	14	17	7
Calgary	10	7	2	0	1	30	21	15	10	4	6	0	0	21	27	8	20	11	8	0	1	51	48	23
Carolina	3	1	1	0	0	6	9	2	5	1	4	0	0	12	15	2	8	2	6	0	0	18	24	4
Chicago	15	9	5	1	0	47	44	19	14	4	9	1	0	26	41	9	29	13	14	2	0	73	85	28
Colorado	10	1	8	1	0	14	40	3	10	0	9	0	1	12	42	1	20	1	17	1	1	26	82	4
Dallas	10	3	7	0	0	27	35	6	10	0	9	0	1	14	35	1	20	3	16	0	1	41	70	7
Detroit	15	2	8	1	4	25	46	9	14	3	9	0	2	37	58	8	29	5	17	1	6	62	104	17
Edmonton	10	2	5	3	0	25	33	7	10	2	7	0	1	20	37	5	20	4	12	3	1	45	70	12
Florida	2	1	1	0	0	4	4	2	4	2	2	0	0	12	13	4	6	3	3	0	0	16	17	6
Los Angeles	10	6	4	0	0	30	38	12	10	3	6	1	0	19	24	7	20	9	10	1	0	49	62	19
Minnesota	9	7	1	1	0	25	11	15	10	3	6	0	1	22	30	7	19	10	7	1	1	45	41	22
Montreal	1	0	1	0	0	1	3	0	4	2	1	1	0	5	6	5	5	2	2	1	0	7	9	5
Nashville	14	7	6	0	1	36	41	15	15	4	10	1	0	34	49	9	29	11	16	1	1	70	90	24
New Jersey	5	3	2	0	0	16	15	6	2	0	1	1	0	4	5	1	7	3	3	1	0	20	17	7
NY Islanders	5	4	0	1	0	17	10	9	2	0	1	0	1	5	7	1	7	4	1	1	1	22	17	9
NY Rangers	5	4	1	0	0	20	10	8	2	0	1	1	0	5	7	1	7	4	2	1	0	25	17	9
Ottawa	2	0	1	1	0	7	9	1	3	0	2	1	0	6	10	1	5	0	3	2	0	13	21	2
Philadelphia	4	0	2	2	0	7	10	2	2	1	1	0	0	3	7	1	6	1	3	2	0	10	17	3
Phoenix	10	5	4	1	0	26	23	11	10	1	6	3	0	21	31	5	20	6	10	4	0	47	54	16
Pittsburgh	4	2	2	0	0	16	10	6	2	0	0	2	0	9	12	2	6	2	2	2	0	25	22	8
St. Louis	14	7	4	1	2	33	33	17	15	3	9	1	2	34	57	9	29	10	13	2	4	67	90	26
San Jose	10	5	4	1	0	29	22	11	10	1	6	0	3	16	42	3	20	6	12	1	3	45	64	14
Tampa Bay	3	1	1	1	0	5	4	3	4	1	3	0	0	5	9	2	7	2	4	1	0	10	13	5
Toronto	1	1	0	0	0	5	3	2	0	0	0	0	0	0	0	0	1	1	0	0	0	5	3	2
Vancouver	10	3	5	2	0	25	37	8	10	2	7	0	1	30	46	5	20	5	12	2	0	55	83	13
Washington	4	1	2	0	1	11	15	3	2	1	1	0	0	7	11	2	6	2	3	0	1	18	26	4
Totals	205	93	83	18	11	533	574	215	205	46	133	15	11	434	694	118	410	139	216	33	22	967	1268	333

Entry Draft
Selections 2006-2000

2006 Pick		2004 Pick		2002 Pick		2001 Pick	
6	Derick Brassard	8	Alexandre Picard	1	Rick Nash	8	Pascal Leclaire
69	Steve Mason	46	Adam Pineault	41	Joakim Lindstrom	38	Tim Jackman
85	Tommy Sestito	59	Kyle Wharton	65	Ole-Kristian Tollefsen	53	Kiel McLeod
113	Ben Wright	93	Dan Lacosta	96	Jeff Genovy	85	Aaron Johnson
129	Robert Nyholm	96	Andrey Plekhanov	98	Ivan Tkachenko	87	Per Mars
136	Nick Sucharski	133	Petr Pohl	119	Jekabs Redlihs	141	Cole Jarrett
142	Maxime Frechette	167	Rob Page	133	Lasse Pirjeta	173	Justin Aikins
159	Jesse Dudas	190	Lennart Petrell	168	Tim Konsorada	187	Artem Vostrikov
189	Derek Dorsett	198	Justin Vienneau	184	Jaroslav Balastik	204	Raffaele Sannitz
194	Matt Marquardt	231	Brian Mcguirk	199	Greg Mauldin	236	Ryan Bowness
		233	Matt Greer	225	Steven Goertzen	242	Andrew Murray
2005 Pick		271	Grant Clitsome	231	Jaroslav Kracik		
6	Gilbert Brule			263	Sergei Mozyakin	2000 Pick	
55	Adam McQuaid	2003 Pick				4	Rostislav Klesla
67	Kris Russell	4	Nikolai Zherdev			69	Ben Knopp
101	Jared Boll	46	Dan Fritsche			133	Petteri Nummelin
131	Tomas Popperle	71	Dmitry Kosmachev			138	Scott Heffernan
177	Derek Reinhart	103	Kevin Jarman			150	Tyler Kolarik
189	Kirill Starkov	104	Philippe Dupuis			169	Shane Bendera
201	Trevor Hendrikx	138	Arsi Piispanen			200	Janne Jokila
		168	Marc Methot			231	Peter Zingoni
		200	Alexander Guskov			278	Martin Paroulek
		233	Mathieu Gravel			286	Andrej Nedorost
		283	Trevor Hendrikx			292	Louis Mandeville

Club Directory

Nationwide Arena

Columbus Blue Jackets
Nationwide Arena
200 W. Nationwide Blvd.
Columbus, Ohio 43215
Phone **614/246-4625**
FAX 614/246-4007
www.BlueJackets.com
Capacity: 18,136

Coaching History

Dave King, 2000-01, 2001-02; Dave King and Doug MacLean, 2002-03; Doug MacLean and Gerard Gallant, 2003-04; Gerard Gallant, 2004-05 to date.

Coach

GALLANT, GERARD
Coach, Columbus Blue Jackets.
Born in Summerside, P.E.I., September 2, 1963.

Former NHL All-Star Gerard Gallant joined the Blue Jackets organization July 18, 2000 and served as an assistant coach for three and a half seasons. He took over as the club's interim head coach on January 1, 2004 and was officially named to the position of head coach on June 25.

Originally the Red Wings' sixth pick, 107th overall, in the 1981 Entry Draft, Gallant spent two seasons with Adirondack, Detroit's AHL affiliate. His NHL career began with the Red Wings in 1984 when he notched six goals and 12 assists for 18 points in 32 games as a rookie. Over the next eight years, he averaged 56 points and 72 games played with Detroit, including four consecutive seasons with 70 or more points from 1986 to 1990. Gallant helped Detroit capture three division titles and in 1988-89 he was named a Second Team NHL All-Star after posting a career-high 39 goals, 54 assists and 93 points in 76 games.

Gallant wrapped up his Red Wings career following the 1992-93 season having registered 207 goals, 260 assists, 467 points and 1,600 penalty minutes in 563 games. He signed with the Tampa Bay Lightning as a free agent and played in 51 games during the 1993-94 season. He concluded his NHL career with 211 goals, 269 assists, 480 points and 1,674 penalty minutes in 615 games.

Gallant spent the next five years coaching at the junior hockey and minor pro levels before joining the Blue Jackets organization. He began his coaching career with the Summerside (PEI) Western Capitals, a Canadian Junior A team, midway through the 1995-96 season. In 1996-97, his first full season with the club, he led the squad to the Royal Bank Cup championship, Canada's Junior A national championship tournament, and a 33-11-11 regular season mark. He remained with the club through 1997-98.

Gallant then served as an assistant coach with the Fort Wayne Komets of the International Hockey League in 1998-99 and the following season joined the Louisville Panthers of the American Hockey League as the club's top assistant coach.

Coaching Record

Season	Team	Games	Regular Season W	L	O/T	Playoffs Games	W	L
2003-04	Columbus (NHL)	45	16	25	4	.....	.....	
2004-05	Columbus (NHL)				Season Cancelled			
2005-06	Columbus (NHL)	82	35	43	4	.....	.....	
	NHL Totals	**127**	**51**	**68**	**8**			

Ownership
Majority Owner/Governor . . . . John H. McConnell
Alternate Governor . . . . John P. McConnell

Executive Staff
President/General Manager/Alt. Governor . . . . Doug MacLean
Executive Vice-President/Asst. General Manager . . . Jim Clark
Sr. Vice-President of Business Operations . . . . Larry Hoepfner
Vice-President of Ticketing . . . . David Paitson
Vice-President of Corporate Development . . . . Paul D'Aiuto
Vice-President of Marketing . . . . Marc Gregory
Vice-President of Public Relations . . . . Todd Sharrock
General Counsel . . . . Greg Kirstein
Chief Financial Officer. T.J. LaMendola

Hockey Operations
Head Coach . . . . Gerard Gallant
Associate Coach . . . . Gary Agnew
Assistant Coach . . . . Gord Murphy
Director of Player Personnel . . . . Don Boyd
Director of Pro Scouting . . . . Bob Strumm
Director of Amateur Scouting . . . . Paul Castron
Player Development . . . . Dean Blais
Manager of Hockey Operations. . . . . Chris MacFarland
Manager of Team Services . . . . Jim Rankin
Video Coordinator . . . . Dan Singleton
Administrative Assistant, Hockey Operations . . . . . Julie Uhler
Amateur Scouts . . . . Sam McMaster, John Williams
Pro Scout . . . . Peter Dineen
European Scout . . . . Kjell Larsson
Regional Scouts . . . . Brian Bates, Denis LeBlanc, John McNamara, Artem Telepin, Bryan Raymond, Andrew Shaw, Milan Tichy
Head Athletic Trainer . . . . Chris Mizer
Strength & Conditioning Coach . . . . Barry Brennan
Massage Therapist . . . . Chris Hannan
Equipment Manager. . . . . Tim LeRoy
Assistant Equipment Manager. . . . . Jamie Healy
Equipment Assistant . . . . Jason Stypinski

Business Operations
Director of Strategic Partnership Marketing . . . . . . Brent Baker
Director of Event Presentation/Production . . . . Kimberly Kershaw
Director of Marketing & Fan Development . . . . J.D. Kershaw
Director of Community Development . . . . Wendy Bradshaw
Director of Creative Services . . . . Jason Rothwell
Director of Human Resources . . . . Kelley Walton
Director of Retail Operations . . . . Chris Weller
Senior Graphic Designer . . . . Will Bennett
Graphic Designer . . . . Andy Scott
Senior Manager of Communications . . . . Karen Davis
Communications Manager . . . . Ryan Holtmann
Communications Coordinator . . . . Brian Dancel
Strategic Partnership Marketing Managers . . . . . . Cheri Wiles, Stephanie Muse
Premium Sales Manager . . . . Joe Jerele
Corporate Development Sr. Account Execs. . . . . . . Steve Sefner
Corporate Development Account Execs. . . . . Jerry Angel, A.J. Poole, Craig Smith
Production Managers . . . . David Bakalik, David Traube
Manager of Event Presentation . . . . Kate McShea
Graphics Coordinator . . . . James Korte
Payroll Administrator . . . . Christine Parthemore
Human Resources Manager . . . . Jennifer Pritz
Fan Development Manager . . . . Joel Siegman
Manager of Marketing . . . . Nate Ferrall
Manager of Marketing, Youth & Amateur Hockey. . . Gordy Haggard
Community Development Manager . . . . Kate Furman
Mascot Coordinator . . . . Jason Zumpano
Retail Operations Warehouse Manager . . . . Rick Matteo
Administrative Asst.–Marketing/Ticketing . . . . Laurie Sanders
Administrative Asst.–Legal . . . . Rachel Phillips
Paralegal. . . . . Ken Erney
Retail Manager . . . . Mark Karr
Retail Associate . . . . Stephen Pawlak

Finance
Controller . . . . Jeff Abbot
Assistant Controller . . . . Jeremy Manly
Staff Accountant . . . . Nora Ludwig
Accounts Payable . . . . Beth Carpenter, Lindsay Wohlheter
MIS Manager . . . . Jim Connolly
PC Specialist . . . . Dallas Solomon
Office Manager . . . . Rachel Durham
Receptionist . . . . Beth Trexler

Ticket Operations
Senior Director of Tickets Sales/Service . . . . Bill Makris
Director of Ticket Operations/Customer Service . . . . Mark Morris
Mgr. of Ticket Operations/Customer Service . . . . . Karen Miller
Inside Sales Manager . . . . Joseph Cote
Group Sales Account Executives . . . . John Clapham, Andy Hire, Valerie Ott, Heather Sweeney
Season Sales Account Executives . . . . Scott Duncan, Cory Rowe
Season Ticket Service Representatives . . . . Amanda Horning, Timothy Hunter
Ticket Operations Coordinator . . . . Elizabeth Lapka

Broadcasting
Director of Broadcasting . . . . Russ Mollohan
FSN Ohio Play-By-Play Announcer . . . . Jeff Rimer
FSN Ohio Color Analyst . . . . Danny Gare
Radio Play-By-Play Announcer . . . . George Matthews
Radio Color Analyst . . . . Bill Davidge

Dallas Stars

2005-06 Results: 53w-23L-5OTL-1SOL 112PTS.
First, Pacific Division

A trio of Stars in the Lone Star State: Mike Modano (center) led the team in scoring in 2005-06. Jere Lehtinen (right) had a career-high 33 goals while maintaining his defensive excellence. Sergei Zubov (left) was a Norris Trophy nominee.

2006-07 Schedule

Oct.	Wed.	4	at Colorado
	Sat.	7	New Jersey
	Thu.	12	at Los Angeles
	Sat.	14	at Los Angeles
	Sun.	15	at Anaheim*
	Tue.	17	at San Jose
	Fri.	20	Chicago
	Sat.	21	at Phoenix
	Mon.	23	Vancouver
	Fri.	27	Detroit
	Sat.	28	Los Angeles
Nov.	Wed.	1	St. Louis
	Fri.	3	at Edmonton
	Mon.	6	at Vancouver
	Tue.	7	at Calgary
	Thu.	9	at Phoenix
	Wed.	15	NY Islanders
	Fri.	17	at Atlanta
	Sat.	18	at Carolina
	Mon.	20	Colorado
	Wed.	22	Nashville
	Fri.	24	Los Angeles
	Mon.	27	at Detroit
	Wed.	29	at Chicago
	Thu.	30	at Washington
Dec.	Sat.	2	Minnesota
	Mon.	4	San Jose
	Wed.	6	Phoenix
	Fri.	8	Edmonton
	Sat.	9	at Phoenix
	Tue.	12	Columbus
	Thu.	14	NY Rangers
	Sat.	16	at Los Angeles*
	Wed.	20	at Anaheim
	Thu.	21	at San Jose
	Sat.	23	Edmonton
	Tue.	26	at Chicago
	Wed.	27	at Colorado
	Fri.	29	Nashville
	Sun.	31	San Jose
Jan.	Wed.	3	at Vancouver

	Thu.	4	at Edmonton
	Sat.	6	at Calgary
	Tue.	9	Phoenix
	Thu.	11	Anaheim
	Mon.	15	Los Angeles*
	Wed.	17	Calgary
	Sat.	20	at Minnesota
	Fri.	26	Pittsburgh
	Sun.	28	at Anaheim*
	Tue.	30	at San Jose
Feb.	Thu.	1	at San Jose
	Sat.	3	at St. Louis
	Tue.	6	Minnesota
	Sat.	10	Anaheim*
	Sun.	11	Colorado*
	Wed.	14	Detroit
	Sun.	18	San Jose*
	Tue.	20	at Minnesota
	Fri.	23	Anaheim
	Sun.	25	Vancouver*
	Tue.	27	at Tampa Bay
Mar.	Thu.	1	at Florida
	Fri.	2	Columbus
	Sun.	4	San Jose*
	Thu.	8	at St. Louis
	Fri.	9	at Columbus
	Sun.	11	Los Angeles*
	Tue.	13	Philadelphia
	Thu.	15	Calgary
	Sat.	17	at Nashville
	Sun.	18	Phoenix
	Wed.	21	at Los Angeles
	Fri.	23	at Anaheim
	Sat.	24	at Phoenix
	Tue.	27	Phoenix
	Fri.	30	at Detroit
	Sat.	31	at Nashville
Apr.	Mon.	2	St. Louis
	Thu.	5	at Columbus
	Fri.	6	Anaheim
	Sun.	8	Chicago*

Denotes afternoon game.

Franchise date: June 5, 1967
Transferred from Minnesota to Dallas, June 9, 1993.

PACIFIC DIVISION

40th NHL Season

Year-by-Year Record

Season	GP	Home W	L	T	OL	Road W	L	T	OL	Overall W	L	T	OL	GF	GA	Pts.	Finished	Playoff Result
2005-06	82	28	11	....	2	25	12	....	4	53	23	....	6	265	218	112	1st, Pacific Div.	Lost Conf. Quarter-Final
2004-05	....	....				....				....								
2003-04	82	26	7	8	0	15	19	5	2	41	26	13	2	194	175	97	2nd, Pacific Div.	Lost Conf. Quarter-Final
2002-03	82	28	5	6	2	18	12	9	2	46	17	15	4	245	169	111	1st, Pacific Div.	Lost Conf. Semi-Final
2001-02	82	18	13	6	4	18	15	7	1	36	28	13	5	215	213	90	4th, Pacific Div.	Out of Playoffs
2000-01	82	26	10	5	0	22	14	3	....	48	24	8	2	241	187	106	1st, Pacific Div.	Lost Conf. Semi-Final
1999-2000	82	21	11	5	4	22	12	5	2	43	23	10	6	211	184	102	1st, Pacific Div.	Lost Final
1998-99	82	29	8	4	....	22	11	8	....	51	19	12	....	236	168	114	1st, Pacific Div.	Won Stanley Cup
1997-98	82	26	8	7	....	23	14	4	....	49	22	11	....	242	167	109	1st, Central Div.	Lost Conf. Final
1996-97	82	25	13	3	....	23	13	5	....	48	26	8	....	252	198	104	1st, Central Div.	Lost Conf. Quarter-Final
1995-96	82	14	18	9	....	12	24	5	....	26	42	14	....	227	280	66	6th, Central Div.	Out of Playoffs
1994-95	48	9	10	5	....	8	13	3	....	17	23	8	....	136	135	42	5th, Central Div.	Lost Conf. Quarter-Final
1993-94	84	23	12	7	....	19	17	6	....	42	29	13	....	286	265	97	3rd, Central Div.	Lost Conf. Semi-Final
1992-93*	84	18	17	7	....	18	21	3	....	36	38	10	....	272	293	82	5th, Norris Div.	Out of Playoffs
1991-92*	80	20	16	4	....	12	26	2	....	32	42	6	....	246	278	70	4th, Norris Div.	Lost Div. Semi-Final
1990-91*	80	19	15	6	....	8	24	8	....	27	39	14	....	256	266	68	4th, Norris Div.	Lost Final
1989-90*	80	26	12	2	....	10	28	2	....	36	40	4	....	284	291	76	4th, Norris Div.	Lost Div. Semi-Final
1988-89*	80	17	15	8	....	10	22	8	....	27	37	16	....	258	278	70	3rd, Norris Div.	Lost Div. Semi-Final
1987-88*	80	10	24	6	....	9	24	7	....	19	48	13	....	242	349	51	5th, Norris Div.	Out of Playoffs
1986-87*	80	17	20	3	....	13	20	7	....	30	40	10	....	296	314	70	5th, Norris Div.	Out of Playoffs
1985-86*	80	21	15	4	....	17	18	5	....	38	33	9	....	327	305	85	2nd, Norris Div.	Lost Div. Semi-Final
1984-85*	80	14	19	7	....	11	24	5	....	25	43	12	....	268	321	62	4th, Norris Div.	Lost Div. Final
1983-84*	80	22	14	4	....	17	17	6	....	39	31	10	....	345	344	88	1st, Norris Div.	Lost Conf. Championship
1982-83*	80	23	6	11	....	17	18	5	....	40	24	16	....	321	290	96	2nd, Norris Div.	Lost Div. Final
1981-82*	80	21	7	12	....	16	16	8	....	37	23	20	....	346	288	94	1st, Norris Div.	Lost Div. Semi-Final
1980-81*	80	23	10	7	....	12	18	10	....	35	28	17	....	291	263	87	3rd, Adams Div.	Lost Final
1979-80*	80	25	8	7	....	11	20	9	....	36	28	16	....	311	253	88	3rd, Adams Div.	Lost Semi-Final
1978-79*	80	19	15	6	....	9	25	6	....	28	40	12	....	257	289	68	4th, Adams Div.	Out Of Playoffs
1977-78*	80	12	24	4	....	6	29	5	....	18	53	9	....	218	325	45	5th, Smythe Div.	Out of Playoffs
1976-77*	80	17	14	9	....	6	25	9	....	23	39	18	....	240	310	64	2nd, Smythe Div.	Lost Prelim. Round
1975-76*	80	15	22	3	....	5	31	4	....	20	53	7	....	195	303	47	4th, Smythe Div.	Out of Playoffs
1974-75*	80	17	20	3	....	6	30	4	....	23	50	7	....	221	341	53	4th, Smythe Div.	Out of Playoffs
1973-74	78	18	15	6	....	5	23	11	....	23	38	17	....	235	275	63	7th, West Div.	Out of Playoffs
1972-73	78	26	6	7	....	11	24	4	....	37	30	11	....	254	230	85	3rd, West Div.	Lost Quarter-Final
1971-72	78	22	11	6	....	15	18	6	....	37	29	12	....	212	191	86	2nd, West Div.	Lost Quarter-Final
1970-71	78	16	15	8	....	12	19	8	....	28	34	16	....	191	223	72	4th, West Div.	Lost Semi-Final
1969-70	76	11	16	11	....	8	19	11	....	19	35	22	....	224	257	60	3rd, West Div.	Lost Quarter-Final
1968-69*	76	11	21	6	....	7	22	9	....	18	43	15	....	189	270	51	6th, West Div.	Out of Playoffs
1967-68*	74	17	12	8	....	10	20	7	....	27	32	15	....	191	226	69	4th, West Div.	Lost Semi-Final

* Minnesota North Stars

2006-07 Player Personnel

FORWARDS	HT	WT	S	Place of Birth	Date	2005-06 Club
BARNABY, Matthew	6-0	189	L	Ottawa, Ont.	5/4/73	Chicago
BARNES, Stu	5-11	180	R	Spruce Grove, Alta.	12/25/70	Dallas
ERIKSSON, Loui	6-1	183	L	Goteborg, Sweden	7/17/85	Iowa
HAGMAN, Niklas	6-0	200	L	Espoo, Finland	12/5/79	Florida-Dallas
HALPERN, Jeff	6-0	198	R	Potomac, MD	5/3/76	Washington
JOKINEN, Jussi	5-11	189	L	Kalajoki, Finland	4/1/83	Dallas
LEHTINEN, Jere	6-0	200	R	Espoo, Finland	6/24/73	Dallas
LESSARD, Junior	6-0	195	R	St-Joseph-de-Beauce, Que.	5/26/80	Dallas-Iowa
LINDROS, Eric	6-4	240	R	London, Ont.	2/28/73	Toronto
MIETTINEN, Antti	5-11	185	R	Hameenlinna, Finland	7/3/80	Dallas
MODANO, Mike	6-3	205	L	Livonia, MI	6/7/70	Dallas
MORROW, Brenden	5-11	210	L	Carlyle, Sask.	1/16/79	Dallas
OTT, Steve	6-0	185	L	Summerside, P.E.I.	8/19/82	Dallas
POLAK, Vojtech	5-11	180	L	Ostrov nad Ohri, Czech.	6/27/85	Dallas-Iowa
SERTICH, Marty	5-8	165	L	Roseville, MN	10/13/82	Colorado College
STEFAN, Patrik	6-2	210	L	Pribram, Czech.	9/16/80	Atlanta
TJARNQVIST, Mathias	6-1	183	L	Umea, Sweden	4/15/79	Dallas-Iowa

DEFENSEMEN	HT	WT	S	Place of Birth	Date	2005-06 Club
BOUCHER, Philippe	6-3	221	R	Ste-Apollinaire, Que.	3/24/73	Dallas
DALEY, Trevor	5-9	197	L	Toronto, Ont.	10/9/83	Dallas
KLEMM, Jon	6-2	200	R	Cranbrook, B.C.	1/8/70	Dallas
MODRY, Jaroslav	6-2	225	L	Ceske Budejovice, Czech.	2/27/71	Atlanta
NIINIMAA, Janne	6-1	220	L	Raahe, Finland	5/22/75	NY Islanders-Dallas
ROBIDAS, Stephane	5-11	188	R	Sherbrooke, Que.	3/3/77	Dallas
SYDOR, Darryl	6-1	205	L	Edmonton, Alta.	5/13/72	Tampa Bay
ZUBOV, Sergei	6-1	200	R	Moscow, USSR	7/22/70	Dallas

GOALTENDERS	HT	WT	C	Place of Birth	Date	2005-06 Club
ELLIS, Dan	6-0	185	L	Orangeville, Ont.	6/19/80	Iowa
SMITH, Mike	6-3	189	L	Kingston, Ont.	3/22/82	Iowa
STEPHAN, Tobias	6-3	178	L	Zurich, Switz.	1/21/84	Kloten
TURCO, Marty	5-11	183	L	Sault Ste. Marie, Ont.	8/13/75	Dallas

Coach

TIPPETT, DAVE
Coach, Dallas Stars. Born in Moosomin, Sask., August 25, 1961.

Dallas Stars general manager Doug Armstrong announced the hiring of Dave Tippett as the club's head coach on May 16, 2002. In his first season behind the bench in 2002-03, he led the Stars to the best record in the Western Conference and the second best in the NHL. In 2005-06, Dallas had the NHL's third-best record.

Before joining the Stars, Tippett had spent the previous three seasons as an assistant coach with the Los Angeles Kings. He served a five-game stint as interim head coach in 2002 while head coach Andy Murray recovered from an auto accident. In all three seasons Tippett was in Los Angeles the Kings qualified for the playoffs. They had reached the postseason just once out of the previous six seasons.

Under Tippett's direction, the Kings power-play led the NHL in 2001-02 with a 20.7 percent success rate. The year before Tippett came aboard the Kings, in 1998-99, the Kings power-play unit ranked 24th in the league. As a highly regarded minor league coach with tremendous work ethic, Tippett posted two 50-win seasons at Houston (International Hockey League) and led the Aeros to the 1999 Turner Cup championship while serving as general manager/head coach. He was also named IHL coach of the year.

Prior to becoming a coach, Tippett played 11 years as a forward in the National Hockey League with the Hartford Whalers, Washington Capitals, Pittsburgh Penguins and Philadelphia Flyers. He ended his playing career in 1995 as a player-assistant coach with the Houston Aeros (IHL). Internationally, he captained the 1984 Canadian Olympic team in Sarajevo, Yugoslavia, and he earned a silver medal as a member of the Canadian Olympic team in Albertville, France, in 1992. He was a member of the 1982 NCAA Division I championship squad at the University of North Dakota with former Stars defenseman Craig Ludwig.

Coaching Record

			Regular Season				Playoffs		
Season	Team	Games	W	L	O/T	Games	W	L
1995-96	Houston (IHL)	42	17	18	7	....	....	....
1996-97	Houston (IHL)	82	44	30	8	13	8	5
1997-98	Houston (IHL)	82	50	22	10	4	1	3
1998-99	Houston (IHL)	82	54	15	13	19	11	8
2002-03	Dallas (NHL)	82	46	21	15	12	6	6
2003-04	Dallas (NHL)	82	41	28	13	5	1	4
2004-05	Dallas (NHL)				Season Cancelled			
2005-06	Dallas (NHL)	82	53	23	6	5	1	4
	NHL Totals	246	140	72	34	22	8	14

2005-06 Scoring
* – rookie

Regular Season

Pos	#	Player	Team	GP	G	A	Pts	+/-	PIM	PP	SH	GW	S	%
C	9	Mike Modano	DAL	78	27	50	77	23	58	12	1	4	207	13.0
C	44	Jason Arnott	DAL	81	32	44	76	13	102	11	1	5	167	19.2
D	56	Sergei Zubov	DAL	78	13	58	71	20	46	9	0	0	141	9.2
L	10	Brenden Morrow	DAL	81	23	42	65	30	183	8	1	4	146	15.8
L	36	* Jussi Jokinen	DAL	81	17	38	55	2	30	8	0	2	107	15.9
R	26	Jere Lehtinen	DAL	80	33	19	52	9	30	14	1	6	216	15.3
D	43	Philippe Boucher	DAL	66	16	27	43	28	77	8	0	3	174	9.2
R	13	Bill Guerin	DAL	70	13	27	40	0	115	3	0	2	210	6.2
C	14	Stu Barnes	DAL	78	15	21	36	9	44	0	1	2	123	12.2
C	39	Niko Kapanen	DAL	81	14	21	35	-10	36	5	2	4	97	14.4
R	20	* Antti Miettinen	DAL	79	11	20	31	0	46	4	0	1	107	10.3
C	29	Steve Ott	DAL	82	5	17	22	1	178	0	0	1	89	5.6
L	15	Niklas Hagman	FLA	30	2	4	6	-8	2	0	0	0	52	3.8
			DAL	54	6	9	15	-2	16	0	1	0	74	8.1
			TOTAL	84	8	13	21	-10	18	0	1	0	126	6.3
D	3	Stephane Robidas	DAL	75	5	15	20	15	67	1	1	0	95	5.3
D	4	Janne Niinimaa	NYI	41	1	9	10	-7	62	0	0	0	23	4.3
			DAL	22	2	4	6	-5	24	1	1	1	26	7.7
			TOTAL	63	3	13	16	-12	86	1	1	1	49	6.1
D	6	Trevor Daley	DAL	81	3	11	14	-2	87	0	0	1	91	3.3
D	42	Jon Klemm	DAL	76	4	7	11	-3	66	0	0	1	57	7.0
D	2	Willie Mitchell	MIN	64	2	6	8	15	87	0	0	0	48	4.2
			DAL	16	0	2	2	4	26	0	0	0	10	0.0
			TOTAL	80	2	8	10	19	113	0	0	0	58	3.4
L	25	Jeremy Stevenson	NSH	35	4	3	7	0	74	0	0	0	36	11.1
			DAL	16	1	0	1	-3	21	0	0	0	12	8.3
			TOTAL	51	5	3	8	-3	95	0	0	0	48	10.4
L	11	Jaroslav Svoboda	DAL	43	4	3	7	-3	22	0	0	2	33	12.1
L	23	Mathias Tjarnqvist	DAL	33	2	4	6	4	18	0	0	1	36	5.6
R	24	Nathan Perrott	TOR	3	0	0	0	-5	2	0	0	0	2	0.0
			DAL	23	2	1	3	2	54	0	0	1	17	11.8
			TOTAL	26	2	1	3	-3	56	0	0	1	19	10.5
R	21	* Junior Lessard	DAL	5	1	0	1	0	12	0	0	0	6	16.7
D	27	Patrick Traverse	DAL	1	0	0	0	0	0	0	0	0	0	0.0
D	38	* Dan Jancevski	DAL	1	0	0	0	1	0	0	0	0	1	0.0
R	28	David Oliver	DAL	3	0	0	0	0	0	0	0	0	1	0.0
L	53	* Vojtech Polak	DAL	3	0	0	0	-1	0	0	0	0	3	0.0

Goaltending

No.	Goaltender	GPI	Mins	Avg	W	L	OT	EN	SO	GA	SA	S%	G	A	PIM
35	Marty Turco	68	3910	2.55	41	19	5	2	3	166	1624	.898	0	2	28
1	Johan Hedberg	19	1079	2.67	12	4	1	1	0	48	472	.898	0	2	6
	Totals	82	5011	2.60	53	23	6	3	3	217	2099	.897			

Playoffs

Pos	#	Player	Team	GP	G	A	Pts	+/-	PIM	PP	SH	GW	OT	S	%
D	56	Sergei Zubov	DAL	5	1	5	6	-1	6	1	0	0	0	11	9.1
L	10	Brenden Morrow	DAL	5	1	4	5	-1	6	0	0	0	0	10	10.0
R	13	Bill Guerin	DAL	5	3	1	4	-2	0	1	0	0	0	18	16.7
R	26	Jere Lehtinen	DAL	5	3	1	4	-1	4	1	0	0	0	17	17.6
C	9	Mike Modano	DAL	5	1	3	4	-1	4	1	0	0	0	12	8.3
L	15	Niklas Hagman	DAL	5	2	1	3	-1	4	0	0	1	0	9	22.2
L	36	* Jussi Jokinen	DAL	5	2	1	3	0	0	1	0	0	0	12	16.7
C	44	Jason Arnott	DAL	5	0	3	3	-1	4	0	0	0	0	17	0.0
C	14	Stu Barnes	DAL	5	1	1	2	0	0	0	0	0	0	4	25.0
D	3	Stephane Robidas	DAL	5	0	2	2	1	2	0	0	0	0	3	0.0
D	42	Jon Klemm	DAL	5	1	1	2	-1	0	0	0	0	0	5	20.0
D	4	Janne Niinimaa	DAL	5	0	2	2	-1	0	0	0	0	0	4	0.0
D	43	Philippe Boucher	DAL	5	0	1	1	1	6	0	0	0	0	13	0.0
C	39	Niko Kapanen	DAL	5	0	1	1	-1	2	0	0	0	0	8	0.0
C	29	Steve Ott	DAL	5	0	1	1	-1	15	0	0	0	0	5	0.0
R	20	* Antti Miettinen	DAL	5	0	1	1	-1	0	0	0	0	0	11	0.0
L	25	Jeremy Stevenson	DAL	1	0	0	0	0	0	0	0	0	0	0	0.0
L	11	Jaroslav Svoboda	DAL	2	0	0	0	0	2	0	0	0	0	1	0.0
D	6	Trevor Daley	DAL	3	0	0	0	-3	0	0	0	0	0	4	0.0
D	2	Willie Mitchell	DAL	5	0	0	0	-1	6	0	0	0	0	6	0.0

Goaltending

No.	Goaltender	GPI	Mins	Avg	W	L	EN	SO	GA	SA	S%	G	A	PIM
35	Marty Turco	5	319	3.39	1	4	0	0	18	136	.868	0	0	2
	Totals	5	320	3.38	1	4	0	0	18	136	.868			

Coaching History

Wren Blair, 1967-68; Wren Blair and John Muckler, 1968-69; Wren Blair and Charlie Burns, 1969-70; Jack Gordon, 1970-71 to 1972-73; Jack Gordon and Parker MacDonald, 1973-74; Jack Gordon and Charlie Burns, 1974-75; Ted Harris, 1975-76, 1976-77; Ted Harris, André Beaulieu and Lou Nanne, 1977-78; Harry Howell and Glen Sonmor, 1978-79; Glen Sonmor, 1979-80 to 1981-82; Glen Sonmor and Murray Oliver, 1982-83; Bill Mahoney, 1983-84, 1984-85; Lorne Henning, 1985-86; Lorne Henning and Glen Sonmor, 1986-87; Herb Brooks, 1987-88; Pierre Page, 1988-89, 1989-90; Bob Gainey, 1990-91 to 1994-95; Bob Gainey and Ken Hitchcock, 1995-96; Ken Hitchcock, 1996-97 to 2000-01; Ken Hitchcock and Rick Wilson, 2001-02; Dave Tippett, 2002-03 to date.

Club Records

Team

(Figures in brackets for season records are games played; records for fewest points, wins, ties, losses, goals, goals against are for 70 or more games)

Most Points **114** 1998-99 (82)
Most Wins **53** 2005-06 (82)
Most Ties **22** 1969-70 (76)
Most Losses **53** 1975-76 (80), 1977-78 (80)
Most Goals **346** 1981-82 (80)
Most Goals Against **349** 1987-88 (80)
Fewest Points **45** 1977-78 (80)
Fewest Wins **18** 1968-69 (76), 1977-78 (80)
Fewest Ties **4** 1989-90 (80)
Fewest Losses **17** 2002-03 (82)
Fewest Goals **189** 1968-69 (76)
Fewest Goals Against **167** 1997-98 (82)
Longest Winning Streak
Overall .... **7** Mar. 16-28/80, Mar. 16-Apr. 2/97, Nov. 22-Dec. 5/97
Home .... **11** Nov. 4-Dec. 27/72
Away .... **7** Three times
Longest Undefeated Streak
Overall .... **17** Jan. 23-Mar. 20/04 (13 wins, 4 ties)
Home .... **13** Oct. 28-Dec. 27/72 (12 wins, 1 tie), Nov. 21/79-Jan. 9/80 (10 wins, 3 ties), Jan. 17-Mar. 17/91 (11 wins, 2 ties)
Away .... **10** Jan. 12-Mar. 4/99 (8 wins, 2 ties)
Longest Losing Streak
Overall .... **10** Feb. 1-20/76
Home .... **6** Jan. 17-Feb. 4/70
Away .... **8** Oct. 19-Nov. 13/75, Jan. 28-Mar. 3/88
Longest Winless Streak
Overall .... **20** Jan. 15-Feb. 28/70 (15 losses, 5 ties)
Home .... **12** Jan. 17-Feb. 25/70 (8 losses, 4 ties)
Away .... **23** Oct. 25/74-Jan. 28/75 (19 losses, 4 ties)
Most Shutouts, Season **11** 2000-01 (82), 2002-03 (82)
Most PIM, Season **2,313** 1987-88 (80)
Most Goals, Game .... **15** Nov. 11/81 (Wpg. 2 at Min. 15)

Individual

Most Seasons .... **17** Mike Modano
Most Games .... **1,179** Mike Modano
Most Goals, Career .... **485** Mike Modano
Most Assists, Career .... **698** Mike Modano
Most Points, Career .... **1,183** Mike Modano (485G, 698A)
Most PIM, Career .... **1,883** Shane Churla
Most Shutouts, Career .... **27** Ed Belfour
Longest Consecutive Games Streak .... **442** Danny Grant (Dec. 4/68-Apr. 7/74)
Most Goals, Season .... **55** Dino Ciccarelli (1981-82), Brian Bellows (1989-90)
Most Assists, Season .... **76** Neal Broten (1985-86)
Most Points, Season .... **114** Bobby Smith (1981-82; 43G, 71A)
Most PIM, Season .... **382** Basil McRae (1987-88)
Most Points, Defenseman, Season .... **77** Craig Hartsburg (1981-82; 17G, 60A)
Most Points, Center, Season .... **114** Bobby Smith (1981-82; 43G, 71A)
Most Points, Right Wing, Season .... **106** Dino Ciccarelli (1981-82; 55G, 51A)
Most Points, Left Wing, Season .... **99** Brian Bellows (1989-90; 55G, 44A)
Most Points, Rookie, Season .... **98** Neal Broten (1981-82; 38G, 60A)
Most Shutouts, Season .... **9** Ed Belfour (1997-98)
Most Goals, Game .... **5** Tim Young (Jan. 15/79)
Most Assists, Game .... **5** Murray Oliver (Oct. 24/71), Larry Murphy (Oct. 17/89)
Most Points, Game .... **7** Bobby Smith (Nov. 11/81; 4G, 3A)

Records include Minnesota North Stars, 1967-68 through 1992-93.

Retired Numbers

7	Neal Broten	1980-1995, 1996-1997
8	Bill Goldsworthy*	1967-1976
19	Bill Masterton*	1967-1968

* Minnesota North Stars

All-time Record vs. Other Clubs

Regular Season

	At Home								On Road								Total							
	GP	W	L	T	OL	GF	GA	PTS	GP	W	L	T	OL	GF	GA	PTS	GP	W	L	T	OL	GF	GA	PTS
Anaheim	31	23	6	2	0	111	59	48	31	16	11	3	1	82	72	36	62	39	17	5	1	193	131	84
Atlanta	5	4	1	0	0	11	9	8	4	4	0	0	0	16	9	8	9	8	1	0	0	27	18	16
Boston	61	18	30	13	0	175	220	49	61	10	41	10	0	148	259	30	122	28	71	23	0	323	479	79
Buffalo	54	27	21	6	0	173	156	60	53	13	29	11	0	142	192	37	107	40	50	17	0	315	348	97
Calgary	64	32	20	11	1	233	199	76	64	16	32	14	2	158	211	48	128	48	52	25	3	391	410	124
Carolina	30	18	10	2	0	120	90	38	32	15	13	4	0	110	101	34	62	33	23	6	0	230	191	72
Chicago	114	54	43	16	1	389	343	125	112	33	64	15	0	301	417	81	226	87	107	31	1	690	760	206
Colorado	43	22	14	5	2	138	121	51	43	13	22	7	1	109	154	34	86	35	36	12	3	247	275	85
Columbus	10	10	0	0	0	35	14	20	10	7	2	0	1	35	27	15	20	17	2	0	1	70	41	35
Detroit	108	52	37	18	1	373	324	123	108	38	54	16	0	344	412	92	216	90	91	34	1	717	736	215
Edmonton	47	25	15	7	0	170	131	57	46	17	20	8	1	152	181	43	93	42	35	15	1	322	312	100
Florida	9	4	2	2	1	29	25	11	10	5	4	1	0	28	22	11	19	9	6	3	1	57	47	22
Los Angeles	88	53	22	13	0	335	238	119	86	29	37	19	1	245	288	78	174	82	59	32	1	580	526	197
Minnesota	10	6	2	1	1	35	23	14	10	5	5	0	0	22	26	10	20	11	7	1	1	57	49	24
Montreal	59	17	30	12	0	153	203	46	59	12	38	9	0	146	254	33	118	29	68	21	0	299	457	79
Nashville	14	12	2	0	0	42	17	24	14	6	7	1	0	29	34	13	28	18	9	1	0	71	51	37
New Jersey	45	26	13	6	0	164	117	58	43	19	21	3	0	132	146	41	88	45	34	9	0	296	263	99
NY Islanders	47	18	20	8	1	139	170	45	48	14	25	8	1	134	176	37	95	32	45	16	2	273	346	82
NY Rangers	61	20	30	11	0	187	221	51	62	15	36	11	0	165	213	41	123	35	66	22	0	352	434	92
Ottawa	11	7	4	0	0	44	28	14	10	6	3	0	1	26	22	13	21	13	7	0	1	70	50	27
Philadelphia	66	27	23	16	0	216	212	70	67	9	42	16	0	150	255	34	133	36	65	32	0	366	467	104
Phoenix	59	29	21	9	0	209	176	67	58	30	24	4	0	197	182	64	117	59	45	13	0	406	358	131
Pittsburgh	64	37	21	6	0	246	213	80	63	19	38	6	0	178	236	44	127	56	59	12	0	424	449	124
St. Louis	117	55	39	22	1	390	337	133	119	33	63	21	2	339	429	89	236	88	102	43	3	729	766	222
San Jose	33	17	10	4	2	94	75	40	34	20	12	1	1	96	83	42	67	37	22	5	3	190	158	82
Tampa Bay	12	7	4	1	0	42	33	15	13	10	1	2	0	37	20	22	25	17	5	3	0	79	53	37
Toronto	97	50	36	11	0	365	306	111	102	36	49	17	0	321	357	89	199	86	85	28	0	686	663	200
Vancouver	73	39	22	12	0	266	214	90	73	31	31	10	1	222	258	73	146	70	53	22	1	488	472	163
Washington	42	22	11	8	1	156	111	53	40	17	15	8	0	129	120	42	82	39	26	16	1	285	231	95
Defunct Clubs	33	19	8	6	0	123	86	44	32	10	16	6	0	84	105	26	65	29	24	12	0	207	191	70
Totals	**1507**	**750**	**517**	**228**	**12**	**5163**	**4471**	**1740**	**1507**	**508**	**755**	**231**	**13**	**4277**	**5261**	**1260**	**3014**	**1258**	**1272**	**459**	**25**	**9440**	**9732**	**3000**

Playoffs

	Series	W	L	GP	W	L	T	GF	GA	Last Mtg.	Rnd.	Result
Anaheim	1	0	1	6	2	4	0	14	14	2003	CSF	L 2-4
Boston	1	1	0	3	3	0	0	20	13	1981	PRE	W 3-0
Buffalo	3	2	1	13	8	5	0	39	37	1999	F	W 4-2
Calgary	1	1	0	6	4	2	0	25	18	1981	SF	W 4-2
Chicago	6	2	4	33	14	19	0	118	120	1991	DSF	W 4-2
Colorado	4	2	2	24	10	14	0	62	66	2006	CQF	L 1-4
Detroit	3	0	3	18	6	12	0	40	55	1998	CF	L 2-4
Edmonton	8	6	2	42	27	15	0	118	104	2003	CQF	W 4-2
Los Angeles	1	1	0	7	4	3	0	26	21	1968	QF	W 4-3
Montreal	2	1	1	13	6	7	0	37	48	1980	QF	W 4-3
New Jersey	1	0	1	6	2	4	0	9	15	2000	F	L 2-4
NY Islanders	1	0	1	5	1	4	0	16	26	1981	F	L 1-4
Philadelphia	2	0	2	11	3	8	0	26	41	1980	SF	L 1-4
Pittsburgh	1	0	1	6	2	4	0	16	28	1991	F	L 2-4
St. Louis	12	6	6	66	34	32	0	197	187	2001	CSF	L 0-4
San Jose	2	2	0	11	8	3	0	31	19	2000	CSF	W 4-1
Toronto	2	2	0	7	6	1	0	35	26	1983	DSF	W 3-1
Vancouver	1	0	1	5	1	4	0	11	18	1994	CSF	L 1-4
Totals	**52**	**26**	**26**	**282**	**141**	**141**	**0**	**840**	**856**			

Calgary totals include Atlanta Flames, 1972-73 to 1979-80. Carolina totals include Hartford, 1979-80 to 1996-97.
Colorado totals include Quebec, 1979-80 to 1994-95.
New Jersey totals include Kansas City, 1974-75 to 1975-76, and Colorado Rockies, 1976-77 to 1981-82.
Phoenix totals include Winnipeg, 1979-80 to 1995-96.

Playoff Results 2006-2001

Year	Round	Opponent	Result	GF	GA
2006	CQF	Colorado	L 1-4	15	18
2004	CQF	Colorado	L 1-4	10	19
2003	CSF	Anaheim	L 2-4	14	14
	CQF	Edmonton	W 4-2	20	11
2001	CSF	St. Louis	L 0-4	6	13
	CQF	Edmonton	W 4-2	16	13

Abbreviations: Round: F - Final; **CF** - conference final; **CSF** - conference semi-final; **CQF** - conference quarter-final; **DSF** - division semi-final; **SF** - semi-final; **QF** - quarter-final; **PRE** - preliminary round.

2005-06 Results

Oct.	5	Los Angeles	5-4		9	at Minnesota	2-1
	8	Colorado	2-3		12	Washington	4-1
	11	Phoenix	3-2		14	at Boston	2-1†
	13	at Calgary	3-2*		16	at Montreal	2-4
	14	at Edmonton	3-2		18	Atlanta	2-5
	16	at Vancouver	2-5		20	Tampa Bay	3-6
	20	Los Angeles	2-7		23	Phoenix	4-1
	22	Calgary	2-1		25	St. Louis	4-3†
	26	San Jose	4-5*		26	at Colorado	3-2†
	28	Edmonton	3-5		28	Detroit	2-1†
	29	at Phoenix	5-3		30	San Jose	3-2*
Nov.	2	Los Angeles	3-6	**Feb.**	1	Nashville	2-1
	4	Chicago	9-1		4	at St. Louis	3-4*
	5	at Colorado	3-2†		6	Nashville	4-2
	7	Edmonton	4-0		9	at Phoenix	5-1
	10	at Nashville	3-5		10	at San Jose	3-6
	12	at San Jose	3-2†		12	at Los Angeles	5-6
	13	at Anaheim	3-1	**Mar.**	2	at Phoenix	2-6
	16	at Anaheim	4-2		4	Colorado	5-3
	18	Columbus	6-3		5	at Chicago	7-2
	23	Anaheim	3-1		7	at Edmonton	4-3†
	25	Phoenix	1-4		9	at Calgary	0-1
	26	at Nashville	3-1		11	at Vancouver	2-1
	30	San Jose	4-1		13	Vancouver	4-2
Dec.	2	Carolina	5-4†		16	at Los Angeles	4-1
	7	Florida	4-3		18	at San Jose	4-3†
	10	at Toronto	2-1		20	Anaheim	1-2
	14	at Buffalo	3-4		22	Minnesota	4-2
	15	at Ottawa	2-0		24	Chicago	3-2†
	18	at Chicago	5-3		26	Calgary	3-2
	19	at Minnesota	1-2		29	Anaheim	2-1
	21	at Columbus	5-3		31	at Anaheim	4-5†
	23	Phoenix	2-3	**Apr.**	1	at Los Angeles	0-1
	26	at St. Louis	6-1		3	San Jose	2-3*
	27	Detroit	1-4		6	at Anaheim	5-3
	29	St. Louis	3-0		8	at Phoenix	3-2†
	31	Los Angeles	2-3		9	at San Jose	1-4
Jan.	2	at Los Angeles	2-3*		11	Columbus	3-2
	4	Vancouver	3-1		15	Minnesota	4-3*
	6	Anaheim	4-3†		17	at Detroit	2-3
	8	at Detroit	6-3		18	at Columbus	4-5*

* – Overtime † – Shootout

Entry Draft
Selections 2006-1992

2006
Pick
27	Ivan Vishnevskiy
90	Aaron Snow
120	Richard Bachman
138	David McIntyre
150	Max Warn

2005
Pick
28	Matt Niskanen
33	James Neal
71	Richard Clune
75	Perttu Lindgren
146	Tom Wandell
160	Matt Watkins
223	Pat McGann

2004
Pick
28	Mark Fistric
34	Johan Fransson
52	Raymond Sawada
56	Nicklas Grossman
86	John Lammers
104	Fredrik Naslund
183	Trevor Ludwig
218	Sergei Kukushkin
248	Lukas Vomela
280	Matt McKnight

2003
Pick
33	Loui Eriksson
36	Vojtech Polak
54	B.J. Crombeen
99	Matt Nickerson
134	Alexander Naurov
144	Eero Kilpelainen
165	Gino Guyer
185	Francis Wathier
195	Drew Bagnall
196	Elias Granath
259	Niko Vainio

2002
Pick
26	Martin Vagner
32	Janos Vas
34	Tobias Stephan
42	Marius Holtet
43	Trevor Daley
78	Geoff Waugh
110	Jarkko A. Immonen
147	David Bararuk
180	Kirill Sidorenko
210	Bryan Hamm
243	Tuomas Mikkonen
273	Ned Havern

2001
Pick
26	Jason Bacasihua
70	Yared Hagos
92	Anthony Aquino
126	Daniel Volrab
161	Mike Smith
167	Michal Blazek
192	Jussi Jokinen
255	Marco Rosa
265	Dale Sullivan
285	Marek Tomica

2000
Pick
25	Steve Ott
60	Dan Ellis
68	Joel Lundqvist
91	Alexei Tereschenko
123	Vadim Khomitsky
139	Ruslan Bernikov
162	Artem Chernov
192	Ladislav Vlcek
219	Marco Tuokko
224	Antti Miettinen

1999
Pick
32	Michael Ryan
66	Dan Jancevski
96	Mathias Tjarnqvist
126	Jeff Bateman
156	Gregor Baumgartner
184	Justin Cox
186	Brett Draney
215	Jeff MacMillan
243	Brian Sullivan
265	Jamie Chamberlain
272	Mikhail Donika

1998
Pick
39	John Erskine
57	Tyler Bouck
86	Gabriel Karlsson
153	Pavel Patera
173	Niko Kapanen
200	Scott Perry

1997
Pick
25	Brenden Morrow
52	Roman Lyashenko
77	Steve Gainey
105	Marcus Kristoffersson
132	Teemu Elomo
160	Alexei Timkin
189	Jeff McKercher
216	Alexei Komarov
242	Brett McLean

1996
Pick
5	Ric Jackman
70	Jon Sim
90	Mike Hurley
112	Ryan Christie
113	Yevgeny Tsybuk
166	Eoin McInerney
194	Joel Kwiatkowski
220	Nick Bootland

1995
Pick
11	Jarome Iginla
37	Patrick Cote
63	Petr Buzek
69	Sergey Gusev
115	Wade Strand
141	Dominic Marleau
173	Jeff Dewar
193	Anatoli Koveshnikov
202	Sergei Luchinkin
219	Stephen Lowe

1994
Pick
20	Jason Botterill
46	Lee Jinman
98	Jamie Wright
124	Marty Turco
150	Evgeny Petrochinin
228	Marty Flichel
254	Jimmy Roy
280	Chris Szysky

1993
Pick
9	Todd Harvey
35	Jamie Langenbrunner
87	Chad Lang
136	Rick Mrozik
139	Per Svartvadet
165	Jeremy Stasiuk
191	Rob Lurtsema
243	Jordan Willis
249	Bill Lang
269	Cory Peterson

1992
Pick
34	Jarkko Varvio
58	Jeff Bes
88	Jere Lehtinen
130	Michael Johnson
154	Kyle Peterson
178	Juha Lind
202	Lars Edstrom
226	Jeff Romfo
250	Jeffrey Moen

Club Directory

American Airlines Center

Dallas Stars
Office Address:
2601 Ave. of the Stars
Frisco, TX 75034
Phone **214/387-5500**
FAX 214/387-5564
Ticket Information 214/GO STARS
www.dallasstars.com
Capacity: 18,532

Chairman of the Board & Owner	Thomas O. Hicks
President	James R. Lites
General Manager	Doug Armstrong
Assistant General Manager	Les Jackson
Assistant General Manager	Frank Provenzano
Head Coach	Dave Tippett
Associate Coach	Rick Wilson
Assistant Coach	Mark Lamb
Assistant Coach	Ulf Dahlen
Director of Player Development/ Goaltending Consultant	Andy Moog
Video Coach	Derek MacKinnon
Director, Hockey Administration and Team Services	Lesa Moake
Director, Amateur Scouting	Tim Bernhardt
Director, Professional Scouting	Doug Overton
Director, European Scouting	Kari Takko
Scout	Bob Gernander
Professional Scout	Paul McIntosh
Professional Scout	Kevin Maxwell
Professional Scout	Scott White
Head Athletic Trainer	Dave Surprenant
Head Equipment Manager	Steve Sumner
Strength and Conditioning Coach	J.J. McQueen
Assistant Athletic Trainer	Tommy Alva
Assistant Equipment Manager	Chris Davidson-Adams
Administrative Assistant, Hockey Operations	Pam Wenzel

Communications
Senior Director, Communications	Rob Scichili
Director, Public Relations	Mark Janko
Manager, Media and Team Services	Jason Rademan

Miscellaneous
Television Networks	FSN Southwest, KDFI
Radio Flagship	WBAP 820 AM
Play-by-Play Announcer (TV/Radio Simulcast)	Ralph Strangis
Color Analyst (TV/Radio Sumilcast)	Daryl Reaugh

Captains' History

Bob Woytowich, 1967-68; Moose Vasko, 1968-69; Claude Larose, 1969-70; Ted Harris, 1970-71 to 1973-74; Bill Goldsworthy, 1974-75, 1975-76; Bill Hogaboam, 1976-77; Nick Beverley, 1977-78; J.P. Parise, 1978-79; Paul Shmyr, 1979-80, 1980-81; Tim Young, 1981-82; Craig Hartsburg, 1982-83; Craig Hartsburg and Brian Bellows, 1983-84; Craig Hartsburg, 1984-85 to 1987-88; Curt Fraser, Bob Rouse and Curt Giles, 1988-89; Curt Giles, 1989-90, 1990-91; Mark Tinordi, 1991-92 to 1993-94; Neal Broten and Derian Hatcher, 1994-95; Derian Hatcher, 1995-96 to 2002-03; Mike Modano, 2003-04 to date.

General Managers' History

Wren Blair, 1967-68 to 1973-74; Jack Gordon, 1974-75 to 1976-77; Lou Nanne, 1977-78 to 1987-88; Jack Ferreira, 1988-89, 1989-90; Bob Clarke 1990-91, 1991-92; Bob Gainey, 1992-93 to 2000-01; Bob Gainey and Doug Armstrong, 2001-02; Doug Armstrong, 2002-03 to date.

General Manager

ARMSTRONG, DOUG
General Manager, Dallas Stars. Born in Sarnia, Ont., September 24, 1964.

Doug Armstrong was in his ninth season as an assistant to Bob Gainey when he was elevated to the position of general manager on January 25, 2002. In his first full season on the job in 2002-03, the Stars had the best record in the Western Conference and the second best in the NHL. In 2005-06, Dallas had the NHL's third-best record.

Armstrong originally joined the club in 1991. As Gainey's assistant, he worked on contract information and season scheduling and handled the day-to-day operations of the hockey department. In five seasons from 1996 to 2001, he helped Gainey build a team that won five straight division championships, as well as the Presidents' Trophy for the best regular-season record in the NHL twice, and the 1999 Stanley Cup. At the international level, Armstrong served as Team Canada's assistant general manger at the 2002 World Championships in Sweden.

A native of Sarnia, Ontario, Armstrong attended Western Michigan University for two years before transferring to Florida State University in Tallahassee, where he earned his B.S. in Business Administration with a major in marketing.

The Stars' first pick (25th overall) in the 1997 NHL Entry Draft, Brenden Morrow established a career high with 65 points (23 goals, 42 assists) in 2005-06.

Detroit Red Wings

In just his third NHL season, Henrik Zetterberg was second on the Red Wings with 39 goals and 85 points in 2005-06. He also picked up an Olympic gold medal with Sweden at the Torino Games.

2005-06 Results: 58w-16L-5oTL-3sOL 124pts.
First, Central Division

2006-07 Schedule

Oct.	Thu.	5	Vancouver
	Sat.	7	at Pittsburgh
	Wed.	11	Phoenix
	Fri.	13	Buffalo
	Mon.	16	at Los Angeles
	Wed.	18	at Anaheim
	Thu.	19	at San Jose
	Sat.	21	at Edmonton
	Wed.	25	San Jose
	Fri.	27	at Dallas
	Sat.	28	at St. Louis
Nov.	Wed.	1	Calgary
	Thu.	2	at Chicago
	Sat.	4	Columbus
	Wed.	8	Edmonton
	Fri.	10	Nashville
	Tue.	14	at Vancouver
	Fri.	17	at Calgary
	Sat.	18	at Edmonton
	Wed.	22	Vancouver
	Fri.	24	St. Louis
	Sat.	25	at Nashville
	Mon.	27	Dallas
Dec.	Fri.	1	at Minnesota
	Sat.	2	San Jose
	Tue.	5	at St. Louis
	Thu.	7	St. Louis
	Sat.	9	Toronto
	Tue.	12	Ottawa
	Thu.	14	at Chicago
	Sat.	16	at New Jersey*
	Mon.	18	at Columbus
	Wed.	20	Columbus
	Fri.	22	Minnesota
	Sat.	23	at Minnesota
	Wed.	27	Minnesota
	Thu.	28	at Columbus
	Sun.	31	Los Angeles
Jan.	Tue.	2	Anaheim
	Thu.	4	at San Jose
	Sat.	6	at Los Angeles
	Sun.	7	at Anaheim*
	Tue.	9	at Colorado
	Thu.	11	at Phoenix
	Sat.	13	Chicago
	Mon.	15	Montreal
	Wed.	17	Nashville
	Fri.	19	at Columbus
	Sat.	20	at Colorado
	Fri.	26	at St. Louis
	Sun.	28	Colorado*
	Tue.	30	at NY Islanders
Feb.	Fri.	2	St. Louis
	Mon.	5	at NY Rangers
	Wed.	7	Phoenix
	Thu.	8	at St. Louis
	Sun.	11	Calgary
	Mon.	12	at Philadelphia
	Wed.	14	at Dallas
	Sat.	17	at Phoenix
	Wed.	21	Chicago
	Fri.	23	Edmonton
	Sat.	24	at Nashville
	Tue.	27	at Chicago
Mar.	Fri.	2	Chicago
	Sun.	4	Colorado*
	Tue.	6	Nashville
	Fri.	9	Los Angeles
	Sun.	11	Boston*
	Tue.	13	at Nashville
	Wed.	14	Nashville
	Sat.	17	at Vancouver
	Tue.	20	at Calgary
	Thu.	22	Columbus
	Sat.	24	St. Louis*
	Mon.	26	Anaheim
	Thu.	29	at Nashville
	Fri.	30	Dallas
Apr.	Sun.	1	at Columbus*
	Tue.	3	Columbus
	Thu.	5	at Chicago
	Sat.	7	Chicago*

* Denotes afternoon game.

Franchise date: September 25, 1926

81st NHL Season

CENTRAL DIVISION

Year-by-Year Record

Season	GP	Home W	L	T	OL	Road W	L	T	OL	Overall W	L	T	OL	GF	GA	Pts.	Finished	Playoff Result
2005-06	82	27	9	....	5	31	7	....	3	58	16	....	8	305	209	124	1st, Central Div.	Lost Conf. Quarter-Final
2004-05																		
2003-04	82	30	7	4	0	18	14	7	2	48	21	11	2	255	189	109	1st, Central Div.	Lost Conf. Semi-Final
2002-03	82	28	6	5	2	20	14	5	2	48	20	10	4	269	203	110	1st, Central Div.	Lost Conf. Quarter-Final
2001-02	82	28	7	5	1	23	10	5	3	51	17	10	4	251	187	116	1st, Central Div.	Won Stanley Cup
2000-01	82	27	9	3	2	22	11	6	2	49	20	9	4	253	202	111	1st, Central Div.	Lost Conf. Quarter-Final
1999-2000	82	28	9	3	1	20	13	7	1	48	22	10	2	278	210	108	2nd, Central Div.	Lost Conf. Semi-Final
1998-99	82	27	12	2		16	20	5		43	32	7		245	202	93	1st, Central Div.	Lost Conf. Semi-Final
1997-98	82	25	8	8		19	15	7		44	23	15		250	196	103	2nd, Central Div.	Won Stanley Cup
1996-97	82	20	12	9		18	14	9		38	26	18		253	197	94	2nd, Central Div.	Won Stanley Cup
1995-96	82	36	3	2		26	10	5		62	13	7		325	181	131	1st, Central Div.	Lost Conf. Championship
1994-95	48	17	4	3		16	7	1		33	11	4		180	117	70	1st, Central Div.	Lost Conf. Quarter-Final
1993-94	84	23	13	6		23	17	2		46	30	8		356	275	100	1st, Central Div.	Lost Conf. Quarter-Final
1992-93	84	25	14	3		22	14	6		47	28	9		369	280	103	2nd, Norris Div.	Lost Div. Semi-Final
1991-92	80	24	12	4		19	13	8		43	25	12		320	256	98	1st, Norris Div.	Lost Div. Final
1990-91	80	26	14	0		8	24	8		34	38	8		273	298	76	3rd, Norris Div.	Lost Div. Semi-Final
1989-90	80	20	14	6		8	24	8		28	38	14		288	323	70	5th, Norris Div.	Out of Playoffs
1988-89	80	20	14	6		14	20	6		34	34	12		313	316	80	1st, Norris Div.	Lost Div. Semi-Final
1987-88	80	24	10	6		17	18	5		41	28	11		322	269	93	1st, Norris Div.	Lost Conf. Championship
1986-87	80	20	14	6		14	22	4		34	36	10		260	274	78	2nd, Norris Div.	Lost Conf. Championship
1985-86	80	10	26	4		7	31	2		17	57	6		266	415	40	5th, Norris Div.	Out of Playoffs
1984-85	80	19	14	7		8	27	5		27	41	12		313	357	66	3rd, Norris Div.	Lost Div. Semi-Final
1983-84	80	18	20	2		13	22	5		31	42	7		298	323	69	3rd, Norris Div.	Lost Div. Semi-Final
1982-83	80	14	19	7		7	25	8		21	44	15		263	344	57	5th, Norris Div.	Out of Playoffs
1981-82	80	15	19	6		6	28	6		21	47	12		270	351	54	6th, Norris Div.	Out of Playoffs
1980-81	80	16	15	9		3	28	9		19	43	18		252	339	56	5th, Norris Div.	Out of Playoffs
1979-80	80	14	21	5		12	22	6		26	43	11		268	306	63	5th, Norris Div.	Out of Playoffs
1978-79	80	15	17	8		8	24	8		23	41	16		252	295	62	5th, Norris Div.	Out of Playoffs
1977-78	80	22	11	7		10	23	7		32	34	14		252	266	78	2nd, Norris Div.	Lost Quarter-Final
1976-77	80	12	22	6		4	33	3		16	55	9		183	309	41	5th, Norris Div.	Out of Playoffs
1975-76	80	17	15	8		9	29	2		26	44	10		226	300	62	4th, Norris Div.	Out of Playoffs
1974-75	80	17	16	7		6	28	6		23	45	12		259	335	58	4th, Norris Div.	Out of Playoffs
1973-74	78	21	12	6		8	27	4		29	39	10		255	319	68	6th, East Div.	Out of Playoffs
1972-73	78	22	12	5		15	17	7		37	29	12		265	243	86	5th, East Div.	Out of Playoffs
1971-72	78	25	11	3		8	24	7		33	35	10		261	262	76	5th, East Div.	Out of Playoffs
1970-71	78	17	15	7		5	30	4		22	45	11		209	308	55	7th, East Div.	Out of Playoffs
1969-70	76	20	11	7		20	10	8		40	21	15		246	199	95	3rd, East Div.	Lost Quarter-Final
1968-69	76	23	8	7		10	23	5		33	31	12		239	221	78	5th, East Div.	Out of Playoffs
1967-68	74	18	15	4		9	20	8		27	35	12		245	257	66	6th, East Div.	Out of Playoffs
1966-67	70	21	11	3		6	28	1		27	39	4		212	241	58	5th,	Out of Playoffs
1965-66	70	20	8	7		11	19	5		31	27	12		221	194	74	4th	Lost Final
1964-65	70	25	7	3		15	16	4		40	23	7		224	175	87	1st	Lost Semi-Final
1963-64	70	23	9	3		7	20	8		30	29	11		191	204	71	4th	Lost Final
1962-63	70	19	10	6		13	15	7		32	25	13		200	194	77	4th	Lost Final
1961-62	70	17	11	7		6	22	7		23	33	14		184	219	60	5th	Out of Playoffs
1960-61	70	15	13	7		10	16	9		25	29	16		195	215	66	4th	Lost Final
1959-60	70	18	14	3		8	15	12		26	29	15		186	197	67	4th	Lost Semi-Final
1958-59	70	13	17	5		12	20	3		25	37	8		167	218	58	6th	Out of Playoffs
1957-58	70	16	11	8		13	18	4		29	29	12		176	207	70	3rd,	Lost Semi-Final
1956-57	70	23	7	5		15	13	7		38	20	12		198	157	88	1st,	Lost Semi-Final
1955-56	70	21	6	8		9	18	8		30	24	16		183	148	76	2nd,	Lost Final
1954-55	70	25	5	5		17	12	6		42	17	11		204	134	95	1st,	Won Stanley Cup
1953-54	70	24	4	7		13	15	7		37	19	14		191	132	88	1st,	Won Stanley Cup
1952-53	70	20	5	10		16	11	8		36	16	18		222	133	90	1st,	Lost Semi-Final
1951-52	70	24	7	4		20	7	8		44	14	12		215	133	100	1st,	Won Stanley Cup
1950-51	70	25	3	7		19	10	6		44	13	13		236	139	101	1st,	Lost Semi-Final
1949-50	70	19	9	7		18	10	7		37	19	14		229	164	88	1st,	Won Stanley Cup
1948-49	60	21	6	3		13	13	4		34	19	7		195	145	75	1st,	Lost Final
1947-48	60	16	9	5		14	9	7		30	18	12		187	148	72	2nd,	Lost Final
1946-47	60	14	10	6		8	17	5		22	27	11		190	193	55	4th,	Lost Semi-Final
1945-46	50	15	5	5		5	15	5		20	20	10		146	159	50	4th,	Lost Semi-Final
1944-45	50	19	5	1		12	9	4		31	14	5		218	161	67	2nd,	Lost Final
1943-44	50	18	5	2		8	13	4		26	18	6		214	177	58	2nd,	Lost Semi-Final
1942-43	50	16	4	5		9	10	6		25	14	11		169	124	61	1st,	Won Stanley Cup
1941-42	48	14	7	3		5	18	1		19	25	4		140	147	42	5th,	Lost Final
1940-41	48	14	5	5		7	11	6		21	16	11		112	102	53	3rd,	Lost Final
1939-40	48	11	10	3		5	16	3		16	26	6		91	126	38	5th,	Lost Semi-Final
1938-39	48	14	4	6		4	16	4		18	24	6		107	128	42	5th,	Out of Playoffs
1937-38	48	8	10	6		4	15	5		12	25	11		99	133	35	4th, Amn. Div.	Out of Playoffs
1936-37	48	14	5	5		11	9	4		25	14	9		128	102	59	1st, Amn. Div.	Won Stanley Cup
1935-36	48	14	5	5		10	11	3		24	16	8		124	103	56	1st, Amn. Div.	Won Stanley Cup
1934-35	48	11	8	5		8	14	2		19	22	7		127	114	45	4th, Amn. Div.	Out of Playoffs
1933-34	48	15	5	4		9	6	9		24	14	10		113	98	58	1st, Amn. Div.	Lost Final
1932-33*	48	17	3	4		8	12	4		25	15	8		111	93	58	2nd, Amn. Div.	Lost Semi-Final
1931-32	48	15	3	6		3	17	4		18	20	10		95	108	46	3rd, Amn. Div.	Lost Quarter-Final
1930-31**	44	10	7	5		6	14	2		16	21	7		102	105	39	4th, Amn. Div.	Out of Playoffs
1929-30	44	9	10	3		5	14	3		14	24	6		117	133	34	4th, Amn. Div.	Out of Playoffs
1928-29	44	11	6	5		8	10	4		19	16	9		72	63	47	3rd, Amn. Div.	Lost Quarter-Final
1927-28	44	10	8	4		9	11	2		19	19	6		88	79	44	4th, Amn. Div.	Out of Playoffs
1926-27***	44	5	16	0		7	12	4		12	28	4		76	105	28	5th, Amn. Div.	Out of Playoffs

* Team name changed to Red Wings. ** Team name changed to Falcons. *** Team named Cougars.

2006-07 Player Personnel

FORWARDS	HT	WT	S	Place of Birth	Date	2005-06 Club
BOOTLAND, Darryl	6-1	194	R	Toronto, Ont.	11/2/81	Grand Rapids
BROOKS, Brendan	5-10	185	R	St. Catherines, Ont.	11/26/78	Peoria
CLEARY, Daniel	6-0	211	L	Carbonear, Nfld.	12/18/78	Detroit
DATSYUK, Pavel	5-11	180	L	Sverdlovsk, USSR	7/20/78	Detroit
DRAPER, Kris	5-11	190	L	Toronto, Ont.	5/24/71	Detroit
ELLIS, Matt	6-1	190	L	Welland, Ont.	8/31/81	Grand Rapids
FILPPULA, Valtteri	5-11	185	L	Vantaa, Finland	3/20/84	Detroit-Grand Rapids
FRANZEN, Johan	6-2	207	L	Landsbro, Sweden	12/23/79	Detroit
HIMELFARB, Eric	5-9	161	R	Thornhill, Ont.	1/1/83	Grand Rapids
HOLMSTROM, Tomas	6-0	200	L	Pitea, Sweden	1/23/73	Detroit
HUDLER, Jiri	5-9	178	L	Olomouc, Czech.	1/4/84	Detroit-Grand Rapids
HUSSEY, Matt	6-2	215	L	New Haven, CT	5/28/79	Pittsburgh-Wilkes-Barre
JOHNSON, Greg	5-11	200	L	Thunder Bay, Ont.	3/16/71	Nashville
KOLANOS, Krys	6-3	206	R	Calgary, Alta.	7/27/81	Phx-San Antonio-Edm-Lowell (AHL)-Wilkes-Barre
KOPECKY, Tomas	6-3	187	L	Ilava, Czech.	2/5/82	Detroit-Grand Rapids
LANG, Robert	6-2	216	R	Teplice, Czech.	12/19/70	Detroit
LANGFELD, Josh	6-3	216	R	Fridley, MN	7/17/77	San Jose-Boston
MALTBY, Kirk	6-0	180	R	Guelph, Ont.	12/22/72	Detroit
McGRATH, Evan	5-11	181	L	Oakville, Ont.	1/14/86	Kitchener
SAMUELSSON, Mikael	6-2	211	L	Mariefred, Sweden	12/23/76	Rapperswil-Detroit
WILLIAMS, Jason	5-11	185	R	London, Ont.	8/11/80	Detroit
ZETTERBERG, Henrik	5-11	176	L	Njurunda, Sweden	10/9/80	Detroit
DEFENSEMEN						
CHELIOS, Chris	6-1	190	R	Chicago, IL	1/25/62	Detroit
FISCHER, Jiri	6-5	225	L	Horovice, Czech.	7/31/80	Detroit
KRONWALL, Niklas	5-11	165	L	Stockholm, Sweden	1/12/81	Detroit-Grand Rapids
LEBDA, Brett	5-11	194	L	Buffalo Grove, IL	1/15/82	Detroit-Grand Rapids
LIDSTROM, Nicklas	6-2	185	L	Vasteras, Sweden	4/28/70	Detroit
LILJA, Andreas	6-3	228	L	Helsingborg, Sweden	7/13/75	Detroit
MARKOV, Danny	6-1	190	L	Moscow, USSR	7/30/76	Nashville
MEECH, Derek	5-11	182	L	Winnipeg, Man.	4/21/84	Grand Rapids
NORTON, Brad	6-4	235	L	Cambridge, MA	2/13/75	Jokerit-Ott-Binghamton
QUINCEY, Kyle	6-1	194	L	Kitchener, Ont.	8/12/85	Detroit-Grand Rapids
SCHNEIDER, Mathieu	5-10	192	L	New York, NY	6/12/69	Detroit
SMITH, Dan	6-3	215	L	Fernie, B.C.	10/19/76	Edmonton-Hamilton

GOALTENDERS	HT	WT	C	Place of Birth	Date	2005-06 Club
HASEK, Dominik	5-11	180	L	Pardubice, Czech.	1/29/65	Ottawa
HOWARD, James	6-0	218	L	Syracuse, NY	3/26/84	Detroit-Grand Rapids
KOOPMANS, Logan	6-2	182	L	Cranbrook, B.C.	5/18/84	Toledo-Grand Rapids
LIV, Stefan	6-0	172	L	Gdynia, Poland	12/21/80	HV 71
MacDONALD, Joey	6-0	200	L	Pictou, N.S.	2/7/80	Grand Rapids-Toledo
MacINTYRE, Drew	6-0	173	L	Charlottetown, P.E.I.	6/24/83	Toledo-Grand Rapids
OSGOOD, Chris	5-10	175	L	Peace River, Alta.	11/26/72	Detroit-Grand Rapids

Coach

BABCOCK, MIKE

Coach, Detroit Red Wings. Born in Manitouwadge, Ont., April 29, 1963.

Mike Babcock became the 26th coach in Detroit Red Wings history on July 14, 2005, bringing a winning track record at all levels of play including college and junior hockey, the American Hockey League, the National Hockey League and the highest level of international competition. He is the only man to coach Team Canada to victories at both the World Junior Championship (1997) and senior World Championship (2004).

In his first season in Detroit, Babcock led the Red Wings to the NHL's best record. Previously, he had spent two seasons with the Mighty Ducks of Anaheim, leading the team to the Stanley Cup finals in his first season behind the bench in 2002–03. He became the first rookie coach to reach the Finals since Florida's Doug MacLean in 1996. With a four-game sweep over Detroit in the first round of the playoffs, the Ducks became the first team since the 1952 Red Wings (over Toronto) to sweep a defending Stanley Cup champion. Babcock led the team to the best regular season in the club's history with 40 wins and 95 points in 2002–03.

Before joining Anaheim, Babcock spent two seasons as head coach of the Cincinnati Mighty Ducks (2000 to 2002), the primary development affiliate for both Detroit and Anaheim in the American Hockey League. He led the club to a franchise-best 41 wins and 95 points in 2000-01. Babcock moved to Cincinnati after a successful six-year run as the head coach of the Spokane Chiefs of the Western Hockey League (1994 through 2000). He was twice named WHL coach of the year (1996 and 2000) after taking the Chiefs to the league finals in both seasons. He began his WHL coaching career with the Moose Jaw Warriors in 1991–92. In Canadian university play, Babcock won a national championship and was named the coach of the year with the Lethbridge Pronghorns in 1993-94. In 1988, he was named head coach at Red Deer College in Red Deer, Alberta. He spent three seasons at the school, winning the Alberta college championship and coach of the year award in 1989.

Babcock played in the WHL for Saskatoon (1980-81) and Kelowna (1982-83), where he was team captain. In between, he spent a year at the University of Saskatoon. Babcock also played four years at McGill University (1983 to 87), twice being named an All-Star defenseman and team captain. He earned his bachelor's degree in physical education and attended graduate school in sports psychology at McGill.

2005-06 Scoring

* – rookie

Regular Season

Pos	#	Player	Team	GP	G	A	Pts	+/–	PIM	PP	SH	GW	S	%
C	13	Pavel Datsyuk	DET	75	28	59	87	26	22	11	0	4	145	19.3
L	40	Henrik Zetterberg	DET	77	39	46	85	29	30	17	1	9	270	14.4
L	14	Brendan Shanahan	DET	82	40	41	81	29	105	14	0	6	289	13.8
D	5	Nicklas Lidstrom	DET	80	16	64	80	21	50	9	0	2	243	6.6
C	20	Robert Lang	DET	72	20	42	62	17	72	8	0	3	171	11.7
L	96	Tomas Holmstrom	DET	81	29	30	59	14	66	11	0	8	140	20.7
D	23	Mathieu Schneider	DET	72	21	38	59	33	86	11	0	4	188	11.2
C	29	Jason Williams	DET	80	21	37	58	4	26	6	0	4	177	11.9
R	37	Mikael Samuelsson	DET	71	23	22	45	27	42	7	0	3	187	12.3
C	19	Steve Yzerman	DET	61	14	20	34	8	18	4	0	3	86	16.3
C	33	Kris Draper	DET	80	10	22	32	3	58	0	1	1	153	6.5
D	15	Jason Woolley	DET	53	1	18	19	3	28	0	0	0	43	2.3
C	39 *	Johan Franzen	DET	80	12	4	16	4	36	0	2	2	119	10.1
R	44	Mark Mowers	DET	46	4	11	15	13	16	0	0	0	65	6.2
R	11	Daniel Cleary	DET	77	3	12	15	5	40	0	0	1	106	2.8
D	3	Andreas Lilja	DET	82	2	13	15	18	98	0	0	1	78	2.6
D	22 *	Brett Lebda	DET	46	3	9	12	9	20	1	0	1	50	6.0
L	18	Kirk Maltby	DET	82	5	6	11	–9	80	0	1	0	115	4.3
D	24	Chris Chelios	DET	81	4	7	11	22	108	1	1	0	83	4.8
D	55 *	Niklas Kronwall	DET	27	1	8	9	11	28	1	0	0	28	3.6
D	2	Jiri Fischer	DET	22	3	5	8	8	33	0	1	1	36	8.3
D	4	Cory Cross	EDM	34	2	3	5	–5	38	0	1	0	20	10.0
			PIT	6	0	1	1	–1	6	0	0	0	1	0.0
			DET	16	1	1	2	3	15	0	0	0	11	9.1
			TOTAL	56	3	5	8	–3	59	0	1	0	32	9.4
C	42	Don MacLean	DET	3	1	1	2	2	0	1	0	1	3	33.3
C	41 *	Valtteri Filppula	DET	4	0	1	1	1	2	0	0	0	1	0.0
C	32 *	Tomas Kopecky	DET	1	0	0	0	1	2	0	0	0	1	0.0
D	45 *	Kyle Quincey	DET	1	0	0	0	0	0	0	0	0	1	0.0
C	26 *	Jiri Hudler	DET	4	0	0	0	0	2	0	0	0	3	0.0

Goaltending

No.	Goaltender	GPI	Mins	Avg	W	L	OT	EN	SO	GA	SA	S%	G	A	PIM
34	Manny Legace	51	2905	2.19	37	8	3	1	7	106	1244	.915	0	1	0
30	Chris Osgood	32	1846	2.76	20	6	5	3	2	85	828	.897	0	0	8
35	* James Howard	4	201	2.99	1	2	0	0	0	10	104	.904	0	0	0
	Totals	**82**	**4972**	**2.47**	**58**	**16**	**8**	**4**	**9**	**205**	**2180**	**.906**			

Playoffs

Pos	#	Player	Team	GP	G	A	Pts	+/–	PIM	PP	SH	GW	OT	S	%
D	23	Mathieu Schneider	DET	6	1	7	8	–1	6	0	0	0	0	17	5.9
L	40	Henrik Zetterberg	DET	6	6	0	6	–2	2	4	0	0	0	23	26.1
C	20	Robert Lang	DET	6	3	3	6	–2	2	2	0	0	0	18	16.7
C	19	Steve Yzerman	DET	4	0	4	4	–2	4	0	0	0	0	10	0.0
L	18	Kirk Maltby	DET	6	2	1	3	2	4	0	0	1	1	12	16.7
L	96	Tomas Holmstrom	DET	6	1	2	3	–1	12	1	0	0	0	10	10.0
C	39 *	Johan Franzen	DET	6	1	2	3	0	4	0	0	0	0	11	9.1
C	13	Pavel Datsyuk	DET	5	0	3	3	0	0	0	0	0	0	11	0.0
D	55 *	Niklas Kronwall	DET	6	0	3	3	0	2	0	0	0	0	7	0.0
L	14	Brendan Shanahan	DET	6	1	1	2	0	6	0	0	0	0	21	4.8
D	5	Nicklas Lidstrom	DET	6	1	1	2	–4	2	1	0	1	0	21	4.8
C	29	Jason Williams	DET	6	1	1	2	–3	6	0	0	0	0	16	6.3
R	11	Daniel Cleary	DET	6	0	1	1	2	6	0	0	0	0	14	0.0
R	37	Mikael Samuelsson	DET	6	0	1	1	–1	6	0	0	0	0	16	0.0
D	3	Andreas Lilja	DET	6	0	1	1	–4	6	0	0	0	0	3	0.0
R	44	Mark Mowers	DET	3	0	0	0	0	0	0	0	0	0	4	0.0
D	24	Chris Chelios	DET	6	0	0	0	2	6	0	0	0	0	3	0.0
C	33	Kris Draper	DET	6	0	0	0	3	6	0	0	0	0	14	0.0
D	22 *	Brett Lebda	DET	6	0	0	0	3	4	0	0	0	0	7	0.0

Goaltending

No.	Goaltender	GPI	Mins	Avg	W	L	EN	SO	GA	SA	S%	G	A	PIM
34	Manny Legace	6	408	2.65	2	4	1	0	18	155	.884	0	0	0
	Totals	**6**	**411**	**2.77**	**2**	**4**	**1**	**0**	**19**	**156**	**.878**			

Coaching Record

			Regular Season			Playoffs		
Season	Team	Games	W	L	O/T	Games	W	L
1991-92	Moose Jaw (WHL)	72	33	36	3	4	0	4
1992-93	Moose Jaw (WHL)	72	27	42	3	....	....	....
1993-94	U. of Lethbridge (CIAU)	28	19	7	2	....	....	....
1994-95	Spokane (WHL)	72	32	36	4	11	6	5
1995-96	Spokane (WHL)	72	50	18	4	9	3	6
1996-97	Spokane (WHL)	65	31	30	4	9	4	5
1997-98	Spokane (WHL)	72	45	23	4	18	10	8
1998-99	Spokane (WHL)	72	19	44	9	....	....	....
1999-2000	Spokane (WHL)	72	47	21	4	20	15	5
2000-01	Cincinnati (WHL)	80	41	26	13	4	1	3
2001-02	Cincinnati (WHL)	80	33	33	14	3	1	2
2002-03	**Anaheim (NHL)**	**82**	**40**	**33**	**9**	**21**	**15**	**6**
2003-04	**Anaheim (NHL)**	**82**	**29**	**43**	**10**	....	....	....
2004-05	**Anaheim (NHL)**			Season Cancelled				
2005-06	**Detroit (NHL)**	**82**	**58**	**16**	**8**	**6**	**2**	**4**
	NHL Totals	**246**	**127**	**92**	**27**	**27**	**17**	**10**

Club Records

Team

(Figures in brackets for season records are games played; records for fewest points, wins, ties, losses, goals, goals against are for 70 or more games)

Most Points 131 1995-96 (82)
Most Wins *62 1995-96 (82)
Most Ties 18 1952-53 (70), 1980-81 (80), 1996-97 (82)
Most Losses 57 1985-86 (80)
Most Goals 369 1992-93 (84)
Most Goals Against 415 1985-86 (80)
Fewest Points 40 1985-86 (80)
Fewest Wins 16 1976-77 (80)
Fewest Ties 4 1966-67 (70)
Fewest Losses 13 1950-51 (70), 1995-96 (82)
Fewest Goals 167 1958-59 (70)
Fewest Goals Against 132 1953-54 (70)

Longest Winning Streak
- Overall .... 9 Five times
- Home .... 14 Jan. 21-Mar. 25/65
- Away .... 12 Mar. 1-Apr. 15/06

Longest Undefeated Streak
- Overall .... 15 Nov. 27-Dec. 28/52 (8 wins, 7 ties)
- Home .... 19 Dec. 31/00-Apr.7/01 (17 wins, 2 ties)
- Away .... 15 Oct. 18-Dec. 20/51 (10 wins, 5 ties)

Longest Losing Streak
- Overall .... 14 Feb. 24-Mar. 25/82
- Home .... 7 Feb. 20-Mar. 25/82
- Away .... 14 Oct. 19-Dec. 21/66

Longest Winless Streak
- Overall .... 19 Feb. 26-Apr. 3/77 (18 losses, 1 tie)
- Home .... 10 Dec. 11/85-Jan. 18/86 (9 losses, 1 tie)
- Away .... 26 Dec. 15/76-Apr. 3/77 (23 losses, 3 ties)

Most Shutouts, Season 13 1953-54 (70)
Most. PIM, Season 2,393 1985-86 (80)
Most Goals, Game .... 15 Jan. 23/44 (NYR 0 at Det. 15)

Individual

Most Seasons .... 25 Gordie Howe
Most Games .... 1,687 Gordie Howe
Most Goals, Career .... 786 Gordie Howe
Most Assists, Career .... 1,063 Steve Yzerman
Most Points, Career .... 1,809 Gordie Howe (786G, 1,023A)
Most PIM, Career .... 2,090 Bob Probert
Most Shutouts, Career .... 85 Terry Sawchuk
Longest Consecutive Games Streak .... 548 Alex Delvecchio (Dec. 13/56-Nov. 11/64)
Most Goals, Season .... 65 Steve Yzerman (1988-89)
Most Assists, Season .... 90 Steve Yzerman (1988-89)
Most Points, Season .... 155 Steve Yzerman (1988-89; 65G, 90A)
Most PIM, Season .... 398 Bob Probert (1987-88)
Most Points, Defenseman, Season .... 80 Nicklas Lidstrom (2005-06; 16G, 64A)
Most Points, Center, Season .... 155 Steve Yzerman (1988-89; 65G, 90A)
Most Points, Right Wing, Season .... 103 Gordie Howe (1968-69; 44G, 59A)
Most Points, Left Wing, Season .... 105 John Ogrodnick (1984-85; 55G, 50A)
Most Points, Rookie, Season .... 87 Steve Yzerman (1983-84; 39G, 48A)
Most Shutouts, Season .... 12 Terry Sawchuk (1951-52, 1953-54, 1954-55), Glenn Hall (1955-56)
Most Goals, Game .... 6 Syd Howe (Feb. 3/44)
Most Assists, Game .... *7 Billy Taylor (Mar. 16/47)
Most Points, Game .... 7 Carl Liscombe (Nov. 5/42; 3G, 4A), Don Grosso (Feb. 3/44; 1G, 6A), Billy Taylor (Mar. 16/47; 7A)

* NHL Record.

Retired Numbers

1	Terry Sawchuk	1949-55, 57-64, 68-69
7	Ted Lindsay	1944-57, 64-65
9	Gordie Howe	1946-1971
10	Alex Delvecchio	1951-1973
12	Sid Abel	1938-43, 45-52

All-time Record vs. Other Clubs

Regular Season

	At Home								On Road								Total							
	GP	W	L	T	OL	GF	GA	PTS	GP	W	L	T	OL	GF	GA	PTS	GP	W	L	T	OL	GF	GA	PTS
Anaheim	24	19	2	3	0	89	52	41	24	12	8	4	0	68	55	28	48	31	10	7	0	157	107	69
Atlanta	4	4	0	0	0	17	8	8	4	3	1	0	0	25	14	6	8	7	1	0	0	42	22	14
Boston	285	154	79	52	0	952	720	360	287	90	153	43	1	761	1007	224	572	244	232	95	1	1713	1727	584
Buffalo	55	32	18	5	0	203	159	69	52	11	33	8	0	153	226	30	107	43	51	13	0	356	385	99
Calgary	61	32	19	10	0	223	180	74	62	21	35	6	0	182	232	48	123	53	54	16	0	405	412	122
Carolina	31	17	7	7	0	119	86	41	31	12	18	1	0	88	107	25	62	29	25	8	0	207	193	66
Chicago	339	206	98	33	2	1161	843	447	342	136	152	51	3	970	1025	326	681	342	250	84	5	2131	1868	773
Colorado	42	26	15	1	0	155	126	53	44	20	20	4	0	149	151	44	86	46	35	5	0	304	277	97
Columbus	14	11	2	0	1	58	37	23	15	12	2	1	0	46	25	25	29	23	4	1	1	104	62	48
Dallas	108	54	38	16	0	412	344	124	108	38	51	18	1	324	373	95	216	92	89	34	1	736	717	219
Edmonton	46	26	15	3	2	177	150	57	46	15	19	10	2	164	177	42	92	41	34	13	4	341	327	99
Florida	8	4	1	3	0	30	21	11	10	6	1	2	1	29	20	15	18	10	2	5	1	59	41	26
Los Angeles	81	38	30	13	0	312	278	89	82	26	41	14	1	256	325	67	163	64	71	27	1	568	603	156
Minnesota	10	6	3	1	0	37	25	13	10	6	1	2	1	29	24	15	20	12	4	3	1	66	49	28
Montreal	280	130	97	53	0	805	717	313	282	67	172	43	0	636	994	177	562	197	269	96	0	1441	1711	490
Nashville	21	14	2	2	3	80	46	33	20	10	7	2	1	58	51	23	41	24	9	4	4	138	97	56
New Jersey	41	26	13	2	0	169	131	54	40	10	21	9	0	103	138	29	81	36	34	11	0	272	269	83
NY Islanders	46	26	18	2	0	166	137	54	46	19	23	4	0	137	164	42	92	45	41	6	0	303	301	96
NY Rangers	286	165	76	45	0	1008	702	375	284	92	134	58	0	738	868	242	570	257	210	103	0	1746	1570	617
Ottawa	9	6	3	0	0	33	19	12	10	6	3	1	0	29	28	13	19	12	6	1	0	62	47	25
Philadelphia	60	32	18	10	0	216	185	74	58	13	34	11	0	168	230	37	118	45	52	21	0	384	415	111
Phoenix	53	25	20	8	0	203	179	58	51	20	17	14	0	162	152	54	104	45	37	22	0	365	331	112
Pittsburgh	66	41	13	12	0	256	179	94	65	17	44	4	0	195	281	38	131	58	57	16	0	451	460	132
St. Louis	114	55	42	17	0	417	342	127	114	38	54	20	2	323	382	98	228	93	96	37	2	740	724	225
San Jose	27	24	2	1	0	111	47	49	28	15	10	3	0	108	94	33	55	39	12	4	0	219	141	82
Tampa Bay	12	10	1	1	0	47	21	21	15	10	4	1	0	67	46	21	27	20	5	2	0	114	67	42
Toronto	322	168	106	46	2	968	792	384	316	105	164	47	0	846	1045	257	638	273	270	93	2	1814	1837	641
Vancouver	68	42	17	8	1	279	193	93	67	27	30	10	0	218	242	64	135	69	47	18	1	497	435	157
Washington	47	21	15	11	0	161	135	53	47	21	21	5	0	151	171	47	94	42	36	16	0	312	306	100
Defunct Clubs	141	76	40	25	0	430	307	177	141	49	63	29	0	364	375	127	282	125	103	54	0	794	682	304
Totals	**2701**	**1490**	**810**	**390**	**11**	**9294**	**7161**	**3381**	**2701**	**927**	**1336**	**425**	**13**	**7547**	**9022**	**2292**	**5402**	**2417**	**2146**	**815**	**24**	**16841**	**16183**	**5673**

Playoffs

	Series	W	L	GP	W	L	T	GF	GA	Last Mtg.	Rnd.	Result
Anaheim	3	2	1	12	8	4	0	36	24	2003	CQF	L 0-4
Boston	7	3	4	33	14	19	0	98	96	1957	SF	L 1-4
Calgary	2	1	1	8	4	4	0	20	16	2004	CSF	L 2-4
Carolina	1	1	0	5	4	1	0	14	7	2002	F	W 4-1
Chicago	14	6	8	69	31	38	0	190	210	1995	CF	W 4-1
Colorado	5	2	3	30	13	17	0	76	79	2002	CF	W 4-3
Dallas	3	3	0	18	12	6	0	55	40	1998	CF	W 4-2
Edmonton	3	0	3	16	4	12	0	43	58	2006	CQF	L 2-4
Los Angeles	2	1	1	10	6	4	0	32	21	2001	CQF	L 2-4
Montreal	12	7	5	62	29	33	0	149	161	1978	QF	L 1-4
Nashville	1	1	0	6	4	2	0	12	9	2004	CQF	W 4-2
New Jersey	1	0	1	4	0	4	0	7	16	1995	F	L 0-4
NY Rangers	5	4	1	23	13	10	0	57	49	1950	F	W 4-3
Philadelphia	1	1	0	4	4	0	0	16	6	1997	F	W 4-0
Phoenix	2	2	0	12	8	4	0	44	28	1998	CQF	W 4-2
St. Louis	7	5	2	40	24	16	0	125	103	2002	CSF	W 4-1
San Jose	2	1	1	11	7	4	0	51	27	1995	CSF	W 4-0
Toronto	23	11	12	117	59	58	0	321	311	1993	DSF	L 3-4
Vancouver	1	1	0	6	4	2	0	22	16	2002	CQF	W 4-2
Washington	1	1	0	4	4	0	0	13	7	1998	F	W 4-0
Defunct Clubs	4	3	1	10	7	2	1	21	13			
Totals	**100**	**56**	**44**	**500**	**259**	**240**	**1**	**1402**	**1297**			

Calgary totals include Atlanta Flames, 1972-73 to 1979-80. Colorado totals include Quebec, 1979-80 to 1994-95. New Jersey totals include Kansas City, 1974-75 to 1975-76, and Colorado Rockies, 1976-77 to 1981-82. Phoenix totals include Winnipeg, 1979-80 to 1995-96. Carolina totals include Hartford, 1979-80 to 1996-97. Dallas totals include Minnesota North Stars, 1967-68 to 1992-93.

Playoff Results 2006-2001

Year	Round	Opponent	Result	GF	GA
2006	CQF	Edmonton	L 2-4	17	19
2004	CSF	Calgary	L 2-4	12	11
	CQF	Nashville	W 4-2	12	9
2003	CQF	Anaheim	L 0-4	6	10
2002	**F**	**Carolina**	**W 4-1**	**14**	**7**
	CF	Colorado	W 4-3	22	13
	CSF	St. Louis	W 4-1	14	11
	CQF	Vancouver	W 4-2	22	16
2001	CQF	Los Angeles	L 2-4	17	15

Abbreviations: Round: F - Final; **CF** - conference final; **CSF** - conference semi-final; **CQF** - conference quarter-final; **DSF** - division semi-final; **SF** - semi-final; **QF** - quarter-final.

2005-06 Results

Oct.	5	St. Louis	5-1
	6	at St. Louis	4-3
	9	Calgary	6-3
	10	Vancouver	2-4
	13	at Los Angeles	5-2
	15	at Phoenix	2-0
	17	San Jose	3-2*
	21	Anaheim	3-2
	22	at Columbus	6-0
	24	at Columbus	6-2
	27	Chicago	5-2
	29	at Chicago	4-2
Nov.	1	Chicago	4-1
	3	Edmonton	3-4*
	5	Phoenix	1-4
	6	at St. Louis	4-1
	9	Los Angeles	5-4*
	11	Minnesota	3-1
	13	at Vancouver	1-4
	16	at Calgary	1-3
	17	at Edmonton	5-6*
	19	St. Louis	2-3
	23	Colorado	7-3
	25	at Anaheim	1-3
	26	at San Jose	7-6
	28	at Los Angeles	5-2
Dec.	1	Calgary	2-3
	4	NY Islanders	1-2
	6	New Jersey	5-2
	9	at Washington	4-3
	12	Pittsburgh	3-1
	13	at Atlanta	6-7
	15	at Florida	2-3*
	17	at Tampa Bay	6-3
	20	Columbus	4-3†
	23	at Chicago	3-2*
	27	at Dallas	4-1
	31	Columbus	5-2
Jan.	3	Minnesota	2-4
	5	St. Louis	3-0
	6	at Nashville	3-1
	8	Dallas	3-6
	10	at Carolina	2-3
	12	Philadelphia	6-3
	14	NY Rangers	4-3
	18	at Columbus	4-0
	21	at Colorado	4-3
	23	Nashville	2-3
	24	Nashville	1-2*
	26	Vancouver	2-1
	28	at Dallas	1-2†
	30	at Minnesota	5-4
Feb.	1	St. Louis	3-2
	4	at Colorado	3-0
	8	Nashville	6-0
	9	at Nashville	3-2
	12	Colorado	6-3
	28	at San Jose	1-5
Mar.	1	at Anaheim	2-0
	4	at Phoenix	7-3
	7	Phoenix	2-5
	9	Los Angeles	7-3
	11	Chicago	6-4
	12	at Chicago	5-3
	15	Anaheim	3-1
	18	at Edmonton	4-3†
	19	at Vancouver	7-3
	21	Nashville	2-3†
	23	San Jose	4-0
	25	Columbus	4-5†
	27	at St. Louis	4-1
	30	at Nashville	4-2
	31	Chicago	2-3*
Apr.	2	at Minnesota	3-2
	3	at Calgary	2-1†
	7	Columbus	6-5†
	8	at Columbus	4-2
	11	Edmonton	2-0
	13	at Chicago	7-3
	15	at St. Louis	3-2
	17	Dallas	3-2
	18	at Nashville	3-6

* – Overtime † – Shootout

Entry Draft
Selections 2006-1992

2006 Pick		2002 Pick		1998 Pick		1994 Pick	
41	Cory Emmerton	58	Jiri Hudler	25	Jiri Fischer	23	Yan Golubovsky
47	Shawn Matthias	63	Tomas Fleischmann	55	Ryan Barnes	49	Mathieu Dandenault
62	Dick Axelsson	95	Valtteri Filppula	56	Tomek Valtonen	75	Sean Gillam
92	Daniel Larsson	131	Johan Berggren	84	Jake McCracken	114	Frederic Deschenes
182	Jan Mursak	166	Logan Koopmans	111	Brent Hobday	127	Doug Battaglia
191	Nick Oslund	197	Jimmy Cuddihy	142	Calle Steen	153	Pavel Agarkov
212	Logan Pyett	229	Derek Meech	151	Adam DeLeeuw	205	Jason Elliot
		260	Pierre-Olivier Beaulieu	171	Pavel Datsyuk	231	Jeff Mikesch
2005 Pick		262	Christian Soderstrom	198	Jeremy Goetzinger	257	Tomas Holmstrom
19	Jakub Kindl	291	Jonathan Ericsson	226	David Petrasek	283	Toivo Suursoo
42	Justin Abdelkader			256	Petja Pietilainen		
80	Christofer Lofberg	**2001 Pick**				**1993 Pick**	
103	Mattias Ritola	62	Igor Grigorenko	**1997 Pick**		22	Anders Eriksson
132	Darren Helm	121	Drew MacIntyre	49	Yuri Butsayev	48	Jon Coleman
137	Johan Ryno	129	Miroslav Blatak	76	Petr Sykora	74	Kevin Hilton
151	Jeff May	157	Andreas Jamtin	102	Quintin Laing	97	John Jakopin
175	Juho Mielonen	195	Nick Pannoni	129	John Wikstrom	100	Benoit Larose
214	Bretton Stamler	258	Dmitri Bykov	157	B.J. Young	126	Norm Maracle
		288	Francois Senez	186	Mike Laceby	152	Tim Spitzig
2004 Pick				213	Steve Willejto	178	Yuri Yeresko
97	Johan Franzen	**2000 Pick**		239	Greg Willers	204	Vitezslav Skuta
128	Evan McGrath	29	Niklas Kronwall			230	Ryan Shanahan
151	Sergei Kolesov	38	Tomas Kopecky	**1996 Pick**		256	James Kosecki
162	Tyler Haskins	102	Stefan Liv	26	Jesse Wallin	282	Gordon Hunt
192	Anton Axelsson	127	Dmitri Semenov	52	Aren Miller		
226	Steven Covington	128	Alexander Seluyanov	108	Johan Forsander	**1992 Pick**	
257	Gennady Stolyarov	130	Aaron Van Leusen	135	Michal Podolka	22	Curtis Bowen
290	Nils Backstrom	187	Per Backer	144	Magnus Nilsson	46	Darren McCarty
		196	Paul Ballantyne	162	Alexandre Jacques	70	Sylvain Cloutier
2003 Pick		228	Jimmie Svensson	189	Colin Beardsmore	118	Mike Sullivan
64	James Howard	251	Todd Jackson	215	Craig Stahl	142	Jason MacDonald
132	Kyle Quincey	260	Yevgeny Bumagin	241	Eugeny Afanasiev	166	Greg Scott
164	Ryan Oulahen					183	Justin Krall
170	Andreas Sundin	**1999 Pick**		**1995 Pick**		189	C. J. Denomme
194	Stefan Blom	120	Jari Tolsa	26	Maxim Kuznetsov	214	Jeff Walker
226	Tomas Kollar	149	Andrei Maximenko	52	Philippe Audet	238	Dan McGillis
258	Vladimir Kutny	181	Kent McDonell	58	Darryl Laplante	262	Ryan Bach
289	Mikael Johansson	210	Henrik Zetterberg	104	Anatoli Ustyugov		
		238	Anton Borodkin	125	Chad Wilchynski		
		266	Ken Davis	126	David Arsenault		
				156	Tyler Perry		
				182	Per Eklund		
				208	Andrei Samokhvalov		
				234	David Engblom		

Club Directory

Joe Louis Arena

Detroit Red Wings
Joe Louis Arena
600 Civic Center Drive
Detroit, MI 48226
Phone **313/396-7535**
FAX PR: 313/567-0296
Media Hotline: 313/396-7599
www.detroitredwings.com
Capacity: 20,066

Owner/Governor	Mike Ilitch
Owner/Secretary-Treasurer	Marian Ilitch
President & CEO Ilitch Holdings/ Alternate Governor Red Wings	Christopher Ilitch
Vice-President Olympia Entertainment/ General Counsel Red Wings	Robert E. Carr
Senior Vice President	Jim Devellano
General Manager	Ken Holland
Assistant General Manager	Jim Nill
Head Coach	Mike Babcock
Assistant Coaches	Paul MacLean, Todd McLellan
Video Coach	Jay Woodcroft
Director of Hockey Administration	Ryan Martin
Consultant	Scotty Bowman
Amateur Scouts	Joe McDonnell, Bruce Haralson, David Kolb, Mark Leach
Minor League Scout	Glenn Merkosky
Part-Time Scout	Marty Stein
Director of European Scouting	Hakan Andersson
European Scout	Vladimir Havluj
Part-Time European Scout	Evgeni Erfilov
Vice-President of Finance	Paul MacDonald
Executive Assistant	Kathi Wyatt
Accounting Assistant	Bridget Merritt
Athletic Therapist	Piet Van Zant
Equipment Manager	Paul Boyer
Assistant Equipment Manager	Chris Scoppetto
Team Masseur	Sergei Tchekmarev
Senior Director of Communications	John Hahn
Media Relations Manager	Mike Brinich
Community Relations Manager	Anne Marie Krappmann
Medical Director	Dr. Donald Weaver
Team Physicians	Dr. Anthony Colucci, Dr. Doug Plagens
Team Dentist	Dr. C.J. Regula
Team Photographer	Dave Reginek
Radio Broadcasters, AM 1270 The Sports Station, WXYT	Ken Kal, Paul Woods
Television Broadcasters, Fox Sports Net – Detroit	Ken Daniels, Mickey Redmond

Coaching History

Art Duncan, 1926-27; Jack Adams, 1927-28 to 1946-47; Tommy Ivan, 1947-48 to 1953-54; Jimmy Skinner, 1954-55 to 1956-57; Jimmy Skinner and Sid Abel, 1957-58; Sid Abel, 1958-59 to 1967-68; Bill Gadsby, 1968-69; Bill Gadsby and Sid Abel, 1969-70; Ned Harkness and Doug Barkley; 1970-71; Doug Barkley and Johnny Wilson, 1971-72; Johnny Wilson, 1972-73; Ted Garvin and Alex Delvecchio, 1973-74; Alex Delvecchio, 1974-75; Doug Barkley and Alex Delvecchio, 1975-76; Alex Delvecchio and Larry Wilson, 1976-77; Bobby Kromm, 1977-78, 1978-79; Bobby Kromm and Ted Lindsay, 1979-80; Ted Lindsay and Wayne Maxner, 1980-81; Wayne Maxner and Billy Dea, 1981-82; Nick Polano, 1982-83 to 1984-85; Harry Neale and Brad Park, 1985-86; Jacques Demers, 1986-87 to 1989-90; Bryan Murray, 1990-91 to 1992-93; Scotty Bowman, 1993-94 to 1997-98; Dave Lewis, Barry Smith (co-coaches) and Scotty Bowman, 1998-99; Scotty Bowman, 1999-2000 to 2001-02; Dave Lewis, 2002-03, 2003-04; Mike Babcock, 2005-06 to date.

General Managers' History

Art Duncan and Duke Keats, 1926-27; Jack Adams, 1927-28 to 1961-62; Sid Abel, 1962-63 to 1969-70; Sid Abel and Ned Harkness, 1970-71; Ned Harkness, 1971-72 to 1973-74; Alex Delvecchio, 1974-75, 1975-76; Alex Delvecchio and Ted Lindsay, 1976-77; Ted Lindsay, 1977-78 to 1979-80; Jimmy Skinner, 1980-81; Jim Devellano, 1982-83 to 1989-90; Bryan Murray, 1990-91 to 1993-94; Jim Devellano (Senior Vice President), 1994-95 to 1996-97; Ken Holland, 1997-98 to date.

Captains' History

Art Duncan, 1926-27; Reg Noble, 1927-28 to 1929-30; George Hay, 1930-31; Carson Cooper, 1931-32; Larry Aurie, 1932-33; Herbie Lewis, 1933-34; Ebbie Goodfellow, 1934-35; Doug Young, 1935-36 to 1937-38; Ebbie Goodfellow, 1938-39 to 1940-41; Ebbie Goodfellow and Syd Howe, 1941-42; Sid Abel, 1942-43; Mud Bruneteau, Flash Hollett (co-captains), 1943-44; Flash Hollett, 1944-45; Flash Hollett and Sid Abel, 1945-46; Sid Abel, 1946-47 to 1951-52; Ted Lindsay, 1952-53 to 1955-56; Red Kelly, 1956-57, 1957-58; Gordie Howe, 1958-59 to 1961-62; Alex Delvecchio, 1962-63 to 1972-73; Alex Delvecchio, Nick Libett, Red Berenson, Gary Bergman, Ted Harris, Mickey Redmond and Larry Johnston, 1973-74; Marcel Dionne, 1974-75; Danny Grant and Terry Harper, 1975-76; Danny Grant and Dennis Polonich, 1976-77; Dan Maloney and Dennis Hextall, 1977-78; Dennis Hextall, Nick Libett and Paul Woods, 1978-79; Dale McCourt, 1979-80; Errol Thompson and Reed Larson, 1980-81; Reed Larson, 1981-82; Danny Gare, 1982-83 to 1985-86; Steve Yzerman, 1986-87 to 2005-06.

General Manager

HOLLAND, KEN
General Manager, Detroit Red Wings. Born in Vernon, B.C., Nov. 10, 1955.

Ken Holland has served in the Red Wings front office since 1985, and has been the club's general manager since July 18, 1997. He has established himself as one of the most innovative and aggressive GMs in the National Hockey League. Detroit's Stanley Cup victory in 2002 marked the team's second championship under his leadership. Holland began his tenure as the club's general manager after serving as assistant general manager for the previous three seasons.

Holland oversees all aspects of hockey operations including all matters relating to player personnel, development, contract negotiations and player movements. He also continues to be Detroit's point person at the NHL Entry Draft, as he has been for the past 13 years.

Holland has deftly handled several different front-office duties for the club over the past 20 years. At the conclusion of his playing days as a goaltender, spending most of his pro career at the American Hockey League level, Holland began his off-ice career in 1985 as a western Canada scout followed by five years as an amateur scouting director before promotions led to his current position as general manager.

A native of Vernon, BC, Holland played in the junior ranks for Medicine Hat (WHL) in 1974-75. He was Toronto's 13th pick (188th overall) in the 1975 draft but never saw action with the Maple Leafs. Holland twice signed with NHL teams as a free agent — in 1980 with Hartford and 1983 with Detroit. He spent most of his pro career with AHL clubs in Binghamton and Springfield, along with Adirondack, but did appear in four NHL games, making his debut with Hartford in 1980-81 and playing three contests for Detroit in 1983-84.

Edmonton Oilers

2005-06 Results: 41W-28L-4OTL-9SOL 95PTS.
Third, Northwest Division

2006-07 Schedule

Oct.	Thu.	5	Calgary
	Sat.	7	at Calgary
	Thu.	12	San Jose
	Sat.	14	at Colorado
	Mon.	16	at Vancouver
	Tue.	17	Vancouver
	Sat.	21	Detroit
	Mon.	23	Phoenix
	Wed.	25	at Anaheim
	Thu.	26	at Phoenix
	Sat.	28	Washington
Nov.	Wed.	1	Nashville
	Fri.	3	Dallas
	Tue.	7	at Montreal
	Wed.	8	at Detroit
	Fri.	10	at Columbus
	Sun.	12	at St. Louis*
	Mon.	13	at Colorado
	Thu.	16	St. Louis
	Sat.	18	Detroit
	Tue.	21	Calgary
	Fri.	24	Chicago
	Tue.	28	Anaheim
	Thu.	30	Colorado
Dec.	Sat.	2	Columbus
	Mon.	4	at Vancouver
	Wed.	6	Carolina
	Fri.	8	at Dallas
	Sun.	10	at Chicago
	Tue.	12	at Nashville
	Thu.	14	Minnesota
	Fri.	15	at Colorado
	Tue.	19	Colorado
	Thu.	21	at Phoenix
	Sat.	23	at Dallas
	Thu.	28	Los Angeles
	Sat.	30	Vancouver
	Sun.	31	at Calgary
Jan.	Tue.	2	Florida
	Thu.	4	Dallas
	Fri.	5	at Vancouver

	Mon.	8	at Los Angeles
	Wed.	10	at San Jose
	Fri.	12	Minnesota
	Sat.	13	at Calgary
	Tue.	16	at Minnesota
	Thu.	18	Anaheim
	Sat.	20	Calgary
	Fri.	26	San Jose
	Sat.	27	Los Angeles
	Wed.	31	Columbus
Feb.	Thu.	1	at Vancouver
	Sat.	3	at Colorado*
	Tue.	6	Vancouver
	Fri.	9	Chicago
	Sun.	11	Atlanta
	Tue.	13	at Boston
	Thu.	15	at Buffalo
	Sat.	17	at Toronto
	Tue.	20	at Ottawa
	Thu.	22	at Columbus
	Fri.	23	at Detroit
	Sun.	25	at Minnesota*
	Tue.	27	Phoenix
Mar.	Thu.	1	Minnesota
	Sat.	3	Calgary
	Wed.	7	Tampa Bay
	Fri.	9	at Anaheim
	Sun.	11	at San Jose*
	Mon.	12	at Los Angeles
	Thu.	15	Minnesota
	Sat.	17	St. Louis
	Mon.	19	Vancouver
	Wed.	21	Colorado
	Fri.	23	Colorado
	Sat.	24	Nashville
	Tue.	27	at Nashville
	Thu.	29	at St. Louis
Apr.	Sun.	1	at Chicago*
	Tue.	3	at Minnesota
	Thu.	5	at Minnesota
	Sat.	7	at Calgary

Denotes afternoon game.

Franchise date: June 22, 1979

NORTHWEST DIVISION

28th NHL Season

Year-by-Year Record

Season	GP	Home W	L	T	OL	Road W	L	T	OL	Overall W	L	T	OL	GF	GA	Pts.	Finished	Playoff Result
2005-06	82	20	15	....	6	21	13	....	7	41	28	....	13	256	251	95	3rd, Northwest Div.	Lost Final
2004-05	....	....				....				....								
2003-04	82	22	12	4	3	14	17	8	2	36	29	12	5	221	208	89	4th, Northwest Div.	Out of Playoffs
2002-03	82	20	12*	5	4	16	14	6	5	36	26	11	9	231	230	92	4th, Northwest Div.	Lost Conf. Quarter-Final
2001-02	82	23	14	4	0	15	14	8	4	38	28	12	4	205	182	92	3rd, Northwest Div.	Out of Playoffs
2000-01	82	23	9	7	2	16	19	5	1	39	28	12	3	243	222	93	2nd, Northwest Div.	Lost Conf. Quarter-Final
1999-2000	82	18	11	9	3	14	15	7	5	32	26	16	8	226	212	88	2nd, Northwest Div.	Lost Conf. Quarter-Final
1998-99	82	17	19	5	....	16	18	7	....	33	37	12	....	230	226	78	2nd, Northwest Div.	Lost Conf. Quarter-Final
1997-98	82	20	16	5	....	15	21	5	....	35	37	10	....	215	224	80	3rd, Pacific Div.	Lost Conf. Semi-Final
1996-97	82	21	16	4	....	15	21	5	....	36	37	9	....	252	247	81	3rd, Pacific Div.	Lost Conf. Semi-Final
1995-96	82	15	21	5	....	15	23	3	....	30	44	8	....	240	304	68	5th, Pacific Div.	Out of Playoffs
1994-95	48	11	12	1	....	6	15	3	....	17	27	4	....	136	183	38	5th, Pacific Div.	Out of Playoffs
1993-94	84	17	22	3	....	8	23	11	....	25	45	14	....	261	305	64	6th, Pacific Div.	Out of Playoffs
1992-93	84	16	21	5	....	10	29	3	....	26	50	8	....	242	337	60	5th, Smythe Div.	Out of Playoffs
1991-92	80	22	13	5	....	14	21	5	....	36	34	10	....	295	297	82	3rd, Smythe Div.	Lost Conf. Championship
1990-91	80	22	15	3	....	15	22	3	....	37	37	6	....	272	272	80	3rd, Smythe Div.	Lost Conf. Championship
1989-90	**80**	**23**	**11**	**6**	....	**15**	**17**	**8**	....	**38**	**28**	**14**	....	**315**	**283**	**90**	**2nd, Smythe Div.**	**Won Stanley Cup**
1988-89	80	21	16	3	....	17	18	5	....	38	34	8	....	325	306	84	3rd, Smythe Div.	Lost Div. Semi-Final
1987-88	**80**	**28**	**8**	**4**	....	**16**	**17**	**7**	....	**44**	**25**	**11**	....	**363**	**288**	**99**	**2nd, Smythe Div.**	**Won Stanley Cup**
1986-87	**80**	**29**	**6**	**5**	....	**21**	**18**	**1**	....	**50**	**24**	**6**	....	**372**	**284**	**106**	**1st, Smythe Div.**	**Won Stanley Cup**
1985-86	80	32	6	2	....	24	11	5	....	56	17	7	....	426	310	119	1st, Smythe Div.	Lost Div. Final
1984-85	**80**	**26**	**7**	**7**	....	**23**	**13**	**4**	....	**49**	**20**	**11**	....	**401**	**298**	**109**	**1st, Smythe Div.**	**Won Stanley Cup**
1983-84	**80**	**31**	**5**	**4**	....	**26**	**13**	**1**	....	**57**	**18**	**5**	....	**446**	**314**	**119**	**1st, Smythe Div.**	**Won Stanley Cup**
1982-83	80	25	9	6	....	22	12	6	....	47	21	12	....	424	315	106	1st, Smythe Div.	Lost Final
1981-82	80	31	5	4	....	17	12	11	....	48	17	15	....	417	295	111	1st, Smythe Div.	Lost Div. Semi-Final
1980-81	80	17	13	10	....	12	22	6	....	29	35	16	....	328	327	74	4th, Smythe Div.	Lost Quarter-Final
1979-80	80	17	14	9	....	11	25	4	....	28	39	13	....	301	322	69	4th, Smythe Div.	Lost Prelim. Round

Shawn Horcoff (left), Ryan Smyth (center) and Fernando Pisani (right) were key contributors to the Oilers' success in 2005-06. Smyth led the team with 36 goals in the regular season. Pisani topped all postseason performers with 14 playoff goals.

2006-07 Player Personnel

FORWARDS

	HT	WT	S	Place of Birth	Date	2005-06 Club
ALMTORP, Jonas	6-1	190	L	Uppsala, Sweden	11/17/83	Brynas
BODIE, Troy	6-4	213	R	Portage La Prairie, Man.	1/25/85	Kelowna
BRODZIAK, Kyle	6-2	198	R	St. Paul, Alta.	5/25/84	Edmonton-Iowa
GOULET, Stephane	6-3	185	L	Levis, Que.	1/7/86	Moncton
HEMSKY, Ales	6-0	192	R	Pardubice, Czech.	8/13/83	Edmonton
HORCOFF, Shawn	6-1	204	L	Trail, B.C.	9/17/78	Edmonton
JACQUES, Jean-Francois	6-4	217	L	Montreal, Que.	4/29/85	Edmonton-Hamilton
JOHANSSON, Fredrik	5-11	183	L	Goteburg, Sweden	2/27/84	Vasteras
LUPUL, Joffrey	6-1	205	R	Fort Saskatchewan, Alta.	9/23/83	Anaheim
MOREAU, Ethan	6-2	220	L	Huntsville, Ont.	9/22/75	Edmonton
PETERSEN, Toby	5-10	197	L	Minneapolis, MN	10/27/78	Edmonton-Iowa
PISANI, Fernando	6-1	205	L	Edmonton, Alta.	12/27/76	Edmonton
POULIOT, Marc-Antoine	6-1	195	R	Quebec City, Que.	5/22/85	Edmonton-Hamilton
RADUNSKE, Brock	6-4	196	L	Kitchener, Ont.	4/5/83	Greenville
REASONER, Marty	6-1	200	L	Honeoye Falls, NY	2/26/77	Edmonton-Boston
REDDOX, Liam	5-9	179	L	East York, Ont.	1/27/86	Peterborough
SCHREMP, Rob	5-11	200	L	Syracuse, NY	7/1/86	London
SMYTH, Ryan	6-1	190	L	Banff, Alta.	2/21/76	Edmonton
SPURGEON, Tyler	5-11	188	L	Edmonton, Alta.	4/10/86	Kelowna
STOLL, Jarret	6-1	201	R	Melville, Sask.	6/25/82	Edmonton
STORTINI, Zachery	6-3	216	R	Elliot Lake, Ont.	9/11/85	Iowa-Milwaukee
SYKORA, Petr	6-0	190	L	Plzen, Czech.	11/19/76	Anaheim-NY Rangers
THORESEN, Patrick	5-10	185	L	Hamar, Norway	11/7/83	Djurgarden-Salzburg
TORRES, Raffi	6-0	216	L	Toronto, Ont.	10/8/81	Edmonton
WINCHESTER, Brad	6-5	215	L	Madison, WI	3/1/81	Edmonton-Hamilton

DEFENSEMEN

	HT	WT	S	Place of Birth	Date	2005-06 Club
BERGERON, Marc-Andre	5-10	197	L	St-Louis-de-France, Que.	10/13/80	Edmonton
GILBERT, Tom	6-2	190	R	Minneapolis, MN	1/10/83	U. of Wisconsin
GREENE, Matt	6-3	223	R	Grand Ledge, MI	5/13/83	Edmonton-Iowa
HEJDA, Jan	6-3	209	L	Prague, Czech.	6/18/78	Mytischi
ROY, Mathieu	6-2	214	R	St-Georges, Que.	8/10/83	Edmonton-Hamilton
SMID, Ladislav	6-3	204	L	Frydlant V Cechach, Czech.	2/1/86	Portland (AHL)
SMITH, Jason	6-3	215	R	Calgary, Alta.	11/2/73	Edmonton
STAIOS, Steve	6-1	200	R	Hamilton, Ont.	7/28/73	Edmonton
SYVRET, Danny	5-11	203	L	Millgrove, Ont.	6/13/85	Edmonton-Hamilton
TJARNQVIST, Daniel	6-2	200	L	Umea, Sweden	10/14/76	Minnesota
YOUNG, Bryan	6-1	191	L	Kitchener, Ont.	8/6/86	Peterborough

GOALTENDERS

	HT	WT	C	Place of Birth	Date	2005-06 Club
DROUIN-DESLAURIERS, Jeff	6-4	189	R	St-Jean-Richelieu, Que.	5/15/84	Hamilton-Greenville
DUBNYK, Devan	6-5	194	L	Regina, Sask.	5/4/86	Kamloops
MARKKANEN, Jussi	6-0	182	L	Imatra, Finland	5/8/75	Edmonton
ROLOSON, Dwayne	6-1	178	L	Simcoe, Ont.	10/12/69	Minnesota-Edmonton

Coaching History

Glen Sather, 1979-80; Bryan Watson and Glen Sather, 1980-81; Glen Sather, 1981-82 to 1988-89; John Muckler, 1989-90, 1990-91; Ted Green, 1991-92, 1992-93; Ted Green and Glen Sather, 1993-94; George Burnett and Ron Low, 1994-95; Ron Low, 1995-96 to 1998-99; Kevin Lowe, 1999-2000; Craig MacTavish, 2000-01 to date.

Coach

MacTAVISH, CRAIG
Coach, Edmonton Oilers. Born in London, Ont., August 15, 1958.

The Edmonton Oilers named Craig MacTavish as their head coach on June 22, 2000. He became the eighth person in the club's NHL history to hold the position. MacTavish joined Kevin Lowe and Glen Sather as head coaches who were former captains of the Oilers. In 2006, he led the Oilers to game seven of the Stanley Cup Final.

MacTavish played for 18 seasons in the NHL, including eight-and-three-quarter campaigns with the Oilers. He was instrumental in helping his teams win four Stanley Cup titles; three with Edmonton and one with the New York Rangers. Although he was the last player in the NHL to play without a helmet, MacTavish was known for his aggressive style, combined with above average skills.

MacTavish retired as a player in 1997 and was immediately named an assistant coach with the New York Rangers. He was with the Rangers for two seasons prior to joining the Oilers' coaching staff as an assistant under Kevin Lowe in 1999-2000. He also served as an assistant coach for Team Canada at the 2005 World Championship.

Coaching Record

Season	Team	Games	Regular Season W	L	O/T	Games	Playoffs W	L
2000-01	Edmonton (NHL)	82	39	31	12	6	2	4
2001-02	Edmonton (NHL)	82	38	32	12	....	....	....
2002-03	Edmonton (NHL)	82	36	35	11	6	2	4
2003-04	Edmonton (NHL)	82	36	34	12	....	....	....
2004-05	Edmonton (NHL)				Season Cancelled			
2005-06	Edmonton (NHL)	82	41	28	13	24	15	9
	NHL Totals	410	190	160	60	36	19	17

2005-06 Scoring

* – rookie

Regular Season

Pos	#	Player	Team	GP	G	A	Pts	+/-	PIM	PP	SH	GW	S	%
R	83	Ales Hemsky	EDM	81	19	58	77	−5	64	7	1	4	178	10.7
C	10	Shawn Horcoff	EDM	79	22	51	73	0	85	3	3	5	167	13.2
C	16	Jarret Stoll	EDM	82	22	46	68	4	74	11	1	4	243	9.1
L	94	Ryan Smyth	EDM	75	36	30	66	−5	58	19	2	3	230	15.7
D	44	Chris Pronger	EDM	80	12	44	56	2	74	10	0	3	155	7.7
L	12	Sergei Samsonov	BOS	55	18	19	37	−3	22	6	0	1	107	16.8
			EDM	19	5	11	16	0	6	4	0	0	36	13.9
			TOTAL	74	23	30	53	−3	28	10	0	1	143	16.1
D	6	Jaroslav Spacek	CHI	45	7	17	24	8	72	1	0	0	80	8.8
			EDM	31	5	14	19	3	24	3	0	0	70	7.1
			TOTAL	76	12	31	43	11	96	4	0	0	150	8.0
L	14	Raffi Torres	EDM	82	27	14	41	4	50	6	0	3	164	16.5
R	34	Fernando Pisani	EDM	80	18	19	37	5	42	4	1	2	131	13.7
D	47	Marc-Andre Bergeron	EDM	75	15	20	35	3	38	8	0	1	144	10.4
R	20	Radek Dvorak	EDM	64	8	20	28	−2	26	2	0	1	131	6.1
D	24	Steve Staios	EDM	82	8	20	28	10	84	1	0	1	140	5.7
L	18	Ethan Moreau	EDM	74	11	16	27	6	87	2	4	4	151	7.3
C	37	Michael Peca	EDM	71	9	14	23	−4	56	2	2	1	108	8.3
C	21	Jason Smith	EDM	76	4	13	17	1	84	0	0	0	79	5.1
D	23	Dick Tarnstrom	PIT	33	5	5	10	−10	52	4	0	0	40	12.5
			EDM	22	1	3	4	−5	24	0	0	0	20	5.0
			TOTAL	55	6	8	14	−15	76	4	0	0	60	10.0
R	27	Georges Laraque	EDM	72	2	10	12	−5	73	0	0	0	50	4.0
D	55	Igor Ulanov	EDM	37	3	6	9	−11	29	1	0	0	29	10.3
L	13	Todd Harvey	EDM	63	5	2	7	−7	32	0	0	0	45	11.1
C	12	Krys Kolanos	PHX	9	2	1	3	2	2	1	0	0	15	13.3
			EDM	6	0	0	0	−1	2	0	0	0	7	0.0
			TOTAL	15	2	1	3	1	4	1	0	0	22	9.1
C	22	Rem Murray	EDM	9	1	1	2	1	2	0	0	0	6	16.7
D	2 *	Matt Greene	EDM	27	0	2	2	−6	43	0	0	0	10	0.0
C	36 *	Marc-Antoine Pouliot	EDM	8	1	0	1	1	6	1	0	0	5	20.0
L	26 *	Brad Winchester	EDM	19	0	1	1	−2	21	0	0	0	19	0.0
D	12 *	Mathieu Roy	EDM	1	0	0	0	−1	0	0	0	0	1	0.0
D	6	Dan Smith	EDM	1	0	0	0	1	7	0	0	0	1	0.0
L	41 *	Jean-Francois Jacques	EDM	7	0	0	0	−3	0	0	0	0	8	0.0
L	15 *	Kyle Brodziak	EDM	10	0	0	0	−4	4	0	0	0	7	0.0
D	28 *	Danny Syvret	EDM	10	0	0	0	1	6	0	0	0	8	0.0

Goaltending

No.	Goaltender	GPI	Mins	Avg	W	L	OT	EN	SO	GA	SA	S%	G	A	PIM
35	Dwayne Roloson	19	1163	2.42	8	7	4	1	1	47	497	.905	0	1	2
29	Ty Conklin	18	922	2.80	8	5	1	1	0	43	359	.880	0	0	2
30	Michael Morrison	21	892	2.83	10	4	2	0	0	42	361	.884	0	0	2
30	Jussi Markkanen	37	2016	3.13	15	12	6	1	0	105	873	.880	0	1	0
	Totals	82	5027	2.89	41	28	13	5	2	242	2095	.884			

Playoffs

Pos	#	Player	Team	GP	G	A	Pts	+/-	PIM	PP	SH	GW	OT	S	%
D	44	Chris Pronger	EDM	24	5	16	21	10	26	3	0	0	0	61	8.2
C	10	Shawn Horcoff	EDM	24	7	12	19	4	12	1	1	2	1	41	17.1
R	34	Fernando Pisani	EDM	24	14	4	18	4	10	3	1	5	1	49	28.6
R	83	Ales Hemsky	EDM	24	6	11	17	−3	14	4	0	2	0	47	12.8
L	94	Ryan Smyth	EDM	24	7	9	16	−2	22	4	0	1	0	60	11.7
L	12	Sergei Samsonov	EDM	24	4	11	15	2	14	1	0	0	0	40	10.0
D	6	Jaroslav Spacek	EDM	24	3	11	14	−3	24	2	0	0	0	43	7.0
C	37	Michael Peca	EDM	24	6	5	11	5	20	0	1	1	0	43	14.0
L	14	Raffi Torres	EDM	22	4	7	11	5	20	1	0	1	0	42	9.5
C	16	Jarret Stoll	EDM	24	4	6	10	−4	24	2	0	1	1	49	8.2
D	24	Steve Staios	EDM	24	1	5	6	0	28	0	0	0	0	28	3.6
D	21	Jason Smith	EDM	24	1	4	5	5	16	0	0	1	0	14	7.1
C	22	Rem Murray	EDM	24	0	4	4	1	0	0	0	0	0	14	0.0
D	47	Marc-Andre Bergeron	EDM	18	2	1	3	0	14	2	0	0	0	17	11.8
L	18	Ethan Moreau	EDM	21	2	1	3	0	40	0	0	0	0	40	5.0
L	26 *	Brad Winchester	EDM	12	1	2	3	−2	4	0	0	0	0	9	11.1
L	13	Todd Harvey	EDM	16	1	1	2	2	6	0	0	0	0	6	16.7
R	27	Georges Laraque	EDM	15	1	1	2	2	4	0	0	0	0	6	16.7
D	23	Dick Tarnstrom	EDM	12	0	2	2	1	10	0	0	0	0	7	0.0
R	20	Radek Dvorak	EDM	16	0	2	2	−1	4	0	0	0	0	32	0.0
C	45	Toby Petersen	EDM	2	1	0	1	1	0	0	0	0	0	3	33.3
D	2 *	Matt Greene	EDM	18	0	1	1	0	34	0	0	0	0	4	0.0

Goaltending

No.	Goaltender	GPI	Mins	Avg	W	L	EN	SO	GA	SA	S%	G	A	PIM
30	Jussi Markkanen	6	360	2.17	3	3	1	1	13	137	.905	0	0	0
35	Dwayne Roloson	18	1160	2.33	12	5	1	1	45	618	.927	0	2	14
29	Ty Conklin	1	6	10.00	0	1	0	0	1	3	.667	0	0	0
	Totals	24	1537	2.38	15	9	2	2	61	760	.920			

Club Records

Team

(Figures in brackets for season records are games played; records for fewest points, wins, ties, losses, goals, goals against are for 70 or more games)

Record		Season(s)
Most Points	119	1983-84 (80), 1985-86 (80)
Most Wins	57	1983-84 (80)
Most Ties	16	1980-81 (80), 1999-2000 (82)
Most Losses	50	1992-93 (84)
Most Goals	*446	1983-84 (80)
Most Goals Against	337	1992-93 (84)
Fewest Points	60	1992-93 (84)
Fewest Wins	25	1993-94 (84)
Fewest Ties	5	1983-84 (80)
Fewest Losses	17	1981-82 (80), 1985-86 (80)
Fewest Goals	205	2001-02 (82)
Fewest Goals Against	182	2001-02 (82)
Longest Winning Streak		
Overall	9	Feb. 20-Mar. 13/01
Home	8	Jan. 19-Feb. 22/85, Feb. 24-Apr. 2/86
Away	8	Dec. 9/86-Jan. 17/87
Longest Undefeated Streak		
Overall	15	Oct. 11-Nov. 9/84 (12 wins, 3 ties)
Home	14	Nov. 15/89-Jan. 6/90 (11 wins, 3 ties)
Away	9	Jan. 17-Mar. 2/82 (6 wins, 3 ties), Nov. 23/82-Jan. 18/83 (7 wins, 2 ties)
Longest Losing Streak		
Overall	11	Oct. 16-Nov. 7/93
Home	9	Oct. 16-Nov. 24/93
Away	9	Nov. 25-Dec. 30/80
Longest Winless Streak		
Overall	14	Oct. 11-Nov. 7/93 (13 losses, 1 tie)
Home	9	Oct. 16-Nov. 24/93 (9 losses)
Away	11	Dec. 18/01-Feb. 8/02 (7 losses, 4 ties)
Most Shutouts, Season	8	1997-98 (82); 2000-01 (82); 2001-02 (82)
Most PIM, Season	2,173	1987-88 (80)
Most Goals, Game	13	Nov. 19/83 (N.J. 4 at Edm. 13), Nov. 8/85 (Van. 0 at Edm. 13)

Individual

Record		Player
Most Seasons	15	Kevin Lowe
Most Games	1,037	Kevin Lowe
Most Goals, Career	583	Wayne Gretzky
Most Assists, Career	1,086	Wayne Gretzky
Most Points, Career	1,669	Wayne Gretzky (583G, 1,086A)
Most PIM, Career	1,747	Kelly Buchberger
Most Shutouts, Career	23	Tommy Salo
Longest Consecutive Games Streak	519	Craig MacTavish (Oct. 11/86-Jan. 2/93)
Most Goals, Season	*92	Wayne Gretzky (1981-82)
Most Assists, Season	*163	Wayne Gretzky (1985-86)
Most Points, Season	*215	Wayne Gretzky (1985-86; 52G, 163A)
Most PIM, Season	286	Steve Smith (1987-88)
Most Points, Defenseman, Season	138	Paul Coffey (1985-86; 48G, 90A)
Most Points, Center, Season	*215	Wayne Gretzky (1985-86; 52G, 163A)
Most Points, Right Wing, Season	135	Jari Kurri (1984-85; 71G, 64A)
Most Points, Left Wing, Season	106	Mark Messier (1982-83; 48G, 58A)
Most Points, Rookie, Season	75	Jari Kurri (1980-81; 32G, 43A)
Most Shutouts, Season	8	Curtis Joseph (1997-98), Tommy Salo (2000-01)
Most Goals, Game	5	Wayne Gretzky (Feb. 18/81, Dec. 30/81, Dec. 15/84, Dec. 6/87), Jari Kurri (Nov. 19/83), Pat Hughes (Feb. 3/84)
Most Assists, Game	*7	Wayne Gretzky (Feb. 15/80, Dec. 11/85, Feb. 14/86)
Most Points, Game	8	Wayne Gretzky (Nov. 19/83; 3G, 5A), (Jan. 4/84; 4G, 4A), Paul Coffey (Mar. 14/86; 2G, 6A)

* NHL Record.

Captains' History

Ron Chipperfield, 1979-80; Blair MacDonald and Lee Fogolin, Jr., 1980-81; Lee Fogolin, Jr., 1981-82, 1982-83; Wayne Gretzky, 1983-84 to 1987-88; Mark Messier, 1988-89 to 1990-91; Kevin Lowe, 1991-92; Craig MacTavish, 1992-93, 1993-94; Shayne Corson, 1994-95; Kelly Buchberger, 1995-96 to 1998-99; Doug Weight, 1999-2000, 2000-01; Jason Smith, 2001-02 to date.

Retired Numbers

3	Al Hamilton	1972-1980
17	Jari Kurri	1980-1990
31	Grant Fuhr	1981-1991
77	Paul Coffey	1980-1987
99	Wayne Gretzky	1979-1988

All-time Record vs. Other Clubs

Regular Season

	At Home								On Road								Total							
	GP	W	L	T	OL	GF	GA	PTS	GP	W	L	T	OL	GF	GA	PTS	GP	W	L	T	OL	GF	GA	PTS
Anaheim	27	19	8	0	0	65	56	38	28	11	15	2	0	74	76	24	55	30	23	2	0	139	132	62
Atlanta	4	2	1	1	0	14	11	5	3	2	1	0	0	8	3	4	7	4	2	1	0	22	14	9
Boston	30	11	15	3	1	102	102	26	30	6	20	3	1	80	126	16	60	17	35	6	2	182	228	42
Buffalo	30	21	6	3	0	121	77	45	30	13	10	7	0	112	109	33	60	34	16	10	0	233	186	78
Calgary	85	44	30	10	1	316	278	99	85	30	46	9	0	283	337	69	170	74	76	19	1	599	615	168
Carolina	31	19	7	5	0	121	92	43	29	11	11	7	0	98	112	29	60	30	18	12	0	219	204	72
Chicago	47	23	19	5	0	173	151	51	46	17	22	7	0	157	173	41	93	40	41	12	0	330	324	92
Colorado	50	27	18	4	1	197	152	59	51	21	26	4	0	183	194	46	101	48	44	8	1	380	346	105
Columbus	10	8	1	0	1	37	20	17	10	5	1	3	1	33	25	14	20	13	2	3	2	70	45	31
Dallas	46	21	14	8	3	181	152	53	47	15	24	7	1	131	170	38	93	36	38	15	4	312	322	91
Detroit	46	21	14	10	1	177	164	53	46	17	24	3	2	150	177	39	92	38	38	13	3	327	341	92
Florida	7	4	2	1	0	24	16	9	9	2	5	2	0	24	24	6	16	6	7	3	0	48	40	15
Los Angeles	79	41	23	15	0	356	278	97	79	35	28	15	1	324	304	86	158	76	51	30	1	680	582	183
Minnesota	15	6	5	3	1	32	31	16	14	9	2	1	2	39	32	21	29	15	7	4	3	71	63	37
Montreal	36	19	17	0	0	122	116	38	30	10	16	4	0	95	105	24	66	29	33	4	0	217	221	62
Nashville	14	8	4	0	2	43	38	18	15	7	5	3	0	44	36	17	29	15	9	3	2	87	74	35
New Jersey	31	14	10	6	1	136	114	35	34	16	13	3	2	113	113	37	65	30	23	9	3	249	227	72
NY Islanders	29	16	8	5	0	107	87	37	32	7	15	9	1	112	131	24	61	23	23	14	1	219	218	61
NY Rangers	28	12	13	3	0	101	94	27	31	14	9	6	2	117	117	36	59	26	22	9	2	218	211	63
Ottawa	12	7	3	2	0	42	30	16	10	5	3	2	0	26	19	12	22	12	6	4	0	68	49	28
Philadelphia	28	14	8	6	0	98	83	34	32	10	20	2	0	88	130	22	60	24	28	8	0	186	213	56
Phoenix	74	47	20	6	1	323	239	101	73	38	26	5	4	321	291	85	147	85	46	11	5	644	530	186
Pittsburgh	30	22	7	1	0	148	98	45	31	13	14	3	1	130	118	30	61	35	21	4	1	278	216	75
St. Louis	46	23	18	4	1	167	153	51	46	17	21	7	1	161	161	42	92	40	39	11	2	328	314	93
San Jose	35	21	7	7	0	117	74	49	34	12	15	5	2	105	119	31	69	33	22	12	2	222	193	80
Tampa Bay	10	7	3	0	0	26	21	14	11	6	3	2	0	35	31	14	21	13	6	2	0	61	52	28
Toronto	44	23	14	6	1	180	141	53	37	15	20	2	0	154	154	32	81	38	34	8	1	334	295	85
Vancouver	85	52	23	7	3	369	267	114	86	41	30	12	3	338	311	97	171	93	53	19	6	707	578	211
Washington	29	15	10	4	0	120	91	34	29	9	18	2	0	93	118	20	58	24	28	6	0	213	209	54
Totals	**1038**	**567**	**328**	**125**	**18**	**4015**	**3226**	**1277**	**1038**	**414**	**463**	**137**	**24**	**3628**	**3816**	**989**	**2076**	**981**	**791**	**262**	**42**	**7643**	**7042**	**2266**

Playoffs

	Series	W	L	GP	W	L	T	GF	GA	Last Mtg.	Rnd.	Result
Anaheim	1	1	0	5	4	1	0	16	13	2006	CF	W 4-1
Boston	2	2	0	9	8	1	0	41	20	1990	F	W 4-1
Calgary	5	4	1	30	19	11	0	132	96	1991	DSF	W 4-3
Carolina	1	0	1	7	3	4	0	16	19	2006	F	L 3-4
Chicago	4	3	1	20	12	8	0	102	77	1992	CF	L 0-4
Colorado	2	1	1	12	5	7	0	30	35	1998	CQF	W 4-3
Dallas	8	2	6	42	15	27	0	104	118	2003	CQF	L 2-4
Detroit	3	3	0	16	12	4	0	58	43	2006	CQF	W 4-2
Los Angeles	7	5	2	36	24	12	0	154	127	1992	DSF	W 4-2
Montreal	1	1	0	3	3	0	0	15	6	1981	PRE	W 3-0
NY Islanders	3	1	2	15	6	9	0	47	58	1984	F	W 4-1
Philadelphia	3	2	1	15	8	7	0	49	44	1987	F	W 4-3
Phoenix	6	6	0	26	22	4	0	120	75	1990	DSF	W 4-3
San Jose	1	1	0	6	4	2	0	19	12	2006	CSF	W 4-2
Vancouver	2	2	0	9	7	2	0	35	20	1992	DF	W 4-2
Totals	**49**	**34**	**15**	**251**	**152**	**99**	**0**	**938**	**763**			

Playoff Results 2006-2001

Year	Round	Opponent	Result	GF	GA
2006	F	Carolina	L 3-4	16	19
	CF	Anaheim	W 4-1	16	13
	CSF	San Jose	W 4-2	19	12
	CQF	Detroit	W 4-2	19	17
2003	CQF	Dallas	L 2-4	11	20
2001	CQF	Dallas	L 2-4	13	16

Abbreviations: Round: F - Final;
CF - conference final; **CQF** - conference quarter-final;
DF - division final; **DSF** - division semi-final;
PRE - preliminary round.

Calgary totals include Atlanta Flames, 1979-80.
Colorado totals include Quebec, 1979-80 to 1994-95.
New Jersey totals include Colorado Rockies, 1979-80 to 1981-82.
Carolina totals include Hartford, 1979-80 to 1996-97.
Dallas totals include Minnesota North Stars, 1979-80 to 1992-93.
Phoenix totals include Winnipeg, 1979-80 to 1995-96.

2005-06 Results

Month	Day	Opponent	Score
Oct.	5	Colorado	4-3
	8	Vancouver	4-3†
	10	at Anaheim	4-2
	11	at Los Angeles	1-3
	14	Dallas	2-3
	15	at Calgary	0-3
	18	Phoenix	3-4*
	20	at Calgary	1-3
	21	Colorado	1-7
	25	at Colorado	3-5
	28	at Dallas	5-3
	29	at Nashville	5-1
Nov.	1	Columbus	5-1
	3	at Detroit	4-3*
	4	at St. Louis	7-2
	7	at Dallas	0-4
	8	at Nashville	2-3
	11	at Columbus	3-1
	13	at Chicago	1-3
	14	at Colorado	5-2
	17	Detroit	6-5*
	19	Chicago	3-4
	21	San Jose	2-1†
	23	at Minnesota	4-3
	25	at Calgary	2-1†
	29	Colorado	2-3
Dec.	1	Vancouver	5-3
	3	Boston	4-5*
	8	at Philadelphia	3-2
	10	at NY Islanders	2-3†
	13	at New Jersey	1-2†
	15	Montreal	5-3
	17	at Vancouver	5-4*
	19	Calgary	5-4
	21	at Vancouver	7-6
	23	Los Angeles	5-3
	26	Minnesota	1-4
	28	Minnesota	2-4
	30	Nashville	4-2
	31	at Calgary	5-6
Jan.	3	Chicago	5-0
	7	Toronto	2-3
	10	at Pittsburgh	3-1
	12	at NY Rangers	4-5*
	14	Ottawa	3-5
	16	Buffalo	1-3
	19	at San Jose	3-2†
	21	at Phoenix	3-4†
	23	Calgary	1-3
	25	at Anaheim	6-3
	26	at Los Angeles	5-3
	29	at Phoenix	4-3†
Feb.	2	Columbus	1-2†
	4	Vancouver	3-1
	6	Anaheim	6-5†
	7	at Colorado	2-5
	10	Minnesota	3-6
	12	St. Louis	4-5†
Mar.	1	St. Louis	2-4
	3	San Jose	3-2
	5	Nashville	3-2*
	7	Dallas	3-4†
	9	at San Jose	2-5
	11	at Columbus	3-4*
	12	at Minnesota	3-4
	14	at Minnesota	2-1
	16	Calgary	3-2*
	18	Detroit	3-4†
	21	Vancouver	1-4
	23	at Vancouver	3-4†
	25	at Vancouver	3-2
	26	at Colorado	4-3†
	28	Minnesota	2-3
	30	Los Angeles	4-0
Apr.	1	Calgary	1-4
	3	Phoenix	7-1
	6	at Minnesota	1-2†
	7	at Chicago	4-3*
	9	at St. Louis	1-2
	11	at Detroit	0-2
	13	Anaheim	2-1
	17	Colorado	4-2

* – Overtime † – Shootout

Entry Draft
Selections 2006-1992

2006
Pick
45	Jeff Petry
75	Theo Peckham
133	Bryan Pitton
140	Cody Wild
170	Alexander Bumagin

2005
Pick
25	Andrew Cogliano
36	Taylor Chorney
81	Danny Syvret
86	Robby Dee
97	Chris Vande Velde
120	Vyacheslav Trukhno
157	Fredrik Pettersson
220	Matthew Glasser

2004
Pick
14	Devan Dubnyk
25	Rob Schremp
44	Roman Tesliuk
57	Geoff Paukovich
112	Liam Reddox
146	Bryan Young
177	Max Gordichuk
209	Stephane Goulet
242	Tyler Spurgeon
274	Bjorn Bjurling

2003
Pick
22	Marc-Antoine Pouliot
51	Colin McDonald
68	Jean-Francois Jacques
72	Mishail Joukov
94	Zachery Stortini
147	Kalle Olsson
154	David Rohlfs
184	Dragan Umicevic
214	Kyle Brodziak
215	Mathieu Roy
248	Josef Hrabal
278	Troy Bodie

2002
Pick
15	Jesse Niinimaki
31	Jeff Drouin-Deslauriers
36	Jarret Stoll
44	Matt Greene
79	Brock Radunske
106	Ivan Koltsov
111	Jonas Almtorp
123	invalid pick
148	Glenn Fisher
181	Mikko Luoma
205	J.F. Dufort
211	Patrick Murphy
244	Dwight Helminen
245	Tomas Micka
274	Fredrik Johansson

2001
Pick
13	Ales Hemsky
43	Doug Lynch
52	Ed Caron
84	Kenny Smith
133	Jussi Markkanen
154	Jake Brenk
185	Mikael Svensk
215	Dan Baum
248	Kari Haakana
272	Ales Pisa
278	Shay Stephenson

2000
Pick
17	Alexei Mikhnov
35	Brad Winchester
83	Alexander Liubimov
113	Lou Dickenson
152	Paul Flache
184	Shaun Norrie
211	Joe Cullen
215	Matthew Lombardi
247	Jason Platt
274	Yevgeny Muratov

1999
Pick
13	Jani Rita
36	Alexei Semenov
41	Tony Salmelainen
81	Adam Hauser
91	Mike Comrie
139	Jonathan Fauteux
171	Chris Legg
199	Christian Chartier
256	Tamas Groschl

1998
Pick
13	Michael Henrich
67	Alex Henry
99	Shawn Horcoff
113	Kristian Antila
128	Paul Elliott
144	Oleg Smirnov
159	Trevor Ettinger
186	Mike Morrison
213	Christian Lefebvre
241	Maxim Spiridonov

1997
Pick
14	Michel Riesen
41	Patrick Dovigi
68	Sergei Yerkovich
94	Jonas Elofsson
121	Jason Chimera
141	Peter Sarno
176	Kevin Bolibruck
187	Chad Hinz
205	Chris Kerr
231	Alexander Fomichev

1996
Pick
6	Boyd Devereaux
19	Matthieu Descoteaux
32	Chris Hajt
59	Tom Poti
114	Brian Urick
141	Bryan Randall
168	David Bernier
170	Brandon Lafrance
195	Fernando Pisani
221	John Hultberg

1995
Pick
6	Steve Kelly
31	Georges Laraque
57	Lukas Zib
83	Mike Minard
109	Jan Snopek
161	Martin Cerven
187	Stephen Douglas
213	Jiri Antonin

1994
Pick
4	Jason Bonsignore
6	Ryan Smyth
32	Mike Watt
53	Corey Neilson
60	Brad Symes
79	Adam Copeland
95	Jussi Tarvainen
110	Jon Gaskins
136	Terry Marchant
160	Curtis Sheptak
162	Dmitri Shulga
179	Chris Wickenheiser
185	Rob Guinn
188	Jason Reid
214	Jeremy Jablonski
266	Ladislav Benysek

1993
Pick
7	Jason Arnott
16	Nick Stajduhar
33	David Vyborny
59	Kevin Paden
60	Alexander Kerch
111	Miroslav Satan
163	Alexander Zhurik
189	Martin Bakula
215	Brad Norton
241	Oleg Maltsev
267	Ilja Byakin

1992
Pick
13	Joe Hulbig
37	Martin Reichel
61	Simon Roy
65	Kirk Maltby
96	Ralph Intranuovo
109	Joaquin Gage
157	Steve Gibson
181	Kyuin Shim
190	Colin Schmidt
205	Marko Tuomainen
253	Bryan Rasmussen

General Managers' History

Larry Gordon, 1979-80; Glen Sather, 1980-81 to 1999-2000; Kevin Lowe, 2000-01 to date.

Vice President and General Manager

LOWE, KEVIN
Executive Vice President/General Manager, Edmonton Oilers.
Born in Lachute, Que., April 15, 1959.

The Edmonton Oilers named Kevin Lowe as their general manager on June 9, 2000, filling the position left vacant when Glen Sather resigned on May 19th. Lowe moved into the front office after spending the 1999-2000 season as coach of the Oilers. In his role as Oilers' g.m., Lowe has worked with Wayne Gretzky as assistant executive director of Canada's gold medal-winning team at the 2002 Winter Olympics and at the 2004 World Cup of Hockey. His Oilers reached the Stanley Cup Final in 2006.

After a brilliant 19-year playing career with the Edmonton Oilers and New York Rangers, Lowe announced his retirement on July 30, 1998 and joined the Edmonton Oilers coaching staff. He replaced Ron Low as head coach on June 18, 1999.

Lowe was the Oilers' first-ever draft pick when he was selected 21st overall in the 1979 NHL Entry Draft. He went on to play in 1,254 regular-season games and 214 playoff games, winning six Stanley Cup championships; the first five with Edmonton (1984, 1985, 1987, 1988, 1990) followed by a sixth title with the Rangers in 1994.

Besides being the first draft choice in Oilers history, Lowe also scored the first goal in team history on October 10, 1979. He holds the Oilers' record for most games played in both the regular season (1,037) and playoffs (172), and became the sixth captain in team history in 1990-91. He was no less a leader off the ice, becoming the only player to win the King Clancy Memorial Trophy and the Budweiser/NHL Man of the Year Award in the same season (1989-90). Both awards are presented for leadership qualities and humanitarian contributions. His work with the Edmonton Christmas Bureau has set the standard for the Oilers' commitment to community involvement.

NHL Coaching Record

Season	Team	Games	Regular Season			Games	Playoffs		L
			W	L	T		W		L
1999-2000	Edmonton	82	32	34	16	5	1		4
	NHL Totals	**82**	**32**	**34**	**16**	**5**	**1**		**4**

Club Directory

Rexall Place

Edmonton Oilers
11230 – 110 Street
Edmonton, Alberta T5G 3H7
Phone **780/414-4000**
Press Box 780/409-3780
Ticketing 780/414-4625
Media Lounge 780/409-3778
FAX 780/409-5848
www.edmontonoilers.com
Capacity: 16,839

Owner	Edmonton Investors Group Ltd.
Governor	Cal Nichols
Alternate Governors	Patrick R. LaForge, Kevin Lowe, William Butler
President & Chief Executive Officer	Patrick R. LaForge
Exec. Vice-President & General Manager	Kevin Lowe
Exec. Vice President, Commercial Operations	Stew MacDonald
Vice-President of Finance and CFO	Darryl Boessenkool
Exec. Assistant to the General Manager	James McGregor
Exec. Assistant to the CFO & Office Manager	Sherry Smith
Security	Gary Goulet

Hockey Operations
Vice-President, Hockey Operations	Kevin Prendergast
Assistant General Manager	Scott Howson
Head Coach	Craig MacTavish
Assistant Coaches	Charlie Huddy, Bill Moores, Craig Simpson
Goaltending Coach	Pete Peeters
Video Coach	Brian Ross
Development Coach	Kelly Buchberger
Director of Research, Analysis and Software Development	Sean Draper
Scouting Staff	Mike Abbamont, Bob Brown, Bill Dandy, Brad Davis, Lorne Davis, Morey Gare, Kent Hawley, Stu MacGregor, Chris McCarthy, Frank Musil, Kent Nilsson, Dave Semenko, John Stevenson

Medical and Training Staff
Head Medical Trainer	Ken Lowe
Head Equipment Manager	Barrie Stafford
Equipment Manager	Lyle Kulchisky
Assistant Equipment Manager	Jeff Lang
Massage Therapist	Stewart Poirier
Team Medical Chief of Staff/Director of Glen Sather Sports Medicine Clinic	Dr. David C. Reid
Team Physicians	Dr. John Clarke, Dr. Dhiron Naidu
Team Dermatologist	Dr. Don Groot
Team Dentists	Dr. Ben Eastwood, Dr. Tony Sneazwell
Fitness Consultants	Dr. Art Quinney, Dr. Gordon Bell
Physical Therapy Consultant	Dr. Dave Magee
Team Optometrist	Dr. Brent Saik

Finance & Administration
Controller	Jason Quilley
Assistant Controller	Sangeeta Sundar
Accounting Supervisor	Corinne Carey
Payroll Manager	Shawna Quigley
Human Resource Manager	Tandy Kustiak
Legal Advisor	Keely Brown
Accounts Payable Coordinator	Yvonne Weleschuk
IT Manager	Terry Rhoades
Systems Administrator	Rod Pruden
Receptionists	Cheryl Thomas, Sandy Langley

Communications & Broadcast
Vice President, Communications & Broadcast	Allan Watt
Manager, Communications & Media Relations	J.J. Hebert
Manager, Corporate Communications	Darren Krill
Information Coordinator	Steve Knowles
Team Services Coordinator	Patrick Garland
Director of Broadcast	Don Metz

Corporate Sales
Vice President, Corporate Sales	Brad MacGregor
Corporate Sales Managers	Daryl Zelinski, Scott Murray, Lisa Munro
Executive Suites Manager	Bob Haromy
Corporate Inventory Specialist	Connie Lloyd
Corporate Sales Coordinators	Bryce Crittenden, Angie Zander, Angela Thompson, Laurie Block
Director, Operations and Events	Craig Tkachuk
Manager, Events	Carmen Day
Facilities Coordinator	Mike Craig

Ticket Sales & Service
V.P., Ticket Sales and Customer Relationships	Eric Upton
Sales Administrative Assistant	Lesli Rentz
Corporate Account Executives	Sheldon Smart, Blair McGeough
Client Service Representatives	Terry Bludd, Tabitha Lidgett, Abe Hajar
Box Office Manager	Ian Weiss
Ticket Inventory Manager	Jamie Schenknecht
Credit Assistant	Tricia Bennett

Marketing & Fan Development
Director, Marketing	Sean Price
Director, Fan Development	Natalie Minckler
Director, Licensing & Special Projects	Nick Wilson
Manager, E-Marketing & Research	Christine Dmytryshyn
Manager, New Media Production	Andreas Schwabe
New Media Production Coordinator	Marc Ciampa
Fan Development Coordinator	Sara Ripko
ICE School Coordinator	Sandy VanRiper
Game Night Director	Glenn Wiun
Game Night Supervisor	Marilyn Riddell

Edmonton Oilers Community Foundation
Executive Director	Gillian Andries
EOCF Coordinator	Jill Metz

Team Information
Television Outlets	Sportsnet , CBXT TV & TSN
Radio Flagship Station	630 CHED (AM); Rod Phillips (Play-by-play) & Morley Scott (Colour)

Florida Panthers

2005-06 Results: 37W-34L-6OTL-5SOL 85PTS.
Fourth, Southeast Division

Year-by-Year Record

Season	GP	Home				Road				Overall				GF	GA	Pts.	Finished	Playoff Result
		W	L	T	OL	W	L	T	OL	W	L	T	OL					
2005-06	82	25	11	....	5	12	23	....	6	37	34	....	11	240	257	85	4th, Southeast Div.	Out of Playoffs
2004-05	....																	
2003-04	82	16	15	7	3	12	20	8	1	28	35	15	4	188	221	75	4th, Southeast Div.	Out of Playoffs
2002-03	82	8	21	7	5	16	15	6	4	24	36	13	9	176	237	70	4th, Southeast Div.	Out of Playoffs
2001-02	82	11	23	4	1	11	21	7	2	22	44	10	6	180	250	60	4th, Southeast Div.	Out of Playoffs
2000-01	82	12	18	7	4	10	20	6	5	22	38	13	9	200	246	66	3rd, Southeast Div.	Out of Playoffs
1999-2000	82	26	9	4	2	17	18	2	4	43	27	6	6	244	209	98	2nd, Southeast Div.	Lost Conf. Quarter-Final
1998-99	82	17	17	7	....	13	17	11	....	30	34	18	....	210	228	78	2nd, Southeast Div.	Out of Playoffs
1997-98	82	11	24	6	....	13	19	9	....	24	43	15	....	203	256	63	6th, Atlantic Div.	Out of Playoffs
1996-97	82	21	12	8	....	14	16	11	....	35	28	19	....	221	201	89	3rd, Atlantic Div.	Lost Conf. Quarter-Final
1995-96	82	25	12	4	....	16	19	6	....	41	31	10	....	254	234	92	3rd, Atlantic Div.	Lost Final
1994-95	48	9	12	3	....	11	10	3	....	20	22	6	....	115	127	46	5th, Atlantic Div.	Out of Playoffs
1993-94	84	15	18	9	....	18	16	8	....	33	34	17	....	233	233	83	5th, Atlantic Div.	Out of Playoffs

2006-07 Schedule

Oct.	Fri.	6	Boston
	Sat.	7	at Atlanta
	Mon.	9	at Toronto
	Wed.	11	Carolina
	Fri.	13	Tampa Bay
	Sat.	14	at Tampa Bay
	Wed.	18	at Washington
	Fri.	20	Philadelphia
	Sat.	21	at Atlanta
	Mon.	23	Atlanta
	Wed.	25	at NY Rangers
	Thu.	26	at New Jersey
	Sat.	28	at NY Islanders
	Tue.	31	San Jose
Nov.	Thu.	2	Toronto
	Wed.	8	NY Rangers
	Fri.	10	at Buffalo
	Sat.	11	at New Jersey
	Mon.	13	Washington
	Thu.	16	Montreal
	Sat.	18	NY Islanders
	Mon.	20	at Boston
	Wed.	22	Tampa Bay
	Fri.	24	Ottawa
	Sat.	25	at Atlanta
	Tue.	28	at Montreal
	Thu.	30	at Ottawa
Dec.	Sat.	2	Atlanta
	Tue.	5	at Pittsburgh
	Thu.	7	Buffalo
	Sat.	9	at NY Islanders
	Sun.	10	at NY Rangers
	Tue.	12	Anaheim
	Thu.	14	at Buffalo
	Sat.	16	at Boston
	Tue.	19	at Toronto
	Thu.	21	NY Rangers
	Sat.	23	Carolina
	Tue.	26	at Carolina
	Wed.	27	Philadelphia
	Fri.	29	Montreal
Jan.	Tue.	2	at Edmonton
	Thu.	4	at Calgary
	Sun.	7	at Vancouver
	Wed.	10	Pittsburgh
	Thu.	11	at Carolina
	Sat.	13	Washington
	Tue.	16	Carolina
	Thu.	18	Toronto
	Sat.	20	at Washington*
	Sat.	27	New Jersey
	Tue.	30	at Pittsburgh
Feb.	Thu.	1	Washington
	Sat.	3	Los Angeles
	Tue.	6	at Colorado
	Thu.	8	at Minnesota
	Sat.	10	Phoenix
	Tue.	13	at Montreal
	Wed.	14	at Ottawa
	Sat.	17	Tampa Bay
	Tue.	20	at Tampa Bay
	Thu.	22	Pittsburgh
	Sat.	24	Boston
	Tue.	27	at Washington
Mar.	Thu.	1	Dallas
	Sat.	3	Tampa Bay
	Tue.	6	at Atlanta
	Thu.	8	at Philadelphia
	Sat.	10	Atlanta
	Tue.	13	at Carolina
	Thu.	15	Buffalo
	Sat.	17	NY Islanders
	Tue.	20	at Philadelphia
	Thu.	22	Ottawa
	Sat.	24	New Jersey
	Tue.	27	at Tampa Bay
	Wed.	28	Atlanta
	Fri.	30	Washington
Apr.	Sun.	1	Carolina*
	Tue.	3	at Washington
	Fri.	6	at Tampa Bay
	Sat.	7	at Carolina

* Denotes afternoon game.

Franchise date: June 14, 1993

EASTERN CONFERENCE
NHL

SOUTHEAST DIVISION

14th NHL Season

Joe Nieuwendyk celebrates one of his 26 goals for Florida last year. Nieuwendyk has topped the 20-goal plateau 15 times in his 18 full NHL seasons. His 26 goals in 2005-06 were the most he has scored since 2000-01.

2006-07 Player Personnel

FORWARDS	HT	WT	S	Place of Birth	Date	2005-06 Club
BERTUZZI, Todd	6-3	245	L	Sudbury, Ont.	2/2/75	Vancouver
CAMPBELL, Gregory	6-0	191	L	London, Ont.	12/17/83	Florida-Rochester
GELINAS, Martin	5-11	195	L	Shawinigan, Que.	6/5/70	Florida
GRATTON, Chris	6-4	220	L	Brantford, Ont.	7/5/75	Florida
HORTON, Nathan	6-2	201	R	Welland, Ont.	5/29/85	Florida
JOKINEN, Olli	6-3	205	L	Kuopio, Finland	12/5/78	Florida
KOLNIK, Juraj	5-10	190	R	Nitra, Czech.	11/13/80	Florida
NIEUWENDYK, Joe	6-2	205	L	Oshawa, Ont.	9/10/66	Florida
OLESZ, Rostislav	6-1	207	L	Bilovec, Czech.	10/10/85	Florida
PELTONEN, Ville	5-9	185	L	Vantaa, Finland	5/24/73	Lugano
ROBERTS, Gary	6-2	215	L	North York, Ont.	5/23/66	Florida
STUMPEL, Jozef	6-3	225	R	Nitra, Czech.	7/20/72	Florida
WEISS, Stephen	5-11	185	L	Toronto, Ont.	4/3/83	Florida
DEFENSEMEN						
ALLEN, Bryan	6-4	220	L	Kingston, Ont.	8/21/80	Vancouver
BOUWMEESTER, Jay	6-4	210	L	Edmonton, Alta.	9/27/83	Florida
JACKMAN, Ric	6-2	197	R	Toronto, Ont.	6/28/78	Pittsburgh-Florida
KWIATKOWSKI, Joel	6-2	210	L	Kindersley, Sask.	3/22/77	Florida
MEZEI, Branislav	6-5	236	L	Nitra, Czech.	10/8/80	Florida
MONTADOR, Steve	6-0	210	R	Vancouver, B.C.	12/21/79	Calgary-Florida
SALEI, Ruslan	6-1	213	L	Minsk, USSR	11/2/74	Anaheim
SEMENOV, Alexei	6-6	235	L	Murmansk, USSR	4/10/81	Yaroslavl-Edm-Fla-Roch
VALLIN, Ari	5-11	194	L	Ylojarvi, Finland	3/21/78	Karpat
VAN RYN, Mike	6-1	202	R	London, Ont.	5/14/79	Florida

GOALTENDERS	HT	WT	C	Place of Birth	Date	2005-06 Club
ANDERSON, Craig	6-2	174	L	Park Ridge, IL	5/21/81	Chicago
AULD, Alex	6-4	200	L	Cold Lake, Alta.	1/7/81	Vancouver
BELFOUR, Ed	5-11	202	L	Carman, Man.	4/21/65	Toronto

General Manager

KEENAN, MIKE
General Manager, Florida Panthers.
Born in Bowmanville, Ont., October 21, 1949.

Mike Keenan became the sixth general manager of the Florida Panthers on May 26, 2004. Previously, he served as interim general manager with Vancouver (1997-98) and as general manager in St. Louis (1994 to 1996) and Chicago (1988 to 1992). During his tenure with these clubs, he traded for players such as Wayne Gretzky (St. Louis), Craig Conroy (St. Louis), Chris Pronger (St. Louis), Todd Bertuzzi (Vancouver), Chris Chelios (Chicago), Michel Goulet (Chicago) and Brent Sutter (Chicago). Serving as both coach and g.m. in Chicago, Keenan posted a mark of 153-126-41 and led the Blackhawks to the Stanley Cup Finals in 1992. His Chicago teams made the playoffs all four years, finishing 33-27 (.550) in the postseason and winning seven of 11 playoff series.

A coaching veteran of 18 seasons, Keenan has spent time behind the bench for seven different NHL clubs including Florida, Boston, Vancouver, St. Louis , NY Rangers, Chicago and Philadelphia. His resume includes three Presidents' Trophies (1985, 1991 and 1994), six division titles (1985, 1986, 1987, 1990, 1991 and 1994), three 50+ win seasons (1984-85, 1985-86 and 1993-94), and five 100+ point seasons (1984-85, 1985-86, 1986-87, 1990-91 and 1993-94). Keenan ranks fifth on the all-time coaching list in both games coached (1,222) and victories (584). Most significantly, he led the Rangers to the 1994 Stanley Cup championship. The Rangers went 52-24-8 under Keenan, going from a non-playoff team to the Presidents' Trophy winner and Stanley Cup champion in a single year. Additionally, Keenan was the general manager/head coach of the championship Team Canada squads that participated in the Canada Cup in 1991 and 1987.

Keenan and Jacques Martin last worked together in Chicago (1988 to 1990), when Keenan served as the team's head coach/general manager and Martin was an assistant coach. Prior to that, the pair worked together when they led the Peterborough Petes to the Memorial Cup Finals in 1980. The duo also played hockey together at St. Lawrence University.

NHL Coaching Record

		Regular Season				Playoffs		
Season	Team	Games	W	L	T	Games	W	L
1984-85	Philadelphia	80	53	20	7	19	12	7
1985-86	Philadelphia	80	53	23	4	5	2	3
1986-87	Philadelphia	80	46	26	8	26	15	11
1987-88	Philadelphia	80	38	33	9	7	3	4
1988-89	Chicago	80	27	41	12	16	9	7
1989-90	Chicago	80	41	33	6	20	10	10
1990-91	Chicago	80	49	23	8	6	2	4
1991-92	Chicago	80	36	29	15	18	12	6
1993-94*	NY Rangers	84	52	24	8	23	16	7
1994-95	St. Louis	48	28	15	5	7	3	4
1995-96	St. Louis	82	32	34	16	13	7	6
1996-97	St. Louis	33	15	17	1	....	....	....
1997-98	Vancouver	63	21	30	12	....	....	....
1998-99	Vancouver	45	15	24	6	....	....	....
2000-01	Boston	74	33	34	7	....	....	....
2001-02	Florida	56	16	32	8	....	....	....
2002-03	Florida	82	24	45	13	....	....	....
2003-04	Florida	15	5	8	2	....	....	....
	NHL Totals	**1222**	**584**	**491**	**147**	**160**	**91**	**69**

* Stanley Cup win.

2005-06 Scoring

* – rookie

Regular Season

Pos	#	Player	Team	GP	G	A	Pts	+/–	PIM	PP	SH	GW	S	%
C	12	Olli Jokinen	FLA	82	38	51	89	14	88	14	1	9	351	10.8
C	25	Joe Nieuwendyk	FLA	65	26	30	56	–2	46	7	0	3	195	13.3
C	15	Jozef Stumpel	FLA	74	15	37	52	11	26	3	1	1	115	13.0
R	16	Nathan Horton	FLA	71	28	19	47	8	89	3	0	1	162	17.3
D	4	Jay Bouwmeester	FLA	82	5	41	46	1	79	0	0	0	189	2.6
L	23	Martin Gelinas	FLA	82	17	24	41	27	80	4	0	3	186	9.1
L	10	Gary Roberts	FLA	58	14	26	40	4	51	4	0	1	122	11.5
C	77	Chris Gratton	FLA	76	17	22	39	6	104	4	1	2	135	12.6
D	26	Mike Van Ryn	FLA	80	8	29	37	15	90	3	0	2	154	5.2
R	13	Juraj Kolnik	FLA	77	15	20	35	1	40	4	1	3	145	10.3
R	11	Jon Sim	PHI	39	7	7	14	–6	28	4	0	2	80	8.8
			FLA	33	10	8	18	–1	26	4	0	3	92	10.9
			TOTAL	72	17	15	32	–7	54	8	0	5	172	9.9
D	55	Ric Jackman	PIT	49	6	22	28	–20	46	3	0	1	95	6.3
			FLA	15	1	1	2	0	6	0	0	0	25	4.0
			TOTAL	64	7	23	30	–20	52	3	0	1	120	5.8
C	9	Stephen Weiss	FLA	41	9	12	21	–2	22	5	0	1	74	12.2
C	85	* Rostislav Olesz	FLA	59	8	13	21	–4	24	0	1	3	105	7.6
D	22	Sean Hill	FLA	78	2	18	20	3	80	1	0	0	110	1.8
D	2	* Lukas Krajicek	FLA	67	2	14	16	1	50	2	0	0	89	2.2
D	20	Joel Kwiatkowski	FLA	73	4	8	12	3	86	1	0	1	87	4.6
C	44	* Gregory Campbell	FLA	64	3	6	9	–11	40	0	0	0	59	5.1
D	7	Steve Montador	CGY	7	1	0	1	0	11	0	0	0	13	7.7
			FLA	51	1	5	6	4	68	0	0	0	42	2.4
			TOTAL	58	2	5	7	4	79	0	0	0	55	3.6
L	43	Serge Payer	FLA	71	2	4	6	–7	26	0	0	0	70	2.9
D	21	Alexei Semenov	EDM	11	1	1	2	–3	17	0	0	0	3	33.3
			FLA	16	1	1	2	–1	21	1	0	0	13	7.7
			TOTAL	27	2	2	4	–4	38	1	0	0	16	12.5
C	42	Mikhail Yakubov	CHI	10	1	2	3	0	8	0	0	1	11	9.1
			FLA	13	0	1	1	–1	4	0	0	0	16	0.0
			TOTAL	23	1	3	4	–1	12	0	0	1	27	3.7
C	57	* Anthony Stewart	FLA	10	2	1	3	2	2	1	0	0	16	12.5
C	51	* Rob Globke	FLA	18	1	0	1	0	6	0	0	0	18	5.6
C	40	* Greg Jacina	FLA	11	0	1	1	–1	4	0	0	0	10	0.0
D	5	Branislav Mezei	FLA	16	0	1	1	3	37	0	0	0	13	0.0
D	33	Jamie Allison	NSH	20	0	1	1	–6	45	0	0	0	3	0.0
			FLA	7	0	0	0	0	11	0	0	0	4	0.0
			TOTAL	27	0	1	1	–6	56	0	0	0	7	0.0
C	37	* Petr Taticek	FLA	3	0	0	0	0	0	0	0	0	3	0.0
D	7	Alexander Karpovtsev	FLA	6	0	0	0	–3	4	0	0	0	4	0.0

Goaltending

No.	Goaltender	GPI	Mins	Avg	W	L	OT	EN	SO	GA	SA	S%	G	A	PIM
1	Roberto Luongo	75	4305	2.97	35	30	9	4	4	213	2488	.914	0	3	2
29	Jamie McLennan	17	678	3.01	2	4	2	1	0	34	360	.906	0	0	0
	Totals	**82**	**5006**	**3.02**	**37**	**34**	**11**	**5**	**4**	**252**	**2853**	**.912**			

Coach

MARTIN, JACQUES
Coach, Florida Panthers. Born in St. Pascal, Ont., October 1, 1952.

Jacques Martin was hired as coach of the Florida Panthers on May 26, 2004, joining the team after eight-and-a-half seasons with the Ottawa Senators. For his career with the Senators, he posted a 341-255-96 regular-season record and stands as the franchise's all-time leader in games coached (692), regular-season wins (341), playoff wins (31) and playoff games coached (69). He is the ninth coach in Panthers history.

Under Martin's guidance, the Senators earned their first Presidents' Trophy and Eastern Conference title, posting a 52-22-8 mark in 2002-03. Martin has been nominated for the Jack Adams Award as coach of the year four times. He won the award in 1998-99 and was nominated in 1996-97, 2000-01 and 2002-03. Martin was named as an associate coach for Team Canada's men's hockey team that won gold at the 2002 Olympic Winter Games in Salt Lake City and served in the same capacity with Team Canada at the World Cup of Hockey in 2004 and at the Olympics again in 2006.

Martin joined Ottawa after spending the first half of the 1995-96 season with the Stanley Cup champion Colorado Avalanche, where he served as an assistant coach. Martin entered the NHL as head coach of the St. Louis Blues in 1986-87 and 1987-88, leading the Blues to the Norris Division championship in his rookie season. He joined the Blues after guiding the Ontario Hockey League's Guelph Platers to the 1986 Memorial Cup championship and winning OHL coach of the year honors for his efforts.

Coaching Record

		Regular Season				Playoffs		
Season	Team	Games	W	L	O/T	Games	W	L
1983-84	Peterborough (OHL)	70	43	23	4	....	....	....
1984-85	Peterborough (OHL)	66	42	20	4	....	....	....
1985-86	Guelph (OHL)	66	41	23	2	....	....	....
1986-87	**St. Louis (NHL)**	**80**	**32**	**33**	**15**	**6**	**2**	**4**
1987-88	**St. Louis (NHL)**	**80**	**34**	**38**	**8**	**10**	**5**	**5**
1993-94	Cornwall (AHL)	80	33	36	11	13	8	5
1995-96	**Ottawa (NHL)**	**38**	**10**	**24**	**4**	....	....	....
1996-97	**Ottawa (NHL)**	**82**	**31**	**36**	**15**	**7**	**3**	**4**
1997-98	**Ottawa (NHL)**	**82**	**34**	**33**	**15**	**11**	**5**	**6**
1998-99	**Ottawa (NHL)**	**82**	**44**	**23**	**15**	**4**	**0**	**4**
1999-2000	**Ottawa (NHL)**	**82**	**41**	**30**	**11**	**6**	**2**	**4**
2000-01	**Ottawa (NHL)**	**82**	**48**	**25**	**9**	**4**	**0**	**4**
2001-02	**Ottawa (NHL)**	**80**	**38**	**33**	**9**	**12**	**7**	**5**
2002-03	**Ottawa (NHL)**	**82**	**52**	**22**	**8**	**18**	**11**	**7**
2003-04	**Ottawa (NHL)**	**82**	**43**	**29**	**10**	**7**	**3**	**4**
2004-05	**Florida (NHL)**			Season Cancelled				
2005-06	**Florida (NHL)**	**82**	**37**	**34**	**11**	....	....	....
	NHL Totals	**934**	**444**	**360**	**130**	**85**	**38**	**47**

Martin stepped aside (with NHL permission) during the final two games of the 2001-02 season in order to allow assistant coach Roger Neilson to reach the 1,000-game plateau, April 11 and 13, 2002.

Club Records

Team

(Figures in brackets for season records are games played; records for fewest points, wins, ties, losses, goals, goals against are for 70 or more games)

Most Points	98	1999-2000 (82)
Most Wins	43	1999-2000 (82)
Most Ties	19	1996-97 (82)
Most Losses	44	2001-02 (82)
Most Goals	254	1995-96 (82)
Most Goals Against	257	2005-06 (82)
Fewest Points	60	2001-02 (82)
Fewest Wins	22	2000-01 (82), 2001-02 (82)
Fewest Ties	6	1999-2000 (82)
Fewest Losses	27	1999-2000 (82)
Fewest Goals	176	2002-03 (82)
Fewest Goals Against	201	1996-97 (82)

Longest Winning Streak

Overall	7	Nov. 2-14/95, Mar. 17-29/06
Home	5	Nov. 5-14/95, Mar. 17-Apr. 1/06
Away	4	Four times

Longest Undefeated Streak

Overall	12	Oct. 5-30/96 (8 wins, 4 ties)
Home	8	Nov. 5-26/95 (7 wins, 1 tie)
Away	7	Two times

Longest Losing Streak

Overall	13	Feb. 7-Mar. 23/98
Home	6	Feb. 25-Mar. 23/98
Away	13	Oct. 27-Dec. 17/05

Longest Winless Streak

Overall	15	Feb. 1-Mar. 23/98 (14 losses, 1 tie)
Home	13	Feb. 5-Mar. 24/03 (11 losses, 2 ties)
Away	16	Jan. 2-Mar. 21/98 (12 losses, 4 ties)

Most Shutouts, Season	7	2002-03 (82)
Most PIM, Season	1,994	2001-02 (82)
Most Goals, Game	10	Nov. 26/97 (Bos. 5 at Fla. 10)

Individual

Most Seasons	9	Paul Laus
Most Games	573	Robert Svehla
Most Goals, Career	157	Scott Mellanby
Most Assists, Career	229	Robert Svehla
Most Points, Career	354	Scott Mellanby (157G, 197A)
Most PIM, Career	1,702	Paul Laus
Most Shutouts, Career	22	Roberto Luongo

Longest Consecutive

Games Streak	300	Robert Svehla (Dec. 23/98-Apr. 14/02)
Most Goals, Season	59	Pavel Bure (2000-01)
Most Assists, Season	53	Viktor Kozlov (1999-2000)
Most Points, Season	94	Pavel Bure (1999-2000; 58G, 36A)
Most PIM, Season	354	Peter Worrell (2001-02)

Most Points, Defenseman,

Season	57	Robert Svehla (1995-96; 8G, 49A)

Most Points, Center,

Season	89	Olli Jokinen (2005-06; 38G, 51A)

Most Points, Right Wing,

Season	94	Pavel Bure (1999-2000; 58G, 36A)

Most Points, Left Wing,

Season	71	Ray Whitney (1999-2000; 29G, 42A)

Most Points, Rookie,

Season	50	Jesse Belanger (1993-94; 17G, 33A)

Most Shutouts, Season	7	Roberto Luongo (2003-04)
Most Goals, Game	4	Mark Parrish (Oct. 30/98); Pavel Bure (Jan. 1/00, Feb. 10/01)
Most Assists, Game	4	Scott Mellanby (Nov. 26/97); Ray Whitney (Oct. 30/00)
Most Points, Game	5	Pavel Bure (Feb. 10/01; 4G, 1A)

Coaching History

Roger Neilson, 1993-94, 1994-95; Doug MacLean, 1995-96, 1996-97; Doug MacLean and Bryan Murray, 1997-98; Terry Murray, 1998-99, 1999-2000; Terry Murray and Duane Sutter, 2000-01; Duane Sutter and Mike Keenan, 2001-02; Mike Keenan, 2002-03; Mike Keenan, Rick Dudley and John Torchetti, 2003-04; Jacques Martin, 2004-05 to date.

Captains' History

Brian Skrudland, 1993-94 to 1996-97; Scott Mellanby, 1997-98 to 2000-01; Pavel Bure, 2001-02; no captain, 2002-03; Olli Jokinen, 2003-04 to date.

General Managers' History

Bob Clarke, 1993-94; Bryan Murray, 1994-95 to 1999-2000; Bryan Murray and Bill Torrey, 2000-01; Bill Torrey and Chuck Fletcher, 2001-02; Rick Dudley, 2002-03, 2003-04; Mike Keenan, 2004-05 to date.

All-time Record vs. Other Clubs

Regular Season

	At Home								On Road								Total							
	GP	W	L	T	OL	GF	GA	PTS	GP	W	L	T	OL	GF	GA	PTS	GP	W	L	T	OL	GF	GA	PTS
Anaheim	8	4	2	2	0	23	17	10	10	5	3	1	1	30	28	12	18	9	5	3	1	53	45	22
Atlanta	17	7	8	1	1	42	52	16	17	4	6	4	3	52	59	15	34	11	14	5	4	94	111	31
Boston	23	10	10	2	1	65	67	23	24	11	9	4	0	62	63	26	47	21	19	6	1	127	130	49
Buffalo	23	12	10	1	0	66	66	25	25	6	15	3	1	42	70	16	48	18	25	4	1	108	136	41
Calgary	9	3	3	2	1	21	22	9	8	3	4	1	0	20	21	7	17	6	7	3	1	41	43	16
Carolina	30	13	6	8	3	86	66	37	29	9	16	3	1	70	87	22	59	22	22	11	4	156	153	59
Chicago	9	5	3	1	0	22	33	7	10	3	5	2	0	30	34	8	19	6	10	3	0	52	67	15
Colorado	11	1	10	0	0	30	48	2	11	4	4	3	0	27	30	11	22	5	14	3	0	57	78	13
Columbus	4	2	0	0	2	13	12	6	4	1	0	0	4	2	6	1	8	3	0	0	6	17	16	8
Dallas	10	4	5	1	0	22	28	9	9	4	2	3	0	25	29	8	19	7	9	3	0	47	57	17
Detroit	10	2	4	2	2	20	29	8	8	1	4	3	0	21	30	5	16	3	8	5	2	41	48	17
Edmonton	9	5	2	2	0	24	24	12	7	2	4	1	0	16	24	5	16	7	6	3	0	40	48	17
Los Angeles	8	4	1	3	0	23	14	11	10	4	6	0	0	30	30	8	18	8	7	3	0	53	44	19
Minnesota	3	1	2	0	0	6	8	2	3	2	1	0	0	11	10	4	6	1	4	1	0	17	18	3
Montreal	24	12	9	3	0	70	63	27	23	10	7	3	3	56	63	26	47	22	16	6	3	126	126	53
Nashville	5	3	0	1	1	18	11	8	5	2	1	2	0	10	8	6	10	5	1	3	1	28	19	14
New Jersey	27	8	14	4	1	58	71	21	26	7	14	3	2	52	79	19	53	15	28	7	3	110	150	40
NY Islanders	27	12	9	6	0	83	81	30	27	12	11	2	2	71	69	28	54	24	20	8	2	154	150	58
NY Rangers	27	11	12	2	2	70	75	26	26	8	14	4	0	59	82	20	53	19	26	6	2	129	157	46
Ottawa	24	10	12	1	1	73	75	22	24	11	9	2	2	68	75	25	53	14	29	7	3	127	170	38
Philadelphia	26	5	18	1	2	59	95	13	27	9	11	6	1	68	75	25	53	14	29	7	3	127	170	38
Phoenix	8	3	5	0	0	23	21	6	11	4	3	3	1	34	31	12	19	7	8	3	1	57	52	18
Pittsburgh	24	14	9	1	0	71	58	29	25	10	10	3	2	77	78	25	49	24	19	4	2	148	136	54
St. Louis	10	3	4	2	1	20	21	9	9	1	7	1	0	12	25	3	19	4	11	3	1	32	46	12
San Jose	9	2	5	0	2	25	27	9	10	2	6	2	0	19	32	6	19	4	8	7	0	44	59	15
Tampa Bay	32	20	6	4	2	99	72	46	32	14	12	6	0	90	70	34	64	34	18	10	2	189	142	80
Toronto	19	5	9	5	0	51	57	15	17	4	3	5	2	40	61	11	36	9	12	10	2	91	118	26
Vancouver	8	3	3	1	1	21	-27	8	9	1	5	2	0	19	25	7	17	4	6	1	1	40	52	15
Washington	32	14	12	4	2	80	79	34	32	12	15	2	3	77	94	31	64	26	25	9	4	157	173	65
Totals	**476**	**196**	**192**	**65**	**23**	**1284**	**1319**	**480**	**476**	**163**	**214**	**77**	**22**	**1180**	**1380**	**425**	**952**	**359**	**406**	**142**	**45**	**2464**	**2699**	**905**

Playoffs

	Series	W	L	GP	W	L	T	GF	GA	Last Mtg.	Rnd.	Result
Boston	1	1	0	5	4	1	0	22	16	1996	CQF	W 4-1
Colorado	1	0	1	4	0	4	0	4	15	1996	F	L 0-4
New Jersey	1	0	1	4	0	4	0	6	12	2000	CQF	L 0-4
NY Rangers	1	0	1	5	1	4	0	10	13	1997	CQF	L 1-4
Philadelphia	1	1	0	6	4	2	0	15	11	1996	CSF	W 4-2
Pittsburgh	1	1	0	7	4	3	0	20	15	1996	CF	W 4-3
Totals	**6**	**3**	**3**	**31**	**13**	**18**	**0**	**77**	**82**			

Colorado totals include Quebec, 1993-94 to 1994-95.
Phoenix totals include Winnipeg, 1993-94 to 1995-96.
Carolina totals include Hartford, 1993-94 to 1996-97.

Playoff Results 2006-2001

(Last playoff appearance: 2000)

Abbreviations: Round: F - Final;
CF - conference final; **CSF** - conference semi-final;
CQF - conference quarter-final.

2005-06 Results

Oct.	5	Atlanta	2-0		3	at New Jersey	0-3
	7	Tampa Bay	2-0		4	at NY Islanders	3-4*
	8	at Tampa Bay	1-2		7	at NY Rangers	0-4
	10	at NY Islanders	3-1		8	at Washington	4-3†
	13	Boston	2-5		12	St. Louis	3-1
	15	Buffalo	3-2		14	Columbus	4-5*
	17	at NY Rangers	0-4		19	at Phoenix	3-6
	18	at New Jersey	3-4		21	at Anaheim	0-1
	20	Washington	3-2		24	at Tampa Bay	3-2*
	25	at Pittsburgh	4-3*		25	Carolina	3-4†
	27	at Philadelphia	4-5*		27	New Jersey	4-0
	31	at Toronto	1-2		30	at Toronto	2-4
Nov.	1	at Montreal	4-5*	Feb.	3	Atlanta	5-2
	3	at Boston	1-4		4	at Atlanta	4-6
	5	at Carolina	0-2		7	at Washington	5-0
	9	NY Rangers	3-4†		11	at Buffalo	3-5
	11	Carolina	0-1		28	at Tampa Bay	8-2
	12	at Philadelphia	4-5	Mar.	2	Montreal	0-1
	15	at Montreal	3-4*		3	at Carolina	2-5
	17	at Ottawa	1-4		6	at Atlanta	3-4†
	19	NY Islanders	3-5		8	Ottawa	6-2
	23	New Jersey	1-5		10	Carolina	5-3
	25	Pittsburgh	6-3		11	Carolina	4-3*
	26	at Atlanta	4-7		15	Philadelphia	0-4
	28	Toronto	1-2		17	NY Islanders	4-2
Dec.	1	Washington	3-2		18	at Washington	4-3†
	3	Chicago	4-3*		20	Tampa Bay	6-5*
	5	Ottawa	3-6		22	Washington	3-2
	7	at Dallas	3-4		24	NY Rangers	3-2†
	8	at San Jose	2-6		27	at Boston	4-3†
	10	at Los Angeles	1-3		29	at Pittsburgh	5-3
	13	Nashville	1-2		31	at Carolina	2-3
	15	Detroit	3-2*	Apr.	1	Tampa Bay	4-2
	17	at Atlanta	1-2		3	at Tampa Bay	1-4
	18	at Washington	3-2		5	Atlanta	2-5
	22	Buffalo	4-1		7	Pittsburgh	1-5
	23	at Carolina	3-4		9	Tampa Bay	6-3
	26	Philadelphia	2-3†		11	at Toronto	5-6†
	28	Boston	6-4		13	at Ottawa	5-4*
	30	Montreal	2-1		15	Washington	1-2†
Jan.	1	at Buffalo	2-1		18	Atlanta	2-1*

* – Overtime † – Shootout

Entry Draft
Selections 2006-1993

2006
Pick
10	Michael Frolik
73	Brady Calla
103	Michael Caruso
116	Derrick Lapoint
155	Peter Aston
193	Marc Cheverie

2005
Pick
20	Kenndal McArdle
32	Tyler Plante
90	Dan Collins
93	Olivier Legault
104	Matt Duffy
161	Brian Foster
164	Roman Derlyuk
224	Zach Bearson

2004
Pick
7	Rostislav Olesz
37	David Shantz
53	David Booth
105	Evan Schafer
152	Bret Nasby
267	Spencer Dillon
283	Luke Beaverson

2003
Pick
3	Nathan Horton
25	Anthony Stewart
38	Kamil Kreps
55	Stefan Meyer
105	Martin Lojek
124	James Pemberton
141	Dan Travis
162	Martin Tuma
171	Denis Stasyuk
223	Dany Roussin
234	Petr Kadlec
264	John Hecimovic
265	Tanner Glass

2002
Pick
3	Jay Bouwmeester
9	Petr Taticek
40	Rob Globke
67	Gregory Campbell
134	Topi Jaakola
158	Vince Bellissimo
169	Jeremy Swanson
196	Mikael Vuorio
200	Denis Yachmenev
232	Peter Hafner

2001
Pick
4	Stephen Weiss
24	Lukas Krajicek
34	Greg Watson
64	Tomas Malec
68	Grant McNeill
117	Mike Woodford
136	Billy Thompson
169	Dustin Johner
200	Toni Koivisto
231	Kyle Bruce
263	Jan Blanar
267	Ivan Majesky

2000
Pick
58	Vladimir Sapozhnikov
77	Robert Fried
82	Sean O'Connor
115	Chris Eade
120	Davis Parley
190	Josh Olson
234	Janis Sprukts
253	Mathew Sommerfeld

1999
Pick
12	Denis Shvidki
40	Alex Auld
70	Niklas Hagman
80	Jean-Francois Laniel
103	Morgan McCormick
109	Rod Sarich
169	Brad Woods
198	Travis Eagles
227	Jonathon Charron

1998
Pick
30	Kyle Rossiter
61	Joe DiPenta
63	Lance Ward
89	Ryan Jardine
117	Jaroslav Spacek
148	Chris Ovington
176	B.J. Ketcheson
203	Ian Jacobs
231	Adrian Wichser

1997
Pick
20	Mike Brown
47	Kristian Huselius
56	Vratislav Cech
74	Nick Smith
95	Ivan Novoseltsev
127	Pat Parthenais
155	Keith Delaney
183	Tyler Palmer
211	Doug Schueller
237	Benoit Cote

1996
Pick
20	Marcus Nilson
60	Chris Allen
65	Oleg Kvasha
82	Joey Tetarenko
129	Andrew Long
156	Gaetan Poirier
183	Alexandre Couture
209	Denis Khloptonov
235	Russell Smith

1995
Pick
10	Radek Dvorak
36	Aaron MacDonald
62	Mike O'Grady
80	Dave Duerden
88	Daniel Tjarnqvist
114	Francois Cloutier
166	Peter Worrell
192	Filip Kuba
218	David Lemanowicz

1994
Pick
1	Ed Jovanovski
27	Rhett Warrener
31	Jason Podollan
36	Ryan Johnson
84	David Nemirovsky
105	Dave Geris
157	Matt O'Dette
183	Jason Boudrias
235	Tero Lehtera
261	Per Gustafsson

1993
Pick
5	Rob Niedermayer
41	Kevin Weekes
57	Chris Armstrong
67	Mikael Tjallden
78	Steve Washburn
83	Bill McCauley
109	Todd MacDonald
135	Alain Nasreddine
161	Trevor Doyle
187	Briane Thompson
213	Chad Cabana
239	John Demarco
265	Eric Montreuil

Chosen third overall in the 2003 NHL Entry Draft, Nathan Horton's 28 goals for the Panthers in 2005-06 ranked second on the team behind Olli Jokinen.

Club Directory

BankAtlantic Center

Florida Panthers
BankAtlantic Center
One Panther Parkway
Sunrise, FL 33323
Phone **954/835-7000**
FAX 954/835-7700
www.floridapanthers.com
Capacity: 19,250

Executive
General Partner/Chairman/
  Chief Executive Officer/Governor . . . . Alan Cohen
Limited Partners . . . . Steve Cohen, David Epstein,
  Jordan Zimmerman, Dr. Elliott Hahn,
  H. Wayne Huizenga, Bernie Kosar,
  Richard Lehman M.D., Al Maroone,
  Michael Maroone, Cliff Viner
Alternate Governor . . . . William A. Torrey
Chief Operating Officer/Alternate Governor . . . . . . Michael R. Yormark
Chief Financial Officer/Vice President, Finance . . . . . Evelyn Lopez
Sr. V.P., Corporate Marketing and
  New Business Development . . . . Pedro Goncalves
Sr. V.P., Sales and Marketing . . . . Chad Johnson
Executive Assistants . . . . Janine Shea & Cathy Stevenson

Hockey Operations
General Manager . . . . Mike Keenan
Head Coach . . . . Jacques Martin
Assistant Coach . . . . Guy Charron
Assistant Coach . . . . George Kingston
Goaltending Coach . . . . Phil Myre
Video Coach . . . . Pierre Groulx
Strength and Conditioning Coach . . . . Andy O'Brien
Director of Hockey Operations . . . . Jack Birch
Director of Hockey Administration . . . . Matt Loughran
Director of Scouting . . . . Scott Luce
Director of Player Development . . . . Duane Sutter
Medical Trainer . . . . Curtis Bell
Massage Therapist . . . . Jim Pizzutelli
Physical Therapist . . . . Steve Dischiavi
Head Equipment Manager . . . . Robert McLean
Assistant Equipment Manager . . . . Chris Moody
Assistant Equipment Manager . . . . Rob Kennedy
Team Services Manager . . . . Austin Guhl

Communication
Manager, Communications . . . . Justin Copertino
Manager, Public Relations . . . . Matt Sacco
Manager, Internet Marketing . . . . Lauren Preziosi
Coordinator, Communications . . . . Brian Goldman

Community Development, Youth Hockey and Broadcasting
V.P., Community Development,
  Youth Hockey & Broadcasting . . . . Randy Moller
Director, Game Presentation . . . . Dennis Docil
Director, Community Dev. and Foundation . . . . Jean Marshall
Manager, Event Production . . . . Phil Crowhurst
Producer, Game Presentation . . . . Richard McClelland
Editor, Game Presentation . . . . Brian Lenihan

Corporate Partnerships
V.P., Corporate Sales . . . . Jarrett Nasca
V.P., Client Services & Retention . . . . Carrie Rubin
Senior Director, Corporate Marketing . . . . Ted Major
Director, Marketing Partnerships . . . . Heather Wright

Sales, Service and Marketing
V.P., Ticket Sales . . . . RJ Martino
V.P., Client Retention . . . . Carrie Rubin
Director, Inside Sales . . . . Ryan Bringger
Director, Premium Seating . . . . Ryan McCoy
Director, Suite Sales & Services . . . . Jason McDonough
Director, New Business Development . . . . Mike Ragan
Director, Ticket Operations . . . . Sammy Wallace
Assistant Director, Ticket Operations . . . . Orvandis Almonte
Manager, Sports Marketing . . . . Nadia Abich

Finance and Business Support
V.P., Human Resources/Payroll . . . . Carol Duncanson
V.P., Information Technology . . . . Kelly Moyer
Controller/Senior Director, Accounting . . . . Phillip Reitz
Director, Purchasing . . . . Laura Barrera
Director, Finance . . . . Michael Fallon

Radio/TV Broadcasting
Play-By-Play Announcer . . . . Dave Strader
Television Analyst . . . . Denis Potvin
Panthers Preview Host . . . . Craig Minervini
Radio Play-By-Pay Announcer . . . . Steve Goldstein
Radio Analyst . . . . Randy Moller

BankAtlantic Centre Building Operations
G.M., BankAtlantic Center/V.P., Operations . . . . . Brett Stefansson
Director, Security & Safety . . . . Bram Bottfield
Director, Operations . . . . Emerson Figueroa
Director, Event Programming . . . . Sid Greenfeig
Director, Event Services . . . . Erik Waldman

Los Angeles Kings

2005-06 Results: 42W-35L-4OTL-1SOL 89PTS.
Fourth, Pacific Division

2006-07 Schedule

Oct.				Jan.		
Fri.	6	at Anaheim		Wed.	3	Columbus
Sat.	7	St. Louis		Sat.	6	Detroit
Tue.	10	NY Islanders		Mon.	8	Edmonton
Thu.	12	Dallas		Thu.	11	San Jose
Sat.	14	Dallas		Sat.	13	at St. Louis*
Mon.	16	Detroit		Mon.	15	at Dallas*
Wed.	18	Minnesota		Tue.	16	at Atlanta
Thu.	19	at Phoenix		Thu.	18	St. Louis
Sun.	22	Anaheim*		Sat.	20	Phoenix
Mon.	23	at Colorado		Fri.	26	at Vancouver
Wed.	25	at Minnesota		Sat.	27	at Edmonton
Fri.	27	at Columbus		Tue.	30	at Calgary
Sat.	28	at Dallas		**Feb.**		
Mon.	30	NY Rangers		Thu.	1	Chicago
Nov.				Sat.	3	at Florida
Wed.	1	Pittsburgh		Tue.	6	at Tampa Bay
Sat.	4	at Phoenix		Thu.	8	at Washington
Tue.	7	at Colorado		Sat.	10	at Nashville
Thu.	9	San Jose		Tue.	13	at Carolina
Sat.	11	Minnesota		Sat.	17	Anaheim
Mon.	13	San Jose		Sun.	18	at Anaheim*
Thu.	16	Philadelphia		Thu.	22	Vancouver
Sat.	18	Phoenix*		Sat.	24	Colorado
Wed.	22	at San Jose		**Mar.**		
Fri.	24	at Dallas		Thu.	1	Anaheim
Sat.	25	Calgary		Sat.	3	Nashville*
Mon.	27	New Jersey		Tue.	6	at Chicago
Thu.	30	at Phoenix		Wed.	7	at Columbus
Dec.				Fri.	9	at Detroit
Sat.	2	Anaheim*		Sun.	11	at Dallas*
Sun.	3	at Anaheim*		Mon.	12	Edmonton
Thu.	7	Nashville		Thu.	15	Chicago
Sat.	9	Colorado		Sat.	17	Columbus
Tue.	12	San Jose		Sun.	18	at Anaheim*
Thu.	14	at San Jose		Wed.	21	Dallas
Sat.	16	Dallas*		Fri.	23	at Chicago
Tue.	19	Calgary		Sat.	24	at Minnesota
Thu.	21	at St. Louis		Tue.	27	at San Jose
Sat.	23	at Nashville		Thu.	29	Vancouver
Tue.	26	Phoenix		**Apr.**		
Thu.	28	at Edmonton		Sun.	1	at San Jose*
Fri.	29	at Calgary		Tue.	3	at Vancouver
Sun.	31	at Detroit		Thu.	5	at Phoenix
				Sat.	7	Phoenix*

* Denotes afternoon game.

Franchise date: June 5, 1967

PACIFIC DIVISION

40th NHL Season

In his first season with the Kings, veteran center Craig Conroy finished second on the club in overall scoring with 66 points (22 goals, 44 assists) in 78 games. He also represented the U.S. at the 2006 Olympic Games in Torino, Italy.

Year-by-Year Record

Season	GP	Home				Road				Overall						Pts.	Finished	Playoff Result
		W	L	T	OL	W	L	T	OL	W	L	T	OL	GF	GA			
2005-06	82	26	14	....	1	16	21	....	4	42	35	....	5	249	270	89	4th, Pacific Div.	Out of Playoffs
2004-05	....	....																
2003-04	82	15	16	9	1	13	13	7	8	28	29	16	9	205	217	81	3rd, Pacific Div.	Out of Playoffs
2002-03	82	19	19	2	1	14	18	4	5	33	37	6	6	203	221	78	3rd, Pacific Div.	Out of Playoffs
2001-02	82	22	12	6	1	18	15	5	3	40	27	11	4	214	190	95	3rd, Pacific Div.	Lost Conf. Quarter-Final
2000-01	82	20	12	8	1	18	16	5	2	38	28	13	3	252	228	92	3rd, Pacific Div.	Lost Conf. Semi-Final
1999-2000	82	21	13	5	2	18	14	7	2	39	27	12	4	245	228	94	2nd, Pacific Div.	Lost Conf. Quarter-Final
1998-99	82	18	20	3	....	14	25	2	....	32	45	5	....	189	222	69	5th, Pacific Div.	Out of Playoffs
1997-98	82	22	16	3	....	16	17	8	....	38	33	11	....	227	225	87	4th, Pacific Div.	Lost Conf. Quarter-Final
1996-97	82	18	16	7	....	10	27	4	....	28	43	11	....	214	268	67	6th, Pacific Div.	Out of Playoffs
1995-96	82	16	16	9	....	8	24	9	....	24	40	18	....	256	302	66	6th, Pacific Div.	Out of Playoffs
1994-95	48	7	11	6	....	9	12	3	....	16	23	9	....	142	174	41	4th, Pacific Div.	Out of Playoffs
1993-94	84	18	16	8	....	9	26	7	....	27	45	12	....	294	322	66	5th, Pacific Div.	Out of Playoffs
1992-93	84	22	15	5	....	17	20	5	....	39	35	10	....	338	340	88	3rd, Smythe Div.	Lost Final
1991-92	80	20	11	9	....	15	20	5	....	35	31	14	....	287	296	84	2nd, Smythe Div.	Lost Div. Semi-Final
1990-91	80	26	9	5	....	20	15	5	....	46	24	10	....	340	254	102	1st, Smythe Div.	Lost Div. Final
1989-90	80	21	16	3	....	13	23	4	....	34	39	7	....	338	337	75	4th, Smythe Div.	Lost Div. Final
1988-89	80	25	12	3	....	17	19	4	....	42	31	7	....	376	335	91	2nd, Smythe Div.	Lost Div. Semi-Final
1987-88	80	19	18	3	....	11	24	5	....	30	42	8	....	318	359	68	4th, Smythe Div.	Lost Div. Semi-Final
1986-87	80	20	17	3	....	11	24	5	....	31	41	8	....	318	341	70	4th, Smythe Div.	Lost Div. Semi-Final
1985-86	80	9	27	4	....	14	22	4	....	23	49	8	....	284	389	54	5th, Smythe Div.	Out of Playoffs
1984-85	80	20	14	6	....	14	18	8	....	34	32	14	....	339	326	82	4th, Smythe Div.	Lost Div. Semi-Final
1983-84	80	13	19	8	....	10	25	5	....	23	44	13	....	309	376	59	5th, Smythe Div.	Out of Playoffs
1982-83	80	20	13	7	....	7	28	5	....	27	41	12	....	308	365	66	5th, Smythe Div.	Out of Playoffs
1981-82	80	19	15	6	....	5	26	9	....	24	41	15	....	314	369	63	4th, Smythe Div.	Lost Div. Final
1980-81	80	22	11	7	....	21	13	6	....	43	24	13	....	337	290	99	2nd, Norris Div.	Lost Prelim. Round
1979-80	80	18	13	9	....	12	23	5	....	30	36	14	....	290	313	74	2nd, Norris Div.	Lost Prelim. Round
1978-79	80	20	13	7	....	14	21	5	....	34	34	12	....	292	286	80	3rd, Norris Div.	Lost Prelim. Round
1977-78	80	18	16	6	....	13	18	9	....	31	34	15	....	243	245	77	3rd, Norris Div.	Lost Prelim. Round
1976-77	80	20	13	7	....	14	18	8	....	34	31	15	....	271	241	83	2nd, Norris Div.	Lost Quarter-Final
1975-76	80	22	13	5	....	16	20	4	....	38	33	9	....	263	265	85	2nd, Norris Div.	Lost Quarter-Final
1974-75	80	22	7	11	....	20	10	10	....	42	17	21	....	269	185	105	2nd, Norris Div.	Lost Prelim. Round
1973-74	78	22	13	4	....	11	20	8	....	33	33	12	....	233	231	78	3rd, West Div.	Lost Quarter-Final
1972-73	78	21	11	7	....	10	25	4	....	31	36	11	....	232	245	73	6th, West Div.	Out of Playoffs
1971-72	78	14	23	2	....	6	26	7	....	20	49	9	....	206	305	49	5th, West Div.	Out of Playoffs
1970-71	78	17	14	8	....	8	26	5	....	25	40	13	....	239	303	63	5th, West Div.	Out of Playoffs
1969-70	76	12	22	4	....	2	30	6	....	14	52	10	....	168	290	38	6th, West Div.	Out of Playoffs
1968-69	76	19	14	5	....	5	28	5	....	24	42	10	....	185	260	58	4th, West Div.	Lost Semi-Final
1967-68	74	20	13	4	....	11	20	6	....	31	33	10	....	200	224	72	2nd, West Div.	Lost Quarter-Final

2006-07 Player Personnel

FORWARDS	HT	WT	S	Place of Birth	Date	2005-06 Club
ARMSTRONG, Derek	6-0	195	R	Ottawa, Ont.	4/23/73	Los Angeles
AVERY, Sean	5-10	185	L	Pickering, Ont.	4/10/80	Los Angeles
BELANGER, Eric	6-0	185	L	Sherbrooke, Que.	12/16/77	Los Angeles
BROWN, Dustin	6-0	195	R	Ithaca, NY	11/4/84	Los Angeles
CAMMALLERI, Michael	5-9	180	L	Richmond Hill, Ont.	6/8/82	Los Angeles
CLARKE, Noah	5-9	185	L	La Verne, CA	6/11/79	Los Angeles-Manchester
CONROY, Craig	6-2	197	R	Potsdam, NY	9/4/71	Los Angeles
COWAN, Jeff	6-2	210	L	Scarborough, Ont.	9/27/76	Los Angeles
FROLOV, Alexander	6-3	210	R	Moscow, USSR	6/19/82	Los Angeles
GAUTHIER, Gabe	5-9	200	L	Buena Park, CA	1/20/84	U. of Denver
GIULIANO, Jeff	5-9	205	L	Nashua, NH	6/20/79	Los Angeles-Manchester
HOGEBOOM, Greg	6-0	190	R	Toronto, Ont.	9/26/82	Manchester-Reading
IVANANS, Raitis	6-3	263	L	Riga, Latvia	1/1/79	Montreal-Hamilton
JACKMAN, Tim	6-4	210	R	Minot, ND	11/14/81	Phoenix-San Antonio-Manchester
KANKO, Petr	5-9	195	L	Pribram, Czech.	2/7/84	Los Angeles-Manchester
KOPITAR, Anze	6-4	220	L	Jesenice, Yugoslavia	8/24/87	Sodertalje-Sodertalje
KOSTOPOULOS, Tom	6-0	200	R	Mississauga, Ont.	1/24/79	Los Angeles
LUKACEVIC, Ned	6-0	185	L	Podgorica, Serbia	2/11/86	Swift Current-Manchester
McCAULEY, Alyn	5-11	200	L	Brockville, Ont.	5/29/77	San Jose
O'SULLIVAN, Patrick	5-11	190	L	Winston Salem, NC	2/1/85	Houston
PARROS, George	6-4	232	R	Washington, PA	12/29/79	Los Angeles
PUSHKAREV, Konstantin	6-0	180	L	Ust-Kamenogorsk, USSR	2/12/85	Los Angeles-Manchester
ROUSSIN, Dany	6-2	195	L	Quebec City, Que.	1/9/85	Manchester-Reading
RYAN, Matt	5-11	182	R	Sharon, Ont.	11/12/83	Los Angeles-Manchester
THORNTON, Scott	6-3	225	L	London, Ont.	1/9/71	San Jose
TUKONEN, Lauri	6-2	200	R	Hyvinkaa, Finland	9/1/86	Manchester
WILLSIE, Brian	6-1	195	R	London, Ont.	3/16/78	Washington
DEFENSEMEN						
BLAKE, Rob	6-4	225	R	Simcoe, Ont.	12/10/69	Colorado
BUCKLEY, Brendan	6-1	205	R	Boston, MA	2/26/77	Peoria
DALLMAN, Kevin	5-11	195	R	Niagara Falls, Ont.	2/26/81	Boston-St. Louis
GLEASON, Tim	6-1	202	L	Clawson, MI	1/29/83	Los Angeles
HARROLD, Peter	5-11	195	R	Kirtland Hills, Ont.	6/8/83	Boston College
MILLER, Aaron	6-4	200	R	Buffalo, NY	8/11/71	Los Angeles
MORMINA, Joey	6-6	220	L	Montreal, Que.	6/29/82	Manchester
NORSTROM, Mattias	6-2	210	L	Stockholm, Sweden	1/2/72	Los Angeles
PETIOT, Richard	6-2	190	L	Daysland, Alta.	8/20/82	Los Angeles-Manchester
SOPEL, Brent	6-1	205	R	Calgary, Alta.	1/7/77	NY Islanders-Los Angeles
VISNOVSKY, Lubomir	5-10	188	L	Topolcany, Czech.	8/11/76	Los Angeles
WEAVER, Mike	5-9	180	R	Bramalea, Ont.	5/2/78	Los Angeles

GOALTENDERS	HT	WT	C	Place of Birth	Date	2005-06 Club
BRUST, Barry	6-2	210	L	Swan River, Man.	8/8/83	Reading-Manchester
CLOUTIER, Dan	6-1	185	L	Mont-Laurier, Que.	4/22/76	Vancouver
FUKUFUJI, Yutaka	6-1	180	L	Tokyo, Japan	9/17/82	Manchester-Reading
GARON, Mathieu	6-2	192	R	Chandler, Que.	1/9/78	Los Angeles
LABARBERA, Jason	6-2	230	L	Burnaby, B.C.	1/18/80	Los Angeles-Manchester
MUNCE, Ryan	6-2	180	L	Mississauga, Ont.	4/16/85	Bakersfield
TAYLOR, Daniel	5-11	179	L	Plymouth, England	4/28/86	Kingston

The Kings have reacquired free agent defenseman Rob Blake, the club's former captain and only Norris Trophy winner. Blake had played with Colorado since the Kings traded him to the Avalanche in February of 2001.

General Managers' History

Larry Regan, 1967-68 to 1972-73; Larry Regan and Jake Milford, 1973-74; Jake Milford, 1974-75 to 1976-77; George Maguire, 1977-78 to 1982-83; George Maguire and Rogie Vachon, 1983-84; Rogie Vachon, 1984-85 to 1991-92; Nick Beverley, 1992-93, 1993-94; Sam McMaster, 1994-95 to 1996-97; Dave Taylor, 1997-98 to 2005-06; Dean Lombardi, 2006-07.

Captains' History

Bob Wall, 1967-68, 1968-69; Larry Cahan, 1969-70, 1970-71; Bob Pulford, 1971-72, 1972-73; Terry Harper, 1973-74, 1974-75; Mike Murphy, 1975-76 to 1980-81; Dave Lewis, 1981-82, 1982-83; Terry Ruskowski, 1983-84, 1984-85; Dave Taylor, 1985-86 to 1988-89; Wayne Gretzky, 1989-90 to 1991-92; Wayne Gretzky and Luc Robitaille, 1992-93; Wayne Gretzky, 1993-94, 1994-95; Wayne Gretzky and Rob Blake, 1995-96; Rob Blake, 1996-97 to 2000-01; Mattias Norstrom, 2001-02 to date.

2005-06 Scoring

* – rookie

Regular Season

Pos	#	Player	Team	GP	G	A	Pts	+/–	PIM	PP	SH	GW	S	%
D	17	Lubomir Visnovsky	L.A.	80	17	50	67	7	50	10	0	3	152	11.2
C	22	Craig Conroy	L.A.	78	22	44	66	13	78	5	3	3	154	14.3
C	38	Pavol Demitra	L.A.	58	25	37	62	21	42	7	5	7	184	13.6
C	13	Michael Cammalleri	L.A.	80	26	29	55	–14	50	15	0	4	206	12.6
L	24	Alexander Frolov	L.A.	69	21	33	54	17	40	4	3	4	174	12.1
R	37	Mark Parrish	NYI	57	24	17	41	–14	16	13	0	5	102	23.5
			L.A.	19	5	3	8	–9	4	3	0	0	35	14.3
			TOTAL	76	29	20	49	–23	20	16	0	5	137	21.2
C	7	Derek Armstrong	L.A.	62	13	28	41	–2	46	7	0	1	100	13.0
D	6	Joseph Corvo	L.A.	81	14	26	40	16	38	7	0	3	190	7.4
C	19	Sean Avery	L.A.	75	15	24	39	–5	257	1	3	1	189	7.9
C	25	Eric Belanger	L.A.	65	17	20	37	–5	62	5	0	1	119	14.3
R	23	Dustin Brown	L.A.	79	14	14	28	–10	80	6	0	2	159	8.8
D	5	Brent Sopel	NYI	57	2	25	27	–9	64	2	0	0	121	1.7
			L.A.	11	0	1	1	–4	6	0	0	0	12	0.0
			TOTAL	68	2	26	28	–13	70	2	0	0	133	1.5
D	14	Mattias Norstrom	L.A.	77	4	23	27	–3	58	2	1	1	83	4.8
L	20	Luc Robitaille	L.A.	65	15	9	24	–6	52	3	0	2	125	12.0
C	97	Jeremy Roenick	L.A.	58	9	13	22	–5	36	2	0	1	111	8.1
R	29	Tom Kostopoulos	L.A.	76	8	14	22	–8	100	0	0	1	74	10.8
D	42	Tim Gleason	L.A.	78	2	19	21	0	77	0	0	0	72	2.8
D	10	Nathan Dempsey	L.A.	53	2	11	13	0	48	0	0	0	58	3.4
L	15	Jeff Cowan	L.A.	46	8	1	9	–8	73	0	0	0	53	15.1
D	43	Mike Weaver	L.A.	53	0	9	9	–3	14	0	0	0	21	0.0
D	3	Aaron Miller	L.A.	56	0	8	8	–6	27	0	0	0	32	0.0
L	53	Jeff Giuliano	L.A.	48	3	4	7	0	26	0	0	2	32	9.4
R	57	* George Parros	L.A.	55	2	3	5	1	138	0	0	0	23	8.7
R	48	* Petr Kanko	L.A.	10	1	0	1	1	0	0	0	0	7	14.3
R	9	* Konstantin Pushkarev	L.A.	1	0	1	1	0	0	0	0	0	0	0.0
C	40	* Matt Ryan	L.A.	12	0	1	1	–4	2	0	0	0	8	0.0
L	49	Ryan Flinn	L.A.	2	0	0	0	0	5	0	0	0	0	0.0
D	2	* Richard Petiot	L.A.	2	0	0	0	–2	2	0	0	0	1	0.0
L	56	* Connor James	L.A.	2	0	0	0	–1	0	0	0	0	1	0.0
L	77	Ken Belanger	L.A.	5	0	0	0	–1	7	0	0	0	0	0.0
L	39	Noah Clarke	L.A.	5	0	0	0	0	0	0	0	0	3	0.0

Goaltending

No.	Goaltender	GPI	Mins	Avg	W	L	OT	EN	SO	GA	SA	S%	G	A	PIM
35	* Jason Labarbera	29	1433	2.89	11	9	2	5	1	69	688	.900	0	1	0
31	Mathieu Garon	63	3446	3.22	31	26	3	4	4	185	1738	.894	0	3	8
45	* Adam Hauser	1	51	7.06	0	0	0	0	0	6	24	.750	0	0	0
	Totals	**82**	**4975**	**3.24**	**42**	**35**	**5**	**9**	**5**	**269**	**2459**	**.891**			

President and General Manager

LOMBARDI, DEAN
President and General Manager, Los Angeles Kings.
Born in Holyoke, MA, March 5, 1958.

The Los Angeles Kings named Dean Lombardi president and general manager on April 21, 2006. Lombardi, formerly a member of the San Jose Sharks front office for 13 years, including seven seasons as general manager, followed by three years as a pro scout for the Philadelphia Flyers from 2003 to 2006, is the eighth general manager in Kings history.

An executive in the San Jose front office since 1990, Lombardi first served as assistant general manager (a post he held the previous two seasons with the Minnesota North Stars) for the expansion Sharks before being elevated to vice president, director of hockey operations in 1992. Four years later, he was promoted to executive vice president and general manager and given the responsibility of turning around the young franchise. During his tenure as general manager in San Jose from 1996 to 2003, Lombardi helped build the Sharks into one of the premier teams in the NHL. Under Lombardi, San Jose reached the playoffs five times – highlighted by two trips to the Western Conference Semifinals – and one Pacific Division title in 2002. The Lombardi-led Sharks in 2002 also tied an NHL-record with six consecutive seasons of improved point totals under on g.m. (Bill Torrey/New York Islanders) while building a roster that became progressively younger in age each season.

During his time as general manager in San Jose, Lombardi made many key personnel and player moves, stocking the Sharks organization with a good mix of veteran stars and up-and-coming youngsters that helped make the Sharks legitimate Stanley Cup contenders.

From the NHL Entry Draft, Lombardi brought to San Jose players like Patrick Marleau, Vesa Toskala, Jonathan Cheechoo, Brad Stuart, Scott Hannan, Marco Sturm, Marcel Goc and Christian Ehrhoff. *The Hockey News* ranked the Sharks' prospects (age 22 and under) as the best in the NHL in 1999-2000 and second best in 2000-01. Lombardi's history in San Jose as it relates to trades and free agency is impressive as well, having brought in such players as Owen Nolan, Teemu Selanne, Adam Graves, Vincent Damphousse, Mike Ricci, Kyle McClaren, Mike Vernon, Todd Harvey, Bryan Marchment and Scott Thornton.

Prior to joining the North Stars, Lombardi spent three seasons as a player representative, including the representation of five members of the 1988 United States Olympic team, and at the time he joined Minnesota's front office Lombardi was only the second former player agent to be employed in an NHL front office (Brian Burke/Vancouver Canucks was the other).

Born in Holyoke, Massachusetts, and raised in nearby Ludlow, Lombardi received his undergraduate degree from the University of New Haven where he finished third in his class. On the ice he was the hockey team's captain his final two seasons, and he received a full athletic scholarship and the school's student-athlete of the year award. In 1985, Lombardi earned his Law Degree (with honors) from Tulane Law School where he specialized in Labor Law.

Club Records

Team

(Figures in brackets for season records are games played; records for fewest points, wins, ties, losses, goals, goals against are for 70 or more games)

Record		
Most Points	**105**	1974-75 (80)
Most Wins	**46**	1990-91 (80)
Most Ties	**21**	1974-75 (80)
Most Losses	**52**	1969-70 (76)
Most Goals	**376**	1988-89 (80)
Most Goals Against	**389**	1985-86 (80)
Fewest Points	**38**	1969-70 (76)
Fewest Wins	**14**	1969-70 (76)
Fewest Ties	**5**	1998-99 (82)
Fewest Losses	**17**	1974-75 (80)
Fewest Goals	**168**	1969-70 (76)
Fewest Goals Against	**185**	1974-75 (80)
Longest Winning Streak		
Overall	**8**	Oct. 21-Nov. 7/72, Feb. 23-Mar. 9/92
Home	**12**	Oct. 10-Dec. 5/92
Away	**8**	Dec. 18/74-Jan. 16/75
Longest Undefeated Streak		
Overall	**11**	Feb. 28-Mar. 24/74 (9 wins, 2 ties)
Home	**13**	Oct. 10-Dec. 8/92 (12 wins, 1 tie)
Away	**11**	Oct. 10-Dec. 11/74 (6 wins, 5 ties)
Longest Losing Streak		
Overall	**11**	Mar. 16-Apr. 4/04
Home	**9**	Feb. 8-Mar. 12/86
Away	**11**	Jan. 11-Feb. 15/70
Longest Winless Streak		
Overall	**17**	Jan. 29-Mar. 5/70 (13 losses, 4 ties)
Home	**9**	Jan. 29-Mar. 5/70 (8 losses, 1 tie), Feb. 8-Mar. 12/86 (9 losses)
Away	**20**	Jan. 11-Apr. 3/70 (16 losses, 4 ties)
Most Shutouts, Season	**10**	2000-01 (82)
Most PIM, Season	**2,247**	1992-93 (84)
Most Goals, Game	**12**	Nov. 29/84 (Van. 1 at L.A. 12)

Individual

Record		
Most Seasons	**17**	Dave Taylor
Most Games	**1,111**	Dave Taylor
Most Goals, Career	**557**	Luc Robitaille
Most Assists, Career	**757**	Marcel Dionne
Most Points Career	**1,307**	Marcel Dionne (550G, 757A)
Most PIM, Career	**1,846**	Marty McSorley
Most Shutouts, Career	**32**	Rogie Vachon
Longest Consecutive Games Streak	**324**	Marcel Dionne (Jan. 7/78-Jan. 9/82)
Most Goals, Season	**70**	Bernie Nicholls (1988-89)
Most Assists, Season	**122**	Wayne Gretzky (1990-91)
Most Points, Season	**168**	Wayne Gretzky (1988-89; 54G, 114A)
Most PIM, Season	**399**	Marty McSorley (1992-93)
Most Points, Defenseman, Season	**76**	Larry Murphy (1980-81; 16G, 60A)
Most Points, Center, Season	**168**	Wayne Gretzky (1988-89; 54G, 114A)
Most Points, Right Wing, Season	**112**	Dave Taylor (1980-81; 47G, 65A)
Most Points, Left Wing, Season	***125**	Luc Robitaille (1992-93; 63G, 62A)
Most Points, Rookie, Season	**84**	Luc Robitaille (1986-87; 45G, 39A)
Most Shutouts, Season	**8**	Rogie Vachon (1976-77)
Most Goals, Game	**4**	Seventeen times
Most Assists, Game	**6**	Bernie Nicholls (Dec. 1/88), Tomas Sandstrom (Oct. 9/93)
Most Points, Game	**8**	Bernie Nicholls (Dec. 1/88; 2G, 6A)

* NHL Record.

Retired Numbers

16	Marcel Dionne	1975-1987
18	Dave Taylor	1977-1994
30	Rogie Vachon	1971-1978
99	Wayne Gretzky	1988-1996

Coaching History

Red Kelly, 1967-68, 1968-69; Hal Laycoe and Johnny Wilson, 1969-70; Larry Regan, 1970-71; Larry Regan and Fred Glover, 1971-72; Bob Pulford, 1972-73 to 1976-77; Ron Stewart, 1977-78; Bob Berry, 1978-79 to 1980-81; Parker MacDonald and Don Perry, 1981-82; Don Perry, 1982-83; Don Perry, Rogie Vachon and Roger Neilson, 1983-84; Pat Quinn, 1984-85, 1985-86; Pat Quinn and Mike Murphy 1986-87; Mike Murphy, Rogie Vachon and Robbie Ftorek, 1987-88; Robbie Ftorek, 1988-89; Tom Webster, 1989-90 to 1991-92; Barry Melrose, 1992-93, 1993-94; Barry Melrose and Rogie Vachon, 1994-95; Larry Robinson, 1995-96 to 1998-99; Andy Murray, 1999-2000 to 2003-04; Andy Murray and John Torchetti, 2005-06; Marc Crawford, 2006-07.

All-time Record vs. Other Clubs

Regular Season

	At Home								On Road								Total							
	GP	W	L	T	OL	GF	GA	PTS	GP	W	L	T	OL	GF	GA	PTS	GP	W	L	T	OL	GF	GA	PTS
Anaheim	34	19	11	4	0	99	85	42	34	11	15	7	1	91	119	30	68	30	26	11	1	190	204	72
Atlanta	5	4	0	0	1	26	15	9	4	3	0	0	1	16	7	7	9	7	0	0	2	42	22	16
Boston	61	21	32	7	1	210	224	50	62	12	44	6	0	175	287	30	123	33	76	13	1	385	511	80
Buffalo	54	22	23	9	0	185	187	53	54	16	29	9	0	158	227	41	108	38	52	18	0	343	414	94
Calgary	93	47	37	9	0	342	320	103	96	28	53	12	3	316	417	71	189	75	90	21	3	658	737	174
Carolina	31	17	11	3	0	131	116	37	31	11	13	5	2	115	114	29	62	28	24	8	2	246	230	66
Chicago	76	35	33	8	0	253	252	78	77	32	35	9	1	227	266	74	153	67	68	17	1	480	518	152
Colorado	45	26	14	5	0	180	145	57	44	18	23	3	0	150	176	39	89	44	37	8	0	330	321	96
Columbus	10	6	3	1	0	24	19	13	10	4	4	0	2	38	30	10	20	10	7	1	2	62	49	23
Dallas	86	38	29	19	0	288	245	95	88	22	51	13	2	238	335	59	174	60	80	32	2	526	580	154
Detroit	82	42	26	14	0	325	256	98	81	30	36	13	2	278	312	75	163	72	62	27	2	603	568	173
Edmonton	79	29	35	15	0	304	324	73	79	23	41	15	0	278	356	61	158	52	76	30	0	582	680	134
Florida	10	6	4	0	0	30	30	12	8	1	4	3	0	14	23	5	18	7	8	3	0	44	53	17
Minnesota	10	4	4	2	0	22	24	10	10	5	2	3	0	25	20	13	20	9	6	5	0	47	44	23
Montreal	65	19	37	9	0	199	256	47	65	8	46	11	0	162	292	27	130	27	83	20	0	361	548	74
Nashville	14	9	4	0	1	45	34	19	14	8	3	3	0	36	23	19	28	17	7	3	1	81	57	38
New Jersey	42	28	8	6	0	201	130	62	43	19	18	5	1	148	142	44	85	47	26	11	1	349	272	106
NY Islanders	45	21	17	7	0	163	143	49	44	15	24	5	0	123	156	35	89	36	41	12	0	286	299	84
NY Rangers	60	23	26	10	1	199	216	57	58	17	35	6	0	172	233	40	118	40	61	16	1	371	449	97
Ottawa	10	8	1	1	0	46	21	17	10	4	5	1	0	29	35	9	20	12	6	2	0	75	56	26
Philadelphia	66	21	37	8	0	193	223	50	63	16	40	7	0	156	244	39	129	37	77	15	0	349	467	89
Phoenix	78	31	32	14	1	307	297	77	80	27	39	11	3	256	316	68	158	58	71	25	4	563	613	145
Pittsburgh	69	44	17	8	0	265	183	96	73	25	38	10	0	233	265	60	142	69	55	18	0	498	448	156
St. Louis	80	37	31	12	0	269	229	86	80	20	49	10	1	203	297	51	160	57	80	22	1	472	526	137
San Jose	41	24	12	4	1	127	105	53	41	13	22	3	3	112	139	32	82	37	34	7	4	239	244	85
Tampa Bay	12	1	9	2	0	25	40	4	10	5	5	0	0	22	23	10	22	6	14	2	0	47	63	14
Toronto	65	34	21	10	0	234	191	78	69	23	34	11	1	225	267	58	134	57	55	21	1	459	458	136
Vancouver	101	53	32	16	0	399	314	122	99	32	50	16	1	308	375	81	200	85	82	32	1	707	689	203
Washington	48	27	14	6	1	189	147	61	46	21	18	7	0	171	185	49	94	48	32	13	1	360	332	110
Defunct Clubs	35	27	6	2	0	141	76	56	34	11	14	9	0	91	109	31	69	38	20	11	0	232	185	87
Totals	**1507**	**723**	**566**	**211**	**7**	**5421**	**4847**	**1664**	**1507**	**480**	**790**	**213**	**24**	**4566**	**5790**	**1197**	**3014**	**1203**	**1356**	**424**	**31**	**9987**	**10637**	**2861**

Playoffs

	Series	W	L	GP	W	L	T	GF	GA	Last Mtg.	Rnd.	Result
Boston	2	0	2	13	5	8	0	38	56	1977	QF	L 2-4
Calgary	6	4	2	26	13	13	0	105	102	1993	DSF	W 4-2
Chicago	1	0	1	5	1	4	0	7	10	1974	QF	L 1-4
Colorado	2	0	2	14	6	8	0	23	33	2002	CQF	L 3-4
Dallas	1	0	1	7	3	4	0	21	26	1968	QF	L 3-4
Detroit	2	1	1	10	4	6	0	21	32	2001	CQF	W 4-2
Edmonton	7	2	5	36	12	24	0	127	154	1992	DSF	L 2-4
Montreal	1	0	1	5	1	4	0	12	15	1993	F	L 1-4
NY Islanders	1	0	1	4	1	3	0	10	21	1980	PRE	L 1-3
NY Rangers	2	0	2	6	1	5	0	14	32	1981	PRE	L 1-3
St. Louis	2	0	2	8	0	8	0	13	32	1998	CQF	L 0-4
Toronto	3	1	2	12	5	7	0	31	41	1993	CF	W 4-3
Vancouver	3	2	1	17	9	8	0	66	60	1993	DF	W 4-2
Defunct Clubs	1	1	0	7	4	3	0	23	25			
Totals	**34**	**11**	**23**	**170**	**65**	**105**	**0**	**511**	**639**			

Calgary totals include Atlanta Flames, 1972-73 to 1979-80.
Carolina totals include Hartford, 1979-80 to 1996-97.
Colorado totals include Quebec, 1979-80 to 1994-95.
Dallas totals include Minnesota North Stars, 1967-68 to 1992-93.
New Jersey totals include Kansas City, 1974-75 to 1975-76, and Colorado Rockies, 1976-77 to 1981-82.
Phoenix totals include Winnipeg, 1979-80 to 1995-96.

Playoff Results 2006-2001

Year	Round	Opponent	Result	GF	GA
2002	CQF	Colorado	L 3-4	13	16
2001	CSF	Colorado	L 3-4	10	17
	CQF	Detroit	W 4-2	15	17

Abbreviations: Round: F - Final; **CF** - conference final; **CSF** - conference semi-final; **CQF** - conference quarter-final; **DF** - division final; **DSF** - division semi-final; **QF** - quarter-final; **PRE** - preliminary round.

2005-06 Results

Oct.	5	at Dallas	4-5	**Jan.**	2	Dallas	3-2*
	6	Phoenix	3-2		5	Phoenix	4-0
	9	Minnesota	2-1*		7	at San Jose	2-3
	11	Edmonton	3-1		9	at Anaheim	2-6
	13	Detroit	2-5		12	at Boston	6-0
	16	Columbus	3-1		14	at Buffalo	1-10
	19	at Colorado	5-4		17	Tampa Bay	1-4
	20	at Dallas	7-2		19	Atlanta	8-6
	23	Calgary	2-3		21	San Jose	3-4*
	25	Anaheim	3-1		23	Anaheim	3-2†
	28	San Jose	4-5		24	at San Jose	1-4
	29	St. Louis	5-2		26	Edmonton	3-5
Nov.	2	at Dallas	6-3		28	Anaheim	2-6
	3	at Phoenix	0-4		30	at Anaheim	3-4*
	5	Nashville	3-2†	**Feb.**	2	at Phoenix	1-2†
	9	at Detroit	4-5*		7	at Minnesota	1-5
	11	at Chicago	4-2		8	at Columbus	4-7
	13	at Columbus	8-2		11	Chicago	5-4*
	15	at Nashville	2-3		12	Dallas	6-5
	17	Vancouver	5-4	**Mar.**	2	Minnesota	3-2
	19	Colorado	4-3		4	Columbus	3-2
	22	at St. Louis	6-3		7	at Minnesota	3-2*
	24	at Nashville	3-4		9	at Detroit	3-7
	26	Chicago	3-2		11	at St. Louis	2-1†
	28	Detroit	2-5		13	at San Jose	3-4
	30	at Chicago	2-3		14	Phoenix	2-6
Dec.	2	at Ottawa	1-5		16	Dallas	1-4
	3	at Montreal	2-3		18	St. Louis	3-1
	6	at Toronto	2-1		20	Colorado	0-5
	8	Carolina	2-3		25	Nashville	6-4
	10	Florida	3-1		27	at Vancouver	4-7
	14	Washington	2-3		29	at Calgary	1-2
	16	at Anaheim	4-3†		30	at Edmonton	0-4
	17	Phoenix	4-1	**Apr.**	1	Dallas	1-0
	19	at Vancouver	4-3†		3	Vancouver	1-0
	21	at Calgary	5-2		4	at Anaheim	2-6
	23	at Edmonton	3-5		6	San Jose	0-5
	26	San Jose	4-3		8	Anaheim	2-4
	28	at Colorado	5-3		13	at Phoenix	0-3
	29	at Phoenix	5-6*		15	Calgary	2-1†
	31	at Dallas	3-2		17	at San Jose	4-0

* – Overtime † – Shootout

Entry Draft
Selections 2006-1992

2006
Pick
11 Jonathan Bernier
17 Trevor Lewis
48 Joe Ryan
74 Jeff Zatkoff
86 Bud Holloway
114 Niclas Andersen
134 David Meckler
144 Martin Nolet
164 Constantin Braun

2005
Pick
11 Anze Kopitar
50 Dany Roussin
60 T.J. Fast
72 Jonathan Quick
139 Patrik Hersley
184 Ryan McGinnis
206 Josh Meyers
226 John Seymour

2004
Pick
11 Lauri Tukonen
95 Paul Baier
110 Ned Lukacevic
143 Eric Neilson
174 Scott Parse
205 Mike Curry
221 Daniel Taylor
238 Yutaka Fukufuji
264 Valtteri Tenkanen

2003
Pick
13 Dustin Brown
26 Brian Boyle
27 Jeff Tambellini
44 Konstantin Pushkarev
82 Ryan Munce
152 Brady Murray
174 Esa Pirnes
231 Matt Zaba
244 Mike Sullivan
274 Marty Guerin

2002
Pick
18 Denis Grebeshkov
50 Sergei Anshakov
66 Petr Kanko
104 Aaron Rome
115 Mark Rooneem
152 Greg Hogeboom
157 Joel Andresen
185 Ryan Murphy
215 Mikhail Lyubushin
248 Tuukka Pulliainen
279 Connor James

2001
Pick
18 Jens Karlsson
30 Dave Steckel
49 Michael Cammalleri
51 Jaroslav Bednar
83 Henrik Juntunen
116 Richard Petiot
152 Terry Denike
153 Tuukka Mantyla
214 Cristobal Huet
237 Mike Gabinet
277 Sebastien Laplante

2000
Pick
20 Alexander Frolov
54 Andreas Lilja
86 Yanick Lehoux*
118 Lubomir Visnovsky
165 Nathan Marsters
201 Yevgeny Fedorov
206 Tim Eriksson
218 Craig Olynick
245 Dan Welch
250 Flavien Conne
282 Carl Grahn

1999
Pick
43 Andrei Shefer
74 Jason Crain
76 Frantisek Kaberle
92 Cory Campbell
104 Brian McGrattan
125 Daniel Johansson
133 Jean-Francois Nogues
193 Kevin Baker
222 George Parros
250 Noah Clarke

1998
Pick
21 Mathieu Biron
46 Justin Papineau
76 Alexei Volkov
103 Kip Brennan
133 Joe Rullier
163 Tomas Zizka
190 Tommi Hannus
217 Jim Henkel
248 Matthew Yeats

1997
Pick
3 Olli Jokinen
15 Matt Zultek
29 Scott Barney
83 Joe Corvo
99 Sean Blanchard
84 Richard Seeley
150 Jeff Katcher
193 Jay Kopischke
220 Konrad Brand

1996
Pick
30 Josh Green
37 Marian Cisar
57 Greg Phillips
84 Mikael Simons
96 Eric Belanger
120 Jesse Black
123 Peter Hogan
190 Stephen Valiquette
193 Kai Nurminen
219 Sebastien Simard

1995
Pick
3 Aki Berg
33 Don MacLean
50 Pavel Rosa
59 Vladimir Tsyplakov
118 Jason Morgan
137 Igor Melyakov
157 Benoit Larose
163 Juha Vuorivirta
215 Brian Stewart

1994
Pick
7 Jamie Storr
33 Matt Johnson
59 Vitali Yachmenev
111 Chris Schmidt
163 Luc Gagne
189 Andrew Dale
215 Jan Nemecek
241 Sergei Shalomai

1993
Pick
42 Shayne Toporowski
68 Jeff Mitchell
94 Bob Wren
105 Frederick Beaubien
117 Jason Saal
120 Tomas Vlasak
146 Jere Karalahti
172 Justin Martin
198 John-Tra Dillabough
224 Martin Strbak
250 Kimmo Timonen
276 Patrick Howald

1992
Pick
39 Justin Hocking
63 Sandy Allan
87 Kevin Brown
111 Jeff Shevalier
135 Rem Murray
207 Magnus Wernblom
231 Ryan Pisiak
255 Jukka Tiilikainen

Club Directory

STAPLES Center

Los Angeles Kings
STAPLES Center
1111 South Figueroa Street
Los Angeles, CA 90015
Phone **213/742-7100**
GM FAX 310/535-4525
www.lakings.com
Capacity: 18,118

Executive
Owner .... Philip F. Anschutz
Owner .... Edward P. Roski
Governor .... Timothy J. Leiweke
President, Business Operations .... Shawn Hunter

Hockey Operations
President/General Manager................. Dean Lombardi
Assistant General Manager................. Ron Hextall
Director of Pro Development .... Mike O'Connell
Director of Amateur Development .... Dave Taylor
Director of Amateur Scouting .... Al Murray
Director of Operations .... Marshall Dickerson
Assistant Director of Amateur Scouting........ Grant Sonier
Scouting Coordinator .... Lee Callans
Executive Assistant, President/G.M. .... Kely Lyon
Royal Ambassador .... Rogie Vachon
Head Coach .... Marc Crawford
Associate Coach .... Mike Johnston
Assistant Coach .... Jamie Kompon
Assistant Coach/Player Development........ Nelson Emerson
Goaltending Coach......................... Bill Ranford
Pro Scouts .... Bob Berry, Rob Laird
Amateur Scouts .... Tony Gasparini, Terry McDonnell,
Brent McEwen, Jan Vopat, Ari Vuori,
Bob Crocker, Mike Donnelly,
Viacheslav Golovin, Victor Tjumenev

Medical
Head Athletic Trainer .... Chris Kingsley
Strength and Conditioning Trainer .... Mike Kadar, BAPE, MT, CSCS
Team Physician .... Dr. Ronald Kvitne
(Kerlan-Jobe Orthopaedic Clinic)
Internist .... Dr. Michael Mellman
Dentist .... Dr. Jeffrey Hoy
Opthamologist .... Dr. Howard Lazerson

Equipment Staff
Equipment Manager .... Darren Granger
Assistant Equipment Manager .... Corey Osmak
Assistant Equipment Manager .... Dana Bryson

Communications
Vice President, Communications and Broadcasting . Michael Altieri
Communications Director .... Jeff Moeller
Communications Manager .... Mike Kalinowski
Communications and Broadcasting Supervisor .... Stephanie Krauss

Broadcasting
TV Play-by-Play Announcer .... Bob Miller
Radio Play-by-Play Announcer .... Nick Nickson
TV Color Commentator...................... Jim Fox
Radio Color Commentator .... Daryl Evans

Miscellaneous
Training center .... Toyota Sports Center
Television .... FSN West
Radio Flagship .... KTLK AM 1150

Coach

CRAWFORD, MARC
Coach, Los Angeles Kings. Born in Belleville, Ont., February 13, 1961.

The Los Angeles Kings named Marc Crawford as the club's 21st head coach on May 22, 2006. He replaced John Torchetti, the Kings' interim head coach after former head coach Andy Murray was relieved of his duties on March 21. Crawford is the third-youngest coach in NHL history to reach 400 career wins (44 years, 355 days), trailing only Scotty Bowman and Glen Sather.

Hired by Vancouver in January of 1999, Crawford became the Canucks' all-time leader in regular-season wins for Vancouver with 246 in 529 regular-season games over seven seasons in Vancouver. In 2003-04, the Canucks won the Northwest Division title (the franchise's first division title since 1992-93) and in 2003 the Canucks advanced to the Western Conference Semifinals.

Crawford began his NHL coaching career with Quebec in 1994 and in his first season he became the youngest coach to win the Jack Adams Award for coach of the year. After the Nordiques relocated to Denver he won the Stanley Cup in 1996 and with the win became the third-youngest coach in NHL history to raise Lord Stanley's Cup. Crawford's four seasons with Colorado/Quebec were marked by incredible success. In addition to the Stanley Cup, the franchise's first, Crawford helped lead them to the Western Conference Finals the following year as his Colorado playoff teams combined to go 26-12 in 1996 and 1997. The franchise also enjoyed a tremendous amount of success in the regular season. Crawford's 1994-95 Nordiques won the first of nine consecutive divisional titles (the streak was snapped by the Crawford-led Canucks in 2003-04) for the club. He was also the head coach for Team Canada at the 1998 Nagano Winter Olympics and an assistant coach at the 1996 World Cup of Hockey.

Crawford coached the Avalanche for two seasons after winning the Cup before leaving following the 1997-98 season. He then spent time providing analysis for CBC's Hockey Night in Canada before being hired as the 15th head coach of the Canucks, where he had played from 1981-82 to 1986-87. As a left winger, Crawford recorded 50 points (19 goals, 31 assists) and 229 penalty minutes in 176 regular season NHL games from 1981 to 1987. He was a rookie on the Canucks team that reached the Stanley Cup Finals in 1982 after being a member of two Memorial Cup teams with Cornwall in 1980 and 1981. He was also named to the Memorial Cup All-Star Team in 1981.

Coaching Record

Season	Team	Games	Regular Season			Playoffs		
			W	L	O/T	Games	W	L
1989-90	Cornwall (OHL)	66	24	38	4	6	2	4
1990-91	Cornwall (OHL)	66	23	42	1	....	....	....
1991-92	St. John's (AHL)	80	39	29	12	16	11	5
1992-93	St. John's (AHL)	80	41	26	13	9	4	5
1993-94	St. John's (AHL)	80	45	23	12	11	6	5
1994-95	Quebec (NHL)	48	30	13	5	6	2	4
1995-96*	Colorado (NHL)	82	47	25	10	22	16	6
1996-97	Colorado (NHL)	82	49	24	9	17	10	7
1997-98	Colorado (NHL)	82	39	26	17	7	3	4
1998-99	Vancouver (NHL)	37	8	23	6	....	....	....
1999-2000	Vancouver (NHL)	82	30	37	15	....	....	....
2000-01	Vancouver (NHL)	82	36	35	11	4	0	4
2001-02	Vancouver (NHL)	82	42	33	7	6	2	4
2002-03	Vancouver (NHL)	82	45	24	13	14	7	7
2003-04	Vancouver (NHL)	82	43	29	10	7	3	4
2004-05	Vancouver (NHL)				Season Cancelled			
2005-06	Vancouver (NHL)	82	42	32	8	....	....	....
	NHL Totals	**823**	**411**	**301**	**111**	**83**	**43**	**40**

* Stanley Cup win.

Minnesota Wild

2005-06 Results: 38W-36L-5OTL-3SOL 84PTS.
Fifth, Northwest Division

Year-by-Year Record

Season	GP	Home W	L	T	OL	Road W	L	T	OL	Overall W	L	T	OL	GF	GA	Pts.	Finished	Playoff Result
2005-06	82	23	16	....	2	15	20	....	6	38	36	....	8	231	215	84	5th, Northwest Div.	Out of Playoffs
2004-05	....																	
2003-04	82	19	13	7	2	11	16	13	1	30	29	20	3	188	183	83	5th, Northwest Div.	Out of Playoffs
2002-03	82	25	13	3	0	17	16	7	1	42	29	10	1	198	178	95	3rd, Northwest Div.	Lost Conf. Championship
2001-02	82	14	14	8	5	12	21	4	4	26	35	12	9	195	238	73	5th, Northwest Div.	Out of Playoffs
2000-01	82	14	13	10	4	11	26	3	1	25	39	13	5	168	210	68	5th, Northwest Div.	Out of Playoffs

2006-07 Schedule

Oct.	Thu.	5	Colorado	Sat.	6	Colorado
	Sat.	7	Nashville	Tue.	9	at Calgary
	Tue.	10	Vancouver	Thu.	11	at Vancouver
	Thu.	12	Washington	Fri.	12	at Edmonton
	Sat.	14	Columbus	Sun.	14	at Chicago
	Wed.	18	at Los Angeles	Tue.	16	Edmonton
	Fri.	20	at Anaheim	Fri.	19	at Chicago
	Sat.	21	at San Jose	Sat.	20	Dallas
	Wed.	25	Los Angeles	Fri.	26	Calgary
	Fri.	27	Anaheim	Sat.	27	at Columbus
	Sun.	29	at Colorado	Sat.	30	at St. Louis
Nov.	Thu.	2	Vancouver	Feb. Thu.	1	at Colorado
	Sat.	4	Nashville	Sat.	3	at Phoenix
	Tue.	7	at San Jose	Tue.	6	at Dallas
	Sat.	11	at Los Angeles	Thu.	8	Florida
	Sun.	12	at Anaheim*	Sat.	10	Carolina
	Tue.	14	at Phoenix	Wed.	14	Vancouver
	Thu.	16	at Nashville	Sat.	17	at Nashville
	Sat.	18	Colorado	Sun.	18	at St. Louis*
	Mon.	20	at Ottawa	Tue.	20	Dallas
	Wed.	22	at Montreal	Thu.	22	at Colorado
	Fri.	24	Phoenix*	Sun.	25	Edmonton*
	Sat.	25	at Columbus	Wed.	28	at Calgary
	Wed.	29	San Jose	Mar. Thu.	1	at Edmonton
Dec.	Fri.	1	Detroit	Sun.	4	at Vancouver
	Sat.	2	at Dallas	Tue.	6	San Jose
	Tue.	5	Chicago	Thu.	8	at Boston
	Thu.	7	Calgary	Fri.	9	at Buffalo
	Sat.	9	Chicago	Sun.	11	Colorado*
	Tue.	12	at Calgary	Tue.	13	at Vancouver
	Thu.	14	at Edmonton	Thu.	15	at Edmonton
	Sat.	16	at Vancouver	Sat.	17	at Calgary
	Tue.	19	Vancouver	Tue.	20	Phoenix
	Fri.	22	at Detroit	Thu.	22	St. Louis
	Sat.	23	Detroit	Sat.	24	Los Angeles
	Tue.	26	at Toronto	Tue.	27	Calgary
	Wed.	27	at Detroit	Thu.	29	Calgary
	Fri.	29	Columbus	Sat.	31	at Colorado*
	Sun.	31	Anaheim*	Apr. Tue.	3	Edmonton
Jan.	Tue.	2	Atlanta	Thu.	5	Edmonton
	Thu.	4	Tampa Bay	Sat.	7	St. Louis

* Denotes afternoon game.

Franchise date: June 25, 1997

NORTHWEST DIVISION

7th NHL Season

Manny Fernandez played in a career-high 58 games for Minnesota last season and won 30 games. He ranked sixth in the NHL in both goals-against average (2.29) and save percentage (.919).

2006-07 Player Personnel

FORWARDS

	HT	WT	S	Place of Birth	Date	2005-06 Club
BOOGAARD, Derek	6-7	250	R	Saskatoon, Sask.	6/23/82	Minnesota
BOUCHARD, Pierre-Marc	5-10	165	L	Sherbrooke, Que.	4/27/84	Minnesota
DEMITRA, Pavol	6-0	206	L	Dubnica, Czech.	11/29/74	Los Angeles
DUPUIS, Pascal	6-0	196	L	Laval, Que.	4/7/79	Minnesota
FOY, Matt	6-2	219	R	Oakville, Ont.	5/18/83	Minnesota-Houston
GABORIK, Marian	6-1	190	L	Trencin, Czech.	2/14/82	Minnesota
IRMEN, Danny	6-0	190	R	Fargo, ND	9/6/84	U. of Minnesota-Houston
KOIVU, Mikko	6-2	205	L	Turku, Finland	3/12/83	Minnesota
MORGAN, Jason	6-1	200	L	St. John's, Nfld.	10/9/76	Chicago-Norfolk
PARRISH, Mark	5-11	200	R	Bloomington, MN	2/2/77	NY Islanders-Los Angeles
RADIVOJEVIC, Branko	6-1	209	R	Piestany, Czech.	11/24/80	Philadelphia
ROLSTON, Brian	6-2	210	L	Flint, MI	2/21/73	Minnesota
SMITH, Wyatt	5-11	200	L	Thief River Falls, MN	2/13/77	NY Islanders-Bridgeport
VEILLEUX, Stephane	6-1	187	L	Beauceville, Que.	11/16/81	Minnesota
WALZ, Wes	5-10	180	R	Calgary, Alta.	5/15/70	Minnesota
WEINHANDL, Mattias	6-0	183	R	Ljungby, Sweden	6/1/80	NY Islanders-Minnesota
WHITE, Todd	5-10	194	L	Kanata, Ont.	5/21/75	Minnesota

DEFENSEMEN

	HT	WT	S	Place of Birth	Date	2005-06 Club
BELLE, Shawn	6-1	230	L	Edmonton, Alta.	1/3/85	Iowa-Houston
BURNS, Brent	6-4	200	R	Ajax, Ont.	3/9/85	Minnesota
CARNEY, Keith	6-1	216	L	Providence, RI	2/3/70	Anaheim-Vancouver
FOSTER, Kurtis	6-5	235	R	Carp, Ont.	11/24/81	Minnesota-Houston
JOHNSSON, Kim	6-1	205	L	Malmo, Sweden	3/16/76	Philadelphia
NUMMELIN, Petteri	5-10	187	L	Turku, Finland	11/25/72	Lugano
REITZ, Erik	6-1	210	R	Detroit, MI	7/29/82	Minnesota-Houston
SCHULTZ, Nick	6-1	207	L	Strasbourg, Sask.	8/25/82	Minnesota
SKOULA, Martin	6-2	195	L	Litomerice, Czech.	10/28/79	Dallas-Minnesota

GOALTENDERS

	HT	WT	C	Place of Birth	Date	2005-06 Club
BACKSTROM, Niklas	6-2	196	L	Helsinki, Finland	2/13/78	Karpat
FERNANDEZ, Manny	6-0	180	L	Etobicoke, Ont.	8/27/74	Minnesota
HARDING, Josh	6-1	180	R	Regina, Sask.	6/18/84	Minnesota-Houston

2005-06 Scoring

*– rookie

Regular Season

Pos	#	Player	Team	GP	G	A	Pts	+/-	PIM	PP	SH	GW	S	%
C	12	Brian Rolston	MIN	82	34	45	79	14	50	15	5	7	293	11.6
R	10	Marian Gaborik	MIN	65	38	28	66	6	64	10	2	7	252	15.1
R	96	Pierre-Marc Bouchard	MIN	80	17	42	59	3	28	7	0	3	118	14.4
C	28	Todd White	MIN	61	19	21	40	-1	18	5	0	0	109	17.4
C	25	Randy Robitaille	MIN	67	12	28	40	-5	54	7	0	2	112	10.7
C	37	Wes Walz	MIN	82	19	18	37	7	61	1	1	0	127	15.0
C	32	Marc Chouinard	MIN	74	14	16	30	1	34	6	2	3	112	12.5
C	26 *	Kurtis Foster	MIN	58	10	18	28	-3	60	6	0	2	124	8.1
R	9	Alexandre Daigle	MIN	46	5	23	28	-6	12	2	0	1	59	8.5
L	11	Pascal Dupuis	MIN	67	10	16	26	-10	40	4	0	2	151	6.6
D	17	Filip Kuba	MIN	65	6	19	25	0	44	1	1	1	69	8.7
C	21 *	Mikko Koivu	MIN	64	6	15	21	-9	40	3	0	0	96	6.3
D	41	Martin Skoula	DAL	61	4	11	15	6	36	3	0	1	78	5.1
			MIN	17	1	5	6	0	10	0	0	0	14	7.1
			TOTAL	78	5	16	21	6	46	3	0	1	92	5.4
D	20	Andrei Zyuzin	MIN	57	7	11	18	-12	50	4	0	1	80	8.8
D	34	Daniel Tjarnqvist	MIN	60	3	15	18	-11	32	3	0	1	54	5.6
L	19	Stephane Veilleux	MIN	71	7	9	16	-13	63	0	0	1	87	8.0
D	8	Brent Burns	MIN	72	4	12	16	-7	32	1	0	1	73	5.5
D	55	Nick Schultz	MIN	79	2	12	14	2	43	0	0	0	45	4.4
R	27	Kyle Wanvig	MIN	51	4	8	12	-8	64	1	0	0	55	7.3
R	18	Mattias Weinhandl	NYI	53	2	4	6	-4	14	0	0	0	40	5.0
			MIN	15	2	3	5	0	10	0	0	0	17	11.8
			TOTAL	68	4	7	11	-4	24	0	0	0	57	7.0
L	24 *	Derek Boogaard	MIN	65	2	4	6	2	158	0	0	1	15	13.3
R	83 *	Matt Foy	MIN	19	2	3	5	-4	16	1	0	0	21	9.5
D	36	Alex Henry	MIN	63	0	5	5	-4	73	0	0	0	41	0.0
C	7	Erik Westrum	MIN	10	0	1	1	-1	2	0	0	0	16	0.0
L	44	Andrei Nazarov	MIN	2	0	0	0	-1	6	0	0	0	0	0.0
D	56 *	Erik Reitz	MIN	5	0	0	0	-2	4	0	0	0	0	0.0
D	23	Scott Ferguson	MIN	15	0	0	0	-3	22	0	0	0	6	0.0

Goaltending

No.	Goaltender	GPI	Mins	Avg	W	L	OT	EN	SO	GA	SA	S%	G	A	PIM
35	Manny Fernandez	58	3411	2.29	30	18	7	3	1	130	1612	.919	0	3	6
29	* Josh Harding	3	185	2.59	2	1	0	0	0	8	83	.904	0	0	0
35	Dwayne Roloson	24	1361	3.00	6	17	1	3	1	68	759	.910	0	0	6
	Totals	**82**	**4974**	**2.56**	**38**	**36**	**8**	**6**	**3**	**212**	**2460**	**.914**			

Coach

LEMAIRE, JACQUES
Coach, Minnesota Wild. Born in LaSalle, Que., September 7, 1945.

The Minnesota Wild announced the signing of Jacques Lemaire as the club's first head coach on June 19, 2000. In 2002-03, he led Minnesota into the playoffs after just three seasons and went all the way to the Western Conference Final. He also won the Jack Adams Award as coach of the year. Prior to joining the Wild, Lemaire had spent parts of the previous two seasons as a senior consultant to the general manager for the Montreal Canadiens, the franchise with which he captured eight Stanley Cup championships as a player.

Lemaire spent five seasons behind the New Jersey Devils bench and compiled a 199-122-57 mark. In 1994-95, he coached the Devils to their first Stanley Cup championship. In his first season with the team (1993-94), he was awarded the Jack Adams Award for the first time.

Lemaire began his NHL coaching career with the Montreal Canadiens in 1983-84. He stepped aside as head coach following the 1984-85 campaign and moved to the front office where he held the position of assistant to the managing director. In that role, Lemaire played a part in Montreal's Stanley Cup championships of 1986 and 1993.

Lemaire spent his entire NHL playing career with Montreal from 1967 to 1979 winning then Stanley Cup eight times. He then began his coaching career in Switzerland where he served as player/coach of the Sierre club. He returned to North America in 1981 and was named the first head coach of the Quebec Major Junior Hockey League's expansion Longueuil Chevaliers. In his only season at the helm (1982-83), Lemaire guided the team to the QMJHL finals.

Coaching Record

Season	Team	Games	Regular Season W	L	O/T	Games	Playoffs W	L
1979-80	Sierre (Switzerland)				UNAVAILABLE			
1980-81	Sierre (Switzerland)				UNAVAILABLE			
1982-83	Longueil (QMJHL)	70	37	29	4	15	9	6
1983-84	Montreal (NHL)	17	7	10	0	15	9	6
1984-85	Montreal (NHL)	80	41	27	12	12	6	6
1993-94	New Jersey (NHL)	84	47	25	12	20	11	9
1994-95*	New Jersey (NHL)	48	22	18	8	20	16	4
1995-96	New Jersey (NHL)	82	37	33	12	....	....	....
1996-97	New Jersey (NHL)	82	45	23	14	10	5	5
1997-98	New Jersey (NHL)	82	48	23	11	6	2	4
2000-01	Minnesota (NHL)	82	25	44	13	....	....	....
2001-02	Minnesota (NHL)	82	26	44	12	....	....	....
2002-03	Minnesota (NHL)	82	42	30	10	18	8	10
2003-04	Minnesota (NHL)	82	30	32	20	....	....	....
2004-05	Minnesota (NHL)				Season Cancelled			
2005-06	Minnesota (NHL)	82	42	35	5	....	....	....
	NHL Totals	**885**	**412**	**344**	**129**	**101**	**57**	**44**

* Stanley Cup win.

Brian Rolston established career highs in goals (34), assists (45) and points (79) in his first season with the Wild in 2005-06.

Club Records

Team
(Figures in brackets for season records are games played.)

Most Points 95 2002-03 (82)
Most Wins 42 2002-03 (82)
Most Ties 20 2003-04 (82)
Most Losses 39 2000-01 (82)
Most Goals 231 2005-06 (82)
Most Goals Against 238 2001-02 (82)
Fewest Points 68 2000-01 (82)
Fewest Wins 25 2000-01 (82)
Fewest Ties 10 2002-03 (82)
Fewest Losses 29 2002-03 (82), 2003-04 (82)
Fewest Goals 168 2000-01 (82)
Fewest Goals Against 178 2002-03 (82)

Longest Winning Streak
Overall . . . . 5 Jan. 18-26/06
Home . . . . 5 Two times
Away . . . . 3 Feb. 2-10/06

Longest Undefeated Streak
Overall . . . . 9 Dec. 13-30/03
(4 wins, 5 ties)
Home . . . . 9 Dec. 13/00-Jan. 10/01
(5 wins, 4 ties)
Away . . . . 7 Dec. 6-30/03
(2 wins, 5 ties)

Longest Losing Streak
Overall . . . . 5 Mar. 11-19/01,
Jan. 28-Feb. 8/02,
Mar. 29-Apr. 5/02
Home . . . . 4 Oct. 29-Nov. 15/00
Away . . . . 6 Feb. 12-Mar. 22/06

Longest Winless Streak
Overall . . . . 12 Mar. 11-Apr. 4/01
(9 losses, 3 ties)
Home . . . . 8 Feb. 26-Mar. 28/01
(5 losses, 3 ties)
Away . . . . 12 Dec. 18/03-Jan. 31/04
(5 losses, 7 ties)
Most Shutouts, Season 7 2003-04 (82)
Most PIM, Season 1,209 2001-02 (82), 2005-06 (82)
Most Goals, Game . . . . 8 Mar. 25/04
(Min. 8 at Chi. 2)

Individual

Most Seasons . . . . 5 Six players
Most Games . . . . 365 Wes Walz
Most Goals, Career . . . . 134 Marian Gaborik
Most Assists, Career . . . . 140 Marian Gaborik
Most Points, Career . . . . 274 Marian Gaborik
(134G, 140A)
Most PIM, Career . . . . 698 Matt Johnson
Most Shutouts, Career . . . . 15 Dwayne Roloson
Longest Consecutive
Games Streak . . . . 288 Antti Laaksonen
(Oct. 6/00-Dec. 29/03)
Most Goals, Season . . . . 38 Marian Gaborik
(2005-06)
Most Assists, Season . . . . 48 Andrew Brunette
(2001-02)
Most Points, Season . . . . 79 Brian Rolston
(2005-06; 34G, 45A)
Most PIM, Season . . . . 201 Matt Johnson
(2002-03)

Most Points, Defenseman,
Season . . . . 34 Lubomir Sekeras
(2000-01; 11G, 23A)
Most Points, Center,
Season . . . . 79 Brian Rolston
(2005-06; 34G, 45A)
Most Points, Right Wing,
Season . . . . 67 Marian Gaborik
(2001-02; 30G, 37A)
Most Points, Left Wing,
Season . . . . 69 Andrew Brunette
(2001-02; 21G, 48A)
Most Points, Rookie,
Season . . . . 36 Marian Gaborik
(2000-01; 18G, 18A)
Most Shutouts, Season . . . . 5 Dwayne Roloson
(2001-02, 2003-04)
Most Goals, Game . . . . 3 Antti Laaksonen
(Nov. 26/00),
Marian Gaborik
(Eight times),
Marc Chouinard
(Oct. 5/05),
Brian Rolston
(Nov. 5/05)
Most Assists, Game . . . . 4 Andrew Brunette
(Mar. 10/02),
Marian Gaborik
(Oct. 26/02)
Pascal Dupuis
(Mar. 25/04)
Most Points, Game . . . . 6 Marian Gaborik
(Oct. 26/02; 2G, 4A)

General Managers' History
Doug Risebrough, 2000-01 to date.

Coaching History
Jacques Lemaire, 2000-01 to date.

Captains' History
Sean O'Donnell, Scott Pellerin, Wes Walz, Brad Bombardir, Darby Hendrickson, 2000-01; Jim Dowd, Filip Kuba, Brad Brown, Andrew Brunette, 2001-02; Brad Bombardir, Matt Johnson, Sergei Zholtok, 2002-03; Brad Brown, Andrew Brunette, Richard Park, Brad Bombardir, Jim Dowd, 2003-04; Alex Henry, Filip Kuba, Willie Mitchell, Brian Rolston, Wes Walz, 2005-06.

All-time Record vs. Other Clubs
Regular Season

	At Home							On Road							Total						
	GP	W	L	T	OL	GF	GA	PTS	GP	W	L	T	OL	GF	GA	PTS	GP	W	L	T	OL	GF	GA	PTS
Anaheim	10	5	2	1	1	21	16	13	10	4	5	0	1	23	26	9	20	9	7	2	2	44	42	22
Atlanta	3	2	0	1	0	8	5	5	2	2	0	0	0	10	6	4	5	4	0	1	0	18	11	9
Boston	3	2	1	0	0	9	5	4	3	3	0	0	0	13	4	6	6	5	1	0	0	22	9	10
Buffalo	4	1	3	0	0	6	10	2	3	1	0	0	2	8	7	4	7	3	4	0	0	14	17	6
Calgary	15	7	6	1	1	36	31	16	14	2	9	3	0	26	35	7	29	9	15	4	1	62	66	23
Carolina	4	1	1	2	0	9	12	4	2	0	2	0	0	0	3	0	6	1	3	2	0	9	15	4
Chicago	10	8	2	0	0	34	21	16	10	5	4	1	0	30	23	11	20	13	6	1	0	64	44	27
Colorado	14	5	7	1	1	34	48	12	15	2	11	2	0	34	49	6	29	7	18	3	1	68	97	18
Columbus	10	7	2	0	1	30	20	15	9	1	5	1	2	11	25	5	19	8	7	1	3	41	45	20
Dallas	10	5	5	0	0	26	22	10	10	3	5	1	1	23	35	8	20	8	10	1	1	49	57	18
Detroit	10	2	5	2	1	24	29	7	10	3	6	1	0	25	37	7	20	5	11	3	1	49	66	14
Edmonton	14	4	8	1	1	32	39	10	15	6	4	3	2	31	32	17	29	10	12	4	3	63	71	27
Florida	3	2	0	1	0	10	1	5	2	0	0	0	2	8	6	4	6	2	0	1	2	18	7	9
Los Angeles	10	2	4	3	1	20	25	8	10	4	3	2	1	24	22	11	20	6	7	5	2	44	47	19
Montreal	3	2	0	0	1	10	8	5	3	1	1	1	0	8	9	3	6	3	1	1	1	18	17	8
Nashville	10	5	2	3	0	29	21	13	10	1	7	2	0	14	27	4	20	6	9	5	0	43	48	17
New Jersey	3	1	1	1	0	7	8	3	4	0	2	1	1	10	16	2	7	1	3	2	1	17	24	5
NY Islanders	3	2	1	0	0	9	9	4	4	2	2	0	0	10	9	4	7	4	3	0	0	19	18	8
NY Rangers	4	1	1	1	1	11	13	4	2	1	0	0	0	8	13	2	6	2	1	1	1	19	26	5
Ottawa	4	1	1	1	1	11	14	4	2	1	1	0	0	5	3	2	6	2	2	1	1	16	17	5
Philadelphia	2	1	0	1	0	5	5	3	5	1	4	0	0	9	13	2	7	2	4	1	0	14	18	5
Phoenix	10	3	4	2	1	20	23	9	10	1	7	1	1	23	29	4	20	4	11	3	2	43	52	17
Pittsburgh	3	2	0	1	0	9	4	5	4	3	1	0	0	17	6	6	7	5	1	1	0	26	11	11
St. Louis	10	5	1	2	2	29	20	14	10	3	3	1	3	15	19	10	20	8	4	3	5	44	39	24
San Jose	10	5	4	1	0	26	23	11	10	5	4	1	0	20	24	11	20	10	8	2	0	46	47	22
Tampa Bay	3	3	0	0	0	13	8	6	4	1	1	0	2	9	8	4	7	4	1	0	2	22	16	9
Toronto	2	1	1	0	0	4	2	2	3	0	3	0	0	3	11	0	5	1	4	0	0	8	15	2
Vancouver	15	7	6	2	0	41	38	16	14	4	3	3	3	32	36	14	29	11	10	5	3	73	74	30
Washington	3	3	0	0	0	6	1	6	3	1	2	0	0	6	7	2	6	4	2	0	0	12	8	8
Totals	205	95	69	28	13	530	482	231	205	66	99	27	13	450	542	172	410	161	168	55	26	980	1024	403

Playoffs

	Series	W	L	GP	W	L	T	GF	GA	Last Mtg.	Rnd.	Result
Anaheim	1	0	1	4	0	4	0	1	9	2003	CF	L 0-4
Colorado	1	1	0	7	4	3	0	16	17	2003	CQF	W 4-3
Vancouver	1	1	0	7	4	3	0	26	17	2003	CSF	W 4-3
Totals	3	2	1	18	8	10	0	43	43			

Playoff Results 2006-2001

Year	Round	Opponent	Result	GF	GA
2003	CF	Anaheim	L 0-4	1	9
	CSF	Vancouver	W 4-3	26	17
	CQF	Colorado	W 4-3	16	17

Abbreviations: Round: CF – conference final; **CSF** – conference semi-final; **CQF** – conference quarter-final.

2005-06 Results

Oct.	5	Calgary	6-3		7	Anaheim	4-1
	8	at Phoenix	1-2		9	Dallas	1-2
	9	at Los Angeles	1-2*		14	Calgary	1-4
	12	Vancouver	6-0		16	Ottawa	1-6
	14	Vancouver	3-5		18	Toronto	5-3
	16	Anaheim	4-1		20	Chicago	4-1
	19	San Jose	6-1		22	at Chicago	3-2
	22	at St. Louis	3-2		24	Phoenix	3-2
	23	at Chicago	2-4		26	Nashville	5-1
	25	Vancouver	1-3		27	at Columbus	3-4
	28	at Columbus	1-2†		30	Detroit	4-5
	29	Columbus	3-1		31	at Colorado	2-3
Nov.	1	at Calgary	0-3	Feb.	2	at San Jose	3-2†
	2	at Vancouver	1-2		4	at Phoenix	6-4
	5	at San Jose	3-1		7	Los Angeles	5-1
	6	at Anaheim	4-3†		9	Colorado	1-2
	8	Phoenix	2-4		10	at Edmonton	6-3
	11	at Detroit	1-3		12	at Vancouver	2-3*
	14	at Calgary	2-3		28	at Colorado	2-4
	19	Nashville	4-2	Mar.	2	at Los Angeles	2-3
	23	Edmonton	3-4		3	at Anaheim	2-4
	25	St. Louis	5-3		5	Colorado	5-3
	30	Columbus	2-3†		7	Los Angeles	2-3*
Dec.	1	at Nashville	1-2		10	at St. Louis	1-2*
	3	at New Jersey	2-3†		12	Edmonton	4-3
	5	at NY Rangers	1-3		14	Edmonton	1-2
	8	at Pittsburgh	5-0		19	Calgary	2-3
	10	at Philadelphia	2-3		21	Calgary	3-1
	11*	Buffalo	2-3		22	at Dallas	2-4
	13	at NY Islanders	4-3		25	San Jose	1-5
	15	Boston	2-3		28	at Edmonton	3-2
	17	Montreal	4-3*		29	at Vancouver	1-2
	19	Dallas	2-1		31	at Vancouver	2-1†
	22	at Colorado	3-4	Apr.	2	Detroit	2-3
	23	Colorado	5-3		4	St. Louis	5-4†
	26	at Edmonton	4-1		6	Edmonton	2-1†
	28	at Edmonton	4-2		7	at Calgary	1-2
	29	at Calgary	2-4		9	at Colorado	5-2
	31	Vancouver	4-3		11	Chicago	2-0
Jan.	3	at Detroit	4-2		13	at Nashville	2-4
	5	Colorado	2-4		15	at Dallas	3-4*

* – Overtime   † – Shootout

Entry Draft
Selections 2006-2000

2006 Pick		2004 Pick		2003 Pick		2001 Pick	
9	James Sheppard	12	A.J. Thelen	20	Brent Burns	6	Mikko Koivu
40	Ondrej Fiala	42	Roman Voloshenko	56	Patrick O'Sullivan	36	Kyle Wanvig
72	Cal Clutterbuck	78	Peter Olvecky	78	Danny Irmen	74	Chris Heid
102	Kyle Medvec	79	Clayton Stoner	157	Marcin Kolusz	93	Stephane Veilleux
132	Niko Hovinen	111	Ryan Jones	187	Miroslav Kopriva	103	Tony Virta
162	Julian Walker	114	Patrick Bordeleau	207	Georgy Misharin	202	Derek Boogaard
192	Chris Hickey	117	Julien Sprunger	219	Adam Courchaine	239	Jake Riddle
		161	Jean-Claude Sawyer	251	Mathieu Melanson		
2005 Pick		175	Aaron Boogaard	281	Jean-Michel Bolduc	**2000 Pick**	
4	Benoit Pouliot	195	Jean-Michel Rizk			3	Marian Gaborik
57	Matt Kassian	206	Anton Khudobin	**2002 Pick**		33	Nick Schultz
65	Kristofer Westblom	272	Kyle Wilson	8	Pierre-Marc Bouchard	99	Marc Cavosie
110	Kyle Bailey			38	Josh Harding	132	Maxim Sushinsky
122	Morten Madsen			72	Mike Erickson	170	Erik Reitz
129	Anthony Aiello			73	Barry Brust	199	Brian Passmore
199	Riley Emmerson			155	Armands Berzins	214	Peter Bartos
				175	Matt Foy	232	Lubomir Sekeras
				204	Niklas Eckerblom	255	Eric Johansson
				237	Christoph Brandner		
				268	Mikhail Tyulyapkin		
				269	Mika Hannula		

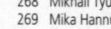

Pavol Demitra joins the Wild for 2006-07, coming over from Los Angeles in exchange for 2003 draft pick Patrick O'Sullivan and a choice in the 2006 Entry Draft.

President and General Manager

RISEBROUGH, DOUG
President/General Manager, Minnesota Wild.
Born in Guelph, Ont., January 29, 1954.

Doug Risebrough was hired as the first executive vice president and general manager of the Minnesota Wild on September 2, 1999. He is responsible for the club's overall hockey operations. His efforts to build a winner through the draft has been exemplified by the success of Marian Gaborik, the club's first-round choice in 2000. The Wild qualified for the playoffs after just three seasons, going all the way to the 2003 Western Conference Final.

After ending his 13-year NHL playing career with the Flames in 1987, Risebrough was named as assistant coach with Calgary and joined Terry Crisp behind the bench. Risebrough was appointed head coach of the Flames on May 18, 1990 and on May 16, 1991, he also assumed the role of general manager. Late in the 1991-92 campaign he directed his energies full-time to general manager, handing the coaching responsibilities over to Guy Charron for the balance of the season. Risebrough served as g.m. in Calgary through the start of the 1995-96 season. He was vice president of hockey operations for the Edmonton Oilers from 1996 to 1999.

Risebrough was Montreal's first selection, seventh overall, in the 1974 Amateur Draft. During his nine years with the Canadiens, he helped his club to four consecutive Stanley Cup championships between 1976 and 1979. He joined the Flames prior to the start of the club's 1982 training camp. During his NHL career, his clubs have won five Stanley Cup titles (1976-1979 as a player and 1989 as an assistant coach with Calgary) and two Presidents' Trophies (1987-88 and 1988-89 as an assistant coach).

NHL Coaching Record

Season	Team	Games	Regular Season			Playoffs		
			W	L	T	Games	W	L
1990-91	Calgary	80	46	26	8	7	3	4
1991-92	Calgary	64	25	30	9	....	....	....
	NHL Totals	**144**	**71**	**56**	**17**	**7**	**3**	**4**

Club Directory

Xcel Energy Center

Minnesota Wild
317 Washington Street
St. Paul, MN 55102
Phone 651/602-6000
FAX 651/293-9574
Tickets 651/222-9453
www.wild.com
Capacity: 18,064

Naegele Sports, LLC
Board Members . . . . Bob Naegele, Jr., Jac Sperling, John Thomas, Rick Pepin
Investors in MSE include (listed in alphabetical order)
Gage Hockey Ventures, LLC (Edwin Gage, Barbara Gage, Geoffrey Gage, Scott Gage, Rick Gage), Trisha and Greg Hoyt, Hubbard Broadcasting, Inc., Horace Irvine III, Bob Naegele, Jr., Bob Naegele III, Glen Nelson, Dick Nicholson, Ford Nicholson, Todd Nicholson, Vance Opperman, Mike Reilly, Jac Sperling, John Thomas, Jill and John Trautz

Executive Management
Chairman	Bob Naegele, Jr.
Vice Chairman	Jac Sperling
President/General Manager	Doug Risebrough
Exec. Vice President, Chief Financial Officer	Pamela Wheelock
Exec. Vice President	Matt Majka
Vice President, Sales and Service	Steve Griggs
Vice President/G.M. of RiverCentre	Jim Ibister
Vice President/G.M. of Xcel Energy Center	Jack Larson
Vice President, Administration	Mike Reeves
Vice President, Communications and Broadcasting	Bill Robertson
Vice President, Minor League Sports Properties	Tom Garrity
Executive Assistant	Stephanie Huseby
Executive Assistant, Hockey Operations	Laura Kinzel

Hockey Operations
Assistant General Manager/Hockey Operations	Tom Lynn
Assistant General Manager/Player Personnel	Tom Thompson
Head Coach	Jacques Lemaire
Assistant Coaches	Mike Ramsey, Mario Tremblay
Goaltending Coach	Bob Mason
Strength and Conditioning Coach	Kirk Olson
Coordinator of Amateur Scouting	Guy Lapointe
Director of Player Development	Barry MacKenzie
Director of Professional Scouting	Blair Mackasey
Senior Amatuer Scout	Paul Charles
Scouting Staff . . . Branislav Gaborik, Christopher Hamel, Jamie Hislop, Ken Hoodikoff, Jiri Koluch, Doug Mosher, Darryl Porter, Glen Sonmor, Thomas Steen, Matti Vaisanen, Ernie Vargas	
Athletic Therapist	Don Fuller
Equipment Manager	Tony DaCosta
Assistant Trainer	Mike Vogt
Assistant Equipment Managers	Brent Proulx, Matt Benz
Video Coordinator	Ian Andersen
Director of Hockey Operations	Chris Snow
Hockey Operations Administrator	Cindy Sweiger
Medical Director	Dr. Sheldon Burns
Orthopedic Surgeon	Dr. Joel Boyd
Nutritionist	Carrie Peterson

Sales and Service
Senior Director, Customer Sales and Service	Jamie Spencer
Manager, Ticket Operations	Chris Turns
Manager, New Business Development	Michael Brinkman
Manager, Group and Event Suites	Cory Effertz
Senior Manager, Customer Service	Maria Troje
Senior Account Service Executive	Jora Deziel
Account Service Executives	Anna Johnson, Joshua Simonson, Natalie Kaess
Administrative Assistant	Tawnya Vidnovic

Retail Operation
Director, Retail Operations	Nikki Braxmeier
Manager, Retail Operations	Scott Sarkis

Corporate Partnerships
Senior Director, Corporate Sales and Service	Carin Anderson
Director, Corporate Sales	Mike Snee
Senior Manager, Corporate Services	Kathleen Borschke
Account Executives	Travis Hoban, Carl Levi, Chris Portas
Corporate Logistics Coordinator	Ed Sauter
Corporate Services Coordinators	Carrie Grubb, Michelle Radzik

Communications and Broadcasting
Manager, Media Relations & Team Services	Aaron Sickman
Manager, Media Relations, Xcel Energy Center	Kathy Ross
Coordinator, Media Relations & Team Services	Wayne Carlson
Broadcast Manager	Maggie Kukar
Radio Operations Coordinator	Kevin Falness
Administrative Assistant	Deb Hanson
Website Content Writer	Glen Andresen
Radio Play-By-Play/Analyst	Bob Kurtz/Tom Reid
Television Play-By-Play/Analyst	Dan Terhaar/Mike Greenlay

Marketing
Senior Director, Marketing	John Maher
Director, Events and Promotions	Wayne Petersen
Manager, Game Presentation	Paul Loomis
Manager, Production Services	Hank Dolan
Manager, Marketing	Emily Gausman

Community Relations
Manager, Community Relations	Amy Woog-Patnode

Finance and Accounting
Controller	Danette Kleinprintz
Senior Financial Analyst	Mitch Helgerson

Administration
Director, Human Resources	Delores Murphy
Facility Manager, 317 on Rice Park	Tim Wolfgram

Information Technology
Director, Information Technology	David Weisbrod
Website Manager	Holly Doyle

Miscellaneous
Radio Network Flagship	WCCO (830 AM)
Television Networks	KSTC.TV Channel 45 (Over-the-Air), Fox Sports Net (Cable)
Team Photographer	Bruce Kluckhohn
Public Address Announcer	Adam Abrams

Montreal Canadiens

2005-06 Results: 42w-31L-6OTL-3SOL 93PTS.
Third, Northeast Division

In his first season with Montreal, Cristobal Huet led the NHL with a .929 save percentage.

2006-07 Schedule

Oct.	Fri.	6	at Buffalo	Sun.	7	New Jersey*
	Sat.	7	at Toronto	Tue.	9	Atlanta
	Wed.	11	at Philadelphia	Thu.	11	at Philadelphia
	Sat.	14	Ottawa	Sat.	13	at Ottawa*
	Tue.	17	Calgary	Mon.	15	at Detroit
	Wed.	18	at Chicago	Tue.	16	Vancouver
	Sat.	21	Colorado	Thu.	18	at Atlanta
	Mon.	23	Buffalo	Sat.	20	Buffalo
	Thu.	26	at Boston	Sat.	27	at Toronto
	Sat.	28	Toronto	Mon.	29	Ottawa
	Tue.	31	Ottawa	**Feb.** Thu.	1	at Pittsburgh
Nov.	Thu.	2	at Carolina	Sat.	3	NY Islanders*
	Sat.	4	New Jersey	Sun.	4	Pittsburgh*
	Tue.	7	Edmonton	Tue.	6	Carolina
	Sat.	11	at Toronto	Thu.	8	at Ottawa
	Mon.	13	at Ottawa	Sat.	10	Ottawa
	Wed.	15	at Tampa Bay	Tue.	13	Florida
	Thu.	16	at Florida	Wed.	14	at New Jersey
	Sat.	18	Atlanta	Sat.	17	Carolina
	Wed.	22	Minnesota	Sun.	18	at Columbus
	Fri.	24	at Buffalo	Tue.	20	Washington
	Sat.	25	Philadelphia	Thu.	22	at Nashville
	Tue.	28	Florida	Sat.	24	at NY Islanders*
	Thu.	30	at Carolina	Mon.	26	Toronto
Dec.	Sat.	2	Toronto	Tue.	27	at NY Rangers
	Mon.	4	Boston	**Mar.** Fri.	2	at Buffalo
	Wed.	6	at New Jersey	Sat.	3	at Boston
	Thu.	7	at NY Islanders	Thu.	8	at Atlanta
	Sat.	9	Buffalo	Sat.	10	at St. Louis
	Tue.	12	Boston	Tue.	13	NY Islanders
	Thu.	14	Tampa Bay	Fri.	16	at Pittsburgh
	Sat.	16	Pittsburgh	Sat.	17	Toronto
	Tue.	19	at Buffalo	Tue.	20	Boston
	Thu.	21	Philadelphia	Thu.	22	at Boston
	Sat.	23	at Boston	Sat.	24	Washington
	Wed.	27	at Washington	Tue.	27	NY Rangers
	Fri.	29	at Florida	Fri.	30	at Ottawa
	Sat.	30	at Tampa Bay	Sat.	31	Buffalo
Jan.	Tue.	2	Tampa Bay	**Apr.** Tue.	3	Boston
	Thu.	4	at Washington	Thu.	5	at NY Rangers
	Sat.	6	NY Rangers*	Sat.	7	at Toronto

* Denotes afternoon game.

Franchise date: November 22, 1917

EASTERN CONFERENCE

NORTHEAST DIVISION

90th NHL Season

Year-by-Year Record

Season	GP	Home W	L	T	OL	Road W	L	T	OL	Overall W	L	T	OL	GF	GA	Pts	Finished	Playoff Result
2005-06	82	24	13		4	18	18		5	42	31		9	243	247	93	3rd, Northeast Div.	Lost Conf. Quarter-Final
2004-05																		
2003-04	82	23	13	4	1	18	17	3	3	41	30		7	208	192	93	4th, Northeast Div.	Lost Conf. Semi-Final
2002-03	82	16	16	5	4	14	19	3	5	30	35	8	9	206	234	77	4th, Northeast Div.	Out of Playoffs
2001-02	82	21	13	6	1	15	18	6	2	36	31	12	3	207	209	87	4th, Northeast Div.	Lost Conf. Semi-Final
2000-01	82	15	20	4	2	13	20	4	4	28	40	8	6	206	232	70	5th, Northeast Div.	Out of Playoffs
1999-2000	82	18	17	5	1	17	17	4	3	35	34	9	4	196	194	83	4th, Northeast Div.	Out of Playoffs
1998-99	82	21	15	5		11	24	6		32	39	11		184	209	75	5th, Northeast Div.	Out of Playoffs
1997-98	82	15	17	9		22	15	4		37	32	13		235	208	87	4th, Northeast Div.	Lost Conf. Semi-Final
1996-97	82	17	17	7		14	19	8		31	36	15		249	276	77	4th, Northeast Div.	Lost Conf. Quarter-Final
1995-96	82	23	12	6		17	20	4		40	32	10		265	248	90	3rd, Northeast Div.	Lost Conf. Quarter-Final
1994-95	48	15	5	4		3	18	3		18	23	7		125	148	43	6th, Northeast Div.	Out of Playoffs
1993-94	84	26	12	4		15	17	10		41	29	14		283	248	96	3rd, Northeast Div.	Lost Conf. Quarter-Final
1992-93	84	27	13	2		21	17	4		48	30	6		326	280	102	**3rd, Adams Div.**	**Won Stanley Cup**
1991-92	80	27	8	5		14	20	6		41	28	11		267	207	93	1st, Adams Div.	Lost Div. Final
1990-91	80	23	12	5		16	18	6		39	30	11		273	249	89	2nd, Adams Div.	Lost Div. Final
1989-90	80	26	8	6		15	20	5		41	28	11		288	234	93	3rd, Adams Div.	Lost Div. Final
1988-89	80	30	6	4		23	12	5		53	18	9		315	218	115	1st, Adams Div.	Lost Final
1987-88	80	26	8	6		19	14	7		45	22	13		298	238	103	1st, Adams Div.	Lost Div. Final
1986-87	80	27	9	4		14	20	6		41	29	10		277	241	92	2nd, Adams Div.	Lost Conf. Championship
1985-86	80	25	11	4		15	22	3		40	33	7		330	280	87	**2nd, Adams Div.**	**Won Stanley Cup**
1984-85	80	24	10	6		17	17	6		41	27	12		309	262	94	1st, Adams Div.	Lost Div. Final
1983-84	80	19	19	2		16	21	3		35	40	5		286	295	75	4th, Adams Div.	Lost Conf. Championship
1982-83	80	25	6	9		17	18	5		42	24	14		350	286	98	2nd, Adams Div.	Lost Div. Semi-Final
1981-82	80	25	6	9		21	11	8		46	17	17		360	223	109	1st, Adams Div.	Lost Div. Semi-Final
1980-81	80	31	7	2		14	15	11		45	22	13		332	232	103	1st, Norris Div.	Lost Prelim. Round
1979-80	80	30	7	3		17	13	10		47	20	13		328	240	107	1st, Norris Div.	Lost Quarter-Final
1978-79	80	29	6	5		23	11	6		52	17	11		337	204	115	**1st, Norris Div.**	**Won Stanley Cup**
1977-78	80	32	4	4		27	6	7		59	10	11		359	183	129	**1st, Norris Div.**	**Won Stanley Cup**
1976-77	80	33	1	6		27	7	6		60	8	12		387	171	132	**1st, Norris Div.**	**Won Stanley Cup**
1975-76	80	32	3	5		26	8	6		58	11	11		337	174	127	**1st, Norris Div.**	**Won Stanley Cup**
1974-75	80	27	8	5		20	6	14		47	14	19		374	225	113	1st, Norris Div.	Lost Semi-Final
1973-74	78	24	12	3		21	12	6		45	24	9		293	240	99	2nd, East Div.	Lost Quarter-inal
1972-73	78	29	4	6		23	6	10		52	10	16		329	184	120	**1st, East Div.**	**Won Stanley Cup**
1971-72	78	29	3	7		17	13	9		46	16	16		307	205	108	3rd, East Div.	Lost Quarter-Final
1970-71	78	29	7	3		13	16	10		42	23	13		291	216	97	**3rd, East Div.**	**Won Stanley Cup**
1969-70	76	21	9	8		17	13	8		38	22	16		244	201	92	5th, East Div.	Out of Playoffs
1968-69	76	26	7	5		20	12	6		46	19	11		271	202	103	**1st, East Div.**	**Won Stanley Cup**
1967-68	74	26	5	6		16	17	4		42	22	10		236	167	94	**1st, East Div.**	**Won Stanley Cup**
1966-67	70	19	9	7		13	16	6		32	25	13		202	188	77	2nd,	Lost Final
1965-66	70	23	11	1		18	10	7		41	21	8		239	173	90	**1st,**	**Won Stanley Cup**
1964-65	70	20	8	7		16	15	4		36	23	11		211	185	83	**2nd,**	**Won Stanley Cup**
1963-64	70	22	7	6		14	14	7		36	21	13		209	167	85	1st,	Lost Semi-Final
1962-63	70	15	10	10		13	9	13		28	19	23		225	183	79	3rd,	Lost Semi-Final
1961-62	70	26	2	7		16	12	7		42	14	14		259	166	98	1st,	Lost Semi-Final
1960-61	70	24	6	5		17	13	5		41	19	10		254	188	92	1st,	Lost Semi-Final
1959-60	70	23	4	8		17	14	4		40	18	12		255	178	92	**1st,**	**Won Stanley Cup**
1958-59	70	21	8	6		18	10	7		39	18	13		258	158	91	**1st,**	**Won Stanley Cup**
1957-58	70	23	8	4		20	9	6		43	17	10		250	158	96	**1st,**	**Won Stanley Cup**
1956-57	70	23	6	6		12	17	6		35	23	12		210	155	82	**2nd,**	**Won Stanley Cup**
1955-56	70	29	5	1		16	10	9		45	15	10		222	131	100	**1st,**	**Won Stanley Cup**
1954-55	70	26	5	4		15	13	7		41	18	11		228	157	93	2nd,	Lost Final
1953-54	70	27	5	3		8	19	8		35	24	11		195	141	81	2nd,	Lost Final
1952-53	70	18	12	5		10	11	14		28	23	19		155	148	75	**2nd,**	**Won Stanley Cup**
1951-52	70	22	8	5		12	18	5		34	26	10		195	164	78	2nd,	Lost Final
1950-51	70	17	10	8		8	20	7		25	30	15		173	184	65	3rd,	Lost Final
1949-50	70	17	8	10		12	14	9		29	22	19		172	150	77	2nd,	Lost Semi-Final
1948-49	60	19	8	3		9	15	6		28	23	9		152	126	65	3rd,	Lost Semi-Final
1947-48	60	13	13	4		7	16	7		20	29	11		147	169	51	5th,	Out of Playoffs
1946-47	60	19	6	5		15	10	5		34	16	10		189	138	78	1st,	Lost Final
1945-46	50	16	6	3		12	11	2		28	17	5		172	134	61	**1st,**	**Won Stanley Cup**
1944-45	50	21	2	2		17	6	2		38	8	4		228	121	80	1st,	Lost Semi-Final
1943-44	50	22	0	3		16	5	4		38	5	7		234	109	83	**1st,**	**Won Stanley Cup**
1942-43	50	14	4	7		5	15	5		19	19	12		181	191	50	4th,	Lost Semi-Final
1941-42	48	12	10	2		6	17	1		18	27	3		134	173	39	6th,	Lost Quarter-Final
1940-41	48	11	9	4		5	17	2		16	26	6		121	147	38	6th,	Lost Quarter-Final
1939-40	48	5	14	5		5	19	0		10	33	5		90	167	25	7th,	Out of Playoffs
1938-39	48	8	11	5		7	13	4		15	24	9		115	146	39	6th,	Lost Quarter-Final
1937-38	48	13	4	7		5	13	6		18	17	13		123	128	49	3rd, Cdn. Div.	Lost Quarter-Final
1936-37	48	16	8	0		8	10	6		24	18	6		115	111	54	1st, Cdn. Div.	Lost Semi-Final
1935-36	48	5	11	8		6	15	3		11	26	11		82	123	33	4th, Cdn. Div.	Out of Playoffs
1934-35	48	11	11	2		8	12	4		19	23	6		110	145	44	3rd, Cdn. Div.	Lost Quarter-Final
1933-34	48	16	6	2		6	14	4		22	20	6		99	101	50	2nd, Cdn. Div.	Lost Quarter-Final
1932-33	48	15	5	4		3	20	1		18	25	5		92	115	41	3rd, Cdn. Div.	Lost Quarter-Final
1931-32	48	18	3	3		7	13	4		25	16	7		128	111	57	1st, Cdn. Div.	Lost Semi-Final
1930-31	44	15	3	4		11	7	4		26	10	8		129	89	60	**1st, Cdn. Div.**	**Won Stanley Cup**
1929-30	44	13	5	4		8	9	5		21	14	9		142	114	51	**2nd, Cdn. Div.**	**Won Stanley Cup**
1928-29	44	12	4	6		10	3	9		22	7	15		71	43	59	1st,	Lost Semi-Final
1927-28	44	12	7	3		14	4	4		26	11	7		116	48	59	1st,	Lost Semi-Final
1926-27	44	14	5	2		13	9	0		28	14	2		99	67	58	2nd, Cdn. Div.	Lost Semi-Final
1925-26	36	5	12	1		6	12	0		11	24	1		79	108	23	7th,	Out of Playoffs
1924-25	30	10	5	0		7	6	2		17	11	2		93	56	36	3rd,	Lost Final
1923-24	24	10	2	0		3	9	0		13	11	0		59	48	26	**2nd,**	**Won Stanley Cup**
1922-23	24	10	2	0		3	7	2		13	9	2		73	61	28	2nd,	Lost NHL Final
1921-22	24	8	3	1		4	8	0		12	11	1		88	94	25	3rd,	Out of Playoffs
1920-21	24	9	3	0		4	8	0		13	11	0		112	99	26	3rd and 2nd*	Out of Playoffs
1919-20	24	8	4	0		5	7	0		13	11	0		129	113	26	2nd and 3rd*	Out of Playoffs
1918-19	18	7	2	0		3	6	0		10	8	0		88	78	20	1st and 2nd*	Cup Final but no Decision
1917-18	22	10	8	0		3	8	0		13	9	0		115	84	26	1st and 3rd*	Lost NHL Final

* Season played in two halves with no combined standing at end.
From 1917-18 through 1925-26, NHL champions played against PCHA/WCHL champions for Stanley Cup.

2006-07 Player Personnel

FORWARDS	HT	WT	S	Place of Birth	Date	2005-06 Club
BEGIN, Steve	6-0	188	L	Trois-Rivieres, Que.	6/14/78	Montreal
BONK, Radek	6-3	213	L	Krnov, Czech.	1/9/76	Montreal
DOWNEY, Aaron	6-1	220	R	Shelburne, Ont.	8/27/74	St. Louis-Montreal
HIGGINS, Christopher	6-0	192	L	Smithtown, NY	6/2/83	Montreal
JOHNSON, Mike	6-2	201	R	Scarborough, Ont.	10/3/74	Phoenix
KOIVU, Saku	5-10	184	L	Turku, Finland	11/23/74	Montreal
KOVALEV, Alex	6-2	229	L	Togliatti, USSR	2/24/73	Montreal
MURRAY, Garth	6-1	213	L	Regina, Sask.	9/17/82	Montreal-Hamilton
PEREZHOGIN, Alexander	6-0	205	L	Ust-Kamenogorsk, USSR	8/10/83	Montreal-Hamilton
PLEKANEC, Tomas	5-11	198	L	Kladno, Czech.	10/31/82	Montreal-Hamilton
RIBEIRO, Mike	6-0	175	L	Montreal, Que.	2/10/80	Montreal
RYDER, Michael	6-0	198	R	Bonavista, Nfld.	3/31/80	Montreal
SAMSONOV, Sergei	5-8	194	R	Moscow, USSR	10/27/78	Boston-Edmonton
DEFENSEMEN						
BOUILLON, Francis	5-8	196	L	New York, NY	10/17/75	Montreal
DANDENAULT, Mathieu	6-1	205	R	Sherbrooke, Que.	2/3/76	Montreal
KOMISAREK, Mike	6-4	241	R	Islip Terrace, NY	1/19/82	Montreal
MARKOV, Andrei	6-0	200	L	Voskresensk, USSR	12/20/78	Montreal
RIVET, Craig	6-2	205	R	North Bay, Ont.	9/13/74	Montreal
SOURAY, Sheldon	6-4	226	L	Elk Point, Alta.	7/13/76	Montreal
STREIT, Mark	6-0	196	L	Englisberg, Switz.	12/11/77	Montreal

GOALTENDERS	HT	WT	C	Place of Birth	Date	2005-06 Club
AEBISCHER, David	6-1	185	L	Fribourg, Switz.	2/7/78	Colorado-Montreal
HUET, Cristobal	6-0	194	L	St. Martin d'Heres, France	9/3/75	Montreal-Hamilton

Coaching History

Jack Laviolette, 1909-10; Adolphe Lecours, 1910-11; Napoleon Dorval, 1911-12, 1912-13; Jimmy Gardner, 1913-14, 1914-15; Newsy Lalonde, 1915-16 to 1920-21; Newsy Lalonde and Léo Dandurand, 1921-22; Léo Dandurand, 1922-23 to 1925-26; Cecil Hart, 1926-27 to 1931-32; Newsy Lalonde, 1932-33, 1933-34; Newsy Lalonde and Léo Dandurand, 1934-35; Sylvio Mantha, 1935-36; Cecil Hart, 1936-37, 1937-38; Cecil Hart and Jules Dugal, 1938-39; Babe Siebert, 1939*; Pit Lepine, 1939-40; Dick Irvin 1940-41 to 1954-55; Toe Blake, 1955-56 to 1967-68; Claude Ruel, 1968-69, 1969-70; Claude Ruel and Al MacNeil, 1970-71; Scotty Bowman, 1971-72 to 1978-79; Bernie Geoffrion and Claude Ruel, 1979-80; Claude Ruel, 1980-81; Bob Berry, 1981-82, 1982-83; Bob Berry and Jacques Lemaire, 1983-84; Jacques Lemaire, 1984-85; Jean Perron, 1985-86 to 1987-88; Pat Burns, 1988-89 to 1991-92; Jacques Demers, 1992-93 to 1994-95; Jacques Demers, Jacques Laperriere, Mario Tremblay, 1995-96; Mario Tremblay, 1996-97; Alain Vigneault, 1997-98 to 1999-2000; Alain Vigneault and Michel Therrien, 2000-01; Michel Therrien, 2001-02; Michel Therrien and Claude Julien, 2002-03; Claude Julien, 2003-04, 2004-05; Claude Julien and Bob Gainey, 2005-06; Guy Carbonneau, 2006-07.

* Named coach in summer but died before 1939-40 season began.

Vice President and General Manager

GAINEY, BOB
Executive Vice President/General Manager, Montreal Canadiens.
Born in Peterborough, Ont., December 13, 1953.

On June 2, 2003, the Montreal Canadiens announced the appointment of Bob Gainey as executive vice president and general manager, effective July 1, 2003. During the 2005-06 season, he also took over behind the bench and coached the Canadiens into the playoffs.

As a player in Montreal, Gainey brought many elements to the Canadiens over his 16-year career. Described as the world's best all-around player by legendary Soviet national team coach Viktor Tikhonov, Gainey was a tenacious competitor, relentless checker and a respected team leader. His presence helped the Canadiens win the Stanley Cup five times in the decade between 1976 and 1986. He won the Conn Smythe Trophy as playoff MVP in 1979 and was a four-time winner of the Selke Trophy as the NHL's best defensive forward. Gainey was captain of the Canadiens from 1981 until his retirement in 1989. He was elected to the Hockey Hall of Fame in 1992.

Gainey spent a year as a player-coach of the Epinal franchise in France before becoming head coach of the Minnesota North Stars in 1990-91. He was given the g.m.'s job in 1992 and was in the dual role when the Stars relocated to Dallas in 1993. Gainey stepped down as coach on January 8, 1996 to focus solely on the duties of general manager and built a powerhouse club that won five straight division titles from 1996-97 to 2000-01, the Presidents' Trophy in 1998 and 1999, and the Stanley Cup in 1999.

NHL Coaching Record

		Regular Season				Playoffs		
Season	Team	Games	W	L	O/T	Games	W	L
1990-91	Minnesota	80	27	39	14	23	14	9
1991-92	Minnesota	80	32	42	6	7	3	4
1992-93	Minnesota	84	36	38	10	....	....	....
1993-94	Dallas	84	42	29	13	9	5	4
1994-95	Dallas	48	17	23	8	5	1	4
1995-96	Dallas	39	11	19	9	....	....	....
2005-06	Montreal	41	23	15	3	6	2	4
	NHL Totals	**456**	**188**	**205**	**63**	**50**	**25**	**25**

2005-06 Scoring

* – rookie

Regular Season

Pos	#	Player	Team	GP	G	A	Pts	+/–	PIM	PP	SH	GW	S	%
R	27	Alex Kovalev	MTL	69	23	42	65	–1	76	9	0	5	206	11.2
C	11	Saku Koivu	MTL	72	17	45	62	1	70	5	0	4	138	12.3
R	73	Michael Ryder	MTL	81	30	25	55	–5	40	18	0	6	243	12.3
C	71	Mike Ribeiro	MTL	79	16	35	51	–6	36	8	0	2	130	12.3
D	79	Andrei Markov	MTL	67	10	36	46	13	74	6	1	1	88	11.4
C	38	Jan Bulis	MTL	73	20	20	40	2	50	6	1	3	131	15.3
D	44	Sheldon Souray	MTL	75	12	27	39	–11	116	7	1	0	202	5.9
C	21	* Chris Higgins	MTL	80	23	15	38	–1	26	7	3	3	148	15.5
D	52	Craig Rivet	MTL	82	7	27	34	–5	109	5	0	1	122	5.7
R	20	Richard Zednik	MTL	67	16	14	30	–2	48	6	0	4	161	9.9
L	35	* Tomas Plekanec	MTL	67	9	20	29	4	32	1	0	0	99	9.1
C	22	Steve Begin	MTL	76	11	12	23	9	113	1	2	2	134	8.2
D	51	Francis Bouillon	MTL	67	3	19	22	–6	34	3	0	1	75	4.0
C	14	Radek Bonk	MTL	61	6	15	21	–3	52	0	2	1	76	7.9
D	25	Mathieu Dandenault	MTL	82	5	15	20	8	83	0	0	1	101	5.0
R	42	* Alexander Perezhogin	MTL	67	9	10	19	5	38	3	0	2	109	8.3
R	37	Niklas Sundstrom	MTL	55	6	9	15	–6	30	0	0	2	54	11.1
R	26	Pierre Dagenais	MTL	32	5	7	12	–5	16	2	0	1	74	6.8
D	32	Mark Streit	MTL	48	2	9	11	–6	28	2	0	0	52	3.8
R	47	Aaron Downey	STL	17	2	0	2	0	45	0	0	0	11	18.2
			MTL	25	1	4	5	2	50	0	0	0	10	10.0
			TOTAL	42	3	4	7	2	95	0	0	0	21	14.3
C	57	Garth Murray	MTL	36	5	1	6	–2	44	0	0	1	25	20.0
D	8	Mike Komisarek	MTL	71	2	4	6	–1	116	0	0	0	66	3.0
L	46	* Andrei Kostitsyn	MTL	12	2	1	3	1	2	0	0	0	9	22.2
D	24	Todd Simpson	CHI	45	0	3	3	–2	116	0	0	0	25	0.0
			MTL	6	0	0	0	0	14	0	0	0	6	0.0
			TOTAL	51	0	3	3	–2	130	0	0	0	31	0.0
R	86	* Jonathan Ferland	MTL	7	1	0	1	–2	2	0	0	0	9	11.1
C	40	* Maxim Lapierre	MTL	1	0	0	0	–1	0	0	0	0	0	0.0
L	3	Raitis Ivanans	MTL	4	0	0	0	–1	9	0	0	0	0	0.0
D	64	* Jean-Philippe Cote	MTL	8	0	0	0	2	4	0	0	0	2	0.0

Goaltending

No.	Goaltender	GPI	Mins	Avg	W	L	OT	EN	SO	GA	SA	S%	G	A	PIM
39	Cristobal Huet	36	2103	2.20	18	11	4	1	7	77	1085	.929	0	0	0
75	* Yann Danis	6	312	2.69	3	2	0	0	1	14	152	.908	0	0	0
60	Jose Theodore	38	2114	3.46	17	15	5	3	0	122	1025	.881	0	1	2
30	David Aebischer	7	418	3.73	4	3	0	1	0	26	240	.892	0	0	0
	Totals	**82**	**4978**	**2.94**	**42**	**31**	**9**	**5**	**8**	**244**	**2507**	**.903**			

Playoffs

Pos	#	Player	Team	GP	G	A	Pts	+/–	PIM	PP	SH	GW	OT	S	%
R	27	Alex Kovalev	MTL	6	4	3	7	3	4	1	0	0	0	15	26.7
D	44	Sheldon Souray	MTL	6	3	2	5	–1	8	2	0	0	0	16	18.8
R	73	Michael Ryder	MTL	6	2	3	5	–4	0	1	0	1	1	13	15.4
C	21	* Chris Higgins	MTL	6	1	3	4	–3	0	0	0	0	0	7	14.3
L	35	* Tomas Plekanec	MTL	6	0	4	4	2	6	0	0	0	0	11	0.0
D	51	Francis Bouillon	MTL	6	1	2	3	0	10	1	0	0	0	15	6.7
R	37	Niklas Sundstrom	MTL	5	0	3	3	3	4	0	0	0	0	4	0.0
D	25	Mathieu Dandenault	MTL	6	0	3	3	1	4	0	0	0	0	8	0.0
C	14	Radek Bonk	MTL	6	2	0	2	–1	2	0	0	1	0	7	28.6
R	20	Richard Zednik	MTL	6	2	0	2	0	4	1	0	0	0	10	20.0
C	38	Jan Bulis	MTL	6	1	1	2	1	2	0	0	0	0	7	14.3
R	42	* Alexander Perezhogin	MTL	6	1	1	2	2	4	0	0	0	0	8	12.5
C	11	Saku Koivu	MTL	3	0	2	2	1	2	0	0	0	0	1	0.0
D	52	Craig Rivet	MTL	6	0	2	2	0	2	0	0	0	0	9	0.0
C	71	Mike Ribeiro	MTL	6	0	2	2	1	0	0	0	0	0	12	0.0
D	79	Andrei Markov	MTL	6	0	1	1	2	4	0	0	0	0	6	0.0
R	47	Aaron Downey	MTL	1	0	0	0	0	0	0	0	0	0	0	0.0
D	32	Mark Streit	MTL	1	0	0	0	0	0	0	0	0	0	0	0.0
C	22	Steve Begin	MTL	2	0	0	0	–1	2	0	0	0	0	6	0.0
D	8	Mike Komisarek	MTL	6	0	0	0	2	10	0	0	0	0	8	0.0
C	57	Garth Murray	MTL	6	0	0	0	2	0	0	0	0	0	4	0.0

Goaltending

No.	Goaltender	GPI	Mins	Avg	W	L	EN	SO	GA	SA	S%	G	A	PIM
39	Cristobal Huet	6	386	2.33	2	4	0	0	15	212	.929	0	0	0
	Totals	**6**	**387**	**2.33**	**2**	**4**	**0**	**0**	**15**	**212**	**.929**			

General Managers' History

Jack Laviolette and Joseph Cattarinich, 1909-1910; George Kennedy, 1910-11 to 1920-21; Leo Dandurand, 1921-22 to 1934-35; Ernest Savard, 1935-36; Cecil Hart, 1936-37 to 1938-39; Jules Dugal, 1939-40; Tom P. Gorman, 1940-41 to 1945-46; Frank J. Selke, 1946-47 to 1963-64; Sam Pollock, 1964-65 to 1977-78; Irving Grundman, 1978-79 to 1982-83; Serge Savard, 1983-84 to 1994-95; Serge Savard and Réjean Houle, 1995-96; Réjean Houle, 1996-97 to 1999-2000; Réjean Houle and Andre Savard, 2000-01; Andre Savard, 2001-02, 2002-03; Bob Gainey, 2003-04 to date.

Captains' History

Jack Laviolette, 1909-10; Newsy Lalonde, 1910-11; Jack Laviolette, 1911-12; Newsy Lalonde, 1912-13; Jimmy Gardner, 1913-14, 1914-15; Howard McNamara, 1915-16; Newsy Lalonde, 1916-17 to 1921-22; Sprague Cleghorn, 1922-23 to 1924-25; Bill Coutu, 1925-26; Sylvio Mantha, 1926-27 to 1931-32; George Hainsworth, 1932-33; Sylvio Mantha, 1933-34 to 1935-36; Babe Siebert, 1936-37 to 1938-39; Walt Buswell, 1939-40; Toe Blake, 1940-41 to 1946-47; Toe Blake and Bill Durnan, 1947-48; Butch Bouchard, 1948-49 to 1955-56; Maurice Richard, 1956-57 to 1959-60; Doug Harvey, 1960-61; Jean Béliveau, 1961-62 to 1970-71; Henri Richard, 1971-72 to 1974-75; Yvan Cournoyer, 1975-76 to 1978-79; Serge Savard, 1979-80, 1980-81; Bob Gainey, 1981-82 to 1988-89; Guy Carbonneau and Chris Chelios (co-captains), 1989-90; Guy Carbonneau, 1990-91 to 1993-94; Kirk Muller and Mike Keane, 1994-95; Mike Keane and Pierre Turgeon, 1995-96; Pierre Turgeon and Vincent Damphousse, 1996-97; Vincent Damphousse, 1997-98, 1998-99; Saku Koivu, 1999-2000 to date.

Club Records

Team

(Figures in brackets for season records are games played; records for fewest points, wins, ties, losses, goals, goals against are for 70 or more games)

Most Points .... *132 — 1976-77 (80)
Most Wins .... 60 — 1976-77 (80)
Most Ties .... 23 — 1962-63 (70)
Most Losses .... 40 — 1983-84 (80), 2000-01 (82)
Most Goals .... 387 — 1976-77 (80)
Most Goals Against .... 295 — 1983-84 (80)
Fewest Points .... 65 — 1950-51 (70)
Fewest Wins .... 25 — 1950-51 (70)
Fewest Ties .... 5 — 1983-84 (80)
Fewest Losses .... *8 — 1976-77 (80)
Fewest Goals .... 155 — 1952-53 (70)
Fewest Goals Against ...... *131 — 1955-56 (70)

Longest Winning Streak
Overall .... 12 — Jan. 6-Feb. 3/68
Home .... 13 — Nov. 2/43-Jan. 8/44, Jan. 30-Mar. 26/77
Away .... 8 — Dec. 18/77-Jan. 18/78, Jan. 21-Feb. 21/82

Longest Undefeated Streak
Overall .... 28 — Dec. 18/77-Feb. 23/78 (23 wins, 5 ties)
Home .... *34 — Nov. 1/76-Apr. 2/77 (28 wins, 6 ties)
Away .... *23 — Nov. 27/74-Mar. 12/75 (14 wins, 9 ties)

Longest Losing Streak
Overall .... 12 — Feb. 13-Mar. 13/26
Home .... 7 — Dec. 16/39-Jan. 18/40, Oct. 28-Nov. 25/00
Away .... 10 — Jan. 16-Mar. 13/26

Longest Winless Streak
Overall .... 12 — Feb. 13-Mar. 13/26 (12 losses), Nov. 28-Dec. 29/35 (8 losses, 4 ties)
Home .... 15 — Dec. 16/39-Mar. 7/40 (12 losses, 3 ties)
Away .... 12 — Nov. 26/33-Jan. 28/34 (8 losses, 4 ties), Oct. 20-Dec. 13/51 (8 losses, 4 ties)

Most Shutouts, Season ...... *22 — 1928-29 (44)
Most PIM, Season .... 1,847 — 1995-96 (82)
Most Goals, Game .... *16 — Mar. 3/20 (Mtl. 16 at Que. 3)

Individual

Most Seasons .... 20 — Henri Richard, Jean Béliveau
Most Games .... 1,256 — Henri Richard
Most Goals, Career .... 544 — Maurice Richard
Most Assists, Career .... 728 — Guy Lafleur
Most Points, Career .... 1,246 — Guy Lafleur (518G, 728A)
Most PIM, Career .... 2,248 — Chris Nilan
Most Shutouts, Career .... 75 — George Hainsworth
Longest Consecutive Games Streak .... 560 — Doug Jarvis (Oct. 8/75-Apr. 4/82)
Most Goals, Season .... 60 — Steve Shutt (1976-77), Guy Lafleur (1977-78)
Most Assists, Season .... 82 — Pete Mahovlich (1974-75)
Most Points, Season .... 136 — Guy Lafleur (1976-77; 56G, 80A)
Most PIM, Season .... 358 — Chris Nilan (1984-85)
Most Points, Defenseman, Season .... 85 — Larry Robinson (1976-77; 19G, 66A)
Most Points, Center, Season .... 117 — Pete Mahovlich (1974-75; 35G, 82A)
Most Points, Right Wing, Season .... 136 — Guy Lafleur (1976-77; 56G, 80A)
Most Points, Left Wing, Season .... 110 — Mats Naslund (1985-86; 43G, 67A)
Most Points, Rookie, Season .... 71 — Mats Naslund (1982-83; 26G, 45A), Kjell Dahlin (1985-86; 32G, 39A)
Most Shutouts, Season ...... *22 — George Hainsworth (1928-29)
Most Goals, Game .... 6 — Newsy Lalonde (Jan. 10/20)
Most Assists, Game .... 6 — Elmer Lach (Feb. 6/43)
Most Points, Game .... 8 — Maurice Richard (Dec. 28/44; 5G, 3A), Bert Olmstead (Jan. 9/54; 4G, 4A)

* NHL Record.

Retired Numbers

1	Jacques Plante	1952-1963
2	Doug Harvey	1947-1961
4	Jean Béliveau	1950-1971
5	Bernard Geoffrion	1950-1964
7	Howie Morenz	1923-1937
9	Maurice Richard	1942-1960
10	Guy Lafleur	1971-1984
12	Dickie Moore	1951-1963
12	Yvan Cournoyer	1963-1979
16	Henri Richard	1955-1975

All-time Record vs. Other Clubs

Regular Season

	At Home								On Road								Total							
	GP	W	L	T	OL	GF	GA	PTS	GP	W	L	T	OL	GF	GA	PTS	GP	W	L	T	OL	GF	GA	PTS
Anaheim	9	4	3	2	0	27	24	10	8	5	3	0	0	27	25	10	17	9	6	2	0	54	49	20
Atlanta	12	8	3	0	1	38	28	17	12	8	2	2	0	33	16	18	24	16	5	2	1	71	44	35
Boston	338	193	97	47	1	1133	796	434	339	127	153	56	3	914	997	313	677	320	250	103	4	2047	1793	747
Buffalo	107	58	35	12	2	401	318	130	106	31	55	19	1	276	327	82	213	89	90	31	3	677	645	212
Calgary	46	26	12	8	0	163	112	60	50	26	16	7	1	166	149	60	96	52	28	15	1	329	261	120
Carolina	77	50	19	7	1	312	226	108	80	36	29	13	2	274	236	87	157	86	48	20	3	586	462	195
Chicago	276	174	54	48	0	1067	653	396	273	125	93	55	0	761	731	305	549	299	147	103	0	1828	1384	701
Colorado	64	38	15	10	1	261	198	87	64	26	32	5	1	223	218	58	128	64	47	15	2	484	416	145
Columbus	4	1	1	1	1	6	6	4	1	1	0	0	0	3	1	2	5	2	1	1	1	9	7	6
Dallas	59	38	12	9	0	254	146	85	59	30	17	12	0	203	153	72	118	68	29	21	0	457	299	157
Detroit	282	172	67	43	0	994	636	387	280	97	129	53	1	717	805	248	562	269	196	96	1	1711	1441	635
Edmonton	30	16	9	4	1	105	95	37	36	17	17	0	2	116	122	36	66	33	26	4	3	221	217	73
Florida	23	10	9	3	1	63	56	24	24	9	12	3	0	63	70	21	47	19	21	6	1	126	126	45
Los Angeles	65	46	8	11	0	292	162	103	65	37	19	9	0	256	199	83	130	83	27	20	0	548	361	186
Minnesota	3	1	1	1	0	9	8	3	3	1	1	0	1	8	10	3	6	2	2	1	1	17	18	6
Nashville	4	4	0	0	0	15	9	8	4	1	2	1	0	7	14	3	8	5	2	1	0	22	23	11
New Jersey	56	33	17	6	0	187	141	72	56	25	27	4	0	197	170	54	112	58	44	10	0	384	311	126
NY Islanders	62	38	15	9	0	223	171	85	62	25	29	6	2	173	193	58	124	63	44	15	2	396	364	143
NY Rangers	292	191	61	40	0	1128	674	422	292	120	117	54	1	852	839	295	584	311	178	94	1	1980	1513	717
Ottawa	37	20	13	4	0	110	105	44	35	16	16	1	2	95	104	35	72	36	29	5	2	205	209	79
Philadelphia	76	36	25	14	1	262	231	87	75	29	29	16	1	224	231	75	151	65	54	30	2	486	462	162
Phoenix	30	25	3	2	0	147	68	52	29	13	9	7	0	112	94	33	59	38	12	9	0	259	162	85
Pittsburgh	84	62	12	10	0	391	214	134	84	42	28	13	1	298	246	98	168	104	40	23	1	689	460	232
St. Louis	59	41	11	7	0	255	161	89	57	28	14	15	0	195	147	71	116	69	25	22	0	450	308	160
San Jose	12	8	2	2	0	42	22	18	11	4	4	2	1	28	33	11	23	12	6	4	1	70	55	29
Tampa Bay	24	12	11	1	0	63	57	25	25	11	9	5	0	71	60	27	49	23	20	6	0	134	117	52
Toronto	337	200	92	43	2	1179	838	445	337	118	173	45	1	880	1023	282	674	318	265	88	3	2059	1861	727
Vancouver	53	38	10	5	0	244	135	81	56	33	14	8	1	204	152	75	109	71	24	13	1	448	287	156
Washington	62	36	17	8	1	233	134	81	61	25	27	9	0	183	169	59	123	61	44	17	1	416	303	140
Defunct Clubs	231	148	58	25	0	779	469	321	230	98	97	35	0	586	606	231	461	246	155	60	0	1365	1075	552
Totals	**2814**	**1727**	**692**	**382**	**13**	**10383**	**6893**	**3849**	**2814**	**1164**	**1173**	**455**	**22**	**8145**	**8140**	**2805**	**5628**	**2891**	**1865**	**837**	**35**	**18528**	**15033**	**6654**

Playoffs

	Series	W	L	GP	W	L	T	GF	GA	Last Mtg.	Rnd.	Result
Boston	30	23	7	152	95	57	0	469	371	2004	CQF	W 4-3
Buffalo	7	4	3	35	18	17	0	124	111	1998	CSF	L 0-4
Calgary	2	1	1	11	6	5	0	31	32	1989	F	L 2-4
Carolina	7	5	2	39	23	16	0	125	106	2006	CQF	L 2-4
Chicago	17	12	5	81	50	29	2	261	185	1976	QF	W 4-0
Colorado	5	3	2	31	17	14	0	105	85	1993	DSF	W 4-2
Dallas	2	1	1	13	7	6	0	48	37	1980	QF	L 3-4
Detroit	12	5	7	62	33	29	0	161	149	1978	QF	W 4-1
Edmonton	1	0	1	3	0	3	0	6	15	1981	PRE	L 0-3
Los Angeles	1	1	0	5	4	1	0	15	12	1993	F	W 4-1
New Jersey	1	0	1	5	1	4	0	11	22	1997	CQF	L 1-4
NY Islanders	4	3	1	22	14	8	0	64	55	1993	CF	W 4-1
NY Rangers	14	7	7	61	34	25	2	188	158	1996	CQF	L 2-4
Philadelphia	4	3	1	21	14	7	0	72	52	1989	CF	W 4-2
Pittsburgh	1	1	0	6	4	2	0	18	15	1998	CQF	W 4-2
St. Louis	3	3	0	12	12	0	0	42	14	1977	QF	W 4-0
Tampa Bay	1	0	1	4	0	4	0	5	14	2004	CSF	L 0-4
Toronto	15	8	7	71	42	29	0	215	160	1979	QF	W 4-0
Vancouver	1	1	0	5	4	1	0	20	9	1975	QF	W 4-1
Defunct Clubs	11*	6	4	28	15	9	4	70	71			
Totals	**139***	**87**	**51**	**667**	**393**	**266**	**8**	**2050**	**1673**			

* 1919 Final incomplete due to influenza epidemic.

Calgary totals include Atlanta Flames, 1972-73 to 1979-80.
Carolina totals include Hartford, 1979-80 to 1996-97.
Colorado totals include Quebec, 1979-80 to 1994-95.
Dallas totals include Minnesota North Stars, 1967-68 to 1992-93.
New Jersey totals include Kansas City, 1974-75 to 1975-76, and Colorado Rockies, 1976-77 to 1981-82.
Phoenix totals include Winnipeg, 1979-80 to 1995-96.

Playoff Results 2006-2001

Year	Round	Opponent	Result	GF	GA
2006	CQF	Carolina	L 2-4	17	15
2004	CSF	Tampa Bay	L 0-4	5	14
	CQF	Boston	W 4-3	19	14
2002	CSF	Carolina	L 2-4	12	21
	CQF	Boston	W 4-2	20	18

Abbreviations: Round: F - Final; **CF** - conference final; **CSF** - conference semi-final; **CQF** - conference quarter-final; **DSF** - division semi-final; **QF** - quarter-final; **PRE** - preliminary round.

2005-06 Results

Oct.	5	at Boston	2-1		14	San Jose	6-2
	6	at NY Rangers	4-3*		16	Dallas	4-2
	8	at Toronto	5-4		19	at Calgary	2-3
	11	Ottawa	2-4		21	at Vancouver	2-6
	12	at Atlanta	2-0		23	at Carolina	3-7
	15	Toronto	2-3		25	at Philadelphia	5-3
	18	Boston	4-3		26	at Ottawa	0-3
	22	NY Islanders	4-3		28	at Toronto	4-3*
	25	Philadelphia	3-2*		31	Carolina	2-8
	27	at Ottawa	3-4*	**Feb.**	2	at Boston	1-3
	29	NY Rangers	2-5		4	Boston	2-0
	31	at NY Rangers	4-1		5	Philadelphia	5-0
Nov.	1	Florida	5-4*		7	Buffalo	2-3*
	4	at Buffalo	3-2		9	at Buffalo	3-2*
	5	Buffalo	3-2		11	Atlanta	1-2†
	8	Tampa Bay	3-2		28	at NY Islanders	5-3
	10	at Pittsburgh	2-3†	**Mar.**	2	at Florida	1-0
	12	Toronto	4-5*		4	at Tampa Bay	6-2
	15	Florida	4-3*		6	at Philadelphia	4-5†
	18	at New Jersey	3-5		7	at Toronto	3-5
	19	Washington	1-5		9	at Boston	3-0
	22	Atlanta	3-2†		11	NY Rangers	1-0
	25	at Buffalo	1-3		13	Tampa Bay	1-2
	26	at Toronto	3-4*		16	Carolina	1-5
	29	at Ottawa	0-4		18	Pittsburgh	4-5
Dec.	1	Buffalo	2-3*		20	at Washington	4-2
	3	Los Angeles	3-2		21	at NY Islanders	1-3
	10	Anaheim	3-5		23	Toronto	5-1
	13	Phoenix	5-2		25	Toronto	6-2
	15	at Edmonton	3-5		26	at Pittsburgh	6-5
	17	at Minnesota	3-4*		28	NY Islanders	2-0
	20	Ottawa	4-3†		30	Washington	3-2*
	23	at Washington	2-4	**Apr.**	1	Boston	2-0
	26	at Atlanta	0-4		4	Boston	5-3
	28	at Tampa Bay	4-3		6	at Ottawa	5-3
	30	at Florida	1-2		8	New Jersey	2-3
	31	at Carolina	3-5		10	Ottawa	3-2
Jan.	3	Pittsburgh	4-6		12	at Buffalo	1-3
	5	at New Jersey	4-5		13	at Boston	4-3
	7	Ottawa	4-1		15	Buffalo	2-4
	11	at Colorado	1-2*		18	New Jersey	3-4

* – Overtime † – Shootout

Entry Draft
Selections 2006-1992

2006 Pick		2002 Pick		1998 Pick		1994 Pick	
20	David Fischer	14	Christopher Higgins	16	Eric Chouinard	18	Brad Brown
49	Ben Maxwell	45	Tomas Linhart	45	Mike Ribeiro	44	Jose Theodore
53	Mathieu Carle	99	Michael Lambert	75	Francois Beauchemin	54	Chris Murray
66	Ryan White	182	Andre Deveaux	132	Andrei Bashkirov	70	Marko Kiprusoff
139	Pavel Valentenko	212	Jonathan Ferland	152	Gordie Dwyer	74	Martin Belanger
199	Cameron Cepek	275	Konstantin Korneev	162	Andrei Markov	96	Arto Kuki
				189	Andrei Kruchinin	122	Jimmy Drolet
2005 Pick		**2001** Pick		201	Craig Murray	148	Joel Irving
5	Carey Price	7	Mike Komisarek	216	Michael Ryder	174	Jessie Rezansoff
45	Guillaume Latendresse	25	Alexander Perezhogin	247	Darcy Harris	200	Peter Strom
121	Juraj Mikus	37	Duncan Milroy			226	Tomas Vokoun
130	Mathieu Aubin	71	Tomas Plekanec	**1997** Pick		252	Chris Aldous
190	Matt D'Agostini	109	Martti Jarventie	11	Jason Ward	278	Ross Parsons
200	Sergei Kostitsyn	171	Eric Himelfarb	37	Gregor Baumgartner		
229	Philippe Paquet	203	Andrew Archer	65	Ilkka Mikkola	**1993** Pick	
		266	Viktor Ujcik	91	Daniel Tetrault	21	Saku Koivu
2004 Pick				118	Konstantin Sidulov	47	Rory Fitzpatrick
18	Kyle Chipchura	**2000** Pick		122	Gennady Razin	73	Sebastien Bordeleau
84	Alexei Yemelin	13	Ron Hainsey	145	Jonathan Desroches	85	Adam Wiesel
100	J.T. Wyman	16	Marcel Hossa	172	Ben Guite	99	Jean-Francois Houle
150	Mikhail Grabovsky	78	Jozef Balej	197	Petr Kubos	113	Jeff Lank
181	Loic Lacasse	79	Tyler Hanchuck	202	Andrei Sidyakin	125	Dion Darling
212	Jon Gleed	109	Johan Eneqvist	228	Jarl Espen Ygranes	151	Darcy Tucker
246	Greg Stewart	114	Christian Larrivee			177	David Ruhly
262	Mark Streit	145	Ryan Glenn	**1996** Pick		203	Alan Letang
278	Alex Dulac-Lemelin	172	Scott Selig	18	Matt Higgins	229	Alexandre Duchesne
		182	Petr Chvojka	44	Mathieu Garon	255	Brian Larochelle
2003 Pick		243	Joni Puurula	71	Arron Asham	281	Russell Guzior
10	Andrei Kostitsyn	275	Jonathan Gauthier	92	Kim Staal		
40	Cory Urquhart			99	Etienne Drapeau	**1992** Pick	
61	Maxim Lapierre	**1999** Pick		127	Daniel Archambault	20	David Wilkie
79	Ryan O'Byrne	39	Alexander Buturlin	154	Brett Clark	33	Valeri Bure
113	Corey Locke	58	Matt Carkner	181	Timo Vertala	44	Keli Corpse
123	Danny Stewart	97	Chris Dyment	207	Mattia Baldi	68	Craig Rivet
177	Chris Heino-Lindberg	107	Evan Lindsay	233	Michel Tremblay	82	Louis Bernard
188	Mark Flood	136	Dusty Jamieson			92	Marc Lamothe
217	Oskari Korpikari	145	Marc-Andre Thinel	**1995** Pick		116	Don Chase
241	Jimmy Bonneau	150	Matt Shasby	8	Terry Ryan	140	Martin Sychra
271	Jaroslav Halak	167	Sean Dixon	60	Miloslav Guren	164	Christian Proulx
		196	Vadim Tarasov	74	Martin Hohenberger	188	Michael Burman
		225	Mikko Hyytia	86	Jonathan Delisle	212	Earl Cronan
		253	Jerome Marois	112	Niklas Anger	236	Trent Cavicchi
				138	Boyd Olson	260	Hiroyuki Miura
				164	Stephane Robidas		
				190	Greg Hart		
				216	Eric Houde		

Coach

CARBONNEAU, GUY
Coach, Montreal Canadiens. Born in Sept-Iles, Que., March 18, 1960.

Guy Carbonneau was hired as an associate coach to Bob Gainey on January 14, 2006 and worked the last 41 games of the 2005-06 regular season. Almost five months later, on May 5, 2006, Carbonneau officially took over head coaching duties from Gainey. When going behind the bench himself and hiring Carbonneau as his assistant, Gainey had announced that Carbonneau would be the Canadiens' new head coach beginning with the 2006-07 season.

Carbonneau began his coaching career as an assistant coach with the Canadiens from November 2000 until the end of the 2001-02 season (144 regular season games and 12 playoff games). He held the position of supervisor of prospect development from August to November 2000. The 18-year NHL veteran had announced his retirement as a player in July 2000, following a brilliant career that saw him win three Stanley Cup championships and three Frank Selke trophies as the NHL's top defensive forward (1988, 1989 and 1992).

Carbonneau was a Canadiens' third round selection, 44th overall in 1979. He spent the first 12 seasons of his career in Montreal winning the Stanley Cup in 1986 and 1993. Captain of the Canadiens for five seasons (1989 to 1994), he also donned a St. Louis Blues jersey in 1994-95, before joining the Dallas Stars where he played from 1995 to 2000 winning a third Stanley Cup in 1998-99. He made the Stanley Cup playoffs 17 out of 18 NHL seasons. Carbonneau also served as an assistant general manager in Dallas from 2002-03 until returning to Montreal during the 2005-06 season.

Coaching Record
No previous head coaching experience.

Club Directory

Bell Centre

Club de Hockey Canadien
1260 de La Gauchetière Street W.
Montréal, QC H3B 5E8
Phone: **514/932-2582**
Media Hotline: 514/989-2835
Fax Lines (all area code 514):
  Communications 932-8285
  Hockey 989-2717
  Press Lounge 932-5258
  Marketing 925-2145
  Community Relations 925-2144
www.canadiens.com
Capacity: 21,273

Executive
Chairman and Governor	George N. Gillett, Jr.
Vice Chairman	Jeff Joyce
President, Canadiens, Bell Centre & Alt. Gov.	Pierre Boivin
Managing Partner & Alternate Governor	Foster Gillett
Assistant to the President	Marie-Claude Pinel
Exec. V.P., Hockey, G.M. & Alt. Gov.	Bob Gainey
Chief Financial Officer & Alt. Gov.	Fred Steer
V.P., Marketing and Sales	Ray Lalonde
V.P., Communications & Community Relations	Donald Beauchamp
V.P., Building Operations	Alain Gauthier
V.P. & G.M., Gillett Entertainment Group	Jacques Aubé
President, Effix – Advertising and Sponsorship Sales	François Seigneur
President, Canadiens Alumni	Réjean Houle

Hockey
Assistant General Manager	Pierre Gauthier
V.P., Hockey Operations	Julien BriseBois
Director of Player Recruitment and Development	Trevor Timmins
Head Coach	Guy Carbonneau
Assistant Coaches	Roland Melanson, Doug Jarvis, Kirk Muller
Professional Scouts	Gordie Roberts, Doug Gibson
Scouting Staff	Patrik Allvin, Elmer Benning, Bill Berglund, Michel Boucher, Vaughn Karpan, Hannu Laine, Dave Mayville, Mike McCann, Denis Morel, Antonin Routa, Nikolai Vakourov, Pat Westrum
Team Services & Hockey Administration Manager	Claudine Crépin
Administrative Assistant to the General Manager	Suzanne Charlebois

Medical and Training Staff
Club Physician and Chief Surgeon	Dr. David Mulder
Consultant, Orthopedic Surgeon	Dr. Eric Lenczner
Dentist	Dr. Jean-François Desjardins
Consultant, Ophthalmologist	Dr. John Little
Consultant, Sports Medicine	Dr. Vincent Lacroix
Head Athletic Therapist	Graham Rynbend
Athletic Therapist	Nick Addey-Jibb
Strength & Conditioning Coordinator	Scott Livingston
Video Supervisor	Mario Leblanc
Equipment Manager	Pierre Gervais
Assistants to the Equipment Manager	Patrick Langlois, Pierre Ouellette
Visiting Team Coordinator	Richard Généreux

Communications
Director of Media Relations	Dominick Saillant
Administrative Assistant to the V.P. Communications	Sylvie Lambert
Communications Coordinator	Michel Lamarche

Community Relations
CEO, Canadiens Children's Foundation	Robert Sirois
Community Relations Manager	Geneviève Paquette
Coordinator, Canadiens Children's Foundation	Marie-Christine Boucher
Community Relations Coordinator	Anne-Marie Bégin
Coordinator, Canadiens Alumni	Normande Herget

Marketing and Sales
Executive Director, Luxury Suites and Services	Richard Primeau
Director, Group Sales and Administration	Pierre Constant
Director, Ticket Sales	Vincent Lucier
Director, Marketing, Media and Broadcast	Jon Trzcienski
Director, Consumer Products	Matt Zalkowitz
Group Manager, Events, Programs and Centennial	Patrick Boivin
Group Manager, Creative Services and Publications	Jean Simard

Building Operations
Director of Ticket Office	Cathy D'Ascoli
Assistant Director of Ticket Office	Lucie Masse
Director of Building Operations	Xavier Luydlin
Director of Concessions	Alec Beaudry
Director of Customer Services	Caroline Hamel
Administrative Assistant to the V.P. Operations	Maryse Cartwright

Finance
Executive Director, Info. & Communication Technology	Pierre-Éric Belzile
Controller	Dennis McKinley
Assistant Controller	Raymond Lamarche
Administrative Assistant, Chief Financial Officer	Christine Ouellette

Team Information
Play-by-play – Radio/TV	Pierre Houde (RDS), Martin McGuire (CKAC), Rick Moffat (CJAD)
Color – Radio/TV	Yvon Pedneault (RDS), Dany Dubé (CKAC), Murray Wilson (CJAD)
Radio/television flagships	RDS (Cable 33), CKAC (730 AM), CJAD (800 AM)

Nashville Predators

2005-06 Results: 49w-25L-5OTL-3SOL 106PTS.
Second, Central Division

Year-by-Year Record

Season	GP	Home W	L	T	OL	Road W	L	T	OL	Overall W	L	T	OL	GF	GA	Pts.	Finished	Playoff Result
2005-06	82	32	8	....	1	17	17	....	7	49	25	....	8	259	227	106	2nd, Central Div.	Lost Conf. Quarter-Final
2004-05	....																	
2003-04	82	22	10	7	2	16	19	4	2	38	29	11	4	216	217	91	3rd, Central Div.	Lost Conf. Quarter-Final
2002-03	82	18	17	5	1	9	18	8	6	27	35	13	7	183	206	74	4th, Central Div.	Out of Playoffs
2001-02	82	17	16	8	0	11	25	5	0	28	41	13	0	196	230	69	4th, Central Div.	Out of Playoffs
2000-01	82	16	18	7	0	18	18	2	3	34	36	9	3	186	200	80	3rd, Central Div.	Out of Playoffs
1999-2000	82	15	21	3	2	13	19	4	5	28	40	7	7	199	240	70	4th, Central Div.	Out of Playoffs
1998-99	82	15	22	4	....	13	25	3	....	28	47	7	....	190	261	63	4th, Central Div.	Out of Playoffs

2006-07 Schedule

Oct.	Thu.	5	Chicago
	Sat.	7	at Minnesota
	Thu.	12	at Chicago
	Sat.	14	Phoenix
	Mon.	16	at NY Islanders
	Wed.	18	at NY Rangers
	Thu.	19	at New Jersey
	Sat.	21	Vancouver
	Thu.	26	San Jose
	Sat.	28	at Calgary
	Tue.	31	at Vancouver
Nov.	Wed.	1	at Edmonton
	Sat.	4	at Minnesota
	Fri.	10	at Detroit
	Sat.	11	Colorado
	Wed.	15	at Columbus
	Thu.	16	Minnesota
	Sat.	18	Columbus
	Mon.	20	at Columbus
	Wed.	22	at Dallas
	Thu.	23	Vancouver
	Sat.	25	Detroit
	Wed.	29	at Philadelphia
	Thu.	30	at St. Louis
Dec.	Sat.	2	Chicago
	Mon.	4	at Phoenix
	Wed.	6	at Anaheim
	Thu.	7	at Los Angeles
	Sat.	9	at San Jose
	Tue.	12	Edmonton
	Thu.	14	Ottawa
	Sat.	16	St. Louis
	Sun.	17	at St. Louis*
	Wed.	20	at Chicago
	Thu.	21	Buffalo
	Sat.	23	Los Angeles
	Tue.	26	St. Louis
	Fri.	29	at Dallas
	Sat.	30	Boston
Jan.	Mon.	1	Colorado*
	Fri.	5	at Chicago
	Sat.	6	St. Louis
	Tue.	9	Anaheim
	Fri.	12	Columbus
	Sat.	13	at Columbus
	Mon.	15	Calgary*
	Wed.	17	at Detroit
	Thu.	18	Columbus
	Sat.	20	Chicago
	Fri.	26	at Chicago
	Sat.	27	at St. Louis
	Sat.	30	at Colorado
Feb.	Thu.	1	at Phoenix
	Sat.	3	Anaheim
	Tue.	6	at Pittsburgh
	Thu.	8	Toronto
	Sat.	10	Los Angeles
	Wed.	14	San Jose
	Fri.	16	at St. Louis
	Sat.	17	Minnesota
	Mon.	19	Phoenix*
	Thu.	22	Montreal
	Sat.	24	Detroit
	Sun.	25	at Columbus
	Wed.	28	at San Jose
Mar.	Sat.	3	at Los Angeles*
	Sun.	4	at Anaheim*
	Tue.	6	at Detroit
	Thu.	8	Calgary
	Sat.	10	Columbus
	Tue.	13	Detroit
	Wed.	14	at Detroit
	Sat.	17	Dallas
	Wed.	21	at Vancouver
	Thu.	22	at Calgary
	Sat.	24	at Edmonton
	Tue.	27	Edmonton
	Thu.	29	Detroit
	Sat.	31	Dallas
Apr.	Tue.	3	Chicago
	Thu.	5	St. Louis
	Sat.	7	at Colorado

* Denotes afternoon game.

Franchise date: June 25, 1997

9th
NHL
Season

CENTRAL
DIVISION

Paul Kariya celebrates a goal with Marek Zidlicky. Kariya topped the Predators with 54 assists and 85 points while Zidlicky led the team's blueliners with 12 goals.

2006-07 Player Personnel

FORWARDS

	HT	WT	S	Place of Birth	Date	2005-06 Club
ABID, Ramzi	6-2	210	L	Montreal, Que.	3/24/80	Atlanta-Chicago (AHL)
ARNOTT, Jason	6-4	220	R	Collingwood, Ont.	10/11/74	Dallas
BROWN, Paul	6-3	184	R	Edmonton, Alta.	7/21/84	Milwaukee-Rockford
ENDICOTT, Shane	6-3	214	L	Saskatoon, Sask.	12/21/81	Pittsburgh-Wilkes-Barre
ERAT, Martin	6-0	195	L	Trebic, Czech.	8/29/81	Nashville
FIDDLER, Vern	5-11	204	L	Edmonton, Alta.	5/9/80	Nashville-Milwaukee
HARTNELL, Scott	6-2	210	L	Regina, Sask.	4/18/82	Nashville
HORDICHUK, Darcy	6-1	215	L	Kamsack, Sask.	8/10/80	Nashville
KARIYA, Paul	5-10	176	L	Vancouver, B.C.	10/16/74	Nashville
LEAHY, Patrick	6-3	200	R	Brighton, MA	6/9/79	Boston-Providence (AHL)
LEGWAND, David	6-2	190	L	Detroit, MI	8/17/80	Nashville-Milwaukee
NICHOL, Scott	5-8	173	R	Edmonton, Alta.	12/31/74	Nashville-Milwaukee
O'REILLY, Cal	6-0	193	L	Toronto, Ont.	9/30/86	Windsor-Milwaukee
RADULOV, Alexander	6-1	188	L	Nizhy Tagil, USSR	7/5/86	Quebec (QMJHL)
SEGAL, Brandon	6-3	213	R	Richmond, B.C.	7/12/83	Milwaukee
SMITHSON, Jerred	6-3	194	R	Vernon, B.C.	2/4/79	Nashville
SULLIVAN, Steve	5-9	155	R	Timmins, Ont.	7/6/74	Nashville
TOOTOO, Jordin	5-9	194	R	Churchill, Man.	2/2/83	Nashville-Milwaukee
UPSHALL, Scottie	6-0	197	L	Fort McMurray, Alta.	10/7/83	Nashville-Milwaukee
VASICEK, Josef	6-5	214	L	Havlickuv Brod, Czech.	9/12/80	Carolina
VIGILANTE, John	5-11	206	L	Dearborn, MI	5/24/85	Plymouth
WIDING, Daniel	6-1	202	R	Gavle, Sweden	4/13/82	TPS-Brynas

DEFENSEMEN

	HT	WT	S	Place of Birth	Date	2005-06 Club
BROOKBANK, Sheldon	6-2	200	R	Lanigan, Sask.	10/3/80	Milwaukee
HAMHUIS, Dan	6-1	200	L	Smithers, B.C.	12/13/82	Nashville
KLEIN, Kevin	6-1	195	L	Kitchener, Ont.	12/13/84	Nashville-Milwaukee
LEHTONEN, Mikko	6-1	194	L	Oulu, Finland	6/12/78	Karpat
SUTER, Ryan	6-1	196	L	Madison, WI	1/21/85	Nashville
TIMONEN, Kimmo	5-10	194	L	Kuopio, Finland	3/18/75	Nashville
WEBER, Shea	6-3	213	R	Sicamous, B.C.	8/14/85	Nashville-Milwaukee
YONKMAN, Nolan	6-6	245	R	Punnichy, Sask.	4/1/81	Washington-Hershey
ZANON, Greg	5-11	211	L	Burnaby, B.C.	6/5/80	Nashville-Milwaukee
ZIDLICKY, Marek	5-11	190	R	Most, Czech.	2/3/77	Nashville

GOALTENDERS

	HT	WT	C	Place of Birth	Date	2005-06 Club
GOEHRING, Karl	5-8	160	L	Apple Valley, MN	8/23/78	Jokerit-San Antonio
MASON, Chris	6-0	195	L	Red Deer, Alta.	4/20/76	Nashville
RINNE, Pekka	6-5	207	L	Kempele, Finland	11/3/82	Nashville-Milwaukee
VOKOUN, Tomas	6-0	195	R	Karlovy Vary, Czech.	7/2/76	Nashville

Vice President and General Manager

POILE, DAVID
Executive Vice President/General Manager, Nashville Predators.
Born in Toronto, Ont., February 14, 1949.

Since joining the Predators as general manager on July 9, 1997, David Poile has made a commitment to building for the future, surrounding himself with one of the youngest and most talented staffs in the National Hockey League. In 2003-04, Nashville reached the playoffs for the first time in franchise history and qualified again in 2005-06. Poile has an impressive reputation as an NHL leader and in 2001 he received the Lester Patrick Trophy for his contributions to hockey in the United States. His father, Norman "Bud" Poile, had won the honor in 1989.

Prior to joining Nashville, Poile spent 15 seasons as vice president/general manager of the Washington Capitals. During his tenure in Washington, the Capitals made 14 postseason appearances, winning their only Patrick Division title in 1989 and advancing to the Conference Finals in 1990. During Poile's 15 years in Washington, the Capitals compiled a record of 594-454-132, finished second in the Patrick Division seven times and recorded 90-or-more points seven different seasons.

Poile started his professional hockey career as an administrative assistant for the Atlanta Flames in 1972, shortly after graduating from Northeastern University in Boston. At Northeastern, he was hockey team captain, leading scorer and most valuable player for two years.

In 1977, he was named assistant general manager of the Atlanta Flames (who moved to Calgary in 1980), serving as the manager and coordinator of the Flames farm club.

Poile is a member of the NHL's general managers committee and was instrumental in the NHL's adoption of the instant replay rule in 1991. He was awarded *Inside Hockey*'s man of the year for his leadership on the issue. He was also twice honored as *The Sporting News* NHL executive of the year following the 1982-83 and 1983-84 seasons. Poile served as general manager of the 1998 and 1999 U.S. national team for the World Championships.

Poile was introduced to hockey by watching his father play seven seasons in the NHL. Bud Poile later became general manager for the Vancouver Canucks and the Philadelphia Flyers, both NHL expansion franchises at the time. He was inducted into the Hockey Hall of Fame in 1990.

2005-06 Scoring

*– rookie

Regular Season

Pos	#	Player	Team	GP	G	A	Pts	+/-	PIM	PP	SH	GW	S	%
L	9	Paul Kariya	NSH	82	31	54	85	−6	40	14	0	3	245	12.7
R	26	Steve Sullivan	NSH	69	31	37	68	2	50	13	4	5	192	16.1
C	81	Mike Sillinger	STL	48	22	19	41	−17	49	11	1	1	131	16.8
			NSH	31	10	12	22	0	14	3	0	1	80	12.5
			TOTAL	79	32	31	63	−17	63	14	1	2	211	15.2
C	94	Yanic Perreault	NSH	69	22	35	57	−3	30	10	0	2	145	15.2
D	44	Kimmo Timonen	NSH	79	11	39	50	−3	74	8	0	1	156	7.1
L	10	Martin Erat	NSH	80	20	29	49	0	76	5	0	1	143	14.0
D	3	Marek Zidlicky	NSH	67	12	37	49	8	82	10	0	1	113	10.6
L	17	Scott Hartnell	NSH	81	25	23	48	8	101	10	2	8	211	11.8
D	2	Dan Hamhuis	NSH	82	7	31	38	11	70	4	1	1	135	5.2
R	18	Adam Hall	NSH	75	14	15	29	0	40	10	0	5	122	11.5
C	11	David Legwand	NSH	44	7	19	26	3	34	0	0	0	109	6.4
R	7	Scottie Upshall	NSH	48	8	16	24	14	34	1	0	2	72	11.1
C	22	Greg Johnson	NSH	68	11	8	19	5	10	0	4	3	76	14.5
R	24	Scott Walker	NSH	33	5	11	16	2	36	1	0	0	57	8.8
D	20	* Ryan Suter	NSH	71	1	15	16	7	66	0	0	0	84	1.2
C	25	Jerred Smithson	NSH	66	5	9	14	9	54	0	0	1	50	10.0
D	19	Brendan Witt	WSH	58	1	10	11	−5	141	0	0	0	62	1.6
			NSH	17	0	3	3	5	68	0	0	0	13	0.0
			TOTAL	75	1	13	14	0	209	0	0	0	75	1.3
L	16	Darcy Hordichuk	NSH	74	7	6	13	9	163	0	0	1	52	13.5
L	38	Vernon Fiddler	NSH	40	8	4	12	−2	42	3	0	2	46	17.4
D	55	Danny Markov	NSH	58	0	11	11	9	62	0	0	0	59	0.0
R	14	Jordin Tootoo	NSH	34	4	6	10	9	55	0	0	0	61	6.6
D	6	* Shea Weber	NSH	28	2	8	10	8	42	2	0	1	46	4.3
C	12	Scott Nichol	NSH	34	3	3	6	3	79	0	0	1	32	9.4
D	4	Mark Eaton	NSH	69	3	1	4	−2	44	0	0	0	28	10.7
D	37	* Greg Zanon	NSH	4	0	2	2	0	6	0	0	0	3	0.0
D	49	Kevin Klein	NSH	2	0	0	0	−1	0	0	0	0	0	0.0

Goaltending

No.	Goaltender	GPI	Mins	Avg	W	L	OT	EN	SO	GA	SA	S%	G	A	PIM
30	Chris Mason	23	1227	2.54	12	5	1	0	2	52	597	.913	1	0	0
29	Tomas Vokoun	61	3601	2.67	36	18	7	1	4	160	1984	.919	0	2	26
35	* Pekka Rinne	2	63	3.81	1	1	0	0	0	4	40	.900	0	0	0
1	* Brian Finley	1	60	7.00	0	1	0	0	0	7	41	.829	0	0	0
	Totals	**82**	**4980**	**2.70**	**49**	**25**	**8**	**1**	**6**	**224**	**2663**	**.916**			

Playoffs

Pos	#	Player	Team	GP	G	A	Pts	+/-	PIM	PP	SH	GW	OT	S	%
L	9	Paul Kariya	NSH	5	2	5	7	0	0	2	0	0	0	12	16.7
D	44	Kimmo Timonen	NSH	5	1	3	4	0	4	1	0	0	0	17	5.9
C	81	Mike Sillinger	NSH	5	2	1	3	−1	12	1	0	0	0	7	28.6
D	6	* Shea Weber	NSH	4	2	0	2	−3	8	1	0	0	0	4	50.0
L	10	Martin Erat	NSH	5	1	1	2	−1	4	0	0	0	0	8	12.5
R	26	Steve Sullivan	NSH	5	0	2	2	−2	0	0	0	0	0	12	0.0
D	2	Dan Hamhuis	NSH	5	0	2	2	4	2	0	0	0	0	9	0.0
R	18	Adam Hall	NSH	5	1	0	1	−3	0	1	0	1	0	7	14.3
L	17	Scott Hartnell	NSH	5	1	0	1	0	4	0	0	0	0	9	11.1
D	3	Marek Zidlicky	NSH	5	0	1	1	0	2	0	0	0	0	7	0.0
C	38	Vernon Fiddler	NSH	2	0	1	1	−1	0	0	0	0	0	1	0.0
C	22	Greg Johnson	NSH	5	0	1	1	1	2	0	0	0	0	3	0.0
C	11	David Legwand	NSH	5	0	1	1	0	8	0	0	0	0	11	0.0
C	94	Yanic Perreault	NSH	1	0	0	0	0	0	0	0	0	0	2	0.0
R	7	Scottie Upshall	NSH	2	0	0	0	0	2	0	0	0	0	4	0.0
C	12	Scott Nichol	NSH	3	0	0	0	−2	2	0	0	0	0	4	0.0
C	25	Jerred Smithson	NSH	5	0	0	0	3	6	0	0	0	0	6	0.0
D	19	Brendan Witt	NSH	5	0	0	0	0	4	0	0	0	0	5	0.0
R	24	Scott Walker	NSH	5	0	0	0	0	2	0	0	0	0	4	0.0
D	55	Danny Markov	NSH	5	0	0	0	−1	6	0	0	0	0	6	0.0
D	4	Mark Eaton	NSH	5	0	0	0	3	0	0	0	0	0	3	0.0

Goaltending

No.	Goaltender	GPI	Mins	Avg	W	L	EN	SO	GA	SA	S%	G	A	PIM
30	Chris Mason	5	296	3.45	1	4	0	0	17	171	.901	0	0	0
	Totals	**5**	**300**	**3.40**	**1**	**4**	**0**	**0**	**17**	**171**	**.901**			

Club Records

Team

(Figures in brackets for season records are games played; records for fewest points, wins, ties, losses, goals, goals against are for 70 or more games)

Most Points **106** 2005-06 (82)
Most Wins **49** 2005-06 (82)
Most Ties **13** 2001-02 (82), 2002-03 (82)
Most Losses **47** 1998-99 (82)
Most Goals **259** 2005-06 (82)
Most Goals Against **261** 1998-99 (82)
Fewest Points **63** 1998-99 (82)
Fewest Wins **27** 2002-03 (82)
Fewest Ties **7** 1998-99 (82), 1999-2000 (82)
Fewest Losses **25** 2005-06 (82)
Fewest Goals **183** 2002-03 (82)
Fewest Goals Against **200** 2000-01 (82)
Longest Winning Streak
Overall .... **6** Nov. 11-Dec. 4/03
Home .... **7** Feb. 13-Mar. 1/03
Away .... **4** Nov. 11-Dec. 4/03, Mar. 20-Apr. 4/04
Longest Undefeated Streak
Overall .... **8** Dec. 18/99-Jan. 1/00 (5 wins, 3 ties)
Home .... **11** Two times
Away .... **4** Two times
Longest Losing Streak
Overall .... **7** Nov. 20-Dec. 2/99
Home .... **6** Jan. 21-Feb. 15/99, Feb. 26-Mar. 21/02
Away .... **5** Five times
Longest Winless Streak
Overall .... **15** Mar. 10-Apr. 6/03 (12 losses (2 in OT), 3 ties)
Home .... **9** Jan. 21-Mar. 2/99 (8 losses, 1 tie)
Away .... **9** Three times
Most Shutouts, Season **6** 2000-01 (82), 2005-06 (82)
Most PIM, Season **1,420** 1998-99 (82)
Most Goals, Game .... **9** Mar. 4/04 (Nsh. 9 at Pit. 4)

Individual

Most Seasons .... **7** Greg Johnson, David Legwand, Kimmo Timonen, Tomas Vokoun, Scott Walker
Most Games .... **502** Greg Johnson
Most Goals, Career .... **96** Scott Walker
Most Assists, Career .... **180** Kimmo Timonen
Most Points, Career .... **247** Scott Walker (96G, 151A)
Most PIM, Career .... **465** Scott Walker
Most Shutouts, Career .... **16** Tomas Vokoun
Longest Consecutive Games Streak .... **269** Karlis Skrastins (Feb. 21/00-Apr. 6/03)
Most Goals, Season .... **31** Paul Kariya (2005-06), Steve Sullivan (2005-06)
Most Assists, Season .... **54** Paul Kariya (2005-06)
Most Points, Season .... **85** Paul Kariya (2005-06; 31G, 54A)
Most PIM, Season .... **242** Patrick Cote (1999-2000)
Most Points, Defenseman, Season .... **53** Marek Zidlicky (2003-04; 14G, 39A)
Most Points, Center, Season .... **62** Cliff Ronning (1999-2000; 26G, 36A) (2000-01; 19G, 43A)
Most Points, Right Wing, Season .... **68** Steve Sullivan (2005-06; 31G, 37A)
Most Points, Left Wing, Season .... **85** Paul Kariya (2005-06; 31G, 54A)
Most Points, Rookie, Season .... **53** Marek Zidlicky (2003-04; 14G, 39A)
Most Shutouts, Season .... **4** Mike Dunham (2000-01)
Most Goals, Game .... **3** Seven times
Most Assists, Game .... **5** Mark Zidlicky (Feb. 18/04)
Most Points, Game .... **5** Mark Zidlicky (Feb. 18/04; 5A), Dan Hamhuis (Mar. 4/04; 1G-4A)

General Managers' History

David Poile, 1998-99 to date.

Coaching History

Barry Trotz, 1998-99 to date.

Captains' History

Tom Fitzgerald, 1998-99 to 2001-02;
Greg Johnson, 2002-03 to 2005-06.

All-time Record vs. Other Clubs

Regular Season

	At Home								On Road								Total							
	GP	W	L	T	OL	GF	GA	PTS	GP	W	L	T	OL	GF	GA	PTS	GP	W	L	T	OL	GF	GA	PTS
Anaheim	14	6	5	2	1	29	34	15	14	3	10	0	1	24	43	7	28	9	15	2	2	53	77	22
Atlanta	3	2	1	0	0	12	6	4	5	1	2	1	1	13	16	4	8	3	3	1	1	25	22	8
Boston	6	2	4	0	0	13	16	4	5	2	2	1	0	9	14	5	11	4	6	1	0	22	30	9
Buffalo	5	2	2	0	1	10	9	5	4	3	0	1	0	16	9	7	9	5	2	1	1	26	18	12
Calgary	15	10	4	1	0	50	29	21	14	5	4	3	2	33	40	15	29	15	8	4	2	83	69	36
Carolina	4	3	1	0	0	9	7	6	6	2	2	1	1	17	19	6	10	5	3	1	1	26	26	12
Chicago	20	11	6	3	0	66	50	25	21	8	12	1	0	53	58	17	41	19	18	4	0	119	108	42
Colorado	14	5	6	3	0	43	50	13	14	5	6	2	1	29	39	13	28	10	12	5	1	72	89	26
Columbus	15	10	3	1	1	49	34	22	14	7	6	0	1	41	36	15	29	17	9	1	2	90	70	37
Dallas	14	7	6	1	0	34	29	15	14	2	11	0	1	17	42	5	28	9	17	1	1	51	71	20
Detroit	20	8	10	2	0	51	58	18	21	5	12	2	2	46	80	14	41	13	22	4	2	97	138	32
Edmonton	15	5	7	3	0	36	44	13	14	6	6	0	2	38	43	14	29	11	13	3	2	74	87	27
Florida	5	1	2	2	0	8	10	4	5	1	3	1	0	11	18	3	10	2	5	3	0	19	28	7
Los Angeles	14	3	8	3	0	23	36	9	14	5	6	0	3	34	45	13	28	8	14	3	3	57	81	22
Minnesota	10	7	1	2	0	27	14	16	10	2	5	3	0	21	29	7	20	9	6	5	0	48	43	23
Montreal	4	2	1	1	0	14	7	5	4	0	3	0	1	9	15	1	8	2	4	1	1	23	22	6
New Jersey	6	1	4	0	1	12	18	3	5	3	1	0	1	14	15	7	11	4	5	0	2	26	33	10
NY Islanders	6	4	2	0	0	16	17	8	4	2	1	0	1	12	11	5	10	6	3	0	1	28	28	13
NY Rangers	5	2	3	0	0	14	19	4	6	3	2	1	0	15	18	7	11	5	5	1	0	29	37	11
Ottawa	4	2	2	0	0	8	11	4	5	1	4	0	0	7	15	2	9	3	6	0	0	15	26	6
Philadelphia	5	1	2	2	0	8	10	4	5	2	2	1	0	9	17	5	10	3	4	3	0	17	27	9
Phoenix	14	7	5	2	0	39	35	16	14	6	7	0	1	43	42	13	28	13	12	2	1	82	77	29
Pittsburgh	7	5	2	0	0	26	14	10	5	2	1	2	0	17	14	6	12	7	3	2	0	43	28	16
St. Louis	21	9	9	3	0	47	52	21	20	7	10	1	2	36	57	17	41	16	19	4	2	83	109	38
San Jose	14	7	6	1	0	34	37	15	14	5	6	1	2	35	36	13	28	12	12	2	2	69	73	28
Tampa Bay	6	2	4	0	0	12	16	4	5	1	2	2	0	13	15	4	11	3	6	2	0	25	31	8
Toronto	1	1	0	0	0	3	2	2	6	3	2	1	0	18	13	7	7	4	2	1	0	21	15	9
Vancouver	15	7	5	1	2	43	41	17	14	3	10	1	0	34	54	7	29	10	15	2	2	77	95	24
Washington	5	3	1	1	0	16	11	7	5	2	3	0	0	13	12	4	10	5	4	1	0	29	23	11
Totals	**287**	**135**	**112**	**34**	**6**	**752**	**716**	**310**	**287**	**97**	**141**	**26**	**23**	**677**	**865**	**243**	**574**	**232**	**253**	**60**	**29**	**1429**	**1581**	**553**

Playoffs

	Series	W	L	GP	W	L	T	GF	GA	Last Mtg.	Rnd.	Result
Detroit	1	0	1	6	2	4	0	9	12	2004	CQF	L 2-4
San Jose	1	0	1	5	1	4	0	10	17	2006	CQF	L 1-4
Totals	**2**	**0**	**2**	**11**	**3**	**8**	**0**	**19**	**29**			

Playoff Results 2006-2001

Year	Round	Opponent	Result	GF	GA
2006	CQF	San Jose	L 1-4	10	17
2004	CQF	Detroit	L 2-4	9	12

Abbreviations: Round: CQF - conference quarter-final.

2005-06 Results

Oct.	5	San Jose	3-2		10	NY Islanders	2-1
	8	Anaheim	3-2†		11	at Atlanta	3-4†
	12	at Colorado	5-4		13	at Carolina	4-5*
	13	at Phoenix	5-4†		15	Pittsburgh	5-4
	15	at St. Louis	4-1		19	New Jersey	3-4†
	20	St. Louis	3-2†		21	Columbus	7-2
	22	San Jose	2-1		23	at Detroit	3-2
	25	Chicago	5-3		24	at Detroit	2-1*
	26	at Columbus	2-3*		26	at Minnesota	1-5
	29	Edmonton	1-5		28	at Columbus	3-4
Nov.	1	at Anaheim	1-4	**Feb.**	1	at Dallas	1-2
	2	at San Jose	2-3*		2	Colorado	4-3*
	5	at Los Angeles	2-3†		4	Chicago	6-0
	8	Edmonton	3-2		6	at Dallas	2-4
	10	Dallas	5-3		8	at Detroit	0-6
	12	St. Louis	3-1		9	Detroit	2-3
	15	Los Angeles	3-2		11	Columbus	5-2
	19	at Minnesota	2-4	**Mar.**	1	at Chicago	0-3
	23	at Columbus	4-2		2	Vancouver	3-1
	24	Los Angeles	4-3		5	at Edmonton	2-3*
	26	Dallas	1-3		7	at Calgary	3-2
	29	Calgary	2-0		9	at Vancouver	3-2*
Dec.	1	Minnesota	2-1		11	at San Jose	2-3*
	3	Philadelphia	4-3†		14	Vancouver	5-0
	7	at Washington	5-2		16	Phoenix	2-0
	8	NY Rangers	1-5		18	Calgary	9-4
	10	at Tampa Bay	3-4		20	St. Louis	4-2
	13	at Florida	3-7		21	at Detroit	3-2†
	15	Chicago	5-3		24	at Anaheim	3-6
	17	Columbus	7-3		25	at Los Angeles	4-6
	20	Colorado	3-2		28	at Phoenix	3-5
	21	at Chicago	6-1		30	Detroit	2-4
	23	at Columbus	5-4	**Apr.**	1	St. Louis	2-1
	27	at Calgary	4-3		3	Columbus	1-3
	28	at Vancouver	3-4		5	at Chicago	3-4
	30	at Edmonton	2-4		6	at St. Louis	3-0
Jan.	1	Anaheim	2-4		8	Chicago	2-1†
	3	at Colorado	0-3		11	at St. Louis	2-0
	4	at St. Louis	4-3		13	Minnesota	4-2
	6	Detroit	1-3		15	Phoenix	5-1
	8	at Chicago	5-1		18	Detroit	6-3

* – Overtime † – Shootout

Entry Draft Selections 2006-1998

2006
Pick
56 Blake Geoffrion
105 Niko Snellman
146 Mark Dekanich
176 Ryan Flynn
206 Viktor Sjodin

2005
Pick
18 Ryan Parent
78 Teemu Laakso
79 Cody Franson
150 Cal O'Reilly
176 Ryan Maki
213 Scott Todd
230 Patric Hornqvist

2004
Pick
15 Alexander Radulov
81 Vaclav Meidl
107 Nick Fugere
139 Kyle Moir
147 Janne Niskala
178 Mike Santorelli
193 Kevin Schaeffer
209 Stanislav Balan
243 Denis Kulyash
258 Pekka Rinne
275 Craig Switzer

2003
Pick
7 Ryan Suter
35 Konstantin Glazachev
37 Kevin Klein
49 Shea Weber
76 Richard Stehlik
89 Paul Brown
92 Alexander Sulzer
98 Grigory Shafigulin
117 Teemu Lassila
133 Rustam Sidikov
210 Andrei Mukhachev
213 Miroslav Hanuljak
268 Lauris Darzins

2002
Pick
6 Scottie Upshall
102 Brandon Segal
138 Patrick Jarrett
172 Mike McKenna
203 Josh Morrow
235 Kaleb Betts
264 Matt Davis
266 Steven Spencer

2001
Pick
12 Dan Hamhuis
33 Timofei Shishkanov
42 Tomas Slovak
75 Denis Platonov
76 Oliver Setzinger
98 Jordin Tootoo
178 Anton Lavrentiev
240 Gustav Grasberg
271 Mikko Lehtonen

2000
Pick
6 Scott Hartnell
36 Daniel Widing
72 Mattias Nilsson
89 Libor Pivko
131 Matt Hendricks
137 Mike Stuart
154 Matt Koalska
173 Tomas Harant
197 Zbynek Irgl
203 Jure Penko
236 Mats Christeen
284 Martin Hohener

1999
Pick
6 Brian Finley
33 Jonas Andersson
52 Adam Hall
54 Andrew Hutchinson
61 Ed Hill
65 Jan Lasak
72 Brett Angel
121 Yevgeny Pavlov
124 Alexandre Krevsun
131 Konstantin Panov
162 Timo Helbling
191 Martin Erat
205 Kyle Kettles
220 Miroslav Durak
248 Darren Haydar

1998
Pick
2 David Legwand
60 Denis Arkhipov
85 Geoff Koch
88 Kent Sauer
138 Martin Beauchesne
147 Craig Brunel
202 Martin Bartek
230 Karlis Skrastins

Coach

TROTZ, BARRY
Coach, Nashville Predators. Born in Winnipeg, Man., July 15, 1962.

Barry Trotz realized his dream of becoming an NHL head coach on August 6, 1997, after serving four seasons as head coach and director of hockey operations for the American Hockey League's Portland Pirates. He and assistant Paul Gardner spent the 1997-98 season scouting in preparation for the inaugural season of the Predators. In his sixth season behind the bench in 2003-04, Trotz led Nashville into the playoffs for the first time. They reached the playoffs again in 2005-06.

Trotz began his coaching career in 1984 as assistant coach with the University of Manitoba for one season, before serving two seasons as the head coach and general manager of the Dauphin Kings Junior Hockey Club from 1985 to 1987. He became head coach of the University of Manitoba during the 1987 season and also served as a scout for the Spokane Chiefs of the Western Hockey League that season. Trotz joined the Washington Capitals organization as their chief western scout during the 1988 season. The Winnipeg, Manitoba native was appointed an assistant coach of the Capitals' American Hockey League affiliate in Baltimore prior to the 1991 season before being named head coach prior to the 1992 season. When the franchise relocated to Portland, he guided the Pirates to two AHL Calder Cup Final appearances in the club's first four seasons. He led the Pirates to a league-best 43-27-10 record, captured the Calder Cup championship and was named the American Hockey League coach of the year following the 1994-95 season.

In 1995, Trotz guided Portland to a new North American professional hockey league record 17-game unbeaten streak (14-0-3) to start the season. He was named head coach for the U.S. team at the American Hockey League All-Star Game in 1996.

Prior to his coaching career, Trotz played junior hockey for the Western Hockey League's Regina Pats from 1979-83. During that time, he recorded 39 goals, 121 assists for 160 points, along with 490 penalty minutes in 204 games.

Coaching Record

		Regular Season				Playoffs		
Season	Team	Games	W	L	O/T	Games	W	L
1992-93	Baltimore (AHL)	80	28	40	12	7	3	4
1993-94	Portland (AHL)	80	43	27	10	8	6	2
1994-95	Portland (AHL)	80	46	22	12	7	3	4
1995-96	Portland (AHL)	80	32	38	10	24	14	10
1996-97	Portland (AHL)	80	37	33	10	5	2	3
1998-99	**Nashville (NHL)**	**82**	**28**	**47**	**7**	....	....	....
1999-2000	**Nashville (NHL)**	**82**	**28**	**47**	**7**	....	....	....
2000-01	**Nashville (NHL)**	**82**	**34**	**39**	**9**	....	....	....
2001-02	**Nashville (NHL)**	**82**	**28**	**41**	**13**	....	....	....
2002-03	**Nashville (NHL)**	**82**	**27**	**42**	**13**	....	....	....
2003-04	**Nashville (NHL)**	**82**	**38**	**33**	**11**	**6**	**2**	**4**
2004-05	**Nashville (NHL)**			Season Cancelled				
2005-06	**Nashville (NHL)**	**82**	**49**	**25**	**8**	**5**	**1**	**4**
	NHL Totals	**574**	**232**	**274**	**68**	**11**	**3**	**8**

Club Directory

Gaylord Entertainment Center

Nashville Predators
Gaylord Entertainment Center
501 Broadway
Nashville, TN 37203
Phone **615/770-2300**
FAX 615/770-2309
Ticket Information 615/770-PUCK
www.nashvillepredators.com
Capacity: 17,113

Owner, Chairman and Governor . . . . Craig Leipold
General Partner . . . . Nashville Predators, LLC
Exec. V.P./G.M. and Alternate Governor . . . . David Poile
Exec. V.P., Finance & Admin./CFO & Alt. Gov. . . . . . . Ed Lang
Exec. V.P., of Business Affairs & Alt. Gov. . . . . Steve Violetta
Sr. V.P., Communications & Development . . . . Gerry Helper

Hockey Operations
Assistant General Manager . . . . Paul Fenton
Director of Hockey Operations . . . . Mike Santos
Head Coach . . . . Barry Trotz
Associate Coach . . . . Brent Peterson
Assistant Coach . . . . Peter Horachek
Goaltending Coach . . . . Mitch Korn
Video Coach . . . . Robert Bouchard
Strength and Conditioning Coach . . . . David Good
Professional Scouts . . . . Nick Beverley, Shawn Dineen
North American Amateur Scouts . . . . Gord Donnelly, Jeff Kealty, Rick Knickle, Glen Sanders, David Westby
European Scouts . . . . Lucas Bergman, Janne Kekalainen, Martin Bakula
Head Athletic Trainer . . . . Dan Redmond
Assistant Athletic Trainer . . . . Eric Claas
Equipment Manager . . . . Pete Rogers
Assistant Equipment Manager . . . . Jeff Camelio
Locker Room Attendant . . . . Craig "Partner" Baugh
Director of Team Services . . . . Gregory Harvey
Hockey Operations Manager . . . . Brandon Walker
Executive Assistant . . . . Caitlin Nierenberg

Medical
Richard W. Garman MD, Blake Garside MD, Donald Griffin MD, Carl Hampf MD, Bryan D. Oslin MD, Michael J. Pagnani MD, Gary S. Solomon PhD, Cristin Wallace DDS, Daniel Weikert MD

Communication/Development
Director of Communications . . . . Ken Anderson
Communications Manager . . . . Tim Darling
Internet Development Manager . . . . Doug Brumley
Community Relations Manager . . . . Rebecca Ward
Youth/Amateur Hockey Coordinator . . . . Andee Boiman
Community Relations Coordinator . . . . Erich Wilhelm
Team Photographer . . . . John Russell

Corporate Sales
Vice President of Corporate Development . . . . Jason Bitsoff
Director of Corporate Development . . . . Delmar Smith
Account Executive – Corporate Partnerships . . . . Tom Moulton
Corporate Partnerships Account Managers . . . . Kyla DeHay, Kristy Estes-Adoff
Executive Assistant . . . . Gerry Pring

Marketing
Vice President of Marketing . . . . Randy Campbell
Director of Marketing . . . . Bryan Shaffer
Marketing and Special Events Manager . . . . Christel Foley
Promotions Manager . . . . Chris Leipold
Entertainment Manager . . . . Adam DeVault
Advertising Manager . . . . Vicki Garrison
Database Marketing Manager . . . . Jason Koettel
Database Coordinator . . . . Shannon Lake
Game Operations Coordinator . . . . Brian Campbell
Media Buyer . . . . Melissa Hindman
Art Director . . . . Jennifer Sheets
Graphic Artist . . . . Chuck Stephens
Executive Assistant . . . . Elaine Lewis

Premium Seating
Vice President of Premium Seating Service . . . . Susie Masotti
Premium Seating Manager . . . . Britt Kincheloe

Finance, Administration, Human Resources
Vice President of Finance . . . . Beth Snider
Director of Human Resources . . . . Angela Briggs
Human Resources Coordinator . . . . Colaina Townsend
Payroll Manager . . . . Susan Charnley
Accountants . . . . Melanie Ainsworth, Stephanie Hackworth, Michael Kruspe

Technical Operations
Director of Technical Operations . . . . Blake Grant
Technical Operations Coordinator . . . . Patrick Abell

Broadcast
Director of Broadcasting . . . . Erik Barnhart
Play-by-Play Announcer . . . . Pete Weber
Color Analyst . . . . Terry Crisp
Manager, Video Production . . . . Mitch Jordan
Associate Producer . . . . Bob Kohl
Videographer/Editor . . . . David White

Ticket Operations
Vice President of Ticket Sales . . . . Scott Wampold
Director of Season Ticket Sales . . . . Nat Harden
Director of Suite and Group Sales . . . . Chris Junghans
Senior Account Executive of Group Sales . . . . Tim Wilson
Account Executives . . . . Chris Burton, Michael Ceccarelli, Brad Gillispie, Todd McNamara, Jenny Moss, Jason Mott, Thomas Tilney, Tiffany Vanek
Ticket Operations/Fan Relations Manager . . . . Brad MacLachlan
Ticket Operations Coordinators . . . . Sara Enwright, Mary Jane Rogers
Fan Relations Coordinators . . . . Paige Belew, Courtney Gray, Chris Harrington, Shannon Lake, Mac Maddox

Miscellaneous
Radio Flagship . . . . WGFX 104.5-FM, WNSR 560-AM
TV Flagship . . . . FSN South

New Jersey Devils

2005-06 Results: 46w-27L-5OTL-4SOL 101PTS.
First, Atlantic Division

2006-07 Schedule

Oct.	Fri.	6	at Carolina	Sun.	7	at Montreal*
	Sat.	7	at Dallas	Wed.	10	St. Louis
	Thu.	12	Toronto	Fri.	12	Atlanta
	Sat.	14	Philadelphia	Sat.	13	at NY Islanders
	Mon.	16	at NY Rangers	Tue.	16	NY Rangers
	Wed.	18	at Pittsburgh	Thu.	18	Tampa Bay
	Thu.	19	Nashville	Sat.	20	Philadelphia*
	Sat.	21	at Ottawa	Fri.	26	at Tampa Bay
	Tue.	24	at Pittsburgh	Sat.	27	at Florida
	Thu.	26	Florida	Tue.	30	at Atlanta
	Sat.	28	Columbus	**Feb.** Thu.	1	at Philadelphia
Nov.	Thu.	2	NY Islanders	Sat.	3	Buffalo
	Sat.	4	at Montreal	Tue.	6	NY Rangers
	Tue.	7	Carolina	Thu.	8	NY Islanders
	Thu.	9	Chicago	Sun.	11	Tampa Bay*
	Sat.	11	Florida	Wed.	14	Montreal
	Tue.	14	at NY Rangers	Fri.	16	Pittsburgh
	Fri.	17	Ottawa	Sat.	17	at NY Islanders
	Sat.	18	at Toronto	Tue.	20	NY Rangers
	Wed.	22	at Phoenix	Thu.	22	at NY Rangers
	Fri.	24	at Anaheim*	Sat.	24	Washington*
	Sat.	25	at San Jose	Sun.	25	at Washington*
	Mon.	27	at Los Angeles	Tue.	27	at Pittsburgh
Dec.	Fri.	1	Pittsburgh	**Mar.** Fri.	2	Toronto
	Sat.	2	at Philadelphia	Sun.	4	Boston
	Wed.	6	Montreal	Tue.	6	at Philadelphia
	Fri.	8	Philadelphia	Thu.	8	at Pittsburgh
	Sat.	9	at Boston	Sat.	10	at Buffalo
	Tue.	12	Buffalo	Wed.	14	Pittsburgh
	Thu.	14	at Boston*	Thu.	15	at Carolina
	Sat.	16	Detroit*	Sat.	17	at Carolina*
	Sun.	17	at NY Rangers	Tue.	20	at Toronto
	Tue.	19	Atlanta	Thu.	22	at Tampa Bay
	Fri.	22	at Washington	Sat.	24	at Florida
	Sat.	23	at Atlanta	Tue.	27	at NY Islanders
	Tue.	26	Pittsburgh	Wed.	28	at Buffalo
	Fri.	29	Washington	Fri.	30	Philadelphia
	Sat.	30	at NY Islanders	**Apr.** Sun.	1	Boston*
Jan.	Tue.	2	NY Rangers	Tue.	3	Ottawa
	Thu.	4	NY Islanders	Thu.	5	at Philadelphia
	Sat.	6	at Ottawa*	Sun.	8	NY Islanders*

Denotes afternoon game.

Franchise date: June 11, 1974

Transferred from Denver to New Jersey, June 30, 1982.
Previously transferred from Kansas City to Denver.

ATLANTIC DIVISION

33rd NHL Season

Brian Gionta took great advantage of NHL rule changes to increase skating room, collecting 48 goals and 41 assists in 2005-06. His 89 points represented a 60-point improvement over the 2003-04 season. Only Eric Staal's 69-point increase was greater.

Year-by-Year Record

Season	GP	Home W	L	T	OL	Road W	L	T	OL	Overall W	L	T	OL	GF	GA	Pts.	Finished	Playoff Result
2005-06	82	27	11	....	3	19	16	....	6	46	27	....	9	242	229	101	1st, Atlantic Div.	Lost Conf. Semi-Final
2004-05	....	....	....	....	....	....	....	....	....	....	....	....	....	....	....	....		
2003-04	82	22	13	5	1	21	12	7	1	43	25	12	2	213	164	100	2nd, Atlantic Div.	Lost Conf. Quarter-Final
2002-03	82	25	11	3	2	21	9	7	4	46	20	10	6	216	166	108	1st, Atlantic Div.	Won Stanley Cup
2001-02	82	22	13	4	2	19	15	5	2	41	28	9	4	205	187	95	3rd, Atlantic Div.	Lost Conf. Quarter-Final
2000-01	82	24	11	6	0	24	8	6	3	48	19	12	3	295	195	111	1st, Atlantic Div.	Lost Final
1999-2000	82	28	9	3	1	17	15	5	4	45	24	8	5	251	203	103	2nd, Atlantic Div.	Won Stanley Cup
1998-99	82	19	14	8	....	28	10	3	....	47	24	11	....	248	196	105	1st, Atlantic Div.	Lost Conf. Quarter-Final
1997-98	82	29	10	2	....	19	13	9	....	48	23	11	....	225	166	107	2nd, Atlantic Div.	Lost Conf. Quarter-Final
1996-97	82	23	9	9	....	22	14	5	....	45	23	14	....	231	182	104	1st, Atlantic Div.	Lost Conf. Semi-Final
1995-96	82	22	17	2	....	15	16	10	....	37	33	12	....	215	202	86	6th, Atlantic Div.	Out of Playoffs
1994-95	48	14	4	6	....	8	14	2	....	22	18	8	....	136	121	52	2nd, Atlantic Div.	Won Stanley Cup
1993-94	84	29	11	2	....	18	14	10	....	47	25	12	....	306	220	106	2nd, Atlantic Div.	Lost Conf. Championship
1992-93	84	24	14	4	....	16	23	3	....	40	37	7	....	308	299	87	4th, Patrick Div.	Lost Div. Semi-Final
1991-92	80	24	12	4	....	14	19	7	....	38	31	11	....	289	259	87	4th, Patrick Div.	Lost Div. Semi-Final
1990-91	80	23	10	7	....	9	23	8	....	32	33	15	....	272	264	79	4th, Patrick Div.	Lost Div. Semi-Final
1989-90	80	22	15	3	....	15	19	6	....	37	34	9	....	295	288	83	2nd, Patrick Div.	Lost Div. Semi-Final
1988-89	80	17	18	5	....	10	23	7	....	27	41	12	....	281	325	66	5th, Patrick Div.	Out of Playoffs
1987-88	80	23	16	1	....	15	20	5	....	38	36	6	....	295	296	82	4th, Patrick Div.	Lost Conf. Championship
1986-87	80	20	17	3	....	9	28	3	....	29	45	6	....	293	368	64	6th, Patrick Div.	Out of Playoffs
1985-86	80	17	21	2	....	11	28	1	....	28	49	3	....	300	374	59	6th, Patrick Div.	Out of Playoffs
1984-85	80	13	21	6	....	9	27	4	....	22	48	10	....	264	346	54	5th, Patrick Div.	Out of Playoffs
1983-84	80	10	28	2	....	7	28	5	....	17	56	7	....	231	350	41	5th, Patrick Div.	Out of Playoffs
1982-83	80	11	20	9	....	6	29	5	....	17	49	14	....	230	338	48	5th, Patrick Div.	Out of Playoffs
1981-82**	80	14	21	5	....	4	28	8	....	18	49	13	....	241	362	49	5th, Smythe Div.	Out of Playoffs
1980-81**	80	15	16	9	....	7	29	4	....	22	45	13	....	258	344	57	5th, Smythe Div.	Out of Playoffs
1979-80**	80	12	20	8	....	7	28	5	....	19	48	13	....	234	308	51	6th, Smythe Div.	Out of Playoffs
1978-79**	80	8	24	8	....	7	29	4	....	15	53	12	....	210	331	42	4th, Smythe Div.	Out of Playoffs
1977-78**	80	17	14	9	....	2	26	12	....	19	40	21	....	257	305	59	2nd, Smythe Div.	Lost Prelim. Round
1976-77**	80	12	20	8	....	8	26	6	....	20	46	14	....	226	307	54	5th, Smythe Div.	Out of Playoffs
1975-76*	80	8	24	8	....	4	32	4	....	12	56	12	....	190	351	36	5th, Smythe Div.	Out of Playoffs
1974-75*	80	12	20	8	....	3	34	3	....	15	54	11	....	184	328	41	5th, Smythe Div.	Out of Playoffs

* Kansas City Scouts. ** Colorado Rockies.

2006-07 Player Personnel

FORWARDS	HT	WT	S	Place of Birth	Date	2005-06 Club
BERGFORS, Nicklas	5-11	190	R	Sodertalje, Sweden	3/7/87	Albany
BRYLIN, Sergei	5-10	190	L	Moscow, USSR	1/13/74	New Jersey
CLARKSON, David	6-1	205	R	Toronto, Ont.	3/31/84	Albany
DAVIS, Patrick	6-2	205	R	Sterling, MI	12/28/86	Kitchener-Windsor-Albany
ELIAS, Patrik	6-1	195	L	Trebic, Czech.	4/13/76	New Jersey
FOSTER, Adrian	6-0	200	L	Lethbridge, Alta.	1/15/82	Albany
GIONTA, Brian	5-7	175	R	Rochester, NY	1/18/79	New Jersey
GIONTA, Stephen	5-7	180	R	Rochester, NY	10/9/83	Boston College-Albany
GOMEZ, Scott	5-11	200	L	Anchorage, AK	12/23/79	New Jersey
JANSSEN, Cam	6-0	205	R	St. Louis, MO	4/15/84	New Jersey-Albany
KHOMUTOV, Ivan	6-3	210	L	Saratov, USSR	3/11/85	Albany
LaCOUTURE, Dan	6-3	215	L	Hyannis, MA	4/18/77	Davos-Boston
LANGENBRUNNER, Jamie	6-1	200	R	Cloquet, MN	7/24/75	New Jersey
LETOURNEAU-LEBLOND, P-L	6-2	210	L	Levis, Que.	6/4/85	Albany-Adirondack
MADDEN, John	5-11	190	L	Barrie, Ont.	5/4/73	New Jersey
MARSHALL, Grant	6-1	200	R	Mississauga, Ont.	6/9/73	New Jersey
MINARD, Chris	6-1	200	L	Thompson, Man.	11/18/81	Albany-Alaska
MOGILNY, Alexander	6-0	210	L	Khabarovsk, USSR	2/18/69	New Jersey-Albany
MONDOU, Benoit	5-9	175	R	Sorel, Que.	5/3/85	Shawinigan
MURPHY, Ryan	6-1	205	L	Van Nuys, CA	3/21/79	Albany
PANDOLFO, Jay	6-1	190	L	Winchester, MA	12/27/74	New Jersey
PAPINEAU, Justin	5-11	205	L	Ottawa, Ont.	1/15/80	Bridgeport
PARISE, Zach	5-11	185	L	Minneapolis, MN	7/28/84	New Jersey
PELLEY, Rod	6-0	200	L	Kitimat, B.C.	9/1/84	Ohio State
PIHLMAN, Tuomas	6-2	210	L	Espoo, Finland	11/13/82	New Jersey-Albany
RASMUSSEN, Erik	6-1	215	L	Minneapolis, MN	3/28/77	New Jersey
RUPP, Mike	6-5	230	L	Cleveland, OH	1/13/80	Phx-CBJ-Syr
RYZNAR, Jason	6-3	200	L	Anchorage, AK	2/19/83	New Jersey-Albany
TALLACKSON, Barry	6-4	210	R	Grafton, ND	4/14/83	New Jersey-Albany
VOROS, Aaron	6-4	200	L	Vancouver, B.C.	7/2/81	Albany
VRANA, Petr	5-10	185	L	Sternberk, Czech.	3/29/85	Albany
WIEMER, Jason	6-1	225	L	Kimberley, B.C.	4/14/76	Calgary-New Jersey
ZAJAC, Travis	6-2	205	R	Winnipeg, Man.	5/13/85	North Dakota-Albany
DEFENSEMEN						
BROOKS, Alex	6-1	195	R	Madison, WI	8/21/76	Albany
CORRENTE, Matthew	6-0	190	R	Mississauga, Ont.	3/17/88	Saginaw
FRASER, Mark	6-3	200	L	Ottawa, Ont.	9/29/86	Kitchener-Albany
GREENE, Andy	5-11	180	L	Trenton, MI	10/30/82	Miami U.
HALE, David	6-2	215	L	Colorado Springs, CO	6/18/81	New Jersey-Albany
HARANT, Tomas	6-3	200	L	Zilina, Czech.	4/28/80	C. Budejovice
HENEGAN, Kyell	6-4	205	L	Montreal, Que.	10/27/87	Shawinigan
LUKOWICH, Brad	6-1	205	L	Cranbrook, B.C.	8/12/76	NY Islanders-New Jersey
MAGNAN, Olivier	6-2	200	L	Sherbrooke, Que.	5/1/86	Rouyn-Noranda
MALAKHOV, Vladimir	6-4	230	L	Sverdlovsk, USSR	8/30/68	New Jersey
MALMIVAARA, Olli	6-7	220	L	Kajaani, Finland	3/13/82	SaiPa
MARTIN, Paul	6-1	190	L	Minneapolis, MN	3/5/81	New Jersey
MATVICHUK, Richard	6-3	215	L	Edmonton, Alta.	2/5/73	New Jersey
McGILLIS, Dan	6-3	220	L	Hawkesbury, Ont.	7/1/72	New Jersey-Albany
MILLER, Bryan	5-10	190	R	Wayne, NJ	2/17/83	Albany
MOTTAU, Mike	6-0	195	L	Quincy, MA	3/19/78	Peoria
ODUYA, Johnny	5-11	200	L	Stockholm, Sweden	10/1/81	Frolunda
RAFALSKI, Brian	5-10	190	R	Dearborn, MI	9/28/73	New Jersey
TULUPOV, Kirill	6-3	220	R	Moscow, USSR	4/23/88	Toronto Rattlers-Leninogorsk
WHITE, Colin	6-4	215	L	New Glasgow, N.S.	12/12/77	New Jersey
ZIMMERMAN, Sean	6-2	200	R	Denver, CO	5/24/87	Spokane-Albany

GOALTENDERS	HT	WT	C	Place of Birth	Date	2005-06 Club
BRODEUR, Martin	6-2	210	L	Montreal, Que.	5/6/72	New Jersey
CLEMMENSEN, Scott	6-3	205	L	Des Moines, IA	7/23/77	New Jersey-Albany
DOYLE, Frank	6-1	185	L	Guelph, Ont.	9/8/80	Albany
PARISE, Jordan	5-11	190	L	Faribault, MN	9/19/82	North Dakota

President and General Manager

LAMORIELLO, LOU
CEO/President/General Manager, New Jersey Devils.
Born in Providence, RI, October 21, 1942.

Lou Lamoriello's life-long dedication to the game of hockey was rewarded in 1992 when he was named a recipient of the Lester Patrick Trophy for outstanding service to hockey in the United States. Lamoriello has been president and general manager of the Devils since 1987-88 following more than 20 years with Providence College as a player, coach and administrator. His trades, signings and draft choices helped lead the Devils to their first Stanley Cup championship in 1995 and were followed by victories again in 2000 and 2003. During the 2005-06 season Lamoriello took over behind the bench and coached the Devils to first place in the Atlantic Division.

A member of the varsity hockey Friars during his undergraduate days, Lamoriello became an assistant coach with the college club after graduating in 1963. He was later named head coach and in the ensuing 15 years, led his teams to a 248-179-13 record and appearances in 10 post-season tournaments, including the 1983 NCAA Final Four. He was hired as president of the Devils on April 30, 1987. He assumed the responsibility of general manager on September 10, 1987. He was G.M. of Team USA for the first World Cup of Hockey in 1996 as the U.S. captured the championship. He was also the G.M. for the 1998 U.S. Olympic team.

NHL Coaching Record

		Regular Season				Playoffs		
Season	Team	Games	W	L	O/T	Games	W	L
2005-06	New Jersey (NHL)	50	32	14	4	9	5	4
	NHL Totals	**50**	**32**	**14**	**4**	**9**	**5**	**4**

Posted an 0-1 playoff record as replacement coach when Jim Schoenfeld was suspended, May 10, 1988. Loss is credited to Schoenfeld's coaching record.

2005-06 Scoring

* – rookie

Regular Season

Pos	#	Player	Team	GP	G	A	Pts	+/–	PIM	PP	SH	GW	S	%
R	14	Brian Gionta	N.J.	82	48	41	89	18	46	24	1	10	291	16.5
C	23	Scott Gomez	N.J.	82	33	51	84	8	42	9	0	5	244	13.5
R	15	Jamie Langenbrunner	N.J.	80	19	34	53	–1	74	8	1	1	243	7.8
D	28	Brian Rafalski	N.J.	82	6	43	49	0	36	3	0	2	126	4.8
C	26	Patrik Elias	N.J.	38	16	29	45	11	20	6	0	3	142	11.3
L	18	Sergei Brylin	N.J.	82	15	22	37	–4	46	4	0	3	126	11.9
D	7	Paul Martin	N.J.	80	5	32	37	1	32	3	0	0	97	5.2
C	11	John Madden	N.J.	82	16	20	36	–7	36	0	1	0	194	8.2
C	9 *	Zach Parise	N.J.	81	14	18	32	–1	28	2	0	5	133	10.5
R	89	Alexander Mogilny	N.J.	34	12	13	25	–7	6	7	0	3	93	12.9
R	22	Viktor Kozlov	N.J.	69	12	13	25	0	16	2	0	1	122	9.8
R	29	Grant Marshall	N.J.	76	8	17	25	–18	70	4	0	3	89	9.0
D	21	Brad Lukowich	NYI	57	1	12	13	–3	32	0	0	1	36	2.8
			N.J.	18	1	7	8	3	8	0	0	0	13	7.7
			TOTAL	75	2	19	21	0	40	0	0	1	49	4.1
L	20	Jay Pandolfo	N.J.	82	10	10	20	2	16	0	0	0	116	8.6
D	5	Colin White	N.J.	73	3	14	17	–2	91	1	0	1	60	5.0
D	8	Ken Klee	TOR	56	3	12	15	–1	66	1	0	1	65	4.6
			N.J.	18	0	0	0	–3	14	0	0	0	5	0.0
			TOTAL	74	3	12	15	–4	80	1	0	1	70	4.3
D	24	Richard Matvichuk	N.J.	62	1	10	11	2	40	0	0	0	43	2.3
C	10	Erik Rasmussen	N.J.	67	5	5	10	–4	32	1	0	0	45	11.1
D	2	Vladimir Malakhov	N.J.	29	4	5	9	–9	26	3	0	0	43	9.3
D	2	Dan McGillis	N.J.	27	0	6	6	–5	36	0	0	0	32	0.0
D	6	Tommy Albelin	N.J.	36	0	6	6	4	2	0	0	0	15	0.0
C	16	Jason Wiemer	CGY	33	1	2	3	–3	65	0	0	0	24	4.2
			N.J.	16	1	0	1	–1	38	0	0	0	13	7.7
			TOTAL	49	2	2	4	–4	103	0	0	0	37	5.4
D	2	David Hale	N.J.	38	0	4	4	5	21	0	0	0	19	0.0
R	27 *	Barry Tallackson	N.J.	10	1	1	2	–2	2	0	0	0	11	9.1
L	19 *	Thomas Pihlman	N.J.	11	1	1	2	–1	10	0	0	0	14	7.1
L	17	Darren Langdon	N.J.	14	0	1	1	–3	22	0	0	0	2	0.0
L	19	Krzysztof Oliwa	N.J.	3	0	0	0	–2	0	0	0	0	1	0.0
L	19 *	Jason Ryznar	N.J.	8	0	0	0	–1	2	0	0	0	1	0.0
R	25 *	Cam Janssen	N.J.	47	0	0	0	–3	91	0	0	0	10	0.0

Goaltending

No.	Goaltender	GPI	Mins	Avg	W	L	OT	EN	SO	GA	SA	S%	G	A	PIM
30	Martin Brodeur	73	4365	2.57	43	23	7	2	5	187	2105	.911	0	3	4
40	Scott Clemmensen	13	627	3.35	3	4	2	1	0	35	295	.881	0	0	0
	Totals	**82**	**5007**	**2.70**	**46**	**27**	**9**	**3**	**5**	**225**	**2403**	**.906**			

Playoffs

Pos	#	Player	Team	GP	G	A	Pts	+/–	PIM	PP	SH	GW	OT	S	%
C	26	Patrik Elias	N.J.	9	6	10	16	5	4	4	0	0	0	32	18.8
R	15	Jamie Langenbrunner	N.J.	9	3	10	13	5	16	1	0	1	0	17	17.6
C	23	Scott Gomez	N.J.	9	5	4	9	–1	6	4	0	1	0	39	12.8
D	28	Brian Rafalski	N.J.	9	1	8	9	3	2	1	0	0	0	9	11.1
R	14	Brian Gionta	N.J.	9	3	4	7	–1	2	1	1	2	0	29	10.3
C	11	John Madden	N.J.	9	4	1	5	2	8	0	2	0	0	27	14.8
L	20	Jay Pandolfo	N.J.	9	1	4	5	1	0	0	1	1	0	4	25.0
C	9 *	Zach Parise	N.J.	9	1	2	3	0	2	0	0	0	0	21	4.8
D	7	Paul Martin	N.J.	9	0	3	3	6	4	0	0	0	0	6	0.0
L	18	Sergei Brylin	N.J.	9	2	0	2	5	2	0	0	0	0	14	14.3
D	2	David Hale	N.J.	8	0	2	2	–1	12	0	0	0	0	3	0.0
D	8	Ken Klee	N.J.	6	1	0	1	–1	6	0	0	0	0	2	50.0
R	29	Grant Marshall	N.J.	7	0	1	1	0	8	0	0	0	0	4	0.0
D	6	Tommy Albelin	N.J.	2	0	0	0	0	2	0	0	0	0	0	0.0
R	22	Viktor Kozlov	N.J.	3	0	0	0	–1	0	0	0	0	0	4	0.0
D	5	Colin White	N.J.	4	0	0	0	0	4	0	0	0	0	1	0.0
D	24	Richard Matvichuk	N.J.	7	0	0	0	5	4	0	0	0	0	1	0.0
C	16	Jason Wiemer	N.J.	8	0	0	0	0	16	0	0	0	0	2	0.0
D	21	Brad Lukowich	N.J.	9	0	0	0	0	4	0	0	0	0	6	0.0
C	10	Erik Rasmussen	N.J.	9	0	0	0	–1	8	0	0	0	0	4	0.0
R	25 *	Cam Janssen	N.J.	9	0	0	0	0	26	0	0	0	0	3	0.0

Goaltending

No.	Goaltender	GPI	Mins	Avg	W	L	EN	SO	GA	SA	S%	G	A	PIM
40	Scott Clemmensen	1	7	.00	0	0	0	0	0	3	1.000	0	0	0
30	Martin Brodeur	9	533	2.25	5	4	1	1	20	261	.923	0	0	2
	Totals	**9**	**543**	**2.32**	**5**	**4**	**1**	**1**	**21**	**265**	**.921**			

Captains' History

Simon Nolet, 1974-75 to 1976-77; Wilf Paiement, 1977-78; Gary Croteau, 1978-79; Mike Christie, Rene Robert and Lanny McDonald, 1979-80; Lanny McDonald, 1980-81; Lanny McDonald and Rob Ramage, 1981-82; Don Lever, 1982-83; Don Lever and Mel Bridgman, 1983-84; Mel Bridgman, 1984-85 to 1986-87; Kirk Muller, 1987-88 to 1990-91; Bruce Driver, 1991-92; Scott Stevens, 1992-93 to 2002-03; Scott Stevens and Scott Neidermayer, 2003-04; no captain, 2005-06.

Coaching History

Bep Guidolin, 1974-75; Bep Guidolin, Sid Abel and Eddie Bush, 1975-76; Johnny Wilson, 1976-77; Pat Kelly, 1977-78; Pat Kelly and Aldo Guidolin, 1978-79; Don Cherry, 1979-80; Bill MacMillan, 1980-81; Bert Marshall and Marshall Johnston, 1981-82; Bill MacMillan, 1982-83; Bill MacMillan and Tom McVie, 1983-84; Doug Carpenter, 1984-85 to 1986-87; Doug Carpenter and Jim Schoenfeld, 1987-88; Jim Schoenfeld, 1988-89; Jim Schoenfeld and John Cunniff, 1989-90; John Cunniff and Tom McVie, 1990-91; Tom McVie, 1991-92; Herb Brooks, 1992-93; Jacques Lemaire, 1993-94 to 1997-98; Robbie Ftorek, 1998-99; Robbie Ftorek and Larry Robinson, 1999-2000; Larry Robinson, 2000-01; Larry Robinson and Kevin Constantine, 2001-02; Pat Burns, 2002-03 to 2004-05; Larry Robinson and Lou Lamoriello, 2005-06; Claude Julien, 2006-07.

Club Records

Team

(Figures in brackets for season records are games played; records for fewest points, wins, ties, losses, goals, goals against are for 70 or more games)

Most Points .... 111 — 2000-01 (82)
Most Wins .... 48 — 1997-98 (82), 2000-01 (82)
Most Ties .... 21 — 1977-78 (80)
Most Losses .... 56 — 1975-76 (80), 1983-84 (80)
Most Goals .... 308 — 1992-93 (84)
Most Goals Against .... 374 — 1985-86 (80)
Fewest Points .... *36 — 1975-76 (80)
41 — 1983-84 (80)
Fewest Wins .... *12 — 1975-76 (80)
17 — 1982-83 (80), 1983-84 (80)
Fewest Ties .... 3 — 1985-86 (80)
Fewest Losses .... 19 — 2000-01 (82)
Fewest Goals .... *184 — 1974-75 (80)
205 — 2001-02 (82)
Fewest Goals Against .... 164 — 2003-04 (82)

Longest Winning Streak
Overall .... 13 — Feb. 26-Mar. 23/01
Home .... 8 — Oct. 9-Nov. 7/87, Jan. 3-Feb. 4/03, Jan. 3-Feb. 7/06
Away .... **10 — Feb. 27-Apr. 7/01

Longest Undefeated Streak
Overall .... 13 — Four times
Home .... 15 — Jan. 8-Mar. 15/97 (9 wins, 6 ties)
Away .... 10 — Feb. 27-Apr. 7/01 (10 wins)

Longest Losing Streak
Overall .... *14 — Dec. 30/75-Jan. 29/76
10 — Oct. 14-Nov. 4/83
Home .... 9 — Dec. 22/85-Feb. 6/86
Away .... 12 — Oct. 19-Dec. 1/83

Longest Winless Streak
Overall .... *27 — Feb. 12-Apr. 4/76 (21 losses, 6 ties)
18 — Oct. 20-Nov. 26/82 (14 losses 4 ties)
Home .... *14 — Feb. 12-Mar. 30/76 (10 losses, 4 ties), Feb. 4-Mar. 31/79 (12 losses, 2 ties)
9 — Dec. 22/85-Feb. 6/86 (9 losses)
Away .... *32 — Nov. 12/77-Mar. 15/78 (22 losses, 10 ties)
14 — Dec. 26/82-Mar. 5/83 (13 losses, 1 tie)

Most Shutouts, Season .... 14 — 2003-04 (82)
Most PIM, Season .... 2,494 — 1988-89 (80)
Most Goals, Game .... 9 — Nine times

Individual

Most Seasons .... 20 — Ken Daneyko
Most Games .... 1,283 — Ken Daneyko
Most Goals, Career .... 347 — John MacLean
Most Assists, Career .... 364 — Scott Niedermayer
Most Points, Career .... 701 — John MacLean (347G, 354A)
Most PIM, Career .... 2,519 — Ken Daneyko
Most Shutouts, Career .... 80 — Martin Brodeur
Longest Consecutive Games Streak ... 388 — Ken Daneyko (Nov. 4/89-Mar. 29/94)
Most Goals, Season .... 48 — Brian Gionta (2005-06)
Most Assists, Season .... 60 — Scott Stevens (1993-94)
Most Points, Season .... 96 — Patrik Elias (2000-01; 40G, 56A)
Most PIM, Season .... 295 — Krzysztof Oliwa (1997-98)
Most Points, Defenseman, Season ... 78 — Scott Stevens (1993-94; 18G, 60A)
Most Points, Center, Season ... 94 — Kirk Muller (1987-88; 37G, 57A)
Most Points, Right Wing, Season ... 89 — Brian Gionta (2005-06; 48G, 41A)
Most Points, Left Wing, Season ... 96 — Patrik Elias (2000-01; 40G, 56A)
Most Points, Rookie, Season ... 70 — Scott Gomez (1999-2000; 19G, 51A)
Most Shutouts, Season .... 11 — Martin Brodeur (2003-04)
Most Goals, Game .... 4 — Five times
Most Assists, Game .... 5 — Greg Adams (Oct. 10/85), Kirk Muller (Mar. 25/87), Tom Kurvers (Feb. 13/89), Scott Gomez (Mar. 30/03)
Most Points, Game .... 6 — Kirk Muller (Nov. 29/86; 3G, 3A)

* Records include Kansas City Scouts and Colorado Rockies, 1974-75 through 1981-82.
** NHL Record.

General Managers' History

Sid Abel, 1974-75, 1975-76; Ray Miron, 1976-77 to 1980-81; Bill MacMillan, 1981-82, 1982-83; Bill MacMillan and Max McNab, 1983-84; Max McNab 1984-85 to 1986-87; Lou Lamoriello, 1987-88 to date.

Retired Numbers

3	Ken Daneyko	1982-2003
4	Scott Stevens	1991-2005

All-time Record vs. Other Clubs

Regular Season

	At Home								On Road								Total							
	GP	W	L	T	OL	GF	GA	PTS	GP	W	L	T	OL	GF	GA	PTS	GP	W	L	T	OL	GF	GA	PTS
Anaheim	8	7	1	0	0	31	14	14	10	5	4	1	0	26	26	11	18	12	5	1	0	57	40	25
Atlanta	12	6	4	1	1	35	24	14	12	7	2	2	1	44	23	17	24	13	6	3	2	79	47	31
Boston	55	17	27	11	0	146	176	45	58	19	29	8	2	179	224	48	113	36	56	19	2	325	400	93
Buffalo	56	21	26	9	0	168	180	51	56	16	32	8	0	169	219	40	112	37	58	17	0	337	399	91
Calgary	46	15	28	3	0	129	166	33	42	6	27	8	1	111	184	21	88	21	55	11	1	240	350	54
Carolina	47	26	17	4	0	162	146	56	46	19	18	8	1	137	144	47	93	45	35	12	1	299	290	103
Chicago	47	20	16	11	0	147	142	51	47	13	24	10	0	130	178	36	94	33	40	21	0	277	320	87
Colorado	37	19	13	4	1	150	125	43	35	13	18	4	0	98	124	30	72	32	31	8	1	248	249	73
Columbus	2	1	0	1	0	5	4	3	5	2	2	0	1	15	16	5	7	3	2	1	1	20	20	8
Dallas	43	21	19	3	0	146	132	45	45	13	25	6	1	117	164	33	88	34	44	9	1	263	296	78
Detroit	40	21	10	9	0	138	103	51	41	13	25	2	1	131	169	29	81	34	35	11	1	269	272	80
Edmonton	34	15	16	3	0	113	113	33	31	11	14	6	0	114	136	28	65	26	30	9	0	227	249	61
Florida	26	16	7	3	0	79	52	35	27	15	8	4	0	71	58	34	53	31	15	7	0	150	110	69
Los Angeles	43	19	19	5	0	142	148	43	42	8	27	6	1	130	201	23	85	27	46	11	1	272	349	66
Minnesota	4	3	0	1	0	16	10	7	3	1	1	1	0	8	7	3	7	4	1	2	0	24	17	10
Montreal	56	27	25	4	0	170	197	58	56	17	32	6	1	141	187	41	112	44	57	10	1	311	384	99
Nashville	5	2	3	0	0	15	14	4	6	5	1	0	0	18	12	10	11	7	4	0	0	33	26	14
NY Islanders	88	37	39	11	1	287	303	86	89	20	56	11	2	256	364	53	177	57	95	22	3	543	667	139
NY Rangers	90	48	35	7	0	311	289	103	88	25	41	20	2	262	334	72	178	73	76	27	2	573	623	175
Ottawa	25	14	9	2	0	71	61	30	26	16	6	3	1	67	54	36	51	30	15	5	1	138	115	66
Philadelphia	87	46	33	8	0	297	288	100	89	25	54	10	0	222	332	60	176	71	87	18	0	519	620	160
Phoenix	29	12	11	6	0	95	87	30	31	7	21	3	0	81	114	17	60	19	32	9	0	176	201	47
Pittsburgh	85	42	29	13	1	311	279	98	83	37	41	4	1	283	306	79	168	79	70	17	2	594	585	177
St. Louis	46	22	17	7	0	146	128	51	47	13	26	7	1	148	195	34	93	35	43	14	1	294	323	85
San Jose	12	7	4	1	0	44	24	15	10	6	2	1	1	32	24	14	22	13	6	2	1	76	48	29
Tampa Bay	28	19	6	2	1	103	54	41	27	13	7	5	2	83	62	33	55	32	13	7	3	186	116	74
Toronto	48	17	15	15	1	161	146	50	50	12	33	5	0	141	188	29	98	29	48	20	1	302	334	79
Vancouver	50	21	21	6	2	154	159	50	47	9	27	11	0	130	175	29	97	30	48	17	2	284	334	79
Washington	81	41	32	7	1	250	230	90	81	26	49	6	0	231	314	58	162	67	81	13	1	481	544	148
Defunct Clubs	8	4	2	2	0	25	19	10	8	2	3	3	0	19	27	7	16	6	5	5	0	44	46	17
Totals	**1238**	**586**	**484**	**159**	**9**	**4047**	**3813**	**1340**	**1238**	**394**	**655**	**169**	**20**	**3594**	**4561**	**977**	**2476**	**980**	**1139**	**328**	**29**	**7641**	**8374**	**2317**

Playoffs

	Series	W	L	GP	W	L	T	GF	GA	Last Mtg.	Rnd.	Result
Anaheim	1	1	0	7	4	3	0	19	12	2003	F	W 4-3
Boston	4	3	1	23	15	8	0	68	60	2003	CQF	W 4-1
Buffalo	1	1	0	7	4	3	0	14	14	1994	CQF	W 4-3
Carolina	3	1	2	17	7	10	0	41	34	2006	CSF	L 1-4
Colorado	1	0	1	7	3	4	0	11	19	2001	F	L 3-4
Dallas	1	1	0	6	4	2	0	15	9	2000	F	W 4-2
Detroit	1	1	0	4	4	0	0	16	7	1995	F	W 4-0
Florida	1	1	0	4	4	0	0	12	6	2000	CQF	W 4-0
Montreal	1	1	0	5	4	1	0	22	11	1997	CQF	W 4-1
NY Islanders	1	1	0	6	4	2	0	23	18	1988	DSF	W 4-2
NY Rangers	4	1	3	23	11	12	0	63	60	2006	CQF	W 4-0
Ottawa	2	1	1	13	6	7	0	29	26	2003	CF	W 4-3
Philadelphia	4	2	2	20	9	11	0	50	49	2004	CQF	L 1-4
Pittsburgh	5	2	3	29	15	14	0	86	80	2001	CF	W 4-1
Tampa Bay	1	1	0	5	4	1	0	14	8	2003	CSF	W 4-1
Toronto	2	2	0	13	8	5	0	37	27	2001	CSF	W 4-3
Washington	2	1	1	13	6	7	0	43	44	1990	DSF	L 2-4
Totals	**35**	**21**	**14**	**202**	**112**	**90**	**0**	**563**	**484**			

Calgary totals include Atlanta Flames, 1974-75 to 1979-80.
Colorado totals include Quebec, 1979-80 to 1994-95.
Phoenix totals include Winnipeg, 1979-80 to 1995-96.
Carolina totals include Hartford, 1979-80 to 1996-97.
Dallas totals include Minnesota North Stars, 1974-75 to 1992-93.

Playoff Results 2006-2001

Year	Round	Opponent	Result	GF	GA
2006	CSF	Carolina	L 1-4	10	17
	CQF	NY Rangers	W 4-0	17	4
2004	CQF	Philadelphia	L 1-4	9	14
2003	**F**	**Anaheim**	**W 4-3**	**19**	**12**
	CF	Ottawa	W 4-3	17	13
	CSF	Tampa Bay	W 4-1	14	8
	CQF	Boston	W 4-1	13	8
2002	CQF	Carolina	L 2-4	11	9
2001	F	Colorado	L 3-4	11	19
	CF	Pittsburgh	W 4-1	17	7
	CSF	Toronto	W 4-3	21	18
	CQF	Carolina	W 4-2	20	8

Abbreviations: Round: F – Final; **CF** – conference final; **CSF** – conference semi-final; **CQF** – conference quarter-final; **DSF** – division semi-final.

2005-06 Results

Month	Day	Opponent	Score	Month	Day	Opponent	Score
Oct.	5	Pittsburgh	5-1		7	at Buffalo	3-2
	7	at Philadelphia	2-5		9	Philadelphia	3-0
	8	NY Rangers	3-2*		13	Vancouver	3-0
	13	at NY Rangers	1-4		15	at Chicago	3-2†
	15	Carolina	1-6		17	at St. Louis	5-3
	18	Florida	4-3		19	at Nashville	4-3†
	20	at Pittsburgh	6-3		21	NY Islanders	3-2†
	22	at Atlanta	3-4		22	at NY Rangers	1-3
	26	Tampa Bay	3-6		24	at NY Islanders	4-0
	28	Buffalo	3-2		26	at Tampa Bay	0-1*
	29	at Boston	5-4†		27	at Florida	0-4
Nov.	1	Pittsburgh	3-4*	**Feb.**	1	Ottawa	5-3
	3	NY Rangers	2-4		3	Carolina	3-0
	5	at NY Rangers	2-3†		4	at Toronto	2-4
	8	NY Islanders	1-4		7	Tampa Bay	7-4
	11	at Washington	4-3		9	at Boston	3-2*
	12	Washington	3-2		11	NY Islanders	1-2
	15	at Buffalo	1-4	**Mar.**	1	Philadelphia	2-1†
	18	Montreal	5-3		2	at NY Islanders	2-3†
	19	at Ottawa	4-5		4	NY Rangers	2-1
	23	at Florida	5-1		7	at NY Islanders	1-2†
	25	at Tampa Bay	8-2		10	at Washington	4-3†
	29	Boston	3-2		11	at Pittsburgh	3-6
	30	at Philadelphia	1-2		14	NY Islanders	1-6
Dec.	3	Minnesota	3-2†		16	Pittsburgh	2-1
	6	at Detroit	2-5		19	Ottawa	0-4
	7	Calgary	1-4		21	at Philadelphia	1-2
	9	Colorado	3-4†		23	at Atlanta	5-6*
	11	at Columbus	2-3*		24	Boston	4-2
	13	Edmonton	2-1†		26	Toronto	3-4
	15	Atlanta	2-3*		28	at Ottawa	3-2†
	17	at Carolina	1-4		30	Buffalo	3-1
	20	at NY Rangers	3-1	**Apr.**	1	at Philadelphia	4-1
	21	at NY Islanders	2-4		2	at Pittsburgh	3-2*
	23	Atlanta	0-1		5	Pittsburgh	6-4
	26	at Toronto	1-2		8	at Montreal	3-2
	28	Washington	7-2		9	NY Rangers	3-2
	29	at Pittsburgh	2-6		11	at Carolina	4-3*
	31	Toronto	3-6		13	Philadelphia	4-1
Jan.	3	Florida	3-0		16	Philadelphia	5-1
	5	Montreal	5-4		18	at Montreal	4-3

* – Overtime † – Shootout

Entry Draft Selections 2006-1992

2006
Pick
30 Matthew Corrente
58 Alexander Vasyunov
67 Kirill Tulupov
77 Vladimir Zharkov
107 T.J. Miller
148 Olivier Magnan
178 Tony Romano
208 Kyle Henegan

2005
Pick
23 Nicklas Bergfors
38 Jeff Frazee
84 Mark Fraser
99 Patrick Davis
155 Mark Fayne
170 Sean Zimmerman
218 Alexander Sundstrom

2004
Pick
20 Travis Zajac
155 Alexander Mikhailishin
185 Josh Disher
216 Pierre-Luc Letourneau-Leblond
217 Tyler Eckford
250 Nathan Perkovich
282 Valeri Klimov

2003
Pick
17 Zach Parise
42 Petr Vrana
93 Ivan Khomutov
167 Zach Tarkir
197 Jason Smith
261 Joey Tenute
292 Arseny Bondarev

2002
Pick
51 Anton Kadeykin
53 Barry Tallackson
64 Jason Ryznar
84 Marek Chvatal
85 Ahren Nittel
117 Cam Janssen
154 Krisjanis Redlihs
187 Eric Johansson
218 Ilkka Pikkarainen
250 Dan Glover
281 Bill Kinkel

2001
Pick
28 Adrian Foster
44 Igor Pohanka
48 Tuomas Pihlman
60 Victor Uchevatov
67 Robin Leblanc
72 Brandon Nolan
128 Andrei Posnov
163 Andreas Salomonsson
194 James Massen
229 Aaron Voros
257 Yevgeny Gamalei

2000
Pick
22 David Hale
39 Teemu Laine
56 Aleksander Suglobov
57 Matt DeMarchi
62 Paul Martin
67 Max Birbraer
76 Mike Rupp
125 Phil Cole
135 Mike Danton
164 Matus Kostur
194 Deryk Engelland
198 Ken Magowan
257 Warren McCutcheon

1999
Pick
27 Ari Ahonen
42 Mike Commodore
50 Brett Clouthier
95 Andre Lakos
100 Teemu Kesa
185 Scott Cameron
214 Chris Hartsburg
242 Justin Dziama

1998
Pick
26 Mike Van Ryn
27 Scott Gomez
37 Christian Berglund
82 Brian Gionta
96 Mikko Jokela
105 Pierre Dagenais
119 Anton But
143 Ryan Flinn
172 Jacques Lariviere
199 Erik Jensen
227 Marko Ahosilta
257 Ryan Held

1997
Pick
24 Jean-Fr. Damphousse
38 Stanislav Gron
104 Lucas Nehrling
131 Jiri Bicek
159 Sascha Goc
188 Mathieu Benoit
215 Scott Clemmensen
241 Jan Srdinko

1996
Pick
10 Lance Ward
38 Wes Mason
41 Josh DeWolf
47 Pierre Dagenais
49 Colin White
63 Scott Parker
91 Josef Boumedienne
101 Josh MacNevin
118 Glenn Crawford
145 Sean Ritchlin
173 Daryl Andrews
199 Willie Mitchell
205 Jay Bertsch
225 Pasi Petrilainen

1995
Pick
18 Petr Sykora
44 Nathan Perrott
70 Sergei Vyshedkevich
78 David Gosselin
79 Alyn McCauley
96 Henrik Rehnberg
122 Chris Mason
148 Adam Young
174 Richard Rochefort
200 Frederic Henry
226 Colin O'Hara

1994
Pick
25 Vadim Sharifijanov
51 Patrik Elias
71 Sheldon Souray
103 Zdenek Skorepa
129 Christian Gosselin
134 Ryan Smart
155 Luciano Caravaggio
181 Jeff Williams
207 Eric Bertrand
233 Steve Sullivan
259 Scott Swanjord
269 Mike Hanson

1993
Pick
13 Denis Pederson
32 Jay Pandolfo
39 Brendan Morrison
65 Krzysztof Oliwa
110 John Guirestante
143 Steve Brule
169 Nikolai Zavarukhin
195 Thomas Cullen
221 Judd Lambert
247 Jimmy Provencher
273 Mike Legg

1992
Pick
18 Jason Smith
42 Sergei Brylin
66 Cale Hulse
90 Vitali Tomilin
94 Scott McCabe
114 Ryan Black
138 Dan Trebil
162 Geordie Kinnear
186 Stephane Yelle
210 Jeff Toms
234 Heath Weenk
258 Vladislav Yakovenko

Coach

JULIEN, CLAUDE
Coach, New Jersey Devils. Born in Orleans, Ont., April 23, 1960.

The New Jersey Devils named Claude Julien to the position of head coach on June 13, 2006. Previously, Julien was head coach of the Montreal Canadiens from January 17, 2003 through January 14, 2006.

Julien joined the Canadiens after spending two-plus seasons as head coach with Hamilton in the American Hockey League. Prior to being named head coach of Montreal, he had led the Bulldogs to a league-leading 33-6-3-3 record (72 points) during the 2002-03 campaign. Despite spending just 45 games in the American Hockey League that season, Julien was named co-winner of the Louis A.R. Pieri Award as the league's outstanding coach. He was also named as head coach for PlanetUSA at the AHL's 2003 All-Star Game.

Julien served as head coach of Hull (QMJHL) from 1996-97 through 1999-00, compiling a 145-118-19 mark in four seasons. During that time, he led the Olympiques to four straight postseason appearances, as well as the 1997 QMJHL and Memorial Cup championships.

A defenseman, Julien's professional career spanned 12 seasons from 1980-81 through 1991-92, including 14 games over the 1984-85 and 1985-86 seasons with Quebec (NHL). His totals include 469 American Hockey League games with Fredericton, Baltimore, Halifax, and Moncton from 1983-84 until 1991-92. Julien played his junior hockey at both Oshawa and Windsor.

Coaching Record

		Regular Season				Playoffs		
Season	Team	Games	W	L	O/T	Games	W	L
1996-97	Hull (QMJHL)	70	48	19	3	14	12	2
1997-98	Hull (QMJHL)	70	32	37	1	11	6	5
1998-99	Hull (QMJHL)	70	23	38	9	23	15	8
1999-00	Hull (QMJHL)	72	42	24	6	15	9	6
2000-01	Hamilton (AHL)	80	28	46	6	....	....	....
2001-02	Hamilton (AHL)	80	37	33	10	15	10	5
2002-03	Hamilton (AHL)	45	33	9	3	....	....	....
2002-03	**Montreal (NHL)**	**36**	**12**	**21**	**3**	....	....	....
2003-04	**Montreal (NHL)**	**82**	**41**	**34**	**7**	**11**	**4**	**7**
2004-05	**Montreal (NHL)**			Season Cancelled				
2005-06	**Montreal (NHL)**	**41**	**19**	**16**	**6**	....	....	....
	NHL Totals	**159**	**72**	**71**	**16**	**11**	**4**	**7**

Club Directory

Continental Airlines Arena

New Jersey Devils
Continental Airlines Arena
50 Route 120 North
P.O. Box 504
East Rutherford, NJ 07073
Phone **201/935-6050**
FAX 201/935-2127
www.newjerseydevils.com
Capacity: 19,040

Chairman/Managing Partner . . . . Jeff Vanderbeek
CEO/President/General Manager . . . . Louis A. Lamoriello
Executive Vice President, Chief Operating Officer . . . . . . Chris Modrzynski
Executive Vice President. . . . . Peter S. McMullen
Vice President, Chief Financial Officer . . . . Scott Struble
Vice President, General Counsel. . . . . Joseph C. Benedetti
Vice President, Ticket Operations . . . . Terry Farmer
Vice President, Corporate Partnerships . . . . Kenneth F. Ferriter
Vice President, Facilities . . . . Mark Gheduzzi
Vice President, Administration . . . . Gordon Lavalette
Vice President, Information/Publications . . . . Mike Levine
Vice President, Marketing/Community Development . . . Jason Siegel

Hockey Club Personnel
Head Coach . . . . Claude Julien
Assistant Coaches . . . . Jacques Laperriere, John MacLean
Goaltending Coach . . . . Jacques Caron
Director, Scouting . . . . David Conte
Assistant Director, Scouting . . . . Claude Carrier
Scouting Staff . . . . Glen Dirk, Milt Fisher, Ferny Flaman, Dan Labraaten, Chris Lamoriello, Vladimir Lokotko, Pierre Mondou, Larry Perris, Marcel Pronovost, Lou Reycroft, Vaclav Slansky, Jr., Steve Smith, Geoff Stevens, Ed Thomlinson, Les Widdifield
Pro Scouting Staff. . . . . Bob Hoffmeyer, Jan Ludvig, Andre Boudrias, Gates Orlando
Special Assignments . . . . Pat Burns, Robbie Ftorek, Kurt Kleinendorst, Larry Robinson
Hockey Operations Video Coordinator . . . . Taran Singleton
Hockey Operations Video Assistant . . . . Mike Ford
Scouting Staff Assistant. . . . . Callie A. Smith
Head Trainer . . . . TBA
Strength/Conditioning Coordinator . . . . Michael Vasalani
Equipment Manager . . . . Rich Matthews
Assistant Equipment Managers . . . . Alex Abasto, Paul Emmick
Massage Therapist. . . . . Tommy Plasko
Team Cardiologist . . . . Dr. Joseph Niznik
Team Dentist. . . . . Dr. H. Hugh Gardy
Team Optometrist . . . . Dr. Paul Berman
Team Orthopedists . . . . Dr. Barry Fisher, Dr. Len Jaffe
Fitness Consultant . . . . Vladimir Bure
Exercise Physiologist . . . . Dr. Garret Caffrey
Physical Therapist . . . . David Feniger
Video Consultant. . . . . Mitch Kaufman
Head Coach, Lowell. . . . . TBA
Goaltending Coach, Lowell . . . . Chris Terreri
Assistant Coach, Lowell . . . . TBA
Athletic Trainer, Lowell . . . . Chris Palmer
Equipment Manager, Lowell . . . . Matthew Mitchell
Assistant Equipment Manager, Lowell . . . . TBA

President's Office
Hockey Ops. Exec. Asst. to CEO/Pres./G.M. . . . . Marie Carnevale
Corporate Exec. Asst. to CEO/Pres./G.M. . . . . Mary K. Morrison
Corporate Staff Assistant. . . . . Christine DellaBarca
Assistant General Counsel . . . . Daniel Pupel
Legal Assistant . . . . Lourdes Garcia

Operations
Receptionist . . . . Jelsa Belotta
Staff Assistant . . . . Pat Maione

Ticket Operations
Director, Ticket Operations . . . . Tom Bates
Ticket Service Managers . . . . Andrea Marchesani, Frank Calandrillo
Director, Group Sales. . . . . Neil Desormeaux
Managers, Group Accounts . . . . Kevin Quinn, John Tierney

Sales
Director, Ticket Sales/Customer Service . . . . David Beck
Assistant Director, Ticket Sales. . . . . Vincent Occhipinti
Account Managers . . . . Brooke Alper, Kelly Baron, Richard Bello, Amanda Brown, Clayton Cantil, Mark Gennarelli, Frank Giasone, Christina Giunta, Kevin Hogan, Bill Idnay, Craig Ishill, Kevin Levy, Dan Millman, Kris Rinaldi, Nicole Rivera, Vincent Russo, Aaron Sanders, Glenn Sperber, Thomas Stocky
Receptionist, Sales. . . . . Katie Catalano

Corporate Partnerships
Director, Corporate Partnerships . . . . Michael DeMartino
Director, Corporate Partner Services. . . . . Matt Dugan
Account Manager, Corporate Partnerships. . . . . Kimberly Torns

Communications
Director, Public Relations . . . . Jeff Altstadter
Manager, Communications . . . . Pete Albietz
Staff Assistant . . . . Daniel Beam

Finance
Assistant Contoller . . . . TBA
Staff Accountants . . . . Mario Deludicibus, Joe Pannia, Kristin Servino
Administrative Assistant. . . . . Eileen Philips

Marketing/Community Development
Director, Merchandising. . . . . David Perricone
Merchandising Assistant . . . . Adam Manger
Director, Grassroots Programs . . . . Michael Merolla
Coordinator, Grassroots Programs . . . . Jason Romano
Director, Game Entertainment . . . . Anthony Gioia
Manager, Game Entertainment . . . . David Schwinger
Game Entertainment Assistant. . . . . Josh Lay
Director, Web Operations/Creative Services . . . . Anthony Bovasso
Coordinator, Web Operations/Creative Services . . . . Greg Orlando
Administrative Assistant. . . . . Heather Hall

Computer Operations
Director, Programming/Computer Operations . . . . Jack Skelley
Programmer/Analyst . . . . Joseph Wyks
Systems Administrator . . . . Mike Tukes
Technical Assistant . . . . Antonio da Silva

Alumni Representatives . . . . Ken Daneyko, Bruce Driver, Rob Skrlac, Randy Velischek

Devils Renaissance Development
Senior Vice President, Development. . . . . Jim Cima
Business Coordinator. . . . . Kim Rossi
Financial Analyst . . . . David Steinfeld
Staff Attorney . . . . Tim Lamoriello

Television/Radio
Television Outlet . . . . FOX Sports Net New York – Mike Emrick, Play-by-Play; Glenn Resch, Color
Radio Outlet . . . . Sports Radio 66 WFAN – Matt Loughlin, Play-by-Play; TBA, Color

New York Islanders

2005-06 Results: 36w-40L-3oTL-3SOL 78PTS.
Fourth, Atlantic Division

2006-07 Schedule

Oct.	Thu.	5	at Phoenix	Tue.	9	at NY Rangers
	Sat.	7	at San Jose	Thu.	11	at Boston
	Tue.	10	at Los Angeles	Sat.	13	New Jersey
	Wed.	11	at Anaheim	Mon.	15	Tampa Bay*
	Sat.	14	Boston	Tue.	16	at Pittsburgh
	Mon.	16	Nashville	Thu.	18	at Philadelphia
	Thu.	19	Pittsburgh	Fri.	26	at Atlanta
	Sat.	21	Carolina	Sat.	27	Buffalo
	Thu.	26	Buffalo	Tue.	30	Detroit
	Sat.	28	Florida	Feb. Thu.	1	at Atlanta
	Tue.	31	Chicago	Sat.	3	at Montreal*
Nov.	Thu.	2	at New Jersey	Sun.	4	at Washington*
	Sat.	4	Atlanta	Wed.	7	Philadelphia
	Mon.	6	Tampa Bay	Thu.	8	at New Jersey
	Thu.	9	at Philadelphia	Sat.	10	at Boston
	Wed.	15	at Dallas	Tue.	13	at Toronto
	Fri.	17	at Tampa Bay	Thu.	15	Boston
	Sat.	18	at Florida	Sat.	17	New Jersey
	Mon.	20	at Toronto	Mon.	19	Pittsburgh*
	Wed.	22	Carolina	Thu.	22	Toronto
	Fri.	24	Pittsburgh*	Sat.	24	Montreal*
	Sat.	25	Washington	Tue.	27	Philadelphia
	Tue.	28	at Pittsburgh	Mar. Thu.	1	St. Louis
	Thu.	30	Philadelphia	Sat.	3	at Washington
Dec.	Sat.	2	at Pittsburgh	Mon.	5	at NY Rangers
	Sun.	3	at NY Rangers*	Thu.	8	NY Rangers
	Tue.	5	Ottawa	Sat.	10	Washington
	Thu.	7	Montreal	Tue.	13	at Montreal
	Sat.	9	Florida	Thu.	15	at Ottawa
	Fri.	15	at Pittsburgh	Sat.	17	at Florida
	Sat.	16	Atlanta	Tue.	20	at Tampa Bay
	Tue.	19	at NY Rangers	Thu.	22	Pittsburgh
	Fri.	22	at Carolina	Sat.	24	at Philadelphia*
	Sat.	23	Columbus	Sun.	25	NY Rangers*
	Tue.	26	NY Rangers	Tue.	27	New Jersey
	Wed.	27	at Ottawa	Fri.	30	at Buffalo
	Sat.	30	New Jersey	Sat.	31	Ottawa
Jan.	Mon.	1	at Buffalo*	Apr. Tue.	3	NY Rangers
	Tue.	2	Philadelphia	Thu.	5	Toronto
	Thu.	4	at New Jersey	Sat.	7	at Philadelphia*
	Sat.	6	at Carolina	Sun.	8	at New Jersey*

Denotes afternoon game.

Franchise date: June 6, 1972

ATLANTIC DIVISION

35th NHL Season

After leading the Sabres in scoring for years, Miroslav Satan topped the Islanders with 35 goals during his first season with the team. His point total of 66 tied Alexei Yashin for the team lead.

Year-by-Year Record

		Home				Road				Overall							
Season	GP	W	L	T	OL	W	L	T	OL	W	L	T	OL	GF	GA	Pts.	Finished	Playoff Result
2005-06	82	20	18	....	3	16	22	....	3	36	40	....	6	230	278	78	4th, Atlantic Div.	Out of Playoffs
2004-05	....																	
2003-04	82	25	11	4	1	13	18	7	3	38	29	11	4	237	210	91	3rd, Atlantic Div.	Lost Conf. Quarter-Final
2002-03	82	18	18	5	0	17	16	6	2	35	34	11	2	224	231	83	3rd, Atlantic Div.	Lost Conf. Quarter-Final
2001-02	82	21	13	5	2	21	15	3	2	42	28	8	4	239	220	96	2nd, Atlantic Div.	Lost Conf. Quarter-Final
2000-01	82	12	27	1	1	9	24	6	2	21	51	7	3	185	268	52	5th, Atlantic Div.	Out of Playoffs
1999-2000	82	10	25	5	1	14	23	4	0	24	48	9	1	194	275	58	5th, Atlantic Div.	Out of Playoffs
1998-99	82	11	23	7	....	13	25	3	....	24	48	10	....	194	244	58	5th, Atlantic Div.	Out of Playoffs
1997-98	82	17	20	4	....	13	21	7	....	30	41	11	....	212	225	71	4th, Atlantic Div.	Out of Playoffs
1996-97	82	19	18	4	....	10	23	8	....	29	41	12	....	240	250	70	7th, Atlantic Div.	Out of Playoffs
1995-96	82	14	21	6	....	8	29	4	....	22	50	10	....	229	315	54	7th, Atlantic Div.	Out of Playoffs
1994-95	48	10	11	3	....	5	17	2	....	15	28	5	....	126	158	35	7th, Atlantic Div.	Out of Playoffs
1993-94	84	23	15	4	....	13	21	8	....	36	36	12	....	282	264	84	4th, Atlantic Div.	Lost Conf. Quarter-Final
1992-93	84	20	19	3	....	20	18	4	....	40	37	7	....	335	297	87	3rd, Patrick Div.	Lost Conf. Championship
1991-92	80	20	15	5	....	14	20	6	....	34	35	11	....	291	299	79	5th, Patrick Div.	Out of Playoffs
1990-91	80	15	19	6	....	10	26	4	....	25	45	10	....	223	290	60	6th, Patrick Div.	Out of Playoffs
1989-90	80	15	17	8	....	16	21	3	....	31	38	11	....	281	288	73	4th, Patrick Div.	Lost Div. Semi-Final
1988-89	80	19	18	3	....	9	29	2	....	28	47	5	....	265	325	61	6th, Patrick Div.	Out of Playoffs
1987-88	80	24	10	6	....	15	21	4	....	39	31	10	....	308	267	88	1st, Patrick Div.	Lost Div. Semi-Final
1986-87	80	20	15	5	....	15	18	7	....	35	33	12	....	279	281	82	3rd, Patrick Div.	Lost Div. Final
1985-86	80	22	11	7	....	17	18	5	....	39	29	12	....	327	284	90	3rd, Patrick Div.	Lost Div. Semi-Final
1984-85	80	26	11	3	....	14	23	3	....	40	34	6	....	345	312	86	3rd, Patrick Div.	Lost Div. Final
1983-84	80	28	11	1	....	22	15	3	....	50	26	4	....	357	269	104	1st, Patrick Div.	Lost Final
1982-83	**80**	**26**	**11**	**3**	**....**	**16**	**15**	**9**	**....**	**42**	**26**	**12**	**....**	**302**	**226**	**96**	**2nd, Patrick Div.**	**Won Stanley Cup**
1981-82	**80**	**33**	**3**	**4**	**....**	**21**	**13**	**6**	**....**	**54**	**16**	**10**	**....**	**385**	**250**	**118**	**1st, Patrick Div.**	**Won Stanley Cup**
1980-81	**80**	**23**	**6**	**11**	**....**	**25**	**12**	**3**	**....**	**48**	**18**	**14**	**....**	**355**	**260**	**110**	**1st, Patrick Div.**	**Won Stanley Cup**
1979-80	**80**	**26**	**9**	**5**	**....**	**13**	**19**	**8**	**....**	**39**	**28**	**13**	**....**	**281**	**247**	**91**	**2nd, Patrick Div.**	**Won Stanley Cup**
1978-79	80	31	3	6	....	20	12	8	....	51	15	14	....	358	214	116	1st, Patrick Div.	Lost Semi-Final
1977-78	80	29	3	8	....	19	14	7	....	48	17	15	....	334	210	111	1st, Patrick Div.	Lost Quarter-Final
1976-77	80	24	11	5	....	23	10	7	....	47	21	12	....	288	193	106	2nd, Patrick Div.	Lost Semi-Final
1975-76	80	24	8	8	....	18	13	9	....	42	21	17	....	297	190	101	2nd, Patrick Div.	Lost Semi-Final
1974-75	80	22	6	12	....	11	19	10	....	33	25	22	....	264	221	88	3rd, Patrick Div.	Lost Semi-Final
1973-74	78	13	17	9	....	6	24	9	....	19	41	18	....	182	247	56	8th, East Div.	Out of Playoffs
1972-73	78	10	25	4	....	2	35	2	....	12	60	6	....	170	347	30	8th, East Div.	Out of Playoffs

2006-07 Player Personnel

FORWARDS

	HT	WT	S	Place of Birth	Date	2005-06 Club
AQUINO, Luciano	5-9	198	L	Mississauga, Ont.	1/26/85	Bram-Bridgeport-Trenton
ASHAM, Arron	5-11	209	R	Portage La Prairie, Man.	4/13/78	NY Islanders
BATES, Shawn	6-0	205	R	Melrose, MA	4/3/75	NY Islanders
BERGENHEIM, Sean	5-11	194	L	Helsinki, Finland	2/8/84	NY Islanders-Bridgeport
BLAKE, Jason	5-10	180	L	Moorhead, MN	9/2/73	NY Islanders
COLLITON, Jeremy	6-2	195	R	Blackie, Alta.	1/13/85	NY Islanders-Bridgeport
COMEAU, Blake	6-1	198	R	Meadow Lake, Sask.	2/18/86	Kelowna-Bridgeport
HILBERT, Andy	5-11	194	L	Lansing, MI	2/6/81	Chi-Norfolk-Pit
HUNTER, Trent	6-3	191	R	Red Deer, Alta.	7/5/80	NY Islanders
KOALSKA, Matt	6-1	196	L	St. Paul, MN	5/16/80	NY Islanders-Bridgeport
MARJAMAKI, Masi	6-2	202	L	Pori, Finland	1/16/85	NY Islanders-Bridgeport
NIELSEN, Frans	5-11	172	L	Herning, Denmark	4/24/84	Timra
NILSSON, Robert	5-11	176	L	Calgary, Alta.	1/10/85	NY Islanders-Bridgeport
NOKELAINEN, Petteri	6-1	187	R	Imatra, Finland	1/16/86	NY Islanders
O'MARRA, Ryan	6-1	193	R	Tokyo, Japan	6/9/87	Erie (OHL)-Bridgeport
REGIER, Steve	6-4	194	L	Edmonton, Alta.	8/31/84	NY Islanders-Bridgeport
SATAN, Miroslav	6-3	190	L	Topolcany, Czech.	10/22/74	NY Islanders
SILLINGER, Mike	5-11	196	R	Regina, Sask.	6/29/71	St. Louis-Nashville
TAMBELLINI, Jeff	5-11	186	L	Calgary, Alta.	4/13/84	L.A.-Manchester-NYI-Bridgeport
YASHIN, Alexei	6-3	225	R	Sverdlovsk, USSR	11/5/73	NY Islanders
YORK, Mike	5-10	185	R	Waterford, MI	1/3/78	NY Islanders

DEFENSEMEN

	HT	WT	S	Place of Birth	Date	2005-06 Club
BERRY, Rick	6-2	210	L	Birtle, Man.	11/4/78	San Antonio-Milwaukee
BOUCHARD, Joel	6-1	209	L	Montreal, Que.	1/23/74	NY Islanders-Bridgeport
CALDWELL, Ryan	6-2	174	L	Deloraine, Man.	6/15/81	NY Islanders-Bridgeport
CAMPOLI, Chris	6-0	190	L	North York, Ont.	7/9/84	NY Islanders
GERVAIS, Bruno	6-0	188	R	Longueuil, Que.	10/3/84	NY Islanders-Bridgeport
HALVARDSSON, Johan	6-3	198	L	Jonkoping, Sweden	12/26/79	HV 71
HILL, Sean	6-0	205	R	Duluth, MN	2/14/70	Florida
MARTINEK, Radek	6-1	200	R	Havlickuv Brod, Czech.	8/31/76	NY Islanders
POTI, Tom	6-3	210	L	Worcester, MA	3/22/77	NY Rangers
ROURKE, Allan	6-1	214	L	Mississauga, Ont.	3/6/80	NY Islanders-Bridgeport
WITT, Brendan	6-2	219	L	Humboldt, Sask.	2/20/75	Washington-Nashville
WOTTON, Mark	6-1	195	L	Foxwarren, Man.	11/16/73	Hershey
ZHITNIK, Alexei	5-11	215	L	Kiev, USSR	10/10/72	NY Islanders

GOALTENDERS

	HT	WT	C	Place of Birth	Date	2005-06 Club
DiPIETRO, Rick	5-11	185	R	Winthrop, MA	9/19/81	NY Islanders
DUBIELEWICZ, Wade	5-10	178	L	Invermere, B.C.	1/30/78	NY Islanders-Bridgeport
THOMPSON, Billy	6-2	200	L	Saskatoon, Sask.	9/24/82	Binghamton

2005-06 Scoring

*– rookie

Regular Season

Pos	#	Player	Team	GP	G	A	Pts	+/-	PIM	PP	SH	GW	S	%
R	81	Miroslav Satan	NYI	82	35	31	66	-8	54	17	0	2	253	13.8
C	79	Alexei Yashin	NYI	82	28	38	66	-14	68	10	0	2	253	11.1
L	55	Jason Blake	NYI	76	28	29	57	0	60	12	-2	2	304	9.2
L	16	Mike York	NYI	75	13	39	52	-9	30	4	1	2	146	8.9
R	7	Trent Hunter	NYI	82	16	19	35	-9	34	5	0	3	221	7.2
C	17	Shawn Bates	NYI	66	15	19	34	-11	60	1	1	4	95	15.8
D	14 *	Chris Campoli	NYI	80	9	25	34	-16	46	2	0	2	123	7.3
D	77	Alexei Zhitnik	NYI	59	5	24	29	4	88	3	0	0	99	5.1
R	45	Arron Asham	NYI	63	9	15	24	-5	103	2	1	0	99	9.1
R	21 *	Robert Nilsson	NYI	53	6	14	20	-6	26	1	0	1	70	8.6
D	24	Radek Martinek	NYI	74	1	16	17	-9	32	0	0	0	79	1.3
L	10 *	Sean Bergenheim	NYI	28	4	5	9	-11	20	0	0	1	63	6.3
D	4	Joel Bouchard	NYI	25	1	8	9	5	23	0	0	0	45	2.2
C	18	Jeffrey Hamilton	NYI	13	2	6	8	0	8	1	0	0	29	6.9
C	28	Wyatt Smith	NYI	42	0	8	8	-7	26	0	0	0	37	0.0
D	6 *	Bruno Gervais	NYI	27	3	4	7	-1	8	0	0	0	21	14.3
D	3 *	Denis Grebeshkov	L.A.	8	0	2	2	-4	12	0	0	0	10	0.0
			NYI	21	0	3	3	-8	8	0	0	0	14	0.0
			TOTAL	29	0	5	5	-12	20	0	0	0	24	0.0
R	49	Eric Godard	NYI	57	2	2	4	-2	115	0	0	0	17	11.8
L	15 *	Jeff Tambellini	L.A.	4	0	0	0	-1	2	0	0	0	6	0.0
			NYI	21	1	3	4	2	8	0	0	0	11	9.1
			TOTAL	25	1	3	4	1	10	0	0	0	17	5.9
R	26	Rob Collins	NYI	8	1	1	2	1	0	0	0	0	8	12.5
C	29 *	Petteri Nokelainen	NYI	15	1	1	2	-1	4	0	0	1	13	7.7
C	27 *	Jeremy Colliton	NYI	19	1	1	2	2	6	0	0	0	9	11.1
D	44	John Erskine	DAL	26	0	0	0	-3	62	0	0	0	9	0.0
			NYI	34	1	0	1	-12	99	0	0	0	23	4.3
			TOTAL	60	1	0	1	-15	161	0	0	0	32	3.1
D	38 *	Allan Rourke	NYI	6	0	1	1	0	0	0	0	0	2	0.0
L	63 *	Cole Jarrett	NYI	1	0	0	0	0	0	0	0	0	1	0.0
L	58 *	Masi Marjamaki	NYI	1	0	0	0	0	0	0	0	0	0	0.0
D	43 *	Ryan Caldwell	NYI	2	0	0	0	-2	2	0	0	0	2	0.0
C	40 *	Matt Koalska	NYI	3	0	0	0	-1	2	0	0	0	3	0.0
L	48 *	Steve Regier	NYI	9	0	0	0	-1	0	0	0	0	4	0.0
R	62	Kevin Colley	NYI	16	0	0	0	-2	52	0	0	0	4	0.0
D	8	Tomi Pettinen	NYI	18	0	0	0	-2	16	0	0	0	7	0.0

Goaltending

No.	Goaltender	GPI	Mins	Avg	W	L	OT	EN	SO	GA	SA	S%	G	A	PIM
34	Wade Dubielewicz	7	310	2.90	2	3	0	1	0	15	145	.897	0	0	0
39	Rick DiPietro	63	3572	3.02	30	24	5	7	1	180	1797	.900	0	1	28
30	Garth Snow	20	1096	3.72	4	13	1	4	0	68	595	.886	0	0	2
	Totals	82	5001	3.30	36	40	6	12	1	275	2549	.892			

Coach

NOLAN, TED
Coach, New York Islanders. Born in Sault Ste. Marie, Ont., April 7, 1958.

Hired as head coach by the New York Islanders on June 8, 2006, Ted Nolan has been a coaching success at every level of professional and amateur hockey, having reached the pinnacle when he was awarded the Jack Adams Award as NHL coach of the year for his work with the Buffalo Sabres in 1996-97. Nolan is noted for his ability to motivate and teach and he has a knack for drawing the most from the talent available on his teams.

After an eight-year absence from competitive coaching, Nolan returned with a sterling debut as head coach and director of hockey operations for the Moncton Wildcats of the Quebec Major Junior Hockey League in 2005-06. He introduced 14 new players to the team, and led Moncton to its first President Cup as QMJHL champion, finishing first overall in the regular season at 52-15-3. The Wildcats advanced to the finals of the Memorial Cup (Canadian Junior championship) where they finished runner-up to Patrick Roy's Quebec Remparts.

Born on the Garden River First Nation Reserve just outside of Sault Ste. Marie, Ontario, Nolan is a member of the First Nations Ojibway tribe. Following his time in Buffalo, Nolan devoted himself to First Nations causes, including teaching hockey to First Nations children. His work in this area earned him the National Aboriginal Achievement Award, the Sault Ste. Marie Medal of Merit and the Order of Ontario.

As a player, Nolan skated for the Ontario Hockey Association's Sault Ste. Marie Greyhounds, the Kansas City Red Wings of the Central Hockey League, and the Adirondack Red Wings, Rochester Americans and Baltimore Skipjacks of the American Hockey League. He also played for the Pittsburgh Penguins and the Detroit Red Wings of the National Hockey League between 1981-82 and 1985-86. He became head coach of the Sault Ste. Marie Greyhounds in 1988, as a midseason replacement and coached there until the end of the 1994 season. Nolan led the Greyhounds to three consecutive Memorial Cup tournament berths, winning the Canadian national junior championship in 1993.

The Hartford Whalers hired Nolan before the 1994 regular season as an assistant coach for one season before accepting the position of head coach of the Buffalo Sabres where he had his best success. In his second season in Buffalo, he led the team to a strong regular season, culminating in the Northeast Division title. He was rewarded with the Jack Adams Award as the league's top coach.

Coaching Record

Season	Team	Games	Regular Season W	L	T	Playoffs Games	W	L
1988-89	S.S. Marie (OHL)	38	12	25	1	....	....	....
1989-90	S.S. Marie (OHL)	66	18	42	6	....	....	....
1990-91	S.S. Marie (OHL)	66	42	21	3	14	12	2
1991-92	S.S. Marie (OHL)	66	41	19	6	19	12	7
1992-93	S.S. Marie (OHL)	66	38	23	5	18	13	5
1993-94	S.S. Marie (OHL)	66	35	24	7	14	10	4
1995-96	**Buffalo (NHL)**	82	33	42	7	....	....	....
1996-97	**Buffalo (NHL)**	82	40	30	12	12	5	7
2005-06	Moncton (QMJHL)	70	52	15	3	21	16	5
	NHL Totals	**164**	**73**	**72**	**19**	**12**	**5**	**7**

In his first season with the Islanders, Mike York recorded 39 assists, leading the club and matching a career high he had established in his last year with the Rangers.

Coaching History

Phil Goyette and Earl Ingarfield, 1972-73; Al Arbour, 1973-74 to 1985-86; Terry Simpson, 1986-87, 1987-88; Terry Simpson and Al Arbour, 1988-89; Al Arbour, 1989-90 to 1993-94; Lorne Henning, 1994-95; Mike Milbury, 1995-96; Mike Milbury and Rick Bowness, 1996-97; Rick Bowness and Mike Milbury, 1997-98; Mike Milbury and Bill Stewart, 1998-99; Butch Goring, 1999-2000; Butch Goring and Lorne Henning, 2000-01; Peter Laviolette, 2001-02, 2002-03; Steve Stirling, 2003-04, 2004-05; Steve Stirling and Brad Shaw, 2005-06; Ted Nolan, 2006-07.

Club Records

Team

(Figures in brackets for season records are games played; records for fewest points, wins, ties, losses, goals, goals against are for 70 or more games)

Most Points 118 1981-82 (80)
Most Wins 54 1981-82 (80)
Most Ties 22 1974-75 (80)
Most Losses 60 1972-73 (78)
Most Goals 385 1981-82 (80)
Most Goals Against 347 1972-73 (78)
Fewest Points 30 1972-73 (78)
Fewest Wins 12 1972-73 (78)
Fewest Ties 4 1983-84 (80)
Fewest Losses 15 1978-79 (80)
Fewest Goals 170 1972-73 (78)
Fewest Goals Against 190 1975-76 (80)
Longest Winning Streak
Overall .... 15 Jan. 21-Feb. 20/82
Home .... 14 Jan. 2-Feb. 25/82
Away .... 8 Feb. 27-Mar. 29/81
Longest Undefeated Streak
Overall .... 15 Three times
Home .... 23 Oct. 17/78-Jan. 27/79 (19 wins, 4 ties), Jan. 2-Apr. 3/82 (21 wins, 2 ties)
Away .... 8 Three times
Longest Losing Streak
Overall .... 12 Dec. 27/72-Jan. 16/73, Nov. 22-Dec. 15/88
Home .... 7 Nov. 13-Dec. 14/99
Away .... 15 Jan. 20-Mar. 31/73
Longest Winless Streak
Overall .... 15 Nov. 22-Dec. 21/72 (12 losses, 3 ties)
Home .... 9 Mar. 2-Apr. 6/99 (7 losses, 2 ties)
Away .... 20 Nov. 3/72-Jan. 13/73 (19 losses, 1 tie)
Most Shutouts, Season 10 1975-76 (80)
Most PIM, Season 1,857 1986-87 (80)
Most Goals, Game .... 11 Dec. 20/83 (Pit. 3 at NYI 11), Mar. 3/84 (NYI 11 at Tor. 6)

Individual

Most Seasons .... 17 Billy Smith
Most Games .... 1,123 Bryan Trottier
Most Goals, Career .... 573 Mike Bossy
Most Assists, Career .... 853 Bryan Trottier
Most Points, Career .... 1,353 Bryan Trottier (500G, 853A)
Most PIM, Career .... 1,879 Mick Vukota
Most Shutouts, Career .... 25 Glenn Resch
Longest Consecutive Games Streak .... 576 Billy Harris (Oct. 7/72-Nov. 30/79)
Most Goals, Season .... 69 Mike Bossy (1978-79)
Most Assists, Season .... 87 Bryan Trottier (1978-79)
Most Points, Season .... 147 Mike Bossy (1981-82; 64G, 83A)
Most PIM, Season .... 356 Brian Curran (1986-87)
Most Points, Defenseman, Season .... 101 Denis Potvin (1978-79; 31G, 70A)
Most Points, Center, Season .... 134 Bryan Trottier (1978-79; 47G, 87A)
Most Points, Right Wing, Season .... 147 Mike Bossy (1981-82; 64G, 83A)
Most Points, Left Wing, Season .... 100 John Tonelli (1984-85; 42G, 58A)
Most Points, Rookie, Season .... 95 Bryan Trottier (1975-76; 32G, 63A)
Most Shutouts, Season .... 7 Glenn Resch (1975-76)
Most Goals, Game .... 5 Bryan Trottier (Dec. 23/78, Feb. 13/82), John Tonelli (Jan. 6/81)
Most Assists, Game .... 6 Mike Bossy (Jan. 6/81)
Most Points, Game .... 8 Bryan Trottier (Dec. 23/78; 5G, 3A)

Captains' History

Ed Westfall, 1972-73 to 1975-76; Ed Westfall and Clark Gillies, 1976-77; Clark Gillies, 1977-78, 1978-79; Denis Potvin, 1979-80 to 1986-87; Brent Sutter, 1987-88 to 1990-91; Brent Sutter and Pat Flatley, 1991-92; Pat Flatley, 1992-93 to 1995-96; no captain, 1996-97; Bryan McCabe and Trevor Linden, 1997-98; Trevor Linden, 1998-99; Kenny Jonsson, 1999-2000, 2000-01; Michael Peca, 2001-02 to 2003-04; Alexei Yashin, 2005-06.

Retired Numbers

5	Denis Potvin	1973-1988
9	Clark Gillies	1974-1986
19	Bryan Trottier	1975-1990
22	Mike Bossy	1977-1987
23	Bob Nystrom	1972-1986
31	Billy Smith	1972-1989

All-time Record vs. Other Clubs

Regular Season

	At Home								On Road								Total							
	GP	W	L	T	OL	GF	GA	PTS	GP	W	L	T	OL	GF	GA	PTS	GP	W	L	T	OL	GF	GA	PTS
Anaheim	8	4	3	1	0	24	23	9	9	4	2	3	0	24	18	11	17	8	5	4	0	48	41	20
Atlanta	12	7	5	0	0	45	29	14	12	7	3	2	0	46	34	16	24	14	8	2	0	91	63	30
Boston	63	26	27	10	0	211	204	62	61	18	31	11	1	171	224	48	124	44	58	21	1	382	428	110
Buffalo	63	27	26	9	1	179	176	64	63	20	33	9	1	171	209	50	126	47	59	18	2	350	385	114
Calgary	52	26	17	9	0	194	145	61	49	14	24	11	0	145	172	39	101	40	41	20	0	339	317	100
Carolina	46	21	21	4	0	135	126	46	47	19	23	5	0	152	160	43	93	40	44	9	0	287	286	89
Chicago	47	18	14	15	0	163	141	51	49	18	26	5	0	164	163	41	96	36	40	20	0	327	304	92
Colorado	33	19	13	1	0	134	113	39	34	11	20	3	0	97	123	25	67	30	33	4	0	231	236	64
Columbus	2	0	2	0	0	7	11	0	5	0	3	1	1	10	17	2	7	0	5	1	1	17	28	2
Dallas	48	26	14	8	0	176	134	60	47	21	18	8	0	170	139	50	95	47	32	16	0	346	273	110
Detroit	46	23	18	4	1	164	137	51	46	18	26	2	0	137	166	38	92	41	44	6	1	301	303	89
Edmonton	32	16	7	9	0	131	112	41	29	8	16	5	0	87	107	21	61	24	23	14	0	218	219	62
Florida	27	13	12	2	0	69	71	28	27	9	12	6	0	81	83	24	54	22	24	8	0	150	154	52
Los Angeles	44	24	15	5	0	156	123	53	45	17	21	7	0	143	163	41	89	41	36	12	0	299	286	94
Minnesota	4	2	2	0	0	9	10	4	3	1	2	0	0	9	9	2	7	3	4	0	0	18	19	6
Montreal	62	31	25	6	0	193	173	68	62	15	38	9	0	171	223	39	124	46	63	15	0	364	396	107
Nashville	4	2	2	0	0	11	12	4	6	2	4	0	0	17	16	4	10	4	6	0	0	28	28	8
New Jersey	89	58	20	11	0	364	256	127	88	40	34	11	3	303	287	94	177	98	54	22	3	667	543	221
NY Rangers	100	55	36	8	1	381	326	119	100	32	57	11	0	292	368	75	200	87	93	19	1	673	694	194
Ottawa	26	5	14	6	1	82	99	17	25	5	15	5	0	65	88	15	51	10	29	11	1	147	187	32
Philadelphia	102	51	36	15	0	365	303	117	99	30	58	11	0	277	355	71	201	81	94	26	0	642	658	188
Phoenix	30	13	9	8	0	113	91	34	30	15	11	4	0	105	96	34	60	28	20	12	0	218	187	68
Pittsburgh	90	48	32	8	2	358	301	106	92	36	40	14	2	322	345	88	182	84	72	22	4	680	646	194
St. Louis	49	25	13	11	0	183	131	61	48	21	17	9	1	159	169	52	97	46	30	20	1	342	300	113
San Jose	11	5	4	2	0	40	35	12	12	6	5	1	0	40	30	13	23	11	9	3	0	80	65	25
Tampa Bay	27	13	12	1	1	81	74	28	28	12	13	2	1	84	75	27	55	25	25	3	2	165	149	55
Toronto	55	31	20	3	1	213	160	66	57	23	29	4	1	192	201	51	112	54	49	7	2	405	361	117
Vancouver	48	26	12	10	0	175	137	62	47	21	23	3	0	153	155	45	95	47	35	13	0	328	292	107
Washington	83	44	37	2	0	308	258	90	83	31	40	11	1	258	275	74	166	75	77	13	1	566	533	164
Defunct Clubs	13	11	0	2	0	75	33	24	13	4	5	4	0	35	41	12	26	15	5	6	0	110	74	36
Totals	**1316**	**670**	**468**	**170**	**8**	**4739**	**3944**	**1518**	**1316**	**478**	**649**	**177**	**12**	**4080**	**4511**	**1145**	**2632**	**1148**	**1117**	**347**	**20**	**8819**	**8455**	**2663**

Playoffs

	Series	W	L	GP	W	L	T	GF	GA	Last Mtg.	Rnd.	Result
Boston	2	2	0	11	8	3	0	49	35	1983	CF	W 4-2
Buffalo	3	3	0	16	12	4	0	59	45	1980	SF	W 4-2
Chicago	2	2	0	6	6	0	0	21	6	1979	QF	W 4-0
Colorado	1	1	0	4	4	0	0	18	9	1982	CF	W 4-0
Dallas	1	1	0	5	4	1	0	26	16	1981	F	W 4-1
Edmonton	3	2	1	15	9	6	0	58	47	1984	F	L 1-4
Los Angeles	1	1	0	4	3	1	0	21	10	1980	PRE	W 3-1
Montreal	4	1	3	22	8	14	0	55	64	1993	CF	L 1-4
New Jersey	1	0	1	6	2	4	0	18	23	1988	DSF	L 2-4
NY Rangers	8	5	3	39	20	19	0	129	132	1994	CQF	L 0-4
Ottawa	1	0	1	5	1	4	0	7	13	2003	CQF	L 1-4
Philadelphia	4	1	3	25	11	14	0	69	83	1987	DF	L 3-4
Pittsburgh	3	3	0	19	11	8	0	67	58	1993	DF	W 4-3
Tampa Bay	1	0	1	5	1	4	0	5	12	2004	CQF	L 1-4
Toronto	3	1	2	17	9	8	0	54	42	2002	CQF	L 3-4
Vancouver	2	2	0	6	6	0	0	26	14	1982	F	W 4-0
Washington	6	5	1	30	18	12	0	99	88	1993	DSF	W 4-2
Totals	**46**	**30**	**16**	**235**	**133**	**102**	**0**	**781**	**697**			

Calgary totals include Atlanta Flames, 1972-73 to 1979-80. Carolina totals include Hartford, 1979-80 to 1996-97.
Colorado totals include Quebec, 1979-80 to 1994-95. Dallas totals include Minnesota North Stars, 1972-73 to 1992-93.
New Jersey totals include Kansas City, 1974-75 to 1975-76, and Colorado Rockies, 1976-77 to 1981-82.
Phoenix totals include Winnipeg, 1979-80 to 1995-96.

Playoff Results 2006-2001

Year	Round	Opponent	Result	GF	GA
2004	CQF	Tampa Bay	L 1-4	5	12
2003	CQF	Ottawa	L 1-4	7	13
2002	CQF	Toronto	L 3-4	21	22

Abbreviations: Round: F – Final; **CF** – conference final; **CQF** – conference quarter-final; **DF** – division final; **DSF** – division semi-final; **SF** – semi-final; **QF** – quarter-final; **PRE** – preliminary round.

2005-06 Results

Oct.	5	at Buffalo	4-6		10	at Nashville	1-2
	8	Carolina	3-2		12	Calgary	3-2
	10	Florida	1-3		14	Vancouver	1-8
	13	at Washington	5-3		17	at Chicago	2-1*
	15	at Philadelphia	1-5		19	at Carolina	3-4
	19	at NY Rangers	3-2†		21	at New Jersey	2-3†
	20	NY Rangers	5-4		24	New Jersey	0-4
	22	at Montreal	3-4		26	Pittsburgh	4-3†
	25	Atlanta	4-3		28	at Boston	4-3
	27	at NY Rangers	1-3		31	Washington	5-3
	29	Buffalo	4-6	Feb.	2	NY Rangers	2-5
Nov.	1	Boston	4-3*		4	at Pittsburgh	5-4†
	3	Pittsburgh	1-5		6	Tampa Bay	2-3*
	5	at Ottawa	0-6		8	at Philadelphia	2-5
	8	at New Jersey	4-1		11	at New Jersey	2-1
	10	at Philadelphia	2-3		28	Montreal	3-5
	12	Boston	5-2	Mar.	2	New Jersey	3-2†
	14	at Pittsburgh	3-2†		4	Philadelphia	4-2
	16	at Atlanta	7-3		6	at Washington	2-5
	17	at Tampa Bay	2-3		7	New Jersey	2-1†
	19	at Florida	5-3		10	Toronto	2-1†
	23	Buffalo	3-4†		11	at Boston	3-1
	25	Ottawa	2-6		14	at New Jersey	6-1
	26	at Philadelphia	4-2		16	at Atlanta	2-4
	29	Philadelphia	3-4		17	at Florida	2-4
Dec.	4	at Detroit	2-1		19	at Tampa Bay	2-5
	6	at St. Louis	6-3		21	Montreal	3-1
	8	at Columbus	3-4†		24	at Pittsburgh	3-4*
	10	Edmonton	3-2†		25	Atlanta	5-1
	13	Minnesota	3-4		28	at Montreal	0-2
	17	Colorado	5-4		29	NY Rangers	1-5
	19	at Toronto	6-9		31	Pittsburgh	0-4
	21	New Jersey	4-2	Apr.	2	Philadelphia	1-4
	23	Ottawa	2-4		5	at Toronto	2-3
	26	at Buffalo	3-6		6	at NY Rangers	1-3
	28	NY Rangers	2-6		8	Washington	5-0
	30	at Ottawa	3-4		11	at NY Rangers	3-2
Jan.	2	Tampa Bay	1-2		13	Toronto	3-4*
	4	Florida	4-3*		15	Pittsburgh	5-4†
	6	at Carolina	1-4		17	at Pittsburgh	1-6
	7	Carolina	0-3		18	Philadelphia	1-4

* – Overtime † – Shootout

Entry Draft
Selections 2006-1992

2006 Pick		2002 Pick		1998 Pick		1994 Pick	
7	Kyle Okposo	22	Sean Bergenheim	9	Mike Rupp	9	Brett Lindros
60	Jesse Joensuu	87	Frans Nielsen	36	Chris Nielsen	38	Jason Holland
70	Robin Figren	149	Marcus Paulsson	95	Andy Burnham	63	Jason Strudwick
100	Rhett Rakhshani	189	Alexei Stonkus	123	Jiri Dopita	90	Brad Lukowich
108	Jase Weslosky	220	Brad Topping	155	Kevin Clauson	112	Mark McArthur
115	Tomas Marcinko	252	Martin Chabada	182	Evgeny Korolev	116	Albert O'Connell
119	Doug Rogers	283	Per Braxenholm	209	Frederik Brindamour	142	Jason Stewart
126	Shane Sims			237	Ben Blais	194	Mike Loach
141	Kim Johansson	**2001 Pick**		242	Jason Doyle	203	Peter Hogardh
160	Andrew Macdonald	101	Cory Stillman	250	Radek Matejovsky	220	Gord Walsh
171	Brian Day	132	Dusan Salficky			246	Kirk Dewaele
173	Stefan Ridderwall	166	Andy Chiodo	**1997 Pick**		272	Dick Tarnstrom
190	Troy Mattila	197	Jan Holub	4	Roberto Luongo		
		228	Mike Bray	5	Eric Brewer	**1993 Pick**	
2005 Pick		260	Bryan Perez	31	Jeff Zehr	23	Todd Bertuzzi
15	Ryan O'Marra	280	Roman Kuhtinov	59	Jarrett Smith	40	Bryan McCabe
46	Dustin Kohn	287	Juha-Pekka Ketola	79	Robert Schnabel	66	Vladimir Chebaturkin
76	Shea Guthrie			85	Petr Mika	92	Warren Luhning
144	Masi Marjamaki	**2000 Pick**		115	Adam Ediger	118	Tommy Salo
180	Tyrell Mason	1	Rick DiPietro	139	Bobby Leavins	144	Peter LeBoutillier
196	Nicholas Tuzzolino	5	Raffi Torres	166	Kris Knoblauch	170	Darren Van Impe
210	Luciano Aquino	101	Arto Tukio	196	Jeremy Symington	196	Rod Hinks
		105	Vladimir Gorbunov	222	Ryan Clark	222	Daniel Johansson
2004 Pick		136	Dmitri Upper			248	Stephane Larocque
16	Petteri Nokelainen	148	Kristofer Ottosson	**1996 Pick**		274	Carl Charland
47	Blake Comeau	202	Ryan Caldwell	3	J.P. Dumont		
82	Sergei Ogorodnikov	264	Dmitri Altarev	29	Dan LaCouture	**1992 Pick**	
115	Wes O'Neill	267	Tomi Pettinen	56	Zdeno Chara	5	Darius Kasparaitis
148	Steve Regier			83	Tyrone Garner	56	Jarrett Deuling
179	Jaroslav Mrazek	**1999 Pick**		109	Bubba Berenzweig	104	Thomas Klimt
210	Emil Axelsson	5	Tim Connolly	128	Petr Sachl	105	Ryan Duthie
227	Chris Campoli	8	Taylor Pyatt	138	Todd Miller	128	Derek Armstrong
244	Jason Pitton	10	Branislav Mezei	165	J.R. Prestifilippo	152	Vladimir Grachev
276	Sylvain Michaud	28	Kristian Kudroc	192	Evgeny Korolev	159	Steve O'Rourke
		78	Mattias Weinhandl	218	Mike Muzechka	176	Jason Widmer
2003 Pick		87	Brian Collins			200	Daniel Paradis
15	Robert Nilsson	101	Juraj Kolnik	**1995 Pick**		224	David Wainwright
48	Dmitri Chernykh	102	Johan Halvardsson	2	Wade Redden	248	Andrei Vasilyev
53	Evgeny Tunik	130	Justin Mapletoft	28	Jan Hlavac		
58	Jeremy Colliton	140	Adam Johnson	41	D.J. Smith		
120	Stefan Blaho	163	Bjorn Melin	106	Vladimir Orszagh		
182	Bruno Gervais	228	Radek Martinek	158	Andrew Taylor		
212	Denis Rehak	255	Brett Henning	210	David MacDonald		
238	Cody Blanshan	268	Tyler Scott	211	Mike Broda		
246	Igor Volkov						

General Managers' History

Bill Torrey, 1972-73 to 1991-92; Don Maloney, 1992-93 to 1994-95; Don Maloney and Mike Milbury, 1995-96; Mike Milbury, 1996-97 to 2005-06; Neil Smith and Garth Snow, 2006-07.

General Manager

SNOW, GARTH
General Manager, New York Islanders. Born in Wrentham, MA, July 28, 1969.

Former Islanders goaltender Garth Snow retired as a player to become the new general manager of the New York Islanders on July 18, 2006. As Islanders g.m., Snow will be the point person for trades and oversee the pro scouting department. Snow becomes part of a hockey operations staff that includes head coach Ted Nolan, player development director Bryan Trottier, chief amateur scout Tony Feltrin and pro scouting director Ken Morrow.

The 2005-06 season marked Snow's fourth with the Islanders and 12th in the NHL. The goaltender was 135-147-44 with a 2.80 goals-against average and .901 save percentage over 368 games with Quebec, Philadelphia, Vancouver, Pittsburgh and the Islanders. Originally selected in the sixth round by Quebec in the 1987 NHL Entry Draft, the native of Wrentham, Mass. signed with the Islanders as a free agent on July 1, 2001.

Club Directory

Nassau Veterans' Memorial Coliseum

New York Islanders Executive Office
1535 Old Country Rd.
Plainview, NY 11803
Phone **516/501-6700**
FAX 516/501-6850
www.newyorkislanders.com
Arena
Nassau Veterans'
Memorial Coliseum
Uniondale, NY 11553
Capacity: 16,234

Owner & Governor . . . . Charles B. Wang

Operations
Sr. Vice President/Chief Financial Officer/
& Alt. Govenor . . . . Arthur McCarthy
Sr. Vice President of Sports Properties/
& Alt. Govenor . . . . Mike Milbury
General Manager/& Alt. Govenor . . . . Garth Snow
Sr. Vice President of Public Relations
and Special Projects . . . . Paul Lancey
Executive Director of Player Personnel . . . . Bryan Trottier

Hockey Operations
Assistant General Manager/
Director of Amateur Scouting . . . . Ryan Jankowski
Manager Hockey Administration . . . . Joanne Holewa
Assistant to General Manager . . . . Kerry Gwydir
Head Coach . . . . Ted Nolan
Assistant Coaches . . . . Daniel Flynn, Daniel Lacroix
Head Athletic Trainer . . . . Garrett Timms
Assistant Athletic Trainer . . . . Nates Goto
Director of Pro Scouting . . . . Ken Morrow
Equipment Manager . . . . Scott Boggs
Assistant Equipment Manager . . . . Richard Krouse
Equipment Assistant . . . . Tom Kitz
Director of Medical Services . . . . Dr. Elliot Pellman
Chief European Scout . . . . Veli-Pekka Kautonen
Scouts . . . . Tony Feltrin, Anders Kallur, Al MacPherson,
Chris O'Sullivan, Karel Pavlik, Mario Saracen

Administration
General Counsel & Alt. Govenor . . . . Roy Reichbach
Assistant General Counsel . . . . Jaimie Wolf
Staff Attorney . . . . Ivy Shen
Human Resources Manager . . . . Mary Molloy
Executive Assistant . . . . Jackie Kraemer
IT Manager . . . . Pawel Tauter
Receptionist . . . . Bonnie Dreher

Finance
Controller . . . . Ralph Sellitti
Assistant Controllers . . . . Jeff LaBonte, Marina Pi
Payroll Manager . . . . Christine Bowler
Payroll Assistant . . . . Michelle Finkelstein
Accounts Payable . . . . Janet Nelson
Staff Accountants . . . . Laura Ferretti, Christopher Vardaro
Accounting Assistant . . . . Nicole Lorenzo
Ticket Manager . . . . Adam Ortiz
Assistant Ticket Manager . . . . Karen Stepnowski

Communications
Vice President of Communications . . . . Chris Botta
Media Relations Coordinator . . . . Corey Witt
Website/Publications Coordinator . . . . Jason Lockhart
Radio Broadcasters . . . . Chris King, Steve Mears
Office Assistant . . . . Todd Aronovitch

Marketing Services
Director of Marketing Services . . . . Jessica Sousa
Creative Services Manager . . . . Thomas Rakoczy
Marketing Account Manager . . . . . . Mary Cedeno, Suzanne Keller
Copywriter . . . . Andrew Miller
Video Production Manager . . . . Susan Schopp

Game Operations
Vice President of Games Operations and Events . . . Tim Beach
Game Operations Manager . . . . Mike Sciortino
Avid Editor . . . . Brian Jones

Marketing
Vice President of Marketing and
Communications, I TV . . . . Joshua Bernstein
Producer, I TV . . . . Victor Francois, Matthew Holota
Associate Producer, I TV . . . . Laura Marciano

Sales
Vice President of Sponsorship . . . . Dave Decina
Vice President of Ticket Sales . . . . John Davis
Sr. Director of Sales . . . . Sean Argaman
Corporate Partnerships Account Manager . . . . . . Steve Beisel, Robert Cohen,
Christopher Lombardo
Corporate Partnership Services Manager . . . . Michelle Winter
Corporate Partnerships Coordinator . . . . Lauren Andrich, Catie Bennett
Corporate Partnerships Assistant . . . . Lori Ogden
Corporate Sales Manager . . . . Doug Cohen
Corporate Account Reps . . . . Steve Alexander, Mike Assortato,
Matthew Chierchie, Bryan Davis,
Robert Felice, Eddie Fisher, Kevin Fox,
Marc Gerstein, Jeff Guida, Tony James,
Rich Pascullo, Adam Robertson, Joe Varrone
Manager of Group Sales . . . . Cliff Gault
Group Sales Representative . . . . Shannon Geerlings, Adam Jacobs,
Christine Myers
Fan Development Manager . . . . Kerry Cornils
Fan Development Representatives . . . . TJ Carpenter, Mike Surrey, Dan Pascullo,
Keith Mitchell
Community Relations Manager . . . . Dana Cipriano
Director of Grassroots Hockey . . . . Steve Webb
Community Relations Coordinator . . . . Nicole D'Addario
Alumni/Community Development . . . . Bob Nystrom
Merchandise Director . . . . Terry Goldstein
Merchandise Assistant . . . . Teressa Farino

Henrik Lundqvist notched 30 victories in 2005-06, breaking the Rangers' rookie record for wins in a season (29), previously held by Jim Henry (1941-42) and Johnny Bower (1953-54).

New York Rangers

2005-06 Results: 44W-26L-8OTL-4SOL 100PTS.
Third, Atlantic Division

Year-by-Year Record

		Home				Road				Overall								
Season	**GP**	**W**	**L**	**T**	**OL**	**W**	**L**	**T**	**OL**	**W**	**L**	**T**	**OL**	**GF**	**GA**	**Pts.**	**Finished**	**Playoff Result**
2005-06	82	25	10	....	6	19	16	....	6	44	26	....	12	257	215	100	3rd, Atlantic Div.	Lost Conf. Quarter-Final
2004-05	....	....	....	....	....	....	....	....	....	....	....	....	....	....	....	....		
2003-04	82	13	21	3	4	14	19	4	4	27	40	7	8	206	250	69	4th, Atlantic Div.	Out of Playoffs
2002-03	82	17	18	4	2	15	18	6	2	32	36	10	4	210	231	78	4th, Atlantic Div.	Out of Playoffs
2001-02	82	19	19	2	1	17	19	2	3	36	38	4	4	227	258	80	4th, Atlantic Div.	Out of Playoffs
2000-01	82	17	20	3	1	16	23	2	0	33	43	5	1	250	290	72	4th, Atlantic Div.	Out of Playoffs
1999-2000	82	15	20	5	1	14	18	7	2	29	38	12	3	218	246	73	4th, Atlantic Div.	Out of Playoffs
1998-99	82	17	19	5	....	16	19	6	....	33	38	11	....	217	227	77	4th, Atlantic Div.	Out of Playoffs
1997-98	82	14	18	9	....	11	21	9	....	25	39	18	....	197	231	68	5th, Atlantic Div.	Out of Playoffs
1996-97	82	21	14	6	....	17	20	4	....	38	34	10	....	258	231	86	4th, Atlantic Div.	Lost Conf. Final
1995-96	82	22	10	9	....	19	17	5	....	41	27	14	....	272	237	96	2nd, Atlantic Div.	Lost Conf. Semi-Final
1994-95	48	11	10	3	....	11	13	0	....	22	23	3	....	139	134	47	4th, Atlantic Div.	Lost Conf. Semi-Final
1993-94	**84**	**28**	**8**	**6**	....	**24**	**16**	**2**	....	**52**	**24**	**8**	....	**299**	**231**	**112**	**1st, Atlantic Div.**	**Won Stanley Cup**
1992-93	84	20	17	5	....	14	22	6	....	34	39	11	....	304	308	79	6th, Patrick Div.	Out of Playoffs
1991-92	80	28	8	4	....	22	17	1	....	50	25	5	....	321	246	105	1st, Patrick Div.	Lost Div. Final
1990-91	80	22	11	7	....	14	20	6	....	36	31	13	....	297	265	85	2nd, Patrick Div.	Lost Div. Semi-Final
1989-90	80	20	11	9	....	16	20	4	....	36	31	13	....	279	267	85	1st, Patrick Div.	Lost Div. Final
1988-89	80	21	17	2	....	16	18	6	....	37	35	8	....	310	307	82	3rd, Patrick Div.	Lost Div. Semi-Final
1987-88	80	22	13	5	....	14	21	5	....	36	34	10	....	300	283	82	5th, Patrick Div.	Out of Playoffs
1986-87	80	18	18	4	....	16	20	4	....	34	38	8	....	307	323	76	4th, Patrick Div.	Lost Div. Semi-Final
1985-86	80	20	18	2	....	16	20	4	....	36	38	6	....	280	276	78	4th, Patick Div.	Lost Conf. Championship
1984-85	80	16	18	6	....	10	26	4	....	26	44	10	....	295	345	62	4th, Patrick Div.	Lost Div. Semi-Final
1983-84	80	27	12	1	....	15	17	8	....	42	29	9	....	314	304	93	4th, Patrick Div.	Lost Div. Semi-Final
1982-83	80	24	13	3	....	11	22	7	....	35	35	10	....	306	287	80	4th, Patrick Div.	Lost Div. Final
1981-82	80	19	15	6	....	20	12	8	....	39	27	14	....	316	306	92	2nd, Patrick Div.	Lost Div. Final
1980-81	80	17	13	10	....	13	23	4	....	30	36	14	....	312	317	74	4th, Patrick Div.	Lost Semi-Final
1979-80	80	22	10	8	....	16	22	2	....	38	32	10	....	308	284	86	3rd, Patrick Div.	Lost Quarter-Final
1978-79	80	19	13	8	....	21	16	3	....	40	29	11	....	316	292	91	3rd, Patrick Div.	Lost Final
1977-78	80	18	15	7	....	12	22	6	....	30	37	13	....	279	280	73	4th, Patrick Div.	Lost Prelim. Round
1976-77	80	17	18	5	....	12	19	9	....	29	37	14	....	272	310	72	4th, Patrick Div.	Out of Playoffs
1975-76	80	16	16	8	....	13	26	1	....	29	42	9	....	262	333	67	4th, Patrick Div.	Out of Playoffs
1974-75	80	21	11	8	....	16	18	6	....	37	29	14	....	319	276	88	2nd, Patrick Div.	Lost Prelim. Round
1973-74	78	26	7	6	....	14	17	8	....	40	24	14	....	300	251	94	3rd, East Div.	Lost Semi-Final
1972-73	78	26	8	5	....	21	15	3	....	47	23	8	....	297	208	102	3rd, East Div.	Lost Semi-Final
1971-72	78	26	6	7	....	22	11	6	....	48	17	13	....	317	192	109	2nd, East Div.	Lost Final
1970-71	78	30	2	7	....	19	16	4	....	49	18	11	....	259	177	109	2nd, East Div.	Lost Semi-Final
1969-70	76	22	8	8	....	16	14	8	....	38	22	16	....	246	189	92	4th, East Div.	Lost Quarter-Final
1968-69	76	27	7	4	....	14	19	5	....	41	26	9	....	231	196	91	3rd, East Div.	Lost Quarter-Final
1967-68	74	22	8	7	....	17	15	5	....	39	23	12	....	226	183	90	2nd, East Div.	Lost Quarter-Final
1966-67	70	18	12	5	....	12	16	7	....	30	28	12	....	188	189	72	4th,	Lost Semi-Final
1965-66	70	12	16	7	....	6	25	4	....	18	41	11	....	195	261	47	6th,	Out of Playoffs
1964-65	70	8	19	8	....	12	19	4	....	20	38	12	....	179	246	52	5th,	Out of Playoffs
1963-64	70	14	13	8	....	8	25	2	....	22	38	10	....	186	242	54	5th,	Out of Playoffs
1962-63	70	12	17	6	....	10	19	6	....	22	36	12	....	211	233	56	5th,	Out of Playoffs
1961-62	70	16	11	8	....	10	21	4	....	26	32	12	....	195	207	64	4th,	Lost Semi-Final
1960-61	70	15	15	5	....	7	23	5	....	22	38	10	....	204	248	54	5th,	Out of Playoffs
1959-60	70	10	15	10	....	7	23	5	....	17	38	15	....	187	247	49	6th,	Out of Playoffs
1958-59	70	14	16	5	....	12	16	7	....	26	32	12	....	201	217	64	5th,	Out of Playoffs
1957-58	70	14	15	6	....	18	10	7	....	32	25	13	....	195	188	77	2nd,	Lost Semi-Final
1956-57	70	15	12	8	....	11	18	6	....	26	30	14	....	184	227	66	4th,	Lost Semi-Final
1955-56	70	20	7	8	....	12	21	2	....	32	28	10	....	204	203	74	3rd,	Lost Semi-Final
1954-55	70	10	12	13	....	7	23	5	....	17	35	18	....	150	210	52	5th,	Out of Playoffs
1953-54	70	18	12	5	....	11	19	5	....	29	31	10	....	161	182	68	5th,	Out of Playoffs
1952-53	70	11	14	10	....	6	23	6	....	17	37	16	....	152	211	50	6th,	Out of Playoffs
1951-52	70	16	13	6	....	7	21	7	....	23	34	13	....	192	219	59	5th,	Out of Playoffs
1950-51	70	14	11	10	....	6	18	11	....	20	29	21	....	169	201	61	5th,	Out of Playoffs
1949-50	70	19	12	4	....	9	19	7	....	28	31	11	....	170	189	67	4th,	Lost Final
1948-49	60	13	12	5	....	5	19	6	....	18	31	11	....	133	172	47	6th,	Out of Playoffs
1947-48	60	11	12	7	....	10	14	6	....	21	26	13	....	176	201	55	4th,	Lost Semi-Final
1946-47	60	11	14	5	....	11	18	1	....	22	32	6	....	167	186	50	5th,	Out of Playoffs
1945-46	50	8	12	5	....	5	16	4	....	13	28	9	....	144	191	35	6th,	Out of Playoffs
1944-45	50	7	11	7	....	4	18	3	....	11	29	10	....	154	247	32	6th,	Out of Playoffs
1943-44	50	4	17	4	....	2	22	1	....	6	39	5	....	162	310	17	6th,	Out of Playoffs
1942-43	50	7	13	5	....	4	18	3	....	11	31	8	....	161	253	30	6th,	Out of Playoffs
1941-42	48	15	8	1	....	14	9	1	....	29	17	2	....	177	143	60	1st,	Lost Semi-Final
1940-41	48	13	7	4	....	8	12	4	....	21	19	8	....	143	125	50	4th,	Lost Quarter-Final
1939-40	**48**	**17**	**4**	**3**	....	**10**	**7**	**7**	....	**27**	**11**	**10**	....	**136**	**77**	**64**	**2nd,**	**Won Stanley Cup**
1938-39	48	13	8	3	....	13	8	3	....	26	16	6	....	149	105	58	2nd,	Lost Semi-Final
1937-38	48	15	5	4	....	12	10	2	....	27	15	6	....	149	96	60	2nd, Amn. Div.	Lost Quarter-Final
1936-37	48	9	7	8	....	10	13	1	....	19	20	9	....	117	106	47	3rd, Amn. Div.	Lost Final
1935-36	48	11	6	7	....	8	11	5	....	19	17	12	....	91	96	50	4th, Amn. Div.	Out of Playoffs
1934-35	48	11	8	5	....	11	12	1	....	22	20	6	....	137	139	50	3rd, Amn. Div.	Lost Semi-Final
1933-34	48	11	7	6	....	10	12	2	....	21	19	8	....	120	113	50	3rd, Amn. Div.	Lost Quarter-Final
1932-33	**48**	**12**	**7**	**5**	....	**11**	**10**	**3**	....	**23**	**17**	**8**	....	**135**	**107**	**54**	**3rd, Amn. Div.**	**Won Stanley Cup**
1931-32	48	13	7	4	....	10	10	4	....	23	17	8	....	134	112	54	1st, Amn. Div.	Lost Final
1930-31	44	10	9	3	....	9	7	6	....	19	16	9	....	106	87	47	3rd, Amn. Div.	Lost Semi-Final
1929-30	44	11	5	6	....	6	12	4	....	17	17	10	....	136	143	44	3rd, Amn. Div.	Lost Semi-Final
1928-29	44	12	6	4	....	9	7	6	....	21	13	10	....	72	65	52	2nd, Amn. Div.	Lost Final
1927-28	**44**	**10**	**8**	**4**	....	**9**	**8**	**5**	....	**19**	**16**	**9**	....	**94**	**79**	**47**	**2nd, Amn. Div.**	**Won Stanley Cup**
1926-27	44	13	5	4	....	12	8	2	....	25	13	6	....	95	72	56	1st, Amn. Div.	Lost Quarter-Final

2006-07 Schedule

Oct.	Thu.	5	Washington
	Sat.	7	at Philadelphia
	Tue.	10	Philadelphia
	Thu.	12	Pittsburgh
	Sat.	14	at Buffalo
	Mon.	16	New Jersey
	Wed.	18	Nashville
	Sat.	21	at Toronto
	Wed.	25	Florida
	Sat.	28	at Phoenix
	Mon.	30	at Los Angeles
Nov.	Wed.	1	at Anaheim
	Thu.	2	at San Jose
	Sun.	5	Buffalo*
	Wed.	8	at Florida
	Fri.	10	at Atlanta
	Sat.	11	at Washington
	Tue.	14	New Jersey
	Wed.	15	at Carolina
	Sat.	18	at Pittsburgh
	Sun.	19	Tampa Bay
	Tue.	21	Carolina
	Sat.	25	at Pittsburgh
	Sun.	26	Buffalo
	Tue.	28	Atlanta
Dec.	Fri.	1	at Buffalo
	Sun.	3	NY Islanders*
	Thu.	7	Pittsburgh
	Sat.	9	at Ottawa*
	Sun.	10	Florida
	Tue.	12	at Philadelphia
	Thu.	14	at Dallas
	Sat.	16	at Toronto
	Sun.	17	New Jersey
	Tue.	19	NY Islanders
	Thu.	21	at Florida
	Sat.	23	at Tampa Bay
	Tue.	26	at NY Islanders
	Fri.	29	at Ottawa
	Sat.	30	Washington
Jan.	Tue.	2	at New Jersey
	Thu.	4	Philadelphia
	Sat.	6	at Montreal*
	Tue.	9	NY Islanders
	Thu.	11	Ottawa
	Sat.	13	Boston*
	Tue.	16	at New Jersey
	Sat.	20	Atlanta*
	Sat.	27	at Philadelphia*
	Mon.	29	at Boston
	Wed.	31	Toronto
Feb.	Sat.	3	at Tampa Bay
	Mon.	5	Detroit
	Tue.	6	at New Jersey
	Fri.	9	Tampa Bay
	Sat.	10	at Washington
	Thu.	15	at Carolina
	Sat.	17	Philadelphia*
	Sun.	18	Chicago*
	Tue.	20	at New Jersey
	Thu.	22	New Jersey
	Sat.	24	Columbus
	Tue.	27	Montreal
Mar.	Thu.	1	Pittsburgh
	Sat.	3	St. Louis*
	Mon.	5	NY Islanders
	Thu.	8	at NY Islanders
	Sat.	10	at Pittsburgh*
	Sun.	11	Carolina*
	Tue.	13	Ottawa
	Fri.	16	at Atlanta
	Sat.	17	Boston
	Mon.	19	Pittsburgh
	Wed.	21	Philadelphia
	Sat.	24	at Boston*
	Sun.	25	at NY Islanders*
	Tue.	27	at Montreal
	Sat.	31	at Philadelphia
Apr.	Sun.	1	Toronto
	Tue.	3	at NY Islanders
	Thu.	5	Montreal
	Sat.	7	at Pittsburgh

* Denotes afternoon game.

Franchise date: May 15, 1926

81st NHL Season

ATLANTIC DIVISION

2006-07 Player Personnel

FORWARDS	HT	WT	S	Place of Birth	Date	2005-06 Club
BETTS, Blair	6-3	207	L	Edmonton, Alta.	2/16/80	NY Rangers
BYERS, Dane	6-3	194	L	Nipawin, Sask.	2/21/86	Prince Albert-Hartford
CALLAHAN, Ryan	5-11	185	R	Rochester, NY	3/21/85	Guelph
CULLEN, Matt	6-1	205	L	Virginia, MN	11/2/76	Carolina
DAWES, Nigel	5-8	190	L	Winnipeg, Man.	2/9/85	Hartford
DUBINSKY, Brandon	6-1	224	L	Anchorage, AK	4/29/86	Portland (WHL)-Hartford
FALARDEAU, Lee	6-4	214	L	Midland, MI	7/22/83	Hartford-Charlotte
GRAHAM, Bruce	6-6	224	L	Moncton, N.B.	12/2/85	Hartford-Charlotte
HALL, Adam	6-3	210	R	Kalamazoo, MI	8/14/80	Nashville
HELMINEN, Dwight	5-10	191	L	Hancock, MI	6/22/83	Hartford
HOLLWEG, Ryan	5-11	213	L	Downey, CA	4/23/83	NY Rangers-Hartford
HOSSA, Marcel	6-3	220	L	Ilava, Czech.	10/12/81	NY Rangers
IMMONEN, Jarkko	5-11	202	R	Rantasalmi, Finland	4/19/82	NY Rangers-Hartford
JAGR, Jaromir	6-3	245	L	Kladno, Czech.	2/15/72	NY Rangers
JESSIMAN, Hugh	6-6	224	R	New York, NY	3/28/84	Hartford-Charlotte
KORPIKOSKI, Lauri	6-1	194	L	Turku, Finland	7/28/86	TPS Jr.-Suomi U20-TPS-Hartford
KOZAK, Rick	6-2	215	R	Winnipeg, Man.	8/19/85	Hartford-Charlotte
MOORE, Greg	6-1	230	R	Lisbon, ME	3/26/84	U. of Maine-Hartford
NYLANDER, Michael	6-1	193	L	Stockholm, Sweden	10/3/72	NY Rangers
ORR, Colton	6-3	225	R	Winnipeg, Man.	3/3/82	Boston-NY Rangers
ORTMEYER, Jed	6-0	193	R	Omaha, NE	9/3/78	NY Rangers
PRUCHA, Petr	6-0	170	R	Chrudim, Czech.	9/14/82	NY Rangers-Hartford
SHANAHAN, Brendan	6-3	218	R	Mimico, Ont.	1/23/69	Detroit
STRAKA, Martin	5-9	178	L	Plzen, Czech.	9/3/72	NY Rangers
WARD, Jason	6-2	204	R	Chapleau, Ont.	1/16/79	NY Rangers
WELLER, Craig	6-3	195	R	Calgary, Alta.	1/17/81	Hartford
DEFENSEMEN						
BARANKA, Ivan	6-3	200	L	Ilava, Czech.	5/19/85	Hartford
GIRARDI, Daniel	6-1	205	R	Welland, Ont.	4/29/84	Hartford-Charlotte
KASPARAITIS, Darius	5-11	218	L	Elektrenai, USSR	10/16/72	NY Rangers
LAMPMAN, Bryce	6-1	199	L	Rochester, MN	8/31/82	NY Rangers-Hartford
LIFFITON, David	6-2	210	L	Windsor, Ont.	10/18/84	NY Rangers-Hartford
MALIK, Marek	6-6	238	L	Ostrava, Czech.	6/24/75	NY Rangers
OZOLINSH, Sandis	6-3	220	L	Riga, Latvia	8/3/72	Anaheim-NY Rangers
PIKKARAINEN, Hannu	6-1	190	L	Helsinki, Finland	10/13/83	HIFK
POCK, Thomas	6-1	200	L	Klagenfurt, Austria	12/2/81	NY Rangers-Hartford
RACHUNEK, Karel	6-2	212	R	Gottwaldov/Zlin, Czech.	8/27/79	Yaroslavl
RICHTER, Martin	6-1	205	R	Prostejov, Czech.	12/6/77	Liberec
ROZSIVAL, Michal	6-2	210	R	Vlasim, Czech.	9/3/78	NY Rangers
TAYLOR, Jake	6-4	220	R	Rochester, MN	8/1/83	Hartford
TYUTIN, Fedor	6-2	204	L	Izhevsk, USSR	7/19/83	NY Rangers
WARD, Aaron	6-2	225	R	Windsor, Ont.	1/17/73	Carolina

GOALTENDERS	HT	WT	C	Place of Birth	Date	2005-06 Club
HOLT, Chris	6-2	218	L	Vancouver, B.C.	6/5/85	NY Rangers-Hartford-Charlotte
LUNDQVIST, Henrik	6-1	194	L	Are, Sweden	3/2/82	NY Rangers
MONTOYA, Al	6-1	194	L	Chicago, IL	2/13/85	Charlotte-Hartford
VALIQUETTE, Stephen	6-5	205	L	Etobicoke, Ont.	8/20/77	Yaroslavl
WEEKES, Kevin	6-1	209	L	Toronto, Ont.	4/4/75	NY Rangers

Coach

RENNEY, TOM
Coach, New York Rangers. Born in Cranbrook, B.C., March 1, 1955.

Tom Renney took over as interim coach of the New York Rangers on February 25, 2004. He was officially named the 33rd head coach in franchise history on July 6. In 2005-06, Renney guided the Rangers to their first playoff berth since 1996-97.

Renney joined the Rangers on July 31, 2000 as director of player personnel and was promoted to vice president, player development on June 21, 2002. In that position, he oversaw all facets of the team's amateur scouting operations, while also assisting with the professional scouting process and player development within the organization. Renney joined the Rangers coaching staff as an assistant coach on July 21, 2003.

From June of 1996 through November, 1997, Renney served as head coach of the Vancouver Canucks. Prior to his return to the National Hockey League in New York, Renney held the position of vice president and head coach of the Canadian national team. Renney rejoined the Canadian Hockey Association in May, 1998. He began his affiliation with the Canadian national team in 1992 and coached Canada's Olympic hockey team to a silver medal at the 1994 Winter Games in Lillehammer, Norway. Later that year, he served as an assistant coach on Team Canada's gold medal-winning team at the World Championships. He won silver again as an assistant coach at the 2005 World Championship. Previously, he won the Memorial Cup with the Kamloops Blazers in 1992.

Coaching Record

		Regular Season				Playoffs, Olympics or World Championships			
Year	Team	Games	W	L	O/T	Games	W	L	T
1990-91	Kamloops (WHL)	72	50	20	2	12	5	7	0
1991-92	Kamloops (WHL)	72	51	17	4	16	11	5	0
1993-94*	Canadian National	63	33	26	4	8	5	2	1
1994-95**	Canadian National	57	37	17	3	8	4	2	2
1995-96***	Canadian National	53	33	12	8	8	4	2	2
1996-97	**Vancouver (NHL)**	**82**	**35**	**40**	**7**	....	....	....	....
1997-98	**Vancouver (NHL)**	**19**	**4**	**13**	**2**	....	....	....	....
1999-00	Canadian National	56	27	23	6	....	....	....	....
2003-04	**NY Rangers (NHL)**	**20**	**5**	**15**	**0**	....	....	....	....
2004-05	**NY Rangers (NHL)**				Season Cancelled				
2005-06	**NY Rangers (NHL)**	**82**	**44**	**26**	**12**	**4**	**0**	**4**	
	NHL Totals	**203**	**88**	**94**	**21**	**4**	**0**	**4**	

* Olympics (silver medal)
** World Championships (bronze)
*** World Championships (silver)

2005-06 Scoring

* – rookie

Regular Season

Pos	#	Player	Team	GP	G	A	Pts	+/–	PIM	PP	SH	GW	S	%
R	68	Jaromir Jagr	NYR	82	54	69	123	34	72	24	0	9	368	14.7
C	92	Michael Nylander	NYR	81	23	56	79	31	76	6	0	4	172	13.4
L	82	Martin Straka	NYR	82	22	54	76	17	42	4	0	4	171	12.9
L	26	Martin Rucinsky	NYR	52	16	39	55	10	56	4	0	4	152	10.5
R	17	Petr Sykora	ANA	34	7	13	20	1	28	1	0	0	118	5.9
			NYR	40	16	15	31	5	22	7	0	0	112	14.3
			TOTAL	74	23	28	51	6	50	8	0	0	230	10.0
R	25	* Petr Prucha	NYR	68	30	17	47	3	32	16	0	2	130	23.1
C	20	Steve Rucchin	NYR	72	13	23	36	6	10	4	1	0	111	11.7
D	3	Michal Rozsival	NYR	82	5	25	30	35	90	3	0	3	115	4.3
R	14	Jason Ward	NYR	81	10	18	28	–4	44	0	2	1	125	8.0
D	51	* Fedor Tyutin	NYR	77	6	19	25	1	58	4	0	2	102	5.9
D	16	Tom Poti	NYR	73	3	20	23	16	70	2	0	2	122	2.5
D	24	Sandis Ozolinsh	ANA	17	3	3	6	–4	8	0	0	2	17	17.6
			NYR	19	3	11	14	2	20	2	0	0	41	7.3
			TOTAL	36	6	14	20	–2	28	2	0	2	58	10.3
C	18	* Dominic Moore	NYR	82	9	9	18	4	28	2	0	1	139	6.5
D	8	Marek Malik	NYR	74	2	16	18	28	78	0	0	2	70	2.9
L	81	Marcel Hossa	NYR	64	10	6	16	–6	28	3	0	0	105	9.5
C	19	Blair Betts	NYR	66	8	2	10	–10	24	0	1	0	94	8.5
R	41	Jed Ortmeyer	NYR	78	5	2	7	2	38	0	0	1	90	5.6
D	34	Jason Strudwick	NYR	65	3	4	7	–10	66	0	0	0	31	9.7
D	6	Darius Kasparaitis	NYR	67	0	6	6	7	97	0	0	0	48	0.0
L	44	* Ryan Hollweg	NYR	52	2	3	5	–3	84	0	0	0	32	6.3
D	24	* Maxim Kondratiev	NYR	29	1	2	3	–2	22	1	0	0	16	6.3
C	38	* Jarkko Immonen	NYR	6	2	0	2	–1	0	1	0	0	8	25.0
D	22	* Thomas Pock	NYR	8	1	1	2	–3	4	0	0	0	15	6.7
L	21	* Chad Wiseman	NYR	1	0	1	1	2	4	0	0	0	1	0.0
R	28	* Colton Orr	BOS	20	0	0	0	0	27	0	0	0	1	0.0
			NYR	15	0	1	1	1	44	0	0	0	0	0.0
			TOTAL	35	0	1	1	1	71	0	0	0	1	0.0
C	39	* Alexandre Giroux	NYR	1	0	0	0	–1	0	0	0	0	0	0.0
D	33	* Bryce Lampman	NYR	1	0	0	0	–1	2	0	0	0	1	0.0
D	55	* David Liffiton	NYR	1	0	0	0	0	2	0	0	0	0	0.0
L	17	Fedor Fedorov	NYR	3	0	0	0	0	6	0	0	0	2	0.0
C	15	Jeff Taffe	PHX	2	0	0	0	0	0	0	0	0	2	0.0
			NYR	2	0	0	0	0	0	0	0	0	1	0.0
			TOTAL	4	0	0	0	0	0	0	0	0	3	0.0

Goaltending

No.	Goaltender	GPI	Mins	Avg	W	L	OT	EN	SO	GA	SA	S%	G	A	PIM
40	* Chris Holt	1	10	0.00	0	0	0	0	0	0	2	1.000	0	0	0
30	* Henrik Lundqvist	53	3112	2.24	30	12	9	2	2	116	1485	.922	0	2	0
80	Kevin Weekes	32	1850	2.95	14	14	3	2	0	91	867	.895	0	1	4
	Totals	**82**	**4997**	**2.53**	**44**	**26**	**12**	**4**	**2**	**211**	**2358**	**.911**			

Playoffs

Pos	#	Player	Team	GP	G	A	Pts	+/–	PIM	PP	SH	GW	OT	S	%
C	19	Blair Betts	NYR	4	1	1	2	–1	2	0	0	0	0	4	25.0
C	20	Steve Rucchin	NYR	4	1	0	1	–2	0	1	0	0	0	9	11.1
R	25	* Petr Prucha	NYR	4	1	0	1	–3	0	1	0	0	0	6	16.7
R	41	Jed Ortmeyer	NYR	4	1	0	1	1	4	0	0	0	0	4	25.0
L	26	Martin Rucinsky	NYR	2	0	1	1	–1	2	0	0	0	0	5	0.0
R	68	Jaromir Jagr	NYR	3	0	1	1	0	2	0	0	0	0	10	0.0
C	92	Michael Nylander	NYR	4	0	1	1	–3	0	0	0	0	0	10	0.0
D	8	Marek Malik	NYR	4	0	1	1	–2	6	0	0	0	0	3	0.0
D	3	Michal Rozsival	NYR	4	0	1	1	–2	8	0	0	0	0	5	0.0
D	51	* Fedor Tyutin	NYR	4	0	1	1	–1	0	0	0	0	0	7	0.0
L	44	* Ryan Hollweg	NYR	4	0	1	1	–1	19	0	0	0	0	2	0.0
R	14	Jason Ward	NYR	1	0	0	0	0	2	0	0	0	0	1	0.0
R	28	* Colton Orr	NYR	1	0	0	0	0	2	0	0	0	0	0	0.0
D	6	Darius Kasparaitis	NYR	2	0	0	0	–1	0	0	0	0	0	1	0.0
D	24	Sandis Ozolinsh	NYR	3	0	0	0	–3	6	0	0	0	0	9	0.0
D	34	Jason Strudwick	NYR	3	0	0	0	–1	0	0	0	0	0	2	0.0
L	82	Martin Straka	NYR	4	0	0	0	–4	2	0	0	0	0	6	0.0
R	17	Petr Sykora	NYR	4	0	0	0	–5	0	0	0	0	0	9	0.0
D	16	Tom Poti	NYR	4	0	0	0	–4	2	0	0	0	0	7	0.0
L	81	Marcel Hossa	NYR	4	0	0	0	–1	6	0	0	0	0	6	0.0
C	18	* Dominic Moore	NYR	4	0	0	0	–1	2	0	0	0	0	8	0.0

Goaltending

No.	Goaltender	GPI	Mins	Avg	W	L	EN	SO	GA	SA	S%	G	A	PIM
80	Kevin Weekes	1	60	4.00	0	1	0	0	4	25	.840	0	0	2
30	* Henrik Lundqvist	3	177	4.41	0	3	0	0	13	79	.835	0	0	0
	Totals	**4**	**240**	**4.25**	**0**	**4**	**0**	**0**	**17**	**104**	**.837**			

Coaching History

Lester Patrick, 1926-27 to 1938-39; Frank Boucher, 1939-40 to 1947-48; Frank Boucher and Lynn Patrick, 1948-49; Lynn Patrick, 1949-50; Neil Colville, 1950-51; Neil Colville and Bill Cook, 1951-52; Bill Cook, 1952-53; Frank Boucher and Muzz Patrick, 1953-54; Muzz Patrick, 1954-55; Phil Watson, 1955-56 to 1958-59; Phil Watson and Alf Pike, 1959-60; Alf Pike, 1960-61; Doug Harvey, 1961-62; Muzz Patrick and Red Sullivan, 1962-63; Red Sullivan, 1963-64, 1964-65; Red Sullivan and Emile Francis, 1965-66; Emile Francis, 1966-67, 1967-68; Bernie Geoffrion and Emile Francis, 1968-69; Emile Francis, 1969-70 to 1972-73; Larry Popein and Emile Francis, 1973-74; Emile Francis, 1974-75; Ron Stewart and John Ferguson, 1975-76; John Ferguson, 1976-77; Jean-Guy Talbot, 1977-78; Fred Shero, 1978-79, 1979-80; Fred Shero and Craig Patrick, 1980-81; Herb Brooks, 1981-82 to 1983-84; Herb Brooks and Craig Patrick, 1984-85; Ted Sator, 1985-86; Ted Sator, Tom Webster and Phil Esposito, 1986-87; Michel Bergeron, 1987-88; Michel Bergeron and Phil Esposito, 1988-89; Roger Neilson, 1989-90 to 1991-92; Roger Neilson and Ron Smith, 1992-93; Mike Keenan, 1993-94; Colin Campbell, 1994-95 to 1996-97; Colin Campbell and John Muckler, 1997-98; John Muckler, 1998-99; John Muckler and John Tortorella, 1999-2000; Ron Low, 2000-01, 2001-02; Bryan Trottier and Glen Sather, 2002-03; Glen Sather and Tom Renney, 2003-04; Tom Renney, 2004-05 to date.

Club Records

Team

(Figures in brackets for season records are games played; records for fewest points, wins, ties, losses, goals, goals against are for 70 or more games)

Most Points **112** 1993-94 (84)
Most Wins **52** 1993-94 (84)
Most Ties **21** 1950-51 (70)
Most Losses **44** 1984-85 (80)
Most Goals **321** 1991-92 (80)
Most Goals Against **345** 1984-85 (80)
Fewest Points **47** 1965-66 (70)
Fewest Wins **17** 1952-53 (70), 1954-55 (70), 1959-60 (70)
Fewest Ties **4** 2001-02 (82)
Fewest Losses **17** 1971-72 (78)
Fewest Goals **150** 1954-55 (70)
Fewest Goals Against **177** 1970-71 (78)

Longest Winning Streak
Overall .... **10** Dec. 19/39-Jan. 13/40, Jan. 19-Feb. 10/73
Home .... **14** Dec. 19/39-Feb. 25/40
Away .... **7** Jan. 12-Feb. 12/35, Oct. 28-Nov. 29/78

Longest Undefeated Streak
Overall .... **19** Nov. 23/39-Jan. 13/40 (14 wins, 5 ties)
Home .... **26** Mar. 29/70-Jan. 31/71 (19 wins, 7 ties)
Away .... **11** Nov. 5/39-Jan. 13/40 (6 wins, 5 ties)

Longest Losing Streak
Overall .... **11** Oct. 30-Nov. 27/43
Home .... **7** Oct. 20-Nov. 14/76, Mar. 24-Apr. 14/93
Away .... **10** Oct. 30-Dec. 23/43, Feb. 2-Mar. 15/61

Longest Winless Streak
Overall .... **21** Jan. 23-Mar. 19/44 (17 losses, 4 ties)
Home .... **10** Jan. 30-Mar. 19/44 (7 losses, 3 ties)
Away .... **16** Oct. 9-Dec. 20/52 (12 losses, 4 ties)

Most Shutouts, Season **13** 1928-29 (44)
Most PIM, Season **2,018** 1989-90 (80)
Most Goals, Game .... **12** Nov. 21/71 (Cal. 1 at NYR 12)

Individual

Most Seasons .... **18** Rod Gilbert
Most Games .... **1,160** Harry Howell
Most Goals, Career .... **406** Rod Gilbert
Most Assists, Career .... **741** Brian Leetch
Most Points, Career .... **1,021** Rod Gilbert (406G, 615A)
Most PIM, Career .... **1,226** Ron Greschner
Most Shutouts, Career .... **49** Ed Giacomin
Longest Consecutive Games Streak .... **560** Andy Hebenton (Oct. 7/55-Mar. 24/63)
Most Goals, Season .... **54** Jaromir Jagr (2005-06)
Most Assists, Season .... **80** Brian Leetch (1991-92)
Most Points, Season .... **123** Jaromir Jagr (2005-06; 54G, 69A)
Most PIM, Season .... **305** Troy Mallette (1989-90)
Most Points, Defenseman, Season .... **102** Brian Leetch (1991-92; 22G, 80A)
Most Points, Center, Season .... **109** Jean Ratelle (1971-72; 46G, 63A)
Most Points, Right Wing, Season .... **123** Jaromir Jagr (2005-06; 54G, 69A)
Most Points, Left Wing, Season .... **106** Vic Hadfield (1971-72; 50G, 56A)
Most Points, Rookie, Season .... **76** Mark Pavelich (1981-82; 33G, 43A)
Most Shutouts, Season .... **13** John Ross Roach (1928-29)
Most Goals, Game .... **5** Don Murdoch (Oct. 12/76), Mark Pavelich (Feb. 23/83)
Most Assists, Game .... **5** Walt Tkaczuk (Feb. 12/72), Rod Gilbert (Mar. 2/75, Mar. 30/75, Oct. 8/76), Don Maloney (Jan. 3/87), Brian Leetch (Apr. 18/95), Wayne Gretzky (Feb. 15/99)
Most Points, Game .... **7** Steve Vickers (Feb. 18/76; 3G, 4A)

Retired Numbers

1	Ed Giacomin	1965-1975
7	Rod Gilbert	1960-1977
11	Mark Messier	1991-97; 2000-04
35	Mike Richter	1989-2003

All-time Record vs. Other Clubs

Regular Season

	At Home								On Road								Total							
	GP	W	L	T	OL	GF	GA	PTS	GP	W	L	T	OL	GF	GA	PTS	GP	W	L	T	OL	GF	GA	PTS
Anaheim	9	3	5	1	0	23	26	7	8	2	6	0	0	25	32	4	17	5	11	1	0	48	58	11
Atlanta	12	4	5	1	2	35	38	11	12	8	3	0	1	42	34	17	24	12	8	1	3	77	72	28
Boston	304	133	116	55	0	929	857	321	300	98	160	42	0	841	1081	238	604	231	276	97	0	1770	1938	559
Buffalo	68	29	24	15	0	220	186	73	70	20	40	10	0	216	284	50	138	49	64	25	0	436	470	123
Calgary	53	25	23	5	0	182	186	55	49	12	27	10	0	148	216	34	102	37	50	15	0	330	402	89
Carolina	47	28	14	4	1	177	120	61	45	16	26	3	0	141	155	35	92	44	40	7	1	318	275	96
Chicago	285	117	113	55	0	841	807	289	287	115	128	43	1	793	872	274	572	232	241	98	1	1634	1679	563
Colorado	35	19	10	4	2	135	101	44	35	13	18	3	1	130	143	30	70	32	28	7	3	265	244	74
Columbus	2	1	0	1	0	7	5	3	5	1	4	0	0	10	20	2	7	2	4	1	0	17	25	5
Dallas	62	36	15	11	0	213	165	83	61	30	19	11	1	221	187	72	123	66	34	22	1	434	352	155
Detroit	284	134	92	58	0	868	738	326	286	76	165	45	0	702	1008	197	570	210	257	103	0	1570	1746	523
Edmonton	31	11	14	6	0	117	117	28	28	13	12	3	0	94	101	29	59	24	26	9	0	211	218	57
Florida	26	14	8	4	0	82	59	32	27	14	9	2	2	75	70	32	53	28	17	6	2	157	129	64
Los Angeles	58	35	17	6	0	233	172	76	60	27	23	10	0	216	199	64	118	62	40	16	0	449	371	140
Minnesota	4	3	1	0	0	13	8	6	4	3	1	0	0	13	11	6	8	6	2	0	0	26	19	12
Montreal	292	118	119	54	1	839	852	291	292	61	191	40	0	674	1128	162	584	179	310	94	1	1513	1980	453
Nashville	6	2	2	1	1	18	15	6	5	3	1	0	1	19	14	7	11	5	3	1	2	37	29	13
New Jersey	88	43	25	20	0	334	262	106	90	35	47	7	1	289	311	78	178	78	72	27	1	623	573	184
NY Islanders	100	57	31	11	1	368	292	126	100	37	55	8	0	326	381	82	200	94	86	19	1	694	673	208
Ottawa	25	12	13	0	0	80	76	24	25	11	10	3	1	68	79	26	50	23	23	3	1	148	155	50
Philadelphia	114	48	40	23	3	364	336	122	113	42	56	14	1	313	366	99	227	90	96	37	4	677	702	221
Phoenix	29	18	9	2	0	128	102	38	31	14	13	4	0	101	107	32	60	32	22	6	0	229	209	70
Pittsburgh	105	54	42	9	0	407	352	117	104	45	41	14	4	381	371	108	209	99	83	23	4	788	723	225
St. Louis	60	44	10	6	0	245	143	94	64	29	25	10	0	207	192	68	124	73	35	16	0	452	335	162
San Jose	10	7	2	1	0	40	29	15	13	9	2	2	0	49	31	20	23	16	4	3	0	89	60	35
Tampa Bay	29	14	11	2	2	91	88	32	27	12	11	3	1	91	92	28	56	26	22	5	3	182	180	60
Toronto	285	122	106	56	1	882	840	301	284	85	159	39	1	746	978	210	569	207	265	95	2	1628	1818	511
Vancouver	55	38	12	5	0	239	142	81	51	33	15	3	0	204	163	69	106	71	27	8	0	443	305	150
Washington	84	40	34	9	1	312	287	90	86	33	43	9	1	276	323	76	170	73	77	18	2	588	610	166
Defunct Clubs	139	87	30	22	0	460	290	196	139	82	34	23	0	441	291	187	278	169	64	45	0	901	581	383
Totals	**2701**	**1296**	**943**	**447**	**15**	**8882**	**7691**	**3054**	**2701**	**979**	**1344**	**361**	**17**	**7852**	**9240**	**2336**	**5402**	**2275**	**2287**	**808**	**32**	**16734**	**16931**	**5390**

Playoffs

	Series	W	L	GP	W	L	T	GF	GA	Last Mtg.	Rnd.	Result
Boston	9	3	6	42	18	22	2	104	114	1973	QF	W 4-1
Buffalo	1	0	1	3	1	2	0	6	11	1978	PRE	L 1-2
Calgary	1	1	0	4	3	1	0	14	8	1980	PRE	W 3-1
Chicago	5	1	4	24	10	14	0	54	66	1973	SF	L 1-4
Colorado	1	1	0	6	4	2	0	25	19	1995	CQF	W 4-2
Detroit	5	1	4	23	10	13	0	49	57	1950	F	L 3-4
Florida	1	1	0	5	4	1	0	13	10	1997	CQF	W 4-1
Los Angeles	2	2	0	6	5	1	0	32	14	1981	PRE	W 3-1
Montreal	14	7	7	61	25	34	2	158	188	1996	CQF	W 4-2
New Jersey	4	3	1	23	12	11	0	60	63	2006	CQF	L 0-4
NY Islanders	8	3	5	39	19	20	0	132	129	1994	CQF	W 4-0
Philadelphia	10	4	6	47	20	27	0	153	157	1997	CF	L 1-4
Pittsburgh	3	0	3	15	3	12	0	45	64	1996	CSF	L 1-4
St. Louis	1	1	0	6	4	2	0	29	22	1981	QF	W 4-2
Toronto	8	5	3	35	19	16	0	86	86	1971	QF	W 4-2
Vancouver	1	1	0	7	4	3	0	21	19	1994	F	W 4-3
Washington	4	2	2	22	11	11	0	71	75	1994	CSF	W 4-1
Defunct Clubs	9	6	3	22	11	7	4	43	29			
Totals	**87**	**42**	**45**	**390**	**183**	**199**	**8**	**1095**	**1131**			

Calgary totals include Atlanta Flames, 1972-73 to 1979-80.
Carolina totals include Hartford, 1979-80 to 1996-97.
Colorado totals include Quebec, 1979-80 to 1994-95.
Dallas totals include Minnesota North Stars, 1967-68 to 1992-93.
New Jersey totals include Kansas City, 1974-75 to 1975-76, and Colorado Rockies, 1976-77 to 1981-82.
Phoenix totals include Winnipeg, 1979-80 to 1995-96.

Playoff Results 2006-2001

Year	Round	Opponent	Result	GF	GA
2006	CQF	New Jersey	L 0-4	4	17

Abbreviations: Round: F – Final;
CF – conference final; **CSF** – conference semi-final;
CQF – conference quarter-final; **SF** – semi-final;
QF – quarter-final; **PRE** – preliminary round.

2005-06 Results

Oct.	5	at Philadelphia	5-3
	6	Montreal	3-4*
	8	at New Jersey	2-3*
	10	at Washington	2-3
	13	New Jersey	4-1
	15	Atlanta	5-1
	17	Florida	4-0
	19	NY Islanders	2-3†
	20	at NY Islanders	4-5
	22	at Buffalo	1-3
	27	NY Islanders	3-1
	29	at Montreal	5-2
	31	Montreal	1-4
Nov.	3	at New Jersey	4-2
	5	New Jersey	3-2†
	7	Pittsburgh	2-3
	9	at Florida	4-3†
	10	at Tampa Bay	5-2
	12	at Pittsburgh	6-1
	15	at Toronto	1-2
	17	at Carolina	1-5
	19	Carolina	4-3
	20	Boston	3-2
	22	at Buffalo	3-2†
	24	at Atlanta	6-3
	26	Washington	3-2†
Dec.	1	Pittsburgh	2-1
	3	at Washington	1-5
	5	Minnesota	3-1
	7	at Chicago	1-2*
	8	at Nashville	5-1
	10	at St. Louis	5-4*
	13	Vancouver	2-3
	18	Colorado	1-2
	20	New Jersey	1-3
	22	Tampa Bay	4-2
	26	at Ottawa	2-6
	28	at NY Islanders	6-2
	31	at Pittsburgh	3-4*
Jan.	3	Tampa Bay	0-1*
	5	Philadelphia	3-4*
	7	Florida	4-0
	10	Calgary	4-2
	12	Edmonton	5-4*
	14	at Detroit	3-4
	16	at Columbus	3-4
	19	at Pittsburgh	4-2
	21	at Boston	3-2†
	22	New Jersey	3-1
	24	Buffalo	1-2
	28	Pittsburgh	7-1
	30	Philadelphia	2-3*
Feb.	1	Pittsburgh	3-1
	2	at NY Islanders	5-2
	4	at Philadelphia	4-3*
	8	Ottawa	5-1
	10	Toronto	4-2
	11	at Toronto	4-2
Mar.	2	at Philadelphia	6-1
	4	at New Jersey	1-2
	6	Carolina	1-2
	8	at Atlanta	2-3†
	11	at Montreal	0-1
	12	Atlanta	2-3*
	14	at Carolina	3-5
	16	Washington	5-4
	18	Toronto	5-2
	20	Boston	5-2
	22	Philadelphia	3-6
	24	at Florida	2-3†
	25	at Tampa Bay	3-4†
	27	Buffalo	5-4†
	29	at NY Islanders	5-1
	30	at Ottawa	1-4
Apr.	4	Philadelphia	3-2†
	6	NY Islanders	3-1
	8	at Boston	4-3*
	9	at New Jersey	2-3
	11	NY Islanders	2-3
	13	at Pittsburgh	3-5
	15	at Philadelphia	1-4
	18	Ottawa	1-5

* – Overtime † – Shootout

Entry Draft
Selections 2006-1992

2006
Pick
21 Bobby Sanguinetti
54 Artem Anisimov
84 Ryan Hillier
104 David Kveton
137 Tomas Zaborsky
174 Eric Hunter
204 Lukas Zeliska

2005
Pick
12 Marc Staal
40 Michael Sauer
56 Marc-Andre Cliche
66 Brodie Dupont
77 Dalyn Flatt
107 Tom Pyatt
147 Trevor Koverko
178 Greg Beller
211 Ryan Russell

2004
Pick
6 Al Montoya
19 Lauri Korpikoski
36 Darin Olver
48 Dane Byers
51 Bruce Graham
60 Brandon Dubinsky
73 Zdenek Bahensky
80 Billy Ryan
127 Ryan Callahan
135 Roman Psurny
169 Jordan Foote
247 Jonathan Paiement
266 Jakub Petruzalek

2003
Pick
12 Hugh Jessiman
50 Ivan Baranka
75 Ken Roche
122 Corey Potter
149 Nigel Dawes
176 Ivan Dornic
179 Philippe Furrer
180 Chris Holt
209 Dylan Reese
243 Jan Marek

2002
Pick
33 Lee Falardeau
81 Marcus Jonasen
127 Nate Guenin
143 Mike Walsh
177 Jake Taylor
194 Kim Hirschovits
226 Joey Crabb
240 Petr Prucha
270 Rob Flynn

2001
Pick
10 Dan Blackburn
40 Fedor Tyutin
79 Garth Murray
113 Bryce Lampman
139 Shawn Collymore
176 Marek Zidlicky
206 Petr Preucil
226 Pontus Petterstrom
226 Pontus Petterstrom
230 Leonid Zhvachkin
238 Ryan Hollweg
269 Juris Stals

2000
Pick
64 Filip Novak
95 Dominic Moore
112 Premysl Duben
140 Nathan Martz
143 Brandon Snee
175 Sven Helfenstein
205 Henrik Lundqvist
238 Danny Eberly
269 Martin Richter

1999
Pick
4 Pavel Brendl
9 Jamie Lundmark
59 David Inman
79 Johan Asplund
90 Patrick Aufiero
137 Garrett Bembridge
177 Jay Dardis
197 Arto Laatikainen
226 Yevgeny Gusakov
251 Petter Henning
254 Alexei Bulatov

1998
Pick
7 Manny Malhotra
40 Randy Copley
66 Jason Labarbera
114 Boyd Kane
122 Patrick Leahy
131 Tomas Kloucek
180 Stefan Lundqvist
207 Johan Witehall
235 Jan Mertzig

1997
Pick
19 Stefan Cherneski
46 Wes Jarvis
73 Burke Henry
93 Tomi Kallarsson
126 Jason McLean
134 Johan Lindbom
136 Mike York
154 Shawn Degagne
175 Johan Holmqvist
182 Mike Mottau
210 Andrew Proskurnicki
236 Richard Miller

1996
Pick
22 Jeff Brown
48 Daniel Goneau
76 Dmitri Subbotin
131 Colin Pepperall
158 Ola Sandberg
185 Jeff Dessner
211 Ryan McKie
237 Ronnie Sundin

1995
Pick
39 Christian Dube
65 Mike Martin
91 Marc Savard
110 Alexei Vasiliev
117 Dale Purinton
143 Peter Slamiar
169 Jeff Heil
195 Ilya Gorokhov
221 Bob Maudie

1994
Pick
26 Dan Cloutier
52 Rudolf Vercik
78 Adam Smith
100 Alexander Korobolin
104 Sylvain Blouin
130 Martin Ethier
135 Yuri Litvinov
156 David Brosseau
182 Alexei Lazarenko
208 Craig Anderson
209 Vitali Yeremeyev
234 Eric Boulton
260 Radoslav Kropac
267 Jamie Butt
286 Kim Johnsson

1993
Pick
8 Niklas Sundstrom
34 Lee Sorochan
61 Maxim Galanov
86 Sergei Olimpiyev
112 Gary Roach
138 Dave Trofimenkoff
162 Sergei Kondrashkin
164 Todd Marchant
190 Ed Campbell
216 Ken Shepard
242 Andrei Kudinov
261 Pavel Komarov
268 Maxim Smelnitsky

1992
Pick
24 Peter Ferraro
48 Mattias Norstrom
72 Eric Cairns
85 Chris Ferraro
120 Dmitri Starostenko
144 David Dal Grande
168 Matt Oates
192 Mickey Elick
216 Daniel Brierley
240 Vladimir Vorobiev

President and General Manager

SATHER, GLEN
President/General Manager, New York Rangers.
Born in High River, Alta., September 2, 1943.

Glen Sather, who spent parts of four seasons with the New York Rangers as a player from 1970 to 1974, became the franchise's 12th president and tenth general manager on June 2, 2000. He also served as coach of the team from January 30, 2003, to February 25, 2004.

Sather joined the Rangers following a 24-year career with the Edmonton Oilers, where he was the architect of five Stanley Cup championships between 1984 and 1990. One of the most respected executives in the National Hockey League, Sather was honored for his tremendous achievements in 1997 by becoming the first member of the Oilers organization to be selected to the Hockey Hall of Fame.

Named coach and vice president of hockey operations for the Oilers when the franchise joined the NHL in June of 1979, Sather became general manager and club president in May of 1980. He coached through the 1988-89 season and also returned for 60 games behind the bench in 1993-94. Sather-coached teams won the Stanley Cup four times in the 1980s. As general manager, Sather was instrumental in the Oilers' fifth Cup triumph in 1990.

He played for six different teams during a 10-year NHL career. He scored 80 goals in 658 games.

NHL Coaching Record

Season	Team	Games	Regular Season W	L	T	Playoffs Games	W	L
1979-80	Edmonton	80	28	39	13	3	0	3
1980-81	Edmonton	62	25	26	11	9	5	4
1981-82	Edmonton	80	48	17	15	5	2	3
1982-83	Edmonton	80	47	21	12	16	11	5
1983-84*	Edmonton	80	57	18	5	19	15	4
1984-85*	Edmonton	80	49	20	11	18	15	3
1985-86	Edmonton	80	56	17	7	10	6	4
1986-87*	Edmonton	80	50	24	6	21	16	5
1987-88*	Edmonton	80	44	25	11	18	16	2
1988-89	Edmonton	80	38	34	8	7	3	4
1993-94	Edmonton	60	22	27	11	....	....	....
2002-03	NY Rangers	28	11	13	4	....	....	....
2003-04	NY Rangers	62	22	33	7	....	....	....
NHL Totals		**932**	**497**	**314**	**121**	**126**	**89**	**37**

* Stanley Cup win.

Club Directory

Madison Square Garden

New York Rangers
14th Floor
2 Pennsylvania Plaza
New York, New York 10121
Phone **212/465-6486**
PR FAX 212/465-6494
www.newyorkrangers.com
Capacity: 18,200

Team Executive Management
Chairman, Madison Square Garden . . . . James L. Dolan
Vice Chairman, Madison Square Garden . . . . Hank J. Ratner
President and COO, MSG Sports . . . . Steve Mills
President and General Manager . . . . Glen Sather

Hockey Administration
President and General Manager . . . . Glen Sather
Assistant G.M. and V.P. Player Personnel . . . . Don Maloney
V.P. Hockey Administration, R & D . . . . Cameron Hope
Manager of Scouting . . . . Victor Saljanin
Executive Assistant to the Pres. and G.M. . . . . Sara Adamson

Coaching
Head Coach . . . . Tom Renney
Assistant Coaches . . . . Perry Pearn, Mike Pelino, Benoit Allaire
Video Coach . . . . Jerry Dineen

Training
Manager, Training Center Operations . . . . Pat Boller
Head Athletic Trainer . . . . Jim Ramsay
Equipment Manager . . . . Acacio Marques
Assistant Equipment Manager . . . . James "Beets" Johnson
Massage Therapist and Assistant Trainer . . . . Bruce Lifrieri
Strength and Conditioning Coach . . . . Reg Grant
Strength and Conditioning Advisor . . . . Daniel Hedin
Mental Skills Coach . . . . John Phelan

Scouting
Pro Scouting Staff . . . . Frank Effinger, Gilles Leger, Peter Stephan
Assistant Director of Player Personnel . . . . Tim Murray
Head Amateur Scout . . . . Gordie Clark
Director of Player Personnel Europe . . . . Christer Rockstrom
Amateur Scouting Staff . . . . Andre Beaulieu, Rich Brown, Ray Clearwater, Pierre Dorion, Jan Gajdosik, Earnie Gare, Vladimir Lutchenko, Shanon Sather

Medical
Team Physician and Orthopedic Surgeon . . . . Dr. Andrew Feldman
Assistant Team Physician . . . . Dr. Tony Maddalo
Medical Consultant . . . . Dr. Ron Weissman
Team Dentists . . . . Dr. Joe Esposito, Dr. Don Salomon, Dr. Jeff Shapiro

Community Relations
V.P, Community Relations & Fan Development . . . . Kerryann Tomlinson
Dir., Special Projects & Community Relations Rep. . . Rod Gilbert
Special Assistant, Prospect Development
and Community Relations . . . . Adam Graves

Marketing
Vice President, Marketing . . . . Jeanie Baumgartner
Vice President, Marketing Services . . . . Janet Duch
Director, Event Presentation . . . . Ryan Halkett
Manager, Event Presentation . . . . Damian Santucci
Manager, Internet Marketing and Development . . . Dan David

Public Relations
Vice President, Public Relations . . . . John Rosasco
Director, Public Relations . . . . Sammy Steinlight
Manager, Public Relations . . . . Jody Sowa
Coordinator, Public Relations . . . . David Martella

Sponsorships
Vice President, Team Sponsorships . . . . Rob Scolaro
Manager, Team Sponsorships . . . . Kelly Jutras
Coordinator, Team Sponsorships . . . . Nathan Finkel

MSG Teams Advertising and Design
Design Director . . . . Joanecy Kagalingan
Art Director . . . . Anthony Spera

Sports Team Operations
Senior Vice President, Sports Team Operations . . . . Mark Piazza
Vice President, Sports Team Operations . . . . Jason Vogel

Team Finance
Senior Vice President, Finance and Controller . . . . . John Cudmore
Manager, Accounting . . . . Jeanine McGrory

Miscellaneous
Television Network . . . . MSG Network
Radio Network . . . . MSG Radio
Manager, Fan Development . . . . Adam Evert

General Managers' History

Lester Patrick, 1926-27 to 1945-46; Frank Boucher, 1946-47 to 1954-55; Muzz Patrick, 1955-56 to 1963-64; Emile Francis, 1964-65 to 1974-75; Emile Francis and John Ferguson, 1975-76; John Ferguson, 1976-77, 1977-78; John Ferguson and Fred Shero, 1978-79; Fred Shero, 1979-80; Fred Shero and Craig Patrick, 1980-81; Craig Patrick, 1981-82 to 1985-86; Phil Esposito, 1986-87 to 1988-89; Neil Smith, 1989-90 to 1999-2000; Glen Sather, 2000-01 to date.

Captains' History

Bill Cook, 1926-27 to 1936-37; Art Coulter, 1937-38 to 1941-42; Ott Heller, 1942-43 to 1944-45; Neil Colville 1945-46 to 1948-49; Buddy O'Connor, 1949-50; Frank Eddolls, 1950-51; Frank Eddolls and Allan Stanley, 1951-52; Allan Stanley, 1952-53; Allan Stanley and Don Raleigh, 1953-54; Don Raleigh, 1954-55; Harry Howell, 1955-56, 1956-57; Red Sullivan, 1957-58 to 1960-61; Andy Bathgate, 1961-62, 1962-63; Andy Bathgate and Camille Henry, 1963-64; Camille Henry and Bob Nevin, 1964-65; Bob Nevin 1965-66 to 1970-71; Vic Hadfield, 1971-72 to 1973-74; Brad Park, 1974-75; Brad Park and Phil Esposito, 1975-76; Phil Esposito, 1976-77, 1977-78; Dave Maloney, 1978-79, 1979-80; Dave Maloney, Walt Tkaczuk and Barry Beck, 1980-81; Barry Beck, 1981-82 to 1985-86; Ron Greschner, 1986-87; Ron Greschner and Kelly Kisio, 1987-88; Kelly Kisio, 1988-89 to 1990-91; Mark Messier, 1991-92 to 1996-97; Brian Leetch, 1997-98 to 1999-2000; Mark Messier, 2000-01 to 2003-04; no captain, 2005-06.

Ottawa Senators

2005-06 Results: 52w-21L-3OTL-6SOL 113PTS.
First, Northeast Division

Year-by-Year Record

Season	GP	Home W	L	T	OL	Road W	L	T	OL	Overall W	L	T	OL	GF	GA	Pts.	Finished	Playoff Result
2005-06	82	29	9	....	3	23	12	....	6	52	21	....	9	314	211	113	1st, Northeast Div.	Lost Conf. Semi-Final
2004-05	....	....				....				....								
2003-04	82	23	8	5	5	20	15	5	1	43	23	10	6	262	189	102	3rd, Northeast Div.	Lost Conf. Quarter-Final
2002-03	82	28	9	3	1	24	12	5	0	52	21	8	1	263	182	113	1st, Northeast Div.	Lost Conf. Championship
2001-02	82	21	13	3	4	18	14	6	3	39	27	9	7	243	208	94	3rd, Northeast Div.	Lost Conf. Semi-Final
2000-01	82	26	7	5	3	22	14	4	1	48	21	9	4	274	205	109	1st, Northeast Div.	Lost Conf. Quarter-Final
1999-2000	82	24	10	5	2	17	18	6	0	41	28	11	2	244	210	95	2nd, Northeast Div.	Lost Conf. Quarter-Final
1998-99	82	22	11	8	....	22	12	7	....	44	23	15	....	239	179	103	1st, Northeast Div.	Lost Conf. Quarter-Final
1997-98	82	18	16	7	....	16	17	8	....	34	33	15	....	193	200	83	5th, Northeast Div.	Lost Conf. Semi-Final
1996-97	82	16	17	8	....	15	19	7	....	31	36	15	....	226	234	77	3rd, Northeast Div.	Lost Conf. Quarter-Final
1995-96	82	8	28	5	....	10	31	0	....	18	59	5	....	191	291	41	6th, Northeast Div.	Out of Playoffs
1994-95	48	5	16	3	....	4	18	2	....	9	34	5	....	117	174	23	7th, Northeast Div.	Out of Playoffs
1993-94	84	8	30	4	....	6	31	5	....	14	61	9	....	201	397	37	7th, Northeast Div.	Out of Playoffs
1992-93	84	9	29	4	....	1	41	0	....	10	70	4	....	202	395	24	6th, Adams Div.	Out of Playoffs

2006-07 Schedule

Oct.	Wed.	4	at Toronto	Wed.	3	Buffalo	
	Thu.	5	Toronto	Sat.	6	New Jersey*	
	Sat.	7	Buffalo	Sun.	7	Philadelphia*	
	Thu.	12	Calgary	Tue.	9	Boston	
	Sat.	14	at Montreal	Thu.	11	at NY Rangers	
	Thu.	19	Colorado	Sat.	13	Montreal*	
	Sat.	21	New Jersey	Tue.	16	Washington	
	Tue.	24	at Toronto	Thu.	18	Vancouver	
	Thu.	26	Toronto	Sat.	20	at Boston	
	Sat.	28	at Boston	Sat.	27	Boston*	
	Tue.	31	at Montreal	Mon.	29	at Montreal	
Nov.	Sat.	4	Carolina	Tue.	30	Washington	
	Mon.	6	at Washington	**Feb.** Sat.	3	Toronto	
	Wed.	8	at Atlanta	Wed.	7	at Buffalo	
	Fri.	10	at Pittsburgh	Thu.	8	Montreal	
	Sat.	11	at Boston	Sat.	10	at Montreal	
	Mon.	13	Montreal	Wed.	14	Florida	
	Wed.	15	at Buffalo	Sat.	17	Atlanta*	
	Fri.	17	at New Jersey	Tue.	20	Edmonton	
	Sat.	18	Buffalo	Thu.	22	at Buffalo	
	Mon.	20	Minnesota	Sat.	24	Buffalo	
	Wed.	22	at Philadelphia	Tue.	27	at Carolina	
	Fri.	24	at Florida	Wed.	28	Carolina	
	Sun.	26	at Tampa Bay*	**Mar.** Fri.	2	at Atlanta	
	Tue.	28	at Carolina	Sun.	4	at Chicago*	
	Thu.	30	Florida	Tue.	6	Pittsburgh	
Dec.	Sat.	2	Tampa Bay	Thu.	8	Toronto	
	Tue.	5	at NY Islanders	Sat.	10	at Toronto	
	Wed.	6	at Washington	Tue.	13	at NY Rangers	
	Sat.	9	NY Rangers*	Thu.	15	NY Islanders	
	Sun.	10	at Columbus	Sat.	17	Philadelphia	
	Tue.	12	at Detroit	Sun.	18	at Pittsburgh	
	Thu.	14	at Nashville	Tue.	20	at St. Louis	
	Sat.	16	at Buffalo	Thu.	22	at Florida	
	Tue.	19	Boston	Sat.	24	at Tampa Bay	
	Thu.	21	Tampa Bay	Tue.	27	Boston	
	Sat.	23	at Philadelphia*	Fri.	30	Montreal	
	Wed.	27	NY Islanders	Sat.	31	at NY Islanders	
	Fri.	29	NY Rangers	**Apr.** Tue.	3	at New Jersey	
	Sat.	30	at Toronto	Thu.	5	Pittsburgh	
Jan.	Mon.	1	Atlanta*	Sat.	7	at Boston	

* Denotes afternoon game.

Though injuries limited him to just 68 games in 2005-06, Jason Spezza collected 90 points on 19 goals and 71 assists. Only Art Ross Trophy winner Joe Thornton (96) had more assists than Spezza.

Franchise date: December 16, 1991

EASTERN
NHL
CONFERENCE

NORTHEAST DIVISION

15th NHL Season

2006-07 Player Personnel

FORWARDS

	HT	WT	S	Place of Birth	Date	2005-06 Club
ALFREDSSON, Daniel	5-11	208	R	Goteborg, Sweden	12/11/72	Ottawa
EAVES, Patrick	6-0	192	R	Calgary, Alta.	5/1/84	Ottawa-Binghamton
FISHER, Mike	6-1	211	R	Peterborough, Ont.	6/5/80	Ottawa
HAMEL, Denis	6-1	201	L	Lachute, Que.	5/10/77	Ottawa-Binghamton
HEATLEY, Dany	6-3	215	L	Freiburg, West Germany	1/21/81	Ottawa
HENNESSY, Josh	6-0	190	L	Brockton, MA	2/7/85	Cleveland
KELLY, Chris	6-0	190	L	Toronto, Ont.	11/11/80	Ottawa
McAMMOND, Dean	5-11	200	L	Grand Cache, Alta.	6/15/73	St. Louis
McGRATTAN, Brian	6-5	238	R	Hamilton, Ont.	9/2/81	Ottawa
NEIL, Chris	6-0	213	R	Markdale, Ont.	6/18/79	Ottawa
PAYER, Serge	6-0	191	L	Rockland, Ont.	5/7/79	Florida
SCHAEFER, Peter	5-11	195	L	Yellow Grass, Sask.	7/12/77	Ottawa
SPEZZA, Jason	6-2	206	R	Mississauga, Ont.	6/13/83	Ottawa
VERMETTE, Antoine	6-1	193	L	St-Agapit, Que.	7/20/82	Ottawa

DEFENSEMEN

	HT	WT	S	Place of Birth	Date	2005-06 Club
ALLISON, Jamie	6-1	210	L	Lindsay, Ont.	5/13/75	Nashville-Florida
CORVO, Joe	6-1	205	R	Oak Park, IL	6/20/77	Los Angeles
HEDLUND, Andy	6-3	215	L	Osseo, MN	5/16/78	Krefeld
MESZAROS, Andrej	6-2	215	L	Povazska Bystrica, Czech.	10/13/85	Ottawa
PHILLIPS, Chris	6-3	215	L	Calgary, Alta.	3/9/78	Ottawa
PREISSING, Tom	6-0	205	R	Arlington Heights, IL	12/3/78	San Jose
REDDEN, Wade	6-2	212	L	Lloydminster, Sask.	6/12/77	Ottawa
SCHUBERT, Christoph	6-3	210	L	Munich, West Germany	2/5/82	Ottawa
VOLCHENKOV, Anton	6-1	227	L	Moscow, USSR	2/25/82	Ottawa

GOALTENDERS

	HT	WT	C	Place of Birth	Date	2005-06 Club
EMERY, Ray	6-2	198	L	Cayuga, Ont.	9/28/82	Ottawa
GERBER, Martin	6-0	185	L	Burgdorf, Switz.	9/3/74	Carolina

2005-06 Scoring

*– rookie

Regular Season

Pos	#	Player	Team	GP	G	A	Pts	+/-	PIM	PP	SH	GW	S	%
L	15	Dany Heatley	OTT	82	50	53	103	29	86	23	2	7	300	16.7
R	11	Daniel Alfredsson	OTT	77	43	60	103	29	50	16	5	8	249	17.3
C	19	Jason Spezza	OTT	68	19	71	90	23	33	7	0	5	156	12.2
L	27	Peter Schaefer	OTT	82	20	30	50	16	40	4	4	2	137	14.6
D	6	Wade Redden	OTT	65	10	40	50	35	63	8	0	4	153	6.5
C	21	Bryan Smolinski	OTT	81	17	31	48	8	46	4	0	5	178	9.6
C	10	Tyler Arnason	CHI	60	13	28	41	5	40	5	0	1	161	8.1
			OTT	19	0	4	4	-4	4	0	0	0	42	0.0
			TOTAL	79	13	32	45	1	44	5	0	1	203	6.4
C	12	Mike Fisher	OTT	68	22	22	44	23	64	2	4	3	150	14.7
D	3	Zdeno Chara	OTT	71	16	27	43	17	135	10	1	3	212	7.5
D	14 *	Andrej Meszaros	OTT	82	10	29	39	34	61	5	0	2	137	7.3
D	2	Brian Pothier	OTT	77	5	30	35	29	59	3	0	0	133	3.8
C	20	Antoine Vermette	OTT	82	21	12	33	17	44	1	6	4	123	17.1
R	25	Chris Neil	OTT	79	16	17	33	9	204	8	0	0	126	12.7
C	22 *	Chris Kelly	OTT	82	10	20	30	21	76	1	0	2	112	8.9
R	44 *	Patrick Eaves	OTT	58	20	9	29	7	22	5	1	4	100	20.0
L	26	Vaclav Varada	OTT	76	5	16	21	2	50	1	0	0	114	4.4
D	4	Chris Phillips	OTT	69	1	18	19	19	90	0	0	0	79	1.3
D	24	Anton Volchenkov	OTT	75	4	13	17	20	53	0	0	0	82	4.9
R	9	Martin Havlat	OTT	18	9	7	16	6	4	2	1	1	57	15.8
D	5 *	Christoph Schubert	OTT	56	4	6	10	4	48	0	1	0	72	5.6
R	16 *	Brian McGrattan	OTT	60	2	3	5	0	141	0	0	0	36	5.6
C	36	Steve Martins	OTT	4	1	1	2	2	0	0	0	0	6	16.7
C	45	Denis Hamel	OTT	4	1	0	1	1	0	0	0	0	9	11.1
D	42	Tomas Malec	OTT	2	0	0	0	4	2	0	0	0	1	0.0
D	33	Brad Norton	OTT	7	0	0	0	1	31	0	0	0	3	0.0
D	17 *	Filip Novak	OTT	11	0	0	0	-2	4	0	0	0	5	0.0

Goaltending

No.	Goaltender	GPI	Mins	Avg	W	L	OT	EN	SO	GA	SA	S%	G	A	PIM
39	Dominik Hasek	43	2584	2.09	28	10	4	1	5	90	1202	.925	0	0	16
1	* Ray Emery	39	2168	2.82	23	11	4	0	3	102	1045	.902	0	1	2
30	Mike Morrison	4	207	3.48	1	0	1	0	0	12	96	.875	0	0	0
	Totals	82	4975	2.47	52	21	9	1	8	205	2344	.913			

Playoffs

Pos	#	Player	Team	GP	G	A	Pts	+/-	PIM	PP	SH	GW	OT	S	%
C	19	Jason Spezza	OTT	10	5	9	14	-1	2	3	0	1	0	23	21.7
R	9	Martin Havlat	OTT	10	7	6	13	0	4	3	0	1	0	27	25.9
L	15	Dany Heatley	OTT	10	3	9	12	1	11	3	0	1	0	32	9.4
D	6	Wade Redden	OTT	9	2	8	10	-2	10	2	0	1	0	19	10.5
R	11	Daniel Alfredsson	OTT	10	2	8	10	2	4	1	0	0	0	24	8.3
L	27	Peter Schaefer	OTT	10	2	5	7	2	14	0	0	0	0	18	11.1
C	21	Bryan Smolinski	OTT	10	3	3	6	3	2	1	0	0	0	23	13.0
C	12	Mike Fisher	OTT	10	2	2	4	1	12	0	1	0	0	20	10.0
D	3	Zdeno Chara	OTT	10	1	3	4	0	23	1	0	0	0	17	5.9
D	24	Anton Volchenkov	OTT	9	0	4	4	1	2	0	0	0	0	10	0.0
D	2	Brian Pothier	OTT	8	2	1	3	1	2	0	0	0	0	10	20.0
D	4	Chris Phillips	OTT	9	2	0	2	-2	6	0	0	0	0	8	25.0
C	20	Antoine Vermette	OTT	10	2	0	2	-1	4	0	0	1	0	17	11.8
L	26	Vaclav Varada	OTT	8	0	2	2	-2	12	0	0	0	0	7	0.0
R	25	Chris Neil	OTT	10	1	0	1	-1	14	0	0	0	0	10	10.0
R	44 *	Patrick Eaves	OTT	10	1	0	1	-3	10	0	0	0	0	20	5.0
D	14 *	Andrej Meszaros	OTT	10	1	0	1	0	18	0	0	0	0	17	5.9
D	5 *	Christoph Schubert	OTT	7	0	1	1	3	4	0	0	0	0	4	0.0
C	22 *	Chris Kelly	OTT	10	0	0	0	-4	2	0	0	0	0	14	0.0

Goaltending

No.	Goaltender	GPI	Mins	Avg	W	L	EN	SO	GA	SA	S%	G	A	PIM
1	* Ray Emery	10	604	2.88	5	5	0	0	29	289	.900	0	1	0
	Totals	10	608	2.86	5	5	0	0	29	289	.900			

General Manager

MUCKLER, JOHN
General Manager, Ottawa Senators. Born in Midland, Ont., April 3, 1934.

John Muckler was named the sixth general manager in Senators history on June 12, 2002. Prior to his arrival in Ottawa, Muckler served as coach of the New York Rangers from 1997-98 to 1999-2000. Previously, he was general manager of the Buffalo Sabres from 1993 to 1997, and was named NHL executive of the year by *The Sporting News* for the 1996-97 season. Muckler is the first g.m. hired by the Senators to have previous NHL experience as a general manager.

Working for Glen Sather, Muckler enjoyed Edmonton's great 1980s run. He was an assistant coach with the Stanley Cup winners in 1984 and 1985, and designated co-coach during the 1987 and 1988 championship seasons. When Sather gave up the Oilers' coaching reins in 1989, Muckler stepped in and led the team to its fifth Stanley Cup in seven years. In 1991, he left the Oilers for the Buffalo Sabres.

Muckler has been involved in professional hockey since the 1949-50 season. He was a defenseman in the minor leagues for 13 seasons, playing the bulk of his career in the old Eastern Hockey League. His professional coaching career began while he was still a player in 1959 when he took over the New York Rovers of the EHL. He had great success with the team in the 1960s when they were known as the Long Island Ducks. Muckler joined the Minnesota North Stars after NHL expansion in 1967 and spent six seasons in the organization, mostly as a coach and g.m. in the minor leagues. His first NHL coaching job came with the North Stars midway through the 1968-69 season. He later worked in the Rangers and Canucks organizations before joining the Oilers as coach of their Wichita farm club in 1981.

NHL Coaching Record

Season	Team		Regular Season					Playoffs		
		Games	W	L	T		Games	W	L
1968-69	Minnesota	35	6	23	6		....	....	....
1989-90*	Edmonton	80	38	28	14		22	16	6
1990-91	Edmonton	80	37	37	6		18	9	9
1991-92	Buffalo	52	22	22	8		7	3	4
1992-93	Buffalo	84	38	36	10		8	4	4
1993-94	Buffalo	84	43	32	9		7	3	4
1994-95	Buffalo.	48	22	19	7		5	1	4
1997-98	NY Rangers	25	8	15	2		....	....	....
1998-99	NY Rangers	82	33	38	11		....	....	....
1999-2000	NY Rangers	78	29	38	11		....	....	....
	NHL Totals	648	276	288	84		67	36	31

* Stanley Cup win.

General Managers' History

Mel Bridgman, 1992-93; Randy Sexton, 1993-94, 1994-95; Randy Sexton and Pierre Gauthier, 1995-96; Pierre Gauthier, 1996-97, 1997-98; Rick Dudley, 1998-99; Marshall Johnston, 1999-2000 to 2001-02; John Muckler, 2002-03 to date.

Club Records

Team

(Figures in brackets for season records are games played; records for fewest points, wins, ties, losses, goals, goals against are for 70 or more games)

Most Points 113   2002-03 (82), 2005-06 (82)
Most Wins 52   2002-03 (82), 2005-06 (82)
Most Ties 15   1996-97 (82), 1997-98 (82), 1998-99 (82)
Most Losses 70   1992-93 (84)
Most Goals 314   2005-06 (82)
Most Goals Against 397   1993-94 (84)
Fewest Points 24   1992-93 (84)
Fewest Wins 10   1992-93 (84)
Fewest Ties 4   1992-93 (84)
Fewest Losses 21   2000-01 (82), 2002-03 (82), 2005-06 (82)
Fewest Goals 191   1995-96 (82)
Fewest Goals Against 179   1998-99 (82)
Longest Winning Streak
  Overall 7   Oct. 25-Nov. 13/01
  Home 8   Nov. 14-Dec. 14/02
  Away 6   Mar. 18-Apr. 5/03
Longest Undefeated Streak
  Overall 11   Three times
  Home 12   Dec. 18/03-Jan. 24/04 (10 wins, 2 ties)
  Away 7   Three times

** NHL records do not include neutral site games

Longest Losing Streak
  Overall 14   Mar. 2-Apr. 7/93
  Home . . . . *11   Oct. 27-Dec. 8/93
  Away . . . . *38   Oct. 10/92-Apr. 3/93**
Longest Winless Streak
  Overall 21   Oct. 10-Nov. 23/92 (20 losses, 1 tie)
  Home . . . . *17   Oct. 28/95-Jan. 27/96 (15 losses, 2 ties)
  Away . . . . *38   Oct. 10/92-Apr. 3/93 (38 losses)
Most Shutouts, Season 10   2001-02 (82)
Most PIM, Season 1,716   1992-93 (84)
Most Goals, Game 11   Nov. 13/01 (Ott. 11 at Wsh. 5)

Individual

Most Seasons 10   Radek Bonk, Daniel Alfredsson
Most Games, Career 706   Daniel Alfredsson
Most Goals, Career 262   Daniel Alfredsson
Most Assists, Career 409   Daniel Alfredsson
Most Points, Career 671   Daniel Alfredsson (262G, 409A)
Most PIM, Career 776   Chris Neil
Most Shutouts, Career 30   Patrick Lalime
Longest Consecutive
  Games Streak 292   Alexei Yashin (Dec. 31/95-Apr. 17/99)

Most Goals, Season 50   Dany Heatley (2005-06)
Most Assists, Season 71   Jason Spezza (2005-06)
Most Points, Season 103   Dany Heatley (2005-06; 50G, 53A), Daniel Alfredsson (2005-06; 43G, 60A)
Most PIM, Season 318   Mike Peluso (1992-93)
Most Points, Defenseman, Season 63   Norm Maciver (1992-93; 17G, 46A)
Most Points, Center, Season 94   Alexei Yashin (1998-99; 44G, 50A)
Most Points, Right Wing, Season 103   Daniel Alfredsson (2005-06; 43G, 60A)
Most Points, Left Wing, Season 103   Dany Heatley (2005-06; 50G, 53A)
Most Points, Rookie, Season 79   Alexei Yashin (1993-94; 30G, 49A)
Most Shutouts, Season 8   Patrick Lalime (2002-03)
Most Goals, Game 4   Four times
Most Assists, Game 5   Marian Hossa (Jan. 4/01)
Most Points, Game 6   Dan Quinn (Oct. 15/95; 3G, 3A), Radek Bonk (Jan. 4/01; 3G, 3A), Daniel Alfredsson (Nov. 2/05; 4G, 2A)

* NHL Record.

Retired Numbers

8   Frank Finnigan   1924-1934

Coaching History

Rick Bowness, 1992-93 to 1994-95; Rick Bowness, Dave Allison and Jacques Martin, 1995-96; Jacques Martin, 1996-97 to 2000-01; Jacques Martin and Roger Neilson, 2001-02; Jacques Martin, 2002-03, 2003-04; Bryan Murray, 2004-05 to date.

Captains' History

Laurie Boschman, 1992-93; Brad Shaw, Mark Lamb and Gord Dineen, 1993-94; Randy Cunneyworth, 1994-95 to 1997-98; Alexei Yashin, 1998-99; Daniel Alfredsson, 1999-2000 to date.

All-time Record vs. Other Clubs

Regular Season

	At Home								On Road								Total							
	GP	W	L	T	OL	GF	GA	PTS	GP	W	L	T	OL	GF	GA	PTS	GP	W	L	T	OL	GF	GA	PTS
Anaheim	9	4	3	1	1	27	23	10	9	3	4	2	0	18	21	8	18	7	7	3	1	45	44	18
Atlanta	12	7	2	1	2	54	32	17	12	8	2	1	1	51	40	18	24	15	4	2	3	105	72	35
Boston	35	16	16	3	0	91	104	35	37	10	21	5	1	101	135	26	72	26	37	8	1	192	239	61
Buffalo	37	13	14	7	3	93	95	36	35	9	20	3	3	66	111	24	72	22	34	10	6	159	206	60
Calgary	10	5	1	3	1	27	24	14	12	4	6	1	1	26	40	10	22	9	7	4	2	53	64	24
Carolina	31	13	12	4	2	88	82	32	29	8	17	4	0	72	87	20	60	21	29	8	2	160	169	52
Chicago	10	4	5	0	1	31	30	9	8	2	4	2	0	18	18	6	18	6	9	2	1	49	48	15
Colorado	18	8	7	3	0	53	64	19	16	3	12	1	0	47	72	7	34	11	19	4	0	100	136	26
Columbus	3	2	0	1	0	12	6	5	2	1	0	1	0	9	7	3	5	3	0	2	0	21	13	8
Dallas	10	4	6	0	0	22	26	8	11	4	7	0	0	28	44	8	21	8	13	0	0	50	70	16
Detroit	10	3	5	1	1	28	29	8	9	3	5	0	1	19	33	7	19	6	10	1	2	47	62	15
Edmonton	10	3	4	2	0	19	26	8	12	3	7	2	0	30	42	8	22	6	12	4	0	49	68	16
Florida	24	11	10	2	1	69	66	25	24	13	10	1	0	75	73	27	48	24	20	3	1	144	139	52
Los Angeles	10	5	3	1	1	35	29	12	10	1	8	1	0	21	46	3	20	6	11	2	1	56	75	15
Minnesota	2	1	1	0	0	4	4	2	4	2	1	1	0	14	11	5	6	3	2	1	0	18	15	7
Montreal	35	18	16	1	0	104	95	37	37	13	19	4	1	105	110	31	72	31	35	5	1	209	205	68
Nashville	5	4	1	0	0	15	7	8	4	2	2	0	0	11	8	4	9	6	3	0	0	26	15	12
New Jersey	26	7	14	3	2	54	67	19	25	9	13	2	1	61	71	21	51	16	27	5	3	115	138	40
NY Islanders	25	15	5	5	0	88	65	35	26	15	5	6	0	99	82	36	51	30	10	11	0	187	147	71
NY Rangers	25	11	11	3	0	79	68	25	25	13	12	0	0	76	80	26	50	24	23	3	0	155	148	51
Philadelphia	26	9	11	6	0	71	79	24	25	8	15	2	0	69	83	18	51	17	26	8	0	140	162	42
Phoenix	12	5	6	1	0	38	36	11	10	5	4	1	0	36	38	11	22	10	10	2	0	74	70	22
Pittsburgh	29	10	14	5	0	80	91	25	29	8	16	4	1	75	102	21	58	18	30	9	1	155	193	46
St. Louis	10	4	6	0	0	23	36	8	9	3	4	2	0	25	27	8	19	7	10	2	0	48	63	16
San Jose	10	4	2	4	0	36	28	12	9	4	5	0	0	16	18	8	19	8	7	4	0	52	46	20
Tampa Bay	25	17	6	1	1	96	55	34	25	15	8	2	0	88	71	32	50	32	16	3	1	184	126	66
Toronto	24	16	6	1	1	81	63	34	26	13	11	2	0	76	68	28	50	29	17	3	1	157	131	62
Vancouver	10	5	3	1	1	24	24	12	12	5	5	1	1	28	36	12	22	10	8	2	*2	52	60	24
Washington	25	13	10	1	1	91	72	28	26	11	11	4	0	76	79	26	51	24	21	5	1	167	151	54
Totals	**518**	**237**	**203**	**60**	**18**	**1531**	**1426**	**552**	**518**	**198**	**254**	**55**	**11**	**1438**	**1649**	**462**	**1036**	**435**	**457**	**115**	**29**	**2969**	**3075**	**1014**

Playoffs

	Series	W	L	GP	W	L	T	GF	GA	Last Mtg.	Rnd.	Result
Buffalo	3	0	3	16	4	12	0	32	42	2006	CSF	L 1-4
New Jersey	2	1	1	13	7	6	0	26	29	2003	CF	L 3-4
NY Islanders	1	1	0	5	4	1	0	13	7	2003	CQF	W 4-1
Philadelphia	2	2	0	11	8	3	0	28	12	2003	CSF	W 4-2
Tampa Bay	1	1	0	5	4	1	0	23	13	2006	CQF	W 4-1
Toronto	4	0	4	24	8	16	0	42	57	2004	CQF	L 3-4
Washington	1	0	1	5	1	4	0	7	18	1998	CSF	L 1-4
Totals	**14**	**5**	**9**	**79**	**36**	**43**	**0**	**171**	**178**			

Playoff Results 2006-2001

Year	Round	Opponent	Result	GF	GA
2006	CSF	Buffalo	L 1-4	13	16
	CQF	Tampa Bay	W 4-1	23	13
2004	CQF	Toronto	L 3-4	11	14
2003	CF	New Jersey	L 3-4	13	17
	CSF	Philadelphia	W 4-2	17	10
	CQF	NY Islanders	W 4-1	13	7
2002	CSF	Toronto	L 3-4	18	16
	CQF	Philadelphia	W 4-1	11	2
2001	CQF	Toronto	L 0-4	3	10

Abbreviations: Round: CF – conference final; **CSF** – conference semi-final; **CQF** – conference quarter-final.

Colorado totals include Quebec, 1992-93 to 1994-95.
Dallas totals include Minnesota North Stars, 1992-93.

Carolina totals include Hartford, 1992-93 to 1996-97.
Phoenix totals include Winnipeg, 1992-93 to 1995-96.

2005-06 Results

Oct. 5 at Toronto 3-2†
8   Buffalo 5-0
10   Toronto 6-5†
11 at Montreal 4-2
15   Boston 5-1
21 at Tampa Bay 4-1
24 at Carolina 2-3
27   Montreal 4-3*
29 at Toronto 8-0
30   Philadelphia 3-5
Nov. 1   Tampa Bay 4-2
3   NY Islanders 6-0
5 at Boston 5-2
8   Buffalo 6-1
15   Carolina 1-2
17   Florida 4-1
19   New Jersey 5-4
22 at Carolina 5-3
25 at NY Islanders 6-2
26   Boston 4-2
29   Montreal 4-0
Dec. 1 at Boston 0-3
2   Los Angeles 5-1
5 at Florida 6-3
9 at Vancouver 2-3†
10 at Calgary 1-2*
12 at Colorado 6-2
15   Dallas 0-2
17   Toronto 8-2
20 at Montreal 3-4†
22 at Philadelphia 3-4
23 at NY Islanders 4-2
26   NY Rangers 6-2
28   Carolina 6-2
30   NY Islanders 4-3
Jan. 2 at Atlanta 3-8
4 at Washington 3-1
5 at Boston 2-4
7 at Montreal 1-4
10   Phoenix 7-2

12   San Jose 0-2
14 at Edmonton 5-3
16 at Minnesota 6-1
19   Anaheim 3-4†
21   Toronto 7-0
23   Toronto 4-3
26   Montreal 3-0
30   Boston 0-5
Feb. 1 at New Jersey 3-5
2 at Pittsburgh 7-2
4 at Buffalo 1-2†
6   Pittsburgh 5-2
8 at NY Rangers 1-5
9   Atlanta 1-2
11   Philadelphia 3-2
Mar. 1 at Pittsburgh 4-3
2   Washington 7-1
4 at Toronto 4-2
6 at Tampa Bay 4-0
8 at Florida 2-6
10 at Atlanta 3-1
12 at Washington 5-2
14   Tampa Bay 4-3
16 at Boston 2-3†
18   Buffalo 4-2
19 at New Jersey 4-0
21   Pittsburgh 5-2
24 at Buffalo 3-1
25 at Philadelphia 3-6
28   New Jersey 2-3†
30   NY Rangers 4-1
Apr. 1   Washington 0-1
3   Atlanta 6-4
5 at Buffalo 4-5*
6   Montreal 3-5
8   Buffalo 2-6
10 at Montreal 2-3
11   Boston 4-3*
13   Florida 4-5*
15 at Toronto 1-5
18 at NY Rangers 5-1

* – Overtime   † – Shootout

Entry Draft Selections 2006-1992

2006

Pick	
28	Nick Foligno
68	Eric Gryba
91	Kaspars Daugavins
121	Pierre-Luc Lessard
151	Ryan Daniels
181	Kevin Koopman
211	Erik Condra

2005

Pick	
9	Brian Lee
70	Vitali Anikeyenko
95	Cody Bass
98	Ilja Zubov
115	Janne Kolehmainen
136	Tomas Kudelka
186	Dmitri Megalinsky
204	Colin Greening

2004

Pick	
23	Andrej Meszaros
58	Kirill Lyamin
77	Shawn Weller
87	Peter Regin
89	Jeff Glass
122	Alexander Nikulin
141	Jim McKenzie
156	Roman Wick
219	Joe Cooper
251	Matthew McIlvane
284	John Wikner

2003

Pick	
29	Patrick Eaves
67	Igor Mirnov
100	Philippe Seydoux
135	Mattias Karlsson
142	Tim Cook
166	Sergei Gimaev
228	Will Colbert
260	Ossi Louhivaara
291	Brian Elliott

2002

Pick	
16	Jakub Klepis
47	Alexei Kaigorodov
75	Arttu Luttinen
113	Scott Dobben
125	Johan Bjork
150	Brock Hooton
246	Josef Vavra
276	Vitali Atyushov

2001

Pick	
2	Jason Spezza
23	Tim Gleason
81	Neil Komadoski
99	Ray Emery
127	Christoph Schubert
162	Stefan Schauer
193	Brooks Laich
218	Jan Platil
223	Brandon Bochenski
235	Neil Petruic
256	Gregg Johnson
286	Toni Dahlman

2000

Pick	
21	Anton Volchenkov
45	Mathieu Chouinard
55	Antoine Vermette
87	Jan Bohac
122	Derrick Byfuglien
156	Greg Zanon
157	Grant Potulny
158	Sean Connolly
188	Jason Maleyko
283	James Demone

1999

Pick	
26	Martin Havlat
48	Simon Lajeunesse
62	Teemu Sainomaa
94	Chris Kelly
154	Andrew Ianiero
164	Martin Prusek
201	Mikko Ruutu
209	Layne Ulmer
213	Alexandre Giroux
269	Konstantin Gorovikov

1998

Pick	
15	Mathieu Chouinard
44	Mike Fisher
58	Chris Bala
74	Julien Vauclair
101	Petr Schastlivy
130	Gavin McLeod
161	Chris Neil
188	Michel Periard
223	Sergei Verenikin
246	Rastislav Pavlikovsky

1997

Pick	
12	Marian Hossa
58	Jani Hurme
66	Josh Langfeld
119	Magnus Arvedson
146	Jeff Sullivan
173	Robin Bacul
203	Nick Gillis
229	Karel Rachunek

1996

Pick	
1	Chris Phillips
81	Antti-Jussi Niemi
136	Andreas Dackell
163	Francois Hardy
212	Erich Goldmann
216	Ivan Ciernik
239	Sami Salo

1995

Pick	
1	Bryan Berard
27	Marc Moro
53	Brad Larsen
89	Kevin Bolibruck
103	Kevin Boyd
131	David Hruska
183	Kaj Linna
184	Ray Schultz
231	Erik Kaminski

1994

Pick	
3	Radek Bonk
29	Stan Neckar
81	Bryan Masotta
131	Mike Gaffney
133	Daniel Alfredsson
159	Doug Sproule
210	Frederic Cassivi
211	Danny Dupont
237	Stephen MacKinnon
274	Antti Tormanen

1993

Pick	
1	Alexandre Daigle
27	Radim Bicanek
53	Patrick Charbonneau
91	Cosmo Dupaul
131	Rick Bodkin
157	Sergei Poleschuk
183	Jason Disher
209	Toby Kvalevog
227	Pavol Demitra
235	Rick Schuwerk

1992

Pick	
2	Alexei Yashin
25	Chad Penney
50	Patrick Traverse
73	Radek Hamr
98	Daniel Guerard
121	Al Sinclair
146	Jaroslav Miklenda
169	Jay Kenney
194	Claude Savoie
217	Jake Grimes
242	Tomas Jelinek
264	Petter Ronnqvist

Coach

MURRAY, BRYAN

Coach, Ottawa Senators. Born in Shawville, Que., December 5, 1942.

Bryan Murray was named head coach of the Ottawa Senators on June 8, 2004. The former NHL coach of the year is the fifth head coach in the Senators' new era. Murray resigned as senior vice president and general manager of Anaheim to take the coaching position in Ottawa. Murray had moulded the Ducks into Western Conference champions in 2002-03.

Murray joined the NHL coaching fraternity with the Washington Capitals on November 11, 1981. He remained at the helm of the Capitals for the following 8 1/2 seasons. Beginning with his first full season behind the Washington bench, the club had winning records and averaged 95 points per season over the next seven years. Murray won the Jack Adams Award in 1983-84 as the NHL's coach of the year. He has also served coaching stints with Detroit, Florida and Anaheim, coaching his 1,000th game in the NHL with Anaheim on November 28, 2001 and earning his 500th victory on January 25, 2002.

Coaching Record

		Regular Season				Playoffs		
Season	Team	Games	W	L	O/T	Games	W	L
1981-82	Washington (NHL)	66	25	28	13	....	....	....
1982-83	Washington (NHL)	80	39	25	16	4	1	3
1983-84	Washington (NHL)	80	48	27	5	8	4	4
1984-85	Washington (NHL)	80	46	25	9	5	2	3
1985-86	Washington (NHL)	80	50	23	7	9	5	4
1986-87	Washington (NHL)	80	38	32	10	7	3	4
1987-88	Washington (NHL)	80	38	33	9	14	7	7
1988-89	Washington (NHL)	80	41	29	10	6	2	4
1989-90	Washington (NHL)	46	18	24	4	....	....	....
1990-91	Detroit (NHL)	80	34	38	8	7	3	4
1991-92	Detroit (NHL)	80	43	25	12	11	4	7
1992-93	Detroit (NHL)	84	47	28	9	7	3	4
1997-98	Florida (NHL)	59	17	31	11	....	....	....
2001-02	Anaheim (NHL)	82	29	45	8	....	....	....
2004-05	Ottawa (NHL)			Season Cancelled				
2005-06	Ottawa (NHL)	82	52	21	9	10	5	5
	NHL Totals	1139	565	434	140	88	39	49

Club Directory

Scotiabank Place

Ottawa Senators
Scotiabank Place
1000 Palladium Drive
Ottawa, Ontario
K2V 1A5
Phone **613/599-0250**
FAX 613/599-0358
www.ottawasenators.com
Capacity: 19,153

Executive

Owner, Governor and Chairman	Eugene Melnyk
President, CEO and Alternate Governor	Roy Mlakar
Chief Operating Officer	Cyril Leeder
General Manager	John Muckler
V.P. and Executive Director, Scotiabank Place	Tom Conroy
Executive Assistant to the President and CEO	Cheryl Blake
Executive Assistant to the COO	Gail Martineau

Hockey Operations

Director of Hockey Administration	Kevin Billet
Head Coach	Bryan Murray
Director of Player Personnel and Pro Scout	Anders Hedberg
Director of Amateur Scouting	Frank Jay
Assistant Coaches	John Paddock, Greg Carvel
Conditioning Coach	Randy Lee
Goaltending Coach and Pro Scout	Ron Low
Video Coach	Tim Pattyson
General Counsel	Rhonda Wing
Law Clerk	Heather Havelock
Assistant to the General Manager	Allison Vaughan
Director of Player Services	Chad Schella
Team Services and Scouting Coordinator	Alex Lepore
Head Athletic Therapist	Gerry Townend
Assistant Athletic Therapist	Andy Playter
Equipment Manager	Scott Allegrino
Assistant Equipment Manager	Chris Cook

Scouts

Scout, Slovakia and Czech Republic	Vaclav Burda
Scouts	Wayne Daniels, George Fargher, Bob Janecyk, Bob Lowes, Bill McCarthy, Lewis Mongelluzzo, Patrick Savard
Pro Scouts	Gord Pell, Nick Polano
Scout, Finland	Mikko Ruutu
Scout, Russia	Boris Shagas

Communications and Publications

Vice-President, Communications	Phil Legault
Director, Communications	Steve Keogh
Director, Publications	Karen Ruttan
Communications & Publications Coordinator	Brian Morris
Translator	Eric Tremblay
Content Editor	Todd Anderson

Broadcasting

Vice-President, Broadcast	Jim Steel

Corporate & Ticket Sales and Service

Senior Vice-President, Corporate & Ticketing Sales	Mark Bonneau
Exec. Ass't. To Sr. V.P., Corporate & Ticketing Sales	Brooke Girard
Director, Corporate Sales	Bill Courchaine
Senior Corporate Account Managers	Steve Chestnut, Mark Clatney
Director, Business Development	Gina Hillcoat
Director, Sales	Jim Orban
Manager, Inside Sales	Chris Atack
Senior Account Manager, Group Sales	Jim Armstrong
Account Manager, Group Sales	Devon Wingate
Account Managers	Matt Berezowski, David Chadala, Chad Elliott, Jodi Gibson, David Jelley, David Leblanc, Mark Morrison, Brad Weir, Chris Zito
Corporate Account Managers	Jason Dashnay, Gianni Farinon, Joe Lowes, Phil Murphy, Tim Williton
Director, Premium Services	Christine Clancy
Manager, Premium Client Services	Tracey Bonner
Corporate Event Account Manager	Deborah Wilson-Desormeaux

Finance

Chief Financial Officer	Erin Crowe
Controller	Derek Winch
Accounting Manager, Ottawa Senators	Chris Dangerfield

Information Technology

Director, Information Technology	Sean Shrubsole
Web Developer	Stéphane Bourbonnais

Marketing

Vice-President, Marketing	Jeff Kyle
Administrative Assistant, Marketing	Kathy Downs
Director, Marketing	Patti Zebchuck
Director, Game Entertainment	Glen Gower
Art Director	Wendy Moenig
Director, E-Marketing	Isabelle Perrault-Lachapelle
Director, Media & Scotiabank Place Marketing	Krista Pogue
Director, Fan and Community Development	Aaron Robinson

Operations and Events

Vice-President & Exec. Dir., Scotiabank Place	Tom Conroy
Assistant to the Vice-President & Executive Director	Linda Julian
Director, Engineering & Operations	Ed Healy

Ottawa Senators Foundation

President	Dave Ready
Executive Assistant and Special Events Officer	Colleen Clark
Director, Corporate & Community Relations	Danielle Robinson

People Department

Director, People Department	Sandi Horner

Miscellaneous

Radio	Team 1200 (English), CJRC 1150 (French)
Television	Rogers Sportsnet, A-Channel and RDS
Team Photographer	Freestyle Photography (André Ringuette)
Anthem singer	Lyndon Slewidge
Mascot	Spartacat

Philadelphia Flyers

2005-06 Results: 45W-26L-5OTL-6SOL 101PTS.
Second, Atlantic Division

2006-07 Schedule

Oct.	Thu.	5	at Pittsburgh	Sun.	7	at Ottawa*
	Sat.	7	NY Rangers	Tue.	9	at Washington
	Tue.	10	at NY Rangers	Thu.	11	Montreal
	Wed.	11	Montreal	Sat.	13	Pittsburgh*
	Sat.	14	at New Jersey	Thu.	18	NY Islanders
	Tue.	17	at Buffalo	Sat.	20	at New Jersey
	Thu.	19	at Tampa Bay	Sat.	27	NY Rangers*
	Fri.	20	at Florida	Sun.	28	at Atlanta*
	Thu.	26	Atlanta	Tue.	30	Tampa Bay
	Sat.	28	Pittsburgh	Feb. Thu.	1	New Jersey
	Mon.	30	Chicago	Sat.	3	at Atlanta
Nov.	Thu.	2	Tampa Bay	Wed.	7	at NY Islanders
	Sat.	4	Washington	Thu.	8	Pittsburgh
	Mon.	6	at Toronto	Sat.	10	St. Louis
	Thu.	9	NY Islanders	Mon.	12	Detroit
	Sat.	11	Buffalo	Thu.	15	Toronto
	Mon.	13	at Pittsburgh	Sat.	17	at NY Rangers*
	Wed.	15	at Anaheim	Mon.	19	Boston
	Thu.	16	at Los Angeles	Tue.	20	at Buffalo
	Sat.	18	at San Jose	Thu.	22	at Carolina
	Mon.	20	Pittsburgh	Sat.	24	Toronto
	Wed.	22	Ottawa	Tue.	27	at NY Islanders
	Fri.	24	Columbus*	Mar. Thu.	1	at Boston
	Sat.	25	at Montreal	Sun.	4	at Pittsburgh*
	Wed.	29	Nashville	Tue.	6	New Jersey
	Thu.	30	at NY Islanders	Thu.	8	Florida
Dec.	Sat.	2	New Jersey	Sat.	10	Boston*
	Fri.	8	at New Jersey	Mon.	12	at Phoenix
	Sat.	9	Washington	Tue.	13	at Dallas
	Tue.	12	NY Rangers	Thu.	15	Atlanta
	Wed.	13	at Pittsburgh	Sat.	17	at Ottawa
	Sat.	16	at Washington	Tue.	20	Florida
	Tue.	19	Carolina	Wed.	21	at NY Rangers
	Thu.	21	at Montreal	Sat.	24	NY Islanders*
	Sat.	23	Ottawa*	Wed.	28	Carolina
	Wed.	27	at Florida	Fri.	30	at New Jersey
	Thu.	28	at Tampa Bay	Sat.	31	NY Rangers
	Sun.	31	at Carolina	Apr. Tue.	3	at Toronto
Jan.	Tue.	2	at NY Islanders	Thu.	5	New Jersey
	Thu.	4	at NY Rangers	Sat.	7	NY Islanders*
	Sat.	6	at Boston*	Sun.	8	Buffalo*

*Denotes afternoon game.

Year-by-Year Record

Season	GP	Home W	L	T	OL	Road W	L	T	OL	Overall W	L	T	OL	GF	GA	Pts.	Finished	Playoff Result
2005-06	82	22	13	....	6	23	13	....	5	45	26	....	11	267	259	101	2nd, Atlantic Div.	Lost Conf. Quarter-Final
2004-05	....	....	....	....	....	....	....	....	....	....	....	....	....	....	....	....		
2003-04	82	24	11	3	3	16	10	12	3	40	21	15	6	229	186	101	1st, Atlantic Div.	Lost Conf. Final
2002-03	82	21	10	8	2	24	15	5	2	45	20	13	4	211	166	107	2nd, Atlantic Div.	Lost Conf. Semi-Final
2001-02	82	20	13	5	3	22	14	5	0	42	27	10	3	234	192	97	1st, Atlantic Div.	Lost Conf. Quarter-Final
2000-01	82	26	11	4	0	17	14	7	3	43	25	11	3	240	207	100	2nd, Atlantic Div.	Lost Conf. Quarter-Final
1999-2000	82	25	6	7	3	20	16	5	0	45	22	12	3	237	179	105	1st, Atlantic Div.	Lost Conf. Championship
1998-99	82	21	9	11	....	16	17	8	....	37	26	19	....	231	196	93	2nd, Atlantic Div.	Lost Conf. Quarter-Final
1997-98	82	24	11	6	....	18	18	5	....	42	29	11	....	242	193	95	2nd, Atlantic Div.	Lost Conf. Quarter-Final
1996-97	82	23	12	6	....	22	12	7	....	45	24	13	....	274	217	103	2nd, Atlantic Div.	Lost Final
1995-96	82	27	9	5	....	18	15	8	....	45	24	13	....	282	208	103	1st, Atlantic Div.	Lost Conf. Semi-Final
1994-95	48	16	7	1	....	12	9	3	....	28	16	4	....	150	132	60	1st, Atlantic Div.	Lost Conf. Championship
1993-94	84	19	20	3	....	16	19	7	....	35	39	10	....	294	314	80	6th, Atlantic Div.	Out of Playoffs
1992-93	84	23	14	5	....	13	23	6	....	36	37	11	....	319	319	83	5th, Patrick Div.	Out of Playoffs
1991-92	80	22	11	7	....	10	26	4	....	32	37	11	....	252	273	75	6th, Patrick Div.	Out of Playoffs
1990-91	80	18	16	6	....	15	21	4	....	33	37	10	....	252	267	76	5th, Patrick Div.	Out of Playoffs
1989-90	80	17	19	4	....	13	20	7	....	30	39	11	....	290	297	71	6th, Patrick Div.	Out of Playoffs
1988-89	80	22	15	3	....	14	21	5	....	36	36	8	....	307	285	80	4th, Patrick Div.	Lost Conf. Championship
1987-88	80	20	14	6	....	18	15	7	....	38	33	9	....	292	292	85	3rd, Patrick Div.	Lost Div. Semi-Final
1986-87	80	29	9	2	....	17	17	6	....	46	26	8	....	310	245	100	1st, Patrick Div.	Lost Final
1985-86	80	33	6	1	....	20	17	3	....	53	23	4	....	335	241	110	1st, Patrick Div.	Lost Div. Semi-Final
1984-85	80	32	4	4	....	21	16	3	....	53	20	7	....	348	241	113	1st, Patrick Div.	Lost Final
1983-84	80	25	10	5	....	19	16	5	....	44	26	10	....	350	290	98	3rd, Patrick Div.	Lost Div. Semi-Final
1982-83	80	29	8	3	....	20	15	5	....	49	23	8	....	326	240	106	1st, Patrick Div.	Lost Div. Semi-Final
1981-82	80	25	10	5	....	13	21	6	....	38	31	11	....	325	313	87	3rd, Patrick Div.	Lost Div. Semi-Final
1980-81	80	23	9	8	....	18	15	7	....	41	24	15	....	313	249	97	2nd, Patrick Div.	Lost Quarter-Final
1979-80	80	27	5	8	....	21	7	12	....	48	12	20	....	327	254	116	1st, Patrick Div.	Lost Final
1978-79	80	26	10	4	....	14	15	11	....	40	25	15	....	281	248	95	2nd, Patrick Div.	Lost Quarter-Final
1977-78	80	29	6	5	....	16	14	10	....	45	20	15	....	296	200	105	2nd, Patrick Div.	Lost Semi-Final
1976-77	80	33	6	1	....	15	10	15	....	48	16	16	....	323	213	112	1st, Patrick Div.	Lost Semi-Final
1975-76	80	36	2	2	....	15	11	14	....	51	13	16	....	348	209	118	1st, Patrick Div.	Lost Final
1974-75	80	32	6	2	....	19	12	9	....	51	18	11	....	293	181	113	1st, Patrick Div.	Won Stanley Cup
1973-74	78	28	6	5	....	22	10	7	....	50	16	12	....	273	164	112	1st, West Div.	Won Stanley Cup
1972-73	78	27	8	4	....	10	22	7	....	37	30	11	....	296	256	85	2nd, West Div.	Lost Semi-Final
1971-72	78	19	13	7	....	7	25	7	....	26	38	14	....	200	236	66	5th, West Div.	Out of Playoffs
1970-71	78	20	10	9	....	8	23	8	....	28	33	17	....	207	225	73	3rd, West Div.	Lost Quarter-Final
1969-70	76	11	14	13	....	6	21	11	....	17	35	24	....	197	225	58	5th, West Div.	Out of Playoffs
1968-69	76	14	16	8	....	6	19	13	....	20	35	21	....	174	225	61	3rd, West Div.	Lost Quarter-Final
1967-68	74	17	13	7	....	14	19	4	....	31	32	11	....	173	179	73	1st, West Div.	Lost Quarter-Final

Franchise date: June 5, 1967

EASTERN NHL CONFERENCE

ATLANTIC DIVISION

40th NHL Season

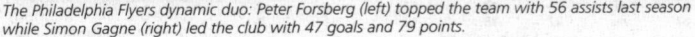

The Philadelphia Flyers dynamic duo: Peter Forsberg (left) topped the team with 56 assists last season while Simon Gagne (right) led the club with 47 goals and 79 points.

2006-07 Player Personnel

FORWARDS	HT	WT	S	Place of Birth	Date	2005-06 Club
CALDER, Kyle	5-11	176	L	Mannville, Alta.	1/5/79	Chicago
CARTER, Jeff	6-3	200	R	London, Ont.	1/1/85	Philadelphia
CORSO, Daniel	5-10	187	L	Montreal, Que.	4/3/78	Frankfurt
CULLEN, Mark	5-11	175	L	Moorhead, MN	10/28/78	Chicago-Norfolk
DIMITRAKOS, Niko	5-10	205	R	Somerville, MA	5/21/79	San Jose-Philadelphia
DOWNIE, Steve	5-10	192	R	Newmarket, Ont.	4/3/87	Windsor-Peterborough
EAGER, Ben	6-2	225	L	Ottawa, Ont.	1/22/84	Phi-Phi (AHL)
ELLISON, Matt	6-0	192	R	Duncan, B.C.	12/8/83	Chi-Phi-Phi (AHL)
FORSBERG, Peter	6-0	205	L	Ornskoldsvik, Sweden	7/20/73	Philadelphia
GAGNE, Simon	6-0	190	L	Ste-Foy, Que.	2/29/80	Philadelphia
KANE, Boyd	6-2	218	L	Swift Current, Sask.	4/18/78	Washington-Hershey
KAPANEN, Sami	5-10	185	L	Vantaa, Finland	6/14/73	Philadelphia
KNUBLE, Mike	6-3	228	R	Toronto, Ont.	7/4/72	Philadelphia
MELOCHE, Eric	5-10	202	R	Montreal, Que.	5/1/76	Philadelphia (AHL)-Norfolk
MURRAY, Marty	5-9	180	L	Deloraine, Man.	2/16/75	Hannover
NEDVED, Petr	6-3	196	L	Liberec, Czech.	12/9/71	Phoenix-Philadelphia
POTULNY, Ryan	6-0	190	L	Grand Forks, ND	9/5/84	U. of Minnesota-Phi
PRIMEAU, Keith	6-5	220	L	Toronto, Ont.	11/24/71	Philadelphia
RICHARDS, Mike	5-11	185	L	Kenora, Ont.	2/11/85	Philadelphia
ROBITAILLE, Randy	5-11	200	L	Ottawa, Ont.	10/12/75	Minnesota
RUZICKA, Stefan	6-0	205	R	Nitra, Czech.	2/17/85	Phi-Phi (AHL)
SANDERSON, Geoff	6-0	190	L	Hay River, N.W.T.	2/1/72	Columbus-Phoenix
TAPPER, Brad	6-0	185	R	Scarborough, Ont.	4/28/78	Hannover
UMBERGER, R.J.	6-2	200	L	Pittsburgh, PA	5/3/82	Phi-Phi (AHL)
VOCE, Tony	5-8	185	L	Philadelphia, PA	10/30/80	Philadelphia (AHL)
DEFENSEMEN						
BAUMGARTNER, Nolan	6-2	205	R	Calgary, Alta.	3/23/76	Vancouver
GAUTHIER, Denis	6-3	224	L	Montreal, Que.	10/1/76	Phoenix-Philadelphia
GRENIER, Martin	6-5	255	L	Laval, Que.	11/2/80	Hartford
HATCHER, Derian	6-5	235	L	Sterling Hts., MI	6/4/72	Philadelphia
JONES, Randy	6-2	200	L	Quispamsis, N.B.	7/23/81	Phi-Phi (AHL)
JONSSON, Lars	6-1	205	L	Borlange, Sweden	1/2/82	HV 71
MEYER, Freddy	5-10	192	L	Sanbornville, NH	1/4/81	Phi-Phi (AHL)
PICARD, Alexandre	6-2	214	L	Gatineau, Que.	7/5/85	Phi-Phi (AHL)
PITKANEN, Joni	6-3	200	L	Oulu, Finland	9/19/83	Philadelphia
PRINTZ, David	6-5	220	L	Stockholm, Sweden	7/24/80	Phi-Phi (AHL)
RATHJE, Mike	6-5	235	L	Mannville, Alta.	5/11/74	Philadelphia

GOALTENDERS	HT	WT	C	Place of Birth	Date	2005-06 Club
BEAUCHEMIN, Rejean	6-1	193	L	Winnipeg, Man.	5/3/85	Trenton-Philadelphia (AHL)
ESCHE, Robert	6-1	210	L	Whitesboro, NY	1/22/78	Philadelphia
HOULE, Martin	5-10	170	L	Montreal, Que.	2/12/85	Philadelphia (AHL)-Trenton
NIITTYMAKI, Antero	6-0	195	L	Turku, Finland	6/18/80	Philadelphia

Coach

HITCHCOCK, KEN

Coach, Philadelphia Flyers. Born in Edmonton, Alta., December 17, 1951.

The Philadelphia Flyers named Ken Hitchcock as their head coach on May 14, 2002. Hitchcock is the 15th head coach in Flyers history. Prior to joining the Flyers, he won a gold medal as an associate coach with Team Canada at the 2002 Winter Olympic Games. (He served the same role with Canada's team at the 2004 World Cup and 2006 Olympics.) Hitchcock served as head coach of the Dallas Stars for parts of seven seasons (1995-96 to 2001-02), compiling a 277-166-60 record in 503 regular season games.

Hitchcock served as head coach of Dallas' International Hockey League affiliate, the Kalamazoo Wings/Michigan K-Wings for three seasons, from the 1993-94 season until being named Stars' head coach on January 8, 1996. Prior to joining the Stars' organization, Hitchcock served three seasons as an assistant coach with the Flyers (1990-91 through 1992-93).

Hitchcock joined the Flyers after six seasons as head coach of the Kamloops Blazers of the Western Hockey League from 1984-85 through 1989-90. His .693 winning percentage as head coach at Kamloops is the second highest in the history of the WHL (291-125-15). His international experience also includes serving as an assistant coach for the Team Canada team that captured the gold medal at the 1987 World Junior Championships.

Coaching Record

			Regular Season				Playoffs	
Season	Team	Games	W	L	O/T	Games	W	L
1984-85	Kamloops (WHL)	71	52	17	2	15	10	5
1985-86	Kamloops (WHL)	72	49	19	4	16	14	2
1986-87	Kamloops (WHL)	72	55	14	3	13	8	5
1987-88	Kamloops (WHL)	72	45	26	1	18	12	6
1988-89	Kamloops (WHL)	72	34	33	5	16	8	8
1989-90	Kamloops (WHL)	72	56	16	0	17	14	3
1993-94	Kalamazoo (IHL)	81	48	26	7	5	1	4
1994-95	Kalamazoo (IHL)	81	43	24	14	16	10	6
1995-96	Michigan (IHL)	40	19	10	11	....	....	....
	Dallas (NHL)	**43**	**15**	**23**	**5**	....	....	....
1996-97	**Dallas (NHL)**	**82**	**48**	**26**	**8**	**7**	**3**	**4**
1997-98	**Dallas (NHL)**	**82**	**49**	**22**	**11**	**17**	**10**	**7**
1998-99*	**Dallas (NHL)**	**82**	**51**	**19**	**12**	**23**	**16**	**7**
1999-2000	**Dallas (NHL)**	**82**	**43**	**29**	**10**	**23**	**14**	**9**
2000-01	**Dallas (NHL)**	**82**	**48**	**26**	**8**	**10**	**4**	**6**
2001-02	**Dallas (NHL)**	**50**	**23**	**21**	**6**	....	....	....
2002-03	**Philadelphia (NHL)**	**82**	**45**	**24**	**13**	**13**	**6**	**7**
2003-04	**Philadelphia (NHL)**	**82**	**40**	**27**	**15**	**18**	**11**	**7**
2004-05	**Philadelphia (NHL)**				Season Cancelled			
2005-06	**Philadelphia (NHL)**	**82**	**45**	**26**	**11**	**6**	**2**	**4**
	NHL Totals	**749**	**407**	**243**	**99**	**117**	**66**	**51**

* Stanley Cup win.

2005-06 Scoring

* – rookie

Regular Season

Pos	#	Player	Team	GP	G	A	Pts	+/–	PIM	PP	SH	GW	S	%
L	12	Simon Gagne	PHI	72	47	32	79	31	38	12	2	7	334	14.1
C	21	Peter Forsberg	PHI	60	19	56	75	21	46	8	1	2	132	14.4
R	22	Mike Knuble	PHI	82	34	31	65	25	80	13	2	6	217	15.7
D	44	Joni Pitkanen	PHI	58	13	33	46	22	78	5	0	3	118	11.0
C	26	Michal Handzus	PHI	73	11	33	44	–2	38	2	1	1	113	9.7
C	17 *	Jeff Carter	PHI	81	23	19	42	10	40	6	2	7	189	12.2
C	20 *	R.J. Umberger	PHI	73	20	18	38	9	18	5	0	2	138	14.5
R	24	Sami Kapanen	PHI	58	12	22	34	–9	12	3	4	2	123	9.8
C	18 *	Mike Richards	PHI	79	11	23	34	6	65	1	3	1	168	6.5
D	34 *	Freddy Meyer	PHI	57	6	21	27	10	33	2	0	0	68	8.8
R	15	Niko Dimitrakos	S.J.	45	4	12	16	0	26	0	0	0	66	6.1
			PHI	19	5	4	9	4	6	1	0	1	27	18.5
			TOTAL	64	9	16	25	4	32	1	0	1	93	9.7
C	93	Petr Nedved	PHX	25	2	9	11	–6	34	1	0	1	43	4.7
			PHI	28	5	9	14	–8	36	2	0	0	47	10.6
			TOTAL	53	7	18	25	–14	70	3	0	1	90	7.8
D	5	Kim Johnsson	PHI	47	6	19	25	5	34	3	0	0	97	6.2
D	37	Eric Desjardins	PHI	45	4	20	24	3	56	3	0	1	88	4.5
D	3	Mike Rathje	PHI	79	3	21	24	22	46	1	1	1	55	5.5
D	2	Derian Hatcher	PHI	77	4	13	17	2	93	1	1	0	98	4.1
L	49	Brian Savage	PHI	66	9	5	14	–18	28	4	1	1	102	8.8
R	19	Branko Radivojevic	PHI	64	8	6	14	–6	44	1	0	1	84	9.5
R	23 *	Matt Ellison	CHI	26	3	9	12	–4	17	1	0	0	47	6.4
			PHI	5	0	1	1	2	2	0	0	0	2	0.0
			TOTAL	31	3	10	13	–2	19	1	0	0	49	6.1
D	23	Denis Gauthier	PHX	45	2	9	11	–4	61	0	0	0	43	4.7
			PHI	17	0	0	0	6	37	0	0	0	13	0.0
			TOTAL	62	2	9	11	2	98	0	0	0	56	3.6
L	87	Donald Brashear	PHI	76	4	5	9	–2	166	0	0	0	73	5.5
L	55 *	Ben Eager	PHI	25	3	5	8	0	18	0	0	0	21	14.3
D	29 *	Randy Jones	PHI	28	0	8	8	–6	16	0	0	0	21	0.0
C	25	Keith Primeau	PHI	9	1	6	7	0	6	1	0	0	12	8.3
R	27	Turner Stevenson	PHI	31	1	3	4	–2	45	0	1	0	26	3.8
D	6	Chris Therien	PHI	47	0	4	4	–7	34	0	0	0	16	0.0
C	11 *	Ryan Potulny	PHI	2	0	1	1	1	0	0	0	0	0	0.0
L	14	Ryan Ready	PHI	7	0	1	1	0	0	0	0	0	9	0.0
R	15	Eric Chouinard	PHI	1	0	0	0	0	2	0	0	0	0	0.0
D	28 *	David Printz	PHI	1	0	0	0	0	0	0	0	0	0	0.0
D	43 *	Wade Skolney	PHI	1	0	0	0	0	2	0	0	0	0	0.0
R	40 *	Stefan Ruzicka	PHI	1	0	0	0	0	2	0	0	0	1	0.0
D	41 *	Alexandre Picard	PHI	6	0	0	0	–2	4	0	0	0	9	0.0
R	36	Pat Kavanagh	PHI	8	0	0	0	–2	2	0	0	0	1	0.0

Goaltending

No.	Goaltender	GPI	Mins	Avg	W	L	OT	EN	SO	GA	SA	S%	G	A	PIM
42	Robert Esche	40	2286	2.97	22	11	5	3	1	113	1099	.897	0	3	4
30	* Antero Niittymaki	46	2690	2.97	23	15	6	4	2	133	1266	.895	0	1	0
	Totals	**82**	**4995**	**3.04**	**45**	**26**	**11**	**7**	**3**	**253**	**2372**	**.893**			

Playoffs

Pos	#	Player	Team	GP	G	A	Pts	+/–	PIM	PP	SH	GW	OT	S	%
C	21	Peter Forsberg	PHI	6	4	4	8	2	6	1	0	2	0	12	33.3
L	12	Simon Gagne	PHI	6	3	1	4	2	2	1	0	0	0	26	11.5
D	37	Eric Desjardins	PHI	6	1	3	4	–3	6	0	0	0	0	10	10.0
R	22	Mike Knuble	PHI	6	1	3	4	1	8	0	0	0	0	17	5.9
C	93	Petr Nedved	PHI	6	2	0	2	–4	8	1	0	0	0	7	28.6
D	2	Derian Hatcher	PHI	6	0	2	2	–4	10	0	0	0	0	5	0.0
C	26	Michal Handzus	PHI	6	0	2	2	–2	2	0	0	0	0	4	0.0
D	44	Joni Pitkanen	PHI	6	0	2	2	0	2	0	0	0	0	10	0.0
R	19	Branko Radivojevic	PHI	5	1	0	1	–1	0	0	0	0	0	6	16.7
C	20 *	R.J. Umberger	PHI	5	1	0	1	–3	2	0	0	0	0	6	16.7
L	49	Brian Savage	PHI	6	1	0	1	–4	4	0	1	0	0	7	14.3
D	23	Denis Gauthier	PHI	6	0	1	1	–5	19	0	0	0	0	3	0.0
D	34 *	Freddy Meyer	PHI	6	0	1	1	–5	8	0	0	0	0	5	0.0
C	18 *	Mike Richards	PHI	6	0	1	1	–5	0	0	0	0	0	9	0.0
L	87	Donald Brashear	PHI	1	0	0	0	0	0	0	0	0	0	1	0.0
L	55 *	Ben Eager	PHI	2	0	0	0	–4	26	0	0	0	0	3	0.0
R	15	Niko Dimitrakos	PHI	5	0	0	0	–2	2	0	0	0	0	4	0.0
D	3	Mike Rathje	PHI	6	0	0	0	–1	6	0	0	0	0	3	0.0
R	24	Sami Kapanen	PHI	6	0	0	0	–4	2	0	0	0	0	12	0.0
C	17 *	Jeff Carter	PHI	6	0	0	0	–4	10	0	0	0	0	10	0.0

Goaltending

No.	Goaltender	GPI	Mins	Avg	W	L	EN	SO	GA	SA	S%	G	A	PIM
30	* Antero Niittymaki	2	73	4.11	0	0	0	0	5	29	.828	0	0	0
42	Robert Esche	6	314	4.20	2	4	0	0	22	176	.875	0	0	2
	Totals	**6**	**388**	**4.18**	**2**	**4**	**0**	**0**	**27**	**205**	**.868**			

Coaching History

Keith Allen, 1967-68, 1968-69; Vic Stasiuk, 1969-70, 1970-71; Fred Shero, 1971-72 to 1977-78; Bob McCammon and Pat Quinn, 1978-79; Pat Quinn, 1979-80, 1980-81; Pat Quinn and Bob McCammon, 1981-82; Bob McCammon, 1982-83, 1983-84; Mike Keenan, 1984-85 to 1987-88; Paul Holmgren, 1988-89 to 1990-91; Paul Holmgren and Bill Dineen, 1991-92; Bill Dineen, 1992-93; Terry Simpson, 1993-94; Terry Murray, 1994-95 to 1996-97; Wayne Cashman and Roger Neilson, 1997-98; Roger Neilson, 1998-99, 1999-2000; Craig Ramsay and Bill Barber, 2000-01; Bill Barber, 2001-02; Ken Hitchcock, 2002-03 to date.

Club Records

Team

(Figures in brackets for season records are games played; records for fewest points, wins, ties, losses, goals, goals against are for 70 or more games)

Most Points	118	1975-76 (80)
Most Wins	53	1984-85 (80), 1985-86 (80)
Most Ties	*24	1969-70 (76)
Most Losses	39	1989-90 (80), 1993-94 (84)
Most Goals	350	1983-84 (80)
Most Goals Against	319	1992-93 (84)
Fewest Points	58	1969-70 (76)
Fewest Wins	17	1969-70 (76)
Fewest Ties	4	1985-86 (80)
Fewest Losses	12	1979-80 (80)
Fewest Goals	173	1967-68 (74)
Fewest Goals Against	164	1973-74 (78)
Longest Winning Streak		
Overall	13	Oct. 19-Nov. 17/85
Home	*20	Jan. 4-Apr. 3/76
Away	8	Dec. 22/82-Jan. 16/83
Longest Undefeated Streak		
Overall	*35	Oct. 14/79-Jan. 6/80 (25 wins, 10 ties)
Home	26	Oct. 11/79-Feb. 3/80 (19 wins, 7 ties)
Away	16	Oct. 20/79-Jan. 6/80 (11 wins, 5 ties)
Longest Losing Streak		
Overall	6	Mar. 25-Apr. 4/70, Dec. 5-17/92, Jan. 25-Feb. 5/94
Home	5	Jan. 30-Feb. 15/69, Dec. 19/89-Jan. 23/90
Away	8	Oct. 25-Nov. 26/72, Mar. 3-29/88
Longest Winless Streak		
Overall	12	Feb. 24-Mar. 16/99 (8 losses, 4 ties)
Home	8	Dec. 19/68-Jan. 18/69 (4 losses, 4 ties), Nov. 17-Dec. 14/91 (4 losses, 4 ties)
Away	19	Oct. 23/71-Jan. 27/72 (15 losses, 4 ties)
Most Shutouts, Season	13	1974-75 (80)
Most PIM, Season	2,621	1980-81 (80)
Most Goals, Game	13	Mar. 22/84 (Pit. 4 at Phi. 13), Oct. 18/84 (Van. 2 at Phi. 13)

Individual

Most Seasons	15	Bobby Clarke
Most Games	1,144	Bobby Clarke
Most Goals, Career	420	Bill Barber
Most Assists, Career	852	Bobby Clarke
Most Points, Career	1,210	Bobby Clarke (358G, 852A)
Most PIM, Career	1,817	Rick Tocchet
Most Shutouts, Career	50	Bernie Parent
Longest Consecutive Game Streak	484	Rod Brind'Amour (Feb. 24/93-Apr. 18/99)
Most Goals, Season	61	Reggie Leach (1975-76)
Most Assists, Season	89	Bobby Clarke (1974-75, 1975-76)
Most Points, Season	123	Mark Recchi (1992-93; 53G, 70A)
Most PIM, Season	*472	Dave Schultz (1974-75)
Most Points, Defenseman, Season	82	Mark Howe (1985-86; 24G, 58A)
Most Points, Center, Season	119	Bobby Clarke (1975-76; 30G, 89A)
Most Points, Right Wing, Season	123	Mark Recchi (1992-93; 53G, 70A)
Most Points, Left Wing, Season	112	Bill Barber (1975-76; 50G, 62A)
Most Points, Rookie, Season	82	Mikael Renberg (1993-94; 38G, 44A)
Most Shutouts, Season	12	Bernie Parent (1973-74, 1974-75)
Most Goals, Game	4	Sixteen times
Most Assists, Game	6	Eric Lindros (Feb. 26/97)
Most Points, Game	8	Tom Bladon (Dec. 11/77; 4G, 4A)

* NHL Record.

Retired Numbers

1	Bernie Parent	1967-1971, 1973-1979
4	Barry Ashbee	1970-1974
7	Bill Barber	1972-1985
16	Bobby Clarke	1969-1984

All-time Record vs. Other Clubs

Regular Season

	At Home								On Road								Total							
	GP	W	L	T	OL	GF	GA	PTS	GP	W	L	T	OL	GF	GA	PTS	GP	W	L	T	OL	GF	GA	PTS
Anaheim	8	3	2	3	0	22	17	9	9	3	3	2	1	28	30	9	17	6	5	5	1	50	47	18
Atlanta	12	8	1	2	1	55	37	19	12	9	2	1	0	42	29	19	24	17	3	3	1	97	66	38
Boston	75	33	31	10	1	247	219	77	78	21	44	11	2	217	286	55	153	54	75	21	3	464	505	132
Buffalo	69	40	16	12	1	234	170	93	65	24	33	8	0	182	215	56	134	64	49	20	1	416	385	149
Calgary	52	34	14	3	1	200	137	72	52	18	25	9	0	172	208	45	104	52	39	12	1	372	345	117
Carolina	45	30	9	5	1	168	113	66	46	23	14	9	0	168	151	55	91	53	23	14	1	336	264	121
Chicago	62	35	16	11	0	204	162	81	61	16	26	19	0	175	207	51	123	51	42	30	0	379	369	132
Colorado	35	22	9	2	2	125	95	48	35	11	11	12	1	122	124	35	70	33	20	14	3	247	219	83
Columbus	2	1	0	1	0	7	3	3	4	2	0	2	0	10	7	6	6	3	0	3	0	17	10	9
Dallas	67	42	9	16	0	255	150	100	66	23	27	16	0	212	216	62	133	65	36	32	0	467	366	162
Detroit	58	34	13	11	0	230	168	79	60	18	32	10	0	185	216	46	118	52	45	21	0	415	384	125
Edmonton	32	20	10	2	0	130	88	42	28	8	14	6	0	83	98	22	60	28	24	8	0	213	186	64
Florida	27	12	8	6	1	75	68	31	26	20	5	1	0	95	59	41	53	32	13	7	1	170	127	72
Los Angeles	63	40	15	7	1	244	156	88	66	37	21	8	0	223	193	82	129	77	36	15	1	467	349	170
Minnesota	5	4	1	0	0	14	5	8	2	0	1	1	0	3	5	1	7	4	2	1	0	17	10	9
Montreal	75	30	28	16	1	231	224	77	76	26	34	14	2	231	262	68	151	56	62	30	3	462	486	145
Nashville	5	2	1	1	1	17	9	6	5	2	0	2	1	10	8	7	10	4	1	3	2	27	17	13
New Jersey	89	54	24	10	1	332	222	119	87	33	45	8	1	288	297	75	176	87	69	18	2	620	519	194
NY Islanders	99	58	28	11	2	355	277	129	102	36	50	15	1	303	365	88	201	94	78	26	3	658	642	217
NY Rangers	113	57	41	14	1	366	313	129	114	43	46	23	2	336	364	111	227	100	87	37	3	702	677	240
Ottawa	25	15	8	2	0	83	69	32	26	11	9	6	0	79	71	28	51	26	17	8	0	162	140	60
Phoenix	31	23	8	0	0	134	83	46	31	16	13	2	0	106	99	34	62	39	21	2	0	240	182	80
Pittsburgh	110	84	17	8	1	462	270	177	110	41	47	22	0	359	383	104	220	125	64	30	1	821	653	281
St. Louis	67	45	12	10	0	264	153	100	69	36	26	7	0	224	196	79	136	81	38	17	0	488	349	179
San Jose	11	6	3	2	0	36	27	14	12	7	3	2	0	31	22	16	23	13	6	4	0	67	49	30
Tampa Bay	27	14	5	7	1	81	56	36	28	16	11	1	0	83	82	33	55	30	16	8	1	164	138	69
Toronto	69	43	18	8	0	258	162	94	69	31	24	14	0	232	216	76	138	74	42	22	0	490	378	170
Vancouver	55	37	17	1	0	238	164	75	51	29	10	12	0	203	144	70	106	66	27	13	0	441	308	145
Washington	85	55	24	6	0	325	224	116	82	35	32	13	2	265	266	85	167	90	56	19	2	590	490	201
Defunct Clubs	34	24	4	6	0	137	67	54	35	13	14	8	0	102	89	34	69	37	18	14	0	239	156	88
Totals	**1507**	**905**	**392**	**193**	**17**	**5529**	**3908**	**2020**	**1507**	**608**	**622**	**264**	**13**	**4769**	**4908**	**1493**	**3014**	**1513**	**1014**	**457**	**30**	**10298**	**8816**	**3513**

Playoffs

	Series	W	L	GP	W	L	T	GF	GA	Last Mtg.	Rnd.	Result
Boston	4	2	2	20	9	11	0	57	60	1978	SF	L 1-4
Buffalo	8	5	3	43	25	18	0	124	123	2006	CQF	L 2-4
Calgary	2	1	1	11	7	4	0	43	28	1981	QF	L 3-4
Chicago	1	0	1	4	0	4	0	8	20	1971	QF	L 0-4
Colorado	2	2	0	11	7	4	0	39	29	1985	CF	W 4-2
Dallas	2	2	0	11	8	3	0	41	26	1980	SF	W 4-1
Detroit	1	0	1	4	0	4	0	6	16	1997	F	L 0-4
Edmonton	3	1	2	15	7	8	0	44	49	1987	F	L 3-4
Florida	1	0	1	6	2	4	0	11	15	1996	CSF	L 2-4
Montreal	4	1	3	21	7	14	0	52	72	1989	CF	L 2-4
New Jersey	4	2	2	20	11	9	0	49	50	2004	CQF	W 4-1
NY Islanders	4	3	1	25	14	11	0	83	69	1987	DF	W 4-3
NY Rangers	10	6	4	47	27	20	0	157	153	1997	CF	W 4-1
Ottawa	2	0	2	11	3	8	0	12	28	2003	CSF	L 2-4
Pittsburgh	3	3	0	18	12	6	0	66	51	2000	CSF	W 4-2
St. Louis	2	0	2	11	3	8	0	20	34	1969	QF	L 0-4
Tampa Bay	2	1	1	13	7	6	0	45	34	2004	CF	L 3-4
Toronto	6	5	1	36	22	14	0	119	85	2004	CSF	W 4-2
Vancouver	1	1	0	3	2	1	0	15	9	1979	PRE	W 2-1
Washington	3	1	2	16	7	9	0	55	65	1989	DSF	W 4-2
Totals	**65**	**36**	**29**	**346**	**180**	**166**	**0**	**1046**	**1016**			

Playoff Results 2006-2001

Year	Round	Opponent	Result	GF	GA
2006	CQF	Buffalo	L 2-4	14	27
2004	CF	Tampa Bay	L 3-4	19	21
	CSF	Toronto	W 4-2	17	13
	CQF	New Jersey	W 4-1	14	9
2003	CSF	Ottawa	L 2-4	10	17
	CQF	Toronto	W 4-3	24	16
2002	CQF	Ottawa	L 1-4	2	11
2001	CQF	Buffalo	L 2-4	13	21

Abbreviations: Round: F – Final; **CF** – conference final; **CSF** – conference semi-final; **CQF** – conference quarter-final; **DF** – division final; **DSF** – division semi-final; **SF** – semi-final; **QF** – quarter-final; **PRE** – preliminary round.

Calgary totals include Atlanta Flames, 1972-73 to 1979-80.
Colorado totals include Quebec, 1979-80 to 1994-95.
Carolina totals include Hartford, 1979-80 to 1996-97.
Dallas totals include Minnesota North Stars, 1967-68 to 1992-93.
New Jersey totals include Kansas City, 1974-75 to 1975-76, and Colorado Rockies, 1976-77 to 1981-82.
Phoenix totals include Winnipeg, 1979-80 to 1995-96.

2005-06 Results

Month	Day	Opponent	Score
Oct.	5	NY Rangers	3-5
	7	New Jersey	5-2
	11	at Toronto	2-4
	14	Pittsburgh	6-5*
	15	NY Islanders	5-1
	22	at Toronto	5-2
	25	at Montreal	2-3*
	27	Florida	5-4*
	28	at Carolina	6-8
	30	at Ottawa	5-3
Nov.	3	Washington	8-1
	5	Atlanta	4-3
	8	Boston	4-3*
	10	NY Islanders	3-2
	12	Florida	5-4
	14	at Tampa Bay	2-5
	16	Pittsburgh	2-3*
	18	Atlanta	5-6*
	19	at Pittsburgh	6-3
	22	Tampa Bay	2-4
	25	at Boston	5-3
	26	NY Islanders	2-4
	29	at NY Islanders	4-3
	30	New Jersey	2-1
Dec.	3	at Nashville	3-4†
	6	Calgary	1-0†
	8	Edmonton	2-3
	10	Minnesota	3-2
	13	at Columbus	3-1
	15	Vancouver	4-5
	17	at St. Louis	5-2
	19	Buffalo	1-2†
	22	Ottawa	4-3
	23	at Pittsburgh	5-4
	26	at Florida	3-2†
	28	at Atlanta	4-3*
	29	at Carolina	4-3*
	31	at Washington	3-4†
Jan.	2	at Boston	1-0
	5	at NY Rangers	4-3*
	6	at Washington	3-1
	9	at New Jersey	0-3
	11	at Chicago	5-2
	12	at Detroit	3-6
	14	Colorado	3-4*
	17	Carolina	3-4†
	19	Boston	2-5
	21	at Pittsburgh	2-1
	23	Pittsburgh	4-2
	25	Montreal	3-5
	28	Tampa Bay	0-6
	30	at NY Rangers	3-2*
Feb.	2	at Buffalo	2-4
	4	NY Rangers	3-4*
	5	at Montreal	0-5
	8	NY Islanders	5-2
	10	Washington	5-4
	11	at Ottawa	2-3
Mar.	1	at New Jersey	1-2†
	2	NY Rangers	1-6
	4	at NY Islanders	2-4
	6	Montreal	5-4†
	8	Carolina	3-2†
	11	Buffalo	5-6
	12	at Pittsburgh	0-2
	15	at Florida	4-0
	17	at Tampa Bay	3-6
	18	at Atlanta	4-2
	21	New Jersey	2-1
	22	at NY Rangers	6-3
	25	Ottawa	6-3
	28	Toronto	2-3
Apr.	1	New Jersey	1-4
	2	at NY Islanders	4-1
	4	at NY Rangers	2-3†
	7	at Buffalo	4-2
	8	Toronto	2-5
	11	Pittsburgh	4-3
	13	at New Jersey	1-4
	15	NY Rangers	4-1
	16	at New Jersey	1-5
	18	at NY Islanders	4-1

* – Overtime † – Shootout

Entry Draft
Selections 2006-1992

2006 Pick		2002 Pick		1998 Pick		1994 Pick	
22	Claude Giroux	4	Joni Pitkanen	22	Simon Gagne	62	Artem Anisimov
39	Andreas Nodl	105	Rosario Ruggeri	42	Jason Beckett	88	Adam Magarrell
42	Michael Ratchuk	126	Konstantin Baranov	51	Ian Forbes	101	Sebastien Vallee
55	Denis Bodrov	161	Dov Grumet-Morris	109	Jean-Philippe Morin	140	Alex Selivanov
79	Jonathan Matsumoto	192	Nikita Korovkin	124	Francis Belanger	166	Colin Forbes
101	Joonas Lehtivuori	193	Joey Mormina	139	Garrett Prosofsky	192	Derek Diener
109	Jakub Kovar	201	Mathieu Brunelle	168	Antero Niittymaki	202	Raymond Giroux
145	Jonathan Rheault			175	Cam Ondrik	218	Johan Hedberg
175	Michael Dupont	**2001**		195	Tomas Divisek	244	Andre Payette
205	Andrei Popov	**Pick**		222	Lubomir Pistek	270	Jan Lipiansky
		27	Jeff Woywitka	243	Petr Hubacek		
2005		95	Patrick Sharp	253	Bruno St. Jacques	**1993**	
Pick		146	Jussi Timonen	258	Sergei Skrobot	**Pick**	
29	Steve Downie	150	Bernd Bruckler			36	Janne Niinimaa
91	Oskars Bartulis	158	Roman Malek	**1997**		71	Vaclav Prospal
119	Jeremy Duchesne	172	Dennis Seidenberg	**Pick**		77	Milos Holan
152	Josh Beaulieu	177	Andrei Razin	30	Jean-Marc Pelletier	114	Vladimir Krechin
174	John Flatters	208	Thierry Douville	50	Pat Kavanagh	140	Mike Crowley
215	Matt Clackson	225	David Printz	62	Kris Mallette	166	Aaron Israel
				103	Mikhail Chernov	192	Paul Healey
2004		**2000**		158	Jordon Flodell	218	Tripp Tracy
Pick		**Pick**		164	Todd Fedoruk	226	E.J. Bradley
92	Rob Bellamy	28	Justin Williams	214	Marko Kauppinen	244	Jeff Staples
101	R.J. Anderson	94	Alexander Drozdetsky	240	Par Styf	270	Ken Hemenway
124	David Laliberte	171	Roman Cechmanek				
144	Chris Zarb	195	Colin Shields	**1996**		**1992**	
149	Gino Pisellini	210	John Eichelberger	**Pick**		**Pick**	
170	Ladislav Scurko	227	Guillaume Lefebvre	15	Dainius Zubrus	7	Ryan Sittler
171	Frederik Cabana	259	Regan Kelly	64	Chester Gallant	15	Jason Bowen
232	Martin Houle	287	Milan Kopecky	124	Per-Ragna Bergqvist	31	Denis Metlyuk
253	Travis Gawryletz			133	Jesse Boulerice	103	Vladislav Buljin
286	Triston Grant	**1999**		187	Roman Malov	127	Roman Zolotov
291	John Carter	**Pick**		213	Jeff Milleker	151	Kirk Daubenspeck
		22	Maxime Ouellet			175	Claude Jr. Jutras
2003		119	Jeff Feniak	**1995**		199	Jonas Hakansson
Pick		160	Konstantin Rudenko	**Pick**		223	Chris Herperger
11	Jeff Carter	200	Pavel Kasparik	22	Brian Boucher	247	Patrice Paquin
24	Mike Richards	208	Vaclav Pletka	48	Shane Kenny		
69	Colin Fraser	224	David Nystrom	100	Radovan Somik		
81	Stefan Ruzicka			132	Dmitri Tertyshny		
85	Alexandre Picard			135	Jamie Sokolsky		
87	Ryan Potulny			152	Martin Spanhel		
95	Rick Kozak			178	Martin Streit		
108	Kevin Romy			204	Ruslan Shafikov		
140	David Tremblay			230	Jeff Lank		
191	Rejean Beauchemin						
193	Ville Hostikka						

Captains' History

Lou Angotti, 1967-68; Ed Van Impe, 1968-69 to 1971-72; Ed Van Impe and Bobby Clarke, 1972-73; Bobby Clarke, 1973-74 to 1978-79; Mel Bridgman, 1979-80, 1980-81; Bill Barber, 1981-82; Bill Barber and Bobby Clarke, 1982-83; Bobby Clarke, 1983-84; Dave Poulin, 1984-85 to 1988-89; Dave Poulin and Ron Sutter, 1989-90; Ron Sutter, 1990-91; Rick Tocchet, 1991-92; no captain, 1992-93; Kevin Dineen, 1993-94; Eric Lindros, 1994-95 to 1998-99; Eric Lindros and Eric Desjardins, 1999-2000; Eric Desjardins, 2000-01; Eric Desjardins and Keith Primeau, 2001-02; Keith Primeau, 2002-03, 2003-04; Keith Primeau and Derian Hatcher, 2005-06.

General Managers' History

Bud Poile, 1967-68, 1968-69; Bud Poile and Keith Allen, 1969-70; Keith Allen, 1970-71 to 1982-83; Bob McCammon, 1983-84; Bob Clarke, 1984-85 to 1989-90; Russ Farwell, 1990-91 to 1993-94; Bob Clarke, 1994-95 to date.

General Manager

CLARKE, BOB
General Manager, Philadelphia Flyers.
Born in Flin Flon, Man., August 13, 1949.

Bob Clarke was named general manager of the Philadelphia Flyers on June 15, 1994. Clarke's appointment marked the second time he has served as the Flyers' general manager. The Flin Flon native was the Flyers' vice president and general manager from 1984 to 1990. During his tenure as the team's general manager, the Flyers have won seven divisional titles, three conference championships, reached the Stanley Cup semifinals seven times and the Finals three times.

Prior to re-joining the Flyers' family in 1994, Clarke served as vice president and general manager of the Florida Panthers. In 1993-94, their first season in the NHL, the Panthers established NHL records for wins (33) and points (83) by an expansion franchise. Clarke also served as the vice president and general manager of the Minnesota North Stars from 1990 to 1992, guiding the team to the Stanley Cup Finals in 1991.

As a player, the former Philadelphia captain led his club to Stanley Cup championships in 1974 and 1975 and captured numerous individual awards, including the Hart Trophy as the league's most valuable player in 1973, 1975 and 1976. The four-time All-Star also received the Bill Masterton Memorial Trophy (perseverance and dedication) in 1972 and the Frank J. Selke Trophy (top defensive forward) in 1983. He appeared in eight All-Star Games and was elected to the Hockey Hall of Fame in 1987. He was awarded the Lester Patrick Trophy in 1979-80 in recognition of his contribution to hockey in the United States. Clarke appeared in 1,144 regular season games, recording 358 goals and 852 assists for 1,210 points. He also added 119 points in 136 playoff games.

Club Directory

Wachovia Center

Philadelphia Flyers
Wachovia Center
3601 South Broad Street
Philadelphia, PA 19148-5290
Phone **215/465-4500**
PR FAX 215/389-9403
www.philadelphiaflyers.com
Capacity: 19,523

Executive Management
Chairman	Ed Snider
President and COO, Comcast-Spectacor	Peter Luukko
General Manager	Bob Clarke
Executive Vice President	Keith Allen
Governor	Ed Snider
Alternate Governors	Bob Clarke, Peter Luukko, Phil Weinberg
Consultant	Ron Ryan
Senior Vice President, Sales	Joe Croce
Vice President, Marketing and Communications	Shawn Tilger
Executive Assistants	Cheri Arnao, Lisa D'Aprile, Kate Dreyer, Mya Gupta
Receptionists	Ann Bachich, Debbie Brown

Hockey Club Personnel
Assistant General Managers	Paul Holmgren, Barry Hanrahan
Head Coach	Ken Hitchcock
Assistant Coaches	Terry Murray, John Stevens
Goaltending Coach	Reggie Lemelin
Director of Player Personnel	Dave Brown
Scouting Staff	John Chapman, Inge Hammarstrom, Steve Leach, Simon Nolet, Dennis Patterson, Chris Pryor, Ilkka Sinisalo, Vaclav Slansky, Evgeny Zimin
Pro Scouts	Ross Fitzpatrick, Al Hill
Video Coordinator	Adam Patterson
Director of Team Services	Bryan Hardenbergh
Executive Assistant	Dianna Taylor
Receptionist	Sharon Allison

Medical/Training Staff
Team Physicians	Bill DeLong, M.D.; Gary Dorshimer, M.D.; Tom Graham, M.D.; Guy Lanzi, D.M.D.; Emanuel Sanfilippo, D.C.
Athletic Trainer/Strength and Conditioning Coach	Jim McCrossin
Assistant Athletic Trainer	Sal Raffa
Massage Therapist	Brad Smith
Head Equipment Manager	Derek Settlemyre
Equipment Managers	Anthony Oratorio, Harry Bricker, Luke Clarke
Training Center Maintenance	Mike Craytor

Communications
Senior Director of Communications	Zack Hill
Director of Media Services and Publications	Joe Klueg
Manager, Communications and New Media	Kevin Kurz
Communications Office Manager	Jill Lipson

Community Relations
Dir. of Comm. Relations & Fan Development	Linda Mantai
Community Relations Manager	Donna Katzman
Fan Development Manager	Rob Baer
Ambassador of Hockey	Bob Kelly
Director of Fan Relations	Joe Kadlec
Ambassadors	Gary Dornhoefer, Bernie Parent

Customer Service
Director of Customer Service	Cindy Stutman
Senior Customer Service Account Manager	Missy Keeler
Customer Service Acc. Mgrs.	Kristen Canterbury, Lauren Cochran, Emily Zoltowski

Game Presentation
Director of Game Presentation	Matthew Coppola
Producer/Director	Artie Halstead

Marketing
Marketing Manager	Lindsey Domers
Publicist	Jennifer Kron

Ticket Sales
Senior Director of Sales	Jim Willits
Sales Manager	Shawn Anderson
Sales Coordinator	Jessica Palmer

Ticketing
Vice President, Ticket Operations	Cecilia Baker
Ticket Office Manager	Linda Fleischer

Finance
Director of Finance	Dave Jablonski
Controller	Justine Kostka
Staff Accountant	Doreen Holmgren
Payroll Accountant	Jim Wineland

Advertising Sales
Vice President of Advertising Sales	Brian Monihan
Senior Director of Sales	Adrian Staiti
National Sales Manager	Louis Harmelin
Advertising Sales Managers	Mike Garrity, Bo Koelle,
Senior Account Executives	Ray Lyons, Joe Watson
Account Executives	Stephanie Bennett, Bryan Collins, Joe Heyer, Andrew Humphreys, Gabe Leibowitz, John Murphy, Rich Rodowicz, Meredith Timberlake
Sponsorship Manager	Maura Thomson
Manager of Television Services	Shannan Archer
Manager of Contract Services	Sheri Wade

Premium Seating
Vice President of Premium Seating	Dennis Shea
Director of Premium Seating	Jimmy Dunk
Sales Manager of Premium Seating	Anthony Monaco
Senior Sales Executive	Chris Genther
Sales Executives	Craig Broderdorp, John Patterson
Director of Client Services	Tamlyn Shusterman

Premium Services
Director of Premium Services	Steve Suppa
Assistant Director, Premium Services	Graig Selgrath
Premium Membership Manager	Debbie Oddi
Membership Sales Manager	Ariel Greenberg

Comcast-Spectacor Foundation – Flyers Charities
Senior Vice President	Mary Ann Saleski
Director	Rita Johanson

Phoenix Coyotes

2005-06 Results: 38w-39L-2OTL-3SOL 81PTS.
Fifth, Pacific Division

Year-by-Year Record

Season	GP	Home W	L	T	OL	Road W	L	T	OL	Overall W	L	T	OL	GF	GA	Pts.	Finished	Playoff Result
2005-06	82	19	18	....	4	19	21	....	1	38	39	....	5	246	271	81	5th, Pacific Div.	Out of Playoffs
2004-05	....	....	....	....	....	....	....	....	....	....	....	....	....	....	....	....		
2003-04	82	11	19	7	4	11	17	11	2	22	36	18	6	188	245	68	5th, Pacific Div.	Out of Playoffs
2002-03	82	17	16	6	2	14	19	5	3	31	35	11	5	204	230	78	4th, Pacific Div.	Out of Playoffs
2001-02	82	27	8	3	3	13	19	6	3	40	27	9	6	228	210	95	2nd, Pacific Div.	Lost Conf. Quarter-Final
2000-01	82	21	11	7	2	14	16	10	1	35	27	17	3	214	212	90	4th, Pacific Div.	Out of Playoffs
1999-2000	82	22	16	2	1	17	15	6	3	39	31	8	4	232	228	90	3rd, Pacific Div.	Lost Conf. Quarter-Final
1998-99	82	23	13	5	....	16	18	7	....	39	31	12	....	205	197	90	2nd, Pacific Div.	Lost Conf. Quarter-Final
1997-98	82	19	16	6	....	16	19	6	....	35	35	12	....	224	227	82	4th, Central Div.	Lost Conf. Quarter-Final
1996-97	82	15	19	7	....	23	18	0	....	38	37	7	....	240	243	83	3rd, Central Div.	Lost Conf. Quarter-Final
1995-96*	82	22	16	3	....	14	24	3	....	36	40	6	....	275	291	78	5th, Central Div.	Lost Conf. Quarter-Final
1994-95*	48	10	10	4	....	6	15	3	....	16	25	7	....	157	177	39	6th, Central Div.	Out of Playoffs
1993-94*	84	15	23	4	....	9	28	5	....	24	51	9	....	245	344	57	6th, Central Div.	Out of Playoffs
1992-93*	84	23	16	3	....	17	21	4	....	40	37	7	....	322	320	87	4th, Smythe Div.	Lost Div. Semi-Final
1991-92*	80	20	14	6	....	13	18	9	....	33	32	15	....	251	244	81	4th, Smythe Div.	Lost Div. Semi-Final
1990-91*	80	17	18	5	....	9	25	6	....	26	43	11	....	260	288	63	5th, Smythe Div.	Out of Playoffs
1989-90*	80	22	13	5	....	15	19	6	....	37	32	11	....	298	290	85	3rd, Smythe Div.	Lost Div. Semi-Final
1988-89*	80	17	18	5	....	9	24	7	....	26	42	12	....	300	355	64	5th, Smythe Div.	Out of Playoffs
1987-88*	80	20	14	6	....	13	22	5	....	33	36	11	....	292	310	77	3rd, Smythe Div.	Lost Div. Semi-Final
1986-87*	80	25	12	3	....	15	20	5	....	40	32	8	....	279	271	88	3rd, Smythe Div.	Lost Div. Final
1985-86*	80	18	19	3	....	8	28	4	....	26	47	7	....	295	372	59	3rd, Smythe Div.	Lost Div. Semi-Final
1984-85*	80	21	13	6	....	22	14	4	....	43	27	10	....	358	332	96	2nd, Smythe Div.,	Lost Div. Final
1983-84*	80	17	15	8	....	14	23	3	....	31	38	11	....	340	374	73	4th, Smythe Div.	Lost Div. Semi-Final
1982-83*	80	22	16	2	....	11	23	6	....	33	39	8	....	311	333	74	4th, Smythe Div.	Lost Div. Semi-Final
1981-82*	80	18	13	9	....	15	20	5	....	33	33	14	....	319	332	80	2nd, Norris Div.	Lost Div. Semi-Final
1980-81*	80	7	25	8	....	2	32	6	....	9	57	14	....	246	400	32	6th, Smythe Div.	Out of Playoffs
1979-80*	80	13	19	8	....	7	30	3	....	20	49	11	....	214	314	51	5th, Smythe Div.	Out of Playoffs

* Winnipeg Jets

2006-07 Schedule

Oct.	Thu.	5	NY Islanders
	Sat.	7	Anaheim
	Mon.	9	at Columbus
	Wed.	11	at Detroit
	Sat.	14	at Nashville
	Tue.	17	at St. Louis
	Thu.	19	Los Angeles
	Sat.	21	Dallas
	Mon.	23	at Edmonton
	Tue.	24	at Calgary
	Thu.	26	Edmonton
	Sat.	28	NY Rangers
Nov.	Fri.	3	at Anaheim
	Sat.	4	Los Angeles
	Thu.	9	Dallas
	Sat.	11	San Jose
	Tue.	14	Minnesota
	Thu.	16	Chicago
	Sat.	18	at Los Angeles*
	Sun.	19	at Anaheim*
	Wed.	22	New Jersey
	Fri.	24	at Minnesota*
	Sat.	25	at St. Louis
	Thu.	30	Los Angeles
Dec.	Mon.	4	Nashville
	Wed.	6	at Dallas
	Thu.	7	at Chicago
	Sat.	9	Dallas
	Mon.	11	at San Jose
	Tue.	12	at Vancouver
	Thu.	14	Columbus
	Sat.	16	Calgary
	Thu.	21	Edmonton
	Sat.	23	Anaheim
	Tue.	26	at Los Angeles
	Thu.	28	at San Jose
	Sat.	30	San Jose
Jan.	Mon.	1	at Washington*
	Thu.	4	at Carolina
	Fri.	5	at Atlanta
	Sun.	7	at Chicago*

	Tue.	9	at Dallas
	Thu.	11	Detroit
	Sat.	13	San Jose
	Mon.	15	St. Louis*
	Wed.	17	at Colorado
	Thu.	18	at San Jose
	Sat.	20	at Los Angeles
	Fri.	26	at Colorado
	Sat.	27	Pittsburgh
	Wed.	31	at Anaheim
Feb.	Thu.	1	Nashville
	Sat.	3	Minnesota
	Tue.	6	at Columbus
	Wed.	7	at Detroit
	Sat.	10	at Florida
	Tue.	13	at Tampa Bay
	Thu.	15	Anaheim
	Sat.	17	Detroit
	Mon.	19	at Nashville*
	Thu.	22	Calgary
	Mon.	26	at Calgary
	Tue.	27	at Edmonton
Mar.	Thu.	1	at Vancouver
	Sat.	3	Columbus
	Wed.	7	at Anaheim
	Thu.	8	Vancouver
	Sat.	10	Chicago
	Mon.	12	Philadelphia
	Thu.	15	San Jose
	Sat.	17	Colorado
	Sun.	18	at Dallas
	Tue.	20	at Minnesota
	Thu.	22	Anaheim
	Sat.	24	Dallas
	Tue.	27	at Dallas
	Thu.	29	Colorado
	Fri.	30	at San Jose
Apr.	Tue.	3	St. Louis
	Thu.	5	Los Angeles
	Sat.	7	at Los Angeles*
	Sun.	8	Vancouver*

Denotes afternoon game.

Franchise date: June 22, 1979
Transferred from Winnipeg to Phoenix, July 1, 1996

WESTERN
CONFERENCE

PACIFIC DIVISION

28th NHL Season

Ladislav Nagy averaged better than a point per game for the Coyotes last season with 56 points in just 51 games. His 41 assists were tops on the team.

2006-07 Player Personnel

FORWARDS	HT	WT	S	Place of Birth	Date	2005-06 Club
COMRIE, Mike	5-10	185	L	Edmonton, Alta.	9/11/80	Phoenix
DOAN, Shane	6-2	216	R	Halkirk, Alta.	10/10/76	Phoenix
FISCHER, Patrick	5-11	194	L	Zug, Switz.	9/6/75	Zug
GRATTON, Josh	6-2	214	L	Brantford, Ont.	9/9/82	Phi-Phi (AHL)-Phx
LARAQUE, Georges	6-3	243	R	Montreal, Que.	12/7/76	Edmonton
LATENDRESSE, Olivier	5-10	195	L	LaSalle, Que.	2/12/86	Val-d'Or
LEHOUX, Yanick	6-1	200	R	Montreal, Que.	4/8/82	Geneve-Basel-Phoenix-Manchester-San Antonio
LISIN, Enver	6-2	190	L	Moscow, USSR	4/22/86	Kazan
MacLEAN, Don	6-2	199	L	Sydney, N.S.	1/14/77	Detroit-Grand Rapids
MUELLER, Peter	6-2	205	R	Bloomington, MN	4/14/88	Everett
NAGY, Ladislav	5-11	192	L	Saca, Czech.	6/1/79	Phoenix
NASH, Tyson	5-11	191	L	Edmonton, Alta.	3/11/75	Phoenix
NOLAN, Owen	6-1	215	R	Belfast, N. Ireland	2/12/72	Did not play
PERREAULT, Joel	6-1	197	R	Montreal, Que.	4/6/83	Portland (AHL)-Phoenix-San Antonio
REINPRECHT, Steve	6-0	195	L	Edmonton, Alta.	5/7/76	Calgary-Phoenix
RHEAUME, Pascal	6-1	220	L	Quebec City, Que.	6/21/73	N.J.-Alb-Phx-San Antonio
RICCI, Mike	6-0	200	L	Scarborough, Ont.	10/27/71	Phoenix
ROENICK, Jeremy	6-1	196	R	Boston, MA	1/17/70	Los Angeles
SAPRYKIN, Oleg	6-1	195	L	Moscow, USSR	2/12/81	Phoenix
SCATCHARD, Dave	6-3	220	R	Hinton, Alta.	2/20/76	Boston-Phoenix
SJOSTROM, Fredrik	6-1	217	L	Fargelanda, Sweden	5/6/83	Phoenix
TAFFE, Jeff	6-3	201	L	Hastings, MN	2/19/81	NYR-Hart-Phx-San Antonio
THOMAS, Bill	6-1	191	R	Pittsburgh, PA	6/20/83	Nebraska-Omaha-Phoenix
ZIGOMANIS, Mike	6-1	200	R	North York, Ont.	1/17/81	Carolina-Lowell (AHL)-St. Louis-Peoria

DEFENSEMEN						
BALLARD, Keith	5-11	208	L	Baudette, MN	11/26/82	Phoenix
BOYNTON, Nick	6-2	211	R	Nobleton, Ont.	1/14/79	Boston
HELMER, Bryan	6-1	200	R	Sault Ste. Marie, Ont.	7/15/72	Grand Rapids
JONES, Matt	6-0	215	L	Downers Grove, IL	8/8/83	Phoenix-San Antonio
JOVANOVSKI, Ed	6-2	210	L	Windsor, Ont.	6/26/76	Vancouver
MICHALEK, Zbynek	6-1	200	R	Jindrichuv Hradec, Czech.	12/23/82	Phoenix
MORRIS, Derek	6-0	220	R	Edmonton, Alta.	8/24/78	Phoenix
ROCHE, Travis	6-1	200	R	Grand Cache, Alta.	6/17/78	Chicago (AHL)
SEIDENBERG, Dennis	6-1	210	L	Schwenningen, W. Germ.	7/18/81	Philadelphia-Phoenix
SPILLER, Matthew	6-5	233	L	Daysland, Alta.	2/7/83	Phoenix-San Antonio
YANDLE, Keith	6-2	195	L	Boston, MA	9/9/86	Moncton

GOALTENDERS	HT	WT	C	Place of Birth	Date	2005-06 Club
JOSEPH, Curtis	5-11	190	L	Keswick, Ont.	4/29/67	Phoenix
LENEVEU, David	6-1	187	L	Fernie, B.C.	5/23/83	Phoenix-San Antonio
MORRISON, Mike	6-3	194	L	Medford, MA	7/11/79	Edmonton-Greenville-Ottawa
SAUVE, Philippe	6-0	188	L	Buffalo, NY	2/27/80	Calgary-Phoenix

Coach

GRETZKY, WAYNE
Coach, Phoenix Coyotes. Born in Brantford, Ont., January 26, 1961.

Phoenix Coyotes chairman and governor Steve Ellman announced on August 8, 2005 that Wayne Gretzky had agreed to a multiyear contract to serve as head coach of the Phoenix Coyotes. In addition to serving as the Coyotes' head coach, Gretzky also continues as managing partner and alternate governor for the Coyotes, a role that he had performed for the previous four seasons. Gretzky officially joined the franchise on February 15, 2001, when the Ellman and Moyes ownership group completed the purchase of the Coyotes.

Gretzky played 20 seasons in the National Hockey League with Edmonton, Los Angeles, St. Louis and the New York Rangers, dominating the game unlike any player in history. Gretzky helped win four Stanley Cup championships and three Canada Cup tournament titles during his illustrious playing career. He became the NHL's all-time leading goal, assist and point producer for a single season and career (both regular season and playoffs). Gretzky won the Art Ross Trophy as the NHL's leading scorer 10 times, the Hart Trophy as the League's MVP nine times (including eight consecutive seasons) and the Conn Smythe Trophies as playoff MVP twice. He earned the Lady Byng Trophy as the NHL's most gentlemanly player five times and made 18 consecutive All-Star Game appearances, securing three All-Star MVP Awards. Gretzky is an eight-time First All-Star Team member and seven-time Second All-Star Team member. He holds virtually every offensive record in the NHL and his tireless support of the game has contributed significantly to the popularity it enjoys today.

On November 22, 1999 – seven months after his retirement – Gretzky was inducted into the Hockey Hall of Fame in Toronto, becoming the tenth and final player in Hockey Hall of Fame history to have the mandatory three-year waiting period for enshrinement waived by the Hall's board of directors.

Gretzky's incredible success in hockey has continued past his playing career. In a managerial role with Team Canada, Gretzky served as executive director for Team Canada, responsible for assembling Canada's best hockey players at the 2002 Olympic Winter Games in Salt Lake City and again in 2004 at the World Cup of Hockey. Under Gretzky's leadership, Team Canada won the gold medal for the first time in 50 years at the 2002 Olympics. Two years later, Team Canada repeated the feat by winning the 2004 World Cup of Hockey championship. Gretzky also served as executive director again at the 2006 Olympics.

Coaching Record

Season	Team	Games	Regular Season				Playoffs		
			W	L	O/T	Games	W	L	
2005-06	Phoenix (NHL)	82	38	39	5	.....	.....	.....	
	NHL Totals	82	38	39	5				

Assistant coach Rick Tocchet posted an 2-3 record as replacement coach when Gretzky was sidelined due to the death of his mother, December 17 to 28, 2005. All games are credited to Gretzky's coaching record.

2005-06 Scoring
*– rookie

Regular Season

Pos	#	Player	Team	GP	G	A	Pts	+/–	PIM	PP	SH	GW	S	%
R	19	Shane Doan	PHX	82	30	36	66	–9	123	17	0	7	254	11.8
C	89	Mike Comrie	PHX	80	30	30	60	2	55	10	0	4	190	15.8
L	17	Ladislav Nagy	PHX	51	15	41	56	8	74	7	1	4	132	11.4
R	12	Mike Johnson	PHX	80	16	38	54	7	50	6	1	3	145	11.0
C	29	Steve Reinprecht	CGY	52	16	19	29	10	24	5	0	1	72	13.9
			PHX	28	12	11	23	1	8	4	1	2	58	20.7
			TOTAL	80	22	30	52	11	32	9	1	3	130	16.9
D	23	Paul Mara	PHX	78	15	32	47	–12	70	8	0	0	157	9.6
L	8	Geoff Sanderson	CBJ	2	0	0	0	–1	0	0	0	0	7	0.0
			PHX	75	25	21	46	–14	58	11	1	1	152	16.4
			TOTAL	77	25	21	46	–15	58	11	1	1	159	15.7
D	2	* Keith Ballard	PHX	82	8	31	39	–18	99	1	3	1	102	7.8
C	38	Dave Scatchard	BOS	16	4	6	10	–2	28	1	0	0	40	10.0
			PHX	47	11	12	23	–11	84	4	0	3	81	13.6
			TOTAL	63	15	18	33	–13	112	5	0	3	121	12.4
L	11	Oleg Kvasha	NYI	49	9	12	21	–2	32	1	0	1	104	8.7
			PHX	15	4	7	11	5	6	0	0	0	32	12.5
			TOTAL	64	13	19	32	3	38	1	0	1	136	9.6
D	53	Derek Morris	PHX	53	6	21	27	–7	54	4	1	2	91	6.6
L	91	Oleg Saprykin	PHX	67	11	14	25	–16	50	3	0	1	126	8.7
D	4	* Zbynek Michalek	PHX	82	9	15	24	4	62	5	0	2	105	8.6
R	20	Fredrik Sjostrom	PHX	75	6	17	23	1	42	1	0	1	109	5.5
C	15	Boyd Devereaux	PHX	78	8	14	22	–13	44	1	0	1	76	10.5
D	22	Dennis Seidenberg	PHI	29	2	5	7	–4	4	1	0	0	34	5.9
			PHX	34	1	10	11	–9	14	1	0	0	49	2.0
			TOTAL	63	3	15	18	–13	18	2	0	0	83	3.6
C	40	Mike Ricci	PHX	78	10	6	16	–22	69	5	1	1	50	20.0
D	5	Jamie Rivers	DET	15	0	1	1	0	12	0	0	0	4	0.0
			PHX	18	0	5	5	2	26	0	0	0	32	0.0
			TOTAL	33	0	6	6	2	38	0	0	0	36	0.0
L	18	Tyson Nash	PHX	50	0	6	6	–7	84	0	0	0	44	0.0
R	21	* Bill Thomas	PHX	9	1	2	3	–2	2	1	0	0	15	6.7
C	26	* Joel Perrault	PHX	5	1	1	2	0	2	0	0	0	7	14.3
D	55	* Matt Jones	PHX	16	0	2	2	–2	14	0	0	0	10	0.0
C	29	* Yanick Lehoux	PHX	3	1	0	1	1	0	0	0	0	5	20.0
C	24	* Josh Gratton	PHI	3	0	0	0	0	14	0	0	0	3	0.0
			PHX	11	1	0	1	–3	30	0	0	0	14	7.1
			TOTAL	14	1	0	1	–3	44	0	0	0	17	5.9
R	9	Brett Hull	PHX	5	0	1	1	–3	0	0	0	0	8	0.0
D	6	Matthew Spiller	PHX	8	0	1	1	–1	13	0	0	0	3	0.0
L	14	Steve Gainey	PHX	20	0	1	1	–3	20	0	0	0	11	0.0
R	28	Pavel Brendl	PHX	2	0	0	0	–3	0	0	0	0	4	0.0
R	29	* Tim Jackman	N.J.	12	0	0	0	1	21	0	0	0	4	0.0
C	22	Pascal Rheaume	N.J.	12	0	0	0	–6	4	0	0	0	11	0.0
			PHX	1	0	0	0	–1	0	0	0	0	0	0.0
			TOTAL	13	0	0	0	–7	4	0	0	0	11	0.0

Goaltending

No.	Goaltender	GPI	Mins	Avg	W	L	OT	EN	SO	GA	SA	S%	G	A	PIM
31	Curtis Joseph	60	3424	2.91	32	21	3	3	4	166	1690	.902	0	1	18
30	* David Leneveu	15	814	3.24	3	8	2	1	0	44	386	.886	0	0	0
33	Brian Boucher	11	512	3.87	3	6	0	3	0	33	268	.877	0	0	2
35	* Philippe Sauve	5	187	5.45	0	4	0	1	0	17	128	.867	0	0	0
	Totals	82	4976	3.23	38	39	5	8	4	268	2480	.892			

Ten-year veteran Ed Jovanovski joins the Coyotes for the 2006-07 season.

Coaching History

Tom McVie and Bill Sutherland, 1979-80; Tom McVie, Bill Sutherland and Mike Smith, 1980-81; Tom Watt, 1981-82, 1982-83; Tom Watt and Barry Long, 1983-84; Barry Long, 1984-85; Barry Long and John Ferguson, 1985-86; Dan Maloney, 1986-87, 1987-88; Dan Maloney and Rick Bowness, 1988-89; Bob Murdoch, 1989-90, 1990-91; John Paddock, 1991-92 to 1993-94; John Paddock and Terry Simpson, 1994-95; Terry Simpson, 1995-96; Don Hay, 1996-97; Jim Schoenfeld, 1997-98, 1998-99; Bob Francis, 1999-2000 to 2002-03; Bob Francis and Rick Bowness, 2003-04; Rick Bowness, 2004-05; Wayne Gretzky, 2005-06 to date.

Club Records

Team

(Figures in brackets for season records are games played; records for fewest points, wins, ties, losses, goals, goals against are for 70 or more games)

Most Points **96** 1984-85 (80)
Most Wins **43** 1984-85 (80)
Most Ties **18** 2003-04 (82)
Most Losses **57** 1980-81 (80)
Most Goals **358** 1984-85 (80)
Most Goals Against **400** 1980-81 (80)
Fewest Points **32** 1980-81 (80)
Fewest Wins **9** 1980-81 (80)
Fewest Ties **6** 1995-96 (82)
Fewest Losses **27** 1984-85 (80), 2000-01 (82), 2001-02 (82)
Fewest Goals **188** 2003-04 (82)
Fewest Goals Against **197** 1998-99 (82)
Longest Winning Streak
Overall .... **9** Mar. 8-27/85
Home .... **9** Dec. 27/92-Jan. 23/93
Away .... **8** Feb. 25-Apr. 6/85
Longest Undefeated Streak
Overall .... **14** Oct. 25-Nov. 28/98 (12 wins, 2 ties)
Home .... **11** Dec. 23/83-Feb. 5/84 (6 wins, 5 ties), Oct. 15-Dec. 20/98 (10 wins, 1 tie)
Away .... **9** Feb. 25-Apr. 7/85 (8 wins, 1 tie), Dec. 7/03-Jan. 9/04 (5 wins, 4 ties)
Longest Losing Streak
Overall .... **10** Nov. 30-Dec. 20/80, Feb. 6-25/94
Home .... **5** Oct. 29-Nov. 13/93 Mar. 13-23/00
Away .... **13** Jan. 26-Apr. 14/94
Longest Winless Streak
Overall .... ***30** Oct. 19-Dec. 20/80 (23 losses, 7 ties)
Home .... **14** Oct. 19-Dec. 14/80 (9 losses, 5 ties)
Away .... **18** Oct. 10-Dec. 20/80 (16 losses, 2 ties)
Most Shutouts, Season **9** 1998-99 (82)
Most PIM, Season **2,278** 1987-88 (80)
Most Goals, Game .... **12** Feb. 25/85 (Wpg. 12 at NYR 5)

Individual

Most Seasons .... **15** Teppo Numminen
Most Games .... **1,098** Teppo Numminen
Most Goals, Career .... **379** Dale Hawerchuk
Most Assists, Career .... **553** Thomas Steen
Most Points, Career .... **929** Dale Hawerchuk (379G, 550A)
Most PIM, Career .... **1,508** Keith Tkachuk
Most Shutouts, Career .... **21** Nikolai Khabibulin
Longest Consecutive Games Streak .... **475** Dale Hawerchuk (Dec. 19/82-Dec. 10/88)
Most Goals, Season .... **76** Teemu Selanne (1992-93)
Most Assists, Season .... **79** Phil Housley (1992-93)
Most Points, Season .... **132** Teemu Selanne (1992-93; 76G, 56A)
Most PIM, Season .... **347** Tie Domi (1993-94)
Most Points, Defenseman, Season .... **97** Phil Housley (1992-93; 18G, 79A)
Most Points, Center, Season .... **130** Dale Hawerchuk (1984-85; 53G, 77A)
Most Points, Right Wing, Season .... **132** Teemu Selanne (1992-93; 76G, 56A)
Most Points, Left Wing, Season .... **98** Keith Tkachuk (1995-96; 50G, 48A)
Most Points, Rookie, Season .... ***132** Teemu Selanne (1992-93; 76G, 56A)
Most Shutouts, Season .... **8** Nikolai Khabibulin (1998-99)
Most Goals, Game .... **5** Willy Lindstrom (Mar. 2/82), Alexei Zhamnov (Apr. 1/95)
Most Assists, Game .... **5** Dale Hawerchuk (Mar. 6/84, Mar. 18/89, Mar. 4/90), Phil Housley (Jan. 18/93), Keith Tkachuk (Feb. 23/01)
Most Points, Game .... **6** Willy Lindstrom (Mar. 2/82; 5G, 1A), Dale Hawerchuk (Dec. 14/83; 3G, 3A, Mar. 5/88; 2G, 4A, Mar. 18/89; 1G, 5A), Thomas Steen (Oct. 24/84; 2G, 4A), Ed Olczyk (Dec. 21/91; 2G, 4A)

* NHL Record.
Records include Winnipeg Jets, 1979-80 through 1995-96.

Winnipeg Jets Retired Numbers

9	Bobby Hull	1972-1980
25	Thomas Steen	1981-1995

Captains' History

Lars-Erik Sjoberg, 1979-80; Morris Lukowich, 1980-81; Dave Christian, 1981-82; Dave Christian and Lucien DeBlois, 1982-83; Lucien DeBlois, 1983-84; Dale Hawerchuk, 1984-85 to 1988-89; Randy Carlyle, Dale Hawerchuk and Thomas Steen (tri-captains), 1989-90; Randy Carlyle and Thomas Steen (co-captains), 1990-91; Troy Murray, 1991-92; Troy Murray and Dean Kennedy, 1992-93; Dean Kennedy and Keith Tkachuk, 1993-94; Keith Tkachuk, 1994-95; Kris King, 1995-96; Keith Tkachuk, 1996-97 to 2000-01; Teppo Numminen, 2001-02, 2002-03; Shane Doan, 2003-04 to date.

All-time Record vs. Other Clubs

Regular Season

	At Home								On Road								Total							
	GP	W	L	T	OL	GF	GA	PTS	GP	W	L	T	OL	GF	GA	PTS	GP	W	L	T	OL	GF	GA	PTS
Anaheim	30	12	13	2	3	83	90	29	31	9	17	3	2	75	93	23	61	21	30	5	5	158	183	52
Atlanta	6	5	0	1	0	21	9	11	4	3	1	0	0	12	6	6	10	8	1	1	0	33	15	17
Boston	30	13	14	3	0	101	102	29	31	5	22	4	0	94	137	14	61	18	36	7	0	195	239	43
Buffalo	29	13	14	2	0	87	92	28	32	7	20	5	0	82	128	19	61	20	34	7	0	169	220	47
Calgary	72	35	26	11	0	270	244	81	73	24	40	9	0	231	300	57	145	59	66	20	0	501	544	138
Carolina	32	15	14	2	1	118	116	33	30	10	13	6	1	89	103	27	62	25	27	8	2	207	219	60
Chicago	52	28	19	5	0	169	160	61	50	13	26	10	1	132	188	37	102	41	45	15	1	301	348	98
Colorado	42	16	19	7	0	147	150	39	43	15	21	5	2	141	155	37	85	31	40	12	2	288	305	76
Columbus	10	6	1	3	0	31	21	15	10	4	5	1	0	23	26	9	20	10	6	4	0	54	47	24
Dallas	58	24	29	4	1	182	197	53	59	21	29	9	0	176	209	51	117	45	58	13	1	358	406	104
Detroit	51	17	20	14	0	152	162	48	53	20	25	8	0	179	203	48	104	37	45	22	0	331	365	96
Edmonton	73	30	36	5	2	291	321	67	74	21	45	6	2	239	323	50	147	51	81	11	4	530	644	117
Florida	11	4	3	3	1	31	34	12	8	5	3	0	0	21	23	10	19	9	6	3	1	52	57	22
Los Angeles	80	42	26	11	1	316	256	96	78	33	30	14	1	297	307	81	158	75	56	25	2	613	563	177
Minnesota	10	6	3	1	0	29	23	13	10	5	3	2	0	23	20	12	20	11	6	3	0	52	43	25
Montreal	29	9	13	7	0	94	112	25	30	3	25	2	0	68	147	8	59	12	38	9	0	162	259	33
Nashville	14	8	4	0	2	42	43	18	14	5	5	2	2	35	39	14	28	13	9	2	4	77	82	32
New Jersey	31	21	7	3	0	114	81	45	29	11	12	6	0	87	95	28	60	32	19	9	0	201	176	73
NY Islanders	30	11	15	4	0	96	105	26	30	9	13	8	0	91	113	26	60	20	28	12	0	187	218	52
NY Rangers	31	13	13	4	1	107	101	31	29	9	17	2	1	102	128	21	60	22	30	6	2	209	229	52
Ottawa	10	4	5	1	0	34	38	9	12	6	5	1	0	36	36	13	22	10	10	2	0	70	74	22
Philadelphia	31	13	16	2	0	99	106	28	31	8	23	0	0	83	134	16	62	21	39	2	0	182	240	44
Pittsburgh	31	14	13	3	1	116	107	32	30	10	20	0	0	86	120	20	61	24	33	3	1	202	227	52
St. Louis	53	27	19	7	0	175	165	61	52	15	26	11	0	144	185	41	105	42	45	18	0	319	350	102
San Jose	39	20	13	3	3	122	110	46	36	17	15	4	0	117	122	38	75	37	28	7	3	239	232	84
Tampa Bay	12	6	6	0	0	29	29	12	10	5	5	0	0	33	33	10	22	11	11	0	0	62	62	22
Toronto	39	20	13	6	0	161	142	46	44	22	20	2	0	165	160	46	83	42	33	8	0	326	302	92
Vancouver	71	34	27	10	0	262	253	78	74	19	45	10	0	205	278	48	145	53	72	20	0	467	531	126
Washington	31	15	9	7	0	113	111	37	31	8	17	5	1	85	119	22	62	23	26	12	1	198	230	59
Totals	**1038**	**481**	**410**	**131**	**16**	**3592**	**3480**	**1109**	**1038**	**342**	**548**	**135**	**13**	**3151**	**3930**	**832**	**2076**	**823**	**958**	**266**	**29**	**6743**	**7410**	**1941**

Playoffs

	Series	W	L	GP	W	L	T	GF	GA	Last Mtg.	Rnd.	Result
Anaheim	1	0	1	7	3	4	0	17	17	1997	CQF	L 3-4
Calgary	3	2	1	13	7	6	0	45	43	1987	DSF	W 4-2
Colorado	1	0	1	5	1	4	0	10	17	2000	CQF	L 1-4
Detroit	2	0	2	12	4	8	0	28	44	1998	CQF	L 2-4
Edmonton	6	0	6	26	4	22	0	75	120	1990	DSF	L 3-4
St. Louis	2	0	2	11	4	7	0	29	39	1999	CQF	L 3-4
San Jose	1	0	1	5	1	4	0	7	13	2002	CQF	L 1-4
Vancouver	2	0	2	13	5	8	0	34	50	1993	DSF	L 2-4
Totals	**18**	**2**	**16**	**92**	**29**	**63**	**0**	**245**	**343**			

Playoff Results 2006-2001

Year	Round	Opponent	Result	GF	GA
2002	CQF	San Jose	L 1-4	7	13

Abbreviations: Round: CQF – conference quarter-final; **DSF** – division semi-final.

Calgary totals include Atlanta Flames, 1979-80.
Colorado totals include Quebec, 1979-80 to 1994-95.
New Jersey totals include Colorado Rockies, 1979-80 to 1981-82.
Carolina totals include Hartford, 1979-80 to 1996-97.
Dallas totals include Minnesota North Stars, 1979-80 to 1992-93.

2005-06 Results

Oct.	5	at Vancouver	2-3
	6	at Los Angeles	2-3
	8	Minnesota	2-1
	11	at Dallas	2-3
	13	Nashville	4-5†
	15	Detroit	0-2
	17	at Calgary	2-0
	18	at Edmonton	4-3*
	20	at Vancouver	2-3
	23	at Anaheim	3-5
	25	St. Louis	5-4*
	27	Calgary	3-2
	29	Dallas	3-5
	30	at Anaheim	2-3
Nov.	3	Los Angeles	4-0
	5	at Detroit	4-1
	6	at Chicago	1-2*
	8	at Minnesota	4-2
	10	Calgary	3-4
	12	Anaheim	2-1*
	16	Colorado	1-3
	19	at San Jose	4-3†
	20	Columbus	5-1
	22	Anaheim	1-2
	25	at Dallas	4-1
	26	Vancouver	2-1
	30	at Anaheim	1-6
Dec.	3	Carolina	8-4
	5	Atlanta	5-2
	11	at Boston	2-1*
	13	at Montreal	2-5
	15	Tampa Bay	1-3
	17	at Los Angeles	1-4
	20	St. Louis	4-5
	22	San Jose	2-1
	23	at Dallas	3-2
	26	at Colorado	4-7
	28	at San Jose	5-4
	29	Los Angeles	6-5*
	31	Colorado	2-5
Jan.	5	at Los Angeles	0-4
	8	Columbus	2-5
	10	at Ottawa	2-7
	12	at Buffalo	2-1†
	14	at Toronto	4-3
	16	Washington	1-6
	19	Florida	6-3
	21	Edmonton	4-3†
	23	at Dallas	1-4
	24	at Minnesota	2-3
	26	at St. Louis	5-3
	28	San Jose	6-2
	29	Edmonton	3-4†
	31	Vancouver	4-7
Feb.	2	Los Angeles	2-1†
	4	Minnesota	4-6
	7	Chicago	1-3
	9	Dallas	1-5
	12	San Jose	4-5*
Mar.	2	Dallas	6-2
	4	Detroit	3-7
	7	at Detroit	5-2
	9	at Columbus	4-5
	11	Anaheim	3-5
	12	at Anaheim	2-5
	14	at Los Angeles	6-2
	16	at Nashville	0-2
	19	at Chicago	3-2
	21	at Columbus	5-2
	23	Chicago	4-3
	25	Anaheim	2-5
	28	Nashville	5-3
	30	at San Jose	5-2
Apr.	1	at San Jose	4-3*
	3	at Edmonton	1-7
	5	at Calgary	2-5
	8	Dallas	2-3†
	10	San Jose	2-3
	11	at Colorado	4-6
	13	Los Angeles	3-0
	15	at Nashville	1-5
	16	at St. Louis	3-0

* – Overtime † – Shootout

Entry Draft Selections 2006-1992

2006

Pick	
8	Peter Mueller
29	Chris Summers
88	Jonas Ahnelov
130	Brett Bennett
131	Martin Latal
152	Jordan Bendfeld
188	Chris Frank
196	Benn Ferriero

2005

Pick	
17	Martin Hanzal
59	Pier-Olivier Pelletier
105	Keith Yandle
148	Anton Krysanov
212	Pat Brosnihan

2004

Pick	
5	Blake Wheeler
35	Logan Stephenson
50	Enver Lisin
103	Roman Tomanek
119	Kevin Porter
168	Kevin Cormier
199	Chad Kolarik
240	Aaron Gagnon
261	Will Engasser
265	Daniel Winnik

2003

Pick	
77	Tyler Redenbach
80	Dmitri Pestunov
115	Liam Lindstrom
178	Ryan Gibbons
208	Randall Gelech
242	Eduard Lewandowski
272	Sean Sullivan
290	Loic Burkhalter

2002

Pick	
19	Jakub Koreis
23	Ben Eager
46	David Leneveu
70	Joe Callahan
80	Matt Jones
97	Lance Monych
132	John Zeiler
186	Jeff Pietrasiak
216	Ladislav Kouba
249	Marcus Smith
280	Russell Spence

2001

Pick	
11	Fredrik Sjostrom
31	Matthew Spiller
45	Martin Podlesak
78	Beat Forster
148	David Klema
180	Scott Polaski
210	Steve Belanger
243	Frantisek Lukes
273	Severin Blindenbacher

2000

Pick	
19	Krys Kolanos
53	Alexander Tatarinov
85	Ramzi Abid
160	Nate Kiser
186	Brent Gauvreau
217	Igor Samoilov
249	Sami Venalainen
281	Peter Fabus

1999

Pick	
15	Scott Kelman
19	Kirill Safronov
53	Brad Ralph
71	Jason Jaspers
116	Ryan Lauzon
123	Preston Mizzi
168	Erik Lewerstrom
234	Goran Bezina
262	Alexei Litvinenko

1998

Pick	
14	Patrick DesRochers
43	Ossi Vaananen
73	Pat O'Leary
100	Ryan Vanbuskirk
115	Jay Leach
116	Josh Blackburn
129	Robert Schnabel
160	Rickard Wallin
187	Erik Westrum
214	Justin Hansen

1997

Pick	
43	Juha Gustafsson
96	Scott McCallum
123	Curtis Suter
151	Robert Francz
207	Alexander Andreyev
233	Wyatt Smith

1996

Pick	
11	Dan Focht
24	Daniel Briere
62	Per-Anton Lundstrom
119	Richard Lintner
139	Robert Esche
174	Trevor Letowski
200	Nicholas Lent
226	Marc-Etienne Hubert

1995

Pick	
7	Shane Doan
32	Marc Chouinard
34	Jason Doig
67	Brad Isbister
84	Justin Kurtz
121	Brian Elder
136	Sylvain Daigle
162	Paul Traynor
188	Jaroslav Obsut
189	Fredrik Loven
214	Rob Deciantis

1994

Pick	
30	Deron Quint
56	Dorian Anneck
58	Tavis Hansen
82	Steve Cheredaryk
108	Craig Mills
143	Steve Vezina
146	Chris Kibermanis
186	Ramil Saifullin
212	Henrik Smangs
238	Mike Mader
264	Jason Issel

1993

Pick	
15	Mats Lindgren
31	Scott Langkow
43	Alexei Budayev
79	Ruslan Batyrshin
93	Ravil Gusmanov
119	Larry Courville
145	Michal Grosek
171	Martin Woods
197	Adrian Murray
217	Vladimir Potapov
223	Ilja Stashenkov
228	Harijs Vitolinsh
285	Russ Hewson

1992

Pick	
17	Sergei Bautin
27	Boris Mironov
60	Jeremy Stevenson
84	Mark Visheau
132	Alexander Alexeyev
155	Artur Oktyabrev
156	Andrei Raisky
204	Nikolai Khabibulin
228	Yevgeny Garanin
229	Teemu Numminen
252	Andrei Karpovstev
254	Ivan Vologzhaninov

General Managers' History

John Ferguson, 1979-80 to 1987-88; John Ferguson and Mike Smith, 1988-89; Mike Smith, 1989-90 to 1992-93; Mike Smith and John Paddock, 1993-94; John Paddock, 1994-95, 1995-96; John Paddock and Bobby Smith, 1996-97; Bobby Smith, 1997-98 to 1999-2000; Bobby Smith and Cliff Fletcher, 2000-01; Cliff Fletcher and Michael Barnett, 2001-02; Michael Barnett, 2002-03 to date.

Vice President and General Manager

BARNETT, MICHAEL
Executive Vice President/General Manager, Phoenix Coyotes.
Born in Olds, Alta., October 9, 1948.

Michael Barnett joined the Coyotes as vice president and general manager on August 28, 2001 after serving as president of International Management Group's (IMG) hockey division since 1990. Barnett is the sixth general manager in franchise history and follows in the footsteps of Brian Burke, Pierre Lacroix and Dean Lombardi as former player agents who have become NHL general managers.

With over 20 years of experience in the game prior to joining the Coyotes, Barnett left IMG as one of hockey's most distinguished and well-respected player agents. Over the years, Barnett earned acclaim for his integrity, vision and success as a negotiator. He developed a reputation within the NHL as one of the most creative and well-informed agents in the industry. He is reunited in Phoenix with his longtime friend Wayne Gretzky, the Coyotes' managing partner. Barnett served as Gretzky's agent for 20 years. He also represented some of the NHL's most high-profile players including Jaromir Jagr, Brett Hull, Paul Coffey, Alexander Mogilny, Owen Nolan, Mats Sundin and Joe Thornton.

Barnett actually began his career in hockey as a player. He played hockey at St. Lawrence University in Canton, New York and later attended the University of Calgary, where he played both intercollegiate hockey and football for three years. In 1973-74, he turned professional with the Chicago Cougars (WHA) playing left wing for their minor league affiliate, the Long Island Cougars (NAHL). The following season (1974-75), while playing for the Roanoke-Valley Rebels (SHL) — the Houston Aeros' (WHA) minor league affiliate — Barnett suffered a career ending eye injury.

In 1980, Barnett opened a Western Canadian sports management agency and began his long-lasting relationship with Gretzky by signing him on as his top client. In 1990, Barnett merged his company with Mark McCormack's IMG and became president of IMG hockey operations.

Club Directory

Glendale Arena

Phoenix Coyotes
5800 W. Glenn Drive, Suite 350
Glendale, AZ 85301
Phone **623/463-8800**
FAX 623/463-8810
Tickets 480/563-PUCK

Glendale Arena
9400 W. Maryland Avenue
Glendale, AZ 85305
Phone 623/772-3200
FAX 623/772-3201
Capacity: 17,799
www.PhoenixCoyotes.com

Club Officers & Executives

Majority Investor	Jerry Moyes
Chief Executive Officer & Governor	Jeff A. Shumway
Managing Partner, Alt. Gov. & Head Coach	Wayne Gretzky
President, Chief Operating Officer & Alt. Gov.	Douglas Moss
Sr. Exec. Vice President of Hockey Operations	Cliff Fletcher
Sr. Exec. Vice President, G.M.& Alt. Gov.	Michael Barnett
Sr. Vice President & Assistant General Manager	Laurence Gilman
Exec. Vice President of Business Development	John Browne
Exec. Vice President & Chief Marketing Officer	Michael Bucek
Sr. Vice President of Media & Player Relations	Richard Nairn
Sr. Vice President of Corporate Communications	Jeff Holbrook
Sr. Vice President of Ticket Sales and Services	Jim Van Stone
Sr. Vice President Chief Financial Officer	Mike Nealy
Executive Assistant to the CEO	Elly Penrod
Executive Assistant to the President	Cheryl Taylor
Administrative Assisstant to the G.M.	Michelle Marquez
Assistant to the CFO	Melissa Rezvani

Hockey Operations

Head Coach	Wayne Gretzky
Associate Coaches	Barry Smith, Ulf Samuelsson
Goaltending Coach	Grant Fuhr
Director of Player Personnel	Tom Kurvers
Director of Player Development	Eddie Mio
Director of Hockey Administration	Jay Neal
Strength & Conditioning Coordinator	Mike Bahn
Athletic Therapist	Chris Broadhurst
Massage Therapist	Jukka Nieminen
Head Equipment Manager	Stan Wilson
Equipment Manager	Tony Silva
Assistant Equipment Manager	Jason Rudee
Video Coordinator	Steve Peters
Power Skating Coach	Mark Ciaccio
Team Travel Coordinator	Rick Braunstein
Manager of Team Services	Lesa Guth
Team Internist	Robert Luberto, D.O.
Team Orthopedic Surgeons	Dr. Doug Freedberg, Dr. Gary Waslewski
Team Dentists	Dr. Lawrence Emmott, Dr. Ron Foeldi
San Antonio (AHL) Head Coach	Pat Conacher
San Antonio (AHL) Assistant Coach	Gord Dineen
Professional Scouts	Patrik Augusta, Greg Malone, Christian Ruuttu, Rich Sutter
Director of Amateur Scouting	Keith Gretzky
Amateur Scouts	Gus Badali, Charles Henry, Willy Lindstrom, Steve Lyons, Blair Reid, Greg Royce, Evzen Slansky, Boris Yemeljanov
Director of Security	Jim O'Neal

Communications

Director of Media Relations & Publications	Kevin Crawley
Manager of Media Relations	TBD

Broadcasting

TV Play-by-Play/Analyst	Curt Keilback/Darren Pang
TV/Radio Host	Todd Walsh
Radio Play-by-Play/Analyst	Bob Heethuis/Louie DeBrusk
Director of Broadcasting	Doug Cannon

Community Relations

Manager of Comm. Relations & Fan Development	Sarah Finecey
Manager of Corporate Communications	Heather Van Peursem

Corporate Sales & Service

Vice President of Corporate Partnerships	Bob McGahie
Director of Corporate Partner & Suite Services	Thea Crum
Corporate Partnership Directors	Judd Norris, Bret Fishkind

Finance & Administration

Vice President and Controller	Joe Leibfried
Assistant Controller	Burlenti Shaban

Marketing

Director of Marketing	Dan Brewster
Manager of Advertising & Media	Ted Santiago
Manager of Creative Services	Scott Jenner
Manager of Promotions	Stacey Cohen
Manager of New Media	Chad Lynch

Game Operations

Executive Producer of Event Presentation	Matt Coy
Creative Director	David Rickles

Ticket Sales & Services

Vice President of Ticket Sales & Service	Shayne Donohue
Director of Ticket Sales & Services	Flavil Hampsten
Director of Ticket Sales Administration	Tudor Waddell
Director of Inside Sales	Al Guido
Director of Ticket Operations	Douglas Vanderheyden

Suite Sales

Vice President of Suite Sales	Ron Campbell
Directors of Suite Sales	Mike Briody, Brian Moss

Charities

Director of Coyotes Charities	Michele Shipitofsky

Technology

Vice President of IT & Strategic Operations	Christine Stoffel

Phoenix Coyotes & Arena Management Group

Executive Director of Human Resources	Julie Atherton
Legal Counsel	Steve Weinreich

Team Information

Broadcast Television Station	KAZT-TV
Regional Sports Network	FSN Arizona
Radio Station	The FAN 1060 AM

Pittsburgh Penguins

2005-06 Results: 22w-46L-8OTL-6SOL 58PTS.
Fifth, Atlantic Division

2006-07 Schedule

Oct.	Thu.	5	Philadelphia		Wed.	10	at Florida
	Sat.	7	Detroit		Sat.	13	at Philadelphia*
	Thu.	12	at NY Rangers		Tue.	16	NY Islanders
	Sat.	14	Carolina		Thu.	18	at Boston
	Wed.	18	New Jersey		Sat.	20	Toronto
	Thu.	19	at NY Islanders		Fri.	26	at Dallas
	Sat.	21	Columbus		Sat.	27	at Phoenix
	Tue.	24	New Jersey		Tue.	30	Florida
	Sat.	28	at Philadelphia	Feb.	Thu.	1	Montreal
Nov.	Wed.	1	at Los Angeles		Sat.	3	Washington*
	Sat.	4	at San Jose		Sun.	4	at Montreal*
	Mon.	6	at Anaheim		Tue.	6	Nashville
	Wed.	8	Tampa Bay		Thu.	8	at Philadelphia
	Fri.	10	Ottawa		Sat.	10	at Toronto
	Sat.	11	at Carolina		Wed.	14	Chicago
	Mon.	13	Philadelphia		Fri.	16	at New Jersey
	Fri.	17	at Buffalo		Sun.	18	Washington*
	Sat.	18	NY Rangers		Mon.	19	at NY Islanders*
	Mon.	20	at Philadelphia		Thu.	22	at Florida
	Wed.	22	Boston		Sun.	25	at Tampa Bay*
	Fri.	24	at NY Islanders*		Tue.	27	New Jersey
	Sat.	25	NY Rangers	Mar.	Thu.	1	at NY Rangers
	Tue.	28	NY Islanders		Fri.	2	at Carolina
Dec.	Fri.	1	at New Jersey		Sun.	4	Philadelphia*
	Sat.	2	NY Islanders		Tue.	6	at Ottawa
	Tue.	5	Florida		Thu.	8	New Jersey
	Thu.	7	at NY Rangers		Sat.	10	NY Rangers*
	Sat.	9	at Atlanta		Tue.	13	Buffalo
	Mon.	11	at Washington		Wed.	14	at New Jersey
	Wed.	13	Philadelphia		Fri.	16	Montreal
	Fri.	15	NY Islanders		Sun.	18	Ottawa
	Sat.	16	at Montreal		Mon.	19	at NY Rangers
	Tue.	19	St. Louis		Thu.	22	at NY Islanders
	Thu.	21	at Atlanta		Sat.	24	Atlanta*
	Tue.	26	at New Jersey		Sun.	25	Boston*
	Wed.	27	Atlanta		Tue.	27	at Washington
	Fri.	29	Toronto		Thu.	29	at Boston
Jan.	Tue.	2	Carolina		Sat.	31	at Toronto
	Fri.	5	at Buffalo	Apr.	Tue.	3	Buffalo
	Sun.	7	Tampa Bay		Thu.	5	at Ottawa
	Tue.	9	at Tampa Bay		Sat.	7	NY Rangers

Denotes afternoon game.

Franchise date: June 5, 1967

EASTERN CONFERENCE

ATLANTIC DIVISION

40th NHL Season

Sidney Crosby ranked sixth in the NHL with 102 points in 2005-06. He spent his rookie season living in Mario Lemieux's house and broke the Penguins superstar's club rookie records for points and assists (63).

Year-by-Year Record

		Home				Road				Overall								
Season	GP	W	L	T	OL	W	L	T	OL	W	L	T	OL	GF	GA	Pts.	Finished	Playoff Result
2005-06	82	12	21	....	8	10	25	....	6	22	46	....	14	244	316	58	5th, Atlantic Div.	Out of Playoffs
2004-05	....	....	....	....	....	....	....	....	....	....	....	....	....	....	....	....		
2003-04	82	13	22	6	0	10	25	2	4	23	47	8	4	190	303	58	5th, Atlantic Div.	Out of Playoffs
2002-03	82	15	22	2	2	12	22	4	3	27	44	6	5	189	255	65	5th, Atlantic Div.	Out of Playoffs
2001-02	82	16	20	4	1	12	21	4	4	28	41	8	5	198	249	69	5th, Atlantic Div.	Out of Playoffs
2000-01	82	24	15	2	0	18	13	7	3	42	28	9	3	281	256	96	3rd, Atlantic Div.	Lost Conf. Championship
1999-2000	82	23	11	7	0	14	20	1	6	37	31	8	6	241	236	88	3rd, Atlantic Div.	Lost Conf. Semi-Final
1998-99	82	21	10	10		17	20	4		38	30	14		242	225	90	3rd, Atlantic Div.	Lost Conf. Semi-Final
1997-98	82	21	10	10		19	14	8		40	24	18		228	188	98	1st, Northeast Div.	Lost Conf. Quarter-Final
1996-97	82	25	11	5		13	25	3		38	36	8		285	280	84	2nd, Northeast Div.	Lost Conf. Quarter-Final
1995-96	82	32	9	0		17	20	4		49	29	4		362	284	102	1st, Northeast Div.	Lost Conf. Championship
1994-95	48	18	5	1		11	11	2		29	16	3		181	158	61	2nd, Northeast Div.	Lost Conf. Semi-Final
1993-94	84	25	9	8		19	18	5		44	27	13		299	285	101	1st, Northeast Div.	Lost Conf. Quarter-Final
1992-93	84	32	6	4		24	15	3		56	21	7		367	268	119	1st, Patrick Div.	Lost Div. Final
1991-92	**80**	**21**	**13**	**6**		**18**	**19**	**3**		**39**	**32**	**9**		**343**	**308**	**87**	**3rd, Patrick Div.**	**Won Stanley Cup**
1990-91	**80**	**25**	**12**	**3**		**16**	**21**	**3**		**41**	**33**	**6**		**342**	**305**	**88**	**1st, Patrick Div.**	**Won Stanley Cup**
1989-90	80	22	15	3		10	25	5		32	40	8		318	359	72	5th, Patrick Div.	Out of Playoffs
1988-89	80	24	13	3		16	20	4		40	33	7		347	349	87	2nd, Patrick Div.	Lost Div. Final
1987-88	80	22	12	6		14	23	3		36	35	9		319	316	81	6th, Patrick Div.	Out of Playoffs
1986-87	80	19	15	6		11	23	6		30	38	12		297	290	72	5th, Patrick Div.	Out of Playoffs
1985-86	80	20	15	5		14	23	3		34	38	8		313	305	76	5th, Patrick Div.	Out of Playoffs
1984-85	80	17	20	3		7	31	2		24	51	5		276	385	53	6th, Patrick Div.	Out of Playoffs
1983-84	80	7	29	4		9	29	2		16	58	6		254	390	38	6th, Patrick Div.	Out of Playoffs
1982-83	80	14	22	4		4	31	5		18	53	9		257	394	45	6th, Patrick Div.	Out of Playoffs
1981-82	80	21	11	8		10	25	5		31	36	13		310	337	75	4th, Patrick Div.	Lost Div. Semi-Final
1980-81	80	21	16	3		9	21	10		30	37	13		302	345	73	3rd, Norris Div.	Lost Prelim. Round
1979-80	80	20	13	7		10	24	6		30	37	13		251	303	73	3rd, Norris Div.	Lost Prelim. Round
1978-79	80	23	12	5		13	19	8		36	31	13		281	279	85	2nd, Norris Div.	Lost Quarter-Final
1977-78	80	16	15	9		9	22	9		25	37	18		254	321	68	4th, Norris Div.	Out of Playoffs
1976-77	80	22	12	6		12	21	7		34	33	13		240	252	81	3rd, Norris Div.	Lost Prelim. Round
1975-76	80	23	11	6		12	22	6		35	33	12		339	303	82	3rd, Norris Div.	Lost Prelim. Round
1974-75	80	25	5	10		12	23	5		37	28	15		326	289	89	3rd, Norris Div.	Lost Quarter-Final
1973-74	78	15	18	6		13	23	3		28	41	9		242	273	65	5th, West Div.	Out of Playoffs
1972-73	78	24	11	4		8	26	5		32	37	9		257	265	73	5th, West Div.	Out of Playoffs
1971-72	78	18	15	6		8	23	8		26	38	14		220	258	66	4th, West Div.	Lost Quarter-Final
1970-71	78	18	12	9		3	25	11		21	37	20		221	240	62	6th, West Div.	Out of Playoffs
1969-70	76	17	13	8		9	25	4		26	38	12		182	238	64	2nd, West Div.	Lost Semi-Final
1968-69	76	12	16	10		8	29	1		20	45	11		189	252	51	5th, West Div.	Out of Playoffs
1967-68	74	15	12	10		12	22	3		27	34	13		195	216	67	5th, West Div.	Out of Playoffs

2006-07 Player Personnel

FORWARDS	HT	WT	S	Place of Birth	Date	2005-06 Club
ARMSTRONG, Colby	6-2	195	R	Lloydminster, Sask.	11/23/82	Pittsburgh-Wilkes-Barre
CARCILLO, Daniel	5-11	202	L	King City, Ont.	1/28/85	Wilkes-Barre-Wheeling
CHRISTENSEN, Erik	6-1	196	L	Edmonton, Alta.	12/17/83	Pittsburgh-Wilkes-Barre
CROSBY, Sidney	5-11	193	L	Cole Harbour, N.S.	8/7/87	Pittsburgh
DIXON, Stephen	5-11	188	L	Halifax, N.S.	9/7/85	Wilkes-Barre
EKMAN, Nils	6-0	185	L	Stockholm, Sweden	3/11/76	San Jose
FILEWICH, Jonathan	6-2	205	R	Kelowna, B.C.	10/2/84	Wilkes-Barre
JAMES, Connor	5-10	168	R	Calgary, Alta.	8/25/82	Los Angeles-Manchester
JENSEN, Joe	5-11	180	L	Maple Grove, MN	2/6/83	St. Cloud State
KENNEDY, Tyler	5-10	183	R	Sault Ste. Marie, Ont.	7/15/86	Sault Ste. Marie
LeCLAIR, John	6-3	226	L	St. Albans, VT	7/5/69	Pittsburgh
MALONE, Ryan	6-4	216	L	Pittsburgh, PA	12/1/79	Pittsburgh
MOORE, Dominic	6-0	195	L	Thornhill, Ont.	8/3/80	NY Rangers
OUELLET, Michel	6-0	201	R	Rimouski, Que.	3/5/82	Pittsburgh-Wilkes-Barre
PETROVICKY, Ronald	5-11	190	R	Zilina, Czechoslovakia	2/15/77	Atlanta
PIVKO, Libor	6-3	214	L	Novy Vicin, Czech.	3/29/80	Milwaukee
RECCHI, Mark	5-10	190	L	Kamloops, B.C.	2/1/68	Pittsburgh-Carolina
ROY, Andre	6-4	221	L	Port Chester, NY	2/8/75	Pittsburgh
RUUTU, Jarkko	6-2	195	L	Vantaa, Finland	8/23/75	Vancouver
STONE, Ryan	6-2	200	L	Calgary, Alta.	3/20/85	Wilkes-Barre
TALBOT, Maxime	5-11	176	L	Lemoyne, Que.	2/11/84	Pittsburgh-Wilkes-Barre
DEFENSEMEN						
BISSONNETTE, Paul	6-3	212	L	Welland, Ont.	3/11/85	Wilkes-Barre-Wheeling
CAIRNS, Eric	6-6	230	L	Oakville, Ont.	6/27/74	Florida-Pittsburgh
CARKNER, Matt	6-4	235	R	Winchester, Ont.	11/3/80	San Jose-Cleveland
DuPONT, Micki	5-10	186	R	Calgary, Alta.	4/15/80	Eisbaren Berlin
EATON, Mark	6-2	212	L	Wilmington, DE	5/6/77	Nashville
FERNHOLM, Daniel	6-4	218	L	Stockholm, Sweden	12/20/83	Wilkes-Barre-Wheeling
GONCHAR, Sergei	6-2	215	L	Chelyabinsk, USSR	4/13/74	Pittsburgh
LANNON, Ryan	6-2	220	L	Worcester, MA	12/14/82	Wilkes-Barre
MELICHAR, Josef	6-2	220	L	Ceske Budejovice, Czech.	1/20/79	Pittsburgh
NASREDDINE, Alain	6-1	201	L	Montreal, Que.	7/10/75	Pittsburgh-Wilkes-Barre
ORPIK, Brooks	6-2	228	L	San Francisco, CA	9/26/80	Pittsburgh
SCUDERI, Rob	6-0	214	L	Syosset, NY	12/30/78	Pittsburgh-Wilkes-Barre
SKOLNEY, Wade	6-0	197	R	Wynyard, Sask.	6/24/81	Phi-Phi (AHL)
WELCH, Noah	6-4	212	L	Brighton, MA	8/26/82	Pittsburgh-Wilkes-Barre
WHITNEY, Ryan	6-4	202	L	Boston, MA	2/19/83	Pittsburgh-Wilkes-Barre

GOALTENDERS	HT	WT	C	Place of Birth	Date	2005-06 Club
EHELECHNER, Patrick	6-2	169	L	Rosenheim, W. Germany	9/23/84	Mannheim-Duisburg
FLEURY, Marc-Andre	6-1	175	L	Sorel, Que.	11/28/84	Pittsburgh-Wilkes-Barre
SABOURIN, Dany	6-2	182	L	Val-d'Or, Que.	9/2/80	Pittsburgh-Wilkes-Barre
THIBAULT, Jocelyn	5-11	169	L	Montreal, Que.	1/12/75	Pittsburgh

Coach

THERRIEN, MICHEL

Coach, Pittsburgh Penguins. Born in Montreal, Que., November 4, 1963.

Michel Therrien took over as head coach of the Pittsburgh Penguins from Ed Olczyk on December 15, 2005. Therrien was promoted from Pittsburgh's top minor-league affiliate in Wilkes-Barre/Scranton, where he guided the Baby Penguins for two and a half seasons after he became the team's second head coach on July 15, 2003.

Therrien was in the midst of the Baby Penguins' most successful season. He guided the team to a 21-1-2-1 start and 45 points in the team's first 25 games in the American Hockey League. Wilkes-Barre/Scranton won its first nine games of the season and did not lose a game in regulation time until its 24th game. The Baby Penguins also established an AHL road winning streak of 15 games, dating back to April 10 of last season. In his first season behind the bench, Therrien led the Penguins to the Calder Cup Finals. He followed the 2003-04 season by setting a new team mark for points in a season (88) in 2004-05.

Prior to joining the Penguins, Therrien spent six seasons in the Montreal Canadiens organization, including a stint as the team's head coach over parts of three seasons. In 2001-02, Therrien led the Canadiens to their first postseason appearance in four seasons. He spent four seasons as a head coach in the American Hockey League with the Canadiens' AHL affiliates, the Fredericton Canadiens and Quebec Citadelles, winning a division championship with the Citadelles in 1999-00.

Prior to joining the Canadiens, Therrien coached Laval and Granby in the Quebec Major Junior Hockey League. He posted a .720 winning percentage in four seasons as a head coach in the QMJHL, reaching the finals three times and was the head coach of the Memorial Cup winning team in Granby in 1995-96. Beginning in 1993-94, Therrien's teams led the QMJHL in points for three straight seasons. Therrien also played three seasons in the AHL (1983 to 1985 and 1986-87) for Nova Scotia, Sherbrooke and Baltimore, recording 89 points (16 goals, 73 assists).

Coaching Record

		Regular Season				Playoffs		
Season	Team	Games	W	L	O/T	Games	W	L
1993-94	Laval (QMJHL)	72	49	22	1	21	14	7
1994-95	Laval (QMJHL)	72	48	22	2	20	14	6
1995-96	Granby (QMJHL)	70	56	12	2	21	17	4
1996-97	Granby (QMJHL)	70	44	20	6	5	1	4
1997-98	Fredericton (AHL)	80	33	32	15	4	1	3
1998-99	Fredericton (AHL)	80	33	36	11	15	9	6
1999-2000	Quebec (AHL)	80	37	34	9	3	0	3
2000-01	Quebec (AHL)	19	12	6	1	....	....	....
	Montreal (NHL)	**62**	**23**	**33**	**6**	....	....	....
2001-02	**Montreal (NHL)**	**82**	**36**	**34**	**12**	**12**	**6**	**6**
2002-03	**Montreal (NHL)**	**46**	**18**	**23**	**5**	....	....	....
2003-04	Wilkes-Barre (AHL)	80	34	36	10	24	12	12
2004-05	Wilkes-Barre (AHL)	80	39	34	7	11	5	6
2005-06	Wilkes-Barre (AHL)	25	21	1	3	....	....	....
2005-06	**Pittsburgh (NHL)**	**51**	**14**	**29**	**8**	....	....	....
	NHL Totals	**241**	**91**	**119**	**31**	**12**	**6**	**6**

2005-06 Scoring

* – rookie

Regular Season

Pos	#	Player	Team	GP	G	A	Pts	+/–	PIM	PP	SH	GW	S	%
C	87	* Sidney Crosby	PIT	81	39	63	102	–1	110	16	0	5	278	14.0
D	55	Sergei Gonchar	PIT	75	12	46	58	–13	100	8	0	2	192	6.3
L	10	John LeClair	PIT	73	22	29	51	–24	61	8	1	0	135	16.3
L	12	Ryan Malone	PIT	77	22	22	44	–22	63	10	5	1	153	14.4
R	33	Ziggy Palffy	PIT	42	11	31	42	5	12	2	0	2	112	9.8
R	20	* Colby Armstrong	PIT	47	16	24	40	15	58	7	2	3	86	18.6
D	19	* Ryan Whitney	PIT	68	6	32	38	–7	85	2	0	1	113	5.3
R	7	* Michel Ouellet	PIT	50	16	16	32	–13	16	11	0	0	87	18.4
C	9	Andy Hilbert	CHI	28	5	4	9	–4	22	0	0	1	50	10.0
			PIT	19	7	11	18	8	16	3	0	1	51	13.7
			TOTAL	47	12	15	27	4	38	3	0	2	101	11.9
L	43	Tomas Surovy	PIT	53	12	13	25	–13	45	3	0	1	107	11.2
C	66	Mario Lemieux	PIT	26	7	15	22	–16	16	3	0	0	77	9.1
R	23	Eric Boguniecki	STL	9	1	4	5	–1	4	1	0	0	12	8.3
			PIT	38	5	6	11	–2	29	1	0	0	36	13.9
			TOTAL	47	6	10	16	–3	33	2	0	0	48	12.5
D	2	Josef Melichar	PIT	72	3	12	15	–2	66	0	1	0	53	5.7
C	16	* Erik Christensen	PIT	33	6	7	13	–3	34	2	0	0	85	7.1
R	28	* Jani Rita	EDM	21	3	0	3	0	6	0	0	0	13	23.1
			PIT	30	3	4	7	–6	4	0	0	0	36	8.3
			TOTAL	51	6	4	10	–6	10	0	0	0	49	12.2
R	71	Konstantin Koltsov	PIT	60	3	6	9	–10	20	0	1	0	72	4.2
D	44	Brooks Orpik	PIT	64	2	7	9	–3	124	0	0	0	32	6.3
C	25	* Maxime Talbot	PIT	48	5	3	8	–12	59	0	2	1	45	11.1
L	11	Lasse Pirjeta	PIT	25	4	3	7	4	18	0	0	0	30	13.3
L	15	Niklas Nordgren	CAR	43	4	2	6	–4	30	0	0	0	32	12.5
			PIT	15	0	0	0	–4	4	0	0	0	6	0.0
			TOTAL	58	4	2	6	–8	34	0	0	0	38	10.5
L	17	* Matt Murley	PIT	41	1	5	6	–9	24	0	0	0	48	2.1
D	4	* Noah Welch	PIT	5	1	3	4	0	2	0	0	0	5	20.0
D	5	Robert Scuderi	PIT	57	0	4	4	–18	36	0	0	0	28	0.0
L	36	Andre Roy	PIT	42	2	1	3	–3	116	0	0	1	11	18.2
C	14	* Shane Endicott	PIT	41	1	1	2	–9	43	0	1	0	44	2.3
D	33	Eric Cairns	FLA	23	0	1	1	1	37	0	0	0	11	0.0
			PIT	27	1	0	1	0	87	0	0	0	8	12.5
			TOTAL	50	1	1	2	1	124	0	0	0	19	5.3
R	37	Ryan Vandenbussche	PIT	20	1	0	1	0	42	0	0	0	5	20.0
C	28	Matt Hussey	PIT	13	0	1	1	–5	0	0	0	0	17	0.0
D	24	Lyle Odelein	PIT	27	0	1	1	–10	50	0	0	0	17	0.0
D	32	Alain Nasreddine	PIT	6	0	0	0	2	8	0	0	0	3	0.0
L	11	Guillaume Lefebvre	PIT	9	0	0	0	–3	9	0	0	0	3	0.0

Goaltending

No.	Goaltender	GPI	Mins	Avg	W	L	OT	EN	SO	GA	SA	S%	G	A	PIM
29	* Marc-Andre Fleury	50	2809	3.25	13	27	6	3	1	152	1485	.898	0	1	0
31	Sebastien Caron	26	1312	3.98	8	9	5	3	1	87	733	.881	0	1	0
41	Jocelyn Thibault	16	807	4.46	1	9	3	1	0	60	484	.876	0	0	2
30	* Dany Sabourin	1	21	11.43	0	1	0	0	0	4	14	.714	0	0	0
	Totals	**82**	**4985**	**3.73**	**22**	**46**	**14**	**7**	**2**	**310**	**2723**	**.886**			

General Managers' History

Jack Riley, 1967-68 to 1969-70; Red Kelly, 1970-71; Red Kelly and Jack Riley, 1971-72; Jack Riley, 1972-73; Jack Riley and Jack Button, 1973-74; Jack Button, 1974-75; Wren Blair, 1975-76; Wren Blair and Baz Bastien, 1976-77; Baz Bastien, 1977-78 to 1982-83; Eddie Johnston, 1983-84 to 1987-88; Tony Esposito, 1988-89; Tony Esposito and Craig Patrick, 1989-90; Craig Patrick, 1990-91 to 2005-06; Ray Shero, 2006-07.

Coaching History

Red Sullivan, 1967-68, 1968-69; Red Kelly, 1969-70 to 1971-72; Red Kelly and Ken Schinkel, 1972-73; Ken Schinkel and Marc Boileau, 1973-74; Marc Boileau, 1974-75; Marc Boileau and Ken Schinkel, 1975-76; Ken Schinkel, 1976-77; Johnny Wilson, 1977-78 to 1979-80; Eddie Johnston, 1980-81 to 1982-83; Lou Angotti, 1983-84; Bob Berry, 1984-85 to 1986-87; Pierre Creamer, 1987-88; Gene Ubriaco, 1988-89; Gene Ubriaco and Craig Patrick, 1989-90; Bob Johnson, 1990-91, 1991-92; Scotty Bowman, 1991-92, 1992-93; Eddie Johnston, 1993-94 to 1995-96; Eddie Johnston and Craig Patrick, 1996-97; Kevin Constantine, 1997-98, 1998-99; Kevin Constantine and Herb Brooks, 1999-2000; Ivan Hlinka, 2000-01; Ivan Hlinka and Rick Kehoe, 2001-02; Rick Kehoe, 2002-03; Ed Olczyk, 2003-04; Ed Olczyk and Michel Therrien, 2005-06; Michel Therrien, 2006-07.

Club Records

Team

(Figures in brackets for season records are games played; records for fewest points, wins, ties, losses, goals, goals against are for 70 or more games)

Most Points	**119**	1992-93 (84)
Most Wins	**56**	1992-93 (84)
Most Ties	**20**	1970-71 (78)
Most Losses	**58**	1983-84 (80)
Most Goals	**367**	1992-93 (84)
Most Goals Against	**394**	1982-83 (80)
Fewest Points	**38**	1983-84 (80)
Fewest Wins	**16**	1983-84 (80)
Fewest Ties	**4**	1995-96 (82)
Fewest Losses	**21**	1992-93 (84)
Fewest Goals	**182**	1969-70 (76)
Fewest Goals Against	**188**	1997-98 (82)
Longest Winning Streak		
Overall	***17**	Mar. 9-Apr. 10/93
Home	**11**	Jan. 5-Mar. 7/91
Away	**7**	Mar. 14-Apr. 9/93
Longest Undefeated Streak		
Overall	**18**	Mar. 9-Apr. 14/93 (17 wins, 1 tie)
Home	**20**	Nov. 30/74-Feb. 22/75 (12 wins, 8 ties)
Away	**8**	Mar. 14-Apr. 14/93 (7 wins, 1 tie)
Longest Losing Streak		
Overall	**18**	Jan. 13-Feb. 22/04
Home	**14**	Dec. 31/03-Feb. 22/04
Away	**18**	Dec. 23/82-Mar. 4/83
Longest Winless Streak		
Overall	**18**	Jan. 2-Feb. 10/83 (17 losses, 1 tie), Jan. 13-Feb. 22/04 (18 losses)
Home	**16**	Dec. 31/03-Mar. 4/04 (15 losses, 1 tie)
Away	**18**	Oct. 25/70-Jan. 14/71 (11 losses, 7 ties), Dec. 23/82-Mar. 4/83 (18 losses)
Most Shutouts, Season	**9**	1998-99 (82)
Most PIM, Season	**2,670**	1988-89 (80)
Most Goals, Game	**12**	Mar. 15/75 (Wsh. 1 at Pit. 12), Dec. 26/91 (Tor. 1 at Pit. 12)

Individual

Most Seasons	**17**	Mario Lemieux
Most Games	**915**	Mario Lemieux
Most Goals, Career	**690**	Mario Lemieux
Most Assists, Career	**1,033**	Mario Lemieux
Most Points, Career	**1,723**	Mario Lemieux (690G, 1,033A)
Most PIM, Career	**1,048**	Kevin Stevens
Most Shutouts, Career	**22**	Tom Barrasso
Longest Consecutive Games Streak	**320**	Ron Schock (Oct. 24/73-Apr. 3/77)
Most Goals, Season	**85**	Mario Lemieux (1988-89)
Most Assists, Season	**114**	Mario Lemieux (1988-89)
Most Points, Season	**199**	Mario Lemieux (1988-89; 85G, 114A)
Most PIM, Season	**409**	Paul Baxter (1981-82)
Most Points, Defenseman, Season	**113**	Paul Coffey (1988-89; 30G, 83A)
Most Points, Center, Season	**199**	Mario Lemieux (1988-89; 85G, 114A)
Most Points, Right Wing, Season	***149**	Jaromir Jagr (1995-96; 62G, 87A)
Most Points, Left Wing, Season	**123**	Kevin Stevens (1991-92; 54G, 69A)
Most Points, Rookie, Season	**102**	Sidney Crosby (2005-06; 39G, 63A)
Most Shutouts, Season	**7**	Tom Barrasso (1997-98)
Most Goals, Game	**5**	Mario Lemieux (Three times)
Most Assists, Game	**6**	Ron Stackhouse (Mar. 8/75), Greg Malone (Nov. 28/79), Mario Lemieux (Three times)
Most Points, Game	**8**	Mario Lemieux (Oct. 15/88; 2G, 6A, Dec. 31/88; 5G, 3A)

* NHL Record.

Captains' History

Ab McDonald, 1967-68; no captain, 1968-69 to 1972-73; Ron Schock, 1973-74 to 1976-77; Jean Pronovost, 1977-78; Orest Kindrachuk, 1978-79 to 1980-81; Randy Carlyle, 1981-82 to 1983-84; Mike Bullard, 1984-85, 1985-86; Mike Bullard and Terry Ruskowski, 1986-87; Dan Frawley and Mario Lemieux, 1987-88; Mario Lemieux, 1988-89 to 1993-94; Ron Francis, 1994-95; Mario Lemieux, 1995-96, 1996-97; Ron Francis, 1997-98; Jaromir Jagr, 1998-99 to 2000-01; Mario Lemieux, 2001-02 to 2003-04; Mario Lemieux and no captain, 2005-06.

Retired Numbers

21	Michel Brière	1969-1970

All-time Record vs. Other Clubs

Regular Season

	At Home								On Road								Total							
	GP	W	L	T	OL	GF	GA	PTS	GP	W	L	T	OL	GF	GA	PTS	GP	W	L	T	OL	GF	GA	PTS
Anaheim	9	5	2	2	0	29	27	12	8	3	4	0	1	24	29	7	17	8	6	2	1	53	56	19
Atlanta	12	9	2	0	1	49	34	19	12	9	3	0	0	43	35	18	24	18	5	0	1	92	69	37
Boston	82	32	34	15	1	280	296	80	80	16	58	6	0	224	355	38	162	48	92	21	1	504	651	118
Buffalo	73	36	18	18	1	271	224	91	73	20	35	17	1	195	281	58	146	56	53	35	2	466	505	149
Calgary	45	24	11	10	0	169	136	58	46	11	27	8	0	140	204	30	91	35	38	18	0	309	340	88
Carolina	48	23	19	6	0	193	182	52	50	22	21	5	2	183	184	51	98	45	40	11	2	376	366	103
Chicago	59	29	23	7	0	210	190	65	61	11	40	10	0	158	240	32	120	40	63	17	0	368	430	97
Colorado	38	16	17	5	0	149	155	37	32	13	16	2	1	122	142	29	70	29	33	7	1	271	297	66
Columbus	3	2	1	0	0	12	9	4	4	2	2	0	0	10	16	4	7	4	3	0	0	22	25	8
Dallas	63	38	19	6	0	236	178	82	64	21	36	6	1	213	246	49	127	59	55	12	1	449	424	131
Detroit	65	44	17	4	0	281	195	92	66	13	40	12	1	179	256	39	131	57	57	16	1	460	451	131
Edmonton	31	15	13	3	0	118	130	33	30	7	22	1	0	98	148	15	61	22	35	4	0	216	278	48
Florida	25	12	9	3	1	78	77	28	24	9	12	1	2	58	71	21	49	21	21	4	3	136	148	49
Los Angeles	73	38	25	10	0	265	233	86	69	17	43	8	1	183	265	43	142	55	68	18	1	448	498	129
Minnesota	4	1	3	0	0	6	17	2	3	0	2	1	0	5	9	1	7	1	5	1	0	11	26	3
Montreal	84	29	41	13	1	246	298	72	84	12	60	10	2	214	391	36	168	41	101	23	3	460	689	108
Nashville	5	1	2	2	0	14	17	4	7	2	5	0	0	14	26	4	12	3	7	2	0	28	43	8
New Jersey	83	42	35	4	2	306	283	90	85	30	41	13	1	279	311	74	168	72	76	17	3	585	594	164
NY Islanders	92	42	34	14	2	345	322	100	90	34	46	8	2	301	358	78	182	76	80	22	4	646	680	178
NY Rangers	104	45	45	14	0	371	381	104	105	42	54	9	0	352	407	93	209	87	99	23	0	723	788	197
Ottawa	29	17	8	4	0	102	75	38	29	14	10	5	0	91	80	33	58	31	18	9	0	193	155	71
Philadelphia	110	47	41	22	0	383	359	116	110	18	80	8	4	270	462	48	220	65	121	30	4	653	821	164
Phoenix	30	20	10	0	0	120	86	40	31	14	14	3	0	107	116	31	61	34	24	3	0	227	202	71
St. Louis	64	32	20	12	0	238	190	76	65	15	42	6	2	171	250	38	129	47	62	18	2	409	440	114
San Jose	9	4	4	1	0	41	32	9	13	6	5	2	0	54	34	14	22	10	9	3	0	95	66	23
Tampa Bay	25	15	6	3	1	95	67	34	25	9	13	2	1	61	80	21	50	24	19	5	2	156	147	55
Toronto	71	36	28	6	1	280	232	79	69	24	32	11	2	218	272	61	140	60	60	17	3	498	504	140
Vancouver	51	33	11	7	0	229	175	73	50	23	22	4	1	187	180	51	101	56	33	11	1	416	355	124
Washington	85	49	29	7	0	335	266	105	88	33	45	9	1	321	367	76	173	82	74	16	1	656	633	181
Defunct Clubs	35	22	6	7	0	148	93	51	34	13	10	11	0	108	101	37	69	35	16	18	0	256	194	88
Totals	**1507**	**758**	**533**	**205**	**11**	**5599**	**4959**	**1732**	**1507**	**463**	**840**	**178**	**26**	**4583**	**5916**	**1130**	**3014**	**1221**	**1373**	**383**	**37**	**10182**	**10875**	**2862**

Playoffs

	Series	W	L	GP	W	L	T	GF	GA	Last Mtg.	Rnd.	Result
Boston	4	2	2	19	10	9	0	67	62	1992	CF	W 4-0
Buffalo	2	2	0	10	6	4	0	26	26	2001	CSF	W 4-3
Chicago	2	1	1	8	4	4	0	23	24	1992	F	W 4-0
Dallas	1	1	0	6	4	2	0	28	16	1991	F	W 4-2
Florida	1	0	1	7	3	4	0	15	20	1996	CF	L 3-4
Montreal	1	0	1	6	2	4	0	15	18	1998	CQF	L 2-4
New Jersey	5	3	2	29	14	15	0	80	86	2001	CF	L 1-4
NY Islanders	3	0	3	19	8	11	0	58	67	1993	DF	L 3-4
NY Rangers	3	3	0	15	12	3	0	64	45	1996	CSF	W 4-1
Philadelphia	3	0	3	18	6	12	0	51	66	2000	CSF	L 2-4
St. Louis	3	1	2	13	6	7	0	40	45	1981	PRE	L 2-3
Toronto	3	0	3	12	4	8	0	27	39	1999	CSF	L 2-4
Washington	7	6	1	42	26	16	0	137	121	2001	CQF	W 4-2
Defunct Clubs	1	1	0	4	4	0	0	13	6			
Totals	**39**	**20**	**19**	**208**	**109**	**99**	**0**	**644**	**641**			

Playoff Results 2006-2001

Year	Round	Opponent	Result	GF	GA
2001	CF	New Jersey	L 1-4	7	17
	CSF	Buffalo	W 4-3	17	17
	CQF	Washington	W 4-2	14	10

Abbreviations: Round: F – Final; **CF** – conference final; **CSF** – conference semi-final; **CQF** – conference quarter-final; **DF** – division final; **PRE** – preliminary round.

Calgary totals include Atlanta Flames, 1972-73 to 1979-80. Carolina totals include Hartford, 1979-80 to 1996-97.
Colorado totals include Quebec, 1979-80 to 1994-95. Dallas totals include Minnesota North Stars, 1967-68 to 1992-93.
New Jersey totals include Kansas City, 1974-75 to 1975-76, and Colorado Rockies, 1976-77 to 1981-82.
Phoenix totals include Winnipeg, 1979-80 to 1995-96.

2005-06 Results

Oct.	5	at New Jersey	1-5
	7	at Carolina	2-3†
	8	Boston	6-7*
	10	at Buffalo	2-3*
	14	at Philadelphia	5-6*
	15	Tampa Bay	1-3
	20	New Jersey	3-6
	22	at Boston	3-6
	25	Florida	3-4*
	27	Atlanta	7-5
	29	Carolina	3-5
Nov.	1	at New Jersey	4-3*
	3	at NY Islanders	5-1
	5	at Boston	3-6
	7	at NY Rangers	3-2
	9	at Atlanta	0-5
	10	Montreal	3-2†
	12	NY Rangers	1-6
	14	NY Islanders	2-3†
	16	at Philadelphia	3-2*
	19	Philadelphia	3-6
	22	Washington	5-4
	25	at Florida	3-6
	27	at Tampa Bay	1-4
	29	Buffalo	2-3
Dec.	1	at NY Rangers	1-2
	3	Calgary	2-3
	8	Minnesota	0-5
	10	Colorado	4-3
	12	at Detroit	1-3
	13	at St. Louis	0-3
	16	Buffalo	3-4*
	17	at Buffalo	3-4
	23	Philadelphia	4-5
	27	Toronto	2-3*
	29	New Jersey	6-2
	31	NY Rangers	4-3*
Jan.	2	at Toronto	2-3*
	3	at Montreal	6-4
	6	at Atlanta	4-6
	7	Atlanta	3-4
	10	Edmonton	1-3
	11	at Columbus	1-6
	13	at Chicago	1-4
	15	at Nashville	4-5
	16	Vancouver	2-4
	19	NY Rangers	2-4
	21	Philadelphia	1-2
	23	at Philadelphia	2-4
	25	Washington	8-1
	26	at NY Islanders	3-4†
	28	at NY Rangers	1-7
Feb.	1	at NY Rangers	1-3
	2	Ottawa	2-7
	4	NY Islanders	4-5†
	6	at Ottawa	2-5
	8	Boston	1-3
	10	at Carolina	4-3
	11	at Washington	6-3
Mar.	1	Ottawa	3-4
	4	Carolina	5-7
	7	Tampa Bay	4-5†
	8	at Washington	3-6
	11	New Jersey	6-3
	12	Philadelphia	2-0
	16	at New Jersey	1-2
	18	at Montreal	5-4
	19	Toronto	0-1
	21	at Ottawa	2-5
	24	NY Islanders	4-3*
	26	Montreal	5-6
	29	Florida	3-5
	31	at NY Islanders	4-0
Apr.	2	New Jersey	2-3*
	5	at New Jersey	4-6
	7	at Florida	5-1
	8	at Tampa Bay	0-1
	11	at Philadelphia	3-4
	13	NY Rangers	5-3
	15	at NY Islanders	4-5†
	17	NY Islanders	6-1
	18	at Toronto	3-5

* – Overtime † – Shootout

Entry Draft
Selections 2006-1992

2006
Pick
2 Jordan Staal
32 Carl Sneep
65 Brian Strait
125 Chad Johnson
185 Timo Seppanen

2005
Pick
1 Sidney Crosby
61 Michael Gergen
62 Kristopher Letang
125 Tommi Leinonen
126 Tim Crowder
194 Jean-Philippe Paquet
195 Joe Vitale

2004
Pick
2 Evgeni Malkin
31 Johannes Salmonsson
61 Alex Goligoski
67 Nick Johnson
85 Brian Gifford
99 Tyler Kennedy
130 Michal Sersen
164 Moises Gutierrez
194 Chris Peluso
222 Jordan Morrison
228 David Brown
259 Brian Ihnacak

2003
Pick
1 Marc-Andre Fleury
32 Ryan Stone
70 Jonathan Filewich
73 Daniel Carcillo
121 Paul Bissonnette
161 Evgeni Isakov
169 Lukas Bolf
199 Andy Chiodo
229 Stephen Dixon
232 Joe Jensen
263 Matt Moulson

2002
Pick
5 Ryan Whitney
35 Ondrej Nemec
69 Erik Christensen
101 Daniel Fernholm
136 Andrew Sertich
137 Cam Paddock
171 Robert Goepfert
202 Patrik Bartschi
234 Maxime Talbot
239 Ryan Lannon
265 Dwight Labrosse

2001
Pick
21 Colby Armstrong
54 Noah Welch
86 Drew Fata
96 Alexandre Rouleau
120 Tomas Surovy
131 Ben Eaves
156 Andy Schneider
217 Tomas Duba
250 Brandon
Crawford-West

2000
Pick
18 Brooks Orpik
52 Shane Endicott
84 Peter Hamerlik
124 Michel Ouellet
146 David Koci
185 Patrick Foley
216 Jim Abbott
248 Steve Crampton
273 Roman Simicek
280 Nick Boucher

1999
Pick
18 Konstantin Koltsov
51 Matt Murley
57 Jeremy Van Hoof
86 Sebastian Caron
115 Ryan Malone
144 Tomas Skvaridlo
157 Vladimir Malenkykh
176 Doug Meyer
204 Tom Kostopoulos
233 Darcy Robinson
261 Andrew McPherson

1998
Pick
23 Milan Kraft
54 Alexander Zevakhin
80 David Cameron
110 Scott Myers
134 Rob Scuderi
169 Jan Fadrny
196 Joel Scherban
224 Mika Lehto
244 Toby Petersen
254 Matt Hussey

1997
Pick
17 Robert Dome
44 Brian Gaffaney
71 Josef Melichar
97 Alexandre Mathieu
124 Harlan Pratt
152 Petr Havelka
179 Mark Moore
208 Andrew Ference
234 Eric Lind

1996
Pick
23 Craig Hillier
28 Pavel Skrbek
72 Boyd Kane
77 Boris Protsenko
105 Michal Rozsival
150 Peter Bergman
186 Eric Meloche
238 Timo Seikkula

1995
Pick
24 Aleksey Morozov
76 Jean-Sebastien Aubin
102 Oleg Belov
128 Jan Hrdina
154 Alexei Kolkunov
180 Derrick Pyke
206 Sergei Voronov
232 Frank Ivankovic

1994
Pick
24 Chris Wells
50 Richard Park
57 Sven Butenschon
73 Greg Crozier
76 Alexei Krivchenkov
102 Tom O'Connor
128 Clint Johnson
154 Valentin Morozov
161 Serge Aubin
180 Drew Palmer
206 Boris Zelenko
232 Jason Godbout
258 Mikhail Kazakevich
284 Brian Leitza

1993
Pick
26 Stefan Bergkvist
52 Domenic Pittis
62 Dave Roche
104 Jonas Andersson-Junkka
130 Chris Kelleher
156 Patrick Lalime
182 Sean Selmser
208 Larry McMorran
234 Timothy Harberts
260 Leonid Toropchenko
286 Hans Jonsson

1992
Pick
19 Martin Straka
43 Marc Hussey
67 Travis Thiessen
91 Todd Klassen
115 Philippe DeRouville
139 Artem Kopot
163 Jan Alinc
187 Fran Bussey
211 Brian Bonin
235 Brian Callahan

General Manager

SHERO, RAY
General Manager, Pittsburgh Penguins. Born in Hartsdale, NY, July 28, 1962.

The Pittsburgh Penguins signed Ray Shero to a five-year contract as their new general manager on May 25, 2006. He is the son of the late Fred Shero, who coached the Philadelphia Flyers for seven years and led them to back-to-back Stanley Cup championships in 1973-74 and 1974-75. Fred Shero also was g.m. and coach of the New York Rangers from 1978-80. Ray Shero played college hockey at St. Lawrence University, serving twice as team captain, and was drafted by the Los Angeles Kings in 1982. He worked as a player agent for seven years before entering NHL management.

Before joining the Penguins, Shero had been assistant general manager of the Nashville Predators for eight seasons, working closely with Predators g.m. David Poile on all aspects of the club's hockey operations. His specific responsibilities included scouting at the amateur and professional levels, contract negotiations, and personnel matters such as arbitration, in addition to overseeing operations of the Predators top minor-league affiliate, the Milwaukee Admirals of the American Hockey League. Before joining the Predators organization, Shero spent six seasons as assistant general manager of the Ottawa Senators – joining the club in its second year of existence as an expansion team.

Both Ottawa and Nashville made significant improvement during Shero's tenure as assistant g.m., building with youth while adhering to a budget and business plan. The Predators went 49-25-8 and established a club record with 106 points in 2005-06, qualifying for the Stanley Cup playoffs for the second straight season. They had the third-best record in the Western Conference and fifth-best in the NHL.

Shero also played an important role in the success of the Milwaukee Admirals, Nashville's top affiliate in the American Hockey League. In 2003-04, the Admirals led the AHL in wins (43) and points (102) and won the Calder Cup by defeating the Wilkes-Barre/Scranton Penguins in the league final. Milwaukee reached the Calder Cup Final again in 2005-06.

Club Directory

Mellon Arena

Pittsburgh Penguins
Mellon Arena
66 Mario Lemieux Place
Pittsburgh, PA 15219
Phone **412/642-1300**
FAX 412/642-1859
Media Relations FAX 412/642-1322
www.pittsburghpenguins.com
Capacity: 16,940

Ownership . . . . Lemieux Group LP

Executive Operations
Chairman . . . . Mario Lemieux
CEO and President . . . . Ken Sawyer
Executive VP/General Manager . . . . Ray Shero
Vice President, Business & Legal Affairs . . . . Ted Black
Vice President & Controller . . . . Kevin Hart
Vice President, Communications . . . . Tom McMillan
Vice President, Sales & Marketing . . . . David Soltesz
Senior Consultant . . . . David Morehouse
Executive Assistants . . . . Fay McNamara, Helen Volkov
Receptionist . . . . Kelly Hart
Mailroom Supervisor . . . . Brett Hart

Hockey Operations
Assistant General Manager . . . . Chuck Fletcher
Senior Advisor/Hockey Operations. . . . . Ed Johnston
Head Coach . . . . Michel Therrien
Assistant Coaches . . . . Andre Savard, Mike Yeo
Strength & Conditioning Coach . . . . Stephane Dube
Director of Amateur Scouting . . . . Jay Heinbuck
Amateur Scouts . . . . Chuck Grillo, Jim Madigan, Matt Recchi
Pro Scouts . . . . Dan MacKinnon, Bill O'Flaherty
Head Coach, Wilkes-Barre/Scranton (AHL) . . Todd Richards
Assistant Coach, Wilkes-Barre/Scranton (AHL) . . . . Dan Bylsma
Team Physician . . . . Dr. Charles Burke
Head Athletic Trainer . . . . Chris Stewart
Assistant Athletic Trainer. . . . . TBA
Head Equipment Manager . . . . TBA
Assistant Equipment Manager. . . . . Paul DeFazio
Director of Team Services . . . . Frank Buonomo
Executive Assistant . . . . Tracey Botsford
Video Coordinator . . . . Paul Fink

Communications/Marketing
Director of Media Relations . . . . Keith Wehner
Manager of Media Relations . . . . Todd Lepovsky
Manager of Media Relations/Publications . . . . Joe Sager
Director of Marketing . . . . Ross Miller
Director of Game Operations/Video Production . . . Chris Devivo
Creative Director . . . . Barb Pilarski
Director of Amateur Hockey . . . . Mark Shuttleworth
Director of Community/Alumni Relations. . . . . Cindy Himes
Exec. Producer, Penguins Radio Network. . . . . . . Ray Walker
Radio Broadcasters . . . . Mike Lange, Phil Bourque
Director of New Media . . . . Jeremy Zimmer
Game Night Producer . . . . Matt Bettinger
Game Night Manager . . . . James Archer
Manager of Arts & Graphics . . . . Dori Minnis
Editors . . . . Steve Finerty, Billy Wareham

Corporate Sales
Senior Director of Corporate Sales . . . . Kim Bogesdorfer
Director of Corporate Sales . . . . Mark DeAndrea
Managers of Corporate Sales . . . . Dee Baker, David Schleter, Danny Smith
Senior Account Service Manager. . . . . Lori Wineland
Account Service Manager . . . . Jamie Greenwald
Account Service Coordinator. . . . . Ronald Hay
Corporate Sales Liason . . . . Pierre Larouche

Finance
Assistant Controller . . . . Mark R. Kuczinski
Senior Accountant . . . . Troy Ussack
Payroll Manager . . . . Andrea Winschel
Accounts Payable . . . . Tawni Love

Ticketing
Senior Director of Ticketing. . . . . James Santilli
Director of Premium Seating/Group Sales . . . . Mike Guiffre
Manager of Premium Sales . . . . Brian Magness
Coordinator of Premium Services . . . . Lydia Tobiasz
Group Sales Account Executive . . . . Mike Zatchey
Director of Ticket Sales and Services . . . . . . Chad Slencak
Ticket Sales Account Executives. . . . . George Birman, Bonnie Golinski, George Murphy, Chuck Pukansky
Inside Sales Representatives . . . . Jeff Blizman, Beth Folcik, Robbie Hofmann, Nicole Kyslinger, Sarah Swartz
Box Office Manager . . . . Carol Coulson
Manager of Box Office Operations . . . . Jason Onufer
Box Office Assistant . . . . Kelly Gabany
Manager of Customer Service . . . . Kathy Davis
Customer Service Representatives . . . . Cori Shrader, Amanda Rameas, Kathleen Unger
Director of Database Marketing . . . . Jill Shipley
Database Manager . . . . Erin Exley

St. Louis Blues

2005-06 Results: 21W-46L-7OTL-8SOL 57PTS.
Fifth, Central Division

2006-07 Schedule

Oct.	Thu.	5	at San Jose	Tue.	9	at Columbus
	Sat.	7	at Los Angeles	Wed.	10	at New Jersey
	Mon.	9	at Anaheim	Sat.	13	Los Angeles*
	Thu.	12	Boston	Mon.	15	at Phoenix*
	Sat.	14	Chicago	Tue.	16	at Anaheim
	Tue.	17	Phoenix	Thu.	18	at Los Angeles
	Fri.	20	Vancouver	Sat.	20	at San Jose
	Sat.	21	at Chicago	Fri.	26	Detroit
	Sat.	28	Detroit	Sat.	27	Nashville
	Mon.	30	Anaheim	Tue.	30	Minnesota
Nov.	Wed.	1	at Dallas	**Feb.** Fri.	2	at Detroit
	Thu.	2	Colorado	Sat.	3	Dallas
	Sat.	4	Calgary	Tue.	6	Toronto
	Thu.	9	Columbus	Thu.	8	Detroit
	Fri.	10	at Chicago	Sat.	10	at Philadelphia
	Sun.	12	Edmonton*	Tue.	13	San Jose
	Tue.	14	at Calgary	Wed.	14	at Columbus
	Thu.	16	at Edmonton	Fri.	16	Nashville
	Fri.	17	at Vancouver	Sun.	18	Minnesota*
	Wed.	22	at Columbus	Tue.	20	Columbus
	Fri.	24	at Detroit	Sun.	25	at Chicago*
	Sat.	25	Phoenix	Tue.	27	Vancouver
	Tue.	28	San Jose	**Mar.** Thu.	1	at NY Islanders
	Thu.	30	Nashville	Sat.	3	at NY Rangers*
Dec.	Fri.	1	at Chicago	Tue.	6	Calgary
	Tue.	5	Detroit	Thu.	8	Dallas
	Thu.	7	at Detroit	Sat.	10	Montreal
	Sat.	9	Columbus	Mon.	12	at Calgary
	Tue.	12	Chicago	Thu.	15	at Vancouver
	Wed.	13	at Colorado	Sat.	17	at Edmonton
	Sat.	16	at Nashville	Tue.	20	Ottawa
	Sun.	17	Nashville*	Thu.	22	at Minnesota
	Tue.	19	at Pittsburgh	Sat.	24	at Detroit*
	Thu.	21	Los Angeles	Sun.	25	at Columbus*
	Sat.	23	Buffalo	Tue.	27	Columbus
	Tue.	26	at Nashville	Thu.	29	Edmonton
	Fri.	29	at Colorado	Sat.	31	Anaheim
	Sat.	30	Colorado	**Apr.** Mon.	2	at Dallas
Jan.	Tue.	2	Chicago	Tue.	3	at Phoenix
	Thu.	4	Chicago	Thu.	5	at Nashville
	Sat.	6	at Nashville	Sat.	7	at Minnesota

* Denotes afternoon game.

Franchise date: June 5, 1967

CENTRAL DIVISION

40th NHL Season

Petr Cajanek established NHL career highs with 71 games played and 31 assists in 2005-06. He tied Scott Young for the team lead in assists and finished second to Young with 41 points.

Year-by-Year Record

		Home				Road				Overall								
Season	GP	W	L	T	OL	W	L	T	OL	W	L	T	OL	GF	GA	Pts.	Finished	Playoff Result
2005-06	82	12	23	....	6	9	23	....	9	21	46	....	15	197	292	57	5th, Central Div.	Out of Playoffs
2004-05		....																
2003-04	82	23	11	7	0	16	19	4	2	39	30	11	2	191	198	91	2nd, Central Div.	Lost Conf. Quarter-Final
2002-03	82	23	11	4	3	18	13	7	3	41	24	11	6	253	222	99	2nd, Central Div.	Lost Conf. Quarter-Final
2001-02	82	27	12	1	1	16	15	7	3	43	27	8	4	227	188	98	2nd, Central Div.	Lost Conf. Semi-Final
2000-01	82	28	5	5	3	15	17	7	2	43	22	12	5	249	195	103	2nd, Central Div.	Lost Conf. Championship
1999-2000	82	24	9	7	1	27	10	4	0	51	19	11	1	248	165	114	1st, Central Div.	Lost Conf. Quarter-Final
1998-99	82	18	17	6	....	19	15	7	....	37	32	13	....	237	209	87	2nd, Central Div.	Lost Conf. Semi-Final
1997-98	82	26	10	5	....	19	19	3	....	45	29	8	....	256	204	98	3rd, Central Div.	Lost Conf. Semi-Final
1996-97	82	17	20	4	....	19	15	7	....	36	35	11	....	236	239	83	4th, Central Div.	Lost Conf. Quarter-Final
1995-96	82	15	17	9	....	17	17	7	....	32	34	16	....	219	248	80	4th, Central Div.	Lost Conf. Semi-Final
1994-95	48	16	6	2	....	12	9	3	....	28	15	5	....	178	135	61	2nd, Central Div.	Lost Conf. Quarter-Final
1993-94	84	23	11	8	....	17	22	3	....	40	33	11	....	270	283	91	4th, Central Div.	Lost Conf. Quarter-Final
1992-93	84	22	13	7	....	15	23	4	....	37	36	11	....	282	278	85	4th, Norris Div.	Lost Div. Final
1991-92	80	25	12	3	....	11	21	8	....	36	33	11	....	279	266	83	3rd, Norris Div.	Lost Div. Semi-Final
1990-91	80	24	9	7	....	23	13	4	....	47	22	11	....	310	250	105	2nd, Norris Div.	Lost Div. Final
1989-90	80	20	15	5	....	17	19	4	....	37	34	9	....	295	279	83	2nd, Norris Div.	Lost Div. Final
1988-89	80	22	11	7	....	11	24	5	....	33	35	12	....	275	285	78	2nd, Norris Div.	Lost Div. Final
1987-88	80	18	17	5	....	16	21	3	....	34	38	8	....	278	294	76	2nd, Norris Div.	Lost Div. Final
1986-87	80	21	12	7	....	11	21	8	....	32	33	15	....	281	293	79	1st, Norris Div.	Lost Div. Semi-Final
1985-86	80	23	11	6	....	14	23	3	....	37	34	9	....	302	291	83	3rd, Norris Div.	Lost Conf. Championship
1984-85	80	21	12	7	....	16	19	5	....	37	31	12	....	299	288	86	1st, Norris Div.	Lost Div. Semi-Final
1983-84	80	23	14	3	....	9	27	4	....	32	41	7	....	293	316	71	2nd, Norris Div.	Lost Div. Final
1982-83	80	16	16	8	....	9	24	7	....	25	40	15	....	285	316	65	4th, Norris Div.	Lost Div. Semi-Final
1981-82	80	22	14	4	....	10	26	4	....	32	40	8	....	315	349	72	3rd Norris Div.	Lost Div. Final
1980-81	80	29	7	4	....	16	11	13	....	45	18	17	....	352	281	107	1st, Smythe Div.	Lost Quarter-Final
1979-80	80	20	13	7	....	14	21	5	....	34	34	12	....	266	278	80	2nd, Smythe Div.	Lost Prelim. Round
1978-79	80	14	20	6	....	4	30	6	....	18	50	12	....	249	348	48	3rd, Smythe Div.	Out of Playoffs
1977-78	80	12	20	8	....	8	27	5	....	20	47	13	....	195	304	53	4th, Smythe Div.	Out of Playoffs
1976-77	80	22	13	5	....	10	26	4	....	32	39	9	....	239	276	73	1st, Smythe Div.	Lost Quarter-Final
1975-76	80	20	12	8	....	9	25	6	....	29	37	14	....	249	290	72	3rd, Smythe Div.	Lost Prelim. Round
1974-75	80	23	13	4	....	12	18	10	....	35	31	14	....	269	267	84	2nd, Smythe Div.	Lost Prelim. Round
1973-74	78	16	14	9	....	10	24	5	....	26	40	12	....	206	248	64	6th, West Div.	Out of Playoffs
1972-73	78	21	11	7	....	11	23	5	....	32	34	12	....	233	251	76	4th, West Div.	Lost Quarter-Final
1971-72	78	17	17	5	....	11	22	6	....	28	39	11	....	208	247	67	3rd, West Div.	Lost Semi-Final
1970-71	78	23	7	9	....	11	18	10	....	34	25	19	....	223	208	87	2nd, West Div.	Lost Quarter-Final
1969-70	76	24	9	5	....	13	18	7	....	37	27	12	....	224	179	86	1st, West Div.	Lost Final
1968-69	76	21	8	9	....	16	17	5	....	37	25	14	....	204	157	88	1st, West Div.	Lost Final
1967-68	74	18	12	7	....	9	19	9	....	27	31	16	....	177	191	70	3rd, West Div.	Lost Final

2006-07 Player Personnel

FORWARDS

	HT	WT	S	Place of Birth	Date	2005-06 Club
BACKES, David	6-2	200	R	Blaine, MN	5/1/84	Minnesota State-Peoria
BIRNER, Michal	6-0	183	L	Litomerice, Czech.	3/2/86	Saginaw
CAJANEK, Petr	5-11	176	L	Gottwaldov/Zlin, Czech.	8/18/75	St. Louis
DISALVATORE, Jon	6-1	200	R	Bangor, ME	3/30/81	St. Louis-Peoria
DRAKE, Dallas	6-1	195	L	Trail, B.C.	2/4/69	St. Louis
GLUMAC, Mike	6-2	205	R	Niagara Falls, Ont.	4/5/80	St. Louis-Peoria
GUERIN, Bill	6-2	210	R	Worcester, MA	11/9/70	Dallas
HINOTE, Dan	6-0	190	R	Leesburg, FL	1/30/77	Colorado
JOHNSON, Ryan	6-1	205	L	Thunder Bay, Ont.	6/14/76	St. Louis
KAHNBERG, Magnus	6-2	190	L	Kallered, Sweden	2/25/80	Frolunda
KING, D.J.	6-3	230	L	Meadow Lake, Sask.	1/27/84	Peoria-Alaska
MAYERS, Jamal	6-1	212	R	Toronto, Ont.	10/24/74	St. Louis
McCLEMENT, Jay	6-1	199	L	Kingston, Ont.	3/2/83	St. Louis-Peoria
ORSZAGH, Vladimir	5-11	195	L	Banska Bystrica, Czech.	5/24/77	Lulea-St. Louis
RAMSAY, Ryan	5-11	200	L	Ajax, Ont.	5/18/83	Peoria-Alaska
RUCINSKY, Martin	6-1	205	L	Most, Czech.	3/11/71	NY Rangers
SEJNA, Peter	5-11	198	L	Liptovsky Mikulas, Czech.	10/5/79	St. Louis-Peoria
SHISHKANOV, Timofei	6-1	209	R	Moscow, USSR	6/10/83	Milwaukee-StL-Peoria
SHKOTOV, Alexei	5-10	175	L	Elektrostal, USSR	6/22/84	Mytischi-Elektrostal
SODERBERG, Carl	6-3	198	L	Malmo, Sweden	10/12/85	Malmo
STEMPNIAK, Lee	6-0	190	R	Buffalo, NY	2/4/83	St. Louis
TKACHUK, Keith	6-2	225	L	Melrose, MA	3/28/72	St. Louis
WEIGHT, Doug	5-11	200	L	Warren, MI	1/21/71	St. Louis-Carolina
WHITFIELD, Trent	5-11	204	L	Estevan, Sask.	6/17/77	St. Louis-Peoria
ZAKHAROV, Konstantin	6-1	190	R	Minsk, USSR	5/2/85	Yunost-Alaska

DEFENSEMEN

	HT	WT	S	Place of Birth	Date	2005-06 Club
BACKMAN, Christian	6-4	198	L	Alingsas, Sweden	4/28/80	St. Louis
BREWER, Eric	6-3	225	L	Vernon, B.C.	4/17/79	St. Louis
FITZGERALD, Zack	6-1	214	L	Two Harbors, MN	6/16/85	Peoria-Alaska
JACKMAN, Barret	6-0	200	L	Trail, B.C.	3/5/81	St. Louis
LYNCH, Doug	6-3	214	L	North Vancouver, B.C.	4/4/83	Peoria-Alaska
MacKENZIE, Aaron	6-0	193	L	Terrace Bay, Ont.	3/7/81	Peoria
McKEE, Jay	6-4	200	L	Kingston, Ont.	9/8/77	Buffalo
MOJZIS, Tomas	6-1	192	L	Kolin, Czech.	5/2/82	Van-Manitoba-Peoria
POLAK, Roman	6-1	198	R	Ostrava, Czech.	4/28/86	Vitkovice Jr.-Vitkovice
SALVADOR, Bryce	6-2	215	L	Brandon, Man.	2/11/76	St. Louis
STUART, Mike	6-0	200	R	Rochester, MN	8/31/80	St. Louis-Peoria
WALKER, Matt	6-3	227	R	Beaverlodge, Alta.	4/7/80	St. Louis
WELLAR, Patrick	6-3	210	L	Carrot River, Sask.	12/4/83	Peoria-Alaska
WIDEMAN, Dennis	6-0	200	R	Kitchener, Ont.	3/20/83	St. Louis-Peoria
WOYWITKA, Jeff	6-2	209	L	Vermilion, Alta.	9/1/83	St. Louis-Peoria

GOALTENDERS

	HT	WT	C	Place of Birth	Date	2005-06 Club
BACASHIHUA, Jason	5-11	175	L	Garden City, MI	9/20/82	St. Louis-Peoria
BECKFORD-TSEU, Chris	6-2	201	L	Toronto, Ont.	6/22/84	Peoria-Alaska
LEGACE, Manny	5-9	162	L	Toronto, Ont.	2/4/73	Detroit-Grand Rapids
SANFORD, Curtis	5-10	187	L	Owen Sound, Ont.	10/5/79	St. Louis-Peoria
SCHWARZ, Marek	5-11	176	R	Mlada Boleslav, Czech.	4/1/86	Sparta Jr.-Sparta-Beroun

2005-06 Scoring
* – rookie

Regular Season

Pos	#	Player	Team	GP	G	A	Pts	+/-	PIM	PP	SH	GW	S	%
R	48	Scott Young	STL	79	18	31	49	–32	52	10	0	1	284	6.3
C	26	Petr Cajanek	STL	71	10	31	41	–22	54	3	0	0	150	6.7
C	37	Dean McAmmond	STL	78	15	22	37	–25	32	4	0	0	116	12.9
L	7	Keith Tkachuk	STL	41	15	21	36	–15	46	10	0	1	133	11.3
R	12 *	Lee Stempniak	STL	57	14	13	27	–10	22	5	0	2	100	14.0
C	9 *	Jay McClement	STL	67	6	21	27	–23	30	1	0	2	76	7.9
R	21	Jamal Mayers	STL	67	15	11	26	–22	129	0	2	1	111	13.5
R	10	Dallas Drake	STL	62	2	24	26	–13	59	1	0	1	88	2.3
D	25 *	Dennis Wideman	STL	67	8	16	24	–31	83	5	1	1	150	5.3
D	55	Christian Backman	STL	52	6	12	18	–15	48	3	0	1	70	8.6
D	38 *	Kevin Dallman	BOS	21	0	1	1	1	8	0	0	0	42	0.0
			STL	46	4	9	13	–15	21	3	0	0	89	4.5
			TOTAL	67	4	10	14	–14	29	3	0	0	131	3.1
R	54 *	Mike Glumac	STL	33	7	5	12	–8	33	5	0	0	55	12.7
R	42	Mark Rycroft	STL	80	6	4	10	–14	46	0	1	2	77	7.8
D	5	Barret Jackman	STL	63	4	6	10	–6	156	0	2	2	56	7.1
D	4	Eric Brewer	STL	32	6	3	9	–17	45	1	0	1	64	9.4
R	32	Vladimir Orszagh	STL	16	4	5	9	–2	14	1	0	0	23	17.4
C	17	Ryan Johnson	STL	65	3	6	9	–21	33	1	1	0	57	5.3
R	22	Jeff Hoggan	STL	52	2	6	8	–16	34	0	0	0	60	3.3
L	20 *	Simon Gamache	NSH	11	0	0	0	–6	0	0	0	0	4	0.0
			STL	15	3	4	7	1	10	0	0	0	32	9.4
			TOTAL	26	3	4	7	–5	10	0	0	0	36	8.3
C	23	Trent Whitfield	STL	30	2	5	7	–3	14	1	0	0	41	4.9
R	20 *	Timofei Shishkanov	STL	22	3	2	5	–1	6	0	0	0	26	11.5
D	27	Bryce Salvador	STL	46	1	4	5	–24	26	0	0	0	23	4.3
D	33	Steve Poapst	PIT	21	0	4	4	–5	10	0	0	0	4	0.0
			STL	41	0	1	1	–21	37	0	0	0	19	0.0
			TOTAL	62	0	5	5	–26	47	0	0	0	23	0.0
D	20	Andy Roach	STL	5	1	2	3	0	0	0	0	0	2	50.0
L	15 *	Peter Sejna	STL	6	1	2	3	1	4	0	0	0	9	11.1
D	29 *	Jeff Woywitka	STL	26	0	2	2	–12	25	0	0	0	23	0.0
D	28	Matt Walker	STL	54	0	2	2	–7	79	0	0	0	59	0.0
C	41	Mike Zigomanis	CAR	21	1	0	1	1	4	0	0	0	16	6.3
			STL	2	0	0	0	0	0	0	0	0	1	0.0
			TOTAL	23	1	0	1	1	4	0	0	0	17	5.9
D	43 *	Mike Stuart	STL	1	0	0	0	0	0	0	0	0	1	0.0
L	53 *	Colin Hemingway	STL	3	0	0	0	0	0	0	0	0	2	0.0
R	62 *	Jon Disalvatore	STL	5	0	0	0	–1	2	0	0	0	3	0.0
R	36	Jesse Boulerice	CAR	26	0	0	0	–3	51	0	0	0	3	0.0
			STL	12	0	0	0	–4	13	0	0	0	2	0.0
			TOTAL	38	0	0	0	–7	64	0	0	0	5	0.0

Goaltending

No.	Goaltender	GPI	Mins	Avg	W	L	OT	EN	SO	GA	SA	S%	G	A	PIM
1	* Curtis Sanford	34	1830	2.66	13	13	5	4	3	81	885	.908	0	0	0
30	* Jason Bacashihua	19	966	3.23	4	10	1	5	0	52	515	.899	0	1	0
40	Patrick Lalime	31	1699	3.64	4	18	8	2	0	103	868	.881	0	0	0
50	Reinhard Divis	12	475	4.67	0	5	1	0	0	37	231	.840	0	0	0
	Totals	82	5001	3.41	21	46	15	11	3	284	2510	.887			

Coaching History

Lynn Patrick and Scotty Bowman, 1967-68; Scotty Bowman, 1968-69, 1969-70; Al Arbour and Scotty Bowman, 1970-71; Sid Abel, Bill McCreary and Al Arbour, 1971-72; Al Arbour and Jean-Guy Talbot, 1972-73; Jean-Guy Talbot and Lou Angotti, 1973-74; Lou Angotti, Lynn Patrick and Garry Young, 1974-75; Garry Young, Lynn Patrick and Leo Boivin, 1975-76; Emile Francis, 1976-77; Leo Boivin and Barclay Plager, 1977-78; Barclay Plager, 1978-79; Barclay Plager and Red Berenson, 1979-80; Red Berenson, 1980-81; Red Berenson and Emile Francis, 1981-82; Emile Francis and Barclay Plager, 1982-83; Jacques Demers, 1983-84 to 1985-86; Jacques Martin, 1986-87, 1987-88; Brian Sutter, 1988-89 to 1991-92; Bob Plager and Bob Berry, 1992-93; Bob Berry, 1993-94; Mike Keenan, 1994-95; 1995-96; Mike Keenan, Jim Roberts and Joel Quenneville, 1996-97; Joel Quenneville, 1997-98 to 2002-03; Joel Quenneville and Mike Kitchen, 2003-04; Mike Kitchen, 2004-05 to date.

Coach

KITCHEN, MIKE
Coach, St. Louis Blues. Born in Newmarket, Ont., February 1, 1956.

Mike Kitchen was named head coach of the St. Louis Blues on February 24, 2004. His first game as head coach was on February 26, 2004 at Colorado. Kitchen spent six and a half seasons as the Blues' assistant coach, joining the staff on September 1, 1998. Prior to joining the Blues, he spent nine seasons as an assistant coach for the Toronto Maple Leafs. He joined the Leafs on August 8, 1989 after spending one season as an assistant coach for Newmarket in the American Hockey League.

Kitchen spent eight seasons in the National Hockey League as a defenseman with the Colorado Rockies and the New Jersey Devils. He appeared in 474 games, while recording 12 goals, 62 assists and 370 penalty minutes. Kansas City originally drafted him as the 38th overall choice in the 1976 Entry Draft.

Prior to playing in the NHL, Kitchen spent three seasons with the Toronto Marlboros of the OHA, accumulating 79 points (14 goals, 65 assists) and 429 penalty minutes in 202 games played. He also spent one season with the Rhode Island Reds of the AHL, registering 10 assists and 14 penalty minutes in 14 games played.

Coaching Record

Season	Team	Games	Regular Season				Playoffs		
			W	L	O/T		Games	W	L
2003-04	St. Louis (NHL)	21	10	7	4		5	1	4
2004-05	St. Louis (NHL)				Season Cancelled				
2005-06	St. Louis (NHL)	82	21	46	15		....	....	....
	NHL Totals	103	31	53	19		5	1	4

Manny Legace joins the Blues after a career year in 2005-06. Legace ranked among the NHL leaders with 37 wins, seven shutouts and a 2.19 goals-against average.

Captains' History

Al Arbour, 1967-68 to 1969-70; Red Berenson and Barclay Plager, 1970-71; Barclay Plager, 1971-72 to 1975-76; no captain, 1976-77; Red Berenson, 1977-78; Barry Gibbs, 1978-79; Brian Sutter, 1979-80 to 1987-88; Bernie Federko, 1988-89; Rick Meagher, 1989-90; Scott Stevens, 1990-91; Garth Butcher, 1991-92; Brett Hull, 1992-93 to 1994-95; Brett Hull, Shayne Corson and Wayne Gretzky, 1995-96; no captain, 1996-97; Chris Pronger, 1997-98 to 2001-02; Al MacInnis, 2002-03, 2003-04; Dallas Drake, 2005-06.

Club Records

Team

(Figures in brackets for season records are games played; records for fewest points, wins, ties, losses, goals, goals against are for 70 or more games)

Record		
Most Points	**114**	1999-2000 (82)
Most Wins	**51**	1999-2000 (82)
Most Ties	**19**	1970-71 (78)
Most Losses	**50**	1978-79 (80)
Most Goals	**352**	1980-81 (80)
Most Goals Against	**349**	1981-82 (80)
Fewest Points	**48**	1978-79 (80)
Fewest Wins	**18**	1978-79 (80)
Fewest Ties	**7**	1983-84 (80)
Fewest Losses	**18**	1980-81 (80)
Fewest Goals	**177**	1967-68 (74)
Fewest Goals Against	**157**	1968-69 (76)
Longest Winning Streak		
Overall	**10**	Jan. 3-23/02
Home	**9**	Jan. 26-Feb. 26/91
Away	***10**	Jan. 21-Mar. 2/00
Longest Undefeated Streak		
Overall	**12**	Nov. 10-Dec. 8/68 (5 wins, 7 ties), Nov. 24-Dec. 26/00 (11 wins, 1 tie)
Home	**11**	Four times
Away	**11**	Jan. 21-Mar. 4/00 (10 wins, 1 tie)
Longest Losing Streak		
Overall	**13**	Mar. 16-Apr. 8/06
Home	**7**	Oct. 22-Nov. 26/05
Away	**10**	Jan. 20-Mar. 8/82, Dec. 29/05-Feb. 1/06
Longest Winless Streak		
Overall	**13**	Mar. 16-Apr. 8/06 (10 losses, 3 OT losses)
Home	**7**	Dec. 28/82-Jan. 25/83 (5 losses, 2 ties), Oct. 22-Nov. 26/05 (6 losses, 1 OT loss)
Away	**17**	Jan. 23-Oct. 9/74 (13 losses, 4 ties)
Most Shutouts, Season	**13**	1968-69 (76)
Most PIM, Season	**2,041**	1990-91 (80)
Most Goals, Game	**11**	Feb. 26/94 (St.L. 11 at Ott. 1)

Individual

Record		
Most Seasons	**13**	Bernie Federko
Most Games	**927**	Bernie Federko
Most Goals, Career	**527**	Brett Hull
Most Assists, Career	**721**	Bernie Federko
Most Points, Career	**1,073**	Bernie Federko (352G, 721A)
Most PIM, Career	**1,786**	Brian Sutter
Most Shutouts, Career	**16**	Glenn Hall
Longest Consecutive Games Streak	**662**	Garry Unger (Feb. 7/71-Apr. 8/79)
Most Goals, Season	**86**	Brett Hull (1990-91)
Most Assists, Season	**90**	Adam Oates (1990-91)
Most Points, Season	**131**	Brett Hull (1990-91) (86G, 45A)
Most PIM, Season	**306**	Bob Gassoff (1975-76)
Most Points, Defenseman, Season	**78**	Jeff Brown (1992-93; 25G, 53A)
Most Points, Center, Season	**115**	Adam Oates (1990-91; 25G, 90A)
Most Points, Right Wing, Season	**131**	Brett Hull (1990-91; 86G, 45A)
Most Points, Left Wing, Season	**102**	Brendan Shanahan (1993-94; 52G, 50A)
Most Points, Rookie, Season	**73**	Jorgen Pettersson (1980-81; 37G, 36A)
Most Shutouts, Season	**8**	Glenn Hall (1968-69)
Most Goals, Game	**6**	Red Berenson (Nov. 7/68)
Most Assists, Game	**5**	Brian Sutter (Nov. 22/83), Bernie Federko (Feb. 27/88), Adam Oates (Jan. 26/91), Dallas Drake (Oct. 29/03)
Most Points, Game	**7**	Red Berenson (Nov. 7/68; 6G, 1A), Garry Unger (Mar. 13/71; 3G, 4A)

* NHL Record.

Retired Numbers

2	Al MacInnis	1994-2004
3	Bob Gassoff	1973-1977
8	Barclay Plager	1967-1977
11	Brian Sutter	1976-1988
24	Bernie Federko	1976-1989

All-time Record vs. Other Clubs

Regular Season

	At Home								On Road								Total							
	GP	W	L	T	OL	GF	GA	PTS	GP	W	L	T	OL	GF	GA	PTS	GP	W	L	T	OL	GF	GA	PTS
Anaheim	24	13	7	3	1	74	63	30	24	13	9	2	0	72	66	28	48	26	16	5	1	146	129	58
Atlanta	3	3	0	0	0	11	1	6	5	2	2	1	0	16	16	5	8	5	2	1	0	27	17	11
Boston	59	27	23	9	0	188	198	63	59	15	35	9	0	161	247	39	118	42	58	18	0	349	445	102
Buffalo	50	29	14	7	0	180	125	65	52	17	29	6	0	164	200	40	102	46	43	13	0	344	325	105
Calgary	66	32	25	9	0	234	204	73	64	28	29	5	2	183	207	63	130	60	54	14	2	417	411	136
Carolina	31	19	9	3	0	119	94	41	32	17	13	2	0	99	96	36	63	36	22	5	0	218	190	77
Chicago	119	59	41	17	2	405	372	137	122	36	64	18	4	355	445	94	241	95	105	35	6	760	817	231
Colorado	42	22	14	4	2	151	129	50	43	14	22	7	0	114	148	35	85	36	36	11	2	265	277	85
Columbus	15	11	3	1	0	57	34	23	14	5	5	2	2	33	33	14	29	16	8	3	2	90	67	37
Dallas	119	65	33	21	0	429	339	151	117	40	54	22	1	337	390	103	236	105	87	43	1	766	729	254
Detroit	114	56	38	20	0	382	323	132	114	42	54	17	1	342	417	102	228	98	92	37	1	724	740	234
Edmonton	46	22	17	7	0	161	161	51	46	19	23	4	0	153	167	42	92	41	40	11	0	314	328	93
Florida	9	7	1	1	0	25	12	15	10	5	3	2	0	21	20	12	19	12	4	3	0	46	32	27
Los Angeles	80	50	19	10	1	297	203	111	80	31	37	12	0	229	269	74	160	81	56	22	1	526	472	185
Minnesota	10	4	3	3	0	19	15	11	10	3	4	2	1	20	29	9	20	7	7	5	1	39	44	20
Montreal	57	14	28	15	0	147	195	43	59	11	41	7	0	161	255	29	116	25	69	22	0	308	450	72
Nashville	20	12	7	1	0	57	36	25	21	9	7	3	2	52	47	23	41	21	14	4	2	109	83	48
New Jersey	47	27	12	7	1	195	148	62	46	17	22	7	0	128	146	41	93	44	34	14	1	323	294	103
NY Islanders	48	18	19	9	2	169	159	47	49	13	25	11	0	131	183	37	97	31	44	20	2	300	342	84
NY Rangers	64	25	28	10	1	192	207	61	60	10	44	6	0	143	245	26	124	35	72	16	1	335	452	87
Ottawa	9	4	3	2	0	27	25	10	10	6	4	0	0	36	23	12	19	10	7	2	0	63	48	22
Philadelphia	69	26	34	7	2	196	224	61	67	12	45	10	0	153	264	34	136	38	79	17	2	349	488	95
Phoenix	52	26	15	11	0	185	144	63	53	19	25	7	2	165	175	47	105	45	40	18	2	350	319	110
Pittsburgh	65	44	15	6	0	250	171	94	64	20	31	12	1	190	238	53	129	64	46	18	1	440	409	147
San Jose	30	18	10	1	1	99	78	38	26	20	5	1	0	89	57	41	56	38	15	2	1	188	135	79
Tampa Bay	11	10	1	0	0	44	24	20	14	5	5	3	1	46	43	14	25	15	6	3	1	90	67	34
Toronto	102	58	29	14	1	348	283	131	99	30	58	11	0	292	369	71	201	88	87	25	1	640	652	202
Vancouver	73	43	21	9	0	273	206	95	74	35	29	9	1	238	217	80	147	78	50	18	1	511	423	175
Washington	41	20	13	8	0	165	127	48	40	15	20	4	1	121	141	35	81	35	33	12	1	286	268	83
Defunct Clubs	32	25	4	3	0	131	55	53	33	11	10	12	0	95	100	34	65	36	14	15	0	226	155	87
Totals	**1507**	**789**	**486**	**218**	**14**	**5210**	**4355**	**1810**	**1507**	**520**	**754**	**214**	**19**	**4339**	**5253**	**1273**	**3014**	**1309**	**1240**	**432**	**33**	**9549**	**9608**	**3083**

Playoffs

	Series	W	L	GP	W	L	T	GF	GA	Last Mtg.	Rnd.	Result
Boston	2	0	2	8	0	8	0	15	48	1972	SF	L 0-4
Buffalo	1	0	1	3	1	2	0	8	7	1976	PRE	L 1-2
Calgary	1	0	1	7	3	4	0	22	28	1986	CF	L 3-4
Chicago	10	3	7	50	22	28	0	142	171	2002	CQF	W 4-1
Colorado	1	0	1	5	1	4	0	11	17	2001	CF	L 1-4
Dallas	12	6	6	66	32	34	0	187	197	2001	CSF	W 4-0
Detroit	7	2	5	40	16	24	0	103	125	2002	CSF	L 1-4
Los Angeles	2	2	0	8	8	0	0	32	13	1998	CQF	W 4-0
Montreal	3	0	3	12	0	12	0	14	42	1977	QF	L 0-4
NY Rangers	1	0	1	6	2	4	0	22	29	1981	QF	L 2-4
Philadelphia	2	2	0	11	8	3	0	34	20	1969	QF	W 4-0
Phoenix	2	2	0	11	7	4	0	39	29	1999	CQF	W 4-3
Pittsburgh	3	2	1	13	7	6	0	45	40	1981	PRE	W 3-2
San Jose	3	1	2	18	8	10	0	47	43	2004	CQF	L 1-4
Toronto	5	3	2	31	17	14	0	88	90	1996	CQF	W 4-2
Vancouver	2	0	2	14	6	8	0	48	44	2003	CQF	L 3-4
Totals	**57**	**23**	**34**	**303**	**138**	**165**	**0**	**857**	**943**			

Calgary totals include Atlanta Flames, 1972-73 to 1979-80.
Colorado totals include Quebec, 1979-80 to 1994-95.
Carolina totals include Hartford, 1979-80 to 1996-97.
Dallas totals include Minnesota North Stars, 1967-68 to 1992-93.
New Jersey totals include Kansas City, 1974-75 to 1975-76, and Colorado Rockies, 1976-77 to 1981-82.
Phoenix totals include Winnipeg, 1979-80 to 1995-96.

Playoff Results 2006-2001

Year	Round	Opponent	Result	GF	GA
2004	CQF	San Jose	L 1-4	9	12
2003	CQF	Vancouver	L 3-4	21	17
2002	CSF	Detroit	L 1-4	11	14
	CQF	Chicago	W 4-1	13	5
2001	CF	Colorado	L 1-4	11	17
	CSF	Dallas	W 4-0	13	6
	CQF	San Jose	W 4-2	16	11

Abbreviations: Round: CF – conference final; **CSF** – conference semi-final; **CQF** – conference quarter-final; **SF** – semi-final; **QF** – quarter-final; **PRE** – preliminary round.

2005-06 Results

Oct.	5	at Detroit	1-5
	6	Detroit	3-4
	8	San Jose	6-7
	11	Chicago	4-1
	15	Nashville	1-4
	19	Anaheim	3-2
	20	at Nashville	2-3†
	22	Minnesota	2-3
	25	at Phoenix	4-5*
	28	at Anaheim	4-6
	29	at Los Angeles	2-5
Nov.	2	Chicago	5-6*
	4	Edmonton	2-7
	6	Detroit	1-4
	9	at Columbus	1-3
	10	Chicago	2-4
	12	at Nashville	1-3
	16	at Columbus	2-0
	19	at Detroit	3-2
	22	Los Angeles	3-6
	25	at Minnesota	3-5
	26	Columbus	3-4
Dec.	1	Columbus	4-1
	6	NY Islanders	3-6
	8	at Tampa Bay	4-5
	10	NY Rangers	4-5*
	13	Pittsburgh	3-0
	16	at Chicago	1-5
	17	Philadelphia	2-5
	20	at Phoenix	5-4
	21	at Anaheim	3-6
	23	at San Jose	2-1†
	26	Dallas	1-6
	28	at Chicago	2-1
	29	at Dallas	0-3
	31	Anaheim	4-5†
Jan.	2	Vancouver	4-1
	4	Nashville	3-4
	5	at Detroit	0-3
	9	at Colorado	1-6
	12	at Florida	1-3
	13	at Atlanta	0-2
	15	at Carolina	2-4
	17	New Jersey	3-5
	19	at Washington	4-5†
	20	at Columbus	3-4†
	23	Vancouver	4-0
	25	at Dallas	3-4†
	26	Phoenix	3-5
	30	Calgary	3-2†
Feb.	1	at Detroit	2-3
	2	Chicago	6-5†
	4	Dallas	4-3*
	8	at Vancouver	4-2
	10	at Calgary	2-3*
	12	at Edmonton	5-4†
Mar.	1	at Edmonton	4-2
	2	at Calgary	1-3
	5	at Vancouver	4-1
	7	Colorado	1-2†
	10	Minnesota	2-1*
	11	Los Angeles	1-2†
	13	Columbus	3-2*
	16	at San Jose	2-5
	18	at Los Angeles	1-3
	20	at Nashville	2-4
	21	San Jose	0-6
	23	Calgary	2-7
	25	Colorado	2-3*
	27	Detroit	1-4
	29	at Chicago	2-3*
	31	Columbus	2-4
Apr.	1	at Nashville	1-2
	4	at Minnesota	4-5†
	6	Nashville	0-3
	8	at Colorado	2-4
	9	Edmonton	2-1
	11	Nashville	0-2
	13	at Columbus	1-4
	15	Detroit	2-3
	16	Phoenix	0-3
	18	at Chicago	2-3*

* – Overtime † – Shootout

Entry Draft Selections 2006-1992

2006

Pick	
1	Erik Johnson
25	Patrik Berglund
31	Tomas Kana
64	Jonas Junland
94	Ryan Turek
106	Reto Berra
124	Andy Sackrison
154	Matthew McCollem
184	Alexander Hellstrom

2005

Pick	
24	T.J. Oshie
37	Scott Jackson
85	Ben Bishop
156	Ryan Reaves
169	Mike Gauthier
171	Nicholas Drazenovic
219	Nikolai Lemtyugov

2004

Pick	
17	Marek Schwarz
49	Carl Soderberg
83	Viktor Alexandrov
116	Michal Birner
136	Nikita Nikitin
180	Roman Polak
211	David Fredriksson
277	Jonathan Michel Boutin

2003

Pick	
30	Shawn Belle
62	David Backes
84	Konstantin Barulin
88	Zack Fitzgerald
101	Konstantin Zakharov
127	Alexandre Bolduc
148	Lee Stempniak
159	Chris Beckford-Tseu
189	Jonathan Lehun
221	Yevgeny Skachkov
253	Andrei Pervyshin
284	Juhamatti Aaltonen

2002

Pick	
48	Alexei Shkotov
62	Andrei Mikhnov
89	Tomas Troliga
120	Robin Jonsson
165	Justin Maiser
191	D.J. King
221	Jonas Johnson
253	Tom Koivisto
284	Ryan MacMurchy

2001

Pick	
57	Jay McClement
89	Tuomas Nissinen
122	Igor Valeev
159	Dmitri Semin
190	Brett Scheffelmaier
253	Petr Cajanek
270	Grant Jacobsen
283	Simon Skoog

2000

Pick	
30	Jeff Taffe
65	Dave Morisset
75	Justin Papineau
96	Antoine Bergeron
129	Troy Riddle
167	Craig Weller
229	Brett Lutes
261	Reinhard Divis
293	Lauri Kinos

1999

Pick	
17	Barret Jackman
85	Peter Smrek
114	Chad Starling
143	Trevor Byrne
180	Tore Vikingstad
203	Phil Osaer
221	Colin Hemingway
232	Alexander Khavanov
260	Brian McMeekin
270	James Desmarais

1998

Pick	
24	Christian Backman
41	Maxim Linnik
83	Matt Walker
157	Brad Voth
170	Andrei Troschinsky
197	Brad Twordik
225	Yevgeny Pastukh
255	John Pohl

1997

Pick	
40	Tyler Rennette
86	Didier Tremblay
98	Jan Horacek
106	Jame Pollock
149	Nicholas Bilotto
177	Ladislav Nagy
206	Bobby Haglund
232	Dmitri Plekhanov
244	Marek Ivan

1996

Pick	
14	Marty Reasoner
67	Gordie Dwyer
95	Jonathan Zukiwsky
97	Andrei Petrakov
159	Stephen Wagner
169	Daniel Corso
177	Reed Low
196	Andrej Podkonicky
203	Tony Hutchins
229	Konstantin Shafranov

1995

Pick	
49	Jochen Hecht
75	Scott Roche
101	Michal Handzus
127	Jeff Ambrosio
153	Denis Hamel
179	Jean-Luc Grand-Pierre
205	Derek Bekar
209	Libor Zabransky

1994

Pick	
68	Stephane Roy
94	Tyler Harlton
120	Edvin Frylen
172	Roman Vopat
198	Steve Noble
224	Marc Stephan
250	Kevin Harper
276	Scott Fankhouser

1993

Pick	
37	Maxim Bets
63	Jamie Rivers
89	Jamal Mayers
141	Todd Kelman
167	Mike Buzak
193	Eric Boguniecki
219	Mike Grier
245	Libor Prochazka
271	Alexander Vasilevski
275	Christer Olsson

1992

Pick	
38	Igor Korolev
62	Vitali Karamnov
64	Vitali Prokhorov
86	Lee Leslie
134	Bob Lachance
158	Ian Laperriere
160	Lance Burns
180	Igor Boldin
182	Nick Naumenko
206	Todd Harris
230	Yuri Gunko
259	Wade Salzman

General Managers' History

Lynn Patrick, 1967-68; Scotty Bowman, 1968-69 to 1970-71; Lynn Patrick, 1971-72; Sid Abel, 1972-73; Charles Catto, 1973-74; Gerry Ehman, 1974-75; Dennis Ball, 1975-76; Emile Francis, 1976-77 to 1982-83; Ron Caron, 1983-84 to 1993-94; Mike Keenan, 1994-95, 1995-96; Mike Keenan and Ron Caron, 1996-97; Larry Pleau, 1997-98 to date.

Vice President and General Manager

PLEAU, LARRY
Senior Vice President/General Manager, St. Louis Blues.
Born in Lynn, MA, June 29, 1947.

Larry Pleau was named general manager on June 9, 1997, becoming the tenth person to hold that position in team history. Under his leadership the Blues won the President's Trophy in 1999-2000 and reached the Western Conference Finals in 2000-01. In international hockey, he served as associate general manager of the silver medal-winning 2002 U.S. Olympic team and as general manager of Team USA at the World Championships in 2003 and 2004 (bronze medal) and at the 2004 World Cup.

Pleau joined the Blues after spending eight seasons with the New York Rangers organization, reaching the position of vice president of player personnel. He joined the Rangers in 1989 as assistant general manager of player development. During Pleau's tenure in New York, the Rangers drafted NHL stars Sergei Zubov, Doug Weight, Alex Kovalev and Niklas Sundstrom. Prior to joining the Rangers, Pleau spent 17 seasons with the Hartford Whalers organization as a player, assistant coach, head coach, general manager and minor league general manager and head coach. He was also instrumental in drafting Ray Ferraro, Ron Francis, Kevin Dineen and Ulf Samuelsson while a member of the Whalers organization.

Pleau played three seasons with the Montreal Canadiens (1969-1972) in the National Hockey League before being the first player signed by the Hartford Whalers of the World Hockey Association. He was a center/left wing for the Whalers from 1972 until his retirement in 1979. He played in 468 regular season games for Hartford, accumulating 157 goals and 215 assists for 372 points. He also played for the 1968 United States Olympic team, the 1969 U.S. national team and went to training camp with Team USA for the 1976 Canada Cup tournament.

NHL Coaching Record

		Regular Season				Playoffs		
Season	Team	Games	W	L	T	Games	W	L
1980-81	Hartford	20	6	12	2	....	....	....
1981-82	Hartford	80	21	41	18	....	....	....
1982-83	Hartford	18	4	13	1	....	....	....
1987-88	Hartford	26	13	13	0	6	2	4
1988-89	Hartford	80	37	38	5	4	0	4
	NHL Totals	**224**	**81**	**117**	**26**	**10**	**2**	**8**

Club Directory

Savvis Center

St. Louis Blues
Savvis Center
1401 Clark Avenue
St. Louis, MO 63103
Phone **314/622-2500**
FAX 314/622-2582
www.stlouisblues.com
Capacity: 19,022

Sports Capital Partners, LLC
Chairman/Governor . . . . . David W. Checketts
Partner/Alternate Governor . . . . . Kenneth W. Munoz
Partner . . . . . Michael McCarthy

Executive
President of Hockey Operations/Alt. Gov. . . . . . John Davidson
CEO of St. Louis Blues Enterprises . . . . . Peter McLoughlin
Sr. V.P. and General Manager . . . . . Larry Pleau
Sr. V.P. of Finance & Hockey Admin. . . . . . Jerry Jasiek
Sr. V.P. and G.M., Savvis Center . . . . . Dennis Petrullo
Vice President of Sales . . . . . Bruce Affleck
Vice President of Marketing . . . . . Jo Ann Miles
Vice President of Sponsorship Sales . . . . . Jim Goessling
Vice President of Human Resources . . . . . Dave Coverstone
Vice President of Building Operations . . . . . Fred Corsi
Exec. Assistant to the President . . . . . Lisa Cwiklowski
Exec. Assistant to the G.M. . . . . . Donna Lembke
Exec. Assistant to the G.M., Savvis Center . . . . . Cherri Haynes

Hockey Operations
Asst. G.M./Dir. of Amateur Scouting . . . . . Jarmo Kekalainen
Dir. of Pro Scouting and Peoria G.M. . . . . . Kevin McDonald
Special Assignments . . . . . Al MacInnis
Head Coach . . . . . Mike Kitchen
Assistant Coach/Goaltending Coach . . . . . Rick Wamsley
Assistant Coach . . . . . Brad Shaw
Strength and Conditioning Coach . . . . . Nelson Ayotte
Video Coach . . . . . Scott Masters

Training
Athletic Trainer . . . . . Ray Barile
Equipment Manager . . . . . Bert Godin
Assistant Equipment Manager . . . . . Steve Wissman
Equipment Assistant . . . . . Ray Halle
Massage Therapist . . . . . Jeff Wright

Scouting
Professional Scouts . . . . . Wayne Mundey, Vaclav Nedomansky, Raimo Summanen
Amateur Scouts . . . . . Mike Antonovich, Craig Channell, Rick Meagher, Ville Siren
Part-Time Amateur Scouts . . . . . Bill Armstrong, Thomas Carlsson, Dan Ginnell, Vladimir Havluj, Jr., Barclay Parneta, Georgi Zhuravlev

Medical
Orthopedic Surgeons . . . . . Drs. Rick Wright, Matt Matava, Jerome Gilden
Internists . . . . . Drs. William Birenbaum, Aaron Birenbaum
Neurosurgeon . . . . . Dr. Ralph Dacey
General Surgery . . . . . Dr. Michael Brunt
Plastic Surgery . . . . . Dr. Tom Francel
Dentist . . . . . Dr. Glenn Edwards
Ophthalmologist . . . . . Dr. Gill Grand
Optometrist . . . . . Dr. Rex Ghormley
Oral Surgeon . . . . . Dr. Ken Kram

Communications
Director of Media Relations and Team Services . . . . Mike Caruso
Communications Coordinator . . . . . Scott Bonanni
Communications Coordinator . . . . . Rich Jankowski
Marketing/Public Relations Assistant . . . . . Donna Ferguson
Team Photographer . . . . . Mark Buckner

Marketing
Senior Director of Corporate Sponsorship . . . . . Chris Arger
Director of Corporate Sponsorship . . . . . Mary Greener
Director of Marketing Programs . . . . . Lou Siville
Event Presentation Director . . . . . Chris Frome
Client Services Manager . . . . . Justine Lundin
Marketing Program Manager . . . . . Josh Hardin
KTRS Radio/Community Relations . . . . . Bob Plager

Sales
Director of Sales . . . . . Jennifer Nevins
Inside Sales Manager . . . . . Theo Hodges
Administrative Assistant . . . . . Brenda Wilbur
Sales Executives . . . . . Kari Palmer, Renee Orr, Kim Derringer, Randy Walker
Group Sales . . . . . Ashley Patey, Jason Roeslein
Customer Service Manager . . . . . Jill Hahn
Customer Service Assistant Manager . . . . . Paula Barnes Munder
Customer Service Representative . . . . . Jill Mahoney
Manager Database/Customer Service Representative . Jason Penning

Finance
Director of MIS/Accounting . . . . . Phil Siddle
Manager of Accounting . . . . . Craig Bryant
Payroll Supervisor . . . . . Pam Di Rie
Payroll Assistant . . . . . Crystal Strasburg
Accountants . . . . . Deann Cromer, Chantay Kane, Carrin Stelmach, Emily Hobbs

Team Broadcasters
Radio Station . . . . . KTRS 550 AM
Radio Broadcasters . . . . . Chris Kerber, Kelly Chase
Television Station . . . . . KPLR-TV, WB11
Regional Sports Network . . . . . FSN Midwest
Television Broadcasters . . . . . John Kelly, Bernie Federko, Dan McLaughlin

San Jose Sharks

2005-06 Results: 44w-27l-4otl-7sol 99pts.
Second, Pacific Division

Year-by-Year Record

Season	GP	Home				Road				Overall					GF	GA	Pts.	Finished	Playoff Result
		W	L	T	OL	W	L	T	OL	W	L	T	OL						
2005-06	82	25	9	....	7	19	18	....	4	44	27	....	11		266	242	99	2nd, Pacific Div.	Lost Conf. Semi-Final
2004-05	....														....	....	....		
2003-04	82	24	8	7	2	19	13	5	4	43	21	12	6		219	183	104	1st, Pacific Div.	Lost Conf. Final
2002-03	82	17	16	5	3	11	21	4	5	28	37	9	8		214	239	73	5th, Pacific Div.	Out of Playoffs
2001-02	82	25	11	3	2	19	16	5	1	44	27	8	3		248	199	99	1st, Pacific Div.	Lost Conf. Semi-Final
2000-01	82	22	14	4	1	18	13	8	2	40	27	12	3		217	192	95	2nd, Pacific Div.	Lost Conf. Quarter-Final
1999-2000	82	21	14	3	3	14	16	7	4	35	30	10	7		225	214	87	4th, Pacific Div.	Lost Conf. Semi-Final
1998-99	82	17	15	9	....	14	18	9	....	31	33	18	....		196	191	80	4th, Pacific Div.	Lost Conf. Quarter-Final
1997-98	82	17	19	5	....	17	19	5	....	34	38	10	....		210	216	78	4th, Pacific Div.	Lost Conf. Quarter-Final
1996-97	82	14	23	4	....	13	24	4	....	27	47	8	....		211	278	62	7th, Pacific Div.	Out of Playoffs
1995-96	82	12	26	3	....	8	29	4	....	20	55	7	....		252	357	47	7th, Pacific Div.	Out of Playoffs
1994-95	48	10	13	1	....	9	12	3	....	19	25	4	....		129	161	42	3rd, Pacific Div.	Lost Conf. Semi-Final
1993-94	84	19	13	10	....	14	22	6	....	33	35	16	....		252	265	82	3rd, Pacific Div.	Lost Conf. Semi-Final
1992-93	84	8	33	1	....	3	38	1	....	11	71	2	....		218	414	24	6th, Smythe Div.	Out of Playoffs
1991-92	80	14	23	3	....	3	35	2	....	17	58	5	....		219	359	39	6th, Smythe Div.	Out of Playoffs

2006-07 Schedule

Oct.	Thu.	5	St. Louis
	Sat.	7	NY Islanders
	Mon.	9	at Calgary
	Thu.	12	at Edmonton
	Fri.	13	at Vancouver
	Tue.	17	Dallas
	Thu.	19	Detroit
	Sat.	21	Minnesota
	Mon.	23	at Columbus
	Wed.	25	at Detroit
	Thu.	26	at Nashville
	Sun.	29	at Tampa Bay*
	Tue.	31	at Florida
Nov.	Thu.	2	NY Rangers
	Sat.	4	Pittsburgh
	Tue.	7	Minnesota
	Thu.	9	at Los Angeles
	Sat.	11	at Phoenix
	Mon.	13	at Los Angeles
	Wed.	15	at Colorado
	Sat.	18	Philadelphia
	Tue.	21	at Anaheim
	Wed.	22	Los Angeles
	Sat.	25	New Jersey
	Tue.	28	at St. Louis
	Wed.	29	at Minnesota
Dec.	Sat.	2	at Detroit
	Mon.	4	at Dallas
	Thu.	7	Colorado
	Sat.	9	Nashville
	Mon.	11	Phoenix
	Tue.	12	at Los Angeles
	Thu.	14	Los Angeles
	Sat.	16	Anaheim
	Thu.	21	Dallas
	Sat.	23	Calgary
	Tue.	26	Anaheim
	Thu.	28	Phoenix
	Sat.	30	at Phoenix
	Sun.	31	at Dallas
Jan.	Thu.	4	Detroit
	Sat.	6	Columbus
	Wed.	10	Edmonton
	Thu.	11	at Los Angeles
	Sat.	13	at Phoenix
	Mon.	15	Colorado
	Thu.	18	Phoenix
	Sat.	20	St. Louis
	Fri.	26	at Edmonton
	Sun.	28	at Vancouver
	Tue.	30	Dallas
Feb.	Thu.	1	Dallas
	Sat.	3	Chicago*
	Tue.	6	Anaheim
	Wed.	7	at Anaheim
	Tue.	13	at St. Louis
	Wed.	14	at Nashville
	Fri.	16	at Columbus
	Sun.	18	at Dallas*
	Wed.	21	at Washington
	Thu.	22	at Chicago
	Sat.	24	at Calgary
	Mon.	26	Anaheim
	Wed.	28	Nashville
Mar.	Fri.	2	at Anaheim
	Sun.	4	at Dallas*
	Tue.	6	at Minnesota
	Fri.	9	Vancouver
	Sun.	11	Edmonton*
	Tue.	13	Chicago
	Thu.	15	at Phoenix
	Fri.	16	Columbus
	Sun.	18	at Colorado
	Wed.	21	at Chicago
	Thu.	22	at Atlanta
	Sat.	24	at Carolina
	Tue.	27	Los Angeles
	Fri.	30	Phoenix
Apr.	Sun.	1	Los Angeles*
	Wed.	4	at Anaheim
	Thu.	5	Calgary
	Sat.	7	Vancouver*

* Denotes afternoon game.

Franchise date: May 9, 1990

WESTERN CONFERENCE

PACIFIC DIVISION

16th NHL Season

Vesa Toskala had the hot hand down the stretch as the Sharks rallied in the second half of the season to climb to fifth overall in the Western Conference. Toskala had a 23-7-4 record in 37 games played in 2005-06.

2006-07 Player Personnel

FORWARDS	HT	WT	S	Place of Birth	Date	2005-06 Club
ARMSTRONG, Riley	5-11	185	R	Saskatoon, Sask.	11/8/84	Cleveland
BELL, Mark	6-4	205	L	St. Paul's, Ont.	8/5/80	Chicago
BERNIER, Steve	6-2	230	R	Quebec City, Que.	3/31/85	San Jose-Cleveland
BROWN, Curtis	6-0	196	L	Unity, Sask.	2/12/76	Chicago
CAVANAGH, Tom	5-10	178	L	Warwick, RI	3/24/82	Cleveland
CHEECHOO, Jonathan	6-1	190	R	Moose Factory, Ont.	7/15/80	San Jose
CLOWE, Ryane	6-2	215	R	St. John's, Nfld.	9/30/82	San Jose-Cleveland
DARCHE, Mathieu	6-1	210	L	St. Laurent, Que.	11/26/76	Duisburg
GOC, Marcel	6-0	195	L	Calw, West Germany	8/24/83	San Jose
GRIER, Mike	6-1	227	R	Detroit, MI	1/5/75	Buffalo
IGGULDEN, Mike	6-3	215	R	St. Catherines, Ont.	11/9/82	Cleveland
KASPAR, Lukas	6-2	198	L	Most, Czech.	9/23/85	Cleveland
KOROLYUK, Alexander	5-9	190	L	Moscow, USSR	1/15/76	Chekhov
MACHO, Michal	6-1	170	R	Martin, Czech.	1/17/82	Bratislava
MARLEAU, Patrick	6-2	220	L	Aneroid, Sask.	9/15/79	San Jose
MICHALEK, Milan	6-2	220	L	Jindrichuv Hradec, Czech.	12/7/84	San Jose
MINK, Graham	6-3	217	R	Stowe, VT	5/21/79	Washington-Hershey
MORRIS, Mike	6-1	182	R	Dorchester, MA	7/14/83	Northeastern
NIEMINEN, Ville	5-11	200	L	Tampere, Finland	4/6/77	NY Rangers-San Jose
OLSON, Glenn	6-4	230	L	Fort McNeil, B.C.	5/1/84	Cleveland-Fresno
PARKER, Scott	6-5	230	R	Hanford, CA	1/29/78	San Jose
PAVELSKI, Joe	5-11	194	L	Plover, WI	7/11/84	U. of Wisconsin
PLIHAL, Tomas	6-1	195	L	Frydlant v Cechach, Czech.	3/28/83	Cleveland
RISSMILLER, Pat	6-4	210	L	Belmont, MA	10/26/78	San Jose-Cleveland
ROME, Ashton	6-1	202	R	Nesbitt, Man.	12/31/85	Red Deer-Kamloops
SETOGUCHI, Devin	5-11	186	R	Taber, Alta.	1/1/87	Saskatoon
SMITH, Mark	5-10	215	L	Edmonton, Alta.	10/24/77	San Jose
STEVENSON, Grant	5-11	170	R	Spruce Grove, Alta.	10/15/81	San Jose-Cleveland
THORNTON, Joe	6-4	223	L	London, Ont.	7/2/79	Boston-San Jose
TREMBLAY, Jonathan	6-3	240	R	Fauquier, Ont.	3/3/84	Tol-Kalamazoo-Quad City
VALETTE, Craig	6-0	190	L	Shellbrook, Sask.	10/7/82	Cleveland
DEFENSEMEN						
BIRON, Mathieu	6-6	220	R	Lac-St-Charles, Que.	4/29/80	Washington
CARLE, Matthew	6-0	182	L	Anchorage, AK	9/25/84	U. of Denver-San Jose
DAVISON, Rob	6-2	225	L	St. Catharines, Ont.	5/1/80	San Jose
EHRHOFF, Christian	6-2	195	L	Moers, West Germany	7/6/82	San Jose
FAHEY, Jim	6-0	205	R	Boston, MA	5/11/79	San Jose
FERGUSON, Scott	6-1	195	L	Camrose, Alta.	1/6/73	Minnesota-Houston
GORGES, Josh	6-1	190	L	Kelowna, B.C.	8/14/84	San Jose-Cleveland
HANNAN, Scott	6-1	220	L	Richmond, B.C.	1/23/79	San Jose
McLAREN, Kyle	6-4	225	L	Humboldt, Sask.	6/18/77	San Jose
MURRAY, Doug	6-3	245	L	Bromma, Sweden	3/12/80	San Jose-Cleveland
SPANG, Dan	6-0	205	L	Winchester, MA	8/18/83	Boston University-Cleveland
STAFFORD, Garrett	6-0	190	R	Los Angeles, CA	1/28/80	Cleveland
STAUBITZ, Brad	6-1	208	R	Bright's Grove, Ont.	7/28/84	Cleveland
TRAVERSE, Patrick	6-4	207	L	Montreal, Que.	3/14/74	Dallas-Iowa
VLASIC, Marc-Edouard	6-1	190	L	Montreal, Que.	3/30/87	Quebec (QMJHL)
WISHART, Ty	6-4	205	L	Belleville, Ont.	5/19/88	Prince George

GOALTENDERS	HT	WT	C	Place of Birth	Date	2005-06 Club
DAKERS, Taylor	6-1	165	L	Richmond, B.C.	9/14/86	Kootenay
GREISS, Thomas	6-1	192	L	Straubing, West Germany	1/29/86	Koln
NABOKOV, Evgeni	6-0	200	L	Ust-Kamenogorsk, USSR	7/25/75	San Jose
PATZOLD, Dimitri	6-0	200	L	Ust-Kamenogorsk, USSR	2/3/83	Cleveland
SCHAEFER, Nolan	6-2	200	R	Yellow Grass, Sask.	1/15/80	San Jose-Cleveland
TOSKALA, Vesa	5-10	190	L	Tampere, Finland	5/20/77	San Jose-Cleveland

Vice President and General Manager

WILSON, DOUG
Executive Vice President/General Manager, San Jose Sharks.
Born in Ottawa, Ont., July 5, 1957.

Doug Wilson is the architect of the current San Jose Sharks team. After missing the playoffs in 2002-03, the Sharks rebounded to capture the Pacific Division title, setting a franchise record with 104 points, earning the second seed in the Western Conference playoffs and reaching the Western Conference Finals for the first time. The Sharks' record of 43-21-12-8 in 2003-04 was the third-best mark in the NHL and the team's 31-point improvement over the previous season was the largest turnaround in the NHL. In 2005-06, the Sharks enjoyed a stellar second half of the season and reached the Western Conference Semi-Final.

Doug Wilson officially took over as the Sharks' executive vice president and general manager on May 13, 2003. In his current role, he has overall authority regarding all hockey-related operations. He oversees all player personnel decisions, negotiates player contracts, coordinates the efforts of the team's scouting department, leads the team in its draft-day preparations and administers the club's player evaluation process at all professional, minor and junior levels.

In his previous role as the team's director of pro development (1997 to 2003), the 16-year NHL veteran's primary responsibilities included evaluating talent at all professional and minor league levels and continuous assessment of the Sharks roster and reserve list. In addition, he provided valuable input assisting the club's player development programs and consulting with the hockey department on all major personnel issues, special assignments and contract negotiations.

A first-round choice (sixth overall) of the Blackhawks in 1977 after a stellar junior career with the Ottawa 67s, Wilson played 14 seasons in Chicago and still ranks as the club's highest scoring defenseman in goals (225), assists (554) and points (779). In addition, he led all Blackhawks defensemen in scoring from 10 consecutive seasons (1980-81 through 1990-91) and captured the 1982 Norris Trophy, symbolic of the NHL's top defenseman, when he tallied 39 goals and 85 points – still Blackhawks single-season records for goals and points by a defenseman.

2005-06 Scoring

* – rookie

Regular Season

Pos	#	Player	Team	GP	G	A	Pts	+/-	PIM	PP	SH	GW	S	%
C	19	Joe Thornton	BOS	23	9	24	33	0	6	3	0	2	60	15.0
			S.J.	58	20	72	92	31	55	8	0	4	135	14.8
			TOTAL	81	29	96	125	31	61	11	0	6	195	14.9
R	14	Jonathan Cheechoo	S.J.	82	56	37	93	23	58	24	2	11	317	17.7
C	12	Patrick Marleau	S.J.	82	34	52	86	–12	26	20	1	4	260	13.1
L	28	Nils Ekman	S.J.	77	21	36	57	20	54	5	0	2	176	11.9
D	42	Tom Preissing	S.J.	74	11	32	43	17	26	2	0	2	131	8.4
R	9 *	Milan Michalek	S.J.	81	17	18	35	1	45	4	0	2	159	10.7
R	26 *	Steve Bernier	S.J.	39	14	13	27	4	35	2	1	1	75	18.7
C	10	Alyn McCauley	S.J.	76	12	14	26	–3	30	4	2	3	105	11.4
C	16	Mark Smith	S.J.	80	9	15	24	3	97	2	1	1	100	9.0
L	15	Ville Nieminen	NYR	48	5	12	17	10	53	0	0	2	73	6.8
			S.J.	22	3	4	7	–3	10	0	1	0	41	7.3
			TOTAL	70	8	16	24	7	63	0	1	2	114	7.0
D	22	Scott Hannan	S.J.	81	6	18	24	7	58	2	0	1	104	5.8
D	44	Christian Ehrhoff	S.J.	64	5	18	23	10	32	2	0	2	124	4.0
D	4	Kyle McLaren	S.J.	77	2	21	23	6	66	0	0	1	67	3.0
C	37 *	Grant Stevenson	S.J.	47	10	12	22	–7	14	5	0	2	67	14.9
C	11 *	Marcel Goc	S.J.	81	8	14	22	–7	22	2	0	2	96	8.3
L	17	Scott Thornton	S.J.	71	10	11	21	–8	84	1	0	2	122	8.2
D	25 *	Matthew Carle	S.J.	12	3	3	6	–2	14	2	0	1	11	27.3
C	34	Pat Rissmiller	S.J.	18	3	3	6	1	8	1	0	1	26	11.5
D	5	Rob Davison	S.J.	69	1	5	6	6	76	0	0	0	36	2.8
D	6 *	Josh Gorges	S.J.	49	0	6	6	5	31	0	0	0	25	0.0
L	29 *	Ryane Clowe	S.J.	18	0	2	2	–2	9	0	0	0	14	0.0
D	21	Jim Fahey	S.J.	21	0	2	2	–11	14	0	0	0	22	0.0
R	27	Scott Parker	S.J.	10	1	0	1	3	38	0	0	0	6	16.7
D	43 *	Matt Carkner	S.J.	1	0	1	1	0	2	0	0	0	0	0.0
D	41 *	Doug Murray	S.J.	34	0	1	1	3	27	0	0	0	21	0.0

Goaltending

No.	Goaltender	GPI	Mins	Avg	W	L	OT	EN	SO	GA	SA	S%	G	A	PIM
31	* Nolan Schaefer	7	352	1.88	5	1	0	1	1	11	138	.920	0	0	2
35	Vesa Toskala	37	2039	2.56	23	7	4	1	2	87	878	.901	0	1	4
20	Evgeni Nabokov	45	2575	3.10	16	19	7	2	1	133	1160	.885	0	1	18
	Totals	**82**	**4996**	**2.82**	**44**	**27**	**11**	**4**	**5**	**235**	**2180**	**.892**			

Evgeni Nabokov and Nolan Schaefer shared a shutout vs. Buffalo on December 2, 2005.

Playoffs

Pos	#	Player	Team	GP	G	A	Pts	+/-	PIM	PP	SH	GW	OT	S	%
C	12	Patrick Marleau	S.J.	11	9	5	14	2	8	4	0	2	0	38	23.7
R	14	Jonathan Cheechoo	S.J.	11	4	5	9	–1	8	1	0	1	0	46	8.7
C	19	Joe Thornton	S.J.	11	2	7	9	–4	12	1	0	1	0	23	8.7
D	44	Christian Ehrhoff	S.J.	11	2	6	8	2	18	1	0	1	0	27	7.4
D	42	Tom Preissing	S.J.	11	1	6	7	0	4	0	0	0	0	18	5.6
R	26 *	Steve Bernier	S.J.	11	1	5	6	4	8	1	0	1	0	14	7.1
R	9 *	Milan Michalek	S.J.	9	1	4	5	4	8	1	0	0	0	23	4.3
L	28	Nils Ekman	S.J.	11	2	2	4	–2	8	1	0	0	0	24	8.3
C	16	Mark Smith	S.J.	11	3	0	3	2	6	1	0	0	0	23	13.0
C	34	Pat Rissmiller	S.J.	11	2	1	3	1	6	0	0	0	0	11	18.2
D	4	Kyle McLaren	S.J.	11	0	3	3	2	4	0	0	0	0	7	0.0
C	11 *	Marcel Goc	S.J.	11	0	3	3	0	0	0	0	0	0	9	0.0
D	25 *	Matthew Carle	S.J.	11	0	3	3	1	4	0	0	0	0	13	0.0
L	17	Scott Thornton	S.J.	11	2	0	2	–1	6	0	0	0	0	23	8.7
L	15	Ville Nieminen	S.J.	11	0	2	2	–1	24	0	0	0	0	18	0.0
C	10	Alyn McCauley	S.J.	6	0	1	1	0	4	0	0	0	0	4	0.0
D	22	Scott Hannan	S.J.	11	0	1	1	0	6	0	0	0	0	12	0.0
D	6 *	Josh Gorges	S.J.	11	0	1	1	–1	4	0	0	0	0	6	0.0
D	5	Rob Davison	S.J.	1	0	0	0	0	0	0	0	0	0	1	0.0
R	29 *	Ryane Clowe	S.J.	1	0	0	0	–1	0	0	0	0	0	0	0.0
C	37 *	Grant Stevenson	S.J.	5	0	0	0	–1	4	0	0	0	0	6	0.0

Goaltending

No.	Goaltender	GPI	Mins	Avg	W	L	EN	SO	GA	SA	S%	G	A	PIM
35	Vesa Toskala	11	686	2.45	6	5	0	1	28	311	.910	0	0	0
20	Evgeni Nabokov	1	12	5.00	0	0	0	0	1	4	.750	0	0	0
	Totals	**11**	**702**	**2.48**	**6**	**5**	**0**	**1**	**29**	**315**	**.908**			

General Managers' History

Jack Ferreira, 1991-92; Chuck Grillo (V.P. Director of Player Personnel), 1992-93 to 1995-96; Dean Lombardi, 1996-97 to 2002-03; Doug Wilson, 2003-04 to date.

Coaching History

George Kingston, 1991-92, 1992-93; Kevin Constantine, 1993-94, 1994-95; Kevin Constantine and Jim Wiley, 1995-96; Al Sims, 1996-97; Darryl Sutter, 1997-98 to 2001-02; Darryl Sutter and Ron Wilson, 2002-03; Ron Wilson, 2003-04 to date.

Club Records

Team

(Figures in brackets for season records are games played; records for fewest points, wins, ties, losses, goals, goals against are for 70 or more games)

Most Points **104** 2003-04 (82)
Most Wins **44** 2001-02 (82), 2005-06 (82)
Most Ties **18** 1998-99 (82)
Most Losses ***71** 1992-93 (84)
Most Goals **266** 2005-06 (82)
Most Goals Against **414** 1992-93 (84)
Fewest Points **24** 1992-93 (84)
Fewest Wins **11** 1992-93 (84)
Fewest Ties ***2** 1992-93 (84)
Fewest Losses **27** 2003-04 (82)
Fewest Goals **196** 1998-99 (82)
Fewest Goals Against **183** 2003-04 (82)
Longest Winning Streak
Overall .... **8** Apr. 3-15/06
Home .... **8** Jan. 24-Mar. 3/04
Away .... **6** Nov. 30-Dec. 19/01
Longest Undefeated Streak
Overall .... **10** Nov. 27-Dec. 19/01 (9 wins, 1 tie)
Home .... **11** Nov. 15-Dec. 29/03 (8 wins, 3 ties)
Away .... **10** Dec. 26/00-Feb. 16/01 (6 wins, 4 ties)
Longest Losing Streak
Overall .... ***17** Jan. 4-Feb. 12/93
Home .... **9** Nov. 19-Dec. 19/92
Away .... **19** Nov. 27/92-Feb. 12/93
Longest Winless Streak
Overall .... **20** Dec. 29/92-Feb. 12/93 (19 losses, 1 tie)
Home .... **9** Nov. 19-Dec. 19/92 (9 losses)
Away .... **19** Nov. 27/92-Feb. 12/93 (19 losses)
Most Shutouts, Season **9** 2000-01 (82), 2001-02 (82)
Most PIM, Season **2,134** 1992-93 (84)
Most Goals, Game .... **10** Jan. 13/96 (S.J. 10 at Pit. 8), Mar. 30/02 (CBJ 2 at S.J. 10)

Individual

Most Seasons .... **11** Mike Rathje
Most Games, Career .... **671** Mike Rathje
Most Goals, Career .... **206** Owen Nolan
Most Assists, Career .... **225** Owen Nolan
Most Points, Career .... **431** Owen Nolan (206G, 225A)
Most PIM, Career .... **1,001** Jeff Odgers
Most Shutouts, Career .... **27** Evgeni Nabokov
Longest Consecutive Games Streak .... **228** Mike Ricci (Nov. 22/97-Oct. 20/00)
Most Goals, Season .... **56** Jonathan Cheechoo (2005-06)
Most Assists, Season .... **72** Joe Thornton (2005-06)
Most Points, Season .... **93** Jonathan Cheechoo (2005-06; 56G, 37A)
Most PIM, Season .... **326** Link Gaetz (1991-92)
Most Points, Defenseman, Season .... **64** Sandis Ozolinsh (1993-94; 26G, 38A)
Most Points, Center, Season .... **92** Joe Thornton (2005-06; 20G, 72A)
Most Points, Right Wing, Season .... **93** Jonathan Cheechoo (2005-06; 56G, 37A)
Most Points, Left Wing, Season .... **66** Johan Garpenlov (1992-93; 22G, 44A)
Most Points, Rookie, Season .... **59** Pat Falloon (1991-92; 25G, 34A)
Most Shutouts, Season .... **9** Evgeni Nabokov (2003-04)
Most Goals, Game .... **4** Owen Nolan (Dec. 19/95)
Most Assists, Game .... **4** Eleven times
Most Points, Game .... **6** Owen Nolan (Oct. 4/99; 3G, 3A)

* NHL Record.

Captains' History

Doug Wilson, 1991-92, 1992-93; Bob Errey, 1993-94; Bob Errey and Jeff Odgers, 1994-95; Jeff Odgers, 1995-96; Todd Gill, 1996-97, 1997-98; Owen Nolan, 1998-99 to 2002-03; Mike Ricci, Vincent Damphousse, Alyn McCauley, Patrick Marleau, 2003-04; Patrick Marleau, 2005-06.

All-time Record vs. Other Clubs

Regular Season

	At Home								On Road								Total							
	GP	W	L	T	OL	GF	GA	PTS	GP	W	L	T	OL	GF	GA	PTS	GP	W	L	T	OL	GF	GA	PTS
Anaheim	34	16	15	2	1	94	89	35	34	19	11	2	2	114	92	42	68	35	26	4	3	208	181	77
Atlanta	5	4	0	1	0	21	10	9	4	2	0	1	1	11	7	6	9	6	0	2	1	32	17	15
Boston	11	4	5	2	0	30	38	10	11	1	7	3	0	32	41	5	22	5	12	5	0	62	79	15
Buffalo	10	5	1	4	0	36	33	14	12	1	11	0	0	32	52	2	22	6	12	4	0	68	85	16
Calgary	36	14	18	4	0	106	108	32	34	10	19	4	1	89	121	25	70	24	37	8	1	195	229	57
Carolina	12	8	4	0	0	54	34	16	11	5	6	0	0	23	34	10	23	13	10	0	0	77	68	26
Chicago	28	15	9	3	1	78	74	34	27	11	12	2	2	85	86	26	55	26	21	5	3	163	160	60
Colorado	26	9	16	1	0	76	96	19	25	6	15	4	0	46	88	16	51	15	31	5	0	122	184	35
Columbus	10	9	0	0	1	42	16	19	10	5	5	0	0	22	29	10	20	14	5	0	1	64	45	29
Dallas	34	13	16	1	4	83	96	31	33	12	16	4	1	75	94	29	67	25	32	5	5	158	190	60
Detroit	28	10	14	3	1	94	108	24	27	2	22	1	2	47	111	7	55	12	36	4	3	141	219	31
Edmonton	34	17	11	5	1	119	105	40	35	7	20	7	1	74	117	22	69	24	31	12	2	193	222	62
Florida	10	6	2	2	0	32	19	14	9	2	2	5	0	27	25	9	19	8	4	7	0	59	44	23
Los Angeles	41	25	13	3	0	139	112	53	41	13	22	4	2	105	127	32	82	38	35	7	2	244	239	85
Minnesota	10	4	4	1	1	24	20	10	10	4	4	1	1	23	26	10	20	8	8	2	2	47	46	20
Montreal	11	5	3	2	1	33	28	13	12	2	8	2	0	22	42	6	23	7	11	4	1	55	70	19
Nashville	14	8	5	1	0	36	35	17	14	6	6	1	1	37	34	14	28	14	11	2	1	73	69	31
New Jersey	10	3	5	1	1	24	32	8	12	4	6	1	1	24	44	10	22	7	11	2	2	48	76	18
NY Islanders	12	5	5	1	1	30	40	12	11	4	5	2	0	35	40	10	23	9	10	3	1	65	80	22
NY Rangers	13	2	9	2	0	31	49	6	10	2	6	1	1	29	40	6	23	4	15	3	1	60	89	12
Ottawa	9	5	4	0	0	18	16	10	10	2	4	4	0	28	36	8	19	7	8	4	0	46	52	18
Philadelphia	12	3	7	2	0	22	31	8	11	3	6	2	0	27	36	8	23	6	13	4	0	49	67	16
Phoenix	36	15	14	4	3	122	117	37	39	16	19	3	1	110	122	36	75	31	33	7	4	232	239	73
Pittsburgh	13	5	6	2	0	34	54	12	9	4	4	1	0	32	41	9	22	9	10	3	0	66	95	21
St. Louis	26	5	18	1	2	57	89	13	30	11	17	1	1	78	99	24	56	16	35	2	3	135	188	37
Tampa Bay	11	4	6	1	0	35	37	9	12	4	6	1	1	31	32	10	23	8	12	2	1	66	69	19
Toronto	15	5	7	3	0	32	40	13	19	5	12	2	0	52	73	12	34	10	19	5	0	84	113	25
Vancouver	36	14	17	5	0	104	112	33	34	11	18	4	1	91	122	27	70	25	35	9	1	195	234	60
Washington	11	7	3	1	0	33	27	15	12	7	5	0	0	36	34	14	23	14	8	1	0	69	61	29
Totals	**558**	**245**	**237**	**58**	**18**	**1639**	**1665**	**566**	**558**	**181**	**294**	**63**	**20**	**1437**	**1845**	**445**	**1116**	**426**	**531**	**121**	**38**	**3076**	**3510**	**1011**

Playoffs

	Series	W	L	GP	W	L	T	GF	GA	Last Mtg.	Rnd.	Result
Calgary	2	1	1	13	6	7	0	38	51	2004	CF	L 2-4
Colorado	3	1	2	19	9	10	0	52	51	2004	CSF	W 4-2
Dallas	2	0	2	11	3	8	0	19	31	2000	CSF	L 1-4
Detroit	2	1	1	11	4	7	0	27	51	1995	CSF	L 0-4
Edmonton	1	0	1	6	2	4	0	12	19	2006	CSF	L 2-4
Nashville	1	1	0	5	4	1	0	17	10	2006	CQF	W 4-1
Phoenix	1	1	0	5	4	1	0	13	7	2002	CQF	W 4-1
St. Louis	3	2	1	18	10	8	0	43	47	2004	CQF	W 4-1
Toronto	1	0	1	7	3	4	0	21	26	1994	CSF	L 3-4
Totals	**16**	**7**	**9**	**95**	**45**	**50**	**0**	**242**	**293**			

Carolina totals include Hartford, 1991-92 to 1996-97.
Dallas totals include Minnesota North Stars, 1991-92 to 1992-93.

Playoff Results 2006-2001

Year	Round	Opponent	Result	GF	GA
2006	CSF	Edmonton	L 2-4	12	19
	CQF	Nashville	W 4-1	17	10
2004	CF	Calgary	L 2-4	12	16
	CSF	Colorado	W 4-2	14	7
	CQF	St. Louis	W 4-1	12	9
2002	CSF	Colorado	L 3-4	21	25
	CQF	Phoenix	W 4-1	13	7
2001	CQF	St. Louis	L 2-4	11	16

Abbreviations: Round: CF – conference final; **CSF** – conference semi-final; **CQF** – conference quarter-final.

Colorado totals include Quebec, 1991-92 to 1994-95.
Phoenix totals include Winnipeg, 1991-92 to 1995-96.

2005-06 Results

Oct.	5	at Nashville	2-3
	7	at Chicago	3-6
	8	at St. Louis	7-6
	12	Columbus	4-1
	15	Chicago	4-3
	17	at Detroit	2-3*
	19	at Minnesota	1-6
	21	at Columbus	1-4
	22	at Nashville	1-2
	26	at Dallas	5-4*
	28	at Los Angeles	5-4
	29	Calgary	3-2†
Nov.	2	Nashville	3-2*
	4	at Anaheim	1-0*
	5	Minnesota	1-3
	8	at Colorado	2-5
	12	Dallas	2-3†
	16	Vancouver	1-3
	19	Phoenix	3-4†
	21	at Edmonton	1-2†
	23	at Calgary	2-3
	24	at Vancouver	2-3
	26	Detroit	6-7
	30	at Dallas	1-4
Dec.	2	at Buffalo	5-0
	3	at Toronto	5-4
	6	Atlanta	5-3
	8	Florida	6-2
	10	Carolina	4-3
	16	Washington	4-1
	18	at Anaheim	4-5
	20	Anaheim	4-2
	22	at Phoenix	1-2
	23	St. Louis	1-2†
	26	at Los Angeles	3-4
	28	Phoenix	4-5
	30	Colorado	5-2
Jan.	5	Columbus	6-3
	7	Los Angeles	3-2
	10	at Boston	6-2
	12	at Ottawa	2-0
	14	at Montreal	2-6
	16	Tampa Bay	3-1
	19	Edmonton	2-3†
	21	at Los Angeles	4-3*
	24	Los Angeles	4-1
	26	Anaheim	0-2
	28	at Phoenix	2-6
	30	at Dallas	2-3*
Feb.	1	at Anaheim	6-4
	2	Minnesota	2-3†
	4	Anaheim	0-2
	6	Calgary	3-4
	8	Chicago	2-1
	10	Dallas	6-3
	12	at Phoenix	5-4*
	28	Detroit	5-1
Mar.	3	at Edmonton	2-3
	4	at Calgary	0-2
	7	at Anaheim	4-5*
	9	Edmonton	5-2
	11	Nashville	3-2*
	13	Los Angeles	4-3
	16	St. Louis	5-2
	18	Dallas	3-4†
	19	Colorado	6-5
	21	at St. Louis	6-0
	23	at Detroit	0-4
	25	at Minnesota	5-1
	26	at Chicago	5-4*
	28	at Columbus	1-4
	30	Phoenix	2-5
Apr.	1	Phoenix	3-4*
	3	at Dallas	3-2*
	5	at Colorado	2-1
	6	at Los Angeles	5-0
	9	Dallas	4-1
	10	at Phoenix	3-2
	12	at Vancouver	5-4*
	13	Vancouver	5-3
	15	Anaheim	6-3
	17	Los Angeles	0-4

* – Overtime † – Shootout

Entry Draft
Selections 2006-1992

2006
Pick
16	Ty Wishart
36	Jamie McGinn
98	James Delory
143	Ashton Rome
202	John McCarthy
203	Jay Barriball

2005
Pick
8	Devin Setoguchi
35	Marc-Edouard Vlasic
112	Alex Stalock
140	Taylor Dakers
149	Derek Joslin
162	P.J. Fenton
183	Will Colbert
193	Tony Lucia

2004
Pick
22	Lukas Kaspar
94	Thomas Greiss
126	Torrey Mitchell
129	Jason Churchill
153	Steven Zalewski
201	Michael Vernace
225	David MacDonald
234	Derek MacIntyre
288	Brian Mahoney-Wilson
289	Christian Jensen

2003
Pick
6	Milan Michalek
16	Steve Bernier
43	Josh Hennessy
47	Matthew Carle
139	Patrick Ehelechner
201	Jonathan Tremblay
205	Joe Pavelski
216	Kai Hospelt
236	Alexander Hult
267	Brian O'Hanley
276	Carter Lee

2002
Pick
27	Mike Morris
52	Dan Spang
86	Jonas Fiedler
139	Kris Newbury
163	Tom Walsh
217	Tim Conboy
288	Michael Hutchins

2001
Pick
20	Marcel Goc
106	Christian Ehrhoff
107	Dimitri Patzold
140	Tomas Plihal
175	Ryane Clowe
182	Tom Cavanagh

2000
Pick
41	Tero Maatta
104	Jon Disalvatore
142	Michal Pinc
166	Nolan Schaefer
183	Michal Macho
246	Chad Wiseman
256	Pasi Saarinen

1999
Pick
14	Jeff Jillson
82	Mark Concannon
111	Willie Levesque
155	Niko Dimitrakos
229	Eric Betournay
241	Doug Murray
257	Hannes Hyvonen

1998
Pick
3	Brad Stuart
29	Jonathan Cheechoo
65	Eric Laplante
98	Rob Davison
104	Miroslav Zalesak
127	Brandon Coalter
145	Mikael Samuelsson
185	Robert Mulick
212	Jim Fahey

1997
Pick
2	Patrick Marleau
23	Scott Hannan
82	Adam Colagiacomo
107	Adam Nittel
163	Joe Dusbabek
192	Cam Severson
219	Mark Smith

1996
Pick
2	Andrei Zyuzin
21	Marco Sturm
55	Terry Friesen
102	Matt Bradley
137	Michel Larocque
164	Jake Deadmarsh
191	Cory Cyrenne
217	David Thibeault

1995
Pick
12	Teemu Riihijarvi
38	Peter Roed
64	Marko Makinen
90	Vesa Toskala
116	Miikka Kiprusoff
130	Michal Bros
140	Timo Hakanen
142	Jaroslav Kudrna
167	Brad Mehalko
168	Robert Jindrich
194	Ryan Kraft
220	Mikko Markkanen

1994
Pick
11	Jeff Friesen
37	Angel Nikolov
66	Alexei Yegorov
89	Vaclav Varada
115	Brian Swanson
141	Alexander Korolyuk
167	Sergei Gorbachev
193	Eric Landry
219	Evgeni Nabokov
240	Tomas Pisa
245	Aniket Dhadphale
271	David Beauregard

1993
Pick
6	Viktor Kozlov
28	Shean Donovan
45	Vlastimil Kroupa
58	Ville Peltonen
80	Alexander Osadchy
106	Andrei Buschan
132	Petri Varis
154	Fredrik Oduya
158	Anatoli Filatov
184	Todd Holt
210	Jonas Forsberg
236	Jeff Salajko
262	Jamie Matthews

1992
Pick
3	Mike Rathje
10	Andrei Nazarov
51	Alexander Cherbayev
75	Jan Caloun
99	Marcus Ragnarsson
123	Michal Sykora
147	Eric Bellerose
171	Ryan Smith
195	Chris Burns
219	Alexander Kholomeyev
243	Victor Ignatjev

Coach

WILSON, RON
Coach, San Jose Sharks. Born in Windsor, Ont., May 28, 1955.

Named head coach of the Sharks on December 4, 2002, Ron Wilson's first full season behind the San Jose bench saw the team rebound from a disappointing 2002-03 campaign in which they finished last in the Pacific Division and 14th in the Western Conference to capture its second Pacific Division title with a franchise-best 104 points. The Sharks finished second overall in the Western Conference and reached the Western Conference Final for the first time. The Sharks reached the Conference Semi-Final in 2005-06 after a stellar second half of the season.

Prior to spending five seasons with the Washington Capitals, Wilson had served as the first head coach of the expansion Mighty Ducks of Anaheim in 1993 and led the team to its first trip to the Stanley Cup playoffs in 1996-97. In four seasons behind the Anaheim bench, he posted a record of 120-145-31.

Throughout his professional and amateur career, Wilson has enjoyed a long-standing relationship with USA Hockey. In 1996, he led Team USA to the gold medal at the inaugural World Cup of Hockey. He coached the team again at the 2004 tournament. Wilson also coached the U.S. national team at the 1994 and 1996 World Championships, where his teams finished fourth and third respectively. Wilson also served as head coach for Team USA at the 1998 Nagano Winter Olympics.

Born in Windsor, Ontario, but raised in Riverside, Rhode Island, Wilson was selected by the Toronto Maple Leafs in the seventh round (132nd overall) of the 1975 NHL Entry Draft. He began his professional career with the Dallas Blackhawks (Central Hockey League) in the spring of 1977 and joined the Maple Leafs for the 1977-78 season. In 177 career games with Toronto and the Minnesota North Stars, Wilson posted 93 points (26 goals, 67 assists). He also played for the U.S. national team in 1975, 1981, 1983 and 1987.

Coaching Record

Season	Team	Games	Regular Season W	L	O/T	Playoffs Games	W	L
1993-94	Anaheim (NHL)	84	33	46	5	....	....	....
1994-95	Anaheim (NHL)	48	16	27	5	....	....	....
1995-96	Anaheim (NHL)	82	35	39	8	....	....	....
1996-97	Anaheim (NHL)	82	36	33	13	11	4	7
1997-98	Washington (NHL)	82	40	30	12	21	12	9
1998-99	Washington (NHL)	82	31	45	6	....	....	....
1999-2000	Washington (NHL)	82	44	26	12	5	1	4
2000-01	Washington (NHL)	82	41	31	10	6	2	4
2001-02	Washington (NHL)	82	36	35	11	....	....	....
2002-03	San Jose (NHL)	57	19	31	7	....	....	....
2003-04	San Jose (NHL)	82	43	27	12	17	10	7
2004-05	San Jose (NHL)			Season Cancelled				
2005-06	San Jose (NHL)	82	44	27	11	11	6	5
NHL Totals		**927**	**418**	**397**	**112**	**71**	**35**	**36**

Club Directory

HP Pavilion at San Jose

San Jose Sharks
HP Pavilion at San Jose
525 West Santa Clara Street
San Jose, CA 95113
Phone **408/287-7070**
FAX 408/999-5797
www.sjsharks.com
Capacity: 17,496

San Jose Sports & Entertainment Enterprises
Board Members: Kevin Compton, Greg Reyes, Greg Jamison, Tom McEnery, Brent Jones
Investors in SJSEE include
Blue Line Associates (Kevin Compton, Greg Reyes, Hasso Plattner, Stratton Sclavos, Gary Valenzuela, Harvey Armstrong), William DelBiaggio, George Gund III, Greg Jamison, Floyd Kvamme, Tom McEnery, Gordon Russell, Rudy Staedler

Executive
President & Chief Executive Officer	Greg Jamison
Executive V.P. of Business Operations	Malcolm Bordelon
Executive V.P. & G.M. (HP Pavilion at San Jose)	Jim Goddard
Executive V.P. & General Counsel	Don Gralnek
Executive V.P. & G.M. (Sharks)	Doug Wilson
Executive V.P. & Chief Financial Officer	Charlie Faas
Vice President of Finance	Ken Caveney
Vice President of Sales & Marketing	Kent Russell
Vice President of Building Operations	Rich Sotelo
Vice President and Assistant G.M. (Sharks)	Wayne Thomas
Executive Assistants	Tricia Sullivan, Michelle Simmons, Niki Hartley

Hockey Operations
Head Coach	Ron Wilson
Assistant Coach	Tim Hunter
Assistant Coach	Rob Zettler
Goaltender Coach	Warren Strelow
Director of Hockey Operations	Joe Will
Special Consultant to the General Manager	John Ferguson
Director of Scouting	Tim Burke
Director of Professional Scouting	Sean Coady
Scouts	Gilles Cote, Pelle Eklund, Pat Funk, Jack Gardiner, Rob Grillo, Brian Gross, Karel Masopust, Cap Raeder, Graeme Townshend
Director of Hockey Administration	Rosemary Tebaldi
Video Scouting Coordinator	TBD
Head Athletic Trainer	Ray Tufts, A.T.,C
Assistant Athletic Trainer and Massage Therapist	Wes Howard, A.T.C., CMT
Strength & Conditioning Coach	TBD
Equipment Manager	Mike Aldrich
Assistant Equipment Manager	Kurt Harvey
Equipment Assistant & Equipment Transportation	Roy Sneesby
Head Coach, Worcester Sharks (AHL)	Roy Sommer
Assistant Coach, Worcester Sharks (AHL)	David Cunniff
Head Athletic Trainer, Worcester Sharks (AHL)	Matt White
Equipment Manager, Worcester Sharks (AHL)	Vinny Ferraiuolo
Asst. Equipment Manager, Worcester Sharks (AHL)	Chuck Rullan
Team Physician	Arthur J. Ting, M.D.
Team Internists	John Chiu, M.D., Greg Whitley, M.D.
Team Dentists	Robert Bonahoom, D.D.S., Don Goudy, D.D.S.
Team Vision Specialist	Vincent S. Zuccaro, O.D., F.A.A.O.
Medical Staff	Steve Franzino, M.D., Robert Millard, M.D., Mark Sontag, M.D.

SVS&E/Business Operations
Senior Director of Communications	Ken Arnold
Director of Broadcasting	Frank Albin
Director of Ticket Sales	John Castro
Director of Advertising & Promotions	Andrew Ebel
Director of Media Relations	Scott Emmert
Director of Fan Development/The Sharks Foundation	Rob Jaynes
Director of Event Presentation	Steve Maroni
Director, Corporate Partnerships	Chris Parker
Director of Suite Sales & Service	Bruce Ross
Director of Communications & Internet Services	Roger Ross
Senior Manager, Corporate Partnerships	Bryan Deierling
Senior Ticket Operations Manager	Scott Fitzsimmons
Senior Service Manager, Corporate Partnerships	Heather Hunter
Managers, Corporate Partnerships	Jennifer Birmingham, Justin Piper, Holly Yip
Account Sales Managers	Patrick Frost, Ted Chuba, Adam King, Adam Requarth
Account Service Managers	Sharon Holman, Sarah Bauerle, Julie Kennedy
Media Relations Manager	Tom Holy
Public Relations Manager	Jim Sparaco
Service Managers, Corporate Partnerships	Janelle Garcia, Ryan Hilgers
Media Relations & Hockey Ops. Coordinator	Ryan Stenn

Finance
Director of Human Resources	Cathy Chandler
Manager of Information Technology	Melanie Putnam
Controller	Stephanie Reitz

Building Operations
Director of Ticket Operations	Daniel DeBoer
Director of Booking & Events	Steve Kirsner
Director of Guest Services	David Cahill
Facilities Technical Director	Greg Carrolan
Director of Building Services	Monte Chavez

Miscellaneous
Television Station	FSN Bay Area
Radio Station Flagship	98.5 K-FOX (KUFX FM)
Television Play-By-Play Broadcaster	Randy Hahn
Television Color Analyst	TBD
Radio Play-By-Play Broadcaster	Dan Rusanowsky
Radio Color Analysts	Jamie Baker, Dave Maley
In Game TV Host	Glen Kuiper
Team Photographers	Don Smith, Rocky Widner
P.A. Announcer	Joe Ike
In Game Host	Danny Miller
Mascot	S.J. Sharkie

Tampa Bay Lightning

2005-06 Results: 43w-33L-2OTL-4SOL 92PTS.
Second, Southeast Division

Year-by-Year Record

Season	GP	Home W	L	T	OL	Road W	L	T	OL	Overall W	L	T	OL	GF	GA	Pts.	Finished	Playoff Result
2005-06	82	25	14	....	2	18	19	....	4	43	33	....	6	252	260	92	2nd, Southeast Div.	Lost Conf. Quarter-Final
2004-05																		
2003-04	**82**	**24**	**10**	**4**	**3**	**22**	**12**	**4**	**3**	**46**	**22**	**8**	**6**	**245**	**192**	**106**	**1st, Southeast Div.**	**Won Stanley Cup**
2002-03	82	22	9	7	3	14	16	9	2	36	25	16	5	219	210	93	1st, Southeast Div.	Lost Conf. Semi-Final
2001-02	82	16	17	5	3	11	23	6	1	27	40	11	4	178	219	69	3rd, Southeast Div.	Out of Playoffs
2000-01	82	17	19	3	2	7	28	3	3	24	47	6	5	201	280	59	5th, Southeast Div.	Out of Playoffs
1999-2000	82	13	20	4	4	6	27	5	3	19	47	9	7	204	310	54	4th, Southeast Div.	Out of Playoffs
1998-99	82	12	25	4	....	7	29	5	....	19	54	9	....	179	292	47	4th, Southeast Div.	Out of Playoffs
1997-98	82	11	23	7	....	6	32	3	....	17	55	10	....	151	269	44	7th, Atlantic Div.	Out of Playoffs
1996-97	82	15	18	8	....	17	22	2	....	32	40	10	....	217	247	74	6th, Atlantic Div.	Out of Playoffs
1995-96	82	22	14	5	....	16	18	7	....	38	32	12	....	238	248	88	5th, Atlantic Div.	Lost Conf. Quarter-Final
1994-95	48	10	14	0	....	7	14	3	....	17	28	3	....	120	144	37	6th, Atlantic Div.	Out of Playoffs
1993-94	84	14	22	6	....	16	21	5	....	30	43	11	....	224	251	71	7th, Atlantic Div.	Out of Playoffs
1992-93	84	12	27	3	....	11	27	4	....	23	54	7	....	245	332	53	6th, Norris Div.	Out of Playoffs

2006-07 Schedule

Oct.							
Thu.	5	at Atlanta		Fri.	5	at Colorado
Sat.	7	Boston		Sun.	7	at Pittsburgh
Mon.	9	Atlanta		Tue.	9	Pittsburgh
Fri.	13	at Florida		Thu.	11	Washington
Sat.	14	Florida		Sat.	13	at Buffalo
Mon.	16	Carolina		Mon.	15	at NY Islanders*
Thu.	19	Philadelphia		Tue.	16	Toronto
Sat.	21	at Washington		Thu.	18	at New Jersey
Thu.	26	Carolina		Sat.	20	at Carolina
Sat.	28	at Carolina		Fri.	26	New Jersey
Sun.	29	San Jose*		Tue.	30	at Philadelphia

Nov.				Feb.		
Wed.	1	Toronto		Thu.	1	at Carolina
Thu.	2	at Philadelphia		Sat.	3	NY Rangers
Sat.	4	at Boston		Tue.	6	Los Angeles
Mon.	6	at NY Islanders		Fri.	9	at NY Rangers
Wed.	8	at Pittsburgh		Sun.	11	at New Jersey*
Sat.	11	Atlanta		Tue.	13	Phoenix
Wed.	15	Montreal		Thu.	15	Washington
Fri.	17	NY Islanders		Sat.	17	at Florida
Sun.	19	at NY Rangers		Tue.	20	Florida
Mon.	20	at Buffalo		Thu.	22	at Atlanta
Wed.	22	at Florida		Fri.	23	Boston
Fri.	24	Atlanta		Sun.	25	Pittsburgh*
Sun.	26	Ottawa*		Tue.	27	Dallas
Tue.	28	Washington	Mar.	Thu.	1	at Washington
Thu.	30	at Boston		Sat.	3	at Florida

Dec.						
Sat.	2	at Ottawa		Tue.	6	at Vancouver
Tue.	5	Buffalo		Wed.	7	at Edmonton
Thu.	7	Atlanta		Sat.	10	at Calgary
Sat.	9	Anaheim		Tue.	13	at Toronto
Tue.	12	at Toronto		Fri.	16	Buffalo
Thu.	14	at Montreal		Sun.	18	at Washington*
Sat.	16	Carolina		Tue.	20	NY Islanders
Tue.	19	at Washington		Thu.	22	New Jersey
Thu.	21	at Ottawa		Sat.	24	Ottawa
Sat.	23	NY Rangers		Tue.	27	Florida
Tue.	26	at Atlanta		Fri.	30	at Carolina
Thu.	28	Philadelphia		Sat.	31	Washington
Sat.	30	Montreal	Apr.	Tue.	3	Carolina

Jan.						
Tue.	2	at Montreal		Fri.	6	Florida
Thu.	4	at Minnesota		Sat.	7	at Atlanta

Denotes afternoon game.

Franchise date: December 16, 1991

EASTERN
NHL
CONFERENCE

SOUTHEAST
DIVISION

15th NHL Season

Brad Richards played in all 82 games for Tampa Bay last season, as he has done four times in his five-year career. He ranked fifth in the NHL with 68 assists last season, and led the Lightning with 91 points.

2006-07 Player Personnel

FORWARDS

	HT	WT	S	Place of Birth	Date	2005-06 Club
AFANASENKOV, Dmitry	6-2	209	R	Arkhangelsk, USSR	5/12/80	Tampa Bay
ALEXEEV, Nikita	6-5	227	L	Murmansk, USSR	12/27/81	Omsk
CRAIG, Ryan	6-2	220	L	Abbotsford, B.C.	1/6/82	Tampa Bay-Springfield
DiMAIO, Rob	5-10	190	R	Calgary, Alta.	2/19/68	Tampa Bay
FEDOTENKO, Ruslan	6-2	195	L	Kiev, Ukraine	1/18/79	Tampa Bay
FRITZ, Mitch	6-8	258	L	Osoyoos, B.C.	11/24/80	Springfield
HEALEY, Eric	6-0	196	L	Hull, MA	1/20/75	Boston-Providence (AHL)
KARLSSON, Andreas	6-4	205	L	Ludvika, Sweden	8/19/75	HV 71
KVAPIL, Marek	5-10	192	R	Ilava, Czech.	1/5/85	Springfield
LECAVALIER, Vincent	6-4	223	L	Ile Bizard, Que.	4/21/80	Tampa Bay
MILLEY, Norm	6-0	211	R	Toronto, Ont.	2/14/80	Tampa Bay-Springfield
PERRIN, Eric	5-9	176	L	Laval, Que.	11/1/75	Bern
PROSPAL, Vaclav	6-1	195	L	Ceske Budejovice, Czech.	2/17/75	Tampa Bay
REID, Darren	6-2	205	R	Lac La Biche, Alta.	5/8/83	Tampa Bay-Springfield
RICHARDS, Brad	6-0	198	L	Murray Harbour, P.E.I.	5/2/80	Tampa Bay
ST. LOUIS, Martin	5-9	185	L	Laval, Que.	6/18/75	Tampa Bay
TARNASKY, Nick	6-2	233	L	Rocky Mtn. House, Alta.	11/25/84	Tampa Bay-Springfield
TAYLOR, Tim	6-1	195	L	Stratford, Ont.	2/6/69	Tampa Bay

DEFENSEMEN

	HT	WT	S	Place of Birth	Date	2005-06 Club
BOYLE, Dan	5-11	190	R	Ottawa, Ont.	7/12/76	Tampa Bay
DELMORE, Andy	6-0	200	L	LaSalle, Ont.	12/26/76	Columbus-Syracuse
EGENER, Mike	6-4	216	L	Lahr, West Germany	9/26/84	Springfield-Johnstown
JANIK, Doug	6-2	209	L	Agawam, MA	3/26/80	Buffalo-Rochester
KUBA, Filip	6-3	205	L	Ostrava, Czech.	12/29/76	Minnesota
O'BRIEN, Doug	6-1	200	L	St. John's, Nfld.	2/16/84	Tampa Bay-Springfield
PRATT, Nolan	6-3	207	L	Fort McMurray, Alta.	8/14/75	Tampa Bay
RANGER, Paul	6-2	215	L	Whitby, Ont.	9/12/84	Tampa Bay-Springfield
RICHARDSON, Luke	6-4	215	L	Ottawa, Ont.	3/26/69	Columbus-Toronto
ROGERS, Andy	6-5	218	L	Calgary, Alta.	8/25/86	Prince George
SARICH, Cory	6-4	210	R	Saskatoon, Sask.	8/16/78	Tampa Bay
SMABY, Matt	6-6	239	L	Minneapolis, MN	10/14/84	North Dakota

GOALTENDERS

	HT	WT	C	Place of Birth	Date	2005-06 Club
BURKE, Sean	6-4	211	L	Windsor, Ont.	1/29/67	Tampa Bay
COLEMAN, Gerald	6-4	205	L	Romeoville, IL	4/3/85	Tampa Bay-Springfield
DENIS, Marc	6-1	193	L	Montreal, Que.	8/1/77	Columbus
HOLMQVIST, Johan	6-3	195	L	Tolfta, Sweden	5/24/78	Brynas
RAMO, Karri	6-2	215	L	Asikkala, Finland	7/1/86	Haukat-Suomi U20-HPK

Coaching History

Terry Crisp, 1992-93 to 1996-97; Terry Crisp, Rick Paterson and Jacques Demers, 1997-98; Jacques Demers, 1998-99; Steve Ludzik, 1999-2000; Steve Ludzik and John Tortorella, 2000-01; John Tortorella, 2001-02 to date.

Coach

TORTORELLA, JOHN
Coach, Tampa Bay Lightning. Born in Boston, MA, June 24, 1958.

John Tortorella took over as head coach in Tampa Bay on January 6, 2001. He led the team to its first Eastern Conference and Stanley Cup championships, as well as its second consecutive Southeast Division championship in 2003-04. He was the winner of the Jack Adams Award as the National Hockey League's top coach after leading the Lightning to franchise records with 46 wins and 106 points before embarking on the successful playoff campaign. He now has 164 wins with the Lightning, ranking him first on the team's all-time wins list.

A 14-year NHL coaching veteran, Tortorella became the fourth head coach in team history when he was named to that position on January 6, 2001. Recognized as one of the top teaching coaches in the game, the Boston native joined the Lightning organization when he was hired on as an associate coach prior to the 2000-01 season.

Tortorella began his playing career at Salem State College before transferring to the University of Maine. He spent three seasons with the Black Bears and was twice named an ECAC All-Star. After playing in Sweden, Tortorella played in the Atlantic Coast Hockey League with Virginia, Hampton Roads, and Erie. He spent two seasons as general manager and head coach of the Virginia Lancers (ACHL) from 1986 to 1988, where he garnered coach of the year honors both years while leading his 1986-87 team to the league championship. He was hired as an assistant coach with the New Haven Nighthawks of the American Hockey League in 1988-89 and became an assistant coach with the Buffalo Sabres the following season. Tortorella remained with the Sabres organization through the 1996-97 season, including two years as coach of their AHL affiliate in Rochester.

Tortorella returned to the NHL in 1997 as an assistant with the Phoenix Coyotes, where he spent two seasons before joining the Rangers for 1999-2000. He served as the Rangers' interim head coach for the final four games of the '99-00 season before joining the Lightning staff.

Coaching Record

Season	Team	Games	Regular Season				Playoffs		
			W	L	O/T		Games	W	L
1995-96	Rochester (AHL)	80	37	38	5		19	15	4
1996-97	Rochester (AHL)	80	40	30	9		10	6	4
1999-2000	NY Rangers (NHL)	4	0	3	1		....	....	....
2000-01	Tampa Bay (NHL)	43	12	30	1		....	....	....
2001-02	Tampa Bay (NHL)	82	27	44	11		....	....	....
2002-03	Tampa Bay (NHL)	82	36	30	16		11	5	6
2003-04	Tampa Bay (NHL)	82	46	28	8		23	16	7
2004-05	Tampa Bay (NHL)			Season Cancelled					
2005-06	Tampa Bay (NHL)	82	43	33	6		5	1	4
	NHL Totals	375	164	168	43		39	22	17

2005-06 Scoring

* – rookie

Regular Season

Pos	#	Player	Team	GP	G	A	Pts	+/-	PIM	PP	SH	GW	S	%
C	19	Brad Richards	T.B.	82	23	68	91	0	32	7	4	0	282	8.2
C	20	Vaclav Prospal	T.B.	81	25	55	80	-3	50	10	0	3	236	10.6
C	4	Vincent Lecavalier	T.B.	80	35	40	75	0	90	13	2	7	309	11.3
R	26	Martin St. Louis	T.B.	80	31	30	61	-3	38	9	3	7	221	14.0
L	33	Fredrik Modin	T.B.	77	31	23	54	5	56	12	1	4	221	14.0
D	22	Dan Boyle	T.B.	79	15	38	53	-8	38	6	0	4	153	9.8
R	17	Ruslan Fedotenko	T.B.	80	26	15	41	-44	44	4	0	6	164	15.9
D	13	Pavel Kubina	T.B.	76	5	33	38	-12	96	4	0	1	155	3.2
C	34	* Ryan Craig	T.B.	48	15	13	28	-4	6	6	0	3	81	18.5
D	5	Darryl Sydor	T.B.	49	4	19	23	-18	30	1	0	0	64	6.3
L	25	Dave Andreychuk	T.B.	42	6	12	18	-13	16	4	1	1	81	7.4
D	54	* Paul Ranger	T.B.	76	1	17	18	5	58	0	0	1	73	1.4
R	18	Rob Dimaio	T.B.	61	4	13	17	-7	30	2	0	1	72	5.6
R	76	Evgeny Artyukhin	T.B.	72	4	13	17	-4	90	1	0	0	79	5.1
L	29	Dimitry Afanasenkov	T.B.	68	9	6	15	-7	16	1	0	0	78	11.5
D	21	Cory Sarich	T.B.	82	1	14	15	-2	79	0	0	0	88	1.1
C	27	Tim Taylor	T.B.	82	7	6	13	-12	22	0	0	0	109	6.4
D	44	Nolan Pratt	T.B.	82	0	9	9	7	60	0	0	0	26	0.0
C	8	Martin Cibak	T.B.	65	2	6	8	-9	22	0	0	0	50	4.0
R	14	* Norm Milley	T.B.	14	3	2	5	-2	4	1	0	0	12	16.7
R	46	* Darren Reid	T.B.	7	0	1	1	-1	2	0	0	0	3	0.0
D	2	* Timo Helbling	T.B.	9	0	1	1	-3	6	0	0	0	5	0.0
C	74	* Nick Tarnasky	T.B.	12	0	1	1	-3	4	0	0	0	9	0.0
L	11	Chris Dingman	T.B.	34	0	1	1	-10	22	0	0	0	24	0.0
R	16	Jim Campbell	T.B.	1	0	0	0	0	2	0	0	0	1	0.0
D	39	* Doug O'Brien	T.B.	5	0	0	0	0	0	0	0	0	2	0.0

Goaltending

No.		Goaltender	GPI	Mins	Avg	W	L	OT	EN	SO	GA	SA	S%	G	A	PIM
50	*	Gerald Coleman	2	43	2.79	0	0	1	0	0	2	17	.882	0	0	0
1		Sean Burke	35	1713	2.80	14	10	4	2	2	80	764	.895	0	1	10
47		John Grahame	57	1713	3.06	29	22	1	8	5	161	1450	.889	0	1	14
40	*	Brian Eklund	1	58	3.10	0	1	0	0	0	3	19	.842	0	0	0
		Totals	82	4997	3.07	43	33	6	10	7	256	2260	.887			

Playoffs

Pos	#	Player	Team	GP	G	A	Pts	+/-	PIM	PP	SH	GW	OT	S	%
C	19	Brad Richards	T.B.	5	3	5	8	-5	6	0	0	0	0	24	12.5
D	54	* Paul Ranger	T.B.	5	2	2	4	0	2	1	0	0	0	13	15.4
R	26	Martin St. Louis	T.B.	5	4	0	4	-2	2	1	0	1	0	15	26.7
D	22	Dan Boyle	T.B.	5	1	3	4	-1	6	0	0	0	0	6	16.7
C	4	Vincent Lecavalier	T.B.	5	1	3	4	0	7	0	0	0	0	17	5.9
D	13	Pavel Kubina	T.B.	5	1	2	3	-6	26	1	0	0	0	9	11.1
L	20	Vaclav Prospal	T.B.	5	0	2	2	1	4	0	0	0	0	5	0.0
R	76	* Evgeny Artyukhin	T.B.	5	1	0	1	-1	6	0	0	0	0	10	10.0
D	5	Darryl Sydor	T.B.	5	0	1	1	-3	0	0	0	0	0	5	0.0
D	21	Cory Sarich	T.B.	5	0	1	1	-1	4	0	0	0	0	5	0.0
L	29	Dimitry Afanasenkov	T.B.	5	0	1	1	-1	2	0	0	0	0	12	0.0
R	18	Rob Dimaio	T.B.	5	0	1	1	-1	2	0	0	0	0	7	0.0
L	11	Chris Dingman	T.B.	5	0	1	1	-1	0	0	0	0	0	4	0.0
C	27	Tim Taylor	T.B.	5	0	1	1	-2	2	0	0	0	0	7	0.0
D	44	Nolan Pratt	T.B.	5	0	0	0	-2	4	0	0	0	0	1	0.0
L	33	Fredrik Modin	T.B.	5	0	0	0	-6	6	0	0	0	0	11	0.0
C	8	Martin Cibak	T.B.	5	0	0	0	-1	0	0	0	0	0	2	0.0
R	17	Ruslan Fedotenko	T.B.	5	0	0	0	-1	20	0	0	0	0	11	0.0
C	34	* Ryan Craig	T.B.	5	0	0	0	-3	10	0	0	0	0	4	0.0

Goaltending

No.	Goaltender	GPI	Mins	Avg	W	L	EN	SO	GA	SA	S%	G	A	PIM
1	Sean Burke	3	109	3.85	0	1	0	0	7	57	.877	0	0	0
47	John Grahame	4	188	4.79	1	3	1	0	15	98	.847	0	0	0
	Totals	5	300	4.60	1	4	1	0	23	156	.853			

General Managers' History

Phil Esposito, 1992-93 to 1997-98; Jacques Demers, 1998-99; Rick Dudley, 1999-2000, 2000-01; Rick Dudley and Jay Feaster, 2001-02; Jay Feaster, 2002-03 to date.

Club Records

Team

(Figures in brackets for season records are games played; records for fewest points, wins, ties, losses, goals, goals against are for 70 or more games)

Most Points	106	2003-04 (82)
Most Wins	46	2003-04 (82)
Most Ties	16	2002-03 (82)
Most Losses	55	1997-98 (82)
Most Goals	252	2005-06 (82)
Most Goals Against	332	1992-93 (84)
Fewest Points	44	1997-98 (82)
Fewest Wins	17	1997-98 (82)
Fewest Ties	6	2000-01 (82)
Fewest Losses	22	2003-04 (82)
Fewest Goals	151	1997-98 (82)
Fewest Goals Against	192	2003-04 (82)
Longest Winning Streak		
Overall	8	Feb. 23-Mar. 6/04
Home	8	Mar. 17-Apr. 8/06
Away	5	Feb. 23-Mar. 6/04
Longest Undefeated Streak		
Overall	13	Mar. 7-Apr. 2/03 (7 wins, 6 ties)
Home	10	Jan. 29-Mar. 12/03 (9 wins, 1 tie)
Away	7	Feb. 23-Mar. 10/04 (6 wins, 1 tie)
Longest Losing Streak		
Overall	13	Jan. 3-Feb. 2/98
Home	10	Jan. 3-Feb. 26/98
Away	11	Oct. 24-Dec. 10/97
Longest Winless Streak		
Overall	16	Oct. 10-Nov. 17/97 (15 losses, 1 tie), Jan. 2-Feb. 5/98 (14 losses, 2 ties)
Home	11	Jan. 2-Feb. 26/98 (10 losses, 1 tie)
Away	17	Dec. 2/99-Feb. 19/00 (14 losses, 3 ties)
Most Shutouts, Season	9	2001-02 (82)
Most PIM, Season	1,823	1997-98 (82)
Most Goals, Game	9	Nov. 8/03 (Pit. 0 at T.B. 9)

Individual

Most Seasons	8	Pavel Kubina
Most Games, Career	547	Vincent Lecavalier
Most Goals, Career	181	Vincent Lecavalier
Most Assists, Career	261	Brad Richards
Most Points, Career	402	Vincent Lecavalier (181G, 221A)
Most PIM, Career	782	Chris Gratton
Most Shutouts, Career	14	Nikolai Khabibulin
Longest Consecutive Games Streak	306	Cory Sarich (Nov. 27/01 to date)
Most Goals, Season	42	Brian Bradley (1992-93)
Most Assists, Season	68	Brad Richards (2005-06)
Most Points, Season	94	Martin St. Louis (2003-04; 38G, 56A)
Most PIM, Season	258	Enrico Ciccone (1995-96)
Most Points, Defenseman, Season	65	Roman Hamrlik (1995-96; 16G, 49A)
Most Points, Center, Season	91	Brad Richards (2005-06; 23G, 68A)
Most Points, Right Wing, Season	94	Martin St. Louis (2003-04; 38G, 56A)
Most Points, Left Wing, Season	80	Cory Stillman (2003-04; 25G, 55A), Vaclav Prospal (2005-06; 25G, 55A)
Most Points, Rookie, Season	62	Brad Richards (2000-01; 21G, 41A)
Most Shutouts, Season	7	Nikolai Khabibulin (2001-02)
Most Goals, Game	4	Chris Kontos (Oct. 7/92)
Most Assists, Game	4	Four times
Most Points, Game	6	Doug Crossman (Nov. 7/92; 3G, 3A)

Captains' History

No captain, 1992-93 to 1994-95; Paul Ysebaert, 1995-96, 1996-97; Paul Ysebaert and Mikael Renberg, 1997-98; Rob Zamuner, 1998-99; Bill Houlder, Chris Gratton and Vincent Lecavalier, 1999-2000; Vincent Lecavalier, 2000-01; no captain, 2001-02; Dave Andreychuk, 2002-03, 2003-04; Dave Andreychuk and no captain, 2005-06.

All-time Record vs. Other Clubs

Regular Season

	At Home								On Road								Total							
	GP	W	L	T	OL	GF	GA	PTS	GP	W	L	T	OL	GF	GA	PTS	GP	W	L	T	OL	GF	GA	PTS
Anaheim	9	4	5	0	0	17	23	8	9	3	5	1	0	22	28	7	18	7	10	1	0	39	51	15
Atlanta	17	11	4	1	1	62	46	24	17	5	9	3	0	47	55	13	34	16	13	4	1	109	101	37
Boston	25	10	10	3	2	73	72	25	25	2	16	6	1	58	95	11	50	12	26	9	3	131	167	36
Buffalo	25	6	14	3	2	53	78	17	25	8	14	2	1	69	74	19	50	14	28	5	3	122	152	36
Calgary	10	5	4	1	0	31	32	11	10	4	5	0	1	24	32	9	20	9	9	1	1	55	64	20
Carolina	30	18	9	3	0	91	78	39	31	6	16	7	2	79	96	21	61	24	25	10	2	170	174	60
Chicago	12	5	3	3	1	29	30	14	14	4	8	2	0	35	45	10	26	9	11	5	1	64	75	24
Colorado	12	8	2	1	1	39	32	18	13	3	8	2	0	28	50	8	25	11	10	3	1	67	82	26
Columbus	4	3	1	0	0	9	5	6	3	1	1	1	0	4	5	3	7	4	2	1	0	13	10	9
Dallas	13	1	10	2	0	20	37	4	12	4	7	1	0	33	42	9	25	5	17	3	0	53	79	13
Detroit	15	4	9	1	1	46	67	10	12	1	10	1	0	21	47	3	27	5	19	2	1	67	114	13
Edmonton	11	3	5	2	1	31	35	9	10	3	7	0	0	21	26	6	21	6	12	2	1	52	61	15
Florida	32	12	13	6	1	70	90	31	32	8	17	4	3	72	99	23	64	20	30	10	4	142	189	54
Los Angeles	10	5	4	0	1	23	22	11	12	9	1	2	0	40	25	20	22	14	5	2	1	63	47	31
Minnesota	3	1	1	1	0	8	9	3	3	0	3	0	0	8	13	0	6	1	4	1	0	16	22	3
Montreal	25	9	10	5	1	60	71	24	24	11	12	1	0	57	63	23	49	20	22	6	1	117	134	47
Nashville	5	2	1	2	0	15	13	6	6	4	2	0	0	16	12	8	11	6	3	2	0	31	25	14
New Jersey	27	9	13	5	0	62	83	23	28	7	19	2	0	54	103	16	55	16	32	7	0	116	186	39
NY Islanders	28	14	12	2	0	75	84	30	27	13	12	1	1	74	81	28	55	27	24	3	1	149	165	58
NY Rangers	27	12	11	3	1	92	91	28	29	13	13	2	1	88	91	29	56	25	24	5	2	180	182	57
Ottawa	25	8	14	2	1	71	88	19	25	8	17	0	0	55	96	16	50	16	31	2	1	126	184	35
Philadelphia	28	11	15	1	1	82	83	24	27	6	14	7	0	56	81	19	55	17	29	8	1	138	164	43
Phoenix	10	5	5	0	0	33	33	10	12	6	6	0	0	29	29	12	22	11	11	0	0	62	62	22
Pittsburgh	25	14	9	2	0	80	61	30	25	7	14	3	1	67	95	18	50	21	23	5	1	147	156	48
St. Louis	14	6	5	3	0	43	46	15	11	1	9	0	1	24	44	3	25	7	14	3	1	67	90	18
San Jose	12	7	4	1	0	32	31	15	11	6	4	1	0	37	35	13	23	13	8	2	0	69	66	28
Toronto	22	5	15	1	1	47	74	12	23	7	14	1	1	59	86	16	45	12	29	2	2	106	160	28
Vancouver	9	3	5	0	1	31	37	7	9	0	6	2	1	17	40	3	18	3	11	2	2	48	77	10
Washington	33	12	19	2	0	79	102	26	33	8	19	4	2	75	113	22	66	20	38	6	2	154	215	48
Totals	**518**	**213**	**232**	**56**	**17**	**1404**	**1553**	**499**	**518**	**158**	**288**	**56**	**16**	**1269**	**1701**	**388**	**1036**	**371**	**520**	**112**	**33**	**2673**	**3254**	**887**

Playoffs

	Series	W	L	GP	W	L	T	GF	GA	Last Mtg.	Rnd.	Result
Calgary	1	1	0	7	4	3	0	13	14	2004	F	W 4-3
Montreal	1	1	0	4	4	0	0	14	5	2004	CSF	W 4-0
New Jersey	1	0	1	5	1	4	0	8	14	2003	CSF	L 1-4
NY Islanders	1	1	0	5	4	1	0	12	5	2004	CQF	W 4-1
Ottawa	1	0	1	5	1	4	0	13	23	2006	CQF	L 1-4
Philadelphia	2	1	1	13	6	7	0	34	45	2004	CF	W 4-3
Washington	1	1	0	6	4	2	0	14	15	2003	CQF	W 4-2
Totals	**8**	**5**	**3**	**45**	**24**	**21**	**0**	**108**	**121**			

Playoff Results 2006-2001

Year	Round	Opponent	Result	GF	GA
2006	CQF	Ottawa	L 1-4	13	23
2004	**F**	**Calgary**	**W 4-3**	**13**	**14**
	CF	Philadelphia	W 4-3	21	19
	CSF	Montreal	W 4-0	14	5
	CQF	NY Islanders	W 4-1	12	5
2003	CSF	New Jersey	L 1-4	8	14
	CQF	Washington	W 4-2	14	15

Abbreviations: Round: F – Final;
CF – conference final; **CSF** – conference semi-final;
CQF – conference quarter-final.

Carolina totals include Hartford, 1992-93 to 1996-97.
Dallas totals include Minnesota North Stars, 1992-93.

Colorado totals include Quebec, 1992-93 to 1994-95.
Phoenix totals include Winnipeg, 1992-93 to 1995-96.

2005-06 Results

Oct.	5	Carolina	5-2
	7	at Florida	0-2
	8	Florida	2-1
	10	Boston	2-4
	13	Buffalo	3-4†
	15	at Pittsburgh	3-1
	16	at Washington	2-3†
	20	at Atlanta	6-0
	21	Ottawa	1-4
	26	at New Jersey	6-3
	28	Washington	4-2
	29	at Atlanta	3-2
Nov.	1	Atlanta	4-6
	3	at Ottawa	2-4
	5	at Toronto	3-5
	8	at Montreal	2-3
	10	NY Rangers	2-5
	11	at Atlanta	2-5
	14	Philadelphia	5-2
	15	at Washington	3-4†
	17	NY Islanders	3-2
	20	at Carolina	5-2
	22	at Philadelphia	4-2
	23	at Washington	4-3†
	25	New Jersey	2-8
	27	Pittsburgh	4-1
	30	Toronto	2-1
Dec.	2	Chicago	3-2†
	8	St. Louis	5-4
	10	Nashville	4-3
	14	at Anaheim	2-4
	15	at Phoenix	3-1
	17	Detroit	3-6
	20	at Carolina	4-6
	22	at NY Rangers	2-4
	23	Buffalo	1-4
	26	Carolina	5-4*
	28	Montreal	3-4
	30	Boston	1-2
Jan.	2	at NY Islanders	2-1
	3	at NY Rangers	1-0*
	5	at Buffalo	1-3
	7	at Boston	3-6
	13	Columbus	4-2
	16	at San Jose	1-3
	17	at Los Angeles	4-1
	20	at Dallas	6-3
	21	at Atlanta	2-0
	24	Florida	2-3*
	26	New Jersey	1-0*
	28	at Philadelphia	6-0
	29	at Washington	1-2
	31	Toronto	3-2†
Feb.	4	Washington	5-0
	6	at NY Islanders	3-2*
	7	at New Jersey	4-7
	9	Carolina	5-3
	11	at Boston	6-5
	28	Florida	2-8
Mar.	4	Montreal	2-6
	6	Ottawa	0-4
	7	at Pittsburgh	5-4†
	9	at Buffalo	5-8
	11	at Toronto	1-5
	13	at Montreal	2-1
	14	at Ottawa	3-4
	17	Philadelphia	6-3
	19	NY Islanders	5-2
	20	at Florida	5-6*
	23	Washington	4-3*
	25	NY Rangers	4-3†
	27	at Carolina	1-2
	30	Atlanta	4-3
Apr.	1	at Florida	2-4
	3	Florida	4-1
	6	Atlanta	3-2†
	8	Pittsburgh	1-0
	9	at Florida	3-6
	11	Atlanta	2-6
	14	at Carolina	4-5†
	15	Carolina	3-2*
	18	Washington	1-4

* – Overtime † – Shootout

Entry Draft
Selections 2006-1992

2006
Pick
15 Riku Helenius
78 Kevin Quick
168 Dane Crowley
198 Denis Kazionov

2005
Pick
30 Vladimir Mihalik
73 Radek Smolenak
89 Chris Lawrence
92 Marek Bartanus
102 Blair Jones
133 Stanislav Lascek
163 Marek Kvapil
165 Kevin Beech
225 John Wessbecker

2004
Pick
30 Andy Rogers
65 Mark Tobin
102 Mike Lundin
158 Brandon Elliott
163 Dusty Collins
188 Jan Zapletal
191 Karri Ramo
245 Justin Keller

2003
Pick
34 Mike Egener
41 Matt Smaby
96 Jonathan Boutin
192 Doug O'Brien
224 Gerald Coleman
227 Jay Rosehill
255 Raimonds Danilics
256 Brady Greco
273 Albert Vishnyakov
286 Zbynek Hrdel
287 Nick Tarnasky

2002
Pick
60 Adam Henrich
100 Dmitri Kazionov
135 Joseph Pearce
162 Gerard Dicaire
170 P.J. Atherton
174 Karri Akkanen
183 Paul Ranger
213 Fredrik Norrena
233 Vasily Koshechkin
255 Ryan Craig
256 Darren Reid
286 Alexei Glukhov
287 John Toffey

2001
Pick
3 Alexander Svitov
47 Alexander Polushin
61 Andreas Holmqvist
94 Evgeni Artyukhin
123 Aaron Lobb
138 Paul Lynch
188 Art Femenella
219 Dennis Packard
222 Jeremy Van Hoof
252 J.F. Soucy
259 Dmitri Bezrukov
261 Vitali Smolyaninov
281 Ilja Solarev
289 Henrik Bergfors

2000
Pick
8 Nikita Alexeev
34 Ruslan Zainullin
81 Alexander Kharitonov
126 Johan Hagglund
161 Pavel Sedov
191 Aaron Gionet
222 Marek Priechodsky
226 Brian Eklund
233 Alexander Polukeyev
263 Thomas Ziegler

1999
Pick
47 Sheldon Keefe
67 Evgeny Konstantinov
75 Brett Scheffelmaier
88 Jimmie Olvestad
127 Kaspars Astashenko
148 Michal Lanicek
182 Fedor Fedorov
187 Ivan Rachunek
216 Erkki Rajamaki
244 Mikko Kuparinen

1998
Pick
1 Vincent Lecavalier
64 Brad Richards
72 Dmitry Afanasenkov
92 Eric Beaudoin
121 Curtis Rich
146 Sergei Kuznetsov
174 Brett Allan
194 Oak Hewer
221 Daniel Hulak
229 Chris Lyness
252 Martin Cibak

1997
Pick
7 Paul Mara
33 Kyle Kos
61 Matt Elich
108 Mark Thompson
109 Jan Sulc
112 Karel Betik
153 Andrei Skopintsev
168 Justin Jack
170 Eero Somervuori
185 Samuel St-Pierre
198 Shawn Skolney
224 Paul Comrie

1996
Pick
16 Mario Larocque
69 Curtis Tipler
125 Jason Robinson
152 Nikolai Ignatov
157 Xavier Delisle
179 Pavel Kubina

1995
Pick
5 Daymond Langkow
30 Mike McBain
56 Shane Willis
108 Konstantin Golokhvastov
134 Eduard Pershin
160 Cory Murphy
186 Joe Cardarelli
212 Zac Bierk

1994
Pick
8 Jason Wiemer
34 Colin Cloutier
55 Vadim Epanchintsev
86 Dmitri Klevakin
137 Daniel Juden
138 Bryce Salvador
164 Chris Maillet
190 Alexei Baranov
216 Yuri Smirnov
242 Shawn Gervais
268 Brian White

1993
Pick
3 Chris Gratton
29 Tyler Moss
55 Allan Egeland
81 Marian Kacir
107 Ryan Brown
133 Kiley Hill
159 Matthieu Raby
185 Ryan Nauss
211 Alexandre Laporte
237 Brett Duncan
263 Mark Szoke

1992
Pick
1 Roman Hamrlik
26 Drew Bannister
49 Brent Gretzky
74 Aaron Gavey
97 Brantt Myhres
122 Martin Tanguay
145 Derek Wilkinson
170 Dennis Maxwell
193 Andrew Kemper
218 Marc Tardif
241 Tom MacDonald

Vice President and General Manager

FEASTER, JAY
Executive Vice President/General Manager, Tampa Bay Lightning.
Born in Williamstown, PA, July 30, 1962.

Jay Feaster joined the Lightning on October 20, 1998 and was named general manager on February 10, 2002. He led Tampa Bay to the Stanley Cup in 2003-04 and was named NHL executive of the year by *The Sporting News*. The Lightning enjoyed a storybook season under Feaster's direction in 2003-04, winning a second consecutive Southeast Division title, capturing the top seed in the Eastern Conference and skating off with Lord Stanley's Cup after a hard-fought seven game series against the Calgary Flames. He has been widely praised for bringing continuity and stability to the Lightning franchise.

Feaster, named the fourth general manager in franchise history on February 10, 2002, joined the Lightning on October 20, 1998, from the Hershey Bears of the American Hockey League. He spent three-plus seasons as Tampa Bay's assistant general manager, overseeing all contractual, collective bargaining and NHL legal issues, as well as the organization's scouting department and its minor league affiliates. As general manager, Feaster has developed the Lightning into one of the most competitive and entertaining teams in the NHL. He also served as co-general manager of Team USA for the 2003 World Championships along with Larry Pleau of St. Louis.

To join the Lightning, Feaster resigned his post as president of the Hershey Bears and vice president of Hershey Sports and Entertainment. In that capacity, Feaster oversaw the operations of the Bears, the Hershey Wildcats professional soccer team and HersheyPark Arena/Stadium. In his nine years with the Bears, he led the team to a division title (1993-94) and a Calder Cup Championship (1997), while establishing three consecutive single-season attendance records (1991-92 to 1993-94) and entering into a five-year affiliation agreement with the NHL's Colorado Avalanche.

While in Hershey, Feaster spent time on the advisory boards of the Big 33 Scholarship Foundation, the Four Diamonds Fund at the Pennsylvania State University Milton S. Hershey Medical Center, and the Central PA Chapter of the National Multiple Sclerosis Society. He also taught business law and hotel law as a visiting faculty member at the Lebanon Valley College in Annville, Pennsylvania. Prior to joining the Hershey Company, Feaster practiced law with the firm of McNees, Wallace & Nurick in Harrisburg, Pennsylvania. He is a Summa Cum Laude graduate of Susquehanna University and a Cum Laude graduate of The Georgetown Law Center in Washington, D.C.

Club Directory

St. Pete Times Forum

Tampa Bay Lightning
St. Pete Times Forum
401 Channelside Drive
Tampa, FL 33602
Phone **813/301-6500**
FAX 813/301-1480
Ticket Info. 813/301-6600
www.tampabaylightning.com
Capacity: 19,758

Executive
Owner . . . . Palace Sports & Entertainment, Bill Davidson
Pres. of Palace Sports & Entertainment/Governor . . . Tom Wilson
Pres. of Tampa Bay Lightning/Alternate Governor . . . Ron Campbell
Executive Vice President/Chief Operating Officer . . . Sean Henry
Executive VP of Corporate Sales & Marketing . . . . . Harry Hutt
Vice President of Business Delvelopment . . . . Rick Salomone
Vice President of Sponsorship Sales . . . . Rob Keith
Sr. Vice President of Ticket Sales . . . . Dave Bullock
Executive Assistants . . . . Michele Colaianni, Julie Stein
Executive Vice President, G.M. & Alt. Gov. . . . . . . Jay H. Feaster
Executive Assistant to General Manager . . . . Elizabeth Sylvia
Sr. Vice President Communications . . . . Bill Wickett
Vice President, Legal Affairs/Legal Counsel . . . . . . Paul Davis
Vice President, Chief Financial Officer . . . . Joe Fada

Hockey Operations
Executive Vice President, G.M. & Alt. Gov. . . . . Jay H. Feaster
Assistant General Manager . . . . Claude Loiselle
Director of Player Personnel . . . . Bill Barber
Assistant to the General Manager . . . . Ryan Belec
Head Coach . . . . John Tortorella
Associate Coach . . . . Craig Ramsay
Assistant Coach . . . . Jeff Reese
Strength & Conditioning Coach . . . . Eric Lawson
Video Coach . . . . Nigel Kirwan
Chief Scout . . . . Jake Goertzen
Scouting Staff . . . . Angelo Bumbacco, Charlie Hodge, Gerry O'Flaherty,
Mikael Andersson, Stephen Baker, Larry Bernard, Dirk Graham,
Dave Heitz, Kari Kettunen, Miroslav Prihoda, Darrell Young,
Glen Zacharias, Cory Schwab, Yuri Yanchenkov
Director of Team Services . . . . Phil Thibodeau
Head Medical Trainer . . . . Thomas Mulligan
Assistant Athletic Trainer . . . . Jason Serbus
Massage Therapist . . . . Mike Griebel
Equipment Manager . . . . Ray Thill
Assistant Equipment Managers . . . . Dana Heinze, Jim Pickard
Head Coach Springfield Falcons . . . . Steve Stirling
Asst Coach Springfield Falcons . . . . Darren Rumble
Head Medical Trainer Springfield Falcons . . . . Adam Rambo
Asst. Equipment Mgr. Springfield Falcons . . . . Casey Taylor
Head Athletic Trainer Johnstown Chiefs . . . . Scott Adams
Team Physician . . . . Dr. Ira Guttentag
Director of Alumni . . . . John Tucker

Premium Services
Director of Premium Services. . . . . Karrie Yager
Premium Services Ticket Manager . . . . Missy Davis
Premium Services Suite Manager . . . . Lakisha Sharpe
Premium Services Manager . . . . Amanda Graul

Finance
Senior Accountants. Doug Riefler, Dave Weber
Accounts Payable . . . . Donna Clark
Staff Accountants . . . . Jane Sheill, Debbie Myers

Internal Support Staff
Vice President, Information Services . . . . David Everett
Assistant Information Services Manager . . . . Rosie Chhuor, Jon Therrien
Database Manager . . . . Nick Gesacion

Box Office
Director of Ticket Operations . . . . Jim Mannino
Assistant Box Office Manager . . . . Alex Bohne

Ticket Sales
Sr. Vice President of Ticket Sales . . . . Dave Bullock
VP of Ticket Sales and Service . . . . Todd Lambert
Director of Group Sales . . . . Brad Lott
Director of Outside Sales . . . . Patrick Duffy
Director of Suite Sales. . . . . Chris Diiorio

Sponsorship Sales & Marketing
Director of Promotions . . . . Mark Gullett
Sr Director of Corporate Partnerships . . . . Arden Robbins
Director of Corporate Partnerships . . . . Giles Dowden
Director of Marketing Partnerships . . . . Alaina Miller
Director of Event Marketing . . . . Holly Brown
Director of Broadcast Production & Game Ops . . . . Jim Ciotoli
In Game Entertainment Coordinator . . . . Hope Reep
Director of Fan Development . . . . David Cole

Communications
Director of Public Relations . . . . Jay Preble
Media Relations Manager . . . . Brian Breseman
Public Relations Coordinator . . . . Brian Dancel
Executive Director of Lightning Foundation . . . . Nancy Crane
Community Relations/Lightning Foundation Mgr. . . . . . . Kathryn Harper
Director of Web Services . . . . Martin Quessenberry

Broadcast Information
Director of Broadcasting & Programming . . . . Jason Dixon
Television . . . . Sun Sports
Television Broadcasters . . . . Rick Peckham, Bobby (the Chief) Taylor,
Television Rinkside Reporter . . . . Paul Kennedy
Radio . . . . WDAE 620 AM, WHOO 1080 AM (Orlando)
WIXC 1060 AM (Melbourne), WDGF 1350 AM (Dade City)
Radio Broadcasters . . . . David Mishkin, Phil Esposito

Tomas Kaberle led the Maple Leafs with 58 assists in 2005-06.

Toronto Maple Leafs

2005-06 Results: 41W-33L-1OTL-7SOL 90PTS.
Fourth, Northeast Division

2006-07 Schedule

Month	Day	Date	Opponent	Month	Day	Date	Opponent
Oct.	Wed.	4	Ottawa		Thu.	4	at Boston
	Thu.	5	at Ottawa		Sat.	6	Buffalo
	Sat.	7	Montreal		Tue.	9	Carolina
	Mon.	9	Florida		Thu.	11	at Buffalo
	Thu.	12	at New Jersey		Sat.	13	Vancouver
	Sat.	14	Calgary		Tue.	16	at Tampa Bay
	Wed.	18	Colorado		Thu.	18	at Florida
	Fri.	20	at Columbus		Sat.	20	at Pittsburgh
	Sat.	21	NY Rangers		Sat.	27	Montreal
	Tue.	24	Ottawa		Tue.	30	at Carolina
	Thu.	26	at Ottawa		Wed.	31	at NY Rangers
	Sat.	28	at Montreal	Feb.	Sat.	3	at Ottawa
	Mon.	30	Atlanta		Tue.	6	at St. Louis
Nov.	Wed.	1	at Tampa Bay		Thu.	8	at Nashville
	Thu.	2	at Florida		Sat.	10	Pittsburgh
	Sat.	4	at Buffalo		Tue.	13	NY Islanders
	Mon.	6	Philadelphia		Thu.	15	at Philadelphia
	Thu.	9	at Boston		Sat.	17	Edmonton
	Sat.	11	Montreal		Tue.	20	Boston
	Thu.	16	at Boston		Thu.	22	at NY Islanders
	Sat.	18	New Jersey		Sat.	24	at Philadelphia
	Mon.	20	NY Islanders		Mon.	26	at Montreal
	Wed.	22	at Buffalo		Tue.	27	Buffalo
	Fri.	24	at Washington	Mar.	Fri.	2	at New Jersey
	Sat.	25	Boston		Sat.	3	Buffalo
	Tue.	28	Boston		Tue.	6	Washington
	Thu.	30	at Atlanta		Thu.	8	at Ottawa
Dec.	Sat.	2	at Montreal		Sat.	10	Ottawa
	Tue.	5	Atlanta		Tue.	13	Tampa Bay
	Thu.	7	at Boston		Fri.	16	at Washington
	Sat.	9	at Detroit		Sat.	17	at Montreal
	Tue.	12	Tampa Bay		Tue.	20	New Jersey
	Fri.	15	at Carolina		Fri.	23	at Buffalo
	Sat.	16	NY Rangers		Sat.	24	Buffalo
	Tue.	19	Florida		Tue.	27	Carolina
	Fri.	22	at Chicago		Thu.	29	at Atlanta
	Sat.	23	Washington		Sat.	31	Pittsburgh
	Tue.	26	Minnesota	Apr.	Sun.	1	at NY Rangers
	Fri.	29	at Pittsburgh		Tue.	3	Philadelphia
	Sat.	30	Ottawa		Thu.	5	at NY Islanders
Jan.	Mon.	1	Boston		Sat.	7	Montreal

* Denotes afternoon game.

Franchise date: November 22, 1917

EASTERN CONFERENCE
NORTHEAST DIVISION

90th NHL Season

Year-by-Year Record

		Home				Road				Overall								
Season	**GP**	**W**	**L**	**T**	**OL**	**W**	**L**	**T**	**OL**	**W**	**L**	**T**	**OL**	**GF**	**GA**	**Pts.**	**Finished**	**Playoff Result**
2005-06	82	26	12	....	3	15	21	....	5	41	33	....	8	257	270	90	4th, Northeast Div.	Out of Playoffs
2004-05	....	....	....	....	....	....	....	....	....	....	....	....	....	....	....	....		
2003-04	82	22	14	3	2	23	10	7	1	45	24	10	3	242	204	103	2nd, Northeast Div.	Lost Conf. Semi-Final
2002-03	82	24	13	4	0	20	15	3	3	44	28	7	3	236	208	98	2nd, Northeast Div.	Lost Conf. Quarter-Final
2001-02	82	24	11	6	0	19	14	4	4	43	25	10	4	249	207	100	2nd, Northeast Div.	Lost Conf. Championship
2000-01	82	19	11	7	4	18	18	4	1	37	29	11	5	232	207	90	3rd, Northeast Div.	Lost Conf. Semi-Final
1999-2000	82	24	12	5	0	21	15	2	3	45	27	7	3	246	222	100	1st, Northeast Div.	Lost Conf. Semi-Final
1998-99	82	23	13	5	....	22	17	2	....	45	30	7	....	268	231	97	2nd, Northeast Div.	Lost Conf. Championship
1997-98	82	16	20	5	....	14	23	4	....	30	43	9	....	194	237	69	6th, Central Div.	Out of Playoffs
1996-97	82	18	20	3	....	12	24	5	....	30	44	8	....	230	273	68	6th, Central Div.	Out of Playoffs
1995-96	82	19	15	7	....	15	21	5	....	34	36	12	....	247	252	80	3rd, Central Div.	Lost Conf. Quarter-Final
1994-95	48	15	7	2	....	6	12	6	....	21	19	8	....	135	146	50	4th, Central Div.	Lost Conf. Quarter-Final
1993-94	84	23	15	4	....	20	14	8	....	43	29	12	....	280	243	98	2nd, Central Div.	Lost Conf. Championship
1992-93	84	25	11	6	....	19	18	5	....	44	29	11	....	288	241	99	3rd, Norris Div.	Lost Conf. Championship
1991-92	80	21	16	3	....	9	27	4	....	30	43	7	....	234	294	67	5th, Norris Div.	Out of Playoffs
1990-91	80	15	21	4	....	8	25	7	....	23	46	11	....	241	318	57	5th, Norris Div.	Out of Playoffs
1989-90	80	24	14	2	....	14	24	2	....	38	38	4	....	337	358	80	3rd, Norris Div.	Lost Div. Semi-Final
1988-89	80	15	20	5	....	13	26	1	....	28	46	6	....	259	342	62	5th, Norris Div.	Out of Playoffs
1987-88	80	14	20	6	....	7	29	4	....	21	49	10	....	273	345	52	4th, Norris Div.	Lost Div. Semi-Final
1986-87	80	22	14	4	....	10	28	2	....	32	42	6	....	286	319	70	4th, Norris Div.	Lost Div. Final
1985-86	80	16	21	3	....	9	27	4	....	25	48	7	....	311	386	57	4th, Norris Div.	Lost Div. Final
1984-85	80	10	28	2	....	10	24	6	....	20	52	8	....	253	358	48	5th, Norris Div.	Out of Playoffs
1983-84	80	17	16	7	....	9	29	2	....	26	45	9	....	303	387	61	5th, Norris Div.	Out of Playoffs
1982-83	80	20	15	5	....	8	25	7	....	28	40	12	....	293	330	68	3rd, Norris Div.	Lost Div. Semi-Final
1981-82	80	12	20	8	....	8	24	8	....	20	44	16	....	298	380	56	5th, Norris Div.	Out of Playoffs
1980-81	80	14	21	5	....	14	16	10	....	28	37	15	....	322	367	71	5th, Adams Div.	Lost Prelim. Round
1979-80	80	17	19	4	....	18	21	1	....	35	40	5	....	304	327	75	4th, Adams Div.	Lost Prelim. Round
1978-79	80	20	12	8	....	14	21	5	....	34	33	13	....	267	252	81	3rd, Adams Div.	Lost Quarter-Final
1977-78	80	21	13	6	....	20	16	4	....	41	29	10	....	271	237	92	3rd, Adams Div.	Lost Semi-Final
1976-77	80	18	13	9	....	15	19	6	....	33	32	15	....	301	285	81	3rd, Adams Div.	Lost Quarter-Final
1975-76	80	23	12	5	....	11	19	10	....	34	31	15	....	294	276	83	3rd, Adams Div.	Lost Quarter-Final
1974-75	80	19	12	9	....	12	21	7	....	31	33	16	....	280	309	78	3rd, Adams Div.	Lost Quarter-Final
1973-74	78	21	11	7	....	14	16	9	....	35	27	16	....	274	230	86	4th, East Div.	Lost Quarter-Final
1972-73	78	20	12	7	....	7	29	3	....	27	41	10	....	247	279	64	6th, East Div.	Out of Playoffs
1971-72	78	21	11	7	....	12	20	7	....	33	31	14	....	209	208	80	4th, East Div.	Lost Quarter-Final
1970-71	78	24	9	6	....	13	24	2	....	37	33	8	....	248	211	82	4th, East Div.	Lost Quarter-Final
1969-70	76	18	13	7	....	11	21	6	....	29	34	13	....	222	242	71	6th, East Div.	Out of Playoffs
1968-69	76	20	8	10	....	15	18	5	....	35	26	15	....	234	217	85	4th, East Div.	Lost Quarter-Final
1967-68	74	24	9	4	....	9	22	6	....	33	31	10	....	209	176	76	5th, East Div.	Out of Playoffs
1966-67	**70**	**21**	**8**	**6**	....	**11**	**19**	**5**	....	**32**	**27**	**11**	....	**204**	**211**	**75**	**3rd,**	**Won Stanley Cup**
1965-66	70	22	9	4	....	12	16	7	....	34	25	11	....	208	187	79	3rd,	Lost Semi-Final
1964-65	70	17	15	3	....	13	11	11	....	30	26	14	....	204	173	74	4th,	Lost Semi-Final
1963-64	**70**	**22**	**7**	**6**	....	**11**	**18**	**6**	....	**33**	**25**	**12**	....	**192**	**172**	**78**	**3rd,**	**Won Stanley Cup**
1962-63	**70**	**21**	**8**	**6**	....	**14**	**15**	**6**	....	**35**	**23**	**12**	....	**221**	**180**	**82**	**1st,**	**Won Stanley Cup**
1961-62	**70**	**25**	**5**	**5**	....	**12**	**17**	**6**	....	**37**	**22**	**11**	....	**232**	**180**	**85**	**2nd,**	**Won Stanley Cup**
1960-61	70	21	6	8	....	18	13	4	....	39	19	12	....	234	176	90	2nd,	Lost Semi-Final
1959-60	70	20	9	6	....	15	17	3	....	35	26	9	....	199	195	79	2nd,	Lost Final
1958-59	70	17	13	5	....	10	19	6	....	27	32	11	....	189	201	65	4th,	Lost Final
1957-58	70	12	16	7	....	9	22	4	....	21	38	11	....	192	226	53	6th,	Out of Playoffs
1956-57	70	12	16	7	....	9	18	8	....	21	34	15	....	174	192	57	5th,	Out of Playoffs
1955-56	70	19	10	6	....	5	23	7	....	24	33	13	....	153	181	61	4th,	Lost Semi-Final
1954-55	70	14	10	11	....	10	14	11	....	24	24	22	....	147	135	70	3rd,	Lost Semi-Final
1953-54	70	22	6	7	....	10	18	7	....	32	24	14	....	152	131	78	3rd,	Lost Semi-Final
1952-53	70	17	12	6	....	10	18	7	....	27	30	13	....	156	167	67	5th,	Out of Playoffs
1951-52	70	17	10	8	....	12	15	8	....	29	25	16	....	168	157	74	3rd,	Lost Semi-Final
1950-51	**70**	**22**	**8**	**5**	....	**19**	**8**	**8**	....	**41**	**16**	**13**	....	**212**	**138**	**95**	**2nd,**	**Won Stanley Cup**
1949-50	70	18	9	8	....	13	18	4	....	31	27	12	....	176	173	74	3rd,	Lost Semi-Final
1948-49	**60**	**12**	**8**	**10**	....	**10**	**17**	**3**	....	**22**	**25**	**13**	....	**147**	**161**	**57**	**4th,**	**Won Stanley Cup**
1947-48	**60**	**22**	**3**	**5**	....	**10**	**12**	**8**	....	**32**	**15**	**13**	....	**182**	**143**	**77**	**1st,**	**Won Stanley Cup**
1946-47	**60**	**20**	**8**	**2**	....	**11**	**11**	**8**	....	**31**	**19**	**10**	....	**209**	**172**	**72**	**2nd,**	**Won Stanley Cup**
1945-46	50	10	13	2	....	9	11	5	....	19	24	7	....	174	185	45	5th,	Out of Playoffs
1944-45	**50**	**13**	**9**	**3**	....	**11**	**13**	**1**	....	**24**	**22**	**4**	....	**183**	**161**	**52**	**3rd,**	**Won Stanley Cup**
1943-44	50	13	11	1	....	10	12	3	....	23	23	4	....	214	174	50	3rd,	Lost Semi-Final
1942-43	50	17	6	2	....	5	13	7	....	22	19	9	....	198	159	53	3rd,	Lost Semi-Final
1941-42	**48**	**18**	**6**	**0**	....	**9**	**12**	**3**	....	**27**	**18**	**3**	....	**158**	**136**	**57**	**2nd,**	**Won Stanley Cup**
1940-41	48	16	5	3	....	12	9	3	....	28	14	6	....	145	99	62	2nd,	Lost Semi-Final
1939-40	48	15	3	6	....	10	14	0	....	25	17	6	....	134	110	56	3rd,	Lost Final
1938-39	48	13	8	3	....	6	12	6	....	19	20	9	....	114	107	47	3rd,	Lost Final
1937-38	48	13	6	5	....	11	9	4	....	24	15	9	....	151	127	57	1st, Cdn. Div.	Lost Final
1936-37	48	14	9	1	....	8	12	4	....	22	21	5	....	119	115	49	3rd, Cdn. Div.	Lost Quarter-Final
1935-36	48	15	4	5	....	8	15	1	....	23	19	6	....	126	106	52	2nd, Cdn. Div.	Lost Final
1934-35	48	16	6	2	....	14	8	2	....	30	14	4	....	157	111	64	1st, Cdn. Div.	Lost Final
1933-34	48	19	2	3	....	7	11	6	....	26	13	9	....	174	119	61	1st, Cdn. Div.	Lost Semi-Final
1932-33	48	16	4	4	....	8	14	2	....	24	18	6	....	119	111	54	1st, Cdn. Div.	Lost Final
1931-32	**48**	**17**	**4**	**3**	....	**6**	**14**	**4**	....	**23**	**18**	**7**	....	**155**	**127**	**53**	**2nd, Cdn. Div.**	**Won Stanley Cup**
1930-31	44	15	4	3	....	7	9	6	....	22	13	9	....	118	99	53	2nd, Cdn. Div.	Lost Quarter-Final
1929-30	44	10	8	4	....	7	13	2	....	17	21	6	....	116	124	40	4th, Cdn. Div.	Out of Playoffs
1928-29	44	15	5	2	....	6	13	3	....	21	18	5	....	85	69	47	3rd, Cdn. Div.	Lost Semi-Final
1927-28	44	9	8	5	....	9	10	3	....	18	18	8	....	89	88	44	4th, Cdn. Div.	Out of Playoffs
1926-27*	44	10	10	2	....	5	14	3	....	15	24	5	....	79	94	35	5th, Cdn. Div.	Out of Playoffs
1925-26	36	11	5	2	....	1	16	1	....	12	21	3	....	92	114	27	6th,	Out of Playoffs
1924-25	30	10	5	0	....	9	6	0	....	19	11	0	....	90	84	38	2nd,	Lost NHL S-Final
1923-24	24	7	5	0	....	3	9	0	....	10	14	0	....	59	85	20	3rd,	Out of Playoffs
1922-23	24	10	1	1	....	3	9	0	....	13	10	1	....	82	88	27	3rd,	Out of Playoffs
1921-22	**24**	**8**	**4**	**0**	....	**5**	**6**	**1**	....	**13**	**10**	**1**	....	**98**	**97**	**27**	**2nd,**	**Won Stanley Cup**
1920-21	24	9	3	0	....	6	6	0	....	15	9	0	....	105	100	30	2nd and 1st***	Lost NHL Final
1919-20**	24	8	4	0	....	4	8	0	....	12	12	0	....	119	106	24	3rd and 2nd***	Out of Playoffs
1918-19	18	5	4	0	....	0	9	0	....	5	13	0	....	64	92	10	3rd and 3rd***	Out of Playoffs
1917-18	**22**	**10**	**1**	**0**	....	**3**	**8**	**0**	....	**13**	**9**	**0**	....	**108**	**109**	**26**	**2nd and 1st***	**Won Stanley Cup**

* Name changed from St. Patricks to Maple Leafs (February, 1927). ** Name changed from Arenas to St. Patricks.
*** Season played in two halves with no combined standing at end.
From 1917-18 through 1925-26, NHL champions played against PCHA/WCHL champions for Stanley Cup.

2006-07 Player Personnel

FORWARDS

	HT	WT	S	Place of Birth	Date	2005-06 Club
ANTROPOV, Nik	6-6	230	L	Ust-Kamenogorsk, USSR	2/18/80	Toronto
BATTAGLIA, Bates	6-2	205	L	Chicago, IL	12/13/75	Toronto (AHL)
BELAK, Wade	6-5	221	R	Saskatoon, Sask.	7/3/76	Toronto
EARL, Robbie	6-0	195	L	Chicago, IL	6/6/85	U. of Wisconsin-Tor (AHL)
FOSTER, Alex	6-1	195	L	Canton, MI	8/26/84	Bowling Green
KILGER, Chad	6-4	224	L	Cornwall, Ont.	11/27/76	Toronto
LEEB, Brad	5-11	187	R	Red Deer, Alta.	8/27/79	Toronto (AHL)
MITCHELL, John	6-1	195	L	Oakville, Ont.	1/22/85	Toronto (AHL)
NEWBURY, Kris	5-10	200	L	Brampton, Ont.	2/19/82	Toronto (AHL)
ONDRUS, Ben	6-0	185	R	Sherwood Park, Alta.	6/25/82	Toronto-Toronto (AHL)
O'NEILL, Jeff	6-1	195	R	Richmond Hill, Ont.	2/23/76	Toronto
PECA, Michael	5-11	190	R	Toronto, Ont.	3/26/74	Edmonton
POHL, John	6-1	196	R	Rochester, MN	6/29/79	Toronto-Toronto (AHL)
PONIKAROVSKY, Alexei	6-4	220	L	Kiev, USSR	4/9/80	Toronto
STAJAN, Matt	6-1	180	L	Mississauga, Ont.	12/19/83	Toronto
STEEN, Alex	6-1	205	L	Winnipeg, Man.	3/1/84	Toronto
SUGLOBOV, Alexander	6-0	200	L	Elektrostal, USSR	1/15/82	N.J.-Alb-Tor-Tor (AHL)
SUNDIN, Mats	6-5	231	L	Bromma, Sweden	2/13/71	Toronto
TLUSTY, Jiri	6-0	196	L	Slany, Czech.	3/16/88	Kladno Jr.-Kladno
TUCKER, Darcy	5-10	178	L	Castor, Alta.	3/15/75	Toronto
WELLWOOD, Kyle	5-10	180	R	Windsor, Ont.	5/16/83	Toronto
WESTRUM, Erik	6-0	204	L	Minneapolis, MN	7/26/79	Minnesota-Houston
WILLIAMS, Jeremy	5-11	184	R	Regina, Sask.	1/26/84	Toronto-Toronto (AHL)

DEFENSEMEN

	HT	WT	S	Place of Birth	Date	2005-06 Club
BELL, Brendan	6-1	205	L	Ottawa, Ont.	3/31/83	Toronto-Toronto (AHL)
BROWN, Brad	6-4	220	R	Baie Verte, Nfld.	12/27/75	Toronto (AHL)
COLAIACOVO, Carlo	6-1	200	L	Toronto, Ont.	1/27/83	Toronto-Toronto (AHL)
GILL, Hal	6-7	250	L	Concord, MA	4/6/75	Boston
HARRISON, Jay	6-4	211	L	Oshawa, Ont.	11/3/82	Toronto-Toronto (AHL)
KABERLE, Tomas	6-1	198	L	Rakovnik, Czech.	3/2/78	Toronto
KRONWALL, Staffan	6-3	209	L	Jarfalla, Sweden	9/10/82	Toronto-Toronto (AHL)
KUBINA, Pavel	6-4	244	R	Celadna, Czech.	4/15/77	Tampa Bay
McCABE, Bryan	6-2	220	L	St. Catharines, Ont.	6/8/75	Toronto
WHITE, Ian	5-10	185	R	Winnipeg, Man.	6/4/84	Toronto-Toronto (AHL)
WOZNIEWSKI, Andy	6-4	220	L	Buffalo Grove, IL	5/25/80	Toronto-Toronto (AHL)

GOALTENDERS

	HT	WT	C	Place of Birth	Date	2005-06 Club
AUBIN, Jean-Sebastien	5-11	180	R	Montreal, Que.	7/19/77	Toronto-Toronto (AHL)
FORD, Todd	6-4	176	L	Calgary, Alta.	5/1/84	Pensacola-Toronto (AHL)
POGGE, Justin	6-3	204	L	Ft. McMurray, Alta.	4/22/86	Calgary (WHL)
RACINE, Jean-Francois	6-3	194	L	St-Hyacinthe, Que.	4/27/82	Toronto (AHL)
RAYCROFT, Andrew	6-0	185	L	Belleville, Ont.	5/4/80	Boston-Providence (AHL)
TELLQVIST, Mikael	5-11	185	L	Sundbyberg, Sweden	9/19/79	Toronto

2005-06 Scoring

*– rookie

Regular Season

Pos	#	Player	Team	GP	G	A	Pts	+/-	PIM	PP	SH	GW	S	%
C	13	Mats Sundin	TOR	70	31	47	78	7	58	16	2	2	220	14.1
D	24	Bryan McCabe	TOR	73	19	49	68	-1	116	13	0	6	207	9.2
D	15	Tomas Kaberle	TOR	82	9	58	67	-1	46	6	0	2	163	5.5
R	16	Darcy Tucker	TOR	74	28	33	61	-12	100	18	0	4	189	14.8
C	41	Jason Allison	TOR	66	17	43	60	-18	76	9	0	2	111	15.3
C	10 *	Alex Steen	TOR	75	18	27	45	-9	42	9	1	3	176	10.2
R	42 *	Kyle Wellwood	TOR	81	11	34	45	0	14	3	0	0	117	9.4
L	23	Alexei Ponikarovsky	TOR	81	21	17	38	15	68	2	4	3	157	13.4
C	92	Jeff O'Neill	TOR	74	19	19	38	-19	64	14	0	6	169	11.2
C	80	Nik Antropov	TOR	57	12	19	31	13	56	2	1	0	113	10.6
L	18	Chad Kilger	TOR	79	17	11	28	-6	63	1	1	2	103	16.5
C	14	Matt Stajan	TOR	80	15	12	27	5	50	3	4	5	83	18.1
C	88	Eric Lindros	TOR	33	11	11	22	-3	43	4	0	2	59	18.6
R	28	Tie Domi	TOR	77	5	11	16	-10	109	0	0	0	67	7.5
D	25	Alexander Khavanov	TOR	64	6	6	12	-11	60	2	1	0	44	13.6
D	22	Luke Richardson	CBJ	44	1	6	7	-18	30	0	0	0	24	4.2
			TOR	21	0	3	3	-1	41	0	0	0	16	0.0
			TOTAL	65	1	9	10	-19	71	0	0	0	40	2.5
C	39	Clarke Wilm	TOR	60	1	7	8	-15	43	0	0	0	50	2.0
D	8	Aki Berg	TOR	75	0	8	8	-5	56	0	0	0	42	0.0
D	45 *	Carlo Colaiacovo	TOR	21	2	5	7	0	17	1	0	0	21	9.5
D	37 *	Ian White	TOR	12	1	5	6	2	10	0	0	0	21	4.8
C	53	John Pohl	TOR	7	3	1	4	2	4	1	0	0	17	17.6
D	3	Wade Belak	TOR	55	0	3	3	-13	109	0	0	0	16	0.0
R	48 *	Jeremy Williams	TOR	1	1	0	1	0	0	0	0	0	1	100.0
R	19 *	Aleksander Suglobov	N.J.	1	1	0	1	-2	0	0	0	0	2	50.0
			TOR	2	0	0	0	-1	0	0	0	0	3	0.0
			TOTAL	3	1	0	1	-3	0	0	0	0	5	20.0
D	43 *	Jay Harrison	TOR	8	0	1	1	5	2	0	0	0	7	0.0
D	56 *	Andy Wozniewski	TOR	13	0	1	1	-8	13	0	0	0	6	0.0
D	44 *	Staffan Kronwall	TOR	34	0	1	1	-3	14	0	0	0	18	0.0
D	36 *	Brendan Bell	TOR	1	0	0	0	0	0	0	0	0	2	0.0
R	46 *	Ben Ondrus	TOR	22	0	0	0	-10	18	0	0	0	17	0.0

Goaltending

No.	Goaltender	GPI	Mins	Avg	W	L	OT	EN	SO	GA	SA	S%	G	A	PIM
30	J-Sebastien Aubin	11	677	2.22	9	0	2	0	1	25	330	.924	0	0	0
32	* Mikael Tellqvist	25	1399	3.13	10	11	2	4	2	73	697	.895	0	0	0
20	Ed Belfour	49	2897	3.29	22	22	4	2	0	159	1476	.892	0	1	12
	Totals	82	4994	3.16	41	33	8	6	3	263	2509	.895			

Coach

MAURICE, PAUL
Coach, Toronto Maple Leafs. Born in Sault Ste. Marie, Ont., January 30, 1967.

The Toronto Maple Leafs named Paul Maurice as the team's new head coach on May 12, 2006. Maurice, who spent eight seasons as head coach of the Hartford Whalers and Carolina Hurricanes, had recently completed his first season in the Leafs organization as head coach of the team's American Hockey League club, the Toronto Marlies.

Maurice, the 26th head coach in Maple Leafs history, became the NHL's youngest head coach at only 28 years of age when he was elevated from assistant coach with the Whalers on November 6, 1995. He followed the club to Carolina where he went on to rank first in franchise history in regular season wins (268), games coached (674), playoff wins (17) and playoff games coached (35). Maurice guided the Hurricanes to four consecutive winning seasons from 1998 to 2002, where they captured Southeast Division titles in 1999 and 2002. His club eliminated the Leafs in six games during the Eastern Conference Final in 2002 to reach the Stanley Cup Final for the first time. He became the sixth-youngest coach in league history to reach the Final.

Maurice played junior hockey with the OHL's Windsor Compuware Spitfires (1984 to 88). He had his career cut short due to an eye injury and began coaching as an assistant with the Detroit Junior Red Wings shortly thereafter. He served six seasons in that capacity before taking over as head coach of the club in the 1993-94 season. Maurice led the team to the 1995 OHL championship and an appearance in the Memorial Cup in Kamloops, British Columbia. That season he finished second in voting to Guelph's Craig Hartsburg for the Matt Leyden Trophy, which is given annually to the OHL's coach of the year.

Coaching Record

Season	Team	Games	Regular Season W	L	O/T	Playoffs Games	W	L
1993-94	Detroit (OHL)	66	42	20	4	17	11	6
1994-95	Detroit (OHL)	66	44	18	4	21	16	5
1995-96	Hartford (NHL)	70	29	33	8	....	....	....
1996-97	Hartford (NHL)	82	32	39	11	....	....	....
1997-98	Carolina (NHL)	82	33	41	8	....	....	....
1998-99	Carolina (NHL)	82	34	30	18	6	2	4
1999-2000	Carolina (NHL)	82	37	35	10	....	....	....
2000-01	Carolina (NHL)	82	38	35	9	6	2	4
2001-02	Carolina (NHL)	82	35	31	16	23	13	10
2002-03	Carolina (NHL)	82	22	49	11	....	....	....
2003-04	Carolina (NHL)	30	8	14	4	....	....	....
2005-06	Toronto (AHL)	80	41	29	10	5	1	4
	NHL Totals	**674**	**268**	**307**	**99**	**35**	**17**	**18**

Coaching History

Dick Carroll, 1917-18, 1918-19; Frank Heffernan and Harry Sproule, 1919-20; Frank Carroll, 1920-21; George O'Donohue, 1921-22; George O'Donohue and Charles Querrie, 1922-23; Charles Querrie, 1923-24; Eddie Powers, 1924-25, 1925-26; Charles Querrie, Mike Rodden and Alex Romeril, 1926-27; Conn Smythe, 1927-28 to 1929-30; Conn Smythe and Art Duncan, 1930-31; Art Duncan and Dick Irvin, 1931-32; Dick Irvin, 1932-33 to 1939-40; Hap Day, 1940-41 to 1949-50; Joe Primeau, 1950-51 to 1952-53; King Clancy, 1953-54 to 1955-56; Howie Meeker, 1956-57; Billy Reay, 1957-58; Billy Reay and Punch Imlach, 1958-59; Punch Imlach, 1959-60 to 1968-69; John McLellan, 1969-70 to 1972-73; Red Kelly, 1973-74 to 1976-77; Roger Neilson, 1977-78, 1978-79; Floyd Smith, Dick Duff and Punch Imlach, 1979-80; Punch Imlach, Joe Crozier and Mike Nykoluk, 1980-81; Mike Nykoluk, 1981-82 to 1983-84; Dan Maloney, 1984-85, 1985-86; John Brophy, 1986-87, 1987-88; John Brophy and George Armstrong, 1988-89; Doug Carpenter, 1989-90; Doug Carpenter and Tom Watt, 1990-91; Tom Watt, 1991-92; Pat Burns, 1992-93 to 1994-95; Pat Burns and Nick Beverley, 1995-96; Mike Murphy, 1996-97, 1997-98; Pat Quinn, 1998-99 to 2005-06; Paul Maurice, 2006-07.

Captains' History

Hap Day, 1927-28 to 1936-37; Charlie Conacher, 1937-38; Red Horner, 1938-39, 1939-40; Syl Apps, 1940-41 to 1942-43; Bob Davidson, 1943-44, 1944-45; Syl Apps, 1945-46 to 1947-48; Ted Kennedy, 1948-49 to 1954-55; Sid Smith, 1955-56; Jimmy Thomson, Ted Kennedy, 1956-57; George Armstrong, 1957-58 to 1968-69; Dave Keon, 1969-70 to 1974-75; Darryl Sittler, 1975-76 to 1980-81; Rick Vaive, 1981-82 to 1985-86; no captain, 1986-87 to 1988-89; Rob Ramage, 1989-90, 1990-91; Wendel Clark, 1991-92 to 1993-94; Doug Gilmour, 1994-95 to 1996-97; Mats Sundin, 1997-98 to date.

Club Records

Team

(Figures in brackets for season records are games played; records for fewest points, wins, ties, losses, goals, goals against are for 70 or more games)

Most Points	103	2003-04 (82)
Most Wins	45	1998-99 (82), 1999-2000 (82), 2003-04 (82)
Most Ties	22	1954-55 (70)
Most Losses	52	1984-85 (80)
Most Goals	337	1989-90 (80)
Most Goals Against	387	1983-84 (80)
Fewest Points	48	1984-85 (80)
Fewest Wins	20	1981-82 (80), 1984-85 (80)
Fewest Ties	4	1989-90 (80)
Fewest Losses	16	1950-51 (70)
Fewest Goals	147	1954-55 (70)
Fewest Goals Against	*131	1953-54 (70)
Longest Winning Streak		
Overall	10	Oct. 7-28/93
Home	9	Nov. 11-Dec. 26/53
Away	7	Three times
Longest Undefeated Streak		
Overall	11	Oct. 15-Nov. 8/50 (8 wins, 3 ties), Jan. 6-Feb. 1/94 (7 wins, 4 ties)
Home	18	Nov. 28/33-Mar. 10/34 (15 wins, 3 ties), Oct. 31/53-Jan. 23/54 (16 wins, 2 ties)
Away	9	Nov. 30/47-Jan. 11/48 (4 wins, 5 ties)
Longest Losing Streak		
Overall	10	Jan. 15-Feb. 8/67
Home	7	Nov. 11-Dec. 5/84
Away	11	Feb. 20-Apr. 1/88
Longest Winless Streak		
Overall	15	Dec. 26/87-Jan. 25/88 (11 losses, 4 ties)
Home	11	Dec. 19/87-Jan. 25/88 (7 losses, 4 ties)
Away	18	Oct. 6/82-Jan. 5/83 (13 losses, 5 ties)
Most Shutouts, Season	13	1953-54 (70)
Most PIM, Season	2,419	1989-90 (80)
Most Goals, Game	14	Mar. 16/57 (NYR 1 at Tor. 14)

Individual

Most Seasons	21	George Armstrong
Most Games	1,187	George Armstrong
Most Goals, Career	389	Darryl Sittler
Most Assists, Career	620	Borje Salming
Most Points, Career	916	Darryl Sittler (389G, 527A)
Most PIM, Career	2,265	Tie Domi
Most Shutouts, Career	62	Turk Broda
Longest Consecutive Games Streak	486	Tim Horton (Feb. 11/61-Feb. 4/68)
Most Goals, Season	54	Rick Vaive (1981-82)
Most Assists, Season	95	Doug Gilmour (1992-93)
Most Points, Season	127	Doug Gilmour (1992-93; 32G, 95A)
Most PIM, Season	365	Tie Domi (1997-98)
Most Points, Defenseman, Season	79	Ian Turnbull (1976-77; 22G, 57A)
Most Points, Center, Season	127	Doug Gilmour (1992-93; 32G, 95A)
Most Points, Right Wing, Season	97	Wilf Paiement (1980-81; 40G, 57A)
Most Points, Left Wing, Season	99	Dave Andreychuk (1993-94; 53G, 46A)
Most Points, Rookie, Season	66	Peter Ihnacak (1982-83; 28G, 38A)
Most Shutouts, Season	13	Harry Lumley (1953-54)
Most Goals, Game	6	Corb Denneny (Jan. 26/21), Darryl Sittler (Feb. 7/76)
Most Assists, Game	6	Babe Pratt (Jan. 8/44), Doug Gilmour (Feb. 13/93)
Most Points, Game	*10	Darryl Sittler (Feb. 7/76; 6G, 4A)

* NHL Record.

Retired Numbers

5	Bill Barilko	1946-1951
6	Ace Bailey	1926-1934

Honored Numbers

1	Turk Broda	1936-43, 45-52
	Johnny Bower	1958-1970
7	King Clancy	1930-1937
	Tim Horton	1949-50, 51-70
9	Charlie Conacher	1929-1938
	Ted Kennedy	1942-55, 56-57
10	Syl Apps	1936-43, 45-48
	George Armstrong	1949-50, 51-71
27	Frank Mahovlich	1956-1968
	Darryl Sittler	1970-1982

All-time Record vs. Other Clubs

Regular Season

	At Home								On Road								Total							
	GP	W	L	T	OL	GF	GA	PTS	GP	W	L	T	OL	GF	GA	PTS	GP	W	L	T	OL	GF	GA	PTS
Anaheim	16	10	2	4	0	53	32	24	11	5	5	1	0	28	34	11	27	15	7	5	0	81	66	35
Atlanta	11	7	2	1	1	42	23	16	11	8	3	0	0	44	17	16	22	15	5	1	1	86	40	32
Boston	303	159	93	51	0	1018	783	369	302	91	161	47	3	794	977	232	605	250	254	98	3	1812	1760	601
Buffalo	71	30	28	12	1	220	242	73	73	20	47	6	0	189	299	46	144	50	75	18	1	409	541	119
Calgary	53	28	17	7	1	202	189	64	62	22	33	5	2	195	240	51	115	50	50	12	3	397	429	115
Carolina	38	15	18	5	0	128	132	35	39	13	19	6	1	125	152	33	77	28	37	11	1	253	284	68
Chicago	315	164	97	54	0	1071	821	382	318	120	156	42	0	831	968	282	633	284	253	96	0	1902	1789	664
Colorado	35	16	15	4	0	118	133	36	30	7	18	5	0	90	116	19	65	23	33	9	0	208	249	55
Columbus	3	2	0	1	0	10	4	5	1	0	0	0	1	3	4	1	4	2	0	1	1	13	8	6
Dallas	102	49	36	17	0	357	321	115	97	36	50	11	0	306	365	83	199	85	86	28	0	663	686	198
Detroit	316	164	105	47	0	1045	846	375	322	108	168	46	0	792	968	262	638	272	273	93	0	1837	1814	637
Edmonton	37	20	15	2	0	154	154	42	44	15	22	6	1	141	180	37	81	35	37	8	1	295	334	79
Florida	17	11	4	2	0	61	40	24	19	9	5	5	0	57	51	23	36	20	9	7	0	118	91	47
Los Angeles	69	35	23	11	0	267	225	81	65	21	34	10	0	191	234	52	134	56	57	21	0	458	459	133
Minnesota	3	3	0	0	0	11	3	6	2	1	1	0	0	4	5	2	5	4	1	0	0	15	8	8
Montreal	337	174	117	45	1	1023	880	394	337	94	200	43	0	838	1179	231	674	268	317	88	1	1861	2059	625
Nashville	6	2	3	1	0	13	18	5	1	0	0	0	1	2	3	1	7	2	3	1	1	15	21	6
New Jersey	50	33	12	5	0	188	141	71	48	16	16	15	1	146	161	48	98	49	28	20	1	334	302	119
NY Islanders	57	30	23	4	0	201	192	64	55	21	30	3	1	160	213	46	112	51	53	7	1	361	405	110
NY Rangers	284	160	85	39	0	978	746	359	285	107	120	56	2	840	882	272	569	267	205	95	2	1818	1628	631
Ottawa	26	11	11	2	2	68	76	26	24	7	14	1	2	63	81	17	50	18	25	3	4	131	157	43
Philadelphia	69	24	30	14	1	216	232	63	69	18	42	8	1	162	258	45	138	42	72	22	2	378	490	108
Phoenix	44	20	22	2	0	160	165	42	39	13	20	6	0	142	161	32	83	33	42	8	0	302	326	74
Pittsburgh	69	34	24	11	0	272	218	79	71	29	36	6	0	232	280	64	140	63	60	17	0	504	498	143
St. Louis	99	58	28	11	2	369	292	129	102	30	58	14	0	283	348	74	201	88	86	25	2	652	640	203
San Jose	19	12	5	2	0	73	52	26	15	7	5	3	0	40	32	17	34	19	10	5	0	113	84	43
Tampa Bay	23	15	7	1	0	86	59	31	22	16	4	1	1	74	47	34	45	31	11	2	1	160	106	65
Vancouver	60	28	21	11	0	219	195	67	65	24	30	11	0	219	229	59	125	52	51	22	0	438	424	126
Washington	50	27	17	6	0	220	172	60	52	18	30	4	0	149	191	40	102	45	47	10	0	369	363	100
Defunct Clubs	232	158	53	21	0	860	515	337	233	84	120	29	0	607	745	197	465	242	173	50	0	1467	1260	534
Totals	**2814**	**1499**	**913**	**393**	**9**	**9703**	**7901**	**3400**	**2814**	**960**	**1447**	**390**	**17**	**7747**	**9420**	**2327**	**5628**	**2459**	**2360**	**783**	**26**	**17450**	**17321**	**5727**

Playoffs

	Series	W	L	GP	W	L	T	GF	GA	Last Mtg.	Rnd.	Result
Boston	13	8	5	62	31	30	1	150	153	1974	QF	L 0-4
Buffalo	1	0	1	5	1	4	0	16	21	1999	CF	L 1-4
Calgary	1	1	0	2	2	0	0	9	5	1979	PRE	W 2-0
Carolina	1	0	1	6	2	4	0	6	10	2002	CF	L 2-4
Chicago	9	6	3	38	22	15	1	111	89	1995	CQF	L 3-4
Dallas	2	0	2	7	1	6	0	26	35	1983	DSF	L 1-3
Detroit	23	12	11	117	58	59	0	311	321	1993	DSF	W 4-3
Los Angeles	3	2	1	12	7	5	0	41	31	1993	CF	L 3-4
Montreal	15	7	8	71	29	42	0	160	215	1979	QF	L 0-4
New Jersey	2	0	2	13	5	8	0	27	37	2001	CSF	L 3-4
NY Islanders	3	2	1	17	8	9	0	42	54	2002	CQF	W 4-3
NY Rangers	8	3	5	35	16	19	0	86	86	1971	QF	L 2-4
Ottawa	4	4	0	24	16	8	0	57	42	2004	CQF	W 4-3
Philadelphia	6	1	5	36	14	22	0	85	119	2004	CSF	L 2-4
Pittsburgh	3	3	0	12	8	4	0	39	27	1999	CSF	W 4-2
St. Louis	5	2	3	31	14	17	0	90	88	1996	CQF	L 2-4
San Jose	1	1	0	7	4	3	0	26	21	1994	CSF	W 4-3
Vancouver	1	0	1	5	1	4	0	9	16	1994	CF	L 1-4
Defunct Clubs	8	6	2	24	12	10	2	59	57			
Totals	**109**	**58**	**51**	**524**	**251**	**269**	**4**	**1350**	**1427**			

Calgary totals include Atlanta Flames, 1972-73 to 1979-80.
Carolina totals include Hartford, 1979-80 to 1996-97.
Colorado totals include Quebec, 1979-80 to 1994-95.
Dallas totals include Minnesota North Stars, 1967-68 to 1992-93.
New Jersey totals include Kansas City, 1974-75 to 1975-76, and Colorado Rockies, 1976-77 to 1981-82.
Phoenix totals include Winnipeg, 1979-80 to 1995-96.

Playoff Results 2006-2001

Year	Round	Opponent	Result	GF	GA
2004	CSF	Philadelphia	L 2-4	13	17
	CQF	Ottawa	W 4-3	14	11
2003	CQF	Philadelphia	L 3-4	16	24
2002	CF	Carolina	L 2-4	6	10
	CSF	Ottawa	W 4-3	16	18
	CQF	NY Islanders	W 4-3	22	21
2001	CSF	New Jersey	L 3-4	18	21
	CQF	Ottawa	W 4-0	10	3

Abbreviations: Round: CF – conference final; **CSF** – conference semi-final; **CQF** – conference quarter-final; **DSF** – division semi-final; **QF** – quarter-final; **PRE** – preliminary round.

2005-06 Results

Oct.	5	Ottawa	2-3†
	8	Montreal	4-5
	10	at Ottawa	5-6†
	11	Philadelphia	4-2
	14	at Atlanta	9-1
	15	at Montreal	3-2
	20	Carolina	5-4*
	22	Philadelphia	2-5
	24	Boston	5-4†
	27	at Boston	1-2
	29	Ottawa	0-8
	31	Florida	2-1
Nov.	3	at Carolina	3-4
	5	Tampa Bay	5-3
	6	at Washington	4-5
	8	Washington	6-4
	11	at Buffalo	2-5
	12	at Montreal	5-4*
	15	NY Rangers	2-1
	17	at Boston	4-1
	19	Atlanta	5-1
	23	Boston	1-5
	25	at Carolina	3-4†
	26	Montreal	4-3*
	28	at Florida	2-1
	30	at Tampa Bay	1-2
Dec.	1	at Atlanta	4-0
	3	San Jose	4-5
	6	Los Angeles	1-2
	10	Dallas	1-2
	12	Anaheim	3-2
	17	at Ottawa	2-8
	19	NY Islanders	9-6
	22	at Boston	1-4
	23	Boston	2-1
	26	New Jersey	2-1
	27	at Pittsburgh	3-2*
	29	Buffalo	4-3†
	31	at New Jersey	6-3
Jan.	2	Pittsburgh	3-2*
	6	at Calgary	0-1
	7	at Edmonton	3-2
	10	at Vancouver	3-4
	14	Phoenix	3-4
	17	at Colorado	3-5
	18	at Minnesota	3-5
	21	at Ottawa	0-7
	23	at Ottawa	3-4
	26	Buffalo	4-8
	28	Montreal	3-4*
	30	at Florida	4-2
	31	at Tampa Bay	2-3†
Feb.	3	at Washington	1-4
	4	New Jersey	4-2
	7	Atlanta	4-1
	10	at NY Rangers	2-4
	11	NY Rangers	2-4
	28	Washington	3-5
Mar.	3	at Buffalo	2-6
	4	Ottawa	2-4
	7	Montreal	5-3
	10	at NY Islanders	1-2†
	11	Tampa Bay	5-1
	14	Boston	5-4†
	16	at Buffalo	1-3
	18	at NY Rangers	2-5
	19	at Pittsburgh	1-0
	21	Carolina	3-2
	23	at Montreal	1-5
	25	at Montreal	2-6
	26	at New Jersey	4-3
	28	at Philadelphia	3-2
Apr.	1	Buffalo	7-0
	3	Buffalo	2-3†
	5	NY Islanders	3-2
	6	at Boston	2-3†
	8	at Philadelphia	5-2
	11	Florida	6-5*
	13	at NY Islanders	4-3*
	15	Ottawa	5-1
	16	at Buffalo	0-6
	18	Pittsburgh	5-3

* – Overtime † – Shootout

Entry Draft
Selections 2006-1992

2006 Pick		2001 Pick		1998 Pick		1995 Pick	
13	Jiri Tlusty	17	Carlo Colaiacovo	10	Nik Antropov	15	Jeff Ware
44	Nikolai Kulemin	39	Karel Pilar	35	Petr Svoboda	54	Ryan Pepperall
99	James Reimer	65	Brendan Bell	69	Jamie Hodson	139	Doug Bonner
111	Korbinian Holzer	82	Jay Harrison	87	Alexei Ponikarovsky	145	Yannick Tremblay
161	Viktor Stalberg	88	Nicolas Corbeil	126	Morgan Warren	171	Marek Melenovsky
166	Tyler Ruegsegger	134	Kyle Wellwood	154	Allan Rourke	197	Mark Murphy
180	Leo Komarov	168	Maxim Kondratiev	181	Jonathan Gagnon	223	Danny Markov
2005		183	Jaroslav Sklenar	215	Dwight Wolfe		
Pick		198	Ivan Kolozvary	228	Michal Travnicek	**1994**	
21	Tuukka Rask	213	Jan Chovan	236	Sergei Rostov	**Pick**	
82	Phil Oreskovic	246	Tomas Mojzis			16	Eric Fichaud
153	Alex Berry	276	Mike Knoepfli	**1997**		48	Sean Haggerty
173	Johan Dahlberg			**Pick**		64	Fredrik Modin
216	Anton Stralman	**2000**		57	Jeff Farkas	126	Mark Deyell
228	Chad Rau	**Pick**		84	Adam Mair	152	Kam White
		24	Brad Boyes	111	Frantisek Mrazek	178	Tommi Rajamaki
2004		51	Kris Vernarsky	138	Eric Gooldy	204	Rob Butler
Pick		70	Mikael Tellqvist	165	Hugo Marchand	256	Sergei Berezin
90	Justin Pogge	90	Jean-Francois Racine	190	Shawn Thornton	282	Doug Nolan
113	Roman Kukumberg	100	Miguel Delisle	194	Russ Bartlett		
157	Dmitri Vorobiev	179	Vadim Sozinov	221	Jonathan Hedstrom	**1993**	
187	Robbie Earl	209	Markus Seikola			**Pick**	
220	Maxim Semenov	223	Lubos Velebny	**1996**		12	Kenny Jonsson
252	Jan Steber	254	Alexander Shinkar	**Pick**		19	Landon Wilson
285	Pierce Norton	265	Jean-Philippe Cote	36	Marek Posmyk	123	Zdenek Nedved
				50	Francis Larivee	149	Paul Vincent
2003		**1999**		66	Mike Lankshear	175	Jeff Andrews
Pick		**Pick**		68	Konstantin Kalmikov	201	David Brumby
57	John Doherty	24	Luca Cereda	86	Jason Sessa	253	Kyle Ferguson
91	Martin Sagat	60	Peter Reynolds	103	Vladimir Antipov	279	Mikhail Lapin
125	Konstantin Volkov	108	Mirko Murovic	110	Peter Cava		
158	John Mitchell	110	Jon Zion	111	Brandon Sugden	**1992**	
220	Jeremy Williams	151	Vaclav Zavoral	140	Dmitri Yakushin	**Pick**	
237	Shaun Landolt	161	Jan Sochor	148	Chris Bogas	8	Brandon Convery
		211	Vladimir Kulikov	151	Lucio DeMartinis	23	Grant Marshall
2002		239	Pierre Hedin	178	Reggie Berg	77	Nikolai Borschevsky
Pick		267	Peter Metcalf	204	Tomas Kaberle	95	Mark Raiter
24	Alexander Steen			230	Jared Hope	101	Janne Gronvall
57	Matt Stajan					106	Chris Deruiter
74	Todd Ford					125	Mikael Hakansson
88	Dominic D'Amour					149	Patrik Augusta
122	David Turon					173	Ryan Vandenbussche
191	Ian White					197	Wayne Clarke
222	Scott May					221	Sergei Simonov
254	Jarkko Immonen					245	Nathan Dempsey
285	Staffan Kronwall						

General Managers' History

Charles Querrie, 1917-18 to 1926-27; Conn Smythe, 1927-28 to 1956-57; Hap Day, 1957-58; Punch Imlach, 1958-59 to 1968-69; Jim Gregory, 1969-70 to 1978-79; Punch Imlach, 1979-80, 1980-81; Punch Imlach and Gerry McNamara, 1981-82; Gerry McNamara, 1982-83 to 1987-88; Gord Stellick, 1988-89; Floyd Smith, 1989-90, 1990-91; Cliff Fletcher, 1991-92 to 1996-97; Ken Dryden, 1997-98, 1998-99; Pat Quinn, 1999-2000 to 2002-03; John Ferguson, 2003-04 to date.

General Manager

FERGUSON, JOHN
General Manager, Toronto Maple Leafs. Born in Montreal, Que., July 7, 1967.

John Ferguson became the 12th person to hold the role of general manager of the Toronto Maple Leafs on August 29, 2003. He is the youngest current general manager in the NHL. In his first year on the job in 2003-04, the Maple Leafs set a club record with 103 points.

Prior to his arrival in Toronto, Ferguson had served as vice-president and director of hockey operations for the St. Louis Blues since February 26, 2001. Prior to that he spent five seasons as assistant general manager with the club. Ferguson was also the president and general manager of the Worcester IceCats, the Blues' top minor league affiliate. He is a former chairman of the American Hockey League's Competition Committee and also served on the league's Legal Affairs Committee.

The son of former Montreal Canadiens great John Ferguson, John Jr. played hockey at Providence College and spent four professional seasons at the American Hockey League level with the Montreal Canadiens and Ottawa Senators organizations from 1989 to 1993. From 1993 to 1996 he was a member of the Ottawa Senators scouting staff as an amateur and professional scout. Before joining the Blues, he served as a player agent.

Club Directory

Air Canada Centre

Toronto Maple Leafs
Air Canada Centre
40 Bay St., Suite 400
Toronto, Ontario M5J 2X2
Phone **416/815-5700**
FAX 416/359-9331
www.mapleleafs.com
Capacity: 18,819

Board of Directors
Lawrence M. Tanenbaum (Chairman of the Board), Robert G. Bertram, James W. Leech, Dean Metcalf, Ivan Fecan, Robert MacLellan, Dale H. Lastman, Richard Peddie

Maple Leaf Sports & Entertainment
Chairman, NHL Governor	Lawrence M. Tanenbaum
President, CEO and Alternate NHL Governor	Richard Peddie
Alternate NHL Governors	John Ferguson, Dale H. Lastman, Dean Metcalf
Executive V.P., Chief Operating Officer	Tom Anselmi
Executive V.P., CFO and Business Development	Ian Clarke
Executive V.P., Venues & Entertainment	Bob Hunter
Senior V.P., General Counsel & Corporate Secretary	Robin Brudner
Senior V.P., Communications & Community Dev.	John Lashway
Senior V.P., People	Mardi Walker
V.P., Corporate Sales & Service	Dave Hopkinson
V.P., Finance	Kevin Nonomura
V.P., Marketing	Beth Robertson
V.P., Operations	Diego Roccasalva
President & General Manager, Toronto Raptors	Bryan Colangelo

Maple Leafs Management
V.P. & General Manager	John Ferguson
Assistant G.M. & Director of Player Personnel	Mike Penny
Head Coach	Paul Maurice
Assistant Coaches	Keith Acton, Dallas Eakins, Randy Ladouceur
Director, Hockey Administration	Jeff Jackson
Player Development Coach	Paul Dennis
Manager, Hockey Admin. & Scouting Coord.	Reid Mitchell
Goaltending Coach	Stephen McKichan
Strength & Conditioning Coordinator	Matt Nichol
Manager, Team Services	Dave Griffiths
Coordinator, Team Services	Brad Lynn
Video Analyst	Chris Dennis
Community Representatives	Wendel Clark, Darryl Sittler, Rick Vaive
Director, Amateur Scouting	Dave Morrison
Professional Scouts	Craig Button, Don Granato, Shawn Simpson
Amateur Scouts	Garth Malarchuk, Mike Palmateer, Clint McConnachie, Allan Power, George Armstrong, Fred Bandel
European Scouts	Thommie Bergman, Peter Ihnacak, Jan Kovac, Nikolai Ladygin, Jari Gronstrand
Travel Coordinator	Mary Speck
Executive Assistant	Ann Clark

Communications and Community Development
Sr. V.P., Communications & Community Dev.	John Lashway
Director, Media Relations	Pat Park
Coordinators, Media Relations	Craig Downey, James Lamont
Manager, Corporate Communications	Rajani Kamath
Director, Community Development	Beverley Deeth
Manager, Community Dev., the Leafs Fund	Jennifer Millard
Manager, Youth Hockey Development	Dave De Freitas
Exec. Asst. to John Lashaway	Rose Politi

Medical and Training Staff
Head Athletic Therapist	Rudy Cantu
Assistant Athletic Therapist	Chris Davie
Equipment Manager	Brian Papineau
Assistant Equipment Managers	Tom Blatchford, Bobby Hastings
Team Doctors	Dr. Noah Forman, Dr. Erin Boynton

Air Canada Centre
Director, Project Development	Dan Arts
Director, Business Operations, MLS	Paul Beirne
Director, Retail Finance	Alldrick Britto
Director, Event Personnel	Brendan Costigan
Director, Media Sales	Bob Doherty
Director, Food and Beverage	Michael Doyle
Director, Sales and Service	Jim Edmands
Director, Labour Relations	Les Fisher
Director, Executive Suite Services	Kristy Fletcher
Director, Business Operations, Toronto Marlies	Chris Gibbs
Director, Security	Pete Gibson
Director, Ticketing	Donna Henderson
Director, Marketing Promotions	Shannon Hosford
Director, Restaurant Operations, Executive Chef	Brad Long
Director, Building Operations & Technical Services	Colin Morrell
Director, Corporate Sales	Tom Pistore
Director, Information Technology	Sasha Puric
Director, Finance	Suzanne Scott
Director, Live Entertainment	Patti-Anne Tarlton
Director, Special Projects	Eric Wong
Director, Consumer Products	Caroline Wright
Legal Counsel	Peter Miller

Television and Radio
AM 640 Toronto Radio, Play-By-Play	Joe Bowen, Dennis Beyak (mid-weeks)
AM 640 Toronto Radio, Analyst	Jim Ralph
Television Play-By-Play	Joe Bowen (mid-weeks)
Television Analyst	Harry Neale
Director, Programming and Production, Leafs TV	Frank Hayward
Senior Broadcast Producer, Leafs TV	Mark Askin
Game Director, Leafs TV	Jacques Primeau
Director, Broadcast & Live Game Prod., Leafs TV	Liana Bristol
Senior Producer, Leafs TV	Chris Clarke
Producers, Leafs TV	Mike Brock, Brian Bileski
Jr. Producers, Leafs TV	Jamie Arnold, Filomena Lowry
Executive Assistant, Leafs TV	Karyn Savoia
Talent, Leafs TV	Joe Bowen, Brian Duff, Paul Hendrick, Greg Millen, Harry Neale, Rick Vaive

Vancouver Canucks

2005-06 Results: 42w-32L-4oTL-4soL 92pts.
Fourth, Northwest Division

2006-07 Schedule

Oct.	Thu.	5	at Detroit	Fri.	5	Edmonton
	Fri.	6	at Columbus	Sun.	7	Florida
	Sun.	8	at Colorado	Thu.	11	Minnesota
	Tue.	10	at Minnesota	Sat.	13	at Toronto
	Fri.	13	San Jose	Tue.	16	at Montreal
	Mon.	16	Edmonton	Thu.	18	at Ottawa
	Tue.	17	at Edmonton	Fri.	19	at Buffalo
	Fri.	20	at St. Louis	Fri.	26	Los Angeles
	Sat.	21	at Nashville	Sun.	28	San Jose
	Mon.	23	at Dallas	Tue.	30	Columbus
	Wed.	25	at Chicago	Feb. Thu.	1	Edmonton
	Fri.	27	Washington	Sat.	3	at Calgary
	Tue.	31	Nashville	Tue.	6	at Edmonton
Nov.	Thu.	2	at Minnesota	Wed.	7	Chicago
	Sat.	4	at Colorado	Sat.	10	Atlanta
	Mon.	6	Dallas	Wed.	14	at Minnesota
	Thu.	9	Anaheim	Fri.	16	at Chicago
	Sat.	11	Calgary	Sun.	18	Colorado
	Tue.	14	Detroit	Tue.	20	at Anaheim
	Fri.	17	St. Louis	Thu.	22	at Los Angeles
	Sun.	19	Chicago	Sun.	25	at Dallas*
	Wed.	22	at Detroit	Tue.	27	at St. Louis
	Thu.	23	at Nashville	Mar. Thu.	1	Phoenix
	Sat.	25	at Colorado	Sun.	4	Minnesota
	Tue.	28	Columbus	Tue.	6	Tampa Bay
	Thu.	30	Anaheim	Thu.	8	at Phoenix
Dec.	Sat.	2	Colorado	Fri.	9	at San Jose
	Mon.	4	Edmonton	Sun.	11	at Anaheim*
	Fri.	8	Carolina	Tue.	13	Minnesota
	Sat.	9	at Calgary	Thu.	15	St. Louis
	Tue.	12	Phoenix	Sat.	17	Detroit
	Thu.	14	Calgary	Mon.	19	at Edmonton
	Sat.	16	Minnesota	Wed.	21	Nashville
	Tue.	19	at Minnesota	Sun.	25	Colorado
	Thu.	21	at Boston	Tue.	27	at Colorado
	Fri.	22	at Columbus	Thu.	29	at Los Angeles
	Tue.	26	at Calgary	Sat.	31	Calgary
	Wed.	27	Calgary	Apr. Tue.	3	Los Angeles
	Sat.	30	at Edmonton	Thu.	5	Colorado
Jan.	Tue.	2	at Calgary	Sat.	7	at San Jose*
	Wed.	3	Dallas	Sun.	8	at Phoenix*

*Denotes afternoon game.

Franchise date: May 22, 1970

WESTERN CONFERENCE

NORTHWEST DIVISION

37th NHL Season

The Sedin twins both had big years in 2005-06, finishing 1-2 on the team in assists. Henrik (left) led the way with 57 helpers and 75 points. Daniel (right) had 49 assist and 71 points.

Year-by-Year Record

Season	GP	Home W	L	T	OL	Road W	L	T	OL	Overall W	L	T	OL	GF	GA	Pts	Finished	Playoff Result
2005-06	82	25	10	....	6	17	22	....	2	42	32	....	8	256	255	92	4th, Northwest Div.	Out of Playoffs
2004-05	....																	
2003-04	82	21	13	7	0	22	11	3	5	43	24	10	5	235	194	101	1st, Northwest Div.	Lost Conf. Quarter-Final
2002-03	82	22	13	6	0	23	10	7	1	45	23	13	1	264	208	104	2nd, Northwest Div.	Lost Conf. Semi-Final
2001-02	82	23	11	5	2	19	19	2	1	42	30	7	3	254	211	94	2nd, Northwest Div.	Lost Conf. Quarter-Final
2000-01	82	21	12	5	3	15	16	6	4	36	28	11	7	239	238	90	3rd, Northwest Div.	Lost Conf. Quarter-Final
1999-2000	82	16	14	5	6	14	15	10	2	30	29	15	8	227	237	83	3rd, Northwest Div.	Out of Playoffs
1998-99	82	14	21	6	....	9	26	6	....	23	47	12	....	192	258	58	4th, Northwest Div.	Out of Playoffs
1997-98	82	15	22	4	....	10	21	10	....	25	43	14	....	224	273	64	7th, Pacific Div.	Out of Playoffs
1996-97	82	20	17	4	....	15	23	3	....	35	40	7	....	257	273	77	4th, Pacific Div.	Out of Playoffs
1995-96	82	15	19	7	....	17	16	8	....	32	35	15	....	278	278	79	3rd, Pacific Div.	Lost Conf. Quarter-Final
1994-95	48	10	8	6	....	8	10	6	....	18	18	12	....	153	148	48	2nd, Pacific Div.	Lost Conf. Semi-Final
1993-94	84	20	19	3	....	21	21	0	....	41	40	3	....	279	276	85	2nd, Pacific Div.	Lost Final
1992-93	84	27	11	4	....	19	18	5	....	46	29	9	....	346	278	101	1st, Smythe Div.	Lost Div. Final
1991-92	80	23	10	7	....	19	16	5	....	42	26	12	....	285	250	96	1st, Smythe Div.	Lost Div. Final
1990-91	80	18	17	5	....	10	26	4	....	28	43	9	....	243	315	65	4th, Smythe Div.	Lost Div. Semi-Final
1989-90	80	13	16	11	....	12	25	3	....	25	41	14	....	245	306	64	5th, Smythe Div.	Out of Playoffs
1988-89	80	19	15	6	....	14	24	2	....	33	39	8	....	251	253	74	4th, Smythe Div.	Lost Div. Semi-Final
1987-88	80	15	20	5	....	10	26	4	....	25	46	9	....	272	320	59	5th, Smythe Div.	Out of Playoffs
1986-87	80	17	19	4	....	12	24	4	....	29	43	8	....	282	314	66	5th, Smythe Div.	Out of Playoffs
1985-86	80	17	18	5	....	6	26	8	....	23	44	13	....	282	333	59	4th, Smythe Div.	Lost Div. Semi-Final
1984-85	80	15	21	4	....	10	25	5	....	25	46	9	....	284	401	59	5th, Smythe Div.	Out of Playoffs
1983-84	80	20	16	4	....	12	23	5	....	32	39	9	....	306	322	73	3rd, Smythe Div.	Lost Div. Semi-Final
1982-83	80	20	12	8	....	10	23	7	....	30	35	15	....	303	309	75	3rd, Smythe Div.	Lost Div. Semi-Final
1981-82	80	20	8	12	....	10	25	5	....	30	33	17	....	290	286	77	2nd, Smythe Div.	Lost Final
1980-81	80	17	12	11	....	11	20	9	....	28	32	20	....	289	301	76	3rd, Smythe Div.	Lost Prelim. Round
1979-80	80	14	17	9	....	13	20	7	....	27	37	16	....	256	281	70	3rd, Smythe Div.	Lost Prelim. Round
1978-79	80	15	18	7	....	10	24	6	....	25	42	13	....	217	291	63	2nd, Smythe Div.	Lost Prelim. Round
1977-78	80	13	15	12	....	7	28	5	....	20	43	17	....	239	320	57	3rd, Smythe Div.	Out of Playoffs
1976-77	80	13	21	6	....	12	21	7	....	25	42	13	....	235	294	63	4th, Smythe Div.	Out of Playoffs
1975-76	80	22	11	7	....	11	21	8	....	33	32	15	....	271	272	81	2nd, Smythe Div.	Lost Prelim. Round
1974-75	80	23	12	5	....	15	20	5	....	38	32	10	....	271	254	86	1st, Smythe Div.	Lost Quarter-Final
1973-74	78	14	18	7	....	10	25	4	....	24	43	11	....	224	296	59	7th, East Div.	Out of Playoffs
1972-73	78	14	18	4	....	5	29	5	....	22	47	9	....	233	339	53	7th, East Div.	Out of Playoffs
1971-72	78	14	20	5	....	6	30	3	....	20	50	8	....	203	297	48	7th, East Div.	Out of Playoffs
1970-71	78	17	18	4	....	7	28	4	....	24	46	8	....	229	296	56	6th, East Div.	Out of Playoffs

2006-07 Player Personnel

FORWARDS

	HT	WT	S	Place of Birth	Date	2005-06 Club
BERNIER, Marc-Andre	6-4	198	R	Laval, Que.	2/5/85	Manitoba-Columbia
BOUCK, Tyler	6-0	196	L	Camrose, Alta.	1/13/80	Vancouver-Manitoba
BROWN, Mike	6-0	210	R	Northbrook, IL	6/24/85	Manitoba
BULIS, Jan	6-1	208	L	Pardubice, Czech.	3/18/78	Montreal
BURROWS, Alexandre	6-1	190	L	Pincourt, Que.	4/11/81	Vancouver-Manitoba
CHOUINARD, Marc	6-5	218	R	Charlesbourg, Que.	5/6/77	Minnesota
COOKE, Matt	6-0	205	L	Belleville, Ont.	9/7/78	Vancouver
GOREN, Lee	6-3	205	R	Winnipeg, Man.	12/26/77	Vancouver-Manitoba
GREEN, Josh	6-3	215	L	Camrose, Alta.	11/16/77	Vancouver-Manitoba
GUENETTE, Francois-Pierre	6-1	183	R	Laval, Que.	1/18/84	Columbia
HANSEN, Jannik	6-0	176	R	Herlev, Denmark	3/15/86	Portland (WHL)
KESLER, Ryan	6-2	195	R	Detroit, MI	8/31/84	Vancouver
KING, Jason	6-1	195	L	Corner Brook, Nfld.	9/14/81	Manitoba
MORAN, Brad	5-11	187	L	Abbotsford, B.C.	3/20/79	Langnau
MORRISON, Brendan	5-11	190	L	Pitt Meadows, B.C.	8/15/75	Vancouver
NASLUND, Markus	5-11	195	L	Ornskoldsvik, Sweden	7/30/73	Vancouver
PYATT, Taylor	6-4	227	L	Thunder Bay, Ont.	8/19/81	Buffalo
REID, Brandon	5-8	185	R	Kirkland, Que.	3/9/81	Rapperswil
RYPIEN, Rick	5-11	170	L	Coleman, Alta	5/16/84	Vancouver-Manitoba
SANTALA, Tommi	6-3	210	R	Helsinki, Finland	6/27/79	Jokerit
SCHULTZ, Jesse	6-0	192	R	Strasbourg, Sask.	9/28/82	Manitoba
SEDIN, Daniel	6-1	200	L	Ornskoldsvik, Sweden	9/26/80	Vancouver
SEDIN, Henrik	6-2	200	L	Ornskoldsvik, Sweden	9/26/80	Vancouver
SMITH, Nathan	6-2	192	L	Edmonton, Alta.	2/9/82	Vancouver-Manitoba

DEFENSEMEN

	HT	WT	S	Place of Birth	Date	2005-06 Club
BIEKSA, Kevin	6-1	195	R	Grimsby, Ont.	6/16/81	Vancouver-Manitoba
BOURDON, Luc	6-2	199	L	Shippagan, N.B.	2/16/87	Val-d'Or-Moncton
EDLER, Alexander	6-3	194	L	Stockholm, Sweden	4/21/86	Kelowna
HESHKA, Shaun	6-1	195	R	Melville, Sask.	7/30/85	Everett
KRAJICEK, Lukas	6-2	185	L	Prostejov, Czech.	3/11/83	Florida
McIVER, Nathan	6-2	195	L	Kinkora, P.E.I.	1/6/85	Manitoba
MITCHELL, Willie	6-3	205	L	Port McNeill, B.C.	4/23/77	Minnesota-Dallas
OHLUND, Mattias	6-2	220	L	Pitea, Sweden	9/9/76	Vancouver
RAHIMI, Daniel	6-3	213	L	Umea, Sweden	4/28/87	Bjorkloven Jr.-Bjorkloven
RULLIER, Joe	6-3	230	R	Montreal, Que.	1/28/80	Hartford-Manchester
RYAN, Prestin	6-0	190	L	Arcola, Sask.	6/29/80	Vancouver-Manitoba
SALO, Sami	6-3	215	R	Turku, Finland	9/2/74	Vancouver
TREMBLAY, Yannick	6-2	200	R	Pointe-aux-Trembles, Que.	11/15/75	Mannheim

GOALTENDERS

	HT	WT	C	Place of Birth	Date	2005-06 Club
FLAHERTY, Wade	6-0	190	L	Terrace, B.C.	1/11/68	Manitoba
LUONGO, Roberto	6-3	205	L	Montreal, Que.	4/4/79	Florida

2005-06 Scoring
*– rookie

Regular Season

Pos	#	Player	Team	GP	G	A	Pts	+/-	PIM	PP	SH	GW	S	%
L	19	Markus Naslund	VAN	81	32	47	79	–19	66	13	0	2	264	12.1
C	33	Henrik Sedin	VAN	82	18	57	75	11	56	5	1	0	113	15.9
R	44	Todd Bertuzzi	VAN	82	25	46	71	–17	120	12	0	3	200	12.5
L	22	Daniel Sedin	VAN	82	22	49	71	7	34	11	0	4	204	10.8
C	7	Brendan Morrison	VAN	82	19	37	56	–1	84	8	0	5	156	12.2
R	77	Anson Carter	VAN	81	33	22	55	–1	41	15	0	7	146	22.6
D	4	Nolan Baumgartner	VAN	70	5	29	34	11	30	4	1	1	73	6.8
D	2	Mattias Ohlund	VAN	78	13	20	33	–6	92	8	1	2	183	7.1
D	6	Sami Salo	VAN	59	10	23	33	9	38	9	0	2	140	7.1
D	55	Ed Jovanovski	VAN	44	8	25	33	–8	58	6	0	2	87	9.2
C	20	Ryan Kesler	VAN	82	10	13	23	1	79	1	0	2	119	8.4
D	3	Keith Carney	ANA	61	2	16	18	13	48	1	0	1	71	2.8
			VAN	18	0	2	2	–5	14	0	0	0	14	0.0
			TOTAL	79	2	18	20	8	62	1	0	1	85	2.4
C	24	Matt Cooke	VAN	45	8	10	18	–8	71	0	0	2	67	11.9
R	18	Richard Park	VAN	60	8	10	18	–2	29	0	1	2	97	8.2
L	37	Jarkko Ruutu	VAN	82	10	7	17	1	142	2	0	2	85	11.8
D	5	Bryan Allen	VAN	77	7	10	17	4	115	1	0	0	88	8.0
D	8	Eric Weinrich	STL	59	1	16	17	–10	44	1	0	0	56	1.8
			VAN	16	0	0	0	–13	8	0	0	0	12	0.0
			TOTAL	75	1	16	17	–23	52	1	0	0	68	1.5
C	16	Trevor Linden	VAN	82	7	9	16	3	55	1	1	0	55	12.7
L	14	* Alexandre Burrows	VAN	43	7	5	12	5	61	0	0	1	49	14.3
D	23	Sean Brown	N.J.	35	1	11	12	–14	27	0	0	0	37	2.7
			VAN	12	0	0	0	–3	8	0	0	0	12	0.0
			TOTAL	47	1	11	12	–17	35	0	0	0	49	2.0
L	36	Josh Green	VAN	33	4	2	6	2	14	0	0	0	35	11.4
D	25	* Kevin Bieksa	VAN	39	0	6	6	–1	77	0	0	0	38	0.0
R	27	Lee Goren	VAN	28	1	2	3	–6	30	0	0	1	37	2.7
D	28	Wade Brookbank	VAN	32	1	2	3	3	81	0	0	0	10	10.0
R	21	Tyler Bouck	VAN	12	1	1	2	1	21	0	0	0	6	16.7
C	15	Rick Rypien	VAN	5	1	0	1	1	4	0	0	0	6	16.7
R	8	* Jozef Balej	VAN	1	0	1	1	1	2	0	0	0	3	0.0
D	45	* Tomas Mojzis	VAN	7	0	1	1	2	12	0	0	0	7	0.0
C	29	* Nathan Smith	VAN	1	0	0	0	0	0	0	0	0	0	0.0
D	41	Prestin Ryan	VAN	1	0	0	0	–1	2	0	0	0	0	0.0
D	52	Sven Butenschon	VAN	8	0	0	0	0	10	0	0	0	4	0.0

Goaltending

No.	Goaltender	GPI	Mins	Avg	W	L	OT	EN	SO	GA	SA	S%	G	A	PIM
34	* Rob McVicar	1	3	0.00	0	0	0	0	0	0	0	.000	0	0	0
35	Alex Auld	67	3859	2.94	33	26	6	3	0	189	1938	.902	0	2	4
39	Dan Cloutier	13	681	3.17	8	3	1	0	0	36	334	.892	0	0	4
1	* Maxime Ouellet	4	222	3.24	0	1	0	1	0	12	113	.894	0	0	2
31	Mika Noronen	4	170	3.53	1	1	0	0	0	10	77	.870	0	0	0
	Totals	82	4978	3.03	42	32	8	4	0	251	2466	.898			

Coach

VIGNEAULT, ALAIN
Coach, Vancouver Canucks. Born in Quebec City, Que., May 14, 1961.

On June 20, 2006, Alain Vigneault became the 16th head coach in Vancouver Canucks history. He previously served in the NHL as head coach of the Montreal Canadiens from 1997 to 2001, becoming the organization's second youngest coach in club history at the age of 36. Vigneault was nominated for the Jack Adams Award as NHL coach of the year following the 1999-2000 season.

Vigneault joined the Canucks from the club's AHL affiliate, the Manitoba Moose, where he led the team to within one game of the conference finals in 2005-06. Prior to joining the Moose, Vigneault spent many years as a head coach in the QMJHL with Trois-Rivieres, Hull, Beauport and PEI. In 1988, Vigneault led the Hull Olympiques into the Memorial Cup and was subsequently named CHL coach of the year. He has also been honoured as coach of the QMJHL's Second All-Star team on three separate occasions. Vigneault has also achieved success on the international stage. He served as an assistant coach with Canada's national junior team in 1989 and 1991, winning a gold medal at the 1991 World Junior Championships in Saskatoon.

As a player, Vigneault was a member of the St. Louis Blues from 1981 to 1983. Drafted by the Blues in the eighth round, 167th overall, in the 1981 Entry Draft, the defenceman recorded two goals, five assists and 82 penalty minutes in his NHL career. Vigneault went on to serve as a scout for the Blues for two seasons and as an assistant coach for the Ottawa Senators from 1992 to 1996.

Coaching Record

Season	Team	Games	Regular Season W	L	T	Playoffs Games	W	L
1986-87	Trois-Rivières (QMJHL)	65	26	37	2	....	....	....
1987-88	Hull (QMJHL)	70	43	23	4	19	12	7
1988-89	Hull (QMJHL)	66	36	25	5	9	5	4
1989-90	Hull (QMJHL)	70	36	29	5	11	4	7
1990-91	Hull (QMJHL)	65	33	25	7	6	2	4
1991-92	Hull (QMJHL)	68	40	23	5	6	2	4
1995-96	Beauport (QMJHL)	31	19	7	5	20	13	7
1996-97	Beauport (QMJHL)	70	24	44	2	4	1	3
1997-98	Montreal (NHL)	82	37	32	13	10	4	6
1998-99	Montreal (NHL)	82	32	39	11	....	....	....
1999-2000	Montreal (NHL)	82	35	38	9	....	....	....
2000-01	Montreal (NHL)	20	5	13	2	....	....	....
2003-04	PEI (QMJHL)	70	40	25	5	11	6	5
2004-05	PEI (QMJHL)	70	24	39	7	....	....	....
2005-06	Manitoba (AHL)	80	44	24	12	13	7	6
	NHL Totals	**266**	**109**	**122**	**35**	**10**	**4**	**6**

The Canucks acquired goaltender Roberto Luongo in a blockbuster deal with the Florida Panthers on June 23, 2006.

Coaching History

Hal Laycoe, 1970-71, 1971-72; Vic Stasiuk, 1972-73; Bill McCreary and Phil Maloney, 1973-74; Phil Maloney, 1974-75, 1975-76; Phil Maloney and Orland Kurtenbach, 1976-77; Orland Kurtenbach, 1977-78; Harry Neale, 1978-79 to 1980-81; Harry Neale and Roger Neilson, 1981-82; Roger Neilson, 1982-83; Roger Neilson and Harry Neale, 1983-84; Bill Laforge and Harry Neale, 1984-85; Tom Watt, 1985-86, 1986-87; Bob McCammon, 1987-88 to 1989-90; Bob McCammon and Pat Quinn, 1990-91; Pat Quinn, 1991-92 to 1993-94; Rick Ley, 1994-95; Rick Ley and Pat Quinn, 1995-96; Tom Renney, 1996-97; Tom Renney and Mike Keenan, 1997-98; Mike Keenan and Marc Crawford, 1998-99; Marc Crawford, 1999-2000 to 2005-06; Alain Vigneault, 2006-07.

Club Records

Team

(Figures in brackets for season records are games played; records for fewest points, wins, ties, losses, goals, goals against are for 70 or more games)

Most Points	**104**	2002-03 (82)
Most Wins	**46**	1992-93 (84)
Most Ties	**20**	1980-81 (80)
Most Losses	**50**	1971-72 (78)
Most Goals	**346**	1992-93 (84)
Most Goals Against	**401**	1984-85 (80)
Fewest Points	**48**	1971-72 (78)
Fewest Wins	**20**	1971-72 (78), 1977-78 (80)
Fewest Ties	**3**	1993-94 (84)
Fewest Losses	**24**	2002-03 (82)
Fewest Goals	**192**	1998-99 (82)
Fewest Goals Against	**194**	2003-04 (82)
Longest Winning Streak		
Overall	**10**	Nov. 9-30/02
Home	**9**	Nov. 6-Dec. 9/92
Away	**8**	Dec. 20/03-Jan. 13/04
Longest Undefeated Streak		
Overall	**14**	Jan.26-Feb. 25/03 (10 wins, 4 ties)
Home	**18**	Nov. 4/92-Jan. 16/93 (16 wins, 2 ties)
Away	**9**	Feb. 4-Mar. 3/03 (6 wins, 3 ties)
Longest Losing Streak		
Overall	**10**	Oct. 23-Nov. 11/97
Home	**6**	Dec. 18/70-Jan. 20/71
Away	**12**	Nov. 28/81-Feb. 6/82
Longest Winless Streak		
Overall	**13**	Nov. 9-Dec. 7/73 (10 losses, 3 ties)
Home	**11**	Dec. 18/70-Feb. 6/71 (10 losses, 1 tie)
Away	**20**	Jan. 2-Apr. 2/86 (14 losses, 6 ties)
Most Shutouts, Season	**8**	1974-75 (80), 2001-02 (82)
Most PIM, Season	**2,326**	1992-93 (84)
Most Goals, Game	**11**	Mar. 28/71 (Cal. 5 at Van. 11), Nov. 25/86 (L.A. 5 at Van. 11), Mar. 1/92 (Cgy. 0 at Van. 11)

Individual

Most Seasons	**14**	Trevor Linden
Most Games	**1,001**	Trevor Linden
Most Goals, Career	**299**	Trevor Linden
Most Assists, Career	**411**	Stan Smyl
Most Points, Career	**696**	Trevor Linden (299G, 397A)
Most PIM, Career	**2,127**	Gino Odjick
Most Shutouts, Career	**20**	Kirk McLean
Longest Consecutive Games Streak	**482**	Trevor Linden (Oct. 4/90-Dec. 7/96)
Most Goals, Season	**60**	Pavel Bure (1992-93, 1993-94)
Most Assists, Season	**62**	André Boudrias (1974-75)
Most Points, Season	**110**	Pavel Bure (1992-93; 60G, 50A)
Most PIM, Season	**372**	Donald Brashear (1997-98)
Most Points, Defenseman, Season	**63**	Doug Lidster (1986-87; 12G, 51A)
Most Points, Center, Season	**91**	Patrik Sundstrom (1983-84; 38G, 53A)
Most Points, Right Wing, Season	**110**	Pavel Bure (1992-93; 60G, 50A)
Most Points, Left Wing, Season	**104**	Markus Naslund (2002-03; 48G, 56A)
Most Points, Rookie, Season	**60**	Ivan Hlinka (1981-82; 23G, 37A), Pavel Bure (1991-92; 34G, 26A)
Most Shutouts, Season	**7**	Dan Cloutier (2001-02)
Most Goals, Game	**4**	Twelve times
Most Assists, Game	**6**	Patrik Sundstrom (Feb. 29/84)
Most Points, Game	**7**	Patrik Sundstrom (Feb. 29/84; 1G, 6A)

Retired Numbers

12	Stan Smyl	1978-1991

General Managers' History

Bud Poile, 1970-71 to 1972-73; Hal Laycoe, 1973-74; Phil Maloney, 1974-75 to 1976-77; Jake Milford, 1977-78 to 1981-82; Harry Neale, 1982-83 to 1984-85; Jack Gordon, 1985-86, 1986-87; Pat Quinn, 1987-88 to 1997-98; Brian Burke, 1998-99 to 2003-04; David Nonis, 2004-05 to date.

Captains' History

Orland Kurtenbach, 1970-71 to 1973-74; no captain, 1974-75; Andre Boudrias, 1975-76; Chris Oddleifson, 1976-77; Don Lever, 1977-78; Don Lever and Kevin McCarthy, 1978-79; Kevin McCarthy, 1979-80 to 1981-82; Stan Smyl, 1982-83 to 1989-90; Dan Quinn, Doug Lidster and Trevor Linden, 1990-91; Trevor Linden, 1991-92 to 1996-97; Mark Messier, 1997-98 to 1999-2000; Markus Naslund, 2000-01 to date.

All-time Record vs. Other Clubs

Regular Season

	At Home								On Road								Total							
	GP	W	L	T	OL	GF	GA	PTS	GP	W	L	T	OL	GF	GA	PTS	GP	W	L	T	OL	GF	GA	PTS
Anaheim	28	16	10	2	0	94	66	34	27	12	8	7	0	79	67	31	55	28	18	9	0	173	133	65
Atlanta	3	1	1	1	0	10	5	3	3	2	1	0	0	12	11	4	6	3	2	1	0	22	16	7
Boston	52	17	26	8	1	171	211	43	52	7	37	7	1	124	217	22	104	24	63	15	2	295	428	65
Buffalo	53	26	16	11	0	197	163	63	52	18	26	8	0	152	186	44	105	44	42	19	0	349	349	107
Calgary	103	38	45	18	2	348	340	96	102	28	59	15	0	291	399	71	205	66	104	33	2	639	739	167
Carolina	30	14	10	6	0	105	81	34	29	12	12	5	0	100	94	29	59	26	22	11	0	205	175	63
Chicago	74	37	22	15	0	227	213	89	73	19	45	7	2	172	273	47	147	56	67	22	2	399	486	136
Colorado	51	20	23	7	1	171	195	48	51	18	23	8	2	144	176	46	102	38	46	15	3	315	371	94
Columbus	10	8	2	0	0	46	30	16	10	5	2	2	1	37	25	13	20	13	4	2	1	83	55	29
Dallas	73	32	30	10	1	258	222	75	73	22	39	12	0	214	266	56	146	54	69	22	1	472	488	131
Detroit	67	30	27	10	0	242	218	70	68	18	41	8	1	193	279	45	135	48	68	18	1	435	497	115
Edmonton	86	33	39	12	2	311	338	80	85	26	49	7	3	267	369	62	171	59	88	19	5	578	707	142
Florida	9	3	1	5	0	25	19	11	8	4	3	1	0	27	21	9	17	7	4	6	0	52	40	20
Los Angeles	99	51	31	16	1	375	308	119	101	32	52	16	1	314	399	81	200	83	83	32	2	689	707	200
Minnesota	14	7	2	3	2	36	32	19	15	6	7	2	0	38	41	14	29	13	9	5	2	74	73	33
Montreal	56	15	33	8	0	152	204	38	53	10	38	5	0	135	244	25	109	25	71	13	0	287	448	63
Nashville	14	10	2	1	1	54	34	22	15	7	7	1	0	41	43	15	29	17	9	2	1	95	77	37
New Jersey	47	27	9	11	0	175	130	65	50	23	21	6	0	159	154	52	97	50	30	17	0	334	284	117
NY Islanders	47	23	21	3	0	155	153	49	48	12	25	10	1	137	175	35	95	35	46	13	1	292	328	84
NY Rangers	51	15	33	3	0	163	204	33	55	12	38	5	0	142	239	29	106	27	71	8	0	305	443	62
Ottawa	12	6	5	1	0	36	28	13	10	4	5	1	0	24	24	9	22	10	10	2	0	60	52	22
Philadelphia	51	10	28	12	1	144	203	33	55	17	36	1	1	164	238	36	106	27	64	13	2	308	441	69
Phoenix	74	45	18	10	1	278	205	101	71	27	33	10	1	253	262	65	145	72	51	20	2	531	467	166
Pittsburgh	50	23	23	4	0	180	187	50	51	11	33	7	0	175	229	29	101	34	56	11	0	355	416	79
St. Louis	74	30	35	9	0	217	238	69	73	21	43	9	0	206	273	51	147	51	78	18	0	423	511	120
San Jose	34	19	10	4	1	122	91	43	36	17	14	5	0	112	104	39	70	36	24	9	1	234	195	82
Tampa Bay	9	7	0	2	0	40	17	16	9	6	3	0	0	37	31	12	18	13	3	2	0	77	48	28
Toronto	65	30	22	11	2	229	219	73	60	21	28	11	0	195	219	53	125	51	50	22	2	424	438	126
Washington	39	18	15	5	1	136	123	42	40	14	21	4	1	120	132	33	79	32	36	9	2	256	255	75
Defunct Clubs	19	14	3	2	0	82	48	30	19	10	8	1	0	71	68	21	38	24	11	3	0	153	116	51
Totals	**1394**	**625**	**542**	**210**	**17**	**4779**	**4525**	**1477**	**1394**	**441**	**757**	**181**	**15**	**4135**	**5258**	**1078**	**2788**	**1066**	**1299**	**391**	**32**	**8914**	**9783**	**2555**

Playoffs

	Series	W	L	GP	W	L	T	GF	GA	Last Mtg.	Rnd.	Result
Buffalo	2	0	2	7	1	6	0	14	28	1981	PRE	L 0-3
Calgary	6	2	4	32	15	17	0	96	101	2004	CQF	L 3-4
Chicago	2	1	1	9	4	5	0	24	24	1995	CSF	L 0-4
Colorado	2	0	2	10	2	8	0	26	40	2001	CQF	L 0-4
Dallas	1	1	0	5	4	1	0	18	11	1994	CSF	W 4-1
Detroit	1	0	1	6	2	4	0	16	22	2002	CQF	L 2-4
Edmonton	2	0	2	9	2	7	0	20	35	1992	DF	L 2-4
Los Angeles	3	1	2	17	8	9	0	60	66	1993	DF	L 2-4
Minnesota	1	0	1	7	3	4	0	17	26	2003	CSF	L 3-4
Montreal	1	0	1	5	1	4	0	9	20	1975	QF	L 1-4
NY Islanders	2	0	2	6	0	6	0	14	26	1982	F	L 0-4
NY Rangers	1	0	1	7	3	4	0	19	21	1994	F	L 3-4
Philadelphia	1	0	1	3	1	2	0	9	15	1979	PRE	L 1-2
Phoenix	2	2	0	13	8	5	0	50	34	1993	DSF	W 4-2
St. Louis	2	2	0	14	8	6	0	44	48	2003	CQF	W 4-3
Toronto	1	1	0	5	4	1	0	16	9	1994	CF	W 4-1
Totals	**30**	**10**	**20**	**155**	**66**	**89**	**0**	**452**	**526**			

Playoff Results 2006-2001

Year	Round	Opponent	Result	GF	GA
2004	CQF	Calgary	L 3-4	16	19
2003	CSF	Minnesota	L 3-4	17	26
	CQF	St. Louis	W 4-3	17	21
2002	CQF	Detroit	L 2-4	16	22
2001	CQF	Colorado	L 0-4	9	16

Abbreviations: Round: F – Final; **CF** – conference final; **CSF** – conference semi-final; **CQF** – conference quarter-final; **DF** – division final; **DSF** – division semi-final; **QF** – quarter-final; **PRE** – preliminary round.

Calgary totals include Atlanta Flames, 1972-73 to 1979-80.
Carolina totals include Hartford, 1979-80 to 1996-97.
Colorado totals include Quebec, 1979-80 to 1994-95.
Dallas totals include Minnesota North Stars, 1970-71 to 1992-93.
New Jersey totals include Kansas City, 1974-75 to 1975-76, and Colorado Rockies, 1976-77 to 1981-82.
Phoenix totals include Winnipeg, 1979-80 to 1995-96.

2005-06 Results

Oct.	5	Phoenix	3-2		7	Calgary	4-3*
	8	at Edmonton	3-4†		10	Toronto	4-3
	10	at Detroit	4-2		13	at New Jersey	0-3
	12	at Minnesota	0-6		14	at NY Islanders	8-1
	14	at Minnesota	5-3		16	at Pittsburgh	4-2
	16	Dallas	5-2		19	Buffalo	4-1
	18	Chicago	6-2		21	Montreal	6-2
	20	Phoenix	3-2		23	at St. Louis	0-4
	22	Colorado	6-4		24	at Columbus	5-6
	25	at Minnesota	3-1		26	at Detroit	1-2
	27	at Colorado	2-6		28	at Colorado	4-3†
	29	at Colorado	3-4*		31	at Phoenix	7-4
Nov.	2	Minnesota	2-1	**Feb.**	3	at Calgary	3-1
	4	Columbus	5-3		4	at Edmonton	1-3
	5	at Calgary	0-1		6	Columbus	7-4
	7	at Calgary	3-4		8	St. Louis	2-4
	10	Colorado	3-5		10	Anaheim	1-3
	13	Detroit	4-1		12	Minnesota	3-2*
	16	at San Jose	3-1		28	at Calgary	2-1
	17	at Los Angeles	4-5	**Mar.**	2	at Nashville	1-3
	20	at Anaheim	3-2		3	at Chicago	5-4†
	22	Chicago	3-1		5	St. Louis	1-4
	24	San Jose	3-2		9	Nashville	2-3*
	26	at Phoenix	1-2		11	Dallas	1-2
	27	at Colorado	2-6		13	at Dallas	2-4
	30	Colorado	5-2		14	at Nashville	0-5
Dec.	1	at Edmonton	3-5		17	at Columbus	3-2
	4	Boston	5-2		19	Detroit	3-7
	9	Ottawa	3-2†		21	at Edmonton	4-1
	13	at NY Rangers	3-2		23	Edmonton	4-3†
	15	at Philadelphia	5-4		25	Edmonton	2-3
	17	Edmonton	4-5*		27	Los Angeles	7-4
	19	Los Angeles	3-4†		29	Minnesota	2-1
	21	Edmonton	6-7		31	Minnesota	1-2†
	23	Calgary	5-6†	**Apr.**	2	at Anaheim	2-6
	26	Calgary	1-2		3	at Los Angeles	0-1
	28	Nashville	4-3		8	Calgary	3-2*
	31	at Minnesota	3-4		10	Anaheim	2-4
Jan.	2	at St. Louis	1-4		12	San Jose	4-5*
	4	at Dallas	1-3		13	at San Jose	3-5
	5	at Chicago	3-2		15	Colorado	4-3*

* – Overtime † – Shootout

Entry Draft
Selections 2006-1992

2006
Pick
14	Michael Grabner
82	Daniel Rahimi
163	Sergei Shirokov
167	Juraj Simek
197	Evan Fuller

2005
Pick
10	Luc Bourdon
51	Mason Raymond
114	Alexandre Vincent
138	Matt Butcher
185	Kris Fredheim
205	Mario Bliznak

2004
Pick
26	Cory Schneider
91	Alexander Edler
125	Andrew Sarauer
159	Mike Brown
189	Julien Ellis-Plante
254	David Schulz
287	Jannik Hansen

2003
Pick
23	Ryan Kesler
60	Marc-Andre Bernier
111	Brandon Nolan
128	Ty Morris
160	Nicklas Danielsson
190	Chad Brownlee
222	Francois-Pierre Guenette
252	Sergei Topol
254	Nathan McIver
285	Matthew Hansen

2002
Pick
49	Kirill Koltsov
55	Denis Grot
68	Brett Skinner
83	Lukas Mensator
114	John Laliberte
151	Rob McVicar
214	Marc-Andre Roy
223	Ilya Krikunov
247	Matt Violin
277	Thomas Nussli
278	Matt Gens

2001
Pick
16	R.J. Umberger
66	Fedor Fedorov
114	Evgeny Gladskikh
151	Kevin Bieksa
212	Jason King
245	Konstantin Mikhailov

2000
Pick
23	Nathan Smith
71	Thatcher Bell
93	Tim Branham
144	Pavel Duma
208	Brandon Reid
241	Nathan Barrett
272	Tim Smith

1999
Pick
2	Daniel Sedin
3	Henrik Sedin
69	Rene Vydareny
129	Ryan Thorpe
172	Josh Reed
189	Kevin Swanson
218	Markus Kankaanpera
271	Darrell Hay

1998
Pick
4	Bryan Allen
31	Artem Chubarov
68	Jarkko Ruutu
81	Justin Morrison
90	Regan Darby
136	David Ytfeldt
140	Rick Bertran
149	Paul Cabana
177	Vincent Malts
204	Greg Mischler
219	Curtis Valentine
232	Jason Metcalfe

1997
Pick
10	Brad Ference
34	Ryan Bonni
36	Harold Druken
64	Kyle Freadrich
90	Chris Stanley
114	David Darguzas
117	Matt Cockell
144	Matt Cooke
148	Larry Shapley
171	Rod Leroux
201	Denis Martynyuk
227	Peter Brady

1996
Pick
12	Josh Holden
75	Zenith Komarniski
93	Jonas Soling
121	Tyler Prosofsky
147	Nolan McDonald
175	Clint Cabana
201	Jeff Scissons
227	Lubomir Vaic

1995
Pick
40	Chris McAllister
61	Larry Courville
66	Peter Schaefer
92	Lloyd Shaw
120	Todd Norman
144	Brent Sopel
170	Stewart Bodtker
196	Tyler Willis
222	Jason Cugnet

1994
Pick
13	Mattias Ohlund
39	Robb Gordon
42	Dave Scatchard
65	Chad Allan
92	Mike Dubinsky
117	Yanick Dube
169	Yuri Kuznetsov
195	Rob Trumbley
221	Bill Muckalt
247	Tyson Nash
273	Robert Longpre

1993
Pick
20	Mike Wilson
46	Rick Girard
98	Dieter Kochan
124	Scott Walker
150	Troy Creurer
176	Yevgeni Babariko
202	Sean Tallaire
254	Bert Robertsson
280	Sergei Tkachenko

1992
Pick
21	Libor Polasek
40	Michael Peca
45	Mike Fountain
69	Jeff Connolly
93	Brent Tully
110	Brian Loney
117	Adrian Aucoin
141	Jason Clark
165	Scott Hollis
213	Sonny Mignacca
237	Mark Wotton
261	Aaron Boh

Vice President and General Manager

NONIS, DAVID
Senior Vice President/General Manager, Vancouver Canucks.
Born in Burnaby, B.C., May 25, 1966.

David Nonis was given his first assignment as general manager of an NHL hockey club when he was named to the position by the Vancouver Canucks on May 6, 2004. Nonis had spent the previous six seasons as senior vice president, director of hockey operations and was the Canucks' chief negotiator of player contracts. In his first act as general manager, Nonis appointed Steve Tambellini assistant general manager.

A native of Vancouver, Nonis broke into the NHL with the Canucks in 1990. In his first years he was primarily responsible for corporate contracts, computer scouting and team services. Prior to being named senior vice president in 1998, Nonis served as the National Hockey League's manager of hockey operations for four seasons. In his role with the NHL, Nonis gained a vast knowledge of the collective bargaining agreement and helped finalize sections of the document when the previous edition was drafted during the 1994-95 season. He also worked with the league's arbitration team, which included helping teams prepare for arbitration, researching salaries and interpreting contract language.

Nonis played for the Burnaby Blackhawks of the British Columbia Junior Hockey League from 1982 to 1984. He then played for the University of Maine where he served as captain for two seasons and graduated with a B.A. in 1988. Nonis played one season professionally in Denmark, then returned to Maine in 1989 to serve as graduate assistant under head coach Shawn Walsh. Nonis earned an MBA from the University of Maine in 1990.

Club Directory

General Motors Place

Vancouver Canucks
General Motors Place
800 Griffiths Way
Vancouver, B.C. V6B 6G1
Phone **604/899-4600**
FAX 604/899-4640
www.canucks.com
Capacity: 18,630

Executive
Chairman, OBSE & Governor, NHL	John E. McCaw Jr.
Deputy Chairman, OBSE & Alt. Gov., NHL	Francesco Aquilini
Senior Vice President, G.M. & Alt. Gov., NHL	David M. Nonis
General Counsel	James Conrad
Vice President, Finance & CFO	Victor de Bonis
Executive Vice President, Business	Jon Festinger
Vice President, People Development	Susanne Haine
Vice President, Broadcast & New Media	Chris Hebb
Vice President & G.M., Arena Operations	Harvey Jones

Hockey Operations
Senior Vice President, G.M. & Alt. Gov., NHL	David M. Nonis
Executive Assistant	Chris Stephens
Vice President & Assistant General Manager	Steve Tambellini
Head Coach	Alain Vigneault
Executive Assistant	Lori Meehan
Assistant Coaches	Rick Bowness, Mike Kelly, Barry Smith
Goaltending Coach	Ian Clark
Strength & Conditioning Coach	Roger Takahashi
Director, Player Development	Stan Smyl
Director, Player Personnel	Lorne Henning
General Manager, Manitoba Moose	Craig Heisinger
Head Coach, Manitoba Moose	Scott Arniel
Assistant Coach, Manitoba Moose	Brad Berry
Senior Editor, Alumni Liaison	Norm Jewison
Director, Media Relations	T.C. Carling
Manager, Media Relations	Ben Brown
Assistant, Media Relations	Stephanie Maniago
Director, Community Partnerships	Debbie Butt
Manager, Community Partnerships	Karen Christiansen
Coordinator, Community Partnerships	Jessica Danylchuk
Assistant, Community Partnerships	Tara Clarke
Manager, Hockey Development	Rod Brathwaite

Scouting Staff
Chief Scout	Ron Delorme
Amateur Scouts	Sergei Chibisov, Barry Dean, Thomas Gradin, Gary Lupul, Mario Marois, Harold Snepsts, Jim Eagle, Tim Lenardon, Branislav Pulis
Professional Scouts	Lucien DeBlois, Eric Crawford, Jack McIlhargey
Manager, Scouting & Player Information	Jonathan Wall

Medical and Training Staff
Medical Trainer	Mike Burnstein
Assistant Medical Trainers	Jon Sanderson, Marty Dudgeon
Equipment Manager	Pat O'Neill
Assistant Equipment Manager	Jamie Hendricks
Assistant Equipment Trainer	Brian Hamilton
Game Dressing Room Attendants	John Jukich, Ron Shute, Brian Brumwell
Team Doctors	Dr. Bill Regan, Dr. Mike Wilkinson, Dr. Rui Avelar
Team Dentist	Dr. Jeffrey Norden
Team Chiropractor	Dr. Sid Sheard
Team Optometrist	Dr. Alan R. Boyco

Marketing and Creative Services
Director, Marketing	Paul Dal Monte
Marketing Manager	Jennifer Murtagh
Marketing Assistant	Michelle Davies
Manager, Creative Services	Ken Jones
Graphic Designers	Kim Sissons, Jenny McCleery
Image Resource Coordinator	Kristina Edmondson

Broadcast
Director, Facilities & In-house Productions	Paul Brettell
Director, Production Services	Mike Hall
Director, Technical Services	Vic Araujo

Business Development
Director, Business Development	David Altman
Director, Business Development	Sharon Butler
Director, Sponsorship Services	Darren Moscovitch
Manager, Suite & Sponsorship Services	Deborah Boren
Manager, Business Development	Lui Garcea

Customer Sales and Service
Director, Customer Sales & Service	Jordan Thorsteinson
Director, Ticket Operations & Customer Service	Mary Nagy
Manager, Customer Accounts	Josh Bender, Martha Vassos, Aysha Martin, David Pan, Chris Wallace

Game Entertainment
Manager, Game Entertainment & Events	Jamie Levchuk
Coordinator, Game Presentation & Events	Cam Goudreau

Finance and Central Services
Controller, Hockey	Patricia Bigonzi
Corporate Controller	Aaron Wilson
Travel Manager	Cathie Moroney
Managers, People Development	Lisa Steiman, Pam Petrie

Authentix, Fan Apparel and Collectibles
Senior Manager, Retail	Kristy Pennock
Retail Operations Manager	Jeff Winslade
Retail Operations Coordinator	Danielle Libonati

Radio and Television
Radio Affiliation	Team 1040
Television Affiliation	Rogers Sportsnet (Channel 22)

Washington Capitals

2005-06 Results: 29w-41L-6OTL-6SOL 70PTS.
Fifth, Southeast Division

2006-07 Schedule

Oct.	Thu.	5	at NY Rangers	Sat.	6	Atlanta	
	Sat.	7	Carolina	Tue.	9	Philadelphia	
	Thu.	12	at Minnesota	Thu.	11	at Tampa Bay	
	Sat.	14	Atlanta	Sat.	13	at Florida	
	Wed.	18	Florida	Tue.	16	at Ottawa	
	Thu.	19	at Atlanta	Thu.	18	at Carolina	
	Sat.	21	Tampa Bay	Sat.	20	Florida*	
	Wed.	25	at Colorado	Fri.	26	at Carolina	
	Fri.	27	at Vancouver	Sat.	27	Carolina	
	Sat.	28	at Edmonton	Tue.	30	at Ottawa	
	Mon.	30	at Calgary	**Feb.** Thu.	1	at Florida	
Nov.	Fri.	3	Atlanta	Sat.	3	at Pittsburgh*	
	Sat.	4	at Philadelphia	Sun.	4	NY Islanders*	
	Mon.	6	Ottawa	Tue.	6	Boston	
	Thu.	9	at Carolina	Thu.	8	Los Angeles	
	Sat.	11	NY Rangers	Sat.	10	NY Rangers	
	Mon.	13	at Florida	Thu.	15	at Tampa Bay	
	Wed.	15	Boston	Sun.	18	at Pittsburgh*	
	Fri.	17	Carolina	Tue.	20	at Montreal	
	Sat.	18	at Boston	Wed.	21	San Jose	
	Wed.	22	Atlanta	Sat.	24	at New Jersey*	
	Fri.	24	Toronto	Sun.	25	New Jersey*	
	Sat.	25	at NY Islanders	Tue.	27	Florida	
	Tue.	28	at Tampa Bay	**Mar.** Thu.	1	Tampa Bay	
	Thu.	30	Dallas	Sat.	3	NY Islanders	
Dec.	Sat.	2	Buffalo	Tue.	6	at Toronto	
	Wed.	6	Ottawa	Fri.	9	Carolina	
	Fri.	8	Anaheim	Sat.	10	at NY Islanders	
	Sat.	9	at Philadelphia	Mon.	12	at Atlanta	
	Mon.	11	Pittsburgh	Thu.	15	at Boston	
	Fri.	15	at Atlanta	Fri.	16	Toronto	
	Sat.	16	Philadelphia	Sun.	18	Tampa Bay*	
	Tue.	19	Tampa Bay	Wed.	21	at Buffalo	
	Fri.	22	New Jersey	Thu.	22	at Carolina	
	Sat.	23	at Toronto	Sat.	24	at Montreal	
	Tue.	26	at Buffalo	Tue.	27	Pittsburgh	
	Wed.	27	Montreal	Fri.	30	at Florida	
	Fri.	29	at New Jersey	Sat.	31	at Tampa Bay	
	Sat.	30	at NY Rangers	**Apr.** Tue.	3	Florida	
Jan.	Mon.	1	Phoenix*	Wed.	4	at Atlanta	
	Thu.	4	Montreal	Sat.	7	Buffalo*	

Denotes afternoon game.

Franchise date: June 11, 1974

EASTERN
CONFERENCE

SOUTHEAST DIVISION

33rd NHL Season

Alex Ovechkin shattered Washington's rookie record of 67 points (held by Bob Carpenter and Chris Valentine) in 2005-06. Ovechkin was third in the NHL with 106 points, and tied for third with 52 goals.

Year-by-Year Record

Season	GP	Home W	L	T	OL	Road W	L	T	OL	Overall W	L	T	OL	GF	GA	Pts.	Finished	Playoff Result
2005-06	82	16	18	....	7	13	23	....	5	29	41	....	12	237	306	70	5th, Southeast Div.	Out of Playoffs
2004-05	....																	
2003-04	82	13	20	6	2	10	26	4	1	23	46	10	3	186	253	59	5th, Southeast Div.	Out of Playoffs
2002-03	82	24	13	2	2	15	16	6	4	39	29	8	6	224	220	92	2nd, Southeast Div.	Lost Conf. Quarter-Final
2001-02	82	21	12	6	2	15	21	5	0	36	33	11	2	228	240	85	2nd, Southeast Div.	Out of Playoffs
2000-01	82	24	9	6	2	17	18	4	2	41	27	10	4	233	211	96	1st, Southeast Div.	Lost Conf. Quarter-Final
1999-2000	82	26	5	8	2	18	19	4	0	44	24	12	2	227	194	102	1st, Southeast Div.	Lost Conf. Quarter-Final
1998-99	82	16	23	2	....	15	22	4	....	31	45	6	....	200	218	68	3rd, Southeast Div.	Out of Playoffs
1997-98	82	23	12	6	....	17	18	6	....	40	30	12	....	219	202	92	3rd, Atlantic Div.	Lost Final
1996-97	82	19	17	5	....	14	23	4	....	33	40	9	....	214	231	75	5th, Atlantic Div.	Out of Playoffs
1995-96	82	21	15	5	....	18	17	6	....	39	32	11	....	234	204	89	4th, Atlantic Div.	Lost Conf. Quarter-Final
1994-95	48	15	6	3	....	7	12	5	....	22	18	8	....	136	120	52	3rd, Atlantic Div.	Lost Conf. Quarter-Final
1993-94	84	17	16	9	....	22	19	1	....	39	35	10	....	277	263	88	3rd, Atlantic Div.	Lost Conf. Semi-Final
1992-93	84	21	15	6	....	22	19	1	....	43	34	7	....	325	286	93	2nd, Patrick Div.	Lost Div. Semi-Final
1991-92	80	25	12	3	....	20	15	5	....	45	27	8	....	330	275	98	2nd, Patrick Div.	Lost Div. Semi-Final
1990-91	80	21	14	5	....	16	22	2	....	37	36	7	....	258	258	81	3rd, Patrick Div.	Lost Div. Final
1989-90	80	19	18	3	....	17	20	3	....	36	38	6	....	284	275	78	3rd, Patrick Div.	Lost Conf. Championship
1988-89	80	25	12	3	....	16	17	7	....	41	29	10	....	305	259	92	1st, Patrick Div.	Lost Div. Semi-Final
1987-88	80	22	14	4	....	16	19	5	....	38	33	9	....	281	249	85	2nd, Patrick Div.	Lost Div. Final
1986-87	80	22	15	3	....	16	17	7	....	38	32	10	....	285	278	86	2nd, Patrick Div.	Lost Div. Semi-Final
1985-86	80	30	8	2	....	20	15	5	....	50	23	7	....	315	272	107	2nd, Patrick Div.	Lost Div. Final
1984-85	80	27	11	2	....	19	14	7	....	46	25	9	....	322	240	101	2nd, Patrick Div.	Lost Div. Final
1983-84	80	26	11	3	....	22	16	2	....	48	27	5	....	308	226	101	2nd, Patrick Div.	Lost Div. Semi-Final
1982-83	80	22	12	6	....	17	13	10	....	39	25	16	....	306	283	94	3rd, Patrick Div.	Lost Div. Semi-Final
1981-82	80	16	16	8	....	10	25	5	....	26	41	13	....	319	338	65	5th, Patrick Div.	Out of Playoffs
1980-81	80	16	17	7	....	10	19	11	....	26	36	18	....	286	317	70	5th, Patrick Div.	Out of Playoffs
1979-80	80	20	14	6	....	7	26	7	....	27	40	13	....	261	293	67	5th, Patrick Div.	Out of Playoffs
1978-79	80	15	19	6	....	9	22	9	....	24	41	15	....	273	338	63	4th, Norris Div.	Out of Playoffs
1977-78	80	10	23	7	....	7	26	7	....	17	49	14	....	195	321	48	5th, Norris Div.	Out of Playoffs
1976-77	80	17	15	8	....	7	27	6	....	24	42	14	....	221	307	62	4th, Norris Div.	Out of Playoffs
1975-76	80	6	26	8	....	5	33	2	....	11	59	10	....	224	394	32	5th, Norris Div.	Out of Playoffs
1974-75	80	7	28	5	....	1	39	0	....	8	67	5	....	181	446	21	5th, Norris Div.	Out of Playoffs

2006-07 Player Personnel

FORWARDS

Player	HT	WT	S	Place of Birth	Date	2005-06 Club
BEECH, Kris	6-2	208	L	Salmon Arm, B.C.	2/5/81	Nsh-Milwaukee-Wsh-Her
BOURQUE, Chris	5-7	177	L	Boston, MA	1/29/86	Hershey
BRADLEY, Matt	6-3	205	R	Stittsville, Ont.	6/13/78	Washington
BRASHEAR, Donald	6-2	235	L	Bedford, IN	1/7/72	Philadelphia
CLARK, Chris	6-0	200	R	South Windsor, CT	3/8/76	Washington
CLYMER, Ben	6-1	201	R	Bloomington, MN	4/11/78	Washington
FATA, Rico	6-0	205	R	Sault Ste. Marie, Ont.	2/12/80	Pit-Wilkes-Barre-Atl-Wsh
FEHR, Eric	6-4	204	R	Winkler, Man.	9/7/85	Washington-Hershey
FLEISCHMANN, Tomas	6-1	188	L	Koprivnice, Czech.	5/16/84	Washington-Hershey
GIROUX, Alexandre	6-3	190	L	Quebec City, Que.	6/16/81	NY Rangers-Hartford
GORDON, Boyd	6-1	201	R	Unity, Sask.	10/19/83	Washington-Hershey
JOHANSSON, Jonas	6-3	215	R	Jonkoping, Sweden	3/18/84	Lulea-Washington-Hershey-South Carolina
KLEPIS, Jakub	6-0	200	R	Prague, Czech.	6/5/84	Washington-Hershey
LAICH, Brooks	6-2	208	L	Wawota, Sask.	6/23/83	Washington-Hershey
OVECHKIN, Alex	6-2	212	R	Moscow, USSR	9/17/85	Washington
PETTINGER, Matt	6-1	210	L	Edmonton, Alta.	10/22/80	Washington
ROBITAILLE, Louis	6-1	192	L	Montreal, Que.	3/16/82	Washington-Hershey
SEMIN, Alexander	6-0	181	L	Krasnoyarsk, USSR	3/3/84	Togliatti-Mytischi
STECKEL, Dave	6-5	215	L	Westbend, WI	3/15/82	Washington-Hershey
SUTHERBY, Brian	6-3	205	L	Edmonton, Alta.	3/1/82	Washington
TENUTE, Joey	5-9	180	L	Hamilton, Ont.	4/2/83	Washington-Hershey
WERNER, Steve	6-0	197	L	Washington, DC	8/8/84	Massachusetts-Hershey
WISEMAN, Chad	6-0	205	L	Burlington, Ont.	3/25/81	NY Rangers-Hartford
ZEDNIK, Richard	6-1	196	L	Banska Bystrica, Czech.	1/6/76	Montreal
ZUBRUS, Dainius	6-4	225	L	Elektrenai, USSR	6/16/78	Washington

DEFENSEMEN

Player	HT	WT	S	Place of Birth	Date	2005-06 Club
CUTTA, Jakub	6-3	210	L	Jablonec nad Nisou, Czech.	12/29/81	Hershey
EMINGER, Steve	6-2	217	R	Woodbridge, Ont.	10/31/83	Washington
GREEN, Mike	6-1	200	R	Calgary, Alta.	10/12/85	Washington-Hershey
HEWARD, Jamie	6-2	215	R	Regina, Sask.	3/30/71	Washington
MORRISONN, Shaone	6-4	210	L	Vancouver, B.C.	12/23/82	Washington
MUIR, Bryan	6-3	224	L	Winnipeg, Man.	6/8/73	Washington
NYCHOLAT, Lawrence	6-0	192	L	Calgary, Alta.	5/7/79	Hershey
POKULOK, Sasha	6-5	220	L	Montreal, Que.	5/25/86	Cornell
POTHIER, Brian	6-0	195	R	New Bedford, MA	4/15/77	Ottawa
SCHULTZ, Jeff	6-6	215	L	Calgary, Alta.	2/25/86	Calgary (WHL)-Hershey

GOALTENDERS

Player	HT	WT	C	Place of Birth	Date	2005-06 Club
CASSIVI, Frederic	6-4	220	L	Sorel, Que.	6/12/75	Washington-Hershey
DAIGNEAULT, Maxime	6-3	202	L	St-Jacques-le-Mineur, Que.	1/23/84	South Carolina-Hershey
JOHNSON, Brent	6-3	196	L	Farmington, MI	3/12/77	Washington
KOLZIG, Olaf	6-3	225	L	Johannesburg, S. Africa	4/6/70	Washington

2005-06 Scoring

* – rookie

Regular Season

Pos	#	Player	Team	GP	G	A	Pts	+/-	PIM	PP	SH	GW	S	%
L	8	* Alex Ovechkin	WSH	81	52	54	106	2	52	21	3	5	425	12.2
R	9	Dainius Zubrus	WSH	71	23	34	57	3	84	13	0	5	181	12.7
C	11	Jeff Halpern	WSH	70	11	33	44	-8	79	6	1	1	151	7.3
R	24	Brian Willsie	WSH	82	19	22	41	-19	77	8	1	2	185	10.3
R	17	Chris Clark	WSH	78	20	19	39	9	110	1	3	0	144	13.9
L	18	Matt Pettinger	WSH	71	20	18	38	-2	39	4	5	2	134	14.9
L	27	Ben Clymer	WSH	77	16	17	33	-7	72	3	0	3	149	10.7
C	16	Brian Sutherby	WSH	76	14	16	30	-17	73	0	2	0	85	16.5
D	6	Jamie Heward	WSH	71	7	21	28	-5	54	4	0	2	140	5.0
D	47	Bryan Muir	WSH	72	8	18	26	-9	72	4	0	2	136	5.9
C	21	* Brooks Laich	WSH	73	7	14	21	-9	26	1	0	1	118	5.9
R	10	Matt Bradley	WSH	74	7	12	19	-8	72	0	1	1	87	8.0
D	44	Steve Eminger	WSH	66	5	13	18	-12	81	1	0	0	50	10.0
D	26	Shaone Morrisonn	WSH	80	1	13	14	7	91	0	0	0	56	1.8
D	34	Mathieu Biron	WSH	52	4	9	13	-19	50	3	0	0	61	6.6
C	25	Andrew Cassels	WSH	31	4	8	12	-3	14	2	0	0	29	13.8
C	23	Ivan Majesky	WSH	57	1	8	9	-2	66	0	1	0	35	2.9
C	20	Rico Fata	PIT	20	0	0	0	-5	10	0	0	0	18	0.0
			ATL	6	0	1	1	-2	4	0	0	0	1	0.0
			WSH	21	3	3	6	3	8	0	0	0	31	9.7
			TOTAL	47	3	4	7	-4	22	0	0	0	50	6.0
D	40	* Nolan Yonkman	WSH	38	0	7	7	1	86	0	0	0	14	0.0
C	20	Petr Sykora	WSH	10	2	2	4	0	6	0	0	0	9	22.2
C	38	* Jakub Klepis	WSH	25	1	3	4	-11	8	0	0	0	26	3.8
C	28	Kris Beech	NSH	5	1	2	3	1	4	0	0	0	6	16.7
			WSH	5	0	0	0	-4	0	0	0	0	6	0.0
			TOTAL	10	1	2	3	-3	4	0	0	0	12	8.3
D	52	* Mike Green	WSH	22	1	2	3	-8	18	0	0	0	13	7.7
C	43	* Tomas Fleischmann	WSH	14	0	2	2	-7	0	0	0	0	11	0.0
L	22	Boyd Kane	WSH	5	0	1	1	0	2	0	0	0	1	0.0
R	15	Boyd Gordon	WSH	25	0	1	1	-4	4	0	0	0	12	0.0
R	51	Stephen Peat	WSH	1	0	0	0	-2	2	0	0	0	2	0.0
R	45	* Jonas Johansson	WSH	1	0	0	0	0	0	0	0	0	1	0.0
C	13	* Joey Tenute	WSH	1	0	0	0	0	0	0	0	0	1	0.0
D	41	* Louis Robitaille	WSH	2	0	0	0	-1	5	0	0	0	0	0.0
L	39	* Graham Mink	WSH	3	0	0	0	0	0	0	0	0	1	0.0
L	70	* Dave Steckel	WSH	7	0	0	0	-1	0	0	0	0	6	0.0
L	36	Colin Forbes	WSH	9	0	0	0	-2	2	0	0	0	10	0.0
R	50	* Eric Fehr	WSH	11	0	0	0	-1	2	0	0	0	10	0.0

Goaltending

No.	Goaltender	GPI	Mins	Avg	W	L	OT	EN	SO	GA	SA	S%	G	A	PIM
1	Brent Johnson	26	1413	3.44	9	12	1	1	1	81	854	.905	0	0	14
37	Olaf Kolzig	59	3506	3.53	20	28	11	8	0	206	1987	.896	0	3	14
30	Frederic Cassivi	1	59	4.07	0	1	0	0	0	4	30	.867	0	0	0
	Totals	82	5006	3.60	29	41	12	9	1	300	2880	.896			

Olaf Kozig has been a member of the of the Capitals organization since the team selected him with its first choice (19th overall) in the 1989 NHL Entry Draft.

Coach

HANLON, GLEN
Coach, Washington Capitals. Born in Brandon, Man., February 20, 1957.

Glen Hanlon was in his second season as an assistant coach when he was promoted to the position of head coach on December 10, 2003. Previously, Hanlon had served as head coach for Washington's minor-league affiliate, the Portland Pirates, for three seasons.

During his first season at the helm of the Pirates in 1999-2000, Hanlon was named the American Hockey League's coach of the year after guiding Portland to a 46-23-10-1 record and a league-best 48-point turnaround. The Pirates finished with 103 points overall, second best in the AHL's New England Division.

In three seasons leading the Pirates, Hanlon guided the club to two Calder Cup playoff appearances. He finished his tenure posting the second-highest win total (110) in Pirates history.

Before arriving in Portland, Hanlon served eight seasons with the Vancouver Canucks as an assistant coach (1994 to 1999) and goaltending coach (1991 to 1994). He helped lead the Canucks to their first 40-win season in franchise history in 1991-92, and the team advanced to the Stanley Cup Finals in 1994. He also served as an assistant coach with the Canadian national team at the 1998 World Championships in Zurich, Switzerland.

Hanlon appeared in 477 NHL games in 14 seasons as a goaltender between 1977 and 1991, playing with the Vancouver Canucks, St. Louis Blues, New York Rangers and Detroit Red Wings. He posted a career record of 167-202-61, a 3.60 goals-against average and 13 shutouts. He also played 35 career NHL playoff games, compiling an 11-15-0 record, a 3.14 goals-against average and four shutouts.

Coaching Record

Season	Team	Games	Regular Season				Playoffs		
			W	L	O/T		Games	W	L
1999-00	Portland (AHL)	80	46	24	10		4	1	3
2000-01	Portland (AHL)	80	34	42	4		3	0	3
2001-02	Portland (AHL)	80	30	35	15		....	....	....
2003-04	**Washington (NHL)**	**54**	15	30	9		....	....	....
2004-05	**Washington (NHL)**			Season Cancelled					
2005-06	**Washington (NHL)**	**82**	29	41	12		....	....	....
	NHL Totals	**136**	**53**	**69**	**14**		....	....	....

Coaching History

Jim Anderson, Red Sullivan and Milt Schmidt, 1974-75; Milt Schmidt and Tom McVie, 1975-76; Tom McVie, 1976-77, 1977-78; Danny Belisle, 1978-79; Danny Belisle and Gary Green, 1979-80; Gary Green, 1980-81; Gary Green, Roger Crozier and Bryan Murray, 1981-82; Bryan Murray, 1982-83 to 1988-89; Bryan Murray and Terry Murray, 1989-90; Terry Murray, 1990-91 to 1992-93; Terry Murray and Jim Schoenfeld, 1993-94; Jim Schoenfeld, 1994-95 to 1996-97; Ron Wilson, 1997-98 to 2001-02; Bruce Cassidy, 2002-03; Bruce Cassidy and Glen Hanlon, 2003-04; Glen Hanlon, 2004-05 to date.

Club Records

Team

(Figures in brackets for season records are games played; records for fewest points, wins, ties, losses, goals, goals against are for 70 or more games)

Most Points	107	1985-86 (80)
Most Wins	50	1985-86 (80)
Most Ties	18	1980-81 (80)
Most Losses	67	1974-75 (80)
Most Goals	330	1991-92 (80)
Most Goals Against	*446	1974-75 (80)
Fewest Points	*21	1974-75 (80)
Fewest Wins	*8	1974-75 (80)
Fewest Ties	5	1974-75 (80), 1983-84 (80)
Fewest Losses	23	1985-86 (80)
Fewest Goals	181	1974-75 (80)
Fewest Goals Against	194	1999-00 (82)

Longest Winning Streak
- Overall....10 Jan. 27-Feb. 18/84
- Home....10 Jan. 4-Feb. 23/00
- Away....6 Feb. 26-Apr. 1/84

Longest Undefeated Streak
- Overall....14 Nov. 24-Dec. 23/82 (9 wins, 5 ties), Jan. 17-Feb. 18/84 (13 wins, 1 tie)
- Home....13 Nov. 25/92-Jan. 31/93 (9 wins, 4 ties), Dec. 27/99-Feb. 23/00 (11 wins, 2 ties)
- Away....10 Nov. 24/82-Jan. 8/83 (6 wins, 4 ties)

Longest Losing Streak
- Overall....*17 Feb. 18-Mar. 26/75
- Home....*11 Feb. 18-Mar. 30/75
- Away....37 Oct. 9/74-Mar. 26/75

Longest Winless Streak
- Overall....25 Nov. 29/75-Jan. 21/76 (22 losses, 3 ties)
- Home....14 Dec. 3/75-Jan. 21/76 (11 losses, 3 ties)
- Away....37 Oct. 9/74-Mar. 26/75 (37 losses)

Most Shutouts, Season....9 1995-96 (82)
Most PIM, Season....2,204 1989-90 (80)
Most Goals, Game....12 Feb. 6/90 (Que. 2 at Wsh. 12), Jan. 11/03 (Fla. 2 at Wsh. 12)

Individual

Most Seasons	15	Calle Johansson
Most Games	983	Calle Johansson
Most Goals, Career	472	Peter Bondra
Most Assists, Career	418	Michal Pivonka
Most Points, Career	825	Peter Bondra (472G, 353A)
Most PIM, Career	2,003	Dale Hunter
Most Shutouts, Career	33	Olaf Kolzig
Longest Consecutive Games Streak	422	Bob Carpenter (Oct. 7/81-Nov. 22/86)
Most Goals, Season	60	Dennis Maruk (1981-82)
Most Assists, Season	76	Dennis Maruk (1981-82)
Most Points, Season	136	Dennis Maruk (1981-82; 60G, 76A)
Most PIM, Season	339	Alan May (1989-90)

Most Points, Defenseman, Season....81 Larry Murphy (1986-87; 23G, 58A)
Most Points, Center, Season....136 Dennis Maruk (1981-82; 60G, 76A)
Most Points, Right Wing, Season....102 Mike Gartner (1984-85; 50G, 52A)
Most Points, Left Wing, Season....106 Alex Ovechkin (2005-06; 52G, 54A)
Most Points, Rookie, Season....106 Alex Ovechkin (2005-06; 52G, 54A)
Most Shutouts, Season....9 Jim Carey (1995-96)
Most Goals, Game....5 Bengt Gustafsson (Jan. 8/84), Peter Bondra (Feb. 5/94)
Most Assists, Game....6 Mike Ridley (Jan. 7/89)
Most Points, Game....7 Dino Ciccarelli (Mar. 18/89; 4G, 3A)

* NHL Record.

Retired Numbers

5	Rod Langway	1982-1993
7	Yvon Labre	1974-1981
32	Dale Hunter	1987-1999

Captains' History

Doug Mohns, 1974-75; Bill Clement and Yvon Labre, 1975-76; Yvon Labre, 1976-77, 1977-78; Guy Charron, 1978-79; Ryan Walter, 1979-80 to 1981-82; Rod Langway, 1982-83 to 1991-92; Rod Langway and Kevin Hatcher, 1992-93; Kevin Hatcher, 1993-94; Dale Hunter, 1994-95 to 1998-99; Adam Oates, 1999-2000, 2000-01; Brendan Witt and Steve Konowalchuk, 2001-02; Steve Konowalchuk, 2002-03, 2003-04; Jeff Halpern, 2005-06.

All-time Record vs. Other Clubs

Regular Season

	At Home								On Road								Total							
	GP	W	L	T	OL	GF	GA	PTS	GP	W	L	T	OL	GF	GA	PTS	GP	W	L	T	OL	GF	GA	PTS
Anaheim	9	4	5	0	0	16	22	8	10	3	6	1	0	25	31	7	19	7	11	1	0	41	53	15
Atlanta	17	11	3	3	0	64	47	25	17	6	8	2	1	50	49	15	34	17	11	5	1	114	96	40
Boston	57	17	27	12	1	160	198	47	58	16	32	9	1	155	213	42	115	33	59	21	2	315	411	89
Buffalo	58	15	33	9	1	146	205	40	58	16	36	6	0	154	226	38	116	31	69	15	1	300	431	78
Calgary	41	21	14	6	0	153	139	48	38	7	24	7	0	93	157	21	79	28	38	13	0	246	296	69
Carolina	51	30	16	4	1	174	132	65	53	26	15	10	2	167	143	64	104	56	31	14	3	341	275	129
Chicago	42	21	15	5	1	148	131	48	40	12	22	6	0	120	151	30	82	33	37	11	1	268	282	78
Colorado	33	18	10	4	1	131	105	41	34	14	15	5	0	116	105	33	67	32	25	9	1	247	210	74
Columbus	3	2	1	0	0	11	7	5	4	3	1	0	0	15	11	6	7	5	1	0	0	26	18	11
Dallas	40	15	17	8	0	120	129	38	42	12	22	8	0	111	156	32	82	27	39	16	0	231	285	70
Detroit	47	21	21	5	0	171	151	47	47	15	20	11	1	135	161	42	94	36	41	16	1	306	312	89
Edmonton	29	18	9	2	0	118	93	38	29	10	15	4	0	91	120	24	58	28	24	6	0	209	213	62
Florida	32	15	9	5	3	94	77	38	32	14	14	4	0	79	80	32	64	29	23	9	3	173	157	70
Los Angeles	46	18	21	7	0	185	171	43	48	15	27	6	0	147	189	36	94	33	48	13	0	332	360	79
Minnesota	3	2	1	0	0	7	6	4	3	0	3	0	0	1	6	0	6	2	4	0	0	8	12	4
Montreal	61	27	25	9	0	169	183	63	62	18	35	8	1	134	233	45	123	45	60	17	1	303	416	108
Nashville	5	3	2	0	0	12	13	6	5	1	3	1	0	11	16	3	10	4	5	1	0	23	29	9
New Jersey	81	49	24	6	2	314	231	106	81	33	38	7	3	230	250	76	162	82	62	13	5	544	481	182
NY Islanders	83	41	31	11	0	275	258	93	83	37	44	2	0	258	308	76	166	78	75	13	0	533	566	169
NY Rangers	86	44	30	9	3	323	276	100	84	35	39	9	1	287	312	80	170	79	69	18	4	610	588	180
Ottawa	26	11	11	4	0	79	76	26	25	11	13	1	0	72	91	23	51	22	24	5	0	151	167	49
Philadelphia	82	34	35	13	0	266	265	81	85	24	55	6	0	224	325	54	167	58	90	19	0	490	590	135
Phoenix	31	18	7	5	1	119	85	42	31	9	15	7	0	111	113	25	62	27	22	12	1	230	198	67
Pittsburgh	88	46	32	9	1	367	321	102	85	29	49	7	0	266	335	65	173	75	81	16	1	633	656	167
St. Louis	40	21	15	4	0	141	121	46	41	13	20	8	0	127	165	34	81	34	35	12	0	268	286	80
San Jose	12	5	7	0	0	34	36	10	11	3	7	1	0	27	33	7	23	8	14	1	0	61	69	17
Tampa Bay	33	21	7	4	1	113	75	47	33	19	11	2	1	102	79	41	66	40	18	6	2	215	154	88
Toronto	52	30	17	4	1	191	149	65	50	17	26	6	1	172	220	41	102	47	43	10	2	363	369	106
Vancouver	40	22	14	4	0	132	120	48	39	16	18	5	0	123	136	37	79	38	32	9	0	255	256	85
Defunct Clubs	10	2	8	0	0	28	42	4	10	4	5	1	0	30	39	9	20	6	13	1	0	58	81	13
Totals	**1238**	**602**	**466**	**153**	**17**	**4261**	**3864**	**1374**	**1238**	**438**	**638**	**150**	**12**	**3633**	**4453**	**1038**	**2476**	**1040**	**1104**	**303**	**29**	**7894**	**8317**	**2412**

Playoffs

	Series	W	L	GP	W	L	T	GF	GA	Last Mtg.	Rnd.	Result
Boston	2	1	1	10	4	6	0	21	28	1998	CQF	W 4-2
Buffalo	1	1	0	6	4	2	0	13	11	1998	CF	W 4-2
Detroit	1	0	1	4	0	4	0	7	13	1998	F	L 0-4
New Jersey	2	1	1	13	7	6	0	44	43	1990	DSF	W 4-2
NY Islanders	6	1	5	30	12	18	0	88	99	1993	DSF	L 2-4
NY Rangers	4	2	2	22	11	11	0	75	71	1994	CSF	L 1-4
Ottawa	1	1	0	5	4	1	0	18	7	1998	CSF	W 4-1
Philadelphia	3	2	1	16	9	7	0	65	55	1989	DSF	L 2-4
Pittsburgh	7	1	6	42	16	26	0	121	137	2001	CQF	L 2-4
Tampa Bay	1	0	1	6	2	4	0	15	14	2003	CQF	L 2-4
Totals	**28**	**10**	**18**	**154**	**69**	**85**	**0**	**467**	**478**			

Calgary totals include Atlanta Flames, 1974-75 to 1979-80. Carolina totals include Hartford, 1979-80 to 1996-97. Colorado totals include Quebec, 1979-80 to 1994-95. Dallas totals include Minnesota North Stars, 1974-75 to 1992-93. New Jersey totals include Kansas City, 1974-75 to 1975-76, and Colorado Rockies, 1976-77 to 1981-82. Phoenix totals include Winnipeg, 1979-80, 1995-96.

Playoff Results 2006-2001

Year	Round	Opponent	Result	GF	GA
2003	CQF	Tampa Bay	L 2-4	15	14
2001	CQF	Pittsburgh	L 2-4	10	14

Abbreviations: Round: F – Final; **CF** – conference final; **CSF** – conference semi-final; **CQF** – conference quarter-final; **DSF** – division semi-final.

2005-06 Results

Oct.	5	Columbus	3-2		12	at Dallas	1-4
	7	Atlanta	3-7		13	at Anaheim	3-2*
	8	at Atlanta	1-8		16	at Phoenix	6-1
	10	NY Rangers	3-2		19	St. Louis	5-4†
	12	at Carolina	2-7		21	Carolina	5-2
	13	NY Islanders	3-5		23	Boston	2-3
	16	Tampa Bay	3-2†		25	at Pittsburgh	1-8
	20	at Florida	2-3		26	at Boston	2-3
	22	Carolina	0-4		29	Tampa Bay	2-1
	26	at Buffalo	3-2		31	at NY Islanders	3-5
	28	at Tampa Bay	2-4	Feb.	3	Toronto	4-1
Nov.	3	at Philadelphia	1-8		4	at Tampa Bay	0-5
	4	Atlanta	3-2†		7	Florida	0-5
	6	Toronto	5-4		10	at Philadelphia	4-5
	8	at Toronto	4-6		11	Pittsburgh	3-6
	11	New Jersey	3-4		28	at Toronto	5-3
	12	at New Jersey	2-3	Mar.	2	at Ottawa	1-7
	15	Tampa Bay	4-3†		4	at Atlanta	2-3*
	17	at Buffalo	5-8		6	NY Islanders	2-3
	19	at Montreal	5-1		8	Pittsburgh	6-3
	22	at Pittsburgh	4-5		10	New Jersey	3-4†
	23	Tampa Bay	3-4†		12	Ottawa	2-5
	26	at NY Rangers	2-3†		14	Buffalo	4-6
	27	Buffalo	2-3		16	at NY Rangers	4-5
Dec.	1	at Florida	2-3		18	Florida	3-4†
	3	NY Rangers	5-1		20	Montreal	2-4
	9	Nashville	2-5		22	at Florida	3-4
	9	Detroit	3-4		23	at Tampa Bay	3-4*
	14	at Los Angeles	3-2		25	at Carolina	3-1
	16	at San Jose	1-4		29	at Carolina	5-1
	18	Florida	2-3		30	at Montreal	2-3*
	22	at Atlanta	6-5†	Apr.	1	at Ottawa	1-0
	23	Montreal	4-2		3	at Carolina	5-6*
	27	Boston	3-4*		5	Carolina	3-4†
	28	at New Jersey	2-7		7	Carolina	3-4
	31	Philadelphia	4-3†		8	at NY Islanders	0-5
Jan.	1	Atlanta	2-5		10	at Boston	2-1*
	4	Ottawa	1-3		13	at Atlanta	3-5
	6	Philadelphia	1-3		15	at Florida	2-1†
	8	Florida	3-4†		17	Atlanta	6-4
	10	Chicago	3-4*		18	at Tampa Bay	4-1

* – Overtime   † – Shootout

Entry Draft
Selections 2006-1992

2006
Pick
4	Nicklas Backstrom
23	Simeon Varlamov
34	Michal Neuvirth
35	Francois Bouchard
52	Keith Seabrook
97	Oskar Osala
122	Luke Lynes
127	Maxime Lacroix
157	Brent Gwidt
177	Mathieu Perreault

2005
Pick
14	Sasha Pokulok
27	Joe Finley
109	Andrew Thomas
118	Patrick McNeill
143	Daren Machesney
181	Tim Kennedy
209	Viktor Dovgan
209	Ineligible Claim

2004
Pick
1	Alex Ovechkin
27	Jeff Schultz
29	Mike Green
33	Chris Bourque
62	Mikhail Yunkov
66	Sami Lepisto
88	Clayton Barthel
132	Oscar Hedman
138	Pasi Salonen
166	Peter Guggisberg
197	Andrew Gordon
230	Justin Mrazek
263	Travis Morin

2003
Pick
18	Eric Fehr
83	Steve Werner
109	Andreas Valdix
155	Josh Robertson
249	Andrew Joudrey
279	Mark Olafson

2002
Pick
12	Steve Eminger
13	Alexander Semin
17	Boyd Gordon
59	Maxime Daigneault
77	Patrick Wellar
92	Derek Krestanovich
109	Jevon Desautels
118	Petr Dvorak
145	Rob Gherson
179	Marian Havel
209	Joni Lindlof
242	Igor Ignatushkin
272	Patric Blomdahl

2001
Pick
58	Nathan Paetsch
90	Owen Fussey
125	Jeff Lucky
160	Artem Ternavsky
191	Zbynek Novak
221	John Oduya
249	Matt Maglione
254	Peter Polcik
275	Röbert Muller
284	Viktor Hubl

2000
Pick
26	Brian Sutherby
43	Matt Pettinger
61	Jakub Cutta
121	Ryan Vanbuskirk
163	Ivan Nepryayev
289	Bjorn Nord

1999
Pick
7	Kris Beech
29	Michal Sivek
31	Charlie Stephens
34	Ross Lupaschuk
37	Nolan Yonkman
132	Roman Tvrdon
175	Kyle Clark
192	David Bornhammar
219	Maxim Orlov
249	Igor Shadilov

1998
Pick
49	Jomar Cruz
59	Todd Hornung
106	Krys Barch
107	Chris Corrinet
118	Mike Siklenka
125	Erik Wendell
179	Nate Forster
193	Rastislav Stana
220	Mike Farrell
251	Blake Evans

1997
Pick
9	Nick Boynton
35	Jean-Francois Fortin
89	Curtis Cruickshank
116	Kevin Caulfield
143	Henrik Petre
200	Pierre-Luc Therrien
226	Matt Oikawa

1996
Pick
4	Alexandre Volchkov
17	Jaroslav Svejkovsky
43	Jan Bulis
58	Sergei Zimakov
74	Dave Weninger
78	Shawn McNeil
85	Justin Davis
126	Matthew Lahey
153	Andrew Van Bruggen
180	Michael Anderson
206	Oleg Orekhovsky
232	Chad Cavanagh

1995
Pick
17	Brad Church
23	Miika Elomo
43	Dwayne Hay
93	Sebastien Charpentier
95	Joel Theriault
105	Benoit Gratton
124	Joel Cort
147	Frederick Jobin
199	Vasili Turkovsky
225	Scott Swanson

1994
Pick
10	Nolan Baumgartner
15	Alexander Kharlamov
41	Scott Cherrey
93	Matt Herr
119	Yanick Jean
145	Dmitri Mekeshkin
171	Daniel Reja
197	Chris Patrick
223	John Tuohy
249	Richard Zednik
275	Sergei Tertyshny

1993
Pick
11	Brendan Witt
17	Jason Allison
69	Patrick Boileau
147	Frank Banham
173	Daniel Hendrickson
174	Andrew Brunette
199	Joel Poirier
225	Jason Gladney
251	Mark Seliger
277	Dany Bousquet

1992
Pick
14	Sergei Gonchar
32	Jim Carey
53	Stefan Ustorf
71	Martin Gendron
119	John Varga
167	Mark Matier
191	Mike Mathers
215	Brian Stagg
239	Gregory Callahan
263	Billy Jo MacPherson

General Managers' History

Milt Schmidt, 1974-75; Milt Schmidt and Max McNab, 1975-76; Max McNab, 1976-77 to 1980-81; Max McNab and Roger Crozier, 1981-82; David Poile, 1982-83 to 1996-97; George McPhee, 1997-98 to date.

Vice President and General Manager

McPHEE, GEORGE
Vice President/General Manager, Washington Capitals.
Born in Guelph, Ont., July 2, 1958.
On June 9, 1997, George McPhee became the fifth general manager of the Washington Capitals. In his first year on the job, McPhee led the Caps to the Stanley Cup Finals for the first time in franchise history. He has begun rebuilding the Capitals with younger players and used the first overall choice at the 2004 NHL Entry Draft to select Alexander Ovechkin.

Prior to joining the Capitals, McPhee spent five years in the front office of the Vancouver Canucks where he served as vice president of hockey operations and alternate governor. He has earned degrees in both law and business and, while attending law school at Rutgers University, interned at the United States Court of International Trade in 1991.

A back injury forced McPhee to retire as an active player at the conclusion of the 1988-89 season, after a seven year playing career with the New York Rangers and New Jersey Devils. McPhee originally signed as a free agent with the Rangers in July, 1982, after graduating from Bowling Green State University with a business degree. McPhee did not waste any time in college, tallying 40 goals and 48 assists in his freshman season and easily winning CCHA rookie of the year honors. His outstanding collegiate hockey career was capped off when he was named the recipient of the Hobey Baker Award as the top U.S. collegiate player in his senior season. McPhee also earned All-America honors as a senior and finished his career at Bowling Green as the CCHA's all-time leading scorer with 114-153-267. He was the first player in CCHA history to make the Conference's all-academic team three straight seasons.

Club Directory

Verizon Center

Washington Capitals
627 N. Globe Road
Arlington, VA 22203
Phone 202/266-2200
PR FAX 202/266-2360
www.washingtoncapitals.com
Capacity: 18,277

Washington Ownership (Lincoln Holdings LLC)
Chairman and Majority Owner	Ted Leonsis
President and Owner	Dick Patrick
Owners	Jack Davies, Richard Fairbank, Raul Fernandez, Joshua M. Freeman, Sheila Johnson, Richard Kay, Jeong Kim, Mark D. Lerner, George Stamas
Director of Office Admin./Exec. Assistant	Michelle Trostle

Hockey Operations
Vice President & General Manager	George McPhee
Director of Legal Affairs/Hockey Admin.	Don Fishman
Head Coach	Glen Hanlon
Assistant Coaches	Jay Leach, Dean Evason
Goaltending Coach	Dave Prior
Video Coach	Blaine Forsythe
Physiologist	Jack Blatherwick
Hockey Operations Assistant	Eric Garvey
Executive Assistant	Katy Headman
Security Representative	James Wiseman

Scouting Staff
Director of Scouting Operations	Kris Wagner
Director of Player Personnel	Brian MacLellan
Professional Scouts	Larry Carriere
Professional Scout	Dave Draper, Steve Richmond
Director of Amateur Scouting	Ross Mahoney
Amateur Scouts	Steve Bowman, Ed McColgan, Ray Payne, Martin Pouliot, Todd Woodcroft
European Scouts	Gleb Chistyakov, Vojtech Kucera, Petri Skriko, Mats Weiderstal

Medical Staff
Head Athletic Trainer	Greg Smith
Assistant Athletic Trainer	Christopher Phillips
Massage Therapist	Curt Millar
Team Physician	Ben Shaffer, MD

Equipment Staff
Head Equipment Manager	Doug Shearer
Assistant Equipment Manager	Craig Leydig
Equipment Assistant	Brian Metzger

Business Operations
Senior Director of Operations	George Parr
Information Technology Manager	Brian McPartland
Mailroom Coordinator	Keith McCombs
Receptionist	Caitlin Wallace

Communications and Marketing
V.P., Communications & Marketing, CCO	Kurt Kehl
Director of Media Relations	Nate Ewell
Manager of Media Relations	Corey Masse
Manager of Community Relations	Elizabeth Wodatch
Director of New Media	Sean Parker
Senior Writer	Mike Vogel
Communications Coordinator	Carolyn Weaver
Website & Publications Coordinator	Andrew Mattice
Director of Game Operations	Mark Tamar
Director of Promotions	Chris Lewis
Manager, Fan Development and Promotions	Gail Rodriguez
Amateur Hockey/Alumni Relations Coordinator	Justin Guiles
Game Operations Coordinator	James Dowd
Mascot Coordinator	Chris Monihan

Finance
VP, Finance	Keith Burrows
Accounts Payable Manager	Jennifer Simpson
Accounting Manager	Jill Ruehle
Staff Accountant	Marta Sokol

Sales
Director of Group Sales	Darren Montgomery
Director, Season Ticket Sales	Anthony Aspaas
Sr. Regional Sales Manager, Groups	Tim Bronaugh
Sr. Regional Sales Managers	Dave Boettinger, Audrius Zubrus
Regional Sales Managers, Groups	Jeff Keeney, Peter Sekulow
Regional Sales Managers	Nova Ackerman, Ian Anderson, Jaclyn Benjamin, Matt MacDonald, Joseph O'Neill, Aaron Pearl, Letitia Petrillo, Jason Rocco, Harry Schroeder, Matt Winkler
Sponsorship Activation Manager	Julie DiBella
Executive Assistant	Lauren Gilmore

Ticket Operations
Director, Ticket Operations	Gary Brosius
Manager, Ticket Operations	Chris Sheap
Coordinator, Ticket Operations	Andre Morales

Guest Services
Director, Guest Services	Greg Monares
Coordinators, Guest Services	Justine Itté, Emily Plourde, Chris Roberts

Broadcasting
Television Rights Holder	Comcast SportsNet
Television Play-by-Play	Joe Beninati
Television Analyst	Craig Laughlin
Television Reporter	Al Koken
Radio Play-by-Play	Steve Kolbe
Radio Analyst	Ken Sabourin

2005-2006 Final Statistics

Standings

Abbreviations: **GP** – games played; **W** – wins; **L** – losses;
OT – overtime and shootout losses; **GF** – goals for; **GA** – goals against; **PTS** – points.

EASTERN CONFERENCE

Northeast Division

	GP	W	L	OT	GF	GA	PTS
Ottawa	82	52	21	9	314	211	113
Buffalo	82	52	24	6	281	239	110
Montreal	82	42	31	9	243	247	93
Toronto	82	41	33	8	257	270	90
Boston	82	29	37	16	230	266	74

Atlantic Division

	GP	W	L	OT	GF	GA	PTS
New Jersey	82	46	27	9	242	229	101
Philadelphia	82	45	26	11	267	259	101
NY Rangers	82	44	26	12	257	215	100
NY Islanders	82	36	40	6	230	278	78
Pittsburgh	82	22	46	14	244	316	58

Southeast Division

	GP	W	L	OT	GF	GA	PTS
Carolina	82	52	22	8	294	260	112
Tampa Bay	82	43	33	6	252	260	92
Atlanta	82	41	33	8	281	275	90
Florida	82	37	34	11	240	257	85
Washington	82	29	41	12	237	306	70

WESTERN CONFERENCE

Central Division

	GP	W	L	OT	GF	GA	PTS
Detroit	82	58	16	8	305	209	124
Nashville	82	49	25	8	259	227	106
Columbus	82	35	43	4	223	279	74
Chicago	82	26	43	13	211	285	65
St. Louis	82	21	46	15	197	292	57

Pacific Division

	GP	W	L	OT	GF	GA	PTS
Dallas	82	53	23	6	265	218	112
San Jose	82	44	27	11	266	242	99
Anaheim	82	43	27	12	254	229	98
Los Angeles	82	42	35	5	249	270	89
Phoenix	82	38	39	5	246	271	81

Northwest Division

	GP	W	L	OT	GF	GA	PTS
Calgary	82	46	25	11	218	200	103
Colorado	82	43	30	9	283	257	95
Edmonton	82	41	28	13	256	251	95
Vancouver	82	42	32	8	256	255	92
Minnesota	82	38	36	8	231	215	84

INDIVIDUAL LEADERS

Goal Scoring

Player	Team	GP	G
Jonathan Cheechoo	San Jose	82	56
Jaromir Jagr	NY Rangers	82	54
Ilya Kovalchuk	Atlanta	78	52
Alex Ovechkin	Washington	81	52
Dany Heatley	Ottawa	82	50
Brian Gionta	New Jersey	82	48
Simon Gagne	Philadelphia	72	47
Eric Staal	Carolina	82	45
Daniel Alfredsson	Ottawa	77	43
Teemu Selanne	Anaheim	80	40
Brendan Shanahan	Detroit	82	40

Assists

Player	Team	GP	A
Joe Thornton	Bos., S.J.	81	96
Jason Spezza	Ottawa	68	71
Jaromir Jagr	NY Rangers	82	69
Marc Savard	Atlanta	82	69
Brad Richards	Tampa Bay	82	68
Nicklas Lidstrom	Detroit	80	64
Sidney Crosby	Pittsburgh	81	63
Daniel Alfredsson	Ottawa	77	60
Pavel Datsyuk	Detroit	75	59
Sergei Zubov	Dallas	78	58
Ales Hemsky	Edmonton	81	58
Tomas Kaberle	Toronto	82	58

Power-play Goals

Player	Team	GP	PP
Ilya Kovalchuk	Atlanta	78	27
Jaromir Jagr	NY Rangers	82	24
Jonathan Cheechoo	San Jose	82	24
Brian Gionta	New Jersey	82	24
Dany Heatley	Ottawa	82	23
Alex Ovechkin	Washington	81	21
Patrick Marleau	San Jose	82	20

Shorthand Goals

Player	Team	GP	SH
Marian Hossa	Atlanta	80	7
Antoine Vermette	Ottawa	82	6
Pavol Demitra	Los Angeles	58	5
Matt Pettinger	Washington	71	5
Daniel Alfredsson	Ottawa	77	5
Ryan Malone	Pittsburgh	77	5
Brian Rolston	Minnesota	82	5

Game-winning Goals

Player	Team	GP	GW
Jonathan Cheechoo	San Jose	82	11
Brian Gionta	New Jersey	82	10
Marek Svatos	Colorado	61	9
Henrik Zetterberg	Detroit	77	9
Jaromir Jagr	NY Rangers	82	9
Olli Jokinen	Florida	82	9

Shots

Player	Team	GP	S
Alex Ovechkin	Washington	81	425
Jaromir Jagr	NY Rangers	82	368
Olli Jokinen	Florida	82	351
Marian Hossa	Atlanta	80	341
Simon Gagne	Philadelphia	72	334

Shooting Percentage

(minimum 82 shots)

Player	Team	GP	G	S	%
Alex Tanguay	Colorado	71	29	125	23.2
Petr Prucha	NY Rangers	68	30	130	23.1
Anson Carter	Vancouver	81	33	146	22.6
Mark Parrish	NYI, L.A	76	29	137	21.2
Tomas Holmstrom	Detroit	81	29	140	20.7

Penalty Minutes

Player	Team	GP	PIM
Sean Avery	Los Angeles	75	257
Brendan Witt	Wsh., Nsh.	75	209
Chris Neil	Ottawa	79	204
Brenden Morrow	Dallas	81	183
Steve Ott	Dallas	82	178

Plus/Minus

Player	Team	GP	+/–
Wade Redden	Ottawa	65	35
Michal Rozsival	NY Rangers	82	35
Jaromir Jagr	NY Rangers	82	34
Andrej Meszaros	Ottawa	82	34
Mathieu Schneider	Detroit	72	33

Jonathan Cheechoo and Joe Thornton became the first teammates to lead the league in goals and assists since Mario Lemieux and Ron Francis accomplished the feat with Pittsburgh in 1995-96.

Individual Leaders

Abbreviations: GP – games played; **G** – goals; **A** – assists; **Pts** – points; **+/–** – difference between Goals For (**GF**) scored when a player is on the ice with his team at even strength or short-handed and Goals Against (**GA**) scored when the same player is on the ice with his team at even strength or on a power play; **PIM** – penalties in minutes; **PP** – power play goals; **SH** – short-handed goals; **GW** – game-winning goals; **GT** – game-tying goals; **S** – shots on goal; **%** – percentage of shots on goal resulting in goals.

Individual Scoring Leaders for Art Ross Trophy

Player	Team	GP	G	A	Pts	+/–	PIM	PP	SH	GW	S	%
Joe Thornton	Bos., S.J.	81	29	96	125	31	61	11	0	6	195	14.9
Jaromir Jagr	NY Rangers	82	54	69	123	34	72	24	0	9	368	14.7
Alex Ovechkin	Washington	81	52	54	106	2	52	21	3	5	425	12.2
Dany Heatley	Ottawa	82	50	53	103	29	86	23	2	7	300	16.7
Daniel Alfredsson	Ottawa	77	43	60	103	29	50	16	5	8	249	17.3
Sidney Crosby	Pittsburgh	81	39	63	102	–1	110	16	0	5	278	14.0
Eric Staal	Carolina	82	45	55	100	–8	81	19	4	4	279	16.1
Ilya Kovalchuk	Atlanta	78	52	46	98	–6	68	27	0	7	323	16.1
Marc Savard	Atlanta	82	28	69	97	7	100	14	1	4	212	13.2
Jonathan Cheechoo	San Jose	82	56	37	93	23	58	24	2	11	317	17.7
Marian Hossa	Atlanta	80	39	53	92	17	67	14	7	7	341	11.4
Brad Richards	Tampa Bay	82	23	68	91	0	32	7	4	0	282	8.2
Teemu Selanne	Anaheim	80	40	50	90	28	44	18	0	5	267	15.0
Jason Spezza	Ottawa	68	19	71	90	23	33	7	0	5	156	12.2
Brian Gionta	New Jersey	82	48	41	89	18	46	24	1	10	291	16.5
Olli Jokinen	Florida	82	38	51	89	14	88	14	1	9	351	10.8
Joe Sakic	Colorado	82	32	55	87	10	60	10	0	6	263	12.2
Pavel Datsyuk	Detroit	75	28	59	87	26	22	11	0	4	145	19.3
Patrick Marleau	San Jose	82	34	52	86	–12	26	20	1	4	260	13.1
Henrik Zetterberg	Detroit	77	39	46	85	29	30	17	1	9	270	14.4
Andy McDonald	Anaheim	82	34	51	85	24	32	13	0	7	229	14.8
Paul Kariya	Nashville	82	31	54	85	–6	40	14	0	3	245	12.7
Scott Gomez	New Jersey	82	33	51	84	10	42	9	0	5	244	13.5
Brendan Shanahan	Detroit	82	40	41	81	29	105	14	0	6	289	13.8

Defencemen Scoring Leaders

Player	Team	GP	G	A	Pts	+/–	PIM	PP	SH	GW	S	%
Nicklas Lidstrom	Detroit	80	16	64	80	21	50	9	0	2	243	6.6
Sergei Zubov	Dallas	78	13	58	71	20	46	9	0	1	141	9.2
Bryan McCabe	Toronto	73	19	49	68	–1	116	13	0	6	207	9.2
Lubomir Visnovsky	Los Angeles	80	17	50	67	7	50	10	0	3	152	11.2
Tomas Kaberle	Toronto	82	9	58	67	–1	46	6	0	2	163	5.5
Scott Niedermayer	Anaheim	82	13	50	63	8	96	9	0	3	181	7.2
Mathieu Schneider	Detroit	72	21	38	59	33	86	11	0	4	188	11.2
Sergei Gonchar	Pittsburgh	75	12	46	58	–13	100	8	0	2	192	6.3
Chris Pronger	Edmonton	80	12	44	56	2	74	10	0	3	155	7.7
Dan Boyle	Tampa Bay	79	15	38	53	–8	38	6	0	4	153	9.8
Rob Blake	Colorado	81	14	37	51	2	94	7	1	1	264	5.3
Kimmo Timonen	Nashville	79	11	39	50	–3	74	8	0	1	156	7.1
Wade Redden	Ottawa	65	10	40	50	35	63	8	0	4	153	6.5

Dany Heatley scored points in each of his first 22 games as a member of the Ottawa Senators, a streak that stretched from October 5, 2005 to November 29 and established a new Senators team record.

CONSECUTIVE SCORING STREAKS

Goals

Games	Player	Team	G
7	Ilya Kovalchuk	Atlanta	11
7	Mike Sillinger	StL., Nsh.	8
7	Alex Ovechkin	Washington	8
6	Jaromir Jagr	NY Rangers	9
6	Petr Prucha	NY Rangers	9
6	Mark Bell	Chicago	8
6	Jere Lehtinen	Dallas	8
6	Rick Nash	Columbus	7
6	Alex Ovechkin	Washington	6
5	Mats Sundin	Toronto	8
5	Alex Ovechkin	Washington	8
5	Keith Tkachuk	St. Louis	7
5	Simon Gagne	Philadelphia	7
5	Marian Gaborik	Minnesota	7
5	Michel Ouellet	Pittsburgh	7
5	Eric Lindros	Toronto	7
5	Mike Knuble	Philadelphia	6
5	Cory Stillman	Carolina	6
5	Ryan Smyth	Edmonton	6
5	Brian Gionta	New Jersey	6
5	Henrik Zetterberg	Detroit	6
5	Ilya Kovalchuk	Atlanta	6
5	Jason Spezza	Ottawa	6
5	Michael Cammalleri	Los Angeles	6
5	Sidney Crosby	Pittsburgh	6
5	Teemu Selanne	Anaheim	5
5	Brian Rolston	Minnesota	5
5	Steve Sullivan	Nashville	5
5	Joe Thornton	Bos., S.J.	5
5	Michael Ryder	Montreal	5
5	Dany Heatley	Ottawa	5

Assists

Games	Player	Team	A
10	Brad Richards	Tampa Bay	16
10	Joe Thornton	Bos., S.J.	15
9	Pavel Datsyuk	Detroit	13
9	Lubomir Visnovsky	Los Angeles	11
8	Daniel Alfredsson	Ottawa	12
8	Joe Thornton	Bos., S.J.	12
8	Craig Conroy	Los Angeles	11
8	Joe Thornton	Boston	10
8	Olli Jokinen	Florida	8
7	Jason Spezza	Ottawa	14
7	Patrick Marleau	San Jose	13
7	Sergei Zubov	Dallas	11
7	Cory Stillman	Carolina	11
7	Vyacheslav Kozlov	Atlanta	10
7	Michael Nylander	NY Rangers	10
7	Pavel Datsyuk	Detroit	10
7	Mike Modano	Dallas	8
7	Dan Boyle	Tampa Bay	8
7	Francois Beauchemin	CBJ, Ana.	8
7	Jason Spezza	Ottawa	8
7	Alex Kovalev	Montreal	7

Points

Games	Player	Team	G	A	PTS
22	Dany Heatley	Ottawa	17	21	38
15	Brian Gionta	New Jersey	12	13	25
14	Joe Thornton	Bos., S.J.	5	17	22
13	Joe Sakic	Colorado	9	15	24
13	Vaclav Prospal	Tampa Bay	8	13	21
12	Jaromir Jagr	NY Rangers	9	14	23
12	Jaromír Jagr	NY Rangers	12	7	19
12	Jon. Cheechoo	San Jose	10	9	19
11	Mats Sundin	Toronto	12	9	21
11	Michael Nylander	NY Rangers	5	15	20
11	Cory Stillman	Carolina	7	12	19
11	Andy McDonald	Anaheim	5	13	18
11	Alex Ovechkin	Washington	5	12	17
11	Steve Yzerman	Detroit	5	9	14
10	Daniel Alfredsson	Ottawa	12	12	24
10	Eric Staal	Carolina	7	13	20
10	Scott Gomez	New Jersey	8	11	19
10	Jason Spezza	Ottawa	2	17	19
10	Brad Richards	Tampa Bay	2	16	18
10	Pavel Datsyuk	Detroit	6	12	18
10	Steve Sullivan	Nashville	5	12	17
10	Pavel Datsyuk	Detroit	4	13	17
10	Sidney Crosby	Pittsburgh	8	9	17
10	Olli Jokinen	Florida	6	10	16
10	Craig Conroy	Los Angeles	4	11	15
10	Mike Modano	Dallas	4	10	14
10	Joe Sakic	Colorado	6	8	14
10	Alex Tanguay	Colorado	3	9	12
10	Brad Richards	Tampa Bay	4	8	12

Individual Rookie Scoring Leaders

Rookie	Team	GP	G	A	Pts	+/−	PIM	PP	SH	GW	S	%
Alex Ovechkin	Washington	81	52	54	106	2	52	21	3	5	425	12.2
Sidney Crosby	Pittsburgh	81	39	63	102	−1	110	16	0	5	278	14.0
Brad Boyes	Boston	82	26	43	69	11	30	8	0	3	203	12.8
Jussi Jokinen	Dallas	81	17	38	55	2	30	8	0	2	107	15.9
Marek Svatos	Colorado	61	32	18	50	0	60	12	0	9	165	19.4
Dion Phaneuf	Calgary	82	20	29	49	5	93	16	0	7	242	8.3
Thomas Vanek	Buffalo	81	25	23	48	−11	72	11	0	4	204	12.3
Petr Prucha	NY Rangers	68	30	17	47	3	32	16	0	2	130	23.1
Alex Steen	Toronto	75	18	27	45	−9	42	9	1	3	176	10.2
Kyle Wellwood	Toronto	81	11	34	45	9	14	3	0	0	117	9.4
Jeff Carter	Philadelphia	81	23	19	42	10	40	6	2	7	189	12.2
Chris Kunitz	Atl., Ana.	69	19	22	41	16	71	5	1	2	149	12.8
Colby Armstrong	Pittsburgh	47	16	24	40	15	58	7	2	3	86	18.6
Ryan Getzlaf	Anaheim	57	14	25	39	6	22	10	0	1	116	12.1
Andrej Meszaros	Ottawa	82	10	29	39	34	61	5	0	2	137	7.3
Keith Ballard	Phoenix	82	8	31	39	−18	99	1	3	1	102	7.8

Goal Scoring

Name	Team	GP	G
Alex Ovechkin	Washington	81	52
Sidney Crosby	Pittsburgh	81	39
Marek Svatos	Colorado	61	32
Petr Prucha	NY Rangers	68	30
Brad Boyes	Boston	82	26
Thomas Vanek	Buffalo	81	25
Chris Higgins	Montreal	80	23
Jeff Carter	Philadelphia	81	23

Assists

Name	Team	GP	A
Sidney Crosby	Pittsburgh	81	63
Alex Ovechkin	Washington	81	54
Brad Boyes	Boston	82	43
Jussi Jokinen	Dallas	81	38
Kyle Wellwood	Toronto	81	34
Ryan Whitney	Pittsburgh	68	32
Keith Ballard	Phoenix	82	31

Power-play Goals

Name	Team	GP	PP
Alex Ovechkin	Washington	81	21
Petr Prucha	NY Rangers	68	16
Sidney Crosby	Pittsburgh	81	16
Dion Phaneuf	Calgary	82	16
Marek Svatos	Colorado	61	12
Michel Ouellet	Pittsburgh	50	11
Thomas Vanek	Buffalo	81	11
Jason Pominville	Buffalo	57	10
Ryan Getzlaf	Anaheim	57	10

Shorthand Goals

Name	Team	GP	SH
Mike Richards	Philadelphia	79	3
Chris Higgins	Montreal	80	3
Alex Ovechkin	Washington	81	3
Keith Ballard	Phoenix	82	3
Colby Armstrong	Pittsburgh	47	2
Maxime Talbot	Pittsburgh	48	2
Jason Pominville	Buffalo	57	2
Johan Franzen	Detroit	80	2
Jeff Carter	Philadelphia	81	2

Game-winning Goals

Name	Team	GP	GW
Marek Svatos	Colorado	61	9
Jeff Carter	Philadelphia	81	7
Dion Phaneuf	Calgary	82	7
Zach Parise	New Jersey	81	5
Alex Ovechkin	Washington	81	5
Sidney Crosby	Pittsburgh	81	5

Shots

Name	Team	GP	S
Alex Ovechkin	Washington	81	425
Sidney Crosby	Pittsburgh	81	278
Dion Phaneuf	Calgary	82	242
Thomas Vanek	Buffalo	81	204
Brad Boyes	Boston	82	203

Shooting Percentage
(minimum 82 shots)

Name	Team	GP	G	S	%
Petr Prucha	NY Rangers	68	30	130	23.1
Patrick Eaves	Ottawa	58	20	100	20.0
Marek Svatos	Colorado	61	32	165	19.4
Colby Armstrong	Pittsburgh	47	16	86	18.6
Michel Ouellet	Pittsburgh	50	16	87	18.4

Penalty Minutes

Name	Team	GP	PIM
Derek Boogaard	Minnesota	65	158
Brian McGrattan	Ottawa	60	141
George Parros	Los Angeles	55	138
Sidney Crosby	Pittsburgh	81	110
Keith Ballard	Phoenix	82	99

Plus/Minus

Name	Team	GP	+/−
Andrej Meszaros	Ottawa	82	34
Chris Kelly	Ottawa	82	21
Chris Kunitz	Atl., Ana.	69	16
Colby Armstrong	Pittsburgh	47	15
Niklas Kronwall	Detroit	27	11
Brad Boyes	Boston	82	11

Three-or-More-Goal Games

Player	Team	Date		Final Score		G
Kevyn Adams	Carolina	Nov.	17	NYR 1	Car. 5	3
Kevyn Adams	Carolina	Dec.	6	Car. 6	Ana. 2	3
Daniel Alfredsson	Ottawa	Nov.	2	Ott. 10	Buf. 4	4
Derek Armstrong	Los Angeles	Dec.	29	L.A. 5	Phx. 6	3
Jason Arnott	Dallas	Nov.	16	Dal. 4	Ana. 2	3
Stu Barnes	Dallas	Nov.	4	Chi. 1	Dal. 9	3
Bryan Berard	Columbus	Jan.	8	CBJ 5	Phx. 2	3
Marc-Andre Bergero	Edmonton	Jan.	14	Ott. 5	Edm. 3	3
Todd Bertuzzi	Vancouver	Nov.	13	Det. 1	Van. 4	3
Todd Bertuzzi	Vancouver	Jan.	14	Van. 8	NYI 1	3
Jason Blake	Ny Islanders	Nov.	26	NYI 4	Phi. 2	3
*Brandon Bochenski	Ottawa	Dec.	5	Ott. 6	Fla. 3	3
*Brad Boyes	Boston	Mar.	18	Car. 2	Bos. 4	3
Jan Bulis	Montreal	Jan.	25	Mtl. 5	Phi. 3	4
*Alexandre Burrows	Vancouver	Mar.	27	L.A. 4	Van. 7	3
Jonathan Cheechoo	San Jose	Dec.	20	Ana. 2	S.J. 4	3
Jonathan Cheechoo	San Jose	Jan.	5	CBJ 3	S.J. 6	3
Jonathan Cheechoo	San Jose	Feb.	1	S.J. 4	Ana. 4	3
Jonathan Cheechoo	San Jose	Mar.	13	L.A. 3	S.J. 4	3
Jonathan Cheechoo	San Jose	Apr.	15	Ana. 3	S.J. 6	3
Marc Chouinard	Minnesota	Oct.	5	Cgy. 3	Min. 6	3
Chris Clark	Washington	Mar.	18	Fla. 4	Wsh. 3	3
Erik Cole	Carolina	Jan.	31	Car. 8	Mtl. 2	3
Craig Conroy	Los Angeles	Nov.	13	L.A. 8	CBJ 2	3
Pavol Demitra	Los Angeles	Nov.	19	Col. 3	L.A. 4	3
Patrik Elias	New Jersey	Apr.	5	Pit. 4	N.J. 6	3
Alexander Frolov	Los Angeles	Nov.	13	L.A. 8	CBJ 2	3
Alexander Frolov	Los Angeles	Jan.	12	L.A. 6	Bos. 0	3
Marian Gaborik	Minnesota	Apr.	9	Min. 5	Col. 2	3
Simon Gagne	Philadelphia	Nov.	5	Atl. 3	Phi. 4	3
Scott Gomez	New Jersey	Dec.	31	Tor. 6	N.J. 3	3
Scott Hartnell	Nashville	Feb.	4	Chi. 0	Nsh. 6	3
Martin Havlat	Ottawa	Nov.	2	Ott. 10	Buf. 4	3
Dany Heatley	Ottawa	Oct.	29	Ott. 8	Tor. 0	4
Jochen Hecht	Buffalo	Jan.	14	L.A. 1	Buf.10	3
Jonathan Hedstrom	Anaheim	Jan.	9	L.A. 2	Ana. 6	3
Shawn Horcoff	Edmonton	Jan.	10	Edm. 3	Pit. 1	3
Nathan Horton	Florida	Dec.	13	Nsh. 3	Fla. 7	3
Jaromir Jagr	Ny Rangers	Oct.	20	NYR 4	NYI 5	3
Jaromir Jagr	Ny Rangers	Nov.	1	NYR 6	Pit. 1	3
Jaromir Jagr	Ny Rangers	Mar.	22	Phi. 6	NYR 3	3
Olli Jokinen	Florida	Nov.	25	Pit. 3	Fla. 6	3
Niko Kapanen	Dallas	Feb.	9	Dal. 5	Phx. 1	3
Paul Kariya	Nashville	Apr.	18	Det. 3	Nsh. 5	3
Chuck Kobasew	Calgary	Jan.	24	Cgy. 4	Col. 7	3
Ilya Kovalchuk	Atlanta	Nov.	11	T.B. 2	Atl. 5	4
Ilya Kovalchuk	Atlanta	Jan.	6	Pit. 4	Atl. 5	3
Vyacheslav Kozlov	Atlanta	Jan.	2	Ott. 3	Atl. 8	3
Fredrik Modin	Tampa Bay	Jan.	28	T.B. 6	Phi. 0	3
Ladislav Nagy	Phoenix	Dec.	3	Car. 4	Phx. 3	3
Rick Nash	Columbus	Apr.	7	CBJ 5	Det. 6	3
Joe Nieuwendyk	Florida	Apr.	11	Fla. 5	Tor. 6	3
Jeff O'Neill	Toronto	Oct.	14	Tor. 9	Atl. 1	3
*Alex Ovechkin	Washington	Jan.	13	Wsh. 3	Ana. 2	3
Ronald Petrovicky	Atlanta	Dec.	9	CBJ 2	Atl. 5	3
*Jason Pominville	Buffalo	Jan.	14	L.A. 1	Buf.10	3
Vaclav Prospal	Tampa Bay	Nov.	14	Phi. 2	T.B. 5	3
Taylor Pyatt	Buffalo	Nov.	17	Wsh. 5	Buf. 8	3
Mark Recchi	Pittsburgh	Mar.	4	Car. 7	Pit. 5	3
*Mike Richards	Philadelphia	Feb.	8	NYI 2	Phi. 5	3
Luc Robitaille	Los Angeles	Jan.	19	Atl. 6	L.A. 8	3
Brian Rolston	Minnesota	Nov.	5	Min. 3	S.J. 1	3
Derek Roy	Buffalo	Mar.	3	Tor. 2	Buf. 6	3
Derek Roy	Buffalo	Mar.	9	T.B. 5	Buf. 6	3
Michael Ryder	Montreal	Feb.	5	Phi. 0	Mtl. 5	3
Miroslav Satan	Ny Islanders	Feb.	4	NYI 5	Pit. 4	3
Mathieu Schneider	Detroit	Nov.	26	Det. 7	S.J. 6	3
Brendan Shanahan	Detroit	Apr.	13	Det. 7	Chi. 3	3
Jon Sim	Florida	Feb.	7	Fla. 5	Wsh. 0	3
Eric Staal	Carolina	Oct.	28	Fla. 4	Car. 8	3
Eric Staal	Carolina	Jan.	15	St.L. 2	Car. 4	3
Martin Straka	Ny Rangers	Mar.	29	NYR 5	NYI 1	3
Steve Sullivan	Nashville	Nov.	10	Det. 4	Nsh. 5	3
Mats Sundin	Toronto	Apr.	11	Fla. 5	Tor. 6	4
*Marek Svatos	Colorado	Oct.	10	Cgy. 3	Col. 7	3
*Marek Svatos	Colorado	Jan.	9	St.L. 1	Col. 6	3
Lubomir Visnovsky	Los Angeles	Nov.	5	L.A. 6	Dal. 3	3
Jason Williams	Detroit	Oct.	22	Det. 6	CBJ 0	3

* indicates rookie

2005-06 Penalty Shots

(For shootout statistics, see page 143.)

Scored

Patrick Marleau (San Jose) scored against Patrick Lalime (St. Louis), October 8. Final Score: San Jose 7 at St. Louis 6.

Ladislav Nagy (Phoenix) scored against Dwayne Roloson (Minnesota), October 8. Final Score: Minnesota 1 at Phoenix 2.

Jay McClement (St. Louis) scored against Nikolai Khabibulin (Chicago), October 11. Final Score: Chicago 1 at St. Louis 4.

Pierre-Marc Bouchard (Minnesota) scored against Dan Cloutier (Vancouver), October 12. Final Score: Vancouver 0 at Minnesota 6.

Ryan Smyth (Edmonton) scored against Patrick Lalime (St. Louis), November 4. Final Score: Edmonton 7 at St. Louis 2.

Erik Cole (Carolina) scored against Martin Biron (Buffalo), November 9. Final Score: Carolina 5 at Buffalo 3.

Jarome Iginla (Calgary) scored against Curtis Joseph (Phoenix), November 10. Final Score: Calgary 4 at Phoenix 3.

Alex Tanguay (Colorado) scored against Miikka Kiprusoff (Calgary), November 12. Final Score: Colorado 3 at Calgary 5.

Trevor Linden (Vancouver) scored against Ilya Bryzgalov (Anaheim), November 20. Final Score: Vancouver 3 at Anaheim 2.

Justin Williams (Carolina) scored against John Grahame (Tampa Bay), November 20. Final Score: Tampa Bay 5 at Carolina 2.

Matt Pettinger (Washington) scored against John Grahame (Tampa Bay), November 23. Final Score: Tampa Bay 4 at Washington 3.

Joe Corvo (Los Angeles) scored against James Howard (Detroit), November 28. Final Score: Detroit 5 at Los Angeles 2.

Antti Miettinen (Dallas) scored against Evgeni Nabokov (San Jose), November 30. Final Score: San Jose 1 at Dallas 4.

Marek Svatos (Colorado) scored against Martin Biron (Buffalo), December 4. Final Score: Buffalo 6 at Colorado 4.

Thomas Vanek (Buffalo) scored against J Giguere (Anaheim), December 8. Final Score: Anaheim 2 at Buffalo 3.

David Vyborny (Columbus) scored against Tomas Vokoun (Nashville), December 17. Final Score: Columbus 3 at Nashville 7.

Joe Sakic (Colorado) scored against Kevin Weekes (NY Rangers), December 18. Final Score: Colorado 2 at NY Rangers 1.

Jonathan Cheechoo (San Jose) scored against J Giguere (Anaheim), December 20. Final Score: Anaheim 2 at San Jose 4.

Ryan Smyth (Edmonton) scored against Tomas Vokoun (Nashville), December 30. Final Score: Nashville 2 at Edmonton 4.

Scott Gomez (New Jersey) scored against Ed Belfour (Toronto), December 31. Final Score: Toronto 6 at New Jersey 3.

Vincent Lecavalier (Tampa Bay) scored against Garth Snow (NY Islanders), January 2. Final Score: Tampa Bay 2 at NY Islanders 1.

Jarkko Ruutu (Vancouver) scored against Craig Anderson (Chicago), January 5. Final Score: Vancouver 3 at Chicago 2.

Steve Sullivan (Nashville) scored against Craig Anderson (Chicago), January 8. Final Score: Nashville 5 at Chicago 1.

Alexander Frolov (Los Angeles) scored against Andrew Raycroft (Boston), January 12. Final Score: Los Angeles 6 at Boston 0.

Frantisek Kaberle (Carolina) scored against Tomas Vokoun (Nashville), January 13. Final Score: Nashville 4 at Carolina 5.

Erik Cole (Carolina) scored against Olaf Kolzig (Washington), January 21. Final Score: Carolina 2 at Washington 5.

Ryan Malone (Pittsburgh) scored against Olaf Kolzig (Washington), January 25. Final Score: Washington 1 at Pittsburgh 8.

Martin Straka (NY Rangers) scored against Rick DiPietro (NY Islanders), February 2. Final Score: NY Rangers 5 at NY Islanders 2.

Marian Gaborik (Minnesota) scored against Vesa Toskala (San Jose), February 2. Final Score: Minnesota 3 at San Jose 2.

Jussi Jokinen (Dallas) scored against Ty Conklin (Edmonton), March 7. Final Score: Dallas 4 at Edmonton 3.

Maxim Afinogenov (Buffalo) scored against Andrew Raycroft (Boston), March 12. Final Score: Boston 2 at Buffalo 6.

Chad Kilger (Toronto) scored against Marc-Andre Fleury (Pittsburgh), March 19. Final Score: Toronto 1 at Pittsburgh 0.

Jonathan Hedstrom (Anaheim) scored against Peter Budaj (Colorado), March 22. Final Score: Colorado 4 at Anaheim 5.

Matthew Lombardi (Calgary) scored against Peter Budaj (Colorado), March 31. Final Score: Colorado 3 at Calgary 6.

Marc Savard (Atlanta) scored against Cam Ward (Carolina), April 1. Final Score: Carolina 2 at Atlanta 5.

Stopped

Robert Esche (Philadelphia) stopped Michael Nylander (NY Rangers), October 5. Final Score: NY Rangers 5 at Philadelphia 3.

Curtis Joseph (Phoenix) stopped Alexandre Daigle (Minnesota), October 8. Final Score: Minnesota 1 at Phoenix 2.

Roberto Luongo (Florida) stopped Miroslav Satan (NY Islanders), October 10. Final Score: Florida 3 at NY Islanders 1.

Miikka Kiprusoff (Calgary) stopped Oleg Saprykin (Phoenix), October 17. Final Score: Phoenix 2 at Calgary 0.

Michael Garnett (Atlanta) stopped Ruslan Fedotenko (Tampa Bay), October 20. Final Score: Tampa Bay 6 at Atlanta 0.

Mathieu Garon (Los Angeles) stopped Marcus Nilson (Calgary), October 23. Final Score: Calgary 3 at Los Angeles 2.

Rick DiPietro (NY Islanders) stopped Patrik Stefan (Atlanta), October 25. Final Score: Atlanta 3 at NY Islanders 4.

Marty Turco (Dallas) stopped Marcel Goc (San Jose), October 26. Final Score: San Jose 5 at Dallas 4.

Roberto Luongo (Florida) stopped Peter Forsberg (Philadelphia), October 27. Final Score: Florida 4 at Philadelphia 5.

Nolan Schaefer (San Jose) stopped Tony Amonte (Calgary), October 29. Final Score: Calgary 2 at San Jose 3.

Nikolai Khabibulin (Chicago) stopped Robert Lang (Detroit), November 1. Final Score: Chicago 1 at Detroit 4.

Jason Labarbera (Los Angeles) stopped David Legwand (Nashville), November 5. Final Score: Nashville 2 at Los Angeles 3.

Rick DiPietro (NY Islanders) stopped Dany Heatley (Ottawa), November 5. Final Score: NY Islanders 0 at Ottawa 6.

Kevin Weekes (NY Rangers) stopped Zigmund Palffy (Pittsburgh), November 7. Final Score: Pittsburgh 3 at NY Rangers 2.

Alexander Auld (Vancouver) stopped Chuck Kobasew (Calgary), November 7. Final Score: Vancouver 3 at Calgary 4.

Martin Biron (Buffalo) stopped Erik Cole (Carolina), November 9. Final Score: Carolina 5 at Buffalo 3.

Marty Turco (Dallas) stopped Steve Sullivan (Nashville), November 10. Final Score: Dallas 3 at Nashville 5.

Roberto Luongo (Florida) stopped Erik Cole (Carolina), November 11. Final Score: Carolina 1 at Florida 0.

Michael Garnett (Atlanta) stopped R.J. Umberger (Philadelphia), November 18. Final Score: Atlanta 6 at Philadelphia 5.

Ilya Bryzgalov (Anaheim) stopped Brett Clark (Colorado), November 18. Final Score: Colorado 3 at Anaheim 2.

Jason Labarbera (Los Angeles) stopped Paul Kariya (Nashville), November 23. Final Score: Los Angeles 3 at Nashville 4.

Sean Burke (Tampa Bay) stopped Brian Gionta (New Jersey), November 25. Final Score: New Jersey 8 at Tampa Bay 2.

Marty Turco (Dallas) stopped Mike Comrie (Phoenix), November 25. Final Score: Phoenix 4 at Dallas 1.

Alexander Auld (Vancouver) stopped Shane Doan (Phoenix), November 26. Final Score: Vancouver 1 at Phoenix 2.

John Grahame (Tampa Bay) stopped Matt Murley (Pittsburgh), November 27. Final Score: Pittsburgh 1 at Tampa Bay 4.

James Howard (Detroit) stopped Shean Donovan (Calgary), December 1. Final Score: Calgary 3 at Detroit 2.

Olaf Kolzig (Washington) stopped Steve Sullivan (Nashville), December 7. Final Score: Nashville 5 at Washington 2.

Martin Brodeur (New Jersey) stopped Marian Hossa (Atlanta), December 15. Final Score: Atlanta 3 at New Jersey 2.

Nikolai Khabibulin (Chicago) stopped Doug Weight (St. Louis), December 16. Final Score: St. Louis 1 at Chicago 5.

Roberto Luongo (Florida) stopped Marian Hossa (Atlanta), December 17. Final Score: Florida 1 at Atlanta 2.

Dwayne Roloson (Minnesota) stopped Niklas Sundstrom (Montreal), December 17. Final Score: Montreal 3 at Minnesota 4.

Marc Denis (Columbus) stopped Steve Sullivan (Nashville), December 23. Final Score: Nashville 5 at Columbus 4.

Cam Ward (Carolina) stopped Chris Phillips (Ottawa), December 28. Final Score: Carolina 2 at Ottawa 6.

Miikka Kiprusoff (Calgary) stopped Brian Rolston (Minnesota), December 29. Final Score: Minnesota 2 at Calgary 4.

Jason Labarbera (Los Angeles) stopped Ladislav Nagy (Phoenix), December 29. Final Score: Los Angeles 5 at Phoenix 6.

Garth Snow (NY Islanders) stopped Peter Schaefer (Ottawa), December 30. Final Score: NY Islanders 3 at Ottawa 4.

Roberto Luongo (Florida) stopped Alex Kovalev (Montreal), December 30. Final Score: Montreal 1 at Florida 2.

Martin Gerber (Carolina) stopped Michael Ryder (Montreal), December 31. Final Score: Montreal 3 at Carolina 5.

Craig Anderson (Chicago) stopped Alexandre Burrows (Vancouver), January 5. Final Score: Vancouver 3 at Chicago 2.

Curtis Sanford (St. Louis) stopped Marian Hossa (Atlanta), January 13. Final Score: St. Louis 0 at Atlanta 2.

John Grahame (Tampa Bay) stopped Sean Avery (Los Angeles), January 17. Final Score: Tampa Bay 4 at Los Angeles 1.

Olaf Kolzig (Washington) stopped Mike Sillinger (St. Louis), January 19. Final Score: St. Louis 4 at Washington 5.

Tomas Vokoun (Nashville) stopped Trevor Letowski (Columbus), January 21. Final Score: Columbus 2 at Nashville 7.

Tim Thomas (Boston) stopped Alex Ovechkin (Washington), January 26. Final Score: Washington 2 at Boston 3.

Cristobal Huet (Montreal) stopped P.J. Axelsson (Boston), February 2. Final Score: Montreal 1 at Boston 3.

Miikka Kiprusoff (Calgary) stopped Alexandre Burrows (Vancouver), February 3. Final Score: Vancouver 3 at Calgary 1.

Ed Belfour (Toronto) stopped Viktor Kozlov (New Jersey), February 4. Final Score: New Jersey 2 at Toronto 4.

Alexander Auld (Vancouver) stopped Rick Nash (Columbus), February 6. Final Score: Columbus 4 at Vancouver 7.

John Grahame (Tampa Bay) stopped Erik Cole (Carolina), February 9. Final Score: Carolina 3 at Tampa Bay 5.

Manny Legace (Detroit) stopped Nils Ekman (San Jose), February 28. Final Score: Detroit 1 at San Jose 5.

Antero Niittymaki (Philadelphia) stopped Robert Nilsson (NY Islanders), March 4. Final Score: Philadelphia 2 at NY Islanders 4.

Philippe Sauve (Phoenix) stopped Nicklas Lidstrom (Detroit), March 4. Final Score: Detroit 7 at Phoenix 3.

Pascal Leclaire (Columbus) stopped Scott Niedermayer (Anaheim), March 5. Final Score: Columbus 3 at Anaheim 2.

Curtis Joseph (Phoenix) stopped Mark Mowers (Detroit), March 7. Final Score: Phoenix 5 at Detroit 2.

Kari Lehtonen (Atlanta) stopped Jason Ward (NY Rangers), March 8. Final Score: NY Rangers 2 at Atlanta 3.

Mathieu Garon (Los Angeles) stopped Keith Tkachuk (St. Louis), March 11. Final Score: Los Angeles 2 at St. Louis 1.

Martin Gerber (Carolina) stopped Martin Straka (NY Rangers), March 14. Final Score: NY Rangers 3 at Carolina 5.

Nikolai Khabibulin (Chicago) stopped Dan Fritsche (Columbus), March 15. Final Score: Columbus 2 at Chicago 3.

Mathieu Garon (Los Angeles) stopped Stu Barnes (Dallas), March 16. Final Score: Dallas 4 at Los Angeles 1.

Manny Legace (Detroit) stopped Scott Hartnell (Nashville), March 21. Final Score: Nashville 3 at Detroit 2.

Ryan Miller (Buffalo) stopped Travis Green (Boston), March 25. Final Score: Buffalo 4 at Boston 5.

Sebastien Caron (Pittsburgh) stopped Sean Bergenheim (NY Islanders), March 31. Final Score: Pittsburgh 4 at NY Islanders 0.

Martin Gerber (Carolina) stopped Jim Slater (Atlanta), April 8. Final Score: Carolina 2 at Atlanta 5.

Mike Morrison (Ottawa) stopped Marco Sturm (Boston), April 11. Final Score: Boston 3 at Ottawa 4.

David Aebischer (Montreal) stopped J-P Dumont (Buffalo), April 15. Final Score: Buffalo 4 at Montreal 2.

Tim Thomas (Boston) stopped Marc Savard (Atlanta), April 15. Final Score: Boston 3 at Atlanta 4.

Jamie McLennan (Florida) stopped Matt Pettinger (Washington), April 15. Final Score: Washington 2 at Florida 1.

Marc-Andre Fleury (Pittsburgh) stopped Miroslav Satan (NY Islanders), April 17. Final Score: NY Islanders 1 at Pittsburgh 6.

Summary

103 penalty shots resulted in 35 goals.

Goaltending Leaders

Minimum 25 games

Goals Against Average

Goaltender	Team	GPI	MINS	GA	Avg
Miikka Kiprusoff	Calgary	74	4380	151	2.07
Dominik Hasek	Ottawa	43	2584	90	2.09
Manny Legace	Detroit	51	2905	106	2.19
Cristobal Huet	Montreal	36	2103	77	2.20
*Henrik Lundqvist	NY Rangers	53	3112	116	2.24

Wins

Goaltender	Team	GPI	MINS	W	L	OT
Martin Brodeur	New Jersey	73	4365	43	23	7
Miikka Kiprusoff	Calgary	74	4380	42	20	11
Marty Turco	Dallas	68	3910	41	19	5
Martin Gerber	Carolina	60	3493	38	14	6
Manny Legace	Detroit	51	2905	37	8	3

Save Percentage

Goaltender	Team	GPI	MINS	GA	SA	S%	W	L	OT
Cristobal Huet	Montreal	36	2103	77	1085	.929	18	11	4
Dominik Hasek	Ottawa	43	2584	90	1202	.925	28	10	4
Miikka Kiprusoff	Calgary	74	4380	151	1951	.923	42	20	11
*Henrik Lundqvist	NY Rangers	53	3112	116	1485	.922	30	12	9
Tomas Vokoun	Nashville	61	3601	160	1984	.919	36	18	7
Manny Fernandez	Minnesota	58	3411	130	1612	.919	30	18	7

Shutouts

Goaltender	Team	GPI	MINS	SO	W	L	OT
Miikka Kiprusoff	Calgary	74	4380	10	42	20	11
Cristobal Huet	Montreal	36	2103	7	18	11	4
Manny Legace	Detroit	51	2905	7	37	8	3
Dominik Hasek	Ottawa	43	2584	5	28	10	4
John Grahame	Tampa Bay	57	3152	5	29	22	1
Martin Brodeur	New Jersey	73	4365	5	43	23	7

Team-by-Team Point Totals

2000-01 to 2005-06

(Ranked by five-year point %)

Team	05-06	03-04	02-03	01-02	00-01	Pts%
Detroit	124	109	110	116	111	.695
Ottawa	113	102	113	94	109	.648
Colorado	95	100	105	99	118	.630
Dallas	112	97	111	90	106	.629
New Jersey	101	100	108	95	111	.628
Philadelphia	101	101	107	97	100	.617
Toronto	90	103	98	100	90	.587
Vancouver	92	101	104	94	90	.587
San Jose	99	104	73	99	95	.573
Edmonton	95	89	92	92	93	.562
Boston	74	104	87	101	88	.554
St. Louis	57	91	99	98	103	.546
Buffalo	110	85	72	82	98	.545
Los Angeles	89	81	78	95	92	.530
Carolina	112	76	61	91	88	.522
Calgary	103	94	75	79	73	.517
Montreal	93	93	77	87	70	.512
Nashville	106	91	74	69	80	.512
Tampa Bay	92	106	93	69	59	.511
Phoenix	81	68	78	95	90	.502
Anaheim	98	76	95	69	66	.492
Minnesota	84	83	95	73	68	.491
Washington	70	60	92	85	96	.491
NY Islanders	78	91	83	96	52	.488
NY Rangers	100	69	78	80	72	.487
Chicago	65	59	79	96	71	.451
Atlanta	90	78	74	54	60	.434
Florida	85	75	70	60	66	.434
Pittsburgh	58	58	65	69	96	.422
Columbus	74	62	69	57	71	.406

Team Record When Scoring First Goal of a Game

Team	FG	W	L	OT
Anaheim	38	26	8	4
Atlanta	32	23	6	3
Boston	40	21	11	8
Buffalo	45	36	5	4
Calgary	50	32	13	5
Carolina	41	36	3	2
Chicago	30	16	10	4
Colorado	49	31	11	7
Columbus	34	19	14	1
Dallas	43	31	10	2
Detroit	47	35	8	4
Edmonton	40	31	4	5
Florida	38	22	9	7
Los Angeles	40	25	11	4
Minnesota	42	27	11	4
Montreal	42	31	8	3
Nashville	46	26	14	6
New Jersey	46	32	8	6
NY Islanders	37	24	12	1
NY Rangers	47	33	7	7
Ottawa	46	40	3	3
Philadelphia	45	31	9	5
Phoenix	37	23	9	5
Pittsburgh	32	19	8	5
San Jose	40	30	8	2
St. Louis	40	16	15	9
Tampa Bay	44	30	12	2
Toronto	44	27	13	4
Vancouver	36	24	8	4
Washington	37	16	13	8

Team Plus/Minus Differential

Team	GF	PPGF	Net GF	GA	PPGA	Net GA	Goal Differential
Ottawa	314	102	212	211	73	138	+74
Detroit	305	102	203	209	67	142	+61
Dallas	265	88	177	218	82	136	+41
NY Rangers	257	83	174	215	79	136	+38
Philadelphia	267	80	187	259	97	162	+25
Anaheim	254	87	167	229	84	145	+22
Carolina	294	95	199	260	81	179	+20
Nashville	259	94	165	227	82	145	+20
Florida	240	63	177	257	91	166	+11
Calgary	218	87	131	200	80	120	+11
San Jose	266	91	175	242	77	165	+10
Atlanta	281	100	181	275	102	173	+8
Colorado	283	89	194	257	69	188	+6
Los Angeles	249	77	172	270	104	166	+6
Buffalo	281	101	180	239	59	180	0
New Jersey	242	78	164	229	63	166	−2
Vancouver	256	96	160	255	93	162	−2
Montreal	243	89	154	247	91	156	−2
Minnesota	231	77	154	215	55	160	−6
Edmonton	256	88	168	251	76	175	−7
Tampa Bay	252	81	171	260	72	188	−17
Boston	230	62	168	266	78	188	−20
Toronto	257	107	150	270	99	171	−21
Phoenix	246	96	150	271	98	173	−23
Washington	237	72	165	306	116	190	−25
Columbus	223	64	159	279	95	184	−25
NY Islanders	230	76	154	278	99	179	−25
Chicago	211	51	160	285	88	197	−37
Pittsburgh	244	94	150	316	113	203	−53
St. Louis	197	75	122	292	82	210	−88

Team Record When Leading, Trailing, Tied

Team	Leading after 1 period W	L	OT	Leading after 2 periods W	L	OT	Trailing after 1 period W	L	OT	Trailing after 2 periods W	L	OT	Tied after 1 period W	L	OT	Tied after 2 periods W	L	OT
Anaheim	22	6	4	31	2	4	8	12	5	3	18	2	13	9	3	9	7	6
Atlanta	20	4	3	22	3	0	8	18	2	8	25	3	13	11	3	11	5	5
Boston	15	4	8	23	5	5	6	11	5	2	21	2	8	22	3	4	11	9
Buffalo	21	1	2	33	1	3	8	14	3	9	21	2	23	9	1	10	2	1
Calgary	22	9	4	33	3	2	8	8	2	4	16	3	16	8	5	9	6	6
Carolina	21	1	2	31	0	2	10	15	3	7	19	5	21	6	3	14	3	1
Chicago	13	5	3	17	0	4	4	25	3	1	32	5	9	13	7	8	11	4
Colorado	21	6	6	30	1	2	5	16	1	2	22	3	17	8	2	11	7	4
Columbus	12	7	1	15	2	0	9	18	2	9	34	3	14	18	1	11	7	1
Dallas	24	2	2	31	5	2	13	15	2	12	17	2	16	6	2	10	1	2
Detroit	27	4	3	38	0	2	10	8	0	3	11	1	21	4	5	17	5	5
Edmonton	16	4	3	21	2	2	7	14	6	9	20	4	18	10	4	11	6	7
Florida	13	1	3	28	2	4	10	18	3	2	21	2	14	15	5	7	11	5
Los Angeles	22	5	1	25	3	0	7	22	1	10	24	1	13	8	3	7	8	4
Minnesota	18	4	1	24	3	2	5	16	2	4	22	4	15	16	5	10	11	2
Montreal	19	4	3	24	5	2	7	17	3	6	21	5	16	10	3	12	5	2
Nashville	24	6	4	30	1	4	11	9	1	9	19	2	14	10	3	6	5	2
New Jersey	27	2	3	31	0	4	6	16	1	7	17	2	13	9	5	8	4	2
NY Islanders	16	8	1	23	3	1	5	21	3	1	29	2	15	11	2	12	8	3
NY Rangers	29	2	4	29	2	3	5	15	1	5	18	3	10	9	7	10	6	6
Ottawa	32	3	3	43	0	2	7	12	5	5	18	5	13	7	1	7	2	3
Philadelphia	23	4	3	30	4	5	10	13	6	4	17	3	12	7	4	11	5	3
Phoenix	17	5	2	24	3	3	6	24	1	7	31	2	15	9	3	7	4	1
Pittsburgh	13	2	3	17	1	3	2	28	6	0	41	10	15	6	5	4	1	1
San Jose	20	4	0	29	2	1	7	9	8	5	16	4	17	14	3	10	9	6
St. Louis	11	9	1	13	8	5	3	27	3	0	32	5	7	10	11	8	8	3
Tampa Bay	20	3	1	26	3	2	6	17	1	4	22	2	13	4	3	8	2	2
Toronto	19	8	2	26	1	3	4	16	3	1	24	4	18	9	3	14	4	1
Vancouver	20	1	1	27	4	2	12	21	0	3	22	1	10	10	7	7	6	5
Washington	8	8	5	18	1	3	4	25	3	5	35	4	17	4	6	5	5	5

Calgary's Miikka Kiprusoff led the NHL with 10 shutouts and a 2.07 goals-against average. His 42 wins ranked second, while his .923 save percentage was third.

Team Statistics

TEAMS' HOME AND ROAD RECORD

Eastern Conference

Team	GP	W	L	OT	GF	GA	PTS	GP	W	L	OT	GF	GA	PTS
			Home							Road				
OTT	41	29	9	3	164	96	61	41	23	12	6	150	115	52
CAR	41	31	8	2	153	127	64	41	21	14	6	141	133	48
BUF	41	27	11	3	152	111	57	41	25	13	3	129	128	53
N.J.	41	27	11	3	125	105	57	41	19	16	6	117	124	44
PHI	41	22	13	6	139	137	50	41	23	13	5	128	122	51
NYR	41	25	10	6	126	94	56	41	19	16	6	131	121	44
MTL	41	24	13	4	127	115	52	41	18	18	5	116	132	41
T.B.	41	25	14	2	125	128	52	41	18	19	4	127	132	40
TOR	41	26	12	3	147	129	55	41	15	21	5	110	141	35
ATL	41	24	13	4	149	135	52	41	17	20	4	132	140	38
FLA	41	25	11	5	128	112	55	41	12	23	6	112	145	30
NYI	41	20	18	3	114	138	43	41	16	22	3	116	140	35
BOS	41	16	15	10	115	125	42	41	13	22	6	115	141	32
WSH	41	16	18	7	126	145	39	41	13	23	5	111	161	31
PIT	41	12	21	8	133	156	32	41	10	25	6	111	160	26
Total	615	349	197	69	2023	1853	767	615	262	277	76	1846	2035	600

Western Conference

Team	GP	W	L	OT	GF	GA	PTS	GP	W	L	OT	GF	GA	PTS
DET	41	27	9	5	148	105	59	41	31	7	3	157	104	65
DAL	41	28	11	2	134	108	58	41	25	12	4	131	110	54
NSH	41	32	8	1	142	94	65	41	17	17	7	117	133	41
CGY	41	30	7	4	108	73	64	41	16	18	7	110	127	39
S.J.	41	25	9	7	142	112	57	41	19	18	4	124	130	42
ANA	41	26	10	5	147	116	57	41	17	17	7	107	113	41
COL	41	25	10	6	151	121	56	41	18	20	3	132	136	39
EDM	41	20	15	6	130	128	46	41	21	13	7	126	123	49
VAN	41	25	10	6	146	123	56	41	17	22	2	110	132	36
L.A.	41	26	14	1	121	120	53	41	16	21	4	128	150	36
MIN	41	23	16	2	129	106	48	41	15	20	6	102	109	36
PHX	41	19	18	4	131	137	42	41	19	21	1	115	134	39
CBJ	41	23	18	0	121	131	46	41	12	25	4	102	148	28
CHI	41	16	19	6	109	127	38	41	10	24	7	102	158	27
ST.L.	41	12	23	6	104	148	30	41	9	23	9	93	144	27
Total	615	357	197	61	1963	1749	775	615	262	278	75	1756	1951	599
	1230	706	394	4130	3986	3602	1542	1230	524	555	5151	3602	3986	1199

TEAMS' DIVISIONAL RECORD

Northeast Division

			Against Own Division							Against Other Divisions				
	GP	W	L	OT	GF	GA	PTS	GP	W	L	OT	GF	GA	PTS
OTT	32	20	8	4	122	84	44	50	32	13	5	192	127	69
BUF	32	21	9	2	108	94	44	50	31	15	4	173	145	66
MTL	32	18	9	5	93	86	41	50	24	22	4	150	161	52
TOR	32	11	16	5	89	131	27	50	30	17	3	168	139	63
BOS	32	10	19	3	80	97	23	50	19	18	13	150	169	51
Total								250	136	85	29	833	741	301

Atlantic Division

	GP	W	L	OT	GF	GA	PTS	GP	W	L	OT	GF	GA	PTS
N.J.	32	16	12	4	84	83	36	50	30	15	5	158	146	65
PHI	32	19	9	4	97	90	42	50	26	17	7	170	169	59
NYR	32	18	9	5	107	79	41	50	26	17	7	150	136	59
NYI	32	15	15	2	81	106	32	50	21	25	4	149	172	46
PIT	32	12	14	6	100	111	30	50	10	32	8	144	205	28
Total								250	113	106	31	771	828	257

Southeast Division

	GP	W	L	OT	GF	GA	PTS	GP	W	L	OT	GF	GA	PTS
CAR	32	18	11	3	103	109	39	50	34	11	5	191	151	73
T.B.	32	16	11	5	102	102	37	50	27	22	1	150	158	55
ATL	32	17	10	5	122	98	39	50	24	23	3	159	177	51
FLA	32	18	11	3	99	88	39	50	19	23	8	141	169	46
WSH	32	11	14	7	89	118	29	50	18	27	5	148	188	41
Total								250	122	106	22	789	843	266

Central Division

	GP	W	L	OT	GF	GA	PTS	GP	W	L	OT	GF	GA	PTS
DET	32	25	3	4	127	71	54	50	33	13	4	178	138	70
NSH	32	23	8	1	110	73	47	50	26	17	7	149	154	59
CBJ	32	14	15	3	90	113	31	50	21	28	1	133	166	43
CHI	32	11	17	4	85	118	26	50	15	26	9	126	167	39
ST.L.	32	7	20	5	66	103	19	50	14	26	10	131	189	38
Total								250	109	110	31	717	814	249

Pacific Division

	GP	W	L	OT	GF	GA	PTS	GP	W	L	OT	GF	GA	PTS
DAL	32	17	11	4	98	97	38	50	36	12	2	167	121	74
S.J.	32	16	10	6	102	100	38	50	28	17	5	164	142	61
ANA	32	18	9	5	105	88	41	50	25	18	7	149	141	57
L.A.	32	14	14	4	92	107	32	50	28	21	1	157	163	57
PHX	32	15	15	2	94	99	32	50	23	24	3	152	172	49
Total								250	140	92	18	789	739	298

Northwest Division

	GP	W	L	OT	GF	GA	PTS	GP	W	L	OT	GF	GA	PTS
CGY	32	20	8	4	96	84	44	50	26	17	7	122	116	59
COL	32	16	12	4	116	106	36	50	27	18	5	167	151	59
EDM	32	15	15	2	92	110	32	50	26	13	11	164	141	63
VAN	32	15	12	5	96	104	35	50	27	20	3	160	151	57
MIN	32	14	17	1	89	85	29	50	24	19	7	142	130	55
Total								250	130	87	33	755	689	293

TEAM STREAKS

Consecutive Wins

Games	Team	From	To
11	New Jersey	Mar. 28	Apr. 18
9	Detroit	Oct. 13	Nov. 1
9	Carolina	Oct. 22	Nov. 11
9	Carolina	Dec. 31	Jan. 19
9	New Jersey	Jan. 3	Jan. 21
8	Nashville	Oct. 5	Oct. 25
8	Calgary	Nov. 1	Nov. 16
8	Colorado	Dec. 31	Jan. 17
8	Buffalo	Mar. 3	Mar. 16
8	Montreal	Mar. 23	Apr. 6
8	Detroit	Apr. 2	Apr. 17
8	San Jose	Apr. 3	Apr. 15

Consecutive Home Wins

Games	Team	From	To
9	Philadelphia	Oct. 7	Nov. 12
9	Carolina	Dec. 31	Jan. 28
8	Calgary	Oct. 20	Nov. 16
8	New Jersey	Jan. 3	Feb. 7
8	Dallas	Jan. 23	Mar. 13
8	Tampa Bay	Mar. 17	Apr. 8
7	Vancouver	Oct. 5	Nov. 4
7	Carolina	Oct. 7	Nov. 5
7	San Jose	Feb. 8	Mar. 16
7	Anaheim	Mar. 7	Apr. 4

Consecutive Road Wins

Games	Team	From	To
12	Detroit	Mar. 1	Apr. 15
9	Buffalo	Nov. 19	Dec. 19
7	Detroit	Oct. 6	Nov. 6
6	Philadelphia	Dec. 13	Dec. 29
6	NY Rangers	Jan. 19	Mar. 2
6	New Jersey	Mar. 28	Apr. 18
5	Carolina	Oct. 22	Nov. 15
5	NY Rangers	Oct. 29	Nov. 12
5	Ottawa	Oct. 29	Nov. 25
5	Dallas	Nov. 12	Dec. 10
5	Boston	Dec. 30	Jan. 30
5	San Jose	Apr. 3	Apr. 12

Atlanta's Marian Hossa led the NHL with seven shorthand goals.

TEAM PENALTIES

Abbreviations: GP – games played; **PEN** – total penalty minutes including bench minutes; **BMI** – total bench minor minutes; **AVG** – average penalty minutes/game calculated by dividing total penalty minutes by games played

Team	GP	PEN	BMI	AVG	Team	GP	PEN	BMI	AVG
N.J.	82	948	10	11.6	ST.L.	82	1373	18	16.7
T.B.	82	959	22	11.7	TOR	82	1398	20	17.0
S.J.	82	1058	14	12.9	CBJ	82	1416	20	17.3
DET	82	1117	14	13.6	ANA	82	1459	14	17.8
CAR	82	1125	18	13.7	OTT	82	1462	20	17.8
BUF	82	1164	20	14.2	L.A.	82	1474	34	18.0
BOS	82	1174	12	14.3	VAN	82	1477	12	18.0
COL	82	1178	26	14.4	CGY	82	1482	18	18.1
NYR	82	1194	12	14.6	DAL	82	1496	12	18.2
PHI	82	1201	14	14.6	WSH	82	1499	26	18.3
EDM	82	1204	22	14.7	PHX	82	1511	18	18.4
MIN	82	1209	20	14.7	NSH	82	1533	16	18.7
NYI	82	1266	18	15.4	CHI	82	1544	26	18.8
FLA	82	1279	24	15.6	PIT	82	1559	20	19.0
MTL	82	1336	22	16.3	**Total**	**1230**	**39439**	**568**	
ATL	82	1344	26	16.4	**Two-Team Avg. PIM/GP**				**32.1**

HOCKEY IS FOR EVERYONE™

Calgary's Dion Phaneuf scored 16 of his 20 goals when the Flames had a man advantage. Among NHL rookies, his 33 power-play points trailed only Alex Ovechkin (52) and Sidney Crosby (47)

TEAMS' POWER-PLAY RECORD

Abbreviations: ADV – total advantages; **PPGF** – power-play goals for; **%** – calculated by dividing number of power-play goals by total advantages.

	Home					Road					Overall				
	Team	**GP**	**ADV**	**PPGF**	**%**	**Team**	**GP**	**ADV**	**PPGF**	**%**	**Team**	**GP**	**ADV**	**PPGF**	**%**
1	BUF	41	236	59	25.0	ATL	41	276	58	21.0	DET	82	461	102	22.1
2	OTT	41	257	64	24.9	DET	41	241	50	20.7	TOR	82	501	107	21.4
3	DET	41	220	52	23.6	TOR	41	239	49	20.5	BUF	82	477	101	21.2
4	TOR	41	262	58	22.1	DAL	41	228	43	18.9	OTT	82	490	102	20.8
5	MTL	41	250	54	21.6	CAR	41	250	47	18.8	MTL	82	463	89	19.2
6	ANA	41	256	55	21.5	NYR	41	209	39	18.7	PIT	82	495	94	19.0
7	PIT	41	261	55	21.1	EDM	41	243	45	18.5	NYR	82	440	83	18.9
8	VAN	41	272	56	20.6	CGY	41	266	49	18.4	ATL	82	528	100	18.9
9	COL	41	247	51	20.6	S.J.	41	243	43	17.7	COL	82	473	89	18.8
10	N.J.	41	221	45	20.4	PHI	41	206	36	17.5	NSH	82	512	94	18.4
11	MIN	41	236	46	19.5	NSH	41	252	44	17.5	VAN	82	526	96	18.3
12	NSH	41	260	50	19.2	BUF	41	241	42	17.4	S.J.	82	500	91	18.2
13	NYR	41	231	44	19.0	T.B.	41	247	42	17.0	CGY	82	478	87	18.2
14	PHX	41	290	55	19.0	COL	41	226	38	16.8	ANA	82	480	87	18.1
15	S.J.	41	257	48	18.7	PIT	41	234	39	16.7	EDM	82	485	88	18.1
16	PHI	41	238	44	18.5	MTL	41	213	35	16.4	PHI	82	444	80	18.0
17	NYI	41	218	39	17.9	OTT	41	233	38	16.3	CAR	82	531	95	17.9
18	CGY	41	212	38	17.9	PHX	41	251	41	16.3	N.J.	82	439	78	17.8
19	EDM	41	242	43	17.8	NYI	41	232	37	15.9	DAL	82	498	88	17.7
20	CAR	41	281	48	17.1	VAN	41	254	40	15.7	PHX	82	541	96	17.7
21	DAL	41	270	45	16.7	FLA	41	210	32	15.2	MIN	82	453	77	17.0
22	ATL	41	252	42	16.7	N.J.	41	218	33	15.1	NYI	82	450	76	16.9
23	BOS	41	213	35	16.4	WSH	41	244	36	14.8	T.B.	82	485	81	16.7
24	T.B.	41	238	39	16.4	ANA	41	224	32	14.3	FLA	82	411	63	15.3
25	FLA	41	201	31	15.4	MIN	41	217	31	14.3	BOS	82	418	62	14.8
26	ST.L.	41	278	42	15.1	ST.L.	41	234	33	14.1	WSH	82	490	72	14.7
27	L.A.	41	296	44	14.9	CBJ	41	215	30	14.0	ST.L.	82	512	75	14.6
28	WSH	41	246	36	14.6	L.A.	41	245	33	13.5	CBJ	82	451	64	14.2
29	CHI	41	206	30	14.6	BOS	41	205	27	13.2	L.A.	82	541	77	14.2
30	CBJ	41	236	34	14.4	CHI	41	211	21	10.0	CHI	82	417	51	12.2
TOTAL		**1230**	**7383**	**1382**	**18.7**		**1230**	**7007**	**1163**	**16.6**		**1230**	**14390**	**2545**	**17.7**

TEAMS' PENALTY KILLING RECORD

Abbreviations: TSH – total times short-handed; **PPGA** – power-play goals against; **%** – calculated by dividing times short minus power-play goals against by times short.

	Home					Road					Overall				
	Team	**GP**	**TSH**	**PPGA**	**%**	**Team**	**GP**	**TSH**	**PPGA**	**%**	**Team**	**GP**	**TSH**	**PPGA**	**%**
1	BUF	41	202	20	90.1	MIN	41	221	27	87.8	MIN	82	436	55	87.4
2	CGY	41	231	26	88.7	EDM	41	262	39	85.1	BUF	82	439	59	86.6
3	BOS	41	244	31	87.3	DET	41	249	39	84.3	DET	82	461	67	85.5
4	NSH	41	265	34	87.2	OTT	41	239	38	84.1	OTT	82	476	73	84.7
5	NYR	41	234	30	87.2	BUF	41	237	39	83.5	NSH	82	533	82	84.6
6	COL	41	232	30	87.1	PHI	41	227	38	83.3	COL	82	447	69	84.6
7	MIN	41	215	28	87.0	CHI	41	292	49	83.2	CGY	82	508	80	84.3
8	DET	41	212	28	86.8	CAR	41	207	35	83.1	EDM	82	478	76	84.1
9	OTT	41	237	35	85.2	ANA	41	255	43	83.1	CHI	82	547	88	83.9
10	VAN	41	243	37	84.8	DAL	41	260	44	83.1	BOS	82	479	78	83.7
11	CHI	41	255	39	84.7	N.J.	41	181	31	82.9	NYR	82	486	79	83.7
12	DAL	41	244	38	84.4	ST.L.	41	233	40	82.8	DAL	82	504	82	83.7
13	FLA	41	250	40	84.0	NSH	41	268	48	82.1	ANA	82	510	84	83.5
14	ANA	41	255	41	83.9	COL	41	215	39	81.9	FLA	82	514	91	82.3
15	MTL	41	237	39	83.5	NYI	41	231	43	81.4	ST.L.	82	461	82	82.2
16	T.B.	41	193	32	83.4	PHX	41	265	50	81.1	N.J.	82	348	63	81.9
17	CBJ	41	244	41	83.2	FLA	41	264	51	80.7	CBJ	82	523	95	81.8
18	EDM	41	216	37	82.9	NYR	41	252	49	80.6	CAR	82	445	81	81.8
19	WSH	41	272	48	82.4	CBJ	41	279	54	80.6	VAN	82	512	93	81.8
20	L.A.	41	228	41	82.0	CGY	41	277	54	80.5	T.B.	82	390	72	81.5
21	TOR	41	231	42	81.8	PIT	41	277	55	80.1	MTL	82	481	91	81.1
22	ST.L.	41	228	42	81.6	BOS	41	235	47	80.0	PHX	82	513	98	80.9
23	S.J.	41	196	36	81.6	S.J.	41	203	41	79.8	S.J.	82	399	77	80.7
24	N.J.	41	167	32	80.8	T.B.	41	197	40	79.7	TOR	82	496	99	80.0
25	CAR	41	238	46	80.7	VAN	41	269	56	79.2	NYI	82	476	99	79.2
26	PHX	41	248	48	80.6	MTL	41	244	52	78.7	ATL	82	491	102	79.2
27	ATL	41	251	49	80.5	TOR	41	265	57	78.5	PHI	82	465	97	79.1
28	PIT	41	256	58	77.3	ATL	41	240	53	77.9	WSH	82	550	116	78.9
29	NYI	41	245	56	77.1	L.A.	41	261	63	75.9	PIT	82	533	113	78.8
30	PHI	41	238	59	75.2	WSH	41	278	68	75.5	L.A.	82	489	104	78.7
TOTAL		**1230**	**7007**	**1163**	**83.4**		**1230**	**7383**	**1382**	**81.3**		**1230**	**14390**	**2545**	**82.3**

SHORTHAND GOALS FOR

	Home			Road			Overall		
	Team	**GP**	**SHGF**	**Team**	**GP**	**SHGF**	**Team**	**GP**	**SHGF**
1	OTT	41	12	OTT	41	13	OTT	82	25
2	PHI	41	9	EDM	41	12	PHI	82	19
3	L.A.	41	9	CAR	41	11	CAR	82	17
4	COL	41	9	PHI	41	10	WSH	82	15
5	TOR	41	8	PIT	41	8	L.A.	82	15
6	WSH	41	7	WSH	41	8	EDM	82	15
7	DAL	41	7	ATL	41	7	TOR	82	14
8	PHX	41	7	BOS	41	7	ATL	82	13
9	MTL	41	7	L.A.	41	6	PIT	82	13
10	NSH	41	6	T.B.	41	6	NSH	82	12
11	MIN	41	6	BUF	41	6	T.B.	82	11
12	CAR	41	6	TOR	41	6	MIN	82	11
13	CBJ	41	6	NSH	41	6	COL	82	11
14	ATL	41	6	S.J.	41	5	MTL	82	10
15	ANA	41	6	MIN	41	5	BUF	82	10
16	CGY	41	6	CBJ	41	4	CBJ	82	10
17	FLA	41	5	ST.L.	41	4	S.J.	82	10
18	T.B.	41	5	VAN	41	4	DAL	82	10
19	DET	41	5	MTL	41	3	BOS	82	9
20	PIT	41	5	ANA	41	3	ANA	82	9
21	S.J.	41	5	CHI	41	3	PHX	82	9
22	BUF	41	4	DAL	41	3	CGY	82	8
23	NYR	41	4	NYI	41	2	DET	82	7
24	CHI	41	3	CGY	41	2	ST.L.	82	6
25	EDM	41	3	COL	41	2	CHI	82	6
26	NYI	41	3	PHX	41	2	VAN	82	6
27	BOS	41	2	DET	41	2	NYI	82	5
28	VAN	41	2	N.J.	41	2	FLA	82	5
29	ST.L.	41	2	NYR	41	0	NYR	82	4
30	N.J.	41	1	FLA	41	0	N.J.	82	3
TOTAL		**1230**	**166**		**1230**	**152**		**1230**	**318**

SHORTHAND GOALS AGAINST

	Home			Road			Overall		
	Team	**GP**	**SHGA**	**Team**	**GP**	**SHGA**	**Team**	**GP**	**SHGA**
1	DET	41	2	MTL	41	1	EDM	82	5
2	EDM	41	2	CBJ	41	2	MTL	82	6
3	CGY	41	2	N.J.	41	3	PHI	82	6
4	PHI	41	3	VAN	41	3	N.J.	82	6
5	N.J.	41	3	MIN	41	3	MIN	82	7
6	DAL	41	3	EDM	41	3	CGY	82	7
7	ST.L.	41	3	PHI	41	3	DAL	82	7
8	MIN	41	4	NYR	41	4	CBJ	82	8
9	L.A.	41	4	DAL	41	4	ST.L.	82	8
10	PHX	41	4	ATL	41	5	NYR	82	9
11	BOS	41	5	OTT	41	5	BOS	82	10
12	FLA	41	5	ST.L.	41	5	ATL	82	10
13	NSH	41	5	S.J.	41	5	DET	82	10
14	CHI	41	5	CGY	41	5	VAN	82	10
15	NYR	41	5	T.B.	41	5	OTT	82	11
16	CAR	41	5	BOS	41	5	T.B.	82	11
17	ATL	41	5	TOR	41	5	S.J.	82	11
18	MTL	41	5	ANA	41	6	PHX	82	11
19	T.B.	41	6	COL	41	6	FLA	82	12
20	CBJ	41	6	PHX	41	7	TOR	82	12
21	OTT	41	6	WSH	41	7	CHI	82	12
22	NYI	41	6	FLA	41	7	L.A.	82	12
23	COL	41	6	CHI	41	7	COL	82	12
24	S.J.	41	6	CAR	41	8	CAR	82	13
25	BUF	41	7	L.A.	41	8	NSH	82	13
26	TOR	41	7	DET	41	8	ANA	82	13
27	VAN	41	7	NSH	41	8	NYI	82	15
28	PIT	41	7	NYI	41	9	PIT	82	16
29	ANA	41	7	PIT	41	9	BUF	82	17
30	WSH	41	11	BUF	41	10	WSH	82	18
TOTAL		**1230**	**152**		**1230**	**166**		**1230**	**318**

Regular-Season Overtime Results

2005-06 to 1985-86

Team	05-06 GP	W	L	SO	03-04 GP	W	L	T	02-03 GP	W	L	T	01-02 GP	W	L	T	00-01 GP	W	L	T	99-00 GP	W	L	T	98-99 GP	W	L	T	97-98 GP	W	L	T	96-97 GP	W	L	T	95-96 GP	W	L	T
ANA	18	3	5	10	22	4	8	10	21	6	6	9	14	3	3	8	20	4	5	11	18	3	3	12	17	1	3	13	20	3	4	13	16	3	0	13	16	6	2	8
ATL	18	5	3	10	18	6	4	8	19	7	5	7	19	3	5	11	16	2	2	12	11	0	4	7																
BOS	22	4	8	10	30	8	7	15	21	6	4	11	24	9	9	6	20	4	8	8	26	1	6	19	17	2	2	13	21	1	3	17	15	3	3	9	19	2	6	11
BUF	17	6	1	10	13	2	4	7	21	3	8	10	16	4	1	11	10	4	1	5	20	5	4	11	23	3	3	17	21	1	1	17	21	5	4	12	15	2	6	7
CGY	15	2	4	9	13	3	3	7	19	2	6	11	17	2	3	12	22	3	4	15	14	4	0	10	16	3	1	12	22	4	3	15	16	3	4	9	16	2	3	11
CAR/HFD	20	4	6	10	25	5	6	14	15	4	3	8	27	6	5	16	18	6	3	9	14	4	0	10	24	1	5	18	12	2	2	8	18	3	4	11	19	1	4	14
CHI	22	7	7	8	23	4	8	11	23	6	4	13	17	3	1	13	15	2	5	8	17	5	2	10	15	1	2	12	18	1	4	13	19	1	5	13	19	1	4	14
COL/QUE	15	3	3	9	28	8	7	13	23	4	6	13	13	4	1	8	20	6	4	10	17	5	1	11	12	2	0	10	22	2	3	17	15	2	3	10	6	1	0	5
CBJ	18	6	1	11	18	6	4	8	28	7	8	13	15	2	5	8	18	3	6	9																				
DAL/MIN	21	3	5	13	18	3	2	13	24	5	4	15	21	3	5	13	16	6	2	8	19	3	6	10	16	3	1	12	17	5	1	11	15	4	3	8	15	1	0	14
DET	15	3	5	7	20	7	2	11	21	7	4	10	24	10	4	10	23	10	4	9	16	4	2	10	10	2	1	7	15	3	2	10	27	7	2	18	11	3	1	7
EDM	26	6	4	16	23	6	5	12	27	7	9	11	19	3	4	12	20	5	3	12	27	3	8	16	20	3	5	12	15	3	2	10	16	1	6	9	14	4	2	8
FLA	23	8	6	9	24	5	4	15	26	4	9	13	16	0	6	10	24	2	9	13	15	3	6	6	21	1	2	18	20	3	2	15	26	3	4	19	13	0	3	10
L.A.	15	4	4	7	27	2	9	16	19	6	7	6	18	3	4	11	19	3	3	13	21	5	4	12	17	5	2	10	16	3	2	11	14	0	3	11	23	3	2	18
MIN	14	1	5	8	24	1	3	20	19	8	1	10	21	0	9	12	22	4	5	13																				
MTL	18	7	6	5	16	5	4	7	19	2	9	8	17	2	3	12	16	2	6	8	17	4	4	9	15	0	4	11	20	3	4	13	21	2	4	15	15	2	3	10
NSH	17	3	5	9	22	7	4	11	24	8	6	10	18	5	0	13	18	4	7	7	16	4	4	5	10	1	2	7												
N.J.	22	4	5	13	21	7	2	12	25	5	7	13	19	6	4	9	20	5	3	12	16	3	5	8	15	3	1	11	16	2	3	11	17	1	2	14	19	7	0	12
NYI	18	3	3	12	17	2	4	11	18	5	2	11	18	6	4	8	12	2	3	7	15	5	1	9	17	1	6	10	13	0	2	11	17	3	2	12	17	2	5	10
NYR	23	4	8	11	18	3	8	7	20	6	4	10	13	5	4	4	11	5	1	5	21	6	3	12	19	5	3	11	24	2	4	18	17	0	2	15	17	2	1	14
OTT	13	2	3	8	19	3	6	10	16	7	1	8	19	3	7	9	16	3	4	9	15	2	2	11	18	1	2	15	17	2	0	15	17	0	2	15	8	0	3	5
PHI	22	7	5	10	23	2	6	15	23	6	4	13	16	3	3	10	19	5	3	11	26	6	3	12	24	2	3	19	15	3	1	11	18	3	2	13	20	4	3	13
PHX/WPG	15	6	2	7	29	5	6	18	20	4	5	11	19	4	6	9	23	3	3	17	16	4	4	8	15	2	1	12	14	0	2	12	16	5	4	7	9	3	2	4
PIT	19	4	8	7	19	7	4	8	14	3	5	6	20	7	5	8	15	3	3	9	17	3	6	8	22	7	1	14	23	3	2	18	13	1	4	8	9	3	2	4
ST.L.	22	3	7	12	24	11	2	11	19	2	8	9	18	6	4	8	23	6	5	12	17	5	1	11	15	1	1	13	12	2	2	8	13	1	1	11	18	1	1	16
S.J.	21	9	4	8	21	3	6	12	23	6	6	11	13	2	3	8	13	2	3	12	16	0	7	9	21	1	2	9	13	0	3	10	16	4	2	10	18	3	3	12
T.B.	18	6	2	10	18	4	6	8	23	2	5	16	19	4	4	11	13	2	5	6	16	0	9	7	12	1	2	9	13	0	3	10	16	4	2	10	18	3	3	12
TOR	18	7	1	10	17	4	3	10	17	7	3	7	17	3	4	10	17	3	4	10	17	7	3	7	14	6	1	7	10	1	0	9	10	1	1	8	18	4	2	12
VAN	16	4	4	8	26	11	5	10	19	5	1	13	14	4	3	7	23	5	7	11	27	4	8	15	13	0	1	12	17	0	3	14	14	5	2	7	20	1	4	15
WSH	21	2	6	13	14	1	3	10	20	6	6	8	19	6	2	11	16	2	4	10	19	5	2	12	11	2	3	6	17	4	1	12	13	2	2	9	16	4	1	11
Totals	**281**	**136**		**145**	**315**	**145**		**170**	**313**	**156**		**157**	**270**	**121**		**149**	**274**	**122**		**152**	**260**	**114**		**146**	**222**	**60**		**162**	**219**	**54**		**165**	**214**	**70**		**144**	**201**	**64**		**137**

2005-06

Home Team Wins:	60
Visiting Team Wins:	76

Team	94-95 GP	W	L	T	93-94 GP	W	L	T	92-93 GP	W	L	T	91-92 GP	W	L	T	90-91 GP	W	L	T	89-90 GP	W	L	T	88-89 GP	W	L	T	87-88 GP	W	L	T	86-87 GP	W	L	T	85-86 GP	W	L	T
ANA	7	2	0	5	12	2	5	5																																
ATL																																								
BOS	8	2	3	3	17	2	2	13	15	5	3	7	20	6	2	12	17	5	0	12	14	3	2	9	19	3	2	14	19	4	4	6	12	4	4	7	17	2	3	12
BUF	9	1	1	7	13	0	4	9	18	4	4	10	16	2	2	12	24	3	2	19	15	4	3	8	13	2	4	7	12	0	1	11	13	1	4	8	12	1	2	9
CGY	9	1	1	7	18	3	2	13	19	4	4	11	19	2	5	12	15	3	4	8	21	3	3	15	17	5	3	9	15	2	4	9	14	1	0	3	12	1	2	9
CAR/HFD	9	1	1	7	14	4	1	9	18	3	9	6	18	2	3	13	9	1	1	7	9	0	0	9	10	1	4	5	13	3	2	7	9	2	0	7	7	1	2	4
CHI	7	2	0	5	16	2	5	9	16	1	3	12	19	2	2	15	12	3	1	8	10	2	2	6	17	2	3	12	15	4	2	9	15	1	0	14	12	3	1	8
COL/QUE	8	0	0	8	15	3	3	9	15	4	1	10	17	0	5	12	18	1	3	14	8	0	1	7	10	2	1	7	9	2	2	5	14	0	4	10	11	4	1	6
CBJ																																								
DAL/MIN	9	0	1	8	22	6	3	13	10	0	0	10	8	0	2	6	17	0	3	14	11	3	4	4	17	0	1	16	16	1	2	13	14	2	2	10	15	4	2	9
DET	4	0	0	4	15	5	2	8	11	2	0	9	16	3	1	12	14	2	4	8	17	2	1	14	16	3	1	12	16	2	3	11	13	2	5	6	13	2	5	6
EDM	7	1	2	4	21	1	6	14	17	5	4	9	12	0	2	10	15	4	5	6	20	5	1	14	15	4	3	8	16	3	2	11	14	5	3	6	14	5	2	7
FLA	9	0	3	6	24	2	5	17																																
L.A.	9	0	0	9	18	3	3	12	13	1	0	12	16	1	1	14	16	4	2	10	12	3	2	7	14	6	1	7	13	3	1	8					14	3	3	8
MIN																																								
MTL	10	1	2	7	19	3	2	14	14	5	3	6	20	6	3	11	17	3	3	11	17	4	2	11	11	2	0	9	16	1	2	13	16	2	4	10	14	1	6	7
NSH																																								
N.J.	11	1	2	8	14	1	1	12	11	4	0	7	17	2	4	11	17	1	1	15	16	3	4	9	17	1	4	12	12	4	2	6	13	3	4	6	10	4	3	3
NYI	7	1	1	5	19	5	2	12	13	3	3	7	16	3	2	11	15	2	3	10	16	3	2	11	11	3	3	5	13	3	0	10	19	4	3	12	17	4	1	12
NYR	3	0	0	3	12	1	1	10	17	2	4	11	11	5	1	5	16	1	2	13	17	2	2	13	10	1	1	8	11	0	1	10	19	5	6	8	13	0	7	6
OTT	7	1	1	5	17	4	4	9	10	0	6	4																												
PHI	8	3	1	4	18	3	5	10	17	4	2	11	17	2	4	11	11	1	0	10	18	2	5	11	14	1	5	8	13	1	3	9	10	1	1	8	9	4	1	4
PHX/WPG	9	0	2	7	15	1	5	9	11	2	2	7	20	1	4	15	14	1	2	11	19	4	4	11	20	6	2	12	21	8	2	11	11	2	1	8	8	0	1	7
PIT	5	1	1	3	13	4	2	9	10	3	2	9	12	2	1	9	12	4	2	6	14	3	3	8	10	2	1	7	16	5	2	9	21	5	4	12	14	3	3	8
ST.L.	7	1	1	5	17	4	2	11	17	2	4	11	15	2	2	11	18	3	4	11					16	3	1	12	14	2	4	8	21	4	2	15	17	5	3	9
S.J.	5	1	0	4	19	2	1	16	14	3	4	7																												
T.B.	7	2	2	3	18	3	4	11	14	3	4	7																												
TOR	8	0	0	8	17	4	1	12	11	0	1	10	11	4	0	7	13	3	4	6	11	3	4	4	11	1	4	6	11	0	1	10	17	4	6	7	17	4	6	7
VAN	13	0	1	12	12	5	4	3	10	1	0	9	17	4	1	12	15	3	3	9	21	2	5	14	14	2	4	8	11	0	2	9	10	2	0	8	16	1	2	13
WSH	9	0	1	8	14	2	2	10	11	2	2	7	12	2	2	8	14	4	3	7	9	2	1	6	16	2	4	10	15	2	4	9	17	5	2	10	11	4	0	7
Totals	**101**	**26**		**75**	**214**	**74**		**140**	**165**	**65**		**100**	**169**	**52**		**117**	**166**	**54**		**112**	**155**	**55**		**100**	**149**	**52**		**97**	**146**	**49**		**97**	**147**	**54**		**93**	**135**	**56**		**79**

Abbreviations: GP – games played; **W** – overtime win; **L** – overtime loss;
SO – game tied after overtime. Game decided in shootout. (2005-06 to date);
T – game tied after overtime. (Up to and including 2003-04.)

Shootout Summary

Team Shootout Statistics

Team	OVERALL									HOME								ROAD							
	GP	W	L	G	S	S%	SA	GA	Sv%	W	L	G	S	S%	SA	GA	Sv%	W	L	G	S	S%	SA	GA	Sv%
ANA	10	3	7	8	31	25.8	31	12	.613	1	3	3	10	30.0	10	5	.500	2	4	5	21	23.8	21	7	.667
ATL	10	5	5	11	36	30.6	34	11	.676	3	2	7	17	41.2	18	6	.667	2	3	4	19	21.0	16	5	.688
BOS	10	2	8	6	36	16.7	36	12	.667	2	6	6	30	20.0	32	10	.688	0	2	0	6	0.0	4	2	.500
BUF	10	5	5	12	32	37.5	30	11	.633	1	2	3	8	37.5	9	4	.556	4	3	9	24	37.5	21	7	.667
CGY	9	2	7	6	29	20.7	26	12	.538	0	3	0	8	0.0	8	5	.375	2	4	6	21	28.6	18	7	.611
CAR	10	8	2	17	34	50.0	36	10	.722	4	0	7	12	58.3	14	2	.857	4	2	10	22	45.4	22	8	.636
CHI	8	2	6	10	31	32.3	29	14	.517	0	2	1	7	14.3	7	3	.571	2	4	9	24	37.5	22	11	.500
COL	9	3	6	6	30	20.0	31	11	.645	1	6	4	20	20.0	21	11	.476	2	0	2	10	20.0	10	0	1.000
CBJ	11	8	3	15	43	34.9	44	9	.795	3	0	4	12	33.3	14	1	.929	5	3	11	31	35.5	30	8	.733
DAL	13	12	1	24	42	57.1	41	9	.780	5	0	11	21	52.4	21	5	.762	7	1	13	21	61.9	20	4	.800
DET	7	4	3	12	25	48.0	25	9	.640	2	2	6	16	37.5	17	6	.647	2	1	6	9	66.7	8	3	.625
EDM	16	7	9	19	53	35.8	54	23	.574	3	4	8	23	34.8	24	10	.583	4	5	11	30	36.7	30	13	.567
FLA	9	4	5	8	31	25.8	31	9	.710	1	4	4	19	21.0	19	7	.632	3	1	4	12	33.3	12	2	.833
L.A.	7	6	1	10	20	50.0	21	3	.857	3	0	6	9	66.7	10	2	.800	3	1	4	11	36.4	11	1	.909
MIN	8	5	3	9	31	29.0	30	7	.767	2	1	4	9	44.4	9	3	.667	3	2	5	22	22.7	21	4	.810
MTL	5	2	3	4	14	28.6	15	4	.733	2	1	3	7	42.9	8	1	.875	0	2	1	7	14.3	7	3	.571
NSH	9	6	3	12	25	48.0	25	8	.680	4	1	7	11	63.6	12	2	.833	2	2	5	14	35.7	13	6	.538
N.J.	13	9	4	18	45	40.0	45	12	.733	4	1	6	18	33.3	20	2	.900	5	3	12	27	44.4	25	10	.600
NYI	12	9	3	19	41	46.3	44	12	.727	6	1	12	19	63.2	23	7	.696	3	2	7	22	31.8	21	5	.762
NYR	11	7	4	18	49	36.7	50	15	.700	4	1	9	26	34.6	28	6	.786	3	3	9	23	39.1	22	9	.591
OTT	8	2	6	4	23	17.4	21	8	.619	1	2	1	8	12.5	9	2	.778	1	4	3	15	20.0	12	6	.500
PHI	10	4	6	11	33	33.3	32	14	.563	3	2	8	18	44.4	19	7	.632	1	4	3	15	20.0	13	7	.462
PHX	7	4	3	7	24	29.2	25	7	.720	2	3	4	17	23.5	18	6	.667	2	0	3	7	42.9	7	1	.857
PIT	7	1	6	6	28	21.4	27	13	.519	1	3	3	16	18.8	17	7	.588	0	3	3	12	25.0	10	6	.400
STL	12	4	8	10	38	26.3	37	16	.568	2	3	5	17	29.4	17	6	.647	2	5	5	21	23.8	20	10	.500
S.J.	8	1	7	7	29	24.1	29	14	.517	1	6	6	26	23.1	26	12	.538	0	1	1	3	33.3	3	2	.333
T.B.	10	6	4	12	27	44.4	27	9	.667	4	1	7	10	70.0	14	4	.714	2	3	5	17	29.4	13	5	.615
TOR	7	3	7	4	24	16.7	24	10	.583	3	2	4	11	36.4	14	3	.786	0	5	0	13	0.0	10	7	.300
VAN	8	4	4	7	23	30.4	24	9	.625	2	3	5	15	33.3	16	7	.563	2	1	2	8	25.0	8	2	.750
WSH	13	7	6	18	54	33.3	57	17	.702	5	1	12	32	37.5	35	10	.657	2	5	6	22	27.3	22	5	.773

Individual Shootout Leaders

Goaltenders

Goaltender Shootout Wins

	Team	W	L
Marty Turco	DAL	8	1
Martin Brodeur	N.J.	8	3
Rick DiPietro	NYI	8	3
Martin Gerber	CAR	7	2
Kari Lehtonen	ATL	5	0
Michael Morrison	OTT	5	2
10 Goaltenders with…		4	

Goaltender Shootout Shots Against

	Team	SA	GA	Sv%
Olaf Kolzig	WSH	44	15	.659
Rick DiPietro	NYI	41	12	.707
Martin Brodeur	N.J.	38	9	.763
Henrik Lundqvist	NYR	37	9	.757
Martin Gerber	CAR	33	10	.697
J-S Giguere	ANA	31	12	.613
Tim Thomas	BOS	31	9	.710
Roberto Luongo	FLA	27	7	.741
Curtis Sanford	STL	25	10	.600
3 Goaltenders with …		24		

Goaltender Shootout Save Percentage

(min. 10 shots faced)	Team	Sv%	SA	GA
Kari Lehtonen	ATL	.850	20	3
Brent Johnson	WSH	.846	13	2
Johan Hedberg	DAL	.824	17	3
Mathieu Garon	L.A.	.812	16	3
David Aebischer	MTL	.800	10	2
Manny Fernandez	MIN	.789	19	4
Pascal Leclaire	CBJ	.778	18	4
Marc Denis	CBJ	.778	18	4
Martin Brodeur	N.J.	.763	38	9
Henrik Lundqvist	NYR	.757	37	9

Marek Malik ended the longest shootout game of the season on November 26, 2005 with a spectacular between-the-legs move to beat Washington's Olaf Kolzig on the game's 30th shootout attempt.

MSG PHOTO

Team Shootout Leaders

Wins

	W	L	Win%
DAL	12	1	.923
N.J.	9	4	.692
NYI	9	3	.750
CAR	8	2	.800
CBJ	8	3	.727
EDM	7	9	.438
NYR	7	4	.636
WSH	7	6	.538
L.A.	6	1	.857
NSH	6	3	.667
T.B.	6	4	.600

Goals Scored

	G	S	S%
DAL	24	42	57.1
NYI	19	41	46.3
EDM	19	53	35.8
N.J.	18	45	40.0
NYR	18	49	36.7
WSH	18	54	33.3
CAR	17	34	50.0
CBJ	15	43	34.9
NSH	12	25	48.0
T.B.	12	27	44.4
BUF	12	32	37.5
DET	12	25	48.0

Fewest Goals Against

	SA	GA	Sv%
L.A.	21	3	.857
MTL	15	4	.733
MIN	30	7	.767
PHX	25	7	.720
NSH	25	8	.680
OTT	21	8	.619
DAL	41	9	.780
CBJ	44	9	.795
T.B.	27	9	.667
DET	25	9	.640
FLA	31	9	.710
VAN	24	9	.625

Winning Percentage

	W	L	Win%
DAL	12	1	.923
L.A.	6	1	.857
CAR	8	2	.800
NYI	9	3	.750
CBJ	8	3	.727
N.J.	9	4	.692
NSH	6	3	.667
NYR	7	4	.636
MIN	5	3	.625
T.B.	6	4	.600

Shootout Abbreviations

- G ....Goals Scored
- GA ......Goals Against
- GDG ...Game Deciding Goal
- S ....Shots Taken
- SA ......Shots Against
- S% ....Goal Scoring %
- Sv%.....Save %

Individual Shootout Leaders – Skaters

Shootout Goals Scored

	Team	G	S	S%
Jussi Jokinen	DAL	10	13	.769
Viktor Kozlov	N.J.	8	12	.667
Miroslav Satan	NYI	7	10	.700
Sergei Zubov	DAL	7	12	.583
Matt Cullen	CAR	6	9	.667
Brad Richards	T.B.	6	9	.667
Jaroslav Balastik	CBJ	6	9	.667
Alex Ovechkin	WSH	6	13	.462
7 Players with …		5		

Shootout Shots Taken

	Team	S	G	S%
Ales Hemsky	EDM	14	5	.357
Jussi Jokinen	DAL	13	10	.769
Alex Ovechkin	WSH	13	6	.462
Ryan Smyth	EDM	13	4	.308
Viktor Kozlov	N.J.	12	8	.667
Sergei Zubov	DAL	12	7	.583
Michael Nylander	NYR	11	5	.454
Miroslav Satan	NYI	10	7	.700
Brian Gionta	N.J.	10	4	.400
Ilya Kovalchuk	ATL	10	1	.100

Shootout Scoring Percentage

(min. 5 shots taken)	Team	S%	S	G
Ray Whitney	CAR	.800	5	4
Jussi Jokinen	DAL	.769	13	10
Vyacheslav Kozlov	ATL	.714	7	5
Jason Williams	DET	.714	7	5
Petr Sykora	NYR	.714	7	5
Paul Kariya	NSH	.714	7	5
Miroslav Satan	NYI	.700	10	7
Viktor Kozlov	N.J.	.667	12	8
Matt Cullen	CAR	.667	9	6
Brad Richards	T.B.	.667	9	6
Jaroslav Balastik	CBJ	.667	9	6

Shootout Game-Deciding Goals

	Team	GDG	S	G
Viktor Kozlov	N.J.	5	12	8
Miroslav Satan	NYI	5	10	7
Sergei Zubov	DAL	4	12	7
Brad Richards	T.B.	4	9	6
Jussi Jokinen	DAL	3	13	10
Jaroslav Balastik	CBJ	3	9	6
Alex Ovechkin	WSH	3	13	6
Petr Sykora	NYR	3	7	5
Pavol Demitra	L.A.	3	5	3
Brian Rolston	MIN	3	7	3

Shootout Register

Skaters

Player	Team	S	G	S%	GDG
Afanasenkov, Dimitry	T.B.	1	0	.000	0
Afinogenov, Maxim	BUF	5	3	.600	2
Alfredsson, Daniel	OTT	8	2	.250	1
Allison, Jason	TOR	3	0	.000	0
Amonte, Tony	CGY	8	3	.375	1
Arnason, Tyler	OTT	3	1	.333	0
Arnott, Jason	DAL	1	0	.000	0
Asham, Arron	NYI	1	0	.000	0
Axelsson, P.J.	BOS	1	0	.000	0
Balastik, Jaroslav	CBJ	9	6	.667	3
Barnaby, Matthew	CHI	2	1	.500	0
Bates, Shawn	NYI	3	2	.667	0
Bell, Mark	CHI	2	0	.000	0
Berard, Bryan	CBJ	1	0	.000	0
Bergeron, Patrice	BOS	9	2	.222	1
Bernier, Steve	S.J.	1	0	.000	0
Bertuzzi, Todd	VAN	5	2	.400	1
Betts, Blair	NYR	1	0	.000	0
Blake, Jason	NYI	5	2	.400	1
Bondra, Peter	ATL	3	0	.000	0
Bouchard, Pierre-Marc	MIN	1	0	.000	0
Bourque, Rene	CHI	5	1	.200	0
Boyes, Brad	BOS	6	2	.333	1
Bradley, Matt	WSH	1	0	.000	0
Briere, Daniel	BUF	4	2	.500	1
Brind'Amour, Rod	CAR	4	1	.250	1
Brunette, Andrew	COL	1	0	.000	0
Brylin, Sergei	N.J.	3	1	.333	1
Byfuglien, Dustin	CHI	1	0	.000	0
Cajanek, Petr	STL	6	1	.167	1
Calder, Kyle	CHI	1	0	.000	0
Cammalleri, Michael	L.A.	1	0	.000	0
Carter, Anson	VAN	1	0	.000	0
Carter, Jeff	PHI	3	0	.000	0
Cassels, Andrew	WSH	2	1	.500	0
Cheechoo, Jonathan	S.J.	6	1	.167	0
Chimera, Jason	CBJ	1	1	1.000	1
Chouinard, Marc	MIN	1	0	.000	0
Christensen, Erik	PIT	1	1	1.000	0
Clark, Chris	WSH	1	0	.000	0
Clymer, Ben	WSH	2	0	.000	0
Cole, Erik	CAR	3	1	.333	1
Comrie, Mike	PHX	4	1	.250	0
Connolly, Tim	BUF	5	2	.400	1
Conroy, Craig	L.A.	1	0	.000	0
Corvo, Joseph	L.A.	3	1	.333	1
Crosby, Sidney	PIT	6	2	.333	1
Cullen, Mark	CHI	1	0	.000	0
Cullen, Matt	CAR	9	6	.667	2
Czerkawski, Mariusz	BOS	2	0	.000	0
Dagenais, Pierre	MTL	2	2	1.000	2
Daigle, Alexandre	MIN	1	0	.000	0
Datsyuk, Pavel	DET	6	3	.500	1
De Vries, Greg	ATL	2	0	.000	0
Demitra, Pavol	L.A.	5	3	.600	3
Dimitrakos, Nicholas	PHI	3	1	.333	0
Doan, Shane	PHX	3	1	.333	0
Drury, Chris	BUF	1	0	.000	0
Dumont, J.P.	BUF	1	0	.000	0
Dvorak, Radek	EDM	2	1	.500	1
Eaves, Patrick	OTT	1	0	.000	0
Ekman, Nils	S.J.	6	2	.333	1
Elias, Patrik	N.J.	5	2	.400	0
Eminger, Steve	WSH	1	0	.000	0
Erat, Martin	NSH	2	2	1.000	2
Fedorov, Sergei	CBJ	5	0	.000	0
Fedotenko, Ruslan	T.B.	1	0	.000	0
Fisher, Mike	OTT	2	0	.000	0
Fleischmann, Tomas	WSH	2	0	.000	0
Forsberg, Peter	PHI	7	3	.429	0
Fritsche, Dan	CBJ	1	0	.000	0
Frolov, Alexander	L.A.	4	3	.750	1
Gaborik, Marian	MIN	6	0	.000	0
Gagne, Simon	PHI	6	2	.333	1
Gamache, Simon	NSH	2	0	.000	0
Gelinas, Martin	FLA	1	0	.000	0
Getzlaf, Ryan	ANA	2	0	.000	0
Gionta, Brian	N.J.	10	4	.400	1
Gomez, Scott	N.J.	3	2	.667	1
Gonchar, Sergei	PIT	1	1	1.000	0
Guerin, Bill	DAL	1	1	1.000	0
Halpern, Jeff	WSH	2	0	.000	0
Handzus, Michal	PHI	4	2	.500	1
Hartigan, Mark	CBJ	2	1	.500	0
Havlat, Martin	OTT	1	0	.000	0
Heatley, Dany	OTT	8	2	.250	1
Hedstrom, Jonathan	ANA	2	1	.500	0
Hejduk, Milan	COL	7	1	.143	1
Hemsky, Ales	EDM	14	5	.357	0
Heward, Jamie	WSH	1	0	.000	0
Hilbert, Andy	PIT	1	0	.000	0
Hollweg, Ryan	NYR	1	0	.000	0
Holmqvist, Mikael	CHI	5	2	.400	1
Holmstrom, Tomas	DET	2	1	.500	1
Horcoff, Shawn	EDM	1	0	.000	0
Horton, Nathan	FLA	7	2	.286	0
Hossa, Marcel	NYR	1	0	.000	0
Hossa, Marian	ATL	9	3	.333	2
Hrdina, Jan	CBJ	2	0	.000	0
Hunter, Trent	NYI	9	5	.556	2
Huselius, Kristian	CGY	3	0	.000	0
Iginla, Jarome	CGY	9	1	.111	0
Isbister, Brad	BOS	1	0	.000	0
Jagr, Jaromir	NYR	8	2	.250	1
Johnson, Mike	PHX	1	0	.000	0
Jokinen, Jussi	DAL	13	10	.769	3
Jokinen, Olli	FLA	9	4	.444	2
Kapanen, Niko	DAL	1	0	.000	0
Kariya, Paul	NSH	7	5	.714	2
Kesler, Ryan	VAN	2	0	.000	0
Klepis, Jakub	WSH	2	0	.000	0
Knuble, Mike	PHI	2	0	.000	0
Kobasew, Chuck	CGY	4	0	.000	0
Koivu, Mikko	MIN	6	4	.667	1
Kolnik, Juraj	FLA	1	0	.000	0
Koltsov, Konstantin	PIT	1	0	.000	0
Kondratiev, Maxim	ANA	1	0	.000	0
Kotalik, Ales	BUF	6	2	.333	0
Kovalchuk, Ilya	ATL	10	1	.100	0
Kovalev, Alex	MTL	4	1	.250	0
Kozlov, Viktor	N.J.	12	8	.667	5
Kozlov, Vyacheslav	ATL	7	5	.714	2
Kuba, Filip	MIN	1	0	.000	0
Kubina, Pavel	T.B.	1	0	.000	0
Kunitz, Chris	ANA	6	2	.333	2
Laaksonen, Antti	COL	3	1	.333	1
Laich, Brooks	WSH	6	2	.333	0
Lang, Robert	DET	2	0	.000	0
Langenbrunner, Jamie	N.J.	3	0	.000	0
Lecavalier, Vincent	T.B.	9	4	.444	1
Leclair, John	PIT	1	0	.000	0
Lehtinen, Jere	DAL	1	0	.000	0
Lemieux, Mario	PIT	3	0	.000	0
Letowski, Trevor	CBJ	4	2	.500	1
Lindros, Eric	TOR	3	1	.333	1
Lombardi, Matthew	CGY	3	1	.333	0
Lundmark, Jamie	CGY	1	0	.000	0
Lupul, Joffrey	ANA	2	0	.000	0
Madden, John	N.J.	2	0	.000	0
Malik, Marek	NYR	1	1	1.000	1
Malone, Ryan	PIT	2	0	.000	0
Marleau, Patrick	S.J.	5	0	.000	0
McAmmond, Dean	STL	6	1	.167	0
McClement, Jay	STL	4	2	.500	0
McDonald, Andy	ANA	6	2	.333	0
Michalek, Milan	S.J.	2	1	.500	0
Miettinen, Antti	DAL	5	2	.400	2
Modano, Mike	DAL	7	3	.429	2
Mogilny, Alexander	N.J.	4	0	.000	0
Moore, Dominic	NYR	1	0	.000	0
Morrow, Brenden	DAL	1	1	1.000	1
Muir, Bryan	WSH	1	1	1.000	0
Murray, Glen	BOS	5	1	.200	0
Nagy, Ladislav	PHX	5	1	.200	1
Nash, Rick	CBJ	8	3	.375	2
Naslund, Markus	VAN	7	2	.286	1
Nedved, Petr	PHI	4	1	.250	1
Niedermayer, Rob	ANA	1	1	1.000	1
Niedermayer, Scott	ANA	1	0	.000	0
Nieminen, Ville	S.J.	1	1	1.000	0
Nieuwendyk, Joe	FLA	7	2	.286	2
Nilsson, Robert	NYI	2	1	.500	1
Nylander, Michael	NYR	11	5	.454	0
O'Neill, Jeff	TOR	1	0	.000	0
Olesz, Rostislav	FLA	1	0	.000	0
Ortmeyer, Jed	NYR	1	0	.000	0
Ouellet, Michel	PIT	3	1	.333	0
Ovechkin, Alex	WSH	13	6	.462	3
Palffy, Ziggy	PIT	2	0	.000	0
Parise, Zach	N.J.	3	1	.333	1
Park, Richard	VAN	1	0	.000	0
Parrish, Mark	L.A.	3	0	.000	0
Peca, Michael	EDM	5	2	.400	0
Perezhogin, Alexander	MTL	3	0	.000	0
Perry, Corey	ANA	2	0	.000	0
Petrovicky, Ronald	ATL	1	0	.000	0
Pettinger, Matt	WSH	7	3	.429	2
Phaneuf, Dion	CGY	1	0	.000	0
Pirjeta, Lasse	PIT	1	0	.000	0
Pisani, Fernando	EDM	7	3	.429	2
Pominville, Jason	BUF	2	0	.000	0
Ponikarovsky, Alexei	TOR	5	1	.200	0
Prospal, Vaclav	T.B.	3	2	.667	1
Prucha, Petr	NYR	5	2	.400	2
Reasoner, Marty	BOS	1	0	.000	0
Recchi, Mark	CAR	4	0	.000	0
Reinprecht, Steve	PHX	3	2	.667	2
Ribeiro, Mike	MTL	1	1	1.000	0
Richards, Brad	T.B.	9	6	.667	4
Richards, Mike	PHI	7	3	.429	1
Rita, Jani	PIT	1	0	.000	0
Robitaille, Luc	L.A.	3	2	.667	1
Robitaille, Randy	MIN	4	1	.250	1
Roenick, Jeremy	L.A.	2	1	.500	0
Rolston, Brian	MIN	7	3	.429	3
Roy, Derek	BUF	2	1	.500	0
Rozsival, Michal	NYR	1	0	.000	0
Rucinsky, Martin	NYR	2	0	.000	0
Ruutu, Jarkko	VAN	4	2	.500	1
Ruutu, Tuomo	CHI	1	1	1.000	1
Ryder, Michael	MTL	4	0	.000	0
Sakic, Joe	COL	7	0	.000	0
Samsonov, Sergei	EDM	6	2	.333	1
Samuelsson, Mikael	DET	1	0	.000	0
Sanderson, Geoff	PHX	5	3	.600	2
Saprykin, Oleg	PHX	2	0	.000	0
Satan, Miroslav	NYI	10	7	.700	5
Savard, Marc	ATL	3	1	.333	0
Sedin, Daniel	VAN	3	1	.333	1
Selanne, Teemu	ANA	7	2	.286	0
Shanahan, Brendan	DET	1	0	.000	0
Sharp, Patrick	CHI	2	0	.000	0
Sillinger, Mike	NSH	5	1	.200	0
Sim, Jon	FLA	1	0	.000	0
Slater, Jim	ATL	1	1	1.000	1
Smyth, Ryan	EDM	13	4	.308	2
Spacek, Jaroslav	EDM	1	1	1.000	0
Spezza, Jason	OTT	2	0	.000	0
St. Louis, Martin	T.B.	3	0	.000	0
Staal, Eric	CAR	4	1	.250	1
Stempniak, Lee	STL	3	2	.667	2
Stevenson, Grant	S.J.	1	0	.000	0
Stillman, Cory	CAR	3	1	.333	1
Stoll, Jarret	EDM	3	1	.333	0
Straka, Martin	NYR	6	1	.167	0
Strudwick, Jason	NYR	1	1	1.000	0
Stuart, Brad	BOS	1	0	.000	0
Stumpel, Jozef	FLA	3	0	.000	0
Sturm, Marco	BOS	6	2	.333	0
Sullivan, Steve	NSH	7	3	.429	2
Sundin, Mats	TOR	7	1	.143	1
Sutherby, Brian	WSH	1	0	.000	0
Svatos, Marek	COL	5	2	.400	0
Sykora, Petr	NYR	7	5	.714	3
Sykora, Petr	WSH	1	1	1.000	0
Tanguay, Alex	COL	6	2	.333	1
Thomas, Bill	PHX	1	0	.000	0
Thornton, Joe	S.J.	5	1	.200	0
Timonen, Kimmo	NSH	1	0	.000	0
Tjarnqvist, Daniel	MIN	1	0	.000	0
Tkachuk, Keith	STL	3	1	.333	0
Torres, Raffi	EDM	5	1	.200	1
Tucker, Darcy	TOR	4	1	.250	1
Turgeon, Pierre	COL	1	0	.000	0
Vanek, Thomas	BUF	6	2	.333	1
Vermette, Antoine	OTT	1	0	.000	0
Vorobiev, Pavel	CHI	3	2	.667	0
Vrbata, Radim	CHI	6	2	.333	1
Vyborny, David	CBJ	7	1	.143	1
Walter, Ben	BOS	1	0	.000	0
Walz, Wes	MIN	1	0	.000	0
Ward, Jason	NYR	1	0	.000	0
Weight, Doug	CAR	6	2	.333	1
Weiss, Stephen	FLA	1	0	.000	0
Wellwood, Kyle	TOR	1	0	.000	0
White, Todd	MIN	2	1	.500	0
Whitney, Ray	CAR	5	4	.800	0
Whitney, Ryan	PIT	2	1	.500	0
Wideman, Dennis	STL	6	2	.333	1
Williams, Jason	DET	7	5	.714	2
Williams, Justin	CAR	2	1	.500	0
Willsie, Brian	WSH	9	3	.333	1
Wright, Tyler	ANA	1	0	.000	0
Yashin, Alexei	NYI	7	2	.286	0
York, Mike	NYI	2	0	.000	0
Young, Scott	STL	1	0	.000	0
Yzerman, Steve	DET	2	1	.500	0
Zetterberg, Henrik	DET	4	2	.500	0
Zherdev, Nikolai	CBJ	3	1	.333	0
Zidlicky, Marek	NSH	5	1	.200	0
Zubov, Sergei	DAL	12	7	.583	4
Zubrus, Dainius	WSH	2	1	.500	0

Jussi Jokinen scored on his first nine shootout attempts and ended the season as the league's shootout leader with 10 goals on 13 shots.

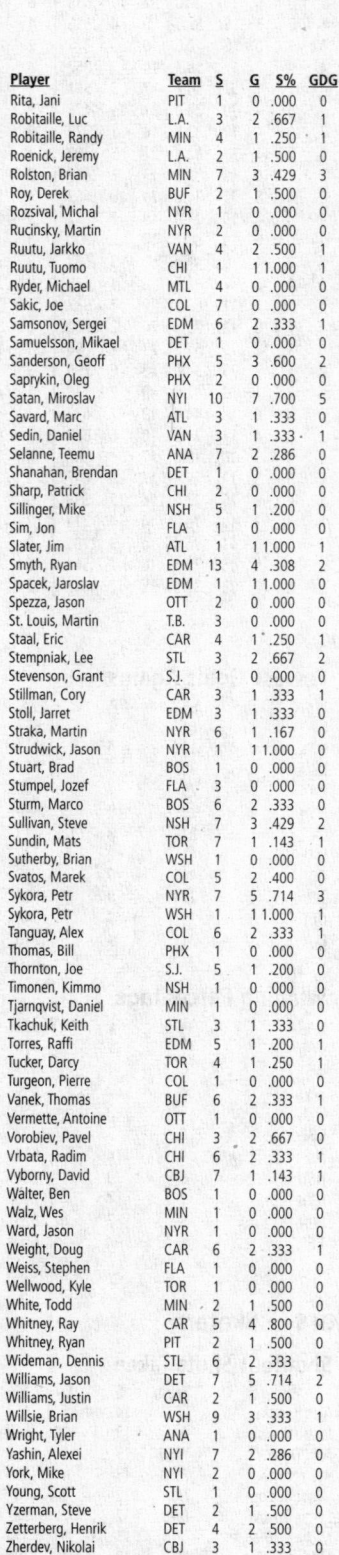

Goaltenders

Goaltender	Team	W	L	SA	GA	Sv %
Aebischer, David	MTL	2	1	10	2	.800
Anderson, Craig	CHI	0	3	7	5	.286
Aubin, J-Sebastien	TOR	0	2	5	2	.600
Auld, Alexander	VAN	4	3	22	7	.682
Bacashihua, Jason	STL	1	0	4	1	.750
Belfour, Ed	TOR	2	4	14	6	.571
Biron, Martin	BUF	2	3	12	5	.583
Boucher, Brian	CGY	1	0	3	0	1.000
Brodeur, Martin	N.J.	8	3	38	9	.763
Budaj, Peter	COL	0	5	14	9	.357
Burke, Sean	T.B.	2	3	11	5	.545
Caron, Sebastien	PIT	0	3	10	6	.400
Clemmensen, Scott	N.J.	1	1	7	3	.571
Cloutier, Dan	VAN	0	1	2	2	.000
Conklin, Ty	EDM	0	1	2	2	.000
Crawford, Corey	CHI	0	1	3	2	.333
Denis, Marc	CBJ	3	1	18	4	.778
DiPietro, Rick	NYI	8	3	41	12	.707
Divis, Reinhard	STL	0	1	3	2	.333
Dubielewicz, Wade	NYI	1	0	3	0	1.000
Dunham, Mike	ATL	0	2	4	3	.250
Emery, Ray	OTT	0	2	5	2	.600
Esche, Robert	PHI	1	2	8	4	.500
Fernandez, Manny	MIN	4	2	19	4	.789
Fleury, Marc-Andre	PIT	0	2	5	4	.200
Garnett, Michael	ATL	0	2	8	4	.500
Garon, Mathieu	L.A.	4	1	16	3	.812
Gerber, Martin	CAR	7	2	33	10	.697
Giguere, J-S	ANA	3	7	31	12	.613
Grahame, John	T.B.	4	1	16	4	.750
Harding, Josh	MIN	1	0	3	1	.667
Hasek, Dominik	OTT	2	4	16	6	.625
Hedberg, Johan	DAL	4	0	17	3	.824
Huet, Cristobal	MTL	1	2	9	3	.667
Johnson, Brent	WSH	3	1	13	2	.846
Joseph, Curtis	PHX	3	2	19	6	.684
Khabibulin, Nikolai	CHI	2	1	15	5	.667
Kiprusoff, Miikka	CGY	1	7	23	12	.478
Kolesnik, Vitaly	COL	1	0	7	0	1.000
Kolzig, Olaf	WSH	4	5	44	15	.659
Labarbera, Jason	L.A.	2	0	5	0	1.000
Lalime, Patrick	STL	0	2	5	3	.400
Leclaire, Pascal	CBJ	4	2	18	4	.778
Legace, Manny	DET	2	2	17	7	.588
Lehtonen, Kari	ATL	5	0	20	3	.850
Leneveu, David	PHX	0	1	3	1	.667
Lundqvist, Henrik	NYR	4	3	37	9	.757
Luongo, Roberto	FLA	4	4	27	7	.741
Markkanen, Jussi	EDM	1	3	16	8	.500
Mason, Chris	NSH	2	0	5	0	1.000
McLennan, Jamie	FLA	0	1	4	2	.500
Miller, Ryan	BUF	3	2	17	5	.706
Morrison, Michael	OTT	5	2	24	6	.750
Munro, Adam	CHI	0	1	4	2	.500
Nabokov, Evgeni	S.J.	0	4	13	8	.385
Niittymaki, Antero	PHI	3	4	24	10	.583
Noronen, Mika	VAN	0	0	1	1	.000
Osgood, Chris	DET	2	1	8	2	.750
Prusek, Martin	CBJ	1	0	8	1	.875
Raycroft, Andrew	BOS	0	1	2	1	.500
Roloson, Dwayne	EDM	1	4	20	9	.550
Sanford, Curtis	STL	3	5	25	10	.600
Sauve, Philippe	PHX	1	0	3	0	1.000
Schaefer, Nolan	S.J.	1	0	4	1	.750
Shields, Steve	ATL	0	1	2	1	.500
Tellqvist, Mikael	TOR	1	1	5	2	.600
Theodore, Jose	COL	1	1	6	1	.833
Thibault, Jocelyn	PIT	1	1	12	3	.750
Thomas, Tim	BOS	2	6	31	9	.710
Toivonen, Hannu	BOS	0	1	3	2	.333
Toskala, Vesa	S.J.	0	3	12	5	.583
Turco, Marty	DAL	8	1	24	6	.750
Vokoun, Tomas	NSH	4	3	20	8	.600
Ward, Cam	CAR	1	0	3	0	1.000
Weekes, Kevin	NYR	3	1	13	6	.538

NHL Record Book

Year-By-Year Final Standings & Leading Scorers

*Stanley Cup winner

1917-18

First Half

Team	GP	W	L	T	GF	GA	PTS
Montreal	14	10	4	0	81	47	20
Toronto	14	8	6	0	71	75	16
Ottawa	14	5	9	0	67	79	10
**Mtl. Wanderers	6	1	5	0	17	35	2

**Montreal Arena burned down and Wanderers forced to withdraw from League. Montreal Canadiens and Toronto each counted a win for defaulted games with Wanderers.

Second Half

Team	GP	W	L	T	GF	GA	PTS
*Toronto	8	5	3	0	37	34	10
Ottawa	8	4	4	0	35	35	8
Montreal	8	3	5	0	34	37	6

Leading Scorers

Player	Club	GP	G	A	PTS	PIM
Joe Malone	Montreal	20	44	4	48	30
Cy Denneny	Ottawa	20	36	10	46	80
Reg Noble	Toronto	20	30	10	40	35
Newsy Lalonde	Montreal	14	23	7	30	51
Corb Denneny	Toronto	21	20	9	29	14
Harry Cameron	Toronto	21	17	10	27	28
Didier Pitre	Montreal	20	17	6	23	29
Eddie Gerard	Ottawa	20	13	7	20	26
Jack Darragh	Ottawa	18	14	5	19	26
Frank Nighbor	Ottawa	10	11	8	19	6
Harry Meeking	Toronto	21	10	9	19	28

1918-19

First Half

Team	GP	W	L	T	GF	GA	PTS
• Montreal	10	7	3	0	57	50	14
Ottawa	10	5	5	0	39	39	10
Toronto	10	3	7	0	42	49	6

Second Half

Team	GP	W	L	T	GF	GA	PTS
Ottawa	8	7	1	0	32	14	14
Montreal	8	3	5	0	31	28	6
Toronto	8	2	6	0	22	43	4

• NHL Champion. Stanley Cup not awarded due to influenza epidemic.

Leading Scorers

Player	Club	GP	G	A	PTS	PIM
Newsy Lalonde	Montreal	17	22	10	32	40
Odie Cleghorn	Montreal	17	22	6	28	22
Frank Nighbor	Ottawa	18	19	9	28	27
Cy Denneny	Ottawa	18	18	4	22	58
Didier Pitre	Montreal	17	14	5	19	12
Alf Skinner	Toronto	17	12	4	16	26
Harry Cameron	Tor., Ott.	14	11	3	14	35
Jack Darragh	Ottawa	14	11	3	14	33
Ken Randall	Toronto	15	8	6	14	27
Sprague Cleghorn	Ottawa	18	7	6	13	27

All-Time Standings of NHL Teams

(ranked by percentage)

Active Clubs

Team	Games	Wins	Losses	Ties	OT Losses	SO Losses	Goals For	Goals Against	Points	Pts %	First Season
Montreal	5628	2891	1865	837	32	3	18528	15033	6654	.589	1917-18
Philadelphia	3014	1513	1014	457	24	6	10298	8816	3513	.577	1967-68
Boston	5468	2593	2034	791	42	8	17683	16155	6027	.548	1924-25
Buffalo	2788	1309	1046	409	19	5	9357	8491	3051	.542	1970-71
Edmonton	2076	981	791	262	33	9	7643	7042	2266	.536	1979-80
Calgary	2632	1188	1035	379	23	7	9009	8511	2785	.523	1972-73
Detroit	5402	2417	2146	815	21	3	16841	16183	5673	.522	1926-27
Colorado	2076	940	845	261	24	6	7183	6949	2171	.515	1979-80
Toronto	5628	2459	2360	783	19	7	17450	17321	5727	.506	1917-18
St. Louis	3014	1309	1240	432	25	8	9549	9608	3083	.505	1967-68
NY Islanders	2632	1148	1117	347	17	3	8819	8455	2663	.501	1972-73
NY Rangers	5402	2275	2287	808	28	4	16734	16931	5390	.496	1926-27
Dallas	3014	1258	1272	459	24	1	9440	9732	3000	.492	1967-68
Chicago	5402	2202	2351	814	29	6	16054	16421	5253	.483	1926-27
Washington	2476	1040	1104	303	23	6	7894	8317	2412	.481	1974-75
Ottawa	1036	435	457	115	23	6	2969	3075	1014	.478	1992-93
Los Angeles	3014	1203	1356	424	30	1	9987	10637	2861	.470	1967-68
Pittsburgh	3014	1221	1373	383	31	6	10182	10875	2862	.470	1967-68
Minnesota	410	161	168	55	23	3	980	1024	403	.465	2000-01
Phoenix	2076	823	958	266	26	3	6743	7410	1941	.460	1979-80
New Jersey	2476	980	1139	328	25	4	7641	8374	2317	.460	1974-75
Anaheim	952	381	427	107	30	7	2474	2667	906	.460	1993-94
Florida	952	359	406	142	40	5	2464	2699	905	.458	1993-94
Carolina	2076	813	972	263	26	2	6397	7133	1917	.454	1979-80
Nashville	574	232	253	60	26	3	1429	1581	553	.453	1998-99
Vancouver	2788	1066	1299	391	28	4	8914	9783	2555	.452	1970-71
San Jose	1116	426	531	121	31	7	3076	3510	1011	.439	1991-92
Tampa Bay	1036	371	520	112	29	4	2673	3254	887	.415	1992-93
Columbus	410	139	216	33	19	3	967	1268	333	.374	2000-01
Atlanta	492	161	258	45	23	5	1289	1692	395	.373	1999-2000

Defunct Clubs

Team	Games	Wins	Losses	Ties	Goals For	Goals Against	Points	Pts %	First Season	Last Season
Ottawa Senators	542	258	221	63	1458	1333	579	.534	1917-18	1933-34
Montreal Maroons	622	271	260	91	1474	1405	633	.509	1924-25	1937-38
NY/Brooklyn Americans	784	255	402	127	1643	2182	637	.406	1925-26	1941-42
Hamilton Tigers	126	47	78	1	414	475	95	.377	1920-21	1924-25
Cleveland Barons	160	47	87	26	470	617	120	.375	1976-77	1977-78
Pittsburgh Pirates	212	67	122	23	376	519	157	.370	1925-26	1929-30
Calif./Oakland Seals	698	182	401	115	1826	2580	479	.343	1967-68	1975-76
St. Louis Eagles	48	11	31	6	86	144	28	.292	1934-35	1934-35
Quebec Bulldogs	24	4	20	0	91	177	8	.167	1919-20	1919-20
Montreal Wanderers	6	1	5	0	17	35	2	.167	1917-18	1917-18
Philadelphia Quakers	44	4	36	4	76	184	12	.136	1930-31	1930-31

Calgary totals include Atlanta Flames, 1972-73 to 1979-80.
Carolina totals include Hartford, 1979-80 to 1996-97.
Colorado totals include Quebec, 1979-80 to 1994-95.
Dallas totals include Minnesota North Stars, 1967-68 to 1992-93.
Detroit totals include Cougars, 1926-27 to 1929-30, and Falcons, 1930-31 to 1931-32.
New Jersey totals include Kansas City, 1974-75 to 1975-76, and Colorado Rockies, 1976-77 to 1981-82.
Phoenix totals include Winnipeg, 1979-80 to 1995-96.
Toronto totals include Arenas, 1917-18 to 1918-19, and St. Patricks, 1919-20 to 1925-26.

1919-20

First Half

Team	GP	W	L	T	GF	GA	PTS
Ottawa	12	9	3	0	59	23	18
Montreal	12	8	4	0	62	51	16
Toronto	12	5	7	0	52	62	10
Quebec	12	2	10	0	44	81	4

Second Half

Team	GP	W	L	T	GF	GA	PTS
*Ottawa	12	10	2	0	62	41	20
Toronto	12	7	5	0	67	44	14
Montreal	12	5	7	0	67	62	10
Quebec	12	2	10	0	47	96	4

Leading Scorers

Player	Club	GP	G	A	PTS	PIM
Joe Malone	Quebec	24	39	10	49	12
Newsy Lalonde	Montreal	23	37	9	46	34
Frank Nighbor	Ottawa	23	26	15	41	18
Corb Denneny	Toronto	24	24	12	36	20
Jack Darragh	Ottawa	23	22	14	36	22
Reg Noble	Toronto	24	24	9	33	52
Amos Arbour	Montreal	22	21	5	26	13
Cully Wilson	Toronto	23	20	6	26	86
Didier Pitre	Montreal	22	14	12	26	6
Punch Broadbent	Ottawa	21	19	6	25	40

1920-21

First Half

Team	GP	W	L	T	GF	GA	PTS
*Ottawa	10	8	2	0	49	23	16
Toronto	10	5	5	0	39	47	10
Montreal	10	4	6	0	37	51	8
Hamilton	10	3	7	0	34	38	6

Second Half

Team	GP	W	L	T	GF	GA	PTS
Toronto	14	10	4	0	66	53	20
Montreal	14	9	5	0	75	48	18
Ottawa	14	6	8	0	48	52	12
Hamilton	14	3	11	0	58	94	6

Leading Scorers

Player	Club	GP	G	A	PTS	PIM
Newsy Lalonde	Montreal	24	33	10	43	36
Babe Dye	Ham., Tor.	24	35	5	40	32
Cy Denneny	Ottawa	24	34	5	39	10
Joe Malone	Hamilton	20	28	9	37	6
Frank Nighbor	Ottawa	24	19	10	29	10
Reg Noble	Toronto	24	19	8	27	54
Harry Cameron	Toronto	24	18	9	27	35
Goldie Prodgers	Hamilton	24	18	9	27	8
Corb Denneny	Toronto	20	19	7	26	29
Jack Darragh	Ottawa	24	11	15	26	20

1921-22

Team	GP	W	L	T	GF	GA	PTS
Ottawa	24	14	8	2	106	84	30
*Toronto	24	13	10	1	98	97	27
Montreal	24	12	11	1	88	94	25
Hamilton	24	7	17	0	88	105	14

Leading Scorers

Player	Club	GP	G	A	PTS	PIM
Punch Broadbent	Ottawa	24	32	14	46	28
Cy Denneny	Ottawa	22	27	12	39	20
Babe Dye	Toronto	24	31	7	38	39
Harry Cameron	Toronto	24	18	17	35	22
Joe Malone	Hamilton	24	24	7	31	4
Corb Denneny	Toronto	24	19	9	28	28
Reg Noble	Toronto	24	17	11	28	14
Sprague Cleghorn	Montreal	24	17	9	26	80
Georges Boucher	Ottawa	23	13	12	25	12
Odie Cleghorn	Montreal	23	21	3	24	26

1922-23

Team	GP	W	L	T	GF	GA	PTS
*Ottawa	24	14	9	1	77	54	29
Montreal	24	13	9	2	73	61	28
Toronto	24	13	10	1	82	88	27
Hamilton	24	6	18	0	81	110	12

Leading Scorers

Player	Club	GP	G	A	PTS	PIM
Babe Dye	Toronto	22	26	11	37	19
Cy Denneny	Ottawa	24	23	11	34	28
Billy Boucher	Montreal	24	24	7	31	55
Jack Adams	Toronto	23	19	9	28	42
Mickey Roach	Hamilton	24	17	10	27	8
Odie Cleghorn	Montreal	24	19	6	25	18
Georges Boucher	Ottawa	24	14	9	23	58
Reg Noble	Toronto	24	12	11	23	47
Cully Wilson	Hamilton	23	16	5	21	46
Aurel Joliat	Montreal	24	12	9	21	37

1923-24

Team	GP	W	L	T	GF	GA	PTS
Ottawa	24	16	8	0	74	54	32
*Montreal	24	13	11	0	59	48	26
Toronto	24	10	14	0	59	85	20
Hamilton	24	9	15	0	63	68	18

Leading Scorers

Player	Club	GP	G	A	PTS	PIM
Cy Denneny	Ottawa	22	22	2	24	10
Georges Boucher	Ottawa	21	13	10	23	38
Billy Boucher	Montreal	23	16	6	22	48
Billy Burch	Hamilton	24	16	6	22	6
Aurel Joliat	Montreal	24	15	5	20	27
Babe Dye	Toronto	19	16	3	19	23
Jack Adams	Toronto	22	14	4	18	51
Reg Noble	Toronto	23	12	5	17	79
Howie Morenz	Montreal	24	13	3	16	20
King Clancy	Ottawa	24	8	8	16	26

1924-25

Team	GP	W	L	T	GF	GA	PTS
Hamilton	30	19	10	1	90	60	39
Toronto	30	19	11	0	90	84	38
• Montreal	30	17	11	2	93	56	36
Ottawa	30	17	12	1	83	66	35
Mtl. Maroons	30	9	19	2	45	65	20
Boston	30	6	24	0	49	119	12

• NHL Champion (Stanley Cup won by Victoria Cougars, WCHL)

Leading Scorers

Player	Club	GP	G	A	PTS	PIM
Babe Dye	Toronto	29	38	8	46	41
Cy Denneny	Ottawa	29	27	15	42	16
Aurel Joliat	Montreal	25	30	11	41	85
Howie Morenz	Montreal	30	28	11	39	46
Red Green	Hamilton	30	19	15	34	81
Jack Adams	Toronto	27	21	10	31	67
Billy Boucher	Montreal	30	17	13	30	92
Billy Burch	Hamilton	27	20	7	27	10
Jimmy Herberts	Boston	30	17	7	24	55
Hooley Smith	Ottawa	30	10	13	23	81

1925-26

Team	GP	W	L	T	GF	GA	PTS
Ottawa	36	24	8	4	77	42	52
*Mtl. Maroons	36	20	11	5	91	73	45
Pittsburgh	36	19	16	1	82	70	39
Boston	36	17	15	4	92	85	38
NY Americans	36	12	20	4	68	89	28
Toronto	36	12	21	3	92	114	27
Montreal	36	11	24	1	79	108	23

Leading Scorers

Player	Club	GP	G	A	PTS	PIM
Nels Stewart	Mtl. Maroons	36	34	8	42	119
Cy Denneny	Ottawa	36	24	12	36	18
Carson Cooper	Boston	36	28	3	31	10
Jimmy Herberts	Boston	36	26	5	31	47
Howie Morenz	Montreal	31	23	3	26	39
Jack Adams	Toronto	36	21	5	26	52
Aurel Joliat	Montreal	35	17	9	26	52
Billy Burch	NY Americans	36	22	3	25	33
Hooley Smith	Ottawa	28	16	9	25	53
Frank Nighbor	Ottawa	35	12	13	25	40

1926-27
Canadian Division

Team	GP	W	L	T	GF	GA	PTS
*Ottawa	44	30	10	4	86	69	64
Montreal	44	28	14	2	99	67	58
Mtl. Maroons	44	20	20	4	71	68	44
NY Americans	44	17	25	2	82	91	36
Toronto	44	15	24	5	79	94	35

American Division

Team	GP	W	L	T	GF	GA	PTS
NY Rangers	44	25	13	6	95	72	56
Boston	44	21	20	3	97	89	45
Chicago	44	19	22	3	115	116	41
Pittsburgh	44	15	26	3	79	108	33
Detroit	44	12	28	4	76	105	28

Leading Scorers

Player	Club	GP	G	A	PTS	PIM
Bill Cook	NY Rangers	44	33	4	37	58
Dick Irvin	Chicago	43	18	18	36	34
Howie Morenz	Montreal	44	25	7	32	49
Frank Fredrickson	Det., Bos.	41	18	13	31	46
Babe Dye	Chicago	41	25	5	30	14
Ace Bailey	Toronto	42	15	13	28	82
Frank Boucher	NY Rangers	44	13	15	28	17
Billy Burch	NY Americans	43	19	8	27	40
Harry Oliver	Boston	42	18	6	24	17
Duke Keats	Bos., Det.	42	16	8	24	52

1927-28
Canadian Division

Team	GP	W	L	T	GF	GA	PTS
Montreal	44	26	11	7	116	48	59
Mtl. Maroons	44	24	14	6	96	77	54
Ottawa	44	20	14	10	78	57	50
Toronto	44	18	18	8	89	88	44
NY Americans	44	11	27	6	63	128	28

American Division

Team	GP	W	L	T	GF	GA	PTS
Boston	44	20	13	11	77	70	51
*NY Rangers	44	19	16	9	94	79	47
Pittsburgh	44	19	17	8	67	76	46
Detroit	44	19	19	6	88	79	44
Chicago	44	7	34	3	68	134	17

Leading Scorers

Player	Club	GP	G	A	PTS	PIM
Howie Morenz	Montreal	43	33	18	51	66
Aurel Joliat	Montreal	44	28	11	39	105
Frank Boucher	NY Rangers	44	23	12	35	15
George Hay	Detroit	42	22	13	35	20
Nels Stewart	Mtl. Maroons	41	27	7	34	104
Art Gagne	Montreal	44	20	10	30	75
Bun Cook	NY Rangers	44	14	14	28	45
Bill Carson	Toronto	32	20	6	26	36
Frank Finnigan	Ottawa	38	20	5	25	34
Bill Cook	NY Rangers	43	18	6	24	42
Duke Keats	Det., Chi.	38	14	10	24	60

1928-29
Canadian Division

Team	GP	W	L	T	GF	GA	PTS
Montreal	44	22	7	15	71	43	59
NY Americans	44	19	13	12	53	53	50
Toronto	44	21	18	5	85	69	47
Ottawa	44	14	17	13	54	67	41
Mtl. Maroons	44	15	20	9	67	65	39

American Division

Team	GP	W	L	T	GF	GA	PTS
*Boston	44	26	13	5	89	52	57
NY Rangers	44	21	13	10	72	65	52
Detroit	44	19	16	9	72	63	47
Pittsburgh	44	9	27	8	46	80	26
Chicago	44	7	29	8	33	85	22

Leading Scorers

Player	Club	GP	G	A	PTS	PIM
Ace Bailey	Toronto	44	22	10	32	78
Nels Stewart	Mtl. Maroons	44	21	8	29	74
Carson Cooper	Detroit	43	18	9	27	14
Howie Morenz	Montreal	42	17	10	27	47
Andy Blair	Toronto	44	12	15	27	41
Frank Boucher	NY Rangers	44	10	16	26	8
Harry Oliver	Boston	43	17	6	23	24
Bill Cook	NY Rangers	43	15	8	23	41
Jimmy Ward	Mtl. Maroons	43	14	8	22	46

Seven players tied with 19 points

1929-30
Canadian Division

Team	GP	W	L	T	GF	GA	PTS
Mtl. Maroons	44	23	16	5	141	114	51
*Montreal	44	21	14	9	142	114	51
Ottawa	44	21	15	8	138	118	50
Toronto	44	17	21	6	116	124	40
NY Americans	44	14	25	5	113	161	33

American Division

Team	GP	W	L	T	GF	GA	PTS
Boston	44	38	5	1	179	98	77
Chicago	44	21	18	5	117	111	47
NY Rangers	44	17	17	10	136	143	44
Detroit	44	14	24	6	117	133	34
Pittsburgh	44	5	36	3	102	185	13

Leading Scorers

Player	Club	GP	G	A	PTS	PIM
Cooney Weiland	Boston	44	43	30	73	27
Frank Boucher	NY Rangers	42	26	36	62	16
Dit Clapper	Boston	44	41	20	61	48
Bill Cook	NY Rangers	44	29	30	59	56
Hec Kilrea	Ottawa	44	36	22	58	72
Nels Stewart	Mtl. Maroons	44	39	16	55	81
Howie Morenz	Montreal	44	40	10	50	72
Normie Himes	NY Americans	44	28	22	50	15
Joe Lamb	Ottawa	44	29	20	49	119
Dutch Gainor	Boston	42	18	31	49	39

1930-31
Canadian Division

Team	GP	W	L	T	GF	GA	PTS
*Montreal	44	26	10	8	129	89	60
Toronto	44	22	13	9	118	99	53
Mtl. Maroons	44	20	18	6	105	106	46
NY Americans	44	18	16	10	76	74	46
Ottawa	44	10	30	4	91	142	24

American Division

Team	GP	W	L	T	GF	GA	PTS
Boston	44	28	10	6	143	90	62
Chicago	44	24	17	3	108	78	51
NY Rangers	44	19	16	9	106	87	47
Detroit	44	16	21	7	102	105	39
Philadelphia	44	4	36	4	76	184	12

Leading Scorers

Player	Club	GP	G	A	PTS	PIM
Howie Morenz	Montreal	39	28	23	51	49
Ebbie Goodfellow	Detroit	44	25	23	48	32
Charlie Conacher	Toronto	37	31	12	43	78
Bill Cook	NY Rangers	43	30	12	42	39
Ace Bailey	Toronto	40	23	19	42	46
Joe Primeau	Toronto	38	9	32	41	18
Nels Stewart	Mtl. Maroons	42	25	14	39	75
Frank Boucher	NY Rangers	44	12	27	39	20
Cooney Weiland	Boston	44	25	13	38	14
Bun Cook	NY Rangers	44	18	17	35	72
Aurel Joliat	Montreal	43	13	22	35	73

1931-32

Canadian Division

Team	GP	W	L	T	GF	GA	PTS
Montreal	48	25	16	7	128	111	57
*Toronto	48	23	18	7	155	127	53
Mtl. Maroons	48	19	22	7	142	139	45
NY Americans	48	16	24	8	95	142	40

American Division

Team	GP	W	L	T	GF	GA	PTS
NY Rangers	48	23	17	8	134	112	54
Chicago	48	18	19	11	86	101	47
Detroit	48	18	20	10	95	108	46
Boston	48	15	21	12	122	117	42

Leading Scorers

Player	Club	GP	G	A	PTS	PIM
Busher Jackson	Toronto	48	28	25	53	63
Joe Primeau	Toronto	46	13	37	50	25
Howie Morenz	Montreal	48	24	25	49	46
Charlie Conacher	Toronto	44	34	14	48	66
Bill Cook	NY Rangers	48	34	14	48	33
Dave Trottier	Mtl. Maroons	48	26	18	44	94
Hooley Smith	Mtl. Maroons	43	11	33	44	49
Babe Siebert	Mtl. Maroons	48	21	18	39	64
Dit Clapper	Boston	48	17	22	39	21
Aurel Joliat	Montreal	48	15	24	39	46

1932-33

Canadian Division

Team	GP	W	L	T	GF	GA	PTS
Toronto	48	24	18	6	119	111	54
Mtl. Maroons	48	22	20	6	135	119	50
Montreal	48	18	25	5	92	115	41
NY Americans	48	15	22	11	91	118	41
Ottawa	48	11	27	10	88	131	32

American Division

Team	GP	W	L	T	GF	GA	PTS
Boston	48	25	15	8	124	88	58
Detroit	48	25	15	8	111	93	58
*NY Rangers	48	23	17	8	135	107	54
Chicago	48	16	20	12	88	101	44

Leading Scorers

Player	Club	GP	G	A	PTS	PIM
Bill Cook	NY Rangers	48	28	22	50	51
Busher Jackson	Toronto	48	27	17	44	43
Baldy Northcott	Mtl. Maroons	48	22	21	43	30
Hooley Smith	Mtl. Maroons	48	20	21	41	66
Paul Haynes	Mtl. Maroons	48	16	25	41	18
Aurel Joliat	Montreal	48	18	21	39	53
Marty Barry	Boston	48	24	13	37	40
Bun Cook	NY Rangers	48	22	15	37	35
Nels Stewart	Boston	47	18	18	36	62
Howie Morenz	Montreal	46	14	21	35	32
Johnny Gagnon	Montreal	48	12	23	35	64
Eddie Shore	Boston	48	8	27	35	102
Frank Boucher	NY Rangers	46	7	28	35	4

1933-34

Canadian Division

Team	GP	W	L	T	GF	GA	PTS
Toronto	48	26	13	9	174	119	61
Montreal	48	22	20	6	99	101	50
Mtl. Maroons	48	19	18	11	117	122	49
NY Americans	48	15	23	10	104	132	40
Ottawa	48	13	29	6	115	143	32

American Division

Team	GP	W	L	T	GF	GA	PTS
Detroit	48	24	14	10	113	98	58
*Chicago	48	20	17	11	88	83	51
NY Rangers	48	21	19	8	120	113	50
Boston	48	18	25	5	111	130	41

Leading Scorers

Player	Club	GP	G	A	PTS	PIM
Charlie Conacher	Toronto	42	32	20	52	38
Joe Primeau	Toronto	45	14	32	46	8
Frank Boucher	NY Rangers	48	14	30	44	4
Marty Barry	Boston	48	27	12	39	12
Cecil Dillon	NY Rangers	48	13	26	39	10
Nels Stewart	Boston	48	21	17	38	68
Busher Jackson	Toronto	38	20	18	38	38
Aurel Joliat	Montreal	48	22	15	37	27
Reg Smith	Mtl. Maroons	47	18	19	37	58
Paul Thompson	Chicago	48	20	16	36	17

1934-35

Canadian Division

Team	GP	W	L	T	GF	GA	PTS
Toronto	48	30	14	4	157	111	64
*Mtl. Maroons	48	24	19	5	123	92	53
Montreal	48	19	23	6	110	145	44
NY Americans	48	12	27	9	100	142	33
St. Louis	48	11	31	6	86	144	28

American Division

Team	GP	W	L	T	GF	GA	PTS
Boston	48	26	16	6	129	112	58
Chicago	48	26	17	5	118	88	57
NY Rangers	48	22	20	6	137	139	50
Detroit	48	19	22	7	127	114	45

Leading Scorers

Player	Club	GP	G	A	PTS	PIM
Charlie Conacher	Toronto	47	36	21	57	24
Syd Howe	St.L., Det.	50	22	25	47	34
Larry Aurie	Detroit	48	17	29	46	24
Frank Boucher	NY Rangers	48	13	32	45	2
Busher Jackson	Toronto	42	22	22	44	27
Herbie Lewis	Detroit	47	16	27	43	26
Art Chapman	NY Americans	47	9	34	43	4
Marty Barry	Boston	48	20	20	40	33
Sweeney Schriner	NY Americans	48	18	22	40	6
Nels Stewart	Boston	47	21	18	39	45
Paul Thompson	Chicago	48	16	23	39	20

1935-36

Canadian Division

Team	GP	W	L	T	GF	GA	PTS
Mtl. Maroons	48	22	16	10	114	106	54
Toronto	48	23	19	6	126	106	52
NY Americans	48	16	25	7	109	122	39
Montreal	48	11	26	11	82	123	33

American Division

Team	GP	W	L	T	GF	GA	PTS
*Detroit	48	24	16	8	124	103	56
Boston	48	22	20	6	92	83	50
Chicago	48	21	19	8	93	92	50
NY Rangers	48	19	17	12	91	96	50

Leading Scorers

Player	Club	GP	G	A	PTS	PIM
Sweeney Schriner	NY Americans	48	19	26	45	8
Marty Barry	Detroit	48	21	19	40	16
Paul Thompson	Chicago	45	17	23	40	19
Bill Thoms	Toronto	48	23	15	38	29
Charlie Conacher	Toronto	44	23	15	38	74
Hooley Smith	Mtl. Maroons	47	19	19	38	75
Doc Romnes	Chicago	48	13	25	38	6
Art Chapman	NY Americans	47	10	28	38	14
Herbie Lewis	Detroit	45	14	23	37	25
Baldy Northcott	Mtl. Maroons	48	15	21	36	41

1936-37

Canadian Division

Team	GP	W	L	T	GF	GA	PTS
Montreal	48	24	18	6	115	111	54
Mtl. Maroons	48	22	17	9	126	110	53
Toronto	48	22	21	5	119	115	49
NY Americans	48	15	29	4	122	161	34

American Division

Team	GP	W	L	T	GF	GA	PTS
*Detroit	48	25	14	9	128	102	59
Boston	48	23	18	7	120	110	53
NY Rangers	48	19	20	9	117	106	47
Chicago	48	14	27	7	99	131	35

Leading Scorers

Player	Club	GP	G	A	PTS	PIM
Sweeney Schriner	NY Americans	48	21	25	46	17
Syl Apps	Toronto	48	16	29	45	10
Marty Barry	Detroit	48	17	27	44	6
Larry Aurie	Detroit	45	23	20	43	20
Busher Jackson	Toronto	46	21	19	40	12
Johnny Gagnon	Montreal	48	20	16	36	38
Bob Gracie	Mtl. Maroons	47	11	25	36	18
Nels Stewart	Bos., NYA	43	23	12	35	37
Paul Thompson	Chicago	47	17	18	35	28
Bill Cowley	Boston	46	13	22	35	4

1937-38

Canadian Division

Team	GP	W	L	T	GF	GA	PTS
Toronto	48	24	15	9	151	127	57
NY Americans	48	19	18	11	110	111	49
Montreal	48	18	17	13	123	128	49
Mtl. Maroons	48	12	30	6	101	149	30

American Division

Team	GP	W	L	T	GF	GA	PTS
Boston	48	30	11	7	142	89	67
NY Rangers	48	27	15	6	149	96	60
*Chicago	48	14	25	9	97	139	37
Detroit	48	12	25	11	99	133	35

Leading Scorers

Player	Club	GP	G	A	PTS	PIM
Gordie Drillon	Toronto	48	26	26	52	4
Syl Apps	Toronto	47	21	29	50	9
Paul Thompson	Chicago	48	22	22	44	14
Georges Mantha	Montreal	47	23	19	42	12
Cecil Dillon	NY Rangers	48	21	18	39	6
Bill Cowley	Boston	48	17	22	39	8
Sweeney Schriner	NY Americans	49	21	17	38	22
Bill Thoms	Toronto	48	14	24	38	14
Clint Smith	NY Rangers	48	14	23	37	0
Nels Stewart	NY Americans	48	19	17	36	29
Neil Colville	NY Rangers	45	17	19	36	11

1938-39

Team	GP	W	L	T	GF	GA	PTS
*Boston	48	36	10	2	156	76	74
NY Rangers	48	26	16	6	149	105	58
Toronto	48	19	20	9	114	107	47
NY Americans	48	17	21	10	119	157	44
Detroit	48	18	24	6	107	128	42
Montreal	48	15	24	9	115	146	39
Chicago	48	12	28	8	91	132	32

Leading Scorers

Player	Club	GP	G	A	PTS	PIM
Toe Blake	Montreal	48	24	23	47	10
Sweeney Schriner	NY Americans	48	13	31	44	20
Bill Cowley	Boston	34	8	34	42	2
Clint Smith	NY Rangers	48	21	20	41	2
Marty Barry	Detroit	48	13	28	41	4
Syl Apps	Toronto	44	15	25	40	4
Tom Anderson	NY Americans	48	13	27	40	14
Johnny Gottselig	Chicago	48	16	23	39	15
Paul Haynes	Montreal	47	5	33	38	27
Roy Conacher	Boston	47	26	11	37	12
Lorne Carr	NY Americans	46	19	18	37	16
Neil Colville	NY Rangers	48	18	19	37	12
Phil Watson	NY Rangers	48	15	22	37	42

1939-40

Team	GP	W	L	T	GF	GA	PTS
Boston	48	31	12	5	170	98	67
*NY Rangers	48	27	11	10	136	77	64
Toronto	48	25	17	6	134	110	56
Chicago	48	23	19	6	112	120	52
Detroit	48	16	26	6	91	126	38
NY Americans	48	15	29	4	106	140	34
Montreal	48	10	33	5	90	168	25

Leading Scorers

Player	Club	GP	G	A	PTS	PIM
Milt Schmidt	Boston	48	22	30	52	37
Woody Dumart	Boston	48	22	21	43	16
Bobby Bauer	Boston	48	17	26	43	2
Gordie Drillon	Toronto	43	21	19	40	13
Bill Cowley	Boston	48	13	27	40	24
Bryan Hextall	NY Rangers	48	24	15	39	52
Neil Colville	NY Rangers	48	19	19	38	22
Syd Howe	Detroit	46	14	23	37	17
Toe Blake	Montreal	48	17	19	36	48
Murray Armstrong	NY Americans	48	16	20	36	12

1940-41

Team	GP	W	L	T	GF	GA	PTS
*Boston	48	27	8	13	168	102	67
Toronto	48	28	14	6	145	99	62
Detroit	48	21	16	11	112	102	53
NY Rangers	48	21	19	8	143	125	50
Chicago	48	16	25	7	112	139	39
Montreal	48	16	26	6	121	147	38
NY Americans	48	8	29	11	99	186	27

Leading Scorers

Player	Club	GP	G	A	PTS	PIM
Bill Cowley	Boston	46	17	45	62	16
Bryan Hextall	NY Rangers	48	26	18	44	16
Gordie Drillon	Toronto	42	23	21	44	2
Syl Apps	Toronto	41	20	24	44	6
Lynn Patrick	NY Rangers	48	20	24	44	12
Syd Howe	Detroit	48	20	24	44	8
Neil Colville	NY Rangers	48	14	28	42	28
Eddie Wiseman	Boston	48	16	24	40	10
Bobby Bauer	Boston	48	17	22	39	2
Sweeney Schriner	Toronto	48	24	14	38	6
Roy Conacher	Boston	40	24	14	38	7
Milt Schmidt	Boston	44	13	25	38	23

1941-42

Team	GP	W	L	T	GF	GA	PTS
NY Rangers	48	29	17	2	177	143	60
*Toronto	48	27	18	3	158	136	57
Boston	48	25	17	6	160	118	56
Chicago	48	22	23	3	145	155	47
Detroit	48	19	25	4	140	147	42
Montreal	48	18	27	3	134	173	39
Brooklyn	48	16	29	3	133	175	35

Leading Scorers

Player	Club	GP	G	A	PTS	PIM
Bryan Hextall	NY Rangers	48	24	32	56	30
Lynn Patrick	NY Rangers	47	32	22	54	18
Don Grosso	Detroit	48	23	30	53	13
Phil Watson	NY Rangers	48	15	37	52	48
Sid Abel	Detroit	48	18	31	49	45
Toe Blake	Montreal	47	17	28	45	19
Bill Thoms	Chicago	47	15	30	45	8
Gordie Drillon	Toronto	48	23	18	41	6
Syl Apps	Toronto	38	18	23	41	0
Tom Anderson	Brooklyn	48	12	29	41	54

1942-43

Team	GP	W	L	T	GF	GA	PTS
*Detroit	50	25	14	11	169	124	61
Boston	50	24	17	9	195	176	57
Toronto	50	22	19	9	198	159	53
Montreal	50	19	19	12	181	191	50
Chicago	50	17	18	15	179	180	49
NY Rangers	50	11	31	8	161	253	30

Leading Scorers

Player	Club	GP	G	A	PTS	PIM
Doug Bentley	Chicago	50	33	40	73	18
Bill Cowley	Boston	48	27	45	72	10
Max Bentley	Chicago	47	26	44	70	2
Lynn Patrick	NY Rangers	50	22	39	61	28
Lorne Carr	Toronto	50	27	33	60	15
Billy Taylor	Toronto	50	18	42	60	2
Bryan Hextall	NY Rangers	50	27	32	59	28
Toe Blake	Montreal	48	23	36	59	28
Elmer Lach	Montreal	45	18	40	58	14
Buddy O'Connor	Montreal	50	15	43	58	2

1943-44

Team	GP	W	L	T	GF	GA	PTS
*Montreal	50	38	5	7	234	109	83
Detroit	50	26	18	6	214	177	58
Toronto	50	23	23	4	214	174	50
Chicago	50	22	23	5	178	187	49
Boston	50	19	26	5	223	268	43
NY Rangers	50	6	39	5	162	310	17

Leading Scorers

Player	Club	GP	G	A	PTS	PIM
Herb Cain	Boston	48	36	46	82	4
Doug Bentley	Chicago	50	38	39	77	22
Lorne Carr	Toronto	50	36	38	74	9
Carl Liscombe	Detroit	50	36	37	73	17
Elmer Lach	Montreal	48	24	48	72	23
Clint Smith	Chicago	50	23	49	72	4
Bill Cowley	Boston	36	30	41	71	12
Bill Mosienko	Chicago	50	32	38	70	10
Art Jackson	Boston	49	28	41	69	8
Gus Bodnar	Toronto	50	22	40	62	18

1944-45

Team	GP	W	L	T	GF	GA	PTS
Montreal	50	38	8	4	228	121	80
Detroit	50	31	14	5	218	161	67
*Toronto	50	24	22	4	183	161	52
Boston	50	16	30	4	179	219	36
Chicago	50	13	30	7	141	194	33
NY Rangers	50	11	29	10	154	247	32

Leading Scorers

Player	Club	GP	G	A	PTS	PIM
Elmer Lach	Montreal	50	26	54	80	37
Maurice Richard	Montreal	50	50	23	73	36
Toe Blake	Montreal	49	29	38	67	15
Bill Cowley	Boston	49	25	40	65	2
Ted Kennedy	Toronto	49	29	25	54	14
Bill Mosienko	Chicago	50	28	26	54	0
Joe Carveth	Detroit	50	26	28	54	6
Ab DeMarco	NY Rangers	50	24	30	54	10
Clint Smith	Chicago	50	23	31	54	0
Syd Howe	Detroit	46	17	36	53	6

1945-46

Team	GP	W	L	T	GF	GA	PTS
*Montreal	50	28	17	5	172	134	61
Boston	50	24	18	8	167	156	56
Chicago	50	23	20	7	200	178	53
Detroit	50	20	20	10	146	159	50
Toronto	50	19	24	7	174	185	45
NY Rangers	50	13	28	9	144	191	35

Leading Scorers

Player	Club	GP	G	A	PTS	PIM
Max Bentley	Chicago	47	31	30	61	6
Gaye Stewart	Toronto	50	37	15	52	8
Toe Blake	Montreal	50	29	21	50	2
Clint Smith	Chicago	50	26	24	50	2
Maurice Richard	Montreal	50	27	21	48	50
Bill Mosienko	Chicago	40	18	30	48	12
Ab DeMarco	NY Rangers	50	20	27	47	20
Elmer Lach	Montreal	50	13	34	47	34
Alex Kaleta	Chicago	49	19	27	46	17
Billy Taylor	Toronto	48	23	18	41	14
Pete Horeck	Chicago	50	20	21	41	34

1946-47

Team	GP	W	L	T	GF	GA	PTS
Montreal	60	34	16	10	189	138	78
*Toronto	60	31	19	10	209	172	72
Boston	60	26	23	11	190	175	63
Detroit	60	22	27	11	190	193	55
NY Rangers	60	22	32	6	167	186	50
Chicago	60	19	37	4	193	274	42

Leading Scorers

Player	Club	GP	G	A	PTS	PIM
Max Bentley	Chicago	60	29	43	72	12
Maurice Richard	Montreal	60	45	26	71	69
Billy Taylor	Detroit	60	17	46	63	35
Milt Schmidt	Boston	59	27	35	62	40
Ted Kennedy	Toronto	60	28	32	60	27
Doug Bentley	Chicago	52	21	34	55	18
Bobby Bauer	Boston	58	30	24	54	4
Roy Conacher	Detroit	60	30	24	54	6
Bill Mosienko	Chicago	59	25	27	52	2
Woody Dumart	Boston	60	24	28	52	12

1947-48

Team	GP	W	L	T	GF	GA	PTS
*Toronto	60	32	15	13	182	143	77
Detroit	60	30	18	12	187	148	72
Boston	60	23	24	13	167	168	59
NY Rangers	60	21	26	13	176	201	55
Montreal	60	20	29	11	147	169	51
Chicago	60	20	34	6	195	225	46

Leading Scorers

Player	Club	GP	G	A	PTS	PIM
Elmer Lach	Montreal	60	30	31	61	72
Buddy O'Connor	NY Rangers	60	24	36	60	8
Doug Bentley	Chicago	60	20	37	57	16
Gaye Stewart	Tor., Chi.	61	27	29	56	83
Max Bentley	Chi., Tor.	59	26	28	54	14
Bud Poile	Tor., Chi.	58	25	29	54	17
Maurice Richard	Montreal	53	28	25	53	89
Syl Apps	Toronto	55	26	27	53	12
Ted Lindsay	Detroit	60	33	19	52	95
Roy Conacher	Chicago	52	22	27	49	4

1948-49

Team	GP	W	L	T	GF	GA	PTS
Detroit	60	34	19	7	195	145	75
Boston	60	29	23	8	178	163	66
Montreal	60	28	23	9	152	126	65
*Toronto	60	22	25	13	147	161	57
Chicago	60	21	31	8	173	211	50
NY Rangers	60	18	31	11	133	172	47

Leading Scorers

Player	Club	GP	G	A	PTS	PIM
Roy Conacher	Chicago	60	26	42	68	8
Doug Bentley	Chicago	58	23	43	66	38
Sid Abel	Detroit	60	28	26	54	49
Ted Lindsay	Detroit	50	26	28	54	97
Jim Conacher	Det., Chi.	59	26	23	49	43
Paul Ronty	Boston	60	20	29	49	11
Harry Watson	Toronto	60	26	19	45	0
Billy Reay	Montreal	60	22	23	45	33
Gus Bodnar	Chicago	59	19	26	45	14
Johnny Peirson	Boston	59	22	21	43	45

1949-50

Team	GP	W	L	T	GF	GA	PTS
*Detroit	70	37	19	14	229	164	88
Montreal	70	29	22	19	172	150	77
Toronto	70	31	27	12	176	173	74
NY Rangers	70	28	31	11	170	189	67
Boston	70	22	32	16	198	228	60
Chicago	70	22	38	10	203	244	54

Leading Scorers

Player	Club	GP	G	A	PTS	PIM
Ted Lindsay	Detroit	69	23	55	78	141
Sid Abel	Detroit	69	34	35	69	46
Gordie Howe	Detroit	70	35	33	68	69
Maurice Richard	Montreal	70	43	22	65	114
Paul Ronty	Boston	70	23	36	59	8
Roy Conacher	Chicago	70	25	31	56	16
Doug Bentley	Chicago	64	20	33	53	28
Johnny Peirson	Boston	57	27	25	52	49
Metro Prystai	Chicago	65	29	22	51	31
Bep Guidolin	Chicago	70	17	34	51	42

1950-51

Team	GP	W	L	T	GF	GA	PTS
Detroit	70	44	13	13	236	139	101
*Toronto	70	41	16	13	212	138	95
Montreal	70	25	30	15	173	184	65
Boston	70	22	30	18	178	197	62
NY Rangers	70	20	29	21	169	201	61
Chicago	70	13	47	10	171	280	36

Leading Scorers

Player	Club	GP	G	A	PTS	PIM
Gordie Howe	Detroit	70	43	43	86	74
Maurice Richard	Montreal	65	42	24	66	97
Max Bentley	Toronto	67	21	41	62	34
Sid Abel	Detroit	69	23	38	61	30
Milt Schmidt	Boston	62	22	39	61	33
Ted Kennedy	Toronto	63	18	43	61	32
Ted Lindsay	Detroit	67	24	35	59	110
Tod Sloan	Toronto	70	31	25	56	105
Red Kelly	Detroit	70	17	37	54	24
Sid Smith	Toronto	70	30	21	51	10
Cal Gardner	Toronto	66	23	28	51	42

1951-52

Team	GP	W	L	T	GF	GA	PTS
*Detroit	70	44	14	12	215	133	100
Montreal	70	34	26	10	195	164	78
Toronto	70	29	25	16	168	157	74
Boston	70	25	29	16	162	176	66
NY Rangers	70	23	34	13	192	219	59
Chicago	70	17	44	9	158	241	43

Leading Scorers

Player	Club	GP	G	A	PTS	PIM
Gordie Howe	Detroit	70	47	39	86	78
Ted Lindsay	Detroit	70	30	39	69	123
Elmer Lach	Montreal	70	15	50	65	36
Don Raleigh	NY Rangers	70	19	42	61	14
Sid Smith	Toronto	70	27	30	57	6
Bernie Geoffrion	Montreal	67	30	24	54	66
Bill Mosienko	Chicago	70	31	22	53	10
Sid Abel	Detroit	62	17	36	53	32
Ted Kennedy	Toronto	70	19	33	52	33
Milt Schmidt	Boston	69	21	29	50	57
Johnny Peirson	Boston	68	20	30	50	30

1952-53

Team	GP	W	L	T	GF	GA	PTS
Detroit	70	36	16	18	222	133	90
*Montreal	70	28	23	19	155	148	75
Boston	70	28	29	13	152	172	69
Chicago	70	27	28	15	169	175	69
Toronto	70	27	30	13	156	167	67
NY Rangers	70	17	37	16	152	211	50

Leading Scorers

Player	Club	GP	G	A	PTS	PIM
Gordie Howe	Detroit	70	49	46	95	57
Ted Lindsay	Detroit	70	32	39	71	111
Maurice Richard	Montreal	70	28	33	61	112
Wally Hergesheimer	NY Rangers	70	30	29	59	10
Alex Delvecchio	Detroit	70	16	43	59	28
Paul Ronty	NY Rangers	70	16	38	54	20
Metro Prystai	Detroit	70	16	34	50	12
Red Kelly	Detroit	70	19	27	46	8
Bert Olmstead	Montreal	69	17	28	45	83
Fleming Mackell	Boston	65	27	17	44	63
Jim McFadden	Chicago	70	23	21	44	29

1953-54

Team	GP	W	L	T	GF	GA	PTS
*Detroit	70	37	19	14	191	132	88
Montreal	70	35	24	11	195	141	81
Toronto	70	32	24	14	152	131	78
Boston	70	32	28	10	177	181	74
NY Rangers	70	29	31	10	161	182	68
Chicago	70	12	51	7	133	242	31

Leading Scorers

Player	Club	GP	G	A	PTS	PIM
Gordie Howe	Detroit	70	33	48	81	109
Maurice Richard	Montreal	70	37	30	67	112
Ted Lindsay	Detroit	70	26	36	62	110
Bernie Geoffrion	Montreal	54	29	25	54	87
Bert Olmstead	Montreal	70	15	37	52	85
Red Kelly	Detroit	62	16	33	49	18
Dutch Reibel	Detroit	69	15	33	48	18
Ed Sandford	Boston	70	16	31	47	42
Fleming Mackell	Boston	67	15	32	47	60
Ken Mosdell	Montreal	67	22	24	46	64
Paul Ronty	NY Rangers	70	13	33	46	18

1954-55

Team	GP	W	L	T	GF	GA	PTS
*Detroit	70	42	17	11	204	134	95
Montreal	70	41	18	11	228	157	93
Toronto	70	24	24	22	147	135	70
Boston	70	23	26	21	169	188	67
NY Rangers	70	17	35	18	150	210	52
Chicago	70	13	40	17	161	235	43

Leading Scorers

Player	Club	GP	G	A	PTS	PIM
Bernie Geoffrion	Montreal	70	38	37	75	57
Maurice Richard	Montreal	67	38	36	74	125
Jean Béliveau	Montreal	70	37	36	73	58
Dutch Reibel	Detroit	70	25	41	66	15
Gordie Howe	Detroit	64	29	33	62	68
Red Sullivan	Chicago	69	19	42	61	51
Bert Olmstead	Montreal	70	10	48	58	103
Sid Smith	Toronto	70	33	21	54	14
Ken Mosdell	Montreal	70	22	32	54	82
Danny Lewicki	NY Rangers	70	29	24	53	8

1955-56

Team	GP	W	L	T	GF	GA	PTS
*Montreal	70	45	15	10	222	131	100
Detroit	70	30	24	16	183	148	76
NY Rangers	70	32	28	10	204	203	74
Toronto	70	24	33	13	153	181	61
Boston	70	23	34	13	147	185	59
Chicago	70	19	39	12	155	216	50

Leading Scorers

Player	Club	GP	G	A	PTS	PIM
Jean Béliveau	Montreal	70	47	41	88	143
Gordie Howe	Detroit	70	38	41	79	100
Maurice Richard	Montreal	70	38	33	71	89
Bert Olmstead	Montreal	70	14	56	70	94
Tod Sloan	Toronto	70	37	29	66	100
Andy Bathgate	NY Rangers	70	19	47	66	59
Bernie Geoffrion	Montreal	59	29	33	62	66
Dutch Reibel	Detroit	68	17	39	56	10
Alex Delvecchio	Detroit	70	25	26	51	24
Dave Creighton	NY Rangers	70	20	31	51	43
Bill Gadsby	NY Rangers	70	9	42	51	84

1956-57

Team	GP	W	L	T	GF	GA	PTS
Detroit	70	38	20	12	198	157	88
*Montreal	70	35	23	12	210	155	82
Boston	70	34	24	12	195	174	80
NY Rangers	70	26	30	14	184	227	66
Toronto	70	21	34	15	174	192	57
Chicago	70	16	39	15	169	225	47

Leading Scorers

Player	Club	GP	G	A	PTS	PIM
Gordie Howe	Detroit	70	44	45	89	72
Ted Lindsay	Detroit	70	30	55	85	103
Jean Béliveau	Montreal	69	33	51	84	105
Andy Bathgate	NY Rangers	70	27	50	77	60
Ed Litzenberger	Chicago	70	32	32	64	48
Maurice Richard	Montreal	63	33	29	62	74
Don McKenney	Boston	69	21	39	60	31
Dickie Moore	Montreal	70	29	29	58	56
Henri Richard	Montreal	63	18	36	54	71
Norm Ullman	Detroit	64	16	36	52	47

1957-58

Team	GP	W	L	T	GF	GA	PTS
*Montreal	70	43	17	10	250	158	96
NY Rangers	70	32	25	13	195	188	77
Detroit	70	29	29	12	176	207	70
Boston	70	27	28	15	199	194	69
Chicago	70	24	39	7	163	202	55
Toronto	70	21	38	11	192	226	53

Leading Scorers

Player	Club	GP	G	A	PTS	PIM
Dickie Moore	Montreal	70	36	48	84	65
Henri Richard	Montreal	67	28	52	80	56
Andy Bathgate	NY Rangers	65	30	48	78	42
Gordie Howe	Detroit	64	33	44	77	40
Bronco Horvath	Boston	67	30	36	66	71
Ed Litzenberger	Chicago	70	32	30	62	63
Fleming Mackell	Boston	70	20	40	60	72
Jean Béliveau	Montreal	55	27	32	59	93
Alex Delvecchio	Detroit	70	21	38	59	22
Don McKenney	Boston	70	28	30	58	22

1958-59

Team	GP	W	L	T	GF	GA	PTS
*Montreal	70	39	18	13	258	158	91
Boston	70	32	29	9	205	215	73
Chicago	70	28	29	13	197	208	69
Toronto	70	27	32	11	189	201	65
NY Rangers	70	26	32	12	201	217	64
Detroit	70	25	37	8	167	218	58

Leading Scorers

Player	Club	GP	G	A	PTS	PIM
Dickie Moore	Montreal	70	41	55	96	61
Jean Béliveau	Montreal	64	45	46	91	67
Andy Bathgate	NY Rangers	70	40	48	88	48
Gordie Howe	Detroit	70	32	46	78	57
Ed Litzenberger	Chicago	70	33	44	77	37
Bernie Geoffrion	Montreal	59	22	44	66	30
Red Sullivan	NY Rangers	70	21	42	63	56
Andy Hebenton	NY Rangers	70	33	29	62	8
Don McKenney	Boston	70	32	30	62	20
Tod Sloan	Chicago	59	27	35	62	79

1959-60

Team	GP	W	L	T	GF	GA	PTS
*Montreal	70	40	18	12	255	178	92
Toronto	70	35	26	9	199	195	79
Chicago	70	28	29	13	191	180	69
Detroit	70	26	29	15	186	197	67
Boston	70	28	34	8	220	241	64
NY Rangers	70	17	38	15	187	247	49

Leading Scorers

Player	Club	GP	G	A	PTS	PIM
Bobby Hull	Chicago	70	39	42	81	68
Bronco Horvath	Boston	68	39	41	80	60
Jean Béliveau	Montreal	60	34	40	74	57
Andy Bathgate	NY Rangers	70	26	48	74	28
Henri Richard	Montreal	70	30	43	73	66
Gordie Howe	Detroit	70	28	45	73	46
Bernie Geoffrion	Montreal	59	30	41	71	36
Don McKenney	Boston	70	20	49	69	28
Vic Stasiuk	Boston	69	29	39	68	121
Dean Prentice	NY Rangers	70	32	34	66	43

1960-61

Team	GP	W	L	T	GF	GA	PTS
Montreal	70	41	19	10	254	188	92
Toronto	70	39	19	12	234	176	90
*Chicago	70	29	24	17	198	180	75
Detroit	70	25	29	16	195	215	66
NY Rangers	70	22	38	10	204	248	54
Boston	70	15	42	13	176	254	43

Leading Scorers

Player	Club	GP	G	A	PTS	PIM
Bernie Geoffrion	Montreal	64	50	45	95	29
Jean Béliveau	Montreal	69	32	58	90	57
Frank Mahovlich	Toronto	70	48	36	84	131
Andy Bathgate	NY Rangers	70	29	48	77	22
Gordie Howe	Detroit	64	23	49	72	30
Norm Ullman	Detroit	70	28	42	70	34
Red Kelly	Toronto	64	20	50	70	12
Dickie Moore	Montreal	57	35	34	69	62
Henri Richard	Montreal	70	24	44	68	91
Alex Delvecchio	Detroit	70	27	35	62	26

1961-62

Team	GP	W	L	T	GF	GA	PTS
Montreal	70	42	14	14	259	166	98
*Toronto	70	37	22	11	232	180	85
Chicago	70	31	26	13	217	186	75
NY Rangers	70	26	32	12	195	207	64
Detroit	70	23	33	14	184	219	60
Boston	70	15	47	8	177	306	38

Leading Scorers

Player	Club	GP	G	A	PTS	PIM
Bobby Hull	Chicago	70	50	34	84	35
Andy Bathgate	NY Rangers	70	28	56	84	44
Gordie Howe	Detroit	70	33	44	77	54
Stan Mikita	Chicago	70	25	52	77	97
Frank Mahovlich	Toronto	70	33	38	71	87
Alex Delvecchio	Detroit	70	26	43	69	18
Ralph Backstrom	Montreal	66	27	38	65	29
Norm Ullman	Detroit	70	26	38	64	54
Bill Hay	Chicago	60	11	52	63	34
Claude Provost	Montreal	70	33	29	62	22

1962-63

Team	GP	W	L	T	GF	GA	PTS
*Toronto	70	35	23	12	221	180	82
Chicago	70	32	21	17	194	178	81
Montreal	70	28	19	23	225	183	79
Detroit	70	32	25	13	200	194	77
NY Rangers	70	22	36	12	211	233	56
Boston	70	14	39	17	198	281	45

Leading Scorers

Player	Club	GP	G	A	PTS	PIM
Gordie Howe	Detroit	70	38	48	86	100
Andy Bathgate	NY Rangers	70	35	46	81	54
Stan Mikita	Chicago	65	31	45	76	69
Frank Mahovlich	Toronto	67	36	37	73	56
Henri Richard	Montreal	67	23	50	73	57
Jean Béliveau	Montreal	69	18	49	67	68
John Bucyk	Boston	69	27	39	66	36
Alex Delvecchio	Detroit	70	20	44	64	8
Bobby Hull	Chicago	65	31	31	62	27
Murray Oliver	Boston	65	22	40	62	38

1963-64

Team	GP	W	L	T	GF	GA	PTS
Montreal	70	36	21	13	209	167	85
Chicago	70	36	22	12	218	169	84
*Toronto	70	33	25	12	192	172	78
Detroit	70	30	29	11	191	204	71
NY Rangers	70	22	38	10	186	242	54
Boston	70	18	40	12	170	212	48

Leading Scorers

Player	Club	GP	G	A	PTS	PIM
Stan Mikita	Chicago	70	39	50	89	146
Bobby Hull	Chicago	70	43	44	87	50
Jean Béliveau	Montreal	68	28	50	78	42
Andy Bathgate	NYR, Tor.	71	19	58	77	34
Gordie Howe	Detroit	69	26	47	73	70
Kenny Wharram	Chicago	70	39	32	71	18
Murray Oliver	Boston	70	24	44	68	41
Phil Goyette	NY Rangers	67	24	41	65	15
Rod Gilbert	NY Rangers	70	24	40	64	62
Dave Keon	Toronto	70	23	37	60	6

1964-65

Team	GP	W	L	T	GF	GA	PTS
Detroit	70	40	23	7	224	175	87
*Montreal	70	36	23	11	211	185	83
Chicago	70	34	28	8	224	176	76
Toronto	70	30	26	14	204	173	74
NY Rangers	70	20	38	12	179	246	52
Boston	70	21	43	6	166	253	48

Leading Scorers

Player	Club	GP	G	A	PTS	PIM
Stan Mikita	Chicago	70	28	59	87	154
Norm Ullman	Detroit	70	42	41	83	70
Gordie Howe	Detroit	70	29	47	76	104
Bobby Hull	Chicago	61	39	32	71	32
Alex Delvecchio	Detroit	68	25	42	67	16
Claude Provost	Montreal	70	27	37	64	28
Rod Gilbert	NY Rangers	70	25	36	61	52
Pierre Pilote	Chicago	68	14	45	59	162
John Bucyk	Boston	68	26	29	55	24
Ralph Backstrom	Montreal	70	25	30	55	41
Phil Esposito	Chicago	70	23	32	55	44

1965-66

Team	GP	W	L	T	GF	GA	PTS
*Montreal	70	41	21	8	239	173	90
Chicago	70	37	25	8	240	187	82
Toronto	70	34	25	11	208	187	79
Detroit	70	31	27	12	221	194	74
Boston	70	21	43	6	174	275	48
NY Rangers	70	18	41	11	195	261	47

Leading Scorers

Player	Club	GP	G	A	PTS	PIM
Bobby Hull	Chicago	65	54	43	97	70
Stan Mikita	Chicago	68	30	48	78	58
Bobby Rousseau	Montreal	70	30	48	78	20
Jean Béliveau	Montreal	67	29	48	77	50
Gordie Howe	Detroit	70	29	46	75	83
Norm Ullman	Detroit	70	31	41	72	35
Alex Delvecchio	Detroit	70	31	38	69	16
Bob Nevin	NY Rangers	69	29	33	62	10
Henri Richard	Montreal	62	22	39	61	47
Murray Oliver	Boston	70	18	42	60	30

1966-67

Team	GP	W	L	T	GF	GA	PTS
Chicago	70	41	17	12	264	170	94
Montreal	70	32	25	13	202	188	77
*Toronto	70	32	27	11	204	211	75
NY Rangers	70	30	28	12	188	189	72
Detroit	70	27	39	4	212	241	58
Boston	70	17	43	10	182	253	44

Leading Scorers

Player	Club	GP	G	A	PTS	PIM
Stan Mikita	Chicago	70	35	62	97	12
Bobby Hull	Chicago	66	52	28	80	52
Norm Ullman	Detroit	68	26	44	70	26
Kenny Wharram	Chicago	70	31	34	65	21
Gordie Howe	Detroit	69	25	40	65	53
Bobby Rousseau	Montreal	68	19	44	63	58
Phil Esposito	Chicago	69	21	40	61	40
Phil Goyette	NY Rangers	70	12	49	61	6
Doug Mohns	Chicago	61	25	35	60	58
Henri Richard	Montreal	65	21	34	55	28
Alex Delvecchio	Detroit	70	17	38	55	10

1967-68

East Division

Team	GP	W	L	T	GF	GA	PTS
*Montreal	74	42	22	10	236	167	94
NY Rangers	74	39	23	12	226	183	90
Boston	74	37	27	10	259	216	84
Chicago	74	32	26	16	212	222	80
Toronto	74	33	31	10	209	176	76
Detroit	74	27	35	12	245	257	66

West Division

Team	GP	W	L	T	GF	GA	PTS
Philadelphia	74	31	32	11	173	179	73
Los Angeles	74	31	33	10	200	224	72
St. Louis	74	27	31	16	177	191	70
Minnesota	74	27	32	15	191	226	69
Pittsburgh	74	27	34	13	195	216	67
Oakland	74	15	42	17	153	219	47

Leading Scorers

Player	Club	GP	G	A	PTS	PIM
Stan Mikita	Chicago	72	40	47	87	14
Phil Esposito	Boston	74	35	49	84	21
Gordie Howe	Detroit	74	39	43	82	53
Jean Ratelle	NY Rangers	74	32	46	78	18
Rod Gilbert	NY Rangers	73	29	48	77	12
Bobby Hull	Chicago	71	44	31	75	39
Norm Ullman	Det., Tor.	71	35	37	72	28
Alex Delvecchio	Detroit	74	22	48	70	14
John Bucyk	Boston	72	30	39	69	8
Kenny Wharram	Chicago	74	27	42	69	18

1968-69

East Division

Team	GP	W	L	T	GF	GA	PTS
*Montreal	76	46	19	11	271	202	103
Boston	76	42	18	16	303	221	100
NY Rangers	76	41	26	9	231	196	91
Toronto	76	35	26	15	234	217	85
Detroit	76	33	31	12	239	221	78
Chicago	76	34	33	9	280	246	77

West Division

Team	GP	W	L	T	GF	GA	PTS
St. Louis	76	37	25	14	204	157	88
Oakland	76	29	36	11	219	251	69
Philadelphia	76	20	35	21	174	225	61
Los Angeles	76	24	42	10	185	260	58
Pittsburgh	76	20	45	11	189	252	51
Minnesota	76	18	43	15	189	270	51

Leading Scorers

Player	Club	GP	G	A	PTS	PIM
Phil Esposito	Boston	74	49	77	126	79
Bobby Hull	Chicago	74	58	49	107	48
Gordie Howe	Detroit	76	44	59	103	58
Stan Mikita	Chicago	74	30	67	97	52
Ken Hodge	Boston	75	45	45	90	75
Yvan Cournoyer	Montreal	76	43	44	87	31
Alex Delvecchio	Detroit	72	25	58	83	8
Red Berenson	St. Louis	76	35	47	82	43
Jean Béliveau	Montreal	69	33	49	82	55
Frank Mahovlich	Detroit	76	49	29	78	38
Jean Ratelle	NY Rangers	75	32	46	78	26

1969-70

East Division

Team	GP	W	L	T	GF	GA	PTS
Chicago	76	45	22	9	250	170	99
*Boston	76	40	17	19	277	216	99
Detroit	76	40	21	15	246	199	95
NY Rangers	76	38	22	16	246	189	92
Montreal	76	38	22	16	244	201	92
Toronto	76	29	34	13	222	242	71

West Division

Team	GP	W	L	T	GF	GA	PTS
St. Louis	76	37	27	12	224	179	86
Pittsburgh	76	26	38	12	182	238	64
Minnesota	76	19	35	22	224	257	60
Oakland	76	22	40	14	169	243	58
Philadelphia	76	17	35	24	197	225	58
Los Angeles	76	14	52	10	168	290	38

Leading Scorers

Player	Club	GP	G	A	PTS	PIM
Bobby Orr	Boston	76	33	87	120	125
Phil Esposito	Boston	76	43	56	99	50
Stan Mikita	Chicago	76	39	47	86	50
Phil Goyette	St. Louis	72	29	49	78	16
Walt Tkaczuk	NY Rangers	76	27	50	77	38
Jean Ratelle	NY Rangers	75	32	42	74	28
Red Berenson	St. Louis	67	33	39	72	38
Jean-Paul Parise	Minnesota	74	24	48	72	72
Gordie Howe	Detroit	76	31	40	71	58
Frank Mahovlich	Detroit	74	38	32	70	59
Dave Balon	NY Rangers	76	33	37	70	100
John McKenzie	Boston	72	29	41	70	114

1970-71

East Division

Team	GP	W	L	T	GF	GA	PTS
Boston	78	57	14	7	399	207	121
NY Rangers	78	49	18	11	259	177	109
*Montreal	78	42	23	13	291	216	97
Toronto	78	37	33	8	248	211	82
Buffalo	78	24	39	15	217	291	63
Vancouver	78	24	46	8	229	296	56
Detroit	78	22	45	11	209	308	55

West Division

Team	GP	W	L	T	GF	GA	PTS
Chicago	78	49	20	9	277	184	107
St. Louis	78	34	25	19	223	208	87
Philadelphia	78	28	33	17	207	225	73
Minnesota	78	28	34	16	191	223	72
Los Angeles	78	25	40	13	239	303	63
Pittsburgh	78	21	37	20	221	240	62
California	78	20	53	5	199	320	45

Leading Scorers

Player	Club	GP	G	A	PTS	PIM
Phil Esposito	Boston	78	76	76	152	71
Bobby Orr	Boston	78	37	102	139	91
John Bucyk	Boston	78	51	65	116	8
Ken Hodge	Boston	78	43	62	105	113
Bobby Hull	Chicago	78	44	52	96	32
Norm Ullman	Toronto	73	34	51	85	24
Wayne Cashman	Boston	77	21	58	79	100
John McKenzie	Boston	65	31	46	77	120
Dave Keon	Toronto	76	38	38	76	4
Jean Béliveau	Montreal	70	25	51	76	40
Fred Stanfield	Boston	75	24	52	76	12

1971-72

East Division

Team	GP	W	L	T	GF	GA	PTS
*Boston	78	54	13	11	330	204	119
NY Rangers	78	48	17	13	317	192	109
Montreal	78	46	16	16	307	205	108
Toronto	78	33	31	14	209	208	80
Detroit	78	33	35	10	261	262	76
Buffalo	78	16	43	19	203	289	51
Vancouver	78	20	50	8	203	297	48

West Division

Team	GP	W	L	T	GF	GA	PTS
Chicago	78	46	17	15	256	166	107
Minnesota	78	37	29	12	212	191	86
St. Louis	78	28	39	11	208	247	67
Pittsburgh	78	26	38	14	220	258	66
Philadelphia	78	26	38	14	200	236	66
California	78	21	39	18	216	288	60
Los Angeles	78	20	49	9	206	305	49

Leading Scorers

Player	Club	GP	G	A	PTS	PIM
Phil Esposito	Boston	76	66	67	133	76
Bobby Orr	Boston	76	37	80	117	106
Jean Ratelle	NY Rangers	63	46	63	109	4
Vic Hadfield	NY Rangers	78	50	56	106	142
Rod Gilbert	NY Rangers	73	43	54	97	64
Frank Mahovlich	Montreal	76	43	53	96	36
Bobby Hull	Chicago	78	50	43	93	24
Yvan Cournoyer	Montreal	73	47	36	83	15
John Bucyk	Boston	78	32	51	83	4
Bobby Clarke	Philadelphia	78	35	46	81	87
Jacques Lemaire	Montreal	77	32	49	81	26

1972-73

East Division

Team	GP	W	L	T	GF	GA	PTS
*Montreal	78	52	10	16	329	184	120
Boston	78	51	22	5	330	235	107
NY Rangers	78	47	23	8	297	208	102
Buffalo	78	37	27	14	257	219	88
Detroit	78	37	29	12	265	243	86
Toronto	78	27	41	10	247	279	64
Vancouver	78	22	47	9	233	339	53
NY Islanders	78	12	60	6	170	347	30

West Division

Team	GP	W	L	T	GF	GA	PTS
Chicago	78	42	27	9	284	225	93
Philadelphia	78	37	30	11	296	256	85
Minnesota	78	37	30	11	254	230	85
St. Louis	78	32	34	12	233	251	76
Pittsburgh	78	32	37	9	257	265	73
Los Angeles	78	31	36	11	232	245	73
Atlanta	78	25	38	15	191	239	65
California	78	16	46	16	213	323	48

Leading Scorers

Player	Club	GP	G	A	PTS	PIM
Phil Esposito	Boston	78	55	75	130	87
Bobby Clarke	Philadelphia	78	37	67	104	80
Bobby Orr	Boston	63	29	72	101	99
Rick MacLeish	Philadelphia	78	50	50	100	69
Jacques Lemaire	Montreal	77	44	51	95	16
Jean Ratelle	NY Rangers	78	41	53	94	12
Mickey Redmond	Detroit	76	52	41	93	24
John Bucyk	Boston	78	40	53	93	12
Frank Mahovlich	Montreal	78	38	55	93	51
Jim Pappin	Chicago	76	41	51	92	82

The Rangers' first 50-goal scorer, Vic Hadfield was fourth in the NHL with 106 points in 1971-72. He finished in between fellow members of the Goal-A-Game (G-A-G) line Jean Ratelle and Rod Gilbert.

1973-74

East Division

Team	GP	W	L	T	GF	GA	PTS
Boston	78	52	17	9	349	221	113
Montreal	78	45	24	9	293	240	99
NY Rangers	78	40	24	14	300	251	94
Toronto	78	35	27	16	274	230	86
Buffalo	78	32	34	12	242	250	76
Detroit	78	29	39	10	255	319	68
Vancouver	78	24	43	11	224	296	59
NY Islanders	78	19	41	18	182	247	56

West Division

Team	GP	W	L	T	GF	GA	PTS
*Philadelphia	78	50	16	12	273	164	112
Chicago	78	41	14	23	272	164	105
Los Angeles	78	33	33	12	233	231	78
Atlanta	78	30	34	14	214	238	74
Pittsburgh	78	28	41	9	242	273	65
St. Louis	78	26	40	12	206	248	64
Minnesota	78	23	38	17	235	275	63
California	78	13	55	10	195	342	36

Leading Scorers

Player	Club	GP	G	A	PTS	PIM
Phil Esposito	Boston	78	68	77	145	58
Bobby Orr	Boston	74	32	90	122	82
Ken Hodge	Boston	76	50	55	105	43
Wayne Cashman	Boston	78	30	59	89	111
Bobby Clarke	Philadelphia	77	35	52	87	113
Rick Martin	Buffalo	78	52	34	86	38
Syl Apps Jr.	Pittsburgh	75	24	61	85	37
Darryl Sittler	Toronto	78	38	46	84	55
Lowell MacDonald	Pittsburgh	78	43	39	82	14
Brad Park	NY Rangers	78	25	57	82	148
Dennis Hextall	Minnesota	78	20	62	82	138

1974-75

PRINCE OF WALES CONFERENCE
Norris Division

Team	GP	W	L	T	GF	GA	PTS
Montreal	80	47	14	19	374	225	113
Los Angeles	80	42	17	21	269	185	105
Pittsburgh	80	37	28	15	326	289	89
Detroit	80	23	45	12	259	335	58
Washington	80	8	67	5	181	446	21

Adams Division

Team	GP	W	L	T	GF	GA	PTS
Buffalo	80	49	16	15	354	240	113
Boston	80	40	26	14	345	245	94
Toronto	80	31	33	16	280	309	78
California	80	19	48	13	212	316	51

CLARENCE CAMPBELL CONFERENCE
Patrick Division

Team	GP	W	L	T	GF	GA	PTS
*Philadelphia	80	51	18	11	293	181	113
NY Rangers	80	37	29	14	319	276	88
NY Islanders	80	33	25	22	264	221	88
Atlanta	80	34	31	15	243	233	83

Smythe Division

Team	GP	W	L	T	GF	GA	PTS
Vancouver	80	38	32	10	271	254	86
St. Louis	80	35	31	14	269	267	84
Chicago	80	37	35	8	268	241	82
Minnesota	80	23	50	7	221	341	53
Kansas City	80	15	54	11	184	328	41

Leading Scorers

Player	Club	GP	G	A	PTS	PIM
Bobby Orr	Boston	80	46	89	135	101
Phil Esposito	Boston	79	61	66	127	62
Marcel Dionne	Detroit	80	47	74	121	14
Guy Lafleur	Montreal	70	53	66	119	37
Pete Mahovlich	Montreal	80	35	82	117	64
Bobby Clarke	Philadelphia	80	27	89	116	125
Rene Robert	Buffalo	74	40	60	100	75
Rod Gilbert	NY Rangers	76	36	61	97	22
Gilbert Perreault	Buffalo	68	39	57	96	36
Rick Martin	Buffalo	68	52	43	95	72

1975-76

PRINCE OF WALES CONFERENCE
Norris Division

Team	GP	W	L	T	GF	GA	PTS
*Montreal	80	58	11	11	337	174	127
Los Angeles	80	38	33	9	263	265	85
Pittsburgh	80	35	33	12	339	303	82
Detroit	80	26	44	10	226	300	62
Washington	80	11	59	10	224	394	32

Adams Division

Team	GP	W	L	T	GF	GA	PTS
Boston	80	48	15	17	313	237	113
Buffalo	80	46	21	13	339	240	105
Toronto	80	34	31	15	294	276	83
California	80	27	42	11	250	278	65

CLARENCE CAMPBELL CONFERENCE
Patrick Division

Team	GP	W	L	T	GF	GA	PTS
Philadelphia	80	51	13	16	348	209	118
NY Islanders	80	42	21	17	297	190	101
Atlanta	80	35	33	12	262	237	82
NY Rangers	80	29	42	9	262	333	67

Smythe Division

Team	GP	W	L	T	GF	GA	PTS
Chicago	80	32	30	18	254	261	82
Vancouver	80	33	32	15	271	272	81
St. Louis	80	29	37	14	249	290	72
Minnesota	80	20	53	7	195	303	47
Kansas City	80	12	56	12	190	351	36

Leading Scorers

Player	Club	GP	G	A	PTS	PIM
Guy Lafleur	Montreal	80	56	69	125	36
Bobby Clarke	Philadelphia	76	30	89	119	136
Gilbert Perreault	Buffalo	80	44	69	113	36
Bill Barber	Philadelphia	80	50	62	112	104
Pierre Larouche	Pittsburgh	76	53	58	111	33
Jean Ratelle	Bos., NYR	80	36	69	105	18
Pete Mahovlich	Montreal	80	34	71	105	76
Jean Pronovost	Pittsburgh	80	52	52	104	24
Darryl Sittler	Toronto	79	41	59	100	90
Syl Apps Jr.	Pittsburgh	80	32	67	99	24

1976-77

PRINCE OF WALES CONFERENCE
Norris Division

Team	GP	W	L	T	GF	GA	PTS
*Montreal	80	60	8	12	387	171	132
Los Angeles	80	34	31	15	271	241	83
Pittsburgh	80	34	33	13	240	252	81
Washington	80	24	42	14	221	307	62
Detroit	80	16	55	9	183	309	41

Adams Division

Team	GP	W	L	T	GF	GA	PTS
Boston	80	49	23	8	312	240	106
Buffalo	80	48	24	8	301	220	104
Toronto	80	33	32	15	301	285	81
Cleveland	80	25	42	13	240	292	63

CLARENCE CAMPBELL CONFERENCE
Patrick Division

Team	GP	W	L	T	GF	GA	PTS
Philadelphia	80	48	16	16	323	213	112
NY Islanders	80	47	21	12	288	193	106
Atlanta	80	34	34	12	264	265	80
NY Rangers	80	29	37	14	272	310	72

Smythe Division

Team	GP	W	L	T	GF	GA	PTS
St. Louis	80	32	39	9	239	276	73
Minnesota	80	23	39	18	240	310	64
Chicago	80	26	43	11	240	298	63
Vancouver	80	25	42	13	235	294	63
Colorado	80	20	46	14	226	307	54

Leading Scorers

Player	Club	GP	G	A	PTS	PIM
Guy Lafleur	Montreal	80	56	80	136	20
Marcel Dionne	Los Angeles	80	53	69	122	12
Steve Shutt	Montreal	80	60	45	105	28
Rick MacLeish	Philadelphia	79	49	48	97	42
Gilbert Perreault	Buffalo	80	39	56	95	30
Tim Young	Minnesota	80	29	66	95	58
Jean Ratelle	Boston	78	33	61	94	22
Lanny McDonald	Toronto	80	46	44	90	77
Darryl Sittler	Toronto	73	38	52	90	89
Bobby Clarke	Philadelphia	80	27	63	90	71

1977-78

PRINCE OF WALES CONFERENCE
Norris Division

Team	GP	W	L	T	GF	GA	PTS
*Montreal	80	59	10	11	359	183	129
Detroit	80	32	34	14	252	266	78
Los Angeles	80	31	34	15	243	245	77
Pittsburgh	80	25	37	18	254	321	68
Washington	80	17	49	14	195	321	48

Adams Division

Team	GP	W	L	T	GF	GA	PTS
Boston	80	51	18	11	333	218	113
Buffalo	80	44	19	17	288	215	105
Toronto	80	41	29	10	271	237	92
Cleveland	80	22	45	13	230	325	57

CLARENCE CAMPBELL CONFERENCE
Patrick Division

Team	GP	W	L	T	GF	GA	PTS
NY Islanders	80	48	17	15	334	210	111
Philadelphia	80	45	20	15	296	200	105
Atlanta	80	34	27	19	274	252	87
NY Rangers	80	30	37	13	279	280	73

Smythe Division

Team	GP	W	L	T	GF	GA	PTS
Chicago	80	32	29	19	230	220	83
Colorado	80	19	40	21	257	305	59
Vancouver	80	20	43	17	239	320	57
St. Louis	80	20	47	13	195	304	53
Minnesota	80	18	53	9	218	325	45

Leading Scorers

Player	Club	GP	G	A	PTS	PIM
Guy Lafleur	Montreal	78	60	72	132	26
Bryan Trottier	NY Islanders	77	46	77	123	46
Darryl Sittler	Toronto	80	45	72	117	100
Jacques Lemaire	Montreal	76	36	61	97	14
Denis Potvin	NY Islanders	80	30	64	94	81
Mike Bossy	NY Islanders	73	53	38	91	6
Terry O'Reilly	Boston	77	29	61	90	211
Gilbert Perreault	Buffalo	79	41	48	89	20
Bobby Clarke	Philadelphia	71	21	68	89	83
Lanny McDonald	Toronto	74	47	40	87	54
Wilf Paiement	Colorado	80	31	56	87	114

1978-79

PRINCE OF WALES CONFERENCE
Norris Division

Team	GP	W	L	T	GF	GA	PTS
*Montreal	80	52	17	11	337	204	115
Pittsburgh	80	36	31	13	281	279	85
Los Angeles	80	34	34	12	292	286	80
Washington	80	24	41	15	273	338	63
Detroit	80	23	41	16	252	295	62

Adams Division

Team	GP	W	L	T	GF	GA	PTS
Boston	80	43	23	14	316	270	100
Buffalo	80	36	28	16	280	263	88
Toronto	80	34	33	13	267	252	81
Minnesota	80	28	40	12	257	289	68

CLARENCE CAMPBELL CONFERENCE

Patrick Division

Team	GP	W	L	T	GF	GA	PTS
NY Islanders	80	51	15	14	358	214	116
Philadelphia	80	40	25	15	281	248	95
NY Rangers	80	40	29	11	316	292	91
Atlanta	80	41	31	8	327	280	90

Smythe Division

Team	GP	W	L	T	GF	GA	PTS
Chicago	80	29	36	15	244	277	73
Vancouver	80	25	42	13	217	291	63
St. Louis	80	18	50	12	249	348	48
Colorado	80	15	53	12	210	331	42

Leading Scorers

Player	Club	GP	G	A	PTS	PIM
Bryan Trottier	NY Islanders	76	47	87	134	50
Marcel Dionne	Los Angeles	80	59	71	130	30
Guy Lafleur	Montreal	80	52	77	129	28
Mike Bossy	NY Islanders	80	69	57	126	25
Bob MacMillan	Atlanta	79	37	71	108	14
Guy Chouinard	Atlanta	80	50	57	107	14
Denis Potvin	NY Islanders	73	31	70	101	58
Bernie Federko	St. Louis	74	31	64	95	14
Dave Taylor	Los Angeles	78	43	48	91	124
Clark Gillies	NY Islanders	75	35	56	91	68

1979-80
PRINCE OF WALES CONFERENCE
Norris Division

Team	GP	W	L	T	GF	GA	PTS
Montreal	80	47	20	13	328	240	107
Los Angeles	80	30	36	14	290	313	74
Pittsburgh	80	30	37	13	251	303	73
Hartford	80	27	34	19	303	312	73
Detroit	80	26	43	11	268	306	63

Adams Division

Team	GP	W	L	T	GF	GA	PTS
Buffalo	80	47	17	16	318	201	110
Boston	80	46	21	13	310	234	105
Minnesota	80	36	28	16	311	253	88
Toronto	80	35	40	5	304	327	75
Quebec	80	25	44	11	248	313	61

CLARENCE CAMPBELL CONFERENCE
Patrick Division

Team	GP	W	L	T	GF	GA	PTS
Philadelphia	80	48	12	20	327	254	116
*NY Islanders	80	39	28	13	281	247	91
NY Rangers	80	38	32	10	308	284	86
Atlanta	80	35	32	13	282	269	83
Washington	80	27	40	13	261	293	67

Smythe Division

Team	GP	W	L	T	GF	GA	PTS
Chicago	80	34	27	19	241	250	87
St. Louis	80	34	34	12	266	278	80
Vancouver	80	27	37	16	256	281	70
Edmonton	80	28	39	13	301	322	69
Winnipeg	80	20	49	11	214	314	51
Colorado	80	19	48	13	234	308	51

Leading Scorers

Player	Club	GP	G	A	PTS	PIM
Marcel Dionne	Los Angeles	80	53	84	137	32
Wayne Gretzky	Edmonton	79	51	86	137	21
Guy Lafleur	Montreal	74	50	75	125	12
Gilbert Perreault	Buffalo	80	40	66	106	57
Mike Rogers	Hartford	80	44	61	105	10
Bryan Trottier	NY Islanders	78	42	62	104	68
Charlie Simmer	Los Angeles	64	56	45	101	65
Blaine Stoughton	Hartford	80	56	44	100	16
Darryl Sittler	Toronto	73	40	57	97	62
Blair MacDonald	Edmonton	80	46	48	94	6
Bernie Federko	St. Louis	79	38	56	94	24

1980-81
PRINCE OF WALES CONFERENCE
Norris Division

Team	GP	W	L	T	GF	GA	PTS
Montreal	80	45	22	13	332	232	103
Los Angeles	80	43	24	13	337	290	99
Pittsburgh	80	30	37	13	302	345	73
Hartford	80	21	41	18	292	372	60
Detroit	80	19	43	18	252	339	56

Adams Division

Team	GP	W	L	T	GF	GA	PTS
Buffalo	80	39	20	21	327	250	99
Boston	80	37	30	13	316	272	87
Minnesota	80	35	28	17	291	263	87
Quebec	80	30	32	18	314	318	78
Toronto	80	28	37	15	322	367	71

CLARENCE CAMPBELL CONFERENCE
Patrick Division

Team	GP	W	L	T	GF	GA	PTS
*NY Islanders	80	48	18	14	355	260	110
Philadelphia	80	41	24	15	313	249	97
Calgary	80	39	27	14	329	298	92
NY Rangers	80	30	36	14	312	317	74
Washington	80	26	36	18	286	317	70

Smythe Division

Team	GP	W	L	T	GF	GA	PTS
St. Louis	80	45	18	17	352	281	107
Chicago	80	31	33	16	304	315	78
Vancouver	80	28	32	20	289	301	76
Edmonton	80	29	35	16	328	327	74
Colorado	80	22	45	13	258	344	57
Winnipeg	80	9	57	14	246	400	32

Leading Scorers

Player	Club	GP	G	A	PTS	PIM
Wayne Gretzky	Edmonton	80	55	109	164	28
Marcel Dionne	Los Angeles	80	58	77	135	70
Kent Nilsson	Calgary	80	49	82	131	26
Mike Bossy	NY Islanders	79	68	51	119	32
Dave Taylor	Los Angeles	72	47	65	112	130
Peter Stastny	Quebec	77	39	70	109	37
Charlie Simmer	Los Angeles	65	56	49	105	62
Mike Rogers	Hartford	80	40	65	105	32
Bernie Federko	St. Louis	78	31	73	104	47
Jacques Richard	Quebec	78	52	51	103	39
Rick Middleton	Boston	80	44	59	103	16
Bryan Trottier	NY Islanders	73	31	72	103	74

1981-82
CLARENCE CAMPBELL CONFERENCE
Norris Division

Team	GP	W	L	T	GF	GA	PTS
Minnesota	80	37	23	20	346	288	94
Winnipeg	80	33	33	14	319	332	80
St. Louis	80	32	40	8	315	349	72
Chicago	80	30	38	12	332	363	72
Toronto	80	20	44	16	298	380	56
Detroit	80	21	47	12	270	351	54

Smythe Division

Team	GP	W	L	T	GF	GA	PTS
Edmonton	80	48	17	15	417	295	111
Vancouver	80	30	33	17	290	286	77
Calgary	80	29	34	17	334	345	75
Los Angeles	80	24	41	15	314	369	63
Colorado	80	18	49	13	241	362	49

PRINCE OF WALES CONFERENCE
Adams Division

Team	GP	W	L	T	GF	GA	PTS
Montreal	80	46	17	17	360	223	109
Boston	80	43	27	10	323	285	96
Buffalo	80	39	26	15	307	273	93
Quebec	80	33	31	16	356	345	82
Hartford	80	21	41	18	264	351	60

Patrick Division

Team	GP	W	L	T	GF	GA	PTS
*NY Islanders	80	54	16	10	385	250	118
NY Rangers	80	39	27	14	316	306	92
Philadelphia	80	38	31	11	325	313	87
Pittsburgh	80	31	36	13	310	337	75
Washington	80	26	41	13	319	338	65

Leading Scorers

Player	Club	GP	G	A	PTS	PIM
Wayne Gretzky	Edmonton	80	92	120	212	26
Mike Bossy	NY Islanders	80	64	83	147	22
Peter Stastny	Quebec	80	46	93	139	91
Dennis Maruk	Washington	80	60	76	136	128
Bryan Trottier	NY Islanders	80	50	79	129	88
Denis Savard	Chicago	80	32	87	119	82
Marcel Dionne	Los Angeles	78	50	67	117	50
Bobby Smith	Minnesota	80	43	71	114	82
Dino Ciccarelli	Minnesota	76	55	51	106	138
Dave Taylor	Los Angeles	78	39	67	106	130

1982-83
CLARENCE CAMPBELL CONFERENCE
Norris Division

Team	GP	W	L	T	GF	GA	PTS
Chicago	80	47	23	10	338	268	104
Minnesota	80	40	24	16	321	290	96
Toronto	80	28	40	12	293	330	68
St. Louis	80	25	40	15	285	316	65
Detroit	80	21	44	15	263	344	57

Smythe Division

Team	GP	W	L	T	GF	GA	PTS
Edmonton	80	47	21	12	424	315	106
Calgary	80	32	34	14	321	317	78
Vancouver	80	30	35	15	303	309	75
Winnipeg	80	33	39	8	311	333	74
Los Angeles	80	27	41	12	308	365	66

PRINCE OF WALES CONFERENCE
Adams Division

Team	GP	W	L	T	GF	GA	PTS
Boston	80	50	20	10	327	228	110
Montreal	80	42	24	14	350	286	98
Buffalo	80	38	29	13	318	285	89
Quebec	80	34	34	12	343	336	80
Hartford	80	19	54	7	261	403	45

Patrick Division

Team	GP	W	L	T	GF	GA	PTS
Philadelphia	80	49	23	8	326	240	106
*NY Islanders	80	42	26	12	302	226	96
Washington	80	39	25	16	306	283	94
NY Rangers	80	35	35	10	306	287	80
New Jersey	80	17	49	14	230	338	48
Pittsburgh	80	18	53	9	257	394	45

Leading Scorers

Player	Club	GP	G	A	PTS	PIM
Wayne Gretzky	Edmonton	80	71	125	196	59
Peter Stastny	Quebec	75	47	77	124	78
Denis Savard	Chicago	78	35	86	121	99
Mike Bossy	NY Islanders	79	60	58	118	20
Marcel Dionne	Los Angeles	80	56	51	107	22
Barry Pederson	Boston	77	46	61	107	47
Mark Messier	Edmonton	77	48	58	106	72
Michel Goulet	Quebec	80	57	48	105	51
Glenn Anderson	Edmonton	72	48	56	104	70
Kent Nilsson	Calgary	80	46	58	104	10
Jari Kurri	Edmonton	80	45	59	104	22

1983-84
CLARENCE CAMPBELL CONFERENCE
Norris Division

Team	GP	W	L	T	GF	GA	PTS
Minnesota	80	39	31	10	345	344	88
St. Louis	80	32	41	7	293	316	71
Detroit	80	31	42	7	298	323	69
Chicago	80	30	42	8	277	311	68
Toronto	80	26	45	9	303	387	61

Smythe Division

Team	GP	W	L	T	GF	GA	PTS
*Edmonton	80	57	18	5	446	314	119
Calgary	80	34	32	14	311	314	82
Vancouver	80	32	39	9	306	328	73
Winnipeg	80	31	38	11	340	374	73
Los Angeles	80	23	44	13	309	376	59

PRINCE OF WALES CONFERENCE
Adams Division

Team	GP	W	L	T	GF	GA	PTS
Boston	80	49	25	6	336	261	104
Buffalo	80	48	25	7	315	257	103
Quebec	80	42	28	10	360	278	94
Montreal	80	35	40	5	286	295	75
Hartford	80	28	42	10	288	320	66

Patrick Division

Team	GP	W	L	T	GF	GA	PTS
NY Islanders	80	50	26	4	357	269	104
Washington	80	48	27	5	308	226	101
Philadelphia	80	44	26	10	350	290	98
NY Rangers	80	42	29	9	314	304	93
New Jersey	80	17	56	7	231	350	41
Pittsburgh	80	16	58	6	254	390	38

Leading Scorers

Player	Club	GP	G	A	PTS	PIM
Wayne Gretzky	Edmonton	74	87	118	205	39
Paul Coffey	Edmonton	80	40	86	126	104
Michel Goulet	Quebec	75	56	65	121	76
Peter Stastny	Quebec	80	46	73	119	73
Mike Bossy	NY Islanders	67	51	67	118	8
Barry Pederson	Boston	80	39	77	116	64
Jari Kurri	Edmonton	64	52	61	113	14
Bryan Trottier	NY Islanders	68	40	71	111	59
Bernie Federko	St. Louis	79	41	66	107	43
Rick Middleton	Boston	80	47	58	105	14

1984-85
CLARENCE CAMPBELL CONFERENCE
Norris Division

Team	GP	W	L	T	GF	GA	PTS
St. Louis	80	37	31	12	299	288	86
Chicago	80	38	35	7	309	299	83
Detroit	80	27	41	12	313	357	66
Minnesota	80	25	43	12	268	321	62
Toronto	80	20	52	8	253	358	48

Smythe Division

Team	GP	W	L	T	GF	GA	PTS
*Edmonton	80	49	20	11	401	298	109
Winnipeg	80	43	27	10	358	332	96
Calgary	80	41	27	12	363	302	94
Los Angeles	80	34	32	14	339	326	82
Vancouver	80	25	46	9	284	401	59

PRINCE OF WALES CONFERENCE
Adams Division

Team	GP	W	L	T	GF	GA	PTS
Montreal	80	41	27	12	309	262	94
Quebec	80	41	30	9	323	275	91
Buffalo	80	38	28	14	290	237	90
Boston	80	36	34	10	303	287	82
Hartford	80	30	41	9	268	318	69

Patrick Division

Team	GP	W	L	T	GF	GA	PTS
Philadelphia	80	53	20	7	348	241	113
Washington	80	46	25	9	322	240	101
NY Islanders	80	40	34	6	345	312	86
NY Rangers	80	26	44	10	295	345	62
New Jersey	80	22	48	10	264	346	54
Pittsburgh	80	24	51	5	276	385	53

Leading Scorers

Player	Club	GP	G	A	PTS	PIM
Wayne Gretzky	Edmonton	80	73	135	208	52
Jari Kurri	Edmonton	73	71	64	135	30
Dale Hawerchuk	Winnipeg	80	53	77	130	74
Marcel Dionne	Los Angeles	80	46	80	126	46
Paul Coffey	Edmonton	80	37	84	121	97
Mike Bossy	NY Islanders	76	58	59	117	38
John Ogrodnick	Detroit	79	55	50	105	30
Denis Savard	Chicago	79	38	67	105	56
Bernie Federko	St. Louis	76	30	73	103	27
Mike Gartner	Washington	80	50	52	102	71

1985-86
CLARENCE CAMPBELL CONFERENCE
Norris Division

Team	GP	W	L	T	GF	GA	PTS
Chicago	80	39	33	8	351	349	86
Minnesota	80	38	33	9	327	305	85
St. Louis	80	37	34	9	302	291	83
Toronto	80	25	48	7	311	386	57
Detroit	80	17	57	6	266	415	40

Smythe Division

Team	GP	W	L	T	GF	GA	PTS
Edmonton	80	56	17	7	426	310	119
Calgary	80	40	31	9	354	315	89
Winnipeg	80	26	47	7	295	372	59
Vancouver	80	23	44	13	282	333	59
Los Angeles	80	23	49	8	284	389	54

PRINCE OF WALES CONFERENCE
Adams Division

Team	GP	W	L	T	GF	GA	PTS
Quebec	80	43	31	6	330	289	92
*Montreal	80	40	33	7	330	280	87
Boston	80	37	31	12	311	288	86
Hartford	80	40	36	4	332	302	84
Buffalo	80	37	37	6	296	291	80

Patrick Division

Team	GP	W	L	T	GF	GA	PTS
Philadelphia	80	53	23	4	335	241	110
Washington	80	50	23	7	315	272	107
NY Islanders	80	39	29	12	327	284	90
NY Rangers	80	36	38	6	280	276	78
Pittsburgh	80	34	38	8	313	305	76
New Jersey	80	28	49	3	300	374	59

Leading Scorers

Player	Club	GP	G	A	PTS	PIM
Wayne Gretzky	Edmonton	80	52	163	215	52
Mario Lemieux	Pittsburgh	79	48	93	141	43
Paul Coffey	Edmonton	79	48	90	138	120
Jari Kurri	Edmonton	78	68	63	131	22
Mike Bossy	NY Islanders	80	61	62	123	14
Peter Stastny	Quebec	76	41	81	122	60
Denis Savard	Chicago	80	47	69	116	111
Mats Naslund	Montreal	80	43	67	110	16
Dale Hawerchuk	Winnipeg	80	46	59	105	44
Neal Broten	Minnesota	80	29	76	105	47

1986-87
CLARENCE CAMPBELL CONFERENCE
Norris Division

Team	GP	W	L	T	GF	GA	PTS
St. Louis	80	32	33	15	281	293	79
Detroit	80	34	36	10	260	274	78
Chicago	80	29	37	14	290	310	72
Toronto	80	32	42	6	286	319	70
Minnesota	80	30	40	10	296	314	70

Smythe Division

Team	GP	W	L	T	GF	GA	PTS
*Edmonton	80	50	24	6	372	284	106
Calgary	80	46	31	3	318	289	95
Winnipeg	80	40	32	8	279	271	88
Los Angeles	80	31	41	8	318	341	70
Vancouver	80	29	43	8	282	314	66

PRINCE OF WALES CONFERENCE
Adams Division

Team	GP	W	L	T	GF	GA	PTS
Hartford	80	43	30	7	287	270	93
Montreal	80	41	29	10	277	241	92
Boston	80	39	34	7	301	276	85
Quebec	80	31	39	10	267	276	72
Buffalo	80	28	44	8	280	308	64

Patrick Division

Team	GP	W	L	T	GF	GA	PTS
Philadelphia	80	46	26	8	310	245	100
Washington	80	38	32	10	285	278	86
NY Islanders	80	35	33	12	279	281	82
NY Rangers	80	34	38	8	307	323	76
Pittsburgh	80	30	38	12	297	290	72
New Jersey	80	29	45	6	293	368	64

Leading Scorers

Player	Club	GP	G	A	PTS	PIM
Wayne Gretzky	Edmonton	79	62	121	183	28
Jari Kurri	Edmonton	79	54	54	108	41
Mario Lemieux	Pittsburgh	63	54	53	107	57
Mark Messier	Edmonton	77	37	70	107	73
Doug Gilmour	St. Louis	80	42	63	105	58
Dino Ciccarelli	Minnesota	80	52	51	103	92
Dale Hawerchuk	Winnipeg	80	47	53	100	54
Michel Goulet	Quebec	75	49	47	96	61
Tim Kerr	Philadelphia	75	58	37	95	57
Raymond Bourque	Boston	78	23	72	95	36

1987-88
CLARENCE CAMPBELL CONFERENCE
Norris Division

Team	GP	W	L	T	GF	GA	PTS
Detroit	80	41	28	11	322	269	93
St. Louis	80	34	38	8	278	294	76
Chicago	80	30	41	9	284	328	69
Toronto	80	21	49	10	273	345	52
Minnesota	80	19	48	13	242	349	51

Smythe Division

Team	GP	W	L	T	GF	GA	PTS
Calgary	80	48	23	9	397	305	105
*Edmonton	80	44	25	11	363	288	99
Winnipeg	80	33	36	11	292	310	77
Los Angeles	80	30	42	8	318	359	68
Vancouver	80	25	46	9	272	320	59

PRINCE OF WALES CONFERENCE
Adams Division

Team	GP	W	L	T	GF	GA	PTS
Montreal	80	45	22	13	298	238	103
Boston	80	44	30	6	300	251	94
Buffalo	80	37	32	11	283	305	85
Hartford	80	35	38	7	249	267	77
Quebec	80	32	43	5	271	306	69

Patrick Division

Team	GP	W	L	T	GF	GA	PTS
NY Islanders	80	39	31	10	308	267	88
Washington	80	38	33	9	281	249	85
Philadelphia	80	38	33	9	292	292	85
New Jersey	80	38	36	6	295	296	82
NY Rangers	80	36	34	10	300	283	82
Pittsburgh	80	36	35	9	319	316	81

Leading Scorers

Player	Club	GP	G	A	PTS	PIM
Mario Lemieux	Pittsburgh	77	70	98	168	92
Wayne Gretzky	Edmonton	64	40	109	149	24
Denis Savard	Chicago	80	44	87	131	95
Dale Hawerchuk	Winnipeg	80	44	77	121	59
Luc Robitaille	Los Angeles	80	53	58	111	82
Peter Stastny	Quebec	76	46	65	111	69
Mark Messier	Edmonton	77	37	74	111	103
Jimmy Carson	Los Angeles	80	55	52	107	45
Hakan Loob	Calgary	80	50	56	106	47
Michel Goulet	Quebec	80	48	58	106	56

1988-89
CLARENCE CAMPBELL CONFERENCE
Norris Division

Team	GP	W	L	T	GF	GA	PTS
Detroit	80	34	34	12	313	316	80
St. Louis	80	33	35	12	275	285	78
Minnesota	80	27	37	16	258	278	70
Chicago	80	27	41	12	297	335	66
Toronto	80	28	46	6	259	342	62

Smythe Division

Team	GP	W	L	T	GF	GA	PTS
*Calgary	80	54	17	9	354	226	117
Los Angeles	80	42	31	7	376	335	91
Edmonton	80	38	34	8	325	306	84
Vancouver	80	33	39	8	251	253	74
Winnipeg	80	26	42	12	300	355	64

PRINCE OF WALES CONFERENCE
Adams Division

Team	GP	W	L	T	GF	GA	PTS
Montreal	80	53	18	9	315	218	115
Boston	80	37	29	14	289	256	88
Buffalo	80	38	35	7	291	299	83
Hartford	80	37	38	5	299	290	79
Quebec	80	27	46	7	269	342	61

Patrick Division

Team	GP	W	L	T	GF	GA	PTS
Washington	80	41	29	10	305	259	92
Pittsburgh	80	40	33	7	347	349	87
NY Rangers	80	37	35	8	310	307	82
Philadelphia	80	36	36	8	307	285	80
New Jersey	80	27	41	12	281	325	66
NY Islanders	80	28	47	5	265	325	61

Leading Scorers

Player	Club	GP	G	A	PTS	PIM
Mario Lemieux	Pittsburgh	76	85	114	199	100
Wayne Gretzky	Los Angeles	78	54	114	168	26
Steve Yzerman	Detroit	80	65	90	155	61
Bernie Nicholls	Los Angeles	79	70	80	150	96
Rob Brown	Pittsburgh	68	49	66	115	118
Paul Coffey	Pittsburgh	75	30	83	113	193
Joe Mullen	Calgary	79	51	59	110	16
Jari Kurri	Edmonton	76	44	58	102	69
Jimmy Carson	Edmonton	80	49	51	100	36
Luc Robitaille	Los Angeles	78	46	52	98	65

1989-90
CLARENCE CAMPBELL CONFERENCE
Norris Division

Team	GP	W	L	T	GF	GA	PTS
Chicago	80	41	33	6	316	294	88
St. Louis	80	37	34	9	295	279	83
Toronto	80	38	38	4	337	358	80
Minnesota	80	36	40	4	284	291	76
Detroit	80	28	38	14	288	323	70

Smythe Division

Team	GP	W	L	T	GF	GA	PTS
Calgary	80	42	23	15	348	265	99
*Edmonton	80	38	28	14	315	283	90
Winnipeg	80	37	32	11	298	290	85
Los Angeles	80	34	39	7	338	337	75
Vancouver	80	25	41	14	245	306	64

PRINCE OF WALES CONFERENCE
Adams Division

Team	GP	W	L	T	GF	GA	PTS
Boston	80	46	25	9	289	232	101
Buffalo	80	45	27	8	286	248	98
Montreal	80	41	28	11	288	234	93
Hartford	80	38	33	9	275	268	85
Quebec	80	12	61	7	240	407	31

Patrick Division

Team	GP	W	L	T	GF	GA	PTS
NY Rangers	80	36	31	13	279	267	85
New Jersey	80	37	34	9	295	288	83
Washington	80	36	38	6	284	275	78
NY Islanders	80	31	38	11	281	288	73
Pittsburgh	80	32	40	8	318	359	72
Philadelphia	80	30	39	11	290	297	71

Leading Scorers

Player	Club	GP	G	A	PTS	PIM
Wayne Gretzky	Los Angeles	73	40	102	142	42
Mark Messier	Edmonton	79	45	84	129	79
Steve Yzerman	Detroit	79	62	65	127	79
Mario Lemieux	Pittsburgh	59	45	78	123	78
Brett Hull	St. Louis	80	72	41	113	24
Bernie Nicholls	L.A., NYR	79	39	73	112	86
Pierre Turgeon	Buffalo	80	40	66	106	29
Pat LaFontaine	NY Islanders	74	54	51	105	38
Paul Coffey	Pittsburgh	80	29	74	103	95
Joe Sakic	Quebec	80	39	63	102	27
Adam Oates	St. Louis	80	23	79	102	30

1990-91
CLARENCE CAMPBELL CONFERENCE
Norris Division

Team	GP	W	L	T	GF	GA	PTS
Chicago	80	49	23	8	284	211	106
St. Louis	80	47	22	11	310	250	105
Detroit	80	34	38	8	273	298	76
Minnesota	80	27	39	14	256	266	68
Toronto	80	23	46	11	241	318	57

Smythe Division

Team	GP	W	L	T	GF	GA	PTS
Los Angeles	80	46	24	10	340	254	102
Calgary	80	46	26	8	344	263	100
Edmonton	80	37	37	6	272	272	80
Vancouver	80	28	43	9	243	315	65
Winnipeg	80	26	43	11	260	288	63

PRINCE OF WALES CONFERENCE
Adams Division

Team	GP	W	L	T	GF	GA	PTS
Boston	80	44	24	12	299	264	100
Montreal	80	39	30	11	273	249	89
Buffalo	80	31	30	19	292	278	81
Hartford	80	31	38	11	238	276	73
Quebec	80	16	50	14	236	354	46

Patrick Division

Team	GP	W	L	T	GF	GA	PTS
*Pittsburgh	80	41	33	6	342	305	88
NY Rangers	80	36	31	13	297	265	85
Washington	80	37	36	7	258	258	81
New Jersey	80	32	33	15	272	264	79
Philadelphia	80	33	37	10	252	267	76
NY Islanders	80	25	45	10	223	290	60

Leading Scorers

Player	Club	GP	G	A	PTS	PIM
Wayne Gretzky	Los Angeles	78	41	122	163	16
Brett Hull	St. Louis	78	86	45	131	22
Adam Oates	St. Louis	61	25	90	115	29
Mark Recchi	Pittsburgh	78	40	73	113	48
John Cullen	Pit., Hfd.	78	39	71	110	101
Joe Sakic	Quebec	80	48	61	109	24
Steve Yzerman	Detroit	80	51	57	108	34
Theoren Fleury	Calgary	79	51	53	104	136
Al MacInnis	Calgary	78	28	75	103	90
Steve Larmer	Chicago	80	44	57	101	79

1991-92
CLARENCE CAMPBELL CONFERENCE
Norris Division

Team	GP	W	L	T	GF	GA	PTS
Detroit	80	43	25	12	320	256	98
Chicago	80	36	29	15	257	236	87
St. Louis	80	36	33	11	279	266	83
Minnesota	80	32	42	6	246	278	70
Toronto	80	30	43	7	234	294	67

Smythe Division

Team	GP	W	L	T	GF	GA	PTS
Vancouver	80	42	26	12	285	250	96
Los Angeles	80	35	31	14	287	296	84
Edmonton	80	36	34	10	295	297	82
Winnipeg	80	33	32	15	251	244	81
Calgary	80	31	37	12	296	305	74
San Jose	80	17	58	5	219	359	39

PRINCE OF WALES CONFERENCE
Adams Division

Team	GP	W	L	T	GF	GA	PTS
Montreal	80	41	28	11	267	207	93
Boston	80	36	32	12	270	275	84
Buffalo	80	31	37	12	289	299	74
Hartford	80	26	41	13	247	283	65
Quebec	80	20	48	12	255	318	52

Patrick Division

Team	GP	W	L	T	GF	GA	PTS
NY Rangers	80	50	25	5	321	246	105
Washington	80	45	27	8	330	275	98
*Pittsburgh	80	39	32	9	343	308	87
New Jersey	80	38	31	11	289	259	87
NY Islanders	80	34	35	11	291	299	79
Philadelphia	80	32	37	11	252	273	75

Leading Scorers

Player	Club	GP	G	A	PTS	PIM
Mario Lemieux	Pittsburgh	64	44	87	131	94
Kevin Stevens	Pittsburgh	80	54	69	123	254
Wayne Gretzky	Los Angeles	74	31	90	121	34
Brett Hull	St. Louis	73	70	39	109	48
Luc Robitaille	Los Angeles	80	44	63	107	95
Mark Messier	NY Rangers	79	35	72	107	76
Jeremy Roenick	Chicago	80	53	50	103	23
Steve Yzerman	Detroit	79	45	58	103	64
Brian Leetch	NY Rangers	80	22	80	102	26
Adam Oates	St.L., Bos.	80	20	79	99	22

1992-93
CLARENCE CAMPBELL CONFERENCE
Norris Division

Team	GP	W	L	T	GF	GA	PTS
Chicago	84	47	25	12	279	230	106
Detroit	84	47	28	9	369	280	103
Toronto	84	44	29	11	288	241	99
St. Louis	84	37	36	11	282	278	85
Minnesota	84	36	38	10	272	293	82
Tampa Bay	84	23	54	7	245	332	53

Smythe Division

Team	GP	W	L	T	GF	GA	PTS
Vancouver	84	46	29	9	346	278	101
Calgary	84	43	30	11	322	282	97
Los Angeles	84	39	35	10	338	340	88
Winnipeg	84	40	37	7	322	320	87
Edmonton	84	26	50	8	242	337	60
San Jose	84	11	71	2	218	414	24

PRINCE OF WALES CONFERENCE
Adams Division

Team	GP	W	L	T	GF	GA	PTS
Boston	84	51	26	7	332	268	109
Quebec	84	47	27	10	351	300	104
*Montreal	84	48	30	6	326	280	102
Buffalo	84	38	36	10	335	297	86
Hartford	84	26	52	6	284	369	58
Ottawa	84	10	70	4	202	395	24

Patrick Division

Team	GP	W	L	T	GF	GA	PTS
Pittsburgh	84	56	21	7	367	268	119
Washington	84	43	34	7	325	286	93
NY Islanders	84	40	37	7	335	297	87
New Jersey	84	40	37	7	308	299	87
Philadelphia	84	36	37	11	319	319	83
NY Rangers	84	34	39	11	304	308	79

Leading Scorers

Player	Club	GP	G	A	PTS	PIM
Mario Lemieux	Pittsburgh	60	69	91	160	38
Pat LaFontaine	Buffalo	84	53	95	148	63
Adam Oates	Boston	84	45	97	142	32
Steve Yzerman	Detroit	84	58	79	137	44
Teemu Selanne	Winnipeg	84	76	56	132	45
Pierre Turgeon	NY Islanders	83	58	74	132	26
Alexander Mogilny	Buffalo	77	76	51	127	40
Doug Gilmour	Toronto	83	32	95	127	100
Luc Robitaille	Los Angeles	84	63	62	125	100
Mark Recchi	Philadelphia	84	53	70	123	95

1993-94
EASTERN CONFERENCE
Northeast Division

Team	GP	W	L	T	GF	GA	PTS
Pittsburgh	84	44	27	13	299	285	101
Boston	84	42	29	13	289	252	97
Montreal	84	41	29	14	283	248	96
Buffalo	84	43	32	9	282	218	95
Quebec	84	34	42	8	277	292	76
Hartford	84	27	48	9	227	288	63
Ottawa	84	14	61	9	201	397	37

Atlantic Division

Team	GP	W	L	T	GF	GA	PTS
*NY Rangers	84	52	24	8	299	231	112
New Jersey	84	47	25	12	306	220	106
Washington	84	39	35	10	277	263	88
NY Islanders	84	36	36	12	282	264	84
Florida	84	33	34	17	233	233	83
Philadelphia	84	35	39	10	294	314	80
Tampa Bay	84	30	43	11	224	251	71

WESTERN CONFERENCE
Central Division

Team	GP	W	L	T	GF	GA	PTS
Detroit	84	46	30	8	356	275	100
Toronto	84	43	29	12	280	243	98
Dallas	84	42	29	13	286	265	97
St. Louis	84	40	33	11	270	283	91
Chicago	84	39	36	9	254	240	87
Winnipeg	84	24	51	9	245	344	57

Pacific Division

Team	GP	W	L	T	GF	GA	PTS
Calgary	84	42	29	13	302	256	97
Vancouver	84	41	40	3	279	276	85
San Jose	84	33	35	16	252	265	82
Anaheim	84	33	46	5	229	251	71
Los Angeles	84	27	45	12	294	322	66
Edmonton	84	25	45	14	261	305	64

Leading Scorers

Player	Club	GP	G	A	PTS	PIM
Wayne Gretzky	Los Angeles	81	38	92	130	20
Sergei Fedorov	Detroit	82	56	64	120	34
Adam Oates	Boston	77	32	80	112	45
Doug Gilmour	Toronto	83	27	84	111	105
Pavel Bure	Vancouver	76	60	47	107	86
Jeremy Roenick	Chicago	84	46	61	107	125
Mark Recchi	Philadelphia	84	40	67	107	46
Brendan Shanahan	St. Louis	81	52	50	102	211
Dave Andreychuk	Toronto	83	53	46	99	98
Jaromir Jagr	Pittsburgh	80	32	67	99	61

1994-95
EASTERN CONFERENCE
Northeast Division

Team	GP	W	L	T	GF	GA	PTS
Quebec	48	30	13	5	185	134	65
Pittsburgh	48	29	16	3	181	158	61
Boston	48	27	18	3	150	127	57
Buffalo	48	22	19	7	130	119	51
Hartford	48	19	24	5	127	141	43
Montreal	48	18	23	7	125	148	43
Ottawa	48	9	34	5	117	174	23

Atlantic Division

Team	GP	W	L	T	GF	GA	PTS
Philadelphia	48	28	16	4	150	132	60
*New Jersey	48	22	18	8	136	121	52
Washington	48	22	18	8	136	120	52
NY Rangers	48	22	23	3	139	134	47
Florida	48	20	22	6	115	127	46
Tampa Bay	48	17	28	3	120	144	37
NY Islanders	48	15	28	5	126	158	35

WESTERN CONFERENCE
Central Division

Team	GP	W	L	T	GF	GA	PTS
Detroit	48	33	11	4	180	117	70
St. Louis	48	28	15	5	178	135	61
Chicago	48	24	19	5	156	115	53
Toronto	48	21	19	8	135	146	50
Dallas	48	17	23	8	136	135	42
Winnipeg	48	16	25	7	157	177	39

Pacific Division

Team	GP	W	L	T	GF	GA	PTS
Calgary	48	24	17	7	163	135	55
Vancouver	48	18	18	12	153	148	48
San Jose	48	19	25	4	129	161	42
Los Angeles	48	16	23	9	142	174	41
Edmonton	48	17	27	4	136	183	38
Anaheim	48	16	27	5	125	164	37

Leading Scorers

Player	Club	GP	G	A	PTS	PIM
Jaromir Jagr	Pittsburgh	48	32	38	70	37
Eric Lindros	Philadelphia	46	29	41	70	60
Alex Zhamnov	Winnipeg	48	30	35	65	20
Joe Sakic	Quebec	47	19	43	62	30
Ron Francis	Pittsburgh	44	11	48	59	18
Theoren Fleury	Calgary	47	29	29	58	112
Paul Coffey	Detroit	45	14	44	58	72
Mikael Renberg	Philadelphia	47	26	31	57	20
John LeClair	Mtl., Phi.	46	26	28	54	30
Mark Messier	NY Rangers	46	14	39	53	40
Adam Oates	Boston	48	12	41	53	8

1995-96
EASTERN CONFERENCE
Northeast Division

Team	GP	W	L	T	GF	GA	PTS
Pittsburgh	82	49	29	4	362	284	102
Boston	82	40	31	11	282	269	91
Montreal	82	40	32	10	265	248	90
Hartford	82	34	39	9	237	259	77
Buffalo	82	33	42	7	247	262	73
Ottawa	82	18	59	5	191	291	41

Atlantic Division

Team	GP	W	L	T	GF	GA	PTS
Philadelphia	82	45	24	13	282	208	103
NY Rangers	82	41	27	14	272	237	96
Florida	82	41	31	10	254	234	92
Washington	82	39	32	11	234	204	89
Tampa Bay	82	38	32	12	238	248	88
New Jersey	82	37	33	12	215	202	86
NY Islanders	82	22	50	10	229	315	54

WESTERN CONFERENCE
Central Division

Team	GP	W	L	T	GF	GA	PTS
Detroit	82	62	13	7	325	181	131
Chicago	82	40	28	14	273	220	94
Toronto	82	34	36	12	247	252	80
St. Louis	82	32	34	16	219	248	80
Winnipeg	82	36	40	6	275	291	78
Dallas	82	26	42	14	227	280	66

Pacific Division

Team	GP	W	L	T	GF	GA	PTS
*Colorado	82	47	25	10	326	240	104
Calgary	82	34	37	11	241	240	79
Vancouver	82	32	35	15	278	278	79
Anaheim	82	35	39	8	234	247	78
Edmonton	82	30	44	8	240	304	68
Los Angeles	82	24	40	18	256	302	66
San Jose	82	20	55	7	252	357	47

Leading Scorers

Player	Club	GP	G	A	PTS	PIM
Mario Lemieux	Pittsburgh	70	69	92	161	54
Jaromir Jagr	Pittsburgh	82	62	87	149	96
Joe Sakic	Colorado	82	51	69	120	44
Ron Francis	Pittsburgh	77	27	92	119	56
Peter Forsberg	Colorado	82	30	86	116	47
Eric Lindros	Philadelphia	73	47	68	115	163
Paul Kariya	Anaheim	82	50	58	108	20
Teemu Selanne	Wpg., Ana.	79	40	68	108	22
Alexander Mogilny	Vancouver	79	55	52	107	16
Sergei Fedorov	Detroit	78	39	68	107	48

1996-97
EASTERN CONFERENCE
Northeast Division

Team	GP	W	L	T	GF	GA	PTS
Buffalo	82	40	30	12	237	208	92
Pittsburgh	82	38	36	8	285	280	84
Ottawa	82	31	36	15	226	234	77
Montreal	82	31	36	15	249	276	77
Hartford	82	32	39	11	226	256	75
Boston	82	26	47	9	234	300	61

Atlantic Division

Team	GP	W	L	T	GF	GA	PTS
New Jersey	82	45	23	14	231	182	104
Philadelphia	82	45	24	13	274	217	103
Florida	82	35	28	19	221	201	89
NY Rangers	82	38	34	10	258	231	86
Washington	82	33	40	9	214	231	75
Tampa Bay	82	32	40	10	217	247	74
NY Islanders	82	29	41	12	240	250	70

WESTERN CONFERENCE
Central Division

Team	GP	W	L	T	GF	GA	PTS
Dallas	82	48	26	8	252	198	104
*Detroit	82	38	26	18	253	197	94
Phoenix	82	38	37	7	240	243	83
St. Louis	82	36	35	11	236	239	83
Chicago	82	34	35	13	223	210	81
Toronto	82	30	44	8	230	273	68

Pacific Division

Team	GP	W	L	T	GF	GA	PTS
Colorado	82	49	24	9	277	205	107
Anaheim	82	36	33	13	245	233	85
Edmonton	82	36	37	9	252	247	81
Vancouver	82	35	40	7	257	273	77
Calgary	82	32	41	9	214	239	73
Los Angeles	82	28	43	11	214	268	67
San Jose	82	27	47	8	211	278	62

Leading Scorers

Player	Club	GP	G	A	PTS	PIM
Mario Lemieux	Pittsburgh	76	50	72	122	65
Teemu Selanne	Anaheim	78	51	58	109	34
Paul Kariya	Anaheim	69	44	55	99	6
John LeClair	Philadelphia	82	50	47	97	58
Wayne Gretzky	NY Rangers	82	25	72	97	28
Jaromir Jagr	Pittsburgh	63	47	48	95	40
Mats Sundin	Toronto	82	41	53	94	59
Ziggy Palffy	NY Islanders	80	48	42	90	43
Ron Francis	Pittsburgh	81	27	63	90	20
Brendan Shanahan	Hfd., Det.	81	47	41	88	131

1997-98

EASTERN CONFERENCE
Northeast Division

Team	GP	W	L	T	GF	GA	PTS
Pittsburgh	82	40	24	18	228	188	98
Boston	82	39	30	13	221	194	91
Buffalo	82	36	29	17	211	187	89
Montreal	82	37	32	13	235	208	87
Ottawa	82	34	33	15	193	200	83
Carolina	82	33	41	8	200	219	74

Atlantic Division

Team	GP	W	L	T	GF	GA	PTS
New Jersey	82	48	23	11	225	166	107
Philadelphia	82	42	29	11	242	193	95
Washington	82	40	30	12	219	202	92
NY Islanders	82	30	41	11	212	225	71
NY Rangers	82	25	39	18	197	231	68
Florida	82	24	43	15	203	256	63
Tampa Bay	82	17	55	10	151	269	44

WESTERN CONFERENCE
Central Division

Team	GP	W	L	T	GF	GA	PTS
Dallas	82	49	22	11	242	167	109
*Detroit	82	44	23	15	250	196	103
St. Louis	82	45	29	8	256	204	98
Phoenix	82	35	35	12	224	227	82
Chicago	82	30	39	13	192	199	73
Toronto	82	30	43	9	194	237	69

Pacific Division

Team	GP	W	L	T	GF	GA	PTS
Colorado	82	39	26	17	231	205	95
Los Angeles	82	38	33	11	227	225	87
Edmonton	82	35	37	10	215	224	80
San Jose	82	34	38	10	210	216	78
Calgary	82	26	41	15	217	252	67
Anaheim	82	26	43	13	205	261	65
Vancouver	82	25	43	14	224	273	64

Leading Scorers

Player	Club	GP	G	A	PTS	PIM
Jaromir Jagr	Pittsburgh	77	35	67	102	64
Peter Forsberg	Colorado	72	25	66	91	94
Pavel Bure	Vancouver	82	51	39	90	48
Wayne Gretzky	NY Rangers	82	23	67	90	28
John LeClair	Philadelphia	82	51	36	87	32
Ziggy Palffy	NY Islanders	82	45	42	87	34
Ron Francis	Pittsburgh	81	25	62	87	20
Teemu Selanne	Anaheim	73	52	34	86	30
Jason Allison	Boston	81	33	50	83	60
Jozef Stumpel	Los Angeles	77	21	58	79	53

1998-99

EASTERN CONFERENCE
Northeast Division

Team	GP	W	L	T	GF	GA	PTS
Ottawa	82	44	23	15	239	179	103
Toronto	82	45	30	7	268	231	97
Boston	82	39	30	13	214	181	91
Buffalo	82	37	28	17	207	175	91
Montreal	82	32	39	11	184	209	75

Atlantic Division

Team	GP	W	L	T	GF	GA	PTS
New Jersey	82	47	24	11	248	196	105
Philadelphia	82	37	26	19	231	196	93
Pittsburgh	82	38	30	14	242	225	90
NY Rangers	82	33	38	11	217	227	77
NY Islanders	82	24	48	10	194	244	58

Southeast Division

Team	GP	W	L	T	GF	GA	PTS
Carolina	82	34	30	18	210	202	86
Florida	82	30	34	18	210	228	78
Washington	82	31	45	6	200	218	68
Tampa Bay	82	19	54	9	179	292	47

WESTERN CONFERENCE
Central Division

Team	GP	W	L	T	GF	GA	PTS
Detroit	82	43	32	7	245	202	93
St Louis	82	37	32	13	237	209	87
Chicago	82	29	41	12	202	248	70
Nashville	82	28	47	7	190	261	63

Pacific Division

Team	GP	W	L	T	GF	GA	PTS
*Dallas	82	51	19	12	236	168	114
Phoenix	82	39	31	12	205	197	90
Anaheim	82	35	34	13	215	206	83
San Jose	82	31	33	18	196	191	80
Los Angeles	82	32	45	5	189	222	69

Northwest Division

Team	GP	W	L	T	GF	GA	PTS
Colorado	82	44	28	10	239	205	98
Edmonton	82	33	37	12	230	226	78
Calgary	82	30	40	12	211	234	72
Vancouver	82	23	47	12	192	258	58

Leading Scorers

Player	Club	GP	G	A	PTS	PIM
Jaromir Jagr	Pittsburgh	81	44	83	127	66
Teemu Selanne	Anaheim	75	47	60	107	30
Paul Kariya	Anaheim	82	39	62	101	40
Peter Forsberg	Colorado	78	30	67	97	108
Joe Sakic	Colorado	73	41	55	96	29
Alexei Yashin	Ottawa	82	44	50	94	54
Eric Lindros	Philadelphia	71	40	53	93	120
Theoren Fleury	Cgy., Col.	75	40	53	93	86
John LeClair	Philadelphia	76	43	47	90	30
Pavol Demitra	St Louis	82	37	52	89	16

1999-2000

EASTERN CONFERENCE
Northeast Division

Team	GP	W	L	T	OTL	GF	GA	PTS
Toronto	82	45	27	7	3	246	222	100
Ottawa	82	41	28	11	2	244	210	95
Buffalo	82	35	32	11	4	213	204	85
Montreal	82	35	34	9	4	196	194	83
Boston	82	24	33	19	6	210	248	73

Atlantic Division

Team	GP	W	L	T	OTL	GF	GA	PTS
Philadelphia	82	45	22	12	3	237	179	105
*New Jersey	82	45	24	8	5	251	203	103
Pittsburgh	82	37	31	8	6	241	236	88
NY Rangers	82	29	38	12	3	218	246	73
NY Islanders	82	24	48	9	1	194	275	58

Southeast Division

Team	GP	W	L	T	OTL	GF	GA	PTS
Washington	82	44	24	12	2	227	194	102
Florida	82	43	27	6	6	244	209	98
Carolina	82	37	35	10	0	217	216	84
Tampa Bay	82	19	47	9	7	204	310	54
Atlanta	82	14	57	7	4	170	313	39

WESTERN CONFERENCE
Central Division

Team	GP	W	L	T	OTL	GF	GA	PTS
St. Louis	82	51	19	11	1	248	165	114
Detroit	82	48	22	10	2	278	210	108
Chicago	82	33	37	10	2	242	245	78
Nashville	82	28	40	7	7	199	240	70

Pacific Division

Team	GP	W	L	T	OTL	GF	GA	PTS
Dallas	82	43	23	10	6	211	184	102
Los Angeles	82	39	27	12	4	245	228	94
Phoenix	82	39	31	8	4	232	228	90
San Jose	82	35	30	10	7	225	214	87
Anaheim	82	34	33	12	3	217	227	83

Northwest Division

Team	GP	W	L	T	OTL	GF	GA	PTS
Colorado	82	42	28	11	1	233	201	96
Edmonton	82	32	26	16	8	226	212	88
Vancouver	82	30	29	15	8	227	237	83
Calgary	82	31	36	10	5	211	256	77

Leading Scorers

Player	Club	GP	G	A	PTS	PIM
Jaromir Jagr	Pittsburgh	63	42	54	96	50
Pavel Bure	Florida	74	58	36	94	16
Mark Recchi	Philadelphia	82	28	63	91	50
Paul Kariya	Anaheim	74	42	44	86	24
Teemu Selanne	Anaheim	79	33	52	85	12
Owen Nolan	San Jose	78	44	40	84	110
Tony Amonte	Chicago	82	43	41	84	48
Mike Modano	Dallas	77	38	43	81	48
Joe Sakic	Colorado	60	28	53	81	28
Steve Yzerman	Detroit	78	35	44	79	34

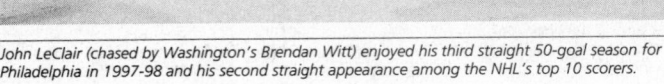

John LeClair (chased by Washington's Brendan Witt) enjoyed his third straight 50-goal season for Philadelphia in 1997-98 and his second straight appearance among the NHL's top 10 scorers.

Then with Ottawa, Alexei Yashin finished sixth in scoring in 1998-99. His 44 goals, 50 assists and 94 points remain career highs.

2000-01

EASTERN CONFERENCE
Northeast Division

Team	GP	W	L	T	OTL	GF	GA	PTS
Ottawa	82	48	21	9	4	274	205	109
Buffalo	82	46	30	5	1	218	184	98
Toronto	82	37	29	11	5	232	207	90
Boston	82	36	30	8	8	227	249	88
Montreal	82	28	40	8	6	206	232	70

Atlantic Division

Team	GP	W	L	T	OTL	GF	GA	PTS
New Jersey	82	48	19	12	3	295	195	111
Philadelphia	82	43	25	11	3	240	207	100
Pittsburgh	82	42	28	9	3	281	256	96
NY Rangers	82	33	43	5	1	250	290	72
NY Islanders	82	21	51	7	3	185	268	52

Southeast Division

Team	GP	W	L	T	OTL	GF	GA	PTS
Washington	82	41	27	10	4	233	211	96
Carolina	82	38	32	9	3	212	225	88
Florida	82	22	38	13	9	200	246	66
Atlanta	82	23	45	12	2	211	289	60
Tampa Bay	82	24	47	6	5	201	280	59

WESTERN CONFERENCE
Central Division

Team	GP	W	L	T	OTL	GF	GA	PTS
Detroit	82	49	20	9	4	253	202	111
St. Louis	82	43	22	12	5	249	195	103
Nashville	82	34	36	9	3	186	200	80
Chicago	82	29	40	8	5	210	246	71
Columbus	82	28	39	9	6	190	233	71

Pacific Division

Team	GP	W	L	T	OTL	GF	GA	PTS
Dallas	82	48	24	8	2	241	187	106
San Jose	82	40	27	12	3	217	192	95
Los Angeles	82	38	28	13	3	252	228	92
Phoenix	82	35	27	17	3	214	212	90
Anaheim	82	25	41	11	5	188	245	66

Northwest Division

Team	GP	W	L	T	OTL	GF	GA	PTS
*Colorado	82	52	16	10	4	270	192	118
Edmonton	82	39	28	12	3	243	222	93
Vancouver	82	36	28	11	7	239	238	90
Calgary	82	27	36	15	4	197	236	73
Minnesota	82	25	39	13	5	168	210	68

Leading Scorers

Player	Club	GP	G	A	PTS	PIM
Jaromir Jagr	Pittsburgh	81	52	69	121	42
Joe Sakic	Colorado	82	54	64	118	30
Patrik Elias	New Jersey	82	40	56	96	51
Alex Kovalev	Pittsburgh	79	44	51	95	96
Jason Allison	Boston	82	36	59	95	85
Martin Straka	Pittsburgh	82	27	68	95	38
Pavel Bure	Florida	82	59	33	92	58
Doug Weight	Edmonton	82	25	65	90	91
Ziggy Palffy	Los Angeles	73	38	51	89	20
Peter Forsberg	Colorado	73	27	62	89	54

2001-02

EASTERN CONFERENCE
Northeast Division

Team	GP	W	L	T	OTL	GF	GA	PTS
Boston	82	43	24	6	9	236	201	101
Toronto	82	43	25	10	4	249	207	100
Ottawa	82	39	27	9	7	243	208	94
Montreal	82	36	31	12	3	207	209	87
Buffalo	82	35	35	11	1	213	200	82

Atlantic Division

Team	GP	W	L	T	OTL	GF	GA	PTS
Philadelphia	82	42	27	10	3	234	192	97
NY Islanders	82	42	28	8	4	239	220	96
New Jersey	82	41	28	9	4	205	187	95
NY Rangers	82	36	38	4	4	227	258	80
Pittsburgh	82	28	41	8	5	198	249	69

Southeast Division

Team	GP	W	L	T	OTL	GF	GA	PTS
Carolina	82	35	26	16	5	217	217	91
Washington	82	36	33	11	2	228	240	85
Tampa Bay	82	27	40	11	4	178	219	69
Florida	82	22	44	10	6	180	250	60
Atlanta	82	19	47	11	5	187	288	54

WESTERN CONFERENCE
Central Division

Team	GP	W	L	T	OTL	GF	GA	PTS
*Detroit	82	51	17	10	4	251	187	116
St. Louis	82	43	27	8	4	227	188	98
Chicago	82	41	27	13	1	216	207	96
Nashville	82	28	41	13	0	196	230	69
Columbus	82	22	47	8	5	164	255	57

Pacific Division

Team	GP	W	L	T	OTL	GF	GA	PTS
San Jose	82	44	27	8	3	248	199	99
Phoenix	82	40	27	9	6	228	210	95
Los Angeles	82	40	27	11	4	214	190	95
Dallas	82	36	28	13	5	215	213	90
Anaheim	82	29	42	8	3	175	198	69

Northwest Division

Team	GP	W	L	T	OTL	GF	GA	PTS
Colorado	82	45	28	8	1	212	169	99
Vancouver	82	42	30	7	3	254	211	94
Edmonton	82	38	28	12	4	205	182	92
Calgary	82	32	35	12	3	201	220	79
Minnesota	82	26	35	12	9	195	238	73

Leading Scorers

Player	Club	GP	G	A	PTS	PIM
Jarome Iginla	Calgary	82	52	44	96	77
Markus Naslund	Vancouver	81	40	50	90	50
Todd Bertuzzi	Vancouver	72	36	49	85	110
Mats Sundin	Toronto	82	41	39	80	94
Jaromir Jagr	Washington	69	31	48	79	30
Joe Sakic	Colorado	82	26	53	79	18
Pavol Demitra	St. Louis	82	35	43	78	46
Adam Oates	Wsh., Phi.	80	14	64	78	28
Mike Modano	Dallas	78	34	43	77	38
Ron Francis	Carolina	80	27	50	77	18

2002-03

EASTERN CONFERENCE
Northeast Division

Team	GP	W	L	T	OTL	GF	GA	PTS
Ottawa	82	52	21	8	1	263	182	113
Toronto	82	44	28	7	3	236	208	98
Boston	82	36	31	11	4	245	237	87
Montreal	82	30	35	8	9	206	234	77
Buffalo	82	27	37	10	8	190	219	72

Atlantic Division

Team	GP	W	L	T	OTL	GF	GA	PTS
*New Jersey	82	46	20	10	6	216	166	108
Philadelphia	82	45	20	13	4	211	166	107
NY Islanders	82	35	34	11	2	224	231	83
NY Rangers	82	32	36	10	4	210	231	78
Pittsburgh	82	27	44	6	5	189	255	65

Southeast Division

Team	GP	W	L	T	OTL	GF	GA	PTS
Tampa Bay	82	36	25	16	5	219	210	93
Washington	82	39	29	8	6	224	220	92
Atlanta	82	31	39	7	5	226	284	74
Florida	82	24	36	13	9	176	237	70
Carolina	82	22	43	11	6	171	240	61

WESTERN CONFERENCE
Central Division

Team	GP	W	L	T	OTL	GF	GA	PTS
Detroit	82	48	20	10	4	269	203	110
St. Louis	82	41	24	11	6	253	222	99
Chicago	82	30	33	13	6	207	226	79
Nashville	82	27	35	13	7	183	206	74
Columbus	82	29	42	8	3	213	263	69

Pacific Division

Team	GP	W	L	T	OTL	GF	GA	PTS
Dallas	82	46	17	15	4	245	169	111
Anaheim	82	40	27	9	6	203	193	95
Los Angeles	82	33	37	6	6	203	221	78
Phoenix	82	31	35	11	5	204	230	78
San Jose	82	28	37	9	8	214	239	73

Northwest Division

Team	GP	W	L	T	OTL	GF	GA	PTS
Colorado	82	42	19	13	8	251	194	105
Vancouver	82	45	23	13	1	264	208	104
Minnesota	82	42	29	10	1	198	178	95
Edmonton	82	36	26	11	9	231	230	92
Calgary	82	29	36	13	4	186	228	75

Leading Scorers

Player	Club	GP	G	A	PTS	PIM
Peter Forsberg	Colorado	75	29	77	106	70
Markus Naslund	Vancouver	82	48	56	104	52
Joe Thornton	Boston	77	36	65	101	109
Milan Hejduk	Colorado	82	50	48	98	52
Todd Bertuzzi	Vancouver	82	46	51	97	144
Pavol Demitra	St. Louis	78	36	57	93	32
Glen Murray	Boston	82	44	48	92	64
Mario Lemieux	Pittsburgh	67	28	63	91	43
Danny Heatley	Atlanta	77	41	48	89	58
Ziggy Palffy	Los Angeles	76	37	48	85	47
Mike Modano	Dallas	79	28	57	85	30

With 41 goals and 39 assists, Mats Sundin finished fourth in the NHL in scoring in 2001-02, the highest finish of his career.

Ziggy Palffy made two appearances among the NHL's top 10 scorers with Los Angeles. He had also finished in the top ten on two previous occasions while with the Islanders.

2003-04
EASTERN CONFERENCE
Northeast Division

Team	GP	W	L	T	OTL	GF	GA	PTS
Boston	82	41	19	15	7	209	188	104
Toronto	82	45	24	10	3	242	204	103
Ottawa	82	43	23	10	6	262	189	102
Montreal	82	41	30	7	4	208	192	93
Buffalo	82	37	34	7	4	220	221	85

Atlantic Division

Team	GP	W	L	T	OTL	GF	GA	PTS
Philadelphia	82	40	21	15	6	229	186	101
New Jersey	82	43	25	12	2	213	164	100
NY Islanders	82	38	29	11	4	237	210	91
NY Rangers	82	27	40	7	8	206	250	69
Pittsburgh	82	23	47	8	4	190	303	58

Southeast Division

Team	GP	W	L	T	OTL	GF	GA	PTS
*Tampa Bay	82	46	22	8	6	245	192	106
Atlanta	82	33	37	8	4	214	243	78
Carolina	82	28	34	14	6	172	209	76
Florida	82	28	35	15	4	188	221	75
Washington	82	23	46	10	3	186	253	59

WESTERN CONFERENCE
Central Division

Team	GP	W	L	T	OTL	GF	GA	PTS
Detroit	82	48	21	11	2	255	189	109
St. Louis	82	39	30	11	2	191	198	91
Nashville	82	38	29	11	4	216	217	91
Columbus	82	25	45	8	4	177	238	62
Chicago	82	20	43	11	8	188	259	59

Pacific Division

Team	GP	W	L	T	OTL	GF	GA	PTS
San Jose	82	43	21	12	6	219	183	104
Dallas	82	41	26	13	2	194	175	97
Los Angeles	82	28	29	16	9	205	217	81
Anaheim	82	29	35	10	8	184	213	76
Phoenix	82	22	36	18	6	188	245	68

Northwest Division

Team	GP	W	L	T	OTL	GF	GA	PTS
Vancouver	82	43	24	10	5	235	194	101
Colorado	82	40	22	13	7	236	198	100
Calgary	82	42	30	7	3	200	176	94
Edmonton	82	36	29	12	5	221	208	89
Minnesota	82	30	29	20	3	188	183	83

Leading Scorers

Player	Club	GP	G	A	PTS	PIM
Martin St. Louis	Tampa Bay	82	38	56	94	24
Ilya Kovalchuk	Atlanta	81	41	46	87	63
Joe Sakic	Colorado	81	33	54	87	42
Markus Naslund	Vancouver	78	35	49	84	58
Marian Hossa	Ottawa	81	36	46	82	46
Patrik Elias	New Jersey	82	38	43	81	44
Daniel Alfredsson	Ottawa	77	32	48	80	24
Cory Stillman	Tampa Bay	81	25	55	80	36
Robert Lang	Wsh., Det.	69	30	49	79	24
Brad Richards	Tampa Bay	82	26	53	79	12
Alex Tanguay	Colorado	69	25	54	79	42

2004-05
SEASON CANCELLED

2005-06
EASTERN CONFERENCE
Northeast Division

Team	GP	W	L	OTL	GF	GA	PTS
Ottawa	82	52	21	9	314	211	113
Buffalo	82	52	24	6	281	239	110
Montreal	82	42	31	9	243	247	93
Toronto	82	41	33	8	257	270	90
Boston	82	29	37	16	230	266	74

Atlantic Division

Team	GP	W	L	OTL	GF	GA	PTS
New Jersey	82	46	27	9	242	229	101
Philadelphia	82	45	26	11	267	259	101
NY Rangers	82	44	26	12	257	215	100
NY Islanders	82	36	40	6	230	278	78
Pittsburgh	82	22	46	14	244	316	58

Southeast Division

Team	GP	W	L	OTL	GF	GA	PTS
*Carolina	82	52	22	8	294	260	112
Tampa Bay	82	43	33	6	252	260	92
Atlanta	82	41	33	8	281	275	90
Florida	82	37	34	11	240	257	85
Washington	82	29	41	12	237	306	70

WESTERN CONFERENCE
Central Division

Team	GP	W	L	OTL	GF	GA	PTS
Detroit	82	58	16	8	305	209	124
Nashville	82	49	25	8	259	227	106
Columbus	82	35	43	4	223	279	74
Chicago	82	26	43	13	211	285	65
St. Louis	82	21	46	15	197	292	57

Pacific Division

Team	GP	W	L	OTL	GF	GA	PTS
Dallas	82	53	23	6	265	218	112
San Jose	82	44	27	11	266	242	99
Anaheim	82	43	27	12	254	229	98
Los Angeles	82	42	35	5	249	270	89
Phoenix	82	38	39	5	246	271	81

Northwest Division

Team	GP	W	L	OTL	GF	GA	PTS
Calgary	82	46	25	11	218	200	103
Colorado	82	43	30	9	283	257	95
Edmonton	82	41	28	13	256	251	95
Vancouver	82	42	32	8	256	255	92
Minnesota	82	38	36	8	231	215	84

Leading Scorers

Player	Club	GP	G	A	PTS	PIM
Joe Thornton	Bos., S.J.	81	29	96	125	61
Jaromir Jagr	NY Rangers	82	54	69	123	72
Alex Ovechkin	Washington	81	52	54	106	52
Dany Heatley	Ottawa	82	50	53	103	86
Daniel Alfredsson	Ottawa	77	43	60	103	50
Sidney Crosby	Pittsburgh	81	39	63	102	110
Eric Staal	Carolina	82	45	55	100	81
Ilya Kovalchuk	Atlanta	78	52	46	98	68
Marc Savard	Atlanta	82	28	69	97	100
Jonathan Cheechoo	San Jose	82	56	37	93	58

> **Note:** Detailed statistics for 2005-06 are listed in the Final Statistics, 2005-06 section of the *NHL Guide & Record Book*. **See page 135.**

The 2003-04 season marked the third straight year that Markus Naslund (above) finished among the NHL's top 10 scorers. His 84 points (35 goals, 49 assists) were 10 less than the league-leading total of Martin St. Louis (below). St. Louis won the Hart Trophy in addition to the Art Ross and helped lead Tampa Bay to its first Stanley Cup title.

Jaromir Jagr (far left) was a close second in the NHL scoring race last season. He had not appeared in the top 10 since winning the scoring title four years in a row through 2000-01. Marc Savard (left) was a two-time scoring champion with the OHL's Oshawa Generals. He cracked the top 10 in the NHL for the first time with Atlanta in 2005-06.

Team Records
Regular Season

FINAL STANDINGS

MOST POINTS, ONE SEASON:
   132 – Montreal Canadiens, 1976-77. 60w-8L-12T. 80GP
   131 – Detroit Red Wings, 1995-96. 62w-13L-7T. 82GP
   129 – Montreal Canadiens, 1977-78. 59w-10L-11T. 80GP

BEST POINTS PERCENTAGE, ONE SEASON:
   .875 – Boston Bruins, 1929-30. 38w-5L-1T. 77PTS in 44GP
   .830 – Montreal Canadiens, 1943-44. 38w-5L-7T. 83PTS in 50GP
   .825 – Montreal Canadiens, 1976-77. 60w-8L-12T. 132PTS in 80GP
   .806 – Montreal Canadiens, 1977-78. 59w-10L-11T. 129PTS in 80GP
   .800 – Montreal Canadiens, 1944-45. 38w-8L-4T. 80PTS in 50GP

FEWEST POINTS, ONE SEASON:
   8 – Quebec Bulldogs, 1919-20. 4w-20L-0T. 24GP
   10 – Toronto Arenas, 1918-19. 5w-13L-0T. 18GP
   12 – Hamilton Tigers, 1920-21. 6w-18L-0T. 24GP
     – Hamilton Tigers, 1922-23. 6w-18L-0T. 24GP
     – Boston Bruins, 1924-25. 6w-24L-0T. 30GP
     – Philadelphia Quakers, 1930-31. 4w-36L-4T. 44GP

FEWEST POINTS, ONE SEASON (MINIMUM 70-GAME SCHEDULE):
   21 – Washington Capitals, 1974-75. 8w-67L-5T. 80GP
   24 – Ottawa Senators, 1992-93. 10w-70L-4T. 84GP
     – San Jose Sharks, 1992-93. 11w-71L-2T. 84GP
   30 – New York Islanders, 1972-73. 12w-60L-6T. 78GP

WORST POINTS PERCENTAGE, ONE SEASON:
   .131 – Washington Capitals, 1974-75. 8w-67L-5T. 21PTS in 80GP
   .136 – Philadelphia Quakers, 1930-31. 4w-36L-4T. 12PTS in 44GP
   .143 – Ottawa Senators, 1992-93. 10w-70L-4T. 24PTS in 84GP
     – San Jose Sharks, 1992-93. 11w-71L-2T. 24PTS in 84GP
   .148 – Pittsburgh Pirates, 1929-30. 5w-36L-3T. 13PTS in 44GP

TEAM WINS

Most Wins

MOST WINS, ONE SEASON:
   62 – Detroit Red Wings, 1995-96. 82GP
   60 – Montreal Canadiens, 1976-77. 80GP
   59 – Montreal Canadiens, 1977-78. 80GP

MOST HOME WINS, ONE SEASON:
   36 – Philadelphia Flyers, 1975-76. 40GP
     – Detroit Red Wings, 1995-96. 41GP
   33 – Boston Bruins, 1970-71. 39GP
     – Boston Bruins, 1973-74. 39GP
     – Montreal Canadiens, 1976-77. 40GP
     – Philadelphia Flyers, 1976-77. 40GP
     – New York Islanders, 1981-82. 40GP
     – Philadelphia Flyers, 1985-86. 40GP

MOST ROAD WINS, ONE SEASON:
   31 – Detroit Red Wings, 2005-06. 41GP
   28 – New Jersey Devils, 1998-99. 41GP
   27 – Montreal Canadiens, 1976-77. 40GP
     – Montreal Canadiens, 1977-78. 40GP
     – St. Louis Blues, 1999-2000. 41GP
   26 – Boston Bruins, 1971-72. 39GP
     – Montreal Canadiens, 1975-76. 40GP
     – Edmonton Oilers, 1983-84. 40GP
     – Detroit Red Wings, 1995-96. 41GP

Fewest Wins

FEWEST WINS, ONE SEASON:
   4 – Quebec Bulldogs, 1919-20. 24GP
     – Philadelphia Quakers, 1930-31. 44GP
   5 – Toronto Arenas, 1918-19. 18GP
     Pittsburgh Pirates, 1929-30. 44GP

FEWEST WINS, ONE SEASON (MINIMUM 70-GAME SCHEDULE):
   8 – Washington Capitals, 1974-75. 80GP
   9 – Winnipeg Jets, 1980-81. 80GP
   10 – Ottawa Senators, 1992-93. 84GP

FEWEST HOME WINS, ONE SEASON:
   2 – Chicago Blackhawks, 1927-28. 22GP
   3 – Boston Bruins, 1924-25. 15GP
     – Chicago Blackhawks, 1928-29. 22GP
     – Philadelphia Quakers, 1930-31. 22GP

FEWEST HOME WINS, ONE SEASON (MINIMUM 70-GAME SCHEDULE):
   6 – Chicago Blackhawks, 1954-55. 35GP
     – Washington Capitals, 1975-76. 40GP
   7 – Boston Bruins, 1962-63. 35GP
     – Washington Capitals, 1974-75. 40GP
     – Winnipeg Jets, 1980-81. 40GP
     – Pittsburgh Penguins, 1983-84. 40GP

FEWEST ROAD WINS, ONE SEASON:
   0 – Toronto Arenas, 1918-19. 9GP
     – Quebec Bulldogs, 1919-20. 12GP
     – Pittsburgh Pirates, 1929-30. 22GP
   1 – Hamilton Tigers, 1921-22. 12GP
     – Toronto St. Patricks, 1925-26. 18GP
     – Philadelphia Quakers, 1930-31. 22GP
     – New York Americans, 1940-41. 24GP
     – Washington Capitals, 1974-75. 40GP
   * – Ottawa Senators, 1992-93. 41GP

FEWEST ROAD WINS, ONE SEASON (MINIMUM 70-GAME SCHEDULE):
   1 – Washington Capitals, 1974-75. 40GP
   * **– Ottawa Senators**, 1992-93. 41GP
   2 – Boston Bruins, 1960-61. 35GP
     – Los Angeles Kings, 1969-70. 38GP
     – New York Islanders, 1972-73. 39GP
     – California Golden Seals, 1973-74. 39GP
     – Colorado Rockies, 1977-78. 40GP
     – Winnipeg Jets, 1980-81. 40GP
     – Quebec Nordiques, 1991-92. 40GP

TEAM LOSSES

Fewest Losses

FEWEST LOSSES, ONE SEASON:
   5 – Ottawa Senators, 1919-20. 24GP
     – Boston Bruins, 1929-30. 44GP
     – Montreal Canadiens, 1943-44. 50GP

FEWEST HOME LOSSES, ONE SEASON:
   0 – Ottawa Senators, 1922-23. 12GP
     – Montreal Canadiens, 1943-44. 25GP
   1 – Toronto Arenas, 1917-18. 11GP
     – Ottawa Senators, 1918-19. 9GP
     – Ottawa Senators, 1919-20. 12GP
     – Toronto St. Patricks, 1922-23. 12GP
     – Boston Bruins, 1929-30. 22GP
     – Boston Bruins, 1930-31. 22GP
     – Montreal Canadiens, 1976-77. 40GP
     – Quebec Nordiques, 1994-95. 24GP

FEWEST ROAD LOSSES, ONE SEASON:
   3 – Montreal Canadiens, 1928-29. 22GP
   4 – Ottawa Senators, 1919-20. 12GP
     – Montreal Canadiens, 1927-28. 22GP
     – Boston Bruins, 1929-30. 20GP
     – Boston Bruins, 1940-41. 24GP

FEWEST LOSSES, ONE SEASON (MINIMUM 70-GAME SCHEDULE):
   8 – Montreal Canadiens, 1976-77. 80GP
   10 – Montreal Canadiens, 1972-73. 78GP
     – Montreal Canadiens, 1977-78. 80GP
   11 – Montreal Canadiens, 1975-76. 80GP

FEWEST HOME LOSSES, ONE SEASON (MINIMUM 70-GAME SCHEDULE):
   1 – Montreal Canadiens, 1976-77. 40GP
   2 – Montreal Canadiens, 1961-62. 35GP
     – New York Rangers, 1970-71. 39GP
     – Philadelphia Flyers, 1975-76. 40GP

FEWEST ROAD LOSSES, ONE SEASON (MINIMUM 70-GAME SCHEDULE):
   6 – Montreal Canadiens, 1972-73. 39GP
     – Montreal Canadiens, 1974-75. 40GP
     – Montreal Canadiens, 1977-78. 40GP
   7 – Detroit Red Wings, 1951-52. 35GP
     – Montreal Canadiens, 1976-77. 40GP
     – Philadelphia Flyers, 1979-80. 40GP
     – Boston Bruins, 2003-04. 41GP
     – Detroit Red Wings, 2005-06. 41GP

Most Losses

MOST LOSSES, ONE SEASON:
   71 – San Jose Sharks, 1992-93. 84GP
   70 – Ottawa Senators, 1992-93. 84GP
   67 – Washington Capitals, 1974-75. 80GP
   61 – Quebec Nordiques, 1989-90. 80GP
     – Ottawa Senators, 1993-94. 84GP

MOST HOME LOSSES, ONE SEASON:
   *32 – San Jose Sharks, 1992-93. 41GP
   29 – Pittsburgh Penguins, 1983-84. 40GP
   * – Ottawa Senators, 1993-94. 41GP

MOST ROAD LOSSES, ONE SEASON:
   *40 – Ottawa Senators, 1992-93. 41GP
   39 – Washington Capitals, 1974-75. 40GP
   37 – California Golden Seals, 1973-74. 39GP
   * – San Jose Sharks, 1992-93. 41GP

* – Does not include neutral site games

TEAM TIES

Most Ties

MOST TIES, ONE SEASON:
 24 – Philadelphia Flyers, 1969-70. 76GP
 23 – Montreal Canadiens, 1962-63. 70GP
  – Chicago Blackhawks, 1973-74. 78GP

MOST HOME TIES, ONE SEASON:
 13 – New York Rangers, 1954-55. 35GP
  – Philadelphia Flyers, 1969-70. 38GP
  – California Golden Seals, 1971-72. 39GP
  – California Golden Seals, 1972-73. 39GP
  – Chicago Blackhawks, 1973-74. 39GP

MOST ROAD TIES, ONE SEASON:
 15 – Philadelphia Flyers, 1976-77. 40GP
 14 – Montreal Canadiens, 1952-53. 35GP
  – Montreal Canadiens, 1974-75. 40GP
  – Philadelphia Flyers, 1975-76. 40GP

Fewest Ties

FEWEST TIES, ONE SEASON (Since 1926-27):
 1 – Boston Bruins, 1929-30. 44GP
 2 – Montreal Canadiens, 1926-27. 44GP
  – New York Americans, 1926-27. 44GP
  – Boston Bruins, 1938-39. 48GP
  – New York Rangers, 1941-42. 48GP
  – San Jose Sharks, 1992-93. 84GP

FEWEST TIES, ONE SEASON (MINIMUM 70-GAME SCHEDULE):
 2 – San Jose Sharks, 1992-93. 84GP
 3 – New Jersey Devils, 1985-86. 80GP
  – Calgary Flames, 1986-87. 80GP
  – Vancouver Canucks, 1993-94. 84GP

WINNING STREAKS

LONGEST WINNING STREAK, ONE SEASON:
 17 Games – Pittsburgh Penguins, Mar. 9 – Apr. 10, 1993.
 15 Games – New York Islanders, Jan. 21 – Feb. 20, 1982.
 14 Games – Boston Bruins, Dec. 3, 1929 – Jan. 9, 1930.

LONGEST HOME WINNING STREAK, ONE SEASON:
 20 Games – Boston Bruins, Dec. 3, 1929 – Mar. 18, 1930.
  – Philadelphia Flyers, Jan. 4 – Apr. 3, 1976.

LONGEST ROAD WINNING STREAK, ONE SEASON:
 12 Games – Detroit Red Wings, Mar.1 – Apr. 15, 2006.
 10 Games – Buffalo Sabres, Dec. 10, 1983 – Jan. 23, 1984.
  – St. Louis Blues, Jan. 21 – Mar. 2, 2000.
  – New Jersey Devils, Feb. 27 – Apr. 7, 2001.
 9 Games – Buffalo Sabres, Nov. 19 – Dec. 19, 2005.

LONGEST WINNING STREAK FROM START OF SEASON:
 10 Games – Toronto Maple Leafs, 1993-94.
 8 Games – Toronto Maple Leafs, 1934-35.
  – Buffalo Sabres, 1975-76.
  – Nashville Predators, 2005-06.
 7 Games – Edmonton Oilers, 1983-84.
  – Quebec Nordiques, 1985-86.
  – Pittsburgh Penguins, 1986-87.
  – Pittsburgh Penguins, 1994-95.

LONGEST HOME WINNING STREAK FROM START OF SEASON:
 11 Games – Chicago Blackhawks, 1963-64.
 10 Games – Ottawa Senators, 1925-26.
 9 Games – Montreal Canadiens, 1953-54.
  – Chicago Blackhawks, 1971-72.

LONGEST ROAD WINNING STREAK FROM START OF SEASON:
 7 Games – Toronto Maple Leafs, Nov. 14 – Dec. 15, 1940.
  – Philadelphia Flyers, Oct. 12 – Nov. 16, 1985.
  – Detroit Red Wings, Oct. 6 – Nov. 6, 2005.

LONGEST WINNING STREAK, INCLUDING PLAYOFFS:
 15 Games – Detroit Red Wings, Feb. 27 – Apr. 5, 1955.
  (9 regular-season games, 6 playoff games)
  – New Jersey Devils, Mar. 28 – Apr. 29, 2006.
  (11 regular-season games, 4 playoff games)

LONGEST HOME WINNING STREAK, INCLUDING PLAYOFFS:
 24 Games – Philadelphia Flyers, Jan. 4 – Apr. 25, 1976.
  (20 regular-season games, 4 playoff games)

LONGEST ROAD WINNING STREAK, INCLUDING PLAYOFFS:
 11 Games – New Jersey Devils, Feb. 27 – Apr. 17, 2001.
  (10 regular-season games, 1 playoff game)

UNDEFEATED STREAKS

LONGEST UNDEFEATED STREAK, ONE SEASON:
 35 Games – Philadelphia Flyers, Oct. 14, 1979 – Jan. 6, 1980. 25w-10T
 28 Games – Montreal Canadiens, Dec. 18, 1977 – Feb. 23, 1978. 23w-5T

LONGEST HOME UNDEFEATED STREAK, ONE SEASON:
 34 Games – Montreal Canadiens, Nov. 1, 1976 – Apr. 2, 1977. 28w-6T
 27 Games – Boston Bruins, Nov. 22, 1970 – Mar. 20, 1971. 26w-1T

LONGEST ROAD UNDEFEATED STREAK, ONE SEASON:
 23 Games – Montreal Canadiens, Nov. 27, 1974 – Mar. 12, 1975. 14w-9T
 17 Games – Montreal Canadiens, Dec. 18, 1977 – Mar. 1, 1978. 14w-3T

LONGEST UNDEFEATED STREAK FROM START OF SEASON:
 15 Games – Edmonton Oilers, 1984-85. 12w-3T
 14 Games – Montreal Canadiens, 1943-44. 11w-3T

LONGEST HOME UNDEFEATED STREAK FROM START OF SEASON:
 26 Games – Philadelphia Flyers, Oct. 11, 1979 – Feb. 3, 1980. 19w-7T

LONGEST ROAD UNDEFEATED STREAK FROM START OF SEASON:
 15 Games – Detroit Red Wings, Oct. 18 – Dec. 20, 1951. 10w-5T

LONGEST UNDEFEATED STREAK, INCLUDING PLAYOFFS:
 21 Games – Pittsburgh Penguins, Mar. 9 – Apr. 22, 1993.
  17w-1T in regular season and 3w in playoffs.

LONGEST HOME UNDEFEATED STREAK, INCLUDING PLAYOFFS:
 38 Games – Montreal Canadiens, Nov. 1, 1976 – Apr. 26, 1977.
  28w-6T in regular season and 4w in playoffs.

LONGEST ROAD UNDEFEATED STREAK, INCLUDING PLAYOFFS:
 13 Games – Philadelphia Flyers, Feb. 26 – Apr. 21, 1977. 6w-4T in
  regular season and 3w in playoffs.
  – Montreal Canadiens, Feb. 26 – Apr. 20, 1980. 6w-4T in
  regular season and 3w in playoffs.
  – New York Islanders, Mar. 16 – May 1, 1980. 3w-3T in regular
  season and 7w in playoffs.

LOSING STREAKS

LONGEST LOSING STREAK, ONE SEASON:
 17 Games – Washington Capitals, Feb. 18 – Mar. 26, 1975.
  – San Jose Sharks, Jan. 4 – Feb. 12, 1993.
 15 Games – Philadelphia Quakers, Nov. 29, 1930 – Jan. 8, 1931.

LONGEST HOME LOSING STREAK, ONE SEASON:
 14 Games – Pittsburgh Penguins, Dec. 31, 2003 – Feb. 22, 2004.
 11 Games – Boston Bruins, Dec. 8, 1924 – Feb. 17, 1925.
  – Washington Capitals, Feb. 18 – Mar. 30, 1975.
  – Ottawa Senators, Oct. 27 – Dec. 8, 1993.
  – Atlanta Thrashers, Jan. 24 – Mar. 16, 2000.

LONGEST ROAD LOSING STREAK, ONE SEASON:
 *38 Games – Ottawa Senators, Oct. 10, 1992 – Apr. 3, 1993.
 37 Games – Washington Capitals, Oct. 9, 1974 – Mar. 26, 1975.

LONGEST LOSING STREAK FROM START OF SEASON:
 11 Games – New York Rangers, 1943-44.
 7 Games – Montreal Canadiens, 1938-39.
  – Chicago Blackhawks, 1947-48.
  – Washington Capitals, 1983-84.
  – Chicago Blackhawks, 1997-98.

LONGEST HOME LOSING STREAK FROM START OF SEASON:
 8 Games – Los Angeles Kings, Oct. 13 – Nov. 6, 1971.

LONGEST ROAD LOSING STREAK FROM START OF SEASON:
 *38 Games – Ottawa Senators, Oct. 10, 1992 – Apr. 3, 1993.

WINLESS STREAKS

LONGEST WINLESS STREAK, ONE SEASON:
 30 Games – Winnipeg Jets, Oct. 19 – Dec. 20, 1980. 23L-7T
 27 Games – Kansas City Scouts, Feb. 12 – Apr. 4, 1976. 21L-6T
 25 Games – Washington Capitals, Nov. 29, 1975 – Jan. 21, 1976. 22L-3T

LONGEST HOME WINLESS STREAK, ONE SEASON:
 17 Games – Ottawa Senators, Oct. 28, 1995 – Jan. 27, 1996. 15L-2T
  – Atlanta Thrashers, Jan. 19 – Mar. 29, 2000. 15L-2T
 16 Games – Pittsburgh Penguins, Dec. 31, 2003 – Mar. 4, 2004. 15L-1T

LONGEST ROAD WINLESS STREAK, ONE SEASON:
 *38 Games – Ottawa Senators, Oct. 10, 1992 – Apr. 3, 1993. 38L
 37 Games – Washington Capitals, Oct. 9, 1974 – Mar. 26, 1975. 37L

LONGEST WINLESS STREAK FROM START OF SEASON:
 15 Games – New York Rangers, 1943-44. 14L-1T
 11 Games – Pittsburgh Pirates, 1927-28. 8L-3T
  – Minnesota North Stars, 1973-74. 5L-6T
  – San Jose Sharks, 1995-96. 7L-4T

LONGEST HOME WINLESS STREAK FROM START OF SEASON:
 11 Games – Pittsburgh Penguins, Oct. 8 – Nov. 19, 1983. 9L-2T

LONGEST ROAD WINLESS STREAK FROM START OF SEASON:
 *38 Games – Ottawa Senators, Oct. 10, 1992 – Apr. 3, 1993. 38L

NON-SHUTOUT STREAKS

LONGEST NON-SHUTOUT STREAK:
  264 Games – Calgary Flames, Nov. 12, 1981 – Jan. 9, 1985.
  261 Games – Los Angeles Kings, Mar. 15, 1986 – Oct. 22, 1989.
  244 Games – Washington Capitals, Oct. 31, 1989 – Nov. 11, 1993.
  236 Games – New York Rangers, Dec. 20, 1989 – Dec. 13, 1992.
  230 Games – Quebec Nordiques, Feb. 10, 1980 – Jan. 12, 1983.

LONGEST NON-SHUTOUT STREAK, INCLUDING PLAYOFFS:
  264 Games – Los Angeles Kings, Mar. 15, 1986 – Apr. 6, 1989.
    (5 playoff games in 1987; 5 in 1988; 2 in 1989).
  262 Games – Chicago Blackhawks, Mar. 14, 1970 – Feb. 21, 1973.
    (8 playoff games in 1970; 18 in 1971; 8 in 1972).
  251 Games – Quebec Nordiques, Feb. 10, 1980 – Jan. 12, 1983.
    (5 playoff games in 1981; 16 in 1982).
  246 Games – Pittsburgh Penguins, Jan. 7, 1989 – Oct. 26, 1991.
    (11 playoff games in 1989; 24 in 1991).

TEAM GOALS

Most Goals

MOST GOALS, ONE SEASON:
  446 – Edmonton Oilers, 1983-84. 80GP
  426 – Edmonton Oilers, 1985-86. 80GP
  424 – Edmonton Oilers, 1982-83. 80GP
  417 – Edmonton Oilers, 1981-82. 80GP
  401 – Edmonton Oilers, 1984-85. 80GP

MOST GOALS, ONE TEAM, ONE GAME:
  16 – Montreal Canadiens, Mar. 3, 1920, at Quebec. Montreal won 16-3.

MOST GOALS, BOTH TEAMS, ONE GAME:
  21 – Montreal Canadiens (14), Toronto St. Patricks (7), Jan. 10, 1920,
    at Montreal.
    – **Edmonton Oilers (12), Chicago Blackhawks (9)**, Dec. 11, 1985,
    at Chicago.
  20 – Edmonton Oilers (12), Minnesota North Stars (8), Jan. 4, 1984,
    at Edmonton.
    – Toronto Maple Leafs (11), Edmonton Oilers (9), Jan. 8, 1986,
    at Toronto.
  19 – Montreal Wanderers (10), Toronto Arenas (9), Dec. 19, 1917,
    at Montreal.
    – Montreal Canadiens (16), Quebec Bulldogs (3), Mar. 3, 1920,
    at Quebec.
    – Montreal Canadiens (13), Hamilton Tigers (6), Feb. 26, 1921,
    at Montreal.
    – Boston Bruins (10), New York Rangers (9), Mar. 4, 1944, at Boston.
    – Detroit Red Wings (10), Boston Bruins (9), Mar. 16, 1944, at Detroit.
    – Vancouver Canucks (10), Minnesota North Stars (9), Oct. 7, 1983,
    at Vancouver.

MOST GOALS, ONE TEAM, ONE PERIOD:
  9 – Buffalo Sabres, Mar. 19, 1981, at Buffalo, second period during
    14-4 win over Toronto.
  8 – Detroit Red Wings, Jan. 23, 1944, at Detroit, third period during
    15-0 over NY Rangers.
    – Boston Bruins, Mar. 16, 1969, at Boston, second period during
    11-3 win over Toronto.
    – New York Rangers, Nov. 21, 1971, at NY Rangers, third period during
    12-1 win over California.
    – Philadelphia Flyers, Mar. 31, 1973, at Philadelphia, second period
    during 10-2 win over NY Islanders.
    – Buffalo Sabres, Dec. 21, 1975, at Buffalo, third period during
    14-2 win over Washington.
    – Minnesota North Stars, Nov. 11, 1981, at Minnesota, second
    period during 15-2 win over Winnipeg.
    – Pittsburgh Penguins, Dec. 17, 1991, at Pittsburgh, second period
    during 10-2 win over San Jose.
    – Washington Capitals, Feb. 3, 1999, at Washington, second period
    during 10-1 win over Tampa Bay.

MOST GOALS, BOTH TEAMS, ONE PERIOD:
  12 – Buffalo Sabres (9), Toronto Maple Leafs (3), Mar. 19, 1981,
    at Buffalo, second period. Buffalo won 14-4.
    – **Edmonton Oilers (6), Chicago Blackhawks (6)**, Dec. 11, 1985,
    at Chicago, second period. Edmonton won 12-9.
  10 – New York Rangers (7), New York Americans (3), Mar. 16, 1939, at
    NY Rangers, third period. NY Rangers won 11-5.
    – Toronto Maple Leafs (6), Detroit Red Wings (4), Mar. 17, 1946,
    at Detroit, third period. Toronto won 11-7.
    – Buffalo Sabres (6), Vancouver Canucks (4), Jan. 8, 1976,
    at Buffalo, third period. Buffalo won 8-5.
    – Buffalo Sabres (5), Montreal Canadiens (5), Oct. 26, 1982,
    at Montreal, first period. Teams tied 7-7.
    – Quebec Nordiques (6), Boston Bruins (4), Dec. 7, 1982,
    at Quebec, second period. Quebec won 10-5.
    – Vancouver Canucks (6), Calgary Flames (4), Jan. 16, 1987,
    at Vancouver, first period. Vancouver won 9-5.
    – Detroit Red Wings (7), Winnipeg Jets (3), Nov. 25, 1987,
    at Detroit, third period. Detroit won 10-8.
    – Chicago Blackhawks (5), St. Louis Blues (5), Mar. 15, 1988,
    at St. Louis, third period. Teams tied 7-7.

MOST CONSECUTIVE GOALS, ONE TEAM, ONE GAME:
  15 – Detroit Red Wings, Jan. 23, 1944, at Detroit during 15-0 win over
    NY Rangers.

Fewest Goals

FEWEST GOALS, ONE SEASON:
  33 – Chicago Blackhawks, 1928-29. 44GP
  45 – Montreal Maroons, 1924-25. 30GP
  46 – Pittsburgh Pirates, 1928-29. 44GP

FEWEST GOALS, ONE SEASON (MINIMUM 70-GAME SCHEDULE):
  133 – Chicago Blackhawks, 1953-54. 70GP
  147 – Toronto Maple Leafs, 1954-55. 70GP
    – Boston Bruins, 1955-56. 70GP
  150 – New York Rangers, 1954-55. 70GP

TEAM POWER-PLAY GOALS

MOST POWER-PLAY GOALS, ONE SEASON:
  119 – Pittsburgh Penguins, 1988-89. 80GP
  113 – Detroit Red Wings, 1992-93. 84GP
  111 – New York Rangers, 1987-88. 80GP
  110 – Pittsburgh Penguins, 1987-88. 80GP
    – Winnipeg Jets, 1987-88. 80GP

TEAM SHORTHAND GOALS

MOST SHORTHAND GOALS, ONE SEASON:
  36 – Edmonton Oilers, 1983-84. 80GP
  28 – Edmonton Oilers, 1986-87. 80GP
  27 – Edmonton Oilers, 1985-86. 80GP
    – Edmonton Oilers, 1988-89. 80GP

TEAM GOALS-PER-GAME

HIGHEST GOALS-PER-GAME AVERAGE, ONE SEASON:
  5.58 – Edmonton Oilers, 1983-84. 446G in 80GP.
  5.38 – Montreal Canadiens, 1919-20. 129G in 24GP.
  5.33 – Edmonton Oilers, 1985-86. 426G in 80GP.
  5.30 – Edmonton Oilers, 1982-83. 424G in 80GP.
  5.23 – Montreal Canadiens, 1917-18. 115G in 22GP.

LOWEST GOALS-PER-GAME AVERAGE, ONE SEASON:
  0.75 – Chicago Blackhawks, 1928-29. 33G in 44GP.
  1.05 – Pittsburgh Pirates, 1928-29. 46G in 44GP.
  1.20 – New York Americans, 1928-29. 53G in 44GP.

TEAM ASSISTS

MOST ASSISTS, ONE SEASON:
  737 – Edmonton Oilers, 1985-86. 80GP
  736 – Edmonton Oilers, 1983-84. 80GP
  706 – Edmonton Oilers, 1981-82. 80GP

FEWEST ASSISTS, ONE SEASON (Since 1926-27):
  45 – New York Rangers, 1926-27. 44GP

FEWEST ASSISTS, ONE SEASON (MINIMUM 70-GAME SCHEDULE):
  206 – Chicago Blackhawks, 1953-54. 70GP

TEAM TOTAL POINTS

MOST SCORING POINTS, ONE SEASON:
  1,182 – Edmonton Oilers, 1983-84. 80GP
  1,163 – Edmonton Oilers, 1985-86. 80GP
  1,123 – Edmonton Oilers, 1981-82. 80GP

MOST SCORING POINTS, ONE TEAM, ONE GAME:
  40 – Buffalo Sabres, Dec. 21, 1975, at Buffalo.
    Buffalo defeated Washington 14-2, and had 26A.
  39 – Minnesota North Stars, Nov. 11, 1981, at Minnesota.
    Minnesota defeated Winnipeg 15-2, and had 24A.
  37 – Detroit Red Wings, Jan. 23, 1944, at Detroit.
    Detroit defeated NY Rangers 15-0, and had 22A.
    – Toronto Maple Leafs, Mar. 16, 1957, at Toronto.
    Toronto defeated NY Rangers 14-1, and had 23A.
    – Buffalo Sabres, Feb. 25, 1978, at Cleveland.
    Buffalo defeated Cleveland 13-3, and had 24A.
    – Calgary Flames, Feb. 10, 1993, at Calgary.
    Calgary defeated San Jose 13-1, and had 24A.

MOST SCORING POINTS, BOTH TEAMS, ONE GAME:
  62 – Edmonton Oilers, Chicago Blackhawks, Dec. 11, 1985, at Chicago.
    Edmonton won 12-9. Edmonton had 24A, Chicago, 17A.
  53 – Quebec Nordiques, Washington Capitals, Feb. 22, 1981, at Washington.
    Quebec won 11-7. Quebec had 22A, Washington, 13A.
    – Edmonton Oilers, Minnesota North Stars, Jan. 4, 1984, at Edmonton.
    Edmonton had 20A, Minnesota, 13A.
    – Minnesota North Stars, St. Louis Blues, Jan. 27, 1984, at St. Louis.
    Minnesota won 10-8. Minnesota had 19A, St. Louis, 16A.
    – Toronto Maple Leafs, Edmonton Oilers, Jan. 8, 1986, at Toronto.
    Toronto won 11-9. Toronto had 17A, Edmonton, 16A.
  52 – Montreal Maroons, New York Americans, Feb. 18, 1936, at
    NY Americans. Teams tied 8-8. NY Americans had 20A, Montreal, 16A.
    (3A allowed for each goal.)
    – Vancouver Canucks, Minnesota North Stars, Oct. 7, 1983, at Vancouver.
    Vancouver won 10-9. Vancouver had 16A, Minnesota, 17A.

MOST SCORING POINTS, ONE TEAM, ONE PERIOD:
23 – New York Rangers, Nov. 21, 1971, at NY Rangers, third period during 12-1 win over California. NY Rangers had 8G, 15A.
– **Buffalo Sabres**, Dec. 21, 1975, at Buffalo, third period during 14-2 win over Washington. Buffalo had 8G, 15A.
– **Buffalo Sabres**, Mar. 19, 1981, at Buffalo, second period during 14-4 win over Toronto. Buffalo had 9G, 14A.
22 – Detroit Red Wings, Jan. 23, 1944, at Detroit, third period during 15-0 win over NY Rangers. Detroit had 8G, 14A.
– Boston Bruins, Mar. 16, 1969, at Boston, second period during 11-3 win over Toronto. Boston had 8G, 14A.
– Minnesota North Stars, Nov. 11, 1981, at Minnesota, second period during 15-2 win over Winnipeg. Minnesota had 8G, 14A.
– Pittsburgh Penguins, Dec. 17, 1991, at Pittsburgh, second period during 10-2 win over San Jose. Pittsburgh had 8G, 14A.
– Washington Capitals, Feb. 3, 1999, at Washington, second period during 10-1 win over Tampa Bay. Washington had 8G, 14A.

MOST SCORING POINTS, BOTH TEAMS, ONE PERIOD:
35 – Edmonton, Oilers, Chicago Blackhawks, Dec. 11, 1985, at Chicago, second period. Edmonton won 12-9. Edmonton had 6G, 12A; Chicago, 6G, 11A.
31 – Buffalo Sabres, Toronto Maple Leafs, Mar. 19, 1981, at Buffalo, second period. Buffalo won 14-4. Buffalo had 9G, 14A; Toronto, 3G, 5A.
29 – Winnipeg Jets, Detroit Red Wings, Nov. 25, 1987, at Detroit, third period. Detroit won 10-8. Detroit had 7G, 13A; Winnipeg, 3G, 6A.
– Chicago Blackhawks, St. Louis Blues, Mar. 15, 1988, at St. Louis, third period. Teams tied 7-7. St. Louis had 5G, 10A; Chicago, 5G, 9A.

FASTEST GOALS

FASTEST SIX GOALS, BOTH TEAMS:
3:00 – Quebec Nordiques, Washington Capitals, Feb. 22, 1981, at Washington. Scorers: Peter Stastny, Quebec, 18:51; Pierre Lacroix, Quebec, 19:57 (first period); Anton Stastny, Quebec, 0:34; Jacques Richard, Quebec, 1:07 and 1:37; Rick Green, Washington, 1:51 (second period). Quebec won 11-7.
3:15 – Montreal Canadiens, Toronto Maple Leafs, Jan. 4, 1944, at Montreal, first period. Scorers: Maurice Richard, Montreal, 14:10; Don Webster, Toronto, 15:13; Fern Majeau, Montreal, 15:41; Phil Watson, Montreal, 15:52; Lorne Carr, Toronto, 16:55; Butch Bouchard, Montreal, 17:25. Montreal won 6-3.

FASTEST FIVE GOALS, BOTH TEAMS:
1:24 – Chicago Blackhawks, Toronto Maple Leafs, Oct. 15, 1983, at Toronto, second period. Scorers: Gaston Gingras, Toronto, 16:49; Denis Savard, Chicago, 17:12; Steve Larmer, Chicago, 17:27; Denis Savard, Chicago, 17:42; John Anderson, Toronto, 18:13. Toronto won 10-8.
1:39 – Detroit Red Wings, Toronto Maple Leafs, Nov. 15, 1944, at Toronto, third period. Scorers: Ted Kennedy, Toronto, 10:36 and 10:55; Harold Jackson, Detroit, 11:48; Steve Wojciechowski, Detroit, 12:02; Don Grosso, Detroit, 12:15. Detroit won 8-4.

FASTEST FIVE GOALS, ONE TEAM:
2:07 – Pittsburgh Penguins, Nov. 22, 1972, at Pittsburgh, third period. Scorers: Bryan Hextall, Jr., 12:00; Jean Pronovost, 12:18; Al McDonough, 13:40; Ken Schinkel, 13:49; Ron Schock, 14:07. Pittsburgh defeated St. Louis 10-4.
2:37 – New York Islanders, Jan. 26, 1982, at NY Islanders, first period. Scorers: Duane Sutter, 1:31; John Tonelli, 2:30; Bryan Trottier, 2:46 and 3:31; Duane Sutter, 4:08. NY Islanders defeated Pittsburgh 9-2.
2:55 – Boston Bruins, Dec. 19, 1974, at Boston. Scorers: Bobby Schmautz, 19:13 (first period); Ken Hodge, 0:18; Phil Esposito, 0:43; Don Marcotte, 0:58; John Bucyk, 2:08 (second period). Boston defeated NY Rangers 11-3.

FASTEST FOUR GOALS, BOTH TEAMS:
0:53 – Chicago Blackhawks, Toronto Maple Leafs, Oct. 15, 1983, at Toronto, second period. Scorers: Gaston Gingras, Toronto, 16:49; Denis Savard, Chicago, 17:12; Steve Larmer, Chicago, 17:27; Denis Savard, Chicago, 17:42. Toronto won 10-8.
0:57 – Quebec Nordiques, Detroit Red Wings, Jan. 27, 1990, at Quebec, first period. Scorers: Paul Gillis, Quebec, 18:01; Claude Loiselle, Quebec, 18:12; Joe Sakic, Quebec, 18:27; Jimmy Carson, Detroit, 18:58. Detroit won 8-6.
1:01 – Colorado Rockies, New York Rangers, Jan. 15, 1980, at NY Rangers, first period. Scorers: Doug Sulliman, NY Rangers, 7:52; Eddie Johnstone, NY Rangers, 7:57; Warren Miller, NY Rangers, 8:20; Rob Ramage, Colorado, 8:53. Teams tied 6-6.
– Chicago Blackhawks, Toronto Maple Leafs, Oct. 15, 1983, at Toronto, second period. Scorers: Denis Savard, Chicago, 17:12; Steve Larmer, Chicago, 17:27; Denis Savard, Chicago, 17:42; John Anderson, Toronto, 18:13. Toronto won 10-8.

FASTEST FOUR GOALS, ONE TEAM:
1:20 – Boston Bruins, Jan. 21, 1945, at Boston, second period. Scorers: Bill Thoms, 6:34; Frank Mario, 7:08 and 7:27; Ken Smith, 7:54. Boston defeated NY Rangers 14-3.

FASTEST THREE GOALS, BOTH TEAMS:
0:15 – Minnesota North Stars, New York Rangers, Feb. 10, 1983, at Minnesota, second period. Scorers: Mark Pavelich, NY Rangers, 19:18; Ron Greschner, NY Rangers, 19:27; Willi Plett, Minnesota, 19:33. Minnesota won 7-5.
0:18 – Montreal Canadiens, New York Rangers, Dec. 12, 1963, at Montreal, first period. Scorers: Dave Balon, Montreal, 0:58; Gilles Tremblay, Montreal, 1:04; Camille Henry, NY Rangers, 1:16. Montreal won 6-4.
– California Golden Seals, Buffalo Sabres, Feb. 1, 1976, at California, third period. Scorers: Jim Moxey, California, 19:38; Wayne Merrick, California, 19:45; Danny Gare, Buffalo, 19:56. Buffalo won 9-5.

FASTEST THREE GOALS, ONE TEAM:
0:20 – Boston Bruins, Feb. 25, 1971, at Boston, third period. Scorers: John Bucyk, 4:50; Ed Westfall, 5:02; Ted Green, 5:10. Boston defeated Vancouver 8-3.
0:21 – Chicago Blackhawks, Mar. 23, 1952, at NY Rangers, third period. Bill Mosienko scored all three goals, at 6:09, 6:20 and 6:30. Chicago defeated NY Rangers 7-6.
– Washington Capitals, Nov. 23, 1990, at Washington, first period. Scorers: Michal Pivonka, 16:18; Stephen Leach, 16:29 and 16:39. Washington defeated Pittsburgh 7-3.

FASTEST THREE GOALS FROM START OF PERIOD, BOTH TEAMS:
1:05 – Hartford Whalers, Montreal Canadiens, Mar. 11, 1989, at Montreal, second period. Scorers: Kevin Dineen, Hartford, 0:11; Guy Carbonneau, Montreal, 0:36; Petr Svoboda, Montreal, 1:05. Montreal won 5-3.

FASTEST THREE GOALS FROM START OF PERIOD, ONE TEAM:
0:53 – Calgary Flames, Feb. 10, 1993, at Calgary, third period. Scorers: Gary Suter, 0:17; Chris Lindberg, 0:40; Ron Stern, 0:53. Calgary defeated San Jose 13-1.

FASTEST TWO GOALS, BOTH TEAMS:
0:02 – St. Louis Blues, Boston Bruins, Dec. 19, 1987, at Boston, third period. Scorers: Ken Linseman, Boston, 19:50; Doug Gilmour, St. Louis, 19:52. St. Louis won 7-5.
0:03 – Chicago Blackhawks, Minnesota North Stars, Nov. 5, 1988, at Minnesota, third period. Scorers: Steve Thomas, Chicago, 6:03; Dave Gagner, Minnesota, 6:06. Teams tied 5-5.

FASTEST TWO GOALS, ONE TEAM:
0:03 – Minnesota Wild, Jan. 21, 2004, at Minnesota, third period. Scorers: Jim Dowd, 19:44; Richard Park, 19:47. Minnesota defeated Chicago 4-2.
0:04 – Montreal Maroons, Jan. 3, 1931, at Montreal, third period. Nels Stewart scored both goals, at 8:24 and 8:28. Mtl. Maroons defeated Boston 5-3.
– Buffalo Sabres, Oct. 17, 1974, at Buffalo, third period. Scorers: Lee Fogolin, Jr., 14:55; Don Luce, 14:59. Buffalo defeated California 6-1.
– Toronto Maple Leafs, Dec. 29, 1988, at Quebec, third period. Scorers: Ed Olczyk, 5:24; Gary Leeman, 5:28. Toronto defeated Quebec 6-5.
– Calgary Flames, Oct. 17, 1989, at Quebec, third period. Scorers: Doug Gilmour, 19:45; Paul Ranheim, 19:49. Teams tied 8-8.
– Winnipeg Jets, Dec. 15, 1995, at Winnipeg, second period. Deron Quint scored both goals, at 7:51 and 7:55. Winnipeg defeated Edmonton 9-4.

FASTEST TWO GOALS FROM START OF GAME, ONE TEAM:
0:24 – Edmonton Oilers, Mar. 28, 1982, at Los Angeles. Scorers: Mark Messier, 0:14; Dave Lumley, 0:24. Edmonton defeated Los Angeles 6-2.
0:27 – Boston Bruins, Feb. 14, 2003, at Florida. Mike Knuble scored both goals, at 0:10 and 0:27. Calgary defeated Hartford 6-1.
0:29 – Pittsburgh Penguins, Dec. 6, 1980, at Pittsburgh. Scorers: George Ferguson, 0:17; Greg Malone, 0:29. Pittsburgh defeated Chicago 6-4.

FASTEST TWO GOALS FROM START OF PERIOD, BOTH TEAMS:
0:14 – New York Rangers, Quebec Nordiques, Nov. 5, 1983, at Quebec, third period. Scorers: Andre Savard, Quebec, 0:08; Pierre Larouche, NY Rangers, 0:14. Teams tied 4-4.
0:25 – St. Louis Blues, Chicago Blackhawks, Feb. 2, 2006 at St. Louis, second period. Scorers: Peter Cajanek, St. Louis, 0:10; Tyler Arnason, Chicago, 0:25. St. Louis won 6-5.
0:28 – Boston Bruins, Montreal Canadiens, Oct. 11, 1989, at Montreal, third period. Scorers: Jim Wiemer, Boston 0:10; Tom Chorske, Montreal 0:28. Montreal won 4-2.

FASTEST TWO GOALS FROM START OF PERIOD, ONE TEAM:
0:21 – Chicago Blackhawks, Nov. 5, 1983, at Minnesota, second period. Scorers: Ken Yaremchuk, 0:12; Darryl Sutter, 0:21. Minnesota defeated Chicago 10-5.
0:24 – Edmonton Oilers, Mar. 28, 1982, at Los Angeles, first period. Scorers: Mark Messier, 0:14; Dave Lumley, 0:24. Edmonton defeated Los Angeles 6-2.
0:29 – Pittsburgh Penguins, Dec. 6, 1980, at Pittsburgh, first period. Scorers: George Ferguson, 0:17; Greg Malone, 0:29. Pittsburgh defeated Chicago 6-4.

Richard Park's goal against Chicago at 19:47 of the third period came just three seconds after Minnesota teammate Jim Dowd had scored and clinched a Wild victory over the Blackhawks.

50, 40, 30, 20-GOAL SCORERS

MOST 50-OR-MORE GOAL SCORERS, ONE SEASON:
- **3 – Edmonton Oilers**, 1983-84. 80GP. Wayne Gretzky, 87; Glenn Anderson, 54; Jari Kurri, 52.
- **– Edmonton Oilers**, 1985-86. 80GP. Jari Kurri, 68; Glenn Anderson, 54; Wayne Gretzky, 52.
- 2 – Boston Bruins, 1970-71. 78GP. Phil Esposito, 76; John Bucyk, 51.
- – Boston Bruins, 1973-74. 78GP. Phil Esposito, 68; Ken Hodge, 50.
- – Philadelphia Flyers, 1975-76. 80GP. Reggie Leach, 61; Bill Barber, 50.
- – Pittsburgh Penguins, 1975-76. 80GP. Pierre Larouche, 53; Jean Pronovost, 52.
- – Montreal Canadiens, 1976-77. 80GP. Steve Shutt, 60; Guy Lafleur, 56.
- – Los Angeles Kings, 1979-80. 80GP. Charlie Simmer, 56; Marcel Dionne, 53.
- – Montreal Canadiens, 1979-80. 80GP. Pierre Larouche, 50; Guy Lafleur, 50.
- – Los Angeles Kings, 1980-81. 80GP. Marcel Dionne, 58; Charlie Simmer, 56.
- – Edmonton Oilers, 1981-82. 80GP. Wayne Gretzky, 92; Mark Messier, 50.
- – New York Islanders, 1981-82. 80GP. Mike Bossy, 64; Bryan Trottier, 50.
- – Edmonton Oilers, 1984-85. 80GP. Wayne Gretzky, 73; Jari Kurri, 71.
- – Washington Capitals, 1984-85. 80GP. Bob Carpenter, 53; Mike Gartner, 50.
- – Edmonton Oilers, 1986-87. 80GP. Wayne Gretzky, 62; Jari Kurri, 54.
- – Calgary Flames, 1987-88. 80GP. Joe Nieuwendyk, 51; Hakan Loob, 50.
- – Los Angeles Kings, 1987-88. 80GP. Jimmy Carson, 55; Luc Robitaille, 53.
- – Los Angeles Kings, 1988-89. 80GP. Bernie Nicholls, 70; Wayne Gretzky, 54.
- – Calgary Flames, 1988-89. 80GP. Joe Nieuwendyk, 51; Joe Mullen, 51.
- – Buffalo Sabres, 1992-93. 84GP. Alexander Mogilny, 76; Pat LaFontaine, 53.
- – Pittsburgh Penguins, 1992-93. 84GP. Mario Lemieux, 69; Kevin Stevens, 55.
- – St. Louis Blues, 1992-93. 84GP. Brett Hull, 54; Brendan Shanahan, 51.
- – St. Louis Blues, 1993-94. 84GP. Brett Hull, 57; Brendan Shanahan, 52.
- – Detroit Red Wings, 1993-94. 84GP. Sergei Fedorov, 56; Ray Sheppard, 52.
- – Pittsburgh Penguins, 1995-96. 82GP. Mario Lemieux, 69; Jaromir Jagr, 62.

MOST 40-OR-MORE GOAL SCORERS, ONE SEASON:
- **4 – Edmonton Oilers**, 1982-83. 80GP. Wayne Gretzky, 71; Glenn Anderson, 48; Mark Messier, 48; Jari Kurri, 45.
- **– Edmonton Oilers**, 1983-84. 80GP. Wayne Gretzky, 87; Glenn Anderson, 54; Jari Kurri, 52; Paul Coffey, 40.
- **– Edmonton Oilers**, 1984-85. 80GP. Wayne Gretzky, 73; Jari Kurri, 71; Mike Krushelnyski, 43; Glenn Anderson, 42.
- **– Edmonton Oilers**, 1985-86. 80GP. Jari Kurri, 68; Glenn Anderson, 54; Wayne Gretzky, 52; Paul Coffey, 48.
- **– Calgary Flames**, 1987-88. 80GP. Joe Nieuwendyk, 51; Hakan Loob, 50; Mike Bullard, 48; Joe Mullen, 40.
- 3 – Boston Bruins, 1970-71. 78GP. Phil Esposito, 76; John Bucyk, 51; Ken Hodge, 43.
- – New York Rangers, 1971-72. 78GP. Vic Hadfield, 50; Jean Ratelle, 46; Rod Gilbert, 43.
- – Buffalo Sabres, 1975-76. 80GP. Danny Gare, 50; Rick Martin, 49; Gilbert Perreault, 44.
- – Montreal Canadiens, 1979-80. 80GP. Guy Lafleur, 50; Pierre Larouche, 50; Steve Shutt, 47.
- – Buffalo Sabres, 1979-80. 80GP. Danny Gare, 56; Rick Martin, 45; Gilbert Perreault, 40.
- – Los Angeles Kings, 1980-81. 80GP. Marcel Dionne, 58; Charlie Simmer, 56; Dave Taylor, 47.
- – Los Angeles Kings, 1984-85. 80GP. Marcel Dionne, 46; Bernie Nicholls, 46; Dave Taylor, 41.
- – New York Islanders, 1984-85. 80GP. Mike Bossy, 58; Brent Sutter, 42; John Tonelli, 42.
- – Chicago Blackhawks, 1985-86. 80GP. Denis Savard, 47; Troy Murray, 45; Al Secord, 40.
- – Chicago Blackhawks, 1987-88. 80GP. Denis Savard, 44; Rick Vaive, 43; Steve Larmer, 41.
- – Edmonton Oilers, 1987-88. 80GP. Craig Simpson, 43; Jari Kurri, 43; Wayne Gretzky, 40.
- – Los Angeles Kings, 1988-89. 80GP. Bernie Nicholls, 70; Wayne Gretzky, 54; Luc Robitaille, 46.
- – Los Angeles Kings, 1990-91. 80GP. Luc Robitaille, 45; Tomas Sandstrom, 45; Wayne Gretzky, 41.
- – Pittsburgh Penguins, 1991-92. 80GP. Kevin Stevens, 54; Mario Lemieux, 44; Joe Mullen, 42.
- – Pittsburgh Penguins, 1992-93. 84GP. Mario Lemieux, 69; Kevin Stevens, 55; Rick Tocchet, 48.
- – Calgary Flames, 1993-94. 84GP. Gary Roberts, 41; Robert Reichel, 40; Theoren Fleury, 40.
- – Pittsburgh Penguins, 1995-96. 82GP. Mario Lemieux, 69; Jaromir Jagr, 62; Petr Nedved, 45.

MOST 30-OR-MORE GOAL SCORERS, ONE SEASON:
- **6 – Buffalo Sabres**, 1974-75. 80GP. Rick Martin, 52; Rene Robert, 40; Gilbert Perreault, 39; Don Luce, 33; Rick Dudley, 31; Danny Gare, 31.
- **– New York Islanders**, 1977-78. 80GP. Mike Bossy, 53; Bryan Trottier, 46; Clark Gillies, 35; Denis Potvin, 30; Bob Nystrom, 30; Bob Bourne, 30.
- **– Winnipeg Jets**, 1984-85. 80GP. Dale Hawerchuk, 53; Paul MacLean, 41; Laurie Boschman, 32; Brian Mullen, 32; Doug Smail, 31; Thomas Steen, 30.
- 5 – Chicago Blackhawks, 1968-69. 76GP
- – Boston Bruins, 1970-71. 78GP
- – Montreal Canadiens, 1971-72. 78GP
- – Philadelphia Flyers, 1972-73. 78GP
- – Boston Bruins, 1973-74. 78GP
- – Montreal Canadiens, 1974-75. 80GP
- – Montreal Canadiens, 1975-76. 80GP
- – Pittsburgh Penguins, 1975-76. 80GP
- – New York Islanders, 1978-79. 80GP
- – Detroit Red Wings, 1979-80. 80GP
- – Philadelphia Flyers, 1979-80. 80GP
- – New York Islanders, 1980-81. 80GP
- – St. Louis Blues, 1980-81. 80GP
- – Chicago Blackhawks, 1981-82. 80GP
- – Edmonton Oilers, 1981-82. 80GP
- – Montreal Canadiens, 1981-82. 80GP
- – Quebec Nordiques, 1981-82. 80GP
- – Washington Capitals, 1981-82. 80GP
- – Edmonton Oilers, 1982-83. 80GP
- – Edmonton Oilers, 1983-84. 80GP
- – Edmonton Oilers, 1984-85. 80GP
- – Los Angeles Kings, 1984-85. 80GP
- – Edmonton Oilers, 1985-86. 80GP
- – Edmonton Oilers, 1986-87. 80GP
- – Edmonton Oilers, 1987-88. 80GP
- – Edmonton Oilers, 1988-89. 80GP
- – Detroit Red Wings, 1991-92. 80GP
- – New York Rangers, 1991-92. 80GP
- – Pittsburgh Penguins, 1991-92. 80GP
- – Detroit Red Wings, 1992-93. 84GP
- – Pittsburgh Penguins, 1992-93. 84GP

MOST 20-OR-MORE GOAL SCORERS, ONE SEASON:
- **11 – Boston Bruins**, 1977-78. 80GP. Peter McNab, 41; Terry O'Reilly, 29; Bobby Schmautz, 27; Stan Jonathan, 27; Jean Ratelle, 25; Rick Middleton, 25; Wayne Cashman, 24; Gregg Sheppard, 23; Brad Park, 22; Don Marcotte, 20; Bob Miller, 20.
- 10 – Boston Bruins, 1970-71. 78GP
- – Montreal Canadiens, 1974-75. 80GP
- – St. Louis Blues, 1980-81. 80GP

Thomas Steen was one of six Winnipeg Jets to reach the 30-goal plateau back in 1984-85. His son Alex had 18 goals as a Maple Leafs rookie last season.

100-POINT SCORERS

MOST 100 OR-MORE-POINT SCORERS, ONE SEASON:
4 – Boston Bruins, 1970-71. 78GP. Phil Esposito, 76G-76A-152PTS;
Bobby Orr, 37G-102A-139PTS; John Bucyk, 51G-65A-116PTS;
Ken Hodge, 43G-62A-105PTS.
– **Edmonton Oilers**, 1982-83. 80GP. Wayne Gretzky, 71G-125A-196PTS;
Mark Messier, 48G-58A-106PTS; Glenn Anderson, 48G-56A-104PTS;
Jari Kurri, 45G-59A-104PTS.
– **Edmonton Oilers**, 1983-84. 80GP. Wayne Gretzky, 87G-118A-205PTS;
Paul Coffey, 40G-86A-126PTS; Jari Kurri, 52G-61A-113PTS;
Mark Messier, 37G-64A-101PTS.
– **Edmonton Oilers**, 1985-86. 80GP. Wayne Gretzky, 52G-163A-215PTS;
Paul Coffey, 48G-90A-138PTS; Jari Kurri, 68G-63A-131PTS;
Glenn Anderson, 54G-48A-102PTS.
– **Pittsburgh Penguins**, 1992-93. 84GP. Mario Lemieux, 69G-91A-160PTS;
Kevin Stevens, 55G-56A-111PTS; Rick Tocchet, 48G-61A-109PTS;
Ron Francis, 24G-76A-100PTS.
3 – Boston Bruins, 1973-74. 78GP. Phil Esposito, 68G-77A-145PTS;
Bobby Orr, 32G-90A-122PTS; Ken Hodge, 50G-55A-105PTS.
– New York Islanders, 1978-79. 80GP. Bryan Trottier, 47G-87A-134PTS;
Mike Bossy, 69G-57A-126PTS; Denis Potvin, 31G-70A-101PTS.
– Los Angeles Kings, 1980-81. 80GP. Marcel Dionne, 58G-77A-135PTS;
Dave Taylor, 47G-65A-112PTS; Charlie Simmer, 56G-49A-105PTS.
– Edmonton Oilers, 1984-85. 80GP. Wayne Gretzky, 73G-135A-208PTS;
Jari Kurri, 71G-64A-135PTS; Paul Coffey, 37G-84A-121PTS.
– New York Islanders, 1984-85. 80GP. Mike Bossy, 58G-59A-117PTS;
Brent Sutter, 42G-60A-102PTS; John Tonelli, 42G-58A-100PTS.
– Edmonton Oilers, 1986-87. 80GP. Wayne Gretzky, 62G-121A-183PTS;
Jari Kurri, 54G-54A-108PTS; Mark Messier, 37G-70A-107PTS.
– Pittsburgh Penguins, 1988-89. 80GP. Mario Lemieux, 85G-114A-199PTS;
Rob Brown, 49G-66A-115PTS; Paul Coffey, 30G-83A-113PTS.
– Pittsburgh Penguins, 1995-96. 82GP. Mario Lemieux, 69G-92A-161PTS;
Jaromir Jagr, 62G-87A-149PTS; Ron Francis, 27G-92A-119PTS.

SHOTS ON GOAL

MOST SHOTS, BOTH TEAMS, ONE GAME:
141 – New York Americans, Pittsburgh Pirates, Dec. 26, 1925, at
NY Americans. NY Americans won 3-1 with 73 shots; Pittsburgh had 68
shots.

MOST SHOTS, ONE TEAM, ONE GAME:
83 – Boston Bruins, Mar. 4, 1941, at Boston. Boston defeated Chicago 3-2.
73 – New York Americans, Dec. 26, 1925, at NY Americans. NY Americans
defeated Pittsburgh 3-1.
– Boston Bruins, Mar. 21, 1991, at Boston. Boston tied Quebec 3-3.
72 – Boston Bruins, Dec. 10, 1970, at Boston. Boston defeated Buffalo 8-2.

MOST SHOTS, ONE TEAM, ONE PERIOD:
33 – Boston Bruins, Mar. 4, 1941, at Boston, second period.
Boston defeated Chicago 3-2.

TEAM GOALS AGAINST

Fewest Goals Against

FEWEST GOALS AGAINST, ONE SEASON:
42 – Ottawa Senators, 1925-26. 36GP.
43 – Montreal Canadiens, 1928-29. 44GP.
48 – Montreal Canadiens, 1923-24. 24GP.
– Montreal Canadiens, 1927-28. 44GP.

**FEWEST GOALS AGAINST, ONE SEASON
(MINIMUM 70-GAME SCHEDULE):**
131 – Toronto Maple Leafs, 1953-54. 70GP.
– **Montreal Canadiens**, 1955-56. 70GP.
132 – Detroit Red Wings, 1953-54. 70GP.
133 – Detroit Red Wings, 1951-52. 70GP.
– Detroit Red Wings, 1952-53. 70GP.

LOWEST GOALS-AGAINST-PER-GAME AVERAGE, ONE SEASON:
0.98 – Montreal Canadiens, 1928-29. 43GA in 44GP.
1.09 – Montreal Canadiens, 1927-28. 48GA in 44GP.
1.17 – Ottawa Senators, 1925-26. 42GA in 36GP.

Most Goals Against

MOST GOALS AGAINST, ONE SEASON:
446 – Washington Capitals, 1974-75. 80GP.
415 – Detroit Red Wings, 1985-86. 80GP.
414 – San Jose Sharks, 1992-93. 84GP.
407 – Quebec Nordiques, 1989-90. 80GP.
403 – Hartford Whalers, 1982-83. 80GP.

HIGHEST GOALS-AGAINST-PER-GAME AVERAGE, ONE SEASON:
7.38 – Quebec Bulldogs, 1919-20. 177GA in 24GP.
6.20 – New York Rangers, 1943-44. 310GA in 50GP.
5.58 – Washington Capitals, 1974-75. 446GA in 80GP.

MOST POWER-PLAY GOALS AGAINST, ONE SEASON:
122 – Chicago Blackhawks, 1988-89. 80GP.
120 – Pittsburgh Penguins, 1987-88. 80GP.
116 – Washington Capitals, 2005-06. 82GP.
115 – New Jersey Devils, 1988-89. 80GP.
– Ottawa Senators, 1992-93. 84GP.
114 – Los Angeles Kings, 1992-93. 84GP.

MOST SHORTHAND GOALS AGAINST, ONE SEASON:
22 – Pittsburgh Penguins, 1984-85. 80GP.
– **Minnesota North Stars**, 1991-92. 80GP.
– **Colorado Avalanche**, 1995-96. 82GP.
21 – Calgary Flames, 1984-85. 80GP.
– Pittsburgh Penguins, 1989-90. 80GP.

SHUTOUTS

MOST SHUTOUTS, ONE SEASON:
22 – Montreal Canadiens, 1928-29. All by George Hainsworth. 44GP.
16 – New York Americans, 1928-29. Roy Worters 13; Flat Walsh 3. 44GP.
15 – Ottawa Senators, 1925-26. All by Alex Connell. 36GP.
– Ottawa Senators, 1927-28. All by Alex Connell. 44GP.
– Boston Bruins, 1927-28. All by Hal Winkler. 44GP.
– Chicago Blackhawks, 1969-70. All by Tony Esposito. 76GP.

MOST CONSECUTIVE SHUTOUTS, ONE SEASON:
6 – Ottawa Senators, Jan. 31 – Feb. 18, 1928. All by Alex Connell.

MOST CONSECUTIVE SHUTOUTS TO START SEASON:
5 – Toronto Maple Leafs, Nov. 13 – 22, 1930. Lorne Chabot 3,
Benny Grant 2.

MOST GAMES SHUTOUT, ONE SEASON:
20 – Chicago Blackhawks, 1928-29. 44GP.

MOST CONSECUTIVE GAMES SHUTOUT:
8 – Chicago Blackhawks, Feb. 7 – 28, 1929.

MOST CONSECUTIVE GAMES SHUTOUT TO START SEASON:
3 – Montreal Maroons, Nov. 11 – 18, 1930.

TEAM PENALTIES

MOST PENALTY MINUTES, ONE SEASON:
2,713 – Buffalo Sabres, 1991-92. 80GP.
2,670 – Pittsburgh Penguins, 1988-89. 80GP.
2,663 – Chicago Blackhawks, 1991-92. 80GP.
2,643 – Calgary Flames, 1991-92. 80GP.
2,621 – Philadelphia Flyers, 1980-81. 80GP.

MOST PENALTIES, BOTH TEAMS, ONE GAME:
85 – Edmonton Oilers (44), Los Angeles Kings (41), Feb. 28, 1990, at
Los Angeles. Edmonton received 26 minors, 7 majors, 6 10-minute
misconducts, 4 game misconducts and 1 match penalty; Los Angeles
received 26 minors, 9 majors, 3 10-minute misconducts and 3 game
misconducts.

MOST PENALTY MINUTES, BOTH TEAMS, ONE GAME:
419 – Ottawa Senators (206), Philadelphia Flyers (213), Mar. 5, 2004, at
Philadelphia. Ottawa received 8 minors, 10 majors, 4 10-minute
misconducts and 10 game misconducts. Philadelphia received 9 minors,
11 majors, 4 10-minute misconducts and 10 game misconducts.

MOST PENALTIES, ONE TEAM, ONE GAME:
44 – Edmonton Oilers, Feb. 28, 1990, at Los Angeles. Edmonton received
26 minors, 7 majors, 6 10-minute misconducts, 4 game misconducts
and 1 match penalty.
42 – Minnesota North Stars, Feb. 26, 1981, at Boston. Minnesota received
18 minors, 13 majors, 4 10-minute misconducts and 7 game misconducts.
– Boston Bruins, Feb. 26, 1981, at Boston vs. Minnesota. Boston received
20 minors, 13 majors, 3 10-minute misconducts and 6 game misconducts.

MOST PENALTY MINUTES, ONE TEAM, ONE GAME:
213 – Philadelphia Flyers, Mar. 5, 2004, at Philadelphia. Philadelphia received
9 minors, 11 majors, 4 10-minute misconducts and 10 game misconducts.

MOST PENALTIES, BOTH TEAMS, ONE PERIOD:
67 – Minnesota North Stars (34), Boston Bruins (33), Feb. 26, 1981, at
Boston, first period. Minnesota received 15 minors, 8 majors, 4 10-minute
misconducts and 7 game misconducts. Boston had 16 minors, 8 majors,
3 10-minute misconducts and 6 game misconducts.

MOST PENALTY MINUTES, BOTH TEAMS, ONE PERIOD:
409 – Ottawa Senators (200), Philadelphia Flyers (209), Mar. 5, 2004, at
Philadelphia, third period. Ottawa received 5 minors, 10 majors, 4 10-
minute misconducts and 10 game misconducts. Philadelphia received 7
minors, 11 majors, 4 10-minute misconducts and 10 game misconducts.

MOST PENALTIES, ONE TEAM, ONE PERIOD:
34 – Minnesota North Stars, Feb. 26, 1981, at Boston, first period.
Minnesota received 15 minors, 8 majors, 4 10-minute misconducts and
7 game misconducts.

MOST PENALTY MINUTES, ONE TEAM, ONE PERIOD:
209 – Philadelphia Flyers, Mar. 5, 2004, at Philadelphia vs. Ottawa, third
period. Philadelphia received 7 minors, 11 majors, 4 10-minute
misconducts and 10 game misconducts.
200 – Ottawa Senators, Mar. 5, 2004, at Philadelphia, third period.
Ottawa received 5 minors, 10 majors, 4 10-minute misconducts and
10 game misconducts.

NHL Individual Scoring Records - History

Six individual scoring records stand as benchmarks in the history of the game: most goals, single-season and career; most assists, single-season and career; and most points, single-season and career. The evolution of these six records is traced here, beginning with 1917-18, the NHL's first season. New research has resulted in changes to scoring records in the NHL's first nine seasons.

MOST GOALS, ONE SEASON

44 —Joe Malone, Montreal, 1917-18.
  Scored goal #44 against Toronto's Harry Holmes on March 2, 1918 and finished season with 44 goals.
50 —Maurice Richard, Montreal, 1944-45.
  Scored goal #45 against Toronto's Frank McCool on February 25, 1945 and finished the season with 50 goals.
50 —Bernie Geoffrion, Montreal, 1960-61.
  Scored goal #50 against Toronto's Cesare Maniago on March 16, 1961 and finished the season with 50 goals.
50 —Bobby Hull, Chicago, 1961-62.
  Scored goal #50 against NY Rangers' Gump Worsley on March 25, 1962 and finished the season with 50 goals.
54 —Bobby Hull, Chicago, 1965-66.
  Scored goal #51 against NY Rangers' Cesare Maniago on March 12, 1966 and finished the season with 54 goals.
58 —Bobby Hull, Chicago, 1968-69.
  Scored goal #55 against Boston's Gerry Cheevers on March 20, 1969 and finished the season with 58 goals.
76 —Phil Esposito, Boston, 1970-71.
  Scored goal #59 against Los Angeles' Denis DeJordy on March 11, 1971 and finished the season with 76 goals.
92 —Wayne Gretzky, Edmonton, 1981-82.
  Scored goal #77 against Buffalo's Don Edwards on February 24, 1982 and finished the season with 92 goals.

MOST ASSISTS, ONE SEASON

10 —Cy Denneny, Ottawa, 1917-18.
  —Reg Noble, Toronto, 1917-18.
  —Harry Cameron, Toronto, 1917-18.
  —Newsy Lalonde, Montreal, 1918-19.
15 —Frank Nighbor, Ottawa, 1919-20.
  —Jack Darragh, Ottawa, 1920-21.
17 —Harry Cameron, Toronto, 1921-22.
18 —Dick Irvin, Chicago, 1926-27.
  —Howie Morenz, Montreal, 1927-28.
36 —Frank Boucher, NY Rangers, 1929-30.
37 —Joe Primeau, Toronto, 1931-32.
45 —Bill Cowley, Boston, 1940-41.
  —Bill Cowley, Boston, 1942-43.
49 —Clint Smith, Chicago, 1943-44.
54 —Elmer Lach, Montreal, 1944-45.
55 —Ted Lindsay, Detroit, 1949-50.
56 —Bert Olmstead, Montreal, 1955-56.
58 —Jean Beliveau, Montreal, 1960-61.
  —Andy Bathgate, NY Rangers/Toronto, 1963-64.
59 —Stan Mikita, Chicago, 1964-65.
62 —Stan Mikita, Chicago, 1966-67.
77 —Phil Esposito, Boston, 1968-69.
87 —Bobby Orr, Boston, 1969-70.
102 —Bobby Orr, Boston, 1970-71.
109 —Wayne Gretzky, Edmonton, 1980-81.
120 —Wayne Gretzky, Edmonton, 1981-82.
125 —Wayne Gretzky, Edmonton, 1982-83.
135 —Wayne Gretzky, Edmonton, 1984-85.
163 —Wayne Gretzky, Edmonton, 1985-86.

MOST POINTS, ONE SEASON

48 —Joe Malone, Montreal, 1917-18.
49 —Joe Malone, Montreal, 1919-20.
51 —Howie Morenz, Montreal, 1927-28.
73 —Cooney Weiland, Boston, 1929-30.
  —Doug Bentley, Chicago, 1942-43.
82 —Herb Cain, Boston, 1943-44.
86 —Gordie Howe, Detroit, 1950-51.
95 —Gordie Howe, Detroit, 1952-53.
96 —Dickie Moore, Montreal, 1958-59.
97 —Bobby Hull, Chicago, 1965-66.
  —Stan Mikita, Chicago, 1966-67.
126 —Phil Esposito, Boston, 1968-69.
152 —Phil Esposito, Boston, 1970-71.
164 —Wayne Gretzky, Edmonton, 1980-81.
212 —Wayne Gretzky, Edmonton, 1981-82.
215 —Wayne Gretzky, Edmonton, 1985-86.

MOST REGULAR-SEASON GOALS, CAREER

44 —Joe Malone, 1917-18, Montreal.
  Malone led the NHL in goals in the league's first season and finished with 44 goals in 22 games in 1917-18.
54 —Cy Denneny, 1918-19, Ottawa.
  Denneny passed Malone during the 1918-19 season, finishing the year with a two-year total of 54 goals. He held the career goal-scoring mark until 1919-20.
143 —Joe Malone, Montreal, Quebec Bulldogs, Hamilton.
  Malone passed Denneny in 1919-20 and remained the NHL's career goal-scoring leader until 1922-23.
248 —Cy Denneny, Ottawa, Boston.
  Denneny passed Malone with goal #144 in 1922-23 and remained the NHL's career goal-scoring leader until his retirement. He finished with a career total of 248 goals.
271 —Howie Morenz, Montreal, Chicago, NY Rangers.
  Morenz passed Denneny with goal #249 in 1933-34 and finished his career with 271 goals.
324 —Nels Stewart, Montreal Maroons, Boston, NY Americans.
  Stewart passed Morenz with goal #272 in 1936-37 and remained the NHL's career goal-scoring leader until his retirement. He finished his career with 324 goals.
544 —Maurice Richard, Montreal.
  Richard passed Nels Stewart with goal #325 on Nov. 8, 1952 and remained the NHL's career goal-scoring leader until his retirement. He finished his career with 544 goals.
801 —Gordie Howe, Detroit, Hartford.
  Howe passed Richard with goal #545 on Nov. 10, 1963 and remained the NHL's career goal-scoring leader until his retirement. He finished his career with 801 goals.
894 —Wayne Gretzky, Edmonton, Los Angeles, St. Louis, NY Rangers.
  Gretzky passed Gordie Howe with goal #802 on March 23, 1994. He retired as the NHL's current goal-scoring leader with 894.

Maurice Richard (above left), Elmer Lach (above center) and Toe Blake (above right) comprised Montreal's famous Punch Line of the early 1940s. This trio led the Canadiens to Stanley Cup titles in 1944 and 1946 and re-wrote the NHL record book during the 1944-45 season. Richard set a record by scoring 50 goals in 50 games that year, while Lach set a new single-season record with 54 assists. Lach would later retire as the NHL's career assist leader, while Richard would set career marks for goals and points. Gordie Howe (far right, receiving the Hart and Art Ross trophies from NHL President Clarence Campbell) would later pass both. Howe would establish new records for goals, assists and points that were later broken by Wayne Gretzky.

MOST REGULAR-SEASON ASSISTS, CAREER

(minimum 100 assists)

100 —Frank Boucher, Ottawa, NY Rangers.
In 1930-31, Boucher became the first NHL player to reach the 100-assist milestone.

263 —Frank Boucher, Ottawa, NY Rangers.
Boucher retired as the NHL's career assist leader in 1938 with 253. He returned to the NHL in 1943-44 and remained the NHL's career assist leader until he was overtaken by Bill Cowley in 1943-44. He finished his career with 263 assists.

353 —Bill Cowley, St. Louis Eagles, Boston.
Cowley passed Boucher with assist #264 in 1943-44. He retired as the NHL's career assist leader in 1947 with 353.

408 —Elmer Lach, Montreal.
Lach passed Cowley with assist #354 in 1951-52. He retired as the NHL's career assist leader in 1954 with 408.

1,049 —Gordie Howe, Detroit, Hartford.
Howe passed Lach with assist #409 in 1957-58. He retired as the NHL's career assist leader in 1980 with 1,049.

1,963 —Wayne Gretzky, Edmonton, Los Angeles, St. Louis, NY Rangers.
Gretzky passed Howe with assist #1,050 in 1988-89. He retired as the NHL's current career assist leader with 1,963.

MOST REGULAR-SEASON POINTS, CAREER

(minimum 100 points)

100 —Joe Malone, Montreal, Quebec Bulldogs, Hamilton.
In 1919-20, Malone became the first player in NHL history to record 100 points.

200 —Cy Denneny, Ottawa.
In 1923-24, Denneny became the first player in NHL history to record 200 points.

300 —Cy Denneny, Ottawa.
In 1926-27, Denneny became the first player in NHL history to record 300 points.

333 —Cy Denneny, Ottawa, Boston.
Denneny retired as the NHL's career point-scoring leader in 1929 with 333 points.

472 —Howie Morenz, Montreal, Chicago, NY Rangers.
Morenz passed Cy Denneny with point #334 in 1931-32. At the time his career ended in 1937, he was the NHL's career point-scoring leader with 472 points.

515 —Nels Stewart, Montreal Maroons, Boston, NY Americans.
Stewart passed Morenz with point #473 in 1938-39. He retired as the NHL's career point-scoring leader in 1940 with 515 points.

528 —Syd Howe, Ottawa, Philadelphia Quakers, Toronto, St. Louis Eagles, Detroit.
Howe passed Nels Stewart with point #516 on March 8, 1945. He retired as the NHL's career point-scoring leader in 1946 with 528 points.

548 —Bill Cowley, St. Louis Eagles, Boston.
Cowley passed Syd Howe with point #529 on Feb. 12, 1947. He retired as the NHL's career point-scoring leader in 1947 with 548 points.

610 —Elmer Lach, Montreal.
Lach passed Bill Cowley with point #549 on Feb. 23, 1952. He remained the NHL's career point-scoring leader until he was overtaken by Maurice Richard in 1953-54. He finished his career with 623 points.

946 —Maurice Richard, Montreal.
Richard passed teammate Elmer Lach with point #611 on Dec. 12, 1953. He remained the NHL's career point-scoring leader until he was overtaken by Gordie Howe in 1959-60. He finished his career with 965 points.

1,850 —Gordie Howe, Detroit, Hartford.
Howe passed Richard with point #947 on Jan. 16, 1960. He retired as the NHL's career point-scoring leader in 1980 with 1,850 points.

2,857 —Wayne Gretzky, Edmonton, Los Angeles, St. Louis, NY Rangers.
Gretzky passed Howe with point #1,851 on Oct. 15, 1989. He retired as the NHL's current career points leader with 2,857.

Individual Records

Regular Season

SEASONS

MOST SEASONS:
26 – **Gordie Howe**, Detroit, 1946-47 – 1970-71; Hartford, 1979-80.
25 – Mark Messier, Edmonton, NY Rangers, Vancouver,
    1979-80 – 2003-04.
24 – Alex Delvecchio, Detroit, 1950-51 – 1973-74.
  – Tim Horton, Toronto, NY Rangers, Pittsburgh, Buffalo,
    1949-50, 1951-52 – 1973-74.
23 – John Bucyk, Detroit, Boston, 1955-56 – 1977-78.
  – Ron Francis, Hartford, Pittsburgh, Carolina, Toronto, 1981-82 – 2003-04.
  – Al MacInnis, Calgary, St. Louis, 1981-82 – 2003-04.
  – Dave Andreychuk, Buffalo, Toronto, New Jersey, Boston,
    Colorado, Tampa Bay, 1982-83 – 2003-04, 2005-06.

GAMES

MOST GAMES:
1,767 – **Gordie Howe**, Detroit, 1946-47 – 1970-71; Hartford, 1979-80.
1,756 – Mark Messier, Edmonton, NY Rangers, Vancouver, 1979-80 – 2003-04.
1,731 – Ron Francis, Hartford, Pittsburgh, Carolina, Toronto, 1981-82 – 2003-04.
1,639 – Dave Andreychuk, Buffalo, Toronto, New Jersey, Boston,
    Colorado, Tampa Bay, 1982-83 – 2003-04, 2005-06.
1,635 – Scott Stevens, Washington, St. Louis, New Jersey, 1982-83 – 2003-04.
1,615 – Larry Murphy, Los Angeles, Washington, Minnesota, Pittsburgh, Toronto,
    Detroit, 1980-81 – 2000-01.

MOST GAMES, INCLUDING PLAYOFFS:
1,992 – **Mark Messier**, Edmonton, NY Rangers, Vancouver,
    1,756 regular-season games, 236 playoff games.
1,924 – Gordie Howe, Detroit, Hartford, 1,767 regular-season games,
    157 playoff games.
1,902 – Ron Francis, Hartford, Pittsburgh, Carolina, Toronto, 1,731 regular-season
    games, 171 playoff games.
1,868 – Scott Stevens, Washington, St. Louis, New Jersey, 1,635 regular-season
    games, 233 playoff games.
1,830 – Larry Murphy, Los Angeles, Washington, Minnesota, Pittsburgh, Toronto,
    Detroit, 1,615 regular-season games, 215 playoff games.

MOST CONSECUTIVE GAMES:
964 – **Doug Jarvis**, Montreal, Washington, Hartford,
    Oct. 8, 1975 – Oct. 10, 1987.
914 – Garry Unger, Toronto, Detroit, St. Louis, Atlanta,
    Feb. 24, 1968 – Dec. 21, 1979.
884 – Steve Larmer, Chicago, Oct. 6, 1982 – Apr. 15, 1993.
776 – Craig Ramsay, Buffalo, Mar. 27, 1973 – Feb. 10, 1983.
630 – Andy Hebenton, NY Rangers, Boston, Oct. 7, 1955 – Mar. 22, 1964.

GOALS

MOST GOALS:
894 – **Wayne Gretzky**, Edmonton, Los Angeles, St. Louis, NY Rangers,
    in 20 seasons. 1,487GP
801 – Gordie Howe, Detroit, Hartford, in 26 seasons. 1,767GP
741 – Brett Hull, Calgary, St. Louis, Dallas, Detroit, Phoenix,
    in 19 seasons. 1,269GP
731 – Marcel Dionne, Detroit, Los Angeles, NY Rangers, in 18 seasons. 1,348GP
717 – Phil Esposito, Chicago, Boston, NY Rangers, in 18 seasons. 1,282GP

MOST GOALS, INCLUDING PLAYOFFS:
1,016 – **Wayne Gretzky**, Edmonton, Los Angeles, St. Louis, NY Rangers,
    894G in 1,487 regular-season games, 122G in 208 playoff games.
869 – Gordie Howe, Detroit, Hartford,
    801G in 1,767 regular-season games, 68G in 157 playoff games.
844 – Brett Hull, Calgary, St. Louis, Dallas, Detroit, Phoenix,
    741G in 1,269 regular-season games, 103G in 202 playoff games.
803 – Mark Messier, Edmonton, NY Rangers, Vancouver,
    694G in 1,756 regular-season games, 109G in 236 playoff games.
778 – Phil Esposito, Chicago, Boston, NY Rangers,
    717G in 1,282 regular-season games, 61G in 130 playoff games.

MOST GOALS, ONE SEASON:
92 – **Wayne Gretzky**, Edmonton, 1981-82. 80GP – 80 game schedule.
87 – Wayne Gretzky, Edmonton, 1983-84. 74GP – 80 game schedule.
86 – Brett Hull, St. Louis, 1990-91. 78GP – 80 game schedule.
85 – Mario Lemieux, Pittsburgh, 1988-89. 76GP – 80 game schedule.
76 – Phil Esposito, Boston, 1970-71. 78GP – 78 game schedule.
  – Alexander Mogilny, Buffalo, 1992-93. 77GP – 84 game schedule.
  – Teemu Selanne, Winnipeg, 1992-93. 84GP – 84 game schedule.
73 – Wayne Gretzky, Edmonton, 1984-85. 80GP – 80 game schedule.
72 – Brett Hull, St. Louis, 1989-90. 80GP – 80 game schedule.
71 – Wayne Gretzky, Edmonton, 1982-83. 80GP – 80 game schedule.
  – Jari Kurri, Edmonton, 1984-85. 73GP – 80 game schedule.
70 – Mario Lemieux, Pittsburgh, 1987-88. 77GP – 80 game schedule.
  – Bernie Nicholls, Los Angeles, 1988-89. 79GP – 80 game schedule.
  – Brett Hull, St. Louis, 1991-92. 73GP – 80 game schedule.

MOST GOALS, ONE SEASON, INCLUDING PLAYOFFS:
100 – **Wayne Gretzky**, Edmonton, 1983-84,
    87G in 74 regular-season games, 13G in 19 playoff games.
97 – Wayne Gretzky, Edmonton, 1981-82,
    92G in 80 regular-season games, 5G in 5 playoff games.
  – Mario Lemieux, Pittsburgh, 1988-89,
    85G in 76 regular-season games, 12G in 11 playoff games.
  – Brett Hull, St. Louis, 1990-91,
    86G in 78 regular-season games, 11G in 13 playoff games.
90 – Wayne Gretzky, Edmonton, 1984-85,
    73G in 80 regular-season games, 17G in 18 playoff games.
  – Jari Kurri, Edmonton, 1984-85,
    71G in 80 regular-season games, 19G in 18 playoff games.
85 – Mike Bossy, NY Islanders, 1980-81,
    68G in 79 regular-season games, 17G in 18 playoff games.
  – Brett Hull, St. Louis, 1989-90,
    72G in 80 regular-season games, 13G in 12 playoff games.
83 – Wayne Gretzky, Edmonton, 1982-83,
    71G in 73 regular-season games, 12G in 16 playoff games.
  – Alexander Mogilny, Buffalo, 1992-93,
    76G in 77 regular-season games, 7G in 7 playoff games.

MOST GOALS, 50 GAMES FROM START OF SEASON:
61 – **Wayne Gretzky**, Edmonton, 1981-82.
    Oct. 7, 1981 – Jan. 22, 1982. (80-game schedule)
  – **Wayne Gretzky**, Edmonton, 1983-84.
    Oct. 5, 1983 – Jan. 25, 1984. (80-game schedule)
54 – Mario Lemieux, Pittsburgh, 1988-89.
    Oct. 7, 1988 – Jan. 31, 1989. (80-game schedule)
53 – Wayne Gretzky, Edmonton, 1984-85.
    Oct. 11, 1984 – Jan. 28, 1985. (80-game schedule)
52 – Brett Hull, St. Louis, 1990-91.
    Oct. 4, 1990 – Jan. 26, 1991. (80-game schedule)
50 – Maurice Richard, Montreal, 1944-45.
    Oct. 28, 1944 – Mar. 18, 1945. (50-game schedule)
  – Mike Bossy, NY Islanders, 1980-81.
    Oct. 11, 1980 – Jan. 24, 1981. (80-game schedule)
  – Brett Hull, St. Louis, 1991-92.
    Oct. 5, 1991 – Jan. 28, 1992. (80-game schedule)

MOST GOALS, ONE GAME:
7 – **Joe Malone**, Quebec, Jan. 31, 1920, at Quebec.
    Quebec 10, Toronto 6.
6 – Newsy Lalonde, Montreal, Jan. 10, 1920, at Montreal.
    Montreal 14, Toronto 7.
  – Joe Malone, Quebec, Mar. 10, 1920, at Quebec.
    Quebec 10, Ottawa 4.
  – Corb Denneny, Toronto, Jan. 26, 1921, at Toronto.
    Toronto 10, Hamilton 3.
  – Cy Denneny, Ottawa, Mar. 7, 1921, at Ottawa.
    Ottawa 12, Hamilton 5.
  – Syd Howe, Detroit, Feb. 3, 1944, at Detroit.
    Detroit 12, NY Rangers 2.
  – Red Berenson, St. Louis, Nov. 7, 1968, at Philadelphia.
    St. Louis 8, Philadelphia 0.
  – Darryl Sittler, Toronto, Feb. 7, 1976, at Toronto.
    Toronto 11, Boston 4.

Only three players in NHL history have played in more games than former Devils star Scott Stevens. Stevens played 1,635 regular-season games and 233 more in the playoffs. No defenseman has ever played more.

The Toronto Maple Leafs Kid Line of Charlie Conacher (left), Joe Primeau (center) and Busher Jackson (left). Jackson was the first player in NHL history to score four goals in one period.

MOST GOALS, ONE ROAD GAME:

6 – Red Berenson, St. Louis, Nov. 7, 1968, at Philadelphia.
St. Louis 8, Philadelphia 0.

5 – Joe Malone, Montreal, Dec. 19, 1917, at Ottawa. Montreal 7, Ottawa 4.
– Red Green, Hamilton, Dec. 5, 1924, at Toronto. Hamilton 10, Toronto 3.
– Babe Dye, Toronto, Dec. 22, 1924, at Boston. Toronto 10, Boston 1.
– Punch Broadbent, Mtl. Maroons, Jan. 7, 1925, at Hamilton.
Mtl. Maroons 6, Hamilton 2.
– Don Murdoch, NY Rangers, Oct. 12, 1976, at Minnesota.
NY Rangers 10, Minnesota 4.
– Tim Young, Minnesota, Jan. 15, 1979, at NY Rangers.
Minnesota 8, NY Rangers 1.
– Willy Lindstrom, Winnipeg, Mar. 2, 1982, at Philadelphia.
Winnipeg 7, Philadelphia 6.
– Bengt Gustafsson, Washington, Jan. 8, 1984, at Philadelphia.
Washington 7, Philadelphia 1.
– Wayne Gretzky, Edmonton, Dec. 15, 1984, at St. Louis.
Edmonton 8, St. Louis 2.
– Dave Andreychuk, Buffalo, Feb. 6, 1986, at Boston. Buffalo 8, Boston 6.
– Mats Sundin, Quebec, Mar. 5, 1992, at Hartford. Quebec 10, Hartford 4.
– Mario Lemieux, Pittsburgh, Apr. 9, 1993, at NY Rangers.
Pittsburgh 10, NY Rangers 4.
– Mike Ricci, Quebec, Feb. 17, 1994, at San Jose. Quebec 8, San Jose 2.
– Alex Zhamnov, Winnipeg, Apr. 1, 1995, at Los Angeles.
Winnipeg 7, Los Angeles 7.

MOST GOALS, ONE PERIOD:

4 – Busher Jackson, Toronto, Nov. 20, 1934, at St. Louis,
third period. Toronto 5, St. Louis 2.
– **Max Bentley**, Chicago, Jan. 28, 1943, at Chicago,
third period. Chicago 10, NY Rangers 1.
– **Clint Smith**, Chicago, Mar. 4, 1945, at Chicago,
third period. Chicago 6, Montreal 4.
– **Red Berenson**, St. Louis, Nov. 7, 1968, at Philadelphia,
second period. St. Louis 8, Philadelphia 0.
– **Wayne Gretzky**, Edmonton, Feb. 18, 1981, at Edmonton,
third period. Edmonton 9, St. Louis 2.
– **Grant Mulvey**, Chicago, Feb. 3, 1982, at Chicago,
first period. Chicago 9, St. Louis 5.
– **Bryan Trottier**, NY Islanders, Feb. 13, 1982, at NY Islanders,
second period. NY Islanders 8, Philadelphia 2.
– **Al Secord**, Chicago, Jan. 7, 1987, at Chicago,
second period. Chicago 6, Toronto 4.
– **Joe Nieuwendyk**, Calgary, Jan. 11, 1989, at Calgary,
second period. Calgary 8, Winnipeg 3.
– **Peter Bondra**, Washington, Feb. 5, 1994, at Washington,
first period. Washington 6, Tampa Bay 3.
– **Mario Lemieux**, Pittsburgh, Jan. 26, 1997, at Montreal,
third period. Pittsburgh 5, Montreal 2.

ASSISTS

MOST ASSISTS:

1,963 – Wayne Gretzky, Edmonton, Los Angeles, St. Louis, NY Rangers,
in 20 seasons. 1,487GP
1,249 – Ron Francis, Hartford, Pittsburgh, Carolina, Toronto, in 23 seasons. 1,731GP
1,193 – Mark Messier, Edmonton, NY Rangers, Vancouver, in 25 seasons. 1,756GP
1,169 – Raymond Bourque, Boston, Colorado, in 22 seasons. 1,612GP
1,135 – Paul Coffey, Edmonton, Pittsburgh, Los Angeles, Detroit, Hartford,
Philadelphia, Chicago, Carolina, Boston, in 21 seasons. 1,409GP

MOST ASSISTS, INCLUDING PLAYOFFS:

2,223 – Wayne Gretzky, Edmonton, Los Angeles, St. Louis, NY Rangers,
1,963A in 1,487 regular-season games, 260A in 208 playoff games.
1,379 – Mark Messier, Edmonton, NY Rangers, Vancouver,
1,193A in 1,756 regular-season games, 186A in 236 playoff games.
1,346 – Ron Francis, Hartford, Pittsburgh, Carolina, Toronto,
1,249A in 1,731 regular-season games, 97A in 171 playoff games.
1,308 – Raymond Bourque, Boston, Colorado,
1,169A in 1,612 regular-season games, 139A in 214 playoff games.
1,272 – Paul Coffey, Edmonton, Pittsburgh, Los Angeles, Detroit,
Hartford, Philadelphia, Chicago, Carolina, Boston,
1,135A in 1,409 regular-season games, 137A in 194 playoff games.

MOST ASSISTS, ONE SEASON:

163 – Wayne Gretzky, Edmonton, 1985-86. 80GP – 80 game schedule.
135 – Wayne Gretzky, Edmonton, 1984-85. 80GP – 80 game schedule.
125 – Wayne Gretzky, Edmonton, 1982-83. 80GP – 80 game schedule.
122 – Wayne Gretzky, Los Angeles, 1990-91. 78GP – 80 game schedule.
121 – Wayne Gretzky, Edmonton, 1986-87. 79GP – 80 game schedule.
120 – Wayne Gretzky, Edmonton, 1981-82. 80GP – 80 game schedule.
118 – Wayne Gretzky, Edmonton, 1983-84. 74GP – 80 game schedule.
114 – Wayne Gretzky, Los Angeles, 1988-89. 78GP – 80 game schedule.
– Mario Lemieux, Pittsburgh, 1988-89. 76GP – 80 game schedule.
109 – Wayne Gretzky, Edmonton, 1980-81. 80GP – 80 game schedule.
– Wayne Gretzky, Edmonton, 1987-88. 64GP – 80 game schedule.
102 – Bobby Orr, Boston, 1970-71. 78GP – 78 game schedule.
– Wayne Gretzky, Los Angeles, 1989-90. 73GP – 80 game schedule.

MOST ASSISTS, ONE SEASON, INCLUDING PLAYOFFS:
174 – Wayne Gretzky, Edmonton, 1985-86,
163A in 80 regular-season games, 11A in 10 playoff games.
165 – Wayne Gretzky, Edmonton, 1984-85,
135A in 80 regular-season games, 30A in 18 playoff games.
151 – Wayne Gretzky, Edmonton, 1982-83,
125A in 80 regular-season games, 26A in 16 playoff games.
150 – Wayne Gretzky, Edmonton, 1986-87,
121A in 79 regular-season games, 29A in 21 playoff games.
140 – Wayne Gretzky, Edmonton, 1983-84,
118A in 74 regular-season games, 22A in 19 playoff games.
– Wayne Gretzky, Edmonton, 1987-88,
109A in 64 regular-season games, 31A in 19 playoff games.
133 – Wayne Gretzky, Los Angeles, 1990-91,
122A in 78 regular-season games, 11A in 12 playoff games.
131 – Wayne Gretzky, Los Angeles, 1988-89,
114A in 78 regular-season games, 17A in 11 playoff games.
127 – Wayne Gretzky, Edmonton, 1981-82,
120A in 80 regular-season games, 7A in 5 playoff games.
123 – Wayne Gretzky, Edmonton, 1980-81,
109A in 80 regular-season games, 14A in 9 playoff games.
121 – Mario Lemieux, Pittsburgh, 1988-89,
114A in 76 regular-season games, 7A in 11 playoff games.

MOST ASSISTS, ONE GAME:
7 – Billy Taylor, Detroit, Mar. 16, 1947, at Chicago. Detroit 10, Chicago 6.
– Wayne Gretzky, Edmonton, Feb. 15, 1980, at Edmonton.
Edmonton 8, Washington 2.
– Wayne Gretzky, Edmonton, Dec. 11, 1985, at Chicago.
Edmonton 12, Chicago 9.
– Wayne Gretzky, Edmonton, Feb. 14, 1986, at Edmonton.
Edmonton 8, Quebec 2.
6 – Six assists have been recorded in one game on 24 occasions since
Elmer Lach of Montreal first accomplished the feat vs. Boston on
Feb. 6, 1943. The most recent player is Eric Lindros of Philadelphia
on Feb. 26, 1997 at Ottawa.

MOST ASSISTS, ONE ROAD GAME:
7 – Billy Taylor, Detroit, Mar. 16, 1947, at Chicago. Detroit 10, Chicago 6.
– Wayne Gretzky, Edmonton, Dec. 11, 1985, at Chicago.
Edmonton 12, Chicago 9.
6 – Bobby Orr, Boston, Jan. 1, 1973, at Vancouver. Boston 8, Vancouver 2.
– Patrik Sundstrom, Vancouver, Feb. 29, 1984, at Pittsburgh.
Vancouver 9, Pittsburgh 5.
– Mario Lemieux, Pittsburgh, Dec. 5, 1992, at San Jose.
Pittsburgh 9, San Jose 4.
– Eric Lindros, Philadelphia, Feb. 26, 1997, at Ottawa.
Philadelphia 8, Ottawa 5.

MOST ASSISTS, ONE PERIOD:
5 – Dale Hawerchuk, Winnipeg, Mar. 6, 1984, at Los Angeles,
second period. Winnipeg 7, Los Angeles 3.
4 – Four assists have been recorded in one period on 65 occasions since
Mickey Roach of Hamilton first accomplished the feat vs. Toronto
on Feb. 23, 1921. The most recent player is Shawn Horcoff of Edmonton
on Nov. 17, 2005 vs. Detroit.

POINTS

MOST POINTS:
2,857 – Wayne Gretzky, Edmonton, Los Angeles, St. Louis, NY Rangers,
in 20 seasons. 1,487GP (894G–1,963A)
1,887 – Mark Messier, Edmonton, NY Rangers, Vancouver,
in 25 seasons. 1,756GP (694G–1,193A)
1,850 – Gordie Howe, Detroit, Hartford, in 26 seasons. 1,767GP (801G–1,049A)
1,798 – Ron Francis, Hartford, Pittsburgh, Carolina, Toronto,
in 23 seasons. 1,731GP (549G–1,249A)
1,771 – Marcel Dionne, Detroit, Los Angeles, NY Rangers,
in 18 seasons. 1,348GP (731G–1,040A)

MOST POINTS, INCLUDING PLAYOFFS:
3,239 – Wayne Gretzky, Edmonton, Los Angeles, St. Louis, NY Rangers,
2,857PTS in 1,487 regular-season games, 382PTS in 208 playoff games.
2,182 – Mark Messier, Edmonton, NY Rangers, Vancouver,
1,887PTS in 1,756 regular-season games, 295PTS in 236 playoff games.
2,010 – Gordie Howe, Detroit, Hartford,
1,850PTS in 1,767 regular-season games, 160PTS in 157 playoff games.
1,941 – Ron Francis, Hartford, Pittsburgh, Carolina, Toronto,
1,798PTS in 1,731 regular-season games, 143PTS in 171 playoff games.
1,940 – Steve Yzerman, Detroit,
1,755PTS in 1,514 regular-season games, 185PTS in 196 playoff games.

MOST POINTS, ONE SEASON:
215 – Wayne Gretzky, Edmonton, 1985-86. 80GP – 80 game schedule.
212 – Wayne Gretzky, Edmonton, 1981-82. 80GP – 80 game schedule.
208 – Wayne Gretzky, Edmonton, 1984-85. 80GP – 80 game schedule.
205 – Wayne Gretzky, Edmonton, 1983-84. 74GP – 80 game schedule.
199 – Mario Lemieux, Pittsburgh, 1988-89. 76GP – 80 game schedule.
196 – Wayne Gretzky, Edmonton, 1982-83. 80GP – 80 game schedule.
183 – Wayne Gretzky, Edmonton, 1986-87. 79GP – 80 game schedule.
168 – Mario Lemieux, Pittsburgh, 1987-88. 77GP – 80 game schedule.
– Wayne Gretzky, Los Angeles, 1988-89. 78GP – 80 game schedule.
164 – Wayne Gretzky, Edmonton, 1980-81. 80GP – 80 game schedule.
163 – Wayne Gretzky, Los Angeles, 1990-91. 78GP – 80 game schedule.
161 – Mario Lemieux, Pittsburgh, 1995-96. 70GP – 82 game schedule.
160 – Mario Lemieux, Pittsburgh, 1992-93. 60GP – 84 game schedule.

MOST POINTS, ONE SEASON, INCLUDING PLAYOFFS:
255 – Wayne Gretzky, Edmonton, 1984-85.
208PTS in 80 regular-season games, 47PTS in 18 playoff games.
240 – Wayne Gretzky, Edmonton, 1983-84,
205PTS in 74 regular-season games, 35PTS in 19 playoff games.
234 – Wayne Gretzky, Edmonton, 1982-83,
196PTS in 80 regular-season games, 38PTS in 16 playoff games.
– Wayne Gretzky, Edmonton, 1985-86,
215PTS in 80 regular-season games, 19PTS in 10 playoff games.
224 – Wayne Gretzky, Edmonton, 1981-82,
212PTS in 80 regular-season games, 12PTS in 5 playoff games.
218 – Mario Lemieux, Pittsburgh, 1988-89,
199PTS in 76 regular-season games, 19PTS in 11 playoff games.
217 – Wayne Gretzky, Edmonton, 1986-87,
183PTS in 79 regular-season games, 34PTS in 21 playoff games.
192 – Wayne Gretzky, Edmonton, 1987-88,
149PTS in 64 regular-season games, 43PTS in 19 playoff games.
190 – Wayne Gretzky, Los Angeles, 1988-89,
168PTS in 78 regular-season games, 22PTS in 11 playoff games.
188 – Mario Lemieux, Pittsburgh, 1995-96,
161PTS in 70 regular-season games, 27PTS in 18 playoff games.
185 – Wayne Gretzky, Edmonton, 1980-81,
164PTS in 80 regular-season games, 21PTS in 9 playoff games.

When his regular-season and playoff totals are combined, Steve Yzerman is the fifth-highest scorer in hockey history. Yzerman scored all his points for the Red Wings in a career that began in 1983-84 and ended after the 2005-06 campaign. He also wore the captain's "C" for Detroit since 1986-87.

MOST POINTS, ONE GAME:
10 – Darryl Sittler, Toronto, Feb. 7, 1976, at Toronto, 6G-4A.
Toronto 11, Boston 4.
  8 – Maurice Richard, Montreal, Dec. 28, 1944, at Montreal, 5G-3A.
Montreal 9, Detroit 1.
   – Bert Olmstead, Montreal, Jan. 9, 1954, at Montreal, 4G-4A.
Montreal 12, Chicago 1.
   – Tom Bladon, Philadelphia, Dec. 11, 1977, at Philadelphia, 4G-4A.
Philadelphia 11, Cleveland 1.
   – Bryan Trottier, NY Islanders, Dec. 23, 1978, at NY Islanders, 5G-3A.
NY Islanders 9, NY Rangers 4.
   – Peter Stastny, Quebec, Feb. 22, 1981, at Washington, 4G-4A.
Quebec 11, Washington 7.
   – Anton Stastny, Quebec, Feb. 22, 1981, at Washington, 3G-5A.
Quebec 11, Washington 7.
   – Wayne Gretzky, Edmonton, Nov. 19, 1983, at Edmonton, 3G-5A.
Edmonton 13, New Jersey 4.
   – Wayne Gretzky, Edmonton, Jan. 4, 1984, at Edmonton, 4G-4A.
Edmonton 12, Minnesota 8.
   – Paul Coffey, Edmonton, Mar. 14, 1986, at Edmonton, 2G-6A.
Edmonton 12, Detroit 3.
   – Mario Lemieux, Pittsburgh, Oct. 15, 1988, at Pittsburgh, 2G-6A.
Pittsburgh 9, St. Louis 2.
   – Bernie Nicholls, Los Angeles, Dec. 1, 1988, at Los Angeles, 2G-6A.
Los Angeles 9, Toronto 3.
   – Mario Lemieux, Pittsburgh, Dec. 31, 1988, at Pittsburgh, 5G-3A.
Pittsburgh 8, New Jersey 6.

MOST POINTS, ONE ROAD GAME:
8 – Peter Stastny, Quebec, Feb. 22, 1981, at Washington. 4G-4A.
Quebec 11, Washington 7.
   – **Anton Stastny**, Quebec, Feb. 22, 1981, at Washington. 3G-5A.
Quebec 11, Washington 7.
  7 – Red Green, Hamilton, Dec. 5, 1924, at Toronto. 5G-2A.
Hamilton 10, Toronto 3.
   – Billy Taylor, Detroit, Mar. 16, 1947, at Chicago. 7A. Detroit 10, Chicago 6.
   – Red Berenson, St. Louis, Nov. 7, 1968, at Philadelphia. 6G-1A.
St. Louis 8, Philadelphia 0.
   – Gilbert Perreault, Buffalo, Feb. 1, 1976, at California. 2G-5A.
Buffalo 9, California 5.
   – Peter Stastny, Quebec, Apr. 1, 1982, at Boston. 3G-4A. Quebec 8, Boston 5.
   – Wayne Gretzky, Edmonton, Nov. 6, 1983, at Winnipeg. 4G-3A.
Edmonton 8, Winnipeg 5.
   – Patrik Sundstrom, Vancouver, Feb. 29, 1984, at Pittsburgh. 1G-6A.
Vancouver 9, Pittsburgh 5.
   – Wayne Gretzky, Edmonton, Dec. 11, 1985, at Chicago. 7A.
Edmonton 12, Chicago 9.
   – Cam Neely, Boston, Oct. 16, 1988, at Chicago. 3G-4A.
Boston 10, Chicago 3.
   – Mario Lemieux, Pittsburgh, Jan. 21, 1989, at Edmonton. 2G-5A.
Pittsburgh 7, Edmonton 4.
   – Dino Ciccarelli, Washington, Mar. 18, 1989, at Hartford. 4G-3A.
Washington 8, Hartford 2.
   – Mats Sundin, Quebec, Mar. 5, 1992, at Hartford. 5G-2A.
Quebec 10, Hartford 4.
   – Mario Lemieux, Pittsburgh, Dec. 5, 1992, at San Jose. 1G-6A.
Pittsburgh 9, San Jose 4.
   – Eric Lindros, Philadelphia, Feb. 26, 1997, at Ottawa. 1G-6A.
Philadelphia 8, Ottawa 5.

MOST POINTS, ONE PERIOD:
6 – Bryan Trottier, NY Islanders, Dec. 23, 1978, at NY Islanders,
second period. 3G-3A. NY Islanders 9, NY Rangers 4.
  5 – Bill Cook, NY Rangers, Mar. 12, 1933, at NY Americans
third period. 3G-2A. NY Rangers 8, NY Americans 2.
   – Les Cunningham, Chicago, Jan. 28, 1940, at Chicago,
third period. 2G-3A. Chicago 8, Montreal 1.
   – Max Bentley, Chicago, Jan. 28, 1943, at Chicago,
third period. 4G-1A. Chicago 10, NY Rangers 1.
   – Leo Labine, Boston, Nov. 28, 1954, at Boston,
second period. 3G-2A. Boston 6, Detroit 2.
   – Darryl Sittler, Toronto, Feb. 7, 1976, at Toronto,
second period. 3G-2A. Toronto 11, Boston 4.
   – Grant Mulvey, Chicago, Feb. 3, 1982, at Chicago,
first period. 4G-1A. Chicago 9, St. Louis 5.
   – Dale Hawerchuk, Winnipeg, Mar. 6, 1984, at Los Angeles,
second period. 5A. Winnipeg 7, Los Angeles 3.
   – Jari Kurri, Edmonton, Oct. 26, 1984, at Edmonton,
second period. 2G-3A. Edmonton 8, Los Angeles 2.
   – Pat Elynuik, Winnipeg, Jan. 20, 1989, at Winnipeg,
second period. 2G-3A. Winnipeg 7, Pittsburgh 3.
   – Ray Ferraro, Hartford, Dec. 9, 1989, at Hartford,
first period. 3G-2A. Hartford 7, New Jersey 3.
   – Stephane Richer, Montreal, Feb. 14, 1990, at Montreal,
first period. 2G-3A. Montreal 10, Vancouver 1.
   – Cliff Ronning, Vancouver, Apr. 15, 1993, at Los Angeles,
third period. 3G-2A. Vancouver 8, Los Angeles 6.
   – Peter Forsberg, Colorado, Mar. 3, 1999, at Florida,
third period. 2G-3A. Colorado 7, Florida 5.

POWER-PLAY AND SHORTHAND GOALS

MOST POWER-PLAY GOALS, CAREER:
274 – Dave Andreychuk, Buffalo, Toronto, New Jersey, Boston, Colorado,
Tampa Bay, in 23 seasons. 1,639GP
265 – Brett Hull, Calgary, St. Louis, Dallas, Detroit, Phoenix,
in 19 seasons. 1,269GP
249 – Phil Esposito, Chicago, Boston, NY Rangers, in 18 seasons. 1,282GP

MOST POWER-PLAY GOALS, ONE SEASON:
34 – Tim Kerr, Philadelphia, 1985-86. 76GP – 80 game schedule.
32 – Dave Andreychuk, Buffalo, Toronto, 1992-93. 83GP – 84 game schedule.
31 – Joe Nieuwendyk, Calgary, 1987-88. 75GP – 80 game schedule.
   – Mario Lemieux, Pittsburgh, 1988-89. 76GP – 80 game schedule.
   – Mario Lemieux, Pittsburgh, 1995-96. 70GP – 82 game schedule.
29 – Michel Goulet, Quebec, 1987-88. 80GP – 80 game schedule.
   – Brett Hull, St. Louis, 1990-91. 78GP – 80 game schedule.
   – Brett Hull, St. Louis, 1992-93. 80GP – 84 game schedule.

MOST SHORTHAND GOALS, ONE SEASON:
13 – Mario Lemieux, Pittsburgh, 1988-89. 76GP – 80 game schedule.
12 – Wayne Gretzky, Edmonton, 1983-84. 74GP – 80 game schedule.
11 – Wayne Gretzky, Edmonton, 1984-85. 80GP – 80 game schedule.
10 – Marcel Dionne, Detroit, 1974-75. 80GP – 80 game schedule.
   – Mario Lemieux, Pittsburgh, 1987-88. 77GP – 80 game schedule.
   – Dirk Graham, Chicago, 1988-89. 80GP – 80 game schedule.

MOST SHORTHAND GOALS, ONE GAME:
3 – Theoren Fleury, Calgary, Mar. 9, 1991, at St. Louis. Calgary 8,
St. Louis 4.

OVERTIME SCORING

MOST OVERTIME GOALS, CAREER:
14 – Sergei Fedorov, Detroit, Anaheim, Columbus.
   – **Jaromir Jagr**, Pittsburgh, Washington, NY Rangers.
   – **Mats Sundin**, Quebec, Toronto.
13 – Steve Thomas, Toronto, Chicago, NY Islanders, New Jersey, Anaheim.
12 – Jaromir Jagr, Pittsburgh, Washington.

MOST OVERTIME ASSISTS, CAREER:
18 – Mark Messier, Edmonton, NY Rangers, Vancouver.
17 – Adam Oates, Detroit, St. Louis, Boston, Washington, Philadelphia,
Anaheim.
   – Nicklas Lidstrom, Detroit.
15 – Wayne Gretzky, Edmonton, Los Angeles, St. Louis, NY Rangers.
   – Doug Gilmour, St. Louis, Calgary, Toronto, New Jersey, Chicago,
Buffalo, Montreal.

MOST OVERTIME POINTS, CAREER:
27 – Sergei Fedorov, Detroit, Anaheim, Columbus. 14G-13A.
26 – Mark Messier, Edmonton, NY Rangers, Vancouver. 8G-18A.
24 – Jaromir Jagr, Pittsburgh, Washington, NY Rangers. 14G-10A.
   – Mats Sundin, Quebec, Toronto. 14G-10A.
23 – Steve Thomas, Toronto, Chicago, NY Islanders, New Jersey, Chicago,
Anaheim. 13G-10A.
22 – Mario Lemieux, Pittsburgh. 11G-11A.
   – Adam Oates, Detroit, St. Louis, Boston, Washington, Philadelphia,
Anaheim. 5G-17A.
   – Pierre Turgeon, Buffalo, NY Islanders, Montreal, St. Louis, Dallas.
11G-11A

Florida's Olli Jokinen had four overtime goals in 2005-06,
tying the single-season record for overtime goals since
the five-minute extra session was adopted in 1983-84.
Patrik Elias, Markus Naslund and Mats Sundin
also share this record.

SCORING BY A CENTER

MOST GOALS BY A CENTER, CAREER
- **894 – Wayne Gretzky**, Edmonton, Los Angeles, St. Louis, NY Rangers, in 20 seasons. 1,487GP
- 731 – Marcel Dionne, Detroit, Los Angeles, NY Rangers, in 18 seasons. 1,348GP
- 717 – Phil Esposito, Chicago, Boston, NY Rangers, in 18 seasons. 1,282GP
- 694 – Mark Messier, Edmonton, NY Rangers, Vancouver, in 25 seasons. 1,756GP
- 692 – Steve Yzerman, Detroit, in 22 seasons. 1,514GP
- 690 – Mario Lemieux, Pittsburgh, in 17 seasons. 915GP

MOST GOALS BY A CENTER, ONE SEASON:
- **92 – Wayne Gretzky**, Edmonton, 1981-82. 80GP – 80 game schedule.
- 87 – Wayne Gretzky, Edmonton, 1983-84. 74GP – 80 game schedule.
- 85 – Mario Lemieux, Pittsburgh, 1988-89. 76GP – 80 game schedule.
- 76 – Phil Esposito, Boston, 1970-71. 78GP – 78 game schedule.
- 73 – Wayne Gretzky, Edmonton, 1984-85. 80GP – 80 game schedule.

MOST ASSISTS BY A CENTER, CAREER:
- **1,963 – Wayne Gretzky**, Edmonton, Los Angeles, St. Louis, NY Rangers, in 20 seasons. 1,487GP
- 1,249 – Ron Francis, Hartford, Pittsburgh, Carolina, Toronto, in 23 seasons. 1,731GP
- 1,193 – Mark Messier, Edmonton, NY Rangers, Vancouver, in 25 seasons. 1,756GP
- 1,079 – Adam Oates, Detroit, St. Louis, Boston, Washington, Philadelphia, Anaheim, Edmonton, in 19 seasons. 1,337GP
- 1,063 – Steve Yzerman, Detroit, in 22 seasons. 1,514GP

MOST ASSISTS BY A CENTER, ONE SEASON:
- **163 – Wayne Gretzky**, Edmonton, 1985-86. 80GP – 80 game schedule.
- 135 – Wayne Gretzky, Edmonton, 1984-85. 80GP – 80 game schedule.
- 125 – Wayne Gretzky, Edmonton, 1982-83. 80GP – 80 game schedule.
- 122 – Wayne Gretzky, Los Angeles, 1990-91. 78GP – 80 game schedule.
- 121 – Wayne Gretzky, Edmonton, 1986-87. 79GP – 80 game schedule.

MOST POINTS BY A CENTER, CAREER:
- **2,857 – Wayne Gretzky**, Edmonton, Los Angeles, St. Louis, NY Rangers, in 20 seasons. 1,487GP (894G-1,963A)
- 1,887 – Mark Messier, Edmonton, NY Rangers, Vancouver, in 25 seasons. 1,756GP (694G-1,193A)
- 1,798 – Ron Francis, Hartford, Pittsburgh, Carolina, Toronto, in 23 seasons. 1,731GP (549G-1,249A)
- 1,771 – Marcel Dionne, Detroit, Los Angeles, NY Rangers, in 18 seasons. 1,348GP (731G-1,040A)
- 1,755 – Steve Yzerman, Detroit, in 22 seasons. 1,514GP (682G-1,063A)

MOST POINTS BY A CENTER, ONE SEASON:
- **215 – Wayne Gretzky**, Edmonton, 1985-86. 80GP – 80 game schedule.
- 212 – Wayne Gretzky, Edmonton, 1981-82. 80GP – 80 game schedule.
- 208 – Wayne Gretzky, Edmonton, 1984-85. 80GP – 80 game schedule.
- 205 – Wayne Gretzky, Edmonton, 1983-84. 74GP – 80 game schedule.
- 199 – Mario Lemieux, Pittsburgh, 1988-89. 76GP – 80 game schedule.

SCORING BY A LEFT WING

MOST GOALS BY A LEFT WING, CAREER:
- **668 – Luc Robitaille**, Los Angeles, Pittsburgh, NY Rangers, Detroit, in 19 seasons. 1,431GP
- 640 – Dave Andreychuk, Buffalo, Toronto, New Jersey, Boston, Colorado, Tampa Bay, in 23 seasons. 1,639GP
- 610 – Bobby Hull, Chicago, Winnipeg, Hartford, in 16 seasons. 1,063GP
- 598 – Brendan Shanahan, New Jersey, St. Louis, Hartford, Detroit, in 18 seasons. 1,350GP
- 556 – John Bucyk, Detroit, Boston, in 23 seasons. 1,540GP

MOST GOALS BY A LEFT WING, ONE SEASON:
- **63 – Luc Robitaille**, Los Angeles, 1992-93. 84GP – 84 game schedule.
- 60 – Steve Shutt, Montreal, 1976-77. 80GP – 80 game schedule.
- 58 – Bobby Hull, Chicago, 1968-69. 74GP – 76 game schedule.
- 57 – Michel Goulet, Quebec, 1982-83. 80GP – 80 game schedule.
- 56 – Charlie Simmer, Los Angeles, 1979-80. 64GP – 80 game schedule.
  - Charlie Simmer, Los Angeles, 1980-81. 65GP – 80 game schedule.
  - Michel Goulet, Quebec, 1983-84. 75GP – 80 game schedule.

MOST ASSISTS BY A LEFT WING, CAREER:
- **813 – John Bucyk**, Detroit, Boston, in 23 seasons. 1,540GP
- 726 – Luc Robitaille, Los Angeles, Pittsburgh, NY Rangers, Detroit, in 19 seasons. 1,431GP
- 698 – Dave Andreychuk, Buffalo, Toronto, New Jersey, Boston, Colorado, Tampa Bay, in 23 seasons. 1,639GP
- 634 – Brendan Shanahan, New Jersey, St. Louis, Hartford, Detroit, in 18 seasons. 1,350GP
- 604 – Michel Goulet, Quebec, Chicago, in 15 seasons. 1,089GP

MOST ASSISTS BY A LEFT WING, ONE SEASON:
- **70 – Joe Juneau**, Boston, 1992-93. 84GP – 84 game schedule.
- 69 – Kevin Stevens, Pittsburgh, 1991-92. 80GP – 80 game schedule.
- 67 – Mats Naslund, Montreal, 1985-86. 80GP – 80 game schedule.
- 65 – John Bucyk, Boston, 1970-71. 78GP – 78 game schedule.
  - Michel Goulet, Quebec, 1983-84. 75GP – 80 game schedule.
- 64 – Mark Messier, Edmonton, 1983-84. 73GP – 80 game schedule.

MOST POINTS BY A LEFT WING, CAREER:
- **1,394 – Luc Robitaille**, Los Angeles, Pittsburgh, NY Rangers, Detroit, in 19 seasons. 1,431GP (668G-726A)
- 1,369 – John Bucyk, Detroit, Boston, in 23 seasons. 1,540GP (556G-813A)
- 1,338 – Dave Andreychuk, Buffalo, Toronto, New Jersey, Boston, Colorado, Tampa Bay, in 23 seasons. 1,639GP (640G-698A)
- 1,232 – Brendan Shanahan, New Jersey, St. Louis, Hartford, Detroit, in 18 seasons. 1,350GP (598G-634A)
- 1,170 – Bobby Hull, Chicago, Winnipeg, Hartford, in 16 seasons. 1,063GP (610G-560A)

MOST POINTS BY A LEFT WING, ONE SEASON:
- **125 – Luc Robitaille**, Los Angeles, 1992-93. 84GP – 84 game schedule.
- 123 – Kevin Stevens, Pittsburgh, 1991-92. 80GP – 80 game schedule.
- 121 – Michel Goulet, Quebec, 1983-84. 75GP – 80 game schedule.
- 116 – John Bucyk, Boston, 1970-71. 78GP – 78 game schedule.
- 112 – Bill Barber, Philadelphia, 1975-76. 80GP – 80 game schedule.

SCORING BY A RIGHT WING

MOST GOALS BY A RIGHT WING, CAREER:
- **801 – Gordie Howe**, Detroit, Hartford, in 26 seasons. 1,767GP
- 741 – Brett Hull, Calgary, St. Louis, Dallas, Detroit, Phoenix, in 19 seasons. 1,269GP
- 708 – Mike Gartner, Washington, Minnesota, NY Rangers, Toronto, Phoenix, in 19 seasons. 1,432GP
- 608 – Dino Ciccarelli, Minnesota, Washington, Detroit, Tampa Bay, Florida, in 19 seasons. 1,232GP
- 601 – Jari Kurri, Edmonton, Los Angeles, NY Rangers, Anaheim, Colorado, in 17 seasons. 1,251GP

MOST GOALS BY A RIGHT WING, ONE SEASON:
- **86 – Brett Hull**, St. Louis, 1990-91. 78GP – 80 game schedule.
- 76 – Alexander Mogilny, Buffalo, 1992-93. 77GP – 84 game schedule.
  - Teemu Selanne, Winnipeg, 1992-93. 84GP – 84 game schedule.
- 72 – Brett Hull, St. Louis, 1989-90. 80GP – 80 game schedule.
- 71 – Jari Kurri, Edmonton, 1984-85. 73GP – 80 game schedule.
- 70 – Brett Hull, St. Louis, 1991-92. 73GP – 80 game schedule.

MOST ASSISTS BY A RIGHT WING, CAREER:
- **1,049 – Gordie Howe**, Detroit, Hartford, in 26 seasons. 1,767GP
- 841 – Jaromir Jagr, Pittsburgh, Washington, NY Rangers, in 15 seasons. 1,109GP
- 797 – Jari Kurri, Edmonton, Los Angeles, NY Rangers, Anaheim, Colorado, in 17 seasons. 1,251GP
- 793 – Guy Lafleur, Montreal, NY Rangers, Quebec, in 17 seasons. 1,126GP
- 781 – Mark Recchi, Pittsburgh, Philadelphia, Montreal, Carolina, in 17 seasons. 1,256GP

MOST ASSISTS BY A RIGHT WING, ONE SEASON:
- **87 – Jaromir Jagr**, Pittsburgh, 1995-96. 82GP – 82 game schedule.
- 83 – Mike Bossy, NY Islanders, 1981-82. 80GP – 80 game schedule.
  - Jaromir Jagr, Pittsburgh, 1998-99. 81GP – 82 game schedule.
- 80 – Guy Lafleur, Montreal, 1976-77. 80GP – 80 game schedule.
- 77 – Guy Lafleur, Montreal, 1978-79. 80GP – 80 game schedule.

Luc Robitaille, who retired after the 2005-06 season, leaves the game as the NHL's highest-scoring left winger, holding both the single-season and career records for goals and points at that position.

MOST POINTS BY A RIGHT WING, CAREER:
1,850 – Gordie Howe, Detroit, Hartford, in 26 seasons. 1,767GP (801G-1,049A)
1,432 – Jaromir Jagr, Pittsburgh, Washington, NY Rangers, in 15 seasons. 1,109GP (591G-841A)
1,398 – Jari Kurri, Edmonton, Los Angeles, NY Rangers, Anaheim, Colorado, in 17 seasons. 1,251GP (601G-797A)
1,390 – Brett Hull, Calgary, St. Louis, Dallas, Detroit, Phoenix, in 19 seasons. 1,269GP (741G-649A)
1,353 – Guy Lafleur, Montreal, NY Rangers, Quebec, in 17 seasons. 1,126GP (560G-793A)

MOST POINTS BY A RIGHT WING, ONE SEASON:
149 – Jaromir Jagr, Pittsburgh, 1995-96. 82GP – 82 game schedule.
147 – Mike Bossy, NY Islanders, 1981-82. 80GP – 80 game schedule.
136 – Guy Lafleur, Montreal, 1976-77. 80GP – 80 game schedule.
135 – Jari Kurri, Edmonton, 1984-85. 73GP – 80 game schedule.
132 – Guy Lafleur, Montreal, 1977-78. 78GP – 80 game schedule.
– Teemu Selanne, Winnipeg, 1992-93. 84GP – 84 game schedule.

SCORING BY A DEFENSEMAN

MOST GOALS BY A DEFENSEMAN, CAREER:
410 – Raymond Bourque, Boston, Colorado, in 22 seasons. 1,612GP
396 – Paul Coffey, Edmonton, Pittsburgh, Los Angeles, Detroit, Hartford, Philadelphia, Chicago, Carolina, Boston, in 21 seasons. 1,409GP
340 – Al MacInnis, Calgary, St. Louis, in 23 seasons. 1,416GP
338 – Phil Housley, Buffalo, Winnipeg, St. Louis, Calgary, New Jersey, Washington, Chicago, Toronto, in 21 seasons. 1,495GP
310 – Denis Potvin, NY Islanders, in 15 seasons. 1,060GP

MOST GOALS BY A DEFENSEMAN, ONE SEASON:
48 – Paul Coffey, Edmonton, 1985-86. 79GP – 80 game schedule.
46 – Bobby Orr, Boston, 1974-75. 80GP – 80 game schedule.
40 – Paul Coffey, Edmonton, 1983-84. 80GP – 80 game schedule.
39 – Doug Wilson, Chicago, 1981-82. 76GP – 80 game schedule.
37 – Bobby Orr, Boston, 1970-71. 78GP – 78 game schedule.
– Bobby Orr, Boston, 1971-72. 76GP – 78 game schedule.
– Paul Coffey, Edmonton, 1984-85. 80GP – 80 game schedule.

MOST GOALS BY A DEFENSEMAN, ONE GAME:
5 – Ian Turnbull, Toronto, Feb. 2, 1977, at Toronto. Toronto 9, Detroit 1.
4 – Harry Cameron, Toronto, Dec. 26, 1917, at Toronto. Toronto 7, Montreal 5.
– Harry Cameron, Montreal, Mar. 3, 1920, at Quebec. Montreal 16, Quebec 3.
– Sprague Cleghorn, Montreal, Jan. 14, 1922, at Montreal. Montreal 10, Hamilton 6.
– John McKinnon, Pittsburgh, Nov. 19, 1929, at Pittsburgh. Pittsburgh 10, Toronto 5.
– Hap Day, Toronto, Nov. 19, 1929, at Pittsburgh. Pittsburgh 10, Toronto 5.
– Tom Bladon, Philadelphia, Dec. 11, 1977, at Philadelphia. Philadelphia 11, Cleveland 1.
– Ian Turnbull, Los Angeles, Dec. 12, 1981, at Los Angeles. Los Angeles 7, Vancouver 5.
– Paul Coffey, Edmonton, Oct. 26, 1984, at Calgary. Edmonton 6, Calgary 5.

MOST ASSISTS BY A DEFENSEMAN, CAREER:
1,169 – Raymond Bourque, Boston, Colorado, in 22 seasons. 1,612GP
1,135 – Paul Coffey, Edmonton, Pittsburgh, Los Angeles, Detroit, Hartford, Philadelphia, Chicago, Carolina, Boston, in 21 seasons. 1,409GP
934 – Al MacInnis, Calgary, St. Louis, in 23 seasons. 1,416GP
929 – Larry Murphy, Los Angeles, Washington, Minnesota, Pittsburgh, Toronto, Detroit, in 21 seasons. 1,615GP
894 – Phil Housley, Buffalo, Winnipeg, St. Louis, Calgary, New Jersey, Washington, Chicago, Toronto, in 21 seasons. 1,495GP

MOST ASSISTS BY A DEFENSEMAN, ONE SEASON:
102 – Bobby Orr, Boston, 1970-71. 78GP – 78 game schedule.
90 – Bobby Orr, Boston, 1973-74. 74GP – 78 game schedule.
– Paul Coffey, Edmonton, 1985-86. 79GP – 80 game schedule.
89 – Bobby Orr, Boston, 1974-75. 80GP – 80 game schedule.
87 – Bobby Orr, Boston, 1969-70. 76GP – 78 game schedule.

MOST ASSISTS BY A DEFENSEMAN, ONE GAME:
6 – Babe Pratt, Toronto, Jan. 8, 1944, at Toronto. Toronto 12, Boston 3.
– Pat Stapleton, Chicago, Mar. 30, 1969, at Chicago. Chicago 9, Detroit 5.
– Bobby Orr, Boston, Jan. 1, 1973, at Vancouver. Boston 8, Vancouver 2.
– Ron Stackhouse, Pittsburgh, Mar. 8, 1975, at Pittsburgh. Pittsburgh 8, Philadelphia 2.
– Paul Coffey, Edmonton, Mar. 14, 1986, at Edmonton. Edmonton 12, Detroit 3.
– Gary Suter, Calgary, Apr. 4, 1986, at Calgary. Calgary 9, Edmonton 3.

MOST POINTS BY A DEFENSEMAN, CAREER:
1,579 – Raymond Bourque, Boston, Colorado, in 22 seasons. 1,612GP (410G-1,169A)
1,531 – Paul Coffey, Edmonton, Pittsburgh, Los Angeles, Detroit, Hartford, Philadelphia, Chicago, Carolina, Boston, in 21 seasons. 1,409GP (396G-1,135A)
1,274 – Al MacInnis, Calgary, St. Louis, in 23 seasons. 1,416GP (340G-934A)
1,232 – Phil Housley, Buffalo, Winnipeg, St. Louis, Calgary, New Jersey, Washington, Chicago, Toronto, in 21 seasons. 1,495GP (338G-894A)
1,216 – Larry Murphy, Los Angeles, Washington, Minnesota, Pittsburgh, Toronto, Detroit, in 21 seasons. 1,615GP (287G-929A)

MOST POINTS BY A DEFENSEMAN, ONE SEASON:
139 – Bobby Orr, Boston, 1970-71. 78GP – 78 game schedule.
138 – Paul Coffey, Edmonton, 1985-86. 79GP – 80 game schedule.
135 – Bobby Orr, Boston, 1974-75. 80GP – 80 game schedule.
126 – Paul Coffey, Edmonton, 1983-84. 80GP – 80 game schedule.
122 – Bobby Orr, Boston, 1973-74. 74GP – 78 game schedule.

MOST POINTS BY A DEFENSEMAN, ONE GAME:
8 – Tom Bladon, Philadelphia, Dec. 11, 1977, at Philadelphia. 4G-4A. Philadelphia 11, Cleveland 1.
– **Paul Coffey**, Edmonton, Mar. 14, 1986, at Edmonton. 2G-6A. Edmonton 12, Detroit 3.
7 – Bobby Orr, Boston, Nov. 15, 1973, at Boston. 3G-4A. Boston 10, NY Rangers 2.

SCORING BY A GOALTENDER

MOST POINTS BY A GOALTENDER, CAREER:
48 – Tom Barrasso, Buffalo, Pittsburgh, Ottawa, Carolina, Toronto, St. Louis, in 19 seasons. 777GP
46 – Grant Fuhr, Edmonton, Toronto, Buffalo, Los Angeles, St. Louis, Calgary, in 19 seasons. 868GP

MOST POINTS BY A GOALTENDER, ONE SEASON:
14 – Grant Fuhr, Edmonton, 1983-84. 45GP – 80 game schedule.
9 – Curtis Joseph, St. Louis, 1991-92. 60GP – 80 game schedule.
8 – Mike Palmateer, Washington, 1980-81. 49GP – 80 game schedule.
– Grant Fuhr, Edmonton, 1987-88. 75GP – 80 game schedule.
– Ron Hextall, Philadelphia, 1988-89. 64GP – 80 game schedule.
– Tom Barrasso, Pittsburgh, 1992-93. 63GP – 84 game schedule.

MOST POINTS BY A GOALTENDER, ONE GAME:
3 – Jeff Reese, Calgary, Feb. 10, 1993, at Calgary. Calgary 13, San Jose 1.

Among NHL defensemen, only Hall of Famers Raymond Bourque and Paul Coffey have had more career goals and points than hard-shooting Al MacInnis, who starred with the Calgary Flames and St. Louis Blues for 23 seasons.

SCORING BY A ROOKIE

MOST GOALS BY A ROOKIE, ONE SEASON:
76 – Teemu Selanne, Winnipeg, 1992-93. 84GP – 84 game schedule.
53 – Mike Bossy, NY Islanders, 1977-78. 73GP – 80 game schedule.
52 – Alex Ovechkin, Washington, 2005-06. 81GP – 82 game schedule.
51 – Joe Nieuwendyk, Calgary, 1987-88. 75GP – 80 game schedule.
45 – Dale Hawerchuk, Winnipeg, 1981-82. 80GP – 80 game schedule.
– Luc Robitaille, Los Angeles, 1986-87. 79GP – 80 game schedule.

MOST GOALS BY A PLAYER IN HIS FIRST NHL SEASON, ONE GAME:
5 – Howie Meeker, Toronto, Jan. 8, 1947, at Toronto. Toronto 10, Chicago 4.
– **Don Murdoch**, NY Rangers, Oct. 12, 1976, at Minnesota.
NY Rangers 10, Minnesota 4.

MOST GOALS BY A PLAYER IN HIS FIRST NHL GAME:
3 – Alex Smart, Montreal, Jan. 14, 1943, at Montreal. Montreal 5, Chicago 1.
– **Real Cloutier**, Quebec, Oct. 10, 1979, at Quebec. Atlanta 5, Quebec 3.

MOST ASSISTS BY A ROOKIE, ONE SEASON:
70 – Peter Stastny, Quebec, 1980-81. 77GP – 80 game schedule.
– Joe Juneau, Boston, 1992-93. 84GP – 84 game schedule.
63 – Bryan Trottier, NY Islanders, 1975-76. 80GP – 80 game schedule.
– Sidney Crosby, Pittsburgh, 2005–06. 81GP – 82 game schedule.
62 – Sergei Makarov, Calgary, 1989-90. 80GP – 80 game schedule.
60 – Larry Murphy, Los Angeles, 1980-81. 80GP – 80 game schedule.

MOST ASSISTS BY A PLAYER IN HIS FIRST NHL SEASON, ONE GAME:
7 – Wayne Gretzky, Edmonton, Feb. 15, 1980, at Edmonton.
Edmonton 8, Washington 2.
6 – Gary Suter, Calgary, Apr. 4, 1986, at Calgary. Calgary 9, Edmonton 3.

MOST ASSISTS BY A PLAYER IN HIS FIRST NHL GAME:
4 – Dutch Reibel, Detroit, Oct. 8, 1953, at Detroit. Detroit 4, NY Rangers 1.
– **Roland Eriksson**, Minnesota, Oct. 6, 1976, at NY Rangers.
NY Rangers 6, Minnesota 5.
3 – Al Hill, Philadelphia, Feb. 14, 1977, at Philadelphia. Philadelphia 6,
St. Louis 4.
– Jarno Kultanen, Boston, Oct. 5, 2000, at Boston. Boston 4, Ottawa 4.
– Stanislav Chistov, Anaheim, Oct. 10, 2002, at St. Louis. Anaheim 4,
St. Louis 3.
– Dominic Moore, NY Rangers, Nov. 1, 2003, at Montreal. NY Rangers 5,
Montreal 1.

MOST POINTS BY A ROOKIE, ONE SEASON:
132 – Teemu Selanne, Winnipeg, 1992-93. 84GP – 84 game schedule.
109 – Peter Stastny, Quebec, 1980-81. 77GP – 80 game schedule.
106 – Alex Ovechkin, Washington, 2005-06. 81GP – 82 game schedule.
103 – Dale Hawerchuk, Winnipeg, 1981-82. 80GP – 80 game schedule.
102 – Joe Juneau, Boston, 1992-93. 84GP – 84 game schedule.
– Sidney Crosby, Pittsburgh, 2005–06. 81GP – 82 game schedule.
100 – Mario Lemieux, Pittsburgh, 1984-85. 73GP – 80 game schedule.

MOST POINTS BY A PLAYER IN HIS FIRST NHL SEASON, ONE GAME:
8 – Peter Stastny, Quebec, Feb. 22, 1981, at Washington. 4G-4A.
Quebec 11, Washington 7.
– **Anton Stastny**, Quebec, Feb. 22, 1981, at Washington. 3G-5A.
Quebec 11, Washington 7.
7 – Wayne Gretzky, Edmonton, Feb. 15, 1980, at Edmonton. 7A.
Edmonton 8, Washington 2.
– Sergei Makarov, Calgary, Feb. 25, 1990, at Calgary. 2G-5A.
Calgary 10, Edmonton 4.
6 – Wayne Gretzky, Edmonton, Mar. 29, 1980, at Toronto. 2G-4A.
Edmonton 8, Toronto 5.
– Gary Suter, Calgary, Apr. 4, 1986, at Calgary. 6A.
Calgary 9, Edmonton 3.

MOST POINTS BY A PLAYER IN HIS FIRST NHL GAME:
5 – Al Hill, Philadelphia, Feb. 14, 1977, at Philadelphia. 2G-3A.
Philadelphia 6, St. Louis 4.
4 – Alex Smart, Montreal, Jan. 14, 1943, at Montreal. 3G-1A.
Montreal 5, Chicago 1.
– Dutch Reibel, Detroit, Oct. 8, 1953, at Detroit. 4A.
Detroit 4, NY Rangers 1.
– Roland Eriksson, Minnesota, Oct. 6, 1976, at NY Rangers. 4A.
NY Rangers 6, Minnesota 5.
– Stanislav Chistov, Anaheim, Oct. 10, 2002, at St. Louis. 1G-3A.
Anaheim 4, St. Louis 3.

SCORING BY A ROOKIE DEFENSEMAN

MOST GOALS BY A ROOKIE DEFENSEMAN, ONE SEASON:
23 – Brian Leetch, NY Rangers, 1988-89. 68GP – 80 game schedule.
22 – Barry Beck, Colorado, 1977-78. 75GP – 80 game schedule.
19 – Reed Larson, Detroit, 1977-78. 75GP – 80 game schedule.
– Phil Housley, Buffalo, 1982-83. 77GP – 80 game schedule.

MOST ASSISTS BY A ROOKIE DEFENSEMAN, ONE SEASON:
60 – Larry Murphy, Los Angeles, 1980-81. 80GP – 80 game schedule.
55 – Chris Chelios, Montreal, 1984-85. 74GP – 80 game schedule.
50 – Stefan Persson, NY Islanders, 1977-78. 66GP – 80 game schedule.
– Gary Suter, Calgary, 1985-86. 80GP – 80 game schedule.
49 – Nicklas Lidstrom, Detroit, 1991-92. 80GP – 80 game schedule.

MOST POINTS BY A ROOKIE DEFENSEMAN, ONE SEASON:
76 – Larry Murphy, Los Angeles, 1980-81. 80GP – 80 game schedule.
71 – Brian Leetch, NY Rangers, 1988-89. 68GP – 80 game schedule.
68 – Gary Suter, Calgary, 1985-86. 80GP – 80 game schedule.
66 – Phil Housley, Buffalo, 1982-83. 77GP – 80 game schedule.
65 – Raymond Bourque, Boston, 1979-80. 80GP – 80 game schedule.

*In 1980-81, Peter Stastny, surrounded here by Michel Goulet and Garry Lariviere,
became the NHL's first rookie to top 100 points. He still shares
the NHL rookie record of 70 assists in a season.*

PER-GAME SCORING AVERAGES

HIGHEST GOALS-PER-GAME AVERAGE, CAREER
(AMONG PLAYERS WITH 200-OR-MORE GOALS)
.762 – **Mike Bossy**, NY Islanders, 1977-78 – 1986-87, with 573G in 752GP.
.756 – Cy Denneny, Ottawa, Boston, 1917-18 – 1928-29, with 248G in 328GP.
.754 – Mario Lemieux, Pittsburgh, 1984-85 – 1996-97,
2000-01 – 2003-04, 2005-06 with 690G in 915GP.
.742 – Babe Dye, Toronto, Hamilton, Chicago, NY Americans,
1919-20 – 1930-31, with 201G in 271GP.
.623 – Pavel Bure, Vancouver, Florida, NY Rangers, 1991-92 – 2002-03,
with 437G in 702GP.

HIGHEST GOALS-PER-GAME AVERAGE, ONE SEASON
(AMONG PLAYERS WITH 20-OR-MORE GOALS):
2.20 – **Joe Malone**, Montreal, 1917-18, with 44G in 20GP.
1.80 – Cy Denneny, Ottawa, 1917-18, with 36G in 20GP.
1.64 – Newsy Lalonde, Montreal, 1917-18, with 23G in 14GP.
1.63 – Joe Malone, Quebec, 1919-20, with 39G in 24GP.
1.61 – Newsy Lalonde, Montreal, 1919-20, with 37G in 23GP.

HIGHEST GOALS-PER-GAME AVERAGE, ONE SEASON
(AMONG PLAYERS WITH 50-OR-MORE GOALS):
1.18 – **Wayne Gretzky**, Edmonton, 1983-84, with 87G in 74GP.
1.15 – Wayne Gretzky, Edmonton, 1981-82, with 92G in 80GP.
 – Mario Lemieux, Pittsburgh, 1992-93, with 69G in 60GP.
1.12 – Mario Lemieux, Pittsburgh, 1988-89, with 85G in 76GP.
1.10 – Brett Hull, St. Louis, 1990-91, with 86G in 78GP.
1.02 – Cam Neely, Boston, 1993-94, with 50G in 49GP.
1.00 – Maurice Richard, Montreal, 1944-45, with 50G in 50GP.

HIGHEST ASSISTS-PER-GAME AVERAGE, CAREER
(AMONG PLAYERS WITH 300-OR-MORE ASSISTS):
1.320 – **Wayne Gretzky**, Edmonton, Los Angeles, St. Louis, NY Rangers,
1979-80 – 1998-99, with 1,963A in 1,487GP.
1.129 – Mario Lemieux, Pittsburgh, 1984-85 – 1996-97,
2000-01 – 2003-04, 2005-06, with 1,033A in 915GP.
.982 – Bobby Orr, Boston, Chicago, 1966-67 – 1978-79, with 645A in 657GP.
.908 – Peter Forsberg, Quebec, Colorado, Philadelphia, 1994-95 – 2000-01,
2002-03 – 2003-04, 2005-06 with 581A in 640GP.
.808 – Peter Stastny, Quebec, New Jersey, St. Louis, 1980-81 – 1994-95, with
789A in 977GP.

HIGHEST ASSISTS-PER-GAME AVERAGE, ONE SEASON
(AMONG PLAYERS WITH 35-OR-MORE ASSISTS):
2.04 – **Wayne Gretzky, Edmonton**, 1985-86, with 163A in 80GP.
1.70 – Wayne Gretzky, Edmonton, 1987-88, with 109A in 64GP.
1.69 – Wayne Gretzky, Edmonton, 1984-85, with 135A in 80GP.
1.59 – Wayne Gretzky, Edmonton, 1983-84, with 118A in 74GP.
1.56 – Wayne Gretzky, Edmonton, 1982-83, with 125A in 80GP.
 – Wayne Gretzky, Los Angeles, 1990-91, with 122A in 78GP.
1.53 – Wayne Gretzky, Edmonton, 1986-87, with 121A in 79GP.
1.52 – Mario Lemieux, Pittsburgh, 1992-93, with 91A in 60GP.
1.50 – Wayne Gretzky, Edmonton, 1981-82, with 120A in 80GP.
 – Mario Lemieux, Pittsburgh, 1988-89, with 114A in 76GP.

HIGHEST POINTS-PER-GAME AVERAGE, CAREER:
(AMONG PLAYERS WITH 500-OR-MORE POINTS):
1.921 – **Wayne Gretzky**, Edmonton, Los Angeles, St. Louis, NY Rangers,
1979-80 – 1998-99, with 2,857PTS (894G-1,963A) in 1,487GP.
1.883 – Mario Lemieux, Pittsburgh, 1984-85 – 1996-97,
2000-01 – 2003-04, 2005-06, with 1,723PTS (690G-1,033A) in 915GP.
1.497 – Mike Bossy, NY Islanders, 1977-78 – 1986-87, with 1,126PTS
(573G-553A) in 752GP.
1.393 – Bobby Orr, Boston, Chicago, 1966-67 – 1978-79, with 915PTS
(270G-645A) in 657GP.
1.314 – Marcel Dionne, Detroit, Los Angeles, NY Rangers, 1971-72 – 1988-89,
with 1,771PTS (731G-1,040A) in 1,348GP.

HIGHEST POINTS-PER-GAME AVERAGE, ONE SEASON
(AMONG PLAYERS WITH 50-OR-MORE POINTS):
2.77 – **Wayne Gretzky**, Edmonton, 1983-84, with 205PTS in 74GP.
2.69 – Wayne Gretzky, Edmonton, 1985-86, with 215PTS in 80GP.
2.67 – Mario Lemieux, Pittsburgh, 1992-93, with 160PTS in 60GP.
2.65 – Wayne Gretzky, Edmonton, 1981-82, with 212PTS in 80GP.
2.62 – Mario Lemieux, Pittsburgh, 1988-89, with 199PTS in 76GP.
2.60 – Wayne Gretzky, Edmonton, 1984-85, with 208PTS in 80GP.
2.45 – Wayne Gretzky, Edmonton, 1982-83, with 196PTS in 80GP.
2.33 – Wayne Gretzky, Edmonton, 1987-88, with 149PTS in 64GP.
2.32 – Wayne Gretzky, Edmonton, 1986-87, with 183PTS in 79GP.
2.30 – Mario Lemieux, Pittsburgh, 1995-96, with 161PTS in 70GP.
2.18 – Mario Lemieux, Pittsburgh, 1987-88, with 168PTS in 77GP.
2.15 – Wayne Gretzky, Los Angeles, 1988-89, with 168PTS in 78GP.
2.09 – Wayne Gretzky, Los Angeles, 1990-91, with 163PTS in 78GP.
2.08 – Mario Lemieux, Pittsburgh, 1989-90, with 123PTS in 59GP.

SCORING PLATEAUS

MOST 20-OR-MORE GOAL SEASONS:
22 – **Gordie Howe**, Detroit, Hartford, in 26 seasons.
20 – Ron Francis, Hartford, Pittsburgh, Carolina, Toronto, in 23 seasons.
19 – Dave Andreychuk, Buffalo, Toronto, New Jersey, Boston, Colorado,
Tampa Bay, in 23 seasons.
17 – Marcel Dionne, Detroit, Los Angeles, NY Rangers, in 18 seasons.
 – Mike Gartner, Washington, Minnesota, NY Rangers, Toronto,
Phoenix, in 18 seasons.
 – Wayne Gretzky, Edmonton, Los Angeles, St. Louis, NY Rangers,
in 20 seasons.
 – Mark Messier, Edmonton, NY Rangers, Vancouver, in 25 seasons.
 – Brett Hull, Calgary, St. Louis, Dallas, Detroit, Phoenix, in 19 seasons.
 – Brendan Shanahan, New Jersey, St. Louis, Hartford, Detroit, in 18 seasons.

MOST CONSECUTIVE 20-OR-MORE GOAL SEASONS:
22 – **Gordie Howe**, Detroit, 1949-50 – 1970-71.
17 – Marcel Dionne, Detroit, Los Angeles, NY Rangers, 1971-72 – 1987-88.
 – Brett Hull, Calgary, St. Louis, Dallas, Detroit, 1987-88 – 2003-04.
 – Brendan Shanahan, New Jersey, St. Louis, Hartford, Detroit,
1988-89 – 2005-06.
16 – Phil Esposito, Chicago, Boston, NY Rangers, 1964-65 – 1979-80.
15 – Mike Gartner, Washington, Minnesota, NY Rangers, Toronto,
1979-80 – 1993-94.
 – Jaromir Jagr, Pittsburgh, Washington, NY Rangers, 1990-91 – 2005-06.
 – Mats Sundin, Quebec, Toronto, 1990-91 – 2005-06.

Marcel Dionne racked up his impressive points total in fewer games than many of the NHL's all-time top scorers. Only Wayne Gretzky, Mario Lemieux, Mike Bossy and Bobby Orr top Dionne's career average of 1.314 points per game.

MOST 30-OR-MORE GOAL SEASONS:
17 – Mike Gartner, Washington, Minnesota, NY Rangers, Toronto, Phoenix, in 19 seasons.
14 – Gordie Howe, Detroit, Hartford, in 26 seasons.
  – Marcel Dionne, Detroit, Los Angeles, NY Rangers, in 18 seasons.
  – Wayne Gretzky, Edmonton, Los Angeles, St. Louis, NY Rangers, in 20 seasons.
  – Jaromir Jagr, Pittsburgh, Washington, NY Rangers, in 15 seasons.
13 – Bobby Hull, Chicago, Winnipeg, Hartford, in 16 seasons.
  – Phil Esposito, Chicago, Boston, NY Rangers, in 18 seasons.
  – Brett Hull, Calgary, St. Louis, Dallas, Detroit, Phoenix, in 19 seasons.

MOST CONSECUTIVE 30-OR-MORE GOAL SEASONS:
15 – Mike Gartner, Washington, Minnesota, NY Rangers, Toronto, 1979-80 – 1993-94.
14 – Jaromir Jagr, Pittsburgh, Washington, NY Rangers, 1991-92 – 2005-06.
13 – Bobby Hull, Chicago, 1959-60 – 1971-72.
  – Phil Esposito, Boston, NY Rangers, 1967-68 – 1979-80.
  – Wayne Gretzky, Edmonton, Los Angeles, 1979-80 – 1991-92.

MOST 40-OR-MORE GOAL SEASONS:
12 – Wayne Gretzky, Edmonton, Los Angeles, St. Louis, NY Rangers, in 20 seasons.
10 – Marcel Dionne, Detroit, Los Angeles, NY Rangers, in 18 seasons.
  – Mario Lemieux, Pittsburgh, in 17 seasons.
9 – Mike Bossy, NY Islanders, in 10 seasons.
  – Mike Gartner, Washington, Minnesota, NY Rangers, Toronto, Phoenix, in 19 seasons.

MOST CONSECUTIVE 40-OR-MORE GOAL SEASONS:
12 – Wayne Gretzky, Edmonton, Los Angeles, 1979-80 – 1990-91.
9 – Mike Bossy, NY Islanders, 1977-78 – 1985-86.
8 – Luc Robitaille, Los Angeles, 1986-87 – 1993-94.
7 – Phil Esposito, Boston, 1968-69 – 1974-75.
  – Michel Goulet, Quebec, 1981-82 – 1987-88.
  – Jari Kurri, Edmonton, 1982-83 – 1988-89.

MOST 50-OR-MORE GOAL SEASONS:
9 – Mike Bossy, NY Islanders, in 10 seasons.
  – Wayne Gretzky, Edmonton, Los Angeles, St. Louis, NY Rangers, in 20 seasons.
6 – Guy Lafleur, Montreal, NY Rangers, Quebec, in 17 seasons.
  – Marcel Dionne, Detroit, Los Angeles, NY Rangers, in 18 seasons.
  – Mario Lemieux, Pittsburgh, in 17 seasons.
5 – Bobby Hull, Chicago, Winnipeg, Hartford, in 16 seasons.
  – Phil Esposito, Chicago, Boston, NY Rangers, in 18 seasons.
  – Brett Hull, Calgary, St. Louis, Dallas, Detroit, Phoenix, in 19 seasons.
  – Steve Yzerman, Detroit, in 22 seasons.
  – Pavel Bure, Vancouver, Florida, NY Rangers, in 12 seasons.

MOST CONSECUTIVE 50-OR-MORE GOAL SEASONS:
9 – Mike Bossy, NY Islanders, 1977-78 – 1985-86.
8 – Wayne Gretzky, Edmonton, 1979-80 – 1986-87.
6 – Guy Lafleur, Montreal, 1974-75 – 1979-80.
5 – Phil Esposito, Boston, 1970-71 – 1974-75.
  – Marcel Dionne, Los Angeles, 1978-79 – 1982-83.
  – Brett Hull, St. Louis, 1989-90 – 1993-94.

MOST 60-OR-MORE GOAL SEASONS:
5 – Mike Bossy, NY Islanders, in 10 seasons.
  – Wayne Gretzky, Edmonton, Los Angeles, St. Louis, NY Rangers, in 20 seasons.
4 – Phil Esposito, Chicago, Boston, NY Rangers, in 18 seasons.
  – Mario Lemieux, Pittsburgh, in 17 seasons.

MOST CONSECUTIVE 60-OR-MORE GOAL SEASONS:
4 – Wayne Gretzky, Edmonton, 1981-82 – 1984-85.
3 – Mike Bossy, NY Islanders, 1980-81 – 1982-83.
  – Brett Hull, St. Louis, 1989-90 – 1991-92.
2 – Phil Esposito, Boston, 1970-71 – 1971-72, 1973-74 – 1974-75.
  – Jari Kurri, Edmonton, 1984-85 – 1985-86.
  – Mario Lemieux, Pittsburgh, 1987-88 – 1988-89.
  – Steve Yzerman, Detroit, 1988-89 – 1989-90.
  – Pavel Bure, Vancouver, 1992-93 – 1993-94.

MOST 100-OR-MORE POINT SEASONS:
15 – Wayne Gretzky, Edmonton, Los Angeles, St. Louis, NY Rangers, in 20 seasons.
10 – Mario Lemieux, Pittsburgh, in 17 seasons.
8 – Marcel Dionne, Detroit, Los Angeles, NY Rangers, in 18 seasons.
7 – Mike Bossy, NY Islanders, in 10 seasons.
  – Peter Stastny, Quebec, New Jersey, St. Louis, in 15 seasons.

MOST CONSECUTIVE 100-OR-MORE POINT SEASONS:
13 – Wayne Gretzky, Edmonton, Los Angeles, 1979-80 – 1991-92.
6 – Bobby Orr, Boston, 1969-70 – 1974-75.
  – Guy Lafleur, Montreal, 1974-75 – 1979-80.
  – Mike Bossy, NY Islanders, 1980-81 – 1985-86.
  – Peter Stastny, Quebec, 1980-81 – 1985-86.
  – Mario Lemieux, Pittsburgh, 1984-85 – 1989-90.
  – Steve Yzerman, Detroit, 1987-88 – 1992-93.

*Of the 12 NHL scoring records listed on this page,
Wayne Gretzky holds or shares nine of them.
He is in second or third on the other three.
Though known as a playmaker, Gretzky
recorded 50 hat tricks in his career,
ten more than any other player.*

THREE-OR-MORE-GOAL GAMES

MOST THREE-OR-MORE GOAL GAMES, CAREER:
50 – Wayne Gretzky, Edmonton, Los Angeles, St. Louis, NY Rangers, in 20 seasons, 37 three-goal games, 9 four-goal games, 4 five-goal games.
40 – Mario Lemieux, Pittsburgh, in 17 seasons, 27 three-goal games, 10 four-goal games, 3 five-goal games.
39 – Mike Bossy, NY Islanders, in 10 seasons, 30 three-goal games, 9 four-goal games.
33 – Brett Hull, Calgary, St. Louis, Dallas, Detroit, Phoenix, in 19 seasons, 30 three-goal games, 3 four-goal games.
32 – Phil Esposito, Chicago, Boston, NY Rangers, in 18 seasons, 27 three-goal games, 5 four-goal games.

MOST THREE-OR-MORE GOAL GAMES, ONE SEASON:
10 – Wayne Gretzky, Edmonton, 1981-82. 6 three-goal games, 3 four-goal games, 1 five-goal game.
  – Wayne Gretzky, Edmonton, 1983-84. 6 three-goal games, 4 four-goal games.
9 – Mike Bossy, NY Islanders, 1980-81. 6 three-goal games, 3 four-goal games.
  – Mario Lemieux, Pittsburgh, 1988-89. 7 three-goal games, 1 four-goal game, 1 five-goal game.
8 – Brett Hull, St. Louis, 1991-92. 8 three-goal games.
7 – Joe Malone, Montreal, 1917-18. 2 three-goal games, 2 four-goal games, 3 five-goal games.
  – Phil Esposito, Boston, 1970-71. 7 three-goal games.
  – Rick Martin, Buffalo, 1975-76. 6 three-goal games, 1 four-goal game.
  – Alexander Mogilny, Buffalo, 1992-93. 5 three-goal games, 2 four-goal games.

SCORING STREAKS

LONGEST CONSECUTIVE GOAL-SCORING STREAK:
16 Games – Punch Broadbent, Ottawa, 1921-22. 27G
14 Games – Joe Malone, Montreal, 1917-18. 35G
13 Games – Newsy Lalonde, Montreal, 1920-21. 24G
   – Charlie Simmer, Los Angeles, 1979-80. 17G
12 Games – Cy Denneny, Ottawa, 1917-18. 23G
   – Dave Lumley, Edmonton, 1981-82. 15G
   – Mario Lemieux, Pittsburgh, 1992-93. 18G

LONGEST CONSECUTIVE ASSIST-SCORING STREAK:
23 Games – Wayne Gretzky, Los Angeles, 1990-91. 48A
18 Games – Adam Oates, Boston, 1992-93. 28A
17 Games – Wayne Gretzky, Edmonton, 1983-84. 38A
   – Paul Coffey, Edmonton, 1985-86. 27A
   – Wayne Gretzky, Los Angeles, 1989-90. 35A
16 Games – Jaromir Jagr, Pittsburgh, 2000-01. 24A

LONGEST CONSECUTIVE POINT-SCORING STREAK:
51 Games – Wayne Gretzky, Edmonton, 1983-84. 61G-92A-153PTS
46 Games – Mario Lemieux, Pittsburgh, 1989-90. 39G-64A-103PTS
39 Games – Wayne Gretzky, Edmonton, 1985-86. 33G-75A-108PTS
30 Games – Wayne Gretzky, Edmonton, 1982-83. 24G-52A-76PTS
   – Mats Sundin, Quebec, 1992-93. 21G-25A-46PTS

LONGEST CONSECUTIVE POINT-SCORING STREAK FROM START OF SEASON:
51 Games – Wayne Gretzky, Edmonton, 1983-84. 61G-92A-153PTS. Streak ended by Los Angeles and goaltender Markus Mattsson on Jan. 28, 1984.

LONGEST CONSECUTIVE POINT-SCORING STREAK BY A DEFENSEMAN:
28 Games – Paul Coffey, Edmonton, 1985-86. 16G-39A-55PTS
19 Games – Raymond Bourque, Boston, 1987-88. 6G-21A-27PTS
17 Games – Raymond Bourque, Boston, 1984-85. 4G-24A-28PTS
   – Brian Leetch, NY Rangers, 1991-92. 5G-24A-29PTS
16 Games – Gary Suter, Calgary, 1987-88. 8G-17A-25PTS
15 Games – Bobby Orr, Boston, 1970-71. 10G-23A-33PTS
   – Bobby Orr, Boston, 1973-74. 8G-15A-23PTS
   – Steve Duchesne, Quebec, 1992-93. 4G-17A-21PTS
   – Chris Chelios, Chicago, 1995-96. 4G-16A-20PTS

FASTEST GOALS AND ASSISTS

FASTEST GOAL FROM START OF A GAME:
0:05 – Doug Smail, Winnipeg, Dec. 20, 1981, at Winnipeg. Winnipeg 5, St. Louis 4.
   – **Bryan Trottier**, NY Islanders, Mar. 22, 1984, at Boston. NY Islanders 3, Boston 3.
   – **Alexander Mogilny**, Buffalo, Dec. 21, 1991, at Toronto. Buffalo 4, Toronto 1.
0:06 – Henry Boucha, Detroit, Jan. 28, 1973, at Montreal. Detroit 4, Montreal 2.
   – Jean Pronovost, Pittsburgh, Mar. 25, 1976, at St. Louis. St. Louis 5, Pittsburgh 2.
0:07 – Charlie Conacher, Toronto, Feb. 6, 1932, at Toronto. Toronto 6, Boston 0.
   – Danny Gare, Buffalo, Dec. 17, 1978, at Buffalo. Buffalo 6, Vancouver 3.
   – Tiger Williams, Los Angeles, Feb. 14, 1987, at Los Angeles. Los Angeles 5, Harford 2.
0:08 – Ron Martin, NY Americans, Dec. 4, 1932, at NY Americans. NY Americans 4, Montreal 2.
   – Chuck Arnason, Colorado, Jan. 28, 1977, at Atlanta. Colorado 3, Atlanta 3.
   – Wayne Gretzky, Edmonton, Dec. 14, 1983, at NY Rangers. Edmonton 9, NY Rangers 4.
   – Gaetan Duchesne, Washington, Mar. 14, 1987, at St. Louis. Washington 3, St. Louis 3.
   – Tim Kerr, Philadelphia, Mar. 7, 1989, at Philadelphia. Philadelphia 4, Edmonton 4.
   – Grant Ledyard, Buffalo, Dec. 4, 1991, at Winnipeg. Buffalo 4, Winnipeg 4.
   – Brent Sutter, Chicago, Feb. 5, 1995, at Vancouver. Chicago 9, Vancouver 4.
   – Paul Kariya, Anaheim, Mar. 9, 1997, at Colorado. Anaheim 2, Colorado 2.
   – Tony Hrkac, Dallas, Nov. 7, 1998, at Los Angeles. Dallas 4, Los Angeles 3.
   – Sergei Fedorov, Detroit, Nov. 21, 1998, at Vancouver. Detroit 4, Vancouver 2.
   – Ronald Petrovicky, Atlanta, Dec. 20, 2003, at Pittsburgh. Atlanta 7, Pittsburgh 4.
   – Mike Modano, Dallas, Dec. 27, 2003, at Columbus. Dallas 4, Columbus 3.
   – Antti Laaksonen, Colorado, Feb. 10, 2006, at Columbus. Colorado 4, Columbus 1.

FASTEST GOAL FROM START OF A PERIOD:
0:04 – Claude Provost, Montreal, Nov. 9, 1957, at Montreal, second period. Montreal 4, Boston 2.
   – **Denis Savard**, Chicago, Jan. 12, 1986, at Chicago, third period. Chicago 4, Hartford 2.

FASTEST GOAL BY A PLAYER IN HIS FIRST NHL GAME:
0:15 – Gus Bodnar, Toronto, Oct. 30, 1943, at Toronto. Toronto 5, NY Rangers 2.
0:18 – Danny Gare, Buffalo, Oct. 10, 1974, at Buffalo. Buffalo 9, Boston 5.
0:20 – Alexander Mogilny, Buffalo, Oct. 5, 1989, at Buffalo. Buffalo 4, Quebec 3.

FASTEST TWO GOALS FROM START OF A GAME:
0:27 – Mike Knuble, Boston, Feb. 14, 2003, at Florida at 0:10 and 0:27. Boston 6, Florida 5.

FASTEST TWO GOALS:
0:04 – Nels Stewart, Mtl. Maroons, Jan. 3, 1931, at Mtl. Maroons at 8:24 and 8:28, third period. Mtl. Maroons 5, Boston 3.
   – **Deron Quint**, Winnipeg, Dec. 15, 1995, at Winnipeg at 7:51 and 7:55, second period. Winnipeg 9, Edmonton 4.
0:05 – Pete Mahovlich, Montreal, Feb. 20, 1971, at Montreal at 12:16 and 12:21, third period. Montreal 7, Chicago 1.
0:06 – Jim Pappin, Chicago, Feb. 16, 1972, at Chicago at 2:57 and 3:03, third period. Chicago 3, Philadelphia 3.
   – Ralph Backstrom, Los Angeles, Nov. 2, 1972, at Los Angeles at 8:30 and 8:36, third period. Los Angeles 5, Boston 2.
   – Lanny McDonald, Calgary, Mar. 22, 1984, at Calgary at 16:23 and 16:29, first period. Detroit 6, Calgary 4.
   – Sylvain Turgeon, Hartford, Mar. 28, 1987, at Hartford at 13:59 and 14:05, second period. Hartford 5, Pittsburgh 4.

FASTEST THREE GOALS:
0:21 – Bill Mosienko, Chicago, Mar. 23, 1952, at NY Rangers, against goaltender Lorne Anderson. Mosienko scored at 6:09, 6:20 and 6:30 of third period, all with both teams at full strength. Chicago 7, NY Rangers 6.
0:44 – Jean Béliveau, Montreal, Nov. 5, 1955, at Montreal, against goaltender Terry Sawchuk. Béliveau scored at 0:42, 1:08 and 1:26 of second period, all with Montreal holding a 6-4 man advantage. Montreal 4, Boston 2.

FASTEST THREE ASSISTS:
0:21 – Gus Bodnar, Chicago, Mar. 23, 1952, at NY Rangers, Bodnar assisted on Bill Mosienko's three goals at 6:09, 6:20 and 6:30 of third period. Chicago 7, NY Rangers 6.
0:44 – Bert Olmstead, Montreal, Nov. 5, 1955, at Montreal, Olmstead assisted on Jean Béliveau's three goals at 0:42, 1:08 and 1:26 of second period. Montreal 4, Boston 2.

SHOTS ON GOAL

MOST SHOTS ON GOAL, ONE SEASON:
550 – Phil Esposito, Boston, 1970-71. 78GP – 78 game schedule.
429 – Paul Kariya, Anaheim, 1998-99. 82GP – 82 game schedule.
426 – Phil Esposito, Boston, 1971-72. 76GP – 78 game schedule.
425 – Alex Ovechkin, Washington, 2005-06. 81GP – 82 game schedule.
414 – Bobby Hull, Chicago, 1968-69. 74GP – 76 game schedule.

PENALTIES

MOST PENALTY MINUTES, CAREER:
3,966 – Tiger Williams, Toronto, Vancouver, Detroit, Los Angeles, Hartford, in 14 seasons. 962GP
3,565 – Dale Hunter, Quebec, Washington, Colorado, in 19 seasons. 1,407GP
3,515 – Tie Domi, Toronto, NY Rangers, Winnipeg, in 16 seasons. 1,020GP
3,381 – Marty McSorley, Pittsburgh, Edmonton, Los Angeles, NY Rangers, San Jose, Boston, in 17 seasons. 961GP
3,300 – Bob Probert, Detroit, Chicago, in 17 seasons. 935GP

MOST PENALTY MINUTES, CAREER, INCLUDING PLAYOFFS:
4,421 – Tiger Williams, Toronto, Vancouver, Detroit, Los Angeles, Hartford, 3,966 in 962 regular-season games; 455 in 83 playoff games.
4,294 – Dale Hunter, Quebec, Washington, Colorado, 3,565 in 1,407 regular-season games; 729 in 186 playoff games.
3,755 – Marty McSorley, Pittsburgh, Edmonton, Los Angeles, NY Rangers, San Jose, Boston, 3,381 in 961 regular-season games; 374 in 115 playoff games.
3,753 – Tie Domi, Toronto, NY Rangers, Winnipeg, 3,515 in 1,020 regular-season games; 238 in 98 playoff games.
3,584 – Chris Nilan, Montreal, NY Rangers, Boston, 3,043 in 688 regular-season games; 541 in 111 playoff games.

MOST PENALTY MINUTES, ONE SEASON:
472 – Dave Schultz, Philadelphia, 1974-75.
409 – Paul Baxter, Pittsburgh, 1981-82.
408 – Mike Peluso, Chicago, 1991-92.
405 – Dave Schultz, Los Angeles, Pittsburgh, 1977-78.

MOST PENALTIES, ONE GAME:
10 – Chris Nilan, Boston, Mar. 31, 1991, at Boston vs. Hartford. 6 minors, 2 majors, 1 10-minute misconduct.
9 – Jim Dorey, Toronto, Oct. 16, 1968, at Toronto vs. Pittsburgh. 4 minors, 2 majors, 2 10-minute misconducts, 1 game misconduct.
   – Dave Schultz, Pittsburgh, Apr. 6, 1978, at Detroit. 5 minors, 2 majors, 2 10-minute misconducts.
   – Randy Holt, Los Angeles, Mar. 11, 1979, at Philadelphia. 1 minor, 3 majors, 2 10-minute misconducts, 3 game misconducts.
   – Russ Anderson, Pittsburgh, Jan. 19, 1980, at Pittsburgh vs. Edmonton. 3 minors, 3 majors, 3 game misconducts.
   – Kim Clackson, Quebec, Mar. 8, 1981, at Quebec vs. Chicago. 4 minors, 3 majors, 2 game misconducts.
   – Terry O'Reilly, Boston, Dec. 19, 1984, at Hartford. 5 minors, 3 majors, 1 game misconduct.
   – Larry Playfair, Los Angeles, Dec. 9, 1986, at NY Islanders. 6 minors, 2 majors, 1 10-minute misconduct.
   – Marty McSorley, Los Angeles, Apr. 14, 1992, at Vancouver. 5 minors, 2 majors, 1 10-minute misconduct, 1 game misconduct.
   – Reed Low, St. Louis, Dec. 31, 2002, at Detroit. 4 minors, 1 major, 1 10-minute misconduct, 3 game misconducts.

MOST PENALTY MINUTES, ONE GAME:
67 – Randy Holt, Los Angeles, Mar. 11, 1979, at Philadelphia. 1 minor, 3 majors, 2 10-minute misconducts, 3 game misconducts.
57 – Brad Smith, Toronto, Nov. 15, 1986, at Toronto vs. Detroit. 1 minor, 3 majors, 2 10-minute misconducts, 2 game misconducts.
   – Reed Low, St. Louis, Feb. 28, 2002, at St. Louis vs. Calgary. 1 minor, 3 majors, 1 10-minute misconduct, 3 game misconducts.

MOST PENALTIES, ONE PERIOD:
 9 – **Randy Holt**, Los Angeles, Mar. 11, 1979, at Philadelphia, first period.
 1 minor, 3 majors, 2 10-minute misconducts, 3 game misconducts.

MOST PENALTY MINUTES, ONE PERIOD:
 67 – **Randy Holt**, Los Angeles, Mar. 11, 1979, at Philadelphia, first period.
 1 minor, 3 majors, 2 10-minute misconducts, 3 game misconducts.

GOALTENDING

MOST GAMES APPEARED IN BY A GOALTENDER, CAREER:
 1,029 – **Patrick Roy**, Montreal, Colorado,1984-85 – 2002-03.
 971 – Terry Sawchuk, Detroit, Boston, Toronto, Los Angeles, NY Rangers, 1949-50 – 1969-70.
 906 – Glenn Hall, Detroit, Chicago, St. Louis, 1952-53 – 1970-71.
 905 – Ed Belfour, Chicago, San Jose, Dallas, Toronto, 1988-89 – 2003-04, 2005-06.
 886 – Tony Esposito, Montreal, Chicago, 1968-69 – 1983-84.

MOST CONSECUTIVE COMPLETE GAMES BY A GOALTENDER:
 502 – **Glenn Hall**, Detroit, Chicago. Played 502 games from beginning of 1955-56 season through first 12 games of 1962-63 season. In his 503rd straight game, Nov. 7, 1962, at Chicago, Hall was removed from the game against Boston with a back injury in the first period.

MOST GAMES APPEARED IN BY A GOALTENDER, ONE SEASON:
 79 – **Grant Fuhr**, St. Louis, 1995-96.
 77 – Martin Brodeur, New Jersey, 1995-96.
 – Bill Ranford, Edmonton, Boston, 1995-96.
 – Arturs Irbe, Carolina, 2000-01.
 – Marc Denis, Columbus, 2002-03.

MOST MINUTES PLAYED BY A GOALTENDER, CAREER:
 60,235 – **Patrick Roy**, Montreal, Colorado, 1984-85 – 2002-03.
 57,194 – Terry Sawchuk, Detroit, Boston, Toronto, Los Angeles, NY Rangers, 1949-50 – 1969-70.

MOST MINUTES PLAYED BY A GOALTENDER, ONE SEASON:
 4,555 – **Martin Brodeur**, New Jersey, 2003-04.
 4,511 – Marc Denis, Columbus, 2002-03.

MOST SHUTOUTS, CAREER:
 103 – **Terry Sawchuk**, Detroit, Boston, Toronto, Los Angeles, NY Rangers, in 21 seasons.
 94 – George Hainsworth, Montreal, Toronto, in 11 seasons.
 84 – Glenn Hall, Detroit, Chicago, St. Louis, in 18 seasons.

MOST SHUTOUTS, ONE SEASON:
 22 – **George Hainsworth**, Montreal, 1928-29. 44GP
 15 – Alec Connell, Ottawa, 1925-26. 36GP
 – Alec Connell, Ottawa, 1927-28. 44GP
 – Hal Winkler, Boston, 1927-28. 44GP
 – Tony Esposito, Chicago, 1969-70. 63GP
 14 – George Hainsworth, Montreal, 1926-27. 44GP

LONGEST SHUTOUT SEQUENCE BY A GOALTENDER:
 461:29 – **Alec Connell**, Ottawa, 1927-28, six consecutive shutouts.
 (Forward passing not permitted in attacking zones in 1927-28.)
 343:05 – George Hainsworth, Montreal, 1928-29, four consecutive shutouts.
 (Forward passing not permitted in attacking zones in 1928-29.)
 332:01 – Brian Boucher, Phoenix, 2003-04, five consecutive shutouts.
 324:40 – Roy Worters, NY Americans, 1930-31, four consecutive shutouts.
 309:21 – Bill Durnan, Montreal, 1948-49, four consecutive shutouts.

MOST WINS BY A GOALTENDER, CAREER:
 551 – **Patrick Roy**, Montreal, Colorado, in 19 seasons. 1,029GP
 457 – Ed Belfour, Chicago, San Jose, Dallas, Toronto, in 16 seasons. 905GP
 447 – Terry Sawchuk, Detroit, Boston, Toronto, Los Angeles, NY Rangers, in 21 seasons. 971GP
 446 – Martin Brodeur, New Jersey, in 13 seasons. 813GP
 437 – Jacques Plante, Montreal, NY Rangers, St. Louis, Toronto, Boston, in 18 seasons. 837GP

MOST WINS BY A GOALTENDER, ONE SEASON:
 47 – **Bernie Parent**, Philadelphia, 1973-74. 73GP
 44 – Bernie Parent, Philadelphia, 1974-75. 68GP
 – Terry Sawchuk, Detroit, 1950-51. 70GP
 – Terry Sawchuk, Detroit, 1951-52. 70GP

LONGEST WINNING STREAK BY A GOALTENDER, ONE SEASON:
 17 – **Gilles Gilbert**, Boston, 1975-76.
 14 – Tiny Thompson, Boston, 1929-30.
 – Ross Brooks, Boston, 1973-74.
 – Don Beaupre, Minnesota, 1985-86.
 – Tom Barrasso, Pittsburgh, 1992-93.

LONGEST UNDEFEATED STREAK BY A GOALTENDER, ONE SEASON:
 32 Games – **Gerry Cheevers**, Boston, 1971-72. 24w-8T
 31 Games – Pete Peeters, Boston, 1982-83. 26w-5T
 27 Games – Pete Peeters, Philadelphia, 1979-80. 22w-5T

LONGEST UNDEFEATED STREAK BY A GOALTENDER IN HIS FIRST NHL SEASON:
 23 Games – **Grant Fuhr**, Edmonton, 1981-82. 15w-8T

LONGEST UNDEFEATED STREAK BY A GOALTENDER FROM START OF CAREER:
 16 Games – **Patrick Lalime**, Pittsburgh, 1996-97. 14w-2T

MOST 30-OR-MORE WIN SEASONS BY A GOALTENDER:
 13 – **Patrick Roy**, Montreal, Colorado, in 19 seasons.
 10 – Martin Brodeur, New Jersey, in 13 seasons.
 9 – Ed Belfour, Chicago, San Jose, Dallas, Toronto, in 16 seasons.
 8 – Tony Esposito, Montreal, Chicago, in 16 seasons.
 7 – Jacques Plante, Montreal, NY Rangers, St. Louis, Toronto, Boston, in 18 seasons.
 – Ken Dryden, Montreal, in 8 seasons.
 – Curtis Joseph, St. Louis, Edmonton, Toronto, Detroit, Phoenix, in 16 seasons.

MOST CONSECUTIVE 30-OR-MORE WIN SEASONS BY A GOALTENDER:
 10 – **Martin Brodeur**, New Jersey, 1995-96 – 2005-06.
 8 – Patrick Roy, Montreal, Colorado, 1995-96 – 2002-03.
 7 – Tony Esposito, Chicago, 1969-70 – 1975-76.
 6 – Jacques Plante, Montreal, 1954-55 – 1959-60.
 5 – Terry Sawchuk, Detroit, 1950-51 – 1954-55.
 – Ken Dryden, Montreal, 1974-75 – 1978-79.

MOST 40-OR-MORE WIN SEASONS BY A GOALTENDER:
 5 – **Martin Brodeur**, New Jersey, in 13 seasons.
 3 – Terry Sawchuk, Detroit, Boston, Toronto, Los Angeles, NY Rangers, in 21 seasons.
 – Jacques Plante, Montreal, NY Rangers, St. Louis, Toronto, Boston, in 18 seasons.
 2 – Bernie Parent, Boston, Philadelphia, Toronto, in 13 seasons.
 – Ken Dryden, Montreal, in 8 seasons.
 – Ed Belfour, Chicago, San Jose, Dallas, Toronto, in 16 seasons.

MOST CONSECUTIVE 40-OR-MORE WIN SEASONS BY A GOALTENDER:
 2 – **Terry Sawchuk**, Detroit, 1950-51 – 1951-52.
 – **Bernie Parent**, Philadelphia, 1973-74 – 1974-75.
 – **Ken Dryden**, Montreal, 1975-76 – 1976-77.
 – **Martin Brodeur**, New Jersey, 1999-2000 – 2000-01.

MOST LOSSES BY A GOALTENDER, CAREER:
 352 – **Gump Worsley**, NY Rangers, Montreal, Minnesota, in 21 seasons. 861GP
 351 – Gilles Meloche, Chicago, California, Cleveland, Minnesota, Pittsburgh, in 18 seasons. 788GP
 346 – John Vanbiesbrouck, NY Rangers, Florida, Philadelphia, NY Islanders, New Jersey, in 20 seasons. 882GP
 332 – Terry Sawchuk, Detroit, Boston, Toronto, Los Angeles, NY Rangers, in 21 seasons. 971GP

MOST LOSSES BY A GOALTENDER, ONE SEASON:
 48 – **Gary Smith**, California, 1970-71. 71GP
 47 – Al Rollins, Chicago, 1953-54. 66GP
 46 – Peter Sidorkiewicz, Ottawa, 1992-93. 64GP
 44 – Harry Lumley, Chicago, 1951-52. 70GP

No goalie has ever won more games in a season than the 47 Bernie Parent won for Philadelphia in 1973-74. Parent played in 73 of the Flyers' 78 games that year iand was 47-13-12 with a 1.89 goals-against average.

Active NHL Players' Three-or-More-Goal Games

Regular Season

Teams named are the ones the players were with at the time of their multiple-scoring games. Players listed alphabetically.

Player	Team	3-Goals	4-Goals	5-Goals
Adams, Kevyn	Carolina	2	—	—
Alfredsson, Daniel	Ottawa	4	1	—
Allison, Jason	Boston	4	—	—
Amonte, Tony	NYR, Chi.	7	—	—
Antropov, Nik	Toronto	1	—	—
Armstrong, Derek	Los Angeles	1	—	—
Arnason, Tyler	Chicago	1	—	—
Arnott, Jason	Edm., N.J., Dal.	5	—	—
Barnes, Stu	Wpg., Pit., Dal.	4	—	—
Battaglia, Bates	Carolina	1	—	—
Belanger, Eric	Los Angeles	1	—	—
Berard, Bryan	Columbus	1	—	—
Bergeron, Marc-Andre	Edmonton	1	—	—
Bertuzzi, Todd	Vancouver	5	—	—
Blake, Jason	NY Islanders	2	—	—
Blake, Rob	Los Angeles	1	—	—
Bochenski, Brandon	Ottawa	1	—	—
Bondra, Peter	Washington	12	5	1
Bonk, Radek	Ottawa	1	—	—
Boyes, Brad	Boston	1	—	—
Brind'Amour, Rod	Phi., Car.	2	—	—
Brown, Curtis	Buffalo	1	—	—
Bulis, Jan	Montreal	—	1	—
Burrows, Alexandre	Vancouver	1	—	—
Carter, Anson	Boston	1	—	—
Cassels, Andrew	Vancouver	1	—	—
Cheechoo, Jonathan	San Jose	5	—	—
Chouinard, Marc	Minnesota	1	—	—
Clark, Chris	Washington	1	—	—
Cole, Erik	Carolina	3	—	—
Conroy, Craig	St.L., L.A.	2	—	—
Czerkawski, Mariusz	Edm., NYI	4	—	—
Daigle, Alexandre	Ott., Phi.	2	—	—
Daze, Eric	Chicago	5	1	—
Demitra, Pavol	St.L., L.A.	4	—	—
Devereaux, Boyd	Edmonton	1	—	—
Donovan, Shean	Atlanta	1	—	—
Dumont, Jean-Pierre	Chi., Buf.	3	—	—
Dvorak, Radek	NY Rangers	1	1	—
Elias, Patrik	New Jersey	6	1	—
Fedorov, Sergei	Detroit	4	1	1
Forsberg, Peter	Colorado	6	—	—
Friesen, Jeff	San Jose	2	—	—
Frolov, Alexander	Los Angeles	2	—	—
Gaborik, Marian	Minnesota	6	—	—
Gagne, Simon	Philadelphia	2	—	—
Gelinas, Martin	Edm., Van.	2	1	—
Gomez, Scott	New Jersey	2	—	—
Gonchar, Sergei	Washington	1	—	—
Gratton, Chris	Tampa Bay	1	—	—
Green, Travis	NY Islanders	1	—	—
Grier, Mike	Edmonton	1	—	—
Guerin, Bill	N.J., Bos.	3	—	—
Handzus, Michal	St. Louis	1	—	—
Hartnell, Scott	Nashville	1	—	—
Harvey, Todd	Dal., S.J.	2	—	—
Havlat, Martin	Ottawa	3	1	—
Heatley, Dany	Atl., Ott.	2	1	—
Hecht, Jochen	Buffalo	1	—	—
Hedstrom, Jonathan	Anaheim	1	—	—
Hejduk, Milan	Colorado	1	—	—
Hlavac, Jan	NYR, Car.	3	—	—
Holik, Bobby	New Jersey	3	—	—
Holmstrom, Tomas	Detroit	1	—	—
Horcoff, Shawn	Edmonton	1	—	—
Horton, Nathan	Florida	1	—	—
Hossa, Marian	Ottawa	3	1	—
Iginla, Jarome	Calgary	3	1	—
Jagr, Jaromir	Pit., NYR	13	1	—
Johansson, Andreas	Nashville	1	—	—
Jokinen, Olli	Florida	1	—	—
Kapanen, Niko	Dallas	1	—	—
Kapanen, Sami	Carolina	3	—	—
Kariya, Paul	Ana., Nsh.	9	—	—
Kobasew, Chuck	Calgary	1	—	—
Koivu, Saku	Montreal	1	—	—
Konowalchuk, Steve	Washington	1	—	—
Kovalchuk, Ilya	Atlanta	4	1	—
Kovalev, Alex	NYR, Pit.	10	—	—
Kozlov, Viktor	Florida	1	—	—
Kozlov, Vyacheslav	Det., Atl.	3	1	—
Laaksonen, Antti	Minnesota	1	—	—
Lang, Robert	Washington	1	—	—
Langkow, Daymond	Phoenix	2	—	—
Laperriere, Ian	Los Angeles	1	—	—
Lapointe, Martin	Det., Bos.	2	—	—
Laraque, Georges	Edmonton	1	—	—

Rick Nash of the Columbus Blue Jackets picked up his first career hat trick against Detroit on April 7, 2006. Nash tied for the NHL lead with 41 goals in 2003-04, and had 31 goals in just 54 games last season.

Player	Team	3-Goals	4-Goals	5-Goals
Lecavalier, Vincent	Tampa Bay	3	—	—
LeClair, John	Philadelphia	8	3	—
Lehtinen, Jere	Dallas	2	—	—
Linden, Trevor	Van., Mtl.	5	—	—
Lindros, Eric	Phi., NYR	12	1	—
Lombardi, Matthew	Calgary	1	—	—
Madden, John	New Jersey	1	1	—
Maltby, Kirk	Detroit	1	—	—
Marleau, Patrick	San Jose	1	—	—
McCauley, Alyn	San Jose	1	—	—
McEachern, Shawn	Ott., Atl.	2	—	—
Mellanby, Scott	St. Louis	—	1	—
Modano, Mike	Min., Dal.	6	1	—
Modin, Fredrik	Tampa Bay	3	—	—
Mogilny, Alexander	Buf., Van., N.J., Tor.	15	2	—
Morozov, Aleksey	Pittsburgh	2	—	—
Morrison, Brendan	Vancouver	1	—	—
Morrow, Brendan	Dallas	1	—	—
Murray, Glen	L.A., Bos.	5	—	—
Murray, Rem	Edmonton	1	—	—
Nagy, Ladislav	Phoenix	2	—	—
Nash, Rick	Columbus	1	—	—
Naslund, Markus	Pit., Van.	8	2	—
Nedved, Petr	Pit., NYR	6	1	—
Nieuwendyk, Joe	Cgy., Dal., Fla.	10	3	1
Nolan, Owen	Que., S.J.	9	1	—
Nylander, Michael	Hfd., Chi.	1	1	—
Odelein, Lyle	Montreal	1	—	—
Oliver, David	Edmonton	1	—	—
O'Neill, Jeff	Hfd., Car., Tor.	3	—	—
Orszagh, Vladimir	Nashville	1	—	—
Ovechkin, Alex	Washington	1	—	—
Ozolinsh, Sandis	Col., Car.	2	—	—
Palffy, Ziggy	NYI, L.A.	8	—	—
Parrish, Mark	Fla., NYI	3	1	—
Peca, Michael	Buffalo	1	—	—
Perreault, Yanic	L.A., Tor., Mtl.	3	1	—
Petersen, Toby	Pittsburgh	1	—	—
Petrovicky, Ronald	Atlanta	1	—	—
Piros, Kamil	Atlanta	1	—	—
Pisani, Fernando	Edmonton	1	—	—
Pominville, Jason	Buffalo	1	—	—
Primeau, Keith	Philadelphia	1	—	—
Prospal, Vaclav	Ana., T.B.	2	—	—
Pyatt, Taylor	Buffalo	1	—	—
Quint, Deron	Columbus	1	—	—
Recchi, Mark	Pit., Mtl., Phi.	6	—	—
Reinprecht, Steve	Col., Phx.	2	—	—
Rheaume, Pascal	Atlanta	—	1	—
Ricci, Mike	Que., S.J.	1	—	1
Richards, Mike	Philadelphia	1	—	—
Roberts, Gary	Cgy., Car., Tor.	12	1	—
Roenick, Jeremy	Chi., Phx.	7	2	—

Player	Team	3-Goals	4-Goals	5-Goals
Rolston, Brian	N.J., Min.	2	—	—
Roy, Derek	Buffalo	2	—	—
Rucinsky, Martin	Montreal	2	—	—
Ryder, Michael	Montreal	1	—	—
Sakic, Joe	Que., Col.	13	1	—
Salo, Sami	Ottawa	1	—	—
Samsonov, Sergei	Boston	1	—	—
Sanderson, Geoff	Har., Buf., CBJ	7	1	—
Satan, Miroslav	Buf., NYI	6	1	—
Savage, Brian	Montreal	6	1	—
Savard, Marc	Calgary	1	1	—
Scatchard, Dave	NY Islanders	2	—	—
Schneider, Mathieu	Detroit	1	—	—
Sedin, Daniel	Vancouver	—	1	—
Selanne, Teemu	Wpg., Ana., S.J.	16	2	—
Shanahan, Brendan	N.J., St.L., Hfd., Det.	16	1	—
Sim, Jon	Florida	1	—	—
Smolinski, Bryan	Bos., L.A.	3	—	—
Smyth, Ryan	Edmonton	4	—	—
Souray, Sheldon	Montreal	1	—	—
St. Louis, Martin	Tampa Bay	3	—	—
Staal, Eric	Carolina	2	—	—
Stillman, Cory	Cgy., St.L.	3	—	—
Straka, Martin	Pit., NYR	5	—	—
Stumpel, Jozef	Bos., L.A.	2	—	—
Sturm, Marco	San Jose	1	—	—
Sullivan, Steve	Tor., Chi., Nsh.	4	1	—
Sundin, Mats	Que., Tor.	5	1	1
Svatos, Marek	Colorado	2	—	—
Sydor, Darryl	Dallas	1	—	—
Tanguay, Alex	Colorado	1	—	—
Tenkrat, Petr	Nashville	1	—	—
Thornton, Joe	Boston	2	—	—
Thornton, Scott	San Jose	1	—	—
Tkachuk, Keith	Phoenix	7	2	—
Turgeon, Pierre	Buf., NYI, Mtl., St.L.	15	—	—
Vasicek, Josef	Carolina	1	—	—
Visnovsky, Lubomir	Los Angeles	1	—	—
Vrbata, Radim	Col., Car.	1	—	—
Vyborny, David	Columbus	1	—	—
Walker, Scott	Nashville	2	—	—
Weight, Doug	Edm., St.L.	1	—	—
Wesley, Glen	Boston	1	—	—
Whitney, Ray	Columbus	1	—	—
Wiemer, Jason	Tampa Bay	1	—	—
Williams, Jason	Detroit	1	—	—
Willis, Shane	Carolina	1	—	—
Wright, Tyler	Columbus	3	—	—
Yashin, Alexei	Ott., NYI	8	—	—
Young, Scott	Que., Col.	4	—	—
Zednik, Richard	Washington	1	—	—
Zhamnov, Alex	Wpg., Chi.	5	—	1
Zubrus, Dainus	Montreal	1	—	—

Top 100 All-Time Goal-Scoring Leaders

* active player

Player	Seasons	Games	Goals	Goals per game
1. **Wayne Gretzky**, Edm., L.A., St.L., NYR .	20	1487	**894**	.601
2. **Gordie Howe**, Det., Hfd.	26	1767	**801**	.453
3. **Brett Hull**, Cgy., St.L., Dal., Det., Phx.	20	1269	**741**	.584
4. **Marcel Dionne**, Det., L.A., NYR	18	1348	**731**	.542
5. **Phil Esposito**, Chi., Bos., NYR	18	1282	**717**	.559
6. **Mike Gartner**, Wsh., Min., NYR, Tor., Phx.	19	1432	**708**	.494
7. **Mark Messier**, Edm., NYR, Van.	25	1756	**694**	.395
8. **Steve Yzerman**, Det.	22	1514	**692**	.457
9. **Mario Lemieux**, Pit.	18	915	**690**	.754
10. **Luc Robitaille**, L.A., Pit., NYR, Det.	19	1431	**668**	.467
11. **Dave Andreychuk**, Buf., Tor., N.J., Bos., Col., T.B.	23	1639	**640**	.390
12. **Bobby Hull**, Chi., Wpg., Hfd.	16	1063	**610**	.574
13. **Dino Ciccarelli**, Min., Wsh., Det., T.B., Fla.	19	1232	**608**	.494
14. **Jari Kurri**, Edm., L.A., NYR, Ana., Col.	17	1251	**601**	.480
* 15. **Brendan Shanahan**, N.J., St.L., Hfd., Det.	18	1350	**598**	.443
* 16. **Jaromir Jagr**, Pit., Wsh., NYR	15	1109	**591**	.533
* 17. **Joe Sakic**, Que., Col.	17	1237	**574**	.464
18. **Mike Bossy**, NYI	10	752	**573**	.762
19. **Guy Lafleur**, Mtl., NYR, Que.	17	1126	**560**	.497
* 20. **Joe Nieuwendyk**, Cgy., Dal., N.J., Tor., Fla.	19	1242	**559**	.450
21. **John Bucyk**, Det., Bos.	23	1540	**556**	.361
22. **Ron Francis**, Hfd., Pit., Car., Tor. .	23	1731	**549**	.317
23. **Michel Goulet**, Que., Chi.	15	1089	**548**	.503
24. **Maurice Richard**, Mtl.	18	978	**544**	.556
25. **Stan Mikita**, Chi.	22	1394	**541**	.388
26. **Frank Mahovlich**, Tor., Det., Mtl.	18	1181	**533**	.451
27. **Bryan Trottier**, NYI, Pit.	18	1279	**524**	.410
28. **Pat Verbeek**, N.J., Hfd., NYR, Dal., Det.	20	1424	**522**	.367
29. **Dale Hawerchuk**, Wpg., Buf., St.L., Phi.	16	1188	**518**	.436
30. **Gilbert Perreault**, Buf.	17	1191	**512**	.430
* 31. **Pierre Turgeon**, Buf., NYI, Mtl., St.L., Dal., Col.	18	1277	**511**	.400
32. **Jean Beliveau**, Mtl.	20	1125	**507**	.451
33. **Joe Mullen**, St.L., Cgy., Pit., Bos. .	17	1062	**502**	.473
34. **Lanny McDonald**, Tor., Col., Cgy. . . .	16	1111	**500**	.450
35. **Glenn Anderson**, Edm., Tor., NYR, St.L.	16	1129	**498**	.441
* **Peter Bondra**, Wsh., Ott., Atl.	15	1044	**498**	.477
* 37. **Mats Sundin**, Que., Tor.	15	1156	**496**	.429
* 38. **Teemu Selanne**, Wpg., Ana., S.J., Col.	13	959	**492**	.513
39. **Jean Ratelle**, NYR, Bos.	21	1281	**491**	.383
40. **Norm Ullman**, Det., Tor.	20	1410	**490**	.348
41. **Brian Bellows**, Min., Mtl., T.B., Ana., Wsh.	17	1188	**485**	.408
* **Mike Modano**, Min., Dal.	17	1179	**485**	.411
* 43. **Jeremy Roenick**, Chi., Phx., Phi., L.A.	17	1182	**484**	.409
* **Mark Recchi**, Pit., Phi., Mtl., Car.	17	1256	**484**	.385
Darryl Sittler, Tor., Phi., Det.	15	1096	**484**	.442
46. **Bernie Nicholls**, L.A., NYR, Edm., N.J., Chi., S.J.	18	1127	**475**	.421
47. **Denis Savard**, Chi., Mtl., T.B.	17	1196	**473**	.395
* **Alexander Mogilny**, Buf., Van., N.J., Tor.	16	990	**473**	.478
49. **Pat LaFontaine**, NYI, Buf., NYR.	15	865	**468**	.541
50. **Alex Delvecchio**, Det.	24	1549	**456**	.294
51. **Theoren Fleury**, Cgy., Col., NYR, Chi.	15	1084	**455**	.420
52. **Doug Gilmour**, St.L., Cgy., Tor., N.J., Chi., Buf., Mtl.	20	1474	**450**	.305
Peter Stastny, Que., N.J., St.L.	15	977	**450**	.461
54. **Rick Middleton**, NYR, Bos.	14	1005	**448**	.446
* 55. **Keith Tkachuk**, Wpg., Phx., St.L.	14	897	**446**	.497
* 56. **Sergei Fedorov**, Det., Ana., CBJ	15	1055	**443**	.420
57. **Steve Larmer**, Chi., NYR.	15	1006	**441**	.438
Rick Vaive, Van., Tor., Chi., Buf.	13	876	**441**	.503
59. **Rick Tocchet**, Phi., Pit., L.A., Bos., Wsh., Phx.	18	1144	**440**	.385
60. **Pavel Bure**, Van., Fla., NYR	12	702	**437**	.623
61. **Vincent Damphousse**, Tor., Edm., Mtl., S.J.	18	1378	**432**	.313
62. **Dave Taylor**, L.A.	17	1111	**431**	.388
63. **Yvan Cournoyer**, Mtl.	16	968	**428**	.442
64. **Brian Propp**, Phi., Bos., Min., Hfd.	15	1016	**425**	.418
65. **Steve Shutt**, Mtl., L.A.	13	930	**424**	.456
66. **Stephane Richer**, Mtl., N.J., T.B., St.L., Pit.	17	1054	**421**	.399
Steve Thomas, Tor., Chi., NYI, N.J., Ana., Det.	20	1235	**421**	.341
68. **Bill Barber**, Phi., T.B.	14	903	**420**	.465
69. **Garry Unger**, Tor., Det., St.L., Atl., L.A., Edm.	16	1105	**413**	.374
John MacLean, N.J., S.J., NYR, Dal.	18	1194	**413**	.346
* 71. **Gary Roberts**, Cgy., Car., Tor., Fla.	19	1087	**411**	.378
72. **Raymond Bourque**, Bos., Col.	22	1612	**410**	.254

A classy superstar who reminded many of Canadiens great Jean Beliveau, Jean Ratelle had 491 goals in his NHL career with the Rangers and Bruins. (Beliveau scored 507 for Montreal.)

Player	Seasons	Games	Goals	Goals per game
73. **Ray Ferraro**, Hfd., NYI, NYR, L.A., Atl., St.L.	18	1258	**408**	.324
74. **Rod Gilbert**, NYR	18	1065	**406**	.381
* **Tony Amonte**, NYR, Chi., Phx., Phi., Cgy.	15	1093	**406**	.371
* 76. **John LeClair**, Mtl., Phi., Pit.	15	946	**404**	.427
77. **John Ogrodnick**, Det., Que., NYR	14	928	**402**	.433
78. **Paul Coffey**, Edm., Pit., L.A., Det., Hfd., Phi., Chi., Car., Bos.	21	1409	**396**	.281
Dave Keon, Tor., Hfd.	18	1296	**396**	.306
80. **Pierre Larouche**, Pit., Mtl., Hfd., NYR	14	812	**395**	.486
Cam Neely, Van., Bos.	13	726	**395**	.544
82. **Tomas Sandstrom**, NYR, L.A., Pit., Det., Ana.	15	983	**394**	.401
83. **Bernie Geoffrion**, Mtl., NYR.	16	883	**393**	.445
84. **Dean Prentice**, NYR, Bos., Det., Pit., Min.	22	1378	**391**	.284
Jean Pronovost, Pit., Atl., Wsh.	14	998	**391**	.392
86. **Rick Martin**, Buf., L.A.	11	685	**384**	.561
* 87. **Rod Brind'Amour**, St.L., Phi., Car.	17	1187	**382**	.322
88. **Reggie Leach**, Bos., Cal., Phi., Det. . . .	13	934	**381**	.408
89. **Claude Lemieux**, Mtl., N.J., Col., Phx., Dal.	20	1197	**379**	.317
Ted Lindsay, Det., Chi.	17	1068	**379**	.355
91. **Butch Goring**, L.A., NYI, Bos.	16	1107	**375**	.339
92. **Rick Kehoe**, Tor., Pit.	14	906	**371**	.409
93. **Tim Kerr**, Phi., NYR, Hfd.	13	655	**370**	.565
94. **Bernie Federko**, St.L., Det.	14	1000	**369**	.369
* 95. **Eric Lindros**, Phi., NYR, Tor.	13	711	**367**	.516
Geoff Courtnall, Bos., Edm., Wsh., St.L., Van.	17	1048	**367**	.350
97. **Jacques Lemaire**, Mtl.	12	853	**366**	.429
98. **Peter McNab**, Buf., Bos., Van., N.J.	14	954	**363**	.381
Brent Sutter, NYI, Chi.	18	1111	**363**	.327
100. **Ivan Boldirev**, Bos., Cal., Chi., Atl., Van., Det.	15	1052	**361**	.343

Top 100 Active Goal-Scoring Leaders

Player	Seasons	Games	Goals	Goals per game
1. **Brendan Shanahan**, N.J., St.L., Hfd., Det.	18	1350	**598**	.443
2. **Jaromir Jagr**, Pit., Wsh., NYR	15	1109	**591**	.533
3. **Joe Sakic**, Que., Col.	17	1237	**574**	.464
4. **Joe Nieuwendyk**, Cgy., Dal., N.J., Tor., Fla.	19	1242	**559**	.450
5. **Pierre Turgeon**, Buf., NYI, Mtl., St.L., Dal., Col.	18	1277	**511**	.400
6. **Peter Bondra**, Wsh., Ott., Atl.	15	1044	**498**	.477
7. **Mats Sundin**, Que., Tor.	15	1156	**496**	.429
8. **Teemu Selanne**, Wpg., Ana., S.J., Col.	13	959	**492**	.513
9. **Mike Modano**, Min., Dal.	17	1179	**485**	.411
10. **Mark Recchi**, Pit., Phi., Mtl., Car.	17	1256	**484**	.385
Jeremy Roenick, Chi., Phx., Phi., L.A.	17	1182	**484**	.409
12. **Alexander Mogilny**, Buf., Van., N.J., Tor.	16	990	**473**	.478
13. **Keith Tkachuk**, Wpg., Phx., St.L.	14	897	**446**	.497
14. **Sergei Fedorov**, Det., Ana., CBJ.	15	1055	**443**	.420
15. **Gary Roberts**, Cgy., Car., Tor., Fla.	19	1087	**411**	.378
16. **Tony Amonte**, NYR, Chi., Phx., Phi., Cgy.	15	1093	**406**	.371
17. **John LeClair**, Mtl., Phi., Pit.	15	946	**404**	.427
18. **Rod Brind'Amour**, St.L., Phi., Car.	17	1187	**382**	.322
19. **Eric Lindros**, Phi., NYR, Tor.	13	711	**367**	.516
20. **Trevor Linden**, Van., NYI, Mtl., Wsh.	17	1243	**356**	.286
21. **Scott Mellanby**, Phi., Edm., Fla., St.L., Atl.	20	1362	**352**	.258
22. **Paul Kariya**, Ana., Col., Nsh.	11	739	**342**	.463
Scott Young, Hfd., Pit., Que., Col., Ana., St.L., Dal.	17	1181	**342**	.290
24. **Geoff Sanderson**, Hfd., Car., Van., Buf., CBJ, Phx.	15	1005	**341**	.339
25. **Bill Guerin**, N.J., Edm., Bos., Dal.	14	949	**328**	.346
26. **Markus Naslund**, Pit., Van.	12	871	**322**	.370
27. **Alexei Yashin**, Ott., NYI	11	792	**319**	.403
28. **Alex Kovalev**, NYR, Pit., Mtl.	13	918	**315**	.343
29. **Petr Nedved**, Van., St.L., NYR, Pit., Edm., Phx., Phi.	14	942	**308**	.327
30. **Bobby Holik**, Hfd., N.J., NYR, Atl.	15	1088	**296**	.272
31. **Miroslav Satan**, Edm., Buf., NYI	10	786	**294**	.374
32. **Glen Murray**, Bos., Pit., L.A.	14	887	**292**	.329
33. **Martin Gelinas**, Edm., Que., Van., Car., Cgy., Fla.	17	1134	**286**	.252
34. **Jarome Iginla**, Cgy.	10	708	**285**	.403
35. **Vyacheslav Kozlov**, Det., Buf., Atl.	14	882	**277**	.314
36. **Jason Arnott**, Edm., N.J., Dal.	12	824	**276**	.335
37. **Keith Primeau**, Det., Hfd., Car., Phi.	15	909	**266**	.293
38. **Daniel Alfredsson**, Ott.	10	706	**262**	.371
39. **Shawn McEachern**, Pit., L.A., Bos., Ott., Atl.	14	911	**256**	.281
40. **Alex Zhamnov**, Wpg., Chi., Phi., Bos.	13	807	**249**	.309
41. **Bryan Smolinski**, Bos., Pit., NYI, L.A., Ott.	13	910	**248**	.273
42. **Brian Leetch**, NYR, Tor., Bos.	18	1205	**247**	.205
43. **Mike Ricci**, Phi., Que., Col., S.J., Phx.	15	1092	**243**	.223
44. **Pavol Demitra**, Ott., St.L., L.A.	12	611	**241**	.394
45. **Doug Weight**, NYR, Edm., St.L., Car.	15	982	**239**	.243
46. **Stu Barnes**, Wpg., Fla., Pit., Buf., Dal.	14	975	**236**	.242
47. **Peter Forsberg**, Que., Col., Phi.	11	640	**235**	.367
48. **Ryan Smyth**, Edm.	11	717	**234**	.326
49. **Marian Hossa**, Ott., Atl.	8	547	**227**	.415
50. **Eric Daze**, Chi.	11	601	**226**	.376
51. **Brian Rolston**, N.J., Col., Bos., Min.	11	818	**224**	.274
Martin Rucinsky, Edm., Que., Col., Mtl., Dal., NYR, St.L., Van.	14	869	**224**	.258
53. **Patrik Elias**, N.J.	10	596	**223**	.374
Todd Bertuzzi, NYI, Van.	10	710	**223**	.314
55. **Ray Whitney**, S.J., Edm., Fla., CBJ, Det., Car.	14	763	**222**	.291
56. **Milan Hejduk**, Col.	7	544	**221**	.406
57. **Jeff O'Neill**, Hfd., Car., Tor.	10	747	**217**	.290
Yanic Perreault, Tor., L.A., Mtl., Nsh.	12	740	**217**	.293
59. **Mariusz Czerkawski**, Bos., Edm., NYI, Mtl., Tor.	12	745	**215**	.289
60. **Martin Straka**, Pit., Ott., NYI, Fla., L.A., NYR	13	812	**214**	.264
61. **Jeff Friesen**, S.J., Ana., N.J., Wsh.	11	821	**212**	.258
62. **Steve Sullivan**, N.J., Tor., Chi., Nsh.	10	666	**206**	.309
63. **Andrew Cassels**, Mtl., Hfd., Cgy., Van., CBJ, Wsh.	16	1015	**204**	.201
64. **Petr Sykora**, N.J., Ana., NYR	9	608	**202**	.332
65. **Rob Blake**, L.A., Col.	16	984	**200**	.203
66. **Mike Sillinger**, Det., Ana., Van., Phi., T.B., Fla., Ott., CBJ, Phx., St.L.	15	908	**198**	.218
67. **Robert Lang**, L.A., Bos., Pit., Wsh., Det.	12	718	**194**	.270
68. **Brian Savage**, Mtl., Phx., St.L., Phi.	12	674	**192**	.285
Travis Green, NYI, Ana., Phx., Tor., Bos.	13	939	**192**	.204

Anson Carter had a career high 33 goals for Vancouver last season playing on a line with the Sedin twins. Carter now has 191 goals in his career.

Player	Seasons	Games	Goals	Goals per game
70. **Anson Carter**, Wsh., Bos., Edm., NYR, L.A., Van.	9	610	**191**	.313
Chris Gratton, T.B., Phi., Buf., Phx., Col., Fla.	12	927	**191**	.206
72. **Jere Lehtinen**, Dal.	10	648	**190**	.293
73. **Mathieu Schneider**, Mtl., NYI, Tor., NYR, L.A., Det.	17	1064	**189**	.178
Joe Thornton, Bos., S.J.	8	590	**189**	.320
Nicklas Lidstrom, Det.	14	1096	**189**	.172
76. **Patrick Marleau**, S.J.	8	640	**187**	.292
77. **Cory Stillman**, Cgy., St.L., T.B., Car.	10	645	**184**	.285
78. **Fredrik Modin**, Tor., T.B.	9	662	**183**	.276
79. **Chris Chelios**, Mtl., Chi., Det.	22	1476	**182**	.123
80. **Vincent Lecavalier**, T.B.	7	547	**181**	.331
81. **Sami Kapanen**, Hfd., Car., Phi.	10	680	**173**	.254
Mark Parrish, Fla., NYI, L.A.	7	518	**173**	.334
83. **Shane Doan**, Wpg., Phx.	10	730	**172**	.236
84. **Steve Konowalchuk**, Wsh., Col.	14	790	**171**	.216
85. **Sergei Samsonov**, Bos., Edm.	8	533	**169**	.317
86. **Dallas Drake**, Det., Wpg., Phx., St.L.	13	884	**168**	.190
87. **Jozef Stumpel**, Bos., L.A., Fla.	14	832	**166**	.200
Steve Rucchin, Ana., NYR	11	688	**166**	.241
89. **Sandis Ozolinsh**, S.J., Col., Car., Fla., Ana., NYR	13	815	**164**	.201
90. **Michael Nylander**, Hfd., Cgy., T.B., Chi., Wsh., Bos., NYR	12	729	**163**	.224
91. **Martin Lapointe**, Det., Bos., Chi.	14	839	**162**	.193
92. **Daymond Langkow**, T.B., Phi., Phx., Cgy.	10	707	**161**	.228
Radek Dvorak, Fla., NYR, Edm.	10	746	**161**	.216
Richard Zednik, Wsh., Mtl.	10	579	**161**	.278
95. **Ilya Kovalchuk**, Atl.	4	305	**160**	.525
Michael Peca, Van., Buf., NYI, Edm.	11	693	**160**	.231
Sergei Gonchar, Wsh., Bos., Pit.	11	744	**160**	.215
98. **Radek Bonk**, Ott., Mtl.	11	750	**158**	.211
99. **Chris Drury**, Col., Cgy., Buf.	7	551	**156**	.283
100. **Darcy Tucker**, Mtl., T.B., Tor.	10	683	**155**	.227

Top 100 All-Time Assist Leaders

* active player

Player	Seasons	Games	Assists	Assists per game
1. **Wayne Gretzky**, Edm., L.A., St.L., NYR .	20	1487	**1963**	1.320
2. **Ron Francis**, Hfd., Pit., Car., Tor.	23	1731	**1249**	.722
3. **Mark Messier**, Edm., NYR, Van.	25	1756	**1193**	.679
4. **Raymond Bourque**, Bos., Col.	22	1612	**1169**	.725
5. **Paul Coffey**, Edm., Pit., L.A., Det., Hfd., Phi., Chi., Car., Bos.	21	1409	**1135**	.806
6. **Adam Oates**, Det., St.L., Bos., Wsh., Phi., Ana., Edm.	19	1337	**1079**	.807
7. **Steve Yzerman**, Det.	22	1514	**1063**	.702
8. **Gordie Howe**, Det., Hfd.	26	1767	**1049**	.594
9. **Marcel Dionne**, Det., L.A., NYR	18	1348	**1040**	.772
10. **Mario Lemieux**, Pit.	18	915	**1033**	1.129
11. **Doug Gilmour**, St.L., Cgy., Tor., N.J., Chi., Buf., Mtl.	20	1474	**964**	.654
12. **Al MacInnis**, Cgy., St.L.	23	1416	**934**	.660
13. **Larry Murphy**, L.A., Wsh., Min., Pit., Tor., Det.	21	1615	**929**	.575
14. **Stan Mikita**, Chi.	22	1394	**926**	.664
* 15. **Joe Sakic**, Que., Col.	17	1237	**915**	.740
16. **Bryan Trottier**, NYI, Pit.	18	1279	**901**	.704
17. **Phil Housley**, Buf., Wpg., St.L., Cgy., N.J., Wsh., Chi., Tor.	21	1495	**894**	.598
18. **Dale Hawerchuk**, Wpg., Buf., St.L., Phi.	16	1188	**891**	.750
19. **Phil Esposito**, Chi., Bos., NYR	18	1282	**873**	.681
20. **Denis Savard**, Chi., Mtl., T.B.	17	1196	**865**	.723
21. **Bobby Clarke**, Phi.	15	1144	**852**	.745
* 22. **Jaromir Jagr**, Pit., Wsh., NYR	15	1109	**841**	.758
23. **Alex Delvecchio**, Det.	24	1549	**825**	.533
24. **Gilbert Perreault**, Buf.	17	1191	**814**	.683
25. **John Bucyk**, Det., Bos.	23	1540	**813**	.528
* 26. **Pierre Turgeon**, Buf., NYI, Mtl., St.L., Dal., Col.	18	1277	**809**	.634
27. **Jari Kurri**, Edm., L.A., NYR, Ana., Col. . .	17	1251	**797**	.637
28. **Guy Lafleur**, Mtl., NYR, Que.	17	1126	**793**	.704
29. **Peter Stastny**, Que., N.J., St.L.	15	977	**789**	.808
* 30. **Brian Leetch**, NYR, Tor., Bos.	18	1205	**781**	.648
* **Mark Recchi**, Pit., Phi., Mtl., Car.	17	1256	**781**	.622
32. **Jean Ratelle**, NYR, Bos.	21	1281	**776**	.606
33. **Vincent Damphousse**, Tor., Edm., Mtl., S.J.	18	1378	**773**	.561
34. **Bernie Federko**, St.L., Det.	14	1000	**761**	.761
35. **Larry Robinson**, Mtl., L.A.	20	1384	**750**	.542
* 36. **Chris Chelios**, Mtl., Chi., Det.	22	1476	**743**	.503
37. **Denis Potvin**, NYI	15	1060	**742**	.700
38. **Norm Ullman**, Det., Tor.	20	1410	**739**	.524
39. **Bernie Nicholls**, L.A., NYR, Edm., N.J., Chi., S.J.	18	1127	**734**	.651
40. **Luc Robitaille**, L.A., Pit., NYR, Det. . . .	19	1431	**726**	.507
41. **Scott Stevens**, Wsh., St.L., N.J.	22	1635	**712**	.435
Jean Beliveau, Mtl.	20	1125	**712**	.633
* 43. **Mike Modano**, Min., Dal.	17	1179	**698**	.592
Dave Andreychuk, Buf., Tor., N.J., Bos., Col., T.B.	23	1639	**698**	.426
45. **Dale Hunter**, Que., Wsh., Col.	19	1407	**697**	.495
46. **Henri Richard**, Mtl.	20	1256	**688**	.548
47. **Brad Park**, NYR, Bos., Det.	17	1113	**683**	.614
48. **Bobby Smith**, Min., Mtl.	15	1077	**679**	.630
* 49. **Mats Sundin**, Que., Tor.	15	1156	**671**	.580
* 50. **Jeremy Roenick**, Chi., Phx., Phi., L.A. . .	17	1182	**658**	.557
51. **Brett Hull**, Cgy., St.L., Dal., Det., Phx. .	20	1269	**650**	.512
* 52. **Doug Weight**, NYR, Edm., St.L., Car. . .	15	982	**646**	.658
53. **Bobby Orr**, Bos., Chi.	12	657	**645**	.982
54. **Gary Suter**, Cgy., Chi., S.J.	17	1145	**641**	.560
55. **Dave Taylor**, L.A.	17	1111	**638**	.574
56. **Borje Salming**, Tor., Det.	17	1148	**637**	.555
Darryl Sittler, Tor., Phi., Det.	15	1096	**637**	.581
58. **Neal Broten**, Min., Dal., N.J., L.A. . . .	17	1099	**634**	.577
Brendan Shanahan, N.J., St.L., Hfd., Det.	18	1350	**634**	.470
60. **Theoren Fleury**, Cgy., Col., NYR, Chi. . .	15	1084	**633**	.584
61. **Mike Gartner**, Wsh., Min., NYR, Tor., Phx.	19	1432	**627**	.438
62. **Andy Bathgate**, NYR, Tor., Det., Pit. . . .	17	1069	**624**	.584
* 63. **Sergei Fedorov**, Det., Ana., CBJ	15	1055	**620**	.588
* 64. **Nicklas Lidstrom**, Det.	14	1096	**617**	.563
65. **Rod Gilbert**, NYR	18	1065	**615**	.577
66. **Michel Goulet**, Que., Chi.	15	1089	**604**	.555
67. **Kirk Muller**, N.J., Mtl., NYI, Tor., Fla., Dal.	19	1349	**602**	.446
68. **Glenn Anderson**, Edm., Tor., NYR, St.L.	16	1129	**601**	.532
* 69. **Rod Brind'Amour**, St.L., Phi., Car. . . .	17	1187	**599**	.505
70. **Dino Ciccarelli**, Min., Wsh., Det., T.B., Fla.	19	1232	**592**	.481
71. **Dave Keon**, Tor., Hfd.	18	1296	**590**	.455
Doug Wilson, Chi., S.J.	16	1024	**590**	.576
* 73. **Peter Forsberg**, Que., Col., Phi.	11	640	**581**	.908

The career leader in games, goals, assists and points for the Hartford Whalers/ Carolina Hurricanes franchise, Ron Francis has more assists than any player in NHL history ... other than Wayne Gretzky.

Player	Seasons	Games	Assists	Assist per game
Dave Babych, Wpg., Hfd., Van., Phi., L.A.	19	1195	**581**	.486
75. **Brian Propp**, Phi., Bos., Min., Hfd.	15	1016	**579**	.570
76. **Steve Larmer**, Chi., NYR.	15	1006	**571**	.568
77. **Frank Mahovlich**, Tor., Det., Mtl.	18	1181	**570**	.483
78. **Craig Janney**, Bos., St.L., S.J., Wpg., Phx., T.B., NYI.	12	760	**563**	.741
Cliff Ronning, St.L., Van., Phx., Nsh., L.A., Min., NYI	18	1137	**563**	.495
80. **Joe Mullen**, St.L., Cgy., Pit., Bos.	17	1062	**561**	.528
81. **Bobby Hull**, Chi., Wpg., Hfd.	16	1063	**560**	.527
* 82. **Alexander Mogilny**, Buf., Van., N.J., Tor.	16	990	**559**	.565
* **Joe Nieuwendyk**, Cgy., Dal., N.J., Tor., Fla.	19	1242	**559**	.450
84. **Mike Bossy**, NYI	10	752	**553**	.735
Thomas Steen, Wpg.	14	950	**553**	.582
86. **Ken Linseman**, Phi., Edm., Bos., Tor. . . .	14	860	**551**	.641
Tom Lysiak, Atl., Chi.	13	919	**551**	.600
* 88. **Teemu Selanne**, Wpg., Ana., S.J., Col. . .	13	959	**549**	.572
89. **Mark Howe**, Hfd., Phi., Det.	16	929	**545**	.587
Pat LaFontaine, NYI, Buf., NYR.	15	865	**545**	.630
91. **Red Kelly**, Det., Tor.	20	1316	**542**	.412
* **Sergei Zubov**, NYR, Pit., Dal.	13	934	**542**	.580
93. **Pat Verbeek**, N.J., Hfd., NYR, Dal., Det.	20	1424	**541**	.380
94. **Rick Middleton**, NYR, Bos.	14	1005	**540**	.537
95. **Brian Bellows**, Min., Mtl., T.B., Ana., Wsh.	17	1188	**537**	.452
* 96. **Andrew Cassels**, Mtl., Hfd., Cgy., Van., CBJ, Wsh.	16	1015	**528**	.520
97. **Steve Duchesne**, L.A., Phi., Que., St.L., Ott., Det.	16	1113	**525**	.472
98. **Dennis Maruk**, Cal., Cle., Min., Wsh. . . .	14	888	**522**	.588
99. **Wayne Cashman**, Bos.	17	1027	**516**	.502
100. **Butch Goring**, L.A., NYI, Bos.	16	1107	**513**	.463

Top 100 Active Assist Leaders

Player	Seasons	Games	Assists	Assists per game
1. Joe Sakic, Que., Col.	17	1237	**915**	.740
2. Jaromir Jagr, Pit., Wsh., NYR	15	1109	**841**	.758
3. Pierre Turgeon, Buf., NYI, Mtl., St.L., Dal., Col.	18	1277	**809**	.634
4. Brian Leetch, NYR, Tor., Bos.	18	1205	**781**	.648
Mark Recchi, Pit., Phi., Mtl., Car.	17	1256	**781**	.622
6. Chris Chelios, Mtl., Chi., Det.	22	1476	**743**	.503
7. Mike Modano, Min., Dal.	17	1179	**698**	.592
8. Mats Sundin, Que., Tor.	15	1156	**671**	.580
9. Jeremy Roenick, Chi., Phx., Phi., L.A.	17	1182	**658**	.557
10. Doug Weight, NYR, Edm., St.L., Car.	15	982	**646**	.658
11. Brendan Shanahan, N.J., St.L., Hfd., Det.	18	1350	**634**	.470
12. Sergei Fedorov, Det., Ana., CBJ	15	1055	**620**	.588
13. Nicklas Lidstrom, Det.	14	1096	**617**	.563
14. Rod Brind'Amour, St.L., Phi., Car.	17	1187	**599**	.505
15. Peter Forsberg, Que., Col., Phi.	11	640	**581**	.908
16. Joe Nieuwendyk, Cgy., Dal., N.J., Tor., Fla.	19	1242	**559**	.450
Alexander Mogilny, Buf., Van., N.J., Tor.	16	990	**559**	.565
18. Teemu Selanne, Wpg., Ana., S.J., Col.	13	959	**549**	.572
19. Sergei Zubov, NYR, Pit., Dal.	13	934	**542**	.580
20. Andrew Cassels, Mtl., Hfd., Cgy., Van., CBJ, Wsh.	16	1015	**528**	.520
21. Teppo Numminen, Wpg., Phx., Dal., Buf.	17	1235	**478**	.387
22. Trevor Linden, Van., NYI, Mtl., Wsh.	17	1243	**474**	.381
23. Eric Lindros, Phi., NYR, Tor.	13	711	**472**	.664
24. Alex Zhamnov, Wpg.; Chi., Phi., Bos.	13	807	**470**	.582
25. Tony Amonte, NYR, Chi., Phx., Phi., Cgy.	15	1093	**464**	.425
26. Scott Mellanby, Phi., Edm., Fla., St.L., Atl.	20	1362	**452**	.332
27. Paul Kariya, Ana., Col., Nsh.	11	739	**448**	.606
28. Eric Desjardins, Mtl., Phi.	17	1143	**439**	.384
29. Rob Blake, L.A., Col.	16	984	**437**	.444
30. Gary Roberts, Cgy., Car., Tor., Fla.	19	1087	**435**	.400
31. Jozef Stumpel, Bos., L.A., Fla.	14	832	**434**	.522
32. Alex Kovalev, NYR, Pit., Mtl.	13	918	**430**	.468
33. Keith Tkachuk, Wpg., Phx., St.L.	14	897	**422**	.470
Mathieu Schneider, Mtl., NYI, Tor., NYR, L.A., Det.	17	1064	**422**	.397
35. Scott Young, Hfd., Pit., Que., Col., Ana., St.L., Dal.	17	1181	**415**	.351
36. Scott Niedermayer, N.J., Ana.	14	974	**414**	.425
37. Alexei Yashin, Ott., NYI	11	792	**412**	.520
38. Daniel Alfredsson, Ott.	10	706	**409**	.579
39. John LeClair, Mtl., Phi., Pit.	15	946	**408**	.431
40. Petr Nedved, Van., St.L., NYR, Pit., Edm., Phx., Phi.	14	942	**397**	.421
41. Martin Straka, Pit., Ott., NYI, Fla., L.A., NYR	13	812	**392**	.483
42. Glen Wesley, Bos., Hfd., Car., Tor.	18	1311	**390**	.297
43. Markus Naslund, Pit., Van.	12	871	**386**	.443
44. Sandis Ozolinsh, S.J., Col., Car., Fla., Ana., NYR.	13	815	**381**	.467
45. Peter Bondra, Wsh., Ott., Atl.	15	1044	**380**	.364
46. Bobby Holik, Hfd., N.J., NYR, Atl.	15	1088	**379**	.348
47. Ray Whitney, S.J., Edm., Fla., CBJ, Det., Car.	14	763	**368**	.482
Jason Arnott, Edm., N.J., Dal.	12	824	**368**	.447
49. Michael Nylander, Hfd., Cgy., T.B., Chi., Wsh., Bos., NYR	12	729	**363**	.498
50. Darryl Sydor, L.A., Dal., CBJ, T.B.	14	1023	**361**	.353
Mike Ricci, Phi., Que., Col., S.J., Phx.	15	1092	**361**	.331
52. Joe Thornton, Bos., S.J.	8	590	**357**	.605
53. Vyacheslav Kozlov, Det., Buf., Atl.	14	882	**353**	.400
Keith Primeau, Det., Hfd., Car., Phi.	15	909	**353**	.388
55. Chris Pronger, Hfd., St.L., Edm.	12	802	**350**	.436
56. Roman Hamrlik, T.B., Edm., NYI, Cgy.	13	924	**343**	.371
57. Pavol Demitra, Ott., St.L., L.A.	12	611	**340**	.556
58. Alexei Zhitnik, L.A., Buf., NYI	13	941	**339**	.360
Martin Rucinsky, Edm., Que., Col., Mtl., Dal., NYR, St.L., Van.	14	869	**339**	.390
60. Robert Lang, L.A., Bos., Pit., Wsh., Det.	12	718	**335**	.467
Bill Guerin, N.J., Edm., Bos., Dal.	14	949	**335**	.353
62. Bryan Smolinski, Bos., Pit., NYI, L.A., Ott.	13	910	**334**	.367
63. Jason Allison, Wsh., Bos., L.A., Tor.	12	552	**331**	.600
64. Saku Koivu, Mtl.	10	569	**323**	.568
Sergei Gonchar, Wsh., Bos., Pit.	11	744	**323**	.434
Shawn McEachern, Pit., L.A., Bos., Ott., Atl.	14	911	**323**	.355
67. Chris Gratton, T.B., Phi., Buf., Phx., Col., Fla.	12	927	**318**	.343
Eric Weinrich, N.J., Hfd., Chi., Mtl., Bos., Phi., St.L., Van.	17	1157	**318**	.275

Peter Forsberg averaged nearly an assist per game (56 in 60) in his first season with Philadelphia in 2005-06 and now has 581 career assists in 640 games.

Player	Seasons	Games	Assists	Assists per game
69. Geoff Sanderson, Hfd., Car., Van., Buf., CBJ, Phx.	15	1005	**317**	.315
70. Stu Barnes, Wpg., Fla., Pit., Buf., Dal.	14	975	**313**	.321
71. Steve Sullivan, N.J., Tor., Chi., Nsh.	10	666	**311**	.467
72. Martin Gelinas, Edm., Que., Van., Car., Cgy., Fla.	17	1134	**310**	.273
73. Todd Bertuzzi, NYI, Van.	10	710	**306**	.431
74. Steve Rucchin, Ana., NYR.	11	688	**302**	.439
75. Vaclav Prospal, Phi., Ott., Fla., T.B., Ana.	9	630	**296**	.470
76. Jeff Friesen, S.J., Ana., N.J., Wsh.	11	821	**292**	.356
77. Dallas Drake, Det., Wpg., Phx., St.L.	13	884	**291**	.329
Patrice Brisebois, Mtl., Col.	15	871	**291**	.334
Miroslav Satan, Edm., Buf., NYI	10	786	**291**	.370
80. Scott Gomez, N.J.	6	476	**287**	.603
Brian Rolston, N.J., Col., Bos., Min.	11	818	**287**	.351
82. Jarome Iginla, Cgy.	10	708	**285**	.403
83. Glen Murray, Bos., Pit., L.A.	14	887	**284**	.320
84. Patrik Elias, N.J.	10	596	**281**	.471
85. Marc Savard, NYR, Cgy., Atl.	8	503	**268**	.533
Brendan Morrison, N.J., Van.	8	553	**268**	.485
87. Craig Conroy, Mtl., St.L., Cgy., L.A.	11	687	**266**	.387
88. Alex Tanguay, Col.	6	450	**263**	.584
Mike Sillinger, Det., Ana., Van., Phi., T.B., Fla., Ott., CBJ, Phx., St.L.	15	908	**263**	.290
90. Janne Niinimaa, Phi., Edm., NYI, Dal.	9	700	**262**	.374
Radek Bonk, Ott., Mtl.	11	750	**262**	.349
Ryan Smyth, Edm.	11	717	**262**	.365
Andrew Brunette, Wsh., Nsh., Atl., Min., Col.	10	624	**262**	.420
94. Brad Richards, T.B.	5	408	**261**	.640
Travis Green, NYI, Ana., Phx., Tor., Bos.	13	939	**261**	.278
96. Petr Sykora, N.J., Ana., NYR	9	608	**259**	.426
97. Todd Marchant, NYR, Edm., CBJ, Ana.	12	835	**257**	.308
98. Marian Hossa, Ott., Atl.	8	547	**255**	.466
99. Milan Hejduk, Col.	7	544	**253**	.465
100. Sami Kapanen, Hfd., Car., Phi.	10	680	**252**	.371

Top 100 All-Time Point Leaders

* active player

An artist on the ice, Denis Savard had 1,338 points (473 goals. 865 assists) in 17 NHL seasons with Chicago, Montreal and Tampa Bay.

Player	Seasons	Games	Goals	Assists	Points	Points per game
1. **Wayne Gretzky**, Edm., L.A., St.L., NYR	20	1487	894	1963	**2857**	1.921
2. **Mark Messier**, Edm., NYR, Van.	25	1756	694	1193	**1887**	1.075
3. **Gordie Howe**, Det., Hfd.	26	1767	801	1049	**1850**	1.047
4. **Ron Francis**, Hfd., Pit., Car., Tor.	23	1731	549	1249	**1798**	1.039
5. **Marcel Dionne**, Det., L.A., NYR	18	1348	731	1040	**1771**	1.314
6. **Steve Yzerman**, Det.	22	1514	692	1063	**1755**	1.159
7. **Mario Lemieux**, Pit.	18	915	690	1033	**1723**	1.883
8. **Phil Esposito**, Chi., Bos., NYR	18	1282	717	873	**1590**	1.240
9. **Raymond Bourque**, Bos., Col.	22	1612	410	1169	**1579**	.980
10. **Paul Coffey**, Edm., Pit., L.A., Det., Hfd., Phi., Chi., Car., Bos.	21	1409	396	1135	**1531**	1.087
* 11. **Joe Sakic**, Que., Col.	17	1237	574	915	**1489**	1.204
12. **Stan Mikita**, Chi.	22	1394	541	926	**1467**	1.052
* 13. **Jaromir Jagr**, Pit., Wsh., NYR	15	1109	591	841	**1432**	1.291
14. **Bryan Trottier**, NYI, Pit.	18	1279	524	901	**1425**	1.114
15. **Adam Oates**, Det., St.L., Bos., Wsh., Phi., Ana., Edm.	19	1337	341	1079	**1420**	1.062
16. **Doug Gilmour**, St.L., Cgy., Tor., N.J., Chi., Buf., Mtl.	20	1474	450	964	**1414**	.959
17. **Dale Hawerchuk**, Wpg., Buf., St.L., Phi.	16	1188	518	891	**1409**	1.186
18. **Jari Kurri**, Edm., L.A., NYR, Ana., Col.	17	1251	601	797	**1398**	1.118
19. **Luc Robitaille**, L.A., Pit., NYR, Det.	19	1431	668	726	**1394**	.974
20. **Brett Hull**, Cgy., St.L., Dal., Det., Phx.	20	1269	741	650	**1391**	1.096
21. **John Bucyk**, Det., Bos.	23	1540	556	813	**1369**	.889
22. **Guy Lafleur**, Mtl., NYR, Que.	17	1126	560	793	**1353**	1.202
23. **Denis Savard**, Chi., Mtl., T.B.	17	1196	473	865	**1338**	1.119
Dave Andreychuk, Buf., Tor., N.J., Bos., Col., T.B.	23	1639	640	698	**1338**	.816
25. **Mike Gartner**, Wsh., Min., NYR, Tor., Phx.	19	1432	708	627	**1335**	.932
26. **Gilbert Perreault**, Buf.	17	1191	512	814	**1326**	1.113
* 27. **Pierre Turgeon**, Buf., NYI, Mtl., St.L., Dal., Col.	18	1277	511	809	**1320**	1.034
28. **Alex Delvecchio**, Det.	24	1549	456	825	**1281**	.827
29. **Al MacInnis**, Cgy., St.L.	23	1416	340	934	**1274**	.900
30. **Jean Ratelle**, NYR, Bos.	21	1281	491	776	**1267**	.989
* 31. **Mark Recchi**, Pit., Phi., Mtl., Car.	17	1256	484	781	**1265**	1.007
32. **Peter Stastny**, Que., N.J., St.L.	15	977	450	789	**1239**	1.268
33. **Phil Housley**, Buf., Wpg., St.L., Cgy., N.J., Wsh., Chi., Tor.	21	1495	338	894	**1232**	.824
* **Brendan Shanahan**, N.J., St.L., Hfd., Det.	18	1350	598	634	**1232**	.913
35. **Norm Ullman**, Det., Tor.	20	1410	490	739	**1229**	.872
36. **Jean Beliveau**, Mtl.	20	1125	507	712	**1219**	1.084
37. **Larry Murphy**, L.A., Wsh., Min., Pit., Tor., Det.	21	1615	287	929	**1216**	.753
38. **Bobby Clarke**, Phi.	15	1144	358	852	**1210**	1.058
39. **Bernie Nicholls**, L.A., NYR, Edm., N.J., Chi., S.J.	18	1127	475	734	**1209**	1.073
40. **Vincent Damphousse**, Tor., Edm., Mtl., S.J.	18	1378	432	773	**1205**	.874
41. **Dino Ciccarelli**, Min., Wsh., Det., T.B., Fla.	19	1232	608	592	**1200**	.974
* 42. **Mike Modano**, Min., Dal.	17	1179	485	698	**1183**	1.003
43. **Bobby Hull**, Chi., Wpg., Hfd.	16	1063	610	560	**1170**	1.101
* 44. **Mats Sundin**, Que., Tor.	15	1156	496	671	**1167**	1.010
45. **Michel Goulet**, Que., Chi.	15	1089	548	604	**1152**	1.058
* 46. **Jeremy Roenick**, Chi., Phx., Phi., L.A.	17	1182	484	658	**1142**	.966
47. **Bernie Federko**, St.L., Det.	14	1000	369	761	**1130**	1.130
48. **Mike Bossy**, NYI	10	752	573	553	**1126**	1.497
49. **Darryl Sittler**, Tor., Phi., Det.	15	1096	484	637	**1121**	1.023
* 50. **Joe Nieuwendyk**, Cgy., Dal., N.J., Tor., Fla.	19	1242	559	559	**1118**	.900
51. **Frank Mahovlich**, Tor., Det., Mtl.	18	1181	533	570	**1103**	.934
52. **Glenn Anderson**, Edm., Tor., NYR, St.L.	16	1129	498	601	**1099**	.973
53. **Theoren Fleury**, Cgy., Col., NYR, Chi.	15	1084	455	633	**1088**	1.004
54. **Dave Taylor**, L.A.	17	1111	431	638	**1069**	.962
55. **Pat Verbeek**, N.J., Hfd., NYR, Dal., Det.	20	1424	522	541	**1063**	.746
* **Sergei Fedorov**, Det., Ana., CBJ.		1055	443	620	**1063**	1.008
Joe Mullen, St.L., Cgy., Pit., Bos.	17	1062	502	561	**1063**	1.001
58. **Denis Potvin**, NYI	15	1060	310	742	**1052**	.992
59. **Henri Richard**, Mtl.	20	1256	358	688	**1046**	.833
* 60. **Teemu Selanne**, Wpg., Ana., S.J., Col.	13	959	492	549	**1041**	1.086
61. **Bobby Smith**, Min., Mtl.	15	1077	357	679	**1036**	.962
* 62. **Alexander Mogilny**, Buf., Van., N.J., Tor.	16	990	473	559	**1032**	1.042
* 63. **Brian Leetch**, NYR, Tor., Bos.	18	1205	247	781	**1028**	.853
64. **Brian Bellows**, Min., Mtl., T.B., Ana., Wsh.	17	1188	485	537	**1022**	.860
65. **Rod Gilbert**, NYR	18	1065	406	615	**1021**	.959
66. **Dale Hunter**, Que., Wsh., Col.	19	1407	323	697	**1020**	.725
67. **Pat LaFontaine**, NYI, Buf., NYR	15	865	468	545	**1013**	1.171
68. **Steve Larmer**, Chi., NYR	15	1006	441	571	**1012**	1.006
69. **Lanny McDonald**, Tor., Col., Cgy.	16	1111	500	506	**1006**	.905
70. **Brian Propp**, Phi., Bos., Min., Hfd.	15	1016	425	579	**1004**	.988
71. **Rick Middleton**, NYR, Bos.	14	1005	448	540	**988**	.983
72. **Dave Keon**, Tor., Hfd.	18	1296	396	590	**986**	.761
* 73. **Rod Brind'Amour**, St.L., Phi., Car.	17	1187	382	599	**981**	.826
74. **Andy Bathgate**, NYR, Tor., Det., Pit.	17	1069	349	624	**973**	.910
75. **Maurice Richard**, Mtl.	18	978	544	421	**965**	.987
76. **Kirk Muller**, N.J., Mtl., NYI, Tor., Fla., Dal.	19	1349	357	602	**959**	.711
77. **Larry Robinson**, Mtl., L.A.	20	1384	208	750	**958**	.692
78. **Rick Tocchet**, Phi., Pit., L.A., Bos., Wsh., Phx.	18	1144	440	512	**952**	.832
79. **Steve Thomas**, Tor., Chi., NYI, N.J., Ana., Det.	20	1235	421	512	**933**	.755
* 80. **Chris Chelios**, Mtl., Chi., Det.	22	1476	182	743	**925**	.627
81. **Neal Broten**, Min., Dal., N.J., L.A.	17	1099	289	634	**923**	.840
82. **Bobby Orr**, Bos., Chi.	12	657	270	645	**915**	1.393
83. **Scott Stevens**, Wsh., St.L., N.J.	22	1635	196	712	**908**	.555
84. **Ray Ferraro**, Hfd., NYI, NYR, L.A., Atl., St.L.	18	1258	408	490	**898**	.714
85. **Brad Park**, NYR, Bos., Det.	17	1113	213	683	**896**	.805
86. **Butch Goring**, L.A., NYI, Bos.	16	1107	375	513	**888**	.802
* 87. **Doug Weight**, NYR, Edm., St.L., Car.	15	982	239	646	**885**	.901
88. **Bill Barber**, Phi., T.B.	14	903	420	463	**883**	.978
* 89. **Peter Bondra**, Wsh., Ott., Atl.	15	1044	498	380	**878**	.841
Dennis Maruk, Cal., Cle., Min., Wsh.	14	888	356	522	**878**	.989
* 91. **Tony Amonte**, NYR, Chi., Phx., Phi., Cgy.	15	1093	406	464	**870**	.796
92. **Cliff Ronning**, St.L., Van., Phx., Nsh., L.A., Min., NYI.	18	1137	306	563	**869**	.764
* 93. **Keith Tkachuk**, Wpg., Phx., St.L.	14	897	446	422	**868**	.968
94. **Ivan Boldirev**, Bos., Cal., Chi., Atl., Van., Det.	15	1052	361	505	**866**	.823
95. **Yvan Cournoyer**, Mtl.	16	968	428	435	**863**	.892
96. **Dean Prentice**, NYR, Bos., Det., Pit., Min.	22	1378	391	469	**860**	.624
97. **Tomas Sandstrom**, NYR, L.A., Pit., Det., Ana.	15	983	394	462	**856**	.871
98. **Ted Lindsay**, Det., Chi.	17	1068	379	472	**851**	.797
* 99. **Gary Roberts**, Cgy., Car., Tor., Fla.	19	1087	411	435	**846**	.778
100. **Gary Suter**, Cgy., Chi., S.J.	17	1145	203	641	**844**	.737

Top 100 Active Point Leaders

Player	Seasons	Games	Goals	Assists	Points	Points per game
1. **Joe Sakic**, Que., Col.	17	1237	574	915	**1489**	1.204
2. **Jaromir Jagr**, Pit., Wsh., NYR.	15	1109	591	841	**1432**	1.291
3. **Pierre Turgeon**, Buf., NYI, Mtl., St.L., Dal., Col.	18	1277	511	809	**1320**	1.034
4. **Mark Recchi**, Pit., Phi., Mtl., Car.	17	1256	484	781	**1265**	1.007
5. **Brendan Shanahan**, N.J., St.L., Hfd., Det.	18	1350	598	634	**1232**	.913
6. **Mike Modano**, Min., Dal. . . .	17	1179	485	698	**1183**	1.003
7. **Mats Sundin**, Que., Tor.	15	1156	496	671	**1167**	1.010
8. **Jeremy Roenick**, Chi., Phx., Phi., L.A.	17	1182	484	658	**1142**	.966
9. **Joe Nieuwendyk**, Cgy., Dal., N.J., Tor., Fla.	19	1242	559	559	**1118**	.900
10. **Sergei Fedorov**, Det., Ana., CBJ.	15	1055	443	620	**1063**	1.008
11. **Teemu Selanne**, Wpg., Ana., S.J., Col.	13	959	492	549	**1041**	1.086
12. **Alexander Mogilny**, Buf., Van., N.J., Tor.	16	990	473	559	**1032**	1.042
13. **Brian Leetch**, NYR, Tor., Bos. .	18	1205	247	781	**1028**	.853
14. **Rod Brind'Amour**, St.L., Phi., Car.	17	1187	382	599	**981**	.826
15. **Chris Chelios**, Mtl., Chi., Det.	22	1476	182	743	**925**	.627
16. **Doug Weight**, NYR, Edm., St.L., Car.	15	982	239	646	**885**	.901
17. **Peter Bondra**, Wsh., Ott., Atl.	15	1044	498	380	**878**	.841
18. **Tony Amonte**, NYR, Chi., Phx., Phi., Cgy.	15	1093	406	464	**870**	.796
19. **Keith Tkachuk**, Wpg., Phx. .	14	897	446	422	**868**	.968
20. **Gary Roberts**, Cgy., Car., Tor., Fla.	19	1087	411	435	**846**	.778
21. **Eric Lindros**, Phi., NYR, Tor.	13	711	367	472	**839**	1.180
22. **Trevor Linden**, Van., NYI, Mtl., Wsh.	17	1243	356	474	**830**	.668
23. **Peter Forsberg**, Que., Col., Phi.	11	640	235	581	**816**	1.275
24. **John LeClair**, Mtl., Phi., Pit.	15	946	404	408	**812**	.858
25. **Nicklas Lidstrom**, Det. . . .	14	1096	189	617	**806**	.735
26. **Scott Mellanby**, Phi., Edm., Fla., St.L., Atl.	20	1362	352	452	**804**	.590
27. **Paul Kariya**, Ana., Col., Nsh. .	11	739	342	448	**790**	1.069
28. **Scott Young**, Hfd., Pit., Que., Col., Ana., St.L., Dal.	17	1181	342	415	**757**	.641
29. **Alex Kovalev**, NYR, Pit., Mtl. .	13	918	315	430	**745**	.812
30. **Andrew Cassels**, Mtl., Hfd., Cgy., Van., CBJ, Wsh. . . .	16	1015	204	528	**732**	.721
31. **Alexei Yashin**, Ott., NYI	11	792	319	412	**731**	.923
32. **Alex Zhamnov**, Wpg., Chi., Phi., Bos.	13	807	249	470	**719**	.891
33. **Markus Naslund**, Pit., Van. . .	12	871	322	386	**708**	.813
34. **Petr Nedved**, Van., St.L., NYR, Pit., Edm., Phx., Phi.	14	942	308	397	**705**	.748
35. **Sergei Zubov**, NYR, Pit., Dal. .	13	934	136	542	**678**	.726
36. **Bobby Holik**, Hfd., N.J., NYR, Atl.	15	1088	296	379	**675**	.620
37. **Daniel Alfredsson**, Ott.	10	706	262	409	**671**	.950
38. **Bill Guerin**, N.J., Edm., Bos., Dal.	14	949	328	335	**663**	.699
39. **Geoff Sanderson**, Hfd., Car., Van., Buf., CBJ, Phx. . .	15	1005	341	317	**658**	.655
40. **Jason Arnott**, Edm., N.J., Dal.	12	824	276	368	**644**	.782
41. **Rob Blake**, L.A., Col.	16	984	200	437	**637**	.647
42. **Vyacheslav Kozlov**, Det., Buf., Atl.	14	882	277	353	**630**	.714
43. **Keith Primeau**, Det., Hfd., Car., Phi.	15	909	266	353	**619**	.681
44. **Mathieu Schneider**, Mtl., NYI, Tor., NYR, L.A., Det. .	17	1064	189	422	**611**	.574
45. **Martin Straka**, Pit., Ott., NYI, Fla., L.A., NYR.	13	812	214	392	**606**	.746
46. **Mike Ricci**, Phi., Que., Col., S.J., Phx.	15	1092	243	361	**604**	.553
47. **Jozef Stumpel**, Bos., L.A., Fla.	14	832	166	434	**600**	.721
48. **Martin Gelinas**, Edm., Que., Van., Car., Cgy., Fla. . .	17	1134	286	310	**596**	.526
49. **Teppo Numminen**, Wpg., Phx., Dal., Buf.	17	1235	113	478	**591**	.479
50. **Ray Whitney**, S.J., Edm., Fla., CBJ, Det., Car.	14	763	222	368	**590**	.773
51. **Miroslav Satan**, Edm., Buf., NYI.	10	786	294	291	**585**	.744
52. **Bryan Smolinski**, Bos., Pit., NYI, L.A., Ott.	13	910	248	334	**582**	.640
53. **Pavol Demitra**, Ott., St.L., L.A.	12	611	241	340	**581**	.951
54. **Shawn McEachern**, Pit., L.A., Bos., Ott., Atl.	14	911	256	323	**579**	.636

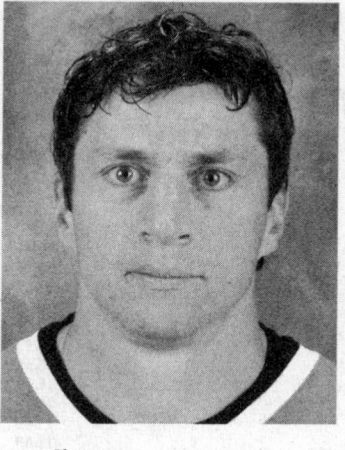

A solid two-way player, Carolina's Rod Brind'Amour recorded 70 points last season (31 goals, 39 assists) and now has 981 in his career.

Player	Seasons	Games	Goals	Assists	Points	Points per game
55. **Glen Murray**, Bos., Pit., L.A. .	14	887	292	284	**576**	.649
56. **Eric Desjardins**, Mtl., Phi. . . .	17	1143	136	439	**575**	.503
57. **Jarome Iginla**, Cgy.	10	708	285	285	**570**	.805
58. **Martin Rucinsky**, Edm., Que., Col., Mtl., Dal., NYR, St.L., Van.	14	869	224	339	**563**	.648
59. **Stu Barnes**, Wpg., Fla., Pit., Buf., Dal.	14	975	236	313	**549**	.563
60. **Joe Thornton**, Bos., S.J.	8	590	189	357	**546**	.925
61. **Sandis Ozolinsh**, S.J., Col., Car., Fla., Ana., NYR .	13	815	164	381	**545**	.669
62. **Scott Niedermayer**, N.J., Ana.	14	974	125	414	**539**	.553
63. **Todd Bertuzzi**, NYI, Van.	10	710	223	306	**529**	.745
64. **Robert Lang**, L.A., Bos., Pit., Wsh., Det.	12	718	194	335	**529**	.737
65. **Michael Nylander**, Hfd., Cgy., T.B., Chi., Wsh., Bos., NYR .	12	729	163	363	**526**	.722
66. **Steve Sullivan**, N.J., Tor., Chi., Nsh.	10	666	206	311	**517**	.776
67. **Glen Wesley**, Bos., Hfd., Car., Tor.	18	1311	126	390	**516**	.394
68. **Brian Rolston**, N.J., Col., Bos., Min.	11	818	224	287	**511**	.625
69. **Chris Gratton**, T.B., Phi., Buf., Phx., Col., Fla.	12	927	191	318	**509**	.549
70. **Patrik Elias**, N.J.	10	596	223	281	**504**	.846
71. **Jeff Friesen**, S.J., Ana., N.J., Wsh.	11	821	212	292	**504**	.614
72. **Ryan Smyth**, Edm.	11	717	234	262	**496**	.692
73. **Jason Allison**, Wsh., Bos., L.A., Tor.	12	552	154	331	**485**	.879
74. **Sergei Gonchar**, Wsh., Bos., Pit.	11	744	160	323	**483**	.649
75. **Marian Hossa**, Ott., Atl.	8	547	227	255	**482**	.881
76. **Milan Hejduk**, Col.	7	544	221	253	**474**	.871
77. **Steve Rucchin**, Ana., NYR . .	11	688	166	302	**468**	.680
78. **Roman Hamrlik**, T.B., Edm., NYI, Cgy.	13	924	124	343	**467**	.505
79. **Yanic Perreault**, Tor., L.A., Mtl., Nsh.	12	740	217	247	**464**	.627
80. **Petr Sykora**, N.J., Ana., NYR .	9	608	202	259	**461**	.758
81. **Mike Sillinger**, Det., Ana., Van., Phi., T.B., Fla., Ott., CBJ, Phx., St.L.	15	908	198	263	**461**	.508
82. **Saku Koivu**, Mtl.	10	569	137	323	**460**	.808
83. **Dallas Drake**, Det., Wpg., Phx., St.L.	13	884	168	291	**459**	.519
84. **Chris Pronger**, Hfd., St.L., Edm.	12	802	106	350	**456**	.569
85. **Jeff O'Neill**, Hfd., Car., Tor. . .	11	747	217	237	**454**	.608
86. **Travis Green**, NYI, Ana., Phx., Tor., Bos.	13	939	192	261	**453**	.482
87. **Darryl Sydor**, L.A., Dal., CBJ, T.B.	14	1023	89	361	**450**	.440
88. **Mariusz Czerkawski**, Bos., Edm., NYI, Mtl., Tor. . .	12	745	215	220	**435**	.584
89. **Cory Stillman**, Cgy., St.L., T.B., Car.	10	645	184	250	**434**	.673
90. **Vaclav Prospal**, Phi., Ott., Fla., T.B., Ana.	9	630	132	296	**428**	.679
91. **Sami Kapanen**, Hfd., Car., Phi.	10	680	173	252	**425**	.625
92. **Alexei Zhitnik**, L.A., Buf., NYI	13	941	86	339	**425**	.452
93. **Radek Bonk**, Ott., Mtl.	11	750	158	262	**420**	.560
94. **Shane Doan**, Wpg., Phx.	10	730	172	245	**417**	.571
95. **Patrick Marleau**, S.J.	8	640	187	226	**413**	.645
96. **Daymond Langkow**, T.B., Phi., Phx., Cgy.	10	707	161	252	**413**	.584
97. **Radek Dvorak**, Fla., NYR, Edm.	10	746	161	251	**412**	.552
98. **Todd Marchant**, NYR, Edm., CBJ, Ana.	12	835	154	257	**411**	.492
99. **Andrew Brunette**, Wsh., Nsh., Atl., Min., Col.	10	624	145	262	**407**	.652
100. **Craig Conroy**, Mtl., St.L., Cgy., L.A.	11	687	140	266	**406**	.591

Top 100 All-Time Games Played Leaders

* active player

	Player	Seasons	Games Played
1.	**Gordie Howe**, Det., Hfd.	26	**1767**
2.	**Mark Messier**, Edm., NYR, Van.	25	**1756**
3.	**Ron Francis**, Hfd., Pit., Car., Tor.	23	**1731**
4.	**Dave Andreychuk**, Buf., Tor., N.J., Bos., Col., T.B.	23	**1639**
5.	**Scott Stevens**, Wsh., St.L., N.J.	22	**1635**
6.	**Larry Murphy**, L.A., Wsh., Min., Pit., Tor., Det.	21	**1615**
7.	**Raymond Bourque**, Bos., Col.	22	**1612**
8.	**Alex Delvecchio**, Det.	24	**1549**
9.	**John Bucyk**, Det., Bos.	23	**1540**
10.	**Steve Yzerman**, Det.	22	**1514**
11.	**Phil Housley**, Buf., Wpg., St.L., Cgy., N.J., Wsh., Chi., Tor.	21	**1495**
12.	**Wayne Gretzky**, Edm., L.A., St.L., NYR	20	**1487**
* 13.	**Chris Chelios**, Mtl., Chi., Det.	22	**1476**
14.	**Doug Gilmour**, St.L., Cgy., Tor., N.J., Chi., Buf., Mtl.	20	**1474**
15.	**Tim Horton**, Tor., NYR, Pit., Buf.	24	**1446**
16.	**Mike Gartner**, Wsh., Min., NYR, Tor., Phx.	19	**1432**
17.	**Luc Robitaille**, L.A., Pit., NYR, Det.	19	**1431**
18.	**Pat Verbeek**, N.J., Hfd., NYR, Dal., Det.	20	**1424**
19.	**Al MacInnis**, Cgy., St.L.	23	**1416**
20.	**Harry Howell**, NYR, Oak., Cal., L.A.	21	**1411**
21.	**Norm Ullman**, Det., Tor.	20	**1410**
22.	**Paul Coffey**, Edm., Pit., L.A., Det., Hfd., Phi., Chi., Car., Bos.	21	**1409**
23.	**Dale Hunter**, Que., Wsh., Col.	19	**1407**
24.	**Stan Mikita**, Chi.	22	**1394**
25.	**Doug Mohns**, Bos., Chi., Min., Atl., Wsh.	22	**1390**
26.	**Larry Robinson**, Mtl., L.A.	20	**1384**
27.	**Vincent Damphousse**, Tor., Edm., Mtl., S.J.	18	**1378**
	Dean Prentice, NYR, Bos., Det., Pit., Min.	22	**1378**
* 29.	**Scott Mellanby**, Phi., Edm., Fla., St.L., Atl.	20	**1362**
30.	**Ron Stewart**, Tor., Bos., St.L., NYR, Van., NYI	21	**1353**
* 31.	**Brendan Shanahan**, N.J., St.L., Hfd., Det.	18	**1350**
32.	**Kirk Muller**, N.J., Mtl., NYI, Tor., Fla., Dal.	19	**1349**
33.	**Marcel Dionne**, Det., L.A., NYR	18	**1348**
34.	**Adam Oates**, Det., St.L., Bos., Wsh., Phi., Ana., Edm.	19	**1337**
35.	**Guy Carbonneau**, Mtl., St.L., Dal.	19	**1318**
36.	**Red Kelly**, Det., Tor.	20	**1316**
* 37.	**Luke Richardson**, Tor., Edm., Phi., CBJ	18	**1312**
* 38.	**Glen Wesley**, Bos., Hfd., Car., Tor.	18	**1311**
39.	**Dave Keon**, Tor., Hfd.	18	**1296**
40.	**Ken Daneyko**, N.J.	20	**1283**
41.	**Phil Esposito**, Chi., Bos., NYR	18	**1282**
42.	**Jean Ratelle**, NYR, Bos.	21	**1281**
43.	**James Patrick**, NYR, Hfd., Cgy., Buf.	21	**1280**
44.	**Bryan Trottier**, NYI, Pit.	18	**1279**
* 45.	**Pierre Turgeon**, Buf., NYI, Mtl., St.L., Dal., Col.	18	**1277**
46.	**Brett Hull**, Cgy., St.L., Dal., Det., Phx.	20	**1269**
47.	**Ray Ferraro**, Hfd., NYI, NYR, L.A., Atl., St.L.	18	**1258**
48.	**Craig Ludwig**, Mtl., NYI, Min., Dal.	17	**1256**
*	**Mark Recchi**, Pit., Phi., Mtl., Car.	17	**1256**
	Henri Richard, Mtl.	20	**1256**
51.	**Kevin Lowe**, Edm., NYR.	19	**1254**
52.	**Jari Kurri**, Edm., L.A., NYR, Ana., Col.	17	**1251**
53.	**Bill Gadsby**, Chi., NYR, Det.	20	**1248**
54.	**Allan Stanley**, NYR, Chi., Bos., Tor., Phi.	21	**1244**
* 55.	**Trevor Linden**, Van., NYI, Mtl., Wsh.	17	**1243**
* 56.	**Joe Nieuwendyk**, Cgy., Dal., N.J., Tor., Fla.	19	**1242**
* 57.	**Joe Sakic**, Que., Col.	17	**1237**
* 58.	**Teppo Numminen**, Wpg., Phx., Dal., Buf.	17	**1235**
	Steve Thomas, Tor., Chi., NYI, N.J., Ana., Det.	20	**1235**
60.	**Dino Ciccarelli**, Min., Wsh., Det., T.B., Fla.	19	**1232**
61.	**Ed Westfall**, Bos., NYI	18	**1226**
62.	**Brad McCrimmon**, Bos., Phi., Cgy., Det., Hfd., Phx.	18	**1222**
63.	**Eric Nesterenko**, Tor., Chi.	21	**1219**
64.	**Marcel Pronovost**, Det., Tor.	21	**1206**
* 65.	**Brian Leetch**, NYR, Tor., Bos.	18	**1205**
66.	**Claude Lemieux**, Mtl., N.J., Col., Phx., Dal.	20	**1197**
67.	**Denis Savard**, Chi., Mtl., T.B.	17	**1196**
68.	**Dave Babych**, Wpg., Hfd., Van., Phi., L.A.	19	**1195**
69.	**John MacLean**, N.J., S.J., NYR, Dal.	18	**1194**
70.	**Gilbert Perreault**, Buf.	17	**1191**
	Marc Bergevin, Chi., NYI, Hfd., T.B., Det., St.L., Pit., Van.	20	**1191**
72.	**Dale Hawerchuk**, Wpg., Buf., St.L., Phi.	16	**1188**
	Brian Bellows, Min., Mtl., T.B., Ana., Wsh.	17	**1188**
	Kevin Dineen, Hfd., Phi., Car., Ott., CBJ	19	**1188**
* 75.	**Rod Brind'Amour**, St.L., Phi., Car.	17	**1187**
	George Armstrong, Tor.	21	**1187**
* 77.	**Jeremy Roenick**, Chi., Phx., Phi., L.A.	17	**1182**
	Kelly Buchberger, Edm., Atl., L.A., Phx., Pit.	18	**1182**
* 79.	**Scott Young**, Hfd., Pit., Que., Col., Ana., St.L., Dal.	17	**1181**
	Frank Mahovlich, Tor., Det., Mtl.	18	**1181**

Chris Chelios completed the 2005-06 season with 1,476 games played. He has a chance to climb as high as eighth on the all-time games-played list this year.

	Player	Seasons	Games Played
* 81.	**Mike Modano**, Min., Dal.	17	**1179**
82.	**Bob Carpenter**, Wsh., NYR, L.A., Bos., N.J.	19	**1178**
83.	**Don Marshall**, Mtl., NYR, Buf., Tor.	19	**1176**
84.	**Sylvain Cote**, Hfd., Wsh., Tor., Chi., Dal.	19	**1171**
85.	**Mike Keane**, Mtl., Col., NYR, Dal., St.L., Van.	16	**1161**
86.	**Bob Gainey**, Mtl.	16	**1160**
87.	**Kevin Hatcher**, Wsh., Dal., Pit., NYR, Car.	17	**1157**
	Eric Weinrich, N.J., Hfd., Chi., Mtl., Bos., Phi., St.L., Van.	17	**1157**
* 89.	**Mats Sundin**, Que., Tor.	15	**1156**
	Shayne Corson, Mtl., Edm., St.L., Tor., Dal.	19	**1156**
91.	**Adam Graves**, Det., Edm., NYR, S.J.	16	**1152**
92.	**Leo Boivin**, Tor., Bos., Det., Pit., Min.	19	**1150**
93.	**Garry Galley**, L.A., Wsh., Bos., Phi., Buf., NYI.	17	**1149**
94.	**Borje Salming**, Tor., Det.	17	**1148**
95.	**Gary Suter**, Cgy., Chi., S.J.	17	**1145**
96.	**Bobby Clarke**, Phi.	15	**1144**
	Rick Tocchet, Phi., Pit., L.A., Bos., Wsh., Phx.	18	**1144**
98.	**Eric Desjardins**, Mtl., Phi.	17	**1143**
99.	**Cliff Ronning**, St.L., Van., Phx., Nsh., L.A., Min., NYI	18	**1137**
* 100.	**Martin Gelinas**, Edm., Que., Van., Car., Cgy., Fla.	17	**1134**

Top 100 Active Games Played Leaders

	Player	Seasons	Games Played
1.	**Chris Chelios**, Mtl., Chi., Det.	22	1476
2.	**Scott Mellanby**, Phi., Edm., Fla., St.L., Atl.	20	1362
3.	**Brendan Shanahan**, N.J., St.L., Hfd., Det.	18	1350
4.	**Luke Richardson**, Tor., Edm., Phi., CBJ	18	1312
5.	**Glen Wesley**, Bos., Hfd., Car., Tor.	18	1311
6.	**Pierre Turgeon**, Buf., NYI, Mtl., St.L., Dal., Col.	18	1277
7.	**Mark Recchi**, Pit., Phi., Mtl., Car.	17	1256
8.	**Trevor Linden**, Van., NYI, Mtl., Wsh.	17	1243
9.	**Joe Nieuwendyk**, Cgy., Dal., N.J., Tor., Fla.	19	1242
10.	**Joe Sakic**, Que., Col.	17	1237
11.	**Teppo Numminen**, Wpg., Phx., Dal., Buf.	17	1235
12.	**Brian Leetch**, NYR, Tor., Bos.	18	1205
13.	**Rod Brind'Amour**, St.L., Phi., Car.	17	1187
14.	**Jeremy Roenick**, Chi., Phx., Phi., L.A.	17	1182
15.	**Scott Young**, Hfd., Pit., Que., Col., Ana., St.L., Dal.	17	1181
16.	**Mike Modano**, Min., Dal.	17	1179
17.	**Mats Sundin**, Que., Tor.	15	1156
18.	**Martin Gelinas**, Edm., Que., Van., Car., Cgy., Fla.	17	1134
19.	**Jaromir Jagr**, Pit., Wsh., NYR	15	1109
20.	**Tom Fitzgerald**, NYI, Fla., Col., Nsh., Chi., Tor., Bos.	17	1097
21.	**Nicklas Lidstrom**, Det.	14	1096
22.	**Tony Amonte**, NYR, Chi., Phx., Phi., Cgy.	15	1093
23.	**Mike Ricci**, Phi., Que., Col., S.J., Phx.	15	1092
24.	**Bobby Holik**, Hfd., N.J., NYR, Atl.	15	1088
25.	**Gary Roberts**, Cgy., Car., Tor., Fla.	19	1087
26.	**Mathieu Schneider**, Mtl., NYI, Tor., NYR, L.A., Det.	17	1064
27.	**Lyle Odelein**, Mtl., N.J., Phx., CBJ, Chi., Dal., Fla., Pit.	16	1056
28.	**Sergei Fedorov**, Det., Ana., CBJ	15	1055
29.	**Peter Bondra**, Wsh., Ott., Atl.	15	1044
30.	**Darryl Sydor**, L.A., Dal., CBJ, T.B.	14	1023
31.	**Tie Domi**, Tor., NYR, Wpg.	16	1020
32.	**Andrew Cassels**, Mtl., Hfd., Cgy., Van., CBJ, Wsh.	16	1015
33.	**Geoff Sanderson**, Hfd., Car., Van., Buf., CBJ, Phx.	15	1005
34.	**Alexander Mogilny**, Buf., Van., N.J., Tor.	16	990
35.	**Rob Blake**, L.A., Col.	16	984
36.	**Doug Weight**, NYR, Edm., St.L., Car.	15	982
37.	**Stu Barnes**, Wpg., Fla., Pit., Buf., Dal.	14	975
38.	**Scott Niedermayer**, N.J., Ana.	13	974
39.	**Teemu Selanne**, Wpg., Ana., S.J., Col.	13	959
40.	**Tommy Albelin**, Que., N.J., Cgy.	18	952
41.	**Bill Guerin**, N.J., Edm., Bos., Dal.	14	949
42.	**John LeClair**, Mtl., Phi., Pit.	15	946
43.	**Petr Nedved**, Van., St.L., NYR, Pit., Edm., Phx., Phi.	14	942
44.	**Alexei Zhitnik**, L.A., Buf., NYI	13	941
45.	**Travis Green**, NYI, Ana., Phx., Tor., Bos.	13	939
46.	**Sergei Zubov**, NYR, Pit., Dal.	13	934
47.	**Chris Gratton**, T.B., Phi., Buf., Phx., Col., Fla.	12	927
48.	**Bryan Marchment**, Wpg., Chi., Hfd., Edm., T.B., S.J., Col., Tor., Cgy.	17	926
49.	**Roman Hamrlik**, T.B., Edm., NYI, Cgy.	13	924
50.	**Derian Hatcher**, Min., Dal., Det., Phi.	14	919
51.	**Alex Kovalev**, NYR, Pit., Mtl.	13	918
52.	**Shawn McEachern**, Pit., L.A., Bos., Ott., Atl.	14	911
53.	**Bryan Smolinski**, Bos., Pit., NYI, L.A., Ott.	13	910
54.	**Keith Primeau**, Det., Hfd., Car., Phi.	15	909
55.	**Mike Sillinger**, Det., Ana., Van., Phi., T.B., Fla., Ott., CBJ, Phx., St.L.	15	908
56.	**Keith Tkachuk**, Wpg., Phx., St.L.	14	897
57.	**Rob DiMaio**, NYI, T.B., Phi., Bos., NYR, Car., Dal.	17	894
58.	**Glen Murray**, Bos., Pit., L.A.	14	887
59.	**Dallas Drake**, Det., Wpg., Phx., St.L.	13	884
60.	**Vyacheslav Kozlov**, Det., Buf., Atl.	14	882
61.	**Keith Carney**, Buf., Chi., Phx., Ana., Van.	12	877
62.	**Bret Hedican**, St.L., Van., Fla., Car.	14	872
63.	**Markus Naslund**, Pit., Van.	12	871
	Patrice Brisebois, Mtl., Col.	15	871
65.	**Martin Rucinsky**, Edm., Que., Col., Mtl., Dal., NYR, St.L., Van.	14	869
66.	**Adam Foote**, Que., Col., CBJ	14	864
67.	**Brad May**, Buf., Van., Phx., Col.	14	858
68.	**Darius Kasparaitis**, NYI, Pit., Col., NYR	13	839
	Martin Lapointe, Det., Bos., Chi.	14	839
70.	**Scott Thornton**, Tor., Edm., Mtl., Dal., S.J.	15	836
71.	**Todd Marchant**, NYR, Edm., CBJ, Ana.	12	835
72.	**Jozef Stumpel**, Bos., L.A., Fla.	14	832
73.	**Jason Arnott**, Edm., N.J., Dal.	12	824
74.	**Jeff Friesen**, S.J., Ana., N.J., Wsh.	11	821
75.	**Brian Rolston**, N.J., Col., Bos., Min.	11	818
76.	**Sandis Ozolinsh**, S.J., Col., Car., Fla., Ana., NYR	13	815
77.	**Martin Straka**, Pit., Ott., NYI, Fla., L.A., NYR	14	812
78.	**Alex Zhamnov**, Wpg., Chi., Phi., Bos.	13	807
79.	**Kris Draper**, Wpg., Det.	15	804

Nicklas Lidstrom has never played fewer than 78 games in any full NHL season over his 14-year career. He has played 1,096 games through 2005-06.

	Player	Seasons	Games Played
80.	**Chris Pronger**, Hfd., St.L., Edm.	12	802
81.	**Kirk Maltby**, Edm., Det.	12	799
82.	**Matthew Barnaby**, Buf., Pit., T.B., NYR, Col., Chi.	13	795
	Richard Matvichuk, Min., Dal., N.J.	13	795
84.	**Alexei Yashin**, Ott., NYI	11	792
85.	**Steve Konowalchuk**, Wsh., Col.	14	790
86.	**Miroslav Satan**, Edm., Buf., NYI	10	786
	Jason Smith, N.J., Tor., Edm.	11	786
88.	**Greg Johnson**, Det., Pit., Chi., Nsh.	12	785
89.	**Bryan McCabe**, NYI, Van., Chi., Tor.	10	781
90.	**Ian Laperriere**, St.L., NYR, L.A., Col.	12	776
91.	**Rob Niedermayer**, Fla., Cgy., Ana.	12	772
92.	**Sean O'Donnell**, L.A., Min., N.J., Bos., Phx., Ana.	11	771
93.	**Donald Brashear**, Mtl., Van., Phi.	12	769
94.	**Chris Therien**, Phi., Dal.	11	764
95.	**Ray Whitney**, S.J., Edm., Fla., CBJ, Det., Car.	14	763
96.	**Mattias Norstrom**, NYR, L.A.	12	761
97.	**Sean Hill**, Mtl., Ana., Ott., Car., St.L., Fla.	15	760
98.	**Niklas Sundstrom**, NYR, S.J., Mtl.	10	750
	Radek Bonk, Ott., Mtl.	11	750
	Mike Rathje, S.J., Phi.	12	750

Goaltending Records

All-Time Shutout Leaders (Minimum 42 Shutouts)

Goaltender	Team	Seasons	Games	Shutouts
Terry Sawchuk (1949-1970)	Detroit	14	734	85
	Boston	2	102	11
	Toronto	3	91	4
	Los Angeles	1	36	2
	NY Rangers	1	8	1
	Total	21	971	**103**
George Hainsworth (1926-1937)	Montreal	7½	318	75
	Toronto	3½	147	19
	Total	11	465	**94**
Glenn Hall (1952-1971)	Detroit	4	148	17
	Chicago	10	618	51
	St. Louis	4	140	16
	Total	18	906	**84**
Jacques Plante (1952-1973)	Montreal	11	556	58
	NY Rangers	2	98	5
	St. Louis	2	69	10
	Toronto	2¾	106	7
	Boston	¼	8	2
	Total	18	837	**82**
Tiny Thompson (1928-1940)	Boston	10¼	468	74
	Detroit	1¾	85	7
	Total	12	553	**81**
Alex Connell (1924-1937)	Ottawa	8	293	64
	Detroit	1	48	6
	NY Americans	1	1	0
	Mtl. Maroons	2	75	11
	Total	12	417	**81**
*Martin Brodeur (1991-2006)	New Jersey	13	813	**80**
Tony Esposito (1968-1984)	Montreal	1	13	2
	Chicago	15	873	74
	Total	16	886	**76**
*Ed Belfour (1988-2006)	Chicago	7⅔	415	30
	San Jose	⅓	13	1
	Dallas	5	307	27
	Toronto	3	170	17
	Total	16	905	**75**
Lorne Chabot (1926-1937)	NY Rangers	2	80	21
	Toronto	5	214	32
	Montreal	1	47	8
	Chicago	1	48	8
	Mtl. Maroons	1	16	2
	NY Americans	1	6	1
	Total	11	411	**72**
Harry Lumley (1943-1960)	Detroit	6½	324	26
	NY Rangers	½	1	0
	Chicago	2	134	5
	Toronto	4	267	34
	Boston	3	78	6
	Total	16	804	**71**
Roy Worters (1925-1937)	Pittsburgh Pirates	3	123	22
	NY Americans	9	360	45
	† Montreal		1	0
	Total	12	484	**67**
*Dominik Hasek (1990-2006)	Chicago	2	25	1
	Buffalo	9	491	55
	Detroit	2	79	7
	Ottawa	1	43	5
	Total	14	638	**68**
Patrick Roy (1984-2003)	Montreal	11½	551	29
	Colorado	6½	478	37
	Total	19	1,029	**66**
Turk Broda (1936-1952)	Toronto	14	629	62
Clint Benedict (1917-1930)	Ottawa	7	158	19
	Mtl. Maroons	6	204	39
	Total	13	362	**58**
John Ross Roach (1921-1935)	Toronto	7	222	13
	NY Rangers	4	89	30
	Detroit	3	180	15
	Total	14	491	**58**
Bernie Parent (1965-1979)	Boston	2	57	1
	Philadelphia	9½	486	50
	Toronto	1½	65	3
	Total	13	608	**54**
Ed Giacomin (1965-1978)	NY Rangers	10¼	539	49
	Detroit	2¾	71	5
	Total	13	610	**54**
Dave Kerr (1930-1941)	Mtl. Maroons	3	101	11
	NY Americans	1	1	0
	NY Rangers	7	324	40
	Total	11	426	**51**
Rogie Vachon (1966-1982)	Montreal	5¼	206	13
	Los Angeles	6¾	389	32
	Detroit	2	109	4
	Boston	2	91	2
	Total	16	795	**51**
Ken Dryden (1970-1979)	Montreal	8	397	46
*Curtis Joseph (1989-2006)	St. Louis	6	280	5
	Edmonton	3	177	14
	Toronto	4	249	17
	Detroit	2	92	7
	Phoenix	1	60	4
	Total	16	558	**47**
*Chris Osgood (1993-2004)	Detroit	9	421	32
	NY Islanders	1¾	103	6
	St. Louis	1¼	76	5
	Total	12	600	**43**
Gump Worsley (1952-1974)	NY Rangers	10	582	24
	Montreal	6½	172	16
	Minnesota	4½	107	3
	Total	21	861	**43**
Charlie Gardiner (1927-1934)	Chicago	7	316	**42**

* Active goalie
† Played 1 game for Montreal in 1929-30.

Ten or More Shutouts, One Season

Number of Shutouts	Goaltender	Team	Season	Length of Schedule
22	George Hainsworth	Montreal	1928-29	44
15	Alex Connell	Ottawa	1925-26	36
	Alex Connell	Ottawa	1927-28	44
	Hal Winkler	Boston	1927-28	44
	Tony Esposito	Chicago	1969-70	76
14	George Hainsworth	Montreal	1926-27	44
13	Clint Benedict	Mtl. Maroons	1926-27	44
	Alex Connell	Ottawa	1926-27	44
	George Hainsworth	Montreal	1927-28	44
	John Ross Roach	NY Rangers	1928-29	44
	Roy Worters	NY Americans	1928-29	44
	Harry Lumley	Toronto	1953-54	70
	Dominik Hasek	Buffalo	1997-98	82
12	Tiny Thompson	Boston	1928-29	44
	Charlie Gardiner	Chicago	1930-31	44
	Terry Sawchuk	Detroit	1951-52	70
	Terry Sawchuk	Detroit	1953-54	70
	Terry Sawchuk	Detroit	1954-55	70
	Glenn Hall	Detroit	1955-56	70
	Bernie Parent	Philadelphia	1973-74	78
	Bernie Parent	Philadelphia	1974-75	80
11	Lorne Chabot	NY Rangers	1927-28	44
	Hap Holmes	Detroit	1927-28	44
	Roy Worters	Pittsburgh Pirates	1927-28	44
	Clint Benedict	Mtl. Maroons	1928-29	44
	Joe Miller	Pittsburgh Pirates	1928-29	44
	Lorne Chabot	Toronto	1928-29	44
	Tiny Thompson	Boston	1932-33	48
	Terry Sawchuk	Detroit	1950-51	70
	Dominik Hasek	Buffalo	2000-01	82
	Martin Brodeur	New Jersey	2003-04	82
10	Lorne Chabot	NY Rangers	1926-27	44
	Dolly Dolson	Detroit	1928-29	44
	John Ross Roach	Detroit	1932-33	48
	Charlie Gardiner	Chicago	1933-34	48
	Tiny Thompson	Boston	1935-36	48
	Frank Brimsek	Boston	1938-39	48
	Bill Durnan	Montreal	1948-49	60
	Harry Lumley	Toronto	1952-53	70
	Gerry McNeil	Montreal	1952-53	70
	Tony Esposito	Chicago	1973-74	78
	Ken Dryden	Montreal	1976-77	80
	Martin Brodeur	New Jersey	1996-97	82
	Martin Brodeur	New Jersey	1997-98	82
	Byron Dafoe	Boston	1998-99	82
	Roman Cechmanek	Philadelphia	2000-01	82
	Ed Belfour	Toronto	2003-04	82
	Miikka Kiprusoff	Calgary	**2005-06**	82

All-Time Win Leaders

(Minimum 230 Wins)

Goaltender	Wins	GP	Dec.	Losses	OT/Ties
Patrick Roy	551	1029	997	315	131
* Ed Belfour	457	905	875	303	115
Terry Sawchuk	447	971	949	330	172
* Martin Brodeur	446	813	798	240	112
Jacques Plante	437	837	827	247	145
* Curtis Joseph	428	858	831	310	93
Tony Esposito	423	886	880	306	151
Glenn Hall	407	906	896	326	163
Grant Fuhr	403	868	812	295	114
Mike Vernon	385	781	750	273	92
John Vanbiesbrouck	374	882	839	346	119
Andy Moog	372	713	669	209	88
Tom Barrasso	369	777	732	277	86
Rogie Vachon	355	795	773	291	127
Gump Worsley	335	861	837	352	150
Harry Lumley	330	803	801	329	142
* Chris Osgood	325	600	579	183	71
* Dominik Hasek	324	638	612	202	86
* Sean Burke	318	797	754	331	105
Billy Smith	305	680	643	233	105
Turk Broda	302	629	627	224	101
Mike Richter	301	666	632	258	73
Ron Hextall	296	608	579	214	69
Mike Liut	294	663	639	271	74
Ed Giacomin	289	610	594	208	97
Dan Bouchard	286	655	631	232	113
Tiny Thompson	284	553	553	194	75
Bernie Parent	271	608	590	198	121
Kelly Hrudey	271	677	624	265	88
Gilles Meloche	270	788	752	351	131
Don Beaupre	268	667	620	277	75
Felix Potvin	266	635	611	260	85
Ken Dryden	258	397	389	57	74
* Olaf Kolzig	254	603	576	248	74
Frank Brimsek	252	514	514	182	80
Johnny Bower	250	552	535	195	90
George Hainsworth	246	465	465	145	74
Pete Peeters	246	489	452	155	51
Kirk McLean	245	612	579	262	72
Bill Ranford	240	647	595	279	76
Reggie Lemelin	236	507	461	162	63
Eddie Johnston	234	592	571	257	80
Glenn Resch	231	571	537	224	82
Gerry Cheevers	230	418	406	102	74

* active player

Active Shutout Leaders

(Minimum 20 Shutouts)

Goaltender	Teams	Seasons	Games	Shutouts
Martin Brodeur	N.J.	13	813	80
Ed Belfour	Chi., S.J., Dal., Tor.	16	905	75
Dominik Hasek	Chi., Buf., Det., Ott.	14	638	68
Curtis Joseph	St.L., Edm., Tor., Det., Phx.	16	858	47
Chris Osgood	Det., NYI, St.L.	12	600	43
Sean Burke	N.J., Hfd., Car., Van., Phi., Fla., Phx., T.B.	17	797	37
Jocelyn Thibault	Que., Col., Mtl., Chi., Pit.	12	552	36
Nikolai Khabibulin	Wpg., Phx., T.B., Chi.	10	526	35
Patrick Lalime	Pit., Ott., St.L.	7	353	33
Olaf Kolzig	Wsh.	14	603	33
Evgeni Nabokov	S.J.	6	303	27
Roberto Luongo	NYI, Fla.	6	341	27
Marty Turco	Dal.	5	253	24
Jose Theodore	Mtl., Col.	10	358	23
Jean-Sebastien Giguere	Hfd., Cgy., Ana.	8	297	21

All-Time Regular-Season Penalty-Minute Leaders

* active player

(Regular season. Minimum 2,000 minutes)

	Player	Seasons	Games	Penalty Minutes	Mins. per game
1.	Tiger Williams, Tor., Van., Det., L.A., Hfd.	14	962	3966	4.12
2.	Dale Hunter, Que., Wsh., Col.	19	1407	3565	2.53
* 3.	Tie Domi, Tor., NYR, Wpg.	16	1020	3515	3.45
4.	Marty McSorley, Pit., Edm., L.A., NYR, S.J., Bos.	17	961	3381	3.52
5.	Bob Probert, Det., Chi.	16	935	3300	3.53
6.	Rob Ray, Buf., Ott.	15	900	3207	3.56
7.	Craig Berube, Phi., Tor., Cgy., Wsh., NYI	17	1054	3149	2.99
8.	Tim Hunter, Cgy., Que., Van., S.J.	16	815	3146	3.86
9.	Chris Nilan, Mtl., NYR, Bos.	13	688	3043	4.42
10.	Rick Tocchet, Phi., Pit., L.A., Bos., Wsh., Phx.	18	1144	2972	2.60

Goals-Against Average Leaders (Minimum 25 games played)

(Exceptions: Minimum 13 games played, 1994-95; minimum 26 games played, 1992-93 to 1993-94; minimum 15 games played, 1917-18 to 1925-26)

Season	Goaltender and Club	GP	Mins.	GA	SO	AVG.
2005-06	Miikka Kiprusoff, Calgary	74	4,380	151	10	2.07
2003-04	Miikka Kiprusoff, Calgary	38	2,301	65	4	1.69
2002-03	Marty Turco, Dallas	55	3,203	92	7	1.72
2001-02	Patrick Roy, Colorado	63	3,773	122	9	1.94
2000-01	Marty Turco, Dallas	26	1,266	40	3	1.90
99-2000	Brian Boucher, Philadelphia	35	2,038	65	4	1.91
1998-99	Ron Tugnutt, Ottawa	43	2,508	75	3	1.79
1997-98	Ed Belfour, Dallas	61	3,581	112	9	1.88
1996-97	Martin Brodeur, New Jersey	67	3,838	120	10	1.88
1995-96	Ron Hextall, Philadelphia	53	3,102	112	4	2.17
1994-95	Dominik Hasek, Buffalo	41	2,416	85	5	2.11
1993-94	Dominik Hasek, Buffalo	58	3,358	109	7	1.95
1992-93	Felix Potvin, Toronto	48	2,781	116	2	2.50
1991-92	Patrick Roy, Montreal	67	3,935	155	5	2.36
1990-91	Ed Belfour, Chicago	74	4,127	170	4	2.47
1989-90	Mike Liut, Hartford, Washington	37	2,161	91	4	2.53
1988-89	Patrick Roy, Montreal	48	2,744	113	4	2.47
1987-88	Pete Peeters, Washington	35	1,896	88	2	2.78
1986-87	Brian Hayward, Montreal	37	2,178	102	1	2.81
1985-86	Bob Froese, Philadelphia	51	2,728	116	5	2.55
1984-85	Tom Barrasso, Buffalo	54	3,248	144	5	2.66
1983-84	Pat Riggin, Washington	41	2,299	102	4	2.66
1982-83	Pete Peeters, Boston	62	3,611	142	8	2.36
1981-82	Denis Herron, Montreal	27	1,547	68	3	2.64
1980-81	Richard Sevigny, Montreal	33	1,777	71	2	2.40
1979-80	Bob Sauve, Buffalo	32	1,880	74	4	2.36
1978-79	Ken Dryden, Montreal	47	2,814	108	5	2.30
1977-78	Ken Dryden, Montreal	52	3,071	105	5	2.05
1976-77	Michel Larocque, Montreal	26	1,525	53	4	2.09
1975-76	Ken Dryden, Montreal	62	3,580	121	8	2.03
1974-75	Bernie Parent, Philadelphia	68	4,041	137	12	2.03
1973-74	Bernie Parent, Philadelphia	73	4,314	136	12	1.89
1972-73	Ken Dryden, Montreal	54	3,165	119	6	2.26
1971-72	Tony Esposito, Chicago	48	2,780	82	9	1.77
1970-71	Jacques Plante, Toronto	40	2,329	73	4	1.88
1969-70	Ernie Wakely, St. Louis	30	1,651	58	4	2.11
1968-69	Jacques Plante, St. Louis	37	2,139	70	5	1.96
1967-68	Gump Worsley, Montreal	40	2,213	73	6	1.98
1966-67	Glenn Hall, Chicago	32	1,664	66	2	2.38
1965-66	Johnny Bower, Toronto	35	1,998	75	3	2.25
1964-65	Johnny Bower, Toronto	34	2,040	81	3	2.38
1963-64	Johnny Bower, Toronto	51	3,009	106	5	2.11
1962-63	Don Simmons, Toronto	28	1,680	69	1	2.46
1961-62	Jacques Plante, Montreal	70	4,200	166	4	2.37
1960-61	Charlie Hodge, Montreal	30	1,800	74	4	2.47
1959-60	Jacques Plante, Montreal	69	4,140	175	3	2.54
1958-59	Jacques Plante, Montreal	67	4,000	144	9	2.16
1957-58	Jacques Plante, Montreal	57	3,386	119	9	2.11
1956-57	Jacques Plante, Montreal	61	3,660	122	9	2.00
1955-56	Jacques Plante, Montreal	64	3,840	119	7	1.86
1954-55	Harry Lumley, Toronto	69	4,140	134	8	1.94
1953-54	Harry Lumley, Toronto	69	4,140	128	13	1.86
1952-53	Terry Sawchuk, Detroit	63	3,780	120	9	1.90
1951-52	Terry Sawchuk, Detroit	70	4,200	133	12	1.90
1950-51	Al Rollins, Toronto	40	2,367	70	5	1.77
1949-50	Bill Durnan, Montreal	64	3,840	141	8	2.20
1948-49	Bill Durnan, Montreal	60	3,600	126	10	2.10
1947-48	Turk Broda, Toronto	60	3,600	143	5	2.38
1946-47	Bill Durnan, Montreal	60	3,600	138	4	2.30
1945-46	Bill Durnan, Montreal	40	2,400	104	4	2.60
1944-45	Bill Durnan, Montreal	50	3,000	121	1	2.42
1943-44	Bill Durnan, Montreal	50	3,000	109	2	2.18
1942-43	Johnny Mowers, Detroit	50	3,010	124	6	2.47
1941-42	Frank Brimsek, Boston	47	2,930	115	3	2.35
1940-41	Turk Broda, Toronto	48	2,970	99	5	2.00
1939-40	Dave Kerr, NY Rangers	48	3,000	77	8	1.54
1938-39	Frank Brimsek, Boston	43	2,610	68	10	1.56
1937-38	Tiny Thompson, Boston	48	2,970	89	7	1.80
1936-37	Normie Smith, Detroit	48	2,980	102	6	2.05
1935-36	Tiny Thompson, Boston	48	2,930	82	10	1.68
1934-35	Lorne Chabot, Chicago	48	2,940	88	8	1.80
1933-34	Wilf Cude, Detroit, Montreal	30	1,920	47	5	1.47
1932-33	Tiny Thompson, Boston	48	3,000	88	11	1.76
1931-32	Charlie Gardiner, Chicago	48	2,989	92	4	1.85
1930-31	Roy Worters, NY Americans	44	2,760	74	8	1.61
1929-30	Tiny Thompson, Boston	44	2,680	98	3	2.19
1928-29	George Hainsworth, Montreal	44	2,800	43	22	0.92
1927-28	George Hainsworth, Montreal	44	2,730	48	13	1.05
1926-27	Clint Benedict, Mtl. Maroons	43	2,748	65	13	1.42
1925-26	Alex Connell, Ottawa	36	2,251	42	15	1.12
1924-25	Georges Vezina, Montreal	30	1,860	56	5	1.81
1923-24	Georges Vezina, Montreal	24	1,459	48	3	1.97
1922-23	Clint Benedict, Ottawa	24	1,478	54	4	2.18
1921-22	Clint Benedict, Ottawa	24	1,508	84	2	3.34
1920-21	Clint Benedict, Ottawa	24	1,457	75	2	3.09
1919-20	Clint Benedict, Ottawa	24	1,444	64	5	2.66
1918-19	Clint Benedict, Ottawa	18	1,113	53	2	2.86
1917-18	Georges Vezina, Montreal	21	1,282	84	1	3.93

All-Time Regular-Season NHL Coaching Register

Regular Season, 1917-2006

Coach	Team	Games Coached	Wins	Losses	O/T	Years	Cup Wins	Career
Abel, Sid	Chicago	140	39	79	22	2		
	Detroit	811	340	339	132	12		
	St. Louis	10	3	6	1	1		
	Kansas City	3	0	3	0	1		
	Total	964	382	427	155	16		1952-76
Adams, Jack	Detroit	964	413	390	161	20	3	1927-47
Allen, Keith	Philadelphia	150	51	67	32	2		1967-69
Allison, Dave	Ottawa	25	2	22	1	1		1995-96
Anderson, Jim	Washington	54	4	45	5	1		1974-75
Angotti, Lou	St. Louis	32	6	20	6	2		
	Pittsburgh	80	16	58	6	1		
	Total	112	22	78	12	3		1973-84
Arbour, Al	St. Louis	107	42	40	25	2		
	NY Islanders	1499	739	537	223	19	4	
	Total	1606	781	577	248	22	4	1970-94
Armstrong, George	Toronto	47	17	26	4	1		1988-89
Babcock, Mike	Anaheim	164	69	76	19	3		
	Detroit	82	58	16	8	1		
	Total	246	127	92	27	4		2002-06
Barber, Bill	Philadelphia	136	73	46	17	2		2000-02
Barkley, Doug	Detroit	77	20	46	11	3		1970-76
Beaulieu, Andre	Minnesota	32	6	23	3	1		1977-78
Belisle, Danny	Washington	96	28	51	17	2		1978-80
Berenson, Red	St. Louis	204	100	72	32	3		1979-82
Bergeron, Michel	Quebec	634	265	283	86	8		
	NY Rangers	158	73	67	18	2		
	Total	792	338	350	104	10		1980-90
Berry, Bob	Los Angeles	240	107	94	39	3		
	Montreal	223	116	71	36	3		
	Pittsburgh	240	88	127	25	3		
	St. Louis	157	73	63	21	2		
	Total	860	384	355	121	11		1978-94
Beverley, Nick	Toronto	17	9	6	2	1		1995-96
Blackburn, Don	Hartford	140	42	63	35	2		1979-81
Blair, Wren	Minnesota	147	48	65	34	3		1967-70
Blake, Toe	Montreal	914	500	255	159	13	8	1955-68
Boileau, Marc	Pittsburgh	151	66	61	24	3		1973-76
Boivin, Leo	St. Louis	97	28	53	16	2		1975-78
Boucher, Frank	NY Rangers	527	181	263	83	11	1	1939-54
Boucher, Georges	Mtl. Maroons	12	6	5	1	1		
	Ottawa	48	13	29	6	1		
	St. Louis	35	9	20	6	1		
	Boston	70	22	32	16	1		
	Total	165	50	86	29	4		1930-50
Bowman, Scotty	St. Louis	238	110	83	45	4		
	Montreal	634	419	110	105	8	5	
	Buffalo	404	210	134	60	7		
	Pittsburgh	164	95	53	16	2	1	
	Detroit	701	410	204	87	9	3	
	Total	2141	1244	584	313	30	9	1967-02
Bowness, Rick	Winnipeg	28	8	17	3	1		
	Boston	80	36	32	12	1		
	Ottawa	235	39	178	18	4		
	NY Islanders	100	38	50	12	2		
	Phoenix	20	2	15	3	2		
	Total	463	123	292	48	10		1988-05
Brooks, Herb	NY Rangers	285	131	113	41	4		
	Minnesota	80	19	48	13	1		
	New Jersey	84	40	37	7	1		
	Pittsburgh	58	29	24	5	1		
	Total	507	219	222	66	7		1981-00
Brophy, John	Toronto	193	64	111	18	3		1986-89
Burnett, George	Edmonton	35	12	20	3	1		1994-95
Burns, Charlie	Minnesota	86	22	50	14	2		1969-75
Burns, Pat	Montreal	320	174	104	42	4		
	Toronto	281	133	107	41	4		
	Boston	254	105	103	46	4		
	New Jersey	164	89	53	22	3	1	
	Total	1019	501	367	151	15	1	1988-05
Bush, Eddie	Kansas City	32	1	23	8	1		1975-76
Campbell, Colin	NY Rangers	269	118	108	43	4		1994-98
Carlyle, Randy	Anaheim	82	43	27	12	1		2005-06
Carpenter, Doug	New Jersey	290	100	166	24	4		
	Toronto	91	39	47	5	2		
	Total	381	139	213	29	6		1984-91
Carroll, Dick	Toronto	40	18	22	0	2	1	1917-19
Carroll, Frank	Toronto	24	15	9	0	1		1920-21
Cashman, Wayne	Philadelphia	61	32	20	9	1		1997-98
Cassidy, Bruce	Washington	110	47	54	9	3		2002-05
Chambers, Dave	Quebec	98	19	64	15	2		1990-92
Charron, Guy	Calgary	16	6	7	3	1		
	Anaheim	49	14	28	7	1		
	Total	65	20	35	10	2		1991-01
Cheevers, Gerry	Boston	376	204	126	46	5		1980-85
Cherry, Don	Boston	400	231	105	64	5		
	Colorado	80	19	48	13	1		
	Total	480	250	153	77	6		1974-80
Clancy, King	Mtl. Maroons	18	6	11	1	1		
	Toronto	210	80	81	49	3		
	Total	228	86	92	50	4		1937-56
Clapper, Dit	Boston	230	102	88	40	4		1945-49
Cleghorn, Odie	Pittsburgh	168	62	86	20	4		1925-29
Cleghorn, Sprague	Mtl. Maroons	48	19	22	7	1		1931-32
Colville, Neil	NY Rangers	93	26	41	26	2		1950-52
Conacher, Charlie	Chicago	162	56	84	22	3		1947-50
Conacher, Lionel	NY Americans	44	14	25	5	1		1929-30
Constantine, Kevin	San Jose	157	55	78	24	3		
	Pittsburgh	188	86	67	35	3		
	New Jersey	31	20	9	2	1		
	Total	376	161	154	61	7		1993-02
Cook, Bill	NY Rangers	117	34	59	24	2		1951-53
Crawford, Marc	Quebec	48	30	13	5	1		
	Colorado	246	135	75	36	3	1	
	Vancouver	529	246	213	70	8		
	Total	823	411	301	111	12	1	1994-06
Creamer, Pierre	Pittsburgh	80	36	35	9	1		1987-88
Creighton, Fred	Atlanta	348	156	136	56	5		
	Boston	73	40	20	13	1		
	Total	421	196	156	69	6		1974-80
Crisp, Terry	Calgary	240	144	63	33	3	1	
	Tampa Bay	391	142	204	45	6		
	Total	631	286	267	78	9	1	1987-98
Crozier, Joe	Buffalo	192	77	80	35	3		
	Toronto	40	13	22	5	1		
	Total	232	90	102	40	4		1971-81
Crozier, Roger	Washington	1	0	1	0	1		1981-82
Cunniff, John	Hartford	13	3	9	1	1		
	New Jersey	133	59	56	18	2		
	Total	146	62	65	19	3		1982-91
Curry, Alex	Ottawa	36	24	8	4	1		1925-26
Dandurand, Leo	Montreal	163	78	76	9	6	1	1921-35
Day, Hap	Toronto	546	259	206	81	10	5	1940-50
Dea, Billy	Detroit	11	3	8	0	1		1981-82
Delvecchio, Alex	Detroit	245	82	131	32	4		1973-77
Demers, Jacques	Quebec	80	25	44	11	1		
	St. Louis	240	106	106	28	3		
	Detroit	320	137	136	47	4		
	Montreal	220	107	86	27	4	1	
	Tampa Bay	147	34	96	17	2		
	Total	1007	409	468	130	14	1	1979-99
Denneny, Cy	Boston	44	26	13	5	1	1	
	Ottawa	48	11	27	10	1		
	Total	92	37	40	15	2	1	1928-33
Dineen, Bill	Philadelphia	140	60	60	20	2		1991-93
Dudley, Rick	Buffalo	188	85	72	31	3		
	Florida	40	13	18	9	2		
	Total	228	98	90	40	5		1989-05
Duff, Dick	Toronto	2	0	2	0	1		1979-80
Dugal, Jules	Montreal	18	9	6	3	1		1938-39
Duncan, Art	Detroit	33	10	21	2	1		
	Toronto	47	21	16	10	2	1	
	Total	80	31	37	12	3	1	1926-32
Dutton, Red	NY Americans	288	90	151	47	6		
	Brooklyn	48	16	29	3	1		
	Total	336	106	180	50	7		1935-42
Eddolls, Frank	Chicago	70	13	40	17	1		1954-55
Esposito, Phil	NY Rangers	45	24	21	0	2		1986-89
Evans, Jack	California	80	27	42	11	1		
	Cleveland	160	47	87	26	2		
	Hartford	374	163	174	37	5		
	Total	614	237	303	74	8		1975-88
Fashoway, Gordie	Oakland	10	4	5	1	1		1967-68
Ferguson, John	NY Rangers	121	43	59	19	2		
	Winnipeg	14	7	6	1	1		
	Total	135	50	65	20	3		1975-86
Filion, Maurice	Quebec	6	1	3	2	1		1980-81
Francis, Bob	Phoenix	390	165	165	60	5		1999-04
Francis, Emile	NY Rangers	654	342	209	103	10		
	St. Louis	124	46	64	14	3		
	Total	778	388	273	117	13		1965-83
Fraser, Curt	Atlanta	279	64	184	31	4		1999-03
Fredrickson, Frank	Pittsburgh	44	5	36	3	1		1929-30
Ftorek, Robbie	Los Angeles	132	65	56	11	2		
	New Jersey	156	88	49	19	2		
	Boston	155	76	65	14	2		
	Total	443	229	170	44	6		1987-03
Gadsby, Bill	Detroit	78	35	31	12	2		1968-70
Gainey, Bob	Minnesota	244	95	119	30	3		
	Dallas	171	70	71	30	3		
	Montreal	41	23	15	3	1		
	Total	456	188	205	63	7		1990-06
Gallant, Gerard	Columbus	127	51	68	8	3		2003-06
Gardiner, Herb	Chicago	32	5	23	4	1		1929-30
Gardner, Jimmy	Hamilton	30	19	10	1	1		1924-25
Garvin, Ted	Detroit	11	2	8	1	1		1973-74
Geoffrion, Bernie	NY Rangers	43	22	18	3	1		
	Atlanta	208	77	92	39	3		
	Montreal	30	15	9	6	1		
	Total	281	114	119	48	5		1968-80

Coach	Team	Games Coached	Wins	Losses	O/T	Years	Cup Wins	Career
Gerard, Eddie	Ottawa	22	9	13	0	1		
	Mtl. Maroons	294	129	122	43	7	1	
	NY Americans	92	34	40	18	2		
	St. Louis	13	2	11	0	1		
	Total	421	174	186	61	11	1	1917-35
Gilbert, Greg	Calgary	121	42	62	17	3		2000-03
Gill, David	Ottawa	132	64	41	27	3	1	1926-29
Glover, Fred	Oakland	152	51	76	25	2		
	California	204	45	131	28	4		
	Los Angeles	68	18	42	8	1		
	Total	424	114	249	61	7		1968-74
Goodfellow, Ebbie	Chicago	140	30	91	19	2		1950-52
Gordon, Jackie	Minnesota	289	116	123	50	5		1970-75
Goring, Butch	Boston	93	42	38	13	2		
	NY Islanders	147	41	92	14	2		
	Total	240	83	130	27	4		1985-01
Gorman, Tommy	NY Americans	80	31	33	16	2		
	Chicago	73	28	28	17	2	1	
	Mtl. Maroons	174	74	71	29	4	1	
	Total	327	133	132	62	8	2	1925-38
Gottselig, Johnny	Chicago	187	62	105	20	4		1944-48
Goyette, Phil	NY Islanders	48	6	38	4	1		1972-73
Graham, Dirk	Chicago	59	16	35	8	1		1998-99
Granato, Tony	Colorado	133	72	44	17	2		2002-04
Green, Gary	Washington	157	50	78	29	3		1979-82
Green, Pete	Ottawa	150	94	52	4	6	3	1919-25
Green, Shorty	NY Americans	44	11	27	6	1		1927-28
Green, Ted	Edmonton	188	65	102	21	3		1991-94
Gretzky, Wayne	Phoenix	82	38	39	5	1		2005-06
Guidolin, Aldo	Colorado	59	12	39	8	1		1978-79
Guidolin, Bep	Boston	104	72	23	9	2		
	Kansas City	125	26	84	15	2		
	Total	229	98	107	24	4		1972-76
Hanlon, Glen	Washington	136	53	69	14	3		2003-06
Harkness, Ned	Detroit	38	12	22	4	1		1970-71
Harris, Ted	Minnesota	179	48	104	27	3		1975-78
Hart, Cecil	Montreal	394	196	125	73	9	2	1926-39
Hartley, Bob	Colorado	359	193	118	48	5	1	
	Atlanta	203	93	89	21	4		
	Total	562	286	207	69	8	1	1998-06
Hartsburg, Craig	Chicago	246	104	102	40	3		
	Anaheim	197	80	88	29	3		
	Total	443	184	190	69	6		1995-01
Harvey, Doug	NY Rangers	70	26	32	12	1		1961-62
Hay, Don	Phoenix	82	38	37	7	1		
	Calgary	68	23	32	13	1		
	Total	150	61	69	20	2		1996-01
Heffernan, Frank	Toronto	12	5	7	0	1		1919-20
Henning, Lorne	Minnesota	158	68	72	18	2		
	NY Islanders	65	19	39	7	2		
	Total	223	87	111	25	4		1985-01
Hitchcock, Ken	Dallas	503	277	166	60	7		
	Philadelphia	246	130	77	39	4		
	Total	749	407	243	99	11	1	1995-06
Hlinka, Ivan	Pittsburgh	86	42	35	9	2		2000-02
Holmgren, Paul	Philadelphia	264	107	126	31	4		
	Hartford	161	54	93	14	4		
	Total	425	161	219	45	8		1988-96
Howell, Harry	Minnesota	11	3	6	2	1		1978-79
Imlach, Punch	Toronto	770	370	275	125	12	4	
	Buffalo	119	32	62	25	2		
	Total	889	402	337	150	14	4	1958-80
Ingarfield, Earl	NY Islanders	30	6	22	2	1		1972-73
Inglis, Bill	Buffalo	56	28	18	10	1		1978-79
Irvin, Dick	Chicago	126	45	62	19	3		
	Toronto	427	216	152	59	9	1	
	Montreal	896	431	313	152	15	3	
	Total	1449	692	527	230	27	4	1928-56
Ivan, Tommy	Detroit	470	262	118	90	7	3	
	Chicago	103	26	56	21	2		
	Total	573	288	174	111	9	3	1947-58
Iverson, Emil	Chicago	21	8	7	6	1		1932-33
Johnson, Bob	Calgary	400	193	155	52	5		
	Pittsburgh	80	41	33	6	1	1	
	Total	480	234	188	58	6	1	1982-91
Johnson, Tom	Boston	208	142	43	23	3	1	1970-73
Johnston, Eddie	Chicago	80	34	27	19	1		
	Pittsburgh	516	232	224	60	7		
	Total	596	266	251	79	8		1979-97
Johnston, Marshall	California	69	13	45	11	2		
	Colorado	56	15	32	9	1		
	Total	125	28	77	20	3		1973-82
Julien, Claude	Montreal	159	72	71	16	4		2002-06
Kasper, Steve	Boston	164	66	78	20	2		1995-97
Keats, Duke	Detroit	11	2	7	2	1		1926-27
Keenan, Mike	Philadelphia	320	190	102	28	4		
	Chicago	320	153	126	41	4		
	NY Rangers	84	52	24	8	1	1	
	St. Louis	163	75	66	22	3		
	Vancouver	108	36	54	18	2		
	Boston	74	33	34	7	1		
	Florida	153	45	85	23	3		
	Total	1222	584	491	147	18	1	1984-04
Kehoe, Rick	Pittsburgh	160	55	91	14	2		2001-03
Kelly, Pat	Colorado	101	22	54	25	2		1977-79
Kelly, Red	Los Angeles	150	55	75	20	2		
	Pittsburgh	274	90	132	52	4		
	Toronto	318	133	123	62	4		
	Total	742	278	330	134	10		1967-77
King, Dave	Calgary	216	109	76	31	3		
	Columbus	204	64	119	21	3		
	Total	420	173	195	52	6		1992-03
Kingston, George	San Jose	164	28	129	7	2		1991-93
Kish, Larry	Hartford	49	12	32	5	1		1982-83
Kitchen, Mike	St. Louis	103	31	53	19	3		2003-06
Kromm, Bobby	Detroit	231	79	111	41	3		1977-80
Kurtenbach, Orland	Vancouver	125	36	62	27	2		1976-78
LaForge, Bill	Vancouver	20	4	14	2	1		1984-85
Lalonde, Newsy	Montreal	207	96	97	14	8		
	NY Americans	44	17	25	2	1		
	Ottawa	88	31	45	12	2		
	Total	339	144	167	28	11		1917-35
Lamorello, Lou	New Jersey	50	32	14	4	1		2005-06
Laperriere, Jacques	Montreal	1	0	1	0	1		1995-96
Lapointe, Ron	Quebec	89	33	50	6	2		1987-89
Laviolette, Peter	NY Islanders	164	77	68	19	2		
	Carolina	134	72	48	14	3	1	
	Total	298	149	116	33	5	1	2001-06
Laycoe, Hal	Los Angeles	24	5	18	1	1		
	Vancouver	156	44	96	16	2		
	Total	180	49	114	17	3		1969-72
Lehman, Hugh	Chicago	21	3	17	1	1		1927-28
Lemaire, Jacques	Montreal	97	48	37	12	2		
	New Jersey	378	199	122	57	5	1	
	Minnesota	410	165	185	60	6		
	Total	885	412	344	129	13	1	1983-05
Lepine, Pit	Montreal	48	10	33	5	1		1939-40
LeSueur, Percy	Hamilton	10	3	7	0	1		1923-24
Lewis, Dave*	Detroit	169	100	48	21	4		1998-06

*Shared a record of 4-1-0 with co-coach Barry Smith in 1998-99

Coach	Team	Games Coached	Wins	Losses	O/T	Years	Cup Wins	Career
Ley, Rick	Hartford	160	69	71	20	2		
	Vancouver	124	47	50	27	2		
	Total	284	116	121	47	4		1989-96
Lindsay, Ted	Detroit	29	5	21	3	2		1979-81
Long, Barry	Winnipeg	205	87	93	25	3		1983-86
Loughlin, Clem	Chicago	144	61	63	20	3		1934-37
Lowe, Ron	Edmonton	341	139	162	40	5		
	NY Rangers	164	69	86	9	2		
	Total	505	208	248	49	7		1994-02
Lowe, Kevin	Edmonton	82	32	34	16	1		1999-00
Ludzik, Steve	Tampa Bay	121	31	76	14	2		1999-01
MacDonald, Parker	Minnesota	61	20	30	11	1		
	Los Angeles	42	13	24	5	1		
	Total	103	33	54	16	2		1973-82
MacLean, Doug	Florida	187	83	71	33	3		
	Columbus	79	24	47	8	2		
	Total	266	107	118	41	5		1995-04
MacMillan, Bill	Colorado	80	22	45	13	1		
	New Jersey	100	19	67	14	2		
	Total	180	41	112	27	3		1980-84
MacNeil, Al	Montreal	55	31	15	9	1	1	
	Atlanta	80	35	32	13	1		
	Calgary	171	72	66	33	3		
	Total	306	138	113	55	5		1970-03
MacTavish, Craig	Edmonton	410	190	160	60	6		2000-06
Magnuson, Keith	Chicago	132	49	57	26	2		1980-82
Mahoney, Bill	Minnesota	93	42	39	12	2		1983-85
Maloney, Dan	Toronto	160	45	100	15	2		
	Winnipeg	212	91	93	28	3		
	Total	372	136	193	43	5		1984-89
Maloney, Phil	Vancouver	232	95	105	32	4		1973-77
Mantha, Sylvio	Montreal	48	11	26	11	1		1935-36
Marshall, Bert	Colorado	24	3	17	4	1		1981-82
Martin, Jacques	St. Louis	160	66	71	23	2		
	Ottawa	692	341	255	96	9		
	Florida	82	37	34	11	2		
	Total	934	444	360	130	13		1986-06
Matheson, Godfrey	Chicago	2	0	2	0	1		1932-33
Maurice, Paul	Hartford	152	61	72	19	2		
	Carolina	522	207	235	80	7		
	Total	674	268	307	99	9		1995-04
Maxner, Wayne	Detroit	129	34	68	27	2		1980-82
McCammon, Bob	Philadelphia	218	119	68	31	4		
	Vancouver	294	102	156	36	4		
	Total	512	221	224	67	8		1978-91
McCreary, Bill	St. Louis	24	6	14	4	1		
	Vancouver	41	9	25	7	1		
	California	32	8	20	4	1		
	Total	97	23	59	15	3		1971-75
McGuire, Pierre	Hartford	67	23	37	7	1		1993-94
McLellan, John	Toronto	310	126	139	45	4		1969-73
McVie, Tom	Washington	204	49	122	33	3		
	Winnipeg	105	20	67	18	2		
	New Jersey	153	57	74	22	3		
	Total	462	126	263	73	8		1975-92
Meeker, Howie	Toronto	70	21	34	15	1		1956-57
Melrose, Barry	Los Angeles	209	79	101	29	3		1992-95

Coach	Team	Games Coached	Wins	Losses	O/T	Years	Cup Wins	Career
Milbury, Mike	Boston	160	90	49	21	2		
	NY Islanders	191	56	111	24	4		
	Total	351	146	160	45	6		1989-99
Molleken, Lorne	Chicago	47	18	21	8	2		1998-00
Muckler, John	Minnesota	35	6	23	6	1		
	Edmonton	160	75	65	20	2	1	
	Buffalo	268	125	109	34	4		
	NY Rangers	185	70	91	24	3		
	Total	648	276	288	84	10	1	1968-00
Muldoon, Pete	Chicago	44	19	22	3	1		1926-27
Munro, Dunc	Mtl. Maroons	76	37	29	10	2		1929-31
Murdoch, Bob	Chicago	80	30	41	9	1		
	Winnipeg	160	63	75	22	2		
	Total	240	93	116	31	3		1987-91
Murphy, Mike	Los Angeles	65	20	37	8	2		
	Toronto	164	60	87	17	2		
	Total	229	80	124	25	4		1986-98
Murray, Andy	Los Angeles	480	215	202	63	7		1999-06
Murray, Bryan	Washington	672	343	246	83	9		
	Detroit	244	124	91	29	3		
	Florida	59	17	31	11	1		
	Anaheim	82	29	45	8	1		
	Ottawa	82	52	21	9	2		
	Total	1139	565	434	140	16		1981-06
Murray, Terry	Washington	325	163	134	28	5		
	Philadelphia	212	118	64	30	3		
	Florida	200	79	90	31	3		
	Total	737	360	288	89	11		1989-01
Nanne, Lou	Minnesota	29	7	18	4	1		1977-78
Neale, Harry	Vancouver	407	142	189	76	6		
	Detroit	35	8	23	4	1		
	Total	442	150	212	80	7		1978-86
Neilson, Roger	Toronto	160	75	62	23	2		
	Buffalo	80	39	20	21	1		
	Vancouver	133	51	61	21	3		
	Los Angeles	28	8	17	3	1		
	NY Rangers	280	141	104	35	4		
	Florida	132	53	56	23	2		
	Philadelphia	185	92	60	33	3		
	Ottawa	2	1	1	0	1		
	Total	1000	460	381	159	17		1977-02
Nolan, Ted	Buffalo	164	73	72	19	2		1995-97
Nykoluk, Mike	Toronto	280	89	144	47	4		1980-84
O'Connell, Mike	Boston	9	3	3	3	1		2002-03
O'Donoghue, George	Toronto	29	15	13	1	2	1	1921-23
O'Reilly, Terry	Boston	227	115	86	26	3		1986-89
Olczyk, Ed	Pittsburgh	113	31	68	14	3		2003-06
Oliver, Murray	Minnesota	41	21	12	8	2		1981-83
Olmstead, Bert	Oakland	64	11	37	16	1		1967-68
Paddock, John	Winnipeg	281	106	138	37	4		1991-95
Page, Pierre	Minnesota	160	63	77	20	2		
	Quebec	230	98	103	29	3		
	Calgary	164	66	78	20	2		
	Anaheim	82	26	43	13	1		
	Total	636	253	301	82	8		1988-98
Park, Brad	Detroit	45	9	34	2	1		1985-86
Paterson, Rick	Tampa Bay	6	0	6	0	1		1997-98
Patrick, Craig	NY Rangers	95	37	45	13	2		
	Pittsburgh	74	29	36	9	2		
	Total	169	66	81	22	4		1980-97
Patrick, Frank	Boston	96	48	36	12	2		1934-36
Patrick, Lester	NY Rangers	604	281	216	107	13	2	1926-39
Patrick, Lynn	NY Rangers	107	40	51	16	2		
	Boston	310	117	130	63	5		
	St. Louis	26	8	15	3	3		
	Total	443	165	196	82	10		1948-76
Patrick, Muzz	NY Rangers	136	43	66	27	4		1953-63
Perron, Jean	Montreal	240	126	84	30	3	1	
	Quebec	47	16	26	5	1		
	Total	287	142	110	35	4	1	1985-89
Perry, Don	Los Angeles	168	52	85	31	3		1981-84
Pike, Alf	NY Rangers	123	36	66	21	2		1959-61
Pilous, Rudy	Chicago	387	162	151	74	6	1	1957-63
Plager, Barclay	St. Louis	178	49	96	33	4		1977-83
Plager, Bob	St. Louis	11	4	6	1	1		1992-93
Pleau, Larry	Hartford	224	81	117	26	5		1980-89
Polano, Nick	Detroit	240	79	127	34	3		1982-85
Popein, Larry	NY Rangers	41	18	14	9	1		1973-74
Powers, Eddie	Toronto	66	31	32	3	2		1924-26
Primeau, Joe	Toronto	210	97	71	42	3	1	1950-53
Pronovost, Marcel	Buffalo	104	52	29	23	2		1977-79
Pulford, Bob	Los Angeles	396	178	150	68	5		
	Chicago	433	185	180	68	7		
	Total	829	363	330	136	12		1972-00
Quenneville, Joel	St. Louis	593	307	209	77	8		
	Colorado	82	43	30	9	2		
	Total	675	350	239	86	10		1996-06
Querrie, Charles	Toronto	72	29	38	5	3		1922-27
Quinn, Mike	Quebec	24	4	20	0	1		1919-20
Quinn, Pat	Philadelphia	262	141	73	48	4		
	Los Angeles	202	75	101	26	3		
	Vancouver	280	141	111	28	5		
	Toronto	574	300	214	60	8		
	Total	1318	657	499	162	19		1978-06
Raeder, Cap	San Jose	1	1	0	0	1		2002-03
Ramsay, Craig	Buffalo	21	4	15	2	1		
	Philadelphia	28	12	12	4	1		
	Total	49	16	27	6	2		1986-01
Randall, Ken	Hamilton	14	6	8	0	1		1923-24
Reay, Billy	Toronto	90	26	50	14	2		
	Chicago	1012	516	335	161	14		
	Total	1102	542	385	175	16		1957-77
Regan, Larry	Los Angeles	88	27	47	14	2		1970-72
Renney, Tom	Vancouver	101	39	53	9	2		
	NY Rangers	102	49	41	12	3		
	Total	203	88	94	21	5		1996-06
Risebrough, Doug	Calgary	144	71	56	17	2		1990-92
Roberts, Jim	Buffalo	45	21	16	8	1		
	Hartford	80	26	41	13	1		
	St. Louis	9	3	3	3	1		
	Total	134	50	60	24	3		1981-97
Robinson, Larry	Los Angeles	328	122	161	45	4		
	New Jersey	173	87	62	24	4	1	
	Total	501	209	223	69	8	1	1995-06
Rodden, Mike	Toronto	2	0	2	0	1		1926-27
Romeril, Alex	Toronto	13	7	5	1	1		1926-27
Ross, Art	Mtl. Wanderers	6	1	5	0	1		
	Hamilton	24	6	18	0	1		
	Boston	728	361	277	90	16	1	
	Total	758	368	300	90	18	1	1917-45
Ruel, Claude	Montreal	305	172	82	51	5	2	1968-81
Ruff, Lindy	Buffalo	656	305	267	84	9		1997-06
Sather, Glen	Edmonton	842	464	268	110	11	4	
	NY Rangers	90	33	46	11	2		
	Total	932	497	314	121	13		1979-04
Sator, Ted	NY Rangers	99	41	48	10	2		
	Buffalo	207	96	89	22	3		
	Total	306	137	137	32	5		1985-89
Savard, Andre	Quebec	24	10	13	1	1		1987-88
Schinkel, Ken	Pittsburgh	203	83	92	28	4		1972-77
Schmidt, Milt	Boston	726	245	360	121	11		
	Washington	44	5	34	5	2		
	Total	770	250	394	126	13		1954-76
Schoenfeld, Jim	Buffalo	43	19	19	5	1		
	New Jersey	124	50	59	15	3		
	Washington	249	113	102	34	4		
	Phoenix	164	74	66	24	2		
	Total	580	256	248	78	10		1985-99
Shaughnessy, Tom	Chicago	21	10	8	3	1		1929-30
Shaw, Brad	NY Islanders	40	18	18	4	1		2005-06
Shero, Fred	Philadelphia	554	308	151	95	7	2	
	NY Rangers	180	82	74	24	3		
	Total	734	390	225	119	10	2	1971-81
Simpson, Joe	NY Americans	144	42	72	30	3		1932-35
Simpson, Terry	NY Islanders	187	81	82	24	3		
	Philadelphia	84	35	39	10	1		
	Winnipeg	97	43	47	7	2		
	Total	368	159	168	41	6		1986-96
Sims, Al	San Jose	82	27	47	8	1		1996-97
Sinden, Harry	Boston	327	153	116	58	6	1	1966-85
Skinner, Jimmy	Detroit	247	123	78	46	4	1	1954-58
Smeaton, Cooper	Philadelphia	44	4	36	4	1		1930-31
Smith, Alf	Ottawa	18	12	6	0	1		1918-19
Smith, Barry*	Detroit	5	4	1	0	1		1998-99
*Results shared with co-coach Dave Lewis								
Smith, Floyd	Buffalo	241	143	62	36	4		
	Toronto	68	30	33	5	1		
	Total	309	173	95	41	5		1971-80
Smith, Mike	Winnipeg	23	2	17	4	1		1980-81
Smith, Ron	NY Rangers	44	15	22	7	1		1992-93
Smythe, Conn	Toronto	134	57	57	20	4		1927-31
Sonmor, Glen	Minnesota	417	174	161	82	7		1978-87
Sproule, Harry	Toronto	12	7	5	0	1		1919-20
Stanley, Barney	Chicago	23	4	17	2	1		1927-28
Stasiuk, Vic	Philadelphia	154	45	68	41	2		
	California	75	21	38	16	1		
	Vancouver	78	22	47	9	1		
	Total	307	88	153	66	4		1969-73
Stewart, Bill	Chicago	69	22	35	12	2	1	1937-39
Stewart, Bill	NY Islanders	37	11	19	7	1		1998-99
Stewart, Ron	NY Rangers	39	15	20	4	1		
	Los Angeles	80	31	34	15	1		
	Total	119	46	54	19	2		1975-86
Stirling, Steve	NY Islanders	124	56	55	13	3		2003-06
Suhonen, Alpo	Chicago	82	29	45	8	1		2000-01
Sullivan, Red	NY Rangers	196	58	103	35	4		
	Pittsburgh	150	47	79	24	2		
	Washington	18	2	16	0	1		
	Total	364	107	198	59	7		1962-74
Sullivan, Mike	Boston	164	70	63	31	3		2003-06
Sutherland, Bill	Winnipeg	32	7	22	3	2		1979-81
Sutter, Brian	St. Louis	320	153	124	43	4		
	Boston	216	120	73	23	3		
	Calgary	246	87	122	37	3		
	Chicago	246	91	118	37	4		
	Total	1028	451	437	140	14		1988-05
Sutter, Darryl	Chicago	216	110	80	26	3		
	San Jose	434	192	182	60	6		
	Calgary	210	107	77	26	4		
	Total	860	409	339	112	12		1992-06
Sutter, Duane	Florida	72	22	42	8	2		2000-02

Coach	Team	Games Coached	Wins	Losses	O/T	Years	Cup Wins	Career
Talbot, Jean-Guy	St. Louis	120	52	53	15	2		
	NY Rangers	80	30	37	13	1		
	Total	**200**	**82**	**90**	**28**	**3**		1972-78
Tessier, Orval	Chicago	213	99	93	21	3		1982-85
Therrien, Michel	Montreal	190	77	90	23	3		
	Pittsburgh	51	14	29	8	1		
	Total	**241**	**91**	**119**	**31**	**4**		2000-06
Thompson, Paul	Chicago	272	104	127	41	7		1938-45
Thompson, Percy	Hamilton	48	13	35	0	2		1920-22
Tippett, Dave	Dallas	246	140	72	34	4		2002-06
Tobin, Bill	Chicago	71	29	29	13	2		1929-32
Torchetti, John	Florida	27	10	13	4	1		
	Los Angeles	12	5	7	0	1		
	Total	**39**	**15**	**20**	**4**	**2**		2003-06
Tortorella, John	NY Rangers	4	0	3	1	1		
	Tampa Bay	371	164	165	42	6	1	
	Total	**375**	**164**	**168**	**43**	**7**	**1**	1999-06
Tremblay, Mario	**Montreal**	159	71	63	25	2		1995-97
Trottier, Bryan	**NY Rangers**	54	21	27	6	1		2002-03
Trotz, Barry	**Nashville**	574	232	274	68	8		1998-06
Ubriaco, Gene	**Pittsburgh**	106	50	47	9	2		1988-90
Vachon, Rogie	**Los Angeles**	10	4	3	3	3		1983-95
Vigneault, Alain	**Montreal**	266	109	122	35	4		1997-01
Waddell, Don	**Atlanta**	10	4	5	1	1		2002-03
Watson, Bryan	**Edmonton**	18	4	9	5	1		1980-81
Watson, Phil	NY Rangers	295	119	124	52	5		
	Boston	84	16	55	13	2		
	Total	**379**	**135**	**179**	**65**	**7**		1955-63
Watt, Tom	Winnipeg	181	72	85	24	3		
	Vancouver	160	52	87	21	2		
	Toronto	149	52	80	17	2		
	Total	**490**	**176**	**252**	**62**	**7**		1981-92
Webster, Tom	NY Rangers	18	5	9	4	1		
	Los Angeles	240	115	94	31	3		
	Total	**258**	**120**	**103**	**35**	**4**		1986-92
Weiland, Cooney	**Boston**	96	58	20	18	2	1	1939-41
White, Bill	**Chicago**	46	16	24	6	1		1976-77
Wiley, Jim	**San Jose**	57	17	37	3	1		1995-96
Wilson, Johnny	Los Angeles	52	9	34	9	1		
	Detroit	145	67	56	22	2		
	Colorado	80	20	46	14	1		
	Pittsburgh	240	91	105	44	3		
	Total	**517**	**187**	**241**	**89**	**7**		1969-80
Wilson, Larry	**Detroit**	36	3	29	4	1		1976-77
Wilson, Rick	**Dallas**	32	13	12	7	1		2001-02
Wilson, Ron	Anaheim	296	120	145	31	4		
	Washington	410	192	167	51	5		
	San Jose	221	106	85	30	4		
	Total	**927**	**418**	**397**	**112**	**13**		1993-05
Yawney, Trent	**Chicago**	82	26	43	13	1		2005-06
Young, Garry	California	12	2	7	3	1		
	St. Louis	98	41	41	16	2		
	Total	**110**	**43**	**48**	**19**	**3**		1972-76

A two-time Stanley Cup winner in Montreal (plus one more in Dallas) and a former captain of the Canadiens (1989 to 1994), Guy Carbonneau (top right) will make his debut as an NHL head coach with Montreal in 2006-07. Carbonneau will be looking to duplicate the success of Jacques Lemaire (below), another former Canadiens great whose first NHL coaching job was in Montreal. Lemaire has gone on to great success with New Jersey and Minnesota. In Buffalo, former team captain Lindy Ruff (bottom right) has coached the Sabres to more wins than any coach in franchise history.

Year-by-Year Individual Regular-Season Leaders

Season	Goals	G	Assists	A	Points	Pts.	Penalty Minutes	PIM
1917-18	Joe Malone	44	Cy Denneny, Reg Noble, Harry Cameron	10	Joe Malone	48	Joe Hall	100
1918-19	Newsy Lalonde	22	Newsy Lalonde, Eddie Gerard	10	Newsy Lalonde	32	Joe Hall	135
1919-20	Joe Malone	39	Frank Nighbor	15	Joe Malone	49	Cully Wilson	86
1920-21	Babe Dye	35	Jack Darragh	15	Newsy Lalonde	43	Bert Corbeau	86
1921-22	Punch Broadbent	32	Harry Cameron	17	Punch Broadbent	46	Sprague Cleghorn	63
1922-23	Babe Dye	26	Edmond Bouchard	12	Babe Dye	37	Georges Boucher	58
1923-24	Cy Denneny	22	Georges Boucher	10	Cy Denneny	24	Bert Corbeau	55
1924-25	Babe Dye	38	Cy Denneny, Red Green	15	Babe Dye	46	Georges Boucher	95
1925-26	Nels Stewart	34	Frank Nighbor	13	Nels Stewart	42	Bert Corbeau	121
1926-27	Bill Cook	33	Dick Irvin	18	Bill Cook	37	Nels Stewart	133
1927-28	Howie Morenz	33	Howie Morenz	18	Howie Morenz	51	Eddie Shore	165
1928-29	Ace Bailey	22	Frank Boucher	16	Ace Bailey	32	Red Dutton	139
1929-30	Cooney Weiland	43	Frank Boucher	36	Cooney Weiland	73	Joe Lamb	119
1930-31	Charlie Conacher	31	Joe Primeau	32	Howie Morenz	51	Harvey Rockburn	118
1931-32	Charlie Conacher, Bill Cook	34	Joe Primeau	37	Busher Jackson	53	Red Dutton	107
1932-33	Bill Cook	28	Frank Boucher	28	Bill Cook	50	Red Horner	144
1933-34	Charlie Conacher	32	Joe Primeau	32	Charlie Conacher	52	Red Horner	126 *
1934-35	Charlie Conacher	36	Art Chapman	34	Charlie Conacher	57	Red Horner	125
1935-36	Charlie Conacher, Bill Thoms	23	Art Chapman	28	Sweeney Schriner	45	Red Horner	167
1936-37	Larry Aurie, Nels Stewart	23	Syl Apps	29	Sweeney Schriner	46	Red Horner	124
1937-38	Gordie Drillon	26	Syl Apps	29	Gordie Drillon	52	Red Horner	82 *
1938-39	Roy Conacher	26	Bill Cowley	34	Toe Blake	47	Red Horner	85
1939-40	Bryan Hextall	24	Milt Schmidt	30	Milt Schmidt	52	Red Horner	87
1940-41	Bryan Hextall	26	Bill Cowley	45	Bill Cowley	62	Jimmy Orlando	99
1941-42	Lynn Patrick	32	Phil Watson	37	Bryan Hextall	56	Pat Egan	124
1942-43	Doug Bentley	33	Bill Cowley	45	Doug Bentley	73	Jimmy Orlando	89 *
1943-44	Doug Bentley	38	Clint Smith	49	Herb Cain	82	Mike McMahon	98
1944-45	Maurice Richard	50	Elmer Lach	54	Elmer Lach	80	Pat Egan	86
1945-46	Gaye Stewart	37	Elmer Lach	34	Max Bentley	61	Jack Stewart	73
1946-47	Maurice Richard	45	Billy Taylor	46	Max Bentley	72	Gus Mortson	133
1947-48	Ted Lindsay	33	Doug Bentley	37	Elmer Lach	61	Bill Barilko	147
1948-49	Sid Abel	28	Doug Bentley	43	Roy Conacher	68	Bill Ezinicki	145
1949-50	Maurice Richard	43	Ted Lindsay	55	Ted Lindsay	78	Bill Ezinicki	144
1950-51	Gordie Howe	43	Gordie Howe, Ted Kennedy	43	Gordie Howe	86	Gus Mortson	142
1951-52	Gordie Howe	47	Elmer Lach	50	Gordie Howe	86	Gus Kyle	127
1952-53	Gordie Howe	49	Gordie Howe	46	Gordie Howe	95	Maurice Richard	112
1953-54	Maurice Richard	37	Gordie Howe	48	Gordie Howe	81	Gus Mortson	132
1954-55	Maurice Richard, Bernie Geoffrion	38	Bert Olmstead	48	Bernie Geoffrion	75	Fern Flaman	150
1955-56	Jean Beliveau	47	Bert Olmstead	56	Jean Beliveau	88	Lou Fontinato	202
1956-57	Gordie Howe	44	Ted Lindsay	55	Gordie Howe	89	Gus Mortson	147
1957-58	Dickie Moore	36	Henri Richard	52	Dickie Moore	84	Lou Fontinato	152
1958-59	Jean Beliveau	45	Dickie Moore	55	Dickie Moore	96	Ted Lindsay	184
1959-60	Bobby Hull, Bronco Horvath	39	Don McKenney	49	Bobby Hull	81	Carl Brewer	150
1960-61	Bernie Geoffrion	50	Jean Beliveau	58	Bernie Geoffrion	95	Pierre Pilote	165
1961-62	Bobby Hull	50	Andy Bathgate	56	Bobby Hull, Andy Bathgate	84	Lou Fontinato	167
1962-63	Gordie Howe	38	Henri Richard	50	Gordie Howe	86	Howie Young	273
1963-64	Bobby Hull	43	Andy Bathgate	58	Stan Mikita	89	Vic Hadfield	151
1964-65	Norm Ullman	42	Stan Mikita	59	Stan Mikita	87	Carl Brewer	177
1965-66	Bobby Hull	54	Stan Mikita, Bobby Rousseau, Jean Beliveau	48	Bobby Hull	97	Reggie Fleming	166
1966-67	Bobby Hull	52	Stan Mikita	62	Stan Mikita	97	John Ferguson	177
1967-68	Bobby Hull	44	Phil Esposito	49	Stan Mikita	87	Barclay Plager	153
1968-69	Bobby Hull	58	Phil Esposito	77	Phil Esposito	126	Forbes Kennedy	219
1969-70	Phil Esposito	43	Bobby Orr	87	Bobby Orr	120	Keith Magnuson	213
1970-71	Phil Esposito	76	Bobby Orr	102	Phil Esposito	152	Keith Magnuson	291
1971-72	Phil Esposito	66	Bobby Orr	80	Phil Esposito	133	Bryan Watson	212
1972-73	Phil Esposito	55	Phil Esposito	75	Phil Esposito	130	Dave Schultz	259
1973-74	Phil Esposito	68	Bobby Orr	90	Phil Esposito	145	Dave Schultz	348
1974-75	Phil Esposito	61	Bobby Orr, Bobby Clarke	89	Bobby Orr	135	Dave Schultz	472
1975-76	Reggie Leach	61	Bobby Clarke	89	Guy Lafleur	125	Steve Durbano	370
1976-77	Steve Shutt	60	Guy Lafleur	80	Guy Lafleur	136	Tiger Williams	338
1977-78	Guy Lafleur	60	Bryan Trottier	77	Guy Lafleur	132	Dave Schultz	405
1978-79	Mike Bossy	69	Bryan Trottier	87	Bryan Trottier	134	Tiger Williams	298
1979-80	Charlie Simmer, Danny Gare, Blaine Stoughton	56	Wayne Gretzky	86	Marcel Dionne, Wayne Gretzky	137	Jimmy Mann	287
1980-81	Mike Bossy	68	Wayne Gretzky	109	Wayne Gretzky	164	Tiger Williams	343
1981-82	Wayne Gretzky	92	Wayne Gretzky	120	Wayne Gretzky	212	Paul Baxter	409
1982-83	Wayne Gretzky	71	Wayne Gretzky	125	Wayne Gretzky	196	Randy Holt	275
1983-84	Wayne Gretzky	87	Wayne Gretzky	118	Wayne Gretzky	205	Chris Nilan	338
1984-85	Wayne Gretzky	73	Wayne Gretzky	135	Wayne Gretzky	208	Chris Nilan	358
1985-86	Jari Kurri	68	Wayne Gretzky	163	Wayne Gretzky	215	Joe Kocur	377
1986-87	Wayne Gretzky	62	Wayne Gretzky	121	Wayne Gretzky	183	Tim Hunter	361
1987-88	Mario Lemieux	70	Wayne Gretzky	109	Mario Lemieux	168	Bob Probert	398
1988-89	Mario Lemieux	85	Mario Lemieux, Wayne Gretzky	114	Mario Lemieux	199	Tim Hunter	375
1989-90	Brett Hull	72	Wayne Gretzky	102	Wayne Gretzky	142	Basil McRae	351
1990-91	Brett Hull	86	Wayne Gretzky	122	Wayne Gretzky	163	Rob Ray	350
1991-92	Brett Hull	70	Wayne Gretzky	90	Mario Lemieux	131	Mike Peluso	408
1992-93	Teemu Selanne, Alexander Mogilny	76	Adam Oates	97	Mario Lemieux	160	Marty McSorley	399
1993-94	Pavel Bure	60	Wayne Gretzky	92	Wayne Gretzky	130	Tie Domi	347
1994-95	Peter Bondra	34	Ron Francis	48	Jaromir Jagr, Eric Lindros	70	Enrico Ciccone	225
1995-96	Mario Lemieux	69	Mario Lemieux, Ron Francis	92	Mario Lemieux	161	Matthew Barnaby	335
1996-97	Keith Tkachuk	52	Mario Lemieux, Wayne Gretzky	72	Mario Lemieux	122	Gino Odjick	371
1997-98	Teemu Selanne, Peter Bondra	52	Jaromir Jagr	67	Jaromir Jagr	102	Donald Brashear	372
1998-99	Teemu Selanne	47	Jaromir Jagr	83	Jaromir Jagr	127	Rob Ray	261
99-2000	Pavel Bure	58	Mark Recchi	63	Jaromir Jagr	96	Denny Lambert	219
2000-01	Pavel Bure	59	Jaromir Jagr, Adam Oates	69	Jaromir Jagr	121	Matthew Barnaby	265
2001-02	Jarome Iginla	52	Adam Oates	64	Jarome Iginla	96	Peter Worell	354
2002-03	Milan Hejduk	50	Peter Forsberg	77	Peter Forsberg	106	Jody Shelley	249
2003-04	Rick Nash, Jarome Iginla, Ilya Kovalchuk	41	Scott Gomez, Martin St. Louis	56	Martin St. Louis	94	Sean Avery	261
2004-05	....		....		....		....	
2005-06	Jonathan Cheechoo	56	Joe Thornton	96	Joe Thornton	125	Sean Avery	257

* Match Misconduct penalty not included in total penalty minutes.
1946-47 was the first season that a Match penalty was automatically written into the player's total penalty minutes as 20 minutes.
Beginning in 1947-48 all penalties, Match, Game Misconduct, and Misconduct, are written as 10 minutes.

One Season Scoring Records

Goals-Per-Game Leaders, One Season

(Among players with 20 goals or more in one season)

Player	Team	Season	Games	Goals	Average
Joe Malone	Montreal	1917-18	20	44	2.20
Cy Denneny	Ottawa	1917-18	20	36	1.80
Newsy Lalonde	Montreal	1917-18	14	23	1.64
Joe Malone	Quebec	1919-20	24	39	1.63
Newsy Lalonde	Montreal	1919-20	23	37	1.61
Reg Noble	Toronto	1917-18	20	30	1.50
Babe Dye	Ham., Tor.	1920-21	24	35	1.46
Cy Denneny	Ottawa	1920-21	24	34	1.42
Joe Malone	Hamilton	1920-21	20	28	1.40
Newsy Lalonde	Montreal	1920-21	24	33	1.38
Punch Broadbent	Ottawa	1921-22	24	32	1.33
Babe Dye	Toronto	1924-25	29	38	1.31
Babe Dye	Toronto	1921-22	24	31	1.29
Newsy Lalonde	Montreal	1918-19	17	22	1.29
Odie Cleghorn	Montreal	1918-19	17	22	1.29
Cy Denneny	Ottawa	1921-22	22	27	1.23
Aurel Joliat	Montreal	1924-25	25	30	1.20
Wayne Gretzky	Edmonton	1983-84	74	87	1.18
Babe Dye	Toronto	1922-23	22	26	1.18
Wayne Gretzky	Edmonton	1981-82	80	92	1.15
Mario Lemieux	Pittsburgh	1992-93	60	69	1.15
Frank Nighbor	Ottawa	1919-20	23	26	1.13
Mario Lemieux	Pittsburgh	1988-89	76	85	1.12
Brett Hull	St. Louis	1990-91	78	86	1.10
Cam Neely	Boston	1993-94	49	50	1.02
Maurice Richard	Montreal	1944-45	50	50	1.00
Reg Noble	Toronto	1919-20	24	24	1.00
Corb Denneny	Toronto	1919-20	24	24	1.00
Joe Malone	Hamilton	1921-22	24	24	1.00
Billy Boucher	Montreal	1922-23	24	24	1.00
Cy Denneny	Ottawa	1923-24	22	22	1.00
Alexander Mogilny	Buffalo	1992-93	77	76	0.99
Mario Lemieux	Pittsburgh	1995-96	70	69	0.99
Cooney Weiland	Boston	1929-30	44	43	0.98
Phil Esposito	Boston	1970-71	78	76	0.97
Jari Kurri	Edmonton	1984-85	73	71	0.97

With 96 assists in 81 games last season, Joe Thornton had one of the greatest seasons for assists in NHL history. Only Wayne Gretzky, Mario Lemieux, Adam Oates and Bobby Orr have averaged more assists per game than Thornton did in 2005-06.

Assists-Per-Game Leaders, One Season

(Among players with 35 assists or more in one season)

Player	Team	Season	Games	Assists	Average
Wayne Gretzky	Edmonton	1985-86	80	163	2.04
Wayne Gretzky	Edmonton	1987-88	64	109	1.70
Wayne Gretzky	Edmonton	1984-85	80	135	1.69
Wayne Gretzky	Edmonton	1983-84	74	118	1.59
Wayne Gretzky	Edmonton	1982-83	80	125	1.56
Wayne Gretzky	Los Angeles	1990-91	78	122	1.56
Wayne Gretzky	Edmonton	1986-87	79	121	1.53
Mario Lemieux	Pittsburgh	1992-93	60	91	1.52
Wayne Gretzky	Edmonton	1981-82	80	120	1.50
Mario Lemieux	Pittsburgh	1988-89	76	114	1.50
Adam Oates	St. Louis	1990-91	61	90	1.48
Wayne Gretzky	Los Angeles	1988-89	78	114	1.46
Wayne Gretzky	Los Angeles	1989-90	73	102	1.40
Wayne Gretzky	Edmonton	1980-81	80	109	1.36
Mario Lemieux	Pittsburgh	1991-92	64	87	1.36
Mario Lemieux	Pittsburgh	1989-90	59	78	1.32
Bobby Orr	Boston	1970-71	78	102	1.31
Mario Lemieux	Pittsburgh	1995-96	70	92	1.31
Mario Lemieux	Pittsburgh	1987-88	77	98	1.27
Bobby Orr	Boston	1973-74	74	90	1.22
Wayne Gretzky	Los Angeles	1991-92	74	90	1.22
Joe Thornton	Bos., S.J.	**2005-06**	81	96	1.19
Ron Francis	Pittsburgh	1995-96	77	92	1.19
Mario Lemieux	Pittsburgh	1985-86	79	93	1.18
Bobby Clarke	Philadelphia	1975-76	76	89	1.17
Peter Stastny	Quebec	1981-82	80	93	1.16
Adam Oates	Boston	1992-93	84	97	1.15
Doug Gilmour	Toronto	1992-93	83	95	1.14
Wayne Gretzky	Los Angeles	1993-94	81	92	1.14
Paul Coffey	Edmonton	1985-86	79	90	1.14
Bobby Orr	Boston	1969-70	76	87	1.14
Bryan Trottier	NY Islanders	1978-79	76	87	1.14
Bobby Orr	Boston	1972-73	63	72	1.14
Bill Cowley	Boston	1943-44	36	41	1.14
Pat LaFontaine	Buffalo	1992-93	84	95	1.13
Steve Yzerman	Detroit	1988-89	80	90	1.13
Paul Coffey	Pittsburgh	1987-88	46	52	1.13
Bobby Orr	Boston	1974-75	80	89	1.11
Bobby Clarke	Philadelphia	1974-75	80	89	1.11
Paul Coffey	Pittsburgh	1988-89	75	83	1.11
Wayne Gretzky	Los Angeles	1992-93	45	49	1.11
Denis Savard	Chicago	1982-83	78	86	1.10
Denis Savard	Chicago	1981-82	80	87	1.09
Denis Savard	Chicago	1987-88	80	87	1.09
Wayne Gretzky	Edmonton	1979-80	79	86	1.09
Ron Francis	Pittsburgh	1994-95	44	48	1.09
Paul Coffey	Edmonton	1983-84	80	86	1.08
Elmer Lach	Montreal	1944-45	50	54	1.08
Peter Stastny	Quebec	1985-86	76	81	1.07
Jaromir Jagr	Pittsburgh	1995-96	82	87	1.06
Mark Messier	Edmonton	1989-90	79	84	1.06
Peter Forsberg	Colorado	1995-96	82	86	1.05
Paul Coffey	Edmonton	1984-85	80	84	1.05
Marcel Dionne	Los Angeles	1979-80	80	84	1.05
Bobby Orr	Boston	1971-72	76	80	1.05
Mike Bossy	NY Islanders	1981-82	80	83	1.04
Adam Oates	Boston	1993-94	77	80	1.04
Phil Esposito	Boston	1968-69	74	77	1.04
Bryan Trottier	NY Islanders	1983-84	68	71	1.04
Jason Spezza	Ottawa	**2005-06**	68	71	1.04
Pete Mahovlich	Montreal	1974-75	80	82	1.03
Kent Nilsson	Calgary	1980-81	80	82	1.03
Peter Stastny	Quebec	1982-83	75	77	1.03
Denis Savard	Chicago	1988-89	58	59	1.02
Jaromir Jagr	Pittsburgh	1998-99	81	83	1.02
Doug Gilmour	Toronto	1993-94	83	84	1.01
Bernie Nicholls	Los Angeles	1988-89	79	80	1.01
Guy Lafleur	Montreal	1979-80	74	75	1.01
Guy Lafleur	Montreal	1976-77	80	80	1.00
Marcel Dionne	Los Angeles	1984-85	80	80	1.00
Brian Leetch	NY Rangers	1991-92	80	80	1.00
Bryan Trottier	NY Islanders	1977-78	77	77	1.00
Mike Bossy	NY Islanders	1983-84	67	67	1.00
Jean Ratelle	NY Rangers	1971-72	63	63	1.00
Steve Yzerman	Detroit	1993-94	58	58	1.00
Ron Francis	Hartford	1985-86	53	53	1.00
Guy Chouinard	Calgary	1980-81	52	52	1.00
Elmer Lach	Montreal	1943-44	48	48	1.00

Points-Per-Game Leaders, One Season

(Among players with 50 points or more in one season)

Player	Team	Season	Games	Points	Average	Player	Team	Season	Games	Points	Average
Wayne Gretzky	Edmonton	1983-84	74	205	2.77	Bobby Orr	Boston	1973-74	74	122	1.65
Wayne Gretzky	Edmonton	1985-86	80	215	2.69	Kent Nilsson	Calgary	1980-81	80	131	1.64
Mario Lemieux	Pittsburgh	1992-93	60	160	2.67	Denis Savard	Chicago	1987-88	80	131	1.64
Wayne Gretzky	Edmonton	1981-82	80	212	2.65	Wayne Gretzky	Los Angeles	1991-92	74	121	1.64
Mario Lemieux	Pittsburgh	1988-89	76	199	2.62	Steve Yzerman	Detroit	1992-93	84	137	1.63
Wayne Gretzky	Edmonton	1984-85	80	208	2.60	Marcel Dionne	Los Angeles	1978-79	80	130	1.63
Wayne Gretzky	Edmonton	1982-83	80	196	2.45	Dale Hawerchuk	Winnipeg	1984-85	80	130	1.63
Wayne Gretzky	Edmonton	1987-88	64	149	2.33	Mark Messier	Edmonton	1989-90	79	129	1.63
Wayne Gretzky	Edmonton	1986-87	79	183	2.32	Bryan Trottier	NY Islanders	1983-84	68	111	1.63
Mario Lemieux	Pittsburgh	1995-96	70	161	2.30	Pat LaFontaine	Buffalo	1991-92	57	93	1.63
Mario Lemieux	Pittsburgh	1987-88	77	168	2.18	Charlie Simmer	Los Angeles	1980-81	65	105	1.62
Wayne Gretzky	Los Angeles	1988-89	78	168	2.15	Guy Lafleur	Montreal	1978-79	80	129	1.61
Wayne Gretzky	Los Angeles	1990-91	78	163	2.09	Bryan Trottier	NY Islanders	1981-82	80	129	1.61
Mario Lemieux	Pittsburgh	1989-90	59	123	2.08	Phil Esposito	Boston	1974-75	79	127	1.61
Wayne Gretzky	Edmonton	1980-81	80	164	2.05	Steve Yzerman	Detroit	1989-90	79	127	1.61
Mario Lemieux	Pittsburgh	1991-92	64	131	2.05	Peter Stastny	Quebec	1985-86	76	122	1.61
Bill Cowley	Boston	1943-44	36	71	1.97	Mario Lemieux	Pittsburgh	1996-97	76	122	1.61
Phil Esposito	Boston	1970-71	78	152	1.95	Michel Goulet	Quebec	1983-84	75	121	1.61
Wayne Gretzky	Los Angeles	1989-90	73	142	1.95	Wayne Gretzky	Los Angeles	1993-94	81	130	1.60
Steve Yzerman	Detroit	1988-89	80	155	1.94	Bryan Trottier	NY Islanders	1977-78	77	123	1.60
Bernie Nicholls	Los Angeles	1988-89	79	150	1.90	Bobby Orr	Boston	1972-73	63	101	1.60
Adam Oates	St. Louis	1990-91	61	115	1.89	Guy Chouinard	Calgary	1980-81	52	83	1.60
Phil Esposito	Boston	1973-74	78	145	1.86	Elmer Lach	Montreal	1944-45	50	80	1.60
Jari Kurri	Edmonton	1984-85	73	135	1.85	Pierre Turgeon	NY Islanders	1992-93	83	132	1.59
Mike Bossy	NY Islanders	1981-82	80	147	1.84	Steve Yzerman	Detroit	1987-88	64	102	1.59
Jaromir Jagr	Pittsburgh	1995-96	82	149	1.82	Mike Bossy	NY Islanders	1978-79	80	126	1.58
Mario Lemieux	Pittsburgh	1985-86	79	141	1.78	Paul Coffey	Edmonton	1983-84	80	126	1.58
Bobby Orr	Boston	1970-71	78	139	1.78	Marcel Dionne	Los Angeles	1984-85	80	126	1.58
Jari Kurri	Edmonton	1983-84	64	113	1.77	Bobby Orr	Boston	1969-70	76	120	1.58
Mario Lemieux	Pittsburgh	2000-01	43	76	1.77	Eric Lindros	Philadelphia	1995-96	73	115	1.58
Pat LaFontaine	Buffalo	1992-93	84	148	1.76	Charlie Simmer	Los Angeles	1979-80	64	101	1.58
Bryan Trottier	NY Islanders	1978-79	76	134	1.76	Teemu Selanne	Winnipeg	1992-93	84	132	1.57
Mike Bossy	NY Islanders	1983-84	67	118	1.76	Jaromir Jagr	Pittsburgh	1998-99	81	127	1.57
Paul Coffey	Edmonton	1985-86	79	138	1.75	Bobby Clarke	Philadelphia	1975-76	76	119	1.57
Phil Esposito	Boston	1971-72	76	133	1.75	Guy Lafleur	Montreal	1975-76	80	125	1.56
Peter Stastny	Quebec	1981-82	80	139	1.74	Dave Taylor	Los Angeles	1980-81	72	112	1.56
Wayne Gretzky	Edmonton	1979-80	79	137	1.73	Denis Savard	Chicago	1982-83	78	121	1.55
Jean Ratelle	NY Rangers	1971-72	63	109	1.73	Ron Francis	Pittsburgh	1995-96	77	119	1.55
Marcel Dionne	Los Angeles	1979-80	80	137	1.71	Joe Thornton	Bos., S.J.	2005-06	81	125	1.54
Herb Cain	Boston	1943-44	48	82	1.71	Mike Bossy	NY Islanders	1985-86	80	123	1.54
Guy Lafleur	Montreal	1976-77	80	136	1.70	Kevin Stevens	Pittsburgh	1991-92	80	123	1.54
Dennis Maruk	Washington	1981-82	80	136	1.70	Bobby Orr	Boston	1971-72	76	117	1.54
Phil Esposito	Boston	1968-69	74	126	1.70	Mike Bossy	NY Islanders	1984-85	76	117	1.54
Guy Lafleur	Montreal	1974-75	70	119	1.70	Kevin Stevens	Pittsburgh	1992-93	72	111	1.54
Mario Lemieux	Pittsburgh	1986-87	63	107	1.70	Doug Bentley	Chicago	1943-44	50	77	1.54
Adam Oates	Boston	1992-93	84	142	1.69	Doug Gilmour	Toronto	1992-93	83	127	1.53
Bobby Orr	Boston	1974-75	80	135	1.69	Marcel Dionne	Los Angeles	1976-77	80	122	1.53
Marcel Dionne	Los Angeles	1980-81	80	135	1.69	Jaromir Jagr	Pittsburgh	99-2000	63	96	1.52
Guy Lafleur	Montreal	1977-78	78	132	1.69	Eric Lindros	Philadelphia	1996-97	52	79	1.52
Guy Lafleur	Montreal	1979-80	74	125	1.69	Eric Lindros	Philadelphia	1994-95	46	70	1.52
Rob Brown	Pittsburgh	1988-89	68	115	1.69	Marcel Dionne	Detroit	1974-75	80	121	1.51
Jari Kurri	Edmonton	1985-86	78	131	1.68	Mike Bossy	NY Islanders	1980-81	79	119	1.51
Brett Hull	St. Louis	1990-91	78	131	1.68	Paul Coffey	Edmonton	1984-85	80	121	1.51
Phil Esposito	Boston	1972-73	78	130	1.67	Dale Hawerchuk	Winnipeg	1987-88	80	121	1.51
Cooney Weiland	Boston	1929-30	44	73	1.66	Paul Coffey	Pittsburgh	1988-89	75	113	1.51
Alexander Mogilny	Buffalo	1992-93	77	127	1.65	Jaromir Jagr	Pittsburgh	1996-97	63	95	1.51
Peter Stastny	Quebec	1982-83	75	124	1.65	Cam Neely	Boston	1993-94	49	74	1.51

Penguins legend Mario Lemieux (seeking open ice behind Montreal's Stephane Quintal) has had some of the greatest points-per-game seasons in NHL history, including 10 seasons in which he ranged between 1.60 and 2.67 points per game.

Never before has the NHL seen two such remarkable rookie performances in the same season: Washington's Alex Ovechkin (far right) became just the third rookie to top both 50 goals and 100 points, while Pittsburgh's Sidney Crosby (right) became the League's youngest 100-point scorer, reaching this milestone as an 18-year-old.

Rookie Scoring Records

All-Time Top 50 Goal-Scoring Rookies

	Rookie	Team	Position	Season	GP	G	A	PTS
1.	* Teemu Selanne	Winnipeg	Right wing	1992-93	84	76	56	132
2.	* Mike Bossy	NY Islanders	Right wing	1977-78	73	53	38	91
3.	* Alex Ovechkin	Washington	Left wing	2005-06	81	52	54	106
4.	* Joe Nieuwendyk	Calgary	Center	1987-88	75	51	41	92
5.	* Dale Hawerchuk	Winnipeg	Center	1981-82	80	45	58	103
	* Luc Robitaille	Los Angeles	Left wing	1986-87	79	45	39	84
7.	Rick Martin	Buffalo	Left wing	1971-72	73	44	30	74
	Barry Pederson	Boston	Center	1981-82	80	44	48	92
9.	Steve Larmer	Chicago	Right wing	1982-83	80	43	47	90
	* Mario Lemieux	Pittsburgh	Center	1984-85	73	43	57	100
11.	Eric Lindros	Philadelphia	Center	1992-93	61	41	34	75
12.	Darryl Sutter	Chicago	Left wing	1980-81	76	40	22	62
	Sylvain Turgeon	Hartford	Left wing	1983-84	76	40	32	72
	Warren Young	Pittsburgh	Left wing	1984-85	80	40	32	72
15.	* Eric Vail	Atlanta	Left wing	1974-75	72	39	21	60
	Anton Stastny	Quebec	Left wing	1980-81	80	39	46	85
	* Peter Stastny	Quebec	Center	1980-81	77	39	70	109
	Steve Yzerman	Detroit	Center	1983-84	80	39	48	87
	Sidney Crosby	Pittsburgh	Center	2005-06	81	39	63	102
20.	* Gilbert Perreault	Buffalo	Center	1970-71	78	38	34	72
	Neal Broten	Minnesota	Center	1981-82	73	38	60	98
	Ray Sheppard	Buffalo	Right wing	1987-88	74	38	27	65
	Mikael Renberg	Philadelphia	Left wing	1993-94	83	38	44	82
24.	Jorgen Pettersson	St. Louis	Left wing	1980-81	62	37	36	73
	Jimmy Carson	Los Angeles	Center	1986-87	80	37	42	79
26.	Mike Foligno	Detroit	Right wing	1979-80	80	36	35	71
	Mike Bullard	Pittsburgh	Center	1981-82	75	36	27	63
	Paul MacLean	Winnipeg	Right wing	1981-82	74	36	25	61
	Tony Granato	NY Rangers	Right wing	1988-89	78	36	27	63
30.	Marian Stastny	Quebec	Right wing	1981-82	74	35	54	89
	Brian Bellows	Minnesota	Right wing	1982-83	78	35	30	65
	Tony Amonte	NY Rangers	Right wing	1991-92	79	35	34	69
33.	Nels Stewart	Mtl. Maroons	Center	1925-26	36	34	8	42
	* Danny Grant	Minnesota	Left wing	1968-69	75	34	31	65
	Norm Ferguson	Oakland	Right wing	1968-69	76	34	20	54
	Brian Propp	Philadelphia	Left wing	1979-80	80	34	41	75
	Wendel Clark	Toronto	Left wing	1985-86	66	34	11	45
	* Pavel Bure	Vancouver	Right wing	1991-92	65	34	26	60
39.	* Willi Plett	Atlanta	Right wing	1976-77	64	33	23	56
	Dale McCourt	Detroit	Center	1977-78	76	33	39	72
	Mark Pavelich	NY Rangers	Center	1981-82	79	33	43	76
	Ron Flockhart	Philadelphia	Center	1981-82	72	33	39	72
	Steve Bozek	Los Angeles	Center	1981-82	71	33	23	56
	Jason Arnott	Edmonton	Center	1993-94	78	33	35	68
45.	Bill Mosienko	Chicago	Right wing	1943-44	50	32	38	70
	Michel Bergeron	Detroit	Right wing	1975-76	72	32	27	59
	* Bryan Trottier	NY Islanders	Center	1975-76	80	32	63	95
	Don Murdoch	NY Rangers	Right wing	1976-77	59	32	24	56
	Jari Kurri	Edmonton	Left wing	1980-81	75	32	43	75
	Bobby Carpenter	Washington	Center	1981-82	80	32	35	67
	Kjell Dahlin	Montreal	Right wing	1985-86	77	32	39	71
	Petr Klima	Detroit	Left wing	1985-86	74	32	24	56
	Darren Turcotte	NY Rangers	Right wing	1989-90	76	32	34	66
	Joe Juneau	Boston	Center	1992-93	84	32	70	102
	Marek Svatos	Colorado	Right wing	2005-06	61	32	18	50

All-Time Top 50 Point-Scoring Rookies

	Rookie	Team	Position	Season	GP	G	A	PTS
1.	* Teemu Selanne	Winnipeg	Right wing	1992-93	84	76	56	132
2.	* Peter Stastny	Quebec	Center	1980-81	77	39	70	109
3.	* Alex Ovechkin	Washington	Left wing	2005-06	81	52	54	106
4.	* Dale Hawerchuk	Winnipeg	Center	1981-82	80	45	58	103
5.	Joe Juneau	Boston	Center	1992-93	84	32	70	102
	Sidney Crosby	Pittsburgh	Center	2005-06	81	39	63	102
7.	* Mario Lemieux	Pittsburgh	Center	1984-85	73	43	57	100
8.	Neal Broten	Minnesota	Center	1981-82	73	38	60	98
9.	* Bryan Trottier	NY Islanders	Center	1975-76	80	32	63	95
10.	Barry Pederson	Boston	Center	1981-82	80	44	48	92
	* Joe Nieuwendyk	Calgary	Center	1987-88	75	51	41	92
12.	* Mike Bossy	NY Islanders	Right wing	1977-78	73	53	38	91
13.	* Steve Larmer	Chicago	Right wing	1982-83	80	43	47	90
14.	Marian Stastny	Quebec	Right wing	1981-82	74	35	54	89
15.	Steve Yzerman	Detroit	Center	1983-84	80	39	48	87
16.	* Sergei Makarov	Calgary	Right wing	1989-90	80	24	62	86
17.	Anton Stastny	Quebec	Left wing	1980-81	80	39	46	85
18.	* Luc Robitaille	Los Angeles	Left wing	1986-87	79	45	39	84
19.	Mikael Renberg	Philadelphia	Left wing	1993-94	83	38	44	82
20.	Jimmy Carson	Los Angeles	Center	1986-87	80	37	42	79
	Sergei Fedorov	Detroit	Center	1990-91	77	31	48	79
	Alexei Yashin	Ottawa	Center	1993-94	83	30	49	79
23.	Marcel Dionne	Detroit	Center	1971-72	78	28	49	77
24.	Larry Murphy	Los Angeles	Defense	1980-81	80	16	60	76
	Mark Pavelich	NY Rangers	Center	1981-82	79	33	43	76
	Dave Poulin	Philadelphia	Center	1983-84	73	31	45	76
27.	Brian Propp	Philadelphia	Left wing	1979-80	80	34	41	75
	Jari Kurri	Edmonton	Left wing	1980-81	75	32	43	75
	Denis Savard	Chicago	Center	1980-81	76	28	47	75
	Mike Modano	Minnesota	Center	1989-90	80	29	46	75
	Eric Lindros	Philadelphia	Center	1992-93	61	41	34	75
32.	Rick Martin	Buffalo	Left wing	1971-72	73	44	30	74
	* Bobby Smith	Minnesota	Center	1978-79	80	30	44	74
34.	Jorgen Pettersson	St. Louis	Left wing	1980-81	62	37	36	73
35.	* Gilbert Perreault	Buffalo	Center	1970-71	78	38	34	72
	Dale McCourt	Detroit	Center	1977-78	76	33	39	72
	Ron Flockhart	Philadelphia	Center	1981-82	72	33	39	72
	Sylvain Turgeon	Hartford	Left wing	1983-84	76	40	32	72
	Warren Young	Pittsburgh	Left wing	1984-85	80	40	32	72
	Carey Wilson	Calgary	Center	1984-85	74	24	48	72
	Alex Zhamnov	Winnipeg	Center	1992-93	68	25	47	72
42.	Mike Foligno	Detroit	Right wing	1979-80	80	36	35	71
	Dave Christian	Winnipeg	Center	1980-81	80	28	43	71
	Mats Naslund	Montreal	Left wing	1982-83	74	26	45	71
	Kjell Dahlin	Montreal	Right wing	1985-86	77	32	39	71
	* Brian Leetch	NY Rangers	Defense	1988-89	68	23	48	71
47.	Bill Mosienko	Chicago	Right wing	1943-44	50	32	38	70
	* Scott Gomez	New Jersey	Center	99-2000	82	19	51	70
49.	Roland Eriksson	Minnesota	Center	1976-77	80	25	44	69
	Tony Amonte	NY Rangers	Right wing	1991-92	79	35	34	69
	Brad Boyes	Boston	Center	2005-06	82	26	43	69

* Calder Trophy Winner

50-Goal Seasons

Mickey Redmond

Reggie Leach

Jonathan Cheechoo

Player	Team	Date of 50th Goal	Score		Goaltender	Player's Game No.	Team Game No.	Total Goals	Total Games	Age When First 50th Scored (Yrs. & Mos.)
Maurice Richard	Mtl.	18-3-45	Mtl. 4	at Bos. 2	Harvey Bennett	50	50	50	50	23.7
Bernie Geoffrion	Mtl.	16-3-61	Tor. 2	at Mtl. 5	Cesare Maniago	62	68	50	64	30.1
Bobby Hull	Chi.	25-3-62	Chi. 1	at NYR 4	Gump Worsley	70	70	50	70	23.2
Bobby Hull	Chi.	2-3-66	Det. 4	at Chi. 5	Hank Bassen	52	57	54	65	
Bobby Hull	Chi.	18-3-67	Chi. 5	at Tor. 9	Bruce Gamble	63	66	52	66	
Bobby Hull	Chi.	5-3-69	NYR 4	at Chi. 4	Ed Giacomin	64	66	58	74	
Phil Esposito	Bos.	20-2-71	Bos. 4	at L.A. 5	Denis DeJordy	58	58	76	78	29.0
John Bucyk	Bos.	16-3-71	Bos. 11	at Det. 4	Roy Edwards	69	69	51	78	35.10
Phil Esposito	Bos.	20-2-72	Bos. 3	at Chi. 1	Tony Esposito	60	60	66	76	
Bobby Hull	Chi.	2-4-72	Det. 1	at Chi. 6	Andy Brown	78	78	50	78	
Vic Hadfield	NYR	2-4-72	Mtl. 6	at NYR 5	Denis DeJordy	78	78	50	78	31.6
Phil Esposito	Bos.	25-3-73	Buf. 1	at Bos. 6	Roger Crozier	75	75	55	78	
Mickey Redmond	Det.	27-3-73	Det. 8	at Tor. 1	Ron Low	73	75	52	76	25.3
Rick MacLeish	Phi.	1-4-73	Phi. 4	at Pit. 5	Cam Newton	78	78	50	78	23.2
Phil Esposito	Bos.	20-2-74	Bos. 5	at Min. 5	Cesare Maniago	56	56	68	78	
Mickey Redmond	Det.	23-3-74	NYR 3	at Det. 5	Ed Giacomin	69	71	51	76	
Ken Hodge	Bos.	6-4-74	Bos. 2	at Mtl. 6	Michel Larocque	75	77	50	76	29.10
Rick Martin	Buf.	7-4-74	St.L. 2	at Buf. 5	Wayne Stephenson	78	78	52	78	22.9
Phil Esposito	Bos.	8-2-75	Bos. 8	at Det. 5	Jim Rutherford	54	54	61	79	
Guy Lafleur	Mtl.	29-3-75	K.C. 1	at Mtl. 4	Denis Herron	66	76	53	70	23.6
Danny Grant	Det.	2-4-75	Wsh. 3	at Det. 8	John Adams	78	78	50	80	29.2
Rick Martin	Buf.	3-4-75	Bos. 2	at Buf. 4	Ken Broderick	67	79	52	68	
Reggie Leach	Phi.	14-3-76	Atl. 1	at Phi. 6	Dan Bouchard	69	69	61	80	25.11
Jean Pronovost	Pit.	24-3-76	Bos. 5	at Pit. 5	Gilles Gilbert	74	74	52	80	30.3
Guy Lafleur	Mtl.	27-3-76	K.C. 2	at Mtl. 8	Denis Herron	76	76	56	80	
Bill Barber	Phi.	3-4-76	Buf. 2	at Phi. 5	Al Smith	79	79	50	80	23.9
Pierre Larouche	Pit.	3-4-76	Wsh. 5	at Pit. 4	Ron Low	75	79	53	76	20.5
Danny Gare	Buf.	4-4-76	Tor. 2	at Buf. 5	Gord McRae	79	80	50	79	21.11
Steve Shutt	Mtl.	1-3-77	Mtl. 5	at NYI 4	Glenn Resch	65	65	60	80	24.8
Guy Lafleur	Mtl.	6-3-77	Mtl. 1	at Buf. 4	Don Edwards	68	68	56	80	
Marcel Dionne	L.A.	2-4-77	Min. 2	at L.A. 7	Pete LoPresti	79	79	53	80	25.8
Guy Lafleur	Mtl.	8-3-78	Wsh. 3	at Mtl. 4	Jim Bedard	63	65	60	78	
Mike Bossy	NYI	1-4-78	Wsh. 2	at NYI 3	Bernie Wolfe	69	72	53	73	21.2
Mike Bossy	NYI	24-2-79	Det. 1	at NYI 3	Rogie Vachon	58	58	69	80	
Marcel Dionne	L.A.	11-3-79	L.A. 3	at Phi. 6	Wayne Stephenson	68	68	59	80	
Guy Lafleur	Mtl.	31-3-79	Pit. 3	at Mtl. 5	Denis Herron	76	76	52	80	
Guy Chouinard	Atl.	6-4-79	NYR 2	at Atl. 9	John Davidson	79	79	50	80	22.5
Marcel Dionne	L.A.	12-3-80	L.A. 2	at Pit. 4	Nick Ricci	70	70	53	80	
Mike Bossy	NYI	16-3-80	NYI 6	at Chi. 1	Tony Esposito	68	71	51	75	
Charlie Simmer	L.A.	19-3-80	Det. 3	at L.A. 4	Jim Rutherford	57	73	56	64	26.0
Pierre Larouche	Mtl.	25-3-80	Chi. 4	at Mtl. 8	Tony Esposito	72	75	50	73	
Danny Gare	Buf.	27-3-80	Det. 1	at Buf. 10	Jim Rutherford	71	75	56	76	
Blaine Stoughton	Hfd.	28-3-80	Hfd. 4	at Van. 4	Glen Hanlon	75	75	56	80	27.0
Guy Lafleur	Mtl.	2-4-80	Mtl. 7	at Det. 2	Rogie Vachon	72	78	50	74	
Wayne Gretzky	Edm.	2-4-80	Min. 1	at Edm. 1	Gary Edwards	78	79	51	79	19.2
Reggie Leach	Phi.	3-4-80	Wsh. 2	at Phi. 4	empty net	75	79	50	76	
Mike Bossy	NYI	24-1-81	Que. 3	at NYI 7	Ron Grahame	50	50	68	79	
Charlie Simmer	L.A.	26-1-81	L.A. 7	at Que. 5	Michel Dion	51	51	56	65	
Marcel Dionne	L.A.	8-3-81	L.A. 4	at Wpg. 1	Markus Mattsson	68	68	58	80	
Wayne Babych	St.L.	12-3-81	St.L. 3	at Mtl. 4	Richard Sevigny	70	68	54	78	22.9
Wayne Gretzky	Edm.	15-3-81	Edm. 3	at Cgy. 3	Pat Riggin	69	69	55	80	
Rick Kehoe	Pit.	16-3-81	Pit. 7	at Edm. 6	Eddie Mio	70	70	55	80	29.7
Jacques Richard	Que.	29-3-81	Mtl. 0	at Que. 4	Richard Sevigny	76	75	52	78	28.6
Dennis Maruk	Wsh.	5-4-81	Det. 2	at Wsh. 7	Larry Lozinski	80	80	50	80	25.3
Wayne Gretzky	Edm.	30-12-81	Phi. 5	at Edm. 7	empty net	39	39	92	80	
Dennis Maruk	Wsh.	21-2-82	Wpg. 3	at Wsh. 6	Doug Soetaert	61	61	60	80	
Mike Bossy	NYI	4-3-82	Tor. 1	at NYI 10	Michel Larocque	66	66	64	80	
Dino Ciccarelli	Min.	8-3-82	St.L. 1	at Min. 8	Mike Liut	67	68	55	76	22.1
Rick Vaive	Tor.	24-3-82	St.L. 3	at Tor. 4	Mike Liut	72	75	54	77	22.10
Blaine Stoughton	Hfd.	28-3-82	Min. 3	at Hfd. 2	Gilles Meloche	76	76	52	80	
Rick Middleton	Bos.	28-3-82	Bos. 5	at Buf. 9	Paul Harrison	72	77	51	75	28.11
Marcel Dionne	L.A.	30-3-82	Cgy. 7	at L.A. 5	Pat Riggin	75	77	50	78	
Mark Messier	Edm.	31-3-82	L.A. 3	at Edm. 7	Mario Lessard	78	79	50	78	21.3
Bryan Trottier	NYI	3-4-82	Phi. 3	at NYI 6	Pete Peeters	79	79	50	80	25.9
Lanny McDonald	Cgy.	18-2-83	Cgy. 1	at Buf. 5	Bob Sauve	60	60	66	80	30.0
Wayne Gretzky	Edm.	19-2-83	Edm. 10	at Pit. 7	Nick Ricci	60	60	71	80	
Michel Goulet	Que.	5-3-83	Hfd. 3	at Que. 10	Mike Veisor	67	67	57	80	22.11
Mike Bossy	NYI	12-3-83	Wsh. 3	at NYI 6	Al Jensen	70	71	60	79	
Marcel Dionne	L.A.	17-3-83	Que. 3	at L.A. 4	Dan Bouchard	71	71	56	80	
Al Secord	Chi.	20-3-83	Tor. 3	at Chi. 7	Mike Palmateer	73	73	54	80	25.0
Rick Vaive	Tor.	30-3-83	Tor. 4	at Det. 2	Gilles Gilbert	76	78	51	78	
Wayne Gretzky	Edm.	7-1-84	Hfd. 3	at Edm. 5	Greg Millen	42	42	87	74	
Michel Goulet	Que.	8-3-84	Que. 8	at Pit. 6	Denis Herron	63	69	56	75	
Rick Vaive	Tor.	14-3-84	Min. 3	at Tor. 3	Gilles Meloche	69	72	52	76	
Mike Bullard	Pit.	14-3-84	Pit. 6	at L.A. 7	Markus Mattsson	71	72	51	76	23.0
Jari Kurri	Edm.	15-3-84	Edm. 2	at Mtl. 3	Rick Wamsley	57	73	52	64	23.10
Glenn Anderson	Edm.	21-3-84	Hfd. 3	at Edm. 5	Greg Millen	76	76	54	80	23.6
Tim Kerr	Phi.	22-3-84	Pit. 4	at Phi. 13	Denis Herron	74	75	54	79	24.3

Player	Team	Date of 50th Goal	Score		Goaltender	Player's Game No.	Team Game No.	Total Goals	Total Games	Age When First 50th Scored (Yrs. & Mos.)
Mike Bossy	NYI	31-3-84	NYI 3	at Wsh. 1	Pat Riggin	67	79	51	67	
Wayne Gretzky	Edm.	26-1-85	Pit. 3	at Edm. 6	Denis Herron	49	49	73	80	
Jari Kurri	Edm.	3-2-85	Hfd. 3	at Edm. 6	Greg Millen	50	53	71	73	
Mike Bossy	NYI	5-3-85	Phi. 5	at NYI 4	Bob Froese	61	65	58	76	
Michel Goulet	Que.	6-3-85	Buf. 3	at Que. 4	Tom Barrasso	62	73	55	69	
Tim Kerr	Phi.	7-3-85	Wsh. 6	at Phi. 9	Pat Riggin	63	65	54	74	
John Ogrodnick	Det.	13-3-85	Det. 6	at Edm. 7	Grant Fuhr	69	69	55	79	25.9
Bob Carpenter	Wsh.	21-3-85	Wsh. 2	at Mtl. 3	Steve Penney	72	72	53	80	21.9
Dale Hawerchuk	Wpg.	29-3-85	Chi. 5	at Wpg. 5	W. Skorodenski	77	77	53	80	21.11
Mike Gartner	Wsh.	7-4-85	Pit. 3	at Wsh. 7	Brian Ford	80	80	50	80	25.5
Jari Kurri	Edm.	4-3-86	Edm. 6	at Van. 2	Richard Brodeur	63	65	68	78	
Mike Bossy	NYI	11-3-86	Cgy. 4	at NYI 8	Reggie Lemelin	67	67	61	80	
Glenn Anderson	Edm.	14-3-86	Det. 3	at Edm. 12	Greg Stefan	63	71	54	72	
Michel Goulet	Que.	17-3-86	Que. 8	at Mtl. 6	Patrick Roy	67	72	53	75	
Wayne Gretzky	Edm.	18-3-86	Wpg. 2	at Edm. 6	Brian Hayward	72	72	52	80	
Tim Kerr	Phi.	20-3-86	Pit. 1	at Phi. 5	Roberto Romano	68	72	58	76	
Wayne Gretzky	Edm.	4-2-87	Edm. 6	at Min. 5	Don Beaupre	55	55	62	79	
Dino Ciccarelli	Min.	7-3-87	Pit. 7	at Min. 3	Gilles Meloche	66	66	52	80	
Mario Lemieux	Pit.	12-3-87	Que. 3	at Pit. 6	Mario Gosselin	53	70	54	63	21.5
Tim Kerr	Phi.	17-3-87	NYR 1	at Phi. 4	J. Vanbiesbrouck	67	71	58	75	
Jari Kurri	Edm.	17-3-87	N.J. 4	at Edm. 7	Craig Billington	69	70	54	79	
Mario Lemieux	Pit.	2-2-88	Wsh. 2	at Pit. 3	Pete Peeters	51	54	70	77	
Steve Yzerman	Det.	1-3-88	Buf. 0	at Det. 4	Tom Barrasso	64	64	50	64	22.10
Joe Nieuwendyk	Cgy.	12-3-88	Buf. 4	at Cgy. 10	Tom Barrasso	66	70	51	75	21.5
Craig Simpson	Edm.	15-3-88	Buf. 4	at Edm. 6	Jacques Cloutier	71	71	56	80	21.1
Jimmy Carson	L.A.	26-3-88	Chi. 5	at L.A. 9	Darren Pang	77	77	55	88	19.8
Luc Robitaille	L.A.	1-4-88	L.A. 6	at Cgy. 3	Mike Vernon	79	79	53	80	21.10
Hakan Loob	Cgy.	3-4-88	Min. 1	at Cgy. 4	Don Beaupre	80	80	50	80	27.9
Stephane Richer	Mtl.	3-4-88	Mtl. 4	at Buf. 4	Tom Barrasso	72	80	50	72	21.10
Mario Lemieux	Pit.	20-1-89	Pit. 3	at Wpg. 7	Pokey Reddick	44	46	85	76	
Bernie Nicholls	L.A.	28-1-89	Edm. 7	at L.A. 6	Grant Fuhr	51	51	70	79	27.7
Steve Yzerman	Det.	5-2-89	Det. 6	at Wpg. 2	Pokey Reddick	55	55	65	80	
Wayne Gretzky	L.A.	4-3-89	Phi. 2	at L.A. 6	Ron Hextall	66	67	54	78	
Joe Nieuwendyk	Cgy.	21-3-89	NYI 1	at Cgy. 4	Mark Fitzpatrick	72	74	51	77	
Joe Mullen	Cgy.	31-3-89	Wpg. 1	at Cgy. 4	Bob Essensa	78	79	51	79	32.1
Brett Hull	St.L.	6-2-90	Tor. 4	at St.L. 6	Jeff Reese	54	54	72	80	25.6
Steve Yzerman	Det.	24-2-90	Det. 3	at NYI 3	Glenn Healy	63	63	62	79	
Cam Neely	Bos.	10-3-90	Bos. 3	at NYI 3	Mark Fitzpatrick	69	71	55	76	24.9
Luc Robitaille	L.A.	31-3-90	L.A. 3	at Van. 6	Kirk McLean	79	79	52	80	25.6
Brian Bellows	Min.	22-3-90	Min. 5	at Det. 1	Tim Cheveldae	75	75	55	80	25.1
Pat LaFontaine	NYI	24-3-90	NYI 5	at Edm. 5	Bill Ranford	71	77	54	74	25.1
Stephane Richer	Mtl.	24-3-90	Mtl. 4	at Hfd. 7	Peter Sidorkiewicz	75	77	51	75	
Gary Leeman	Tor.	28-3-90	NYI 6	at Tor. 3	Mark Fitzpatrick	78	78	51	80	26.1
Brett Hull	St.L.	25-1-91	St.L. 9	at Det. 4	David Gagnon	49	49	86	78	
Cam Neely	Bos.	26-3-91	Bos. 7	at Que. 4	empty net	67	78	51	69	
Theoren Fleury	Cgy.	26-3-91	Van. 2	at Cgy. 7	Bob Mason	77	77	51	79	22.9
Steve Yzerman	Det.	30-3-91	NYR 5	at Det. 6	Mike Richter	79	79	51	80	
Brett Hull	St.L.	28-1-92	St.L. 3	at L.A. 3	Kelly Hrudey	50	50	70	73	
Jeremy Roenick	Chi.	7-3-92	Chi. 2	at Bos. 1	Daniel Berthiaume	67	67	53	80	22.2
Kevin Stevens	Pit.	24-3-92	Pit. 3	at Det. 4	Tim Cheveldae	74	74	54	80	26.11
Gary Roberts	Cgy.	31-3-92	Edm. 2	at Cgy. 5	Bill Ranford	73	77	53	76	25.10
Alexander Mogilny	Buf.	3-2-93	Hfd. 2	at Buf. 3	Sean Burke	46	53	76	77	23.11
Teemu Selanne	Wpg.	28-2-93	Min. 4	at Wpg. 7	Darcy Wakaluk	63	63	76	84	22.6
Pavel Bure	Van.	1-3-93	Van. 5	at Buf. 2*	Grant Fuhr	63	63	60	83	21.11
Steve Yzerman	Det.	10-3-93	Det. 6	at Edm. 3	Bill Ranford	70	70	58	84	
Luc Robitaille	L.A.	15-3-93	L.A. 4	at Buf. 2	Grant Fuhr	69	69	63	84	
Brett Hull	St.L.	20-3-93	St.L. 2	at L.A. 3	Robb Stauber	73	73	54	80	
Mario Lemieux	Pit.	21-3-93	Pit. 6	at Edm. 4**	Ron Tugnutt	48	72	69	60	
Kevin Stevens	Pit.	21-3-93	Pit. 6	at Edm. 4**	Ron Tugnutt	62	72	55	72	
Dave Andreychuk	Tor.	23-3-93	Tor. 5	at Wpg. 4	Bob Essensa	72	73	54	83	29.6
Pat LaFontaine	Buf.	28-3-93	Ott. 1	at Buf. 3	Peter Sidorkiewicz	75	75	53	84	
Pierre Turgeon	NYI	2-4-93	NYI 3	at NYR 2	Mike Richter	75	76	58	83	23.8
Mark Recchi	Phi.	3-4-93	T.B. 2	at Phi. 6	J-C Bergeron	77	77	53	84	25.2
Jeremy Roenick	Chi.	15-4-93	Tor. 2	at Chi. 3	Felix Potvin	84	84	50	84	
Brendan Shanahan	St.L.	15-4-93	T.B. 5	at St.L. 6	Pat Jablonski	71	84	51	71	24.3
Cam Neely	Bos.	7-3-94	Wsh. 3	at Bos. 6	Don Beaupre	44	66	50	49	
Sergei Fedorov	Det.	15-3-94	Van. 2	at Det. 5	Kirk McLean	67	69	56	82	24.3
Pavel Bure	Van.	23-3-94	Van. 6	at L.A. 3	empty net	65	73	60	76	
Adam Graves	NYR	23-3-94	NYR 5	at Edm. 3	Bill Ranford	74	74	51	84	25.11
Dave Andreychuk	Tor.	24-3-94	S.J. 2	at Tor. 1	Arturs Irbe	73	74	53	83	
Brett Hull	St.L.	25-3-94	Dal. 3	at St.L. 5	Andy Moog	71	74	52	81	
Ray Sheppard	Det.	29-3-94	Hfd. 2	at Det. 6	Sean Burke	74	76	52	82	27.10
Brendan Shanahan	St.L.	12-4-94	St.L. 5	at Dal. 9	Andy Moog	80	83	52	81	23.11
Mike Modano	Dal.	12-4-94	St.L. 5	at Dal. 9	Curtis Joseph	75	83	50	76	
Mario Lemieux	Pit.	23-2-96	Hfd. 4	at Pit. 5	Sean Burke	50	59	69	70	
Jaromir Jagr	Pit.	23-2-96	Hfd. 4	at Pit. 5	Sean Burke	59	59	62	82	24.0
Alexander Mogilny	Van.	29-2-96	St.L. 2	at Van. 2	Grant Fuhr	60	63	55	79	
Peter Bondra	Wsh.	3-4-96	Wsh. 5	at Buf. 1	Andrei Trefilov	62	77	52	67	28.1
Joe Sakic	Col.	7-4-96	Col. 4	at Dal. 1	empty net	79	79	51	82	26.7
John LeClair	Phi.	10-4-96	Phi. 5	at N.J. 1	Corey Schwab	80	80	51	82	26.7
Keith Tkachuk	Wpg.	12-4-96	L.A. 3	at Wpg. 5	empty net	75	81	50	76	24.0
Paul Kariya	Ana.	14-4-96	Wpg. 2	at Ana. 2	N. Khabibulin	82	82	50	82	21.5
Keith Tkachuk	Phx.	6-4-97	Phx. 1	at Col. 2	Patrick Roy	78	79	52	81	
Teemu Selanne	Ana.	9-4-97	L.A. 1	at Ana. 4	empty net	77	81	51	78	
Mario Lemieux	Pit.	11-4-97	Pit. 2	at Fla. 4	J. Vanbiesbrouck	75	81	50	76	

Jaromir Jagr

Alex Ovechkin

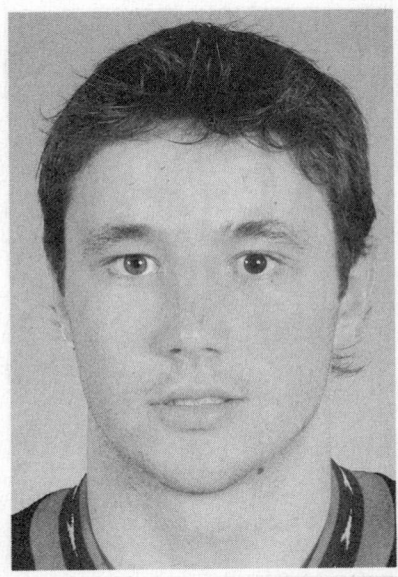

Ilya Kovalchuk

Dany Heatley

Bryan Trottier

Bobby Orr

Player	Team	Date of 50th Goal	Score			Goaltender	Player's Game No.	Team Game No.	Total Goals	Total Games	Age When First 50th Scored (Yrs. & Mos.)
John LeClair	Phi.	13-4-97	N.J. 4	at	Phi. 5	Mike Dunham	82	82	50	82	
Teemu Selanne	Ana.	25-3-98	Ana. 3	at	Chi. 2	Jeff Hackett	66	71	52	73	
John LeClair	Phi.	13-4-98	Phi. 1	at	Buf. 2	Dominik Hasek	79	79	51	82	
Pavel Bure	Van.	17-4-98	Cgy. 4	at	Van. 2	Dwayne Roloson	81	81	51	82	
Peter Bondra	Wsh.	18-4-98	Wsh. 4	at	Car. 3	Mike Fountain	75	80	52	76	
Pavel Bure	Fla.	18-3-00	Fla. 4	at	NYI 2	empty net	63	71	58	74	
Pavel Bure	Fla.	16-3-01	Pit. 6	at	Fla. 3	Johan Hedberg	72	72	59	82	
Joe Sakic	Col.	4-4-01	Ana. 1	at	Col. 1	J-S Giguere	80	80	54	82	
Jaromir Jagr	Pit.	4-4-01	T.B. 2	at	Pit. 4	Kevin Weekes	80	80	52	81	
Jarome Iginla	Cgy.	7-4-02	Cgy. 2	at	Chi. 3	Jocelyn Thibault	79	79	52	82	24.9
Milan Hejduk	Col.	6-4-03	St. L. 2	at	Col. 5	Brent Johnson	82	82	50	82	27.1
Jaromir Jagr	NYR	24-3-06	NYR 2	at	Fla. 3	Roberto Luongo	70	70	54	82	
Ilya Kovalchuk	Atl.	6-4-06	Atl. 2	at	T.B. 3	Sean Burke	72	76	52	78	22.11
Jonathan Cheechoo	S.J.	10-4-06	S.J. 3	at	Phx. 2	David LeNeveu	78	78	56	82	25.8
Alex Ovechkin	Wsh.	13-4-06	Wsh. 3	at	Atl. 5	Mike Dunham	78	79	52	81	20.6
Dany Heatley	Ott.	18-4-06	Ott. 5	at	NYR 1	Henrik Lundqvist	82	82	50	82	25.2

* neutral site game played at Hamilton; ** neutral site game played at Cleveland

100-Point Seasons

Player	Team	Date of 100th Point	G or A	Score			Player's Game No.	Team Game No.	G - A	PTS	Total Games	Age when first 100th point scored (Yrs. & Mos.)
Phil Esposito	Bos.	2-3-69	(G)	Pit. 0	at	Bos. 4	60	62	49-77	126	74	27.1
Bobby Hull	Chi.	20-3-69	(G)	Chi. 5	at	Bos. 5	71	71	58-49	107	76	30.2
Gordie Howe	Det.	30-3-69	(G)	Det. 5	at	Chi. 9	76	76	44-59	103	76	41.0
Bobby Orr	Bos.	15-3-70	(G)	Det. 5	at	Bos. 5	67	67	33-87	120	76	22.11
Phil Esposito	Bos.	6-2-71	(A)	Buf. 3	at	Bos. 4	51	51	76-76	152	78	
Bobby Orr	Bos.	20-2-71	(A)	Bos. 4	at	L.A. 5	58	58	37-102	139	78	
John Bucyk	Bos.	13-3-71	(G)	Bos. 6	at	Van. 3	68	68	51-65	116	78	35.10
Ken Hodge	Bos.	21-3-71	(A)	Buf. 7	at	Bos. 5	72	72	43-62	105	78	26.9
Jean Ratelle	NYR	18-2-72	(A)	NYR 2	at	Cal. 2	58	58	46-63	109	63	31.4
Phil Esposito	Bos.	19-2-72	(A)	Bos. 6	at	Min. 4	59	59	66-67	133	76	
Bobby Orr	Bos.	2-3-72	(A)	Van. 3	at	Bos. 7	64	64	37-80	117	76	
Vic Hadfield	NYR	25-3-72	(A)	NYR 3	at	Mtl. 3	74	74	50-56	106	78	31.5
Phil Esposito	Bos.	3-3-73	(A)	Bos. 1	at	Mtl. 5	64	64	55-75	130	78	
Bobby Clarke	Phi.	29-3-73	(G)	Atl. 2	at	Phi. 4	76	76	37-67	104	78	23.7
Bobby Orr	Bos.	31-3-73	(G)	Bos. 3	at	Tor. 7	62	77	29-72	101	63	
Rick MacLeish	Phi.	1-4-73	(G)	Phi. 4	at	Pit. 5	78	78	50-50	100	78	23.3
Phil Esposito	Bos.	13-2-74	(A)	Bos. 9	at	Cal. 6	53	53	68-77	145	78	
Bobby Orr	Bos.	12-3-74	(A)	Buf. 0	at	Bos. 4	62	66	32-90	122	74	
Ken Hodge	Bos.	24-3-74	(A)	Mtl. 3	at	Bos. 6	72	72	50-55	105	76	
Phil Esposito	Bos.	8-2-75	(A)	Bos. 8	at	Det. 5	54	54	61-66	127	79	
Bobby Orr	Bos.	13-2-75	(A)	Bos. 1	at	Buf. 3	57	57	46-89	135	80	
Guy Lafleur	Mtl.	7-3-75	(G)	Wsh. 4	at	Mtl. 8	56	66	53-66	119	70	24.6
Pete Mahovlich	Mtl.	9-3-75	(G)	Mtl. 5	at	NYR 3	67	67	35-82	117	80	29.5
Marcel Dionne	Det.	9-3-75	(G)	Det. 5	at	Phi. 8	67	67	47-74	121	80	23.7
Bobby Clarke	Phi.	22-3-75	(A)	Min. 0	at	Phi. 4	72	72	27-89	116	80	
Rene Robert	Buf.	5-4-75	(A)	Buf. 4	at	Tor. 2	74	80	40-60	100	74	26.4
Guy Lafleur	Mtl.	10-3-76	(G)	Mtl. 5	at	Chi. 1	69	69	56-69	125	80	
Bobby Clarke	Phi.	11-3-76	(A)	Buf. 1	at	Phi. 6	64	68	30-89	119	76	
Bill Barber	Phi.	18-3-76	(A)	Van. 2	at	Phi. 3	71	71	50-62	112	80	23.8
Gilbert Perreault	Buf.	21-3-76	(A)	K.C. 1	at	Buf. 3	73	73	44-69	113	80	25.4
Pierre Larouche	Pit.	24-3-76	(G)	Bos. 5	at	Pit. 5	70	74	53-58	111	76	20.4
Pete Mahovlich	Mtl.	28-3-76	(A)	Mtl. 2	at	Bos. 2	77	77	34-71	105	80	
Jean Ratelle	Bos.	30-3-76	(A)	Buf. 4	at	Bos. 4	77	77	36-69	105	80	
Jean Pronovost	Pit.	3-4-76	(A)	Wsh. 5	at	Pit. 4	79	79	52-52	104	80	30.4
Darryl Sittler	Tor.	3-4-76	(A)	Bos. 4	at	Tor. 2	78	79	41-59	100	79	25.7
Guy Lafleur	Mtl.	26-2-77	(A)	Cle. 3	at	Mtl. 5	63	63	56-80	136	80	
Marcel Dionne	L.A.	5-3-77	(G)	Pit. 3	at	L.A. 3	67	67	53-69	122	80	
Steve Shutt	Mtl.	27-3-77	(A)	Mtl. 6	at	Det. 0	77	77	60-45	105	80	24.9
Bryan Trottier	NYI	25-2-78	(A)	Chi. 1	at	NYI 7	59	60	46-77	123	77	21.7
Guy Lafleur	Mtl.	28-2-78	(G)	Det. 3	at	Mtl. 9	69	61	60-72	132	78	
Darryl Sittler	Tor.	12-3-78	(A)	Tor. 7	at	Pit. 1	67	67	45-72	117	80	
Guy Lafleur	Mtl.	27-2-79	(A)	Mtl. 3	at	NYI 7	61	61	52-77	129	80	
Bryan Trottier	NYI	6-3-79	(A)	Buf. 3	at	NYI 2	59	63	47-87	134	76	
Marcel Dionne	L.A.	8-3-79	(G)	L.A. 4	at	Buf. 6	66	66	59-71	130	80	
Mike Bossy	NYI	11-3-79	(G)	NYI 4	at	Bos. 4	66	66	69-57	126	80	22.2
Bob MacMillan	Atl.	15-3-79	(A)	Atl. 4	at	Phi. 5	68	69	37-71	108	79	26.6
Guy Chouinard	Atl.	30-3-79	(G)	L.A. 3	at	Atl. 5	75	75	50-57	107	80	22.5
Denis Potvin	NYI	8-4-79	(A)	NYI 5	at	NYR 2	73	80	31-70	101	73	25.5

Player	Team	Date of 100th Point	G or A	Score			Player's Game No.	Team Game No.	G - A — PTS	Total Games	Age when first 100th point scored (Yrs. & Mos.)
Marcel Dionne	L.A.	6-2-80	(A)	L.A. 3	at	Hfd. 7	53	53	53-84 — 137	80	
Guy Lafleur	Mtl.	10-2-80	(A)	Mtl. 3	at	Bos. 2	55	55	50-75 — 125	74	
Wayne Gretzky	Edm.	24-2-80	(A)	Bos. 4	at	Edm. 2	61	62	51-86 — 137	79	19.2
Bryan Trottier	NYI	30-3-80	(A)	NYI 9	at	Que. 6	75	77	42-62 — 104	78	
Gilbert Perreault	Buf.	1-4-80	(A)	Buf. 5	at	Atl. 2	77	77	40-66 — 106	80	
Mike Rogers	Hfd.	4-4-80	(A)	Que. 2	at	Hfd. 9	79	79	44-61 — 105	80	25.5
Charlie Simmer	L.A.	5-4-80	(G)	Van. 5	at	L.A. 3	64	80	56-45 — 101	64	26.0
Blaine Stoughton	Hfd.	6-4-80	(A)	Det. 3	at	Hfd. 5	80	80	56-44 — 100	80	27.0
Wayne Gretzky	Edm.	6-2-81	(A)	Wpg. 4	at	Edm. 10	53	53	55-109 — 164	80	
Marcel Dionne	L.A.	12-2-81	(A)	L.A. 5	at	Chi. 5	58	58	58-77 — 135	80	
Charlie Simmer	L.A.	14-2-81	(A)	Bos. 5	at	L.A. 4	59	59	56-49 — 105	65	
Kent Nilsson	Cgy.	27-2-81	(G)	Hfd. 1	at	Cgy. 5	64	64	49-82 — 131	80	24.6
Mike Bossy	NYI	3-3-81	(G)	Edm. 8	at	NYI 8	65	66	68-51 — 119	79	
Dave Taylor	L.A.	14-3-81	(A)	Min. 4	at	L.A. 10	63	70	47-65 — 112	72	25.3
Mike Rogers	Hfd.	22-3-81	(G)	Tor. 3	at	Hfd. 3	74	74	40-65 — 105	80	
Bernie Federko	St.L.	28-3-81	(A)	Buf. 4	at	St.L. 7	74	76	31-73 — 104	78	24.10
Rick Middleton	Bos.	28-3-81	(A)	Chi. 2	at	Bos. 5	76	76	44-59 — 103	80	27.4
Jacques Richard	Que.	29-3-81	(G)	Mtl. 0	at	Que. 4	75	76	52-51 — 103	78	28.6
Bryan Trottier	NYI	29-3-81	(G)	NYI 5	at	Wsh. 4	69	76	31-72 — 103	73	
Peter Stastny	Que.	29-3-81	(A)	Mtl. 0	at	Que. 4	73	76	39-70 — 109	77	24.6
Wayne Gretzky	Edm.	27-12-81	(G)	L.A. 3	at	Edm. 10	38	38	92-120 — 212	80	
Mike Bossy	NYI	13-2-82	(A)	Phi. 2	at	NYI 8	55	55	64-83 — 147	80	
Peter Stastny	Que.	16-2-82	(A)	Wpg. 3	at	Que. 7	60	60	46-93 — 139	80	
Dennis Maruk	Wsh.	20-2-82	(G)	Wsh. 3	at	Min. 7	60	60	60-76 — 136	80	26.3
Bryan Trottier	NYI	23-2-82	(G)	Chi. 1	at	NYI 5	61	61	50-79 — 129	80	
Denis Savard	Chi.	27-2-82	(A)	Chi. 5	at	L.A. 3	64	64	32-87 — 119	80	21.1
Bobby Smith	Min.	3-3-82	(A)	Det. 4	at	Min. 6	66	66	43-71 — 114	80	24.1
Marcel Dionne	L.A.	6-3-82	(G)	L.A. 6	at	Hfd. 7	64	66	50-67 — 117	78	
Dave Taylor	L.A.	20-3-82	(A)	Pit. 5	at	L.A. 7	71	72	39-67 — 106	78	
Dale Hawerchuk	Wpg.	24-3-82	(G)	L.A. 3	at	Wpg. 5	74	74	45-58 — 103	80	18.11
Dino Ciccarelli	Min.	27-3-82	(A)	Min. 6	at	Bos. 5	72	76	55-52 — 107	76	21.8
Glenn Anderson	Edm.	28-3-82	(A)	Edm. 6	at	L.A. 2	78	78	38-67 — 105	80	21.7
Mike Rogers	NYR	2-4-82	(G)	Pit. 7	at	NYR 5	79	79	38-65 — 103	80	
Wayne Gretzky	Edm.	5-1-83	(A)	Edm. 8	at	Wpg. 3	42	42	71-125 — 196	80	
Mike Bossy	NYI	3-3-83	(A)	Tor. 1	at	NYI 5	66	67	60-58 — 118	79	
Peter Stastny	Que.	5-3-83	(A)	Hfd. 3	at	Que. 10	62	67	47-77 — 124	75	
Denis Savard	Chi.	6-3-83	(A)	Mtl. 4	at	Chi. 5	65	67	35-86 — 121	78	
Mark Messier	Edm.	23-3-83	(G)	Edm. 4	at	Wpg. 7	73	76	48-58 — 106	77	22.2
Barry Pederson	Bos.	26-3-83	(A)	Hfd. 4	at	Bos. 7	73	76	46-61 — 107	77	22.0
Marcel Dionne	L.A.	26-3-83	(A)	Edm. 9	at	L.A. 3	75	75	56-51 — 107	80	
Michel Goulet	Que.	27-3-83	(A)	Que. 6	at	Buf. 6	77	77	57-48 — 105	80	22.11
Glenn Anderson	Edm.	29-3-83	(A)	Edm. 7	at	Van. 4	70	78	48-56 — 104	72	
Jari Kurri	Edm.	29-3-83	(A)	Edm. 7	at	Van. 4	78	78	45-59 — 104	80	22.10
Kent Nilsson	Cgy.	29-3-83	(G)	L.A. 3	at	Cgy. 5	78	78	46-58 — 104	80	
Wayne Gretzky	Edm.	18-12-83	(G)	Edm. 7	at	Wpg. 5	34	34	87-118 — 205	74	
Paul Coffey	Edm.	4-3-84	(A)	Mtl. 1	at	Edm. 6	68	68	40-86 — 126	80	22.9
Michel Goulet	Que.	4-3-84	(A)	Que. 1	at	Buf. 1	62	67	56-65 — 121	75	
Jari Kurri	Edm.	7-3-84	(G)	Chi. 4	at	Edm. 7	53	69	52-61 — 113	64	
Peter Stastny	Que.	8-3-84	(A)	Que. 8	at	Pit. 6	69	69	46-73 — 119	80	
Mike Bossy	NYI	8-3-84	(G)	Tor. 5	at	NYI 9	56	68	51-67 — 118	67	
Barry Pederson	Bos.	14-3-84	(A)	Bos. 4	at	Det. 2	71	71	39-77 — 116	80	
Bryan Trottier	NYI	18-3-84	(A)	NYI 4	at	Hfd. 5	62	73	40-71 — 111	68	
Bernie Federko	St.L.	20-3-84	(A)	Wpg. 3	at	St.L. 9	75	76	41-66 — 107	79	
Rick Middleton	Bos.	27-3-84	(G)	Bos. 6	at	Que. 4	77	77	47-58 — 105	80	
Dale Hawerchuk	Wpg.	27-3-84	(A)	Wpg. 3	at	L.A. 3	77	77	37-65 — 102	80	
Mark Messier	Edm.	27-3-84	(G)	Edm. 9	at	Cgy. 2	72	79	37-64 — 101	73	
Wayne Gretzky	Edm.	29-12-84	(A)	Det. 3	at	Edm. 6	35	35	73-135 — 208	80	
Jari Kurri	Edm.	29-1-85	(G)	Edm. 4	at	Cgy. 2	48	51	71-64 — 135	73	
Mike Bossy	NYI	23-2-85	(G)	Bos. 1	at	NYI 7	56	60	58-59 — 117	76	
Dale Hawerchuk	Wpg.	25-2-85	(A)	Wpg. 12	at	NYR 5	64	64	53-77 — 130	80	
Marcel Dionne	L.A.	5-3-85	(A)	Pit. 0	at	L.A. 6	66	66	46-80 — 126	80	
Brent Sutter	NYI	12-3-85	(A)	NYI 6	at	St.L. 5	68	68	42-60 — 102	72	22.10
John Ogrodnick	Det.	22-3-85	(A)	NYR 3	at	Det. 5	73	73	55-50 — 105	79	25.9
Paul Coffey	Edm.	26-3-85	(A)	Edm. 7	at	NYI 5	74	74	37-84 — 121	80	
Denis Savard	Chi.	29-3-85	(A)	Chi. 5	at	Wpg. 5	75	76	38-67 — 105	79	
Peter Stastny	Que.	2-4-85	(A)	Bos. 4	at	Que. 6	74	77	32-68 — 100	75	
Bernie Federko	St.L.	4-4-85	(A)	NYR 5	at	St.L. 4	74	78	30-73 — 103	76	
John Tonelli	NYI	6-4-85	(G)	N.J. 5	at	NYI 5	80	80	42-58 — 100	80	28.1
Paul MacLean	Wpg.	6-4-85	(A)	Wpg. 6	at	Edm. 5	78	79	41-60 — 101	79	27.1
Bernie Nicholls	L.A.	6-4-85	(A)	Van. 4	at	L.A. 4	80	80	46-54 — 100	80	22.9
Mike Gartner	Wsh.	7-4-85	(G)	Pit. 3	at	Wsh. 7	80	80	50-52 — 102	80	25.6
Mario Lemieux	Pit.	7-4-85	(G)	Pit. 3	at	Wsh. 7	73	80	43-57 — 100	73	19.6
Wayne Gretzky	Edm.	4-1-86	(A)	Hfd. 3	at	Edm. 4	39	39	52-163 — 215	80	
Mario Lemieux	Pit.	15-2-86	(G)	Van. 4	at	Pit. 9	55	56	48-93 — 141	79	
Paul Coffey	Edm.	19-2-86	(A)	Tor. 5	at	Edm. 9	59	60	48-90 — 138	79	
Peter Stastny	Que.	1-3-86	(A)	Buf. 8	at	Que. 4	66	68	41-81 — 122	76	
Jari Kurri	Edm.	2-3-86	(G)	Phi. 1	at	Edm. 2	62	64	68-63 — 131	78	
Mike Bossy	NYI	8-3-86	(A)	Wsh. 6	at	NYI 2	65	65	61-62 — 123	80	
Denis Savard	Chi.	12-3-86	(A)	Buf. 7	at	Chi. 6	69	69	47-69 — 116	80	
Mats Naslund	Mtl.	13-3-86	(A)	Mtl. 2	at	Bos. 3	70	70	43-67 — 110	80	26.4
Michel Goulet	Que.	24-3-86	(A)	Que. 1	at	Min. 0	70	75	53-50 — 103	75	
Glenn Anderson	Edm.	25-3-86	(G)	Edm. 7	at	Det. 2	66	74	54-48 — 102	72	
Neal Broten	Min.	26-3-86	(A)	Min. 6	at	Tor. 1	76	76	29-76 — 105	80	26.4
Dale Hawerchuk	Wpg.	31-3-86	(A)	Wpg. 5	at	L.A. 3	78	78	46-59 — 105	80	
Bernie Federko	St.L.	5-4-86	(G)	Chi. 5	at	St.L. 7	79	79	34-68 — 102	80	

Pat LaFontaine

Doug Gilmour

Pavel Bure

Joe Thornton

Daniel Alfredsson

Sidney Crosby

Player	Team	Date of 100th Point	G or A	Score			Player's Game No.	Team Game No.	G - A PTS		Total Games	Age when first 100th point scored (Yrs. & Mos.)
Wayne Gretzky	Edm.	11-1-87	(A)	Cgy. 3	at	Edm. 5	42	42	62-121	183	79	
Jari Kurri	Edm.	14-3-87	(A)	Buf. 3	at	Edm. 5	67	68	54-54	108	79	
Mario Lemieux	Pit.	18-3-87	(A)	St.L. 4	at	Pit. 5	55	72	54-53	107	63	
Mark Messier	Edm.	19-3-87	(A)	Edm. 4	at	Cgy. 5	71	71	37-70	107	77	
Dino Ciccarelli	Min.	30-3-87	(A)	NYR 6	at	Min. 5	78	78	52-51	103	80	
Doug Gilmour	St.L.	2-4-87	(A)	Buf. 3	at	St.L. 5	78	78	42-63	105	80	23.10
Dale Hawerchuk	Wpg.	5-4-87	(A)	Wpg. 3	at	Cgy. 1	80	80	47-53	100	80	
Mario Lemieux	Pit.	20-1-88	(G)	Pit. 8	at	Chi. 3	45	48	70-98	168	77	
Wayne Gretzky	Edm.	11-2-88	(A)	Edm. 7	at	Van. 2	43	56	40-109	149	64	
Denis Savard	Chi.	12-2-88	(A)	St.L. 3	at	Chi. 4	57	57	44-87	131	80	
Dale Hawerchuk	Wpg.	23-2-88	(G)	Wpg. 4	at	Pit. 3	61	61	44-77	121	80	
Steve Yzerman	Det.	27-2-88	(A)	Det. 4	at	Que. 5	63	63	50-52	102	64	22.10
Peter Stastny	Que.	8-3-88	(A)	Hfd. 4	at	Que. 6	63	67	46-65	111	76	
Mark Messier	Edm.	15-3-88	(A)	Buf. 4	at	Edm. 6	68	71	37-74	111	77	
Jimmy Carson	L.A.	26-3-88	(A)	Chi. 5	at	L.A. 9	77	77	55-52	107	80	19.8
Hakan Loob	Cgy.	26-3-88	(A)	Van. 1	at	Cgy. 6	76	76	50-56	106	80	27.9
Mike Bullard	Cgy.	26-3-88	(A)	Van. 1	at	Cgy. 6	76	76	48-55	103	79	27.1
Michel Goulet	Que.	27-3-88	(A)	Pit. 6	at	Que. 3	76	76	48-58	106	80	
Luc Robitaille	L.A.	30-3-88	(G)	Cgy. 7	at	L.A. 9	78	78	53-58	111	80	22.1
Mario Lemieux	Pit.	31-12-88	(A)	N.J. 6	at	Pit. 8	36	38	85-114	199	76	
Wayne Gretzky	L.A.	21-1-89	(A)	L.A. 4	at	Hfd. 5	47	48	54-114	168	78	
Bernie Nicholls	L.A.	21-1-89	(A)	L.A. 4	at	Hfd. 5	48	48	70-80	150	79	
Steve Yzerman	Det.	27-1-89	(G)	Tor. 1	at	Det. 8	50	50	65-90	155	80	
Rob Brown	Pit.	16-3-89	(A)	Pit. 2	at	N.J. 1	60	72	49-66	115	68	·20.11
Paul Coffey	Pit.	20-3-89	(A)	Pit. 2	at	Min. 7	69	74	30-83	113	75	
Joe Mullen	Cgy.	23-3-89	(A)	L.A. 2	at	Cgy. 4	74	75	51-59	110	79	32.1
Jari Kurri	Edm.	29-3-89	(A)	Edm. 5	at	Van. 2	75	79	44-58	102	76	
Jimmy Carson	Edm.	2-4-89	(A)	Edm. 2	at	Cgy. 4	80	80	49-51	100	80	
Mario Lemieux	Pit.	28-1-90	(G)	Pit. 2	at	Buf. 7	50	50	45-78	123	59	
Wayne Gretzky	L.A.	30-1-90	(A)	N.J. 2	at	L.A. 5	51	51	40-102	142	73	
Steve Yzerman	Det.	19-2-90	(A)	Mtl. 5	at	Det. 5	61	61	62-65	127	79	
Mark Messier	Edm.	20-2-90	(A)	Edm. 4	at	Van. 2	62	62	45-84	129	79	
Brett Hull	St.L.	3-3-90	(A)	NYI 4	at	St.L. 5	67	67	72-41	113	80	25.7
Bernie Nicholls	NYR	12-3-90	(A)	L.A. 6	at	NYR 2	70	71	39-73	112	79	
Pierre Turgeon	Buf.	25-3-90	(G)	N.J. 4	at	Buf. 3	76	76	40-66	106	80	20.7
Paul Coffey	Pit.	25-3-90	(A)	Pit. 2	at	Hfd. 4	77	77	29-74	103	80	
Pat LaFontaine	NYI	27-3-90	(G)	Cgy. 4	at	NYI 2	72	78	54-51	105	74	25.1
Adam Oates	St.L.	29-3-90	(A)	Pit. 4	at	St.L. 5	79	79	23-79	102	80	27.7
Joe Sakic	Que.	31-3-90	(G)	Hfd. 3	at	Que. 2	79	79	39-63	102	80	20.8
Ron Francis	Hfd.	31-3-90	(G)	Hfd. 3	at	Que. 2	79	79	32-69	101	80	27.0
Luc Robitaille	L.A.	1-4-90	(A)	L.A. 4	at	Cgy. 8	80	80	52-49	101	80	
Wayne Gretzky	L.A.	30-1-91	(A)	N.J. 4	at	L.A. 2	50	51	41-122	163	78	
Brett Hull	St.L.	23-2-91	(A)	Bos. 2	at	St.L. 9	60	62	86-45	131	78	
Mark Recchi	Pit.	5-3-91	(G)	Van. 1	at	Pit. 4	66	67	40-73	113	78	23.1
Steve Yzerman	Det.	10-3-91	(G)	Det. 4	at	St.L. 1	72	72	51-57	108	80	
John Cullen	Hfd.	16-3-91	(G)	N.J. 2	at	Hfd. 6	71	71	39-71	110	78	26.7
Adam Oates	St.L.	17-3-91	(A)	St.L. 4	at	Chi. 6	54	73	25-90	115	61	
Joe Sakic	Que.	19-3-91	(A)	Edm. 7	at	Que. 6	74	74	48-61	109	80	
Steve Larmer	Chi.	24-3-91	(G)	Min. 4	at	Chi. 5	76	76	44-57	101	80	29.9
Theoren Fleury	Cgy.	28-3-91	(A)	Van. 2	at	Cgy. 7	77	77	51-53	104	79	22.9
Al MacInnis	Cgy.	28-3-91	(A)	Edm. 4	at	Cgy. 4	78	78	28-75	103	78	27.8
Brett Hull	St.L.	2-3-92	(G)	St.L. 5	at	Van. 3	66	66	70-39	109	73	
Wayne Gretzky	L.A.	3-3-92	(A)	Phi. 1	at	L.A. 4	60	66	31-90	121	74	
Kevin Stevens	Pit.	7-3-92	(A)	Pit. 3	at	L.A. 5	66	66	54-69	123	80	26.11
Mario Lemieux	Pit.	10-3-92	(A)	Cgy. 2	at	Pit. 5	53	67	44-87	131	64	
Luc Robitaille	L.A.	17-3-92	(A)	Wpg. 4	at	L.A. 5	73	73	44-63	107	80	
Mark Messier	NYR	22-3-92	(G)	N.J. 3	at	NYR 6	74	75	35-72	107	79	
Jeremy Roenick	Chi.	29-3-92	(A)	Tor. 1	at	Chi. 5	77	77	53-50	103	80	22.2
Steve Yzerman	Det.	14-4-92	(G)	Det. 7	at	Min. 4	79	80	45-58	103	79	
Brian Leetch	NYR	16-4-92	(G)	Pit. 1	at	NYR 7	80	80	22-80	102	80	24.1
Mario Lemieux	Pit.	31-12-92	(G)	Tor. 3	at	Pit. 3	38	39	69-91	160	60	
Pat LaFontaine	Buf.	10-2-93	(A)	Buf. 6	at	Wpg. 2	55	55	53-95	148	84	
Adam Oates	Bos.	14-2-93	(A)	Bos. 3	at	T.B. 3	58	58	45-97	142	84	
Steve Yzerman	Det.	24-2-93	(A)	Det. 7	at	Buf. 10	64	64	58-79	137	84	
Pierre Turgeon	NYI	28-2-93	(G)	NYI 7	at	Hfd. 6	62	63	58-74	132	83	
Doug Gilmour	Tor.	3-3-93	(A)	Min. 1	at	Tor. 3	64	64	32-95	127	83	
Alexander Mogilny	Buf.	5-3-93	(A)	Hfd. 4	at	Buf. 2	58	65	76-51	127	77	24.1
Mark Recchi	Phi.	7-3-93	(G)	Phi. 3	at	N.J. 7	66	66	53-70	123	84	
Teemu Selanne	Wpg.	9-3-93	(G)	Wpg. 4	at	T.B. 2	68	68	76-56	132	84	22.7
Luc Robitaille	L.A.	15-3-93	(A)	L.A. 4	at	Buf. 2	69	69	63-62	125	84	
Kevin Stevens	Pit.	23-3-93	(A)	S.J. 2	at	Pit. 7	63	73	55-56	111	72	
Mats Sundin	Que.	27-3-93	(A)	Phi. 3	at	Que. 8	71	75	47-67	114	80	22.1
Pavel Bure	Van.	1-4-93	(G)	Van. 5	at	T.B. 3	77	77	60-50	110	83	22.0
Jeremy Roenick	Chi.	4-4-93	(G)	St.L. 4	at	Chi. 5	79	79	50-57	107	84	
Craig Janney	St.L.	4-4-93	(G)	St.L. 4	at	Chi. 5	79	79	24-82	106	84	25.7
Rick Tocchet	Pit.	7-4-93	(G)	Mtl. 3	at	Pit. 4	77	81	48-61	109	80	28.11
Joe Sakic	Que.	8-4-93	(A)	Que. 2	at	Bos. 6	75	81	48-57	105	78	
Ron Francis	Pit.	9-4-93	(A)	Pit. 10	at	NYR 4	82	82	24-76	100	84	
Brett Hull	St.L.	11-4-93	(G)	Min. 1	at	St.L. 5	78	82	54-47	101	80	
Theoren Fleury	Cgy.	11-4-93	(G)	Cgy. 3	at	Van. 6	82	82	34-66	100	83	
Joe Juneau	Bos.	14-4-93	(A)	Bos. 4	at	Ott. 2	84	84	32-70	102	84	25.3
Wayne Gretzky	L.A.	14-2-94	(A)	Bos. 3	at	L.A. 2	56	56	38-92	130	81	

Player	Team	Date of 100th Point	G or A	Score			Player's Game No.	Team Game No.	G - A	PTS	Total Games	Age when first 100th point scored (Yrs. & Mos.)
Sergei Fedorov	Det.	1-3-94	(A)	Cgy. 2	at	Det. 5	63	63	56-64 — 120		82	24.2
Doug Gilmour	Tor.	23-3-94	(G)	Tor. 1	at	Fla. 1	74	74	27-84 — 111		83	
Adam Oates	Bos.	26-3-94	(A)	Mtl. 3	at	Bos. 6	68	75	32-80 — 112		77	
Mark Recchi	Phi.	27-3-94	(A)	Ana. 3	at	Phi. 2	76	76	40-67 — 107		84	
Pavel Bure	Van.	28-3-94	(A)	Tor. 2	at	Van. 3	68	76	60-47 — 107		76	
Jeremy Roenick	Chi.	31-3-94	(A)	Chi. 3	at	Wsh. 6	78	78	46-61 — 107		84	
Brendan Shanahan	St.L.	12-4-94	(G)	St.L. 5	at	Dal. 9	80	83	52-50 — 102		81	25.2
Mario Lemieux	Pit.	16-1-96	(G)	Col. 5	at	Pit. 2	38	44	69-92 — 161		70	
Jaromir Jagr	Pit.	6-2-96	(G)	Bos. 5	at	Pit. 6	52	52	62-87 — 149		82	23.11
Ron Francis	Pit.	9-3-96	(A)	N.J. 4	at	Pit. 3	61	66	27-92 — 119		77	
Peter Forsberg	Col.	9-3-96	(A)	Col. 7	at	Van. 5	68	68	30-86 — 116		82	22.7
Joe Sakic	Col.	17-3-96	(A)	Edm. 1	at	Col. 8	70	70	51-69 — 120		82	
Teemu Selanne	Ana.	25-3-96	(A)	Ana. 1	at	Det. 5	70	73	40-68 — 108		79	
Alexander Mogilny	Van.	25-3-96	(A)	L.A. 1	at	Van. 4	72	75	55-52 — 107		79	
Eric Lindros	Phi.	25-3-96	(A)	Hfd. 0	at	Phi. 3	65	73	47-68 — 115		73	23.0
Wayne Gretzky	St.L.	28-3-96	(A)	N.J. 4	at	St.L. 4	76	75	23-79 — 102		80	
Doug Weight	Edm.	30-3-96	(G)	Tor. 4	at	Edm. 3	76	76	25-79 — 104		82	25.3
Sergei Fedorov	Det.	2-4-96	(A)	Det. 3	at	S.J. 6	72	76	39-68 — 107		78	
Paul Kariya	Ana.	7-4-96	(G)	Ana. 5	at	S.J. 3	78	78	50-58 — 108		82	21.5
Mario Lemieux	Pit.	8-3-97	(A)	Phi. 2	at	Pit. 3	61	65	50-72 — 122		76	
Teemu Selanne	Ana.	1-4-97	(A)	Chi. 3	at	Ana. 3	74	78	51-58 — 109		78	
Jaromir Jagr	Pit.	15-4-98	(G)	T.B. 1	at	Pit. 5	76	80	35-67 — 102 .		77	
Jaromir Jagr	Pit.	13-3-99	(G)	Phi. 0	at	Pit. 4	65	65	44-83 — 127		81	
Teemu Selanne	Ana.	5-4-99	(A)	Ana. 2	at	Det. 3	69	76	47-60 — 107		75	
Paul Kariya	Ana.	17-4-99	(A)	Ana. 3	at	S.J. 3	82	82	39-62 — 101		82	
Jaromir Jagr	Pit.	10-3-01	(G)	Cgy. 3	at	Pit. 6	68	68	52-69 — 121		81	
Joe Sakic	Col.	18-3-01	(G)	Min. 3	at	Col. 4	72	72	54-64 — 118		82	
Markus Naslund	Van.	27-3-03	(A)	Phx. 1	at	Van. 5	78	78	48-56 — 104		82	
Peter Forsberg	Col.	31-3-03	(A)	S.J. 1	at	Col. 3	72	79	29-77 — 106		79	
Joe Thornton	Bos.	4-4-03	(A)	Buf. 5	at	Bos. 8	77	82	36-65 — 101		77	
Jaromir Jagr	NYR	18-3-06		A	Tor. 2	at NYR 5	67	67	54-69 — 123		82	
Joe Thornton	S.J.	21-3-06		A	S.J. 6	at St.L. 0	66	67	29-96 — 125		81	
Alex Ovechkin	Wsh.	10-4-06		G	Wsh. 2	at Bos. 1	77	78	52-54 — 106		81	20.6
Dany Heatley	Ott.	13-4-06		A	Fla. 5	at Ott. 4	80	80	50-53 — 103		82	25.2
Daniel Alfredsson	Ott.	15-4-06		A	Fla. 5	at Ott. 4	76	81	43-60 — 103		77	33.4
Eric Staal	Car.	15-4-06		A	Car. 2	at T.B. 3	81	81	45-55 — 100		82	21.5
Sidney Crosby	Pit.	17-4-06		A	NYI 1	at Pit. 6	80	81	39-63 — 102		81	18.8

Eric Staal

The NHL's first two 50-goal scorers were Maurice Richard (left) and Bernie Geoffrion (center). Bobby Hull was the NHL's third 50-goal scorer, and later became the first to top 50 goals and 100 points in the same season.

Five-or-more-Goal Games

Player	Team	Date	Score				Opposing Goaltender
SEVEN GOALS							
Joe Malone	Quebec Bulldogs	Jan. 31/20	Tor. 6	at	Que. 10		Ivan Mitchell
SIX GOALS							
Newsy Lalonde	Montreal	Jan. 10/20	Tor. 7	at	Mtl. 14		Ivan Mitchell
Joe Malone	Quebec Bulldogs	Mar. 10/20	Ott. 4	at	Que. 10		Clint Benedict
Corb Denneny	Toronto St. Pats	Jan. 26/21	Ham. 3	at	Tor. 10		Howard Lockhart
Cy Denneny	Ottawa Senators	Mar. 7/21	Ham. 5	at	Ott. 12		Howard Lockhart
Syd Howe	Detroit	Feb. 3/44	NYR 2	at	Det. 12		Ken McAuley
Red Berenson	St. Louis	Nov. 7/68	St.L. 8	at	Phi. 0		Doug Favell
Darryl Sittler	Toronto	Feb. 7/76	Bos. 4	at	Tor. 11		Dave Reece
FIVE GOALS							
Joe Malone	Montreal	Dec. 19/17	Mtl. 7	at	Ott. 4		Clint Benedict
Harry Hyland	Mtl. Wanderers	Dec. 19/17	Tor. 9	at	Mtl. W. 10		Art Brooks, Sammy Hebert
Joe Malone	Montreal	Jan. 12/18	Ott. 4	at	Mtl. 9		Clint Benedict
Joe Malone	Montreal	Feb. 2/18	Tor. 2	at	Mtl. 11		Hap Holmes
Mickey Roach	Toronto St. Pats	Mar. 6/20	Que. 2	at	Tor. 11		Howard Lockhart
Newsy Lalonde	Montreal	Feb. 16/21	Ham. 5	at	Mtl. 10		Howard Lockhart
Babe Dye	Toronto St. Pats	Dec. 16/22	Mtl. 2	at	Tor. 7		Georges Vezina
Red Green	Hamilton Tigers	Dec. 5/24	Ham. 10	at	Tor. 3		John Ross Roach
Babe Dye	Toronto St. Pats	Dec. 22/24	Tor. 10	at	Bos. 1		Hec Fowler
Punch Broadbent	Mtl. Maroons	Jan. 7/25	Mtl. 6	at	Ham. 2		Jake Forbes
Pit Lepine	Montreal	Dec. 14/29	Ott. 4	at	Mtl. 6		Alex Connell
Howie Morenz	Montreal	Mar. 18/30	NYA 3	at	Mtl. 8		Roy Worters
Charlie Conacher	Toronto	Jan. 19/32	NYA 3	at	Tor. 11		Roy Worters, Al Shields
Ray Getliffe	Montreal	Feb. 6/43	Bos. 3	at	Mtl. 8		Frank Brimsek
Maurice Richard	Montreal	Dec. 28/44	Det. 1	at	Mtl. 9		Harry Lumley
Howie Meeker	Toronto	Jan. 8/47	Chi. 4	at	Tor. 10		Paul Bibeault
Bernie Geoffrion	Montreal	Feb. 19/55	NYR 2	at	Mtl. 10		Gump Worsley
Bobby Rousseau	Montreal	Feb. 1/64	Det. 3	at	Mtl. 9		Roger Crozier
Yvan Cournoyer	Montreal	Feb. 15/75	Chi. 3	at	Mtl. 12		Mike Veisor
Don Murdoch	NY Rangers	Oct. 12/76	NYR 10	at	Min. 4		Gary Smith
Ian Turnbull	Toronto	Feb. 2/77	Det. 1	at	Tor. 9		Ed Giacomin (2), Jim Rutherford (3)
Bryan Trottier	NY Islanders	Dec. 23/78	NYR 4	at	NYI 9		Wayne Thomas (4), John Davidson (1)
Tim Young	Minnesota	Jan. 15/79	Min. 8	at	NYR 1		Doug Soetaert (3), Wayne Thomas (2)
John Tonelli	NY Islanders	Jan. 6/81	Tor. 3	at	NYI 6		Jiri Crha (4), empty net (1)
Wayne Gretzky	Edmonton	Feb. 18/81	St.L. 2	at	Edm. 9		Mike Liut (3), Ed Staniowski (2)
Wayne Gretzky	Edmonton	Dec. 30/81	Phi. 5	at	Edm. 7		Pete Peeters (4), empty net (1)
Grant Mulvey	Chicago	Feb. 3/82	St.L. 5	at	Chi. 9		Mike Liut (4), Gary Edwards (1)
Bryan Trottier	NY Islanders	Feb. 13/82	Phi. 2	at	NYI 8		Pete Peeters
Willy Lindstrom	Winnipeg	Mar. 2/82	Wpg. 7	at	Phi. 6		Pete Peeters
Mark Pavelich	NY Rangers	Feb. 23/83	Hfd. 3	at	NYR 11		Greg Millen
Jari Kurri	Edmonton	Nov. 19/83	N.J. 4	at	Edm. 13		Glenn Resch (3), Ron Low (2)
Bengt Gustafsson	Washington	Jan. 8/84	Wsh. 7	at	Phi. 1		Pelle Lindbergh
Pat Hughes	Edmonton	Feb. 3/84	Cgy. 5	at	Edm. 10		Don Edwards (3), Reggie Lemelin (2)
Wayne Gretzky	Edmonton	Dec. 15/84	Edm. 8	at	St.L. 2		Rick Wamsley (4), Mike Liut (1)
Dave Andreychuk	Buffalo	Feb. 6/86	Buf. 8	at	Bos. 6		Pat Riggin (1), Doug Keans (4)
Wayne Gretzky	Edmonton	Dec. 6/87	Min. 4	at	Edm. 10		Don Beaupre (4), Kari Takko (1)
Mario Lemieux	Pittsburgh	Dec. 31/88	N.J. 6	at	Pit. 8		Bob Sauve (3), Chris Terreri (2)
Joe Nieuwendyk	Calgary	Jan. 11/89	Wpg. 3	at	Cgy. 8		Daniel Berthiaume
Mats Sundin	Quebec	Mar. 5/92	Que. 10	at	Hfd. 4		Peter Sidorkiewicz (3), Kay Whitmore (2)
Mario Lemieux	Pittsburgh	Apr. 9/93	Pit. 10	at	NYR 4		Corey Hirsch (3), Mike Richter (2)
Peter Bondra	Washington	Feb. 5/94	T.B. 3	at	Wsh. 6		Daren Puppa (4), Pat Jablonski (1)
Mike Ricci	Quebec	Feb. 17/94	Que. 8	at	S.J. 2		Arturs Irbe (3), Jimmy Waite (2)
Alex Zhamnov	Winnipeg	Apr. 1/95	Wpg. 7	at	L.A. 7		Kelly Hrudey (3), Grant Fuhr (2)
Mario Lemieux	Pittsburgh	Mar. 26/96	St.L. 4	at	Pit. 8		Grant Fuhr (1), Jon Casey (4)
Sergei Fedorov	Detroit	Dec. 26/96	Wsh. 4	at	Det. 5		Jim Carey

Players' 500th Goals

Regular Season

Player	Team	Date	Game No.	Score			Opposing Goaltender	Total Goals	Total Games
Maurice Richard	Montreal	Oct. 19/57	863	Chi. 1	at	Mtl. 3	Glenn Hall	544	978
Gordie Howe	Detroit	Mar. 14/62	1,045	Det. 2	at	NYR 3	Gump Worsley	801	1,767
Bobby Hull	Chicago	Feb. 21/70	861	NYR. 2	at	Chi. 4	Ed Giacomin	610	1,063
Jean Béliveau	Montreal	Feb. 11/71	1,101	Min. 2	at	Mtl. 6	Gilles Gilbert	507	1,125
Frank Mahovlich	Montreal	Mar. 21/73	1,105	Van. 2	at	Mtl. 3	Dunc Wilson	533	1,181
Phil Esposito	Boston	Dec. 22/74	803	Det. 4	at	Bos. 5	Jim Rutherford	717	1,282
John Bucyk	Boston	Oct. 30/75	1,370	St.L. 2	at	Bos. 3	Yves Bélanger	556	1,540
Stan Mikita	Chicago	Feb. 27/77	1,221	Van. 4	at	Chi. 3	Cesare Maniago	541	1,394
Marcel Dionne	Los Angeles	Dec. 14/82	887	L.A. 2	at	Wsh. 7	Al Jensen	731	1,348
Guy Lafleur	Montreal	Dec. 20/83	918	Mtl. 6	at	N.J. 0	Glenn Resch	560	1,126
Mike Bossy	NY Islanders	Jan. 2/86	647	Bos. 5	at	NYI 7	empty net	573	752
Gilbert Perreault	Buffalo	Mar. 9/86	1,159	N.J. 3	at	Buf. 4	Alain Chevrier	512	1,191
Wayne Gretzky	Edmonton	Nov. 22/86	575	Van. 2	at	Edm. 5	empty net	894	1,487
Lanny McDonald	Calgary	Mar. 21/89	1,107	NYI 1	at	Cgy. 4	Mark Fitzpatrick	500	1,111
Bryan Trottier	NY Islanders	Feb. 13/90	1,104	Cgy. 4	at	NYI 2	Rick Wamsley	524	1,279
Mike Gartner	NY Rangers	Oct. 14/91	936	Wsh. 5	at	NYR 3	Mike Liut	708	1,432
Michel Goulet	Chicago	Feb. 16/92	951	Cgy. 5	at	Chi. 5	Jeff Reese	548	1,089
Jari Kurri	Los Angeles	Oct. 17/92	833	Bos. 6	at	L.A. 8	empty net	601	1,251
Dino Ciccarelli	Detroit	Jan. 8/94	946	Det. 6	at	L.A. 3	Kelly Hrudey	608	1,232
Mario Lemieux	Pittsburgh	Oct. 26/95	605	Pit. 7	at	NYI 5	Tommy Soderstrom	690	915
Mark Messier	NY Rangers	Nov. 6/95	1,141	Cgy. 2	at	NYR 4	Rick Tabaracci	694	1,756
Steve Yzerman	Detroit	Jan. 17/96	906	Col. 2	at	Det. 3	Patrick Roy	692	1,514
Dale Hawerchuk	St. Louis	Jan. 31/96	1,103	St.L. 4	at	Tor. 0	Felix Potvin	518	1,188
Brett Hull	St. Louis	Dec. 22/96	693	L.A. 4	at	St.L. 7	Stephane Fiset	741	1,269
Joe Mullen	Pittsburgh	Mar. 14/97	1,052	Pit. 3	at	Col. 6	Patrick Roy	502	1,062
Dave Andreychuk	New Jersey	Mar. 15/97	1,070	Wsh. 2	at	N.J. 3	Bill Ranford	640	1,639
Luc Robitaille	Los Angeles	Jan. 7/99	928	Buf. 2	at	L.A. 4	Dwayne Roloson	668	1,431
Pat Verbeek	Detroit	Mar. 22/00	1,285	Cgy. 2	at	Det. 2	Fred Brathwaite	522	1,424
Ron Francis	Carolina	Jan. 2/02	1,533	Bos. 6	at	Car. 3	Byron Dafoe	549	1,731
*Brendan Shanahan	Detroit	Mar. 23/02	1,100	Det. 2	at	Col. 0	Patrick Roy	598	1,350
*Joe Sakic	Colorado	Dec. 11/02	1,044	Col. 1	at	Van. 3	Dan Cloutier	574	1,237
*Joe Nieuwendyk	New Jersey	Jan. 17/03	1,094	N.J. 2	at	Car. 1	Kevin Weekes	559	1,242
*Jaromir Jagr	Washington	Feb. 4/03	928	Wsh. 5	at	T.B. 1	John Grahame	591	1,109
*Pierre Turgeon	Colorado	Nov. 8/05	1,229	S.J. 2	at	Col. 5	Vesa Toskala	511	1,277

*Active

Pierre Turgeon displays the puck he shot past San Jose's Vesa Toskala on November 8, 2005 to become the NHL's newest 500-goal scorer. As many as six players could score their 500th in 2006-07.

Players' 1,000th Points

Regular Season

Player	Team	Date	Game No.	G or A	Score			Total Points G-A-PTS	Total Games
Gordie Howe	Detroit	Nov. 27/60	938	(A)	Tor. 0	at	Det. 2	801-1,049–1,850	1,767
Jean Béliveau	Montreal	Mar. 3/68	911	(G)	Mtl. 2	at	Det. 5	507-712–1,219	1,125
Alex Delvecchio	Detroit	Feb. 16/69	1,143	(A)	L.A. 3	at	Det. 6	456-825–1,281	1,549
Bobby Hull	Chicago	Dec. 13/70	909	(A)	Min. 2	at	Chi. 5	610-560–1,170	1,063
Norm Ullman	Toronto	Oct. 16/71	1,113	(A)	NYR 5	at	Tor. 3	490-739–1,229	1,410
Stan Mikita	Chicago	Oct. 15/72	924	(A)	St.L. 3	at	Chi. 1	541-926–1,467	1,394
John Bucyk	Boston	Nov. 9/72	1,144	(G)	Det. 3	at	Bos. 8	556-813–1,369	1,540
Frank Mahovlich	Montreal	Feb. 17/73	1,090	(A)	Phi. 7	at	Mtl. 6	533-570–1,103	1,181
Henri Richard	Montreal	Dec. 20/73	1,194	(A)	Mtl. 2	at	Buf. 2	358-688–1,046	1,256
Phil Esposito	Boston	Feb. 15/74	745	(A)	Bos. 4	at	Van. 2	717-873–1,590	1,282
Rod Gilbert	NY Rangers	Feb. 19/77	1,027	(G)	NYR 2	at	NYI 5	406-615–1,021	1,065
Jean Ratelle	Boston	Apr. 3/77	1,007	(A)	Tor. 4	at	Bos. 7	491-776–1,267	1,281
Marcel Dionne	Los Angeles	Jan. 7/81	740	(G)	L.A. 5	at	Hfd. 3	731-1,040–1,771	1,348
Guy Lafleur	Montreal	Mar. 4/81	720	(G)	Mtl. 9	at	Wpg. 3	560-793–1,353	1,126
Bobby Clarke	Philadelphia	Mar. 19/81	922	(G)	Bos. 3	at	Phi. 5	358-852–1,210	1,144
Gilbert Perreault	Buffalo	Apr. 3/82	871	(A)	Buf. 5	at	Mtl. 4	512-814–1,326	1,191
Darryl Sittler	Philadelphia	Jan. 20/83	927	(A)	Cgy. 2	at	Phi. 5	484-637–1,121	1,096
Wayne Gretzky	Edmonton	Dec. 19/84	424	(A)	L.A. 3	at	Edm. 7	894-1,963–2,875	1,487
Bryan Trottier	NY Islanders	Jan. 29/85	726	(A)	Min. 4	at	NYI 4	524-901–1,425	1,279
Mike Bossy	NY Islanders	Jan. 24/86	656	(G)	NYI 7	at	Wsh. 5	573-553–1,126	752
Denis Potvin	NY Islanders	Apr. 4/87	987	(G)	Buf. 6	at	NYI 6	310-742–1,052	1,060
Bernie Federko	St. Louis	Mar. 19/88	855	(A)	Hfd. 5	at	St.L. 3	369-761–1,130	1,000
Lanny McDonald	Calgary	Mar. 7/89	1,101	(G)	Wpg. 5	at	Cgy. 9	500-506–1,006	1,111
Peter Stastny	Quebec	Oct. 19/89	682	(G)	Que. 5	at	Chi. 3	450-789–1,239	977
Jari Kurri	Edmonton	Jan. 2/90	716	(A)	Edm. 6	at	St.L. 4	601-797–1,398	1,251
Denis Savard	Chicago	Mar. 11/90	727	(A)	St.L. 6	at	Chi. 4	473-865–1,338	1,196
Paul Coffey	Pittsburgh	Dec. 22/90	770	(A)	Pit. 4	at	NYI 3	396-1,135–1,531	1,409
Mark Messier	Edmonton	Jan. 13/91	822	(A)	Edm. 5	at	Phi. 3	694-1,193–1,887	1,756
Dave Taylor	Los Angeles	Feb. 5/91	930	(A)	L.A. 3	at	Phi. 2	431-638–1,069	1,111
Michel Goulet	Chicago	Feb. 23/91	878	(G)	Chi. 3	at	Min. 3	548-604–1,152	1,089
Dale Hawerchuk	Buffalo	Mar. 8/91	781	(G)	Chi. 5	at	Buf. 3	518-891–1,409	1,188
Bobby Smith	Minnesota	Nov. 30/91	986	(A)	Min. 4	at	Tor. 3	357-679–1,036	1,077
Mike Gartner	NY Rangers	Jan. 4/92	971	(A)	NYR 4	at	NJ. 6	708-627–1,335	1,432
Raymond Bourque	Boston	Feb. 29/92	933	(A)	Wsh. 5	at	Bos. 5	410-1,169–1,579	1,612
Mario Lemieux	Pittsburgh	Mar. 24/92	513	(A)	Pit. 3	at	Det. 4	690-1,033–1,723	915
Glenn Anderson	Toronto	Feb. 22/93	954	(G)	Tor. 8	at	Van. 4	498-601–1,099	1,129
Steve Yzerman	Detroit	Feb. 24/93	737	(A)	Det. 7	at	Buf. 10	692-1,063–1,755	1,514
Ron Francis	Pittsburgh	Oct. 28/93	893	(G)	Que. 7	at	Pit. 3	549-1,249–1,798	1,731
Bernie Nicholls	New Jersey	Feb. 13/94	858	(G)	N.J. 3	at	T.B. 3	475-734–1,209	1,127
Dino Ciccarelli	Detroit	Mar. 9/94	957	(G)	Det. 5	at	Cgy. 1	608-592–1,200	1,232
Brian Propp	Hartford	Mar. 19/94	1,008	(G)	Hfd. 3	at	Phi. 3	425-579–1,004	1,016
Joe Mullen	Pittsburgh	Feb. 7/95	935	(A)	Fla. 3	at	Pit. 7	502-561–1,063	1,062
Steve Larmer	NY Rangers	Mar. 8/95	983	(A)	N.J. 4	at	NYR 6	441-571–1,012	1,006
Doug Gilmour	Toronto	Dec. 23/95	935	(A)	Edm. 1	at	Tor. 6	450-964–1,414	1,474
Larry Murphy	Toronto	Mar. 27/96	1,228	(G)	Tor. 6	at	Van. 2	287-929–1,216	1,615
Dave Andreychuk	New Jersey	Apr. 7/96	998	(G)	NYR 2	at	N.J. 4	640-698–1,338	1,639
Adam Oates	Washington	Oct. 8/97	830	(A)	Wsh. 4	at	NYI 3	341-1,079–1,420	1,337
Phil Housley	Washington	Nov. 8/97	1,081	(A)	Edm. 1	at	Wsh. 2	338-894–1,232	1,495
Dale Hunter	Washington	Jan. 9/98	1,308	(A)	Phi. 1	at	Wsh. 4	323-697–1,020	1,407
Pat LaFontaine	NY Islanders	Jan. 22/98	847	(G)	Phi. 4	at	NYR 3	468-545–1,013	865
Luc Robitaille	Los Angeles	Jan. 29/98	882	(G)	Cgy. 3	at	L.A. 5	668-726–1,394	1,431
Al MacInnis	St. Louis	Apr. 7/98	1,056	(A)	St.L. 3	at	Det. 5	340-934–1,274	1,416
Brett Hull	Dallas	Nov. 14/98	815	(G)	Dal. 3	at	Bos. 1	741-650–1,391	1,269
Brian Bellows	Washington	Jan. 2/99	1,147	(A)	Tor. 2	at	Wsh. 5	485-537–1,022	1,188
*Pierre Turgeon	St. Louis	Oct. 9/99	881	(G)	St.L. 4	at	Edm. 3	511-809–1,320	1,277
*Joe Sakic	Colorado	Dec. 27/99	810	(A)	St.L. 1	at	Col. 5	574-915–1,489	1,237
Pat Verbeek	Detroit	Feb. 27/00	1,275	(A)	T.B. 1	at	Det. 3	522-541–1,063	1,424
V. Damphousse	San Jose	Oct. 14/00	1,090	(A)	Bos. 2	at	S.J. 5	432-773–1,205	1,378
*Jaromir Jagr	Pittsburgh	Dec. 30/00	763	(G)	Ott. 3	at	Pit. 5	591-841–1,432	1,109
*Mark Recchi	Philadelphia	Mar. 13/01	920	(A)	St.L. 2	at	Phi. 5	484-781–1,265	1,256
Theoren Fleury	NY Rangers	Oct. 29/01	960	(A)	Dal. 2	at	NYR 4	455-633–1,088	1,084
*B. Shanahan	Detroit	Jan. 12/02	1,073	(A)	Dal. 2	at	Det. 5	598-634–1,232	1,350
*Jeremy Roenick	Philadelphia	Jan. 30/02	961	(G)	Phi. 1	at	Ott. 3	484-658–1,142	1,182
*Mike Modano	Dallas	Nov. 15/02	965	(A)	Col. 2	at	Dal. 4	485-698–1,183	1,179
*Joe Nieuwendyk	New Jersey	Feb. 23/03	1,094	(G)	N.J. 4	at	Pit. 3	559-559–1,118	1,242
*Mats Sundin	Toronto	Mar. 10/03	994	(G)	Tor. 3	at	Edm. 2	496-671–1,167	1,156
*Sergei Fedorov	Anaheim	Feb. 14/04	965	(A)	Ana. 2	at	Van. 1	443-620–1,063	1,055
*Alexander Mogilny	Toronto	Mar. 15/04	946	(A)	Tor. 6	at	Buf. 5	473-559–1,032	990
*Brian Leetch	Boston	Oct. 18/05	1,151	(A)	Bos. 3	at	Mtl. 4	247-781–1,028	1,205
*Teemu Selanne	Anaheim	Jan. 30/06	928	(G)	L.A. 3	at	Ana. 4	492-549–1,041	959

*Active

Brian Leetch (top) became the seventh defenseman in NHL history to score 1,000 points on October 18, 2005. Teemu Selanne (above) also reached the milestone last season.

Individual Awards

Hart Memorial Trophy

Art Ross Trophy

Calder Memorial Trophy

James Norris Memorial Trophy

HART MEMORIAL TROPHY

An annual award "to the player adjudged to be the most valuable to his team." Winner selected in a poll by the Professional Hockey Writers' Association in the 30 NHL cities at the end of the regular schedule.

History: The Hart Memorial Trophy was presented by the National Hockey League in 1960 after the original Hart Trophy was retired to the Hockey Hall of Fame. The original Hart Trophy was donated to the NHL in 1923 by Dr. David A. Hart, father of Cecil Hart, former manager-coach of the Montreal Canadiens.

2005-06 Winner: Joe Thornton, Boston Bruins/San Jose Sharks
Runners-up: Jaromir Jagr, New York Rangers
Miikka Kiprusoff, Calgary Flames

Center Joe Thornton of the San Jose Sharks captured the Hart Memorial Trophy in a close battle with Jaromir Jagr of the New York Rangers. Thornton was named on all 129 ballots and received 67 first-place votes for a total of 1,058 points. Jagr was selected on 128 ballots, including 48 first-place votes, and had a total of 974 points. Calgary Flames goalie Miikka Kiprusoff was third with 10 first-place votes and 561 points. Carolina's Eric Staal and Ottawa's Daniel Alfredsson finished out the top five, although neither received a first-place vote. Four other players who received first-place votes were Washington's Alex Ovechkin (sixth overall in voting), Detroit's Nicklas Lidstrom (seventh), Anaheim's Scott Niedermayer (eighth) and Nashville's Tomas Vokoun (16th). Thornton, a first-time Hart Trophy nominee and the first Hart nominee in Sharks history, collected a league-leading 125 points (29 goals, 96 assists). He had 92 points in 58 games after being acquired by the Sharks on November 30, leading San Jose to a 36-15-7 record and a late-season surge to fifth in the Western Conference standings. Thornton was also named to the NHL First All-Star Team at center for the first time in his career.

ART ROSS TROPHY

An annual award "to the player who leads the league in scoring points at the end of the regular season."

History: Arthur Howey Ross, former manager-coach of the Boston Bruins, presented the trophy to the National Hockey League in 1947. If two players finish the schedule with the same number of points, the trophy is awarded in the following manner: 1. Player with most goals. 2. Player with fewer games played. 3. Player scoring first goal of the season.

2005-06 Winner: Joe Thornton, Boston Bruins/San Jose Sharks
Runners-up: Jaromir Jagr, New York Rangers
Alex Ovechkin, Washington Capitals

Center Joe Thornton of the San Jose Sharks won the Art Ross Trophy for the first time. His win marked the fourth season in a row that the award was won by a first-time winner following four straight wins by Jaromir Jagr from 1998 through 2001. Thornton established career highs with 96 assists and 125 points for the highest single-season scoring since Jagr had 127 points in 1997-98 and edged out the New York Rangers star who finished the 2005-06 season with 123 points (54 goals, 69 assists). Washington Capitals rookie sensation Alex Ovechkin finished third in the scoring race with 52 goals and 54 assists for 106 points. Ottawa Senators teammates Dany Heatley and Daniel Alfredsson, as well as Pittsburgh rookie Sidney Crosby and Carolina's Eric Staal also reached the 100-point plateau. Thornton's 125 points are the most in NHL history by a player who played with two teams in one season.

CALDER MEMORIAL TROPHY

An annual award "to the player selected as the most proficient in his first year of competition in the National Hockey League." Winner selected in a poll by the Professional Hockey Writers' Association at the end of the regular schedule.

History: From 1936-37 until his death in 1943, Frank Calder, NHL President, bought a trophy each year to be given permanently to the outstanding rookie. After Calder's death, the NHL presented the Calder Memorial Trophy in his memory and the trophy is to be kept in perpetuity. To be eligible for the award, a player cannot have played more than 25 games in any single preceding season nor in six or more games in each of any two preceding seasons in any major professional league. Beginning in 1990-91, to be eligible for this award a player must not have attained his twenty-sixth birthday by September 15th of the season in which he is eligible.

2005-06 Winner: Alex Ovechkin, Washington Capitals
Runners-up: Sidney Crosby, Pittsburgh Penguins
Dion Phaneuf, Calgary Flames

Left winger Alex Ovechkin of the Washington Capitals captured the Calder Memorial Trophy in a near-unanimous vote. Ovechkin received 124 of 129 first-place votes and five second-place votes for a total of 1,275 points. Pittsburgh's Sidney Crosby was also named on all 129 ballots, taking four first-place votes and 95 second-place votes among his total of 831 points. Dion Phaneuf of Calgary finished third in the voting with 580 points, while New York Rangers goalie Henrik Lundqvist finished fourth with 455 points and one first-place vote.

Ovechkin's prolific scoring and sensational moves dominated headlines and highlight reels throughout the season. The first pick in the 2004 Entry Draft led all rookies in scoring with 106 points and became the second rookie in history to tally 50 goals and 100 points in a season, following Winnipeg's Teemu Selanne in 1992-93. Ovechkin also led the NHL in shots with 425, the most ever for a rookie, and ranked third among all players in points. His 52 goals tied for third in the league and ranked third all-time among rookies behind Selanne (76) and Mike Bossy (53). Ovechkin also became the first rookie since Ed Belfour in 1990-91 to be named to the NHL First All-Star Team.

JAMES NORRIS MEMORIAL TROPHY

An annual award "to the defense player who demonstrates throughout the season the greatest all-round ability in the position." Winner selected in a poll by the Professional Hockey Writers' Association at the end of the regular schedule.

History: The James Norris Memorial Trophy was presented in 1953 by the four children of the late James Norris in memory of the former owner-president of the Detroit Red Wings.

2005-06 Winner: Nicklas Lidstrom, Detroit Red Wings
Runners-up: Scott Niedermayer, Anaheim Mighty Ducks
Sergei Zubov, Dallas Stars

For the fourth time in five seasons, Nicklas Lidstrom of the Detroit Red Wings was the winner of the James Norris Memorial Trophy. Lidstrom was named on all 129 ballots and received 91 first-place votes for 1,152 points. 2003-04 winner Scott Niedermayer of Anaheim finished second in voting with 29 first-place votes and 817 points. Sergei Zubov of Dallas finished third with 464 points. Ottawa's Zdeno Chara had five first-place votes in a fourth-place finish (430 points), while Detroit's Mathieu Schneider had four first-place votes but finished sixth (111 points.)

Lidstrom led all defensemen in scoring with a career-high 80 points (16 goals, 64 assists). He ranked third in the NHL in ice time per game (28:06) and posted a +21 rating. Lidstrom and Niedermayer were named to the NHL First All-Star Team.

Vezina Trophy

Lady Byng Memorial Trophy

Frank J. Selke Trophy

Conn Smythe Trophy

VEZINA TROPHY

An annual award "to the goalkeeper adjudged to be the best at his position" as voted by the general managers of each of the 30 clubs.

History: Leo Dandurand, Louis Letourneau and Joe Cattarinich, former owners of the Montreal Canadiens, presented the trophy to the National Hockey League in 1926-27 in memory of Georges Vezina, outstanding goalkeeper of the Canadiens who collapsed during an NHL game on November 28, 1925, and died of tuberculosis a few months later. Until the 1981-82 season, the goalkeeper(s) of the team allowing the fewest number of goals during the regular season were awarded the Vezina Trophy.

2005-06 Winner: Miikka Kiprusoff, Calgary Flames
Runners-up: Martin Brodeur, New Jersey Devils
Henrik Lundqvist, New York Rangers

Miikka Kiprusoff of the Calgary Flames captured the Vezina Trophy for the first time after finishing as runner-up in his first time as a finalist for the award in 2003-04. Kiprusoff received votes on all 30 ballots, including 25 first-place votes, for 140 points. New Jersey's Martin Brodeur, winner of the Vezina the past two seasons, was named on 20 of 30 ballots, including two first-place votes, for 48 points. New York Rangers rookie Henrik Lundqvist also received two first-place votes and a total of 41 points. Tomas Vokoun of Nashville received the final first-place vote.

Kiprusoff led all netminders in goals-against average (2.07) and shutouts (10), ranked second in victories (42) and third in save percentage (.923). He also captured the William Jennings Trophy as the goaltender on the club allowing the fewest goals during the regular season and was named to the NHL First All-Star Team.

CONN SMYTHE TROPHY

An annual award "to the most valuable player for his team in the playoffs." Winner selected by the Professional Hockey Writers' Association at the conclusion of the final game in the Stanley Cup Finals.

History: Presented by Maple Leaf Gardens Limited in 1964 to honor Conn Smythe, the former coach, manager, president and owner-governor of the Toronto Maple Leafs.

2005-06 Winner: Cam Ward, Carolina Hurricanes

Carolina Hurricanes goalie Cam Ward is the first rookie to win the Conn Smythe Trophy since Philadelphia Flyers goalie Ron Hextall in 1987, and the first rookie goalie to lead his team to the Stanley Cup since Patrick Roy in 1986. Ward tied Hextall and Roy's record for rookie playoff goalie wins by leading the postseason with 15 victories. His two shutouts and 2.14 goals-against average in 23 games ranked him second. In the Finals, Ward allowed the Edmonton Oilers just 16 goals in seven games and had a sparkling .921 save percentage. After taking over from an ailing Martin Gerber in round one, Ward reeled off seven straight victories to begin his playoff career.

LADY BYNG MEMORIAL TROPHY

An annual award "to the player adjudged to have exhibited the best type of sportsmanship and gentlemanly conduct combined with a high standard of playing ability." Winner selected in a poll by the Professional Hockey Writers' Association at the end of the regular schedule.

History: Lady Byng, wife of Canada's Governor-General at the time, presented the Lady Byng Trophy in the 1924-25 season. After Frank Boucher of the New York Rangers won the award seven times in eight seasons, he was given the trophy to keep and Lady Byng donated another trophy in 1936. After Lady Byng's death in 1949, the National Hockey League presented a new trophy, changing the name to Lady Byng Memorial Trophy.

2005-06 Winner: Pavel Datsyuk, Detroit Red Wings
Runners-up: Brad Richards, Tampa Bay Lightning
Patrick Marleau, San Jose Sharks

Detroit Red Wings center Pavel Datsyuk won the Lady Byng Memorial Trophy in his first time as a finalist. Datsyuk was named on 94 of 128 ballots and received 41 first-place votes for 669 points, well ahead of 2004 Lady Byng winner Brad Richards of the Tampa Bay Lightning (12 first-place votes, 442 points) and Patrick Marleau of the San Jose Sharks (13 and 356). Datsyuk led the Red Wings in scoring with a career-high 87 points (28 goals, 59 assists), the most by a Detroit player since Brendan Shanahan's 88 points in 1996-97. Datsyuk also became the first Red Wing with 50 assists since Steve Yzerman in 1996-97. He had just 22 penalty minutes in 75 games.

FRANK J. SELKE TROPHY

An annual award "to the forward who best excels in the defensive aspects of the game." Winner selected in a poll by the Professional Hockey Writers' Association at the end of the regular schedule.

History: Presented to the National Hockey League in 1977 by the Board of Governors of the NHL in honor of Frank J. Selke, one of the great architects of Montreal and Toronto championship teams.

2005-06 Winner: Rod Brind'Amour, Carolina Hurricanes
Runners-up: Jere Lehtinen, Dallas Stars
Mike Fisher, Ottawa Senators

Carolina Hurricanes center Rod Brind'Amour captured the Frank J. Selke Award for the first time. Brind'Amour, who was named on 108 of 129 ballots, outdistanced the field by receiving 80 first-place votes and 954 points. Three-time Selke winner Jere Lehtinen of the Dallas Stars was second with nine first-place votes and 567 points. Mike Fisher of the Ottawa Senators finished third with 179 points, including five first-place votes.

Brind'Amour's trademark tenacity and versatility helped the Hurricanes to a franchise-best 112-point season and the second seed in the Eastern Conference. The Carolina captain led all NHL forwards in ice time per game at 24:17, more than a minute and a half ahead of second-place Brad Richards of Tampa Bay (22:45). Brind'Amour also excelled in the face-off circle, leading all players in face-offs taken with 2,145 and placing third in face-off winning percentage at 59.1 percent.

WILLIAM M. JENNINGS TROPHY

An annual award "to the goalkeeper(s) having played a minimum of 25 games for the team with the fewest goals scored against it." Winners selected on regular-season play.

History: The Jennings Trophy was presented in 1981-82 by the National Hockey League's Board of Governors to honor the late William M. Jennings, longtime governor and president of the New York Rangers and one of the great builders of hockey in the United States.

2005-06 Winner: Miikka Kiprusoff, Calgary Flames
Runners-up: Manny Legace/Chris Osgood, Detroit Red Wings
Dominik Hasek/Ray Emery, Ottawa Senators

The Calgary Flames' Miikka Kiprusoff captured the William M. Jennings Trophy for the first time. The winner of the Vezina Trophy and a finalist for the Hart Trophy, Kiprusoff led all goaltenders in average (2.07) and shutouts (10), ranked second in games (74) and victories (42) and third in save percentage (.923). He backstopped the Flames to their first division title since 1994-95 by posting an 8-0-3 record in April with a 1.01 goals-against average and two shutouts. The Flames allowed a league-low 200 goals en route to a 46-25-11 record. Detroit had the NHL's second-best defensive record with 209 goals against, while Ottawa was third with 211.

William M. Jennings Trophy

Jack Adams Award

Bill Masterton Trophy

Lester Patrick Trophy

Lester B. Pearson Award

JACK ADAMS AWARD

An annual award presented by the National Hockey League Broadcasters' Association to "the NHL coach adjudged to have contributed the most to his team's success." Winner selected by a poll among members of the NHL Broadcasters' Association at the end of the regular season.

History: The award was presented by the NHL Broadcasters' Association in 1974 to commemorate the late Jack Adams, coach and general manager of the Detroit Red Wings, whose lifetime dedication to hockey serves as an inspiration to all who aspire to further the game.

2005-06 Winner: **Lindy Ruff, Buffalo Sabres**
Runners-up: **Peter Laviolette, Carolina Hurricanes**
Tom Renney, New York Rangers

Buffalo Sabres coach Lindy Ruff captured the Jack Adams Award in the closest voting for the trophy since it was first awarded in 1973-74. Ruff edged out Carolina Hurricanes coach Peter Laviolette by just one point, 155-154. Both men received 20 first-place votes. Tom Renney of the New York Rangers had 13 first-place votes and 127 points. The razor-thin margin between Ruff and Laviolette was reflective of their clubs' competition this season; Carolina earned the Eastern Conference's second seed with 112 points, two more than the fourth-seeded Sabres, and the clubs staged a seven-game Eastern Conference Final.

The NHL's longest-serving active coach, Ruff guided the Sabres to a 52-24-6 record for 110 points, a 25-point improvement over 2003-04, and franchise records for wins and points. The Sabres scored 281 goals, their highest total since 1993-94, but did not place a single player among the leagues top 60 scorers.

BILL MASTERTON MEMORIAL TROPHY

An annual award under the trusteeship of the Professional Hockey Writers' Association to "the National Hockey League player who best exemplifies the qualities of perseverance, sportsmanship and dedication to hockey." Winner selected by a poll among the 30 chapters of the PHWA at the end of the regular season. A $2,500 grant from the PHWA is awarded annually to the Bill Masterton Scholarship Fund, based in Bloomington, MN, in the name of the Masterton Trophy winner.

History: The trophy was presented by the NHL Writers' Association in 1968 to commemorate the late Bill Masterton, a player with the Minnesota North Stars, who exhibited to a high degree the qualities of perseverance, sportsmanship and dedication to hockey, and who died January 15, 1968.

2005-06 Winner: **Teemu Selanne, Mighty Ducks of Anaheim**

Anaheim Mighty Ducks right winger Teemu Selanne is the 2005-06 recipient of the Bill Masterton Memorial Trophy. Plagued by knee injuries for many seasons, Selanne endured the least productive season of his NHL career with the Colorado Avalanche in 2003-04. He underwent reconstructive surgery in 2004 and spent the lockout season of 2004-05 rehabilitating his knee. Selanne signed a one-year free-agent contract with Anaheim in August of 2005 and turned in a spectacular season to begin his second stint with the club. He led the Ducks with 40 goals and 90 points, finishing 13th in the NHL in scoring. Without question the most popular player in franchise history, the relationship between Selanne and Ducks fans is truly unusual in modern-day sports, with Selanne spending countless hours signing autographs and visiting with fans.

LESTER PATRICK TROPHY

An annual award "for outstanding service to hockey in the United States." Eligible recipients are players, officials, coaches, executives and referees. Winners are selected by an award committee consisting of the commissioner of the NHL, an NHL governor, a representative of the New York Rangers, a member of the Hockey Hall of Fame builder's section, a member of the Hockey Hall of Fame player's section, a member of the U.S. Hockey Hall of Fame, a member of the NHL Broadcasters' Association and a member of the Professional Hockey Writers' Association. Each except the League Commissioner is rotated annually. The winner receives a miniature of the trophy.

History: Presented by the New York Rangers in 1966 to honor the late Lester Patrick, longtime general manager and coach of the New York Rangers, whose teams finished out of the playoffs only once in his first 16 years with the club.

2005-06 Winner: **To be announced**

LESTER B. PEARSON AWARD

The Lester B. Pearson Award is presented annually to the "most outstanding player" in the NHL as voted by fellow members of the National Hockey League Players' Association. The winner receives $20,000, and the two finalists receive $10,000 each to donate to the grassroots hockey program of their choice, through the NHLPA's Goals & Dreams Fund.

History: The award was first presented in 1970-71 by the NHLPA in honor of the late Lester B. Pearson, former Prime Minister of Canada.

2005-06 Winner: **Jaromir Jagr, New York Rangers**
Runners-up: **Thornton, Boston Bruins/San Jose Sharks**
Alex Ovechkin, Washington Capitals

Jaromir Jagr, appeared in 82 games for the New York Rangers, finishing in the NHL's top three in goals (second 54), assists (third 69), points (second 123), and plus/minus (tied for third +34). Rangers fans enjoyed his first full season in New York as he helped the team to its first playoff berth since 1996-97. As a three-time winner of the Award, Jagr ties Guy Lafleur's three Pearsons, and trails only Wayne Gretzky (five), Mario Lemieux (four) on the all-time list.

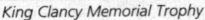

King Clancy Memorial Trophy

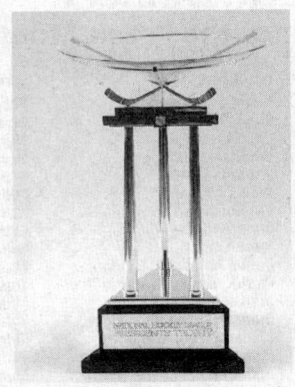

Presidents' Trophy

Maurice "Rocket" Richard Trophy

Bud Light Plus-Minus Award

KING CLANCY MEMORIAL TROPHY

An annual award "to the player who best exemplifies leadership qualities on and off the ice and has made a noteworthy humanitarian contribution in his community."

History: The King Clancy Memorial Trophy was presented to the National Hockey League by the Board of Governors in 1988 to honor the late Frank "King" Clancy.

2005-06 Winner: **Olaf Kolzig, Washington Capitals**

Washington Capitals goalie Olaf Kolzig has been a driving force in the community since he arrived in Washington, D.C. more than 15 years ago. He has worked closely with the Children's National Medical Center and, more recently, become one of the United States leading spokesmen in raising awareness and funds for autism research.

Every year since 1999, Kolzig has purchased 10 Capitals season tickets and donated them to patients at Children's Hospital. Each game, Olie's All-Stars receive T-shirts and sit in a special section in the lower level of the Verizon Center. Kolzig also helped raise more than $650,000 for the hospital through Olie and Eliot's Great Saves and the Olie Kolzig Children's Hospital Golf & Tennis Classic.

Since learning four years ago that his son Carson is autistic, Kolzig has dedicated himself to helping others cope with the disorder. Kolzig is a founding member of Athletes against Autism (Triple A), a group of athletes, personally touched by autism, who are harnessing their efforts into one voice in order to raise awareness and funds for autism research, treatment and education programs. Kolzig also has created the Carson Kolzig Foundation, which focuses primarily on development, research, education and awareness programs for children with autism as well as other youth education and sports-related activities. In 2005, Kolzig had the idea to host an Autism Awareness Night at a Capitals game to benefit Triple Cure Autism Now and the American Special Hockey Association. Thanks to his vision, five other NHL teams either have hosted or will host Autism Awareness Nights.

Kolzig has been recognized for his performance both on and off the ice. He won the Vezina Trophy as the league's top goaltender in 1999-2000, and won the 2000-01 NHL Foundation Player Award for his community efforts. In January 2001, Kolzig was named a Washingtonian of the Year by *Washingtonian Magazine*; he has also been featured as an NHL Good Guy in national media, including The Sporting News and NHL.com. Olaf and his wife Christin were recipients of the Children's National Medical Center's Chairman's Special Award in 2000.

PRESIDENTS' TROPHY

An annual award to the club finishing the regular-season with the best overall record.

History: Presented to the National Hockey League in 1985-86 by the NHL Board of Governors to recognize the team compiling the top regular-season record.

2005-06 Winner: **Detroit Red Wings**
Runners-up: **Ottawa Senators**
                      Dallas Stars

The Detroit Red Wings won the President's Trophy for the third time in four seasons and the fifth time since 1995. The Red Wings led the NHL with a record of 56-16-8, which was good for 124 points. They also had the league's best road record at 31-7-3 and were second in the NHL with 305 goals scored. Detroit has won the Central Division four seasons in a row, five times in the last six seasons and eight times in the last 11. Ottawa won the Northeast Division title for the fourth time in seven seasons, and earned the top seed in the Eastern Conference with a 52-21-9 record for 113 points. Dallas won the Pacific Division title for the seventh time in nine seasons, posting a record of 53-23-6 and 112 points.

MAURICE "ROCKET" RICHARD TROPHY

An annual award "presented to the player finishing the regular season as the League's goal-scoring leader."

History: A gift to the NHL from the Montreal Canadiens in 1999, the Maurice "Rocket" Richard Trophy honors one of the game's greatest stars. During his 18-year career with the Canadiens from 1942-43 through 1959-60, Richard was the first player in NHL history to score 50 goals in a season and 500 in his career. He played on eight Stanley Cup champions and led the League in goal scoring five times.

2005-06 Winner: **Jonathan Cheechoo, San Jose Sharks**
Runners-up: **Jaromir Jagr, New York Rangers**
                      Alex Ovechkin, Washington Capitals
                      Ilya Kovalchuk, Atlanta Thrashers

Right winger Jonathan Cheechoo of the San Jose Sharks tallied a team-record 56 goals to lead the NHL and win the Maurice "Rocket" Richard Trophy for the first time. Cheechoo scored 11 goals in the final 10 games of the season to overtake the Ranger's Jaromir Jagr (54 goals) for the honor. Scoring in pivotal moments, Cheechoo led the NHL in game-winning goals (11), home-ice goals (31) and divisional goals (29). With his three-goal, two-assist performance against Anaheim on April 15, Cheechoo became the first player to record five or more hat tricks in one season since Mario Lemieux notched six in 1995-96. Jaromir Jagr's 54 goals marked the first time he reached 50 since scoring 52 in 2000-01, and rank second only to his 62-goal season of 1995-96. Atlanta's Ilya Kovalchuk, who tied for the Richard Trophy in 2003-04, established a career high with 52 goals, tying him for third in the league with rookie sensation and fellow Russian Alex Ovechkin. Ottawa's Dany Heatley also reached the 50-goal plateau in 2005-06.

BUD LIGHT PLUS-MINUS AWARD

An annual award "to the player, having played a minimum of 60 games, who leads the League in plus/minus statistics" at the end of the regular season.

History: This award was first presented to the NHL in 1997-98 by Anheuser-Busch Inc. to recognize the League leader in plus-minus statistics. Plus-minus statistics are calculated by giving a player a "plus" when on-ice for an even-strength or short-handed goal scored by his team. He receives a "minus" when on-ice for an even-strength or short-handed goal scored by the opposing team. A plus-minus award has been presented since the 1982-83 season.

2005-06 Winner: **Wade Redden, Ottawa Senators**
                      Michal Rozsival, New York Rangers
Runners-up: **Andrej Meszaros, Ottawa Senators**
                      Jaromir Jagr, New York Rangers

Two defensemen, Wade Redden of the Ottawa Senators and Michal Rozsival of the New York Rangers, were co-winners of the Bud Light Plus-Minus Award. Both players had a plus-minus rating of +35. Redden, who established career highs with 40 assists and 50 points, achieved his rating in only 65 games and helped Ottawa to a first-place finish in the Northeast Division and Eastern Conference (52-21-9, 113 points.) Rozsival played in all 82 games for the first time in his career and also set career highs in assists (25) and points (30). He helped the Rangers to their first playoff appearance since 1996-97 with a record of 44-26-12 and 100 points. Redden and Rozsival were each followed by a teammate in the plus-minus standings, as Ottawa rookie Andrej Meszaros and Rangers veteran Jaromir Jagr both finished the season at +34.

MBNA Roger Crozier
Saving Grace Award

Bud Light NHL All-Star Game
MVP Award

MBNA ROGER CROZIER SAVING GRACE AWARD

An award "presented to the goaltender having played a minimum of 25 games with the NHL's best save percentage during the regular season." The winner receives a monetary award to be donated to the youth hockey or educational program of his choice.

History: This award was first presented to the league in 1999-2000 by MBNA Corporation. It is named for Roger Crozier, one of the NHL's top goaltenders during his career. Crozier joined MBNA America Bank in 1983. He passed away on Jan. 11, 1996. Save percentage is calculated by dividing total saves by total shots faced.

2005-06 Winner: **Cristobal Huet, Montreal Canadiens**
Runner-up: **Dominik Hasek, Ottawa Senators**

Cristobal Huet of the Montreal Canadiens won the MBNA Roger Crozier Saving Grace Award by compiling a .929 save percentage (1,085 shots, 1,008 saves) in 36 games. Huet edged Dominik Hasek of the Ottawa Senators, who finished with a .925 save percentage (1,202 shots, 1,112 saves) in 43 appearances. Miikka Kiprusoff of Calgary finished third with a save percentage of .923 (1,951 shots, 1,800 saves) in 74 games. In his first year with the Canadiens, Huet took over the number-one goaltending position and posted a career-best 2.20 goals-against average, which ranked fourth in the NHL behind Kiprusoff (2.07), Hasek (2.09) and Detroit's Manny Legace (2.19). Huets seven shutouts tied him with Legace for second in the NHL behind Kiprusoff's 10.

NHL/SHERATON ROAD PERFORMER AWARD

An award "to the players who accumulate the most road points." The player with the most road points at the end of each month is recognized as the monthly winner. At season's end, the player who accrues the most road points during the regular season wins year-end honors. Sheraton will donate one million Starpoints® to the charity of the player's choice. Points can be used for travel expenses including hotel stays, airline tickets and more.

History: This award was introduced for the 2003-04 season by the NHL and Sheraton Hotels & Resorts Worldwide, Inc

2005-06 Winner: **Jaromir Jagr, New York Rangers**
Runners-up: **Joe Thornton, Boston Bruins/San Jose Sharks**
Ilya Kovalchuk, Atlanta

New York Rangers right winger Jaromir Jagr, with 64 points (31 goals, 33 assists) in 41 road games, captured the NHL/Sheraton Hotels Road Performer Award. Jagr finished 10 points ahead of runner-up Joe Thornton of the San Jose Sharks (9 goals, 45 assists in 38 road games). Ilya Kovalchuk of the Atlanta Thrashers finished third with 53 points (27 goals, 26 assists) in 38 games played. Jagr's 31 goals also topped all road performers, with Washington Capitals rookie Alex Ovechkin finishing next with 28. Kovalchuk and New Jersey's Brian Gionta each had 27 goals on the road. Jagr receives a Sheraton Sweet Sleeper Bed™ and Sheraton Hotels & Resorts donated a million Starpoints to charity on his behalf.

BUD LIGHT NHL ALL-STAR GAME MVP AWARD

1962	Eddie Shack, Tor.	1976	Pete Mahovlich, Mtl.
1963	Frank Mahovlich, Tor.	1977	Rick Martin, Buf.
1964	Jean Beliveau, Mtl.	1978	Billy Smith, NYI
1965	Gordie Howe, Det.	1980	Reggie Leach, Phi.
1967	Henri Richard, Mtl.	1981	Mike Liut, St.L.
1968	Bruce Gamble, Tor.	1982	Mike Bossy, NYI
1969	Frank Mahovlich, Det.	1983	Wayne Gretzky, Edm.
1970	Bobby Hull, Chi.	1984	Don Maloney, NYR
1971	Bobby Hull, Chi.	1985	Mario Lemieux, Pit.
1972	Bobby Orr, Bos.	1986	Grant Fuhr, Edm.
1973	Greg Polis, Pit.	1988	Mario Lemieux, Pit.
1974	Garry Unger, St.L.	1989	Wayne Gretzky, L.A.
1975	Syl Apps Jr., Pit.	1990	Mario Lemieux, Pit.

1991	Vincent Damphousse, Tor.
1992	Brett Hull, St.L.
1993	Mike Gartner, NYR
1994	Mike Richter, NYR
1996	Raymond Bourque, Bos.
1997	Mark Recchi, Mtl.
1998	Teemu Selanne, Ana.
1999	Wayne Gretzky, NYR
2000	Pavel Bure, Fla.
2001	Bill Guerin, Bos.
2002	Eric Daze, Chi.
2003	Dany Heatley, Atl.
2004	Joe Sakic, Col.

2005-06
NHL Player of the Week/Month Award Winners

Player of the Week/Month

Period Ending	Offensive Player	Defensive Player
Oct. 9	Marc Savard, Atlanta	Roberto Luongo, Florida
Oct. 16	Steve Sullivan, Nashville	Bryan McCabe, Toronto
Oct. 23	Craig Conroy, Los Angeles	Manny Legace, Detroit
Oct. 30	Eric Staal, Carolina	Henrik Lundqvist, NY Rangers
October	**Eric Staal, Carolina**	**Manny Legace, Detroit**
Nov. 6	Daniel Alfredsson, Ottawa	Miikka Kiprusoff, Calgary
Nov. 13	Ilya Kovalchuk, Atlanta	Marty Turco, Dallas
Nov. 20	Bryan McCabe, Toronto	Curtis Sanford, St. Louis
Nov. 27	Jason Spezza, Ottawa	Mike Morrison, Edmonton
November	**Daniel Alfredsson, Ottawa**	**Marty Turco, Dallas**
Dec. 4	Patrick Marleau, San Jose	Tomas Vokoun, Nashville
Dec. 11	Joe Thornton, San Jose	Miikka Kiprusoff, Calgary
Dec. 18	Brendan Shanahan, Detroit	Roberto Luongo, Florida
Dec. 25	Marian Hossa, Atlanta	Ryan Miller, Buffalo
December	**Jaromir Jagr, NY Rangers**	**Mathieu Garon, Los Angeles**
Jan. 1	Alex Ovechkin, Washington	Manny Fernandez, Minnesota
Jan. 8	Ilya Kovalchuk, Atlanta	Antero Niittymaki, Philadelphia
		David Aebischer, Colorado
Jan. 15	Eric Staal, Carolina	Martin Brodeur, New Jersey
Jan. 22	Alex Ovechkin, Washington	Henrik Lundqvist, NY Rangers
Jan. 29	David Vyborny, Columbus	Marty Turco, Dallas
January	**Alex Ovechkin, Washington**	**Martin Brodeur, New Jersey**
Feb. 5	Henrik Sedin, Vancouver	Ryan Miller, Buffalo
Feb. 12	Patrick Marleau, San Jose	Manny Legace, Detroit
February	**No Players of the Month named for February due to Olympic Break**	
Mar. 5	Eric Staal, Carolina	Cristobal Huet, Montreal
Mar. 12	Olli Jokinen, Florida	Rick DiPietro, NY Islanders
Mar. 19	Michael Nylander, NY Rangers	Tomas Vokoun, Nashville
Mar. 26	Teemu Selanne, Anaheim	Vesa Toskala, San Jose
March	**Jaromir Jagr, NY Rangers**	**Ray Emery, Ottawa**
Apr. 2	Steve Reinprecht, Phoenix	Cristobal Huet, Montreal
Apr. 9	Scott Gomez, New Jersey	Vesa Toskala, San Jose
Apr. 16	Joe Thornton, San Jose	Miikka Kiprusoff, Calgary
		Jonathan Cheechoo, San Jose

Rookie of the Month

Month	Player
October	**Sidney Crosby, Pittsburgh**
November	**Dion Phaneuf, Calgary**
December	**Alex Ovechkin, Washington**
January	**Alex Ovechkin, Washington**
March	**Ray Emery, Ottawa**

NATIONAL HOCKEY LEAGUE INDIVIDUAL AWARD WINNERS

ART ROSS TROPHY

	Winner	Runner-up
2006	Joe Thornton, Bos., S.J.	Jaromir Jagr, NYR
2005	....	....
2004	Martin St. Louis, T.B.	Ilya Kovalchuk, Atl.
2003	Peter Forsberg, Col.	Markus Naslund, Van.
2002	Jarome Iginla, Cgy.	Markus Naslund, Van.
2001	Jaromir Jagr, Pit.	Joe Sakic, Col.
2000	Jaromir Jagr, Pit.	Pavel Bure, Fla.
1999	Jaromir Jagr, Pit.	Teemu Selanne, Ana.
1998	Jaromir Jagr, Pit.	Peter Forsberg, Col.
1997	Mario Lemieux, Pit.	Teemu Selanne, Ana.
1996	Mario Lemieux, Pit.	Jaromir Jagr, Pit.
1995	Jaromir Jagr, Pit.	Eric Lindros, Phi.
1994	Wayne Gretzky, L.A.	Sergei Fedorov, Det.
1993	Mario Lemieux, Pit.	Pat LaFontaine, Buf.
1992	Mario Lemieux, Pit.	Kevin Stevens, Pit.
1991	Wayne Gretzky, L.A.	Brett Hull, St.L.
1990	Wayne Gretzky, L.A.	Mark Messier, Edm.
1989	Mario Lemieux, Pit.	Wayne Gretzky, L.A.
1988	Mario Lemieux, Pit.	Wayne Gretzky, Edm.
1987	Wayne Gretzky, Edm.	Jari Kurri, Edm.
1986	Wayne Gretzky, Edm.	Mario Lemieux, Pit.
1985	Wayne Gretzky, Edm.	Jari Kurri, Edm.
1984	Wayne Gretzky, Edm.	Paul Coffey, Edm.
1983	Wayne Gretzky, Edm.	Peter Stastny, Que.
1982	Wayne Gretzky, Edm.	Mike Bossy, NYI
1981	Wayne Gretzky, Edm.	Marcel Dionne, L.A.
1980	Marcel Dionne, L.A.	Wayne Gretzky, Edm.
1979	Bryan Trottier, NYI	Marcel Dionne, L.A.
1978	Guy Lafleur, Mtl.	Bryan Trottier, NYI
1977	Guy Lafleur, Mtl.	Marcel Dionne, L.A.
1976	Guy Lafleur, Mtl.	Bobby Clarke, Phi.
1975	Bobby Orr, Bos.	Phil Esposito, Bos.
1974	Phil Esposito, Bos.	Bobby Orr, Bos.
1973	Phil Esposito, Bos.	Bobby Clarke, Phi.
1972	Phil Esposito, Bos.	Bobby Orr, Bos.
1971	Phil Esposito, Bos.	Bobby Orr, Bos.
1970	Bobby Orr, Bos.	Phil Esposito, Bos.
1969	Phil Esposito, Bos.	Bobby Hull, Chi.
1968	Stan Mikita, Chi.	Phil Esposito, Bos.
1967	Stan Mikita, Chi.	Bobby Hull, Chi.
1966	Bobby Hull, Chi.	Stan Mikita, Chi.
1965	Stan Mikita, Chi.	Norm Ullman, Det.
1964	Stan Mikita, Chi.	Bobby Hull, Chi.
1963	Gordie Howe, Det.	Andy Bathgate, NYR
1962	Bobby Hull, Chi.	Andy Bathgate, NYR
1961	Bernie Geoffrion, Mtl.	Jean Beliveau, Mtl.
1960	Bobby Hull, Chi.	Bronco Horvath, Bos.
1959	Dickie Moore, Mtl.	Jean Beliveau, Mtl.
1958	Dickie Moore, Mtl.	Henri Richard, Mtl.
1957	Gordie Howe, Det.	Ted Lindsay, Det.
1956	Jean Beliveau, Mtl.	Gordie Howe, Det.
1955	Bernie Geoffrion, Mtl.	Maurice Richard, Mtl.
1954	Gordie Howe, Det.	Maurice Richard, Mtl.
1953	Gordie Howe, Det.	Ted Lindsay, Det.
1952	Gordie Howe, Det.	Ted Lindsay, Det.
1951	Gordie Howe, Det.	Maurice Richard, Mtl.
1950	Ted Lindsay, Det.	Sid Abel, Det.
1949	Roy Conacher, Chi.	Doug Bentley, Chi.
1948*	Elmer Lach, Mtl.	Buddy O'Connor, NYR
1947	Max Bentley, Chi.	Maurice Richard, Mtl.
1946	Max Bentley, Chi.	Gaye Stewart, Tor.
1945	Elmer Lach, Mtl.	Maurice Richard, Mtl.
1944	Herb Cain, Bos.	Doug Bentley, Chi.
1943	Doug Bentley, Chi.	Bill Cowley, Bos.
1942	Bryan Hextall, NYR	Lynn Patrick, NYR
1941	Bill Cowley, Bos.	Bryan Hextall, NYR
1940	Milt Schmidt, Bos.	Woody Dumart, Bos.
1939	Toe Blake, Mtl.	Sweeney Schriner, NYA
1938	Gordie Drillon, Tor.	Syl Apps, Tor.
1937	Sweeney Schriner, NYA	Syl Apps, Tor.
1936	Sweeney Schriner, NYA	Marty Barry, Det.
1935	Charlie Conacher, Tor.	Syd Howe, St.L., Det.
1934	Charlie Conacher, Tor.	Joe Primeau, Tor
1933	Bill Cook, NYR	Busher Jackson, Tor.
1932	Busher Jackson, Tor.	Joe Primeau, Tor.
1931	Howie Morenz, Mtl.	Ebbie Goodfellow, Det.
1930	Cooney Weiland, Bos.	Frank Boucher, NYR
1929	Ace Bailey, Tor.	Nels Stewart, Mtl.M
1928	Howie Morenz, Mtl.	Aurel Joliat, Mtl.
1927	Bill Cook, NYR	Dick Irvin, Chi.
1926	Nels Stewart, Mtl.M.	Cy Denneny, Ott.
1925	Babe Dye, Tor.	Cy Denneny, Ott.
1924	Cy Denneny, Ott.	Billy Boucher, Mtl.
1923	Babe Dye, Tor.	Cy Denneny, Ott.
1922	Punch Broadbent, Ott.	Cy Denneny, Ott.
1921	Newsy Lalonde, Mtl.	Babe Dye, Ham., Tor.
1920	Joe Malone, Que.	Newsy Lalonde, Mtl.
1919	Newsy Lalonde, Mtl.	Odie Cleghorn, Mtl.
1918	Joe Malone, Mtl.	Cy Denneny, Ott.

* Trophy first awarded in 1948.
Scoring leaders listed from 1918 to 1947.

NHL/SHERATON ROAD PERFORMER AWARD

2006	Jaromir Jagr	NY Rangers
2005	....	....
2004	Joe Sakic	Colorado

HART MEMORIAL TROPHY

	Winner	Runner-up
2006	Joe Thornton, Bos., S.J.	Jaromir Jagr, NYR
2005	....	....
2004	Martin St. Louis, T.B.	Jarome Iginla, Cgy.
2003	Peter Forsberg, Col.	Markus Naslund, Van.
2002	Jose Theodore, Mtl.	Jarome Iginla, Cgy.
2001	Joe Sakic, Col.	Mario Lemieux, Pit.
2000	Chris Pronger, St.L.	Jaromir Jagr, Pit.
1999	Jaromir Jagr, Pit.	Alexei Yashin, Ott.
1998	Dominik Hasek, Buf.	Jaromir Jagr, Pit.
1997	Dominik Hasek, Buf.	Paul Kariya, Ana.
1996	Mario Lemieux, Pit.	Mark Messier, NYR
1995	Eric Lindros, Phi.	Jaromir Jagr, Pit.
1994	Sergei Fedorov, Det.	Dominik Hasek, Buf.
1993	Mario Lemieux, Pit.	Doug Gilmour, Tor.
1992	Mark Messier, NYR	Patrick Roy, Mtl.
1991	Brett Hull, St.L.	Wayne Gretzky, L.A.
1990	Mark Messier, Edm.	Raymond Bourque, Bos.
1989	Wayne Gretzky, L.A.	Mario Lemieux, Pit.
1988	Mario Lemieux, Pit.	Grant Fuhr, Edm.
1987	Wayne Gretzky, Edm.	Raymond Bourque, Bos.
1986	Wayne Gretzky, Edm.	Mario Lemieux, Pit.
1985	Wayne Gretzky, Edm.	Dale Hawerchuk, Wpg.
1984	Wayne Gretzky, Edm.	Rod Langway, Wsh.
1983	Wayne Gretzky, Edm.	Pete Peeters, Bos.
1982	Wayne Gretzky, Edm.	Bryan Trottier, NYI
1981	Wayne Gretzky, Edm.	Mike Liut, St.L.
1980	Wayne Gretzky, Edm.	Marcel Dionne, L.A.
1979	Bryan Trottier, NYI	Guy Lafleur, Mtl
1978	Guy Lafleur, Mtl.	Bryan Trottier, NYI
1977	Guy Lafleur, Mtl.	Bobby Clarke, Phi.
1976	Bobby Clarke, Phi.	Denis Potvin, NYI
1975	Bobby Clarke, Phi.	Rogie Vachon, L.A.
1974	Phil Esposito, Bos.	Bernie Parent, Phi.
1973	Bobby Clarke, Phi.	Phil Esposito, Bos.
1972	Bobby Orr, Bos.	Ken Dryden, Mtl.
1971	Bobby Orr, Bos.	Phil Esposito, Bos.
1970	Bobby Orr, Bos.	Tony Esposito, Chi.
1969	Phil Esposito, Bos.	Jean Beliveau, Mtl.
1968	Stan Mikita, Chi.	Jean Beliveau, Mtl.
1967	Stan Mikita, Chi.	Ed Giacomin, NYR
1966	Bobby Hull, Chi.	Jean Beliveau, Mtl.
1965	Bobby Hull, Chi.	Norm Ullman, Det.
1964	Jean Beliveau, Mtl.	Bobby Hull, Chi.
1963	Gordie Howe, Det.	Stan Mikita, Chi.
1962	Jacques Plante, Mtl.	Doug Harvey, NYR
1961	Bernie Geoffrion, Mtl.	Johnny Bower, Tor.
1960	Gordie Howe, Det.	Bobby Hull, Chi.
1959	Andy Bathgate, NYR	Gordie Howe, Det.
1958	Gordie Howe, Det.	Andy Bathgate, NYR
1957	Gordie Howe, Det.	Jean Beliveau, Mtl.
1956	Jean Beliveau, Mtl.	Tod Sloan, Tor.
1955	Ted Kennedy, Tor.	Harry Lumley, Tor.
1954	Al Rollins, Chi.	Red Kelly, Det.
1953	Gordie Howe, Det.	Al Rollins, Chi.
1952	Gordie Howe, Det.	Elmer Lach, Mtl.
1951	Milt Schmidt, Bos.	Maurice Richard, Mtl.
1950	Chuck Rayner, NYR	Ted Kennedy, Tor.
1949	Sid Abel, Det.	Bill Durnan, Mtl.
1948	Buddy O'Connor, NYR	Frank Brimsek, Bos.
1947	Maurice Richard, Mtl.	Milt Schmidt, Bos.
1946	Max Bentley, Chi.	Gaye Stewart, Tor.
1945	Elmer Lach, Mtl.	Maurice Richard, Mtl.
1944	Babe Pratt, Tor.	Bill Cowley, Bos.
1943	Bill Cowley, Bos.	Doug Bentley, Chi.
1942	Tom Anderson, Bro.	Syl Apps, Tor.
1941	Bill Cowley, Bos.	Dit Clapper, Bos.
1940	Ebbie Goodfellow, Det.	Syl Apps, Tor.
1939	Toe Blake, Mtl.	Syl Apps, Tor.
1938	Eddie Shore, Bos.	Paul Thompson, Chi.
1937	Babe Siebert, Mtl.	Lionel Conacher, Mtl.M
1936	Eddie Shore, Bos.	Hooley Smith, Mtl.M
1935	Eddie Shore, Bos.	Charlie Conacher, Tor.
1934	Aurel Joliat, Mtl.	Lionel Conacher, Chi.
1933	Eddie Shore, Bos.	Bill Cook, NYR
1932	Howie Morenz, Mtl.	Ching Johnson, NYR
1931	Howie Morenz, Mtl.	Eddie Shore, Bos.
1930	Nels Stewart, Mtl.M.	Lionel Hitchman, Bos.
1929	Roy Worters, NYA	Ace Bailey, Tor.
1928	Howie Morenz, Mtl.	Roy Worters, Pit.
1927	Herb Gardiner, Mtl.	Bill Cook, NYR
1926	Nels Stewart, Mtl.M.	Sprague Cleghorn, Bos.
1925	Billy Burch, Ham.	Howie Morenz, Mtl.
1924	Frank Nighbor, Ott.	Sprague Cleghorn, Mtl.

BUD LIGHT PLUS-MINUS AWARD

2006	Wade Redden	Ottawa
	Michal Roszival	NY Rangers
2005	....	....
2004	Marek Malik	Vancouver
	Martin St. Louis	Tampa Bay
2003	Peter Forsberg	Colorado
	Milan Hejduk	Colorado
2002	Chris Chelios	Detroit
2001	Patrik Elias	New Jersey
	Joe Sakic	Colorado
2000	Chris Pronger	St. Louis
1999	John LeClair	Philadelphia
1998	Chris Pronger	St. Louis
1997	John LeClair	Philadelphia

WILLIAM M. JENNINGS TROPHY

	Winner	Runner-up
2006	Miikka Kiprusoff, Cgy.	Manny Legace, Det.
		Chris Osgood, Det.
2005	....	....
2004	Martin Brodeur, N.J.	Marty Turco, Dal.
2003	Martin Brodeur, N.J.	Marty Turco, Dal.
	Roman Cechmanek, Phi.	Ron Tugnutt, Dal.
	Robert Esche, Phi.	
2002	Patrick Roy, Col.	Tommy Salo, Edm.
2001	Dominik Hasek, Buf.	Ed Belfour, Dal.
		Marty Turco, Dal.
2000	Roman Turek, St.L.	John Vanbiesbrouck, Phi.
		Brian Boucher, Phi.
1999	Ed Belfour, Dal.	Dominik Hasek, Buf.
	Roman Turek, Dal.	
1998	Martin Brodeur, N.J.	Ed Belfour, Dal.
1997	Martin Brodeur, N.J.	Chris Osgood, Det.
	Mike Dunham, N.J.	Mike Vernon, Det.
1996	Chris Osgood, Det.	Martin Brodeur, N.J.
	Mike Vernon, Det.	
1995	Ed Belfour, Chi.	Mike Vernon, Det.
		Chris Osgood, Det.
1994	Dominik Hasek, Buf.	Martin Brodeur, N.J.
	Grant Fuhr, Buf.	Chris Terreri, N.J.
1993	Ed Belfour, Chi.	Felix Potvin, Tor.
		Grant Fuhr, Tor.
1992	Patrick Roy, Mtl.	Ed Belfour, Chi.
1991	Ed Belfour, Chi.	Patrick Roy, Mtl.
1990	Andy Moog, Bos.	Patrick Roy, Mtl.
	Reggie Lemelin, Bos.	Brian Hayward, Mtl.
1989	Patrick Roy, Mtl.	Mike Vernon, Cgy.
	Brian Hayward, Mtl.	Rick Wamsley, Cgy.
1988	Patrick Roy, Mtl.	Clint Malarchuk, Wsh.
	Brian Hayward, Mtl.	Pete Peeters, Wsh.
1987	Patrick Roy, Mtl.	Ron Hextall, Phi.
	Brian Hayward, Mtl.	
1986	Bob Froese, Phi.	Al Jensen, Wsh.
	Darren Jensen, Phi.	Pete Peeters, Wsh.
1985	Tom Barrasso, Buf.	Pat Riggin, Wsh.
	Bob Sauve, Buf.	
1984	Al Jensen, Wsh.	Tom Barrasso, Buf.
	Pat Riggin, Wsh.	Bob Sauve, Buf.
1983	Roland Melanson, NYI	Pete Peeters, Bos.
	Billy Smith, NYI	
1982	Rick Wamsley, Mtl.	Billy Smith, NYI
	Denis Herron, Mtl.	Roland Melanson, NYI

BILL MASTERTON MEMORIAL TROPHY

2006	Teemu Selanne	Anaheim
2005	....	....
2004	Bryan Berard	Chicago
2003	Steve Yzerman	Detroit
2002	Saku Koivu	Montreal
2001	Adam Graves	NY Rangers
2000	Ken Daneyko	New Jersey
1999	John Cullen	Tampa Bay
1998	Jamie McLennan	St. Louis
1997	Tony Granato	San Jose
1996	Gary Roberts	Calgary
1995	Pat LaFontaine	Buffalo
1994	Cam Neely	Boston
1993	Mario Lemieux	Pittsburgh
1992	Mark Fitzpatrick	NY Islanders
1991	Dave Taylor	Los Angeles
1990	Gord Kluzak	Boston
1989	Tim Kerr	Philadelphia
1988	Bob Bourne	Los Angeles
1987	Doug Jarvis	Hartford
1986	Charlie Simmer	Boston
1985	Anders Hedberg	NY Rangers
1984	Brad Park	Detroit
1983	Lanny McDonald	Calgary
1982	Glenn Resch	Colorado
1981	Blake Dunlop	St. Louis
1980	Al MacAdam	Minnesota
1979	Serge Savard	Montreal
1978	Butch Goring	Los Angeles
1977	Ed Westfall	NY Islanders
1976	Rod Gilbert	NY Rangers
1975	Don Luce	Buffalo
1974	Henri Richard	Montreal
1973	Lowell MacDonald	Pittsburgh
1972	Bobby Clarke	Philadelphia
1971	Jean Ratelle	NY Rangers
1970	Pit Martin	Chicago
1969	Ted Hampson	Oakland
1968	Claude Provost	Montreal

MAURICE "ROCKET" RICHARD TROPHY

2006	Jonathan Cheechoo	San Jose
2005	....	....
2004	Rick Nash	Columbus
	Jarome Iginla	Calgary
	Ilya Kovalchuk	Atlanta
2003	Milan Hejduk	Colorado
2002	Jarome Iginla	Calgary
2001	Pavel Bure	Florida
2000	Pavel Bure	Florida
1999	Teemu Selanne	Anaheim

LADY BYNG MEMORIAL TROPHY

	Winner	Runner-up
2006	Pavel Datsyuk, Det.	Brad Richards, T.B.
2005	....	....
2004	Brad Richards, T.B.	Daniel Alfredsson, Ott.
2003	Alexander Mogilny, Tor.	Nicklas Lidstrom, Det.
2002	Ron Francis, Car.	Joe Sakic, Col.
2001	Joe Sakic, Col.	Nicklas Lidstrom, Det.
2000	Pavol Demitra, St.L.	Nicklas Lidstrom, Det.
1999	Wayne Gretzky, NYR.	Nicklas Lidstrom, Det.
1998	Ron Francis, Pit.	Teemu Selanne, Ana.
1997	Paul Kariya, Ana.	Teemu Selanne, Ana.
1996	Paul Kariya, Ana.	Adam Oates, Bos.
1995	Ron Francis, Pit.	Adam Oates, Bos.
1994	Wayne Gretzky, L.A.	Adam Oates, Bos.
1993	Pierre Turgeon, NYI	Adam Oates, Bos.
1992	Wayne Gretzky, L.A.	Joe Sakic, Que.
1991	Wayne Gretzky, L.A.	Brett Hull, St.L.
1990	Brett Hull, St.L.	Wayne Gretzky, L.A.
1989	Joe Mullen, Cgy.	Wayne Gretzky, L.A.
1988	Mats Naslund, Mtl.	Wayne Gretzky, Edm.
1987	Joe Mullen, Cgy.	Wayne Gretzky, Edm.
1986	Mike Bossy, NYI	Jari Kurri, Edm.
1985	Jari Kurri, Edm.	Joe Mullen, St.L.
1984	Mike Bossy, NYI	Rick Middleton, Bos.
1983	Mike Bossy, NYI	Rick Middleton, Bos.
1982	Rick Middleton, Bos.	Mike Bossy, NYI
1981	Rick Kehoe, Pit.	Wayne Gretzky, Edm.
1980	Wayne Gretzky, Edm.	Marcel Dionne, L.A.
1979	Bob MacMillan, Atl.	Marcel Dionne, L.A.
1978	Butch Goring, L.A.	Peter McNab, Bos.
1977	Marcel Dionne, L.A.	Jean Ratelle, Bos.
1976	Jean Ratelle, NYR-Bos.	Jean Pronovost, Pit.
1975	Marcel Dionne, Det.	John Bucyk, Bos.
1974	John Bucyk, Bos.	Lowell MacDonald, Pit.
1973	Gilbert Perreault, Buf.	Jean Ratelle, NYR
1972	Jean Ratelle, NYR	John Bucyk, Bos.
1971	John Bucyk, Bos.	Dave Keon, Tor.
1970	Phil Goyette, St.L.	John Bucyk, Bos.
1969	Alex Delvecchio, Det.	Ted Hampson, Oak.
1968	Stan Mikita, Chi.	John Bucyk, Bos.
1967	Stan Mikita, Chi.	Dave Keon, Tor.
1966	Alex Delvecchio, Det.	Bobby Rousseau, Mtl.
1965	Bobby Hull, Chi.	Alex Delvecchio, Det.
1964	Kenny Wharram, Chi.	Dave Keon, Tor.
1963	Dave Keon, Tor.	Camille Henry, NYR
1962	Dave Keon, Tor.	Claude Provost, Mtl.
1961	Red Kelly, Tor.	Norm Ullman, Det.
1960	Don McKenney, Bos.	Andy Hebenton, NYR
1959	Alex Delvecchio, Det.	Andy Hebenton, NYR
1958	Camille Henry, NYR	Don Marshall, Mtl.
1957	Andy Hebenton, NYR	Dutch Reibel, Det.
1956	Dutch Reibel, Det.	Floyd Curry, Mtl.
1955	Sid Smith, Tor.	Danny Lewicki, NYR
1954	Red Kelly, Det.	Don Raleigh, NYR
1953	Red Kelly, Det.	Wally Hergesheimer, NYR
1952	Sid Smith, Tor.	Red Kelly, Det.
1951	Red Kelly, Det.	Woody Dumart, Bos.
1950	Edgar Laprade, NYR	Red Kelly, Det.
1949	Bill Quackenbush, Det.	Harry Watson, Tor.
1948	Buddy O'Connor, NYR	Syl Apps, Tor.
1947	Bobby Bauer, Bos.	Syl Apps, Tor.
1946	Toe Blake, Mtl.	Clint Smith, Chi.
1945	Bill Mosienko, Chi.	Syd Howe, Det.
1944	Clint Smith, Chi.	Herb Cain, Bos.
1943	Max Bentley, Chi.	Buddy O'Connor, Mtl.
1942	Syl Apps, Tor.	Gordie Drillon, Tor.
1941	Bobby Bauer, Bos.	Gordie Drillon, Tor.
1940	Bobby Bauer, Bos.	Clint Smith, NYR
1939	Clint Smith, NYR	Marty Barry, Det.
1938	Gordie Drillon, Tor.	Clint Smith, NYR
1937	Marty Barry, Det.	Gordie Drillon, Tor.
1936	Doc Romnes, Chi.	Sweeney Schriner, NYA
1935	Frank Boucher, NYR	Russ Blinco, Mtl.M
1934	Frank Boucher, NYR	Joe Primeau, Tor.
1933	Frank Boucher, NYR	Joe Primeau, Tor.
1932	Joe Primeau, Tor.	Frank Boucher, NYR
1931	Frank Boucher, NYR	Normie Himes, NYA
1930	Frank Boucher, NYR	Normie Himes, NYA
1929	Frank Boucher, NYR	Harold Darragh, Pit.
1928	Frank Boucher, NYR	George Hay, Det.
1927	Billy Burch, NYA	Dick Irvin, Chi.
1926	Frank Nighbor, Ott.	Billy Burch, NYA
1925	Frank Nighbor, Ott.	none

KING CLANCY MEMORIAL TROPHY

2006	Olaf Kolzig	Washington
2005	....	....
2004	Jarome Iginla	Calgary
2003	Brendan Shanahan	Detroit
2002	Ron Francis	Carolina
2001	Shjon Podein	Colorado
2000	Curtis Joseph	Toronto
1999	Rob Ray	Buffalo
1998	Kelly Chase	St. Louis
1997	Trevor Linden	Vancouver
1996	Kris King	Winnipeg
1995	Joe Nieuwendyk	Calgary
1994	Adam Graves	NY Rangers
1993	Dave Poulin	Boston
1992	Raymond Bourque	Boston
1991	Dave Taylor	Los Angeles
1990	Kevin Lowe	Edmonton
1989	Bryan Trottier	NY Islanders
1988	Lanny McDonald	Calgary

VEZINA TROPHY

	Winner	Runner-up
2006	Miikka Kiprusoff, Cgy.	Martin Brodeur, N.J.
2005	....	....
2004	Martin Brodeur, N.J.	Miikka Kiprusoff, Cgy.
2003	Martin Brodeur, N.J.	Marty Turco, Dal.
2002	Jose Theodore, Mtl.	Patrick Roy, Col.
2001	Dominik Hasek, Buf.	Roman Cechmanek, Phi.
2000	Olaf Kolzig, Wsh.	Roman Turek, St.L.
1999	Dominik Hasek, Buf.	Curtis Joseph, Tor.
1998	Dominik Hasek, Buf.	Martin Brodeur, N.J.
1997	Dominik Hasek, Buf.	Martin Brodeur, N.J.
1996	Jim Carey, Wsh.	Chris Osgood, Det.
1995	Dominik Hasek, Buf.	Ed Belfour, Chi.
1994	Dominik Hasek, Buf.	John Vanbiesbrouck, Fla.
1993	Ed Belfour, Chi.	Tom Barrasso, Pit.
1992	Patrick Roy, Mtl.	Kirk McLean, Van.
1991	Ed Belfour, Chi.	Patrick Roy, Mtl.
1990	Patrick Roy, Mtl.	Daren Puppa, Buf.
1989	Patrick Roy, Mtl.	Mike Vernon, Cgy.
1988	Grant Fuhr, Edm.	Tom Barrasso, Buf.
1987	Ron Hextall, Phi.	Mike Liut, Hfd.
1986	John Vanbiesbrouck, NYR	Bob Froese, Phi.
1985	Pelle Lindbergh, Phi.	Tom Barrasso, Buf.
1984	Tom Barrasso, Buf.	Reggie Lemelin, Cgy.
1983	Pete Peeters, Bos.	Roland Melanson, NYI
1982	Billy Smith, NYI	Grant Fuhr, Edm.
1981	Richard Sevigny, Mtl.	Pete Peeters, Phi.
	Denis Herron, Mtl.	Rick St. Croix, Phi.
	Michel Larocque, Mtl.	
1980	Bob Sauve, Buf.	Gerry Cheevers, Bos.
	Don Edwards, Buf.	Gilles Gilbert, Bos.
1979	Ken Dryden, Mtl.	Glenn Resch, NYI
	Michel Larocque, Mtl.	Billy Smith, NYI
1978	Ken Dryden, Mtl.	Bernie Parent, Phi.
	Michel Larocque, Mtl.	Wayne Stephenson, Phi.
1977	Ken Dryden, Mtl.	Glenn Resch, NYI
	Michel Larocque, Mtl.	Billy Smith, NYI
1976	Ken Dryden, Mtl.	Glenn Resch, NYI
		Billy Smith, NYI
1975	Bernie Parent, Phi.	Rogie Vachon, L.A.
		Gary Edwards, L.A.
1974	Bernie Parent, Phi. (tie)	Gilles Gilbert, Bos.
	Tony Esposito, Chi. (tie)	
1973	Ken Dryden, Mtl.	Ed Giacomin, NYR
		Gilles Villemure, NYR
1972	Tony Esposito, Chi.	Cesare Maniago, Min.
	Gary Smith, Chi.	Gump Worsley, Min.
1971	Ed Giacomin, NYR	Tony Esposito, Chi.
	Gilles Villemure, NYR	
1970	Tony Esposito, Chi.	Jacques Plante, St.L.
		Ernie Wakely, St.L.
1969	Jacques Plante, St.L.	Ed Giacomin, NYR
	Glenn Hall, St.L.	
1968	Gump Worsley, Mtl.	Johnny Bower, Tor.
	Rogie Vachon, Mtl.	Bruce Gamble, Tor.
1967	Glenn Hall, Chi.	Charlie Hodge, Mtl.
	Denis DeJordy, Chi.	
1966	Gump Worsley, Mtl.	Glenn Hall, Chi.
	Charlie Hodge, Mtl.	
1965	Terry Sawchuk, Tor.	Roger Crozier, Det.
	Johnny Bower, Tor.	
1964	Charlie Hodge, Mtl.	Glenn Hall, Chi.
1963	Glenn Hall, Chi.	Johnny Bower, Tor.
		Don Simmons, Tor.
1962	Jacques Plante, Mtl.	Johnny Bower, Tor.
1961	Johnny Bower, Tor.	Glenn Hall, Chi.
1960	Jacques Plante, Mtl.	Glenn Hall, Chi.
1959	Jacques Plante, Mtl.	Johnny Bower, Tor.
		Ed Chadwick, Tor.
1958	Jacques Plante, Mtl.	Gump Worsley, NYR
		Marcel Paille, NYR
1957	Jacques Plante, Mtl.	Glenn Hall, Det.
1956	Jacques Plante, Mtl.	Glenn Hall, Det.
1955	Terry Sawchuk, Det.	Harry Lumley, Tor.
1954	Harry Lumley, Tor.	Terry Sawchuk, Det.
1953	Terry Sawchuk, Det.	Gerry McNeil, Mtl.
1952	Terry Sawchuk, Det.	Al Rollins, Tor.
1951	Al Rollins, Tor.	Terry Sawchuk, Det.
1950	Bill Durnan, Mtl.	Harry Lumley, Det.
1949	Bill Durnan, Mtl.	Harry Lumley, Det.
1948	Turk Broda, Tor.	Harry Lumley, Det.
1947	Bill Durnan, Mtl.	Turk Broda, Tor.
1946	Bill Durnan, Mtl.	Frank Brimsek, Bos.
1945	Bill Durnan, Mtl.	Frank McCool, Tor. (tie)
		Harry Lumley, Det. (tie)
1944	Bill Durnan, Mtl.	Paul Bibeault, Tor.
1943	Johnny Mowers, Det.	Turk Broda, Tor.
1942	Frank Brimsek, Bos.	Turk Broda, Tor.
1941	Turk Broda, Tor.	Frank Brimsek, Bos. (tie)
		Johnny Mowers, Det. (tie)
1940	Dave Kerr, NYR	Frank Brimsek, Bos.
1939	Frank Brimsek, Bos.	Dave Kerr, NYR
1938	Tiny Thompson, Bos.	Dave Kerr, NYR
1937	Normie Smith, Det.	Dave Kerr, NYR
1936	Tiny Thompson, Bos.	Mike Karakas, Chi.
1935	Lorne Chabot, Chi.	Alex Connell, Mtl.M
1934	Charlie Gardiner, Chi.	Wilf Cude, Det.
1933	Tiny Thompson, Bos.	John Ross Roach, Det.
1932	Charlie Gardiner, Chi.	Alex Connell, Det.
1931	Roy Worters, NYA	Charlie Gardiner, Chi.
1930	Tiny Thompson, Bos.	Charlie Gardiner, Chi.
1929	George Hainsworth, Mtl.	Tiny Thompson, Bos.
1928	George Hainsworth, Mtl.	Alex Connell, Ott.
1927	George Hainsworth, Mtl.	Clint Benedict, Mtl.M

CALDER MEMORIAL TROPHY

	Winner	Runner-up
2006	Alex Ovechkin, Wsh.	Sidney Crosby, Pit.
2005	....	
2004	Andrew Raycroft, Bos.	Michael Ryder, Mtl.
2003	Barret Jackman, St.L.	Henrik Zetterberg, Det.
2002	Dany Heatley, Atl.	Ilya Kovalchuk, Atl.
2001	Evgeni Nabokov, S.J.	Brad Richards, T.B.
2000	Scott Gomez, N.J.	Brad Stuart, S.J.
1999	Chris Drury, Col.	Marian Hossa, Ott.
1998	Sergei Samsonov, Bos.	Mattias Ohlund, Van.
1997	Bryan Berard, NYI	Jarome Iginla, Cgy.
1996	Daniel Alfredsson, Ott.	Eric Daze, Chi.
1995	Peter Forsberg, Que.	Jim Carey, Wsh.
1994	Martin Brodeur, N.J.	Jason Arnott, Edm.
1993	Teemu Selanne, Wpg.	Joe Juneau, Bos.
1992	Pavel Bure, Van.	Nicklas Lidstrom, Det
1991	Ed Belfour, Chi.	Sergei Fedorov, Det.
1990	Sergei Makarov, Cgy.	Mike Modano, Min.
1989	Brian Leetch, NYR	Trevor Linden, Van.
1988	Joe Nieuwendyk, Cgy.	Ray Sheppard, Buf.
1987	Luc Robitaille, L.A.	Ron Hextall, Phi.
1986	Gary Suter, Cgy.	Wendel Clark, Tor.
1985	Mario Lemieux, Pit.	Chris Chelios, Mtl.
1984	Tom Barrasso, Buf.	Steve Yzerman, Det.
1983	Steve Larmer, Chi.	Phil Housley, Buf.
1982	Dale Hawerchuk, Wpg.	Barry Pederson, Bos.
1981	Peter Stastny, Que.	Larry Murphy, L.A.
1980	Raymond Bourque, Bos.	Mike Foligno, Det.
1979	Bobby Smith, Min	Ryan Walter, Wsh.
1978	Mike Bossy, NYI	Barry Beck, Col.
1977	Willi Plett, Atl.	Don Murdoch, NYR
1976	Bryan Trottier, NYI	Glenn Resch, NYI
1975	Eric Vail, Atl.	Pierre Larouche, Pit.
1974	Denis Potvin, NYI	Tom Lysiak, Atl.
1973	Steve Vickers, NYR	Bill Barber, Phi.
1972	Ken Dryden, Mtl.	Rick Martin, Buf.
1971	Gilbert Perreault, Buf.	Jude Drouin, Min.
1970	Tony Esposito, Chi.	Bill Fairbairn, NYR
1969	Danny Grant, Min.	Norm Ferguson, Oak.
1968	Derek Sanderson, Bos.	Jacques Lemaire, Mtl.
1967	Bobby Orr, Bos.	Ed Van Impe, Chi.
1966	Brit Selby, Tor.	Bert Marshall, Det.
1965	Roger Crozier, Det.	Ron Ellis, Tor.
1964	Jacques Laperriere, Mtl.	John Ferguson, Mtl.
1963	Kent Douglas, Tor.	Doug Barkley, Det.
1962	Bobby Rousseau, Mtl.	Cliff Pennington, Bos.
1961	Dave Keon, Tor.	Bob Nevin, Tor.
1960	Bill Hay, Chi.	Murray Oliver, Det.
1959	Ralph Backstrom, Mtl.	Carl Brewer, Tor.
1958	Frank Mahovlich, Tor.	Bobby Hull, Chi.
1957	Larry Regan, Bos.	Ed Chadwick, Tor.
1956	Glenn Hall, Det.	Andy Hebenton, NYR
1955	Ed Litzenberger, Chi.	Don McKenney, Bos.
1954	Camille Henry, NYR	Dutch Reibel, Det.
1953	Gump Worsley, NYR	Gord Hannigan, Tor.
1952	Bernie Geoffrion, Mtl.	Hy Buller, NYR
1951	Terry Sawchuk, Det.	Al Rollins, Tor.
1950	Jack Gelineau, Bos.	Phil Maloney, Bos.
1949	Pentti Lund, NYR	Allan Stanley, NYR
1948	Jim McFadden, Det.	Pete Babando, Bos.
1947	Howie Meeker, Tor.	Jim Conacher, Det.
1946	Edgar Laprade, NYR	George Gee, Chi.
1945	Frank McCool, Tor.	Ken Smith, Bos.
1944	Gus Bodnar, Tor.	Bill Durnan, Mtl.
1943	Gaye Stewart, Tor.	Glen Harmon, Mtl.
1942	Grant Warwick, NYR	Buddy O'Connor, Mtl.
1941	John Quilty, Mtl.	Johnny Mowers, Det.
1940	Kilby MacDonald, NYR	Wally Stanowski, Tor.
1939	Frank Brimsek, Bos.	Roy Conacher, Bos.
1938	Cully Dahlstrom, Chi.	Murph Chamberlain, Tor.
1937	Syl Apps, Tor.	Gordie Drillon, Tor.
1936	Mike Karakas, Chi.	Bucko McDonald, Det.
1935	Sweeney Schriner, NYA	Bert Connelly, NYR
1934	Russ Blinco, Mtl.M.	none
1933	Carl Voss, Det.	none

FRANK J. SELKE TROPHY

	Winner	Runner-up
2006	Rod Brind'Amour, Car.	Jere Lehtinen, Dal.
2005	....	....
2004	Kris Draper, Det.	John Madden, N.J.
2003	Jere Lehtinen, Dal.	John Madden, N.J.
2002	Michael Peca, NYI	Craig Conroy, Cgy.
2001	John Madden, N.J.	Joe Sakic, Col.
2000	Steve Yzerman, Det.	Michal Handzus, St.L.
1999	Jere Lehtinen, Dal.	Magnus Arvedson, Ott.
1998	Jere Lehtinen, Dal.	Michael Peca, Buf.
1997	Michael Peca, Buf.	Peter Forsberg, Col.
1996	Sergei Fedorov, Det.	Ron Francis, Pit.
1995	Ron Francis, Pit.	Esa Tikkanen, St.L.
1994	Sergei Fedorov, Det.	Doug Gilmour, Tor.
1993	Doug Gilmour, Tor.	Dave Poulin, Bos.
1992	Guy Carbonneau, Mtl.	Sergei Fedorov, Det.
1991	Dirk Graham, Chi.	Esa Tikkanen, Edm.
1990	Rick Meagher, St.L.	Guy Carbonneau, Mtl.
1989	Guy Carbonneau, Mtl.	Esa Tikkanen, Edm.
1988	Guy Carbonneau, Mtl.	Steve Kasper, Bos.
1987	Dave Poulin, Phi.	Guy Carbonneau, Mtl.
1986	Troy Murray, Chi.	Ron Sutter, Phi.
1985	Craig Ramsay, Buf.	Doug Jarvis, Wsh.
1984	Doug Jarvis, Wsh.	Bryan Trottier, NYI
1983	Bobby Clarke, Phi.	Jari Kurri, Edm.
1982	Steve Kasper, Bos.	Bob Gainey, Mtl.
1981	Bob Gainey, Mtl.	Craig Ramsay, Buf.
1980	Bob Gainey, Mtl.	Craig Ramsay, Buf.
1979	Bob Gainey, Mtl.	Don Marcotte, Bos.
1978	Bob Gainey, Mtl.	Craig Ramsay, Buf.

CONN SMYTHE TROPHY

2006	Cam Ward	Carolina
2005	....	....
2004	Brad Richards	Tampa Bay
2003	Jean-Sebastien Giguere	Anaheim
2002	Nicklas Lidstrom	Detroit
2001	Patrick Roy	Colorado
2000	Scott Stevens	New Jersey
1999	Joe Nieuwendyk	Dallas
1998	Steve Yzerman	Detroit
1997	Mike Vernon	Detroit
1996	Joe Sakic	Colorado
1995	Claude Lemieux	New Jersey
1994	Brian Leetch	NY Rangers
1993	Patrick Roy	Montreal
1992	Mario Lemieux	Pittsburgh
1991	Mario Lemieux	Pittsburgh
1990	Bill Ranford	Edmonton
1989	Al MacInnis	Calgary
1988	Wayne Gretzky	Edmonton
1987	Ron Hextall	Philadelphia
1986	Patrick Roy	Montreal
1985	Wayne Gretzky	Edmonton
1984	Mark Messier	Edmonton
1983	Billy Smith	NY Islanders
1982	Mike Bossy	NY Islanders
1981	Butch Goring	NY Islanders
1980	Bryan Trottier	NY Islanders
1979	Bob Gainey	Montreal
1978	Larry Robinson	Montreal
1977	Guy Lafleur	Montreal
1976	Reggie Leach	Philadelphia
1975	Bernie Parent	Philadelphia
1974	Bernie Parent	Philadelphia
1973	Yvan Cournoyer	Montreal
1972	Bobby Orr	Boston
1971	Ken Dryden	Montreal
1970	Bobby Orr	Boston
1969	Serge Savard	Montreal
1968	Glenn Hall	St. Louis
1967	Dave Keon	Toronto
1966	Roger Crozier	Detroit
1965	Jean Beliveau	Montreal

JAMES NORRIS MEMORIAL TROPHY

	Winner	Runner-up
2006	Nicklas Lidstrom, Det.	Scott Niedermayer, Ana.
2005	....	....
2004	Scott Niedermayer, N.J.	Zdeno Chara, Ott.
2003	Nicklas Lidstrom, Det.	Al MacInnis, St.L.
2002	Nicklas Lidstrom, Det.	Chris Chelios, Det.
2001	Nicklas Lidstrom, Det.	Raymond Bourque, Col.
2000	Chris Pronger, St.L.	Nicklas Lidstrom, Det.
1999	Al MacInnis, St.L.	Nicklas Lidstrom, Det.
1998	Rob Blake, L.A.	Nicklas Lidstrom, Det.
1997	Brian Leetch, NYR	V. Konstantinov, Det.
1996	Chris Chelios, Chi.	Raymond Bourque, Bos.
1995	Paul Coffey, Det.	Chris Chelios, Chi.
1994	Raymond Bourque, Bos.	Scott Stevens, N.J.
1993	Chris Chelios, Chi.	Raymond Bourque, Bos.
1992	Brian Leetch, NYR	Raymond Bourque, Bos.
1991	Raymond Bourque, Bos.	Al MacInnis, Cgy.
1990	Raymond Bourque, Bos.	Al MacInnis, Cgy.
1989	Chris Chelios, Mtl	Paul Coffey, Pit.
1988	Raymond Bourque, Bos.	Scott Stevens, Wsh.
1987	Raymond Bourque, Bos.	Mark Howe, Phi.
1986	Paul Coffey, Edm.	Mark Howe, Phi.
1985	Paul Coffey, Edm.	Raymond Bourque, Bos.
1984	Rod Langway, Wsh.	Paul Coffey, Edm.
1983	Rod Langway, Wsh.	Mark Howe, Phi.
1982	Doug Wilson, Chi.	Raymond Bourque, Bos.
1981	Randy Carlyle, Pit.	Denis Potvin, NYI
1980	Larry Robinson, Mtl.	Borje Salming, Tor.
1979	Denis Potvin, NYI	Larry Robinson, Mtl.
1978	Denis Potvin, NYI	Brad Park, Bos.
1977	Larry Robinson, Mtl.	Borje Salming, Tor.
1976	Denis Potvin, NYI	Brad Park, NYR-Bos.
1975	Bobby Orr, Bos.	Denis Potvin, NYI
1974	Bobby Orr, Bos.	Brad Park, NYR
1973	Bobby Orr, Bos.	Guy Lapointe, Mtl.
1972	Bobby Orr, Bos.	Brad Park, NYR
1971	Bobby Orr, Bos.	Brad Park, NYR
1970	Bobby Orr, Bos.	Brad Park, NYR
1969	Bobby Orr, Bos.	Tim Horton, Tor.
1968	Bobby Orr, Bos.	J.C. Tremblay, Mtl
1967	Harry Howell, NYR	Pierre Pilote, Chi.
1966	Jacques Laperriere, Mtl.	Pierre Pilote, Chi.
1965	Pierre Pilote, Chi.	Jacques Laperriere, Mtl.
1964	Pierre Pilote, Chi.	Tim Horton, Tor.
1963	Pierre Pilote, Chi.	Carl Brewer, Tor.
1962	Doug Harvey, NYR	Pierre Pilote, Chi.
1961	Doug Harvey, Mtl.	Marcel Pronovost, Det.
1960	Doug Harvey, Mtl.	Allan Stanley, Tor.
1959	Tom Johnson, Mtl.	Bill Gadsby, NYR
1958	Doug Harvey, Mtl.	Bill Gadsby, NYR
1957	Doug Harvey, Mtl.	Red Kelly, Det.
1956	Doug Harvey, Mtl.	Bill Gadsby, NYR
1955	Doug Harvey, Mtl.	Red Kelly, Det.
1954	Red Kelly, Det.	Doug Harvey, Mtl.

MBNA ROGER CROZIER SAVING GRACE AWARD

	Winner	Runner-up
2006	Cristobal Huet, Mtl.	Dominik Hasek, Ott.
2005	....	....
2004	Dwayne Roloson, Min.	Miikka Kiprusoff, Cgy.
2003	Marty Turco, Dal.	Dwayne Roloson, Min.
2002	Jose Theodore, Mtl.	Patrick Roy, Col.
2001	Marty Turco, Dal.	Mike Dunham, N.J.
2000	Ed Belfour, Dal.	Jose Theodore, Mtl.

LESTER PATRICK TROPHY

2006	To be announced
2005	....
2004	Mike Emrick
	John Davidson
	Ray Miron
2003	Raymond Bourque
	Ron DeGregorio
	Willie O'Ree
2002	1960 U.S. Olympic Hockey Team
	Herb Brooks
	Larry Pleau
2001	Scotty Bowman
	David Poile
	Gary Bettman
2000	Mario Lemieux
	Craig Patrick
	Lou Vairo
1999	Harry Sinden
	1998 U.S. Olympic Women's Hockey Team
1998	Peter Karmanos
	Neal Broten
	John Mayasich
	Max McNab
1997	*Seymour H. Knox III
	Bill Cleary
	Pat LaFontaine
1996	George Gund
	Ken Morrow
	Milt Schmidt
1995	Joe Mullen
	Brian Mullen
	Bob Fleming
1994	Wayne Gretzky
	Robert Ridder
1993	*Frank Boucher
	*Mervyn "Red" Dutton
	Bruce McNall
	Gil Stein
1992	Al Arbour
	Art Berglund
	Lou Lamoriello
1991	Rod Gilbert
	Mike Ilitch
1990	Len Ceglarski
1989	Dan Kelly
	Lou Nanne
	*Lynn Patrick
	Bud Poile
1988	Keith Allen
	Fred Cusick
	Bob Johnson
1987	*Hobey Baker
	Frank Mathers
1986	John MacInnes
	Jack Riley
1985	Jack Butterfield
	Arthur M. Wirtz
1984	John A. Ziegler, Jr.
	*Arthur Howie Ross
1983	Bill Torrey
1982	Emile P. Francis
1981	Charles M. Schulz
1980	Bobby Clarke
	Edward M. Snider
	Frederick A. Shero
	1980 U.S. Olympic Hockey Team
1979	Bobby Orr
1978	Phil Esposito
	Tom Fitzgerald
	William T. Tutt
	William W. Wirtz
1977	John P. Bucyk
	Murray A. Armstrong
	John Mariucci
1976	Stanley Mikita
	George A. Leader
	Bruce A. Norris
1975	Donald M. Clark
	William L. Chadwick
	Thomas N. Ivan
1974	Alex Delvecchio
	Murray Murdoch
	*Weston W. Adams, Sr.
	*Charles L. Crovat
1973	Walter L. Bush, Jr.
1972	Clarence S. Campbell
	John A. "Snooks" Kelly
	Ralph "Cooney" Weiland
	*James D. Norris
1971	William M. Jennings
	*John B. Sollenberger
	*Terrance G. Sawchuk
1970	Edward W. Shore
	*James C. V. Hendy
1969	Robert M. Hull
	*Edward J. Jeremiah
1968	Thomas F. Lockhart
	*Walter A. Brown
	*Gen. John R. Kilpatrick
1967	Gordon Howe
	*Charles F. Adams
	*James Norris, Sr.
1966	J.J. "Jack" Adams

* awarded posthumously

PRESIDENTS' TROPHY

	Winner	Runner-up
2006	Detroit Red Wings	Ottawa Senators
2005	....	
2004	Detroit Red Wings	Tampa Bay Lightning
2003	Ottawa Senators	Dallas Stars
2002	Detroit Red Wings	Boston Bruins
2001	Colorado Avalanche	Detroit Red Wings
2000	St. Louis Blues	Detroit Red Wings
1999	Dallas Stars	New Jersey Devils
1998	Dallas Stars	New Jersey Devils
1997	Colorado Avalanche	Dallas Stars
1996	Detroit Red Wings	Colorado Avalanche
1995	Detroit Red Wings	Quebec Nordiques
1994	New York Rangers	New Jersey Devils
1993	Pittsburgh Penguins	Boston Bruins
1992	New York Rangers	Washington Capitals
1991	Chicago Blackhawks	St. Louis Blues
1990	Boston Bruins	Calgary Flames
1989	Calgary Flames	Montreal Canadiens
1988	Calgary Flames	Montreal Canadiens
1987	Edmonton Oilers	Philadelphia Flyers
1986	Edmonton Oilers	Philadelphia Flyers

LESTER B. PEARSON AWARD

2006	Jaromir Jagr	NY Rangers
2005	....	
2004	Martin St. Louis	Tampa Bay
2003	Markus Naslund	Vancouver
2002	Jarome Iginla	Calgary
2001	Joe Sakic	Colorado
2000	Jaromir Jagr	Pittsburgh
1999	Jaromir Jagr	Pittsburgh
1998	Dominik Hasek	Buffalo
1997	Dominik Hasek	Buffalo
1996	Mario Lemieux	Pittsburgh
1995	Eric Lindros	Philadelphia
1994	Sergei Fedorov	Detroit
1993	Mario Lemieux	Pittsburgh
1992	Mark Messier	NY Rangers
1991	Brett Hull	St. Louis
1990	Mark Messier	Edmonton
1989	Steve Yzerman	Detroit
1988	Mario Lemieux	Pittsburgh
1987	Wayne Gretzky	Edmonton
1986	Mario Lemieux	Pittsburgh
1985	Wayne Gretzky	Edmonton
1984	Wayne Gretzky	Edmonton
1983	Wayne Gretzky	Edmonton
1982	Wayne Gretzky	Edmonton
1981	Mike Liut	St. Louis
1980	Marcel Dionne	Los Angeles
1979	Marcel Dionne	Los Angeles
1978	Guy Lafleur	Montreal
1977	Guy Lafleur	Montreal
1976	Guy Lafleur	Montreal
1975	Bobby Orr	Boston
1974	Phil Esposito	Boston
1973	Bobby Clarke	Philadelphia
1972	Jean Ratelle	NY Rangers
1971	Phil Esposito	Boston

JACK ADAMS AWARD

	Winner	Runner-up
2006	Lindy Ruff, Buf.	Peter Laviolette, NYR
2005	....	
2004	John Tortorella, T.B.	Ron Wilson, S.J.
2003	Jacques Lemaire, Min.	John Tortorella, T.B.
2002	Bob Francis, Phx.	Brian Sutter, Chi.
2001	Bill Barber, Phi.	Scotty Bowman, Det.
2000	Joel Quenneville, St.L.	Alain Vigneault, Mtl.
1999	Jacques Martin, Ott.	Pat Quinn, Tor.
1998	Pat Burns, Bos.	Larry Robinson, L.A.
1997	Ted Nolan, Buf.	Ken Hitchcock, Dal.
1996	Scotty Bowman, Det.	Doug MacLean, Fla.
1995	Marc Crawford, Que.	Scotty Bowman, Det.
1994	Jacques Lemaire, N.J.	Kevin Constantine, S.J.
1993	Pat Burns, Tor.	Brian Sutter, Bos.
1992	Pat Quinn, Van.	Roger Neilson, NYR
1991	Brian Sutter, St.L.	Tom Webster, L.A.
1990	Bob Murdoch, Wpg.	Mike Milbury, Bos.
1989	Pat Burns, Mtl.	Bob McCammon, Van.
1988	Jacques Demers, Det.	Terry Crisp, Cgy.
1987	Jacques Demers, Det.	Jack Evans, Hfd.
1986	Glen Sather, Edm.	Jacques Demers, St.L.
1985	Mike Keenan, Phi.	Barry Long, Wpg.
1984	Bryan Murray, Wsh.	Scotty Bowman, Buf.
1983	Orval Tessier, Chi.	
1982	Tom Watt, Wpg.	
1981	Red Berenson, St.L.	Bob Berry, L.A.
1980	Pat Quinn, Phi.	
1979	Al Arbour, NYI	Fred Shero, NYR
1978	Bobby Kromm, Det.	Don Cherry, Bos.
1977	Scotty Bowman, Mtl.	Tom McVie, Wsh.
1976	Don Cherry, Bos.	
1975	Bob Pulford, L.A.	
1974	Fred Shero, Phi.	

NHL Entry Draft

History

Year	Location	Date	Players Drafted
1963	Queen Elizabeth Hotel, Montreal	June 5	21
1964	Queen Elizabeth Hotel, Montreal	June 11	24
1965	Queen Elizabeth Hotel, Montreal	April 27	11
1966	Mount Royal Hotel, Montreal	April 25	24
1967	Queen Elizabeth Hotel, Montreal	June 7	18
1968	Queen Elizabeth Hotel, Montreal	June 13	24
1969	Queen Elizabeth Hotel, Montreal	June 12	84
1970	Queen Elizabeth Hotel, Montreal	June 11	115
1971	Queen Elizabeth Hotel, Montreal	June 10	117
1972	Queen Elizabeth Hotel, Montreal	June 8	152
1973	Mount Royal Hotel, Montreal	May 15	168
1974	NHL Montreal Office	May 28	247
1975	NHL Montreal Office	June 3	217
1976	NHL Montreal Office	June 1	135
1977	NHL Montreal Office	June 14	185
1978	Queen Elizabeth Hotel, Montreal	June 15	234
1979	Queen Elizabeth Hotel, Montreal	August 9	126
1980	Montreal Forum	June 11	210
1981	Montreal Forum	June 10	211
1982	Montreal Forum	June 9	252
1983	Montreal Forum	June 8	242
1984	Montreal Forum	June 9	250
1985	Toronto Convention Centre	June 15	252
1986	Montreal Forum	June 21	252
1987	Joe Louis Arena, Detroit	June 13	252
1988	Montreal Forum	June 11	252
1989	Met Sports Center, Minnesota	June 17	252
1990	B.C. Place, Vancouver	June 16	250
1991	Memorial Auditorium, Buffalo	June 22	264
1992	Montreal Forum	June 20	264
1993	Le Colisee, Quebec	June 26	286
1994	Hartford Civic Center	June 28-29	286
1995	Edmonton Coliseum	July 8	234
1996	Kiel Center, St. Louis	June 22	241
1997	Civic Arena, Pittsburgh	June 21	246
1998	Marine Midland Arena, Buffalo	June 27	258
1999	FleetCenter, Boston	June 26	272
2000	Saddledome, Calgary	June 24-25	293
2001	National Car Rental Center, Florida	June 23-24	289
2002	Air Canada Centre, Toronto	June 22-23	290
2003	Gaylord Entertainment Center, Nashville	June 21-22	292
2004	RBC Center, Carolina	June 26-27	291
2005	Sheraton Hotel and Towers, Ottawa	July 30	230
2006	General Motors Place, Vancouver	June 24	213

First Selections

Year	Player	Pos	Team	Drafted From	Age
1963	Garry Monahan	LW	Montreal	St. Michael's Juveniles	16.7
1964	Claude Gauthier		Detroit	Comite des jeunes (Rosemont)	
1965	Andre Veilleux	RW	NY Rangers	Montreal Ranger Jr. B	
1966	Barry Gibbs	D	Boston	Estevan Bruins	17.7
1967	Rick Pagnutti	D	Los Angeles	Garson Native Sons	20.6
1968	Michel Plasse	G	Montreal	Drummondville Rangers	20.0
1969	Rejean Houle	LW	Montreal	Montreal Jr. Canadiens	19.8
1970	Gilbert Perreault	C	Buffalo	Montreal Jr. Canadiens	19.7
1971	Guy Lafleur	RW	Montreal	Quebec Remparts	19.9
1972	Billy Harris	RW	NY Islanders	Toronto Marlboros	20.4
1973	Denis Potvin	D	NY Islanders	Ottawa 67's	19.7
1974	Greg Joly	D	Washington	Regina Pats	20.0
1975	Mel Bridgman	C	Philadelphia	Victoria Cougars	20.1
1976	Rick Green	D	Washington	London Knights	20.3
1977	Dale McCourt	C	Detroit	St. Catharines Fincups	20.4
1978	Bobby Smith	C	Minnesota	Ottawa 67's	20.4
1979	Rob Ramage	D	Colorado	London Knights	20.5
1980	Doug Wickenheiser	C	Montreal	Regina Pats	19.2
1981	Dale Hawerchuk	C	Winnipeg	Cornwall Royals	18.2
1982	Gord Kluzak	D	Boston	Nanaimo Islanders	18.3
1983	Brian Lawton	C	Minnesota	Mount St. Charles HS	18.11
1984	Mario Lemieux	C	Pittsburgh	Laval Voisins	18.8
1985	Wendel Clark	LW/D	Toronto	Saskatoon Blades	18.7
1986	Joe Murphy	C	Detroit	Michigan State Spartans	18.8
1987	Pierre Turgeon	C	Buffalo	Granby Bisons	17.10
1988	Mike Modano	C	Minnesota	Prince Albert Raiders	18.0
1989	Mats Sundin	RW	Quebec	Nacka (Sweden)	18.4
1990	Owen Nolan	RW	Quebec	Cornwall Royals	18.4
1991	Eric Lindros	C	Quebec	Oshawa Generals	18.3
1992	Roman Hamrlik	D	Tampa Bay	ZPS Zlin (Czech.)	18.2
1993	Alexandre Daigle	C	Ottawa	Victoriaville Tigres	18.5
1994	Ed Jovanovski	D	Florida	Windsor Spitfires	18.0
1995	Bryan Berard	D	Ottawa	Detroit Jr. Red Wings	18.4
1996	Chris Phillips	D	Ottawa	Prince Albert Raiders	18.3
1997	Joe Thornton	C	Boston	Sault Ste. Marie Greyhounds	17.11
1998	Vincent Lecavalier	C	Tampa Bay	Rimouski Oceanic	18.2
1999	Patrik Stefan	C	Atlanta	Long Beach Ice Dogs (IHL)	18.9
2000	Rick DiPietro	G	NY Islanders	Boston University Terriers	18.9
2001	Ilya Kovalchuk	LW	Atlanta	Spartak (Russia)	18.2
2002	Rick Nash	LW	Columbus	London Knights	18.0
2003	Marc-Andre Fleury	G	Pittsburgh	Cape Breton Screaming Eagles	18.0
2004	Alex Ovechkin	LW	Washington	Dynamo Moscow (Russia)	18.9
2005	Sidney Crosby	C	Pittsburgh	Rimouski Oceanic	17.11
2006	Erik Johnson	D	St. Louis	U.S. National U-18	18.3

Draft Summary

Following is a summary of the players drafted from the Ontario Hockey League (OHL), Quebec Major Junior Hockey League (QMJHL), Western Hockey League (WHL), United States colleges, United States high schools, European and other North American leagues since 1969. "Other" may include Canadian and U.S. Jr. A and Jr. B, minor professional leagues (AHL, IHL), midget and other teams playing in leagues not listed above.

Year	Total Picks	OHL Picks	%	QMJHL Picks	%	WHL Picks	%	College Picks	%	Hi School Picks	%	Int'l Picks	%	Other Picks	%
1969	84	36	42.9	11	13.1	20	23.8	7	8.3	-	-	1	1.2	9	10.7
1970	115	51	44.3	13	11.3	22	19.1	16	13.9	-	-	-	-	13	11.3
1971	117	41	35.0	13	11.1	28	23.9	22	18.8	-	-	-	-	13	11.1
1972	152	46	30.3	30	19.7	44	28.9	21	13.8	-	-	-	-	11	7.2
1973	168	56	33.3	24	14.3	49	29.2	25	14.9	-	-	-	-	14	8.3
1974	247	69	27.9	40	16.2	66	26.7	41	16.6	-	-	6	2.4	25	10.1
1975	217	55	25.3	28	12.9	57	26.3	59	27.2	-	-	6	2.8	12	5.5
1976	135	47	34.8	18	13.3	33	24.4	26	19.3	-	-	8	5.9	3	2.2
1977	185	42	22.7	40	21.6	44	23.8	49	26.5	-	-	5	2.7	5	2.7
1978	234	59	25.2	22	9.4	48	20.5	73	31.2	-	-	16	6.8	16	6.8
1979	126	48	38.1	19	15.1	37	29.4	15	11.9	-	-	6	4.8	1	0.8
1980	210	73	34.8	24	11.4	41	19.5	42	20.0	7	3.3	13	6.2	10	4.8
1981	211	59	28.0	28	13.3	37	17.5	21	10.0	17	8.1	32	15.2	17	8.1
1982	252	60	23.8	17	6.7	55	21.8	20	7.9	47	18.7	35	13.9	18	7.1
1983	242	57	23.6	24	9.9	41	16.9	14	5.8	35	14.5	34	14.0	37	15.3
1984	250	55	22.0	16	6.4	37	14.8	22	8.8	44	17.6	40	16.0	36	14.4
1985	252	59	23.4	15	6.0	48	19.0	20	7.9	48	19.0	31	12.3	31	12.3
1986	252	66	26.2	22	8.7	32	12.7	22	8.7	40	15.9	28	11.1	42	16.7
1987	252	32	12.7	17	6.7	36	14.3	40	15.9	69	27.4	38	15.1	20	7.9
1988	252	32	12.7	22	8.7	30	11.9	48	19.0	56	22.2	39	15.5	25	9.9
1989	252	39	15.5	16	6.3	44	17.5	48	19.0	47	18.7	38	15.1	20	7.9
1990	250	39	15.6	14	5.6	33	13.2	38	15.2	57	22.8	53	21.2	16	6.4
1991	264	43	16.3	25	9.5	40	15.2	43	16.3	37	14.0	55	20.8	21	8.0
1992	264	57	21.6	22	8.3	45	17.0	9	3.4	25	9.5	84	31.8	22	8.3
1993	286	60	21.0	23	8.0	44	15.4	17	5.9	33	11.5	78	27.3	31	10.8
1994	286	45	15.7	28	9.8	66	23.1	6	2.1	28	9.8	80	28.0	33	11.5
1995	234	54	23.1	35	15.0	55	23.5	5	2.1	2	0.9	69	29.5	14	6.0
1996	241	51	21.2	31	12.9	54	22.4	25	10.4	6	2.5	58	24.1	16	6.6
1997	246	52	21.1	19	7.7	63	25.6	26	10.6	4	1.6	63	25.6	19	7.7
1998	258	50	19.4	41	15.9	44	17.1	27	10.5	7	2.7	75	29.1	14	5.4
1999	272	52	19.1	20	7.4	40	14.7	36	13.2	9	3.3	94	34.6	21	7.7
2000	293	39	13.3	21	7.2	41	14.0	35	11.9	7	2.4	123	42.0	27	9.2
2001	289	41	14.2	26	9.0	45	15.6	24	8.3	8	2.8	119	41.2	26	9.0
2002	290	35	12.1	23	7.9	43	14.8	41	14.1	6	2.1	110	37.9	32	11.0
2003	292	44	15.1	38	13.0	41	14.0	23	7.9	10	3.4	93	31.8	43	14.7
2004	291	42	14.4	27	9.3	44	15.1	28	9.6	18	6.2	88	30.2	44	15.1
2005	230	43	18.7	23	10.0	43	18.7	13	5.6	18	7.8	50	21.7	40	17.4
2006	213	29	13.6	25	11.7	24	11.2	18	8.4	19	8.9	63	29.5	35	16.4
Total	1829	21.5	875	10.3	1590	18.7	1047	12.3	685	8.0	1668	19.5	797	9.3

Total Players Drafted (1969-2006): 8,704

2006 was a good year for the Staal family. Marc (left) won a gold medal with Team Canada at the World Junior Championship, Eric (center) won the Stanley Cup with Carolina and Jordan (right) was selected second overall by Pittsburgh in the 2006 NHL Entry Draft.

Ontario Hockey League Draft Selections by Club

Total	Club	'06	'05	'04	'03	'02	'01	'00	'99	'98	'97	'96	'95	'94	'93	'92	'91	'90	'89	'88	'87	'86	'85	'84	'83	'82	'81	'80	'79	'78	'77	'76	'69 to '75
161	Peterborough	1	2	5	5	1	2	1	4	1	5	4	5	2	4	4	3	4	2	2	5	2	9	3	7	5	3	10	9	6	4	1	38
146	Oshawa	2	–	3	3	3	1	2	3	4	3	1	10	1	4	4	3	4	2	4	2	3	6	6	5	5	7	3	5	3	1	–	29
138	London	1	3	6	4	2	2	1	4	8	1	4	1	1	4	3	1	3	3	6	2	3	1	7	3	5	5	2	6	3	4	5	30
136	Kitchener	0	4	2	1	4	1	–	5	3	2	4	2	4	1	3	5	7	1	2	3	6	4	8	5	5	4	4	4	3	1	2	26
132	Ottawa	1	2	3	2	–	3	2	6	2	5	2	1	1	4	6	5	5	–	1	2	3	3	2	2	9	4	8	3	5	5	5	39
107	Sudbury	2	4	0	1	1	2	–	5	5	3	1	2	2	10	2	8	2	1	–	1	3	5	2	–	4	2	7	3	4	4	5	29
104	Sault Ste. Marie	0	1	3	1	2	1	1	1	4	1	4	4	3	4	3	7	2	1	3	2	1	7	5	4	6	1	8	3	3	5	1	5	26
97	Kingston	4	2	–	1	1	2	–	4	1	4	4	3	2	5	3	2	2	–	1	1	4	3	3	1	2	5	8	2	9	4	6	36
76	Windsor	2	3	2	2	2	2	2	1	5	1	4	3	–	3	–	1	2	5	–	7	3	2	2	3	5	3	2	4	1	2	–
67	Guelph	1	2	2	1	2	4	1	3	5	1	6	5	7	2	2	–	4	–	2	8	3	5	1	–	–	–	–	–	–	–	–
64	Saginaw/N. Bay	2	3	1	2	2	3	2	2	1	1	2	7	2	5	2	4	1	3	3	3	3	4	–	–	–	–	–	–	–	–	–	–
57	Belleville	2	2	–	–	2	3	1	5	2	5	–	3	3	–	4	1	2	4	–	2	5	4	4	3	–	–	–	–	–	–	–	–
53	Plymouth	2	3	3	3	3	3	6	2	4	3	6	2	7	2	2	–	–	–	–	–	–	–	–	–	–	–	–	–	–	–	–	–
29	Sarnia	1	3	–	5	2	1	3	1	3	2	7	1	–	–	–	–	–	–	–	–	–	–	–	–	–	–	–	–	–	–	–	–
28	Brampton	4	4	2	4	3	3	6	2	–	–	–	–	–	–	–	–	–	–	–	–	–	–	–	–	–	–	–	–	–	–	–	–
27	Owen Sound	2	2	1	1	1	–	1	–	1	2	3	3	4	2	1	1	–	–	–	–	–	–	–	–	–	–	–	–	–	–	–	–
22	Barrie	1	–	1	1	1	3	6	3	4	2	–	–	–	–	–	–	–	–	–	–	–	–	–	–	–	–	–	–	–	–	–	–
17	Erie	0	2	2	–	2	2	3	2	1	3	–	–	–	–	–	–	–	–	–	–	–	–	–	–	–	–	–	–	–	–	–	–
16	St. Michael's	0	–	4	5	1	5	1	–	–	–	–	–	–	–	–	–	–	–	–	–	–	–	–	–	–	–	–	–	–	–	–	–
9	Mississauga	1	1	3	2	–	–	2	–	–	–	–	–	–	–	–	–	–	–	–	–	–	–	–	–	–	–	–	–	–	–	–	–

Teams no longer operating

Total	Club	'06	'05	'04	'03	'02	'01	'00	'99	'98	'97	'96	'95	'94	'93	'92	'91	'90	'89	'88	'87	'86	'85	'84	'83	'82	'81	'80	'79	'78	'77	'76	'69 to '75
97	Toronto	–	–	–	–	–	–	–	–	–	–	–	–	–	–	–	–	–	2	2	1	4	3	4	4	6	2	10	4	5	7	4	38
72	Niagara Falls	–	–	–	–	–	–	–	–	6	2	3	4	4	4	4	–	–	–	–	–	–	6	6	8	5	3	2	–	30			
62	Hamilton	–	–	–	–	–	–	–	–	–	–	–	2	–	–	4	4	6	3	–	–	–	–	–	1	8	–	3	12				
52	St. Catharines	–	–	–	–	–	–	–	–	–	–	–	–	–	–	–	–	–	–	–	–	–	–	–	–	–	6	4	10				
37	Cornwall	–	–	–	–	–	–	–	–	5	3	3	2	3	3	2	2	3	4	7	–	–	–	–	–	–	–	18					
27	Brantford	–	–	–	–	–	–	–	–	–	–	–	–	–	–	–	–	2	7	2	5	8	3	–	–	–	–	18					
20	Montreal	–	–	–	–	–	–	–	–	–	–	–	–	–	–	–	–	–	–	–	–	–	–	–	–	–	–	–					
5	Newmarket	–	–	–	–	–	–	–	–	–	–	–	2	3	–	–	–																

Quebec Major Junior Hockey League Draft Selections by Club

Total	Club	'06	'05	'04	'03	'02	'01	'00	'99	'98	'97	'96	'95	'94	'93	'92	'91	'90	'89	'88	'87	'86	'85	'84	'83	'82	'81	'80	'79	'78	'77	'76	'69 to '75
74	Shawinigan	1	1	3	2	2	1	1	1	3	1	4	2	1	1	3	2	–	2	–	1	2	–	2	5	5	2	2	–	–	3	–	11
72	Gatineau/Hull	2	–	4	4	5	2	–	4	3	–	3	3	1	3	3	3	2	2	3	4	–	1	3	–	1	3	–	3	–	2	2	11
72	Lewiston/Sher.	2	5	2	1	–	3	–	–	5	1	–	4	2	3	–	–	–	–	–	–	–	–	–	2	5	1	4	3	6	5	26	
54	Drummondville	2	2	1	1	–	1	1	–	2	2	3	4	1	2	2	4	–	1	4	2	2	2	1	–	3	1	6	3	1	1	5	17
51	Chicoutimi	0	4	–	1	3	1	1	–	1	2	–	2	3	1	1	–	1	1	2	2	1	3	–	3	1	6	3	1	1	5	–	17
28	Halifax	3	1	3	6	–	3	2	–	3	3	1	3	–	–	–	–	–	–	–	–	–	–	–	–	–	–	–	–	–	–	–	–
22	Rimouski	0	2	3	4	–	4	2	2	5	–	–	–	–	–	–	–	–	–	–	–	–	–	–	–	–	–	–	–	–	–	–	–
21	Val-d'Or	0	2	1	1	1	2	2	3	–	2	4	2	1	–	–	–	–	–	–	–	–	–	–	–	–	–	–	–	–	–	–	–
19	Quebec	2	2	1	3	1	3	–	3	4	–	–	–	–	–	–	–	–	–	–	–	–	–	–	–	–	–	–	–	–	–	–	–
18	PEI/Mtl. Rocket	0	2	8	1	3	1	1	2	–	–	–	–	–	–	–	–	–	–	–	–	–	–	–	–	–	–	–	–	–	–	–	–
17	Baie-Comeau	3	–	3	2	1	3	2	–	3	–	–	–	–	–	–	–	–	–	–	–	–	–	–	–	–	–	–	–	–	–	–	–
17	Moncton	3	1	2	3	2	–	2	2	1	1	–	–	–	–	–	–	–	–	–	–	–	–	–	–	–	–	–	–	–	–	–	–
14	Rouyn-Noranda	3	1	–	2	–	–	4	1	3	–	–	–	–	–	–	–	–	–	–	–	–	–	–	–	–	–	–	–	–	–	–	–
13	Cape Breton	1	–	3	2	2	1	1	–	3	–	–	–	–	–	–	–	–	–	–	–	–	–	–	–	–	–	–	–	–	–	–	–
9	Acadie-Bathurst	2	–	3	2	–	2	–	–	–	–	–	–	–	–	–	–	–	–	–	–	–	–	–	–	–	–	–	–	–	–	–	–
1	Saint John	1	–	–	–	–	–	–	–	–	–	–	–	–	–	–	–	–	–	–	–	–	–	–	–	–	–	–	–	–	–	–	–

Teams no longer operating

Total	Club	'06	'05	'04	'03	'02	'01	'00	'99	'98	'97	'96	'95	'94	'93	'92	'91	'90	'89	'88	'87	'86	'85	'84	'83	'82	'81	'80	'79	'78	'77	'76	'69 to '75
54	Laval	–	–	–	–	–	3	1	2	4	5	2	1	4	3	3	1	3	5	–	2	1	2	–	–	1	2	4	1	10			
47	Quebec	–	–	–	–	–	–	–	–	–	–	–	–	–	–	–	–	–	–	3	2	1	2	2	3	1	7	3	19				
47	Trois Rivieres	–	–	–	–	–	–	–	–	–	1	2	1	3	3	1	–	3	–	3	1	2	2	2	3	6	2	18					
45	Cornwall	–	–	–	–	–	–	–	–	–	–	–	–	–	–	–	–	–	5	5	1	6	1	3	21								
32	Montreal	–	–	–	–	–	–	–	–	–	–	–	–	–	–	–	–	–	3	–	3	4	2	3	1	16							
30	Granby	–	–	–	–	1	3	2	5	1	–	2	–	2	–	4	2	2	3	1	2	–	–	2									
30	Victoriaville	–	–	–	3	1	3	2	1	2	3	1	1	6	2	1	–	4	–	–	–	5	–	–	–	3	1	9					
28	Sorel	–	–	–	–	–	–	–	–	–	–	–	–	–	–	–	–	–	–	–	5	–	–	–	3	1	9						
27	Verdun	–	–	–	–	–	–	–	–	–	–	3	–	1	3	0	3	–	3	3	–	3	3	1	–	7							
21	Beauport	–	–	–	–	–	–	3	3	7	3	1	3	1	–	–	–	–	–	–	–	–	–	–	–								
16	St. Jean	–	–	–	–	–	–	–	1	1	2	1	3	–	1	3	0	1	1	–	–	–	–	–	–								
15	St. Hyacinthe	–	–	–	–	–	–	–	–	4	–	4	1	2	1	3	–	–	–	–	–	–	–	–	–								
12	Longueuil	–	–	–	–	–	–	–	–	–	–	3	2	–	1	2	1	2	1	–	–	–	–	–	–								2
2	St. Jerome	–	–	–	–	–	–	–	–	–	–	–	–	–	–	–	–	–	–	–	–	–	–	–	2								

2006 NHL Entry Draft Order of Selection

1. A weighted lottery system was used to determine the order of selection for non-playoff teams in all seven rounds of the 2006 NHL Entry Draft. The St. Louis Blues won the Draft Drawing and with it the first overall selection.

    The weighted lottery was structured as follows: only the five teams with the fewest points had the chance to win the first overall selection; no team could move up more than four spots and no team could move backward more than one.
    1. St. Louis
    2. Pittsburgh
    3. Chicago
    4. Washington
    5. Boston
    6. Columbus
    7. New York
    8. Phoenix
    9. Minnesota
    10. Florida
    11. Los Angeles
    12. Atlanta
    13. Toronto
    14. Vancouver

2. Playoff teams that neither won their Divisions nor won the Stanley Cup picked 15th to 24th in ascending order of regular-season points:
    15. Tampa Bay
    16. Montreal
    17. Edmonton
    18. Colorado
    19. Anaheim
    20. San Jose
    21. NY Rangers
    22. Philadelphia
    23. Nashville
    24. Buffalo

3. Regular-season Division champions that did not win the Stanley Cup picked 25th to 29th in ascending order of regular-season points:
    25. New Jersey
    26. Calgary
    27. Dallas
    28. Ottawa
    29. Detroit

4. The Stanley Cup winner picked 30th:
    30. Carolina

Nashville's Steve Sullivan (top) was drafted by New Jersey from Sault Ste. Marie of the OHL with the 233rd pick in 1994. Carolina's Ray Whitney was selected by San Jose from Spokane of the WHL with the 23rd pick in 1991.

Western Hockey League Draft Selections by Club

Total	Club	'06	'05	'04	'03	'02	'01	'00	'99	'98	'97	'96	'95	'94	'93	'92	'91	'90	'89	'88	'87	'86	'85	'84	'83	'82	'81	'80	'79	'78	'77	'76	'69 to '75
105	Kamloops	1	2	5	2	5	2	4	4	1	3	4	5	9	2	3	6	4	5	1	3	4	4	4	4	2	–	–	–	–	4	4	10
105	Regina	1	1	0	2	1	2	2	4	2	3	4	2	3	–	4	–	1	5	–	2	3	4	4	8	6	5	3	1	4	1	3	23
104	Medicine Hat	2	4	2	3	3	2	–	1	3	2	7	2	6	1	3	3	1	4	1	5	2	6	1	2	1	2	4	–	4	5	3	19
104	Portland	1	3	2	1	2	–	6	1	3	3	1	2	3	4	4	1	1	4	1	3	4	2	5	7	7	6	8	7	8	4	–	40
102	Saskatoon	0	4	1	–	–	4	1	4	2	2	2	2	4	2	3	2	2	3	4	4	5	1	3	5	5	3	2	2	1	4	3	20
97	Brandon	1	2	0	3	4	2	–	–	4	5	2	6	5	2	1	1	1	–	3	3	1	2	3	1	2	2	5	10	1	3	–	23
91	Seattle	1	3	2	5	1	5	4	6	2	8	1	5	5	4	2	3	6	2	4	2	1	3	1	–	6	–	3	2	4	–	–	15
86	Lethbridge	1	–	2	2	2	1	3	–	1	5	1	3	3	4	3	7	4	3	3	–	1	5	1	2	7	4	1	4	5	3	2	26
80	Prince Albert	0	2	4	2	1	4	2	3	3	5	3	4	3	5	2	6	4	3	3	1	6	6	2	2	4	–	–	–	–	–	–	4
58	Moose Jaw	1	3	3	3	3	3	5	1	2	4	4	4	3	2	3	2	1	3	–	3	1	4	–	–	–	–	–	–	–	–	–	–
58	Swift Current	2	1	2	2	4	1	3	1	2	2	1	4	4	5	1	1	2	2	2	5	–	–	–	–	–	–	–	–	–	–	–	–
57	Spokane	1	4	1	–	3	3	2	1	1	4	5	4	4	4	7	5	1	2	3	1	–	–	–	–	–	1	–	–	–	–	–	1
51	Tri-City	0	2	4	1	3	2	2	1	4	1	6	6	2	2	5	3	3	4	–	–	–	–	–	–	–	–	–	–	–	–	–	–
41	Red Deer	1	1	1	4	4	6	1	1	5	3	4	2	5	3	–	–	–	–	–	–	–	–	–	–	–	–	–	–	–	–	–	–
30	Calgary	1	2	5	3	2	1	4	6	3	–	3	–	–	–	–	–	–	–	–	–	–	–	–	–	–	–	–	–	–	–	–	–
28	Kelowna	0	2	4	4	1	1	1	2	2	7	4	–	–	–	–	–	–	–	–	–	–	–	–	–	–	–	–	–	–	–	–	–
25	Prince George	4	1	2	2	–	4	–	2	4	2	2	2	–	–	–	–	–	–	–	–	–	–	–	–	–	–	–	–	–	–	–	–
15	Kootenay	1	3	2	1	3	2	1	2	–	–	–	–	–	–	–	–	–	–	–	–	–	–	–	–	–	–	–	–	–	–	–	–
8	Vancouver	1	3	2	1	1	–	–	–	–	–	–	–	–	–	–	–	–	–	–	–	–	–	–	–	–	–	–	–	–	–	–	–
4	Everett	4	–	–	–	–	–	–	–	–	–	–	–	–	–	–	–	–	–	–	–	–	–	–	–	–	–	–	–	–	–	–	–
Teams no longer operating																																	
70	Victoria	–	–	–	–	–	–	–	–	–	–	–	–	2	2	1	–	2	4	4	2	1	2	4	3	2	6	8	1	3	3	4	27
66	Calgary	–	–	–	–	–	–	–	–	–	–	–	–	–	–	–	–	–	–	–	–	2	3	3	3	4	5	2	–	3	4	4	22
62	New Westm'r	–	–	–	–	–	–	–	–	–	–	–	–	–	–	–	–	–	–	1	2	1	1	2	–	–	–	1	5	6	8	5	25
39	Flin Flon	–	–	–	–	–	–	–	–	–	–	–	–	–	–	–	–	–	–	–	–	–	–	–	–	–	–	–	–	5	1	3	9
38	Edmonton	–	–	–	–	–	–	–	–	–	4	–	–	–	–	–	–	–	–	–	–	–	–	–	–	–	–	–	2	–	–	2	4
34	Winnipeg	–	–	–	–	–	–	–	–	–	–	–	–	–	–	–	–	–	–	–	–	–	–	–	1	4	1	–	–	–	4	–	9
13	Billings	–	–	–	–	–	–	–	–	–	–	–	–	–	–	–	–	–	–	–	–	–	–	–	–	–	2	4	3	4	–	–	13
12	Estevan	–	–	–	–	–	–	–	–	–	–	–	–	–	–	–	–	–	–	–	–	–	–	–	–	–	–	–	–	–	–	–	0
12	Tacoma	–	–	–	–	–	–	–	–	–	–	–	2	5	2	3	–	–	–	–	–	–	–	–	–	–	–	–	–	–	–	–	0
11	Kelowna	–	–	–	–	–	–	–	–	–	–	–	–	–	–	–	–	–	–	–	–	–	5	4	2	–	–	–	–	–	–	–	0
6	Nanaimo	–	–	–	–	–	–	–	–	–	–	–	–	–	–	–	–	–	–	–	–	–	–	–	1	5	–	–	–	–	–	–	5
2	Vancouver	–	–	–	–	–	–	–	–	–	–	–	–	–	–	–	–	–	–	–	–	–	–	–	–	–	–	–	–	–	–	–	0

U.S. College Hockey Draft Selections by School

Total	Club	'06	'05	'04	'03	'02	'01	'00	'99	'98	'97	'96	'95	'94	'93	'92	'91	'90	'89	'88	'87	'86	'85	'84	'83	'82	'81	'80	'79	'78	'77	'76	'69 to '75
67	Minnesota	1	1	0	2	3	–	3	3	1	2	3	2	–	–	–	–	–	1	1	1	2	–	–	1	1	1	3	2	5	5	4	21
66	Michigan	2	1	3	2	3	2	1	2	3	1	3	–	1	1	2	4	5	3	2	1	–	1	1	–	–	–	4	–	6	1	3	14
51	Boston U.	1	–	1	–	3	2	1	3	2	1	1	1	–	1	1	2	2	1	3	2	2	1	1	–	–	1	–	1	5	4	1	12
48	Michigan State	1	–	2	1	4	–	2	2	1	1	1	–	1	1	1	4	5	4	4	1	1	–	2	–	2	–	2	–	–	–	1	5
46	Michigan Tech	–	–	–	–	–	1	–	–	–	–	1	–	2	1	–	2	1	2	1	1	2	2	2	–	1	–	4	1	2	1	4	13
43	Denver	–	2	1	–	1	–	–	1	–	3	–	–	–	–	–	–	–	1	1	4	2	1	–	–	1	–	1	2	2	2	2	10
41	Wisconsin	–	–	–	–	–	–	3	2	–	–	–	–	–	–	–	1	–	1	–	1	–	1	1	–	2	3	–	1	–	3	2	11
39	North Dakota	1	–	1	1	1	–	1	1	–	2	–	–	–	–	–	1	1	2	–	–	–	–	1	–	–	1	3	3	2	1	–	10
37	Boston College	1	1	1	1	3	2	3	–	3	3	2	–	–	–	–	–	–	2	–	2	1	–	–	–	1	1	2	–	5	–	1	10
36	Providence	2	–	0	1	1	–	2	–	2	1	–	–	–	–	–	–	1	–	–	–	1	1	–	2	1	4	5	–	4	3	2	19
34	Cornell	–	1	2	2	1	–	2	2	–	1	–	–	–	–	–	–	2	5	2	1	–	2	1	–	1	1	1	–	1	1	1	6
34	Harvard	–	1	–	–	3	2	2	1	2	1	3	–	1	2	–	–	–	2	1	1	–	2	–	1	1	–	–	–	2	2	–	5
33	Clarkson	1	–	–	–	–	–	1	1	3	–	–	–	–	1	1	2	3	1	1	1	–	–	1	1	1	1	1	1	2	2	–	8
32	Colorado	–	1	0	2	1	1	2	1	3	–	–	1	–	–	–	–	2	–	1	–	1	–	3	–	–	–	1	–	2	2	1	6
31	New Hampshire	–	–	1	–	1	–	2	1	–	1	–	–	–	–	–	–	–	–	1	–	–	–	2	1	1	1	2	1	1	4	–	10
31	Notre Dame	1	–	2	–	2	1	1	2	–	2	1	–	–	–	–	–	–	–	–	–	–	–	–	–	–	–	1	1	3	–	2	7
28	Bowling Green	1	1	–	–	1	1	–	1	1	1	–	–	–	–	1	3	1	2	3	–	–	–	–	1	–	–	1	1	1	1	2	6
25	RPI	–	–	–	–	–	1	2	2	–	1	–	–	–	–	1	3	–	–	2	2	–	1	–	1	1	2	1	–	3	1	–	8
24	Lake Superior	–	–	–	–	1	–	–	1	–	1	1	–	–	1	–	1	3	2	3	–	3	–	1	–	–	–	–	–	3	–	–	3
24	W. Michigan	1	–	–	–	1	–	–	–	1	1	–	–	–	2	–	4	1	1	1	1	2	–	2	2	–	–	2	–	–	2	–	4
23	St. Lawrence	–	–	–	–	1	–	–	1	–	1	1	–	–	1	–	2	1	1	1	1	1	1	1	–	3	–	–	–	4	1	–	8
22	Maine	1	–	1	2	–	–	1	4	1	1	1	–	–	1	–	–	1	2	3	–	1	–	–	1	1	–	–	–	–	–	–	1
22	Northern Mich.	–	–	2	2	–	–	1	–	–	–	1	–	–	–	–	1	–	2	1	4	–	–	–	–	1	2	1	–	4	–	–	8
21	Ohio State	–	1	0	1	2	2	–	1	–	1	1	–	–	1	1	1	1	–	2	2	–	–	1	–	–	–	–	–	1	2	–	3
20	Miami U.	1	1	2	–	1	1	–	–	1	–	–	–	–	1	1	2	–	2	4	2	–	1	–	–	–	–	–	–	–	–	–	0
20	Vermont	–	1	–	–	–	2	–	–	–	–	1	–	1	–	–	1	–	–	1	–	–	2	1	1	–	1	1	–	1	1	–	4
16	Yale	1	–	2	–	3	–	–	–	–	–	–	–	–	1	–	–	–	1	–	2	1	–	–	–	–	–	1	–	2	–	–	3
13	Brown	–	–	1	–	–	–	1	–	–	–	–	–	–	–	–	1	–	–	–	–	–	–	–	–	1	–	–	–	2	3	–	6
13	Colgate	1	–	1	–	1	–	–	–	–	–	–	–	–	–	–	2	2	1	1	–	–	–	–	–	–	–	–	1	2	–	–	3
13	Minn.-Duluth	–	–	–	–	–	–	–	–	1	–	–	–	–	–	–	1	2	1	2	–	–	–	–	–	–	1	–	–	1	1	–	3
10	Northeastern	–	–	–	–	–	–	–	1	1	–	–	–	–	–	–	–	1	1	–	–	1	1	–	1	–	–	1	–	1	–	–	2
10	Princeton	–	–	–	–	–	1	–	–	1	–	–	–	–	1	–	–	–	1	–	1	–	–	–	1	–	1	1	–	1	–	–	3

Colleges with fewer than 10 players selected: 9 - Dartmouth; 8 - Ferris State, Merrimack; 7 - Mass.-Lowell, St.Cloud State; 6 - Illinois-Chicago, St. Louis; 5 - Pennsylvania, Union College; 4 - Alaska-Anchorage, Mass.-Amherst, Nebraska-Omaha; 3 - Babson College, Alaska-Fairbanks; 2 - Minnesota State (Mankato); 1 - Air Force, American International College, Army, Bemidji State, Greenway, Hamilton, St. Anselem College, St. Thomas, Salem State, San Diego U., Wisconsin-River Falls.

U.S. High and Prep Schools Draft Selections by School (10 or more players drafted)

Total	School	'06	'05	'04	'03	'02	'01	'00	'99	'98	'97	'96	'95	'94	'93	'92	'91	'90	'89	'88	'87	'86	'85	'84	'83	'82	'81	'80
21	Cushing Acad. (MA)	1	1	2	–	–	1	–	–	–	1	1	–	2	2	–	1	3	2	3	–	–	–	1	–	–	–	–
21	Northwood Prep (NY)	–	–	1	–	–	–	1	–	–	–	–	–	1	1	–	1	3	1	1	4	2	2	–	1	2	–	–
17	Belmont Hill (MA)	1	–	–	–	–	–	–	–	–	–	–	–	1	–	2	1	2	3	1	2	1	2	–	1	–	–	–
16	Edina (MN)	–	–	–	–	–	–	–	–	–	–	–	–	–	–	1	–	1	2	2	1	–	–	2	2	4	1	–
15	Hill-Murray (MN)	–	–	–	–	–	–	–	–	–	–	–	–	1	–	–	–	3	2	–	3	3	–	3	–	–	–	–
14	Catholic Memorial (MA)	–	–	2	–	–	–	–	–	1	–	–	–	2	1	2	–	–	2	1	1	–	2	–	–	–	–	–
13	Deerfield (IL)	–	–	1	1	1	–	2	1	–	–	–	–	–	–	–	1	–	2	1	1	–	1	1	–	–	–	–
13	St. Sebastian's (MA)	1	–	–	4	1	1	–	–	1	–	–	–	1	2	2	–	–	–	–	–	–	–	–	–	–	–	–
12	Culver Mil. Acad. (IN)	–	–	–	–	–	–	–	–	–	–	–	–	–	2	2	1	2	2	1	2	–	–	–	–	–	–	–
12	Mount St. Charles (RI)	–	–	–	–	–	–	–	–	–	–	–	–	–	–	–	–	1	1	2	1	2	–	1	3	–	1	–
11	Canterbury (CT)	–	–	–	1	–	–	–	–	–	–	–	–	–	1	2	–	2	–	3	–	2	–	–	–	–	–	–
11	Hotchkiss (CT)	–	–	1	–	–	1	–	–	–	–	2	1	3	–	–	–	1	–	1	–	–	1	–	–	–	–	–
10	Choate (CT)	–	–	–	–	–	–	1	–	–	–	–	–	–	–	1	1	1	–	3	2	–	1	–	–	–	–	–
10	Matignon (MA)	–	–	–	–	–	–	–	–	–	–	–	–	–	–	–	1	–	–	–	3	–	–	3	–	1	1	1
10	Roseau (MN)	–	–	–	–	–	–	–	–	–	–	–	–	–	–	–	1	3	1	–	–	1	–	1	1	1	–	1
10	Thayer Acad. (MA)	–	2	1	–	–	–	–	2		–	–	–	–	–	2	–	–	–	2	–	1	–	–	–	–	–	–

U.S. College and High School Firsts

1967 – First U.S. College Player Drafted

Michigan Tech center Al Karlander was selected 17th overall by the Detroit Red Wings.

1979 – First U.S. College First- Round Selection

Minnesota-born defenseman Mike Ramsey (currently an assistant coach with the Minnesota Wild) was selected 11th overall by the Buffalo Sabres.

1980 – First U.S. High School Player Drafted

Center Jay North of Bloomington-Jefferson H.S. was taken 62nd overall by the Buffalo Sabres in 1980.

1981 – First U.S. High School First- Round Selection

Center Bob Carpenter of St. John's prep school was selected third overall by Washington in 1981.

1983 – First U.S. High School Player Drafted First Overall

Minnesota North Stars selected left winger Brian Lawton from Mount St. Charles H.S. first overall in 1983.

1986 – First U.S. College Player Drafted First Overall

Detroit selected right winger Joe Murphy from Michigan State first overall in 1986.

2005 – Most U.S. College Players Selected in the First Round

The 2005 draft saw eight U.S. college players selected in the first round, the most in Entry Draft history. Seven were selected in the first round in 2003 and 1986, six in 2000, five in 2002, four in 2001 and three in each of the 1986 and 1999 Entry Drafts.

Record-Setting 10 U.S.-Born Players Selected in First Round of 2006 Entry Draft

A record 10 U.S.-born players were among the 30 players selected in the first round of the 2006 NHL Entry Draft at General Motors Place in Vancouver, surpassing the previous record of eight set in 2005.

Of these 10 players, two were selected from each of the Ontario Hockey League, the United States Hockey League and the U.S. National Under-18 Team. One player was selected from each of the Central Collegiate Hockey Association, the Western Collegiate Hockey Association, the Western Hockey League and a U.S. High School.

Previously, the largest number of U.S.-born players selected in the first round had been eight in 2005 and seven in both 2003 and 1986.

International

Total	Country	'06	'05	'04	'03	'02	'01	'00	'99	'98	'97	'96	'95	'94	'93	'92	'91	'90	'89	'88	'87	'86	'85	'84	'83	'82	'81	'80	'79	'78	'77	'76	'69 to '75
503	USSR/CIS/Russia	16	11	24	32	33	36	44	29	22	16	17	27	35	31	45	25	14	18	11	2	1	2	1	5	3	–	–	2	–	5	–	57
428	Sweden	18	15	18	19	24	14	24	19	14	16	8	17	18	11	11	7	9	14	15	9	16	14	10	14	14	9	5	8	2	5	–	57
399	CzRep/Slovakia	11	15	24	20	21	28	28	20	20	17	14	21	18	15	17	9	21	8	5	11	6	8	13	9	13	4	–	1	2	–	–	20
302	Finland	13	8	14	12	26	29	19	17	12	11	7	12	8	9	8	6	9	3	7	6	10	4	10	9	5	12	4	–	2	3	2	28
42	Switzerland	3	–	4	5	4	5	7	3	2	3	1	–	1	2	–	1	–	–	1	–	–	–	–	–	–	–	–	–	–	–	–	–
40	Germany	2	1	1	4	1	7	1	–	1	3	1	3	2	1	–	–	2	1	–	1	2	1	–	–	2	–	–	–	–	–	–	4
7	Norway	–	–	–	1	–	–	–	1	–	–	–	–	–	–	1	2	–	1	–	–	–	–	–	–	–	–	–	–	–	–	–	–
4	Denmark	–	–	2	–	–	–	–	–	–	–	–	–	–	–	–	–	–	–	–	–	–	–	–	–	–	–	–	–	–	–	–	–
2	Japan	–	–	–	1	–	–	–	–	–	–	–	1	–	–	–	–	–	–	–	–	–	–	–	–	–	–	–	–	–	–	–	–
2	Poland	–	–	–	1	–	–	–	–	–	–	–	1	–	–	–	–	–	–	–	–	–	–	–	–	–	–	–	–	–	–	–	–
1	Scotland	–	1	–	–	–	–	–	–	–	–	–	–	–	–	–	–	–	–	–	–	–	–	–	–	–	–	–	–	–	–	–	–
1	Hungary	–	–	–	–	1	–	–	–	–	–	–	–	–	–	–	–	–	–	–	–	–	–	–	–	–	–	–	–	–	–	–	–

Czech Republic and Slovakia

Total	Club	'06	'05	'04	'03	'02	'01	'00	'99	'98	'97	'96	'95	'94	'93	'92	'91	'90	'89	'88	'87	'86	'85	'84	'83	'82	'81	'80	'79	'78	'77	'76	'69 to '75
34	Chemo. Litv.[1]	–	–	3	2	–	1	–	1	1	2	2	2	4	2	3	1	2	–	–	–	2	1	3	–	–	–	–	–	–	–	–	3
31	HC Ceske Bud.[2]	2	2	1	2	–	2	3	1	2	1	3	2	1	–	2	1	–	1	1	–	–	–	–	–	–	–	–	–	–	–	–	2
29	Dukla Trencin	1	1	4	3	–	2	3	2	–	1	2	1	–	2	2	–	2	1	1	–	–	1	–	–	–	–	–	–	–	–	–	–
28	Dukla Jihlava	–	–	–	–	–	1	–	–	2	2	1	1	2	3	1	1	3	–	1	3	4	2	–	–	1	–	–	–	–	–	–	–
28	Sparta Praha	1	2	4	1	1	2	–	1	1	–	1	–	1	–	2	1	2	1	1	2	1	–	–	–	–	–	–	–	–	–	–	–
27	Slavia Praha	–	1	1	2	2	5	3	2	5	4	–	–	1	–	–	–	–	–	–	–	–	–	–	–	–	–	–	–	–	–	–	–
23	HC Kladno[3]	3	1	1	1	–	1	1	2	–	2	–	1	–	2	–	1	–	–	–	–	–	–	–	–	–	–	–	–	–	–	–	–
22	Slovan Bratis.	–	–	–	3	1	–	2	2	1	1	1	–	3	–	–	–	1	1	1	–	2	–	1	1	–	–	–	–	–	–	–	4
21	ZPS Zlin[4]	–	1	2	–	2	–	2	2	1	–	2	–	1	3	2	–	1	–	1	–	1	–	–	–	–	–	–	–	–	–	–	1
19	HC Vitkovice[5]	1	1	2	–	2	–	1	1	1	1	3	1	1	3	–	–	–	–	–	–	–	–	–	–	–	–	–	–	–	–	–	3
15	HC Kosice[6]	1	1	–	2	–	1	1	1	1	–	–	–	–	–	–	–	1	–	–	–	1	–	–	–	–	–	–	–	–	–	–	–
13	HC Pardubice[7]	–	–	–	3	1	–	–	1	1	2	–	–	–	–	–	2	–	1	2	–	–	–	–	–	–	–	–	–	–	–	–	–
13	HC Vsetin	1	–	1	1	3	2	1	1	–	2	1	–	–	–	–	–	–	–	–	–	–	–	–	–	–	–	–	–	–	–	–	–
13	Interconex Plzen[8]	–	–	–	2	1	1	–	1	1	–	3	–	1	1	–	1	–	1	–	–	–	–	–	–	–	–	–	–	–	–	–	–
8	Zelezarny Trinec	1	–	1	1	1	1	2	–	–	–	–	–	–	–	–	–	–	–	–	–	–	–	–	–	–	–	–	–	–	–	–	–
8	Zetor Brno	–	–	–	–	–	–	1	–	2	–	–	3	–	1	–	–	–	–	–	–	–	–	–	–	–	–	–	–	–	–	–	–
7	AC Nitra	–	–	1	–	1	–	1	–	1	1	–	–	–	–	–	–	–	–	–	–	–	–	–	–	–	–	–	–	–	–	–	–
7	HC Olomouc[9]	–	1	–	–	–	2	1	–	2	–	–	–	–	–	–	–	–	–	–	–	–	–	–	–	–	–	–	–	–	–	–	–
7	ZTK Zvolen	–	–	–	–	2	2	–	1	1	–	1	–	–	–	–	–	–	–	–	–	–	–	–	–	–	–	–	–	–	–	–	–
6	ZTS Martin	–	1	–	1	–	2	–	–	1	–	1	–	–	–	–	–	–	–	–	–	–	–	–	–	–	–	–	–	–	–	–	–
4	HC Karlovy Vary	–	–	1	1	1	–	–	–	–	–	–	–	–	–	–	–	–	–	–	–	–	–	–	–	–	–	–	–	–	–	–	–
4	HC Liberec	–	1	1	–	2	–	–	–	–	–	–	–	–	–	–	–	–	–	–	–	–	–	–	–	–	–	–	–	–	–	–	–
3	Havirov	–	–	1	–	–	1	1	–	–	–	–	–	–	–	–	–	–	–	–	–	–	–	–	–	–	–	–	–	–	–	–	–
3	ZPA Presov	–	1	–	–	1	1	–	–	–	–	–	–	–	–	–	–	–	–	–	–	–	–	–	–	–	–	–	–	–	–	–	–

Former club names: [1]–CHZ Litvinov, [2]–Motor Ceske Budejovice, [3]–Poldi Kladno, [4]–TJ Gottwaldov, TJ Zlin, [5]–TJ Vitkovice, [6]–VSZ Kosice, [7]–Tesla Pardubice, [8]–Skoda Plzen, [9]–DS Olomouc. **Teams with two players selected:** Ingstav Brno, IS Banska Bystrica, Dubnica, Michalovce, Partizan Liptovsky Mikulas, VTJ Pisek, Skalica, Spisska Nova Ves. **Teams with one player selected:** Banik Sokolov, KLH Chomutov, Havlickuv Brod, Ostrava, KC SKP Poprad, Povazska Bystrica, Topolcany, HK Trnava, KHM Zvolen.

Finland

Total	Club	'06	'05	'04	'03	'02	'01	'00	'99	'98	'97	'96	'95	'94	'93	'92	'91	'90	'89	'88	'87	'86	'85	'84	'83	'82	'81	'80	'79	'78	'77	'76	'69 to '75
39	HIFK Helsinki	4	1	2	–	5	2	2	4	2	1	–	1	–	2	–	–	1	2	2	1	1	–	–	–	1	–	3
36	Jokerit	2	–	1	2	6	4	3	3	1	1	–	1	–	3	–	2	–	1	1	–	–	1	2	–	–
34	TPS Turku	–	–	1	1	1	3	3	1	3	3	1	3	2	3	–	–	1	1	–	6	1	–	–	2	1	–	5
33	Ilves	3	3	–	2	4	3	1	2	–	2	–	–	1	1	–	1	1	1	–	1	1	–	–	–	5
24	Karpat	–	2	2	3	3	–	1	1	–	1	–	1	–	2	2	1	–	1	–	1	–	–
20	Tappara	–	–	1	1	2	2	1	–	2	1	1	–	1	–	1	–	4	–	–	–	1	–	1	2	3
18	Lukko	–	–	1	1	3	1	2	–	1	1	1	–	1	–	–	–	–	–	–	–	–	–	–	–	–
16	Assat	2	–	1	–	1	1	1	1	–	2	2	1	–	–	–	–	–	–	–	–	–	–	–	–	–
16	Blues Espoo	–	1	1	–	1	2	–	2	–	1	2	1	1	–	–	–	–	–	–	–	–	–	–	–	–
12	HPK	1	–	1	3	1	1	1	–	1	–	–	–	–	–	–	–	–	–	–	–	–	–	–	–	–
11	JyP Jyvaskyla	–	1	–	2	1	–	3	–	1	2	–	–	–	–	–	–	–	–	–	–	–	–	–	–	–
10	KalPa Kuopio	1	–	1	–	2	1	–	1	–	2	1	–	–	–	–	–	–	–	–	–	–	–	–	–	1
8	Reipas Lahti	–	–	1	–	–	–	1	1	1	1	–	1	–	–	–	–	–	–	–	–	–	–	–	–	–
7	SaiPa Lappeen.	–	1	1	1	–	1	1	–	–	–	–	–	–	–	–	–	–	–	–	–	–	–	–	–	–
3	Kiekoo-67	–	–	–	3	–	–	–	–	–	–	–	–	–	–	–	–	–	–	–	–	–	–	–	–	–

Teams with two players selected: KooKoo Kouvola, Sapko Savonlinna, Sport Vaasa, TuTo.
Teams with one player selected: Ahmat Hyvinkaa, Hermes Kokkola, Junkkarit Kalajoki, GrIFK Kauniainen, LeKi, S-Kiekko Seinajoki.

New Jersey selected Zach Parise (top) from the University of North Dakota with the 17th pick in 2003 Entry Draft. Ottawa selected Slovak Andrej Meszaros from Dukla Trencin with the 23rd selection in 2004.

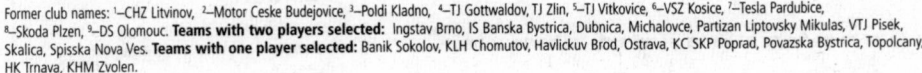

USSR/CIS/Russia

Total	Club	'06	'05	'04	'03	'02	'01	'00	'99	'98	'97	'96	'95	'94	'93	'92	'91	'90	'89	'88	'87	'86	'85	'84	'83	'82	'81	'80	'79	'78	'77	'76	'69 to '75
61	CSKA Moscow	1	1	3	3	–	–	–	3	1	–	3	2	5	3	7	4	3	8	5	1	1	1	–	4	1	–	–	–	1	–	–	2
45	Dynamo Moscow	–	–	1	1	–	–	2	2	1	1	1	7	1	2	10	7	4	3	2	–	–	–	–	–	–	–	–	–	–	–	–	–
33	Krylja Sovetov	1	1	2	–	1	1	1	2	1	1	2	3	5	1	3	4	2	1	1	–	–	–	–	–	–	–	–	–	–	–	–	–
28	Lokomotiv Yaro. 2	3	2	–	3	1	1	9	–	4	2	2	1	–	–	–	–	–	–	–	–	–	–	–	–	–	–	–	–	–	–	–	–
22	Lokomotiv Yaro.[1]	–	–	–	4	2	–	1	1	3	1	1	5	1	–	–	2	1	–	–	–	–	–	–	–	–	–	–	–	–	–	–	–
22	Spartak Moscow	–	–	–	–	–	6	–	1	–	–	–	1	6	–	4	1	–	–	–	1	–	1	–	–	1	–	–	–	–	–	–	1
19	Traktor Chelyabinsk	1	2	–	–	1	–	–	–	1	1	–	1	1	7	2	–	–	2	–	–	–	–	–	–	–	–	–	–	–	–	–	–
18	Lada Togliatti	2	–	2	–	2	–	2	2	1	3	1	–	–	2	1	–	–	–	–	–	–	–	–	–	–	–	–	–	–	–	–	–
16	Dynamo 2	–	–	–	1	–	–	4	–	3	3	–	–	2	1	2	–	–	–	–	–	–	–	–	–	–	–	–	–	–	–	–	–
16	Elektrostal	–	–	–	2	9	1	–	–	–	1	–	–	–	–	3	–	–	–	–	–	–	–	–	–	–	–	–	–	–	–	–	–
14	Voskresensk	–	–	–	1	–	1	1	–	2	–	–	–	1	–	2	1	3	1	–	–	–	–	–	1	–	–	–	–	–	–	–	–
13	Severstal Cher.[2]	1	–	–	2	–	–	1	5	–	–	1	1	–	1	1	–	–	–	–	–	–	–	–	–	–	–	–	–	–	–	–	–
11	CSKA Moscow 2	2	1	1	2	–	–	–	–	–	2	2	–	1	–	–	–	–	–	–	–	–	–	–	–	–	–	–	–	–	–	–	–
11	HC CSKA	–	–	–	–	4	–	5	2	–	–	–	–	–	–	–	–	–	–	–	–	–	–	–	–	–	–	–	–	–	–	–	–
11	SKA St. Pete.[3]	–	–	–	–	–	2	1	2	–	–	–	–	1	–	1	2	–	–	–	–	–	–	–	–	1	–	–	–	1	–	–	–
11	Sokol Kiev	–	–	–	–	–	–	–	–	–	–	–	2	–	1	3	2	1	–	1	–	–	–	1	–	–	–	–	–	–	–	–	–
10	Pardaugava Riga[4]	–	–	–	–	–	–	–	–	–	–	–	–	–	1	4	1	–	2	1	–	–	–	–	–	–	–	–	–	–	–	–	–
9	Avangard Omsk	–	–	–	–	1	3	1	–	–	–	1	–	3	–	–	–	–	–	–	–	–	–	–	–	–	–	–	–	–	–	–	–
9	THC Tver	–	–	3	3	–	1	2	–	–	–	–	–	–	–	–	–	–	–	–	–	–	–	–	–	–	–	–	–	–	–	–	–
9	Ufa	–	–	–	1	–	–	1	–	–	1	1	1	2	2	–	–	–	–	–	–	–	–	–	–	–	–	–	–	–	–	–	–
9	Ust-Kamenogorsk	–	–	–	1	–	–	–	1	2	–	–	1	2	1	1	–	–	–	–	–	–	–	–	–	–	–	–	–	–	–	–	–
7	Magnitogorsk	1	–	1	1	1	3	–	–	–	–	–	–	–	–	–	–	–	–	–	–	–	–	–	–	–	–	–	–	–	–	–	–
7	Novokuznetsk	–	–	1	1	–	1	2	2	–	–	–	–	–	–	–	–	–	–	–	–	–	–	–	–	–	–	–	–	–	–	–	–
6	Lada Togliatti 2	–	1	–	–	–	2	2	1	–	–	–	–	–	–	–	–	–	–	–	–	–	–	–	–	–	–	–	–	–	–	–	–
6	Nizhnekamsk	–	–	1	–	–	2	2	–	–	1	–	–	–	–	–	–	–	–	–	–	–	–	–	–	–	–	–	–	–	–	–	–
5	AK Bars Kazan	–	–	–	1	–	1	1	–	1	–	–	–	1	–	–	–	–	–	–	–	–	–	–	–	–	–	–	–	–	–	–	–
5	Avangard Omsk 2	–	–	1	1	–	3	–	–	–	–	–	–	–	–	–	–	–	–	–	–	–	–	–	–	–	–	–	–	–	–	–	–
5	CSK VVS Samara	–	–	1	1	–	1	–	1	–	–	–	1	–	–	–	–	–	–	–	–	–	–	–	–	–	–	–	–	–	–	–	–
5	Perm	–	–	–	–	1	1	1	–	–	–	–	1	1	–	–	–	–	–	–	–	–	–	–	–	–	–	–	–	–	–	–	–
5	Tivali Minsk[5]	–	–	1	–	–	–	–	–	–	–	–	–	1	2	–	–	–	–	1	–	–	–	–	–	–	–	–	–	–	–	–	–
4	Dyn-Energ. Yekat.[6]	–	–	–	1	–	–	–	1	1	–	1	–	–	–	–	–	–	–	–	–	–	–	–	–	–	–	–	–	–	–	–	–
4	Krylja Sovetov 2	–	–	–	–	3	–	–	–	–	–	–	–	–	1	–	–	–	–	–	–	–	–	–	–	–	–	–	–	–	–	–	–
4	Nizhny Novgorod[7]	–	–	–	–	–	–	1	–	–	–	–	–	–	–	2	–	1	–	–	–	–	–	–	–	–	–	–	–	–	–	–	–
3	Ak-Bars Kazan 2	–	–	–	1	–	1	–	1	–	–	–	–	–	–	–	–	–	–	–	–	–	–	–	–	–	–	–	–	–	–	–	–
3	Kristall Saratov	–	–	1	–	–	1	–	–	–	–	–	–	–	1	–	–	–	–	–	–	–	–	–	–	–	–	–	–	–	–	–	–
3	Severstal Cher. 2	–	–	–	–	1	–	1	1	–	–	–	–	–	–	–	–	–	–	–	–	–	–	–	–	–	–	–	–	–	–	–	–

Former club names: [1]–Torpedo Yaroslavl, [2]–Metallurg Cherepovets, [3]–SKA Leningrad, [4]–Dynamo Riga, HC Riga, [5]–Dynamo Minsk, [6]–Avtomobilist Yekaterinburg, [7]–Torpedo Gorky.
Teams with two players selected: Dizelist Penza, Metallurg Novokuznetsk 2, Salavat Yulayev Ufa 2, Spartak Moscow 2, Torpedo Nizhny Novgorod 2, Yunost Minsk.
Teams with one player selected: Amur Khabarovsk, Argus Moscow, HC CSKA Moscow 2, Dynamo Khazov, Dynamo-81 Riga, Gazovik Tyumen, HK Gomel, Izohets St. Petersburg, Kapitan Stupino, Khimik Novopolotsk, Khimik Voskresensk 2, Mechel Chelyabinsk, Metallurg Magnitogorsk 2, Metalurgs Liepaja, Mostovik Kurgan, Neftekhimik Nizhnekamsk 2, SKA St. Petersburg 2, Spartak St. Petersburg, Sibir Novosibirsk 2, Stalkers-Juniors, Torpedo Nizhny Novgorod 2, THC Tver, Vityaz Podolsk, Vityaz Podolsk 2.

Sweden

Total	Club	'06	'05	'04	'03	'02	'01	'00	'99	'98	'97	'96	'95	'94	'93	'92	'91	'90	'89	'88	'87	'86	'85	'84	'83	'82	'81	'80	'79	'78	'77	'76	'69 to '75
38	Djurgarden	1	1	2	–	2	1	4	1	–	2	2	3	–	1	1	2	1	1	–	2	1	–	1	2	1	–	2	1	–	–	1	5
37	Vastra Frolunda	3	3	4	2	3	3	4	2	1	–	1	1	3	–	1	–	–	1	1	1	–	1	2	–	–	–	–	–	–	–	–	0
36	MoDo	–	1	1	–	3	–	3	7	–	3	3	–	–	5	2	2	–	–	–	1	–	–	2	–	1	–	–	1	–	–	1	3
33	Farjestad	1	–	–	–	2	1	–	1	6	3	–	2	–	1	2	1	–	1	–	–	–	2	1	1	1	2	1	–	2	2	–	8
30	Leksand	1	1	–	2	–	–	5	–	2	–	1	–	2	2	–	2	–	1	2	1	1	2	2	–	1	–	–	1	–	–	–	2
24	AIK Solna	–	–	–	–	1	1	–	3	1	1	–	–	1	–	1	1	1	–	–	–	–	4	–	1	3	2	–	1	1	–	1	8
24	Brynas Gavle	1	–	–	2	–	2	1	1	2	1	1	–	–	1	–	–	–	–	–	4	–	–	2	1	–	1	1	1	1	–	–	4
24	Sodertalje	2	3	1	2	–	1	1	–	1	–	–	–	–	1	–	–	–	2	–	–	2	2	2	1	1	1	–	–	1	–	–	3
22	HV 71	–	1	2	1	1	–	1	3	4	1	2	–	2	–	–	–	1	–	1	1	–	–	–	–	–	1	–	–	–	–	–	1
16	Malmo	1	1	1	1	4	–	1	1	–	–	2	–	1	1	1	–	–	–	1	–	–	–	–	–	–	–	–	–	–	–	–	0
14	Vasteras	3	–	1	–	1	–	1	–	–	–	–	–	1	1	–	1	1	2	2	–	–	–	–	–	–	–	–	–	–	–	–	0
11	Lulea	–	–	1	–	–	–	2	–	1	1	–	–	–	–	1	–	–	–	1	1	1	–	–	–	–	1	1	–	–	–	–	2
10	Hammarby	1	–	–	–	3	–	1	–	–	1	–	–	–	1	1	–	–	–	–	–	–	–	–	–	–	–	1	1	–	–	–	2
10	Skelleftea	–	–	–	–	–	–	–	–	–	1	–	–	–	1	–	–	–	–	1	–	–	–	1	2	1	1	–	–	–	–	1	3
9	Rogle	–	–	–	–	–	–	–	1	–	–	–	1	2	2	–	–	–	–	2	1	–	–	–	–	–	–	–	–	–	–	–	0
8	Bjorkloven	2	1	–	–	–	–	–	–	–	–	–	–	–	–	–	–	–	–	1	–	–	1	–	–	–	1	2	–	–	–	–	3
8	Timra	–	–	–	–	1	–	–	1	–	–	–	–	1	–	–	–	–	–	–	–	1	1	–	–	–	2	1	–	–	–	–	3
7	Huddinge	1	–	–	–	1	1	–	1	–	–	2	–	–	–	–	1	–	–	–	–	–	–	–	–	–	–	–	–	–	–	–	0
6	Mora	–	–	–	1	–	1	–	–	–	1	1	–	–	–	–	–	–	–	–	–	1	–	–	1	–	–	–	–	–	–	–	0
6	Orebro	–	–	1	–	–	–	–	–	–	–	–	–	–	–	–	–	–	–	–	1	–	1	–	1	–	–	–	–	1	–	1	2
4	Nacka	–	–	–	–	–	–	–	–	–	–	–	–	–	–	2	–	–	1	–	–	1	–	–	–	–	–	–	–	–	–	–	0
4	Troja/Ljungby	–	–	–	1	–	–	–	1	–	–	–	–	–	–	–	–	–	–	1	–	–	1	–	–	–	–	–	–	–	–	–	0
3	Boden	–	–	–	–	–	–	–	–	–	–	–	–	1	–	–	–	–	–	–	–	1	–	–	–	–	–	–	–	–	–	–	0
3	Falun	–	–	–	–	–	–	–	–	–	–	–	–	–	–	–	1	–	–	1	–	–	–	–	–	–	1	–	–	–	–	–	1
3	Grums	–	–	–	–	–	–	1	1	–	–	–	–	1	–	–	–	–	–	–	–	–	–	–	–	–	–	–	–	–	–	–	0
3	Linkoping	1	1	1	–	–	–	–	–	–	–	–	–	–	–	–	–	–	–	–	–	–	–	–	–	–	–	–	–	–	–	–	0
3	Morrum	–	–	–	–	2	1	–	–	–	–	–	–	–	–	–	–	–	–	–	–	–	–	–	–	–	–	–	–	–	–	–	0
3	Pitea	–	–	–	–	–	–	–	–	–	–	–	–	1	–	–	–	1	–	–	–	–	–	–	–	1	–	–	–	–	–	–	1
3	Stocksund	–	–	2	–	–	–	–	–	–	–	–	–	–	–	–	–	–	–	–	–	–	–	–	–	1	–	–	–	–	–	–	1
3	Team Kiruna	–	–	–	–	–	–	–	–	–	–	–	–	–	1	–	–	–	–	–	–	–	–	–	–	1	–	–	–	1	–	–	2

Teams with two players selected: Hasten, Ostersund. **Teams with one player selected:** Almtuna, Arboga, Arvika, Bofors, Danderyd Hockey, Fagersta, Jamtland, Karskoga, Kumla, Stocksund, S/G Hockey 83 Gavle, Skovde, Sunne, Talje, Tingsryd, Tunabro, Uppsala, Vallentuna, Vasby.

2006 Entry Draft Analysis

Country of Origin

Country	Players Drafted
Canada	83
USA	60
Czech Republic	8
Sweden	18
Russia	15
Finland	13
Slovakia	4
Germany	3
Latvia	2
Estonia	1
Slovenia	1
Switzerland	3
Austria	2

Birth Year

Year	Players Drafted
1988	127
1987	62
1986	23
1985	1

Position

Position	Players Drafted
Defense	66
Center	60
Right Wing	28
Left Wing	33
Goaltender	26

Note: Players drafted in the international category played outside North America in their draft year.

European-born players drafted from the OHL, QMJHL, WHL, U.S. colleges or other North American leagues are not counted as International players.

See Country of Origin above.

European Draft Firsts

1969 – First European (and Finn) Selected The first European-trained player selected was left winger Tommi Salmelainen taken 66th overall by the St. Louis Blues in 1969.

1974 – First Swede Selected Center Per Alexandersson was selected by the Toronto Maple Leafs 49th overall in 1974. Four other Swedish-born players were selected that year, including defenseman Stefan Persson (214th overall, NY Islanders) who became the first European to play on a Stanley Cup winner. (four times, 1980-83).

1975 – First Russian Selected The Philadelphia Flyers selected center Viktor Khatulev 160th overall in 1975.

1976 – First European Taken in the First Round The California Seals selected Swedish defenseman Bjorn Johansson with their first pick, fifth overall, in the 1976 Amateur Draft.

1976 – First Swiss Selected The St. Louis Blues selected center Jacques Soguel 121st overall in 1976.

1978 – First Czechoslovak Selected The Detroit Red Wings selected left winger Ladislav Svozil 194th overall in 1978

1978 – First German Selected The first German players were also drafted in 1978. The Atlanta Flames selected goaltender Bernard Englbrecht 196th overall and St. Louis selected forward Gerd Truntschka 200th overall.

1989 – First European Taken First Overall The Quebec Nordiques selected Swedish center Mats Sundin first overall in 1989.

Notes on 2006 First-Round Selections

1. ST. LOUIS • **ERIK JOHNSON** • D • An offensive-minded defenseman who is also a solid positional player in the defensive zone, Erik Johnson is respected by teammates and opponents. At 6'4" and 222 pounds, he is a physical presence who is very strong on his feet. He's a powerful skater with long smooth strides who has tremendous acceleration in open ice. Johnson makes the transition from defense to offense quickly and has a hard accurate shot from the point. He is a graduate of the U.S. National Team Development Program.

2. PITTSBURGH • **JORDAN STAAL** • C • A premier forward with a powerful shot and good agility, Jordan Staal is an excellent skater with a wide base style that makes him solid on his skates. Standing 6'4"and weighing 215 pounds, he uses his tremendous size and long reach to protect the puck. He sees the ice well and is able to move the puck through traffic. Jordan's brother Eric was taken second overall in the 2003 Entry Draft, while Marc Staal went twelfth in 2005.

3. CHICAGO • **JONATHAN TOEWS** • C/W • An extremely smart and versatile player, Jonathan Toews has played both wing and center and has very good poise and patience with the puck. He possesses excellent acceleration, quickness and agility and an excellent shot with a quick release. Toews is not overly physical, but works hard and leads by example. He was captain of Canada's Under-18 team in 2005 and won a gold medal at the 2006 World Junior Championship.

4. WASHINGTON • **NICKLAS BACKSTROM** • C • A very mobile skater with acceleration, speed and balance, Nicklas Backstrom is a creative offensive talent with an excellent work ethic and incredible hockey sense. Backstrom is a natural scorer with smooth hands and a quick release. He's a finesse player who can play tough. Backstrom was named best forward on Brynas in 2006 and was the Swedish elite league's rookie of the year.

5. BOSTON • **PHIL KESSEL** • C • A very fast skater who can surprise opponents with an extra gear, Phil Kessel can separate himself from pursuers in an instant and turn players inside out one-on-one. Kessel has a heavy and accurate shot and is an excellent passer and playmaker. He is also good on face-offs and does not shy away along the boards. Kessel is a graduate of the U.S. National Team Development Program who starred at the 2005 World Under-18 Championship.

6. COLUMBUS • **DERICK BRASSARD** • C • A very good skater who can change direction quickly in tight quarters, Derick Brassard can carry the puck end to end. He sees the ice well and reads the play smartly with very good decision making in all areas of the ice. Brassard can beat defenders one-on-one and has a very accurate wrist and slap shot. He is not a very physical player, but is smart in breaking up plays.

7. NYI ISLANDERS • **KYLE OKPOSO** • RW • A strong skater with a good burst of speed, Kyle Okposo comes off the boards and out of the corners using his strength and good balance. He drives hard to the net and is difficult to contain. Okposo likes the physical game and has a "no quit" attitude. He's capable of dominating offensively and knows his defensive responsibilities. He was a 2005-06 USHL All-Star as a rookie.

8. PHOENIX• **PETER MUELLER** • C • An efficient player with offensive talent and defensive responsibility, Peter Mueller has deceptive speed and the uncanny ability to be in the right spot at the right time. He has a heavy shot with a quick release and is good at creating space for his teammates. Mueller is a graduate of the U.S. National Team Development program who went on to play in the WHL.

9. MINNESOTA • **JAMES SHEPPARD** • C • A good skater with a long fluid stride and size-15 feet, James Sheppard is strong on his feet and attains good speed when under way. He is strong along the boards and in the corners while having good playmaking skills and can also score. Sheppard has a good wrist and slap shot which he releases quickly on the go. He will take a check to make a play and has very good vision.

10. FLORIDA • **MICHAEL FROLIK** • C/W • An excellent skater with acceleration, speed and good balance, Michael Frolik is a finesse player loaded with skills. He is a good passer and playmaker with excellent hands and a good hockey sense. Frolik reads the game exceptionally well and has a good selection of shots, though he often prefers to pass. He plays with confidence and works hard in all zones.

11. LOS ANGELES • **JONATHAN BERNIER** • G • A strong skater with excellent balance, Jonathan Bernier has both quick reactions and recovery. He has very quick feet and pads with excellent controlled lateral movement. Bernier has good net coverage, plays his angles well and does a good job of blocking passes from behind the net. He uses the paddle-down technique on wraparounds and has good rebound control. Bernier also goes behind the net well to stop dump-ins.

12. ATLANTA • **BRYAN LITTLE** • C • A highly skilled playmaker who sees the ice well, Bryan Little uses good hands and good passing ability to move the puck through traffic. He possesses a good shot that he gets away quickly and is a good face-off man who is often used for important draws. Little is not big (5'10", 200 pounds) but protects the puck well and plays a competitive two-way game. He is able to force turnovers and is a threat to score shorthanded.

13. TORONTO • **JIRI TLUSTY** • C/W • An excellent skater who is fast and mobile, Jiri Tlusty is strong on his feet and has outstanding acceleration. He's a very good puckhandler with good soft hands who likes to go directly for the net. Tlusty is a sniper who likes to shoot a lot and can score in many ways. He's a hard-working competitor who does not shy away from the physical part of the game. Tlusty captained the Czech team to a bronze medal at the 2006 Under-18 Championship.

14. VANCOUVER • **MICHAEL GRABNER** • RW • A fast skater who is good at getting to holes and loose pucks, Michael Grabner has excellent acceleration and can be at full speed in three strides. He has very good balance and mobility in all directions, possesses very quick hands and has a creative scoring touch. Grabner plays with hustle both at home and on the road, and though he is not overly aggressive, he will bump and finish checks and compete for loose pucks.

15. TAMPA BAY • **RIKU HELENIUS** • G • A product of the Ilves system that produced 2005 first-round draft choice Tuukka Rask and is gaining a reputation as a goalie factory, Riku Helenius is a big goaltender (6'3", 202 pounds) who uses his size to advantage. He plays the butterfly, has a good glove and reads the game well. Helenius plays the angles well and though he needs to improve his footwork and puckhandling skills, he shows lots of desire and determination.

16. SAN JOSE • **TY WISHART** • D • Standing 6'4" and weighing 205 pounds, Ty Wishart is very solid and steady in his one-on-one play and adept at angling and forcing opposing players to the outside. He has good speed and agility for a player his size and is a strong backwards skater. Wishart does not have an overpowering shot from the point, but has a high percentage of getting his shots through. He is not a punishing hitter, but clears out the front of the net well.

17. LOS ANGELES • **TREVOR LEWIS** • C • A strong skater with excellent acceleration and quickness, Trevor Lewis can intimidate defensemen with his ability to change directions at top speed. He can shoot the puck on the fly and does not hesitate to pull the trigger every chance he gets. Lewis has good puck skills and maneuvers very well in traffic. He's good on face-offs, is an effective forechecker and is a good passer.

18. COLORADO • **CHRIS STEWART** • RW • A power forward who possesses a long powerful stride, Chris Stewart is solid on his skates with good balance and agility. He sees the ice well and is a solid competitor who fights through checks. Stewart is an aggressive forechecker who finishes his checks with authority. His brother Anthony was a first-round selection of the Florida Panthers in 2003.

19. ANAHEIM • **MARK MITERA** • D • Strong on his skates and hard to knock off the puck, Mark Mitera is a good skater with a smooth stride and a good backwards skater who pivots well and has good agility. Mitera is not an offensive-minded defenseman, but he makes a crisp first pass and likes to make long lead passes. He can rush the puck and possesses a quick, accurate wrist/snap shot from the point.

20. MONTREAL • **DAVID FISCHER** • D • Minnesota high school star David Fischer is a strong skater with a wide base and quick first two steps. His pivots and turns are sharp, allowing him to gain time and space. He reads and reacts very well to the play at hand and makes good use of his body when protecting the puck. Fischer has soft hands and a lot of confidence in his skills when rushing the puck.

21. NY RANGERS • **BOBBY SANGUINETTI** • D • A good skater with a long smooth stride and good agility and balance, Bobby Sanguinetti is an offensive defenseman who moves the puck well. He makes hard accurate outlet passes, sees the ice well and is able to move the puck through traffic. Sanguinetti will carry the puck, has the ability to go end to end with it, and the mobility to recover quickly. He's a steady competitor who gives a consistent effort.

22. PHILADELPHIA • **CLAUDE GIROUX** • RW • A clever playmaker who excels at killing penalties, Claude Giroux is a good skater who reads the play well and is able to move the puck through traffic. He has very good hands and handles the puck well in a crowd. Giroux is quick to jump into openings and carries the puck with confidence. He has a very good hockey sense and a quick and accurate wrist shot. Giroux is not physical, but is not afraid of getting involved.

23. WASHINGTON • **SIMEON VARLAMOV** • G • With strong legs, excellent reflexes and an extremely quick glove hand, Semen Varlamov is a fine competitor who plays with intensity and communicates well with his defensemen. He plays the butterfly, but needs to improve his puckhandling outside the crease. Varlamov was selected as the best goaltender at the 2006 Five Nations Under-18 tournament.

24. BUFFALO • **DENNIS PERSSON** • D • A good skater with good offensive instincts, Dennis Persson likes to join the offensive rush. He sees the ice very well and finds his forwards with long first passes. Persson reads the game very well and can carry the puck out of danger. He has a good shot from the blueline and is a good team player who works hard to improve his overall game and has a good attitude.

25. ST. LOUIS • **PATRIK BERGLUND**• C • A cool creative playmaker with a good understanding of the game, Patrik Berglund is a good skater who needs to improve his first-step quickness. He has smooth hands and a good quick wrist shot. Berglund creates a lot of scoring chances and looks composed on the ice. He is a hard-working competitor with great offensive instincts and can play a physical and aggressive game when needed, though he could improve his intensity.

26. CALGARY • **LELAND IRVING** • G • A butterfly goalie with good balance and agility, Leland Irving's positional play is very good. He uses the paddle-down technique on wraparounds and stands square to the shooter when playing at the top of the crease. Irving moves very well laterally and is tough to beat low down. He has a quick glove hand and good natural instincts. He makes proper decisions with the puck and does not get rattled when opponents crash the net.

27. DALLAS • **IVAN VISHNEVSKY** • D • A combination of skillful puckhandling, good on-ice vision and good hands, plus a quick wrist shot and powerful slapshot, make Ivan Vishnevsky a dangerous offensive defenseman. He is an excellent skater, both forward and backwards, and his tremendous acceleration allows him to pull away from defenders. Vishnevsky sees the ice very well and has the ability to move the puck through a crowd.

28. OTTAWA • **NICK FOLIGNO** • LW • The son of former NHLer Mike Foligno, Nick Foligno is a gritty, hard-working and aggressive forward who is an unselfish playmaker. He's a solid skater with good balance who has good hands and can handle the puck well in traffic. Foligno is an excellent passer and is defensively responsible. He goes hard to the net and battles tough in front, where he is difficult to move. Foligno is also a very good shot blocker.

29. PHOENIX • **CHRIS SUMMERS** • D • A very good skater with agility, mobility and lateral quickness, Chris Summers has very quick feet and very good balance. He's a very good passer who hits the open man and also has a good shot from the blueline. Summers has a good hockey sense and reads and anticipates the play well in the defensive zone. He is a graduate of the U.S. National Team Development Program.

30. NEW JERSEY • **MATTHEW CORRENTE** • D • With superior mobility, a smooth stride and exceptional lateral movement, Matthew Corrente is a very good skater with good balance and agility. He has a variety of shots that he gets away quickly from the point and he makes good outlet passes to initiate breakouts. Corrente is not a punishing hitter, but will take the body and finish his checks. He has good strength.

Players selected first through tenth in the 2006 NHL Entry Draft. (All rows left to right):
Top row: 1. Erik Johnson, D, St. Louis;
2. Jordan Staal, C, Pittsburgh.
Second row: 3. Jonathan Toews, C/W, Chicago;
4. Nicklas Backstrom, C, Washington.
Third row: 5. Phil Kessel, C, Boston;
6. Derick Brassard, C, Columbus.
Fourth row: 7. Kyle Okposo, RW, NY Islanders;
8. Peter Mueller, C, Phoenix.
Bottom row: 9. James Sheppard, C, Minnesota;
10. Michael Frolik, C/W, Florida.

2006 NHL ENTRY DRAFT

Pick	Claimed by	Amateur Club	Position

FIRST ROUND

Pick	Claimed by	Amateur Club	Position
1	St.L. Erik Johnson	USA U-18	D
2	Pit. Jordan Staal	Peterborough	C
3	Chi. Jonathan Toews	U. of North Dakota	C
4	Wsh. Nicklas Backstrom	Brynas	C
5	Bos. Phil Kessel	U. of Minnesota	C
6	CBJ Derick Brassard	Drummondville	C
7	NYI Kyle Okposo	Des Moines	RW
8	Phx. Peter Mueller	Everett	C
9	Min. James Sheppard	Cape Breton	C
10	Fla. Michael Frolik	Kladno	C
11	L.A. Jonathan Bernier	Lewiston	G
12	Atl. Bryan Little	Barrie	C
13	Tor. Jiri Tlusty	Kladno	C
14	Van. Michael Grabner	Spokane	RW
15	T.B. Riku Helenius	Ilves	G
16	S.J. Ty Wishart	Prince George	D
17	L.A. Trevor Lewis	Des Moines	C
18	Col. Chris Stewart	Kingston	RW
19	Ana. Mark Mitera	U. of Michigan	D
20	Mtl. David Fischer	Apple Valley	D
21	NYR Bobby Sanguinetti	Owen Sound	D
22	Phi. Claude Giroux	Gatineau	RW
23	Wsh. Semen Varlamov	Yaroslavl 2	G
24	Buf. Dennis Persson	Vasteras	D
25	St.L. Patrik Berglund	Vasteras	C
26	Cgy. Leland Irving	Everett	G
27	Dal. Ivan Vishnevskiy	Rouyn Noranda	D
28	Ott. Nick Foligno	Sudbury	LW
29	Phx. Chris Summers	USA U-18	D
30	N.J. Matthew Corrente	Saginaw	D

SECOND ROUND

Pick	Claimed by	Amateur Club	Position
31	St.L. Tomas Kana	Vitkovice	C
32	Pit. Carl Sneep	Brainerd	D
33	Chi. Igor Makarov	Krylja	RW
34	Wsh. Michal Neuvirth	Sparta Jr.	G
35	Wsh. Francois Bouchard	Baie Comeau	RW
36	S.J. Jamie Mcginn	Ottawa	LW
37	Bos. Yuri Alexandrov	Cherepovets	D
38	Ana. Bryce Swan	Halifax	RW
39	Phi. Andreas Nodl	Sioux Falls	RW
40	Min. Ondrej Fiala	Everett	C
41	Det. Cory Emmerton	Kingston	C
42	Phi. Michael Ratchuk	USA U-18	D
43	Atl. Riley Holzapfel	Moose Jaw	C
44	Tor. Nikolai Kulemin	Magnitogorsk	W
45	Edm. Jeff Petry	Des Moines	D
46	Buf. Jhonas Enroth	Sodertalje	G
47	Det. Shawn Matthias	Belleville	C
48	L.A. Joe Ryan	Quebec	D
49	Mtl. Ben Maxwell	Kootenay	C
50	Bos. Milan Lucic	Vancouver	LW
51	Col. Nigel Williams	USA U-18	D
52	Wsh. Keith Seabrook	Burnaby	D
53	Mtl. Mathieu Carle	Acadie-Bathurst	D
54	NYR Artem Anisimov	Yaroslavl	C
55	Phi. Denis Bodrov	Togliatti	D
56	Nsh. Blake Geoffrion	USA U-18	LW
57	Buf. Mike Weber	Windsor	D
58	N.J. Alexander Vasyunov	Yaroslavl 2	LW
59	Col. Codey Burki	Brandon	C
60	NYI Jesse Joensuu	Assat	W
61	Chi. Simon Danis-Pepin	U. of Maine	D
62	Det. Dick Axelsson	Huddinge	W
63	Car. Jamie Mcbain	USA U-18	D

THIRD ROUND

Pick	Claimed by	Amateur Club	Position
64	St.L. Jonas Junland	Linkoping	D
65	Pit. Brian Strait	USA U-18	D
66	Mtl. Ryan White	Calgary	C
67	N.J. Kirill Tulupov	Alemetjevsk	D
68	Ott. Eric Gryba	Green Bay	D
69	CBJ Steve Mason	London	G
70	NYI Robin Figren	Frolunda Jr.	W
71	Bos. Brad Marchand	Moncton	C
72	Min. Cal Clutterbuck	Oshawa	RW
73	Fla. Brady Calla	Everett	RW
74	L.A. Jeff Zatkoff	Miami U.	G
75	Edm. Theo Peckham	Owen Sound	D
76	Chi. Tony Lagerstrom	Sodertalje Jr.	C
77	N.J. Vladimir Zharkov	CSKA 2	RW
78	T.B. Kevin Quick	Salisbury	D
79	Phi. Jonathan Matsumoto	Bowling Green	C
80	Atl. Michael Forney	Thief River Falls	LW
81	Col. Michael Carman	USA U-18	C
82	Van. Daniel Rahimi	Bjorkloven Jr.	D
83	Ana. John Degray	Brampton	D
84	NYR Ryan Hillier	Halifax	LW
85	CBJ Tommy Sestito	Plymouth	LW
86	L.A. Bud Holloway	Seattle	C
87	Cgy. John Armstrong	Plymouth	C
88	Phx. Jonas Ahnelov	Frolunda	D
89	Cgy. Aaron Marvin	Warroad	C
90	Dal. Aaron Snow	Brampton	LW
91	Ott. Kaspars Daugavins	Riga	LW
92	Det. Daniel Larsson	Hammarby	G
93	Car. Harrison Reed	Sarnia	RW

FOURTH ROUND

Pick	Claimed by	Amateur Club	Position
94	St.L. Ryan Turek	Omaha	C
95	Chi. Ben Shutron	Kingston	D
96	Chi. Joseph Palmer	USA U-18	G
97	Wsh. Oskar Osala	Mississauga	LW
98	S.J. James Delory	Oshawa	D
99	Tor. James Reimer	Red Deer	G
100	NYI Rhett Rakhshani	USA U-18	RW
101	Phi. Joonas Lehtivuori	Ilves Jr.	D
102	Min. Kyle Medvec	Apple Valley	D
103	Fla. Michael Caruso	Guelph	D
104	NYR David Kveton	Vsetin	RW
105	Nsh. Niko Snellman	Ilves Jr.	W
106	St.L. Reto Berra	Zurich/Kusnacht	G
107	N.J. T.J. Miller	Penticton	D
108	NYI Jase Weslosky	Sherwood Park	G
109	Phi. Jakub Kovar	Budejovice Jr.	G
110	Col. Kevin Montgomery	USA U-18	D
111	Tor. Korbinian Holzer	Bad Tolz	D
112	Ana. Matt Beleskey	Belleville	LW
113	CBJ Ben Wright	Lethbridge	D
114	L.A. Niclas Andersen	Leksand	C
115	NYI Tomas Marcinko	Kosice	C
116	Fla. Derrick Lapoint	Eau Claire North	D
117	Buf. Felix Schutz	Saint John	C
118	Cgy. Hugo Carpentier	Rouyn Noranda	C
119	NYI Doug Rogers	St. Sebastian's	C
120	Dal. Richard Bachman	Cushing Academy	G
121	Ott. Pierre-Luc Lessard	Gatineau	D
122	Wsh. Luke Lynes	Brampton	C
123	Car. Bobby Hughes	Kingston	C

FIFTH ROUND

Pick	Claimed by	Amateur Club	Position
124	St.L. Andy Sackrison	St. Louis Park	C
125	Pit. Chad Johnson	Alaska-Fairbanks	G
126	NYI Shane Sims	Des Moines	D
127	Wsh. Maxime Lacroix	Quebec	LW
128	Bos. Andrew Bodnarchuk	Halifax	D
129	CBJ Robert Nyholm	IFK Jr.	RW
130	Phx. Brett Bennett	USA U-18	G
131	Phx. Martin Latal	Kladno	RW
132	Min. Niko Hovinen	Jokerit	G
133	Edm. Bryan Pitton	Brampton	G
134	L.A. David Meckler	Yale	C
135	Atl. Alex Kangas	Sioux Falls	G
136	CBJ Nick Sucharski	Michigan State	LW
137	NYR Tomas Zaborsky	Trencin	W
138	Dal. David Mcintyre	Newmarket	C
139	Mtl. Pavel Valentenko	Neftekamsk	D
140	Edm. Cody Wild	Providence	D
141	NYI Kim Johansson	Malmo Jr.	C
142	CBJ Maxime Frechette	Drummondville	D
143	S.J. Ashton Rome	Kamloops	RW
144	L.A. Martin Nolet	Champlain	D
145	Phi. Jonathan Rheault	Providence	RW
146	Nsh. Mark Dekanich	Colgate	G
147	Buf. Alex Biega	Salisbury	D
148	N.J. Olivier Magnan	Rouyn Noranda	D
149	Cgy. Juuso Puustinen	Kalpa Jr.	RW
150	Dal. Max Warn	IFK Jr.	LW
151	Ott. Ryan Daniels	Saginaw	G
152	Phx. Jordan Bendfeld	Medicine Hat	D
153	Car. Stefan Chaput	Lewiston	C

SIXTH ROUND

Pick	Claimed by	Amateur Club	Position
154	St.L. Matthew Mccollem	Belmont Hill	LW
155	Fla. Peter Aston	Windsor	C
156	Chi. Jan-Mikael Juutilainen	Jokerit Jr.	C
157	Wsh. Brent Gwidt	Lakeland H.S.	C
158	Bos. Levi Nelson	Swift Current	C
159	CBJ Jesse Dudas	Prince George	D
160	NYI Andrew Macdonald	Moncton	D
161	Tor. Viktor Stahlberg	Frolunda	LW
162	Min. Julian Walker	Basel	W
163	Van. Sergei Shirokov	CSKA	W
164	L.A. Constantin Braun	Eisbaren	LW
165	Atl. Jonas Enlund	IFK Jr.	C
166	Tor. Tyler Ruegsegger	Shattuck-St. Mary's	C
167	Van. Juraj Simek	Kloten	W
168	T.B. Dane Crowley	Swift Current	D
169	Chi. Chris Auger	Wellington	C
170	Edm. Alexander Bumagin	Togliatti	W
171	NYI Brian Day	Governor Dummer	RW
172	Ana. Petteri Wirtanen	HPK	C
173	NYI Stefan Ridderwall	Djurgarden Jr	G
174	NYR Eric Hunter	Prince George	C
175	Phi. Michael Dupont	Baie Comeau	G
176	Nsh. Ryan Flynn	USA U-18	RW
177	Wsh. Mathieu Perreault	Acadie-Bathurst	C
178	N.J. Tony Romano	NY Bobcats	C
179	Cgy. Jordan Fulton	Breck School	C
180	Tor. Leo Komarov	Assat	C
181	Ott. Kevin Koopman	Beaver Valley Jr B	D
182	Det. Jan Mursak	Budejovice Jr.	LW
183	Car. Nick Dodge	Clarkson	RW

Pick	Claimed by	Amateur Club	Position

SEVENTH ROUND

Pick	Claimed by	Amateur Club	Position
184	St.L.	Alexander Hellstrom	Bjorkloven	D
185	Pit.	Timo Seppanen	IFK	D
186	Chi.	Peter Leblanc	Hamilton	C
187	Cgy.	Devin Didiomete	Sudbury	LW
188	Phx.	Chris Frank	Western Michigan	D
189	CBJ	Derek Dorsett	Medicine Hat	RW
190	NYI	Troy Mattila	Springfield	LW
191	Det.	Nick Oslund	Burnsville	RW
192	Min.	Chris Hickey	Cretin Derham Hall	C
193	Fla.	Marc Cheverie	Nanaimo	G
194	CBJ	Matt Marquardt	Moncton	LW
195	Atl.	Jesse Martin	Spruce Grove	C
196	Phx.	Benn Ferriero	Boston College	C
197	Van.	Evan Fuller	Prince George	RW
198	T.B.	Denis Kazionov	Tver	LW
199	Mtl.	Cameron Cepek	Portland	D
200	Atl.	Arturs Kulda	CSKA 2	D
201	Col.	Billy Sauer	U. of Michigan	G
202	S.J.	John Mccarthy	Boston U.	LW
203	S.J.	Jay Barriball	Sioux Falls	LW
204	NYR	Lukas Zeliska	Trinec Jr.	C
205	Phi.	Andrei Popov	Chelyabinsk	RW
206	Nsh.	Viktor Sjodin	Vasteras Jr	W
207	Buf.	Benjamin Breault	Baie Comeau	C
208	N.J.	Kyle Henegan	Shawinigan	D
209	Cgy.	Per Jonsson	Farjestad Jr.	F
210	Atl.	Will O'Neill	Tabor Academy	D
211	Ott.	Erik Condra	U. of Notre Dame	RW
212	Det.	Logan Pyett	Regina	D
213	Car.	Justin Krueger	Penticton	D

First Two Rounds
2005–2003

2005

FIRST ROUND

Pick	Claimed by	Amateur Club	Position
1	Pit.	Sidney Crosby	Rimouski	C
2	Ana.	Bobby Ryan	Owen Sound	RW
3	Car.	Jack Johnson	USA U-18	D
4	Min.	Benoit Pouliot	Sudbury	LW
5	Mtl.	Carey Price	Tri-City	G
6	CBJ	Gilbert Brule	Vancouver	C
7	Chi.	Jack Skille	USA U-18	RW
8	S.J.	Devin Setoguchi	Saskatoon	RW
9	Ott.	Brian Lee	Moorhead	D
10	Van.	Luc Bourdon	Val D'or	D
11	L.A.	Anze Kopitar	Sodertalje Jr.	C
12	NYR	Marc Staal	Sudbury	D
13	Buf.	Marek Zagrapan	Chicoutimi	C
14	Wsh.	Sasha Pokulok	Cornell	D
15	NYI	Ryan O'Marra	Erie	C
16	Atl.	Alex Bourret	Lewiston	RW
17	Phx.	Martin Hanzal	C. Budejovice	D
18	Nsh.	Ryan Parent	Guelph	D
19	Det.	Jakub Kindl	Kitchener	D
20	Fla.	Kenndal McArdle	Moose Jaw	LW
21	Tor.	Tuukka Rask	Ilves Jr.	G
22	Bos.	Matt Lashoff	Kitchener	D
23	N.J.	Nicklas Bergfors	Sodertalje	RW
24	St.L.	T.J. Oshie	Warroad	C
25	Edm.	Andrew Cogliano	St. Mike's B's	C
26	Cgy.	Matt Pelech	Sarnia	D
27	Wsh.	Joe Finley	Sioux Falls	D
28	Dal.	Matt Niskanen	Virginia	D
29	Phi.	Steve Downie	Windsor	RW
30	T.B.	Vladimir Mihalik	Presov	D

SECOND ROUND

Pick	Claimed by	Amateur Club	Position
31	Ana.	Brendan Mikkelson	Portland	D
32	Fla.	Tyler Plante	Brandon	G
33	Dal.	James Neal	Plymouth	LW
34	Col.	Ryan Stoa	USA U-18	C
35	S.J.	Marc-Edouard Vlasic	Quebec	D
36	Edm.	Taylor Chorney	Shat.-St. Mary's	D
37	St.L.	Scott Jackson	Seattle	D
38	N.J.	Jeff Frazee	USA U-18	G
39	Bos.	Petr Kalus	Vitkovice Jr.	LW
40	NYR	Michael Sauer	Portland	D
41	Atl.	Ondrej Pavelec	Kladno Jr.	G
42	Det.	Justin Abdelkader	Cedar Rapids	LW
43	Chi.	Michael Blunden	Erie	RW
44	Col.	Paul Stastny	U. of Denver	C
45	Mtl.	Guillaume Latendresse	Drummondville	RW
46	NYI	Dustin Kohn	Calgary	D
47	Col.	Tom Fritsche	Ohio State	LW
48	Buf.	Philip Gogulla	Koln	RW
49	Atl.	Chad Denny	Lewiston	D
50	L.A.	Dany Roussin	Rimouski	LW
51	Van.	Mason Raymond	Camrose	LW
52	Col.	Chris Durand	Seattle	C
53	Atl.	Andrew Kozek	South Surrey	W
54	Chi.	Dan Bertram	Boston College	RW
55	CBJ	Adam McQuaid	Sudbury	D
56	NYR	Marc-Andre Cliche	Lewiston	RW

57	Min.	Matt Kassian	Kamloops	LW
58	Car.	Nathan Hagemo	U. of Minnesota	D
59	Phx.	Pier-Olivier Pelletier	Drummondville	G
60	L.A.	T.J. Fast	Camrose	D
61	Pit.	Michael Gergen	Shat.-St. Mary's	W

2004

FIRST ROUND

Pick	Claimed by	Amateur Club	Position
1	Wsh.	Alex Ovechkin	Dynamo	LW
2	Pit.	Evgeni Malkin	Magnitogorsk	C
3	Chi.	Cam Barker	Medicine Hat	D
4	Car.	Andrew Ladd	Calgary	LW
5	Phx.	Blake Wheeler	Breck	RW
6	NYR	Al Montoya	U. of Michigan	G
7	Fla.	Rostislav Olesz	Vitkovice	LW
8	CBJ	Alexandre Picard	Lewiston	LW
9	Ana.	Ladislav Smid	Liberec	D
10	Atl.	Boris Valabik	Kitchener	D
11	L.A.	Lauri Tukonen	Blues Espoo	RW
12	Min.	A.J. Thelen	Michigan State	D
13	Buf.	Drew Stafford	U. of North Dakota	RW
14	Edm.	Devan Dubnyk	Kamloops	G
15	Nsh.	Alexander Radulov	Tver	LW
16	NYI	Petteri Nokelainen	SaiPa	C
17	St.L.	Marek Schwarz	Sparta Praha	G
18	Mtl.	Kyle Chipchura	Prince Albert	C
19	NYR	Lauri Korpikoski	TPS Turku Jr.	LW
20	N.J.	Travis Zajac	Salmon Arm	C
21	Col.	Wojtek Wolski	Brampton	LW
22	S.J.	Lukas Kaspar	Litvinov	RW
23	Ott.	Andrej Meszaros	Trencin	D
24	Cgy.	Kris Chucko	Salmon Arm	RW
25	Edm.	Rob Schremp	London	C
26	Van.	Cory Schneider	Phillips-Andover	G
27	Wsh.	Jeff Schultz	Calgary	D
28	Dal.	Mark Fistric	Vancouver	D
29	Wsh.	Mike Green	Saskatoon	D
30	T.B.	Andy Rogers	Calgary	D

SECOND ROUND

Pick	Claimed by	Amateur Club	Position
31	Pit.	Johannes Salmonsson	Djurgarden	LW
32	Chi.	Dave Bolland	London	C/RW
33	Wsh.	Christopher Bourque	Cushing Academy	LW
34	Dal.	Johan Fransson	Lulea	D
35	Phx.	Logan Stephenson	Tri-City	D
36	NYR	Darin Olver	Northern Michigan	C
37	Fla.	David Shantz	Mississauga	G
38	Car.	Justin Peters	St. Michael's	G
39	Ana.	Jordan Smith	Sault Ste. Marie	D
40	Atl.	Grant Lewis	Dartmouth	D
41	Chi.	Bryan Bickell	Ottawa	LW
42	Min.	Roman Voloshenko	Krylja Sovetov	LW
43	Buf.	Michael Funk	Portland	D
44	Edm.	Roman Teslyuk	Kamloops	D
45	Chi.	Ryan Garlock	Windsor	C
46	CBJ	Adam Pineault	Boston College	RW
47	NYI	Blake Comeau	Kelowna	RW
48	NYR	Dane Byers	Prince Albert	LW
49	St.L.	Carl Soderberg	Malmo	C
50	Phx.	Enver Lisin	Saratov	RW
51	NYR	Bruce Graham	Moncton	C
52	Dal.	Raymond Sawada	Nanaimo	RW
53	Fla.	David Booth	Michigan State	LW
54	Chi.	Jakub Sindel	Sparta Praha	C
55	Col.	Victor Oreskovich	Green Bay	RW
56	Dal.	Niklas Grossman	Sodertalje Jr.	D
57	Edm.	Geoff Paukovich	U.S. Nat'l U-18	LW
58	Ott.	Kirill Lyamin	CSKA Moscow	D
59	CBJ	Kyle Wharton	Ottawa	D
60	NYR	Brandon Dubinsky	Portland	C
61	Pit.	Alex Goligoski	Sioux Falls	D
62	Wsh.	Michail Yunkov	Krylja	C
63	Bos.	David Krejci	Kladno Jr.	C
64	Bos.	Martins Karsums	Moncton	RW
65	T.B.	Mark Tobin	Rimouski	LW

2003

FIRST ROUND

Pick	Claimed by	Amateur Club	Position
1	Pit.	Marc-Andre Fleury	Cape Breton	G
2	Car.	Eric Staal	Peterborough	C
3	Fla.	Nathan Horton	Oshawa	C
4	CBJ	Nikolai Zherdev	CSKA Moscow	W
5	Buf.	Thomas Vanek	U. of Minnesota	LW
6	S.J.	Milan Michalek	Budejovice	RW
7	Nsh.	Ryan Suter	U.S. National U-18	D
8	Atl.	Braydon Coburn	Portland	D
9	Cgy.	Dion Phaneuf	Red Deer	D
10	Mtl.	Andrei Kostitsyn	CSKA Moscow 2	RW
11	Phi.	Jeff Carter	Sault Ste. Marie	C
12	NYR	Hugh Jessiman	Dartmouth	RW
13	L.A.	Dustin Brown	Guelph	RW
14	Chi.	Brent Seabrook	Lethbridge	D
15	NYI	Robert Nilsson	Leksand	C
16	S.J.	Steve Bernier	Moncton	RW
17	N.J.	Zach Parise	North Dakota	C
18	Wsh.	Eric Fehr	Brandon	RW

Selected 25th overall in the 2003 NHL Entry Draft, Anthony Stewart made his debut with the Florida Panthers on October 18, 2005. Colorado selected his brother Chris with the 18th pick in 2006.

19	Ana.	Ryan Getzlaf	Calgary	C
20	Min.	Brent Burns	Brampton	RW
21	Bos.	Mark Stuart	Colorado College	D
22	Edm.	Marc-Antoine Pouliot	Rimouski	C
23	Van.	Ryan Kesler	Ohio State	C
24	Phi.	Mike Richards	Kitchener	C
25	Fla.	Anthony Stewart	Kingston	C
26	L.A.	Brian Boyle	St. Sebastian's H.S.	C
27	L.A.	Jeff Tambellini	U. of Michigan	LW
28	Ana.	Corey Perry	London	RW
29	Ott.	Patrick Eaves	Boston College	RW
30	St.L.	Shawn Belle	Tri-City	D

SECOND ROUND

Pick	Claimed by	Amateur Club	Position
31	Car.	Danny Richmond	U. of Michigan	D
32	Pit.	Ryan Stone	Brandon	C
33	Dal.	Loui Eriksson	Vastra Frolunda Jr.	LW
34	T.B.	Mike Egener	Calgary	D
35	Nsh.	Konstantin Glazachev	Yaroslavl	LW
36	Dal.	Vojtech Polak	Karlovy Vary	LW
37	Nsh.	Kevin Klein	St. Michael's	D
38	Fla.	Kamil Kreps	Brampton	C
39	Cgy.	Tim Ramholt	Zurich	D
40	Mtl.	Cory Urquhart	Montreal	C
41	T.B.	Matt Smaby	Shattuck St. Mary's H.S.	D
42	N.J.	Petr Vrana	Halifax	LW
43	S.J.	Joshua Hennessy	Quebec	C
44	L.A.	Konstantin Pushkarev	Ust-Kamenogorsk	RW
45	Bos.	Patrice Bergeron	Acadie-Bathurst	C
46	CBJ	Dan Fritsche	Sarnia	C
47	S.J.	Matthew Carle	River City	D
48	NYI	Dmitri Chernykh	Khimik Voskresensk	RW
49	Nsh.	Shea Weber	Kelowna	D
50	NYR	Ivan Baranka	Dubnica Jr.	D
51	Col.	Colin McDonald	New England	RW
52	Chi.	Corey Crawford	Moncton	G
53	NYI	Yevgeni Tunik	Elektrostal	C
54	Dal.	Brandon Crombeen	Barrie	RW
55	Fla.	Stefan Meyer	Medicine Hat	LW
56	Min.	Patrick O'Sullivan	Mississauga	C
57	Tor.	John Doherty	Phillips-Andover	D
58	NYI	Jeremy Colliton	Prince Albert	C
59	Chi.	Michal Barinka	Budejovice	D
60	Van.	Marc-Andre Bernier	Halifax	RW
61	Mtl.	Maxim Lapierre	Montreal	C
62	St.L.	David Backes	Lincoln	C
63	Col.	David Liffiton	Plymouth	D
64	Det.	James Howard	U. of Maine	G
65	Buf.	Branislav Fabry	Bratislava Jr.	LW
66	Bos.	Masi Marjamaki	Red Deer	LW
67	Ott.	Igor Mirnov	Dynamo	LW
68	Edm.	Jean-Francois Jacques	Baie-Comeau	LW

First Round and Other Notable Selections 2002–1969

2002

FIRST ROUND

Pick	Claimed by	Player	Amateur Club	Position
1	CBJ	Rick Nash	London	LW
2	Atl.	Kari Lehtonen	Jokerit	G
3	Fla.	Jay Bouwmeester	Medicine Hat	D
4	Phi.	Joni Pitkanen	Karpat	D
5	Pit.	Ryan Whitney	Boston U.	D
6	Nsh.	Scottie Upshall	Kamloops	RW
7	Ana.	Joffrey Lupul	Medicine Hat	C
8	Min.	Pierre-Marc Bouchard	Chicoutimi	C
9	Fla.	Petr Taticek	Sault Ste. Marie	C
10	Cgy.	Eric Nystrom	U. of Michigan	LW
11	Buf.	Keith Ballard	U. of Minnesota	D
12	Wsh.	Steve Eminger	Kitchener	D
13	Wsh.	Alexander Semin	Chelyabinsk	LW
14	Mtl.	Christopher Higgins	Yale	C
15	Edm.	Jesse Niinimaki	Ilves Tampere	C
16	Ott.	Jakub Klepis	Portland	C
17	Wsh.	Boyd Gordon	Red Deer	RW
18	L.A.	Denis Grebeshkov	Yaroslavl	D
19	Phx.	Jakub Koreis	Plzen	C
20	Buf.	Dan Paille	Guelph	LW
21	Chi.	Anton Babchuk	Elektrostal	D
22	NYI	Sean Bergenheim	Jokerit	C
23	Phx.	Ben Eager	Oshawa	LW
24	Tor.	Alexander Steen	Vastra Frolunda	C
25	Car.	Cam Ward	Red Deer	G
26	Dal.	Martin Vagner	Hull	D
27	S.J.	Mike Morris	St. Sebastian's H.S.	RW
28	Col.	Jonas Johansson	HV 71 Jonkoping Jr.	RW
29	Bos.	Hannu Toivonen	HPK Jr.	G
30	Atl.	Jim Slater	Michigan State	C

OTHER NOTABLE SELECTIONS

Pick	Claimed by	Player	Amateur Club	Position
36	Edm.	Jarret Stoll	Kootenay	C
43	Dal.	Trevor Daley	Sault Ste. Marie	D
44	Edm.	Matt Greene	Green Bay	D
46	Phx.	David Leneveu	Cornell	G
57	Tor.	Matt Stajan	Belleville	C
58	Det.	Jiri Hudler	Vsetin	C
117	N.J.	Cam Janssen	Windsor	RW
133	CBJ	Lasse Pirjeta	Karpat	D
213	T.B.	Fredrik Norrena	TPS Turku	G
240	NYR	Petr Prucha	Pardubice	RW
254	Tor.	Jarkko Immonen	Assat	C
259	Bos.	Jan Stastny	U. of Notre Dame	C

2001

FIRST ROUND

Pick	Claimed by	Player	Amateur Club	Position
1	Atl.	Ilya Kovalchuk	Spartak	LW
2	Ott.	Jason Spezza	Windsor	C
3	T.B.	Alexander Svitov	Avangard Omsk	C
4	Fla.	Stephen Weiss	Plymouth	C
5	Ana.	Stanislav Chistov	Avangard Omsk	LW
6	Min.	Mikko Koivu	TPS Turku	C
7	Mtl.	Mike Komisarek	U. of Michigan	D
8	CBJ	Pascal Leclaire	Halifax	G
9	Chi.	Tuomo Ruutu	Jokerit	C/LW
10	NYR	Dan Blackburn	Kootenay	G
11	Phx.	Fredrik Sjostrom	Vastra Frolunda	RW
12	Nsh.	Dan Hamhuis	Prince George	D
13	Edm.	Ales Hemsky	Hull	RW
14	Cgy.	Chuck Kobasew	Boston College	C
15	Car.	Igor Knyazev	Spartak	D
16	Van.	R.J. Umberger	Ohio State	C
17	Tor.	Carlo Colaiacovo	Erie	D
18	L.A.	Jens Karlsson	Vastra Frolunda	RW
19	Bos.	Shaone Morrisonn	Kamloops	D
20	S.J.	Marcel Goc	Schwenningen	C
21	Pit.	Colby Armstrong	Red Deer	RW
22	Buf.	Jiri Novotny	Budejovice	C
23	Ott.	Tim Gleason	Windsor	D
24	Fla.	Lukas Krajicek	Peterborough	D
25	Mtl.	Alexander Perezhogin	Avangard Omsk	C
26	Dal.	Jason Bacashihua	Chicago (NAHL)	G
27	Phi.	Jeff Woywitka	Red Deer	D
28	N.J.	Adrian Foster	Saskatoon	C
29	Chi.	Adam Munro	Erie	G
30	L.A.	Dave Steckel	Ohio State	C

OTHER NOTABLE SELECTIONS

Pick	Claimed by	Player	Amateur Club	Position
39	Tor.	Karel Pilar	Litvinov	D
49	L.A.	Mike Cammalleri	U. of Michigan	C
66	Van.	Fedor Fedorov	Sudbury	LW
98	Nsh.	Jordin Tootoo	Brandon	RW
106	S.J.	Christoph Ehrhoff	Krefeld	D
132	NYI	Dusan Salficky	Plzen	G
172	Phi.	Dennis Seidenberg	Mannheim	D
176	Nsh.	Marek Zidlicky	HIFK	D
189	Atl.	Pasi Nurminen	Jokerit	G
214	L.A.	Cristobal Huet	Lugano	G
232	Ana.	Martin Gerber	Langnau	G
253	St.L.	Petr Cajanek	Zlin	RW

2000

FIRST ROUND

Pick	Claimed by	Player	Amateur Club	Position
1	NYI	Rick DiPietro	Boston U.	G
2	Atl.	Dany Heatley	U. of Wisconsin	RW
3	Min.	Marian Gaborik	Dukla Trencin	RW
4	CBJ	Rostislav Klesla	Brampton	D
5	NYI	Raffi Torres	Brampton	LW
6	Nsh.	Scott Hartnell	Prince Albert	LW
7	Bos.	Lars Jonsson	Leksand	D
8	T.B.	Nikita Alexeev	Erie	RW
9	Cgy.	Brent Krahn	Calgary	G
10	Chi.	Mikhail Yakubov	Lada Togliatti	C
11	Chi.	Pavel Vorobiev	Yaroslavl	RW
12	Ana.	Alexei Smirnov	Tver	LW
13	Mtl.	Ron Hainsey	U. of Mass-Lowell	D
14	Col.	Vaclav Nedorost	Budejovice	C
15	Buf.	Artem Kryukov	Yaroslavl	C
16	Mtl.	Marcel Hossa	Portland	LW
17	Edm.	Alexei Mikhnov	Yaroslavl	LW
18	Pit.	Brooks Orpik	Boston College	D
19	Phx.	Krys Kolanos	Boston College	C
20	L.A.	Alexander Frolov	Yaroslavl 2	LW
21	Ott.	Anton Volchenkov	HC Moscow	D
22	N.J.	David Hale	Sioux City	D
23	Van.	Nathan Smith	Swift Current	C
24	Tor.	Brad Boyes	Erie	C
25	Dal.	Steve Ott	Windsor	C
26	Wsh.	Brian Sutherby	Moose Jaw	C
27	Bos.	Martin Samuelsson	MoDo Ornskoldsvik	RW
28	Phi.	Justin Williams	Plymouth	RW
29	Det.	Niklas Kronwall	Djurgarden	D
30	St.L.	Jeff Taffe	U. of Minnesota	C

OTHER NOTABLE SELECTIONS

Pick	Claimed by	Player	Amateur Club	Position
33	Min.	Nick Schultz	Prince Albert	D
43	Wsh.	Matt Pettinger	Calgary	LW
44	Ana.	Ilya Bryzgalov	Lada Togliatti	G
46	Cgy.	Jarrett Stoll	Kootenay	C
54	L.A.	Andreas Lilja	Malmo	D
76	N.J.	Michael Rupp	Erie	LW
97	Car.	Niclas Wallin	Brynas	D
118	L.A.	Lubomir Visnovsky	Bratislava	D
155	Cgy.	Travis Moen	Kelowna	LW
159	Col.	John-Michael Liles	Michigan State	D
171	Phi.	Roman Cechmanek	Vsetin	G
232	Min.	Lubomir Sekeras	Trinec	D

1999

FIRST ROUND

Pick	Claimed by	Player	Amateur Club	Position
1	Atl.	Patrik Stefan	Long Beach	C
2	Van.	Daniel Sedin	MoDo Ornskoldsvik	LW
3	Van.	Henrik Sedin	MoDo Ornskoldsvik	C
4	NYR	Pavel Brendl	Calgary	RW
5	NYI	Tim Connolly	Erie	C
6	Nsh.	Brian Finley	Barrie	G
7	Wsh.	Kris Beech	Calgary	C
8	NYI	Taylor Pyatt	Sudbury	LW
9	NYR	Jamie Lundmark	Moose Jaw	C
10	NYI	Branislav Mezei	Belleville	D
11	Cgy.	Oleg Saprykin	Seattle	LW
12	Fla.	Denis Shvidki	Barrie	RW
13	Edm.	Jani Rita	Jokerit	LW
14	S.J.	Jeff Jillson	U. of Michigan	D
15	Phx.	Scott Kelman	Seattle	C
16	Car.	David Tanabe	U. of Wisconsin	D
17	St.L.	Barret Jackman	Regina	D
18	Pit.	Konstantin Koltsov	Cherepovets	RW
19	Phx.	Kirill Safronov	St. Petersburg	D
20	Buf.	Barrett Heisten	U. of Maine	LW
21	Bos.	Nick Boynton	Ottawa	D
22	Phi.	Maxime Ouellet	Quebec	G
23	Chi.	Steve McCarthy	Kootenay	D
24	Tor.	Luca Cereda	Ambri	C
25	Col.	Mikhail Kuleshov	Cherepovets	LW
26	Ott.	Martin Havlat	Trinec	LW
27	N.J.	Ari Ahonen	JyP HT Jr.	G
28	NYI	Kristian Kudroc	Michalovce	D

OTHER NOTABLE SELECTIONS

Pick	Claimed by	Player	Amateur Club	Position
42	N.J.	Mike Commodore	North Dakota	D
70	Fla.	Niklas Hagman	HIFK Helsinki	LW
76	L.A.	Frantisek Kaberle	MoDo Ornskoldsvik	D
83	Ana.	Niclas Havelid	Malmo	D
91	Edm.	Mike Comrie	U. of Michigan	C
115	Pit.	Ryan Malone	Omaha	LW
191	Nsh.	Martin Erat	ZPS Zlin Jr.	LW
210	Det.	Henrik Zetterberg	Timra	LW
212	Col.	Radim Vrbata	Hull	RW
230	Ana.	Petr Tenkrat	Kladno	RW
232	St.L.	Alexander Khavanov	Dynamo	D
247	Bos.	Mikko Eloranta	TPS Turku	LW

1998

FIRST ROUND

Pick	Claimed by	Player	Amateur Club	Position
1	T.B.	Vincent Lecavalier	Rimouski	C
2	Nsh.	David Legwand	Plymouth	C
3	S.J.	Brad Stuart	Regina	D
4	Van.	Bryan Allen	Oshawa	D
5	Ana.	Vitaly Vishnevski	Yaroslavl 2	D
6	Cgy.	Rico Fata	London	RW
7	NYR	Manny Malhotra	Guelph	C
8	Chi.	Mark Bell	Ottawa	C
9	NYI	Mike Rupp	Erie	RW
10	Tor.	Nik Antropov	Ust-Kamenogorsk	C
11	Car.	Jeff Heerema	Sarnia	RW
12	Col.	Alex Tanguay	Halifax	LW
13	Edm.	Michael Henrich	Barrie	RW
14	Phx.	Patrick DesRochers	Sarnia	G
15	Ott.	Mathieu Chouinard	Shawinigan	G
16	Mtl.	Eric Chouinard	Quebec	LW
17	Col.	Martin Skoula	Barrie	D
18	Buf.	Dmitri Kalinin	Chelyabinsk	D
19	Col.	Robyn Regehr	Kamloops	D
20	Col.	Scott Parker	Kelowna	RW
21	L.A.	Mathieu Biron	Shawinigan	D
22	Phi.	Simon Gagne	Quebec	LW
23	Pit.	Milan Kraft	Keramika Plzen Jr.	C
24	St.L.	Christian Backman	Vastra Frolunda Jr.	D
25	Det.	Jiri Fischer	Hull	D
26	N.J.	Mike Van Ryn	U. of Michigan	D
27	N.J.	Scott Gomez	Tri-City	C

OTHER NOTABLE SELECTIONS

Pick	Claimed by	Player	Amateur Club	Position
29	S.J.	Jonathan Cheechoo	Belleville	RW
43	Phx.	Ossi Vaananen	Jokerit Jr.	D
44	Ott.	Mike Fisher	Sudbury	C
48	Bos.	Jonathan Girard	Laval	D
60	Nsh.	Denis Arkhipov	Ak Bars Kazan	C
64	T.B.	Brad Richards	Rimouski	C
91	Car.	Josef Vasicek	Slavia Praha Jr.	C
99	Edm.	Shawn Horcoff	Michigan State	C
117	Fla.	Jaroslav Spacek	Farjestad Karlstad	D
135	Bos.	Andrew Raycroft	Sudbury	G
150	Ana.	Trent Hunter	Prince George	RW
171	Det.	Pavel Datsyuk	Yekateringburg	C
216	Mtl.	Michael Ryder	Hull	RW
230	Nsh.	Karlis Skrastins	TPS Turku	D

1997

FIRST ROUND

Pick	Claimed by	Player	Amateur Club	Position
1	Bos.	Joe Thornton	Sault Ste. Marie	C
2	S.J.	Patrick Marleau	Seattle	C
3	L.A.	Olli Jokinen	HIFK Helsinki	C
4	NYI	Roberto Luongo	Val-d'Or	G
5	NYI	Eric Brewer	Prince George	D
6	Cgy.	Daniel Tkaczuk	Barrie	C
7	T.B.	Paul Mara	Sudbury	D
8	Bos.	Sergei Samsonov	Detroit	LW
9	Wsh.	Nick Boynton	Ottawa	D
10	Van.	Brad Ference	Spokane	D
11	Mtl.	Jason Ward	Erie	RW
12	Ott.	Marian Hossa	Dukla Trencin	RW
13	Chi.	Daniel Cleary	Belleville	RW
14	Edm.	Michel Riesen	Biel-Bienne	RW
15	L.A.	Matt Zultek	Ottawa	LW
16	Chi.	Ty Jones	Spokane	RW
17	Pit.	Robert Dome	Las Vegas (IHL)	RW
18	Ana.	Mikael Holmqvist	Djurgarden	C
19	NYR	Stefan Cherneski	Brandon	RW
20	Fla.	Mike Brown	Red Deer	LW
21	Buf.	Mika Noronen	Tappara Tampere	G
22	Car.	Nikos Tselios	Belleville	D
23	S.J.	Scott Hannan	Kelowna	D
24	N.J.	J-F Damphousse	Moncton	G
25	Dal.	Brenden Morrow	Portland	LW
26	Col.	Kevin Grimes	Kingston	D

OTHER NOTABLE SELECTIONS

Pick	Claimed by	Player	Amateur Club	Position
27	Bos.	Ben Clymer	Minnesota-Duluth	LW
70	Cgy.	Erik Andersson	U. of Denver	C
95	Fla.	Ivan Novoseltsev	Krylja Sovetov	RW
119	Ott.	Magnus Arvedson	Farjestad Karlstad	LW
130	Chi.	Kyle Calder	Regina	LW
136	NYR	Mike York	Michigan State	LW
144	Van.	Matt Cooke	Windsor	C
177	St.L.	Ladislav Nagy	Dragon Presov	LW
191	Bos.	Antti Laaksonen	U. of Denver	LW
242	Chi.	Brett McLean	Kelowna	C

Pick	Claimed by	Amateur Club	Position

1996

FIRST ROUND

Pick	Claimed by		Amateur Club	Position
1	Ott.	Chris Phillips	Prince Albert	D
2	S.J.	Andrei Zyuzin	Salavat Yulayev Ufa	D
3	NYI	J.P. Dumont	Val-d'Or	RW
4	Wsh.	Alexandre Volchkov	Barrie	C
5	Dal.	Ric Jackman	Sault Ste. Marie	D
6	Edm.	Boyd Devereaux	Kitchener	C
7	Buf.	Erik Rasmussen	U. of Minnesota	LW/C
8	Bos.	Johnathan Aitken	Medicine Hat	D
9	Ana.	Ruslan Salei	Las Vegas (IHL)	D
10	N.J.	Lance Ward	Red Deer	D
11	Phx.	Dan Focht	Tri-City	D
12	Van.	Josh Holden	Regina	C
13	Cgy.	Derek Morris	Regina	D
14	St.L.	Marty Reasoner	Boston College	C
15	Phi.	Dainius Zubrus	Pembroke Jr. A	RW
16	T.B.	Mario Larocque	Hull	D
17	Wsh.	Jaroslav Svejkovsky	Tri-City	RW
18	Mtl.	Matt Higgins	Moose Jaw	C
19	Edm.	Matthieu Descoteaux	Shawinigan	D
20	Fla.	Marcus Nilson	Djurgarden	LW
21	S.J.	Marco Sturm	Landshut	LW
22	NYR	Jeff Brown	Sarnia	D
23	Pit.	Craig Hillier	Ottawa	G
24	Phx.	Daniel Briere	Drummondville	C
25	Col.	Peter Ratchuk	Shattuck St. Mary's H.S.	D
26	Det.	Jesse Wallin	Red Deer	D

OTHER NOTABLE SELECTIONS

Pick	Claimed by		Amateur Club	Position
35	Ana.	Matt Cullen	St. Cloud State	C
49	N.J.	Colin White	Hull	D
56	NYI	Zdeno Chara	Dukla Trencin	D
59	Edm.	Tom Poti	Cushing Academy	D
65	Fla.	Oleg Kvasha	CSKA Moscow	LW/C
79	Col.	Mark Parrish	St. Cloud State	RW
136	Ott.	Andreas Dackell	Brynas Gavle	RW
139	Phx.	Robert Esche	Detroit	G
174	Phx.	Trevor Letowski	Sarnia	RW
179	T.B.	Pavel Kubina	Vitkovice	D
204	Tor.	Tomas Kaberle	Kladno	D

1995

FIRST ROUND

Pick	Claimed by		Amateur Club	Position
1	Ott.	Bryan Berard	Detroit	D
2	NYI	Wade Redden	Brandon	D
3	L.A.	Aki Berg	Kiekko-67 Turku	D
4	Ana.	Chad Kilger	Kingston	C
5	T.B.	Daymond Langkow	Tri-City	C
6	Edm.	Steve Kelly	Prince Albert	C
7	Wpg.	Shane Doan	Kamloops	RW
8	Mtl.	Terry Ryan	Tri-City	LW
9	Bos.	Kyle McLaren	Tacoma	D
10	Fla.	Radek Dvorak	HC Ceske Budejovice	RW
11	Dal.	Jarome Iginla	Kamloops	RW
12	S.J.	Teemu Riihijarvi	Kiekko-Espoo	LW
13	Hfd.	Jean-Sebastien Giguere	Halifax	G
14	Buf.	Jay McKee	Niagara Falls	D
15	Tor.	Jeff Ware	Oshawa	D
16	Buf.	Martin Biron	Beauport	G
17	Wsh.	Brad Church	Prince Albert	LW
18	N.J.	Petr Sykora	Detroit	RW
19	Chi.	Dmitri Nabokov	Krylja Sovetov	C/LW
20	Cgy.	Denis Gauthier	Drummondville	D
21	Bos.	Sean Brown	Belleville	D
22	Phi.	Brian Boucher	Tri-City	G
23	Wsh.	Miika Elomo	Kiekko-67 Turku	LW
24	Pit.	Aleksey Morozov	Krylja Sovetov	RW
25	Col.	Marc Denis	Chicoutimi	G
26	Det.	Maxim Kuznetsov	Dynamo	D

OTHER NOTABLE SELECTIONS

Pick	Claimed by		Amateur Club	Position
31	Edm.	Georges Laraque	St-Jean	RW
45	Chi.	Christian Laflamme	Beauport	D
59	L.A.	Vladimir Tsyplakov	Fort Wayne IHL	LW
67	Wpg.	Brad Isbister	Portland	LW
79	N.J.	Alyn McCauley	Ottawa	C
87	Hfd.	Sami Kapanen	HIFK Helsinki	RW
91	NYR	Marc Savard	Oshawa	C
101	St.L.	Michal Handzus	IS Banska Bystrica	C
116	S.J.	Miikka Kiprusoff	TPS Turku Jr.	G
128	Pit.	Jan Hrdina	Seattle	C
145	Tor.	Yannick Tremblay	Beauport	D
166	Fla.	Peter Worrell	Hull	LW
177	Bos.	P.J. Axelsson	Vastra Frolunda	LW
223	Tor.	Danny Markov	Spartak	D

1994

FIRST ROUND

Pick	Claimed by		Amateur Club	Position
1	Fla.	Ed Jovanovski	Windsor	D
2	Ana.	Oleg Tverdovsky	Krylja Sovetov	D
3	Ott.	Radek Bonk	Las Vegas (IHL)	C
4	Edm.	Jason Bonsignore	Niagara Falls	C
5	Hfd.	Jeff O'Neill	Guelph	RW
6	Edm.	Ryan Smyth	Moose Jaw	LW
7	L.A.	Jamie Storr	Owen Sound	G
8	T.B.	Jason Wiemer	Portland	C
9	NYI	Brett Lindros	Kingston	RW
10	Wsh.	Nolan Baumgartner	Kamloops	D
11	S.J.	Jeff Friesen	Regina	LW
12	Que.	Wade Belak	Saskatoon	D/RW
13	Van.	Mattias Ohlund	Pitea	D
14	Chi.	Ethan Moreau	Niagara Falls	LW
15	Wsh.	Alexander Kharlamov	CSKA Moscow	C
16	Tor.	Eric Fichaud	Chictoutimi	G
17	Buf.	Wayne Primeau	Owen Sound	C
18	Mtl.	Brad Brown	North Bay	D
19	Cgy.	Chris Dingman	Brandon	LW
20	Dal.	Jason Botterill	U. of Michigan	LW
21	Bos.	Evgeni Ryabchikov	Molot Perm	G
22	Que.	Jeffrey Kealty	Catholic Memorial H.S.	D
23	Det.	Yan Golubovsky	Dynamo 2	D
24	Pit.	Chris Wells	Seattle	C
25	N.J.	Vadim Sharifijanov	Salavat Yulayev Ufa	LW
26	NYR	Dan Cloutier	Sault Ste. Marie	G

OTHER NOTABLE SELECTIONS

Pick	Claimed by		Amateur Club	Position
27	Fla.	Rhett Warrener	Saskatoon	D
43	Buf.	Curtis Brown	Moose Jaw	C/LW
49	Det.	Mathieu Dandenault	Sherbrooke	RW/D
51	N.J.	Patrik Elias	Kladno	C
64	Tor.	Fredrik Modin	Timra	LW
87	Que.	Milan Hejduk	Pardubice	RW
124	Dal.	Marty Turco	Cambridge Jr. A	G
132	Ana.	Bates Battaglia	Caledon Jr. A	LW
133	Ott.	Daniel Alfredsson	Vastra Frolunda	RW
210	N.J.	Steve Sullivan	Sault Ste. Marie	RW
219	S.J.	Evgeni Nabokov	Ust-Kamengorsk	G
272	NYI	Dick Tarnstrom	AIK Solna	D

Drafted directly out of high school in 1993, Hal Gill joined the Bruins in 1997 after four years at Providence College. The 6'7" defenseman has signed with the Toronto Maple Leafs for 2006-07.

1993

FIRST ROUND

Pick	Claimed by		Amateur Club	Position
1	Ott.	Alexandre Daigle	Victoriaville	C
2	Hfd.	Chris Pronger	Peterborough	D
3	T.B.	Chris Gratton	Kingston	C
4	Ana.	Paul Kariya	U. of Maine	LW
5	Fla.	Rob Niedermayer	Medicine Hat	C
6	Det.	Benoit Larose	Laval	D
7	S.J.	Viktor Kozlov	Dynamo	C
8	Edm.	Jason Arnott	Oshawa	C
9	NYR	Niklas Sundstrom	MoDo Ornskoldsvik	RW
10	Dal.	Todd Harvey	Detroit	RW/C
11	Que.	Jocelyn Thibault	Sherbrooke	G
12	Wsh.	Brendan Witt	Seattle	D
13	Tor.	Kenny Jonsson	Rogle Angelholm	D
14	N.J.	Denis Pederson	Prince Albert	C/RW
15	Que.	Adam Deadmarsh	Portland	RW
16	Wpg.	Mats Lindgren	Skelleftea	C/LW
17	Edm.	Nick Stajduhar	London	D
18	Wsh.	Jason Allison	London	C
19	Cgy.	Jesper Mattsson	Malmo	C
20	Tor.	Landon Wilson	Dubuque Jr. A	RW
21	Van.	Mike Wilson	Sudbury	D
22	Mtl.	Saku Koivu	TPS Turku	C
23	Det.	Anders Eriksson	MoDo Ornskoldsvik	D
24	NYI	Todd Bertuzzi	Guelph	RW
25	Chi.	Eric Lecompte	Hull	LW
26	Bos.	Kevyn Adams	Miami of Ohio	C
—	Pit.	Stefan Bergkvist	Leksand	D

OTHER NOTABLE SELECTIONS

Pick	Claimed by		Amateur Club	Position
28	S.J.	Shean Donovan	Ottawa	RW
71	Phi.	Vaclav Prospal	Motor Ceske Budejovice	C
72	Hfd.	Marek Malik	Vitkovice	D
90	Chi.	Eric Daze	Beauport	RW
111	Edm.	Miroslav Satan	Dukla Trencin	LW
118	NYI	Tommy Salo	Vasteras	G
124	Van.	Scott Walker	Owen Sound	RW
151	Mtl.	Darcy Tucker	Kamloops	RW
164	NYR	Todd Marchant	Clarkson	C
207	Bos.	Hal Gill	Nashoba H.S.	D
219	St.L.	Mike Grier	St. Sebastian's H.S.	RW
227	Ott.	Pavol Demitra	Dukla Trencin	LW
252	Cgy.	German Titov	TPS Turku	LW

1992

FIRST ROUND

Pick	Claimed by		Amateur Club	Position
1	T.B.	Roman Hamrlik	ZPS Zlin	D
2	Ott.	Alexei Yashin	Dynamo	C
3	S.J.	Mike Rathje	Medicine Hat	D
4	Que.	Todd Warriner	Windsor	LW
5	NYI	Darius Kasparaitis	Dynamo	D
6	Cgy.	Cory Stillman	Windsor	LW
7	Phi.	Ryan Sittler	Nichols H.S.	LW
8	Tor.	Brandon Convery	Sudbury	C
9	Hfd.	Robert Petrovicky	Dukla Trencin	C
10	S.J.	Andrei Nazarov	Dynamo	LW
11	Buf.	David Cooper	Medicine Hat	D
12	Chi.	Sergei Krivokrasov	CSKA Moscow	RW
13	Edm.	Joe Hulbig	St. Sebastian's H.S.	LW
14	Wsh.	Sergei Gonchar	Chelyabinsk	D
15	Phi.	Jason Bowen	Tri-City	D
16	Bos.	Dmitri Kvartalnov	San Diego (IHL)	LW
17	Wpg.	Sergei Bautin	Dynamo	D
18	N.J.	Jason Smith	Regina	D
19	Pit.	Martin Straka	HC Skoda Plzen	C
20	Mtl.	David Wilkie	Kamloops	D
21	Van.	Libor Polasek	Vitkovice	C
22	Det.	Curtis Bowen	Ottawa	LW
23	Tor.	Grant Marshall	Ottawa	RW
24	NYR	Peter Ferraro	Waterloo Jr. A	LW

OTHER NOTABLE SELECTIONS

Pick	Claimed by		Amateur Club	Position
27	Wpg.	Boris Mironov	CSKA Moscow	D
33	Mtl.	Valeri Bure	Spokane	RW
36	Chi.	Jeff Shantz	Regina	C
38	St.L.	Igor Korolev	Dynamo	C
40	Van.	Michael Peca	Ottawa	C
42	N.J.	Sergei Brylin	CSKA Moscow	C
46	Det.	Darren McCarty	Belleville	RW
48	NYR	Mattias Norstrom	AIK Solna	D
65	Edm.	Kirk Maltby	Owen Sound	RW
78	Cgy.	Robert Svehla	Dukla Trencin	D
83	Buf.	Matthew Barnaby	Beauport	LW
158	St.L.	Ian Laperriere	Drummondville	C/RW
186	N.J.	Stephane Yelle	Oshawa	C
204	Wpg.	Nikolai Khabibulin	CSKA Moscow	G

1991

FIRST ROUND

Pick	Claimed by		Amateur Club	Position
1	Que.	Eric Lindros	Oshawa	C
2	S.J.	Pat Falloon	Spokane	RW
3	N.J.	Scott Niedermayer	Kamloops	D
4	NYI	Scott Lachance	Boston U.	D
5	Wpg.	Aaron Ward	U. of Michigan	D
6	Phi.	Peter Forsberg	MoDo Ornskoldsvik	C
7	Van.	Alek Stojanov	Hamilton	RW
8	Min.	Richard Matvichuk	Saskatoon	D
9	Hfd.	Patrick Poulin	St-Hyacinthe	C
10	Det.	Martin Lapointe	Laval	RW
11	N.J.	Brian Rolston	Detroit Compuware Jr. A	C/RW
12	Edm.	Tyler Wright	Swift Current	C
13	Buf.	Philippe Boucher	Granby	D
14	Wsh.	Pat Peake	Detroit	C
15	NYR	Alex Kovalev	Dynamo	RW
16	Pit.	Markus Naslund	MoDo Ornskoldsvik	LW
17	Mtl.	Brent Bilodeau	Seattle	D
18	Bos.	Glen Murray	Sudbury	RW
19	Cgy.	Niklas Sundblad	AIK Solna	RW
20	Edm.	Martin Rucinsky	CHZ Litvinov	LW
21	Wsh.	Trevor Halverson	North Bay	LW
22	Chi.	Dean McAmmond	Prince Albert	LW

OTHER NOTABLE SELECTIONS

Pick	Claimed by		Amateur Club	Position
23	S.J.	Ray Whitney	Spokane	LW
26	NYI	Ziggy Palffy	AC Nitra	RW
30	S.J.	Sandis Ozolinsh	Dynamo Riga	D
40	Bos.	Jozef Stumpel	AC Nitra	C
52	Cgy.	Sandy McCarthy	Laval	RW
58	Wsh.	Steve Konowalchuk	Portland	LW
59	Hfd.	Michael Nylander	Huddinge	C
71	Chi.	Igor Kravchuk	CSKA Moscow	D
81	L.A.	Alexei Zhitnik	Sokol Kiev	D
103	Que.	Bill Lindsay	Tri-City	RW
106	Bos.	Mariusz Czerkawski	GKS Tychy	RW
122	Phi.	Dmitry Yushkevich	Yaroslavl	D
203	Wpg.	Igor Ulanov	Khimik Voskresensk	D

1990

FIRST ROUND

Pick	Claimed by		Amateur Club	Position
1	Que.	Owen Nolan	Cornwall	RW
2	Van.	Petr Nedved	Seattle	C
3	Det.	Keith Primeau	Niagara Falls	C
4	Phi.	Mike Ricci	Peterborough	C
5	Pit.	Jaromir Jagr	Kladno	RW
6	NYI	Scott Scissons	Saskatoon	C
7	L.A.	Darryl Sydor	Kamloops	D
8	Min.	Derian Hatcher	North Bay	D
9	Wsh.	John Slaney	Cornwall	D
10	Tor.	Drake Berehowsky	Kingston	D
11	Cgy.	Trevor Kidd	Brandon	G
12	Mtl.	Turner Stevenson	Seattle	RW
13	NYR	Michael Stewart	Michigan State	D
14	Buf.	Brad May	Niagara Falls	LW
15	Hfd.	Mark Greig	Lethbridge	RW
16	Chi.	Karl Dykhuis	Hull	D
17	Edm.	Scott Allison	Prince Albert	C
18	Van.	Shawn Antoski	North Bay	LW
19	Wpg.	Keith Tkachuk	Malden Catholic H.S.	LW
20	N.J.	Martin Brodeur	St-Hyacinthe	G
21	Bos.	Bryan Smolinski	Michigan State	C

OTHER NOTABLE SELECTIONS

Pick	Claimed by		Amateur Club	Position
23	Van.	Jiri Slegr	CHZ Litvinov	D
31	Tor.	Felix Potvin	Chicoutimi	G
34	NYR	Doug Weight	Lake Superior State	C
36	Hfd.	Geoff Sanderson	Swift Current	LW
45	Det.	Vyacheslav Kozlov	Khimik Voskresensk	RW
85	NYR	Sergei Zubov	CSKA Moscow	D
86	Van.	Gino Odjick	Laval	RW
97	Buf.	Richard Smehlik	Vitkovice	D
133	L.A.	Robert Lang	CHZ Litvinov	C
156	Wsh.	Peter Bondra	Kosice	RW
177	Wsh.	Ken Klee	Bowling Green	D
244	NYR	Sergei Nemchinov	Krylja Sovetov	LW

1989

FIRST ROUND

Pick	Claimed by		Amateur Club	Position
1	Que.	Mats Sundin	Nacka	C
2	NYI	Dave Chyzowski	Kamloops	LW
3	Tor.	Scott Thornton	Belleville	C
4	Wpg.	Stu Barnes	Tri-City	C
5	N.J.	Bill Guerin	Springfield Jr. B	RW
6	Chi.	Adam Bennett	Sudbury	D
7	Min.	Doug Zmolek	John Marshall H.S.	D
8	Van.	Jason Herter	North Dakota	D
9	St.L.	Jason Marshall	Vernon Jr. A	D
10	Hfd.	Bobby Holik	Dukla Jihlava	C
11	Det.	Mike Sillinger	Regina	C
12	Tor.	Rob Pearson	Belleville	RW
13	Mtl.	Lindsay Vallis	Seattle	D
14	Buf.	Kevin Haller	Regina	D
15	Edm.	Jason Soules	Niagara Falls	D
16	Pit.	Jamie Heward	Regina	D
17	Bos.	Shayne Stevenson	Kitchener	RW
18	N.J.	Jason Miller	Medicine Hat	LW
19	Wsh.	Olie Kolzig	Tri-City	G
20	NYR	Steven Rice	Kitchener	RW
21	Tor.	Steve Bancroft	Belleville	D

OTHER NOTABLE SELECTIONS

Pick	Claimed by		Amateur Club	Position
22	Que.	Adam Foote	Sault Ste. Marie	D
23	NYI	Travis Green	Spokane	C
53	Det.	Nicklas Lidstrom	Vasteras	D
62	Wpg.	Kris Draper	Canadian National	C
73	Hfd.	Jim McKenzie	Victoria	LW
74	Det.	Sergei Fedorov	CSKA Moscow	C
82	Wsh.	Trent Klatt	Osseo H.S.	RW
113	Van.	Pavel Bure	CSKA Moscow	RW
116	Det.	Dallas Drake	Northern Michigan	RW
183	Buf.	Donald Audette	Laval	RW
196	Min.	Arturs Irbe	Dynamo Riga	G
221	Det.	Vladimir Konstantinov	CSKA Moscow	D

1988

FIRST ROUND

Pick	Claimed by		Amateur Club	Position
1	Min.	Mike Modano	Prince Albert	C
2	Van.	Trevor Linden	Medicine Hat	RW
3	Que.	Curtis Leschyshyn	Saskatoon	D
4	Pit.	Darrin Shannon	Windsor	LW
5	Que.	Daniel Dore	Drummondville	RW
6	Tor.	Scott Pearson	Kingston	LW
7	L.A.	Martin Gelinas	Hull	LW
8	Chi.	Jeremy Roenick	Thayer Academy	C
9	St.L.	Rod Brind'Amour	Notre Dame Jr. A	C
10	Wpg.	Teemu Selanne	Jokerit	RW
11	Hfd.	Chris Govedaris	Toronto	LW
12	N.J.	Corey Foster	Peterborough	D
13	Buf.	Joel Savage	Victoria	RW
14	Phi.	Claude Boivin	Drummondville	LW
15	Wsh.	Reggie Savage	Victoriaville	C
16	NYI	Kevin Cheveldayoff	Brandon	D
17	Det.	Kory Kocur	Saskatoon	RW
18	Bos.	Rob Cimetta	Toronto	W
19	Edm.	Francois Leroux	St-Jean	D
20	Mtl.	Eric Charron	Trois-Rivieres	D
21	Cgy.	Jason Muzzatti	Michigan State	G

OTHER NOTABLE SELECTIONS

Pick	Claimed by		Amateur Club	Position
27	Tor.	Tie Domi	Peterborough	RW
60	Bos.	Steve Heinze	Lawrence Academy	RW
67	Pit.	Mark Recchi	Kamloops	RW
68	NYR	Tony Amonte	Thayer Academy	RW
89	Buf.	Alexander Mogilny	CSKA Moscow	RW
97	Buf.	Rob Ray	Cornwall	RW
120	Wsh.	Dmitri Khristich	Sokol Kiev	LW/C
163	NYI	Marty McInnis	Milton Academy	RW
198	St.L.	Bret Hedican	North St. Paul H.S.	D
234	Que.	Claude Lapointe	Laval	LW/C

1987

FIRST ROUND

Pick	Claimed by		Amateur Club	Position
1	Buf.	Pierre Turgeon	Granby	C
2	N.J.	Brendan Shanahan	London	LW
3	Bos.	Glen Wesley	Portland	D
4	L.A.	Wayne McBean	Medicine Hat	D
5	Pit.	Chris Joseph	Seattle	D
6	Min.	Dave Archibald	Portland	C/LW
7	Tor.	Luke Richardson	Peterborough	D
8	Chi.	Jimmy Waite	Chicoutimi	G
9	Que.	Bryan Fogarty	Kingston	D
10	NYR	Jay More	New Westminster	D
11	Det.	Yves Racine	Longueuil	D
12	St.L.	Keith Osborne	North Bay	RW
13	NYI	Dean Chynoweth	Medicine Hat	D
14	Bos.	Stephane Quintal	Granby	D
15	Que.	Joe Sakic	Swift Current	C
16	Wpg.	Bryan Marchment	Belleville	D
17	Mtl.	Andrew Cassels	Ottawa	C
18	Hfd.	Jody Hull	Peterborough	RW
19	Cgy.	Bryan Deasley	U. of Michigan	LW
20	Phi.	Darren Rumble	Kitchener	D
21	Edm.	Peter Soberlak	Swift Current	LW

OTHER NOTABLE SELECTIONS

Pick	Claimed by		Amateur Club	Position
25	Cgy.	Stephane Matteau	Hull	LW
33	Mtl.	John LeClair	Bellows Academy	LW
38	Mtl.	Eric Desjardins	Granby	D
44	Mtl.	Mathieu Schneider	Cornwall	D
71	Tor.	Joe Sacco	Medford H.S.	RW
108	Van.	Garry Valk	Sherwood Park Jr. A	RW
110	Pit.	Shawn McEachern	Matignon H.S.	RW
159	St.L.	Guy Hebert	Hamilton College	G
166	Cgy.	Theoren Fleury	Moose Jaw	RW

1986

FIRST ROUND

Pick	Claimed by		Amateur Club	Position
1	Det.	Joe Murphy	Michigan State	RW
2	L.A.	Jimmy Carson	Verdun	C
3	N.J.	Neil Brady	Medicine Hat	C
4	Pit.	Zarley Zalapski	Canadian National	D
5	Buf.	Shawn Anderson	Canadian National	D
6	Tor.	Vincent Damphousse	Laval	C
7	Van.	Dan Woodley	Portland	RW
8	Wpg.	Pat Elynuik	Prince Albert	RW
9	NYR	Brian Leetch	Avon Old Farms H.S.	D
10	St.L.	Jocelyn Lemieux	Laval	RW
11	Hfd.	Scott Young	Boston U.	RW
12	Min.	Warren Babe	Lethbridge	LW
13	Bos.	Craig Janney	Boston College	C
14	Chi.	Everett Sanipass	Verdun	LW
15	Mtl.	Mark Pederson	Medicine Hat	LW
16	Cgy.	George Pelawa	Bemidji H.S.	RW
17	NYI	Tom Fitzgerald	Austin Prep	RW
18	Que.	Ken McRae	Sudbury	C
19	Wsh.	Jeff Greenlaw	Canadian National	LW
20	Phi.	Kerry Huffman	Guelph	D
21	Edm.	Kim Issel	Prince Albert	RW

OTHER NOTABLE SELECTIONS

Pick	Claimed by		Amateur Club	Position
22	Det.	Adam Graves	Windsor	LW
27	Mtl.	Benoit Brunet	Hull	LW
29	Wpg.	Teppo Numminen	Tappara Tampere	D
47	Buf.	Bob Corkum	U. of Maine	C
57	Mtl.	Jyrki Lumme	Ilves Tampere	D
67	Pit.	Rob Brown	Kamloops	RW
72	NYR	Mark Janssens	Regina	C
85	Det.	Johan Garpenlov	Nacka	LW
114	NYR	Darren Turcotte	North Bay	C
141	Mtl.	Lyle Odelein	Moose Jaw	D
143	NYI	Rich Pilon	Prince Albert AAA	D
167	Phi.	Murray Baron	Vernon Jr. A	D

1985

FIRST ROUND

Pick	Claimed by		Amateur Club	Position
1	Tor.	Wendel Clark	Saskatoon	LW/D
2	Pit.	Craig Simpson	Michigan State	LW
3	N.J.	Craig Wolanin	Kitchener	D
4	Van.	Jim Sandlak	London	RW
5	Hfd.	Dana Murzyn	Calgary	D
6	NYI	Brad Dalgarno	Hamilton	RW
7	NYR	Ulf Dahlen	Ostersund	LW
8	Det.	Brent Fedyk	Regina	LW
9	L.A.	Craig Duncanson	Sudbury	LW
10	L.A.	Dan Gratton	Oshawa	C
11	Chi.	Dave Manson	Prince Albert	D
12	Mtl.	Jose Charbonneau	Drummondville	RW
13	NYI	Derek King	Sault Ste. Marie	LW
14	Buf.	Calle Johansson	Vastra Frolunda	D
15	Que.	David Latta	Kitchener	LW
16	Mtl.	Tom Chorske	Minneapolis SW H.S.	LW
17	Cgy.	Chris Biotti	Belmont Hill H.S.	D
18	Wpg.	Ryan Stewart	Kamloops	C
19	Wsh.	Yvon Corriveau	Toronto	LW
20	Edm.	Scott Metcalfe	Kingston	LW
21	Phi.	Glen Seabrooke	Peterborough	C

OTHER NOTABLE SELECTIONS

Pick	Claimed by		Amateur Club	Position
24	N.J.	Sean Burke	Toronto	G
27	Cgy.	Joe Nieuwendyk	Cornell	C
28	NYR	Mike Richter	Northwood Prep	G
32	N.J.	Eric Weinrich	North Yarmouth Academy	D
35	Buf.	Benoit Hogue	St-Jean	C
44	St.L.	Nelson Emerson	Stratford Jr.A	RW
52	Bos.	Bill Ranford	New Westminster	G
81	Wpg.	Fredrik Olausson	Farjestad Karlstad	D
113	Det.	Randy McKay	Michigan Tech	RW
119	Buf.	Joe Reekie	Cornwall	D
188	Edm.	Kelly Buchberger	Moose Jaw	RW
214	Van.	Igor Larionov	CSKA Moscow	C

1984

FIRST ROUND

Pick	Claimed by		Amateur Club	Position
1	Pit.	Mario Lemieux	Laval	C
2	N.J.	Kirk Muller	Guelph	LW
3	Chi.	Eddie Olczyk	Team USA	C
4	Tor.	Al Iafrate	Belleville	D
5	Mtl.	Petr Svoboda	CHZ Litvinov	D
6	L.A.	Craig Redmond	U. of Denver	D
7	Det.	Shawn Burr	Kitchener	LW/C
8	Mtl.	Shayne Corson	Brantford	LW
9	Pit.	Doug Bodger	Kamloops	D
10	Van.	J.J. Daigneault	Longueuil	D
11	Hfd.	Sylvain Cote	Quebec	D
12	Cgy.	Gary Roberts	Ottawa	LW
13	Min.	David Quinn	Kent H.S.	D
14	NYR	Terry Carkner	Peterborough	D

Pick	Claimed by		Amateur Club	Position
15	Que.	Trevor Stienburg	Guelph	RW
16	Pit.	Roger Belanger	Kingston	C
17	Wsh.	Kevin Hatcher	North Bay	D
18	Buf.	Mikael Andersson	Vastra Frolunda	LW
19	Bos.	Dave Pasin	Prince Albert	RW
20	NYI	Duncan MacPherson	Saskatoon	D
21	Edm.	Selmar Odelein	Regina	D

OTHER NOTABLE SELECTIONS

Pick	Claimed by		Amateur Club	Position
25	Tor.	Todd Gill	Windsor	D
27	Phi.	Scott Mellanby	Henry Carr Jr. B	RW
29	Mtl.	Stephane Richer	Granby	RW
38	Cgy.	Paul Ranheim	Edina H.S.	LW
51	Mtl.	Patrick Roy	Granby	G
59	Wsh.	Michal Pivonka	Kladno	C
60	Buf.	Ray Sheppard	Cornwall	RW
117	Cgy.	Brett Hull	Penticton Jr. A	RW
119	NYR	Kjell Samuelsson	Leksand	D
134	St.L.	Cliff Ronning	New Westminster	C
166	Bos.	Don Sweeney	St. Paul's H.S.	D
171	L.A.	Luc Robitaille	Hull	LW
180	Cgy.	Gary Suter	U. of Wisconsin	D

1983

FIRST ROUND

Pick	Claimed by		Amateur Club	Position
1	Min.	Brian Lawton	Mount St. Charles H.S.	LW
2	Hfd.	Sylvain Turgeon	Hull	LW
3	NYI	Pat LaFontaine	Verdun	C
4	Det.	Steve Yzerman	Peterborough	C
5	Buf.	Tom Barrasso	Acton-Boxborough	G
6	N.J.	John MacLean	Oshawa	RW
7	Tor.	Russ Courtnall	Victoria	RW
8	Wpg.	Andrew McBain	North Bay	RW
9	Van.	Cam Neely	Portland	RW
10	Buf.	Normand Lacombe	New Hampshire	RW
11	Buf.	Adam Creighton	Ottawa	C
12	NYR	Dave Gagner	Brantford	C
13	Cgy.	Dan Quinn	Belleville	C
14	Wpg.	Bobby Dollas	Laval	D
15	Pit.	Bob Errey	Peterborough	LW
16	NYI	Gerald Diduck	Lethbridge	D
17	Mtl.	Alfie Turcotte	Portland	C
18	Chi.	Bruce Cassidy	Ottawa	D
19	Edm.	Jeff Beukeboom	Sault Ste. Marie	D
20	Hfd.	David Jensen	Lawrence Academy	C
21	Bos.	Nevin Markwart	Regina	LW

OTHER NOTABLE SELECTIONS

Pick	Claimed by		Amateur Club	Position
26	Mtl.	Claude Lemieux	Trois-Rivieres	RW
46	Det.	Bob Probert	Brantford	LW
60	Chi.	Marc Bergevin	Chicoutimi	D
82	Edm.	Esa Tikkanen	HIFK Helsinki	LW
88	Det.	Petr Klima	Dukla Jihlava	W
91	Det.	Joe Kocur	Saskatoon	RW
103	L.A.	Garry Galley	Bowling Green	D
114	Van.	Dave Lowry	London	LW
125	Phi.	Rick Tocchet	Sault Ste. Marie	RW
150	N.J.	Viacheslav Fetisov	CSKA Moscow	D
207	Chi.	Dominik Hasek	Pardubice	G
223	Buf.	Uwe Krupp	Koln	D
241	Cgy.	Sergei Makarov	CSKA Moscow	RW

1982

FIRST ROUND

Pick	Claimed by		Amateur Club	Position
1	Bos.	Gord Kluzak	Billings	D
2	Min.	Brian Bellows	Kitchener	LW
3	Tor.	Gary Nylund	Portland	D
4	Phi.	Ron Sutter	Lethbridge	C
5	Wsh.	Scott Stevens	Kitchener	D
6	Buf.	Phil Housley	South St. Paul H.S.	D
7	Chi.	Ken Yaremchuk	Portland	C
8	N.J.	Rocky Trottier	Nanaimo	RW
9	Buf.	Paul Cyr	Victoria	LW
10	Pit.	Rich Sutter	Lethbridge	RW
11	Van.	Michel Petit	Sherbrooke	D
12	Wpg.	Jim Kyte	Cornwall	D
13	Que.	David Shaw	Kitchener	D
14	Hfd.	Paul Lawless	Windsor	LW
15	NYR	Chris Kontos	Toronto	LW/C
16	Buf.	Dave Andreychuk	Oshawa	LW
17	Det.	Murray Craven	Medicine Hat	LW
18	N.J.	Ken Daneyko	Seattle	D
19	Mtl.	Alain Heroux	Chicoutimi	LW
20	Edm.	Jim Playfair	Portland	D
21	NYI	Pat Flatley	U. of Wisconsin	RW

OTHER NOTABLE SELECTIONS

Pick	Claimed by		Amateur Club	Position
36	NYR	Tomas Sandstrom	Farjestad Karlstad	RW
43	N.J.	Pat Verbeek	Sudbury	RW
45	Tor.	Ken Wregget	Lethbridge	G
56	Hfd.	Kevin Dineen	U. of Denver	RW
60	Bos.	Dave Reid	Peterborough	LW
67	Hfd.	Ulf Samuelsson	Leksand	D
75	Wpg.	Dave Ellett	Ottawa Jr. A	D
80	Min.	Bob Rouse	Nanaimo	D
88	Hfd.	Ray Ferraro	Penticton Jr. A.	C
119	Phi.	Ron Hextall	Brandon	G
120	NYR	Tony Granato	Northwood Prep	RW
134	St.L.	Doug Gilmour	Cornwall	C
140	Phi.	Dave Brown	Saskatoon	RW
181	Que.	Mike Hough	Kitchener	LW
183	NYR	Kelly Miller	Michigan State	LW

1981

FIRST ROUND

Pick	Claimed by		Amateur Club	Position
1	Wpg.	Dale Hawerchuk	Cornwall	C
2	L.A.	Doug Smith	Ottawa	C
3	Wsh.	Bob Carpenter	St. John's Prep	C
4	Hfd.	Ron Francis	Sault Ste. Marie	C
5	Col.	Joe Cirella	Oshawa	D
6	Tor.	Jim Benning	Portland	D
7	Mtl.	Mark Hunter	Brantford	RW
8	Edm.	Grant Fuhr	Victoria	G
9	NYR	James Patrick	Prince Albert	D
10	Van.	Garth Butcher	Regina	D
11	Que.	Randy Moller	Lethbridge	D
12	Chi.	Tony Tanti	Oshawa	RW
13	Min.	Ron Meighan	Niagara Falls	D
14	Bos.	Normand Leveille	Chicoutimi	LW
15	Cgy.	Al MacInnis	Kitchener	D
16	Phi.	Steve Smith	Sault Ste. Marie	D
17	Buf.	Jiri Dudacek	Kladno	RW
18	Mtl.	Gilbert Delorme	Chicoutimi	D
19	Mtl.	Jan Ingman	Farjestad Karlstad	LW
20	St.L.	Marty Ruff	Lethbridge	D
21	NYI	Paul Boutilier	Sherbrooke	D

OTHER NOTABLE SELECTIONS

Pick	Claimed by		Amateur Club	Position
40	Mtl.	Chris Chelios	Moose Jaw	D
56	Cgy.	Mike Vernon	Calgary	G
72	NYR	John Vanbiesbrouck	Sault Ste. Marie	G
108	Col.	Bruce Driver	U. of Wisconsin	D
111	Edm.	Steve Smith	London	D
116	Que.	Mike Eagles	Kitchener	C/LW
145	Mtl.	Tom Kurvers	Minnesota-Duluth	D
152	Wsh.	Gaetan Duchesne	Quebec	LW

1980

FIRST ROUND

Pick	Claimed by		Amateur Club	Position
1	Mtl.	Doug Wickenheiser	Regina	C
2	Wpg.	Dave Babych	Portland	D
3	Chi.	Denis Savard	Montreal	C
4	L.A.	Larry Murphy	Peterborough	D
5	Wsh.	Darren Veitch	Regina	D
6	Edm.	Paul Coffey	Kitchener	D
7	Van.	Rick Lanz	Oshawa	D
8	Hfd.	Fred Arthur	Cornwall	D
9	Pit.	Mike Bullard	Brantford	C
10	L.A.	Jim Fox	Ottawa	RW
11	Det.	Mike Blaisdell	Regina	RW
12	St.L.	Rik Wilson	Kingston	D
13	Cgy.	Denis Cyr	Montreal	RW
14	NYR	Jim Malone	Toronto	C
15	Chi.	Jerome Dupont	Toronto	D
16	Min.	Brad Palmer	Victoria	LW
17	NYI	Brent Sutter	Red Deer Jr. A.	C
18	Bos.	Barry Pederson	Victoria	C
19	Col.	Paul Gagne	Windsor	LW
20	Buf.	Steve Patrick	Brandon	RW
21	Phi.	Mike Stothers	Kingston	D

OTHER NOTABLE SELECTIONS

Pick	Claimed by		Amateur Club	Position
37	Min.	Don Beaupre	Sudbury	G
38	NYI	Kelly Hrudey	Medicine Hat	G
39	Cgy.	Steve Konroyd	Oshawa	D
46	Det.	Mark Osborne	Niagara Falls	LW
61	Mtl.	Craig Ludwig	North Dakota	D
69	Edm.	Jari Kurri	Jokerit	RW
73	L.A.	Bernie Nicholls	Kingston	C
80	NYI	Greg Gilbert	Toronto	LW
81	Bos.	Steve Kasper	Verdun	C
106	Col.	Aaron Broten	Minnesota-Duluth	LW/C
120	Chi.	Steve Larmer	Niagara Falls	RW
124	Mtl.	Mike McPhee	RPI	LW
128	Wpg.	Brian Mullen	U.S. Jr. National	RW
132	Edm.	Andy Moog	Billings	G
133	Van.	Doug Lidster	Colorado College	D
167	Buf.	Randy Cunneyworth	Ottawa	LW

Don Beaupre was the first goaltender selected in the 1980 NHL Entry Draft. He entered the NHL as a rookie that season and played until 1996-97.

1979

FIRST ROUND

Pick	Claimed by		Amateur Club	Position
1	Col.	Rob Ramage	London	D
2	St.L.	Perry Turnbull	Portland	C
3	Det.	Mike Foligno	Sudbury	RW
4	Wsh.	Mike Gartner	Niagara Falls	RW
5	Van.	Rick Vaive	Sherbrooke	RW
6	Min.	Craig Hartsburg	Sault Ste. Marie	D
7	Chi.	Keith Brown	Portland	D
8	Bos.	Raymond Bourque	Verdun	D
9	Tor.	Laurie Boschman	Brandon	C
10	Min.	Tom McCarthy	Oshawa	LW
11	Buf.	Mike Ramsey	U. of Minnesota	D
12	Atl.	Paul Reinhart	Kitchener	D
13	NYR	Doug Sulliman	Kitchener	RW
14	Phi.	Brian Propp	Brandon	LW
15	Bos.	Brad McCrimmon	Brandon	D
16	L.A.	Jay Wells	Kingston	D
17	NYI	Duane Sutter	Lethbridge	RW
18	Hfd.	Ray Allison	Brandon	RW
19	Wpg.	Jimmy Mann	Sherbrooke	RW
20	Que.	Michel Goulet	Quebec	LW
21	Edm.	Kevin Lowe	Quebec	D

OTHER NOTABLE SELECTIONS

Pick	Claimed by		Amateur Club	Position
26	Van.	Brent Ashton	Saskatoon	LW
30	L.A.	Mark Hardy	Montreal	D
32	Buf.	Lindy Ruff	Lethbridge	D/LW
37	Mtl.	Mats Naslund	Brynas Gavle	LW
40	Wpg.	Dave Christian	North Dakota	RW
41	Que.	Dale Hunter	Sudbury	C
42	Min.	Neal Broten	Minnesota-Duluth	C
44	Mtl.	Guy Carbonneau	Chicoutimi	C
48	Edm.	Mark Messier	St. Albert Jr. A.	C
54	Atl.	Tim Hunter	Seattle	RW
66	Det.	John Ogrodnick	New Westminster	LW
69	Edm.	Glenn Anderson	U. of Denver	RW
75	Atl.	Jim Peplinski	Toronto	RW
83	Que.	Anton Stastny	Slovan Bratislava	LW
89	Van.	Dirk Graham	Regina	RW/LW
103	Wpg.	Thomas Steen	Leksand	C
120	Bos.	Mike Krushelnyski	Montreal	LW/C

1978

FIRST ROUND

Pick	Claimed by		Amateur Club	Position
1	Min.	Bobby Smith	Ottawa	C
2	Wsh.	Ryan Walter	Seattle	C/LW
3	St.L.	Wayne Babych	Portland	RW
4	Van.	Bill Derlago	Brandon	C
5	Col.	Mike Gillis	Kingston	LW
6	Phi.	Behn Wilson	Kingston	D
7	Phi.	Ken Linseman	Kingston	C
8	Mtl.	Danny Geoffrion	Cornwall	RW
9	Det.	Willie Huber	Hamilton	D
10	Chi.	Tim Higgins	Ottawa	RW
11	Atl.	Brad Marsh	London	D
12	Det.	Brent Peterson	Portland	C
13	Buf.	Larry Playfair	Portland	D
14	Phi.	Danny Lucas	Sault Ste. Marie	RW
15	NYI	Steve Tambellini	Lethbridge	C
16	Bos.	Al Secord	Hamilton	LW
17	Mtl.	Dave Hunter	Sudbury	LW
18	Wsh.	Tim Coulis	Hamilton	LW

OTHER NOTABLE SELECTIONS

Pick	Claimed by		Amateur Club	Position
19	Min.	Steve Payne	Ottawa	LW
21	Tor.	Joel Quenneville	Windsor	D
26	NYR	Don Maloney	Kitchener	LW
32	Buf.	Tony McKegney	Kingston	LW
40	Van.	Stan Smyl	New Westminster	RW
54	Min.	Curt Giles	Minnesota-Duluth	D
55	Wsh.	Bengt-Ake Gustafsson	Farjestad Karlstad	RW
93	NYR	Tom Laidlaw	Northern Michigan	D
103	Mtl.	Keith Acton	Peterborough	C
109	St.L.	Paul MacLean	Hull	RW
153	Bos.	Craig MacTavish	University of Lowell	C
173	St.L.	Risto Siltanen	Ilves Tampere	D
179	Chi.	Darryl Sutter	Lethbridge	LW
231	Mtl.	Chris Nilan	Northeastern	RW

1977

FIRST ROUND

Pick	Claimed by		Amateur Club	Position
1	Det.	Dale McCourt	St. Catharines	C
2	Col.	Barry Beck	New Westminster	D
3	Wsh.	Robert Picard	Montreal	D
4	Van.	Jere Gillis	Sherbrooke	LW
5	Cle.	Mike Crombeen	Kingston	RW
6	Chi.	Doug Wilson	Ottawa	D
7	Min.	Brad Maxwell	New Westminster	D
8	NYR	Lucien DeBlois	Sorel	C
9	St.L.	Scott Campbell	London	D
10	Mtl.	Mark Napier	Toronto	RW
11	Tor.	John Anderson	Toronto	RW
12	Tor.	Trevor Johansen	Toronto	D
13	NYR	Ron Duguay	Sudbury	C/RW
14	Buf.	Ric Seiling	St. Catharines	RW/C
15	NYI	Mike Bossy	Laval	RW
16	Bos.	Dwight Foster	Kitchener	RW
17	Phi.	Kevin McCarthy	Winnipeg	D
18	Mtl.	Norm Dupont	Montreal	LW

OTHER NOTABLE SELECTIONS

Pick	Claimed by		Amateur Club	Position
25	Min.	Dave Semenko	Brandon	LW
33	NYI	John Tonelli	Toronto	LW
36	Mtl.	Rod Langway	New Hampshire	D
43	Mtl.	Alain Cote	Chicoutimi	LW
54	Mtl.	Gordie Roberts	Victoria	D
62	NYR	Mario Marois	Quebec	D
66	Pit.	Mark Johnson	U. of Wisconsin	C
102	Pit.	Greg Millen	Peterborough	G
118	Atl.	Bobby Gould	New Hampshire	RW
135	Phi.	Pete Peeters	Medicine Hat	G
162	Mtl.	Craig Laughlin	Clarkson	RW

1976

FIRST ROUND

Pick	Claimed by		Amateur Club	Position
1	Wsh.	Rick Green	London	D
2	Pit.	Blair Chapman	Saskatoon	RW
3	Min.	Glen Sharpley	Hull	C
4	Det.	Fred Williams	Saskatoon	C
5	Cal.	Bjorn Johansson	Orebro	D
6	NYR	Don Murdoch	Medicine Hat	RW
7	St.L.	Bernie Federko	Saskatoon	C
8	Atl.	Dave Shand	Peterborough	D
9	Chi.	Real Cloutier	Quebec	RW
10	Atl.	Harold Phillipoff	New Westminster	LW
11	K.C.	Paul Gardner	Oshawa	C
12	Mtl.	Peter Lee	Ottawa	RW
13	Mtl.	Rod Schutt	Sudbury	LW
14	NYI	Alex McKendry	Sudbury	W
15	Wsh.	Greg Carroll	Medicine Hat	C
16	Bos.	Clayton Pachal	New Westminster	C/LW
17	Phi.	Mark Suzor	Kingston	D
18	Mtl.	Bruce Baker	Ottawa	RW

OTHER NOTABLE SELECTIONS

Pick	Claimed by		Amateur Club	Position
20	St.L.	Brian Sutter	Lethbridge	LW
22	Det.	Reed Larson	Minnesota-Duluth	D
30	Tor.	Randy Carlyle	Sudbury	D
42	NYR	Mike McEwen	Toronto	D
45	Chi.	Thomas Gradin	MoDo Ornskoldsvik	C
47	Pit.	Morris Lukowich	Medicine Hat	LW
56	St.L.	Mike Liut	Bowling Green	G
64	Atl.	Kent Nilsson	Djurgarden	C
68	NYI	Ken Morrow	Bowling Green	D
133	Mtl.	Ron Wilson	St. Catharines	C

1975

FIRST ROUND

Pick	Claimed by		Amateur Club	Position
1	Phi.	Mel Bridgman	Victoria	C
2	K.C.	Barry Dean	Medicine Hat	LW
3	Cal.	Ralph Klassen	Saskatoon	C
4	Min.	Bryan Maxwell	Medicine Hat	D
5	Det.	Rick Lapointe	Victoria	D
6	Tor.	Don Ashby	Calgary	C
7	Chi.	Greg Vaydik	Medicine Hat	C
8	Atl.	Richard Mulhern	Sherbrooke	D
9	Mtl.	Robin Sadler	Edmonton	D
10	Van.	Rick Blight	Brandon	RW
11	NYI	Pat Price	Saskatoon	D
12	NYR	Wayne Dillon	Toronto	C
13	Pit.	Gord Laxton	New Westminster	G
14	Bos.	Doug Halward	Peterborough	D
15	Mtl.	Pierre Mondou	Montreal	C
16	L.A.	Tim Young	Ottawa	C

OTHER NOTABLE SELECTIONS

Pick	Claimed by		Amateur Club	Position
17	Buf.	Bob Sauve	Laval	G
21	Cal.	Dennis Maruk	London	C
24	Tor.	Doug Jarvis	Peterborough	C
43	Chi.	Mike O'Connell	Kingston	D
57	Cal.	Greg Smith	Colorado College	D
80	Atl.	Willi Plett	St. Catharines	RW
108	Phi.	Paul Holmgren	U. of Minnesota	RW
210	L.A.	Dave Taylor	Clarkson	RW

1974

FIRST ROUND

Pick	Claimed by		Amateur Club	Position
1	Wsh.	Greg Joly	Regina	D
2	K.C.	Wilf Paiement	St. Catharines	RW
3	Cal.	Rick Hampton	St. Catharines	LW/D
4	NYI	Clark Gillies	Regina	LW
5	Mtl.	Cam Connor	Flin Flon	RW
6	Min.	Doug Hicks	Flin Flon	D
7	Mtl.	Doug Risebrough	Kitchener	C
8	Pit.	Pierre Larouche	Sorel	C
9	Det.	Bill Lochead	Oshawa	LW
10	Mtl.	Rick Chartraw	Kitchener	D/RW
11	Buf.	Lee Fogolin Jr.	Oshawa	D
12	Mtl.	Mario Tremblay	Montreal	RW
13	Tor.	Jack Valiquette	Sault Ste. Marie	C
14	NYR	Dave Maloney	Kitchener	D
15	Mtl.	Gord McTavish	Sudbury	C
16	Chi.	Grant Mulvey	Calgary	RW
17	Cal.	Ron Chipperfield	Brandon	C
18	Bos.	Don Larway	Swift Current	RW

OTHER NOTABLE SELECTIONS

Pick	Claimed by		Amateur Club	Position
22	NYI	Bryan Trottier	Swift Current	C
25	Bos.	Mark Howe	Toronto	D
29	Buf.	Danny Gare	Calgary	RW
31	Tor.	Tiger Williams	Swift Current	LW
32	NYR	Ron Greschner	New Westminster	D
38	K.C.	Bob Bourne	Saskatoon	C
39	Cal.	Charlie Simmer	Sault Ste. Marie	LW
52	Chi.	Bob Murray	Cornwall	D
59	Van.	Harold Snepsts	Edmonton	D
70	Chi.	Terry Ruskowski	Swift Current	C
125	Phi.	Reggie Lemelin	Sherbrooke	G
199	Mtl.	Dave Lumley	New Hampshire	RW
214	NYI	Stefan Persson	Brynas Gavle	D

1973

FIRST ROUND

Pick	Claimed by		Amateur Club	Position
1	NYI	Denis Potvin	Ottawa	D
2	Atl.	Tom Lysiak	Medicine Hat	C
3	Van.	Dennis Ververgaert	London	RW
4	Tor.	Lanny McDonald	Medicine Hat	RW
5	St.L.	John Davidson	Calgary	G
6	Bos.	Andre Savard	Quebec	C
7	Pit.	Blaine Stoughton	Flin Flon	RW
8	Mtl.	Bob Gainey	Peterborough	LW
9	Van.	Bob Dailey	Toronto	D
10	Tor.	Bob Neely	Peterborough	LW
11	Det.	Terry Richardson	New Westminster	G
12	Buf.	Morris Titanic	Sudbury	LW
13	Chi.	Darcy Rota	Edmonton	LW
14	NYR	Rick Middleton	Oshawa	RW
15	Tor.	Ian Turnbull	Ottawa	D
16	Atl.	Vic Mercredi	New Westminster	C

OTHER NOTABLE SELECTIONS

Pick	Claimed by		Amateur Club	Position
21	Atl.	Eric Vail	Sudbury	LW
27	Pit.	Colin Campbell	Peterborough	D
30	NYR	Pat Hickey	Hamilton	LW
33	NYI	Dave Lewis	Saskatoon	D
49	NYI	Andre St. Laurent	Montreal	C
85	Atl.	Ken Houston	Chatham Jr. B	RW
130	Cal.	Larry Patey	Braintree H.S.	C
134	Pit.	Gord Lane	New Westminster	D
162	Atl.	Greg Fox	U. of Michigan	D

1972

FIRST ROUND

Pick	Claimed by		Amateur Club	Position
1	NYI	Billy Harris	Toronto	RW
2	Atl.	Jacques Richard	Quebec	LW
3	Van.	Don Lever	Niagara Falls	LW
4	Mtl.	Steve Shutt	Toronto	LW
5	Buf.	Jim Schoenfeld	Niagara Falls	D
6	Mtl.	Michel Larocque	Ottawa	G
7	Phi.	Bill Barber	Kitchener	LW
8	Mtl.	Dave Gardner	Toronto	C
9	St.L.	Wayne Merrick	Ottawa	C
10	NYR	Al Blanchard	Kitchener	LW
11	Tor.	George Ferguson	Toronto	C
12	Min.	Jerry Byers	Kitchener	LW
13	Chi.	Phil Russell	Edmonton	D
14	Mtl.	John Van Boxmeer	Guelph	D
15	NYR	Bob MacMillan	St. Catharines	RW
16	Bos.	Mike Bloom	St. Catharines	LW

OTHER NOTABLE SELECTIONS

Pick	Claimed by		Amateur Club	Position
17	NYI	Lorne Henning	New Westminster	C
23	Phi.	Tom Bladon	Edmonton	D
33	NYI	Bob Nystrom	Calgary	RW
39	Phi.	Jimmy Watson	Calgary	D
55	Phi.	Al MacAdam	University of PEI	RW
85	Buf.	Peter McNab	U. of Denver	C
97	NYI	Richard Brodeur	Cornwall	G
139	Tor.	Pat Boutette	Minnesota-Duluth	C/RW
144	NYI	Garry Howatt	Flin Flon	LW

1971

FIRST ROUND

Pick	Claimed by		Amateur Club	Position
1	Mtl.	Guy Lafleur	Quebec	RW
2	Det.	Marcel Dionne	St. Catharines	C
3	Van.	Jocelyn Guevremont	Montreal	D
4	St.L.	Gene Carr	Flin Flon	C
5	Buf.	Rick Martin	Montreal	LW
6	Bos.	Ron Jones	Edmonton	D
7	Mtl.	Chuck Arnason	Flin Flon	RW
8	Phi.	Larry Wright	Regina	C
9	Phi.	Pierre Plante	Drummondville	RW
10	NYR	Steve Vickers	Toronto	LW
11	Mtl.	Murray Wilson	Ottawa	LW
12	Chi.	Dan Spring	Edmonton	C
13	NYR	Steve Durbano	Toronto	D
14	Bos.	Terry O'Reilly	Oshawa	RW

OTHER NOTABLE SELECTIONS

Pick	Claimed by		Amateur Club	Position
17	Van.	Bobby Lalonde	Montreal	C
19	Buf.	Craig Ramsay	Peterborough	LW
20	Mtl.	Larry Robinson	Kitchener	D
22	Tor.	Rick Kehoe	Hamilton	RW
33	Buf.	Bill Hajt	Saskatoon	D
48	L.A.	Neil Komadoski	Winnipeg	D
55	NYR	Jerry Butler	Hamilton	RW

1970

FIRST ROUND

Pick	Claimed by		Amateur Club	Position
1	Buf.	Gilbert Perreault	Montreal	C
2	Van.	Dale Tallon	Toronto	D
3	Bos.	Reggie Leach	Flin Flon	RW
4	Bos.	Rick MacLeish	Peterborough	C
5	Mtl.	Ray Martyniuk	Flin Flon	G
6	Mtl.	Chuck Lefley	Canadian National	LW
7	Pit.	Greg Polis	Estevan	LW
8	Tor.	Darryl Sittler	London	C
9	Bos.	Ron Plumb	Peterborough	D
10	Cal.	Chris Oddleifson	Winnipeg	C
11	NYR	Norm Gratton	Montreal	LW
12	Det.	Serge Lajeunesse	Montreal	D/RW
13	Bos.	Bob Stewart	Oshawa	D
14	Chi.	Dan Maloney	London	LW

OTHER NOTABLE SELECTIONS

Pick	Claimed by		Amateur Club	Position
18	Phi.	Bill Clement	Ottawa	C
22	Tor.	Errol Thompson	Charlottetown Sr.	LW
25	NYR	Mike Murphy	Toronto	RW
27	Bos.	Dan Bouchard	London	G
32	Phi.	Bob Kelly	Oshawa	LW
40	Det.	Yvon Lambert	Drummondville	LW
59	L.A.	Billy Smith	Cornwall	G
70	Chi.	Gilles Meloche	Verdun	G
88	Oak.	Terry Murray	Ottawa	D
103	Tor.	Ron Low	Dauphin Jr. A	G

1969

FIRST ROUND

Pick	Claimed by		Amateur Club	Position
1	Mtl.	Rejean Houle	Montreal	W
2	Mtl.	Marc Tardif	Montreal	LW
3	Bos.	Don Tannahill	Niagara Falls	LW
4	Bos.	Frank Spring	Edmonton	RW
5	Min.	Dick Redmond	St. Catharines	D
6	Phi.	Bob Currier	Cornwall	C
7	Oak.	Tony Featherstone	Peterborough	RW
8	NYR	Andre Dupont	Montreal	D
9	Tor.	Ernie Moser	Estevan	RW
10	Det.	Jim Rutherford	Hamilton	G
11	Bos.	Ivan Boldirev	Oshawa	C
12	NYR	Pierre Jarry	Ottawa	LW

OTHER NOTABLE SELECTIONS

Pick	Claimed by		Amateur Club	Position
17	Phi.	Bobby Clarke	Flin Flon	C
18	Oak.	Ron Stackhouse	Peterborough	D
25	Min.	Gilles Gilbert	London	G
26	Pit.	Michel Briere	Shawinigan	C
51	L.A.	Butch Goring	Dauphin Jr. A	C
52	Phi.	Dave Schultz	Sorel	LW
55	Tor.	Brian Spencer	Swift Current	LW
64	Phi.	Don Saleski	Regina	RW

NHL All-Stars

Active Players' All-Star Selection Records

	First Team Selections	Second Team Selections	Total
GOALTENDERS			
Dominik Hasek	(6) 1993-94; 1994-95; 1996-97; 1997-98; 1998-99; 2000-01.	(0)	6
Martin Brodeur	(2) 2002-03; 2003-04.	(3) 1996-97; 1997-98; 2005-06.	5
Ed Belfour	(2) 1990-91; 1992-93.	(1) 1994-95	3
Olie Kolzig	(1) 99-2000.	(0)	1
Miikka Kiprusoff	(1) 2005-06.	(0)	1
Chris Osgood	(0)	(1) 1995-96.	1
Jose Theodore	(0)	(1) 2001-02.	1
Marty Turco	(0)	(1) 2002-03.	1
Roberto Luongo	(0)	(1) 2003-04.	1
DEFENSEMEN			
Chris Chelios	(5) 1988-89; 1992-93; 1994-95; 1995-96; 2001-02.	(2) 1990-91; 1996-97.	7
Nicklas Lidstrom	(7) 1997-98; 1998-99; 99-2000; 2000-01; 2001-02; 2002-03; 2005-06.		7
Brian Leetch	(2) 1991-92; 1996-97.	(3) 1990-91; 1993-94; 1995-96.	5
Rob Blake	(1) 1997-98.	(3) 99-2000; 2000-01; 2001-02.	4
Chris Pronger	(1) 99-2000.	(2) 1997-98; 2003-04.	3
Scott Niedermayer	(2) 2003-04; 2005-06.	(1) 2002-03.	3
Zdeno Chara	(1) 2003-04.	(1) 2005-06.	2
Sergei Gonchar	(0)	(2) 2001-02; 2002-03.	2
Sandis Ozolinsh	(1) 1996-97.	(0)	1
Derian Hatcher	(0)	(1) 2002-03.	1
Bryan McCabe	(0)	(1) 2003-04.	1
Sergei Zubov	(0)	(1) 2005-06.	1
CENTERS			
Peter Forsberg	(3) 1997-98; 1998-99; 2002-03.	(0)	3
Joe Sakic	(3) 2000-01; 2001-02; 2003-04.	(0)	3
Eric Lindros	(1) 1994-95.	(1) 1995-96.	2
Joe Thornton	(1) 2005-06.	(1) 2002-03.	2
Mats Sundin	(0)	(2) 2001-02; 2003-04.	2
Sergei Fedorov	(1) 1993-94.	(0)	1
Alex Zhamnov	(0)	(1) 1994-95.	1
Alexei Yashin	(0)	(1) 1998-99.	1
Mike Modano	(0)	(1) 99-2000.	1
Eric Staal	(0)	(1) 2005-06.	1
RIGHT WINGERS			
Jaromir Jagr	(7) 1994-95; 1995-96; 1997-98; 1998-99; 99-2000; 2000-01; 2005-06.	(1) 1996-97.	8
Teemu Selanne	(2) 1992-93; 1996-97.	(2) 1997-98; 1998-99.	4
Jarome Iginla	(1) 2001-02.	(1) 2003-04.	2
Alexander Mogilny	(0)	(2) 1992-93; 1995-96.	1
Todd Bertuzzi	(1) 2002-03.	(0)	1
Martin St. Louis	(1) 2003-04.	(0)	1
Mark Recchi	(0)	(1) 1991-92.	1
Bill Guerin	(0)	(1) 2001-02.	1
Milan Hejduk	(0)	(1) 2002-03.	1
Daniel Alfredsson	(0)	(1) 2005-06.	1
LEFT WINGERS			
Paul Kariya	(3) 1995-96; 1996-97; 1998-99.	(2) 99-2000; 2002-03.	5
John LeClair	(2) 1994-95; 1997-98.	(3) 1995-96; 1996-97; 1998-99.	5
Markus Naslund	(3) 2001-02; 2002-03; 2003-04.	(0)	3
Brendan Shanahan	(2) 1993-94; 99-2000.	(1) 2001-02.	3
Keith Tkachuk	(0)	(2) 1994-95; 1997-98.	2
Patrik Elias	(1) 2000-01.	(0)	1
Alex Ovechkin	(1) 2005-06.	(0)	1
Ilya Kovalchuk	(0)	(1) 2003-04.	1
Dany Heatley	(0)	(1) 2005-06.	1

Leading NHL All-Stars 1930-31 to 2005-06

Player	Pos	Team	NHL Seasons	First Team Selections	Second Team Selections	Total Selections
Howe, Gordie	RW	Detroit	26	12	9	21
Bourque, Raymond	D	Bos., Col.	22	13	6	19
Gretzky, Wayne	C	Edm., L.A., NYR	20	8	7	15
Richard, Maurice	RW	Montreal	18	8	6	14
Hull, Bobby	LW	Chicago	16	10	2	12
Harvey, Doug	D	Mtl., NYR	19	10	1	11
Hall, Glenn	G	Det., Chi., St.L.	18	7	4	11
Beliveau, Jean	C	Montreal	20	6	4	10
Seibert, Earl	D	NYR, Chi.	15	4	6	10
Orr, Bobby	D	Boston	12	8	1	9
Lindsay, Ted	LW	Detroit	17	8	1	9
Lemieux, Mario	C	Pittsburgh	17	5	4	9
Mahovlich, Frank	LW	Tor., Det., Mtl.	18	3	6	9
Shore, Eddie	D	Boston	14	7	1	8
Esposito, Phil	C	Boston	18	6	2	8
Kelly, Red	D	Detroit	20	6	2	8
Mikita, Stan	C	Chicago	22	6	2	8
Bossy, Mike	RW	NY Islanders	10	5	3	8
Pilote, Pierre	D	Chicago	14	5	3	8
Robitaille, Luc	LW	Los Angeles	19	5	3	8
Coffey, Paul	D	Edm., Pit., Det.	21	4	4	8
Brimsek, Frank	G	Boston	10	2	6	8
* Jagr, Jaromir	RW	Pit., NYR	15	7	1	8
Potvin, Denis	D	NY Islanders	15	5	2	7
Park, Brad	D	NYR, Bos.	17	5	2	7
* Chelios, Chris	D	Mtl., Chi.	22	5	2	7
MacInnis, Al	D	Cgy., St.L.	23	4	3	7
Plante, Jacques	G	Mtl., Tor.	18	3	4	7
Gadsby, Bill	D	Chi., NYR, Det.	20	3	4	7
Sawchuk, Terry	G	Detroit	21	3	4	7
* Lidstrom, Niklas	D	Detroit	14	7	0	7
Durnan, Bill	G	Montreal	7	6	0	6
* Hasek, Dominik	G	Buffalo	13	6	0	6
Lafleur, Guy	RW	Montreal	17	6	0	6
Dryden, Ken	G	Montreal	8	5	1	6
Roy, Patrick	G	Montreal	19	4	2	6
Clapper, Dit	RW/D	Boston	20	3	3	6
Robinson, Larry	D	Montreal	20	3	3	6
Horton, Tim	D	Toronto	24	3	3	6
Salming, Borje	D	Toronto	17	1	5	6
Cowley, Bill	C	Boston	13	4	1	5
Jackson, Busher	LW	Toronto	15	4	1	5
Messier, Mark	LW/C	Edm., NYR	25	4	1	5
* Kariya, Paul	LW	Anaheim	11	3	2	5
Conacher, Charlie	RW	Toronto	12	3	2	5
Stewart, Jack	D	Detroit	12	3	2	5
Blake, Toe	LW	Montreal	14	3	2	5
Lach, Elmer	C	Montreal	14	3	2	5
Quackenbush, Bill	D	Det., Bos.	14	3	2	5
Goulet, Michel	LW	Quebec	15	3	2	5
Esposito, Tony	G	Chicago	16	3	2	5
Reardon, Ken	D	Montreal	7	2	3	5
Apps, Syl	C	Toronto	10	2	3	5
* LeClair, John	LW	Mtl., Phi.	15	2	3	5
Giacomin, Ed	G	NY Rangers	13	2	3	5
* Leetch, Brian	D	NY Rangers	17	2	3	5
Kurri, Jari	RW	Edmonton	17	2	3	5
Stevens, Scott	D	Wsh., N.J.	21	2	3	5
* Brodeur, Martin	G	New Jersey	13	2	3	5

* Active

Position Leaders in All-Star Selections

Position	Player	First Team	Second Team	Total		Position	Player	First Team	Second Team	Total
GOAL	Glenn Hall	7	4	11		LEFT WING	Bobby Hull	10	2	12
	Frank Brimsek	2	6	8			Ted Lindsay	8	1	9
	Jacques Plante	3	4	7			Frank Mahovlich	3	6	9
	Terry Sawchuk	3	4	7			Luc Robitaille	5	3	8
	Bill Durnan	6	0	6						
	* Dominik Hasek	6	0	6		RIGHT WING	Gordie Howe	12	9	21
	Ken Dryden	5	1	6			Maurice Richard	8	6	14
	Patrick Roy	4	2	6			* Jaromir Jagr	7	1	8
							Mike Bossy	5	3	8
DEFENSE	Raymond Bourque	13	6	19			Guy Lafleur	6	0	6
	Doug Harvey	10	1	11						
	Earl Seibert	4	6	10		CENTER	Wayne Gretzky	8	7	15
	Bobby Orr	8	1	9			Jean Beliveau	6	4	10
	Eddie Shore	7	1	8			Mario Lemieux	5	4	9
	Red Kelly	6	2	8			Phil Esposito	6	2	8
	Pierre Pilote	5	3	8			Stan Mikita	6	2	8
	Paul Coffey	4	4	8						

* active player

All-Star Teams

1930-2006

Voting for the NHL All-Star Team is conducted among the representatives of the Professional Hockey Writers' Association at the end of the season.

Following is a list of the First and Second All-Star Teams since their inception in 1930-31.

2005-06

First Team		Second Team
Miikka Kiprusoff, Cgy.	G	Martin Brodeur, N.J.
Nicklas Lidstrom, Det.	D	Zdeno Chara, Ott.
Scott Niedermayer, Ana.	D	Sergei Zubov, Dal.
Joe Thornton, Bos., S.J.	C	Eric Staal, Car.
Jaromir Jagr, NYR	RW	Daniel Alfredsson, Ott.
Alex Ovechkin, Wsh.	LW	Dany Heatley, Ott.

2004-05

No All-Star Teams selected

2003-04

First Team		Second Team
Martin Brodeur, N.J.	G	Roberto Luongo, Fla.
Scott Niedermayer, N.J.	D	Chris Pronger, St.L.
Zdeno Chara, Ott.	D	Bryan McCabe, Tor.
Joe Sakic, Col.	C	Mats Sundin, Tor.
Martin St. Louis, T.B.	RW	Jarome Iginla, Cgy.
Markus Naslund, Van.	LW	Ilya Kovalchuk, Atl.

2002-03

First Team		Second Team
Martin Brodeur, N.J.	G	Marty Turco, Dal.
Al MacInnis, St.L.	D	Sergei Gonchar, Wsh.
Nicklas Lidstrom, Det.	D	Derian Hatcher, Dal.
Peter Forsberg, Col.	C	Joe Thornton, Bos.
Todd Bertuzzi, Van.	RW	Milan Hejduk, Col.
Markus Naslund, Van.	LW	Paul Kariya, Ana.

2001-02

First Team		Second Team
Patrick Roy, Col.	G	Jose Theodore, Mtl.
Nicklas Lidstrom, Det.	D	Rob Blake, L.A. Col.
Chris Chelios, Det.	D	Sergei Gonchar, Wsh.
Joe Sakic, Col.	C	Mats Sundin, Tor.
Jarome Iginla, Cgy.	RW	Bill Guerin, Bos.
Markus Naslund, Van.	LW	Brendan Shanahan, Det.

2000-01

First Team		Second Team
Dominik Hasek, Buf.	G	Roman Cechmanek, Phi.
Nicklas Lidstrom, Det.	D	Rob Blake, L.A. Col.
Raymond Bourque, Col.	D	Scott Stevens, N.J.
Joe Sakic, Col.	C	Mario Lemieux, Pit.
Jaromir Jagr, Pit.	RW	Pavel Bure, Fla.
Patrik Elias, N.J.	LW	Luc Robitaille, L.A.

1999-2000

First Team		Second Team
Olaf Kolzig, Wsh.	G	Roman Turek, St.L.
Chris Pronger, St.L.	D	Rob Blake, L.A.
Nicklas Lidstrom, Det.	D	Eric Desjardins, Phi.
Steve Yzerman, Det.	C	Mike Modano, Dal.
Jaromir Jagr, Pit.	RW	Pavel Bure, Fla.
Brendan Shanahan, Det.	LW	Paul Kariya, Ana.

1998-99

First Team		Second Team
Dominik Hasek, Buf.	G	Byron Dafoe, Bos.
Al MacInnis, St.L.	D	Raymond Bourque, Bos.
Nicklas Lidstrom, Det.	D	Eric Desjardins, Phi.
Peter Forsberg, Col.	C	Alexei Yashin, Ott.
Jaromir Jagr, Pit.	RW	Teemu Selanne, Ana.
Paul Kariya, Ana.	LW	John LeClair, Phi.

1997-98

First Team		Second Team
Dominik Hasek, Buf.	G	Martin Brodeur, N.J.
Nicklas Lidstrom, Det.	D	Chris Pronger, St.L.
Rob Blake, L.A.	D	Scott Niedermayer, N.J.
Peter Forsberg, Col.	C	Wayne Gretzky, NYR
Jaromir Jagr, Pit.	RW	Teemu Selanne, Ana.
John LeClair, Phi.	LW	Keith Tkachuk, Phx.

1996-97

First Team		Second Team
Dominik Hasek, Buf.	G	Martin Brodeur, N.J.
Brian Leetch, NYR	D	Chris Chelios, Chi.
Sandis Ozolinsh, Col.	D	Scott Stevens, N.J.
Mario Lemieux, Pit.	C	Wayne Gretzky, NYR
Teemu Selanne, Ana.	RW	Jaromir Jagr, Pit.
Paul Kariya, Ana.	LW	John LeClair, Phi.

1995-96

First Team		Second Team
Jim Carey, Wsh.	G	Chris Osgood, Det.
Chris Chelios, Chi.	D	V. Konstantinov, Det.
Raymond Bourque, Bos.	D	Brian Leetch, NYR
Mario Lemieux, Pit.	C	Eric Lindros, Phi.
Jaromir Jagr, Pit.	RW	Alexander Mogilny, Van.
Paul Kariya, Ana.	LW	John LeClair, Phi.

1994-95

First Team		Second Team
Dominik Hasek, Buf.	G	Ed Belfour, Chi.
Paul Coffey, Det.	D	Raymond Bourque, Bos.
Chris Chelios, Chi.	D	Larry Murphy, Pit.
Eric Lindros, Phi.	C	Alexei Zhamnov, Wpg.
Jaromir Jagr, Pit.	RW	Theoren Fleury, Cgy.
John LeClair, Mtl., Phi.	LW	Keith Tkachuk, Wpg.

1993-94

First Team		Second Team
Dominik Hasek, Buf.	G	John Vanbiesbrouck, Fla.
Raymond Bourque, Bos.	D	Al MacInnis, Cgy.
Scott Stevens, N.J.	D	Brian Leetch, NYR
Sergei Fedorov, Det.	C	Wayne Gretzky, L.A.
Pavel Bure, Van.	RW	Cam Neely, Bos.
Brendan Shanahan, St.L.	LW	Adam Graves, NYR

1992-93

First Team		Second Team
Ed Belfour, Chi.	G	Tom Barrasso, Pit.
Chris Chelios, Chi.	D	Larry Murphy, Pit.
Raymond Bourque, Bos.	D	Al Iafrate, Wsh.
Mario Lemieux, Pit.	C	Pat LaFontaine, Buf.
Teemu Selanne, Wpg.	RW	Alexander Mogilny, Buf.
Luc Robitaille, L.A.	LW	Kevin Stevens, Pit.

1991-92

First Team		Second Team
Patrick Roy, Mtl.	G	Kirk McLean, Van.
Brian Leetch, NYR	D	Phil Housley, Wpg.
Raymond Bourque, Bos.	D	Scott Stevens, N.J.
Mark Messier, NYR	C	Mario Lemieux, Pit.
Brett Hull, St.L.	RW	Mark Recchi, Pit., Phi.
Kevin Stevens, Pit.	LW	Luc Robitaille, L.A.

1990-91

First Team		Second Team
Ed Belfour, Chi.	G	Patrick Roy, Mtl.
Raymond Bourque, Bos.	D	Chris Chelios, Chi.
Al MacInnis, Cgy.	D	Brian Leetch, NYR
Wayne Gretzky, L.A.	C	Adam Oates, St.L.
Brett Hull, St.L.	RW	Cam Neely, Bos.
Luc Robitaille, L.A.	LW	Kevin Stevens, Pit.

1989-90

First Team		Second Team
Patrick Roy, Mtl.	G	Daren Puppa, Buf.
Raymond Bourque, Bos.	D	Paul Coffey, Pit.
Al MacInnis, Cgy.	D	Doug Wilson, Chi.
Mark Messier, Edm.	C	Wayne Gretzky, L.A.
Brett Hull, St.L.	RW	Cam Neely, Bos.
Luc Robitaille, L.A.	LW	Brian Bellows, Min.

1988-89

First Team		Second Team
Patrick Roy, Mtl.	G	Mike Vernon, Cgy.
Chris Chelios, Mtl.	D	Al MacInnis, Cgy.
Paul Coffey, Pit.	D	Raymond Bourque, Bos.
Mario Lemieux, Pit.	C	Wayne Gretzky, L.A.
Joe Mullen, Cgy.	RW	Jari Kurri, Edm.
Luc Robitaille, L.A.	LW	Gerard Gallant, Det.

1987-88

First Team		Second Team
Grant Fuhr, Edm.	G	Patrick Roy, Mtl.
Raymond Bourque, Bos.	D	Gary Suter, Cgy.
Scott Stevens, Wsh.	D	Brad McCrimmon, Cgy.
Mario Lemieux, Pit.	C	Wayne Gretzky, Edm.
Hakan Loob, Cgy.	RW	Cam Neely, Bos.
Luc Robitaille, L.A.	LW	Michel Goulet, Que.

1986-87

First Team		Second Team
Ron Hextall, Phi.	G	Mike Liut, Hfd.
Raymond Bourque, Bos.	D	Larry Murphy, Wsh.
Mark Howe, Phi.	D	Al MacInnis, Cgy.
Wayne Gretzky, Edm.	C	Mario Lemieux, Pit.
Jari Kurri, Edm.	RW	Tim Kerr, Phi.
Michel Goulet, Que.	LW	Luc Robitaille, L.A.

1985-86

First Team		Second Team
John Vanbiesbrouck, NYR	G	Bob Froese, Phi.
Paul Coffey, Edm.	D	Larry Robinson, Mtl.
Mark Howe, Phi.	D	Raymond Bourque, Bos.
Wayne Gretzky, Edm.	C	Mario Lemieux, Pit.
Mike Bossy, NYI	RW	Jari Kurri, Edm.
Michel Goulet, Que.	LW	Mats Naslund, Mtl.

1984-85

First Team		Second Team
Pelle Lindbergh, Phi.	G	Tom Barrasso, Buf.
Paul Coffey, Edm.	D	Rod Langway, Wsh.
Raymond Bourque, Bos.	D	Doug Wilson, Chi.
Wayne Gretzky, Edm.	C	Dale Hawerchuk, Wpg.
Jari Kurri, Edm.	RW	Mike Bossy, NYI
John Ogrodnick, Det.	LW	John Tonelli, NYI

1983-84

First Team		Second Team
Tom Barrasso, Buf.	G	Pat Riggin, Wsh.
Rod Langway, Wsh.	D	Paul Coffey, Edm.
Raymond Bourque, Bos.	D	Denis Potvin, NYI
Wayne Gretzky, Edm.	C	Bryan Trottier, NYI
Mike Bossy, NYI	RW	Jari Kurri, Edm.
Michel Goulet, Que.	LW	Mark Messier, Edm.

1982-83

First Team		Second Team
Pete Peeters, Bos.	G	Roland Melanson, NYI
Mark Howe, Phi.	D	Raymond Bourque, Bos.
Rod Langway, Wsh.	D	Paul Coffey, Edm.
Wayne Gretzky, Edm.	C	Denis Savard, Chi.
Mike Bossy, NYI	RW	Lanny McDonald, Cgy.
Mark Messier, Edm.	LW	Michel Goulet, Que.

First Team		Second Team
1981-82		
Billy Smith, NYI	G	Grant Fuhr, Edm.
Doug Wilson, Chi.	D	Paul Coffey, Edm.
Raymond Bourque, Bos.	D	Brian Engblom, Mtl.
Wayne Gretzky, Edm.	C	Bryan Trottier, NYI
Mike Bossy, NYI	RW	Rick Middleton, Bos.
Mark Messier, Edm.	LW	John Tonelli, NYI
1980-81		
Mike Liut, St.L.	G	Mario Lessard, L.A.
Denis Potvin, NYI	D	Larry Robinson, Mtl.
Randy Carlyle, Pit.	D	Raymond Bourque, Bos.
Wayne Gretzky, Edm.	C	Marcel Dionne, L.A.
Mike Bossy, NYI	RW	Dave Taylor, L.A.
Charlie Simmer, L.A.	LW	Bill Barber, Phi.
1979-80		
Tony Esposito, Chi.	G	Don Edwards, Buf.
Larry Robinson, Mtl.	D	Borje Salming, Tor.
Raymond Bourque, Bos.	D	Jim Schoenfeld, Buf.
Marcel Dionne, L.A.	C	Wayne Gretzky, Edm.
Guy Lafleur, Mtl.	RW	Danny Gare, Buf.
Charlie Simmer, L.A.	LW	Steve Shutt, Mtl.
1978-79		
Ken Dryden, Mtl.	G	Glenn Resch, NYI
Denis Potvin, NYI	D	Borje Salming, Tor.
Larry Robinson, Mtl.	D	Serge Savard, Mtl.
Bryan Trottier, NYI	C	Marcel Dionne, L.A.
Guy Lafleur, Mtl.	RW	Mike Bossy, NYI
Clark Gillies, NYI	LW	Bill Barber, Phi.
1977-78		
Ken Dryden, Mtl.	G	Don Edwards, Buf.
Denis Potvin, NYI	D	Larry Robinson, Mtl.
Brad Park, Bos.	D	Borje Salming, Tor.
Bryan Trottier, NYI	C	Darryl Sittler, Tor.
Guy Lafleur, Mtl.	RW	Mike Bossy, NYI
Clark Gillies, NYI	LW	Steve Shutt, Mtl.
1976-77		
Ken Dryden, Mtl.	G	Rogie Vachon, L.A.
Larry Robinson, Mtl.	D	Denis Potvin, NYI
Borje Salming, Tor.	D	Guy Lapointe, Mtl.
Marcel Dionne, L.A.	C	Gilbert Perreault, Buf.
Guy Lafleur, Mtl.	RW	Lanny McDonald, Tor.
Steve Shutt, Mtl.	LW	Rick Martin, Buf.
1975-76		
Ken Dryden, Mtl.	G	Glenn Resch, NYI
Denis Potvin, NYI	D	Borje Salming, Tor.
Brad Park, Bos.	D	Guy Lapointe, Mtl.
Bobby Clarke, Phi.	C	Gilbert Perreault, Buf.
Guy Lafleur, Mtl.	RW	Reggie Leach, Phi.
Bill Barber, Phi.	LW	Rick Martin, Buf.
1974-75		
Bernie Parent, Phi.	G	Rogie Vachon, L.A.
Bobby Orr, Bos.	D	Guy Lapointe, Mtl.
Denis Potvin, NYI	D	Borje Salming, Tor.
Bobby Clarke, Phi.	C	Phil Esposito, Bos.
Guy Lafleur, Mtl.	RW	René Robert, Buf.
Rick Martin, Buf.	LW	Steve Vickers, NYR
1973-74		
Bernie Parent, Phi.	G	Tony Esposito, Chi.
Bobby Orr, Bos.	D	Bill White, Chi.
Brad Park, NYR	D	Barry Ashbee, Phi.
Phil Esposito, Bos.	C	Bobby Clarke, Phi.
Ken Hodge, Bos.	RW	Mickey Redmond, Det.
Rick Martin, Buf.	LW	Wayne Cashman, Bos.

First Team		Second Team
1972-73		
Ken Dryden, Mtl.	G	Tony Esposito, Chi.
Bobby Orr, Bos.	D	Brad Park, NYR
Guy Lapointe, Mtl.	D	Bill White, Chi.
Phil Esposito, Bos.	C	Bobby Clarke, Phi.
Mickey Redmond, Det.	RW	Yvan Cournoyer, Mtl.
Frank Mahovlich, Mtl.	LW	Dennis Hull, Chi.
1971-72		
Tony Esposito, Chi.	G	Ken Dryden, Mtl.
Bobby Orr, Bos.	D	Bill White, Chi.
Brad Park, NYR	D	Pat Stapleton, Chi.
Phil Esposito, Bos.	C	Jean Ratelle, NYR
Rod Gilbert, NYR	RW	Yvan Cournoyer, Mtl.
Bobby Hull, Chi.	LW	Vic Hadfield, NYR
1970-71		
Ed Giacomin, NYR	G	Jacques Plante, Tor.
Bobby Orr, Bos.	D	Brad Park, NYR
J.C. Tremblay, Mtl.	D	Pat Stapleton, Chi.
Phil Esposito, Bos.	C	Dave Keon, Tor.
Ken Hodge, Bos.	RW	Yvan Cournoyer, Mtl.
John Bucyk, Bos.	LW	Bobby Hull, Chi.
1969-70		
Tony Esposito, Chi.	G	Ed Giacomin, NYR
Bobby Orr, Bos.	D	Carl Brewer, Det.
Brad Park, NYR	D	Jacques Laperriere, Mtl.
Phil Esposito, Bos.	C	Stan Mikita, Chi.
Gordie Howe, Det.	RW	John McKenzie, Bos.
Bobby Hull, Chi.	LW	Frank Mahovlich, Det.
1968-69		
Glenn Hall, St.L.	G	Ed Giacomin, NYR
Bobby Orr, Bos.	D	Ted Green, Bos.
Tim Horton, Tor.	D	Ted Harris, Mtl.
Phil Esposito, Bos.	C	Jean Béliveau, Mtl.
Gordie Howe, Det.	RW	Yvan Cournoyer, Mtl.
Bobby Hull, Chi.	LW	Frank Mahovlich, Det.
1967-68		
Gump Worsley, Mtl.	G	Ed Giacomin, NYR
Bobby Orr, Bos.	D	J.C. Tremblay, Mtl.
Tim Horton, Tor.	D	Jim Neilson, NYR
Stan Mikita, Chi.	C	Phil Esposito, Bos.
Gordie Howe, Det.	RW	Rod Gilbert, NYR
Bobby Hull, Chi.	LW	John Bucyk, Bos.
1966-67		
Ed Giacomin, NYR	G	Glenn Hall, Chi.
Pierre Pilote, Chi.	D	Tim Horton, Tor.
Harry Howell, NYR	D	Bobby Orr, Bos.
Stan Mikita, Chi.	C	Norm Ullman, Det.
Kenny Wharram, Chi.	RW	Gordie Howe, Det.
Bobby Hull, Chi.	LW	Don Marshall, NYR
1965-66		
Glenn Hall, Chi.	G	Gump Worsley, Mtl.
Jacques Laperriere, Mtl.	D	Allan Stanley, Tor.
Pierre Pilote, Chi.	D	Pat Stapleton, Chi.
Stan Mikita, Chi.	C	Jean Béliveau, Mtl.
Gordie Howe, Det.	RW	Bobby Rousseau, Mtl.
Bobby Hull, Chi.	LW	Frank Mahovlich, Tor.
1964-65		
Roger Crozier, Det.	G	Charlie Hodge, Mtl.
Pierre Pilote, Chi.	D	Bill Gadsby, Det.
Jacques Laperriere, Mtl.	D	Carl Brewer, Tor.
Norm Ullman, Det.	C	Stan Mikita, Chi.
Claude Provost, Mtl.	RW	Gordie Howe, Det.
Bobby Hull, Chi.	LW	Frank Mahovlich, Tor.

First Team		Second Team
1963-64		
Glenn Hall, Chi.	G	Charlie Hodge, Mtl.
Pierre Pilote, Chi.	D	Moose Vasko, Chi.
Tim Horton, Tor.	D	Jacques Laperriere, Mtl.
Stan Mikita, Chi.	C	Jean Béliveau, Mtl.
Kenny Wharram, Chi.	RW	Gordie Howe, Det.
Bobby Hull, Chi.	LW	Frank Mahovlich, Tor.
1962-63		
Glenn Hall, Chi.	G	Terry Sawchuk, Det.
Pierre Pilote, Chi.	D	Tim Horton, Tor.
Carl Brewer, Tor.	D	Moose Vasko, Chi.
Stan Mikita, Chi.	C	Henri Richard, Mtl.
Gordie Howe, Det.	RW	Andy Bathgate, NYR
Frank Mahovlich, Tor.	LW	Bobby Hull, Chi.
1961-62		
Jacques Plante, Mtl.	G	Glenn Hall, Chi.
Doug Harvey, NYR	D	Carl Brewer, Tor.
Jean-Guy Talbot, Mtl.	D	Pierre Pilote, Chi.
Stan Mikita, Chi.	C	Dave Keon, Tor.
Andy Bathgate, NYR	RW	Gordie Howe, Det.
Bobby Hull, Chi.	LW	Frank Mahovlich, Tor.
1960-61		
Johnny Bower, Tor.	G	Glenn Hall, Chi.
Doug Harvey, Mtl.	D	Allan Stanley, Tor.
Marcel Pronovost, Det.	D	Pierre Pilote, Chi.
Jean Béliveau, Mtl.	C	Henri Richard, Mtl.
Bernie Geoffrion, Mtl.	RW	Gordie Howe, Det.
Frank Mahovlich, Tor.	LW	Dickie Moore, Mtl.
1959-60		
Glenn Hall, Chi.	G	Jacques Plante, Mtl.
Doug Harvey, Mtl.	D	Allan Stanley, Tor.
Marcel Pronovost, Det.	D	Pierre Pilote, Chi.
Jean Béliveau, Mtl.	C	Bronco Horvath, Bos.
Gordie Howe, Det.	RW	Bernie Geoffrion, Mtl.
Bobby Hull, Chi.	LW	Dean Prentice, NYR
1958-59		
Jacques Plante, Mtl.	G	Terry Sawchuk, Det.
Tom Johnson, Mtl.	D	Marcel Pronovost, Det.
Bill Gadsby, NYR	D	Doug Harvey, Mtl.
Jean Béliveau, Mtl.	C	Henri Richard, Mtl.
Andy Bathgate, NYR	RW	Gordie Howe, Det.
Dickie Moore, Mtl.	LW	Alex Delvecchio, Det.
1957-58		
Glenn Hall, Chi.	G	Jacques Plante, Mtl.
Doug Harvey, Mtl.	D	Fern Flaman, Bos.
Bill Gadsby, NYR	D	Marcel Pronovost, Det.
Henri Richard, Mtl.	C	Jean Béliveau, Mtl.
Gordie Howe, Det.	RW	Andy Bathgate, NYR
Dickie Moore, Mtl.	LW	Camille Henry, NYR
1956-57		
Glenn Hall, Det.	G	Jacques Plante, Mtl.
Doug Harvey, Mtl.	D	Fern Flaman, Bos.
Red Kelly, Det.	D	Bill Gadsby, NYR
Jean Béliveau, Mtl.	C	Ed Litzenberger, Chi.
Gordie Howe, Det.	RW	Maurice Richard, Mtl.
Ted Lindsay, Det.	LW	Real Chevrefils, Bos.
1955-56		
Jacques Plante, Mtl.	G	Glenn Hall, Det.
Doug Harvey, Mtl.	D	Red Kelly, Det.
Bill Gadsby, NYR	D	Tom Johnson, Mtl.
Jean Béliveau, Mtl.	C	Tod Sloan, Tor.
Maurice Richard, Mtl.	RW	Gordie Howe, Det.
Ted Lindsay, Det.	LW	Bert Olmstead, Mtl.

First Team		Second Team

1954-55

First Team		Second Team
Harry Lumley, Tor.	G	Terry Sawchuk, Det.
Doug Harvey, Mtl.	D	Bob Goldham, Det.
Red Kelly, Det.	D	Fern Flaman, Bos.
Jean Béliveau, Mtl.	C	Ken Mosdell, Mtl.
Maurice Richard, Mtl.	RW	Bernie Geoffrion, Mtl.
Sid Smith, Tor.	LW	Danny Lewicki, NYR

1953-54

Harry Lumley, Tor.	G	Terry Sawchuk, Det.
Red Kelly, Det.	D	Bill Gadsby, Chi.
Doug Harvey, Mtl.	D	Tim Horton, Tor.
Ken Mosdell, Mtl.	C	Ted Kennedy, Tor.
Gordie Howe, Det.	RW	Maurice Richard, Mtl.
Ted Lindsay, Det.	LW	Ed Sandford, Bos.

1952-53

Terry Sawchuk, Det.	G	Gerry McNeil, Mtl.
Red Kelly, Det.	D	Bill Quackenbush, Bos.
Doug Harvey, Mtl.	D	Bill Gadsby, Chi.
Fleming MacKell, Bos.	C	Alex Delvecchio, Det.
Gordie Howe, Det.	RW	Maurice Richard, Mtl.
Ted Lindsay, Det.	LW	Bert Olmstead, Mtl.

1951-52

Terry Sawchuk, Det.	G	Jim Henry, Bos.
Red Kelly, Det.	D	Hy Buller, NYR
Doug Harvey, Mtl.	D	Jimmy Thomson, Tor.
Elmer Lach, Mtl.	C	Milt Schmidt, Bos.
Gordie Howe, Det.	RW	Maurice Richard, Mtl.
Ted Lindsay, Det.	LW	Sid Smith, Tor.

1950-51

Terry Sawchuk, Det.	G	Chuck Rayner, NYR
Red Kelly, Det.	D	Jimmy Thomson, Tor.
Bill Quackenbush, Bos.	D	Leo Reise Jr., Det.
Milt Schmidt, Bos.	C	Sid Abel, Det.
		Ted Kennedy (tied), Tor.
Gordie Howe, Det.	RW	Maurice Richard, Mtl.
Ted Lindsay, Det.	LW	Sid Smith, Tor.

1949-50

Bill Durnan, Mtl.	G	Chuck Rayner, NYR
Gus Mortson, Tor.	D	Leo Reise Jr., Det.
Ken Reardon, Mtl.	D	Red Kelly, Det.
Sid Abel, Det.	C	Ted Kennedy, Tor.
Maurice Richard, Mtl.	RW	Gordie Howe, Det.
Ted Lindsay, Det.	LW	Tony Leswick, NYR

1948-49

Bill Durnan, Mtl.	G	Chuck Rayner, NYR
Bill Quackenbush, Det.	D	Glen Harmon, Mtl.
Jack Stewart, Det.	D	Ken Reardon, Mtl.
Sid Abel, Det.	C	Doug Bentley, Chi.
Maurice Richard, Mtl.	RW	Gordie Howe, Det.
Roy Conacher, Chi.	LW	Ted Lindsay, Det.

1947-48

Turk Broda, Tor.	G	Frank Brimsek, Bos.
Bill Quackenbush, Det.	D	Ken Reardon, Mtl.
Jack Stewart, Det.	D	Neil Colville, NYR
Elmer Lach, Mtl.	C	Buddy O'Connor, NYR
Maurice Richard, Mtl.	RW	Bud Poile, Chi.
Ted Lindsay, Det.	LW	Gaye Stewart, Chi.

1946-47

Bill Durnan, Mtl.	G	Frank Brimsek, Bos.
Ken Reardon, Mtl.	D	Jack Stewart, Det.
Butch Bouchard, Mtl.	D	Bill Quackenbush, Det.
Milt Schmidt, Bos.	C	Max Bentley, Chi.
Maurice Richard, Mtl.	RW	Bobby Bauer, Bos.
Doug Bentley, Chi.	LW	*Woody Dumart, Bos.*

1945-46

Bill Durnan, Mtl.	G	Frank Brimsek, Bos.
Jack Crawford, Bos.	D	Ken Reardon, Mtl.
Butch Bouchard, Mtl.	D	Jack Stewart, Det.
Max Bentley, Chi.	C	Elmer Lach, Mtl.
Maurice Richard, Mtl.	RW	Bill Mosienko, Chi.
Gaye Stewart, Tor.	LW	Toe Blake, Mtl.
Dick Irvin, Mtl.	Coach	Johnny Gottselig, Chi.

1944-45

First Team		Second Team
Bill Durnan, Mtl.	G	Mike Karakas, Chi.
Butch Bouchard, Mtl.	D	Glen Harmon, Mtl.
Flash Hollett, Det.	D	Babe Pratt, Tor.
Elmer Lach, Mtl.	C	Bill Cowley, Bos.
Maurice Richard, Mtl.	RW	Bill Mosienko, Chi.
Toe Blake, Mtl.	LW	Syd Howe, Det.
Dick Irvin, Mtl.	Coach	Jack Adams, Det.

1943-44

Bill Durnan, Mtl.	G	Paul Bibeault, Tor.
Earl Seibert, Chi.	D	Butch Bouchard, Mtl.
Babe Pratt, Tor.	D	Dit Clapper, Bos.
Bill Cowley, Bos.	C	Elmer Lach, Mtl.
Lorne Carr, Tor.	RW	Maurice Richard, Mtl.
Doug Bentley, Chi.	LW	Herb Cain, Bos.
Dick Irvin, Mtl.	Coach	Hap Day, Tor.

1942-43

Johnny Mowers, Det.	G	Frank Brimsek, Bos.
Earl Seibert, Chi.	D	Jack Crawford, Bos.
Jack Stewart, Det.	D	Flash Hollett, Bos.
Bill Cowley, Bos.	C	Syl Apps, Tor.
Lorne Carr, Tor.	RW	Bryan Hextall, NYR
Doug Bentley, Chi.	LW	Lynn Patrick, NYR
Jack Adams, Det.	Coach	Art Ross, Bos.

1941-42

Frank Brimsek, Bos.	G	Turk Broda, Tor.
Earl Seibert, Chi.	D	Pat Egan, Bro.
Tom Anderson, Bro.	D	Bucko McDonald, Tor.
Syl Apps, Tor.	C	Phil Watson, NYR
Bryan Hextall, NYR	RW	Gordie Drillon, Tor.
Lynn Patrick, NYR	LW	Sid Abel, Det.
Frank Boucher, NYR	Coach	Paul Thompson, Chi.

1940-41

Turk Broda, Tor.	G	Frank Brimsek, Bos.
Dit Clapper, Bos.	D	Earl Seibert, Chi.
Wally Stanowski, Tor.	D	Ott Heller, NYR
Bill Cowley, Bos.	C	Syl Apps, Tor.
Bryan Hextall, NYR	RW	Bobby Bauer, Bos.
Sweeney Schriner, Tor.	LW	Woody Dumart, Bos.
Cooney Weiland, Bos.	Coach	Dick Irvin, Mtl.

1939-40

Dave Kerr, NYR	G	Frank Brimsek, Bos.
Dit Clapper, Bos.	D	Art Coulter, NYR
Ebbie Goodfellow, Det.	D	Earl Seibert, Chi.
Milt Schmidt, Bos.	C	Neil Colville, NYR
Bryan Hextall, NYR	RW	Bobby Bauer, Bos.
Toe Blake, Mtl.	LW	Woody Dumart, Bos.
Paul Thompson, Chi.	Coach	Frank Boucher, NYR

1938-39

Frank Brimsek, Bos.	G	Earl Robertson, NYA
Eddie Shore, Bos.	D	Earl Seibert, Chi.
Dit Clapper, Bos.	D	Art Coulter, NYR
Syl Apps, Tor.	C	Neil Colville, NYR
Gordie Drillon, Tor.	RW	Bobby Bauer, Bos.
Toe Blake, Mtl.	LW	Johnny Gottselig, Chi.
Art Ross, Bos.	Coach	Red Dutton, NYA

1937-38

Tiny Thompson, Bos.	G	Dave Kerr, NYR
Eddie Shore, Bos.	D	Art Coulter, NYR
Babe Siebert, Mtl.	D	Earl Seibert, Chi.
Bill Cowley, Bos.	C	Syl Apps, Tor.
Cecil Dillon, NYR	RW	
Gordie Drillon, Tor.	(tied)	
Paul Thompson, Chi.	LW	Toe Blake, Mtl.
Lester Patrick, NYR	Coach	Art Ross, Bos.

1936-37

Normie Smith, Det.	G	Wilf Cude, Mtl.
Babe Siebert, Mtl.	D	Earl Seibert, Chi.
Ebbie Goodfellow, Det.	D	Lionel Conacher, Mtl. M.
Marty Barry, Det.	C	Art Chapman, NYA
Larry Aurie, Det.	RW	Cecil Dillon, NYR
Busher Jackson, Tor.	LW	Sweeney Schriner, NYA
Jack Adams, Det.	Coach	Cecil Hart, Mtl.

1935-36

First Team		Second Team
Tiny Thompson, Bos.	G	Wilf Cude, Mtl.
Eddie Shore, Bos.	D	Earl Seibert, Chi.
Babe Siebert, Bos.	D	Ebbie Goodfellow, Det.
Hooley Smith, Mtl. M.	C	Bill Thoms, Tor.
Charlie Conacher, Tor.	RW	Cecil Dillon, NYR
Sweeney Schriner, NYA	LW	Paul Thompson, Chi.
Lester Patrick, NYR	Coach	Tommy Gorman, Mtl. M.

1934-35

Lorne Chabot, Chi.	G	Tiny Thompson, Bos.
Eddie Shore, Bos.	D	Cy Wentworth, Mtl. M.
Earl Seibert, Chi.	D	Art Coulter, Chi.
Frank Boucher, NYR	C	Cooney Weiland, Det.
Charlie Conacher, Tor.	RW	Dit Clapper, Bos.
Busher Jackson, Tor.	LW	Aurel Joliat, Mtl.
Lester Patrick, NYR	Coach	Dick Irvin, Tor.

1933-34

Charlie Gardiner, Chi.	G	Roy Worters, NYA
King Clancy, Tor.	D	Eddie Shore, Bos.
Lionel Conacher, Chi.	D	Ching Johnson, NYR
Frank Boucher, NYR	C	Joe Primeau, Tor.
Charlie Conacher, Tor.	RW	Bill Cook, NYR
Busher Jackson, Tor.	LW	Aurel Joliat, Mtl.
Lester Patrick, NYR	Coach	Dick Irvin, Tor.

1932-33

John Ross Roach, Det.	G	Charlie Gardiner, Chi.
Eddie Shore, Bos.	D	King Clancy, Tor.
Ching Johnson, NYR	D	Lionel Conacher, Mtl. M.
Frank Boucher, NYR	C	Howie Morenz, Mtl.
Bill Cook, NYR	RW	Charlie Conacher, Tor.
Baldy Northcott, Mtl M.	LW	Busher Jackson, Tor.
Lester Patrick, NYR	Coach	Dick Irvin, Tor.

1931-32

Charlie Gardiner, Chi.	G	Roy Worters, NYA
Eddie Shore, Bos.	D	Sylvio Mantha, Mtl.
Ching Johnson, NYR	D	King Clancy, Tor.
Howie Morenz, Mtl.	C	Hooley Smith, Mtl. M.
Bill Cook, NYR	RW	Charlie Conacher, Tor.
Busher Jackson, Tor.	LW	Aurel Joliat, Mtl.
Lester Patrick, NYR	Coach	Dick Irvin, Tor.

1930-31

Charlie Gardiner, Chi.	G	Tiny Thompson, Bos.
Eddie Shore, Bos.	D	Sylvio Mantha, Mtl.
King Clancy, Tor.	D	Ching Johnson, NYR
Howie Morenz, Mtl.	C	Frank Boucher, NYR
Bill Cook, NYR	RW	Dit Clapper, Bos.
Aurel Joliat, Mtl.	LW	Bun Cook, NYR
Lester Patrick, NYR	Coach	Dick Irvin, Chi.

A future Hall of Famer, Chicago's Doug Bentley played in each of the first five NHL All-Star Games, collecting two goals and an assist.

All-Star Game Results

Year	Venue	Score	Coaches	Attendance
2004	Minnesota	East 6, West 4	Pat Quinn, Dave Lewis	19,434
2003	Florida	West 6, East 5	Marc Crawford, Jacques Martin	19,250
2002	Los Angeles	World 8, North America 5	Scotty Bowman, Pat Quinn	18,118
2001	Colorado	North America 14, World 12	Joel Quenneville, Jacques Martin	18,646
2000	Toronto	World 9, North America 4	Scotty Bowman, Pat Quinn	19,300
1999	Tampa Bay	North America 8, World 6	Lindy Ruff, Ken Hitchcock	19,758
1998	Vancouver	North America 8, World 7	Jacques Lemaire, Ken Hitchcock	18,422
1997	San Jose	East 11, West 7	Doug MacLean, Ken Hitchcock	17,422
1996	Boston	East 5, West 4	Doug MacLean, Scotty Bowman	17,565
1994	NY Rangers	East 9, West 8	Jacques Demers, Barry Melrose	18,200
1993	Montreal	Wales 16, Campbell 6	Scotty Bowman, Mike Keenan	17,137
1992	Philadelphia	Campbell 10, Wales 6	Bob Gainey, Scotty Bowman	17,380
1991	Chicago	Campbell 11, Wales 5	John Muckler, Mike Milbury	18,472
1990	Pittsburgh	Wales 12, Campbell 7	Pat Burns, Terry Crisp	16,236
1989	Edmonton	Campbell 9, Wales 5	Glen Sather, Terry O'Reilly	17,503
1988	St. Louis	Wales 6, Campbell 5 OT	Mike Keenan, Glen Sather	17,878
1986	Hartford	Wales 4, Campbell 3 OT	Mike Keenan, Glen Sather	15,100
1985	Calgary	Wales 6, Campbell 4	Al Arbour, Glen Sather	16,825
1984	New Jersey	Wales 7, Campbell 6	Al Arbour, Glen Sather	18,939
1983	NY Islanders	Campbell 9, Wales 3	Roger Neilson, Al Arbour	15,230
1982	Washington	Wales 4, Campbell 2	Al Arbour, Glen Sonmor	18,130
1981	Los Angeles	Campbell 4, Wales 1	Pat Quinn, Scotty Bowman	15,761
1980	Detroit	Wales 6, Campbell 3	Scotty Bowman, Al Arbour	21,002
1978	Buffalo	Wales 3, Campbell 2 OT	Scotty Bowman, Fred Shero	16,433
1977	Vancouver	Wales 4, Campbell 3	Scotty Bowman, Fred Shero	15,607
1976	Philadelphia	Wales 7, Campbell 5	Floyd Smith, Fred Shero	16,436
1975	Montreal	Wales 7, Campbell 1	Bep Guidolin, Fred Shero	16,080
1974	Chicago	West 6, East 4	Billy Reay, Scotty Bowman	16,426
1973	NY Rangers	East 5, West 4	Tom Johnson, Billy Reay	16,986
1972	Minnesota	East 3, West 2	Al MacNeil, Billy Reay	15,423
1971	Boston	West 2, East 1	Scotty Bowman, Harry Sinden	14,790
1970	St. Louis	East 4, West 1	Claude Ruel, Scotty Bowman	16,587
1969	Montreal	East 3, West 3	Toe Blake, Scotty Bowman	16,260
1968	Toronto	Toronto 4, All-Stars 3	Punch Imlach, Toe Blake	15,753
1967	Montreal	Montreal 3, All-Stars 0	Toe Blake, Sid Abel	14,284
1965	Montreal	All-Stars 5, Montreal 2	Billy Reay, Toe Blake	13,529
1964	Toronto	All-Stars 3, Toronto 2	Sid Abel, Punch Imlach	14,232
1963	Toronto	All-Stars 3, Toronto 3	Sid Abel, Punch Imlach	14,034
1962	Toronto	Toronto 4, All-Stars 1	Punch Imlach, Rudy Pilous	14,236
1961	Chicago	All-Stars 3, Chicago 1	Sid Abel, Rudy Pilous	14,534
1960	Montreal	All-Stars 2, Montreal 1	Punch Imlach, Toe Blake	13,949

Year	Venue	Score	Coaches	Attendance
1959	Montreal	Montreal 6, All-Stars 1	Toe Blake, Punch Imlach	13,818
1958	Montreal	Montreal 6, All-Stars 3	Toe Blake, Milt Schmidt	13,989
1957	Montreal	All-Stars 5, Montreal 3	Milt Schmidt, Toe Blake	13,003
1956	Montreal	All-Stars 1, Montreal 1	Jim Skinner, Toe Blake	13,095
1955	Detroit	Detroit 3, All-Stars 1	Jim Skinner, Dick Irvin	10,111
1954	Detroit	All-Stars 2, Detroit 2	King Clancy, Jim Skinner	10,689
1953	Montreal	All-Stars 3, Montreal 1	Lynn Patrick, Dick Irvin	14,153
1952	Detroit	1st Team 1, 2nd Team 1	Tommy Ivan, Dick Irvin	10,680
1951	Toronto	1st Team 2, 2nd Team 2	Joe Primeau, Dick Irvin	11,469
1950	Detroit	Detroit 7, All-Stars 1	Tommy Ivan, Lynn Patrick	9,166
1949	Toronto	All-Stars 3, Toronto 1	Tommy Ivan, Hap Day	13,541
1948	Chicago	All-Stars 3, Toronto 1	Tommy Ivan, Hap Day	12,794
1947	Toronto	All-Stars 4, Toronto 3	Dick Irvin, Hap Day	14,169

There was no All-Star contest during the calendar year of 1966 because the game was moved from the start of season to mid-season. In 1979, the Challenge Cup series between the Soviet Union and Team NHL replaced the All-Star Game. In 1987, Rendez-Vous '87, two games between the Soviet Union and Team NHL replaced the All-Star Game. Rendez-Vous '87 scores: game one, NHL All-Stars 4, Soviet Union 3; game two, Soviet Union 5, NHL All-Stars 3. No All-Star Games were played in 1995, 2005 and 2006.

NHL ALL-ROOKIE TEAM

Voting for the NHL All-Rookie Team is conducted among the representatives of the Professional Hockey Writers' Association at the end of the season. The rookie all-star team was first selected for the 1982-83 season.

2005-06
Goal — Henrik Lundqvist, NY Rangers
Defense — Andrej Meszaros, Ottawa
Defense — Dion Phaneuf, Calgary
Forward — Brad Boyes, Boston
Forward — Sidney Crosby, Pittsburgh
Forward — Alex Ovechkin, Washington

2004-05
No All-Rookie Team selected

2003-04
Goal — Andrew Raycroft, Boston
Defense — John-Michael Liles, Colorado
Defense — Joni Pitkanen, Philadelphia
Forward — Trent Hunter, NY Islanders
Forward — Ryan Malone, Pittsburgh
Forward — Michael Ryder, Montreal

2002-03
Goal — Sebastian Caron, Pittsburgh
Defense — Jay Bouwmeester, Florida
Defense — Barret Jackman, St. Louis
Forward — Tyler Arnason, Chicago
Forward — Rick Nash, Columbus
Forward — Henrik Zetterberg, Detroit

2001-02
Goal — Dan Blackburn, NY Rangers
Defense — Nick Boynton, Boston
Defense — Rostislav Klesla, Columbus
Forward — Dany Heatley, Atlanta
Forward — Ilya Kovalchuk, Atlanta
Forward — Kristian Huselius, Florida

2000-01
Goal — Evgeni Nabokov, San Jose
Defense — Lubomir Visnovsky, Los Angeles
Defense — Colin White, New Jersey
Forward — Martin Havlat, Ottawa
Forward — Brad Richards, Tampa Bay
Forward — Shane Willis, Carolina

1999-2000
Brian Boucher, Philadelphia
Brian Rafalski, New Jersey
Brad Stuart, San Jose
Simon Gagne, Philadelphia
Scott Gomez, New Jersey
Michael York, NY Rangers

1998-99
Jamie Storr, Los Angeles
Tom Poti, Edmonton
Sami Salo, Ottawa
Chris Drury, Colorado
Milan Hejduk, Colorado
Marian Hossa, Ottawa

1997-98
Jamie Storr, Los Angeles
Mattias Ohlund, Vancouver
Derek Morris, Calgary
Sergei Samsonov, Boston
Patrik Elias, New Jersey
Mike Johnson, Toronto

1996-97
Patrick Lalime, Pittsburgh
Bryan Berard, NY Islanders
Janne Niinimaa, Philadelphia
Jarome Iginla, Calgary
Jim Campbell, St. Louis
Sergei Berezin, Toronto

1995-96
Corey Hirsch, Vancouver
Ed Jovanovski, Florida
Kyle McLaren, Boston
Daniel Alfredsson, Ottawa
Eric Daze, Chicago
Petr Sykora, New Jersey

1994-95
Jim Carey, Washington
Chris Therien, Philadelphia
Kenny Jonsson, Toronto
Peter Forsberg, Quebec
Jeff Friesen, San Jose
Paul Kariya, Anaheim

1993-94
Martin Brodeur, New Jersey
Chris Pronger, Hartford
Boris Mironov, Wpg./Edm.
Jason Arnott, Edmonton
Mikael Renberg, Philadelphia
Oleg Petrov, Montreal

1992-93
Felix Potvin, Toronto
Vladimir Malakhov, NY Islanders
Scott Niedermayer, New Jersey
Eric Lindros, Philadelphia
Teemu Selanne, Winnipeg
Joe Juneau, Boston

1991-92
Dominik Hasek, Chicago
Nicklas Lidstrom, Detroit
Vladimir Konstantinov, Detroit
Kevin Todd, New Jersey
Tony Amonte, NY Rangers
Gilbert Dionne, Montreal

1990-91
Ed Belfour, Chicago
Eric Weinrich, New Jersey
Rob Blake, Los Angeles
Sergei Fedorov, Detroit
Ken Hodge, Boston
Jaromir Jagr, Pittsburgh

1989-90
Bob Essensa, Winnipeg
Brad Shaw, Hartford
Geoff Smith, Edmonton
Mike Modano, Minnesota
Sergei Makarov, Calgary
Rod Brind'Amour, St. Louis

1988-89
Peter Sidorkiewicz, Hartford
Brian Leetch, NY Rangers
Zarley Zalapski, Pittsburgh
Trevor Linden, Vancouver
Tony Granato, NY Rangers
David Volek, NY Islanders

1987-88
Darren Pang, Chicago
Glen Wesley, Boston
Calle Johansson, Buffalo
Joe Nieuwendyk, Calgary
Ray Sheppard, Buffalo
Iain Duncan, Winnipeg

1986-87
Ron Hextall, Philadelphia
Steve Duchesne, Los Angeles
Brian Benning, St. Louis
Jimmy Carson, Los Angeles
Jim Sandlak, Vancouver
Luc Robitaille, Los Angeles

1985-86
Patrick Roy, Montreal
Gary Suter, Calgary
Dana Murzyn, Hartford
Mike Ridley, NY Rangers
Kjell Dahlin, Montreal
Wendel Clark, Toronto

1984-85
Steve Penney, Montreal
Chris Chelios, Montreal
Bruce Bell, Quebec
Mario Lemieux, Pittsburgh
Tomas Sandstrom, NY Rangers
Warren Young, Pittsburgh

1983-84
Tom Barrasso, Buffalo
Thomas Eriksson, Philadelphia
Jamie Macoun, Calgary
Steve Yzerman, Detroit
Hakan Loob, Calgary
Sylvain Turgeon, Hartford

1982-83
Pelle Lindbergh, Philadelphia
Scott Stevens, Washington
Phil Housley, Buffalo
Dan Daoust, Mtl./Tor.
Steve Larmer, Chicago
Mats Naslund, Montreal

All-Star Game Records 1947 through 2006

TEAM RECORDS

MOST GOALS, BOTH TEAMS, ONE GAME:
26 — North America 14, World 12, 2001 at Colorado
22 — Wales 16, Campbell 6, 1993 at Montreal
19 — Wales 12, Campbell 7, 1990 at Pittsburgh
18 — East 11, West 7, 1997 at San Jose
17 — East 9, West 8, 1994 at NY Rangers
16 — Campbell 11, Wales 5, 1991 at Chicago
— Campbell 10, Wales 6, 1992 at Philadelphia
15 — North America 8, World 7, 1998 at Vancouver

FEWEST GOALS, BOTH TEAMS, ONE GAME:
2 — First Team All-Stars 1, Second Team All-Stars 1, 1952 at Detroit
— NHL All-Stars 1, Montreal Canadiens 1, 1956 at Montreal
3 — NHL All-Stars 2, Montreal Canadiens 1, 1960 at Montreal
— Montreal Canadiens 3, NHL All-Stars 0, 1967 at Montreal
— West 2, East 1, 1971 at Boston

MOST GOALS, ONE TEAM, ONE GAME:
16 — Wales 16, Campbell 6, 1993 at Montreal
14 — North America 14, World 12, 2001 at Colorado
12 — Wales 12, Campbell 7, 1990 at Pittsburgh
— World 12, North America 14, 2001 at Colorado
11 — Campbell 11, Wales 5, 1991 at Chicago
— East 11, West 7, 1997 at San Jose

FEWEST GOALS, ONE TEAM, ONE GAME:
0 — NHL All-Stars 0, Montreal Canadiens 3, 1967 at Montreal
1 — 17 times (1981, 1975, 1971, 1970, 1962, 1961, 1960, 1959, both teams 1956, 1955, 1953, both teams 1952, 1950, 1949, 1948)

MOST SHOTS, BOTH TEAMS, ONE GAME (SINCE 1955):
102 — 1994 at NY Rangers — East 9 (56 shots),
West 8 (46 shots)
98 — 2001 at Colorado — North America 14 (53 shots),
World 12 (45 shots)
90 — 1993 at Montreal — Wales 16 (49 shots),
Campbell 6 (41 shots)
89 — 2002 at Los Angeles — World 8 (39 shots),
North America 5 (50 shots)

FEWEST SHOTS, BOTH TEAMS, ONE GAME (SINCE 1955):
52 — 1978 at Buffalo — Campbell 2 (12 shots)
Wales 3 (40 shots)
53 — 1960 at Montreal — NHL All-Stars 2 (27 shots)
Montreal Canadiens 1 (26 shots)
55 — 1956 at Montreal — NHL All-Stars 1 (28 shots)
Montreal Canadiens 1 (27 shots)
— 1971 at Boston — West 2 (28 shots)
East 1 (27 shots)

MOST SHOTS, ONE TEAM, ONE GAME (SINCE 1955):
56 — 1994 at NY Rangers — East (9-8 vs. West)
53 — 2001 at Colorado — North America (14-12 vs. World)
50 — 2002 at Los Angeles — North America (5-8 vs. World)
49 — 1993 at Montreal — Wales (16-6 vs. Campbell)
— 1999 at Tampa Bay — North America (8-6 vs. World)

FEWEST SHOTS, ONE TEAM, ONE GAME (SINCE 1955):
12 — 1978 at Buffalo — Campbell (2-3 vs. Wales)
17 — 1970 at St. Louis — West (1-4 vs. East)
23 — 1961 at Chicago — Chicago Black Hawks (1-3 vs. NHL All-Stars)
24 — 1976 at Philadelphia — Campbell (5-7 vs. Wales)

MOST POWER-PLAY GOALS, BOTH TEAMS, ONE GAME (SINCE 1950):
3 — 1953 at Montreal — NHL All-Stars 3 (2 power-play goals),
Montreal Canadiens 1 (1 power-play goal)
— 1954 at Detroit — NHL All-Stars 1 (1 power-play goal)
Detroit Red Wings 2 (2 power-play goals)
— 1958 at Montreal — NHL All-Stars 3 (1 power-play goal)
Montreal Canadiens 6 (2 power-play goals)

FEWEST POWER-PLAY GOALS, BOTH TEAMS, ONE GAME (SINCE 1950):
0 — 22 times (1952, 1959, 1960, 1967, 1968, 1969, 1972, 1973, 1976, 1980, 1981, 1984, 1985, 1992, 1994, 1996, 1999, 2000, 2001, 2002, 2003, 2004)

FASTEST TWO GOALS, BOTH TEAMS, FROM START OF GAME:
0:37 — 1970 at St. Louis — Jacques Laperriere of East scored at 0:20 and Dean Prentice of West scored at 0:37. Final score: East 4, West 1.
2:15 — 1998 at Vancouver — Teemu Selanne scored at 0:53 and Jaromir Jagr scored at 2:15 for World. Final score: North America 8, World 7.
3:37 — 1993 at Montreal — Mike Gartner scored at 3:15 and at 3:37 for Wales. Final score: Wales 16, Campbell 6.

FASTEST TWO GOALS, BOTH TEAMS:
0:08 — 1997 at San Jose — Owen Nolan scored at 18:54 and 19:02 of second period for West. Final Score: East 11, West 7.
0:10 — 1976 at Philadelphia — Dennis Ververgaert scored at 4:33 and at 4:43 of third period for Campbell. Final score: Wales 7, Campbell 5.
0:13 — 1998 at Vancouver — Teemu Selanne scored at 4:00 of first period for World and John LeClair scored at 4:13 for North America. Final score: North America 8, World 7.

FASTEST THREE GOALS, BOTH TEAMS:
1:08 — 1993 at Montreal — all by Wales — Mike Gartner scored at 3:15 and at 3:37 of first period; Peter Bondra scored at 4:23. Final score: Wales 16, Campbell 6.
1:14 — 1994 at NY Rangers — Bob Kudelski scored at 9:46 of first period for East; Sergei Fedorov scored at 10:20 for West; Eric Lindros scored at 11:00 for East. Final score: East 9, West 8.
1:23 — 1999 at Tampa Bay — Mats Sundin scored at 2:57 of third period for World; Darryl Sydor scored at 4:02 for North America; Sergei Zubov scored at 4:20 for World. Final score: North America 8, World 6.

FASTEST FOUR GOALS, BOTH TEAMS:
2:24 — 1997 at San Jose — Brendan Shanahan scored at 16:38 of second period for West; Dale Hawerchuk scored at 17:28 for East; Owen Nolan scored at 18:54 and 19:02 for West. Final score: East 11, West 7.
2:57 — 2002 at Los Angeles — Sergei Fedorov scored at 16:59 of third period for World; Markus Naslund scored at 18:17 for World; Alex Zhamnov scored at 19:12 for World; Sami Kapanen scored at 19:56 for World. Final score: World 8, North America 5.
3:04 — 1997 at San Jose — Mark Recchi scored at 15:32 of first period for East; Dale Hawerchuk scored at 16:19 for East; Pavel Bure scored at 17:36 for West; Paul Kariya scored at 18:36 for West. Final score: East 11, West 7.

FASTEST TWO GOALS, ONE TEAM, FROM START OF GAME:
2:15 — 1998 at Vancouver — World — Teemu Selanne scored at 0:53 and Jaromir Jagr scored at 2:15. Final score: North America 8, World 7.
3:37 — 1993 at Montreal — Wales — Mike Gartner scored at 3:15 and at 3:37. Final score: Wales 16, Campbell 6.
4:19 — 1980 at Detroit — Wales — Larry Robinson scored at 3:58 and Steve Payne scored at 4:19. Final score: Wales 6, Campbell 3.

FASTEST TWO GOALS, ONE TEAM:
0:08 — 1997 at San Jose — West — Owen Nolan scored at 18:54 and at 19:02 of second period. Final score: East 11, West 7.
0:10 — 1976 at Philadelphia — Campbell — Dennis Ververgaert scored at 4:33 and at 4:43 of third period. Final score: Wales 7, Campbell 5.
0:14 — 1989 at Edmonton — Campbell — Steve Yzerman and Gary Leeman scored at 17:21 and 17:35 of second period. Final score: Campbell 9, Wales 5.

FASTEST THREE GOALS, ONE TEAM:
1:08 — 1993 at Montreal — Wales — Mike Gartner scored at 3:15 and 3:37 of first period; Peter Bondra scored at 4:23. Final score: Wales 16, Campbell 6.
1:32 — 1980 at Detroit — Wales — Ron Stackhouse scored at 11:40 of third period; Craig Hartsburg scored at 12:40; Reed Larson scored at 13:12. Final score: Wales 6, Campbell 3.
1:39 — 2002 at Los Angeles — Markus Naslund scored at 18:17 of third period; Alex Zhamnov scored at 19:12; Sami Kapanen scored at 19:56. Final score: World 8, North America 5.

FASTEST FOUR GOALS, ONE TEAM:
2:57 — 2002 at Los Angeles — World — Sergei Fedorov scored at 16:59 of third period; Markus Naslund scored at 18:17; Alex Zhamnov scored at 19:12; Sami Kapanen scored at 19:56. Final score: World 8, North America 5.
4:19 — 1992 at Philadelphia — Campbell — Brian Bellows scored at 7:40 of second period; Jeremy Roenick scored at 8:13; Theoren Fleury scored at 11:06, Brett Hull scored at 11:59. Final score: Campbell 10, Wales 6.
4:26 — 1980 at Detroit — Wales — Ron Stackhouse scored at 11:40 of third period; Craig Hartsburg scored at 12:40; Reed Larson scored at 13:12; Real Cloutier scored at 16:06. Final score: Wales 6, Campbell 3.

MOST GOALS, BOTH TEAMS, ONE PERIOD:
10 — 1997 at San Jose — Second period — East (6), West (4).
Final score: East 11, West 7.
— 2001 at Colorado — Second period — North America (6), World (4).
Final score: North America 14, World 12.
— 2001 at Colorado — Third period — North America (5), World (5).
Final score: North America 14, World 12.
9 — 1990 at Pittsburgh — First period — Wales (7), Campbell (2).
Final score: Wales 12, Campbell 7.

MOST GOALS, ONE TEAM, ONE PERIOD:
7 — 1990 at Pittsburgh — First period — Wales. Final score: Wales 12, Campbell 7.
6 — 1983 at NY Islanders — Third period — Campbell.
Final score: Campbell 9, Wales 3.
  — 1992 at Philadelphia — Second period — Campbell.
Final score: Campbell 10, Wales 6.
  — 1993 at Montreal — First period — Wales.
Final score: Wales 16, Campbell 6.
  — 1993 at Montreal — Second period — Wales.
Final score: Wales 16, Campbell 6.
  — 1997 at San Jose — Second period — East.
Final score: East 11, West 7.
  — 2001 at Colorado — Second period — North America.
Final score: North America 14, World 12.

MOST SHOTS, BOTH TEAMS, ONE PERIOD:
39 — 1994 at NY Rangers — Second period — West (21), East (18).
Final score: East 9, West 8.
  — 2001 at Colorado — Third period — World (23), North America (16).
Final score: North America 14, World 12.
36 — 1990 at Pittsburgh — Third period — Campbell (22), Wales (14).
Final score: Wales 12, Campbell 7.
  — 1994 at NY Rangers — First period — East (19), West (17).
Final score: East 9, West 8.
  — 2002 at Los Angeles — Third period — North America (20), World (16).
Final score: World 8, North America 5.

MOST SHOTS, ONE TEAM, ONE PERIOD:
23 — 2001 at Colorado — Third period — World.
Final score: North America 14, World 12.
22 — 1990 at Pittsburgh — Third period — Campbell.
Final score: Wales 12, Campbell 7.
  — 1991 at Chicago — Third period — Wales.
Final score: Campbell 11, Wales 5.
  — 1993 at Montreal — First period — Wales.
Final score: Wales 16, Campbell 6.

FEWEST SHOTS, BOTH TEAMS, ONE PERIOD:
9 — 1971 at Boston — Third period — East (2), West (7).
Final score: West 2, East 1.
  — 1980 at Detroit — Second period — Campbell (4), Wales (5).
Final score: Wales 6, Campbell 3.
13 — 1982 at Washington — Third period — Campbell (6), Wales (7).
Final score: Wales 4, Campbell 3.
14 — 1978 at Buffalo — First period — Campbell (7), Wales (7).
Final score: Wales 3, Campbell 2.
  — 1986 at Hartford — First period — Campbell (6), Wales (8).
Final score: Wales 4, Campbell 3.

FEWEST SHOTS, ONE TEAM, ONE PERIOD:
2 — 1971 at Boston — Third period — East.
Final score: West 2, East 1.
  — 1978 at Buffalo — Second period — Campbell.
Final score: Wales 3, Campbell 2.
3 — 1978 at Buffalo — Third period — Campbell.
Final score: Wales 3, Campbell 2.
4 — 1955 at Detroit — First period — NHL All-Stars.
Final score: Detroit Red Wings 3, NHL All-Stars 1.
  — 1980 at Detroit — Second period — Campbell.
Final score: Wales 6, Campbell 3.

INDIVIDUAL RECORDS

Games

MOST GAMES PLAYED:
23 — **Gordie Howe** from 1948 through 1980
19 — Raymond Bourque from 1981 through 2001
18 — Wayne Gretzky from 1980 through 1999
15 — Frank Mahovlich from 1959 through 1974
  — Mark Messier from 1982 through 2004

Goals

MOST GOALS (CAREER):
13 — **Wayne Gretzky** in 18GP
  — **Mario Lemieux** in 10GP
10 — Gordie Howe in 23GP
8 — Frank Mahovlich in 15GP
  — Luc Robitaille in 8GP
  — Teemu Selanne in 9GP

MOST GOALS, ONE GAME:
4 — **Wayne Gretzky,** Campbell, 1983
  — **Mario Lemieux,** Wales, 1990
  — **Vince Damphousse,** Campbell, 1991
  — **Mike Gartner,** Wales, 1993
  — **Dany Heatley,** East, 2003
3 — Ted Lindsay, Detroit, 1950
  — Mario Lemieux, Wales, 1988
  — Pierre Turgeon, Wales, 1993
  — Mark Recchi, East, 1997
  — Owen Nolan, West, 1997
  — Teemu Selanne, World, 1998
  — Pavel Bure, World, 2000
  — Bill Guerin, North America, 2001
  — Joe Sakic, West, 2004

MOST GOALS, ONE PERIOD:
4 — **Wayne Gretzky,** Campbell, Third period, 1983
3 — Mario Lemieux, Wales, First period, 1990
  — Vince Damphousse, Campbell, Third period, 1991
  — Mike Gartner, Wales, First period, 1993

Assists

MOST ASSISTS (CAREER):
14 — **Mark Messier** in 15GP
13 — Raymond Bourque in 19GP
12 — Adam Oates in 5GP
  — Mats Sundin in 8GP
  — Joe Sakic in 11GP
  — Wayne Gretzky in 18GP

MOST ASSISTS, ONE GAME:
5 — **Mats Naslund,** Wales, 1988
4 — Raymond Bourque, Wales, 1985
  — Adam Oates, Campbell, 1991
  — Adam Oates, Wales, 1993
  — Mark Recchi, Wales, 1993
  — Pierre Turgeon, East, 1994
  — Fredrik Modin, World, 2001

MOST ASSISTS, ONE PERIOD:
4 — **Adam Oates,** Wales, First period, 1993
3 — Mark Messier, Campbell, Third period, 1983

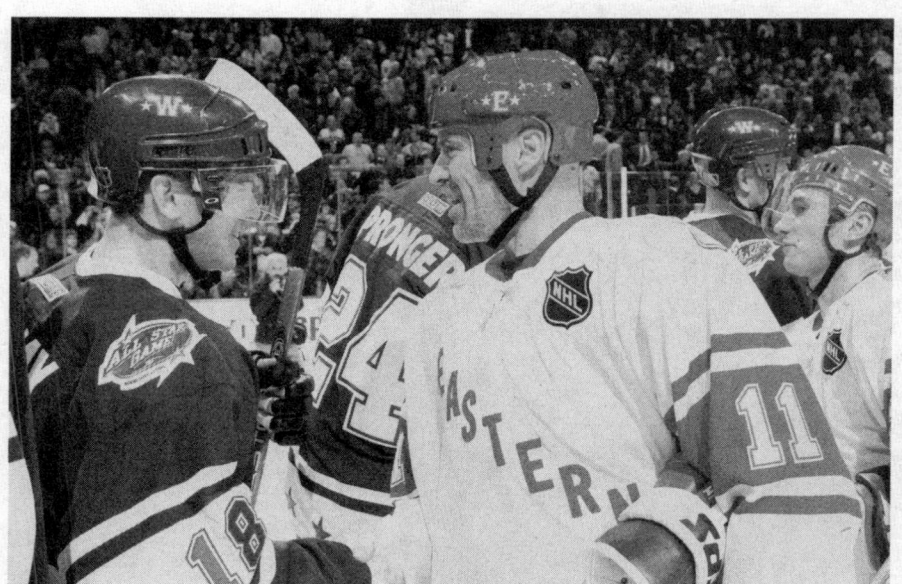

Mark Messier shakes hands with Alex Tanguay following the 2004 NHL All-Star Game in Minnesota. Messier picked up his record-breaking 14th All-Star assist on Adrian Aucoin's goal in a 6-4 victory by the Eastern Conference.

Points

MOST POINTS, CAREER:
25 — Wayne Gretzky (13G-12A in 18GP)
23 — Mario Lemieux (13G-10A in 10GP)
20 — Mark Messier (6G-14A in 15GP)
19 — Gordie Howe (10G-9A in 23GP)
18 — Joe Sakic (6G-12A in 11GP)

MOST POINTS, ONE GAME:
 6 — Mario Lemieux, Wales, 1988 (3G-3A)
 5 — Mats Naslund, Wales, 1988 (5A)
  — Adam Oates, Campbell, 1991 (1G-4A)
  — Mike Gartner, Wales, 1993 (4G-1A)
  — Mark Recchi, Wales, 1993 (1G-4A)
  — Pierre Turgeon, Wales, 1993 (3G-2A)
  — Bill Guerin, North America, 2001 (3G-2A)
  — Dany Heatley, East, 2003 (4G-1A)

MOST POINTS, ONE PERIOD:
 4 — Wayne Gretzky, Campbell, Third period, 1983 (4G)
  — Mike Gartner, Wales, First period, 1993 (3G-1A)
  — Adam Oates, Wales, First period, 1993 (4A)
 3 — Gordie Howe, NHL All-Stars, Second period, 1965 (1G-2A)
  — Pete Mahovlich, Wales, First period, 1976 (1G-2A)
  — Mark Messier, Campbell, Third period, 1983 (3A)
  — Mario Lemieux, Wales, Second period, 1988 (1G-2A)
  — Mario Lemieux, Wales, First period, 1990 (3G)
  — Vince Damphousse, Campbell, Third period, 1991 (3G)
  — Mark Recchi, Wales, Second period, 1993 (1G-2A)
  — Tony Amonte, North America, Second period, 2001 (2G-1A)
  — Daniel Alfredsson, East, Second period, 2004 (2G-1A)

Power-Play Goals

MOST POWER-PLAY GOALS, CAREER:
 6 — Gordie Howe in 23GP
 3 — Bobby Hull in 12GP
  — Maurice Richard in 13GP

Fastest Goals

FASTEST GOAL FROM START OF GAME:
0:19 — Ted Lindsay, Detroit, 1950
0:20 — Jacques Laperriere, East, 1970
0:21 — Mario Lemieux, Wales, 1990
0:35 — Vincent Damphousse, North America, 2002
0:36 — Chico Maki, West, 1971

FASTEST GOAL FROM START OF A PERIOD:
0:17 — Raymond Bourque, North America, 1999 (second period)
0:19 — Ted Lindsay, Detroit, 1950 (first period)
  — Rick Tocchet, Wales, 1993 (second period)
0:20 — Jacques Laperriere, East, 1970 (first period)
0:21 — Mario Lemieux, Wales, 1990 (first period)
0:26 — Wayne Gretzky, Campbell, 1982 (second period)

FASTEST TWO GOALS (ONE PLAYER) FROM START OF GAME:
3:37 — Mike Gartner, Wales, 1993, at 3:15 and 3:37.
4:00 — Teemu Selanne, World, 1998, at 0:53 and 4:00
5:25 — Wally Hergesheimer, NHL All-Stars, 1953, at 4:06 and 5:25.

FASTEST TWO GOALS (ONE PLAYER) FROM START OF A PERIOD:
3:37 — Mike Gartner, Wales, 1993, at 3:15 and 3:37 of first period.
4:00 — Teemu Selanne, World, 1998, at 0:53 and 4:00 of first period.
4:43 — Dennis Ververgaert, Campbell, 1976, at 4:33 and 4:43 of third period.

FASTEST TWO GOALS (ONE PLAYER):
0:08 — Owen Nolan, West, 1997. Scored at 18:54 and 19:02 of second period.
0:10 — Dennis Ververgaert, Campbell, 1976. Scored at 4:33 and 4:43 of third period.
0:22 — Mike Gartner, Wales, 1993. Scored at 3:15 and 3:37 of first period.

Penalties

MOST PENALTY MINUTES:
25 — Gordie Howe in 23GP
21 — Gus Mortson in 9GP
16 — Harry Howell in 7GP

Goaltenders

MOST GAMES PLAYED:
13 — Glenn Hall from 1955 through 1969
11 — Terry Sawchuk from 1950 through 1968
  — Patrick Roy from 1988 through 2003
 8 — Jacques Plante from 1956 through 1970
  — Martin Brodeur from 1996 through 2004

MOST MINUTES PLAYED:
540 — Glenn Hall in 13GP
467 — Terry Sawchuk in 11GP
370 — Jacques Plante in 8GP
230 — Patrick Roy in 11GP
209 — Turk Broda in 4GP

MOST GOALS AGAINST:
29 — Patrick Roy in 11GP
22 — Glenn Hall in 13GP
21 — Mike Vernon in 5GP
19 — Terry Sawchuk in 11GP
18 — Jacques Plante in 8GP
  — Andy Moog in 4GP

BEST GOALS-AGAINST-AVERAGE AMONG THOSE WITH AT LEAST TWO GAMES PLAYED:
0.68 — Gilles Villemure in 3GP
1.49 — Gerry McNeil in 3GP
1.50 — Johnny Bower in 4GP
1.51 — Frank Brimsek in 3GP
1.64 — Gump Worsley in 4GP

This group of NHL All-Stars dropped a 4-1 decision to the Stanley Cup champion Toronto Maple Leafs in the 1962 game. Glenn Hall (in street clothes, standing second from the right) played earlier in the game. His 13 All-Star Game appearances top all NHL goaltenders.

Hockey Hall of Fame

(Year of induction is listed after each Honoured Members name)

Location: BCE Place, at the corner of Front and Yonge Streets in the heart of downtown Toronto. Easy access from all major highways running into Toronto. Close to TTC and Union Station.

Telephone: administration (416) 360-7735; information (416) 360-7765.

Public Hours of Operation: Open every day except Christmas Day, New Year's Day and Induction Day (November 13, 2006). Please call our information number (above) or visit our website (below) for times.

The Hockey Hall of Fame can be booked for private functions after hours.

Website address: www.hhof.com

History: The Hockey Hall of Fame was established in 1943. Members were first honoured in 1945. On August 26, 1961, the Hockey Hall of Fame opened its doors to the public in a building located on the grounds of the Canadian National Exhibition in Toronto. The Hockey Hall of Fame relocated to its new site at BCE Place and welcomed the hockey world on June 18, 1993.

Honour Roll: There are 343 Honoured Members in the Hockey Hall of Fame. 234 have been inducted as players, 95 as builders and 14 as Referees/Linesmen. In addition, there are 76 media honourees.

Founding/Premiere Sponsors: Imperial Oil, International Ice Hockey Federation, MCI Canada, Molson Canada, National Hockey League, National Hockey League Players' Association, Panasonic Canada, Pepsi-Cola Canada, Sun Media (Toronto)/The Toronto Sun, The Sports Network (TSN/RDS).

In statistical terms, Patrick Roy is the greatest goaltender in NHL history. The former Canadiens and Avalanche superstar enters the Hockey Hall of Fame as the NHL's career leader in games played, minutes played and wins in both the regular season and playoffs.

PLAYERS

* Abel, Sidney Gerald 1969
* Adams, John James "Jack" 1959
* Apps, Charles Joseph Sylvanus "Syl" 1961
  Armstrong, George Edward 1975
* Bailey, Irvine Wallace "Ace" 1975
* Bain, Donald H. "Dan" 1949
* Baker, Hobart "Hobey" 1945
  Barber, William Charles "Bill" 1990
* Barry, Martin J. "Marty" 1965
  Bathgate, Andrew James "Andy" 1978
* Bauer, Robert Theodore "Bobby" 1996
  Béliveau, Jean Arthur 1972
* Benedict, Clinton S. 1965
* Bentley, Douglas Wagner 1964
* Bentley, Maxwell H. L. 1966
* Blake, Hector "Toe" 1966
  Boivin, Leo Joseph 1986
* Boon, Richard R. "Dickie" 1952
  Bossy, Michael 1991
  Bouchard, Emile Joseph "Butch" 1966
* Boucher, Frank 1958
* Boucher, Georges "Buck" 1960
  Bourque, Raymond 2004
  Bower, John William 1976
* Bowie, Russell 1947
* Brimsek, Francis Charles 1966
* Broadbent, Harry L. "Punch" 1962
* Broda, Walter Edward "Turk" 1967
  Bucyk, John Paul 1981
* Burch, Billy 1974
* Cameron, Harold Hugh "Harry" 1962
  Cheevers, Gerald Michael "Gerry" 1985
* Clancy, Francis Michael "King" 1958
* Clapper, Aubrey "Dit" 1947
  Clarke, Robert "Bobby" 1987
* Cleghorn, Sprague 1958
  Coffey, Paul 2004
* Colville, Neil MacNeil 1967
* Conacher, Charles W. 1961
* Conacher, Lionel Pretoria 1994
* Conacher, Roy Gordon 1998
* Connell, Alex 1958
* Cook, Fred "Bun" 1995
* Cook, William Osser 1952
* Coulter, Arthur Edmund 1974
  Cournoyer, Yvan Serge 1982
* Cowley, William Mailes 1968
* Crawford, Samuel Russell "Rusty" 1962
* Darragh, John Proctor "Jack" 1962
* Davidson, Allan M. "Scotty" 1950
* Day, Clarence Henry "Hap" 1961
  Delvecchio, Alex 1977
* Denneny, Cyril "Cy" 1959
  Dionne, Marcel 1992
* Drillon, Gordon Arthur 1975

* Drinkwater, Charles Graham 1950
  Dryden, Kenneth Wayne 1983
  Duff, Dick 2006
* Dumart, Woodrow "Woody" 1992
* Dunderdale, Thomas 1974
* Durnan, William Ronald 1964
* Dutton, Mervyn A. "Red" 1958
* Dye, Cecil Henry "Babe" 1970
  Esposito, Anthony James "Tony" 1988
  Esposito, Philip Anthony 1984
* Farrell, Arthur F. 1965
  Federko, Bernie 2002
  Fetisov, Viacheslav 2001
  Flaman, Ferdinand Charles "Fern" 1990
* Foyston, Frank 1958
* Fredrickson, Frank 1958
  Fuhr, Grant 2003
  Gadsby, William Alexander 1970
  Gainey, Bob 1992
* Gardiner, Charles Robert "Chuck" 1945
* Gardiner, Herbert Martin "Herb" 1958
* Gardner, James Henry "Jimmy" 1962
  Gartner, Michael Alfred 2001
* Geoffrion, Jos. A. Bernard "Boom Boom" 1972
* Gerard, Eddie 1945
  Giacomin, Edward "Eddie" 1987
  Gilbert, Rodrigue Gabriel "Rod" 1982
  Gillies, Clark 2002
* Gilmour, Hamilton Livingstone "Billy" 1962
* Goheen, Frank Xavier "Moose" 1952
* Goodfellow, Ebenezer R. "Ebbie" 1963
  Goulet, Michel 1998
* Grant, Michael "Mike" 1950
* Green, Wilfred "Shorty" 1962
  Gretzky, Wayne Douglas 1999
* Griffis, Silas Seth "Si" 1950
* Hainsworth, George 1961
  Hall, Glenn Henry 1975
* Hall, Joseph Henry 1961
* Harvey, Douglas Norman 1973
  Hawerchuk, Dale Martin 2001
* Hay, George 1958
* Hern, William Milton "Riley" 1962
  Hextall, Bryan Aldwyn 1969
* Holmes, Harry "Hap" 1972
* Hooper, Charles Thomas "Tom" 1962
* Horner, George Reginald "Red" 1965
* Horton, Miles Gilbert "Tim" 1977
  Howe, Gordon 1972
* Howe, Sydney Harris 1965
  Howell, Henry Vernon "Harry" 1979
  Hull, Robert Marvin 1983
* Hutton, John Bower "Bouse" 1962
* Hyland, Harry M. 1962
* Irvin, James Dickenson "Dick" 1958

* Jackson, Harvey "Busher" 1971
* Johnson, Ernest "Moose" 1952
* Johnson, Ivan "Ching" 1958
  Johnson, Thomas Christian 1970
* Joliat, Aurel 1947
* Keats, Gordon "Duke" 1958
  Kelly, Leonard Patrick "Red" 1969
  Kennedy, Theodore Samuel "Teeder" 1966
  Keon, David Michael 1986
* Kharlamov, Valeri 2005
  Kurri, Jari 2001
  Lach, Elmer James 1966
  Lafleur, Guy Damien 1988
  LaFontaine, Pat 2003
* Lalonde, Edouard Charles "Newsy" 1950
  Langway, Rod Corry 2002
  Laperriere, Jacques 1987
  Lapointe, Guy 1993
  Laprade, Edgar 1993
* Laviolette, Jean Baptiste "Jack" 1962
* Lehman, Hugh 1958
  Lemaire, Jacques Gerard 1984
  Lemieux, Mario 1997
* LeSueur, Percy 1961
* Lewis, Herbert A. 1989
  Lindsay, Robert Blake Theodore "Ted" 1966
  Lumley, Harry 1980
* MacKay, Duncan "Mickey" 1952
  Mahovlich, Frank William 1981
* Malone, Joseph "Joe" 1950
* Mantha, Sylvio 1960
* Marshall, John "Jack" 1965
* Maxwell, Fred G. "Steamer" 1962
  McDonald, Lanny 1992
* McGee, Frank 1945
* McGimsie, William George "Billy" 1962
* McNamara, George 1958
  Mikita, Stanley 1983
  Moore, Richard Winston "Dickie" 1974
* Moran, Patrick Joseph "Paddy" 1958
  Morenz, Howie 1945
* Mosienko, William "Billy" 1965
  Mullen, Joseph P. 2000
  Murphy, Larry 2004
  Neely, Cam 2005
* Nighbor, Frank 1947
* Noble, Edward Reginald "Reg" 1962
* O'Connor, Herbert William "Buddy" 1988
* Oliver, Harry 1967
  Olmstead, Murray Bert "Bert" 1985
  Orr, Robert Gordon 1979
  Parent, Bernard Marcel 1984
  Park, Douglas Bradford "Brad" 1988
* Patrick, Joseph Lynn 1980
* Patrick, Lester 1947

Perreault, Gilbert 1990
* Phillips, Tommy 1945
Pilote, Joseph Albert Pierre Paul 1975
* Pitre, Didier "Pit" 1962
* Plante, Joseph Jacques Omer 1978
Potvin, Denis 1991
* Pratt, Walter "Babe" 1966
* Primeau, A. Joseph 1963
Pronovost, Joseph René Marcel 1978
Pulford, Bob 1991
* Pulford, Harvey 1945
* Quackenbush, Hubert George "Bill" 1976
* Rankin, Frank 1961
Ratelle, Joseph Gilbert Yvan Jean "Jean" 1985
* Rayner, Claude Earl "Chuck" 1973
Reardon, Kenneth Joseph 1966
Richard, Joseph Henri 1979
* Richard, Joseph Henri Maurice "Rocket" 1961
* Richardson, George Taylor 1950
Roberts, Gordon 1971
Robinson, Larry 1995
* Ross, Arthur Howey 1949
Roy, Patrick 2006
* Russel, Blair 1965
* Russell, Ernest 1965
* Ruttan, J.D. "Jack" 1962
Salming, Borje Anders 1996
Savard, Denis Joseph 2000
Savard, Serge 1986
* Sawchuk, Terrance Gordon "Terry" 1971
* Scanlan, Fred 1965
Schmidt, Milton Conrad "Milt" 1961
* Schriner, David "Sweeney" 1962
* Seibert, Earl Walter 1963
* Seibert, Oliver Levi 1961
* Shore, Edward W. "Eddie" 1947
Shutt, Stephen 1993
* Siebert, Albert C. "Babe" 1964
* Simpson, Harold Edward "Bullet Joe" 1962
Sittler, Darryl Glen 1989
* Smith, Alfred E. 1962
Smith, Clint 1991
* Smith, Reginald "Hooley" 1972
* Smith, Thomas James 1973
Smith, William John "Billy" 1993
Stanley, Allan Herbert 1981
* Stanley, Russell "Barney" 1962
Stastny, Peter 1998
* Stewart, John Sherratt "Black Jack" 1964
* Stewart, Nelson "Nels" 1952
* Stuart, Bruce 1961
* Stuart, Hod 1945
* Taylor, Frederick "Cyclone" (O.B.E.) 1947
* Thompson, Cecil R. "Tiny" 1959
Tretiak, Vladislav 1989
* Trihey, Col. Harry J. 1950
Trottier, Bryan 1997
Ullman, Norman V. Alexander "Norm" 1982
* Vezina, Georges 1945
* Walker, John Phillip "Jack" 1960
* Walsh, Martin "Marty" 1962
* Watson, Harry E. 1962
* Watson, Harry 1994
* Weiland, Ralph "Cooney" 1971
* Westwick, Harry 1962
* Whitcroft, Fred 1962
* Wilson, Gordon Allan "Phat" 1962
Worsley, Lorne John "Gump" 1980
* Worters, Roy 1969

BUILDERS

* Adams, Charles 1960
* Adams, Weston W. 1972
* Ahearn, Thomas Franklin "Frank" 1962
* Ahearne, John Francis "Bunny" 1977
* Allan, Sir Montagu (C.V.O.) 1945
Allen, Keith 1992
Arbour, Alger Joseph "Al" 1996
* Ballard, Harold Edwin 1977
* Bauer, Father David 1989
* Bickell, John Paris 1978
Bowman, Scotty 1991
* Brooks, Herb 2006
* Brown, George V. 1961
* Brown, Walter A. 1962
* Buckland, Frank 1975
Bush, Walter 2000
Butterfield, Jack Arlington 1980
* Calder, Frank 1947
* Campbell, Angus D. 1964
* Campbell, Clarence Sutherland 1966
* Cattarinich, Joseph 1977

Costello, Murray 2005
* Dandurand, Joseph Viateur "Leo" 1963
* Dilio, Francis Paul 1964
* Dudley, George S. 1958
* Dunn, James A. 1968
Fletcher, Cliff 2004
Francis, Emile 1982
* Gibson, Dr. John L. "Jack" 1976
* Gorman, Thomas Patrick "Tommy" 1963
* Griffiths, Frank A. 1993
* Hanley, William 1986
* Hay, Charles 1974
* Hendy, James C. 1968
* Hewitt, Foster 1965
* Hewitt, William Abraham 1947
Hotchkiss, Harley 2006
* Hume, Fred J. 1962
Illitch, Mike 2003
* Imlach, George "Punch" 1984
* Ivan, Thomas N. 1974
* Jennings, William M. 1975
* Johnson, Bob 1992
* Juckes, Gordon W. 1979
* Kilpatrick, Gen. John Reed 1960
Kilrea, Brian Blair 2003
* Knox, Seymour H. III 1993
* Leader, George Alfred 1969
* LeBel, Robert 1970
* Lockhart, Thomas F. 1965
* Loicq, Paul 1961
* Mariucci, John 1985
* Mathers, Frank 1992
* McLaughlin, Major Frederic 1963
* Milford, John "Jake" 1984
* Molson, Hon. Hartland de Montarville 1973
Morrison, Ian "Scotty" 1999
* Murray, Monsignor Athol 1998
* Neilson, Roger 2002
* Nelson, Francis 1947
* Norris, Bruce A. 1969
* Norris, Sr., James 1958
* Norris, James Dougan 1962
* Northey, William M. 1947
* O'Brien, John Ambrose 1962
O'Neill, Brian 1994
* Page, Fred 1993
Patrick, Craig 2001
* Patrick, Frank 1950
* Pickard, Allan W. 1958
* Pilous, Rudy 1985
* Poile, Norman "Bud" 1990
Pollock, Samuel Patterson Smyth 1978
* Raymond, Sen. Donat 1958
* Robertson, John Ross 1947
* Robinson, Claude C. 1947
* Ross, Philip D. 1976
* Sabetzki, Dr. Gunther 1995
Sather, Glen 1997
* Selke, Frank J. 1960
Sinden, Harry James 1983
* Smith, Frank D. 1962
* Smythe, Conn 1958
Snider, Edward M. 1988
* Stanley of Preston, Lord (G.C.B.) 1945
* Sutherland, Cap. James T. 1947
* Tarasov, Anatoli V. 1974
Torrey, Bill 1995
* Turner, Lloyd 1958
* Tutt, William Thayer 1978
* Voss, Carl Potter 1974
* Waghorne, Fred 1961
* Wirtz, Arthur Michael 1971
* Wirtz, William W. "Bill" 1976
Ziegler, John A. Jr. 1987

REFEREES/LINESMEN

Armstrong, Neil 1991
Ashley, John George 1981
Chadwick, William L. 1964
* D'Amico, John 1993
* Elliott, Chaucer 1961
Hayes, George William 1988
* Hewitson, Robert W. 1963
* Ion, Fred J. "Mickey" 1961
Pavelich, Matt 1987
* Rodden, Michael J. "Mike" 1962
* Smeaton, J. Cooper 1961
* Storey, Roy Alvin "Red" 1967
Udvari, Frank Joseph 1973
Van Hellemond, Andy 1999

Elmer Ferguson
Memorial Award Winners

In recognition of distinguished members of the newspaper profession whose words have brought honor to journalism and to hockey. Selected by the Professional Hockey Writers' Association.

* Barton, Charlie, Buffalo-Courier Express 1985
* Beauchamp, Jacques, Montreal Matin/Journal de Montréal 1984
* Brennan, Bill, Detroit News 1984
* Burchard, Jim, New York World Telegram 1984
* Burnett, Red, Toronto Star 1984
* Carroll, Dink, Montreal Gazette 1984
* Coleman, Jim, Southam Newspapers 1984
Conway, Russ, Eagle-Tribune 1999
* Damata, Ted, Chicago Tribune 1984
Delano, Hugh, New York Post 1991
Desjardins, Marcel, Montréal La Presse 1984
Duhatschek, Eric, Calgary Herald/Globe and Mail 2001
* Dulmage, Jack, Windsor Star 1984
Dunnell, Milt, Toronto Star 1984
Dupont, Kevin Paul, Boston Globe 2002
Elliott, Helene, Los Angeles Times 2005
Farber, Michael, Montreal Gazette/Sports Illustrated 2003
* Ferguson, Elmer, Montreal Herald/Star 1984
* Fitzgerald, Tom, Boston Globe 1984
Frayne, Trent, Toronto Telegram/Globe and Mail/Sun 1984
Gatecliff, Jack, St. Catharines Standard 1995
Gross, George, Toronto Telegram/Sun 1985
Johnston, Dick, Buffalo News 1986
Kelley, Jim, Buffalo News 2004
* Laney, Al, New York Herald-Tribune 1984
* Larochelle, Claude, Le Soleil 1989
L'Esperance, Zotique, Journal de Montréal/ le Petit Journal 1985
* MacLeod, Rex, Toronto Globe and Mail/Star 1987
Matheson, Jim, Edmonton Journal 2000
* Mayer, Charles, Journal de Montréal/la Patrie 1985
* McKenzie, Ken, The Hockey News 1997
Monahan, Leo, Boston Daily Record/Record-American/ Herald American 1986
Moriarty, Tim, UPI/Newsday 1986
Morrison, Scott, Toronto Sun/Rogers Sportsnet 2006
* Nichols, Joe, New York Times 1984
* O'Brien, Andy, Weekend Magazine 1985
Orr, Frank, Toronto Star 1989
Olan, Ben, New York Associated Press 1987
* O'Meara, Basil, Montreal Star 1984
Pedneault, Yvon, La Presse/Journal de Montréal 1998
* Proudfoot, Jim, Toronto Star 1988
Raymond, Bertrand, Journal de Montréal 1990
Rosa, Fran, Boston Globe 1987
Strachan, Al, Globe and Mail/Toronto Sun 1993
* Vipond, Jim, Toronto Globe and Mail 1984
Walter, Lewis, Detroit Times 1984
* Young, Scott, Toronto Globe and Mail/Telegram 1988

Foster Hewitt
Memorial Award Winners

In recognition of members of the radio and television industry who made outstanding contributions to their profession and the game during their career in hockey broadcasting. Selected by the NHL Broadcasters' Association.

Cole, Bob, Hockey Night in Canada 1996
Cusick, Fred, Boston 1984
* Darling, Ted, Buffalo 1994
* Gallivan, Danny, Montreal 1984
Garneau, Richard, Montreal 1999
* Hart, Gene, Philadelphia 1997
* Hewitt, Foster, Toronto 1984
Irvin, Dick, Montreal 1988
Kaiton, Chuck, Hartford/Carolina 2004
* Kelly, Dan, St. Louis 1989
Lange, Mike, Pittsburgh 2001
Lecavelier, René, Montreal 1984
Lynch, Budd, Detroit 1985
Maher, Peter, Calgary 2006
Martyn, Bruce, Detroit 1991
McDonald, Jiggs, Los Angeles, Atlanta, NY Islanders 1990
McFarlane, Brian, Hockey Night in Canada 1995
* McKnight, Wes, Toronto 1986
Meeker, Howie, Hockey Night in Canada 1998
Messina, Sal, New York 2005
Miller, Bob, Los Angeles 2000
Pettit, Lloyd, Chicago 1986
Phillips, Rod, Edmonton 2003
Robson, Jim, Vancouver 1992
Shaver, Al, Minnesota 1993
* Smith, Doug, Montreal 1985
Tremblay, Gilles, La Soirée du Hockey 2002
Wilson, Bob, Boston 1987

* Deceased

7th Annual Hockey Hall of Fame Game
Saturday, November 11, 2006
Montreal Canadiens vs. Toronto Maple Leafs
at Air Canada Centre in Toronto.

United States Hockey Hall of Fame

There are 127 enshrined members consisting of 78 players, 25 coaches, 20 administrators, one player/administrator, one referee and two teams. A special Wayne Gretzky Award pays tribute to international individuals who have made major contributions to hockey in the United States.

PLAYERS

* Abel, Clarence "Taffy" 1973
* Baker, Hobart "Hobey" 1973
* Bartholome, Earl 1977
* Bessone, Peter 1978
Blake, Robert 1985
Boucha, Henry 1995
* Brimsek, Frank 1973
Broten, Neal 2000
Cavanagh, Joe 1994
* Chaisson, Ray 1974
* Chase, John P. 1973
Christian, Dave 2001
Christian, Roger 1989
Christian, William "Bill" 1984
Christiansen, Keith 2005
Cleary, Robert 1981
Cleary, William 1976
* Conroy, Anthony 1975
Coppo, Paul 2004
Curran, Mike 1998
* Dahlstrom, Carl "Cully" 1973
* Desjardins, Victor 1974
* Desmond, Richard 1988
* Dill, Robert 1979
Dougherty, Richard "Dick" 2003
* Everett, Doug 1974
Fusco, Mark 2002
Fusco, Scott 2002
Ftorek, Robbie 1991
* Garrison, John B. 1973
Garrity, Jack 1986
* Goheen, Frank "Moose" 1973
Grant, Wally 1994
* Harding, Austin "Austie" 1975
Housley, Phil 2004
Howe, Mark 2003
* Iglehart, Stewart 1975
Johnson, Mark 2004
Johnson, Paul 2001
* Johnson, Virgil 1974
* Karakas, Mike 1973
Kirrane, Jack 1987
LaFontaine, Pat 2003
* Lane, Myles J. 1973
Langevin, David R. 1993
Langway, Rod 1999
Larson, Reed 1996
* Linder, Joseph 1975
* LoPresti, Sam L. 1973
MacDonald, Lane 2005
* Mariucci, John 1973
Matchefts, John 1991
* Mather, Bruce 1998
Mayasich, John 1976
McCartan, Jack 1983
* Moe, William 1974
Morrow, Ken 1995
* Moseley, Fred 1975
Mullen, Joe 1998
* Murray, Sr., Hugh "Muzz" 1987
* Nelson, Hubert "Hub" 1978
* Nyrop, William D. 1997
* Olson, Eddie 1977
* Owen, Jr., George 1973
* Palmer, Winthrop 1973
Paradise, Robert 1989
* Purpur, Clifford "Fido" 1974
Ramsey, Mike 2001
* Riley, Joe 2002
Riley, William 1977
Roberts, Gordie 1999
* Roberts, Moe 2005
* Romnes, Elwin "Doc" 1973
* Rondeau, Richard 1985
Sheehy, Timothy K. 1997
* Williams, Thomas 1981
* Winters, Frank "Coddy" 1973
* Yackel, Ken 1986

COACHES

* Almquist, Oscar 1983
Bessone, Amo 1992
* Brooks, Herb 1990
Ceglarski, Len 1992
* Cunniff, John 2003
* Fullerton, James 1992
Gambucci, Sergio 1996
* Gordon, Malcolm K. 1973
Harkness, Nevin D. "Ned" 1994
Heyliger, Victor 1974
* Holt, Jr. Charles E. 1997
Ikola, Willard 1990
* Jeremiah, Edward J. 1973
* Johnson, Bob 1991
* Kelley, John "Snooks" 1974
Kelley, John H. "Jack" 1993
Patrick, Craig 1996
* Pleban, Jon "Connie" 1990
Riley, Jack 1979
* Ross, Larry 1988
* Thompson, Clifford, R. 1973
* Stewart, William 1982
Williamson, Murray 2005
* Winsor, Alfred "Ralph" 1973
Woog, Doug 2002

ADMINISTRATORS

* Brown, George V. 1973
* Brown, Walter A. 1973
Bush, Walter 1980
* Clark, Donald 1978
Claypool, James 1995
* Gibson, J.C. "Doc" 1973
Ilitch, Mike 2004
* Jennings, William M. 1981
* Kahler, Nick 1980
* Lockhart, Thomas F. 1973
* Marvin, Cal 1982
Palazzari, Doug 2000
Pleau, Larry 2000
* Ridder, Robert 1976
* Schulz, Charles M. 1993
Trumble, Harold 1985
* Tutt, William Thayer 1973
* Watson, Sid 1999
Wirtz, William W. "Bill" 1984
* Wright, Lyle Z.1973

PLAYER/ADMINISTRATOR

Nanne, Lou 1998

REFEREE

Chadwick, William 1974

TEAMS

1960 Olympic Team, 2000
1980 Olympic Team, 2003

WAYNE GRETZKY INTERNATIONAL AWARD

Wayne Gretzky 1999
The Howe family 2000
Scotty Morrison 2001
Scotty Bowman 2002
Bobby Hull 2003
* Herb Brooks 2004

*Deceased

The architect of 1980's "The Miracle on Ice," coach Herb Brooks was inducted into the U.S. Hockey Hall of Fame in 1990. This year, he will be inducted into the Builders category of the Hockey Hall of Fame in Toronto.

International Ice Hockey Federation Hall of Fame

The IIHF Hall of Fame was founded in 1997.

Candidates for election as Honoured Members in the player category shall be chosen on the basis of their playing ability, sportsmanship, character and their contribution to their team or teams and to the game of ice hockey in general.

Candidates for election as Honoured Members in the builder category shall be chosen on the basis of their coaching, managerial or executive ability, where applicable, their sportsmanship and character, and their contribution to their organization or organizations and to the game of ice hockey in general.

Candidates for election as Honoured Members in the referee or linesman category shall be chosen on the basis of their officiating ability, sportsmanship, character and their contribution to the game of ice hockey in general. The Paul Loicq Award, named for the longtime former IIHF president, is presented to honor a person for his service to the international hockey community.

Inductees' names are followed by their country and year of induction.

PLAYERS

Balderis, Helmut, LAT, 1998
Ball, Rudi, GER, 2004
Bergqvist, Sven, SWE, 1999
Bjorn, Lars, SWE, 1998
Bobrov, Vsevolod, RUS, 1997
Bourbonnais, Roger, CAN, 1999
Bubnik, Vlastimil, CzRep, 1997
Cattini, Ferdinand, SUI, 1998
Cattini, Hans, SUI, 1998
Christian, Bill, USA, 1998
Cleary, Bill, USA, 1997
Cosby, Gerry, USA, 1997
Craig, Jim, USA, 1999
Curran, Mike, USA, 1999
Davydov, Vitaly, RUS, 2004
Drobny, Jaroslav, CzRep, 1997
Dzurilla, Vladimir, SVK, 1998
Erhardt, Carl, G.B., 1998
Fetisov, Vyacheslav, RUS, 2005
Firsov, Anatoli, RUS, 1998
Golonka, Josef, SVK, 1998
Gretzky, Wayne, CAN, 2000
Gruth, Henryk, POL, 2006
Gustafsson, Bengt-Ake, SWE, 2003
Gut, Karel, CzRep, 1998
Hedberg, Anders, SWE, 1997
Hlinka, Ivan, CzRep, 2002
Holecek, Jiri, CzRep, 1998
Holik, Jiri, CzRep, 1999
Holmqvist, Leif, SWE, 1999
Huck, Fran, CAN, 1999
Jaenecke, Gustav, GER, 1998
Johnson, Mark, USA, 1999
Johnston, Marshall, CAN, 1998
Jonsson, Tomas, SWE, 2000
Jutila, Timo, FIN, 2003
Keinonen, Matti, FIN, 2002
Kharlamov, Valeri, RUS, 1998
Kiessling, Udo, GER, 2000
Kuhnhackl, Erich, GER, 1997
Kurri, Jari, FIN, 2000
Kuzkin, Viktor, RUS, 2005
Lacarriere, Jacques, FRA, 1998
Loob, Hakan, SWE, 1998
Lundquist, Vic, CAN, 1997
Machac, Oldrich, CzRep, 1999
MacKenzie, Barry, CAN, 1999

Makarov, Sergei, RUS, 2001
Malecek, Josef, CzRep, 2003
Maltsev, Alexander, RUS, 1999
Marjamaki, Pekka, FIN, 1998
Martin, Seth, CAN, 1997
Martinec, Vladimir, CzRep, 2001
Mayasich, John, USA, 1997
Mayorov, Boris, RUS, 1999
McCartan, Jack, USA, 1998
McLeod, Jackie, CAN, 1999
Mikhailov, Boris, RUS, 2000
Nanne, Lou, USA, 2004
Naslund, Mats, SWE, 2005
Nedomansky, Vaclav, CzRep, 1997
Nilsson, Kent, SWE, 2006
Nilsson, Nisse, SWE, 2002
O'Malley, Terry, CAN, 1998
Oksanen, Lasse, FIN, 1999
Pana, Eduard, ROM, 1998
Patton, Peter, G.B., 2002
Petrov, Vladimir, RUS, 2006
Pettersson, Ronald, SWE, 2004
Pospisil, Frantisek, CzRep, 1999

Puschnig, Josef, AUT, 1999
Ragulin, Alexander, RUS, 1997
Rampf, Hans, GER, 2001
Salming, Borje, SWE, 1998
Schloder, Alois, GER, 2005
Sinden, Harry, CAN, 1997
Sologubov, Nikolai, RUS, 2004
Stastny, Peter, SVK, 2000
Sterner, Ulf, SWE, 2001
Stoltz, Roland, SWE, 1999
Tikal, Frantisek, CzRep, 2004
Torriani, Bibi, SUI, 1997
Tretiak, Vladislav, RUS, 1997
Tumba, Sven, SWE, 1997
Valtonen, Jorma, FIN, 1999
Vasiliev, Valeri, RUS, 1998
Wahlsten, Vladimir, FIN, 2006
Watson, Harry, CAN, 1998
Yakushev, Alexander, RUS, 2003
Ylonen, Urpo, FIN, 1997
Zabrodsky, Vladimir, CzRep, 1997
Ziesche, Joachim, GER, 1999

BUILDERS

Ahearne, Bunny, G.B., 1997
Aljancic Sr., Ernest, SLO, 2002
Bauer, Father David, CAN, 1997
Berglund, Curt, SWE, 2003
Brooks, Herb, USA, 1999
Brown, Walter, USA, 1997
Buckna, Mike, CAN, 2004
Calcaterra, Enrico, ITA, 1999
Chernyshev, Arkady, RUS, 1999
Eklow, Rudolf, SWE, 1999
Grunander, Arne, SWE, 1997
Henschel, Heinz, GER, 2003
Hewitt, William, CAN, 1998
Holmes, Derek, CAN, 1999
Horsky, Ladislav, SVK, 2004

Hviid, Jorgen, DEN, 2005
Johannessen, Tore, NOR, 1999
Juckes, Gordon, CAN, 1997
Kawabuchi, Tsutomu, JPN, 2004
Khorozov, Anatoli, UKR, 2006
King, Dave, CAN, 2001
Kostka, Vladimir, CzRep, 1997
LeBel, Bob, CAN, 1997
Lindblad, Harry, FIN, 1999
Loicq, Paul, BEL, 1997
Luhti, Cesar W., SUI, 1998
Magnus, Louis, FRA, 1997
Pasztor, Gyorgy, HUN, 2001
Renwick, Gordon, CAN, 2002
Ridder, Bob, USA, 1998
Riley, Jack, USA, 1998
Sabetzki, Dr. Gunther, GER, 1997
Starovoitov, Andrei, RUS, 1997
Starsi, Jan, SVK, 1999
Stromberg, Arne, SWE, 1998
Stubb, Goran, FIN, 2000
Subrt, Miroslav, CzRep, 2004
Tarasov, Anatoli, RUS, 1997
Tikhonov, Viktor, RUS, 1998
Tomita, Shoichi, JPN, 2006
Trumble, Hal, USA, 1999
Tsutsumi, Yoshiaki, JPN, 1999
Tutt, Thayer, USA, 2002
Unsinn, Xaver, GER, 1998
Wasservogel, Walter, AUT, 1997
Yurzinov, Vladimir, RUS, 2002

REFEREES

Adamec, Quido, CzRep, 2005
Dahlberg, Ove, SWE, 2004
Karandin, Yuri, RUS, 2004
Kompalla, Josef, GER, 2003
Wiitala, Unto, FIN, 2003

PAUL LOICQ AWARD

Montag, Wolf-Dieter, GER, 1998
Neumayer, Roman, GER, 1999
Kukushkin, Vsevolod, RUS, 2000
Kataoka, Isao, JPN, 2001
Marsh, Pat, G.B., 2002
Nagobads, George, USA, 2003
Kukulowicz, Aggie, CAN, 2004
Hrabcek, Rita, AUS, 2005
Tovland, Bo, SWE, 2006

The Soviet national team photographed after winning the Izvestia Tournament in 1968. Six members of the 19-man squad are now in the IIHF Hall of Fame: Vitali Davydov, Anatoli Firsov, Viktor Kuzkin, Boris Mayorov, Alexander Ragulin and Alexander Yakushev.

Results

2006
Stanley Cup Playoffs

CONFERENCE QUARTER-FINALS
(Best-of-seven series)

Eastern Conference

Series 'A'
Fri. Apr. 21	Tampa Bay 1	at	Ottawa 4
Sun. Apr. 23	Tampa Bay 4	at	Ottawa 3
Tue. Apr. 25	Ottawa 8	at	Tampa Bay 4
Thu. Apr. 27	Ottawa 5	at	Tampa Bay 2
Sat. Apr. 29	Tampa Bay 2	at	Ottawa 3

(Ottawa won series 4-1)

Series 'B'
Sat. Apr. 22	Montreal 6	at	Carolina 1
Mon. Apr. 24	Montreal 6	at	Carolina 5*
Wed. Apr. 26	Carolina 2	at	Montreal 1**
Fri. Apr. 28	Carolina 3	at	Montreal 2
Sun. Apr. 30	Montreal 1	at	Carolina 2
Tue. May 2	Carolina 2	at	Montreal 1***

*Michael Ryder scored at 22:32 of overtime
**Eric Staal scored at 3:38 of overtime
***Cory Stillman scored at 1:19 of overtime
(Carolina won series 4-2)

Series 'C'
Sat. Apr. 22	NY Rangers 1	at	New Jersey 6
Mon. Apr. 24	NY Rangers 1	at	New Jersey 4
Wed. Apr. 26	New Jersey 3	at	NY Rangers 0
Sat. Apr. 29	New Jersey 4	at	NY Rangers 2

(New Jersey won series 4-0)

Series 'D'
Sat. Apr. 22	Philadelphia 2	at	Buffalo 3*
Mon. Apr. 24	Philadelphia 2	at	Buffalo 8
Wed. Apr. 26	Buffalo 2	at	Philadelphia 4
Fri. Apr. 28	Buffalo 4	at	Philadelphia 5
Sun. Apr. 30	Philadelphia 0	at	Buffalo 3
Tue. May 2	Buffalo 7	at	Philadelphia 1

*Daniel Briere scored at 27:31 of overtime
(Buffalo won series 4-2)

Western Conference

Series 'E'
Fri. Apr. 21	Edmonton 2	at	Detroit 3*
Sun. Apr. 23	Edmonton 4	at	Detroit 2
Tue. Apr. 25	Detroit 3	at	Edmonton 4**
Thu. Apr. 27	Detroit 4	at	Edmonton 2
Sat. Apr. 29	Edmonton 3	at	Detroit 2
Mon. May 1	Detroit 3	at	Edmonton 4

*Kirk Maltby scored at 22:39 of overtime
**Jarret Stoll scored at 28:44 of overtime
(Edmonton won series 4-2)

Series 'F'
Sat. Apr. 22	Colorado 5	at	Dallas 2
Mon. Apr. 24	Colorado 5	at	Dallas 4*
Wed. Apr. 26	Dallas 3	at	Colorado 4**
Fri. Apr. 28	Dallas 4	at	Colorado 1
Sun. Apr. 30	Colorado 3	at	Dallas 2***

*Joe Sakic scored at 4:36 of overtime
**Alex Tanguay scored at 1:09 of overtime
***Andrew Brunette scored at 13:55 of overtime
(Colorado won series 4-1)

Series 'G'
Fri. Apr. 21	Anaheim 1	at	Calgary 2*
Sun. Apr. 23	Anaheim 4	at	Calgary 3
Tue. Apr. 25	Calgary 5	at	Anaheim 2
Thu. Apr. 27	Calgary 2	at	Anaheim 2**
Sat. Apr. 29	Anaheim 2	at	Calgary 3
Mon. May 1	Calgary 1	at	Anaheim 2
Wed. May 3	Anaheim 3	at	Calgary 0

*Darren McCarty scored at 9:45 of overtime
**Sean O'Donnell scored at 1:36 of overtime
(Anaheim won series 4-3)

Series 'H'
Fri. Apr. 21	San Jose 3	at	Nashville 4
Sun. Apr. 23	San Jose 3	at	Nashville 0
Tue. Apr. 25	Nashville 1	at	San Jose 4
Thu. Apr. 27	Nashville 4	at	San Jose 5
Sun. Apr. 30	San Jose 2	at	Nashville 1

(San Jose won series 4-1)

CONFERENCE SEMI-FINALS
(Best-of-seven series)

Eastern Conference

Series 'I'
Fri. May 5	Buffalo 7	at	Ottawa 6*
Mon. May 8	Buffalo 2	at	Ottawa 1
Wed. May 10	Ottawa 2	at	Buffalo 3**
Thu. May 11	Ottawa 2	at	Buffalo 1
Sat. May 13	Buffalo 3	at	Ottawa 2***

*Chris Drury scored at 0:18 of overtime
**Jean-Pierre Dumont scored at 5:05 of overtime
***Jason Pominville scored at 2:26 of overtime
(Buffalo won series 4-1)

Series 'J'
Sat. May 6	New Jersey 0	at	Carolina 6
Mon. May 8	New Jersey 2	at	Carolina 3*
Wed. May 10	Carolina 3	at	New Jersey 2
Sat. May 13	Carolina 1	at	New Jersey 5
Sun. May 14	New Jersey 1	at	Carolina 4

*Niclas Wallin scored at 3:09 of overtime
(Carolina won series 4-1)

Western Conference

Series 'K'
Sun. May 7	Edmonton 1	at	San Jose 2
Mon. May 8	Edmonton 1	at	San Jose 2
Wed. May 10	San Jose 2	at	Edmonton 3*
Fri. May 12	San Jose 3	at	Edmonton 6
Sun. May 14	Edmonton 6	at	San Jose 3
Wed. May 17	San Jose 0	at	Edmonton 2

*Shawn Horcoff scored at 42:24 of overtime
(Edmonton won series 4-2)

Series 'L'
Fri. May 5	Colorado 0	at	Anaheim 5
Sun. May 7	Colorado 0	at	Anaheim 3
Tue. May 9	Anaheim 4	at	Colorado 3*
Thu. May 11	Anaheim 4	at	Colorado 1

*Joffrey Lupul scored at 16:30 of overtime
(Anaheim won series 4-0)

CONFERENCE FINALS
(Best-of-seven series)

Eastern Conference

Series 'M'
Sat. May 20	Buffalo 3	at	Carolina 2
Mon. May 22	Buffalo 3	at	Carolina 4
Wed. May 24	Carolina 3	at	Buffalo 4
Fri. May 26	Carolina 4	at	Buffalo 0
Sun. May 28	Buffalo 3	at	Carolina 4*
Tue. May 30	Carolina 1	at	Buffalo 2**
Thu. June 1	Buffalo 2	at	Carolina 4

*Cory Stillman scored at 8:46 of overtime
**Daniel Briere scored at 4:22 of overtime
(Carolina won series 4-3)

Western Conference

Series 'N'
Fri. May 19	Edmonton 3	at	Anaheim 1
Sun. May 21	Edmonton 3	at	Anaheim 1
Tue. May 23	Anaheim 4	at	Edmonton 5
Thu. May 25	Anaheim 6	at	Edmonton 3
Sat. May 27	Edmonton 2	at	Anaheim 1

(Edmonton won series 4-1)

STANLEY CUP FINAL
(Best-of-seven series)

Series 'O'
Mon. June 5	Edmonton 4	at	Carolina 5
Wed. June 7	Edmonton 0	at	Carolina 5
Sat. June 10	Carolina 1	at	Edmonton 2
Mon. June 12	Carolina 2	at	Edmonton 1
Wed. June 14	Edmonton 4	at	Carolina 3*
Sat. June 17	Carolina 0	at	Edmonton 4
Mon. June 19	Edmonton 1	at	Carolina 3

*Fernando Pisani scored at 3:31 of overtime
(Carolina won series 4-3)

Team Playoff Records

	GP	W	L	GF	GA	%
Carolina	25	16	9	73	60	.640
Edmonton	24	15	9	70	61	.625
Buffalo	18	11	7	60	49	.611
Anaheim	16	9	7	46	36	.563
San Jose	11	6	5	29	29	.545
New Jersey	9	5	4	27	21	.556
Ottawa	10	5	5	36	29	.500
Colorado	9	4	5	22	31	.444
Calgary	7	3	4	16	17	.429
Montreal	6	2	4	17	15	.333
Detroit	6	2	4	17	19	.333
Philadelphia	6	2	4	14	27	.333
Dallas	5	1	4	15	18	.200
Nashville	5	1	4	10	17	.200
Tampa Bay	5	1	4	13	23	.200
NY Rangers	4	0	4	4	17	.000

Individual Leaders

Abbreviations: GP – games played; **G** – goals; **A** – assists; **Pts** – points; **+/–** – difference between Goals For (**GF**) scored when a player is on the ice with his team at even strength or short-handed and Goals Against (**GA**) scored when the same player is on the ice with his team at even strength or on a power play; **PIM** – penalties in minutes; **PP** – power play goals; **SH** – short-handed goals; **GW** – game-winning goals; **OT** – overtime goals; **S** – shots on goal; **%** – percentage of shots resulting in goals.

Playoff Scoring Leaders

Player	Team	GP	G	A	PTS	+/–	PIM	PP	SH	GW	OT	S	%
Eric Staal	Carolina	25	9	19	28	0	8	7	0	1	1	87	10.3
Cory Stillman	Carolina	25	9	17	26	12	14	4	0	3	2	75	12.0
Chris Pronger	Edmonton	24	5	16	21	10	26	3	0	0	0	61	8.2
Daniel Briere	Buffalo	18	8	11	19	0	12	3	0	2	2	47	17.0
Shawn Horcoff	Edmonton	24	7	12	19	4	12	1	1	2	1	41	17.1
Fernando Pisani	Edmonton	24	14	4	18	4	10	3	1	5	1	49	28.6
Rod Brind'Amour	Carolina	25	12	6	18	9	16	6	0	4	0	75	16.0
Chris Drury	Buffalo	18	9	9	18	5	10	5	1	1	1	42	21.4
Justin Williams	Carolina	25	7	11	18	12	34	0	1	1	0	71	9.9
Matt Cullen	Carolina	25	4	14	18	2	12	2	0	1	0	56	7.1
Ales Hemsky	Edmonton	24	6	11	17	–3	14	4	0	2	0	47	12.8
Ryan Smyth	Edmonton	24	7	9	16	–2	22	4	0	1	0	60	11.7
Mark Recchi	Carolina	25	7	9	16	–5	18	2	0	2	0	45	15.6
Patrik Elias	New Jersey	9	6	10	16	5	4	4	0	0	0	32	18.8
Doug Weight	Carolina	23	3	13	16	–3	20	1	0	0	0	35	8.6
Ray Whitney	Carolina	24	9	6	15	–1	14	5	0	1	0	40	22.5
Derek Roy	Buffalo	18	5	10	15	7	16	1	1	0	0	33	15.2
Sergei Samsonov	Edmonton	24	4	11	15	2	14	1	0	0	0	40	10.0
Patrick Marleau	San Jose	11	9	5	14	2	8	4	0	2	0	38	23.7
J.P. Dumont	Buffalo	18	7	7	14	1	14	3	0	1	1	25	28.0
Teemu Selanne	Anaheim	16	6	8	14	0	6	1	0	2	0	53	11.3
Jason Spezza	Ottawa	10	5	9	14	–1	2	3	0	1	0	23	21.7
Jaroslav Spacek	Edmonton	24	3	11	14	–3	24	2	0	0	0	43	7.0

Playoff Defencemen Scoring Leaders

Player	Team	GP	G	A	PTS	+/–	PIM	PP	SH	GW	OT	S	%
Chris Pronger	Edmonton	24	5	16	21	10	26	3	0	0	0	61	8.2
Jaroslav Spacek	Edmonton	24	3	11	14	–3	24	2	0	0	0	43	7.0
Frantisek Kaberle	Carolina	25	4	9	13	–7	8	3	0	1	0	35	11.4
Scott Niedermayer	Anaheim	16	2	9	11	1	14	1	1	1	0	48	4.2
Bret Hedican	Carolina	25	2	9	11	6	42	0	0	0	0	23	8.7
Wade Redden	Ottawa	9	2	8	10	–2	10	2	0	1	0	19	10.5
*Francois Beauchemin	Anaheim	16	3	6	9	0	11	3	0	0	0	35	8.6
Brian Rafalski	New Jersey	9	1	8	9	3	2	1	0	0	0	9	11.1
Christian Ehrhoff	San Jose	11	2	6	8	2	18	1	0	1	0	27	7.4
Henrik Tallinder	Buffalo	14	2	6	8	14	16	0	0	0	0	12	16.7
Mathieu Schneider	Detroit	6	1	7	8	–1	6	0	0	0	0	17	5.9

GOALTENDING LEADERS

Goals Against Average

Goaltender	Team	GP	Mins	GA	Avg.
Ilja Bryzgalov	Anaheim	11	659	16	1.46
Cam Ward	Carolina	23	1320	47	2.14
Miikka Kiprusoff	Calgary	7	428	16	2.24
Martin Brodeur	New Jersey	9	533	20	2.25
Dwayne Roloson	Edmonton	18	1160	45	2.33

Wins

Goaltender	Team	GP	Mins	W	L
Cam Ward	Carolina	23	1320	15	8
Dwayne Roloson	Edmonton	18	1160	12	5
Ryan Miller	Buffalo	18	1123	11	7
Ilja Bryzgalov	Anaheim	11	659	6	4
Vesa Toskala	San Jose	11	686	6	5

Save Percentage

Goaltender	Team	GP	Mins	GA	SA	S%	W	L
Ilja Bryzgalov	Anaheim	11	659	16	285	.944	6	4
Dwayne Roloson	Edmonton	18	1160	45	618	.927	12	5
Martin Brodeur	New Jersey	9	533	20	261	.923	5	4
Miikka Kiprusoff	Calgary	7	428	16	202	.921	3	4
Cam Ward	Carolina	23	1320	47	584	.920	15	8

Shutouts

Goaltender	Team	GP	Mins	SO
Ilja Bryzgalov	Anaheim	11	659	3
Cam Ward	Carolina	23	1320	2
Martin Gerber	Carolina	6	221	1
Jussi Markkanen	Edmonton	6	360	1
Martin Brodeur	New Jersey	9	533	1
Vesa Toskala	San Jose	11	686	1
Ryan Miller	Buffalo	18	1123	1
Dwayne Roloson	Edmonton	18	1160	1

Goals

Name	Team	GP	G
Fernando Pisani	Edmonton	24	14
Rod Brind'Amour	Carolina	25	12
Patrick Marleau	San Jose	11	9
Joffrey Lupul	Anaheim	16	9
Chris Drury	Buffalo	18	9
Ray Whitney	Carolina	24	9
Cory Stillman	Carolina	25	9
Eric Staal	Carolina	25	9
Daniel Briere	Buffalo	18	8
Martin Havlat	Ottawa	10	7
J.P. Dumont	Buffalo	18	7
Ryan Smyth	Edmonton	24	7
Shawn Horcoff	Edmonton	24	7
Mark Recchi	Carolina	25	7
Justin Williams	Carolina	25	7

Assists

Name	Team	GP	A
Eric Staal	Carolina	25	19
Cory Stillman	Carolina	25	17
Chris Pronger	Edmonton	24	16
Matt Cullen	Carolina	25	14
Doug Weight	Carolina	23	13
Shawn Horcoff	Edmonton	24	12
Daniel Briere	Buffalo	18	11
Sergei Samsonov	Edmonton	24	11
Jaroslav Spacek	Edmonton	24	11
Ales Hemsky	Edmonton	24	11
Justin Williams	Carolina	25	11
Jamie Langenbrunner	New Jersey	9	10
Patrik Elias	New Jersey	9	10
Todd Marchant	Anaheim	16	10
Derek Roy	Buffalo	18	10

Power-play Goals

Name	Team	GP	PP
Eric Staal	Carolina	25	7
Rod Brind'Amour	Carolina	25	6
Chris Drury	Buffalo	18	5
Ray Whitney	Carolina	24	5

Game-winning Goals

Name	Team	GP	GW
Fernando Pisani	Edmonton	24	5
Rod Brind'Amour	Carolina	25	4
Ales Kotalik	Buffalo	18	3
Cory Stillman	Carolina	25	3
Peter Forsberg	Philadelphia	6	2
Brian Gionta	New Jersey	9	2
Patrick Marleau	San Jose	11	2
Teemu Selanne	Anaheim	16	2
Samuel Pahlsson	Anaheim	16	2
Daniel Briere	Buffalo	18	2
Shawn Horcoff	Edmonton	24	2
Ales Hemsky	Edmonton	24	2
Mark Recchi	Carolina	25	2

Short-handed Goals

Name	Team	GP	SH
John Madden	New Jersey	9	2
21 players with one			

Overtime Goals

Name	Team	GP	OT
Daniel Briere	Buffalo	18	2
Cory Stillman	Carolina	25	2
16 players with one			

Shots

Name	Team	GP	S
Eric Staal	Carolina	25	87
Rod Brind'Amour	Carolina	25	75
Cory Stillman	Carolina	25	75
Justin Williams	Carolina	25	71
Joffrey Lupul	Anaheim	16	62

Plus/Minus

Name	Team	GP	+/–
Henrik Tallinder	Buffalo	14	14
Todd Marchant	Anaheim	16	14
Toni Lydman	Buffalo	18	14
Cory Stillman	Carolina	25	12
Justin Williams	Carolina	25	12

TEAMS' PLAYOFF HOME/ROAD RECORD

	HOME						ROAD					
	GP	W	L	GF	GA	%	GP	W	L	GF	GA	%
CAR	14	10	4	51	36	.714	11	6	5	22	24	.545
EDM	11	8	3	36	28	.727	13	7	6	34	33	.538
BUF	8	6	2	24	16	.750	10	5	5	36	33	.500
ANA	8	4	4	18	16	.500	8	5	3	28	20	.625
S.J.	5	4	1	16	13	.800	6	2	4	13	16	.333
N.J.	4	3	1	17	6	.750	5	2	3	10	15	.400
OTT	6	2	4	19	19	.333	4	3	1	17	10	.750
COL	4	1	3	9	15	.250	5	3	2	13	16	.600
CGY	4	2	2	8	10	.500	3	1	2	8	7	.333
MTL	3	0	3	4	7	.000	3	2	1	13	8	.667
DET	3	1	2	7	9	.333	3	1	2	10	10	.333
PHI	3	2	1	10	13	.667	3	0	3	4	14	.000
DAL	3	0	3	8	13	.000	2	1	1	7	5	.500
NSH	3	1	2	5	8	.333	2	0	2	5	9	.000
T.B.	2	0	2	6	13	.000	3	1	2	7	10	.333
NYR	2	0	2	2	7	.000	2	0	2	2	10	.000
Total	**83**	**44**	**39**	**240**	**229**	**.530**	**83**	**39**	**44**	**229**	**240**	**.470**

TEAMS' POWER-PLAY RECORD

Abbreviations: ADV-total advantages; **PPGF**-power play goals for; **%** arrived by dividing number of power-play goals by total advantages.

	HOME					ROAD					OVERALL			
Team	GP	ADV	PPGF	%	Team	GP	ADV	PPGF	%	Team	GP	ADV	PPGF	%
1 CAR	14	81	25	30.9	OTT	4	20	7	35.0	OTT	10	56	14	25.0
2 MTL	3	11	3	27.3	DET	3	24	6	25.0	CAR	25	129	31	24.0
3 N.J.	4	36	9	25.0	MTL	3	16	3	18.8	MTL	6	27	6	22.2
4 NSH	3	21	5	23.8	DAL	2	11	2	18.2	DET	6	40	8	20.0
5 T.B.	2	15	3	20.0	EDM	13	65	11	16.9	N.J.	9	58	11	19.0
6 OTT	6	36	7	19.4	CGY	3	18	3	16.7	NSH	5	32	6	18.8
7 EDM	11	76	13	17.1	S.J.	6	38	6	15.8	EDM	24	141	24	17.0
8 BUF	8	53	9	17.0	BUF	10	46	7	15.2	BUF	18	99	16	16.2
9 DAL	3	20	3	15.0	CAR	11	48	6	12.5	DAL	5	31	5	16.1
10 S.J.	5	34	5	14.7	COL	5	25	3	12.0	S.J.	11	72	11	15.3
11 ANA	8	60	8	13.3	NSH	2	11	1	9.1	CGY	7	43	6	14.0
12 NYR	2	8	1	12.5	PHI	3	11	1	9.1	T.B.	5	31	4	12.9
13 DET	3	16	2	12.5	N.J.	5	22	2	9.1	ANA	16	102	11	10.8
14 CGY	4	25	3	12.0	NYR	2	13	1	7.7	PHI	6	29	3	10.3
15 PHI	3	18	2	11.1	ANA	8	42	3	7.1	COL	9	52	5	9.6
16 COL	4	27	2	7.4	T.B.	3	16	1	6.3	NYR	4	21	2	9.5
Total	**83**	**537**	**100**	**18.6**		**83**	**426**	**63**	**14.8**		**83**	**963**	**163**	**16.9**

TEAMS' PENALTY KILLING RECORD

Abbreviations: TSH – Total times short-handed; **PPGA** – power-play goals against; **%** arrived by dividing times short-handed minus power-play goals against by times short.

	HOME					ROAD					OVERALL			
Team	GP	TSH	PPGA	%	Team	GP	TSH	PPGA	%	Team	GP	TSH	PPGA	%
1 MTL	3	12	1	91.7	ANA	8	53	6	88.7	ANA	16	96	11	88.5
2 OTT	6	30	3	90.0	DAL	2	14	2	85.7	OTT	10	55	7	87.3
3 COL	4	19	2	89.5	CGY	3	25	4	84.0	CGY	7	44	6	86.4
4 CGY	4	19	2	89.5	OTT	4	25	4	84.0	EDM	24	158	22	86.1
5 EDM	11	73	8	89.0	COL	5	31	5	83.9	COL	9	50	7	86.0
6 CAR	14	72	8	88.9	EDM	13	85	14	83.5	CAR	25	137	20	85.4
7 ANA	8	43	5	88.4	BUF	10	59	10	83.1	PHI	6	41	7	82.9
8 N.J.	4	22	3	86.4	PHI	3	27	5	81.5	BUF	18	92	16	82.6
9 PHI	3	14	2	85.7	CAR	11	65	12	81.5	DAL	5	28	5	82.1
10 BUF	8	33	6	81.8	NSH	2	16	3	81.3	S.J.	11	62	12	80.6
11 S.J.	5	25	5	80.0	S.J.	6	37	7	81.1	MTL	6	30	6	80.0
12 DAL	3	14	3	78.6	DET	3	24	5	79.2	DET	6	37	8	78.4
13 DET	3	13	3	76.9	T.B.	3	16	4	75.0	NSH	5	37	9	75.7
14 NYR	2	8	2	75.0	MTL	3	18	5	72.2	N.J.	9	45	11	75.6
15 NSH	3	21	6	71.4	NYR	2	19	6	68.4	NYR	4	27	8	70.4
16 T.B.	2	8	4	50.0	N.J.	5	23	8	65.2	T.B.	5	24	8	66.7
Total	**83**	**426**	**63**	**85.2**		**83**	**537**	**100**	**81.4**		**83**	**963**	**163**	**83.1**

SHORT HAND GOALS

	GOALS FOR			GOALS AGAINST		
Team	GP	GF	Team	GP	GA
BUF	18	5	N.J.	9	0
N.J.	9	4	MTL	6	0
EDM	24	3	DET	6	0
CGY	7	2	NSH	5	0
COL	9	2	EDM	24	1
CAR	25	2	COL	9	1
DAL	5	1	CGY	7	1
NSH	5	1	T.B.	5	1
PHI	6	1	DAL	5	1
OTT	10	1	CAR	25	2
ANA	16	1	BUF	18	2
NYR	4	0	S.J.	11	2
T.B.	5	0	PHI	6	2
MTL	6	0	OTT	10	3
DET	6	0	NYR	4	3
S.J.	11	0	ANA	16	4
Total		**23**	**Total**		**23**

TEAM PENALTIES

Abbreviations: GP – games played; **PEN** – total penalty minutes, including bench penalties; **BMI** – total bench minor minutes; **AVG** – average penalty minutes per game. 89 games played.

Team	GP	PEN	BMI	AVG
MTL	6	68	0	11.3
BUF	18	220	0	12.2
CAR	25	319	8	12.8
DAL	5	64	0	12.8
S.J.	11	144	2	13.1
DET	6	84	0	14.0
N.J.	9	140	2	15.6
EDM	24	385	10	16.0
OTT	10	164	2	16.4
ANA	16	267	4	16.7
NSH	5	88	0	17.6
NYR	4	71	2	17.8
CGY	7	129	4	18.4
COL	9	166	2	18.4
PHI	6	129	4	21.5
T.B.	5	125	2	25.0
Total	**83**	**2563**	**42**	
Two-Team average PIM/GP				**30.9**

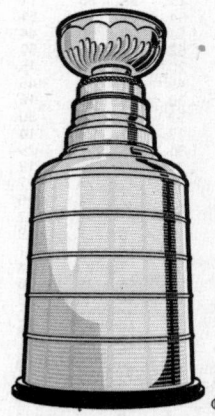

After scoring 18 goals in 80 regular-season games, Edmonton Oilers hometown hero Fernando Pisani led all playoff performers with 14 goals in 24 games.

Stanley Cup Record Book

History: The Stanley Cup, the oldest trophy competed for by professional athletes in North America, was donated by Frederick Arthur, Lord Stanley of Preston and son of the Earl of Derby, in 1893. Lord Stanley purchased the trophy for 10 guineas ($50 at that time) for presentation to the amateur hockey champions of Canada. Since 1906, when Canadian teams began to pay their players openly, the Stanley Cup has been the symbol of professional hockey supremacy. It has been competed for only by NHL teams since 1926-27 and has been under the exclusive control of the NHL since 1947.

Stanley Cup Standings

1918-2006
(ranked by Cup wins)

Teams	Cup Wins	Yrs.	Series	Wins	Losses	Games	Wins	Losses	Ties	Goals For	Goals Against	Winning %
Montreal[1,2]	23	75	138	86	51	667	393	266	8	2050	1673	.595
Toronto[3]	13	64	109	58	51	524	251	269	4	1350	1427	.483
Detroit	10	54	100	56	44	500	259	340	1	1402	1297	.519
Boston	5	62	104	47	57	512	242	264	6	1488	1516	.479
Edmonton	5	20	49	34	15	251	152	99	0	938	763	.606
NY Rangers	4	49	87	42	45	390	183	199	5	1095	1131	.476
NY Islanders	4	20	46	30	16	235	133	102	0	781	697	.566
Chicago	3	53	90	40	50	411	188	218	5	1176	1311	.464
New Jersey[4]	3	17	35	21	14	202	112	90	0	563	484	.554
Philadelphia	2	31	65	36	29	346	180	166	0	1046	1016	.520
Pittsburgh	2	21	39	20	19	208	109	99	0	644	641	.524
Colorado[5]	2	19	41	24	17	233	126	107	0	689	651	.541
Dallas[6]	1	27	52	26	26	282	141	141	0	840	856	.500
Calgary[7]	1	23	37	15	22	189	87	102	0	595	643	.460
Tampa Bay	1	4	8	5	3	45	24	21	0	108	121	.533
Carolina[8]	1	12	19	8	11	109	51	58	0	277	314	.469
St. Louis	0	34	57	23	34	303	138	165	0	857	943	.455
Buffalo	0	26	45	19	26	227	110	117	0	684	684	.485
Los Angeles	0	23	34	11	23	170	65	105	0	511	649	.382
Vancouver	0	20	30	10	20	155	66	89	0	452	526	.426
Washington	0	18	28	10	18	154	69	85	0	467	478	.448
Phoenix[9]	0	16	18	2	16	92	29	63	0	245	343	.315
San Jose	0	9	16	7	9	95	45	50	0	242	293	.474
Ottawa[10]	0	9	14	5	9	79	36	43	0	171	178	.456
Anaheim	0	4	10	6	4	52	28	24	0	122	123	.538
Florida	0	3	6	3	3	31	13	18	0	77	82	.419
Minnesota	0	1	3	2	1	18	8	10	0	43	43	.444
Nashville	0	2	2	0	2	11	3	8	0	19	29	.273
Atlanta	0	0	0	0	0	0	0	0	0	0	0	.000
Columbus	0	0	0	0	0	0	0	0	0	0	0	.000

1 Montreal also won the Stanley Cup in 1916.
2 1919 final incomplete due to influenza epidemic.
3 Toronto Blueshirts also won the Stanley Cup in 1914.
4 Includes totals of Colorado Rockies 1976-82.
5 Includes totals of Quebec Nordiques 1979-95.
6 Includes totals of Minnesota North Stars 1967-93.
7 Includes totals of Atlanta Flames 1972-80.
8 Includes totals of Hartford Whalers 1979-97.
9 Includes totals of Winnipeg Jets 1979-96.
10 Modern Ottawa Senators franchise only, 1992 to date.

Stanley Cup Winners Prior to Formation of NHL in 1917

Season	Champions	Manager	Coach
1916-17	Seattle Metropolitans	Pete Muldoon	Pete Muldoon
1915-16	Montreal Canadiens	George Kennedy	George Kennedy
1914-15	Vancouver Millionaires	Frank Patrick	Frank Patrick
1913-14	Toronto Blueshirts	Jack Marshall	Scotty Davidson*
1912-13**	Quebec Bulldogs	M.J. Quinn	Joe Malone*
1911-12	Quebec Bulldogs	M.J. Quinn	C. Nolan*
1910-11	Ottawa Senators		Percy LeSueur*
1909-10	Montreal Wanderers (Mar. 1910)	Dickie Boon	Pud Glass*
1909-10	Ottawa Senators (Jan. 1910)		Bruce Stuart*
1908-09	Ottawa Senators		Bruce Stuart*
1907-08	Montreal Wanderers		Cecil Blachford
1906-07	Montreal Wanderers (Mar. 1907)	Dickie Boon	Cecil Blachford
1906-07	Kenora Thistles (Jan./Mar. 1907)	F.A. Hudson	Tom Phillips*
1905-06	Montreal Wanderers (Mar. 1906)	Cecil Blachford*	
1905-06	Ottawa Silver Seven (Feb. 1906)		Alf Smith
1904-05	Ottawa Silver Seven		Alf Smith
1903-04	Ottawa Silver Seven		Alf Smith
1902-03	Ottawa Silver Seven (Mar. 1903)		Alf Smith
1902-03	Montreal A.A.A. (Feb. 1903)		C. McKerrow
1901-02	Montreal A.A.A. (Mar. 1902)		C. McKerrow
1901-02	Winnipeg Victorias (Jan. 1902)		
1900-01	Winnipeg Victorias		Dan Bain*
1899-1900	Montreal Shamrocks		Harry Trihey*
1898-99	Montreal Shamrocks (Mar. 1899)		Harry Trihey*
1898-99	Montreal Victorias (Feb. 1899)		Mike Grant*
1897-98	Montreal Victorias		Frank Richardson
1896-97	Montreal Victorias		Mike Grant*
1895-96	Montreal Victorias (Dec. 1896)		Mike Grant*
1895-96	Winnipeg Victorias (Feb. 1896)		Jack Armitage
1894-95	Montreal Victorias		Mike Grant*
1893-94	Montreal A.A.A.		
1892-93	Montreal A.A.A.		

* In the early years the teams were frequently run by the Captain. *Indicates Captain
** Victoria defeated Quebec in challenge series. No official recognition.

Stanley Cup Winners

Year	W-L-T in Finals	Winner	Coach	Finalist	Coach
2006	4-3	Carolina	Peter Laviolette	Edmonton	Craig MacTavish
2005	....	....		....	
2004	4-3	Tampa Bay	John Tortorella	Calgary	Darryl Sutter
2003	4-3	New Jersey	Pat Burns	Anaheim	Mike Babcock
2002	4-1	Detroit	Scotty Bowman	Carolina	Paul Maurice
2001	4-3	Colorado	Bob Hartley	New Jersey	Larry Robinson
2000	4-2	New Jersey	Larry Robinson	Dallas	Ken Hitchcock
1999	4-2	Dallas	Ken Hitchcock	Buffalo	Lindy Ruff
1998	4-0	Detroit	Scotty Bowman	Washington	Ron Wilson
1997	4-0	Detroit	Scotty Bowman	Philadelphia	Terry Murray
1996	4-0	Colorado	Marc Crawford	Florida	Doug MacLean
1995	4-0	New Jersey	Jacques Lemaire	Detroit	Scotty Bowman
1994	4-3	NY Rangers	Mike Keenan	Vancouver	Pat Quinn
1993	4-1	Montreal	Jacques Demers	Los Angeles	Barry Melrose
1992	4-0	Pittsburgh	Scotty Bowman	Chicago	Mike Keenan
1991	4-2	Pittsburgh	Bob Johnson	Minnesota	Bob Gainey
1990	4-1	Edmonton	John Muckler	Boston	Mike Milbury
1989	4-2	Calgary	Terry Crisp	Montreal	Pat Burns
1988	4-0	Edmonton	Glen Sather	Boston	Terry O'Reilly
1987	4-3	Edmonton	Glen Sather	Philadelphia	Mike Keenan
1986	4-1	Montreal	Jean Perron	Calgary	Bob Johnson
1985	4-1	Edmonton	Glen Sather	Philadelphia	Mike Keenan
1984	4-1	Edmonton	Glen Sather	NY Islanders	Al Arbour
1983	4-0	NY Islanders	Al Arbour	Edmonton	Glen Sather
1982	4-0	NY Islanders	Al Arbour	Vancouver	Roger Neilson
1981	4-1	NY Islanders	Al Arbour	Minnesota	Glen Sonmor
1980	4-2	NY Islanders	Al Arbour	Philadelphia	Pat Quinn
1979	4-1	Montreal	Scotty Bowman	NY Rangers	Fred Shero
1978	4-2	Montreal	Scotty Bowman	Boston	Don Cherry
1977	4-0	Montreal	Scotty Bowman	Boston	Don Cherry
1976	4-0	Montreal	Scotty Bowman	Philadelphia	Fred Shero
1975	4-2	Philadelphia	Fred Shero	Buffalo	Floyd Smith
1974	4-2	Philadelphia	Fred Shero	Boston	Bep Guidolin
1973	4-2	Montreal	Scotty Bowman	Chicago	Billy Reay
1972	4-2	Boston	Tom Johnson	NY Rangers	Emile Francis
1971	4-3	Montreal	Al MacNeil	Chicago	Billy Reay
1970	4-0	Boston	Harry Sinden	St. Louis	Scotty Bowman
1969	4-0	Montreal	Claude Ruel	St. Louis	Scotty Bowman
1968	4-0	Montreal	Toe Blake	St. Louis	Scotty Bowman
1967	4-2	Toronto	Punch Imlach	Montreal	Toe Blake
1966	4-2	Montreal	Toe Blake	Detroit	Sid Abel
1965	4-3	Montreal	Toe Blake	Chicago	Billy Reay
1964	4-3	Toronto	Punch Imlach	Detroit	Sid Abel
1963	4-1	Toronto	Punch Imlach	Detroit	Sid Abel
1962	4-2	Toronto	Punch Imlach	Chicago	Rudy Pilous
1961	4-2	Chicago	Rudy Pilous	Detroit	Sid Abel
1960	4-0	Montreal	Toe Blake	Toronto	Punch Imlach
1959	4-1	Montreal	Toe Blake	Toronto	Punch Imlach
1958	4-2	Montreal	Toe Blake	Boston	Milt Schmidt
1957	4-1	Montreal	Toe Blake	Boston	Milt Schmidt
1956	4-1	Montreal	Toe Blake	Detroit	Jimmy Skinner
1955	4-3	Detroit	Jimmy Skinner	Montreal	Dick Irvin
1954	4-3	Detroit	Tommy Ivan	Montreal	Dick Irvin
1953	4-1	Detroit	Dick Irvin	Boston	Lynn Patrick
1952	4-0	Detroit	Tommy Ivan	Montreal	Dick Irvin
1951	4-1	Toronto	Joe Primeau	Montreal	Dick Irvin
1950	4-3	Detroit	Tommy Ivan	NY Rangers	Lynn Patrick
1949	4-0	Toronto	Hap Day	Detroit	Tommy Ivan
1948	4-0	Toronto	Hap Day	Detroit	Tommy Ivan
1947	4-2	Toronto	Hap Day	Montreal	Dick Irvin
1946	4-1	Montreal	Dick Irvin	Boston	Dit Clapper
1945	4-3	Toronto	Hap Day	Detroit	Jack Adams
1944	4-0	Montreal	Dick Irvin	Chicago	Paul Thompson
1943	4-0	Detroit	Jack Adams	Boston	Art Ross
1942	4-3	Toronto	Hap Day	Detroit	Jack Adams
1941	4-0	Boston	Cooney Weiland	Detroit	Ebbie Goodfellow
1940	4-2	NY Rangers	Frank Boucher	Toronto	Dick Irvin
1939	4-1	Boston	Art Ross	Toronto	Dick Irvin
1938	3-1	Chicago	Bill Stewart	Toronto	Dick Irvin
1937	3-2	Detroit	Jack Adams	NY Rangers	Lester Patrick
1936	3-1	Detroit	Jack Adams	Toronto	Dick Irvin
1935	3-0	Mtl. Maroons	Tommy Gorman	Toronto	Dick Irvin
1934	3-1	Chicago	Tommy Gorman	Detroit	Herbie Lewis
1933	3-1	NY Rangers	Lester Patrick	Toronto	Lester Patrick
1932	3-0	Toronto	Dick Irvin	NY Rangers	Lester Patrick
1931	3-2	Montreal	Cecil Hart	Chicago	Dick Irvin
1930	2-0	Montreal	Cecil Hart	Boston	Art Ross
1929	2-0	Boston	Cy Denneny	NY Rangers	Lester Patrick
1928	3-2	NY Rangers	Lester Patrick	Mtl. Maroons	Eddie Gerard
1927	2-0-2	Ottawa	Dave Gill	Boston	Art Ross
The National Hockey League assumed control of Stanley Cup competition after 1926					
1926	3-1	Mtl. Maroons	Eddie Gerard	Victoria	Lester Patrick
1925	3-2	Victoria	Lester Patrick	Montreal	Leo Dandurand
1924	2-0	Montreal	Leo Dandurand	Cgy. Tigers	Eddie Oatman
1923	2-0	Ottawa	Pete Green	Edm. Eskimos	Ken McKenzie
1922	3-2	Tor. St. Pats	George O'Donoghue	Van. Millionaires	Lloyd Cook/Frank Patrick
1921	3-2	Ottawa	Pete Green	Van. Millionaires	Lloyd Cook/Frank Patrick
1920	3-2	Ottawa	Pete Green	Seattle	Pete Muldoon
1919	2-2-1	No decision - series between Montreal and Seattle cancelled due to influenza epidemic			
1918	3-2	Tor. Arenas	Dick Carroll	Van. Millionaires	Frank Patrick

Championship Trophies

PRINCE OF WALES TROPHY

Beginning with the 1993-94 season, the club which advances to the Stanley Cup Finals as the winner of the Eastern Conference Championship is presented with the Prince of Wales Trophy.

History: His Royal Highness, the Prince of Wales, donated the trophy to the National Hockey League in 1925. It was originally awarded to the winner of the first game played in Madison Square Garden, December 15, 1925 (Montreal Canadiens 3 at NY Americans 1). It was then awarded to the NHL playoff champion in 1925-26 and 1926-27. From 1927-28 through 1937-38, the award was presented to the regular-season champion of the American Division of the NHL. (The team finishing first in the Canadian Division received the O'Brien Trophy during these years.) From 1938-39, when the NHL reverted to one section, to 1966-67, it was presented to the team winning the NHL regular-season championship. With expansion in 1967-68, it again became a divisional trophy, awarded to the regular-season champions of the East Division through to the end of the 1973-74 season. Beginning in 1974-75, it was awarded to the regular-season winner of the conference bearing the name of the trophy. From 1981-82 to 1992-93 the trophy was presented to the playoff champion in the Wales Conference. Since 1993-94, the trophy has been presented to the playoff champion in the Eastern Conference.

2005-06 Winner: Carolina Hurricanes

The Carolina Hurricanes won their second Prince of Wales Trophy on June 1, 2006 after defeating the Buffalo Sabres 4-2 in game seven of the Eastern Conference Championship series. Before defeating the Sabres, the Hurricanes had series wins over the Montreal Canadiens and the New Jersey Devils.

PRINCE OF WALES TROPHY WINNERS

2005-06	Carolina	1976-77	Montreal	1948-49	Detroit
2003-04	Tampa Bay	1975-76	Montreal	1947-48	Toronto
2002-03	New Jersey	1974-75	Buffalo	1946-47	Montreal
2001-02	Carolina	1973-74	Boston	1945-46	Montreal
2000-01	New Jersey	1972-73	Montreal	1944-45	Montreal
99-2000	New Jersey	1971-72	Boston	1943-44	Montreal
1998-99	Buffalo	1970-71	Boston	1942-43	Detroit
1997-98	Washington	1969-70	Chicago	1941-42	NY Rangers
1996-97	Philadelphia	1968-69	Montreal	1940-41	Boston
1995-96	Florida	1967-68	Montreal	1939-40	Boston
1994-95	New Jersey	1966-67	Chicago	1938-39	Boston
1993-94	NY Rangers	1965-66	Montreal	1937-38	Boston
1992-93	Montreal	1964-65	Detroit	1936-37	Detroit
1991-92	Pittsburgh	1963-64	Montreal	1935-36	Detroit
1990-91	Pittsburgh	1962-63	Toronto	1934-35	Boston
1989-90	Boston	1961-62	Montreal	1933-34	Detroit
1988-89	Montreal	1960-61	Montreal	1932-33	Boston
1987-88	Boston	1959-60	Montreal	1931-32	NY Rangers
1986-87	Philadelphia	1958-59	Montreal	1930-31	Boston
1985-86	Montreal	1957-58	Montreal	1929-30	Boston
1984-85	Philadelphia	1956-57	Detroit	1928-29	Boston
1983-84	NY Islanders	1955-56	Montreal	1927-28	Boston
1982-83	NY Islanders	1954-55	Detroit	1926-27	Ottawa
1981-82	NY Islanders	1953-54	Detroit	1925-26	Mtl. Maroons
1980-81	Montreal	1952-53	Detroit	Dec. 15/25	Montreal
1979-80	Buffalo	1951-52	Detroit	1923-24	Montreal*
1978-79	Montreal	1950-51	Detroit		
1977-78	Montreal	1949-50	Detroit		

* Engraved by Montreal Canadiens in 1925-26.

Prince of Wales Trophy

Clarence S. Campbell Bowl

Stanley Cup

CLARENCE S. CAMPBELL BOWL

Beginning with the 1993-94 season, the club which advances to the Stanley Cup Finals as the winner of the Western Conference Championship is presented with the Clarence S. Campbell Bowl.

History: Presented by the member clubs in 1968 for perpetual competition by the National Hockey League in recognition of the services of Clarence S. Campbell, President of the NHL from 1946 to 1977. From 1967-68 through 1973-74, the trophy was awarded to the regular-season champions of the West Division. Beginning in 1974-75, it was awarded to the regular-season winner of the conference bearing the name of the trophy. From 1981-82 to 1992-93 the trophy was presented to the playoff champion in the Campbell Conference. Since 1993-94, the trophy has been presented to the playoff champion in the Western Conference. The trophy itself is a hallmark piece made of sterling silver and was crafted by a British silversmith in 1878.

2005-06 Winner: Edmonton Oilers

The Edmonton Oilers won their first Clarence Campbell Bowl since 1990 on May 27, 2006 after defeating the Mighty Ducks of Anaheim 2-1 in game five of the Western Conference Championship series. Before defeating the Mighty Ducks, the Oilers had series wins over the Detroit Red Wings and the San Jose Sharks.

CLARENCE S. CAMPBELL BOWL WINNERS

2005-06	Edmonton	1991-92	Chicago	1978-79	NY Islanders
2003-04	Calgary	1990-91	Minnesota	1977-78	NY Islanders
2002-03	Anaheim	1989-90	Edmonton	1976-77	Philadelphia
2001-02	Detroit	1988-89	Calgary	1975-76	Philadelphia
2000-01	Colorado	1987-88	Edmonton	1974-75	Philadelphia
99-2000	Dallas	1986-87	Edmonton	1973-74	Philadelphia
1998-99	Dallas	1985-86	Calgary	1972-73	Chicago
1997-98	Detroit	1984-85	Edmonton	1971-72	Chicago
1996-97	Detroit	1983-84	Edmonton	1970-71	Chicago
1995-96	Colorado	1982-83	Edmonton	1969-70	St. Louis
1994-95	Detroit	1981-82	Vancouver	1968-69	St. Louis
1993-94	Vancouver	1980-81	NY Islanders	1967-68	Philadelphia
1992-93	Los Angeles	1979-80	Philadelphia		

Stanley Cup Winners

Rosters and Final Series Scores

2005-06 — Carolina Hurricanes — Rod Brind'Amour (Captain), Craig Adams, Kevyn Adams, Anton Babchuk, Erik Cole, Mike Commodore, Matt Cullen, Martin Gerber, Bret Hedican, Andrew Hutchinson, Frantisek Kaberle, Chad LaRose, Andrew Ladd, Mark Recchi, Eric Staal, Cory Stillman, Oleg Tverdovsky, Josef Vasicek, Niclas Wallin, Aaron Ward, Cam Ward, Doug Weight, Glen Wesley, Ray Whitney, Justin Williams, Peter Karmanos Jr. (Owner), Thomas Thewes (Owner), Jim Rutherford (President and General Manager), Jason Karmanos (Vice President and Assistant General Manager), Mike Amendola (Chief Financial Officer), Peter Laviolette (Head Coach), Kevin McCarthy, Jeff Daniels (Assistant Coaches), Greg Stefan (Goaltending Coach), Chris Huffine (Video Coordinator), Skip Cunningham, Wally Tatomir, Bob Gorman (Equipment Managers), Peter Friesen (Head Athletic Therapist and Strength and Conditioning Coach), Chris Stewart (Associate Athletic Trainer), Brian Tatum (Team Services Manager), Kelly Kirwin (Event Coordinator for Hockey Operations), Marshall Johnston (Director of Professional Scouting), Claude Larose, Ron Smith (Professional Scouts), Sheldon Ferguson (Director of Amateur Scouting), Tony MacDonald, Albert Marshall, Martin Madden (Amateur Scouts), Tom Rowe (Head Coach, Lowell Lock Monsters), Mike Sundheim (Director of Media Relations), Kyle Hanlin (Manager of Media Relations).

Scores: June 5, at Carolina - Carolina 5, Edmonton 4; June 7, at Carolina - Carolina 5, Edmonton 0; June 10, at Edmonton - Edmonton 2, Carolina 1; June 12, at Edmonton - Carolina 2, Edmonton 1; June 14, at Carolina - Edmonton 4, Carolina 3; June 17, at Edmonton - Edmonton 4, Carolina 0; June 19, at Carolina - Carolina 3, Edmonton 1.

2003-04 — Tampa Bay Lightning — Dave Andreychuk (Captain), Dimitry Afanasenkov, Dan Boyle, Martin Cibak, Ben Clymer, Jassen Cullimore, Chris Dingman, Ruslan Fedotenko, John Grahame, Nikolai Khabibulin, Pavel Kubina, Vincent Lecavalier, Brad Lukowich, Fredrik Modin, Stan Neckar, Eric Perrin, Nolan Pratt, Brad Richards, Andre Roy, Martin St. Louis, Cory Sarich, Cory Stillman, Darryl Sydor, Tim Taylor, Bill Davidson (Owner), Tom Wilson (Governor), Ron Campbell (President), Jay Feaster (General Manager), Bill Barber (Director of Player Personnel), John Tortorella (Head Coach), Craig Ramsay (Assistant Coach), Jeff Reese (Assistant Coach), Eric Lawson (Strength and Conditioning Coach), Nigel Kinwan (Video Coach), Jack Goertzen (Head Scout), Rick Paterson (Chief Professional Scout), Mikael Andersson, Stephen Baker, Larry Bernard, Dirk Graham, Dave Heitz, Karri Kettunen, Yuri Yanchenkov, Darrell Young, Glen Zacharias (Scouts), Phil Thibodeau (Director of Team Services), Thomas Mulligan (Trainer), Adam Rambo (Assistant Trainer), Mike Griebel (Massage Therapist), Ray Thill (Equipment Manager), Dana Heinze, Jim Pickard (Assistant Equipment Managers).

Scores: May 25, at Tampa Bay - Calgary 4, Tampa Bay 1; May 27, at Tampa Bay - Tampa Bay 4, Calgary 1; May 29, at Calgary - Calgary 3, Tampa Bay 0; May 31, at Calgary - Tampa Bay 1, Calgary 0; June 3, at Tampa Bay - Calgary 3, Tampa Bay 2; June 5, at Calgary - Tampa Bay 3, Calgary 2; June 7, at Tampa Bay - Tampa Bay 2, Calgary 1.

2002-03 — New Jersey Devils — Scott Stevens (Captain), Tommy Albelin, Jiri Bicek, Martin Brodeur, Sergei Brylin, Ken Daneyko, Patrik Elias, Jeff Friesen, Brian Gionta, Scott Gomez, Jamie Langenbrunner, John Madden, Grant Marshall, Jim McKenzie, Scott Niedermayer, Joe Nieuwendyk, Jay Pandolfo, Brian Rafalski, Pascal Rheaume, Mike Rupp, Corey Schwab, Richard Smehlik, Turner Stevenson, Oleg Tverdovsky, Colin White, Lou Lamoriello (CEO/President/General Manager), Pat Burns (Head Coach), Bob Carpenter (Assistant Coach), John MacLean (Assistant Coach), Jacques Caron (Goaltending Coach), Larry Robinson (Special Assignment Coach), David Conte (Director, Scouting), Claude Carrier (Assistant Director, Scouting), Chris Lamoriello (Scout/Albany GM), Milt Fisher (Scout), Dan Labraaten (Scout), Marcel Pronovost (Scout), Bob Hoffmeyer (Pro Scout), Jan Ludvig (Pro Scout), Dr. Barry Fisher (Orthopedist), Vladimir Bure (Fitness Consultant), Taran Singleton (Hockey Operations), Bill Murray (Medical Trainer), Michael Vasalani (Strength/Conditioning Coordinator), Rich Matthews (Equipment Manager), Juergen Merz (Massage Therapist), Alex Abasto (Assistant Equipment Manager).

Scores: May 27, at New Jersey - New Jersey 3, Anaheim 0; May 29, at New Jersey - New Jersey 3, Anaheim 0; May 31, at Anaheim - Anaheim 3, New Jersey 2; June 2, at Anaheim - Anaheim 1, New Jersey 0; June 5, at New Jersey - New Jersey 6, Anaheim 3; June 7, at Anaheim - Anaheim 5, New Jersey 2; June 9, at New Jersey - New Jersey 3, Anaheim 0.

2001-02 — Detroit Red Wings — Steve Yzerman (Captain), Chris Chelios, Mathieu Dandenault, Pavel Datsyuk, Boyd Devereaux, Kris Draper, Steve Duchesne, Sergei Fedorov, Jiri Fischer, Dominik Hasek, Tomas Holmstrom, Brett Hull, Igor Larionov, Manny Legace, Nicklas Lidstrom, Kirk Maltby, Darren McCarty, Fredrik Olausson, Luc Robitaille, Brendan Shanahan, Jiri Slegr, Jason Williams, Michael Ilitch (Owner/Governor) Marian Ilitch (Owner/Secretary Treasurer), Ronald Ilitch, Michael Ilitch Jr., Lisa Ilitch Murray, Atanas Ilitch, Carole Ilitch Trepeck, Jim Devellano (Senior Vice President), Christopher Ilitch (Vice President), Denise Ilitch (Alternate Governor), Ken Holland (General Manager), Jim Nill (Assistant General Manager), Scotty Bowman (Head Coach), Dave Lewis (Associate Coach), Barry Smith (Associate Coach), Jim Berard (Goaltending Consultant), Joe Kocur (Video Coordinator), John Wharton (Athletic Trainer), Paul Boyer (Equipment Manager), Piet Van Zant (Assistant Athletic Trainer), Tim Abbott (Assistant Equipment Manager), Sergei Tchekmarev (Masseur), Dan Belisle (Pro Scout), Mark Howe (Pro Scout), Bob McCammon (Pro Scout), Hakan Andersson (Director of European Scouting), Mark Leach (Scout), Bruce Haralson (Scout), Joe McDonnell (Scout), Glenn Merkosky (Scout).

Scores: June 4, at Detroit - Carolina 3, Detroit 2; June 6, at Detroit - Detroit 3, Carolina 1; June 8, at Carolina - Detroit 3, Carolina 2; June 10, at Carolina - Detroit 3, Carolina 0; June 13, at Detroit - Detroit 3, Carolina 1.

2000-01 — Colorado Avalanche — Joe Sakic (Captain), David Aebischer, Rob Blake, Raymond Bourque, Greg de Vries, Chris Dingman, Chris Drury, Adam Foote, Peter Forsberg, Milan Hejduk, Dan Hinote, Jon Klemm, Eric Messier, Bryan Muir, Ville Nieminen, Scott Parker, Shjon Podein, Nolan Pratt, Dave Reid, Steve Reinprecht, Patrick Roy, Martin Skoula, Alex Tanguay, Stephane Yelle, E. Stanley Kroenke (Owner/Governor), Pierre Lacroix (President and General Manager), Bob Hartley (Head Coach), Jacques Cloutier (Assistant Coach), Bryan Trottier (Assistant Coach), Paul Fixter (Video Coach), Francois Giguere (Vice President of Hockey Operations), Brian MacDonald (Assistant General Manager), Michel Goulet (Vice President of Player Personnel), Jean Martineau (Vice President of Communications/Team Services), Pat Karns (Head Athletic Trainer), Matthew Sokolowski (Assistant Athletic Trainer), Wayne Flemming (Equipment Manager), Mark Miller (Equipment Manager), Dave Randolph (Assistant Equipment Manager), Paul Goldberg (Strength and Conditioning Coach), Gregorio Pradera (Massage Therapist), Brad Smith (Pro Scout), Jim Hammett (Chief Scout), Garth Joy, Steve Lyons, Joni Lehto, Orval Tessier (Scouts), Charlotte Grahame (Director of Hockey Operations).

Scores: May 26, at Colorado - Colorado 5, New Jersey 0; May 29, at Colorado - New Jersey 2, Colorado 1; May 31, at New Jersey - Colorado 3, New Jersey 1; June 2, at New Jersey - New Jersey 3, Colorado 2; June 4, at Colorado - New Jersey 4, Colorado 1; June 7, at New Jersey - Colorado 4, New Jersey 0; June 9, at Colorado - Colorado 3, New Jersey 1.

1999-2000 — New Jersey Devils — Scott Stevens (Captain), Jason Arnott, Brad Bombardir, Martin Brodeur, Steve Brule, Sergei Brylin, Ken Daneyko, Patrik Elias, Scott Gomez, Bobby Holik, Steve Kelly, Claude Lemieux, John Madden, Vladimir Malakhov, Randy McKay, Alexander Mogilny, Sergei Nemchinov, Scott Niedermayer, Krzysztof Oliwa, Jay Pandolfo, Brian Rafalski, Ken Sutton, Petr Sykora, Chris Terreri, Colin White, Dr. John J. McMullen (Owner/Chairman), Peter S. McMullen (Owner), Lou Lamoriello (President/General Manager), Larry Robinson (Head Coach), Viacheslav Fetisov (Assistant Coach), Bob Carpenter (Assistant Coach), Jacques Caron (Goaltending Coach), John Cunniff (AHL Coach), David Conte (Director of Scouting), Milt Fisher (Scout), Claude Carrier (Assistant Director of Scouting), Dan Labraaten (Scout), Marcel Pronovost (Scout), Bob Hoffmeyer (Pro Scout), Dr. Barry Fisher (Orthopedist), Dennis Gendron (AHL Assistant Coach), Robbie Ftorek (Coach), Vladimir Bure (Consultant), Taran Singleton (Hockey Operations), Marie Carnevale (Hockey Operations), Callie Smith (Hockey Operations), Bill Murray (Medical Trainer), Michael Vasalani (Strength/Conditioning Coordinator), Dana McGuane (Equipment Manager), Juergen Merz (Massage Therapist), Harry Bricker (Assistant Equipment Manager), Lou Centanni (Assistant Equipment Manager).

Scores: May 30, at New Jersey - New Jersey 7, Dallas 3; June 1, at New Jersey - Dallas 2, New Jersey 1; June 3, at Dallas - New Jersey 2, Dallas 1; June 5, at Dallas - New Jersey 3, Dallas 1; June 8, at New Jersey - Dallas 1 - New Jersey 0; at Dallas, New Jersey 2 - Dallas 1.

1998-99 — Dallas Stars — Derian Hatcher (Captain), Ed Belfour, Guy Carbonneau, Shawn Chambers, Benoit Hogue, Tony Hrkac, Brett Hull, Mike Keane, Jamie Langenbrunner, Jere Lehtinen, Craig Ludwig, Grant Marshall, Richard Matvichuk, Mike Modano, Joe Nieuwendyk, Derek Plante, Dave Reid, Jon Sim, Brian Skrudland, Blake Sloan, Darryl Sydor, Roman Turek, Pat Verbeek, Sergei Zubov, Thomas Hicks (Chairman of the Board and Owner), Jim Lites (President), Bob Gainey (Vice President, Hockey Operations and General Manager), Doug Armstrong (Assistant General Manager), Craig Button (Director of Player Personnel), Ken Hitchcock (Head Coach), Doug Jarvis (Assistant Coach), Rick Wilson (Assistant Coach), Rick McLaughlin (Vice President and Chief Financial Officer), Jeff Cogen (Vice President, Marketing and Promotion), Bill Strong (Vice President, Marketing and Broadcasting), Tim Bernhardt (Director of Amateur Scouting), Doug Overton (Director of Pro Scouting), Bob Gernander (Chief Scout), Stu MacGregor (Western Scout), Dave Suprenant (Medical Trainer), Dave Smith (Equipment Manager), Rich Matthews (Equipment Manager), J.J. McQueen (Strength and Conditioning Coach), Rick St. Croix (Goaltending Consultant), Dan Stuchal (Director of Team Services), Larry Kelly (Director of Public Relations).

Scores: June 8, at Dallas - Buffalo 3, Dallas 2; June 10, at Dallas - Dallas 4, Buffalo 2; June 12, at Buffalo - Dallas 2, Buffalo 1; June 15, at Buffalo - Buffalo 2, Dallas 1; June 17, at Dallas - Dallas 2, Buffalo 0; June 19, at Buffalo - Dallas 2, Buffalo 1.

1997-98 — Detroit Red Wings — Steve Yzerman (Captain), Doug Brown, Mathieu Dandenault, Kris Draper, Anders Eriksson, Sergei Fedorov, Viacheslav Fetisov, Brent Gilchrist, Kevin Hodson, Tomas Holmstrom, Mike Knuble, Joe Kocur, Vladimir Konstantinov, Vyacheslav Kozlov, Martin Lapointe, Igor Larionov, Nicklas Lidstrom, Jamie Macoun, Kirk Maltby, Darren McCarty, Dmitri Mironov, Larry Murphy, Chris Osgood, Bob Rouse, Brendan Shanahan, Aaron Ward, Mike Ilitch, (Owner/Chairman), Marian Ilitch (Owner), Atanas Ilitch (Vice President), Christopher Ilitch (Vice President), Denise Ilitch, Ronald Ilitch, Michael Ilitch Jr., Lisa Ilitch Murray, Carole Ilitch Trepeck, Jim Devellano (Senior Vice President), Scotty Bowman (Head Coach), Ken Holland (General Manager), Don Waddell (Assistant General Manager), Barry Smith (Associate Coach), Dave Lewis (Associate Coach), Jim Bedard (Goaltending Consultant), Jim Nill (Director of Player Development), Dan Belisle (Pro Scout), Mark Howe (Pro Scout), Hakan Andersson (Director of European Scouting), Mark Leach (USA Scout), Moe McDonnell (Eastern Scout), Bruce Haralson (Western Scout), John Wharton (Athletic Trainer), Paul Boyer (Equipment Manager) Tim Abbott (Assistant Equipment Manager), Bob Huddleston (Masseur), Sergei Mnatsakanov (Masseur), Wally Crossman (Dressing Room Assistant).

Scores: June 9, at Detroit — Detroit 2, Washington 1; June 11, at Detroit — Detroit 5, Washington 4; June 13, at Washington — Detroit 2, Washington 1; June 16, at Washington — Detroit 4, Washington 1.

1996-97 — Detroit Red Wings — Steve Yzerman (Captain), Doug Brown, Mathieu Dandenault, Kris Draper, Sergei Fedorov, Viacheslav Fetisov, Kevin Hodson, Tomas Holmstrom, Joe Kocur, Vladimir Konstantinov, Vyacheslav Kozlov, Martin Lapointe, Igor Larionov, Nicklas Lidstrom, Kirk Maltby, Darren McCarty, Larry Murphy, Chris Osgood, Jamie Pushor, Bob Rouse, Tomas Sandstrom, Brendan Shanahan, Tim Taylor, Mike Vernon, Aaron Ward, Mike Ilitch (Owner/Chairman), Marian Ilitch (Owner), Atanas Ilitch (Vice President), Christopher Ilitch (Vice President), Denise Ilitch Lites, Ronald Ilitch, Michael Ilitch, Jr., Lisa Ilitch Murray, Carole Ilitch Trepeck, Jim Devellano (Senior Vice President), Scotty Bowman (Head Coach/Director of Player Personnel), Ken Holland (Assistant General Manager), Barry Smith (Associate Coach), Dave Lewis (Associate Coach), Mike Krushelnyski (Assistant Coach). Jim Nill (Director of Player Development), Dan Belisle (Pro Scout), Mark Howe (Pro Scout), Hakan Andersson (Director of European Scouting), John Wharton (Athletic Trainer), Paul Boyer (Equipment Manager) Tim Abbott (Assistant Equipment Manager), Sergei Mnatsakanov (Masseur).

Scores: May 31, at Philadelphia — Detroit 4, Philadelphia 2; June 3, at Philadelphia — Detroit 4, Philadelphia 2; June 5, at Detroit — Detroit 6, Philadelphia 1; June 7, at Detroit — Detroit 2, Philadelphia 1.

1995-96 — Colorado Avalanche — Joe Sakic (Captain), Rene Corbet, Adam Deadmarsh, Stephane Fiset, Adam Foote, Peter Forsberg, Alexei Gusarov, Dave Hannan, Valeri Kamensky, Mike Keane, Jon Klemm, Uwe Krupp, Sylvain Lefebvre, Claude Lemieux, Curtis Leschyshyn, Troy Murray, Sandis Ozolinsh, Mike Ricci, Patrick Roy, Warren Rychel, Chris Simon, Craig Wolanin, Stephane Yelle, Scott Young, Charlie Lyons (Chairman, CEO), Pierre Lacroix (Exec. V.P., G.M.), Marc Crawford (Head Coach), Joel Quenneville (Assistant Coach), Jacques Cloutier (Assistant Coach), Francois Giguere (Assistant General Manager), Michel Goulet (Director of Player Personnel), Dave Draper (Chief Scout), Jean Martineau (Director of Public Relations), Pat Karns (Trainer), Matthew Sokolowski (Assistant Trainer), Rob McLean (Equipment Manager), Mike Kramer (Assistant Equipment Manager), Brock Gibbins (Assistant Equipment Manager), Skip Allen (Strength and Conditioning Coach), Paul Fixter (Video Coordinator), Leo Vyssokov (Massage Therapist).

Scores: June 4, at Colorado — Colorado 3, Florida 1; June 6, at Colorado — Colorado 8, Florida 1; June 8, at Florida — Colorado 3, Florida 2; June 10, at Florida — Colorado 1, Florida 0.

1994-95 — New Jersey Devils — Scott Stevens (Captain), Tommy Albelin, Martin Brodeur, Neal Broten, Sergei Brylin, Bob Carpenter, Shawn Chambers, Tom Chorske, Danton Cole, Ken Daneyko, Kevin Dean, Jim Dowd, Bruce Driver (Alternate Captain), Bill Guerin, Bobby Holik, Claude Lemieux, John MacLean (Alternate Captain), Chris McAlpine, Randy McKay, Scott Niedermayer, Mike Peluso, Stephane Richer, Brian Rolston, Chris Terreri, Valeri Zelepukin, Dr. John J. McMullen (Owner/Chairman), Peter S. McMullen (Owner), Lou Lamoriello (President/General Manager), Jacques Lemaire (Head Coach), Jacques Caron (Goaltender Coach), Dennis Gendron (Assistant Coach), Larry Robinson (Assistant Coach), Robbie Ftorek (AHL Coach), Alex Abasto (Assistant Equipment Manager), Bob Huddleston (Massage Therapist), David Nichols (Equipment Manager), Ted Schuch (Medical Trainer), Mike Vasalani (Strength Coach), David Conte (Director of Scouting) Claude Carrier (Scout), Milt Fisher (Scout), Dan Labraaten (Scout), Marcel Pronovost (Scout).

Scores: June 17, at Detroit — New Jersey 2, Detroit 1; June 20, at Detroit — New Jersey 4, Detroit 2; June 22, at New Jersey — New Jersey 5, Detroit 2; June 24, at New Jersey — New Jersey 5, Detroit 2.

1993-94 — New York Rangers — Mark Messier (Captain), Brian Leetch, Kevin Lowe, Adam Graves, Steve Larmer, Glenn Anderson, Jeff Beukeboom, Greg Gilbert, Mike Hartman, Glenn Healy, Mike Hudson, Alexander Karpovtsev, Joe Kocur, Alexei Kovalev, Nick Kypreos, Doug Lidster, Stephane Matteau, Craig MacTavish, Sergei Nemchinov, Brian Noonan, Ed Olczyk, Mike Richter, Esa Tikkanen, Jay Wells, Sergei Zubov, Neil Smith (President, General Manager and Governor), Robert Gutkowski, Stanley Jaffe, Kenneth Munoz (Governors), Larry Pleau (Assistant General Manager), Mike Keenan (Head Coach), Colin Campbell (Associate Coach), Dick Todd (Assistant Coach), Matthew Loughren (Manager, Team Operations), Barry Watkins (Director, Communications), Christer Rockstrom, Tony Feltrin, Martin Madden, Herb Hammond, Darwin Bennett (Scouts), Dave Smith, Joe Murphy, Mike Folga, Bruce Lifrieri (Trainers).

Scores: May 31, at New York — Vancouver 3, NY Rangers 2; June 2, at New York — NY Rangers 3, Vancouver 1; June 4, at Vancouver — NY Rangers 5, Vancouver 1; June 7, at Vancouver — NY Rangers 4, Vancouver 2; June 9, at New York — Vancouver 6, at NY Rangers 3; June 11, at Vancouver — Vancouver 4, NY Rangers 1; June 14, at New York — NY Rangers 3, Vancouver 2.

1992-93 — Montreal Canadiens — Guy Carbonneau (Captain), Patrick Roy, Mike Keane, Eric Desjardins, Stephan Lebeau, Mathieu Schneider, J-J Daigneault, Denis Savard, Lyle Odelein, Todd Ewen, Kirk Muller, John LeClair, Gilbert Dionne, Benoit Brunet, Patrice Brisebois, Paul DiPietro, Andre Racicot, Donald Dufresne, Mario Roberge, Sean Hill, Ed Ronan, Kevin Haller, Vincent Damphousse, Brian Bellows, Gary Leeman, Rob Ramage, Ronald Corey (President), Serge Savard (Managing Director & Vice-President Hockey), Jacques Demers (Head Coach), Jacques Laperriere (Assistant Coach), Charles Thiffault (Assistant Coach), Francois Allaire (Goaltending Instructor), Jean Béliveau (Senior Vice-President, Corporate Affairs), Fred Steer (Vice-President, Finance & Adminstration), Aldo Giampaolo (Vice-President, Operations), Bernard Brisset (Vice-President, Marketing & Communications), André Boudrias (Assistant to the Managing Director & Director of Scouting), Jacques Lemaire (Assistant to the Managing Director), Gaeten Lefebvre (Athletic Trainer), John Shipman (Assistant to the Athletic Trainer), Eddy Palchak (Equipment Manager), Pierre Gervais (Assistant to the Equipment Manager), Robert Boulanger (Assistant to the Equipment Manager), Pierre Ouellete (Assistant to the Equipment Manager).
Scores: June 1, at Montreal — Los Angeles 4, Montreal 1; June 2, at Montreal — Montreal 3, Los Angeles 2; June 5, at Los Angeles — Montreal 4, Los Angeles 3; June 7, at Los Angeles — Montreal 3, Los Angeles 2; June 9, at Montreal — Montreal 4, Los Angeles 1.

1991-92 — Pittsburgh Penguins — Mario Lemieux (Captain), Ron Francis, Bryan Trottier, Kevin Stevens, Bob Errey, Phil Bourque, Troy Loney, Rick Tocchet, Joe Mullen, Jaromir Jagr, Jiri Hrdina, Shawn McEachern, Ulf Samuelsson, Kjell Samuelsson, Larry Murphy, Gordie Roberts, Jim Paek, Paul Stanton, Tom Barrasso, Ken Wregget, Jay Caufield, Jamie Leach, Wendell Young, Grant Jennings, Peter Taglianetti, Jock Callander, Dave Michayluk, Mike Needham, Jeff Chychrun, Ken Priestlay, Jeff Daniels, Howard Baldwin (Owner and President), Morris Belzberg (Owner), Thomas Ruta (Owner), Donn Patton (Executive Vice President and Chief Financial Officer), Paul Martha (Executive Vice President and General Counsel), Craig Patrick (Executive Vice President and General Manager), Bob Johnson (Coach), Scotty Bowman (Director of Player Development and Coach), Barry Smith, Rick Kehoe, Pierre McGuire, Gilles Meloche, Rick Paterson (Assistant Coaches), Steve Latin (Equipment Manager), Skip Thayer (Trainer), John Welday (Strength and Conditioning Coach), Greg Malone, Les Binkley, Charlie Hodge, John Gill, Ralph Cox (Scouts).
Scores: May 26, at Pittsburgh — Pittsburgh 5, Chicago 4; May 28, at Pittsburgh — Pittsburgh 3, Chicago 1; May 30, at Chicago — Pittsburgh 1, Chicago 0; June 1, at Chicago — Pittsburgh 6, Chicago 5.

1990-91 — Pittsburgh Penguins — Mario Lemieux (Captain), Paul Coffey, Randy Hillier, Bob Errey, Tom Barrasso, Phil Bourque, Jay Caufield, Ron Francis, Randy Gilhen, Jiri Hrdina, Jaromir Jagr, Grant Jennings, Troy Loney, Joe Mullen, Larry Murphy, Jim Paek, Frank Pietrangelo, Barry Pederson, Mark Recchi, Gordie Roberts, Ulf Samuelsson, Paul Stanton, Kevin Stevens, Peter Taglianetti, Bryan Trottier, Scott Young, Wendell Young, Edward J. DeBartolo, Sr. (Owner), Marie D. DeBartolo York (President), Paul Martha (Vice-President & General Counsel), Craig Patrick (General Manager), Scotty Bowman (Director of Player Development & Recruitment), Bob Johnson (Coach), Rick Kehoe (Assistant Coach), Gilles Meloche (Goaltending Coach & Scout), Rick Paterson (Assistant Coach), Barry Smith (Assistant Coach), Steve Latin (Equipment Manager), Skip Thayer (Trainer), John Welday (Strength & Conditioning Coach), Greg Malone (Scout).
Scores: May 15, at Pittsburgh — Minnesota 5, Pittsburgh 4; May 17, at Pittsburgh — Pittsburgh 4, Minnesota 1; May 19, at Minnesota — Minnesota 3, Pittsburgh 1; May 21, at Minnesota — Pittsburgh 5, Minnesota 3; May 23, at Pittsburgh — Pittsburgh 6, Minnesota 4; May 25, at Minnesota — Pittsburgh 8, Minnesota 0.

1989-90 — Edmonton Oilers — Kevin Lowe, Steve Smith, Jeff Beukeboom, Mark Lamb, Joe Murphy, Glenn Anderson, Mark Messier (Captain), Adam Graves, Craig MacTavish, Kelly Buchberger, Jari Kurri, Craig Simpson, Martin Gelinas, Randy Gregg, Charlie Huddy, Geoff Smith, Reijo Ruotsalainen, Craig Muni, Bill Ranford, Dave Brown, Pokey Reddick, Petr Klima, Esa Tikkanen, Grant Fuhr, Peter Pocklington (Owner), Glen Sather (President/General Manager), John Muckler (Coach), Ted Green (Co-Coach), Ron Low (Ass't Coach), Bruce MacGregor (Ass't General Manager), Barry Fraser (Director of Player Personnel), John Blackwell (Director of Operations, AHL), Ace Bailey, Ed Chadwick, Lorne Davis, Harry Howell, Matti Vaisanen and Albert Reeves (Scouts), Bill Tuele (Director of Public Relations), Werner Baum (Controller), Dr. Gordon Cameron (Medical Chief of Staff), Dr. David Reid (Team Physician), Barrie Stafford (Athletic Trainer), Ken Lowe (Athletic Therapist), Stuart Poirier (Massage Therapist), Lyle Kulchisky (Ass't Trainer).
Scores: May 15, at Boston — Edmonton 3, Boston 2; May 18, at Boston — Edmonton 7, Boston 2; May 20, at Edmonton — Boston 2, Edmonton 1; May 22, at Edmonton — Edmonton 5, Boston 1; May 24, at Boston — Edmonton 4, Boston 1.

1988-89 — Calgary Flames — Mike Vernon, Rick Wamsley, Al MacInnis, Brad McCrimmon, Dana Murzyn, Ric Nattress, Joe Mullen, Lanny McDonald (Co-captain), Gary Roberts, Colin Patterson, Hakan Loob, Theoren Fleury, Jiri Hrdina, Tim Hunter (Ass't. captain), Gary Suter, Mark Hunter, Jim Peplinski (Co-captain), Joe Nieuwendyk, Brian MacLellan, Joel Otto, Jamie Macoun, Doug Gilmour, Rob Ramage. Norman Green, Harley Hotchkiss, Norman Kwong, Sonia Scurfield, B.J. Seaman, D.K. Seaman (Owners), Cliff Fletcher (President and General Manager), Al MacNeil (Ass't General Manager), Al Coates (Ass't to the President), Terry Crisp (Head Coach), Doug Risebrough, Tom Watt (Ass't Coaches), Glenn Hall (Goaltending Consultant), Jim Murray (Trainer), Bob Stewart (Equipment Manager), Al Murray (Ass't Trainer).
Scores: May 14, at Calgary — Calgary 3, Montreal 2; May 17, at Calgary— Montreal 4, Calgary 2; May 19, at Montreal — Montreal 4, Calgary 3; May 21, at Montreal — Calgary 4, Montreal 2; May 23, at Calgary — Calgary 3, Montreal 2; May 25, at Montreal — Calgary 4, Montreal 2.

1987-88 — Edmonton Oilers — Keith Acton, Glenn Anderson, Jeff Beukeboom, Geoff Courtnall, Grant Fuhr, Randy Gregg, Wayne Gretzky (Captain), Dave Hannan, Charlie Huddy, Mike Krushelnyski, Jari Kurri, Normand Lacombe, Kevin Lowe, Craig MacTavish, Kevin McClelland, Marty McSorley, Mark Messier, Craig Muni, Bill Ranford, Craig Simpson, Steve Smith, Esa Tikkanen, Peter Pocklington (Owner), Glen Sather (General Manager/Coach), John Muckler (Co-Coach), Ted Green (Ass't Coach), Bruce MacGregor (Ass't General Manager), Barry Fraser (Director of Player Personnel), Bill Tuele (Director of Public Relations), Dr. Gordon Cameron (Team Physician), Peter Millar (Athletic Therapist), Barrie Stafford (Trainer), Juergen Mers (Massage Therapist), Lyle Kulchisky (Ass't Trainer).
Scores: May 18, at Edmonton — Edmonton 2, Boston 1; May 20, at Edmonton — Edmonton 4, Boston 2; May 22, at Boston — Edmonton 6, Boston 3; May 24, at Boston — Boston 3, Edmonton 3 (suspended due to power failure); May 26, at Edmonton — Edmonton 6, Boston 3.

1986-87 — Edmonton Oilers — Glenn Anderson, Jeff Beukeboom, Kelly Buchberger, Paul Coffey, Grant Fuhr, Randy Gregg, Wayne Gretzky (Captain), Charlie Huddy, Dave Hunter, Mike Krushelnyski, Jari Kurri, Moe Lemay, Kevin Lowe, Craig MacTavish, Kevin McClelland, Marty McSorley, Mark Messier, Andy Moog, Craig Muni, Kent Nilsson, Jaroslav Pouzar, Reijo Ruotsalainen, Steve Smith, Esa Tikkanen, Peter Pocklington (Owner), Glen Sather (General Manager/Coach), John Muckler (Co-Coach), Ted Green (Ass't. Coach), Ron Low (Ass't. Coach), Bruce MacGregor (Ass't. General Manager), Barry Fraser (Director of Player Personnel), Peter Millar (Athletic Therapist), Barrie Stafford (Trainer), Lyle Kulchisky (Ass't Trainer).
Scores: May 17, at Edmonton — Edmonton 4, Philadelphia 2; May 20, at Edmonton — Edmonton 3, Philadelphia 2; May 22, at Philadelphia — Philadelphia 5, Edmonton 3; May 24, at Philadelphia — Edmonton 4, Philadelphia 1; May 26, at Edmonton — Philadelphia 4, Edmonton 3; May 28, at Philadelphia — Philadelphia 3, Edmonton 2; May 31, at Edmonton — Edmonton 3, Philadelphia 1.

1985-86 — Montreal Canadiens — Bob Gainey (Captain), Doug Soetaert, Patrick Roy, Rick Green, David Maley, Ryan Walter, Serge Boisvert, Mario Tremblay, Bobby Smith, Craig Ludwig, Tom Kurvers, Kjell Dahlin, Larry Robinson, Guy Carbonneau, Chris Chelios, Petr Svoboda, Mats Naslund, Lucien DeBlois, Steve Rooney, Gaston Gingras, Mike Lalor, Chris Nilan, John Kordic, Claude Lemieux, Mike McPhee, Brian Skrudland, Stephane Richer, Ronald Corey (President), Serge Savard (General Manager), Jean Perron (Coach), Jacques Laperrière (Ass't. Coach), Jean Béliveau (Vice President), Francois-Xavier Seigneur (Vice President), Fred Steer (Vice President), Jacques Lemaire (Ass't. General Manager), André Boudrias (Ass't. General Manager), Claude Ruel (Scouting), Yves Belanger (Athletic Therapist), Gaetan Lefebvre (Ass't. Athletic Therapist), Eddy Palchak (Trainer), Sylvain Toupin (Ass't. Trainer).
Scores: May 16, at Calgary — Calgary 5, Montreal 2; May 18, at Calgary — Montreal 3, Calgary 2; May 20, at Montreal — Montreal 5, Calgary 3; May 22, at Montreal — Montreal 1, Calgary 0; May 24, at Calgary — Montreal 4, Calgary 3.

1984-85 — Edmonton Oilers — Glenn Anderson, Billy Carroll, Paul Coffey, Lee Fogolin, Grant Fuhr, Randy Gregg, Wayne Gretzky (Captain), Charlie Huddy, Pat Hughes, Dave Hunter, Don Jackson, Mike Krushelnyski, Jari Kurri, Willy Lindstrom, Kevin Lowe, Dave Lumley, Kevin McClelland, Larry Melnyk, Mark Messier, Andy Moog, Mark Napier, Jaroslav Pouzar, Dave Semenko, Esa Tikkanen, Peter Pocklington (Owner), Glen Sather (General Manager/Coach), John Muckler (Ass't. Coach), Ted Green (Ass't. Coach), Bruce MacGregor (Ass't. General Manager), Barry Fraser (Director of Player Personnel/Chief Scout), Peter Millar (Athletic Therapist), Barrie Stafford, Lyle Kulchisky (Trainers)
Scores: May 21, at Philadelphia — Philadelphia 4, Edmonton 1; May 23, at Philadelphia — Edmonton 3, Philadelphia 1; May 25, at Edmonton — Edmonton 4, Philadelphia 3; May 28, at Edmonton — Edmonton 5, Philadelphia 3; May 30, at Edmonton — Edmonton 8, Philadelphia 3.

1983-84 — Edmonton Oilers — Glenn Anderson, Paul Coffey, Pat Conacher, Lee Fogolin, Grant Fuhr, Randy Gregg, Wayne Gretzky (Captain), Charlie Huddy, Pat Hughes, Dave Hunter, Don Jackson, Jari Kurri, Willy Lindstrom, Ken Linseman, Kevin Lowe, Dave Lumley, Kevin McClelland, Mark Messier, Andy Moog, Jaroslav Pouzar, Dave Semenko, Peter Pocklington (Owner), Glen Sather (General Manager/Coach), John Muckler (Ass't. Coach), Ted Green (Ass't. Coach), Bruce MacGregor (Ass't. General Manager), Barry Fraser (Director of Player Personnel/Chief Scout), Peter Millar (Athletic Therapist), Barrie Stafford (Trainer)
Scores: May 10, at New York — Edmonton 1, NY Islanders 0; May 12, at New York — NY Islanders 6, Edmonton 1; May 15, at Edmonton — Edmonton 7, NY Islanders 2; May 17, at Edmonton — Edmonton 7, NY Islanders 2; May 19, at Edmonton — Edmonton 5, NY Islanders 2.

1982-83 — New York Islanders — Mike Bossy, Bob Bourne, Paul Boutilier, Billy Carroll, Greg Gilbert, Clark Gillies, Butch Goring, Mats Hallin, Tomas Jonsson, Anders Kallur, Gord Lane, Dave Langevin, Mike McEwen, Roland Melanson, Wayne Merrick, Ken Morrow, Bob Nystrom, Stefan Persson, Denis Potvin (Captain), Billy Smith, Brent Sutter, Duane Sutter, John Tonelli, Bryan Trottier, Al Arbour (Coach), Lorne Henning (Ass't. Coach), Bill Torrey (General Manager), Ron Waske, Jim Pickard (Trainers)
Scores: May 10, at Edmonton — NY Islanders 2, Edmonton 0; May 12, at Edmonton — NY Islanders 6, Edmonton 3; May 14, at New York — NY Islanders 5, Edmonton 1; May 17, at New York — NY Islanders 4, Edmonton 2

1981-82 — New York Islanders — Mike Bossy, Bob Bourne, Billy Carroll, Butch Goring, Greg Gilbert, Clark Gillies, Tomas Jonsson, Anders Kallur, Gord Lane, Dave Langevin, Hector Marini, Mike McEwen, Roland Melanson, Wayne Merrick, Ken Morrow, Bob Nystrom, Stefan Persson, Denis Potvin (Captain), Billy Smith, Brent Sutter, Duane Sutter, John Tonelli, Bryan Trottier, Al Arbour (Coach), Lorne Henning (Ass't. Coach), Bill Torrey (General Manager), Jim Devellano (ass't. general manager/dir. of scouting), Ron Waske, Jim Pickard (Trainers)
Scores: May 8, at New York — NY Islanders 6, Vancouver 5; May 11, at New York — NY Islanders 6, Vancouver 4; May 13, at Vancouver — NY Islanders 3, Vancouver 0; May 16, at Vancouver — NY Islanders 3, Vancouver 1

1980-81 — New York Islanders — Denis Potvin (Captain), Mike McEwen, Ken Morrow, Gord Lane, Bob Lorimer, Stefan Persson, Dave Langevin, Mike Bossy, Bryan Trottier, Butch Goring, Wayne Merrick, Clark Gillies, John Tonelli, Bob Nystrom, Billy Carroll, Bob Bourne, Hector Marini, Anders Kallur, Duane Sutter, Garry Howatt, Lorne Henning, Billy Smith, Roland Melanson, Al Arbour (Coach), Bill Torrey (General Manager), Jim Devellano (Chief Scout), Ron Waske, Jim Pickard (Trainers).
Scores: May 12, at New York — NY Islanders 6, Minnesota 3; May 14, at New York — NY Islanders 6, Minnesota 3; May 17, at Minnesota — NY Islanders 7, Minnesota 5; May 19, at Minnesota— Minnesota 4, NY Islanders 2; May 21, at New York — NY Islanders 5, Minnesota 1.

1979-80 — New York Islanders — Gord Lane, Jean Potvin, Bob Lorimer, Denis Potvin (Captain), Stefan Persson, Ken Morrow, Dave Langevin, Duane Sutter, Garry Howatt, Clark Gillies, Lorne Henning, Wayne Merrick, Bob Bourne, Steve Tambellini, Bryan Trottier, Mike Bossy, Bob Nystrom, John Tonelli, Anders Kallur, Butch Goring, Alex McKendry, Glenn Resch, Billy Smith, Al Arbour (Coach), Bill Torrey (General Manager), Jim Devellano (Chief Scout), Ron Waske, Jim Pickard (Trainers).
Scores: May 13, at Philadelphia — NY Islanders 4, Philadelphia 3; May 15, at Philadelphia — Philadelphia 8, NY Islanders 3; May 17, at New York — NY Islanders 6, Philadelphia 2; May 19, at New York — NY Islanders 5, Philadelphia 2; May 22 at Philadelphia — Philadelphia 6, NY Islanders 3; May 24, at New York — NY Islanders 5, Philadelphia 4.

1978-79 — Montreal Canadiens — Ken Dryden, Larry Robinson, Serge Savard, Guy Lapointe, Brian Engblom, Gilles Lupien, Rick Chartraw, Guy Lafleur, Steve Shutt, Jacques Lemaire, Yvan Cournoyer (Captain), Réjean Houle, Pierre Mondou, Bob Gainey, Doug Jarvis, Yvon Lambert, Doug Risebrough, Pierre Larouche, Mario Tremblay, Cam Connor, Pat Hughes, Rod Langway, Mark Napier, Michel Larocque, Richard Sévigny, Scotty Bowman (Coach), Irving Grundman (Managing Director), Eddy Palchak, Pierre Meilleur (Trainers).
Scores: May 13, at Montreal — NY Rangers 4, Montreal 1; May 15, at Montreal — Montreal 6, NY Rangers 2; May 17, at New York — Montreal 4, NY Rangers 1; May 19, at New York — Montreal 4, NY Rangers 3; May 21, at Montreal — Montreal 4, NY Rangers 1.

1977-78 — Montreal Canadiens — Ken Dryden, Larry Robinson, Serge Savard, Guy Lapointe, Bill Nyrop, Pierre Bouchard, Brian Engblom, Gilles Lupien, Rick Chartraw, Guy Lafleur, Steve Shutt, Jacques Lemaire, Yvan Cournoyer (Captain), Réjean Houle, Pierre Mondou, Bob Gainey, Doug Jarvis, Yvon Lambert, Doug Risebrough, Pierre Larouche, Mario Tremblay, Michel Larocque, Murray Wilson, Scotty Bowman (Coach), Sam Pollock (General Manager), Eddy Palchak, Pierre Meilleur (Trainers).
Scores: May 13, at Montreal — Montreal 4, Boston 1; May 16, at Montreal — Montreal 3, Boston 2; May 18, at Boston — Boston 4, Montreal 0; May 21, at Boston — Boston 4, Montreal 3; May 23, at Montreal — Montreal 4, Boston 1; May 25, at Boston — Montreal 4, Boston 1.

1976-77 — Montreal Canadiens — Ken Dryden, Guy Lapointe, Larry Robinson, Serge Savard, Jimmy Roberts, Rick Chartraw, Bill Nyrop, Pierre Bouchard, Brian Engblom, Yvan Cournoyer (Captain), Guy Lafleur, Jacques Lemaire, Steve Shutt, Pete Mahovlich, Murray Wilson, Doug Jarvis, Yvon Lambert, Bob Gainey, Doug Risebrough, Mario Tremblay, Rejean Houle, Pierre Mondou, Mike Polich, Michel Larocque, Scotty Bowman (Coach), Sam Pollock (General Manager), Eddy Palchak, Pierre Meilleur (Trainers).
Scores: May 7, at Montreal — Montreal 7, Boston 3; May 10, at Montreal — Montreal 3, Boston 0; May 12, at Boston — Montreal 4, Boston 2; May 14, at Boston — Montreal 2, Boston 1.

1975-76 — Montreal Canadiens — Ken Dryden, Serge Savard, Guy Lapointe, Larry Robinson, Bill Nyrop, Pierre Bouchard, Jimmy Roberts, Guy Lafleur, Steve Shutt, Pete Mahovlich, Yvan Cournoyer (Captain), Jacques Lemaire, Yvon Lambert, Bob Gainey, Doug Jarvis, Doug Risebrough, Murray Wilson, Mario Tremblay, Rick Chartraw, Michel Larocque, Scotty Bowman (Coach), Sam Pollock (General Manager), Eddy Palchak, Pierre Meilleur (Trainers).
Scores: May 9, at Montreal — Montreal 4, Philadelphia 3; May 11, at Montreal — Montreal 2, Philadelphia 1; May 13, at Philadelphia — Montreal 3, Philadelphia 2; May 16, at Philadelphia — Montreal 5, Philadelphia 3.

1974-75 — Philadelphia Flyers — Bernie Parent, Wayne Stephenson, Ed Van Impe, Tom Bladon, André Dupont, Joe Watson, Jimmy Watson, Ted Harris, Larry Goodenough, Rick MacLeish, Bobby Clarke (Captain), Bill Barber, Reggie Leach, Gary Dornhoefer, Ross Lonsberry, Bob Kelly, Terry Crisp, Don Saleski, Dave Schultz, Orest Kindrachuk, Bill Clement, Fred Shero (Coach), Keith Allen (general manager), Frank Lewis, Jim McKenzie (Trainers).
Scores: May 15, at Philadelphia — Philadelphia 4, Buffalo 1; May 18, at Philadelphia — Philadelphia 2, Buffalo 1; May 20, at Buffalo — Buffalo 5, Philadelphia 4; May 22, at Buffalo — Buffalo 4, Philadelphia 2; May 25, at Philadelphia — Philadelphia 5, Buffalo 1; May 27, at Buffalo — Philadelphia 2, Buffalo 0.

1973-74 — Philadelphia Flyers — Bernie Parent, Ed Van Impe, Tom Bladon, André Dupont, Joe Watson, Jimmy Watson, Barry Ashbee, Bill Barber, Dave Schultz, Don Saleski, Gary Dornhoefer, Terry Crisp, Bobby Clarke (Captain), Simon Nolet, Ross Lonsberry, Rick MacLeish, Bill Flett, Orest Kindrachuk, Bill Clement, Bob Kelly, Bruce Cowick, Al MacAdam, Bobby Taylor, Fred Shero (Coach), Keith Allen (General Manager), Frank Lewis, Jim McKenzie (Trainers).
Scores: May 7, at Boston — Boston 3, Philadelphia 2; May 9, at Boston — Philadelphia 3, Boston 2; May 12, at Philadelphia — Philadelphia 4, Boston 1; May 14, at Philadelphia — Philadelphia 4, Boston 2; May 16, at Boston — Boston 5, Philadelphia 1; May 19, at Philadelphia — Philadelphia 1, Boston 0.

1972-73 — Montreal Canadiens — Ken Dryden, Guy Lapointe, Serge Savard, Larry Robinson, Jacques Laperrière, Bob Murdoch, Pierre Bouchard, Jimmy Roberts, Yvan Cournoyer, Frank Mahovlich, Jacques Lemaire, Pete Mahovlich, Marc Tardif, Henri Richard (Captain), Réjean Houle, Guy Lafleur, Chuck Lefley, Claude Larose, Murray Wilson, Steve Shutt, Michel Plasse, Scotty Bowman (Coach), Sam Pollock (General Manager), Eddy Palchak, Bob Williams (Trainers).
Scores: April 29, at Montreal — Montreal 8, Chicago 3; May 1, at Montreal — Montreal 4, Chicago 1; May 3, at Chicago — Chicago 7, Montreal 4; May 6, at Chicago — Montreal 4, Chicago 0; May 8, at Montreal — Chicago 8, Montreal 7; May 10, at Chicago — Montreal 6, Chicago 4.

1971-72 — Boston Bruins — Gerry Cheevers, Eddie Johnston, Bobby Orr, Ted Green, Carol Vadnais, Dallas Smith, Don Awrey, Phil Esposito, Ken Hodge, John Bucyk, Mike Walton, Wayne Cashman, Garnet Bailey, Derek Sanderson, Fred Stanfield, Ed Westfall, John McKenzie, Don Marcotte, Garry Peters, Chris Hayes, Tom Johnson (Coach), Milt Schmidt (General Manager), Dan Canney, John Forristall (Trainers).
Scores: April 30, at Boston — Boston 6, NY Rangers 5; May 2, at Boston — Boston 2, NY Rangers 1; May 4, at New York — NY Rangers 5, Boston 2; May 7, at New York — Boston 3, NY Rangers 2; May 9, at Boston — NY Rangers 3, Boston 2; May 11, at New York — Boston 3, NY Rangers 0.

1970-71 — Montreal Canadiens — Ken Dryden, Rogie Vachon, Jacques Laperrière, J.C. Tremblay, Guy Lapointe, Terry Harper, Pierre Bouchard, Jean Béliveau (Captain), Marc Tardif, Yvan Cournoyer, Réjean Houle, Claude Larose, Henri Richard, Phil Roberto, Pete Mahovlich, Leon Rochefort, John Ferguson, Bobby Sheehan, Jacques Lemaire, Frank Mahovlich, Bob Murdoch, Chuck Lefley, Al MacNeil (Coach), Sam Pollock (General Manager), Yvon Belanger, Eddy Palchak (Trainers).
Scores: May 4, at Chicago — Chicago 2, Montreal 1; May 6, at Chicago — Chicago 5, Montreal 3; May 9, at Montreal — Montreal 4, Chicago 2; May 11, at Montreal — Montreal 5, Chicago 2; May 13, at Chicago — Chicago 2, Montreal 0; May 16, at Montreal — Montreal 4, Chicago 3; May 18, at Chicago — Montreal 3, Chicago 2.

1969-70 — Boston Bruins — Gerry Cheevers, Eddie Johnston, Bobby Orr, Rick Smith, Dallas Smith, Bill Speer, Gary Doak, Don Awrey, Phil Esposito, Ken Hodge, John Bucyk, Wayne Carleton, Wayne Cashman, Derek Sanderson, Fred Stanfield, Ed Westfall, John McKenzie, Jim Lorentz, Don Marcotte, Bill Lesuk, Danny Schock, Harry Sinden (Coach), Milt Schmidt (General Manager), Dan Canney, John Forristall (Trainers).
Scores: May 3, at St. Louis — Boston 6, St. Louis 1; May 5, at St. Louis — Boston 6, St. Louis 2; May 7, at Boston — Boston 4, St. Louis 1; May 10, at Boston — Boston 4, St. Louis 3.

1968-69 — Montreal Canadiens — Gump Worsley, Rogie Vachon, Jacques Laperrière, J.C. Tremblay, Ted Harris, Serge Savard, Terry Harper, Larry Hillman, Jean Béliveau (Captain), Ralph Backstrom, Dick Duff, Yvan Cournoyer, Claude Provost, Bobby Rousseau, Henri Richard, John Ferguson, Christian Bordeleau, Mickey Redmond, Jacques Lemaire, Lucien Grenier, Tony Esposito, Claude Ruel (Coach), Sam Pollock (General Manager), Larry Aubut, Eddy Palchak (Trainers).
Scores: April 27, at Montreal — Montreal 3, St. Louis 1; April 29, at Montreal — Montreal 3, St. Louis 1; May 1 at St. Louis — Montreal 4, St. Louis 0; May 4, at St. Louis — Montreal 2, St. Louis 1.

1967-68 — Montreal Canadiens — Gump Worsley, Rogie Vachon, Jacques Laperrière, J.C. Tremblay, Ted Harris, Serge Savard, Terry Harper, Carol Vadnais, Jean Béliveau (Captain), Gilles Tremblay, Ralph Backstrom, Dick Duff, Claude Larose, Yvan Cournoyer, Claude Provost, Bobby Rousseau, Henri Richard, John Ferguson, Danny Grant, Jacques Lemaire, Mickey Redmond, Toe Blake (Coach), Sam Pollock (General Manager), Larry Aubut, Eddy Palchak (Trainers).
Scores: May 5, at St. Louis — Montreal 3, St. Louis 2; May 7, at St. Louis — Montreal 1, St. Louis 0; May 9, at Montreal — Montreal 4, St. Louis 3; May 11, at Montreal — Montreal 3, St. Louis 2.

1966-67 — Toronto Maple Leafs — Johnny Bower, Terry Sawchuk, Larry Hillman, Marcel Pronovost, Tim Horton, Bob Baun, Aut Erickson, Allan Stanley, Red Kelly, Ron Ellis, George Armstrong (Captain), Pete Stemkowski, Dave Keon, Mike Walton, Jim Pappin, Bob Pulford, Brian Conacher, Eddie Shack, Frank Mahovlich, Milan Marcetta, Larry Jeffrey, Bruce Gamble, Punch Imlach (Manager-Coach), Bob Haggart (Trainer).
Scores: April 20, at Montreal — Toronto 2, Montreal 6; April 22, at Montreal — Toronto 3, Montreal 0; April 25, at Toronto — Toronto 3, Montreal 2; April 27, at Toronto — Toronto 2, Montreal 6; April 29, at Montreal — Toronto 4, Montreal 1; May 2, at Toronto — Toronto 3, Montreal 1.

1965-66 — Montreal Canadiens — Gump Worsley, Charlie Hodge, J.C. Tremblay, Ted Harris, Jean-Guy Talbot, Terry Harper, Jacques Laperrière, Noel Price, Jean Béliveau (Captain), Ralph Backstrom, Dick Duff, Gilles Tremblay, Claude Larose, Yvan Cournoyer, Claude Provost, Bobby Rousseau, Henri Richard, Dave Balon, John Ferguson, Leon Rochefort, Jimmy Roberts, Toe Blake (Coach), Sam Pollock (general manager), Larry Aubut, Andy Galley (Trainers).
Scores: April 24, at Montreal — Detroit 3, Montreal 2; April 26, at Montreal — Detroit 5, Montreal 2; April 28, at Detroit — Montreal 4, Detroit 2; May 1, at Detroit — Montreal 2, Detroit 1; May 3, at Montreal — Montreal 5, Detroit 1; May 5, at Detroit — Montreal 3, Detroit 2.

1964-65 — Montreal Canadiens — Gump Worsley, Charlie Hodge, J.C. Tremblay, Ted Harris, Jean-Guy Talbot, Terry Harper, Jacques Laperrière, Jean Gauthier, Noel Picard, Jean Béliveau (Captain), Ralph Backstrom, Dick Duff, Claude Larose, Yvan Cournoyer, Claude Provost, Bobby Rousseau, Henri Richard, Dave Balon, John Ferguson, Red Berenson, Jimmy Roberts, Toe Blake (Coach), Sam Pollock (general manager), Larry Aubut, Andy Galley (Trainers).
Scores: April 17, at Montreal — Montreal 3, Chicago 2; April 20, at Montreal — Montreal 2, Chicago 0; April 22, at Chicago — Montreal 1, Chicago 3; April 25, at Chicago — Montreal 1, Chicago 5; April 7, at Montreal — Montreal 6, Chicago 0; April 29, at Chicago — Montreal 1, Chicago 2; May 1, at Montreal — Montreal 4, Chicago 0.

1963-64 — Toronto Maple Leafs — Johnny Bower, Don Simmons, Carl Brewer, Tim Horton, Bob Baun, Allan Stanley, Larry Hillman, Al Arbour, Red Kelly, Gerry Ehman, Andy Bathgate, George Armstrong (Captain), Ron Stewart, Dave Keon, Billy Harris, Don McKenney, Jim Pappin, Bob Pulford, Eddie Shack, Frank Mahovlich, Ed Litzenberger, Punch Imlach (Manager-Coach), Bob Haggert (Trainer).
Scores April 11, at Toronto — Toronto 3, Detroit 2; April 14, at Toronto — Toronto 3, Detroit 4; April 16, at Detroit — Toronto 3, Detroit 4; April 18, at Detroit — Toronto 4, Detroit 2; April 21, at Toronto — Toronto 1, Detroit 2; April 23, at Detroit — Toronto 4, Detroit 3; April 25, at Toronto — Toronto 4, Detroit 0.

1962-63 — Toronto Maple Leafs — Johnny Bower, Don Simmons, Carl Brewer, Tim Horton, Kent Douglas, Allan Stanley, Bob Baun, Larry Hillman, Red Kelly, Dick Duff, George Armstrong (Captain), Bob Nevin, Ron Stewart, Dave Keon, Billy Harris, Bob Pulford, Eddie Shack, Ed Litzenberger, Frank Mahovlich, John MacMillan, Punch Imlach (Manager-Coach), Bob Haggert (Trainer).
Scores: April 9, at Toronto — Toronto 4, Detroit 2; April 11, at Toronto — Toronto 4, Detroit 2; April 14, at Detroit — Toronto 2, Detroit 3; April 16, at Detroit — Toronto 4, Detroit 2; April 18, at Toronto — Toronto 3, Detroit 1.

1961-62 — Toronto Maple Leafs — Johnny Bower, Don Simmons, Carl Brewer, Tim Horton, Bob Baun, Allan Stanley, Al Arbour, Larry Hillman, Red Kelly, Dick Duff, George Armstrong (Captain), Frank Mahovlich, Bob Nevin, Ron Stewart, Billy Harris, Bert Olmstead, Bob Pulford, Eddie Shack, Dave Keon, Ed Litzenberger, John MacMillan, Punch Imlach (Manager-Coach), Bob Haggert (Trainer).
Scores: April 10, at Toronto — Toronto 4, Chicago 1; April 12, at Toronto — Toronto 3, Chicago 2; April 15, at Chicago — Toronto 0, Chicago 3; April 17, at Chicago — Toronto 1, Chicago 4; April 19, at Toronto —Toronto 8, Chicago 4; April 22, at Chicago — Toronto 2, Chicago 1.

1960-61 — Chicago Black Hawks — Glenn Hall, Al Arbour, Pierre Pilote, Moose Vasko, Jack Evans, Dollard St. Laurent, Reggie Fleming, Tod Sloan, Ron Murphy, Ed Litzenberger (Captain), Bill Hay, Wayne Hillman, Bobby Hull, Ab McDonald, Eric Nesterenko, Kenny Wharram, Earl Balfour, Stan Mikita, Murray Balfour, Chico Maki, Wayne Hicks, Tommy Ivan (Manager), Rudy Pilous (Coach), Nick Garen (Trainer).
Scores: April 6, at Chicago — Chicago 3, Detroit 2; April 8, at Detroit — Detroit 3, Chicago 1; April 10, at Chicago — Chicago 3, Detroit 1; April 12, at Detroit — Detroit 2, Chicago 1; April 14, at Chicago — Chicago 6, Detroit 3; April 16, at Detroit — Chicago 5, Detroit 1.

1959-60 — Montreal Canadiens — Jacques Plante, Charlie Hodge, Doug Harvey, Tom Johnson, Bob Turner, Jean-Guy Talbot, Albert Langlois, Ralph Backstrom, Jean Béliveau, Marcel Bonin, Bernie Geoffrion, Phil Goyette, Bill Hicke, Don Marshall, Ab McDonald, Dickie Moore, André Pronovost, Claude Provost, Henri Richard, Maurice Richard (Captain), Frank Selke (Manager), Toe Blake (Coach), Hector Dubois, Larry Aubut (Trainers).
Scores: April 7, at Montreal — Montreal 4, Toronto 2; April 9, at Montreal — Montreal 2, Toronto 1; April 12, at Toronto — Montreal 5, Toronto 2; April 14, at Toronto — Montreal 4, Toronto 0.

1958-59 — Montreal Canadiens — Jacques Plante, Charlie Hodge, Doug Harvey, Tom Johnson, Bob Turner, Jean-Guy Talbot, Albert Langlois, Bernie Geoffrion, Ralph Backstrom, Bill Hicke, Maurice Richard (Captain), Dickie Moore, Claude Provost, Ab McDonald, Henri Richard, Marcel Bonin, Phil Goyette, Don Marshall, André Pronovost, Jean Béliveau, Frank Selke (Manager), Toe Blake (Coach), Hector Dubois, Larry Aubut (Trainers).
Scores: April 9, at Montreal — Montreal 5, Toronto 3; April 11, at Montreal — Montreal 3, Toronto 1; April 14, at Toronto — Toronto 3, Montreal 2; April 16, at Toronto — Montreal 3, Toronto 2; April 18, at Montreal — Montreal 5, Toronto 3.

1957-58 — Montreal Canadiens — Jacques Plante, Gerry McNeil, Doug Harvey, Tom Johnson, Bob Turner, Dollard St-Laurent, Jean-Guy Talbot, Albert Langlois, Jean Béliveau, Bernie Geoffrion, Maurice Richard (Captain), Dickie Moore, Claude Provost, Floyd Curry, Bert Olmstead, Henri Richard, Marcel Bonin, Phil Goyette, Don Marshall, André Pronovost, Connie Broden, Ab McDonald, Frank Selke (Manager), Toe Blake (Coach), Hector Dubois, Larry Aubut (Trainers).
Scores: April 8, at Montreal —Montreal 2, Boston 1; April 10, at Montreal — Boston 5, Montreal 2; April 13, at Boston — Montreal 3, Boston 0; April 15, at Boston — Montreal 3, Boston 1; April 17, at Montreal — Montreal 3, Boston 2; April 20, at Boston — Montreal 5, Boston 3.

1956-57 — Montreal Canadiens — Jacques Plante, Gerry McNeil, Doug Harvey, Tom Johnson, Bob Turner, Dollard St-Laurent, Jean-Guy Talbot, Jean Béliveau, Bernie Geoffrion, Floyd Curry, Dickie Moore, Maurice Richard (Captain), Claude Provost, Bert Olmstead, Henri Richard, Phil Goyette, Don Marshall, André Pronovost, Connie Broden, Frank Selke (Manager), Toe Blake (Coach), Hector Dubois, Larry Aubut (Trainers).
Scores: April 6, at Montreal — Montreal 5, Boston 1; April 9, at Montreal — Montreal 1, Boston 0; April 11, at Boston — Montreal 4, Boston 2; April 14, at Boston — Boston 2, Montreal 0; April 16, at Montreal — Montreal 5, Boston 1.

1955-56 — Montreal Canadiens — Jacques Plante, Doug Harvey, Butch Bouchard (Captain), Bob Turner, Tom Johnson, Jean-Guy Talbot, Dollard St-Laurent, Jean Béliveau, Bernie Geoffrion, Bert Olmstead, Floyd Curry, Jackie Leclair, Maurice Richard, Dickie Moore, Henri Richard, Ken Mosdell, Don Marshall, Claude Provost, Frank Selke (Manager), Toe Blake (Coach), Hector Dubois (Trainer).
Scores: March 31, at Montreal — Montreal 6, Detroit 4; April 3, at Montreal — Montreal 5, Detroit 1; April 5, at Detroit — Detroit 3, Montreal 1; April 8, at Detroit — Montreal 3, Detroit 0; April 10, at Montreal — Montreal 3, Detroit 1.

1954-55 — Detroit Red Wings — Terry Sawchuk, Red Kelly, Bob Goldham, Marcel Pronovost, Benny Woit, Jim Hay, Larry Hillman, Ted Lindsay (Captain), Tony Leswick, Gordie Howe, Alex Delvecchio, Marty Pavelich, Glen Skov, Earl Reibel, Johnny Wilson, Bill Dineen, Vic Stasiuk, Marcel Bonin, Jack Adams (Manager), Jimmy Skinner (Coach), Carl Mattson (Trainer).
Scores: April 3, at Detroit — Detroit 4, Montreal 2; April 5, at Detroit — Detroit 7, Montreal 1, April 7, at Montreal — Montreal 4, Detroit 2; April 9, at Montreal — Montreal 5, Detroit 3; April 10, at Detroit — Detroit 5, Montreal 1; April 12, at Montreal — Montreal 6, Detroit 3; April 14, at Detroit — Detroit 3, Montreal 1.

1953-54 — Detroit Red Wings — Terry Sawchuk, Red Kelly, Bob Goldham, Benny Woit, Marcel Pronovost, Al Arbour, Keith Allen, Ted Lindsay (Captain), Tony Leswick, Gordie Howe, Marty Pavelich, Alex Delvecchio, Gilles Dube, Metro Prystai, Glen Skov, Johnny Wilson, Bill Dineen, Jimmy Peters, Earl Reibel, Vic Stasiuk, Jack Adams (Manager), Tommy Ivan (Coach), Carl Mattson (Trainer).
Scores: April 4, at Detroit — Detroit 3, Montreal 1; April 6, at Detroit — Montreal 3, Detroit 1; April 8, at Montreal — Detroit 5, Montreal 2; April 10, at Montreal — Detroit 2, Montreal 0; April 11, at Detroit — Montreal 1, Detroit 0; April 13, at Montreal — Montreal 4, Detroit 1; April 16, at Detroit — Detroit 2, Montreal 1.

1952-53 — Montreal Canadiens — Gerry McNeil, Jacques Plante, Doug Harvey, Butch Bouchard (Captain), Tom Johnson, Dollard St. Laurent, Bud MacPherson, Maurice Richard, Elmer Lach, Paul Meger, Bert Olmstead, Bernie Geoffrion, Floyd Curry, Paul Masnick, Billy Reay, Dickie Moore, Ken Mosdell, Dick Gamble, John McCormack, Lorne Davis, Calum MacKay, Eddie Mazur, Frank Selke (Manager), Dick Irvin (Coach), Hector Dubois (Trainer).
Scores: April 9, at Montreal — Montreal 4, Boston 2; April 11, at Montreal — Boston 4, Montreal 1; April 12, at Boston — Montreal 3, Boston 0; April 14, at Boston — Montreal 7, Boston 3; April 16, at Montreal — Montreal 1, Boston 0.

1951-52 — Detroit Red Wings — Terry Sawchuk, Bob Goldham, Benny Woit, Red Kelly, Leo Reise Jr., Marcel Pronovost, Ted Lindsay, Tony Leswick, Gordie Howe, Metro Prystai, Marty Pavelich, Sid Abel (Captain), Glen Skov, Alex Delvecchio, John Wilson, Vic Stasiuk, Larry Zeidel, Jack Adams (Manager) Tommy Ivan (Coach), Carl Mattson (Trainer).
Scores: April 10, at Montreal — Detroit 3, Montreal 1; April 12, at Montreal — Detroit 2, Montreal 1; April 13, at Detroit — Detroit 3, Montreal 0; April 15, at Detroit — Detroit 3, Montreal 0.

1950-51 — Toronto Maple Leafs — Turk Broda, Al Rollins, Jimmy Thomson, Gus Mortson, Bill Barilko, Bill Juzda, Fern Flaman, Hugh Bolton, Ted Kennedy (Captain), Sid Smith, Tod Sloan, Cal Gardner, Howie Meeker, Harry Watson, Max Bentley, Joe Klukay, Danny Lewicki, Ray Timgren, Fleming Mackell, John McCormack, Bob Hassard, Conn Smythe (Manager), Joe Primeau (Coach), Tim Daly (Trainer).
Scores: April 11, at Toronto — Toronto 3, Montreal 2; April 14, at Toronto — Toronto 3, Montreal 2; April 17, at Montreal — Toronto 2, Montreal 1; April 19, at Montreal — Toronto 3, Montreal 2; April 21, at Toronto — Toronto 3, Montreal 2.

1949-50 — Detroit Red Wings — Harry Lumley, Jack Stewart, Leo Reise Jr., Clare Martin, Doug McKay, Al Dewsbury, Lee Fogolin, Marcel Pronovost, Red Kelly, Gord Haidy, Ted Lindsay, Sid Abel (Captain), Gordie Howe, George Gee, Jimmy Peters, Marty Pavelich, Jim McFadden, Pete Babando, Max McNab, Gerry Couture, Joe Carveth, Steve Black, Johnny Wilson, Larry Wilson, Jack Adams (Manager), Tommy Ivan (Coach), Carl Mattson (Trainer).
Scores: April 11, at Detroit — Detroit 4, NY Rangers 1; April 13, at Toronto* — NY Rangers 3, Detroit 1; April 15, at Toronto — Detroit 4, NY Rangers 3; April 18, at Detroit — NY Rangers 4, Detroit 3; April 20, at Detroit — NY Rangers 2, Detroit 1; April 22, at Detroit — Detroit 5, NY Rangers 4; April 23, at Detroit — Detroit 4, NY Rangers 3.

* Ice was unavailable in Madison Square Garden and Rangers elected to play second and third games on Toronto ice.

Bobby Clarke and Bill Barber helped lead the Philadelphia Flyers to back-to-back Stanley Cup titles in 1974 and 1975. The Flyers reached the Finals for a third straight year in 1976, but were defeated by the Montreal Canadiens.

1948-49 — Toronto Maple Leafs — Turk Broda, Jimmy Thomson, Gus Mortson, Bill Barilko, Garth Boesch, Bill Juzda, Ted Kennedy (Captain), Howie Meeker, Vic Lynn, Harry Watson, Bill Ezinicki, Cal Gardner, Max Bentley, Joe Klukay, Sid Smith, Don Metz, Ray Timgren, Fleming Mackell, Harry Taylor, Bob Dawes, Tod Sloan, Conn Smythe (Manager), Hap Day (Coach), Tim Daly (Trainer).
Scores: April 8, at Detroit — Toronto 3, Detroit 2; April 10, at Detroit — Toronto 3, Detroit 1; April 13, at Toronto — Toronto 3, Detroit 1; April 16, at Toronto — Toronto 3, Detroit 1.

1947-48 — Toronto Maple Leafs — Turk Broda, Jimmy Thomson, Wally Stanowski, Garth Boesch, Bill Barilko, Gus Mortson, Phil Samis, Syl Apps (Captain), Bill Ezinicki, Harry Watson, Ted Kennedy, Howie Meeker, Vic Lynn, Nick Metz, Max Bentley, Joe Klukay, Les Costello, Don Metz, Sid Smith, Conn Smythe (Manager), Hap Day (Coach), Tim Daly (Trainer).
Scores: April 7, at Toronto — Toronto 5, Detroit 3; April 10, at Toronto — Toronto 4, Detroit 2; April 11, at Detroit — Toronto 2, Detroit 0; April 14, at Detroit — Toronto 7, Detroit 2.

1946-47 — Toronto Maple Leafs — Turk Broda, Garth Boesch, Gus Mortson, Jimmy Thomson, Wally Stanowski, Bill Barilko, Harry Watson, Bud Poile, Ted Kennedy, Syl Apps (Captain), Don Metz, Nick Metz, Bill Ezinicki, Vic Lynn, Howie Meeker, Gaye Stewart, Joe Klukay, Gus Bodnar, Bob Goldham, Conn Smythe (Manager), Hap Day (Coach), Tim Daly (Trainer).
Scores: April 8, at Montreal — Montreal 6, Toronto 0; April 10, at Montreal — Toronto 4, Montreal 0; April 12, at Toronto — Toronto 4, Montreal 2; April 15, at Toronto — Toronto 2, Montreal 1; April 17, at Montreal — Montreal 3, Toronto 1; April 19, at Toronto — Toronto 2, Montreal 1.

1945-46 — Montreal Canadiens — Elmer Lach, Toe Blake (Captain), Maurice Richard, Bob Fillion, Dutch Hiller, Murph Chamberlain, Ken Mosdell, Buddy O'Connor, Glen Harmon, Jimmy Peters, Butch Bouchard, Billy Reay, Ken Reardon, Leo Lamoureux, Frank Eddolls, Gerry Plamondon, Bill Durnan, Tommy Gorman (Manager), Dick Irvin (Coach), Ernie Cook (Trainer).
Scores: March 30, at Montreal — Montreal 4, Boston 3; April 2, at Montreal — Montreal 3, Boston 2; April 4, at Boston — Montreal 4, Boston 2; April 7, at Boston — Boston 3, Montreal 2; April 9, at Montreal — Montreal 6, Boston 3.

1944-45 — Toronto Maple Leafs — Don Metz, Frank McCool, Wally Stanowski, Reg Hamilton, Moe Morris, John McCreedy, Tom O'Neill, Ted Kennedy, Babe Pratt, Gus Bodnar, Art Jackson, Jack McLean, Mel Hill, Nick Metz, Bob Davidson (Captain), Sweeney Schriner, Lorne Carr, Conn Smythe (Manager), Frank Selke (Business Manager), Hap Day (Coach), Tim Daly (Trainer).
Scores: April 6, at Detroit — Toronto 1, Detroit 0; April 8, at Detroit — Toronto 2, Detroit 0; April 12, at Toronto — Toronto 1, Detroit 0; April 14, at Toronto — Detroit 5, Toronto 3; April 19, at Detroit — Detroit 2, Toronto 0; April 21, at Toronto — Detroit 1, Toronto 0; April 22, at Detroit — Toronto 2, Detroit 1.

1943-44 — Montreal Canadiens — Toe Blake (Captain), Maurice Richard, Elmer Lach, Ray Getliffe, Murph Chamberlain, Phil Watson, Butch Bouchard, Glen Harmon, Buddy O'Connor, Gerry Heffernan, Mike McMahon, Leo Lamoureux, Fern Majeau, Bob Fillion, Bill Durnan, Tommy Gorman (Manager), Dick Irvin (Coach), Ernie Cook (Trainer).
Scores: April 4, at Montreal — Montreal 5, Chicago 1; April 6, at Chicago — Montreal 3, Chicago 1; April 9, at Chicago — Montreal 3, Chicago 2; April 13, at Montreal — Montreal 5, Chicago 4.

1942-43 — Detroit Red Wings — Jack Stewart, Jimmy Orlando, Sid Abel (Captain), Alex Motter, Harry Watson, Joe Carveth, Mud Bruneteau, Eddie Wares, Johnny Mowers, Cully Simon, Don Grosso, Carl Liscombe, Connie Brown, Syd Howe, Les Douglas, Harold Jackson, Joe Fisher, Jack Adams (Manager), Ebbie Goodfellow (Playing Coach), Honey Walker (Trainer).
Scores: April 1, at Detroit — Detroit 6, Boston 2; April 4, at Detroit — Detroit 4, Boston 3; April 7, at Boston — Detroit 4, Boston 0; April 8, at Boston — Detroit 2, Boston 0.

1941-42 — Toronto Maple Leafs — Wally Stanowski, Syl Apps (Captain), Bob Goldham, Gordie Drillon, Hank Goldup, Ernie Dickens, Sweeney Schriner, Bucko McDonald, Bob Davidson, Nick Metz, Bingo Kampman, Don Metz, Gaye Stewart, Turk Broda, John McCreedy, Lorne Carr, Pete Langelle, Billy Taylor, Conn Smythe (Manager), Hap Day (Coach), Frank Selke (Business Manager), Tim Daly (Trainer).
Scores: April 4, at Toronto — Detroit 3, Toronto 2; April 7, at Toronto — Detroit 4, Toronto 2; April 9, at Detroit — Detroit 5, Toronto 2; April 12, at Detroit — Toronto 4, Detroit 3; April 14, at Toronto — Toronto 9, Detroit 3; April 16, at Detroit — Toronto 3, Detroit 0; April 18, at Toronto — Toronto 3, Detroit 1.

1940-41 — Boston Bruins — Bill Cowley, Des Smith, Dit Clapper (Captain), Frank Brimsek, Flash Hollett, Jack Crawford, Bobby Bauer, Pat McReavy, Herb Cain, Mel Hill, Milt Schmidt, Woody Dumart, Roy Conacher, Terry Reardon, Art Jackson, Eddie Wiseman, Art Ross (Manager), Cooney Weiland (Coach), Win Green (Trainer).
Scores: April 6, at Boston — Detroit 2, Boston 3; April 8, at Boston — Detroit 1, Boston 2; April 10, at Detroit — Boston 4, Detroit 2; April 12, at Detroit — Boston 3, Detroit 1.

1939-40 — New York Rangers — Dave Kerr, Art Coulter (Captain), Ott Heller, Alex Shibicky, Mac Colville, Neil Colville, Phil Watson, Lynn Patrick, Clint Smith, Muzz Patrick, Babe Pratt, Bryan Hextall, Kilby MacDonald, Dutch Hiller, Alf Pike, Stan Smith, Lester Patrick (Manager), Frank Boucher (Coach), Harry Westerby (Trainer).
Scores: April 2, at New York — NY Rangers 2, Toronto 1; April 3, at New York — NY Rangers 6, Toronto 2; April 6, at Toronto — NY Rangers 1, Toronto 2; April 9, at Toronto — NY Rangers 0, Toronto 3; April 11, at Toronto — NY Rangers 2, Toronto 1; April 13, at Toronto — NY Rangers 3, Toronto 2.

1938-39 — Boston Bruins — Bobby Bauer, Mel Hill, Flash Hollett, Roy Conacher, Gord Pettinger, Charlie Sands, Milt Schmidt, Woody Dumart, Jack Crawford, Ray Getliffe, Frank Brimsek, Eddie Shore, Dit Clapper, Bill Cowley, Jack Portland, Red Hamill, Cooney Weiland (Captain), Art Ross (Manager-Coach), Win Green (Trainer).
Scores: April 6, at Boston — Toronto 1, Boston 2; April 9, at Boston — Toronto 3, Boston 2; April 11, at Toronto — Toronto 1, Boston 3; April 13, at Toronto — Toronto 0, Boston 2; April 16, at Boston — Toronto 1, Boston 3.

1937-38 — Chicago Black Hawks — Art Wiebe, Carl Voss, Harold Jackson, Mike Karakas, Mush March, Jack Shill, Earl Seibert, Cully Dahlstrom, Alex Levinsky, Johnny Gottselig (Captain), Lou Trudel, Pete Palangio, Bill MacKenzie, Doc Romnes, Paul Thompson, Roger Jenkins, Alfie Moore, Bert Connelly, Virgil Johnson, Paul Goodman, Bill Stewart (Manager-Coach), Eddie Froelich (Trainer).
Scores: April 5, at Toronto — Chicago 3, Toronto 1; April 7, at Toronto — Chicago 1, Toronto 5; April 10, at Chicago — Chicago 2, Toronto 1; April 12, at Chicago — Chicago 4, Toronto 1.

1936-37 — Detroit Red Wings — Normie Smith, Pete Kelly, Larry Aurie, Herbie Lewis, Hec Kilrea, Mud Bruneteau, Syd Howe, Wally Kilrea, Jimmy Franks, Bucko McDonald, Gord Pettinger, Ebbie Goodfellow, John Gallagher, Ralph Bowman, John Sorrell, Marty Barry, Earl Robertson, John Sherf, Howie Mackie, Rolly Roulston, Doug Young (Captain), Jack Adams (Manager-Coach), Honey Walker (Trainer).
Scores: April 6, at New York — Detroit 1, NY Rangers 5; April 8, at Detroit — Detroit 4, NY Rangers 2; April 11, at Detroit — Detroit 0, NY Rangers 1; April 13, at Detroit — Detroit 1, NY Rangers 0; April 15, at Detroit — Detroit 3, NY Rangers 0.

1935-36 — Detroit Red Wings — John Sorrell, Syd Howe, Marty Barry, Herbie Lewis, Mud Bruneteau, Wally Kilrea, Hec Kilrea, Gord Pettinger, Bucko McDonald, Ralph Bowman, Pete Kelly, Doug Young (Captain), Ebbie Goodfellow, Normie Smith, Larry Aurie, Jack Adams (Manager-Coach), Honey Walker (Trainer).
Scores: April 5, at Detroit — Detroit 3, Toronto 1; April 7, at Detroit — Detroit 9, Toronto 4; April 9, at Toronto — Detroit 3, Toronto 4; April 11, at Toronto — Detroit 3, Toronto 2.

1934-35 — Montreal Maroons — Lionel Conacher, Cy Wentworth, Alex Connell, Toe Blake, Stewart Evans, Earl Robinson, Bill Miller, Dave Trottier, Jimmy Ward, Baldy Northcott, Hooley Smith, Russ Blinco, Al Shields, Sammy McManus, Gus Marker, Bob Gracie, Herb Cain, Tommy Gorman (Manager-Coach), Bill O'Brien (Trainer).
Scores: April 4, at Toronto — Mtl. Maroons 3, Toronto 2; April 6, at Toronto — Mtl. Maroons 3, Toronto 1; April 9, at Montreal — Mtl. Maroons 4, Toronto 1.

1933-34 — Chicago Black Hawks — Clarence Abel, Rosie Couture, Lou Trudel, Lionel Conacher, Paul Thompson, Leroy Goldsworthy, Art Coulter, Roger Jenkins, Don McFadyen, Tom Cook, Doc Romnes, Johnny Gottselig, Mush March, Johnny Sheppard, Charlie Gardiner (Captain), Bill Kendall, Tommy Gorman (Manager-Coach), Eddie Froelich (Trainer).
Scores: April 3, at Detroit — Chicago 2, Detroit 1; April 5, at Detroit — Chicago 4, Detroit 1; April 8, at Chicago — Detroit 5, Chicago 2; April 10, at Chicago — Chicago 1, Detroit 0.

1932-33 — New York Rangers — Ching Johnson, Butch Keeling, Frank Boucher, Art Somers, Babe Siebert, Bun Cook, Andy Aitkenhead, Ott Heller, Oscar Asmundson, Gord Pettinger, Doug Brennan, Cecil Dillon, Bill Cook (Captain), Murray Murdoch, Earl Seibert, Lester Patrick (Manager-Coach), Harry Westerby (Trainer).
Scores: April 4, at New York — NY Rangers 5, Toronto 1; April 8, at Toronto — NY Rangers 3, Toronto 1; April 11, at Toronto — Toronto 3, NY Rangers 2; April 13, at Toronto — NY Rangers 1, Toronto 0.

1931-32 — Toronto Maple Leafs — Charlie Conacher, Busher Jackson, King Clancy, Andy Blair, Red Horner, Lorne Chabot, Alex Levinsky, Joe Primeau, Harold Darragh, Baldy Cotton, Frank Finnigan, Hap Day (Captain), Ace Bailey, Bob Gracie, Fred Robertson, Earl Miller, Conn Smythe (Manager), Dick Irvin (Coach), Tim Daly (Trainer).
Scores: April 5, at New York — Toronto 6, NY Rangers 4; April 7, at Boston* — Toronto 6, NY Rangers 2; April 9, at Toronto — Toronto 6, NY Rangers 4.

* Ice was unavailable in Madison Square Garden and Rangers elected to play the second game on neutral ice.

1930-31 — Montreal Canadiens — George Hainsworth, Wildor Larochelle, Marty Burke, Sylvio Mantha (Captain), Howie Morenz, Johnny Gagnon, Aurel Joliat, Armand Mondou, Pit Lepine, Albert Leduc, Georges Mantha, Art Lesieur, Nick Wasnie, Bert McCaffrey, Gus Rivers, Jean Pusie, Léo Dandurand (Manager), Cecil Hart (Coach), Ed Dufour (Trainer).
Scores: April 3, at Chicago — Montreal 2, Chicago 1; April 5, at Chicago — Chicago 2, Montreal 1; April 9, at Montreal — Chicago 3, Montreal 2; April 11, at Montreal — Montreal 4, Chicago 2; April 14, at Montreal — Montreal 2, Chicago 0.

1929-30 — Montreal Canadiens — George Hainsworth, Marty Burke, Sylvio Mantha (Captain), Howie Morenz, Bert McCaffrey, Aurel Joliat, Albert Leduc, Pit Lepine, Wildor Larochelle, Nick Wasnie, Gerry Carson, Armand Mondou, Georges Mantha, Gus Rivers, Léo Dandurand (Manager), Cecil Hart (Coach), Ed Dufour (Trainer).
Scores: April 1, at Boston — Montreal 3, Boston 0; April 3, at Montreal — Montreal 4, Boston 3.

1928-29 — Boston Bruins — Tiny Thompson, Eddie Shore, Lionel Hitchman (Captain), Percy Galbraith, Eric Pettinger, Frank Fredrickson, Mickey Mackay, Red Green, Dutch Gainor, Harry Oliver, Eddie Rodden, Dit Clapper, Cooney Weiland, Lloyd Klein, Cy Denneny, Bill Carson, George Owen, Myles Lane, Art Ross (Manager-Coach), Win Green (Trainer).
Scores: March 28, at Boston — Boston 2, NY Rangers 0; March 29, at New York — Boston 2, NY Rangers 1.

1927-28 — New York Rangers — Lorne Chabot, Clarence Abel, Leo Bourgeault, Ching Johnson, Bill Cook (Captain), Bun Cook, Frank Boucher, Bill Boyd, Murray Murdoch, Paul Thompson, Alex Gray, Joe Miller, Patsy Callighen, Lester Patrick (Manager-Coach), Harry Westerby (Trainer).
Scores: April 5, at Montreal — Mtl. Maroons 2, NY Rangers 0; April 7, at Montreal — NY Rangers 2, Mtl. Maroons 1; April 10, at Montreal — Mtl. Maroons 2, NY Rangers 0; April 12, at Montreal — NY Rangers 1, Mtl. Maroons 0; April 14, at Montreal — NY Rangers 2, Mtl. Maroons 1.

1926-27 — Ottawa Senators — Alex Connell, King Clancy, Georges Boucher, Ed Gorman, Frank Finnigan, Alex Smith, Hec Kilrea, Hooley Smith, Cy Denneny, Frank Nighbor, Jack Adams, Milt Halliday, Dave Gill (Manager-Coach).
Scores: April 7, at Boston — Ottawa 0, Boston 0; April 9, at Boston — Ottawa 3, Boston 1; April 11, at Ottawa — Boston 1, Ottawa 1; April 13, at Ottawa — Ottawa 3, Boston 1.

1925-26 — Montreal Maroons — Clint Benedict, Reg Noble, Frank Carson, Dunc Munro, Nels Stewart, Punch Broadbent, Babe Siebert, Chuck Dinsmore, Merlyn Phillips, Hobie Kitchen, Sam Rothschild, Albert Holway, George Horne, Bernie Brophy, Eddie Gerard (Manager-Coach), Bill O'Brien (Trainer).
Scores: March 30, at Montreal — Mtl. Maroons 3, Victoria 0; April 1, at Montreal — Mtl. Maroons 3, Victoria 0; April 3, at Montreal — Victoria 3, Mtl. Maroons 2; April 6, at Montreal — Mtl. Maroons 2, Victoria 0.

The series in the spring of 1926 ended the annual playoffs between the champions of the East and the champions of the West. Since 1926-27 the annual playoffs in the National Hockey League have decided the Stanley Cup champions.

1924-25 — Victoria Cougars — Hap Holmes, Clem Loughlin, Gord Fraser, Frank Fredrickson, Jack Walker, Gizzy Hart, Harold Halderson, Frank Foyston, Wally Elmer, Harry Meeking, Jocko Anderson, Lester Patrick (Manager-Coach).
Scores: March 21, at Victoria — Victoria 5, Montreal 2; March 23, at Vancouver — Victoria 3, Montreal 1; March 27, at Victoria — Montreal 4, Victoria 2; March 30, at Victoria — Victoria 6, Montreal 1.

One hundred years ago this season, the Kenora Thistles of Kenora, Ontario (population, 6,000) became the team from the smallest town ever to win the Stanley Cup. The 1907 Thistles were: (back row, left to right) Russell Phillips, J.F. McGillivray, James Link, Fred Hudson, Joe Hall, (middle, left to right) Roxy Beaudro, Tom Hooper, Tommy Phillips, Billy McGimsie, (front, left to right) Si Griffis, Eddie Giroux and Art Ross.

1923-24 — Montreal Canadiens — Georges Vezina, Sprague Cleghorn (Captain), Billy Coutu, Howie Morenz, Aurel Joliat, Billy Boucher, Odie Cleghorn, Sylvio Mantha, Bobby Boucher, Billy Bell, Billy Cameron, Joe Malone, Charles Fortier, Leo Dandurand (Manager-Coach).
Scores: March 22, at Montreal — Montreal 6, Cgy. Tigers 1; March 25, at Ottawa* — Montreal 3, Cgy. Tigers 0.
* Game transferred to Ottawa to benefit from artificial ice surface.

1922-23 — Ottawa Senators — Georges Boucher, Lionel Hitchman, Frank Nighbor, King Clancy, Harry Helman, Clint Benedict, Jack Darragh, Eddie Gerard, Cy Denneny, Punch Broadbent, Tommy Gorman (Manager), Pete Green (Coach), F. Dolan (Trainer).
Scores: March 29, at Vancouver — Ottawa 2, Edm. Eskimos 1; March 31, at Vancouver — Ottawa 1, Edm. Eskimos 0.

1921-22 — Toronto St. Patricks — Ted Stackhouse, Corb Denneny, Rod Smylie, Lloyd Andrews, John Ross Roach, Harry Cameron, Billy Stuart, Babe Dye, Ken Randall, Reg Noble, Eddie Gerard (borrowed for one game from Ottawa), Stan Jackson, Ivan Mitchell, Charlie Querrie (Manager), George O'Donoghue (Coach).
Scores: March 17, at Toronto — Van. Millionaires 4, Toronto 3; March 20, at Toronto — Toronto 2, Van. Millionaires 1; March 23, at Toronto — Van. Millionaires 3, Toronto 0; March 25, at Toronto — Toronto 6, Van. Millionaires 0; March 28, at Toronto — Toronto 5, Van. Millionaires 1.

1920-21 — Ottawa Senators — Jack MacKell, Jack Darragh, Morley Bruce, Georges Boucher, Eddie Gerard, Clint Benedict, Sprague Cleghorn, Frank Nighbor, Punch Broadbent, Cy Denneny, Leth Graham, Tommy Gorman (Manager), Pete Green (Coach), F. Dolan (Trainer).
Scores: March 21, at Vancouver — Van. Millionaires 2, Ottawa 1; March 24, at Vancouver — Ottawa 4, Van. Millionaires 3; March 28, at Vancouver — Van. Millionaires 2; March 31, at Vancouver — Van. Millionaires 3, Ottawa 2; April 4, at Vancouver — Ottawa 2, Van. Millionaires 1

1919-20 — Ottawa Senators — Jack MacKell, Jack Darragh, Morley Bruce, Horrace Merrill, Georges Boucher, Eddie Gerard, Clint Benedict, Sprague Cleghorn, Frank Nighbor, Punch Broadbent, Cy Denneny, Tommy Gorman (Manager), Pete Green (Coach).
Scores: March 22, at Ottawa — Ottawa 3, Seattle 2; March 24, at Ottawa — Ottawa 3, Seattle 0; March 27, at Ottawa — Seattle 3, Ottawa 1; March 30, at Toronto* — Seattle 5, Ottawa 2; April 1, at Toronto* — Ottawa 6, Seattle 1.

* Games transferred to Toronto to benefit from artificial ice surface.

1918-19 — No decision, Series halted by Spanish influenza epidemic, illness of several players and death of Joe Hall of Montreal Canadiens from flu. Five games had been played when the series was halted, each team having won two and tied one. The results are shown:
Scores: March 19, at Seattle — Seattle 7, Montreal 0; March 22, at Seattle — Montreal 4, Seattle 2; March 24, at Seattle — Seattle 7, Montreal 2; March 26, at Seattle — Montreal 0, Seattle 0; March 30, at Seattle — Montreal 4, Seattle 3.

1917-18 — Toronto Arenas — Rusty Crawford, Harry Meeking, Ken Randall, Corb Denneny, Harry Cameron, Jack Adams, Alf Skinner, Harry Mummery, Hap Holmes, Reg Noble, Sammy Hebert, Jack Marks, Jack Coughlin, Charlie Querrie (Manager), Dick Carroll (Coach), Frank Carroll (Trainer).
Scores: March 20, at Toronto — Toronto 5, Van. Millionaires 3; March 23, at Toronto — Van. Millionaires 6, Toronto 4; March 26, at Toronto — Toronto 6, Van. Millionaires 3; March 28, at Toronto — Van. Millionaires 8, Toronto 1; March 30, at Toronto — Toronto 2, Van. Millionaires 1.

1916-17 — Seattle Metropolitans — Hap Holmes, Ed Carpenter, Cully Wilson, Jack Walker, Bernie Morris, Frank Foyston, Roy Rickey, Jim Riley, Bobby Rowe (Captain), Peter Muldoon (Manager).
Scores: March 17, at Seattle — Montreal 8, Seattle 4; March 20, at Seattle — Seattle 6, Montreal 1; March 23, at Seattle — Seattle 4, Montreal 1; March 25, at Seattle — Seattle 9, Montreal 1.

1915-16 — Montreal Canadiens — Georges Vezina, Bert Corbeau, Jack Laviolette, Newsy Lalonde, Louis Berlinquette, Goldie Prodgers, Howard McNamara (Captain), Didier Pitre, Skene Ronan, Amos Arbour, Skinner Poulin, Jack Fournier, George Kennedy (Manager).
Scores: March 20, at Montreal — Portland 2, Montreal 0; March 22, at Montreal — Montreal 2, Portland 1; March 25, at Montreal — Montreal 6, Portland 3; March 28, at Montreal — Portland 6, Montreal 5; March 30, at Montreal — Montreal 2, Portland 1.

1914-15 — Vancouver Millionaires — Ken Mallen, Frank Nighbor, Cyclone Taylor, Hugh Lehman, Lloyd Cook, Mickey Mackay, Barney Stanley, Jim Seaborn, Si Griffis (Captain), Johnny Matz, Frank Patrick (Playing Manager).
Scores: March 22, at Vancouver — Van. Millionaires 6, Ottawa 2; March 24, at Vancouver — Van. Millionaires 8, Ottawa 3; March 26, at Vancouver — Van. Millionaires 12, Ottawa 3.

1913-14 — Toronto Blueshirts — Con Corbeau, Roy McGiffen, Jack Walker, George McNamara, Cully Wilson, Frank Foyston, Harry Cameron, Hap Holmes, Scotty Davidson (Captain), Harriston, Jack Marshall (Playing Manager), Frank and Dick Carroll (Trainers).
Scores: March 14, at Toronto — Toronto 5, Victoria 2; March 17, at Toronto — Toronto 6, Victoria 5; March 19, at Toronto — Toronto 2, Victoria 1.

1912-13 — Quebec Bulldogs — Joe Malone, Joe Hall, Paddy Moran, Harry Mummery, Tommy Smith, Jack Marks, Rusty Crawford, Billy Creighton, Jeff Malone, Rocket Power, M.J. Quinn (Manager), D. Beland (Trainer).
Scores: March 8, at Quebec — Que. Bulldogs 14, Sydney 3; March 10, at Quebec — Que. Bulldogs 6, Sydney 2.
Victoria challenged Quebec but the Bulldogs refused to put the Stanley Cup in competition so the two teams played an exhibition series with Victoria winning two games to one by scores of 7-5, 3-6, 6-1. It was the first meeting between the Eastern champions and the Western champions. The following year, and until the Western Hockey League disbanded after the 1926 playoffs, the Cup went to the winner of the series between East and West.

1911-12 — Quebec Bulldogs — Goldie Prodgers, Joe Hall, Walter Rooney, Paddy Moran, Jack Marks, Jack McDonald, Eddie Oatman, George Leonard, Joe Malone (Captain), C. Nolan (Coach), M.J. Quinn (Manager), D. Beland (Trainer).
Scores: March 11, at Quebec — Que. Bulldogs 9, Moncton 3; March 13, at Quebec — Que. Bulldogs 8, Moncton 0.
Prior to 1912, teams could challenge the Stanley Cup champions for the title, thus there was more than one Championship Series played in most of the seasons between 1894 and 1911.

1910-11 — Ottawa Senators — Hamby Shore, Percy LeSueur (Captain), Jack Darragh, Bruce Stuart, Marty Walsh, Bruce Ridpath, Fred Lake, Dubbie Kerr, Alex Currie, Horace Gaul.
Scores: March 13, at Ottawa — Ottawa 7, Galt 4; March 16, at Ottawa — Ottawa 13, Port Arthur 4.

1909-10 (March) — Montreal Wanderers — Cecil Blachford, Moose Johnson, Ernie Russell, Riley Hern, Harry Hyland, Jack Marshall, Pud Glass (Captain), Jimmy Gardner, Dickie Boon (Manager).
Scores: March 12, at Montreal — Mtl. Wanderers 7, Berlin (Kitchener) 3.

1909-10 (January) — Ottawa Senators — Dubbie Kerr, Fred Lake, Percy LeSueur, Ken Mallen, Bruce Ridpath, Gord Roberts, Hamby Shore, Bruce Stuart, Marty Walsh.
Scores: January 5, at Ottawa — Ottawa 12, Galt 3; January 7, at Ottawa — Ottawa 3, Galt 1; January 18, at Ottawa — Ottawa 8, Edmonton 4; January 20, at Ottawa — Ottawa 13, Edmonton 7.

1908-09 — Ottawa Senators — Fred Lake, Percy LeSueur, Cyclone Taylor, Billy Gilmour, Dubbie Kerr, Edgar Dey, Marty Walsh, Bruce Stuart (Captain).
Scores: Ottawa, as champions of the Eastern Canada Hockey Association took over the Stanley Cup in 1909 and, although a challenge was accepted by the Cup trustees from Winnipeg Shamrocks, games could not be arranged because of the lateness of the season. No other challenges were made in 1909. The following season — 1909-10 — however, the Senators accepted two challenges as defending Cup Champions. The first was against Galt in a two-game, total-goals series, and the second against Edmonton, also a two-game, total-goals series. Results: January 5, at Ottawa —Ottawa 12, Galt 3; January 7, at Ottawa — Ottawa 3, Galt 1. January 18, at Ottawa — Ottawa 8, Edm. Eskimos 4; January 20, at Ottawa — Ottawa 13, Edm. Eskimos 7.

1907-08 — Montreal Wanderers — Riley Hern, Art Ross, Walter Smaill, Pud Glass, Bruce Stuart, Ernie Russell, Moose Johnson, Cecil Blachford (Captain), Tom Hooper, Larry Gilmour, Ernie Liffiton, Dickie Boon (Manager).
Scores: Wanderers accepted four challenges for the Cup: January 9, at Montreal — Mtl. Wanderers 9, Ott. Victorias 3; January 13, at Montreal — Mtl. Wanderers 13, Ott. Victorias 1; March 10, at Montreal — Mtl. Wanderers 11, Wpg. Maple Leafs 5; March 12, at Montreal — Mtl. Wanderers 9, Wpg. Maple Leafs 3; March 14, at Montreal — Mtl. Wanderers 6, Toronto (OPHL) 4. At start of following season, 1908-09, Wanderers were challenged by Edmonton. Results: December 28, at Montreal — Mtl. Wanderers 7, Edm. Eskimos 3; December 30, at Montreal — Edm. Eskimos 7, Mtl. Wanderers 6. Total goals: Mtl. Wanderers 13, Edm. Eskimos 10.

1906-07 — (March 25) — Montreal Wanderers — Billy Strachan, Riley Hern, Lester Patrick, Hod Stuart, Pud Glass, Ernie Russell, Cecil Blachford (Captain), Moose Johnson, Rod Kennedy, Jack Marshall, Dickie Boon (Manager).

1906-07 — (March 18) — Kenora Thistles — Eddie Giroux, Si Griffis, Tom Hooper, Fred Whitcroft, Alf Smith, Harry Westwick, Roxy Beaudro, Tom Phillips (Captain), Russell Phillips.
Scores: March 16, at Winnipeg — Kenora 8, Brandon 6; March 18, at Winnipeg — Kenora 4, Brandon 1; March 23, at Winnipeg — Mtl. Wanderers 7, Kenora 2; March 25, at Winnipeg — Kenora 6, Mtl. Wanderers 5. Total goals: Mtl. Wanderers 12, Kenora 8.

1906-07 — (January) — Kenora Thistles — Eddie Giroux, Art Ross, Si Griffis, Tom Hooper, Billy McGimsie, Roxy Beaudro, Tommy Phillips (Captain), Joe Hall, Russell Phillips.
Scores: January 17, at Montreal — Kenora 4, Mtl. Wanderers 2; Jan. 21, at Montreal — Kenora 8, Mtl. Wanderers 6.

1905-06 — (March) — Montreal Wanderers — Henri Menard, Billy Strachan, Rod Kennedy, Lester Patrick, Pud Glass, Ernie Russell, Moose Johnson, Cecil Blachford (Captain), Josh Arnold, Dickie Boon (Manager).
Scores: March 14, at Montreal — Mtl. Wanderers 9, Ottawa 1; March 17, at Ottawa — Ottawa 9, Mtl. Wanderers 3. Total goals: Mtl. Wanderers 12, Ottawa 10. Wanderers accepted a challenge from New Glasgow, N.S., prior to the start of the 1906-07 season. Results: December 27, at Montreal — Mtl. Wanderers 10, New Glasgow 3; December 29, at Montreal — Mtl. Wanderers 7, New Glasgow 2.

1905-06 — (February) — Ottawa Silver Seven — Harvey Pulford (Captain), Arthur Moore, Harry Westwick, Frank McGee, Alf Smith (Playing Coach), Billy Gilmour, Billy Hague, Percy LeSueur, Harry Smith, Tommy Smith, Dion, Ebbs.
Scores: February 27, at Ottawa — Ottawa 16, Queen's University 7; February 28, at Ottawa — Ottawa 12, Queen's University 7; March 6, at Ottawa — Ottawa 6, Smiths Falls 5; March 8, at Ottawa — Ottawa 8, Smiths Falls 2.

1904-05 — Ottawa Silver Seven — Dave Finnie, Harvey Pulford (Captain), Arthur Moore, Harry Westwick, Frank McGee, Alf Smith (Playing Coach), Billy Gilmour, Frank White, Horace Gaul, Hamby Shore, Bones Allen.
Scores: January 13, at Ottawa — Ottawa 9, Dawson City 2; January 16, at Ottawa — Ottawa 23, Dawson City 2; March 7, at Ottawa — Rat Portage 9, Ottawa 3; March 9, at Ottawa — Ottawa 4, Rat Portage 2; March 11, at Ottawa — Ottawa 5, Rat Portage 4.

1903-04 — Ottawa Silver Seven — Suddy Gilmour, Arthur Moore, Frank McGee, Bouse Hutton, Billy Gilmour, Jim McGee, Harry Westwick, Harvey Pulford (Captain), Scott, Alf Smith (Playing Coach).
Scores: December 30, at Ottawa — Ottawa 9, Wpg. Rowing Club 1; January 1, at Ottawa — Wpg. Rowing Club 6, Ottawa 2; January 4, at Ottawa — Ottawa 2, Wpg. Rowing Club 0. February 23, at Ottawa — Ottawa 6, Tor. Marlboros 3; February 25, at Ottawa — Ottawa 11, Tor. Marlboros 2; March 2, at Montreal — Ottawa 5, Mtl. Wanderers 5. Following the tie game, a new two-game series was ordered to be played in Ottawa but the Wanderers refused unless the tie game was replayed in Montreal. When no settlement could be reached, the series was abandoned and Ottawa retained the Cup and accepted a two-game challenge from Brandon. Results: (both games at Ottawa), March 9, Ottawa 6, Brandon 3; March 11, Ottawa 9, Brandon 3.

1902-03 — (March) — Ottawa Silver Seven — Suddy Gilmour, Percy Sims, Bouse Hutton, Dave Gilmour, Billy Gilmour, Harry Westwick, Frank McGee, F.H. Wood, A.A. Fraser, Charles Spittal, Harvey Pulford (Captain), Arthur Moore, Alf Smith (coach.)
Scores: March 7, at Montreal — Ottawa 1, Mtl. Victorias 1; March 10, at Ottawa — Ottawa 8, Mtl. Victorias 0. Total goals: Ottawa 9, Mtl. Victorias 1; March 12, at Ottawa — Ottawa 6, Rat Portage 2; March 14, at Ottawa — Ottawa 4, Rat Portage 2.

1902-03 — (February) — Montreal AAA — Tom Hodge, Dickie Boon, Billy Nicholson, Tommy Phillips, Art Hooper, Billy Bellingham, Charles Liffiton, Jack Marshall, Jimmy Gardner, Cecil Blachford, George Smith.
Scores: January 29, at Montreal — Mtl. AAA 8, Wpg. Victorias 1; January 31, at Montreal — Wpg. Victorias 2, Mtl. AAA 2; February 2, at Montreal — Wpg. Victorias 4, Mtl. AAA 2; February 4, at Montreal — Mtl. AAA 5, Wpg. Victorias 1.

1901-02 — (March) — Montreal AAA — Tom Hodge, Dickie Boon, Billy Nicholson, Archie Hooper, Billy Bellingham, Charles Liffiton, Jack Marshall, Roland Elliott, Jimmy Gardner.
Scores: March 13, at Winnipeg — Wpg. Victorias 1, Mtl. AAA 0; March 15, at Winnipeg — Mtl. AAA 5, Wpg. Victorias 0; March 17, at Winnipeg — Mtl. AAA 2, Wpg. Victorias 1.

1901-02 — (January) — Winnipeg Victorias — Burke Wood, Tony Gingras, Charles Johnstone, Rod Flett, Magnus Flett, Dan Bain (Captain), Fred Scanlon, F. Cadham, G. Brown.
Scores: January 21, at Winnipeg — Wpg. Victorias 5, Tor. Wellingtons 3; January 23, at Winnipeg — Wpg. Victorias 5, Tor. Wellingtons 3.

1900-01 — Winnipeg Victorias — Burke Wood, Jack Marshall, Tony Gingras, Charles Johnstone, Rod Flett, Magnus Flett, Dan Bain (Captain), Art Brown, George Carruthers.
Scores: January 29, at Montreal — Wpg. Victorias 4, Mtl. Shamrocks 3; January 31, at Montreal — Wpg. Victorias 2, Mtl. Shamrocks 1.

1899-1900 — Montreal Shamrocks — Joe McKenna, Frank Tansey, Frank Wall, Art Farrell, Fred Scanlon, Harry Trihey (Captain), Jack Brannen.
Scores: February 12, at Montreal — Mtl. Shamrocks 4, Wpg. Victorias 3; February 14, at Montreal — Wpg. Victorias 3, Mtl. Shamrocks 2; February 16, at Montreal — Mtl. Shamrocks 5, Wpg. Victorias 4; March 5, at Montreal — Mtl. Shamrocks 10, Halifax 2; March 7, at Montreal — Mtl. Shamrocks 11, Halifax 0.

1898-99 — (March) — Montreal Shamrocks — Joe McKenna, Frank Tansey, Frank Wall, Harry Trihey (Captain), Art Farrell, Fred Scanlon, Jack Brannen, John Dobby, Charles Hoerner.
Scores: March 14, at Montreal — Mtl. Shamrocks 6, Queen's University 2.

1898-99 — (February) — Montreal Victorias — Gordon Lewis, Mike Grant, Graham Drinkwater, Cam Davidson, Bob McDougall, Ernie McLea, Frank Richardson, Jack Ewing, Russell Bowie, Douglas Acer, Fred McRobie.
Scores: February 15, at Montreal — Mtl. Victorias 2, Wpg. Victorias 1; February 18, at Montreal — Mtl. Victorias 3, Wpg. Victorias 2.

1897-98 — Montreal Victorias — Gordon Lewis, Hartland McDougall, Mike Grant, Graham Drinkwater, Cam Davidson, Bob McDougall, Ernie McLea, Frank Richardson (Captain), Jack Ewing. The Victorias as champions of the Amateur Hockey Association, retained the Cup and were not called upon to defend it.

1896-97 — Montreal Victorias — Gordon Lewis, Harold Henderson, Mike Grant (Captain), Cam Davidson, Graham Drinkwater, Bob McDougall, Ernie McLea, Shirley Davidson, Hartland McDougall, Jack Ewing, Percy Molson, David Gillilan, McLellan.
Scores: December 27, at Montreal — Mtl. Victorias 15, Ott. Capitals 2.

1895-96 — (December) — Montreal Victorias — Harold Henderson, Mike Grant (Captain), Bob McDougall, Graham Drinkwater, Shirley Davidson, Ernie McLea, W. Wallace, Robert Jones, Cam Davidson, David Gillilan, Stanley Willett.
Scores: December 30, at Winnipeg — Mtl. Victorias 6, Wpg. Victorias 5.

1895-96 — (February) — Winnipeg Victorias — Whitey Merritt, Rod Flett, Fred Higginbotham, Jack Armitage (Captain), Tote Campbell, Dan Bain, Bobby Benson, Attie Howard.
Scores: February 14, at Montreal — Wpg. Victorias 2, Mtl. Victorias 0.

1894-95 — Montreal Victorias — Robert Jones, Harold Henderson, Mike Grant (Captain), Shirley Davidson, Bob McDougall, Norman Rankin, Graham Drinkwater, Roland Elliot, William Pullan, Hartland McDougall, Art Fenwick, A. McDougall.
Montreal Victorias, as champions of the Amateur Hockey Association, were prepared to defend the Stanley Cup. However, the Stanley Cup trustees had already accepted a challenge match between the 1894 champion Montreal AAA and Queen's University. It was declared that if Montreal AAA defeated Queen's University, Montreal Victorias would be declared Stanley Cup champions. If Queen's University won, the Cup would go to the university club. In a game played March 9, 1895, Montreal AAA defeated Queen's University 5-1. As a result, Montreal Victorias were awarded the Stanley Cup.

1893-94 — Montreal AAA — Herb Collins, Allan Cameron, George James, Billy Barlow, Clare Mussen, Archie Hodgson, Haviland Routh, Alex Irving, James Stewart, E. O'Brien, A.C. (Toad) Wand, A.B. Kingan.
Scores: March 17, at Mtl. Victorias — Mtl. AAA 3, Mtl. Victorias 2; March 22, at Montreal — Mtl. AAA 3, Ott. Capitals 1.

1892-93 — Montreal AAA — Tom Paton, James Stewart, Allan Cameron, Haviland Routh, Archie Hodgson, Billy Barlow, A.B. Kingan, G.S. Lowe.
In accordance with the terms governing the presentation of the Stanley Cup, it was awarded for the first time to the Montreal AAA as champions of the Amateur Hockey Association in 1893. Once Montreal AAA had been declared holders of the Stanley Cup, any Canadian hockey team could challenge for the trophy.

All-Time NHL Playoff Formats

1917-18 — The regular-season was split into two halves. The winners of both halves faced each other in a two-game, total-goals series for the NHL championship and the right to meet the PCHA champion in the best-of-five Stanley Cup Finals.

1918-19 — Same as 1917-18, except that the Stanley Cup Finals was extended to a best-of-seven series.

1919-20 — Same as 1917-1918, except that Ottawa won both halves of the split regular-season schedule to earn an automatic berth into the best-of-five Stanley Cup Finals against the PCHA champions.

1921-22 — The top two teams at the conclusion of the regular-season faced each other in a two-game, total-goals series for the NHL championship. The NHL champion then moved on to play the winner of the PCHA-WCHL playoff series in the best-of-five Stanley Cup Finals.

1922-23 — The top two teams at the conclusion of the regular-season faced each other in a two-game, total-goals series for the NHL championship. The NHL champion then moved on to play the PCHA champion in the best-of-three Stanley Cup Semi-Finals, and the winner of the Semi-Finals played the WCHL champion, which had been given a bye, in the best-of-three Stanley Cup Finals.

1923-24 — The top two teams at the conclusion of the regular-season faced each other in a two-game, total-goals series for the NHL championship. The NHL champion then moved on to play the loser of the PCHA-WCHL playoff (the winner of the PCHA-WCHL playoff earned a bye into the Stanley Cup Finals) in the best-of-three Stanley Cup Semi-Finals. The winner of this series met the PCHA-WCHL playoff winner in the best-of-three Stanley Cup Finals.

1924-25 — The first place team (Hamilton) at the conclusion of the regular-season was supposed to play the winner of a two-game, total-goals series between the second (Toronto) and third (Montreal) place clubs. However, Hamilton refused to abide by this new format, demanding greater compensation than offered by the League. Thus, Toronto and Montreal played their two-game, total-goals series, and the winner (Montreal) earned the NHL title and then played the WCHL champion (Victoria) in the best-of-five Stanley Cup Finals.

1925-26 — The format which was intended for 1924-25 went into effect. The winner of the two-game, total-goals series between the second and third place teams squared off against the first place team in the two-game, total-goals NHL championship series. The NHL champion then moved on to play the WHL champion in the best-of-five Stanley Cup Finals.

After the 1925-26 season, the NHL was the only major professional hockey league still in existence and consequently took over sole control of the Stanley Cup competition.

1926-27 — The 10-team league was divided into two divisions — Canadian and American — of five teams apiece. In each division, the winner of the two-game, total-goals series between the second and third place teams faced the first place team in a two-game, total-goals series for the division title. The two division title winners then met in the best-of-five Stanley Cup Finals.

1928-29 — Both first place teams in the two divisions played each other in a best-of-five series. Both second place teams in the two divisions played each other in a two-game, total-goals series as did the two third place teams. The winners of these latter two series then played each other in a best-of-three series for the right to meet the winner of the series between the two first place clubs. This Stanley Cup Final was a best-of-three.

Series A: First in Canadian Division vs. first in American (best-of-five)
Series B: Second in Canadian Division vs. second in American (two-game, total-goals)
Series C: Third in Canadian Division vs. third in American (two-game, total-goals)
Series D: Winner of Series B vs. winner of Series C (best-of-three)
Series E: Winner of Series A vs. winner of Series D (best-of-three) for Stanley Cup

1931-32 — Same as 1928-29, except that Series D was changed to a two-game, total-goals format and Series E was changed to best-of-five.

1936-37 — Same as 1931-32, except that Series B, C, and D were each best-of-three.

1938-39 — With the NHL reduced to seven teams, the two-division system was replaced by one seven-team league. Based on final regular-season standings, the following playoff format was adopted:

Series A: First vs. Second (best-of-seven)
Series B: Third vs. Fourth (best-of-three)
Series C: Fifth vs. Sixth (best-of-three)
Series D: Winner of Series B vs. winner of Series C (best-of-three)
Series E: Winner of Series A vs. winner of Series D (best-of-seven)

1942-43 — With the NHL reduced to six teams (the "original six"), only the top four finishers qualified for playoff action. The best-of-seven Semi-Finals pitted Team #1 vs. Team #3 and Team #2 vs. Team #4. The winners of each Semi-Final series met in the best-of-seven Stanley Cup Finals.

1967-68 — When it doubled in size from 6 to 12 teams, the NHL once again was divided into two divisions — East and West — of six teams apiece. The top four clubs in each division qualified for the playoffs (all series were best-of-seven):

Series A: Team #1 (East) vs. Team #3 (East)
Series B: Team #2 (East) vs. Team #4 (East)
Series C: Team #1 (West) vs. Team #3 (West)
Series D: Team #2 (West) vs. Team #4 (West)
Series E: Winner of Series A vs. winner of Series B
Series F: Winner of Series C vs. winner of Series D
Series G: Winner of Series E vs. Winner of Series F

1970-71 — Same as 1967-68 except that Series E matched the winners of Series A and D, and Series F matched the winners of Series B and C.

1971-72 — Same as 1970-71, except that Series A and C matched Team #1 vs. Team #4, and Series B and D matched Team #2 vs. Team #3.

1974-75 — With the League now expanded to 18 teams in four divisions, a completely new playoff format was introduced. First, the #2 and #3 teams in each of the four divisions were pooled together in the Preliminary round. These eight (#2 and #3) clubs were ranked #1 to #8 based on regular-season record:

Series A: Team #1 vs. Team #8 (best-of-three)
Series B: Team #2 vs. Team #7 (best-of-three)
Series C: Team #3 vs. Team #6 (best-of-three)
Series D: Team #4 vs. Team #5 (best-of-three)
The winners of this Preliminary round then pooled together with the four division winners, which had received byes into this Quarter-Final round. These eight teams were again ranked #1 to #8 based on regular-season record:
Series E: Team #1 vs. Team #8 (best-of-seven)
Series F: Team #2 vs. Team #7 (best-of-seven)
Series G: Team #3 vs. Team #6 (best-of-seven)
Series H: Team #4 vs. Team #5 (best-of-seven)
The four Quarter-Finals winners, which moved on to the Semi-Finals, were then ranked #1 to #4 based on regular season record:
Series I: Team #1 vs. Team #4 (best-of-seven)
Series J: Team #2 vs. Team #3 (best-of-seven)
Series K: Winner of Series I vs. winner of Series J (best-of-seven)

1977-78 — Same as 1974-75, except that the Preliminary round consisted of the #2 teams in the four divisions and the next four teams based on regular-season record (not their standings within their divisions).

1979-80 — With the addition of four WHA franchises, the League expanded its playoff structure to include 16 of its 21 teams. The four first place teams in the four divisions automatically earned playoff berths. Among the 17 other clubs, the top 12, according to regular-season record, also earned berths. All 16 teams were then pooled together and ranked #1 to #16 based on regular-season record:

Series A: Team #1 vs. Team #16 (best-of-five)
Series B: Team #2 vs. Team #15 (best-of-five)
Series C: Team #3 vs. Team #14 (best-of-five)
Series D: Team #4 vs. Team #13 (best-of-five)
Series E: Team #5 vs. Team #12 (best-of-five)
Series F: Team #6 vs. Team #11 (best-of-five)
Series G: Team #7 vs. Team #10 (best-of-five)
Series H: Team #8 vs. Team # 9 (best-of-five)

The eight Preliminary round winners, ranked #1 to #8 based on regular-season record, moved on to the Quarter-Finals:
Series I: Team #1 vs. Team #8 (best-of-seven)
Series J: Team #2 vs. Team #7 (best-of-seven)
Series K: Team #3 vs. Team #6 (best-of-seven)
Series L: Team #4 vs. Team #5 (best-of-seven)
The four Quarter-Finals winners, ranked #1 to #4 based on regular-season record, moved on to the semi-finals:
Series M: Team #1 vs. Team #4 (best-of-seven)
Series N: Team #2 vs. Team #3 (best-of-seven)
Series O: Winner of Series M vs. winner of Series N (best-of-seven)

1981-82 — The first four teams in each division earned playoff berths. In each division, the first-place team opposed the fourth-place team and the second-place team opposed the third-place team in a best-of-five Division Semi-Final series (DSF). In each division, the two winners of the DSF met in a best-of-seven Division Final series (DF). The two DF winners in each conference met in a best-of-seven Conference Final series (CF). In the Prince of Wales Conference, the Adams Division winner opposed the Patrick Division winner; in the Clarence Campbell Conference, the Smythe Division winner opposed the Norris Division winner. The two CF winners met in a best-of-seven Stanley Cup Final (F) series.

1986-87 — Division Semi-Final series changed from best-of-five to best-of-seven.

1993-94 — The NHL's playoff draw is conference-based rather than division-based. At the conclusion of the regular season, the top eight teams in each of the Eastern and Western Conferences qualify for the playoffs. The teams that finish in first place in each of the League's divisions are seeded first and second in each conference's playoff draw and are assured of home-ice advantage in the first two playoff rounds. The remaining teams are seeded based on their regular-season point totals. In each conference, the team seeded #1 plays #8; #2 vs. #7; #3 vs. #6; and #4 vs. #5. All series are best-of-seven with home ice rotating on a 2-2-1-1-1 basis, with the exception of matchups between Central and Pacific Division teams. These matchups will be played on a 2-3-2 basis to reduce travel. In a 2-3-2 series, the team with the most points will have its choice to start the series at home or on the road. The Eastern Conference champion will face the Western Conference champion in the Stanley Cup Final.

1994-95 — Same as 1993-94, except that in first, second or third-round playoff series involving Central and Pacific Division teams, the team with the better record has the choice of using either a 2-3-2 or a 2-2-1-1-1 format. When a 2-3-2 format is selected, the higher-ranked team also has the choice of playing games 1, 2, 6 and 7 at home or playing games 3, 4 and 5 at home. The format for the Stanley Cup Final remains 2-2-1-1-1.

1998-99 — The NHL's clubs are re-aligned into two conferences each consisting of three divisions. The number of teams qualifying for the Stanley Cup Playoffs remains unchanged at 16.

First-round playoff berths will be awarded to the first-place team in each division as well as to the next five best teams based on regular-season point totals in each conference. The three division winners in each conference will be seeded first through third, in order of points, for the playoffs and the next five best teams, in order of points, will be seeded fourth through eighth. In each conference, the team seeded #1 will play #8; #2 vs. #7; #3 vs. #6; and #4 vs. #5 in the quarterfinal round. Home-ice in the Conference Quarter-Finals is granted to those teams seeded first through fourth in each conference.

In the Conference Semi-Finals and Conference Finals, teams will be re-seeded according to the same criteria as the Conference Quarter-Finals. Higher seeded teams will have home-ice advantage.

Home-ice advantage for the Stanley Cup Finals will be determined by points.

All series remain best-of-seven.

The Carolina Hurricanes went seven games in each of the last two rounds of the 2006 playoffs during their successful 25-game Stanley Cup marathon. Eric Staal, Justin Williams and Kevyn Adams played in all 107 of Carolina's games last year. Mark Recchi, acquired in a late-season trade from Pittsburgh, played a total of 108.

Team Records
1918-2006

GAMES PLAYED

MOST GAMES PLAYED BY ALL TEAMS, ONE PLAYOFF YEAR:
92 — 1991. There were 51 DSF, 24 DF, 11 CF and 6 F games.
90 — 1994. There were 48 CQF, 23 CSF, 12 CF and 7 F games.
— 2002. There were 47 CQF, 25 CSF, 13 CF and 5 F games.

MOST GAMES PLAYED, ONE TEAM, ONE PLAYOFF YEAR:
26 — Philadelphia Flyers, 1987. Won DSF 4-2 vs. NY Rangers, DF 4-3 vs. NY Islanders, CF 4-2 vs. Montreal, and lost F 4-3 vs. Edmonton.
— **Calgary Flames,** 2004. Won DSF 4-3 vs. Vancouver, DF 4-2 vs. Detroit, CF 4-2 vs. San Jose, and lost F 4-3 vs. Tampa Bay.
25 — New Jersey Devils, 2001. Won CQF 4-2 vs. Carolina, CSF 4-3 vs. Toronto, CF 4-1 vs. Pittsburgh, and lost F 4-3 vs. Colorado.
— Carolina Hurricanes, 2006. Won CQF 4-2 vs. Montreal, CSF 4-1 vs. New Jersey, CF 4-3 vs. Buffalo, and F 4-3 vs. Edmonton

PLAYOFF APPEARANCES

MOST STANLEY CUP CHAMPIONSHIPS:
23 — Montreal Canadiens (1924-30-31-44-46-53-56-57-58-59-60-65-66-68-69-71-73-76-77-78-79-86-93)
13 — Toronto Maple Leafs (1918-22-32-42-45-47-48-49-51-62-63-64-67)
10 — Detroit Red Wings (1936-37-43-50-52-54-55-97-98-02)

MOST CONSECUTIVE STANLEY CUP CHAMPIONSHIPS:
5 — Montreal Canadiens (1956-57-58-59-60)
4 — Montreal Canadiens (1976-77-78-79)
— NY Islanders (1980-81-82-83)

MOST FINAL SERIES APPEARANCES:
32 — Montreal Canadiens in 88-year history.
22 — Detroit Red Wings in 79-year history.
21 — Toronto Maple Leafs in 88-year history.

MOST CONSECUTIVE FINAL SERIES APPEARANCES:
10 — Montreal Canadiens, (1951-60, inclusive)
5 — Montreal Canadiens, (1965-69, inclusive)
— NY Islanders, (1980-84, inclusive)

MOST YEARS IN PLAYOFFS:
75 — Montreal Canadiens in 88-year history.
64 — Toronto Maple Leafs in 88-year history.
62 — Boston Bruins in 81-year history.

MOST CONSECUTIVE PLAYOFF APPEARANCES:
29 — Boston Bruins (1968-96, inclusive)
28 — Chicago Blackhawks (1970-97, inclusive)
25 — St. Louis Blues (1980-2004, inclusive)
24 — Montreal Canadiens (1971-94, inclusive)
21 — Montreal Canadiens (1949-69, inclusive)

TEAM WINS

MOST HOME WINS, ONE TEAM, ONE PLAYOFF YEAR:
12 — New Jersey Devils, 2003 in 13 home games.
11 — Edmonton Oilers, 1988 in 11 home games.
10 — Edmonton Oilers, 1985 in 10 home games.
— Montreal Canadiens, 1986 in 11 home games.
— Montreal Canadiens, 1993 in 11 home games.
— Carolina Hurricanes, 2006 in 14 home games.

MOST ROAD WINS, ONE TEAM, ONE PLAYOFF YEAR:
10 — New Jersey Devils, 1995. Won three at Boston in CQF; two at Pittsburgh in CSF; three at Philadelphia in CF; and two at Detroit in F.
— **New Jersey Devils,** 2000. Won two at Florida in CQF; two at Toronto in CSF; three at Philadelphia in CF; and three at Dallas in F.
— **Calgary Flames,** 2004. Won three at Vancouver in DSF; two at Detroit in DF; three at San Jose in CF; and two at Tampa Bay in F.
8 — NY Islanders, 1980. Won two at Los Angeles in PR; three at Boston in QF; two at Buffalo in SF; and one at Philadelphia in F.
— Philadelphia Flyers, 1987. Won two at NY Rangers in DSF; two at NY Islanders in DF; three at Montreal in CF; and one at Edmonton in F.
— Edmonton Oilers, 1990. Won one at Winnipeg in DSF; two at Los Angeles in DF; two at Chicago in CF and three at Boston in F.
— Pittsburgh Penguins, 1992. Won two at Washington in DSF; two at NY Rangers in DF; two at Boston in CF; and two at Chicago in F.
— Vancouver Canucks, 1994. Won three at Calgary in CQF; two at Dallas in CSF; one at Toronto in CF; and two at NY Rangers in F.
— Colorado Avalanche, 1996. Won two at Vancouver in CQF; two at Chicago in CSF; two at Detroit in CF; and two at Florida in F.
— Detroit Red Wings, 1998. Won two at Phoenix in CQF; three at St. Louis in CSF; one at Dallas in CF; and two at Washington in F.
— Colorado Avalanche, 1999. Won three at San Jose in CQF; three at Detroit in CSF; and two at Dallas in CF.
— New Jersey Devils, 2001. Won two at Carolina in CQF; two at Toronto in CSF; two at Pittsburgh in CF; and two at Colorado in F.
— Detroit Red Wings, 2002. Won three at Vancouver in CQF; one at St. Louis in CSF; two at Colorado in CF; and two at Carolina in F.

MOST ROAD WINS, ALL TEAMS, ONE PLAYOFF YEAR:
46 — 1987. Of 87 games played, road teams won 46 (22 DSF, 14 DF, 8 CF and 2 in F).

MOST OVERTIME WINS, ONE TEAM, ONE PLAYOFF YEAR:
10 — Montreal Canadiens, 1993. Won two vs. Quebec in DSF; three vs. Buffalo in DF; two vs. NY Islanders in CF; and three vs. Los Angeles in F.
7 — Carolina Hurricanes, 2002. Won two vs. New Jersey in CQF; one vs. Montreal in CSF; three vs. Toronto in CF; and one vs. Detroit in F.
— Anaheim Mighty Ducks, 2003. Won two vs. Detroit in CQF; two vs. Dallas in CSF; one vs. Minnestoa in CF; and two vs. New Jersey in F.

MOST OVERTIME WINS AT HOME, ONE TEAM, ONE PLAYOFF YEAR:
4 — St. Louis Blues, 1968. Won one vs. Philadelphia in QF; three vs. Minnesota in SF.
— **Montreal Canadiens, 1993.** Won one vs. Quebec in DSF; one vs. Buffalo in DF, one vs. NY Islanders in CF; one vs. Los Angeles in F.

MOST OVERTIME WINS ON THE ROAD, ONE TEAM, ONE PLAYOFF YEAR:
6 — Montreal Canadiens, 1993. Won one vs. Quebec in DSF; two vs. Buffalo in DF; one vs. NY Islanders in CF; two vs. Los Angeles in F.

TEAM LOSSES

MOST LOSSES, ONE TEAM, ONE PLAYOFF YEAR:
11 — Philadelphia Flyers, 1987. Lost two vs. NY Rangers in DSF; three vs. NY Islanders in DF; two vs. Montreal in CF; four vs. Edmonton in F.
— **Calgary Flames, 2004.** Lost three vs. Vancouver in CQF; two vs. Detroit in CSF; two vs. San Jose in CF; four vs. Tampa Bay in F

MOST HOME LOSSES, ONE TEAM, ONE PLAYOFF YEAR:
7 — Calgary Flames, 2004. Lost two vs. Vancouver in DSF; one vs. Detroit in DF; two vs. San Jose in CF; two vs. Tampa Bay in F.
6 — Philadelphia Flyers, 1987. Lost one vs. NY Rangers in DSF; two vs. NY Islanders in DF; two vs. Montreal in CF; one vs. Edmonton in F.
— **Washington Capitals, 1998.** Lost two vs. Boston in CQF; two vs. Buffalo in CF; two vs. Detroit in F.
— **Colorado Avalanche, 1999.** Lost two vs. San Jose in CQF; two vs. Detroit in CSF; two vs. Dallas in CF.
— **New Jersey Devils, 2001.** Lost one vs. Carolina in CQF; two vs. Toronto in CSF; one vs. Pittsburgh in CF; two vs Colorado in F.
— **Minnesota Wild, 2003.** Lost two vs. Colorado in CQF; two vs. Vancouver in CSF; two vs. Anaheim in CF.

MOST ROAD LOSSES, ONE TEAM, ONE PLAYOFF YEAR:
7 — New Jersey Devils, 2003. Lost one at Boston in CQF; one at Tampa Bay in CSF; two at Ottawa in CF; three at Anaheim in F.

MOST OVERTIME LOSSES, ONE TEAM, ONE PLAYOFF YEAR:
4 — Montreal Canadiens, 1951. Lost four vs. Toronto in F.
— **St. Louis Blues, 1968.** Lost one vs. Philadelphia in QF; one vs. Minnesota in SF; two vs. Montreal in F.
— **New York Rangers, 1979.** Lost one vs. Philadelphia in QF; two vs. NY Islanders in SF; one vs. Montreal in F.
— **Los Angeles Kings, 1991.** Lost one vs. Vancouver in DSF; three vs. Edmonton in DF.
— **Los Angeles Kings, 1993.** Lost one vs. Toronto in CF; three vs. Montreal in F.
— **New Jersey Devils, 1994.** Lost one vs. Buffalo in CQF; one vs. Boston in CSF; two vs. NY Rangers in CF.
— **Chicago Blackhawks, 1995.** Lost one vs. Toronto in CQF; three vs. Detroit in CF.
— **Philadelphia Flyers, 1996.** Lost two vs. Tampa Bay in CQF; two vs. Florida in CSF.
— **Dallas Stars, 1999.** Lost two vs. St. Louis in CSF; one vs. Colorado in CF; one vs. Buffalo in F.
— **Detroit Red Wings, 2002.** Lost one vs. Vancouver in CQF; two vs. Colorado in CF; one vs. Carolina in F.
— **New Jersey Devils, 2003.** Lost two vs. Ottawa in CF; two vs. Anaheim in F.

MOST OVERTIME LOSSES AT HOME, ONE TEAM, ONE PLAYOFF YEAR:
4 — Detroit Red Wings, 2002. Lost one vs. Vancouver in CQF; two vs. Colorado in CF; one vs. Carolina in F.

MOST OVERTIME LOSSES ON THE ROAD, ONE TEAM, ONE PLAYOFF YEAR:
3 — Los Angeles Kings, 1991. Lost one at Vancouver in DSF; two at Edmonton in DF.
— **Chicago Blackhawks, 1995.** Lost one at Toronto in CQF; two at Detroit in CF.
— **St. Louis Blues, 1996.** Lost two at Toronto in CQF; one at Detroit in CSF.
— **Dallas Stars, 1999.** Lost two at St. Louis in CSF; one at Colorado in CF.
— **New Jersey Devils, 2003.** Lost one at Ottawa in CF; two at Anaheim in F.

PLAYOFF WINNING STREAKS

LONGEST PLAYOFF WINNING STREAK:
14 — Pittsburgh Penguins. Streak started May 9, 1992 as Pittsburgh won the first of three straight games in DF vs. NY Rangers. Continued with four wins vs. Boston in 1992 CF and four wins vs. Chicago in 1992 F. Pittsburgh then won the first three games of 1993 DSF vs. New Jersey. New Jersey ended the streak April 25, 1993, at New Jersey with a 4-1 win vs. Pittsburgh in the fourth game of 1993 DSF.
12 — Edmonton Oilers. Streak started May 15, 1984 as Edmonton won the first of three straight games in DF vs. NY Islanders. Continued with three wins vs. Los Angeles in 1985 DSF and four wins vs. Winnipeg in 1985 DF. Edmonton then won the first two games of 1985 CF vs. Chicago. Chicago ended the streak May 9, 1985, at Chicago with a 5-2 win vs. Edmonton in the third game of 1985 CF.

MOST CONSECUTIVE WINS, ONE TEAM, ONE PLAYOFF YEAR:
11 — Chicago Blackhawks in 1992. Chicago won last three games of DSF vs. St. Louis to win series 4-2, defeated Detroit 4-0 in DF and Edmonton 4-0 in CF.
— **Pittsburgh Penguins** in 1992. Pittsburgh won last three games of DF vs. NY Rangers to win series 4-2, defeated Boston 4-0 in CF and Chicago 4-0 in F.
— **Montreal Canadiens** in 1993. Montreal won last four games of DSF vs. Quebec to win series 4-2, defeated Buffalo 4-0 in DF and won first three games of CF vs. NY Islanders.

PLAYOFF LOSING STREAKS

LONGEST PLAYOFF LOSING STREAK:
16 — Chicago Black Hawks. Streak started April 20, 1975 at Chicago with a 6-2 loss in fourth game of QF vs. Buffalo, won by Buffalo 4-1. Continued with four consecutive losses vs. Montreal, in 1976 QF and two straight losses vs. NY Islanders in 1977 best-of-three PRE. Chicago then lost four games vs. Boston in 1978 QF and four games vs. NY Islanders in 1979 QF. Chicago ended the streak April 8, 1980, at Chicago with a 3-2 win vs. St. Louis in the opening game of 1980 PRE.
— **Los Angeles Kings.** Streak started June 3, 1993 at Montreal with a 3-2 loss in second game of F vs. Montreal, won by Montreal 4-1. Los Angeles failed to qualify for the playoffs for the next four years. Then Los Angeles lost four games vs. St. Louis in 1998 CQF; missed the 1999 playoffs and lost four games vs. Detroit in 2002 CQF. Los Angeles then lost the first two games of 2001 CQF vs. Detroit. Los Angeles ended the streak April 15, 2001, at Los Angeles with a 2-1 win vs. Detroit in the third game of 2001 CQF.

Red Wings coach Jim Skinner kisses the Cup after Detroit's victory in 1955 as Marguerite Norris, Clarence Campbell and several players (including Gordie Howe) smile with approval. Detroit has won the Stanley Cup 10 times in all.

MOST GOALS IN A SERIES, ONE TEAM

MOST GOALS, ONE TEAM, ONE PLAYOFF SERIES:
44 — **Edmonton Oilers** in 1985. Edmonton won best-of-seven CF 4-2, outscoring Chicago 44-25.
35 — Edmonton Oilers in 1983. Edmonton won best-of-seven DF 4-1, outscoring Calgary 35-13.
— Calgary Flames in 1995. Calgary lost best-of-seven CQF 4-3, outscoring San Jose 35-26.

MOST GOALS, ONE TEAM, TWO-GAME SERIES:
11 — **Buffalo Sabres** in 1977. Buffalo won best-of-three PRE 2-0, outscoring Minnesota 11-3.
— **Toronto Maple Leafs** in 1978. Toronto won best-of-three PRE 2-0, outscoring Los Angeles 11-3.

MOST GOALS, ONE TEAM, THREE-GAME SERIES:
23 — **Chicago Blackhawks** in 1985. Chicago won best-of-five DSF 3-0, outscoring Detroit 23-8.
20 — Minnesota North Stars in 1981. Minnesota won best-of-five PRE 3-0, outscoring Boston 20-13.
— NY Islanders in 1981. NY Islanders won best-of-five PRE 3-0, outscoring Toronto 20-4.

MOST GOALS, ONE TEAM, FOUR-GAME SERIES:
28 — **Boston Bruins** in 1972. Boston won best-of-seven SF 4-0, outscoring St. Louis 28-8.

MOST GOALS, ONE TEAM, FIVE-GAME SERIES:
35 — **Edmonton Oilers** in 1983. Edmonton won best-of-seven DF 4-1, outscoring Calgary 35-13.
32 — Edmonton Oilers in 1987. Edmonton won best-of-seven DSF 4-1, outscoring Los Angeles 32-20.
30 — Calgary Flames in 1988. Calgary won best-of-seven DSF 4-1, outscoring Los Angeles 30-18.

MOST GOALS, ONE TEAM, SIX-GAME SERIES:
44 — **Edmonton Oilers** in 1985. Edmonton won best-of-seven CF 4-2, outscoring Chicago 44-25.
33 — Montreal Canadiens in 1973. Montreal won best-of-seven F 4-2, outscoring Chicago 33-23.
— Chicago Blackhawks in 1985. Chicago won best-of-seven DF 4-2, outscoring Minnesota 33-29.
— Los Angeles Kings in 1993. Los Angeles won best-of-seven DSF 4-2, outscoring Calgary 33-28.

MOST GOALS, ONE TEAM, SEVEN-GAME SERIES:
35 — **Calgary Flames** in 1995. Calgary lost best-of-seven CQF 4-3, outscoring San Jose 35-26.
33 — Philadelphia Flyers in 1976. Philadelphia won best-of-seven QF 4-3, outscoring Toronto 33-23.
— Boston Bruins in 1983. Boston won best-of-seven DF 4-3, outscoring Buffalo 33-23.
— Edmonton Oilers in 1984. Edmonton won best-of-seven DF 4-3, outscoring Calgary 33-27.

FEWEST GOALS IN A SERIES, ONE TEAM

FEWEST GOALS, ONE TEAM, TWO-GAME SERIES:
0 — **Toronto St. Patricks** in 1921. Toronto lost two-game, total-goals NHL F 7-0 vs. Ottawa.
— **New York Americans** in 1929. NY Americans lost two-game, total-goals QF 1-0 vs. NY Rangers.
— **New York Rangers** in 1931. NY Rangers lost two-game, total-goals SF 3-0 vs. Chicago.
— **Chicago Black Hawks** in 1935. Chicago lost two-game, total-goals SF 1-0 vs. Mtl. Maroons.
— **Montreal Maroons** in 1937. Mtl. Maroons lost best-of-three SF 2-0, outscored by NY Rangers 5-0.
— **New York Americans** in 1939. NY Americans lost best-of-three QF 2-0, outscored by Toronto 5-0.

FEWEST GOALS, ONE TEAM, THREE-GAME SERIES:
1 — **Montreal Maroons** in 1936. Mtl. Maroons lost best-of-five SF 3-0, outscored by Detroit 6-1.

FEWEST GOALS, ONE TEAM, FOUR-GAME SERIES:
1 — **Minnesota Wild** in 2003. Minnesota lost best-of-seven CF 4-0, outscored by Anaheim 9-1.

FEWEST GOALS, ONE TEAM, FIVE-GAME SERIES:
2 — **Philadelphia Flyers** in 2002. Ottawa won best-of-seven CQF 4-1, while outscoring Philadelphia 11-2.

FEWEST GOALS, ONE TEAM, SIX-GAME SERIES:
5 — **Boston Bruins** in 1951. Toronto won best-of-seven SF 4-1 with 1 tie, outscoring Boston 17-5.

FEWEST GOALS, ONE TEAM, SEVEN-GAME SERIES:
9 — **Toronto Maple Leafs,** in 1945. Toronto won best-of-seven F 4-3; teams tied in scoring 9-9.
— **Detroit Red Wings,** in 1945. Toronto won best-of-seven F 4-3; teams tied in scoring 9-9.

Roy Worters of the New York Americans surrendered just one goal in the 1929 playoffs, but it was enough to knock his team out of the postseason. Worters' Americans were beaten 1-0 by the rival Rangers in a two-game, total-goals quarterfinal series.

MOST GOALS IN A SERIES, BOTH TEAMS

MOST GOALS, BOTH TEAMS, ONE PLAYOFF SERIES:
69 — **Edmonton Oilers (44), Chicago Black Hawks (25)** in 1985. Edmonton won best-of-seven CF 4-2.
62 — Chicago Black Hawks (33), Minnesota North Stars (29) in 1985. Chicago won best-of-seven DF 4-2.
61 — Los Angeles Kings (33), Calgary Flames (28) in 1993. Los Angeles won best-of-seven DSF 4-2.
— Calgary Flames (35), San Jose Sharks (26) in 1995. San Jose won best-of-seven CQF 4-3.

MOST GOALS, BOTH TEAMS, TWO-GAME SERIES:
17 — **Toronto St. Patricks (10), Montreal Canadiens (7)** in 1918. Toronto won two-game total-goals NHL F.
15 — Boston Bruins (10), Chicago Black Hawks (5) in 1927. Boston won two-game total-goals QF.
— Pittsburgh Penguins (9), St. Louis Blues (6) in 1975. Pittsburgh won best-of-three PRE 2-0.

MOST GOALS, BOTH TEAMS, THREE-GAME SERIES:
33 — **Minnesota North Stars (20), Boston Bruins (13)** in 1981. Minnesota won best-of-five PRE 3-0.
31 — Chicago Black Hawks (23), Detroit Red Wings (8) in 1985. Chicago won best-of-five DSF 3-0.
28 — Toronto Maple Leafs (18), New York Rangers (10) in 1932. Toronto won best-of-five F 3-0.

MOST GOALS, BOTH TEAMS, FOUR-GAME SERIES:
36 — **Boston Bruins (28), St. Louis Blues (8)** in 1972. Boston won best-of-seven SF 4-0.
— **Minnesota North Stars (18), Toronto Maple Leafs (18)** in 1983. Minnesota won best-of-five DSF 3-1.
— **Edmonton Oilers (25), Chicago Black Hawks (11)** in 1983. Edmonton won best-of-seven CF 4-0.
35 — New York Rangers (23), Los Angeles Kings (12) in 1981. NY Rangers won best-of-five PRE 3-1.

MOST GOALS, BOTH TEAMS, FIVE-GAME SERIES:
52 — Edmonton Oilers (32), Los Angeles Kings (20) in 1987. Edmonton won best-of-seven DSF 4-1.
50 — Los Angeles Kings (27), Edmonton Oilers (23) in 1982. Los Angeles won best-of-five DSF 3-2.
48 — Edmonton Oilers (35), Calgary Flames (13) in 1983. Edmonton won best-of-seven DF 4-1.
— Calgary Flames (30), Los Angeles Kings (18) in 1988. Calgary won best-of-seven DSF 4-1.

MOST GOALS, BOTH TEAMS, SIX-GAME SERIES:
69 — Edmonton Oilers (44), Chicago Black Hawks (25) in 1985. Edmonton won best-of-seven CF 4-2.
62 — Chicago Black Hawks (33), Minnesota North Stars (29) in 1985. Chicago won best-of-seven DF 4-2.
61 — Los Angeles Kings (33), Calgary Flames (28) in 1993. Los Angeles won best-of-seven DSF 4-2.

MOST GOALS, BOTH TEAMS, SEVEN-GAME SERIES:
61 — Calgary Flames (35), San Jose Sharks (26) in 1995. San Jose won best-of-seven CQF 4-3.
60 — Edmonton Oilers (33), Calgary Flames (27) in 1984. Edmonton won best-of-seven DF 4-3.

FEWEST GOALS IN A SERIES, BOTH TEAMS

FEWEST GOALS, BOTH TEAMS, TWO-GAME SERIES:
1 — New York Rangers (1), New York Americans (0) in 1929. NY Rangers won two-game total-goals QF.
— **Montreal Maroons (1), Chicago Black Hawks (0)** in 1935. Mtl. Maroons won two-game total-goals SF.

FEWEST GOALS, BOTH TEAMS, THREE-GAME SERIES:
7 — Boston Bruins (5), Montreal Canadiens (2) in 1929. Boston won best-of-five SF 3-0.
— **Detroit Red Wings (6), Montreal Maroons (1)** in 1936. Detroit won best-of-five SF 3-0.

FEWEST GOALS, BOTH TEAMS, FOUR-GAME SERIES:
9 — Toronto Maple Leafs (7), Boston Bruins (2) in 1935. Toronto won best-of-five SF 3-1.

FEWEST GOALS, BOTH TEAMS, FIVE-GAME SERIES:
11 — Montreal Maroons (6), New York Rangers (5) in 1928. NY Rangers won best-of-five F 3-2.

FEWEST GOALS, BOTH TEAMS, SIX-GAME SERIES:
16 — Carolina Hurricanes (10), Toronto Maple Leafs (6) in 2002. Carolina won best-of-seven CF 4-2.

FEWEST GOALS, BOTH TEAMS, SEVEN-GAME SERIES:
18 — Toronto Maple Leafs (9), Detroit Red Wings (9) in 1945. Toronto won best-of-seven F 4-3.

MOST GOALS IN A GAME OR PERIOD

MOST GOALS, ONE TEAM, ONE GAME:
13 — Edmonton Oilers April 9, 1987, vs. Los Angeles at Edmonton. Edmonton won 13-3.
12 — Los Angeles Kings, April 10, 1990, vs. Calgary at Los Angeles. Los Angeles won 12-4.
11 — Montreal Canadiens, March 30, 1944, vs. Toronto at Montreal. Montreal won 11-0.
— Edmonton Oilers, May 4, 1985, vs. Chicago at Edmonton. Edmonton won 11-2.

MOST GOALS, ONE TEAM, ONE PERIOD:
7 — Montreal Canadiens (6), March 30, 1944, vs. Toronto at Montreal, third period. Montreal won 11-0.

MOST GOALS, BOTH TEAMS, ONE GAME:
18 — Los Angeles Kings (10), Edmonton Oilers (8), April 7, 1982, at Edmonton. Los Angeles won best-of-five DSF 3-2.
17 — Pittsburgh Penguins (10), Philadelphia Flyers (7), April 25, 1989, at Pittsburgh. Pittsburgh won best-of-seven DF 4-3.
16 — Edmonton Oilers (13), Los Angeles Kings (3), April 9, 1987, at Edmonton. Edmonton won best-of-seven DSF 4-1.
— Los Angeles Kings (12), Calgary Flames (4), April 10, 1990, at Los Angeles. Los Angeles won best-of-seven DF 4-2.

MOST GOALS, BOTH TEAMS, ONE PERIOD:
9 — New York Rangers (6), Philadelphia Flyers (3), April 24, 1979, third period, at Philadelphia. NY Rangers won 8-3.
— **Los Angeles Kings (5), Calgary Flames (4),** April 10, 1990, second period, at Los Angeles. Los Angeles won 12-4.
8 — Chicago Black Hawks (5), Montreal Canadiens (3), May 8, 1973, second period, at Montreal. Chicago won 8-7.
— Chicago Black Hawks (5), Edmonton Oilers (3), May 12, 1985, first period, at Chicago. Chicago won 8-6.
— Edmonton Oilers (6), Winnipeg Jets (2), April 6, 1988, third period, at Edmonton. Edmonton won 7-4.
— Hartford Whalers (5), Montreal Canadiens (3), April 10, 1988, third period, at Montreal. Hartford won 7-5.
— Vancouver Canucks (5), New York Rangers (3), June 9, 1994, third period, at NY Rangers. Vancouver won 6-3.

TEAM POWER-PLAY GOALS

MOST POWER-PLAY GOALS BY ALL TEAMS, ONE PLAYOFF YEAR:
199 — 1988 in 83 games.

MOST POWER-PLAY GOALS, ONE TEAM, ONE PLAYOFF YEAR:
35 — Minnesota North Stars, 1991 in 23 games.
32 — Edmonton Oilers, 1988 in 18 games.
31 — New York Islanders, 1981 in 18 games.

MOST POWER-PLAY GOALS, ONE TEAM, ONE SERIES:
15 — New York Islanders in 1980 F vs. Philadelphia. NY Islanders won series 4-2.
— **Minnesota North Stars** in 1991 DSF vs. Chicago. Minnesota won series 4-2.
13 — New York Islanders in 1981 QF vs. Edmonton. NY Islanders won series 4-2.
— Calgary Flames in 1986 CF vs. St. Louis. Calgary won series 4-3.
12 — Toronto Maple Leafs in 1976 QF vs. Philadelphia. Philadelphia won series 4-3.

MOST POWER-PLAY GOALS, BOTH TEAMS, ONE SERIES:
21 — New York Islanders (15), Philadelphia Flyers (6) in 1980 best-of-seven F won by NY Islanders 4-2.
— **New York Islanders (13), Edmonton Oilers (8)** in 1981 best-of-seven QF won by NY Islanders 4-2.
— **Philadelphia Flyers (11), Pittsburgh Penguins (10)** in 1989 best-of-seven DF won by Philadelphia 4-3.
— **Minnesota North Stars (15), Chicago Black Hawks (6)** in 1991 best-of-seven DSF won by Minnesota 4-2.
20 — Toronto Maple Leafs (12), Philadelphia Flyers (8) in 1976 best-of-seven QF won by Philadelphia 4-3.

MOST POWER-PLAY GOALS, ONE TEAM, ONE GAME:
6 — Boston Bruins, April 2, 1969, at Boston vs. Toronto. Boston won 10-0.

MOST POWER-PLAY GOALS, BOTH TEAMS, ONE GAME:
8 — Minnesota North Stars (4), St. Louis Blues (4), April 24, 1991, at Minnesota. Minnesota won 8-4.
7 — Minnesota North Stars (4), Edmonton Oilers (3), May 14, 1985, at Edmonton. Edmonton won 10-5.
— Philadelphia Flyers (4), NY Rangers (3), April 13, 1985, at NY Rangers. Philadelphia won 6-5.
— Chicago Black Hawks (5), Edmonton Oilers (2), May 14, 1985, at Edmonton. Edmonton won 10-5.
— Edmonton Oilers (5), Los Angeles Kings (2), April 9, 1987, at Edmonton. Edmonton won 13-3.
— Vancouver Canucks (4), Calgary Flames (3), April 9, 1989, at Vancouver. Vancouver won 5-3.

MOST POWER-PLAY GOALS, ONE TEAM, ONE PERIOD:
4 — Toronto Maple Leafs, March 26, 1936, second period vs. Boston at Toronto. Toronto won 8-3.
— **Minnesota North Stars,** April 28, 1984, second period vs. Edmonton at Minnesota. Minnesota won 8-5.
— **Boston Bruins,** April 11, 1991, third period vs. Hartford at Boston. Boston won 6-1.
— **Minnesota North Stars,** April 24, 1991, second period vs. St. Louis at Minnesota. Minnesota won 8-4.
— **St. Louis Blues,** April 27, 1998, third period at Los Angeles. St. Louis won 4-3.

MOST POWER-PLAY GOALS, BOTH TEAMS, ONE PERIOD:
5 — Minnesota North Stars (4), Edmonton Oilers (1), April 28, 1984, at Minnesota. Edmonton won 8-5.
— **Vancouver Canucks (3), Calgary Flames (2),** April 9, 1989, at Vancouver. Vancouver won 5-3.
— **Minnesota North Stars (4), St. Louis Blues (1),** April 24, 1991, at Minnesota. Minnesota won 8-4.

TEAM SHORTHAND GOALS

MOST SHORTHAND GOALS BY ALL TEAMS, ONE PLAYOFF YEAR:
33 — 1988, in 83 games.

MOST SHORTHAND GOALS, ONE TEAM, ONE PLAYOFF YEAR:
10 — Edmonton Oilers, 1983, in 16 games.
9 — New York Islanders, 1981, in 19 games.
8 — Philadelphia Flyers, 1989, in 19 games.

MOST SHORTHAND GOALS, ONE TEAM, ONE SERIES:

6 — Calgary Flames in 1995 vs. San Jose in best-of-seven CQF won by San Jose 4-3.
— Vancouver Canucks in 1995 vs. St. Louis in best-of-seven CQF won by Vancouver 4-3.
5 — NY Rangers in 1979 vs. Philadelphia in best-of-seven QF won by NY Rangers 4-1.
— Edmonton Oilers in 1983 vs. Calgary in best-of-seven DF won by Edmonton 4-1.

MOST SHORTHAND GOALS, BOTH TEAMS, ONE SERIES:

7 — Boston Bruins (4), NY Rangers (3), in 1958 SF won by Boston 4-2.
— Edmonton Oilers (5), Calgary Flames (2), in 1983 DF won by Edmonton 4-1.
— Vancouver Canucks (6), St. Louis Blues (1), in 1995 CQF won by Vancouver 4-3.

MOST SHORTHAND GOALS, ONE TEAM, ONE GAME:

3 — Boston Bruins, April 11, 1981, at Minnesota North Stars. Minnesota won 6-3.
— New York Islanders, April 17, 1983, at NY Rangers. NY Rangers won 7-6.
— Toronto Maple Leafs, May 8, 1994, at San Jose Sharks. Toronto won 8-3.

MOST SHORTHAND GOALS, BOTH TEAMS, ONE GAME:

4 — Boston Bruins (3), Minnesota North Stars (1), April 11, 1981, at Minnesota. Minnesota won 6-3.
— New York Islanders (3), New York Rangers (1), April 17, 1983, at NY Rangers. NY Rangers won 7-6.
— Toronto Maple Leafs (3), San Jose Sharks (1), May 8, 1994, at San Jose. Toronto won 8-3.
3 — Toronto Maple Leafs (2), Detroit Red Wings (1), April 5, 1947, at Toronto. Toronto won 6-1.
— New York Rangers (2), Boston Bruins (1), April 1, 1958, at Boston. NY Rangers won 5-2.
— Minnesota North Stars (2), Philadelphia Flyers (1), May 4, 1980, at Minnesota. Philadelphia won 5-3.
— Winnipeg Jets (2), Edmonton Oilers (1), April 9, 1988, at Winnipeg. Winnipeg won 6-4.
— New York Islanders (2), New Jersey Devils (1), April 14, 1988, at New Jersey. New Jersey won 6-5.
— Montreal Canadiens (2), New Jersey Devils (1), April 17, 1997, at New Jersey. New Jersey won 5-2.
— Dallas Stars (2), San Jose Sharks (1), May 5, 2000, at San Jose. Dallas won 5-4.

MOST SHORTHAND GOALS, ONE TEAM, ONE PERIOD:

2 — Toronto Maple Leafs, April 5, 1947, first period vs. Detroit at Toronto. Toronto won 6-1.
— Toronto Maple Leafs, April 13, 1965, first period vs. Montreal at Toronto. Montreal won 4-3.
— Boston Bruins, April 20, 1969, first period vs. Montreal at Boston. Boston won 3-2.
— Boston Bruins, April 8, 1970, second period vs. NY Rangers at Boston. Boston won 8-2.
— Boston Bruins, April 30, 1972, first period vs. NY Rangers at Boston. Boston won 6-5.
— Chicago Black Hawks, May 3, 1973, first period vs. Montreal at Chicago. Chicago won 7-4.
— Montreal Canadiens, April 23, 1978, first period at Detroit. Montreal won 8-0.
— New York Islanders, April 8, 1980, second period vs. Los Angeles at NY Islanders. NY Islanders won 8-1.
— Los Angeles Kings, April 9, 1980, first period at NY Islanders. Los Angeles won 6-3.
— Boston Bruins, April 13, 1980, second period at Pittsburgh. Boston won 8-3.
— Minnesota North Stars, May 4, 1980, second period vs. Philadelphia at Minnesota. Philadelphia won 5-3.
— Boston Bruins, April 11, 1981, third period at Minnesota North Stars. Minnesota won 6-3.
— New York Islanders, May 12, 1981, first period vs. Minnesota North Stars at NY Islanders. NY Islanders won 6-3.
— Montreal Canadiens, April 7, 1982, third period vs. Quebec at Montreal. Montreal won 5-1.
— Edmonton Oilers, April 24, 1983, third period vs. Chicago at Edmonton. Edmonton won 8-4.
— Winnipeg Jets, April 14, 1985, second period at Calgary. Winnipeg won 5-3.
— Boston Bruins, April 6, 1988, first period vs. Buffalo at Boston. Boston won 7-3.
— New York Islanders, April 14, 1988, third period at New Jersey. New Jersey won 6-5.
— Detroit Red Wings, April 29, 1993, second period at Toronto. Detroit won 7-3.
— Toronto Maple Leafs, May 8, 1994, third period at San Jose. Toronto won 8-3.
— Calgary Flames, May 11, 1995, first period at San Jose. Calgary won 9-2.
— Vancouver Canucks, May 15, 1995, second period at St. Louis. Vancouver won 6-5.
— Montreal Canadiens, April 17, 1997, second period at New Jersey. New Jersey won 5-2.
— Philadelphia Flyers, April 26, 1997, first period vs. Pittsburgh at Philadelphia. Philadelphia won 6-3.
— Phoenix Coyotes, April 24, 1998, second period at Detroit. Phoenix won 7-4.
— Buffalo Sabres, April 27, 1998, second period vs. Philadelphia at Buffalo. Buffalo won 6-1.
— San Jose Sharks, April 30, 1999, third period at Colorado. San Jose won 7-3.
— Detroit Red Wings, April 27, 2002, second period at Vancouver. Detroit won 6-4.

MOST SHORTHAND GOALS, BOTH TEAMS, ONE PERIOD:

3 — Toronto Maple Leafs (2), Detroit Red Wings (1), April 5, 1947, first period at Toronto. Toronto won 6-1.
— Toronto Maple Leafs (2), San Jose Sharks (1), May 8, 1994, third period at San Jose. Toronto won 8-3.

FASTEST GOALS

FASTEST FIVE GOALS, BOTH TEAMS:

3:06 — Minnesota North Stars, Chicago Black Hawks, April 21, 1985, at Chicago. Keith Brown scored for Chicago at 1:12 of the second period; Ken Yaremchuk, Chicago, 1:27; Dino Ciccarelli, Minnesota, 2:48; Tony McKegney, Minnesota, 4:07; and Curt Fraser, Chicago, 4:18. Chicago won 6-2 and won best-of-seven DF 4-2.
3:20 — Minnesota North Stars, Philadelphia Flyers, April 29, 1980, at Philadelphia. Paul Shmyr scored for Minnesota at 13:20 of the first period; Steve Christoff, Minnesota, 13:59; Ken Linseman, Philadelphia, 14:54; Tom Gorence, Philadelphia, 15:36; and Ken Linseman, Philadelphia, 16:40. Minnesota won 6-5. Philadelphia won best-of-seven SF 4-1.
4:00 — Los Angeles Kings, Detroit Red Wings, April 15, 2000, at Detroit. Brendan Shanahan scored for Detroit at 0:55 of the first period; Martin Lapointe, Detroit, 1:33; Luc Robitaille, Los Angeles, 2:04; Kris Draper, Detroit, 3:32; and Ziggy Palffy, Los Angeles, 4:55. Detroit won 8-5 and won best-of-seven CQF 4-0.

FASTEST FIVE GOALS, ONE TEAM:

3:36 — Montreal Canadiens, March 30, 1944, at Montreal vs. Toronto. Toe Blake scored at 7:58 and 8:37 of the third period; Maurice Richard, 9:17; Ray Getliffe, 10:33; and Buddy O'Connor, 11:34. Canadiens won 11-0 and won best-of-seven SF 4-1.

FASTEST FOUR GOALS, BOTH TEAMS:

1:33 — Toronto Maple Leafs, Philadelphia Flyers, April 20, 1976, at Philadelphia. Don Saleski scored for Philadelphia at 10:04 of the second period; Bob Neely, Toronto, 10:42; Gary Dornhoefer, Philadelphia, 11:24; and Don Saleski, Philadelphia, 11:37. Philadelphia won 7-1 and won best-of-seven SF 4-3.
1:34 — Calgary Flames, Montreal Canadiens, May 20, 1986, at Montreal. Joel Otto scored for Calgary at 17:59 of the first period; Bobby Smith, Montreal, 18:25; Mats Naslund, Montreal, 19:17; and Bob Gainey, Montreal, 19:33. Montreal won 5-3 and won best-of-seven F 4-1.
1:38 — Boston Bruins, Philadelphia Flyers, April 26, 1977, at Philadelphia. Gregg Sheppard scored for Boston at 14:01 of the second period; Mike Milbury, Boston, 15:01; Gary Dornhoefer, Philadelphia, 15:16; and Jean Ratelle, Boston, 15:39. Boston won 5-4 and won best-of-seven SF 4-0.

FASTEST FOUR GOALS, ONE TEAM:

2:35 — Montreal Canadiens, March 30, 1944, at Montreal. Toe Blake scored at 7:58 and 8:37 of the third period; Maurice Richard, 9:17; and Ray Getliffe, 10:33. Montreal won 11-0 and won best-of-seven SF 4-1.

FASTEST THREE GOALS, BOTH TEAMS:

0:21 — Chicago Black Hawks, Edmonton Oilers, May 7, 1985, at Edmonton. Behn Wilson scored for Chicago at 19:22 of the third period; Jari Kurri, 19:36; and Glenn Anderson, Edmonton, 19:43. Edmonton won 7-3 and won best-of-seven CF 4-2.
0:27 — Phoenix Coyotes, Detroit Red Wings, April 24, 1998, at Detroit. Jeremy Roenick scored for Phoenix at 13:24 of the second period; Mathieu Dandenault, Detroit, 13:32; and Keith Tkachuk, Phoenix, 13:51. Phoenix won 7-4. Detroit won best-of-seven CQF 4-2.
0:30 — Pittsburgh Penguins, Chicago Blackhawks, June 1, 1992, at Chicago. Dirk Graham scored for Chicago at 6:21 of the first period; Kevin Stevens, Pittsburgh, 6:33; and Dirk Graham, Chicago, 6:51. Pittsburgh won 6-5 and won best-of-seven F 4-0.

FASTEST THREE GOALS, ONE TEAM:

0:23 — Toronto Maple Leafs, April 12, 1979, at Toronto vs. Atlanta Flames. Darryl Sittler scored at 4:04 and 4:16 of the first period; and Ron Ellis, 4:27. Toronto won 7-4 and won best-of-three PRE 2-0.
0:38 — New York Rangers, April 12, 1986, at NY Rangers vs. Philadelphia. Jim Weimer scored at 12:29 of the third period; Bob Brooke, 12:43; and Ron Greschner, 13:07. NY Rangers won 5-2 and won best-of-five DSF 3-2.
— Colorado Avalanche, April 18, 2001, at Vancouver. Peter Forsberg scored at 9:11 of the third period; Joe Sakic, 9:28; and Eric Messier, 9:49. Colorado won 5-1 and won best-of-seven CQF 4-0.

FASTEST TWO GOALS, BOTH TEAMS:

0:05 — Pittsburgh Penguins, Buffalo Sabres, April 14, 1979, at Buffalo. Gilbert Perreault scored for Buffalo at 12:59 of the first period; and Jim Hamilton, Pittsburgh, 13:04. Pittsburgh won 4-3 and won best-of-three PRE 2-1.
0:08 — St. Louis Blues, Minnesota North Stars, April 9, 1989, at Minnesota. Bernie Federko scored for St. Louis at 2:28 of the third period; and Perry Berezan, Minnesota, 2:36. Minnesota won 5-4. St. Louis won best-of-seven DSF 4-1.
— Phoenix Coyotes, Detroit Red Wings, April 24, 1998, at Detroit. Jeremy Roenick scored for Phoenix at 13:24 of the second period; and Mathieu Dandenault, Detroit, 13:32. Phoenix won 7-4. Detroit won best-of-seven CQF 4-2.

FASTEST TWO GOALS, ONE TEAM:

0:05 — Detroit Red Wings, April 11, 1965, at Detroit vs. Chicago. Norm Ullman scored at 17:35 and 17:40 of the second period. Detroit won 4-2. Chicago won best-of-seven SF 4-3.

Cam Ward took over from Martin Gerber during the first round of the 2006 playoffs and sparked the Hurricanes to seven straight victories. Ward tied a rookie record with 15 postseason victories and won the Conn Smythe Trophy as playoff MVP.

OVERTIME

SHORTEST OVERTIME:
0:09 — Montreal Canadiens, Calgary Flames, May 18, 1986, at Calgary. Montreal won 3-2 on Brian Skrudland's goal at 0:09 of the first overtime period. Montreal won best-of-seven F 4-1.
0:11 — New York Islanders, New York Rangers, April 11, 1975, at NY Rangers. NY Islanders won 4-3 on J.P. Parise's goal at 0:11 of the first overtime period. NY Islanders won best-of-three PRE 2-1.

LONGEST OVERTIME:
116:30 — Detroit Red Wings, Montreal Maroons, March 24, 1936, at Montreal. Mtl. Maroons won 1-0 on Mud Bruneteau's goal at 16:30 of the sixth overtime period. Detroit won best-of-five SF 3-0.

MOST OVERTIME GAMES, ONE PLAYOFF YEAR:
28 — 1993. Of 85 games played, 28 went into overtime.
26 — 2001. Of 86 games played, 26 went into overtime.
22 — 2003. Of 89 games played, 22 went into overtime.
21 — 1999. Of 86 games played, 21 went into overtime.

FEWEST OVERTIME GAMES, ONE PLAYOFF YEAR:
0 — 1963. None of the 16 games went into overtime, the only year since 1926 that no overtime was required in any playoff series.

MOST OVERTIME GAMES, ONE SERIES:
5 — Toronto Maple Leafs, Montreal Canadiens in 1951. Toronto won best-of-seven F 4-1.
4 — Toronto Maple Leafs, Boston Bruins in 1933. Toronto won best-of-five SF 3-2.
— Boston Bruins, NY Rangers in 1939. Boston won best-of-seven SF 4-3.
— St. Louis Blues, Minnesota North Stars in 1968. St. Louis won best-of-seven SF 4-3.
— Dallas Stars, St. Louis Blues in 1999. Dallas won best-of-seven CSF 4-2.
— Dallas Stars, Edmonton Oilers in 2001. Dallas won best-of-seven CQF 4-2.

TEAM HAT-TRICKS

MOST HAT-TRICKS, BY ALL TEAMS, ONE PLAYOFF YEAR:
12 — 1983 in 66 games.
— **1988** in 83 games.
11 — 1985 in 70 games.
— 1992 in 86 games.

MOST HAT-TRICKS, ONE TEAM, ONE PLAYOFF YEAR:
6 — Edmonton Oilers in 16 games, 1983.
— **Edmonton Oilers** in 18 games, 1985.

SHUTOUTS

MOST SHUTOUTS, ONE PLAYOFF YEAR, ALL TEAMS:
25 — 2002. Of 90 games played, Detroit had 6; Ottawa had 4; Carolina, Colorado, St. Louis and Toronto had 3 each; while Los Angeles, New Jersey and Philadelphia had 1 each.
23 — 2004. Of 89 games played, Tampa Bay, Calgary had 5 each; Toronto, and San Jose had 3 each; while Boston, Colorado, Detroit, Montreal, Nashville, NY Islanders and Philadelphia had 1 each.
19 — 2001. Of 86 games played, Colorado, New Jersey had 4 each, Toronto had 3, Pittsburgh and Los Angeles had 2 each, while Buffalo, Washington, Detroit and San Jose had 1 each.

FEWEST SHUTOUTS, ONE PLAYOFF YEAR, ALL TEAMS:
0 — 1959. 18 games played.

MOST SHUTOUTS, BOTH TEAMS, ONE SERIES:
5 — Toronto Maple Leafs (3), Detroit Red Wings (2), in 1945. Toronto won best-of-seven F 4-3.
— **Toronto Maple Leafs (3), Detroit Red Wings (2),** in 1950. Toronto won best-of-seven SF 4-3.

TEAM PENALTIES

FEWEST PENALTIES, BOTH TEAMS, BEST-OF-SEVEN SERIES:
19 — Detroit Red Wings, Toronto Maple Leafs in 1945. Detroit received 10 minors, Toronto received 9 minors. Detroit won best-of-seven F 4-3.

FEWEST PENALTIES, ONE TEAM, BEST-OF-SEVEN SERIES:
9 — Toronto Maple Leafs in 1945 vs. Detroit. Toronto received 9 minors. Detroit won best-of-seven F 4-3.

MOST PENALTIES, BOTH TEAMS, ONE SERIES:
218 — New Jersey Devils, Washington Capitals in 1988. New Jersey received 97 minors, 11 majors, 9 misconducts and 1 match penalty. Washington received 80 minors, 11 majors, 8 misconducts and 1 match penalty. New Jersey won best-of-seven DF 4-3.

MOST PENALTY MINUTES, BOTH TEAMS, ONE SERIES:
654 — New Jersey Devils (349), Washington Capitals (305) in 1988. New Jersey won best-of-seven DF 4-3.

MOST PENALTIES, ONE TEAM, ONE SERIES:
118 — New Jersey Devils in 1988 vs. Washington. New Jersey received 97 minors, 11 majors, 9 misconducts and 1 match penalty. New Jersey won best-of-seven DF 4-3.

MOST PENALTY MINUTES, ONE TEAM, ONE SERIES:
349 — New Jersey Devils in 1988 vs. Washington. New Jersey won best-of-seven DF 4-3.

MOST PENALTIES, BOTH TEAMS, ONE GAME:
66 — Detroit Red Wings (33), St. Louis Blues (33), April 12, 1991, at St. Louis. St. Louis won 6-1.
63 — Minnesota North Stars (34), Chicago Blackhawks (29), April 6, 1990, at Chicago. Chicago won 5-3.
62 — New Jersey Devils (32), Washington Capitals (30), April 22, 1988, at New Jersey. New Jersey won 10-4.

MOST PENALTY MINUTES, BOTH TEAMS, ONE GAME:
298 — Detroit Red Wings (152), St. Louis Blues (146), April 12, 1991, at St. Louis. Detroit received 33 penalties; St. Louis received 33 penalties. St. Louis won 6-1.
267 — New York Rangers (142), Los Angeles Kings (125), April 9, 1981, at Los Angeles. NY Rangers received 31 penalties; Los Angeles received 28 penalties. Los Angeles won 5-4.

MOST PENALTIES, ONE TEAM, ONE GAME:
34 — Minnesota North Stars, April 6, 1990, at Chicago. Chicago won 5-3.
33 — Detroit Red Wings, April 12, 1991, at St. Louis. St. Louis won 6-1.
— St. Louis Blues, April 12, 1991, at St. Louis vs. Detroit. St. Louis won 6-1.

MOST PENALTY MINUTES, ONE TEAM, ONE GAME:
152 — Detroit Red Wings, April 12, 1991, at St. Louis. St. Louis won 6-1.
146 — St. Louis Blues, April 12, 1991, at St. Louis vs. Detroit. St. Louis won 6-1.
142 — New York Rangers, April 9, 1981, at Los Angeles. Los Angeles won 5-4.

MOST PENALTIES, BOTH TEAMS, ONE PERIOD:
43 — New York Rangers (24), Los Angeles Kings (19), April 9, 1981, first period at Los Angeles. Los Angeles won 5-4.

MOST PENALTY MINUTES, BOTH TEAMS, ONE PERIOD:
248 — New York Islanders (124), Boston Bruins (124), April 17, 1980, first period at Boston. NY Islanders won 5-4.

MOST PENALTIES, ONE TEAM, ONE PERIOD:
24 — New York Rangers, April 9, 1981, first period at Los Angeles. Los Angeles won 5-4.

MOST PENALTY MINUTES, ONE TEAM, ONE PERIOD:
125 — New York Rangers, April 9, 1981, first period at Los Angeles. Los Angeles won 5-4.

Individual Records

GAMES PLAYED

MOST YEARS IN PLAYOFFS:
21 — Raymond Bourque, Boston, Colorado (1980-96 inclusive; 98-2001 inclusive)
— Chris Chelios, Montreal, Chicago, Detroit (1984-97 inclusive; 1999-2004 inclusive, 2006)
20 — Gordie Howe, Detroit, Hartford
— Larry Robinson, Montreal, Los Angeles
— Larry Murphy, Los Angeles, Washington, Minnesota, Pittsburgh, Toronto, Detroit
— Scott Stevens, Washington, St. Louis, New Jersey

MOST CONSECUTIVE YEARS IN PLAYOFFS:
20 — Larry Robinson, Montreal, Los Angeles (1973-92, inclusive).
19 — Brett Hull, Calgary, St. Louis, Dallas, Detroit (1986-2004, inclusive).
18 — Larry Murphy, Los Angeles, Washington, Minnesota, Pittsburgh, Toronto, Detroit (1984-2001, inclusive).
17 — Brad Park, NY Rangers, Boston, Detroit (1969-85, inclusive).
— Raymond Bourque, Boston (1980-96, inclusive).

MOST PLAYOFF GAMES:
247 — Patrick Roy, Montreal, Colorado
236 — Mark Messier, Edmonton, NY Rangers
233 — Claude Lemieux, Montreal, New Jersey, Colorado, Phoenix
— Scott Stevens, Washington, St. Louis, New Jersey
231 — Guy Carbonneau, Montreal, St. Louis, Dallas
228 — Chris Chelios, Montreal, Chicago, Detroit

GOALS

MOST GOALS IN PLAYOFFS (CAREER):
122 — Wayne Gretzky, Edmonton, Los Angeles, St. Louis, NY Rangers
109 — Mark Messier, Edmonton, NY Rangers
106 — Jari Kurri, Edmonton, Los Angeles, NY Rangers, Anaheim
103 — Brett Hull, Calgary, St. Louis, Dallas, Detroit
93 — Glenn Anderson, Edmonton, Toronto, NY Rangers, St. Louis

MOST GOALS, ONE PLAYOFF YEAR:
19 — Reggie Leach, Philadelphia, 1976. 16 games.
— Jari Kurri, Edmonton, 1985. 18 games.
18 — Joe Sakic, Colorado, 1996. 22 games.
17 — Newsy Lalonde, Montreal, 1919. 10 games.
— Mike Bossy, NY Islanders, 1981. 18 games.
— Steve Payne, Minnesota, 1981. 19 games.
— Mike Bossy, NY Islanders, 1982. 19 games.
— Mike Bossy, NY Islanders, 1983. 19 games
— Wayne Gretzky, Edmonton, 1985. 18 games.
— Kevin Stevens, Pittsburgh, 1991. 24 games.

MOST GOALS IN ONE SERIES (OTHER THAN FINAL):
12 — Jari Kurri, Edmonton, in 1985 CF, 6 games vs. Chicago.
11 — Newsy Lalonde, Montreal, in 1919 NHL F, 5 games vs. Ottawa.
10 — Tim Kerr, Philadelphia, in 1989 DF, 7 games vs. Pittsburgh.
9 — Reggie Leach, Philadelphia, in 1976 SF, 5 games vs. Boston.
— Bill Barber, Philadelphia, in 1980 SF, 5 games vs. Minnesota.
— Mike Bossy, NY Islanders, in 1983 CF, 6 games vs. Boston.
— Mario Lemieux, Pittsburgh, in 1989 DF, 7 games vs. Philadelphia.

MOST GOALS IN FINAL SERIES (NHL PLAYERS ONLY):
9 — Babe Dye, Toronto, in 1922, 5 games vs. Van. Millionaires.
8 — Alf Skinner, Toronto, in 1918, 5 games vs. Van. Millionaires.
7 — Jean Beliveau, Montreal, in 1956, 5 games vs. Detroit.
— Mike Bossy, NY Islanders, in 1982, 4 games vs. Vancouver.
— Wayne Gretzky, Edmonton, in 1985, 5 games vs. Philadelphia.

MOST GOALS, ONE GAME:
5 — Newsy Lalonde, Montreal, March 1, 1919, at Montreal. Final score: Montreal 6, Ottawa 3.
— Maurice Richard, Montreal, March 23, 1944, at Montreal. Final score: Montreal 5, Toronto 1.
— Darryl Sittler, Toronto, April 22, 1976, at Toronto. Final score: Toronto 8, Philadelphia 5.
— Reggie Leach, Philadelphia, May 6, 1976, at Philadelphia. Final score: Philadelphia 6, Boston 3.
— Mario Lemieux, Pittsburgh, April 25, 1989, at Pittsburgh. Final score: Pittsburgh 10, Philadelphia 7.

MOST GOALS, ONE PERIOD:
4 — Tim Kerr, Philadelphia, April 13, 1985, at NY Rangers, second period. Final score: Philadelphia 6, NY Rangers 5.
— Mario Lemieux, Pittsburgh, April 25, 1989, at Pittsburgh vs. Philadelphia, first period. Final score: Pittsburgh 10, Philadelphia 7.

ASSISTS

MOST ASSISTS IN PLAYOFFS (CAREER):
260 — Wayne Gretzky, Edmonton, Los Angeles, St. Louis, NY Rangers
186 — Mark Messier, Edmonton, NY Rangers
139 — Raymond Bourque, Boston, Colorado
137 — Paul Coffey, Edmonton, Pittsburgh, Los Angeles, Detroit, Philadelphia, Carolina
128 — Doug Gilmour, St. Louis, Calgary, Toronto, New Jersey, Buffalo, Montreal

MOST ASSISTS, ONE PLAYOFF YEAR:
31 — Wayne Gretzky, Edmonton, 1988. 19 games.
30 — Wayne Gretzky, Edmonton, 1985. 18 games.
29 — Wayne Gretzky, Edmonton, 1987. 21 games.
28 — Mario Lemieux, Pittsburgh, 1991. 23 games.
26 — Wayne Gretzky, Edmonton, 1983. 16 games.

MOST ASSISTS IN ONE SERIES (OTHER THAN FINAL):
14 — Rick Middleton, Boston, in 1983 DF, 7 games vs. Buffalo.
— Wayne Gretzky, Edmonton, in 1985 CF, 6 games vs. Chicago.
13 — Wayne Gretzky, Edmonton, in 1987 DSF, 5 games vs. Los Angeles.
— Doug Gilmour, Toronto, in 1994 CSF, 7 games vs. San Jose.
11 — Al MacInnis, Calgary, in 1984 DF, 7 games vs. Edmonton.
— Mark Messier, Edmonton, in 1989 DSF, 7 games vs. Los Angeles.
— Mike Ridley, Washington, in 1992 DSF, 7 games vs. Pittsburgh.
— Ron Francis, Pittsburgh, in 1995 CQF, 7 games vs. Washington.
10 — Fleming Mackell, Boston, in 1958 SF, 6 games vs. NY Rangers.
— Stan Mikita, Chicago, in 1962 SF, 6 games vs. Montreal.
— Bob Bourne, NY Islanders, in 1983 DF, 6 games vs. NY Rangers.
— Wayne Gretzky, Edmonton, in 1988 DSF, 5 games vs. Winnipeg.
— Mario Lemieux, Pittsburgh, in 1992 DSF, 6 games vs. Washington.

MOST ASSISTS IN FINAL SERIES:
10 — Wayne Gretzky, Edmonton, in 1988, 4 games plus suspended game vs. Boston.
9 — Jacques Lemaire, Montreal, in 1973, 6 games vs. Chicago.
— Wayne Gretzky, Edmonton, in 1987, 7 games vs. Philadelphia.
— Larry Murphy, Pittsburgh, in 1991, 6 games vs. Minnesota.

MOST ASSISTS, ONE GAME:
6 — Mikko Leinonen, NY Rangers, April 8, 1982, at NY Rangers. Final score: NY Rangers 7, Philadelphia 3.
— Wayne Gretzky, Edmonton, April 9, 1987, at Edmonton. Final score: Edmonton 13, Los Angeles 3.
5 — Toe Blake, Montreal, March 23, 1944, at Montreal. Final score: Montreal 5, Toronto 1.
— Maurice Richard, Montreal, March 27, 1956, at Montreal. Final score: Montreal 7, NY Rangers 0.
— Bert Olmstead, Montreal, March 30, 1957, at Montreal. Final score: Montreal 8, NY Rangers 3.
— Don McKenney, Boston, April 5, 1958, at Boston. Final score: Boston 8, NY Rangers 2.
— Stan Mikita, Chicago, April 4, 1973, at Chicago. Final score: Chicago 7, St. Louis 1.
— Wayne Gretzky, Edmonton, April 8, 1981, at Montreal. Final score: Edmonton 6, Montreal 3.
— Paul Coffey, Edmonton, May 14, 1985, at Edmonton. Final score: Edmonton 10, Chicago 5.
— Doug Gilmour, St. Louis, April 15, 1986, at Minnesota. Final score: St. Louis 6, Minnesota 3.
— Risto Siltanen, Quebec, April 14, 1987, at Hartford. Final score: Quebec 7, Hartford 5.
— Patrik Sundstrom, New Jersey, April 22, 1988, at New Jersey. Final score: New Jersey 10, Washington 4.
— Geoff Courtnall, St. Louis, April 23, 1998, at St. Louis. Final score: St. Louis 6, Los Angeles 3.

MOST ASSISTS, ONE PERIOD:
3 — Three assists by one player in one period of a playoff game has been recorded on 74 occasions. Chris Chelios of the Detroit Red Wings is the most recent to equal this mark with 3 assists in the second period at Vancouver, April 27, 2002. Final score: Detroit 6, Vancouver 4.
— Wayne Gretzky has had 3 assists in one period 5 times; Raymond Bourque, 3 times; Toe Blake, Jean Beliveau, Doug Harvey and Bobby Orr, twice each. Joe Primeau of Toronto was the first player to be credited with 3 assists in one period of a playoff game; third period at Boston vs. NY Rangers, April 7, 1932. Final score: Toronto 6, NY Rangers 2.

POINTS

MOST POINTS IN PLAYOFFS (CAREER):
382 — Wayne Gretzky, Edmonton, Los Angeles, St. Louis, NY Rangers, 122G, 260A
295 — Mark Messier, Edmonton, NY Rangers, 109G, 186A
233 — Jari Kurri, Edmonton, Los Angeles, NY Rangers, Anaheim, 106G, 127A
214 — Glenn Anderson, Edmonton, Toronto, NY Rangers, St. Louis, 93G, 121A
196 — Paul Coffey, Edmonton, Pittsburgh, Los Angeles, Detroit, Philadelphia, Carolina, 59G, 137A

MOST POINTS, ONE PLAYOFF YEAR:
47 — Wayne Gretzky, Edmonton, in 1985. 17 goals, 30 assists in 18 games.
44 — Mario Lemieux, Pittsburgh, in 1991. 16 goals, 28 assists in 23 games.
43 — Wayne Gretzky, Edmonton, in 1988. 12 goals, 31 assists in 19 games.
40 — Wayne Gretzky, Los Angeles, in 1993. 15 goals, 25 assists in 24 games.
38 — Wayne Gretzky, Edmonton, in 1983. 12 goals, 26 assists in 16 games.

MOST POINTS IN ONE SERIES (OTHER THAN FINAL):
19 — Rick Middleton, Boston, in 1983 DF, 7 games vs. Buffalo. 5 goals, 14 assists.
18 — Wayne Gretzky, Edmonton, in 1985 CF, 6 games vs. Chicago. 4 goals, 14 assists.
17 — Mario Lemieux, Pittsburgh, in 1992 DSF, 6 games vs. Washington. 7 goals, 10 assists.
16 — Barry Pederson, Boston, in 1983 DF, 7 games vs. Buffalo. 7 goals, 9 assists.
— Doug Gilmour, Toronto, in 1994 CSF, 7 games vs. San Jose. 3 goals, 13 assists.
15 — Jari Kurri, Edmonton, in 1985 CF, 6 games vs. Chicago. 12 goals, 3 assists.
— Wayne Gretzky, Edmonton, in 1987 DSF, 5 games vs. Los Angeles. 2 goals, 13 assists.
— Tim Kerr, Philadelphia, in 1989 DF, 7 games vs. Pittsburgh. 10 goals, 5 assists.
— Mario Lemieux, Pittsburgh, in 1991 CF, 6 games vs. Boston. 6 goals, 9 assists.

MOST POINTS IN FINAL SERIES:
13 — Wayne Gretzky, Edmonton, in 1988, 4 games plus suspended game vs. Boston. 3 goals, 10 assists.
12 — Gordie Howe, Detroit, in 1955, 7 games vs. Montreal. 5 goals, 7 assists.
— Yvan Cournoyer, Montreal, in 1973, 6 games vs. Chicago. 6 goals, 6 assists.
— Jacques Lemaire, Montreal, in 1973, 6 games vs. Chicago. 3 goals, 9 assists.
— Mario Lemieux, Pittsburgh, in 1991, 5 games vs. Minnesota. 5 goals, 7 assists.

MOST POINTS, ONE GAME:
8 — Patrik Sundstrom, New Jersey, April 22, 1988, at New Jersey in 10-4 win over Washington. Sundstrom had 3 goals, 5 assists.
— **Mario Lemieux, Pittsburgh,** April 25, 1989, at Pittsburgh in 10-7 win over Philadelphia. Lemieux had 5 goals, 3 assists.
7 — Wayne Gretzky, Edmonton, April 17, 1983, at Calgary in 10-2 win. Gretzky had 4 goals, 3 assists.
— Wayne Gretzky, Edmonton, April 25,1985, at Winnipeg in 8-3 win. Gretzky had 3 goals, 4 assists.
— Wayne Gretzky, Edmonton, April 9, 1987, at Edmonton in 13-3 win over Los Angeles. Gretzky had 1 goal, 6 assists.
6 — Dickie Moore, Montreal, March 25, 1954, at Montreal in 8-1 win over Boston. Moore had 2 goals, 4 assists.
— Phil Esposito, Boston, April 2, 1969, at Boston in 10-0 win over Toronto. Esposito had 4 goals, 2 assists.
— Darryl Sittler, Toronto, April 22, 1976, at Toronto in 8-5 win over Philadelphia. Sittler had 5 goals, 1 assist.
— Guy Lafleur, Montreal, April 11, 1977, at Montreal in 7-2 win over St. Louis. Lafleur had 3 goals, 3 assists.
— Mikko Leinonen, NY Rangers, April 8, 1982, at NY Rangers in 7-3 win over Philadelphia. Leinonen had 6 assists.
— Paul Coffey, Edmonton, May 14, 1985, at Edmonton in 10-5 win over Chicago. Coffey had 1 goal, 5 assists.
— John Anderson, Hartford, April 12, 1986, at Hartford in 9-4 win over Quebec. Anderson had 2 goals, 4 assists.
— Mario Lemieux, Pittsburgh, April 23, 1992, at Pittsburgh in 6-4 win over Washington. Lemieux had 3 goals, 3 assists.
— Geoff Courtnall, St. Louis, April 23, 1998, at St. Louis in 8-3 win over Los Angeles. Courtnall had 1 goal, 5 assists.

MOST POINTS, ONE PERIOD:
4 — Maurice Richard, Montreal, March 29, 1945, at Montreal, third period, in 10-3 win vs. Toronto. 3 goals, 1 assist.
— **Dickie Moore,** Montreal, March 25, 1954, at Montreal, first period, in 8-1 win vs. Boston. 2 goals, 2 assists.
— **Barry Pederson,** Boston, April 8, 1982, at Boston, second period, in 7-3 win vs. Buffalo. 3 goals, 1 assist.
— **Peter McNab,** Boston, April 11, 1982, at Buffalo, second period, in 5-2 win vs. Buffalo. 1 goal, 3 assists.
— **Tim Kerr,** Philadelphia, April 13, 1985, at NY Rangers, second period, in 6-5 win vs. NY Rangers. 4 goals.
— **Ken Linseman,** Boston, April 14, 1985, at Boston, second period, in 7-6 win vs. Montreal. 2 goals, 2 assists.
— **Wayne Gretzky,** Edmonton, April 12, 1987, at Los Angeles, third period, in 6-3 win vs. Los Angeles. 1 goal, 3 assists.
— **Glenn Anderson,** Edmonton, April 6, 1988, at Edmonton, third period, in 7-4 win vs. Winnipeg. 3 goals, 1 assist.
— **Mario Lemieux,** Pittsburgh, April 25, 1989, at Pittsburgh, first period, in 10-7 win vs. Philadelphia. 4 goals.
— **Dave Gagner,** Minnesota North Stars, April 8, 1991, at Minnesota, first period, in 6-5 loss vs. Chicago. 2 goals, 2 assists.
— **Mario Lemieux,** Pittsburgh, April 23, 1992, at Pittsburgh, second period, in 6-4 win vs. Washington. 2 goals, 2 assists.
— **Alexander Mogilny,** New Jersey, April 28, 2001, at New Jersey, second period, in 6-5 win vs. Toronto. 1 goal, 3 assists.

POWER-PLAY GOALS

MOST POWER-PLAY GOALS IN PLAYOFFS (CAREER):
38 — Brett Hull, St. Louis, Dallas, Detroit
35 — Mike Bossy, NY Islanders
34 — Dino Ciccarelli, Minnesota, Washington, Detroit
— Wayne Gretzky, Edmonton, Los Angeles, St. Louis, NY Rangers
29 — Mario Lemieux, Pittsburgh

MOST POWER-PLAY GOALS, ONE PLAYOFF YEAR:
9 — Mike Bossy, NY Islanders, 1981. 18 games vs. Toronto, Edmonton, NY Rangers and Minnesota.
— **Cam Neely, Boston,** 1991. 19 games vs. Hartford, Montreal and Pittsburgh.
8 — Tim Kerr, Philadelphia, 1989. 19 games.
— John Druce, Washington, 1990. 15 games.
— Brian Propp, Minnesota, 1991. 23 games.
— Mario Lemieux, Pittsburgh, 1992. 15 games.

MOST POWER-PLAY GOALS, ONE PLAYOFF SERIES:
6 — Chris Kontos, Los Angeles, 1989 DSF vs. Edmonton, won by Los Angeles 4-3.
5 — Andy Bathgate, Detroit, 1966 SF vs. Chicago, won by Detroit 4-2.
— Denis Potvin, NY Islanders, 1981 QF vs. Edmonton, won by NY Islanders 4-2.
— Ken Houston, Calgary, 1981 QF vs. Philadelphia, won by Calgary 4-3.
— Rick Vaive, Chicago, 1988 DSF vs. St. Louis, won by St. Louis 4-1.
— Tim Kerr, Philadelphia, 1989 DF vs. Pittsburgh, won by Philadelphia 4-3.
— Mario Lemieux, Pittsburgh, 1989 DF vs. Philadelphia, won by Philadelphia 4-3.
— John Druce, Washington, 1990 DF vs. NY Rangers, won by Washington 4-1.
— Pat LaFontaine, Buffalo, 1992 DSF vs. Boston, won by Boston 4-3.
— Adam Graves, NY Rangers, 1996 CQF vs Montreal, won by NY Rangers 4-2.

MOST POWER-PLAY GOALS, ONE GAME:
3 — Syd Howe, Detroit, March 23, 1939, at Detroit vs. Montreal. Detroit won 7-3.
— **Sid Smith, Toronto,** April 10, 1949, at Detroit. Toronto won 3-1.
— **Phil Esposito, Boston,** April 2, 1969, at Boston vs. Toronto. Boston won 10-0.
— **John Bucyk, Boston,** April 21, 1974, at Boston vs. Chicago. Boston won 8-6.
— **Denis Potvin, NY Islanders,** April 17, 1981, at NY Islanders vs. Edmonton. NY Islanders won 6-3.
— **Tim Kerr, Philadelphia,** April 13, 1985, at NY Rangers. Philadelphia won 6-5.
— **Jari Kurri, Edmonton,** April 9, 1987, at Edmonton vs. Los Angeles. Edmonton won 13-3.
— **Mark Johnson, New Jersey,** April 22, 1988, at New Jersey vs. Washington. New Jersey won 10-4.
— **Dino Ciccarelli, Detroit,** April 29, 1993, at Toronto. Detroit won 7-3.
— **Dino Ciccarelli, Detroit,** May 11, 1995, at Dallas. Detroit won 5-1.
— **Valeri Kamensky, Colorado,** April 24, 1997, at Colorado vs. Chicago. Colorado won 7-0.

MOST POWER-PLAY GOALS, ONE PERIOD:
3 — Tim Kerr, Philadelphia, April 13, 1985, at NY Rangers, second period in 6-5 win.
2 — Two power-play goals have been scored by one player in one period on 55 occasions. Charlie Conacher of Toronto was the first to score two power-play goals in one period, setting the mark with two power-play goals in the second period at Toronto vs. Boston, March 26, 1936. Final score: Toronto 8, Boston 3. Brad Richards of the Tampa Bay Lightning is the most recent to equal this mark with two power-play goals in the second period at Calgary, June 5, 2004. Final score: Tampa Bay 3, Calgary 2.

SHORTHAND GOALS

MOST SHORTHAND GOALS IN PLAYOFFS (CAREER):
14 — Mark Messier, Edmonton, NY Rangers
11 — Wayne Gretzky, Edmonton, Los Angeles, St. Louis
10 — Jari Kurri, Edmonton, Los Angeles, NY Rangers
8 — Ed Westfall, Boston, NY Islanders
— Hakan Loob, Calgary

MOST SHORTHAND GOALS, ONE PLAYOFF YEAR:
3 — Derek Sanderson, Boston, 1969. 1 vs. Toronto in QF, won by Boston 4-0; 2 vs. Montreal in SF, won by Montreal, 4-2.
— **Bill Barber, Philadelphia,** 1980. All vs. Minnesota in SF, won by Philadelphia 4-1.
— **Lorne Henning, NY Islanders,** 1980. 1 vs. Boston in QF, won by NY Islanders 4-1; 1 vs. Buffalo in SF, won by NY Islanders 4-2, 1 vs. Philadelphia in F, won by NY Islanders 4-2.
— **Wayne Gretzky, Edmonton,** 1983. 2 vs. Winnipeg in DSF, won by Edmonton 3-0; 1 vs. Calgary in DF, won by Edmonton 4-1.
— **Wayne Presley, Chicago,** 1989. All vs. Detroit in DSF, won by Chicago 4-2.
— **Todd Marchant, Edmonton,** 1997. 1 vs. Dallas in CQF, won by Edmonton 4-3; 2 vs. Colorado in CSF, won by Colorado 4-1.

Joffrey Lupul joined hockey legends Newsy Lalonde and Maurice Richard as the only players to score all four-or-more of their teams' goals in a single playoff game. Lupul's four-goal effort led Anaheim past Colorado 4-3 in overtime on May 9, 2006.

MOST SHORTHAND GOALS, ONE PLAYOFF SERIES:
3 — **Bill Barber, Philadelphia,** 1980 SF vs. Minnesota, won by Philadelphia 4-1.
— **Wayne Presley, Chicago,** 1989 DSF vs. Detroit, won by Chicago 4-2.
2 — Mac Colville, NY Rangers, 1940 SF vs. Boston, won by NY Rangers 4-2.
— Jerry Toppazzini, Boston, 1958 SF vs. NY Rangers, won by Boston 4-2.
— Dave Keon, Toronto, 1963 F vs. Detroit, won by Toronto 4-1.
— Bob Pulford, Toronto, 1964 F vs. Detroit, won by Toronto 4-3.
— Serge Savard, Montreal, 1968 F vs. St. Louis, won by Montreal 4-0.
— Derek Sanderson, Boston, 1969 SF vs. Montreal, won by Montreal 4-2.
— Bryan Trottier, NY Islanders, 1980 PR vs. Los Angeles, won by NY Islanders 3-1.
— Bobby Lalonde, Boston, 1981 PR vs. Minnesota, won by Minnesota 3-0.
— Butch Goring, NY Islanders, 1981 SF vs. NY Rangers, won by NY Islanders 4-0.
— Wayne Gretzky, Edmonton, 1983 DSF vs. Winnipeg, won by Edmonton 3-0.
— Mark Messier, Edmonton, 1983 DF vs. Calgary, won by Edmonton 4-1.
— Jari Kurri, Edmonton, 1983 CF vs. Chicago, won by Edmonton 4-0.
— Wayne Gretzky, Edmonton, 1985 DF vs. Winnipeg, won by Edmonton 4-0.
— Kevin Lowe, Edmonton, 1987 F vs. Philadelphia, won by Edmonton 4-3.
— Bob Gould, Washington, 1988 DSF vs. Philadelphia, won by Washington 4-3.
— Dave Poulin, Philadelphia, 1989 DF vs. Pittsburgh, won by Philadelphia 4-3.
— Russ Courtnall, Montreal, 1991 DF vs. Boston, won by Boston 4-3.
— Sergei Fedorov, Detroit, 1992 DSF vs. Minnesota, won by Detroit 4-3.
— Mark Messier, NY Rangers, 1992 DSF vs. New Jersey, won by NY Rangers 4-3.
— Tom Fitzgerald, NY Islanders, 1993 DF vs. Pittsburgh, won by NY Islanders 4-3.
— Mark Osborne, Toronto, 1994 CSF vs. San Jose, won by Toronto 4-3.
— Tony Amonte, Chicago, 1997 CQF vs. Colorado, won by Colorado 4-2.
— Brian Rolston, New Jersey, 1997 CQF vs. Montreal, won by New Jersey 4-1.
— Rod Brind'Amour, Philadelphia, 1997 CQF vs. Pittsburgh, won by Philadelphia 4-1.
— Todd Marchant, Edmonton, 1997 CSF vs. Colorado, won by Colorado 4-1.
— Jeremy Roenick, Phoenix, 1998 CQF vs. Detroit, won by Detroit 4-2.
— Vincent Damphousse, San Jose, 1999 CQF vs. Colorado, won by Colorado 4-2.
— Dixon Ward, Buffalo, 1999 CF vs. Toronto, won by Buffalo 4-1.
— Curtis Brown, Buffalo, 2001 CSF vs. Pittsburgh, won by Pittsburgh 4-3.
— John Madden, New Jersey, 2006 CQF vs. NY Rangers, won by New Jersey 4-0.

MOST SHORTHAND GOALS, ONE GAME:
2 — **Dave Keon, Toronto,** April 18, 1963, at Toronto, in 3-1 win vs. Detroit.
— **Bryan Trottier, NY Islanders,** April 8, 1980, at NY Islanders, in 8-1 win vs. Los Angeles.
— **Bobby Lalonde, Boston,** April 11, 1981, at Minnesota, in 6-3 loss vs. Minnesota.
— **Wayne Gretzky, Edmonton,** April 6, 1983, at Edmonton, in 6-3 win vs. Winnipeg.
— **Jari Kurri, Edmonton,** April 24, 1983, at Edmonton, in 8-3 win vs. Chicago.
— **Wayne Gretzky, Edmonton,** April 25, 1985, at Winnipeg, in 8-3 win by Edmonton.
— **Mark Messier, NY Rangers,** April 21, 1992, at NY Rangers, in 7-3 loss vs. New Jersey.
— **Tom Fitzgerald, NY Islanders,** May 8, 1993, at NY Islanders, in 6-5 win vs. Pittsburgh.
— **Rod Brind'Amour, Philadelphia,** April 26, 1997, at Philadelphia, in 6-3 win vs. Pittsburgh.
— **Jeremy Roenick, Phoenix,** April 24, 1998, at Detroit, in 7-4 win by Phoenix.
— **Vincent Damphousse, San Jose,** April 30, 1999, at Colorado, in 7-3 win by San Jose.
— **John Madden, New Jersey,** April 24, 2006, at New Jersey, in 4-1 win vs. NY Rangers.

MOST SHORTHAND GOALS, ONE PERIOD:
2 — **Bryan Trottier, NY Islanders,** April 8, 1980, second period, at NY Islanders, in 8-1 win vs. Los Angeles.
— **Bobby Lalonde, Boston,** April 11, 1981, third period, at Minnesota, in 6-3 loss vs. Minnesota.
— **Jari Kurri, Edmonton,** April 24, 1983, third period, at Edmonton, in 8-4 win vs. Chicago.
— **Rod Brind'Amour, Philadelphia,** April 26, 1997, first period, at Philadelphia, in 6-3 win vs. Pittsburgh.
— **Jeremy Roenick, Phoenix,** April 24, 1998, second period, at Detroit, in 7-4 win by Phoenix.
— **Vincent Damphousse, San Jose,** April 30, 1999, third period, at Colorado, in 7-3 win vs. Colorado.

GAME-WINNING GOALS

MOST GAME-WINNING GOALS IN PLAYOFFS, CAREER:
24 — **Wayne Gretzky, Edmonton, Los Angeles, St. Louis, NY Rangers**
— **Brett Hull, St. Louis, Dallas, Detroit**
19 — Claude Lemieux, Montreal, New Jersey, Colorado
18 — Maurice Richard, Montreal
— Joe Sakic, Colorado

MOST GAME-WINNING GOALS, ONE PLAYOFF YEAR:
7 — **Brad Richards, Tampa Bay,** 2004. 23 games.
6 — Joe Sakic, Colorado, 1996. 22 games.
— Joe Nieuwendyk, Dallas, 1999. 23 games.
5 — Mike Bossy, NY Islanders, 1983. 19 games.
— Jari Kurri, Edmonton, 1987. 21 games.
— Bobby Smith, Minnesota, 1991. 23 games.
— Mario Lemieux, Pittsburgh, 1992. 15 games.
— Fernando Pisani, Edmonton, 2006. 24 games.

MOST GAME-WINNING GOALS, ONE PLAYOFF SERIES:
4 — **Mike Bossy, NY Islanders,** 1983 CF vs. Boston, won by NY Islanders 4-2.

OVERTIME GOALS

MOST OVERTIME GOALS IN PLAYOFFS, CAREER:
7 — **Joe Sakic, Colorado** (2 in 1996; 1 in 1998; 1 in 2001; 2 in 2004; 1 in 2006)
6 — Maurice Richard, Montreal
5 — Glenn Anderson, Edmonton, Toronto, St. Louis
4 — Bob Nystrom, NY Islanders
— Dale Hunter, Quebec, Washington
— Wayne Gretzky, Edmonton, Los Angeles
— Stephane Richer, Montreal, New Jersey
— Joe Murphy, Edmonton, Chicago
— Esa Tikkanen, Edmonton, NY Rangers
— Jaromir Jagr, Pittsburgh
— Kirk Muller, Montreal, Dallas
— Jeremy Roenick, Chicago, Philadelphia
— Chris Drury, Colorado, Buffalo

MOST OVERTIME GOALS, ONE PLAYOFF YEAR:
3 — **Mel Hill, Boston,** 1939. All vs. NY Rangers in best-of-seven SF, won by Boston 4-3.
— **Maurice Richard, Montreal,** 1951. 2 vs. Detroit in best-of-seven SF, won by Montreal 4-2; 1 vs. Toronto best-of-seven F, won by Toronto 4-1.

MOST OVERTIME GOALS, ONE PLAYOFF SERIES:
3 — **Mel Hill, Boston,** 1939, SF vs. NY Rangers, won by Boston 4-3. Hill scored at 59:25 of overtime March 21 for a 2-1 win; at 8:24 of overtime, March 23 for a 3-2 win; and at 48:00 of overtime, April 2 for a 2-1 win.

Joe Sakic backhands the puck past Marty Turco to give Colorado a 5-4 overtime win versus Dallas on April 24, 2006. The goal was Sakic's seventh career playoff overtime tally, surpassing Maurice Richard as the all-time leader.

SCORING BY A DEFENSEMAN

MOST GOALS BY A DEFENSEMAN, ONE PLAYOFF YEAR:
12 — Paul Coffey, Edmonton, 1985. 18 games.
11 — Brian Leetch, NY Rangers, 1994. 23 games.
9 — Bobby Orr, Boston, 1970. 14 games.
   — Brad Park, Boston, 1978. 15 games.
8 — Denis Potvin, NY Islanders, 1981. 18 games.
   — Raymond Bourque, Boston, 1983. 17 games.
   — Denis Potvin, NY Islanders, 1983. 20 games.
   — Paul Coffey, Edmonton, 1984. 19 games.

MOST GOALS BY A DEFENSEMAN, ONE GAME:
3 — Bobby Orr, Boston, April 11, 1971, at Montreal. Final score: Boston 5, Montreal 2.
   — **Dick Redmond, Chicago,** April 4, 1973, at Chicago. Final score: Chicago 7, St. Louis 1.
   — **Denis Potvin, NY Islanders,** April 17, 1981, at NY Islanders. Final score: NY Islanders 6, Edmonton 3.
   — **Paul Reinhart, Calgary,** April 14, 1983, at Edmonton. Final score: Edmonton 6, Calgary 3.
   — **Doug Halward, Vancouver,** April 7, 1984, at Vancouver. Final score: Vancouver 7, Calgary 0.
   — **Paul Reinhart, Calgary,** April 8, 1984, at Vancouver. Final score: Calgary 5, Vancouver 1.
   — **Al Iafrate, Washington,** April 26, 1993, at Washington. Final score: Washington 6, NY Islanders 4.
   — **Eric Desjardins, Montreal,** June 3, 1993, at Montreal. Final score: Montreal 3, Los Angeles 2.
   — **Gary Suter, Chicago,** April 24, 1994, at Chicago. Final score: Chicago 4, Toronto 3.
   — **Brian Leetch, NY Rangers,** May 22, 1995, at Philadelphia. Final score: Philadelphia 4, NY Rangers 3.
   — **Andy Delmore, Philadelphia,** May 7, 2000, at Philadelphia. Final score: Philadelphia 6, Pittsburgh 3.

MOST ASSISTS BY A DEFENSEMAN, ONE PLAYOFF YEAR:
25 — Paul Coffey, Edmonton, 1985. 18 games.
24 — Al MacInnis, Calgary, 1989. 22 games.
23 — Brian Leetch, NY Rangers, 1994. 23 games.
19 — Bobby Orr, Boston, 1972. 15 games.
18 — Raymond Bourque, Boston, 1988. 23 games.
   — Raymond Bourque, Boston, 1991. 19 games.
   — Larry Murphy, Pittsburgh, 1991. 23 games.

MOST ASSISTS BY A DEFENSEMAN, ONE GAME:
5 — Paul Coffey, Edmonton, May 14, 1985 at Edmonton vs. Chicago. Edmonton won 10-5.
   — **Risto Siltanen, Quebec,** April 14, 1987 at Hartford. Quebec won 7-5.

MOST POINTS BY A DEFENSEMAN, ONE PLAYOFF YEAR:
37 — Paul Coffey, Edmonton, 1985. 12 goals, 25 assists in 18 games.
34 — Brian Leetch, NY Rangers, 1994. 11 goals, 23 assists in 23 games.
31 — Al MacInnis, Calgary, 1989. 7 goals, 24 assists in 22 games.
25 — Denis Potvin, NY Islanders, 1981. 8 goals, 17 assists in 18 games.
   — Raymond Bourque, Boston, 1991. 7 goals, 18 assists in 19 games.

MOST POINTS BY A DEFENSEMAN, ONE GAME:
6 — Paul Coffey, Edmonton, May 14, 1985 at Edmonton vs. Chicago. 1 goal, 5 assists. Edmonton won 10-5.
5 — Eddie Bush, Detroit, April 9, 1942, at Detroit vs. Toronto. 1 goal, 4 assists. Detroit won 5-2.
   — Bob Dailey, Philadelphia, May 1, 1980, at Philadelphia vs. Minnesota. 1 goal, 4 assists. Philadelphia won 7-0.
   — Denis Potvin, NY Islanders, April 17, 1981, at NY Islanders vs. Edmonton. 3 goals, 2 assists. NY Islanders won 6-3.
   — Risto Siltanen, Quebec, April 14, 1987, at Hartford. 5 assists. Quebec won 7-5.

SCORING BY A ROOKIE

MOST GOALS BY A ROOKIE, ONE PLAYOFF YEAR:
14 — Dino Ciccarelli, Minnesota, 1981. 19 games.
11 — Jeremy Roenick, Chicago, 1990. 20 games.
10 — Claude Lemieux, Montreal, 1986. 20 games.
9 — Pat Flatley, NY Islanders, 1984. 21 games.
8 — Steve Christoff, Minnesota, 1980. 14 games.
   — Brad Palmer, Minnesota, 1981. 19 games.
   — Mike Krushelnyski, Boston, 1983. 17 games.
   — Bob Joyce, Boston, 1988. 23 games.

MOST POINTS BY A ROOKIE, ONE PLAYOFF YEAR:
21 — Dino Ciccarelli, Minnesota, 1981. 14 goals, 7 assists in 19 games.
20 — Don Maloney, NY Rangers, 1979. 7 goals, 13 assists in 18 games.

THREE-OR-MORE-GOAL GAMES

MOST THREE-OR-MORE-GOAL GAMES IN PLAYOFFS, CAREER:
10 — Wayne Gretzky, Edmonton, Los Angeles, NY Rangers. Eight three-goal games; two four-goal games.
7 — Maurice Richard, Montreal. Four three-goal games; two four-goal games; one five-goal game.
   — Jari Kurri, Edmonton. Six three-goal games; one four-goal game.
6 — Dino Ciccarelli, Minnesota, Washington, Detroit. Five three-goal games; one four-goal game.
5 — Mike Bossy, NY Islanders. Four three-goal games; one four-goal game.

MOST THREE-OR-MORE-GOAL GAMES, ONE PLAYOFF YEAR:
4 — Jari Kurri, Edmonton, 1985. 1 four-goal game, 3 three-goal games.
3 — Mark Messier, Edmonton, 1983. 3 three-goal games.
   — Mike Bossy, NY Islanders, 1983. 1 four-goal game, 2 three-goal games
2 — Newsy Lalonde, Montreal, 1919. 1 five-goal game, 1 four-goal game.
   — Maurice Richard, Montreal, 1944. 1 five-goal game; 1 three-goal game.
   — Doug Bentley, Chicago, 1944. 2 three-goal games.
   — Norm Ullman, Detroit, 1964. 2 three-goal games.
   — Phil Esposito, Boston, 1970. 2 three-goal games.
   — Pit Martin, Chicago, 1973. 2 three-goal games.
   — Rick MacLeish, Philadelphia, 1975. 2 three-goal games.
   — Lanny McDonald, Toronto, 1977. 1 four-goal game; 1 three-goal game.
   — Wayne Gretzky, Edmonton, 1981. 2 three-goal games.
   — Wayne Gretzky, Edmonton, 1983. 2 four-goal games.
   — Wayne Gretzky, Edmonton, 1985. 2 three-goal games.
   — Petr Klima, Detroit, 1988. 2 three-goal games.
   — Cam Neely, Boston, 1991. 2 three-goal games.
   — Wayne Gretzky, NY Rangers, 1997. 2 three-goal games.
   — Daniel Alfredsson, Ottawa, 1998. 2 three-goal games.
   — Patrick Marleau, San Jose, 2004. 2 three-goal games.

MOST THREE-OR-MORE-GOAL GAMES, ONE PLAYOFF SERIES:
3 — Jari Kurri, Edmonton, 1985 CF vs. Chicago, won by Edmonton 4-2. Kurri scored 3 goals May 7 at Edmonton in 7-3 win, 3 goals May 14 at Edmonton in 10-5 win and 4 goals May 16 at Chicago in 8-2 win.
2 — Doug Bentley, Chicago, 1944 SF vs. Detroit, won by Chicago 4-1. Bentley scored 3 goals Mar. 28 at Chicago in 7-1 win and 3 goals Mar. 30 at Detroit in 5-2 win.
   — Norm Ullman, Detroit, 1964 SF vs. Chicago, won by Detroit 4-3. Ullman scored 3 goals Mar. 29 at Chicago in 5-4 win and 3 goals April 7 at Detroit in 7-2 win.
   — Mark Messier, Edmonton, 1983 DF vs. Calgary, won by Edmonton 4-1. Messier scored 4 goals April 14 at Edmonton in 6-3 win and 3 goals April 17 at Calgary in 10-2 win.
   — Mike Bossy, NY Islanders, 1983 CF vs. Boston, won by NY Islanders 4-2. Bossy scored 3 goals May 3 at NY Islanders in 8-3 win and 4 goals May 7 at New York in 8-4 win.

SCORING STREAKS

LONGEST CONSECUTIVE GOAL-SCORING STREAK, ONE PLAYOFF YEAR:
10 Games — Reggie Leach, Philadelphia, 1976. Streak started April 17 at Toronto and ended May 9 at Montreal. He scored one goal in each of eight games; two in one game; and five in another; a total of 15 goals.

LONGEST CONSECUTIVE POINT-SCORING STREAK, ONE PLAYOFF YEAR:
18 games — Bryan Trottier, NY Islanders, 1981. 11 goals, 18 assists, 29 points.
17 games — Wayne Gretzky, Edmonton, 1988. 12 goals, 29 assists, 41 points.
   — Al MacInnis, Calgary, 1989. 7 goals, 19 assists, 26 points.

LONGEST CONSECUTIVE POINT-SCORING STREAK, MORE THAN ONE PLAYOFF YEAR:
27 games — Bryan Trottier, NY Islanders, 1980, 1981 and 1982. 7 games in 1980 (3 goals, 5 assists, 8 points), 18 games in 1981 (11 goals, 18 assists, 29 points), and two games in 1982 (2 goals, 3 assists, 5 points). Total points, 42.
19 games — Wayne Gretzky, Edmonton, Los Angeles, 1988 and 1989. 17 games in 1988 (12 goals, 29 assists, 41 points with Edmonton), 2 games in 1989 (1 goal, 2 assists, 3 points with Los Angeles). Total points, 44.
   — Al MacInnis, Calgary, 1989 and 1990. 17 games in 1989 (7 goals, 19 assists, 26 points), and two games in 1990 (2 goals, 1 assist, 3 points). Total points, 29.

FASTEST GOALS

FASTEST GOAL FROM START OF GAME:
0:06 — Don Kozak, Los Angeles, April 17, 1977, at Los Angeles vs. Boston and goaltender Gerry Cheevers. Los Angeles won 7-4.
0:07 — Bob Gainey, Montreal, May 5, 1977, at NY Islanders vs. goaltender Chico Resch. Montreal won 2-1.
   — Terry Murray, Philadelphia, April 12, 1981, at Quebec vs. goaltender Dan Bouchard. Quebec won 4-3 in overtime.

FASTEST GOAL FROM START OF PERIOD (OTHER THAN FIRST):
0:06 — Pelle Eklund, Philadelphia, April 25, 1989, at Pittsburgh vs. goaltender Tom Barrasso, second period. Pittsburgh won 10-7.
0:09 — Bill Collins, Minnesota, April 9, 1968, at Minnesota vs. Los Angeles and goaltender Wayne Rutledge, third period. Minnesota won 7-5.
   — Dave Balon, Minnesota, April 25, 1968, at St. Louis vs. goaltender Glenn Hall, third period. Minnesota won 5-1.
   — Murray Oliver, Minnesota, April 8, 1971, at St. Louis vs. goaltender Ernie Wakely, third period. St. Louis won 4-2.
   — Clark Gillies, NY Islanders, April 15, 1977, at Buffalo vs. goaltender Don Edwards, third period. NY Islanders won 4-3.
   — Eric Vail, Atlanta, April 11, 1978, at Atlanta vs. Detroit and goaltender Ron Low, third period. Detroit won 5-3.
   — Stan Smyl, Vancouver, April 10, 1979, at Philadelphia vs. goaltender Wayne Stephenson, third period. Vancouver won 3-2.
   — Wayne Gretzky, Edmonton, April 6, 1983, at Edmonton vs. Winnipeg and goaltender Brian Hayward, second period. Edmonton won 6-3.
   — Mark Messier, Edmonton, April 16, 1984, at Calgary vs. goaltender Don Edwards, third period. Edmonton won 5-3.
   — Brian Skrudland, Montreal, May 18, 1986, at Calgary vs. goaltender Mike Vernon, first overtime period. Montreal won 3-2.

FASTEST TWO GOALS:
0:05 — Norm Ullman, Detroit, April 11, 1965, at Detroit vs. Chicago and goaltender Glenn Hall. Ullman scored at 17:35 and 17:40 of second period. Detroit won 4-2.

FASTEST TWO GOALS FROM START OF A GAME:
1:08 — **Dick Duff, Toronto,** April 9, 1963, at Toronto vs. Detroit and goaltender Terry Sawchuk. Duff scored at 0:49 and 1:08. Toronto won 4-2.

FASTEST TWO GOALS FROM START OF A PERIOD:
0:35 — **Pat LaFontaine, NY Islanders,** May 19, 1984, at Edmonton vs. goaltender Andy Moog. LaFontaine scored at 0:13 and 0:35 of third period. Edmonton won 5-2.

PENALTIES

MOST PENALTY MINUTES IN PLAYOFFS, CAREER:
729 — Dale Hunter, Quebec, Washington, Colorado
541 — Chris Nilan, Montreal, NY Rangers, Boston
529 — Claude Lemieux, Montreal, New Jersey, Colorado, Phoenix
471 — Rick Tocchet, Philadelphia, Pittsburgh, Boston, Phoenix
466 — Willi Plett, Atlanta, Calgary, Minnesota, Boston

MOST PENALTIES, ONE GAME:
8 — **Forbes Kennedy, Toronto,** April 2, 1969, at Boston. Kennedy was assessed 4 minors, 2 majors, 1 10-minute misconduct, 1 game misconduct. Boston won 10-0.
— **Kim Clackson, Pittsburgh,** April 14, 1980, at Boston. Clackson was assessed 5 minors, 2 majors, 1 10-minute misconduct. Boston won 6-2.

MOST PENALTY MINUTES, ONE GAME:
42 — **Dave Schultz, Philadelphia,** April 22, 1976, at Toronto. Schultz was assessed 1 minor, 2 majors, 1 10-minute misconduct and 2 game-misconducts. Toronto won 8-5.

MOST PENALTIES, ONE PERIOD AND MOST PENALTY MINUTES, ONE PERIOD:
6 Penalties; 39 Minutes — **Ed Hospodar, NY Rangers,** April 9, 1981, at Los Angeles, first period. Hospodar was assessed 2 minors, 1 major, 1 10-minute misconduct, 2 game misconducts. Los Angeles won 5-4.

GOALTENDING

MOST PLAYOFF GAMES APPEARED IN BY A GOALTENDER, CAREER:
247 — Patrick Roy, Montreal, Colorado
161 — Ed Belfour, Chicago, Dallas, Toronto
153 — Martin Brodeur, New Jersey
150 — Grant Fuhr, Edmonton, Buffalo, St. Louis
138 — Mike Vernon, Calgary, Detroit, San Jose, Florida

MOST MINUTES PLAYED BY A GOALTENDER, CAREER:
15,209 — Patrick Roy, Montreal, Colorado
9,945 — Ed Belfour, Chicago, Dallas, Toronto
9,533 — Martin Brodeur, New Jersey
8,834 — Grant Fuhr, Edmonton, Buffalo, St. Louis
8,214 — Mike Vernon, Calgary, Detroit, San Jose, Florida

MOST MINUTES PLAYED BY A GOALTENDER, ONE PLAYOFF YEAR:
1,655 — Miikka Kiprusoff, Calgary, 2004. 26 games.
1,544 — Kirk McLean, Vancouver, 1994. 24 games.
— Ed Belfour, Dallas, 1999. 23 games.
1,540 — Ron Hextall, Philadelphia, 1987. 26 games.
1,505 — Martin Brodeur, New Jersey, 2001. 25 games.

MOST SHUTOUTS IN PLAYOFFS (CAREER):
23 — Patrick Roy, Montreal, Colorado
21 — Martin Brodeur, New Jersey
16 — Curtis Joseph, St. Louis, Edmonton, Toronto

MOST SHUTOUTS, ONE PLAYOFF YEAR:
7 — Martin Brodeur, New Jersey, 2003. 24 games.
6 — Dominik Hasek, Detroit, 2002. 23 games.
5 — Jean-Sebastien Giguere, Anaheim, 2003. 21 games.
— Nikolai Khabibulin, Tampa Bay, 2004. 23 games.
— Miikka Kiprusoff, Calgary, 2004. 26 games.

MOST SHUTOUTS, ONE PLAYOFF SERIES:
3 — **Clint Benedict, Mtl. Maroons,** 1926 F vs. Victoria. 4 games.
— **Dave Kerr, NY Rangers,** 1940 SF vs. Boston. 6 games.
— **Frank McCool, Toronto,** 1945 F vs. Detroit. 7 games.
— **Turk Broda, Toronto,** 1950 SF vs. Detroit. 7 games.
— **Felix Potvin, Toronto,** 1994 CQF vs. Chicago. 6 games.
— **Martin Brodeur, New Jersey,** 1995 CQF vs. Boston. 7 games.
— **Brent Johnson, St. Louis,** 2002 CQF vs. Chicago. 5 games.
— **Patrick Lalime, Ottawa,** 2002 CQF vs. Philadelphia. 5 games.
— **Jean-Sebastien Giguere, Anaheim,** 2003 CF vs. Minnesota. 4 games.
— **Martin Brodeur, New Jersey,** 2003 F vs. Anaheim. 7 games.
— **Ed Belfour, Toronto,** 2004 CQF vs. Ottawa. 7 games.
— **Nikolai Khabibulin, Tampa Bay,** 2004 CQF vs. NY Islanders. 5 games.

MOST WINS BY A GOALTENDER, (CAREER):
151 — Patrick Roy, Montreal, Colorado
92 — Grant Fuhr, Edmonton, Buffalo, St. Louis
89 — Martin Brodeur, New Jersey
88 — Billy Smith, NY Islanders
— Ed Belfour, Chicago, Dallas, Toronto

MOST WINS BY A GOALTENDER, ONE PLAYOFF YEAR:
16 — Sixteen wins by a goaltender in one playoff year has been recorded on 16 occasions. Nikolai Khabibulin of the Tampa Bay Lightning is the most recent to equal this mark, posting a record of 16 wins and 7 losses in 23 games in 2004. It was first accomplished by Grant Fuhr in 1988.

MOST CONSECUTIVE WINS BY A GOALTENDER, MORE THAN ONE PLAYOFF YEAR:
14 — **Tom Barrasso, Pittsburgh,** 1992, 1993; 3 wins vs. NY Rangers in 1992 DF, won by Pittsburgh 4-2; 4 wins vs. Boston in 1992 CF, won by Pittsburgh 4-0; 4 wins vs. Chicago in 1992 F, won by Pittsburgh 4-0; 3 wins vs. New Jersey in 1993 DSF, won by Pittsburgh 4-1.

MOST CONSECUTIVE WINS BY A GOALTENDER, ONE PLAYOFF YEAR:
11 — **Ed Belfour, Chicago,** 1992. 3 wins vs. St. Louis in DSF, won by Chicago 4-2; 4 wins vs. Detroit in DF, won by Chicago 4-0; and 4 wins vs. Edmonton in CF, won by Chicago 4-0.
— **Tom Barrasso, Pittsburgh,** 1992. 3 wins vs. NY Rangers in DF, won by Pittsburgh 4-2; 4 wins vs. Boston in CF, won by Pittsburgh 4-0; and 4 wins vs. Chicago in F, won by Pittsburgh 4-0.
— **Patrick Roy, Montreal,** 1993. 4 wins vs. Quebec in DSF, won by Montreal 4-2; 4 wins vs. Buffalo in DF, won by Montreal 4-0; and 3 wins vs. NY Islanders in CF, won by Montreal 4-1.

LONGEST SHUTOUT SEQUENCE:
270:08 — **George Hainsworth, Montreal,** 1930. Hainsworth's shutout streak began after Murray Murdoch scored a goal for the NY Rangers at 15:34 of the first period in the first game of a SF series on March 28, 1930. Hainsworth did not allow another goal in the final 113:18 of that game, won by Montreal 2-1 at 8:52 of the 4th overtime period. Hainsworth then shutout the NY Rangers in the next and final game of the series on March 30, 1930, won by Montreal 2-0. The streak continued with a 3-0 win over Boston in the opening game of the F series on April 1, 1930. His streak ended on April 3, 1930 when Boston's Eddie Shore scored at 16:50 of the second period in the second game of the F series.

MOST CONSECUTIVE SHUTOUTS:
3 — **Clint Benedict, Mtl. Maroons,** 1926. Benedict shut out Ottawa 1-0, Mar. 27; he then shut out Victoria twice, 3-0, Mar. 30; 3-0, Apr. 1. Mtl. Maroons won NHL F vs. Ottawa 2 goals to 1 and won the best-of-five F vs. Victoria 3-1.
— **John Ross Roach, NY Rangers,** 1929. Roach shut out NY Americans twice, 0-0, Mar. 19; 1-0, Mar. 21; he then shut out Toronto 1-0, Mar. 24. NY Rangers won QF vs. NY Americans 1 goal to 0 and won the best-of-three SF vs. Toronto 2-0.
— **Frank McCool, Toronto,** 1945. McCool shut out Detroit 1-0, April 6; 2-0, April 8; 1-0, April 12. Toronto won the best-of-seven F 4-3.
— **Brent Johnson, St. Louis,** 2002. Johnson shut out Chicago three times; 2-0, April 20; 4-0, April 21; 1-0, April 23. St. Louis won the best-of-seven CQF 4-1.
— **Patrick Lalime, Ottawa,** 2002. Lalime shut out Philadelphia three times; 3-0, April 20; 3-0, April 22; 3-0, April 24. Ottawa won the best-of-seven CQF 4-1.
— **Jean-Sebastien Giguere, Anaheim,** 2003. Giguere shut out Minnesota 1-0, May 10; 2-0, May 12; 4-0, May 14. Anaheim won the best-of-seven CF 4-0.

Early Playoff Records

1893-1918
Team Records

MOST GOALS, BOTH TEAMS, ONE GAME:
25 — **Ottawa Silver Seven, Dawson City** at Ottawa, Jan. 16, 1905. Ottawa 23, Dawson City 2. Ottawa won best-of-three series 2-0.

MOST GOALS, ONE TEAM, ONE GAME:
23 — **Ottawa Silver Seven** at Ottawa, Jan. 16, 1905. Ottawa defeated Dawson City 23-2.

MOST GOALS, BOTH TEAMS, BEST-OF-THREE SERIES:
42 — **Ottawa Silver Seven, Queen's University** at Ottawa, 1906. Ottawa defeated Queen's 16-7, Feb. 27, and 12-7, Feb. 28.

MOST GOALS, ONE TEAM, BEST-OF-THREE SERIES:
32 — **Ottawa Silver Seven** in 1905 at Ottawa. Defeated Dawson City 9-2, Jan. 13, and 23-2, Jan. 16.

MOST GOALS, BOTH TEAMS, BEST-OF-FIVE SERIES:
39 — **Toronto Arenas, Vancouver Millionaires** at Toronto, 1918. Toronto won 5-3, Mar. 20; 6-3, Mar. 26; 2-1, Mar. 30. Vancouver won 6-4, Mar. 23, and 8-1, Mar. 28. Toronto scored 18 goals; Vancouver 21.

MOST GOALS, ONE TEAM, BEST-OF-FIVE SERIES:
26 — **Vancouver Millionaires** in 1915 at Vancouver. Defeated Ottawa Senators 6-2, Mar. 22; 8-3, Mar. 24; and 12-3, Mar. 26.

Individual Records

MOST GOALS IN PLAYOFFS:
63 — **Frank McGee, Ottawa Silver Seven,** in 22 playoff games. Seven goals in four games, 1903; 21 goals in eight games, 1904; 18 goals in four games, 1905; 17 goals in six games, 1906.

MOST GOALS, ONE PLAYOFF SERIES:
15 — **Frank McGee, Ottawa Silver Seven,** in two games in 1905 at Ottawa. Scored one goal, Jan. 13, in 9-2 victory over Dawson City and 14 goals, Jan. 16, in 23-2 victory.

MOST GOALS, ONE PLAYOFF GAME:
14 — **Frank McGee, Ottawa Silver Seven,** at Ottawa, Jan. 16, 1905, in 23-2 victory over Dawson City.

FASTEST THREE GOALS:
40 Seconds — **Marty Walsh, Ottawa Senators,** at Ottawa, March 16, 1911, at 3:00, 3:10, and 3:40 of third period. Ottawa defeated Port Arthur 13-4.

All-Time Playoff Goal Leaders since 1918

(40 or more goals)

Player	Teams	Yrs.	GP	G
Wayne Gretzky	Edm., L.A., St.L., NYR	16	208	122
Mark Messier	Edm., NYR, Van.	17	236	109
Jari Kurri	Edm., L.A., NYR, Ana., Col.	15	200	106
Brett Hull	Cgy., St.L., Dal., Det., Phx.	19	202	103
Glenn Anderson	Edm., Tor., NYR, St.L.	15	225	93
Mike Bossy	NYI	10	129	85
Maurice Richard	Mtl.	15	133	82
*Joe Sakic	Que., Col.	12	162	82
Claude Lemieux	Mtl., N.J., Col., Phx., Dal.	17	233	80
Jean Beliveau	Mtl.	17	162	79
Mario Lemieux	Pit.	8	107	76
Dino Ciccarelli	Min., Wsh., Det., T.B., Fla.	14	141	73
Esa Tikkanen	Edm., NYR, St.L., N.J., Van., Fla., Wsh.	13	186	72
Bryan Trottier	NYI, Pit.	17	221	71
Steve Yzerman	Det.	20	196	70
Gordie Howe	Det., Hfd.	20	157	68
*Jaromir Jagr	Pit., Wsh., NYR	13	149	67
*Joe Nieuwendyk	Cgy., Dal., N.J., Tor., Fla.	16	158	66
Denis Savard	Chi., Mtl., T.B.	16	169	66
Yvan Cournoyer	Mtl.	12	147	64
Brian Propp	Phi., Bos., Min., Hfd.	13	160	64
Bobby Smith	Min., Mtl.	13	184	64
Bobby Hull	Chi., Wpg., Hfd.	14	119	62
Phil Esposito	Chi., Bos., NYR	15	130	61
*Peter Forsberg	Que., Col., Phi.	11	139	61
Jacques Lemaire	Mtl.	11	145	61
Joe Mullen	St.L., Cgy., Pit., Bos.	15	143	60
Doug Gilmour	St.L., Cgy., Tor., N.J., Chi., Buf., Mtl.	17	182	60
Stan Mikita	Chi.	18	155	59
Paul Coffey	Edm., Pit., L.A., Det., Hfd., Phi., Chi., Car., Bos.	16	194	59
Guy Lafleur	Mtl., NYR, Que.	14	128	58
Bernie Geoffrion	Mtl., NYR	16	132	58
Luc Robitaille	L.A., Pit., NYR, Det.	15	159	58
Cam Neely	Van., Bos.	9	93	57
Steve Larmer	Chi., NYR	13	140	56
Denis Potvin	NYI	14	185	56
Rick MacLeish	Phi., Hfd., Pit., Det.	11	114	54
Steve Thomas	Tor., Chi., NYI, N.J., Ana., Det.	16	174	54
Bill Barber	Phi., T.B.	11	129	53
Stephane Richer	Mtl., N.J., T.B., St.L., Pit.	13	134	53
*Brendan Shanahan	N.J., St.L., Hfd., Det.	16	157	53
Rick Tocchet	Phi., Pit., L.A., Bos., Wsh., Phx.	13	145	52
*Mike Modano	Min., Dal.	13	149	52
*Jeremy Roenick	Chi., Phx., Phi., L.A.	15	136	51
Frank Mahovlich	Tor., Det., Mtl.	14	137	51
Brian Bellows	Min., Mtl., T.B., Ana., Wsh.	13	143	51
Steve Shutt	Mtl., L.A.	12	99	50
*Rod Brind'Amour	St.L., Phi., Car.	11	141	50
*Sergei Fedorov	Det., Ana., CBJ	13	162	50
Henri Richard	Mtl.	18	180	49
Reggie Leach	Bos., Cal., Phi., Det.	8	94	47
Ted Lindsay	Det., Chi.	16	133	47
*Mark Recchi	Pit., Phi., Mtl., Car.	11	135	47
Clark Gillies	NYI, Buf.	13	164	47
Kevin Stevens	Pit., Bos., L.A., NYR, Phi.	7	103	46
Dickie Moore	Mtl., Tor., St.L.	14	135	46
Ron Francis	Hfd., Pit., Car., Tor.	17	171	46
Rick Middleton	NYR, Bos.	12	114	45
Lanny McDonald	Tor., Col., Cgy.	13	117	44
*Scott Young	Hfd., Pit., Que., Col., Ana., St.L., Dal.	14	141	44
Ken Linseman	Phi., Edm., Bos., Tor.	11	113	43
Mike Gartner	Wsh., Min., NYR, Tor., Phx.	15	122	43
Dave Andreychuk	Buf., Tor., N.J., Bos., Col., T.B.	18	162	43
*Vyacheslav Kozlov	Det., Buf., Atl.	9	114	42
Bernie Nicholls	L.A., NYR, Edm., N.J., Chi., S.J.	13	118	42
Bobby Clarke	Phi.	13	136	42
*John LeClair	Mtl., Phi., Pit.	14	154	42
Adam Oates	Det., St.L., Bos., Wsh., Phi., Ana., Edm.	15	163	42
Dale Hunter	Que., Wsh., Col.	18	186	42
John Bucyk	Det., Bos.	14	124	41
Vincent Damphousse	Tor., Edm., Mtl., S.J.	14	140	41
Raymond Bourque	Bos., Col.	21	214	41
Tim Kerr	Phi., NYR, Hfd.	10	81	40
Peter McNab	Buf., Bos., Van., N.J.	10	107	40
Bob Bourne	NYI, L.A.	13	139	40
John Tonelli	NYI, Cgy., L.A., Chi., Que.	13	172	40

*Active

All-Time Playoff Assist Leaders since 1918

(60 or more assists)

Player	Teams	Yrs.	GP	A
Wayne Gretzky	Edm., L.A., St.L., NYR	16	208	260
Mark Messier	Edm., NYR, Van.	17	236	186
Raymond Bourque	Bos., Col.	21	214	139
Paul Coffey	Edm., Pit., L.A., Det., Hfd., Phi., Chi., Car., Bos.	16	194	137
Doug Gilmour	St.L., Cgy., Tor., N.J., Chi., Buf., Mtl.	17	182	128
Jari Kurri	Edm., L.A., NYR, Ana., Col.	15	200	127
Al MacInnis	Cgy., St.L.	19	177	121
Glenn Anderson	Edm., Tor., NYR, St.L.	15	225	121
Larry Robinson	Mtl., L.A.	20	227	116
Steve Yzerman	Det.	20	196	115
Larry Murphy	L.A., Wsh., Min., Pit., Tor., Det.	20	215	115
Adam Oates	Det., St.L., Bos., Wsh., Phi., Ana., Edm.	15	163	114
*Sergei Fedorov	Det., Ana., CBJ	13	162	113
Bryan Trottier	NYI, Pit.	17	221	113
Denis Savard	Chi., Mtl., T.B.	16	169	109
Denis Potvin	NYI	14	185	108
*Chris Chelios	Mtl., Chi., Det.	21	228	107
*Peter Forsberg	Que., Col., Phi.	11	139	101
Jean Beliveau	Mtl.	17	162	97
Ron Francis	Hfd., Pit., Car., Tor.	17	171	97
Mario Lemieux	Pit.	8	107	96
*Joe Sakic	Que., Col.	12	162	96
Bobby Smith	Min., Mtl.	13	184	96
Gordie Howe	Det., Hfd.	20	157	92
Scott Stevens	Wsh., St.L., N.J.	20	233	92
Stan Mikita	Chi.	18	155	91
Brad Park	NYR, Bos., Det.	17	161	90
*Jaromir Jagr	Pit., Wsh., NYR	13	149	88
Brett Hull	Cgy., St.L., Dal., Det., Phx.	19	202	87
Craig Janney	Bos., St.L., S.J., Wpg., Phx., T.B., NYI	11	120	86
*Sergei Zubov	NYR, Pit., Dal.	11	147	84
Brian Propp	Phi., Bos., Min., Hfd.	13	160	84
*Nicklas Lidstrom	Det.	14	174	83
Henri Richard	Mtl.	18	180	80
*Mike Modano	Min., Dal.	13	149	79
Jacques Lemaire	Mtl.	11	145	78
Claude Lemieux	Mtl., N.J., Col., Phx., Dal.	17	233	78
Ken Linseman	Phi., Edm., Bos., Tor.	11	113	77
Bobby Clarke	Phi.	13	136	77
Guy Lafleur	Mtl., NYR, Que.	14	128	76
Phil Esposito	Chi., Bos., NYR	15	130	76
Dale Hunter	Que., Wsh., Col.	18	186	76
Mike Bossy	NYI	10	129	75
Steve Larmer	Chi., NYR	13	140	75
John Tonelli	NYI, Cgy., L.A., Chi., Que.	13	172	75
Peter Stastny	Que., N.J., St.L.	12	93	72
Bernie Nicholls	L.A., NYR, Edm., N.J., Chi., S.J.	13	118	72
Brian Bellows	Min., Mtl., T.B., Ana., Wsh.	13	143	71
Gilbert Perreault	Buf.	11	90	70
Geoff Courtnall	Bos., Edm., Wsh., St.L., Van.	15	156	70
*Brian Leetch	NYR, Tor., Bos.	8	95	69
Dale Hawerchuk	Wpg., Buf., St.L., Phi.	15	97	69
Alex Delvecchio	Det.	14	121	69
Luc Robitaille	L.A., Pit., NYR, Det.	15	159	69
Bobby Hull	Chi., Wpg., Hfd.	14	119	67
*Sandis Ozolinsh	S.J., Col., Car., Fla., Ana., NYR	10	137	67
Frank Mahovlich	Tor., Det., Mtl.	14	137	67
Igor Larionov	Van., S.J., Det., Fla., N.J.	13	150	67
Bobby Orr	Bos., Chi.	8	74	66
Bernie Federko	St.L., Det.	11	91	66
Jean Ratelle	NYR, Bos.	15	123	66
*Mark Recchi	Pit., Phi., Mtl., Car.	11	135	66
*Brendan Shanahan	N.J., St.L., Hfd., Det.	16	157	66
Charlie Huddy	Edm., L.A., Buf., St.L.	14	183	66
*Jeremy Roenick	Chi., Phx., Phi., L.A.	15	136	65
Dickie Moore	Mtl., Tor., St.L.	14	135	64
Doug Harvey	Mtl., NYR, Det., St.L.	15	137	64
Neal Broten	Min., Dal., N.J., L.A.	13	135	63
Vincent Damphousse	Tor., Edm., Mtl., S.J.	14	140	63
Yvan Cournoyer	Mtl.	12	147	63
*Pierre Turgeon	Buf., NYI, Mtl., St.L., Dal., Col.	15	109	62
John Bucyk	Det., Bos.	14	124	62
Doug Wilson	Chi., S.J.	12	95	61
Steve Duchesne	L.A., Phi., Que., St.L., Ott., Det.	14	121	61
Kevin Stevens	Pit., Bos., L.A., NYR, Phi.	7	103	60
*Patrik Elias	N.J.	9	111	60
*Trevor Linden	Van., NYI, Mtl., Wsh.	11	112	60
Bernie Geoffrion	Mtl., NYR	16	132	60
Rick Tocchet	Phi., Pit., L.A., Bos., Wsh., Phx.	13	145	60
Esa Tikkanen	Edm., NYR, St.L., N.J., Van., Fla., Wsh.	13	186	60

All-Time Playoff Point Leaders since 1918

(105 or more points)

Player	Teams	Yrs.	GP	G	A	Pts.
Wayne Gretzky	Edm., L.A., St.L., NYR	16	208	122	260	382
Mark Messier	Edm., NYR, Van.	17	236	109	186	295
Jari Kurri	Edm., L.A., NYR, Ana., Col.	15	200	106	127	233
Glenn Anderson	Edm., Tor., NYR, St.L.	15	225	93	121	214
Paul Coffey	Edm., Pit., L.A., Det., Hfd., Phi., Chi., Car., Bos.	16	194	59	137	196
Brett Hull	Cgy., St.L., Dal., Det., Phx.	19	202	103	87	190
Doug Gilmour	St.L., Cgy., Tor., N.J., Chi., Buf., Mtl.	17	182	60	128	188
Steve Yzerman	Det.	20	196	70	115	185
Bryan Trottier	NYI, Pit.	17	221	71	113	184
Raymond Bourque	Bos., Col.	21	214	41	139	180
*Joe Sakic	Que., Col.	12	162	82	96	178
Jean Beliveau	Mtl.	17	162	79	97	176
Denis Savard	Chi., Mtl., T.B.	16	169	66	109	175
Mario Lemieux	Pit.	8	107	76	96	172
Denis Potvin	NYI	14	185	56	108	164
*Sergei Fedorov	Det., Ana., CBJ	13	162	50	113	163
*Peter Forsberg	Que., Col., Phi.	11	139	61	101	162
Mike Bossy	NYI	10	129	85	75	160
Gordie Howe	Det., Hfd.	20	157	68	92	160
Al MacInnis	Cgy., St.L.	19	177	39	121	160
Bobby Smith	Min., Mtl.	13	184	64	96	160
Claude Lemieux	Mtl., N.J., Col., Phx., Dal.	17	233	80	78	158
Adam Oates	Det., St.L., Bos., Wsh., Phi., Ana., Edm.	15	163	42	114	156
*Jaromir Jagr	Pit., Wsh., NYR	13	149	67	88	155
Larry Murphy	L.A., Wsh., Min., Pit., Tor., Det.	20	215	37	115	152
Stan Mikita	Chi.	18	155	59	91	150
Brian Propp	Phi., Bos., Min., Hfd.	13	160	64	84	148
Larry Robinson	Mtl., L.A.	20	227	28	116	144
Ron Francis	Hfd., Pit., Car., Tor.	17	171	46	97	143
Jacques Lemaire	Mtl.	11	145	61	78	139
Phil Esposito	Chi., Bos., NYR	15	130	61	76	137
*Chris Chelios	Mtl., Chi., Det.	21	228	30	107	137
Guy Lafleur	Mtl., NYR, Que.	14	128	58	76	134
Esa Tikkanen	Edm., NYR, St.L., N.J., Van., Fla., Wsh.	13	186	72	60	132
Steve Larmer	Chi., NYR	13	140	56	75	131
*Mike Modano	Min., Dal.	13	149	52	79	131
Bobby Hull	Chi., Wpg., Hfd.	14	119	62	67	129
Henri Richard	Mtl.	18	180	49	80	129
Yvan Cournoyer	Mtl.	12	147	64	63	127
Luc Robitaille	L.A., Pit., NYR, Det.	15	159	58	69	127
Maurice Richard	Mtl.	15	133	82	44	126
Brad Park	NYR, Bos., Det.	17	161	35	90	125
Brian Bellows	Min., Mtl., T.B., Ana., Wsh.	13	143	51	71	122
Ken Linseman	Phi., Edm., Bos., Tor.	11	113	43	77	120
Bobby Clarke	Phi.	13	136	42	77	119
*Brendan Shanahan	N.J., St.L., Hfd., Det.	16	157	53	66	119
Bernie Geoffrion	Mtl., NYR	16	132	58	60	118
Frank Mahovlich	Tor., Det., Mtl.	14	137	51	67	118
Dino Ciccarelli	Min., Wsh., Det., T.B., Fla.	14	141	73	45	118
*Nicklas Lidstrom	Det.	14	174	35	83	118
Dale Hunter	Que., Wsh., Col.	18	186	42	76	118
Scott Stevens	Wsh., St.L., N.J.	20	233	26	92	118
*Jeremy Roenick	Chi., Phx., Phi., L.A.	15	136	51	65	116
*Joe Nieuwendyk	Cgy., Dal., N.J., Tor., Fla.	16	158	66	50	116
John Tonelli	NYI, Cgy., L.A., Chi., Que.	13	172	40	75	115
Bernie Nicholls	L.A., NYR, Edm., N.J., Chi., S.J.	13	118	42	72	114
*Mark Recchi	Pit., Phi., Mtl., Car.	11	135	47	66	113
Rick Tocchet	Phi., Pit., L.A., Bos., Wsh., Phx.	13	145	52	60	112
Craig Janney	Bos., St.L., S.J., Wpg., Phx., T.B., NYI	11	120	24	86	110
Dickie Moore	Mtl., Tor., St.L.	14	135	46	64	110
Geoff Courtnall	Bos., Edm., Wsh., St.L., Van.	15	156	39	70	109
Bill Barber	Phi., T.B.	11	129	53	55	108
Rick MacLeish	Phi., Hfd., Pit., Det.	11	114	54	53	107
*Rod Brind'Amour	St.L., Phi., Car.	11	141	50	57	107
*Sergei Zubov	NYR, Pit., Dal.	11	147	23	84	107
Steve Thomas	Tor., Chi., NYI, N.J., Ana., Det.	16	174	54	53	107
Kevin Stevens	Pit., Bos., L.A., NYR, Phi.	7	103	46	60	106
Joe Mullen	St.L., Cgy., Pit., Bos.	15	143	60	46	106
Peter Stastny	Que., N.J., St.L.	12	93	33	72	105

Bruins defenseman Fern Flaman clears the puck away from Montreal's Elmer Lach as teammates Murray Henderson (#8), Woody Dumart and goalie Frank Brimsek look on. Lach was the top playoff scorer when Montreal beat Boston for the Cup in 1946.

Leading Playoff Scorers, 1918–2006

Season	Player and Club	Games Played	Goals	Assists	Points
2005-06	Eric Staal, Carolina	25	9	19	28
2004-05	....	....	....	....	....
2003-04	Brad Richards, Tampa Bay	23	12	14	26
2002-03	Jamie Langenbrunner, New Jersey	24	11	7	18
	Scott Niedermayer, New Jersey	24	2	16	18
2001-02	Peter Forsberg, Colorado	20	9	18	27
2000-01	Joe Sakic, Colorado	21	13	13	26
99-2000	Brett Hull, Dallas	23	11	13	24
1998-99	Peter Forsberg, Colorado	19	8	16	24
1997-98	Steve Yzerman, Detroit	22	6	18	24
1996-97	Eric Lindros, Philadelphia	19	12	14	26
1995-96	Joe Sakic, Colorado	22	18	16	34
1994-95	Sergei Fedorov, Detroit	17	7	17	24
1993-94	Brian Leetch, NY Rangers	23	11	23	34
1992-93	Wayne Gretzky, Los Angeles	24	15	25	40
1991-92	Mario Lemieux, Pittsburgh	15	16	18	34
1990-91	Mario Lemieux, Pittsburgh	23	16	28	44
1989-90	Craig Simpson, Edmonton	22	16	15	31
	Mark Messier, Edmonton	22	9	22	31
1988-89	Al MacInnis, Calgary	22	7	24	31
1987-88	Wayne Gretzky, Edmonton	19	12	31	43
1986-87	Wayne Gretzky, Edmonton	21	5	29	34
1985-86	Doug Gilmour, St. Louis	19	9	12	21
	Bernie Federko, St. Louis	19	7	14	21
1984-85	Wayne Gretzky, Edmonton	18	17	30	47
1983-84	Wayne Gretzky, Edmonton	19	13	22	35
1982-83	Wayne Gretzky, Edmonton	16	12	26	38
1981-82	Bryan Trottier, NY Islanders	19	6	23	29
1980-81	Mike Bossy, NY Islanders	18	17	18	35
1979-80	Bryan Trottier, NY Islanders	21	12	17	29
1978-79	Jacques Lemaire, Montreal	16	11	12	23
	Guy Lafleur, Montreal	16	10	13	23
1977-78	Guy Lafleur, Montreal	15	10	11	21
	Larry Robinson, Montreal	15	4	17	21
1976-77	Guy Lafleur, Montreal	14	9	17	26
1975-76	Reggie Leach, Philadelphia	16	19	5	24
1974-75	Rick MacLeish, Philadelphia	17	11	9	20
1973-74	Rick MacLeish, Philadelphia	17	13	9	22
1972-73	Yvan Cournoyer, Montreal	17	15	10	25
1971-72	Phil Esposito, Boston	15	9	15	24
	Bobby Orr, Boston	15	5	19	24
1970-71	Frank Mahovlich, Montreal	20	14	13	27
1969-70	Phil Esposito, Boston	14	13	14	27
1968-69	Phil Esposito, Boston	10	8	10	18
1967-68	Bill Goldsworthy, Minnesota	14	8	7	15
1966-67	Jim Pappin, Toronto	12	7	8	15
1965-66	Norm Ullman, Detroit	12	6	9	15
1964-65	Bobby Hull, Chicago	14	10	7	17
1963-64	Gordie Howe, Detroit	14	9	10	19
1962-63	Gordie Howe, Detroit	11	7	9	16
	Norm Ullman, Detroit	11	4	12	16
1961-62	Stan Mikita, Chicago	12	6	15	21
1960-61	Gordie Howe, Detroit	11	4	11	15
	Pierre Pilote, Chicago	12	3	12	15
1959-60	Henri Richard, Montreal	8	3	9	12
	Bernie Geoffrion, Montreal	8	2	10	12
1958-59	Dickie Moore, Montreal	11	5	12	17
1957-58	Fleming Mackell, Boston	12	5	14	19
1956-57	Bernie Geoffrion, Montreal	11	11	7	18
1955-56	Jean Béliveau, Montreal	10	12	7	19
1954-55	Gordie Howe, Detroit	11	9	11	20
1953-54	Dickie Moore, Montreal	11	5	8	13
1952-53	Ed Sandford, Boston	11	8	3	11
1951-52	Ted Lindsay, Detroit	8	5	2	7
	Floyd Curry, Montreal	11	4	3	7
	Metro Prystai, Detroit	8	2	5	7
	Gordie Howe, Detroit	8	2	5	7
1950-51	Maurice Richard, Montreal	11	9	4	13
	Max Bentley, Toronto	11	2	11	13
1949-50	Pentti Lund, NY Rangers	12	6	5	11
1948-49	Gordie Howe, Detroit	11	8	3	11
1947-48	Ted Kennedy, Toronto	9	8	6	14
1946-47	Maurice Richard, Montreal	10	6	5	11
1945-46	Elmer Lach, Montreal	9	5	12	17
1944-45	Joe Carveth, Detroit	14	5	6	11
1943-44	Toe Blake, Montreal	9	7	11	18
1942-43	Carl Liscombe, Detroit	10	6	8	14
1941-42	Don Grosso, Detroit	12	8	6	14
	Syl Apps, Toronto	13	5	9	14
1940-41	Milt Schmidt, Boston	11	5	6	11
1939-40	Phil Watson, NY Rangers	12	3	6	9
	Neil Colville, NY Rangers	12	2	7	9
1938-39	Bill Cowley, Boston	12	3	11	14
1937-38	Johnny Gottselig, Chicago	10	5	3	8
	Gordie Drillon, Toronto	7	7	1	8
1936-37	Marty Barry, Detroit	10	4	7	11
1935-36	Frank Boll, Toronto	9	7	3	10
1934-35	Baldy Northcott, Mtl. Maroons	7	4	1	5
	Busher Jackson, Toronto	7	3	2	5
	Cy Wentworth, Mtl. Maroons	7	3	2	5
	Charlie Conacher, Toronto	7	1	4	5
1933-34	Larry Aurie, Detroit	9	3	7	10
1932-33	Cecil Dillon, NY Rangers	8	8	2	10
1931-32	Frank Boucher, NY Rangers	7	3	6	9
1930-31	Cooney Weiland, Boston	5	6	3	9
1929-30	Marty Barry, Boston	6	3	3	6
	Cooney Weiland, Boston	6	1	5	6
1928-29	Andy Blair, Toronto	4	3	0	3
	Butch Keeling, NY Rangers	6	3	0	3
	Ace Bailey, Toronto	4	1	2	3
1927-28	Frank Boucher, NY Rangers	9	7	3	10
1926-27	Harry Oliver, Boston	8	4	2	6
	Percy Galbraith, Boston	8	3	3	6
1925-26	Nels Stewart, Mtl. Maroons	8	6	3	9
1924-25	Howie Morenz, Montreal	6	7	1	8
1923-24	Howie Morenz, Montreal	6	7	3	10
1922-23	Punch Broadbent, Ottawa	8	6	1	7
1921-22	Babe Dye, Toronto	7	11	1	12
1920-21	Cy Denneny, Ottawa	7	4	2	6
1919-20	Frank Nighbor, Ottawa	5	6	1	7
	Jack Darragh, Ottawa	5	5	2	7
1918-19	Newsy Lalonde, Montreal	10	17	2	19
1917-18	Alf Skinner, Toronto	7	8	3	11

Three-or-more-Goal Games, Playoffs 1918–2006

Player	Team	Date	City	Total Goals	Opposing Goaltender	Score
Wayne Gretzky (10)	Edm.	Apr. 11/81	Edm.	3	Richard Sevigny	Edm. 6 Mtl. 2
		Apr. 19/81	Edm.	3	Billy Smith	Edm. 5 NYI 2
		Apr. 6/83	Edm.	4	Brian Hayward	Edm. 6 Wpg. 3
		Apr. 17/83	Cgy.	4	Reggie Lemelin	Edm. 10 Cgy. 2
		Apr. 25/85	Wpg.	3	Brian Hayward (2) / Marc Behrend (1)	Edm. 8 Wpg. 3
		May 25/85	Edm.	3	Pelle Lindbergh	Edm. 4 Phi. 3
		Apr. 24/86	Cgy.	3	Mike Vernon	Edm. 7 Cgy. 4
	L.A.	May 29/93	Tor.	3	Felix Potvin	L.A. 5 Tor. 4
	NYR	Apr. 23/97	NYR	3	John Vanbiesbrouck	NYR 3 Fla. 2
		May 18/97	Phi.	3	Garth Snow	NYR 5 Phi. 4
Maurice Richard (7)	Mtl.	Mar. 23/44	Mtl.	5	Paul Bibeault	Mtl. 5 Tor. 1
		Apr. 6/44	Chi.	3	Mike Karakas	Mtl. 3 Chi. 1
		Mar. 29/45	Mtl.	4	Frank McCool	Mtl. 10 Tor. 3
		Apr. 14/53	Bos.	3	Gord Henry	Mtl. 7 Bos. 3
		Mar. 20/56	Mtl.	3	Gump Worsley	Mtl. 7 NYR 1
		Apr. 6/57	Mtl.	3	Don Simmons	Mtl. 5 Bos. 1
		Apr. 1/58	Det.	3	Terry Sawchuk	Mtl. 4 Det. 3
Jari Kurri (7)	Edm.	Apr. 4/84	Edm.	3	Doug Soetaert (1) / Mike Veisor (2)	Edm. 9 Wpg. 2
		Apr. 25/85	Wpg.	3	Brian Hayward (2) / Marc Behrend (1)	Edm. 8 Wpg. 3
		May 7/85	Edm.	3	Murray Bannerman	Edm. 7 Chi. 3
		May 14/85	Edm.	3	Murray Bannerman	Edm. 10 Chi. 5
		May 16/85	Chi.	4	Murray Bannerman	Edm. 8 Chi. 2
		Apr. 9/87	Edm.	4	Rollie Melanson (2) / Darren Eliot (2)	Edm. 13 L.A. 3
		May 18/90	Bos.	3	Andy Moog (2) / Reggie Lemelin (1)	Edm. 7 Bos. 2
Dino Ciccarelli (6)	Min.	May 5/81	Min.	3	Pat Riggin	Min. 7 Cgy. 4
		Apr. 10/82	Min.	3	Murray Bannerman	Min. 7 Chi. 1
	Wsh.	Apr. 5/90	N.J.	3	Sean Burke	Wsh. 5 N.J. 4
		Apr. 25/92	Pit.	4	Tom Barrasso (1) / Ken Wregget (3)	Wsh. 7 Pit. 2
	Det.	Apr. 29/93	Tor.	3	Felix Potvin (2) / Daren Puppa (1)	Det. 7 Tor. 3
		May 11/95	Dal.	3	Andy Moog (2) / Darcy Wakaluk (1)	Det. 5 Dal. 1
Mike Bossy (5)	NYI	Apr. 16/79	NYI	3	Tony Esposito	NYI 6 Chi. 2
		May 8/82	NYI	3	Richard Brodeur	NYI 6 Van. 5
		Apr. 10/83	Wsh.	3	Al Jensen	NYI 6 Wsh. 3
		May 3/83	NYI	3	Pete Peeters	NYI 8 Bos. 3
		May 7/83	NYI	3	Pete Peeters	NYI 8 Bos. 4
Phil Esposito (4)	Bos.	Apr. 2/69	Bos.	4	Bruce Gamble	Bos. 10 Tor. 0
		Apr. 8/70	Bos.	3	Ed Giacomin	Bos. 8 NYR 2
		Apr. 19/70	Chi.	3	Tony Esposito	Bos. 6 Chi. 3
		Apr. 8/75	Bos.	3	Tony Esposito (2) / Michel Dumas (1)	Bos. 8 Chi. 2
Mark Messier (4)	Edm.	Apr. 14/83	Edm.	3	Reggie Lemelin	Edm. 6 Cgy. 3
		Apr. 17/83	Cgy.	3	Reggie Lemelin (1) / Don Edwards (2)	Edm. 10 Cgy. 2
		Apr. 26/83	Edm.	3	Murray Bannerman	Edm. 8 Chi. 2
	NYR	May 25/94	N.J.	3	Martin Brodeur (2) / ENG (1)	NYR 4 N.J. 2
Steve Yzerman (4)	Det.	Apr. 6/89	Det.	3	Alain Chevrier	Chi. 5 Det. 4
		Apr. 4/91	St.L.	3	Vincent Riendeau (2) / Pat Jablonski (1)	Det. 6 St.L. 3
		May 8/96	St.L.	3	Jon Casey	St.L. 5 Det. 4
		Apr. 21/99	Det.	3	Guy Hebert (2) / Pat Jablonski (1)	Det. 5 Ana. 3
Bernie Geoffrion (3)	Mtl.	Mar. 27/52	Mtl.	3	Jim Henry	Mtl. 4 Bos. 0
		7/55	Mtl.	3	Terry Sawchuk	Mtl. 4 Det. 2
		Mar. 30/57	Mtl.	3	Gump Worsley	Mtl. 8 NYR 3
Norm Ullman (3)	Det.	Mar. 29/64	Chi.	3	Glenn Hall	Det. 5 Chi. 4
		Apr. 7/64	Det.	3	Glenn Hall / Denis DeJordy (1)	Det. 7 Chi. 2
		Apr. 11/65	Det.	3	Glenn Hall	Det. 4 Chi. 2
John Bucyk (3)	Bos.	May 3/70	St.L.	3	Jacques Plante (1) / Ernie Wakely (2)	Bos. 6 St.L. 1
		Apr. 20/72	Bos.	3	Jacques Caron (1) / Ernie Wakely (2)	Bos. 10 St.L. 2
		Apr. 21/74	Bos.	3	Tony Esposito	Bos. 8 Chi. 6
Rick MacLeish (3)	Phi.	Apr. 11/74	Phi.	3	Phil Myre	Phi. 5 Atl. 1
		Apr. 13/75	Phi.	3	Gord McRae	Phi. 6 Tor. 3
		May 13/75	Phi.	3	Glenn Resch	Phi. 4 NYI 1
Denis Savard (3)	Chi.	Apr. 19/82	Chi.	3	Mike Liut	Chi. 7 Stl. 4
		Apr. 10/86	Chi.	4	Ken Wregget	Tor. 6 Chi. 4
				3	Greg Millen	Chi. 6 St.L. 3
Tim Kerr (3)	Phi.	Apr. 13/85	NYR	3	Glen Hanlon	Phi. 6 NYR 5
		Apr. 20/87	Phi.	3	Kelly Hrudey	Phi. 4 NYI 2
		Apr. 19/89	Pit.	3	Tom Barrasso	Phi. 4 Pit. 2
Cam Neely (3)	Bos.	Apr. 9/87	Mtl.	3	Patrick Roy	Mtl. 4 Bos. 3
		Apr. 5/91	Bos.	3	Peter Sidorkiewicz	Bos. 4 Hfd. 3
		Apr. 25/91	Bos.	3	Patrick Roy	Bos. 4 Mtl. 1
Petr Klima (3)	Det.	Apr. 7/88	Tor.	3	Alan Bester (2) / Ken Wregett (1)	Det. 6 Tor. 2
		Apr. 21/88	St.L.	3	Greg Millen	Det. 6 St.L. 0
	Edm.	May 4/91	Edm.	3	Jon Casey	Edm. 7 Min. 2
Esa Tikkanen (3)	Edm.	May 22/88	Edm.	3	Reggie Lemelin	Edm. 6 Bos. 3
		Apr. 16/91	Cgy.	3	Mike Vernon	Edm. 5 Cgy. 4
	L.A.	Apr. 26/92	L.A.	3	Kelly Hrudey (2) / Tom Askey (1)	Edm. 5 L.A. 2
Mike Gartner (3)	NYR	Apr. 13/90	NYR	3	Mark Fitzpatrick (2) / Glenn Healy (1)	NYR 6 NYI 5
		Apr. 27/92	NYR	3	Chris Terreri	NYR 8 N.J. 5
	Tor.	Apr. 25/96	Tor.	3	Jon Casey	Tor. 5 St.L. 4
Mario Lemieux (3)	Pit.	Apr. 25/89	Pit.	5	Ron Hextall	Pit. 10 Phi. 7
		Apr. 23/92	Pit.	3	Don Beaupre	Pit. 6 Wsh. 4
		May 11/96	Pit.	3	Mike Richter	Pit. 7 NYR 3
Patrick Marleau (3)	S.J.	Apr. 10/04	S.J.	3	Chris Osgood	S.J. 3 St.L. 1
		Apr. 22/04	S.J.	3	David Aebischer	S.J. 5 Col. 2
		Apr. 27/06	S.J.	3	Chris Mason	Nsh. 4 S.J. 5
Newsy Lalonde (2)	Mtl.	Mar. 1/19	Mtl.	5	Clint Benedict	Mtl. 6 Ott. 3
		Mar. 22/19	Sea.	4	Hap Holmes	Mtl. 4 Sea. 2
Howie Morenz (2)	Mtl.	Mar. 22/24	Mtl.	3	Charles Reid	Mtl. 6 Cgy.T. 1
		Mar. 27/25	Mtl.	3	Hap Holmes	Mtl. 4 Vic. 2
Doug Bentley (2)	Chi.	Mar. 28/44	Chi.	3	Connie Dion	Chi. 7 Det. 1
		Mar. 30/44	Det.	3	Connie Dion	Chi. 2 Det. 2
Toe Blake (2)	Mtl.	Mar. 22/38	Mtl.	3	Mike Karakas	Mtl. 6 Chi. 4
		Mar. 26/46	Chi.	3	Mike Karakas	Mtl. 7 Chi. 2
Ted Kennedy (2)	Tor.	Apr. 14/45	Tor.	3	Harry Lumley	Det. 5 Tor. 3
		Mar. 27/48	Tor.	4	Frank Brimsek	Tor. 5 Bos. 3
F. St. Marseille (2)	St.L.	Apr. 28/70	St.L.	3	Al Smith	St.L. 5 Pit. 0
		Apr. 6/72	Min.	3	Cesare Maniago	Min. 5 St.L. 5
Bobby Hull (2)	Chi.	Apr. 7/63	Det.	3	Terry Sawchuk	Det. 7 Chi. 4
		Apr. 9/72	Pit.	3	Jim Rutherford	Chi. 6 Pit. 5
Pit Martin (2)	Chi.	Apr. 4/73	Chi.	3	Wayne Stephenson	Chi. 7 St.L. 1
		May 10/73	Chi.	3	Ken Dryden	Mtl. 8 Chi. 4
Yvan Cournoyer (2)	Mtl.	May 5/73	Mtl.	3	Dave Dryden	Mtl. 7 Buf. 3
		Apr. 11/74	Mtl.	3	Ed Giacomin	Mtl. 4 NYR 1
Guy Lafleur (2)	Mtl.	May 1/75	Mtl.	3	Roger Crozier (1) / Gerry Desjardins (2)	Mtl. 7 Buf. 0
		Apr. 11/77	Mtl.	3	Ed Staniowski	Mtl. 7 St.L. 2
Lanny McDonald (2)	Tor.	Apr. 9/77	Pit.	3	Denis Herron	Tor. 5 Pit. 2
		Apr. 17/77	Tor.	4	Wayne Stephenson	Phi. 6 Tor. 5
Bill Barber (2)	Phi.	May 4/80	Min.	3	Gilles Meloche	Phi. 5 Min. 3
		9/81	Phi.	3	Dan Bouchard	Phi. 8 Que. 5
Bryan Trottier (2)	NYI	Apr. 8/80	NYI	3	Doug Keans	NYI 8 L.A. 1
		9/81	NYI	3	Michel Larocque	NYI 5 Tor. 1
Butch Goring (2)	L.A.	Apr. 9/77	L.A.	3	Phil Myre	L.A. 4 Atl. 2
	NYI	May 17/81	Min.	3	Gilles Meloche	NYI 7 Min. 5
Paul Reinhart (2)	Cgy.	Apr. 14/83	Edm.	3	Andy Moog	Edm. 6 Cgy. 3
		8/84	Van	3	Richard Brodeur	Cgy. 5 Van. 1
Brian Propp (2)	Phi.	Apr. 22/81	Phi.	3	Pat Riggin	Phi. 9 Cgy. 4
		Apr. 21/85	Phi.	3	Billy Smith	Phi. 5 NYI 2
Peter Stastny (2)	Que.	Apr. 5/83	Bos.	3	Pete Peeters	Bos. 4 Que. 3
		Apr. 11/87	Que.	3	Mike Liut (2) / Steve Weeks (1)	Que. 5 Hfd. 1
Michel Goulet (2)	Que.	Apr. 23/85	Que.	3	Steve Penney	Que. 7 Mtl. 6
		Apr. 12/87	Que.	3	Mike Liut	Que. 4 Hfd. 1
Glenn Anderson (2)	Edm.	Apr. 26/83	Edm.	4	Murray Bannerman	Edm. 8 Chi. 2
		6/88	Wpg.	3	Daniel Berthiaume	Edm. 7 Wpg. 4
Peter Zezel (2)	Phi.	Apr. 13/86	NYR	3	John Vanbiesbrouck	Phi. 7 NYR 1
	St.L.	Apr. 11/89	St.L.	3	Jon Casey (2) / Kari Takko (1)	St.L. 6 Min. 1
Geoff Courtnall (2)	Van.	Apr. 4/91	L.A.	3	Kelly Hrudey	Van. 6 L.A. 5
		Apr. 30/92	Van.	3	Rick Tabaracci	Van. 5 Win. 0
Joe Sakic (2)	Que.	May 6/95	Que.	3	Mike Richter	Que. 5 NYR 4
	Col.	Apr. 25/96	Col.	3	Corey Hirsch	Col. 5 Van. 4
Daniel Alfredsson (2)	Ott.	Apr. 28/98	Ott.	3	Martin Brodeur	Ott. 4 N.J. 3
		May 11/98	Ott.	3	Olaf Kolzig	Ott. 4 Wsh. 3
Harry Meeking	Tor.	Mar. 11/18	Tor.	3	Georges Vezina	Tor. 7 Mtl. 3
Alf Skinner	Tor.	Mar. 23/18	Tor.	3	Hugh Lehman	Van.M. 6 Tor. 4
Joe Malone	Mtl.	Feb. 23/19	Mtl.	3	Clint Benedict	Mtl. 8 Ott. 4
Odie Cleghorn	Mtl.	Feb. 27/19	Ott.	3	Clint Benedict	Mtl. 5 Ott. 4
Jack Darragh	Ott.	Apr. 1/20	Tor.	3	Hap Holmes	Ott. 6 Sea. 1
George Boucher	Ott.	Mar. 10/21	Ott.	3	Jake Forbes	Ott. 5 Tor. 0
Babe Dye	Tor.	Mar. 28/22	Tor.	4	Hugh Lehman	Tor. 5 Van.M. 1
Percy Galbraith	Bos.	Mar. 31/27	Bos.	3	Hugh Lehman	Bos. 4 Chi. 4
Busher Jackson	Tor.	Apr. 5/32	NYR	3	John Ross Roach	Tor. 6 NYR 4
Frank Boucher	NYR	Apr. 9/32	Tor.	3	Lorne Chabot	Tor. 6 NYR 4
Charlie Conacher	Tor.	Mar. 26/36	Tor.	3	Tiny Thompson	Tor. 8 Bos. 3
Syd Howe	Det.	Mar. 23/39	Det.	3	Claude Bourque	Det. 7 Mtl. 3
Bryan Hextall	NYR	Apr. 3/40	NYR	3	Turk Broda	NYR 6 Tor. 2
Joe Benoit	Mtl.	Mar. 22/41	Mtl.	3	Sam LoPresti	Mtl. 4 Chi. 3
Syl Apps	Tor.	Mar. 25/41	Tor.	3	Frank Brimsek	Tor. 7 Bos. 2
Jack McGill	Bos.	Mar. 29/42	Bos.	3	Johnny Mowers	Det. 6 Bos. 4
Don Metz	Tor.	Apr. 14/42	Tor.	3	Johnny Mowers	Tor. 9 Det. 3
Mud Bruneteau	Det.	Apr. 1/43	Det.	3	Frank Brimsek	Det. 6 Bos. 2
Don Grosso	Det.	Apr. 7/43	Bos.	3	Frank Brimsek	Det. 4 Bos. 0
Carl Liscombe	Det.	Apr. 3/45	Bos.	4	Paul Bibeault	Det. 5 Bos. 3
Billy Reay	Mtl.	Apr. 1/47	Bos.	3	Frank Brimsek	Mtl. 5 Bos. 3
Gerry Plamondon	Mtl.	Mar. 24/49	Det.	3	Harry Lumley	Mtl. 4 Det. 3
Sid Smith	Tor.	Apr. 10/49	Det.	3	Harry Lumley	Tor. 3 Det. 1
Pentti Lund	NYR	Apr. 2/50	NYR	3	Bill Durnan	NYR 4 Mtl. 1
Ted Lindsay	Det.	Apr. 5/55	Det.	3	Charlie Hodge (1) / Jacques Plante (3)	Det. 7 Mtl. 1
Gordie Howe	Det.	Apr. 10/55	Det.	3	Jacques Plante	Det. 5 Mtl. 1

Three-or-more-Goal Games, Playoffs — *continued*

Player	Team	Date	City	Total Goals	Opposing Goaltender	Score	
Phil Goyette	Mtl.	Mar. 25/58	Mtl.	3	Terry Sawchuk	Mtl. 8	Det. 1
Jerry Toppazzini	Bos.	Apr. 5/58	Bos.	3	Gump Worsley	Bos. 8	NYR 2
Bob Pulford	Tor.	Apr. 19/62	Tor.	3	Glenn Hall	Tor. 8	Chi. 4
Dave Keon	Tor.	Apr. 9/64	Mtl.	3	Charlie Hodge (2) ENG (1)	Tor. 3	Mtl. 1
Henri Richard	Mtl.	Apr. 20/67	Mtl.	3	Terry Sawchuk (2) Johnny Bower (1)	Mtl. 6	Tor. 2
Rosaire Paiement	Phi.	Apr. 13/68	Phi.	3	Glenn Hall (1) Seth Martin (2)	Phi. 6	St.L. 1
Jean Beliveau	Mtl.	Apr. 20/68	Mtl.	3	Denis DeJordy	Mtl. 4	Chi. 1
Red Berenson	St.L.	Apr. 15/69	St.L.	3	Gerry Desjardins	St.L. 4	L.A. 0
Ken Schinkel	Pit.	Apr. 11/70	Oak.	3	Gary Smith	Pit. 5	Oak. 2
Jim Pappin	Chi.	Apr. 11/71	Phi.	3	Bruce Gamble	Chi. 6	Phi. 2
Bobby Orr	Bos.	Apr. 11/71	Mtl.	3	Ken Dryden	Bos. 5	Mtl. 2
Jacques Lemaire	Mtl.	Apr. 20/71	Mtl.	3	Gump Worsley	Mtl. 7	Min. 2
Vic Hadfield	NYR	Apr. 22/71	NYR	3	Tony Esposito	NYR 4	Chi. 1
Fred Stanfield	Bos.	Apr. 18/72	Bos.	3	Jacques Caron	Bos. 6	St.L. 1
Ken Hodge	Bos.	Apr. 30/72	Bos.	3	Ed Giacomin	Bos. 6	NYR 5
Dick Redmond	Chi.	Apr. 4/73	Chi.	3	Wayne Stephenson	Chi. 7	St.L. 1
Steve Vickers	NYR	Apr. 10/73	Bos.	3	Ross Brooks (2) Eddie Johnston (1)	NYR 6	Bos. 3
Tom Williams	L.A.	Apr. 14/74	L.A.	3	Mike Veisor	L.A. 5	Chi. 1
Marcel Dionne	L.A.	Apr. 15/76	L.A.	3	Gilles Gilbert	L.A. 6	Bos. 4
Don Saleski	Phi.	Apr. 22/76	Phi.	3	Wayne Thomas	Phi. 7	Tor. 1
Darryl Sittler	Tor.	Apr. 22/76	Tor.	5	Bernie Parent	Tor. 8	Phi. 5
Reggie Leach	Phi.	May 6/76	Phi.	5	Gilles Gilbert	Phi. 6	Bos. 3
Jim Lorentz	Buf.	Apr. 7/77	Min.	3	Pete LoPresti (2) Gary Smith (1)	Buf. 7	Min. 1
Bobby Schmautz	Bos.	Apr. 11/77	Bos.	3	Rogie Vachon	Bos. 8	L.A. 3
Billy Harris	NYI	Apr. 23/77	Mtl.	3	Ken Dryden	Mtl. 4	NYI 3
George Ferguson	Tor.	Apr. 11/78	Tor.	3	Rogie Vachon	Tor. 7	L.A. 3
Jean Ratelle	Bos.	May 3/79	Bos.	3	Ken Dryden	Bos. 4	Mtl. 3
Stan Jonathan	Bos.	May 8/79	Bos.	3	Ken Dryden	Bos. 5	Mtl. 2
Ron Duguay	NYR	Apr. 20/80	NYR	3	Pete Peeters	NYR 4	Phi. 2
Steve Shutt	Mtl.	Apr. 22/80	Mtl.	3	Gilles Meloche	Mtl. 6	Min. 3
Gilbert Perreault	Buf.	May 6/80	NYI	3	Billy Smith (2) ENG (1)	Buf. 7	NYI 4
Paul Holmgren	Phi.	May 15/80	Phi.	3	Billy Smith	Phi. 8	NYI 3
Steve Payne	Min.	Apr. 8/81	Bos.	3	Rogie Vachon	Min. 5	Bos. 4
Denis Potvin	NYI	Apr. 17/81	NYI	3	Andy Moog	NYI 6	Edm. 3
Barry Pederson	Bos.	Apr. 8/82	Bos.	3	Don Edwards	Bos. 7	Buf. 3
Duane Sutter	NYI	Apr. 15/83	NYI	3	Glen Hanlon	NYI 5	NYR 0
Doug Halward	Van.	Apr. 7/84	Van.	3	Reggie Lemelin (2) Don Edwards (1)	Van. 7	Cgy. 0
Jorgen Pettersson	St.L.	Apr. 8/84	Det.	3	Eddie Mio	St.L. 3	Det. 2
Clark Gillies	NYI	May 12/84	NYI	3	Grant Fuhr	NYI 6	Edm. 1
Ken Linseman	Bos.	Apr. 14/85	Bos.	3	Steve Penney	Bos. 7	Mtl. 6
Dave Andreychuk	Buf.	Apr. 14/85	Buf.	3	Dan Bouchard	Buf. 7	Que. 4
Greg Paslawski	St.L.	Apr. 15/86	Min.	3	Don Beaupre	St.L. 6	Min. 3
Doug Risebrough	Cgy.	May 4/86	Cgy.	3	Rick Wamsley	Cgy. 8	St.L. 2
Mike McPhee	Mtl.	Apr. 11/87	Bos.	3	Doug Keans	Mtl. 5	Bos. 4
John Ogrodnick	Que.	Apr. 14/87	Hfd.	3	Mike Liut	Que. 7	Hfd. 5
Pelle Eklund	Phi.	May 10/87	Mtl.	3	Patrick Roy (1) Brian Hayward (2)	Phi. 6	Mtl. 3
John Tucker	Buf.	Apr. 9/88	Bos.	4	Andy Moog	Buf. 6	Bos. 2
Tony Hrkac	St.L.	Apr. 10/88	St.L.	3	Darren Pang	St.L. 6	Chi. 5
Hakan Loob	Cgy.	Apr. 10/88	Cgy.	3	Glenn Healy	Cgy. 7	L.A. 3
Ed Olczyk	Tor.	Apr. 12/88	Tor.	3	Greg Stefan (2) Glen Hanlon (1)	Tor. 6	Det. 5
Aaron Broten	N.J.	Apr. 20/88	N.J.	3	Pete Peeters	N.J. 5	Wsh. 2
Mark Johnson	N.J.	Apr. 22/88	Wsh.	4	Pete Peeters	N.J. 10	Wsh. 4
Patrik Sundstrom	N.J.	Apr. 22/88	Wsh.	3	Pete Peeters (2) Clint Malarchuk (1)	N.J. 10	Wsh. 4
Bob Brooke	Min.	Apr. 5/89	St.L.	3	Greg Millen	St.L. 4	Min. 3
Chris Kontos	L.A.	Apr. 6/89	L.A.	3	Grant Fuhr	L.A. 5	Edm. 2
Wayne Presley	Chi.	Apr. 13/89	Chi.	3	Greg Stefan (1) Glen Hanlon (2)	Chi. 7	Det. 1
Tony Granato	L.A.	Apr. 10/90	L.A.	3	Mike Vernon (1) Rick Wamsley (2)	L.A. 12	Cgy. 4
Tomas Sandstrom	L.A.	Apr. 10/90	L.A.	3	Mike Vernon (1) Rick Wamsley (2)	L.A. 12	Cgy. 4
Dave Taylor	L.A.	Apr. 10/90	L.A.	3	Mike Vernon (1) Rick Wamsley (2)	L.A. 12	Cgy. 4
Bernie Nicholls	NYR	Apr. 19/90	NYR	3	Mike Liut	NYR 7	Wsh. 3
John Druce	Wsh.	Apr. 21/90	NYR	3	John Vanbiesbrouck	Wsh. 6	NYR 3
Adam Oates	St.L.	Apr. 12/91	St.L.	3	Tim Chevaldae	St.L. 6	Det. 1
Luc Robitaille	L.A.	Apr. 26/91	L.A.	3	Grant Fuhr	L.A. 5	Edm. 2
Ray Sheppard	Det.	Apr. 24/92	Min.	3	Jon Casey	Min. 5	Det. 2
Pavel Bure	Van.	Apr. 28/92	Van.	3	Rick Tabaracci	Van. 8	Wpg. 3
Joe Murphy	Edm.	May 6/92	Edm.	3	Kirk McLean	Edm. 5	Van. 2
Ron Francis	Pit.	May 9/92	Pit.	3	Mike Richter (2) John V'brouck (1)	Pit. 5	NYR 4
Kevin Stevens	Pit.	May 21/92	Bos.	4	Andy Moog	Pit. 5	Bos. 2
Dirk Graham	Chi.	Jun. 1/92	Chi.	3	Tom Barrasso	Pit. 6	Chi. 5
Brian Noonan	Chi.	Apr. 18/93	Chi.	3	Curtis Joseph	St.L. 4	Chi. 3
Dale Hunter	Wsh.	Apr. 20/93	Wsh.	3	Glenn Healy	NYI 5	Wsh. 4
Teemu Selanne	Wpg.	Apr. 23/93	Wpg.	3	Kirk McLean	Wpg. 5	Van. 4
Ray Ferraro	NYI	Apr. 26/93	Wsh.	4	Don Beaupre	Wsh. 6	NYI 4
Al Iafrate	Wsh.	Apr. 26/93	Wsh.	3	Glenn Healy (2) Mark Fitzpatrick (1)	Wsh. 6	NYI 4
Paul DiPietro	Mtl.	Apr. 28/93	Mtl.	3	Ron Hextall	Mtl. 6	Que. 2
Wendel Clark	Tor.	May 27/93	L.A.	3	Kelly Hrudey	L.A. 5	Tor. 4
Eric Desjardins	Mtl.	Jun. 3/93	Mtl.	3	Kelly Hrudey	Mtl. 3	L.A. 2
Tony Amonte	Chi.	Apr. 23/94	Chi.	4	Felix Potvin	Chi. 5	Tor. 4
Gary Suter	Chi.	Apr. 24/94	Chi.	3	Felix Potvin	Chi. 4	Tor. 3
Ulf Dahlen	S.J.	May 6/94	S.J.	3	Felix Potvin	S.J. 5	Tor. 2
Mike Sullivan	Cgy.	May 11/95	S.J.	3	Arturs Irbe (2) Wade Flaherty (1)	Cgy. 9	S.J. 2
Theoren Fleury	Cgy.	May 13/95	S.J.	4	Arturs Irbe (3) ENG (1)	Cgy. 6	S.J. 4
Brendan Shanahan	St.L.	May 13/95	Van.	3	Kirk McLean	St.L. 5	Van. 2
John LeClair	Phi.	May 21/95	Phi.	3	Mike Richter	Phi. 5	NYR 4
Brian Leetch	NYR	May 22/95	Phi.	3	Ron Hextall	Phi. 4	NYR 3
Trevor Linden	Van.	Apr. 25/96	Col.	3	Patrick Roy	Col. 5	Van. 4
Jaromir Jagr	Pit.	May 11/96	Pit.	3	Mike Richter	Pit. 7	NYR 3
Peter Forsberg	Col.	Jun. 6/96	Col.	3	John Vanbiesbrouck	Col. 8	Fla. 1
Valeri Zelepukin	N.J.	Apr. 22/97	Mtl.	3	Jocelyn Thibault	N.J. 6	Mtl. 4
Valeri Kamensky	Col.	Apr. 24/97	Col.	3	Jeff Hackett (2) Chris Terreri (1)	Col. 7	Chi. 0
Eric Lindros	Phi.	May 20/97	NYR	3	Mike Richter	Phi. 6	NYR 3
Matthew Barnaby	Buf.	May 10/98	Buf.	3	Andy Moog (2) ENG (1)	Buf. 6	Mtl. 3
Martin Straka	Pit.	Apr. 25/99	Pit.	3	Martin Brodeur	Pit. 4	N.J. 2
Martin Lapointe	Det.	Apr. 15/00	Det.	3	Stephane Fiset (2) Jamie Storr (1)	Det. 8	L.A. 5
Doug Weight	Edm.	Apr. 16/00	Edm.	3	Ed Belfour	Edm. 5	Dal. 2
Bill Guerin	Edm.	Apr. 18/00	Edm.	3	Ed Belfour	Dal. 4	Edm. 3
Scott Young	St.L.	Apr. 23/00	S.J.	3	Steve Shields	St.L. 6	S.J. 2
Andy Delmore	Phi.	May 7/00	Phi.	3	Ron Tugnutt (2) Peter Skudra (1)	Phi. 6	Pit. 3
Brett Hull	Det.	Apr. 27/02	Van.	3	Peter Skudra	Det. 6	Van. 4
Keith Tkachuk	St.L.	May 7/02	St.L.	3	Dominik Hasek	St.L. 6	Det. 1
Darren McCarty	Det.	May 18/02	Det.	3	Patrick Roy	Det. 5	Col. 3
Alexander Mogilny	Tor.	Apr. 9/03	Phi.	3	Roman Cechmanek (2) ENG (1)	Tor. 5	Phi. 3
Mike Sillinger	St.L.	Apr. 12/04	St.L.	3	Evgeni Nabokov (2) ENG (1)	St.L. 4	S.J. 1
Keith Primeau	Phi.	May 2/04	Phi.	3	Ed Belfour (2) Trevor Kidd (1)	Phi. 7	Tor. 2
Jean-Pierre Dumont	Buf.	Apr. 24/06	Buf.	3	Antero Niitymaki (1) Robert Esche (2)	Phi. 2	Buf. 8
John Madden	N.J.	Apr. 24/06	N.J.	3	Kevin Weekes	NYR 1	N.J. 4
Jason Pominville	Buf.	Apr. 24/06	Buf.	3	Antero Niittymaki (2) Robert Esche (1)	Phi. 2	Buf. 8
Joffrey Lupul	Ana.	May 9/06	Col.	4	Jose Theodore	Ana. 4	Col. 3

Henrik Timander congratulates Jason Pominville after his third goal in Buffalo's 8-2 victory over Philadelphia during the 2006 playoffs. Pominville topped all rookie scorers with five goals and 10 points in the postseason.

Overtime Games since 1918

Abbreviations: Teams/Cities: — **Ana.** - Anaheim; **Atl.** - Atlanta; **Bos.** - Boston; **Buf.** - Buffalo; **Cgy.** - Calgary; **Cgy. T.** - Calgary Tigers (Western Canada Hockey League); **Chi.** - Chicago; **Col.** - Colorado; **Dal.** - Dallas; **Det.** - Detroit; **Edm.** - Edmonton; **Edm. E.** - Edmonton Eskimos (WCHL); **Fla.** - Florida; **Hfd.** - Hartford; **L.A.** - Los Angeles; **Min.** - Minnesota; **Mtl.** - Montreal; **Mtl. M.** - Montreal Maroons; **N.J.** - New Jersey; **NYA** - NY Americans; **NYI** - New York Islanders; **NYR** - New York Rangers; **Oak.** - Oakland; **Ott.** - Ottawa; **Phi.** - Philadelphia; **Phx.** - Phoenix; **Pit.** - Pittsburgh; **Que.** - Quebec; **St.L.** - St. Louis; **Sea.** - Seattle Metropolitans (Pacific Coast Hockey Association); **S.J.** - San Jose; **T.B.** - Tampa Bay; **Tor.** - Toronto; **Van.** - Vancouver; **Van. M.** - Vancouver Millionaires (PCHA); **Vic.** - Victoria Cougars (WCHL); **Wpg.** - Winnipeg; **Wsh.** - Washington.

SERIES — **CF** - conference final; **CQF** - conference quarter-final; **CSF** - conference semi-final; **DF** - division final; **DSF** - division semi-final; **F** - final; **PRE** - preliminary round; **QF** - quarter-final; **SF** - semi-final.

Date	City	Series	Score		Scorer	Overtime	Series Winner
Mar. 26/19	Sea.	F	Mtl. 0	Sea. 0	no scorer	20:00	....
Mar. 30/19	Sea.	F	Mtl. 4	Sea. 3	Odie Cleghorn	15:57	....
Mar. 20/22	Tor.	F	Tor. 2	Van. M. 1	Babe Dye	4:50	Tor.
Mar. 29/23	Van.	F	Ott. 2	Edm. E. 1	Cy Denneny	2:08	Ott.
Mar. 31/27	Mtl.	QF	Mtl. 1	Mtl. M. 0	Howie Morenz	12:05	Mtl.
Apr. 7/27	Bos.	F	Ott. 0	Bos. 0	no scorer	20:00	Ott.
Apr. 11/27	Ott.	F	Bos. 1	Ott. 1	no scorer	20:00	Ott.
Apr. 3/28	Mtl.	QF	Mtl. M. 1	Mtl. 0	Russell Oatman	8:20	Mtl. M.
Apr. 7/28	Mtl.	F	NYR 2	Mtl. M. 1	Frank Boucher	7:05	NYR
Mar. 21/29	NYR	QF	NYR 1	NYA 0	Butch Keeling	29:50	NYR
Mar. 26/29	Tor.	SF	NYR 2	Tor. 1	Frank Boucher	2:03	NYR
Mar. 20/30	Mtl.	SF	Bos. 2	Mtl. M. 1	Harry Oliver	45:35	Bos.
Mar. 25/30	Bos.	SF	Mtl. M. 1	Bos. 0	Archie Wilcox	26:27	Bos.
Mar. 26/30	Mtl.	QF	Chi. 2	Mtl. 2	Howie Morenz (Mtl.)	51:43	Mtl.
Mar. 28/30	Mtl.	SF	Mtl. 2	NYR 1	Gus Rivers	68:52	Mtl.
Mar. 24/31	Bos.	SF	Bos. 5	Mtl. 4	Cooney Weiland	18:56	Mtl.
Mar. 26/31	Chi.	QF	Chi. 2	Tor. 1	Stew Adams	19:20	Chi.
Mar. 28/31	Mtl.	SF	Mtl. 4	Bos. 3	Georges Mantha	5:10	Mtl.
Apr. 1/31	Mtl.	SF	Mtl. 3	Bos. 2	Wildor Larochelle	19:00	Mtl.
Apr. 5/31	Chi.	F	Chi. 2	Mtl. 1	Johnny Gottselig	24:50	Mtl.
Apr. 9/31	Mtl.	F	Chi. 3	Mtl. 2	Cy Wentworth	53:50	Mtl.
Mar. 26/32	Mtl.	SF	NYR 4	Mtl. 3	Fred Cook	59:32	NYR
Apr. 2/32	Tor.	SF	Tor. 3	Mtl. M. 2	Bob Gracie	17:59	Tor.
Mar. 25/33	Bos.	SF	Bos. 2	Tor. 1	Marty Barry	14:14	Tor.
Mar. 28/33	Bos.	SF	Tor. 1	Bos. 0	Busher Jackson	15:03	Tor.
Mar. 30/33	Tor.	SF	Bos. 2	Tor. 1	Eddie Shore	4:23	Tor.
Apr. 3/33	Tor.	SF	Tor. 1	Bos. 0	Ken Doraty	104:46	Tor.
Apr. 13/33	Tor.	F	NYR 1	Tor. 0	Bill Cook	7:33	NYR
Mar. 22/34	Tor.	SF	Det. 2	Tor. 1	Herbie Lewis	1:33	Det.
Mar. 25/34	Chi.	QF	Chi. 1	Mtl. 1	Mush March (Chi)	11:05	Chi.
Apr. 3/34	Det.	F	Chi. 2	Det. 1	Paul Thompson	21:10	Chi.
Apr. 10/34	Chi.	F	Chi. 1	Det. 0	Mush March	30:05	Chi.
Mar. 23/35	Bos.	SF	Bos. 1	Tor. 0	Dit Clapper	33:26	Tor.
Mar. 26/35	Chi.	QF	Mtl. M. 1	Chi. 0	Baldy Northcott	4:02	Mtl. M.
Mar. 30/35	Tor.	SF	Tor. 2	Bos. 1	Pep Kelly	1:36	Tor.
Apr. 4/35	Tor.	F	Mtl. M. 3	Tor. 2	Dave Trottier	5:28	Mtl. M.
Mar. 24/36	Mtl.	SF	Det. 1	Mtl. M. 0	Mud Bruneteau	116:30	Det.
Apr. 9/36	Tor.	F	Tor. 4	Det. 3	Buzz Boll	0:31	Det.
Mar. 25/37	NYR	QF	NYR 2	Tor. 1	Babe Pratt	13:05	NYR
Apr. 1/37	Mtl.	SF	Det. 2	Mtl. 1	Hec Kilrea	51:49	Det.
Mar. 22/38	NYR	QF	NYA 2	NYR 1	John Sorrell	21:25	NYA
Mar. 24/38	Tor.	SF	Tor. 1	Bos. 0	George Parsons	21:31	Tor.
Mar. 26/38	Mtl.	QF	Chi. 3	Mtl. 2	Paul Thompson	11:49	Chi.
Mar. 27/38	NYR	QF	NYA 3	NYR 2	Lorne Carr	60:40	NYA
Mar. 29/38	Bos.	SF	Tor. 3	Bos. 2	Gordie Drillon	10:04	Tor.
Mar. 31/38	Chi.	SF	Chi. 1	NYA 0	Cully Dahlstrom	33:01	Chi.
Mar. 21/39	NYR	SF	Bos. 2	NYR 1	Mel Hill	59:25	Bos.
Mar. 23/39	Bos.	SF	Bos. 3	NYR 2	Mel Hill	8:24	Bos.
Mar. 26/39	Det.	QF	Det. 1	Mtl. 0	Marty Barry	7:47	Det.
Mar. 30/39	Bos.	SF	NYR 2	Bos. 1	Clint Smith	17:19	Bos.
Apr. 1/39	Tor.	SF	Tor. 5	Det. 4	Gordie Drillon	5:42	Tor.
Apr. 2/39	Bos.	SF	Bos. 2	NYR 1	Mel Hill	48:00	Bos.
Apr. 9/39	Bos.	F	Tor. 3	Bos. 2	Doc Romnes	10:38	Bos.
Mar. 19/40	Det.	QF	Det. 2	NYA 1	Syd Howe	0:25	Det.
Mar. 19/40	Tor.	QF	Tor. 3	Chi. 2	Syl Apps	6:35	Tor.
Apr. 2/40	NYR	F	NYR 2	Tor. 1	Alf Pike	15:30	NYR
Apr. 11/40	Tor.	F	NYR 2	Tor. 1	Muzz Patrick	31:43	NYR
Apr. 13/40	Tor.	F	NYR 3	Tor. 2	Bryan Hextall	2:07	NYR
Mar. 20/41	Det.	QF	Det. 2	NYR 1	Gus Giesebrecht	12:01	Det.
Mar. 22/41	Mtl.	QF	Mtl. 4	Chi. 3	Charlie Sands	34:04	Chi.
Mar. 29/41	Bos.	SF	Tor. 2	Bos. 1	Pete Langelle	17:31	Bos.
Mar. 30/41	Chi.	SF	Det. 2	Chi. 1	Gus Giesebrecht	9:15	Det.
Mar. 22/42	Chi.	QF	Bos. 2	Chi. 1	Des Smith	6:51	Bos.
Mar. 21/43	Bos.	SF	Bos. 5	Mtl. 4	Don Gallinger	12:30	Bos.
Mar. 23/43	Det.	SF	Tor. 3	Det. 2	Jack McLean	70:18	Det.
Mar. 25/43	Mtl.	SF	Bos. 3	Mtl. 2	Busher Jackson	3:20	Bos.
Mar. 30/43	Tor.	SF	Det. 3	Tor. 2	Adam Brown	9:21	Det.
Mar. 30/43	Bos.	SF	Bos. 5	Mtl. 4	Ab DeMarco	3:41	Bos.
Apr. 13/44	Mtl.	F	Mtl. 5	Chi. 4	Toe Blake	9:12	Mtl.
Mar. 27/45	Tor.	SF	Tor. 4	Mtl. 3	Gus Bodnar	12:36	Tor.
Mar. 29/45	Det.	SF	Det. 3	Bos. 2	Mud Bruneteau	17:12	Det.
Apr. 21/45	Tor.	F	Det. 1	Tor. 0	Eddie Bruneteau	14:16	Tor.
Mar. 28/46	Bos.	SF	Bos. 4	Det. 3	Don Gallinger	9:51	Bos.
Mar. 30/46	Mtl.	F	Mtl. 4	Bos. 3	Maurice Richard	9:08	Mtl.
Apr. 2/46	Mtl.	F	Mtl. 3	Bos. 2	Jimmy Peters	16:55	Mtl.
Apr. 7/46	Bos.	F	Bos. 3	Mtl. 2	Terry Reardon	15:13	Mtl.
Mar. 26/47	Tor.	SF	Tor. 3	Det. 2	Howie Meeker	3:05	Tor.
Mar. 27/47	Mtl.	SF	Mtl. 2	Bos. 1	Ken Mosdell	5:38	Mtl.
Apr. 3/47	Mtl.	SF	Mtl. 4	Bos. 3	John Quilty	36:40	Mtl.
Apr. 15/47	Tor.	F	Tor. 2	Mtl. 1	Syl Apps	16:36	Tor.
Mar. 24/48	Tor.	SF	Tor. 5	Bos. 4	Nick Metz	17:03	Tor.
Mar. 22/49	Det.	SF	Det. 2	Mtl. 1	Max McNab	44:52	Det.
Mar. 24/49	Det.	SF	Mtl. 4	Det. 3	Gerry Plamondon	2:59	Det.
Mar. 26/49	Tor.	SF	Bos. 5	Tor. 4	Woody Dumart	16:14	Tor.
Apr. 8/49	Det.	F	Tor. 3	Det. 2	Joe Klukay	17:31	Tor.
Apr. 4/50	Tor.	SF	Det. 2	Tor. 1	Leo Reise Jr.	20:38	Det.
Apr. 4/50	Mtl.	SF	Mtl. 3	NYR 2	Elmer Lach	15:19	NYR
Apr. 9/50	Det.	SF	Det. 1	Tor. 0	Leo Reise Jr.	8:39	Det.
Apr. 18/50	Det.	F	NYR 4	Det. 3	Don Raleigh	8:34	Det.
Apr. 20/50	Det.	F	NYR 2	Det. 1	Don Raleigh	1:38	Det.
Apr. 23/50	Det.	F	Det. 4	NYR 3	Pete Babando	28:31	Det.
Mar. 27/51	Det.	SF	Mtl. 3	Det. 2	Maurice Richard	61:09	Mtl.
Mar. 29/51	Det.	SF	Mtl. 1	Det. 0	Maurice Richard	42:20	Mtl.
Mar. 31/51	Tor.	SF	Bos. 1	Tor. 1	no scorer	20:00	Tor.
Apr. 11/51	Tor.	F	Tor. 3	Mtl. 2	Sid Smith	5:51	Tor.
Apr. 14/51	Tor.	F	Mtl. 3	Tor. 2	Maurice Richard	2:55	Tor.
Apr. 17/51	Mtl.	F	Tor. 2	Mtl. 1	Ted Kennedy	4:47	Tor.
Apr. 19/51	Mtl.	F	Tor. 3	Mtl. 2	Harry Watson	5:15	Tor.
Apr. 21/51	Tor.	F	Tor. 3	Mtl. 2	Bill Barilko	2:53	Tor.
Apr. 6/52	Bos.	SF	Mtl. 3	Bos. 2	Paul Masnick	27:49	Mtl.
Mar. 29/53	Bos.	SF	Bos. 2	Det. 1	Jack McIntyre	12:29	Bos.
Mar. 29/53	Chi.	SF	Chi. 2	Mtl. 1	Al Dewsbury	5:18	Mtl.
Apr. 16/53	Mtl.	F	Mtl. 1	Bos. 0	Elmer Lach	1:22	Mtl.
Apr. 1/54	Det.	SF	Det. 4	Tor. 3	Ted Lindsay	21:01	Det.
Apr. 11/54	Det.	F	Mtl. 1	Det. 0	Ken Mosdell	5:45	Det.
Apr. 16/54	Det.	F	Det. 2	Mtl. 1	Tony Leswick	4:29	Det.
Mar. 29/55	Bos.	SF	Mtl. 4	Bos. 3	Don Marshall	3:05	Mtl.
Mar. 24/56	Tor.	SF	Det. 5	Tor. 4	Ted Lindsay	4:22	Det.
Mar. 28/57	NYR	SF	NYR 4	Mtl. 3	Andy Hebenton	13:38	Mtl.
Apr. 4/57	Mtl.	SF	Mtl. 4	NYR 3	Maurice Richard	1:11	Mtl.
Mar. 27/58	NYR	SF	Bos. 4	NYR 3	Jerry Toppazzini	4:46	Bos.
Mar. 30/58	Det.	SF	Mtl. 2	Det. 1	André Pronovost	11:52	Mtl.
Apr. 17/58	Mtl.	F	Mtl. 3	Bos. 2	Maurice Richard	5:45	Mtl.
Mar. 28/59	Tor.	SF	Tor. 3	Bos. 2	Gerry Ehman	5:02	Tor.
Mar. 31/59	Tor.	SF	Tor. 3	Bos. 2	Frank Mahovlich	11:21	Tor.
Apr. 14/59	Tor.	F	Tor. 3	Mtl. 2	Dick Duff	10:06	Mtl.
Mar. 26/60	Mtl.	SF	Mtl. 4	Chi. 3	Doug Harvey	8:38	Mtl.
Mar. 27/60	Det.	SF	Tor. 5	Det. 4	Frank Mahovlich	43:00	Tor.
Mar. 29/60	Det.	SF	Det. 2	Tor. 1	Gerry Melnyk	1:54	Tor.
Mar. 22/61	Tor.	SF	Tor. 3	Det. 2	George Armstrong	24:51	Det.
Mar. 26/61	Chi.	SF	Chi. 2	Mtl. 1	Murray Balfour	52:12	Chi.
Apr. 5/62	Tor.	SF	Tor. 3	NYR 2	Red Kelly	24:23	Tor.
Apr. 2/64	Det.	SF	Chi. 3	Det. 2	Murray Balfour	8:21	Det.
Apr. 14/64	Tor.	F	Det. 4	Tor. 3	Larry Jeffrey	7:52	Tor.
Apr. 23/64	Det.	F	Tor. 4	Det. 3	Bob Baun	1:43	Tor.
Apr. 6/65	Tor.	SF	Tor. 3	Mtl. 2	Dave Keon	4:17	Mtl.
Apr. 13/65	Tor.	SF	Mtl. 4	Tor. 3	Claude Provost	16:33	Mtl.
May 5/66	Det.	F	Mtl. 3	Det. 2	Henri Richard	2:20	Mtl.
Apr. 13/67	NYR	SF	Mtl. 2	NYR 1	John Ferguson	6:28	Mtl.
Apr. 25/67	Tor.	F	Tor. 3	Mtl. 2	Bob Pulford	28:26	Tor.
Apr. 10/68	St.L.	QF	St.L. 3	Phi. 2	Larry Keenan	24:10	St.L.
Apr. 16/68	St.L.	QF	Phi. 2	St.L. 1	Don Blackburn	31:18	St.L.
Apr. 16/68	Min.	QF	Min. 4	L.A. 3	Milan Marcetta	9:11	Min.
Apr. 22/68	Min.	SF	Min. 3	St.L. 2	Parker MacDonald	3:41	St.L.
Apr. 27/68	St.L.	SF	St.L. 4	Min. 3	Gary Sabourin	1:32	St.L.
Apr. 28/68	Mtl.	SF	Mtl. 4	Chi. 3	Jacques Lemaire	2:14	Mtl.
Apr. 29/68	St.L.	SF	St.L. 3	Min. 2	Bill McCreary	17:27	St.L.
May 3/68	St.L.	SF	St.L. 2	Min. 1	Ron Schock	22:50	St.L.
May 5/68	St.L.	F	Mtl. 3	St.L. 2	Jacques Lemaire	1:41	Mtl.
May 9/68	Mtl.	F	Mtl. 4	St.L. 3	Bobby Rousseau	1:13	Mtl.
Apr. 2/69	Oak.	QF	L.A. 5	Oak. 4	Ted Irvine	0:19	L.A.
Apr. 10/69	Mtl.	SF	Mtl. 3	Bos. 2	Ralph Backstrom	0:42	Mtl.
Apr. 13/69	Mtl.	SF	Mtl. 4	Bos. 3	Mickey Redmond	4:55	Mtl.
Apr. 24/69	Bos.	SF	Mtl. 2	Bos. 1	Jean Béliveau	31:28	Mtl.
Apr. 12/70	Oak.	QF	Pit. 3	Oak. 2	Michel Briere	8:28	Pit.
May 10/70	Bos.	F	Bos. 4	St.L. 3	Bobby Orr	0:40	Bos.
Apr. 15/71	Tor.	QF	NYR 2	Tor. 1	Bob Nevin	9:07	NYR
Apr. 18/71	Chi.	SF	NYR 2	Chi. 1	Pete Stemkowski	1:37	Chi.
Apr. 27/71	Chi.	SF	Chi. 3	NYR 2	Bobby Hull	6:35	Chi.
Apr. 29/71	NYR	SF	NYR 3	Chi. 2	Pete Stemkowski	41:29	Chi.
May 4/71	Chi.	F	Chi. 2	Mtl. 1	Jim Pappin	21:11	Mtl.
Apr. 6/72	Bos.	QF	Tor. 4	Bos. 3	Jim Harrison	2:58	Bos.
Apr. 6/72	Min.	QF	Min. 6	St.L. 5	Bill Goldsworthy	1:36	St.L.
Apr. 9/72	Pit.	QF	Chi. 6	Pit. 5	Pit Martin	0:12	Chi.
Apr. 16/72	Min.	QF	St.L. 2	Min. 1	Kevin O'Shea	10:07	St.L.
Apr. 1/73	Mtl.	QF	Buf. 3	Mtl. 2	René Robert	9:18	Mtl.
Apr. 10/73	Phi.	QF	Phi. 3	Min. 2	Gary Dornhoefer	8:35	Phi.
Apr. 14/73	Mtl.	SF	Phi. 5	Mtl. 4	Rick MacLeish	2:56	Mtl.
Apr. 17/73	Mtl.	SF	Mtl. 4	Phi. 3	Larry Robinson	6:45	Mtl.
Apr. 14/74	Tor.	QF	Bos. 4	Tor. 3	Ken Hodge	1:27	Bos.
Apr. 14/74	Atl.	QF	Phi. 4	Atl. 3	Dave Schultz	5:40	Phi.
Apr. 16/74	Mtl.	QF	NYR 3	Mtl. 2	Ron Harris	4:07	NYR
Apr. 23/74	Chi.	SF	Chi. 4	Bos. 3	Jim Pappin	3:48	Bos.
Apr. 28/74	NYR	SF	NYR 2	Phi. 1	Rod Gilbert	4:20	Phi.
May 9/74	Bos.	F	Phi. 3	Bos. 2	Bobby Clarke	12:01	Phi.
Apr. 8/75	L.A.	PRE	L.A. 3	Tor. 2	Mike Murphy	8:53	Tor.
Apr. 10/75	Tor.	PRE	Tor. 3	L.A. 2	Blaine Stoughton	10:19	Tor.
Apr. 10/75	Chi.	PRE	Chi. 4	Bos. 3	Ivan Boldirev	7:33	Chi.
Apr. 11/75	NYR	PRE	NYI 4	NYR 3	Jean-Paul Parise	0:11	NYI
Apr. 17/75	Chi.	QF	Chi. 5	Buf. 4	Stan Mikita	2:31	Buf.
Apr. 19/75	Tor.	QF	Phi. 4	Tor. 3	André Dupont	1:45	Phi.
Apr. 22/75	Mtl.	QF	Mtl. 5	Van. 4	Guy Lafleur	17:06	Mtl.
Apr. 27/75	Buf.	SF	Buf. 6	Mtl. 5	Danny Gare	4:42	Buf.
May 1/75	Phi.	SF	Phi. 5	NYI 4	Bobby Clarke	2:56	Phi.
May 6/75	Buf.	SF	Buf. 5	Mtl. 4	René Robert	5:56	Buf.
May 7/75	NYI	SF	NYI 4	Phi. 3	Jude Drouin	1:53	Phi.
May 20/75	Buf.	F	Buf. 5	Phi. 4	René Robert	18:29	Phi.
Apr. 8/76	Buf.	PRE	Buf. 3	St.L. 2	Danny Gare	11:43	Buf.

Overtime Games since 1918 — *continued*

Date	City	Series	Score		Scorer	Overtime	Series Winner
Apr. 9/76	Buf.	PRE	Buf. 2	St.L. 1	Don Luce	14:27	Buf.
Apr. 13/76	Bos.	QF	L.A. 3	Bos. 2	Butch Goring	0:27	Bos.
Apr. 13/76	Buf.	QF	Buf. 3	NYI 2	Danny Gare	14:04	NYI
Apr. 22/76	L.A.	QF	L.A. 4	Bos. 3	Butch Goring	18:28	Bos.
Apr. 29/76	Phi.	SF	Phi. 2	Bos. 1	Reggie Leach	13:38	Phi.
Apr. 15/77	Tor.	QF	Phi. 4	Tor. 3	Rick MacLeish	2:55	Phi.
Apr. 17/77	Tor.	QF	Phi. 6	Tor. 5	Reggie Leach	19:10	Phi.
Apr. 24/77	Phi.	SF	Bos. 4	Phi. 3	Rick Middleton	2:57	Bos.
Apr. 26/77	Phi.	SF	Bos. 5	Phi. 4	Terry O'Reilly	30:07	Bos.
May 3/77	Mtl.	SF	NYI 4	Mtl. 3	Billy Harris	3:58	Mtl.
May 14/77	Bos.	F	Mtl. 2	Bos. 1	Jacques Lemaire	4:32	Mtl.
Apr. 11/78	Phi.	PRE	Phi. 3	Col. 2	Mel Bridgman	0:23	Phi.
Apr. 13/78	NYR	PRE	NYR 4	Buf. 3	Don Murdoch	1:37	Buf.
Apr. 19/78	Bos.	QF	Bos. 4	Chi. 3	Terry O'Reilly	1:50	Bos.
Apr. 19/78	NYI	QF	NYI 3	Tor. 2	Mike Bossy	2:50	Tor.
Apr. 21/78	Chi.	QF	Bos. 4	Chi. 3	Peter McNab	10:17	Bos.
Apr. 25/78	NYI	QF	NYI 2	Tor. 1	Bob Nystrom	8:02	Tor.
Apr. 29/78	NYI	QF	Tor. 2	NYI 1	Lanny McDonald	4:13	Tor.
May 2/78	Bos.	SF	Bos. 3	Phi. 2	Rick Middleton	1:43	Bos.
May 16/78	Mtl.	F	Mtl. 3	Bos. 2	Guy Lafleur	13:09	Mtl.
May 21/78	Bos.	F	Bos. 4	Mtl. 3	Bobby Schmautz	6:22	Mtl.
Apr. 12/79	L.A.	PRE	NYR 2	L.A. 1	Phil Esposito	6:11	NYR
Apr. 14/79	Buf.	PRE	Pit. 4	Buf. 3	George Ferguson	0:47	Pit.
Apr. 16/79	Phi.	QF	Phi. 3	NYR 2	Ken Linseman	0:44	NYR
Apr. 18/79	NYI	QF	NYI 1	Chi. 0	Mike Bossy	2:31	NYI
Apr. 21/79	Tor.	QF	Mtl. 4	Tor. 3	Cam Connor	25:25	Mtl.
Apr. 22/79	Tor.	QF	Mtl. 5	Tor. 4	Larry Robinson	4:14	Mtl.
Apr. 28/79	NYI	SF	NYI 4	NYR 3	Denis Potvin	8:02	NYR
May 3/79	NYR	SF	NYI 3	NYR 2	Bob Nystrom	3:40	NYR
May 3/79	Bos.	SF	Bos. 4	Mtl. 3	Jean Ratelle	3:46	Mtl.
May 10/79	Mtl.	SF	Mtl. 5	Bos. 4	Yvon Lambert	9:33	Mtl.
May 19/79	NYR	F	Mtl. 4	NYR 3	Serge Savard	7:25	Mtl.
Apr. 8/80	NYR	PRE	NYR 2	Atl. 1	Steve Vickers	0:33	NYR
Apr. 8/80	Phi.	PRE	Phi. 4	Edm. 3	Bobby Clarke	8:06	Phi.
Apr. 8/80	Chi.	PRE	Chi. 3	St.L. 2	Doug Lecuyer	12:34	Chi.
Apr. 11/80	Hfd.	PRE	Mtl. 4	Hfd. 3	Yvon Lambert	0:29	Mtl.
Apr. 11/80	Tor.	PRE	Min. 4	Tor. 3	Al MacAdam	0:32	Min.
Apr. 11/80	L.A.	PRE	NYI 4	L.A. 3	Ken Morrow	6:55	NYI
Apr. 11/80	Edm.	PRE	Phi. 3	Edm. 2	Ken Linseman	23:56	Phi.
Apr. 16/80	Bos.	QF	NYI 2	Bos. 1	Clark Gillies	1:02	NYI
Apr. 17/80	Bos.	QF	NYI 5	Bos. 4	Bob Bourne	1:24	NYI
Apr. 21/80	NYI	QF	Bos. 4	NYI 3	Terry O'Reilly	17:13	NYI
May 1/80	Buf.	SF	NYI 2	Buf. 1	Bob Nystrom	21:20	NYI
May 13/80	Phi.	F	NYI 4	Phi. 3	Denis Potvin	4:07	NYI
May 24/80	NYI	F	NYI 5	Phi. 4	Bob Nystrom	7:11	NYI
Apr. 8/81	Buf.	PRE	Buf. 3	Van. 2	Alan Haworth	5:00	Buf.
Apr. 8/81	Bos.	PRE	Min. 5	Bos. 4	Steve Payne	3:34	Min.
Apr. 11/81	Chi.	PRE	Cgy. 5	Chi. 4	Willi Plett	35:17	Cgy.
Apr. 12/81	Que.	PRE	Que. 4	Phi. 3	Dale Hunter	0:37	Phi.
Apr. 14/81	St.L.	PRE	St.L. 4	Pit. 3	Mike Crombeen	25:16	St.L.
Apr. 16/81	Buf.	QF	Min. 4	Buf. 3	Steve Payne	0:22	Min.
Apr. 20/81	Min.	QF	Buf. 5	Min. 4	Craig Ramsay	16:32	Min.
Apr. 20/81	Edm.	QF	NYI 5	Edm. 4	Ken Morrow	5:41	NYI
Apr. 7/82	Min.	DSF	Chi. 3	Min. 2	Greg Fox	3:34	Chi.
Apr. 8/82	Edm.	DSF	Edm. 3	L.A. 2	Wayne Gretzky	6:20	L.A.
Apr. 8/82	Van.	DSF	Van. 2	Cgy. 1	Tiger Williams	14:20	Van.
Apr. 10/82	Pit.	DSF	Pit. 2	NYI 1	Rick Kehoe	4:14	NYI
Apr. 10/82	L.A.	DSF	L.A. 6	Edm. 5	Daryl Evans	2:35	L.A.
Apr. 13/82	Mtl.	DSF	Que. 3	Mtl. 2	Dale Hunter	0:22	Que.
Apr. 13/82	NYI	DSF	NYI 4	Pit. 3	John Tonelli	6:19	NYI
Apr. 16/82	Van.	DF	L.A. 3	Van. 2	Steve Bozek	4:33	Van.
Apr. 18/82	Que.	DF	Que. 3	Bos. 2	Wilf Paiement	11:44	Que.
Apr. 18/82	NYR	DF	NYI 4	NYR 3	Bryan Trottier	3:00	NYI
Apr. 18/82	L.A.	DF	Van. 4	L.A. 3	Colin Campbell	1:23	Van.
Apr. 21/82	St.L.	DF	St.L. 3	Chi. 2	Bernie Federko	3:28	Chi.
Apr. 23/82	Que.	DF	Bos. 6	Que. 5	Peter McNab	10:54	Que.
Apr. 27/82	Chi.	CF	Van. 2	Chi. 1	Jim Nill	28:58	Van.
May 1/82	Que.	CF	NYI 5	Que. 4	Wayne Merrick	16:52	NYI
May 8/82	NYI	F	NYI 6	Van. 5	Mike Bossy	19:58	NYI
Apr. 5/83	Bos.	DSF	Bos. 4	Que. 3	Barry Pederson	1:46	Bos.
Apr. 6/83	Cgy.	DSF	Cgy. 4	Van. 3	Eddy Beers	12:27	Cgy.
Apr. 7/83	Min.	DSF	Min. 5	Tor. 4	Bobby Smith	5:03	Min.
Apr. 10/83	Tor.	DSF	Min. 5	Tor. 4	Dino Ciccarelli	8:05	Min.
Apr. 10/83	Van.	DSF	Cgy. 4	Van. 3	Greg Meredith	1:06	Cgy.
Apr. 18/83	Min.	DF	Chi. 4	Min. 3	Rich Preston	10:34	Chi.
Apr. 24/83	Bos.	DF	Bos. 3	Buf. 2	Brad Park	1:52	Bos.
Apr. 5/84	Edm.	DSF	Edm. 5	Wpg. 4	Randy Gregg	0:21	Edm.
Apr. 7/84	Det.	DSF	St.L. 4	Det. 3	Mark Reeds	37:07	St.L.
Apr. 8/84	Det.	DSF	St.L. 3	Det. 2	Jorgen Pettersson	2:42	St.L.
Apr. 10/84	NYI	DSF	NYI 3	NYR 2	Ken Morrow	8:56	NYI
Apr. 13/84	Min.	DF	St.L. 4	Min. 3	Doug Gilmour	16:16	Min.
Apr. 13/84	Edm.	DF	Cgy. 6	Edm. 5	Carey Wilson	3:42	Edm.
Apr. 13/84	NYI	DF	NYI 5	Wsh. 4	Anders Kallur	7:35	NYI
Apr. 16/84	Mtl.	DF	Que. 4	Mtl. 3	Bo Berglund	3:00	Mtl.
Apr. 20/84	Cgy.	DF	Cgy. 5	Edm. 4	Lanny McDonald	1:04	Edm.
Apr. 22/84	Min.	DF	Min. 4	St.L. 3	Steve Payne	6:00	Min.
Apr. 10/85	Phi.	DSF	Phi. 5	NYR 4	Mark Howe	8:01	Phi.
Apr. 10/85	Wsh.	DSF	Wsh. 4	NYI 3	Alan Haworth	2:28	NYI
Apr. 10/85	Edm.	DSF	Edm. 3	L.A. 2	Lee Fogolin	3:01	Edm.
Apr. 10/85	Wpg.	DSF	Wpg. 5	Cgy. 4	Brian Mullen	7:56	Wpg.
Apr. 11/85	Wsh.	DSF	Wsh. 2	NYI 1	Mike Gartner	21:23	NYI
Apr. 13/85	L.A.	DSF	Edm. 4	L.A. 3	Glenn Anderson	0:46	Edm.
Apr. 18/85	Mtl.	DF	Que. 2	Mtl. 1	Mark Kumpel	12:23	Que.
Apr. 23/85	Que.	DF	Que. 7	Mtl. 6	Dale Hunter	18:36	Que.
Apr. 25/85	Min.	DF	Chi. 7	Min. 6	Darryl Sutter	21:57	Chi.
Apr. 28/85	Chi.	DF	Min. 5	Chi. 4	Dennis Maruk	1:14	Chi.
Apr. 30/85	Min.	DF	Chi. 6	Min. 5	Darryl Sutter	15:41	Chi.
May 2/85	Mtl.	DF	Que. 3	Mtl. 2	Peter Stastny	2:22	Que.
May 5/85	Que.	CF	Que. 2	Phi. 1	Peter Stastny	6:20	Phi.
Apr. 9/86	Que.	DSF	Hfd. 3	Que. 2	Sylvain Turgeon	2:36	Hfd.
Apr. 12/86	Wpg.	DSF	Cgy. 4	Wpg. 3	Lanny McDonald	8:25	Cgy.
Apr. 17/86	Wsh.	DF	NYR 4	Wsh. 3	Brian MacLellan	1:16	NYR
Apr. 20/86	Edm.	DF	Edm. 6	Cgy. 5	Glenn Anderson	1:04	Cgy.
Apr. 23/86	Hfd.	DF	Hfd. 2	Mtl. 1	Kevin Dineen	1:07	Mtl.
Apr. 23/86	NYR	DF	NYR 6	Wsh. 5	Bob Brooke	2:40	NYR
Apr. 26/86	St L.	DF	St L. 4	Tor. 3	Mark Reeds	7:11	St L.
Apr. 29/86	Mtl.	DF	Mtl. 2	Hfd. 1	Claude Lemieux	5:55	Mtl.
May 5/86	NYR	CF	Mtl. 4	NYR 3	Claude Lemieux	9:41	Mtl.
May 12/86	St L.	CF	St L. 6	Cgy. 5	Doug Wickenheiser	7:30	Cgy.
May 18/86	Cgy.	F	Mtl. 3	Cgy. 2	Brian Skrudland	0:09	Mtl.
Apr. 8/87	Hfd.	DSF	Hfd. 3	Que. 2	Paul MacDermid	2:20	Que.
Apr. 9/87	Mtl.	DSF	Mtl. 4	Bos. 3	Mats Naslund	2:38	Mtl.
Apr. 9/87	St.L.	DSF	Tor. 3	St.L. 2	Rick Lanz	10:17	Tor.
Apr. 11/87	Wpg.	DSF	Cgy. 3	Wpg. 2	Mike Bullard	3:53	Wpg.
Apr. 11/87	Chi.	DSF	Det. 4	Chi. 3	Shawn Burr	4:51	Det.
Apr. 16/87	Que.	DSF	Que. 5	Hfd. 4	Peter Stastny	6:05	Que.
Apr. 18/87	Wsh.	DSF	NYI 3	Wsh. 2	Pat LaFontaine	68:47	NYI
Apr. 21/87	Edm.	DF	Edm. 3	Wpg. 2	Glenn Anderson	0:36	Edm.
Apr. 26/87	Que.	DF	Mtl. 3	Que. 2	Mats Naslund	5:30	Mtl.
Apr. 27/87	Tor.	DF	Tor. 3	Det. 2	Mike Allison	9:31	Det.
May 4/87	Phi.	CF	Phi. 4	Mtl. 3	Ilkka Sinislao	9:11	Phi.
May 20/87	Edm.	F	Edm. 3	Phi. 2	Jari Kurri	6:50	Edm.
Apr. 6/88	NYI	DSF	NYI 4	N.J. 3	Pat LaFontaine	6:11	N.J.
Apr. 10/88	Phi.	DSF	Phi. 5	Wsh. 4	Murray Craven	1:18	Wsh.
Apr. 10/88	N.J.	DSF	NYI 5	N.J. 4	Brent Sutter	15:07	N.J.
Apr. 10/88	Buf.	DSF	Buf. 6	Bos. 5	John Tucker	5:32	Bos.
Apr. 12/88	Det.	DSF	Tor. 6	Det. 5	Ed Olczyk	0:34	Det.
Apr. 16/88	Wsh.	DSF	Wsh. 5	Phi. 4	Dale Hunter	5:57	Wsh.
Apr. 21/88	Cgy.	DF	Edm. 5	Cgy. 4	Wayne Gretzky	7:54	Edm.
May 4/88	Bos.	CF	N.J. 3	Bos. 2	Doug Brown	17:46	Bos.
May 9/88	Det.	CF	Edm. 4	Det. 3	Jari Kurri	11:02	Edm.
Apr. 5/89	St.L.	DSF	St.L. 4	Min. 3	Brett Hull	11:55	St.L.
Apr. 5/89	Cgy.	DSF	Van. 4	Cgy. 3	Paul Reinhart	2:47	Cgy.
Apr. 6/89	St.L.	DSF	St.L. 4	Min. 3	Rick Meagher	5:30	St.L.
Apr. 6/89	Det.	DSF	Chi. 5	Det. 4	Duane Sutter	14:36	Chi.
Apr. 8/89	Hfd.	DSF	Mtl. 5	Hfd. 4	Stephane Richer	5:01	Mtl.
Apr. 8/89	Phi.	DSF	Wsh. 4	Phi. 3	Kelly Miller	0:51	Phi.
Apr. 9/89	Hfd.	DSF	Mtl. 4	Hfd. 3	Russ Courtnall	15:12	Mtl.
Apr. 15/89	Cgy.	DSF	Cgy. 4	Van. 3	Joel Otto	19:21	Cgy.
Apr. 18/89	Cgy.	DF	Cgy. 4	L.A. 3	Doug Gilmour	7:47	Cgy.
Apr. 19/89	Mtl.	DF	Mtl. 3	Bos. 2	Bobby Smith	12:24	Mtl.
Apr. 20/89	St.L.	DF	St.L. 5	Chi. 4	Tony Hrkac	33:49	Chi.
Apr. 21/89	Phi.	DF	Pit. 4	Phi. 3	Phil Bourque	12:08	Phi.
May 8/89	Chi.	CF	Cgy. 2	Chi. 1	Al MacInnis	15:05	Cgy.
May 9/89	Mtl.	CF	Phi. 2	Mtl. 1	Dave Poulin	5:02	Mtl.
May 19/89	Mtl.	F	Mtl. 4	Cgy. 3	Ryan Walter	38:08	Cgy.
Apr. 5/90	N.J.	DSF	Wsh. 5	N.J. 4	Dino Ciccarelli	5:34	Wsh.
Apr. 6/90	Edm.	DSF	Edm. 3	Wpg. 2	Mark Lamb	4:21	Edm.
Apr. 8/90	Tor.	DSF	St.L. 6	Tor. 5	Sergio Momesso	6:04	St.L.
Apr. 8/90	L.A.	DSF	L.A. 2	Cgy. 1	Tony Granato	8:37	L.A.
Apr. 9/90	Mtl.	DSF	Mtl. 2	Buf. 1	Brian Skrudland	12:35	Mtl.
Apr. 9/90	NYI	DSF	NYI 4	NYR 3	Brent Sutter	20:59	NYR
Apr. 10/90	Wpg.	DSF	Wpg. 4	Edm. 3	Dave Ellett	21:08	Edm.
Apr. 14/90	L.A.	DSF	L.A. 4	Cgy. 3	Mike Krushelnyski	23:14	L.A.
Apr. 15/90	Hfd.	DSF	Hfd. 3	Bos. 2	Kevin Dineen	12:30	Bos.
Apr. 21/90	Bos.	DF	Bos. 5	Mtl. 4	Garry Galley	3:42	Bos.
Apr. 24/90	L.A.	DF	Edm. 6	L.A. 5	Joe Murphy	4:42	Edm.
Apr. 25/90	Wsh.	DF	Wsh. 4	NYR 3	Rod Langway	0:34	Wsh.
Apr. 27/90	NYR	DF	Wsh. 2	NYR 1	John Druce	6:48	Wsh.
May 15/90	Bos.	F	Edm. 3	Bos. 2	Petr Klima	55:13	Edm.
Apr. 4/91	Chi.	DSF	Min. 4	Chi. 3	Brian Propp	4:14	Min.
Apr. 5/91	Pit.	DSF	Pit. 5	N.J. 4	Jaromir Jagr	8:52	Pit.
Apr. 6/91	L.A.	DSF	L.A. 3	Van. 2	Wayne Gretzky	11:08	L.A.
Apr. 8/91	Van.	DSF	Van. 2	L.A. 1	Cliff Ronning	3:12	L.A.
Apr. 11/91	NYR	DSF	Wsh. 5	NYR 4	Dino Ciccarelli	6:44	Wsh.
Apr. 11/91	Mtl.	DSF	Mtl. 4	Buf. 3	Russ Courtnall	5:56	Mtl.
Apr. 14/91	Edm.	DSF	Cgy. 2	Edm. 1	Theoren Fleury	4:40	Edm.
Apr. 16/91	Cgy.	DSF	Edm. 5	Cgy. 4	Esa Tikkanen	6:58	Edm.
Apr. 18/91	L.A.	DF	L.A. 4	Edm. 3	Luc Robitaille	2:13	Edm.
Apr. 19/91	Bos.	DF	Mtl. 4	Bos. 3	Stephane Richer	0:27	Bos.
Apr. 19/91	Pit.	DF	Pit. 7	Wsh. 6	Kevin Stevens	8:10	Pit.
Apr. 20/91	L.A.	DF	Edm. 4	L.A. 3	Petr Klima	24:48	Edm.
Apr. 22/91	Edm.	DF	Edm. 4	L.A. 3	Esa Tikkanen	20:48	Edm.
Apr. 27/91	Mtl.	DF	Mtl. 3	Bos. 2	Shayne Corson	17:47	Bos.
Apr. 28/91	Edm.	DF	Edm. 4	L.A. 3	Craig MacTavish	16:57	Edm.
May 3/91	Bos.	CF	Bos. 5	Pit. 4	Vladimir Ruzicka	8:14	Pit.
Apr. 21/92	Bos.	DSF	Bos. 3	Buf. 2	Adam Oates	11:14	Bos.
Apr. 22/92	Min.	DSF	Det. 5	Min. 4	Yves Racine	1:15	Det.
Apr. 22/92	St.L.	DSF	St.L. 5	Chi. 4	Brett Hull	23:33	Chi.
Apr. 25/92	Buf.	DSF	Bos. 5	Buf. 4	Ted Donato	2:08	Bos.
Apr. 28/92	Min.	DSF	Det. 1	Min. 0	Sergei Fedorov	16:13	Det.
Apr. 29/92	Hfd.	DSF	Hfd. 2	Mtl. 1	Yvon Corriveau	0:24	Mtl.
May 1/92	Mtl.	DSF	Mtl. 3	Hfd. 2	Russ Courtnall	25:26	Mtl.
May 3/92	Van.	DF	Edm. 4	Van. 3	Joe Murphy	8:36	Edm.
May 5/92	Mtl.	DF	Bos. 3	Mtl. 2	Peter Douris	3:12	Bos.
May 7/92	Pit.	DF	NYR 6	Pit. 5	Kris King	1:29	Pit.
May 9/92	Pit.	DF	Pit. 5	NYR 4	Ron Francis	2:47	Pit.
May 17/92	Pit.	CF	Pit. 4	Bos. 3	Jaromir Jagr	9:44	Pit.

The Montreal Canadiens celebrate with the Stanley Cup after winning 10 straight overtime games in the 1993 playoffs. In all, a record 28 of 85 games played required overtime that year. The Canadiens had a record of 10-1 in extended time.

Date	City	Series	Score		Scorer	Overtime	Series Winner
May 20/92	Edm.	CF	Chi. 4	Edm. 3	Jeremy Roenick	2:45	Chi.
Apr. 18/93	Bos.	DSF	Buf. 5	Bos. 4	Bob Sweeney	11:03	Buf.
Apr. 18/93	Que.	DSF	Que. 3	Mtl. 2	Scott Young	16:49	Mtl.
Apr. 20/93	Wsh.	DSF	NYI 5	Wsh. 4	Brian Mullen	34:50	NYI
Apr. 22/93	Mtl.	DSF	Mtl. 2	Que. 1	Vincent Damphousse	10:30	Mtl.
Apr. 22/93	Buf.	DSF	Buf. 4	Bos. 3	Yuri Khmylev	1:05	Buf.
Apr. 22/93	NYI	DSF	NYI 4	Wsh. 3	Ray Ferraro	4:46	NYI
Apr. 24/93	Buf.	DSF	Buf. 6	Bos. 5	Brad May	4:48	Buf.
Apr. 24/93	NYI	DSF	NYI 4	Wsh. 3	Ray Ferraro	25:40	NYI
Apr. 25/93	St.L.	DSF	St.L. 4	Chi. 3	Craig Janney	10:43	St.L.
Apr. 26/93	Mtl.	DSF	Mtl. 5	Que. 4	Kirk Muller	8:17	Mtl.
Apr. 27/93	Det.	DSF	Tor. 5	Det. 4	Mike Foligno	2:05	Tor.
Apr. 27/93	Van.	DSF	Wpg. 4	Van. 3	Teemu Selanne	6:18	Van.
Apr. 29/93	Wpg.	DSF	Van. 4	Wpg. 3	Greg Adams	4:30	Van.
May 1/93	Det.	DSF	Tor. 4	Det. 3	Nikolai Borschevsky	2:35	Tor.
May 3/93	Tor.	DF	Tor. 2	St.L. 1	Doug Gilmour	23:16	Tor.
May 4/93	Mtl.	DF	Mtl. 4	Buf. 3	Guy Carbonneau	2:50	Mtl.
May 5/93	Tor.	DF	St.L. 2	Tor. 1	Jeff Brown	23:03	Tor.
May 6/93	Buf.	DF	Mtl. 4	Buf. 3	Gilbert Dionne	8:28	Mtl.
May 8/93	Buf.	DF	Mtl. 4	Buf. 3	Kirk Muller	11:37	Mtl.
May 11/93	Van.	DF	L.A. 4	Van. 3	Gary Shuchuk	26:31	L.A.
May 14/93	Pit.	DF	NYI 4	Pit. 3	Dave Volek	5:16	NYI
May 18/93	Mtl.	CF	Mtl. 4	NYI 3	Stephan Lebeau	26:21	Mtl.
May 20/93	NYI	CF	Mtl. 2	NYI 1	Guy Carbonneau	12:34	Mtl.
May 25/93	Tor.	CF	Tor. 3	L.A. 2	Glenn Anderson	19:20	L.A.
May 27/93	L.A.	CF	L.A. 5	Tor. 4	Wayne Gretzky	1:41	L.A.
Jun. 3/93	Mtl.	F	Mtl. 3	L.A. 2	Eric Desjardins	0:51	Mtl.
Jun. 5/93	L.A.	F	Mtl. 4	L.A. 3	John LeClair	0:34	Mtl.
Jun. 7/93	L.A.	F	Mtl. 3	L.A. 2	John LeClair	14:37	Mtl.
Apr. 20/94	Tor.	CQF	Tor. 1	Chi. 0	Todd Gill	2:15	Tor.
Apr. 22/94	St.L.	CQF	Dal. 5	St.L. 4	Paul Cavallini	8:34	Dal.
Apr. 24/94	Chi.	CQF	Chi. 4	Tor. 3	Jeremy Roenick	1:23	Tor.
Apr. 25/94	Bos.	CQF	Mtl. 2	Bos. 1	Kirk Muller	17:18	Bos.
Apr. 26/94	Cgy.	CQF	Van. 2	Cgy. 1	Geoff Courtnall	7:15	Van.
Apr. 27/94	Buf.	CQF	Buf. 1	N.J. 0	Dave Hannan	65:43	N.J.
Apr. 28/94	Van.	CQF	Van. 3	Cgy. 2	Trevor Linden	16:43	Van.
Apr. 30/94	Cgy.	CQF	Van. 4	Cgy. 3	Pavel Bure	22:20	Van.
May 3/94	N.J.	CSF	Bos. 6	N.J. 5	Don Sweeney	9:08	N.J.
May 7/94	Bos.	CSF	N.J. 5	Bos. 4	Stephane Richer	14:19	N.J.
May 8/94	Van.	CSF	Van. 2	Dal. 1	Sergio Momesso	11:01	Van.
May 12/94	Tor.	CSF	Tor. 3	S.J. 2	Mike Gartner	8:53	Tor.
May 15/94	NYR	CF	N.J. 4	NYR 3	Stephane Richer	35:23	NYR
May 16/94	Tor.	CF	Tor. 3	Van. 2	Peter Zezel	16:55	Van.
May 19/94	N.J.	CF	NYR 3	N.J. 2	Stephane Matteau	26:13	NYR
May 24/94	N.J.	CF	Van. 4	Tor. 3	Greg Adams	20:14	Van.
May 27/94	NYR	CF	NYR 2	N.J. 1	Stephane Matteau	24:24	NYR
May 31/94	NYR	F	Van. 3	NYR 2	Greg Adams	19:26	NYR
May 7/95	Phi.	CQF	Phi. 4	Buf. 3	Karl Dykhuis	10:06	Phi.
May 9/95	Cgy.	CQF	S.J. 5	Cgy. 4	Ulf Dahlen	12:21	S.J.
May 12/95	NYR	CQF	NYR 3	Que. 2	Steve Larmer	8:09	NYR
May 12/95	N.J.	CQF	N.J. 1	Bos. 0	Randy McKay	8:51	N.J.
May 14/95	Pit.	CQF	Pit. 6	Wsh. 5	Luc Robitaille	4:30	Pit.
May 15/95	St.L.	CQF	Van. 6	St.L. 5	Cliff Ronning	1:48	Van.
May 17/95	Tor.	CQF	Tor. 5	Chi. 4	Randy Wood	10:00	Chi.
May 19/95	Cgy.	CQF	S.J. 5	Cgy. 4	Ray Whitney	21:54	S.J.
May 21/95	Phi.	CSF	Phi. 5	NYR 4	Eric Desjardins	7:03	Phi.
May 21/95	Chi.	CSF	Chi. 2	Van. 1	Joe Murphy	9:04	Chi.
May 22/95	Phi.	CSF	Phi. 4	NYR 3	Kevin Haller	0:25	Phi.
May 25/95	Van.	CSF	Chi. 3	Van. 2	Chris Chelios	6:22	Chi.
May 26/95	N.J.	CSF	N.J. 2	Pit. 1	Neal Broten	18:36	N.J.
May 27/95	Van.	CSF	Chi. 4	Van. 3	Chris Chelios	5:35	Chi.
Jun. 1/95	Det.	CF	Det. 2	Chi. 1	Nicklas Lidstrom	1:01	Det.
Jun. 6/95	Chi.	CF	Det. 4	Chi. 3	Vladimir Konstantinov	29:25	Det.
Jun. 7/95	N.J.	CF	Phi. 3	N.J. 2	Eric Lindros	4:19	N.J.
Jun. 11/95	Det.	CF	Det. 2	Chi. 1	Vyacheslav Kozlov	22:25	Det.
Apr. 16/96	NYR	CQF	Mtl. 3	NYR 2	Vincent Damphousse	5:04	NYR
Apr. 18/96	Tor.	CQF	Tor. 5	St.L. 4	Mats Sundin	4:02	St.L.
Apr. 18/96	Phi.	CQF	Phi. 2	T.B. 1	Brian Bellows	9:05	Phi.
Apr. 21/96	St.L.	CQF	St.L. 3	Tor. 2	Glenn Anderson	1:24	St.L.
Apr. 21/96	T.B.	CQF	T.B. 5	Phi. 4	Alexander Selivanov	2:04	Phi.
Apr. 23/96	Cgy.	CQF	Chi. 2	Cgy. 1	Joe Murphy	50:02	Chi.
Apr. 24/96	Wsh.	CQF	Pit. 3	Wsh. 2	Petr Nedved	79:15	Pit.
Apr. 25/96	Col.	CQF	Col. 5	Van. 4	Joe Sakic	0:51	Col.
Apr. 25/96	Tor.	CQF	Tor. 5	St.L. 4	Mike Gartner	7:31	St.L.
May 2/96	Col.	CSF	Chi. 3	Col. 2	Jeremy Roenick	6:29	Col.
May 6/96	Chi.	CSF	Col. 3	Chi. 2	Sergei Krivokrasov	0:46	Col.
May 8/96	St.L.	CSF	St.L. 5	Det. 4	Igor Kravchuk	3:23	Det.
May 8/96	Chi.	CSF	Col. 3	Chi. 2	Joe Sakic	44:33	Col.
May 9/96	Fla.	CSF	Fla. 3	Phi. 2	Dave Lowry	4:06	Fla.
May 12/96	Phi.	CSF	Fla. 2	Phi. 1	Mike Hough	28:05	Fla.
May 13/96	Chi.	CSF	Col. 4	Chi. 3	Sandis Ozolinsh	25:18	Col.
May 16/96	Det.	CSF	Det. 1	St.L. 0	Steve Yzerman	21:15	Det.
May 19/96	Det.	CF	Col. 3	Det. 2	Mike Keane	17:31	Col.
Jun. 10/96	Fla.	F	Col. 1	Fla. 0	Uwe Krupp	44:31	Col.
Apr. 20/97	Chi.	CQF	Col. 3	Chi. 2	Sergei Krivokrasov	31:03	Col.
Apr. 20/97	Edm.	CQF	Edm. 4	Dal. 3	Kelly Buchberger	9:15	Edm.
Apr. 22/97	NYR	CQF	NYR 4	Fla. 3	Esa Tikkanen	16:29	NYR
Apr. 23/97	Ott.	CQF	Ott. 1	Buf. 0	Daniel Alfredsson	2:34	Buf.
Apr. 24/97	Mtl.	CQF	Mtl. 4	N.J. 3	Patrice Brisebois	47:37	N.J.
Apr. 25/97	Fla.	CQF	NYR 3	Fla. 2	Esa Tikkanen	12:02	NYR
Apr. 25/97	Dal.	CQF	Edm. 1	Dal. 0	Ryan Smyth	20:22	Edm.
Apr. 27/97	Phx.	CQF	Ana. 3	Phx. 2	Paul Kariya	7:29	Ana.
Apr. 29/97	Buf.	CQF	Buf. 3	Ott. 2	Derek Plante	5:24	Buf.
Apr. 29/97	Dal.	CQF	Edm. 4	Dal. 3	Todd Marchant	12:26	Edm.
May 2/97	Det.	CSF	Det. 2	Ana. 1	Martin Lapointe	0:59	Det.
May 4/97	Det.	CSF	Det. 3	Ana. 2	Vyacheslav Kozlov	41:31	Det.
May 8/97	Ana.	CSF	Det. 3	Ana. 2	Brendan Shanahan	37:03	Det.
May 9/97	Phi.	CSF	Buf. 5	Phi. 4	Ed Ronan	6:24	Phi.
May 9/97	Edm.	CSF	Col. 3	Edm. 2	Claude Lemieux	8:35	Col.
May 11/97	N.J.	CSF	NYR 2	N.J. 1	Adam Graves	14:08	NYR
Apr. 22/98	N.J.	CQF	Ott. 2	N.J. 1	Bruce Gardiner	5:58	Ott.
Apr. 23/98	Pit.	CQF	Mtl. 3	Pit. 2	Benoit Brunet	18:43	Mtl.
Apr. 24/98	Wsh.	CQF	Bos. 4	Wsh. 3	Darren Van Impe	20:54	Wsh.
Apr. 26/98	Ott.	CQF	Ott. 2	N.J. 1	Alexei Yashin	2:47	Ott.
Apr. 26/98	Bos.	CQF	Wsh. 3	Bos. 2	Joe Juneau	26:31	Wsh.
Apr. 26/98	Edm.	CQF	Col. 5	Edm. 4	Joe Sakic	15:25	Edm.

Overtime Games since 1918 — *continued*

Date	City	Series	Score		Scorer	Overtime	Series Winner
Apr. 28/98	S.J.	CQF	S.J. 1	Dal. 0	Andrei Zyuzin	6:31	Dal.
May 1/98	Phi.	CQF	Buf. 3	Phi. 2	Michal Grosek	5:40	Buf.
May 2/98	S.J.	CQF	Dal. 3	S.J. 2	Mike Keane	3:43	Dal.
May 3/98	Bos.	CQF	Wsh. 3	Bos. 2	Brian Bellows	15:24	Wsh.
May 3/98	Buf.	CSF	Buf. 3	Mtl. 2	Geoff Sanderson	2:37	Buf.
May 11/98	Edm.	CSF	Dal. 1	Edm. 0	Benoit Hogue	13:07	Dal.
May 12/98	Mtl.	CSF	Buf. 5	Mtl. 4	Michael Peca	21:24	Buf.
May 12/98	St.L.	CSF	Det. 3	St.L. 2	Brendan Shanahan	31:12	Det.
May 25/98	Wsh.	CF	Wsh. 3	Buf. 2	Todd Krygier	3:01	Wsh.
May 28/98	Buf.	CF	Wsh. 4	Buf. 3	Peter Bondra	9:37	Wsh.
Jun. 3/98	Dal.	CF	Dal. 3	Det. 2	Jamie Langenbrunner	0:46	Det.
Jun. 4/98	Buf.	CF	Wsh. 3	Buf. 2	Joe Juneau	6:24	Wsh.
Jun. 11/98	Det.	F	Det. 5	Wsh. 4	Kris Draper	15:24	Det.
Apr. 23/99	Ott.	CQF	Buf. 3	Ott. 2	Miroslav Satan	30:35	Buf.
Apr. 24/99	Car.	CQF	Car. 3	Bos. 2	Ray Sheppard	17:05	Bos.
Apr. 24/99	Phx.	CQF	Phx. 4	St.L. 3	Shane Doan	8:58	St.L.
Apr. 26/99	S.J.	CQF	Col. 2	S.J. 1	Milan Hejduk	7:53	Col.
Apr. 27/99	Edm.	CQF	Dal. 3	Edm. 2	Joe Nieuwendyk	57:34	Dal.
Apr. 30/99	Tor.	CQF	Tor. 2	Phi. 1	Yanic Perreault	11:51	Tor.
Apr. 30/99	Car.	CQF	Bos. 4	Car. 3	Anson Carter	34:45	Bos.
Apr. 30/99	Phx.	CQF	St.L. 2	Phx. 1	Scott Young	5:43	St.L.
May 2/99	Pit.	CQF	Pit. 3	N.J. 2	Jaromir Jagr	8:59	Pit.
May 3/99	S.J.	CQF	Col. 3	S.J. 2	Milan Hejduk	13:12	Col.
May 4/99	Phx.	CQF	St.L. 1	Phx. 0	Pierre Turgeon	17:59	St.L.
May 7/99	Col.	CSF	Det. 3	Col. 2	Kirk Maltby	4:18	Col.
May 8/99	Dal.	CSF	Dal. 5	St.L. 4	Joe Nieuwendyk	8:22	Dal.
May 10/99	St.L.	CSF	St.L. 3	Dal. 2	Pavol Demitra	2:43	Dal.
May 12/99	St.L.	CSF	St.L. 3	Dal. 2	Pierre Turgeon	5:52	Dal.
May 13/99	Pit.	CSF	Tor. 3	Pit. 2	Sergei Berezin	2:18	Tor.
May 17/99	Pit.	CSF	Tor. 4	Pit. 3	Garry Valk	1:57	Tor.
May 17/99	St.L.	CSF	Dal. 2	St.L. 1	Mike Modano	2:21	Dal.
May 28/99	Col.	CF	Col. 3	Dal. 2	Chris Drury	19:29	Dal.
Jun. 8/99	Dal.	F	Buf. 3	Dal. 2	Jason Woolley	15:30	Dal.
Jun. 19/99	Buf.	F	Dal. 2	Buf. 1	Brett Hull	54:51	Dal.
Apr. 15/00	Pit.	CQF	Pit. 2	Wsh. 1	Jaromir Jagr	5:49	Pit.
Apr. 18/00	Buf.	CQF	Buf. 3	Phi. 2	Stu Barnes	4:42	Phi.
Apr. 22/00	Tor.	CQF	Tor. 2	Ott. 1	Steve Thomas	14:47	Tor.
May 2/00	Pit.	CSF	Phi. 4	Pit. 3	Andy Delmore	11:01	Phi.
May 3/00	Det.	CSF	Col. 3	Det. 2	Chris Drury	10:21	Col.
May 4/00	Pit.	CSF	Phi. 2	Pit. 1	Keith Primeau	92:01	Phi.
May 23/00	Dal.	CF	Dal. 3	Col. 2	Joe Nieuwendyk	12:10	Dal.
Jun. 8/00	N.J.	F	Dal. 1	N.J. 0	Mike Modano	46:21	N.J.
Jun. 10/00	Dal.	F	N.J. 2	Dal. 1	Jason Arnott	28:20	N.J.
Apr. 11/01	Dal.	CQF	Dal. 2	Edm. 1	Jamie Langenbrunner	2:08	Dal.
Apr. 13/01	Ott.	CQF	Tor. 1	Ott. 0	Mats Sundin	10:49	Tor.
Apr. 14/01	Phi.	CQF	Buf. 4	Phi. 3	Jay McKee	18:02	Buf.
Apr. 15/01	Edm.	CQF	Dal. 3	Edm. 2	Benoit Hogue	19:48	Dal.
Apr. 16/01	Tor.	CQF	Tor. 3	Ott. 2	Cory Cross	2:16	Tor.
Apr. 16/01	Van.	CQF	Col. 4	Van. 3	Peter Forsberg	2:50	Col.
Apr. 17/01	Buf.	CQF	Buf. 4	Phi. 3	Curtis Brown	6:13	Buf.
Apr. 17/01	Edm.	CQF	Edm. 2	Dal. 1	Mike Comrie	17:19	Dal.
Apr. 18/01	Car.	CQF	Car. 3	N.J. 2	Rod Brind'Amour	:46	N.J.
Apr. 18/01	Pit.	CQF	Wsh. 4	Pit. 3	Jeff Halpern	4:01	Pit.
Apr. 18/01	L.A.	CQF	L.A. 4	Det. 3	Eric Belanger	2:36	L.A.
Apr. 19/01	Dal.	CQF	Dal. 4	Edm. 3	Kirk Muller	8:01	Dal.
Apr. 19/01	St.L.	CQF	St.L. 3	S.J. 2	Bryce Salvador	9:54	St.L.
Apr. 23/01	Pit.	CQF	Pit. 4	Wsh. 3	Martin Straka	13:04	Pit.
Apr. 23/01	L.A.	CQF	L.A. 3	Det. 2	Adam Deadmarsh	4:48	L.A.
Apr. 26/01	Col.	CSF	L.A. 4	Col. 3	Jaroslav Modry	14:23	Col.
Apr. 28/01	N.J.	CSF	N.J. 6	Tor. 5	Randy McKay	5:31	N.J.
May 1/01	Tor.	CSF	N.J. 3	Tor. 2	Brian Rafalski	7:00	N.J.
May 1/01	St.L.	CSF	St.L. 3	Dal. 2	Cory Stillman	29:26	St.L.
May 5/01	Buf.	CSF	Buf. 3	Pit. 2	Stu Barnes	8:34	Pit.
May 6/01	L.A.	CSF	L.A. 1	Col. 0	Glen Murray	22:41	Col.
May 8/01	Pit.	CSF	Pit. 3	Buf. 2	Martin Straka	11:29	Pit.
May 10/01	Buf.	CSF	Pit. 3	Buf. 2	Darius Kasparaitis	13:01	Pit.
May 16/01	St.L.	CF	St.L. 4	Col. 3	Scott Young	30:27	Col.
May 18/01	St.L.	CF	Col. 4	St.L. 3	Stephane Yelle	4:23	Col.
May 21/01	Col.	CF	Col. 2	St.L. 1	Joe Sakic	:24	Col.
Apr. 17/02	Phi.	CQF	Phi. 1	Ott. 0	Ruslan Fedotenko	7:47	Ott.
Apr. 17/02	Det.	CQF	Van. 4	Det. 3	Henrik Sedin	13:59	Det.
Apr. 19/02	Car.	CQF	Car. 2	N.J. 1	Bates Battaglia	15:26	Car.
Apr. 24/02	Car.	CQF	Car. 3	N.J. 2	Josef Vasicek	8:16	Car.
Apr. 25/02	Col.	CQF	L.A. 1	Col. 0	Craig Johnson	2:19	Col.
Apr. 26/02	Phi.	CQF	Ott. 2	Phi. 1	Martin Havlat	7:33	Ott.
May 4/02	Tor.	CSF	Tor. 3	Ott. 2	Gary Roberts	44:30	Tor.
May 7/02	Mtl.	CSF	Mtl. 2	Car. 1	Donald Audette	2:26	Car.
May 9/02	Mtl.	CSF	Car. 4	Mtl. 3	Niclas Wallin	3:14	Car.
May 13/02	S.J.	CSF	Col. 2	S.J. 1	Peter Forsberg	2:47	Col.
May 19/02	Car.	CF	Car. 2	Tor. 1	Niclas Wallin	13:42	Car.
May 20/02	Det.	CF	Col. 4	Det. 3	Chris Drury	2:17	Det.
May 21/02	Tor.	CF	Car. 2	Tor. 1	Jeff O'Neill	6:01	Car.
May 22/02	Col.	CF	Det. 2	Col. 1	Fredrik Olausson	12:44	Det.
May 27/02	Det.	CF	Col. 2	Det. 1	Peter Forsberg	6:24	Det.
May 28/02	Tor.	CF	Car. 2	Tor. 1	Martin Gelinas	8:05	Car.
Jun. 4/02	Det.	F	Car. 3	Det. 2	Ron Francis	:58	Det.
Jun. 8/02	Car.	F	Det. 3	Car. 2	Igor Larionov	54:47	Det.
Apr. 10/03	Det.	CQF	Ana. 2	Det. 1	Paul Kariya	43:18	Ana.
Apr. 14/03	NYI	CQF	Ott. 3	NYI 2	Todd White	22:25	Ott.
Apr. 14/03	Tor.	CQF	Tor. 4	Phi. 3	Tomas Kaberle	27:20	Phi.
Apr. 15/03	Wsh.	CQF	T.B. 4	Wsh. 3	Vincent Lecavalier	2:29	T.B.
Apr. 16/03	Tor.	CQF	Phi. 3	Tor. 2	Mark Recchi	53:54	Phi.
Apr. 16/03	Ana.	CQF	Ana. 3	Det. 2	Steve Rucchin	6:53	Ana.
Apr. 20/03	Wsh.	CQF	T.B. 2	Wsh. 1	Martin St. Louis	44:03	T.B.
Apr. 21/03	Tor.	CQF	Tor. 2	Phi. 1	Travis Green	30:51	Phi.
Apr. 21/03	Min.	CQF	Min. 3	Col. 2	Richard Park	4:22	Min.
Apr. 22/03	Col.	CQF	Min. 3	Col. 2	Andrew Brunette	3:25	Min.
Apr. 24/03	Dal.	CSF	Ana. 4	Dal. 3	Petr Sykora	80:48	Ana.
Apr. 25/03	Van.	CSF	Van. 4	Min. 3	Trent Klatt	3:42	Min.
Apr. 26/03	N.J.	CSF	N.J. 3	T.B. 2	Jamie Langenbrunner	2:09	N.J.
Apr. 26/03	Dal.	CSF	Ana. 3	Dal. 2	Mike Leclerc	1:44	Ana.
Apr. 29/03	Phi.	CSF	Ott. 3	Phi. 2	Wade Redden	6:43	Ott.
May 2/03	Min.	CSF	Van. 3	Min. 2	Brent Sopel	15:52	Min.
May 2/03	N.J.	CSF	N.J. 2	T.B. 1	Grant Marshall	51:12	N.J.
May 10/03	Min.	CF	Ana. 1	Min. 0	Petr Sykora	28:06	Ana.
May 10/03	Ott.	CF	Ott. 3	N.J. 2	Shaun Van Allen	3:08	N.J.
May 21/03	N.J.	CF	Ott. 2	N.J. 1	Chris Phillips	15:51	N.J.
May 31/03	Ana.	F	Ana. 3	N.J. 2	Ruslan Salei	6:59	N.J.
Jun. 2/03	Ana.	F	Ana. 1	N.J. 0	Steve Thomas	0:39	N.J.
Apr. 8/04	S.J.	CQF	S.J. 1	St.L. 0	Niko Dimitrakos	9:16	S.J.
Apr. 9/04	Bos.	CQF	Bos. 2	Mtl. 1	Patrice Bergeron	1:26	Mtl.
Apr. 12/04	Dal.	CQF	Dal. 4	Col. 3	Steve Ott	2:11	Col.
Apr. 13/04	Mtl.	CQF	Bos. 4	Mtl. 3	Glen Murray	29:27	Mtl.
Apr. 14/04	Dal.	CQF	Col. 3	Dal. 2	Marek Svatos	25:21	Col.
Apr. 16/04	T.B.	CQF	T.B. 3	NYI 2	Martin St. Louis	4:07	T.B.
Apr. 17/04	Cgy.	CQF	Van. 5	Cgy. 4	Brendan Morrison	42:28	Cgy.
Apr. 18/04	Ott.	CQF	Ott. 2	Tor. 1	Mike Fisher	21:47	Tor.
Apr. 19/04	Van.	CQF	Cgy. 3	Van. 2	Martin Gelinas	1:25	Cgy.
Apr. 22/04	Det.	CSF	Cgy. 2	Det. 1	Marcus Nilson	2:39	Cgy.
Apr. 27/04	Mtl.	CSF	T.B. 4	Mtl 3	Brad Richards	1:05	T.B.
Apr. 28/04	Col	CSF	Col. 1	S.J. 0	Joe Sakic	5:15	S.J.
May 1/04	S.J.	CSF	Col. 2	S.J. 1	Joe Sakic	1:54	S.J.
May 3/04	Cgy	CSF	Cgy. 1	Det. 0	Martin Gelinas	19:13	Cgy.
May 4/04	Phi.	CSF	Phi. 3	Tor. 2	Jeremy Roenick	7:39	Phi.
May 9/04	S.J.	CF	Cgy. 4	S.J. 3	Steve Montador	18:43	Cgy.
May 20/04	Phi.	CF	Phi. 5	T.B. 4	Simon Gagne	18:18	T.B.
Jun. 3/04	T.B.	F	Cgy. 3	T.B. 2	Oleg Saprykin	14:40	T.B.
Jun. 5/04	Cgy.	F	T.B. 3	Cgy. 2	Martin St. Louis	20:33	T.B.
Apr. 21/06	Det.	CQF	Det. 3	Edm. 2	Kirk Maltby	22:39	Edm.
Apr. 21/06	Cgy.	CQF	Cgy. 2	Ana. 1	Darren McCarty	9:45	Ana.
Apr. 22/06	Buf.	CQF	Buf. 3	Phi. 2	Daniel Briere	27:31	Buf.
Apr. 24/06	Car.	CQF	Mtl. 6	Car. 5	Michael Ryder	22:32	Car.
Apr. 24/06	Dal.	CQF	Col. 5	Dal. 4	Joe Sakic	4:36	Col.
Apr. 25/06	Edm.	CQF	Edm. 4	Det. 3	Jarret Stoll	28:44	Edm.
Apr. 26/06	Mtl.	CQF	Car. 2	Mtl. 1	Eric Staal	3:38	Car.
Apr. 26/06	Col.	CQF	Col. 4	Dal. 3	Alex Tanguay	1:09	Col.
Apr. 27/06	Ana.	CQF	Ana. 3	Cgy. 2	Sean O'Donnell	1:36	Ana.
Apr. 30/06	Dal.	CQF	Col. 3	Dal. 2	Andrew Brunette	13:55	Col.
May 2/06	Mtl.	CQF	Car. 2	Mtl. 1	Cory Stillman	1:99	Car.
May 5/06	Ott.	CSF	Buf. 7	Ott. 6	Chris Drury	0:18	Buf.
May 8/06	Car.	CSF	Car. 3	N.J. 2	Niclas Wallin	3:09	Car.
May 9/06	Col.	CSF	Ana. 4	Col. 3	Joffrey Lupul	16:30	Ana.
May 10/06	Buf.	CSF	Buf. 3	Ott. 2	J.P. Dumont	5:05	Buf.
May 10/06	Edm.	CSF	Edm. 3	S.J. 2	Shawn Horcoff	42:24	Edm.
May 13/06	Ott.	CSF	Buf. 3	Ott. 2	Jason Pominville	2:26	Buf.
May 28/06	Car.	CF	Car. 4	Buf. 3	Cory Stillman	8:46	Car.
May 30/06	Buf.	CF	Buf. 2	Car. 1	Daniel Briere	4:22	Car.
June 14/06	Car.	F	Edm. 4	Car. 3	Fernando Pisani	3:31	Car.

Ten Longest Overtime Games

Date	City	Series	Score		Scorer	Overtime	Series Winner
Mar. 24/36	Mtl.	SF	Det. 1	Mtl. M. 0	Mud Bruneteau	116:30	Det.
Apr. 3/33	Tor.	SF	Tor. 1	Bos. 0	Ken Doraty	104:46	Tor.
May 4/00	Pit.	CSF	Phi. 2	Pit. 1	Keith Primeau	92:01	Phi.
Apr. 24/03	Dal.	CSF	Ana. 4	Dal. 3	Petr Sykora	80:48	Ana.
Apr. 24/96	Wsh.	CQF	Pit. 3	Wsh. 2	Petr Nedved	79:15	Pit.
Mar. 23/43	Det.	SF	Tor. 3	Det. 2	Jack McLean	70:18	Det.
Mar. 28/30	Mtl.	SF	Mtl. 2	NYR 1	Gus Rivers	68:52	Mtl.
Apr. 18/87	Wsh.	DSF	NYI 3	Wsh. 2	Pat LaFontaine	68:47	NYI
Apr. 27/94	Buf.	CQF	Buf. 1	N.J. 0	Dave Hannan	65:43	N.J.
Mar. 27/51	Det.	SF	Mtl. 3	Det. 2	Maurice Richard	61:09	Mtl.

Overtime Record of Current Teams

(Listed by number of OT games played)

Team	Overall				Home				Last OT Game	Road				Last OT Game
	GP	W	L	T	GP	W	L	T		GP	W	L	T	
Montreal	128	71	57	2	61	37	23	1	May 2/06	67	34	34	1	Apr. 24/06
Toronto	106	54	51	1	68	36	31	1	May 4/04	38	18	20	0	Apr. 18/04
Boston	100	40	57	3	46	21	24	1	Apr. 9/04	54	19	33	2	Apr. 13/04
Detroit	78	34	44	0	46	17	29	0	Apr. 21/06	32	17	15	0	Apr. 25/06
NY Rangers	63	30	33	0	27	12	15	0	Apr. 22/97	36	18	18	0	May 11/97
Chicago	62	30	30	2	30	16	13	1	Apr. 20/97	32	14	17	1	May 2/96
Philadelphia[1]	59	28	31	0	26	13	13	0	May 20/04	33	15	18	0	Apr. 22/06
Dallas[1]	57	24	33	0	29	11	18	0	Apr. 30/06	28	13	15	0	Apr. 26/06
Colorado[2]	53	31	22	0	21	10	11	0	May 9/06	32	21	11	0	Apr. 30/06
Buffalo	52	30	22	0	29	19	10	0	May 30/06	23	11	12	0	May 28/06
St. Louis	50	27	23	0	26	20	6	0	May 18/01	24	7	17	0	Apr. 8/04
Edmonton	42	24	18	0	23	13	10	0	May 10/06	19	11	8	0	Jun. 14/06
NY Islanders	40	29	11	0	18	14	4	0	Apr. 14/03	22	15	7	0	Apr. 16/04
Calgary[3]	39	17	22	0	18	6	12	0	Apr. 26/06	21	11	10	0	Apr. 27/06
Los Angeles	35	17	18	0	19	11	8	0	May 6/01	16	6	10	0	Apr. 25/02
Vancouver	35	17	18	0	15	6	9	0	Apr. 19/04	20	11	9	0	Apr. 17/04
New Jersey[4]	34	10	24	0	14	5	9	0	May 21/03	20	5	15	0	May 8/06
Washington	31	14	17	0	12	5	7	0	Apr. 20/03	19	9	10	0	Apr. 23/01
Carolina[5]	30	18	12	0	18	11	7	0	Jun. 14/06	12	7	5	0	May 30/06
Pittsburgh	28	15	13	0	18	10	8	0	May 8/01	10	5	5	0	May 10/01
Ottawa	19	9	10	0	8	4	4	0	May 13/06	11	5	6	0	May 10/06
San Jose	14	4	10	0	8	2	6	0	May 9/04	6	2	4	0	May 10/06
Anaheim	14	10	4	0	5	4	1	0	Apr. 27/06	9	6	3	0	May 9/06
Phoenix[6]	12	5	7	0	8	3	5	0	May 4/99	4	2	2	0	Apr. 27/93
Tampa Bay	11	7	4	0	3	2	1	0	Jun. 3/04	8	5	3	0	Jun. 5/04
Florida	5	2	3	0	3	1	2	0	Apr. 25/97	2	1	1	0	Apr. 22/97
Minnesota	5	2	3	0	3	1	2	0	May 10/03	2	1	1	0	Apr. 25/03

[1] Totals include those of Minnesota North Stars 1967-93.
[2] Totals include those of Quebec 1979-95.
[3] Totals include those of Atlanta Flames 1972-80.
[4] Totals include those of Kansas City and Colorado Rockies 1974-82.
[5] Totals include those of Hartford 1979-97.
[6] Totals include those of Winnipeg 1979-96.

Chris Pronger celebrates the first penalty shot goal in the history of the Stanley Cup Finals during game one between Edmonton and Carolina on June 5, 2006.

Penalty Shots in Stanley Cup Playoff Games

Date	Player	Goaltender	Scored	Final Score				Series
Mar. 25/37	Lionel Conacher, Mtl. Maroons	Tiny Thompson, Boston	No	Mtl. M.	0	at	Bos. 4	QF
Apr. 15/37	Alex Shibicky, NY Rangers	Earl Robertson, Detroit	No	NYR	0	at	Det. 3	F
Mar. 24/38	Mush March, Chicago	Wilf Cude, Montreal	No	Mtl.	0	at	Chi. 4	QF
Mar. 29/38	Lorne Carr, NY Americans	Mike Karakas, Chicago	No	Chi.	1	at	NYA 3	SF
Apr. 10/38	Art Wiebe, Chicago	Turk Broda, Toronto	No	Tor.	1	at	Chi. 2	F
Mar. 24/42	Charlie Sands, Montreal	Johnny Mowers, Detroit	No	Det.	0	at	Mtl. 5	QF
Apr. 13/44	Virgil Johnson, Chicago	Bill Durnan, Montreal	No	Chi.	4	at	Mtl. 5*	F
Apr. 9/68	Wayne Connelly, Minnesota	Terry Sawchuk, Los Angeles	Yes	L.A.	5	at	Min. 7	QF
Apr. 27/68	Jim Roberts, St. Louis	Cesare Maniago, Minnesota	No	St.L.	4	at	Min. 3	SF
May 16/71	Frank Mahovlich, Montreal	Tony Esposito, Chicago	No	Chi.	3	at	Mtl. 4	F
May 7/75	Bill Barber, Philadelphia	Glenn Resch, NY Islanders	No	Phi.	3	at	NYI 4*	SF
Apr. 20/79	Mike Walton, Chicago	Glenn Resch, NY Islanders	No	NYI	4	at	Chi. 0	QF
Apr. 9/81	Peter McNab, Boston	Don Beaupre, Minnesota	No	Min.	5	at	Bos. 4*	PR
Apr. 17/81	Anders Hedberg, NY Rangers	Mike Liut, St. Louis	Yes	NYR	6	at	St.L. 4	QF
Apr. 9/83	Denis Potvin, NY Islanders	Pat Riggin, Washington	No	NYI	6	at	Wsh. 2	DSF
Apr. 28/84	Wayne Gretzky, Edmonton	Don Beaupre, Minnesota	Yes	Edm.	8	at	Min. 5	CF
May 1/84	Mats Naslund, Montreal	Billy Smith, NY Islanders	No	Mtl.	1	at	NYI 3	CF
Apr. 14/85	Bob Carpenter, Washington	Billy Smith, NY Islanders	No	Wsh.	4	at	NYI. 5	DF
May 28/85	Ron Sutter, Philadelphia	Grant Fuhr, Edmonton	No	Phi.	3	at	Edm. 5	F
May 30/85	Dave Poulin, Philadelphia	Grant Fuhr, Edmonton	No	Phi.	3	at	Edm. 8	F
Apr. 9/88	John Tucker, Buffalo	Andy Moog, Boston	Yes	Bos.	2	at	Buf. 6	DSF
Apr. 9/88	Petr Klima, Detroit	Allan Bester, Toronto	Yes	Det.	6	at	Tor. 3	DSF
Apr. 8/89	Neal Broten, Minnesota	Greg Millen, St. Louis	Yes	St.L.	5	at	Min. 3	DSF
Apr. 4/90	Al MacInnis, Calgary	Kelly Hrudey, Los Angeles	Yes	L.A.	5	at	Cgy. 3	DSF
Apr. 5/90	Randy Wood, NY Islanders	Mike Richter, NY Rangers	No	NYI	1	at	NYR 2	DSF
May 3/90	Kelly Miller, Washington	Andy Moog, Boston	No	Wsh.	3	at	Bos. 5	CF
May 18/90	Petr Klima, Edmonton	Reggie Lemelin, Boston	No	Edm.	7	at	Bos. 2	F
Apr. 6/91	Basil McRae, Minnesota	Ed Belfour, Chicago	Yes	Min.	2	at	Chi. 5	DSF
Apr. 10/91	Steve Duchesne, Los Angeles	Kirk McLean, Vancouver	Yes	L.A.	6	at	Van. 1	DSF
May 11/92	Jaromir Jagr, Pittsburgh	John Vanbiesbrouck, NYR	Yes	Pit.	3	at	NYR 2	DF
May 13/92	Shawn McEachern, Pittsburgh	John Vanbiesbrouck, NYR.	No	NYR	1	at	Pit. 5	DF
June 7/94	Pavel Bure, Vancouver	Mike Richter, NYR	No	NYR	4	at	Van. 2	F
May 9/95	Patrick Poulin, Chicago	Felix Potvin, Toronto	No	Tor.	3	at	Chi. 0	CQF
May 10/95	Michal Pivonka, Washington	Tom Barrasso, Pittsburgh	No	Pit.	2	at	Wsh. 6	CQF
Apr. 24/96	Joe Juneau, Washington	Ken Wregget, Pittsburgh	No	Pit.	3	at	Wsh. 2**	CQF
May 11/97	Eric Lindros, Philadelphia	Steve Shields, Buffalo	Yes	Phi.	6	at	Buf. 3	CSF
Apr. 23/98	Aleksey Morozov, Pittsburgh	Andy Moog, Montreal	No	Mtl.	3	at	Pit. 2**	CQF
Apr. 22/99	Mats Sundin, Toronto	John Vanbiesbrouck, Phi.	No	Phi.	3	at	Tor. 0	CQF
May 29/99	Mats Sundin, Toronto	Dominik Hasek, Buffalo	Yes	Tor.	2	at	Buf. 5	CF
Apr. 16/00	Eric Desjardins, Philadelphia	Dominik Hasek, Buffalo	No	Phi.	2	at	Buf. 0	CQF
Apr. 11/01	Mark Recchi, Philadelphia	Dominik Hasek, Buffalo	No	Buf.	2	at	Phi. 1	CQF
May 2/01	Martin Straka, Pittsburgh	Dominik Hasek, Buffalo	No	Buf.	5	at	Pit. 2	CSF
May 12/01	Joe Sakic, Colorado	Roman Turek, St. Louis	Yes	St.L.	1	at	Col. 4	CF
Apr. 21/02	Todd Bertuzzi, Vancouver	Dominik Hasek, Detroit	No	Det.	3	at	Van. 1	CQF
Apr. 24/02	Shawn Bates, NY Islanders	Curtis Joseph, Toronto	Yes	Tor.	3	at	NYI 4	CQF
Apr. 26/02	Mike Johnson, Phoenix	Evgeni Nabokov, San Jose	Yes	Phx.	1	at	S.J. 4	CQF
Apr. 15/03	Dainius Zubrus, Washington	Nikolai Khabibulin, Tampa Bay	No	T.B.	4	at	Wsh. 3	CQF
Apr. 21/03	Robert Reichel, Toronto	Roman Cechmanek, Philadelphia	No	Phi.	1	at	Tor. 1	CQF
Apr. 7/04	Steve Sullivan, Nashville	Manny Legace, Detroit	No	Nsh.	1	at	Det. 3	CQF
Apr. 28/06	Derek Roy, Buffalo	Robert Esche, Philadelphia	No	Buf.	4	at	Phi. 5	CQF
June 5/06	Chris Pronger, Edmonton***	Cam Ward, Carolina	Yes	Edm.	4	at	Car. 5	F

* Game was decided in overtime, but shot taken during regulation time.

** Shot taken in overtime.

*** First penalty shot scored in Stanley Cup Final history

Carolina's Cory Stillman scored the series winner in overtime for Carolina versus Montreal in the 2006 Eastern Conference quarterfinals. Stillman and Buffalo's Daniel Briere were the only players to score two overtime goals in last year's playoffs.

NHL Playoff Coaching Records

Coach	Team	Games Coached	Wins	Losses	Ties	Playoff Years	Cup Wins	Career
Abel, Sid	Chicago	7	3	4	0	1		
	Detroit	69	29	40	0	8		
	Total	76	32	44	0	9		1952-76
Adams, Jack	Detroit	105	52	52	1	15	3	1927-47
Allen, Keith	Philadelphia	11	3	8	0	2		1967-69
Arbour, Al	St. Louis	11	4	7	0	1		
	NY Islanders	198	119	79	0	15	4	
	Total	209	123	86	0	16	4	1970-94
Babcock, Mike	Anaheim	21	15	6	0	1		
	Detroit	6	2	4	0	1		
	Total	27	17	10	0	2		2002-06
Barber, Bill	Philadelphia	11	3	8	0	2		2000-02
Berenson, Red	St. Louis	14	5	9	0	2		1979-82
Bergeron, Michel	Quebec	68	31	37	0	7		1980-90
Berry, Bob	Los Angeles	10	2	8	0	3		
	Montreal	8	2	6	0	2		
	St. Louis	15	7	8	0	2		
	Total	33	11	22	0	7		1978-94
Beverley, Nick	Toronto	6	2	4	0	1		1995-96
Blackburn, Don	Hartford	3	0	3	0	1		1979-81
Blair, Wren	Minnesota	14	7	7	0	1		1967-70
Blake, Toe	Montreal	119	82	37	0	13	8	1955-68
Boileau, Marc	Pittsburgh	9	5	4	0	1		1973-76
Boivin, Leo	St. Louis	3	1	2	0	1		1975-78
Boucher, Frank	NY Rangers	27	13	14	0	4	1	1939-54
Boucher, Georges	Mtl. Maroons	2	0	2	0	1		1930-50
Bowman, Scotty	St. Louis	52	26	26	0	4		
	Montreal	98	70	28	0	8	5	
	Buffalo	36	18	18	0	5		
	Pittsburgh	33	23	10	0	2	1	
	Detroit	134	86	48	0	9	3	
	Total	353	223	130	0	28	9	1967-02
Bowness, Rick	Boston	15	8	7	0	1		1988-05
Brooks, Herb	NY Rangers	24	12	12	0	3		
	New Jersey	5	1	4	0	1		
	Pittsburgh	11	6	5	0	1		
	Total	40	19	21	0	5		1981-00
Brophy, John	Toronto	19	9	10	0	2		1986-89
Burns, Charlie	Minnesota	6	2	4	0	1		1969-75
Burns, Pat	Montreal	56	30	26	0	4		
	Toronto	46	23	23	0	3		
	Boston	18	8	10	0	3		
	New Jersey	29	17	12	0	2	1	
	Total	149	78	71	0	11	1	1988-05
Campbell, Colin	NY Rangers	36	18	18	0	3		1994-98
Carlyle, Randy	Anaheim	16	9	7	0	1		2005-06
Carpenter, Doug	Toronto	5	1	4	0	1		1984-91
Carroll, Dick	Toronto	7	4	3	0	1	1	1917-19
Cassidy, Bruce	Washington	6	2	4	0	1		2002-04
Cheevers, Gerry	Boston	34	15	19	0	4		1980-85
Cherry, Don	Boston	55	31	24	0	5		1974-80
Clancy, King	Toronto	14	2	12	0	3		1937-56
Clapper, Dit	Boston	25	8	17	0	4		1945-49
Cleghorn, Odie	Pittsburgh	4	1	2	1	2		1925-29
Cleghorn, Sprague	Mtl. Maroons	4	1	1	2	1		1931-32
Constantine, Kevin	San Jose	25	11	14	0	2		
	Pittsburgh	19	8	11	0	2		
	New Jersey	6	2	4	0	1		
	Total	50	21	29	0	5		1993-02
Crawford, Marc	Quebec	6	2	4	0	1		
	Colorado	46	29	17	0	3	1	
	Vancouver	31	12	19	0	4		
	Total	83	43	40	0	8	1	1994-06
Creighton, Fred	Atlanta	9	2	7	0	4		1974-80
Crisp, Terry	Calgary	37	22	15	0	3	1	
	Tampa Bay	6	2	4	0	1		
	Total	43	24	19	0	4	1	1987-98
Crozier, Joe	Buffalo	6	2	4	0	1		1971-81
Cunniff, John	New Jersey	6	2	4	0	1		1982-91
Curry, Alex	Ottawa	2	0	1	1	1		1925-26
Dandurand, Leo	Montreal	16	10	6	0	4	1	1921-35
Day, Hap	Toronto	80	49	31	0	9	5	1940-50
Demers, Jacques	St. Louis	33	16	17	0	3		
	Detroit	38	20	18	0	3		
	Montreal	27	19	8	0	2	1	
	Total	98	55	43	0	8	1	1979-99
Denneny, Cy	Boston	5	5	0	0	1	1	1928-33
Dudley, Rick	Buffalo	12	4	8	0	2		1989-04
Dugal, Jules	Montreal	3	1	2	0	1		1938-39
Duncan, Art	Toronto	2	0	1	1	1		1926-32
Dutton, Red	NY Americans	16	6	10	0	4		1935-42
Esposito, Phil	NY Rangers	10	2	8	0	2		1986-89
Evans, Jack	Hartford	16	8	8	0	2		1975-88
Ferguson, John	Winnipeg	3	0	3	0	1		1975-86
Francis, Bob	Phoenix	10	2	8	0	2		1999-04
Francis, Emile	NY Rangers	75	34	41	0	9		
	St. Louis	14	5	9	0	2		
	Total	89	39	50	0	11		1965-83
Ftorek, Robbie	Los Angeles	16	5	11	0	2		
	New Jersey	7	3	4	0	1		
	Boston	6	2	4	0	1		
	Total	29	10	19	0	4		1987-02
Gainey, Bob	Minnesota	30	17	13	0	2		
	Dallas	14	6	8	0	2		
	Montreal	6	2	4	0	1		
	Total	50	25	25	0	5		1990-06
Geoffrion, Bernie	Atlanta	4	0	4	0	1		1968-80
Gerard, Eddie	Mtl. Maroons	25	11	9	5	5	1	1917-35
Gill, David	Ottawa	8	3	2	3	2	1	1926-29
Glover, Fred	Oakland	11	3	8	0	2		1968-74
Gordon, Jackie	Minnesota	25	11	14	0	3		1970-75
Goring, Butch	Boston	3	0	3	0	1		1985-01
Gorman, Tommy	NY Americans	2	0	1	1	1		
	Chicago	8	6	1	1	1	1	
	Mtl. Maroons	15	7	6	2	3	1	
	Total	25	13	8	4	5	2	1925-38
Gottselig, Johnny	Chicago	4	0	4	0	1		1944-48
Granato, Tony	Colorado	18	9	9	0	2		2002-04
Green, Pete	Ottawa	26	14	9	3	6	3	1919-25
Green, Ted	Edmonton	16	8	8	0	1		1991-94
Guidolin, Bep	Boston	21	11	10	0	2		1972-76
Harris, Ted	Minnesota	2	0	2	0	1		1975-78
Hart, Cecil	Montreal	37	16	17	4	8	2	1926-39
Hartley, Bob	Colorado	80	49	31	0	4	1	1998-06
Hartsburg, Craig	Chicago	16	8	8	0	2		
	Anaheim	4	0	4	0	1		
	Total	20	8	12	0	3		1995-01
Harvey, Doug	NY Rangers	6	2	4	0	1		1961-62
Hay, Don	Phoenix	7	3	4	0	1		1996-01
Henning, Lorne	Minnesota	5	2	3	0	1		1985-01
Hitchcock, Ken	Dallas	80	47	33	0	5	1	
	Philadelphia	37	19	18	0	3		
	Total	117	66	51	0	8	1	1995-06
Hlinka, Ivan	Pittsburgh	18	9	9	0	1		2000-02
Holmgren, Paul	Philadelphia	19	10	9	0	1		1988-96
Imlach, Punch	Toronto	92	44	48	0	11	4	1958-80
Inglis, Bill	Buffalo	3	1	2	0	1		1978-79
Irvin, Dick	Chicago	9	5	3	1	2		
	Toronto	66	33	32	1	9	1	
	Montreal	115	62	53	0	14	3	
	Total	190	100	88	2	24	4	1928-56
Ivan, Tommy	Detroit	67	36	31	0	7	3	1947-58
Johnson, Bob	Calgary	52	25	27	0	5		
	Pittsburgh	24	16	8	0	1	1	
	Total	76	41	35	0	6	1	1982-91
Johnson, Tom	Boston	22	15	7	0	2	1	1970-73
Johnston, Eddie	Chicago	7	3	4	0	1		
	Pittsburgh	46	22	24	0	5		
	Total	53	25	28	0	6		1979-97
Julien, Claude	Montreal	11	4	7	0	1		2002-06
Kasper, Steve	Boston	5	1	4	0	1		1995-97
Keenan, Mike	Philadelphia	57	32	25	0	4		
	Chicago	60	33	27	0	4		
	NY Rangers	23	16	7	0	1	1	
	St. Louis	20	10	10	0	2		
	Total	160	91	69	0	11	1	1984-04
Kelly, Pat	Colorado	2	0	2	0	1		1977-79
Kelly, Red	Los Angeles	18	7	11	0	2		
	Pittsburgh	14	6	8	0	2		
	Toronto	30	11	19	0	4		
	Total	62	24	38	0	8		1967-77
King, Dave	Calgary	20	8	12	0	3		1992-02
Kitchen, Mike	St. Louis	5	1	4	0	1		2003-06
Kromm, Bobby	Detroit	7	3	4	0	1		1977-80
Lalonde, Newsy	Montreal	16	7	6	3	4		
	Ottawa	2	0	1	1	1		
	Total	18	7	7	4	5		1917-35
Lamorello, Lou	New Jersey	9	5	4	0	1		2005-06
Laviolette, Peter	NY Islanders	12	4	8	0	2		
	Carolina	25	16	9	0	1	1	
	Total	37	20	17	0	3	1	2001-06
Lemaire, Jacques	Montreal	27	15	12	0	2		
	New Jersey	56	34	22	0	4	1	
	Minnesota	18	8	10	0	1		
	Total	101	57	44	0	7	1	1983-06
Lewis, Dave	Detroit	16	6	10	0	2		1998-05
Ley, Rick	Hartford	13	5	8	0	2		
	Vancouver	11	4	7	0	1		
	Total	24	9	15	0	3		1989-96
Long, Barry	Winnipeg	11	3	8	0	2		1983-86
Loughlin, Clem	Chicago	4	1	2	1	2		1934-37
Low, Ron	Edmonton	28	10	18	0	3		1994-02
Lowe, Kevin	Edmonton	5	1	4	0	1		1999-00
MacLean, Doug	Florida	27	13	14	0	2		1995-04
MacNeil, Al	Montreal	20	12	8	0	1	1	
	Atlanta	4	1	3	0	1		
	Calgary	19	9	10	0	2		
	Total	43	22	21	0	4	1	1970-82

Coach	Team	Games Coached	Wins	Losses	Ties	Playoff Years	Cup Wins	Career
MacTavish, Craig	Edmonton	36	19	17	0	3		2000-06
Magnuson, Keith	Chicago	3	0	3	0	1		1980-82
Mahoney, Bill	Minnesota	16	7	9	0	1		1983-85
Maloney, Dan	Toronto	10	6	4	0	1		
	Winnipeg	15	5	10	0	2		
	Total	25	11	14	0	3		1984-89
Maloney, Phil	Vancouver	7	1	6	0	2		1973-77
Martin, Jacques	St. Louis	16	7	9	0	2		
	Ottawa	69	31	38	0	8		
	Total	85	38	47	0	10		1986-06
Maurice, Paul	Carolina	35	17	18	0	3		1995-04
McCammon, Bob	Philadelphia	10	1	9	0	3		
	Vancouver	7	3	4	0	1		
	Total	17	4	13	0	4		1978-91
McLellan, John	Toronto	11	3	8	0	2		1969-73
McVie, Tom	New Jersey	14	6	8	0	2		1975-92
Melrose, Barry	Los Angeles	24	13	11	0	1		1992-95
Milbury, Mike	Boston	40	23	17	0	2		1989-98
Muckler, John	Edmonton	40	25	15	0	2	1	
	Buffalo	27	11	16	0	4		
	Total	67	36	31	0	6	1	1968-00
Muldoon, Pete	Chicago	2	0	1	1	1		1926-27
Munro, Dunc	Mtl. Maroons	4	1	3	0	1		1929-31
Murdoch, Bob	Chicago	5	1	4	0	1		
	Winnipeg	7	3	4	0	1		
	Total	12	4	8	0	2		1987-91
Murphy, Mike	Los Angeles	5	1	4	0	1		1986-98
Murray, Andy	Los Angeles	24	10	14	0	3		1999-06
Murray, Bryan	Washington	53	24	29	0	7		
	Detroit	25	10	15	0	3		
	Ottawa	10	5	5	0	1		
	Total	88	39	49	0	11		1981-06
Murray, Terry	Washington	39	18	21	0	4		
	Philadelphia	46	28	18	0	3		
	Florida	4	0	4	0	1		
	Total	89	46	43	0	8		1989-01
Neale, Harry	Vancouver	14	3	11	0	4		1978-86
Neilson, Roger	Toronto	19	8	11	0	2		
	Buffalo	8	4	4	0	1		
	Vancouver	21	12	9	0	2		
	NY Rangers	29	13	16	0	3		
	Philadelphia	29	14	15	0	3		
	Total	106	51	55	0	11		1977-02
Nolan, Ted	Buffalo	12	5	7	0	1		1995-97
Nykoluk, Mike	Toronto	7	1	6	0	2		1980-84
O'Connell, Mike	Boston	5	1	4	0	1		2002-06
O'Donoghue, George	Toronto	7	4	2	1	1	1	1921-23
O'Reilly, Terry	Boston	37	17	19	1	3		1986-89
Oliver, Murray	Minnesota	13	5	8	0	2		1981-83
Paddock, John	Winnipeg	13	5	8	0	2		1991-95
Page, Pierre	Minnesota	12	4	8	0	2		
	Quebec	6	2	4	0	1		
	Calgary	4	0	4	0	1		
	Total	22	6	16	0	4		1988-98
Patrick, Craig	NY Rangers	17	7	10	0	2		
	Pittsburgh	5	1	4	0	1		
	Total	22	8	14	0	3		1980-97
Patrick, Frank	Boston	6	2	4	0	2		1934-36
Patrick, Lester	NY Rangers	65	32	26	7	12	2	1926-39
Patrick, Lynn	NY Rangers	12	7	5	0	1		
	Boston	28	9	18	1	4		
	Total	40	16	23	1	5		1948-76
Perron, Jean	Montreal	48	30	18	0	3	1	1985-89
Perry, Don	Los Angeles	10	4	6	0	1		1981-84
Pilous, Rudy	Chicago	41	19	22	0	5	1	1957-63
Plager, Barclay	St. Louis	4	1	3	0	1		1977-83
Pleau, Larry	Hartford	10	2	8	0	2		1980-89
Polano, Nick	Detroit	7	1	6	0	2		1982-85
Powers, Eddie	Toronto	2	0	2	0	1		1924-26
Primeau, Joe	Toronto	15	8	6	1	2	1	1950-53
Pronovost, Marcel	Buffalo	8	3	5	0	1		1977-79
Pulford, Bob	Los Angeles	26	10	16	0	4		
	Chicago	45	17	28	0	6		
	Total	71	27	44	0	10		1972-00
Quenneville, Joel	St. Louis	68	34	34	0	7		
	Colorado	9	4	5	0	1		
	Total	77	38	39	0	8		1996-06
Quinn, Pat	Philadelphia	39	22	17	0	3		
	Los Angeles	3	0	3	0	1		
	Vancouver	61	31	30	0	5		
	Toronto	80	41	39	0	6		
	Total	183	94	89	0	15		1978-06
Reay, Billy	Chicago	116	56	60	0	12		1957-77
Renney, Tom	NY Rangers	4	0	4	0	1		1996-06
Risebrough, Doug	Calgary	7	3	4	0	1		1990-92
Roberts, Jim	Hartford	7	3	4	0	1		1981-97
Robinson, Larry	Los Angeles	4	0	4	0	1		
	New Jersey	48	31	17	0	2	1	
	Total	52	31	21	0	3	1	1995-06
Ross, Art	Boston	65	27	33	5	11	1	1917-45
Ruel, Claude	Montreal	27	18	9	0	3	1	1968-81
Ruff, Lindy	Buffalo	72	43	29	0	5		1997-06
Sather, Glen	Edmonton	127	89	37	1	10	4	1979-04
Sator, Ted	NY Rangers	16	8	8	0	1		
	Buffalo	11	3	8	0	2		
	Total	27	11	16	0	3		1985-89
Schinkel, Ken	Pittsburgh	6	2	4	0	2		1972-77
Schmidt, Milt	Boston	34	15	19	0	4		1954-76
Schoenfeld, Jim	New Jersey	20	11	9	0	1		
	Washington	24	10	14	0	3		
	Phoenix	13	5	8	0	2		
	Total	57	26	31	0	6		1985-99
Shero, Fred	Philadelphia	83	48	35	0	6	2	
	NY Rangers	27	15	12	0	2		
	Total	110	63	47	0	8	2	1971-81
Simpson, Terry	NY Islanders	20	9	11	0	2		
	Winnipeg	6	2	4	0	1		
	Total	26	11	15	0	3		1986-96
Sinden, Harry	Boston	43	24	19	0	5	1	1966-85
Skinner, Jimmy	Detroit	26	14	12	0	3	1	1954-58
Smith, Alf	Ottawa	5	1	4	0	1		1918-19
Smith, Floyd	Buffalo	32	16	16	0	3		1971-80
Smythe, Conn	Toronto	4	2	2	0	1		1927-31
Sonmor, Glen	Minnesota	43	25	18	0	3		1978-87
Stasiuk, Vic	Philadelphia	4	0	4	0	1		1969-73
Stewart, Bill	Chicago	10	7	3	0	1	1	1937-39
Stewart, Ron	Los Angeles	2	0	2	0	1		1975-78
Stirling, Steve	NY Islanders	5	1	4	0	1		2003-06
Sullivan, Mike	Boston	7	3	4	0	1		2003-06
Sutter, Brian	St. Louis	41	20	21	0	4		
	Boston	22	7	15	0	3		
	Chicago	5	1	4	0	1		
	Total	68	28	40	0	8		1988-05
Sutter, Darryl	Chicago	26	11	15	0	3		
	San Jose	42	18	24	0	5		
	Calgary	33	18	15	0	2		
	Total	101	47	54	0	10		1992-06
Talbot, Jean-Guy	St. Louis	5	1	4	0	1		
	NY Rangers	3	1	2	0	1		
	Total	8	2	6	0	2		1972-78
Tessier, Orval	Chicago	18	9	9	0	2		1982-85
Therrien, Michel	Montreal	12	6	6	0	1		2000-06
Thompson, Paul	Chicago	19	7	12	0	4		1938-45
Tippett, Dave	Dallas	22	8	14	0	3		2002-06
Tobin, Bill	Chicago	4	1	2	1	2		1929-32
Tortorella, John	Tampa Bay	39	22	17	0	3	1	1999-06
Tremblay, Mario	Montreal	11	3	8	0	2		1995-97
Trotz, Barry	Nashville	11	3	8	0	2		1998-06
Ubriaco, Gene	Pittsburgh	11	7	4	0	1		1988-90
Vigneault, Alain	Montreal	10	4	6	0	1		1997-01
Watson, Phil	NY Rangers	16	4	12	0	3		1955-63
Watt, Tom	Winnipeg	7	1	6	0	2		
	Vancouver	3	0	3	0	1		
	Total	10	1	9	0	3		1981-92
Webster, Tom	Los Angeles	28	12	16	0	3		1986-92
Weiland, Cooney	Boston	17	10	7	0	2	1	1939-41
White, Bill	Chicago	2	0	2	0	1		1976-77
Wilson, Johnny	Pittsburgh	12	4	8	0	1		1969-80
Wilson, Ron	Anaheim	11	4	7	0	1		
	Washington	32	15	17	0	3		
	San Jose	28	16	12	0	2		
	Total	71	35	36	0	6		1993-06
Young, Garry	St. Louis	2	0	2	0	1		1972-76

Key to Prospect, NHL Player and Goaltender Registers

Demographics: Position, shooting side (catching hand for goaltenders), height, weight, place and date of birth as well as draft information, if any, is located on this line.

Major and tier-II junior, NCAA, minor pro, European and NHL clubs form a permanent part of each player's data panel. If a player sees action with more than one club in any of the above categories, a separate line is included for each one.

Olympic Team statistics are also listed.

Player's NHL organization as of August 15, 2006. This includes players under contract, unsigned draft choices and other players on reserve lists. Free agents as of this date show a blank here.

The complete career data panels of players with NHL experience who announced their retirement before the start of the 2006-07 season are included in the 2006-07 Player Register. These newly-retired players also show a blank here.

Each NHL club's minor-pro affiliates are listed on page 14.

Season	Club	League	GP	G	A	Pts	PIM	PP	SH	GW	S	%	+/-	TF	F%	Min	GP	G	A	Pts	PIM	PP	SH	GW	Min
											Regular Season									Playoffs				
COLE, Erik													(KOHL, AIR-ihk)			**CAR.**								
Left wing. Shoots left. 2", 200 lbs. Born, Oswego, NY, November 6, 1978. Carolina's 3rd choice, 71st overall, in 1998 Entry Draft.																								
1995-96	Oswego	High-NY	40	49	41	90		....							....										
1996-97	Des Moines	USHL	48	30	34	64	140	....							....		5	2	0	2	6				
1997-98	Clarkson Knights	ECAC	34	11	20	31	55	....							....										
1998-99	Clarkson Knights	ECAC	36	*22	20	42	50	....							....										
99-2000	Clarkson Knights	ECAC	33	19	11	30	46	....							....										
	Cincinnati	IHL		4	3	7	2	....							....		7	1	1	2	2				
2000-01	Cincinnati	IHL	63	23	20	43	28	....							....		5	1	0	1	2				
2001-02	Carolina	NHL	81	16	24	40	35	3	0	2	159	10.1	−10	17	47.1	16:04	23	6	3	9	30	1	0	1	18:27
2002-03	Carolina	NHL	53	14	13	27	72	6	2	3	125	11.2	1	56	39.3	17:08									
2003-04	Carolina	NHL	80	18	24	42	93	2	2	3	172	10.5	−4	15	46.7	18:06									
2004-05	Eisbaren Berlin	Germany	39	6	21	27	76										8	5	1	6	7				
2005-06 ♦	Carolina	NHL	60	30	29	59	54	3	3	8	164	18.3	19	19	36.8	19:18	2	0	0	0	1	0	0	0	15:29
	United States	Olympics	6	1	2	3	0																		
	NHL Totals		274	78	90	168	254	14	7	16	620	12.6		107	41.1	17:34	25	6	3	9	30	1	0	1	18:13

ECAC Rookie of the Year (1998) (co-winner - Willie Mitchell) • ECAC First All-Star Team (1999) • NCAA East Second All-American Team (1999) • ECAC Second All-Star Team (2000)
Signed as a free agent by **Eisbaren Berlin** (Germany), October 24, 2004.

Diamond (♦) indicates member of Stanley Cup-winning team.

Asterisk (*) indicates league leader in this statistical category.

"Did not play" Indicates that a player did not participate in a professional, junior or college league for an entire season.

Dates for trades or free agent signings often differ depending upon source. Signings can be reported based on when contracts are filed with NHL Central Registry or on the date a club announces that it has made a trade or come to terms with a free agent.

All trades, free agent signings and other transactions involving NHL clubs are listed in chronological order. First draft selection for players who re-enter the NHL Entry Draft is noted here. Other special notes are also listed here. These are highlighted with a bullet (•).

All-Star Team selections and awards are listed below player's year-by-year data.

NHL All-Star Game appearances are listed above trade notes.

Pronunciation of Player Names

United Press International phonetic style.

AY	long A as in mate
A	short A as in cat
AI	nasal A as on air
AH	short A as in father
AW	broad A as in talk
EE	long E as in meat
EH	short E as in get
UH	hollow E as in the
AY	French long E with acute accent as in Pathe
IH	middle E as in pretty
EW	EW dipthong as in few
IGH	long I as in time
EE	French long I as in machine
IH	short I as in pity
OH	long O as in note
AH	short O as in hot
AW	broad O as in fought
OI	OI dipthong as in noise
OO	long double OO as in fool
U	short double O as in foot
OW	OW dipthong as in how
EW	long U as in mule
OO	long U as in rule
U	middle U as in put
UH	short U as in shut or hurt
K	hard C as in cat
S	soft C as in cease
SH	soft CH as in machine
CH	hard CH or TCH as in catch
Z	hard S as in bells
S	soft S as in sun
G	hard G as in gang
J	soft G as in general
ZH	soft J as in French version of Joliet
KH	gutteral CH as in Scottish version of Loch

THIS 75TH EDITION OF THE *NHL Official Guide & Record Book* is the eighth to include additional statistical categories for forwards and defensemen in the National Hockey League. These categories are, from left to right in the sample panel above, power-play goals (PP), shorthand goals (SH), game-winning goals (GW), shots on goal (S), percentage of shots that score (%), plus-minus rating (+/–), total faceoffs taken (TF), faceoff winning percentage (F%), and average time-on-ice per game played (Min).

To integrate this data, the Player Register has been is split into two sections. The Prospect Register presents data on players who have yet to play in the NHL. The NHL Player Register, containing more information and a photo of each player, lists all active players who have appeared in an NHL regular-season or playoff game at any time.

Goaltenders, whether prospects or active NHLers, are included in one register. With the addition of the shootout to NHL regular-season play, the column formerly used to record tie games for goaltenders has been renamed "O/T." For NHL goaltenders in 2005-06, it lists overtime losses and shootout losses; previous to 2005-06, it lists tie games.

Registers (with their starting page) are presented in the following order: Prospects (279), NHL Players (367), Goaltenders (605), Retired Players (630) and Retired Goaltenders (665).

League abbreviations, page 346. Late additions to the Registers, page 611.

Some information is unavailable at press time. Readers are encouraged to contribute. See page 5 for contact names and addresses.

2006-07 Prospect Register

Note: The 2006-07 Prospect Register lists forwards and defensemen only. Goaltenders are listed separately. The Prospect Register lists every player drafted in the 2006 Entry Draft, players on NHL Reserve Lists and other players who have not yet played in the NHL. Trades and roster changes are current as of August 15, 2006.
Abbreviations: A – assists; **G** – goals; **GP** – games played; **PIM** – penalties in minutes; **Pts** – points; ***** – league-leading total.
NHL Player Register begins on page 347.
Goaltender Register begins on page 587.
League Abbreviations are listed on page 346.

AALTONEN, Juhamatti (AL-toh-nehn, YOO-haw-MAH-tee) ST.L.
Right wing. Shoots right. 6', 180 lbs. Born, Ii, Finland, June 4, 1985.
(St. Louis' 12th choice, 284th overall, in 2003 Entry Draft).

			Regular Season					Playoffs				
Season	Club	League	GP	G	A	Pts	PIM	GP	G	A	Pts	PIM
2000-01	Karpat Oulu U18	Fin-U18	3	0	1	1	0	....	....	....	....	....
2001-02	Karpat Oulu U18	Fin-U18	23	9	11	20	28	2	0	0	0	0
2002-03	Karpat Oulu U18	Fin-U18	2	5	1	6	6	....	....	....	....	....
	Karpat Oulu Jr.	Fin-Jr.	33	19	3	22	30	1	0	0	0	7
	Karpat Oulu	Finland	1	0	0	0	0	....	....	....	....	....
2003-04	Karpat Oulu Jr.	Fin-Jr.	32	30	15	45	-32	3	1	0	1	2
	Karpat Oulu	Finland	8	0	0	0	2	....	....	....	....	....
2004-05	Karpat Oulu Jr.	Fin-Jr.	34	27	23	50	38	5	0	2	2	22
	Karpat Oulu	Finland	6	0	0	0	0	....	....	....	....	....
2005-06	Karpat Oulu	Finland	50	13	12	25	28	9	0	0	0	0

ABDELKADER, Justin (abdehl-KAY-durh, JUHS-tihn) DET.
Left wing. Shoots left. 6'1", 195 lbs. Born, Muskegon, MI, February 25, 1987.
(Detroit's 2nd choice, 42nd overall, in 2005 Entry Draft).

			Regular Season					Playoffs				
Season	Club	League	GP	G	A	Pts	PIM	GP	G	A	Pts	PIM
2003-04	Muskegon M.S.	High-MI	28	37	43	80	....	....	....	....	....	....
2004-05	Cedar Rapids	USHL	60	27	25	52	86	11	0	4	4	8
2005-06	Michigan State	CCHA	44	10	12	22	83	....	....	....	....	....

AHNELOV, Jonas (AH-neh-lawv, YOH-nuhs) PHX.
Defense. Shoots left. 6'3", 205 lbs. Born, Huddinge, Sweden, December 11, 1987.
(Phoenix's 3rd choice, 88th overall, in 2006 Entry Draft).

			Regular Season					Playoffs				
Season	Club	League	GP	G	A	Pts	PIM	GP	G	A	Pts	PIM
2003-04	Huddinge IK U18	Swe-U18	6	0	3	3	8	....	....	....	....	....
	Huddinge Jr.	Swe-Jr.	9	0	1	1	6	....	....	....	....	....
2004-05	Huddinge IK U18	Swe-U18	2	0	0	0	2	....	....	....	....	....
	Huddinge Jr.	Swe-Jr.	29	3	3	6	94	3	0	0	0	2
2005-06	Frolunda Jr.	Swe-Jr.	29	4	11	15	84	7	2	4	6	22
	Frolunda	Sweden	15	0	0	0	2	....	....	....	....	....

AIELLO, Anthony (igh-EHL-oh, AN-thu-nee) MIN.
Defense. Shoots left. 6'1", 202 lbs. Born, Braintree, MA, May 19, 1986.
(Minnesota's 6th choice, 129th overall, in 2005 Entry Draft).

			Regular Season					Playoffs				
Season	Club	League	GP	G	A	Pts	PIM	GP	G	A	Pts	PIM
2003-04	Thayer Academy	High-MA	33	11	26	37	....	....	....	....	....	....
2004-05	Thayer Academy	High-MA	30	7	27	34	42	....	....	....	....	....
2005-06	Boston College	H-East	40	1	8	9	50	....	....	....	....	....

AKKANEN, Karri (ah-KAHN-uhn, KAH-ree)
Right wing. Shoots right. 6'6", 226 lbs. Born, Tampere, Finland, January 29, 1984.
(Tampa Bay's 6th choice, 174th overall, in 2002 Entry Draft).

			Regular Season					Playoffs				
Season	Club	League	GP	G	A	Pts	PIM	GP	G	A	Pts	PIM
2000-01	Ilves Tampere U18	Fin-U18	32	5	10	15	20	....	....	....	....	....
2001-02	Ilves Tampere U18	Fin-U18	15	6	6	12	30	4	0	1	1	4
	Ilves Tampere Jr.	Fin-Jr.	5	0	1	1	4	....	....	....	....	....
2002-03	Ilves Tampere Jr.	Fin-Jr.	24	7	20	27	81	....	....	....	....	....
	Ilves Tampere U18	Fin-U18	11	1	6	7	65	....	....	....	....	....
	Ilves Tampere	Finland	21	0	1	1	0	....	....	....	....	....
2003-04	Suomi U20	Finland-2	4	0	0	0	4	....	....	....	....	....
	Ilves Tampere Jr.	Fin-Jr.	4	0	1	1	22	....	....	....	....	....
	Tappara Jr.	Fin-Jr.	31	4	8	12	58	14	4	3	7	16
2004-05	Tappara Jr.	Fin-Jr.	29	6	6	12	42	4	0	0	0	16
2005-06	HCM Tampere	Finland-3	5	1	2	3	4	....	....	....	....	....

ALBERS, Paul (AL-buhrs, PAWL) MIN.
Defense. Shoots left. 6'1", 189 lbs. Born, Melville, Sask., October 15, 1985.

			Regular Season					Playoffs				
Season	Club	League	GP	G	A	Pts	PIM	GP	G	A	Pts	PIM
2001-02	Calgary Hitmen	WHL	54	1	5	6	32	5	0	0	0	6
2002-03	Calgary Hitmen	WHL	72	4	20	24	51	5	0	0	0	0
2003-04	Calgary Hitmen	WHL	8	0	1	1	6	....	....	....	....	....
	Regina Pats	WHL	54	5	18	23	30	4	0	0	0	2
2004-05	Regina Pats	WHL	23	0	4	4	6	....	....	....	....	....
	Vancouver Giants	WHL	48	4	19	23	42	6	2	3	5	0
2005-06	Vancouver Giants	WHL	70	17	45	62	33	18	3	*16	19	8

Signed as a free agent by **Minnesota**, July 5, 2006.

ALEN, Juha (AL-ehn, YOO-haw) VAN.
Defense. Shoots left. 6'4", 218 lbs. Born, Tampere, Finland, October 25, 1981.
(Anaheim's 4th choice, 90th overall, in 2003 Entry Draft).

			Regular Season					Playoffs				
Season	Club	League	GP	G	A	Pts	PIM	GP	G	A	Pts	PIM
1998-99	KooVee Jr.	Fin-Jr.	36	6	7	13	42	....	....	....	....	....
99-2000	KooVee Jr.	Fin-Jr.	22	2	4	6	28	....	....	....	....	....
2000-01	Ilves Tampere Jr.	Fin-Jr.	42	2	12	14	62	....	....	....	....	....
2001-02	Soo Indians	NAHL	54	10	10	20	46	2	0	1	1	0
2002-03	Northern Mich.	CCHA	40	4	19	23	64	....	....	....	....	....
2003-04	Cincinnati	AHL	59	2	3	5	64	9	0	0	0	14
2004-05	Ilves Tampere	Finland	7	0	0	0	16	2	0	0	0	0
2005-06	Ilves Tampere	Finland	52	5	5	10	104	4	0	0	0	6

• Missed majority of 2004-05 season recovering from off-season foot injury. Traded to **Vancouver** by **Anaheim** with Keith Carney for Brett Skinner and NY Islanders' 2nd round choice (previously acquired - Anaheim selected Bryce Swan) in 2006 Entry Draft, March 9, 2006.

ALEXANDROV, Viktor (al-ehx-AN-drawv, VIHK-tohr) ST.L.
Left wing. Shoots left. 5'11", 183 lbs. Born, Ust-Kamenogorsk, USSR, December 28, 1985.
(St. Louis' 3rd choice, 83rd overall, in 2004 Entry Draft).

			Regular Season					Playoffs				
Season	Club	League	GP	G	A	Pts	PIM	GP	G	A	Pts	PIM
2001-02	Ust-Kamenogorsk	Russia-2	45	12	17	29	48	2	0	1	1	2
2002-03	Yaroslavl	Russia	2	0	0	0	2	....	....	....	....	....
	Energiya Kemerovo	Russia-2	15	2	4	6	12	....	....	....	....	....
	Novokuznetsk	Russia	11	0	0	0	4	....	....	....	....	....
2003-04	Novokuznetsk	Russia	57	5	4	9	26	4	1	1	2	4
2004-05	Novokuznetsk	Russia	50	8	10	18	16	4	1	1	2	0
2005-06	SKA St. Petersburg	Russia	41	4	6	10	55	....	....	....	....	....
	St. Petersburg 2	Russia-3	1	0	3	3	0	....	....	....	....	....

ALEXANDROV, Yuri (al-ehx-AN-drawv, YOO-ree) BOS.
Defense. Shoots left. 6', 185 lbs. Born, Cherepovets, Russia, June 24, 1988.
(Boston's 2nd choice, 37th overall, in 2006 Entry Draft).

			Regular Season					Playoffs				
Season	Club	League	GP	G	A	Pts	PIM	GP	G	A	Pts	PIM
2003-04	Cherepovets 2	Russia-3	32	0	2	2	10	4	0	0	0	0
2004-05	Cherepovets 2	Russia-3			STATISTICS NOT AVAILABLE							
2005-06	Cherepovets	Russia	37	1	0	1	18	2	0	0	0	2

ALMTORP, Jonas (AHLM-tohrp, YOH-nuhs) EDM.
Center. Shoots left. 6'1", 190 lbs. Born, Uppsala, Sweden, November 17, 1983.
(Edmonton's 7th choice, 111th overall, in 2002 Entry Draft).

			Regular Season					Playoffs				
Season	Club	League	GP	G	A	Pts	PIM	GP	G	A	Pts	PIM
99-2000	MoDo U18	Swe-U18	22	*19	12	31	*55	....	....	....	....	....
	Malmo Jr.	Swe-Jr.	7	1	0	1	0	....	....	....	....	....
2000-01	MoDo U18	Swe-U18	12	11	1	12	30	....	....	....	....	....
	Malmo Jr.	Swe-Jr.	27	19	7	26	38	7	6	1	7	10
2001-02	MODO	Sweden	3	0	0	0	0	....	....	....	....	....
	Malmo Jr.	Swe-Jr.	37	26	18	44	102	2	1	1	2	4
2002-03	MODO	Sweden	28	1	1	2	22	....	....	....	....	....
	Ornskoldsviks SK	Sweden-2	12	5	4	9	49	....	....	....	....	....
	Malmo Jr.	Swe-Jr.	5	2	2	4	12	....	....	....	....	....
2003-04	MODO	Sweden	20	0	0	0	4	3	0	0	0	0
	Sundsvall	Sweden-2	32	9	9	18	65	....	....	....	....	....
	Malmo Jr.	Swe-Jr.	5	0	0	0	14	....	....	....	....	....
2004-05	Brynas IF Gavle	Sweden	3	0	0	0	0	....	....	....	....	....
	Almtuna	Sweden-2	44	16	20	36	56	3	0	3	3	2
2005-06	Brynas IF Gavle	Sweden	50	6	6	12	42	4	0	1	1	4

ALTAREV, Dmitri (al-ta-REHV, dih-MEE-tree) NYI

Left wing. Shoots left. 6'3", 191 lbs. Born, Penza, USSR, August 12, 1980.
(NY Islanders' 8th choice, 264th overall, in 2000 Entry Draft).

			Regular Season					Playoffs				
Season	Club	League	GP	G	A	Pts	PIM	GP	G	A	Pts	PIM
1997-98	Dizelist Penza 2	Russia-3	57	15	8	23	83	....	....	....	....	....
1998-99	Dizelist Penza 2	Russia-4	35	4	3	7	30	....	....	....	....	....
	Dizelist Penza	Russia-2	6	2	0	2	8	....	....	....	....	....
99-2000	Dizelist Penza 2	Russia-3	44	10	8	18	25	....	....	....	....	....
2000-01	Nizhny Novgorod	Russia	36	1	2	3	26	....	....	....	....	....
2001-02	Nizh. Novgorod 2	Russia-3	10	5	6	11	12	....	....	....	....	....
	Nizhny Novgorod	Russia	32	2	3	5	42	....	....	....	....	....
2002-03	Dizel Penza	Russia-3	47	22	26	48	106	....	....	....	....	....
2003-04	Dizel Penza	Russia-2	56	19	20	39	86	4	1	0	1	8
2004-05	Dizel Penza	Russia-2	52	13	11	24	72	4	1	0	1	8
2005-06	Dizel Penza	Russia-2	52	19	23	42	84	13	5	5	10	37

ANDERSEN, Niclas (AN-duhr-suhn, NIHK-las) L.A.

Defense. Shoots left. 6'1", 207 lbs. Born, Grums, Sweden, April 28, 1988.
(Los Angeles' 6th choice, 114th overall, in 2006 Entry Draft).

			Regular Season					Playoffs				
Season	Club	League	GP	G	A	Pts	PIM	GP	G	A	Pts	PIM
2003-04	Grums IK	Sweden-3	30	4	5	9	45	....	....	....	....	....
2004-05	Leksands IF Jr.	Swe-Jr.	26	3	2	5	91	5	0	2	2	2
2005-06	Leksands IF U18	Swe-U18	3	0	3	3	8	2	0	0	0	10
	Leksands IF Jr.	Swe-Jr.	36	5	6	11	214	....	....	....	....	....
	Leksands IF	Sweden	8	0	0	0	8	....	....	....	....	....
	Leksands IF	Sweden-Q	3	0	0	0	2	....	....	....	....	....

ANDERSON, R.J. (AN-duhr-suhn, AHR-JAY) PHI.

Defense. Shoots right. 5'11", 180 lbs. Born, Maple Wood, MN, July 16, 1986.
(Philadelphia's 2nd choice, 101st overall, in 2004 Entry Draft).

			Regular Season					Playoffs				
Season	Club	League	GP	G	A	Pts	PIM	GP	G	A	Pts	PIM
2002-03	Centennial	High-MN	24	6	35	41	10	....	....	....	....	....
2003-04	Centennial	High-MN	30	29	56	85	34	....	....	....	....	....
	Team Northeast	UMEHL	24	9	16	25	....	....	....	....	....	....
2004-05	Centennial	High-MN	28	23	36	59	....	....	....	....	....	....
2005-06	U. of Minnesota	WCHA	37	0	4	4	32	....	....	....	....	....

ANDERSSON, Johan (AN-duhr-suhn, YOH-hahn) CHI.

Center. Shoots left. 6'1", 201 lbs. Born, Motala, Sweden, May 18, 1984.
(Chicago's 6th choice, 181st overall, in 2003 Entry Draft).

			Regular Season					Playoffs				
Season	Club	League	GP	G	A	Pts	PIM	GP	G	A	Pts	PIM
2000-01	IF Troja-Ljungby	Sweden-2	3	0	0	0	0	....	....	....	....	....
2001-02	IF Troja-Ljungby	Sweden-2	42	2	0	2	10	5	2	0	2	2
2002-03	IF Troja-Ljungby	Sweden-2	20	8	4	12	16	....	....	....	....	....
2003-04	IF Troja-Ljungby	Sweden-2	43	13	11	24	94	....	....	....	....	....
2004-05	Linkopings HC Jr.	Swe-Jr.	2	0	2	2	4	....	....	....	....	....
	IF Troja-Ljungby	Sweden-2	21	6	5	11	37	....	....	....	....	....
	Linkopings HC	Sweden	29	1	2	3	14	4	0	0	0	2
2005-06	Linkopings HC Jr.	Swe-Jr.	1	1	1	2	2	....	....	....	....	....
	Linkopings HC	Sweden	50	2	7	9	40	13	0	0	0	39

ANGELIDIS, Mike (AN-gehl-EE-dihs, MIGHK) CAR.

Left wing. Shoots left. 6'1", 220 lbs. Born, Woodbridge, Ont., June 27, 1985.

			Regular Season					Playoffs				
Season	Club	League	GP	G	A	Pts	PIM	GP	G	A	Pts	PIM
2002-03	Owen Sound	OHL	65	7	10	17	81	4	1	1	2	0
2003-04	Owen Sound	OHL	66	9	9	18	118	7	4	1	5	4
2004-05	Owen Sound	OHL	41	9	10	19	126	8	3	2	5	10
2005-06	Owen Sound	OHL	68	53	25	78	167	11	5	9	14	38

OHL First All-Star Team (2006)

Signed as a free agent by **Carolina**, July 21, 2006.

ANIKEYENKO, Vitali (ah-nih-KEH-ehn-koh, vih-TAL-ee) OTT.

Defense. Shoots right. 6'3", 200 lbs. Born, Kiev, USSR, January 2, 1987.
(Ottawa's 2nd choice, 70th overall, in 2005 Entry Draft).

			Regular Season					Playoffs				
Season	Club	League	GP	G	A	Pts	PIM	GP	G	A	Pts	PIM
2003-04	Yaroslavl 2	Russia-3	40	2	9	11	68	....	....	....	....	....
2004-05	Yaroslavl 2	Russia-3	58	3	11	14	62	....	....	....	....	....
2005-06	Yaroslavl 2	Russia-3	19	3	5	8	20	....	....	....	....	....
	Yaroslavl	Russia	26	0	1	1	28	1	0	0	0	0

ANISIMOV, Artem (a-NEE-see-mawv, ahr-TEHM) NYR

Center. Shoots left. 6'3", 187 lbs. Born, Yaroslavl, Russia, May 24, 1988.
(NY Rangers' 2nd choice, 54th overall, in 2006 Entry Draft).

			Regular Season					Playoffs				
Season	Club	League	GP	G	A	Pts	PIM	GP	G	A	Pts	PIM
2004-05	Yaroslavl 2	Russia-3	24	3	5	8	10	....	....	....	....	....
2005-06	Yaroslavl	Russia	10	0	1	1	4	....	....	....	....	....
	Yaroslavl 2	Russia-3	32	15	12	27	28	....	....	....	....	....

ANSHAKOV, Sergei (an-sha-KAHV, SAIR-gay) PIT.

Left wing. Shoots left. 6'3", 179 lbs. Born, Moscow, USSR, January 13, 1984.
(Los Angeles' 2nd choice, 50th overall, in 2002 Entry Draft).

			Regular Season					Playoffs				
Season	Club	League	GP	G	A	Pts	PIM	GP	G	A	Pts	PIM
2000-01	Dyn'o Moscow 18	Exhib.	6	7	1	8	2	....	....	....	....	....
2001-02	HK CSKA 2	Russia-3	3	3	1	4	0	....	....	....	....	....
	HK CSKA Moscow	Russia-2	46	20	12	22	10	....	....	....	....	....
2002-03	CSKA Moscow	Russia	25	1	2	3	4	....	....	....	....	....
2003-04	CSKA Moscow	Russia	33	3	2	5	12	....	....	....	....	....
2004-05	CSKA Moscow	Russia	11	0	0	0	2	....	....	....	....	....
	Ufa	Russia	23	9	3	12	4	....	....	....	....	....
2005-06	Ufa	Russia	6	1	1	2	12	....	....	....	....	....
	Dynamo Moscow	Russia	1	0	0	0	0	....	....	....	....	....
	HK MVD-THK Tver	Russia-3	1	2	0	2	0	....	....	....	....	....
	MVD	Russia	12	1	3	4	2	2	0	1	1	0

Traded to **Pittsburgh** by **Los Angeles** with Martin Strbak for Martin Straka, November 30, 2003.
Loaned to **Ufa** (Russia) by **CSKA Moscow** (Russia), December 20, 2004.

ANTTILA, Marko (AN-tih-la, MAHR-koh) CHI.

Right wing. Shoots right. 6'8", 226 lbs. Born, Lempaala, Finland, May 27, 1985.
(Chicago's 17th choice, 260th overall, in 2004 Entry Draft).

			Regular Season					Playoffs				
Season	Club	League	GP	G	A	Pts	PIM	GP	G	A	Pts	PIM
2002-03	LeKi Lempaala U18	Fin-U18	11	17	8	25	41	....	....	....	....	....
2003-04	LeKi Lempaala Jr.	Fin-Jr.	12	11	11	22	26	....	....	....	....	....
	LeKi Lempaala	Finland-4	21	18	18	36	20	....	....	....	....	....
2004-05	Ilves Tampere Jr.	Fin-Jr.	27	14	6	20	44	9	5	7	12	14
	Ilves Tampere	Finland	28	2	1	3	10	3	0	0	0	0
2005-06	Ilves Tampere Jr.	Fin-Jr.	10	4	2	6	6	2	1	1	2	4
	Ilves Tampere	Finland	50	4	3	7	46	4	0	0	0	0

AQUINO, Luciano (a-KEE-noh, LEW-CHI-a-noh) NYI

Center/Left wing. Shoots left. 5'9", 198 lbs. Born, Mississauga, Ont., January 26, 1985.
(NY Islanders' 7th choice, 210th overall, in 2005 Entry Draft).

			Regular Season					Playoffs				
Season	Club	League	GP	G	A	Pts	PIM	GP	G	A	Pts	PIM
2003-04	U. of Maine	H-East	20	4	5	9	8	....	....	....	....	....
2004-05	Brampton	OHL	65	25	46	71	80	....	....	....	....	....
2005-06	Brampton	OHL	32	28	44	72	32	11	8	13	21	23
	Bridgeport	AHL	9	0	2	2	6	....	....	....	....	....
	Trenton Titans	ECHL	3	0	1	1	0	....	....	....	....	....

ARCHER, Andrew (AHR-chuhr, AN-droo) MTL.

Defense. Shoots right. 6'4", 212 lbs. Born, Calgary, Alta., May 15, 1983.
(Montreal's 7th choice, 203rd overall, in 2001 Entry Draft).

			Regular Season					Playoffs				
Season	Club	League	GP	G	A	Pts	PIM	GP	G	A	Pts	PIM
99-2000	Oshawa Generals	OHL	47	0	1	1	24	3	0	1	1	2
2000-01	Oshawa Generals	OHL	2	0	0	0	4	....	....	....	....	....
	Guelph Storm	OHL	50	0	2	2	59	4	0	0	0	4
2001-02	Guelph Storm	OHL	58	3	10	13	76	9	0	2	2	16
2002-03	Guelph Storm	OHL	65	2	16	18	138	11	2	2	4	18
2003-04	Hamilton Bulldogs	AHL	30	0	1	1	23	3	0	0	0	0
	Columbus	ECHL	6	0	1	1	19	....	....	....	....	....
2004-05	Hamilton Bulldogs	AHL	68	1	10	11	112	3	0	0	0	2
2005-06	Hamilton Bulldogs	AHL	42	0	3	3	62	....	....	....	....	....

• Missed majority of 2003-04 season recovering from hernia injury suffered in training camp, September 15, 2003.

ARMSTRONG, John (ahrm-STRAWNG, JAWN) CGY.

Center. Shoots right. 6'2", 188 lbs. Born, Unionville, Ont., February 26, 1988.
(Calgary's 2nd choice, 87th overall, in 2006 Entry Draft).

			Regular Season					Playoffs				
Season	Club	League	GP	G	A	Pts	PIM	GP	G	A	Pts	PIM
2004-05	Plymouth Whalers	OHL	52	6	13	19	39	4	0	0	0	4
2005-06	Plymouth Whalers	OHL	65	14	23	37	75	13	4	7	11	18

ARMSTRONG, Riley (AHRM-strawng, RIGH-lee) S.J.

Right wing. Shoots right. 5'11", 185 lbs. Born, Saskatoon, Sask., November 8, 1984.

			Regular Season					Playoffs				
Season	Club	League	GP	G	A	Pts	PIM	GP	G	A	Pts	PIM
2001-02	Yorkton Terriers	SMHL	42	43	34	77	....	....	....	....	....	....
2002-03	Kootenay Ice	WHL	65	6	10	16	69	10	0	1	1	14
2003-04	Everett Silvertips	WHL	69	18	26	44	119	21	5	4	9	46
2004-05	Cleveland Barons	AHL	70	8	11	19	117	....	....	....	....	....
2005-06	Cleveland Barons	AHL	64	4	5	9	67	....	....	....	....	....

Signed as a free agent by **San Jose**, September 15, 2004.

ARSENE, Dean (ahr-SEH-nee, DEEN) WSH.

Defense. Shoots left. 6'2", 200 lbs. Born, Abbotsford, B.C., July 12, 1980.

			Regular Season					Playoffs				
Season	Club	League	GP	G	A	Pts	PIM	GP	G	A	Pts	PIM
1996-97	Regina Pats	WHL	62	0	8	8	53	3	0	0	0	2
1997-98	Regina Pats	WHL	31	2	7	9	47	....	....	....	....	....
	Edmonton Ice	WHL	43	0	12	12	90	....	....	....	....	....
1998-99	Kootenay Ice	WHL	68	1	4	5	111	4	0	0	0	4
99-2000	Kootenay Ice	WHL	66	4	7	11	150	21	1	2	3	59
2000-01	Kootenay Ice	WHL	68	1	10	11	178	11	0	1	1	34
2001-02	Charlotte	ECHL	63	3	10	13	101	5	0	2	2	16
2002-03	Hartford Wolf Pack	AHL	50	1	3	4	94	....	....	....	....	....
2003-04	Reading Royals	ECHL	46	0	6	6	118	15	1	5	6	34
	Hershey Bears	AHL	22	0	2	2	44	....	....	....	....	....
2004-05	Hershey Bears	AHL	56	1	5	6	140	....	....	....	....	....
2005-06	Hershey Bears	AHL	68	2	5	7	181	21	0	1	1	29

Signed as a free agent by **Washington**. July 26, 2006.

ASTON, Peter (AS-tuhn, PEE-tuhr) FLA.

Defense. Shoots right. 6'1", 205 lbs. Born, Toronto, Ont., February 24, 1986.
(Florida's 5th choice, 155th overall, in 2006 Entry Draft).

			Regular Season					Playoffs				
Season	Club	League	GP	G	A	Pts	PIM	GP	G	A	Pts	PIM
2002-03	Pickering Panthers	OPJHL	45	4	20	24	52	....	....	....	....	....
2003-04	Peterborough	OHL	36	2	3	5	17	....	....	....	....	....
2004-05	Peterborough	OHL	52	0	15	15	16	14	0	4	4	6
2005-06	Peterborough	OHL	16	4	15	19	10	....	....	....	....	....
	Windsor Spitfires	OHL	49	12	21	33	21	7	2	1	3	2

ATHERTON, P.J. (A-thur-tuhn, PEE-JAY) T.B.

Defense. Shoots right. 6'1", 204 lbs. Born, Edina, MN, August 16, 1982.
(Tampa Bay's 5th choice, 170th overall, in 2002 Entry Draft).

			Regular Season					Playoffs				
Season	Club	League	GP	G	A	Pts	PIM	GP	G	A	Pts	PIM
99-2000	Edina Hornets	High-MN	38	7	15	22	....	....	....	....	....	....
	Cedar Rapids	USHL	5	0	1	1	4	....	....	....	....	....
2000-01	Cedar Rapids	USHL	43	4	9	13	99	4	2	0	2	10
2001-02	Cedar Rapids	USHL	51	7	22	29	101	8	0	0	0	14
2002-03	U. of Minnesota	WCHA	20	2	2	4	20	....	....	....	....	....
2003-04	U. of Minnesota	WCHA	28	0	2	2	36	....	....	....	....	....
2004-05	U. of Minnesota	WCHA	17	2	2	4	22	....	....	....	....	....
2005-06	U. of Minnesota	WCHA	41	1	6	7	68	....	....	....	....	....
	Springfield Falcons	AHL	9	1	3	4	4	....	....	....	....	....

ATYUSHOV, Vitali (a-tew-SHAWF, vih-TAL-ee) OTT.

Defense. Shoots left. 6'1", 205 lbs. Born, Penza, USSR, July 4, 1979.
(Ottawa's 8th choice, 276th overall, in 2002 Entry Draft).

			Regular Season					Playoffs				
Season	Club	League	GP	G	A	Pts	PIM	GP	G	A	Pts	PIM
1997-98	Krylja Sovetov	Russia	4	0	0	0	2	....	....	....	....	....
1998-99	Dizelist Penza 2	Russia-4	2	1	1	2	2	....	....	....	....	....
	Dizelist Penza	Russia-2	22	0	0	0	22	....	....	....	....	....
	Krylja Sovetov	Russia	17	1	0	1	20	....	....	....	....	....
	Krylja Sovetov	Russia-Q	21	0	5	5	50	....	....	....	....	....
99-2000	Perm	Russia	38	4	0	4	50	3	0	0	0	12
2000-01	Perm	Russia	44	3	9	12	32	....	....	....	....	....
2001-02	Perm	Russia	51	4	8	12	66	....	....	....	....	....
2002-03	Ak Bars Kazan	Russia	33	0	9	9	12	2	0	0	0	0
2003-04	Magnitogorsk	Russia	56	5	9	14	26	14	2	3	5	6
2004-05	Magnitogorsk	Russia	58	6	18	24	42	5	2	0	2	0
2005-06	Magnitogorsk	Russia	51	7	12	19	64	11	2	0	2	4

AUBIN, Mathieu (oh-BEHN, MAT-yew) MTL.

Center. Shoots right. 6'3", 204 lbs. Born, Sorel, Que., September 18, 1986.
(Montreal's 4th choice, 130th overall, in 2005 Entry Draft).

			Regular Season					Playoffs				
Season	Club	League	GP	G	A	Pts	PIM	GP	G	A	Pts	PIM
2001-02	Antoine-Girouard	QAAA	19	5	10	15	10	....	....	....	....	....
2002-03	Antoine-Girouard	QAAA	42	19	35	54	28	....	....	....	....	....
	Sherbrooke	QMJHL	1	0	0	0	0	....	....	....	....	....
2003-04	Lewiston	QMJHL	68	19	23	42	34	7	1	1	2	2
2004-05	Lewiston	QMJHL	49	19	26	45	24	8	3	6	9	6
2005-06	Lewiston	QMJHL	70	47	56	103	63	6	3	4	7	4

AUFFREY, Matt (AWF-ree, MAT) ANA.

Right wing. Shoots right. 6'2", 203 lbs. Born, Cincinnati, OH, January 3, 1986.
(Anaheim's 5th choice, 172nd overall, in 2004 Entry Draft).

			Regular Season					Playoffs				
Season	Club	League	GP	G	A	Pts	PIM	GP	G	A	Pts	PIM
2001-02	Syracuse	OPJHL	....	33	39	72	....	....	....	....	....	....
2002-03	USNTDP	U-17	23	3	9	12	18	....	....	....	....	....
	USNTDP	NAHL	40	8	9	17	50	....	....	....	....	....
2003-04	USNTDP	U-18	44	13	14	27	....	....	....	....	....	....
	USNTDP	NAHL	10	1	2	3	8	....	....	....	....	....
2004-05	U. of Wisconsin	WCHA	25	3	5	8	18	....	....	....	....	....
2005-06	U. of Wisconsin	WCHA	1	0	0	0	0	....	....	....	....	....
	Kitchener Rangers	OHL	59	24	26	50	82	5	1	2	3	12
	Portland Pirates	AHL	2	0	1	1	6	....	....	....	....	....

AUGER, Chris (AW-zhay, KRIHS) CHI.

Center. Shoots left. 5'10", 161 lbs. Born, Belleville, Ont., December 16, 1987.
(Chicago's 8th choice, 169th overall, in 2006 Entry Draft).

			Regular Season					Playoffs				
Season	Club	League	GP	G	A	Pts	PIM	GP	G	A	Pts	PIM
2004-05	Wellington Dukes	OPJHL	44	25	30	55	16	14	9	11	20	37
2005-06	Wellington Dukes	OPJHL	47	41	51	92	46	12	8	14	22	2

OPJHL East MVP (2006)

Signed Letter of Intent to attend **U. of Mass.-Lowell** (Hockey East) in fall of 2006.

AXELSSON, Anton (AHX-ehl-suhn, AN-tawn) DET.

Left wing. Shoots left. 6', 183 lbs. Born, Ytterby, Sweden, January 16, 1986.
(Detroit's 5th choice, 192nd overall, in 2004 Entry Draft).

			Regular Season					Playoffs				
Season	Club	League	GP	G	A	Pts	PIM	GP	G	A	Pts	PIM
2003-04	V.Frolunda Jr.	Swe-Jr.	28	7	10	17	14	10	2	3	5	2
2004-05	Frolunda Jr.	Swe-Jr.	33	12	30	42	14	6	2	5	7	0
2005-06	Frolunda Jr.	Swe-Jr.	12	6	11	17	2	1	0	1	1	0
	Frolunda	Sweden	39	3	3	6	8	11	0	0	0	6

AXELSSON, Dick (AHX-ehl-suhn, DIHK) DET.

Wing. Shoots left. 6'2", 198 lbs. Born, Stockholm, Sweden, April 25, 1987.
(Detroit's 3rd choice, 62nd overall, in 2006 Entry Draft).

			Regular Season					Playoffs				
Season	Club	League	GP	G	A	Pts	PIM	GP	G	A	Pts	PIM
2003-04	Huddinge IK U18	Swe-U18	13	3	1	4	38	....	....	....	....	....
2004-05	Huddinge IK U18	Swe-U18	1	0	0	0	0	....	....	....	....	....
	Huddinge IK Jr.	Swe-Jr.	31	12	4	16	34	3	1	0	1	0
2005-06	Huddinge IK Jr.	Swe-Jr.	28	19	15	34	157	....	....	....	....	....
	Huddinge IK	Sweden-3	31	23	6	29	14	5	1	2	3	6

AXELSSON, Emil (AHX-ehl-suhn, eh-MIHL) NYI

Defense. Shoots left. 6'3", 198 lbs. Born, Orebro, Sweden, March 19, 1986.
(NY Islanders' 7th choice, 210th overall, in 2004 Entry Draft).

			Regular Season					Playoffs				
Season	Club	League	GP	G	A	Pts	PIM	GP	G	A	Pts	PIM
2002-03	HC Orebro 90 Jr.	Swe-Jr.	27	7	9	16	2	....	....	....	....	....
2003-04	HC Orebro 90	Sweden-2	49	4	0	4	116	....	....	....	....	....
2004-05	Linkopings HC Jr.	Swe-Jr.	21	0	1	1	32	....	....	....	....	....
2005-06	IFK Arboga IK	Sweden-2	39	1	2	3	30	....	....	....	....	....

BABY, Stephen (BAH-bee, STEE-vehn) ATL.

Right wing. Shoots right. 6'5", 235 lbs. Born, Chicago, IL, January 31, 1980.
(Atlanta's 8th choice, 188th overall, in 1999 Entry Draft).

			Regular Season					Playoffs				
Season	Club	League	GP	G	A	Pts	PIM	GP	G	A	Pts	PIM
1997-98	Green Bay	USHL	56	17	17	34	85	4	1	3	4	8
1998-99	Green Bay	USHL	55	23	24	47	83	6	1	1	2	4
99-2000	Cornell Big Red	ECAC	31	4	10	14	52	....	....	....	....	....
2000-01	Cornell Big Red	ECAC	32	8	20	28	47	....	....	....	....	....
2001-02	Cornell Big Red	ECAC	35	9	23	32	42	....	....	....	....	....
2002-03	Cornell Big Red	ECAC	36	8	*33	41	60	....	....	....	....	....
2003-04	Chicago Wolves	AHL	68	14	12	26	72	10	1	4	5	6
2004-05	Chicago Wolves	AHL	64	6	3	9	115	6	0	0	0	12
2005-06	Chicago Wolves	AHL	39	7	15	22	44	....	....	....	....	....

ECAC Second All-Star Team (2002, 2003) • NCAA East Second All-American Team (2003)

BACKES, David (BA-kuhs, DAY-vihd) ST.L.

Center. Shoots right. 6'2", 200 lbs. Born, Blaine, MN, May 1, 1984.
(St. Louis' 2nd choice, 62nd overall, in 2003 Entry Draft).

			Regular Season					Playoffs				
Season	Club	League	GP	G	A	Pts	PIM	GP	G	A	Pts	PIM
99-2000	Spring Lake Park	High-MN	24	17	20	37	....	....	....	....	....	....
2000-01	Spring Lake Park	High-MN	24	29	46	75	....	....	....	....	....	....
2001-02	Chicago Steel	USHL	25	31	36	67	....	2	1	1	2	....
	Lincoln Stars	USHL	30	11	10	21	54	3	0	0	0	2
2002-03	Lincoln Stars	USHL	57	28	41	69	126	7	4	1	5	17
2003-04	Minnesota State	WCHA	39	16	21	37	66	....	....	....	....	....
2004-05	Minnesota State	WCHA	38	17	23	40	55	....	....	....	....	....
2005-06	Minnesota State	WCHA	38	13	29	42	91	....	....	....	....	....
	Peoria Rivermen	AHL	12	5	5	10	10	3	1	1	2	8

USHL First All-Star Team (2003) • WCHA All-Rookie Team (2004) • WCHA Second All-Star Team (2006) • NCAA West Second All-American Team (2006)

BACKSTROM, Nicklas (BAK-struhm, NIHK-las) WSH.

Center. Shoots left. 6', 183 lbs. Born, Gavle, Sweden, November 23, 1987.
(Washington's 1st choice, 4th overall, in 2006 Entry Draft).

			Regular Season					Playoffs				
Season	Club	League	GP	G	A	Pts	PIM	GP	G	A	Pts	PIM
2001-02	Brynas U18	Swe-U18	2	0	0	0	0	....	....	....	....	....
2002-03	Brynas U18	Swe-U18	STATISTICS NOT AVAILABLE									
2003-04	Brynas U18	Swe-U18	6	9	5	14	4	3	0	3	3	0
	Brynas IF Gavle Jr.	Swe-Jr.	21	2	6	8	2	5	0	0	0	4
2004-05	Brynas IF Gavle Jr.	Swe-Jr.	29	17	17	34	24	....	....	....	....	....
	Brynas IF Gavle	Sweden	19	0	0	0	2	....	....	....	....	....
	Brynas IF Gavle	Sweden	19	0	0	0	2	....	....	....	....	....
2005-06	Brynas IF Gavle Jr.	Swe-Jr.	....	....	....	....	....	1	0	0	0	2
	Brynas IF Gavle	Sweden	46	10	16	26	30	4	1	0	1	2

BACKSTROM, Nils (BAK-struhm, NIHLS) DET.

Defense. Shoots right. 6', 183 lbs. Born, Stockholm, Sweden, June 29, 1986.
(Detroit's 8th choice, 290th overall, in 2004 Entry Draft).

			Regular Season					Playoffs				
Season	Club	League	GP	G	A	Pts	PIM	GP	G	A	Pts	PIM
2003-04	Stocksund Jr.	Swe-Jr.	12	1	6	7	26	....	....	....	....	....
2004-05	Djurgarden Jr.	Swe-Jr.	31	0	5	5	75	....	....	....	....	....
2005-06	Djurgarden Jr.	Swe-Jr.	41	7	11	18	70	4	0	1	1	4
	Djurgarden	Sweden	1	0	0	0	0	....	....	....	....	....

BAGNALL, Drew (BAG-nuhl, DROO) FLA.

Defense. Shoots left. 6'3", 205 lbs. Born, Oakbank, Man., October 26, 1983.
(Dallas' 9th choice, 195th overall, in 2003 Entry Draft).

			Regular Season					Playoffs				
Season	Club	League	GP	G	A	Pts	PIM	GP	G	A	Pts	PIM
2000-01	Battlefords	SJHL	58	7	20	27	205	....	....	....	....	....
2001-02	Battlefords	SJHL	60	16	23	39	247	....	....	....	....	....
2002-03	Battlefords	SJHL	55	17	46	63	248	4	0	1	1	4
2003-04	St. Lawrence	ECAC	40	5	13	18	61	....	....	....	....	....
2004-05	St. Lawrence	ECACHL	37	7	12	19	68	....	....	....	....	....
2005-06	St. Lawrence	ECACHL	24	1	9	10	32	....	....	....	....	....

Traded to **Florida** by **Dallas** with Dallas' 2nd round compensatory choice (later traded to Phoenix - Phoenix selected Enver Lisin) in 2004 Entry Draft for Valeri Bure, March 8, 2004.

BAHENSKY, Zdenek (ba-HEHN-skee, z'DEHN-ehk) NYR

Right wing. Shoots left. 6'2", 195 lbs. Born, Most, Czech., January 3, 1986.
(NY Rangers' 7th choice, 73rd overall, in 2004 Entry Draft).

			Regular Season					Playoffs				
Season	Club	League	GP	G	A	Pts	PIM	GP	G	A	Pts	PIM
2001-02	Litvinov U17	CzR-U17	46	16	17	33	102	2	0	0	0	0
2002-03	Litvinov U17	CzR-U17	3	2	3	5	4	....	....	....	....	....
	Litvinov Jr.	CzRep-Jr.	31	4	2	6	8	....	....	....	....	....
2003-04	Litvinov Jr.	CzRep-Jr.	52	14	15	29	204	2	1	1	2	14
2004-05	Saskatoon Blades	WHL	66	14	17	31	101	4	0	0	0	2
2005-06	Saskatoon Blades	WHL	65	19	36	55	76	10	2	5	7	16

BAIER, Paul (BAI-uhr, PAWL) L.A.

Defense. Shoots right. 6'3", 212 lbs. Born, Summit, NJ, February 2, 1985.
(Los Angeles' 2nd choice, 95th overall, in 2004 Entry Draft).

			Regular Season					Playoffs				
Season	Club	League	GP	G	A	Pts	PIM	GP	G	A	Pts	PIM
2002-03	Deerfield Academy	High-MA	25	2	15	17	24	....	....	....	....	....
2003-04	Deerfield Academy	High-MA	23	6	4	10	22	....	....	....	....	....
2004-05	Brown U.	ECACHL	32	2	8	10	24	....	....	....	....	....
2005-06	Brown U.	ECACHL	30	0	6	6	18	....	....	....	....	....

BAILEY, Jason (BAY-lee, JAY-sohn) ANA.

Right wing. Shoots right. 6', 205 lbs. Born, Ottawa, Ont., June 4, 1987.
(Anaheim's 3rd choice, 63rd overall, in 2005 Entry Draft).

			Regular Season					Playoffs				
Season	Club	League	GP	G	A	Pts	PIM	GP	G	A	Pts	PIM
2003-04	Nepean Raiders	CJHL	45	14	14	28	119	18	2	7	9	35
2004-05	USNTDP	U-18	26	3	2	5	91	....	....	....	....	....
	USNTDP	NAHL	13	2	4	6	50	....	....	....	....	....
2005-06	U. of Michigan	CCHA	27	5	2	7	57	....	....	....	....	....

BAILEY, Kyle (BAY-lee, KIGHL) MIN.

Center. Shoots right. 6'2", 188 lbs. Born, Ponoka, Alta., October 15, 1986.
(Minnesota's 4th choice, 110th overall, in 2005 Entry Draft).

			Regular Season					Playoffs				
Season	Club	League	GP	G	A	Pts	PIM	GP	G	A	Pts	PIM
2002-03	Leduc Oil Kings	AMHL	35	23	19	42	56	....	....	....	....	....
	Portland	WHL	4	1	1	2	0	6	0	0	0	0
2003-04	Portland	WHL	70	9	15	24	85	5	0	1	1	0
2004-05	Portland	WHL	67	11	22	33	116	7	0	2	2	11
2005-06	Portland	WHL	66	18	35	53	145	7	2	4	6	6

BAINES, Ajay (BAYNZ, AY-JAY)

Center. Shoots left. 5'10", 179 lbs. Born, Kamloops, B.C., March 25, 1978.

			Regular Season					Playoffs				
Season	Club	League	GP	G	A	Pts	PIM	GP	G	A	Pts	PIM
1994-95	Kamloops	BCAHA	52	45	79	124	139	....	....	....	....	....
1995-96	Kamloops Blazers	WHL	68	14	29	43	43	....	....	....	....	....
1996-97	Kamloops Blazers	WHL	70	32	43	75	106	5	4	1	5	6
1997-98	Kamloops Blazers	WHL	72	34	25	59	88	....	....	....	....	....
1998-99	Kamloops Blazers	WHL	72	33	32	65	145	15	7	6	13	20
99-2000	Greenville Grrrowl	ECHL	67	24	31	55	102	15	2	5	7	13
2000-01	Norfolk Admirals	AHL	73	18	18	36	92	9	0	1	1	2
2001-02	Norfolk Admirals	AHL	80	16	28	44	70	4	0	1	1	0
2002-03	Norfolk Admirals	AHL	74	8	14	22	108	9	2	1	3	18
2003-04	Norfolk Admirals	AHL	80	15	27	42	81	8	1	3	4	13
2004-05	Norfolk Admirals	AHL	70	7	16	23	60	6	3	2	5	16
2005-06	Norfolk Admirals	AHL	32	4	4	8	45	....	....	....	....	....
	Omaha	AHL	24	8	4	12	26	....	....	....	....	....

Signed as a free agent by **Chicago**, August 1, 2001.

BALAN, Stanislav (BAY-luhn, STAN-ihs-lahv) NSH.

Center. Shoots left. 6'2", 161 lbs. Born, Hodonin, Czech., January 30, 1986.
(Nashville's 8th choice, 209th overall, in 2004 Entry Draft).

			Regular Season					Playoffs				
Season	Club	League	GP	G	A	Pts	PIM	GP	G	A	Pts	PIM
2001-02	HC Zlin Jr.	CzRep-Jr.	48	21	23	44	60	4	1	1	2	0
2002-03	HC Zlin Jr.	CzRep-Jr.	35	24	21	45	59	3	2	0	2	16
2003-04	HC Zlin Jr.	CzRep-Jr.	53	23	33	56	122	5	2	0	2	31
	HC Hame Zlin	CzRep	4	1	0	1	2	....	....	....	....	....
2004-05	SHK Hodonin	CzRep-3	5	3	2	5	20	....	....	....	....	....
	HC Zlin Jr.	CzRep-Jr.	37	10	13	23	131	2	0	0	0	2
2005-06	Portland	WHL	67	14	23	37	102	12	1	4	5	18

BALDWIN, Gord (BAHLD-wihn, GOHRD) CGY.

Defense. Shoots left. 6'5", 205 lbs. Born, Winnipeg, Man., March 1, 1987.
(Calgary's 2nd choice, 69th overall, in 2005 Entry Draft).

			Regular Season					Playoffs				
Season	Club	League	GP	G	A	Pts	PIM	GP	G	A	Pts	PIM
2003-04	Wpg. Thrashers	MMHL	39	5	16	21	66	....	....	....	....	....
2004-05	Medicine Hat	WHL	66	3	8	11	73	....	....	....	....	....
2005-06	Medicine Hat	WHL	71	4	20	24	119	13	0	9	9	22

BARANKA, Ivan (ba-RAN-kuh, IGH-vuhn) NYR

Defense. Shoots left. 6'3", 200 lbs. Born, Ilava, Czech., May 19, 1985.
(NY Rangers' 2nd choice, 50th overall, in 2003 Entry Draft).

			Regular Season					Playoffs				
Season	Club	League	GP	G	A	Pts	PIM	GP	G	A	Pts	PIM
2002-03	Dubnica Jr.	Slovak-Jr.	27	1	7	8	44	....	....	....	....	....
	Dubnica	Slovak-2	2	0	0	0	0	....	....	....	....	....
2003-04	Everett Silvertips	WHL	58	3	12	15	69	20	3	5	8	26
2004-05	Everett Silvertips	WHL	64	7	16	23	64	11	3	1	4	6
	Hartford Wolf Pack	AHL	....	....	....	....	....	1	0	0	0	0
2005-06	Hartford Wolf Pack	AHL	59	5	16	21	87	....	....	....	....	....

BARANOV, Konstantin (buh-RA-nawf, kawn-stuhn-TEEN) PHI.

Right wing. Shoots left. 6'2", 185 lbs. Born, Omsk, USSR, January 11, 1982.
(Philadelphia's 3rd choice, 126th overall, in 2002 Entry Draft).

			Regular Season					Playoffs				
Season	Club	League	GP	G	A	Pts	PIM	GP	G	A	Pts	PIM
1998-99	Omsk 2	Russia-4	23	18	8	26	40	....	....	....	....	....
	Avangard Omsk	Russia	1	0	0	0	0	2	0	0	0	0
99-2000	Omsk 2	Russia-3	33	15	8	23	46	....	....	....	....	....
	Avangard Omsk	Russia	1	0	0	0	2	....	....	....	....	....
2000-01	Kristall Saratov	Russia-2	26	6	9	15	26	....	....	....	....	....
	Ufa	Russia	8	1	0	1	4	....	....	....	....	....
2001-02	Avangard Omsk	Russia	5	0	0	0	6	....	....	....	....	....
	Mechel	Russia	6	1	2	3	2	....	....	....	....	....
	Lada Togliatti	Russia	20	2	4	6	18	3	0	2	2	0
2002-03	Avangard Omsk	Russia	6	0	1	1	2	....	....	....	....	....
	Ufa	Russia	11	2	2	4	0	....	....	....	....	....
	CSKA Moscow	Russia	14	4	1	5	10	....	....	....	....	....
	Omsk 2	Russia-3	3	4	6	10	2	....	....	....	....	....
2003-04	Avangard Omsk	Russia	51	6	10	16	50	11	2	2	4	6
2004-05	Omsk 2	Russia-3	7	5	7	12	20	....	....	....	....	....
	Avangard Omsk	Russia	21	3	2	5	16	....	....	....	....	....
2005-06	Dynamo Moscow	Russia	19	0	5	5	10	....	....	....	....	....
	SKA St. Petersburg	Russia	12	1	2	3	18	3	0	0	0	2

BARCH, Krys (BAHRCH, KRIHS) DAL.

Right wing. Shoots left. 6'2", 200 lbs. Born, Guelph, Ont., March 26, 1980.
(Washington's 3rd choice, 106th overall, in 1998 Entry Draft).

			Regular Season					Playoffs				
Season	Club	League	GP	G	A	Pts	PIM	GP	G	A	Pts	PIM
1995-96	Georgetown	OPJHL	41	6	8	14	10	....	....	....	....	....
1996-97	Georgetown	OPJHL	51	18	26	44	58	....	....	....	....	....
1997-98	London Knights	OHL	65	9	27	36	62	16	4	3	7	16
1998-99	London Knights	OHL	66	18	20	38	66	25	9	17	26	15
99-2000	London Knights	OHL	56	23	26	49	78	....	....	....	....	....
	Portland Pirates	AHL	....	....	....	....	....	4	0	2	2	2
2000-01	Portland Pirates	AHL	76	10	15	25	91	2	0	0	0	0
2001-02	Portland Pirates	AHL	29	3	8	11	28	....	....	....	....	....
	Richmond	ECHL	25	6	4	10	43	....	....	....	....	....
2002-03	Portland Pirates	AHL	36	1	7	8	49	....	....	....	....	....
2003-04			DID NOT PLAY									
2004-05	Norfolk Admirals	AHL	9	1	0	1	37	....	....	....	....	....
	Greenville Grrrowl	ECHL	55	11	19	30	154	3	0	0	0	36
2005-06	Iowa Stars	AHL	43	7	6	13	129	7	0	1	1	37
	Greenville Grrrowl	ECHL	14	10	4	14	75	....	....	....	....	....

Signed as a free agent by **Dallas**, July 18, 2006.

BARNES, Joe (BAHRNZ, JOH) CAR.

Center. Shoots left. 6'3", 212 lbs. Born, Winnipeg, Man., June 16, 1986.
(Carolina's 3rd choice, 64th overall, in 2005 Entry Draft).

			Regular Season					Playoffs				
Season	Club	League	GP	G	A	Pts	PIM	GP	G	A	Pts	PIM
2001-02	Winnipeg Sharks	MMHL	STATISTICS NOT AVAILABLE									
	Saskatoon Blades	WHL	1	0	0	0	0	....	....	....	....	....
2002-03	Saskatoon Blades	WHL	54	9	7	16	48	....	....	....	....	....
2003-04	Saskatoon Blades	WHL	58	5	17	22	90	....	....	....	....	....
2004-05	Saskatoon Blades	WHL	72	30	32	62	73	4	0	1	1	0
2005-06	Saskatoon Blades	WHL	55	25	27	52	55	7	2	4	6	8

BARRETT, Nathan (BAIR-uht, NAY-thun)

Center. Shoots left. 6', 189 lbs. Born, Vancouver, B.C., August 3, 1981.
(Vancouver's 6th choice, 241st overall, in 2000 Entry Draft).

			Regular Season					Playoffs				
Season	Club	League	GP	G	A	Pts	PIM	GP	G	A	Pts	PIM
1996-97	Langley Lions	BCAHA	90	107	109	216	96	....	....	....	....	....
1997-98	Tri-City Americans	WHL	47	1	1	2	23	....	....	....	....	....
1998-99	Tri-City Americans	WHL	33	9	9	18	19	....	....	....	....	....
	Lethbridge	WHL	22	12	9	21	19	4	1	0	1	0
99-2000	Lethbridge	WHL	72	44	38	82	38	....	....	....	....	....
2000-01	Lethbridge	WHL	70	46	53	99	66	5	1	1	2	6
2001-02	Lethbridge	WHL	72	45	*62	*107	100	4	0	1	1	6
2002-03	St. John's	AHL	69	9	22	31	35	....	....	....	....	....
2003-04	St. John's	AHL	49	17	21	38	41	....	....	....	....	....
2004-05	St. John's	AHL	61	17	22	39	34	3	0	1	1	0
2005-06	Norfolk Admirals	AHL	78	30	31	61	68	4	1	2	3	4

WHL East Second All-Star Team (2001) • WHL East First All-Star Team (2002)

Signed as a free agent by **Toronto**, July 31, 2002.

BARRIBALL, Jay (BEHR-ih-bahl, JAY) S.J.

Left wing. Shoots left. 5'9", 155 lbs. Born, Prior Lake, MN, May 27, 1987.
(San Jose's 6th choice, 203rd overall, in 2006 Entry Draft).

			Regular Season					Playoffs				
Season	Club	League	GP	G	A	Pts	PIM	GP	G	A	Pts	PIM
2004-05	Holy Angels	High-MN	30	32	49	81	....	....	....	....	....	....
2005-06	Holy Angels	High-MN	20	28	38	66	....	....	....	....	....	....
	Sioux Falls	USHL	13	5	7	12	2	5	2	1	3	0

BARTANUS, Marek (bahr-TA-nuhs, MAHR-ehk) T.B.

Right wing. Shoots right. 6'3", 209 lbs. Born, Liptovsky Mikulas, Czech., February 13, 1987.
(Tampa Bay's 4th choice, 92nd overall, in 2005 Entry Draft).

			Regular Season					Playoffs				
Season	Club	League	GP	G	A	Pts	PIM	GP	G	A	Pts	PIM
2003-04	HC Kosice U18	Svk-U18	4	3	2	5	2	....	....	....	....	....
	HC Kosice Jr.	Slovak-Jr.	41	23	11	34	40	3	1	2	3	8
2004-05	HC Kosice	Slovakia	24	2	1	3	2	....	....	....	....	....
	VTJ Trebisov	Slovak-2	1	0	0	0	0	....	....	....	....	....
	HC Kosice Jr.	Slovak-Jr.	34	14	14	28	99	8	1	1	2	16
2005-06	Owen Sound	OHL	49	7	12	19	47	10	2	4	6	8

BARTULIS, Oskars (bahr-TEW-lihs, AWHS-kahrs) PHI.

Defense. Shoots left. 6'2", 185 lbs. Born, Ogre, Latvia, January 21, 1987.
(Philadelphia's 2nd choice, 91st overall, in 2005 Entry Draft).

			Regular Season					Playoffs				
Season	Club	League	GP	G	A	Pts	PIM	GP	G	A	Pts	PIM
2001-02	Prizma '83 Riga	EEHL-B	3	1	0	1	2	....	....	....	....	....
	Prizma '83 Riga	Latvia	6	0	1	1	2	....	....	....	....	....
2002-03	Prizma '83 Riga	EEHL-B	12	5	5	10	12	....	....	....	....	....
	Vilki Riga	Latvia	....	0	1	1	12	....	....	....	....	....
2003-04	CSKA Moscow 2	Russia-3	65	3	9	12	....	....	....	....	....	....
2004-05	Moncton Wildcats	QMJHL	62	5	19	24	55	12	1	1	2	16
2005-06	Moncton Wildcats	QMJHL	54	6	25	31	84	21	1	9	10	22

QMJHL All-Rookie Team (2005) • Canadian Major Junior All-Rookie Team (2005)

BASS, Cody (BAS, KOH-dee) OTT.

Center. Shoots right. 6', 191 lbs. Born, Owen Sound, Ont., January 7, 1987.
(Ottawa's 3rd choice, 95th overall, in 2005 Entry Draft).

			Regular Season					Playoffs				
Season	Club	League	GP	G	A	Pts	PIM	GP	G	A	Pts	PIM
2003-04	Mississauga	OHL	61	3	7	10	30	24	2	3	5	21
2004-05	Mississauga	OHL	66	11	17	28	103	5	1	1	2	8
2005-06	Mississauga	OHL	67	16	25	41	152	....	....	....	....	....
	Binghamton	AHL	9	1	0	1	2	....	....	....	....	....

BEARSON, Zach (BEER-suhn, ZAK) FLA.

Right wing. Shoots right. 6'1", 180 lbs. Born, Houston, TX, June 13, 1987.
(Florida's 8th choice, 224th overall, in 2005 Entry Draft).

			Regular Season					Playoffs				
Season	Club	League	GP	G	A	Pts	PIM	GP	G	A	Pts	PIM
2002-03	Team Illinois	MWEHL	....	21	29	50	....	....	....	....	....	....
2003-04	Waterloo	USHL	53	7	11	18	65	9	4	1	5	12
2004-05	Waterloo	USHL	51	18	18	36	56	5	0	1	1	2
2005-06	Waterloo	USHL	56	13	21	34	73	....	....	....	....	....

Signed Letter of Intent to attend **U. of Wisconsin** (WCHA) in fall of 2006.

BEAULIEU, Josh (BOI-loh, JAWSH) PHI.

Center. Shoots left. 6', 180 lbs. Born, Windsor, Ont., January 10, 1987.
(Philadelphia's 4th choice, 152nd overall, in 2005 Entry Draft).

			Regular Season					Playoffs				
Season	Club	League	GP	G	A	Pts	PIM	GP	G	A	Pts	PIM
2003-04	London Knights	OHL	41	3	6	9	32	9	0	0	0	5
2004-05	London Knights	OHL	65	9	13	22	159	13	2	3	5	13
2005-06	London Knights	OHL	60	15	13	28	140	18	4	5	9	12

BEAVERSON, Luke (BEE-vuhr-suhn, LEWK) FLA.

Defense. Shoots left. 6'3", 208 lbs. Born, St. Paul, MN, December 11, 1984.
(Florida's 7th choice, 283rd overall, in 2004 Entry Draft).

			Regular Season					Playoffs				
Season	Club	League	GP	G	A	Pts	PIM	GP	G	A	Pts	PIM
2003-04	Green Bay	USHL	57	1	6	7	141	....	....	....	....	....
2004-05	Alaska-Anchorage	WCHA	37	0	2	2	48	....	....	....	....	....
2005-06	Alaska-Anchorage	WCHA	34	1	3	4	53	....	....	....	....	....

BELESKEY, Matt (beh-LEH-skee, MAT) ANA.

Left wing. Shoots left. 5'11", 202 lbs. Born, Windsor, Ont., June 7, 1988.
(Anaheim's 4th choice, 112th overall, in 2006 Entry Draft).

			Regular Season					Playoffs				
Season	Club	League	GP	G	A	Pts	PIM	GP	G	A	Pts	PIM
2004-05	Belleville Bulls	OHL	68	10	13	23	118	5	0	0	0	18
2005-06	Belleville Bulls	OHL	61	20	20	40	119	6	1	2	3	10

BELLAMY, Rob (BEHL-ah-mee, RAWB) **PHI.**

Right wing. Shoots right. 6', 190 lbs. Born, Providence, RI, May 30, 1985.
(Philadelphia's 1st choice, 92nd overall, in 2004 Entry Draft).

			Regular Season					Playoffs				
Season	**Club**	**League**	**GP**	**G**	**A**	**Pts**	**PIM**	**GP**	**G**	**A**	**Pts**	**PIM**
2002-03	Berkshire Bears	High-MA	32	21	21	42	128	....	....	....	....	....
2003-04	N.E. Jr. Coyotes	EJHL	36	19	21	40	95	....	....	....	....	....
2004-05	U. of Maine	H-East	28	3	4	7	34	....	....	....	....	....
2005-06	U. of Maine	H-East	40	6	9	15	77	....	....	....	....	....

BELLE, Shawn (BEHL, SHAWN) **MIN.**

Defense. Shoots left. 6'1", 230 lbs. Born, Edmonton, Alta., January 3, 1985.
(St. Louis' 1st choice, 30th overall, in 2003 Entry Draft).

			Regular Season					Playoffs				
Season	**Club**	**League**	**GP**	**G**	**A**	**Pts**	**PIM**	**GP**	**G**	**A**	**Pts**	**PIM**
99-2000	K of C Squires	AMBHL	34	7	20	27	36	....	....	....	....	....
2000-01	K of C Squires	AMBHL	39	18	30	48	69	....	....	....	....	....
	Regina Pats	WHL	4	0	3	3	0	....	....	....	....	....
	Tri-City Americans	WHL	2	0	1	1	0	....	....	....	....	....
2001-02	Tri-City Americans	WHL	64	1	17	18	51	5	2	1	3	2
2002-03	Tri-City Americans	WHL	66	7	14	21	79	....	....	....	....	....
2003-04	Tri-City Americans	WHL	55	9	20	29	68	11	3	5	8	15
2004-05	Tri-City Americans	WHL	62	13	32	45	76	5	1	1	2	6
2005-06	Iowa Stars	AHL	45	1	2	3	63	....	....	....	....	....
	Houston Aeros	AHL	16	1	1	2	18	8	1	0	1	4

Rights traded to **Dallas** by **St. Louis** for Jason Bacashihua, June 25, 2004. Traded to **Minnesota** by **Dallas** with Martin Skoula for Willie Mitchell and a 2nd round choice in 2007 Entry Draft, March 9, 2006.

BELLEMARE, Thomas (BEHL-mahr, TAW-muhs) **CGY.**

Right wing. Shoots right. 6'3", 222 lbs. Born, Shawinigan, Que., January 11, 1984.
(Calgary's 7th choice, 206th overall, in 2003 Entry Draft).

			Regular Season					Playoffs				
Season	**Club**	**League**	**GP**	**G**	**A**	**Pts**	**PIM**	**GP**	**G**	**A**	**Pts**	**PIM**
2002-03	Drummondville	QMJHL	67	5	3	8	474	....	....	....	....	....
2003-04	Drummondville	QMJHL	60	2	5	7	181	7	0	0	0	2
2004-05	Texas Wildcatters	ECHL	29	0	1	1	82	....	....	....	....	....
	Charlotte	ECHL	36	4	2	6	117	15	0	2	2	20
2005-06	Omaha	AHL	2	0	0	0	5	....	....	....	....	....
	Las Vegas	ECHL	51	6	3	9	115	....	....	....	....	....

BELLER, Greg (BEHL-uhr, GREHG) **NYR**

Wing. Shoots left. 6'3", 213 lbs. Born, Vancouver, B.C., January 22, 1987.
(NY Rangers' 8th choice, 178th overall, in 2005 Entry Draft).

			Regular Season					Playoffs				
Season	**Club**	**League**	**GP**	**G**	**A**	**Pts**	**PIM**	**GP**	**G**	**A**	**Pts**	**PIM**
2004-05	Lake of the Woods	High-MN	21	23	25	48	38	....	....	....	....	....
	Borderland	SJHL	6	2	5	7	0	2	0	1	1	2
2005-06	Green Bay	USHL	3	1	0	1	2	....	....	....	....	....

• Missed majority of 2005-06 season recovering from collarbone injury suffered during the pre-season and re-injured in a game on November 29, 2005. Signed Letter of Intent to attend **Yale** (ECACHL) in fall of 2006.

BELLISSIMO, Vince (behl-IHS-ih-moh, VIHNTS) **CAR.**

Center. Shoots right. 6', 199 lbs. Born, Toronto, Ont., December 14, 1982.
(Florida's 6th choice, 158th overall, in 2002 Entry Draft).

			Regular Season					Playoffs				
Season	**Club**	**League**	**GP**	**G**	**A**	**Pts**	**PIM**	**GP**	**G**	**A**	**Pts**	**PIM**
99-2000	St. Mike's B's	OPJHL	47	30	29	59	31	....	....	....	....	....
2000-01	St. Mike's B's	OPJHL	47	32	64	96	28	6	6	8	14	
2001-02	Topeka	USHL	61	37	39	76	33	....	....	....	....	....
2002-03	Western Mich.	CCHA	37	19	17	36	18	....	....	....	....	....
2003-04	Western Mich.	CCHA	38	13	27	40	42	....	....	....	....	....
2004-05	Western Mich.	CCHA	35	17	20	37	81	....	....	....	....	....
	San Antonio	AHL	12	3	3	6	2	....	....	....	....	....
2005-06	Lowell	AHL	47	8	6	14	20	....	....	....	....	....
	Florida Everblades	ECHL	19	13	10	23	2	8	5	8	13	4

USHL First All-Star Team (2002) • USHL Top Forward (2002) • CCHA All-Rookie Team (2003)

Signed as a free agent by **Carolina**, September 15, 2005.

BENDFELD, Jordan (BENHD-felhd, JOHR-dahn) **PHX.**

Defense. Shoots right. 6'2", 222 lbs. Born, Leduc, Alta., February 9, 1988.
(Phoenix's 6th choice, 152nd overall, in 2006 Entry Draft).

			Regular Season					Playoffs				
Season	**Club**	**League**	**GP**	**G**	**A**	**Pts**	**PIM**	**GP**	**G**	**A**	**Pts**	**PIM**
2003-04	Leduc Oil Kings	AMHL	36	0	9	9	22	....	....	....	....	....
2004-05	Leduc Oil Kings	AMHL	21	1	5	6	96	....	....	....	....	....
	Medicine Hat	WHL	16	0	0	0	4	2	0	0	0	2
2005-06	Medicine Hat	WHL	65	2	10	12	92	13	0	4	4	27

BENOIT, Andre (behn-WAH, AWN-dray) **MTL.**

Defense. Shoots left. 5'11", 190 lbs. Born, St. Albert, Ont., January 6, 1984.

			Regular Season					Playoffs				
Season	**Club**	**League**	**GP**	**G**	**A**	**Pts**	**PIM**	**GP**	**G**	**A**	**Pts**	**PIM**
2000-01	Kitchener Rangers	OHL	65	16	19	35	37	....	....	....	....	....
2001-02	Kitchener Rangers	OHL	62	13	32	45	77	4	1	0	1	8
2002-03	Kitchener Rangers	OHL	65	22	45	67	77	21	1	16	17	16
2003-04	Kitchener Rangers	OHL	65	24	51	75	67	5	1	1	2	6
2004-05	Kitchener Rangers	OHL	67	24	53	77	72	15	5	13	18	6
2005-06	Hamilton Bulldogs	AHL	70	7	19	26	60	....	....	....	....	....

Signed as a free agent by **Montreal**. January 9, 2006.

BERGFORS, Nicklas (BUHRG-fohrs, NIHK-las) **N.J.**

Right wing. Shoots right. 5'11", 190 lbs. Born, Sodertalje, Sweden, March 7, 1987.
(New Jersey's 1st choice, 23rd overall, in 2005 Entry Draft).

			Regular Season					Playoffs				
Season	**Club**	**League**	**GP**	**G**	**A**	**Pts**	**PIM**	**GP**	**G**	**A**	**Pts**	**PIM**
2002-03	Sodertalje SK U18	Swe-U18	4	4	4	8	0	....	....	....	....	....
	Sodertalje SK Jr.	Swe-Jr.	13	1	5	6	4	....	....	....	....	....
2003-04	Sodertalje SK U18	Swe-U18	5	14	4	18	4	2	0	1	1	6
	Sodertalje SK Jr.	Swe-Jr.	31	13	17	30	22	2	1	1	2	0
2004-05	Sodertalje SK Jr.	Swe-Jr.	21	18	16	34	25	3	0	3	3	4
	Sodertalje SK	Sweden	25	1	0	1	2	2	0	0	0	0
2005-06	Albany River Rats	AHL	65	17	23	40	10	....	....	....	....	....

BERGLUND, Patrik (BUHRG-luhnd, PAT-rihk) **ST.L.**

Center. Shoots left. 6'4", 187 lbs. Born, Vesteras, Sweden, June 2, 1988.
(St. Louis' 2nd choice, 25th overall, in 2006 Entry Draft).

			Regular Season					Playoffs				
Season	**Club**	**League**	**GP**	**G**	**A**	**Pts**	**PIM**	**GP**	**G**	**A**	**Pts**	**PIM**
2002-03	Vasteras U18	Swe-U18	1	0	1	1	0	....	....	....	....	....
2003-04	Vasteras U18	Swe-U18	10	4	1	5	18	....	....	....	....	....
2004-05	Vasteras U18	Swe-U18	5	2	1	3	4	3	0	1	1	6
	Vasteras Jr.	Swe-Jr.	25	5	5	10	14	....	....	....	....	....
2005-06	Vasteras Jr.	Swe-Jr.	27	17	12	29	38	....	....	....	....	....
	VIK Vasteras HK	Sweden-2	21	3	1	4	4	....	....	....	....	....

BERNIER, Marc-Andre (BAIRN-yay, MAHRK-AWN-dray) **VAN.**

Right wing. Shoots right. 6'4", 198 lbs. Born, Laval, Que., February 5, 1985.
(Vancouver's 2nd choice, 60th overall, in 2003 Entry Draft).

			Regular Season					Playoffs				
Season	**Club**	**League**	**GP**	**G**	**A**	**Pts**	**PIM**	**GP**	**G**	**A**	**Pts**	**PIM**
99-2000	Laval-Laurentides	QAAA	15	2	3	5	10	9	1	0	1	2
2000-01	Laval-Laurentides	QAAA	26	6	12	18	16	8	3	2	5	6
2001-02	Halifax	QMJHL	49	0	6	6	20	2	0	0	0	0
2002-03	Halifax	QMJHL	67	29	29	58	43	21	9	8	17	8
2003-04	Cape Breton	QMJHL	58	27	23	50	27	5	1	3	4	2
2004-05	Halifax	QMJHL	65	27	23	50	51	12	4	5	9	8
2005-06	Manitoba Moose	AHL	16	0	0	0	7	....	....	....	....	....
	Columbia Inferno	ECHL	44	6	17	23	34	....	....	....	....	....

BERNIKOV, Ruslan (BAIR-nih-kahf, roos-LAHN) **DAL.**

Right wing. Shoots left. 6'3", 216 lbs. Born, Vidnoye, USSR, December 4, 1977.
(Dallas' 6th choice, 139th overall, in 2000 Entry Draft).

			Regular Season					Playoffs				
Season	**Club**	**League**	**GP**	**G**	**A**	**Pts**	**PIM**	**GP**	**G**	**A**	**Pts**	**PIM**
1996-97	Dyn'o Moscow 2	Russia-3	32	11	4	15	20	....	....	....	....	....
	Dynamo Moscow	Russia	2	0	0	0	0	....	....	....	....	....
1997-98	Yekaterinburg 2	Russia-3	2	1	1	2	0	....	....	....	....	....
	Yekaterinburg	Russia	43	7	7	14	55	....	....	....	....	....
1998-99	Dynamo Moscow	Russia	6	0	1	1	2	....	....	....	....	....
	Krylja Sovetov	Russia	20	3	1	4	24	....	....	....	....	....
	CSKA Moscow	Russia	1	0	0	0	0	....	....	....	....	....
	Cherepovets	Russia	5	0	0	0	0	1	0	0	0	0
99-2000	Dynamo Moscow	Russia	6	2	1	3	2	....	....	....	....	....
	Amur Khabarovsk	Russia	14	3	6	9	10	5	3	1	4	2
2000-01	Amur Khabarovsk	Russia	33	1	4	5	40	....	....	....	....	....
2001-02	Amur Khabarovsk	Russia	38	7	10	17	20	....	....	....	....	....
2002-03	Krylja Sovetov	Russia	50	15	10	25	40	....	....	....	....	....
2003-04	Lada Togliatti	Russia	49	8	10	18	51	6	0	0	0	4
2004-05	Lada Togliatti	Russia	16	3	1	4	14	....	....	....	....	....
	Cherepovets	Russia	33	9	6	15	8	....	....	....	....	....
2005-06	Mytischi	Russia	21	2	3	5	40	....	....	....	....	....
	Ak Bars Kazan	Russia	5	0	0	0	0	....	....	....	....	....
	Ufa	Russia	16	3	2	5	26	6	1	0	1	4

BERRY, Alex (BAIR-ee, AL-ehx) **TOR.**

Right wing. Shoots right. 6'2", 212 lbs. Born, Danvers, MA, March 6, 1986.
(Toronto's 3rd choice, 153rd overall, in 2005 Entry Draft).

			Regular Season					Playoffs				
Season	**Club**	**League**	**GP**	**G**	**A**	**Pts**	**PIM**	**GP**	**G**	**A**	**Pts**	**PIM**
2003-04	Cushing	High-MA	31	19	16	35	50	....	....	....	....	....
2004-05	Junior Bruins	EJHL	53	17	25	42	170	....	....	....	....	....
2005-06	Massachusetts	H-East	24	1	1	2	33	....	....	....	....	....

BERTI, Adam (BUHR-tee, A-duhm) **CHI.**

Left wing. Shoots left. 6'3", 207 lbs. Born, Scarborough, Ont., July 1, 1986.
(Chicago's 6th choice, 68th overall, in 2004 Entry Draft).

			Regular Season					Playoffs				
Season	**Club**	**League**	**GP**	**G**	**A**	**Pts**	**PIM**	**GP**	**G**	**A**	**Pts**	**PIM**
2002-03	Oshawa Generals	OHL	15	3	3	6	12	....	....	....	....	....
2003-04	Oshawa Generals	OHL	66	17	29	46	44	7	0	2	2	4
2004-05	Oshawa Generals	OHL	66	23	28	51	53	....	....	....	....	....
2005-06	Oshawa Generals	OHL	23	16	18	34	28	....	....	....	....	....
	Erie Otters	OHL	39	17	12	29	24	....	....	....	....	....

BERTRAM, Dan (BUHR-truhm, DAN) **CHI.**

Right wing. Shoots right. 5'10", 177 lbs. Born, Calgary, Alta., January 14, 1987.
(Chicago's 3rd choice, 54th overall, in 2005 Entry Draft).

			Regular Season					Playoffs				
Season	**Club**	**League**	**GP**	**G**	**A**	**Pts**	**PIM**	**GP**	**G**	**A**	**Pts**	**PIM**
2003-04	Camrose Kodiaks	AJHL	44	22	33	55	....	....	....	....	....	....
2004-05	Boston College	H-East	39	9	8	17	58	....	....	....	....	....
2005-06	Boston College	H-East	39	10	16	26	38	....	....	....	....	....

AJHL Rookie of the Year (2004)

BETTS, Kaleb (BEHTZ, KAHL-uhb) **NSH.**

Center. Shoots left. 5'10", 180 lbs. Born, Maple Ridge, B.C., January 10, 1983.
(Nashville's 6th choice, 235th overall, in 2002 Entry Draft).

			Regular Season					Playoffs				
Season	**Club**	**League**	**GP**	**G**	**A**	**Pts**	**PIM**	**GP**	**G**	**A**	**Pts**	**PIM**
2000-01	Chilliwack Chiefs	BCHL	58	17	20	37	79	....	....	....	....	....
2001-02	Chilliwack Chiefs	BCHL	54	35	37	72	92	....	....	....	....	....
2002-03	Nebraska-Omaha	CCHA	DID NOT PLAY – ACADEMICALLY INELIGIBLE									
2003-04	Nebraska-Omaha	CCHA	35	9	13	22	48	....	....	....	....	....
2004-05	Nebraska-Omaha	CCHA	32	5	11	16	88	....	....	....	....	....
2005-06	Nebraska-Omaha	CCHA	32	6	12	18	59	....	....	....	....	....

BEZRUKOV, Dmitri (behz-ROO-kahv, dih-MEE-tree) T.B.

Left wing. Shoots left. 6'3", 187 lbs. Born, Kazan, USSR, November 9, 1977.
(Tampa Bay's 11th choice, 259th overall, in 2001 Entry Draft).

			Regular Season					Playoffs				
Season	Club	League	GP	G	A	Pts	PIM	GP	G	A	Pts	PIM
1997-98	Nizhnekamsk 2	Russia-3	8	0	1	1	6	....	....	....	....	....
	Nizhnekamsk	Russia	14	5	3	8	4	....	....	....	....	....
1998-99	Nizhnekamsk 2	Russia-4	1	3	0	3	0	....	....	....	....	....
	Nizhnekamsk	Russia	39	4	6	10	18	3	1	0	1	2
99-2000	Nizhnekamsk 2	Russia-3	4	0	0	0	6	....	....	....	....	....
	Leninogorsk	Russia-2	8	2	1	3	8	....	....	....	....	....
	Nizhnekamsk	Russia	28	5	6	11	45	3	0	1	1	2
2000-01	Nizhnekamsk	Russia	35	7	10	17	54	4	0	2	2	2
2001-02	Nizhnekamsk	Russia	38	5	6	11	45	....	....	....	....	....
2002-03	Spartak Moscow	Russia	51	10	12	22	24	....	....	....	....	....
2003-04	Nizhnekamsk	Russia	17	1	3	4	10	....	....	....	....	....
	Cherepovets	Russia	8	0	0	0	0	....	....	....	....	....
	Cherepovets 2	Russia-3	12	7	10	17	20	....	....	....	....	....
2004-05	Perm	Russia	27	1	3	4	18	....	....	....	....	....
	Nizhny Novgorod	Russia-2	18	7	5	12	16	6	0	1	1	4
2005-06	Nizhny Novgorod	Russia-2	25	4	4	8	32	....	....	....	....	....
	Almetjevsk 2	Russia-3	3	2	0	2	0	....	....	....	....	....
	Almetjevsk	Russia-2	18	3	4	7	18	8	0	0	0	8

BICKELL, Bryan (bih-KEHL, BRIGH-uhn) CHI.

Left wing. Shoots left. 6'4", 226 lbs. Born, Bowmanville, Ont., March 9, 1986.
(Chicago's 3rd choice, 41st overall, in 2004 Entry Draft).

			Regular Season					Playoffs				
Season	Club	League	GP	G	A	Pts	PIM	GP	G	A	Pts	PIM
2000-01	Tor. Red Wings	GTHL	68	24	26	50	20	5	3	1	4	4
2001-02	Tor. Red Wings	GTHL	65	31	41	72	76	2	2	2	4	0
2002-03	Ottawa 67's	OHL	50	7	10	17	4	20	5	3	8	12
2003-04	Ottawa 67's	OHL	59	20	16	36	76	7	3	0	3	11
2004-05	Ottawa 67's	OHL	66	22	32	54	95	21	5	12	17	32
2005-06	Ottawa 67's	OHL	41	28	22	50	41	....	....	....	....	....
	Windsor Spitfires	OHL	26	17	16	33	19	7	5	5	10	10

BIEGA, Alex (bee-AY-guh, AL-ehx) BUF.

Defense. Shoots right. 5'10", 191 lbs. Born, Montreal, Que., April 4, 1988.
(Buffalo's 5th choice, 147th overall, in 2006 Entry Draft).

			Regular Season					Playoffs				
Season	Club	League	GP	G	A	Pts	PIM	GP	G	A	Pts	PIM
2004-05	Salisbury School	High-CT	27	9	22	31	45	....	....	....	....	....
2005-06	Salisbury School	High-CT	28	10	17	27	51	....	....	....	....	....

BIRNER, Michal (BUHR-nuhr, MEE-khahl) ST.L.

Left wing. Shoots left. 6', 183 lbs. Born, Litomerice, Czech., March 2, 1986.
(St. Louis' 4th choice, 116th overall, in 2004 Entry Draft).

			Regular Season					Playoffs				
Season	Club	League	GP	G	A	Pts	PIM	GP	G	A	Pts	PIM
2000-01	Slavia U17	CzR-U17	48	16	24	40	20	7	0	1	1	6
2001-02	Slavia U17	CzR-U17	46	24	34	58	28	21	1	0	1	0
2002-03	Slavia U17	CzR-U17	5	5	6	11	14	5	4	3	7	20
	HC Slavia Praha Jr.	CzRep-Jr.	31	4	8	12	10	3	1	0	1	2
2003-04	HC Slavia Praha	CzRep	1	0	0	0	0	....	....	....	....	....
	HC Slavia Praha Jr.	CzRep-Jr.	55	25	35	60	112	2	0	1	1	4
2004-05	Barrie Colts	OHL	28	4	10	14	12	....	....	....	....	....
	Saginaw Spirit	OHL	31	7	21	28	29	....	....	....	....	....
2005-06	Saginaw Spirit	OHL	60	31	54	85	91	4	1	3	4	8

BISSONNETTE, Paul (bih-sawn-EHT, PAWL) PIT.

Defense. Shoots left. 6'3", 212 lbs. Born, Welland, Ont., March 11, 1985.
(Pittsburgh's 5th choice, 121st overall, in 2003 Entry Draft).

			Regular Season					Playoffs				
Season	Club	League	GP	G	A	Pts	PIM	GP	G	A	Pts	PIM
2001-02	North Bay	OHL	57	3	3	6	21	5	0	0	0	2
2002-03	Saginaw Spirit	OHL	67	7	16	23	57	....	....	....	....	....
2003-04	Saginaw Spirit	OHL	67	5	14	19	96	....	....	....	....	....
2004-05	Saginaw Spirit	OHL	28	1	6	7	46	....	....	....	....	....
	Owen Sound	OHL	35	2	11	13	46	8	1	3	4	2
2005-06	Wilkes-Barre	AHL	55	1	5	6	60	11	0	1	1	4
	Wheeling Nailers	ECHL	14	3	7	10	4	....	....	....	....	....

BITZ, Byron (BIHTZ, BIGH-ruhn) BOS.

Right wing. Shoots right. 6'3", 200 lbs. Born, Saskatoon, Sask., July 21, 1984.
(Boston's 4th choice, 107th overall, in 2003 Entry Draft).

			Regular Season					Playoffs				
Season	Club	League	GP	G	A	Pts	PIM	GP	G	A	Pts	PIM
2000-01	Saskatoon	SMBHL	40	17	35	52	....	....	....	....	....	....
2001-02	Saskatoon	SMHL	41	25	48	73	69	11	12	10	22	9
2002-03	Nanaimo Clippers	BCHL	58	27	46	73	59	....	....	....	....	....
2003-04	Cornell Big Red	ECAC	31	5	16	21	36	....	....	....	....	....
2004-05	Cornell Big Red	ECACHL	29	5	10	15	20	....	....	....	....	....
2005-06	Cornell Big Red	ECACHL	35	10	18	28	52	....	....	....	....	....

BLANCHARD, Nicolas (BLAN-shard, NIHK-o-las) CAR.

Center. Shoots left. 6'3", 176 lbs. Born, Granby, Que., May 31, 1987.
(Carolina's 8th choice, 192nd overall, in 2005 Entry Draft).

			Regular Season					Playoffs				
Season	Club	League	GP	G	A	Pts	PIM	GP	G	A	Pts	PIM
2003-04	Antoine-Girouard	QAAA	42	24	28	52	28	13	9	6	15	4
2004-05	Chicoutimi	QMJHL	69	13	26	39	31	17	2	2	4	10
2005-06	Chicoutimi	QMJHL	60	15	29	44	51	9	1	2	3	4

BLATAK, Miroslav (BLAT-ak, MEER-oh-slav) DET.

Defense. Shoots left. 5'11", 172 lbs. Born, Gottwaldov/Zlin, Czech., May 25, 1982.
(Detroit's 3rd choice, 129th overall, in 2001 Entry Draft).

			Regular Season					Playoffs				
Season	Club	League	GP	G	A	Pts	PIM	GP	G	A	Pts	PIM
99-2000	HC Vsetin U17	CzR-U17	30	0	0	0	12	....	....	....	....	....
	HC Vsetin Jr.	CzRep-Jr.	12	0	2	2	10	....	....	....	....	....
2000-01	HC Vsetin U17	CzR-U17	33	7	8	15	56	....	....	....	....	....
	HC Vsetin Jr.	CzRep-Jr.	12	2	4	6	54	7	0	6	6	6
	Zlin	CzRep	8	0	2	2	0	6	0	0	0	0
2001-02	Jihlava Jr.	CzRep-Jr.	3	0	0	0	0	....	....	....	....	....
	HC Zlin Jr.	CzRep-Jr.	3	0	0	0	8	....	....	....	....	....
	HC Dukla Jihlava	CzRep-2	1	0	0	0	0	2	0	0	0	0
	Zlin	CzRep	39	4	7	11	18	11	1	2	3	8
2002-03	HC Hame Zlin	CzRep	49	4	12	16	34	....	....	....	....	....
2003-04	HC Hame Zlin	CzRep	50	5	10	15	34	17	3	3	6	10
2004-05	HC Hame Zlin	CzRep	52	4	8	12	30	17	2	4	6	18
2005-06	HC Hame Zlin	CzRep	47	8	13	21	34	6	1	2	3	8

BLIZNAK, Mario (BLIZH-nak, MAHR-ee-oh) VAN.

Center. Shoots left. 6', 185 lbs. Born, Trencin, Czech., March 6, 1987.
(Vancouver's 6th choice, 205th overall, in 2005 Entry Draft).

			Regular Season					Playoffs				
Season	Club	League	GP	G	A	Pts	PIM	GP	G	A	Pts	PIM
2003-04	Dubnica U18	Svk-U18	46	25	26	51	62	....	....	....	....	....
	Dubnica Jr.	Slovak-Jr.	2	1	0	1	2	....	....	....	....	....
2004-05	Dubnica U18	Svk-U18	14	5	8	13	45	....	....	....	....	....
	Dubnica Jr.	Slovak-Jr.	36	22	17	39	38	....	....	....	....	....
	Dubnica	Slovakia	19	0	0	0	14	....	....	....	....	....
2005-06	Vancouver Giants	WHL	69	9	12	21	29	18	4	1	5	14

BLOM, Stefan (BLAWM, STEH-fan) DET.

Defense. Shoots left. 6'2", 189 lbs. Born, Stockholm, Sweden, July 30, 1985.
(Detroit's 5th choice, 194th overall, in 2003 Entry Draft).

			Regular Season					Playoffs				
Season	Club	League	GP	G	A	Pts	PIM	GP	G	A	Pts	PIM
2002-03	Hammarby U18	Swe-U18	18	3	0	0	4	....	....	....	....	....
	Hammarby Jr.	Swe-Jr.	27	4	2	6	12	2	0	0	0	0
2003-04	Djurgarden Jr.	Swe-Jr.	33	2	5	7	16	....	....	....	....	....
2004-05	Hammarby Jr.	Swe-Jr.	18	0	2	2	16	....	....	....	....	....
	Arlanda	Sweden-3	10	0	2	2	8	....	....	....	....	....
2005-06	Arlanda	Sweden-3	26	1	7	8	16	....	....	....	....	....

BLUNDEN, Michael (BLUHN-dehn, MIGHK-uhl) CHI.

Right wing. Shoots right. 6'3", 207 lbs. Born, Toronto, Ont., December 15, 1986.
(Chicago's 2nd choice, 43rd overall, in 2005 Entry Draft).

			Regular Season					Playoffs				
Season	Club	League	GP	G	A	Pts	PIM	GP	G	A	Pts	PIM
2002-03	Erie Otters	OHL	63	10	7	17	55	....	....	....	....	....
2003-04	Erie Otters	OHL	52	22	17	39	53	3	0	0	0	0
2004-05	Erie Otters	OHL	61	22	19	41	75	2	0	0	0	2
2005-06	Erie Otters	OHL	60	46	38	84	63	....	....	....	....	....
	Norfolk Admirals	AHL	11	1	5	6	2	1	0	0	0	0

BOBROV, Viktor (bawb-RAWV, VIHK-tohr) CGY.

Center. Shoots left. 6'1", 176 lbs. Born, Novocheboksarsk, USSR, January 1, 1984.
(Calgary's 7th choice, 146th overall, in 2002 Entry Draft).

			Regular Season					Playoffs				
Season	Club	League	GP	G	A	Pts	PIM	GP	G	A	Pts	PIM
99-2000	Nizh. Novgorod 2	Russia-3	6	6	1	7	0	....	....	....	....	....
2000-01	CSKA Moscow 2	Russia-3	31	30	17	47	32	4	4	3	7	4
2001-02	HK CSKA 2	Russia-3	36	11	16	27	20	....	....	....	....	....
2002-03	Elektrostal	Russia-2	48	7	7	14	16	....	....	....	....	....
2003-04	Kristall Elektrostal	Russia-2	60	6	10	16	38	....	....	....	....	....
2004-05	CSKA Moscow 2	Russia-3	STATISTICS NOT AVAILABLE									
2005-06	HK Dmitrov	Russia-2	55	8	10	18	22	4	0	1	1	2

BODIE, Troy (BOH-dee, TROI) EDM.

Right wing. Shoots right. 6'4", 213 lbs. Born, Portage La Prairie, Man., January 25, 1985.
(Edmonton's 12th choice, 278th overall, in 2003 Entry Draft).

			Regular Season					Playoffs				
Season	Club	League	GP	G	A	Pts	PIM	GP	G	A	Pts	PIM
2001-02	Central Plains	MMMHL	40	22	21	43	10	....	....	....	....	....
2002-03	Kelowna Rockets	WHL	35	4	4	8	36	11	1	1	2	2
2003-04	Kelowna Rockets	WHL	71	8	12	20	112	17	7	3	10	6
2004-05	Kelowna Rockets	WHL	72	24	24	48	96	24	4	13	17	26
2005-06	Kelowna Rockets	WHL	72	28	25	53	117	12	5	4	9	8

BODNARCHUK, Andrew (BAWD-nahr-chuhk, an-DROO) BOS.

Defense. Shoots left. 5'10", 172 lbs. Born, Drumheller, Alta., July 11, 1988.
(Boston's 5th choice, 128th overall, in 2006 Entry Draft).

			Regular Season					Playoffs				
Season	Club	League	GP	G	A	Pts	PIM	GP	G	A	Pts	PIM
2003-04	Dartmouth	NSMHL	58	16	23	39	81	....	....	....	....	....
2004-05	St. Paul's School	High-NH	36	3	15	18	....	....	....	....	....	....
2005-06	Halifax	QMJHL	68	6	17	23	136	11	0	2	2	22

BODROV, Denis (bawd-RAWV, DEH-nihs) PHI.

Defense. Shoots left. 6', 185 lbs. Born, Moscow, Russia, August 22, 1986.
(Philadelphia's 4th choice, 55th overall, in 2006 Entry Draft).

			Regular Season					Playoffs				
Season	Club	League	GP	G	A	Pts	PIM	GP	G	A	Pts	PIM
2002-03	Lada Togliatti 2	Russia-3	9	0	0	0	2	....	....	....	....	....
2003-04	Lada Togliatti 2	Russia-3	45	3	4	7	58	....	....	....	....	....
2004-05	CSK VVS Samara	Russia-2	33	1	6	7	57	....	....	....	....	....
2005-06	Lada Togliatti	Russia	35	2	2	4	42	8	0	0	0	8

BOIS, Danny (BOIZ, DA-nee) **OTT.**

Right wing. Shoots right. 6'1", 197 lbs. Born, Thunder Bay, Ont., June 1, 1983.
(Colorado's 2nd choice, 97th overall, in 2001 Entry Draft).

			Regular Season					Playoffs				
Season	Club	League	GP	G	A	Pts	PIM	GP	G	A	Pts	PIM
1998-99	Thunder Bay Kings	TBMHL	15	7	12	19	28	....	....	....	....	....
99-2000	Wellington Dukes	OPJHL	37	15	20	35	115	....	....	....	....	....
2000-01	London Knights	OHL	66	21	16	37	218	5	2	1	3	19
2001-02	London Knights	OHL	62	16	14	30	256	12	2	2	4	47
2002-03	London Knights	OHL	56	19	13	32	207	13	4	6	10	38
2003-04	London Knights	OHL	52	14	25	39	242	7	4	4	8	29
2004-05	Binghamton	AHL	72	2	4	6	287	6	0	1	1	2
2005-06	Binghamton	AHL	79	18	17	35	224	....	....	....	....	....

Signed as a free agent by **Ottawa**, April 30, 2004.

BOLF, Lukas (BAWLF, LOO-kahsh) **PIT.**

Defense. Shoots left. 6'1", 190 lbs. Born, Vrchlabi, Czech., February 20, 1985.
(Pittsburgh's 7th choice, 169th overall, in 2003 Entry Draft).

			Regular Season					Playoffs				
Season	Club	League	GP	G	A	Pts	PIM	GP	G	A	Pts	PIM
99-2000	Karlovy Vary Jr.	CzRep-Jr.	43	2	7	9	57	....	....	....	....	....
2000-01	Sparta U17	CzR-U17	42	4	13	17	54	....	....	....	....	....
2001-02	HPK U18	Fin-U18	6	1	5	6	12	1	0	0	0	0
	HPK Jr.	Fin-Jr.	25	0	4	4	18	5	0	0	0	2
	Sparta Jr.	CzRep-Jr.	21	2	3	5	35	....	....	....	....	....
2002-03	Sparta Jr.	CzRep-Jr.	28	3	7	10	....	....	....	....	....	....
2003-04	Barrie Colts	OHL	56	2	18	20	42	12	0	2	2	26
2004-05	Barrie Colts	OHL	56	6	25	31	59	6	0	2	2	8
2005-06	Sparta Jr.	CzRep-Jr.	7	1	6	7	8	....	....	....	....	....
	HC Sparta Praha	CzRep	10	0	0	0	2	....	....	....	....	....
	Jind. Hradec	CzRep-2	10	0	0	0	14	....	....	....	....	....
	HC Vsetin	CzRep	25	0	1	1	14	....	....	....	....	....
	HC Vsetin	CzRep-Q	....	....	....	....	....	6	0	0	0	4

BOLL, Jared (BAWL, JAIR-ehd) **CBJ**

Right wing. Shoots right. 6'2", 190 lbs. Born, Crystal Lake, IL, May 13, 1986.
(Columbus' 4th choice, 101st overall, in 2005 Entry Draft).

			Regular Season					Playoffs				
Season	Club	League	GP	G	A	Pts	PIM	GP	G	A	Pts	PIM
2003-04	Lincoln Stars	USHL	57	6	8	14	*176	....	....	....	....	....
2004-05	Lincoln Stars	USHL	59	23	24	47	*294	4	1	3	4	25
2005-06	Plymouth Whalers	OHL	65	19	22	41	205	13	2	4	6	21

BOLLAND, Dave (BOHL-uhnd, DAYV) **CHI.**

Center. Shoots right. 6', 170 lbs. Born, Toronto, Ont., June 5, 1986.
(Chicago's 2nd choice, 32nd overall, in 2004 Entry Draft).

			Regular Season					Playoffs				
Season	Club	League	GP	G	A	Pts	PIM	GP	G	A	Pts	PIM
2000-01	Tor. Red Wings	GTHL	95	79	67	146		....	....	....	....	....
2001-02	Tor. Red Wings	GTHL	36	35	35	70	40	....	....	....	....	....
2002-03	London Knights	OHL	64	7	10	17	21	14	2	1	3	2
2003-04	London Knights	OHL	65	37	30	67	58	15	3	10	13	18
2004-05	London Knights	OHL	66	34	51	85	97	18	11	14	25	30
2005-06	London Knights	OHL	59	*57	73	130	104	15	*15	9	24	41

OHL First All-Star Team (2006)

BOLT, Bobby (BOHLT, BAW-bee) **ANA.**

Left wing. Shoots left. 6'3", 223 lbs. Born, Thunder Bay, Ont., April 29, 1987.
(Anaheim's 4th choice, 127th overall, in 2005 Entry Draft).

			Regular Season					Playoffs				
Season	Club	League	GP	G	A	Pts	PIM	GP	G	A	Pts	PIM
2003-04	Strathroy Rockets	OHA-B	39	5	14	19	41	....	....	....	....	....
	London Knights	OHL	8	1	0	1	2	....	....	....	....	....
2004-05	Kingston	OHL	67	11	14	25	92	....	....	....	....	....
2005-06	Kingston	OHL	68	5	10	15	89	6	0	0	0	4

BONNEAU, Jimmy (BAW-noh, JIHM-mee) **MTL.**

Left wing. Shoots left. 6'3", 217 lbs. Born, Baie-Comeau, Que., March 22, 1985.
(Montreal's 10th choice, 241st overall, in 2003 Entry Draft).

			Regular Season					Playoffs				
Season	Club	League	GP	G	A	Pts	PIM	GP	G	A	Pts	PIM
2000-01	Jonquiere Elites	QAAA	1	0	0	0	0	....	....	....	....	....
2001-02	Jonquiere Elites	QAAA	40	5	10	15	55	3	1	1	2	2
2002-03	Montreal Rocket	QMJHL	65	1	5	6	261	7	0	0	0	12
2003-04	PEI Rocket	QMJHL	70	7	12	19	263	11	1	0	1	12
2004-05	PEI Rocket	QMJHL	70	11	11	22	234	....	....	....	....	....
2005-06	Long Beach	ECHL	65	1	5	6	137	....	....	....	....	....

BOOTH, David (BOOTH, DAY-vihd) **FLA.**

Left wing. Shoots left. 6', 212 lbs. Born, Detroit, MI, November 24, 1984.
(Florida's 3rd choice, 53rd overall, in 2004 Entry Draft).

			Regular Season					Playoffs				
Season	Club	League	GP	G	A	Pts	PIM	GP	G	A	Pts	PIM
2000-01	Det. Compuware	NAHL	42	17	13	30	44	2	1	0	1	2
2001-02	USNTDP	U-18	40	12	6	18	17	....	....	....	....	....
	USNTDP	USHL	12	4	3	7	6	....	....	....	....	....
	USNTDP	NAHL	6	1	3	4	18	....	....	....	....	....
2002-03	Michigan State	CCHA	39	17	19	36	53	....	....	....	....	....
2003-04	Michigan State	CCHA	30	8	10	18	30	....	....	....	....	....
2004-05	Michigan State	CCHA	29	7	9	16	30	....	....	....	....	....
2005-06	Michigan State	CCHA	37	13	22	35	50	....	....	....	....	....

CCHA All-Rookie Team (2003)

BORER, Casey (BOHR-uhr, KAY-see) **CAR.**

Defense. Shoots left. 6'2", 197 lbs. Born, Minneapolis, MN, July 28, 1985.
(Carolina's 3rd choice, 69th overall, in 2004 Entry Draft).

			Regular Season					Playoffs				
Season	Club	League	GP	G	A	Pts	PIM	GP	G	A	Pts	PIM
2002-03	USNTDP	U-18	46	2	2	4	36	....	....	....	....	....
	USNTDP	NAHL	10	1	2	3	10	....	....	....	....	....
2003-04	St. Cloud State	WCHA	31	0	8	8	18	....	....	....	....	....
2004-05	St. Cloud State	WCHA	35	0	11	11	40	....	....	....	....	....
2005-06	St. Cloud State	WCHA	42	3	8	11	24	....	....	....	....	....

BOUCHARD, Francois (BOO-shahrd, frahn-SWUH) **WSH.**

Right wing. Shoots left. 6', 180 lbs. Born, Sherbrooke, Que., April 26, 1988.
(Washington's 4th choice, 35th overall, in 2006 Entry Draft).

			Regular Season					Playoffs				
Season	Club	League	GP	G	A	Pts	PIM	GP	G	A	Pts	PIM
2004-05	Baie-Comeau	QMJHL	54	11	13	24	13	6	1	1	2	2
2005-06	Baie-Comeau	QMJHL	69	33	69	102	66	4	1	0	1	6

BOURDON, Luc (BOOR-duhn, LEWK) **VAN.**

Defense. Shoots left. 6'2", 199 lbs. Born, Shippagan, N.B., February 16, 1987.
(Vancouver's 1st choice, 10th overall, in 2005 Entry Draft).

			Regular Season					Playoffs				
Season	Club	League	GP	G	A	Pts	PIM	GP	G	A	Pts	PIM
2003-04	Val-d'Or Foreurs	QMJHL	64	2	6	8	58	7	1	0	1	4
2004-05	Val-d'Or Foreurs	QMJHL	70	13	19	32	117	....	....	....	....	....
2005-06	Val-d'Or Foreurs	QMJHL	20	2	18	20	54	....	....	....	....	....
	Moncton Wildcats	QMJHL	10	1	7	8	8	16	0	3	3	22

BOURQUE, Chris (BOHRK, KRIHS) **WSH.**

Center. Shoots left. 5'7", 177 lbs. Born, Boston, MA, January 29, 1986.
(Washington's 4th choice, 33rd overall, in 2004 Entry Draft).

			Regular Season					Playoffs				
Season	Club	League	GP	G	A	Pts	PIM	GP	G	A	Pts	PIM
2002-03	Cushing	High-MA	28	31	26	57	49	....	....	....	....	....
2003-04	Cushing	High-MA	31	37	53	90	96	....	....	....	....	....
2004-05	Boston University	H-East	35	10	13	23	50	....	....	....	....	....
	Portland Pirates	AHL	6	1	1	2	2	....	....	....	....	....
2005-06	Hershey Bears	AHL	52	8	28	36	40	1	0	0	0	0

Hockey East All-Rookie Team (2005)

BOURRET, Alex (BUHR-ray, AL-ehx) **ATL.**

Right wing. Shoots left. 5'10", 210 lbs. Born, Drummondville, Que., October 5, 1986.
(Atlanta's 1st choice, 16th overall, in 2005 Entry Draft).

			Regular Season					Playoffs				
Season	Club	League	GP	G	A	Pts	PIM	GP	G	A	Pts	PIM
2001-02	Magog	QAAA	40	26	34	60	105	....	....	....	....	....
2002-03	Sherbrooke	QMJHL	61	13	15	28	73	12	1	1	2	10
2003-04	Lewiston	QMJHL	65	22	41	63	94	7	4	5	9	20
2004-05	Lewiston	QMJHL	65	31	55	86	172	8	6	8	14	25
2005-06	Shawinigan	QMJHL	67	44	70	114	133	7	3	4	7	14

QMJHL Second All-Star Team (2005, 2006)

BOYCHUK, Johnny (BOI-chuhk, JAW-nee) **COL.**

Defense. Shoots right. 6'3", 225 lbs. Born, Edmonton, Alta., January 19, 1984.
(Colorado's 2nd choice, 61st overall, in 2002 Entry Draft).

			Regular Season					Playoffs				
Season	Club	League	GP	G	A	Pts	PIM	GP	G	A	Pts	PIM
1998-99	Edm. Cycle	AMBHL	36	8	20	28	59	....	....	....	....	....
99-2000	Edm. Cycle	AMHL	35	6	17	23	59	....	....	....	....	....
2000-01	Calgary Hitmen	WHL	66	4	8	12	61	12	1	1	2	17
2001-02	Calgary Hitmen	WHL	70	8	32	40	85	7	1	1	2	6
2002-03	Calgary Hitmen	WHL	40	8	18	26	58	....	....	....	....	....
	Moose Jaw	WHL	27	5	17	22	32	13	2	6	8	29
2003-04	Moose Jaw	WHL	62	13	20	33	71	10	1	9	10	9
2004-05	Hershey Bears	AHL	80	3	12	15	69	....	....	....	....	....
2005-06	Lowell	AHL	74	6	26	32	73	....	....	....	....	....

BOYD, Dustin (BOID, DUHS-tihn) **CGY.**

Center. Shoots left. 6', 188 lbs. Born, Winnipeg, Man., July 16, 1986.
(Calgary's 3rd choice, 98th overall, in 2004 Entry Draft).

			Regular Season					Playoffs				
Season	Club	League	GP	G	A	Pts	PIM	GP	G	A	Pts	PIM
2001-02	Winnipeg Warriors	MMMHL	40	50	57	107	16	....	....	....	....	....
2002-03	Moose Jaw	WHL	63	11	17	28	15	13	0	3	3	2
2003-04	Moose Jaw	WHL	72	18	20	38	40	10	2	2	4	8
2004-05	Moose Jaw	WHL	66	26	35	61	57	5	1	2	3	2
2005-06	Moose Jaw	WHL	64	48	42	90	34	22	7	11	18	10

WHL East First All-Star Team (2006)

BOYLE, Brian (BOIL, BRIGH-uhn) **L.A.**

Center. Shoots left. 6'6", 222 lbs. Born, Dorchester, MA, December 18, 1984.
(Los Angeles' 2nd choice, 26th overall, in 2003 Entry Draft).

			Regular Season					Playoffs				
Season	Club	League	GP	G	A	Pts	PIM	GP	G	A	Pts	PIM
2000-01	St. Sebastian's	High-MA	25	20	19	39		....	....	....	....	....
2001-02	St. Sebastian's	High-MA	28	21	26	47	22	....	....	....	....	....
2002-03	St. Sebastian's	High-MA	31	32	31	62	46	....	....	....	....	....
2003-04	Boston College	H-East	35	5	3	8	36	....	....	....	....	....
2004-05	Boston College	H-East	40	19	8	27	64	....	....	....	....	....
2005-06	Boston College	H-East	42	22	*30	52	90	....	....	....	....	....

Hockey East First All-Star Team (2006) • NCAA East Second All-American Team (2006)

BRADFORD, Brock (BRAD-fohrd, BRAHK) **BOS.**

Center. Shoots right. 5'8", 168 lbs. Born, Burnaby, B.C., January 7, 1987.
(Boston's 8th choice, 217th overall, in 2005 Entry Draft).

			Regular Season					Playoffs				
Season	Club	League	GP	G	A	Pts	PIM	GP	G	A	Pts	PIM
2002-03	Richmond	PIJHL	18	12	12	24	....	....	....	....	....	....
	Coquitlam Express	BCHL	36	11	23	34	14	....	....	....	....	....
2003-04	Coquitlam Express	BCHL	57	36	49	85	....	....	....	....	....	....
2004-05	Omaha Lancers	USHL	60	24	33	57	16	5	0	1	1	0
2005-06	Boston College	H-East	42	6	12	18	8	....	....	....	....	....

BRASSARD, Derick (bra-SAHRD, DAIR-ihk) **CBJ**

Center. Shoots left. 6', 180 lbs. Born, Hull, Que., September 22, 1987.
(Columbus' 1st choice, 6th overall, in 2006 Entry Draft).

			Regular Season					Playoffs				
Season	Club	League	GP	G	A	Pts	PIM	GP	G	A	Pts	PIM
2004-05	Drummondville	QMJHL	69	25	51	76	25	6	1	5	6	6
2005-06	Drummondville	QMJHL	58	44	72	116	92	7	5	4	9	10

BRAUN, Constantin — (BRAWN, kawn-stuhn-TIHN) — L.A.

Left wing. Shoots left. 6'3", 198 lbs. Born, Lampertheim, Germany, March 11, 1988.
(Los Angeles' 9th choice, 164th overall, in 2006 Entry Draft).

			Regular Season					Playoffs				
Season	Club	League	GP	G	A	Pts	PIM	GP	G	A	Pts	PIM
2003-04	Mannheim Jr.	Ger-Jr.	30	12	5	17	42	....	....	....	....	....
2004-05	Eisb. Jrs. Berlin	German-3	1	0	0	0	0	....	....	....	....	....
	Eisb. Jrs. Berl. Jr.	Ger-Jr.	29	14	20	34	125	6	5	4	9	16
2005-06	Eisb. Jrs. Berl. Jr.	Ger-Jr.	7	8	4	12	14	1	1	0	1	6
	Eisbaren Berlin	Germany	6	0	0	0	0	....	....	....	....	....
	Eisb. Jrs. Berlin	German-3	24	13	10	23	34	....	....	....	....	....

BREAULT, Benjamin — (BRAWLT, BEHN-jah-mihn) — BUF.

Center. Shoots left. 5'10", 177 lbs. Born, Pembroke, Ont., February 21, 1988.
(Buffalo's 6th choice, 207th overall, in 2006 Entry Draft).

			Regular Season					Playoffs				
Season	Club	League	GP	G	A	Pts	PIM	GP	G	A	Pts	PIM
2004-05	Baie-Comeau	QMJHL	54	13	27	40	27	4	2	0	2	0
2005-06	Baie-Comeau	QMJHL	68	30	38	68	60	4	0	2	2	4

BRENT, Tim — (BREHNT, TIHM) — ANA.

Center. Shoots right. 6', 196 lbs. Born, Cambridge, Ont., March 10, 1984.
(Anaheim's 3rd choice, 75th overall, in 2004 Entry Draft).

			Regular Season					Playoffs				
Season	Club	League	GP	G	A	Pts	PIM	GP	G	A	Pts	PIM
99-2000	Cambridge	OHA-B	40	19	16	35	42	....	....	....	....	....
2000-01	St. Michael's	OHL	64	9	19	28	31	18	2	8	10	6
2001-02	St. Michael's	OHL	61	19	40	59	52	14	7	12	19	20
2002-03	St. Michael's	OHL	60	24	42	66	74	19	7	17	24	14
2003-04	St. Michael's	OHL	53	26	41	67	105	18	4	13	17	24
2004-05	Cincinnati	AHL	46	5	13	18	42	12	0	1	1	6
2005-06	Portland Pirates	AHL	37	15	9	24	32	15	4	4	8	16

• Re-entered NHL Entry Draft. Originally Anaheim's 2nd choice, 37th overall, in 2002 Entry Draft.

BROOKBANK, Sheldon — (BRUK-bank, SHEHL-dohn) — NSH.

Defense. Shoots right. 6'2", 200 lbs. Born, Lanigan, Sask., October 3, 1980.

			Regular Season					Playoffs				
Season	Club	League	GP	G	A	Pts	PIM	GP	G	A	Pts	PIM
2000-01	Humboldt Broncos	SJHL	59	14	35	49	281	....	....	....	....	....
2001-02	Grand Rapids	AHL	6	0	1	1	24	....	....	....	....	....
	Mississippi	ECHL	62	8	21	29	137	10	1	4	5	27
2002-03	Grand Rapids	AHL	69	2	11	13	136	15	1	3	4	28
2003-04	Cincinnati	AHL	74	2	9	11	216	9	0	2	2	20
2004-05	Cincinnati	AHL	60	1	11	12	181	11	0	0	0	40
2005-06	Milwaukee	AHL	73	9	26	35	232	21	1	8	9	49

Signed as a free agent by **Anaheim**, July 21, 2003. Signed as a free agent by **Nashville**, August 4, 2005.

BROOKS, Alex — (BROOKS, AL-ehx) — N.J.

Defense. Shoots right. 6'1", 195 lbs. Born, Madison, WI, August 21, 1976.

			Regular Season					Playoffs				
Season	Club	League	GP	G	A	Pts	PIM	GP	G	A	Pts	PIM
1993-94	Madison Capitols	USHL	13	3	11	14	....	....	....	....	....	....
1994-95	Madison West	High-WI	24	13	28	41	....	....	....	....	....	....
1995-96	Green Bay	USHL	46	3	22	25	....	....	....	....	....	....
1996-97	U. of Wisconsin	WCHA	DID NOT PLAY – INJURED									
1997-98	U. of Wisconsin	WCHA	40	1	4	5	72	....	....	....	....	....
1998-99	U. of Wisconsin	WCHA	37	0	3	3	73	....	....	....	....	....
99-2000	U. of Wisconsin	WCHA	41	4	10	14	78	....	....	....	....	....
2000-01	U. of Wisconsin	WCHA	41	3	16	19	76	....	....	....	....	....
2001-02	Jokerit Helsinki	Finland	53	1	3	4	109	12	0	0	0	11
2002-03	Albany River Rats	AHL	66	0	7	7	56	....	....	....	....	....
2003-04	Albany River Rats	AHL	77	2	6	8	100	....	....	....	....	....
2004-05	Albany River Rats	AHL	63	0	6	6	83	....	....	....	....	....
2005-06	Albany River Rats	AHL	58	1	4	5	81	....	....	....	....	....

• Missed entire 1996-97 season recovering from back injury suffered during off-season training, August, 1996. Signed as a free agent by **New Jersey**, July 12, 2002.

BROOKS, Brendan — (BROOKS, BREHN-duhn) — DET.

Center. Shoots right. 5'10", 185 lbs. Born, St. Catherines, Ont., November 26, 1978.

			Regular Season					Playoffs				
Season	Club	League	GP	G	A	Pts	PIM	GP	G	A	Pts	PIM
1997-98	Owen Sound	OHL	25	3	10	13	6	....	....	....	....	....
	North Bay	OHL	32	7	5	12	26	....	....	....	....	....
	Mississippi	ECHL	1	0	1	1	0	....	....	....	....	....
1998-99	Quad City	UHL	61	18	17	35	67	15	3	1	4	8
99-2000	Quad City	UHL	73	26	26	52	102	14	6	3	9	35
2000-01	Dayton Bombers	ECHL	65	29	18	47	95	8	2	3	5	20
	Cincinnati	IHL	1	0	0	0	0	....	....	....	....	....
	Lowell	AHL	5	0	1	1	17	....	....	....	....	....
2001-02	Manchester	AHL	9	0	2	2	10	....	....	....	....	....
2004-05	Worcester IceCats	AHL	79	20	18	38	36	....	....	....	....	....
2005-06	Peoria Rivermen	AHL	79	14	13	27	61	4	1	0	1	4

Signed as a free agent by **Detroit**, August 7, 2006.

BROPHEY, Evan — (BROH-fee, EH-vehn) — CHI.

Center/Left wing. Shoots left. 6'1", 203 lbs. Born, Kitchener, Ont., December 3, 1986.
(Chicago's 4th choice, 68th overall, in 2005 Entry Draft).

			Regular Season					Playoffs				
Season	Club	League	GP	G	A	Pts	PIM	GP	G	A	Pts	PIM
2002-03	Barrie Colts	OHL	61	12	14	26	36	6	0	0	0	2
2003-04	Barrie Colts	OHL	67	14	11	25	63	12	4	3	7	4
2004-05	Barrie Colts	OHL	10	3	7	10	13	....	....	....	....	....
	Belleville Bulls	OHL	53	25	36	61	42	5	2	1	3	2
2005-06	Belleville Bulls	OHL	22	9	17	26	39	....	....	....	....	....
	Plymouth Whalers	OHL	40	10	25	35	42	13	4	7	11	18

BROSNIHAN, Pat — (BRAWS-nih-han, PAT) — PHX.

Right wing. Shoots right. 6'4", 214 lbs. Born, Worcester, MA, August 20, 1986.
(Phoenix's 5th choice, 212th overall, in 2005 Entry Draft).

			Regular Season					Playoffs				
Season	Club	League	GP	G	A	Pts	PIM	GP	G	A	Pts	PIM
2003-04	Worcester	High-MA	25	28	26	54	30	....	....	....	....	....
2004-05	Worcester	High-MA	26	20	44	64	48	....	....	....	....	....
2005-06	Yale	ECACHL	19	0	1	1	31	....	....	....	....	....

BROUWER, Troy — (BROW-uhr, TROI) — CHI.

Right wing. Shoots right. 6'3", 220 lbs. Born, Vancouver, B.C., August 17, 1985.
(Chicago's 13th choice, 214th overall, in 2004 Entry Draft).

			Regular Season					Playoffs				
Season	Club	League	GP	G	A	Pts	PIM	GP	G	A	Pts	PIM
2001-02	Moose Jaw	WHL	13	0	0	0	7	....	....	....	....	....
2002-03	Moose Jaw	WHL	59	9	12	21	54	13	1	2	3	14
2003-04	Moose Jaw	WHL	72	23	26	49	111	10	3	0	3	12
2004-05	Moose Jaw	WHL	71	22	25	47	132	5	1	2	3	8
2005-06	Moose Jaw	WHL	72	49	53	*102	122	17	10	4	14	34

WHL East First All-Star Team (2006)

BROWN, Mike — (BROWN, MIGHK) — VAN.

Right wing. Shoots right. 6', 210 lbs. Born, Northbrook, IL, June 24, 1985.
(Vancouver's 4th choice, 159th overall, in 2004 Entry Draft).

			Regular Season					Playoffs				
Season	Club	League	GP	G	A	Pts	PIM	GP	G	A	Pts	PIM
2000-01	Chicago Chill	USAHA	66	27	23	50	....	....	....	....	....	....
2001-02	USNTDP	U-17	17	6	4	10	13	....	....	....	....	....
	USNTDP	NAHL	46	5	11	16	56	....	....	....	....	....
2002-03	USNTDP	U-18	34	5	3	8	16	....	....	....	....	....
	USNTDP	NAHL	9	0	3	3	29	....	....	....	....	....
2003-04	U. of Michigan	CCHA	42	8	5	13	51	....	....	....	....	....
2004-05	U. of Michigan	CCHA	35	3	5	8	95	....	....	....	....	....
2005-06	Manitoba Moose	AHL	73	7	8	15	139	13	1	2	3	17

BROWN, Paul — (BROWN, PAWL) — NSH.

Right wing. Shoots right. 6'3", 184 lbs. Born, Edmonton, Alta., July 21, 1984.
(Nashville's 6th choice, 89th overall, in 2003 Entry Draft).

			Regular Season					Playoffs				
Season	Club	League	GP	G	A	Pts	PIM	GP	G	A	Pts	PIM
99-2000	Prince George	BCAHA	65	84	120	204	260	....	....	....	....	....
	Regina Pats	WHL	3	0	0	0	0	....	....	....	....	....
2000-01	Regina Pats	WHL	33	3	1	4	83	....	....	....	....	....
	Kamloops Blazers	WHL	30	6	11	17	118	2	0	0	0	4
2001-02	Kamloops Blazers	WHL	37	7	12	19	130	1	0	0	0	0
2002-03	Kamloops Blazers	WHL	67	21	36	57	231	6	3	0	3	20
2003-04	Kamloops Blazers	WHL	59	11	20	31	222	5	0	1	1	13
2004-05	Milwaukee	AHL	20	3	2	5	90	7	2	0	2	25
	Trenton Titans	ECHL	20	2	4	6	63	12	5	6	11	32
2005-06	Milwaukee	AHL	41	3	1	4	59	18	0	0	0	27
	Rockford IceHogs	UHL	3	0	0	0	4	....	....	....	....	....

• Missed majority of 2001-02 season recovering from off-season ankle injury, August 20, 2001.

BROWNLEE, Chad — (BROWN-lee, CHAD) — VAN.

Defense. Shoots right. 6'2", 184 lbs. Born, Kelowna, B.C., July 12, 1984.
(Vancouver's 6th choice, 190th overall, in 2003 Entry Draft).

			Regular Season					Playoffs				
Season	Club	League	GP	G	A	Pts	PIM	GP	G	A	Pts	PIM
2001-02	Vernon Vipers	BCHL	55	6	12	18	62	....	....	....	....	....
2002-03	Vernon Vipers	BCHL	58	8	16	24	63	18	2	7	9	14
2003-04	Minnesota State	WCHA	35	2	1	3	44	....	....	....	....	....
2004-05	Minnesota State	WCHA	36	1	1	2	60	....	....	....	....	....
2005-06	Minnesota State	WCHA	29	1	1	2	47	....	....	....	....	....

BUCKLEY, Brendan — (BUHK-lee, BREHN-duhn) — L.A.

Defense. Shoots right. 6'1", 205 lbs. Born, Boston, MA, February 26, 1977.
(Anaheim's 3rd choice, 117th overall, in 1996 Entry Draft).

			Regular Season					Playoffs				
Season	Club	League	GP	G	A	Pts	PIM	GP	G	A	Pts	PIM
1994-95	Boston Jr. Bruins	Exhib.	48	22	43	65	164	....	....	....	....	....
1995-96	Boston College	H-East	34	0	4	4	72	....	....	....	....	....
1996-97	Boston College	H-East	38	2	6	8	90	....	....	....	....	....
1997-98	Boston College	H-East	41	1	12	13	69	....	....	....	....	....
1998-99	Boston College	H-East	43	1	13	14	75	....	....	....	....	....
99-2000	Cincinnati	AHL	4	0	0	0	6	....	....	....	....	....
	Quad City	UHL	61	1	10	11	73	9	1	0	1	10
2000-01	Wilkes-Barre	AHL	63	2	8	10	62	21	0	2	2	33
2001-02	Wilkes-Barre	AHL	80	1	19	20	116	....	....	....	....	....
2002-03	Wilkes-Barre	AHL	80	2	6	8	99	6	0	0	0	2
2003-04	Wilkes-Barre	AHL	45	2	4	6	61	....	....	....	....	....
	Syracuse Crunch	AHL	30	0	4	4	40	7	0	0	0	14
2004-05	Worcester IceCats	AHL	63	3	13	16	128	....	....	....	....	....
2005-06	Peoria Rivermen	AHL	73	2	9	11	104	4	0	0	0	4

Signed as a free agent by **Pittsburgh**, September 28, 2000. Traded to **Columbus** by **Pittsburgh** for Pauli Levokari, February 10, 2004. Signed as a free agent by **Worcester** (AHL), October 25, 2004. Signed as a free agent by **Los Angeles**, July 10, 2006.

BUMAGIN, Alexander — (buh-MAH-gihn, al-ehx-AN-duhr) — EDM.

Wing. Shoots left. 6', 180 lbs. Born, Togliatti, Russia, March 1, 1987.
(Edmonton's 5th choice, 170th overall, in 2006 Entry Draft).

			Regular Season					Playoffs				
Season	Club	League	GP	G	A	Pts	PIM	GP	G	A	Pts	PIM
2002-03	Lada Togliatti 2	Russia-3	9	4	1	5	2	....	....	....	....	....
2003-04	Lada Togliatti 2	Russia-3	22	4	9	13	12	4	0	1	1	4
2004-05	Lada Togliatti	Russia	7	2	0	2	2	....	....	....	....	....
	Lada Togliatti 2	Russia-3	STATISTICS NOT AVAILABLE									
	Lada Togliatti	Russia	7	2	0	2	2	....	....	....	....	....
2005-06	Lada Togliatti	Russia	40	9	12	21	28	8	0	3	3	4

BURAVCHIKOV, Vyacheslav — (burh-AV-chih-kawf, VYACH-ih-slav) — BUF.

Defense. Shoots left. 6', 189 lbs. Born, Moscow, USSR, May 22, 1987.
(Buffalo's 7th choice, 191st overall, in 2005 Entry Draft).

			Regular Season					Playoffs				
Season	Club	League	GP	G	A	Pts	PIM	GP	G	A	Pts	PIM
2003-04	Krylja Sovetov 2	Russia-3	STATISTICS NOT AVAILABLE									
2004-05	Krylja Sovetov 2	Russia-3	15	5	6	11	22	....	....	....	....	....
	Krylja Sovetov	Russia-2	26	4	1	5	14	3	0	0	0	2
2005-06	Mytischi	Russia	43	1	2	3	24	9	1	0	1	4

BURISH, Adam (BUHR-ish, A-duhm) **CHI.**

Right wing. Shoots right. 6'1", 189 lbs. Born, Madison, WI, January 6, 1983.
(Chicago's 9th choice, 282nd overall, in 2002 Entry Draft).

			Regular Season					Playoffs				
Season	Club	League	GP	G	A	Pts	PIM	GP	G	A	Pts	PIM
2000-01	Edgewood	High-WI	22	25	30	55	22	....	....	....	....	....
2001-02	Green Bay	USHL	61	24	33	57	122	1	0	0	0	0
2002-03	U. of Wisconsin	WCHA	19	0	6	6	32	....	....	....	....	....
2003-04	U. of Wisconsin	WCHA	43	6	13	19	63	....	....	....	....	....
2004-05	U. of Wisconsin	WCHA	41	13	7	20	41	....	....	....	....	....
2005-06	U. of Wisconsin	WCHA	42	9	24	33	67	....	....	....	....	....

BURKI, Codey (BUHR-kee, KOH-dee) **COL.**

Center. Shoots left. 6', 190 lbs. Born, Winnipeg, Man., November 17, 1987.
(Colorado's 3rd choice, 59th overall, in 2006 Entry Draft).

			Regular Season					Playoffs				
Season	Club	League	GP	G	A	Pts	PIM	GP	G	A	Pts	PIM
2004-05	Brandon	WHL	68	10	13	23	48	24	6	5	11	13
2005-06	Brandon	WHL	70	27	34	61	69	6	0	3	3	2

BUT, Anton (BOOT, AN-tawn) **T.B.**

Left wing. Shoots left. 6'1", 201 lbs. Born, Kharkov, USSR, July 3, 1980.
(New Jersey's 7th choice, 119th overall, in 1998 Entry Draft).

			Regular Season					Playoffs				
Season	Club	League	GP	G	A	Pts	PIM	GP	G	A	Pts	PIM
1995-96	Yaroslavl 2	CIS-2	60	30	12	42	10	....	....	....	....	....
1996-97	Yaroslavl 2	Russia-3	70	30	20	50	20	....	....	....	....	....
1997-98	Yaroslavl 2	Russia-2	48	12	5	17	28	....	....	....	....	....
1998-99	Yaroslavl 2	Russia-3	22	12	8	20	59	....	....	....	....	....
	Torpedo Yaroslavl	Russia	5	0	0	0	0	....	....	....	....	....
99-2000	Yaroslavl 2	Russia-3	1	0	0	0	2	....	....	....	....	....
	Torpedo Yaroslavl	Russia	26	2	5	7	16	8	2	1	3	0
2000-01	Yaroslavl	Russia	42	14	6	20	14	11	1	3	4	8
2001-02	Yaroslavl	Russia	48	14	11	25	14	6	0	1	1	2
2002-03	Yaroslavl	Russia	44	16	13	29	16	9	1	2	3	6
2003-04	Yaroslavl	Russia	51	11	10	21	24	3	0	0	0	0
2004-05	Yaroslavl	Russia	60	12	22	34	58	8	3	3	6	0
2005-06	Yaroslavl	Russia	49	16	21	37	26	11	2	1	3	2

Rights traded to **Tampa Bay** by **New Jersey** with Josef Boumedienne and Sascha Goc for Andrei Zyuzin, November 9, 2001.

BUTCHER, Matt (BUH-chuhr, MAT) **VAN.**

Center. Shoots left. 6'1", 185 lbs. Born, Bellingham, WA, January 1, 1987.
(Vancouver's 4th choice, 138th overall, in 2005 Entry Draft).

			Regular Season					Playoffs				
Season	Club	League	GP	G	A	Pts	PIM	GP	G	A	Pts	PIM
2003-04	Chilliwack Chiefs	BCHL	48	7	18	25	73	11	3	1	4	14
2004-05	Chilliwack Chiefs	BCHL	59	27	28	55	94	....	....	....	....	....
2005-06	Chilliwack Chiefs	BCHL	57	38	63	101	109	10	12	11	23	12

Signed Letter of Intent to attend **Northern Michigan U.** (CCHA) in fall of 2006.

BUTLER, Chris (BUHT-luhr, KRIHS) **BUF.**

Defense. Shoots left. 6'1", 178 lbs. Born, St. Louis, MO, October 27, 1986.
(Buffalo's 4th choice, 96th overall, in 2005 Entry Draft).

			Regular Season					Playoffs				
Season	Club	League	GP	G	A	Pts	PIM	GP	G	A	Pts	PIM
2003-04	Sioux City	USHL	55	3	6	9	37	7	0	1	1	6
2004-05	Sioux City	USHL	60	6	22	28	90	13	1	6	7	10
2005-06	U. of Denver	WCHA	35	7	15	22	28	....	....	....	....	....

USHL First All-Star Team (2005) • WCHA All-Rookie Team (2006)

BUTURLIN, Alexander (boo-tuhr-LIHN, AL-ehx-an-DEHR)

Right wing. Shoots left. 5'11", 182 lbs. Born, Moscow, USSR, September 3, 1981.
(Montreal's 1st choice, 39th overall, in 1999 Entry Draft).

			Regular Season					Playoffs				
Season	Club	League	GP	G	A	Pts	PIM	GP	G	A	Pts	PIM
1997-98	CSKA Moscow 2	Russia-3	50	12	15	27	46	....	....	....	....	....
	CSKA Moscow	Russia	2	0	0	0	0	....	....	....	....	....
1998-99	CSKA Moscow	Russia	16	1	0	1	6	3	1	0	1	2
99-2000	Sarnia Sting	OHL	57	20	27	47	46	7	4	2	6	12
2000-01	Sarnia Sting	OHL	57	28	37	65	27	4	3	1	4	0
2001-02	Ufa	Russia	32	3	3	6	42	....	....	....	....	....
2002-03	Lada Togliatti	Russia	49	6	14	20	71	10	3	0	3	4
2003-04	Lada Togliatti	Russia	53	7	13	20	78	6	0	1	1	4
2004-05	Lada Togliatti	Russia	56	9	11	20	46	10	3	6	9	8
2005-06	Lada Togliatti	Russia	51	8	10	18	80	8	1	2	3	16

BYERS, Dane (BIGH-uhrs, DAYN) **NYR**

Left wing. Shoots left. 6'3", 194 lbs. Born, Nipawin, Sask., February 21, 1986.
(NY Rangers' 4th choice, 48th overall, in 2004 Entry Draft).

			Regular Season					Playoffs				
Season	Club	League	GP	G	A	Pts	PIM	GP	G	A	Pts	PIM
2002-03	Prince Albert	WHL	49	8	6	14	46	....	....	....	....	....
2003-04	Prince Albert	WHL	51	9	8	17	134	6	1	2	3	17
2004-05	Prince Albert	WHL	65	11	9	20	181	17	4	6	10	18
2005-06	Prince Albert	WHL	71	21	27	48	157	....	....	....	....	....
	Hartford Wolf Pack	AHL	5	0	2	2	6	....	....	....	....	....

BYRNE, Trevor (BUHR-ne, TREH-vuhr) **WSH.**

Defense. Shoots left. 6'3", 205 lbs. Born, Weymouth, MA, May 7, 1980.
(St. Louis' 4th choice, 143rd overall, in 1999 Entry Draft).

			Regular Season					Playoffs				
Season	Club	League	GP	G	A	Pts	PIM	GP	G	A	Pts	PIM
1997-98	Deerfield Academy	High-MA	25	5	14	19	16	....	....	....	....	....
1998-99	Deerfield Academy	High-MA	25	9	19	28	22	....	....	....	....	....
99-2000	Dartmouth	ECAC	30	3	9	12	40	....	....	....	....	....
2000-01	Dartmouth	ECAC	34	5	21	26	52	....	....	....	....	....
2001-02	Dartmouth	ECAC	32	5	16	21	38	....	....	....	....	....
2002-03	Dartmouth	ECAC	34	8	16	24	28	....	....	....	....	....
2003-04	Worcester IceCats	AHL	63	7	13	20	22	9	2	2	4	2
	Peoria Rivermen	ECHL	6	0	0	0	0	....	....	....	....	....
2004-05	Worcester IceCats	AHL	40	1	6	7	18	....	....	....	....	....
	Peoria Rivermen	ECHL	33	6	12	18	28	....	....	....	....	....
2005-06	Peoria Rivermen	AHL	51	3	18	21	47	3	0	1	1	0
	Wheeling Nailers	ECHL	2	0	3	3	0	....	....	....	....	....

ECAC Second All-Star Team (2001, 2002, 2003)
Signed as a free agent by **Washington**, July 25, 2006.

CABANA, Frederik (kah-BAH-nuh, FREHD-uhr-ihk) **PHI.**

Center/Left wing. Shoots left. 6', 182 lbs. Born, Fleurimont, Que., May 16, 1986.
(Philadelphia's 7th choice, 171st overall, in 2004 Entry Draft).

			Regular Season					Playoffs				
Season	Club	League	GP	G	A	Pts	PIM	GP	G	A	Pts	PIM
2001-02	Magog	QAAA	37	20	16	36	124	7	1	4	5	12
2002-03	Halifax	QMJHL	62	4	10	14	65	24	7	1	8	50
2003-04	Halifax	QMJHL	70	17	21	38	78	....	....	....	....	....
2004-05	Halifax	QMJHL	59	10	24	34	47	11	6	6	12	11
2005-06	Halifax	QMJHL	68	17	24	41	85	11	1	3	4	17

CALLA, Brady (KAL-luh, BRAY-dee) **FLA.**

Right wing. Shoots right. 6', 190 lbs. Born, North Vancouver, B.C., March 14, 1988.
(Florida's 2nd choice, 73rd overall, in 2006 Entry Draft).

			Regular Season					Playoffs				
Season	Club	League	GP	G	A	Pts	PIM	GP	G	A	Pts	PIM
2004-05	Everett Silvertips	WHL	68	11	10	21	38	11	1	1	2	0
2005-06	Everett Silvertips	WHL	66	8	25	33	52	11	1	2	3	4

CALLAHAN, Joe (kal-AH-han, JOH) **PHX.**

Defense. Shoots right. 6'3", 221 lbs. Born, Brockton, MA, December 20, 1982.
(Phoenix's 4th choice, 70th overall, in 2002 Entry Draft).

			Regular Season					Playoffs				
Season	Club	League	GP	G	A	Pts	PIM	GP	G	A	Pts	PIM
2001-02	Yale	ECAC	31	3	8	11	20	....	....	....	....	....
2002-03	Yale	ECAC	32	2	11	13	38	....	....	....	....	....
2003-04	Yale	ECAC	31	6	14	20	38	....	....	....	....	....
	Springfield Falcons	AHL	13	0	4	4	12	....	....	....	....	....
2004-05	Utah Grizzlies	AHL	75	4	7	11	66	....	....	....	....	....
2005-06	San Antonio	AHL	80	1	5	6	88	....	....	....	....	....

CALLAHAN, Ryan (kal-AH-han, RIGH-uhn) **NYR**

Right wing. Shoots right. 5'11", 185 lbs. Born, Rochester, NY, March 21, 1985.
(NY Rangers' 9th choice, 127th overall, in 2004 Entry Draft).

			Regular Season					Playoffs				
Season	Club	League	GP	G	A	Pts	PIM	GP	G	A	Pts	PIM
2002-03	Guelph Storm	OHL	59	14	17	31	47	11	0	3	3	2
2003-04	Guelph Storm	OHL	68	36	32	68	86	22	*13	8	21	20
2004-05	Guelph Storm	OHL	60	28	26	54	108	4	1	1	2	6
2005-06	Guelph Storm	OHL	62	52	32	84	126	13	7	17	24	20

OHL Second All-Star Team (2006)

CARCILLO, Daniel (KAR-sihl-oh, DAN-yuhl) **PIT.**

Left wing. Shoots left. 5'11", 202 lbs. Born, King City, Ont., January 28, 1985.
(Pittsburgh's 4th choice, 73rd overall, in 2003 Entry Draft).

			Regular Season					Playoffs				
Season	Club	League	GP	G	A	Pts	PIM	GP	G	A	Pts	PIM
2001-02	Milton Merchants	OHA-B	47	15	16	31	162	....	....	....	....	....
2002-03	Sarnia Sting	OHL	68	29	37	66	157	6	0	4	4	14
2003-04	Sarnia Sting	OHL	61	30	29	59	148	4	1	2	3	12
2004-05	Sarnia Sting	OHL	12	2	7	9	40	....	....	....	....	....
	Mississauga	OHL	20	8	10	18	75	5	3	1	4	18
2005-06	Wilkes-Barre	AHL	51	11	13	24	311	11	1	0	1	47
	Wheeling Nailers	ECHL	6	3	2	5	32	....	....	....	....	....

CARD, Mike (KARD, MIGHK) **BUF.**

Defense. Shoots right. 6', 201 lbs. Born, Kitchener, Ont., February 18, 1986.
(Buffalo's 7th choice, 241st overall, in 2004 Entry Draft).

			Regular Season					Playoffs				
Season	Club	League	GP	G	A	Pts	PIM	GP	G	A	Pts	PIM
2002-03	Kelowna Rockets	WHL	61	7	22	29	41	19	2	6	8	12
2003-04	Kelowna Rockets	WHL	72	6	12	18	47	17	2	4	6	20
2004-05	Kelowna Rockets	WHL	72	10	35	45	85	24	2	5	7	38
2005-06	Kelowna Rockets	WHL	64	12	43	55	103	12	0	3	3	8

CAREFOOT, Mitch (KAIR-fut, MIHTCH) **ATL.**

Center. Shoots left. 6'1", 210 lbs. Born, Dauphin, Man., January 2, 1985.
(Atlanta's 8th choice, 237th overall, in 2004 Entry Draft).

			Regular Season					Playoffs				
Season	Club	League	GP	G	A	Pts	PIM	GP	G	A	Pts	PIM
2002-03	Salmon Arm	BCHL	56	19	36	55	51	11	4	3	7	26
2003-04	Cornell Big Red	ECAC	31	6	1	7	14	....	....	....	....	....
2004-05	Cornell Big Red	ECACHL	31	4	7	11	8	....	....	....	....	....
2005-06	Cornell Big Red	ECACHL	33	6	4	10	28	....	....	....	....	....

CARLE, Mathieu (KARL, MA-tyew) **MTL.**

Defense. Shoots right. 6', 208 lbs. Born, Gatineau, Que., September 30, 1987.
(Montreal's 3rd choice, 53rd overall, in 2006 Entry Draft).

			Regular Season					Playoffs				
Season	Club	League	GP	G	A	Pts	PIM	GP	G	A	Pts	PIM
2004-05	Acadie-Bathurst	QMJHL	69	4	29	33	53	....	....	....	....	....
2005-06	Acadie-Bathurst	QMJHL	67	18	51	69	122	17	1	14	15	29

CARMAN, Michael (KAR-mahn, MIGH-kuhl) **COL.**

Center. Shoots left. 6', 180 lbs. Born, Augusta, GA, April 14, 1988.
(Colorado's 4th choice, 81st overall, in 2006 Entry Draft).

			Regular Season					Playoffs				
Season	Club	League	GP	G	A	Pts	PIM	GP	G	A	Pts	PIM
2003-04	Holy Angels	High-MN	29	19	40	59		....	....	....	....	....
2004-05	USNTDP	U-17	14	2	9	11	40	....	....	....	....	....
	USNTDP	NAHL	39	12	15	27	38	10	2	4	6	10
2005-06	USNTDP	U-18	43	15	23	38	78	....	....	....	....	....
	USNTDP	NAHL	17	6	10	16	24	....	....	....	....	....

Signed Letter of Intent to attend **U. of Minnesota** (WCHA) in fall of 2006.

CARPENTIER, Hugo (kar-PUHNT-yay, HEW-goh) **CGY.**

Center. Shoots left. 6'1", 200 lbs. Born, Hull, PQ, March 17, 1988.
(Calgary's 4th choice, 118th overall, in 2006 Entry Draft).

			Regular Season					Playoffs				
Season	Club	League	GP	G	A	Pts	PIM	GP	G	A	Pts	PIM
2004-05	Rouyn-Noranda	QMJHL	49	6	9	15	32	5	0	1	1	6
2005-06	Rouyn-Noranda	QMJHL	70	31	39	70	64	5	1	2	3	4

CARSON, Brett (KAR-suhn, BREHT) **CAR.**

Defense. Shoots right. 6'4", 220 lbs. Born, Regina, Sask., November 29, 1985.
(Carolina's 4th choice, 109th overall, in 2004 Entry Draft).

			Regular Season					Playoffs				
Season	Club	League	GP	G	A	Pts	PIM	GP	G	A	Pts	PIM
99-2000	Pipestone Valley	SSMHL	8	0	0	0	0	....	....	....	....	....
2000-01	Pipestone Valley	SSMHL	31	5	17	22	20	....	....	....	....	....
2001-02	Yorkton Terriers	SMHL	41	16	37	53	32	....	....	....	....	....
	Moose Jaw	WHL	6	0	0	0	0	12	2	0	2	0
2002-03	Moose Jaw	WHL	28	1	4	5	28	....	....	....	....	....
	Calgary Hitmen	WHL	30	3	6	9	4	5	2	1	3	0
2003-04	Calgary Hitmen	WHL	71	5	27	32	49	7	0	0	0	6
2004-05	Calgary Hitmen	WHL	61	8	16	24	61	8	2	2	4	8
2005-06	Calgary Hitmen	WHL	72	11	29	40	62	13	1	6	7	20

WHL East First All-Star Team (2006)

CARTER, Ryan (KAR-tuhr, RIGH-uhn) **ANA.**

Left wing. Shoots left. 6'1", 200 lbs. Born, White Bear Lake, MN, August 3, 1983.

			Regular Season					Playoffs				
Season	Club	League	GP	G	A	Pts	PIM	GP	G	A	Pts	PIM
2002-03	Green Bay	USHL	55	19	17	36	94	....	....	....	....	....
2003-04	Green Bay	USHL	59	22	23	45	131	....	....	....	....	....
2004-05	Minnesota State	WCHA	37	15	8	23	44	....	....	....	....	....
2005-06	Minnesota State	WCHA	39	19	16	35	71	....	....	....	....	....

Signed as a free agent by **Anaheim**, July 12, 2006.

CARUSO, Michael (kah-ROO-soh, MIGH-kuhl) **FLA.**

Defense. Shoots left. 6'2", 191 lbs. Born, Mississauga, Ont., July 5, 1988.
(Florida's 3rd choice, 103rd overall, in 2006 Entry Draft).

			Regular Season					Playoffs				
Season	Club	League	GP	G	A	Pts	PIM	GP	G	A	Pts	PIM
2004-05	Guelph Storm	OHL	56	0	3	3	31	4	0	0	0	2
2005-06	Guelph Storm	OHL	66	1	15	16	85	15	1	2	3	24

CAVANAGH, Tom (KAV-a-naw, TAWM) **S.J.**

Left wing. Shoots left. 5'10", 178 lbs. Born, Warwick, RI, March 24, 1982.
(San Jose's 6th choice, 182nd overall, in 2001 Entry Draft).

			Regular Season					Playoffs				
Season	Club	League	GP	G	A	Pts	PIM	GP	G	A	Pts	PIM
1997-98	Toll Gate Titans	High-RI	15	5	17	22	6	4	2	8	10	4
1998-99	Toll Gate Titans	High-RI	15	9	20	29	26	5	5	4	9	6
99-2000	Toll Gate Titans	High-RI	18	25	29	*54	28	5	0	12	12	9
2000-01	Exeter	High-NH	31	*42	40	82	34	....	....	....	....	....
2001-02	Harvard Crimson	ECAC	34	8	17	25	4	....	....	....	....	....
2002-03	Harvard Crimson	ECAC	34	14	13	27	31	....	....	....	....	....
2003-04	Harvard Crimson	ECAC	36	16	20	36	26	....	....	....	....	....
2004-05	Harvard Crimson	ECACHL	34	10	19	29	22	....	....	....	....	....
2005-06	Cleveland Barons	AHL	62	10	11	21	36	....	....	....	....	....

ECACHL Second All-Star Team 2005)

CAVANAUGH, Dan (KAV-a-naw, DAN)

Center. Shoots right. 6'1", 190 lbs. Born, Springfield, MA, March 3, 1980.
(Calgary's 2nd choice, 38th overall, in 1999 Entry Draft).

			Regular Season					Playoffs				
Season	Club	League	GP	G	A	Pts	PIM	GP	G	A	Pts	PIM
1995-96	N.E. Jr. Whalers	EJHL	43	8	7	15	....	....	....	....	....	....
1996-97	N.E. Jr. Coyotes	EJHL	56	23	46	69	....	....	....	....	....	....
1997-98	N.E. Jr. Coyotes	EJHL	38	31	*47	*78	58	13	8	12	30	....
1998-99	Boston University	H-East	36	6	8	14	60	....	....	....	....	....
99-2000	Boston University	H-East	40	9	25	34	62	....	....	....	....	....
2000-01	Boston University	H-East	35	7	21	28	43	....	....	....	....	....
2001-02	Houston Aeros	AHL	70	3	16	19	41	5	0	0	0	0
2002-03	Houston Aeros	AHL	77	13	13	26	126	23	2	2	4	20
2003-04	Houston Aeros	AHL	73	16	23	39	94	2	0	1	1	2
2004-05	Houston Aeros	AHL	66	8	14	22	128	5	0	0	0	13
2005-06	Philadelphia	AHL	26	2	6	8	36	....	....	....	....	....
	Springfield Falcons	AHL	39	4	15	19	61	....	....	....	....	....

Rights traded to **Minnesota** by **Calgary** with Calgary's 8th round choice (Jake Riddle) in 2001 Entry Draft for Mike Vernon, June 23, 2000.

CAVOSIE, Marc (kuh-VOI-see, MAHRK)

Center. Shoots left. 6', 173 lbs. Born, Albany, NY, August 6, 1981.
(Minnesota's 3rd choice, 99th overall, in 2000 Entry Draft).

			Regular Season					Playoffs				
Season	Club	League	GP	G	A	Pts	PIM	GP	G	A	Pts	PIM
1995-96	Albany	High-NY	22	8	27	31	....	....	....	....	....	....
1996-97	Albany	High-NY	28	26	45	71	....	....	....	....	....	....
1997-98	Albany	High-NY	28	38	33	71	....	....	....	....	....	....
1998-99	Albany	High-NY	28	23	20	43	32	....	....	....	....	....
99-2000	RPI Engineers	ECAC	29	11	17	28	10	....	....	....	....	....
2000-01	RPI Engineers	ECAC	28	13	16	29	47	....	....	....	....	....
2001-02	RPI Engineers	ECAC	36	23	*27	*50	44	....	....	....	....	....
2002-03	Houston Aeros	AHL	54	5	14	19	24	19	3	5	8	12
2003-04	Houston Aeros	AHL	75	10	21	31	37	2	1	0	1	0
2004-05	Houston Aeros	AHL	60	3	17	20	10	4	0	0	0	2
2005-06	Philadelphia	AHL	63	8	21	29	28	....	....	....	....	....

ECAC First All-Star Team (2002) • ECAC Player of the Year (2002)

Signed as a free agent by **Rogle** (Sweden), August 16, 2006.

CEPEK, Cameron (SEE-pehk, KAM-ih-RUHN) **MTL.**

Defense. Shoots right. 6'1", 187 lbs. Born, Huntington Beach, CA, January 12, 1988.
(Montreal's 6th choice, 199th overall, in 2006 Entry Draft).

			Regular Season					Playoffs				
Season	Club	League	GP	G	A	Pts	PIM	GP	G	A	Pts	PIM
2004-05	Portland	WHL	66	2	2	4	104	7	0	0	0	4
2005-06	Portland	WHL	21	2	8	10	71	12	0	1	1	10

CEREDA, Luca (suh-REH-duh, LOO-ka) **TOR.**

Center. Shoots left. 6'2", 202 lbs. Born, Lugano, Switz., September 7, 1981.
(Toronto's 1st choice, 24th overall, in 1999 Entry Draft).

			Regular Season					Playoffs				
Season	Club	League	GP	G	A	Pts	PIM	GP	G	A	Pts	PIM
1996-97	HC Ambri-Piotta	Swiss	35	13	8	21	....	....	....	....	....	....
1997-98	HC Ambri-Piotta	Swiss	28	17	27	44	24	....	....	....	....	....
1998-99	Ambri Jr.	Swiss-Jr.	3	4	3	7	20	....	....	....	....	....
	HC Ambri-Piotta	Swiss	38	6	10	16	8	15	0	6	6	4
99-2000	HC Ambri-Piotta	Swiss	44	1	5	6	14	9	0	1	1	2
2000-01	Ottawa 67's	OHL	DID NOT PLAY									
2001-02	St. John's	AHL	71	5	8	13	23	11	2	1	3	10
2002-03	St. John's	AHL	68	7	18	25	26	....	....	....	....	....
2003-04	St. John's	AHL	22	0	2	2	8	....	....	....	....	....
	SC Bern	Swiss	9	1	3	4	22	15	4	0	4	4
2004-05	SC Bern	Swiss	37	1	1	2	6	11	0	1	1	2
2005-06	HC Ambri-Piotta	Swiss	42	6	16	22	51	7	1	1	2	4

• Missed entire 2000-01 season recovering from heart surgery, October 19, 2000. • Loaned to **Bern** (Swiss) by **Toronto**, January 21, 2004.

CHAPUT, Stefan (sha-PEW, STEH-fan) **CAR.**

Center. Shoots left. 6'2", 190 lbs. Born, Montreal, Que., March 11, 1988.
(Carolina's 4th choice, 153rd overall, in 2006 Entry Draft).

			Regular Season					Playoffs				
Season	Club	League	GP	G	A	Pts	PIM	GP	G	A	Pts	PIM
2003-04	West Island Lions	QAAA	29	7	12	19	32	7	1	3	4	4
2004-05	West Island Lions	QAAA	39	29	25	54	86	5	2	2	4	16
	Lewiston	QMJHL	8	2	3	5	2	8	1	0	1	2
2005-06	Lewiston	QMJHL	69	19	29	48	44	6	0	1	1	4

CHARLEBOIS, Joe (SHAHR-luh-bwah, JOH) **CHI.**

Defense. Shoots right. 6'1", 210 lbs. Born, Potsdam, NY, February 18, 1986.
(Chicago's 10th choice, 188th overall, in 2005 Entry Draft).

			Regular Season					Playoffs				
Season	Club	League	GP	G	A	Pts	PIM	GP	G	A	Pts	PIM
2002-03	Cornwall Colts	CJHL	59	2	18	20	....	....	....	....	....	....
2003-04	USNTDP	U-18	35	0	2	2	10	....	....	....	....	....
	USNTDP	NAHL	12	1	0	1	6	7	0	1	1	4
2004-05	Sioux City	USHL	59	1	24	25	146	7	1	1	2	6
2005-06	New Hampshire	H-East	32	2	3	5	35	....	....	....	....	....

CHERNYKH, Dmitri (TCHAIR-nihk, dih-MEE-tree) **NYI**

Right wing. Shoots left. 6', 180 lbs. Born, Voskresensk, USSR, February 27, 1985.
(NY Islanders' 2nd choice, 48th overall, in 2003 Entry Draft).

			Regular Season					Playoffs				
Season	Club	League	GP	G	A	Pts	PIM	GP	G	A	Pts	PIM
2001-02	Voskresensk 2	Russia-3	28	9	6	15	32	....	....	....	....	....
	Voskresensk	Russia-2	7	0	0	0	2	....	....	....	....	....
2002-03	Voskresensk	Russia-2	29	5	4	9	29	....	....	....	....	....
	Voskresensk 2	Russia-3	1	0	0	0	18	....	....	....	....	....
2003-04	CSKA Moscow	Russia	27	2	2	4	0	....	....	....	....	....
2004-05	Mechel	Russia-2	22	1	5	6	6	4	1	0	1	0
2005-06	Yuzhny Ural Orsk	Russia-2	15	1	1	2	4	....	....	....	....	....
	Novopolotsk	BelOpen	31	5	7	12	37	....	....	....	....	....

CHIPCHURA, Kyle (chip-CHUHR-a, KIGHL) **MTL.**

Center. Shoots left. 6'2", 197 lbs. Born, Westlock, Alta., February 19, 1986.
(Montreal's 1st choice, 18th overall, in 2004 Entry Draft).

			Regular Season					Playoffs				
Season	Club	League	GP	G	A	Pts	PIM	GP	G	A	Pts	PIM
2000-01	Spruce Grove	AMBHL	36	26	34	60	48	....	....	....	....	....
2001-02	Ft. Saskatchewan	AMHL	33	15	36	51	78	17	16	20	36	....
2002-03	Prince Albert	WHL	63	9	21	30	89	....	....	....	....	....
2003-04	Prince Albert	WHL	64	15	33	48	118	6	2	4	6	12
2004-05	Prince Albert	WHL	28	14	18	32	32	14	4	7	11	25
2005-06	Prince Albert	WHL	59	21	34	55	81	....	....	....	....	....
	Hamilton Bulldogs	AHL	8	1	2	3	6	....	....	....	....	....

WHL East Second All-Star Team (2006)

CHORNEY, Taylor (CHOHR-nee, TAY-luhr) **EDM.**

Defense. Shoots left. 5'11", 182 lbs. Born, Thunder Bay, Ont., April 27, 1987.
(Edmonton's 2nd choice, 36th overall, in 2005 Entry Draft).

			Regular Season					Playoffs				
Season	Club	League	GP	G	A	Pts	PIM	GP	G	A	Pts	PIM
2003-04	Shat.-St. Mary's	High-MN	74	12	44	56	58	....	....	....	....	....
2004-05	Shat.-St. Mary's	High-MN	50	4	30	34	52	....	....	....	....	....
2005-06	North Dakota	WCHA	44	3	15	18	54	....	....	....	....	....

CHRISTIE, Matt (KRIHS-tee, MAT) **ANA.**

Center. Shoots left. 5'10", 195 lbs. Born, Toronto, Ont., February 22, 1985.
(Anaheim's 7th choice, 236th overall, in 2004 Entry Draft).

			Regular Season					Playoffs				
Season	Club	League	GP	G	A	Pts	PIM	GP	G	A	Pts	PIM
2002-03	Aurora Tigers	OPJHL	40	21	30	51	22	15	6	7	13	10
2003-04	Miami U.	CCHA	41	21	14	35	22	....	....	....	....	....
2004-05	Miami U.	CCHA	33	15	21	36	14	....	....	....	....	....
2005-06	Miami U.	CCHA	39	7	17	24	10	....	....	....	....	....

CHUCKO, Kris (CHUH-koh, KRIHS) **CGY.**

Left wing. Shoots right. 6'2", 190 lbs. Born, Burnaby, B.C., March 13, 1986.
(Calgary's 1st choice, 24th overall, in 2004 Entry Draft).

			Regular Season					Playoffs				
Season	Club	League	GP	G	A	Pts	PIM	GP	G	A	Pts	PIM
2002-03	Salmon Arm	BCHL	59	14	19	33	80	11	5	3	8	12
2003-04	Salmon Arm	BCHL	53	32	55	87	161	14	10	9	19	36
2004-05	U. of Minnesota	WCHA	44	10	11	21	61	....	....	....	....	....
2005-06	U. of Minnesota	WCHA	33	4	9	13	40	....	....	....	....	....

CLACKSON, Matt (KLAK-suhn, MA-thyew) **PHI.**

Left wing. Shoots right. 5'11", 196 lbs. Born, Saskatoon, Sask., April 26, 1985.
(Philadelphia's 6th choice, 215th overall, in 2005 Entry Draft).

			Regular Season					Playoffs				
Season	Club	League	GP	G	A	Pts	PIM	GP	G	A	Pts	PIM
2002-03	Pittsburgh Hornets	MWEHL	64	22	22	44	169	....	....	....	....	....
2003-04	Chicago Steel	USHL	42	5	4	9	108	5	0	1	1	8
2004-05	Chicago Steel	USHL	56	10	15	25	270	....	....	....	....	....
2005-06	Western Mich.	CCHA	34	1	1	2	52	....	....	....	....	....

CLARKSON, David (KLAHRK-suhn, DAYV-ihd) N.J.

Right wing. Shoots right. 6'1", 205 lbs. Born, Toronto, Ont., March 31, 1984.

			Regular Season					Playoffs				
Season	Club	League	GP	G	A	Pts	PIM	GP	G	A	Pts	PIM
2001-02	Belleville Bulls	OHL	22	2	7	9	34	8	1	1	2	6
2002-03	Belleville Bulls	OHL	3	0	0	0	11	....	....	....	....	....
	Kitchener Rangers	OHL	54	17	11	28	122	21	4	3	7	23
2003-04	Kitchener Rangers	OHL	55	22	17	39	173	....	....	....	....	....
2004-05	Kitchener Rangers	OHL	51	33	21	54	145	15	6	2	8	40
2005-06	Albany River Rats	AHL	56	13	21	34	233	....	....	....	....	....

Signed as a free agent by **New Jersey**, August 12, 2005.

CLICHE, Marc-Andre (Kligh-SHAY, MAHRK-AWN-dray) NYR

Right wing. Shoots right. 6'1", 190 lbs. Born, Rouyn-Noranda, Que., March 23, 1987.
(NY Rangers' 3rd choice, 56th overall, in 2005 Entry Draft.)

			Regular Season					Playoffs				
Season	Club	League	GP	G	A	Pts	PIM	GP	G	A	Pts	PIM
2003-04	Lewiston	QMJHL	52	8	10	18	17	7	1	2	3	0
2004-05	Lewiston	QMJHL	19	4	4	8	8	....	....	....	....	....
2005-06	Lewiston	QMJHL	66	37	45	82	60	6	2	2	4	0

CLITSOME, Grant (KLIHT-suhm, GRANT) CBJ

Defense. Shoots left. 6', 208 lbs. Born, Gloucester, Ont., April 14, 1985.
(Columbus' 12th choice, 271st overall, in 2004 Entry Draft.)

			Regular Season					Playoffs				
Season	Club	League	GP	G	A	Pts	PIM	GP	G	A	Pts	PIM
2003-04	Nepean Raiders	CJHL	55	13	26	39	67	17	1	10	11	6
2004-05	Clarkson Knights	ECACHL	39	2	11	13	36	....	....	....	....	....
2005-06	Clarkson Knights	ECACHL	34	2	17	19	20	....	....	....	....	....

CLOUTHIER, Brett (KLOO-tyay, BREHT)

Left wing. Shoots left. 6'5", 225 lbs. Born, Ottawa, Ont., June 9, 1981.
(New Jersey's 3rd choice, 50th overall, in 1999 Entry Draft.)

			Regular Season					Playoffs				
Season	Club	League	GP	G	A	Pts	PIM	GP	G	A	Pts	PIM
1997-98	Kanata Valley	CJHL	50	12	10	22	135	....	....	....	....	....
1998-99	Kingston	OHL	64	8	14	22	227	5	1	1	2	4
99-2000	Kingston	OHL	65	13	26	39	*266	5	2	0	2	17
2000-01	Kingston	OHL	68	28	29	57	165	4	1	0	1	10
2001-02	Albany River Rats	AHL	62	4	0	4	109	....	....	....	....	....
2002-03	Albany River Rats	AHL	74	6	7	13	220	....	....	....	....	....
2003-04	Albany River Rats	AHL	39	1	0	1	122	....	....	....	....	....
	Cincinnati	ECHL	12	3	3	6	14	....	....	....	....	....
2004-05	Albany River Rats	AHL	46	0	4	4	168	....	....	....	....	....
	Augusta Lynx	ECHL	11	1	1	2	14	....	....	....	....	....
2005-06	Binghamton	AHL	79	2	4	6	202	....	....	....	....	....

Signed as a free agent by **Ottawa**, August 19, 2005. Signed as a free agent by **Sheffield** (Britain), August 16, 2006.

CLUNE, Richard (KLOON, RIH-chuhrd) DAL.

Left wing. Shoots left. 5'11", 195 lbs. Born, Toronto, Ont., April 25, 1987.
(Dallas' 3rd choice, 71st overall, in 2005 Entry Draft.)

			Regular Season					Playoffs				
Season	Club	League	GP	G	A	Pts	PIM	GP	G	A	Pts	PIM
2003-04	Sarnia Sting	OHL	58	3	13	16	72	5	0	1	1	0
2004-05	Sarnia Sting	OHL	68	21	13	34	103	....	....	....	....	....
2005-06	Sarnia Sting	OHL	61	20	32	52	126	....	....	....	....	....

CLUTTERBUCK, Cal (CLUH-tuhr-buhck, KAL) MIN.

Right wing. Shoots right. 5'10", 203 lbs. Born, Welland, Ont., November 18, 1987.
(Minnesota's 3rd choice, 72nd overall, in 2006 Entry Draft.)

			Regular Season					Playoffs				
Season	Club	League	GP	G	A	Pts	PIM	GP	G	A	Pts	PIM
2004-05	St. Michael's	OHL	38	10	6	16	55	....	....	....	....	....
	Oshawa Generals	OHL	27	9	9	18	42	....	....	....	....	....
2005-06	Oshawa Generals	OHL	66	35	33	68	139	....	....	....	....	....

COGLIANO, Andrew (kawg-LEE-a-noh, AN-droo) EDM.

Center. Shoots left. 5'9", 178 lbs. Born, Toronto, Ont., June 14, 1987.
(Edmonton's 1st choice, 25th overall, in 2005 Entry Draft.)

			Regular Season					Playoffs				
Season	Club	League	GP	G	A	Pts	PIM	GP	G	A	Pts	PIM
2002-03	Vaughan	GTHL	58	39	54	93	122	....	....	....	....	....
2003-04	St. Mike's B's	OPJHL	36	26	47	73	14	24	11	20	31	12
2004-05	St. Mike's B's	OPJHL	49	36	*66	*102	33	25	*22	*24	*46	20
2005-06	U. of Michigan	CCHA	39	12	16	28	38	....	....	....	....	....

CCHA All-Rookie Team (2006)

COLBERT, Will (KOHL-buhrt, WIHL) S.J.

Defense. Shoots left. 6'3", 212 lbs. Born, Arnprior, Ont., February 6, 1985.
(San Jose's 7th choice, 183rd overall, in 2005 Entry Draft).

			Regular Season					Playoffs				
Season	Club	League	GP	G	A	Pts	PIM	GP	G	A	Pts	PIM
2001-02	Pembroke	CJHL	52	2	6	8	20	....	....	....	....	....
2002-03	Ottawa 67's	OHL	56	1	6	7	23	23	1	5	6	7
2003-04	Ottawa 67's	OHL	55	3	18	21	28	7	0	4	4	0
2004-05	Ottawa 67's	OHL	68	6	26	32	65	21	3	8	11	8
2005-06	St. FX University	AUAA	28	3	8	11	10	....	....	....	....	....

• Re-entered NHL Entry Draft. Originally Ottawa's 7th choice, 228th overall, in 2003 Entry Draft.
CIS All-Rookie Team (2006)

COLE, Phil (KOHL, FIHL)

Defense. Shoots left. 6'4", 205 lbs. Born, Winnipeg, Man., September 6, 1982.
(New Jersey's 8th choice, 125th overall, in 2000 Entry Draft.)

			Regular Season					Playoffs				
Season	Club	League	GP	G	A	Pts	PIM	GP	G	A	Pts	PIM
1997-98	Winnipeg Sharks	MMMHL	45	0	18	18	68	5	0	4	4	2
1998-99	Lethbridge	WHL	45	2	1	3	64	4	0	0	0	0
99-2000	Lethbridge	WHL	51	1	6	7	112	....	....	....	....	....
2000-01	Lethbridge	WHL	63	6	15	21	129	1	0	0	0	2
2001-02	Lethbridge	WHL	33	3	13	16	87	....	....	....	....	....
	Vancouver Giants	WHL	6	0	1	1	18	....	....	....	....	....
	Medicine Hat	WHL	15	1	5	6	49	....	....	....	....	....
2002-03	Albany River Rats	AHL	4	0	0	0	6	....	....	....	....	....
	Columbus	ECHL	51	4	5	9	135	....	....	....	....	....
2003-04	Cincinnati	ECHL	12	1	0	1	33	....	....	....	....	....
	Albany River Rats	AHL	39	1	3	4	80	....	....	....	....	....
2004-05	Albany River Rats	AHL	18	0	0	0	16	....	....	....	....	....
	Augusta Lynx	ECHL	42	1	4	5	80	....	....	....	....	....
2005-06	Philadelphia	AHL	10	0	0	0	20	....	....	....	....	....
	Augusta Lynx	ECHL	48	1	11	12	91	2	0	0	0	0

COLLINS, Chris (KAW-lihns, KRIHS) BOS.

Wing. Shoots right. 5'10", 190 lbs. Born, Fairport, NY, June 8, 1984.

			Regular Season					Playoffs				
Season	Club	League	GP	G	A	Pts	PIM	GP	G	A	Pts	PIM
2001-02	Des Moines	USHL	60	26	39	65	112	3	1	2	3	10
2002-03	Boston College	H-East	39	11	12	23	53	....	....	....	....	....
2003-04	Boston College	H-East	41	9	10	19	42	....	....	....	....	....
2004-05	Boston College	H-East	40	9	8	17	58	....	....	....	....	....
2005-06	Boston College	H-East	40	*31	29	*60	26	....	....	....	....	....

Hockey East First All-Star Team (2006) • NCAA East First All-American Team (2006)
Signed as a free agent by **Boston**, July 11, 2006.

COLLINS, Dan (KAW-lihns, DAN) FLA.

Right wing. Shoots right. 6'1", 185 lbs. Born, Syracuse, NY, February 26, 1987.
(Florida's 3rd choice, 90th overall, in 2005 Entry Draft.)

			Regular Season					Playoffs				
Season	Club	League	GP	G	A	Pts	PIM	GP	G	A	Pts	PIM
2002-03	Syracuse	OPJHL	35	14	12	26	58	....	....	....	....	....
2003-04	Plymouth Whalers	OHL	59	9	13	22	30	9	0	1	1	0
2004-05	Plymouth Whalers	OHL	68	25	21	46	60	4	0	0	0	6
2005-06	Plymouth Whalers	OHL	44	26	23	49	56	4	3	2	5	2

COLLINS, Dusty (KAW-lihns, DUHS-tee) T.B.

Center/Left wing. Shoots left. 6'3", 213 lbs. Born, Payson, AZ, February 28, 1985.
(Tampa Bay's 5th choice, 163rd overall, in 2004 Entry Draft.)

			Regular Season					Playoffs				
Season	Club	League	GP	G	A	Pts	PIM	GP	G	A	Pts	PIM
2001-02	USNTDP	U-17	17	2	4	6	10	....	....	....	....	....
	USNTDP	NAHL	46	4	6	10	28	....	....	....	....	....
2002-03	USNTDP	U-18	44	5	8	13	20	....	....	....	....	....
	USNTDP	NAHL	9	1	3	4	11	....	....	....	....	....
2003-04	Northern Mich.	CCHA	37	1	5	6	30	....	....	....	....	....
2004-05	Northern Mich.	CCHA	25	2	1	3	28	....	....	....	....	....
2005-06	Northern Mich.	CCHA	35	4	6	10	45	....	....	....	....	....

COMEAU, Blake (KOH-moh, BLAYK) NYI

Right wing. Shoots right. 6'1", 198 lbs. Born, Meadow Lake, Sask., February 18, 1986.
(NY Islanders' 2nd choice, 47th overall, in 2004 Entry Draft.)

			Regular Season					Playoffs				
Season	Club	League	GP	G	A	Pts	PIM	GP	G	A	Pts	PIM
2001-02	Sask. Contacts	SMHL	42	27	33	60	72	....	....	....	....	....
	Kelowna Rockets	WHL	3	0	0	0	4	....	....	....	....	....
2002-03	Kelowna Rockets	WHL	54	5	18	23	77	19	2	1	3	20
2003-04	Kelowna Rockets	WHL	71	10	23	33	123	17	4	2	6	23
2004-05	Kelowna Rockets	WHL	65	24	23	47	108	24	6	12	18	34
2005-06	Kelowna Rockets	WHL	60	21	53	74	85	12	4	9	13	22
	Bridgeport	AHL	....	....	....	....	....	7	0	3	3	0

WHL West First All-Star Team (2006)

CONBOY, Tim (KAWN-boy, TIHM) CAR.

Defense. Shoots right. 6'1", 205 lbs. Born, Farmington, MN, March 22, 1982.
(San Jose's 6th choice, 217th overall, in 2002 Entry Draft.)

			Regular Season					Playoffs				
Season	Club	League	GP	G	A	Pts	PIM	GP	G	A	Pts	PIM
99-2000	Brainerd	High-MN	22	20	26	46	....	....	....	....	....	....
2000-01	Rochester	USHL	51	5	9	14	256	....	....	....	....	....
2001-02	Rochester	USHL	14	1	6	7	65	....	....	....	....	....
	Topeka	USHL	29	4	15	19	128	....	....	....	....	....
2002-03	St. Cloud State	WCHA	31	3	12	15	48	....	....	....	....	....
2003-04	St. Cloud State	WCHA	32	5	5	10	68	....	....	....	....	....
	Cleveland Barons	AHL	....	....	....	....	....	3	0	3	3	4
2004-05	Cleveland Barons	AHL	61	4	11	15	134	....	....	....	....	....
2005-06	Cleveland Barons	AHL	78	6	14	20	124	....	....	....	....	....

Signed as a free agent by **Carolina**, July 21, 2006.

CONDRA, Erik (KAWN-druh, AIR-ihk) OTT.

Right wing. Shoots right. 5'11", 180 lbs. Born, Trenton, MI, August 6, 1986.
(Ottawa's 7th choice, 211th overall, in 2006 Entry Draft.)

			Regular Season					Playoffs				
Season	Club	League	GP	G	A	Pts	PIM	GP	G	A	Pts	PIM
2004-05	Lincoln Stars	USHL	60	30	30	60	56	4	0	2	2	4
2005-06	U. of Notre Dame	CCHA	36	6	28	34	32	....	....	....	....	....

CONNER, Chris (KAWN-uhr, KRIHS)

Wing. Shoots left. 5'7", 180 lbs. Born, Westland, MI, December 23, 1983.

			Regular Season					Playoffs				
Season	Club	League	GP	G	A	Pts	PIM	GP	G	A	Pts	PIM
2002-03	Michigan Tech	WCHA	38	13	24	37	8	....	....	....	....	....
2003-04	Michigan Tech	WCHA	38	25	14	39	12	....	....	....	....	....
2004-05	Michigan Tech	WCHA	37	14	10	24	6	....	....	....	....	....
2005-06	Michigan Tech	WCHA	38	17	12	29	18	....	....	....	....	....
	Iowa Stars	AHL	15	2	3	5	0	7	1	1	2	2

Signed as a free agent by **Dallas**, July 13, 2006.

COOK, Tim (KUK, TIHM) **OTT.**

Defense. Shoots right. 6'4", 190 lbs. Born, Montclair, NJ, March 13, 1984.
(Ottawa's 5th choice, 142nd overall, in 2003 Entry Draft).

			Regular Season					Playoffs				
Season	Club	League	GP	G	A	Pts	PIM	GP	G	A	Pts	PIM
2000-01	Hotchkiss	High-CT	22	2	10	12	22	....	....	....	....	....
2001-02	Omaha Lancers	USHL	42	2	4	6	39	5	0	1	1	2
2002-03	River City Lancers	USHL	59	3	12	15	62	10	0	2	2	18
2003-04	U. of Michigan	CCHA	24	0	2	2	28	....	....	....	....	....
2004-05	U. of Michigan	CCHA	36	0	0	0	54	....	....	....	....	....
2005-06	U. of Michigan	CCHA	40	1	2	3	37	....	....	....	....	....

COOPER, Joe (KOO-puhr, JOH) **OTT.**

Right wing. Shoots right. 6'1", 199 lbs. Born, Toronto, Ont., June 7, 1985.
(Ottawa's 9th choice, 219th overall, in 2004 Entry Draft).

			Regular Season					Playoffs				
Season	Club	League	GP	G	A	Pts	PIM	GP	G	A	Pts	PIM
2002-03	St. Mike's B's	OPJHL	44	15	30	45	121	....	....	....	....	....
2003-04	Miami U.	CCHA	34	1	0	1	66	....	....	....	....	....
2004-05	Miami U.	CCHA	36	1	7	8	43	....	....	....	....	....
2005-06	Miami U.	CCHA	39	3	7	10	64	....	....	....	....	....

CORBIN, J.D. (KOHR-bihn, JAY-DEE) **COL.**

Left wing. Shoots left. 5'10", 185 lbs. Born, Littleton, CO, March 23, 1985.
(Colorado's 8th choice, 249th overall, in 2004 Entry Draft).

			Regular Season					Playoffs				
Season	Club	League	GP	G	A	Pts	PIM	GP	G	A	Pts	PIM
2001-02	USNTDP	U-17	14	3	9	12	26	....	....	....	....	....
	USNTDP	NAHL	29	3	4	7	20	....	....	....	....	....
2002-03	USNTDP	U-18	41	7	12	19	....	....	....	....	....	....
	USNTDP	NAHL	10	1	1	2	4	....	....	....	....	....
2003-04	U. of Denver	WCHA	39	3	6	9	18	....	....	....	....	....
2004-05	U. of Denver	WCHA	41	1	18	19	22	....	....	....	....	....
2005-06	U. of Denver	WCHA	38	5	15	20	16	....	....	....	....	....

CORMIER, Kevin (KOHR-mee-ay, KEH-vihn) **PHX.**

Left wing. Shoots left. 6'3", 249 lbs. Born, Moncton, N.B., January 27, 1986.
(Phoenix's 6th choice, 168th overall, in 2004 Entry Draft).

			Regular Season					Playoffs				
Season	Club	League	GP	G	A	Pts	PIM	GP	G	A	Pts	PIM
2003-04	Moncton	MJrHL	42	3	2	5	235	4	0	0	0	52
	Halifax	QMJHL	1	0	0	0	5	....	....	....	....	....
2004-05	Halifax	QMJHL	60	2	5	7	235	9	0	0	0	8
2005-06	Halifax	QMJHL	69	16	11	27	202	11	0	1	1	18

CORRENTE, Matthew (kohr-REHN-tay, MA-thew) **N.J.**

Defense. Shoots right. 6', 190 lbs. Born, Mississauga, Ont., March 17, 1988.
(New Jersey's 1st choice, 30th overall, in 2006 Entry Draft).

			Regular Season					Playoffs				
Season	Club	League	GP	G	A	Pts	PIM	GP	G	A	Pts	PIM
2004-05	Saginaw Spirit	OHL	62	6	9	15	89	....	....	....	....	....
2005-06	Saginaw Spirit	OHL	61	6	24	30	172	4	1	1	2	8

COTE, Riley (COH-tay, RIGH-lee) **PHI.**

Left wing. Shoots left. 6'1", 210 lbs. Born, Winnipeg, Man., March 16, 1982.

			Regular Season					Playoffs				
Season	Club	League	GP	G	A	Pts	PIM	GP	G	A	Pts	PIM
1998-99	Prince Albert	WHL	37	3	2	5	63	9	0	0	0	9
99-2000	Prince Albert	WHL	67	6	7	13	71	3	1	0	1	2
2000-01	Prince Albert	WHL	64	17	35	52	114	....	....	....	....	....
2001-02	Prince Albert	WHL	67	28	23	51	134	....	....	....	....	....
2002-03	St. John's	AHL	6	0	0	0	5	....	....	....	....	....
	Memphis	CHL	51	8	6	14	241	14	1	0	1	54
2003-04	Syracuse Crunch	AHL	9	0	0	0	19	....	....	....	....	....
	Dayton Bombers	ECHL	57	6	11	17	258	....	....	....	....	....
2004-05	Philadelphia	AHL	61	4	7	11	280	13	0	0	0	6
2005-06	Philadelphia	AHL	70	3	1	4	259	....	....	....	....	....

Signed as a free agent by **Philadelphia**, August 23, 2005.

COUTURE, Derek (coh-TYOOR, DAI-ihk) **CGY.**

Right wing. Shoots right. 6'2", 202 lbs. Born, Calgary, Alta., April 24, 1984.

			Regular Season					Playoffs				
Season	Club	League	GP	G	A	Pts	PIM	GP	G	A	Pts	PIM
2001-02	Saskatoon Blades	WHL	61	6	10	16	159	7	0	0	0	10
2002-03	Saskatoon Blades	WHL	70	17	20	37	160	6	1	2	3	13
2003-04	Saskatoon Blades	WHL	45	3	9	12	99	....	....	....	....	....
2004-05	Seattle	WHL	71	20	18	38	154	12	3	6	9	18
2005-06	Omaha	AHL	66	7	12	19	88	....	....	....	....	....

Signed as a free agent by **Calgary**, August 5, 2005.

CRABB, Joey (KRAB, JOH-ee)

Right wing. Shoots right. 6'1", 187 lbs. Born, Anchorage, AK, April 3, 1983.
(NY Rangers' 7th choice, 226th overall, in 2002 Entry Draft).

			Regular Season					Playoffs				
Season	Club	League	GP	G	A	Pts	PIM	GP	G	A	Pts	PIM
99-2000	USNTDP	NAHL	55	13	10	23	69	3	1	0	1	4
2000-01	USNTDP	U-18	39	10	10	20	22	....	....	....	....	....
	USNTDP	USHL	21	2	3	5	18	....	....	....	....	....
2001-02	Green Bay	USHL	61	15	27	42	94	7	4	8	12	21
2002-03	Colorado College	WCHA	35	4	4	8	40	....	....	....	....	....
2003-04	Colorado College	WCHA	39	15	12	27	20	....	....	....	....	....
2004-05	Colorado College	WCHA	43	16	16	32	44	....	....	....	....	....
2005-06	Colorado College	WCHA	42	18	25	43	45	....	....	....	....	....

CRACKNELL, Adam (krak-NEHL, A-duhm) **CGY.**

Right wing. Shoots right. 6'2", 211 lbs. Born, Prince Albert, Sask., July 15, 1985.
(Calgary's 10th choice, 279th overall, in 2004 Entry Draft).

			Regular Season					Playoffs				
Season	Club	League	GP	G	A	Pts	PIM	GP	G	A	Pts	PIM
2002-03	Kootenay Ice	WHL	67	7	4	11	37	11	0	0	0	2
2003-04	Kootenay Ice	WHL	72	26	35	61	63	4	1	1	2	2
2004-05	Kootenay Ice	WHL	72	19	29	48	65	16	8	8	16	6
2005-06	Kootenay Ice	WHL	72	42	51	93	85	6	1	4	5	6
	Omaha	AHL	6	1	2	3	2	....	....	....	....	....

WHL West Second All-Star Team (2006)

CROMBEEN, B.J. (KRAWM-been, BRAN-duhn) **DAL.**

Right wing. Shoots right. 6'2", 200 lbs. Born, Denver, CO, July 10, 1985.
(Dallas' 3rd choice, 54th overall, in 2003 Entry Draft).

			Regular Season					Playoffs				
Season	Club	League	GP	G	A	Pts	PIM	GP	G	A	Pts	PIM
2000-01	Newmarket	OPJHL	35	14	14	28	63	....	....	....	....	....
2001-02	Barrie Colts	OHL	60	12	13	25	118	20	1	1	2	31
2002-03	Barrie Colts	OHL	63	22	24	46	133	6	1	0	1	8
2003-04	Barrie Colts	OHL	62	21	29	50	154	12	5	7	12	35
2004-05	Barrie Colts	OHL	63	31	18	49	111	6	2	4	6	35
2005-06	Iowa Stars	AHL	52	5	7	12	97	5	1	0	1	9
	Idaho Steelheads	ECHL	8	5	3	8	5	....	....	....	....	....

CROWDER, Tim (KROW-duhr, TIHM) **PIT.**

Right wing. Shoots right. 6'2", 180 lbs. Born, Victoria, B.C., October 16, 1986.
(Pittsburgh's 5th choice, 126th overall, in 2005 Entry Draft).

			Regular Season					Playoffs				
Season	Club	League	GP	G	A	Pts	PIM	GP	G	A	Pts	PIM
2002-03	Powell River Kings	BCHL	52	6	6	12	....	....	....	....	....	....
2003-04	Powell River Kings	BCHL	57	21	34	55	44	7	3	3	6	8
2004-05	South Surrey	BCHL	56	23	27	50	30	....	....	....	....	....
2005-06	Michigan State	CCHA	44	17	13	30	29	....	....	....	....	....

CROWLEY, Dane (CROW-lee, DAYN) **T.B.**

Defense. Shoots right. 6'2", 210 lbs. Born, Winnipeg, Man., January 22, 1987.
(Tampa Bay's 3rd choice, 168th overall, in 2006 Entry Draft).

			Regular Season					Playoffs				
Season	Club	League	GP	G	A	Pts	PIM	GP	G	A	Pts	PIM
2003-04	Saskatoon Blades	WHL	28	1	3	4	28	....	....	....	....	....
2004-05	Saskatoon Blades	WHL	52	1	3	4	101	4	0	0	0	8
2005-06	Saskatoon Blades	WHL	42	0	9	9	85	....	....	....	....	....
	Swift Current	WHL	29	1	11	12	64	4	0	2	2	23

CULLEN, Joe (KUH-lehn, JOH)

Center. Shoots left. 6'1", 210 lbs. Born, Virginia, MN, February 14, 1981.
(Edmonton's 7th choice, 211th overall, in 2000 Entry Draft).

			Regular Season					Playoffs				
Season	Club	League	GP	G	A	Pts	PIM	GP	G	A	Pts	PIM
1997-98	Moorhead Spuds	High-MN	23	18	18	36	....	....	....	....	....	....
1998-99	USNTDP	U-18	6	2	0	2	4	....	....	....	....	....
	USNTDP	USHL	52	11	15	26	33	....	....	....	....	....
99-2000	Colorado College	WCHA	29	4	6	10	30	....	....	....	....	....
2000-01	Colorado College	WCHA	34	8	12	20	38	....	....	....	....	....
2001-02	Colorado College	WCHA	43	9	12	21	42	....	....	....	....	....
2002-03	Colorado College	WCHA	42	20	15	35	56	....	....	....	....	....
2003-04	Toronto	AHL	69	14	16	30	30	3	0	0	0	2
2004-05	Edmonton	AHL	30	3	9	12	16	....	....	....	....	....
	San Antonio	AHL	38	3	3	6	20	....	....	....	....	....
2005-06	Binghamton	AHL	72	7	11	18	56	....	....	....	....	....

Loaned to **San Antonio** (AHL) by **Edmonton** (AHL), January 3, 2005. Signed as a free agent by **Ottawa**, September 17, 2005.

CUMISKEY, Kyle (kuh-MIHS-kee, KIGHL) **COL.**

Defense. Shoots left. 5'10", 185 lbs. Born, Abbotsford, B.C., December 2, 1986.
(Colorado's 9th choice, 222nd overall, in 2005 Entry Draft).

			Regular Season					Playoffs				
Season	Club	League	GP	G	A	Pts	PIM	GP	G	A	Pts	PIM
2002-03	Penticton Panthers	BCHL	59	10	11	21	36	....	....	....	....	....
2003-04	Kelowna Rockets	WHL	54	2	7	9	20	17	0	0	0	0
2004-05	Kelowna Rockets	WHL	72	4	36	40	47	24	0	13	13	12
2005-06	Kelowna Rockets	WHL	51	6	24	30	52	12	0	6	6	8

CUNNING, Cam (KUH-nihng, KAM) **CGY.**

Left wing. Shoots left. 6'2", 215 lbs. Born, Powell River, B.C., June 4, 1985.
(Calgary's 8th choice, 240th overall, in 2003 Entry Draft).

			Regular Season					Playoffs				
Season	Club	League	GP	G	A	Pts	PIM	GP	G	A	Pts	PIM
2002-03	Kamloops Blazers	WHL	71	7	12	19	54	6	1	0	1	2
2003-04	Kamloops Blazers	WHL	65	14	13	27	62	5	1	1	2	10
2004-05	Kamloops Blazers	WHL	39	14	8	22	63	....	....	....	....	....
	Vancouver Giants	WHL	30	3	7	10	19	6	1	3	4	14
2005-06	Red Deer Rebels	WHL	40	19	13	32	52	....	....	....	....	....
	Omaha	AHL	30	2	4	6	24	....	....	....	....	....

CURRY, Mike (KUH-ree) **L.A.**

Right wing. Shoots right. 6'3", 190 lbs. Born, Fort Benning, GA, September 20, 1984.
(Los Angeles' 6th choice, 205th overall, in 2004 Entry Draft).

			Regular Season					Playoffs				
Season	Club	League	GP	G	A	Pts	PIM	GP	G	A	Pts	PIM
2002-03	Sioux City	USHL	52	6	13	19	58	4	1	2	3	2
2003-04	Sioux City	USHL	60	20	20	40	119	7	2	5	7	16
2004-05	U. Minn-Duluth	WCHA	22	3	6	9	35	....	....	....	....	....
2005-06	U. Minn-Duluth	WCHA	36	2	3	5	68	....	....	....	....	....

CURRY, Sean (KUH-ree, SHAWN)

Defense. Shoots right. 6'4", 230 lbs. Born, Burnsville, MN, April 29, 1982.
(Carolina's 6th choice, 211th overall, in 2001 Entry Draft).

			Regular Season					Playoffs				
Season	Club	League	GP	G	A	Pts	PIM	GP	G	A	Pts	PIM
99-2000	Burnsville	High-MN	23	8	18	26	....	....	....	....	....	....
2000-01	Tri-City Americans	WHL	72	5	12	17	113	....	....	....	....	....
2001-02	Tri-City Americans	WHL	36	6	6	12	84	....	....	....	....	....
	Medicine Hat	WHL	24	4	13	17	43	....	....	....	....	....
2002-03	Lowell	AHL	35	0	2	2	62	....	....	....	....	....
	Florida Everblades	ECHL	32	1	6	7	77	1	0	0	0	0
2003-04	Lowell	AHL	74	1	8	9	66	....	....	....	....	....
2004-05	Lowell	AHL	61	2	7	9	103	7	0	1	1	4
2005-06	Providence Bruins	AHL	72	4	4	8	144	6	0	1	1	20

D'AGOSTINI, Matt (DAG-uh-stee-noh, MAT) **MTL.**

Right wing. Shoots right. 6', 181 lbs. Born, Sault Ste. Marie, Ont., October 23, 1986.
(Montreal's 5th choice, 190th overall, in 2005 Entry Draft).

			Regular Season					Playoffs				
Season	Club	League	GP	G	A	Pts	PIM	GP	G	A	Pts	PIM
2003-04	Soo North Stars	GNML	36	36	23	59	41	....	....	....	....	....
2004-05	Guelph Storm	OHL	59	24	22	46	29	4	0	2	2	8
2005-06	Guelph Storm	OHL	66	25	54	79	81	15	8	20	28	16

DAHLBERG, Johan (DAHL-buhrg, YO-han) TOR.

Left wing. Shoots left. 6’2”, 194 lbs. Born, Kramfors, Sweden , February 3, 1987.
(Toronto’s 4th choice, 173rd overall, in 2005 Entry Draft).

			Regular Season					Playoffs				
Season	**Club**	**League**	**GP**	**G**	**A**	**Pts**	**PIM**	**GP**	**G**	**A**	**Pts**	**PIM**
2002-03	Kramfors	Sweden-3	19	2	0	2	19	....	....	....	....	....
2003-04	MODO U18	Swe-U18	14	3	2	5	64	3	0	0	0	14
	MODO Jr.	Swe-Jr.	1	0	0	0	0	....	....	....	....	....
2004-05	MODO Jr.	Swe-Jr.	33	10	5	15	78	4	0	0	0	4
2005-06	MODO Jr.	Swe-Jr.	41	18	9	27	194	2	1	0	1	12
	MODO	Sweden	2	0	0	0	0	....	....	....	....	....

D’AMOUR, Dominic (dah-MOHR, DOHM-ihn-ihk) TOR.

Defense. Shoots left. 6’3”, 202 lbs. Born, LaSalle, Que., January 28, 1984.
(Toronto’s 4th choice, 88th overall, in 2002 Entry Draft).

			Regular Season					Playoffs				
Season	**Club**	**League**	**GP**	**G**	**A**	**Pts**	**PIM**	**GP**	**G**	**A**	**Pts**	**PIM**
99-2000	Charles-Lemoyne	QAAA	35	3	8	11	47	16	1	1	2	14
2000-01	Charles-Lemoyne	QAAA	11	1	4	5	36	....	....	....	....	....
	Rouyn-Noranda	QMJHL	18	0	0	0	10	....	....	....	....	....
2001-02	Hull Olympiques	QMJHL	68	5	5	10	225	12	0	3	3	32
2002-03	Hull Olympiques	QMJHL	65	5	25	30	211	17	2	3	5	51
2003-04	Gatineau	QMJHL	61	15	38	53	211	15	3	6	9	*41
2004-05	St. John’s	AHL	26	1	1	2	60	1	0	0	0	0
	Pensacola	ECHL	22	4	8	12	33	4	0	0	0	2
2005-06	Toronto Marlies	AHL	30	1	3	4	25	....	....	....	....	....

DANIELSSON, Nicklas (DAN-yehl-suhn, NIHK-las) VAN.

Right wing. Shoots right. 6’1”, 169 lbs. Born, Uppsala, Sweden, December 7, 1984.
(Vancouver’s 5th choice, 160th overall, in 2003 Entry Draft).

			Regular Season					Playoffs				
Season	**Club**	**League**	**GP**	**G**	**A**	**Pts**	**PIM**	**GP**	**G**	**A**	**Pts**	**PIM**
2001-02	Calgary Bruins	CBHL	9	6	8	14	12	....	....	....	....	....
	Brynas IF Gavle Jr.	Swe-Jr.	42	15	14	29	74	....	....	....	....	....
	Cardiff Devils	Britain-2	13	3	5	8	2	....	....	....	....	....
2002-03	Brynas IF Gavle Jr.	Swe-Jr.	21	21	12	33	24	2	1	0	1	2
	Brynas IF Gavle	Sweden	26	0	4	4	10	....	....	....	....	....
	Brynas IF Gavle	Sweden-Q	6	0	0	0	4	....	....	....	....	....
2003-04	Brynas IF Gavle	Sweden	47	6	0	6	22	....	....	....	....	....
	Brynas IF Gavle Jr.	Swe-Jr.	10	8	8	16	12	5	3	1	4	48
	Almtuna	Sweden-2	4	1	1	2	6	....	....	....	....	....
2004-05	Brynas IF Gavle	Sweden	30	0	1	1	2	....	....	....	....	....
2005-06	Almtuna	Sweden-2	38	15	20	35	147	....	....	....	....	....

DANILICS, Raimonds (da-NIH-likhs, RAY-mawndz) T.B.

Forward. Shoots right. 6’3”, 180 lbs. Born, Riga, Latvia, July 17, 1985.
(Tampa Bay’s 7th choice, 255th overall, in 2003 Entry Draft).

			Regular Season					Playoffs				
Season	**Club**	**League**	**GP**	**G**	**A**	**Pts**	**PIM**	**GP**	**G**	**A**	**Pts**	**PIM**
2000-01	Daugavpils Jr.	Latvia-Jr.	20	6	8	14	....	....	....	....	....	....
	Prizma Riga	Latvia	2	0	0	0	0	....	....	....	....	....
2001-02	Daugavpils Jr.	Latvia-Jr.	16	4	5	9	10	....	....	....	....	....
2002-03	Daugavpils Jr.	Latvia-Jr.	14	4	5	9	18	....	....	....	....	....
	Daugavpils	EEHL-B	18	7	15	22	29	....	....	....	....	....
2003-04	Lukko Rauma Jr.	Fin-Jr.	27	0	0	0	12	....	....	....	....	....
2004-05	Texas Tornado	NAHL	13	0	5	5	9	....	....	....	....	....
	Tri-City Storm	USHL	7	2	0	2	6	....	....	....	....	....
	Bismarck Bobcats	NAHL	25	3	9	12	0	2	0	1	1	0
2005-06	HK Riga 2000	Latvia	....	14	14	28	18	....	....	....	....	....
	HK Riga 2000	BelOpen	20	1	1	2	16	....	....	....	....	....

DANIS-PEPIN, Simon (da-NEE-peh-PEH, see-MOHN) CHI.

Defense. Shoots right. 6’7”, 217 lbs. Born, Montreal, Que., April 11, 1988.
(Chicago’s 3rd choice, 61st overall, in 2006 Entry Draft).

			Regular Season					Playoffs				
Season	**Club**	**League**	**GP**	**G**	**A**	**Pts**	**PIM**	**GP**	**G**	**A**	**Pts**	**PIM**
2003-04	Gatineau Intrepide	QAAA	33	2	14	16	20	2	0	0	0	0
2004-05	Gatineau Intrepide	QAAA	39	6	31	37	64	14	6	7	13	25
2005-06	N.H. Jr. Monarchs	EJHL	2	0	0	0	0	....	....	....	....	....
	U. of Maine	H-East	23	0	5	5	14	....	....	....	....	....

DARZINS, Lauris (DAHR-zihnzh, LOW-rihs) NSH.

Forward. Shoots right. 6’3”, 192 lbs. Born, Riga, Latvia, January 28, 1985.
(Nashville’s 13th choice, 268th overall, in 2003 Entry Draft).

			Regular Season					Playoffs				
Season	**Club**	**League**	**GP**	**G**	**A**	**Pts**	**PIM**	**GP**	**G**	**A**	**Pts**	**PIM**
2001-02	Lukko Rauma U18	Fin-U18	7	4	1	5	4	....	....	....	....	....
	Lukko Rauma Jr.	Fin-Jr.	5	1	0	1	0	....	....	....	....	....
2002-03	Lukko Rauma U18	Fin-U18	13	10	10	20	6	....	....	....	....	....
	Lukko Rauma Jr.	Fin-Jr.	13	6	4	10	6	....	....	....	....	....
2003-04	Lukko Rauma Jr.	Fin-Jr.	35	17	8	25	14	....	....	....	....	....
2004-05	Kelowna Rockets	WHL	53	19	15	34	38	24	7	7	14	10
2005-06	Kelowna Rockets	WHL	47	13	20	33	26	6	5	1	6	2

DASILVA, Daniel (duh-SIHL-vah, DAN-yehl) COL.

Right wing. Shoots right. 6’1”, 195 lbs. Born, Saskatoon, Sask., April 30, 1985.

			Regular Season					Playoffs				
Season	**Club**	**League**	**GP**	**G**	**A**	**Pts**	**PIM**	**GP**	**G**	**A**	**Pts**	**PIM**
2002-03	Portland	WHL	64	9	13	22	81	7	0	4	4	16
2003-04	Portland	WHL	65	36	20	56	120	5	0	1	1	6
2004-05	Portland	WHL	71	31	42	73	127	5	1	1	2	6
2005-06	Lowell	AHL	25	3	2	5	27	....	....	....	....	....
	San Diego Gulls	ECHL	4	5	3	8	2	....	....	....	....	....

Signed as a free agent by **Colorado**, October 11, 2005.

DAUGAVINS, Kaspars (DAH-gah-vihnsh, KAS-purz) OTT.

Left wing. Shoots left. 5’11”, 181 lbs. Born, Riga, Latvia, May 18, 1988.
(Ottawa’s 3rd choice, 91st overall, in 2006 Entry Draft).

			Regular Season					Playoffs				
Season	**Club**	**League**	**GP**	**G**	**A**	**Pts**	**PIM**	**GP**	**G**	**A**	**Pts**	**PIM**
2003-04	HK Riga 2000	EEHL	2	0	1	1	0	....	....	....	....	....
	Prizma/Riga 86	Latvia	14	6	6	12	10	2	1	1	2	4
2004-05	CSKA Moscow 2	Russia-3	STATISTICS NOT AVAILABLE									
2005-06	HK Riga 2000	Latvia	....	4	6	10	16	....	....	....	....	....
	HK Riga 2000	BelOpen	45	4	11	15	16	....	....	....	....	....

DAVIS, Nathan (DAY-vihs, NAY-thuhn) CHI.

Center/Left wing. Shoots left. 6’, 194 lbs. Born, Cleveland, OH, May 23, 1986.
(Chicago’s 6th choice, 113th overall, in 2005 Entry Draft).

			Regular Season					Playoffs				
Season	**Club**	**League**	**GP**	**G**	**A**	**Pts**	**PIM**	**GP**	**G**	**A**	**Pts**	**PIM**
2002-03	USNTDP	NAHL	20	2	3	5	23	....	....	....	....	....
2003-04	USNTDP	U-18	46	7	8	15	16	....	....	....	....	....
	USNTDP	NAHL	11	3	6	9	17	....	....	....	....	....
2004-05	Miami U.	CCHA	38	14	11	25	30	....	....	....	....	....
2005-06	Miami U.	CCHA	37	20	20	40	34	....	....	....	....	....

CCHA First All-Star Team (2006)

DAVIS, Patrick (DAY-vihs, PAT-rihk) N.J.

Left wing. Shoots right. 6’2”, 205 lbs. Born, Sterling, MI, December 28, 1986.
(New Jersey’s 4th choice, 99th overall, in 2005 Entry Draft).

			Regular Season					Playoffs				
Season	**Club**	**League**	**GP**	**G**	**A**	**Pts**	**PIM**	**GP**	**G**	**A**	**Pts**	**PIM**
2002-03	Detroit Belle Tire	MWEHL	STATISTICS NOT AVAILABLE									
	Sioux City	USHL	16	3	2	5	8	1	0	0	0	2
2003-04	Kitchener Rangers	OHL	27	8	10	18	21	....	....	....	....	....
2004-05	Kitchener Rangers	OHL	59	20	30	50	41	14	3	4	7	20
2005-06	Kitchener Rangers	OHL	22	13	4	17	30	....	....	....	....	....
	Windsor Spitfires	OHL	38	22	29	51	64	7	2	6	8	12
	Albany River Rats	AHL	3	0	0	0	2	....	....	....	....	....

DAWES, Nigel (DAWZ, NIGH-juhl) NYR

Left wing. Shoots left. 5’8”, 190 lbs. Born, Winnipeg, Man., February 9, 1985.
(NY Rangers’ 5th choice, 149th overall, in 2003 Entry Draft).

			Regular Season					Playoffs				
Season	**Club**	**League**	**GP**	**G**	**A**	**Pts**	**PIM**	**GP**	**G**	**A**	**Pts**	**PIM**
2000-01	Winnipeg Warriors	MMMHL	36	55	41	96	74	....	....	....	....	....
2001-02	Kootenay Ice	WHL	54	15	19	34	14	22	9	6	15	8
2002-03	Kootenay Ice	WHL	72	47	45	92	54	11	4	8	12	6
2003-04	Kootenay Ice	WHL	56	47	23	70	31	4	1	2	3	10
	Hartford Wolf Pack	AHL	4	0	0	0	0	....	....	....	....	....
2004-05	Kootenay Ice	WHL	63	50	26	76	30	12	5	10	15	5
2005-06	Hartford Wolf Pack	AHL	77	35	31	66	21	13	6	6	12	9

WHL West Second All-Star Team (2003) • WHL West First All-Star Team (2004, 2005)

DAY, Brian (DAY, BRIGH-uhn) NYI

Right wing. Shoots right. 6’, 186 lbs. Born, Boston, MA, August 4, 1988.
(NY Islanders’ 11th choice, 171st overall, in 2006 Entry Draft).

			Regular Season					Playoffs				
Season	**Club**	**League**	**GP**	**G**	**A**	**Pts**	**PIM**	**GP**	**G**	**A**	**Pts**	**PIM**
2003-04	Gov. Dummer	High-MA	25	8	15	23	....	....	....	....	....	....
2004-05	Gov. Dummer	High-MA	25	11	13	24	....	....	....	....	....	....
2005-06	Gov. Dummer	High-MA	28	9	13	22	34	....	....	....	....	....

DEE, Robby (DEE, RAWB-ee) EDM.

Center/Wing. Shoots left. 6’1”, 185 lbs. Born, Minneapolis, MN, April 9, 1987.
(Edmonton’s 4th choice, 86th overall, in 2005 Entry Draft).

			Regular Season					Playoffs				
Season	**Club**	**League**	**GP**	**G**	**A**	**Pts**	**PIM**	**GP**	**G**	**A**	**Pts**	**PIM**
2004-05	Breck Mustangs	High-MN	28	49	38	87	14	....	....	....	....	....
2005-06	Omaha Lancers	USHL	32	6	6	12	20	3	1	0	1	2

Signed Letter of Intent to attend **U. of Maine** (Hockey East) in fall of 2006.

DEGRAY, John (DIH-gray, JAWN) ANA.

Defense. Shoots left. 6’4”, 204 lbs. Born, Richmond Hill, Ont., March 14, 1988.
(Anaheim’s 3rd choice, 83rd overall, in 2006 Entry Draft).

			Regular Season					Playoffs				
Season	**Club**	**League**	**GP**	**G**	**A**	**Pts**	**PIM**	**GP**	**G**	**A**	**Pts**	**PIM**
2003-04	Richmond Hill	OMHA	76	5	35	40	107	....	....	....	....	....
2004-05	Brampton	OHL	52	2	8	10	51	6	0	0	0	2
2005-06	Brampton	OHL	68	0	10	10	103	11	0	0	0	8

DELORY, James (deh-LOR-ee, JAYMZ) S.J.

Defense. Shoots right. 6’4”, 212 lbs. Born, Scarborough, Ont., March 3, 1988.
(San Jose’s 3rd choice, 98th overall, in 2006 Entry Draft).

			Regular Season					Playoffs				
Season	**Club**	**League**	**GP**	**G**	**A**	**Pts**	**PIM**	**GP**	**G**	**A**	**Pts**	**PIM**
2004-05	Oshawa Generals	OHL	61	1	4	5	82	....	....	....	....	....
2005-06	Oshawa Generals	OHL	67	6	26	32	136	....	....	....	....	....

DeMARCHI, Matt (dih-MAHR-shee, MAT)

Defense. Shoots left. 6’3”, 190 lbs. Born, Bemidji, MN, May 4, 1981.
(New Jersey’s 4th choice, 57th overall, in 2000 Entry Draft).

			Regular Season					Playoffs				
Season	**Club**	**League**	**GP**	**G**	**A**	**Pts**	**PIM**	**GP**	**G**	**A**	**Pts**	**PIM**
1997-98	North Iowa	USHL	34	1	2	3	66	10	0	1	1	19
1998-99	North Iowa	USHL	53	4	14	18	131	....	....	....	....	....
99-2000	U. of Minnesota	WCHA	39	1	6	7	82	....	....	....	....	....
2000-01	U. of Minnesota	WCHA	39	4	9	13	*149	....	....	....	....	....
2001-02	U. of Minnesota	WCHA	36	3	8	11	112	....	....	....	....	....
2002-03	U. of Minnesota	WCHA	44	8	9	17	130	....	....	....	....	....
2003-04	Albany River Rats	AHL	52	4	10	14	78	....	....	....	....	....
2004-05	Albany River Rats	AHL	61	1	6	7	85	....	....	....	....	....
2005-06	Albany River Rats	AHL	56	2	11	13	72	....	....	....	....	....

NCAA Championship All-Tournament Team (2003)

DEMEN-WILLAUME, Richard (deh-MEHN-WIHL-awm, RIH-kahrd) COL.

Defense. Shoots left. 6’3”, 196 lbs. Born, Asa, Sweden, January 28, 1986.
(Colorado’s 4th choice, 154th overall, in 2004 Entry Draft).

			Regular Season					Playoffs				
Season	**Club**	**League**	**GP**	**G**	**A**	**Pts**	**PIM**	**GP**	**G**	**A**	**Pts**	**PIM**
2001-02	V.Frolunda U18	Swe-U18	13	2	2	4	14	3	1	0	1	2
	V.Frolunda Jr.	Swe-Jr.	1	0	0	0	0	....	....	....	....	....
2002-03	V.Frolunda Jr.	Swe-Jr.	22	0	6	6	14	5	0	1	1	6
	V.Frolunda U18	Swe-U18	1	0	0	0	2	7	1	2	3	4
2003-04	V.Frolunda Jr.	Swe-Jr.	35	6	7	13	22	....	....	....	....	....
2004-05	Frolunda	Sweden	9	0	0	0	0	1	0	0	0	0
	Frolunda Jr.	Swe-Jr.	32	3	12	15	63	6	1	1	2	22
2005-06	Frolunda Jr.	Swe-Jr.	10	4	8	12	8	6	3	5	8	31
	Frolunda	Sweden	42	2	1	3	26	....	....	....	....	....

DENISOV, Denis (den-NEES-ahf, deh-NEES) BUF.

Left wing. Shoots left. 6', 183 lbs. Born, Kalinin, USSR, December 31, 1981.
(Buffalo's 4th choice, 149th overall, in 2000 Entry Draft).

			Regular Season					Playoffs				
Season	Club	League	GP	G	A	Pts	PIM	GP	G	A	Pts	PIM
1997-98	HK CSKA Moscow	Russia	7	0	0	0	4	....	....	....	....	....
1998-99	HK CSKA Moscow	Russia-2	42	1	6	7	16	....	....	....	....	....
99-2000	HK Moscow	Russia-2	39	1	8	9	16	....	....	....	....	....
2000-01	HK Moscow	Russia-2	41	0	3	3	6	....	....	....	....	....
2001-02	Krylja Sovetov	Russia	47	3	4	7	37	....	....	....	....	....
	Krylja Sovetov 2	Russia-3	3	0	1	1	18	....	....	....	....	....
2002-03	Ufa	Russia	50	2	8	10	12	3	0	1	1	0
2003-04	Ak Bars Kazan	Russia	51	4	11	15	34	7	0	0	0	4
2004-05	Ak Bars Kazan	Russia	57	4	7	11	30	4	0	0	0	2
2005-06	Ak Bars Kazan	Russia	22	0	2	2	51	2	0	0	0	4

DENNY, Chad (DEHN-ee, CHAD) ATL.

Defense. Shoots left. 6'2", 220 lbs. Born, Sydney, N.S., March 27, 1987.
(Atlanta's 3rd choice, 49th overall, in 2005 Entry Draft).

			Regular Season					Playoffs				
Season	Club	League	GP	G	A	Pts	PIM	GP	G	A	Pts	PIM
2003-04	Lewiston	QMJHL	41	3	6	9	19	7	0	0	0	11
2004-05	Lewiston	QMJHL	53	8	18	26	98	8	2	2	4	14
2005-06	Lewiston	QMJHL	62	19	28	47	150	6	0	3	3	10

DERLYUK, Roman (duhr-LYUHK, ROH-muhn) FLA.

Defense. Shoots left. 6'3", 198 lbs. Born, Leningrad, USSR, October 27, 1986.
(Florida's 7th choice, 164th overall, in 2005 Entry Draft).

			Regular Season					Playoffs				
Season	Club	League	GP	G	A	Pts	PIM	GP	G	A	Pts	PIM
2003-04	Lokom. St. Pete.	Russia-3	STATISTICS NOT AVAILABLE									
2004-05	Spartak St. Pet.	Russia-2	51	0	3	3	74	....	....	....	....	....
2005-06	SKA St. Petersburg	Russia	32	0	3	3	63	2	1	0	1	0
	St. Petersburg 2	Russia-3	2	0	1	1	0	....	....	....	....	....

DESBIENS, Guillaume (deh-BYEHN, gwee-AHM) ATL.

Right wing. Shoots left. 6'2", 210 lbs. Born, Alma, Que., April 20, 1985.
(Atlanta's 3rd choice, 116th overall, in 2003 Entry Draft).

			Regular Season					Playoffs				
Season	Club	League	GP	G	A	Pts	PIM	GP	G	A	Pts	PIM
2001-02	Rouyn-Noranda	QMJHL	65	14	10	24	115	4	1	1	2	9
2002-03	Rouyn-Noranda	QMJHL	64	15	18	33	233	4	0	0	0	4
2003-04	Rouyn-Noranda	QMJHL	58	20	21	41	199	11	2	2	4	24
2004-05	Rouyn-Noranda	QMJHL	56	27	16	43	206	10	1	4	5	25
2005-06	Chicago Wolves	AHL	3	0	0	0	7	....	....	....	....	....
	Gwinnett	ECHL	65	33	27	60	187	17	10	6	16	38

DEVEAUX, Andre (de-VOH, AWN-dray) T.B.

Center. Shoots right. 6'3", 240 lbs. Born, Freeport, Bahamas, February 23, 1984.
(Montreal's 4th choice, 182nd overall, in 2002 Entry Draft).

			Regular Season					Playoffs				
Season	Club	League	GP	G	A	Pts	PIM	GP	G	A	Pts	PIM
2000-01	Belleville Bulls	OHL	58	3	6	9	65	10	3	6	9	6
2001-02	Belleville Bulls	OHL	64	8	13	21	89	11	1	2	3	30
2002-03	Belleville Bulls	OHL	34	6	12	18	93	....	....	....	....	....
	Owen Sound	OHL	29	9	10	19	33	4	2	2	4	6
2003-04	Owen Sound	OHL	64	16	30	46	151	7	3	3	6	21
2004-05	Springfield Falcons	AHL	73	4	8	12	210	....	....	....	....	....
2005-06	Springfield Falcons	AHL	59	6	5	11	135	....	....	....	....	....
	Johnstown Chiefs	ECHL	11	4	7	11	36	5	1	1	2	2

Signed as a free agent by **Tampa Bay**, September 15, 2004.

DICAIRE, Gerard (dih-KAIR, zhehr-AHR)

Defense. Shoots left. 6'2", 190 lbs. Born, Faro, Yukon, September 14, 1982.
(Tampa Bay's 4th choice, 162nd overall, in 2002 Entry Draft).

			Regular Season					Playoffs				
Season	Club	League	GP	G	A	Pts	PIM	GP	G	A	Pts	PIM
1997-98	Tumble Ridge	NWJHL	35	15	28	43	63	....	....	....	....	....
1998-99	Prince George	BCHL	51	6	22	28	28	....	....	....	....	....
99-2000	Seattle	WHL	68	11	25	36	38	7	0	1	1	6
2000-01	Seattle	WHL	69	15	36	51	33	9	0	2	2	2
2001-02	Seattle	WHL	41	4	25	29	25	....	....	....	....	....
	Kootenay Ice	WHL	25	2	21	23	9	22	1	14	15	24
2002-03	Kootenay Ice	WHL	72	15	44	59	79	11	2	6	8	12
2003-04	Utah Grizzlies	AHL	53	2	7	9	36	....	....	....	....	....
2004-05	Springfield Falcons	AHL	47	3	4	7	20	....	....	....	....	....
2005-06	Springfield Falcons	AHL	40	1	7	8	12	....	....	....	....	....
	Johnstown Chiefs	ECHL	27	4	10	14	14	....	....	....	....	....

• Re-entered NHL Entry Draft. Originally Buffalo's 2nd choice, 48th overall, in 2000 Entry Draft.

WHL West Second All-Star Team (2001, 2003)

DiCASMIRRO, Nate (dee-CAZ-MIHR-oh, NAYT) BOS.

Left wing. Shoots left. 5'11", 205 lbs. Born, Atikokan, Ont, September 27, 1978.

			Regular Season					Playoffs				
Season	Club	League	GP	G	A	Pts	PIM	GP	G	A	Pts	PIM
1996-97	North Iowa	USHL	51	18	22	40	86	12	0	6	6	22
1997-98	North Iowa	USHL	52	29	45	74	118	11	5	5	10	34
1998-99	St. Cloud State	WCHA	34	6	8	14	46	....	....	....	....	....
99-2000	St. Cloud State	WCHA	40	19	24	43	26	....	....	....	....	....
2000-01	St. Cloud State	WCHA	32	9	20	29	26	....	....	....	....	....
2001-02	St. Cloud State	WCHA	41	17	33	50	58	....	....	....	....	....
	Hamilton Bulldogs	AHL	1	0	0	0	0	10	0	5	5	6
2002-03	Hamilton Bulldogs	AHL	49	5	12	17	22	16	2	1	3	8
2003-04	Toronto	AHL	71	17	18	35	37	2	0	1	1	0
2004-05	Edmonton	AHL	77	7	18	25	48	....	....	....	....	....
2005-06	Grand Rapids	AHL	72	16	36	52	97	16	3	3	6	20

USHL First All-Star Team (1998) • USHL MVP (1998) • WCHA Second All-Star Team (2002)

Signed as a free agent by **Edmonton**, May 28, 2002. Signed as a free agent by **Boston**, July 17, 2006.

DIDIOMETE, Devin (dih-dee-OH-meht, DEH-vihn) CGY.

Left wing. Shoots left. 5'11", 200 lbs. Born, Stratford, Ont., May 9, 1988.
(Calgary's 7th choice, 187th overall, in 2006 Entry Draft).

			Regular Season					Playoffs				
Season	Club	League	GP	G	A	Pts	PIM	GP	G	A	Pts	PIM
2004-05	Sudbury Wolves	OHL	58	7	8	15	113	11	0	1	1	11
2005-06	Sudbury Wolves	OHL	60	15	21	36	202	10	0	4	4	26

DILLON, Spencer (DIH-luhn, SPEHN-suhr) FLA.

Defense. Shoots right. 6'4", 190 lbs. Born, Santa Cruz, CA, January 7, 1985.
(Florida's 6th choice, 267th overall, in 2004 Entry Draft).

			Regular Season					Playoffs				
Season	Club	League	GP	G	A	Pts	PIM	GP	G	A	Pts	PIM
2003-04	Salmon Arm	BCHL	42	0	7	7	160	14	0	2	2	22
2004-05	Green Bay	USHL	54	1	2	3	91	....	....	....	....	....
2005-06	Northern Mich.	CCHA	6	0	1	1	14	....	....	....	....	....

• Missed majority of 2005-06 season due to injury.

DIXON, Stephen (DIHX-uhn, STEE-vehn) PIT.

Center. Shoots left. 5'11", 188 lbs. Born, Halifax, N.S., September 7, 1985.
(Pittsburgh's 9th choice, 229th overall, in 2003 Entry Draft).

			Regular Season					Playoffs				
Season	Club	League	GP	G	A	Pts	PIM	GP	G	A	Pts	PIM
2001-02	Cape Breton	QMJHL	64	16	15	31	12	16	3	5	8	12
2002-03	Cape Breton	QMJHL	72	28	42	70	54	4	0	0	0	6
2003-04	Cape Breton	QMJHL	55	22	50	72	33	5	1	0	1	0
2004-05	Cape Breton	QMJHL	45	17	34	51	40	....	....	....	....	....
2005-06	Wilkes-Barre	AHL	80	12	17	29	45	11	0	1	1	4

DOBRYSHKIN, Yuri (doh-BRIHSH-kihn, yew-REE) ATL.

Left wing. Shoots right. 6', 190 lbs. Born, Penza, USSR, July 19, 1979.
(Atlanta's 7th choice, 159th overall, in 1999 Entry Draft).

			Regular Season					Playoffs				
Season	Club	League	GP	G	A	Pts	PIM	GP	G	A	Pts	PIM
1996-97	Krylja Sovetov 2	Russia-3	35	13	5	18	42	....	....	....	....	....
	Krylja Sovetov	Russia	2	0	0	0	0	2	0	0	0	0
1997-98	Krylja Sovetov 2	Russia-3	26	12	5	17	68	....	....	....	....	....
	Krylja Sovetov	Russia	22	4	0	4	12	....	....	....	....	....
1998-99	Krylja Sovetov	Russia	50	11	5	16	86	....	....	....	....	....
99-2000	Ak Bars Kazan	Russia	27	6	9	15	24	17	2	0	2	10
2000-01	Ak Bars Kazan	Russia	40	10	5	15	32	4	2	0	2	2
2001-02	Ak Bars Kazan	Russia	38	9	8	17	22	11	0	2	2	6
2002-03	Cherepovets	Russia	49	19	7	26	82	12	5	2	7	12
2003-04	Cherepovets	Russia	53	11	7	18	75	....	....	....	....	....
2004-05	Magnitogorsk	Russia	54	14	6	20	42	2	0	0	0	0
2005-06	Magnitogorsk	Russia	15	3	1	4	22	8	0	0	0	0
	Magnitogorsk 2	Russia-3	2	3	1	4	2	....	....	....	....	....

DODGE, Nick (DAWGE, NIHK) CAR.

Right wing. Shoots right. 5'10", 175 lbs. Born, Oakville, Ont., May 1, 1986.
(Carolina's 5th choice, 183rd overall, in 2006 Entry Draft).

			Regular Season					Playoffs				
Season	Club	League	GP	G	A	Pts	PIM	GP	G	A	Pts	PIM
2004-05	Clarkson Knights	ECACHL	37	6	12	18	42	....	....	....	....	....
2005-06	Clarkson Knights	ECACHL	38	16	25	41	72	....	....	....	....	....

DOELL, Kevin (DOH-ehl, KEH-vihn) ATL.

Center. Shoots left. 5'11", 190 lbs. Born, Saskatoon, Sask., July 15, 1979.

			Regular Season					Playoffs				
Season	Club	League	GP	G	A	Pts	PIM	GP	G	A	Pts	PIM
99-2000	U. of Denver	WCHA	40	8	15	23	18	....	....	....	....	....
2000-01	U. of Denver	WCHA	36	9	10	19	26	....	....	....	....	....
2001-02	U. of Denver	WCHA	41	20	23	43	28	....	....	....	....	....
2002-03	U. of Denver	WCHA	41	25	26	51	34	....	....	....	....	....
2003-04	Chicago Wolves	AHL	8	1	1	2	6	1	0	0	0	0
	Gwinnett	ECHL	63	33	41	74	88	13	1	6	7	12
2004-05	Chicago Wolves	AHL	45	4	8	12	69	....	....	....	....	....
	Gwinnett	ECHL	11	6	9	15	14	8	2	1	3	14
2005-06	Chicago Wolves	AHL	78	17	34	51	72	....	....	....	....	....

ECHL All-Rookie Team (2004) • ECHL Rookie of the Year (2004)

Signed as a free agent by **Atlanta**, June 30, 2004.

DOHERTY, John (DOH-her-tee, JAWN) TOR.

Defense. Shoots right. 6'4", 235 lbs. Born, Malden, MA, March 25, 1984.
(Toronto's 1st choice, 57th overall, in 2003 Entry Draft).

			Regular Season					Playoffs				
Season	Club	League	GP	G	A	Pts	PIM	GP	G	A	Pts	PIM
2001-02	Andover	High-MA	24	5	18	23	....	....	....	....	....	....
2002-03	Andover	High-MA	24	12	12	24	40	....	....	....	....	....
	N.H. Jr. Monarchs	EJHL	11	1	4	5	36	....	....	....	....	....
2003-04	New Hampshire	H-East	16	1	2	3	6	....	....	....	....	....
2004-05	New Hampshire	H-East	4	0	0	0	2	....	....	....	....	....
	Des Moines	USHL	39	9	7	16	96	....	....	....	....	....
2005-06	Quinnipiac	ECACHL	DID NOT PLAY – TRANSFERRED COLLEGES									

DONALLY, Ryan (DAWN-ah-lee, RIGH-uhn) CGY.

Left wing. Shoots left. 6'5", 227 lbs. Born, Tecumseh, Ont., February 4, 1985.
(Calgary's 3rd choice, 97th overall, in 2003 Entry Draft).

			Regular Season					Playoffs				
Season	Club	League	GP	G	A	Pts	PIM	GP	G	A	Pts	PIM
2001-02	Windsor Spitfires	OHL	53	6	7	13	77	16	0	2	2	6
2002-03	Windsor Spitfires	OHL	65	11	15	26	108	7	0	1	1	8
2003-04	Windsor Spitfires	OHL	44	8	14	22	93	....	....	....	....	....
2004-05	Windsor Spitfires	OHL	29	2	3	5	87	....	....	....	....	....
	Kitchener Rangers	OHL	21	1	2	3	45	13	0	0	0	12
2005-06	Kitchener Rangers	OHL	8	0	0	0	29	....	....	....	....	....
	Sudbury Wolves	OHL	39	5	5	10	76	10	0	1	1	27

DONIKA, Mikhail (DAW-nih-ka, mih-kigh-EHL) DAL.

Defense. Shoots left. 6', 185 lbs. Born, Yaroslavl, USSR, May 15, 1979.
(Dallas' 11th choice, 272nd overall, in 1999 Entry Draft).

			Regular Season					Playoffs				
Season	Club	League	GP	G	A	Pts	PIM	GP	G	A	Pts	PIM
1996-97	Yaroslavl 2	Russia-3	15	3	5	8	6	....	....	....	....	....
	Torpedo Yaroslavl	Russia	22	1	0	1	6	2	0	0	0	0
1997-98	Yaroslavl 2	Russia-2	19	1	2	3	32	....	....	....	....	....
	Torpedo Yaroslavl	Russia	30	0	2	2	14	....	....	....	....	....
1998-99	Yaroslavl 2	Russia-3	6	2	1	3	4	....	....	....	....	....
	Torpedo Yaroslavl	Russia	37	0	1	1	10	....	....	....	....	....
99-2000	Torpedo Yaroslavl	Russia	35	0	1	1	22	10	0	0	0	4
2000-01	Dynamo Moscow	Russia	43	1	3	4	12	....	....	....	....	....
2001-02	Amur Khabarovsk	Russia	51	1	3	4	66	....	....	....	....	....
2002-03	Spartak Moscow	Russia	51	4	7	11	16	....	....	....	....	....
2003-04	Spartak Moscow	Russia-2	55	4	14	18	14	12	2	1	3	2
2004-05	Spartak Moscow	Russia	49	0	2	2	34	....	....	....	....	....
2005-06	Perm	Russia	26	0	0	0	18	....	....	....	....	....
	Sibir Novosibirsk	Russia	14	1	3	4	8	3	0	1	1	0

DORNIC, Ivan (DOHR-nihch, ee-VAHN) NYR

Center. Shoots right. 6', 195 lbs. Born, Bratislava, Czech., April 12, 1985.
(NY Rangers' 6th choice, 176th overall, in 2003 Entry Draft).

			Regular Season					Playoffs				
Season	Club	League	GP	G	A	Pts	PIM	GP	G	A	Pts	PIM
2001-02	Bratislava Jr.	Slovak-Jr.	17	7	7	14	33	....	....	....	....	....
2002-03	Bratislava Jr.	Slovak-Jr.	33	13	13	26	45	....	....	....	....	....
	Bratislava	Slovakia	8	1	0	1	0	....	....	....	....	....
2003-04	Portland	WHL	54	6	8	14	28	5	0	0	0	4
2004-05	Portland	WHL	8	0	1	1	5	....	....	....	....	....
	HK Trnava	Slovak-2	6	3	2	5	2	3	0	0	0	4
	Bratislava Jr.	Slovak-Jr.	10	7	5	12	26	1	0	1	1	2
	Bratislava	Slovakia	24	2	2	4	2	16	2	0	2	2
2005-06	Bratislava	Slovakia	31	2	2	4	26	....	....	....	....	....
	HK 36 Skalica	Slovakia	19	1	2	3	6	6	1	1	2	0

DORSETT, Derek (DORH-seht, DAIR-ihk) CBJ

Right wing. Shoots right. 5'11", 176 lbs. Born, Kindersley, Sask., December 20, 1986.
(Columbus' 9th choice, 189th overall, in 2006 Entry Draft).

			Regular Season					Playoffs				
Season	Club	League	GP	G	A	Pts	PIM	GP	G	A	Pts	PIM
2004-05	Medicine Hat	WHL	51	5	11	16	108	13	5	1	6	35
2005-06	Medicine Hat	WHL	68	25	23	48	279	13	8	4	12	53

DOVGAN, Viktor (DAWV-guhn, VIHK-tohr) WSH.

Defense. Shoots left. 6'1", 205 lbs. Born, Moscow, USSR, February 27, 1987.
(Washington's 7th choice, 209th overall, in 2005 Entry Draft).

			Regular Season					Playoffs				
Season	Club	League	GP	G	A	Pts	PIM	GP	G	A	Pts	PIM
2003-04	CSKA Moscow 2	Russia-3	STATISTICS NOT AVAILABLE									
2004-05	CSKA Moscow 2	Russia-3	STATISTICS NOT AVAILABLE									
2005-06	CSKA Moscow 2	Russia-3	STATISTICS NOT AVAILABLE									
	CSK VVS Samara	Russia-2	8	1	2	3	20	3	0	1	1	4

DOWELL, Jake (DOW-uhl, JAYK) CHI.

Center. Shoots left. 5'11", 200 lbs. Born, Eau Claire, WI, March 4, 1985.
(Chicago's 10th choice, 140th overall, in 2004 Entry Draft).

			Regular Season					Playoffs				
Season	Club	League	GP	G	A	Pts	PIM	GP	G	A	Pts	PIM
2000-01	Eau Claire Mem.	High-WI	24	25	30	55	....	....	....	....	....	....
2001-02	USNTDP	U-17	11	5	1	6	14	....	....	....	....	....
	USNTDP	NAHL	44	5	12	17	51	....	....	....	....	....
2002-03	USNTDP	U-18	54	8	17	25	54	....	....	....	....	....
	USNTDP	NAHL	9	2	2	4	13	....	....	....	....	....
2003-04	U. of Wisconsin	WCHA	37	6	13	19	48	....	....	....	....	....
2004-05	U. of Wisconsin	WCHA	38	12	14	26	74	....	....	....	....	....
2005-06	U. of Wisconsin	WCHA	43	5	15	20	42	....	....	....	....	....

DOWNIE, Steve (DOW-nee, STEEV) PHI.

Right wing. Shoots right. 5'10", 192 lbs. Born, Newmarket, Ont., April 3, 1987.
(Philadelphia's 1st choice, 29th overall, in 2005 Entry Draft).

			Regular Season					Playoffs				
Season	Club	League	GP	G	A	Pts	PIM	GP	G	A	Pts	PIM
2002-03	Aurora Tigers	OPJHL	34	12	13	25	55	....	....	....	....	....
2003-04	Windsor Spitfires	OHL	49	7	9	16	90	4	0	1	1	27
2004-05	Windsor Spitfires	OHL	61	21	52	73	179	11	4	5	9	49
2005-06	Windsor Spitfires	OHL	1	3	0	3	4	....	....	....	....	....
	Peterborough	OHL	34	16	34	50	109	19	6	15	21	38

DRAZENOVIC, Nicholas (DRAY-zehn-oh-vihk, NIHK-oh-las) ST.L.

Center. Shoots left. 6', 172 lbs. Born, Prince George, B.C., January 14, 1987.
(St. Louis' 6th choice, 171st overall, in 2005 Entry Draft).

			Regular Season					Playoffs				
Season	Club	League	GP	G	A	Pts	PIM	GP	G	A	Pts	PIM
2003-04	Prince George	WHL	65	7	30	37	38	....	....	....	....	....
2004-05	Prince George	WHL	72	18	38	56	24	....	....	....	....	....
2005-06	Prince George	WHL	71	30	33	63	51	5	0	0	0	4

DROZDETSKY, Alexander (drawz-DEHT-skee, al-ehx-AN-duhr) PHI.

Right wing. Shoots left. 6', 180 lbs. Born, Moscow, USSR, November 10, 1981.
(Philadelphia's 2nd choice, 94th overall, in 2000 Entry Draft).

			Regular Season					Playoffs				
Season	Club	League	GP	G	A	Pts	PIM	GP	G	A	Pts	PIM
1997-98	St. Petersburg 2	Russia-3	19	0	1	1	0	....	....	....	....	....
1998-99	St. Petersburg 2	Russia-4	24	5	3	8	12	....	....	....	....	....
99-2000	St. Petersburg 2	Russia-3	4	4	1	5	2	....	....	....	....	....
	SKA St. Petersburg	Russia	32	2	0	2	10	4	0	0	0	0
2000-01	SKA St. Petersburg	Russia	42	6	7	13	74	....	....	....	....	....
2001-02	CSKA Moscow	Russia	49	11	6	17	26	....	....	....	....	....
2002-03	CSKA Moscow	Russia	46	14	13	27	30	....	....	....	....	....
2003-04	Ak Bars Kazan	Russia	57	16	15	31	62	1	0	0	0	2
2004-05	Ak Bars Kazan	Russia	32	3	4	7	28	....	....	....	....	....
	Ak Bars Kazan 2	Russia-3	....	10	8	18	....	....	....	....	....	....
	Nizhnekamsk	Russia	7	5	1	6	4	....	....	....	....	....
2005-06	Avangard Omsk	Russia	30	6	6	12	26	....	....	....	....	....
	SKA St. Petersburg	Russia	16	4	10	14	6	3	0	0	0	0

DUBINSKY, Brandon (DOO-bihn-skee, BRAN-duhn) NYR

Center. Shoots left. 6'1", 224 lbs. Born, Anchorage, AK, April 29, 1986.
(NY Rangers' 6th choice, 60th overall, in 2004 Entry Draft).

			Regular Season					Playoffs				
Season	Club	League	GP	G	A	Pts	PIM	GP	G	A	Pts	PIM
2001-02	Alaska All-Stars	AASHA	37	14	24	38	....	....	....	....	....	....
2002-03	Portland	WHL	44	8	18	26	35	7	2	2	4	10
2003-04	Portland	WHL	71	30	48	78	137	5	0	2	2	6
2004-05	Portland	WHL	68	23	36	59	160	7	4	5	9	8
2005-06	Portland	WHL	51	21	46	67	98	12	5	10	15	24
	Hartford Wolf Pack	AHL	....	....	....	....	....	11	5	5	10	14

WHL West Second All-Star Team (2004, 2006)

DUDAS, Jesse (DOO-dah, JEH-see) CBJ

Defense. Shoots right. 6'1", 214 lbs. Born, St. Albert, Alta., March 31, 1988.
(Columbus' 8th choice, 159th overall, in 2006 Entry Draft).

			Regular Season					Playoffs				
Season	Club	League	GP	G	A	Pts	PIM	GP	G	A	Pts	PIM
2004-05	Lethbridge	WHL	44	1	3	4	28	2	0	1	1	0
2005-06	Lethbridge	WHL	18	0	7	7	12	....	....	....	....	....
	Prince George	WHL	6	0	4	4	15	....	....	....	....	....

DUFFY, Matt (DUHF-ee, MAT) FLA.

Defense. Shoots right. 6'2", 180 lbs. Born, Portland, ME, March 21, 1986.
(Florida's 5th choice, 104th overall, in 2005 Entry Draft).

			Regular Season					Playoffs				
Season	Club	League	GP	G	A	Pts	PIM	GP	G	A	Pts	PIM
2003-04	N.H. Jr. Monarchs	EJHL	33	9	13	22	....	....	....	....	....	....
2004-05	N.H. Jr. Monarchs	EJHL	54	19	26	45	147	....	....	....	....	....
2005-06	U. of Maine	H-East	28	3	5	8	43	....	....	....	....	....

DUPONT, Brodie (DOO-pohnt, BROH-dee) NYR

Center. Shoots left. 6'2", 206 lbs. Born, Russell, Man., February 17, 1987.
(NY Rangers' 4th choice, 66th overall, in 2005 Entry Draft).

			Regular Season					Playoffs				
Season	Club	League	GP	G	A	Pts	PIM	GP	G	A	Pts	PIM
2003-04	Swan Valley	MJHL	51	25	16	41	88	12	5	1	6	36
	Calgary Hitmen	WHL	2	0	1	1	0	....	....	....	....	....
2004-05	Calgary Hitmen	WHL	70	14	11	25	111	12	2	8	10	21
2005-06	Calgary Hitmen	WHL	72	30	23	53	123	13	4	5	9	24

DUPUIS, Philippe (doo-PWEE, fihl-EEP) CBJ

Center. Shoots right. 6', 196 lbs. Born, Laval, Que., April 24, 1985.
(Columbus' 5th choice, 104th overall, in 2003 Entry Draft).

			Regular Season					Playoffs				
Season	Club	League	GP	G	A	Pts	PIM	GP	G	A	Pts	PIM
2000-01	Laval-Laurentides	QAAA	46	16	27	43	74	8	1	5	6	30
2001-02	Hull Olympiques	QMJHL	67	7	14	21	59	12	6	5	11	14
2002-03	Hull Olympiques	QMJHL	68	22	34	56	89	20	2	4	6	22
2003-04	Gatineau	QMJHL	60	18	37	55	77	15	6	10	16	14
2004-05	Rouyn-Noranda	QMJHL	62	34	50	84	60	10	5	3	8	8
2005-06	Moncton Wildcats	QMJHL	56	32	76	108	52	19	14	18	32	14

DURAND, Chris (DUHR-and, KRIHS) COL.

Center. Shoots right. 6'1", 186 lbs. Born, Saskatoon, Sask., January 21, 1987.
(Colorado's 4th choice, 52nd overall, in 2005 Entry Draft).

			Regular Season					Playoffs				
Season	Club	League	GP	G	A	Pts	PIM	GP	G	A	Pts	PIM
2002-03	Sask. Contacts	SMHL	39	9	18	27	38	....	....	....	....	....
2003-04	Seattle	WHL	60	17	26	43	71	....	....	....	....	....
2004-05	Seattle	WHL	66	19	34	53	76	12	0	1	1	14
2005-06	Seattle	WHL	71	14	20	34	105	7	5	3	8	12

DWYER, Patrick (DWIGH-uhr, PAT-rihk) CAR.

Right wing. Shoots right. 5'11", 185 lbs. Born, Great Falls, MT, June 22, 1983.
(Atlanta's 3rd choice, 116th overall, in 2002 Entry Draft).

			Regular Season					Playoffs				
Season	Club	League	GP	G	A	Pts	PIM	GP	G	A	Pts	PIM
2000-01	Great Falls	NWJHL	40	33	57	90	106	12	10	12	22	....
2001-02	Western Mich.	CCHA	38	17	17	34	26	....	....	....	....	....
2002-03	Western Mich.	CCHA	33	9	10	19	20	....	....	....	....	....
2003-04	Western Mich.	CCHA	35	13	13	26	22	....	....	....	....	....
2004-05	Western Mich.	CCHA	36	6	16	22	56	....	....	....	....	....
2005-06	Chicago Wolves	AHL	73	16	29	45	49	....	....	....	....	....

CCHA All-Rookie Team (2002) • CCHA Rookie of the Year (2002)

Signed as a free agent by **Carolina**, July 7, 2006.

DYMENT, Chris (DIGH-mehnt, KRIHS)

Defense. Shoots right. 6'3", 207 lbs. Born, Reading, MA, October 24, 1979.
(Montreal's 3rd choice, 97th overall, in 1999 Entry Draft).

			Regular Season					Playoffs				
Season	Club	League	GP	G	A	Pts	PIM	GP	G	A	Pts	PIM
1997-98	Reading	High-MA	22	22	22	44	15	....	....	....	....	....
1998-99	Boston University	H-East	25	1	5	6	16	....	....	....	....	....
99-2000	Boston University	H-East	42	11	20	31	42	....	....	....	....	....
2000-01	Boston University	H-East	37	1	10	11	38	....	....	....	....	....
2001-02	Boston University	H-East	38	7	18	25	24	....	....	....	....	....
2002-03	Houston Aeros	AHL	40	2	3	5	64	17	0	1	1	8
2003-04	Houston Aeros	AHL	13	1	0	1	12	....	....	....	....	....
	Springfield Falcons	AHL	23	0	1	1	16	....	....	....	....	....
2004-05	Providence Bruins	AHL	48	3	4	7	112	5	0	0	0	0
2005-06	Providence Bruins	AHL	32	4	7	11	47	5	0	0	0	4

Hockey East First All-Star Team (2000) • NCAA East Second All-American Team (2000) • Hockey East Second All-Star Team (2002)

Traded to **Minnesota** by **Montreal** for Minnesota's 5th round choice (later traded to Calgary – Calgary selected Jiri Cetkovsky) in 2002 Entry Draft, May 25, 2002. Traded to **Phoenix** by **Minnesota** for Michael Schutte, December 9, 2003. Signed as a free agent by **Boston**, September 8, 2004.

EARL, Robbie (UHRL, RAW-bee) TOR.

Left wing. Shoots left. 6', 195 lbs. Born, Chicago, IL, June 6, 1985.
(Toronto's 4th choice, 187th overall, in 2004 Entry Draft).

			Regular Season					Playoffs				
Season	Club	League	GP	G	A	Pts	PIM	GP	G	A	Pts	PIM
2000-01	L.A. Jr. Kings	Cal-Am	29	48	22	70	....	....	....	....	....	....
2001-02	USNTDP	U-17	15	8	9	17	....	....	....	....	....	....
	USNTDP	NAHL	43	14	7	21	43	....	....	....	....	....
2002-03	USNTDP	U-18	43	16	8	24	58	....	....	....	....	....
	USNTDP	NAHL	10	4	5	9	18	....	....	....	....	....
2003-04	U. of Wisconsin	WCHA	42	14	13	27	46	....	....	....	....	....
2004-05	U. of Wisconsin	WCHA	41	20	24	44	62	....	....	....	....	....
2005-06	U. of Wisconsin	WCHA	42	24	26	50	56	....	....	....	....	....
	Toronto Marlies	AHL	1	0	0	0	0	3	0	0	0	0

WCHA All-Rookie Team (2004) • WCHA Second All-Star Team (2005)

ECKFORD, Tyler (EHK-fuhrd, TIGH-luhr) N.J.

Defense. Shoots left. 6'1", 205 lbs. Born, Vancouver, B.C., September 8, 1985.
(New Jersey's 5th choice, 217th overall, in 2004 Entry Draft).

			Regular Season					Playoffs				
Season	Club	League	GP	G	A	Pts	PIM	GP	G	A	Pts	PIM
2003-04	South Surrey	BCHL	58	7	30	37	101	13	2	8	10	34
2004-05	South Surrey	BCHL	60	22	43	65	93	25	4	15	19	46
2005-06	Alaska-Fairbanks	CCHA	38	3	15	18	43	....	....	....	....	....

CCHA All-Rookie Team (2006)

EDLER, Alexander (EHD-luhr, al-EHX-AN-duhr) VAN.

Defense. Shoots left. 6'3", 194 lbs. Born, Stockholm, Sweden, April 21, 1986.
(Vancouver's 2nd choice, 91st overall, in 2004 Entry Draft).

			Regular Season					Playoffs				
Season	Club	League	GP	G	A	Pts	PIM	GP	G	A	Pts	PIM
2001-02	Jamtland	Exhib.	8	0	1	1	2	....	....	....	....	....
2002-03	Jamtland	Exhib.	8	2	1	3	0	....	....	....	....	....
2003-04	Jamtland Jr.	Swe-Jr.	6	0	3	3	6	....	....	....	....	....
	Jamtland	Sweden-3	24	3	6	9	20	....	....	....	....	....
2004-05	MODO Jr.	Swe-Jr.	33	8	15	23	40	5	1	0	1	6
2005-06	Kelowna Rockets	WHL	62	13	40	53	44	12	3	5	8	12

EGENER, Mike (EHG-eh-nuhr, MIGHK) T.B.

Defense. Shoots left. 6'4", 216 lbs. Born, Lahr, West Germany, September 26, 1984.
(Tampa Bay's 1st choice, 34th overall, in 2003 Entry Draft).

			Regular Season					Playoffs				
Season	Club	League	GP	G	A	Pts	PIM	GP	G	A	Pts	PIM
99-2000	Calgary Bruins	CMHA	27	4	9	13	88	....	....	....	....	....
2000-01	Calgary Hitmen	WHL	52	1	0	1	91	6	0	0	0	5
2001-02	Calgary Hitmen	WHL	68	2	7	9	175	6	0	0	0	23
2002-03	Calgary Hitmen	WHL	40	2	8	10	210	3	1	0	1	8
2003-04	Calgary Hitmen	WHL	64	1	16	17	228	7	1	1	2	47
2004-05	Springfield Falcons	AHL	45	3	2	5	183	....	....	....	....	....
2005-06	Springfield Falcons	AHL	38	2	1	3	142	....	....	....	....	....
	Johnstown Chiefs	ECHL	18	2	2	4	66	....	....	....	....	....

ELLIOTT, Brandon (EHL-lee-awt, BRAN-duhn) T.B.

Defense. Shoots left. 6'4", 225 lbs. Born, Orangeville, Ont., March 8, 1984.
(Tampa Bay's 4th choice, 158th overall, in 2004 Entry Draft).

			Regular Season					Playoffs				
Season	Club	League	GP	G	A	Pts	PIM	GP	G	A	Pts	PIM
2001-02	Orangeville	OHA-B		STATISTICS NOT AVAILABLE								
	Mississauga	OHL	7	0	0	0	14	....	....	....	....	....
2002-03	Collingwood Blues	OPJHL		STATISTICS NOT AVAILABLE								
2003-04	Collingwood Blues	OPJHL	25	6	15	21	138	....	....	....	....	....
	Mississauga	OHL	30	0	4	4	89	13	0	0	0	32
2004-05	Mississauga	OHL	22	1	4	5	74	....	....	....	....	....
	Springfield Falcons	AHL	2	0	0	0	7	....	....	....	....	....
	Victoria	ECHL	13	0	2	2	41	....	....	....	....	....
2005-06	Johnstown Chiefs	ECHL	68	10	7	17	207	5	0	0	0	0

ELLIS, Matt (EH-lihs, MAT) DET.

Left wing. Shoots left. 6'1", 190 lbs. Born, Welland, Ont., August 31, 1981.

			Regular Season					Playoffs				
Season	Club	League	GP	G	A	Pts	PIM	GP	G	A	Pts	PIM
1998-99	St. Michael's	OHL	47	10	8	18	6	....	....	....	....	....
99-2000	St. Michael's	OHL	59	15	20	35	20	....	....	....	....	....
2000-01	St. Michael's	OHL	68	21	24	45	19	18	4	8	12	6
2001-02	St. Michael's	OHL	66	38	51	89	20	15	8	6	14	6
2002-03	Toledo Storm	ECHL	71	27	32	59	34	7	3	5	8	0
2003-04	Grand Rapids	AHL	64	5	10	15	23	4	0	0	0	2
2004-05	Grand Rapids	AHL	79	18	23	41	59	....	....	....	....	....
2005-06	Grand Rapids	AHL	74	20	28	48	61	16	4	1	5	20

Signed as a free agent by **Detroit**, May 10, 2002.

EMMERSON, Riley (EHM-uhr-sohn, RIGH-lee) MIN.

Right wing. Shoots left. 6'6", 250 lbs. Born, Burnaby, B.C., February 7, 1986.
(Minnesota's 7th choice, 199th overall, in 2005 Entry Draft).

			Regular Season					Playoffs				
Season	Club	League	GP	G	A	Pts	PIM	GP	G	A	Pts	PIM
2003-04	Chilliwack Chiefs	BCHL	52	0	6	6	137	6	0	0	0	0
2004-05	Tri-City Americans	WHL	35	0	0	0	61	....	....	....	....	....
2005-06	Tri-City Americans	WHL	66	1	1	2	109	2	0	0	0	0

EMMERTON, Cory (EHM-uhr-tuhn, KOHR-ee) DET.

Center. Shoots left. 5'11", 177 lbs. Born, St. Thomas, Ont., June 1, 1988.
(Detroit's 1st choice, 41st overall, in 2006 Entry Draft).

			Regular Season					Playoffs				
Season	Club	League	GP	G	A	Pts	PIM	GP	G	A	Pts	PIM
2004-05	Kingston	OHL	58	17	21	38	8	....	....	....	....	....
2005-06	Kingston	OHL	66	26	64	90	32	6	2	0	2	6

ENGASSER, Will (EHN-gahs-uhr, WIHL-yuhm) PHX.

Left wing. Shoots left. 6'2", 237 lbs. Born, Edina, MN, September 25, 1985.
(Phoenix's 9th choice, 261st overall, in 2004 Entry Draft).

			Regular Season					Playoffs				
Season	Club	League	GP	G	A	Pts	PIM	GP	G	A	Pts	PIM
2000-01	Blake Bears	High-MN	5	1	2	3	....	....	....	....	....	....
2001-02	Blake Bears	High-MN	26	7	24	31	....	....	....	....	....	....
2002-03	Blake Bears	High-MN	28	17	26	43	52	....	....	....	....	....
2003-04	Blake Bears	High-MN	28	22	30	52	20	....	....	....	....	....
	Team Southwest	UMEHL	24	9	5	14	....	....	....	....	....	....
2004-05	Yale	ECACHL	21	2	0	2	10	....	....	....	....	....
2005-06	Yale	ECACHL	18	2	2	4	6	....	....	....	....	....

ENLUND, Jonas (EHN-luhnd, YOH-nuhs) ATL.

Center. Shoots left. 6', 185 lbs. Born, Helsinki, Finland, November 3, 1987.
(Atlanta's 5th choice, 165th overall, in 2006 Entry Draft).

			Regular Season					Playoffs				
Season	Club	League	GP	G	A	Pts	PIM	GP	G	A	Pts	PIM
2002-03	HIFK Helsinki U18	Fin-U18	24	11	3	14	0	2	1	0	1	0
2003-04	HIFK Helsinki U18	Fin-U18	30	15	16	31	30	7	3	5	8	2
	HIFK Helsinki Jr.	Fin-Jr.	3	0	0	0	0	....	....	....	....	....
2004-05	HIFK Helsinki U18	Fin-U18	....	....	....	....	....	7	4	3	7	8
	HIFK Helsinki Jr.	Fin-Jr.	38	15	15	30	18	2	1	1	2	0
2005-06	Suomi U20	Finland-2	4	1	1	2	0	....	....	....	....	....
	HIFK Helsinki Jr.	Fin-Jr.	37	24	18	42	14	....	....	....	....	....

ENSTROM, Tobias (EHN-stuhm, toh-BEE-uhs) ATL.

Defense. Shoots left. 5'9", 175 lbs. Born, Nordingra, Sweden, November 5, 1984.
(Atlanta's 8th choice, 239th overall, in 2003 Entry Draft).

			Regular Season					Playoffs				
Season	Club	League	GP	G	A	Pts	PIM	GP	G	A	Pts	PIM
99-2000	MoDo U18	Swe-U18	3	0	0	0	0	....	....	....	....	....
2000-01	MoDo U18	Swe-U18	16	7	6	13	18	....	....	....	....	....
	Malmo Jr.	Swe-Jr.	1	0	0	0	0	....	....	....	....	....
2001-02	Malmo Jr.	Swe-Jr.	21	1	7	8	10	2	1	1	2	2
2002-03	Malmo Jr.	Swe-Jr.	7	4	6	10	31	....	....	....	....	....
	MODO	Sweden	42	1	5	6	16	6	0	1	1	4
2003-04	MODO	Sweden	33	1	4	5	6	6	1	1	2	2
2004-05	MODO	Sweden	49	4	10	14	24	2	0	0	0	0
2005-06	MODO	Sweden	47	4	7	11	48	4	0	1	1	25

ERIKSSON, Loui (AIR-ihk-suhn, LOO-ee) DAL.

Left wing. Shoots left. 6'1", 183 lbs. Born, Goteborg, Sweden, July 17, 1985.
(Dallas' 1st choice, 33rd overall, in 2003 Entry Draft).

			Regular Season					Playoffs				
Season	Club	League	GP	G	A	Pts	PIM	GP	G	A	Pts	PIM
2000-01	V.Frolunda U18	Swe-U18	9	5	3	8	4	....	....	....	....	....
	V.Frolunda Jr.	Swe-Jr.	1	0	0	0	0	....	....	....	....	....
2001-02	V.Frolunda U18	Swe-U18	1	1	0	1	0	....	....	....	....	....
	V.Frolunda Jr.	Swe-Jr.	35	7	15	22	2	8	2	3	5	2
2002-03	V.Frolunda Jr.	Swe-Jr.	30	16	15	31	10	8	4	6	10	4
2003-04	V.Frolunda	Sweden	46	8	5	13	4	10	1	5	6	0
2004-05	Frolunda	Sweden	39	5	9	14	4	12	0	0	0	0
2005-06	Iowa Stars	AHL	78	31	29	60	27	7	2	5	7	0

ESTRADA, Kevin (eh-STRA-duh, KEH-vihn) CAR.

Right wing. Shoots left. 5'11", 185 lbs. Born, Surrey, B.C., May 28, 1982.
(Carolina's 3rd choice, 91st overall, in 2001 Entry Draft).

			Regular Season					Playoffs				
Season	Club	League	GP	G	A	Pts	PIM	GP	G	A	Pts	PIM
1997-98	Chilliwack Chiefs	BCHL	35	1	5	6	17	....	....	....	....	....
1998-99	Chilliwack Chiefs	BCHL	58	13	29	42	58	....	....	....	....	....
99-2000	Chilliwack Chiefs	BCHL	45	9	20	29	29	30	6	27	33	14
2000-01	Chilliwack Chiefs	BCHL	59	34	*84	*118	65	....	....	....	....	....
2001-02	Michigan State	CCHA	40	4	7	11	24	....	....	....	....	....
2002-03	Michigan State	CCHA	35	7	4	11	16	....	....	....	....	....
2003-04	Michigan State	CCHA	34	6	10	16	43	....	....	....	....	....
2004-05	Michigan State	CCHA	26	3	1	4	16	....	....	....	....	....
2005-06	Lowell	AHL	59	5	10	15	36	....	....	....	....	....
	Florida Everblades	ECHL	7	1	5	6	6	8	1	4	5	4

EVANS, Blake (EH-vans, BLAYK)

Center. Shoots left. 6'1", 210 lbs. Born, Smiley, Sask., July 2, 1980.
(Washington's 10th choice, 251st overall, in 1998 Entry Draft).

			Regular Season					Playoffs				
Season	Club	League	GP	G	A	Pts	PIM	GP	G	A	Pts	PIM
1995-96	Sask. Contacts	SMHL	41	15	23	38	84	....	....	....	....	....
1996-97	Spokane Chiefs	WHL	53	4	7	11	19	7	0	0	0	0
1997-98	Spokane Chiefs	WHL	16	6	5	11	29	....	....	....	....	....
	Tri-City Americans	WHL	57	13	29	42	102	....	....	....	....	....
1998-99	Tri-City Americans	WHL	72	18	29	47	131	12	0	4	4	16
99-2000	Tri-City Americans	WHL	72	27	43	70	110	4	1	0	1	6
2000-01	Tri-City Americans	WHL	40	28	31	59	70	....	....	....	....	....
	Regina Pats	WHL	27	24	19	43	50	6	6	2	8	8
2001-02	Worcester IceCats	AHL	28	4	5	9	18	3	0	0	0	2
	Peoria Rivermen	ECHL	43	17	20	37	26	....	....	....	....	....
2002-03	Worcester IceCats	AHL	78	13	21	34	79	3	0	0	0	0
2003-04	Worcester IceCats	AHL	80	21	23	44	91	10	2	3	5	10
2004-05	Worcester IceCats	AHL	67	14	24	38	60	....	....	....	....	....
2005-06	Peoria Rivermen	AHL	80	14	19	33	81	4	1	1	2	6

WHL East Second All-Star Team (2001)

Signed as a free agent by **St. Louis**, April 11, 2001.

EVSEEV, Vladislav (yehv-SAY-ehv, VLA-dih-slav) BOS.

Left wing. Shoots left. 6'2", 196 lbs. Born, Moscow, USSR, September 10, 1984.
(Boston's 2nd choice, 56th overall, in 2002 Entry Draft).

			Regular Season					Playoffs				
Season	Club	League	GP	G	A	Pts	PIM	GP	G	A	Pts	PIM
99-2000	Dyn'o Moscow 2	Russia-3	5	2	3	5	6	....	....	....	....	....
2000-01	Dyn'o Moscow 2	Russia-3	6	5	2	7	6	....	....	....	....	....
2001-02	CSKA Moscow 2	Russia-3	8	2	1	3	2	....	....	....	....	....
	HK CSKA Moscow	Russia-2	15	2	5	7	10	....	....	....	....	....
2002-03	Dynamo Moscow	Russia	22	1	1	2	2	1	0	0	0	0
2003-04	Vityaz Podolsk	Russia-2	8	1	2	3	2	7	0	0	0	2
2004-05	Dynamo Moscow	Russia	12	1	1	2	2	....	....	....	....	....
	Ufa	Russia	5	0	0	0	2	....	....	....	....	....
2005-06	Cherepovets	Russia	30	3	0	3	18	....	....	....	....	....

EZHOV, Denis (YEHZH-awf, DEH-nihs) BUF.

Defense. Shoots left. 5'11", 200 lbs. Born, Togliatti, USSR, February 28, 1985.
(Buffalo's 5th choice, 114th overall, in 2003 Entry Draft).

			Regular Season					Playoffs				
Season	Club	League	GP	G	A	Pts	PIM	GP	G	A	Pts	PIM
99-2000	Lada Togliatti 2	Russia-3	4	0	0	0	4	....	....	....	....	....
2000-01	Lada Togliatti 2	Russia-3	STATISTICS NOT AVAILABLE									
2001-02	Lada Togliatti 2	Russia-3	4	2	4	6	6	....	....	....	....	....
	Lada Togliatti	Russia	15	0	0	0	6	....	....	....	....	....
2002-03	Lada Togliatti 2	Russia-3	15	2	7	9	4	....	....	....	....	....
	CSK VVS Samara	Russia-2	9	0	1	1	8	....	....	....	....	....
2003-04	Novokuznetsk	Russia	19	0	1	1	2	3	0	0	0	0
	CSKA Moscow 2	Russia-3	4	1	2	3	2	....	....	....	....	....
2004-05	Novokuznetsk	Russia	28	0	0	0	16	4	0	0	0	2
2005-06	Mytischi	Russia	24	1	0	1	10	....	....	....	....	....
	Kristall Elektrostal	Russia-3	STATISTICS NOT AVAILABLE									

FABRY, Branislav (FA-bree, BRAN-ih-slav) BUF.

Left wing. Shoots left. 6', 185 lbs. Born, Bratislava, Czech., January 15, 1985.
(Buffalo's 2nd choice, 65th overall, in 2003 Entry Draft).

			Regular Season					Playoffs				
Season	Club	League	GP	G	A	Pts	PIM	GP	G	A	Pts	PIM
2000-01	Bratislava Jr.	Slovak-Jr.	47	22	25	47	....	....	....	....	....	....
2001-02	Bratislava Jr.	Slovak-Jr.	48	29	37	66	....	....	....	....	....	....
2002-03	Bratislava Jr.	Slovak-Jr.	32	12	15	27	84	....	....	....	....	....
	Bratislava	Slovakia	8	0	0	0	0	....	....	....	....	....
2003-04	Bratislava Jr.	Slovak-Jr.	4	5	2	7	14	....	....	....	....	....
	Bratislava	Slovakia	44	1	6	7	2	5	0	0	0	0
2004-05	MsHK SKP Zilina	Slovakia	12	0	1	1	2	....	....	....	....	....
	Bratislava	Slovakia	10	0	0	0	0	....	....	....	....	....
	HK Trnava	Slovak-2	11	3	4	7	2	....	....	....	....	....
	Bratislava Jr.	Slovak-Jr.	21	9	12	21	44	3	1	0	1	0
2005-06	Presov	Slovak-2	13	4	7	11	10	5	0	1	1	18

FALARDEAU, Lee (FAL-ahr-doh, LEE) NYR

Center. Shoots left. 6'4", 214 lbs. Born, Midland, MI, July 22, 1983.
(NY Rangers' 1st choice, 33rd overall, in 2002 Entry Draft).

			Regular Season					Playoffs				
Season	Club	League	GP	G	A	Pts	PIM	GP	G	A	Pts	PIM
99-2000	USNTDP	U-17	6	4	3	7	....	....	....	....	....	....
	USNTDP	USHL	5	0	0	0	4	....	....	....	....	....
	USNTDP	NAHL	47	5	10	15	20	3	0	1	1	0
2000-01	USNTDP	U-18	40	7	19	26	22	....	....	....	....	....
	USNTDP	USHL	21	3	2	5	4	....	....	....	....	....
2001-02	Michigan State	CCHA	34	4	10	14	24	....	....	....	....	....
2002-03	Michigan State	CCHA	39	9	6	15	39	....	....	....	....	....
2003-04	Michigan State	CCHA	35	5	5	10	28	....	....	....	....	....
2004-05	Charlotte	ECHL	55	18	17	35	52	14	7	1	8	14
	Hartford Wolf Pack	AHL	3	0	0	0	0	....	....	....	....	....
2005-06	Hartford Wolf Pack	AHL	64	5	17	22	71	11	0	3	3	6
	Charlotte	ECHL	6	2	2	4	4	....	....	....	....	....

FAST, T.J. (FAST, TEE-JAY) L.A.

Defense. Shoots left. 6'1", 190 lbs. Born, Calgary, Alta., September 2, 1987.
(Los Angeles' 3rd choice, 60th overall, in 2005 Entry Draft).

			Regular Season					Playoffs				
Season	Club	League	GP	G	A	Pts	PIM	GP	G	A	Pts	PIM
2003-04	Cgy. North Stars	AMHL	31	7	7	14	42	....	....	....	....	....
2004-05	Camrose Kodiaks	AJHL	58	8	28	36	40	....	....	....	....	....
2005-06	U. of Denver	WCHA	39	1	6	7	26	....	....	....	....	....

AJHL All-Rookie Team (2005)

FATA, Drew (FA-tuh, DROO)

Defense. Shoots left. 6'1", 220 lbs. Born, Sault Ste. Marie, Ont., July 28, 1983.
(Pittsburgh's 3rd choice, 86th overall, in 2001 Entry Draft).

			Regular Season					Playoffs				
Season	Club	League	GP	G	A	Pts	PIM	GP	G	A	Pts	PIM
1998-99	S.S. Marie AA	NOHA	46	4	16	20	55	....	....	....	....	....
99-2000	St. Mike's B's	OPJHL	49	9	18	27	144	....	....	....	....	....
2000-01	St. Michael's	OHL	58	5	15	20	134	18	1	3	4	26
2001-02	St. Michael's	OHL	67	7	21	28	175	15	1	9	10	38
2002-03	St. Michael's	OHL	35	6	13	19	66	....	....	....	....	....
	Kingston	OHL	34	2	17	19	64	....	....	....	....	....
2003-04	Wilkes-Barre	AHL	23	1	2	3	26	....	....	....	....	....
	Wheeling Nailers	ECHL	28	6	10	16	61	4	0	0	0	8
2004-05	Wilkes-Barre	AHL	32	1	1	2	88	5	0	1	1	37
	Wheeling Nailers	ECHL	22	0	1	1	55	....	....	....	....	....
2005-06	Wilkes-Barre	AHL	28	1	12	13	98	11	0	0	0	16
	Wheeling Nailers	ECHL	34	10	8	18	145	....	....	....	....	....

FAYNE, Mark (FAYN, MAHRK) N.J.

Defense. Shoots right. 6'3", 195 lbs. Born, Nashua, NH, May 15, 1987.
(New Jersey's 5th choice, 155th overall, in 2005 Entry Draft).

			Regular Season					Playoffs				
Season	Club	League	GP	G	A	Pts	PIM	GP	G	A	Pts	PIM
2003-04	Nobles	High-MA	20	3	5	8	14	....	....	....	....	....
2004-05	Nobles	High-MA	24	1	17	18	16	....	....	....	....	....
2005-06	Nobles	High-MA	29	10	24	34	....	....	....	....	....	....

FEMENELLA, Art (feh-meh-NEHL-uh, AHRT) T.B.

Defense. Shoots right. 6'7", 255 lbs. Born, Annandale, NJ, June 6, 1982.
(Tampa Bay's 7th choice, 188th overall, in 2001 Entry Draft).

			Regular Season					Playoffs				
Season	Club	League	GP	G	A	Pts	PIM	GP	G	A	Pts	PIM
1998-99	USNTDP	NAHL	51	0	2	2	135	....	....	....	....	....
99-2000	USNTDP	USHL	3	0	0	0	7	....	....	....	....	....
	USNTDP	NAHL	54	0	8	8	156	2	0	0	0	6
2000-01	Sioux City	USHL	52	1	1	2	*252	3	0	0	0	2
2001-02	Sioux City	USHL	56	1	10	11	215	12	0	1	1	32
2002-03	Sioux City	USHL	48	1	6	7	197	....	....	....	....	....
2003-04	U. of Vermont	ECAC	27	1	0	1	67	....	....	....	....	....
2004-05	U. of Vermont	ECACHL	21	0	0	0	32	....	....	....	....	....
2005-06	U. of Vermont	H-East	10	0	0	0	31	....	....	....	....	....

FENTON, P.J. (FEHN-tuhn, PAWL) S.J.

Left wing. Shoots left. 5'11", 177 lbs. Born, Springfield, MA, August 26, 1985.
(San Jose's 6th choice, 162nd overall, in 2005 Entry Draft).

			Regular Season					Playoffs				
Season	Club	League	GP	G	A	Pts	PIM	GP	G	A	Pts	PIM
2002-03	N.E. Jr. Coyotes	EJHL	35	8	17	25	....	....	....	....	....	....
2003-04	N.E. Jr. Coyotes	EJHL	37	16	17	33	61	....	....	....	....	....
2004-05	Massachusetts	H-East	36	12	12	24	24	....	....	....	....	....
2005-06	Massachusetts	H-East	35	5	12	17	61	....	....	....	....	....

Hockey East All-Rookie Team (2005)

FERNHOLM, Daniel (FUHRN-hohlm, DAN-yehl) PIT.

Defense. Shoots left. 6'4", 218 lbs. Born, Stockholm, Sweden, December 20, 1983.
(Pittsburgh's 4th choice, 101st overall, in 2002 Entry Draft).

			Regular Season					Playoffs				
Season	Club	League	GP	G	A	Pts	PIM	GP	G	A	Pts	PIM
99-2000	Mora IK Jr.	Swe-Jr.	33	3	3	6	8	1	0	0	0	0
2000-01	Mora IK Jr.	Swe-Jr.	3	0	1	1	2	....	....	....	....	....
	Mora IK	Sweden-2	2	0	0	0	0	....	....	....	....	....
2001-02	Djurgarden Jr.	Swe-Jr.	8	6	13	19	12	3	0	0	0	0
2002-03	Huddinge IK	Sweden-2	39	6	10	16	20	2	1	0	1	0
	Huddinge IK Jr.	Swe-Jr.	1	0	0	0	2	....	....	....	....	....
2003-04	Djurgarden	Sweden	37	4	7	11	28	4	0	0	0	4
	Hammarby	Sweden-2	15	1	3	4	6	....	....	....	....	....
2004-05	Djurgarden Jr.	Swe-Jr.	2	0	0	0	4	....	....	....	....	....
	HC Forst Bolzano	Italy	7	0	2	2	2	....	....	....	....	....
	Djurgarden	Sweden	31	3	2	5	22	11	0	0	0	14
2005-06	Wilkes-Barre	AHL	27	1	6	7	10	....	....	....	....	....
	Wheeling Nailers	ECHL	29	2	4	6	20	9	1	3	4	6

FERRIERO, Benn (fuh-RAIR-oh, BEHN) PHX.

Center. Shoots right. 5'10", 191 lbs. Born, Boston, MA, April 29, 1987.
(Phoenix's 8th choice, 196th overall, in 2006 Entry Draft).

			Regular Season					Playoffs				
Season	Club	League	GP	G	A	Pts	PIM	GP	G	A	Pts	PIM
2001-02	Gov. Dummer	High-MA	STATISTICS NOT AVAILABLE									
2002-03	Gov. Dummer	High-MA	....	8	10	18	....	....	....	....	....	....
2003-04	Gov. Dummer	High-MA	28	19	24	43	....	....	....	....	....	....
2004-05	Gov. Dummer	High-MA	28	15	27	42	....	....	....	....	....	....
2005-06	Boston College	H-East	42	16	9	25	36	....	....	....	....	....

Hockey East All-Rookie Team (2006)

FESTERLING, Brett (FEHS-tuhr-lihng, BREHT) ANA.

Defense. Shoots left. 6'1", 180 lbs. Born, Quesnel, B.C., March 3, 1986.

			Regular Season					Playoffs				
Season	Club	League	GP	G	A	Pts	PIM	GP	G	A	Pts	PIM
2001-02	Tri-City Americans	WHL	3	0	0	0	0	....	....	....	....	....
2002-03	Tri-City Americans	WHL	55	3	8	11	26	....	....	....	....	....
2003-04	Tri-City Americans	WHL	54	1	9	10	34	11	1	1	2	2
2004-05	Tri-City Americans	WHL	33	3	11	14	20	....	....	....	....	....
	Vancouver Giants	WHL	32	2	4	6	10	5	0	0	0	6
2005-06	Vancouver Giants	WHL	67	1	6	7	35	18	0	1	1	10

Signed as a free agent by **Anaheim**, September 14, 2005.

FIALA, Ondrej (fee-A-la, AWN-dray) MIN.

Center. Shoots left. 6'1", 200 lbs. Born, Stenberk, Czech., November 4, 1987.
(Minnesota's 2nd choice, 40th overall, in 2006 Entry Draft).

			Regular Season					Playoffs				
Season	Club	League	GP	G	A	Pts	PIM	GP	G	A	Pts	PIM
2000-01	HC Olomouc U17	CzR-U17	6	1	2	3	2	1	0	0	0	0
2001-02	HC Havirov U17	CzR-U17	16	6	9	15	8	....	....	....	....	....
	HC Trinec U17	CzR-U17	27	6	12	18	16	6	2	2	4	2
2002-03	HC Trinec U17	CzR-U17	40	26	30	56	54	2	1	1	2	2
	HC Trinec Jr.	CzRep-Jr.	2	0	0	0	0	6	1	0	1	2
2003-04	HC Trinec U17	CzR-U17	3	1	0	1	4	2	1	0	1	0
	HC Trinec Jr.	CzRep-Jr.	28	9	7	16	16	2	0	0	0	0
2004-05	HC Trinec Jr.	CzRep-Jr.	29	6	6	12	77	....	....	....	....	....
	HC Kladno Jr.	CzRep-Jr.	11	3	5	8	12	10	2	3	5	2
	HC Ocelari Trinec	CzRep	3	0	0	0	0	....	....	....	....	....
2005-06	Everett Silvertips	WHL	51	21	14	35	26	8	4	4	8	4

FIEDLER, Jonas (FIHD-luhr, YOH-nahsh) CAR.

Right wing. Shoots right. 6'2", 177 lbs. Born, Jihlava, Czech., May 29, 1984.
(Carolina's 7th choice, 235th overall, in 2004 Entry Draft).

			Regular Season					Playoffs				
Season	Club	League	GP	G	A	Pts	PIM	GP	G	A	Pts	PIM
99-2000	Jihlava Jr.	CzRep-Jr.	48	11	11	22	48	....	....	....	....	....
2000-01	Jihlava Jr.	CzRep-Jr.	44	29	33	62	167	....	....	....	....	....
2001-02	Plymouth Whalers	OHL	68	8	12	20	27	6	0	1	1	4
2002-03	Plymouth Whalers	OHL	63	7	21	28	59	18	5	9	14	10
2003-04	Plymouth Whalers	OHL	63	18	28	46	83	9	1	6	7	16
2004-05	Plymouth Whalers	OHL	61	19	18	37	71	4	1	0	1	2
	Florida Everblades	ECHL	2	0	0	0	0	....	....	....	....	....
2005-06	HC Dukla Jihlava	CzRep-2	46	8	9	17	122	6	0	2	2	22

• Re-entered NHL Entry Draft. Originally San Jose's 3rd choice, 86th overall, in 2002 Entry Draft.

FIGREN, Robin (FIH-grehn, RAW-bihn) NYI

Wing. Shoots right. 5'11", 176 lbs. Born, Stockholm, Sweden, March 7, 1988.
(NY Islanders' 3rd choice, 70th overall, in 2006 Entry Draft).

			Regular Season					Playoffs				
Season	Club	League	GP	G	A	Pts	PIM	GP	G	A	Pts	PIM
2003-04	Hammarby U18	Swe-U18	11	5	5	10	22	....	....	....	....	....
2004-05	Frolunda U18	Swe-U18	12	13	8	21	94	7	4	4	8	10
	Frolunda Jr.	Swe-Jr.	4	1	2	3	0	....	....	....	....	....
2005-06	Frolunda Jr.	Swe-Jr.	38	10	18	28	72	7	4	2	6	6
	Frolunda	Sweden	2	0	0	0	0	....	....	....	....	....
	Frolunda U18	Swe-U18	1	1	0	1	2	2	2	0	2	0

FILEWICH, Jonathan (FIGHL-uh-which, JAWN-ah-thun) PIT.

Right wing. Shoots right. 6'2", 205 lbs. Born, Kelowna, B.C., October 2, 1984.
(Pittsburgh's 3rd choice, 70th overall, in 2003 Entry Draft).

			Regular Season					Playoffs				
Season	Club	League	GP	G	A	Pts	PIM	GP	G	A	Pts	PIM
1998-99	Sherwood Park	AMBHL	36	29	43	72	90	....	....	....	....	....
99-2000	Sherwood Park	AMHL	33	28	20	48	59	....	....	....	....	....
	Prince George	WHL	3	0	0	0	0	....	....	....	....	....
2000-01	Prince George	WHL	61	9	16	25	32	....	....	....	....	....
2001-02	Prince George	WHL	66	13	19	32	23	7	2	0	2	2
2002-03	Prince George	WHL	51	27	27	54	45	5	1	1	2	2
2003-04	Prince George	WHL	72	30	25	55	52	....	....	....	....	....
2004-05	Lethbridge	WHL	68	42	38	80	26	5	1	1	2	2
2005-06	Wilkes-Barre	AHL	73	22	14	36	40	11	6	4	10	6

FINGER, Jeff (FIHN-guhr, JEHF) COL.

Defense. Shoots right. 6'2", 195 lbs. Born, Hancock, MI, December 18, 1979.
(Colorado's 11th choice, 240th overall, in 1999 Entry Draft).

			Regular Season					Playoffs				
Season	Club	League	GP	G	A	Pts	PIM	GP	G	A	Pts	PIM
1997-98	Green Bay	USHL	51	5	9	14	208	4	0	0	0	18
1998-99	Green Bay	USHL	54	11	28	39	199	6	0	3	3	14
99-2000	Green Bay	USHL	55	13	35	48	15	14	3	11	14	40
2000-01	St. Cloud State	WCHA	41	4	5	9	84	....	....	....	....	....
2001-02	St. Cloud State	WCHA	42	6	20	26	105	....	....	....	....	....
2002-03	St. Cloud State	WCHA	24	5	8	13	46	....	....	....	....	....
2003-04	Hershey Bears	AHL	63	2	9	11	88	....	....	....	....	....
	Reading Royals	ECHL	10	2	5	7	24	....	....	....	....	....
2004-05	Hershey Bears	AHL	75	4	12	16	125	....	....	....	....	....
2005-06	Lowell	AHL	70	3	20	23	116	....	....	....	....	....

FINLEY, Joe (FIHN-lee, JOH) WSH.

Defense. Shoots left. 6'7", 229 lbs. Born, Edina, MN, June 29, 1987.
(Washington's 2nd choice, 27th overall, in 2005 Entry Draft).

			Regular Season					Playoffs				
Season	Club	League	GP	G	A	Pts	PIM	GP	G	A	Pts	PIM
2004-05	Sioux Falls	USHL	55	3	10	13	181	....	....	....	....	....
2005-06	North Dakota	WCHA	43	0	3	3	96	....	....	....	....	....

FISCHER, David (FIH-shuhr, DAY-vihd) MTL.

Defense. Shoots right. 6'4", 187 lbs. Born, Minneapolis, MN, February 19, 1988.
(Montreal's 1st choice, 20th overall, in 2006 Entry Draft).

			Regular Season					Playoffs				
Season	Club	League	GP	G	A	Pts	PIM	GP	G	A	Pts	PIM
2003-04	Apple Valley	High-MN	27	2	9	11	10	....	....	....	....	....
2004-05	Apple Valley	High-MN	28	8	20	28	36	....	....	....	....	....
2005-06	Apple Valley	High-MN	28	8	31	39	22	....	....	....	....	....

Signed Letter of Intent to attend **U. of Minnesota** (WCHA) in fall of 2006.

FISCHER, Patrick (FIH-shuhr, PAT-rihk) PHX.

Left wing. Shoots left. 5'11", 194 lbs. Born, Zug, Switz., September 6, 1975.

			Regular Season					Playoffs				
Season	Club	League	GP	G	A	Pts	PIM	GP	G	A	Pts	PIM
1993-94	EV Zug	Swiss	32	3	5	8	14	9	0	2	2	6
1994-95	EV Zug	Swiss	36	10	18	28	30	12	2	3	5	14
1995-96	EV Zug	Swiss	36	10	17	27	24	....	....	....	....	....
1996-97	EV Zug	Swiss	43	20	18	38	26	....	....	....	....	....
1997-98	HC Lugano	Swiss	40	15	28	43	38	....	....	....	....	....
1998-99	HC Lugano	Swiss	45	11	17	28	73	....	....	....	....	....
99-2000	HC Davos	Swiss	44	19	17	36	107	5	2	2	4	0
2000-01	HC Davos	Swiss	42	13	27	40	54	....	....	....	....	....
2001-02	HC Davos	Swiss	38	8	22	30	36	....	....	....	....	....
2002-03	HC Davos	Swiss	44	17	21	38	87	....	....	....	....	....
2003-04	EV Zug	Swiss	46	12	23	35	70	5	1	4	5	0
2004-05	EV Zug	Swiss	44	17	18	35	64	9	2	5	7	12
2005-06	EV Zug	Swiss	44	21	32	53	72	....	....	....	....	....
	Switzerland	Olympics	6	1	1	2	4	....	....	....	....	....

Signed as a free agent by **Phoenix**, April 28, 2006.

FISTRIC, Mark (FIHST-rihc, MAHRK) DAL.

Defense. Shoots left. 6'2", 232 lbs. Born, Edmonton, Alta., June 1, 1986.
(Dallas' 1st choice, 28th overall, in 2004 Entry Draft).

			Regular Season					Playoffs				
Season	Club	League	GP	G	A	Pts	PIM	GP	G	A	Pts	PIM
2000-01	Edmonton MLAC	AMBHL	34	13	13	26	144	....	....	....	....	....
2001-02	Edmonton MLAC	AMHL	30	8	10	18	85	....	....	....	....	....
	Vancouver Giants	WHL	4	0	2	2	0	....	....	....	....	....
2002-03	Vancouver Giants	WHL	63	2	7	9	81	4	0	0	0	8
2003-04	Vancouver Giants	WHL	72	1	11	12	192	11	0	2	2	10
2004-05	Vancouver Giants	WHL	15	1	5	6	32	6	1	1	2	16
2005-06	Vancouver Giants	WHL	60	7	22	29	148	18	1	9	10	30

FITZGERALD, Zack (fihtz-JAIR-uhld, ZAK) ST.L.

Defense. Shoots left. 6'1", 214 lbs. Born, Two Harbors, MN, June 16, 1985.
(St. Louis' 4th choice, 88th overall, in 2003 Entry Draft).

			Regular Season					Playoffs				
Season	Club	League	GP	G	A	Pts	PIM	GP	G	A	Pts	PIM
2000-01	Duluth East	High-MN	26	1	7	8	44	....	....	....	....	....
2001-02	Seattle	WHL	61	3	7	10	214	10	0	2	2	19
2002-03	Seattle	WHL	64	8	14	22	232	15	0	4	4	33
2003-04	Seattle	WHL	58	4	15	19	163	....	....	....	....	....
2004-05	Seattle	WHL	65	7	18	25	*244	9	0	3	3	24
2005-06	Peoria Rivermen	AHL	13	1	1	2	47	....	....	....	....	....
	Alaska Aces	ECHL	12	1	1	2	108	....	....	....	....	....

FLACHE, Paul (FLAK, PAWL)

Defense. Shoots right. 6'5", 220 lbs. Born, Toronto, Ont., March 4, 1982.
(Atlanta's 5th choice, 144th overall, in 2002 Entry Draft).

			Regular Season					Playoffs				
Season	Club	League	GP	G	A	Pts	PIM	GP	G	A	Pts	PIM
1998-99	Cobourg Cougars	OPJHL	41	1	6	7	50	....	....	....	....	....
99-2000	Brampton	OHL	54	1	0	1	59	6	0	0	0	8
2000-01	Brampton	OHL	68	8	16	24	100	9	1	1	2	18
2001-02	Brampton	OHL	68	9	35	44	148	....	....	....	....	....
2002-03	Greenville Grrrowl	ECHL	46	1	9	10	64	4	0	4	4	6
2003-04	Gwinnett	ECHL	62	3	15	18	114	10	2	2	4	4
	Chicago Wolves	AHL	9	2	2	4	12	....	....	....	....	....
2004-05	Chicago Wolves	AHL	61	3	12	15	172	....	....	....	....	....
	Gwinnett	ECHL	3	1	2	3	4	....	....	....	....	....
2005-06	Bridgeport	AHL	40	1	5	6	67	....	....	....	....	....

• Re-entered NHL Entry Draft. Originally Edmonton's 5th choice, 152nd overall, in 2000 Entry Draft.

FLATT, Dalyn (FLAT, DA-lihn) NYR

Defense. Shoots left. 6'3", 215 lbs. Born, Winnipeg, Man., October 7, 1986.
(NY Rangers' 5th choice, 77th overall, in 2005 Entry Draft).

			Regular Season					Playoffs				
Season	Club	League	GP	G	A	Pts	PIM	GP	G	A	Pts	PIM
2001-02	Interlake Lightning	MMHL	51	2	16	18	148	....	....	....	....	....
	Saskatoon Blades	WHL	2	0	0	0	0	....	....	....	....	....
2002-03	Swan Valley	MJHL	51	1	12	13	286	....	....	....	....	....
2003-04	Saskatoon Blades	WHL	41	0	2	2	91	....	....	....	....	....
2004-05	Saskatoon Blades	WHL	72	1	18	19	237	4	0	0	0	12
2005-06	Saskatoon Blades	WHL	9	0	0	0	20	....	....	....	....	....
	Kootenay Ice	WHL	49	0	4	4	131	6	1	1	2	12

FLATTERS, John (FLAT-uhrs, JAWN) PHI.

Defense. Shoots left. 6'1", 203 lbs. Born, Calgary, Alta., June 17, 1987.
(Philadelphia's 5th choice, 174th overall, in 2005 Entry Draft).

			Regular Season					Playoffs				
Season	Club	League	GP	G	A	Pts	PIM	GP	G	A	Pts	PIM
2003-04	Notre Dame	SMHL	43	1	11	12	116	....	....	....	....	....
2004-05	Red Deer Rebels	WHL	53	0	2	2	117	7	0	0	0	2
2005-06	Red Deer Rebels	WHL	14	0	1	1	45	....	....	....	....	....
	Vancouver Giants	WHL	51	3	3	6	95	3	0	0	0	2

FLOOD, Mark (FLUD, MAHRK) CBJ

Defense. Shoots right. 6'1", 190 lbs. Born, Charlottetown, PEI, September 29, 1984.
(Montreal's 8th choice, 188th overall, in 2003 Entry Draft).

			Regular Season					Playoffs				
Season	Club	League	GP	G	A	Pts	PIM	GP	G	A	Pts	PIM
2000-01	Charlotwn AAA	PEIHA	STATISTICS NOT AVAILABLE									
	Charlotwn Abbies	MJrHL	11	0	2	2	2	....	....	....	....	....
2001-02	Peterborough	OHL	57	1	4	5	21	6	0	0	0	2
2002-03	Peterborough	OHL	68	5	24	29	18	7	1	2	3	0
2003-04	Peterborough	OHL	68	15	29	44	30	....	....	....	....	....
2004-05	Peterborough	OHL	60	4	38	42	14	14	2	7	9	0
2005-06	Syracuse Crunch	AHL	9	1	1	2	2	....	....	....	....	....
	Dayton Bombers	ECHL	50	11	14	25	20	....	....	....	....	....

Signed as a free agent by **Columbus**, August 22, 2005.

FLYNN, Ryan (FLIHN, RIGH-uhn) NSH.

Right wing. Shoots right. 6'2", 212 lbs. Born, St. Paul, MN, March 22, 1988.
(Nashville's 4th choice, 176th overall, in 2006 Entry Draft).

			Regular Season					Playoffs				
Season	Club	League	GP	G	A	Pts	PIM	GP	G	A	Pts	PIM
2003-04	Centennial	High-MN	30	29	39	68		....	....	....	....	....
2004-05	USNTDP	U-17	14	4	5	9	12	....	....	....	....	....
	USNTDP	NAHL	41	11	8	19	31	9	2	4	6	7
2005-06	USNTDP	U-18	42	10	12	22	57	....	....	....	....	....
	USNTDP	NAHL	17	6	5	11	20	....	....	....	....	....

Signed Letter of Intent to attend **U. of Minnesota** (WCHA) in fall of 2006.

FOLIGNO, Nick (foh-LIHG-noh, NIHK) OTT.

Left wing. Shoots left. 6', 188 lbs. Born, Buffalo, NY, October 31, 1987.
(Ottawa's 1st choice, 28th overall, in 2006 Entry Draft).

			Regular Season					Playoffs				
Season	Club	League	GP	G	A	Pts	PIM	GP	G	A	Pts	PIM
2003-04	USNTDP	U-17	18	7	9	16	28	....	....	....	....	....
	USNTDP	NAHL	43	8	12	20	44	7	2	1	3	8
2004-05	USNTDP	U-18	4	2	1	3	0	....	....	....	....	....
	Sudbury Wolves	OHL	65	10	28	38	111	12	5	5	10	16
2005-06	Sudbury Wolves	OHL	65	24	46	70	146	10	1	3	4	28

FOOTE, Jordan (FUT, JOHN-dan) NYR

Left wing. Shoots left. 6'3", 213 lbs. Born, Edmonton, Alta., March 7, 1985.
(NY Rangers' 11th choice, 169th overall, in 2004 Entry Draft).

			Regular Season					Playoffs				
Season	Club	League	GP	G	A	Pts	PIM	GP	G	A	Pts	PIM
2003-04	Nanaimo Clippers	BCHL	58	23	26	49	73	....	....	....	....	....
2004-05	Michigan Tech	WCHA	13	1	1	2	6	....	....	....	....	....
2005-06	Michigan Tech	WCHA	31	2	0	2	33	....	....	....	....	....

FORD, Matthew (FOHRD, MA-thew) CHI.

Right wing. Shoots right. 6'1", 203 lbs. Born, West Hills, CA, October 9, 1984.
(Chicago's 16th choice, 256th overall, in 2004 Entry Draft).

			Regular Season					Playoffs				
Season	Club	League	GP	G	A	Pts	PIM	GP	G	A	Pts	PIM
2003-04	Sioux Falls	USHL	60	*37	31	68	60	....	....	....	....	....
2004-05	U. of Wisconsin	WCHA	21	5	5	10	18	....	....	....	....	....
2005-06	U. of Wisconsin	WCHA	31	5	2	7	14	....	....	....	....	....

FORNEY, Michael (fohr-NEE, MIGH-kuhl) ATL.

Left wing. Shoots right. 6'2", 185 lbs. Born, Thief River Falls, MN, May 14, 1988.
(Atlanta's 3rd choice, 80th overall, in 2006 Entry Draft).

			Regular Season					Playoffs				
Season	Club	League	GP	G	A	Pts	PIM	GP	G	A	Pts	PIM
2002-03	Thief River Falls	High-MN	28	4	10	14	....	....	....	....	....	....
2003-04	Thief River Falls	High-MN	24	14	22	36	....	....	....	....	....	....
2004-05	Thief River Falls	High-MN	28	34	33	67	....	....	....	....	....	....
2005-06	Thief River Falls	High-MN	21	23	37	60	28	....	....	....	....	....
	Des Moines	USHL	3	0	0	0	0	....	....	....	....	....

Signed Letter of Intent to attend **U. of North Dakota** (WCHA) in fall of 2006.

FORREST, J.D. (FOH-rehst, JAY-DEE) CAR.

Defense. Shoots left. 5'9", 185 lbs. Born, Auburn, NY, April 15, 1981.
(Carolina's 5th choice, 181st overall, in 2000 Entry Draft).

			Regular Season					Playoffs				
Season	Club	League	GP	G	A	Pts	PIM	GP	G	A	Pts	PIM
1997-98	USNTDP	U-17	23	3	9	12	2	....	....	....	....	....
	USNTDP	USHL	5	2	0	2	17	....	....	....	....	....
	USNTDP	NAHL	41	2	16	18	20	5	0	1	1	2
1998-99	USNTDP	U-18	6	1	2	3	10	....	....	....	....	....
	USNTDP	USHL	48	5	21	26	34	....	....	....	....	....
	USNTDP	NAHL	2	1	0	1	4	....	....	....	....	....
99-2000	USNTDP	USHL	8	0	0	0	2	....	....	....	....	....
	USNTDP	NAHL	49	6	28	34	46	3	0	0	0	6
2000-01	Boston College	H-East	38	6	17	23	40	....	....	....	....	....
2001-02	Boston College	H-East	35	8	19	27	28	....	....	....	....	....
2002-03	Boston College	H-East	34	6	25	31	28	....	....	....	....	....
2003-04	Boston College	H-East	37	4	13	17	26	....	....	....	....	....
2004-05	SaiPa	Finland	53	7	12	19	44	....	....	....	....	....
2005-06	Assat Pori	Finland	43	6	5	11	69	14	0	4	4	14

Hockey East Second All-Star Team (2003) • NCAA East Second All-American Team (2003)

Signed as a free agent by **SaiPa** (Finland), May 21, 2004. Signed as a free agent by **Carolina**, July 20, 2006.

FOSTER, Adrian (FAW-stuhr, AY-dree-uhn) N.J.

Center. Shoots left. 6', 200 lbs. Born, Lethbridge, Alta., January 15, 1982.
(New Jersey's 1st choice, 28th overall, in 2001 Entry Draft).

			Regular Season					Playoffs				
Season	Club	League	GP	G	A	Pts	PIM	GP	G	A	Pts	PIM
1997-98	Calgary Buffaloes	AMHL	36	26	54	80	50	9	3	14	17	18
1998-99	Calgary Canucks	AJHL	18	15	17	32	18	....	....	....	....	....
99-2000	Saskatoon Blades	WHL	7	1	2	3	6	....	....	....	....	....
2000-01	Saskatoon Blades	WHL	5	0	5	5	4	....	....	....	....	....
2001-02	Saskatoon Blades	WHL	13	9	3	12	18	....	....	....	....	....
	Brandon	WHL	14	5	10	15	23	15	4	11	15	14
2002-03	Albany River Rats	AHL	9	3	0	3	4	....	....	....	....	....
2003-04	Albany River Rats	AHL	44	8	13	21	25	....	....	....	....	....
2004-05	Albany River Rats	AHL	51	6	11	17	27	....	....	....	....	....
2005-06	Albany River Rats	AHL	8	2	1	3	18	....	....	....	....	....

• Missed majority of 1998-99 season recovering from ankle injury. • Missed majority of 1999-2000, 2000-01, 2001-02 and 2002-03 seasons recovering from abdominal injury, October, 1999. • Missed majority of 2005-06 season recovering from head injury.

FOSTER, Alex (FAW-stuhr, al-EHX) TOR.

Center. Shoots left. 6'1", 195 lbs. Born, Canton, MI, August 26, 1984.

			Regular Season					Playoffs				
Season	Club	League	GP	G	A	Pts	PIM	GP	G	A	Pts	PIM
2002-03	Danville Wings	USHL	43	9	18	27	38	....	....	....	....	....
2003-04	Danville Wings	USHL	55	23	30	53	91	6	1	2	3	6
2004-05	Bowling Green	CCHA	34	8	23	31	31	....	....	....	....	....
2005-06	Bowling Green	CCHA	38	11	40	51	40	....	....	....	....	....

CCHA Second All-Star Team (2006)

Signed as a free agent by **Toronto**, March 8, 2006.

FRANK, Chris (FRANK, KRIHS) PHX.

Defense. Shoots left. 6'1", 231 lbs. Born, Lynnwood, WA, January 8, 1986.
(Phoenix's 7th choice, 188th overall, in 2006 Entry Draft).

			Regular Season					Playoffs				
Season	Club	League	GP	G	A	Pts	PIM	GP	G	A	Pts	PIM
2003-04	Cowichan Valley	BCHL	55	3	16	19	277	6	1	0	1	26
2004-05	Cowichan Valley	BCHL	55	6	30	36	207	....	....	....	....	....
2005-06	Western Mich.	CCHA	38	2	2	4	127	....	....	....	....	....

FRANSON, Cody (FRAN-suhn, KOH-dee) NSH.

Defense. Shoots right. 6'4", 205 lbs. Born, Salmon Arm, B.C., August 8, 1987.
(Nashville's 3rd choice, 79th overall, in 2005 Entry Draft).

			Regular Season					Playoffs				
Season	Club	League	GP	G	A	Pts	PIM	GP	G	A	Pts	PIM
2002-03	Sicamous	BCAHA	65	44	82	126	42	....	....	....	....	....
	Vancouver Giants	WHL	3	0	0	0	0	....	....	....	....	....
2003-04	Beaver Valley	KIJHL	48	10	22	32	70	....	....	....	....	....
	Trail Smoke Eaters	BCHL	2	0	1	1	0	....	....	....	....	....
	Vancouver Giants	WHL	2	0	0	0	0	....	....	....	....	....
2004-05	Vancouver Giants	WHL	64	2	11	13	44	4	0	1	1	0
2005-06	Vancouver Giants	WHL	71	15	40	55	61	18	5	15	20	12

WHL West Second All-Star Team (2006)

FRANSSON, Johan (FRAN-suhn, YOH-hahn) DAL.

Defense. Shoots left. 6'1", 183 lbs. Born, Kalix, Sweden, February 18, 1985.
(Dallas' 2nd choice, 34th overall, in 2004 Entry Draft).

			Regular Season					Playoffs				
Season	Club	League	GP	G	A	Pts	PIM	GP	G	A	Pts	PIM
2000-01	Kalix HF	Sweden-3	19	0	6	6	8	....	....	....	....	....
2001-02	Lulea HF U18	Swe-U18	5	2	0	2	0	....	....	....	....	....
	Lulea HF Jr.	Swe-Jr.	29	4	4	8	28	5	0	1	1	8
2002-03	Lulea HF Jr.	Swe-Jr.	24	2	4	6	67	....	....	....	....	....
	Lulea HF U18	Swe-U18	2	0	0	0	2	....	....	....	....	....
	Lulea HF	Sweden	3	0	0	0	0	....	....	....	....	....
2003-04	Lulea HF Jr.	Swe-Jr.	5	0	2	2	10	....	....	....	....	....
	Lulea HF	Sweden	44	3	3	6	28	2	0	0	0	4
2004-05	Lulea HF Jr.	Swe-Jr.	1	1	1	2	0	7	1	2	3	4
	Lulea HF	Sweden	43	1	6	7	30	3	0	0	0	0
2005-06	Lulea HF	Sweden	50	3	5	8	74	6	1	1	2	6

FRASER, Colin (FRAY-zuhr, KAW-lihn) CHI.

Center. Shoots left. 6'1", 182 lbs. Born, Sicamous, B.C., January 28, 1985.
(Philadelphia's 3rd choice, 69th overall, in 2003 Entry Draft).

			Regular Season					Playoffs				
Season	Club	League	GP	G	A	Pts	PIM	GP	G	A	Pts	PIM
2000-01	Port Coquitlam	PIJHL	38	16	24	40	90	8	2	2	4	21
2001-02	Red Deer Rebels	WHL	67	11	31	42	126	23	2	1	3	39
2002-03	Red Deer Rebels	WHL	69	15	37	52	192	22	7	6	13	40
2003-04	Red Deer Rebels	WHL	70	24	29	53	174	19	5	9	14	24
2004-05	Red Deer Rebels	WHL	63	24	43	67	148	7	2	5	7	8
	Norfolk Admirals	AHL	3	0	0	0	20	6	1	0	1	2
2005-06	Norfolk Admirals	AHL	75	12	13	25	145	4	0	0	0	7

Canadian Major Junior Humanitarian Player of the Year (2005)

Traded to **Chicago** by **Philadelphia** with Jim Vandermeer and Los Angeles' 2nd round choice (previously acquired, Chicago selected Bryan Bickell) in 2004 Entry Draft for Alex Zhamnov and Washington's 4th round choice (previously acquired, Philadelphia selected R.J. Anderson) in 2004 Entry Draft, February 19, 2004.

FRASER, Mark (FRAY-zuhr, MAHRK) N.J.

Defense. Shoots left. 6'3", 200 lbs. Born, Ottawa, Ont., September 29, 1986.
(New Jersey's 3rd choice, 84th overall, in 2005 Entry Draft).

			Regular Season					Playoffs				
Season	Club	League	GP	G	A	Pts	PIM	GP	G	A	Pts	PIM
2004-05	Gloucester	CJHL	STATISTICS NOT AVAILABLE									
	Kitchener Rangers	OHL	58	0	8	8	96	15	0	3	3	26
2005-06	Kitchener Rangers	OHL	59	0	5	5	129	5	0	1	1	4
	Albany River Rats	AHL	4	0	0	0	2	....	....	....	....	....

FRECHETTE, Maxime (freh-SHEHT, max-EEM) CBJ

Defense. Shoots right. 6'4", 200 lbs. Born, Sorel, Que., May 9, 1988.
(Columbus' 7th choice, 142nd overall, in 2006 Entry Draft).

			Regular Season					Playoffs				
Season	Club	League	GP	G	A	Pts	PIM	GP	G	A	Pts	PIM
2004-05	Drummondville	QMJHL	50	2	3	5	50	1	0	0	0	0
2005-06	Drummondville	QMJHL	13	0	0	0	24	....	....	....	....	....

• Missed majority of 2005-06 season recovering from shoulder injury.

FREDHEIM, Kris (FREHD-highm, KRIHS) VAN.

Defense. Shoots right. 6'1", 170 lbs. Born, Campbell River, B.C., February 23, 1987.
(Vancouver's 5th choice, 185th overall, in 2005 Entry Draft).

			Regular Season					Playoffs				
Season	Club	League	GP	G	A	Pts	PIM	GP	G	A	Pts	PIM
2003-04	Notre Dame	SMHL	41	9	21	30	38	....	....	....	....	....
2004-05	Notre Dame	SJHL	50	2	15	17	28	....	....	....	....	....
2005-06	Notre Dame	SJHL	52	12	23	35	75	11	2	9	11	15

Signed Letter of Intent to attend **Colorado College** (WCHA) in fall of 2006.

FREDRIKSSON, David (FREHD-rihk-suhn, DAY-vihd) ST.L.

Right wing. Shoots left. 6'2", 214 lbs. Born, Jonkoping, Sweden, October 4, 1985.
(St. Louis' 7th choice, 211th overall, in 2004 Entry Draft).

			Regular Season					Playoffs				
Season	Club	League	GP	G	A	Pts	PIM	GP	G	A	Pts	PIM
2001-02	HV 71 Jr.	Swe-Jr.	14	6	2	8	20	....	....	....	....	....
2002-03	HV 71 Jr.	Swe-Jr.	27	9	10	19	24	8	10	0	10	10
	HV 71 Jonkoping	Sweden	1	0	0	0	0	....	....	....	....	....
2003-04	HV 71 Jr.	Swe-Jr.	18	9	3	12	42	2	1	0	1	2
	HV 71 Jonkoping	Sweden	9	0	0	0	2	6	0	0	0	0
2004-05	HV 71 Jr.	Swe-Jr.	19	8	5	13	48	....	....	....	....	....
	Morrums GoIS IK	Sweden-2	2	1	0	1	2	....	....	....	....	....
	HV 71 Jonkoping	Sweden	18	0	0	0	0	....	....	....	....	....
2005-06	HV 71 Jr.	Swe-Jr..	4	6	3	9	8	....	....	....	....	....
	HV 71 Jonkoping	Sweden	37	5	4	9	34	3	0	0	0	4

FRITSCHE, Tom (FRIHCH, TAWM) COL.

Left wing. Shoots left. 5'11", 183 lbs. Born, Parma, OH, September 30, 1986.
(Colorado's 3rd choice, 47th overall, in 2005 Entry Draft).

			Regular Season					Playoffs				
Season	Club	League	GP	G	A	Pts	PIM	GP	G	A	Pts	PIM
2002-03	USNTDP	U-17	19	7	11	18	16	....	....	....	....	....
	USNTDP	NAHL	44	14	9	23	43	....	....	....	....	....
2003-04	USNTDP	U-18	46	19	23	42	46	....	....	....	....	....
	USNTDP	NAHL	11	5	4	9	0	....	....	....	....	....
2004-05	Ohio State	CCHA	42	11	*34	45	38	....	....	....	....	....
2005-06	Ohio State	CCHA	37	11	19	30	16	....	....	....	....	....

CCHA All-Rookie Team (2005) • CCHA Second All-Star Team (2005)

FRITZ, Mitch (FRIHTZ, MIHTCH) T.B.

Left wing. Shoots left. 6'8", 258 lbs. Born, Osoyoos, B.C., November 24, 1980.

			Regular Season					Playoffs				
Season	Club	League	GP	G	A	Pts	PIM	GP	G	A	Pts	PIM
1998-99	Kelowna Rockets	WHL	52	9	0	9	156	2	0	0	0	0
99-2000	Kelowna Rockets	WHL	58	4	2	6	204	5	0	0	0	0
2000-01	Lowell	AHL	5	0	0	0	20	....	....	....	....	....
	Tallahassee	ECHL	42	5	3	8	79	....	....	....	....	....
2001-02	Hamilton Bulldogs	AHL	13	0	0	0	37	....	....	....	....	....
	Columbus	ECHL	45	3	7	10	284	....	....	....	....	....
	Saint John Flames	AHL	11	0	0	0	34	....	....	....	....	....
2002-03	Milwaukee	AHL	13	1	2	3	33	....	....	....	....	....
	Columbus	ECHL	33	2	4	6	144	....	....	....	....	....
2003-04	Worcester IceCats	AHL	4	0	0	0	10	4	0	0	0	4
	Columbus	ECHL	64	3	9	12	149	....	....	....	....	....
2004-05	Springfield Falcons	AHL	45	3	1	4	179	....	....	....	....	....
2005-06	Springfield Falcons	AHL	69	6	5	11	212	....	....	....	....	....

Yanick Dupre Memorial Award (AHL Man of the Year) (2006)

Signed as a free agent by **Tampa Bay**, August 5, 2005.

FROLIK, Michael (FROH-lihk, MIGH-kuhl) FLA.

Center. Shoots left. 6'1", 185 lbs. Born, Kladno, Czech., February 17, 1988.
(Florida's 1st choice, 10th overall, in 2006 Entry Draft).

			Regular Season					Playoffs				
Season	Club	League	GP	G	A	Pts	PIM	GP	G	A	Pts	PIM
2002-03	HC Kladno U17	CzR-U17	46	37	21	58	36	9	9	1	10	18
	HC Kladno Jr.	CzRep-Jr.	....	....	....	....	....	1	0	0	0	2
2003-04	HC Kladno U17	CzR-U17	1	0	1	1	2	....	....	....	....	....
	HC Kladno Jr.	CzRep-Jr.	53	21	23	44	22	7	3	1	4	6
2004-05	HC Kladno U17	CzR-U17	....	....	....	....	....	1	1	0	1	0
	HC Kladno Jr.	CzRep-Jr.	15	9	11	20	18	5	1	0	1	0
	HC Rabat Kladno	CzRep	27	3	1	4	6	1	0	0	0	0
2005-06	HC Kladno Jr.	CzRep-Jr.	3	1	2	3	0	6	3	9	12	6
	HC Rabat Kladno	CzRep	48	2	7	9	32	....	....	....	....	....

FULLER, Evan (FUL-lehr, EN-vuhn) VAN.

Right wing. Shoots right. 6'1", 196 lbs. Born, Salmon Arm, B.C., June 1, 1988.
(Vancouver's 5th choice, 197th overall, in 2006 Entry Draft).

			Regular Season					Playoffs				
Season	Club	League	GP	G	A	Pts	PIM	GP	G	A	Pts	PIM
2004-05	Prince George	WHL	55	5	3	8	66	....	....	....	....	....
2005-06	Prince George	WHL	56	2	5	7	87	5	0	0	0	7

FULTON, Jordan (FUL-tuhn, JOHR-dahn) CGY.

Center. Shoots left. 6', 191 lbs. Born, St. Louis Park, MN, September 12, 1987.
(Calgary's 6th choice, 179th overall, in 2006 Entry Draft).

			Regular Season					Playoffs				
Season	Club	League	GP	G	A	Pts	PIM	GP	G	A	Pts	PIM
2002-03	Breck Mustangs	High-MN	26	24	7	31	12	....	....	....	....	....
2003-04	Breck Mustangs	High-MN	31	30	36	66	24	....	....	....	....	....
2004-05	Breck Mustangs	High-MN	28	29	41	70	68	....	....	....	....	....
2005-06	Breck Mustangs	High-MN	28	45	36	81	76	....	....	....	....	....

Signed Letter of Intent to attend **U. of Minnesota-Duluth** (WCHA) in fall of 2006.

FUNK, Michael (FUHNK, MIGH-kuhl) BUF.

Defense. Shoots left. 6'4", 199 lbs. Born, Abbotsford, B.C., August 15, 1986.
(Buffalo's 2nd choice, 43rd overall, in 2004 Entry Draft).

			Regular Season					Playoffs				
Season	Club	League	GP	G	A	Pts	PIM	GP	G	A	Pts	PIM
2001-02	Abbotsford Hawks	BCAHA	72	9	24	33	84	....	....	....	....	....
2002-03	Portland	WHL	68	1	15	16	54	7	0	1	1	15
2003-04	Portland	WHL	71	3	25	28	86	5	0	1	1	6
2004-05	Portland	WHL	71	8	22	30	84	7	1	1	2	4
2005-06	Portland	WHL	70	11	36	47	88	5	0	0	0	8

FURRER, Philippe (FUHR-ruhr, fihl-EEP) NYR

Defense. Shoots left. 6'1", 198 lbs. Born, Bern, Switz., June 16, 1985.
(NY Rangers' 7th choice, 179th overall, in 2003 Entry Draft).

			Regular Season					Playoffs				
Season	Club	League	GP	G	A	Pts	PIM	GP	G	A	Pts	PIM
2000-01	SC Bern Jr.	Swiss-Jr.	....	....	....	....	....	3	0	0	0	0
2001-02	SC Bern Jr.	Swiss-Jr.	29	5	11	16	31	1	0	0	0	0
	SC Bern	Swiss	10	0	0	0	0	....	....	....	....	....
2002-03	SC Bern Jr.	Swiss-Jr.	11	1	11	12	12	....	....	....	....	....
	SC Bern	Swiss	27	0	1	1	6	13	0	0	0	2
2003-04	SC Bern	Swiss	DID NOT PLAY – INJURED									
2004-05	SC Bern	Swiss	37	3	3	6	14	11	1	1	2	4
2005-06	SC Bern	Swiss	29	1	0	1	14	....	....	....	....	....
	SC Langenthal	Swiss-2	2	0	0	0	0	....	....	....	....	....

• Missed entire 2003-04 season recovering from hip injury suffered during 2002-03 season.

GAUTHIER, Gabe (GOH-tyay, GAYB) L.A.

Left wing. Shoots left. 5'9", 200 lbs. Born, Buena Park, CA, January 20, 1984.

			Regular Season					Playoffs				
Season	Club	League	GP	G	A	Pts	PIM	GP	G	A	Pts	PIM
2002-03	U. of Denver	WCHA	41	8	8	16	30	....	....	....	....	....
2003-04	U. of Denver	WCHA	42	18	25	43	32	....	....	....	....	....
2004-05	U. of Denver	WCHA	41	23	29	52	44	....	....	....	....	....
2005-06	U. of Denver	WCHA	38	15	24	39	35	....	....	....	....	....

Signed as a free agent by **Los Angeles**, July 7, 2006.

GAUTHIER, Mike (GOH-tyay, MIGHK) ST.L.

Defense. Shoots right. 6'3", 185 lbs. Born, Vancouver, B.C., March 26, 1987.
(St. Louis' 5th choice, 169th overall, in 2005 Entry Draft).

			Regular Season					Playoffs				
Season	Club	League	GP	G	A	Pts	PIM	GP	G	A	Pts	PIM
2002-03	Delta Ice Hawks	PIJHL	36	6	15	21	288	....	....	....	....	....
	Prince Albert	WHL	3	0	0	0	2	....	....	....	....	....
2003-04	Prince Albert	WHL	52	1	0	1	130	5	0	0	0	2
2004-05	Prince Albert	WHL	40	2	1	3	93	13	0	0	0	18
2005-06	Prince Albert	WHL	69	4	8	12	169	....	....	....	....	....

GAWRYLETZ, Travis (GAW-reh-lehtz, TRA-vihs) PHI.

Defense. Shoots right. 6'2", 190 lbs. Born, Trail, B.C., November 2, 1985.
(Philadelphia's 9th choice, 253rd overall, in 2004 Entry Draft).

			Regular Season					Playoffs				
Season	Club	League	GP	G	A	Pts	PIM	GP	G	A	Pts	PIM
2002-03	Trail Smoke Eaters	BCHL	56	4	28	32	42	14	6	6	12	10
2003-04	Trail Smoke Eaters	BCHL	51	9	21	30	51	10	1	3	4	6
2004-05	U. Minn-Duluth	WCHA	35	4	1	5	26	....	....	....	....	....
2005-06	U. Minn-Duluth	WCHA	32	0	7	7	12	....	....	....	....	....

BCHL All-Rookie Team (2003) • BCHL Interior Division First All-Star Team (2004)

GELECH, Randall (GEH-lehkh, RAN-duhl) PHX.

Center. Shoots right. 6'3", 220 lbs. Born, Wynard, Sask., February 2, 1984.
(Phoenix's 5th choice, 208th overall, in 2003 Entry Draft).

			Regular Season					Playoffs				
Season	Club	League	GP	G	A	Pts	PIM	GP	G	A	Pts	PIM
2000-01	Kelowna Rockets	WHL	51	1	9	10	19	6	0	0	0	4
2001-02	Kelowna Rockets	WHL	48	6	2	8	33	15	2	1	3	15
2002-03	Kelowna Rockets	WHL	67	25	20	45	93	19	8	4	12	17
2003-04	Kelowna Rockets	WHL	71	30	19	49	117	17	10	4	14	22
2004-05	Utah Grizzlies	AHL	76	15	12	27	72	....	....	....	....	....
2005-06	San Antonio	AHL	75	9	12	21	39	....	....	....	....	....

Memorial Cup Tournament All-Star Team (2004)

GENEROUS, Matt (GEHN-uhr-uhs, MAT) BUF.

Defense. Shoots right. 6'3", 185 lbs. Born, Methuen, MA, May 4, 1985.
(Buffalo's 8th choice, 208th overall, in 2005 Entry Draft).

			Regular Season					Playoffs				
Season	Club	League	GP	G	A	Pts	PIM	GP	G	A	Pts	PIM
2003-04	N.E. Jr. Falcons	EJHL	43	6	9	15	134	....	....	....	....	....
2004-05	N.E. Jr. Falcons	EJHL	49	8	16	24	105	....	....	....	....	....
2005-06	St. Lawrence	ECACHL	34	4	11	15	34	....	....	....	....	....

ECACHL All-Rookie Team (2006)

GENOWAY, Colby (JEHN-oh-way, KOHL-bee) ANA.

Right wing. Shoots right. 6'1", 201 lbs. Born, Morden, Man., December 12, 1983.

			Regular Season					Playoffs				
Season	Club	League	GP	G	A	Pts	PIM	GP	G	A	Pts	PIM
2002-03	North Dakota	WCHA	31	1	2	3	24	....	....	....	....	....
2003-04	North Dakota	WCHA	40	11	23	34	22	....	....	....	....	....
2004-05	North Dakota	WCHA	42	13	31	44	38	....	....	....	....	....
	Hartford Wolf Pack	AHL	4	0	0	0	0	....	....	....	....	....
2005-06	Hartford Wolf Pack	AHL	77	26	35	61	78	13	4	8	12	10

Signed as a free agent by **Anaheim**, July 11, 2006.

GEOFFRION, Blake (JEHF-REE-ohn, BLAYK) NSH.

Left wing. Shoots left. 6'1", 190 lbs. Born, Plantation, FL, February 3, 1988.
(Nashville's 1st choice, 56th overall, in 2006 Entry Draft).

			Regular Season					Playoffs				
Season	Club	League	GP	G	A	Pts	PIM	GP	G	A	Pts	PIM
2003-04	Culver Academy	High-IN	45	....	....	65	....	....	....	....	....	....
2004-05	USNTDP	U-17	11	2	3	5	24	....	....	....	....	....
	USNTDP	NAHL	37	7	15	22	62	10	2	5	7	23
2005-06	USNTDP	U-18	41	12	14	26	38	....	....	....	....	....
	USNTDP	NAHL	13	6	9	15	30	....	....	....	....	....

Signed Letter of Intent to attend **U. of Wisconsin** (WCHA) in fall of 2006.

GERBE, Nathan (GUHR-bee, NAY-thuhn) BUF.

Center. Shoots left. 5'5", 160 lbs. Born, Oxford, MI, July 24, 1987.
(Buffalo's 5th choice, 142nd overall, in 2005 Entry Draft).

			Regular Season					Playoffs				
Season	Club	League	GP	G	A	Pts	PIM	GP	G	A	Pts	PIM
2002-03	River City Lancers	USHL	25	3	3	6	49	7	1	1	2	2
2003-04	USNTDP	U-17	32	14	12	26	66	....	....	....	....	....
	USNTDP	NAHL	26	11	7	18	87	....	....	....	....	....
2004-05	USNTDP	U-18	26	6	11	17	48	....	....	....	....	....
	USNTDP	NAHL	12	7	5	12	25	....	....	....	....	....
2005-06	Boston College	H-East	39	11	7	18	75	....	....	....	....	....

GERGEN, Michael (GUHR-gehn, MIGHK-uhl) PIT.

Left wing. Shoots left. 5'10", 185 lbs. Born, Hastings, MN, February 17, 1987.
(Pittsburgh's 2nd choice, 61st overall, in 2005 Entry Draft).

			Regular Season					Playoffs				
Season	Club	League	GP	G	A	Pts	PIM	GP	G	A	Pts	PIM
2003-04	Shat.-St. Mary's	High-MN	71	29	26	55	52	....	....	....	....	....
2004-05	Shat.-St. Mary's	High-MN	69	64	53	117	110	....	....	....	....	....
2005-06	U. Minn-Duluth	WCHA	39	14	8	22	63	....	....	....	....	....

GIFFORD, Brian (GIH-fuhrd, BRIGH-uhn) PIT.

Center. Shoots left. 6'1", 173 lbs. Born, Fargo, ND, November 12, 1985.
(Pittsburgh's 5th choice, 85th overall, in 2004 Entry Draft).

			Regular Season					Playoffs				
Season	Club	League	GP	G	A	Pts	PIM	GP	G	A	Pts	PIM
2002-03	Moorhead Spuds	High-MN	30	18	20	38	32	....	....	....	....	....
2003-04	Moorhead Spuds	High-MN	26	19	37	56	26	....	....	....	....	....
2004-05	Indiana Ice	USHL	55	13	10	23	80	3	1	0	1	0
2005-06	Indiana Ice	USHL	56	12	14	26	55	5	0	2	2	0

GILBERT, Tom (GIHL-buhrt, TAWM) EDM.

Defense. Shoots right. 6'2", 190 lbs. Born, Minneapolis, MN, January 10, 1983.
(Colorado's 5th choice, 129th overall, in 2002 Entry Draft).

			Regular Season					Playoffs				
Season	Club	League	GP	G	A	Pts	PIM	GP	G	A	Pts	PIM
99-2000	Bloomington-Jeff.	High-MN	18	7	18	25	....	....	....	....	....	....
2000-01	Bloomington-Jeff.	High-MN	23	20	18	38	....	....	....	....	....	....
	Chicago Steel	USHL	1	0	0	0	0	....	....	....	....	....
2001-02	Chicago Steel	USHL	57	13	15	28	62	4	0	0	0	4
2002-03	U. of Wisconsin	WCHA	39	7	13	20	36	....	....	....	....	....
2003-04	U. of Wisconsin	WCHA	39	6	15	21	36	....	....	....	....	....
2004-05	U. of Wisconsin	WCHA	41	8	9	17	48	....	....	....	....	....
2005-06	U. of Wisconsin	WCHA	43	12	19	31	32	....	....	....	....	....

WCHA First All-Star Team (2006) • NCAA West Second All-American Team (2006)

Traded to **Edmonton** by **Colorado** for Tommy Salo and Edmonton's 6th round choice (Justin Mercier) in 2005 Entry Draft, March 8, 2004.

GIMAEV, Sergei (gih-MIGH-ehv, SAIR-gay) OTT.

Defense. Shoots left. 6'1", 183 lbs. Born, Moscow, USSR, February 16, 1984.
(Ottawa's 6th choice, 166th overall, in 2003 Entry Draft).

			Regular Season					Playoffs				
Season	Club	League	GP	G	A	Pts	PIM	GP	G	A	Pts	PIM
2001-02	CSKA Moscow 2	Russia-3	36	0	10	10	50	....	....	....	....	....
2002-03	Cherepovets	Russia	11	0	0	0	4	....	....	....	....	....
2003-04	Cherepovets	Russia	50	1	3	4	32	....	....	....	....	....
2004-05	Cherepovets	Russia	5	0	1	1	2	....	....	....	....	....
	Sibir Novosibirsk	Russia	31	1	6	7	34	....	....	....	....	....
2005-06	Dynamo Moscow	Russia	46	1	3	4	36	2	0	0	0	0

GIONTA, Stephen (jee-OHN-tuh, STEE-vehn) N.J.

Right wing. Shoots right. 5'7", 180 lbs. Born, Rochester, NY, October 9, 1983.

			Regular Season					Playoffs				
Season	Club	League	GP	G	A	Pts	PIM	GP	G	A	Pts	PIM
2002-03	Boston College	H-East	33	5	10	15	36	....	....	....	....	....
2003-04	Boston College	H-East	41	9	15	24	36	....	....	....	....	....
2004-05	Boston College	H-East	38	8	11	19	44	....	....	....	....	....
2005-06	Boston College	H-East	37	11	21	32	66	....	....	....	....	....
	Albany River Rats	AHL	3	5	1	6	2	....	....	....	....	....

Signed to a ATO (tryout) contract by **Albany** (AHL), April 12, 2006. Signed as a free agent by **New Jersey**, August, 2006.

GIRARDI, Daniel (jih-RAHR-dee, DAN-yehl) NYR

Defense. Shoots right. 6'1", 205 lbs. Born, Welland, Ont., April 29, 1984.

			Regular Season					Playoffs				
Season	Club	League	GP	G	A	Pts	PIM	GP	G	A	Pts	PIM
2000-01	Barrie Colts	OHL	6	0	0	0	0	....	....	....	....	....
2001-02	Barrie Colts	OHL	21	0	1	1	0	20	0	0	0	0
2002-03	Guelph Storm	OHL	36	1	13	14	20	11	0	9	9	14
	Barrie Colts	OHL	31	3	13	16	24	....	....	....	....	....
2003-04	Guelph Storm	OHL	68	8	39	47	55	22	2	17	19	10
2004-05	Guelph Storm	OHL	38	5	20	25	24	....	....	....	....	....
	London Knights	OHL	31	4	10	14	14	18	0	6	6	10
2005-06	Hartford Wolf Pack	AHL	66	8	31	39	44	13	4	5	9	8
	Charlotte	ECHL	7	1	4	5	6	....	....	....	....	....

Signed as a free agent by **NY Rangers**, July 1, 2006.

GIROUX, Claude (zhih-ROO, KLOHD) PHI.

Right wing. Shoots right. 5'10", 169 lbs. Born, Hearst, Ont., January 12, 1988.
(Philadelphia's 1st choice, 22nd overall, in 2006 Entry Draft).

			Regular Season					Playoffs				
Season	Club	League	GP	G	A	Pts	PIM	GP	G	A	Pts	PIM
2004-05	Cumberland	CJHL	48	13	27	40	30	....	....	....	....	....
2005-06	Gatineau	QMJHL	69	39	64	103	64	17	5	15	20	24

GLADSKIKH, Evgeny (glad-SKEEKH, ehv-GEH-nee) VAN.

Right wing. Shoots left. 6', 198 lbs. Born, Magnitogorsk, USSR, April 24, 1982.
(Vancouver's 3rd choice, 114th overall, in 2001 Entry Draft).

			Regular Season					Playoffs				
Season	Club	League	GP	G	A	Pts	PIM	GP	G	A	Pts	PIM
1998-99	Magnitogorsk 2	Russia-4	16	3	3	6	6	....	....	....	....	....
99-2000	Magnitogorsk 2	Russia-3	39	17	2	19	24	....	....	....	....	....
	Magnitogorsk	Russia	1	0	0	0	0	....	....	....	....	....
2000-01	Magnitogorsk 2	Russia-3	11	10	7	17	6	....	....	....	....	....
	Magnitogorsk	Russia	31	3	5	8	10	12	0	2	2	2
2001-02	Magnitogorsk	Russia	32	5	6	11	6	4	0	0	0	4
2002-03	Magnitogorsk	Russia	42	4	7	11	18	3	0	0	0	2
2003-04	Magnitogorsk	Russia	47	13	13	26	22	14	3	1	4	10
2004-05	Magnitogorsk 2	Russia-3	2	0	2	2	0	....	....	....	....	....
	Magnitogorsk	Russia	42	11	12	23	24	4	1	0	1	4
2005-06	Magnitogorsk	Russia	43	12	8	20	20	7	1	1	2	2

GLASS, Tanner (GLAS, TA-nuhr) FLA.

Forward. Shoots left. 6', 196 lbs. Born, Regina, Sask., November 29, 1983.
(Florida's 13th choice, 265th overall, in 2003 Entry Draft).

			Regular Season					Playoffs				
Season	Club	League	GP	G	A	Pts	PIM	GP	G	A	Pts	PIM
2000-01	Yorkton Mallers	SMHL	39	31	29	60	120	4	3	1	4	10
2001-02	Penticton Panthers	BCHL	57	11	28	39	171	....	....	....	....	....
2002-03	Penticton Panthers	BCHL	32	15	25	40	108	....	....	....	....	....
	Nanaimo Clippers	BCHL	18	8	14	22	46	....	....	....	....	....
2003-04	Dartmouth	ECAC	26	4	7	11	18	....	....	....	....	....
2004-05	Dartmouth	ECACHL	33	7	8	15	32	....	....	....	....	....
2005-06	Dartmouth	ECACHL	33	12	16	28	56	....	....	....	....	....

GLASSER, Matthew (GLAS-uhr, MA-thyew) EDM.

Left wing. Shoots left. 5'10", 175 lbs. Born, Saskatoon, Sask., January 11, 1987.
(Edmonton's 8th choice, 220th overall, in 2005 Entry Draft).

			Regular Season					Playoffs				
Season	Club	League	GP	G	A	Pts	PIM	GP	G	A	Pts	PIM
2003-04	Fort McMurray	AJHL	55	13	12	25	24	....	....	....	....	....
2004-05	Fort McMurray	AJHL	62	25	24	49	14	....	....	....	....	....
2005-06	Fort McMurray	AJHL	58	15	20	35	36	17	5	2	7	38

GLAZACHEV, Konstantin (GLAH-zuh-chehv, kawn-stuhn-TIHN) NSH.

Left wing. Shoots right. 6', 186 lbs. Born, Arkhangelsk, USSR, February 18, 1985.
(Nashville's 2nd choice, 35th overall, in 2003 Entry Draft).

			Regular Season					Playoffs				
Season	Club	League	GP	G	A	Pts	PIM	GP	G	A	Pts	PIM
2001-02	Yaroslavl 2	Russia-3	7	5	6	11	6	....	....	....	....	....
2002-03	Yaroslavl 2	Russia-3	STATISTICS NOT AVAILABLE									
	Yaroslavl	Russia	13	3	4	7	4	4	0	0	0	0
2003-04	Yaroslavl	Russia	35	4	3	7	4	2	0	0	0	0
	Yaroslavl 2	Russia-3	9	6	5	11	8	....	....	....	....	....
2004-05	Sibir Novosibirsk	Russia	24	4	9	13	6	....	....	....	....	....
	Yaroslavl	Russia	9	0	3	3	2	....	....	....	....	....
	Yaroslavl 2	Russia-3	20	17	9	26	14	....	....	....	....	....
2005-06	Yaroslavl	Russia	29	7	4	11	8	9	0	2	2	0

GLEED, Jon (GLEED, JAWN) MTL.

Defense. Shoots right. 6'2", 210 lbs. Born, Milton, Ont., January 3, 1984.
(Montreal's 6th choice, 212th overall, in 2004 Entry Draft).

			Regular Season					Playoffs				
Season	Club	League	GP	G	A	Pts	PIM	GP	G	A	Pts	PIM
2001-02	Brampton Capitals	OPJHL	45	3	15	18	39	....	....	....	....	....
2002-03	Cornell Big Red	ECAC	12	0	1	1	10	....	....	....	....	....
2003-04	Cornell Big Red	ECAC	28	3	3	6	18	....	....	....	....	....
2004-05	Cornell Big Red	ECACHL	30	1	5	6	43	....	....	....	....	....
2005-06	Cornell Big Red	ECACHL	28	1	7	8	26	....	....	....	....	....

GLENCROSS, Curtis (GLEHN-kraws, KUHR-tis) ANA.

Center. Shoots left. 6'1", 186 lbs. Born, Kindersley, Sask., December 28, 1982.

			Regular Season					Playoffs				
Season	Club	League	GP	G	A	Pts	PIM	GP	G	A	Pts	PIM
2001-02	Brooks Bandits	AJHL	....	42	26	68	....	....	....	....	....	....
2002-03	Alaska-Anchorage	WCHA	35	11	12	23	79	....	....	....	....	....
2003-04	Alaska-Anchorage	WCHA	37	21	13	34	79	....	....	....	....	....
	Cincinnati	AHL	7	2	1	3	6	9	1	6	7	10
2004-05	Cincinnati	AHL	51	6	3	9	63	12	2	0	2	10
2005-06	Portland Pirates	AHL	41	15	10	25	85	19	4	6	10	37

Signed as a free agent by **Anaheim**, March 25, 2004.

GLOVER, Dan (GLUH-vuhr, DAN) N.J.

Defense. Shoots left. 6'2", 175 lbs. Born, Delburne, Alta., May 4, 1983.
(New Jersey's 10th choice, 250th overall, in 2002 Entry Draft).

			Regular Season					Playoffs				
Season	Club	League	GP	G	A	Pts	PIM	GP	G	A	Pts	PIM
2000-01	Red Deer Chiefs	AMHL	35	1	5	6	40	....	....	....	....	....
2001-02	Camrose Kodiaks	AJHL	55	1	10	11	110	....	....	....	....	....
2002-03	Camrose Kodiaks	AJHL	61	5	14	19	118	27	0	6	6	32
2003-04	Cornell Big Red	ECAC	23	1	2	3	20	....	....	....	....	....
2004-05	Cornell Big Red	ECACHL	15	0	1	1	6	....	....	....	....	....
2005-06	Cornell Big Red	ECACHL	28	3	2	5	39	....	....	....	....	....

GOGULLA, Philip (GOH-goo-lah, FIL-uhp) BUF.

Right wing. Shoots left. 6'2", 176 lbs. Born, Dusseldorf, West Germany, July 31, 1987.
(Buffalo's 2nd choice, 48th overall, in 2005 Entry Draft).

			Regular Season					Playoffs				
Season	Club	League	GP	G	A	Pts	PIM	GP	G	A	Pts	PIM
2002-03	Krefelder EV Jr.	Ger-Jr.	32	11	23	34	42	2	0	0	0	2
2003-04	Krefelder EV Jr.	Ger-Jr.	35	35	44	79	22	2	0	2	2	27
2004-05	Essen	German-2	3	0	0	0	0	....	....	....	....	....
	Koln Jr.	Ger-Jr.	7	4	5	9	18	....	....	....	....	....
	Kolner Haie	Germany	47	1	1	2	14	7	0	0	0	2
2005-06	Kolner Haie	Germany	48	7	15	22	49	9	3	2	5	40

GOLIGOSKI, Alex (goh-lih-GAW-skee, AL-ehx) PIT.

Defense. Shoots right. 5'11", 180 lbs. Born, Grand Rapids, MN, July 30, 1985.
(Pittsburgh's 3rd choice, 61st overall, in 2004 Entry Draft).

			Regular Season					Playoffs				
Season	Club	League	GP	G	A	Pts	PIM	GP	G	A	Pts	PIM
2002-03	Grand Rapids	High-MN	28	14	20	34	22	....	....	....	....	....
2003-04	Grand Rapids	High-MN	26	25	31	56	16	....	....	....	....	....
	Sioux Falls	USHL	10	0	2	2	6	....	....	....	....	....
2004-05	U. of Minnesota	WCHA	33	5	15	20	44	....	....	....	....	....
2005-06	U. of Minnesota	WCHA	41	11	28	39	63	....	....	....	....	....

WCHA All-Rookie Team (2005) • WCHA Second All-Star Team (2006)

GORBUNOV, Vladimir (gohr-buh-NAHF, vla-DIH-meer) NYI

Right wing. Shoots left. 6', 174 lbs. Born, Moscow, USSR, April 22, 1982.
(NY Islanders' 4th choice, 105th overall, in 2000 Entry Draft).

			Regular Season					Playoffs				
Season	Club	League	GP	G	A	Pts	PIM	GP	G	A	Pts	PIM
99-2000	HK Moscow	Russia-2	22	11	7	18	32	....	....	....	....	....
2000-01	HK Moscow	Russia-2	43	10	14	24	63	....	....	....	....	....
2001-02	HK CSKA Moscow	Russia-2	46	16	18	34	22	....	....	....	....	....
	CSKA Moscow 2	Russia-3	3	1	1	2	0	....	....	....	....	....
2002-03	CSKA Moscow	Russia	35	5	5	10	46	....	....	....	....	....
	CSKA Moscow 2	Russia-3	STATISTICS NOT AVAILABLE									
2003-04	CSKA Moscow	Russia	34	4	7	11	56	....	....	....	....	....
2004-05	Ufa	Russia	1	0	0	0	0	....	....	....	....	....
	HK MVD Tver	Russia-2	36	4	15	19	48	11	2	1	3	8
2005-06	MVD	Russia	44	3	4	7	146	4	2	0	2	8

GORDON, Andrew (GOHR-duhn, AN-droo) WSH.

Right wing. Shoots right. 5'11", 180 lbs. Born, Halifax, N.S., December 13, 1985.
(Washington's 11th choice, 197th overall, in 2004 Entry Draft).

			Regular Season					Playoffs				
Season	Club	League	GP	G	A	Pts	PIM	GP	G	A	Pts	PIM
2002-03	Notre Dame	SJHL	58	20	27	47	12	....	....	....	....	....
2003-04	Notre Dame	SJHL	55	20	44	64	12	....	....	....	....	....
2004-05	St. Cloud State	WCHA	38	9	8	17	6	....	....	....	....	....
2005-06	St. Cloud State	WCHA	42	20	20	40	22	....	....	....	....	....

GOULET, Stephane (goo-LAY, STEH-fan) EDM.

Right wing. Shoots left. 6'3", 185 lbs. Born, Levis, Que., January 7, 1986.
(Edmonton's 8th choice, 208th overall, in 2004 Entry Draft).

			Regular Season					Playoffs				
Season	Club	League	GP	G	A	Pts	PIM	GP	G	A	Pts	PIM
2002-03	Levis	QAAA	42	39	29	68	70	....	....	....	....	....
2003-04	Quebec Remparts	QMJHL	54	6	8	14	14	5	0	0	0	2
2004-05	Moncton Wildcats	QMJHL	69	22	25	47	37	12	3	7	10	12
2005-06	Moncton Wildcats	QMJHL	67	51	42	93	80	13	7	8	15	16

GRABNER, Michael (GRAB-nuhr, MIGH-kuhl) VAN.

Right wing. Shoots left. 6', 170 lbs. Born, Villach, Austria, October 5, 1987.
(Vancouver's 1st choice, 14th overall, in 2006 Entry Draft).

			Regular Season					Playoffs				
Season	Club	League	GP	G	A	Pts	PIM	GP	G	A	Pts	PIM
2002-03	EC Villacher SV Jr.	Austria-Jr.	13	6	4	10	4	....	....	....	....	....
2003-04	EC Villacher SV Jr.	Austria-Jr.	23	32	5	37	58	....	....	....	....	....
	EC Villacher SV	Austria	18	2	1	3	0	....	....	....	....	....
2004-05	Spokane Chiefs	WHL	58	13	11	24	18	....	....	....	....	....
2005-06	Spokane Chiefs	WHL	67	36	14	50	28	....	....	....	....	....

GRABOVSKY, Mikhail (gra-BAWV-skee, mih-kigh-EHL) MTL.

Center. Shoots left. 5'11", 181 lbs. Born, Potsdam, East Germany, January 31, 1984.
(Montreal's 4th choice, 150th overall, in 2004 Entry Draft).

			Regular Season					Playoffs				
Season	Club	League	GP	G	A	Pts	PIM	GP	G	A	Pts	PIM
2001-02	HC Minsk	Belarus	26	10	7	17	16	....	....	....	....	....
2002-03	HC Minsk	Belarus	STATISTICS NOT AVAILABLE									
2003-04	Nizhnekamsk	Russia	45	6	11	17	26	5	0	0	0	4
2004-05	Nizhnekamsk	Russia	60	16	20	36	32	3	2	0	2	2
	Yunost-Minsk	BelOpen	....	....	....	....	....	5	2	4	6	6
2005-06	Dynamo Moscow	Russia	48	10	17	27	28	4	0	0	0	4
	Yunost-Minsk	BelOpen	8	6	8	14	10	....	....	....	....	....

GRACIK, Juraj (GRAH-chihk, YUH-righ) ATL.

Right wing. Shoots right. 6'3", 190 lbs. Born, Topolcany, Czech., August 14, 1986.
(Atlanta's 5th choice, 142nd overall, in 2004 Entry Draft).

			Regular Season					Playoffs				
Season	Club	League	GP	G	A	Pts	PIM	GP	G	A	Pts	PIM
2002-03	Topolcany Jr.	Slovak-Jr.	24	10	7	17	28	....	....	....	....	....
2003-04	Topolcany Jr.	Slovak-Jr.	28	22	12	34	78	....	....	....	....	....
	Topolcany	Slovak-2	28	16	8	24	8	4	1	0	1	0
2004-05	Tri-City Americans	WHL	33	4	2	6	18	....	....	....	....	....
2005-06	Tri-City Americans	WHL	53	22	23	45	36	....	....	....	....	....

GRAGNANI, Marc-Andre (GRUH-na-nee, MAHRK-AWN-dray) BUF.

Defense. Shoots left. 6'1", 180 lbs. Born, Montreal, Que., March 11, 1987.
(Buffalo's 3rd choice, 87th overall, in 2005 Entry Draft).

			Regular Season					Playoffs				
Season	**Club**	**League**	**GP**	**G**	**A**	**Pts**	**PIM**	**GP**	**G**	**A**	**Pts**	**PIM**
2002-03	West Island Lions	QAAA	34	3	15	18	22	....	....	....	....	....
2003-04	PEI Rocket	QMJHL	61	2	13	15	42	11	0	0	0	4
2004-05	PEI Rocket	QMJHL	68	10	29	39	48	....	....	....	....	....
2005-06	PEI Rocket	QMJHL	62	16	55	71	75	6	1	4	5	14

GRAHAM, Bruce (GRAY-uhm, BROOS) NYR

Center. Shoots left. 6'6", 224 lbs. Born, Moncton, N.B., December 2, 1985.
(NY Rangers' 5th choice, 51st overall, in 2004 Entry Draft).

			Regular Season					Playoffs				
Season	**Club**	**League**	**GP**	**G**	**A**	**Pts**	**PIM**	**GP**	**G**	**A**	**Pts**	**PIM**
2001-02	Moncton Flyers	NBMHL	STATISTICS NOT AVAILABLE									
	Moncton Wildcats	QMJHL	3	0	0	0	0	....	....	....	....	....
2002-03	Moncton Wildcats	QMJHL	66	15	13	28	80	6	0	2	2	0
2003-04	Moncton Wildcats	QMJHL	68	24	33	57	89	18	0	14	14	4
2004-05	Moncton Wildcats	QMJHL	47	23	19	42	56	12	4	5	9	19
2005-06	Hartford Wolf Pack	AHL	25	2	5	7	15	....	....	....	....	....
	Charlotte	ECHL	23	6	12	18	40	2	0	0	0	0

GRANATH, Elias (GRA-nuth, EHL-ee-ahs) DAL.

Defense. Shoots left. 6'1", 174 lbs. Born, Borlange, Sweden, September 6, 1985.
(Dallas' 10th choice, 196th overall, in 2003 Entry Draft).

			Regular Season					Playoffs				
Season	**Club**	**League**	**GP**	**G**	**A**	**Pts**	**PIM**	**GP**	**G**	**A**	**Pts**	**PIM**
2001-02	Leksands IF U18	Swe-U18	11	0	1	1	8	4	0	0	0	2
	Leksands IF Jr.	Swe-Jr.	6	0	0	0	0	1	0	0	0	0
2002-03	Leksands IF Jr.	Swe-Jr.	29	0	4	4	49	....	....	....	....	....
	Leksands IF U18	Swe-U18	6	0	2	2	0	2	0	1	1	8
2003-04	Leksands IF Jr.	Swe-Jr.	25	4	4	8	34	....	....	....	....	....
	Leksands IF	Sweden-Q	10	0	0	0	4	....	....	....	....	....
2004-05	Leksands IF	Sweden-2	35	3	3	6	24	....	....	....	....	....
	Leksands IF Jr.	Swe-Jr.	5	0	2	2	8	5	1	0	1	2
2005-06	Leksands IF Jr.	Swe-Jr.	3	1	1	2	2	....	....	....	....	....
	Leksands IF	Sweden	46	0	0	0	55	....	....	....	....	....

GRANT, Triston (GRANT, TRIHS-tuhn) PHI.

Left wing. Shoots left. 6'1", 223 lbs. Born, Brandon, Man., February 2, 1984.
(Philadelphia's 10th choice, 286th overall, in 2004 Entry Draft).

			Regular Season					Playoffs				
Season	**Club**	**League**	**GP**	**G**	**A**	**Pts**	**PIM**	**GP**	**G**	**A**	**Pts**	**PIM**
2000-01	Neepawa Natives	MJHL	STATISTICS NOT AVAILABLE									
	Lethbridge	WHL	23	2	0	2	75	5	0	0	0	11
2001-02	Lethbridge	WHL	36	8	1	9	110	....	....	....	....	....
	Vancouver Giants	WHL	21	2	4	6	53	....	....	....	....	....
2002-03	Vancouver Giants	WHL	72	10	10	20	200	4	0	0	0	10
2003-04	Vancouver Giants	WHL	69	10	8	18	267	11	1	1	2	33
2004-05	Vancouver Giants	WHL	70	20	12	32	193	6	1	0	1	8
2005-06	Philadelphia	AHL	64	2	3	5	193	....	....	....	....	....

GRECO, Brady (GREH-koh, BRAY-dee) T.B.

Defense. Shoots right. 6'3", 202 lbs. Born, Bryan, OH, March 4, 1983.
(Tampa Bay's 8th choice, 256th overall, in 2003 Entry Draft).

			Regular Season					Playoffs				
Season	**Club**	**League**	**GP**	**G**	**A**	**Pts**	**PIM**	**GP**	**G**	**A**	**Pts**	**PIM**
1997/00	Edgewood	High-WI	66	29	33	62	....	....	....	....	....	....
2000-01	Billings Bulls	AWHL	STATISTICS NOT AVAILABLE									
2001-02	Michigan Tech	WCHA	24	1	9	10	28	....	....	....	....	....
2002-03	Chicago Steel	USHL	57	9	20	29	225	....	....	....	....	....
2003-04	Colorado College	WCHA	28	7	5	12	22	....	....	....	....	....
2004-05	Colorado College	WCHA	26	4	2	6	36	....	....	....	....	....
2005-06	Springfield Falcons	AHL	2	0	0	0	0	....	....	....	....	....
	Johnstown Chiefs	ECHL	29	5	5	10	65	....	....	....	....	....

• Statistics for **Edgewood** (High-WI) are career totals for 1997-2000 seasons.

GREENE, Andy (GREEN, AN-dee) N.J.

Defense. Shoots left. 5'11", 180 lbs. Born, Trenton, MI, October 30, 1982.

			Regular Season					Playoffs				
Season	**Club**	**League**	**GP**	**G**	**A**	**Pts**	**PIM**	**GP**	**G**	**A**	**Pts**	**PIM**
2002-03	Miami U.	CCHA	41	4	19	23	64	....	....	....	....	....
2003-04	Miami U.	CCHA	41	7	19	26	78	....	....	....	....	....
2004-05	Miami U.	CCHA	38	7	27	34	66	....	....	....	....	....
2005-06	Miami U.	CCHA	39	9	22	31	48	....	....	....	....	....

CCHA First All-Star Team (2005, 2006) • NCAA West First All-American Team (2006)

Signed as a free agent by **New Jersey**, April 4, 2006.

GREENING, Colin (GREEN-ihng, CAW-lihn) OTT.

Center/Left wing. Shoots left. 6'2", 191 lbs. Born, St. John's, Nfld., March 9, 1986.
(Ottawa's 8th choice, 204th overall, in 2005 Entry Draft).

			Regular Season					Playoffs				
Season	**Club**	**League**	**GP**	**G**	**A**	**Pts**	**PIM**	**GP**	**G**	**A**	**Pts**	**PIM**
2002-03	St. John's	NFAHA	60	24	34	58	48	....	....	....	....	....
2003-04	Upper Canada	High-ON	53	30	43	73	40	....	....	....	....	....
2004-05	Upper Canada	High-ON	35	24	22	46	24	....	....	....	....	....
2005-06	Nanaimo Clippers	BCHL	56	27	35	62	46	5	3	0	3	2

Signed Letter of Intent to attend **Cornell** (ECACHL) in fall of 2006.

GREER, Matt (GREER, MAT) CBJ

Left wing. Shoots right. 6'2", 190 lbs. Born, St. Paul, MN, November 21, 1985.
(Columbus' 11th choice, 233rd overall, in 2004 Entry Draft).

			Regular Season					Playoffs				
Season	**Club**	**League**	**GP**	**G**	**A**	**Pts**	**PIM**	**GP**	**G**	**A**	**Pts**	**PIM**
2003-04	White Bear	High-MN	27	25	19	44	....	....	....	....	....	....
2004-05	Des Moines	USHL	60	14	18	32	16	....	....	....	....	....
2005-06	U. Minn-Duluth	WCHA	40	2	3	5	12	....	....	....	....	....

GRENZY, Michael (GREHN-zee, MIGH-kuhl) CHI.

Defense. Shoots left. 6'4", 215 lbs. Born, Niagara Falls, NY, February 6, 1984.
(Chicago's 9th choice, 275th overall, in 2003 Entry Draft).

			Regular Season					Playoffs				
Season	**Club**	**League**	**GP**	**G**	**A**	**Pts**	**PIM**	**GP**	**G**	**A**	**Pts**	**PIM**
99-2000	Toronto Marlboros	MTHL	56	7	34	41	....	....	....	....	....	....
2000-01	USNTDP	U-17	13	0	0	0	....	....	....	....	....	....
	USNTDP	NAHL	56	0	1	1	25	....	....	....	....	....
2001-02	USNTDP	U-18	25	0	5	5	4	....	....	....	....	....
	USNTDP	USHL	2	0	0	0	0	....	....	....	....	....
	USNTDP	NAHL	24	0	1	1	34	....	....	....	....	....
2002-03	Chicago Steel	USHL	51	3	13	16	48	....	....	....	....	....
2003-04	Clarkson Knights	ECAC	22	2	3	5	36	....	....	....	....	....
2004-05	Clarkson Knights	ECACHL	37	4	7	11	26	....	....	....	....	....
2005-06	Clarkson Knights	ECACHL	36	3	19	22	18	....	....	....	....	....

GRIGORENKO, Igor (grih-goh-REHN-koh, EE-gohr) DET.

Right wing. Shoots right. 5'10", 178 lbs. Born, Togliatti, USSR, April 9, 1983.
(Detroit's 1st choice, 62nd overall, in 2001 Entry Draft).

			Regular Season					Playoffs				
Season	**Club**	**League**	**GP**	**G**	**A**	**Pts**	**PIM**	**GP**	**G**	**A**	**Pts**	**PIM**
1998-99	Lada Togliatti 2	Russia-4	19	3	3	6	2	....	....	....	....	....
99-2000	Lada Togliatti 2	Russia-3	38	17	18	35	36	....	....	....	....	....
2000-01	Lada Togliatti 2	Russia-3	6	5	4	9	....	....	....	....	....	....
	CSK VVS Samara	Russia-2	39	10	10	20	....	....	....	....	....	....
	Lada Togliatti	Russia	....	....	....	....	....	5	1	0	1	4
2001-02	Lada Togliatti	Russia	41	8	9	17	58	4	1	0	1	2
2002-03	Lada Togliatti	Russia	47	19	11	30	82	10	1	*6	7	10
2003-04	Lada Togliatti 2	Russia-3	6	2	2	4	0	2	0	1	1	0
	Lada Togliatti	Russia	....	....	....	....	....	3	0	0	0	0
2004-05	Lada Togliatti	Russia	11	0	1	1	6	....	....	....	....	....
	Ufa	Russia	30	11	7	18	22	....	....	....	....	....
2005-06	Cherepovets	Russia	50	13	20	33	26	4	1	1	2	8

• Missed majority of 2003-04 season recovering from injuries suffered in automobile accident, May 16, 2003.

GROSSMAN, Nicklas (GROHS-man, NIH-kluhs) DAL.

Defense. Shoots left. 6'4", 187 lbs. Born, Stockholm, Sweden, January 22, 1985.
(Dallas' 4th choice, 56th overall, in 2004 Entry Draft).

			Regular Season					Playoffs				
Season	**Club**	**League**	**GP**	**G**	**A**	**Pts**	**PIM**	**GP**	**G**	**A**	**Pts**	**PIM**
2002-03	Sodertalje SK Jr.	Swe-Jr.	34	1	1	2	32	....	....	....	....	....
2003-04	Sodertalje SK Jr.	Swe-Jr.	33	1	2	3	32	2	0	0	0	0
	Sodertalje SK	Sweden	1	0	0	0	0	....	....	....	....	....
2004-05	Sodertalje SK Jr.	Swe-Jr.	12	3	6	9	8	1	0	0	0	0
	Sodertalje SK	Sweden	31	0	2	2	14	9	0	0	0	0
2005-06	Iowa Stars	AHL	61	2	3	5	49	7	0	1	1	4

GROT, Denis (GROHT, DEH-nihs) VAN.

Defense. Shoots left. 6', 185 lbs. Born, Minsk, USSR, June 1, 1984.
(Vancouver's 2nd choice, 55th overall, in 2002 Entry Draft).

			Regular Season					Playoffs				
Season	**Club**	**League**	**GP**	**G**	**A**	**Pts**	**PIM**	**GP**	**G**	**A**	**Pts**	**PIM**
2000-01	Yaroslavl 2	Russia-3	34	5	1	6	10	....	....	....	....	....
	Russia	Nat-Tm	5	0	2	2	8	....	....	....	....	....
2001-02	Yaroslavl 2	Russia-3	14	1	0	1	10	....	....	....	....	....
	Elektrostal 2	Russia-3	3	0	1	1	2	....	....	....	....	....
	Elektrostal	Russia-2	33	1	1	2	42	....	....	....	....	....
2002-03	HK Lipetsk	Russia-2	27	4	4	8	28	....	....	....	....	....
2003-04	Yaroslavl	Russia	31	0	2	2	4	3	0	0	0	2
2004-05	Yaroslavl 2	Russia-3	20	2	3	5	22	....	....	....	....	....
	Yaroslavl	Russia	1	0	0	0	2	....	....	....	....	....
	Sibir Novosibirsk	Russia	23	0	4	4	32	....	....	....	....	....
	Amur Khabarovsk	Russia-2	9	1	5	6	2	12	0	0	0	31
2005-06	Spartak Moscow	Russia	48	1	4	5	28	3	0	0	0	0

GRYBA, Eric (GREE-buh, AIR-ihk) OTT.

Defense. Shoots right. 6'3", 215 lbs. Born, Saskatoon, Sask., April 14, 1988.
(Ottawa's 2nd choice, 68th overall, in 2006 Entry Draft).

			Regular Season					Playoffs				
Season	**Club**	**League**	**GP**	**G**	**A**	**Pts**	**PIM**	**GP**	**G**	**A**	**Pts**	**PIM**
2003-04	Sask. Contacts	SMHL	39	1	10	11	89	10	4	8	12	20
2004-05	Sask. Contacts	SMHL	32	11	29	40	83	11	5	7	12	22
2005-06	Green Bay	USHL	56	3	12	15	205	3	1	1	2	27

Signed Letter of Intent to attend **Boston U.** (Hockey East) in fall of 2006.

GUENETTE, Francois-Pierre (gwih-NEHT, frahn-SWUH-PEE-air) VAN.

Center. Shoots right. 6'1", 183 lbs. Born, Laval, Que., January 18, 1984.
(Vancouver's 7th choice, 222nd overall, in 2003 Entry Draft).

			Regular Season					Playoffs				
Season	**Club**	**League**	**GP**	**G**	**A**	**Pts**	**PIM**	**GP**	**G**	**A**	**Pts**	**PIM**
99-2000	Laval-Laurentides	QAAA	33	15	18	33	14	9	3	6	9	2
2000-01	Laval-Laurentides	QAAA	41	17	27	44	47	8	3	8	11	4
2001-02	Halifax	QMJHL	35	2	11	13	14	11	3	4	7	0
2002-03	Halifax	QMJHL	72	38	49	87	24	24	10	17	27	12
2003-04	Cape Breton	QMJHL	69	34	51	85	26	5	0	2	2	2
2004-05	Halifax	QMJHL	70	21	38	59	46	13	4	11	15	4
2005-06	Columbia Inferno	ECHL	68	12	30	42	34	....	....	....	....	....

GUERIN, Marty (GAIR-ihn, MAHR-tee) L.A.

Right wing. Shoots right. 6'1", 190 lbs. Born, Manchester, NH, May 25, 1983.
(Los Angeles' 10th choice, 274th overall, in 2003 Entry Draft).

			Regular Season					Playoffs				
Season	**Club**	**League**	**GP**	**G**	**A**	**Pts**	**PIM**	**GP**	**G**	**A**	**Pts**	**PIM**
2000-01	Omaha Lancers	USHL	42	3	5	8	24	7	0	0	0	0
2001-02	Omaha Lancers	USHL	31	12	11	33	16	....	....	....	....	....
	Des Moines	USHL	7	2	1	3	2	....	....	....	....	....
2002-03	Des Moines	USHL	60	27	33	60	30	4	1	3	4	6
2003-04	Miami U.	CCHA	41	14	19	33	18	....	....	....	....	....
2004-05	Miami U.	CCHA	34	15	19	34	42	....	....	....	....	....
2005-06	Miami U.	CCHA	39	8	8	16	36	....	....	....	....	....

GUGGISBERG, Peter (GUH-gihs-buhrg, PEE-tuhr) WSH.

Right wing. Shoots right. 5'11", 183 lbs. Born, Davos, Switz., January 20, 1985.
(Washington's 10th choice, 166th overall, in 2004 Entry Draft).

			Regular Season					Playoffs				
Season	Club	League	GP	G	A	Pts	PIM	GP	G	A	Pts	PIM
2000-01	Langnau Jr.	Swiss-Jr.	12	3	3	6	0	2	1	0	1	2
2001-02	Langnau Jr.	Swiss-Jr.	15	12	4	16	2	4	2	3	5	4
	Langnau	Swiss	....	....	....	....	....	6	0	1	1	0
2002-03	Langnau Jr.	Swiss-Jr.	10	7	10	17	0	5	2	1	3	32
	Langnau	Swiss	34	6	7	13	0	....	....	....	....	....
2003-04	HC Davos	Swiss	39	11	9	20	2	6	0	0	0	4
2004-05	HC Davos	Swiss	36	12	7	19	8	15	3	5	8	4
2005-06	HC Davos	Swiss	43	7	9	16	10	15	3	2	5	2

GUTHRIE, Shea (GUHTH-ree, SHAY) NYI

Wing. Shoots right. 6', 187 lbs. Born, Almonte, Ont., July 30, 1987.
(NY Islanders' 3rd choice, 76th overall, in 2005 Entry Draft).

			Regular Season					Playoffs				
Season	Club	League	GP	G	A	Pts	PIM	GP	G	A	Pts	PIM
2004-05	St. George's	High-RI	25	31	26	57	20	....	....	....	....	....
2005-06	Clarkson Knights	ECACHL	33	9	17	26	60	....	....	....	....	....

ECACHL All-Rookie Team (2006)

GWIDT, Brent (GWIGHT, BREHNT) WSH.

Center. Shoots left. 6'2", 198 lbs. Born, Minocqua, WI, February 20, 1988.
(Washington's 9th choice, 157th overall, in 2006 Entry Draft).

			Regular Season					Playoffs				
Season	Club	League	GP	G	A	Pts	PIM	GP	G	A	Pts	PIM
2004-05	Lakeland Union	High-WI	15	25	10	35	10	....	....	....	....	....
2005-06	Lakeland Union	High-WI	21	41	23	64	43	....	....	....	....	....

HAGEMO, Nate (HAG-eh-moh, NAYT) CAR.

Defense. Shoots right. 5'11", 192 lbs. Born, Minneapolis, MN, October 8, 1986.
(Carolina's 2nd choice, 58th overall, in 2005 Entry Draft).

			Regular Season					Playoffs				
Season	Club	League	GP	G	A	Pts	PIM	GP	G	A	Pts	PIM
2002-03	USNTDP	U-17	32	3	6	9	30	....	....	....	....	....
	USNTDP	NAHL	38	2	6	8	65	....	....	....	....	....
2003-04	USNTDP	U-18	42	8	15	23	49	....	....	....	....	....
	USNTDP	NAHL	9	0	4	4	10	....	....	....	....	....
2004-05	U. of Minnesota	WCHA	25	2	7	9	22	....	....	....	....	....
2005-06	U. of Minnesota	WCHA	3	0	0	0	6	....	....	....	....	....

• Missed remainder of 2005-06 season after suffering a shoulder/neck injury early in the season.

HAGOS, Yared (HA-gohs, YAIR-ehd) DAL.

Center. Shoots left. 6'1", 202 lbs. Born, Stockholm, Sweden, March 27, 1983.
(Dallas' 2nd choice, 70th overall, in 2001 Entry Draft).

			Regular Season					Playoffs				
Season	Club	League	GP	G	A	Pts	PIM	GP	G	A	Pts	PIM
1998-99	AIK Solna Jr.	Swe-Jr.	32	8	12	20	22	....	....	....	....	....
99-2000	AIK Solna U18	Swe-U18	13	4	6	10	6	....	....	....	....	....
	AIK Solna Jr.	Swe-Jr.	17	6	4	10	10	....	....	....	....	....
2000-01	AIK Solna Jr.	Swe-Jr.	24	8	13	21	46	2	2	1	3	2
	AIK Solna	Sweden	....	....	....	....	....	5	0	0	0	0
2001-02	AIK Solna Jr.	Swe-Jr.	1	0	3	3	2	1	0	2	2	0
	AIK Solna	Sweden	45	4	6	10	36	....	....	....	....	....
	AIK Solna	Sweden-Q	9	0	0	0	12	....	....	....	....	....
2002-03	AIK Solna	Sweden-2	49	10	22	32	67	4	0	1	1	2
	AIK Solna Jr.	Swe-Jr.	1	0	1	1	0	....	....	....	....	....
2003-04	Timra IK	Sweden	48	9	11	20	75	10	3	1	4	6
2004-05	Timra IK	Sweden	49	6	15	21	38	7	1	0	1	2
2005-06	Iowa Stars	AHL	57	7	15	22	40	....	....	....	....	....

HALVARDSSON, Johan (HAL-vahrds-sohn, YOH-hahn) NYI

Defense. Shoots left. 6'3", 198 lbs. Born, Jonkoping, Sweden, December 26, 1979.
(NY Islanders' 8th choice, 102nd overall, in 1999 Entry Draft).

			Regular Season					Playoffs				
Season	Club	League	GP	G	A	Pts	PIM	GP	G	A	Pts	PIM
1997-98	HV 71 Jr.	Swe-Jr.	28	5	5	10	65	....	....	....	....	....
1998-99	HV 71 Jonkoping	Sweden	17	1	2	3	33	....	....	....	....	....
99-2000	HV 71 Jonkoping	Sweden	46	0	3	3	75	5	0	0	0	8
2000-01	HV 71 Jonkoping	Sweden	33	0	0	0	24	....	....	....	....	....
2001-02	HV 71 Jonkoping	Sweden	3	0	0	0	0	....	....	....	....	....
2002-03	HV 71 Jonkoping	Sweden	39	0	1	1	14	7	0	0	0	0
2003-04	IK Oskarshamn	Sweden-2	32	3	4	7	94	....	....	....	....	....
	HV 71 Jonkoping	Sweden	11	0	4	4	39	17	1	3	4	41
2004-05	HV 71 Jonkoping	Sweden	36	2	3	5	46	....	....	....	....	....
2005-06	HV 71 Jonkoping	Sweden	37	1	1	2	34	10	0	0	0	8

• Missed majority of 2001-02 season recovering from knee injury suffered in game vs. Sodertalje (Sweden), September 23, 2001.

HAMILTON, Mike (HAM-ihl-tuhn, MIGHK) ATL.

Left wing. Shoots left. 6'1", 200 lbs. Born, Vancouver, B.C., May 2, 1983.
(Atlanta's 6th choice, 175th overall, in 2003 Entry Draft).

			Regular Season					Playoffs				
Season	Club	League	GP	G	A	Pts	PIM	GP	G	A	Pts	PIM
99-2000	Peninsula Panthers	VIJHL	44	33	42	75	94	....	....	....	....	....
2000-01	Peninsula Panthers	VIJHL	19	15	20	35	106	....	....	....	....	....
	Victoria Salsa	BCHL	31	2	5	7	18	....	....	....	....	....
2001-02	Victoria Salsa	BCHL	13	5	2	7	14	....	....	....	....	....
	Merritt	BCHL	45	23	36	59	64	....	....	....	....	....
2002-03	Merritt	BCHL	56	42	51	95	133	....	....	....	....	....
2003-04	U. of Maine	H-East	29	7	6	13	40	....	....	....	....	....
2004-05	U. of Maine	H-East	38	3	15	18	49	....	....	....	....	....
2005-06	U. of Maine	H-East	30	1	10	11	56	....	....	....	....	....

HAMILTON, Ryan (HAM-ihl-tuhn, RIGH-uhn) MIN.

Left wing. Shoots left. 6'2", 230 lbs. Born, Oshawa, Ont., April 15, 1985.

			Regular Season					Playoffs				
Season	Club	League	GP	G	A	Pts	PIM	GP	G	A	Pts	PIM
2001-02	Moose Jaw	WHL	10	0	1	1	6	3	0	0	0	0
2002-03	Moose Jaw	WHL	5	0	0	0	2	....	....	....	....	....
	Couchiching	OPJHL	11	5	8	13	2	....	....	....	....	....
	Peterborough Bees	OPJHL	27	3	10	13	43	....	....	....	....	....
	Trenton Sting	OPJHL	17	3	8	11	24	....	....	....	....	....
	Barrie Colts	OHL	24	3	2	5	10	6	1	0	1	0
2003-04	Kingston	OPJHL	14	1	5	6	23	....	....	....	....	....
	Barrie Colts	OHL	46	17	10	27	21	7	0	1	1	8
2004-05	Barrie Colts	OHL	37	13	11	24	6	6	2	0	2	2
2005-06	Barrie Colts	OHL	63	46	26	72	58	14	8	9	17	11
	Houston Aeros	AHL	....	....	....	....	....	1	0	0	0	0

Signed as a free agent by **Minnesota**, July 5, 2006.

HANNULA, Mika (HAH-noo-lah, MEE-kah) MIN.

Right wing. Shoots left. 5'11", 180 lbs. Born, Huddinge, Sweden, April 2, 1979.
(Minnesota's 10th choice, 269th overall, in 2002 Entry Draft).

			Regular Season					Playoffs				
Season	Club	League	GP	G	A	Pts	PIM	GP	G	A	Pts	PIM
1996-97	AIK Solna Jr.	Swe-Jr.	26	4	4	8	58	....	....	....	....	....
1997-98	Djurgarden Jr.	Swe-Jr.	14	10	6	16	22	2	1	1	2	0
	Lukko Rauma Jr.	Fin-Jr.	6	2	0	2	36	....	....	....	....	....
1998-99	Lidingo HC	Sweden-2	32	10	0	10	47	....	....	....	....	....
99-2000	Hammarby	Sweden-2	43	10	10	20	53	2	0	0	0	2
2000-01	Malmo Jr.	Swe-Jr.	1	1	1	2	0	....	....	....	....	....
	Malmo	Sweden	45	2	9	11	26	8	3	2	5	14
2001-02	Malmo	Sweden	41	10	7	17	14	5	2	1	3	0
2002-03	Malmo	Sweden	49	15	15	30	72	....	....	....	....	....
2003-04	Houston Aeros	AHL	67	9	18	27	59	....	....	....	....	....
2004-05	Malmo	Sweden	47	14	9	23	71	....	....	....	....	....
2005-06	HV 71 Jonkoping	Sweden	45	13	18	31	62	12	3	8	11	22
	Sweden	Olympics	8	0	0	0	2	....	....	....	....	....

Signed as a free agent by **Malmo** (Sweden), May 12, 2004.

HANSEN, Jannik (HAHN-suhn, YAH-nih) VAN.

Left wing. Shoots right. 6', 176 lbs. Born, Herlev, Denmark, March 15, 1986.
(Vancouver's 7th choice, 287th overall, in 2004 Entry Draft).

			Regular Season					Playoffs				
Season	Club	League	GP	G	A	Pts	PIM	GP	G	A	Pts	PIM
2002-03	Rodovre	Denmark	15	0	0	0	0	....	....	....	....	....
	Malmo U18	Swe-U18	12	8	7	15	2	3	2	0	2	0
2003-04	Rodovre	Denmark	35	12	7	19	48	....	....	....	....	....
2004-05	Rodovre	Denmark	32	17	17	34	40	5	3	1	4	24
2005-06	Portland	WHL	64	24	40	64	67	12	7	6	13	16

HANZAL, Martin (HAHN-zuhl, MAHR-tihn) PHX.

Center. Shoots left. 6'5", 208 lbs. Born, Pisek, Czech., February 20, 1987.
(Phoenix's 1st choice, 17th overall, in 2005 Entry Draft).

			Regular Season					Playoffs				
Season	Club	League	GP	G	A	Pts	PIM	GP	G	A	Pts	PIM
2002-03	C. Budejovice U17	CzR-U17	47	24	30	54	28	7	1	3	4	25
2003-04	C. Budejovice U17	CzR-U17	2	0	2	2	2	2	1	0	1	4
	C. Budejovice Jr.	CzRep-Jr.	53	15	7	22	32	....	....	....	....	....
2004-05	C. Budejovice Jr.	CzRep-Jr.	37	22	22	44	80	2	1	2	3	2
	C. Budejovice	CzRep-2	15	1	2	3	2	6	0	0	0	6
2005-06	C. Budejovice Jr.	CzRep-Jr.	7	3	5	8	20	....	....	....	....	....
	C. Budejovice	CzRep	19	0	1	1	10	....	....	....	....	....
	BK Mlada Boleslav	CzRep-2	5	2	0	2	0	....	....	....	....	....
	Omaha Lancers	USHL	19	4	15	19	30	5	1	0	1	4

HARANT, Tomas (HAH-rant, TAW-mahsh) N.J.

Defense. Shoots left. 6'3", 200 lbs. Born, Zilina, Czech., April 28, 1980.
(Nashville's 8th choice, 173rd overall, in 2000 Entry Draft).

			Regular Season					Playoffs				
Season	Club	League	GP	G	A	Pts	PIM	GP	G	A	Pts	PIM
1995-96	HKP Zilina Jr.	Slovak-Jr.	46	3	9	12	142	....	....	....	....	....
1996-97	HKP Zilina Jr.	Slovak-Jr.	44	1	4	5	18	....	....	....	....	....
1997-98	HK SKP Zilina Jr.	Slovak-Jr.	41	5	7	12	72	....	....	....	....	....
	HK SKP Zilina	Slovak-2	5	0	0	0	0	....	....	....	....	....
1998-99	HK SKP Zilina Jr.	Slovak-Jr.	33	1	6	7	108	....	....	....	....	....
99-2000	HK SKP PChZ Zilina	Slovak-2	26	0	3	3	34	....	....	....	....	....
2000-01	HC Trinec Jr.	CzRep-Jr.	5	1	2	3	8	1	0	0	0	4
	HC Ocelari Trinec	CzRep	15	1	2	3	14	....	....	....	....	....
2001-02	MsHK SKP Zilina	Slovakia	51	2	3	5	46	4	0	0	0	4
2002-03	MsHK SKP Zilina	Slovakia	28	2	3	5	86	4	1	0	1	24
	HC Havirov	CzRep	19	0	1	1	40	....	....	....	....	....
2003-04	Dynamo Moscow	Russia	31	1	0	1	18	3	0	0	0	0
2004-05	Dynamo Moscow	Russia	1	0	0	0	2	....	....	....	....	....
	Karlovy Vary	CzRep	37	1	5	6	57	....	....	....	....	....
2005-06	C. Budejovice	CzRep	45	2	7	9	90	10	4	2	6	40

Signed as a free agent by **New Jersey**, July 4, 2006.

HARRINGTON, Chris (HAYR-ihng-tuhn, KRIHS) TOR.

Defense. Shoots right. 6', 182 lbs. Born, St. Cloud, MN, May 7, 1982.

			Regular Season					Playoffs				
Season	Club	League	GP	G	A	Pts	PIM	GP	G	A	Pts	PIM
2000-01	Omaha Lancers	USHL	50	7	11	18	66	10	2	6	8	12
2001-02	Omaha Lancers	USHL	57	9	33	42	68	13	3	3	6	32
2002-03	U. of Minnesota	WCHA	45	4	14	18	60	....	....	....	....	....
2003-04	U. of Minnesota	WCHA	41	5	24	29	42	....	....	....	....	....
2004-05	U. of Minnesota	WCHA	43	2	24	26	98	....	....	....	....	....
2005-06	U. of Minnesota	WCHA	40	3	33	36	64	....	....	....	....	....

Signed as a free agent by **Toronto**. April 19, 2006.

HARROLD, Peter (HAIR-ohld, PEE-tuhr) L.A.

Defense. Shoots right. 5'11", 195 lbs. Born, Kirtland Hills, Ont., June 8, 1983.

			Regular Season					Playoffs				
Season	Club	League	GP	G	A	Pts	PIM	GP	G	A	Pts	PIM
2003-04	Boston College	H-East	40	2	12	14	12	....	....	....	....	....
2004-05	Boston College	H-East	35	4	10	14	22	....	....	....	....	....
2005-06	Boston College	H-East	42	7	23	30	32	....	....	....	....	....

Hockey East First All-Star Team (2006) • NCAA East First All-American Team (2006)
Signed as a free agent by **Los Angeles**. April 12, 2006.

HAUHTONEN, Janne (HOWKH-tih-nehn, YAH-nee) **CBJ**

Center. Shoots right. 6'3", 205 lbs. Born, Pori, Finland, July 5, 1979.

			Regular Season					Playoffs				
Season	Club	League	GP	G	A	Pts	PIM	GP	G	A	Pts	PIM
99-2000	JYP Jyvaskyla	Finland	15	2	1	3	6	....	....	....	....	....
2000-01	JYP Jyvaskyla	Finland	55	6	10	16	44	....	....	....	....	....
2001-02	JYP Jyvaskyla	Finland	56	5	11	16	84	....	....	....	....	....
2002-03	JYP Jyvaskyla	Finland	46	6	13	19	69	7	0	2	2	12
2003-04	JYP Jyvaskyla	Finland	47	3	12	15	30	2	1	0	1	25
2004-05	JYP Jyvaskyla	Finland	51	6	17	23	54	3	0	0	0	0
2005-06	HIFK Helsinki	Finland	49	19	27	46	36	....	....	....	....	....

Signed as a free agent by **Columbus**, July 21, 2006.

HEDLUND, Andy (HEHD-luhnd, AN-dee) **OTT.**

Defense. Shoots left. 6'3", 215 lbs. Born, Osseo, MN, May 16, 1978.

			Regular Season					Playoffs				
Season	Club	League	GP	G	A	Pts	PIM	GP	G	A	Pts	PIM
1997-98	Fargo-Moorhead	USHL	56	4	12	16	135	4	0	4	4	0
1998-99	Minnesota State	WCHA	34	1	2	3	34	....	....	....	....	....
99-2000	Minnesota State	WCHA	36	4	2	6	58	....	....	....	....	....
2000-01	Minnesota State	WCHA	38	6	6	12	64	....	....	....	....	....
2001-02	Minnesota State	WCHA	37	5	10	15	48	....	....	....	....	....
	Trenton Titans	ECHL	2	0	0	0	0	6	0	0	0	6
2002-03	Trenton Titans	ECHL	13	1	2	3	14	....	....	....	....	....
	Binghamton	AHL	59	1	7	8	48	10	0	0	0	0
2003-04	Binghamton	AHL	80	4	19	23	108	2	0	0	0	2
2004-05	Binghamton	AHL	75	2	13	15	103	6	0	2	2	25
2005-06	Krefeld Pinguine	Germany	52	12	22	34	100	5	0	2	2	6

Signed as a free agent by **Trenton** (ECHL), March 28, 2002. Signed as a free agent by **Binghamton** (AHL), November 3, 2002. Signed as a free agent by **Ottawa**, December 18, 2003.

HEDMAN, Anton (HEHD-man, AN-tawn) **BOS.**

Forward. Shoots left. 6'2", 207 lbs. Born, Stockholm, Sweden, May 15, 1986.
(Boston's 7th choice, 255th overall, in 2004 Entry Draft).

			Regular Season					Playoffs				
Season	Club	League	GP	G	A	Pts	PIM	GP	G	A	Pts	PIM
2003-04	Stocksund Jr.	Swe-Jr.	14	5	5	10	14	....	....	....	....	....
2004-05	Djurgarden Jr.	Swe-Jr.	32	14	9	23	119	....	....	....	....	....
2005-06	Sudbury Wolves	OHL	60	18	16	34	126	8	1	3	4	19

HEDMAN, Oscar (HEHD-man, AWS-kuhr) **WSH.**

Defense. Shoots left. 6', 209 lbs. Born, Ornskoldsvik, Sweden, April 21, 1986.
(Washington's 8th choice, 132nd overall, in 2004 Entry Draft).

			Regular Season					Playoffs				
Season	Club	League	GP	G	A	Pts	PIM	GP	G	A	Pts	PIM
2002-03	MODO U18	Swe-U18	14	4	5	9	8	6	2	1	3	32
	Malmo Jr.	Swe-Jr.	5	0	1	1	2	....	....	....	....	....
2003-04	Malmo Jr.	Swe-Jr.	25	7	11	18	28	8	3	3	6	6
	MODO U18	Swe-U18	3	3	1	4	2	2	0	3	3	0
	MODO	Sweden	24	1	2	3	6	6	0	0	0	0
2004-05	MODO Jr.	Swe-Jr.	7	2	2	4	12	5	0	1	1	4
	MODO	Sweden	43	1	3	4	18	4	0	0	0	0
2005-06	MODO Jr.	Swe-Jr.	7	3	2	5	10	....	....	....	....	....
	MODO	Sweden	44	3	2	5	30	5	0	1	1	0

HEID, Chris (HIGHD, KRIHS)

Defense. Shoots left. 6'2", 205 lbs. Born, Langley, B.C., March 14, 1983.
(Minnesota's 3rd choice, 74th overall, in 2001 Entry Draft).

			Regular Season					Playoffs				
Season	Club	League	GP	G	A	Pts	PIM	GP	G	A	Pts	PIM
1998-99	Kamloops	BCAHA	58	26	34	60	65	....	....	....	....	....
	Spokane Chiefs	WHL	1	0	0	0	0	....	....	....	....	....
99-2000	Spokane Chiefs	WHL	44	1	7	8	25	6	0	0	0	4
2000-01	Spokane Chiefs	WHL	51	2	15	17	76	12	0	4	4	12
2001-02	Spokane Chiefs	WHL	69	7	28	35	56	11	1	4	5	8
2002-03	Spokane Chiefs	WHL	60	9	36	45	66	11	2	11	13	10
2003-04	Houston Aeros	AHL	58	3	10	13	35	....	....	....	....	....
2004-05	Houston Aeros	AHL	19	0	5	5	20	....	....	....	....	....
	Louisiana	ECHL	17	2	6	8	14	....	....	....	....	....
	Pensacola	ECHL	....	....	....	....	....	4	0	1	1	2
2005-06	Houston Aeros	AHL	4	0	1	1	14	....	....	....	....	....
	Cleveland Barons	AHL	4	0	2	2	8	....	....	....	....	....
	Pensacola	ECHL	50	4	16	20	69	....	....	....	....	....
	Fresno Falcons	ECHL	....	....	....	....	....	16	2	2	4	8

HEJDA, Jan (HAY-dah, YAHN) **EDM.**

Defense. Shoots left. 6'3", 209 lbs. Born, Prague, Czech., June 18, 1978.
(Buffalo's 4th choice, 106th overall, in 2003 Entry Draft).

			Regular Season					Playoffs				
Season	Club	League	GP	G	A	Pts	PIM	GP	G	A	Pts	PIM
1997-98	HC Slavia Praha	CzRep	44	2	5	7	51	5	0	0	0	6
1998-99	HC Slavia Praha	CzRep	34	1	2	3	38	....	....	....	....	....
99-2000	HC Slavia Praha	CzRep	26	1	2	3	14	....	....	....	....	....
	HC Femax Havirov	CzRep	7	0	2	2	6	....	....	....	....	....
	HC Stadion Liberec	CzRep-2	1	0	0	0	4	....	....	....	....	....
2000-01	HC Slavia Praha	CzRep	38	2	6	8	70	11	3	0	3	12
	SK Kadan	CzRep-2	8	1	0	1	6	....	....	....	....	....
2001-02	HC Slavia Praha	CzRep	42	9	8	17	52	9	1	1	2	14
2002-03	HC Slavia Praha	CzRep	52	6	11	17	44	17	5	8	13	12
2003-04	CSKA Moscow	Russia	60	1	5	6	26	....	....	....	....	....
2004-05	CSKA Moscow	Russia	60	2	11	13	59	....	....	....	....	....
2005-06	Mytischi	Russia	50	3	12	15	56	9	2	3	5	24

Rights traded to **Edmonton** by **Buffalo** for a 7th round choice in 2007 Entry Draft, July 10, 2006.

HELLSTROM, Alexander (HEHL-struhm, al-ehx-AN-duhr) **ST.L.**

Defense. Shoots left. 6'2", 207 lbs. Born, Falun, Sweden, April 17, 1987.
(St. Louis' 9th choice, 184th overall, in 2006 Entry Draft).

			Regular Season					Playoffs				
Season	Club	League	GP	G	A	Pts	PIM	GP	G	A	Pts	PIM
2003-04	Bjorkloven U18	Swe-U18	7	0	2	2	8	....	....	....	....	....
2004-05	Bjorkloven U18	Swe-U18	STATISTICS NOT AVAILABLE									
	Bjorkloven Jr.	Swe-Jr.	3	0	2	2	2	....	....	....	....	....
	IF Bjorkloven Umea	Sweden-2	15	0	1	1	8	....	....	....	....	....
2005-06	Bjorkloven Jr.	Swe-Jr.	11	1	3	4	20	6	0	3	3	4
	IF Bjorkloven Umea	Sweden-2	31	1	0	1	45	....	....	....	....	....

HELM, Darren (HEHLM, DAIR-ehn) **DET.**

Center/Left wing. Shoots left. 5'11", 172 lbs. Born, Winnipeg, Man., January 21, 1987.
(Detroit's 5th choice, 132nd overall, in 2005 Entry Draft).

			Regular Season					Playoffs				
Season	Club	League	GP	G	A	Pts	PIM	GP	G	A	Pts	PIM
2003-04	Selkirk Fishermen	MJBHL	34	39	32	71	34	....	....	....	....	....
2004-05	Medicine Hat	WHL	72	10	14	24	27	13	2	6	8	10
2005-06	Medicine Hat	WHL	70	41	38	79	37	13	5	4	9	2

WHL East First All-Star Team (2006)

HELMINEN, Dwight (HEHL-mih-nehn, DWIGHT) **NYR**

Center. Shoots left. 5'10", 191 lbs. Born, Hancock, MI, June 22, 1983.
(Edmonton's 12th choice, 244th overall, in 2002 Entry Draft).

			Regular Season					Playoffs				
Season	Club	League	GP	G	A	Pts	PIM	GP	G	A	Pts	PIM
1998-99	Det. Compuware	MNHL	32	9	7	16	....	....	....	....	....	....
99-2000	USNTDP	USHL	30	5	7	12	10	....	....	....	....	....
	USNTDP	NAHL	30	7	10	17	8	....	....	....	....	....
2000-01	USNTDP	U-18	42	9	36	45	20	....	....	....	....	....
	USNTDP	USHL	24	12	7	19	8	....	....	....	....	....
	USNTDP	NAHL	1	0	1	1	2	....	....	....	....	....
2001-02	U. of Michigan	CCHA	39	10	8	18	10	....	....	....	....	....
2002-03	U. of Michigan	CCHA	39	17	16	33	34	....	....	....	....	....
2003-04	U. of Michigan	CCHA	41	17	11	28	4	....	....	....	....	....
2004-05	Hartford Wolf Pack	AHL	41	2	7	9	10	....	....	....	....	....
	Charlotte	ECHL	28	5	16	21	10	15	7	3	10	2
2005-06	Hartford Wolf Pack	AHL	77	32	24	56	40	13	3	5	8	10

Traded to **NY Rangers** by **Edmonton** with Stephen Valiquette and Edmonton's 2nd round compensatory choice (Dane Byers) in 2004 Entry Draft and future considerations for Petr Nedved and Jussi Markkanen, March 3, 2004.

HEMINGWAY, Brett (HEH-mihng-way, BREHT) **COL.**

Right wing. Shoots right. 6'1", 185 lbs. Born, Yorkton, Sask., September 28, 1983.
(Colorado's 6th choice, 225th overall, in 2003 Entry Draft).

			Regular Season					Playoffs				
Season	Club	League	GP	G	A	Pts	PIM	GP	G	A	Pts	PIM
2000-01	Port Coquitlam	PIJHL	36	22	19	41	24	....	....	....	....	....
2001-02	Coquitlam Express	BCHL	60	45	39	84	31	....	....	....	....	....
2002-03	Coquitlam Express	BCHL	60	42	50	92	50	7	7	5	12	4
2003-04	New Hampshire	H-East	34	7	12	19	8	....	....	....	....	....
2004-05	New Hampshire	H-East	42	22	21	43	14	....	....	....	....	....
2005-06	New Hampshire	H-East	38	19	22	41	22	....	....	....	....	....

Hockey East All-Rookie Team (2004)

HENDRIKX, Trevor (HEHN-drihx, TREH-vuhr) **CBJ**

Defense. Shoots right. 6'2", 205 lbs. Born, Russell, Ont., March 29, 1985.
(Columbus' 8th choice, 201st overall, in 2005 Entry Draft).

			Regular Season					Playoffs				
Season	Club	League	GP	G	A	Pts	PIM	GP	G	A	Pts	PIM
2000-01	Gloucester	OPJHL	26	2	3	5	25	....	....	....	....	....
2001-02	Peterborough	OHL	46	1	3	4	37	5	0	0	0	4
2002-03	Peterborough	OHL	56	1	8	9	128	7	0	0	0	4
2003-04	Peterborough	OHL	63	8	24	32	208	....	....	....	....	....
2004-05	Peterborough	OHL	68	15	33	48	100	14	5	7	12	14
2005-06	Peterborough	OHL	60	9	47	56	123	19	5	10	15	40

• Re-entered NHL Entry Draft. Originally Columbus' 10th choice, 283rd overall, in 2003 Entry Draft.

HENDRY, Jordan (HEHN-dree, JOHR-dan) **CHI.**

Defense. Shoots left. 6', 205 lbs. Born, Nokomis, Sask., February 23, 1984.

			Regular Season					Playoffs				
Season	Club	League	GP	G	A	Pts	PIM	GP	G	A	Pts	PIM
2002-03	Alaska-Fairbanks	CCHA	35	3	5	8	10	....	....	....	....	....
2003-04	Alaska-Fairbanks	CCHA	36	4	9	13	38	....	....	....	....	....
2004-05	Alaska-Fairbanks	CCHA	3	0	1	1	21	....	....	....	....	....
2005-06	Alaska-Fairbanks	CCHA	38	4	10	14	74	....	....	....	....	....
	Norfolk Admirals	AHL	13	1	4	5	13	3	0	0	0	2

Signed as a free agent by **Chicago**, July 17, 2006.

HENEGAN, Kyell (HEH-neh-gan, KIGHL) **N.J.**

Defense. Shoots left. 6'4", 205 lbs. Born, Montreal, Que., October 27, 1987.
(New Jersey's 8th choice, 208th overall, in 2006 Entry Draft).

			Regular Season					Playoffs				
Season	Club	League	GP	G	A	Pts	PIM	GP	G	A	Pts	PIM
2004-05	Shawinigan	QMJHL	45	1	3	4	50	1	0	0	0	0
2005-06	Shawinigan	QMJHL	68	3	4	7	200	10	0	1	1	38

HENNESSY, Josh (HEHN-eh-see, JAW-sh) **OTT.**

Center. Shoots left. 6', 190 lbs. Born, Brockton, MA, February 7, 1985.
(San Jose's 3rd choice, 43rd overall, in 2003 Entry Draft).

			Regular Season					Playoffs				
Season	Club	League	GP	G	A	Pts	PIM	GP	G	A	Pts	PIM
2000-01	Milton Academy	High-MA	28	20	30	50	20	....	....	....	....	....
2001-02	Quebec Remparts	QMJHL	70	20	20	40	24	9	3	9	12	8
2002-03	Quebec Remparts	QMJHL	72	33	51	84	44	11	6	9	15	10
2003-04	Quebec Remparts	QMJHL	59	40	42	82	55	....	....	....	....	....
2004-05	Quebec Remparts	QMJHL	68	35	50	85	39	12	2	9	11	6
2005-06	Cleveland Barons	AHL	80	24	39	63	60	....	....	....	....	....

Traded to **Chicago** by **San Jose** with Tom Preissing for Mark Bell, July 9, 2006. Traded to **Ottawa** by **Chicago** with Tom Preissing, Michal Barinka and a 2nd round choice in 2008 Entry Draft for Martin Havlat and Bryan Smolinski, July 10, 2006.

HENRICH, Adam (HEHN-rihch, A-duhm) **T.B.**

Left wing. Shoots left. 6'4", 231 lbs. Born, Thornhill, Ont., January 19, 1984.
(Tampa Bay's 1st choice, 60th overall, in 2002 Entry Draft).

			Regular Season					Playoffs				
Season	Club	League	GP	G	A	Pts	PIM	GP	G	A	Pts	PIM
99-2000	Don Mills Flyers	GTHL	54	30	52	82	86	....	....	....	....	....
2000-01	Brampton	OHL	48	5	4	9	27	9	0	0	0	6
2001-02	Brampton	OHL	66	33	30	63	92	....	....	....	....	....
2002-03	Brampton	OHL	63	31	33	64	84	11	4	1	5	25
2003-04	Brampton	OHL	65	29	29	58	146	12	5	1	6	24
2004-05	Springfield Falcons	AHL	63	10	16	26	97	....	....	....	....	....
	Johnstown Chiefs	ECHL	6	2	1	3	15	....	....	....	....	....
2005-06	Springfield Falcons	AHL	12	0	3	3	14	....	....	....	....	....
	Johnstown Chiefs	ECHL	51	18	23	41	78	5	2	4	6	8

HENSICK, T.J. (HEHN-sihk, TEE-JAY) **COL.**

Center. Shoots right. 5'10", 185 lbs. Born, Lansing, MI, December 10, 1985.
(Colorado's 5th choice, 88th overall, in 2005 Entry Draft).

			Regular Season					Playoffs				
Season	Club	League	GP	G	A	Pts	PIM	GP	G	A	Pts	PIM
2001-02	USNTDP	U-17	17	10	5	15	....	....	....	....	....	....
	USNTDP	NAHL	46	15	25	40	10	....	....	....	....	....
2002-03	USNTDP	U-18	48	24	24	48	11	....	....	....	....	....
	USNTDP	NAHL	10	6	7	13	0	....	....	....	....	....
2003-04	U. of Michigan	CCHA	43	12	*34	46	38	....	....	....	....	....
2004-05	U. of Michigan	CCHA	39	23	32	55	24	....	....	....	....	....
2005-06	U. of Michigan	CCHA	41	17	35	52	44	....	....	....	....	....

CCHA All-Rookie Team (2004) • CCHA First All-Star Team (2004, 2005) • CCHA Rookie of the Year (2004) • NCAA West First All-American Team (2005) • CCHA Second All-Star Team (2006)

HERSLEY, Patrik (HUHRS-lee, PAT-rihk) **L.A.**

Defense. Shoots right. 6'3", 205 lbs. Born, Malmo, Sweden, June 23, 1986.
(Los Angeles' 5th choice, 139th overall, in 2005 Entry Draft).

			Regular Season					Playoffs				
Season	Club	League	GP	G	A	Pts	PIM	GP	G	A	Pts	PIM
2002-03	Malmo U18	Swe-U18	9	3	4	7	53	4	1	2	3	4
	Malmo Jr.	Swe-Jr.	16	0	2	2	4	1	0	0	0	0
2003-04	Malmo U18	Swe-U18	2	2	0	2	4	....	....	....	....	....
	Malmo Jr.	Swe-Jr.	17	1	4	5	16	8	0	2	2	2
2004-05	Malmo Jr.	Swe-Jr.	31	8	14	22	104	3	2	1	3	6
	Malmo	Sweden	8	0	1	1	0	....	....	....	....	....
	Malmo	Sweden-Q	6	0	0	0	2	....	....	....	....	....
2005-06	Malmo Jr.	Swe-Jr.	13	10	9	19	38	....	....	....	....	....
	Malmo	Sweden-2	41	6	8	14	38	....	....	....	....	....

HESHKA, Shaun (HEHSH-kah, SHAWN) **VAN.**

Defense. Shoots right. 6'1", 195 lbs. Born, Melville, Sask., July 30, 1985.

			Regular Season					Playoffs				
Season	Club	League	GP	G	A	Pts	PIM	GP	G	A	Pts	PIM
2002-03	Melville	SJHL	53	6	14	20	53	....	....	....	....	....
2003-04	Everett Silvertips	WHL	66	3	7	10	25	21	0	2	2	8
2004-05	Everett Silvertips	WHL	72	12	26	38	21	11	2	0	2	6
2005-06	Everett Silvertips	WHL	66	10	49	59	91	14	3	10	13	10

WHL West First All-Star Team (2006)

Signed as a free agent by **Vancouver**, July 24, 2006.

HICKEY, Chris (HIHK-ee, KRIHS) **MIN.**

Center. Shoots right. 6'3", 190 lbs. Born, St. Paul, MN, September 2, 1988.
(Minnesota's 7th choice, 192nd overall, in 2006 Entry Draft).

			Regular Season					Playoffs				
Season	Club	League	GP	G	A	Pts	PIM	GP	G	A	Pts	PIM
2003-04	Cretin-Derham	High-MN	27	19	13	32	32	....	....	....	....	....
2004-05	Cretin-Derham	High-MN	28	25	21	46	48	....	....	....	....	....
2005-06	Cretin-Derham	High-MN	31	37	28	65	36	....	....	....	....	....

HILLIER, Ryan (HIHL-lee-uhr, RIGH-uhn) **NYR**

Left wing. Shoots left. 6', 197 lbs. Born, Halifax, N.S., January 25, 1988.
(NY Rangers' 3rd choice, 84th overall, in 2006 Entry Draft).

			Regular Season					Playoffs				
Season	Club	League	GP	G	A	Pts	PIM	GP	G	A	Pts	PIM
2003-04	Dartmouth	NSMHL	55	31	36	67	97	....	....	....	....	....
2004-05	Halifax	QMJHL	21	1	1	2	13	7	0	2	2	2
2005-06	Halifax	QMJHL	68	19	38	57	76	11	2	2	4	12

HIMELFARB, Eric (HIH-muhl-FAHRB, AIR-ihk) **DET.**

Center. Shoots right. 5'9", 161 lbs. Born, Thornhill, Ont., January 1, 1983.
(Montreal's 6th choice, 171st overall, in 2001 Entry Draft).

			Regular Season					Playoffs				
Season	Club	League	GP	G	A	Pts	PIM	GP	G	A	Pts	PIM
1998-99	Don Mills Flyers	GTHL	40	40	31	71	42	....	....	....	....	....
99-2000	Sarnia Sting	OHL	62	14	33	47	26	7	1	4	5	4
2000-01	Sarnia Sting	OHL	49	31	44	75	48	4	1	7	8	4
2001-02	Sarnia Sting	OHL	67	35	48	83	67	5	1	4	5	11
2002-03	Barrie Colts	OHL	67	31	44	75	81	6	1	0	1	6
2003-04	Grand Rapids	AHL	7	2	3	5	2	4	0	3	3	0
	Kingston	OHL	67	37	70	107	80	5	4	4	8	8
2004-05	Grand Rapids	AHL	76	19	24	43	59	....	....	....	....	....
2005-06	Grand Rapids	AHL	62	10	18	28	24	16	0	0	0	12

Traded to **Barrie** (OHL) by **Sarnia** (OHL) with Riley Moher for Tyler Hanchuk, Aaron Power and Joey Tenute, August 20, 2002. Signed as a free agent by **Detroit**, July 21, 2004.

HJALMARSSON, Niklas (HJAHL-mahr-suhn, NIHK-las) **CHI.**

Defense. Shoots left. 6'1", 196 lbs. Born, Eksjo, Sweden , June 6, 1987.
(Chicago's 5th choice, 108th overall, in 2005 Entry Draft).

			Regular Season					Playoffs				
Season	Club	League	GP	G	A	Pts	PIM	GP	G	A	Pts	PIM
2003-04	HV 71 Jr.	Swe-Jr.	15	1	3	4	14	2	0	0	0	8
2004-05	HV 71 U18	Swe-U18	3	0	2	2	4	....	....	....	....	....
	HV 71 Jr.	Swe-Jr.	31	4	11	15	87	....	....	....	....	....
	HV 71 Jonkoping	Sweden	14	0	0	0	0	....	....	....	....	....
2005-06	HV 71 Jr.	Swe-Jr..	7	3	2	5	12	....	....	....	....	....
	HV 71 Jonkoping	Sweden	4	1	2	3	0	12	0	1	1	4

HOBSON, Adam (HAWB-sohn, A-duhm) **CHI.**

Center. Shoots left. 6', 209 lbs. Born, Lund, Sweden, January 9, 1987.
(Chicago's 12th choice, 203rd overall, in 2005 Entry Draft).

			Regular Season					Playoffs				
Season	Club	League	GP	G	A	Pts	PIM	GP	G	A	Pts	PIM
2002-03	Abbotsford Pilots	PIJHL	38	20	28	48	....	....	....	....	....	....
	Spokane Chiefs	WHL	1	0	0	0	2	....	....	....	....	....
2003-04	Spokane Chiefs	WHL	63	4	5	9	35	4	0	0	0	0
2004-05	Spokane Chiefs	WHL	72	10	27	37	47	....	....	....	....	....
2005-06	Spokane Chiefs	WHL	72	23	27	50	124	....	....	....	....	....

HOFFMAN, Mike (HAWF-muhn, MIGHK)

Right wing. Shoots right. 6'4", 240 lbs. Born, Weymouth, MA, September 20, 1980.

			Regular Season					Playoffs				
Season	Club	League	GP	G	A	Pts	PIM	GP	G	A	Pts	PIM
2002-03	Connecticut	MAAC	28	2	8	10	24	....	....	....	....	....
2003-04	Connecticut	MAAC	3	0	0	0	2	....	....	....	....	....
	Worcester IceCats	AHL	15	0	0	0	20	....	....	....	....	....
	Peoria Rivermen	ECHL	25	2	7	9	16	8	0	1	1	6
2004-05	Cleveland Barons	AHL	58	1	7	8	170	....	....	....	....	....
2005-06	Toronto Marlies	AHL	54	2	5	7	103	1	0	0	0	0

Signed as a free agent by **Cleveland** (AHL), September 22, 2004. Signed as a free agent by **Toronto**, August 12, 2005.

HOGEBOOM, Greg (HOH-guh-BOOM, GREHG) **L.A.**

Right wing. Shoots right. 6', 190 lbs. Born, Toronto, Ont., September 26, 1982.
(Los Angeles' 6th choice, 152nd overall, in 2002 Entry Draft).

			Regular Season					Playoffs				
Season	Club	League	GP	G	A	Pts	PIM	GP	G	A	Pts	PIM
99-2000	Wexford Raiders	OPJHL	48	32	47	79	44	....	....	....	....	....
2000-01	Miami U.	CCHA	38	8	5	13	20	....	....	....	....	....
2001-02	Miami U.	CCHA	36	14	9	23	22	....	....	....	....	....
2002-03	Miami U.	CCHA	41	24	18	42	16	....	....	....	....	....
2003-04	Miami U.	CCHA	41	19	23	42	16	....	....	....	....	....
	Manchester	AHL	3	0	1	1	0	....	....	....	....	....
2004-05	Manchester	AHL	14	1	0	1	10	....	....	....	....	....
2005-06	Manchester	AHL	42	9	10	19	18	1	0	0	0	0
	Reading Royals	ECHL	19	9	18	27	4	....	....	....	....	....

CCHA Second All-Star Team (2004)

HOLLOWAY, Bud (HAHL-OH-way, BUHD) **L.A.**

Center. Shoots right. 6', 190 lbs. Born, Wapella, Sask., March 1, 1988.
(Los Angeles' 5th choice, 86th overall, in 2006 Entry Draft).

			Regular Season					Playoffs				
Season	Club	League	GP	G	A	Pts	PIM	GP	G	A	Pts	PIM
2003-04	Yorkton Harvest	SMHL	43	15	21	36	22	....	....	....	....	....
	Seattle	WHL	2	0	0	0	0	....	....	....	....	....
2004-05	Seattle	WHL	67	4	11	15	27	12	0	1	1	0
2005-06	Seattle	WHL	72	21	13	34	18	7	3	2	5	4

HOLMQVIST, Andreas (HOHLM-kvihst, ahn-DRAY-uhs) **T.B.**

Defense. Shoots right. 6'4", 195 lbs. Born, Stockholm, Sweden, July 23, 1981.
(Tampa Bay's 3rd choice, 61st overall, in 2001 Entry Draft).

			Regular Season					Playoffs				
Season	Club	League	GP	G	A	Pts	PIM	GP	G	A	Pts	PIM
99-2000	Hammarby Jr.	Swe-Jr.	33	8	12	20	16	6	1	2	3	4
2000-01	Hammarby Jr.	Swe-Jr.	47	6	15	21	40	....	....	....	....	....
2001-02	Hammarby	Sweden-2	42	11	13	24	97	....	....	....	....	....
2002-03	Linkopings HC	Sweden	43	4	9	13	28	....	....	....	....	....
	Linkopings HC	Sweden-Q	10	0	0	0	4	....	....	....	....	....
2003-04	Hamilton Bulldogs	AHL	4	0	0	0	0	....	....	....	....	....
	Pensacola	ECHL	63	4	33	37	16	5	0	4	4	0
2004-05	Springfield Falcons	AHL	42	3	9	12	22	....	....	....	....	....
2005-06	Linkopings HC	Sweden	46	6	16	22	64	13	1	3	4	24

HOLTET, Marius (HOHL-teht, MAIR-ee-uhs) **DAL.**

Center. Shoots right. 6', 183 lbs. Born, Hamar, Norway, August 31, 1984.
(Dallas' 4th choice, 42nd overall, in 2002 Entry Draft).

			Regular Season					Playoffs				
Season	Club	League	GP	G	A	Pts	PIM	GP	G	A	Pts	PIM
2000-01	Farjestad U18	Swe-U18	5	3	1	4	16	....	....	....	....	....
	Farjestad Jr.	Swe-Jr.	18	2	2	4	18	....	....	....	....	....
2001-02	Farjestad Jr.	Swe-Jr.	37	12	7	19	70	....	....	....	....	....
2002-03	Skare BK Karlstad	Sweden-3	STATISTICS NOT AVAILABLE									
	Bofors	Sweden-2	14	1	1	2	8	2	0	0	0	2
2003-04	Bofors	Sweden-2	43	11	3	14	90	5	2	0	2	4
2004-05	Louisiana	ECHL	4	0	0	0	0	....	....	....	....	....
	Houston Aeros	AHL	54	7	5	12	48	1	0	0	0	0
2005-06	Iowa Stars	AHL	68	9	13	22	61	7	2	0	2	2

HOLZAPFEL, Riley (HOHL-za-fehl, RIGH-lee) **ATL.**

Center. Shoots left. 5'11", 175 lbs. Born, Regina, Sask., August 18, 1988.
(Atlanta's 2nd choice, 43rd overall, in 2006 Entry Draft).

			Regular Season					Playoffs				
Season	Club	League	GP	G	A	Pts	PIM	GP	G	A	Pts	PIM
2004-05	Moose Jaw	WHL	63	15	13	28	32	5	1	2	3	8
2005-06	Moose Jaw	WHL	64	19	38	57	46	22	7	9	16	20

HOLZER, Korbinian (HOHL-zuhr, kohr-BEEHN-yuhn) **TOR.**

Defense. Shoots right. 6'3", 190 lbs. Born, Munich, Germany, February 16, 1988.
(Toronto's 4th choice, 111th overall, in 2006 Entry Draft).

			Regular Season					Playoffs				
Season	Club	League	GP	G	A	Pts	PIM	GP	G	A	Pts	PIM
2004-05	EC Bad Tolz Jr.	Ger-Jr.	34	7	11	18	66	5	0	2	2	2
2005-06	EC Bad Tolz Jr.	Ger-Jr.	2	1	1	2	6	....	....	....	....	....
	Tolzer Lowen	German-2	46	3	3	6	94	....	....	....	....	....

HOOTON, Brock (HOO-tuhn, BRAWK) **OTT.**

Right wing. Shoots right. 6'2", 208 lbs. Born, Smithers, B.C., March 20, 1983.
(Ottawa's 6th choice, 150th overall, in 2002 Entry Draft).

			Regular Season					Playoffs				
Season	Club	League	GP	G	A	Pts	PIM	GP	G	A	Pts	PIM
1998-99	Smithers Selects	BCAHA	40	30	55	85	30	....	....	....	....	....
99-2000	Campbell River	VIJHL	40	8	17	25	8	....	....	....	....	....
2000-01	Quesnel	BCHL	60	11	26	37	....	....	....	....	....	....
2001-02	Quesnel	BCHL	60	34	50	84	33	....	....	....	....	....
2002-03	St. Cloud State	WCHA	26	1	6	7	14	....	....	....	....	....
2003-04	St. Cloud State	WCHA	35	5	10	15	4	....	....	....	....	....
2004-05	St. Cloud State	WCHA	38	5	7	12	10	....	....	....	....	....
2005-06	St. Cloud State	WCHA	42	7	20	27	29	....	....	....	....	....

HOPE, Joey (HOHP, JOH-ee)

Defense. Shoots right. 6', 180 lbs. Born, Anchorage, AK, January 1, 1982.

			Regular Season					Playoffs				
Season	Club	League	GP	G	A	Pts	PIM	GP	G	A	Pts	PIM
1998-99	USNTDP	NAHL	43	4	7	11	125	....	....	....	....	....
99-2000	USNTDP	U-18	6	2	3	5	4	....	....	....	....	....
	USNTDP	USHL	47	5	13	18	66	....	....	....	....	....
2000-01	Prince George	WHL	13	1	3	4	6	....	....	....	....	....
	Portland	WHL	56	6	24	30	103	13	1	7	8	10
2001-02	Portland	WHL	64	9	27	36	124	3	0	2	2	8
2002-03	Portland	WHL	54	12	27	39	142	....	....	....	....	....
2003-04	Philadelphia	AHL	48	0	4	4	32	9	0	1	1	6
	Trenton Titans	ECHL	4	0	2	2	0	....	....	....	....	....
2004-05	Philadelphia	AHL	16	2	2	4	12	....	....	....	....	....
2005-06	Philadelphia	AHL	38	1	2	3	30	....	....	....	....	....

Signed as a free agent by **Philadelphia**, July 14, 2003.

HORNQVIST, Patric (HOHRN-kwihst, PAT-rihk) NSH.

Right wing. Shoots left. 5'11", 187 lbs. Born, Sollentuna, Sweden, January 1, 1987.
(Nashville's 7th choice, 230th overall, in 2005 Entry Draft).

			Regular Season					Playoffs				
Season	Club	League	GP	G	A	Pts	PIM	GP	G	A	Pts	PIM
2003-04	Vasby Jr.	Swe-Jr.	10	7	10	17	30	....	....	....	....	....
	Vasby	Sweden-3	32	8	5	13	26	....	....	....	....	....
2004-05	Vasby	Sweden-3	28	12	12	24	36	....	....	....	....	....
	Djurgarden Jr.	Swe-Jr.	5	3	0	3	2	....	....	....	....	....
2005-06	Djurgarden Jr.	Swe-Jr.	4	2	1	3	2	4	1	2	3	2
	Djurgarden	Sweden	47	5	2	7	36	....	....	....	....	....

HOSPELT, Kai (HAWS-pehlt, KIGH) S.J.

Forward. Shoots left. 6'1", 187 lbs. Born, Cologne, West Germany, August 23, 1985.
(San Jose's 8th choice, 216th overall, in 2003 Entry Draft).

			Regular Season					Playoffs				
Season	Club	League	GP	G	A	Pts	PIM	GP	G	A	Pts	PIM
2000-01	Kolner EC Jr.	Ger-Jr.	35	25	18	43	16	....	....	....	....	....
2001-02	Koln Jr.	Ger-Jr.	40	51	55	106	10	5	6	2	8	4
2002-03	Koln Jr.	Ger-Jr.	29	39	42	81	20	3	2	5	7	2
	Kolner Haie	Germany	21	0	2	2	0	6	0	1	1	0
2003-04	Kolner Haie	Germany	47	2	2	4	18	6	0	0	0	2
2004-05	Kolner Haie	Germany	23	1	1	2	6	....	....	....	....	....
2005-06	Kolner Haie	Germany	47	5	5	10	12	9	1	1	2	0

HRABAL, Josef (huh-RA-buhl, YOH-sehf) EDM.

Defense. Shoots left. 6'1", 176 lbs. Born, Prerov, Czech., August 17, 1985.
(Edmonton's 11th choice, 248th overall, in 2003 Entry Draft).

			Regular Season					Playoffs				
Season	Club	League	GP	G	A	Pts	PIM	GP	G	A	Pts	PIM
2001-02	HC Vsetin U17	CzR-U17	38	4	2	6	18	....	....	....	....	....
2002-03	HC Vsetin Jr.	CzRep-Jr.	30	6	7	13	12	9	2	4	6	10
	HC Vsetin	CzRep	6	0	0	0	4	....	....	....	....	....
2003-04	HC Vsetin	CzRep	13	0	0	0	2	....	....	....	....	....
	HC Vsetin Jr.	CzRep-Jr.	46	12	8	20	54	7	1	0	1	2
2004-05	HC Vsetin	CzRep	23	0	2	2	8	....	....	....	....	....
	HC Kometa Brno	CzRep-2	1	0	0	0	0	....	....	....	....	....
	HC Olomouc	CzRep-2	7	0	0	0	6	....	....	....	....	....
	HC Vsetin Jr.	CzRep-Jr.	19	6	8	14	42	8	3	4	7	16
2005-06	HC Vsetin	CzRep	34	3	9	12	34	....	....	....	....	....
	HC Vsetin Jr.	CzRep-Jr.	1	1	0	1	2	....	....	....	....	....
	HC Vsetin	CzRep-Q	....	....	....	....	....	6	0	2	2	2

HRDEL, Zbynek (HUHR-duhl, ZBIGH-nek) T.B.

Center. Shoots right. 6'4", 197 lbs. Born, Pisek, Czech., August 19, 1985.
(Tampa Bay's 10th choice, 286th overall, in 2003 Entry Draft).

			Regular Season					Playoffs				
Season	Club	League	GP	G	A	Pts	PIM	GP	G	A	Pts	PIM
2000-01	Sparta U17	CzR-U17	46	11	11	22	22	....	....	....	....	....
2001-02	Sparta U17	CzR-U17	31	24	19	43	42	6	4	3	7	2
2002-03	Rimouski Oceanic	QMJHL	65	10	14	24	131	....	....	....	....	....
2003-04	Rimouski Oceanic	QMJHL	54	15	31	46	41	9	4	6	10	4
2004-05	Rimouski Oceanic	QMJHL	56	23	35	58	47	13	8	7	15	10
2005-06	Springfield Falcons	AHL	46	5	10	15	22	....	....	....	....	....
	Johnstown Chiefs	ECHL	15	6	5	11	10	4	1	2	3	8

HROMAS, Karel (huh-ROM-mahs, KAH-rehl) CHI.

Left wing. Shoots left. 6'2", 205 lbs. Born, Beroun, Czech., January 27, 1986.
(Chicago's 8th choice, 123rd overall, in 2004 Entry Draft).

			Regular Season					Playoffs				
Season	Club	League	GP	G	A	Pts	PIM	GP	G	A	Pts	PIM
2000-01	Sparta U17	CzR-U17	34	4	18	22	6	....	....	....	....	....
2001-02	Sparta U17	CzR-U17	39	19	15	34	55	6	3	2	5	6
2002-03	Sparta U17	CzR-U17	1	3	1	4	0	....	....	....	....	....
	Sparta Jr.	CzRep-Jr.	32	6	7	13	14	3	0	1	1	4
2003-04	Sparta Jr.	CzRep-Jr.	21	10	10	20	16	....	....	....	....	....
	HC Sparta Praha	CzRep	13	0	0	0	0	2	0	0	0	0
2004-05	Everett Silvertips	WHL	65	18	11	29	22	11	2	2	4	4
2005-06	Everett Silvertips	WHL	52	11	11	22	14	14	2	0	2	10

HUGHES, Bobby (HEWZ, BAW-bee) CAR.

Center. Shoots left. 5'10", 170 lbs. Born, Richmond Hill, Ont., November 11, 1987.
(Carolina's 3rd choice, 123rd overall, in 2006 Entry Draft).

			Regular Season					Playoffs				
Season	Club	League	GP	G	A	Pts	PIM	GP	G	A	Pts	PIM
2004-05	Kingston	OHL	66	17	38	55	36	....	....	....	....	....
2005-06	Kingston	OHL	56	35	40	75	47	6	1	1	2	4

HULT, Alexander (HUHLT, al-EHX-AN-duhr) S.J.

Center. Shoots left. 6'1", 200 lbs. Born, Falun, Sweden, November 19, 1984.
(San Jose's 9th choice, 236th overall, in 2003 Entry Draft).

			Regular Season					Playoffs				
Season	Club	League	GP	G	A	Pts	PIM	GP	G	A	Pts	PIM
2000-01	HV 71 U18	Swe-U18	13	4	12	16	24	....	....	....	....	....
2001-02	HV 71 U18	Swe-U18	1	0	0	0	2	....	....	....	....	....
	HV 71 Jr.	Swe-Jr.	35	11	7	18	87	....	....	....	....	....
	HV 71 Jonkoping	Sweden	....	....	....	....	....	1	0	0	0	0
2002-03	HV 71 Jr.	Swe-Jr.	24	11	14	25	24	....	....	....	....	....
	HV 71 Jonkoping	Sweden	1	0	0	0	2	....	....	....	....	....
	Tranas AIF	Sweden-2	5	1	0	1	0	....	....	....	....	....
2003-04	IK Oskarshamn	Sweden-2	29	2	7	9	22	....	....	....	....	....
	HV 71 Jonkoping	Sweden	3	0	0	0	2	....	....	....	....	....
	Djurgarden Jr.	Swe-Jr.	11	6	10	16	16	....	....	....	....	....
	Djurgarden	Sweden	8	0	0	0	0	3	0	0	0	0
2004-05	Almtuna	Sweden-2	30	3	3	6	16	....	....	....	....	....
	IK Comet Halden	Norway	18	2	7	9	56	....	....	....	....	....
	IK Comet Halden	Norway-Q	5	2	3	5	2	....	....	....	....	....
2005-06	Mora IK Jr.	Swe-Jr.	4	3	2	5	27	....	....	....	....	....
	HK Dmitrov	Russia-2	24	4	6	10	16	4	0	0	0	2

HUNT, Jamie (HUHNT, JAY-mee) WSH.

Defense. Shoots left. 6'2", 195 lbs. Born, Calgary, Alta., April 20, 1984.

			Regular Season					Playoffs				
Season	Club	League	GP	G	A	Pts	PIM	GP	G	A	Pts	PIM
2002-03	Calgary Canucks	AJHL	63	8	20	28	35	....	....	....	....	....
2003-04	Mercyhurst	AH	27	3	16	19	4	....	....	....	....	....
2004-05	Mercyhurst	AH	38	5	12	17	36	....	....	....	....	....
2005-06	Mercyhurst	AH	33	12	33	45	49	....	....	....	....	....

Signed as a free agent by **Washington**, March 31, 2006.

HUNTER, Dylan (HUHN-tuhr, DIH-luhn) BUF.

Left wing. Shoots left. 5'11", 198 lbs. Born, Quebec City, Que., May 21, 1985.
(Buffalo's 8th choice, 273rd overall, in 2004 Entry Draft).

			Regular Season					Playoffs				
Season	Club	League	GP	G	A	Pts	PIM	GP	G	A	Pts	PIM
2001-02	London Knights	OHL	54	6	21	27	38	6	1	1	2	10
2002-03	London Knights	OHL	68	11	31	42	41	14	3	3	6	8
2003-04	London Knights	OHL	64	26	53	79	47	15	4	10	14	10
2004-05	London Knights	OHL	67	31	73	104	64	18	10	11	21	16
2005-06	London Knights	OHL	62	32	85	117	50	19	13	23	36	16

OHL First All-Star Team (2005) • OHL Second All-Star Team (2006)

HUNTER, Eric (HUHN-tuhr, AIR-ihk) NYR

Center. Shoots left. 6'1", 188 lbs. Born, Winnipeg, Man., August 11, 1986.
(NY Rangers' 6th choice, 174th overall, in 2006 Entry Draft).

			Regular Season					Playoffs				
Season	Club	League	GP	G	A	Pts	PIM	GP	G	A	Pts	PIM
2002-03	Prince George	WHL	66	16	18	34	70	5	1	0	1	6
2003-04	Prince George	WHL	70	19	23	42	122	....	....	....	....	....
2004-05	Prince George	WHL	47	12	18	30	57	....	....	....	....	....
2005-06	Prince George	WHL	71	40	32	72	125	5	3	1	4	10

• Re-entered NHL Entry Draft. Originally Chicago's 15th choice, 229th overall, in 2004 Entry Draft.

HUNTER, J.J. (HUHN-tuhr, JAY-JAY)

Right wing. Shoots left. 6'1", 185 lbs. Born, Shaunavon, Sask., July 6, 1980.

			Regular Season					Playoffs				
Season	Club	League	GP	G	A	Pts	PIM	GP	G	A	Pts	PIM
1998-99	Kelowna Rockets	WHL	66	18	32	50	61	6	1	2	3	2
99-2000	Kelowna Rockets	WHL	66	22	26	48	61	5	1	0	1	2
2000-01	Kelowna Rockets	WHL	12	1	5	6	4	....	....	....	....	....
	Prince Albert	WHL	58	28	17	45	40	....	....	....	....	....
2001-02	Hamilton Bulldogs	AHL	1	0	0	0	0	1	0	0	0	0
	Columbus	ECHL	60	23	22	45	59	....	....	....	....	....
2002-03	Hamilton Bulldogs	AHL	2	0	0	0	2	....	....	....	....	....
	Columbus	ECHL	70	17	36	53	82	....	....	....	....	....
2003-04	Columbus	ECHL	4	2	1	3	2	....	....	....	....	....
	Toronto	AHL	56	12	16	28	53	3	1	1	2	2
2004-05	Edmonton	AHL	64	13	11	24	51	....	....	....	....	....
2005-06	Hamilton Bulldogs	AHL	34	4	7	11	55	....	....	....	....	....

Signed as a free agent by **Edmonton**, August 19, 2002.

HUNWICK, Matt (HUHN-wihk, MAT) BOS.

Defense. Shoots left. 5'11", 187 lbs. Born, Warren, MI, May 21, 1985.
(Boston's 6th choice, 224th overall, in 2004 Entry Draft).

			Regular Season					Playoffs				
Season	Club	League	GP	G	A	Pts	PIM	GP	G	A	Pts	PIM
2001-02	USNTDP	U-17	14	3	4	7	6	....	....	....	....	....
	USNTDP	NAHL	29	2	1	3	30	....	....	....	....	....
2002-03	USNTDP	U-18	40	6	16	22	40	....	....	....	....	....
	USNTDP	NAHL	8	2	2	4	23	....	....	....	....	....
2003-04	U. of Michigan	CCHA	41	1	14	15	62	....	....	....	....	....
2004-05	U. of Michigan	CCHA	40	6	19	25	60	....	....	....	....	....
2005-06	U. of Michigan	CCHA	41	11	19	30	70	....	....	....	....	....

CCHA All-Rookie Team (2004) • CCHA Second All-Star Team (2005, 2006)

HUSKINS, Kent (HUHS-kihns, KEHNT) ANA.

Defense. Shoots left. 6'3", 215 lbs. Born, Ottawa, Ont., May 4, 1979.
(Chicago's 3rd choice, 156th overall, in 1998 Entry Draft).

			Regular Season					Playoffs				
Season	Club	League	GP	G	A	Pts	PIM	GP	G	A	Pts	PIM
1995-96	Kanata Valley	CJHL	49	6	21	27	18	....	....	....	....	....
1996-97	Kanata Valley	CJHL	53	11	36	47	89	....	....	....	....	....
1997-98	Clarkson Knights	ECAC	35	2	8	10	46	....	....	....	....	....
1998-99	Clarkson Knights	ECAC	37	5	11	16	28	....	....	....	....	....
99-2000	Clarkson Knights	ECAC	28	2	16	18	30	....	....	....	....	....
2000-01	Clarkson Knights	ECAC	35	6	28	34	22	....	....	....	....	....
2001-02	Norfolk Admirals	AHL	65	4	11	15	44	4	0	1	1	0
2002-03	Norfolk Admirals	AHL	80	5	22	27	48	9	2	2	4	4
2003-04	San Antonio	AHL	79	5	14	19	42	....	....	....	....	....
2004-05	Manitoba Moose	AHL	65	5	11	16	41	14	0	2	2	12
2005-06	Portland Pirates	AHL	80	8	23	31	64	18	3	6	9	14

ECAC First All-Star Team (2000, 2001) • NCAA East First All-American Team (2001)

Signed as a free agent by **Florida**, August 14, 2003. Signed as a free agent by **Manitoba** (AHL), September 16, 2004. Signed as a free agent by **Anaheim**, August 30, 2005.

HYNES, Shane (HIGHNZ, SHAYN) ANA.

Right wing. Shoots right. 6'3", 224 lbs. Born, Montreal, Que., November 7, 1983.
(Anaheim's 3rd choice, 86th overall, in 2003 Entry Draft).

			Regular Season					Playoffs				
Season	Club	League	GP	G	A	Pts	PIM	GP	G	A	Pts	PIM
99-2000	Cgy. AAA Flames	AMHL	30	8	12	20	20	....	....	....	....	....
2000-01	Cgy. AAA Flames	AMHL	28	18	21	38	76	....	....	....	....	....
2001-02	Nanaimo Clippers	BCHL	50	38	36	74	183	....	....	....	....	....
2002-03	Cornell Big Red	ECAC	32	11	9	20	36	....	....	....	....	....
2003-04	Cornell Big Red	ECAC	30	9	9	18	54	....	....	....	....	....
2004-05	Cornell Big Red	ECACHL	33	7	21	28	40	....	....	....	....	....
2005-06	• Portland Pirates	AHL	12	1	3	4	32	....	....	....	....	....

BCHL All-Rookie Team (2002)

• Missed majority of 2005-06 season recovering from a knee injury.

IGGULDEN, Mike (IHG-gul-den, MIGHK) S.J.

Right wing. Shoots right. 6'3", 215 lbs. Born, St. Catherines, Ont., November 9, 1982.

			Regular Season					Playoffs				
Season	Club	League	GP	G	A	Pts	PIM	GP	G	A	Pts	PIM
2001-02	Cornell Big Red	ECAC	30	1	3	4	6	....	....	....	....	....
2002-03	Cornell Big Red	ECAC	15	0	2	2	19	....	....	....	....	....
2003-04	Cornell Big Red	ECAC	30	2	8	10	10	....	....	....	....	....
2004-05	Cornell Big Red	ECACHL	35	10	8	18	8	....	....	....	....	....
	Rochester	AHL	6	1	0	1	7	....	....	....	....	....
2005-06	Cleveland Barons	AHL	77	22	26	48	57	....	....	....	....	....

Signed to an ATO (tryout) contract by **Rochester** (AHL), April 5, 2004. Signed to a PTO (tryout) contract by **Cleveland** (AHL), September 19, 2005. Signed as a free agent by **San Jose**, January 16, 2006.

IGNATUSHKIN, Igor (ihg-nah-TOOSH-kihn, EE-gohr) WSH.

Center. Shoots left. 5'11", 175 lbs. Born, Elektrostal, USSR, April 7, 1984.
(Washington's 12th choice, 242nd overall, in 2002 Entry Draft).

			Regular Season					Playoffs				
Season	Club	League	GP	G	A	Pts	PIM	GP	G	A	Pts	PIM
99-2000	Elektrostal 2	Russia-3	5	0	0	0	0	....	....	....	....	....
2000-01	Team Center 84	Exhib.	5	1	1	2	0	....	....	....	....	....
	Elektrostal 2	Russia-3	STATISTICS NOT AVAILABLE									
2001-02	Elektrostal 2	Russia-3	6	2	3	5	6	....	....	....	....	....
	Elektrostal	Russia-2	46	1	4	5	20	....	....	....	....	....
2002-03	Elektrostal	Russia-2	36	9	10	19	8	....	....	....	....	....
2003-04	Kristall Elektrostal	Russia-2	49	6	2	8	22	....	....	....	....	....
2004-05	Kristall Elektrostal	Russia-2	45	9	3	12	28	....	....	....	....	....
	Leninogorsk	Russia-2	6	1	1	2	6	4	1	0	1	4
2005-06	Mytischi	Russia	7	0	0	0	2	....	....	....	....	....
	Kristall Elektrostal	Russia-3	STATISTICS NOT AVAILABLE									

IHNACAK, Brian (ih-NAH-chehk, BRIGH-uhn) PIT.

Center. Shoots right. 5'11", 178 lbs. Born, Toronto, Ont., April 10, 1985.
(Pittsburgh's 12th choice, 259th overall, in 2004 Entry Draft).

			Regular Season					Playoffs				
Season	Club	League	GP	G	A	Pts	PIM	GP	G	A	Pts	PIM
2001-02	St. Mike's B's	OPJHL	48	6	13	19	22	....	....	....	....	....
2002-03	St. Mike's B's	OPJHL	46	40	46	86	66	10	8	7	15	8
2003-04	Brown U.	ECAC	31	10	20	30	20	....	....	....	....	....
2004-05	Brown U.	ECACHL	30	12	11	23	30	....	....	....	....	....
2005-06	Brown U.	ECACHL	15	3	6	9	31	....	....	....	....	....

ECAC All-Rookie Team (2004) • ECAC Rookie of the Year (2004) (co-winner - David McKee)

IRMEN, Danny (UHR-mehn, DA-nee) MIN.

Center. Shoots right. 6', 190 lbs. Born, Fargo, ND, September 6, 1984.
(Minnesota's 3rd choice, 78th overall, in 2003 Entry Draft).

			Regular Season					Playoffs				
Season	Club	League	GP	G	A	Pts	PIM	GP	G	A	Pts	PIM
2001-02	Lincoln Stars	USHL	61	17	36	53	....	....	....	....	....	....
2002-03	Lincoln Stars	USHL	45	21	34	55	78	10	8	6	14	17
2003-04	U. of Minnesota	WCHA	44	14	8	22	40	....	....	....	....	....
2004-05	U. of Minnesota	WCHA	44	24	19	43	66	....	....	....	....	....
2005-06	U. of Minnesota	WCHA	30	16	22	38	40	....	....	....	....	....
	Houston Aeros	AHL	4	0	2	2	0	7	0	0	0	4

USHL Second All-Star Team (2003) • USHL Playoff MVP (2003)

ISAKOV, Evgeni (ih-SA-kawf, ehv-GEH-nee) PIT.

Right wing. Shoots left. 6'1", 196 lbs. Born, Krasnoyarsk, USSR, October 13, 1984.
(Pittsburgh's 6th choice, 161st overall, in 2003 Entry Draft).

			Regular Season					Playoffs				
Season	Club	League	GP	G	A	Pts	PIM	GP	G	A	Pts	PIM
99-2000	Rubin Tyumen 2	Russia-3	7	0	2	2	16	....	....	....	....	....
2000-01	Rubin Tyumen 2	Russia-3	....	....	....	....	....	....	....	....	....	....
	Gazovik Tyumen	Russia-3	11	1	1	2	12	....	....	....	....	....
2001-02	Gazovik Tyumen	Russia-2	19	2	2	4	2	....	....	....	....	....
	Elektrostal	Russia-2	29	3	2	5	24	....	....	....	....	....
	Elektrostal 2	Russia-3	11	3	3	6	43	....	....	....	....	....
2002-03	Cherepovets	Russia	36	0	3	3	12	1	0	0	0	0
2003-04	Cherepovets	Russia	38	3	2	5	18	....	....	....	....	....
	Cherepovets 2	Russia-3	14	4	8	12	48	....	....	....	....	....
2004-05	Kristall Saratov	Russia-2	1	0	0	0	0	....	....	....	....	....
	Tyumen 2	Russia-3	2	1	3	4	14	....	....	....	....	....
	Gazovik Tyumen	Russia-2	4	0	2	2	2	3	0	0	0	2
2005-06	Gazovik Tyumen	Russia-2	46	9	12	21	90	3	0	0	0	6

ISTOMIN, Denis (ihst-OH-mihn, DEH-nihs) CHI.

Right wing. Shoots left. 6', 196 lbs. Born, Chelyabinsk, USSR, January 12, 1987.
(Chicago's 7th choice, 117th overall, in 2005 Entry Draft).

			Regular Season					Playoffs				
Season	Club	League	GP	G	A	Pts	PIM	GP	G	A	Pts	PIM
2003-04	Magnitogorsk 2	Russia-3	3	2	1	3	2	....	....	....	....	....
2004-05	Chelyabinsk 2	Russia-3	1	0	0	0	0	....	....	....	....	....
	Chelyabinsk	Russia-2	42	11	5	16	24	8	1	1	2	4
2005-06	Vityaz Chekhov	Russia	46	4	4	8	6	....	....	....	....	....
	Nizhny Novgorod	Russia-2	4	0	3	3	2	3	2	1	3	0

JACKSON, Scott (JAK-suhn, SKAWT) ST.L.

Defense. Shoots left. 6'3", 200 lbs. Born, Salmon Arm, B.C., February 5, 1987.
(St. Louis' 2nd choice, 37th overall, in 2005 Entry Draft).

			Regular Season					Playoffs				
Season	Club	League	GP	G	A	Pts	PIM	GP	G	A	Pts	PIM
2002-03	Sicamous Eagles	KIJHL	45	2	20	22	20	....	....	....	....	....
	Seattle	WHL	2	0	0	0	2	....	....	....	....	....
2003-04	Seattle	WHL	66	4	9	13	17	....	....	....	....	....
2004-05	Seattle	WHL	72	6	16	22	46	12	1	2	3	4
2005-06	Seattle	WHL	57	3	23	26	48	7	1	4	5	12

JARMAN, Kevin (JAR-muhn, KEH-vihn) CBJ

Left wing. Shoots left. 6', 184 lbs. Born, Toronto, Ont., March 12, 1985.
(Columbus' 4th choice, 103rd overall, in 2003 Entry Draft).

			Regular Season					Playoffs				
Season	Club	League	GP	G	A	Pts	PIM	GP	G	A	Pts	PIM
2001-02	Stouffville Spirit	OPJHL	44	20	13	33	53	....	....	....	....	....
2002-03	Stouffville Spirit	OPJHL	46	41	39	80	49	11	5	3	8	6
2003-04	Massachusetts	H-East	34	4	6	10	28	....	....	....	....	....
2004-05	Massachusetts	H-East	37	7	14	21	52	....	....	....	....	....
2005-06	Massachusetts	H-East	29	1	6	7	40	....	....	....	....	....

JENSEN, Christian (JEHN-suhn, KRIHS-tyehn) S.J.

Defense. Shoots right. 6'3", 190 lbs. Born, Brooklyn, NY, January 6, 1986.
(San Jose's 10th choice, 289th overall, in 2004 Entry Draft).

			Regular Season					Playoffs				
Season	Club	League	GP	G	A	Pts	PIM	GP	G	A	Pts	PIM
2003-04	New Jersey Jrs.	AtJHL	48	6	23	29	62	....	....	....	....	....
2004-05	Jersey Hitmen	EJHL	48	1	9	10	22	....	....	....	....	....
2005-06	Chicago Steel	USHL	24	0	4	4	8	....	....	....	....	....
	Waterloo	USHL	18	1	4	5	14	....	....	....	....	....

• Signed Letter of Intent to attend **RPI** (ECACHL) in fall of 2006.

JENSEN, Joe (JEHN-suhn, JOH) PIT.

Center. Shoots left. 5'11", 180 lbs. Born, Maple Grove, MN, February 6, 1983.
(Pittsburgh's 10th choice, 232nd overall, in 2003 Entry Draft).

			Regular Season					Playoffs				
Season	Club	League	GP	G	A	Pts	PIM	GP	G	A	Pts	PIM
2000-01	Sioux City	USHL	56	14	20	34	59	8	2	4	6	12
2001-02	Sioux City	USHL	57	20	26	46	135	3	0	0	0	6
2002-03	St. Cloud State	WCHA	37	9	9	18	14	....	....	....	....	....
2003-04	St. Cloud State	WCHA	38	10	14	24	42	....	....	....	....	....
2004-05	St. Cloud State	WCHA	40	12	14	26	36	....	....	....	....	....
2005-06	St. Cloud State	WCHA	38	14	18	32	14	....	....	....	....	....

JESSIMAN, Hugh (JEHS-ih-muhn, HEW) NYR

Right wing. Shoots right. 6'6", 224 lbs. Born, New York, NY, March 28, 1984.
(NY Rangers' 1st choice, 12th overall, in 2003 Entry Draft).

			Regular Season					Playoffs				
Season	Club	League	GP	G	A	Pts	PIM	GP	G	A	Pts	PIM
2001-02	Brunswick Bruins	High-CT	18	25	27	52	40	....	....	....	....	....
2002-03	Dartmouth	ECAC	34	23	24	47	48	....	....	....	....	....
2003-04	Dartmouth	ECAC	34	16	17	33	71	....	....	....	....	....
2004-05	Dartmouth	ECACHL	12	1	1	2	18	....	....	....	....	....
2005-06	Hartford Wolf Pack	AHL	46	7	11	18	66	2	0	0	0	0
	Charlotte	ECHL	25	13	10	23	56	....	....	....	....	....

ECAC All-Rookie Team (2003) • ECAC Rookie of the Year (2003) • ECAC Second All-Star Team (2004)

JOENSUU, Jesse (YOH-ehn-soo, YEH-see) NYI

Wing. Shoots left. 6'4", 207 lbs. Born, Pori, Finland, October 5, 1987.
(NY Islanders' 2nd choice, 60th overall, in 2006 Entry Draft).

			Regular Season					Playoffs				
Season	Club	League	GP	G	A	Pts	PIM	GP	G	A	Pts	PIM
2002-03	Assat Pori U18	Fin-U18	26	8	10	18	53	3	1	2	3	0
	Assat Pori Jr.	Fin-Jr.	3	0	1	1	2	....	....	....	....	....
2003-04	Assat Pori U18	Fin-U18	6	7	2	9	8	....	....	....	....	....
	Assat Pori Jr.	Fin-Jr.	28	7	9	16	18	3	0	1	1	2
	Assat Pori	Finland	6	0	0	0	0	....	....	....	....	....
2004-05	Assat Pori	Finland	39	1	1	2	4	....	....	....	....	....
	Assat Pori Jr.	Fin-Jr.	17	7	13	20	20	2	1	1	2	2
	Assat Pori	Finland	39	1	1	2	4	....	....	....	....	....
2005-06	Assat Pori	Finland	51	4	8	12	57	14	0	2	2	12
	Suomi U20	Finland-2	2	1	0	1	12	....	....	....	....	....

JOHANSSON, Fredrik (yoh-HAHN-suhn, FREHD-rihk) EDM.

Center. Shoots left. 5'11", 183 lbs. Born, Goteburg, Sweden, February 27, 1984.
(Edmonton's 14th choice, 274th overall, in 2002 Entry Draft).

			Regular Season					Playoffs				
Season	Club	League	GP	G	A	Pts	PIM	GP	G	A	Pts	PIM
2000-01	V.Frolunda Jr.	Swe-Jr.	22	3	4	7	8	3	0	1	1	4
	V.Frolunda U18	Swe-U18	6	5	1	6	4	....	....	....	....	....
2001-02	V.Frolunda Jr.	Swe-Jr.	42	13	23	36	39	....	....	....	....	....
	V.Frolunda U18	Swe-U18	1	0	1	1	0	....	....	....	....	....
2002-03	V.Frolunda Jr.	Swe-Jr.	30	13	34	47	24	3	0	2	2	2
	V.Frolunda	Sweden	9	0	0	0	2	5	0	0	0	0
2003-04	V.Frolunda Jr.	Swe-Jr.	7	1	2	3	4	4	2	4	6	0
	Halmstad	Sweden-2	1	0	0	0	0	....	....	....	....	....
	V.Frolunda	Sweden	48	1	3	4	6	10	0	0	0	0
2004-05	Vasteras	Sweden-2	46	15	15	30	32	5	0	3	3	8
2005-06	VIK Vasteras HK	Sweden-2	41	7	15	22	26	....	....	....	....	....

JOHANSSON, Kim (yoh-HAHN-suhn, KIHM) NYI

Wing. Shoots left. 6'1", 172 lbs. Born, Malmo, Sweden, January 21, 1988.
(NY Islanders' 9th choice, 141st overall, in 2006 Entry Draft).

			Regular Season					Playoffs				
Season	Club	League	GP	G	A	Pts	PIM	GP	G	A	Pts	PIM
2003-04	Malmo U18	Swe-U18	3	0	0	0	2	....	....	....	....	....
2004-05	Malmo U18	Swe-U18	14	4	1	5	14	2	1	1	2	4
	Malmo Jr.	Swe-Jr.	4	0	0	0	2	....	....	....	....	....
2005-06	Malmo U18	Swe-U18	6	1	2	3	27	6	1	0	1	16
	Malmo Jr.	Swe-Jr.	39	5	10	15	28	....	....	....	....	....

JOHANSSON, Mikael (yoh-HAHN-suhn), MIGH-kuhl) DET.

Center. Shoots left. 5'10", 176 lbs. Born, Arvika, Sweden, June 27, 1985.
(Detroit's 8th choice, 289th overall, in 2003 Entry Draft).

			Regular Season					Playoffs				
Season	Club	League	GP	G	A	Pts	PIM	GP	G	A	Pts	PIM
2001-02	Truro Bearcats	MJrHL	31	1	13	14	34	6	0	0	0	6
2002-03	Arvika HC	Sweden-3	30	13	28	41	89	....	....	....	....	....
2003-04	Skare BK Karlstad	Sweden-3	10	1	5	6	6	....	....	....	....	....
2004-05	Bofors	Sweden-2	45	5	7	12	22	5	0	0	0	0
2005-06	Farjestad	Sweden	46	1	5	6	16	18	0	2	2	4

JOHNER, Dustin (JAW-nuhr, DUHS-tihn) FLA.

Center. Shoots right. 5'11", 181 lbs. Born, Estevan, Sask., March 6, 1983.
(Florida's 8th choice, 169th overall, in 2001 Entry Draft).

			Regular Season					Playoffs				
Season	Club	League	GP	G	A	Pts	PIM	GP	G	A	Pts	PIM
1998-99	Red Deer Rebels	AMBHL	36	35	29	64	42	....	....	....	....	....
99-2000	Red Deer Chiefs	AMHL	36	24	31	55	80	....	....	....	....	....
	Seattle	WHL	6	0	1	1	0	....	....	....	....	....
2000-01	Seattle	WHL	72	25	31	56	45	9	1	5	6	6
2001-02	Seattle	WHL	71	33	48	81	71	8	4	3	7	8
2002-03	Seattle	WHL	71	36	41	77	97	15	7	6	13	14
2003-04	Seattle	WHL	71	26	31	57	54	....	....	....	....	....
	South Carolina	ECHL	4	2	4	6	0	7	4	3	7	4
2004-05	Lowell	AHL	23	4	8	12	12	11	1	0	1	4
	Las Vegas	ECHL	51	22	26	48	42	....	....	....	....	....
2005-06	Omaha	AHL	5	0	0	0	2	....	....	....	....	....
	Las Vegas	ECHL	9	2	2	4	8	....	....	....	....	....
	Rochester	AHL	16	1	1	2	8	....	....	....	....	....
	Florida Everblades	ECHL	36	15	21	36	24	8	5	4	9	4

Signed as a free agent by **Calgary**, July 6, 2004. Traded to **Florida** by **Calgary** with Steve Montador for Kristian Huselius, December 2, 2005.

JOHNSON, Erik (JAWN-suhn, AIR-ihk) ST.L.

Defense. Shoots right. 6'4", 222 lbs. Born, Bloomington, MN, March 21, 1988.
(St. Louis' 1st choice, 1st overall, in 2006 Entry Draft).

			Regular Season					Playoffs				
Season	Club	League	GP	G	A	Pts	PIM	GP	G	A	Pts	PIM
2003-04	Holy Angels	High-MN	31	13	21	34	....	....	....	....	....	....
2004-05	USNTDP	U-17	26	5	9	14	14	....	....	....	....	....
	USNTDP	NAHL	31	6	6	12	12	....	....	....	....	....
2005-06	USNTDP	U-18	36	12	22	34	78	....	....	....	....	....
	USNTDP	NAHL	11	4	11	15	10	....	....	....	....	....

Signed Letter of Intent to attend **U. of Minnesota** (WCHA) in fall of 2006.

JOHNSON, Jack (JAWN-suhn, JAK) CAR.

Defense. Shoots left. 6'1", 201 lbs. Born, Indianapolis, IN, January 13, 1987.
(Carolina's 1st choice, 3rd overall, in 2005 Entry Draft).

			Regular Season					Playoffs				
Season	Club	League	GP	G	A	Pts	PIM	GP	G	A	Pts	PIM
2002-03	Shat.-St. Mary's	High-MN	48	15	27	42	....	....	....	....	....	....
2003-04	USNTDP	U-17	31	12	9	21	78	....	....	....	....	....
	USNTDP	NAHL	29	3	12	15	93	....	....	....	....	....
2004-05	USNTDP	U-18	26	5	9	14	86	....	....	....	....	....
	USNTDP	NAHL	12	7	10	17	57	....	....	....	....	....
2005-06	U. of Michigan	CCHA	38	10	22	32	149	....	....	....	....	....

CCHA All-Rookie Team (2006)

JOHNSON, Nick (JAWN-suhn, NIHK) PIT.

Right wing. Shoots right. 6'1", 183 lbs. Born, Calgary, Alta., December 24, 1985.
(Pittsburgh's 4th choice, 67th overall, in 2004 Entry Draft).

			Regular Season					Playoffs				
Season	Club	League	GP	G	A	Pts	PIM	GP	G	A	Pts	PIM
2002-03	St. Albert Saints	AJHL	60	21	30	51	10	....	....	....	....	....
2003-04	St. Albert Saints	AJHL	51	35	36	71	33	4	0	2	2	0
2004-05	Dartmouth	ECACHL	35	18	17	35	16	....	....	....	....	....
2005-06	Dartmouth	ECACHL	33	15	10	25	24	....	....	....	....	....

ECACHL All-Rookie Team 2005)

JONES, Blair (JOHNZ, BLAYR) T.B.

Center. Shoots right. 6'3", 210 lbs. Born, Central Butte, Sask., September 27, 1986.
(Tampa Bay's 5th choice, 102nd overall, in 2005 Entry Draft).

			Regular Season					Playoffs				
Season	Club	League	GP	G	A	Pts	PIM	GP	G	A	Pts	PIM
2002-03	Bethune	SBHL		STATISTICS NOT AVAILABLE								
	Red Deer Rebels	WHL	37	3	4	7	17	10	1	0	1	0
2003-04	Red Deer Rebels	WHL	72	9	22	31	55	19	1	5	6	24
2004-05	Red Deer Rebels	WHL	39	7	18	25	48	....	....	....	....	....
	Moose Jaw	WHL	29	7	18	25	30	5	2	5	7	8
2005-06	Moose Jaw	WHL	72	35	50	85	85	22	9	12	21	45

WHL East Second All-Star Team (2006)

JONES, David (JOHNZ, DAY-vihd) COL.

Right wing. Shoots right. 6'2", 220 lbs. Born, Guelph, Ont., August 10, 1984.
(Colorado's 8th choice, 288th overall, in 2003 Entry Draft).

			Regular Season					Playoffs				
Season	Club	League	GP	G	A	Pts	PIM	GP	G	A	Pts	PIM
2000-01	PoCo Bucs	PIJHL	40	18	11	29	33	....	....	....	....	....
2001-02	Coquitlam Express	BCHL	59	19	32	51	62	....	....	....	....	....
2002-03	Coquitlam Express	BCHL	35	9	19	28	55	7	2	6	8	8
2003-04	Coquitlam Express	BCHL	53	33	60	93	78	7	3	6	9	4
2004-05	Dartmouth	ECACHL	34	9	5	14	26	....	....	....	....	....
2005-06	Dartmouth	ECACHL	33	17	17	34	38	....	....	....	....	....

ECACHL Second All-Star Team (2006)

JONES, Ryan (JOHNZ, RIGH-uhn) MIN.

Right wing. Shoots right. 6'1", 200 lbs. Born, Chatham, Ont., June 14, 1984.
(Minnesota's 5th choice, 111th overall, in 2004 Entry Draft).

			Regular Season					Playoffs				
Season	Club	League	GP	G	A	Pts	PIM	GP	G	A	Pts	PIM
2002-03	Chatham Maroons	OHA-B	38	12	11	23	42	....	....	....	....	....
2003-04	Chatham Maroons	OHA-B	46	39	30	69	64	17	17	9	26	25
2004-05	Miami U.	CCHA	38	8	7	15	79	....	....	....	....	....
2005-06	Miami U.	CCHA	39	22	13	35	72	....	....	....	....	....

CCHA Second All-Star Team (2006)

JONSSON, Lars (YAWN-suhn, LARZ) PHI.

Defense. Shoots left. 6'1", 205 lbs. Born, Borlange, Sweden, January 2, 1982.
(Boston's 1st choice, 7th overall, in 2000 Entry Draft).

			Regular Season					Playoffs				
Season	Club	League	GP	G	A	Pts	PIM	GP	G	A	Pts	PIM
1998-99	Leksands IF Jr.	Swe-Jr.	40	4	8	12	42	....	....	....	....	....
99-2000	Leksands IF Jr.	Swe-Jr.	34	16	22	38	50	2	0	0	0	0
	Leksands IF	Sweden	5	0	0	0	4	....	....	....	....	....
2000-01	Leksands IF Jr.	Swe-Jr.	7	1	3	4	6	....	....	....	....	....
	Leksands IF	Sweden	31	2	1	3	12	....	....	....	....	....
2001-02	Leksands IF Jr.	Swe-Jr.	3	2	1	3	4	1	0	0	0	0
	Leksands IF	Sweden-2	28	1	7	8	59	....	....	....	....	....
2002-03	Leksands IF	Sweden	21	0	0	0	12	5	0	0	0	2
	IF Bjorkloven Umea	Sweden-2	9	3	4	7	10	....	....	....	....	....
	IFK Arboga IK	Sweden-2	4	0	0	0	4	....	....	....	....	....
2003-04	Leksands IF	Sweden	50	3	9	12	30	....	....	....	....	....
	Leksands IF	Sweden-Q	4	1	0	1	2	....	....	....	....	....
2004-05	Timra IK	Sweden	50	5	6	11	32	7	0	0	0	2
2005-06	HV 71 Jonkoping	Sweden	50	11	16	27	46	11	2	3	5	14

Signed as a free agent by **Philadephia**, July 1, 2006.

JONSSON, Per (JAWN-suhn, PAIR) CGY.

Forward. Shoots left. 6', 172 lbs. Born, Karlstad, Sweden, April 20, 1988.
(Calgary's 8th choice, 209th overall, in 2006 Entry Draft).

			Regular Season					Playoffs				
Season	Club	League	GP	G	A	Pts	PIM	GP	G	A	Pts	PIM
2004-05	Farjestad U18	Swe-U18	12	2	2	4	10	2	0	0	0	2
2005-06	Farjestad U18	Swe-U18	14	3	1	4	38	8	1	1	2	22

JOSEPH, Shane (JOH-sehf, SHAYN)

Center. Shoots right. 5'9", 170 lbs. Born, Brooks, Alta., July 23, 1981.

			Regular Season					Playoffs				
Season	Club	League	GP	G	A	Pts	PIM	GP	G	A	Pts	PIM
1997-98	Medicine Hat	AMHL	35	23	34	57	20	....	....	....	....	....
1998-99	Bow Valley Eagles	AJHL	60	36	34	70	14	....	....	....	....	....
99-2000	Minnesota State	WCHA	5	0	0	0	0	....	....	....	....	....
2000-01	Minnesota State	WCHA	16	0	5	5	2	....	....	....	....	....
2001-02	Minnesota State	WCHA	38	20	11	31	0	....	....	....	....	....
2002-03	Minnesota State	WCHA	41	29	36	65	6	....	....	....	....	....
2003-04	Minnesota State	WCHA	39	19	24	43	2	....	....	....	....	....
	Cleveland Barons	AHL	12	4	5	9	0	9	5	4	9	0
2004-05	Cleveland Barons	AHL	67	10	22	32	8	....	....	....	....	....
2005-06	Cleveland Barons	AHL	75	11	20	31	18	....	....	....	....	....

WCHA First All-Star Team (2003) • NCAA West Second All-American Team (2003)

• Missed majority of 1999-2000 season recovering from knee injury suffered in game vs. St. Clouid State (WCHA), November 11, 1999. Signed to a PTO (tryout) contract by **Cleveland** (AHL), March 17, 2004. Signed as a free agent by **San Jose**, June 27, 2004. Signed as a free agent by **Augsburger** (Germany), August 14, 2006.

JOSLIN, Derek (JAWS-lihn, DEH-rihk) S.J.

Defense. Shoots left. 6'1", 191 lbs. Born, Richmond Hill, Ont., March 17, 1987.
(San Jose's 5th choice, 149th overall, in 2005 Entry Draft).

			Regular Season					Playoffs				
Season	Club	League	GP	G	A	Pts	PIM	GP	G	A	Pts	PIM
2002-03	Vaughan	GTHL	60	9	18	27	72	....	....	....	....	....
2003-04	Aurora Tigers	OPJHL	36	4	12	16	....	....	....	....	....	....
	Ottawa 67's	OHL	7	0	0	0	4	....	....	....	....	....
2004-05	Ottawa 67's	OHL	68	6	24	30	44	21	0	3	3	24
2005-06	Ottawa 67's	OHL	68	11	37	48	40	6	1	5	6	10
	Cleveland Barons	AHL	2	0	0	0	0	....	....	....	....	....

JOUDREY, Andrew (JOO-dree, AN-droo) WSH.

Center. Shoots left. 5'11", 191 lbs. Born, Halifax, N.S., July 15, 1984.
(Washington's 5th choice, 249th overall, in 2003 Entry Draft).

			Regular Season					Playoffs				
Season	Club	League	GP	G	A	Pts	PIM	GP	G	A	Pts	PIM
2000-01	Dartmouth	NSMHL	82	51	70	121	....	....	....	....	....	....
2001-02	Notre Dame	SJHL	57	24	38	62	14	....	....	....	....	....
2002-03	Notre Dame	SJHL	53	27	51	78	16	....	....	....	....	....
2003-04	U. of Wisconsin	WCHA	42	7	15	22	2	....	....	....	....	....
2004-05	U. of Wisconsin	WCHA	41	7	17	24	18	....	....	....	....	....
2005-06	U. of Wisconsin	WCHA	37	8	10	18	14	....	....	....	....	....

JOUKOV, Mishail (ZHOO-kawv, mee-shigh-EHL) EDM.

Left wing. Shoots left. 6'3", 187 lbs. Born, Leningrad, USSR, January 3, 1985.
(Edmonton's 4th choice, 72nd overall, in 2003 Entry Draft).

			Regular Season					Playoffs				
Season	Club	League	GP	G	A	Pts	PIM	GP	G	A	Pts	PIM
2000-01	Mora IK Jr.	Swe-Jr.	28	9	14	23	6	9	2	4	6	0
2001-02	IFK Arboga IK	Sweden-2	37	4	9	13	12	3	1	0	1	2
2002-03	IFK Arboga IK	Sweden-2	41	9	14	23	30	3	3	1	4	0
2003-04	Vasteras	Sweden-2	44	5	12	17	16	....	....	....	....	....
	HV 71 Jonkoping	Sweden	3	0	0	0	0	....	....	....	....	....
2004-05	Ak Bars Kazan 2	Russia-3	....	8	11	19		....	....	....	....	....
	Spartak Moscow	Russia	13	1	2	3	2	....	....	....	....	....
	Ak Bars Kazan	Russia	2	0	0	0	0	....	....	....	....	....
2005-06	Ak Bars Kazan	Russia	38	1	7	8	8	4	0	1	1	0

JUNLAND, Jonas (YUHN-land, YOH-nuhs) ST.L.

Defense. Shoots left. 6'2", 198 lbs. Born, Linkoping, Sweden, November 15, 1987.
(St. Louis' 4th choice, 64th overall, in 2006 Entry Draft).

			Regular Season					Playoffs				
Season	Club	League	GP	G	A	Pts	PIM	GP	G	A	Pts	PIM
2002-03	Linkopings HC U18	Swe-U18	7	0	0	0	6	....	....	....	....	....
2003-04	Linkopings HC U18	Swe-U18	4	0	0	0	4	....	....	....	....	....
	Linkopings HC Jr.	Swe-Jr.	19	1	0	1	12	....	....	....	....	....
2004-05	Linkopings HC U18	Swe-U18	11	6	5	11	35	....	....	....	....	....
	Linkopings HC Jr.	Swe-Jr.	32	3	5	8	96	....	....	....	....	....
2005-06	Linkopings HC Jr.	Swe-Jr.	32	17	23	40	44	....	....	....	....	....
	Linkopings HC U18	Swe-U18	1	5	0	5	2	....	....	....	....	....
	Linkopings HC	Sweden	4	0	0	0	0	....	....	....	....	....

JUUTILAINEN, Jan-Mikael (yoo-tih-LIGH-nehn, YAHN-mih-KAYL) **CHI.**

Center. Shoots left. 5'11", 183 lbs. Born, Espoo, Finland, January 5, 1988.
(Chicago's 7th choice, 156th overall, in 2006 Entry Draft).

			Regular Season					Playoffs				
Season	**Club**	**League**	**GP**	**G**	**A**	**Pts**	**PIM**	**GP**	**G**	**A**	**Pts**	**PIM**
2004-05	Jokerit U18	Fin-U18	30	15	6	21	4	7	1	1	2	0
	Jokerit Helsinki Jr.	Fin-Jr.	1	0	0	0	0	....	....	....	....	....
2005-06	Jokerit U18	Fin-U18	16	8	13	21	28	6	6	7	13	2
	Jokerit Helsinki Jr.	Fin-Jr.	36	3	12	15	35	4	0	0	0	2
	Suomi U20	Finland-2	1	0	0	0	0	....	....	....	....	....

KAHNBERG, Magnus (KAHN-buhrg, MAG-nuhs) **ST.L.**

Left wing. Shoots left. 6'2", 190 lbs. Born, Kallered, Sweden, February 25, 1980.
(Carolina's 6th choice, 212th overall, in 2000 Entry Draft).

			Regular Season					Playoffs				
Season	**Club**	**League**	**GP**	**G**	**A**	**Pts**	**PIM**	**GP**	**G**	**A**	**Pts**	**PIM**
1997-98	V.Frolunda U18	Swe-U18	11	15	6	21	6	8	5	8	13	6
	V.Frolunda Jr.	Swe-Jr.	28	6	7	13	8	2	0	0	0	0
1998-99	V.Frolunda Jr.	Swe-Jr.	34	23	18	41	4	4	1	1	2	0
99-2000	V.Frolunda Jr.	Swe-Jr.	35	45	21	66	30	6	7	4	11	4
	V.Frolunda	Sweden	4	0	0	0	0	....	....	....	....	....
2000-01	V.Frolunda U18	Swe-U18	1	8	1	9	0	....	....	....	....	....
	V.Frolunda Jr.	Swe-Jr.	2	*2	1	3	2	....	....	....	....	....
	V.Frolunda	Sweden	50	8	6	14	6	5	0	0	0	2
2001-02	V.Frolunda	Sweden	50	14	11	25	24	10	5	0	5	2
2002-03	V.Frolunda	Sweden	50	14	20	34	22	15	2	6	8	12
2003-04	V.Frolunda	Sweden	50	*33	16	*49	20	10	5	2	7	10
2004-05	Frolunda	Sweden	46	15	8	23	22	13	5	1	6	4
2005-06	Frolunda	Sweden	45	18	15	33	26	17	4	3	7	16

Traded to **St. Louis** by **Carolina** with Jesse Boulerice, Mike Zigomanis, Carolina's 1st round choice (later traded to New Jersey - New Jersey selected Matthew Corrente) in 2006 Entry Draft, Toronto's 4th round choice (previously acquired, St. Louis selected Reto Berra) in 2006 Entry Draft and Chicago's 4th round choice (previously acquired) in 2007 Entry Draft for Doug Weight and Erkki Rajamaki, January 30, 2006.

KAIGORODOV, Alexei (kay-goh-ROH-dahv, al-EHX-ay) **OTT.**

Center. Shoots left. 6'1", 183 lbs. Born, Chelyabinsk, USSR, July 29, 1983.
(Ottawa's 2nd choice, 47th overall, in 2002 Entry Draft).

			Regular Season					Playoffs				
Season	**Club**	**League**	**GP**	**G**	**A**	**Pts**	**PIM**	**GP**	**G**	**A**	**Pts**	**PIM**
1998-99	Magnitogorsk 2	Russia-4	10	6	4	10	2	....	....	....	....	....
99-2000	Magnitogorsk 2	Russia-3	19	2	3	5	8	....	....	....	....	....
2000-01	Magnitogorsk 2	Russia-3	45	12	30	42	26	....	....	....	....	....
2001-02	Magnitogorsk	Russia	46	4	12	16	20	9	0	3	3	2
2002-03	Magnitogorsk	Russia	46	8	14	22	20	3	0	1	1	0
2003-04	Magnitogorsk	Russia	49	4	12	16	24	14	2	2	4	4
2004-05	Magnitogorsk	Russia	57	15	34	49	40	5	0	3	3	2
2005-06	Magnitogorsk	Russia	50	9	21	30	42	11	0	1	1	6

KAIP, Rylan (KAYP, RIH-luhn) **ATL.**

Center. Shoots left. 6', 195 lbs. Born, Wilcox, Sask., March 19, 1984.
(Atlanta's 9th choice, 269th overall, in 2003 Entry Draft).

			Regular Season					Playoffs				
Season	**Club**	**League**	**GP**	**G**	**A**	**Pts**	**PIM**	**GP**	**G**	**A**	**Pts**	**PIM**
2000-01	Notre Dame	SJHL	5	0	0	0	0	1	0	0	0	0
2001-02	Notre Dame	SJHL	61	14	18	32	77	....	....	....	....	....
2002-03	Notre Dame	SJHL	57	20	36	56	164	6	1	6	7	21
2003-04	Notre Dame	SJHL	54	30	36	66	133	4	1	1	2	6
2004-05	North Dakota	WCHA	22	0	4	4	20	....	....	....	....	....
2005-06	North Dakota	WCHA	42	3	5	8	76	....	....	....	....	....

KALETA, Patrick (ka-LEH-tuh, PAT-rihk) **BUF.**

Right wing. Shoots right. 5'11", 195 lbs. Born, Buffalo, NY, June 8, 1986.
(Buffalo's 5th choice, 176th overall, in 2004 Entry Draft).

			Regular Season					Playoffs				
Season	**Club**	**League**	**GP**	**G**	**A**	**Pts**	**PIM**	**GP**	**G**	**A**	**Pts**	**PIM**
2002-03	Peterborough	OHL	67	7	9	16	67	7	0	0	0	6
2003-04	Peterborough	OHL	67	14	14	28	124	....	....	....	....	....
2004-05	Peterborough	OHL	62	24	28	52	146	14	3	3	6	30
2005-06	Peterborough	OHL	68	16	35	51	121	19	8	10	18	43

KALUS, Petr (KA-luhs, PEE-tuhr) **BOS.**

Left wing. Shoots left. 6'1", 186 lbs. Born, Ostrava, Czech., June 29, 1987.
(Boston's 2nd choice, 39th overall, in 2005 Entry Draft).

			Regular Season					Playoffs				
Season	**Club**	**League**	**GP**	**G**	**A**	**Pts**	**PIM**	**GP**	**G**	**A**	**Pts**	**PIM**
2002-03	HC Ostrava U17	CzR-U17	18	3	19	22	14	....	....	....	....	....
	HC Vitkovice U17	CzR-U17	10	3	1	4	37	....	....	....	....	....
	HC Vitkovice Jr.	CzRep-Jr.	11	0	0	0	4	....	....	....	....	....
2003-04	HC Vitkovice U17	CzR-U17	9	7	5	12	60	7	3	5	8	2
	HC Vitkovice Jr.	CzRep-Jr.	41	8	8	16	67	....	....	....	....	....
2004-05	HC Vitkovice Jr.	CzRep-Jr.	39	20	11	31	161	2	2	0	2	25
	HC Vitkovice Steel	CzRep	1	0	0	0	0	....	....	....	....	....
2005-06	Regina Pats	WHL	60	36	22	58	87	6	4	1	5	6

KANA, Tomas (KA-nah, TAW-mahsh) **ST.L.**

Center. Shoots right. 6', 202 lbs. Born, Opava, Czech., November 29, 1987.
(St. Louis' 3rd choice, 31st overall, in 2006 Entry Draft).

			Regular Season					Playoffs				
Season	**Club**	**League**	**GP**	**G**	**A**	**Pts**	**PIM**	**GP**	**G**	**A**	**Pts**	**PIM**
2002-03	HC Vitkovice U17	CzR-U17	44	20	14	34	72	2	2	0	2	4
	HC Vitkovice Jr.	CzRep-Jr.	3	2	0	2	4	....	....	....	....	....
2003-04	HC Vitkovice U17	CzR-U17	8	2	9	11	33	7	4	5	9	18
	HC Vitkovice Jr.	CzRep-Jr.	50	12	7	19	78	....	....	....	....	....
2004-05	HC Vitkovice Jr.	CzRep-Jr.	46	12	22	34	155	2	0	0	0	2
	HC Vitkovice Steel	CzRep	1	0	0	0	0	....	....	....	....	....
2005-06	HC Vitkovice Jr.	CzRep-Jr.	5	4	3	7	16	....	....	....	....	....
	HC Vitkovice Steel	CzRep	42	5	9	14	50	6	0	1	1	2

KARLSSON, Mattias (KARL-suhn, MA-tee-uhs) **OTT.**

Defense. Shoots left. 6'2", 192 lbs. Born, Stora, Sweden, April 15, 1985.
(Ottawa's 4th choice, 135th overall, in 2003 Entry Draft).

			Regular Season					Playoffs				
Season	**Club**	**League**	**GP**	**G**	**A**	**Pts**	**PIM**	**GP**	**G**	**A**	**Pts**	**PIM**
2001-02	Brynas U18	Swe-U18	5	2	1	3	6	....	....	....	....	....
	Brynas IF Gavle Jr.	Swe-Jr.	13	0	1	1	12	....	....	....	....	....
2002-03	Brynas IF Gavle Jr.	Swe-Jr.	27	11	6	17	93	2	0	0	0	4
	Brynas IF Gavle	Sweden	3	0	0	0	0	....	....	....	....	....
	Brynas IF Gavle	Sweden-Q	3	0	0	0	0	....	....	....	....	....
2003-04	Brynas IF Gavle Jr.	Swe-Jr.	20	5	8	13	67	5	0	4	4	10
	Brynas IF Gavle	Sweden	39	0	0	0	6	....	....	....	....	....
2004-05	Brynas IF Gavle Jr.	Swe-Jr.	13	3	5	8	40	....	....	....	....	....
	Almtuna	Sweden-2	22	0	2	2	18	....	....	....	....	....
	Brynas IF Gavle	Sweden	9	0	0	0	2	....	....	....	....	....
	Brynas IF Gavle	Sweden-Q	1	0	0	0	0	....	....	....	....	....
2005-06	Almtuna Jr.	Swe-Jr.	2	0	1	1	4	....	....	....	....	....
	Almtuna	Sweden-2	32	3	4	7	40	....	....	....	....	....

KARSUMS, Martins (KAHR-suhmz, MAHR-tihnsh) **BOS.**

Right wing. Shoots right. 5'10", 180 lbs. Born, Riga, Latvia, February 26, 1986.
(Boston's 2nd choice, 64th overall, in 2004 Entry Draft).

			Regular Season					Playoffs				
Season	**Club**	**League**	**GP**	**G**	**A**	**Pts**	**PIM**	**GP**	**G**	**A**	**Pts**	**PIM**
2000-01	Prizma '83 Riga Jr.	Latvia-Jr.	2	0	0	0	0	....	....	....	....	....
	Lido Nafta Jr.	Latvia-Jr.	18	8	6	14	....	....	....	....	....	....
2001-02	Prizma '83 Riga	EEHL-B	16	7	8	15	4	....	....	....	....	....
	Prizma '83 Riga	Latvia	6	4	1	5	4	....	....	....	....	....
2002-03	HK Riga 2000	EEHL	2	0	0	0	0	....	....	....	....	....
	Vilki Riga	Latvia	STATISTICS NOT AVAILABLE									
2003-04	Moncton Wildcats	QMJHL	60	30	23	53	76	20	8	9	17	14
2004-05	Moncton Wildcats	QMJHL	30	14	12	26	31	2	0	0	0	0
2005-06	Moncton Wildcats	QMJHL	49	34	31	65	89	21	15	11	26	22

QMJHL All-Rookie Team (2004)

KASPAR, Lukas (kas-PAHR, LOO-kahsh) **S.J.**

Right wing. Shoots left. 6'2", 198 lbs. Born, Most, Czech., September 23, 1985.
(San Jose's 1st choice, 22nd overall, in 2004 Entry Draft).

			Regular Season					Playoffs				
Season	**Club**	**League**	**GP**	**G**	**A**	**Pts**	**PIM**	**GP**	**G**	**A**	**Pts**	**PIM**
2000-01	Litvinov U17	CzR-U17	48	27	19	46	64	6	2	3	5	0
2001-02	Litvinov U17	CzR-U17	48	35	41	76	143	2	1	1	2	0
2002-03	Litvinov Jr.	CzRep-Jr.	26	14	14	28	40	....	....	....	....	....
	Litvinov	CzRep	9	1	1	2	2	....	....	....	....	....
2003-04	Litvinov Jr.	CzRep-Jr.	23	21	14	35	56	1	0	0	0	0
	Litvinov	CzRep	37	4	2	6	10	....	....	....	....	....
	Usti n. L.	CzRep-2	1	1	0	1	0	....	....	....	....	....
	SK HC Banik Most	CzRep-3	....	....	....	....	....	1	0	0	0	2
2004-05	Ottawa 67's	OHL	59	21	30	51	45	21	6	14	20	8
2005-06	Cleveland Barons	AHL	76	14	22	36	88	....	....	....	....	....

KASSIAN, Matt (KAS-ee-uhn, MAT) **MIN.**

Left wing. Shoots left. 6'4", 247 lbs. Born, Edmonton, Alta., October 28, 1986.
(Minnesota's 2nd choice, 57th overall, in 2005 Entry Draft).

			Regular Season					Playoffs				
Season	**Club**	**League**	**GP**	**G**	**A**	**Pts**	**PIM**	**GP**	**G**	**A**	**Pts**	**PIM**
2002-03	Sherwood Park	AJHL	33	5	7	12	38	....	....	....	....	....
2003-04	Vancouver Giants	WHL	37	1	0	1	42	3	0	0	0	4
2004-05	Vancouver Giants	WHL	41	0	3	3	89	....	....	....	....	....
	Kamloops Blazers	WHL	28	3	0	3	83	6	1	2	3	14
2005-06	Kamloops Blazers	WHL	67	5	6	11	147	....	....	....	....	....

KAZIONOV, Denis (ka-zee-OH-nawv, DEH-nihs) **T.B.**

Left wing. Shoots left. 6'3", 187 lbs. Born, Perm, Russia, December 8, 1987.
(Tampa Bay's 4th choice, 198th overall, in 2006 Entry Draft).

			Regular Season					Playoffs				
Season	**Club**	**League**	**GP**	**G**	**A**	**Pts**	**PIM**	**GP**	**G**	**A**	**Pts**	**PIM**
2003-04	CSKA Moscow 2	Russia-3	2	0	1	1	2	....	....	....	....	....
2004-05	Dyn'o Moscow 2	Russia-3	STATISTICS NOT AVAILABLE									
2005-06	MVD	Russia	26	0	0	0	12	3	0	0	0	0
	HK MVD-THK Tver	Russia-3	31	6	13	19	34	....	....	....	....	....

KAZIONOV, Dmitri (ka-zee-OH-nahv, dih-MEE-tree) **T.B.**

Center. Shoots left. 6'3", 185 lbs. Born, Moscow, USSR, May 13, 1984.
(Tampa Bay's 2nd choice, 100th overall, in 2002 Entry Draft).

			Regular Season					Playoffs				
Season	**Club**	**League**	**GP**	**G**	**A**	**Pts**	**PIM**	**GP**	**G**	**A**	**Pts**	**PIM**
99-2000	Dyn'o Moscow 2	Russia-3	2	1	0	1	0	....	....	....	....	....
2000-01	THK Tver	Russia-2	33	1	1	2	6	....	....	....	....	....
2001-02	HK CSKA Moscow	Russia-2	2	0	1	1	0	....	....	....	....	....
	HK CSKA 2	Russia-3	10	1	0	1	4	....	....	....	....	....
	Lada Togliatti	Russia	3	0	0	0	0	....	....	....	....	....
	Lada Togliatti 2	Russia-3	16	10	9	19	0	....	....	....	....	....
2002-03	Lada Togliatti	Russia	5	0	1	1	4	....	....	....	....	....
	Lada Togliatti 2	Russia-3	34	14	13	27	26	....	....	....	....	....
2003-04	Lada Togliatti 2	Russia-3	5	3	2	5	0	4	0	0	0	0
	Lada Togliatti	Russia	47	5	5	10	34	5	0	0	0	4
2004-05	Lada Togliatti	Russia	46	3	7	10	32	2	0	0	0	0
2005-06	Lada Togliatti	Russia	13	0	3	3	18	....	....	....	....	....
	Dynamo Moscow	Russia	27	2	2	4	24	4	1	0	1	6

KELLER, Justin (KEHL-uhr, JUHS-tihn) **T.B.**

Left wing. Shoots left. 5'11", 185 lbs. Born, Nelson, B.C., March 4, 1986.
(Tampa Bay's 8th choice, 245th overall, in 2004 Entry Draft).

			Regular Season					Playoffs				
Season	**Club**	**League**	**GP**	**G**	**A**	**Pts**	**PIM**	**GP**	**G**	**A**	**Pts**	**PIM**
2001-02	Spokane Chiefs	WHL	25	7	6	13	10	....	....	....	....	....
	Saskatoon Blades	WHL	36	7	6	13	6	2	0	0	0	2
2002-03	Saskatoon Blades	WHL	2	0	0	0	0	....	....	....	....	....
	Regina Pats	WHL	16	3	3	6	6	....	....	....	....	....
2003-04	Kelowna Rockets	WHL	72	25	21	46	44	17	4	5	9	18
2004-05	Kelowna Rockets	WHL	72	31	22	53	103	23	12	10	22	44
2005-06	Kelowna Rockets	WHL	72	*51	37	88	82	12	3	6	9	14

WHL West First All-Star Team (2006)

KELMAN, Scott (KEHL-man, SCAWT) **CAR.**

Center. Shoots left. 6'3", 215 lbs. Born, Winnipeg, Man., May 7, 1981.
(Phoenix's 1st choice, 15th overall, in 1999 Entry Draft).

			Regular Season					Playoffs				
Season	Club	League	GP	G	A	Pts	PIM	GP	G	A	Pts	PIM
1996-97	Winnipeg Legion	MAHA	35	21	44	65	78	....	....	....	....	....
	Seattle	WHL	5	0	1	1	0	....	....	....	....	....
1997-98	Seattle	WHL	61	13	17	30	35	5	0	0	0	4
1998-99	Seattle	WHL	66	19	54	73	95	11	4	3	7	37
99-2000	Seattle	WHL	64	13	42	55	104	2	0	0	0	2
2000-01	Seattle	WHL	10	5	6	11	10	....	....	....	....	....
	Moose Jaw	WHL	60	15	18	33	130	4	0	1	1	12
2001-02	Moose Jaw	WHL	3	1	0	1	2	....	....	....	....	....
	Tri-City Americans	WHL	68	33	50	83	80	5	1	1	2	12
2002-03	Jackson Bandits	ECHL	51	14	18	32	93	1	0	0	0	4
	San Antonio	AHL	1	0	0	0	0	....	....	....	....	....
2003-04	San Antonio	AHL	17	1	4	5	14	....	....	....	....	....
	Augusta Lynx	ECHL	47	15	32	47	104	....	....	....	....	....
2004-05	San Antonio	AHL	24	1	1	2	25	....	....	....	....	....
	Laredo Bucks	CHL	41	14	21	35	56	....	....	....	....	....
2005-06	Manitoba Moose	AHL	3	0	2	2	2	....	....	....	....	....
	Hershey Bears	AHL	2	0	0	0	0	....	....	....	....	....
	Lowell	AHL	19	6	7	13	49	....	....	....	....	....
	Gwinnett	ECHL	46	14	33	47	104	....	....	....	....	....
	Fresno Falcons	ECHL	....	....	....	....	....	13	1	5	6	28

Signed as a free agent by **Carolina**, July 21, 2006.

KENNEDY, Tim (KEH-nuh-dee, TIHM) **BUF.**

Left wing. Shoots left. 5'9", 170 lbs. Born, Buffalo, NY, April 30, 1986.
(Washington's 6th choice, 181st overall, in 2005 Entry Draft).

			Regular Season					Playoffs				
Season	Club	League	GP	G	A	Pts	PIM	GP	G	A	Pts	PIM
2003-04	Sioux City	USHL	56	9	10	19	42	7	2	2	4	6
2004-05	Sioux City	USHL	54	30	31	61	112	13	*6	*11	*17	18
2005-06	Michigan State	CCHA	29	4	15	19	31	....	....	....	....	....

USHL Second All-Star Team (2005)

Traded to **Buffalo** by **Washington** for Buffalo's 6th round choice (Mathieu Perreault) in 2006 Entry Draft, July 30, 2005.

KENNEDY, Tyler (KEH-nuh-dee, TIGH-luhr) **PIT.**

Center. Shoots right. 5'10", 183 lbs. Born, Sault Ste. Marie, Ont., July 15, 1986.
(Pittsburgh's 6th choice, 99th overall, in 2004 Entry Draft).

			Regular Season					Playoffs				
Season	Club	League	GP	G	A	Pts	PIM	GP	G	A	Pts	PIM
2002-03	Sault Ste. Marie	OHL	61	5	10	15	28	4	0	0	0	0
2003-04	Sault Ste. Marie	OHL	63	16	26	42	28	....	....	....	....	....
2004-05	Sault Ste. Marie	OHL	61	21	36	57	37	4	1	3	4	4
2005-06	Sault Ste. Marie	OHL	64	22	48	70	60	4	1	2	3	2

KESA, Teemu (KEH-sah, TEE-moo)

Defense. Shoots right. 6'1", 211 lbs. Born, Helsinki, Finland, June 7, 1981.
(New Jersey's 5th choice, 100th overall, in 1999 Entry Draft).

			Regular Season					Playoffs				
Season	Club	League	GP	G	A	Pts	PIM	GP	G	A	Pts	PIM
1996-97	Tappara Jr.	Fin-Jr.	32	1	5	6	58	4	1	0	4	29
1997-98	Ilves Tampere U18	Fin-U18	33	8	1	9	78	....	....	....	....	....
1998-99	Ilves Tampere U18	Fin-U18	26	4	5	9	146	....	....	....	....	....
	Ilves Tampere Jr.	Fin-Jr.	6	0	1	1	10	10	0	0	0	12
99-2000	Ilves Tampere Jr.	Fin-Jr.	32	2	7	9	92	....	....	....	....	....
	Ilves Tampere	Finland	5	0	0	0	8	....	....	....	....	....
2000-01	Ilves Tampere Jr.	Fin-Jr.	4	1	0	1	41	....	....	....	....	....
	Sport Vaasa	Finland-2	1	0	1	1	0	....	....	....	....	....
2001-02	Lukko Rauma	Finland	34	2	0	2	32	....	....	....	....	....
	Lukko Rauma Jr.	Fin-Jr.	3	0	4	4	4	....	....	....	....	....
2002-03	Lukko Rauma	Finland	37	1	0	1	22	....	....	....	....	....
2003-04	Lukko Rauma	Finland	49	2	2	4	62	....	....	....	....	....
2004-05	Albany River Rats	AHL	60	3	7	10	61	....	....	....	....	....
2005-06	Albany River Rats	AHL	19	0	2	2	39	....	....	....	....	....

KESSEL, Phil (KEH-sehl, FIHL) **BOS.**

Center. Shoots right. 6', 189 lbs. Born, Madison, WI, October 2, 1987.
(Boston's 1st choice, 5th overall, in 2006 Entry Draft).

			Regular Season					Playoffs				
Season	Club	League	GP	G	A	Pts	PIM	GP	G	A	Pts	PIM
2003-04	USNTDP	U-17	32	31	18	49	8	....	....	....	....	....
	USNTDP	NAHL	30	21	12	33	18	....	....	....	....	....
2004-05	USNTDP	U-18	31	41	32	73	16	....	....	....	....	....
	USNTDP	NAHL	14	11	14	25	21	....	....	....	....	....
2005-06	U. of Minnesota	WCHA	39	18	33	51	28	....	....	....	....	....

KHOMITSKY, Vadim (khoh-MIHT-skee, va-DEEM) **DAL.**

Defense. Shoots left. 6'1", 185 lbs. Born, Voskresensk, USSR, July 21, 1982.
(Dallas' 5th choice, 123rd overall, in 2000 Entry Draft).

			Regular Season					Playoffs				
Season	Club	League	GP	G	A	Pts	PIM	GP	G	A	Pts	PIM
1998-99	Voskresensk	Russia	9	0	0	0	10	....	....	....	....	....
99-2000	Voskresensk	Russia-2	17	0	0	0	31	....	....	....	....	....
	HK Moscow	Russia-2	11	0	1	1	10	....	....	....	....	....
2000-01	HK Moscow	Russia-2	44	2	7	9	89	....	....	....	....	....
2001-02	HK CSKA Moscow	Russia-2	68	2	18	20	63	....	....	....	....	....
2002-03	CSKA Moscow	Russia	51	3	2	5	58	....	....	....	....	....
2003-04	CSKA Moscow	Russia	54	3	3	6	46	....	....	....	....	....
2004-05	CSKA Moscow	Russia	60	1	5	6	105	....	....	....	....	....
2005-06	CSKA Moscow	Russia	51	5	6	11	110	7	0	0	0	6

KHOMUTOV, Ivan (khoh-moo-TAWF, ee-VAHN) **N.J.**

Center. Shoots left. 6'3", 210 lbs. Born, Saratov, USSR, March 11, 1985.
(New Jersey's 3rd choice, 93rd overall, in 2003 Entry Draft).

			Regular Season					Playoffs				
Season	Club	League	GP	G	A	Pts	PIM	GP	G	A	Pts	PIM
2001-02	HK CSKA 2	Russia-3	30	11	8	19	14	....	....	....	....	....
2002-03	Elektrostal	Russia-2	20	1	1	2	8	....	....	....	....	....
2003-04	London Knights	OHL	40	9	12	21	25	15	3	1	4	7
2004-05	Albany River Rats	AHL	66	6	11	17	30	....	....	....	....	....
2005-06	Albany River Rats	AHL	60	9	20	29	44	....	....	....	....	....

KINCH, Matt (KIHNCH, MATT) **NYR**

Defense. Shoots left. 5'11", 185 lbs. Born, Red Deer, Alta., February 17, 1980.
(Buffalo's 8th choice, 146th overall, in 1999 Entry Draft).

			Regular Season					Playoffs				
Season	Club	League	GP	G	A	Pts	PIM	GP	G	A	Pts	PIM
1995-96	Red Deer	AMHL	35	6	17	23	31	....	....	....	....	....
	Calgary Hitmen	WHL	1	0	1	1	2	....	....	....	....	....
1996-97	Calgary Hitmen	WHL	64	10	22	32	31	....	....	....	....	....
1997-98	Calgary Hitmen	WHL	55	7	24	31	13	18	3	2	5	4
1998-99	Calgary Hitmen	WHL	68	14	69	83	16	21	8	15	23	59
99-2000	Calgary Hitmen	WHL	62	14	61	75	24	13	2	12	14	8
2000-01	Calgary Hitmen	WHL	70	18	66	84	52	12	3	6	9	6
2001-02	Hartford Wolf Pack	AHL	40	1	7	8	4	....	....	....	....	....
	Charlotte	ECHL	26	3	12	15	13	5	3	2	5	0
2002-03	Hartford Wolf Pack	AHL	66	7	22	29	28	2	0	0	0	0
2003-04	Hartford Wolf Pack	AHL	67	1	19	20	38	1	0	0	0	0
2004-05	Salzburg	Austria	37	1	12	13	18	....	....	....	....	....
2005-06	Langnau	Swiss	25	1	4	5	14	....	....	....	....	....
	ERC Ingolstadt	Germany	16	1	2	3	16	7	0	0	0	4

WHL East First All-Star Team (1999, 2001) • Memorial Cup Tournament All-Star Team (1999) • Canadian Major Junior Sportsman of the Year (1999) • WHL East Second All-Star Team (2000) • Canadian Major Junior First All-Star Team (2001)

Signed as a free agent by **NY Rangers**, June 26, 2001. Signed as a free agent by **Salzburg** (Austria), September, 2004.

KINDL, Jakub (KEEHN-duhl, YA-kuhb) **DET.**

Defense. Shoots left. 6'3", 200 lbs. Born, Sumperk, Czech., February 10, 1987.
(Detroit's 1st choice, 19th overall, in 2005 Entry Draft).

			Regular Season					Playoffs				
Season	Club	League	GP	G	A	Pts	PIM	GP	G	A	Pts	PIM
2002-03	HC Pardubice U17	CzR-U17	3	0	3	3	10	....	....	....	....	....
	HC Pardubice Jr.	CzRep-Jr.	27	0	3	3	46	....	....	....	....	....
	Pardubice	CzRep	1	0	0	0	0	....	....	....	....	....
2003-04	HC Pardubice U17	CzR-U17	2	0	1	1	6	....	....	....	....	....
	HC Pardubice Jr.	CzRep-Jr.	48	4	14	18	108	....	....	....	....	....
	Hr. Kralove	CzRep-2	1	0	0	0	0	1	0	0	0	0
2004-05	Kitchener Rangers	OHL	62	3	11	14	92	12	0	0	0	22
2005-06	Kitchener Rangers	OHL	60	12	46	58	112	5	1	0	1	10
	Grand Rapids	AHL	3	0	1	1	2	....	....	....	....	....

KING, D.J. (KIHNG, DEE-JAY) **ST.L.**

Center. Shoots left. 6'3", 230 lbs. Born, Meadow Lake, Sask., January 27, 1984.
(St. Louis' 6th choice, 191st overall, in 2002 Entry Draft).

			Regular Season					Playoffs				
Season	Club	League	GP	G	A	Pts	PIM	GP	G	A	Pts	PIM
2000-01	Beardy's	SMHL	52	30	28	58	120	....	....	....	....	....
2001-02	Lethbridge	WHL	65	10	14	24	104	....	....	....	....	....
2002-03	Lethbridge	WHL	55	15	17	32	139	....	....	....	....	....
2003-04	Lethbridge	WHL	35	8	15	23	102	....	....	....	....	....
	Kelowna Rockets	WHL	28	5	2	7	80	17	1	6	7	16
2004-05	Worcester IceCats	AHL	74	6	8	14	178	....	....	....	....	....
2005-06	Peoria Rivermen	AHL	67	5	6	11	160	2	0	0	0	2
	Alaska Aces	ECHL	5	0	4	4	4	....	....	....	....	....

KLIMOV, Valeri (KLEE-mawf, VAL-uhr-ee) **N.J.**

Defense. Shoots left. 6'3", 200 lbs. Born, Moscow, USSR, July 17, 1986.
(New Jersey's 7th choice, 282nd overall, in 2004 Entry Draft).

			Regular Season					Playoffs				
Season	Club	League	GP	G	A	Pts	PIM	GP	G	A	Pts	PIM
2001-02	Spartak Moscow 2	Russia-3	24	1	1	2	6	....	....	....	....	....
2002-03	Spartak Moscow 2	Russia-3	5	2	1	3	8	....	....	....	....	....
2003-04	Spartak Moscow 2	Russia-3	4	1	0	1	0	....	....	....	....	....
2004-05	Spartak Moscow	Russia	6	0	0	0	2	....	....	....	....	....
2005-06	Spartak Moscow 2	Russia-3	17	1	4	5	20	....	....	....	....	....
	Spartak Moscow	Russia	23	1	0	1	4	2	0	0	0	2

KLUBERTANZ, Kyle (KLOO-buhr-tanz, KIGHL) **ANA.**

Defense. Shoots right. 6', 186 lbs. Born, Madison, WI, September 23, 1985.
(Anaheim's 3rd choice, 74th overall, in 2004 Entry Draft).

			Regular Season					Playoffs				
Season	Club	League	GP	G	A	Pts	PIM	GP	G	A	Pts	PIM
2002-03	Green Bay	USHL	60	8	26	34	74	....	....	....	....	....
2003-04	Green Bay	USHL	57	6	21	27	124	....	....	....	....	....
2004-05	U. of Wisconsin	WCHA	41	3	15	18	64	....	....	....	....	....
2005-06	U. of Wisconsin	WCHA	43	4	17	21	44	....	....	....	....	....

WCHA All-Rookie Team (2005)

KNYAZEV, Igor (kuh-NYA-zhev, EE-gohr) **PHX.**

Defense. Shoots left. 6', 208 lbs. Born, Elektrostal, USSR, January 27, 1983.
(Carolina's 1st choice, 15th overall, in 2001 Entry Draft).

			Regular Season					Playoffs				
Season	Club	League	GP	G	A	Pts	PIM	GP	G	A	Pts	PIM
99-2000	Spartak Moscow 2	Russia-3	13	2	4	6	74	....	....	....	....	....
	Spartak Moscow	Russia-2	26	1	1	2	6	....	....	....	....	....
2000-01	Spartak Moscow	Russia-2	53	6	5	11	101	....	....	....	....	....
2001-02	Spartak Moscow	Russia	3	0	0	0	8	....	....	....	....	....
	Spartak Moscow 2	Russia-3	2	0	1	1	0	....	....	....	....	....
	Ak Bars Kazan	Russia	14	0	1	1	4	3	0	0	0	0
2002-03	Lowell	AHL	68	2	5	7	68	....	....	....	....	....
2003-04	Springfield Falcons	AHL	72	1	6	7	61	....	....	....	....	....
2004-05	Voskresensk	Russia	29	0	2	2	57	....	....	....	....	....
2005-06	Mytischi	Russia	21	3	1	4	36	....	....	....	....	....

Traded to **Phoenix** by **Carolina** with David Tanabe for Danny Markov and future considerations (Edmonton's 3rd round choice (previously acquired, later traded to NY Rangers - NY Rangers selected Billy Ryan) in 2004 Entry Draft), June 21, 2003. Signed as a free agent by **Voskresensk** (Russia), September, 2004.

KOCI, David (KOH-chee, DAY-vihd) CHI.

Defense. Shoots left. 6'6", 228 lbs. Born, Prague, Czech., May 12, 1981.
(Pittsburgh's 5th choice, 146th overall, in 2000 Entry Draft).

			Regular Season					Playoffs				
Season	Club	League	GP	G	A	Pts	PIM	GP	G	A	Pts	PIM
1997-98	Sparta Jr.	CzRep-Jr.	41	2	9	11	105	....	....	....	....	....
1998-99	Hvezda Praha Jr.	CzRep-Jr.	22	1	3	4	36	....	....	....	....	....
	Sparta Jr.	CzRep-Jr.	7	0	0	0	4	....	....	....	....	....
99-2000	Sparta Jr.	CzRep-Jr.	47	0	6	6	124	....	....	....	....	....
2000-01	Prince George	WHL	70	2	7	9	155	6	0	0	0	20
2001-02	Wilkes-Barre	AHL	26	1	3	4	98	....	....	....	....	....
	Wheeling Nailers	ECHL	33	2	4	6	105	....	....	....	....	....
2002-03	Wilkes-Barre	AHL	9	0	0	0	4	....	....	....	....	....
	Wheeling Nailers	ECHL	48	0	1	1	103	....	....	....	....	....
2003-04	Wilkes-Barre	AHL	78	1	7	8	298	10	0	0	0	24
2004-05	Wilkes-Barre	AHL	68	1	8	9	311	....	....	....	....	....
2005-06	Wilkes-Barre	AHL	13	0	0	0	59	....	....	....	....	....

• Missed majority of 2005-06 season recovering from an injury. Signed as a free agent by **Chicago**, July 17, 2006.

KOHN, Dustin (KOHN, DUHS-tihn) NYI

Defense. Shoots left. 6'1", 182 lbs. Born, Edmonton, Alta., February 2, 1987.
(NY Islanders' 2nd choice, 46th overall, in 2005 Entry Draft).

			Regular Season					Playoffs				
Season	Club	League	GP	G	A	Pts	PIM	GP	G	A	Pts	PIM
2003-04	Calgary Hitmen	WHL	52	3	6	9	13	7	0	1	1	2
2004-05	Calgary Hitmen	WHL	71	8	35	43	61	12	0	4	4	6
2005-06	Calgary Hitmen	WHL	38	2	12	14	20	....	....	....	....	....
	Brandon	WHL	31	2	13	15	30	6	0	4	4	10
	Bridgeport	AHL	2	0	0	0	0	....	....	....	....	....

KOISTINEN, Ville (KOIS-tih-nehn, VIHL-ee) NSH.

Defense. Shoots left. 5'11", 190 lbs. Born, Oulu, Finland, June 17, 1982.

			Regular Season					Playoffs				
Season	Club	League	GP	G	A	Pts	PIM	GP	G	A	Pts	PIM
2000-01	Ilves Tampere	Finland	6	0	0	0	0	5	0	1	1	0
2001-02	Ilves Tampere	Finland	53	1	8	9	42	....	....	....	....	....
2002-03	Ilves Tampere	Finland	18	4	1	5	8	....	....	....	....	....
2003-04	Ilves Tampere	Finland	54	7	16	23	51	7	0	2	2	0
2004-05	Ilves Tampere	Finland	52	6	14	20	69	3	0	0	0	0
2005-06	Ilves Tampere	Finland	56	8	26	34	70	4	0	1	1	2

Signed as a free agent by **Nashville**, May 11, 2006.

KOJEVNIKOV, Alexander (kuh-ZHEHV-nih-kahv al-ehx-AN-duhr) CHI.

Left wing. Shoots left. 6'3", 199 lbs. Born, Moscow, USSR, April 12, 1984.
(Chicago's 3rd choice, 93rd overall, in 2002 Entry Draft).

			Regular Season					Playoffs				
Season	Club	League	GP	G	A	Pts	PIM	GP	G	A	Pts	PIM
2001-02	Krylja Sovetov 2	Russia-3	32	12	15	27	59	....	....	....	....	....
2002-03	Krylja Sovetov	Russia	5	0	0	0	4	....	....	....	....	....
	Krylja Sovetov 2	Russia-3	3	1	2	3	28	....	....	....	....	....
2003-04	Val-d'Or Foreurs	QMJHL	19	10	4	14	22	....	....	....	....	....
	Quebec Remparts	QMJHL	16	3	4	7	16	4	0	2	2	4
2004-05	Greenville Grrrowl	ECHL	56	11	7	18	46	....	....	....	....	....
	Dayton Bombers	ECHL	2	0	1	1	2	....	....	....	....	....
2005-06	Vityaz Chekhov	Russia	2	0	0	0	0	....	....	....	....	....
	Leninogorsk	Russia-2	3	0	0	0	2	....	....	....	....	....
	Perm	Russia	1	0	0	0	0	....	....	....	....	....
	Novopolotsk	BelOpen	19	10	1	11	83	....	....	....	....	....

KOKOREV, Dmitri (KOH-koh-rehf, DEH-mee-tree) CGY.

Defense. Shoots left. 6'3", 198 lbs. Born, Moscow, USSR, January 9, 1979.
(Calgary's 4th choice, 51st overall, in 1997 Entry Draft).

			Regular Season					Playoffs				
Season	Club	League	GP	G	A	Pts	PIM	GP	G	A	Pts	PIM
1996-97	Dyn'o Moscow 2	Russia-3	27	2	4	6	24	....	....	....	....	....
	Dynamo Moscow	Russia	1	0	0	0	0	....	....	....	....	....
1997-98	Dynamo Moscow	Russia	24	1	2	3	20	....	....	....	....	....
1998-99	Dynamo Moscow	Russia	26	0	1	1	20	8	1	0	1	0
	Dyn'o Moscow 2	Russia-3	14	0	2	2	20	....	....	....	....	....
99-2000	THK Tver	Russia-2	20	6	3	9	32	....	....	....	....	....
	Dynamo Moscow	Russia	22	0	1	1	14	1	0	0	0	0
2000-01	Dynamo Moscow	Russia	5	0	1	1	4	....	....	....	....	....
2001-02	CSKA Moscow 2	Russia-3	11	2	2	4	22	....	....	....	....	....
	CSKA Moscow	Russia	32	1	3	4	32	....	....	....	....	....
2002-03	Sibir Novosibirsk	Russia	26	0	1	1	59	....	....	....	....	....
2003-04	Spartak Moscow	Russia-2	15	0	0	0	10	....	....	....	....	....
	Kristall Elektrostal	Russia-2	10	0	1	1	16	....	....	....	....	....
2004-05	Vityaz Chekhov	Russia-2	48	4	11	15	64	15	1	3	4	22
2005-06	Khimik	Russia-2	24	1	9	10	85	2	0	0	0	29

KOLARIK, Chad (koh-LAHR-ihk, CHAD) PHX.

Center. Shoots right. 5'10", 175 lbs. Born, Abington, PA, January 26, 1986.
(Phoenix's 7th choice, 199th overall, in 2004 Entry Draft).

			Regular Season					Playoffs				
Season	Club	League	GP	G	A	Pts	PIM	GP	G	A	Pts	PIM
2002-03	USNTDP	U-17	21	14	10	24	4	....	....	....	....	....
	USNTDP	NAHL	44	16	22	38	43	....	....	....	....	....
2003-04	USNTDP	U-18	45	18	20	38	16	....	....	....	....	....
	USNTDP	NAHL	10	3	4	7	4	....	....	....	....	....
2004-05	U. of Michigan	CCHA	42	18	17	35	53	....	....	....	....	....
2005-06	U. of Michigan	CCHA	41	12	26	38	30	....	....	....	....	....

KOLARIK, Tyler (koh-LAHR-ihk, TIGH-luhr)

Center. Shoots right. 5'10", 185 lbs. Born, Philadelphia, PA, January 26, 1981.
(Columbus' 5th choice, 150th overall, in 2000 Entry Draft).

			Regular Season					Playoffs				
Season	Club	League	GP	G	A	Pts	PIM	GP	G	A	Pts	PIM
99-2000	Deerfield Academy	High-MA	26	31	22	53	8	....	....	....	....	....
	NY/Mid-Atlantic	MBHL	3	4	3	7	0	....	....	....	....	....
2000-01	Harvard Crimson	ECAC	32	13	15	28	36	....	....	....	....	....
2001-02	Harvard Crimson	ECAC	32	9	21	30	32	....	....	....	....	....
2002-03	Harvard Crimson	ECAC	30	15	13	28	20	....	....	....	....	....
2003-04	Harvard Crimson	ECAC	36	12	18	30	24	....	....	....	....	....
2004-05	Syracuse Crunch	AHL	2	0	0	0	0	....	....	....	....	....
	Dayton Bombers	ECHL	49	16	16	32	67	....	....	....	....	....
2005-06	Syracuse Crunch	AHL	67	10	8	18	145	6	1	0	1	10
	Dayton Bombers	ECHL	2	0	0	0	4	....	....	....	....	....

KOLEHMAINEN, Janne (koh-leh-MAYN-ehn, YA-nee) OTT.

Left wing. Shoots left. 6'3", 209 lbs. Born, Lappeenranta, Finland, March 22, 1986.
(Ottawa's 5th choice, 115th overall, in 2005 Entry Draft).

			Regular Season					Playoffs				
Season	Club	League	GP	G	A	Pts	PIM	GP	G	A	Pts	PIM
2002-03	SaiPa U18	Fin-U18	23	11	8	19	77	....	....	....	....	....
	SaiPa Jr.	Fin-Jr.	1	0	0	0	0	....	....	....	....	....
2003-04	SaiPa U18	Fin-U18	6	3	1	4	18	....	....	....	....	....
	SaiPa Jr.	Fin-Jr.	30	4	7	11	26	4	3	0	3	4
	SaiPa	Finland	6	0	0	0	2	....	....	....	....	....
2004-05	SaiPa Jr.	Fin-Jr.	13	2	4	6	24	2	1	1	2	0
	SaiPa	Finland	29	1	1	2	8	....	....	....	....	....
2005-06	SaiPa Jr.	Fin-Jr.	12	3	2	5	12	3	2	0	2	14
	Suomi U20	Finland-2	3	0	0	0	2	....	....	....	....	....
	SaiPa	Finland	36	0	2	2	45	8	0	1	1	4

KOLESOV, Sergei (KOH-leh-sawf, SAIR-gay) DET.

Defense. Shoots left. 6'4", 187 lbs. Born, Novopolotsk, USSR, May 22, 1986.
(Detroit's 3rd choice, 151st overall, in 2004 Entry Draft).

			Regular Season					Playoffs				
Season	Club	League	GP	G	A	Pts	PIM	GP	G	A	Pts	PIM
2003-04	Dynamo Minsk	Belarus	STATISTICS NOT AVAILABLE									
2004-05	Dynamo Minsk	BelOpen	37	2	6	8	24	....	....	....	....	....
	Yunost-Minsk	BelOpen	1	0	0	0	2	9	0	0	0	4
2005-06	Cedar Rapids	USHL	50	2	8	10	66	8	0	0	0	10

KOLLAR, Tomas (koh-LAHR, TAW-mash) DET.

Left wing. Shoots left. 6'2", 211 lbs. Born, Stockholm, Sweden, April 20, 1982.
(Detroit's 6th choice, 226th overall, in 2003 Entry Draft).

			Regular Season					Playoffs				
Season	Club	League	GP	G	A	Pts	PIM	GP	G	A	Pts	PIM
99-2000	Hammarby Jr.	Swe-Jr.	42	10	15	25	52	....	....	....	....	....
2000-01	Hammarby Jr.	Swe-Jr.	8	2	4	6	12	....	....	....	....	....
	Hammarby	Sweden-2	23	3	2	5	10	....	....	....	....	....
2001-02	Hammarby	Sweden-2	46	9	9	18	24	2	3	0	3	2
	Hammarby Jr.	Swe-Jr.	3	0	3	3	6	2	1	0	1	0
2002-03	Hammarby	Sweden-2	27	10	8	18	45	....	....	....	....	....
2003-04	Djurgarden	Sweden	50	6	8	14	22	4	0	0	0	0
2004-05	Skelleftea AIK HK	Sweden-2	17	9	5	14	16	....	....	....	....	....
	Djurgarden	Sweden	32	1	6	7	46	12	0	1	1	30
2005-06	Sodertalje SK	Sweden	50	7	8	15	111	....	....	....	....	....
	Sodertalje SK	Sweden-Q	9	2	3	5	45	....	....	....	....	....

KOLTSOV, Ivan (kohlt-SAHV, ee-VAHN) EDM.

Defense. Shoots left. 6'2", 182 lbs. Born, Cherepovets, USSR, March 7, 1984.
(Edmonton's 6th choice, 106th overall, in 2002 Entry Draft).

			Regular Season					Playoffs				
Season	Club	League	GP	G	A	Pts	PIM	GP	G	A	Pts	PIM
2001-02	Cherepovets 2	Russia-3	27	2	2	4	24	....	....	....	....	....
2002-03	Leninogorsk	Russia-2	1	0	1	1	2	....	....	....	....	....
	Cherepovets 2	Russia-3	34	4	7	11	26	....	....	....	....	....
2003-04	Cherepovets 2	Russia-3	14	2	2	4	20	....	....	....	....	....
2004-05	HK Lipetsk	Russia-2	10	2	0	2	2	....	....	....	....	....
	HK Belgorod	Russia-2	30	1	2	3	32	....	....	....	....	....
2005-06	Dizel Penza	Russia-2	40	0	4	4	22	8	0	0	0	4

KOLTSOV, Kirill (kohlt-SAHV, kih-RIHL) VAN.

Defense. Shoots left. 5'11", 183 lbs. Born, Chelyabinsk, USSR, February 1, 1983.
(Vancouver's 1st choice, 49th overall, in 2002 Entry Draft).

			Regular Season					Playoffs				
Season	Club	League	GP	G	A	Pts	PIM	GP	G	A	Pts	PIM
1998-99	Streetsville Derbys	OPJHL	20	5	7	12	4	....	....	....	....	....
99-2000	Omsk 2	Russia-3	27	0	7	7	30	....	....	....	....	....
	Avangard Omsk	Russia	2	0	0	0	0	....	....	....	....	....
2000-01	Avangard Omsk	Russia	39	0	1	1	20	16	1	3	4	12
2001-02	Avangard Omsk	Russia	41	1	5	6	34	11	1	0	1	8
2002-03	Avangard Omsk	Russia	45	4	8	12	54	12	1	3	4	8
2003-04	Manitoba Moose	AHL	74	7	25	32	62	....	....	....	....	....
2004-05	Manitoba Moose	AHL	28	3	14	17	42	....	....	....	....	....
	Avangard Omsk	Russia	22	2	2	4	46	10	0	1	1	18
2005-06	Avangard Omsk	Russia	43	9	8	17	98	13	4	5	9	10

KOLUSZ, Marcin (KOH-loosh, MART-sihn) MIN.

Right wing. Shoots left. 6'1", 180 lbs. Born, Limanowa, Poland, January 18, 1985.
(Minnesota's 4th choice, 157th overall, in 2003 Entry Draft).

			Regular Season					Playoffs				
Season	Club	League	GP	G	A	Pts	PIM	GP	G	A	Pts	PIM
2000-01	Nowy Targ	Poland	5	0	0	0	2	....	....	....	....	....
2001-02	Nowy Targ Jr.	Poland-Jr.	11	13	5	18	22	....	....	....	....	....
2002-03	Nowy Targ	Poland	30	2	4	6	10	2	0	0	0	0
2003-04	Vancouver Giants	WHL	64	6	12	18	19	6	1	0	1	0
2004-05	Nowy Targ	Poland	28	5	8	13	12	7	0	5	5	16
2005-06	HC Ocelari Trinec	CzRep	2	1	0	1	0	....	....	....	....	....
	Prostejov	CzRep-2	10	1	1	2	4	....	....	....	....	....
	HC Havirov	CzRep-2	5	0	0	0	4	....	....	....	....	....
	Nowy Targ	Poland	18	11	10	21	4	9	4	2	6	27

KOMADOSKI, Neil (koh-mah-DAW-skee, NEEL) OTT.

Defense. Shoots left. 6'1", 215 lbs. Born, Chesterfield, MO, February 10, 1982.
(Ottawa's 3rd choice, 81st overall, in 2001 Entry Draft).

			Regular Season					Playoffs				
Season	Club	League	GP	G	A	Pts	PIM	GP	G	A	Pts	PIM
1997-98	Aurora Tigers	OPJHL	1	0	0	0	0	....	....	....	....	....
1998-99	USNTDP	NAHL	49	3	11	14	222	....	....	....	....	....
99-2000	USNTDP	U-18	6	0	2	2	12	....	....	....	....	....
	USNTDP	USHL	50	7	8	15	202	....	....	....	....	....
	USNTDP	NAHL	1	1	0	1	0	....	....	....	....	....
2000-01	U. of Notre Dame	CCHA	30	2	5	7	106	....	....	....	....	....
2001-02	U. of Notre Dame	CCHA	37	2	9	11	100	....	....	....	....	....
2002-03	U. of Notre Dame	CCHA	40	1	23	24	46	....	....	....	....	....
2003-04	U. of Notre Dame	CCHA	39	5	15	20	48	....	....	....	....	....
	Binghamton	AHL	3	0	0	0	2	1	0	0	0	0
2004-05	Binghamton	AHL	36	2	1	3	68	....	....	....	....	....
2005-06	Binghamton	AHL	41	0	5	5	71	....	....	....	....	....

KOMAROV, Leo (koh-mah-RAWV, L'YAY-oh) TOR.

Center. Shoots left. 5'10", 187 lbs. Born, Narva, Estonia, January 23, 1987.
(Toronto's 7th choice, 180th overall, in 2006 Entry Draft).

			Regular Season					Playoffs				
Season	Club	League	GP	G	A	Pts	PIM	GP	G	A	Pts	PIM
2003-04	Sport Vaasa U18	Fin-U18	30	9	15	24	8	....	....	....	....	....
2004-05	Assat Pori U18	Fin-U18	9	4	5	9	62	....	....	....	....	....
	Assat Pori Jr.	Fin-Jr.	38	8	6	13	59	2	0	0	0	2
2005-06	Suomi U20	Finland-2	5	0	3	3	4	....	....	....	....	....
	Assat Pori Jr.	Fin-Jr.	10	5	6	11	59	2	2	1	3	10
	Assat Pori	Finland	44	3	3	6	106	14	1	3	4	22

KONSORADA, Tim (kawn-sohr-A-duh, TIHM) CBJ

Right wing. Shoots right. 6', 201 lbs. Born, Ft. Saskatchewan, Alta., March 21, 1984.
(Columbus' 8th choice, 168th overall, in 2002 Entry Draft).

			Regular Season					Playoffs				
Season	Club	League	GP	G	A	Pts	PIM	GP	G	A	Pts	PIM
1998-99	Ft. Saskatchewan	ABHL	36	26	45	71	8	....	....	....	....	....
99-2000	Ft. Saskatchewan	AMHL	34	11	23	34	6	....	....	....	....	....
	Brandon	WHL	5	1	2	3	0	....	....	....	....	....
2000-01	Brandon	WHL	67	9	14	23	33	5	2	3	5	11
2001-02	Brandon	WHL	71	17	28	45	36	19	2	11	13	8
2002-03	Brandon	WHL	72	22	48	70	74	17	4	10	14	19
2003-04	Brandon	WHL	25	3	18	21	23	11	2	5	7	8
2004-05	Brandon	WHL	71	29	58	87	43	19	4	11	15	14
2005-06	Syracuse Crunch	AHL	20	3	2	5	7	3	0	0	0	0
	Dayton Bombers	ECHL	54	16	32	48	8	....	....	....	....	....

KONTIOLA, Petri (KAWN-tee-oh-la, PEH-tree) CHI.

Center. Shoots right. 6', 198 lbs. Born, Seinajoki, Finland, October 4, 1984.
(Chicago's 12th choice, 196th overall, in 2004 Entry Draft).

			Regular Season					Playoffs				
Season	Club	League	GP	G	A	Pts	PIM	GP	G	A	Pts	PIM
2001-02	Tappara U18	Fin-U18	22	5	3	8	8	2	1	0	1	2
2002-03	Tappara Jr.	Fin-Jr.	36	7	10	17	12	8	3	3	6	0
2003-04	Suomi U20	Finland-2	6	1	1	2	4	....	....	....	....	....
	Tappara Jr.	Fin-Jr.	12	3	12	15	8	10	4	4	8	10
	Tappara Tampere	Finland	39	4	9	13	29	3	1	1	2	0
2004-05	Tappara Jr.	Fin-Jr.	1	1	0	1	0	....	....	....	....	....
	Tappara Tampere	Finland	54	8	17	25	24	8	2	2	4	2
2005-06	Tappara Tampere	Finland	56	9	*35	44	55	6	1	3	4	0

KOOPMAN, Kevin (KOOP-man, KEH-vihn) OTT.

Defense. Shoots right. 6'3", 200 lbs. Born, Hope, B.C., June 30, 1988.
(Ottawa's 6th choice, 181st overall, in 2006 Entry Draft).

			Regular Season					Playoffs				
Season	Club	League	GP	G	A	Pts	PIM	GP	G	A	Pts	PIM
2004-05	Beaver Valley	KIJHL	41	4	14	18	45	....	....	....	....	....
2005-06	Beaver Valley	KIJHL	38	14	25	39	64	....	....	....	....	....
	Vernon Vipers	BCHL	8	1	0	1	9	....	....	....	....	....

KIJHL MVP (2006)

KOPITAR, Anze (KOH-pee-tahr, AN-zheh) L.A.

Center. Shoots left. 6'4", 220 lbs. Born, Jesenice, Yugoslavia, August 24, 1987.
(Los Angeles' 1st choice, 11th overall, in 2005 Entry Draft).

			Regular Season					Playoffs				
Season	Club	League	GP	G	A	Pts	PIM	GP	G	A	Pts	PIM
2002-03	Jesenice U18	Sloven-U18	14	38	38	76	10	....	....	....	....	....
	Jesenice Jr.	Sloven-Jr.	20	15	12	27	8	....	....	....	....	....
	Kranjska Gora	Slovenia	11	4	4	8	4	....	....	....	....	....
2003-04	Jesenice Jr.	Sloven-Jr.	25	32	28	60	16	....	....	....	....	....
	Kranjska Gora	Slovenia	21	14	11	25	10	4	1	1	2	0
2004-05	Sodertalje SK U18	Swe-U18	1	1	2	3	0	1	0	0	0	2
	Sodertalje SK Jr.	Swe-Jr.	30	28	21	49	26	2	1	1	2	0
	Sodertalje SK	Sweden	5	0	0	0	0	10	0	0	0	0
2005-06	Sodertalje SK	Sweden	47	8	12	20	28	....	....	....	....	....
	Sodertalje SK	Sweden-Q	10	7	4	11	6	....	....	....	....	....

KOREIS, Jakub (KOHR-ays, YA-kuhb) PHX.

Center. Shoots left. 6'3", 214 lbs. Born, Plzen, Czech, June 26, 1984.
(Phoenix's 1st choice, 19th overall, in 2002 Entry Draft).

			Regular Season					Playoffs				
Season	Club	League	GP	G	A	Pts	PIM	GP	G	A	Pts	PIM
99-2000	HC Plzen U17	CzR-U17	41	21	22	43	44	....	....	....	....	....
	HC Plzen Jr.	CzRep-Jr.	3	2	1	3	2	....	....	....	....	....
2000-01	HC Plzen U17	CzR-U17	9	7	10	17	28	....	....	....	....	....
	HC Plzen Jr.	CzRep-Jr.	43	14	15	29	83	....	....	....	....	....
2001-02	HC Plzen Jr.	CzRep-Jr.	23	14	14	28	38	....	....	....	....	....
	HC Keramika Plzen	CzRep	20	3	0	3	10	....	....	....	....	....
2002-03	HC Keramika Plzen	CzRep	23	1	6	7	8	....	....	....	....	....
	HC Plzen Jr.	CzRep-Jr.	10	3	5	8	28	....	....	....	....	....
2003-04	Guelph Storm	OHL	48	11	28	39	85	22	8	10	18	24
2004-05	Utah Grizzlies	AHL	79	5	6	11	96	....	....	....	....	....
2005-06	San Antonio	AHL	70	3	5	8	74	....	....	....	....	....

KORHONEN, Risto (KOHR-hoh-nehn, REE-stoh) CAR.

Defense. Shoots left. 6'3", 202 lbs. Born, Sotkamo, Finland, November 27, 1986.
(Carolina's 7th choice, 159th overall, in 2005 Entry Draft).

			Regular Season					Playoffs				
Season	Club	League	GP	G	A	Pts	PIM	GP	G	A	Pts	PIM
2001-02	Hokki Kajaani	Finland-3	3	0	0	0	0	....	....	....	....	....
2002-03	Karpat Oulu U18	Fin-U18	10	1	6	7	10	1	0	0	0	2
	Karpat Oulu Jr.	Fin-Jr.	24	1	2	3	22	2	0	0	0	0
2003-04	Karpat Oulu U18	Fin-U18	6	0	2	2	18	....	....	....	....	....
	Karpat Oulu Jr.	Fin-Jr.	36	1	3	4	30	5	0	0	0	6
2004-05	Karpat Oulu Jr.	Fin-Jr.	36	5	12	17	73	5	1	1	2	2
2005-06	HPK Jr.	Fin-Jr.	13	0	5	5	28	3	0	0	0	6
	Suomi U20	Finland-2	5	0	0	0	8	....	....	....	....	....
	HPK Hameenlinna	Finland	22	0	0	0	18	8	0	0	0	16

KORNEEV, Konstantin (kor-NEE-ehv, kawn-stuhn-TIHN) MTL.

Defense. Shoots right. 5'11", 176 lbs. Born, Moscow, USSR, June 5, 1984.
(Montreal's 6th choice, 275th overall, in 2002 Entry Draft).

			Regular Season					Playoffs				
Season	Club	League	GP	G	A	Pts	PIM	GP	G	A	Pts	PIM
99-2000	Krylja Sovetov 2	Russia-3	1	0	0	0	0	....	....	....	....	....
2000-01	Russia Jr.	Exhib.	12	0	4	4	10	....	....	....	....	....
2001-02	Krylja Sovetov 2	Russia-3	26	9	19	28	44	....	....	....	....	....
	Krylja Sovetov	Russia	4	0	2	2	0	2	0	0	0	2
2002-03	Krylja Sovetov	Russia	49	2	8	10	28	....	....	....	....	....
2003-04	Ak Bars Kazan	Russia	55	1	4	5	8	8	0	1	1	2
2004-05	Ak Bars Kazan 2	Russia-3	....	6	16	22	....	....	....	....	....	....
	Ak Bars Kazan	Russia	35	0	4	4	10	1	0	0	0	0
2005-06	Ak Bars Kazan	Russia	30	1	3	4	14	4	0	0	0	0

KORPIKARI, Oskari (kohr-pih-KAH-ree, AWS-kahr-ee) MTL.

Defense. Shoots left. 6'2", 208 lbs. Born, Oulu, Finland, April 5, 1984.
(Montreal's 9th choice, 217th overall, in 2003 Entry Draft).

			Regular Season					Playoffs				
Season	Club	League	GP	G	A	Pts	PIM	GP	G	A	Pts	PIM
2001-02	Karpat Oulu U18	Fin-U18	22	7	3	10	16	2	0	0	0	0
	Karpat Oulu Jr.	Fin-Jr.	5	0	0	0	0	....	....	....	....	....
2002-03	Karpat Oulu Jr.	Fin-Jr.	23	3	7	10	8	2	0	0	0	0
	Karpat Oulu	Finland	23	0	1	1	4	15	0	0	0	6
2003-04	Suomi U20	Finland-2	1	0	0	0	0	....	....	....	....	....
	Karpat Oulu Jr.	Fin-Jr.	7	3	1	4	8	....	....	....	....	....
	Karpat Oulu	Finland	35	0	1	1	14	7	0	0	0	2
2004-05	Karpat Oulu Jr.	Fin-Jr.	13	6	6	12	10	5	1	4	5	4
	Karpat Oulu	Finland	21	0	0	0	10	....	....	....	....	....
2005-06	Karpat Oulu	Finland	56	1	1	2	60	11	0	1	1	2

KORPIKOSKI, Lauri (kohr-pih-KAWS-kee, LOW-ree) NYR

Left wing. Shoots left. 6'1", 194 lbs. Born, Turku, Finland, July 28, 1986.
(NY Rangers' 2nd choice, 19th overall, in 2004 Entry Draft).

			Regular Season					Playoffs				
Season	Club	League	GP	G	A	Pts	PIM	GP	G	A	Pts	PIM
2002-03	TPS Turku U18	Fin-U18	21	7	4	11	10	....	....	....	....	....
2003-04	TPS Turku U18	Fin-U18	....	....	....	....	....	4	5	3	8	16
	TPS Turku Jr.	Fin-Jr.	36	12	8	20	20	4	0	2	2	4
2004-05	TPS Turku Jr.	Fin-Jr.	3	3	0	3	0	....	....	....	....	....
	TPS Turku	Finland	41	0	6	6	12	6	1	0	1	0
2005-06	TPS Turku Jr.	Fin-Jr.	1	1	0	1	2	....	....	....	....	....
	Suomi U20	Finland-2	3	1	3	4	0	....	....	....	....	....
	TPS Turku	Finland	51	3	4	7	16	2	0	1	1	0
	Hartford Wolf Pack	AHL	5	2	1	3	0	11	1	0	1	2

KORSUNOV, Vladimir (KOHR-suhn-ahv, vla-DIH-meer) ANA.

Defense. Shoots left. 6'2", 202 lbs. Born, Moscow, USSR, March 16, 1983.
(Anaheim's 5th choice, 105th overall, in 2001 Entry Draft).

			Regular Season					Playoffs				
Season	Club	League	GP	G	A	Pts	PIM	GP	G	A	Pts	PIM
99-2000	Spartak Moscow 2	Russia-3	22	1	11	12	60	....	....	....	....	....
2000-01	Spartak Moscow 2	Russia-3	2	1	0	1	8	....	....	....	....	....
2001-02	Spartak Moscow	Russia	40	0	3	3	28	....	....	....	....	....
2002-03	Spartak Moscow	Russia	42	1	4	5	50	....	....	....	....	....
2003-04	Spartak Moscow	Russia-2	56	1	8	9	66	5	1	0	1	6
2004-05	Spartak Moscow	Russia	43	4	7	11	54	....	....	....	....	....
2005-06	Spartak Moscow	Russia	42	0	6	6	36	3	0	0	0	2
	Spartak Moscow 2	Russia-3	6	0	2	2	8	....	....	....	....	....

KOSMACHEV, Dmitry (kaws-ma-CHEHV, dih-MEE-tree) CBJ

Defense. Shoots right. 6'3", 209 lbs. Born, Nizhny Novgorod, USSR, June 7, 1985.
(Columbus' 3rd choice, 71st overall, in 2003 Entry Draft).

			Regular Season					Playoffs				
Season	Club	League	GP	G	A	Pts	PIM	GP	G	A	Pts	PIM
2001-02	HK CSKA 2	Russia-3	6	1	0	1	2	....	....	....	....	....
	HK CSKA Moscow	Russia-2	49	0	1	1	12	....	....	....	....	....
2002-03	CSKA Moscow	Russia	27	0	0	0	2	....	....	....	....	....
2003-04	CSKA Moscow	Russia	34	0	2	2	12	....	....	....	....	....
2004-05	Nizhny Novgorod	Russia-2	34	3	4	7	22	15	0	1	1	0
2005-06	Mytischi	Russia	38	2	2	4	14	9	0	0	0	4
	Kristall Elektrostal	Russia-3	STATISTICS NOT AVAILABLE									

KOSTITSYN, Sergei (kaws-TIHT-sihn, SAIR-gay) MTL.

Left wing. Shoots left. 6', 197 lbs. Born, Novopolotsk, USSR, March 20, 1987.
(Montreal's 6th choice, 200th overall, in 2005 Entry Draft).

			Regular Season					Playoffs				
Season	Club	League	GP	G	A	Pts	PIM	GP	G	A	Pts	PIM
2003-04	HK Gomel	EEHL	6	0	1	1	0	....	....	....	....	....
	HK Gomel 2	EEHL-B	6	7	2	9	14	....	....	....	....	....
	Yunior Minsk	EEHL-B	STATISTICS NOT AVAILABLE									
	Yunior Minsk	Belarus	3	0	0	0	0	....	....	....	....	....
	HK Gomel	Belarus	22	5	4	9	4	11	1	2	3	8
2004-05	HK Gomel	BelOpen	40	4	10	14	24	4	2	0	2	12
2005-06	London Knights	OHL	63	26	52	78	78	19	13	24	37	*44

KOVERKO, Trevor (KOH-vehr-koh, TREH-vuhr) NYR

Defense. Shoots left. 6'3", 203 lbs. Born, Toronto, Ont., March 22, 1987.
(NY Rangers' 7th choice, 147th overall, in 2005 Entry Draft).

			Regular Season					Playoffs				
Season	Club	League	GP	G	A	Pts	PIM	GP	G	A	Pts	PIM
2003-04	North York	OPJHL	42	2	7	9	82	....	....	....	....	....
2004-05	Owen Sound	OHL	66	1	12	13	83	8	0	2	2	2
2005-06	Owen Sound	OHL	38	0	3	3	49	11	0	0	0	18

KOZAK, Rick (KOH-zak, RIHK) **NYR**

Right wing. Shoots right. 6'2", 215 lbs. Born, Winnipeg, Man., August 19, 1985.
(Philadelphia's 7th choice, 95th overall, in 2003 Entry Draft).

			Regular Season					Playoffs				
Season	Club	League	GP	G	A	Pts	PIM	GP	G	A	Pts	PIM
2000-01	Norman	MMMHL	31	17	27	44	166	....	....	....	....	....
2001-02	Swan Valley	MJHL	35	14	21	35	103	4	0	0	0	4
	Prince George	WHL	4	0	0	0	11	....	....	....	....	....
2002-03	Swan Valley	MJHL	25	17	20	37	99	....	....	....	....	....
	Brandon	WHL	38	9	6	15	87	16	6	5	11	51
2003-04	Brandon	WHL	25	5	3	8	83	....	....	....	....	....
	Kamloops Blazers	WHL	29	9	6	15	77	5	1	0	1	12
	Hartford Wolf Pack	AHL	2	0	1	1	0	....	....	....	....	....
2004-05	Kamloops Blazers	WHL	12	3	0	3	33	....	....	....	....	....
	Prince Albert	WHL	39	11	13	24	152	17	6	3	9	58
2005-06	Hartford Wolf Pack	AHL	3	0	0	0	4	....	....	....	....	....
	Charlotte	ECHL	28	7	9	16	68	3	0	0	0	6

Traded to **NY Rangers** by **Philadelphia** with Philadelphia's 2nd round choice (later traded to Atlanta - Atlanta selected Ondrej Pavelec) in 2005 Entry Draft for Vladimir Malakhov, March 8, 2004.

KOZEK, Andrew (KOH-zehk, AN-droo) **ATL.**

Wing. Shoots left. 5'10", 190 lbs. Born, Revelstoke, B.C., May 26, 1986.
(Atlanta's 4th choice, 53rd overall, in 2005 Entry Draft).

			Regular Season					Playoffs				
Season	Club	League	GP	G	A	Pts	PIM	GP	G	A	Pts	PIM
2003-04	South Surrey	BCHL	58	19	22	41	67	....	....	....	....	....
2004-05	South Surrey	BCHL	60	48	49	97	81	....	....	....	....	....
2005-06	North Dakota	WCHA	46	7	6	13	22	....	....	....	....	....

KREJCI, Dave (KRIGH-chee, DAYV) **BOS.**

Center. Shoots right. 5'11", 176 lbs. Born, Sternberk, Czech., April 28, 1986.
(Boston's 1st choice, 63rd overall, in 2004 Entry Draft).

			Regular Season					Playoffs				
Season	Club	League	GP	G	A	Pts	PIM	GP	G	A	Pts	PIM
2000-01	HC Olomouc U17	CzR-U17	26	2	6	8	4	3	1	1	2	0
2001-02	HC Trinec U17	CzR-U17	48	32	27	59	30	6	2	4	6	2
2002-03	HC Trinec U17	CzR-U17	22	12	24	36	42	....	....	....	....	....
	HC Trinec Jr.	CzRep-Jr.	12	4	5	9	2	12	5	5	10	8
2003-04	HC Kladno Jr.	CzRep-Jr.	50	23	37	60	37	7	3	6	9	4
2004-05	Gatineau	QMJHL	62	22	41	63	31	10	2	7	9	10
2005-06	Gatineau	QMJHL	55	27	54	81	54	17	10	22	32	24

KREPS, Kamil (KREHPS, KA-mihl) **FLA.**

Center. Shoots right. 6'1", 190 lbs. Born, Litomerice, Czech., November 18, 1984.
(Florida's 3rd choice, 38th overall, in 2003 Entry Draft).

			Regular Season					Playoffs				
Season	Club	League	GP	G	A	Pts	PIM	GP	G	A	Pts	PIM
99-2000	Litvinov Jr.	CzRep-Jr.	48	18	16	34	10	....	....	....	....	....
2000-01	Litvinov Jr.	CzRep-Jr.	47	16	23	39	6	6	2	6	8	10
2001-02	Brampton	OHL	68	19	24	43	14	....	....	....	....	....
2002-03	Brampton	OHL	53	19	42	61	12	11	3	5	8	4
2003-04	Brampton	OHL	57	19	27	46	19	12	7	8	15	2
2004-05	San Antonio	AHL	58	5	6	11	11	....	....	....	....	....
	Texas Wildcatters	ECHL	12	5	6	11	6	....	....	....	....	....
2005-06	Rochester	AHL	61	13	19	32	20	....	....	....	....	....

KRIKUNOV, Ilya (krih-koo-NAWF, IHL-yah) **VAN.**

Left wing. Shoots left. 5'11", 169 lbs. Born, Elektrostal, USSR, February 27, 1984.
(Vancouver's 8th choice, 223rd overall, in 2002 Entry Draft).

			Regular Season					Playoffs				
Season	Club	League	GP	G	A	Pts	PIM	GP	G	A	Pts	PIM
2000-01	Elektrostal 2	Russia-3	4	0	0	0	2	....	....	....	....	....
2001-02	Elektrostal 2	Russia-3	5	3	6	9	4	....	....	....	....	....
	Elektrostal	Russia-2	48	12	10	22	28	....	....	....	....	....
2002-03	Elektrostal	Russia-2	48	19	9	28	34	....	....	....	....	....
2003-04	Voskresensk	Russia	50	10	9	19	14	....	....	....	....	....
2004-05	Voskresensk	Russia	58	9	14	23	20	....	....	....	....	....
2005-06	Mytischi	Russia	46	10	5	15	57	8	1	1	2	2
	Kristall Elektrostal	Russia-3	STATISTICS NOT AVAILABLE									

KRUCHININ, Andrei (kroo-CHIHN-ihn, AWN-dray) **MTL.**

Defense. Shoots left. 5'11", 187 lbs. Born, Karaganda, USSR, May 18, 1978.
(Montreal's 7th choice, 189th overall, in 1998 Entry Draft).

			Regular Season					Playoffs				
Season	Club	League	GP	G	A	Pts	PIM	GP	G	A	Pts	PIM
1996-97	Lada Togliatti	Russia	19	0	1	1	8	11	0	0	0	0
1997-98	Lada Togliatti	Russia	43	0	4	4	73	....	....	....	....	....
1998-99	Lada Togliatti	Russia	41	1	4	5	56	6	0	1	1	2
99-2000	Lada Togliatti	Russia	25	1	2	3	24	6	1	0	1	4
	CSK VVS Samara	Russia	6	1	0	1	0	....	....	....	....	....
2000-01	Perm	Russia	14	1	3	4	10	....	....	....	....	....
	Lada Togliatti	Russia	14	0	2	2	12	3	0	0	0	0
2001-02	Avangard Omsk	Russia	21	0	0	0	6	....	....	....	....	....
	Nizhnekamsk	Russia	17	1	3	4	8	....	....	....	....	....
2002-03	Nizhnekamsk	Russia	30	1	6	7	16	....	....	....	....	....
2003-04	Nizhnekamsk	Russia	49	2	6	8	53	5	1	1	2	4
2004-05	Lada Togliatti	Russia	32	3	4	7	24	7	0	1	1	2
2005-06	Lada Togliatti	Russia	35	6	5	11	67	8	0	2	2	4

KRUEGER, Justin (KROO-guhr, JUHS-tihn) **CAR.**

Defense. Shoots right. 6'2", 205 lbs. Born, Winnipeg, Man., October 6, 1986.
(Carolina's 6th choice, 213th overall, in 2006 Entry Draft).

			Regular Season					Playoffs				
Season	Club	League	GP	G	A	Pts	PIM	GP	G	A	Pts	PIM
2002-03	HC Davos Jr.	Swiss-Jr.	12	0	0	0	4	2	0	0	0	0
2003-04	HC Davos Jr.	Swiss-Jr.	33	2	0	2	14	....	....	....	....	....
2004-05	HC Davos Jr.	Swiss-Jr.	38	5	12	17	76	4	1	2	3	2
2005-06	Penticton Vees	BCHL	55	7	15	22	25	....	....	....	....	....

Signed Letter of Intent to attend **Cornell** (ECACHL) in fall of 2006.

KRYSANOV, Anton (KREE-sa-nahf, AN-tawn) **PHX.**

Center. Shoots left. 6'3", 198 lbs. Born, Togliatti, USSR, March 25, 1987.
(Phoenix's 4th choice, 148th overall, in 2005 Entry Draft).

			Regular Season					Playoffs				
Season	Club	League	GP	G	A	Pts	PIM	GP	G	A	Pts	PIM
2002-03	Lada Togliatti 2	Russia-3	9	1	3	4	2	....	....	....	....	....
2003-04	Lada Togliatti 2	Russia-3	18	2	3	5	2	....	....	....	....	....
2004-05	Lada Togliatti 2	Russia-3	34	13	13	26	32	....	....	....	....	....
	Lada Togliatti	Russia	15	1	0	1	2	....	....	....	....	....
2005-06	Lada Togliatti	Russia	46	3	3	6	24	8	0	0	0	2

KRYUKOV, Artem (KREE-oo-kahf, AHR-tehm) **BUF.**

Center. Shoots left. 6'3", 180 lbs. Born, Novosibirsk, USSR, March 5, 1982.
(Buffalo's 1st choice, 15th overall, in 2000 Entry Draft).

			Regular Season					Playoffs				
Season	Club	League	GP	G	A	Pts	PIM	GP	G	A	Pts	PIM
1997-98	Torpedo Yaroslavl	Russia	7	0	0	0	2	....	....	....	....	....
1998-99	Yaroslavl 2	Russia-3	20	2	2	4	6	....	....	....	....	....
99-2000	Yaroslavl 2	Russia-3	14	1	1	2	12	....	....	....	....	....
	Torpedo Yaroslavl	Russia	3	0	0	0	4	....	....	....	....	....
2000-01	Yaroslavl 2	Russia-3	6	0	0	0	2	11	0	0	0	8
	SKA St. Petersburg	Russia	14	0	2	2	14	....	....	....	....	....
2001-02	Yaroslavl	Russia	15	1	3	4	10	6	1	0	1	8
2002-03	Sibir Novosibirsk	Russia	9	0	0	0	27	....	....	....	....	....
2003-04	Yaroslavl 2	Russia-3	30	5	4	9	26	....	....	....	....	....
	Yaroslavl	Russia	4	0	2	2	0	....	....	....	....	....
2004-05	Yaroslavl	Russia	60	8	9	17	44	7	1	0	1	4
2005-06	Yaroslavl	Russia	33	1	2	3	42	1	0	0	0	0
	Yaroslavl 2	Russia-3	6	3	3	6	18	....	....	....	....	....

KUCHEJDA, David (koo-HAY-dah, DAH-vihd) **CHI.**

Right wing. Shoots left. 5'10", 187 lbs. Born, Havirov, Czech., June 12, 1987.
(Chicago's 11th choice, 202nd overall, in 2005 Entry Draft).

			Regular Season					Playoffs				
Season	Club	League	GP	G	A	Pts	PIM	GP	G	A	Pts	PIM
2002-03	C. Budejovice U17	CzR-U17	45	23	29	52	34	6	3	4	7	6
2003-04	C. Budejovice U17	CzR-U17	3	2	1	3	31	2	1	0	1	16
	C. Budejovice Jr.	CzRep-Jr.	47	7	12	19	40	....	....	....	....	....
2004-05	C. Budejovice	CzRep-2	1	0	0	0	0	....	....	....	....	....
	C. Budejovice Jr.	CzRep-Jr.	42	12	28	40	142	2	1	1	2	2
2005-06	Sault Ste. Marie	OHL	67	19	21	40	80	4	0	1	1	8

KUDELKA, Tomas (koo-DEHL-kah, TAW-mash) **OTT.**

Defense. Shoots left. 6'2", 176 lbs. Born, Gottwaldov, Czech., March 10, 1987.
(Ottawa's 6th choice, 136th overall, in 2005 Entry Draft).

			Regular Season					Playoffs				
Season	Club	League	GP	G	A	Pts	PIM	GP	G	A	Pts	PIM
2002-03	HC Zlin U17	CzR-U17	45	1	16	17	28	3	1	0	1	12
2003-04	HC Zlin U17	CzR-U17	1	0	0	0	2	3	0	0	0	0
	HC Zlin Jr.	CzRep-Jr.	51	1	12	13	95	7	0	0	0	0
	HC Hame Zlin	CzRep	3	0	0	0	0	....	....	....	....	....
2004-05	HC Zlin Jr.	CzRep-Jr.	38	9	8	17	38	....	....	....	....	....
	HC Hame Zlin	CzRep	4	0	0	0	6	....	....	....	....	....
2005-06	Lethbridge	WHL	64	6	25	31	77	6	1	1	2	12
	Binghamton	AHL	5	0	0	0	4	....	....	....	....	....

KUHTINOV, Roman (kukh-TEEN-nawv, ROH-muhn) **NYI**

Defense. Shoots left. 6'1", 207 lbs. Born, Belgorod, USSR, December 1, 1975.
(NY Islanders' 7th choice, 280th overall, in 2001 Entry Draft).

			Regular Season					Playoffs				
Season	Club	League	GP	G	A	Pts	PIM	GP	G	A	Pts	PIM
1997-98	Raichikhinsk	Russia-3	36	18	8	26	46	....	....	....	....	....
1998-99	Novokuznetsk	Russia	42	2	9	11	26	6	0	0	0	2
99-2000	Novokuznetsk	Russia	37	2	6	8	28	14	1	1	2	8
2000-01	Novokuznetsk	Russia	44	7	10	17	36	....	....	....	....	....
2001-02	Ufa	Russia	51	11	10	21	74	....	....	....	....	....
2002-03	Ufa	Russia	50	4	7	11	72	3	2	0	2	4
2003-04	Cherepovets	Russia	54	2	6	8	46	....	....	....	....	....
2004-05	Magnitogorsk	Russia	53	3	8	11	24	5	0	0	0	2
2005-06	Magnitogorsk	Russia	32	0	4	4	18	....	....	....	....	....

KUIPER, Nick (KIGH-puhr, NIHK)

Defense. Shoots right. 6'3", 215 lbs. Born, Beaconsfield, Que., February 12, 1982.

			Regular Season					Playoffs				
Season	Club	League	GP	G	A	Pts	PIM	GP	G	A	Pts	PIM
1998-99	Lac St-Louis Lions	QAAA	42	3	23	26	36	5	0	3	3	4
99-2000	Hawkesbury	CJHL	46	7	22	29	40	....	....	....	....	....
2000-01	Hawkesbury	CJHL	32	7	10	17	22	....	....	....	....	....
	Massachusetts	H-East	13	0	1	1	2	....	....	....	....	....
2001-02	Massachusetts	H-East	32	2	9	11	10	....	....	....	....	....
2002-03	Massachusetts	H-East	36	3	3	6	34	....	....	....	....	....
2003-04	Massachusetts	H-East	37	5	5	10	72	....	....	....	....	....
2004-05	Norfolk Admirals	AHL	73	3	5	8	109	5	0	0	0	2
2005-06	Norfolk Admirals	AHL	70	2	7	9	104	1	0	0	0	0

Signed as a free agent by **Chicago**, March 31, 2004.

KUKUMBERG, Roman (KOO-kuhm-buhrg, ROH-muhn)

Center. Shoots right. 6'1", 198 lbs. Born, Bratislava, Czech., April 8, 1980.
(Toronto's 2nd choice, 113th overall, in 2004 Entry Draft).

			Regular Season					Playoffs				
Season	Club	League	GP	G	A	Pts	PIM	GP	G	A	Pts	PIM
2001-02	Dukla Trencin	Slovakia	46	12	9	21	20	4	0	0	0	2
2002-03	Dukla Trencin	Slovakia	53	18	18	36	60	12	6	5	11	12
2003-04	Dukla Trencin	Slovakia	51	16	20	36	93	11	4	8	12	14
2004-05	Nizhnekamsk	Russia	55	10	11	21	40	3	0	0	0	4
2005-06	Toronto Marlies	AHL	54	2	6	8	30	....	....	....	....	....

Signed as a free agent by **Nizhnekamsk** (Russia), June 28, 2006.

KUKUSHKIN, Sergei (koo-KOOSH-kihn, SAIR-gay) **DAL.**

Center. Shoots left. 6'2", 187 lbs. Born, Minsk, USSR, July 24, 1985.
(Dallas' 8th choice, 218th overall, in 2004 Entry Draft).

			Regular Season					Playoffs				
Season	Club	League	GP	G	A	Pts	PIM	GP	G	A	Pts	PIM
2003-04	Yunost Minsk	Belarus	STATISTICS NOT AVAILABLE									
2004-05	N.E. Jr. Falcons	EJHL	21	9	13	22	30	....	....	....	....	....
	Indiana Ice	USHL	19	1	2	3	50	....	....	....	....	....
2005-06	Kapitan Stupino	Russia-2	45	21	11	32	67	8	4	3	7	10

KULDA , Arturs (KOOL-da, AHR-tuhrs) ATL.

Defense. Shoots left. 6'2", 194 lbs. Born, Riga, Latvia, July 25, 1988.
(Atlanta's 7th choice, 200th overall, in 2006 Entry Draft).

			Regular Season					Playoffs				
Season	Club	League	GP	G	A	Pts	PIM	GP	G	A	Pts	PIM
2003-04	Prizma/Riga 86	Latvia	11	0	0	0	8	2	0	0	0	0
2004-05	CSKA Moscow 2	Russia-3	STATISTICS NOT AVAILABLE									
2005-06	CSKA Moscow 2	Russia-3	44	5	12	17	....	....	....	....	....	....

KULEMIN, Nikolai (koo-LAY-mihn, NIH-koh-ligh) TOR.

Wing. Shoots left. 6'1", 183 lbs. Born, Magnitogorsk, Russia, July 14, 1986.
(Toronto's 2nd choice, 44th overall, in 2006 Entry Draft).

			Regular Season					Playoffs				
Season	Club	League	GP	G	A	Pts	PIM	GP	G	A	Pts	PIM
2003-04	Magnitogorsk 2	Russia-3	43	8	18	26	91	....	....	....	....	....
2004-05	Magnitogorsk 2	Russia-3	43	9	13	22	44	....	....	....	....	....
2005-06	Magnitogorsk	Russia	31	5	7	12	8	11	2	4	6	6
	Magnitogorsk 2	Russia-3	4	3	1	4	6	....	....	....	....	....

KULYASH, Denis (kuh-L'YASH, DEH-nihs) NSH.

Defense. Shoots left. 6'2", 199 lbs. Born, Omsk, USSR, May 31, 1983.
(Nashville's 9th choice, 243rd overall, in 2004 Entry Draft).

			Regular Season					Playoffs				
Season	Club	League	GP	G	A	Pts	PIM	GP	G	A	Pts	PIM
2003-04	CSK VVS Samara 2	Russia-3	STATISTICS NOT AVAILABLE									
	CSKA Moscow	Russia	10	1	0	1	8	....	....	....	....	....
2004-05	CSKA Moscow	Russia	59	8	10	18	58	....	....	....	....	....
2005-06	Dynamo Moscow	Russia	44	12	5	17	117	4	0	2	2	6
	Russia	Olympics	DID NOT PLAY – INJURED									

KUNES, Tim (KOONZ, TIHM) CAR.

Defense. Shoots left. 6'1", 170 lbs. Born, Red Bank, NJ, February 12, 1987.
(Carolina's 6th choice, 145th overall, in 2005 Entry Draft).

			Regular Season					Playoffs				
Season	Club	League	GP	G	A	Pts	PIM	GP	G	A	Pts	PIM
2003-04	N.E. Jr. Falcons	EJHL	45	4	19	23	20	....	....	....	....	....
2004-05	N.E. Jr. Falcons	EJHL	50	12	28	40	51	....	....	....	....	....
2005-06	Boston College	H-East	28	1	3	4	31	....	....	....	....	....

KVAPIL, Marek (kuh-VAH-puhl, MAHR-ehk) T.B.

Right wing. Shoots right. 5'10", 192 lbs. Born, Ilava, Czech., January 5, 1985.
(Tampa Bay's 7th choice, 163rd overall, in 2005 Entry Draft).

			Regular Season					Playoffs				
Season	Club	League	GP	G	A	Pts	PIM	GP	G	A	Pts	PIM
2002-03	HC Slavia Praha Jr.	CzRep-Jr.	33	9	4	13	4	2	0	0	0	0
2003-04	HC Slavia Praha Jr.	CzRep-Jr.	42	19	17	36	43	2	1	0	1	0
	HC Slavia Praha	CzRep	11	0	0	0	0	....	....	....	....	....
	HC Kometa Brno	CzRep-2	4	0	2	2	4	....	....	....	....	....
2004-05	HC Slavia Praha Jr.	CzRep-Jr.	8	6	4	10	8	....	....	....	....	....
	Saginaw Spirit	OHL	53	25	37	62	14	....	....	....	....	....
2005-06	Springfield Falcons	AHL	79	18	27	45	24	....	....	....	....	....

KVETON, David (KVEH-tuhn, DAY-vihd) NYR

Right wing. Shoots left. 5'11", 180 lbs. Born, Novy Jincin, Czech., January 3, 1988.
(NY Rangers' 4th choice, 104th overall, in 2006 Entry Draft).

			Regular Season					Playoffs				
Season	Club	League	GP	G	A	Pts	PIM	GP	G	A	Pts	PIM
2003-04	HC Vsetin U17	CzR-U17	14	9	11	20	35	....	....	....	....	....
	HC Vsetin Jr.	CzRep-Jr.	41	12	11	23	14	5	2	3	5	2
	TJ Novy Jicin	CzRep-3	1	0	1	1	0	....	....	....	....	....
	HC Vsetin	CzRep	1	0	0	0	0	....	....	....	....	....
2004-05	HC Vsetin U17	CzR-U17	1	1	0	1	0	....	....	....	....	....
	HC Vsetin Jr.	CzRep-Jr.	36	21	27	48	66	8	6	5	11	4
	TJ Novy Jicin	CzRep-3	7	0	1	1	6	....	....	....	....	....
	HC Vsetin	CzRep	6	1	0	1	0	....	....	....	....	....
2005-06	HC Vsetin Jr.	CzRep-Jr.	1	1	1	2	0	1	0	1	1	0
	HC Sareza Ostrava	CzRep-2	7	2	1	3	2	....	....	....	....	....
	HC Vsetin	CzRep	45	6	4	10	18	....	....	....	....	....
	TJ Novy Jicin	CzRep-3	....	....	....	....	....	5	5	0	5	18
	HC Vsetin	CzRep-Q	....	....	....	....	....	3	1	1	2	2

LAAKSO, Teemu (LAK-soh, TEE-moo) NSH.

Defense. Shoots right. 6', 200 lbs. Born, Tuusula, Finland, August 27, 1987.
(Nashville's 2nd choice, 78th overall, in 2005 Entry Draft).

			Regular Season					Playoffs				
Season	Club	League	GP	G	A	Pts	PIM	GP	G	A	Pts	PIM
2002-03	KJT Jarvenpaa U18	Fin-U18	18	2	5	7	24	....	....	....	....	....
2003-04	HIFK Helsinki Jr.	Fin-Jr.	41	3	6	9	20	3	0	1	1	0
2004-05	HIFK Helsinki U18	Fin-U18	....	....	....	....	....	1	0	0	0	0
	HIFK Helsinki Jr.	Fin-Jr.	20	5	4	9	18	....	....	....	....	....
	HIFK Helsinki	Finland	15	0	2	2	2	....	....	....	....	....
2005-06	HIFK Helsinki Jr.	Fin-Jr.	6	1	2	3	32	....	....	....	....	....
	Suomi U20	Finland-2	6	2	0	2	10	....	....	....	....	....
	HIFK Helsinki	Finland	47	2	1	3	20	8	1	0	1	0

LACROIX, Maxime (luh-KWAH, max-EEM) WSH.

Left wing. Shoots left. 6', 180 lbs. Born, Quebec City, Que., June 5, 1987.
(Washington's 8th choice, 127th overall, in 2006 Entry Draft).

			Regular Season					Playoffs				
Season	Club	League	GP	G	A	Pts	PIM	GP	G	A	Pts	PIM
2003-04	St-Francois	QAAA	42	21	21	42	47	8	3	1	4	8
2004-05	Quebec Remparts	QMJHL	49	6	8	14	34	13	0	0	0	8
2005-06	Quebec Remparts	QMJHL	70	25	22	47	79	23	7	5	12	21

LAGERSTROM, Tony (LA-guhr-struhm, TOH-nee) CHI.

Center. Shoots left. 6'1", 183 lbs. Born, Stockholm, Sweden, July 19, 1988.
(Chicago's 4th choice, 76th overall, in 2006 Entry Draft).

			Regular Season					Playoffs				
Season	Club	League	GP	G	A	Pts	PIM	GP	G	A	Pts	PIM
2003-04	Huddinge IK U18	Swe-U18	12	5	1	6	6	....	....	....	....	....
2004-05	Sodertalje SK U18	Swe-U18	2	3	2	5	4	1	0	0	0	0
	Sodertalje SK Jr.	Swe-Jr.	28	13	11	24	16	3	2	1	3	2
2005-06	Sodertalje SK U18	Swe-U18	7	9	5	14	2	1	0	0	0	0
	Sodertalje SK Jr.	Swe-Jr.	37	14	19	33	69	4	1	2	3	14
	Sodertalje SK	Sweden	1	0	0	0	0	....	....	....	....	....

LALIBERTE, John (la-LIH-buhr-tee, JAWN) VAN.

Right wing. Shoots left. 6'2", 190 lbs. Born, Portland, ME, August 5, 1983.
(Vancouver's 5th choice, 114th overall, in 2002 Entry Draft).

			Regular Season					Playoffs				
Season	Club	League	GP	G	A	Pts	PIM	GP	G	A	Pts	PIM
99-2000	Thornton	High-ME	STATISTICS NOT AVAILABLE									
	Exeter Snow Devils	EJHL	32	37	40	77	60	....	....	....	....	....
2000-01	Exeter Snow Devils	EJHL	53	33	42	75	42	....	....	....	....	....
2001-02	N.H. Jr. Monarchs	EJHL	35	39	44	*83	60	....	8	12	20	....
2002-03	Boston University	H-East	26	5	6	11	12	....	....	....	....	....
2003-04	Boston University	H-East	35	5	11	16	20	....	....	....	....	....
2004-05	Boston University	H-East	40	12	18	30	45	....	....	....	....	....
2005-06	Boston University	H-East	33	11	21	32	28	....	....	....	....	....

LAMBERT, Michael (lam-BAIR, MIGH-kuhl) MTL.

Left wing. Shoots left. 6'2", 203 lbs. Born, Trois-Rivieres, Que., March 10, 1984.
(Montreal's 3rd choice, 99th overall, in 2002 Entry Draft).

			Regular Season					Playoffs				
Season	Club	League	GP	G	A	Pts	PIM	GP	G	A	Pts	PIM
1998-99	Cap-d-Madeleine	QAAA	3	0	0	0	0	....	....	....	....	....
99-2000	Cap-d-Madeleine	QAAA	42	20	16	36	38	1	0	2	2	0
2000-01	Acadie-Bathurst	QMJHL	23	2	5	7	15	....	....	....	....	....
	Montreal Rocket	QMJHL	33	6	12	18	14	....	....	....	....	....
2001-02	Montreal Rocket	QMJHL	71	29	24	53	111	7	1	6	7	15
2002-03	Montreal Rocket	QMJHL	71	28	32	60	53	7	2	2	4	10
2003-04	PEI Rocket	QMJHL	67	42	42	84	53	11	6	7	13	6
2004-05	Hamilton Bulldogs	AHL	40	3	4	7	18	....	....	....	....	....
	Long Beach	ECHL	18	5	4	9	26	7	5	1	6	14
2005-06	Hamilton Bulldogs	AHL	39	10	7	17	25	....	....	....	....	....
	Long Beach	ECHL	20	11	7	18	16	5	2	1	3	12

LAMMERS, John (LA-muhrs, JAWN) DAL.

Left wing. Shoots left. 5'11", 184 lbs. Born, Bowmanville, Ont., January 29, 1986.
(Dallas' 5th choice, 86th overall, in 2004 Entry Draft).

			Regular Season					Playoffs				
Season	Club	League	GP	G	A	Pts	PIM	GP	G	A	Pts	PIM
2001-02	Langley Bantams	BCAHA	64	51	69	120	30	....	....	....	....	....
	Lethbridge	WHL	5	0	0	0	0	....	....	....	....	....
2002-03	Lethbridge	WHL	53	17	15	32	11	....	....	....	....	....
2003-04	Lethbridge	WHL	62	21	24	45	31	....	....	....	....	....
2004-05	Lethbridge	WHL	66	17	30	47	43	5	0	0	0	2
2005-06	Everett Silvertips	WHL	70	38	37	75	25	15	5	6	11	12

LANNON, Ryan (LA-nuhn, RIGH-uhn) PIT.

Defense. Shoots left. 6'2", 220 lbs. Born, Worcester, MA, December 14, 1982.
(Pittsburgh's 10th choice, 239th overall, in 2002 Entry Draft).

			Regular Season					Playoffs				
Season	Club	League	GP	G	A	Pts	PIM	GP	G	A	Pts	PIM
1998-99	USNTDP	NAHL	56	3	4	7	36	....	....	....	....	....
99-2000	Cushing	High-MA	STATISTICS NOT AVAILABLE									
2000-01	Cushing	High-MA	STATISTICS NOT AVAILABLE									
2001-02	Harvard Crimson	ECAC	34	0	2	2	38	....	....	....	....	....
2002-03	Harvard Crimson	ECAC	34	3	11	14	39	....	....	....	....	....
2003-04	Harvard Crimson	ECAC	35	0	9	9	36	....	....	....	....	....
2004-05	Harvard Crimson	ECACHL	33	1	12	13	34	....	....	....	....	....
2005-06	Wilkes-Barre	AHL	74	2	8	10	65	11	0	0	0	8

LAPOINT, Derrick (luh-POYNT, DAIR-rihk) FLA.

Defense. Shoots left. 6'2", 175 lbs. Born, Eau Claire, MA, May 13, 1988.
(Florida's 4th choice, 116th overall, in 2006 Entry Draft).

			Regular Season					Playoffs				
Season	Club	League	GP	G	A	Pts	PIM	GP	G	A	Pts	PIM
2004-05	Eau Claire North	High-WI	23	9	28	37	14					
2005-06	Eau Claire North	High-WI	23	6	26	32	34					

LARMAN, Drew (LAHR-man, DROO) FLA.

Center. Shoots right. 6'3", 188 lbs. Born, Canton, MI, May 15, 1985.

			Regular Season					Playoffs				
Season	Club	League	GP	G	A	Pts	PIM	GP	G	A	Pts	PIM
2002-03	Sarnia Sting	OHL	67	4	14	18	25	....	....	....	....	....
2003-04	Sarnia Sting	OHL	68	9	18	27	13	5	0	1	1	0
2004-05	Sarnia Sting	OHL	12	2	0	2	6	....	....	....	....	....
	London Knights	OHL	58	11	10	21	28	18	3	4	7	8
2005-06	Rochester	AHL	44	7	8	15	24	....	....	....	....	....
	Florida Everblades	ECHL	6	0	0	0	4	8	4	2	6	4

Signed as a free agent by **Florida**, September 28, 2005.

LASCEK, Stanislav (LASH-chehk, STAHN-ihs-lahv) T.B.

Right wing. Shoots left. 6', 195 lbs. Born, Martin, Czech., January 17, 1986.
(Tampa Bay's 6th choice, 133rd overall, in 2005 Entry Draft).

			Regular Season					Playoffs				
Season	Club	League	GP	G	A	Pts	PIM	GP	G	A	Pts	PIM
2002-03	HKm Zvolen	Slovakia	1	0	0	0	2	....	....	....	....	....
	HKm Zvolen B	Slovak-2	19	2	4	6	29	....	....	....	....	....
2003-04	Chicoutimi	QMJHL	59	17	40	57	49	18	5	13	18	30
2004-05	Chicoutimi	QMJHL	53	18	72	90	42	17	4	18	22	26
2005-06	Chicoutimi	QMJHL	64	47	88	135	96	9	4	13	17	8

QMJHL Second All-Star Team (2006)

LASHOFF, Matt (LASH-awf, MAT) BOS.

Defense. Shoots left. 6'1", 201 lbs. Born, East Greenbush, NY, September 29, 1986.
(Boston's 1st choice, 22nd overall, in 2005 Entry Draft).

			Regular Season					Playoffs				
Season	Club	League	GP	G	A	Pts	PIM	GP	G	A	Pts	PIM
2002-03	USNTDP	U-17	16	1	3	4	14	....	....	....	....	....
	USNTDP	NAHL	46	2	5	7	53	....	....	....	....	....
2003-04	Kitchener Rangers	OHL	62	5	19	24	94	5	0	1	1	0
2004-05	Kitchener Rangers	OHL	44	4	18	22	44	13	0	3	3	18
2005-06	Kitchener Rangers	OHL	56	7	40	47	146	5	1	1	2	12
	Providence Bruins	AHL	7	1	1	2	6	6	0	0	0	6

LATAL, Martin (LAH-tuhl, MAHR-tihn) PHX.

Right wing. Shoots left. 5'11", 174 lbs. Born, Olomouc, Czech., March 17, 1988.
(Phoenix's 5th choice, 131st overall, in 2006 Entry Draft).

			Regular Season					Playoffs				
Season	Club	League	GP	G	A	Pts	PIM	GP	G	A	Pts	PIM
2002-03	Sparta U17	CzR-U17	24	2	6	8	12	2	0	0	0	0
2003-04	HC Kladno U17	CzR-U17	48	15	16	31	69	2	0	1	1	0
	HC Kladno Jr.	CzRep-Jr.	1	0	0	0	0	....	....	....	....	....
2004-05	HC Kladno U17	CzR-U17	3	3	3	6	22	4	3	1	4	10
	HC Kladno Jr.	CzRep-Jr.	41	7	8	15	86	6	1	1	2	12
2005-06	HC Plzen Jr.	CzRep-Jr.	6	2	1	3	2	....	....	....	....	....
	Plzen	CzRep	5	0	0	0	4	....	....	....	....	....
	HC Kladno Jr.	CzRep-Jr.	24	14	9	23	62	7	4	1	5	8
	HC Rabat Kladno	CzRep	20	0	0	0	0	....	....	....	....	....

LATENDRESSE, Guillaume (lah-TEHN-drehs, gee-OHM) MTL.

Right wing. Shoots left. 6'2", 225 lbs. Born, Ste-Catherine, Que., May 24, 1987.
(Montreal's 2nd choice, 45th overall, in 2005 Entry Draft).

			Regular Season					Playoffs				
Season	Club	League	GP	G	A	Pts	PIM	GP	G	A	Pts	PIM
2003-04	Drummondville	QMJHL	53	24	25	49	66	....	....	....	....	....
2004-05	Drummondville	QMJHL	65	29	49	78	76	6	6	4	10	7
2005-06	Drummondville	QMJHL	51	43	40	83	105	5	3	2	5	8

QMJHL All-Rookie Team (2004)

LATENDRESSE, Olivier (la-TEHN-drehs, oh-LIHV-ee-ay) PHX.

Center. Shoots left. 5'10", 195 lbs. Born, LaSalle, Que., February 12, 1986.

			Regular Season					Playoffs				
Season	Club	League	GP	G	A	Pts	PIM	GP	G	A	Pts	PIM
2002-03	Val-d'Or Foreurs	QMJHL	55	11	14	25	22	8	0	2	2	0
2003-04	Val-d'Or Foreurs	QMJHL	53	19	46	65	44	7	1	5	6	14
2004-05	Val-d'Or Foreurs	QMJHL	68	27	47	74	34	....	....	....	....	....
2005-06	Val-d'Or Foreurs	QMJHL	70	41	84	125	83	4	5	2	7	2

Signed as a free agent by **Phoenix**, September 15, 2004.

LaVALLEE, Jordan (LAV-alee, JOHR-dahn) ATL.

Left wing. Shoots left. 6'3", 215 lbs. Born, Corvallis, OR, May 11, 1986.
(Atlanta's 5th choice, 116th overall, in 2005 Entry Draft).

			Regular Season					Playoffs				
Season	Club	League	GP	G	A	Pts	PIM	GP	G	A	Pts	PIM
2002-03	Quebec Remparts	QMJHL	55	3	6	9	54	11	0	1	1	0
2003-04	Quebec Remparts	QMJHL	69	11	16	27	111	5	2	0	2	6
2004-05	Quebec Remparts	QMJHL	64	40	26	66	108	13	5	2	7	26
2005-06	Quebec Remparts	QMJHL	37	18	19	37	34	23	7	8	15	30

LAVRENTIEV, Anton (lahv-REHN-tee-yehv, AN-tawn) NSH.

Defense. Shoots right. 6'4", 196 lbs. Born, Kazan, USSR, August 25, 1983.
(Nashville's 7th choice, 178th overall, in 2001 Entry Draft).

			Regular Season					Playoffs				
Season	Club	League	GP	G	A	Pts	PIM	GP	G	A	Pts	PIM
2000-01	Ak Bars Kazan 2	Russia-3	STATISTICS NOT AVAILABLE									
2001-02	Sudbury Wolves	OHL	10	0	0	0	17	....	....	....	....	....
	Ak Bars Kazan 2	Russia-3	STATISTICS NOT AVAILABLE									
2002-03	Yuzhny Ural Orsk	Russia-2	13	0	1	1	14	....	....	....	....	....
2003-04	HK Rybinsk	Russia-2	31	2	1	3	49	....	....	....	....	....
2004-05	Novopolotsk	BelOpen	23	2	3	5	26	1	0	0	0	2
2005-06	Naber. Chelny	Russia-3	70	8	6	14	214	....	....	....	....	....

LAWRENCE, Chris (LOH-rehnts, KRIHS) T.B.

Center. Shoots right. 6'4", 212 lbs. Born, Toronto, Ont., February 5, 1987.
(Tampa Bay's 3rd choice, 89th overall, in 2005 Entry Draft).

			Regular Season					Playoffs				
Season	Club	League	GP	G	A	Pts	PIM	GP	G	A	Pts	PIM
2003-04	Sault Ste. Marie	OHL	62	7	6	13	34	....	....	....	....	....
2004-05	Sault Ste. Marie	OHL	68	11	40	51	57	7	3	3	6	4
2005-06	Sault Ste. Marie	OHL	29	3	14	17	31	....	....	....	....	....
	Mississauga	OHL	38	20	16	36	60	....	....	....	....	....

LAWSON, Kyle (LAW-suhn, KIGHL) CAR.

Defense. Shoots right. 5'11", 192 lbs. Born, Southfield, MI, January 11, 1987.
(Carolina's 9th choice, 198th overall, in 2005 Entry Draft).

			Regular Season					Playoffs				
Season	Club	League	GP	G	A	Pts	PIM	GP	G	A	Pts	PIM
2003-04	Det. Honeybaked	MWEHL	61	17	41	58	68	....	....	....	....	....
	Texarkana Bandits	NAHL	....	....	....	....	....	3	0	1	1	0
2004-05	USNTDP	U-18	23	2	12	14	6	....	....	....	....	....
	USNTDP	NAHL	8	1	3	4	0	....	....	....	....	....
2005-06	Tri-City Storm	USHL	49	9	13	22	40	1	0	0	0	0

Signed Letter of Intent to attend **Notre Dame** (CCHA) in fall of 2006.

LAWSON, Lucas (LAW-suhn, LOO-kuhs)

Center. Shoots left. 6'1", 195 lbs. Born, Braeside, Ont., August 10, 1979.

			Regular Season					Playoffs				
Season	Club	League	GP	G	A	Pts	PIM	GP	G	A	Pts	PIM
1998-99	Kanata Valley	CJHL	50	40	45	85	124	3	2	10	12	0
99-2000	U. of Maine	H-East	23	2	3	5	12	....	....	....	....	....
2000-01	U. of Maine	H-East	39	9	11	20	16	....	....	....	....	....
2001-02	U. of Maine	H-East	44	18	13	31	37	....	....	....	....	....
2002-03	U. of Maine	H-East	39	21	16	37	18	....	....	....	....	....
	Hartford Wolf Pack	AHL	....	....	....	....	....	2	0	0	0	0
2003-04	Hartford Wolf Pack	AHL	32	3	4	7	27	5	0	0	0	0
	Charlotte	ECHL	26	11	13	24	10	....	....	....	....	....
2004-05	Hartford Wolf Pack	AHL	51	4	11	15	32	3	0	0	0	0
2005-06	JYP Jyvaskyla	Finland	24	1	9	10	20	....	....	....	....	....
	Hamilton Bulldogs	AHL	8	1	2	3	0	....	....	....	....	....
	Long Beach	ECHL	13	2	8	10	35	2	0	0	0	0

Hockey East Second All-Star Team (2003)

Signed as a free agent by **NY Rangers**, April 4, 2003. Signed as a free agent by **Jyvaskyla** (Finland), August 31, 2005.

LEBLANC, Peter (luh-BLAHNK, PEE-tuhr) CHI.

Center. Shoots left. 5'9", 196 lbs. Born, Hamilton, Ont., February 3, 1988.
(Chicago's 9th choice, 186th overall, in 2006 Entry Draft).

			Regular Season					Playoffs				
Season	Club	League	GP	G	A	Pts	PIM	GP	G	A	Pts	PIM
2004-05	Hamilton	OPJHL	49	14	22	36	....	....	....	....	....	....
2005-06	Hamilton	OPJHL	22	10	12	22	25	....	....	....	....	....

OPJHL Rookie of the Year (2005)

• Missed majority of 2005-06 season due to mononucleosis. Signed Letter of Intent to attend **U. of New Hampshire** (Hockey East) in fall of 2006.

LEE, Brian (LEE, BRIGH-uhn) OTT.

Defense. Shoots right. 6'2", 202 lbs. Born, Fargo, ND, March 26, 1987.
(Ottawa's 1st choice, 9th overall, in 2005 Entry Draft).

			Regular Season					Playoffs				
Season	Club	League	GP	G	A	Pts	PIM	GP	G	A	Pts	PIM
2003-04	Moorhead Spuds	High-MN	29	10	38	48	....	....	....	....	....	....
2004-05	Moorhead Spuds	High-MN	25	12	26	38	....	....	....	....	....	....
	Lincoln Stars	USHL	12	0	3	3	4	4	2	3	5	2
2005-06	North Dakota	WCHA	44	4	23	27	44	....	....	....	....	....

WCHA All-Rookie Team (2006)

LEE, Carter (LEE, KAHR-tuhr) S.J.

Right wing. Shoots right. 6'1", 190 lbs. Born, Toms River, NJ, July 2, 1984.
(San Jose's 11th choice, 276th overall, in 2003 Entry Draft).

			Regular Season					Playoffs				
Season	Club	League	GP	G	A	Pts	PIM	GP	G	A	Pts	PIM
2001-02	Christian Bros.	High-NJ	34	10	9	19	45	....	....	....	....	....
2002-03	Canterbury	High-CT	35	38	22	60	40	....	....	....	....	....
2003-04	Canterbury	High-CT	30	19	26	45	40	....	....	....	....	....
2004-05	Northeastern	H-East	11	2	1	3	4	....	....	....	....	....
2005-06	Northeastern	H-East	9	0	1	1	21	....	....	....	....	....

LEHMAN, Scott (LAY-man, SKAWT) ATL.

Defense. Shoots left. 6'1", 205 lbs. Born, Fort McMurray, Alta., January 6, 1986.
(Atlanta's 3rd choice, 76th overall, in 2004 Entry Draft).

			Regular Season					Playoffs				
Season	Club	League	GP	G	A	Pts	PIM	GP	G	A	Pts	PIM
2002-03	St. Michael's	OHL	53	3	10	13	50	19	1	3	4	34
2003-04	St. Michael's	OHL	66	5	27	32	189	18	2	2	4	38
2004-05	St. Michael's	OHL	57	2	19	21	189	10	2	2	4	31
2005-06	St. Michael's	OHL	68	5	50	55	175	4	0	2	2	15

LEHTIVUORI, Joonas (leh-tee-VWOO-aw-ree, YOH-nuhs) PHI.

Defense. Shoots left. 5'11", 167 lbs. Born, Tempere, Finland, July 19, 1988.
(Philadelphia's 6th choice, 101st overall, in 2006 Entry Draft).

			Regular Season					Playoffs				
Season	Club	League	GP	G	A	Pts	PIM	GP	G	A	Pts	PIM
2004-05	Ilves Tampere U18	Fin-U18	25	5	11	16	12	5	1	1	2	8
2005-06	Ilves Tampere U18	Fin-U18	2	0	1	1	0	6	1	4	5	4
	Ilves Tampere Jr.	Fin-Jr.	39	9	16	25	22	3	0	0	0	4
	Ilves Tampere	Finland	1	0	0	0	0	....	....	....	....	....

LEHTONEN, Mikko (LEH-tih-nehn, MEE-koh) BOS.

Right wing. Shoots right. 6'3", 196 lbs. Born, Espoo, Finland, April 1, 1987.
(Boston's 3rd choice, 83rd overall, in 2005 Entry Draft).

			Regular Season					Playoffs				
Season	Club	League	GP	G	A	Pts	PIM	GP	G	A	Pts	PIM
2002-03	Blues Espoo U18	Fin-U18	11	1	3	4	2	1	0	0	0	0
2003-04	Blues Espoo U18	Fin-U18	20	8	7	15	22	....	....	....	....	....
	Blues Espoo Jr.	Fin-Jr.	19	3	0	3	0	5	0	0	0	0
2004-05	Blues Espoo U18	Fin-U18	2	0	2	2	0	....	....	....	....	....
	Blues Espoo Jr.	Fin-Jr.	37	6	9	15	38	6	3	1	4	0
	Blues Espoo	Finland	1	0	0	0	0	....	....	....	....	....
2005-06	Blues Espoo Jr.	Fin-Jr.	15	3	4	7	12	10	5	2	7	6
	Suomi U20	Finland-2	3	1	0	1	2	....	....	....	....	....
	Blues Espoo	Finland	25	4	0	4	0	....	....	....	....	....

LEHTONEN, Mikko (LEHT-oh-nehn, MEE-koh) NSH.

Defense. Shoots left. 6'1", 194 lbs. Born, Oulu, Finland, June 12, 1978.
(Nashville's 9th choice, 271st overall, in 2001 Entry Draft).

			Regular Season					Playoffs				
Season	Club	League	GP	G	A	Pts	PIM	GP	G	A	Pts	PIM
1995-96	Karpat Oulu U18	Fin-U18	15	4	5	9	30	....	....	....	....	....
1996-97	Karpat Oulu Jr.	Fin-Jr.	35	6	19	25	82	....	....	....	....	....
1997-98	Karpat Oulu Jr.	Fin-Jr.	34	8	12	20	56	....	....	....	....	....
	Karpat Oulu U18	Fin-U18	11	5	7	12	31	....	....	....	....	....
1998-99	Karpat Oulu Jr.	Fin-Jr.	35	13	22	35	65	....	....	....	....	....
	Karpat Oulu	Finland-2	2	0	0	0	0	....	....	....	....	....
	Karpat Oulu U18	Fin-U18	13	6	14	20	14	....	....	....	....	....
99-2000	Karpat Oulu	Finland-2	45	5	10	15	26	6	0	0	0	4
2000-01	Karpat Oulu	Finland	54	6	9	15	58	9	0	3	3	4
2001-02	Karpat Oulu	Finland	55	8	11	19	32	4	1	1	2	4
2002-03	Karpat Oulu	Finland	55	5	12	17	50	15	3	1	4	22
2003-04	Karpat Oulu	Finland	53	5	13	18	62	12	2	4	6	8
2004-05	Karpat Oulu	Finland	53	11	17	28	28	12	3	3	6	12
2005-06	Karpat Oulu	Finland	43	6	8	14	46	10	2	2	4	12

LEINONEN, Tommi (LEIH-noh-nehn, TAW-mee) PIT.

Defense. Shoots left. 6'2", 191 lbs. Born, Kajaani, Finland, May 14, 1987.
(Pittsburgh's 4th choice, 125th overall, in 2005 Entry Draft).

			Regular Season					Playoffs				
Season	Club	League	GP	G	A	Pts	PIM	GP	G	A	Pts	PIM
2003-04	Karpat Oulu U18	Fin-U18	28	9	3	12	30	2	0	0	0	0
2004-05	Karpat Oulu U18	Fin-U18	1	0	0	0	0	....	....	....	....	....
	Karpat Oulu Jr.	Fin-Jr.	36	9	11	20	16	1	0	0	0	0
2005-06	Karpat Oulu Jr.	Fin-Jr.	27	8	7	15	28	9	0	3	3	8
	Suomi U20	Finland-2	6	1	0	1	4	....	....	....	....	....
	Karpat Oulu	Finland	3	0	0	0	0	....	....	....	....	....

LEMIEUX, Francis (lehm-YOO, FRAN-sihs) MTL.

Center. Shoots right. 5'11", 185 lbs. Born, Sherbrooke, Que., February 22, 1984.

			Regular Season					Playoffs				
Season	Club	League	GP	G	A	Pts	PIM	GP	G	A	Pts	PIM
2001-02	Chicoutimi	QMJHL	66	17	22	39	44	3	0	0	0	0
2002-03	Chicoutimi	QMJHL	66	28	35	63	36	4	0	0	0	2
2003-04	Chicoutimi	QMJHL	70	22	44	66	49	18	6	4	10	10
2004-05	Chicoutimi	QMJHL	70	32	50	82	52	13	4	5	9	6
2005-06	Hamilton Bulldogs	AHL	67	18	23	41	76	....	....	....	....	....

Signed as a free agent by **Montreal**, December 8, 2005.

LEMTYUGOV, Nikolai (LEHM-tyuh-gawf, NIH-koh-ligh) ST.L.

Right wing. Shoots left. 6', 183 lbs. Born, Miass, USSR, January 15, 1986.
(St. Louis' 7th choice, 219th overall, in 2005 Entry Draft).

			Regular Season					Playoffs				
Season	Club	League	GP	G	A	Pts	PIM	GP	G	A	Pts	PIM
2003-04	CSKA Moscow 2	Russia-3	STATISTICS NOT AVAILABLE									
2004-05	CSKA Moscow 2	Russia-3	STATISTICS NOT AVAILABLE									
	CSKA Moscow	Russia	11	1	1	2	16	....	....	....	....	....
2005-06	CSKA Moscow	Russia	37	9	11	20	45	7	1	1	2	8

LEPISTO, Sami (LEH-pihs-toh, SA-mee) WSH.

Defense. Shoots left. 5'11", 176 lbs. Born, Espoo, Finland, October 17, 1984.
(Washington's 6th choice, 66th overall, in 2004 Entry Draft).

			Regular Season					Playoffs				
Season	Club	League	GP	G	A	Pts	PIM	GP	G	A	Pts	PIM
2001-02	Jokerit U18	Fin-U18	20	8	14	22	36	8	4	8	12	12
	Jokerit Helsinki Jr.	Fin-Jr.	14	0	5	5	2	....	....	....	....	....
2002-03	Jokerit Helsinki Jr.	Fin-Jr.	36	5	14	19	34	11	1	5	6	8
2003-04	Suomi U20	Finland-2	1	0	0	0	0	....	....	....	....	....
	Jokerit Helsinki	Finland	53	3	4	7	20	8	0	1	1	4
2004-05	Jokerit Helsinki	Finland	55	7	18	25	44	12	1	7	8	12
2005-06	Jokerit Helsinki	Finland	56	8	21	29	68	....	....	....	....	....

LESSARD, Pierre-Luc (leh-SAHRD, PEE-air-LEWK) OTT.

Defense. Shoots left. 6', 180 lbs. Born, Thetford Mines, Que., January 16, 1988.
(Ottawa's 4th choice, 121st overall, in 2006 Entry Draft).

			Regular Season					Playoffs				
Season	Club	League	GP	G	A	Pts	PIM	GP	G	A	Pts	PIM
2004-05	Gatineau	QMJHL	48	3	6	9	9	10	0	2	2	0
2005-06	Gatineau	QMJHL	55	7	25	32	38	17	2	10	12	12

LETANG, Kristopher (leh-TANG, KRIHS-tuh-fuhr) PIT.

Defense. Shoots right. 5'11", 190 lbs. Born, Montreal, Que., April 24, 1987.
(Pittsburgh's 3rd choice, 62nd overall, in 2005 Entry Draft).

			Regular Season					Playoffs				
Season	Club	League	GP	G	A	Pts	PIM	GP	G	A	Pts	PIM
2002-03	Antoine-Girouard	QAAA	42	2	10	12	34	....	....	....	....	....
2003-04	Antoine-Girouard	QAAA	39	12	41	53	94	13	7	9	16	38
2004-05	Val-d'Or Foreurs	QMJHL	70	13	19	32	79	....	....	....	....	....
2005-06	Val-d'Or Foreurs	QMJHL	60	25	43	68	156	5	1	5	6	20

QMJHL All-Rookie Team (2005) • Canadian Major Junior All-Rookie Team (2005) • QMJHL First All-Star Team (2006)

LETOURNEAU-LEBLOND, Pierre-Luc (leh-TOOR-noh-leh-BLAWN) N.J.

Left wing. Shoots left. 6'2", 210 lbs. Born, Levis, Que., June 4, 1985.
(New Jersey's 4th choice, 216th overall, in 2004 Entry Draft).

			Regular Season					Playoffs				
Season	Club	League	GP	G	A	Pts	PIM	GP	G	A	Pts	PIM
2003-04	Baie-Comeau	QMJHL	62	2	3	5	198	4	0	0	0	6
2004-05	Baie-Comeau	QMJHL	67	1	6	7	229	6	0	1	1	10
2005-06	Albany River Rats	AHL	27	1	1	2	130	....	....	....	....	....
	Adirondack	UHL	31	3	6	9	165	6	0	1	1	29

LEWANDOWSKI, Eduard (luh-wan-DOW-skee, EHD-wahrd) PHX.

Left wing. Shoots left. 6'1", 205 lbs. Born, Krasnoturjinsk, USSR, May 3, 1980.
(Phoenix's 6th choice, 242nd overall, in 2003 Entry Draft).

			Regular Season					Playoffs				
Season	Club	League	GP	G	A	Pts	PIM	GP	G	A	Pts	PIM
1997-98	Wilhelmshaven	German-2	48	19	12	31	46	....	....	....	....	....
1998-99	Wilhelmshaven	German-3	49	35	21	56	96	....	....	....	....	....
99-2000	Wilhelmshaven	German-2	48	15	26	41	104	....	....	....	....	....
2000-01	Wilhelmshaven	German-2	47	22	30	52	97	....	....	....	....	....
2001-02	Eisbaren Berlin	Germany	59	7	15	22	57	4	0	0	0	2
2002-03	Kolner Haie	Germany	46	6	14	20	46	13	3	3	6	43
2003-04	Kolner Haie	Germany	52	16	17	33	85	5	1	2	3	16
2004-05	Kolner Haie	Germany	49	19	20	39	49	6	1	1	2	33
2005-06	Kolner Haie	Germany	52	20	26	46	48	9	3	5	8	31
	Germany	Olympics	5	0	2	2	0	....	....	....	....	....

LEWIS, Grant (LOO-ihs, GRANT) ATL.

Defense. Shoots right. 6'3", 195 lbs. Born, Pittsburgh, PA, January 20, 1985.
(Atlanta's 2nd choice, 40th overall, in 2004 Entry Draft).

			Regular Season					Playoffs				
Season	Club	League	GP	G	A	Pts	PIM	GP	G	A	Pts	PIM
2002-03	Pittsburgh Forge	NAHL	50	2	7	9	59	....	....	....	....	....
2003-04	Dartmouth	ECAC	34	3	22	25	57	....	....	....	....	....
2004-05	Dartmouth	ECACHL	33	5	17	22	32	....	....	....	....	....
2005-06	Dartmouth	ECACHL	29	4	11	15	53	....	....	....	....	....

ECAC All-Rookie Team (2004) • ECAC First All-Star Team (2004) • ECACHL Second All-Star Team (2006)

LEWIS, Trevor (LOO-his, TREH-vuhr) L.A.

Center. Shoots right. 6'1", 192 lbs. Born, Salt Lake City, UT, January 8, 1987.
(Los Angeles' 2nd choice, 17th overall, in 2006 Entry Draft).

			Regular Season					Playoffs				
Season	Club	League	GP	G	A	Pts	PIM	GP	G	A	Pts	PIM
2004-05	Des Moines	USHL	52	10	12	22	70	....	....	....	....	....
2005-06	Des Moines	USHL	56	35	40	75	69	11	3	13	16	16

USHL Player of the Year (2006)

Signed Letter of Intent to attend **U. of Michigan** (CCHA) in fall of 2006.

LINDGREN, Perttu (LIHND-gruhn, PUHR-too) DAL.

Center. Shoots left. 6', 185 lbs. Born, Tampere, Finland, August 26, 1987.
(Dallas' 4th choice, 75th overall, in 2005 Entry Draft).

			Regular Season					Playoffs				
Season	Club	League	GP	G	A	Pts	PIM	GP	G	A	Pts	PIM
2003-04	Ilves Tampere U18	Fin-U18	24	11	17	28	26	....	....	....	....	....
	Ilves Tampere Jr.	Fin-Jr.	2	0	0	0	0	....	....	....	....	....
2004-05	Ilves Tampere Jr.	Fin-Jr.	38	12	29	41	2	10	7	10	17	4
	Ilves Tampere	Finland	2	0	0	0	0	....	....	....	....	....
2005-06	Ilves Tampere Jr.	Fin-Jr.	2	1	0	1	0	....	....	....	....	....
	Suomi U20	Finland-2	3	0	3	3	0	....	....	....	....	....
	Ilves Tampere	Finland	51	13	24	37	16	4	0	0	0	0

LINDSTROM, Liam (LIHND-struhm, LEE-uhm) PHX.

Center. Shoots left. 6', 194 lbs. Born, Edmonton, Alta., January 12, 1985.
(Phoenix's 3rd choice, 115th overall, in 2003 Entry Draft).

			Regular Season					Playoffs				
Season	Club	League	GP	G	A	Pts	PIM	GP	G	A	Pts	PIM
2000-01	Mora IK U18	Swe-U18	14	3	4	7	14	....	....	....	....	....
	Mora IK Jr.	Swe-Jr.	1	0	0	0	2	1	0	0	0	0
2001-02	Mora IK U18	Swe-U18	2	2	0	2	0	1	1	0	1	4
	Mora IK Jr.	Swe-Jr.	25	5	8	13	12	....	....	....	....	....
2002-03	Mora IK U18	Swe-U18	4	3	1	4	8	....	....	....	....	....
	Mora IK Jr.	Swe-Jr.	20	3	7	10	57	....	....	....	....	....
	Mora IK	Sweden-2	13	0	0	0	0	....	....	....	....	....
2003-04	Sundsvall	Sweden-2	26	0	0	0	4	2	0	0	0	0
2004-05	Sundsvall	Sweden-2	51	5	4	9	30	....	....	....	....	....
2005-06	Hammarby	Sweden-2	46	4	4	8	40	....	....	....	....	....

LINDSTROM, Sanny (LIHND-struhm, SAN-nee) COL.

Defense. Shoots left. 6'2", 205 lbs. Born, Stockholm, Sweden, December 24, 1979.
(Colorado's 4th choice, 112th overall, in 1999 Entry Draft).

			Regular Season					Playoffs				
Season	Club	League	GP	G	A	Pts	PIM	GP	G	A	Pts	PIM
1997-98	Huddinge IK	Sweden-2	32	6	6	12	46	....	....	....	....	....
1998-99	Huddinge IK	Sweden-2	37	4	4	8	65	....	....	....	....	....
99-2000	Hershey Bears	AHL	42	1	2	3	57	....	....	....	....	....
	Baton Rouge	ECHL	11	1	2	3	16	....	....	....	....	....
2000-01	Hershey Bears	AHL	24	0	0	0	61	....	....	....	....	....
	Quad City	UHL	5	1	1	2	10	....	....	....	....	....
2001-02	Quad City	UHL	38	4	23	27	71	12	0	3	3	20
	Hershey Bears	AHL	2	0	0	0	0	....	....	....	....	....
2002-03	Timra IK	Sweden	39	1	1	2	81	9	0	1	1	0
2003-04	Timra IK	Sweden	48	1	3	4	91	10	2	0	2	24
2004-05	Timra IK	Sweden	50	5	6	11	109	7	0	1	1	10
2005-06	Timra IK	Sweden	50	2	4	6	83	....	....	....	....	....

• Missed majority of 2000-01 season recovering from knee injury suffered in practice, March 5, 2000.

LISIN, Enver (LIH-sihn, EHN-vuhr) PHX.

Right wing. Shoots left. 6'2", 190 lbs. Born, Moscow, USSR, April 22, 1986.
(Phoenix's 3rd choice, 50th overall, in 2004 Entry Draft).

			Regular Season					Playoffs				
Season	Club	League	GP	G	A	Pts	PIM	GP	G	A	Pts	PIM
2001-02	Dyn'o Moscow 2	Russia-3	6	3	0	3	14	....	....	....	....	....
2002-03	Dyn'o Moscow 2	Russia-3	STATISTICS NOT AVAILABLE									
2003-04	Dyn'o Moscow 2	Russia-3	STATISTICS NOT AVAILABLE									
	Kristall Saratov	Russia-2	35	10	6	16	30	4	1	0	1	0
2004-05	Ak Bars Kazan 2	Russia-3	....	4	3	7	....	....	....	....	....	....
	Ak Bars Kazan	Russia	53	8	4	12	4	3	0	0	0	0
2005-06	Ak Bars Kazan	Russia	43	7	5	12	26	13	3	1	4	6

LITTLE, Bryan (LIH-tuhl, BRIGH-uhn) ATL.

Center. Shoots right. 5'10", 200 lbs. Born, Edmonton, Alta., November 12, 1987.
(Atlanta's 1st choice, 12th overall, in 2006 Entry Draft).

			Regular Season					Playoffs				
Season	Club	League	GP	G	A	Pts	PIM	GP	G	A	Pts	PIM
2004-05	Barrie Colts	OHL	62	36	32	68	34	4	5	1	6	2
2005-06	Barrie Colts	OHL	64	42	67	109	99	14	8	15	23	19

LOCKE, Corey (LAWK, KOHR-ee) MTL.

Center. Shoots left. 5'9", 173 lbs. Born, Toronto, Ont., May 8, 1984.
(Montreal's 5th choice, 113th overall, in 2003 Entry Draft).

			Regular Season					Playoffs				
Season	Club	League	GP	G	A	Pts	PIM	GP	G	A	Pts	PIM
2000-01	Newmarket	OPJHL	49	34	51	85	16	16	10	12	22	14
2001-02	Ottawa 67's	OHL	55	18	25	43	18	13	6	7	13	10
2002-03	Ottawa 67's	OHL	66	*63	*88	*151	83	23	*19	19	*38	30
2003-04	Ottawa 67's	OHL	65	*51	67	*118	82	7	7	3	10	10
2004-05	Hamilton Bulldogs	AHL	78	16	27	43	20	4	0	0	0	2
2005-06	Hamilton Bulldogs	AHL	77	19	40	59	67	....	....	....	....	....

OHL First All-Star Team (2003, 2004) • OHL Player of the Year (2003, 2004) • Canadian Major Junior First All-Star Team (2003, 2004) • Canadian Major Junior Player of the Year (2003)

LOFBERG, Christofer (LAWF-buhrg, KRIHS-tah-fuhr) DET.

Center. Shoots right. 6'3", 189 lbs. Born, Stockholm, Sweden, October 11, 1986.
(Detroit's 3rd choice, 80th overall, in 2005 Entry Draft).

			Regular Season					Playoffs				
Season	Club	League	GP	G	A	Pts	PIM	GP	G	A	Pts	PIM
2002-03	AIK Solna U18	Swe-U18	13	8	4	12	18	....	....	....	....	....
	AIK Solna Jr.	Swe-Jr.	3	1	0	1	0	4	0	0	0	0
2003-04	Huddinge IK U18	Swe-U18	2	1	0	1	0	....	....	....	....	....
	Huddinge IK Jr.	Swe-Jr.	36	3	12	15	20	....	....	....	....	....
2004-05	Djurgarden Jr.	Swe-Jr.	30	21	13	34	49	....	....	....	....	....
	Djurgarden	Sweden	1	0	0	0	0	....	....	....	....	....
2005-06	Djurgarden Jr.	Swe-Jr.	11	7	6	13	10	4	2	1	3	4
	Djurgarden	Sweden	43	2	0	2	24	....	....	....	....	....

LOGINOV, Denis (LOG-gih-nawv, DEH-nihs) ATL.

Center. Shoots left. 6'1", 210 lbs. Born, Kazan, USSR, May 5, 1985.
(Atlanta's 7th choice, 203rd overall, in 2003 Entry Draft).

			Regular Season					Playoffs				
Season	Club	League	GP	G	A	Pts	PIM	GP	G	A	Pts	PIM
99-2000	Ak Bars Kazan 2	Russia-3	4	0	0	0	0	....	....	....	....	....
2000-01	Ak Bars Kazan 2	Russia-3	STATISTICS NOT AVAILABLE									
2001-02	Ak Bars Kazan 2	Russia-3	38	6	10	16	40	....	....	....	....	....
	Team Volga	Exhib.	3	0	3	3	27	....	....	....	....	....
2002-03	Ak Bars Kazan 2	Russia-3	52	17	24	41	98	....	....	....	....	....
	Perm	Russia	1	0	0	0	0	....	....	....	....	....
2003-04	Ak Bars Kazan	Russia	16	2	1	3	0	7	1	0	1	6
2004-05	Ak Bars Kazan	Russia	2	0	0	0	0	....	....	....	....	....
2005-06	Almetjevsk	Russia-2	7	1	0	1	8	....	....	....	....	....
	Ak Bars Kazan	Russia	16	1	1	2	10	....	....	....	....	....

LOJEK, Martin (LOI-yehk, MAHR-tehn) FLA.

Defense. Shoots right. 6'5", 220 lbs. Born, Brno, Czech., August 19, 1985.
(Florida's 5th choice, 105th overall, in 2003 Entry Draft).

			Regular Season					Playoffs				
Season	Club	League	GP	G	A	Pts	PIM	GP	G	A	Pts	PIM
2000-01	HC Pardubice Jr.	CzRep-Jr.	48	2	2	4	42	7	0	0	0	6
2001-02	HC Pardubice Jr.	CzRep-Jr.	40	2	4	6	24	7	1	0	1	2
2002-03	Brampton	OHL	65	1	13	14	47	11	0	1	1	6
2003-04	Brampton	OHL	68	3	17	20	37	12	0	4	4	2
2004-05	Brampton	OHL	58	1	12	13	58	6	0	0	0	6
2005-06	Rochester	AHL	15	1	1	2	16	....	....	....	....	....
	Florida Everblades	ECHL	45	3	11	14	40	2	0	0	0	0

LOUHIVAARA, Ossi (loo-hih-VAH-rah, AW-see) OTT.

Right wing. Shoots right. 6', 179 lbs. Born, Kotka, Finland, August 31, 1983.
(Ottawa's 8th choice, 260th overall, in 2003 Entry Draft).

			Regular Season					Playoffs				
Season	Club	League	GP	G	A	Pts	PIM	GP	G	A	Pts	PIM
99-2000	Titaanit Kotka	Finland-3	1	0	0	0	0	....	....	....	....	....
2000-01	Titaanit Kotka	Finland-3	32	10	12	22	10	3	1	2	3	2
2001-02	Titaanit Kotka	Finland-3	34	13	14	27	10	3	1	1	2	0
	HC Banik Most	CzRep-3	....	....	....	....	....	2	1	2	3	2
2002-03	KooKoo Kouvola	Finland-2	44	20	15	35	20	9	1	3	4	4
2003-04	KooKoo Kouvola	Finland-2	41	13	17	30	4	9	1	1	2	2
2004-05	JYP Jyvaskyla	Finland	56	4	9	13	12	3	0	0	0	0
2005-06	JYP Jyvaskyla	Finland	53	7	11	18	30	3	0	2	2	2

LOVE, Mitchell (LUHV, MIH-chuhl) COL.

Defense. Shoots left. 6', 200 lbs. Born, Quesnel, B.C., June 15, 1984.

			Regular Season					Playoffs				
Season	Club	League	GP	G	A	Pts	PIM	GP	G	A	Pts	PIM
2000-01	Moose Jaw	WHL	51	5	4	9	97	4	0	0	0	2
2001-02	Moose Jaw	WHL	16	0	1	1	40	....	....	....	....	....
	Swift Current	WHL	52	5	11	16	132	12	0	0	0	37
2002-03	Swift Current	WHL	70	2	15	17	327	4	1	0	1	16
2003-04	Everett Silvertips	WHL	70	12	15	27	163	21	2	6	8	47
2004-05	Everett Silvertips	WHL	59	9	20	29	142	4	0	2	2	6
2005-06	Lowell	AHL	27	0	4	4	68	....	....	....	....	....

Signed as a free agent by **Colorado**, October 25, 2005.

LUCIA, Tony (Loo-CHEE-ah, TOH-nee) S.J.

Left wing. Shoots left. 6', 165 lbs. Born, Wayzata, MN, August 23, 1987.
(San Jose's 8th choice, 193rd overall, in 2005 Entry Draft).

			Regular Season					Playoffs				
Season	Club	League	GP	G	A	Pts	PIM	GP	G	A	Pts	PIM
2003-04	Wayzata	High-MN	31	13	22	35	....	....	....	....	....	....
2004-05	Wayzata	High-MN	24	27	36	63	32	....	....	....	....	....
	Omaha Lancers	USHL	11	1	0	1	0	....	....	....	....	....
2005-06	Omaha Lancers	USHL	56	12	23	35	25	5	0	0	0	2

Signed Letter of Intent to attend **U. of Minnesota** (WCHA) in fall of 2006.

LUCIC, Milan (LOO-sihc, MEE-lan) BOS.

Left wing. Shoots left. 6'2", 204 lbs. Born, Vancouver, B.C., June 7, 1988.
(Boston's 3rd choice, 50th overall, in 2006 Entry Draft).

			Regular Season					Playoffs				
Season	Club	League	GP	G	A	Pts	PIM	GP	G	A	Pts	PIM
2004-05	Coquitlam Express	BCHL	50	9	14	23	100	....	....	....	....	....
	Vancouver Giants	WHL	1	0	0	0	2	2	0	0	0	0
2005-06	Vancouver Giants	WHL	62	9	10	19	149	18	3	4	7	23

LUDWIG, Trevor (LUHD-wihg, TREH-vuhr) DAL.

Defense. Shoots left. 6'1", 200 lbs. Born, Rhinelander, WI, May 24, 1985.
(Dallas' 7th choice, 183rd overall, in 2004 Entry Draft).

			Regular Season					Playoffs				
Season	Club	League	GP	G	A	Pts	PIM	GP	G	A	Pts	PIM
2002-03	Texas Tornado	NAHL	55	4	5	9	39	....	....	....	....	....
2003-04	Texas Tornado	NAHL	54	5	25	30	50	....	....	....	....	....
2004-05	Providence College	H-East	33	1	6	7	36	....	....	....	....	....
2005-06	Providence College	H-East	27	0	2	2	6	....	....	....	....	....

NAHL All-Rookie Team (2003) • NAHL First All-Star Team (2004)

LUKACEVIC, Ned (loo-kuh-SAY-vihk, NEHD) L.A.

Left wing. Shoots left. 6', 185 lbs. Born, Podgorica, Serbia, February 11, 1986.
(Los Angeles' 3rd choice, 110th overall, in 2004 Entry Draft).

			Regular Season					Playoffs				
Season	Club	League	GP	G	A	Pts	PIM	GP	G	A	Pts	PIM
2000-01	Port Coquitlam	BCAHA	60	42	48	90	....	....	....	....	....	....
2001-02	Port Coquitlam	BCAHA	70	40	55	95	60	....	....	....	....	....
	Spokane Chiefs	WHL	1	1	0	1	0	....	....	....	....	....
2002-03	Spokane Chiefs	WHL	31	0	4	4	29	4	0	1	1	0
2003-04	Spokane Chiefs	WHL	72	19	14	33	65	4	1	1	2	2
2004-05	Spokane Chiefs	WHL	71	18	28	46	52	....	....	....	....	....
2005-06	Swift Current	WHL	63	25	28	53	71	4	1	0	1	5
	Manchester	AHL	....	....	....	....	....	7	1	0	1	4

LUKES, Frantisek (LOO-kehsh, FRAHN-tih-sehk)

Left wing. Shoots right. 5'9", 173 lbs. Born, Kadan, Czech., September 25, 1982.
(Phoenix's 8th choice, 243rd overall, in 2001 Entry Draft).

			Regular Season					Playoffs				
Season	Club	League	GP	G	A	Pts	PIM	GP	G	A	Pts	PIM
99-2000	Litvinov Jr.	CzRep-Jr.	36	15	13	28	....	....	....	....	....	....
2000-01	St. Michael's	OHL	61	23	33	56	37	18	4	9	13	12
2001-02	St. Michael's	OHL	63	27	37	64	50	15	7	11	18	16
2002-03	St. Michael's	OHL	62	27	46	73	55	19	8	15	23	28
2003-04	Springfield Falcons	AHL	63	8	20	28	30	....	....	....	....	....
2004-05	Utah Grizzlies	AHL	12	0	2	2	20	....	....	....	....	....
	Idaho Steelheads	ECHL	59	18	22	40	30	3	0	1	1	10
2005-06	San Antonio	AHL	26	1	5	6	4	....	....	....	....	....
	Laredo Bucks	CHL	40	5	28	33	18	15	5	9	14	6

LUNDBOHM, Bryan (LUHND-bawm, BRIGH-uhn)

Right wing. Shoots left. 5'10", 184 lbs. Born, Roseau, MN, August 24, 1977.

			Regular Season					Playoffs				
Season	Club	League	GP	G	A	Pts	PIM	GP	G	A	Pts	PIM
1996-97	Lincoln Stars	USHL	52	12	33	45	33	14	8	4	12	20
1997-98	Lincoln Stars	USHL	55	26	38	64	10	9	2	7	9	0
1998-99	North Dakota	WCHA	32	2	9	11	4	....	....	....	....	....
99-2000	North Dakota	WCHA	44	22	22	44	14	....	....	....	....	....
2000-01	North Dakota	WCHA	46	*32	37	69	38	....	....	....	....	....
2001-02	Milwaukee	AHL	79	11	23	34	63	....	....	....	....	....
2002-03	Milwaukee	AHL	80	9	17	26	63	6	1	5	6	0
2003-04	HC Sierre	Swiss-2	10	6	8	14	8	....	....	....	....	....
	Milwaukee	AHL	28	6	8	14	8	....	....	....	....	....
2004-05	Fort Worth	CHL	26	10	20	30	28	....	....	....	....	....
	Grand Rapids	AHL	3	0	0	0	0	....	....	....	....	....
	Milwaukee	AHL	47	7	12	19	36	4	0	0	0	0
2005-06	Houston Aeros	AHL	78	9	21	30	46	8	3	5	8	4

USHL First All-Star Team (1998) • WCHA First All-Star Team (2001) • NCAA West Second All-American Team (2001) • NCAA Championship All-Tournament Team (2001)

Signed as a free agent by **Nashville**, May 1, 2001. Signed as a free agent by **Sierre** (Swiss-2), September 5, 2003. Signed as a free agent by **Milwaukee** (AHL), November 25, 2003. • Missed majority of 2003-04 season recovering from groin injury suffered in game vs. Philadelphia (AHL), January 31, 2004. Signed as a free agent by **Fort Worth** (CHL), October 19, 2004. Signed as a free agent by **Grand Rapids** (AHL), November 17, 2004. Signed as a free agent by **Milwaukee** (AHL), December 28, 2004.

LUNDIN, Mike (LUHN-dihn, MIGHK) T.B.

Defense. Shoots left. 6'1", 195 lbs. Born, Burnsville, MN, September 24, 1984.
(Tampa Bay's 3rd choice, 102nd overall, in 2004 Entry Draft).

			Regular Season					Playoffs				
Season	Club	League	GP	G	A	Pts	PIM	GP	G	A	Pts	PIM
2002-03	Apple Valley	High-MN	27	8	20	27	....	....	....	....	....	....
2003-04	U. of Maine	H-East	44	3	16	19	34	....	....	....	....	....
2004-05	U. of Maine	H-East	40	1	13	14	2	....	....	....	....	....
2005-06	U. of Maine	H-East	36	3	13	16	4	....	....	....	....	....

LUNDQVIST, Joel (LOOND-kvihst, JOHL) DAL.

Center. Shoots left. 6', 185 lbs. Born, Are, Sweden, March 2, 1982.
(Dallas' 3rd choice, 68th overall, in 2000 Entry Draft).

			Regular Season					Playoffs				
Season	Club	League	GP	G	A	Pts	PIM	GP	G	A	Pts	PIM
1997-98	Rogle Jr.	Swe-Jr.	59	36	40	76	....	....	....	....	....	....
1998-99	V.Frolunda U18	Swe-U18	32	26	38	64	37	4	3	1	4	2
99-2000	V.Frolunda U18	Swe-U18	4	2	4	6	4	....	....	....	....	....
	V.Frolunda Jr.	Swe-Jr.	25	7	12	19	2	6	2	3	5	2
2000-01	V.Frolunda Jr.	Swe-Jr.	18	14	27	41	12	....	....	....	....	....
	IF Molndal Hockey	Sweden-2	26	18	13	31	22	....	....	....	....	....
	V.Frolunda	Sweden	9	0	0	0	0	....	....	....	....	....
2001-02	V.Frolunda	Sweden	46	12	14	26	28	10	1	3	4	8
	V.Frolunda Jr.	Swe-Jr.	....	....	....	....	....	1	0	0	0	0
2002-03	V.Frolunda	Sweden	50	17	20	37	113	16	6	3	9	12
2003-04	V.Frolunda	Sweden	49	9	14	23	48	10	2	2	4	8
2004-05	Frolunda	Sweden	50	7	12	19	38	13	2	5	7	57
2005-06	Frolunda	Sweden	49	10	22	32	87	17	3	4	7	34

LUTTINEN, Arttu (LOO-tuh-nehn, AHR-too) OTT.

Center. Shoots left. 5'11", 205 lbs. Born, Helsinki, Finland, September 3, 1983.
(Ottawa's 3rd choice, 75th overall, in 2002 Entry Draft).

			Regular Season					Playoffs				
Season	Club	League	GP	G	A	Pts	PIM	GP	G	A	Pts	PIM
99-2000	HIFK Helsinki U18	Fin-U18	17	5	9	14	10	2	0	0	0	2
2000-01	HIFK Helsinki U18	Fin-U18	20	14	20	34	141	3	0	3	3	2
	Ilves Tampere U18	Fin-U18	20	14	20	34	141	....	....	....	....	....
	HIFK Helsinki Jr.	Fin-Jr.	8	4	2	6	4	8	0	1	1	2
2001-02	HIFK Helsinki Jr.	Fin-Jr.	24	16	17	33	60	1	0	0	0	0
2002-03	HIFK Helsinki Jr.	Fin-Jr.	10	8	9	17	52	8	4	6	10	20
	FPS Forssa	Finland-2	2	0	1	1	4	....	....	....	....	....
	HIFK Helsinki	Finland	41	4	4	8	10	1	0	0	0	0
2003-04	HIFK Helsinki Jr.	Fin-Jr.	1	0	0	0	0	....	....	....	....	....
	Ahmat Hyvinkaa	Finland-2	4	3	2	5	2	....	....	....	....	....
	Haukat Jarvenpaa	Finland-2	1	0	0	0	0	....	....	....	....	....
	HIFK Helsinki	Finland	50	1	7	8	12	12	0	0	0	0
2004-05	HIFK Helsinki	Finland	56	12	13	25	67	5	1	0	1	0
2005-06	HIFK Helsinki	Finland	56	18	26	44	66	12	4	3	7	39

LYAMIN, Kirill (L'YAH-mihn, kih-RIHL) OTT.

Defense. Shoots left. 6'2", 208 lbs. Born, Moscow, USSR, January 13, 1986.
(Ottawa's 2nd choice, 58th overall, in 2004 Entry Draft).

			Regular Season					Playoffs				
Season	Club	League	GP	G	A	Pts	PIM	GP	G	A	Pts	PIM
2001-02	Moscow 18	Exhib.	5	0	3	3	4	....	....	....	....	....
2002-03	CSKA Moscow 2	Russia-3	5	0	0	0	10	....	....	....	....	....
	Moscow 18	Exhib.	5	0	0	0	6	....	....	....	....	....
2003-04	CSKA Moscow 2	Russia-3	STATISTICS NOT AVAILABLE									
	CSKA Moscow	Russia	28	0	3	3	12	....	....	....	....	....
2004-05	CSKA Moscow 2	Russia-3	STATISTICS NOT AVAILABLE									
2005-06	CSKA Moscow	Russia	25	0	1	1	28	2	0	0	0	0

LYNES, Luke (LIGHNZ, LEWK) WSH.

Center. Shoots left. 6', 195 lbs. Born, Rochester Hills, MI, November 28, 1987.
(Washington's 7th choice, 122nd overall, in 2006 Entry Draft).

			Regular Season					Playoffs				
Season	Club	League	GP	G	A	Pts	PIM	GP	G	A	Pts	PIM
2003-04	Culver Academy	High-IN	46	32	29	61	....	....	....	....	....	....
2004-05	Brampton	OHL	68	11	13	24	60	6	0	0	0	4
2005-06	Brampton	OHL	65	34	28	62	61	11	2	6	8	10

LYUBUSHIN, Mikhail (l'yoo-BOOSH-ihn, mih-kigh-EHL) L.A.

Defense. Shoots left. 6'1", 183 lbs. Born, Moscow, USSR, July 24, 1983.
(Los Angeles' 9th choice, 215th overall, in 2002 Entry Draft).

			Regular Season					Playoffs				
Season	Club	League	GP	G	A	Pts	PIM	GP	G	A	Pts	PIM
99-2000	Vityaz Podolsk 2	Russia-3	24	2	2	4	69	....	....	....	....	....
2000-01	Krylja Sovetov	Russia-2	2	0	1	1	0	1	0	0	0	0
2001-02	Krylja Sovetov 2	Russia-3	20	3	6	9	24	....	....	....	....	....
	THK Tver	Russia-2	22	1	0	1	18	....	....	....	....	....
	Krylja Sovetov	Russia	13	0	1	1	14	3	0	0	0	0
2002-03	Krylja Sovetov	Russia	49	0	6	6	26	....	....	....	....	....
2003-04	Dynamo Moscow	Russia	38	1	2	3	18	2	0	0	0	2
2004-05	Voskresensk	Russia	21	1	2	3	16	....	....	....	....	....
	Vityaz Chekhov	Russia-2	8	0	2	2	6	14	1	0	1	8
2005-06	Cherepovets	Russia	23	1	4	5	10	....	....	....	....	....
	Avangard Omsk	Russia	26	0	1	1	20	8	0	0	0	4

MacARTHUR, Clarke (muh-KAR-thuhr, KLAHRK) BUF.

Left wing. Shoots left. 6', 180 lbs. Born, Lloydminster, Alta., April 6, 1985.
(Buffalo's 3rd choice, 74th overall, in 2003 Entry Draft).

			Regular Season					Playoffs				
Season	Club	League	GP	G	A	Pts	PIM	GP	G	A	Pts	PIM
99-2000	Lloydminster	CABHL	24	19	45	64	51	5	9	6	15	4
2000-01	Strathcona	AMBHL	38	36	63	99	44	8	6	2	8	10
2001-02	Drayton Valley	AJHL	61	22	40	62	33	16	5	8	13	34
2002-03	Medicine Hat	WHL	70	23	52	75	104	11	3	6	9	8
2003-04	Medicine Hat	WHL	62	35	40	75	93	20	8	10	18	16
2004-05	Medicine Hat	WHL	58	30	44	74	100	13	3	8	11	18
	Rochester	AHL	....	....	....	....	....	3	0	1	1	0
2005-06	Rochester	AHL	69	21	32	53	71	....	....	....	....	....

Memorial Cup Tournament All-Star Team (2004) • WHL East First All-Star Team (2005)

MacDONALD, Andrew (MAK-DAWN-uhld, an-DROO) NYI

Defense. Shoots left. 6', 188 lbs. Born, Judique, N.S., September 7, 1986.
(NY Islanders' 10th choice, 160th overall, in 2006 Entry Draft).

			Regular Season					Playoffs				
Season	Club	League	GP	G	A	Pts	PIM	GP	G	A	Pts	PIM
2003-04	Truro Bearcats	MJrHL	50	8	20	28	43	10	0	0	0	....
2004-05	Truro Bearcats	MJrHL	56	11	22	33	60	17	6	7	13	....
2005-06	Moncton Wildcats	QMJHL	68	6	40	46	62	21	2	11	13	10

MacDONALD, David (MAK-DAWN-uhld, DAY-vihd) S.J.

Defense. Shoots right. 6'3", 200 lbs. Born, Halifax, N.S., April 30, 1985.
(San Jose's 7th choice, 225th overall, in 2004 Entry Draft).

			Regular Season					Playoffs				
Season	Club	League	GP	G	A	Pts	PIM	GP	G	A	Pts	PIM
2003-04	N.E. Jr. Coyotes	EJHL	37	1	5	6	81	....	....	....	....	....
2004-05	Harvard Crimson	ECACHL	33	0	2	2	22	....	....	....	....	....
2005-06	Harvard Crimson	ECACHL	22	0	3	3	24	....	....	....	....	....

MACHO, Michal (MA-khoh, MEE-khahl) S.J.

Center. Shoots right. 6'1", 170 lbs. Born, Martin, Czech., January 17, 1982.
(San Jose's 5th choice, 183rd overall, in 2000 Entry Draft).

			Regular Season					Playoffs				
Season	Club	League	GP	G	A	Pts	PIM	GP	G	A	Pts	PIM
1995-96	Martin U18	Svk-U18	12	0	6	6	2	....	....	....	....	....
1996-97	Martin U18	Svk-U18	52	43	44	87	50	....	....	....	....	....
1997-98	Martin U18	Svk-U18	46	41	54	95	58	....	....	....	....	....
	Martin Jr.	Slovak-Jr.	9	3	4	7	0	....	....	....	....	....
1998-99	King's-Edgehill	High-NS	50	45	55	100	....	....	....	....	....	....
	Martin Jr.	Slovak-Jr.	2	2	3	5	0	....	....	....	....	....
99-2000	Martin Jr.	Slovak-Jr.	30	38	44	82	....	....	....	....	....	....
	Martin	Slovak-2	8	1	5	6	4	....	....	....	....	....
2000-01	MHC Martin	Slovakia	37	5	10	15	12	3	1	1	2	2
2001-02	MHC Martin	Slovakia	40	12	8	20	20	....	....	....	....	....
2002-03	Bratislava	Slovakia	51	5	4	9	26	12	1	0	1	0
2003-04	Bratislava	Slovakia	33	7	7	14	14	12	5	3	8	26
2004-05	Bratislava	Slovakia	44	8	20	28	14	12	0	0	0	2
2005-06	Bratislava	Slovakia	48	10	5	15	10	4	0	0	0	0

MACIAS, Raymond (mah-CHEE-ahs, RAY-muhnd) COL.

Defense. Shoots right. 6'2", 195 lbs. Born, Long Beach, CA, September 18, 1986.
(Colorado's 6th choice, 124th overall, in 2005 Entry Draft).

			Regular Season					Playoffs				
Season	Club	League	GP	G	A	Pts	PIM	GP	G	A	Pts	PIM
2002-03	L.A. Jr. Kings	Cal-Am	49	37	26	63	100	....	....	....	....	....
	Kamloops Blazers	WHL	4	0	0	0	0	2	0	0	0	0
2003-04	Kamloops Blazers	WHL	69	12	17	29	14	5	2	0	2	0
2004-05	Kamloops Blazers	WHL	69	12	35	47	18	2	0	0	0	0
2005-06	Kamloops Blazers	WHL	68	12	26	38	34	....	....	....	....	....

MacKENZIE, Aaron (muh-KEHN-zee, AIR-ruhn) ST.L.

Defense. Shoots left. 6', 193 lbs. Born, Terrace Bay, Ont., March 7, 1981.

			Regular Season					Playoffs				
Season	Club	League	GP	G	A	Pts	PIM	GP	G	A	Pts	PIM
1998-99	Thunder Bay Flyers	USHL	49	8	12	20	123	3	0	1	1	0
99-2000	U. of Denver	WCHA	40	1	9	10	56	....	....	....	....	....
2000-01	U. of Denver	WCHA	37	2	6	8	45	....	....	....	....	....
2001-02	U. of Denver	WCHA	39	5	18	23	30	....	....	....	....	....
2002-03	U. of Denver	WCHA	41	11	21	32	33	....	....	....	....	....
2003-04	Worcester IceCats	AHL	66	5	9	14	108	10	0	2	2	10
2004-05	Worcester IceCats	AHL	75	2	13	15	106	....	....	....	....	....
2005-06	Peoria Rivermen	AHL	51	2	7	9	35	4	0	0	0	6

WCHA First All-Star Team (2003)

Signed as a free agent by **Worcester** (AHL), October 6, 2003. Signed as a free agent by **St. Louis**, June 29, 2004.

MacMURCHY, Ryan (mak-MUHR-chee, RIGH-uhn) ST.L.

Right wing. Shoots right. 5'11", 190 lbs. Born, Regina, Sask., April 27, 1983.
(St. Louis' 9th choice, 284th overall, in 2002 Entry Draft).

			Regular Season					Playoffs				
Season	Club	League	GP	G	A	Pts	PIM	GP	G	A	Pts	PIM
1998-99	Regina Capitals	SMHL	40	18	15	33	....	....	....	....	....	....
99-2000	Regina Capitals	SMHL	38	23	44	67	....	....	....	....	....	....
2000-01	Vernon Vipers	BCHL	30	4	6	10	....	....	....	....	....	....
2001-02	Notre Dame	AJHL	61	32	52	84	63	11	2	5	7	13
2002-03	U. of Wisconsin	WCHA	39	10	14	24	69	....	....	....	....	....
2003-04	U. of Wisconsin	WCHA	43	15	13	28	95	....	....	....	....	....
2004-05	U. of Wisconsin	WCHA	40	11	22	33	88	....	....	....	....	....
2005-06	U. of Wisconsin	WCHA	42	8	17	25	90	....	....	....	....	....

MACRI, Vince (MA-kree, VIHNS)

Defense. Shoots right. 6'3", 210 lbs. Born, Bethpage, NY, May 21, 1981.

			Regular Season					Playoffs				
Season	Club	League	GP	G	A	Pts	PIM	GP	G	A	Pts	PIM
99-2000	Exeter	High-NH	....	10	21	31	....	....	....	....	....	....
2000-01	Brown U.	ECAC	16	1	1	2	16	....	....	....	....	....
2001-02	Brown U.	ECAC	25	1	5	6	40	....	....	....	....	....
2002-03	Brown U.	ECAC	34	4	6	10	49	....	....	....	....	....
2003-04	Brown U.	ECAC	31	6	9	52	....	....	....	....	....	....
	Bridgeport	AHL	3	0	1	1	5	....	....	....	....	....
2004-05	Bridgeport	AHL	27	1	0	1	4	....	....	....	....	....
	Atlantic City	ECHL	49	5	9	14	99	1	0	0	0	0
2005-06	Bridgeport	AHL	50	1	7	8	41	....	....	....	....	....
	Fresno Falcons	ECHL	17	0	4	4	24	18	3	2	5	28

Signed as a free agent by **NY Islanders**, August 16, 2004.

MADILL, Mike (MA-dihl, MIGHK) MIN.

Defense. Shoots right. 6', 189 lbs. Born, Kirkland, Que., May 9, 1982.

			Regular Season					Playoffs				
Season	Club	League	GP	G	A	Pts	PIM	GP	G	A	Pts	PIM
2002-03	St. Lawrence	ECAC	35	1	8	9	26	....	....	....	....	....
2003-04	St. Lawrence	ECAC	41	2	4	6	47	....	....	....	....	....
2004-05	St. Lawrence	ECACHL	38	6	15	21	30	....	....	....	....	....
2005-06	St. Lawrence	ECACHL	40	5	22	27	54	....	....	....	....	....

Signed as a free agent by **Minnesota**, July 5, 2006.

MADSEN, Morten (MAD-sehn, MOHR-tuhn) MIN.

Right wing. Shoots right. 6'2", 191 lbs. Born, Rodovre, Denmark, January 16, 1987.
(Minnesota's 5th choice, 122nd overall, in 2005 Entry Draft).

			Regular Season					Playoffs				
Season	Club	League	GP	G	A	Pts	PIM	GP	G	A	Pts	PIM
2003-04	V.Frolunda U18	Swe-U18	11	13	8	21	0	7	3	1	4	4
	V.Frolunda Jr.	Swe-Jr.	16	3	2	5	0	1	0	0	0	0
2004-05	Frolunda U18	Swe-U18	2	1	2	3	0	6	7	7	14	6
	Frolunda Jr.	Swe-Jr.	32	7	14	21	14	6	3	2	5	0
2005-06	Frolunda Jr.	Swe-Jr.	36	10	32	42	60	7	5	3	8	4
	Frolunda	Sweden	5	0	0	0	2	....	....	....	....	....

MAGNAN, Olivier (MAHG-nah, oh-LIHV-ee-ay) N.J.

Defense. Shoots left. 6'2", 200 lbs. Born, Sherbrooke, Que., May 1, 1986.
(New Jersey's 6th choice, 148th overall, in 2006 Entry Draft).

			Regular Season					Playoffs				
Season	Club	League	GP	G	A	Pts	PIM	GP	G	A	Pts	PIM
2004-05	Rouyn-Noranda	QMJHL	70	5	15	20	82	10	0	2	2	14
2005-06	Rouyn-Noranda	QMJHL	69	14	27	41	97	5	0	1	1	6

MAKAROV, Igor (mak-AH-rawv, EE-gohr) CHI.

Right wing. Shoots right. 6'1", 183 lbs. Born, Moscow, Russia, September 19, 1987.
(Chicago's 2nd choice, 33rd overall, in 2006 Entry Draft).

			Regular Season					Playoffs				
Season	Club	League	GP	G	A	Pts	PIM	GP	G	A	Pts	PIM
2003-04	Krylja Sovetov 2	Russia-3	1	0	0	0	0	....	....	....	....	....
2004-05	Krylja Sovetov 2	Russia-3	38	13	15	28	44	....	....	....	....	....
	Krylja Sovetov	Russia-2	6	2	2	4	4	1	0	0	0	0
2005-06	Krylja Sovetov	Russia-2	35	9	7	16	20	17	3	4	7	20

MAKI, Ryan (MA-kee, RIGH-uhn) NSH.

Right wing. Shoots right. 6'1", 203 lbs. Born, Medford, NJ, April 23, 1985.
(Nashville's 5th choice, 176th overall, in 2005 Entry Draft).

			Regular Season					Playoffs				
Season	Club	League	GP	G	A	Pts	PIM	GP	G	A	Pts	PIM
2001-02	USNTDP	U-17	17	3	11	14	6	....	....	....	....	....
	USNTDP	NAHL	31	4	11	15	24	....	....	....	....	....
2002-03	USNTDP	U-18	42	5	6	11	18	....	....	....	....	....
	USNTDP	NAHL	10	1	0	1	8	....	....	....	....	....
2003-04	Harvard Crimson	ECAC	34	4	4	8	18	....	....	....	....	....
2004-05	Harvard Crimson	ECACHL	30	10	9	19	20	....	....	....	....	....
2005-06	Harvard Crimson	ECACHL	33	10	12	22	32	....	....	....	....	....

MAKI, Tomi (MA-kee, TAW-mee) CGY.

Right wing. Shoots left. 5'11", 187 lbs. Born, Helsinki, Finland, August 19, 1983.
(Calgary's 4th choice, 108th overall, in 2001 Entry Draft).

			Regular Season					Playoffs				
Season	Club	League	GP	G	A	Pts	PIM	GP	G	A	Pts	PIM
99-2000	Jokerit Helsinki Jr.	Fin-Jr.	33	6	1	7	12	3	0	0	0	0
2000-01	Jokerit U18	Fin-U18	10	4	10	14	4	6	4	3	7	0
	Jokerit Helsinki Jr.	Fin-Jr.	39	7	8	15	10	2	0	0	0	2
2001-02	Jokerit Helsinki Jr.	Fin-Jr.	29	12	13	25	12	1	0	0	0	2
	Kiekko-Vantaa	Finland-2	5	0	0	0	0	....	....	....	....	....
	Jokerit Helsinki	Finland	8	0	1	1	2	....	....	....	....	....
2002-03	Jokerit Helsinki Jr.	Fin-Jr.	14	4	4	8	12	11	3	3	6	4
	Kiekko-Vantaa	Finland-2	3	1	0	1	4	....	....	....	....	....
	Jokerit Helsinki	Finland	18	2	2	4	4	1	0	0	0	0
2003-04	Jokerit Helsinki	Finland	50	5	5	10	14	8	0	0	0	0
2004-05	Jokerit Helsinki	Finland	51	1	4	5	14	12	1	1	2	2
2005-06	Omaha	AHL	80	12	17	29	33	....	....	....	....	....

MALENKYKH, Vladimir (MAH-lihn-keh, vla-DIH-meer) **PIT.**

Defense. Shoots left. 6'1", 190 lbs. Born, Togliatti, USSR, October 1, 1980.
(Pittsburgh's 7th choice, 157th overall, in 1999 Entry Draft).

			Regular Season					Playoffs				
Season	Club	League	GP	G	A	Pts	PIM	GP	G	A	Pts	PIM
1997-98	Lada Togliatti 2	Russia-3	39	6	4	10	112	....	....	....	....	....
1998-99	Lada Togliatti 2	Russia-4	38	6	3	9	68	....	....	....	....	....
	Lada Togliatti	Russia	9	0	0	0	2	....	....	....	....	....
99-2000	Lada Togliatti 2	Russia-3	34	7	9	16	98	....	....	....	....	....
	CSK VVS Samara	Russia	7	0	1	1	14	....	....	....	....	....
	Lada Togliatti	Russia	1	0	0	0	0	....	....	....	....	....
	CSK VVS Samara 2	Russia-3	1	0	1	1	2	....	....	....	....	....
2000-01	Lada Togliatti	Russia	25	1	1	2	14	5	0	0	0	26
2001-02	Lada Togliatti	Russia	47	5	4	9	88	4	0	0	0	2
2002-03	Lada Togliatti	Russia	30	3	1	4	36	10	0	0	0	6
2003-04	Lada Togliatti	Russia	44	2	4	6	42	3	0	0	0	0
2004-05	Lada Togliatti	Russia	37	1	4	5	20	....	....	....	....	....
2005-06	Magnitogorsk	Russia	36	0	2	2	8	11	0	1	1	16
	Magnitogorsk 2	Russia-3	5	1	1	2	2	....	....	....	....	....

MALKIN, Evgeni (MAHL-kihn, ehv-GEH-nee) **PIT.**

Center. Shoots left. 6'3", 186 lbs. Born, Magnitogorsk, USSR, July 31, 1986.
(Pittsburgh's 1st choice, 2nd overall, in 2004 Entry Draft).

			Regular Season					Playoffs				
Season	Club	League	GP	G	A	Pts	PIM	GP	G	A	Pts	PIM
2003-04	Magnitogorsk 2	Russia-3	2	1	0	1	8	....	....	....	....	....
	Magnitogorsk	Russia	34	3	9	12	12	....	....	....	....	....
2004-05	Magnitogorsk 2	Russia-3	2	1	1	2	2	....	....	....	....	....
	Magnitogorsk	Russia	52	12	20	32	24	5	0	4	4	0
2005-06	Magnitogorsk	Russia	46	21	26	47	46	11	5	10	15	41
	Russia	Olympics	7	2	4	6	31	....	....	....	....	....

MALMIVAARA, Olli (mal-MIH-vah-ruh, OH-lee) **N.J.**

Defense. Shoots left. 6'7", 220 lbs. Born, Kajaani, Finland, March 13, 1982.
(Chicago's 6th choice, 117th overall, in 2000 Entry Draft).

			Regular Season					Playoffs				
Season	Club	League	GP	G	A	Pts	PIM	GP	G	A	Pts	PIM
1998-99	Jokerit U18	Fin-U18	35	1	8	9	10	7	0	0	0	2
99-2000	Jokerit U18	Fin-U18	14	6	6	12	14	1	0	0	0	2
	Jokerit U18	Fin-U18	27	3	3	6	12	12	0	2	2	2
2000-01	Jokerit Helsinki Jr.	Fin-Jr.	33	10	13	23	24	2	0	0	0	0
	Kiekko-Vantaa	Finland-2	4	1	0	1	2	....	....	....	....	....
	Jokerit Helsinki	Finland	5	0	0	0	2	....	....	....	....	....
2001-02	Jokerit Helsinki Jr.	Fin-Jr.	2	0	1	1	0	....	....	....	....	....
	Jokerit Helsinki	Finland	53	0	6	6	16	11	0	0	0	2
2002-03	Jokerit Helsinki Jr.	Fin-Jr.	1	0	0	0	0	....	....	....	....	....
	Kiekko-Vantaa	Finland-2	2	1	1	2	2	....	....	....	....	....
	Jokerit Helsinki	Finland	42	1	0	1	22	5	0	0	0	0
2003-04	Jokerit Helsinki	Finland	25	1	0	1	2	....	....	....	....	....
	SaiPa	Finland	11	1	0	1	6	....	....	....	....	....
2004-05	SaiPa	Finland	56	9	1	10	89	....	....	....	....	....
2005-06	SaiPa	Finland	54	11	9	20	134	8	1	0	1	12

MALONEY, Brian (muh-LOH-nee, BRIGH-uhn) **OTT.**

Left wing. Shoots left. 6'1", 205 lbs. Born, Bassano, Alta., September 27, 1978.

			Regular Season					Playoffs				
Season	Club	League	GP	G	A	Pts	PIM	GP	G	A	Pts	PIM
1997-98	Olds Grizzlys	AJHL	31	21	13	34	....	....	....	....	....	....
	Chilliwack Chiefs	BCHL	27	4	12	16	36	....	....	....	....	....
1998-99	Chilliwack Chiefs	BCHL	60	40	75	115	121	....	....	....	....	....
99-2000	Michigan State	CCHA	42	12	19	31	87	....	....	....	....	....
2000-01	Michigan State	CCHA	41	15	22	37	86	....	....	....	....	....
2001-02	Michigan State	CCHA	37	17	16	33	71	....	....	....	....	....
2002-03	Michigan State	CCHA	39	19	16	35	48	....	....	....	....	....
	Chicago Wolves	AHL	4	0	1	1	11	....	....	....	....	....
2003-04	Chicago Wolves	AHL	69	9	11	20	56	10	1	1	2	17
2004-05	Chicago Wolves	AHL	77	7	10	17	164	18	2	1	3	38
2005-06	Chicago Wolves	AHL	68	16	18	34	143	....	....	....	....	....

Signed as a free agent by **Atlanta**, April 2, 2003. Signed as a free agent by **Ottawa**, July 27, 2006.

MANCARI, Mark (man-KAH-ree, MAHRK) **BUF.**

Right wing. Shoots right. 6'3", 225 lbs. Born, London, Ont., July 11, 1985.
(Buffalo's 6th choice, 207th overall, in 2004 Entry Draft).

			Regular Season					Playoffs				
Season	Club	League	GP	G	A	Pts	PIM	GP	G	A	Pts	PIM
2001-02	Ottawa 67's	OHL	34	3	3	6	10	2	0	1	1	0
2002-03	Ottawa 67's	OHL	61	8	11	19	20	11	2	1	3	2
2003-04	Ottawa 67's	OHL	67	29	36	65	56	7	5	3	8	11
2004-05	Ottawa 67's	OHL	64	36	32	68	86	21	*14	10	24	24
2005-06	Rochester	AHL	71	18	24	42	80	....	....	....	....	....

MANSON, Lane (MAN-suhn, LAYN) **ATL.**

Defense. Shoots left. 6'9", 245 lbs. Born, Watrous, Sask., February 14, 1984.
(Atlanta's 4th choice, 124th overall, in 2002 Entry Draft).

			Regular Season					Playoffs				
Season	Club	League	GP	G	A	Pts	PIM	GP	G	A	Pts	PIM
99-2000	North Battleford	SMBHL	41	7	12	19	110	....	....	....	....	....
2000-01	North Battleford	MMMHL	40	14	12	26	180	....	....	....	....	....
2001-02	Moose Jaw	WHL	67	4	3	7	88	12	0	1	1	6
2002-03	Moose Jaw	WHL	66	0	5	5	192	13	0	0	0	12
2003-04	Moose Jaw	WHL	72	3	9	12	253	10	0	2	2	18
2004-05	Gwinnett	ECHL	71	5	12	17	127	8	0	3	3	20
2005-06	Gwinnett	ECHL	66	2	7	9	169	9	0	0	0	39

MANTYMAA, Ville (man-T'YUH-mah, VIHL-ee) **ANA.**

Defense. Shoots right. 6'3", 183 lbs. Born, Seinajoki, Finland, March 8, 1985.
(Anaheim's 9th choice, 280th overall, in 2003 Entry Draft).

			Regular Season					Playoffs				
Season	Club	League	GP	G	A	Pts	PIM	GP	G	A	Pts	PIM
2000-01	Tappara U18	Fin-U18	2	0	0	0	0	....	....	....	....	....
2001-02	Tappara U18	Fin-U18	1	0	0	0	2	....	....	....	....	....
	Tappara Jr.	Fin-Jr.	32	4	2	6	24	....	....	....	....	....
2002-03	Tappara Jr.	Fin-Jr.	33	3	12	15	26	8	2	0	2	4
	Tappara Tampere	Finland	8	0	0	0	0	1	0	0	0	0
2003-04	Suomi U20	Finland-2	5	0	1	1	2	....	....	....	....	....
	Tappara Jr.	Fin-Jr.	21	1	7	8	14	14	0	3	3	8
	Pelicans Lahti	Finland	2	0	0	0	0	....	....	....	....	....
	Tappara Tampere	Finland	19	0	2	2	8	....	....	....	....	....
2004-05	Tappara Jr.	Fin-Jr.	13	0	6	6	14	4	0	1	1	2
	Tappara Tampere	Finland	32	1	1	2	18	8	0	1	1	0
2005-06	Tappara Jr.	Fin-Jr.	19	8	10	18	14	....	....	....	....	....
	Kiekko-Vantaa	Finland-2	3	1	1	2	2	....	....	....	....	....
	Tappara Tampere	Finland	32	1	0	1	18	6	0	1	1	0

MARCHAND, Brad (mahr-SHAHND, BRAD) **BOS.**

Center. Shoots left. 5'9", 183 lbs. Born, Halifax, N.S., May 11, 1988.
(Boston's 4th choice, 71st overall, in 2006 Entry Draft).

			Regular Season					Playoffs				
Season	Club	League	GP	G	A	Pts	PIM	GP	G	A	Pts	PIM
2003-04	Dartmouth	NSMHL	60	47	47	94	104	....	....	....	....	....
2004-05	Moncton Wildcats	QMJHL	61	9	20	29	52	11	1	0	1	7
2005-06	Moncton Wildcats	QMJHL	68	29	37	66	83	20	5	14	19	34

MARCINKO, Tomas (mahr-TSIHN-koh, TAW-mahsh) **NYI**

Center. Shoots right. 6'4", 187 lbs. Born, Poprad, Slovakia, April 11, 1988.
(NY Islanders' 6th choice, 115th overall, in 2006 Entry Draft).

			Regular Season					Playoffs				
Season	Club	League	GP	G	A	Pts	PIM	GP	G	A	Pts	PIM
2003-04	HC Kosice U18	Slovak-U18	42	19	23	42	60	2	0	0	0	4
	HC Kosice Jr.	Slovak-Jr.	7	0	2	2	4	3	0	1	1	0
2004-05	HC Kosice Jr.	Slovak-Jr.	38	11	18	29	28	8	1	2	3	6
	HC Kosice	Slovakia	6	0	0	0	0	....	....	....	....	....
	HC Kosice	Slovakia	6	0	0	0	0	....	....	....	....	....
2005-06	HC Kosice Jr.	Slovak-Jr.	35	26	21	47	50	3	1	0	1	4
	HKm Humenne	Slovak-2	9	3	5	8	10	....	....	....	....	....
	HC Kosice	Slovakia	18	2	0	2	2	5	0	0	0	0

MAREK, Jan (MAIR-ehk, YAHN) **NYR**

Center. Shoots right. 5'10", 185 lbs. Born, Jindrichuv Hradec, Czech., December 31, 1979.
(NY Rangers' 10th choice, 243rd overall, in 2003 Entry Draft).

			Regular Season					Playoffs				
Season	Club	League	GP	G	A	Pts	PIM	GP	G	A	Pts	PIM
1998-99	Trinec	CzRep	32	2	2	4	2	6	0	0	0	0
99-2000	HC Trinec Jr.	CzRep-Jr.	6	5	5	10	10	1	0	0	0	0
	HC Slezan Opava	CzRep-2	3	0	1	1	4	....	....	....	....	....
	Jind. Hradec	CzRep-2	4	0	3	3	10	....	....	....	....	....
	HC Ocelari Trinec	CzRep	32	1	5	6	4	2	0	0	0	0
2000-01	HC Ocelari Trinec	CzRep	38	7	4	11	2	....	....	....	....	....
2001-02	HC Ocelari Trinec	CzRep	52	13	27	40	44	6	1	3	4	6
2002-03	HC Ocelari Trinec	CzRep	51	*32	30	62	42	12	6	4	10	22
2003-04	HC Sparta Praha	CzRep	50	21	30	51	62	11	4	9	13	26
2004-05	HC Sparta Praha	CzRep	38	7	21	28	26	5	2	2	4	2
2005-06	HC Sparta Praha	CzRep	48	22	32	*54	66	17	4	4	8	24

MARQUARDT, Matt (MAR-kwart, MAT) **CBJ**

Left wing. Shoots left. 6'2", 222 lbs. Born, North Bay, Ont., July 19, 1987.
(Columbus' 10th choice, 194th overall, in 2006 Entry Draft).

			Regular Season					Playoffs				
Season	Club	League	GP	G	A	Pts	PIM	GP	G	A	Pts	PIM
2003-04	Huntsville Wildcats	OPJHL	STATISTICS NOT AVAILABLE									
	Brockville Braves	CJHL	11	1	2	3	17	....	....	....	....	....
2004-05	Brockville Braves	CJHL	55	19	22	41	78	7	2	1	3	8
2005-06	Moncton Wildcats	QMJHL	68	16	9	25	69	20	5	3	8	12

CJHL Rookie of the Year (2005)

MARR, Steve (MAHR, STEEV) **CGY.**

Defense. Shoots left. 6'2", 218 lbs. Born, Kamloops, B.C., June 6, 1984.

			Regular Season					Playoffs				
Season	Club	League	GP	G	A	Pts	PIM	GP	G	A	Pts	PIM
2001-02	Medicine Hat	WHL	63	0	0	0	50	....	....	....	....	....
2002-03	Medicine Hat	WHL	54	3	11	14	95	11	0	1	1	22
2003-04	Medicine Hat	WHL	71	2	9	11	80	20	1	2	3	*50
2004-05	Medicine Hat	WHL	54	11	8	19	105	13	2	3	5	22
2005-06	Omaha	AHL	32	0	0	0	31	....	....	....	....	....
	Las Vegas	ECHL	23	1	3	4	24	....	....	....	....	....

Signed as a free agent by **Calgary**, August 5, 2005.

MARSH, Tyson (MAHRSH, TIGH-suhn) **TOR.**

Defense. Shoots left. 6'1", 190 lbs. Born, Quesnel, B.C, June 20, 1984.

			Regular Season					Playoffs				
Season	Club	League	GP	G	A	Pts	PIM	GP	G	A	Pts	PIM
2000-01	Quesnel	BCHL	52	4	2	6	25	....	....	....	....	....
2001-02	Vancouver Giants	WHL	69	2	14	16	85	....	....	....	....	....
2002-03	Vancouver Giants	WHL	68	3	15	18	143	3	0	1	1	4
2003-04	Vancouver Giants	WHL	67	3	18	21	102	11	0	3	3	4
2004-05	St. John's	AHL	21	0	1	1	30	....	....	....	....	....
	Pensacola	ECHL	23	1	2	3	29	4	0	0	0	2
2005-06	Toronto Marlies	AHL	12	0	0	0	23	....	....	....	....	....

Signed as a free agent by **Toronto**, September 18, 2002. @FNOT = • Missed majority of 2005-06 season recovering from an abdominal injury.

MARTIN, Jesse (MAHR-tihn, JEH-see) **ATL.**

Center. Shoots left. 5'11", 170 lbs. Born, Edmonton, Alta., September 7, 1988.
(Atlanta's 6th choice, 195th overall, in 2006 Entry Draft).

			Regular Season					Playoffs				
Season	Club	League	GP	G	A	Pts	PIM	GP	G	A	Pts	PIM
2003-04	K of C Pats	AMHL	34	10	11	21	6	....	....	....	....	....
2004-05	K of C Pats	AMHL	30	17	28	45	70	8	4	8	12	....
2005-06	Spruce Grove	AJHL	40	15	29	44	122	....	....	....	....	....

MARVIN, Aaron (MAHR-vihn, Air-uhn) CGY.

Forward. Shoots left. 6'2", 191 lbs. Born, Warrod, MN, May 27, 1988.
(Calgary's 3rd choice, 89th overall, in 2006 Entry Draft).

			Regular Season					Playoffs				
Season	Club	League	GP	G	A	Pts	PIM	GP	G	A	Pts	PIM
2004-05	Warroad Warriors	High-MN	31	23	25	48	18					
2005-06	Warroad Warriors	High-MN	23	9	21	30	40					

MASON, Tyrell (MAY-sohn, TIGH-rehl) NYI

Defense. Shoots left. 6'1", 167 lbs. Born, Grand Prairie, Alta., March 12, 1986.
(NY Islanders' 5th choice, 180th overall, in 2005 Entry Draft).

			Regular Season					Playoffs				
Season	Club	League	GP	G	A	Pts	PIM	GP	G	A	Pts	PIM
2003-04	Salmon Arm	BCHL	59	7	29	36	36					
2004-05	Salmon Arm	BCHL	51	6	36	42	78					
2005-06	Clarkson Knights	ECACHL	38	1	5	6	38					

MATSUMOTO, Jonathan (mat-suh-MOH-toh, JAWN-ah-thun) PHI.

Center. Shoots left. 6', 184 lbs. Born, Ottawa, Ont., October 13, 1986.
(Philadelphia's 5th choice, 79th overall, in 2006 Entry Draft).

			Regular Season					Playoffs				
Season	Club	League	GP	G	A	Pts	PIM	GP	G	A	Pts	PIM
2002-03	Cumberland	CJHL	8	2	3	5	2	10	4	7	11	2
2003-04	Cumberland	CJHL	51	31	32	63	26	7	5	5	10	6
2004-05	Bowling Green	CCHA	36	18	14	32	22					
2005-06	Bowling Green	CCHA	36	20	28	48	43					

MATTHIAS, Shawn (muh-TIGH-uhs, SHAWN) DET.

Center. Shoots left. 6'3", 211 lbs. Born, Mississauga, Ont., February 19, 1988.
(Detroit's 2nd choice, 47th overall, in 2006 Entry Draft).

			Regular Season					Playoffs				
Season	Club	League	GP	G	A	Pts	PIM	GP	G	A	Pts	PIM
2004-05	Belleville Bulls	OHL	37	1	1	2	15	3	0	0	0	0
2005-06	Belleville Bulls	OHL	67	13	21	34	42	6	3	0	3	2

MATTILA, Troy (mah-TIHL-luh, TROI) NYI

Left wing. Shoots left. 6'2", 176 lbs. Born, Rockford, IL, January 12, 1988.
(NY Islanders' 13th choice, 190th overall, in 2006 Entry Draft).

			Regular Season					Playoffs				
Season	Club	League	GP	G	A	Pts	PIM	GP	G	A	Pts	PIM
2002-03	Rockford Icemen	High-IL	34	20	28	48	4					
2003-04	Rockford Icemen	High-IL	69	*100	*77	*177	34					
2004-05	Rockford Icemen	High-IL	64	*146	*76	*222	10					
2005-06	Minnesota Blades	Exhib.	8	7	4	11	....					
	Springfield-IL	NAHL	54	14	22	36	13	4	0	1	1	2

MAXIMENKO, Andrei (max-EE-mehn-koh, AWN-dray) DET.

Left wing. Shoots right. 5'11", 172 lbs. Born, Moscow, USSR, January 10, 1981.
(Detroit's 2nd choice, 149th overall, in 1999 Entry Draft).

			Regular Season					Playoffs				
Season	Club	League	GP	G	A	Pts	PIM	GP	G	A	Pts	PIM
1997-98	Krylja Sovetov 2	Russia-3	42	2	4	6	12					
1998-99	Krylja Sovetov	Russia	28	1	2	3	24					
99-2000	Krylja Sovetov 2	Russia-3	6	4	2	6	26					
	Krylja Sovetov	Russia-2	39	6	7	13	41					
2000-01	Krylja Sovetov	Russia-2	28	2	5	7	8					
2001-02	THK Tver	Russia-2	20	3	7	10	6					
	Krylja Sovetov 2	Russia-3	7	3	5	8	2					
	Perm	Russia	9	0	1	1	2					
2002-03	Kristall Saratov	Russia-2	47	12	12	24	36					
2003-04	Krylja Sovetov	Russia-2	19	2	3	5	8					
2004-05	Kristall Saratov	Russia-2	16	4	2	6	8					
	Almetjevsk	Russia-2	27	4	8	12	14	3	0	0	0	2
2005-06	Almetjevsk	Russia-2	36	7	6	13	32					
	Almetjevsk 2	Russia-3	3	3	2	5	8					

MAXWELL, Ben (MAX-wehl, BEHN) MTL.

Center. Shoots left. 6'1", 183 lbs. Born, North Vancouver, B.C., March 30, 1988.
(Montreal's 2nd choice, 49th overall, in 2006 Entry Draft).

			Regular Season					Playoffs				
Season	Club	League	GP	G	A	Pts	PIM	GP	G	A	Pts	PIM
2003-04	North Delta Ice	PIJHL	40	17	28	45	46	5	3	6	9	0
	South Surrey	BCHL	2	0	0	0	0					
	Kootenay Ice	WHL	3	0	1	1	2	1	0	0	0	0
2004-05	Kootenay Ice	WHL	68	8	10	18	37	16	0	1	1	6
2005-06	Kootenay Ice	WHL	69	28	32	60	52	6	3	5	8	0

MAY, Jeff (MAY, JEHF) DET.

Defense. Shoots left. 6'1", 186 lbs. Born, Richmond, B.C., April 4, 1987.
(Detroit's 7th choice, 151st overall, in 2005 Entry Draft).

			Regular Season					Playoffs				
Season	Club	League	GP	G	A	Pts	PIM	GP	G	A	Pts	PIM
2002-03	Richmond	BCAHA	55	11	26	37	143					
	Prince Albert	WHL	5	0	0	0	2					
2003-04	Prince Albert	WHL	40	0	3	3	19	3	0	0	0	4
2004-05	Prince Albert	WHL	67	3	19	22	66	17	2	3	5	13
2005-06	Prince Albert	WHL	72	2	28	30	104					

McARDLE, Kenndal (mih-KAHR-duhl, KEHN-dahl) FLA.

Left wing. Shoots left. 5'11", 190 lbs. Born, Toronto, Ont., January 4, 1987.
(Florida's 1st choice, 20th overall, in 2005 Entry Draft).

			Regular Season					Playoffs				
Season	Club	League	GP	G	A	Pts	PIM	GP	G	A	Pts	PIM
2002-03	Burnaby	BCAHA	30	1	9	10	131					
	Moose Jaw	WHL	2	0	0	0	0					
2003-04	Moose Jaw	WHL	54	8	8	16	57	10	3	2	5	6
2004-05	Moose Jaw	WHL	70	37	37	74	122	5	1	0	1	16
2005-06	Moose Jaw	WHL	72	28	43	71	135	22	6	10	16	43

McBAIN, Jamie (mihk-BAYN, JAY-mee) CAR.

Defense. Shoots right. 6'1", 190 lbs. Born, Edina, MN, February 25, 1988.
(Carolina's 1st choice, 63rd overall, in 2006 Entry Draft).

			Regular Season					Playoffs				
Season	Club	League	GP	G	A	Pts	PIM	GP	G	A	Pts	PIM
2003-04	Shat.-St. Mary's	High-MN	73	6	27	33	....					
2004-05	USNTDP	U-17	14	1	6	7	16					
	USNTDP	NAHL	38	2	7	9	22	10	0	3	3	4
2005-06	USNTDP	U-18	41	9	16	25	35					
	USNTDP	NAHL	14	0	5	5	6					

Signed Letter of Intent to attend **U. of Wisconsin** (WCHA) in fall of 2006.

McCARTHY, John (mih-KAHR-thee, JAWN) S.J.

Left wing. Shoots left. 6', 200 lbs. Born, Boston, MA, August 9, 1986.
(San Jose's 5th choice, 202nd overall, in 2006 Entry Draft).

			Regular Season					Playoffs				
Season	Club	League	GP	G	A	Pts	PIM	GP	G	A	Pts	PIM
2004-05	Des Moines	USHL	60	8	10	18	32					
2005-06	Boston University	H-East	33	2	2	4	12					

McCLELLAN, Steve (muh-KLEHL-uhn, STEEV) COL.

Defense. Shoots left. 6'1", 180 lbs. Born, Boston, MA, April 22, 1985.
(Colorado's 9th choice, 281st overall, in 2004 Entry Draft).

			Regular Season					Playoffs				
Season	Club	League	GP	G	A	Pts	PIM	GP	G	A	Pts	PIM
2001-02	Catholic Memorial	High-MA	20	4	16	20	....					
2002-03	Catholic Memorial	High-MA	28	3	9	12	....					
2003-04	Catholic Memorial	High-MA	25	8	18	26	14					
2004-05	Cushing	High-MA	34	6	20	26	....					
2005-06	Northeastern	H-East	9	0	0	0	6					

McCOLLEM, Matthew (mih-KAHL-uhm, MA-thew) ST.L.

Left wing. Shoots left. 6', 185 lbs. Born, Somerville, MA, May 6, 1988.
(St. Louis' 8th choice, 154th overall, in 2006 Entry Draft).

			Regular Season					Playoffs				
Season	Club	League	GP	G	A	Pts	PIM	GP	G	A	Pts	PIM
2004-05	Belmont Hill	High-MA	....	2	7	9	....					
2005-06	Belmont Hill	High-MA	28	17	11	28	48					

Signed Letter of Intent to attend **Harvard** (ECACHL) in fall of 2006.

McCULLOCH, Scott (muh-KUHL-uh, SKAWT) CHI.

Left wing. Shoots left. 6'1", 212 lbs. Born, Edmonton, Alta., March 10, 1986.
(Chicago's 11th choice, 165th overall, in 2004 Entry Draft).

			Regular Season					Playoffs				
Season	Club	League	GP	G	A	Pts	PIM	GP	G	A	Pts	PIM
2003-04	Grand Prairie	AJHL	44	23	26	49	85	16	12	8	20	18
2004-05	Colorado College	WCHA	11	4	3	7	6					
2005-06	Colorado College	WCHA	42	5	7	12	67					

McCUTCHEON, Mark (mih-KUH-chuhn, MAHRK) COL.

Center. Shoots right. 6', 190 lbs. Born, Ithaca, NY, May 21, 1984.
(Colorado's 3rd choice, 146th overall, in 2003 Entry Draft).

			Regular Season					Playoffs				
Season	Club	League	GP	G	A	Pts	PIM	GP	G	A	Pts	PIM
2001-02	N.E. Jr. Coyotes	EJHL	36	24	26	50	84					
2002-03	N.E. Jr. Coyotes	EJHL	35	27	22	49	76	10	8	5	13	24
2003-04	Cornell Big Red	ECAC	32	0	4	4	12					
2004-05	Cornell Big Red	ECACHL	22	0	5	5	12					
2005-06	Cornell Big Red	ECACHL	34	9	6	15	34					

McDONALD, Colin (mihk-DAW-nuhld, KAW-lihn) EDM.

Right wing. Shoots right. 6'2", 190 lbs. Born, New Haven, CT, September 30, 1984.
(Edmonton's 2nd choice, 51st overall, in 2003 Entry Draft).

			Regular Season					Playoffs				
Season	Club	League	GP	G	A	Pts	PIM	GP	G	A	Pts	PIM
2001-02	N.E. Jr. Coyotes	EJHL	39	16	20	36	50					
2002-03	N.E. Jr. Coyotes	EJHL	44	28	40	*68	59					
2003-04	Providence College	H-East	37	10	6	16	47					
2004-05	Providence College	H-East	26	11	5	16	14					
2005-06	Providence College	H-East	36	9	19	28	29					

Hockey East All-Rookie Team (2004)

McGINN, Jamie (mih-GIHN, JAY-mee) S.J.

Left wing. Shoots left. 5'11", 179 lbs. Born, Fergus, Ont., August 5, 1988.
(San Jose's 2nd choice, 36th overall, in 2006 Entry Draft).

			Regular Season					Playoffs				
Season	Club	League	GP	G	A	Pts	PIM	GP	G	A	Pts	PIM
2004-05	Ottawa 67's	OHL	59	10	12	22	35	18	4	7	11	0
2005-06	Ottawa 67's	OHL	65	26	31	57	113	6	2	2	4	4

McGINNIS, Ryan (mih-GIHN-ihs, RIGH-uhn) L.A.

Defense. Shoots left. 6'1", 197 lbs. Born, Flint, MI, March 3, 1987.
(Los Angeles' 6th choice, 184th overall, in 2005 Entry Draft).

			Regular Season					Playoffs				
Season	Club	League	GP	G	A	Pts	PIM	GP	G	A	Pts	PIM
2003-04	Plymouth Whalers	OHL	32	2	2	4	31	2	0	0	0	0
2004-05	Plymouth Whalers	OHL	66	0	6	6	93	4	0	1	1	2
2005-06	Plymouth Whalers	OHL	65	3	23	26	135	11	1	6	7	20

McGRATH, Evan (muh-GRATH, EH-vuhn) DET.

Center. Shoots left. 5'11", 181 lbs. Born, Oakville, Ont., January 14, 1986.
(Detroit's 2nd choice, 128th overall, in 2004 Entry Draft).

			Regular Season					Playoffs				
Season	Club	League	GP	G	A	Pts	PIM	GP	G	A	Pts	PIM
2001-02	Oakville Blades	OPJHL	49	43	44	87	24					
2002-03	Kitchener Rangers	OHL	64	16	31	47	40	21	6	2	8	6
2003-04	Kitchener Rangers	OHL	68	15	36	51	28	5	2	1	3	2
2004-05	Kitchener Rangers	OHL	67	28	59	87	51	15	7	6	13	6
2005-06	Kitchener Rangers	OHL	67	37	77	114	63	5	1	3	4	4

OHL All-Rookie Team (2003)

McGUIRK, Brian (muh-GUHRK, BRIGH-uhn) **CBJ**

Left wing. Shoots left. 6', 191 lbs. Born, Danvers, MA, July 11, 1985.
(Columbus' 10th choice, 231st overall, in 2004 Entry Draft).

			Regular Season					Playoffs				
Season	Club	League	GP	G	A	Pts	PIM	GP	G	A	Pts	PIM
2003-04	Gov. Dummer	High-MA	25	16	16	32	....	....	....	....	....	....
2004-05	Boston University	H-East	33	0	1	1	18	....	....	....	....	....
2005-06	Boston University	H-East	39	5	4	9	18	....	....	....	....	....

McILVANE, Matthew (MAK-uhl-vay-nee, MA-thew) **OTT.**

Center. Shoots right. 6', 202 lbs. Born, Downers Grove, IL, November 2, 1985.
(Ottawa's 10th choice, 251st overall, in 2004 Entry Draft).

			Regular Season					Playoffs				
Season	Club	League	GP	G	A	Pts	PIM	GP	G	A	Pts	PIM
2003-04	Chicago Steel	USHL	59	22	24	46	53	3	1	2	3	0
2004-05	Ohio State	CCHA	42	1	5	6	30	....	....	....	....	....
2005-06	Ohio State	CCHA	37	3	10	13	45	....	....	....	....	....

McINTYRE, David (mih-IHN-tighr, DAY-vihd) **DAL.**

Center. Shoots left. 5'11", 171 lbs. Born, Oakville, Ont., February 4, 1987.
(Dallas' 4th choice, 138th overall, in 2006 Entry Draft).

			Regular Season					Playoffs				
Season	Club	League	GP	G	A	Pts	PIM	GP	G	A	Pts	PIM
2004-05	Newmarket	OPJHL	46	17	14	31	33	16	8	7	15	20
2005-06	Newmarket	OPJHL	46	42	50	92	143	11	4	8	12	42

Signed Letter of Intent to attend **Colgate** (ECACHL) in fall of 2006.

McIVER, Nathan (mih-KEE-vuhr, NAY-thun) **VAN.**

Defense. Shoots left. 6'2", 195 lbs. Born, Kinkora, P.E.I., January 6, 1985.
(Vancouver's 9th choice, 254th overall, in 2003 Entry Draft).

			Regular Season					Playoffs				
Season	Club	League	GP	G	A	Pts	PIM	GP	G	A	Pts	PIM
2001-02	Summerside	MJrHL	47	4	4	8	91	5	0	0	0	9
2002-03	St. Michael's	OHL	68	5	10	15	121	19	0	4	4	41
2003-04	St. Michael's	OHL	57	4	11	15	183	16	0	1	1	22
2004-05	St. Michael's	OHL	67	4	22	26	160	3	0	1	1	13
2005-06	Manitoba Moose	AHL	66	1	6	7	155	12	0	0	0	28

McKENZIE, Jim (MIHK-ehn-zee, JIHM) **OTT.**

Right wing. Shoots right. 6'2", 209 lbs. Born, St. Paul, MN, June 10, 1984.
(Ottawa's 7th choice, 141st overall, in 2004 Entry Draft).

			Regular Season					Playoffs				
Season	Club	League	GP	G	A	Pts	PIM	GP	G	A	Pts	PIM
2000-01	Hill-Murray	High-MN	27	9	13	22	....	....	....	....	....	....
2001-02	USNTDP	U-18	13	7	8	15	10	....	....	....	....	....
	USNTDP	USHL	2	0	1	1	9	....	....	....	....	....
	USNTDP	NAHL	4	0	2	2	4	....	....	....	....	....
	Green Bay	USHL	17	1	2	3	34	....	....	....	....	....
2002-03	Sioux Falls	USHL	45	6	18	24	108	....	....	....	....	....
2003-04	Sioux Falls	USHL	59	26	38	64	168	....	....	....	....	....
2004-05	Michigan State	CCHA	34	11	7	18	44	....	....	....	....	....
2005-06	Michigan State	CCHA	43	11	17	28	85	....	....	....	....	....

McKNIGHT, Matt (mihk-NIGHT, MAT) **DAL.**

Forward. Shoots right. 6'2", 190 lbs. Born, Red Deer, Alta., June 14, 1984.
(Dallas' 10th choice, 280th overall, in 2004 Entry Draft).

			Regular Season					Playoffs				
Season	Club	League	GP	G	A	Pts	PIM	GP	G	A	Pts	PIM
2003-04	Camrose Kodiaks	AJHL	42	20	36	56	31	....	....	....	....	....
2004-05	U. Minn-Duluth	WCHA	30	6	13	19	16	....	....	....	....	....
2005-06	U. Minn-Duluth	WCHA	40	9	16	25	24	....	....	....	....	....

McLEOD, Cody (mih-KLOWD, KOH-dee) **COL.**

Left wing. Shoots left. 6'2", 210 lbs. Born, Binscarth, Man., June 26, 1984.

			Regular Season					Playoffs				
Season	Club	League	GP	G	A	Pts	PIM	GP	G	A	Pts	PIM
2001-02	Portland	WHL	47	10	3	13	86	5	0	0	0	0
2002-03	Portland	WHL	71	15	18	33	153	7	1	1	2	13
2003-04	Portland	WHL	69	13	18	31	227	5	2	2	4	6
2004-05	Portland	WHL	70	31	29	60	195	7	0	3	3	8
	Adirondack	UHL	1	0	0	0	0	5	0	0	0	11
2005-06	Lowell	AHL	33	4	5	9	87	....	....	....	....	....
	San Diego Gulls	ECHL	16	4	5	9	48	2	2	1	3	14

Signed as a free agent by **Colorado**, July 6, 2006.

McLEOD, Kiel (muk-KLOWD, KIGHL)

Center. Shoots right. 6'6", 230 lbs. Born, Ft. Saskatchewan, Alta., December 30, 1982.
(Columbus' 3rd choice, 53rd overall, in 2001 Entry Draft).

			Regular Season					Playoffs				
Season	Club	League	GP	G	A	Pts	PIM	GP	G	A	Pts	PIM
1997-98	North Delta	BCAHA	55	57	55	112	202	....	....	....	....	....
1998-99	Kelowna Rockets	WHL	55	12	15	27	48	6	0	1	1	2
99-2000	Kelowna Rockets	WHL	59	17	13	30	100	5	2	1	3	2
2000-01	Kelowna Rockets	WHL	65	38	28	66	94	4	4	1	5	8
2001-02	Kelowna Rockets	WHL	41	17	31	48	62	15	3	10	13	14
2002-03	Kelowna Rockets	WHL	68	39	51	90	163	8	5	5	10	4
2003-04	Springfield Falcons	AHL	77	7	11	18	71	....	....	....	....	....
2004-05	Utah Grizzlies	AHL	73	13	12	25	107	....	....	....	....	....
2005-06	San Antonio	AHL	28	0	1	1	33	....	....	....	....	....
	Philadelphia	AHL	34	2	2	4	36	....	....	....	....	....
	Trenton Titans	ECHL	8	5	4	9	15	2	0	1	1	2

WHL West Second All-Star Team (2003)

Signed as a free agent by **Phoenix**, June 9, 2003. Traded to **Philadelphia** by **Phoenix** for Eric Chouinard, December 28, 2005.

McNEILL, Patrick (muhk-NEEL, PAT-rihk) **WSH.**

Defense. Shoots left. 6', 195 lbs. Born, Strathroy, Ont., March 17, 1987.
(Washington's 4th choice, 118th overall, in 2005 Entry Draft).

			Regular Season					Playoffs				
Season	Club	League	GP	G	A	Pts	PIM	GP	G	A	Pts	PIM
2002-03	Strathroy Rockets	OHA-B	45	6	13	19	53	....	....	....	....	....
2003-04	Saginaw Spirit	OHL	57	3	11	14	28	....	....	....	....	....
2004-05	Saginaw Spirit	OHL	66	7	26	33	31	....	....	....	....	....
2005-06	Saginaw Spirit	OHL	68	21	56	77	64	4	1	3	4	6

OHL Second All-Star Team (2006)

McQUAID, Adam (muhk-WAYD, A-duhm) **CBJ**

Defense. Shoots right. 6'3", 206 lbs. Born, Charlottetown, P.E.I., October 12, 1986.
(Columbus' 2nd choice, 55th overall, in 2005 Entry Draft).

			Regular Season					Playoffs				
Season	Club	League	GP	G	A	Pts	PIM	GP	G	A	Pts	PIM
2003-04	Sudbury Wolves	OHL	47	3	6	9	25	7	0	1	1	2
2004-05	Sudbury Wolves	OHL	66	3	16	19	98	8	0	2	2	10
2005-06	Sudbury Wolves	OHL	68	3	14	17	107	10	0	1	1	16

MECKLER, David (MEHK-luhr, DAY-vihd) **L.A.**

Center. Shoots right. 6', 184 lbs. Born, Highland Park, IL, July 9, 1987.
(Los Angeles' 7th choice, 134th overall, in 2006 Entry Draft).

			Regular Season					Playoffs				
Season	Club	League	GP	G	A	Pts	PIM	GP	G	A	Pts	PIM
2004-05	Waterloo	USHL	60	30	15	45	32	5	3	2	5	2
2005-06	Yale	ECACHL	31	7	3	10	28	....	....	....	....	....

MEDVEC, Kyle (MEHD-vek, KIGHL) **MIN.**

Defense. Shoots left. 6'5", 202 lbs. Born, Westminster, CO, June 16, 1988.
(Minnesota's 4th choice, 102nd overall, in 2006 Entry Draft).

			Regular Season					Playoffs				
Season	Club	League	GP	G	A	Pts	PIM	GP	G	A	Pts	PIM
2003-04	Apple Valley	High-MN	27	1	12	13	30	....	....	....	....	....
2004-05	Apple Valley	High-MN	23	4	16	20	18	....	....	....	....	....
2005-06	Apple Valley	High-MN	28	13	22	35	44	....	....	....	....	....
	Sioux City	USHL	3	0	0	0	0	....	....	....	....	....

MEECH, Derek (MEECH, DAIR-ihk) **DET.**

Defense. Shoots left. 5'11", 182 lbs. Born, Winnipeg, Man., April 21, 1984.
(Detroit's 7th choice, 229th overall, in 2002 Entry Draft).

			Regular Season					Playoffs				
Season	Club	League	GP	G	A	Pts	PIM	GP	G	A	Pts	PIM
99-2000	Winnipeg Warriors	MMMHL	36	15	40	55	24	....	....	....	....	....
	Red Deer Rebels	WHL	5	1	0	1	2	....	....	....	....	....
2000-01	Red Deer Rebels	WHL	60	2	7	9	40	22	0	0	0	9
2001-02	Red Deer Rebels	WHL	71	8	19	27	33	13	1	1	2	6
2002-03	Red Deer Rebels	WHL	65	6	16	22	53	12	1	1	2	12
2003-04	Red Deer Rebels	WHL	62	10	28	38	40	19	4	7	11	10
2004-05	Grand Rapids	AHL	78	6	8	14	40	....	....	....	....	....
2005-06	Grand Rapids	AHL	79	4	16	20	85	16	0	2	2	4

WHL East Second All-Star Team (2004)

MEGALINSKY, Dmitri (meh-gahl-IHN-skee, dih-MEE-tree) **OTT.**

Defense. Shoots left. 6'2", 212 lbs. Born, Perm, USSR, April 15, 1985.
(Ottawa's 7th choice, 186th overall, in 2005 Entry Draft).

			Regular Season					Playoffs				
Season	Club	League	GP	G	A	Pts	PIM	GP	G	A	Pts	PIM
2003-04	HK Voronezh	Russia-2	42	4	8	12	159	....	....	....	....	....
	Yaroslavl	Russia	1	0	0	0	0	....	....	....	....	....
	Yaroslavl 2	Russia-3	11	0	4	4	16	....	....	....	....	....
2004-05	Yaroslavl	Russia	1	0	0	0	2	....	....	....	....	....
	Yaroslavl 2	Russia-3	30	6	12	18	82	....	....	....	....	....
2005-06	Yaroslavl 2	Russia-3	12	4	10	14	6	....	....	....	....	....
	Yaroslavl	Russia	20	0	1	1	8	8	0	0	0	6

MELIN, Bjorn (MEH-lihn, b-YOHRN) **ANA.**

Right wing. Shoots right. 6'1", 205 lbs. Born, Jonkoping, Sweden, July 4, 1981.
(NY Islanders' 11th choice, 163rd overall, in 1999 Entry Draft).

			Regular Season					Playoffs				
Season	Club	League	GP	G	A	Pts	PIM	GP	G	A	Pts	PIM
1997-98	HV 71 Jr.	Swe-Jr.	8	0	3	3	2	....	....	....	....	....
1998-99	HV 71 Jr.	Swe-Jr.	30	12	7	19	50	....	....	....	....	....
99-2000	HV 71 Jr.	Swe-Jr.	24	19	16	35	70	....	....	....	....	....
	HV 71 Jonkoping	Sweden	23	3	0	3	2	5	0	0	0	0
2000-01	HV 71 Jr.	Swe-Jr.	10	6	5	11	66	....	....	....	....	....
	HV 71 Jonkoping	Sweden	43	2	1	3	26	....	....	....	....	....
2001-02	HV 71 Jonkoping	Sweden	50	7	9	16	40	8	0	0	0	6
2002-03	HV 71 Jonkoping	Sweden	48	7	9	16	44	7	0	2	2	6
2003-04	HV 71 Jonkoping	Sweden	47	7	11	18	28	19	4	8	12	10
2004-05	Malmo	Sweden	46	9	10	19	22	....	....	....	....	....
	Malmo	Sweden-Q	10	1	2	3	8	....	....	....	....	....
2005-06	HV 71 Jonkoping	Sweden	49	17	19	36	48	10	4	1	5	16

Rights traded to **Anaheim** by **NY Islanders** with Ben Guite for Dave Roche, March 19, 2002.

MELYAKOV, Igor (mehl-yuh-KAHF) **L.A.**

Left wing. Shoots left. 5'10", 190 lbs. Born, Lipetsk, USSR, December 23, 1976.
(Los Angeles' 6th choice, 137th overall, in 1995 Entry Draft).

			Regular Season					Playoffs				
Season	Club	League	GP	G	A	Pts	PIM	GP	G	A	Pts	PIM
1993-94	Torpedo Yaroslavl	CIS	39	4	3	7	10	4	0	0	0	0
1994-95	Torpedo Yaroslavl	CIS	50	6	8	14	34	4	0	1	1	0
1995-96	Torpedo Yaroslavl	CIS	39	5	1	6	6	3	0	0	0	2
1996-97	Torpedo Yaroslavl	Russia	8	0	0	0	0	....	....	....	....	....
	Nizhny Novgorod	Russia	12	2	3	5	10	....	....	....	....	....
1997-98	Nizhny Novgorod	Russia	13	3	3	6	6	....	....	....	....	....
1998-99	Nizhny Novgorod	Russia-2	36	13	17	30	14	....	....	....	....	....
99-2000	Nizhny Novgorod	Russia	34	1	8	9	10	5	1	0	1	4
2000-01	Nizhny Novgorod	Russia	24	2	3	5	10	....	....	....	....	....
2001-02	HK Lipetsk	Russia-2	68	16	37	53	94	....	....	....	....	....
2002-03	Voskresensk	Russia-2	48	9	22	31	16	....	....	....	....	....
2003-04	Nizhny Novgorod	Russia	45	5	10	15	18	....	....	....	....	....
	Nizh. Novgorod 2	Russia-3	4	1	6	7	4	....	....	....	....	....
2004-05	Nizhny Novgorod	Russia-2	52	14	30	44	32	11	2	4	6	18
2005-06	Magnitogorsk	Russia	25	7	8	15	10	3	0	0	0	2

MERCIER, Justin (MUHR-see-uhr, JUHS-tihn) **COL.**

Forward. Shoots left. 5'11", 190 lbs. Born, Erie, PA, June 25, 1987.
(Colorado's 8th choice, 168th overall, in 2005 Entry Draft).

			Regular Season					Playoffs				
Season	Club	League	GP	G	A	Pts	PIM	GP	G	A	Pts	PIM
2003-04	St. Louis	USHL	60	12	9	21	....	....	....	....	....	....
2004-05	USNTDP	U-18	26	1	7	8	31	....	....	....	....	....
	USNTDP	NAHL	16	4	3	7	33	....	....	....	....	....
2005-06	Miami U.	CCHA	35	3	7	10	32	....	....	....	....	....

METHOT, Marc (meh-TOH, MAHRK) **CBJ**

Defense. Shoots left. 6'3", 224 lbs. Born, Ottawa, Ont., June 21, 1985.
(Columbus' 7th choice, 168th overall, in 2003 Entry Draft).

			Regular Season					Playoffs				
Season	Club	League	GP	G	A	Pts	PIM	GP	G	A	Pts	PIM
2001-02	Kanata Laser	CJHL	50	3	10	13	22	....	....	....	....	....
2002-03	London Knights	OHL	68	2	13	15	46	14	2	4	6	6
2003-04	London Knights	OHL	63	2	9	11	66	15	0	3	3	18
2004-05	London Knights	OHL	67	4	12	16	88	18	2	1	3	32
2005-06	Syracuse Crunch	AHL	70	1	12	13	75	5	0	0	0	8

MEYER, Stefan (MAY-uhr, steh-FAN) **FLA.**

Left wing. Shoots left. 6'1", 194 lbs. Born, Medicine Hat, Alta., July 20, 1985.
(Florida's 4th choice, 55th overall, in 2003 Entry Draft).

			Regular Season					Playoffs				
Season	Club	League	GP	G	A	Pts	PIM	GP	G	A	Pts	PIM
2000-01	Notre Dame	SBHL	50	36	52	88	71	....	....	....	....	....
2001-02	Medicine Hat	WHL	67	18	22	40	48	....	....	....	....	....
2002-03	Medicine Hat	WHL	70	36	16	52	90	11	3	3	6	14
2003-04	Medicine Hat	WHL	72	34	41	75	69	19	7	10	17	27
2004-05	Medicine Hat	WHL	69	34	43	77	104	13	2	4	6	8
2005-06	Rochester	AHL	68	12	16	28	139	....	....	....	....	....

MEYERS, Josh (MIGH-uhrs, JAWSH) **L.A.**

Defense. Shoots right. 6'2", 180 lbs. Born, Alexandria, MN, December 7, 1985.
(Los Angeles' 7th choice, 206th overall, in 2005 Entry Draft).

			Regular Season					Playoffs				
Season	Club	League	GP	G	A	Pts	PIM	GP	G	A	Pts	PIM
2003-04	Minnesota Blizzard	NAHL	27	2	12	14	....	....	....	....	....	....
2004-05	Sioux City	USHL	57	8	24	32	92	13	1	9	10	18
2005-06	U. Minn-Duluth	WCHA	27	3	7	10	20	....	....	....	....	....

MIELONEN, Juho (MEE-eh-loh-nuhn, YEW-ho) **DET.**

Defense. Shoots right. 6'2", 180 lbs. Born, Savonlinna, Finland, March 1, 1987.
(Detroit's 8th choice, 175th overall, in 2005 Entry Draft).

			Regular Season					Playoffs				
Season	Club	League	GP	G	A	Pts	PIM	GP	G	A	Pts	PIM
2002-03	Ilves Tampere U18	Fin-U18	11	0	1	1	8	....	....	....	....	....
2003-04	Ilves Tampere U18	Fin-U18	15	7	2	9	12	....	....	....	....	....
	Ilves Tampere Jr.	Fin-Jr.	34	1	2	3	30	3	0	0	0	8
2004-05	Ilves Tampere U18	Fin-U18	1	1	0	1	2	....	....	....	....	....
	Ilves Tampere Jr.	Fin-Jr.	37	2	9	11	32	9	0	1	1	6
2005-06	Ilves Tampere Jr.	Fin-Jr.	7	1	2	3	6	3	0	0	0	4
	Suomi U20	Finland-2	3	0	0	0	2	....	....	....	....	....
	Ilves Tampere	Finland	17	0	1	1	4	....	....	....	....	....

MIHALIK, Vladimir (mih-HAHL-ihk, vla-DIH-meer) **T.B.**

Defense. Shoots left. 6'7", 234 lbs. Born, Presov, Czech., January 29, 1987.
(Tampa Bay's 1st choice, 30th overall, in 2005 Entry Draft).

			Regular Season					Playoffs				
Season	Club	League	GP	G	A	Pts	PIM	GP	G	A	Pts	PIM
2003-04	Presov	Svk-U18	6	4	4	8	4	....	....	....	....	....
	Presov Jr.	Slovak-Jr.	23	6	10	16	44	....	....	....	....	....
2004-05	PHK Presov Jr.	Slovak-Jr.	23	6	10	16	44	....	....	....	....	....
	PHK Presov	Slovak-2	32	3	1	4	24	6	0	1	1	2
2005-06	Red Deer Rebels	WHL	62	3	9	12	86	....	....	....	....	....

MIKHAILISHIN, Alexander (mih-khigh-LIHSH-ihn) **N.J.**

Defense. Shoots left. 6'4", 210 lbs. Born, Neustrelitz, East Germany, February 24, 1986.
(New Jersey's 2nd choice, 155th overall, in 2004 Entry Draft).

			Regular Season					Playoffs				
Season	Club	League	GP	G	A	Pts	PIM	GP	G	A	Pts	PIM
2001-02	Spartak Moscow 2	Russia-3	15	0	0	0	2	....	....	....	....	....
2002-03	Spartak Moscow 2	Russia-3	7	1	1	2	4	....	....	....	....	....
2003-04	Spartak Moscow 2	Russia-3	STATISTICS NOT AVAILABLE									
2004-05	Spartak Moscow	Russia	6	0	1	1	4	....	....	....	....	....
2005-06	Spartak Moscow 2	Russia-3	23	2	0	2	72	....	....	....	....	....

MIKHNOV, Alexei (MIHKH-nahf, al-EHX-ay) **EDM.**

Left wing. Shoots left. 6'5", 200 lbs. Born, Kiev, USSR, August 31, 1982.
(Edmonton's 1st choice, 17th overall, in 2000 Entry Draft).

			Regular Season					Playoffs				
Season	Club	League	GP	G	A	Pts	PIM	GP	G	A	Pts	PIM
1997-98	Torpedo Yaroslavl	Russia	6	0	0	0	0	....	....	....	....	....
1998-99	Yaroslavl 2	Russia-3	14	2	2	4	4	....	....	....	....	....
99-2000	Yaroslavl 2	Russia-3	53	24	17	41	10	....	....	....	....	....
2000-01	HK Moscow	Russia-2	4	0	0	0	2	....	....	....	....	....
	THK Tver	Russia-2	22	5	11	16	6	....	....	....	....	....
2001-02	Dyn'o Moscow 2	Russia-3	8	8	6	14	0	....	....	....	....	....
	Dynamo Moscow	Russia	35	2	1	3	4	3	0	0	0	2
	Ufa	Russia	1	0	0	0	0	....	....	....	....	....
2002-03	Sibir Novosibirsk	Russia	51	7	9	16	10	....	....	....	....	....
2003-04	Sibir Novosibirsk	Russia	58	14	8	22	22	....	....	....	....	....
2004-05	Sibir Novosibirsk	Russia	26	2	3	5	12	....	....	....	....	....
	Yaroslavl 2	Russia-3	2	1	0	1	0	....	....	....	....	....
	Yaroslavl	Russia	18	0	9	9	4	7	0	0	0	4
2005-06	Yaroslavl	Russia	40	14	7	21	18	11	4	4	8	4

MIKKELSON, Brendan (MIGHK-ehl-sohn, BREHN-duhn) **ANA.**

Defense. Shoots left. 6'2", 200 lbs. Born, Regina, Sask., June 22, 1987.
(Anaheim's 2nd choice, 31st overall, in 2005 Entry Draft).

			Regular Season					Playoffs				
Season	Club	League	GP	G	A	Pts	PIM	GP	G	A	Pts	PIM
2003-04	Portland	WHL	65	3	12	15	43	5	1	0	1	0
2004-05	Portland	WHL	70	5	10	15	60	7	1	2	3	0
2005-06	Portland	WHL	3	1	1	2	4	....	....	....	....	....
	Vancouver Giants	WHL	19	1	8	9	37	....	....	....	....	....

• Missed majority of 2005-06 season recovering from shoulder and knee injuries.

MIKUS, Juraj (MEE-kuhsh, YUHR-ay) **MTL.**

Right wing. Shoots right. 6'1", 198 lbs. Born, Skalica, Czech., February 22, 1987.
(Montreal's 3rd choice, 121st overall, in 2005 Entry Draft).

			Regular Season					Playoffs				
Season	Club	League	GP	G	A	Pts	PIM	GP	G	A	Pts	PIM
2003-04	HK 36 Skalica U18	Svk-U18	34	18	17	35	26	9	10	5	15	12
	HK 36 Skalica Jr.	Slovak-Jr.	8	3	7	10	16	....	....	....	....	....
	HK 36 Skalica	Slovakia	2	1	0	1	0	4	0	0	0	0
2004-05	HK 36 Skalica U18	Svk-U18	3	1	7	8	2	....	....	....	....	....
	HK 36 Skalica Jr.	Slovak-Jr.	30	17	18	35	40	9	6	8	14	18
	HK 36 Skalica	Slovakia	46	6	6	12	16	....	....	....	....	....
2005-06	HK 36 Skalica Jr.	Slovak-Jr.	4	1	0	1	2	2	1	2	3	2
	HK 36 Skalica	Slovakia	47	4	7	11	56	7	2	1	3	14

MILLER, Bryan (MIHL-luhr, BRIGH-uhn) **N.J.**

Defense. Shoots right. 5'10", 190 lbs. Born, Wayne, NJ, February 17, 1983.

			Regular Season					Playoffs				
Season	Club	League	GP	G	A	Pts	PIM	GP	G	A	Pts	PIM
2001-02	Boston University	H-East	34	4	15	19	12	....	....	....	....	....
2002-03	Boston University	H-East	42	5	18	23	48	....	....	....	....	....
2003-04	Boston University	H-East	38	5	15	20	24	....	....	....	....	....
2004-05	Boston University	H-East	39	6	20	26	42	....	....	....	....	....
	Albany River Rats	AHL	8	0	2	2	0	....	....	....	....	....
2005-06	Albany River Rats	AHL	40	3	15	18	36	....	....	....	....	....

Signed as a free agent by **New Jersey**, August 6, 2005.

MILLER, Drew (MIHL-luhr, DROO) **ANA.**

Left wing. Shoots left. 6'2", 170 lbs. Born, Dover, NJ, February 17, 1984.
(Anaheim's 6th choice, 186th overall, in 2003 Entry Draft).

			Regular Season					Playoffs				
Season	Club	League	GP	G	A	Pts	PIM	GP	G	A	Pts	PIM
2000-01	Capital Centre	NAHL	37	4	3	7	22	....	....	....	....	....
2001-02	Capital Centre	NAHL	54	18	16	34	56	....	....	....	....	....
2002-03	Capital Centre	NAHL	11	10	9	19	....	....	....	....	....	....
	River City Lancers	USHL	49	14	11	25	22	11	5	4	9	6
2003-04	Michigan State	CCHA	41	4	6	10	39	....	....	....	....	....
2004-05	Michigan State	CCHA	40	17	16	33	20	....	....	....	....	....
2005-06	Michigan State	CCHA	44	18	25	43	30	....	....	....	....	....

MILLER, T.J. (MIHL-luhr, TEE-JAY) **N.J.**

Defense. Shoots left. 6'4", 200 lbs. Born, Placetia, CA, September 15, 1986.
(New Jersey's 5th choice, 107th overall, in 2006 Entry Draft).

			Regular Season					Playoffs				
Season	Club	League	GP	G	A	Pts	PIM	GP	G	A	Pts	PIM
2004-05	South Surrey	BCHL	53	3	9	12	85	....	....	....	....	....
2005-06	Penticton Vees	BCHL	60	16	32	48	73	....	....	....	....	....

MILROY, Duncan (MIHL-roi, DUHN-can) **MTL.**

Right wing. Shoots right. 6'1", 203 lbs. Born, Edmonton, Alta., February 8, 1983.
(Montreal's 3rd choice, 37th overall, in 2001 Entry Draft).

			Regular Season					Playoffs				
Season	Club	League	GP	G	A	Pts	PIM	GP	G	A	Pts	PIM
1998-99	Edm. Maple Leafs	AMHL	34	34	36	70	73	....	....	....	....	....
	Swift Current	WHL	3	0	0	0	0	....	....	....	....	....
99-2000	Swift Current	WHL	68	15	15	30	20	12	3	5	8	12
2000-01	Swift Current	WHL	68	38	54	92	51	19	9	12	21	6
2001-02	Swift Current	WHL	26	20	11	31	20	....	....	....	....	....
	Kootenay Ice	WHL	38	25	31	56	24	22	*17	*20	*37	26
2002-03	Kootenay Ice	WHL	61	34	44	78	40	11	5	3	8	8
2003-04	Hamilton Bulldogs	AHL	50	4	10	14	14	10	3	1	4	4
2004-05	Hamilton Bulldogs	AHL	76	15	18	33	18	3	0	0	0	2
2005-06	Hamilton Bulldogs	AHL	77	16	19	35	63	....	....	....	....	....

MINARD, Chris (mih-NAHRD, KRIHS) **N.J.**

Center. Shoots left. 6'1", 200 lbs. Born, Thompson, Man., November 18, 1981.

			Regular Season					Playoffs				
Season	Club	League	GP	G	A	Pts	PIM	GP	G	A	Pts	PIM
1997-98	Owen Sound	OHL	9	0	1	1	1	1	0	0	0	2
1998-99	Owen Sound	OHL	43	6	9	15	18	....	....	....	....	....
99-2000	Owen Sound	OHL	38	12	14	26	39	....	....	....	....	....
	St. Michael's	OHL	28	5	14	19	6	....	....	....	....	....
2000-01	St. Michael's	OHL	40	11	8	19	28	....	....	....	....	....
	Oshawa Generals	OHL	28	12	12	24	18	....	....	....	....	....
2001-02	Oshawa Generals	OHL	67	36	35	71	20	5	2	3	5	6
2002-03	Pensacola	ECHL	72	15	17	32	71	4	0	0	0	6
2003-04	San Angelo Saints	CHL	64	39	36	75	51	5	1	1	2	2
2004-05	Alaska Aces	ECHL	69	49	29	78	54	15	4	4	8	12
	Milwaukee	AHL	1	0	0	0	0	....	....	....	....	....
2005-06	Albany River Rats	AHL	37	7	12	19	26	....	....	....	....	....
	Alaska Aces	ECHL	33	26	16	42	38	22	14	5	19	54

Signed as a free agent by **New Jersey**, September, 2005.

MIRNOV, Igor (mihr-NAWF, EE-gohr) **OTT.**

Left wing. Shoots left. 5'11", 191 lbs. Born, Chita, USSR, September 19, 1984.
(Ottawa's 2nd choice, 67th overall, in 2003 Entry Draft).

			Regular Season					Playoffs				
Season	Club	League	GP	G	A	Pts	PIM	GP	G	A	Pts	PIM
2001-02	Dyn'o Moscow 2	Russia-3	30	33	17	50	34	....	....	....	....	....
	Dynamo Moscow	Russia	6	0	0	0	0	....	....	....	....	....
2002-03	Dynamo Moscow	Russia	50	3	7	10	49	5	0	0	0	2
2003-04	Dynamo Moscow	Russia	53	11	10	21	26	3	0	0	0	2
2004-05	Dynamo Moscow	Russia	55	13	13	26	50	9	2	4	6	0
2005-06	Dynamo Moscow	Russia	32	8	10	18	36	4	0	2	2	4

MISHARIN, Georgy (mih-SHAHR-ihn, g'YOHR-gee) **MIN.**

Defense. Shoots left. 6', 198 lbs. Born, Yekaterinburg, USSR, May 11, 1985.
(Minnesota's 6th choice, 207th overall, in 2003 Entry Draft).

			Regular Season					Playoffs				
Season	Club	League	GP	G	A	Pts	PIM	GP	G	A	Pts	PIM
2001-02	Yekaterinburg 2	Russia-3	STATISTICS NOT AVAILABLE									
	Magnitogorsk 2	Russia-3	STATISTICS NOT AVAILABLE									
2002-03	Yekaterinburg	Russia-2	28	1	3	4	16	....	....	....	....	....
2003-04	Saginaw Spirit	OHL	65	5	22	27	42	....	....	....	....	....
2004-05	Nizhnekamsk	Russia	47	1	3	4	38	3	0	0	0	4
2005-06	CSKA Moscow	Russia	50	4	9	13	46	7	0	0	0	31

MITCHELL, John (MIH-chuhl, JAWN) TOR.

Center. Shoots left. 6'1", 195 lbs. Born, Oakville, Ont., January 22, 1985.
(Toronto's 4th choice, 158th overall, in 2003 Entry Draft).

			Regular Season					Playoffs				
Season	Club	League	GP	G	A	Pts	PIM	GP	G	A	Pts	PIM
2000-01	Waterloo Siskens	OPJHL	47	15	29	44	33	....	....	....	....	....
2001-02	Plymouth Whalers	OHL	62	9	9	18	23	6	1	0	1	4
2002-03	Plymouth Whalers	OHL	68	18	37	55	31	18	2	10	12	8
2003-04	Plymouth Whalers	OHL	65	28	54	82	45	9	6	6	12	6
2004-05	Plymouth Whalers	OHL	63	25	50	75	59	4	1	1	2	0
	St. John's	AHL	2	0	0	0	0	....	....	....	....	....
2005-06	Toronto Marlies	AHL	51	5	12	17	22	2	0	0	0	0

MITCHELL, Torrey (MIH-chuhl, TOHR-ee) S.J.

Center. Shoots right. 5'11", 175 lbs. Born, Montreal, Que., January 30, 1985.
(San Jose's 3rd choice, 126th overall, in 2004 Entry Draft).

			Regular Season					Playoffs				
Season	Club	League	GP	G	A	Pts	PIM	GP	G	A	Pts	PIM
2002-03	Hotchkiss	High-CT	26	19	30	49	33	....	....	....	....	....
2003-04	Hotchkiss	High-CT	25	25	37	62	42	....	....	....	....	....
2004-05	U. of Vermont	ECACHL	38	11	19	30	74	....	....	....	....	....
2005-06	U. of Vermont	H-East	38	12	28	40	34	....	....	....	....	....

ECACHL All-Rookie Team (2005)

MITERA, Mark (MIH-tair-a, MAHRK) ANA.

Defense. Shoots left. 6'3", 202 lbs. Born, Royal Oak, MI, October 22, 1987.
(Anaheim's 1st choice, 19th overall, in 2006 Entry Draft).

			Regular Season					Playoffs				
Season	Club	League	GP	G	A	Pts	PIM	GP	G	A	Pts	PIM
2003-04	USNTDP	U-17	16	2	6	8	22	....	....	....	....	....
	USNTDP	NAHL	43	2	13	15	69	7	0	2	2	10
2004-05	USNTDP	U-18	45	5	10	15	91	....	....	....	....	....
	USNTDP	NAHL	16	2	6	8	32	....	....	....	....	....
2005-06	U. of Michigan	CCHA	39	0	10	10	59	....	....	....	....	....

MONDOU, Benoit (mawn-DOO, BEHN-wah) N.J.

Center. Shoots right. 5'9", 175 lbs. Born, Sorel, Que., May 3, 1985.
(Boston's 9th choice, 247th overall, in 2003 Entry Draft).

			Regular Season					Playoffs				
Season	Club	League	GP	G	A	Pts	PIM	GP	G	A	Pts	PIM
2001-02	Baie-Comeau	QMJHL	64	25	45	70	36	5	1	5	6	4
2002-03	Baie-Comeau	QMJHL	25	5	16	21	12	....	....	....	....	....
	Shawinigan	QMJHL	35	6	35	41	21	9	3	8	11	8
2003-04	Shawinigan	QMJHL	68	34	61	95	32	10	4	9	13	2
2004-05	Shawinigan	QMJHL	57	16	43	59	44	4	2	3	5	9
2005-06	Shawinigan	QMJHL	59	46	52	98	57	8	5	4	9	6

QMJHL All-Rookie Team (2002) • Canadian Major Junior Sportsman of the Year (2004)

Signed as a free agent by **New Jersey**, June 24, 2006.

MONTGOMERY, Kevin (mawnt-GUH-muhr-ree, KEH-vihn) COL.

Defense. Shoots left. 6'1", 185 lbs. Born, Rochester, NY, April 4, 1988.
(Colorado's 4th choice, 110th overall, in 2006 Entry Draft).

			Regular Season					Playoffs				
Season	Club	League	GP	G	A	Pts	PIM	GP	G	A	Pts	PIM
2003-04	Syracuse Jr. Stars	EmJHL	62	7	28	35	....	....	....	....	....	....
2004-05	USNTDP	U-17	8	1	4	5	4	....	....	....	....	....
	USNTDP	NAHL	38	4	12	16	46	9	1	3	4	6
2005-06	USNTDP	U-18	42	2	10	12	61	....	....	....	....	....
	USNTDP	NAHL	17	4	6	10	15	....	....	....	....	....

Signed Letter of Intent to attend **Ohio State** (CCHA) in fall of 2006.

MONYCH, Lance (MOH-nihch, LANTS) PHX.

Right wing. Shoots right. 6'3", 203 lbs. Born, Red Deer, Alta., July 25, 1984.
(Phoenix's 6th choice, 97th overall, in 2002 Entry Draft).

			Regular Season					Playoffs				
Season	Club	League	GP	G	A	Pts	PIM	GP	G	A	Pts	PIM
99-2000	Brandon Hawks	MBHL	30	32	34	66	98	....	....	....	....	....
	Brandon	WHL	3	0	0	0	0	....	....	....	....	....
2000-01	Brandon	WHL	53	14	8	22	34	6	1	0	1	0
2001-02	Brandon	WHL	71	18	30	48	96	19	4	3	7	20
2002-03	Brandon	WHL	70	19	26	45	111	17	7	3	10	20
2003-04	Brandon	WHL	58	29	26	55	71	11	2	6	8	8
2004-05	Brandon	WHL	64	30	36	66	88	24	*19	7	26	44
2005-06	San Antonio	AHL	37	0	0	0	16	....	....	....	....	....
	Stockton Thunder	ECHL	26	11	10	21	14	....	....	....	....	....
	Laredo Bucks	CHL	3	4	0	4	0	....	....	....	....	....

MOORE, Greg (MOOR, GREHG) NYR

Right wing. Shoots right. 6'1", 230 lbs. Born, Lisbon, ME, March 26, 1984.
(Calgary's 5th choice, 143rd overall, in 2003 Entry Draft).

			Regular Season					Playoffs				
Season	Club	League	GP	G	A	Pts	PIM	GP	G	A	Pts	PIM
99-2000	St. Dominic Saints	High-ME	31	32	40	72	....	....	....	....	....	....
2000-01	USNTDP	U-17	13	4	6	10	1	....	....	....	....	....
	USNTDP	NAHL	56	8	12	20	22	....	....	....	....	....
2001-02	USNTDP	U-18	35	8	20	28	14	....	....	....	....	....
	USNTDP	USHL	12	2	2	4	4	....	....	....	....	....
	USNTDP	NAHL	6	3	2	5	2	....	....	....	....	....
2002-03	U. of Maine	H-East	33	9	7	16	10	....	....	....	....	....
2003-04	U. of Maine	H-East	39	15	8	23	44	....	....	....	....	....
2004-05	U. of Maine	H-East	40	14	9	23	16	....	....	....	....	....
2005-06	U. of Maine	H-East	42	28	17	45	47	....	....	....	....	....
	Hartford Wolf Pack	AHL	2	1	1	2	2	13	2	5	7	6

Hockey East First All-Star Team (2006) • NCAA East First All-American Team (2006)

Traded to **NY Rangers** by **Calgary** with Jamie McLennan and Blair Betts for Chris Simon and NY Rangers' 7th round choice (Matt Schneider) in 2004 Entry Draft, March 6, 2004.

MORIN, Travis (moh-REHN, TRA-vihs) WSH.

Center. Shoots left. 6'2", 175 lbs. Born, Minneapolis, MN, January 9, 1984.
(Washington's 13th choice, 263rd overall, in 2004 Entry Draft).

			Regular Season					Playoffs				
Season	Club	League	GP	G	A	Pts	PIM	GP	G	A	Pts	PIM
2001-02	Chicago Steel	USHL	20	5	8	13	....	4	0	0	0	2
2002-03	Chicago Steel	USHL	60	21	26	47	46	....	....	....	....	....
2003-04	Minnesota State	WCHA	38	9	12	21	14	....	....	....	....	....
2004-05	Minnesota State	WCHA	36	12	19	31	20	....	....	....	....	....
2005-06	Minnesota State	WCHA	39	20	22	42	16	....	....	....	....	....

MORMINA, Joey (mohr-MEE-nah, JOH-ee) L.A.

Defense. Shoots left. 6'6", 220 lbs. Born, Montreal, Que., June 29, 1982.
(Philadelphia's 6th choice, 193rd overall, in 2002 Entry Draft).

			Regular Season					Playoffs				
Season	Club	League	GP	G	A	Pts	PIM	GP	G	A	Pts	PIM
2000-01	Holderness School	High-NH	29	15	15	30	....	....	....	....	....	....
2001-02	Colgate	ECAC	34	2	13	15	28	....	....	....	....	....
2002-03	Colgate	ECAC	40	4	9	13	52	....	....	....	....	....
2003-04	Colgate	ECAC	28	2	10	12	26	....	....	....	....	....
2004-05	Colgate	ECACHL	39	8	8	16	50	....	....	....	....	....
2005-06	Manchester	AHL	61	0	13	13	70	7	0	0	0	4

Signed as a free agent by **Los Angeles**, August 24, 2005.

MORRIS, Mike (MOHR-his, MIGHK) S.J.

Right wing. Shoots right. 6'1", 182 lbs. Born, Dorchester, MA, July 14, 1983.
(San Jose's 1st choice, 27th overall, in 2002 Entry Draft).

			Regular Season					Playoffs				
Season	Club	League	GP	G	A	Pts	PIM	GP	G	A	Pts	PIM
2000-01	St. Sebastian's	High-MA	28	20	28	48	18	....	....	....	....	....
2001-02	St. Sebastian's	High-MA	31	29	29	58	26	....	....	....	....	....
2002-03	Northeastern	H-East	26	9	12	21	16	....	....	....	....	....
2003-04	Northeastern	H-East	34	10	20	30	14	....	....	....	....	....
2004-05	Northeastern	H-East	34	19	20	39	22	....	....	....	....	....
2005-06	Northeastern	H-East	DID NOT PLAY – INJURED									

Hockey East Second All-Star Team (2005)

• Missed 2005-06 season due to head injury originally suffered in 2004.

MORRISON, Jordan (MOHR-ih-suhn, JOHN-dan)

Center. Shoots left. 5'11", 167 lbs. Born, Scarborough, Ont., June 4, 1986.
(Pittsburgh's 10th choice, 222nd overall, in 2004 Entry Draft).

			Regular Season					Playoffs				
Season	Club	League	GP	G	A	Pts	PIM	GP	G	A	Pts	PIM
2002-03	Peterborough	OHL	59	6	8	14	14	7	3	1	4	0
2003-04	Peterborough	OHL	66	15	30	45	52	....	....	....	....	....
2004-05	Peterborough	OHL	67	23	41	64	51	14	2	10	12	6
2005-06	Peterborough	OHL	67	31	37	68	74	19	6	13	19	23

MORRISON, Justin (MOHR-ih-suhn, JUHS-tihn)

Right wing. Shoots right. 6'3", 205 lbs. Born, Los Angeles, CA, September 10, 1979.
(Vancouver's 4th choice, 81st overall, in 1998 Entry Draft).

			Regular Season					Playoffs				
Season	Club	League	GP	G	A	Pts	PIM	GP	G	A	Pts	PIM
1996-97	Omaha Lancers	USHL	62	12	24	36	44	10	2	4	6	8
1997-98	Colorado College	WCHA	42	4	9	13	8	....	....	....	....	....
1998-99	Colorado College	WCHA	38	23	15	38	33	....	....	....	....	....
99-2000	Colorado College	WCHA	38	7	19	26	28	....	....	....	....	....
2000-01	Colorado College	WCHA	41	21	14	35	42	....	....	....	....	....
2001-02	Manitoba Moose	AHL	64	10	9	19	37	7	1	0	1	4
2002-03	Columbia Inferno	ECHL	40	20	35	55	39	2	0	0	0	4
	Manitoba Moose	AHL	30	10	6	16	13	14	2	3	5	4
2003-04	Manitoba Moose	AHL	66	18	18	36	27	....	....	....	....	....
2004-05	Manitoba Moose	AHL	71	11	10	21	33	14	1	5	6	10
2005-06	Chicago Wolves	AHL	58	22	17	39	38	....	....	....	....	....

MORROW, Thomas (MOHR-roh, TAW-muhs) BUF.

Defense. Shoots left. 6'6", 198 lbs. Born, St. Paul, MN, October 21, 1983.
(Buffalo's 6th choice, 150th overall, in 2003 Entry Draft).

			Regular Season					Playoffs				
Season	Club	League	GP	G	A	Pts	PIM	GP	G	A	Pts	PIM
2000-01	Hill-Murray	High-MN	30	2	12	14	....	....	....	....	....	....
2001-02	Hill-Murray	High-MN	31	3	27	39	....	....	....	....	....	....
2002-03	Tri-City Storm	USHL	23	1	3	4	64	....	....	....	....	....
	Des Moines	USHL	34	1	6	7	40	....	....	....	....	....
2003-04	Boston University	H-East	38	0	3	3	34	....	....	....	....	....
2004-05	Boston University	H-East	28	0	1	1	40	....	....	....	....	....
2005-06	Boston University	H-East	34	0	5	5	34	....	....	....	....	....

MOSS, Dave (MAWS, DAYV) CGY.

Left wing. Shoots left. 6'3", 203 lbs. Born, Dearborn, MI, December 28, 1981.
(Calgary's 9th choice, 220th overall, in 2001 Entry Draft).

			Regular Season					Playoffs				
Season	Club	League	GP	G	A	Pts	PIM	GP	G	A	Pts	PIM
99-2000	Catholic Central	High-MI	28	18	20	28	20	....	....	....	....	....
2000-01	St. Louis Jr. Blues	CSJHL	9	2	2	4	2	....	....	....	....	....
	Cedar Rapids	USHL	51	20	18	38	14	4	0	1	1	2
2001-02	U. of Michigan	CCHA	43	4	9	13	10	....	....	....	....	....
2002-03	U. of Michigan	CCHA	43	14	17	31	37	....	....	....	....	....
2003-04	U. of Michigan	CCHA	38	8	12	20	18	....	....	....	....	....
2004-05	U. of Michigan	CCHA	38	10	20	30	26	....	....	....	....	....
2005-06	Omaha	AHL	63	21	27	48	28	....	....	....	....	....

MOULSON, Matt (MOWL-suhn, MAT) PIT.

Left wing. Shoots left. 6'1", 195 lbs. Born, North York, Ont., November 1, 1983.
(Pittsburgh's 11th choice, 263rd overall, in 2003 Entry Draft).

			Regular Season					Playoffs				
Season	Club	League	GP	G	A	Pts	PIM	GP	G	A	Pts	PIM
2001-02	Guelph	OHA-B	42	56	46	102	80	....	....	....	....	....
2002-03	Cornell Big Red	ECAC	33	13	10	23	22	....	....	....	....	....
2003-04	Cornell Big Red	ECAC	32	18	17	35	37	....	....	....	....	....
2004-05	Cornell Big Red	ECACHL	34	22	20	42	33	....	....	....	....	....
2005-06	Cornell Big Red	ECACHL	35	18	20	38	14	....	....	....	....	....

ECACHL First All-Star Team (2005) • NCAA East Second All-American Team (2005) • ECACHL Second All-Star Team (2006)

MOZYAKIN, Sergei (mohz-YA-kihn, SAIR-gay) **CBJ**

Left wing. Shoots right. 5'10", 165 lbs. Born, Yaroslavl, USSR, March 30, 1981.
(Columbus' 13th choice, 263rd overall, in 2002 Entry Draft).

			Regular Season					Playoffs				
Season	Club	League	GP	G	A	Pts	PIM	GP	G	A	Pts	PIM
1998-99	Val-d'Or Foreurs	QMJHL	4	0	1	1	2	....	....	....	....	....
99-2000	HK Moscow 2	Russia-3	6	9	3	12	6	....	....	....	....	....
	HK Moscow	Russia-2	44	23	25	48	10	....	....	....	....	....
2000-01	HK Moscow	Russia-2	37	22	28	50	18	....	....	....	....	....
	CSKA Moscow	Russia	9	0	2	2	0	....	....	....	....	....
2001-02	HK CSKA Moscow	Russia-2	54	34	30	64	10	12	9	12	21	4
2002-03	CSKA Moscow	Russia	33	12	15	27	18	....	....	....	....	....
2003-04	CSKA Moscow	Russia	45	21	19	40	6	....	....	....	....	....
2004-05	CSKA Moscow	Russia	49	11	12	23	22	....	....	....	....	....
2005-06	CSKA Moscow	Russia	51	20	*31	*51	28	7	1	2	3	4

MRAZEK, Jaroslav (muh-RA-zehk, YAHR-roh-slav) **NYI**

Defense. Shoots left. 6'3", 198 lbs. Born, Pisek, Czech., January 14, 1986.
(NY Islanders' 6th choice, 179th overall, in 2004 Entry Draft).

			Regular Season					Playoffs				
Season	Club	League	GP	G	A	Pts	PIM	GP	G	A	Pts	PIM
2003-04	Sparta Jr.	CzRep-Jr.	37	3	6	9	36	....	....	....	....	....
	HC Sparta Praha	CzRep	1	0	0	0	0	1	0	0	0	0
2004-05	St. Michael's	OHL	57	0	2	2	54	10	0	3	3	8
2005-06	St. Michael's	OHL	61	0	12	12	84	4	0	1	1	2

MUELLER, Peter (MEW-luhr, PEE-tuhr) **PHX.**

Center. Shoots right. 6'2", 205 lbs. Born, Bloomington, MN, April 14, 1988.
(Phoenix's 1st choice, 8th overall, in 2006 Entry Draft).

			Regular Season					Playoffs				
Season	Club	League	GP	G	A	Pts	PIM	GP	G	A	Pts	PIM
2003-04	USNTDP	U-17	17	4	9	13	25	....	....	....	....	....
	USNTDP	NAHL	43	10	16	26	26	7	3	2	5	4
2004-05	USNTDP	U-18	43	27	27	64	75	....	....	....	....	....
	USNTDP	NAHL	14	11	13	24	16	....	....	....	....	....
2005-06	Everett Silvertips	WHL	52	26	32	58	44	15	7	6	13	10

MUKHACHEV, Andrei (moo-khah-CHEHV, AWN-dray) **NSH.**

Defense. Shoots left. 6'3", 196 lbs. Born, Ekaterinburg, USSR, July 21, 1980.
(Nashville's 11th choice, 210th overall, in 2003 Entry Draft).

			Regular Season					Playoffs				
Season	Club	League	GP	G	A	Pts	PIM	GP	G	A	Pts	PIM
1998-99	HK CSKA Moscow	Russia-2	38	0	2	2	30	....	....	....	....	....
99-2000	HK Moscow	Russia-2	40	2	9	11	44	....	....	....	....	....
2000-01	CSKA Moscow 2	Russia-3	8	1	5	6	18	....	....	....	....	....
	HK Moscow	Russia-2	40	2	9	11	44	....	....	....	....	....
2001-02	HK CSKA Moscow	Russia-2	39	3	9	12	28	12	2	5	7	10
2002-03	CSKA Moscow	Russia	50	3	7	10	30	....	....	....	....	....
2003-04	CSKA Moscow	Russia	38	2	4	6	28	....	....	....	....	....
2004-05	CSKA Moscow	Russia	21	0	2	2	14	....	....	....	....	....
2005-06	CSKA Moscow	Russia	48	1	4	5	71	7	0	0	0	4

MURATOV, Yevgeny (muhr-A-tahf, ehv-GEH-nee) **EDM.**

Left wing. Shoots right. 5'10", 178 lbs. Born, Nizhny Tagil, USSR, January 28, 1981.
(Edmonton's 10th choice, 274th overall, in 2000 Entry Draft).

			Regular Season					Playoffs				
Season	Club	League	GP	G	A	Pts	PIM	GP	G	A	Pts	PIM
1997-98	Nizhnekamsk 2	Russia-3	39	7	7	14	2	....	....	....	....	....
1998-99	Nizhnekamsk 2	Russia-4	37	26	9	35	32	....	....	....	....	....
	Nizhnekamsk	Russia	4	0	0	0	0	3	1	0	1	2
99-2000	Nizhnekamsk	Russia	29	9	7	16	2	....	....	....	....	....
	Ak Bars Kazan	Russia	8	2	2	4	2	9	0	0	0	2
2000-01	Nizhnekamsk	Russia	42	9	8	17	14	4	0	0	0	0
2001-02	Nizhnekamsk	Russia	45	5	13	18	4	....	....	....	....	....
2002-03	Nizhnekamsk	Russia	51	10	11	21	41	....	....	....	....	....
2003-04	Nizhnekamsk	Russia	20	1	6	7	8	....	....	....	....	....
2004-05	Novokuznetsk	Russia	58	15	13	28	12	4	1	2	3	0
2005-06	SKA St. Petersburg	Russia	49	13	10	23	16	3	0	1	1	0

MURPHY, Colin (MUHR-fee, COHL-ihn)

Left wing. Shoots left. 6', 195 lbs. Born, Fort McMurray, Alta., April 11, 1980.

			Regular Season					Playoffs				
Season	Club	League	GP	G	A	Pts	PIM	GP	G	A	Pts	PIM
2001-02	Michigan Tech	WCHA	38	8	19	27	40	....	....	....	....	....
2002-03	Michigan Tech	WCHA	37	20	20	40	42	....	....	....	....	....
2003-04	Michigan Tech	WCHA	33	15	17	32	28	....	....	....	....	....
2004-05	Michigan Tech	WCHA	37	11	*42	53	40	....	....	....	....	....
	St. John's	AHL	12	1	7	8	34	5	1	3	4	17
2005-06	Toronto Marlies	AHL	53	16	17	33	44	4	0	0	0	0

WCHA First All-Star Team (2005) • NCAA West Second All-American Team (2005)

Signed as a free agent by **Toronto**, March 18, 2005.

MURPHY, Ryan (MUHR-fee, RIGH-yan) **N.J.**

Left wing. Shoots left. 6'1", 205 lbs. Born, Van Nuys, CA, March 21, 1979.
(Carolina's 4th choice, 113th overall, in 1999 Entry Draft).

			Regular Season					Playoffs				
Season	Club	League	GP	G	A	Pts	PIM	GP	G	A	Pts	PIM
1995-96	Thornhill Islanders	MTJHL	32	13	16	29	49	1	0	0	0	0
1996-97	Thornhill Islanders	MTJHL	41	22	32	54	36	12	7	8	15	....
1997-98	Bowling Green	CCHA	36	3	9	12	27	....	....	....	....	....
1998-99	Bowling Green	CCHA	34	10	23	33	38	....	....	....	....	....
99-2000	Bowling Green	CCHA	36	9	10	19	63	....	....	....	....	....
2000-01	Bowling Green	CCHA	38	23	15	38	22	....	....	....	....	....
2001-02	Florida Everblades	ECHL	66	13	18	31	38	6	1	2	3	4
2002-03	Lowell	AHL	12	1	2	3	4	....	....	....	....	....
	Florida Everblades	ECHL	58	28	17	45	47	1	0	0	0	0
2003-04	Albany River Rats	AHL	71	10	9	19	28	....	....	....	....	....
2004-05	Albany River Rats	AHL	75	13	23	36	44	....	....	....	....	....
2005-06	Albany River Rats	AHL	17	4	2	6	12	....	....	....	....	....

Signed as a free agent by **New Jersey**, July 30, 2003.

MURRAY, Andrew (MUHR-ree, AN-droo) **CBJ**

Center. Shoots left. 6'2", 210 lbs. Born, Selkirk, Man., November 6, 1981.
(Columbus' 11th choice, 242nd overall, in 2001 Entry Draft).

			Regular Season					Playoffs				
Season	Club	League	GP	G	A	Pts	PIM	GP	G	A	Pts	PIM
99-2000	Selkirk Steelers	MJHL	63	29	48	77	....	....	....	....	....	....
2000-01	Selkirk Steelers	MJHL	64	46	56	102	72	5	3	0	3	6
2001-02	Bemidji State	CHA	35	15	15	30	22	....	....	....	....	....
2002-03	Bemidji State	CHA	36	9	18	27	38	....	....	....	....	....
2003-04	Bemidji State	CHA	25	6	14	20	41	....	....	....	....	....
2004-05	Bemidji State	CHA	32	16	22	38	30	....	....	....	....	....
2005-06	Syracuse Crunch	AHL	77	13	16	29	73	6	0	1	1	17

CHA All-Rookie Team (2002)

MURRAY, Brady (MUHR-ree, BRAY-dee) **L.A.**

Center. Shoots left. 5'9", 180 lbs. Born, Brandon, Man., August 17, 1984.
(Los Angeles' 6th choice, 152nd overall, in 2003 Entry Draft).

			Regular Season					Playoffs				
Season	Club	League	GP	G	A	Pts	PIM	GP	G	A	Pts	PIM
2001-02	Shat.-St. Mary's	High-MN	60	58	92	150	50	....	....	....	....	....
2002-03	Salmon Arm	BCHL	59	42	59	101	30	....	....	....	....	....
2003-04	North Dakota	WCHA	37	19	27	46	32	....	....	....	....	....
2004-05	North Dakota	WCHA	25	8	12	20	22	....	....	....	....	....
2005-06	Rapperswil	Swiss	36	3	9	12	28	10	3	2	5	10

WCHA All-Rookie Team (2004) • WCHA Rookie of the Year (2004)

MURSAK , Jan (MUHR-sak, YAHN) **DET.**

Left wing. Shoots right. 5'11", 167 lbs. Born, Maribor, Slovenia, January 20, 1988.
(Detroit's 5th choice, 182nd overall, in 2006 Entry Draft).

			Regular Season					Playoffs				
Season	Club	League	GP	G	A	Pts	PIM	GP	G	A	Pts	PIM
2002-03	HK Maribor U18	Sloven-U18	13	27	18	45	14	....	....	....	....	....
2003-04	HK Maribor U18	Sloven-U18	22	27	17	44	14	....	....	....	....	....
	HK Maribor Jr.	Sloven-Jr.	19	8	8	16	37	....	....	....	....	....
	HK Maribor	Slovenia	14	3	3	6	16	....	....	....	....	....
2004-05	HK Maribor Jr.	Sloven-Jr.	19	17	16	33	39	....	....	....	....	....
	HK Maribor	Slovenia	24	16	29	45	10	....	....	....	....	....
2005-06	C. Budejovice Jr.	CzRep-Jr.	43	15	15	30	32	5	0	2	2	2

NASBY, Bret (NAZ-bee, BREHT) **FLA.**

Defense. Shoots right. 6'3", 188 lbs. Born, Grimsby, Ont., March 22, 1986.
(Florida's 5th choice, 152nd overall, in 2004 Entry Draft).

			Regular Season					Playoffs				
Season	Club	League	GP	G	A	Pts	PIM	GP	G	A	Pts	PIM
2002-03	Grimsby	OHA-C	53	6	14	20	63	....	....	....	....	....
2003-04	Oshawa Generals	OHL	56	0	7	7	41	7	0	3	3	6
2004-05	Oshawa Generals	OHL	66	4	13	17	71	....	....	....	....	....
2005-06	Oshawa Generals	OHL	20	5	9	14	42	....	....	....	....	....
	Erie Otters	OHL	32	4	13	17	30	....	....	....	....	....

NASLUND, Fredrik (NAZ-luhnd, FREHD-uhr-ihk) **DAL.**

Left wing. Shoots right. 6'4", 211 lbs. Born, Stockholm, Sweden, February 11, 1986.
(Dallas' 6th choice, 104th overall, in 2004 Entry Draft).

			Regular Season					Playoffs				
Season	Club	League	GP	G	A	Pts	PIM	GP	G	A	Pts	PIM
2002-03	Vasteras Jr.	Swe-Jr.	34	12	9	21	8	....	....	....	....	....
2003-04	Vasteras Jr.	Swe-Jr.	17	13	15	28	6	3	0	1	1	4
	Vasteras	Sweden-2	32	2	4	6	0	....	....	....	....	....
2004-05	Vasteras	Sweden-2	3	0	0	0	0	....	....	....	....	....
	Vasteras Jr.	Swe-Jr.	21	7	7	14	2	....	....	....	....	....
2005-06	Peterborough	OHL	66	9	21	30	30	19	6	5	11	6

NAUROV, Alexander (naw-OO-rawf, ahl-ehx-AN-duhr) **DAL.**

Right wing. Shoots right. 5'11", 191 lbs. Born, Saratov, USSR, March 4, 1985.
(Dallas' 5th choice, 134th overall, in 2003 Entry Draft).

			Regular Season					Playoffs				
Season	Club	League	GP	G	A	Pts	PIM	GP	G	A	Pts	PIM
2001-02	Yaroslavl 2	Russia-3	12	0	0	0	16	....	....	....	....	....
2002-03	Yaroslavl 2	Russia-3	STATISTICS NOT AVAILABLE									
2003-04	Yaroslavl 2	Russia-3	24	9	5	14	73	....	....	....	....	....
2004-05	Yaroslavl 2	Russia-3	35	19	16	35	61	....	....	....	....	....
	Yaroslavl	Russia	11	2	2	4	2	....	....	....	....	....
2005-06	Kristall Saratov	Russia-2	52	11	13	24	42	....	....	....	....	....

NEAL, James (NEEL, JAYMS) **DAL.**

Left wing. Shoots left. 6'2", 185 lbs. Born, Oshawa, Ont., September 3, 1987.
(Dallas' 2nd choice, 33rd overall, in 2005 Entry Draft).

			Regular Season					Playoffs				
Season	Club	League	GP	G	A	Pts	PIM	GP	G	A	Pts	PIM
2003-04	Bowmanville	OPJHL	43	28	27	55	....	....	....	....	....	....
	Plymouth Whalers	OHL	9	2	4	6	0	....	....	....	....	....
2004-05	Plymouth Whalers	OHL	67	18	26	44	32	4	1	1	2	6
2005-06	Plymouth Whalers	OHL	66	21	37	58	109	13	9	7	16	33

NELSON, Levi (NELH-sohn, LEE-vigh) **BOS.**

Center. Shoots left. 5'11", 167 lbs. Born, Calgary, Alta., April 28, 1988.
(Boston's 6th choice, 158th overall, in 2006 Entry Draft).

			Regular Season					Playoffs				
Season	Club	League	GP	G	A	Pts	PIM	GP	G	A	Pts	PIM
2004-05	Cgy. North Stars	AMHL	35	15	13	28	70	....	....	....	....	....
	Swift Current	WHL	2	1	0	1	0	....	....	....	....	....
2005-06	Swift Current	WHL	63	21	17	38	63	4	0	0	0	4

NEPRYAYEV, Ivan (neh-pree-YIGH-ehv, IGH-van) **WSH.**

Center. Shoots left. 6'1", 180 lbs. Born, Yaroslavl, USSR, February 4, 1982.
(Washington's 5th choice, 163rd overall, in 2000 Entry Draft).

			Regular Season					Playoffs				
Season	Club	League	GP	G	A	Pts	PIM	GP	G	A	Pts	PIM
1997-98	Torpedo Yaroslavl	Russia	6	0	0	0	0	....	....	....	....	....
1998-99	Yaroslavl 2	Russia-3	15	1	0	1	0	....	....	....	....	....
99-2000	Yaroslavl 2	Russia-3	40	8	14	22	....	....	....	....	....	....
2000-01	Yaroslavl	Russia	10	0	0	0	2	....	....	....	....	....
2001-02	Yaroslavl 2	Russia-3	2	1	0	1	18	....	....	....	....	....
	Yaroslavl	Russia	36	3	8	11	28	....	....	....	....	....
2002-03	Yaroslavl	Russia	26	3	6	9	12	6	1	0	1	0
2003-04	Yaroslavl 2	Russia-3	13	5	10	15	12	....	....	....	....	....
2004-05	Yaroslavl	Russia	56	10	10	20	73	9	1	0	1	16
2005-06	Yaroslavl	Russia	43	7	16	23	70	11	0	0	0	8
	Russia	Olympics	2	0	0	0	2	....	....	....	....	....

NEWBURY, Kris (new-BUHR-ee, KRIHS) **TOR.**

Center. Shoots left. 5'10", 200 lbs. Born, Brampton, Ont., February 19, 1982.
(San Jose's 4th choice, 139th overall, in 2002 Entry Draft).

			Regular Season					Playoffs				
Season	Club	League	GP	G	A	Pts	PIM	GP	G	A	Pts	PIM
1996-97	Brampton Capitals	OPJHL	28	9	4	13	36	....	....	....	....	....
1997-98	Brampton Capitals	OPJHL	46	11	21	32	161	....	....	....	....	....
1998-99	Belleville Bulls	OHL	51	6	8	14	89	....	....	....	....	....
99-2000	Belleville Bulls	OHL	34	6	18	24	72	....	....	....	....	....
	Sarnia Sting	OHL	27	6	8	14	44	7	0	3	3	16
2000-01	Sarnia Sting	OHL	64	28	30	58	126	4	1	3	4	20
2001-02	Sarnia Sting	OHL	66	42	62	104	141	5	1	3	4	15
2002-03	Sarnia Sting	OHL	64	34	58	92	149	6	4	4	8	16
2003-04	St. John's	AHL	72	5	15	20	153	....	....	....	....	....
2004-05	St. John's	AHL	55	4	9	13	103	5	0	0	0	36
	Pensacola	ECHL	6	2	4	6	20	....	....	....	....	....
2005-06	Toronto Marlies	AHL	74	22	37	59	215	5	0	1	1	12

OHL Second All-Star Team (2002)

Signed as a free agent by **St. John's** (AHL), October 2, 2003. Signed as a free agent by **Toronto**, July 17, 2006.

NICKERSON, Matt (NIH-kuhr-suhn, MAT) **DAL.**

Defense. Shoots right. 6'4", 230 lbs. Born, Old Lyme, CT, January 11, 1985.
(Dallas' 4th choice, 99th overall, in 2003 Entry Draft).

			Regular Season					Playoffs				
Season	Club	League	GP	G	A	Pts	PIM	GP	G	A	Pts	PIM
2000-01	Victoria Salsa	BCHL	....	....	....	....	196	....	....	....	....	....
2001-02	Texas Tornado	NAHL	47	1	12	13	97	6	0	0	0	6
2002-03	Texas Tornado	NAHL	47	6	23	29	277	6	0	1	1	*18
2003-04	Clarkson Knights	ECAC	38	5	9	14	*179	....	....	....	....	....
2004-05	Victoriaville Tigres	QMJHL	48	1	11	12	182	6	0	1	1	27
2005-06	Assat Pori	Finland	36	5	8	13	*236	14	1	0	1	50

NIELSEN, Frans (NEEL-sehn, FRAHNS) **NYI**

Center. Shoots left. 5'11", 172 lbs. Born, Herning, Denmark, April 24, 1984.
(NY Islanders' 2nd choice, 87th overall, in 2002 Entry Draft).

			Regular Season					Playoffs				
Season	Club	League	GP	G	A	Pts	PIM	GP	G	A	Pts	PIM
99-2000	Herning IK Jr.	Den-Jr.	36	18	16	34	6	....	....	....	....	....
2000-01	Herning IK	Denmark	38	18	19	37	6	....	....	....	....	....
2001-02	Malmo	Sweden	20	0	1	1	0	....	....	....	....	....
	Malmo Jr.	Swe-Jr.	29	15	27	42	8	7	3	7	10	2
2002-03	Malmo	Sweden	47	3	6	9	10	....	....	....	....	....
	Malmo Jr.	Swe-Jr.	2	1	3	4	0	....	....	....	....	....
2003-04	Malmo	Sweden	50	9	7	16	28	....	....	....	....	....
	Malmo	Sweden-Q	10	3	5	8	2	....	....	....	....	....
2004-05	Malmo	Sweden	49	8	7	15	6	....	....	....	....	....
	Malmo	Sweden-Q	10	7	2	9	0	....	....	....	....	....
2005-06	Timra IK	Sweden	50	5	13	18	22	....	....	....	....	....

NIKITIN, Nikita (nih-KEE-tihn, nih-KEE-tuh) **ST.L.**

Defense. Shoots left. 6'3", 178 lbs. Born, Omsk, USSR, June 16, 1986.
(St. Louis' 5th choice, 136th overall, in 2004 Entry Draft).

			Regular Season					Playoffs				
Season	Club	League	GP	G	A	Pts	PIM	GP	G	A	Pts	PIM
2002-03	Omsk 2	Russia-3	34	3	7	10	4	....	....	....	....	....
2003-04	Omsk 2	Russia-3	34	3	8	11	22	....	....	....	....	....
2004-05	Omsk 2	Russia-3	31	3	8	11	20	....	....	....	....	....
	Avangard Omsk	Russia	12	0	0	0	2	3	0	0	0	0
2005-06	Avangard Omsk	Russia	43	1	2	3	22	13	1	2	3	6
	Omsk 2	Russia-3	1	0	0	0	0	....	....	....	....	....

NIKULIN, Alexander (nih-KOO-lihn, al-EHX-AN-duhr) **OTT.**

Center. Shoots left. 6'1", 195 lbs. Born, Moscow, USSR, August 25, 1985.
(Ottawa's 6th choice, 122nd overall, in 2004 Entry Draft).

			Regular Season					Playoffs				
Season	Club	League	GP	G	A	Pts	PIM	GP	G	A	Pts	PIM
2002-03	CSKA Moscow 2	Russia-3	46	22	14	36	....	....	....	....	....	....
2003-04	CSKA Moscow 2	Russia-3	47	21	20	41	46	....	....	....	....	....
2004-05	CSKA Moscow	Russia	16	3	3	6	0	....	....	....	....	....
2005-06	CSKA Moscow	Russia	51	10	12	22	22	7	1	0	1	2

NIKULIN, Ilja (nih-KOO-lihn, ihl-YUH) **ATL.**

Defense. Shoots left. 6'3", 210 lbs. Born, Moscow, USSR, March 12, 1982.
(Atlanta's 2nd choice, 31st overall, in 2000 Entry Draft).

			Regular Season					Playoffs				
Season	Club	League	GP	G	A	Pts	PIM	GP	G	A	Pts	PIM
1998-99	Dyn'o Moscow 2	Russia-3	23	0	2	2	18	....	....	....	....	....
99-2000	Dyn'o Moscow 2	Russia-3	4	2	1	3	10	....	....	....	....	....
	THK Tver	Russia-2	39	3	6	9	84	....	....	....	....	....
2000-01	Dynamo Moscow	Russia	44	0	4	4	61	....	....	....	....	....
2001-02	Dyn'o Moscow 2	Russia-3	2	0	1	1	2	....	....	....	....	....
	Dynamo Moscow	Russia	47	2	1	3	44	3	0	0	0	0
2002-03	Dynamo Moscow	Russia	40	1	4	5	46	5	0	1	1	4
2003-04	Dynamo Moscow	Russia	54	1	5	6	56	3	0	0	0	2
2004-05	Dynamo Moscow	Russia	50	1	9	10	65	10	0	3	3	8
2005-06	Ak Bars Kazan	Russia	49	9	9	18	48	13	4	0	4	36

NISKALA, Janne (NIHS-kah-lah, YAH-nee) **NSH.**

Defense. Shoots left. 5'11", 199 lbs. Born, Vasteras, Sweden, September 22, 1981.
(Nashville's 5th choice, 147th overall, in 2004 Entry Draft).

			Regular Season					Playoffs				
Season	Club	League	GP	G	A	Pts	PIM	GP	G	A	Pts	PIM
1997-98	Lukko Rauma U18	Fin-U18	34	7	16	23	40	....	....	....	....	....
1998-99	Lukko Rauma U18	Fin-U18	14	7	4	11	42	....	....	....	....	....
	Lukko Rauma Jr.	Fin-Jr.	2	0	0	0	12	....	....	....	....	....
99-2000	Lukko Rauma Jr.	Fin-Jr.	40	14	15	29	50	8	0	2	2	8
2000-01	Lukko Rauma Jr.	Fin-Jr.	13	4	8	12	40	....	....	....	....	....
	Lukko Rauma	Finland	18	0	0	0	0	....	....	....	....	....
	Jaa-Kotkat	Finland-2	13	4	1	5	43	....	....	....	....	....
	Manchester Storm	Britain	16	0	1	1	14	....	....	....	....	....
2001-02	Lukko Rauma Jr.	Fin-Jr.	3	1	1	2	2	....	....	....	....	....
	Lukko Rauma	Finland	55	7	13	20	81	....	....	....	....	....
2002-03	Lukko Rauma	Finland	46	4	5	9	40	....	....	....	....	....
2003-04	Lukko Rauma	Finland	55	21	15	36	73	4	0	0	0	16
2004-05	Lukko Rauma	Finland	44	9	12	21	63	9	5	2	7	4
2005-06	EV Zug	Swiss	43	12	17	29	50	7	0	2	2	10

NISKANEN, Matt (NIHS-kah-nehn, MAT) **DAL.**

Defense. Shoots right. 6', 194 lbs. Born, Virginia, MN, December 6, 1986.
(Dallas' 1st choice, 28th overall, in 2005 Entry Draft).

			Regular Season					Playoffs				
Season	Club	League	GP	G	A	Pts	PIM	GP	G	A	Pts	PIM
2003-04	Virginia Blue Devils	High-MN	....	24	37	61	....	....	....	....	....	....
2004-05	Virginia Blue Devils	High-MN	29	27	38	65	34	....	....	....	....	....
2005-06	U. Minn-Duluth	WCHA	38	1	13	14	40	....	....	....	....	....

NITTEL, Ahren (NIH-tuhl, AH-rehn)

Left wing. Shoots left. 6'3", 225 lbs. Born, Waterloo, Ont., December 6, 1983.
(New Jersey's 5th choice, 85th overall, in 2002 Entry Draft).

			Regular Season					Playoffs				
Season	Club	League	GP	G	A	Pts	PIM	GP	G	A	Pts	PIM
99-2000	Streetsville Derbys	OPJHL	11	1	5	6	10	....	....	....	....	....
2000-01	Windsor Spitfires	OHL	46	6	4	10	56	7	3	1	4	16
2001-02	Windsor Spitfires	OHL	52	19	11	30	100	9	4	1	5	23
2002-03	Windsor Spitfires	OHL	22	5	4	9	30	....	....	....	....	....
	Oshawa Generals	OHL	20	15	7	22	25	13	5	2	7	10
2003-04	Albany River Rats	AHL	42	4	3	7	24	....	....	....	....	....
	Adirondack	UHL	2	1	0	1	0	....	....	....	....	....
2004-05	Albany River Rats	AHL	50	25	11	36	18	....	....	....	....	....
2005-06	Albany River Rats	AHL	45	14	11	25	51	....	....	....	....	....

NODL, Andreas (NOHD'L, ahn-DRAY-uhs) **PHI.**

Right wing. Shoots left. 6'1", 196 lbs. Born, Vienna, Austria, February 28, 1987.
(Philadelphia's 2nd choice, 39th overall, in 2006 Entry Draft).

			Regular Season					Playoffs				
Season	Club	League	GP	G	A	Pts	PIM	GP	G	A	Pts	PIM
2001-02	Wien Jr.	Austria-Jr.	1	0	0	0	0	....	....	....	....	....
2002-03	Wien Jr.	Austria-Jr.	STATISTICS NOT AVAILABLE									
2003-04	Vienna Capitals	Austria	25	15	22	37	26	....	....	....	....	....
	Wien Jr.	Austria-Jr.	15	11	10	21	47	....	....	....	....	....
2004-05	Sioux Falls	USHL	44	7	9	16	24	....	....	....	....	....
	Sioux Falls	USHL	44	7	9	16	24	....	....	....	....	....
2005-06	Sioux Falls	USHL	58	29	30	59	16	14	6	9	15	6

NOLAN, Brandon (NOH-lan, BRAN-duhn)

Center. Shoots left. 6'1", 185 lbs. Born, Sault Ste. Marie, Ont., July 18, 1983.
(Vancouver's 3rd choice, 111th overall, in 2003 Entry Draft).

			Regular Season					Playoffs				
Season	Club	League	GP	G	A	Pts	PIM	GP	G	A	Pts	PIM
99-2000	St. Catharines	OHA-B	47	18	13	31	10	....	....	....	....	....
2000-01	Oshawa Generals	OHL	52	15	23	38	21	....	....	....	....	....
2001-02	Oshawa Generals	OHL	57	30	28	58	78	5	2	4	6	4
2002-03	Oshawa Generals	OHL	68	36	52	88	57	13	10	7	17	4
2003-04	Manitoba Moose	AHL	48	7	10	17	18	....	....	....	....	....
	Columbia Inferno	ECHL	19	5	10	15	38	3	0	1	1	17
2004-05	Manitoba Moose	AHL	48	4	8	12	16	....	....	....	....	....
2005-06	Manitoba Moose	AHL	18	3	8	11	10	....	....	....	....	....
	Columbia Inferno	ECHL	43	20	31	51	94	....	....	....	....	....

• Re-entered NHL Entry Draft. Originally New Jersey's 6th choice, 72nd overall, in 2001 Entry Draft.

OHL Second All-Star Team (2003)

NOLET, Martin (noh-LAY, MAHR-tihn) **L.A.**

Defense. Shoots right. 6'3", 209 lbs. Born, Quebec, PQ, October 2, 1986.
(Los Angeles' 8th choice, 144th overall, in 2006 Entry Draft).

			Regular Season					Playoffs				
Season	Club	League	GP	G	A	Pts	PIM	GP	G	A	Pts	PIM
2002-03	St-Francois	QAAA	31	3	3	6	62	....	....	....	....	....
2003-04	St-Francois	QAAA	31	5	11	16	91	8	2	2	4	24
2004-05	Champlain College	QJHL	43	4	23	27	97	14	2	3	5	14
2005-06	Champlain College	QJHL	19	5	7	12	26	10	1	1	2	24

• Missed majority of 2005-06 season recovering from off-season shoulder surgery. Signed Letter of Intent to attend **U. of Massachusetts** (Hockey East) in fall of 2006.

NORDQVIST, Jonas (NAWRD-kvihst, YOH-nuhs) **CHI.**

Center. Shoots left. 6'3", 202 lbs. Born, Leksand, Sweden, April 26, 1982.
(Chicago's 3rd choice, 49th overall, in 2000 Entry Draft).

			Regular Season					Playoffs				
Season	Club	League	GP	G	A	Pts	PIM	GP	G	A	Pts	PIM
1997-98	Leksands IF Jr.	Swe-Jr.	42	26	35	61	....	....	....	....	....	....
1998-99	Leksands IF Jr.	Swe-Jr.	32	14	25	39	....	....	....	....	....	....
99-2000	Leksands IF Jr.	Swe-Jr.	34	15	24	39	32	2	0	0	0	2
	Leksands IF	Sweden	3	0	0	0	0	....	....	....	....	....
	Leksands IF U18	Swe-U18	2	0	2	2	0	4	3	5	8	0
2000-01	Leksands IF Jr.	Swe-Jr.	10	6	13	19	6	5	1	6	7	2
	Leksands IF	Sweden	42	3	4	7	4	....	....	....	....	....
2001-02	Leksands IF Jr.	Swe-Jr.	8	14	7	21	6	1	0	1	1	0
	Leksands IF	Sweden-2	40	8	7	15	16	....	....	....	....	....
2002-03	Rogle	Sweden-2	27	12	19	32	4	....	....	....	....	....
2003-04	Lulea HF	Sweden	47	13	11	24	18	3	0	0	0	2
2004-05	Lulea HF	Sweden	49	16	16	32	12	4	1	1	2	0
2005-06	Lulea HF	Sweden	46	19	22	41	30	6	1	2	3	6

NORTON, Pierce (NOHR-tuhn, PIHRS) TOR.

Right wing. Shoots right. 6'2", 200 lbs. Born, Boston, MA, June 7, 1985.
(Toronto's 6th choice, 285th overall, in 2004 Entry Draft).

			Regular Season					Playoffs				
Season	Club	League	GP	G	A	Pts	PIM	GP	G	A	Pts	PIM
2002-03	Thayer Academy	High-MA	29	16	18	34	....	....	....	....	....	....
2003-04	Thayer Academy	High-MA	34	21	34	55	84	....	....	....	....	....
2004-05	Thayer Academy	High-MA	29	*30	20	50	....	....	....	....	....	....
2005-06	Providence College	H-East	35	1	2	3	22	....	....	....	....	....

NYHOLM, Robert (NYOO-hohlm, RAW-buhrt) CBJ

Right wing. Shoots left. 6'1", 194 lbs. Born, Pietarsaari, Finland, March 7, 1988.
(Columbus' 5th choice, 129th overall, in 2006 Entry Draft).

			Regular Season					Playoffs				
Season	Club	League	GP	G	A	Pts	PIM	GP	G	A	Pts	PIM
2003-04	Lepplax U18	Fin-U18	26	76	32	108	36	....	....	....	....	....
2004-05	HIFK Helsinki U18	Fin-U18	1	1	0	1	2	3	0	2	2	6
	HIFK Helsinki Jr.	Fin-Jr.	33	6	5	11	35	....	....	....	....	....
2005-06	HIFK Helsinki U18	Fin-U18	2	2	3	5	4	7	4	3	7	4
	HIFK Helsinki Jr.	Fin-Jr.	39	11	9	20	24	....	....	....	....	....

O'BRIEN, Shane (oh-BRIGH-uhn, SHAYN) ANA.

Defense. Shoots left. 6'2", 237 lbs. Born, Port Hope, Ont., August 9, 1983.
(Anaheim's 8th choice, 250th overall, in 2003 Entry Draft).

			Regular Season					Playoffs				
Season	Club	League	GP	G	A	Pts	PIM	GP	G	A	Pts	PIM
99-2000	Port Hope	OPJHL	47	6	27	33	110	....	....	....	....	....
2000-01	Kingston	OHL	61	2	12	14	89	4	0	1	1	6
2001-02	Kingston	OHL	67	10	23	33	132	1	0	0	0	2
2002-03	Kingston	OHL	28	8	15	23	100	....	....	....	....	....
	St. Michael's	OHL	34	8	11	19	108	19	4	10	14	*79
2003-04	Cincinnati	AHL	60	2	8	10	163	9	0	2	2	20
2004-05	Cincinnati	AHL	77	5	20	25	319	12	1	3	4	57
2005-06	Portland Pirates	AHL	77	8	33	41	287	19	6	16	22	*81

O'BYRNE, Ryan (oh-BUHRN, RIGH-uhn) MTL.

Defense. Shoots right. 6'5", 234 lbs. Born, Victoria, B.C., July 19, 1984.
(Montreal's 4th choice, 79th overall, in 2003 Entry Draft).

			Regular Season					Playoffs				
Season	Club	League	GP	G	A	Pts	PIM	GP	G	A	Pts	PIM
2001-02	Victoria Salsa	BCHL	52	2	9	11	91	....	....	....	....	....
2002-03	Victoria Salsa	BCHL	32	3	6	9	94	....	....	....	....	....
	Nanaimo Clippers	BCHL	9	2	4	6	24	....	....	....	....	....
2003-04	Cornell Big Red	ECAC	31	0	2	2	71	....	....	....	....	....
2004-05	Cornell Big Red	ECACHL	33	3	7	10	68	....	....	....	....	....
2005-06	Cornell Big Red	ECACHL	28	7	6	13	69	....	....	....	....	....

ODUYA, Johnny (oh-DOO-yuh, jaw-KNEE) N.J.

Defense. Shoots left. 5'11", 200 lbs. Born, Stockholm, Sweden, October 1, 1981.
(Washington's 6th choice, 221st overall, in 2001 Entry Draft).

			Regular Season					Playoffs				
Season	Club	League	GP	G	A	Pts	PIM	GP	G	A	Pts	PIM
1996-97	Hammarby Jr.	Swe-Jr.	13	0	0	0	....	....	....	....	....	....
1997-98	Hammarby Jr.	Swe-Jr.	26	3	11	14	70	....	....	....	....	....
1998-99	Hammarby Jr.	Swe-Jr.	38	14	31	45	45	....	....	....	....	....
99-2000	Hammarby Jr.	Swe-Jr.	32	3	18	21	48	6	1	2	3	4
	Hammarby	Sweden-2	1	0	0	0	0	1	0	0	0	0
2000-01	Moncton Wildcats	QMJHL	44	11	38	49	147	....	....	....	....	....
	Victoriaville Tigres	QMJHL	24	3	16	19	112	13	4	9	13	10
2001-02	Hammarby	Sweden-2	46	11	14	25	66	2	1	0	1	4
2002-03	Hammarby	Sweden-2	48	15	25	40	200	....	....	....	....	....
2003-04	Djurgarden	Sweden	42	4	4	8	*173	4	0	0	0	6
2004-05	Djurgarden	Sweden	49	2	4	6	139	12	0	2	2	39
2005-06	Frolunda	Sweden	47	8	11	19	95	17	1	2	3	16

Signed as a free agent by **New Jersey**, July 17, 2006.

OGORODNIKOV, Sergei (oh-goh-RAWD-nee-kawf, SAIR-gay) NYI

Center. Shoots left. 6', 178 lbs. Born, Irkutsk, USSR, January 21, 1986.
(NY Islanders' 3rd choice, 82nd overall, in 2004 Entry Draft).

			Regular Season					Playoffs				
Season	Club	League	GP	G	A	Pts	PIM	GP	G	A	Pts	PIM
2002-03	Dyn'o Moscow 2	Russia-3	STATISTICS NOT AVAILABLE									
2003-04	Dyn'o Moscow 2	Russia-3	STATISTICS NOT AVAILABLE									
	THK Tver	Russia-2	21	8	3	11	14	....	....	....	....	....
2004-05	CSKA Moscow	Russia	18	2	4	6	2	....	....	....	....	....
2005-06	CSKA Moscow	Russia	3	0	0	0	2	....	....	....	....	....
	Ufa	Russia	14	0	3	3	8	6	0	0	0	4
	CSKA Moscow 2	Russia-3	STATISTICS NOT AVAILABLE									

O'HANLEY, Brian (oh-HAN-lee, BRIGH-uhn) S.J.

Defense. Shoots left. 6', 177 lbs. Born, Quincy, MA, December 18, 1984.
(San Jose's 10th choice, 267th overall, in 2003 Entry Draft).

			Regular Season					Playoffs				
Season	Club	League	GP	G	A	Pts	PIM	GP	G	A	Pts	PIM
2001-02	Bos. College High	High-MA	24	22	13	35	20	....	....	....	....	....
2002-03	Bos. College High	High-MA	23	22	21	43	12	....	....	....	....	....
2003-04	Salisbury School	High-CT	26	11	28	39	....	....	....	....	....	....
2004-05	Boston College	H-East	35	2	11	13	18	....	....	....	....	....
2005-06	Boston College	H-East	40	2	4	6	14	....	....	....	....	....

OKPOSO, Kyle (awk-POH-soh, KIGHL) NYI

Right wing. Shoots right. 6', 195 lbs. Born, St. Paul, MN, April 16, 1988.
(NY Islanders' 1st choice, 7th overall, in 2006 Entry Draft).

			Regular Season					Playoffs				
Season	Club	League	GP	G	A	Pts	PIM	GP	G	A	Pts	PIM
2004-05	Shat.-St. Mary's	High-MN	65	47	45	92	72	....	....	....	....	....
2005-06	Des Moines	USHL	50	27	31	58	56	11	5	11	16	8

USHL Rookie of the Year (2006)

OLSON, Glenn (OHL-suhn, GLEHN) S.J.

Left wing. Shoots left. 6'4", 230 lbs. Born, Fort McNeil, B.C., May 1, 1984.

			Regular Season					Playoffs				
Season	Club	League	GP	G	A	Pts	PIM	GP	G	A	Pts	PIM
2002-03	Cowichan Valley	BCHL	41	1	4	5	168	....	....	....	....	....
2003-04	Kootenay Ice	WHL	41	2	1	3	126	4	0	0	0	8
2004-05	Cleveland Barons	AHL	6	0	1	1	12	....	....	....	....	....
	Fresno Falcons	ECHL	10	0	1	1	105	....	....	....	....	....
	Johnstown Chiefs	ECHL	4	0	0	0	9	....	....	....	....	....
2005-06	Cleveland Barons	AHL	34	1	1	2	118	....	....	....	....	....
	Fresno Falcons	ECHL	17	0	1	1	67	....	....	....	....	....

Signed as a free agent by **San Jose**, September 18, 2003.

OLSSON, Kalle (OHL-suhn, KAL-ay) EDM.

Right wing. Shoots left. 6', 183 lbs. Born, Munkedal, Sweden, January 31, 1985.
(Edmonton's 6th choice, 147th overall, in 2003 Entry Draft).

			Regular Season					Playoffs				
Season	Club	League	GP	G	A	Pts	PIM	GP	G	A	Pts	PIM
2000-01	Lysekils HK Viking	Sweden-4	30	5	5	10	12	....	....	....	....	....
2001-02	V.Frolunda Jr.	Swe-Jr.	35	10	10	20	10	8	1	5	6	4
2002-03	V.Frolunda Jr.	Swe-Jr.	30	22	13	35	18	6	4	3	7	4
2003-04	V.Frolunda Jr.	Swe-Jr.	30	13	13	26	28	5	2	1	3	2
	V.Frolunda	Sweden	4	1	0	1	0	2	0	0	0	0
2004-05	Frolunda	Sweden	1	0	0	0	2	....	....	....	....	....
	Vaxjo Lakers HC	Sweden-2	2	0	1	1	0	....	....	....	....	....
	Frolunda Jr.	Swe-Jr.	33	15	16	31	50	6	2	2	4	0
2005-06	VIK Vasteras HK	Sweden-2	40	10	5	15	14	....	....	....	....	....

OLVECKY, Peter (ohl-VEH-tskee, PEE-tuhr) MIN.

Center. Shoots left. 6'2", 204 lbs. Born, Trencin, Czech., October 11, 1985.
(Minnesota's 3rd choice, 78th overall, in 2004 Entry Draft).

			Regular Season					Playoffs				
Season	Club	League	GP	G	A	Pts	PIM	GP	G	A	Pts	PIM
2003-04	Dukla Trencin Jr.	Slovak-Jr.	40	16	20	36	74	2	0	0	0	12
	Dukla Trencin	Slovakia	16	0	0	0	18	....	....	....	....	....
	Dukla Trencin U18	Svk-U18	2	0	0	0	0	....	....	....	....	....
2004-05	SHK 37 Piestany	Slovak-2	1	0	0	0	10	....	....	....	....	....
	Dukla Trencin Jr.	Slovak-Jr.	8	1	3	4	10	2	1	4	5	4
	Dukla Trencin	Slovakia	45	10	9	19	49	12	1	0	1	6
2005-06	Houston Aeros	AHL	67	14	18	32	56	7	1	3	4	4

OLVER, Darin (AWL-vuhr, DAIR-uhn) NYR

Center. Shoots left. 6', 170 lbs. Born, Burnaby, B.C., March 5, 1985.
(NY Rangers' 3rd choice, 36th overall, in 2004 Entry Draft).

			Regular Season					Playoffs				
Season	Club	League	GP	G	A	Pts	PIM	GP	G	A	Pts	PIM
2002-03	Chilliwack Chiefs	BCHL	59	34	55	89	57	....	....	....	....	....
2003-04	Northern Mich.	CCHA	41	13	21	34	26	....	....	....	....	....
2004-05	Northern Mich.	CCHA	40	9	*34	43	30	....	....	....	....	....
2005-06	Northern Mich.	CCHA	36	15	20	35	32	....	....	....	....	....

O'MARRA, Ryan (oh-MAHR-ah, RIGH-uhn) NYI

Center. Shoots right. 6'1", 193 lbs. Born, Tokyo, Japan, June 9, 1987.
(NY Islanders' 1st choice, 15th overall, in 2005 Entry Draft).

			Regular Season					Playoffs				
Season	Club	League	GP	G	A	Pts	PIM	GP	G	A	Pts	PIM
2002-03	Miss. Senators	GTHL	76	51	60	111	83	....	....	....	....	....
	Georgetown	OPJHL	3	0	2	2	0	....	....	....	....	....
	Streetsville Derbys	OPJHL	6	0	1	1	2	....	....	....	....	....
2003-04	Erie Otters	OHL	63	16	16	32	33	9	5	5	10	6
2004-05	Erie Otters	OHL	64	25	38	63	60	6	4	1	5	0
2005-06	Erie Otters	OHL	61	27	50	77	134	....	....	....	....	....
	Bridgeport	AHL	8	4	1	5	4	3	0	1	1	2

O'NEILL, Wes (oh-NEEL, WEHS) NYI

Defense. Shoots left. 6'4", 200 lbs. Born, Windsor, Ont., March 3, 1986.
(NY Islanders' 4th choice, 115th overall, in 2004 Entry Draft).

			Regular Season					Playoffs				
Season	Club	League	GP	G	A	Pts	PIM	GP	G	A	Pts	PIM
2000-01	Chatham Maroons	OHA-B	51	6	9	15	50	....	....	....	....	....
2001-02	Chatham Maroons	OHA-B	51	9	36	45	....	....	....	....	....	....
2002-03	Green Bay	USHL	50	2	15	17	79	....	....	....	....	....
2003-04	U. of Notre Dame	CCHA	39	2	10	12	28	....	....	....	....	....
2004-05	U. of Notre Dame	CCHA	38	6	14	20	52	....	....	....	....	....
2005-06	U. of Notre Dame	CCHA	35	6	19	25	40	....	....	....	....	....

O'NEILL, Will (oh-NEEL, WIHL) ATL.

Defense. Shoots left. 6', 193 lbs. Born, Boston, MA, April 28, 1988.
(Atlanta's 8th choice, 210th overall, in 2006 Entry Draft).

			Regular Season					Playoffs				
Season	Club	League	GP	G	A	Pts	PIM	GP	G	A	Pts	PIM
2004-05	Tabor Academy	High-MA	....	1	16	17	....	....	....	....	....	....
2005-06	Tabor Academy	High-MA	28	5	25	30	38	....	....	....	....	....

O'REILLY, Cal (oh-RIGH-lee, KAL) NSH.

Center. Shoots left. 6', 193 lbs. Born, Toronto, Ont., September 30, 1986.
(Nashville's 4th choice, 150th overall, in 2005 Entry Draft).

			Regular Season					Playoffs				
Season	Club	League	GP	G	A	Pts	PIM	GP	G	A	Pts	PIM
2002-03	St. Mary's Lincolns	OJHL-B	46	11	19	30	2	....	....	....	....	....
2003-04	Windsor Spitfires	OHL	61	3	18	21	2	3	0	1	1	0
2004-05	Windsor Spitfires	OHL	68	24	50	74	16	11	4	5	9	4
2005-06	Windsor Spitfires	OHL	68	18	81	99	8	7	3	8	11	0
	Milwaukee	AHL	2	0	0	0	0	10	0	1	1	0

ORESKOVIC, Phil (oh-rehs-KOH-vich, FIHL) TOR.

Defense. Shoots right. 6'3", 217 lbs. Born, North York, Ont., January 26, 1987.
(Toronto's 2nd choice, 82nd overall, in 2005 Entry Draft).

			Regular Season					Playoffs				
Season	Club	League	GP	G	A	Pts	PIM	GP	G	A	Pts	PIM
2003-04	Brampton	OHL	66	0	7	7	64	12	0	2	2	16
2004-05	Brampton	OHL	61	1	6	7	147	6	0	0	0	4
2005-06	Brampton	OHL	65	3	9	12	202	11	0	0	0	34

ORESKOVICH, Victor
(oh-rehs-KOH-vihvh, VIHK-tohr) **COL.**

Right wing. Shoots right. 6'3", 216 lbs. Born, Whitby, Ont., August 15, 1986.
(Colorado's 2nd choice, 55th overall, in 2004 Entry Draft).

			Regular Season					Playoffs				
Season	Club	League	GP	G	A	Pts	PIM	GP	G	A	Pts	PIM
2002-03	Milton IceHawks	OPJHL	49	28	46	74	51	....	....	....	....	....
2003-04	Green Bay	USHL	58	11	26	37	33	....	....	....	....	....
2004-05	U. of Notre Dame	CCHA	37	1	2	3	69	....	....	....	....	....
2005-06	U. of Notre Dame	CCHA	10	2	1	3	8	....	....	....	....	....
	Kitchener Rangers	OHL	19	6	10	16	16	5	0	2	2	4

ORLOV, Maxim
(ohr-LAHF, max-EEM) **WSH.**

Center. Shoots left. 6', 176 lbs. Born, Moscow, USSR, March 31, 1981.
(Washington's 9th choice, 219th overall, in 1999 Entry Draft).

			Regular Season					Playoffs				
Season	Club	League	GP	G	A	Pts	PIM	GP	G	A	Pts	PIM
1998-99	CSKA Moscow	Russia	2	0	0	0	2	1	0	0	0	0
99-2000	CSKA Moscow	Russia	25	0	0	0	2	2	0	0	0	2
2000-01	CSKA Moscow	Russia	41	5	4	9	14	....	....	....	....	....
2001-02	CSKA Moscow 2	Russia-3	7	7	4	11	4	....	....	....	....	....
	CSKA Moscow	Russia	35	3	5	8	14	....	....	....	....	....
2002-03	MGU Moscow	Russia-3	2	0	0	0	0	....	....	....	....	....
	Leninogorsk	Russia-2	25	3	8	11	24	....	....	....	....	....
2003-04	Leninogorsk	Russia-2	35	5	9	14	39	2	0	0	0	0
2004-05	Kristall Saratov	Russia-2	47	13	23	36	46	4	0	0	0	2
2005-06	Ufa 2	Russia-3	20	8	8	16	10	....	....	....	....	....
	Ufa	Russia	5	0	0	0	0	....	....	....	....	....

ORPIK, Andrew
(OHR-pihk, AN-droo) **BUF.**

Defense. Shoots right. 6'3", 200 lbs. Born, East Amherst, NY, March 12, 1986.
(Buffalo's 9th choice, 227th overall, in 2005 Entry Draft).

			Regular Season					Playoffs				
Season	Club	League	GP	G	A	Pts	PIM	GP	G	A	Pts	PIM
2003-04	Thayer Academy	High-MA	32	9	8	17	18	....	....	....	....	....
2004-05	Thayer Academy	High-MA	31	8	12	20	24	....	....	....	....	....
2005-06	Boston College	H-East	40	3	5	8	32	....	....	....	....	....

OSALA, Oskar
(OH-sa-la, AWS-kuhr) **WSH.**

Left wing. Shoots left. 6'4", 217 lbs. Born, Vassa, Finland, December 26, 1987.
(Washington's 6th choice, 97th overall, in 2006 Entry Draft).

			Regular Season					Playoffs				
Season	Club	League	GP	G	A	Pts	PIM	GP	G	A	Pts	PIM
2003-04	Sport Vaasa U18	Fin-U18	25	19	18	37	32	....	....	....	....	....
	Sport Vaasa Jr.	Fin-Jr.	2	0	0	0	4	....	....	....	....	....
	Sport Vaasa	Finland-2	5	0	0	0	0	....	....	....	....	....
2004-05	Sport Vaasa U18	Fin-U18	4	4	2	6	16	....	....	....	....	....
	Sport Vaasa Jr.	Fin-Jr.	19	13	14	27	28	2	0	0	0	2
	Sport Vaasa	Finland-2	21	1	4	5	6	7	0	0	0	6
2005-06	Mississauga	OHL	68	17	26	43	86	....	....	....	....	....

OSHIE, T.J.
(OH-shee, TEE-JAY) **ST.L.**

Center. Shoots right. 5'10", 170 lbs. Born, Mt. Vernon, WA, December 23, 1986.
(St. Louis' 1st choice, 24th overall, in 2005 Entry Draft).

			Regular Season					Playoffs				
Season	Club	League	GP	G	A	Pts	PIM	GP	G	A	Pts	PIM
2004-05	Warroad Warriors	High-MN	31	37	62	99	22	....	....	....	....	....
	Sioux Falls	USHL	11	3	2	5	6	....	....	....	....	....
2005-06	North Dakota	WCHA	44	24	21	45	33	....	....	....	....	....

WCHA All-Rookie Team (2006)

OSLUND, Nick
(OZ-luhnd, NIHK) **DET.**

Right wing. Shoots right. 6'3", 195 lbs. Born, Burnsville, MN, November 15, 1987.
(Detroit's 6th choice, 191st overall, in 2006 Entry Draft).

			Regular Season					Playoffs				
Season	Club	League	GP	G	A	Pts	PIM	GP	G	A	Pts	PIM
2004-05	Burnsville	High-MN	27	29	18	47	28	....	....	....	....	....
2005-06	Burnsville	High-MN	26	22	30	52	30	....	....	....	....	....

O'SULLIVAN, Patrick
(oh-SUHL-ih-van, PAT-rihk) **L.A.**

Center. Shoots left. 5'11", 190 lbs. Born, Winston Salem, NC, February 1, 1985.
(Minnesota's 2nd choice, 56th overall, in 2003 Entry Draft).

			Regular Season					Playoffs				
Season	Club	League	GP	G	A	Pts	PIM	GP	G	A	Pts	PIM
99-2000	Strathroy Rockets	OHA-B	45	6	13	19	53	....	....	....	....	....
2000-01	USNTDP	U-17	8	8	10	18	12	....	....	....	....	....
	USNTDP	NAHL	56	22	35	57	57	....	....	....	....	....
2001-02	Mississauga	OHL	68	34	58	92	61	....	....	....	....	....
	USNTDP	USHL	1	1	0	1	2	....	....	....	....	....
2002-03	Mississauga	OHL	56	40	41	81	57	5	2	9	11	18
2003-04	Mississauga	OHL	53	43	39	82	32	24	12	11	23	16
2004-05	Mississauga	OHL	57	31	59	90	63	5	0	4	4	6
2005-06	Houston Aeros	AHL	78	47	46	93	64	8	5	5	10	4

AHL All-Rookie Team (2006) • Dudley "Red" Garrett Memorial Trophy (Top Rookie - AHL) (2006)

Traded to **Los Angeles** by **Minnesota** with Edmonton's 1st round choice (previously acquired; Los Angeles selected Trevor Lewis) in 2006 Entry Draft for Pavol Demitra, June 24, 2006.

OTTOSSON, Kristofer
(AW-toh-suhn, KRIHS-tuh-fuhr) **NYI**

Right wing. Shoots left. 5'10", 187 lbs. Born, Stockholm, Sweden, January 9, 1976.
(NY Islanders' 6th choice, 148th overall, in 2000 Entry Draft).

			Regular Season					Playoffs				
Season	Club	League	GP	G	A	Pts	PIM	GP	G	A	Pts	PIM
1993-94	Djurgarden Jr.	Swe-Jr.	13	3	6	9	4	....	....	....	....	....
1994-95	Djurgarden Jr.	Swe-Jr.	15	8	23	31	2	....	....	....	....	....
	Djurgarden	Sweden	30	0	0	0	2	3	0	0	0	0
1995-96	Djurgarden Jr.	Swe-Jr.	15	5	12	17	4	....	....	....	....	....
	Djurgarden	Sweden	32	1	0	1	2	2	0	0	0	0
1996-97	Djurgarden Jr.	Swe-Jr.	2	1	1	2	0	....	....	....	....	....
	Arlanda HC Marsta	Sweden-2	6	6	0	6	0	....	....	....	....	....
	Djurgarden	Sweden	20	0	0	0	2	....	....	....	....	....
	Huddinge IK	Sweden-2	13	1	3	4	2	2	0	1	1	0
1997-98	Huddinge IK	Sweden-2	16	10	13	23	6	14	7	7	14	8
1998-99	Huddinge IK	Sweden-2	27	12	17	29	14	14	3	2	5	2
	Djurgarden	EuroHL	1	0	0	0	0	....	....	....	....	....
99-2000	Djurgarden	Sweden	47	25	15	40	12	13	7	2	9	2
2000-01	Djurgarden	Sweden	46	17	24	41	14	14	*7	4	11	4
2001-02	Djurgarden	Sweden	41	13	8	21	12	4	0	0	0	0
2002-03	Djurgarden	Sweden	46	19	19	38	30	12	1	4	5	0
2003-04	Djurgarden	Sweden	50	7	12	19	16	4	0	1	1	4
2004-05	Djurgarden	Sweden	34	4	9	13	8	11	1	3	4	6
2005-06	Djurgarden	Sweden	31	6	11	17	22	....	....	....	....	....

OULAHEN, Ryan
(OO-la-hehn, RIGH-uhn) **DET.**

Center. Shoots left. 6'1", 180 lbs. Born, Newmarket, Ont., March 26, 1985.
(Detroit's 3rd choice, 164th overall, in 2003 Entry Draft).

			Regular Season					Playoffs				
Season	Club	League	GP	G	A	Pts	PIM	GP	G	A	Pts	PIM
2000-01	Wexford Raiders	OMHA	66	38	58	96	18	....	....	....	....	....
2001-02	Newmarket	OPJHL	48	18	17	35	4	....	....	....	....	....
2002-03	Brampton	OHL	61	21	22	43	6	11	2	1	3	2
2003-04	Brampton	OHL	57	17	18	35	26	12	3	7	10	6
2004-05	Brampton	OHL	64	27	31	58	22	5	1	4	5	4
2005-06	Grand Rapids	AHL	75	9	10	19	20	16	0	0	0	2

OYSTRICK, Nathan
(OI-strihk, NAY-thun) **ATL.**

Defense. Shoots left. 6', 200 lbs. Born, Regina, Sask., December 17, 1982.
(Atlanta's 7th choice, 198th overall, in 2002 Entry Draft).

			Regular Season					Playoffs				
Season	Club	League	GP	G	A	Pts	PIM	GP	G	A	Pts	PIM
99-2000	Reg. Pat Cdns.	SMHL	43	6	22	28	214	....	....	....	....	....
2000-01	South Surrey	BCHL	STATISTICS NOT AVAILABLE									
2001-02	South Surrey	BCHL	50	15	42	57	142	....	....	....	....	....
2002-03	Northern Mich.	CCHA	34	2	10	12	26	....	....	....	....	....
2003-04	Northern Mich.	CCHA	39	8	20	28	98	....	....	....	....	....
2004-05	Northern Mich.	CCHA	40	7	13	20	87	....	....	....	....	....
2005-06	Northern Mich.	CCHA	38	9	20	29	58	....	....	....	....	....
	Chicago Wolves	AHL	2	0	1	1	4	....	....	....	....	....

CCHA Second All-Star Team (2004) • CCHA First All-Star Team (2005, 2006) • NCAA West Second All-American Team (2006)

PACKARD, Dennis
(PA-kuhrd, DEH-nihs) **BOS.**

Left wing. Shoots left. 6'4", 235 lbs. Born, St. Catherines, Ont., February 9, 1982.
(Tampa Bay's 8th choice, 219th overall, in 2001 Entry Draft).

			Regular Season					Playoffs				
Season	Club	League	GP	G	A	Pts	PIM	GP	G	A	Pts	PIM
99-2000	USNTDP	U-18	6	0	1	1	2	....	....	....	....	....
	USNTDP	USHL	55	11	14	25	85	....	....	....	....	....
2000-01	Harvard Crimson	ECAC	33	4	4	8	28	....	....	....	....	....
2001-02	Harvard Crimson	ECAC	32	9	10	19	34	....	....	....	....	....
2002-03	Harvard Crimson	ECAC	30	8	8	16	32	....	....	....	....	....
2003-04	Harvard Crimson	ECAC	36	11	11	22	16	....	....	....	....	....
2004-05	Springfield Falcons	AHL	47	2	8	10	25	....	....	....	....	....
	Johnstown Chiefs	ECHL	15	3	4	7	6	....	....	....	....	....
2005-06	Springfield Falcons	AHL	46	3	6	9	34	....	....	....	....	....
	Johnstown Chiefs	ECHL	16	2	9	11	12	5	0	1	1	4

Signed as a free agent by **Boston**, July 17, 2006.

PAGE, Rob
(PAYJ, RAWB) **CBJ**

Defense. Shoots right. 6'1", 188 lbs. Born, Edina, MN, July 9, 1985.
(Columbus' 7th choice, 167th overall, in 2004 Entry Draft).

			Regular Season					Playoffs				
Season	Club	League	GP	G	A	Pts	PIM	GP	G	A	Pts	PIM
2003-04	Blake Bears	High-MN	28	8	21	29	18	....	....	....	....	....
2004-05	Yale	ECACHL	32	2	9	11	68	....	....	....	....	....
2005-06	Yale	ECACHL	25	0	6	6	36	....	....	....	....	....

PAINCHAUD, Chad
(PAYN-show, CHAD) **ATL.**

Left wing. Shoots left. 5'11", 195 lbs. Born, Mississauga, Ont., May 27, 1986.
(Atlanta's 4th choice, 106th overall, in 2004 Entry Draft).

			Regular Season					Playoffs				
Season	Club	League	GP	G	A	Pts	PIM	GP	G	A	Pts	PIM
2002-03	Mississauga Reps	GTHL	52	47	47	94	....	....	....	....	....	....
2003-04	Mississauga	OHL	68	17	25	42	25	24	4	6	10	23
2004-05	Mississauga	OHL	8	3	3	6	11	....	....	....	....	....
	Sarnia Sting	OHL	49	18	16	34	22	....	....	....	....	....
2005-06	Sarnia Sting	OHL	49	31	34	65	65	....	....	....	....	....

PALIN, Brett
(PAY-lihn, BREHT) **CGY.**

Defense. Shoots right. 6'2", 204 lbs. Born, Nanaimo, B.C., June 23, 1984.

			Regular Season					Playoffs				
Season	Club	League	GP	G	A	Pts	PIM	GP	G	A	Pts	PIM
2000-01	Kelowna Rockets	WHL	39	0	0	0	25	....	....	....	....	....
2001-02	Kelowna Rockets	WHL	70	0	1	1	88	15	0	0	0	4
2002-03	Kelowna Rockets	WHL	71	1	17	18	118	19	0	4	4	12
2003-04	Kelowna Rockets	WHL	72	1	16	17	106	17	0	5	5	24
2004-05	Kelowna Rockets	WHL	72	4	21	25	71	24	4	6	10	52
2005-06	Omaha	AHL	64	0	5	5	46	....	....	....	....	....

Signed as a free agent by **Calgary**, August 5, 2005.

PANOV, Konstantin (PAN-ahv, KAWN-stan-tihn) NSH.

Left wing. Shoots left. 6', 195 lbs. Born, Chelyabinsk, USSR, June 29, 1980.
(Nashville's 10th choice, 131st overall, in 1999 Entry Draft).

			Regular Season					Playoffs				
Season	Club	League	GP	G	A	Pts	PIM	GP	G	A	Pts	PIM
1996-97	Yunior-T Kurgan	Russia-3	25	18	30	48	22	....	....	....	....	....
1997-98	Yunior-T Kurgan	Russia-3	20	7	3	10	6	....	....	....	....	....
	Chelyabinsk	Russia	6	2	0	2	4	2	0	0	0	0
1998-99	Kamloops Blazers	WHL	62	33	30	63	62	13	5	3	8	10
99-2000	Kamloops Blazers	WHL	64	43	30	73	47	....	....	....	....	....
2000-01	Kamloops Blazers	WHL	69	44	56	100	54	4	1	0	1	2
2001-02	Milwaukee	AHL	15	1	5	6	2	....	....	....	....	....
2002-03	Milwaukee	AHL	67	11	20	31	30	2	0	0	0	0
	Toledo Storm	ECHL	2	1	0	1	0	....	....	....	....	....
2003-04	Khabarovsk 2	Russia-3	8	8	6	14	5	....	....	....	....	....
	Amur Khabarovsk	Russia	29	0	1	1	10	....	....	....	....	....
2004-05	Chelyabinsk	Russia-2	51	13	22	35	32	8	2	1	3	12
2005-06	Chelyabinsk	Russia-2	40	15	12	27	62	14	8	5	13	37

WHL West Second All-Star Team (2000) • WHL West First All-Star Team (2001)

PAQUET, Jean-Philippe (pah-KEHT, ZHAWN-fihl-EEP) PIT.

Defense. Shoots left. 6'2", 202 lbs. Born, St-George, Que., January 7, 1987.
(Pittsburgh's 6th choice, 194th overall, in 2005 Entry Draft).

			Regular Season					Playoffs				
Season	Club	League	GP	G	A	Pts	PIM	GP	G	A	Pts	PIM
2003-04	Shawinigan	QMJHL	49	0	8	8	45	10	0	1	1	8
2004-05	Shawinigan	QMJHL	70	5	20	25	96	4	1	2	3	2
2005-06	Shawinigan	QMJHL	47	5	20	25	84	10	2	2	4	20

PAQUET, Philippe (pah-KEHT, fihl-EEP) MTL.

Defense. Shoots right. 6'3", 205 lbs. Born, Quebec City, Que., March 12, 1987.
(Montreal's 7th choice, 229th overall, in 2005 Entry Draft).

			Regular Season					Playoffs				
Season	Club	League	GP	G	A	Pts	PIM	GP	G	A	Pts	PIM
2003-04	St-Francois	QAAA	39	6	14	20	136	7	0	3	3	10
2004-05	Salisbury School	High-CT	26	1	4	5	10	....	....	....	....	....
2005-06	Clarkson Knights	ECACHL	37	2	5	7	91	....	....	....	....	....

PARDY, Adam (PAHR-dee, A-duhm) CGY.

Defense. Shoots left. 6'5", 211 lbs. Born, Bonavista, Nfld., March 29, 1984.
(Calgary's 6th choice, 173rd overall, in 2004 Entry Draft).

			Regular Season					Playoffs				
Season	Club	League	GP	G	A	Pts	PIM	GP	G	A	Pts	PIM
2002-03	Yarmouth	MJrHL	1	0	0	0	2	....	....	....	....	....
	Antigonish	MJrHL	31	5	16	21	42	....	....	....	....	....
	Cape Breton	QMJHL	7	0	1	1	2	2	0	0	0	0
2003-04	Cape Breton	QMJHL	68	4	12	16	137	5	0	1	1	8
2004-05	Cape Breton	QMJHL	69	12	27	39	163	5	2	2	4	8
2005-06	Omaha	AHL	24	0	0	0	18	....	....	....	....	....
	Las Vegas	ECHL	41	1	11	12	55	10	2	1	3	12

PARENT, Ryan (PAIR-ehnt, RIGH-uhn) NSH.

Defense. Shoots left. 6'2", 183 lbs. Born, Prince Albert, Sask., March 17, 1987.
(Nashville's 1st choice, 18th overall, in 2005 Entry Draft).

			Regular Season					Playoffs				
Season	Club	League	GP	G	A	Pts	PIM	GP	G	A	Pts	PIM
2002-03	Waterloo Siskins	OHA-B	41	2	8	10	35	....	....	....	....	....
2003-04	Guelph Storm	OHL	58	1	5	6	18	22	0	0	0	2
2004-05	Guelph Storm	OHL	66	2	17	19	36	4	0	1	1	4
2005-06	Guelph Storm	OHL	60	4	17	21	122	15	1	4	5	24
	Milwaukee	AHL	....	....	....	....	....	10	0	0	0	4

OHL Second All-Star Team (2006)

PARENTEAU, Pierre (pair-ehn-TOH, PEE-air) ANA.

Center. Shoots right. 5'11", 195 lbs. Born, Hull, Que., March 24, 1983.
(Anaheim's 11th choice, 264th overall, in 2001 Entry Draft).

			Regular Season					Playoffs				
Season	Club	League	GP	G	A	Pts	PIM	GP	G	A	Pts	PIM
99-2000	Charles-Lemoyne	QAAA	40	25	40	65	18	16	4	9	13	8
2000-01	Moncton Wildcats	QMJHL	45	10	19	29	38	....	....	....	....	....
	Chicoutimi	QMJHL	28	10	13	23	14	7	4	7	11	2
2001-02	Chicoutimi	QMJHL	68	51	67	118	120	4	3	1	4	10
2002-03	Chicoutimi	QMJHL	31	20	35	55	56	....	....	....	....	....
	Sherbrooke	QMJHL	28	13	35	48	84	12	8	11	19	6
2003-04	Cincinnati	AHL	66	14	16	30	20	7	1	2	3	6
2004-05	Cincinnati	AHL	76	17	24	41	58	9	2	0	2	8
2005-06	Portland Pirates	AHL	56	22	27	49	42	19	5	17	22	24
	Augusta Lynx	ECHL	2	0	1	1	0	....	....	....	....	....

PAROULEK, Martin (PAHR-oh-lehk, MAHR-tihn) CBJ

Right wing. Shoots right. 6', 193 lbs. Born, Uherske Hradiste, Czech., November 4, 1979.
(Columbus' 9th choice, 278th overall, in 2000 Entry Draft).

			Regular Season					Playoffs				
Season	Club	League	GP	G	A	Pts	PIM	GP	G	A	Pts	PIM
1998-99	HC Vsetin Jr.	CzRep-Jr.	45	25	19	44	....	....	....	....	....	....
	HC Slovnaft Vsetin	CzRep	11	1	1	2	....	7	0	1	1	0
99-2000	Vsetin	CzRep	48	11	14	25	24	8	1	1	2	4
2000-01	HC Draci Sumperk	CzRep-2	14	0	1	1	27	....	....	....	....	....
	HC Slovnaft Vsetin	CzRep	28	10	4	14	16	14	3	3	6	10
2001-02	Syracuse Crunch	AHL	59	11	14	25	31	9	1	1	2	4
2002-03	Syracuse Crunch	AHL	9	0	1	1	6	....	....	....	....	....
	HC Sparta Praha	CzRep	16	1	4	5	16	9	1	1	2	8
2003-04	HC Sparta Praha	CzRep	17	2	1	3	4	....	....	....	....	....
	Plzen	CzRep	19	7	10	17	16	12	1	3	4	12
2004-05	Beroun	CzRep-2	1	0	0	0	0	....	....	....	....	....
	Plzen	CzRep	38	7	11	18	49	....	....	....	....	....
2005-06	Plzen	CzRep	4	0	0	0	6	....	....	....	....	....
	HC Ocelari Trinec	CzRep	36	3	7	10	20	....	....	....	....	....

• Released by **Syracuse** (AHL) and signed as a free agent by **Sparta Praha** (CzRep) with Columbus retaining NHL rights, January 13, 2003.

PARSE, Scott (PARS, SKAWT) L.A.

Forward. Shoots right. 6'1", 185 lbs. Born, Kalamazoo, MI, September 5, 1984.
(Los Angeles' 5th choice, 174th overall, in 2004 Entry Draft).

			Regular Season					Playoffs				
Season	Club	League	GP	G	A	Pts	PIM	GP	G	A	Pts	PIM
2002-03	Tri-City Storm	USHL	48	21	23	44	32	3	2	1	3	8
2003-04	Nebraska-Omaha	CCHA	39	16	19	35	52	....	....	....	....	....
2004-05	Nebraska-Omaha	CCHA	39	19	30	49	32	....	....	....	....	....
2005-06	Nebraska-Omaha	CCHA	41	20	*41	*61	40	....	....	....	....	....

USHL All-Rookie Team (2003) • CCHA First All-Star Team (2005) • CCHA Player of the Year (2006) • NCAA West First All-American Team (2006)

PARSHIN, Denis (PAHR-shihn, DEH-nihs) COL.

Right wing. Shoots left. 5'9", 146 lbs. Born, Rybinsk, USSR, February 1, 1986.
(Colorado's 3rd choice, 72nd overall, in 2004 Entry Draft).

			Regular Season					Playoffs				
Season	Club	League	GP	G	A	Pts	PIM	GP	G	A	Pts	PIM
2002-03	CSKA Moscow 2	Russia-3	4	1	0	1	2	....	....	....	....	....
2003-04	CSKA Moscow	Russia	27	2	4	6	4	....	....	....	....	....
	CSKA Moscow 2	Russia-3	STATISTICS NOT AVAILABLE									
2004-05	CSKA Moscow	Russia	42	3	4	7	18	....	....	....	....	....
2005-06	CSKA Moscow 2	Russia-3	STATISTICS NOT AVAILABLE									
	CSKA Moscow	Russia	37	2	8	10	22	6	0	2	2	2

PAUKOVICH, Geoff (paw-KOH-vihch, JEHF) EDM.

Left wing. Shoots left. 6'4", 208 lbs. Born, Englewood, CO, April 24, 1986.
(Edmonton's 4th choice, 57th overall, in 2004 Entry Draft).

			Regular Season					Playoffs				
Season	Club	League	GP	G	A	Pts	PIM	GP	G	A	Pts	PIM
2002-03	Tri-City Storm	USHL	31	1	3	4	29	....	....	....	....	....
2003-04	USNTDP	U-18	44	6	9	15	46	....	....	....	....	....
	USNTDP	NAHL	11	4	2	6	31	....	....	....	....	....
2004-05	U. of Denver	WCHA	41	12	10	22	120	....	....	....	....	....
2005-06	U. of Denver	WCHA	37	4	6	10	72	....	....	....	....	....

PAVELSKI, Joe (pah-VEHL-skee, JOH) S.J.

Center. Shoots left. 5'11", 194 lbs. Born, Plover, WI, July 11, 1984.
(San Jose's 7th choice, 205th overall, in 2003 Entry Draft).

			Regular Season					Playoffs				
Season	Club	League	GP	G	A	Pts	PIM	GP	G	A	Pts	PIM
2002-03	Waterloo	USHL	60	36	33	69	32	7	5	7	12	8
2003-04	Waterloo	USHL	54	21	31	52	58	12	6	6	12	10
2004-05	U. of Wisconsin	WCHA	41	16	29	45	26	....	....	....	....	....
2005-06	U. of Wisconsin	WCHA	43	23	33	56	34	....	....	....	....	....

USHL All-Rookie Team (2003) • USHL First All-Star Team (2003) • USHL Rookie of the Year (2003) • WCHA All-Rookie Team (2005) • WCHA Second All-Star Team (2006) • NCAA West Second All-American Team (2006)

PECKER, Cory (PEH-kuhr, KOH-ree) OTT.

Center. Shoots right. 5'11", 192 lbs. Born, Montreal, Que., March 20, 1981.
(Calgary's 7th choice, 166th overall, in 1999 Entry Draft).

			Regular Season					Playoffs				
Season	Club	League	GP	G	A	Pts	PIM	GP	G	A	Pts	PIM
1996-97	Lac St-Louis Lions	QAAA	40	30	40	70	....	7	4	2	6	....
1997-98	Sault Ste. Marie	OHL	29	3	4	7	15	....	....	....	....	....
1998-99	Sault Ste. Marie	OHL	68	25	34	59	24	5	1	2	3	2
99-2000	Sault Ste. Marie	OHL	65	33	36	69	38	12	6	8	14	8
2000-01	Sault Ste. Marie	OHL	31	24	16	40	37	....	....	....	....	....
	Erie Otters	OHL	30	17	22	39	32	15	14	9	23	16
2001-02	Erie Otters	OHL	56	*53	46	99	108	21	*25	17	*42	36
2002-03	Cincinnati	AHL	77	20	13	33	66	....	....	....	....	....
2003-04	Cincinnati	AHL	54	6	10	16	32	....	....	....	....	....
	Binghamton	AHL	14	3	5	8	27	1	0	0	0	0
2004-05	Cincinnati	AHL	49	4	8	12	51	....	....	....	....	....
	San Diego Gulls	ECHL	3	1	0	1	0	....	....	....	....	....
	Manitoba Moose	AHL	12	1	1	2	8	5	1	0	1	4
2005-06	San Antonio	AHL	3	0	1	1	2	....	....	....	....	....
	Binghamton	AHL	24	9	14	23	20	....	....	....	....	....
	Phoenix	ECHL	18	11	12	23	39	....	....	....	....	....

OHL Second All-Star Team (2001) • OHL First All-Star Team (2002) • Memorial Cup Tournament All-Star Team (2002)

• Missed majority of 1997-98 season after being diagnosed with Chron's Disease. Signed as a free agent by **Anaheim**, July 8, 2002. Loaned to **Manitoba** (AHL) by **Anaheim** (Cincinnati-AHL) for cash, March 17, 2005. Signed as a free agent by **Ottawa**, July 25, 2006.

PECKHAM, Theo (PEHK-am, THEE-oh) EDM.

Defense. Shoots left. 6'1", 216 lbs. Born, Richmond Hill, Ont., November 10, 1987.
(Edmonton's 2nd choice, 75th overall, in 2006 Entry Draft).

			Regular Season					Playoffs				
Season	Club	League	GP	G	A	Pts	PIM	GP	G	A	Pts	PIM
2003-04	North York	OPJHL	29	1	4	5	46	....	....	....	....	....
2004-05	Owen Sound	OHL	61	1	9	10	209	8	0	0	0	8
2005-06	Owen Sound	OHL	67	6	9	15	236	11	1	6	7	32

PELECH, Matt (PEH-lihk, MAT) CGY.

Defense. Shoots right. 6'3", 227 lbs. Born, Toronto, Ont., September 4, 1987.
(Calgary's 1st choice, 26th overall, in 2005 Entry Draft).

			Regular Season					Playoffs				
Season	Club	League	GP	G	A	Pts	PIM	GP	G	A	Pts	PIM
2002-03	Vaughan	GTHL	44	3	13	16	113	....	....	....	....	....
2003-04	Sarnia Sting	OHL	62	4	6	10	39	5	0	1	1	12
2004-05	Sarnia Sting	OHL	31	1	5	6	74	....	....	....	....	....
2005-06	Sarnia Sting	OHL	18	0	2	2	59	....	....	....	....	....
	London Knights	OHL	34	1	7	8	80	19	0	0	0	48

PELLETIER, Pascal PEHL-tyay, pas-KAL) BOS.

Right wing. Shoots right. 5'11", 197 lbs. Born, Labrador City, Nfld., June 16, 1983.

			Regular Season					Playoffs				
Season	Club	League	GP	G	A	Pts	PIM	GP	G	A	Pts	PIM
2000-01	Baie-Comeau	QMJHL	70	15	44	59	176	11	2	11	13	6
2001-02	Baie-Comeau	QMJHL	56	12	25	37	115	5	3	4	7	0
2002-03	Baie-Comeau	QMJHL	67	46	55	101	113	12	5	7	12	14
2003-04	Shawinigan	QMJHL	64	39	52	91	85	11	3	9	12	20
2004-05	Louisiana	ECHL	61	10	28	38	75	....	....	....	....	....
	Gwinnett	ECHL	6	0	1	1	2	5	0	2	2	2
2005-06	Gwinnett	ECHL	21	18	12	30	18	....	....	....	....	....
	Providence Bruins	AHL	53	20	26	46	42	6	2	4	6	23

Signed as a free agent by **Boston**, August 7, 2006.

PELLEY, Rod (PEHL-lee, RAWD) N.J.

Left wing. Shoots left. 6', 200 lbs. Born, Kitimat, B.C., September 1, 1984.

			Regular Season					Playoffs				
Season	Club	League	GP	G	A	Pts	PIM	GP	G	A	Pts	PIM
2002-03	Ohio State	CCHA	43	8	3	11	26	....	....	....	....	....
2003-04	Ohio State	CCHA	42	10	12	22	38	....	....	....	....	....
2004-05	Ohio State	CCHA	41	22	19	41	54	....	....	....	....	....
2005-06	Ohio State	CCHA	39	7	7	14	42	....	....	....	....	....

Signed as a free agent by **New Jersey**, July 17, 2006.

PELTIER, Derek (PEHL-tyay, DAIR-ihk) COL.

Defense. Shoots left. 5'11", 190 lbs. Born, Plymounth, MN, March 14, 1985.
(Colorado's 5th choice, 184th overall, in 2004 Entry Draft).

			Regular Season					Playoffs				
Season	Club	League	GP	G	A	Pts	PIM	GP	G	A	Pts	PIM
2003-04	Cedar Rapids	USHL	55	7	26	33	34	4	0	0	0	4
2004-05	U. of Minnesota	WCHA	43	6	13	19	22	....	....	....	....	....
2005-06	U. of Minnesota	WCHA	41	1	17	18	30	....	....	....	....	....

PELUSO, Chris (puh-LOO-soh, KRIHS) PIT.

Defense. Shoots left. 5'11", 180 lbs. Born, Wadena, MN, August 21, 1986.
(Pittsburgh's 9th choice, 194th overall, in 2004 Entry Draft).

			Regular Season					Playoffs				
Season	Club	League	GP	G	A	Pts	PIM	GP	G	A	Pts	PIM
2003-04	Brainerd	High-MN	25	10	33	43	....	....	....	....	....	....
2004-05	Sioux Falls	USHL	53	1	7	8	54	....	....	....	....	....
2005-06	Sioux Falls	USHL	57	5	19	24	49	14	0	4	4	8

PEMBERTON, James (PEHM-buhr-tuhn, JAYMZ) FLA.

Defense. Shoots right. 6'4", 215 lbs. Born, Providence, RI, October 2, 1983.
(Florida's 6th choice, 124th overall, in 2003 Entry Draft).

			Regular Season					Playoffs				
Season	Club	League	GP	G	A	Pts	PIM	GP	G	A	Pts	PIM
1998-99	Mount St. Charles	High-RI	15	0	1	1	6	6	0	1	1	4
99-2000	Mount St. Charles	High-RI	18	2	11	13	10	6	0	7	7	0
2000-01	Mount St. Charles	High-RI	18	5	14	19	8	5	1	8	9	6
2001-02	N.E. Jr. Coyotes	EJHL	32	9	13	22	59	13	8	5	13	10
2002-03	Providence College	H-East	33	2	9	11	18	....	....	....	....	....
2003-04	Providence College	H-East	37	0	8	8	30	....	....	....	....	....
2004-05	Providence College	H-East	35	3	9	12	22	....	....	....	....	....
2005-06	Providence College	H-East	30	6	9	15	42	....	....	....	....	....

PERKOVICH, Nathan (puhr-KOH-vihch, NAY-thun) N.J.

Right wing. Shoots right. 6'5", 195 lbs. Born, Canton, MI, October 15, 1985.
(New Jersey's 6th choice, 250th overall, in 2004 Entry Draft).

			Regular Season					Playoffs				
Season	Club	League	GP	G	A	Pts	PIM	GP	G	A	Pts	PIM
2003-04	Cedar Rapids	USHL	35	1	7	8	23	4	1	0	1	0
2004-05	Chicago Steel	USHL	37	6	2	8	55	7	2	2	4	4
2005-06	Chicago Steel	USHL	56	28	24	52	121	....	....	....	....	....

PERREAULT, Mathieu (PAIR-oh, MA-tyew) WSH.

Center. Shoots left. 5'8", 151 lbs. Born, Drummondville, Que., January 5, 1988.
(Washington's 10th choice, 177th overall, in 2006 Entry Draft).

			Regular Season					Playoffs				
Season	Club	League	GP	G	A	Pts	PIM	GP	G	A	Pts	PIM
2004-05	Magog Catonniers	QAAA	41	25	47	72	68	9	5	10	15	12
2005-06	Acadie-Bathurst	QMJHL	62	18	34	52	42	17	10	11	21	8

PERSSON, Dennis (PAIR-suhn, DEH-nihs) BUF.

Defense. Shoots left. 6'1", 181 lbs. Born, Nykoping, Sweden, June 2, 1988.
(Buffalo's 1st choice, 24th overall, in 2006 Entry Draft).

			Regular Season					Playoffs				
Season	Club	League	GP	G	A	Pts	PIM	GP	G	A	Pts	PIM
2004-05	Vasteras U18	Swe-U18	3	0	1	1	2	4	0	1	1	0
	Vasteras Jr.	Swe-Jr.	27	3	3	6	24	....	....	....	....	....
2005-06	Vasteras Jr.	Swe-Jr.	28	11	15	26	22	....	....	....	....	....
	VIK Vasteras HK	Sweden-2	19	0	2	2	6	....	....	....	....	....

PERVYSHIN, Andrei (pair-VIHSH-ihn, AWN-dray) ST.L.

Defense. Shoots left. 5'8", 156 lbs. Born, Arkhangelsk, USSR, February 2, 1985.
(St. Louis' 11th choice, 253rd overall, in 2003 Entry Draft).

			Regular Season					Playoffs				
Season	Club	League	GP	G	A	Pts	PIM	GP	G	A	Pts	PIM
2003-04	Spartak Moscow	Russia-2	59	3	6	9	14	13	0	1	1	4
2004-05	Ak Bars Kazan 2	Russia-3	....	0	1	1	....	....	....	....	....	....
	Ak Bars Kazan	Russia	52	0	3	3	10	2	0	0	0	0
2005-06	Ak Bars Kazan	Russia	48	3	7	10	22	13	0	3	3	14

PESONEN, Janne (PEHS-oh-nihn, YAH-nee) ANA.

Left wing. Shoots left. 5'11", 180 lbs. Born, Suomussalmi, Finland, May 11, 1982.
(Anaheim's 8th choice, 269th overall, in 2004 Entry Draft).

			Regular Season					Playoffs				
Season	Club	League	GP	G	A	Pts	PIM	GP	G	A	Pts	PIM
1998-99	Hokki Kajaani	Finland-3	2	0	0	0	0	....	....	....	....	....
99-2000	Karpat Oulu U18	Fin-U18	33	6	12	18	30	3	0	1	1	0
2000-01	Karpat Oulu Jr.	Fin-Jr.	41	9	22	31	18	6	1	1	2	0
2001-02	Karpat Oulu Jr.	Fin-Jr.	42	12	19	31	18	3	2	0	2	2
	Karpat Oulu	Finland	9	2	0	2	0	1	0	0	0	0
2002-03	Hokki Kajaani	Finland-2	40	15	21	36	62	3	2	0	2	4
2003-04	Karpat Oulu	Finland	56	17	13	30	28	15	1	1	2	4
2004-05	Karpat Oulu	Finland	55	11	18	29	42	12	2	0	2	0
2005-06	Karpat Oulu	Finland	53	8	14	22	34	11	4	0	4	8

PESTUNOV, Dmitri (pehs-too-NAWF, dih-MEE-tree) PHX.

Center. Shoots left. 5'9", 196 lbs. Born, Ust-Kamenogorsk, USSR, January 22, 1985.
(Phoenix's 2nd choice, 80th overall, in 2003 Entry Draft).

			Regular Season					Playoffs				
Season	Club	League	GP	G	A	Pts	PIM	GP	G	A	Pts	PIM
2002-03	Magnitogorsk	Russia	32	4	0	4	0	....	....	....	....	....
2003-04	Magnitogorsk	Russia	51	6	7	13	40	14	0	3	3	25
	Magnitogorsk 2	Russia-3	6	3	15	18	2	3	0	2	2	4
2004-05	Magnitogorsk	Russia	37	4	4	8	46	....	....	....	....	....
	Spartak Moscow	Russia	12	1	1	2	14	....	....	....	....	....
2005-06	Magnitogorsk	Russia	48	6	13	19	58	4	0	1	1	0

Signed as a free agent by **Spartak Moscow** (Russia), February 16, 2005.

PETERS, Geoff (PEE-tuhrs, JEHF) ANA.

Center. Shoots left. 6'1", 205 lbs. Born, Hamilton, Ont., April 30, 1978.
(Chicago's 3rd choice, 46th overall, in 1996 Entry Draft).

			Regular Season					Playoffs				
Season	Club	League	GP	G	A	Pts	PIM	GP	G	A	Pts	PIM
1993-94	Wexford Raiders	MTHL	34	39	26	65	26	....	....	....	....	....
	Wexford Raiders	MTJHL	1	0	0	0	0	....	....	....	....	....
1994-95	Niagara Falls	OHL	57	11	9	20	37	6	2	0	2	4
1995-96	Niagara Falls	OHL	64	25	34	59	51	10	4	4	8	8
1996-97	Erie Otters	OHL	28	12	10	22	39	5	1	3	4	7
1997-98	Erie Otters	OHL	31	15	11	26	36	....	....	....	....	....
	North Bay	OHL	20	11	14	25	22	....	....	....	....	....
	Indianapolis Ice	IHL	2	0	0	0	10	....	....	....	....	....
1998-99	Canada	Nat-Tm	38	9	4	13	50	....	....	....	....	....
	Portland Pirates	AHL	4	1	1	2	9	....	....	....	....	....
99-2000	Cleveland	IHL	68	10	4	14	87	7	0	3	3	4
2000-01	Norfolk Admirals	AHL	73	11	10	21	48	6	0	1	1	6
2001-02	Trenton Titans	ECHL	43	13	21	34	55	....	....	....	....	....
	Columbus	ECHL	22	5	13	18	7	....	....	....	....	....
	Rochester	AHL	10	1	4	5	18	2	0	1	1	0
2002-03	Manchester	Britain	4	0	1	1	4	....	....	....	....	....
	Reading Royals	ECHL	40	15	13	28	40	....	....	....	....	....
	Milwaukee	AHL	8	0	0	0	7	....	....	....	....	....
2003-04	Rochester	AHL	46	7	4	11	109	16	0	4	4	27
2004-05	Rochester	AHL	57	9	8	17	125	9	0	2	2	18
2005-06	Portland Pirates	AHL	64	23	22	45	89	19	4	6	10	30

Signed as a free agent by **Manchester** (Britain), August 22, 2002. Signed as a free agent by **Reading** (ECHL) after **Manchester** (Britain) folded, November 11, 2002. Signed as a free agent by **Anaheim**, August 30, 2005.

PETERS, Warren (PEE-tuhrz, WAHR-ihn) CGY.

Center. Shoots left. 6', 200 lbs. Born, Saskatoon, Sask., July 10, 1982.

			Regular Season					Playoffs				
Season	Club	League	GP	G	A	Pts	PIM	GP	G	A	Pts	PIM
1998-99	Saskatoon Blades	WHL	53	8	6	14	111	....	....	....	....	....
99-2000	Saskatoon Blades	WHL	70	11	17	28	97	10	1	2	3	13
2000-01	Saskatoon Blades	WHL	63	27	14	41	111	....	....	....	....	....
2001-02	Saskatoon Blades	WHL	72	34	26	60	115	7	1	4	5	13
2002-03	Saskatoon Blades	WHL	71	31	44	75	108	6	1	6	7	6
	Portland Pirates	AHL	1	0	0	0	0	....	....	....	....	....
2003-04	Utah Grizzlies	AHL	55	4	4	8	63	....	....	....	....	....
	Idaho Steelheads	ECHL	21	6	7	13	33	....	....	....	....	....
2004-05	Idaho Steelheads	ECHL	69	23	23	46	131	4	0	1	1	12
2005-06	Omaha	AHL	77	15	10	25	133	....	....	....	....	....

Signed as a free agent by **Calgary**, August 5, 2005.

PETRELL, Lennart (peh-TREHL, LEH-nahrt) CBJ

Center. Shoots left. 6'3", 198 lbs. Born, Helsinki, Finland, April 13, 1984.
(Columbus' 8th choice, 190th overall, in 2004 Entry Draft).

			Regular Season					Playoffs				
Season	Club	League	GP	G	A	Pts	PIM	GP	G	A	Pts	PIM
2000-01	K-Kissat Jr.	Fin-Jr.	4	3	2	5	0	....	....	....	....	....
	K-Kissat	Finland-4	1	0	0	0	0	....	....	....	....	....
2001-02	HIFK Helsinki U18	Fin-U18	18	10	8	18	12	8	2	0	2	2
	HIFK Helsinki Jr.	Fin-Jr.	5	0	0	0	0	....	....	....	....	....
2002-03	HIFK Helsinki Jr.	Fin-Jr.	28	2	2	4	35	7	3	1	4	29
2003-04	Suomi U20	Finland-2	7	1	0	1	0	....	....	....	....	....
	HIFK Helsinki Jr.	Fin-Jr.	33	11	17	28	28	10	6	7	13	2
	HIFK Helsinki	Finland	8	0	0	0	2	1	0	0	0	0
2004-05	HIFK Helsinki Jr.	Fin-Jr.	12	5	5	10	10	2	0	1	1	0
	HIFK Helsinki	Finland	35	3	2	5	35	4	0	1	1	2
2005-06	HIFK Helsinki	Finland	51	12	8	20	88	10	1	2	3	20

PETROCHININ, Evgeny (peht-roh-CHIH-nihn, ehv-GEH-nee) CBJ

Defense. Shoots left. 6'2", 190 lbs. Born, Murmansk, USSR, February 7, 1976.
(Dallas' 5th choice, 150th overall, in 1994 Entry Draft).

			Regular Season					Playoffs				
Season	Club	League	GP	G	A	Pts	PIM	GP	G	A	Pts	PIM
1993-94	Spartak Moscow	CIS	2	0	0	0	0	....	....	....	....	....
1994-95	Spartak Moscow	CIS	45	0	2	2	14	....	....	....	....	....
1995-96	Spartak Moscow	CIS	50	5	17	22	18	5	3	0	3	0
1996-97	Spartak Moscow	Russia	32	5	6	11	52	....	....	....	....	....
1997-98	Spartak Moscow	Russia	46	12	6	18	100	....	....	....	....	....
1998-99	Spartak Moscow	Russia	21	4	6	10	14	....	....	....	....	....
	Ak Bars Kazan	Russia	6	0	2	2	2	9	1	1	2	24
99-2000	Magnitogorsk	Russia	33	7	10	17	38	14	2	1	3	26
2000-01	Cherepovets	Russia	40	8	7	15	38	9	2	0	2	40
2001-02	Cherepovets	Russia	35	35	2	8	10	1	0	0	0	0
2002-03	Cherepovets	Russia	29	3	6	9	14	10	1	0	1	0
2003-04	Cherepovets	Russia	43	4	9	13	85	....	....	....	....	....
	Cherepovets 2	Russia-3	1	0	2	2	0	....	....	....	....	....
2004-05	Magnitogorsk	Russia	48	3	4	7	14	3	0	0	0	2
2005-06	Magnitogorsk 2	Russia-3	1	0	0	0	0	....	....	....	....	....
	Vityaz Chekhov	Russia	18	0	3	3	6	....	....	....	....	....

Rights traded to **Columbus** by **Dallas** for Kirk Muller, September 28, 2001.

PETRUIC, Neil (peh-TROO-ihk, NEEL) OTT.

Defense. Shoots left. 6'1", 194 lbs. Born, Regina, Sask., July 30, 1982.
(Ottawa's 10th choice, 235th overall, in 2001 Entry Draft).

			Regular Season					Playoffs				
Season	Club	League	GP	G	A	Pts	PIM	GP	G	A	Pts	PIM
99-2000	Kindersley Klippers	SJHL	68	5	25	30	....	....	....	....	....	....
2000-01	Kindersley Klippers	SJHL	68	18	24	42	123	....	....	....	....	....
2001-02	U. Minn-Duluth	WCHA	40	3	6	9	54	....	....	....	....	....
2002-03	U. Minn-Duluth	WCHA	40	6	8	14	78	....	....	....	....	....
2003-04	U. Minn-Duluth	WCHA	45	4	10	14	56	....	....	....	....	....
2004-05	U. Minn-Duluth	WCHA	32	1	8	9	63	....	....	....	....	....
2005-06	Binghamton	AHL	51	1	3	4	31	....	....	....	....	....
	Charlotte	ECHL	10	2	4	6	6	....	....	....	....	....

SJHL First All-Star Team (2001)

PETRUZALEK, Jakub (peh-troo-ZAL-ehk, YA-kuhb) NYR

Right wing. Shoots right. 5'9", 172 lbs. Born, Most, Czech., April 24, 1985.
(NY Rangers' 13th choice, 266th overall, in 2004 Entry Draft).

			Regular Season					Playoffs				
Season	Club	League	GP	G	A	Pts	PIM	GP	G	A	Pts	PIM
2002-03	Litvinov Jr.	CzRep-Jr.	21	17	13	30	10	....	....	....	....	....
	Litvinov	CzRep	5	0	0	0	0	....	....	....	....	....
2003-04	Litvinov Jr.	CzRep-Jr.	53	38	51	89	110	2	0	0	0	2
	Litvinov	CzRep	7	0	0	0	2	....	....	....	....	....
	SK HC Banik Most	CzRep-3	1	0	0	0	0	....	....	....	....	....
2004-05	Ottawa 67's	OHL	59	23	40	63	64	21	8	10	18	30
2005-06	Litvinov Jr.	CzRep-Jr.	3	4	2	6	4	....	....	....	....	....
	Litvinov	CzRep	19	1	1	2	6	....	....	....	....	....
	Barrie Colts	OHL	24	11	20	31	28	14	8	11	19	14

PETRY, Jeff (PEH-tree, JEHF) EDM.

Defense. Shoots right. 6'2", 176 lbs. Born, Ann Arbor, MI, December 9, 1987.
(Edmonton's 1st choice, 45th overall, in 2006 Entry Draft).

			Regular Season					Playoffs				
Season	Club	League	GP	G	A	Pts	PIM	GP	G	A	Pts	PIM
2004-05	St. Mary's Prep	High-MI	23	2	8	10	....	6	2	5	7	....
2005-06	Det. Caesers	MWEHL	33	7	21	28	24	....	....	....	....	....
	Des Moines	USHL	48	1	14	15	68	11	2	5	7	8

PETTERSSON, Fredrik (PEH-tuhr-sohn, FREHD-rihk) EDM.

Left wing. Shoots right. 5'10", 183 lbs. Born, Goteborg, Sweden , June 10, 1987.
(Edmonton's 7th choice, 157th overall, in 2005 Entry Draft).

			Regular Season					Playoffs				
Season	Club	League	GP	G	A	Pts	PIM	GP	G	A	Pts	PIM
2002-03	V.Frolunda U18	Swe-U18	12	5	7	12	6	....	....	....	....	....
2003-04	V.Frolunda U18	Swe-U18	14	13	8	21	6	7	6	3	9	8
	V.Frolunda Jr.	Swe-Jr.	6	4	1	5	2	2	0	0	0	0
2004-05	Frolunda U18	Swe-U18	2	1	2	3	10	6	4	5	9	10
	Frolunda Jr.	Swe-Jr.	24	9	8	17	32	6	5	3	8	16
2005-06	Calgary Hitmen	WHL	59	22	21	43	47	13	5	5	10	18

PIISPANEN, Arsi (pihz-PAH-nehn, AHR-see) CBJ

Right wing. Shoots right. 6'3", 172 lbs. Born, Jyvaskyla, Finland, July 23, 1985.
(Columbus' 6th choice, 138th overall, in 2003 Entry Draft).

			Regular Season					Playoffs				
Season	Club	League	GP	G	A	Pts	PIM	GP	G	A	Pts	PIM
2000-01	Jokerit U18	Fin-U18	3	0	2	2	0	....	....	....	....	....
2001-02	Jokerit U18	Fin-U18	26	7	19	26	8	8	4	3	7	12
	Jokerit Helsinki Jr.	Fin-Jr.	1	0	0	0	0	....	....	....	....	....
2002-03	Jokerit U18	Fin-U18	10	12	6	18	2	6	2	3	5	2
	Jokerit Helsinki Jr.	Fin-Jr.	31	8	9	17	8	7	1	2	3	0
2003-04	Suomi U20	Finland-2	8	2	2	4	0	....	....	....	....	....
	Jokerit Helsinki Jr.	Fin-Jr.	36	5	25	30	12	10	3	3	6	2
	Jokerit Helsinki	Finland	5	0	0	0	0	4	0	0	0	0
2004-05	JYP Jyvaskyla Jr.	Fin-Jr.	1	0	0	0	0	....	....	....	....	....
	JYP Jyvaskyla	Finland	52	2	10	12	12	3	0	1	1	0
2005-06	JYP Jyvaskyla	Finland	52	9	8	17	14	3	1	1	2	2

PIKKARAINEN, Hannu (pih-kar-AY-nihn) NYR

Defense. Shoots left. 6'1", 190 lbs. Born, Helsinki, Finland, October 13, 1983.

			Regular Season					Playoffs				
Season	Club	League	GP	G	A	Pts	PIM	GP	G	A	Pts	PIM
2000-01	HIFK Helsinki U18	Fin-U18	20	1	10	11	59	4	1	1	2	6
	HIFK Helsinki Jr.	Fin-Jr.	19	4	7	11	6	7	0	0	0	2
2001-02	HIFK Helsinki Jr.	Fin-Jr.	44	8	14	22	24	4	0	2	2	0
2002-03	HIFK Helsinki	Finland	47	1	3	4	8	4	0	0	0	0
	HIFK Helsinki Jr.	Fin-Jr.	11	3	11	14	16	6	1	4	5	4
2003-04	HIFK Helsinki Jr.	Fin-Jr.	12	3	9	12	32	5	1	5	6	0
	Salamat	Finland-2	2	0	1	1	2	....	....	....	....	....
	HIFK Helsinki	Finland	16	0	0	0	6	13	0	0	0	2
2004-05	HIFK Helsinki	Finland	49	7	13	20	36	5	0	0	0	0
2005-06	HIFK Helsinki	Finland	47	5	13	18	60	12	0	0	0	2

Signed as a free agent by **NY Rangers**, August 18, 2005.

PIKKARAINEN, Ilkka (pih-kar-AY-nihn, IHL-kah)

Right wing. Shoots right. 6'2", 200 lbs. Born, Sonkajarvi, Finland, April 19, 1981.
(New Jersey's 9th choice, 218th overall, in 2002 Entry Draft).

			Regular Season					Playoffs				
Season	Club	League	GP	G	A	Pts	PIM	GP	G	A	Pts	PIM
1998-99	HIFK Helsinki U18	Fin-U18	24	6	12	18	26	2	1	0	1	27
	HIFK Helsinki Jr.	Fin-Jr.	13	6	1	7	12	....	....	....	....	....
99-2000	HIFK Helsinki Jr.	Fin-Jr.	28	3	2	5	14	3	1	1	2	2
2000-01	HIFK Helsinki Jr.	Fin-Jr.	38	27	31	58	186	9	2	5	7	26
	HIFK Helsinki	Finland	4	0	0	0	8	2	0	0	0	0
2001-02	HIFK Helsinki	Finland	54	9	9	18	111	....	....	....	....	....
2002-03	HIFK Helsinki	Finland	47	11	12	23	40	....	....	....	....	....
2003-04	Albany River Rats	AHL	63	8	10	18	118	....	....	....	....	....
2004-05	Albany River Rats	AHL	71	12	12	24	102	....	....	....	....	....
2005-06	Albany River Rats	AHL	62	9	11	20	85	....	....	....	....	....

PINEAULT, Adam (pih-NOH, A-duhm) CBJ

Right wing. Shoots right. 6'1", 201 lbs. Born, Holyoke, MA, May 23, 1986.
(Columbus' 2nd choice, 46th overall, in 2004 Entry Draft).

			Regular Season					Playoffs				
Season	Club	League	GP	G	A	Pts	PIM	GP	G	A	Pts	PIM
2000-01	Junior Bruins	EJHL	57	30	35	65	56	....	....	....	....	....
2001-02	USNTDP	U-17	20	5	4	9	14	....	....	....	....	....
	USNTDP	NAHL	38	11	4	15	11	....	....	....	....	....
2002-03	USNTDP	U-17	43	13	15	28	76	....	....	....	....	....
	USNTDP	U-18	4	4	3	7	6	....	....	....	....	....
	USNTDP	NAHL	9	5	4	9	13	....	....	....	....	....
2003-04	Boston College	H-East	30	4	4	8	32	....	....	....	....	....
2004-05	Moncton Wildcats	QMJHL	61	26	20	46	64	12	2	6	8	18
2005-06	Moncton Wildcats	QMJHL	55	29	30	59	94	21	14	8	22	25

PISELLINI, Gino (pih-sehl-EE-nee, JEE-noh) PHI.

Right wing. Shoots right. 6', 210 lbs. Born, Melrose Park, IL, August 5, 1986.
(Philadelphia's 5th choice, 149th overall, in 2004 Entry Draft).

			Regular Season					Playoffs				
Season	Club	League	GP	G	A	Pts	PIM	GP	G	A	Pts	PIM
2003-04	Plymouth Whalers	OHL	68	15	15	30	214	9	0	3	3	23
2004-05	Plymouth Whalers	OHL	59	4	6	10	137	4	0	1	1	9
2005-06	Plymouth Whalers	OHL	63	15	16	31	194	13	0	3	3	28

PITTON, Jason (PIH-tuhn, JAY-suhn) NYI

Left wing. Shoots left. 6'2", 196 lbs. Born, Mississauga, Ont., May 23, 1986.
(NY Islanders' 9th choice, 244th overall, in 2004 Entry Draft).

			Regular Season					Playoffs				
Season	Club	League	GP	G	A	Pts	PIM	GP	G	A	Pts	PIM
2002-03	Brampton Capitals	OPJHL	47	23	18	41	46	....	....	....	....	....
	Sault Ste. Marie	OHL	1	0	0	0	0	....	....	....	....	....
2003-04	Sault Ste. Marie	OHL	67	9	11	20	37	....	....	....	....	....
2004-05	Sault Ste. Marie	OHL	68	23	19	42	35	7	2	2	4	4
2005-06	Sault Ste. Marie	OHL	37	18	9	27	29	....	....	....	....	....
	Guelph Storm	OHL	31	10	5	15	21	15	5	3	8	18

PLATIL, Jan (PLA-tihl, YAN)

Defense. Shoots left. 6'2", 195 lbs. Born, Kladno, Czech., February 9, 1983.
(Ottawa's 8th choice, 218th overall, in 2001 Entry Draft).

			Regular Season					Playoffs				
Season	Club	League	GP	G	A	Pts	PIM	GP	G	A	Pts	PIM
1998-99	HC Kladno Jr.	CzRep-Jr.	46	8	12	20	....	....	....	....	....	....
99-2000	HC Kladno Jr.	CzRep-Jr.	39	5	6	11	....	....	....	....	....	....
2000-01	Barrie Colts	OHL	60	6	18	24	114	5	0	0	0	12
2001-02	Barrie Colts	OHL	68	13	34	47	136	20	1	5	6	51
2002-03	Barrie Colts	OHL	61	15	36	51	163	6	1	5	6	8
2003-04	Binghamton	AHL	66	1	3	4	142	....	....	....	....	....
2004-05	Binghamton	AHL	72	1	3	4	198	6	0	1	1	4
2005-06	Binghamton	AHL	65	5	14	19	212	....	....	....	....	....

PLATONOV, Denis (PLAH-tah-nahv, DIHN-ihs) NSH.

Right wing. Shoots left. 6'3", 205 lbs. Born, Saratov, USSR, November 6, 1981.
(Nashville's 4th choice, 75th overall, in 2001 Entry Draft).

			Regular Season					Playoffs				
Season	Club	League	GP	G	A	Pts	PIM	GP	G	A	Pts	PIM
1997-98	Kristall Saratov 2	Russia-3	20	4	2	6	34	....	....	....	....	....
1998-99	Kristall Saratov	Russia-2	14	1	0	1	61	....	....	....	....	....
99-2000	Kristall Saratov 2	Russia-3	5	0	0	0	37	....	....	....	....	....
	Kristall Saratov	Russia-2	32	9	4	13	60	....	....	....	....	....
2000-01	Kristall Saratov	Russia-2	51	14	6	20	75	....	....	....	....	....
2001-02	Kristall Saratov	Russia-2	50	18	14	32	96	....	....	....	....	....
2002-03	Ak Bars Kazan	Russia	47	8	9	17	49	5	0	0	0	2
2003-04	Milwaukee	AHL	3	0	0	0	0	....	....	....	....	....
	Ak Bars Kazan	Russia	28	5	3	8	18	8	1	0	1	2
	Ak Bars Kazan 2	Russia-3	STATISTICS NOT AVAILABLE									
2004-05	Ak Bars Kazan	Russia	38	3	7	10	10	....	....	....	....	....
	Nizhnekamsk	Russia	11	3	1	4	34	3	0	1	1	2
2005-06	Magnitogorsk	Russia	49	11	8	19	60	8	4	0	4	6

Assigned to **Kazan** (Russia) by **Nashville**, October 29, 2003.

PLATT, Jason (PLAT, JAY-suhn)

Defense. Shoots left. 6'1", 210 lbs. Born, San Francisco, CA, April 29, 1981.
(Edmonton's 9th choice, 247th overall, in 2000 Entry Draft).

			Regular Season					Playoffs				
Season	Club	League	GP	G	A	Pts	PIM	GP	G	A	Pts	PIM
1998-99	Omaha Lancers	USHL	56	2	9	11	65	11	0	0	0	8
99-2000	Omaha Lancers	USHL	49	1	6	7	65	4	0	0	0	9
2000-01	Providence College	H-East	26	0	2	2	12	....	....	....	....	....
2001-02	Providence College	H-East	36	2	5	7	60	....	....	....	....	....
2002-03	Providence College	H-East	30	1	7	8	41	....	....	....	....	....
2003-04	Providence College	H-East	34	2	5	7	36	....	....	....	....	....
	Toronto	AHL	1	0	0	0	0	....	....	....	....	....
2004-05	Edmonton	AHL	44	1	1	2	28	....	....	....	....	....
2005-06	Iowa Stars	AHL	60	0	5	5	43	7	0	1	1	2

PLEKHANOV, Andrey (plih-KHAH-nahv, AWN-dray) CBJ

Defense. Shoots right. 6'1", 187 lbs. Born, Nizhnekamsk, USSR, July 12, 1986.
(Columbus' 5th choice, 96th overall, in 2004 Entry Draft).

			Regular Season					Playoffs				
Season	Club	League	GP	G	A	Pts	PIM	GP	G	A	Pts	PIM
2003-04	Nizhnekamsk 2	Russia-3	STATISTICS NOT AVAILABLE									
2004-05	Nizhnekamsk	Russia	2	0	0	0	2	....	....	....	....	....
	Leninogorsk	Russia-2	1	0	0	0	4	....	....	....	....	....
	Perm 2	Russia-3	2	0	0	0	4	....	....	....	....	....
2005-06	Nizhnekamsk	Russia	45	1	2	33	22	5	0	0	0	0

PLIHAL, Tomas (PLEE-hahl, TAW-mahsh) S.J.

Center. Shoots left. 6'1", 195 lbs. Born, Frydlant v Cechach, Czech., March 28, 1983.
(San Jose's 4th choice, 140th overall, in 2001 Entry Draft).

			Regular Season					Playoffs				
Season	Club	League	GP	G	A	Pts	PIM	GP	G	A	Pts	PIM
99-2000	Liberec U17	CzR-U17	38	22	14	36	....	....	....	....	....	....
	Liberec Jr.	CzRep-Jr.	2	0	0	0	0	....	....	....	....	....
2000-01	HC Liberec U17	CzR-U17	18	3	5	8	....	....	....	....	....	....
	HC Liberec Jr.	CzRep-Jr.	33	16	12	28	....	....	....	....	....	....
2001-02	Kootenay Ice	WHL	72	32	54	86	28	22	4	10	14	14
2002-03	Kootenay Ice	WHL	67	35	42	77	113	11	2	4	6	18
2003-04	Cleveland Barons	AHL	51	4	12	16	16	6	0	3	3	2
2004-05	Cleveland Barons	AHL	62	17	11	28	26	....	....	....	....	....
2005-06	Cleveland Barons	AHL	74	11	19	30	53	....	....	....	....	....

George Parsons Trophy (Memorial Cup Tournament Most Sportsmanlike Player) (2002)

PODLESAK, Martin (PAWD-leh-shahk, MAHR-tihn)

Center. Shoots left. 6'6", 219 lbs. Born, Melnik, Czech., September 26, 1982.
(Phoenix's 3rd choice, 45th overall, in 2001 Entry Draft).

			Regular Season					Playoffs				
Season	Club	League	GP	G	A	Pts	PIM	GP	G	A	Pts	PIM
99-2000	Sparta Jr.	CzRep-Jr.	24	6	5	11	....	11	6	2	8	....
2000-01	Tri-City Americans	WHL	39	13	13	26	36	....	....	....	....	....
	Lethbridge	WHL	21	8	6	14	23	3	1	1	2	2
2001-02	Lethbridge	WHL	34	14	20	34	33	....	....	....	....	....
2002-03	Springfield Falcons	AHL	3	0	0	0	4	....	....	....	....	....
2003-04	Springfield Falcons	AHL	57	5	9	14	21	....	....	....	....	....
2004-05	Utah Grizzlies	AHL	10	0	1	1	24	....	....	....	....	....
2005-06	San Antonio	AHL	12	2	6	8	6	....	....	....	....	....

• Missed majority of 2002-03 season recovering from head injury suffered in game vs. Manchester (AHL), October 23, 2002. • Missed majority of 2004-05 season recovering from shoulder injury suffered in game vs. Houston (AHL), November 28, 2004.

POHANKA, Igor (poh-HAHN-kah, EE-gohr)

Center. Shoots left. 6'2", 210 lbs. Born, Piestany, Czech., July 5, 1983.
(New Jersey's 2nd choice, 44th overall, in 2001 Entry Draft).

			Regular Season					Playoffs				
Season	Club	League	GP	G	A	Pts	PIM	GP	G	A	Pts	PIM
1996-97	HK VTJ Piestany Jr.	Slovak-Jr.	3	1	3	4	4	....	....	....	....	....
1997-98	Bratislava Jr.	Slovak-Jr.	40	19	22	41	6	....	....	....	....	....
1998-99	Bratislava Jr.	Slovak-Jr.	40	14	21	35	36	....	....	....	....	....
99-2000	Bratislava Jr.	Slovak-Jr.	57	36	41	77	62	....	....	....	....	....
2000-01	Prince Albert	WHL	70	16	33	49	24	....	....	....	....	....
2001-02	Prince Albert	WHL	58	25	43	68	18	....	....	....	....	....
2002-03	Prince Albert	WHL	56	25	31	56	28	....	....	....	....	....
2003-04	Cincinnati	AHL	42	5	6	11	6	4	0	0	0	0
	San Diego Gulls	ECHL	11	1	5	6	10	3	0	2	2	0
2004-05	Cincinnati	AHL	35	5	3	8	18	....	....	....	....	....
2005-06	Portland Pirates	AHL	67	11	24	35	29	9	0	2	2	2

Traded to **Anaheim** by **New Jersey** with Petr Sykora, Mike Commodore and Jean-Francois Damphousse for Jeff Friesen, Oleg Tverdovsky and Maxim Balmochnykh, July 6, 2002.

POHL, Petr (PAWL, PEE-tuhr) **CBJ**

Right wing. Shoots right. 5'11", 188 lbs. Born, Prostejov, Czech., August 28, 1986.
(Columbus' 6th choice, 133rd overall, in 2004 Entry Draft).

			Regular Season					Playoffs				
Season	Club	League	GP	G	A	Pts	PIM	GP	G	A	Pts	PIM
2001-02	HC Vitkovice U17	CzR-U17	38	34	19	53	65	2	1	0	1	4
	HC Vitkovice Jr.	CzRep-Jr.	10	0	2	2	2	....	....	....	....	....
2002-03	HC Vitkovice Jr.	CzRep-Jr.	36	13	22	35	30	2	1	0	1	6
2003-04	Gatineau	QMJHL	70	23	27	50	16	8	0	2	2	2
2004-05	Gatineau	QMJHL	62	27	32	59	16	10	6	4	10	4
2005-06	Acadie-Bathurst	QMJHL	62	27	43	70	44	17	6	10	16	12

POKULOK, Sasha (poh-KUH-lawk, SA-shuh) **WSH.**

Defense. Shoots left. 6'5", 220 lbs. Born, Montreal, Que., May 25, 1986.
(Washington's 1st choice, 14th overall, in 2005 Entry Draft).

			Regular Season					Playoffs				
Season	Club	League	GP	G	A	Pts	PIM	GP	G	A	Pts	PIM
2003-04	Notre Dame	SJHL	39	7	16	23	34	....	....	....	....	....
2004-05	Cornell Big Red	ECACHL	26	3	7	10	33	....	....	....	....	....
2005-06	Cornell Big Red	ECACHL	27	4	9	13	49	....	....	....	....	....

ECAC All-Rookie Team (2005)

POLAK, Roman (POH-lahk, ROH-muhn) **ST.L.**

Defense. Shoots right. 6'1", 198 lbs. Born, Ostrava, Czech., April 28, 1986.
(St. Louis' 6th choice, 180th overall, in 2004 Entry Draft).

			Regular Season					Playoffs				
Season	Club	League	GP	G	A	Pts	PIM	GP	G	A	Pts	PIM
2001-02	HC Ostrava Jr.	CzRep-Jr.	46	4	9	13	84	....	....	....	....	....
2002-03	HC Ostrava Jr.	CzRep-Jr.	32	3	12	15	34	....	....	....	....	....
2003-04	HC Vitkovice Jr.	CzRep-Jr.	52	4	8	12	48	....	....	....	....	....
2004-05	Kootenay Ice	WHL	65	5	18	23	85	9	0	0	0	6
2005-06	HC Vitkovice Jr.	CzRep-Jr.	1	0	0	0	4	....	....	....	....	....
	HC Vitkovice Steel	CzRep	37	0	1	1	16	6	0	0	0	6

POLUSHIN, Alexander (puh-LOOSH-ihn, al-ehx-AN-duhr) **T.B.**

Center. Shoots left. 6'2", 212 lbs. Born, Kirovo-Chepetsk, USSR, May 8, 1983.
(Tampa Bay's 2nd choice, 47th overall, in 2001 Entry Draft).

			Regular Season					Playoffs				
Season	Club	League	GP	G	A	Pts	PIM	GP	G	A	Pts	PIM
99-2000	Dyn'o Moscow 2	Russia-3	18	4	3	7	14	....	....	....	....	....
	Spartak Moscow	Russia-2	14	1	0	1	2	....	....	....	....	....
2000-01	THK Tver	Russia-2	38	10	5	15	10	....	....	....	....	....
2001-02	HK CSKA Moscow	Russia-2	55	28	21	49	18	....	....	....	....	....
2002-03	CSKA Moscow	Russia	47	5	6	11	22	....	....	....	....	....
2003-04	CSKA Moscow	Russia	13	5	2	7	4	....	....	....	....	....
2004-05	CSKA Moscow	Russia	17	3	4	7	4	....	....	....	....	....
2005-06	Cherepovets	Russia	42	8	5	13	14	1	0	0	0	0

POPOV, Andrei (PAH-pawv, AWN-dray) **PHI.**

Right wing. Shoots left. 6', 187 lbs. Born, Chelyabinsk, Russia, July 15, 1988.
(Philadelphia's 10th choice, 205th overall, in 2006 Entry Draft).

			Regular Season					Playoffs				
Season	Club	League	GP	G	A	Pts	PIM	GP	G	A	Pts	PIM
2003-04	Chelyabinsk 2	Russia-3	6	3	0	3	4	....	....	....	....	....
2004-05	Chelyabinsk 2	Russia-3	17	7	1	8	4	....	....	....	....	....
2005-06	Chelyabinsk 2	Russia-3	2	1	4	5	0	....	....	....	....	....
	Chelyabinsk	Russia-2	37	8	8	16	26	5	2	0	2	2

PORTER, Chris (POHR-tuhr, KRIHS) **CHI.**

Center. Shoots left. 6'1", 202 lbs. Born, Toronto, Ont., May 29, 1984.
(Chicago's 10th choice, 282nd overall, in 2003 Entry Draft).

			Regular Season					Playoffs				
Season	Club	League	GP	G	A	Pts	PIM	GP	G	A	Pts	PIM
2001-02	Shat.-St. Mary's	High-MN	75	10	25	35	32	....	....	....	....	....
2002-03	Lincoln Stars	USHL	59	13	22	35	74	10	4	3	7	10
2003-04	North Dakota	WCHA	41	10	15	25	46	....	....	....	....	....
2004-05	North Dakota	WCHA	45	12	3	15	36	....	....	....	....	....
2005-06	North Dakota	WCHA	46	7	16	23	40	....	....	....	....	....

PORTER, Kevin (POHR-tuhr, KEH-vihn) **PHX.**

Left wing. Shoots left. 5'11", 194 lbs. Born, Detroit, MI, March 12, 1986.
(Phoenix's 5th choice, 119th overall, in 2004 Entry Draft).

			Regular Season					Playoffs				
Season	Club	League	GP	G	A	Pts	PIM	GP	G	A	Pts	PIM
2002-03	USNTDP	U-17	19	9	11	20	8	....	....	....	....	....
	USNTDP	U-18	13	1	2	3	2	....	....	....	....	....
	USNTDP	NAHL	40	19	9	28	17	....	....	....	....	....
2003-04	USNTDP	U-18	44	5	21	26	26	....	....	....	....	....
	USNTDP	NAHL	11	3	8	11	4	....	....	....	....	....
2004-05	U. of Michigan	CCHA	39	11	13	24	51	....	....	....	....	....
2005-06	U. of Michigan	CCHA	39	17	21	38	30	....	....	....	....	....

POSPISIL, Tomas (PAWS-pih-shihl, TAW-mash) **ATL.**

Left wing. Shoots right. 6', 190 lbs. Born, Sumperk, Czech., August 25, 1987.
(Atlanta's 6th choice, 135th overall, in 2005 Entry Draft).

			Regular Season					Playoffs				
Season	Club	League	GP	G	A	Pts	PIM	GP	G	A	Pts	PIM
2002-03	HC Trinec U17	CzR-U17	41	24	28	52	44	2	0	1	1	2
	HC Trinec Jr.	CzRep-Jr.	2	0	0	0	0	2	0	0	0	0
2003-04	HC Trinec U17	CzR-U17	3	3	3	6	14	5	5	2	7	26
	HC Trinec Jr.	CzRep-Jr.	45	14	11	25	40	2	1	1	2	0
2004-05	HC Ocelari Trinec	CzRep	14	0	0	0	0	....	....	....	....	....
	HC Trinec Jr.	CzRep-Jr.	38	19	18	37	44	5	4	1	5	27
2005-06	Sarnia Sting	OHL	60	25	30	55	61	....	....	....	....	....

POTULNY, Grant (poh-TUHL-nee, GRANT) **OTT.**

Center. Shoots left. 6'3", 205 lbs. Born, Grand Forks, ND, March 4, 1980.
(Ottawa's 7th choice, 157th overall, in 2000 Entry Draft).

			Regular Season					Playoffs				
Season	Club	League	GP	G	A	Pts	PIM	GP	G	A	Pts	PIM
1998-99	Lincoln Stars	USHL	46	7	11	18	76	10	2	1	3	7
99-2000	Lincoln Stars	USHL	56	25	30	55	85	10	3	4	7	4
2000-01	U. of Minnesota	WCHA	42	22	11	33	38	....	....	....	....	....
2001-02	U. of Minnesota	WCHA	43	15	19	34	38	....	....	....	....	....
2002-03	U. of Minnesota	WCHA	23	15	8	23	12	....	....	....	....	....
2003-04	U. of Minnesota	WCHA	38	16	10	26	28	....	....	....	....	....
	Binghamton	AHL	3	0	1	1	0	2	0	0	0	0
2004-05	Binghamton	AHL	50	4	6	10	104	6	0	0	0	2
2005-06	Binghamton	AHL	78	23	23	46	122	....	....	....	....	....

NCAA Championship All-Tournament Team (2002) • NCAA Championship Tournament MVP (2002)

POULIOT, Benoit (POO-lee-oh, BEHN-wah) **MIN.**

Left wing. Shoots left. 6'3", 183 lbs. Born, Alfred, Ont., September 29, 1986.
(Minnesota's 1st choice, 4th overall, in 2005 Entry Draft).

			Regular Season					Playoffs				
Season	Club	League	GP	G	A	Pts	PIM	GP	G	A	Pts	PIM
2002-03	Clarence Beavers	OHA-B	38	13	17	30	86	5	0	2	2	8
	Hawkesbury	CJHL	1	1	0	1	0	....	....	....	....	....
2003-04	Hawkesbury	CJHL	45	21	21	42	85	6	3	7	10	10
	Sudbury Wolves	OHL	4	2	2	4	0	4	2	1	3	0
2004-05	Sudbury Wolves	OHL	67	29	38	67	102	12	6	8	14	20
2005-06	Sudbury Wolves	OHL	51	35	30	65	141	8	8	3	11	16
	Houston Aeros	AHL	....	....	....	....	....	2	0	0	0	2

OHL First All-Star Team (2005) • OHL Rookie of the Year (2005) • Canadian Major Junior All-Rookie Team (2005) • Canadian Major Junior Rookie of the Year (2005)

PRUDDEN, Josh (PROO-dehn, JAWSH)

Left wing. Shoots left. 5'11", 190 lbs. Born, Andover, MA, January 10, 1980.

			Regular Season					Playoffs				
Season	Club	League	GP	G	A	Pts	PIM	GP	G	A	Pts	PIM
99-2000	New Hampshire	H-East	16	2	3	5	12	....	....	....	....	....
2000-01	New Hampshire	H-East	37	8	8	16	28	....	....	....	....	....
2001-02	New Hampshire	H-East	36	14	16	30	32	....	....	....	....	....
2002-03	New Hampshire	H-East	42	9	13	22	52	....	....	....	....	....
2003-04	Atlantic City	ECHL	60	18	34	52	54	4	0	0	0	2
2004-05	Cleveland Barons	AHL	73	14	8	22	54	....	....	....	....	....
2005-06	Cleveland Barons	AHL	76	9	12	21	46	....	....	....	....	....

Signed as a free agent by **San Jose**, August 15, 2005.

PRUST, Brandon (PROOST, BRAN-duhn) **CGY.**

Center/Left wing. Shoots left. 5'11", 191 lbs. Born, London, Ont., March 16, 1984.
(Calgary's 2nd choice, 70th overall, in 2004 Entry Draft).

			Regular Season					Playoffs				
Season	Club	League	GP	G	A	Pts	PIM	GP	G	A	Pts	PIM
2001-02	London Nationals	OHA-B	52	17	35	52	38	....	....	....	....	....
2002-03	London Knights	OHL	65	12	17	29	94	14	2	1	3	21
2003-04	London Knights	OHL	64	19	33	52	269	15	7	13	20	33
2004-05	London Knights	OHL	48	10	20	30	174	15	3	5	8	*71
2005-06	Omaha	AHL	79	12	14	26	294	....	....	....	....	....

PSURNY, Roman (P'SHUHR-nee, ROH-muhn) **NYR**

Left wing. Shoots left. 6'1", 180 lbs. Born, Gottwaldov/Zlin, Czech., February 23, 1986.
(NY Rangers' 10th choice, 135th overall, in 2004 Entry Draft).

			Regular Season					Playoffs				
Season	Club	League	GP	G	A	Pts	PIM	GP	G	A	Pts	PIM
2000-01	HC Zlin U17	CzR-U17	42	19	36	55	57	6	3	3	6	6
2002-03	HC Zlin U17	CzR-U17	22	17	27	44	20	3	1	1	2	4
	HC Zlin Jr.	CzRep-Jr.	15	3	7	10	0	....	....	....	....	....
2003-04	HC Zlin Jr.	CzRep-Jr.	52	18	33	51	104	5	0	0	0	2
	HC Hame Zlin	CzRep	9	0	0	0	0	....	....	....	....	....
2004-05	Medicine Hat	WHL	69	21	28	49	64	13	1	4	5	16
2005-06	Medicine Hat	WHL	66	24	30	54	54	13	4	7	11	10

PUUSTINEN, Juuso (POOS-tih-nehn, YUH-soh) **CGY.**

Right wing. Shoots right. 6'1", 185 lbs. Born, Kuopio, Finland, April 5, 1988.
(Calgary's 5th choice, 149th overall, in 2006 Entry Draft).

			Regular Season					Playoffs				
Season	Club	League	GP	G	A	Pts	PIM	GP	G	A	Pts	PIM
2004-05	KalPa Kuopio U18	Fin-U18	26	14	15	29	81	6	1	2	3	4
	KalPa Kuopio Jr.	Fin-Jr.	1	0	0	0	0	....	....	....	....	....
2005-06	KalPa Kuopio U18	Fin-U18	7	8	7	15	18	1	0	0	0	2
	KalPa Kuopio Jr.	Fin-Jr.	29	9	5	14	46	5	0	0	0	0

PYATT, Tom (PEE-yat, TAWM) **NYR**

Center. Shoots left. 5'11", 182 lbs. Born, Thunder Bay, Ont., February 14, 1987.
(NY Rangers' 6th choice, 107th overall, in 2005 Entry Draft).

			Regular Season					Playoffs				
Season	Club	League	GP	G	A	Pts	PIM	GP	G	A	Pts	PIM
2003-04	Saginaw Spirit	OHL	67	9	9	18	21	....	....	....	....	....
2004-05	Saginaw Spirit	OHL	57	18	30	48	14	....	....	....	....	....
2005-06	Saginaw Spirit	OHL	58	24	29	53	29	4	1	2	3	4

PYETT, Logan (PIGH-et, LOH-guhn) DET.

Defense. Shoots right. 5'10", 199 lbs. Born, Regina, Sask., May 26, 1988.
(Detroit's 7th choice, 212th overall, in 2006 Entry Draft).

			Regular Season					Playoffs				
Season	Club	League	GP	G	A	Pts	PIM	GP	G	A	Pts	PIM
2003-04	Regina Pat Cdns.	SMHL	44	18	27	45	34	....	....	....	....	....
	Regina Pats	WHL	2	0	1	1	0	3	0	0	0	0
2004-05	Regina Pats	WHL	67	5	19	24	67	....	....	....	....	....
2005-06	Regina Pats	WHL	71	10	35	45	89	6	1	6	7	12

QUICK, Kevin (KWIHK, KEH-vihn) T.B.

Defense. Shoots left. 6', 175 lbs. Born, Buffalo, NY, March 29, 1988.
(Tampa Bay's 2nd choice, 78th overall, in 2006 Entry Draft).

			Regular Season					Playoffs				
Season	Club	League	GP	G	A	Pts	PIM	GP	G	A	Pts	PIM
2004-05	Salisbury School	High-CT	27	3	9	12	3	....	....	....	....	....
2005-06	Salisbury School	High-CT	28	3	20	23	6	....	....	....	....	....

RABBIT, Wacey (RA-biht, WAY-see) BOS.

Center. Shoots left. 5'9", 169 lbs. Born, Lethbridge, Alta., November 16, 1986.
(Boston's 6th choice, 154th overall, in 2005 Entry Draft).

			Regular Season					Playoffs				
Season	Club	League	GP	G	A	Pts	PIM	GP	G	A	Pts	PIM
2001-02	Cgy. North Stars	AMHL	35	24	28	52	....	....	....	....	....	....
	Saskatoon Blades	WHL	3	0	1	1	0	....	....	....	....	....
2002-03	Saskatoon Blades	WHL	62	21	24	45	33	5	1	3	4	6
2003-04	Saskatoon Blades	WHL	60	9	8	17	51	....	....	....	....	....
2004-05	Saskatoon Blades	WHL	70	22	45	67	70	4	1	2	3	0
2005-06	Saskatoon Blades	WHL	64	28	28	56	45	10	5	3	8	4

RADULOV, Alexander (rah-DOO-lahf, al-EHX-AN-duhr) NSH.

Left wing. Shoots left. 6'1", 188 lbs. Born, Nizhy Tagil, USSR, July 5, 1986.
(Nashville's 1st choice, 15th overall, in 2004 Entry Draft).

			Regular Season					Playoffs				
Season	Club	League	GP	G	A	Pts	PIM	GP	G	A	Pts	PIM
2002-03	Dyn'o Moscow 2	Russia-3		Statistics not available								
2003-04	Dyn'o Moscow 2	Russia-3	•	Statistics not available								
	THK Tver	Russia-2	42	15	16	31	102	....	....	....	....	....
	Dynamo Moscow	Russia	1	0	0	0	2	....	....	....	....	....
2004-05	Quebec Remparts	QMJHL	65	32	43	75	64	13	6	5	11	15
2005-06	Quebec Remparts	QMJHL	62	61	*91	*152	101	23	21	*34	*55	30

QMJHL All-Rookie Team (2005) • QMJHL First All-Star Team (2006) • QMJHL Player of the Year (2006) • Canadian Major Junior First All-Star Team (2006) • Canadian Major Junior Player of the Year (2006)

RADUNSKE, Brock (ra-DOON-skee, BRAWK) EDM.

Left wing. Shoots left. 6'4", 196 lbs. Born, Kitchener, Ont., April 5, 1983.
(Edmonton's 5th choice, 79th overall, in 2002 Entry Draft).

			Regular Season					Playoffs				
Season	Club	League	GP	G	A	Pts	PIM	GP	G	A	Pts	PIM
99-2000	Aurora Tigers	OPJHL	42	6	14	20	23	4	4	8	12	2
2000-01	Newmarket	OPJHL	48	30	39	69	65	....	....	....	....	....
2001-02	Michigan State	CCHA	41	4	9	13	28	....	....	....	....	....
2002-03	Michigan State	CCHA	36	11	18	29	30	....	....	....	....	....
2003-04	Michigan State	CCHA	42	12	10	22	60	....	....	....	....	....
2004-05	Greenville Grrrowl	ECHL	39	12	17	29	52	....	....	....	....	....
	Edmonton	AHL	8	1	1	2	2	....	....	....	....	....
2005-06	Greenville Grrrowl	ECHL	63	38	16	54	58	6	1	2	3	14

RAHIMI, Daniel (RA-hih-mee, DAN-yehl) VAN.

Defense. Shoots left. 6'3", 213 lbs. Born, Umea, Sweden, April 28, 1987.
(Vancouver's 2nd choice, 82nd overall, in 2006 Entry Draft).

			Regular Season					Playoffs				
Season	Club	League	GP	G	A	Pts	PIM	GP	G	A	Pts	PIM
2003-04	Bjorkloven U18	Swe-U18	10	0	3	3	14	....	....	....	....	....
2004-05	Bjorkloven U18	Swe-U18		Statistics not available								
	Bjorkloven Jr.	Swe-Jr.	3	1	0	1	8	....	....	....	....	....
2005-06	Bjorkloven Jr.	Swe-Jr.	40	3	10	13	78	6	3	2	5	37
	IF Bjorkloven Umea	Sweden-2	6	0	0	0	4	....	....	....	....	....

RAKHSHANI, Rhett (rahk-SHAH-nee, REHT) NYI

Right wing. Shoots right. 5'10", 170 lbs. Born, Orange, CA, March 6, 1988.
(NY Islanders' 4th choice, 100th overall, in 2006 Entry Draft).

			Regular Season					Playoffs				
Season	Club	League	GP	G	A	Pts	PIM	GP	G	A	Pts	PIM
2003-04	California Wave	Cal-Am	56	54	67	121	....	....	....	....	....	....
2004-05	USNTDP	U-17	14	6	5	11	32	....	....	....	....	....
	USNTDP	NAHL	40	12	15	27	21	9	1	4	5	2
2005-06	USNTDP	U-18	43	11	12	23	30	....	....	....	....	....
	USNTDP	NAHL	16	13	13	26	35	....	....	....	....	....

RAMHOLT, Tim (RAM-hohlt, TIHM) CGY.

Defense. Shoots left. 6'1", 194 lbs. Born, Zurich, Switz., November 2, 1984.
(Calgary's 2nd choice, 39th overall, in 2003 Entry Draft).

			Regular Season					Playoffs				
Season	Club	League	GP	G	A	Pts	PIM	GP	G	A	Pts	PIM
99-2000	Zurich/Kusn Jr.	Swiss-Jr.	35	2	9	11	26	4	0	2	2	4
	Grasshopper	Swiss-2	2	0	0	0	0	....	....	....	....	....
2000-01	GC Zurich	Swiss-2	37	0	2	2	38	3	0	0	0	4
	GC Zurich Jr.	Swiss-Jr.	17	3	6	9	10	....	....	....	....	....
2001-02	ZSC Lions Zurich	Swiss	37	3	0	3	14	17	0	3	3	2
	GCK/ZSC Zurich Jr.	Swiss-Jr.	5	2	2	4	4	....	....	....	....	....
	GC Zurich	Swiss-2	3	0	0	0	0	....	....	....	....	....
2002-03	ZSC Lions Zurich	Swiss	30	2	0	2	12	9	0	1	1	0
	GC Zurich	Swiss-2	12	0	4	4	6	....	....	....	....	....
2003-04	Cape Breton	QMJHL	51	9	27	36	26	5	0	1	1	4
2004-05	ZSC Lions Zurich	Swiss	41	1	3	4	38	15	0	0	0	10
2005-06	Kloten Flyers	Swiss	42	0	1	1	48	11	0	1	1	8

RAMSAY, Ryan (RAM-zee, RIGH-uhn) ST.L.

Center. Shoots left. 5'11", 200 lbs. Born, Ajax, Ont., May 18, 1983.

			Regular Season					Playoffs				
Season	Club	League	GP	G	A	Pts	PIM	GP	G	A	Pts	PIM
2000-01	Peterborough	OHL	36	16	10	26	67	....	....	....	....	....
	Kitchener Rangers	OHL	22	5	18	23	39	....	....	....	....	....
2001-02	Kitchener Rangers	OHL	54	24	24	48	87	4	1	0	1	4
2002-03	Plymouth Whalers	OHL	59	33	55	88	97	11	2	4	6	18
2003-04	Plymouth Whalers	OHL	61	29	48	77	132	9	1	1	2	18
2004-05	Worcester IceCats	AHL	46	6	12	18	93	....	....	....	....	....
	Peoria Rivermen	ECHL	2	1	2	3	2	....	....	....	....	....
2005-06	Peoria Rivermen	AHL	52	14	11	25	80	2	0	1	1	0
	Alaska Aces	ECHL	17	8	12	20	30	....	....	....	....	....

Signed as a free agent by **St. Louis**, August 2, 2005.

RATCHUK, Michael (RAT-chuhk, MIGH-kuhl) PHI.

Defense. Shoots left. 5'10", 175 lbs. Born, Buffalo, NY, February 20, 1988.
(Philadelphia's 3rd choice, 42nd overall, in 2006 Entry Draft).

			Regular Season					Playoffs				
Season	Club	League	GP	G	A	Pts	PIM	GP	G	A	Pts	PIM
2004-05	USNTDP	U-17	15	1	4	5	16	....	....	....	....	....
	USNTDP	NAHL	33	3	6	9	14	10	1	1	2	2
2005-06	USNTDP	U-18	39	8	14	22	52	....	....	....	....	....
	USNTDP	NAHL	16	4	4	8	4	....	....	....	....	....

Signed Letter of Intent to attend **Michigan State** (CCHA) in fall of 2006.

RAU, Chad (ROW, CHAD) TOR.

Center. Shoots right. 5'11", 185 lbs. Born, Eden Prairie, MN, January 18, 1987.
(Toronto's 6th choice, 228th overall, in 2005 Entry Draft).

			Regular Season					Playoffs				
Season	Club	League	GP	G	A	Pts	PIM	GP	G	A	Pts	PIM
2004-05	Des Moines	USHL	57	31	40	71	32	....	....	....	....	....
2005-06	Colorado College	WCHA	42	13	17	30	8	....	....	....	....	....

USHL All-Rookie Team (2005) • USHL First All-Star Team (2005) • USHL Rookie of the Year (2005)

RAYMOND, Mason (RAY-muhnd, MAY-sohn) VAN.

Left wing. Shoots left. 6', 165 lbs. Born, Calgary, Alta., September 17, 1985.
(Vancouver's 2nd choice, 51st overall, in 2005 Entry Draft).

			Regular Season					Playoffs				
Season	Club	League	GP	G	A	Pts	PIM	GP	G	A	Pts	PIM
2003-04	Camrose Kodiaks	AJHL	....	27	35	62	....	....	....	....	....	....
2004-05	Camrose Kodiaks	AJHL	55	*41	41	82	80	15	8	*12	20	....
2005-06	U. Minn-Duluth	WCHA	40	11	17	28	30	....	....	....	....	....

AJHL MVP (2005) • WCHA All-Rookie Team (2006)

REAVES, Ryan (REEVS, RIGH-uhn) ST.L.

Right wing. Shoots right. 6'1", 193 lbs. Born, Winnipeg, Man., January 20, 1987.
(St. Louis' 4th choice, 156th overall, in 2005 Entry Draft).

			Regular Season					Playoffs				
Season	Club	League	GP	G	A	Pts	PIM	GP	G	A	Pts	PIM
2004-05	Brandon	WHL	64	7	9	16	79	23	2	4	6	43
2005-06	Brandon	WHL	68	14	14	28	91	6	0	1	1	8

REDDOX, Liam (REH-dawks, LEE-uhm) EDM.

Left wing. Shoots left. 5'9", 179 lbs. Born, East York, Ont., January 27, 1986.
(Edmonton's 5th choice, 112th overall, in 2004 Entry Draft).

			Regular Season					Playoffs				
Season	Club	League	GP	G	A	Pts	PIM	GP	G	A	Pts	PIM
2002-03	Wellington Dukes	OPJHL	45	32	32	64	29	....	....	....	....	....
	Peterborough	OHL	4	0	0	0	0	....	....	....	....	....
2003-04	Peterborough	OHL	68	31	33	64	24	....	....	....	....	....
2004-05	Peterborough	OHL	68	36	46	82	38	14	3	10	13	10
2005-06	Peterborough	OHL	68	19	45	64	74	19	5	9	14	20

OHL All-Rookie Team (2004)

REDENBACH, Tyler (REH-dehn-bak, TIGH-luhr) BOS.

Center. Shoots left. 6', 195 lbs. Born, Melville, Sask., September 25, 1984.
(Phoenix's 1st choice, 77th overall, in 2003 Entry Draft).

			Regular Season					Playoffs				
Season	Club	League	GP	G	A	Pts	PIM	GP	G	A	Pts	PIM
2000-01	North Kamloops	BCAHA	49	60	66	126	22	....	....	....	....	....
2001-02	Prince George	WHL	65	3	18	21	30	7	0	1	1	2
2002-03	Prince George	WHL	36	8	34	42	29	....	....	....	....	....
	Swift Current	WHL	24	9	17	26	6	4	0	4	4	4
2003-04	Swift Current	WHL	71	31	*74	*105	52	5	1	1	2	14
2004-05	Swift Current	WHL	42	14	23	37	49	....	....	....	....	....
	Lethbridge	WHL	23	5	21	26	14	5	0	2	2	6
2005-06	Providence Bruins	AHL	78	26	32	58	42	6	1	2	3	37

WHL East Second All-Star Team (2004)

Signed as a free agent by **Boston**, September 7, 2005.

REDLIHS, Jekabs (REHD-lihs, YEH-kabs)

Defense. Shoots left. 6'2", 185 lbs. Born, Riga, Latvia, March 29, 1982.
(Columbus' 6th choice, 119th overall, in 2002 Entry Draft).

			Regular Season					Playoffs				
Season	Club	League	GP	G	A	Pts	PIM	GP	G	A	Pts	PIM
1998-99	Dynamo Riga 18	Latvia-Jr.		Statistics not available								
99-2000	HC Essamika Jr.	EEHL	16	1	4	5	6	....	....	....	....	....
	Metalurgs Liepaja	Latvia	1	0	0	0	0	....	....	....	....	....
	Metalurgs Liepaja	EEHL	11	0	0	0	2	....	....	....	....	....
2000-01	Metalurgs Liepaja	EEHL	31	1	3	4	....	....	....	....	....	....
	Metalurgs Liepaja	Latvia	23	4	5	9	....	....	....	....	....	....
2001-02	NY Apple Core	EJHL	38	3	16	19	24	....	....	....	....	....
2002-03	Boston University	H-East	40	4	12	16	12	....	....	....	....	....
2003-04	Boston University	H-East	23	2	4	6	53	....	....	....	....	....
2004-05	Boston University	H-East	40	1	0	1	32	....	....	....	....	....
2005-06	Boston University	H-East	27	1	5	6	34	....	....	....	....	....
	Syracuse Crunch	AHL	4	0	0	0	6	....	....	....	....	....

Hockey East All-Rookie Team (2003)

REDLIHS, Krisjanis (REHD-lihs, krihs-JA-nihs)

Defense. Shoots left. 6'3", 190 lbs. Born, Riga, Latvia, January 15, 1981.
(New Jersey's 7th choice, 154th overall, in 2002 Entry Draft).

			Regular Season					Playoffs				
Season	Club	League	GP	G	A	Pts	PIM	GP	G	A	Pts	PIM
1998-99	Dynamo Riga 18	Latvia-Jr.	STATISTICS NOT AVAILABLE									
99-2000	Metalurgs Liepaja	EEHL	12	1	3	4	0	....	....	....	....	....
2000-01	Metalurgs Liepaja	EEHL	27	2	2	4	....	....	....	....	....	....
	Metalurgs Liepaja	Latvia	22	1	6	7	....	....	....	....	....	....
2001-02	Metalurgs Liepaja	EEHL	32	0	2	2	....	11	1	1	2	....
	Metalurgs Liepaja	Latvia	13	0	6	6	4	3	2	2	4	0
2002-03	Albany River Rats	AHL	61	1	9	10	20	....	....	....	....	....
2003-04	Albany River Rats	AHL	66	9	10	19	16	....	....	....	....	....
2004-05	Albany River Rats	AHL	46	0	10	10	12	....	....	....	....	....
2005-06	Albany River Rats	AHL	66	3	21	24	30	....	....	....	....	....
	Latvia	Olympics	5	0	0	0	2	....	....	....	....	....

REED, Harrison (REED, HAIR-rih-suhn) **CAR.**

Right wing. Shoots right. 6', 178 lbs. Born, Newmarket, Ont., January 18, 1988.
(Carolina's 2nd choice, 93rd overall, in 2006 Entry Draft).

			Regular Season					Playoffs				
Season	Club	League	GP	G	A	Pts	PIM	GP	G	A	Pts	PIM
2004-05	Petrolia Jets	OJHL-B	43	11	18	29	43	....	....	....	....	....
	London Knights	OHL	6	0	0	0	0	4	0	1	1	0
2005-06	Sarnia Sting	OHL	68	26	24	50	50	....	....	....	....	....

REESE, Dylan (REES, DIH-luhn) **NYR**

Defense. Shoots right. 6', 205 lbs. Born, Pittsburgh, PA, August 29, 1984.
(NY Rangers' 9th choice, 209th overall, in 2003 Entry Draft).

			Regular Season					Playoffs				
Season	Club	League	GP	G	A	Pts	PIM	GP	G	A	Pts	PIM
2000-01	Pittsburgh Hornets	MWEHL	66	14	42	66	....	....	....	....	....	....
2001-02	Pittsburgh Forge	NAHL	48	7	16	23	70	7	0	2	2	4
2002-03	Pittsburgh Forge	NAHL	56	11	30	41	98	5	2	3	5	6
2003-04	Harvard Crimson	ECAC	21	1	4	5	18	....	....	....	....	....
2004-05	Harvard Crimson	ECACHL	34	7	12	19	44	....	....	....	....	....
2005-06	Harvard Crimson	ECACHL	33	4	15	19	36	....	....	....	....	....

ECACHL Second All-Star Team (2006)

REGIN, Peter (REE-gihn-JEHN-sehn, PEE-tuhr) **OTT.**

Center. Shoots left. 6'1", 185 lbs. Born, Herning, Denmark, April 16, 1986.
(Ottawa's 4th choice, 87th overall, in 2004 Entry Draft).

			Regular Season					Playoffs				
Season	Club	League	GP	G	A	Pts	PIM	GP	G	A	Pts	PIM
2002-03	Herning IK	Denmark	24	0	1	1	4	10	1	3	4	4
2003-04	Herning IK	Denmark	33	9	11	20	14	....	....	....	....	....
2004-05	Herning Blue Fox	Denmark	36	19	27	46	43	16	5	8	13	2
2005-06	Timra IK	Sweden	44	4	7	11	14	....	....	....	....	....

REHAK, Denis (REH-hahk, DEH-nihs) **NYI**

Defense. Shoots left. 6'2", 196 lbs. Born, Trencin, Czech., May 14, 1985.
(NY Islanders' 7th choice, 212th overall, in 2003 Entry Draft).

			Regular Season					Playoffs				
Season	Club	League	GP	G	A	Pts	PIM	GP	G	A	Pts	PIM
2002-03	Dukla Trencin Jr.	Slovak-Jr.	24	0	1	1	8	....	....	....	....	....
2003-04	Prince George	WHL	25	0	3	3	12	....	....	....	....	....
	Dukla Trencin U18	Svk-U18	3	1	0	1	4	....	....	....	....	....
2004-05	VSK Technika Brno	CzRep-3	1	0	0	0	0	....	....	....	....	....
	HC Ytong Brno Jr.	CzRep-Jr.	46	4	15	19	38	....	....	....	....	....
2005-06	Trebic	CzRep-2	45	1	8	9	40	....	....	....	....	....

RHEAULT, Jonathan (RAY-oh, JAWN-ah-thun) **PHI.**

Right wing. Shoots right. 5'10", 202 lbs. Born, Arlington, TX, August 1, 1986.
(Philadelphia's 8th choice, 145th overall, in 2006 Entry Draft).

			Regular Season					Playoffs				
Season	Club	League	GP	G	A	Pts	PIM	GP	G	A	Pts	PIM
2003-04	N.H. Jr. Monarchs	EJHL	....	49	46	*95	....	....	....	....	....	....
2004-05	Providence College	H-East	36	11	8	19	36	....	....	....	....	....
2005-06	Providence College	H-East	35	16	14	30	29	....	....	....	....	....

RIAZANTSEV, Alexander (ree-ZAHNT-sehv, al-ehx-AN-duhr) **WSH.**

Defense. Shoots right. 6', 210 lbs. Born, Moscow, USSR, March 15, 1980.
(Colorado's 10th choice, 167th overall, in 1998 Entry Draft).

			Regular Season					Playoffs				
Season	Club	League	GP	G	A	Pts	PIM	GP	G	A	Pts	PIM
1996-97	SAK Moscow	Russia-3	18	0	0	0	8	....	....	....	....	....
	Spartak Moscow	Russia	20	1	2	3	4	....	....	....	....	....
1997-98	Spartak Moscow 2	Russia-3	31	3	8	11	26	....	....	....	....	....
	Victoriaville Tigres	QMJHL	22	6	9	15	14	4	0	0	0	0
1998-99	Victoriaville Tigres	QMJHL	64	17	40	57	57	6	0	3	3	10
	Hershey Bears	AHL	2	0	0	0	0	....	....	....	....	....
99-2000	Victoriaville Tigres	QMJHL	48	17	45	62	45	6	2	5	7	20
	Hershey Bears	AHL	2	0	1	1	2	6	1	1	2	0
2000-01	Hershey Bears	AHL	66	5	18	23	26	11	0	0	0	2
2001-02	Hershey Bears	AHL	76	5	19	24	28	5	0	1	1	4
2002-03	Hershey Bears	AHL	57	5	10	15	65	....	....	....	....	....
	Milwaukee	AHL	14	3	4	7	9	5	0	4	4	2
2003-04	Yaroslavl 2	Russia-3	1	0	0	0	0	....	....	....	....	....
	Yaroslavl	Russia	41	3	8	11	60	....	....	....	....	....
2004-05	Yaroslavl	Russia	53	4	15	19	32	4	0	1	1	4
2005-06	Dynamo Moscow	Russia	39	3	7	10	34	4	0	1	1	29

Traded to **Nashville** by **Colorado** for Nashville's 7th round choice (Linus Videll) in 2003 Entry Draft, March 11, 2003. Traded to **Washington** by **Nashville** for Mike Farrell, July 14, 2003.

RICHTER, Martin (RIHKH-tuhr, MAHR-tihn) **NYR**

Defense. Shoots right. 6'1", 205 lbs. Born, Prostejov, Czech., December 6, 1977.
(NY Rangers' 9th choice, 269th overall, in 2000 Entry Draft).

			Regular Season					Playoffs				
Season	Club	League	GP	G	A	Pts	PIM	GP	G	A	Pts	PIM
1995-96	HC Olomouc	CzRep	3	0	0	0	0	1	0	0	0	0
1996-97	HC Olomouc	CzRep	27	1	0	1	26	....	....	....	....	....
1997-98	Karlovy Vary	CzRep	42	1	2	3	32	....	....	....	....	....
1998-99	Karlovy Vary	CzRep	51	3	6	9	44	....	....	....	....	....
99-2000	Karlovy Vary	CzRep	24	0	5	5	18	....	....	....	....	....
	SaiPa	Finland	26	1	3	4	54	....	....	....	....	....
2000-01	SaiPa	Finland	41	4	5	9	80	....	....	....	....	....
	Hartford Wolf Pack	AHL	1	0	0	0	0	....	....	....	....	....
2001-02	Hartford Wolf Pack	AHL	29	1	1	2	36	....	....	....	....	....
	HC Sparta Praha	CzRep	8	0	0	0	14	13	0	0	0	10
2002-03	HC Sparta Praha	CzRep	34	2	7	9	77	8	0	0	0	10
2003-04	HC Sparta Praha	CzRep	16	2	2	4	16	....	....	....	....	....
	CSKA Moscow	Russia	14	0	0	0	33	....	....	....	....	....
2004-05	HC Sparta Praha	CzRep	44	4	9	13	32	5	1	1	2	4
2005-06	Liberec	CzRep	47	6	20	26	64	5	0	1	1	8

RIDDLE, Troy (RIH-duhl, TROI)

Center. Shoots right. 5'10", 175 lbs. Born, Minneapolis, MN, August 24, 1981.
(St. Louis' 5th choice, 129th overall, in 2000 Entry Draft).

			Regular Season					Playoffs				
Season	Club	League	GP	G	A	Pts	PIM	GP	G	A	Pts	PIM
1997-98	St. Margaret's	High-MN	29	33	35	68	....	....	....	....	....	....
1998-99	St. Margaret's	High-MN	29	54	45	99	....	....	....	....	....	....
99-2000	Des Moines	USHL	53	36	30	66	95	8	2	2	4	31
2000-01	U. of Minnesota	WCHA	38	16	14	30	49	....	....	....	....	....
2001-02	U. of Minnesota	WCHA	44	16	31	47	46	....	....	....	....	....
2002-03	U. of Minnesota	WCHA	45	26	26	52	50	....	....	....	....	....
2003-04	U. of Minnesota	WCHA	44	24	25	49	52	....	....	....	....	....
2004-05	Worcester IceCats	AHL	42	9	6	15	35	....	....	....	....	....
	Peoria Rivermen	ECHL	14	4	8	12	16	....	....	....	....	....
2005-06	Peoria Rivermen	AHL	55	11	11	22	47	....	....	....	....	....
	Alaska Aces	ECHL	7	2	2	4	6	21	4	3	7	28

USHL Second All-Star Team (2000) • USHL Rookie of the Year (2000)

RITOLA, Mattias (RIH-toh-lah, MAT-tee-ahs) **DET.**

Right wing. Shoots left. 6', 192 lbs. Born, Borlange, Sweden, March 14, 1987.
(Detroit's 4th choice, 103rd overall, in 2005 Entry Draft).

			Regular Season					Playoffs				
Season	Club	League	GP	G	A	Pts	PIM	GP	G	A	Pts	PIM
2003-04	V.Frolunda U18	Swe-U18	11	4	11	15	35	7	2	7	9	12
	V.Frolunda Jr.	Swe-Jr.	24	7	4	11	8	5	0	1	1	0
2004-05	Frolunda Jr.	Swe-Jr.	9	2	6	8	6	....	....	....	....	....
	Leksands IF U18	Swe-U18	STATISTICS NOT AVAILABLE									
	Leksands IF Jr.	Swe-Jr.	18	8	10	18	14	5	1	1	2	2
2005-06	Leksands IF Jr.	Swe-Jr.	14	4	2	6	16	....	....	....	....	....
	Leksands IF	Sweden	30	0	3	3	10	....	....	....	....	....
	Leksands IF	Sweden-Q	8	0	0	0	4	....	....	....	....	....

ROBERTSON, Josh (RAW-buhrt-suhn, JAWSH) **WSH.**

Center. Shoots left. 5'11", 186 lbs. Born, Whitman, MA, August 25, 1984.
(Washington's 4th choice, 155th overall, in 2003 Entry Draft).

			Regular Season					Playoffs				
Season	Club	League	GP	G	A	Pts	PIM	GP	G	A	Pts	PIM
2000-01	Whitman-Hanson	High-MA	28	30	28	58	....	....	....	....	....	....
2001-02	Whitman-Hanson	High-MA	30	50	55	105	....	....	....	....	....	....
2002-03	Proctor Academy	High-NH	34	37	44	81	....	....	....	....	....	....
2003-04	Proctor Academy	High-NH	20	23	37	60	....	....	....	....	....	....
2004-05	Northeastern	H-East	22	4	3	7	0	....	....	....	....	....
2005-06	Northeastern	H-East	21	1	9	10	0	....	....	....	....	....

ROBINS, Bobby (RAW-bihns, BAW-bee) **OTT.**

Right wing. Shoots right. 6'1", 220 lbs. Born, Peshtigo, WI, October 17, 1981.

			Regular Season					Playoffs				
Season	Club	League	GP	G	A	Pts	PIM	GP	G	A	Pts	PIM
2001-02	Tri-City Storm	USHL	60	16	14	30	176	....	....	....	....	....
2002-03	U. Mass-Lowell	H-East	26	5	3	8	24	....	....	....	....	....
2003-04	U. Mass-Lowell	H-East	32	5	7	12	49	....	....	....	....	....
2004-05	U. Mass-Lowell	H-East	34	9	9	18	86	....	....	....	....	....
2005-06	U. Mass-Lowell	H-East	35	13	18	31	*94	....	....	....	....	....
	Binghamton	AHL	16	4	3	7	19	....	....	....	....	....

Signed as a free agent by **Ottawa**, July 13, 2006.

ROCHE, Ken (ROHCH, KEHN) **NYR**

Center. Shoots left. 6', 207 lbs. Born, Boston, MA, January 2, 1984.
(NY Rangers' 3rd choice, 75th overall, in 2003 Entry Draft).

			Regular Season					Playoffs				
Season	Club	League	GP	G	A	Pts	PIM	GP	G	A	Pts	PIM
2000-01	St. Sebastian's	High-MA	31	20	18	38	....	....	....	....	....	....
2001-02	St. Sebastian's	High-MA	31	27	33	60	....	....	....	....	....	....
2002-03	St. Sebastian's	High-MA	29	25	28	53	16	....	....	....	....	....
2003-04	Boston University	H-East	38	9	9	18	14	....	....	....	....	....
2004-05	Boston University	H-East	39	5	6	11	37	....	....	....	....	....
2005-06	Boston University	H-East	39	17	14	31	30	....	....	....	....	....

ROGERS, Andy (RAW-juhrs, AN-dee) **T.B.**

Defense. Shoots left. 6'5", 218 lbs. Born, Calgary, Alta., August 25, 1986.
(Tampa Bay's 1st choice, 30th overall, in 2004 Entry Draft).

			Regular Season					Playoffs				
Season	Club	League	GP	G	A	Pts	PIM	GP	G	A	Pts	PIM
2000-01	Calgary AA Gold	CMHA	32	2	7	9	32	....	....	....	....	....
2001-02	Calgary AAA Gold	CBHL	30	1	13	14	80	....	....	....	....	....
2002-03	Calgary Hitmen	WHL	25	0	3	3	17	....	....	....	....	....
2003-04	Calgary Hitmen	WHL	64	1	3	4	89	7	0	0	0	11
2004-05	Calgary Hitmen	WHL	18	1	4	5	36	....	....	....	....	....
	Prince George	WHL	30	1	5	6	49	....	....	....	....	....
2005-06	Prince George	WHL	21	0	3	3	51	....	....	....	....	....

ROGERS, Doug (RAW-juhrs, DUHG) NYI

Center. Shoots right. 6', 175 lbs. Born, Watertown, MA, January 20, 1988.
(NY Islanders' 7th choice, 119th overall, in 2006 Entry Draft).

			Regular Season					Playoffs				
Season	Club	League	GP	G	A	Pts	PIM	GP	G	A	Pts	PIM
2003-04	St. Sebastian's	High-MA	28	24	24	48	....	....	....	....	....	....
2004-05	St. Sebastian's	High-MA	28	17	26	43	....	....	....	....	....	....
2005-06	St. Sebastian's	High-MA	28	24	38	62	20	....	....	....	....	....

ROHLFS, David (ROHLFS, DAY-vihd) EDM.

Right wing. Shoots right. 6'3", 219 lbs. Born, Ann Arbor, MI, June 4, 1984.
(Edmonton's 7th choice, 154th overall, in 2003 Entry Draft).

			Regular Season					Playoffs				
Season	Club	League	GP	G	A	Pts	PIM	GP	G	A	Pts	PIM
2000-01	Det. Compuware	MWEHL	70	35	21	56	....	....	....	....	....	....
	Det. Compuware	NAHL	4	0	1	1	0	....	....	....	....	....
2001-02	Det. Compuware	NAHL	60	13	10	23	36	....	....	....	....	....
2002-03	Det. Compuware	NAHL	53	30	14	44	36	5	2	1	3	8
2003-04	U. of Michigan	CCHA	43	7	6	13	26	....	....	....	....	....
2004-05	U. of Michigan	CCHA	34	5	5	10	14	....	....	....	....	....
2005-06	U. of Michigan	CCHA	40	2	10	12	43	....	....	....	....	....

ROMANO, Tony (roh-MAHN-oh, TOH-nee) N.J.

Center. Shoots right. 5'10", 170 lbs. Born, Smithtown, NY, January 5, 1988.
(New Jersey's 7th choice, 178th overall, in 2006 Entry Draft).

			Regular Season					Playoffs				
Season	Club	League	GP	G	A	Pts	PIM	GP	G	A	Pts	PIM
2004-05	New York Bobcats	AtJHL	....	47	54	101	....	....	....	....	....	....
2005-06	New York Bobcats	AtJHL	40	*50	52	*102	38	....	....	....	....	....

ROME, Aaron (ROHM, AIR-uhn) ANA.

Defense. Shoots left. 6'1", 230 lbs. Born, Nesbitt, Man., September 27, 1983.
(Los Angeles' 4th choice, 104th overall, in 2002 Entry Draft).

			Regular Season					Playoffs				
Season	Club	League	GP	G	A	Pts	PIM	GP	G	A	Pts	PIM
1998-99	Sask. Contacts	SMHL	STATISTICS NOT AVAILABLE									
	Saskatoon Blades	WHL	1	0	0	0	0	....	....	....	....	....
99-2000	Saskatoon Blades	WHL	47	0	6	6	22	1	0	0	0	0
2000-01	Saskatoon Blades	WHL	3	0	0	0	2	....	....	....	....	....
	Kootenay Ice	WHL	53	2	8	10	43	11	1	3	4	6
2001-02	Kootenay Ice	WHL	33	4	13	17	55	....	....	....	....	....
	Swift Current	WHL	37	3	11	14	113	10	1	4	5	23
2002-03	Swift Current	WHL	61	12	44	56	201	4	1	0	1	20
2003-04	Swift Current	WHL	41	7	26	33	122	....	....	....	....	....
	Moose Jaw	WHL	28	3	16	19	88	8	0	6	6	17
2004-05	Cincinnati	AHL	75	2	14	16	130	12	3	3	6	33
2005-06	Portland Pirates	AHL	64	5	19	24	87	18	1	4	5	33

WHL East Second All-Star Team (2004)

Signed as a free agent by **Anaheim**, June 7, 2004.

ROME, Ashton (ROHM, ASH-tuhn) S.J.

Right wing. Shoots right. 6'1", 202 lbs. Born, Nesbitt, Man., December 31, 1985.
(San Jose's 4th choice, 143rd overall, in 2006 Entry Draft).

			Regular Season					Playoffs				
Season	Club	League	GP	G	A	Pts	PIM	GP	G	A	Pts	PIM
2002-03	Moose Jaw	WHL	61	5	10	15	103	13	1	1	2	6
2003-04	Moose Jaw	WHL	72	15	22	37	139	10	6	2	8	18
2004-05	Moose Jaw	WHL	41	10	17	27	84	....	....	....	....	....
	Red Deer Rebels	WHL	31	9	10	19	39	7	3	1	4	14
2005-06	Red Deer Rebels	WHL	14	11	6	17	27	....	....	....	....	....
	Kamloops Blazers	WHL	51	19	28	47	103	....	....	....	....	....

• Re-entered NHL Entry Draft. Originally Boston's 3rd choice, 108th overall, in 2004 Entry Draft.

ROMY, Kevin (ROH-mee, KEH-vihn) PHI.

Center. Shoots left. 5'11", 180 lbs. Born, La Chaux-de-Fonds, Switz., January 31, 1985.
(Philadelphia's 8th choice, 108th overall, in 2003 Entry Draft).

			Regular Season					Playoffs				
Season	Club	League	GP	G	A	Pts	PIM	GP	G	A	Pts	PIM
2000-01	Chaux-de-Fonds Jr.	Swiss-Jr.	24	28	16	44	42	....	....	....	....	....
	Chaux-de-Fonds	Swiss	17	0	0	0	0	2	0	0	0	0
2001-02	Chaux-de-Fonds	Swiss-2	35	10	13	23	16	10	5	5	10	6
	Chaux-de-Fonds Jr.	Swiss-Jr.	1	0	0	0	0	....	....	....	....	....
2002-03	Geneve	Swiss	35	2	2	4	18	6	0	0	0	2
	Chaux-de-Fonds	Swiss-2	1	0	0	0	0	....	....	....	....	....
2003-04	Geneve	Swiss	39	6	7	13	10	12	1	2	3	6
2004-05	Geneve	Swiss	41	10	12	22	18	4	0	0	0	2
2005-06	Geneve	Swiss	2	2	1	3	0	....	....	....	....	....
	HC Lugano	Swiss	36	9	7	16	57	15	2	1	3	8

ROONEEM, Mark (ROO-neem, MAHRK) MIN.

Left wing. Shoots left. 6'2", 185 lbs. Born, Hinton, Alta., January 9, 1983.
(Los Angeles' 5th choice, 115th overall, in 2002 Entry Draft).

			Regular Season					Playoffs				
Season	Club	League	GP	G	A	Pts	PIM	GP	G	A	Pts	PIM
1998-99	Spruce Grove	AMBHL	36	32	30	62	183	....	....	....	....	....
99-2000	Kamloops Blazers	WHL	50	3	8	11	39	4	0	0	0	4
2000-01	Kamloops Blazers	WHL	62	8	9	17	77	4	1	0	1	8
2001-02	Kamloops Blazers	WHL	69	18	23	41	77	4	0	0	0	10
2002-03	Kamloops Blazers	WHL	40	9	6	15	60	....	....	....	....	....
	Calgary Hitmen	WHL	31	2	8	10	43	5	0	2	2	0
2003-04	Calgary Hitmen	WHL	52	22	18	40	61	7	1	2	3	4
2004-05	Houston Aeros	AHL	1	0	0	0	0	....	....	....	....	....
	Louisiana	ECHL	57	17	10	27	72	....	....	....	....	....
	Pensacola	ECHL	8	2	7	9	6	4	0	1	1	2
2005-06	Houston Aeros	AHL	6	1	0	1	10	....	....	....	....	....
	Pensacola	ECHL	38	7	8	15	31	....	....	....	....	....

Signed as a free agent by **Minnesota**, June 4, 2004.

ROSEHILL, Jay (ROHZ-hihl, JAY) T.B.

Defense. Shoots left. 6'3", 210 lbs. Born, Olds, Alta., July 16, 1985.
(Tampa Bay's 6th choice, 227th overall, in 2003 Entry Draft).

			Regular Season					Playoffs				
Season	Club	League	GP	G	A	Pts	PIM	GP	G	A	Pts	PIM
2002-03	Olds Grizzlys	AJHL	59	1	4	5	219	....	....	....	....	....
2003-04	Olds Grizzlys	AJHL	42	4	12	16	172	14	2	2	4	....
2004-05	U. Minn-Duluth	WCHA	34	0	5	5	103	....	....	....	....	....
2005-06	Springfield Falcons	AHL	45	1	2	3	68	....	....	....	....	....
	Johnstown Chiefs	ECHL	5	0	0	0	13	5	0	0	0	4

ROUSSIN, Dany (roo-SEH, DA-nee) L.A.

Center. Shoots left. 6'2", 195 lbs. Born, Quebec City, Que., January 9, 1985.
(Los Angeles' 2nd choice, 50th overall, in 2005 Entry Draft).

			Regular Season					Playoffs				
Season	Club	League	GP	G	A	Pts	PIM	GP	G	A	Pts	PIM
2000-01	Ste-Foy	QAAA	38	27	27	54	42	16	8	13	21	16
2001-02	Sherbrooke	QMJHL	66	10	14	24	38	....	....	....	....	....
2002-03	Sherbrooke	QMJHL	33	8	8	16	18	....	....	....	....	....
	Rimouski Oceanic	QMJHL	38	12	26	38	69	....	....	....	....	....
2003-04	Rimouski Oceanic	QMJHL	66	*59	58	117	70	9	2	10	12	12
2004-05	Rimouski Oceanic	QMJHL	69	54	62	116	66	13	11	9	20	8
2005-06	Manchester	AHL	29	4	2	6	24	3	1	1	2	0
	Reading Royals	ECHL	41	22	23	45	14	1	0	1	1	0

• Re-entered NHL Entry Draft. Originally Florida's 10th choice, 223rd overall, in 2003 Entry Draft.

QMJHL First All-Star Team (2004) • QMJHL Second All-Star Team (2005)

ROY, Jimmy (ROI, JIHM-mee)

Center. Shoots right. 5'11", 170 lbs. Born, Sioux Lookout, Ont., September 22, 1975.
(Dallas' 7th choice, 254th overall, in 1994 Entry Draft).

			Regular Season					Playoffs				
Season	Club	League	GP	G	A	Pts	PIM	GP	G	A	Pts	PIM
1993-94	Thunder Bay Flyers	USHL	46	21	33	54	101	....	....	....	....	....
1994-95	Michigan Tech	WCHA	38	5	11	16	62	....	....	....	....	....
1995-96	Michigan Tech	WCHA	42	17	17	34	84	....	....	....	....	....
1996-97	Canada	Nat-Tm	55	10	17	27	82	....	....	....	....	....
1997-98	Manitoba Moose	IHL	61	8	10	18	133	3	0	0	0	6
1998-99	Manitoba Moose	IHL	78	10	16	26	185	5	0	1	1	6
99-2000	Manitoba Moose	IHL	74	12	9	21	187	1	0	0	0	16
2000-01	Manitoba Moose	IHL	77	18	13	31	150	12	1	1	2	22
2001-02	Manitoba Moose	AHL	73	16	22	38	167	7	2	0	2	28
2002-03	Manitoba Moose	AHL	50	5	10	15	95	14	4	4	8	27
2003-04	Manitoba Moose	AHL	78	13	16	29	186	....	....	....	....	....
2004-05	Manitoba Moose	AHL	50	10	7	17	187	13	2	1	3	39
2005-06	Manitoba Moose	AHL	62	9	8	17	144	4	0	0	0	9

RUDENKO, Konstantin (roo-DEHN-koh, KOHN-stan-tihn) PHI.

Left wing. Shoots right. 5'11", 180 lbs. Born, Ust-Kamenogorsk, USSR, July 23, 1981.
(Philadelphia's 3rd choice, 160th overall, in 1999 Entry Draft).

			Regular Season					Playoffs				
Season	Club	League	GP	G	A	Pts	PIM	GP	G	A	Pts	PIM
1997-98	Omsk 2	Russia-3	22	7	8	15	4	....	....	....	....	....
1998-99	Cherepovets	Russia	28	15	9	24	67	....	....	....	....	....
	Cherepovets 2	Russia-3	3	0	1	1	4	....	....	....	....	....
99-2000	St. Petersburg 2	Russia-3	7	2	4	6	2	....	....	....	....	....
	SKA St. Petersburg	Russia	19	1	1	2	10	1	0	0	0	0
2000-01	Yaroslavl	Russia	18	2	3	5	28	9	2	1	3	8
2001-02	Yaroslavl 2	Russia-3	2	1	1	2	2	....	....	....	....	....
	Yaroslavl	Russia	8	0	2	2	12	1	0	0	0	0
2002-03	Yaroslavl	Russia	20	3	4	7	20	2	0	0	0	0
2003-04	Yaroslavl	Russia	43	10	12	22	18	3	0	0	0	0
	Yaroslavl 2	Russia-3	4	4	2	6	4	....	....	....	....	....
2004-05	Yaroslavl 2	Russia-3	20	13	14	27	42	....	....	....	....	....
	Yaroslavl	Russia	21	1	0	1	8	2	0	0	0	0
2005-06	Yaroslavl	Russia	49	11	17	28	55	11	1	2	3	0

RUEGSEGGER, Tyler (ROOG-suh-guhr, TIGH-luhr) TOR.

Center. Shoots right. 5'11", 170 lbs. Born, Denver, CO, January 19, 1988.
(Toronto's 6th choice, 166th overall, in 2006 Entry Draft).

			Regular Season					Playoffs				
Season	Club	League	GP	G	A	Pts	PIM	GP	G	A	Pts	PIM
2004-05	Shat.-St. Mary's	High-MN	69	26	54	80	30	....	....	....	....	....
2005-06	Shat.-St. Mary's	High-MN	60	38	51	89	70	....	....	....	....	....

Signed Letter of Intent to attend **U. of Denver** (WCHA) in fall of 2006.

RUGGERI, Rosario (ROO-gee-AIR-ee, roh-ZAHR-ee-oh) PHI.

Defense. Shoots left. 6'1", 202 lbs. Born, Montreal, Que., June 8, 1984.
(Philadelphia's 2nd choice, 105th overall, in 2002 Entry Draft).

			Regular Season					Playoffs				
Season	Club	League	GP	G	A	Pts	PIM	GP	G	A	Pts	PIM
99-2000	Lac St-Louis Lions	QAAA	40	0	7	7	70	....	....	....	....	....
2000-01	Lac St-Louis Lions	QAAA	24	6	11	17	117	5	1	3	4	4
	Montreal Rocket	QMJHL	9	0	0	0	8	....	....	....	....	....
2001-02	Chicoutimi	QMJHL	60	2	15	17	131	4	1	1	2	10
2002-03	Chicoutimi	QMJHL	70	10	37	47	64	3	0	0	0	21
2003-04	Chicoutimi	QMJHL	65	12	36	48	98	18	2	2	4	28
2004-05	Philadelphia	AHL	5	0	0	0	0	....	....	....	....	....
	Trenton Titans	ECHL	49	2	12	14	77	20	0	2	2	26
2005-06	Philadelphia	AHL	2	0	0	0	2	....	....	....	....	....
	Trenton Titans	ECHL	32	2	8	10	28	....	....	....	....	....

RULLIER, Joe (ROO-yay, JOH) VAN.

Defense. Shoots right. 6'3", 230 lbs. Born, Montreal, Que., January 28, 1980.
(Los Angeles' 5th choice, 133rd overall, in 1998 Entry Draft).

			Regular Season					Playoffs				
Season	Club	League	GP	G	A	Pts	PIM	GP	G	A	Pts	PIM
1996-97	Montreal-Bourassa	QAAA	24	5	10	15	....	....	....	....	....	....
	Rimouski Oceanic	QMJHL	23	0	3	3	87	4	0	0	0	11
1997-98	Rimouski Oceanic	QMJHL	55	1	10	11	176	16	1	4	5	34
1998-99	Rimouski Oceanic	QMJHL	54	7	32	39	202	11	2	3	5	26
99-2000	Rimouski Oceanic	QMJHL	49	3	32	35	161	14	1	8	9	34
2000-01	Lowell	AHL	63	1	1	2	162	4	0	1	1	2
2001-02	Manchester	AHL	62	2	2	4	133	3	0	0	0	5
2002-03	Manchester	AHL	62	3	6	9	166	3	0	0	0	2
2003-04	Manchester	AHL	73	3	12	15	186	6	0	0	0	4
2004-05	Manchester	AHL	71	3	13	16	322	6	0	2	2	27
2005-06	Hartford Wolf Pack	AHL	51	6	22	28	123	....	....	....	....	....
	Manchester	AHL	16	2	1	3	37	7	0	3	3	14

Signed as a free agent by **NY Rangers**, August 10, 2005. Signed as a free agent by **Vancouver**, July 24, 2006.

RUMSEY, Myles (RUHM-see, MIGH-uhls) CGY.

Defense. Shoots right. 6'1", 200 lbs. Born, Winnipeg, Man., November 5, 1986.
(Calgary's 8th choice, 221st overall, in 2005 Entry Draft).

			Regular Season					Playoffs				
Season	Club	League	GP	G	A	Pts	PIM	GP	G	A	Pts	PIM
2002-03	Wpg. South Blues	MJHL	56	1	10	11	88	....	....	....	....	....
	Swift Current	WHL	3	0	0	0	0	....	....	....	....	....
2003-04	Swift Current	WHL	66	0	4	4	61	5	0	0	0	5
2004-05	Swift Current	WHL	57	2	4	6	102	....	....	....	....	....
2005-06	Swift Current	WHL	67	0	12	12	116	4	0	0	0	6

RUSSELL, Kris (RUH-sehl, KRIHS) CBJ

Defense. Shoots left. 5'10", 167 lbs. Born, Caroline, Alta., May 2, 1987.
(Columbus' 3rd choice, 67th overall, in 2005 Entry Draft).

			Regular Season					Playoffs				
Season	Club	League	GP	G	A	Pts	PIM	GP	G	A	Pts	PIM
2003-04	Medicine Hat	WHL	55	4	15	19	30	20	3	2	5	4
2004-05	Medicine Hat	WHL	72	26	35	61	37	10	2	1	3	4
2005-06	Medicine Hat	WHL	55	14	33	47	18	13	4	8	12	11

WHL East Second All-Star Team (2005) • WHL East First All-Star Team (2006) • WHL Defenseman of the Year (2006)

RUSSELL, Ryan (RUH-sehl, RIGH-uhn) NYR

Center. Shoots left. 5'10", 165 lbs. Born, Caroline, Alta., May 2, 1987.
(NY Rangers' 9th choice, 211th overall, in 2005 Entry Draft).

			Regular Season					Playoffs				
Season	Club	League	GP	G	A	Pts	PIM	GP	G	A	Pts	PIM
2003-04	Kootenay Ice	WHL	67	3	9	12	27	4	0	0	0	0
2004-05	Kootenay Ice	WHL	66	32	21	53	18	16	6	7	13	12
2005-06	Kootenay Ice	WHL	72	33	42	75	30	6	3	5	8	2

RYABYKIN, Dmitri (ryah-BEE-kihn, dih-MEE-tree) CGY.

Defense. Shoots right. 6'1", 203 lbs. Born, Chirchik, USSR, March 24, 1976.
(Calgary's 2nd choice, 45th overall, in 1994 Entry Draft).

			Regular Season					Playoffs				
Season	Club	League	GP	G	A	Pts	PIM	GP	G	A	Pts	PIM
1994-95	Dynamo Moscow	CIS	48	0	0	0	12	11	0	2	2	0
1995-96	Dynamo Moscow	CIS	47	3	1	4	49	13	1	1	2	6
1996-97	Dynamo Moscow	Russia	34	1	10	11	12	4	0	0	0	8
1997-98	Dynamo Moscow	Russia	34	1	4	5	16	....	....	....	....	....
	Dynamo Moscow	EuroHL	7	1	1	2	6	....	....	....	....	....
1998-99	Avangard Omsk	Russia	40	3	10	13	42	5	0	0	0	42
99-2000	Avangard Omsk	Russia	36	5	10	15	42	8	3	2	5	2
2000-01	Avangard Omsk	Russia	43	3	8	11	101	16	3	4	7	16
2001-02	Avangard Omsk	Russia	17	4	7	11	60	11	4	3	7	6
2002-03	Avangard Omsk	Russia	51	7	18	25	113	12	1	2	3	33
2003-04	Avangard Omsk	Russia	57	8	12	20	94	11	1	4	5	4
2004-05	Omsk 2	Russia-3	1	0	1	1	0	....	....	....	....	....
	Avangard Omsk	Russia	43	5	12	17	109	10	2	2	4	12
2005-06	Avangard Omsk	Russia	50	6	13	19	65	13	1	5	6	12

RYAN, Billy (RIGH-uhn, BIHL-lee) NYR

Center. Shoots left. 6', 171 lbs. Born, Boston, MA, October 23, 1985.
(NY Rangers' 8th choice, 80th overall, in 2004 Entry Draft).

			Regular Season					Playoffs				
Season	Club	League	GP	G	A	Pts	PIM	GP	G	A	Pts	PIM
2002-03	Cushing	High-MA	29	14	33	47	10	....	....	....	....	....
2003-04	Cushing	High-MA	37	35	55	90	40	....	....	....	....	....
2004-05	U. of Maine	H-East	34	6	9	15	30	....	....	....	....	....
2005-06	U. of Maine	H-East	36	10	18	28	46	....	....	....	....	....

RYAN, Bobby (RIGH-uhn, BAW-bee) ANA.

Right wing. Shoots right. 6'2", 213 lbs. Born, Cherry Hill, NJ, March 17, 1987.
(Anaheim's 1st choice, 2nd overall, in 2005 Entry Draft).

			Regular Season					Playoffs				
Season	Club	League	GP	G	A	Pts	PIM	GP	G	A	Pts	PIM
2003-04	Owen Sound	OHL	65	22	17	39	52	7	1	2	3	2
2004-05	Owen Sound	OHL	62	37	52	89	51	8	2	7	9	8
2005-06	Owen Sound	OHL	59	31	64	95	44	11	5	7	12	14
	Portland Pirates	AHL	....	....	....	....	....	19	1	7	8	22

OHL First All-Star Team (2005)

RYAN, Joe (RIGH-uhn, JOH) L.A.

Defense. Shoots right. 6'1", 189 lbs. Born, Winchester, MA, October 19, 1987.
(Los Angeles' 3rd choice, 48th overall, in 2006 Entry Draft).

			Regular Season					Playoffs				
Season	Club	League	GP	G	A	Pts	PIM	GP	G	A	Pts	PIM
2003-04	Quebec Remparts	QMJHL	57	0	9	9	98	5	0	0	0	8
2004-05	Quebec Remparts	QMJHL	63	4	9	13	134	13	0	2	2	28
2005-06	Quebec Remparts	QMJHL	61	6	18	24	202	23	2	8	10	29

RYAN, Michael (RIGH-uhn, MIGH-kuhl) BUF.

Center. Shoots left. 6'1", 180 lbs. Born, Boston, MA, May 16, 1980.
(Dallas' 1st choice, 32nd overall, in 1999 Entry Draft).

			Regular Season					Playoffs				
Season	Club	League	GP	G	A	Pts	PIM	GP	G	A	Pts	PIM
1997-98	Bos. College High	High-MA	23	22	14	36	28	....	....	....	....	....
1998-99	Bos. College High	High-MA	21	20	24	44	22	....	....	....	....	....
99-2000	Northeastern	H-East	32	4	9	13	47	....	....	....	....	....
2000-01	Northeastern	H-East	33	17	12	29	52	....	....	....	....	....
2001-02	Northeastern	H-East	36	24	15	39	54	....	....	....	....	....
2002-03	Northeastern	H-East	34	18	14	32	30	....	....	....	....	....
2003-04	Rochester	AHL	45	3	9	12	31	....	....	....	....	....
2004-05	Rochester	AHL	59	11	11	22	20	5	0	1	1	4
2005-06	Rochester	AHL	56	15	22	37	70	....	....	....	....	....

Traded to **Buffalo** by **Dallas** with Dallas's 2nd round choice (Branislav Fabry) in 2003 Entry Draft for Stu Barnes, March 10, 2003.

RYBIN, Maxim (ray-bihn, max-EEM) ANA.

Left wing. Shoots right. 5'8", 182 lbs. Born, Zhukovsky, USSR, June 15, 1981.
(Anaheim's 4th choice, 141st overall, in 1999 Entry Draft).

			Regular Season					Playoffs				
Season	Club	League	GP	G	A	Pts	PIM	GP	G	A	Pts	PIM
1996-97	SAK Moscow	Russia-3	5	0	0	0	4	....	....	....	....	....
	Spartak Moscow	Russia	6	0	0	0	0	....	....	....	....	....
1997-98	Spartak Moscow 2	Russia-3	25	13	5	18	26	....	....	....	....	....
	Spartak Moscow	Russia	5	0	0	0	2	....	....	....	....	....
1998-99	Spartak Moscow	Russia	53	15	12	27	83	....	....	....	....	....
99-2000	Sarnia Sting	OHL	66	29	27	56	47	7	4	1	5	2
2000-01	Sarnia Sting	OHL	67	34	36	70	60	4	0	3	3	2
2001-02	Ufa	Russia	41	6	4	10	30	....	....	....	....	....
2002-03	Cherepovets	Russia	3	0	1	1	2	....	....	....	....	....
	Spartak Moscow	Russia	29	9	4	13	65	....	....	....	....	....
2003-04	Cherepovets	Russia	53	14	14	28	24	....	....	....	....	....
	Cherepovets 2	Russia-3	3	2	2	4	2	....	....	....	....	....
2004-05	Cherepovets	Russia	12	0	1	1	6	....	....	....	....	....
	Spartak Moscow	Russia	30	2	15	17	20	....	....	....	....	....
2005-06	Avangard Omsk	Russia	45	2	6	8	10	13	0	1	1	30
	Omsk 2	Russia-3	1	2	0	2	0	....	....	....	....	....

RYDER, Dan (RIGH-duhr, DAN) CGY.

Center. Shoots right. 5'10", 192 lbs. Born, Bonavista, Nfld., January 12, 1987.
(Calgary's 3rd choice, 74th overall, in 2005 Entry Draft).

			Regular Season					Playoffs				
Season	Club	League	GP	G	A	Pts	PIM	GP	G	A	Pts	PIM
2003-04	Peterborough	OHL	63	20	32	52	16	....	....	....	....	....
2004-05	Peterborough	OHL	68	29	53	82	55	....	....	....	....	....
2005-06	Peterborough	OHL	65	38	44	82	57	19	*15	16	31	22

RYNO, Johan (RYUH-noh, YO-han) DET.

Right wing. Shoots left. 6'4", 198 lbs. Born, Orebro, Sweden, June 5, 1986.
(Detroit's 6th choice, 137th overall, in 2005 Entry Draft).

			Regular Season					Playoffs				
Season	Club	League	GP	G	A	Pts	PIM	GP	G	A	Pts	PIM
2003-04	IFK Hallsberg	Sweden-3	28	9	18	27	30	....	....	....	....	....
2004-05	IFK Arboga IK	Sweden-2	2	0	0	0	0	....	....	....	....	....
	IFK Kumla Jr.	Swe-Jr.	29	20	18	38	14	....	....	....	....	....
2005-06	IK Oskarshamn	Sweden-2	34	13	10	23	64	....	....	....	....	....

SACKRISON, Andy (sak-RIH-suhn, an-DEE) ST.L.

Center. Shoots left. 6'1", 178 lbs. Born, St. Louis Park, MN, November 12, 1987.
(St. Louis' 7th choice, 124th overall, in 2006 Entry Draft).

			Regular Season					Playoffs				
Season	Club	League	GP	G	A	Pts	PIM	GP	G	A	Pts	PIM
2004-05	St. Louis Park	High-MN	26	18	15	33	....	....	....	....	....	....
2005-06	St. Louis Park	High-MN	25	41	26	67	32	....	....	....	....	....

Signed Letter of Intent to attend **Minnesota State** (WCHA) in fall of 2006.

SAGAT, Martin (SHA-gat, MAHR-tehn) TOR.

Left wing. Shoots right. 6'3", 191 lbs. Born, Handlova, Czech., November 11, 1984.
(Toronto's 2nd choice, 91st overall, in 2003 Entry Draft).

			Regular Season					Playoffs				
Season	Club	League	GP	G	A	Pts	PIM	GP	G	A	Pts	PIM
2002-03	Dukla Trencin Jr.	Slovak-Jr.	37	18	20	38	49	3	1	3	4	4
	Dukla Trencin	Slovakia	17	0	0	0	0	2	0	0	0	0
2003-04	Kootenay Ice	WHL	57	11	32	43	39	4	0	2	2	2
2004-05	Kootenay Ice	WHL	72	17	46	63	51	16	8	14	22	18
2005-06	Toronto Marlies	AHL	60	13	8	21	22	5	0	0	0	8

ST. JACQUES, Chris (SAINT ZHAWK, KRIHS) TOR.

Center. Shoots right. 5'8", 181 lbs. Born, Edmonton, Alta., January 22, 1983.

			Regular Season					Playoffs				
Season	Club	League	GP	G	A	Pts	PIM	GP	G	A	Pts	PIM
99-2000	Medicine Hat	WHL	61	21	18	39	65	....	....	....	....	....
2000-01	Medicine Hat	WHL	70	37	36	73	84	....	....	....	....	....
2001-02	Medicine Hat	WHL	45	30	38	68	50	....	....	....	....	....
2002-03	Medicine Hat	WHL	70	31	*65	96	78	11	2	14	16	17
2003-04	Medicine Hat	WHL	64	33	59	92	80	20	12	*15	*27	18
2004-05	Pensacola	ECHL	66	18	29	47	74	3	0	1	1	6
	St. John's	AHL	4	0	0	0	2	....	....	....	....	....
2005-06	Toronto Marlies	AHL	20	1	3	4	12	....	....	....	....	....
	Pensacola	ECHL	34	10	17	27	45	....	....	....	....	....

Signed as a free agent by **Toronto**, June 2, 2004.

SALCIDO, Brian (sal-SEE-doh, BRIGH-uhn) ANA.

Defense. Shoots left. 6'2", 195 lbs. Born, Los Angeles, CA, April 14, 1985.
(Anaheim's 5th choice, 141st overall, in 2005 Entry Draft).

			Regular Season					Playoffs				
Season	Club	League	GP	G	A	Pts	PIM	GP	G	A	Pts	PIM
2002-03	Shat.-St. Mary's	High-MN	53	8	35	43	....	....	....	....	....	....
2003-04	Colorado College	WCHA	12	1	0	1	48	....	....	....	....	....
2004-05	Colorado College	WCHA	38	7	23	30	52	....	....	....	....	....
2005-06	Colorado College	WCHA	42	8	32	40	69	....	....	....	....	....

WCHA Second All-Star Team (2006)

SALMONSSON, Johannes (sal-MUHN-suhn, yoh-HA-nuhs) PIT.

Left wing. Shoots left. 6'2", 183 lbs. Born, Uppsala, Sweden, February 7, 1986.
(Pittsburgh's 2nd choice, 31st overall, in 2004 Entry Draft).

			Regular Season					Playoffs				
Season	Club	League	GP	G	A	Pts	PIM	GP	G	A	Pts	PIM
2002-03	Almtuna	Sweden-2	26	10	14	24	4	....	....	....	....	....
2003-04	Djurgarden Jr.	Swe-Jr.	6	4	9	13	6	....	....	....	....	....
	Djurgarden	Sweden	25	0	3	3	4	....	....	....	....	....
	Almtuna	Sweden-2	2	0	0	0	0	....	....	....	....	....
2004-05	Almtuna	Sweden-2	8	0	2	2	6	....	....	....	....	....
	Djurgarden Jr.	Swe-Jr.	4	2	0	2	4	....	....	....	....	....
	Djurgarden	Sweden	30	2	2	4	6	9	0	0	0	0
2005-06	Spokane Chiefs	WHL	54	12	15	27	30	....	....	....	....	....

SALONEN, Pasi — (SAH-loh-nehn, PA-see) — WSH.

Left wing. Shoots left. 5'11", 187 lbs. Born, Helsinki, Finland, December 18, 1985.
(Washington's 9th choice, 138th overall, in 2004 Entry Draft).

			Regular Season					Playoffs				
Season	Club	League	GP	G	A	Pts	PIM	GP	G	A	Pts	PIM
2000-01	HIFK Helsinki U18	Fin-U18	28	6	8	14	4	....	....	....	....	....
2001-02	HIFK Helsinki U18	Fin-U18	16	10	14	24	39	8	6	4	10	4
	HIFK Helsinki Jr.	Fin-Jr.	19	5	6	11	2	....	....	....	....	....
2002-03	HIFK Helsinki Jr.	Fin-Jr.	32	16	11	27	10	10	8	3	11	2
2003-04	Suomi U20	Finland-2	3	0	0	0	0	....	....	....	....	....
	HIFK Helsinki Jr.	Fin-Jr.	30	12	10	22	60	9	4	4	8	8
	HIFK Helsinki	Finland	3	0	0	0	0	....	....	....	....	....
2004-05		DID NOT PLAY – INJURED										
2005-06	HIFK Helsinki Jr.	Fin-Jr.	10	4	2	6	4	....	....	....	....	....
	HIFK Helsinki	Finland	49	5	9	14	6	8	0	0	0	0

SANFORD, James — (SAN-fohrd, JAYMZ) — MTL.

Defense. Shoots left. 5'9", 190 lbs. Born, Alma, NB, June 18, 1984.

			Regular Season					Playoffs				
Season	Club	League	GP	G	A	Pts	PIM	GP	G	A	Pts	PIM
2000-01	Victoriaville Tigres	QMJHL	41	0	6	6	60	....	....	....	....	....
	Moncton Wildcats	QMJHL	26	4	5	9	40	....	....	....	....	....
2001-02	Moncton Wildcats	QMJHL	72	19	39	58	151	....	....	....	....	....
2002-03	Moncton Wildcats	QMJHL	72	16	45	61	139	6	4	5	9	15
2003-04	Moncton Wildcats	QMJHL	61	16	37	53	126	20	5	11	16	18
2004-05	Hamilton Bulldogs	AHL	31	2	8	10	20	....	....	....	....	....
	Peoria Rivermen	ECHL	24	2	9	11	16	....	....	....	....	....
2005-06	Hamilton Bulldogs	AHL	54	10	18	28	39	....	....	....	....	....
	Long Beach	ECHL	8	0	4	4	12	4	2	4	6	17

Signed as a free agent by **Hamilton** (AHL), October 10, 2004. Signed as a free agent by **Montreal**, March 2, 2006.

SANGUINETTI, Bobby — (san-GIH-neh-tee, BAW-bee) — NYR

Defense. Shoots right. 6'1", 178 lbs. Born, Trenton, NJ, February 29, 1988.
(NY Rangers' 1st choice, 21st overall, in 2006 Entry Draft).

			Regular Season					Playoffs				
Season	Club	League	GP	G	A	Pts	PIM	GP	G	A	Pts	PIM
2003-04	Lawrenceville	High-NJ	26	4	17	21	....	....	....	....	....	....
2004-05	Owen Sound	OHL	67	4	20	24	12	5	0	2	2	0
2005-06	Owen Sound	OHL	68	14	51	65	44	11	5	10	15	4

SANNITZ, Raffaele — (ZAH-nihts, ra-FIGH-ehl-lay) — CBJ

Center. Shoots left. 6'1", 212 lbs. Born, Mendrisio, Switz., May 18, 1983.
(Columbus' 9th choice, 204th overall, in 2001 Entry Draft).

			Regular Season					Playoffs				
Season	Club	League	GP	G	A	Pts	PIM	GP	G	A	Pts	PIM
1997-98	HC Lugano Jr.	Swiss-Jr.	33	7	12	19	54	....	....	....	....	....
1998-99	HC Lugano Jr.	Swiss-Jr.	38	5	12	17	62	....	....	....	....	....
	HC Lugano	Swiss	8	0	1	1	0	....	....	....	....	....
99-2000	HC Lugano Jr.	Swiss-Jr.	33	13	16	29	47	....	....	....	....	....
	HC Lugano	Swiss	1	0	0	0	2	....	....	....	....	....
2000-01	HC Sierre	Swiss-2	2	0	0	0	0	....	....	....	....	....
	HC Lugano Jr.	Swiss-Jr.	35	22	30	52	152	2	0	0	0	0
	HC Lugano	Swiss	13	1	0	1	0	2	0	0	0	0
2001-02	HC Lugano Jr.	Swiss-Jr.	14	14	13	27	18	3	3	2	5	4
	HC Lugano	Swiss	38	3	4	7	37	12	1	1	2	2
2002-03	HC Lugano	Swiss	14	1	1	2	37	....	....	....	....	....
2003-04	HC Lugano	Swiss	48	7	9	16	20	16	2	1	3	8
	EHC Chur	Swiss-2	2	2	1	3	2	....	....	....	....	....
2004-05	Dayton Bombers	ECHL	2	0	3	3	0	....	....	....	....	....
	Syracuse Crunch	AHL	53	6	3	9	38	....	....	....	....	....
2005-06	HC Lugano	Swiss	33	5	9	14	85	17	4	8	12	16

• Missed majority of 2002-03 season recovering from shoulder injury suffered in game vs. Kloten (Swiss), October 12, 2002.

SANTORELLI, Mike — (san-toh-REHL-ee, MIGHK) — NSH.

Center. Shoots right. 5'11", 180 lbs. Born, Vancouver, B.C., December 14, 1985.
(Nashville's 6th choice, 178th overall, in 2004 Entry Draft).

			Regular Season					Playoffs				
Season	Club	League	GP	G	A	Pts	PIM	GP	G	A	Pts	PIM
2003-04	Vernon Vipers	BCHL	60	43	53	96	26	5	0	2	2	0
2004-05	Northern Mich.	CCHA	40	16	14	30	22	....	....	....	....	....
2005-06	Northern Mich.	CCHA	40	15	18	33	24	....	....	....	....	....

CCHA All-Rookie Team (2005)

SARAUER, Andrew — (suh-ROW-uhr, AN-droo) — VAN.

Left wing. Shoots left. 6'4", 194 lbs. Born, Saskatoon, Sask., November 17, 1984.
(Vancouver's 3rd choice, 125th overall, in 2004 Entry Draft).

			Regular Season					Playoffs				
Season	Club	League	GP	G	A	Pts	PIM	GP	G	A	Pts	PIM
2002-03	Victoria Salsa	BCHL	57	11	17	28	73	....	....	....	....	....
2003-04	Langley Hornets	BCHL	57	43	32	75	71	....	....	....	....	....
2004-05	Northern Mich.	CCHA	25	3	4	7	10	....	....	....	....	....
2005-06	Northern Mich.	CCHA	18	2	3	5	8	....	....	....	....	....

SAUER, Michael — (SOW-uhr, MIGHK-uhl) — NYR

Defense. Shoots right. 6'3", 206 lbs. Born, St. Cloud, MN, August 7, 1987.
(NY Rangers' 2nd choice, 40th overall, in 2005 Entry Draft).

			Regular Season					Playoffs				
Season	Club	League	GP	G	A	Pts	PIM	GP	G	A	Pts	PIM
2003-04	St. Cloud Tech	High-MN	18	12	16	28	34	....	....	....	....	....
2004-05	Portland	WHL	32	2	11	13	10	....	....	....	....	....
2005-06	Portland	WHL	59	8	23	31	68	12	4	2	6	8

• Missed majority of 2004-05 season due to hip injury.

SAUNDERS, Nathan — (SAWN-duhrs, NAY-thun) — ANA.

Defense. Shoots right. 6'4", 216 lbs. Born, Charlottetown, P.E.I., April 25, 1985.
(Anaheim's 5th choice, 119th overall, in 2003 Entry Draft).

			Regular Season					Playoffs				
Season	Club	League	GP	G	A	Pts	PIM	GP	G	A	Pts	PIM
2001-02	Moncton Wildcats	QMJHL	54	4	11	15	88	....	....	....	....	....
2002-03	Moncton Wildcats	QMJHL	69	1	13	14	241	6	2	3	5	12
2003-04	Moncton Wildcats	QMJHL	68	4	26	30	267	20	1	1	2	34
2004-05	Moncton Wildcats	QMJHL	70	5	23	28	198	12	2	2	4	24
2005-06	Portland Pirates	AHL	20	1	0	1	75	9	0	0	0	19

SAWADA, Raymond — (suh-WAW-duh, RAY-mawnd) — DAL.

Right wing. Shoots right. 6'2", 195 lbs. Born, Richmond, B.C., February 19, 1985.
(Dallas' 3rd choice, 52nd overall, in 2004 Entry Draft).

			Regular Season					Playoffs				
Season	Club	League	GP	G	A	Pts	PIM	GP	G	A	Pts	PIM
2002-03	Richmond	PIJHL	36	7	17	24	155	....	....	....	....	....
2003-04	Nanaimo Clippers	BCHL	54	20	32	52	93	25	6	16	22	22
2004-05	Cornell Big Red	ECACHL	35	4	5	9	48	....	....	....	....	....
2005-06	Cornell Big Red	ECACHL	35	7	13	20	20	....	....	....	....	....

SCALZO, Mario — (SCAL-zoh, MAHR-ee-oh) — DAL.

Defense. Shoots left. 5'9", 187 lbs. Born, St-Hubert, Que., November 11, 1984.

			Regular Season					Playoffs				
Season	Club	League	GP	G	A	Pts	PIM	GP	G	A	Pts	PIM
2001-02	Antoine-Girouard	QAAA	40	8	27	35	50	....	....	....	....	....
	Victoriaville Tigres	QMJHL	1	0	1	1	0	1	0	0	0	0
2002-03	Victoriaville Tigres	QMJHL	72	10	34	44	134	4	0	3	3	6
2003-04	Victoriaville Tigres	QMJHL	68	16	52	68	113	....	....	....	....	....
2004-05	Victoriaville Tigres	QMJHL	39	11	19	30	73	....	....	....	....	....
	Rimouski Oceanic	QMJHL	23	13	31	44	31	13	7	14	21	10
2005-06	Iowa Stars	AHL	74	4	29	33	42	7	0	2	2	8

QMJHL All-Rookie Team (2003) • QMJHL Second All-Star Team (2004) • QMJHL First All-Star Team (2005) • Memorial Cup All-Star Team (2005)

Signed as a free agent by **Dallas**, August 5, 2005.

SCHAEFFER, Kevin — (SHAY-fuhr, KEH-vihn) — NSH.

Defense. Shoots right. 6', 203 lbs. Born, Huntington, NY, October 16, 1984.
(Nashville's 7th choice, 193rd overall, in 2004 Entry Draft).

			Regular Season					Playoffs				
Season	Club	League	GP	G	A	Pts	PIM	GP	G	A	Pts	PIM
2002-03	NY Apple Core	EJHL	65	20	38	58	60	....	....	....	....	....
2003-04	Boston University	H-East	38	5	12	17	20	....	....	....	....	....
2004-05	Boston University	H-East	41	2	12	14	26	....	....	....	....	....
2005-06	Boston University	H-East	40	4	9	13	18	....	....	....	....	....

SCHELL, Brad — (SHEHL, BRAD) — ATL.

Center. Shoots left. 6'1", 190 lbs. Born, Scott, Sask., August 5, 1984.
(Atlanta's 6th choice, 167th overall, in 2002 Entry Draft).

			Regular Season					Playoffs				
Season	Club	League	GP	G	A	Pts	PIM	GP	G	A	Pts	PIM
99-2000	North Battleford	SMHL	62	38	42	80	28	....	....	....	....	....
	Spokane Chiefs	WHL	1	0	0	0	0	....	....	....	....	....
2000-01	Spokane Chiefs	WHL	60	7	6	13	10	12	0	2	2	2
2001-02	Spokane Chiefs	WHL	70	20	36	56	16	11	0	8	8	6
2002-03	Spokane Chiefs	WHL	37	8	13	21	26	10	0	5	5	2
2003-04	Spokane Chiefs	WHL	71	35	57	92	47	4	1	0	1	0
2004-05	Gwinnett	ECHL	72	14	39	53	28	8	2	4	6	4
2005-06	Chicago Wolves	AHL	10	1	2	3	2	....	....	....	....	....
	Gwinnett	ECHL	59	23	56	79	30	17	1	12	13	8

WHL West Second All-Star Team (2004)

• Missed majority of 2002-03 season recovering from off-season back surgery.

SCHEVJEV, Maxim — (shehv-YAWF-yehv, MAX-ihm) — BUF.

Center. Shoots left. 6', 178 lbs. Born, Noginsk, USSR, July 5, 1984.
(Buffalo's 7th choice, 178th overall, in 2002 Entry Draft).

			Regular Season					Playoffs				
Season	Club	League	GP	G	A	Pts	PIM	GP	G	A	Pts	PIM
99-2000	Elektrostal 2	Russia-3	11	0	1	1	2	....	....	....	....	....
2000-01	Elektrostal	Russia-2	7	0	0	0	6	....	....	....	....	....
2001-02	Elektrostal 2	Russia-3	6	1	2	3	2	....	....	....	....	....
	Elektrostal	Russia-2	49	6	9	15	34	....	....	....	....	....
2002-03	Amur Khabarovsk	Russia	21	0	0	0	10	....	....	....	....	....
	Khabarovsk 2	Russia-3	5	2	1	3	4	....	....	....	....	....
2003-04	Kristall Elektrostal	Russia-2	26	4	5	9	20	....	....	....	....	....
	Voskresensk	Russia	18	1	0	1	2	....	....	....	....	....
2004-05	Kristall Elektrostal	Russia-2	48	4	7	11	109	....	....	....	....	....
2005-06	Yuzhny Ural Orsk	Russia-2	38	3	10	13	38	....	....	....	....	....
	Yuzhny Ural Orsk 2	Russia-3	3	1	3	4	0	....	....	....	....	....
	Kristall Elektrostal	Russia-3		STATISTICS NOT AVAILABLE								

SCHNEIDER, Andy — (SHNIGH-duhr, AN-dee) — PIT.

Defense. Shoots left. 6'1", 215 lbs. Born, Grand Forks, ND, July 31, 1981.
(Pittsburgh's 7th choice, 156th overall, in 2001 Entry Draft).

			Regular Season					Playoffs				
Season	Club	League	GP	G	A	Pts	PIM	GP	G	A	Pts	PIM
1998-99	Lincoln Stars	USHL	9	0	4	4	8	4	0	0	0	2
99-2000	Lincoln Stars	USHL	46	7	10	17	102	10	6	4	10	27
2000-01	Lincoln Stars	USHL	54	12	24	36	134	....	....	....	....	....
2001-02	North Dakota	WCHA	35	3	11	14	65	....	....	....	....	....
2002-03	North Dakota	WCHA	43	11	30	41	52	....	....	....	....	....
2003-04	North Dakota	WCHA	39	2	10	12	54	....	....	....	....	....
2004-05	North Dakota	WCHA	42	2	8	10	58	....	....	....	....	....
2005-06	Wilkes-Barre	AHL	50	3	13	16	54	....	....	....	....	....
	Wheeling Nailers	ECHL	4	0	1	1	2	....	....	....	....	....

SCHREMP, Rob — (SHREHMP, RAWB) — EDM.

Center. Shoots left. 5'11", 200 lbs. Born, Syracuse, NY, July 1, 1986.
(Edmonton's 2nd choice, 25th overall, in 2004 Entry Draft).

			Regular Season					Playoffs				
Season	Club	League	GP	G	A	Pts	PIM	GP	G	A	Pts	PIM
2000-01	Syracuse	OPJHL	49	32	46	78	....	....	....	....	....	....
2001-02	Syracuse	OPJHL	47	41	47	88	93	1	1	2	3	0
2002-03	Mississauga	OHL	65	26	48	74	25	2	1	0	1	0
2003-04	USNTDP	U-18	2	0	0	0	8	....	....	....	....	....
	Mississauga	OHL	3	2	4	6	0	....	....	....	....	....
	London Knights	OHL	60	28	41	69	18	15	7	6	13	2
2004-05	London Knights	OHL	62	41	49	90	54	18	13	16	29	16
2005-06	London Knights	OHL	57	*57	*88	*145	74	19	10	*37	*47	35

OHL All-Rookie Team (2003) • OHL Rookie of the Year (2003) • OHL First All-Star Team (2006)

SCHULTZ, Jeff (SHUHLTZ, JEHF) **WSH.**

Defense. Shoots left. 6'6", 215 lbs. Born, Calgary, Alta., February 25, 1986.
(Washington's 2nd choice, 27th overall, in 2004 Entry Draft).

			Regular Season					Playoffs				
Season	Club	League	GP	G	A	Pts	PIM	GP	G	A	Pts	PIM
2000-01	Calgary Hawks	CBHL	27	7	8	15	20	....	....	....	....	....
2001-02	Calgary Rangers	CBHL	27	5	18	23	42	....	....	....	....	....
2002-03	Calgary Hitmen	WHL	50	2	1	3	4	4	0	0	0	0
2003-04	Calgary Hitmen	WHL	72	11	24	35	33	7	1	1	2	0
2004-05	Calgary Hitmen	WHL	72	2	27	29	31	12	2	1	3	6
2005-06	Calgary Hitmen	WHL	68	7	33	40	36	13	4	6	10	6
	Hershey Bears	AHL	....	....	....	....	....	7	1	3	4	4

WHL East Second All-Star Team (2006)

SCHULTZ, Jesse (SHUHLTZ, JEH-see) **VAN.**

Right wing. Shoots right. 6', 192 lbs. Born, Strasbourg, Sask., September 28, 1982.

			Regular Season					Playoffs				
Season	Club	League	GP	G	A	Pts	PIM	GP	G	A	Pts	PIM
99-2000	Tri-City Americans	WHL	62	10	6	16	34	4	1	1	2	2
2000-01	Tri-City Americans	WHL	30	5	8	13	16	....	....	....	....	....
	Prince Albert	WHL	35	14	18	32	14	....	....	....	....	....
2001-02	Prince Albert	WHL	45	18	24	42	16	....	....	....	....	....
	Kelowna Rockets	WHL	28	10	12	22	14	....	....	....	....	....
2002-03	Kelowna Rockets	WHL	72	53	51	104	47	19	*12	16	*28	21
2003-04	Manitoba Moose	AHL	2	0	1	1	0	....	....	....	....	....
	Columbia Inferno	ECHL	52	27	21	48	72	4	1	2	3	2
2004-05	Manitoba Moose	AHL	70	9	15	24	33	14	3	2	5	2
2005-06	Manitoba Moose	AHL	80	37	30	67	63	13	5	7	12	10

WHL West First All-Star Team (2003)

Signed as a free agent by **Vancouver**, July 30, 2003.

SCHUTZ, Felix (SCHUTZ, FEEL-ihx) **BUF.**

Center. Shoots left. 5'11", 187 lbs. Born, Erding, Germany, November 3, 1987.
(Buffalo's 4th choice, 117th overall, in 2006 Entry Draft).

			Regular Season					Playoffs				
Season	Club	League	GP	G	A	Pts	PIM	GP	G	A	Pts	PIM
2003-04	Mannheim Jr.	Ger-Jr.	30	22	22	44	12	....	....	....	....	....
2004-05	EV Landshut Jr.	Ger-Jr.	9	6	8	14	33	2	2	3	5	0
	Landshut Cann.	German-2	24	1	2	3	8	5	0	0	0	2
2005-06	Saint John	QMJHL	65	21	31	52	61	....	....	....	....	....

SEABROOK, Keith (SEE-bruk, KEETH) **WSH.**

Defense. Shoots right. 6', 198 lbs. Born, Delta, B.C., August 2, 1988.
(Washington's 5th choice, 52nd overall, in 2006 Entry Draft).

			Regular Season					Playoffs				
Season	Club	League	GP	G	A	Pts	PIM	GP	G	A	Pts	PIM
2003-04	Coquitlam Express	BCHL	58	8	20	28	70	....	....	....	....	....
2005-06	Burnaby Express	BCHL	57	10	24	34	81	....	....	....	....	....

Signed Letter of Intent to attend **U. of Denver** (WCHA) in fall of 2006.

SEDOV, Pavel (se-DAHF, PAH-vehl) **T.B.**

Right wing. Shoots left. 6'3", 200 lbs. Born, Voskresensk, USSR, January 12, 1982.
(Tampa Bay's 5th choice, 161st overall, in 2000 Entry Draft).

			Regular Season					Playoffs				
Season	Club	League	GP	G	A	Pts	PIM	GP	G	A	Pts	PIM
99-2000	Voskresensk	Russia-2	10	0	0	0	2	....	....	....	....	....
	Voskresensk 2	Russia-3	21	5	5	-10	26	....	....	....	....	....
2000-01	Voskresensk	Russia-2	38	2	1	3	10	....	....	....	....	....
2001-02	Voskresensk 2	Russia-3	12	4	1	5	0	....	....	....	....	....
	Voskresensk	Russia-2	18	3	1	4	0	....	....	....	....	....
2002-03	Voskresensk 2	Russia-3	7	2	4	6	4	....	....	....	....	....
	Voskresensk	Russia-2	25	1	5	6	6	....	....	....	....	....
2003-04	THK Tver	Russia-2	26	2	6	8	6	....	....	....	....	....
	Voskresensk	Russia	10	1	0	1	2	....	....	....	....	....
	Voskresensk 2	Russia-3	STATISTICS NOT AVAILABLE									
2004-05	HK Tver	Russia-3	STATISTICS NOT AVAILABLE									
	HK Dmitrov	Russia-3	STATISTICS NOT AVAILABLE									
	HK Ryazan	Russia-4	STATISTICS NOT AVAILABLE									
2005-06			DID NOT PLAY									

SEELEY, Richard (SEE-lee, RIH-chuhrd)

Defense. Shoots left. 6'2", 205 lbs. Born, Powell River, B.C., April 30, 1979.
(Los Angeles' 6th choice, 137th overall, in 1997 Entry Draft).

			Regular Season					Playoffs				
Season	Club	League	GP	G	A	Pts	PIM	GP	G	A	Pts	PIM
1995-96	Powell River	BCJHL	44	1	8	9	42	....	....	....	....	....
1996-97	Lethbridge	WHL	3	0	0	0	11	....	....	....	....	....
	Prince Albert	WHL	18	0	1	1	9	4	0	0	0	2
1997-98	Prince Albert	WHL	65	8	21	29	114	....	....	....	....	....
1998-99	Prince Albert	WHL	61	10	48	58	110	14	1	11	12	14
99-2000	Lowell	AHL	36	5	1	6	37	....	....	....	....	....
2000-01	Lowell	AHL	55	2	8	10	102	....	....	....	....	....
	Trenton Titans	ECHL	9	0	2	2	18	....	....	....	....	....
2001-02	Manchester	AHL	61	2	10	12	78	5	0	0	0	6
2002-03	Manchester	AHL	69	4	14	18	127	3	0	1	1	0
2003-04	Manchester	AHL	56	2	9	11	80	6	0	0	0	0
2004-05	Bridgeport	AHL	47	2	6	8	108	....	....	....	....	....
	Norfolk Admirals	AHL	12	0	0	0	17	6	1	0	1	8
2005-06	Manchester	AHL	63	3	13	16	109	3	0	0	0	19

Signed as a free agent by **NY Islanders**, August 13, 2004.

SEGAL, Brandon (SEE-guhl, BRAN-duhn) **NSH.**

Right wing. Shoots right. 6'3", 213 lbs. Born, Richmond, B.C., July 12, 1983.
(Nashville's 2nd choice, 102nd overall, in 2002 Entry Draft).

			Regular Season					Playoffs				
Season	Club	League	GP	G	A	Pts	PIM	GP	G	A	Pts	PIM
99-2000	Calgary Hitmen	WHL	44	2	6	8	76	13	1	1	2	13
	Delta Ice Hawks	PIJHL	....	....	....	....	....	3	0	1	1	2
2000-01	Calgary Hitmen	WHL	72	16	11	27	103	12	1	1	2	17
2001-02	Calgary Hitmen	WHL	71	43	40	83	122	7	1	4	5	16
2002-03	Calgary Hitmen	WHL	71	31	27	58	104	5	2	2	4	4
2003-04	Calgary Hitmen	WHL	28	18	12	30	29	....	....	....	....	....
	Milwaukee	AHL	44	11	10	21	54	13	2	1	3	21
2004-05	Milwaukee	AHL	59	7	8	15	45	3	1	0	1	11
	Rockford IceHogs	UHL	10	5	4	9	27	11	11	5	16	10
2005-06	Milwaukee	AHL	79	18	15	33	126	21	1	2	3	16

SEITSONEN, Aki (SIGHT-soh-nehn, AH-kee) **CGY.**

Center. Shoots right. 6'3", 206 lbs. Born, Riihimaki, Finland, February 5, 1986.
(Calgary's 4th choice, 118th overall, in 2004 Entry Draft).

			Regular Season					Playoffs				
Season	Club	League	GP	G	A	Pts	PIM	GP	G	A	Pts	PIM
2002-03	HPK U18	Fin-U18	28	15	18	33	6	2	1	1	2	0
	HPK Jr.	Fin-Jr.	1	1	0	1	0	....	....	....	....	....
2003-04	Prince Albert	WHL	71	16	24	40	18	5	0	0	0	0
2004-05	Prince Albert	WHL	67	24	28	52	14	17	5	9	14	10
2005-06	Prince Albert	WHL	66	20	15	35	22	....	....	....	....	....
	Omaha	AHL	7	0	0	0	2	....	....	....	....	....

SEKERA, Andrej (SEH-kuhr-ah, AWN-dray) **BUF.**

Defense. Shoots left. 6', 191 lbs. Born, Bojnice, Czech., June 8, 1986.
(Buffalo's 3rd choice, 71st overall, in 2004 Entry Draft).

			Regular Season					Playoffs				
Season	Club	League	GP	G	A	Pts	PIM	GP	G	A	Pts	PIM
2001-02	Dukla Trencin Jr.	Slovak-Jr.	52	5	10	15	10	....	....	....	....	....
2002-03	Dukla Trencin Jr.	Slovak-Jr.	48	9	15	24	20	....	....	....	....	....
2003-04	Dukla Trencin	Slovakia	3	0	0	0	2	....	....	....	....	....
	Dukla Trencin Jr.	Slovak-Jr.	42	5	12	17	40	2	0	1	1	4
	Dukla Trencin U18	Svk-U18	5	0	0	0	0	....	....	....	....	....
2004-05	Owen Sound	OHL	51	7	21	28	18	6	0	4	4	4
2005-06	Owen Sound	OHL	51	21	34	55	54	11	5	8	13	9

OHL All-Rookie Team (2005) • OHL First All-Star Team (2006)

SELUYANOV, Alexander (sehl-oo-YA-nahf, al-ehx-AN-duhr) **DET.**

Defense. Shoots right. 5'11", 172 lbs. Born, Ufa, USSR, March 24, 1982.
(Detroit's 5th choice, 128th overall, in 2000 Entry Draft).

			Regular Season					Playoffs				
Season	Club	League	GP	G	A	Pts	PIM	GP	G	A	Pts	PIM
1997-98	Novoil Ufa	Russia-3	19	0	1	1	8	....	....	....	....	....
1998-99	Novoil Ufa	Russia-4	20	3	3	6	8	....	....	....	....	....
99-2000	Ufa 2	Russia-3	18	3	4	7	10	....	....	....	....	....
	Ufa	Russia	13	1	2	3	4	....	....	....	....	....
2000-01	Ufa	Russia	30	0	3	3	10	....	....	....	....	....
2001-02	CSK VVS Samara	Russia-2	30	2	7	9	58	....	....	....	....	....
	Lada Togliatti	Russia	6	0	0	0	0	....	....	....	....	....
2002-03	Lada Togliatti	Russia	26	2	4	6	12	4	0	0	0	4
	CSK VVS Samara	Russia-2	16	4	4	8	34	....	....	....	....	....
2003-04	Lada Togliatti 2	Russia-3	5	0	1	1	10	4	2	0	2	6
	Lada Togliatti	Russia	43	1	3	4	20	2	0	0	0	0
2004-05	Lada Togliatti	Russia	52	6	5	11	41	8	1	0	1	6
2005-06	Magnitogorsk	Russia	50	3	5	8	44	11	1	0	1	4

SEMENOV, Maxim (seh-MEH-nahv, mahx-EEM) **TOR.**

Defense. Shoots left. 6', 180 lbs. Born, Kamenogorsk, Kazakhstan, February 9, 1984.
(Toronto's 5th choice, 220th overall, in 2004 Entry Draft).

			Regular Season					Playoffs				
Season	Club	League	GP	G	A	Pts	PIM	GP	G	A	Pts	PIM
2002-03	Lada Togliatti 2	Russia-3	18	0	4	4	26	....	....	....	....	....
	Lada Togliatti	Russia	23	0	0	0	16	6	0	1	1	10
2003-04	Lada Togliatti	Russia	59	2	5	7	50	6	0	0	0	0
	Lada Togliatti 2	Russia-3	....	....	....	....	....	4	0	1	1	29
2004-05	Lada Togliatti	Russia	59	2	4	6	79	9	0	0	0	6
2005-06	Lada Togliatti	Russia	23	0	2	2	24	....	....	....	....	....
	Mytischi	Russia	28	2	8	10	76	9	1	0	1	8

SEMIN, Dmitri (SEH-min, dih-MEE-tree) **ST.L.**

Center. Shoots left. 5'10", 185 lbs. Born, Moscow, USSR, August 14, 1983.
(St. Louis' 4th choice, 159th overall, in 2001 Entry Draft).

			Regular Season					Playoffs				
Season	Club	League	GP	G	A	Pts	PIM	GP	G	A	Pts	PIM
99-2000	Spartak Moscow 2	Russia-3	27	9	10	19	10	....	....	....	....	....
	Spartak Moscow	Russia-2	1	0	0	0	0	....	....	....	....	....
2000-01	Spartak Moscow	Russia	21	6	3	9	4	11	2	3	5	4
2001-02	Spartak Moscow 2	Russia-3	4	5	0	5	4	....	....	....	....	....
	Spartak Moscow	Russia	44	2	6	8	14	....	....	....	....	....
2002-03	Spartak Moscow	Russia	51	9	13	22	30	....	....	....	....	....
2003-04	Spartak Moscow	Russia-2	60	15	23	38	34	13	2	2	4	2
2004-05	Spartak Moscow	Russia	53	7	7	14	34	....	....	....	....	....
2005-06	Spartak Moscow	Russia	51	12	14	26	38	3	0	1	1	0

SEPPANEN, Timo (SEH-pah-nehn, TEE-moh) **PIT.**

Defense. Shoots left. 6'1", 209 lbs. Born, Helsinki, Finland, July 22, 1987.
(Pittsburgh's 5th choice, 185th overall, in 2006 Entry Draft).

			Regular Season					Playoffs				
Season	Club	League	GP	G	A	Pts	PIM	GP	G	A	Pts	PIM
2002-03	HIFK Helsinki U18	Fin-U18	24	2	5	7	12	2	2	0	2	0
2003-04	HIFK Helsinki U18	Fin-U18	7	2	5	7	32	4	0	2	2	6
	HIFK Helsinki Jr.	Fin-Jr.	29	0	4	4	6	7	0	0	0	2
2004-05	HIFK Helsinki U18	Fin-U18	....	....	....	....	....	7	2	3	5	26
	HIFK Helsinki Jr.	Fin-Jr.	39	3	4	7	32	3	0	0	0	4
2005-06	Suomi U20	Finland-2	6	2	2	4	10	....	....	....	....	....
	HIFK Helsinki Jr.	Fin-Jr.	30	7	11	18	65	....	....	....	....	....
	HIFK Helsinki	Finland	21	0	0	0	2	5	0	1	1	0

SERSEN, Michal (suhr-SEHN, MEE-khahl) **PIT.**

Defense. Shoots left. 6'1", 200 lbs. Born, Celnica, Czech., December 28, 1985.
(Pittsburgh's 7th choice, 130th overall, in 2004 Entry Draft).

			Regular Season					Playoffs				
Season	Club	League	GP	G	A	Pts	PIM	GP	G	A	Pts	PIM
2002-03	Bratislava Jr.	Slovak-Jr.	33	5	4	9	51	....	....	....	....	....
	Bratislava	Slovakia	17	0	0	0	0	....	....	....	....	....
2003-04	Rimouski Oceanic	QMJHL	45	7	18	25	30	9	1	5	6	6
2004-05	Rimouski Oceanic	QMJHL	67	9	33	42	74	13	0	8	8	18
2005-06	Quebec Remparts	QMJHL	63	22	57	79	76	23	3	18	21	36

QMJHL Second All-Star Team (2006)

SERTICH, Andrew (SUHR-tihch, AN-droo) PIT.

Left wing. Shoots left. 6', 175 lbs. Born, Coleraine, MN, May 6, 1983.
(Pittsburgh's 5th choice, 136th overall, in 2002 Entry Draft).

			Regular Season					Playoffs				
Season	Club	League	GP	G	A	Pts	PIM	GP	G	A	Pts	PIM
1998/00	Greenway Raiders	High-MN	47	39	58	97	•	....	....	....	....	....
2000-01	Greenway Raiders	High-MN	31	35	45	80	14	....	....	....	....	....
2001-02	Greenway Raiders	High-MN	26	24	48	72	35	....	....	....	....	....
	Sioux Falls	USHL	13	2	4	6	0	2	0	0	0	2
2002-03	U. of Minnesota	WCHA	44	5	9	14	12	....	....	....	....	....
2003-04	U. of Minnesota	WCHA	43	8	14	22	14	....	....	....	....	....
2004-05	U. of Minnesota	WCHA	44	6	9	15	8	....	....	....	....	....
2005-06	U. of Minnesota	WCHA	41	8	8	16	22	....	....	....	....	....

• Statistics for 1998/00 **Greenway** (High-MN) are totals for 1998-2000 seasons.

SERTICH, Marty (SUHR-tihch, MAHR-tee) DAL.

Center. Shoots left. 5'8", 165 lbs. Born, Roseville, MN, October 13, 1982.

			Regular Season					Playoffs				
Season	Club	League	GP	G	A	Pts	PIM	GP	G	A	Pts	PIM
2001-02	Sioux Falls	USHL	61	19	33	52	30	3	1	0	1	0
2002-03	Colorado College	WCHA	42	9	20	29	26	....	....	....	....	....
2003-04	Colorado College	WCHA	39	11	28	39	12	....	....	....	....	....
2004-05	Colorado College	WCHA	42	27	37	*64	26	....	....	....	....	....
2005-06	Colorado College	WCHA	42	14	36	50	55	....	....	....	....	....

Signed as a free agent by **Dallas**, July 10, 2006.

SESTITO, Tommy (sehs-TEE-toh, TAW-mee) CBJ

Left wing. Shoots left. 6'4", 209 lbs. Born, Utica, NY, September 28, 1987.
(Columbus' 3rd choice, 85th overall, in 2006 Entry Draft).

			Regular Season					Playoffs				
Season	Club	League	GP	G	A	Pts	PIM	GP	G	A	Pts	PIM
2003-04	Syracuse Jr. Stars	EmJHL	31	13	16	29	137	6	5	6	11	32
2004-05	Plymouth Whalers	OHL	35	1	3	4	88	....	....	....	....	....
2005-06	Plymouth Whalers	OHL	57	10	10	20	176	13	5	2	7	29

SETOGUCHI, Devin (SEHT-oh-GOO-chee, DEH-vihn) S.J.

Right wing. Shoots right. 5'11", 186 lbs. Born, Taber, Alta., January 1, 1987.
(San Jose's 1st choice, 8th overall, in 2005 Entry Draft).

			Regular Season					Playoffs				
Season	Club	League	GP	G	A	Pts	PIM	GP	G	A	Pts	PIM
2003-04	Saskatoon Blades	WHL	66	13	18	31	53	....	....	....	....	....
2004-05	Saskatoon Blades	WHL	69	33	31	64	34	4	0	1	1	0
2005-06	Saskatoon Blades	WHL	65	36	47	83	69	10	8	4	12	8

WHL East Second All-Star Team (2006)

SEYDOUX, Philippe (SAY-doo, fihl-EEP) OTT.

Defense. Shoots left. 6'2", 185 lbs. Born, Bern, Switz., February 23, 1985.
(Ottawa's 3rd choice, 100th overall, in 2003 Entry Draft).

			Regular Season					Playoffs				
Season	Club	League	GP	G	A	Pts	PIM	GP	G	A	Pts	PIM
2000-01	SC Bern Jr.	Swiss-Jr.	30	1	3	4	8	4	1	2	0	6
2001-02	SC Bern Jr.	Swiss-Jr.	35	8	17	25	94	7	3	5	0	24
	SC Bern	Swiss	7	0	0	0	0	2	0	0	0	0
2002-03	Kloten Flyers Jr.	Swiss-Jr.	14	2	10	12	50	....	....	....	....	....
	Kloten Flyers	Swiss	14	0	1	1	4	5	0	0	0	6
2003-04	Kloten Flyers	Swiss	24	2	3	5	20	....	....	....	....	....
2004-05	Kloten Flyers	Swiss	28	1	8	9	22	5	0	0	0	2
2005-06	Kloten Flyers	Swiss	44	1	7	8	48	11	0	0	0	4

SEYMOUR, John (SEE-mohr, JAWN) L.A.

Left wing. Shoots left. 6'3", 176 lbs. Born, Scarborough, Ont., June 16, 1987.
(Los Angeles' 8th choice, 226th overall, in 2005 Entry Draft).

			Regular Season					Playoffs				
Season	Club	League	GP	G	A	Pts	PIM	GP	G	A	Pts	PIM
2002-03	Peterborough	OMHA	48	13	13	26	59	....	....	....	....	....
	Peterborough Bees	OPJHL	1	0	0	0	0	....	....	....	....	....
2003-04	Brampton	OHL	40	0	3	3	16	10	0	0	0	2
2004-05	Brampton	OHL	63	1	4	5	64	6	0	0	0	0
2005-06	Brampton	OHL	50	3	4	7	60	11	0	0	0	6

SHADILOV, Igor (sha-DEE-lahf, EE-gor) WSH.

Defense. Shoots left. 6'2", 189 lbs. Born, Moscow, USSR, June 7, 1980.
(Washington's 10th choice, 249th overall, in 1999 Entry Draft).

			Regular Season					Playoffs				
Season	Club	League	GP	G	A	Pts	PIM	GP	G	A	Pts	PIM
1996-97	Dyn'o Moscow 2	Russia-3	30	3	7	10	30	....	....	....	....	....
1997-98	Dynamo Moscow	Russia	38	1	0	1	6	....	....	....	....	....
1998-99	Dyn'o Moscow 2	Russia-3	28	2	9	11	15	....	....	....	....	....
	Dynamo Moscow	Russia	2	0	0	0	0	....	....	....	....	....
	Krylja Sovetov	Russia	9	0	0	0	0	....	....	....	....	....
99-2000	THK Tver	Russia-2	14	0	3	3	6	....	....	....	....	....
	Dynamo Moscow	Russia	26	0	2	2	8	16	0	0	0	2
2000-01	Dynamo Moscow	Russia	34	1	5	6	12	....	....	....	....	....
2001-02	Cherepovets	Russia	33	7	3	10	10	4	0	0	0	2
2002-03	Cherepovets	Russia	32	3	3	6	28	12	1	3	4	4
2003-04	Dynamo Moscow	Russia	56	4	8	12	16	3	0	1	1	2
2004-05	Dynamo Moscow	Russia	34	0	5	5	12	....	....	....	....	....
2005-06	Ak Bars Kazan	Russia	49	3	9	12	20	13	1	1	2	6

SHAFIGULIN, Grigory (sha-fih-GOO-lihn, grih-GOH-ree) NSH.

Center. Shoots left. 6'2", 185 lbs. Born, Chelyabinsk, USSR, January 13, 1985.
(Nashville's 8th choice, 98th overall, in 2003 Entry Draft).

			Regular Season					Playoffs				
Season	Club	League	GP	G	A	Pts	PIM	GP	G	A	Pts	PIM
2000-01	Chelyabinsk 2	Russia-3	6	3	2	5	8	....	....	....	....	....
2001-02	Yaroslavl 2	Russia-3	19	2	2	4	12	....	....	....	....	....
2002-03	Yaroslavl 2	Russia-3	33	18	12	30	46	7	0	4	4	31
	Yaroslavl	Russia	11	0	1	1	4	8	0	0	0	4
2003-04	Yaroslavl 2	Russia-3	11	3	8	11	22	....	....	....	....	....
	Yaroslavl	Russia	29	3	0	3	4	2	0	0	0	0
2004-05	Yaroslavl 2	Russia-3	1	0	2	2	2	....	....	....	....	....
	Yaroslavl	Russia	46	5	6	11	49	9	0	0	0	10
2005-06	Yaroslavl	Russia	32	3	6	9	20	3	0	0	0	6
	Yaroslavl 2	Russia-3	7	1	3	4	18	....	....	....	....	....

SHANNON, Ryan (SHA-nohn, RIGH-uhn) ANA.

Center. Shoots right. 5'9", 178 lbs. Born, Darien, CT, March 2, 1983.

			Regular Season					Playoffs				
Season	Club	League	GP	G	A	Pts	PIM	GP	G	A	Pts	PIM
2001-02	Boston College	H-East	38	8	17	25	12	....	....	....	....	....
2002-03	Boston College	H-East	36	14	24	38	4	....	....	....	....	....
2003-04	Boston College	H-East	42	15	27	42	22	....	....	....	....	....
2004-05	Boston College	H-East	38	14	31	45	22	....	....	....	....	....
	Cincinnati	AHL	4	1	0	1	2	....	....	....	....	....
2005-06	Portland Pirates	AHL	71	27	59	86	44	19	11	11	22	8

AHL All-Rookie Team (2006)

Signed as a free agent by **Anaheim**, April, 2006.

SHARROW, Jim (SHA-row, JIHM) ATL.

Defense. Shoots right. 6'2", 195 lbs. Born, Framingham, MA, January 31, 1985.
(Atlanta's 2nd choice, 110th overall, in 2003 Entry Draft).

			Regular Season					Playoffs				
Season	Club	League	GP	G	A	Pts	PIM	GP	G	A	Pts	PIM
2001-02	USNTDP	U-17	17	2	11	13	2	....	....	....	....	....
	USNTDP	NAHL	44	3	5	8	28	....	....	....	....	....
2002-03	Halifax	QMJHL	70	2	14	16	54	25	2	4	6	24
2003-04	Halifax	QMJHL	52	12	26	38	67	....	....	....	....	....
2004-05	Halifax	QMJHL	69	16	31	47	76	13	5	6	11	6
2005-06	Chicago Wolves	AHL	47	2	17	19	17	....	....	....	....	....
	Gwinnett	ECHL	23	3	7	10	12	....	....	....	....	....

QMJHL All-Rookie Team (2003)

SHASTIN, Yegor (SHAS-tihn, yeh-GOHR) CGY.

Left wing. Shoots left. 5'9", 172 lbs. Born, Kiev, USSR, September 10, 1982.
(Calgary's 5th choice, 124th overall, in 2001 Entry Draft).

			Regular Season					Playoffs				
Season	Club	League	GP	G	A	Pts	PIM	GP	G	A	Pts	PIM
1997-98	Omsk 2	Russia-3	4	0	1	1	0	....	....	....	....	....
1998-99	Omsk 2	Russia-4	19	11	17	28	30	....	....	....	....	....
	Avangard Omsk	Russia	4	0	0	0	0	4	0	1	1	0
99-2000	Omsk 2	Russia-3	11	6	5	11	20	....	....	....	....	....
	Avangard Omsk	Russia	26	2	4	6	20	7	3	1	4	16
2000-01	Omsk 2	Russia-3	14	13	9	22	62	....	....	....	....	....
	Avangard Omsk	Russia	35	3	11	14	59	9	1	0	1	18
2001-02	Avangard Omsk	Russia	26	2	5	7	10	11	1	0	1	8
2002-03	HC Ambri-Piotta	Swiss	44	2	3	5	18	3	1	0	1	2
	HC Sierre	Swiss-2	2	1	0	1	0	....	....	....	....	....
2003-04	Sibir Novosibirsk	Russia	57	7	5	12	28	....	....	....	....	....
2004-05	Omsk 2	Russia-3	2	1	0	1	0	....	....	....	....	....
	Avangard Omsk	Russia	7	0	0	0	2	....	....	....	....	....
	St. Petersburg 2	Russia-3	2	2	2	4	4	....	....	....	....	....
	SKA St. Petersburg	Russia	21	3	3	6	12	....	....	....	....	....
2005-06	Nizhnekamsk	Russia	30	1	3	4	22	....	....	....	....	....
	Nizhny Novgorod	Russia-2	6	4	1	5	2	6	1	5	6	4

SHEFER, Andrei (SHEH-fuhr, AWN-dray) L.A.

Left wing. Shoots left. 6'1", 194 lbs. Born, Yekaterinburg, USSR, July 26, 1981.
(Los Angeles' 1st choice, 43rd overall, in 1999 Entry Draft).

			Regular Season					Playoffs				
Season	Club	League	GP	G	A	Pts	PIM	GP	G	A	Pts	PIM
1997-98	Yekaterinburg 2	Russia-3	16	3	3	6	18	....	....	....	....	....
1998-99	Cherepovets 3	Russia-4	6	2	2	4	18	....	....	....	....	....
	Cherepovets 2	Russia-3	21	6	5	11	20	....	....	....	....	....
	Cherepovets	Russia	8	1	0	1	4	....	....	....	....	....
99-2000	Halifax	QMJHL	72	34	42	76	30	10	0	5	5	4
2000-01	SKA St. Petersburg	Russia	11	6	1	7	4	....	....	....	....	....
	Cherepovets	Russia	20	1	1	2	10	6	1	0	1	0
2001-02	Cherepovets 2	Russia-3	3	1	2	3	2	....	....	....	....	....
	Cherepovets	Russia	8	0	0	0	6	....	....	....	....	....
	SKA St. Petersburg	Russia	28	4	4	8	10	....	....	....	....	....
2002-03	Cherepovets	Russia	37	2	4	6	10	10	0	0	0	0
	Cherepovets 2	Russia-3	3	1	2	3	2	....	....	....	....	....
2003-04	Cherepovets	Russia	55	4	6	10	46	....	....	....	....	....
2004-05	Cherepovets	Russia	46	1	11	12	18	....	....	....	....	....
2005-06	Cherepovets	Russia	45	2	1	3	32	4	0	1	1	0

SHEPPARD, James (sheh-PUHRD, JAYMZ) MIN.

Center. Shoots left. 6'1", 204 lbs. Born, Halifax, N.S., April 25, 1988.
(Minnesota's 1st choice, 9th overall, in 2006 Entry Draft).

			Regular Season					Playoffs				
Season	Club	League	GP	G	A	Pts	PIM	GP	G	A	Pts	PIM
2003-04	Dartmouth	NSMHL	61	38	54	92	46	....	....	....	....	....
2004-05	Cape Breton	QMJHL	65	14	31	45	40	5	1	3	4	2
2005-06	Cape Breton	QMJHL	66	30	54	84	78	9	2	5	7	12

SHINKAR, Alexander (shihn-KAHR, al-ehx-AN-duhr) TOR.

Right wing. Shoots left. 6'2", 192 lbs. Born, Ufa, USSR, July 3, 1981.
(Toronto's 9th choice, 254th overall, in 2000 Entry Draft).

			Regular Season					Playoffs				
Season	Club	League	GP	G	A	Pts	PIM	GP	G	A	Pts	PIM
1997-98	Novoil Ufa	Russia-3	22	6	2	8	4	....	....	....	....	....
1998-99	Cherepovets 2	Russia-3	25	7	2	9	8	....	....	....	....	....
	Cherepovets 3	Russia-4	8	0	4	4	4	....	....	....	....	....
99-2000	Cherepovets	Russia	18	1	1	2	2	8	0	0	0	0
2000-01	SKA St. Petersburg	Russia	43	7	4	11	50	....	....	....	....	....
2001-02	Ufa	Russia	27	3	3	6	8	....	....	....	....	....
	SKA St. Petersburg	Russia	18	3	4	7	10	....	....	....	....	....
2002-03	Cherepovets	Russia	32	3	1	4	12	11	0	1	1	6
2003-04	Ufa	Russia	15	2	0	2	16	....	....	....	....	....
	SKA St. Petersburg	Russia	12	4	1	5	0	....	....	....	....	....
2004-05	SKA St. Petersburg	Russia	57	16	14	30	22	....	....	....	....	....
2005-06	SKA St. Petersburg	Russia	44	5	8	13	26	2	0	0	0	2
	St. Petersburg 2	Russia-3	1	0	1	1	0	....	....	....	....	....

SHIROKOV, Sergei (sheer-OH-kawv, SAIR-gay) **VAN.**

Wing. Shoots right. 5'10", 176 lbs. Born, Moscow, Russia, March 10, 1986.
(Vancouver's 3rd choice, 163rd overall, in 2006 Entry Draft).

			Regular Season					Playoffs				
Season	Club	League	GP	G	A	Pts	PIM	GP	G	A	Pts	PIM
2001-02	HK CSKA 2	Russia-3	18	2	3	5	0	....	....	....	....	....
2002-03	CSKA Moscow 2	Russia-3	2	0	0	0	0	....	....	....	....	....
2003-04	CSKA Moscow 2	Russia-3	66	39	41	80	66	....	....	....	....	....
2004-05	CSKA Moscow	Russia	8	0	0	0	0	....	....	....	....	....
	CSKA Moscow 2	Russia-3	25	16	13	29	47	....	....	....	....	....
	CSKA Moscow	Russia	8	0	0	0	0	....	....	....	....	....
2005-06	CSKA Moscow	Russia	39	7	7	14	26	4	0	0	0	0

SHKOTOV, Alexei (SHKOH-tahv, al-EHX-ay) **ST.L.**

Right wing. Shoots left. 5'10", 175 lbs. Born, Elektrostal, USSR, June 22, 1984.
(St. Louis' 1st choice, 48th overall, in 2002 Entry Draft).

			Regular Season					Playoffs				
Season	Club	League	GP	G	A	Pts	PIM	GP	G	A	Pts	PIM
2000-01	Elektrostal 2	Russia-3	2	0	0	0	0	....	....	....	....	....
2001-02	Elektrostal 2	Russia-3	4	4	5	9	2	....	....	....	....	....
	Elektrostal	Russia-2	52	17	9	26	40	....	....	....	....	....
2002-03	CSKA Moscow	Russia	33	5	1	6	20	....	....	....	....	....
2003-04	Moncton Wildcats	QMJHL	7	2	4	6	2	....	....	....	....	....
	Quebec Remparts	QMJHL	36	25	36	61	24	5	3	1	4	4
2004-05	Worcester IceCats	AHL	23	6	6	12	18	....	....	....	....	....
	Voskresensk	Russia	21	6	1	7	6	....	....	....	....	....
2005-06	Mytischi	Russia	32	6	10	16	34	9	0	3	3	8
	Kristall Elektrostal	Russia-3	STATISTICS NOT AVAILABLE									

SHUTRON, Ben (SHOO-trawn, BEHN) **CHI.**

Defense. Shoots right. 5'11", 192 lbs. Born, Ottawa, Ont., June 14, 1988.
(Chicago's 5th choice, 95th overall, in 2006 Entry Draft).

			Regular Season					Playoffs				
Season	Club	League	GP	G	A	Pts	PIM	GP	G	A	Pts	PIM
2004-05	Kingston	OHL	63	7	20	27	28	....	....	....	....	....
2005-06	Kingston	OHL	67	10	29	39	134	6	0	2	2	14

SIDDALL, Matt (sih-DUHL, MAT) **ATL.**

Right wing. Shoots right. 6'1", 210 lbs. Born, North Vancouver, B.C., September 26, 1984.
(Atlanta's 9th choice, 270th overall, in 2004 Entry Draft).

			Regular Season					Playoffs				
Season	Club	League	GP	G	A	Pts	PIM	GP	G	A	Pts	PIM
2003-04	Powell River Kings	BCHL	45	25	36	61	216	7	4	2	6	10
2004-05	Northern Mich.	CCHA	33	4	4	8	62	....	....	....	....	....
2005-06	Northern Mich.	CCHA	36	6	6	12	72	....	....	....	....	....

SIDORENKO, Kirill (sih-dohr-EHN-koh, KIH-rihl) **DAL.**

Center. Shoots left. 6'3", 187 lbs. Born, Omsk, USSR, March 30, 1983.
(Dallas' 9th choice, 180th overall, in 2002 Entry Draft).

			Regular Season					Playoffs				
Season	Club	League	GP	G	A	Pts	PIM	GP	G	A	Pts	PIM
1998-99	Omsk 2	Russia-4	2	0	0	0	2	....	....	....	....	....
99-2000	Omsk 2	Russia-3	26	2	11	13	14	....	....	....	....	....
2000-01	Omsk 2	Russia-3	30	8	7	15	44	....	....	....	....	....
2001-02	Mostovik Kurgan	Russia-2	50	11	6	17	64	....	....	....	....	....
2002-03	Sibir Novosibirsk	Russia	30	1	1	2	2	....	....	....	....	....
2003-04	Energiya Kemerovo	Russia-2	14	1	1	2	6	....	....	....	....	....
	Zauralje Kurgan	Russia-2	32	3	3	6	6	4	0	0	0	27
2004-05	Omsk 2	Russia-3	18	7	4	11	12	....	....	....	....	....
	CSK VVS Samara	Russia-2	16	2	2	4	0	....	....	....	....	....
2005-06	CSK VVS Samara	Russia-2	47	8	11	19	62	....	....	....	....	....
	Krylja Sovetov	Russia-2	6	3	3	6	8	17	1	3	4	4

SIDYAKIN, Andrei (sihd-YA-kihn, AWN-dray) **MTL.**

Right wing. Shoots left. 5'11", 169 lbs. Born, Ufa, USSR, January 20, 1979.
(Montreal's 10th choice, 202nd overall, in 1997 Entry Draft).

			Regular Season					Playoffs				
Season	Club	League	GP	G	A	Pts	PIM	GP	G	A	Pts	PIM
1994-95	Ufa	CIS	7	0	1	1	0	....	....	....	....	....
1995-96	Ufa	CIS	25	1	0	1	4	3	0	0	0	2
1996-97	Ufa	Russia	29	3	5	8	4	....	....	....	....	....
1997-98	Ufa	Russia	42	5	4	9	32	....	....	....	....	....
1998-99	Ufa	Russia	36	6	4	10	14	2	0	0	0	2
99-2000	Ufa	Russia	38	7	2	9	32	....	....	....	....	....
2000-01	Ufa	Russia	44	10	13	23	42	....	....	....	....	....
2001-02	Ufa	Russia	43	9	7	16	20	....	....	....	....	....
2002-03	Cherepovets	Russia	38	8	8	16	20	2	0	0	0	4
2003-04	Cherepovets	Russia	19	1	2	3	12	....	....	....	....	....
	Cherepovets 2	Russia-3	4	2	3	5	0	....	....	....	....	....
	Ufa	Russia	29	8	8	16	28	....	....	....	....	....
2004-05	Ufa	Russia	57	8	20	28	54	....	....	....	....	....
2005-06	Ufa	Russia	51	18	20	38	54	6	4	0	4	8

SIFERS, Jaime (SIH-fuhrs, JAY-mee) **TOR.**

Defense. Shoots right. 5'11", 210 lbs. Born, Stratford, CT, January 18, 1983.

			Regular Season					Playoffs				
Season	Club	League	GP	G	A	Pts	PIM	GP	G	A	Pts	PIM
2002-03	U. of Vermont	ECAC	34	4	14	18	66	....	....	....	....	....
2003-04	U. of Vermont	ECAC	35	4	14	18	93	....	....	....	....	....
2004-05	U. of Vermont	ECACHL	36	4	12	16	57	....	....	....	....	....
2005-06	U. of Vermont	H-East	38	3	15	18	60	....	....	....	....	....
	Toronto Marlies	AHL	2	0	0	0	2	....	....	....	....	....

Signed as a free agent by **Toronto**, July 20, 2006.

SIGALET, Jonathan (sihg-A-leht, JAWN-ah-thuhn) **BOS.**

Defense. Shoots left. 6'1", 185 lbs. Born, Vancouver, B.C., February 12, 1986.
(Boston's 4th choice, 100th overall, in 2005 Entry Draft).

			Regular Season					Playoffs				
Season	Club	League	GP	G	A	Pts	PIM	GP	G	A	Pts	PIM
2002-03	Salmon Arm	BCHL	52	13	39	52	34	....	....	....	....	....
2003-04	Bowling Green	CCHA	37	3	12	15	26	....	....	....	....	....
2004-05	Bowling Green	CCHA	35	3	13	16	36	....	....	....	....	....
2005-06	Providence Bruins	AHL	75	9	27	36	59	6	2	1	3	9

SIMEK, Juraj (SEE-mehk, YUHR-ay) **VAN.**

Wing. Shoots left. 6'1", 189 lbs. Born, Presov, Slovakia, September 29, 1987.
(Vancouver's 4th choice, 167th overall, in 2006 Entry Draft).

			Regular Season					Playoffs				
Season	Club	League	GP	G	A	Pts	PIM	GP	G	A	Pts	PIM
2002-03	SC Bern Jr.	Swiss-Jr.	2	1	0	1	0	2	0	0	0	0
2003-04	Kloten Flyers Jr.	Swiss-Jr.	36	8	6	14	28	....	....	....	....	....
2004-05	Kloten Flyers Jr.	Swiss-Jr.	39	17	13	30	62	9	2	3	5	10
	Kloten Flyers	Swiss	18	0	0	0	0	....	....	....	....	....
	Kloten Flyers	Swiss	18	0	0	0	0	....	....	....	....	....
2005-06	Kloten Flyers Jr.	Swiss-Jr.	45	24	44	68	202	....	....	....	....	....
	Kloten Flyers	Swiss	8	0	1	1	4	....	....	....	....	....
	EHC Biel-Bienne	Swiss-2	3	0	0	0	2	....	....	....	....	....

SIMS, Shane (SIHMZ, SHAYN) **NYI**

Defense. Shoots right. 5'11", 192 lbs. Born, East Amherst, NY, April 30, 1988.
(NY Islanders' 8th choice, 126th overall, in 2006 Entry Draft).

			Regular Season					Playoffs				
Season	Club	League	GP	G	A	Pts	PIM	GP	G	A	Pts	PIM
2004-05	Buffalo Lightning	OPJHL	48	14	26	40	47	....	....	....	....	....
2005-06	Des Moines	USHL	59	10	12	22	80	11	2	0	2	12

SINDEL, Jakub (SHIHN-dehl, YA-kuhb) **CHI.**

Center. Shoots right. 6', 172 lbs. Born, Jihlava, Czech., January 24, 1986.
(Chicago's 5th choice, 54th overall, in 2004 Entry Draft).

			Regular Season					Playoffs				
Season	Club	League	GP	G	A	Pts	PIM	GP	G	A	Pts	PIM
99-2000	Slavia U17	CzR-U17	32	10	6	16	6	....	....	....	....	....
2000-01	Slavia U17	CzR-U17	26	12	15	27	2	6	1	0	1	0
2001-02	Slavia U17	CzR-U17	34	32	14	46	34	2	0	1	1	2
	HC Slavia Praha Jr.	CzRep-Jr.	14	7	4	11	10	....	....	....	....	....
2002-03	HC Slavia Praha Jr.	CzRep-Jr.	35	12	11	23	39	2	0	1	1	0
2003-04	HC Sparta Praha	CzRep	34	5	1	6	14	13	1	1	2	2
	Sparta Jr.	CzRep-Jr.	13	8	14	22	4	....	....	....	....	....
	HC Dukla Jihlava	CzRep-2	1	0	0	0	0	....	....	....	....	....
2004-05	Sparta Jr.	CzRep-Jr.	9	5	16	21	16	....	....	....	....	....
	HC Sparta Praha	CzRep	10	0	2	2	0	....	....	....	....	....
	Trebic	CzRep-2	5	0	0	0	0	....	....	....	....	....
	Brandon	WHL	35	16	13	29	12	24	7	4	11	22
2005-06	HC Sparta Praha	CzRep	12	1	1	2	6	....	....	....	....	....
	Plzen	CzRep	31	11	8	19	18	....	....	....	....	....

SIPOTZ, Brian (SIHP-awtz, BRIGH-uhn)

Defense. Shoots right. 6'7", 235 lbs. Born, South Bend, IN, September 16, 1981.
(Atlanta's 3rd choice, 100th overall, in 2001 Entry Draft).

			Regular Season					Playoffs				
Season	Club	League	GP	G	A	Pts	PIM	GP	G	A	Pts	PIM
99-2000	Culver Academy	High-IN	45	14	22	36	56	....	....	....	....	....
2000-01	Miami U.	CCHA	32	0	1	1	48	....	....	....	....	....
2001-02	Miami U.	CCHA	25	0	1	1	28	....	....	....	....	....
2002-03	Miami U.	CCHA	26	0	0	0	24	....	....	....	....	....
2003-04	Miami U.	CCHA	36	0	3	3	39	....	....	....	....	....
2004-05	Chicago Wolves	AHL	75	2	6	8	31	18	1	2	3	6
	Gwinnett	ECHL	2	0	0	0	0	....	....	....	....	....
2005-06	Chicago Wolves	AHL	57	2	12	14	41	....	....	....	....	....

SJODIN, Viktor (shoh-DEEN, VIHK-tohr) **NSH.**

Wing. Shoots right. 6', 207 lbs. Born, Uppsala, Sweden, April 21, 1988.
(Nashville's 5th choice, 206th overall, in 2006 Entry Draft).

			Regular Season					Playoffs				
Season	Club	League	GP	G	A	Pts	PIM	GP	G	A	Pts	PIM
2004-05	Vasteras U18	Swe-U18	6	2	2	4	10	4	1	2	3	2
	Vasteras Jr.	Swe-Jr.	18	3	6	9	20	....	....	....	....	....
2005-06	Vasteras Jr.	Swe-Jr.	31	12	5	17	79	....	....	....	....	....

SKILLE, Jack (SKIH-lee, JAK) **CHI.**

Right wing. Shoots right. 6'1", 206 lbs. Born, Madison, WI, May 19, 1987.
(Chicago's 1st choice, 7th overall, in 2005 Entry Draft).

			Regular Season					Playoffs				
Season	Club	League	GP	G	A	Pts	PIM	GP	G	A	Pts	PIM
2003-04	USNTDP	U-17	33	14	10	24	30	....	....	....	....	....
	USNTDP	NAHL	28	11	9	20	31	....	....	....	....	....
2004-05	USNTDP	U-18	26	9	11	20	36	....	....	....	....	....
	USNTDP	NAHL	16	6	11	17	20	....	....	....	....	....
2005-06	U. of Wisconsin	WCHA	41	13	8	21	37	....	....	....	....	....

SKINNER, Brett (SKIH-nuhr, BREHT) **ANA.**

Defense. Shoots left. 6'1", 195 lbs. Born, Brandon, Man., June 28, 1983.
(Vancouver's 3rd choice, 68th overall, in 2002 Entry Draft).

			Regular Season					Playoffs				
Season	Club	League	GP	G	A	Pts	PIM	GP	G	A	Pts	PIM
1998-99	Brandon Kings	MMBHL	29	3	18	21	20	....	....	....	....	....
99-2000	Brandon Kings	MMMHL	40	8	27	35	48	....	....	....	....	....
2000-01	Trail Smoke Eaters	BCHL	59	11	24	35	43	....	....	....	....	....
2001-02	Des Moines	USHL	44	9	38	47	25	3	0	1	1	0
2002-03	U. of Denver	WCHA	37	4	13	17	27	....	....	....	....	....
2003-04	U. of Denver	WCHA	44	7	23	30	32	....	....	....	....	....
2004-05	U. of Denver	WCHA	43	4	36	40	30	....	....	....	....	....
2005-06	Manitoba Moose	AHL	65	4	21	25	33	13	0	4	4	19

USHL First All-Star Team (2002) • USHL Defenseman of the Year (2002) • WCHA First All-Star Team (2005) • NCAA West Second All-American Team (2005) • NCAA Championship All-Tournament Team (2005)

Traded to **Anaheim** by **Vancouver** with NY Islanders' 2nd round choice (previously acquired, Anahein selected Bryce Swan) in 2006 Entry Draft for Keith Carney and Juha Alen, March 9, 2006.

SKLADANY, Frantisek (sklah-DAH-nee, FRAN-tih-shehk)

Left wing. Shoots left. 6', 185 lbs. Born, Martin, Czech., April 22, 1982.
(Colorado's 4th choice, 143rd overall, in 2001 Entry Draft).

			Regular Season					Playoffs				
Season	Club	League	GP	G	A	Pts	PIM	GP	G	A	Pts	PIM
1995-96	Martin Jr.	Slovak-Jr.	8	2	1	3	2	....	....	....	....	....
1996-97	Martin Jr.	Slovak-Jr.	46	29	28	57	18	....	....	....	....	....
1997-98	Martin Jr.	Slovak-Jr.	53	46	37	83	18	....	....	....	....	....
1998-99	Martin Jr.	Slovak-Jr.	10	2	4	6	4	....	....	....	....	....
	Martin	Slovakia	1	0	0	0	0	....	....	....	....	....
99-2000	Martin Jr.	Slovak-Jr.	3	2	3	5	0	....	....	....	....	....
	Martin	Slovak-2	13	1	4	5	2	....	....	....	....	....
2000-01	Boston University	H-East	35	4	5	9	4	....	....	....	....	....
2001-02	Boston University	H-East	33	13	13	26	23	....	....	....	....	....
2002-03	Boston University	H-East	41	14	21	35	34	....	....	....	....	....
2003-04	Boston University	H-East	37	3	21	24	16	....	....	....	....	....
2004-05	Hershey Bears	AHL	15	0	0	0	2	....	....	....	....	....
	Quad City	UHL	50	9	11	20	33	7	1	1	2	4
2005-06	Lowell	AHL	52	1	10	11	28	....	....	....	....	....
	San Diego Gulls	ECHL	9	2	3	5	6	....	....	....	....	....

SLOVAK, Tomas (SLOHW-vahk, TAW-mawsh)

Defense. Shoots right. 6'1", 203 lbs. Born, Kosice, Czech., April 5, 1983.
(Nashville's 3rd choice, 42nd overall, in 2001 Entry Draft).

			Regular Season					Playoffs				
Season	Club	League	GP	G	A	Pts	PIM	GP	G	A	Pts	PIM
1997-98	HC Kosice Jr.	Slovak-Jr.	47	1	6	7	24	....	....	....	....	....
1998-99	HC VSZ Kosice Jr.	Slovak-Jr.	45	6	14	20	65	....	....	....	....	....
99-2000	HC VSZ Kosice Jr.	Slovak-Jr.	55	16	28	44	117	....	....	....	....	....
	HC VSZ Kosice	Slovakia	2	0	0	0	0	....	....	....	....	....
2000-01	HC VSZ Kosice	Slovakia	43	5	5	10	28	3	1	0	1	2
2001-02	Kelowna Rockets	WHL	53	2	24	26	41	15	0	0	0	8
2002-03	Kelowna Rockets	WHL	65	18	53	71	86	19	2	*20	22	26
2003-04	Hershey Bears	AHL	42	3	8	11	16	....	....	....	....	....
	Reading Royals	ECHL	20	3	7	10	32	....	....	....	....	....
2004-05	Hershey Bears	AHL	1	0	0	0	2	....	....	....	....	....
	HC Kosice	Slovakia	33	3	11	14	42	10	1	2	3	24
2005-06	Lowell	AHL	59	0	8	8	61	....	....	....	....	....
	San Diego Gulls	ECHL	8	0	3	3	4	....	....	....	....	....

WHL West First All-Star Team (2003)

Traded to **Colorado** by **Nashville** for Sergei Soin, June 21, 2003. Assigned to **Kosice** (Slovakia) by **Colorado**, November 2, 2004. Signed as a free agent by **Mora** (Sweden), July 1, 2006.

SMABY, Matt (SMA-bee, MAT) T.B.

Defense. Shoots left. 6'6", 239 lbs. Born, Minneapolis, MN, October 14, 1984.
(Tampa Bay's 2nd choice, 41st overall, in 2003 Entry Draft).

			Regular Season					Playoffs				
Season	Club	League	GP	G	A	Pts	PIM	GP	G	A	Pts	PIM
2001-02	Shat.-St. Mary's	High-MN	65	7	18	25	134	....	....	....	....	....
2002-03	Shat.-St. Mary's	High-MN	57	3	20	23	114	....	....	....	....	....
2003-04	North Dakota	WCHA	39	1	6	7	81	....	....	....	....	....
2004-05	North Dakota	WCHA	44	1	2	3	86	....	....	....	....	....
2005-06	North Dakota	WCHA	46	4	15	19	*113	....	....	....	....	....

SMID, Ladislav (SHMIHD, LA-dih-slahv) EDM.

Defense. Shoots left. 6'3", 204 lbs. Born, Frydlant V Cechach, Czech., February 1, 1986.
(Anaheim's 1st choice, 9th overall, in 2004 Entry Draft).

			Regular Season					Playoffs				
Season	Club	League	GP	G	A	Pts	PIM	GP	G	A	Pts	PIM
2001-02	HC Liberec Jr.	CzRep-Jr.	17	1	3	3	10	....	....	....	....	....
2002-03	HC Liberec Jr.	CzRep-Jr.	32	1	14	15	12	8	2	1	3	31
	Liberec	CzRep	4	0	0	0	0	....	....	....	....	....
2003-04	HC Liberec Jr.	CzRep-Jr.	14	4	10	14	*38	2	1	0	1	6
	Liberec	CzRep	45	1	1	2	51	....	....	....	....	....
	Beroun	CzRep-2	....	....	....	....	....	3	1	1	2	4
2004-05	HC Liberec Jr.	CzRep-Jr.	3	0	1	1	4	....	....	....	....	....
	Liberec	CzRep	39	1	3	4	14	12	0	0	0	6
2005-06	Portland Pirates	AHL	71	3	25	28	48	16	0	1	1	16

Traded to **Edmonton** by **Anaheim** with Joffrey Lupul, a 1st round choice in 2007 Entry Draft, a 2nd round choice in 2008 Entry Draft and future considerations for Chris Pronger, July 3, 2006.

SMITH, Jordan (SMIHTH, JOHN-dan)

Defense. Shoots right. 6'2", 215 lbs. Born, Sault Ste. Marie, Ont., November 4, 1985.
(Anaheim's 2nd choice, 39th overall, in 2004 Entry Draft).

			Regular Season					Playoffs				
Season	Club	League	GP	G	A	Pts	PIM	GP	G	A	Pts	PIM
2001-02	Soo Thunderbirds	NOJHL	8	1	2	3	12	....	....	....	....	....
	Sault Ste. Marie	OHL	19	0	0	0	25	2	0	0	0	2
2002-03	Sault Ste. Marie	OHL	60	2	8	10	107	4	0	0	0	6
2003-04	Sault Ste. Marie	OHL	68	6	20	26	140	....	....	....	....	....
2004-05	Sault Ste. Marie	OHL	64	5	27	32	126	7	1	4	5	7
	Cincinnati	AHL	5	0	1	1	19	9	0	1	1	35
2005-06	Portland Pirates	AHL	55	6	8	14	145	....	....	....	....	....

OHL Second All-Star Team (2005)

• Missed remainder of 2005-06 season after suffering an eye injury in game vs. Manchester (AHL), February 24, 2006.

SMITH, Kenny (SMIHTH, KEHN-nee)

Defense. Shoots right. 6'2", 209 lbs. Born, Stoneham, MA, December 31, 1981.
(Edmonton's 4th choice, 84th overall, in 2001 Entry Draft).

			Regular Season					Playoffs				
Season	Club	League	GP	G	A	Pts	PIM	GP	G	A	Pts	PIM
1998-99	USNTDP	NAHL	29	2	5	7	32	....	....	....	....	....
99-2000	USNTDP	USHL	27	4	6	10	77	....	....	....	....	....
	USNTDP	NAHL	4	1	0	1	4	....	....	....	....	....
2000-01	Harvard Crimson	ECAC	21	0	2	2	37	....	....	....	....	....
2001-02	Harvard Crimson	ECAC	33	3	10	13	48	....	....	....	....	....
2002-03	Harvard Crimson	ECAC	33	4	11	15	52	....	....	....	....	....
2003-04	Harvard Crimson	ECAC	34	4	7	11	44	....	....	....	....	....
2004-05	Greenville Grrrowl	ECHL	64	3	6	9	68	4	0	0	0	0
	Edmonton	AHL	5	0	0	0	4	....	....	....	....	....
2005-06	Portland Pirates	AHL	48	0	8	8	29	7	0	1	1	2
	Greenville Grrrowl	ECHL	11	1	3	4	15	....	....	....	....	....

SMOLENAK, Radek (SMOH-lehn-ahk, RA-dehk) T.B.

Left wing. Shoots left. 6'2", 206 lbs. Born, Prague, Czech., December 3, 1986.
(Tampa Bay's 2nd choice, 73rd overall, in 2005 Entry Draft).

			Regular Season					Playoffs				
Season	Club	League	GP	G	A	Pts	PIM	GP	G	A	Pts	PIM
2001-02	HC Kladno U17	CzR-U17	47	29	20	49	38	....	....	....	....	....
2002-03	HC Kladno U17	CzR-U17	41	39	27	66	50	9	7	3	10	18
	HC Kladno Jr.	CzRep-Jr.	4	2	0	2	6	....	....	....	....	....
2003-04	HC Kladno Jr.	CzRep-Jr.	54	27	25	52	51	7	3	4	7	0
2004-05	Kingston	OHL	67	32	28	60	58	....	....	....	....	....
2005-06	Kingston	OHL	65	42	42	84	109	6	1	3	4	20

SMYTH, Adam (SMIHTH, A-duhm) ATL.

Right wing. Shoots right. 6'1", 225 lbs. Born, Wiarton, Ont., September 8, 1983.

			Regular Season					Playoffs				
Season	Club	League	GP	G	A	Pts	PIM	GP	G	A	Pts	PIM
2000-01	Ottawa 67's	OHL	24	2	2	4	63	....	....	....	....	....
2001-02	Ottawa 67's	OHL	50	4	3	7	205	13	3	1	4	24
2002-03	Ottawa 67's	OHL	48	6	3	9	128	15	5	3	8	29
2003-04	Ottawa 67's	OHL	2	0	2	2	8	....	....	....	....	....
	Owen Sound	OHL	48	11	11	22	152	7	1	0	1	14
	Port Huron	UHL	4	0	0	0	2	7	0	0	0	21
2004-05	Chicago Wolves	AHL	3	0	0	0	2	....	....	....	....	....
	Gwinnett	ECHL	49	6	10	16	217	8	3	2	5	28
2005-06	Chicago Wolves	AHL	2	0	0	0	11	....	....	....	....	....
	Gwinnett	ECHL	64	8	12	20	286	6	0	0	0	2

Signed as a free agent by **Atlanta**, August 9, 2005.

SNEEP, Carl (SNEEP, KARL) PIT.

Defense. Shoots right. 6'4", 210 lbs. Born, St. Louis Park, MN, November 5, 1987.
(Pittsburgh's 2nd choice, 32nd overall, in 2006 Entry Draft).

			Regular Season					Playoffs				
Season	Club	League	GP	G	A	Pts	PIM	GP	G	A	Pts	PIM
2004-05	Brainerd	High-MN	26	20	21	41	25	....	....	....	....	....
2005-06	Brainerd	High-MN	26	14	23	37	34	....	....	....	....	....
	Lincoln Stars	USHL	13	1	3	4	9	9	0	1	1	6

Signed Letter of Intent to attend **Boston College** (Hockey East) in fall of 2006.

SNELLMAN , Niko (SNEHL-mahn, NEE-koh) NSH.

Wing. Shoots left. 6'1", 191 lbs. Born, Tampere, Finland, March 12, 1988.
(Nashville's 2nd choice, 105th overall, in 2006 Entry Draft).

			Regular Season					Playoffs				
Season	Club	League	GP	G	A	Pts	PIM	GP	G	A	Pts	PIM
2004-05	Ilves Tampere U18	Fin-U18	22	5	1	6	44	5	0	0	0	2
2005-06	Ilves Tampere U18	Fin-U18	6	3	8	11	28	6	2	5	7	64
	Ilves Tampere Jr.	Fin-Jr.	23	4	4	8	74	3	0	0	0	4

SNOW, Aaron (SNOH, Air-uhn) DAL.

Left wing. Shoots left. 6', 199 lbs. Born, Windsor, Ont., May 20, 1988.
(Dallas' 2nd choice, 90th overall, in 2006 Entry Draft).

			Regular Season					Playoffs				
Season	Club	League	GP	G	A	Pts	PIM	GP	G	A	Pts	PIM
2003-04	Tecumseh Chiefs	OJHL-B	53	19	21	40	64	....	....	....	....	....
2004-05	Brampton	OHL	61	8	7	15	35	6	1	0	1	2
2005-06	Brampton	OHL	68	30	38	68	107	11	4	4	8	22

SOBOTKA, Vladimir (soh-BAWT-kah, vla-DIH-meer) BOS.

Center. Shoots left. 5'10", 183 lbs. Born, Trebic, Czech., July 2, 1987.
(Boston's 5th choice, 106th overall, in 2005 Entry Draft).

			Regular Season					Playoffs				
Season	Club	League	GP	G	A	Pts	PIM	GP	G	A	Pts	PIM
2002-03	Slavia U17	CzR-U17	46	16	24	40	48	8	1	1	2	29
2003-04	Slavia U17	CzR-U17	35	24	41	65	109	7	7	12	19	8
	HC Slavia Praha Jr.	CzRep-Jr.	18	6	6	12	16	....	....	....	....	....
	HC Slavia Praha	CzRep	1	0	0	0	0	....	....	....	....	....
2004-05	HC Slavia Praha Jr.	CzRep-Jr.	27	12	21	33	93	....	....	....	....	....
	HC Slavia Praha	CzRep	18	0	1	1	8	....	....	....	....	....
	Havl. Brod	CzRep-3	7	3	0	3	31	7	1	5	6	0
2005-06	HC Slavia Praha Jr.	CzRep-Jr.	8	10	4	14	42	....	....	....	....	....
	HC Slavia Praha	CzRep	33	1	9	10	28	11	2	3	5	10

SODERBERG, Carl (SOH-dehr-buhrg, KARL) ST.L.

Center. Shoots left. 6'3", 198 lbs. Born, Malmo, Sweden, October 12, 1985.
(St. Louis' 2nd choice, 49th overall, in 2004 Entry Draft).

			Regular Season					Playoffs				
Season	Club	League	GP	G	A	Pts	PIM	GP	G	A	Pts	PIM
2000-01	Skane	Exhib.	8	1	2	3	2	....	....	....	....	....
	Malmo U18	Swe-U18	3	1	1	2	0	....	....	....	....	....
2001-02	Malmo U18	Swe-U18	13	9	20	29	18	....	....	....	....	....
	Malmo Jr.	Swe-Jr.	4	0	2	2	2	7	0	2	2	4
2002-03	Malmo U18	Swe-U18	4	6	3	9	25	....	....	....	....	....
	Malmo Jr.	Swe-Jr.	28	17	18	35	22	6	2	4	6	8
2003-04	Malmo	Sweden	24	1	1	2	8	....	....	....	....	....
	Malmo U18	Swe-U18	27	23	25	48	30	6	1	2	3	10
	Malmo	Sweden-Q	8	1	1	2	4	....	....	....	....	....
2004-05	Morrums GoIS IK	Sweden-2	14	5	6	11	8	....	....	....	....	....
	Malmo Jr.	Swe-Jr.	12	13	6	19	43	3	2	1	3	12
	Malmo	Sweden	38	0	5	5	8	....	....	....	....	....
	Malmo	Sweden-Q	7	0	0	0	0	....	....	....	....	....
2005-06	Malmo	Sweden-2	49	20	27	47	47	....	....	....	....	....

SOIN, Sergei (SOY-ihn, SAIR-gay) NSH.

Center/Left wing. Shoots left. 6', 175 lbs. Born, Moscow, USSR, March 31, 1982.
(Colorado's 3rd choice, 50th overall, in 2000 Entry Draft).

			Regular Season					Playoffs				
Season	Club	League	GP	G	A	Pts	PIM	GP	G	A	Pts	PIM
1997-98	Krylja Sovetov 2	Russia-3	2	0	0	0	0	....	....	....	....	....
1998-99	Krylja Sovetov	Russia	34	1	4	5	12	....	....	....	....	....
99-2000	Krylja Sovetov 2	Russia-3	8	2	3	5	12	....	....	....	....	....
	Krylja Sovetov	Russia-2	32	8	8	16	28	14	0	2	2	6
2000-01	Krylja Sovetov 2	Russia-3	8	2	3	5	12	....	....	....	....	....
	Krylja Sovetov	Russia-2	19	6	3	9	8	11	2	2	4	2
2001-02	Krylja Sovetov 2	Russia-3	5	2	6	8	20	....	....	....	....	....
	Krylja Sovetov	Russia	41	5	7	12	8	....	....	....	....	....
2002-03	Krylja Sovetov	Russia	49	8	6	14	40	....	....	....	....	....
2003-04	CSKA Moscow	Russia	49	1	6	7	32	....	....	....	....	....
2004-05	CSKA Moscow	Russia	19	3	3	6	10	....	....	....	....	....
2005-06	Cherepovets	Russia	48	5	12	17	36	4	1	1	2	0

Traded to **Nashville** by **Colorado** for Tomas Slovak, June 21, 2003.

SOMERVUORI, Eero (soh-muhr-VOH-ree, AIR-oh) T.B.

Right wing. Shoots right. 5'10", 190 lbs. Born, Jarvenpaa, Finland, February 7, 1979.
(Tampa Bay's 9th choice, 170th overall, in 1997 Entry Draft).

			Regular Season					Playoffs				
Season	Club	League	GP	G	A	Pts	PIM	GP	G	A	Pts	PIM
1994-95	Jokerit U18	Fin-U18	15	8	10	18	4	....	....	....	....	....
	Jokerit Helsinki Jr.	Fin-Jr.	11	1	2	3	2	....	....	....	....	....
1995-96	Jokerit Helsinki Jr.	Fin-Jr.	28	14	12	26	10	9	4	1	5	4
	Jokerit U18	Fin-U18	13	10	13	23	6	....	....	....	....	....
	Haukat Jarvenpaa	Finland-2	1	0	0	0	0	....	....	....	....	....
	Jokerit Helsinki	Finland	6	1	2	3	0	....	....	....	....	....
1996-97	Jokerit U18	Fin-U18	1	0	0	0	2	....	....	....	....	....
	Jokerit Helsinki Jr.	Fin-Jr.	28	20	19	39	30	5	3	0	3	4
	Jokerit Helsinki	EuroHL	3	0	0	0	0	2	2	0	0	0
	Jokerit Helsinki	Finland	35	1	1	2	2	5	0	0	0	0
1997-98	Jokerit Helsinki Jr.	Fin-Jr.	14	4	8	12	2	4	0	2	2	4
	Jokerit Helsinki	EuroHL	5	0	0	0	0	....	....	....	....	....
	Jokerit Helsinki	Finland	42	3	7	10	12	8	2	1	3	6
1998-99	Jokerit Helsinki Jr.	Fin-Jr.	4	1	1	2	2	4	3	0	3	2
	Jokerit Helsinki	EuroHL	6	0	0	0	0	1	0	0	0	0
	Jokerit Helsinki	Finland	50	7	8	15	24	3	1	0	1	6
99-2000	Jokerit Helsinki	Finland	54	6	6	12	10	11	1	0	1	0
2000-01	HPK Hameenlinna	Finland	56	14	6	20	35	....	....	....	....	....
2001-02	HPK Hameenlinna	Finland	56	25	23	48	34	8	2	2	4	6
2002-03	HPK Hameenlinna	Finland	56	21	24	45	42	13	2	3	5	0
2003-04	Hamilton Bulldogs	AHL	79	19	14	33	14	10	2	3	5	0
2004-05	Karpat Oulu	Finland	56	16	26	42	14	12	2	1	3	4
2005-06	HC Ambri-Piotta	Swiss	21	5	11	16	2	....	....	....	....	....

Signed as a free agent by **Oulu** (Finland), August 1, 2004.

SOUTHERN, Dirk (SUH-thuhrn, DUHRK) ANA.

Center. Shoots right. 6', 177 lbs. Born, Winnipeg, Man., August 9, 1983.
(Anaheim's 7th choice, 218th overall, in 2003 Entry Draft).

			Regular Season					Playoffs				
Season	Club	League	GP	G	A	Pts	PIM	GP	G	A	Pts	PIM
2001-02	Lincoln Stars	USHL	60	22	36	58	46	4	1	1	2	2
2002-03	Northern Mich.	CCHA	41	11	22	33	55	....	....	....	....	....
2003-04	Northern Mich.	CCHA	37	10	15	25	32	....	....	....	....	....
2004-05	Northern Mich.	CCHA	32	11	19	30	28	....	....	....	....	....
2005-06	Northern Mich.	CCHA	39	11	23	34	34	....	....	....	....	....

CCHA All-Rookie Team (2003)

SPANG, Dan (SPANG, DAN) S.J.

Defense. Shoots left. 6', 205 lbs. Born, Winchester, MA, August 18, 1983.
(San Jose's 2nd choice, 52nd overall, in 2002 Entry Draft).

			Regular Season					Playoffs				
Season	Club	League	GP	G	A	Pts	PIM	GP	G	A	Pts	PIM
2000-01	Winchester High	High-MA	24	8	37	45	14	....	....	....	....	....
2001-02	Winchester High	High-MA	6	9	8	17	14	....	....	....	....	....
2002-03	Boston University	H-East	27	3	6	9	14	....	....	....	....	....
2003-04	Boston University	H-East	38	5	9	14	12	....	....	....	....	....
2004-05	Boston University	H-East	41	3	13	16	22	....	....	....	....	....
2005-06	Boston University	H-East	40	9	22	31	14	....	....	....	....	....
	Cleveland Barons	AHL	8	0	0	0	8	....	....	....	....	....

Hockey East First All-Star Team (2006) • NCAA East First All-American Team (2006)

• Missed majority of 2001-02 season recovering from head injuries suffered in automobile accident, October, 2001.

SPRUKTS, Janis (SPRUKTS, YAN-ish) FLA.

Center. Shoots left. 6'3", 224 lbs. Born, Riga, Latvia, January 31, 1982.
(Florida's 7th choice, 234th overall, in 2000 Entry Draft).

			Regular Season					Playoffs				
Season	Club	League	GP	G	A	Pts	PIM	GP	G	A	Pts	PIM
99-2000	Lukko Rauma Jr.	Fin-Jr.	26	2	5	7	6	3	0	0	0	0
	HC Essamika Jr.	EEHL-2	2	4	4	8	0	....	....	....	....	....
2000-01	Lukko Rauma Jr.	Fin-Jr.	36	15	22	37	24	3	0	0	0	0
	Lukko Rauma	Finland	9	0	0	0	2	....	....	....	....	....
2001-02	Acadie-Bathurst	QMJHL	63	35	44	79	46	16	14	8	22	12
2002-03	Sport Vaasa	Finland-2	21	5	6	11	8	....	....	....	....	....
	Acadie-Bathurst	QMJHL	30	9	29	38	12	11	3	5	8	0
2003-04	ASK Ogre	Latvia	5	2	4	6	0	....	....	....	....	....
	Odense IK	Denmark	2	0	1	1	2	....	....	....	....	....
2004-05	HK Riga 2000	BelOpen	21	7	9	16	10	3	0	0	0	2
	HK Riga 2000	Latvia	3	2	3	5	0	9	3	4	7	2
2005-06	HPK Hameenlinna	Finland	35	18	10	28	14	13	3	4	7	14

• Released by **Vaasa** (Finland-2) and returned to **Acadie-Bathurst** (QMJHL), January 3, 2003.

SPRUNGER, Julien (SRUHN-guhr, JEW-lee-ehn) MIN.

Right wing. Shoots right. 6'4", 197 lbs. Born, Fribourg, Switz., January 4, 1986.
(Minnesota's 7th choice, 117th overall, in 2004 Entry Draft).

			Regular Season					Playoffs				
Season	Club	League	GP	G	A	Pts	PIM	GP	G	A	Pts	PIM
2002-03	Fribourg Jr.	Swiss-Jr.	24	21	19	40	32	....	....	....	....	....
	Fribourg	Swiss	2	0	0	0	0	....	....	....	....	....
	HC Dudingen	Swiss-3	9	7	1	8	....	2	1	1	2	....
2003-04	Fribourg	Swiss	42	2	3	5	14	4	0	0	0	4
2004-05	Fribourg Jr.	Swiss-Jr.	4	3	4	7	4	....	....	....	....	....
	Chaux-de-Fonds	Swiss-2	1	0	0	0	0	....	....	....	....	....
	Fribourg	Swiss	41	9	7	16	35	11	2	1	3	14
2005-06	Fribourg Jr.	Swiss-Jr.	2	2	1	3	6	....	....	....	....	....
	Fribourg	Swiss	38	19	14	33	36	10	5	2	7	25
	Fribourg	Swiss-Q	....	....	....	....	....	5	2	1	3	4

SPURGEON, Tyler (SPUHR-juhn, TIGH-luhr) EDM.

Center. Shoots left. 5'11", 188 lbs. Born, Edmonton, Alta., April 10, 1986.
(Edmonton's 9th choice, 242nd overall, in 2004 Entry Draft).

			Regular Season					Playoffs				
Season	Club	League	GP	G	A	Pts	PIM	GP	G	A	Pts	PIM
2001-02	Edmonton MLAC	AMHL	35	39	36	75	12	....	....	....	....	....
	Kelowna Rockets	WHL	2	0	1	1	0	....	....	....	....	....
2002-03	Kelowna Rockets	WHL	50	7	6	13	21	19	2	5	7	6
2003-04	Kelowna Rockets	WHL	49	8	16	24	24	17	4	5	9	9
2004-05	Kelowna Rockets	WHL	72	21	41	62	32	24	11	6	17	12
2005-06	Kelowna Rockets	WHL	39	7	17	24	22	12	0	3	3	14

STAAL, Jordan (STAHL, JOHR-dahn) PIT.

Center. Shoots left. 6'4", 215 lbs. Born, Thunder Bay, Ont., September 10, 1988.
(Pittsburgh's 1st choice, 2nd overall, in 2006 Entry Draft).

			Regular Season					Playoffs				
Season	Club	League	GP	G	A	Pts	PIM	GP	G	A	Pts	PIM
2004-05	Peterborough	OHL	66	9	19	28	29	14	5	5	10	16
2005-06	Peterborough	OHL	68	28	40	68	69	19	10	6	16	16

STAAL, Marc (STAHL, MAHRK) NYR

Defense. Shoots left. 6'4", 204 lbs. Born, Thunder Bay, Ont., January 13, 1987.
(NY Rangers' 1st choice, 12th overall, in 2005 Entry Draft).

			Regular Season					Playoffs				
Season	Club	League	GP	G	A	Pts	PIM	GP	G	A	Pts	PIM
2003-04	Sudbury Wolves	OHL	61	1	13	14	34	7	1	2	3	2
2004-05	Sudbury Wolves	OHL	65	6	20	26	53	12	0	4	4	15
2005-06	Sudbury Wolves	OHL	57	11	38	49	60	10	0	8	8	8
	Hartford Wolf Pack	AHL	....	....	....	....	....	12	0	2	2	8

OHL First All-Star Team (2006)

STAFFORD, Drew (STA-fuhrd, DROO) BUF.

Right wing. Shoots right. 6'1", 202 lbs. Born, Milwaukee, WI, October 30, 1985.
(Buffalo's 1st choice, 13th overall, in 2004 Entry Draft).

			Regular Season					Playoffs				
Season	Club	League	GP	G	A	Pts	PIM	GP	G	A	Pts	PIM
2001-02	Shat.-St. Mary's	High-MN	45	35	53	88	30	....	....	....	....	....
2002-03	Shat.-St. Mary's	High-MN	65	49	67	116	....	....	....	....	....	....
2003-04	North Dakota	WCHA	36	11	21	32	30	....	....	....	....	....
2004-05	North Dakota	WCHA	42	13	25	38	34	....	....	....	....	....
2005-06	North Dakota	WCHA	42	24	24	48	63	....	....	....	....	....

STAFFORD, Garrett (STA-fuhrd, GAIR-reht) S.J.

Defense. Shoots right. 6', 190 lbs. Born, Los Angeles, CA, January 28, 1980.

			Regular Season					Playoffs				
Season	Club	League	GP	G	A	Pts	PIM	GP	G	A	Pts	PIM
1996-97	Des Moines	USHL	37	1	10	11	40	5	0	0	0	0
1997-98	Des Moines	USHL	53	6	17	23	89	12	1	3	4	42
1998-99	Des Moines	USHL	56	8	33	41	54	13	2	2	4	18
99-2000	New Hampshire	H-East	38	3	9	12	28	....	....	....	....	....
2000-01	New Hampshire	H-East	37	5	21	26	44	....	....	....	....	....
2001-02	New Hampshire	H-East	36	5	22	27	42	....	....	....	....	....
2002-03	New Hampshire	H-East	23	1	15	16	24	....	....	....	....	....
2003-04	Cleveland Barons	AHL	73	12	34	46	71	6	0	0	0	6
2004-05	Cleveland Barons	AHL	68	6	18	24	55	....	....	....	....	....
2005-06	Cleveland Barons	AHL	80	11	28	39	86	....	....	....	....	....

AHL All-Rookie Team (2004) • AHL Second All-Star Team (2004)

Signed as a free agent by **Cleveland** (AHL), October 10, 2003. Signed as a free agent by **San Jose**, December 9, 2003.

STALBERG, Viktor (STAHL-buhrg, VIHK-tohr) TOR.

Left wing. Shoots left. 6'3", 191 lbs. Born, Stockholm, Sweden, January 17, 1986.
(Toronto's 5th choice, 161st overall, in 2006 Entry Draft).

			Regular Season					Playoffs				
Season	Club	League	GP	G	A	Pts	PIM	GP	G	A	Pts	PIM
2003-04	Molndal U18	Swe-U18	13	14	13	27	....	....	....	....	....	....
	Molndal Jr.	Swe-Jr.	18	25	10	35	....	....	....	....	....	....
	IF Molndal Hockey	Sweden-4	....	11	9	20	....	....	....	....	....	....
2004-05	Molndal Jr.	Swe-Jr.	11	16	7	23	....	....	....	....	....	....
	IF Molndal Hockey	Sweden-3	29	6	9	15	54	....	....	....	....	....
2005-06	Frolunda Jr.	Swe-Jr.	41	27	26	53	89	7	6	5	11	6

STAMLER, Bretton (STAM-lehr, BREH-tuhn) DET.

Defense. Shoots right. 6'1", 201 lbs. Born, Calgary, Alta., March 10, 1987.
(Detroit's 9th choice, 214th overall, in 2005 Entry Draft).

			Regular Season					Playoffs				
Season	Club	League	GP	G	A	Pts	PIM	GP	G	A	Pts	PIM
2002-03	Sherwood Park	AMHL	34	3	8	11	22	....	....	....	....	....
2003-04	Seattle	WHL	61	0	9	9	27	....	....	....	....	....
2004-05	Seattle	WHL	72	4	9	13	106	1	0	0	0	0
2005-06	Seattle	WHL	56	5	10	15	102	7	0	4	4	8

STARKOV, Kirill (stahr-KAWF, kih-RIHL) **CBJ**

Center. Shoots left. 6', 194 lbs. Born, Yekateringburg, USSR, March 31, 1987.
(Columbus' 7th choice, 189th overall, in 2005 Entry Draft).

			Regular Season					Playoffs				
Season	Club	League	GP	G	A	Pts	PIM	GP	G	A	Pts	PIM
2002-03	Esbjerg Oilers	Denmark	28	2	4	6	6	14	0	0	0	0
2003-04	V.Frolunda U18	Swe-U18	9	6	6	12	2	7	2	3	5	2
	V.Frolunda Jr.	Swe-Jr.	25	3	10	13	4	5	2	0	2	0
2004-05	Frolunda U18	Swe-U18	1	0	0	0	4	3	2	1	3	0
	Frolunda Jr.	Swe-Jr.	34	18	12	30	6	6	2	2	4	2
2005-06	Frolunda Jr.	Swe-Jr.	19	8	16	24	16	6	3	4	7	2
	Frolunda	Sweden	34	1	2	3	4	....	....	....	....	....

STASTNY, Paul (STAS-nee, PAWL) **COL.**

Center. Shoots left. 6', 201 lbs. Born, Quebec City, Que., December 27, 1985.
(Colorado's 2nd choice, 44th overall, in 2005 Entry Draft).

			Regular Season					Playoffs				
Season	Club	League	GP	G	A	Pts	PIM	GP	G	A	Pts	PIM
2003-04	River City Lancers	USHL	56	30	*47	77	46	3	1	2	3	0
2004-05	U. of Denver	WCHA	42	17	28	45	30	....	....	....	....	....
2005-06	U. of Denver	WCHA	39	19	34	53	79	....	....	....	....	....

WCHA All-Rookie Team (2005) • WCHA Rookie of the Year (2005) • NCAA Championship All-Tournament Team (2005) • WCHA First All-Star Team (2006) • NCAA West Second All-American Team (2006)

STASYUK, Denis (stah-S'YUHK, DEH-nihs) **FLA.**

Center. Shoots left. 6'1", 165 lbs. Born, Novokuznetsk, USSR, September 2, 1985.
(Florida's 9th choice, 171st overall, in 2003 Entry Draft).

			Regular Season					Playoffs				
Season	Club	League	GP	G	A	Pts	PIM	GP	G	A	Pts	PIM
2002-03	Novokuznetsk 2	Russia-3	STATISTICS NOT AVAILABLE									
	Novokuznetsk	Russia	11	1	0	1	0	....	....	....	....	....
2003-04	Novokuznetsk	Russia	5	0	0	0	0	....	....	....	....	....
	Novokuznetsk 2	Russia-3	STATISTICS NOT AVAILABLE									
2004-05	Amur Khabarovsk	Russia-2	44	11	10	21	12	10	1	2	3	6
2005-06	Novokuznetsk	Russia	41	7	2	9	18	3	0	0	0	0

STAUBITZ, Brad (STAW-bihtz, BRAD) **S.J.**

Defense. Shoots right. 6'1", 208 lbs. Born, Bright's Grove, Ont., July 28, 1984.

			Regular Season					Playoffs				
Season	Club	League	GP	G	A	Pts	PIM	GP	G	A	Pts	PIM
2001-02	Sault Ste. Marie	OHL	45	0	3	3	46	3	0	0	0	2
2002-03	Sault Ste. Marie	OHL	55	2	6	8	116	4	0	0	0	7
2003-04	Sault Ste. Marie	OHL	66	6	18	24	140	....	....	....	....	....
2004-05	Sault Ste. Marie	OHL	40	2	11	13	101	....	....	....	....	....
	Ottawa 67's	OHL	30	5	8	13	80	21	4	16	20	70
2005-06	Cleveland Barons	AHL	71	0	6	6	245	....	....	....	....	....

Signed as a free agent by **San Jose**, September 19, 2005.

STEBER, Jan (STEH-buhr, YAHN) **TOR.**

Left wing. Shoots right. 6'3", 202 lbs. Born, Ostrava, Czech., October 19, 1985.
(Toronto's 5th choice, 252nd overall, in 2004 Entry Draft).

			Regular Season					Playoffs				
Season	Club	League	GP	G	A	Pts	PIM	GP	G	A	Pts	PIM
2000-01	HC Trinec Jr.	CzRep-Jr.	44	16	11	27	12	8	0	1	1	27
2001-02	HC Trinec Jr.	CzRep-Jr.	48	18	14	32	16	6	2	2	4	2
2002-03	HC Trinec Jr.	CzRep-Jr.	31	10	8	18	29	3	1	1	2	2
2003-04	Halifax	QMJHL	69	16	15	31	45	....	....	....	....	....
2004-05	Halifax	QMJHL	63	17	17	34	58	13	3	5	8	8
2005-06	Pensacola	ECHL	49	11	8	19	24	....	....	....	....	....

STEEVES, Ryan (STEEVZ, RIGH-uhn) **COL.**

Center/Left wing. Shoots left. 6', 195 lbs. Born, Ottawa, Ont., December 31, 1982.
(Colorado's 8th choice, 227th overall, in 2002 Entry Draft).

			Regular Season					Playoffs				
Season	Club	League	GP	G	A	Pts	PIM	GP	G	A	Pts	PIM
1998-99	Ott. Jr. Senators	CJHL	51	17	12	29	45	....	....	....	....	....
99-2000	Ott. Jr. Senators	CJHL	55	36	39	75	87	....	....	....	....	....
2000-01	Yale	ECAC	23	3	2	5	10	....	....	....	....	....
2001-02	Yale	ECAC	31	9	13	22	20	....	....	....	....	....
2002-03	Yale	ECAC	32	15	23	38	36	....	....	....	....	....
2003-04	Yale	ECAC	31	10	16	26	44	....	....	....	....	....
2004-05	Hershey Bears	AHL	75	6	5	11	24	....	....	....	....	....
2005-06	Lowell	AHL	69	10	7	17	39	....	....	....	....	....

STEFANISHION, Matt (STEH-fan-IH-shuhn, MAT) **WSH.**

Right wing. Shoots right. 6'3", 210 lbs. Born, Daysland, Alta., October 5, 1983.

			Regular Season					Playoffs				
Season	Club	League	GP	G	A	Pts	PIM	GP	G	A	Pts	PIM
2002-03	Melville	SJHL	60	21	30	51	235	....	....	....	....	....
2003-04	Estevan Bruins	SJHL	52	32	45	77	175	....	....	....	....	....
2004-05	Ferris State	CCHA	34	12	9	21	75	....	....	....	....	....
2005-06	Ferris State	CCHA	23	9	4	13	50	....	....	....	....	....

Signed as a free agent by **Washington**, April 1, 2006.

STEHLIK, Richard (SHTEH-lihk, RIH-chuhrd) **NSH.**

Defense. Shoots left. 6'4", 242 lbs. Born, Skalica, Czech., June 22, 1984.
(Nashville's 5th choice, 76th overall, in 2003 Entry Draft).

			Regular Season					Playoffs				
Season	Club	League	GP	G	A	Pts	PIM	GP	G	A	Pts	PIM
99-2000	HK 36 Skalica Jr.	Slovak-Jr.	50	10	5	15	....	....	....	....	....	....
2000-01	HK 36 Skalica	Slovakia	45	1	1	2	14	3	0	0	0	2
2001-02	HK 36 Skalica	Slovakia	35	1	0	1	12	....	....	....	....	....
2002-03	Sherbrooke	QMJHL	43	8	16	24	105	12	1	5	6	20
2003-04	Lewiston	QMJHL	44	11	25	36	109	7	0	1	1	12
2004-05	HK 36 Skalica	Slovakia	40	8	3	11	28	....	....	....	....	....
	Dukla Trencin	Slovakia	13	1	5	6	33	12	3	3	6	62
2005-06	HC Sparta Praha	CzRep	42	3	7	10	79	17	0	2	2	18

STEPHENSON, Logan (STEE-vehn-suhn, LOH-guhn) **PHX.**

Defense. Shoots left. 6'3", 197 lbs. Born, Saskatoon, Sask., February 19, 1986.
(Phoenix's 2nd choice, 35th overall, in 2004 Entry Draft).

			Regular Season					Playoffs				
Season	Club	League	GP	G	A	Pts	PIM	GP	G	A	Pts	PIM
2001-02	Notre Dame	SMHL	37	4	2	6	74	....	....	....	....	....
	Tri-City Americans	WHL	....	....	....	....	....	3	0	0	0	0
2002-03	Tri-City Americans	WHL	50	0	6	6	121	....	....	....	....	....
2003-04	Tri-City Americans	WHL	69	3	8	11	112	11	1	1	2	10
2004-05	Tri-City Americans	WHL	59	6	9	15	86	5	0	0	0	2
2005-06	Tri-City Americans	WHL	71	10	43	53	162	5	1	0	1	18

WHL West Second All-Star Team (2006)

STEPHENSON, Shay (STEE-vehn-suhn, SHAY) **L.A.**

Left wing. Shoots left. 6'4", 200 lbs. Born, Outlook, Sask., September 13, 1983.
(Carolina's 7th choice, 198th overall, in 2003 Entry Draft).

			Regular Season					Playoffs				
Season	Club	League	GP	G	A	Pts	PIM	GP	G	A	Pts	PIM
99-2000	Notre Dame	SMHL	42	23	7	30	46	....	....	....	....	....
2000-01	Red Deer Rebels	WHL	44	1	4	5	30	22	0	0	0	15
2001-02	Red Deer Rebels	WHL	59	9	10	19	55	23	0	3	3	14
2002-03	Red Deer Rebels	WHL	67	17	15	32	84	23	6	5	11	33
2003-04	Red Deer Rebels	WHL	60	11	19	30	34	19	5	7	12	16
2004-05	Sundsvall	Sweden-2	30	11	9	20	66	....	....	....	....	....
2005-06	Manchester	AHL	6	0	0	0	4	....	....	....	....	....
	Reading Royals	ECHL	62	19	22	41	42	4	0	2	2	8

• Re-entered NHL Entry Draft. Originally Edmonton's 11th choice, 278th overall, in 2001 Entry Draft.

Signed as a free agent by **Sundsvall** (Sweden-2), August 25, 2004. Signed as a free agent by **Los Angeles**, August 17, 2005.

STEPP, Joel (STEHP, JOHL)

Center. Shoots left. 6', 215 lbs. Born, Estevan, Sask., February 11, 1983.
(Anaheim's 3rd choice, 69th overall, in 2001 Entry Draft).

			Regular Season					Playoffs				
Season	Club	League	GP	G	A	Pts	PIM	GP	G	A	Pts	PIM
1998-99	Estevan	SMBHL	60	65	70	135	120	....	....	....	....	....
	Red Deer Rebels	WHL	2	0	0	0	0	....	....	....	....	....
99-2000	Red Deer Rebels	WHL	65	11	13	24	59	4	1	0	1	8
2000-01	Red Deer Rebels	WHL	70	24	13	37	89	22	6	3	9	24
2001-02	Red Deer Rebels	WHL	70	27	26	53	59	23	11	11	22	24
2002-03	Red Deer Rebels	WHL	24	4	11	15	18	23	6	7	13	26
2003-04	Cincinnati	AHL	65	7	7	14	28	9	1	1	2	2
2004-05	San Diego Gulls	ECHL	12	7	0	7	10	....	....	....	....	....
	Cincinnati	AHL	63	3	9	12	23	12	1	0	1	8
2005-06	Portland Pirates	AHL	17	2	1	3	21	....	....	....	....	....
	Augusta Lynx	ECHL	38	13	26	39	26	....	....	....	....	....
	Chicago Wolves	AHL	1	0	0	0	0	....	....	....	....	....
	Gwinnett	ECHL	16	3	12	15	10	9	4	5	9	4

• Missed majority of 2002-03 season recovering from wrist surgery, September 12, 2002. Traded to **Atlanta** by **Anaheim** for Jani Hurme, March 1, 2006.

STERLING, Brett (STUHR-lihng, BRET) **ATL.**

Left wing. Shoots left. 5'7", 185 lbs. Born, Los Angeles, CA, April 24, 1984.
(Atlanta's 5th choice, 145th overall, in 2003 Entry Draft).

			Regular Season					Playoffs				
Season	Club	League	GP	G	A	Pts	PIM	GP	G	A	Pts	PIM
99-2000	L.A. Jr. Kings	SCAHA	35	45	25	70	....	....	....	....	....	....
2000-01	USNTDP	U-17	13	....	....	....	....	....	....	....	....	....
	USNTDP	NAHL	47	29	15	44	72	....	....	....	....	....
2001-02	USNTDP	U-18	31	21	15	36	18	....	....	....	....	....
	USNTDP	USHL	10	6	3	9	8	....	....	....	....	....
	USNTDP	NAHL	9	2	1	3	10	....	....	....	....	....
2002-03	Colorado College	WCHA	36	27	11	38	30	....	....	....	....	....
2003-04	Colorado College	WCHA	30	16	12	28	40	....	....	....	....	....
2004-05	Colorado College	WCHA	43	*34	29	63	74	....	....	....	....	....
2005-06	Colorado College	WCHA	42	31	24	55	66	....	....	....	....	....

WCHA All-Rookie Team (2003) • WCHA First All-Star Team (2005, 2006) • NCAA West First All-American Team (2005, 2006)

STEWART, Chris (STEW-ahrt, KRIHS) **COL.**

Right wing. Shoots right. 6'1", 228 lbs. Born, Toronto, Ont., October 30, 1987.
(Colorado's 1st choice, 18th overall, in 2006 Entry Draft).

			Regular Season					Playoffs				
Season	Club	League	GP	G	A	Pts	PIM	GP	G	A	Pts	PIM
2004-05	Kingston	OHL	64	18	12	30	45	....	....	....	....	....
2005-06	Kingston	OHL	62	37	50	87	118	6	2	0	2	13

STEWART, Greg (STEW-ahrt, GREHG) **MTL.**

Left wing. Shoots left. 6'2", 197 lbs. Born, Kitchener, Ont., May 21, 1986.
(Montreal's 7th choice, 246th overall, in 2004 Entry Draft).

			Regular Season					Playoffs				
Season	Club	League	GP	G	A	Pts	PIM	GP	G	A	Pts	PIM
2003-04	Peterborough	OHL	58	4	6	10	76	....	....	....	....	....
2004-05	Peterborough	OHL	68	16	18	34	111	14	3	3	6	20
2005-06	Peterborough	OHL	60	24	15	39	83	19	1	6	7	30

STOA, Ryan (STOH-ah, RIGH-uhn) **COL.**

Center. Shoots left. 6'3", 200 lbs. Born, Bloomington, MN, April 13, 1987.
(Colorado's 1st choice, 34th overall, in 2005 Entry Draft).

			Regular Season					Playoffs				
Season	Club	League	GP	G	A	Pts	PIM	GP	G	A	Pts	PIM
2003-04	USNTDP	U-17	18	9	8	17	....	....	....	....	....	....
	USNTDP	NAHL	42	10	12	22	26	7	7	1	8	2
2004-05	USNTDP	U-18	23	4	11	15	16	....	....	....	....	....
	USNTDP	NAHL	15	10	13	23	20	....	....	....	....	....
2005-06	U. of Minnesota	WCHA	41	10	15	25	43	....	....	....	....	....

STOESZ, Myles (STOHZ, MIGH-uhls) **ATL.**

Right wing. Shoots right. 6'2", 210 lbs. Born, Steinbach, Man., February 15, 1987.
(Atlanta's 8th choice, 207th overall, in 2005 Entry Draft).

			Regular Season					Playoffs				
Season	Club	League	GP	G	A	Pts	PIM	GP	G	A	Pts	PIM
2003-04	Spokane Chiefs	WHL	43	1	1	2	133	0	0	0	0	0
2004-05	Spokane Chiefs	WHL	67	1	8	9	238	....	....	....	....	....
2005-06	Spokane Chiefs	WHL	56	0	2	2	260	....	....	....	....	....

STOKES, Ryan (STOHKS, RIGH-uhn) **MIN.**

Defense. Shoots left. 6'4", 220 lbs. Born, Sarnia, Ont., June 23, 1983.

			Regular Season					Playoffs				
Season	Club	League	GP	G	A	Pts	PIM	GP	G	A	Pts	PIM
2001-02	Barrie Colts	OHL	53	0	5	5	31	20	0	0	0	16
2002-03	Mississauga	OHL	59	2	7	9	139	5	0	1	1	22
2003-04	Mississauga	OHL	66	4	20	24	179	24	2	9	11	74
2004-05	Houston Aeros	AHL	7	0	0	0	7	....	....	....	....	....
	Pensacola	ECHL	59	1	15	16	119	....	....	....	....	....
2005-06	Houston Aeros	AHL	75	2	3	5	164	6	0	1	1	10

Signed as a free agent by **Minnesota**, May 25, 2004.

STOLYAROV, Gennady (stohl-yah-RAWF, gehn-AH-dee) **DET.**

Right wing. Shoots left. 6'4", 187 lbs. Born, Moscow, USSR, August 20, 1986.
(Detroit's 7th choice, 257th overall, in 2004 Entry Draft).

			Regular Season					Playoffs				
Season	Club	League	GP	G	A	Pts	PIM	GP	G	A	Pts	PIM
2003-04	Dyn'o Moscow 2	Russia-3	STATISTICS NOT AVAILABLE									
	THK Tver	Russia-2	24	3	1	4	4	....	....	....	....	....
2004-05	Vityaz Chekhov	Russia-2	25	0	1	1	2	....	....	....	....	....
2005-06	Kapitan Stupino	Russia-2	17	3	5	8	20	5	1	2	3	36
	Dynamo Moscow	Russia	12	0	0	0	4	3	0	1	1	0

STONE, Ryan (STOHN, RIGH-uhn) **PIT.**

Center. Shoots left. 6'2", 200 lbs. Born, Calgary, Alta., March 20, 1985.
(Pittsburgh's 2nd choice, 32nd overall, in 2003 Entry Draft).

			Regular Season					Playoffs				
Season	Club	League	GP	G	A	Pts	PIM	GP	G	A	Pts	PIM
2000-01	Cgy. North Stars	AMHL	34	37	28	55	90	....	....	....	....	....
2001-02	Brandon	WHL	65	11	27	38	128	19	0	3	3	39
2002-03	Brandon	WHL	54	14	31	45	158	12	4	2	6	20
2003-04	Brandon	WHL	50	20	38	58	125	11	1	3	4	24
2004-05	Brandon	WHL	70	33	*66	99	127	24	4	*23	27	48
2005-06	Wilkes-Barre	AHL	75	14	22	36	109	11	4	7	11	12

WHL East First All-Star Team (2005)

STONER, Clayton (STOH-nuhr, KLAY-tuhn) **MIN.**

Defense. Shoots left. 6'3", 215 lbs. Born, Port McNeill, B.C., February 19, 1985.
(Minnesota's 4th choice, 79th overall, in 2004 Entry Draft).

			Regular Season					Playoffs				
Season	Club	League	GP	G	A	Pts	PIM	GP	G	A	Pts	PIM
2000-01	Campbell River	VIJHL	47	4	16	20	57	....	....	....	....	....
2001-02	Campbell River	VIJHL	42	12	35	47	199	....	....	....	....	....
2002-03	Tri-City Americans	WHL	58	4	12	16	85	....	....	....	....	....
2003-04	Tri-City Americans	WHL	71	7	24	31	109	11	1	1	2	8
2004-05	Tri-City Americans	WHL	60	12	34	46	81	4	0	3	3	2
2005-06	Houston Aeros	AHL	73	6	18	24	92	3	1	1	2	7

WHL West Second All-Star Team (2005)

STONKUS, Alexei (STAWN-kuhs, al-EHX-ay) **NYI**

Defense. Shoots left. 5'11", 175 lbs. Born, Yaroslavl, USSR, May 6, 1984.
(NY Islanders' 4th choice, 189th overall, in 2002 Entry Draft).

			Regular Season					Playoffs				
Season	Club	League	GP	G	A	Pts	PIM	GP	G	A	Pts	PIM
2000-01	Russia Jr.	Exhib.	8	1	1	2	14	....	....	....	....	....
	Yaroslavl 2	Russia-3	....	....	....	....	....	6	0	0	0	2
2001-02	Yaroslavl 2	Russia-3	12	3	3	6	8	....	....	....	....	....
	Elektrostal 2	Russia-3	4	1	0	1	6	....	....	....	....	....
	Elektrostal	Russia-2	31	1	3	4	26	....	....	....	....	....
2002-03	Yaroslavl	Russia	11	0	0	0	2	....	....	....	....	....
2003-04	Yaroslavl	Russia	2	0	0	0	0	....	....	....	....	....
2004-05	Yaroslavl 2	Russia-3	7	0	1	1	6	....	....	....	....	....
2005-06	Yaroslavl 2	Russia-3	14	1	2	3	8	....	....	....	....	....
	Dynamo Minsk	BelOpen	3	0	0	0	0	....	....	....	....	....
	Kristall Saratov	Russia-2	5	1	0	1	2	....	....	....	....	....

STORTINI, Zachery (stohr-TEE-nee, ZA-kuh-ree) **EDM.**

Right wing. Shoots right. 6'3", 216 lbs. Born, Elliot Lake, Ont., September 11, 1985.
(Edmonton's 5th choice, 94th overall, in 2003 Entry Draft).

			Regular Season					Playoffs				
Season	Club	League	GP	G	A	Pts	PIM	GP	G	A	Pts	PIM
2000-01	Newmarket	OPJHL	34	3	10	13	68	....	....	....	....	....
2001-02	Sudbury Wolves	OHL	65	8	6	14	187	5	1	0	1	24
2002-03	Sudbury Wolves	OHL	62	13	16	29	222	....	....	....	....	....
2003-04	Sudbury Wolves	OHL	62	21	16	37	151	7	1	1	2	14
	Toronto	AHL	2	0	0	0	7	3	0	0	0	4
2004-05	Sudbury Wolves	OHL	58	13	27	40	186	12	2	5	7	27
2005-06	Iowa Stars	AHL	27	2	1	3	108	....	....	....	....	....
	Milwaukee	AHL	37	0	7	7	153	....	....	....	....	....

STRACHAN, Tyson (STRAWN, TIGH-suhn) **CAR.**

Defense. Shoots right. 6'3", 205 lbs. Born, Melfort, Sask., October 30, 1984.
(Carolina's 6th choice, 137th overall, in 2003 Entry Draft).

			Regular Season					Playoffs				
Season	Club	League	GP	G	A	Pts	PIM	GP	G	A	Pts	PIM
2001-02	Tisdale Trojans	SMHL	42	5	18	23	70	....	....	....	....	....
	Melville	SJHL	2	0	0	0	0	....	....	....	....	....
2002-03	Vernon Vipers	BCHL	56	6	22	28	99	....	....	....	....	....
2003-04	Ohio State	CCHA	30	2	5	7	8	....	....	....	....	....
2004-05	Ohio State	CCHA	31	1	4	5	32	....	....	....	....	....
2005-06	Ohio State	CCHA	23	3	2	5	37	....	....	....	....	....

STRAIT, Brian (STRAYT, BRIGH-uhn) **PIT.**

Defense. Shoots left. 6', 200 lbs. Born, Boston, MA, January 4, 1988.
(Pittsburgh's 3rd choice, 65th overall, in 2006 Entry Draft).

			Regular Season					Playoffs				
Season	Club	League	GP	G	A	Pts	PIM	GP	G	A	Pts	PIM
2003-04	Northfield Mt.H.	High-MA	30	5	15	20	....	....	....	....	....	....
2004-05	USNTDP	U-17	18	1	5	6	8	....	....	....	....	....
	USNTDP	NAHL	42	4	8	12	42	10	0	2	2	2
2005-06	USNTDP	U-18	40	2	7	9	31	....	....	....	....	....
	USNTDP	NAHL	15	0	5	5	41	....	....	....	....	....

STRALMAN, Anton (STROHL-muhn, AN-tawn) **TOR.**

Defense. Shoots right. 6'1", 180 lbs. Born, Tibro, Sweden , August 1, 1986.
(Toronto's 5th choice, 216th overall, in 2005 Entry Draft).

			Regular Season					Playoffs				
Season	Club	League	GP	G	A	Pts	PIM	GP	G	A	Pts	PIM
2002-03	Skovde IK Jr.	Swe-Jr.	46	20	9	29	38	....	....	....	....	....
2003-04	Skovde IK	Sweden-3	27	4	8	12	18	....	....	....	....	....
2004-05	Skovde IK	Sweden-2	50	10	11	21	40	....	....	....	....	....
2005-06	Timra IK	Sweden	45	1	4	5	28	....	....	....	....	....
	Timra IK Jr.	Swe-Jr.	....	....	....	....	....	3	0	0	0	4

STUART, Colin (STEW-ahrt, CAW-lihn) **ATL.**

Left wing. Shoots left. 6'2", 205 lbs. Born, Rochester, MN, July 8, 1982.
(Atlanta's 5th choice, 135th overall, in 2001 Entry Draft).

			Regular Season					Playoffs				
Season	Club	League	GP	G	A	Pts	PIM	GP	G	A	Pts	PIM
1998-99	Roch. Lourdes	High-MN	23	22	32	54	....	....	....	....	....	....
99-2000	Lincoln Stars	USHL	53	18	19	37	38	9	1	3	4	2
2000-01	Colorado College	WCHA	41	2	7	9	26	....	....	....	....	....
2001-02	Colorado College	WCHA	43	13	9	22	34	....	....	....	....	....
2002-03	Colorado College	WCHA	42	13	11	24	56	....	....	....	....	....
2003-04	Colorado College	WCHA	30	10	12	22	38	....	....	....	....	....
2004-05	Chicago Wolves	AHL	39	3	2	5	12	....	....	....	....	....
	Gwinnett	ECHL	5	1	3	4	4	....	....	....	....	....
2005-06	Chicago Wolves	AHL	78	13	14	27	65	....	....	....	....	....

SUBBOTIN, Dmitri (soo-BOH-tihn, dih-MEE-tree) **CBJ**

Left wing. Shoots left. 6'1", 183 lbs. Born, Tomsk, USSR, October 20, 1977.
(NY Rangers' 3rd choice, 76th overall, in 1996 Entry Draft).

			Regular Season					Playoffs				
Season	Club	League	GP	G	A	Pts	PIM	GP	G	A	Pts	PIM
1993-94	Yekaterinburg	CIS	12	0	3	3	4	....	....	....	....	....
1994-95	Yekaterinburg	CIS	52	9	6	15	75	2	0	0	0	2
1995-96	CSKA Moscow	CIS	41	6	5	11	62	3	0	0	0	0
1996-97	CSKA Moscow	Russia-2	8	1	0	1	8	....	....	....	....	....
	HK CSKA Moscow	Russia	17	5	3	8	22	2	0	0	0	2
1997-98	HK CSKA Moscow	Russia	16	1	1	2	47	....	....	....	....	....
1998-99	Dynamo Moscow	Russia	1	0	1	1	0	....	....	....	....	....
	Lada Togliatti	Russia	31	8	3	11	47	7	0	0	0	4
99-2000	Lada Togliatti	Russia	27	10	4	14	26	7	1	1	2	4
	Lada Togliatti 2	Russia-3	2	0	1	1	0	....	....	....	....	....
2000-01	Dynamo Moscow	Russia	39	11	15	26	48	....	....	....	....	....
2001-02	Magnitogorsk	Russia	38	8	3	11	18	9	0	2	2	10
2002-03	Cherepovets	Russia	10	0	1	1	31	....	....	....	....	....
	CSKA Moscow	Russia	20	3	9	12	6	....	....	....	....	....
2003-04	CSKA Moscow	Russia	20	0	3	3	14	....	....	....	....	....
	Avangard Omsk	Russia	26	6	6	12	36	11	2	3	5	6
2004-05	Avangard Omsk	Russia	55	5	6	11	66	7	0	0	0	10
2005-06	Ufa	Russia	5	0	1	1	8	....	....	....	....	....
	MVD	Russia	27	6	8	14	52	4	1	3	4	4

Claimed by **Columbus** from **NY Rangers** in Expansion Draft, June 23, 2000.

SUCHARSKI, Nick (soo-CHAR-skee, NIHK) **CBJ**

Left wing. Shoots left. 6'1", 165 lbs. Born, Toronto, Ont., November 15, 1987.
(Columbus' 6th choice, 136th overall, in 2006 Entry Draft).

			Regular Season					Playoffs				
Season	Club	League	GP	G	A	Pts	PIM	GP	G	A	Pts	PIM
2003-04	Wexford Raiders	OPJHL	43	15	29	44	48	....	....	....	....	....
2004-05	Wexford Raiders	OPJHL	46	26	27	53	78	13	6	10	16	20
2005-06	Michigan State	CCHA	36	2	5	7	18	....	....	....	....	....

SUGDEN, Brandon (SUHG-duhn, BRAN-duhn) **CBJ**

Right wing. Shoots right. 6'4", 231 lbs. Born, Toronto, Ont., June 23, 1978.
(Toronto's 8th choice, 111th overall, in 1996 Entry Draft).

			Regular Season					Playoffs				
Season	Club	League	GP	G	A	Pts	PIM	GP	G	A	Pts	PIM
1994-95	Tor. Red Wings	MTHL	53	12	24	36	162	....	....	....	....	....
	St. Mike's B's	MTJHL	15	0	3	3	69	....	....	....	....	....
1995-96	London Knights	OHL	55	2	7	9	*264	....	....	....	....	....
1996-97	London Knights	OHL	31	4	10	14	158	....	....	....	....	....
	Sudbury Wolves	OHL	20	0	4	4	70	....	....	....	....	....
1997-98	Sudbury Wolves	OHL	11	2	3	5	62	....	....	....	....	....
	Barrie Colts	OHL	49	6	21	27	191	6	0	0	0	18
1998-99	Cincinnati	IHL	6	0	2	2	51	....	....	....	....	....
	Dayton Bombers	ECHL	44	0	1	1	233	1	0	0	0	17
99-2000	Dayton Bombers	ECHL	13	0	1	1	110	....	....	....	....	....
2000-01	Worcester IceCats	AHL	11	0	0	0	56	....	....	....	....	....
	Tallahassee	ECHL	12	1	0	1	75	....	....	....	....	....
	Peoria Rivermen	ECHL	1	0	0	0	0	....	....	....	....	....
2001-02			DID NOT PLAY									
2002-03	Verdun Dragons	QSPHL	16	0	2	2	120	7	0	1	1	40
2003-04	Syracuse Crunch	AHL	62	3	5	8	283	3	0	0	0	2
2004-05	Syracuse Crunch	AHL	45	1	0	1	252	....	....	....	....	....
2005-06	Syracuse Crunch	AHL	46	2	4	6	195	2	0	0	0	2

Signed as a free agent by **St. Louis**, June 29, 1998. • Suspended for life by ECHL for throwing his stick into the crowd during game vs. Dayton (ECHL), January 26, 2001. Signed as a free agent by **Columbus**, April 19, 2004.

SULLIVAN, Mike (SUHL-ih-vuhn, MIGHK) **L.A.**

Center. Shoots left. 6'4", 190 lbs. Born, Scarborough, Ont., September 14, 1984.
(Los Angeles' 9th choice, 244th overall, in 2003 Entry Draft).

			Regular Season					Playoffs				
Season	Club	League	GP	G	A	Pts	PIM	GP	G	A	Pts	PIM
2001-02	Uxbridge Bruins	OHA-C	42	22	27	49	20	....	....	....	....	....
2002-03	Stouffville Spirit	OPJHL	42	24	39	64	14	....	....	....	....	....
2003-04	Clarkson Knights	ECAC	40	8	11	19	14	....	....	....	....	....
2004-05	Clarkson Knights	ECACHL	37	8	9	17	20	....	....	....	....	....
2005-06	Clarkson Knights	ECACHL	36	15	11	26	30	....	....	....	....	....

SULLIVAN, Sean (SUHL-ih-vuhn, SHAWN) **PHX.**

Defense. Shoots left. 6', 188 lbs. Born, Boston, MA, March 29, 1984.
(Phoenix's 7th choice, 272nd overall, in 2003 Entry Draft).

			Regular Season					Playoffs				
Season	Club	League	GP	G	A	Pts	PIM	GP	G	A	Pts	PIM
2001-02	St. Sebastian's	High-MA	31	3	11	14	4	....	....	....	....	....
2002-03	St. Sebastian's	High-MA	41	9	30	39	59	....	....	....	....	....
2003-04	Boston University	H-East	36	2	5	7	14	....	....	....	....	....
2004-05	Boston University	H-East	41	1	3	4	10	....	....	....	....	....
2005-06	Boston University	H-East	40	3	14	17	32	....	....	....	....	....

SULZER, Alexander (ZUHLT-suhr, ahl-ehx-AN-duhr) NSH.

Defense. Shoots left. 6'1", 207 lbs. Born, Kaufbeuren, West Germany, May 30, 1984.
(Nashville's 7th choice, 92nd overall, in 2003 Entry Draft).

			Regular Season					Playoffs				
Season	Club	League	GP	G	A	Pts	PIM	GP	G	A	Pts	PIM
2000-01	ESV Kaufbeuren	German-3	38	3	6	9	20	....	....	....	....	....
	Kaufbeuren Jr.	Ger-Jr.	1	0	2	2	2	....	....	....	....	....
2001-02	ESV Kaufbeuren	German-3	19	1	9	10	14	....	....	....	....	....
	Kaufbeuren Jr.	Ger-Jr.	1	0	0	0	4	....	....	....	....	....
2002-03	ESV Kaufbeuren	German-2	26	5	3	8	38	1	0	1	1	4
	Hamburg Freezers	Germany	18	0	1	1	18	5	0	0	0	12
2003-04	Dusseldorf	Germany	46	4	1	5	56	4	0	0	0	8
2004-05	Dusseldorf	Germany	42	5	6	11	68	....	....	....	....	....
	EV Duisburg	German-2	....	....	....	....	....	7	0	3	3	6
2005-06	Dusseldorf	Germany	48	3	15	18	82	13	3	6	9	22
	Germany	Olympics	5	0	1	1	2	....	....	....	....	....

SUMMERS, Chris (SUHM-mehrs, KRIHS) PHX.

Defense. Shoots left. 6'2", 180 lbs. Born, Ann Arbor, MI, February 5, 1988.
(Phoenix's 2nd choice, 29th overall, in 2006 Entry Draft).

			Regular Season					Playoffs				
Season	Club	League	GP	G	A	Pts	PIM	GP	G	A	Pts	PIM
2004-05	USNTDP	U-17	13	2	2	4	10	....	....	....	....	....
	USNTDP	NAHL	31	2	5	7	20	7	1	0	1	0
2005-06	USNTDP	U-18	42	4	9	13	67	....	....	....	....	....
	USNTDP	NAHL	17	2	2	4	20	....	....	....	....	....

Signed Letter of Intent to attend **U. of Michigan** (CCHA) in fall of 2006.

SUNDIN, Andreas (suhn-DEEN, an-DRAY-uhs) DET.

Left wing. Shoots left. 6', 185 lbs. Born, Linkoping, Sweden, March 15, 1984.
(Detroit's 4th choice, 170th overall, in 2003 Entry Draft).

			Regular Season					Playoffs				
Season	Club	League	GP	G	A	Pts	PIM	GP	G	A	Pts	PIM
2001-02	Linkopings HC Jr.	Swe-Jr.	19	31	13	44	8	....	....	....	....	....
2002-03	Linkopings HC Jr.	Swe-Jr.	4	4	3	7	6	....	....	....	....	....
	Linkopings HC	Sweden	8	0	1	1	0	....	....	....	....	....
	Linkopings HC	Sweden-Q	7	1	0	1	0	....	....	....	....	....
2003-04	Linkopings HC Jr.	Swe-Jr.	22	16	16	32	14	....	....	....	....	....
	Vasteras	Sweden-2	13	4	5	9	0	....	....	....	....	....
	Linkopings HC	Sweden	28	0	0	0	0	5	0	0	0	0
2004-05	Linkopings HC	Sweden	2	0	0	0	0	....	....	....	....	....
2005-06	Nybro Vikings IF	Sweden-2	34	3	3	6	6	....	....	....	....	....

SUNDSTROM, Alexander (SUHND-struhm, al-ehx-AN-duhr) N.J.

Center. Shoots left. 5'11", 190 lbs. Born, Vancouver, B.C., March 14, 1987.
(New Jersey's 7th choice, 218th overall, in 2005 Entry Draft).

			Regular Season					Playoffs				
Season	Club	League	GP	G	A	Pts	PIM	GP	G	A	Pts	PIM
2003-04	Bjorkloven U18	Swe-U18	7	2	1	3	4	....	....	....	....	....
	Bjorkloven Jr.	Swe-Jr.	STATISTICS NOT AVAILABLE									
2004-05	Bjorkloven U18	Swe-U18	STATISTICS NOT AVAILABLE									
	Bjorkloven Jr.	Swe-Jr.	STATISTICS NOT AVAILABLE									
	IF Bjorkloven Umea	Sweden-2	9	0	0	0	0	....	....	....	....	....
2005-06	Bjorkloven Jr.	Swe-Jr.	29	17	14	31	22	5	1	0	1	4
	IF Bjorkloven Umea	Sweden-2	3	0	0	0	0	....	....	....	....	....

SUTTER, Brett (SUH-tuhr, BREHT) CGY.

Center/Left wing. Shoots left. 5'11", 194 lbs. Born, Viking, Alta., June 2, 1987.
(Calgary's 7th choice, 179th overall, in 2005 Entry Draft).

			Regular Season					Playoffs				
Season	Club	League	GP	G	A	Pts	PIM	GP	G	A	Pts	PIM
2003-04	Kootenay Ice	WHL	44	5	7	12	26	4	0	0	0	4
2004-05	Kootenay Ice	WHL	70	8	11	19	70	16	1	2	3	16
2005-06	Kootenay Ice	WHL	16	8	7	15	21	....	....	....	....	....
	Red Deer Rebels	WHL	57	9	26	35	80	....	....	....	....	....

SVAGROVSKY, David (shva-GRAWF-skee, DAY-vihd) COL.

Right wing. Shoots right. 6'3", 205 lbs. Born, Prague, Czech., December 21, 1984.
(Colorado's 2nd choice, 131st overall, in 2003 Entry Draft).

			Regular Season					Playoffs				
Season	Club	League	GP	G	A	Pts	PIM	GP	G	A	Pts	PIM
99-2000	HC Slavia Praha Jr.	CzRep-Jr.	31	1	3	4	12	....	....	....	....	....
2000-01	HC Slavia Praha Jr.	CzRep-Jr.	48	20	29	49	82	7	5	1	6	10
2001-02	HC Slavia Praha Jr.	CzRep-Jr.	44	7	6	13	38	....	....	....	....	....
2002-03	Seattle	WHL	68	17	25	42	47	15	4	6	10	12
2003-04	Seattle	WHL	52	6	11	17	42	....	....	....	....	....
2004-05	Colorado Eagles	CHL	35	1	3	4	55	....	....	....	....	....
2005-06	Lowell	AHL	27	0	1	1	17	....	....	....	....	....
	San Diego Gulls	ECHL	26	3	5	8	33	....	....	....	....	....

SWAN, Bryce (SWAHN, BRIGHS) ANA.

Center. Shoots right. 6'2", 191 lbs. Born, Alderpoint, N.S., October 6, 1987.
(Anaheim's 2nd choice, 38th overall, in 2006 Entry Draft).

			Regular Season					Playoffs				
Season	Club	League	GP	G	A	Pts	PIM	GP	G	A	Pts	PIM
2004-05	Halifax	QMJHL	36	3	3	6	39	11	2	0	2	10
2005-06	Halifax	QMJHL	34	14	11	25	54	11	2	5	7	8

SWANSON, Jeremy (SWAWN-suhn, JAIR-eh-mee) FLA.

Defense. Shoots left. 6', 199 lbs. Born, Nipigon, Ont., June 21, 1984.
(Florida's choice, 169th overall, in 2002 Entry Draft).

			Regular Season					Playoffs				
Season	Club	League	GP	G	A	Pts	PIM	GP	G	A	Pts	PIM
99-2000	Thunder Bay Kings	TBMHL	48	8	16	24	19	....	....	....	....	....
2000-01	Sault Ste. Marie	OHL	54	1	6	7	60	....	....	....	....	....
2001-02	Barrie Colts	OHL	67	8	16	24	78	20	1	4	5	12
2002-03	Barrie Colts	OHL	68	7	34	41	129	....	....	....	....	....
2003-04	Barrie Colts	OHL	66	6	28	34	120	12	0	5	5	16
2004-05	San Antonio	AHL	21	1	3	4	22	....	....	....	....	....
	Texas Wildcatters	ECHL	44	1	6	7	62	....	....	....	....	....
2005-06	Rochester	AHL	11	0	0	0	23	....	....	....	....	....
	Florida Everblades	ECHL	14	1	3	4	12	....	....	....	....	....

OHL Second All-Star Team (2004)

SWITZER, Craig (SWIHT-zuhr, KRAYG) NSH.

Defense. Shoots left. 6'1", 195 lbs. Born, Calgary, Alta., October 16, 1984.
(Nashville's 11th choice, 275th overall, in 2004 Entry Draft).

			Regular Season					Playoffs				
Season	Club	League	GP	G	A	Pts	PIM	GP	G	A	Pts	PIM
2003-04	Salmon Arm	BCHL	57	14	40	54	117	14	0	12	12	16
2004-05	New Hampshire	H-East	41	1	13	14	22	....	....	....	....	....
2005-06	New Hampshire	H-East	40	2	14	16	54	....	....	....	....	....

TARATUKHIN, Andrei (tahr-a-TOO-khin, AWN-dray) CGY.

Center. Shoots left. 6', 198 lbs. Born, Omsk, USSR, February 22, 1983.
(Calgary's 2nd choice, 41st overall, in 2001 Entry Draft).

			Regular Season					Playoffs				
Season	Club	League	GP	G	A	Pts	PIM	GP	G	A	Pts	PIM
99-2000	Omsk 2	Russia-3	27	10	6	16	16	....	....	....	....	....
	Avangard Omsk	Russia	....	....	....	....	....	1	1	0	1	0
2000-01	Omsk 2	Russia-3	41	19	28	47	69	....	....	....	....	....
2001-02	Mostovik Kurgan	Russia-2	44	13	22	35	30	....	....	....	....	....
	Yaroslavl 2	Russia-3	5	5	2	7	12	....	....	....	....	....
2002-03	Avangard Omsk	Russia	21	0	1	1	4	7	1	0	1	18
	Omsk 2	Russia-3	15	4	13	17	20	....	....	....	....	....
2003-04	Avangard Omsk	Russia	8	0	0	0	4	....	....	....	....	....
	Omsk 2	Russia-3	9	6	5	11	6	....	....	....	....	....
	Mechel	Russia-2	15	3	12	15	12	12	1	4	5	6
2004-05	Ufa 2	Russia-3	1	0	1	1	0	....	....	....	....	....
	Ufa	Russia	54	7	5	12	73	....	....	....	....	....
2005-06	Yaroslavl	Russia	40	9	15	24	85	11	2	2	4	24
	Russia	Olympics	5	0	0	0	2	....	....	....	....	....

TARKIR, Zach (TAHR-kihr, ZAK) N.J.

Defense. Shoots right. 6', 180 lbs. Born, Fresno, CA, June 28, 1984.
(New Jersey's 4th choice, 167th overall, in 2003 Entry Draft).

			Regular Season					Playoffs				
Season	Club	League	GP	G	A	Pts	PIM	GP	G	A	Pts	PIM
2001-02	Great Falls	AWHL	24	3	5	8	....	8	0	3	3	....
2002-03	Chilliwack Chiefs	BCHL	53	5	28	33	86	....	....	....	....	....
2003-04	Northern Mich.	CCHA	36	2	3	5	40	....	....	....	....	....
2004-05	Northern Mich.	CCHA	35	2	8	10	51	....	....	....	....	....
2005-06	Northern Mich.	CCHA	39	3	11	14	57	....	....	....	....	....

TAYLOR, Jake (TAY-luhr, JAIK) NYR

Defense. Shoots right. 6'4", 220 lbs. Born, Rochester, MN, August 1, 1983.
(NY Rangers' 5th choice, 177th overall, in 2002 Entry Draft).

			Regular Season					Playoffs				
Season	Club	League	GP	G	A	Pts	PIM	GP	G	A	Pts	PIM
2000-01	Roch. Lourdes	High-MN	29	9	15	24	34	....	....	....	....	....
	Green Bay	USHL	5	0	0	0	8	....	....	....	....	....
2001-02	Green Bay	USHL	56	1	2	3	147	7	0	0	0	11
2002-03	Green Bay	USHL	60	8	8	16	160	....	....	....	....	....
2003-04	U. of Minnesota	WCHA	39	2	6	8	68	....	....	....	....	....
2004-05	Hartford Wolf Pack	AHL	43	0	3	3	156	....	....	....	....	....
	Charlotte	ECHL	11	0	2	2	31	....	....	....	....	....
2005-06	Hartford Wolf Pack	AHL	66	1	11	12	128	5	0	0	0	6

TAYLOR, Justin (TAY-luhr, JUHS-tihn) CGY.

Left wing. Shoots left. 6'4", 200 lbs. Born, Edmonton, Alta., January 1, 1983.

			Regular Season					Playoffs				
Season	Club	League	GP	G	A	Pts	PIM	GP	G	A	Pts	PIM
99-2000	Medicine Hat	WHL	39	1	5	6	11	....	....	....	....	....
2000-01	Sherwood Park	AJHL	21	6	8	14	19	....	....	....	....	....
2001-02	Sherwood Park	AJHL	55	13	15	28	49	7	2	3	5	14
2002-03	Camrose Kodiaks	AJHL	45	11	24	35	71	17	7	11	18	34
2003-04	Red Deer Rebels	WHL	57	16	22	38	39	19	6	10	16	13
2004-05	Lowell	AHL	62	8	3	11	35	....	....	....	....	....
2005-06	Omaha	AHL	73	16	19	35	48	....	....	....	....	....

Signed as a free agent by **Calgary**, July 6, 2004.

TENKANEN, Valtteri (TEHN-kah-nehn, vahl-TEH-ree) L.A.

Center. Shoots left. 5'11", 183 lbs. Born, Jamsa, Finland, March 27, 1985.
(Los Angeles' 10th choice, 264th overall, in 2004 Entry Draft).

			Regular Season					Playoffs				
Season	Club	League	GP	G	A	Pts	PIM	GP	G	A	Pts	PIM
2001-02	JYP Jyvaskyla U18	Fin-U18	25	14	12	26	2	7	1	0	1	0
	JYP Jyvaskyla Jr.	Fin-Jr.	3	0	1	1	0	....	....	....	....	....
2002-03	JYP Jyvaskyla U18	Fin-U18	1	2	1	3	0	....	....	....	....	....
	JYP Jyvaskyla Jr.	Fin-Jr.	30	8	7	15	14	4	1	1	2	0
2003-04	Suomi U20	Finland-2	2	0	1	1	0	....	....	....	....	....
	JYP Jyvaskyla Jr.	Fin-Jr.	10	3	2	5	2	9	2	3	5	0
	JYP Jyvaskyla	Finland	25	1	3	4	2	2	0	0	0	0
2004-05	JYP Jyvaskyla Jr.	Fin-Jr.	12	1	5	6	14	6	2	1	3	25
	JYP Jyvaskyla	Finland	10	0	1	1	0	....	....	....	....	....
2005-06	JYP Jyvaskyla	Finland	35	0	6	6	4	3	0	1	1	0

TERESCHENKO, Alexei (teh-REH-shehn-koh, al-EHX-ay) DAL.

Center. Shoots left. 5'11", 176 lbs. Born, Mozhaisk, USSR, December 16, 1980.
(Dallas' 4th choice, 91st overall, in 2000 Entry Draft).

			Regular Season					Playoffs				
Season	Club	League	GP	G	A	Pts	PIM	GP	G	A	Pts	PIM
1996-97	Dyn'o Moscow 2	Russia-3	9	0	0	0	2	....	....	....	....	....
1997-98	Dynamo Moscow	Russia	26	6	7	13	30	....	....	....	....	....
1998-99	Dyn'o Moscow 2	Russia-3	28	4	17	21	20	....	....	....	....	....
	THK Tver	Russia-2	12	3	4	7	4	....	....	....	....	....
	Dynamo Moscow	Russia	1	0	1	1	0	2	0	0	0	0
99-2000	Dynamo Moscow	Russia	27	1	1	2	10	17	1	1	2	8
2000-01	Dynamo Moscow	Russia	39	3	2	5	18	....	....	....	....	....
2001-02	Yaroslavl 2	Russia-3	1	0	0	0	0	....	....	....	....	....
	Dynamo Moscow	Russia	40	3	6	9	20	3	0	0	0	0
2002-03	Dynamo Moscow	Russia	40	7	9	16	14	5	1	0	1	2
2003-04	Dynamo Moscow	Russia	47	8	12	20	26	3	0	0	0	4
2004-05	Dynamo Moscow	Russia	31	3	6	9	8	10	0	1	1	2
2005-06	Ak Bars Kazan	Russia	36	3	12	15	12	10	0	4	4	12

TERNAVSKY, Artem (tuhr-NAV-skee, ahr-TEHM) WSH.

Defense. Shoots left. 6'3", 213 lbs. Born, Magnitogorsk, USSR, June 2, 1983.
(Washington's 4th choice, 160th overall, in 2001 Entry Draft).

			Regular Season					Playoffs				
Season	Club	League	GP	G	A	Pts	PIM	GP	G	A	Pts	PIM
99-2000	CSKA Moscow 2	Russia-3	2	0	1	1	0	....	....	....	....	....
	HK Moscow 2	Russia-3	25	0	4	4	42	....	....	....	....	....
2000-01	Sherbrooke	QMJHL	65	3	15	18	143	....	....	....	....	....
2001-02	Mostovik Kurgan	Russia-2	25	0	0	0	46	....	....	....	....	....
2002-03	Sibir Novosibirsk	Russia	42	1	1	2	20	....	....	....	....	....
2003-04	Ufa	Russia	12	0	0	0	4	....	....	....	....	....
	Magnitogorsk 2	Russia-3	7	1	0	1	0	....	....	....	....	....
2004-05	Nizhny Novgorod	Russia-2	16	0	1	1	18	....	....	....	....	....
	Motor Barnaul	Russia-2	8	0	1	1	14	....	....	....	....	....
2005-06	Karaganda	Kazakh.	17	1	1	2	12	....	....	....	....	....
	Karaganda	Russia-2	39	3	2	5	26	6	0	1	1	2

TESLIUK, Roman (tehs-L'YUHK, ROH-muhn)

Defense. Shoots right. 6'1", 195 lbs. Born, Severomorsk, USSR, January 21, 1986.
(Edmonton's 3rd choice, 44th overall, in 2004 Entry Draft).

			Regular Season					Playoffs				
Season	Club	League	GP	G	A	Pts	PIM	GP	G	A	Pts	PIM
2002-03	CSKA Moscow 2	Russia-3	6	0	2	2	6	....	....	....	....	....
2003-04	Kamloops Blazers	WHL	70	5	9	14	118	5	0	1	1	2
2004-05	Kamloops Blazers	WHL	70	9	20	29	109	6	4	1	5	6
2005-06	Kamloops Blazers	WHL	72	14	16	30	109	....	....	....	....	....

THELEN, A.J. (THAY-lehn, AY-JAY) MIN.

Defense. Shoots left. 6'3", 210 lbs. Born, Shakopee, Minn., March 11, 1986.
(Minnesota's 1st choice, 12th overall, in 2004 Entry Draft).

			Regular Season					Playoffs				
Season	Club	League	GP	G	A	Pts	PIM	GP	G	A	Pts	PIM
2000-01	Shat.-St. Mary's	High-MN	40	22	17	39	....	....	....	....	....	....
2001-02	Shat.-St. Mary's	High-MN	62	20	33	53	....	....	....	....	....	....
2002-03	USNTDP	U-17	20	4	1	5	8	....	....	....	....	....
	USNTDP	U-18	3	0	0	0	0	....	....	....	....	....
	USNTDP	NAHL	44	2	7	9	72	....	....	....	....	....
2003-04	Michigan State	CCHA	41	11	18	29	50	....	....	....	....	....
2004-05	Michigan State	CCHA	33	0	11	11	48	....	....	....	....	....
2005-06	Prince Albert	WHL	72	13	23	36	79	....	....	....	....	....
	Houston Aeros	AHL	1	0	0	0	2	....	....	....	....	....

CCHA All-Rookie Team (2004) • CCHA First All-Star Team (2004) • NCAA West Second All-American Team (2004)

THOMAS, Andrew (TAW-mas, AN-droo) WSH.

Defense. Shoots right. 6'2", 196 lbs. Born, West Bend, WI, November 14, 1985.
(Washington's 3rd choice, 109th overall, in 2005 Entry Draft).

			Regular Season					Playoffs				
Season	Club	League	GP	G	A	Pts	PIM	GP	G	A	Pts	PIM
2003-04	Waterloo	USHL	57	1	6	7	86	12	0	2	2	28
2004-05	U. of Denver	WCHA	42	2	5	7	78	....	....	....	....	....
2005-06	U. of Denver	WCHA	38	1	3	4	65	....	....	....	....	....

THOMPSON, Nate (TAWM-suhn, NAYT) BOS.

Center. Shoots left. 6', 206 lbs. Born, Anchorage, AK, October 5, 1984.
(Boston's 8th choice, 183rd overall, in 2003 Entry Draft).

			Regular Season					Playoffs				
Season	Club	League	GP	G	A	Pts	PIM	GP	G	A	Pts	PIM
2001-02	Seattle	WHL	69	13	26	39	42	11	1	3	4	13
2002-03	Seattle	WHL	61	10	24	34	48	15	5	4	9	6
2003-04	Seattle	WHL	65	13	23	36	24	....	....	....	....	....
2004-05	Seattle	WHL	58	19	15	34	39	12	1	2	3	2
	Providence Bruins	AHL	....	....	....	....	....	11	0	1	1	6
2005-06	Providence Bruins	AHL	74	8	10	18	58	3	0	0	0	10

THORESEN, Patrick (THOR-eh-sehn, PAT-rihk) EDM.

Center. Shoots left. 5'10", 185 lbs. Born, Hamar, Norway, November 7, 1983.

			Regular Season					Playoffs				
Season	Club	League	GP	G	A	Pts	PIM	GP	G	A	Pts	PIM
99-2000	Storhamar	Norway	25	1	8	9	4	....	....	....	....	....
2000-01	Storhamar	Norway	40	18	27	45	24	....	....	....	....	....
2001-02	Moncton Wildcats	QMJHL	60	30	43	73	50	....	....	....	....	....
2002-03	Baie-Comeau	QMJHL	71	33	*75	108	57	12	2	8	10	8
2003-04	Djurgarden	Sweden	3	0	0	0	2	....	....	....	....	....
	Morrums GoIS IK	Sweden-2	38	19	22	41	40	....	....	....	....	....
2004-05	Djurgarden	Sweden	30	10	7	17	33	12	2	2	4	29
2005-06	Djurgarden	Sweden	50	17	19	36	44	....	....	....	....	....
	Salzburg	Austria	....	....	....	....	....	9	4	7	11	12

Signed as a free agent by **Edmonton**, June 12, 2006.

TIMKIN, Alexei (TIHM-kihn, al-EHX-ay) DAL.

Right wing. Shoots left. 6'2", 194 lbs. Born, Kirov, USSR, April 21, 1979.
(Dallas' 6th choice, 160th overall, in 1997 Entry Draft).

			Regular Season					Playoffs				
Season	Club	League	GP	G	A	Pts	PIM	GP	G	A	Pts	PIM
1996-97	Yaroslavl 2	Russia-3	47	16	6	22	54	....	....	....	....	....
	Torpedo Yaroslavl	Russia	3	0	1	1	0	....	....	....	....	....
1997-98	Torpedo Yaroslavl	Russia	16	4	5	9	14	....	....	....	....	....
1998-99	Kirovo-Chepetsk	Russia-3	30	4	3	7	36	....	....	....	....	....
	St. Petersburg 2	Russia-4	1	0	0	0	2	....	....	....	....	....
99-2000	Kirovo-Chepetsk	Russia-3	49	29	13	42	26	....	....	....	....	....
2000-01	Kirovo-Chepetsk	Russia-3	STATISTICS NOT AVAILABLE									
2003-04	Kirovo-Chepetsk	Russia-2	3	0	1	1	4	....	....	....	....	....
	Karaganda	Russia-2	11	0	1	1	6	....	....	....	....	....
2005-06	Kirovo-Chepetsk	Russia-2	37	6	6	12	22	3	0	1	1	4
	HK Dmitrov	Russia-2	2	0	0	0	2	....	....	....	....	....

TIMONEN, Jussi (TEEM-oh-nehn, YU-see) PHI.

Defense. Shoots left. 6', 200 lbs. Born, Kuopio, Finland, June 29, 1983.
(Philadelphia's 3rd choice, 146th overall, in 2001 Entry Draft).

			Regular Season					Playoffs				
Season	Club	League	GP	G	A	Pts	PIM	GP	G	A	Pts	PIM
99-2000	KalPa Kuopio U18	Fin-U18	14	3	2	5	10	....	....	....	....	....
	KalPa Kuopio Jr.	Fin-Jr.	19	1	0	1	6	4	0	0	0	4
2000-01	KalPa Kuopio U18	Fin-U18	4	1	4	5	10	....	....	....	....	....
	KalPa Kuopio Jr.	Fin-Jr.	38	6	7	13	22	....	....	....	....	....
	KalPa Kuopio	Finland-3	7	0	1	1	2	2	1	0	1	0
2001-02	KalPa Kuopio Jr.	Fin-Jr.	10	1	1	2	10	....	....	....	....	....
	KalPa Kuopio	Finland-2	41	3	8	11	10	8	0	2	2	0
2002-03	TPS Turku Jr.	Fin-Jr.	2	0	0	0	0	....	....	....	....	....
	TuTo Turku	Finland-2	3	0	0	0	0	....	....	....	....	....
	TPS Turku	Finland	39	1	0	1	10	7	0	2	2	4
2003-04	TPS Turku	Finland	20	0	0	0	4	....	....	....	....	....
	Jukurit Mikkeli	Finland-2	25	7	9	16	10	13	0	4	4	0
2004-05	SaiPa	Finland	54	1	5	6	53	....	....	....	....	....
2005-06	SaiPa	Finland	52	0	7	7	30	8	1	0	1	27

TKACHENKO, Ivan (t'kuh-CHEHN-koh, ee-VAHN) CBJ

Left wing. Shoots left. 5'10", 183 lbs. Born, Yaroslavl, USSR, November 9, 1979.
(Columbus' 5th choice, 98th overall, in 2002 Entry Draft).

			Regular Season					Playoffs				
Season	Club	League	GP	G	A	Pts	PIM	GP	G	A	Pts	PIM
1997-98	Yaroslavl 2	Russia-2	STATISTICS NOT AVAILABLE									
	Torpedo Yaroslavl	Russia	....	....	....	....	....	1	0	0	0	0
1998-99	Yaroslavl 2	Russia-3	28	15	13	28	26	....	....	....	....	....
99-2000	Yaroslavl 2	Russia-3	1	1	0	1	0	....	....	....	....	....
	Motor Zavolzhje	Russia-2	43	15	14	29	22	....	....	....	....	....
	Nizhnekamsk 2	Russia-3	8	6	3	9	24	....	....	....	....	....
	Nizhnekamsk	Russia	5	1	0	1	0	4	0	1	1	0
2000-01	Nizhnekamsk	Russia	28	2	2	4	14	4	0	1	1	0
2001-02	Yaroslavl 2	Russia-3	1	0	1	1	2	....	....	....	....	....
	Yaroslavl	Russia	44	13	20	33	57	9	5	2	7	4
2002-03	Yaroslavl	Russia	44	11	6	17	57	10	2	3	5	6
2003-04	Yaroslavl	Russia	56	7	11	18	22	3	0	0	0	0
2004-05	Yaroslavl	Russia	59	15	15	30	30	9	2	3	5	8
2005-06	Yaroslavl	Russia	45	10	21	31	30	11	1	2	3	16
	Yaroslavl 2	Russia-3	1	0	1	1	2	....	....	....	....	....

TLUSTY, Jiri (T'LOO-stee, YIH-ree) TOR.

Center. Shoots left. 6', 196 lbs. Born, Slany, Czech., March 16, 1988.
(Toronto's 1st choice, 13th overall, in 2006 Entry Draft).

			Regular Season					Playoffs				
Season	Club	League	GP	G	A	Pts	PIM	GP	G	A	Pts	PIM
2001-02	HC Kladno U17	CzR-U17	1	0	0	0	0	....	....	....	....	....
2002-03	HC Kladno U17	CzR-U17	48	28	17	45	22	10	5	4	9	12
2003-04	HC Kladno U17	CzR-U17	1	0	0	0	2	1	0	0	0	2
	HC Kladno Jr.	CzRep-Jr.	51	10	3	13	12	1	0	0	0	0
2004-05	HC Kladno Jr.	CzRep-Jr.	42	15	12	27	54	10	2	2	4	8
2005-06	HC Kladno Jr.	CzRep-Jr.	6	4	2	6	2	6	7	6	13	6
	HC Rabat Kladno	CzRep	44	7	3	10	51	....	....	....	....	....

TOBIN, Mark (TOH-bihn, MAHRK)

Left wing. Shoots left. 6'3", 211 lbs. Born, St. John's, Nfld., November 26, 1985.
(Tampa Bay's 2nd choice, 65th overall, in 2004 Entry Draft).

			Regular Season					Playoffs				
Season	Club	League	GP	G	A	Pts	PIM	GP	G	A	Pts	PIM
2002-03	Rimouski Oceanic	QMJHL	68	8	8	16	176	....	....	....	....	....
2003-04	Rimouski Oceanic	QMJHL	69	22	16	38	112	9	4	1	5	12
2004-05	Rimouski Oceanic	QMJHL	68	22	28	50	107	13	6	3	9	23
2005-06	Rimouski Oceanic	QMJHL	67	26	25	51	109	....	....	....	....	....

TOEWS, Jonathan (TAYVES, JAWN-ah-thun) CHI.

Center. Shoots left. 6'2", 198 lbs. Born, Winnipeg, Man., April 29, 1988.
(Chicago's 1st choice, 3rd overall, in 2006 Entry Draft).

			Regular Season					Playoffs				
Season	Club	League	GP	G	A	Pts	PIM	GP	G	A	Pts	PIM
2004-05	Shat.-St. Mary's	High-MN	64	48	62	110	38	....	....	....	....	....
2005-06	North Dakota	WCHA	42	22	17	39	22	....	....	....	....	....

TOFFEY, John (TAW-fee, JAWN) T.B.

Center. Shoots left. 6'3", 205 lbs. Born, Barnstable, MA, November 26, 1982.
(Tampa Bay's 13th choice, 287th overall, in 2002 Entry Draft).

			Regular Season					Playoffs				
Season	Club	League	GP	G	A	Pts	PIM	GP	G	A	Pts	PIM
1997/00	St. Sebastian's	High-MA	65	29	27	56	....	....	....	....	....	....
2000-01	St. Sebastian's	High-MA	22	22	24	46	....	....	....	....	....	....
2001-02	Ohio State	CCHA	24	2	3	5	4	....	....	....	....	....
2002-03	Walpole Stars	EJHL	19	7	8	15	10	....	....	....	....	....
2003-04	Massachusetts	H-East	20	2	3	5	16	....	....	....	....	....
2004-05	Massachusetts	H-East	20	0	1	1	14	....	....	....	....	....
2005-06	Johnstown Chiefs	ECHL	61	6	5	11	46	....	....	....	....	....

• Statistics for 1997/00 **St. Sebastian's** (High-MA) are totals for 1997-2000 seasons.

TOLKUNOV, Dmitri (tohl-ku-NAWF, di-MEE-tree) FLA.

Defense. Shoots right. 6'2", 200 lbs. Born, Kiev, USSR, May 5, 1979.

			Regular Season					Playoffs				
Season	Club	League	GP	G	A	Pts	PIM	GP	G	A	Pts	PIM
1996-97	Hull Olympiques	QMJHL	34	3	8	11	99	....	....	....	....	....
	Beauport Harfangs	QMJHL	27	3	7	10	18	4	0	1	1	4
1997-98	Quebec Remparts	QMJHL	66	10	25	35	81	14	3	9	12	22
1998-99	Quebec Remparts	QMJHL	69	11	57	68	110	13	2	7	9	22
99-2000	Cleveland	IHL	65	3	12	15	54	8	0	0	0	2
2000-01	Norfolk Admirals	AHL	78	5	18	23	93	9	0	1	1	4
2001-02	Norfolk Admirals	AHL	51	1	18	19	20	4	0	0	0	2
2002-03	Norfolk Admirals	AHL	47	1	17	18	39	....	....	....	....	....
2003-04	Yaroslavl 2	Russia-3	14	4	3	7	11	....	....	....	....	....
	Yaroslavl	Russia	6	0	0	0	4	....	....	....	....	....
	Amur Khabarovsk	Russia	27	1	2	3	28	....	....	....	....	....
2004-05	Sibir Novosibirsk	Russia	3	0	0	0	2	....	....	....	....	....
	Amur Khabarovsk	Russia-2	29	2	8	10	32	9	1	0	1	12
2005-06	Novokuznetsk	Russia	43	3	7	10	73	3	0	0	0	4

QMJHL Second All-Star Team (1999)

Signed as a free agent by **Chicago**, October 8, 1998. Traded to **Florida** by **Chicago** for NY Islanders' 9th round choice (previously acquired – later traded to San Jose – San Jose selected Carter Lee) in 2003 Entry Draft, June 21, 2003. Signed as a free agent by **Yaroslavl** (Russia), September 8, 2003, with **Florida** retaining NHL rights.

TOLPEKO, Denis (tohl-PEH-koh, DEH-nihs) PHI.

Center. Shoots left. 6', 190 lbs. Born, Moscow, Russia, January 29, 1985.

			Regular Season					Playoffs				
Season	Club	League	GP	G	A	Pts	PIM	GP	G	A	Pts	PIM
2003-04	Seattle	WHL	72	13	16	29	63	....	....	....	....	....
2004-05	Seattle	WHL	54	13	18	31	48	12	1	0	1	10
2005-06	Regina Pats	WHL	53	20	31	51	66	6	0	4	4	16

Signed as a free agent by **Philadelphia**, July 5, 2006.

TOPOL, Sergei (TOH-puhl, SAIR-gay) VAN.

Center. Shoots left. 6'2", 183 lbs. Born, Omsk, USSR, February 15, 1985.
(Vancouver's 8th choice, 252nd overall, in 2003 Entry Draft).

			Regular Season					Playoffs				
Season	Club	League	GP	G	A	Pts	PIM	GP	G	A	Pts	PIM
2002-03	Omsk 2	Russia-3	45	16	5	21	18	....	....	....	....	....
2003-04	Omsk 2	Russia-3	39	25	14	39	10	....	....	....	....	....
	Avangard Omsk	Russia	9	0	0	0	2	....	....	....	....	....
2004-05	Mechel	Russia-2	19	1	0	1	6	....	....	....	....	....
	Mechel 2	Russia-3	5	2	1	3	8	....	....	....	....	....
	Omsk 2	Russia-3	18	6	4	10	4	....	....	....	....	....
	Avangard Omsk	Russia	2	1	0	1	0	....	....	....	....	....
2005-06	Omsk 2	Russia-3	33	24	15	39	26	....	....	....	....	....
	Avangard Omsk	Russia	17	1	0	1	12	....	....	....	....	....

TREMBLAY, Jonathan (TRAHM-blay, JAWN-ah-thuhn) S.J.

Right wing. Shoots right. 6'3", 240 lbs. Born, Fauquier, Ont., March 3, 1984.
(San Jose's 6th choice, 201st overall, in 2003 Entry Draft).

			Regular Season					Playoffs				
Season	Club	League	GP	G	A	Pts	PIM	GP	G	A	Pts	PIM
2001-02	Timmins Majors	GNML	STATISTICS NOT AVAILABLE									
	Acadie-Bathurst	QMJHL	2	0	0	0	5	1	0	0	0	0
2002-03	Acadie-Bathurst	QMJHL	62	0	1	1	232	9	0	0	0	45
2003-04	Acadie-Bathurst	QMJHL	60	3	0	3	*316	....	....	....	....	....
2004-05	Cleveland Barons	AHL	1	0	0	0	0	....	....	....	....	....
	Johnstown Chiefs	ECHL	46	2	3	5	136	....	....	....	....	....
2005-06	Toledo Storm	ECHL	1	0	0	0	0	....	....	....	....	....
	Kalamazoo Wings	UHL	8	0	0	0	20	....	....	....	....	....
	Quad City	UHL	37	0	2	2	62	....	....	....	....	....

TROJOVSKY, Matej (troh-YAWV-skee, MAH-tehzh) CAR.

Right wing. Shoots right. 6'5", 220 lbs. Born, Plzen, Czech., October 12, 1984.
(Carolina's 5th choice, 130th overall, in 2003 Entry Draft).

			Regular Season					Playoffs				
Season	Club	League	GP	G	A	Pts	PIM	GP	G	A	Pts	PIM
99-2000	HC Plzen Jr.	CzRep-Jr.	36	2	13	15	58	5	0	1	1	2
2000-01	Lincoln Stars	USHL	17	1	0	1	29	....	....	....	....	....
2001-02	Regina Pats	WHL	67	3	10	13	154	6	0	1	1	18
2002-03	Regina Pats	WHL	70	3	6	9	229	5	0	0	0	6
2003-04	Swift Current	WHL	61	3	6	9	201	3	0	0	0	10
2004-05	Swift Current	WHL	30	3	3	6	119	....	....	....	....	....
	Prince George	WHL	27	2	1	3	80	....	....	....	....	....
2005-06	Plzen	CzRep	13	0	0	0	22	....	....	....	....	....
	Beroun	CzRep-2	19	3	2	5	69	....	....	....	....	....

TRUBACHEV, Yuri (troo-bah-CHEHV, YOO-ree) CGY.

Center. Shoots left. 5'9", 187 lbs. Born, Cherepovets, USSR, March 9, 1983.
(Calgary's 7th choice, 164th overall, in 2001 Entry Draft).

			Regular Season					Playoffs				
Season	Club	League	GP	G	A	Pts	PIM	GP	G	A	Pts	PIM
1997-98	Cherepovets 2	Russia-3	1	0	0	0	0	....	....	....	....	....
1998-99	Cherepovets 3	Russia-4	9	5	1	6	0	....	....	....	....	....
	Cherepovets 2	Russia-3	2	0	0	0	0	....	....	....	....	....
99-2000	Cherepovets 2	Russia-3	42	13	19	32	76	....	....	....	....	....
2000-01	SKA St. Petersburg	Russia	34	6	5	11	24	....	....	....	....	....
2001-02	Cherepovets 2	Russia-3	5	3	3	6	2	....	....	....	....	....
	Cherepovets	Russia	32	2	1	3	6	4	0	2	2	0
2002-03	Cherepovets	Russia	48	5	7	12	26	12	1	2	3	6
2003-04	Cherepovets	Russia	59	8	10	18	50	....	....	....	....	....
2004-05	Cherepovets	Russia	59	12	15	27	44	....	....	....	....	....
2005-06	Cherepovets	Russia	47	7	13	20	69	4	1	0	1	2

TRUKHNO, Vyacheslav (trookh-NOH, VYACH-ih-slav) EDM.

Left wing. Shoots left. 6'1", 196 lbs. Born, Khimki, USSR, February 22, 1987.
(Edmonton's 6th choice, 120th overall, in 2005 Entry Draft).

			Regular Season					Playoffs				
Season	Club	League	GP	G	A	Pts	PIM	GP	G	A	Pts	PIM
2002-03	Rungstead IK	Denmark-2	1	2	3	5	0	....	....	....	....	....
	Rungstead	Denmark	27	7	4	11	8	12	0	1	1	8
2003-04	Rungstead	Denmark	35	12	11	23	18	7	0	0	0	8
2004-05	PEI Rocket	QMJHL	64	25	34	59	57	....	....	....	....	....
2005-06	PEI Rocket	QMJHL	60	28	68	96	81	3	2	2	4	0

QMJHL All-Rookie Team (2005) • Canadian Major Junior All-Rookie Team (2005)

TUKONEN, Lauri (too-KOH-nehn, LOW-ree) L.A.

Right wing. Shoots right. 6'2", 200 lbs. Born, Hyvinkaa, Finland, September 1, 1986.
(Los Angeles' 1st choice, 11th overall, in 2004 Entry Draft).

			Regular Season					Playoffs				
Season	Club	League	GP	G	A	Pts	PIM	GP	G	A	Pts	PIM
2001-02	Ahmat Jr.	Fin-Jr.	2	4	0	4	2	....	....	....	....	....
	HC Sunne	Sweden-3	2	4	0	4	2	....	....	....	....	....
	Ahmat Hyvinkaa	Finland-2	24	7	4	11	6	....	....	....	....	....
2002-03	Ahmat Jr.	Fin-Jr.	4	3	1	4	2	....	....	....	....	....
	Ahmat Hyvinkaa	Finland-2	12	2	2	4	2	....	....	....	....	....
	Blues Espoo Jr.	Fin-Jr.	17	6	6	12	18	5	0	0	0	10
2003-04	Suomi U20	Finland-2	6	0	0	0	6	....	....	....	....	....
	Blues Espoo Jr.	Fin-Jr.	14	14	9	23	4	....	....	....	....	....
	Blues Espoo	Finland	35	3	3	6	16	7	0	0	0	0
2004-05	Blues Espoo Jr.	Fin-Jr.	2	0	0	0	2	....	....	....	....	....
	Blues Espoo	Finland	43	5	5	10	10	....	....	....	....	....
2005-06	Manchester	AHL	62	14	22	36	20	....	....	....	....	....

TULUPOV, Kirill (too-LOO-pawv, kih-RIHL) N.J.

Defense. Shoots right. 6'3", 220 lbs. Born, Moscow, USSR, April 23, 1988.
(New Jersey's 3rd choice, 67th overall, in 2006 Entry Draft).

			Regular Season					Playoffs				
Season	Club	League	GP	G	A	Pts	PIM	GP	G	A	Pts	PIM
2004-05	Toronto Rattlers	Exhib.	57	7	16	23	33	....	....	....	....	....
2005-06	Toronto Rattlers	Exhib.	40	16	28	44	30	....	....	....	....	....
	Leninogorsk	Russia-2	8	1	1	2	14	3	0	2	2	8

TUMA, Martin (TOO-ma, MAHR-tehn) FLA.

Defense. Shoots left. 6'4", 209 lbs. Born, Most, Czech., September 14, 1985.
(Florida's 8th choice, 162nd overall, in 2003 Entry Draft).

			Regular Season					Playoffs				
Season	Club	League	GP	G	A	Pts	PIM	GP	G	A	Pts	PIM
2000-01	Litvinov Jr.	CzRep-Jr.	45	4	12	16	62	6	0	3	3	8
2001-02	Litvinov Jr.	CzRep-Jr.	39	2	1	3	104	2	0	0	0	0
	Litvinov	CzRep	1	0	0	0	2	....	....	....	....	....
2002-03	Litvinov Jr.	CzRep-Jr.	34	1	3	4	123	....	....	....	....	....
2003-04	Sault Ste. Marie	OHL	57	0	5	5	48	....	....	....	....	....
2004-05	Sault Ste. Marie	OHL	61	10	13	23	107	7	0	3	3	6
	San Antonio	AHL	5	0	1	1	0	....	....	....	....	....
2005-06	Rochester	AHL	12	0	2	2	38	....	....	....	....	....
	Florida Everblades	ECHL	48	0	6	6	75	1	0	0	0	0

TUNIK, Evgeny (TOO-nihk, yehv-GEH-nee) NYI

Center. Shoots left. 6'2", 198 lbs. Born, Kraskovo, USSR, November 17, 1984.
(NY Islanders' 3rd choice, 53rd overall, in 2003 Entry Draft).

			Regular Season					Playoffs				
Season	Club	League	GP	G	A	Pts	PIM	GP	G	A	Pts	PIM
99-2000	Elektrostal 2	Russia-3	3	0	0	0	4	....	....	....	....	....
2000-01	Elektrostal	Russia-2	8	2	0	2	2	....	....	....	....	....
2001-02	Elektrostal 2	Russia-3	14	13	6	19	18	....	....	....	....	....
	Elektrostal	Russia-2	22	5	0	5	8	....	....	....	....	....
2002-03	Elektrostal	Russia-2	42	14	10	24	24	....	....	....	....	....
	Elektrostal 2	Russia-3	1	0	0	0	0	....	....	....	....	....
2003-04	St. Petersburg 2	Russia-3	9	6	5	11	54	1	0	0	0	2
	SKA St. Petersburg	Russia	32	3	1	4	26	....	....	....	....	....
2004-05	St. Petersburg 2	Russia-3	15	8	6	14	64	....	....	....	....	....
	SKA St. Petersburg	Russia	4	0	0	0	8	....	....	....	....	....
	Kristall Elektrostal	Russia-2	12	3	2	5	18	....	....	....	....	....
	Leninogorsk	Russia-2	6	0	0	0	32	1	1	0	1	0
2005-06	Bridgeport	AHL	61	4	14	18	44	....	....	....	....	....

TUOMAINEN, Miikka (too-oh-MAY-nehn, MEE-kah) ATL.

Left wing. Shoots left. 6'3", 220 lbs. Born, Turku, Finland, May 22, 1986.
(Atlanta's 7th choice, 204th overall, in 2004 Entry Draft).

			Regular Season					Playoffs				
Season	Club	League	GP	G	A	Pts	PIM	GP	G	A	Pts	PIM
2001-02	TuTo Turku U18	Fin-U18	14	8	5	13	14	....	....	....	....	....
	TuTo Turku Jr.	Fin-Jr.	1	1	0	1	0	....	....	....	....	....
2002-03	TuTo Turku U18	Fin-U18	24	3	4	7	52	4	0	0	0	0
	TuTo Turku Jr.	Fin-Jr.	2	0	0	0	4	....	....	....	....	....
	TuTo Turku	Finland-2	6	0	0	0	0	....	....	....	....	....
2003-04	TuTo Turku Jr.	Fin-Jr.	20	10	7	17	6	....	....	....	....	....
	TuTo Turku U18	Fin-U18	20	10	7	17	6	....	....	....	....	....
	TuTo Turku	Finland-2	30	4	3	7	2	....	....	....	....	....
2004-05	TuTo Turku Jr.	Fin-Jr.	5	1	4	5	0	....	....	....	....	....
	TuTo Turku	Finland-2	42	4	4	8	22	7	1	0	1	2
2005-06	Lukko Rauma Jr.	Fin-Jr.	16	5	3	8	4	9	5	3	8	8
	Suomi U20	Finland-2	2	0	0	0	2	....	....	....	....	....
	Lukko Rauma	Finland	33	2	2	4	12	....	....	....	....	....

TUREK, Ryan (TOOR-ehk, RIGH-uhn) ST.L.

Center. Shoots right. 5'11", 170 lbs. Born, Southfield, MI, September 22, 1987.
(St. Louis' 5th choice, 94th overall, in 2006 Entry Draft).

			Regular Season					Playoffs				
Season	Club	League	GP	G	A	Pts	PIM	GP	G	A	Pts	PIM
2004-05	Omaha Lancers	USHL	45	3	8	11	52	4	1	0	1	2
2005-06	Omaha Lancers	USHL	52	17	11	28	71	5	1	1	2	2

Signed Letter of Intent to attend **Michigan State** (CCHA) in fall of 2006.

TURNER, Brennan (TUHR-nuhr, BREH-nan) CHI.

Defense. Shoots left. 6'3", 221 lbs. Born, Winnipeg, Man., December 5, 1986.
(Chicago's 8th choice, 134th overall, in 2005 Entry Draft).

			Regular Season					Playoffs				
Season	Club	League	GP	G	A	Pts	PIM	GP	G	A	Pts	PIM
2003-04	Notre Dame	SJHL	35	2	8	10	110	....	....	....	....	....
2004-05	Notre Dame	SJHL	41	5	12	17	207	8	0	1	1	25
2005-06	Yale	ECACHL	16	0	2	2	53	....	....	....	....	....

TURON, David (TUHR-awn, DAY-vihd)

Defense. Shoots right. 6'3", 202 lbs. Born, Havirov, Czech., October 4, 1983.
(Toronto's 5th choice, 122nd overall, in 2002 Entry Draft).

			Regular Season					Playoffs				
Season	Club	League	GP	G	A	Pts	PIM	GP	G	A	Pts	PIM
99-2000	SK Karvina Jr.	CzRep-Jr.	2	0	0	0	0	....	....	....	....	....
	HC Havirov Jr.	CzRep-Jr.	41	14	11	25	54	....	....	....	....	....
2000-01	HC Havirov Jr.	CzRep-Jr.	43	12	7	19	26	....	....	....	....	....
	HC Femax Havirov	CzRep	4	0	0	0	4	....	....	....	....	....
2001-02	HC Havirov Jr.	CzRep-Jr.	41	5	11	16	75	....	....	....	....	....
	HC Femax Havirov	CzRep	14	0	1	1	10	....	....	....	....	....
2002-03	Portland	WHL	36	3	6	9	38	7	0	2	2	0
2003-04	Memphis	CHL	42	8	7	15	57	....	....	....	....	....
	St. John's	AHL	11	0	1	1	2	....	....	....	....	....
2004-05	St. John's	AHL	1	0	0	0	2	....	....	....	....	....
	Pensacola	ECHL	50	3	9	12	32	....	....	....	....	....
	Louisiana	ECHL	8	0	4	4	4	....	....	....	....	....
2005-06	Toronto Marlies	AHL	24	2	4	6	33	....	....	....	....	....
	Pensacola	ECHL	38	3	8	11	32	....	....	....	....	....

• Missed majority of 2002-03 season recovering from shoulder injury suffered in training camp, September 26, 2002.

TUZZOLINO, Nicholas (Tootz-OH-lee-noh, NIHK-o-las) NYI

Defense. Shoots right. 6'5", 225 lbs. Born, Buffalo, NY, January 19, 1986.
(NY Islanders' 6th choice, 196th overall, in 2005 Entry Draft).

			Regular Season					Playoffs				
Season	Club	League	GP	G	A	Pts	PIM	GP	G	A	Pts	PIM
2002-03	Buffalo Lightning	OPJHL	46	4	13	17	135	....	....	....	....	....
2003-04	Lincoln Stars	USHL	55	2	1	3	55	....	....	....	....	....
2004-05	Sarnia Sting	OHL	67	2	20	22	128	....	....	....	....	....
2005-06	Sarnia Sting	OHL	37	7	20	27	95	....	....	....	....	....
	Sudbury Wolves	OHL	26	3	8	11	41	10	0	3	3	22

UMICEVIC, Dragan (oo-mih-CHAY-vihk, DRA-guhn) **EDM.**

Left wing. Shoots right. 6', 191 lbs. Born, Köping, Sweden, October 9, 1984.
(Edmonton's 8th choice, 184th overall, in 2003 Entry Draft).

			Regular Season					Playoffs				
Season	**Club**	**League**	**GP**	**G**	**A**	**Pts**	**PIM**	**GP**	**G**	**A**	**Pts**	**PIM**
99-2000	Koping HC	Sweden-3	STATISTICS NOT AVAILABLE									
2000-01	Sodertalje SK U18	Swe-U18	16	8	5	13	49					
	Sodertalje SK Jr.	Swe-Jr.	1	0	0	0	0					
2001-02	Sodertalje SK Jr.	Swe-Jr.	36	20	31	51	41					
	Sodertalje SK	Sweden	3	1	0	1	0					
2002-03	Sodertalje SK	Sweden	22	2	3	5	4					
	Sodertalje SK Jr.	Swe-Jr.	24	19	14	33	28					
2003-04	Sodertalje SK Jr.	Swe-Jr.	9	3	5	8	24					
	IF Bjorkloven Umea	Sweden-2	21	8	8	16	45					
	Sodertalje SK	Sweden	8	0	0	0	0					
2004-05	Sodertalje SK Jr.	Swe-Jr.	4	2	9	11	4					
	Sodertalje SK	Sweden	47	6	13	19	20	10	0	1	1	6
2005-06	Sodertalje SK	Sweden	43	6	16	22	14					
	Sodertalje SK	Sweden-Q	10	2	0	2	6					

UPPER, Dmitri (OO-puhr, dih-MEE-tree) **NYI**

Center. Shoots right. 6'1", 185 lbs. Born, Ust-Kamenogorsk, USSR, July 27, 1978.
(NY Islanders' 5th choice, 136th overall, in 2000 Entry Draft).

			Regular Season					Playoffs				
Season	**Club**	**League**	**GP**	**G**	**A**	**Pts**	**PIM**	**GP**	**G**	**A**	**Pts**	**PIM**
1997-98	Ust-Kamenogorsk	Russia-2	47	16	12	28	44					
1998-99	Ust-Kam'gorsk 2	Russia-4	29	10	11	21	44					
	Nizhny Novgorod	Russia-2	11	4	10	14	16	17	6	6	12	49
99-2000	Nizhny Novgorod	Russia	36	14	6	20	50	5	1	1	2	4
2000-01	Nizhny Novgorod	Russia	6	0	2	2	4					
	Ak Bars Kazan	Russia	31	7	4	11	6	1	0	0	0	0
2001-02	Spartak Moscow	Russia	51	16	9	25	74					
2002-03	Spartak Moscow	Russia	43	7	13	20	63					
2003-04	CSKA Moscow	Russia	58	10	9	19	48					
2004-05	CSKA Moscow	Russia	41	7	3	10	30					
2005-06	CSKA Moscow	Russia	51	11	14	25	54	7	2	0	2	8
	Kazakhstan	Olympics	5	0	1	1	8					

URQUHART, Cory (UHRK-hahrt, KOHR-ee) **MTL.**

Center. Shoots left. 6'3", 201 lbs. Born, Halifax, N.S., October 1, 1984.
(Montreal's 2nd choice, 40th overall, in 2003 Entry Draft).

			Regular Season					Playoffs				
Season	**Club**	**League**	**GP**	**G**	**A**	**Pts**	**PIM**	**GP**	**G**	**A**	**Pts**	**PIM**
1997-98	East Hants	NSBHL	60	35	46	81	24					
1998-99	East Hants	NSBHL	62	54	60	114	74					
99-2000	Dalhousie	NSMHL	21	15	14	29	12					
2000-01	Quebec Remparts	QMJHL	60	25	24	49	32	2	0	0	0	2
2001-02	Quebec Remparts	QMJHL	36	8	10	18	4					
	Montreal Rocket	QMJHL	34	9	9	18	6	7	3	2	5	0
2002-03	Montreal Rocket	QMJHL	71	35	43	78	28	7	9	6	15	6
2003-04	PEI Rocket	QMJHL	67	35	44	79	52	10	6	7	13	14
2004-05	Hamilton Bulldogs	AHL	1	0	0	0	0					
	Long Beach	ECHL	63	16	15	31	14	6	0	0	0	2
2005-06	Hamilton Bulldogs	AHL	2	0	1	1	2					
	Long Beach	ECHL	67	26	26	52	42	7	4	0	4	8

UTKIN, Dmitri (OOT-kihn, dih-MEE-tree) **BOS.**

Left wing. Shoots left. 6', 170 lbs. Born, Yaroslavl, USSR, June 10, 1984.
(Boston's 5th choice, 228th overall, in 2002 Entry Draft).

			Regular Season					Playoffs				
Season	**Club**	**League**	**GP**	**G**	**A**	**Pts**	**PIM**	**GP**	**G**	**A**	**Pts**	**PIM**
2000-01	Yaroslavl 2	Russia-3	49	12	1	13	10					
2001-02	Yaroslavl 2	Russia-3	32	15	7	22	33					
2002-03	Yaroslavl	Russia	4	0	1	1	0					
2003-04	Spartak Moscow	Russia-2	57	10	10	20	8	13	3	3	6	2
2004-05	Keramin Minsk	BelOpen	8	2	0	2	31					
	HK Brest	BelOpen	20	4	12	16	4					
	HK Riga 2000	BelOpen	....	....	....	....	....	3	0	0	0	0
	HK Riga 2000	Latvia	....	....	....	....	....	6	3	2	5	0
2005-06	Spartak Moscow	Russia	33	3	1	4	4	2	0	0	0	0
	Spartak Moscow 2	Russia-3	10	5	2	7	8					

VAGNER, Martin (VAHG-nuhr, MAHR-tihn) **CAR.**

Defense. Shoots left. 6'1", 214 lbs. Born, Jaromer, Czech., March 16, 1984.
(Carolina's 8th choice, 268th overall, in 2004 Entry Draft).

			Regular Season					Playoffs				
Season	**Club**	**League**	**GP**	**G**	**A**	**Pts**	**PIM**	**GP**	**G**	**A**	**Pts**	**PIM**
99-2000	Sparta Jr.	CzRep-Jr.	46	2	8	10	34					
2000-01	HC Pardubice Jr.	CzRep-Jr.	53	2	12	14	46					
2001-02	Hull Olympiques	QMJHL	64	6	28	34	81	8	0	1	1	10
2002-03	Hull Olympiques	QMJHL	53	1	12	13	98	20	1	4	5	38
2003-04	Gatineau	QMJHL	38	6	12	18	85	13	0	3	3	16
2004-05	Acadie-Bathurst	QMJHL	48	3	10	13	84					
2005-06	Pardubice	CzRep	36	0	0	0	14					
	Hr. Kralove	CzRep-2	12	0	1	1	12					

• Re-entered NHL Entry Draft. Originally Dallas' 1st choice, 26th overall, in 2002 Entry Draft.

QMJHL All-Rookie Team (2002)

VALABIK, Boris (vuh-LA-bihk, BOHR-ihs) **ATL.**

Defense. Shoots left. 6'7", 230 lbs. Born, Nitra, Czech., February 14, 1986.
(Atlanta's 1st choice, 10th overall, in 2004 Entry Draft).

			Regular Season					Playoffs				
Season	**Club**	**League**	**GP**	**G**	**A**	**Pts**	**PIM**	**GP**	**G**	**A**	**Pts**	**PIM**
2002-03	HKM Nitra Jr.	Slovak-Jr.	46	2	12	14	145					
2003-04	Kitchener Rangers	OHL	68	3	13	16	278	5	0	0	0	8
2004-05	Kitchener Rangers	OHL	43	0	4	4	231	15	0	0	0	56
2005-06	Kitchener Rangers	OHL	52	1	9	10	216	5	0	2	2	14

OHL All-Rookie Team (2004) • Canadian Major Junior All-Rookie Team (2004)

VALCAK, Patrik (VAHL-chahk, PAT-rihk) **BOS.**

Center. Shoots left. 6'1", 185 lbs. Born, Ostrava, Czech., December 16, 1984.
(Boston's 6th choice, 129th overall, in 2003 Entry Draft).

			Regular Season					Playoffs				
Season	**Club**	**League**	**GP**	**G**	**A**	**Pts**	**PIM**	**GP**	**G**	**A**	**Pts**	**PIM**
2000-01	HC Ostrava Jr.	CzRep-Jr.	44	13	16	29	34					
2001-02	HC Ostrava Jr.	CzRep-Jr.	45	9	16	25	44					
2002-03	HC Ostrava Jr.	CzRep-Jr.	38	14	18	32	131					
2003-04	Lethbridge	WHL	35	2	9	11	28					
	Kelowna Rockets	WHL	22	0	1	1	13	11	0	0	0	6
2004-05	Lincoln Stars	USHL	4	1	2	3	2					
	HC Havirov	CzRep-2	2	0	1	1	6					
	HC Ostrava Jr.	CzRep-Jr.	5	2	3	5	4					
	HC Sareza Ostrava	CzRep-2	26	1	6	7	32	2	0	0	0	2
2005-06	HC Vsetin	CzRep	3	0	0	0	0					
	HC Sareza Ostrava	CzRep-2	15	1	4	5	4					
	Jind. Hradec	CzRep-2	15	2	4	6	20					
	SK Kadan	CzRep-2	13	1	2	3	6					

VALDIX, Andreas (VAHL-dihx, an-DRAY-uhs) **WSH.**

Left wing. Shoots left. 5'11", 170 lbs. Born, Malmo, Sweden, December 6, 1984.
(Washington's 3rd choice, 109th overall, in 2003 Entry Draft).

			Regular Season					Playoffs				
Season	**Club**	**League**	**GP**	**G**	**A**	**Pts**	**PIM**	**GP**	**G**	**A**	**Pts**	**PIM**
99-2000	Malmo Jr.	Swe-Jr.	14	3	7	10	39					
2000-01	Malmo U18	Swe-U18	6	2	2	4	12					
	Malmo Jr.	Swe-Jr.	19	3	3	6	8	3	2	2	4	4
2001-02	Malmo U18	Swe-U18	39	13	13	26	86	7	0	3	3	6
	Malmo	Sweden	1	0	0	0	0					
2002-03	Malmo U18	Swe-U18	11	10	12	22	16	6	2	5	7	8
	Malmo	Sweden	39	2	0	2	10					
2003-04	Malmo U18	Swe-U18	9	4	3	7	4					
	Malmo	Sweden	47	2	3	5	8					
2004-05	Malmo	Sweden	26	0	1	1	2					
	Halmstad	Sweden-2	24	4	5	9	14	2	0	0	0	6
2005-06	Nybro Vikings IF	Sweden-2	42	4	8	12	73					

VALENTENKO, Pavel (val-ehn-TEHN-koh, PAH-vehl) **MTL.**

Defense. Shoots left. 6'2", 202 lbs. Born, Moscow, Russia, October 20, 1987.
(Montreal's 5th choice, 139th overall, in 2006 Entry Draft).

			Regular Season					Playoffs				
Season	**Club**	**League**	**GP**	**G**	**A**	**Pts**	**PIM**	**GP**	**G**	**A**	**Pts**	**PIM**
2002-03	Lada Togliatti 2	Russia-3	6	0	0	0	4					
2003-04	Nizhnekamsk 2	Russia-3	26	0	1	1	28					
2004-05	Nizhnekamsk 2	Russia-3	STATISTICS NOT AVAILABLE									
2005-06	Nizhnekamsk 2	Russia-3	STATISTICS NOT AVAILABLE									
	Nizhnekamsk	Russia	2	0	0	0	2					

VALETTE, Craig (va-LEHT, KRAIG) **S.J.**

Center. Shoots left. 6', 190 lbs. Born, Shellbrook, Sask., October 7, 1982.

			Regular Season					Playoffs				
Season	**Club**	**League**	**GP**	**G**	**A**	**Pts**	**PIM**	**GP**	**G**	**A**	**Pts**	**PIM**
1998-99	Sask. Contacts	SMHL	36	19	22	41	....					
99-2000	Saskatoon Blades	WHL	47	2	1	3	25	3	0	0	0	0
2000-01	Saskatoon Blades	WHL	24	2	0	2	19					
	Portland	WHL	39	8	6	14	39	16	0	2	2	27
2001-02	Portland	WHL	67	8	14	22	160	7	2	1	3	6
2002-03	Portland	WHL	71	30	26	56	192	7	5	4	9	18
2003-04	Cleveland Barons	AHL	56	6	10	16	77	5	0	0	0	2
2004-05	Cleveland Barons	AHL	79	6	6	12	94					
2005-06	Cleveland Barons	AHL	69	5	6	11	95					

Signed as a free agent by **San Jose**, April 4, 2003.

VALLIN, Ari (VAHL-ihn, AH-ree) **FLA.**

Defense. Shoots left. 5'11", 194 lbs. Born, Ylojarvi, Finland, March 21, 1978.

			Regular Season					Playoffs				
Season	**Club**	**League**	**GP**	**G**	**A**	**Pts**	**PIM**	**GP**	**G**	**A**	**Pts**	**PIM**
1996-97	Tappara Tampere	Finland	21	0	0	0	8	3	0	0	0	0
1997-98	Tappara Tampere	Finland	44	2	2	4	16	4	0	3	3	0
1998-99	HPK Hameenlinna	Finland	49	6	3	9	24	8	0	1	1	8
99-2000	Tappara Tampere	Finland	54	4	8	12	36	4	0	0	0	8
2000-01	HPK Hameenlinna	Finland	53	5	7	12	34					
2001-02	Jokerit Helsinki	Finland	45	4	20	24	24	12	1	4	5	2
2002-03	Jokerit Helsinki	Finland	53	5	11	16	34	8	0	1	1	4
2003-04	Karpat Oulu	Finland	54	7	10	17	36	15	3	2	5	8
2004-05	Karpat Oulu	Finland	55	2	15	17	40	12	2	2	4	10
2005-06	Karpat Oulu	Finland	50	7	23	30	84					

Signed as a free agent by **Florida**, July 6, 2006.

VAN DER GULIK, David (VAN-DUHR-GOO-lihk, DAY-vihd) **CGY.**

Right wing. Shoots left. 5'11", 175 lbs. Born, Abbotsford, B.C., April 20, 1983.
(Calgary's 10th choice, 206th overall, in 2002 Entry Draft).

			Regular Season					Playoffs				
Season	**Club**	**League**	**GP**	**G**	**A**	**Pts**	**PIM**	**GP**	**G**	**A**	**Pts**	**PIM**
99-2000	Chilliwack Chiefs	BCHL	41	35	46	81	....					
2000-01	Chilliwack Chiefs	BCHL	60	42	38	80	....					
2001-02	Chilliwack Chiefs	BCHL	56	38	62	100	90	13	8	11	19	....
2002-03	Boston University	H-East	40	10	10	20	56					
2003-04	Boston University	H-East	35	13	7	20	74					
2004-05	Boston University	H-East	41	18	13	31	48					
2005-06	Boston University	H-East	25	11	11	22	26					

Hockey East All-Rookie Team (2003)

VANDE VELDE, Chris (VAN-deh-VEHLD, KRIHS) **EDM.**

Center. Shoots left. 6'1", 190 lbs. Born, Moorhead, MN, March 15, 1987.
(Edmonton's 5th choice, 97th overall, in 2005 Entry Draft).

			Regular Season					Playoffs				
Season	**Club**	**League**	**GP**	**G**	**A**	**Pts**	**PIM**	**GP**	**G**	**A**	**Pts**	**PIM**
2003-04	Moorhead Spuds	High-MN	29	19	24	43	....					
2004-05	Moorhead Spuds	High-MN	30	35	32	67	28					
	Lincoln Stars	USHL	7	1	4	5	0	4	0	2	2	0
2005-06	Lincoln Stars	USHL	56	16	20	36	70	9	1	3	4	10

Signed Letter of Intent to attend **U. of North Dakota** (WCHA) in fall of 2006.

VANDERMEER, Peter (VAN-duhr-meer, PEE-tuhr) WSH.

Left wing. Shoots left. 6', 210 lbs. Born, Carolina, Alta., October 14, 1975.

			Regular Season					Playoffs				
Season	Club	League	GP	G	A	Pts	PIM	GP	G	A	Pts	PIM
1992-93	Red Deer	AMHL	34	26	30	56	172	....	....	....	....	....
	Red Deer Rebels	WHL	2	0	0	0	2	....	....	....	....	....
1993-94	Red Deer Rebels	WHL	54	4	9	13	170	....	....	....	....	....
1994-95	Red Deer Rebels	WHL	61	16	16	32	218	....	....	....	....	....
1995-96	Red Deer Rebels	WHL	63	21	40	61	207	....	....	....	....	....
1996-97	Columbus Chill	ECHL	30	6	11	17	195	7	2	1	3	26
1997-98	Columbus Chill	ECHL	20	4	7	11	78	....	....	....	....	....
	Richmond	ECHL	18	2	5	7	165	....	....	....	....	....
	Rochester	AHL	30	4	2	6	140	4	1	0	1	13
1998-99	Rochester	AHL	2	1	0	1	16	16	1	0	1	38
	Binghamton	UHL	62	15	21	36	*390	5	2	2	4	0
99-2000	Wilkes-Barre	AHL	4	0	0	0	7	....	....	....	....	....
	Richmond	ECHL	58	31	25	56	*457	3	0	1	1	20
	Providence Bruins	AHL	....	....	....	....	....	9	0	3	3	2
2000-01	Providence Bruins	AHL	62	19	18	37	240	4	0	0	0	16
2001-02	Philadelphia	AHL	61	5	1	6	313	5	0	0	0	8
	Trenton Titans	ECHL	2	0	1	1	2	....	....	....	....	....
2002-03	Philadelphia	AHL	77	5	8	13	335	....	....	....	....	....
2003-04	Philadelphia	AHL	71	5	8	13	*398	12	1	0	1	29
2004-05	Grand Rapids	AHL	73	4	13	17	310	....	....	....	....	....
2005-06	Hamilton Bulldogs	AHL	67	6	6	12	276	....	....	....	....	....

Signed as a free agent by **Philadelphia**, July 6, 2001. Signed as a free agent by **Detroit**, August 16, 2004. Signed as a free agent by **Montreal**, August 2, 2005. Signed as a free agent by **Washington**, July 21, 2006.

VANNELLI, Michael (vuh-NEHL-ee, MIGH-kuhl) ATL.

Defense. Shoots right. 6'2", 190 lbs. Born, St. Paul, MN, October 2, 1983.
(Atlanta's 4th choice, 136th overall, in 2003 Entry Draft).

			Regular Season					Playoffs				
Season	Club	League	GP	G	A	Pts	PIM	GP	G	A	Pts	PIM
2001-02	Cretin-Derham	High-MN	28	0	5	5	16	....	....	....	....	....
	Sioux Falls	USHL	37	0	5	5	24	....	....	....	....	....
2002-03	Sioux Falls	USHL	60	13	34	47	88	....	....	....	....	....
2003-04	U. of Minnesota	WCHA	27	2	9	11	10	....	....	....	....	....
2004-05	U. of Minnesota	WCHA	40	4	12	16	33	....	....	....	....	....
2005-06	U. of Minnesota	WCHA	40	7	10	17	44	....	....	....	....	....

USHL First All-Star Team (2003)

VANTUCH, Lukas (VAHN-tooh, LEW-kahsh) BOS.

Right wing. Shoots left. 6'3", 200 lbs. Born, Jihlava, Czech., July 20, 1987.
(Boston's 7th choice, 172nd overall, in 2005 Entry Draft).

			Regular Season					Playoffs				
Season	Club	League	GP	G	A	Pts	PIM	GP	G	A	Pts	PIM
2002-03	HC Liberec U17	CzR-U17	38	11	12	23	36	....	....	....	....	....
	HC Liberec Jr.	CzRep-Jr.	1	0	0	0	2	....	....	....	....	....
2003-04	HC Liberec U17	CzR-U17	32	16	19	35	75	....	....	....	....	....
	HC Liberec Jr.	CzRep-Jr.	1	0	0	0	0	....	....	....	....	....
2004-05	HC Liberec Jr.	CzRep-Jr.	45	16	20	36	58	5	0	3	3	12
2005-06	Calgary Hitmen	WHL	68	4	15	19	70	13	0	1	1	6

VAS, Janos (VAHSH, YAH-nohsh) DAL.

Left wing. Shoots left. 6'1", 183 lbs. Born, Dunaujvaros, Hungary, January 29, 1984.
(Dallas' 2nd choice, 32nd overall, in 2002 Entry Draft).

			Regular Season					Playoffs				
Season	Club	League	GP	G	A	Pts	PIM	GP	G	A	Pts	PIM
99-2000	Dunaferr SE	Hungary	2	2	0	0	0	....	....	....	....	....
2000-01	Malmo Jr.	Swe-Jr.	23	4	4	8	12	....	....	....	....	....
	Malmo U18	Swe-U18	3	2	0	2	4	....	....	....	....	....
2001-02	Malmo Jr.	Swe-Jr.	36	15	19	34	52	7	8	2	10	4
2002-03	Malmo Jr.	Swe-Jr.	17	5	12	17	14	....	....	....	....	....
	IK Pantern Malmo	Sweden-3	STATISTICS NOT AVAILABLE									
	IF Troja-Ljungby	Sweden-2	17	2	2	4	20	....	....	....	....	....
	Malmo	Sweden	14	1	0	1	2	....	....	....	....	....
2003-04	Malmo U18	Swe-U18	15	5	3	8	14	8	5	2	7	33
	Malmo	Sweden	6	0	0	0	0	....	....	....	....	....
	IK Pantern Malmo	Sweden-3	3	0	2	2	0	....	....	....	....	....
	Malmo	Sweden-Q	1	0	0	0	0	....	....	....	....	....
2004-05	Halmstad	Sweden-2	39	9	8	17	10	2	0	1	1	2
2005-06	Iowa Stars	AHL	35	2	9	11	18	7	1	1	2	2
	Idaho Steelheads	ECHL	10	4	5	9	15	....	....	....	....	....

VASYUNOV, Alexander (vahs-YUH-nawv, al-ehx-AN-duhr) N.J.

Left wing. Shoots right. 6', 189 lbs. Born, Yaroslavl, Russia, April 22, 1988.
(New Jersey's 2nd choice, 58th overall, in 2006 Entry Draft).

			Regular Season					Playoffs				
Season	Club	League	GP	G	A	Pts	PIM	GP	G	A	Pts	PIM
2004-05	Yaroslavl 2	Russia-3	28	10	2	12	6	....	....	....	....	....
2005-06	Yaroslavl 2	Russia-3	29	29	6	35	14	....	....	....	....	....
	Yaroslavl	Russia	2	0	0	0	2	....	....	....	....	....

VERNACE, Michael (vuhr-NACE, MIGH-kuhl) COL.

Defense. Shoots left. 6'2", 200 lbs. Born, Toronto, Ont., May 26, 1986.
(San Jose's 6th choice, 201st overall, in 2004 Entry Draft).

			Regular Season					Playoffs				
Season	Club	League	GP	G	A	Pts	PIM	GP	G	A	Pts	PIM
2003-04	Bramalea Blues	OPJHL	33	3	12	15	16	....	....	....	....	....
	Brampton	OHL	2	1	1	2	0	11	2	3	5	8
2004-05	Brampton	OHL	68	12	38	50	42	6	2	2	4	0
2005-06	Brampton	OHL	68	10	62	72	54	11	1	5	6	6

OHL All-Rookie Team (2005)

Traded to **Colorado** by **San Jose** for Colorado's 6th round choice in 2007 Entry Draft, June 1, 2006.

VERSTEEG, Kris (vuhr-STEEG, KRIHS) BOS.

Right wing. Shoots right. 5'9", 160 lbs. Born, Lethbridge, Alta., May 13, 1986.
(Boston's 4th choice, 134th overall, in 2004 Entry Draft).

			Regular Season					Playoffs				
Season	Club	League	GP	G	A	Pts	PIM	GP	G	A	Pts	PIM
2002-03	Lethbridge	WHL	57	8	10	18	32	....	....	....	....	....
2003-04	Lethbridge	WHL	68	16	33	49	85	....	....	....	....	....
2004-05	Lethbridge	WHL	68	22	30	52	68	5	0	1	1	4
2005-06	Kamloops Blazers	WHL	14	6	6	12	24	....	....	....	....	....
	Red Deer Rebels	WHL	57	10	26	36	103	....	....	....	....	....
	Providence Bruins	AHL	13	2	4	6	13	3	0	0	0	6

VESCE, Ryan (veks-KEE, RIGH-uhn) OTT.

Center. Shoots right. 5'8", 165 lbs. Born, Lloyd Harbor, NY, April 7, 1982.

			Regular Season					Playoffs				
Season	Club	League	GP	G	A	Pts	PIM	GP	G	A	Pts	PIM
2000-01	Cornell Big Red	ECAC	33	7	20	27	10	....	....	....	....	....
2001-02	Cornell Big Red	ECAC	35	10	20	30	10	....	....	....	....	....
2002-03	Cornell Big Red	ECAC	36	19	26	45	16	....	....	....	....	....
2003-04	Cornell Big Red	ECAC	27	10	16	26	14	....	....	....	....	....
2004-05	Rogle	Sweden-2	43	20	25	45	51	....	....	....	....	....
2005-06	Springfield Falcons	AHL	80	18	49	67	50	....	....	....	....	....

Signed as a free agent by **Ottawa**, July 17, 2006.

VIDELL, Linus (vih-DEHL, LIH-nuhs) COL.

Left wing. Shoots left. 6'3", 214 lbs. Born, Skarpnack, Sweden, May 5, 1985.
(Colorado's 5th choice, 204th overall, in 2003 Entry Draft).

			Regular Season					Playoffs				
Season	Club	League	GP	G	A	Pts	PIM	GP	G	A	Pts	PIM
2001-02	AIK Solna U18	Swe-U18	14	12	5	17	12	4	7	1	8	....
2002-03	Brynas IF Gavle Jr.	Swe-Jr.	19	4	7	11	4	....	....	....	....	....
	Sodertalje SK U18	Swe-U18	1	0	0	0	2	....	....	....	....	....
	Sodertalje SK Jr.	Swe-Jr.	9	4	2	6	0	3	0	1	1	0
2003-04	Sodertalje SK Jr.	Swe-Jr.	27	20	15	35	6	2	0	0	0	0
	Sodertalje SK	Sweden	23	0	2	2	0	....	....	....	....	....
2004-05	Sodertalje SK	Sweden	5	0	0	0	0	....	....	....	....	....
	Halmstad	Sweden-2	27	6	9	15	6	....	....	....	....	....
	Sodertalje SK Jr.	Swe-Jr.	13	6	4	10	0	3	0	2	2	0
2005-06	Sodertalje SK Jr.	Swe-Jr.	2	3	1	4	0	....	....	....	....	....
	AIK Solna	Sweden-2	20	6	7	13	4	....	....	....	....	....
	Sodertalje SK	Sweden	31	1	3	4	4	....	....	....	....	....
	Sodertalje SK	Sweden-Q	7	1	0	1	0	....	....	....	....	....

VIENNEAU, Justin (vee-EHN-oo, JUHS-tihn)

Defense. Shoots left. 6'4", 205 lbs. Born, Saint John, N.B., February 20, 1986.
(Columbus' 9th choice, 198th overall, in 2004 Entry Draft).

			Regular Season					Playoffs				
Season	Club	League	GP	G	A	Pts	PIM	GP	G	A	Pts	PIM
2002-03	Shawinigan	QMJHL	62	0	8	8	150	9	0	1	1	10
2003-04	Shawinigan	QMJHL	53	0	7	7	129	11	0	1	1	19
2004-05	Shawinigan	QMJHL	60	4	11	15	146	4	0	0	0	6
2005-06	Shawinigan	QMJHL	54	1	14	15	164	10	0	2	2	15
	Syracuse Crunch	AHL	1	0	0	0	2	....	....	....	....	....

VIGILANTE, John (vih-jihl-AN-tee, JAWN) NSH.

Left wing. Shoots left. 5'11", 206 lbs. Born, Dearborn, MI, May 24, 1985.

			Regular Season					Playoffs				
Season	Club	League	GP	G	A	Pts	PIM	GP	G	A	Pts	PIM
2002-03	Plymouth Whalers	OHL	65	15	24	39	31	18	6	3	9	8
2003-04	Plymouth Whalers	OHL	66	30	38	68	25	9	1	7	8	8
2004-05	Plymouth Whalers	OHL	68	24	38	62	17	4	0	0	0	0
2005-06	Plymouth Whalers	OHL	55	24	53	77	34	13	4	12	16	0

Signed as a free agent by **Nashville**. December 7, 2005.

VIITANEN, Mikko (vee-EE-tan-ehn, MEE-koh)

Defense. Shoots left. 6'3", 220 lbs. Born, Nurmijarvi, Finland, February 18, 1982.
(Colorado's 6th choice, 149th overall, in 2001 Entry Draft).

			Regular Season					Playoffs				
Season	Club	League	GP	G	A	Pts	PIM	GP	G	A	Pts	PIM
1998-99	HPK U18	Fin-U18	36	3	6	9	40	....	....	....	....	....
	HPK Jr.	Fin-Jr.	1	0	0	0	0	....	....	....	....	....
99-2000	Chicago Freeze	NAHL	53	4	6	10	126	....	....	....	....	....
2000-01	Ahmat Jr.	Fin-Jr.	9	3	4	7	41	....	....	....	....	....
	Ahmat Hyvinkaa	Finland-2	41	3	9	12	66	3	0	0	0	0
2001-02	Blues Espoo Jr.	Fin-Jr.	10	1	3	4	16	....	....	....	....	....
	Blues Espoo	Finland	3	0	0	0	6	....	....	....	....	....
	Jukurit Mikkeli	Finland-2	21	0	3	3	26	....	....	....	....	....
2002-03	KJT Jarvenpaa	Finland-2	9	0	1	1	56	....	....	....	....	....
	Blues Espoo	Finland	1	0	0	0	0	....	....	....	....	....
	Blues Espoo Jr.	Fin-Jr.	1	0	0	0	0	1	0	0	0	25
2003-04	Hershey Bears	AHL	20	1	1	2	14	....	....	....	....	....
	Reading Royals	ECHL	47	0	4	4	21	13	0	1	1	8
2004-05	Hershey Bears	AHL	22	0	1	1	6	....	....	....	....	....
	Reading Royals	ECHL	52	3	3	6	47	8	0	0	0	8
2005-06	Lowell	AHL	72	1	7	8	56	....	....	....	....	....

VISHNEVSKIY, Ivan (vihsh-NEHV-skee, ee-VAHN) DAL.

Defense. Shoots left. 5'11", 176 lbs. Born, Barnaul, Russia, February 18, 1988.
(Dallas' 1st choice, 27th overall, in 2006 Entry Draft).

			Regular Season					Playoffs				
Season	Club	League	GP	G	A	Pts	PIM	GP	G	A	Pts	PIM
2003-04	Lada Togliatti 2	Russia-3	16	0	0	0	10	....	....	....	....	....
2004-05	Lada Togliatti 2	Russia-3	STATISTICS NOT AVAILABLE									
2005-06	Rouyn-Noranda	QMJHL	54	13	35	48	57	5	2	1	3	2

VISHNYAKOV, Albert (vihsh-nyeh-KAWF, al-BAIRT) T.B.

Left wing. Shoots right. 6'1", 178 lbs. Born, Almyetevsk, USSR, December 30, 1983.
(Tampa Bay's 9th choice, 273rd overall, in 2003 Entry Draft).

			Regular Season					Playoffs				
Season	Club	League	GP	G	A	Pts	PIM	GP	G	A	Pts	PIM
99-2000	Almetjevsk 2	Russia-3	41	11	5	16	68	....	....	....	....	....
2000-01	Almetjevsk	Russia-2	29	0	0	0	2	....	....	....	....	....
2001-02	Ak Bars Kazan	Russia	9	0	1	1	2	....	....	....	....	....
	Nizhny Novgorod	Russia	6	1	0	1	0	....	....	....	....	....
	Nizh. Novgorod 2	Russia-3	4	2	2	4	10	....	....	....	....	....
2002-03	Ak Bars Kazan	Russia	47	7	6	13	47	5	1	0	1	0
2003-04	Nizhnekamsk	Russia	10	2	3	5	10	....	....	....	....	....
	Ak Bars Kazan	Russia	10	1	1	2	8	....	....	....	....	....
	Ak Bars Kazan 2	Russia-3	STATISTICS NOT AVAILABLE									
2004-05	Dynamo Moscow	Russia	28	1	2	3	10	....	....	....	....	....
2005-06	Dynamo Moscow	Russia	48	9	3	12	78	3	0	0	0	0

VITALE, Joe (vih-TA-lee, JOH) PIT.

Center. Shoots right. 5'11", 205 lbs. Born, St. Louis, MO, August 20, 1985.
(Pittsburgh's 7th choice, 195th overall, in 2005 Entry Draft).

			Regular Season					Playoffs				
Season	Club	League	GP	G	A	Pts	PIM	GP	G	A	Pts	PIM
2003-04	St. Louis Jr. Blues	CSJHL	43	21	29	50	42	....	....	....	....	....
2004-05	Sioux Falls	USHL	53	11	20	31	62	....	....	....	....	....
2005-06	Northeastern	H-East	31	8	8	16	71	....	....	....	....	....

VLASIC, Marc-Edouard (vih-LASH-ihc, MAHRK-EHD-wahrd) **S.J.**

Defense. Shoots left. 6'1", 190 lbs. Born, Montreal, Que., March 30, 1987.
(San Jose's 2nd choice, 35th overall, in 2005 Entry Draft).

			Regular Season					Playoffs				
Season	Club	League	GP	G	A	Pts	PIM	GP	G	A	Pts	PIM
2003-04	Quebec Remparts	QMJHL	41	1	9	10	4	5	0	1	1	0
2004-05	Quebec Remparts	QMJHL	70	5	25	30	33	13	2	7	9	2
2005-06	Quebec Remparts	QMJHL	66	16	57	73	57	23	5	24	29	10

VOCE, Tony (VOHS, TOH-nee) **PHI.**

Center. Shoots left. 5'8", 185 lbs. Born, Philadelphia, PA, October 30, 1980.

			Regular Season					Playoffs				
Season	Club	League	GP	G	A	Pts	PIM	GP	G	A	Pts	PIM
1998-99	Lawrence	High-MA	....	39	30	*69	....	....	....	....	....	....
99-2000	Lawrence	High-MA	....	26	33	*59	....	....	....	....	....	....
2000-01	Boston College	H-East	42	12	14	26	40	....	....	....	....	....
2001-02	Boston College	H-East	38	26	22	48	65	....	....	....	....	....
2002-03	Boston College	H-East	37	*23	23	46	56	....	....	....	....	....
2003-04	Boston College	H-East	42	*29	18	47	48	....	....	....	....	....
2004-05	Philadelphia	AHL	73	22	17	39	85	4	0	0	0	4
2005-06	Philadelphia	AHL	67	28	27	55	87	....	....	....	....	....

Hockey East First All-Star Team (2002, 2004) • NCAA East First All-American Team (2004)

Signed as a free agent by **Philadelphia**, July 13, 2004.

VOJTA, Jakub (VOI-tah, YA-kuhb) **CAR.**

Defense. Shoots right. 6', 194 lbs. Born, Usti nad Labem, Czech., February 8, 1987.
(Carolina's 4th choice, 94th overall, in 2005 Entry Draft).

			Regular Season					Playoffs				
Season	Club	League	GP	G	A	Pts	PIM	GP	G	A	Pts	PIM
2002-03	Sparta U17	CzR-U17	47	14	24	38	87	1	0	0	0	12
2003-04	Sparta U17	CzR-U17	4	0	2	2	0	3	1	2	3	2
	Sparta Jr.	CzRep-Jr.	39	3	3	6	20	....	....	....	....	....
2004-05	Sparta Jr.	CzRep-Jr.	38	2	7	9	42	8	1	1	2	8
2005-06	Ottawa 67's	OHL	65	2	22	24	114	6	0	1	1	6

VOLKOV, Igor (VOHL-kawf, EE-gohr) **NYI**

Right wing. Shoots left. 6', 189 lbs. Born, Ufa, USSR, January 24, 1983.
(NY Islanders' 9th choice, 246th overall, in 2003 Entry Draft).

			Regular Season					Playoffs				
Season	Club	League	GP	G	A	Pts	PIM	GP	G	A	Pts	PIM
2000-01	Ufa	Russia	30	1	1	2	4	....	....	....	....	....
2001-02	Ufa	Russia	43	3	1	4	8	....	....	....	....	....
2002-03	Ufa	Russia	41	9	5	14	32	3	1	0	1	4
2003-04	Ufa	Russia	45	11	13	24	38	....	....	....	....	....
2004-05	Ufa	Russia	43	15	12	27	38	....	....	....	....	....
	Dynamo Moscow	Russia	10	0	1	1	0	4	1	0	1	0
2005-06	Ufa	Russia	46	18	13	31	22	6	1	1	2	16

VOLKOV, Konstantin (VOHL-kawf, kawn-stuhn-TIHN) **TOR.**

Right wing. Shoots left. 6', 174 lbs. Born, Kolpino, USSR, February 7, 1985.
(Toronto's 3rd choice, 125th overall, in 2003 Entry Draft).

			Regular Season					Playoffs				
Season	Club	League	GP	G	A	Pts	PIM	GP	G	A	Pts	PIM
2000-01	SKA St. Petersburg	Russia	2	0	1	1	0	....	....	....	....	....
2001-02	Dyn'o Moscow 2	Russia-3	21	3	7	10	10	....	....	....	....	....
2002-03	Dyn'o Moscow 2	Russia-3	29	13	17	30	2	....	....	....	....	....
2003-04	THK Tver	Russia-2	18	0	6	6	6	....	....	....	....	....
	CSK VVS Samara	Russia-2	22	6	6	12	16	....	....	....	....	....
	Lada Togliatti 2	Russia-3	10	2	7	9	10	11	0	10	10	4
2004-05	Lada Togliatti	Russia	1	0	0	0	0	....	....	....	....	....
2005-06	Vityaz Chekhov	Russia	28	3	2	5	8	....	....	....	....	....

VOLOSHENKO, Roman (voh-loh-SHEHN-koh, ROH-muhn) **MIN.**

Left wing. Shoots right. 6'1", 207 lbs. Born, Brest, USSR, May 12, 1986.
(Minnesota's 2nd choice, 42nd overall, in 2004 Entry Draft).

			Regular Season					Playoffs				
Season	Club	League	GP	G	A	Pts	PIM	GP	G	A	Pts	PIM
2001-02	Krylja Sovetov 2	Russia-3	8	2	3	5	0	....	....	....	....	....
2002-03	Krylja Sovetov	Russia	5	0	1	1	2	....	....	....	....	....
	Krylja Sovetov 2	Russia-3	6	3	1	4	2	....	....	....	....	....
2003-04	Krylja Sovetov	Russia-2	46	7	8	15	40	4	1	1	2	4
2004-05	Krylja Sovetov 2	Russia-3	1	0	0	0	2	....	....	....	....	....
	Krylja Sovetov	Russia-2	38	16	13	29	22	3	0	1	1	2
2005-06	Houston Aeros	AHL	69	33	27	60	36	7	0	1	1	0

VOMELA, Lukas (voh-MEH-luh, LOO-kahsh) **DAL.**

Defense. Shoots left. 6'3", 189 lbs. Born, Ceske Budejovice, Czech., September 25, 1985.
(Dallas' 9th choice, 248th overall, in 2004 Entry Draft).

			Regular Season					Playoffs				
Season	Club	League	GP	G	A	Pts	PIM	GP	G	A	Pts	PIM
2000-01	C. Budejovice U17	CzR-U17	39	1	1	2	8	....	....	....	....	....
2001-02	C. Budejovice U17	CzR-U17	47	9	9	18	87	....	....	....	....	....
	C. Budejovice Jr.	CzRep-Jr.	1	0	0	0	0	....	....	....	....	....
2002-03	C. Budejovice Jr.	CzRep-Jr.	36	2	2	4	24	....	....	....	....	....
	C. Budejovice	CzRep	1	0	0	0	4	....	....	....	....	....
2003-04	C. Budejovice	CzRep	15	0	1	1	8	....	....	....	....	....
	C. Budejovice Jr.	CzRep-Jr.	21	1	7	8	45	....	....	....	....	....
2004-05	C. Budejovice	CzRep-2	2	0	0	0	0	....	....	....	....	....
	Jind. Hradec	CzRep-3	5	0	3	3	0	....	....	....	....	....
	C. Budejovice Jr.	CzRep-Jr.	30	3	10	13	68	2	0	1	1	4
2005-06	C. Budejovice	CzRep	1	0	0	0	0	....	....	....	....	....
	Jind. Hradec	CzRep-2	49	1	4	5	42	....	....	....	....	....

VOROBIEV, Dmitri (voh-roh-BEE-ehf, dih-MEE-tree) **TOR.**

Defense. Shoots left. 6'2", 211 lbs. Born, Togliatti, USSR, October 18, 1985.
(Toronto's 3rd choice, 157th overall, in 2004 Entry Draft).

			Regular Season					Playoffs				
Season	Club	League	GP	G	A	Pts	PIM	GP	G	A	Pts	PIM
2002-03	Lada Togliatti 2	Russia-3	31	3	5	8	12	....	....	....	....	....
2003-04	Lada Togliatti 2	Russia-3	10	1	1	2	4	....	....	....	....	....
	Lada Togliatti	Russia	23	1	0	1	12	4	0	0	0	4
2004-05	Lada Togliatti	Russia	53	2	6	8	30	10	0	0	0	8
2005-06	Lada Togliatti	Russia	42	1	7	8	73	8	0	0	0	8

VOROS, Aaron (VOH-ruhs, AIR-uhn) **N.J.**

Center. Shoots left. 6'4", 200 lbs. Born, Vancouver, B.C., July 2, 1981.
(New Jersey's 10th choice, 229th overall, in 2001 Entry Draft).

			Regular Season					Playoffs				
Season	Club	League	GP	G	A	Pts	PIM	GP	G	A	Pts	PIM
99-2000	Victoria Salsa	BCHL	58	14	21	35	285	....	....	....	....	....
2000-01	Victoria Salsa	BCHL	57	34	34	68	196	30	16	15	31	....
2001-02	Alaska-Fairbanks	CCHA	37	18	12	30	*101	....	....	....	....	....
2002-03	Alaska-Fairbanks	CCHA	16	2	5	7	42	....	....	....	....	....
2003-04	Alaska-Fairbanks	CCHA	36	16	8	24	*132	....	....	....	....	....
	Albany River Rats	AHL	9	2	1	3	14	....	....	....	....	....
2004-05	Albany River Rats	AHL	71	11	17	28	220	....	....	....	....	....
2005-06	Albany River Rats	AHL	73	16	14	30	180	....	....	....	....	....

CCHA All-Rookie Team (2002)

• Missed majority of 2002-03 season recovering from leg surgery, January 30, 2003.

VOROSHNIN, Pavel (vo-rohsh-NIHN, PAH-vehl) **BUF.**

Defense. Shoots left. 6'3", 175 lbs. Born, Chelyabinsk, USSR, March 23, 1984.
(Buffalo's 7th choice, 172nd overall, in 2003 Entry Draft).

			Regular Season					Playoffs				
Season	Club	League	GP	G	A	Pts	PIM	GP	G	A	Pts	PIM
2001-02	Chelyabinsk	Russia-2	32	0	2	2	10	....	....	....	....	....
2002-03	Mississauga	OHL	68	9	27	36	81	1	0	0	0	2
2003-04	Mississauga	OHL	18	0	4	4	6	....	....	....	....	....
	Owen Sound	OHL	40	3	18	21	36	7	0	2	2	4
2004-05	Metallurg Serov	Russia-2	34	0	1	1	12	....	....	....	....	....
2005-06	Lada Togliatti	Russia	33	0	1	1	18	8	0	1	1	0

VRANA, Petr (vuh-RA-nuh, PEE-tuhr) **N.J.**

Center. Shoots left. 5'10", 185 lbs. Born, Sternberk, Czech., March 29, 1985.
(New Jersey's 2nd choice, 42nd overall, in 2003 Entry Draft).

			Regular Season					Playoffs				
Season	Club	League	GP	G	A	Pts	PIM	GP	G	A	Pts	PIM
2001-02	HC Havirov Jr.	CzRep-Jr.	38	11	12	23	....	....	....	....	....	....
	HC Femax Havirov	CzRep	6	0	0	0	4	....	....	....	....	....
2002-03	Halifax	QMJHL	72	37	46	83	32	24	5	15	20	12
2003-04	Halifax	QMJHL	48	13	25	38	56	....	....	....	....	....
2004-05	Halifax	QMJHL	60	16	35	51	77	12	10	4	14	12
2005-06	Albany River Rats	AHL	74	12	23	35	91	....	....	....	....	....

QMJHL All-Rookie Team (2003) • QMJHL Rookie of the Year (2003)

WALKER, Julian (WAH-kuhr, JEW-lee-ehn) **MIN.**

Wing. Shoots right. 6'2", 216 lbs. Born, Bern, Switz., September 10, 1986.
(Minnesota's 6th choice, 162nd overall, in 2006 Entry Draft).

			Regular Season					Playoffs				
Season	Club	League	GP	G	A	Pts	PIM	GP	G	A	Pts	PIM
2001-02	SC Bern Jr.	Swiss-Jr.	....	....	....	....	....	1	0	0	0	0
2002-03	SC Bern Jr.	Swiss-Jr.	34	2	5	7	14	3	0	0	0	4
2003-04	SC Bern Jr.	Swiss-Jr.	35	15	15	30	91	7	2	3	5	8
2004-05	SC Bern Jr.	Swiss-Jr.	42	25	32	57	84	9	1	11	12	10
	SC Langenthal	Swiss-2	3	0	0	0	0	....	....	....	....	....
2005-06	EHC Basel Jr.	Swiss-Jr.	6	3	2	5	6	....	....	....	....	....
	EHC Olten	Swiss-2	2	0	0	0	2	....	....	....	....	....
	EHC Basel	Swiss	36	2	0	2	41	5	1	0	1	6

WANDELL, Tom (VAHN-dehl, TAWM) **DAL.**

Center. Shoots left. 6'1", 183 lbs. Born, Sodertalje, Sweden, January 29, 1987.
(Dallas' 5th choice, 146th overall, in 2005 Entry Draft).

			Regular Season					Playoffs				
Season	Club	League	GP	G	A	Pts	PIM	GP	G	A	Pts	PIM
2002-03	Sodertalje SK U18	Swe-U18	13	8	7	15	6	....	....	....	....	....
2003-04	Sodertalje SK U18	Swe-U18	6	5	7	12	6	2	0	0	0	0
	Sodertalje SK Jr.	Swe-Jr.	33	7	15	22	14	2	0	0	0	0
2004-05	Sodertalje SK Jr.	Swe-Jr.	5	1	2	3	4	....	....	....	....	....
2005-06	Sodertalje SK Jr.	Swe-Jr.	41	19	20	39	45	4	1	0	1	2
	Sodertalje SK	Sweden	6	0	0	0	0	....	....	....	....	....
	Sodertalje SK	Sweden-Q	1	1	0	1	0	....	....	....	....	....

WARN, Max (VAHRN, MAX) **DAL.**

Left wing. Shoots left. 6'2", 194 lbs. Born, Helsinki, Finland, June 10, 1988.
(Dallas' 5th choice, 150th overall, in 2006 Entry Draft).

			Regular Season					Playoffs				
Season	Club	League	GP	G	A	Pts	PIM	GP	G	A	Pts	PIM
2004-05	HIFK Helsinki U18	Fin-U18	22	6	9	15	30	7	1	3	4	4
	HIFK Helsinki Jr.	Fin-Jr.	4	0	0	0	0	2	0	0	0	0
2005-06	HIFK Helsinki U18	Fin-U18	7	5	4	9	6	7	4	2	6	6
	HIFK Helsinki Jr.	Fin-Jr.	24	3	10	13	39	....	....	....	....	....

WATHIER, Francis (waw-TEE-ay, FRAN-sihs) **DAL.**

Left wing. Shoots left. 6'3", 198 lbs. Born, St Isidore, Ont., December 7, 1984.
(Dallas' 8th choice, 185th overall, in 2003 Entry Draft).

			Regular Season					Playoffs				
Season	Club	League	GP	G	A	Pts	PIM	GP	G	A	Pts	PIM
2001-02	Hull Olympiques	QMJHL	63	1	3	4	68	12	1	2	3	30
2002-03	Hull Olympiques	QMJHL	72	9	18	27	143	20	1	6	7	20
2003-04	Gatineau	QMJHL	51	9	16	25	127	15	0	2	2	23
2004-05	Gatineau	QMJHL	67	15	20	35	96	10	0	2	2	8
2005-06	Iowa Stars	AHL	11	0	1	1	26	....	....	....	....	....

• Missed majority of 2005-06 season recovering from two shoulder injuries.

WATKINS, Matt (WAHT-kihns, MAT) **DAL.**

Right wing. Shoots left. 5'10", 180 lbs. Born, Aylesbury, Sask., November 22, 1986.
(Dallas' 6th choice, 160th overall, in 2005 Entry Draft).

			Regular Season					Playoffs				
Season	Club	League	GP	G	A	Pts	PIM	GP	G	A	Pts	PIM
2003-04	Tisdale Trojans	SMHL	44	34	37	71	52	....	....	....	....	....
2004-05	Vernon Vipers	BCHL	60	36	38	74	53	....	....	....	....	....
2005-06	North Dakota	WCHA	46	5	4	9	45	....	....	....	....	....

WATSON, Greg (WAWT-suhn, GREHG)

Center. Shoots left. 6', 205 lbs. Born, Eastend, Sask., March 2, 1983.
(Florida's 3rd choice, 34th overall, in 2001 Entry Draft).

			Regular Season					Playoffs				
Season	Club	League	GP	G	A	Pts	PIM	GP	G	A	Pts	PIM
1998-99	Calgary Buffaloes	AMHL	71	23	23	46	120	....	....	....	....	....
	Prince Albert	WHL	2	0	0	0	5	....	....	....	....	....
99-2000	Prince Albert	WHL	67	10	5	15	63	6	0	2	2	2
2000-01	Prince Albert	WHL	71	22	28	50	72	....	....	....	....	....
2001-02	Prince Albert	WHL	51	22	30	52	88	....	....	....	....	....
2002-03	Prince Albert	WHL	39	11	15	26	58	....	....	....	....	....
	Brandon	WHL	30	6	14	20	37	17	3	8	11	12
2003-04	Binghamton	AHL	69	4	7	11	72	2	0	0	0	2
2004-05	Binghamton	AHL	57	3	4	7	68	1	0	0	0	0
2005-06	Binghamton	AHL	28	6	6	12	27	....	....	....	....	....

Traded to **Ottawa** by **Florida** with Billy Thompson for Jani Hurme, October 1, 2002.

WATT, J.D. (WAHT , JAY-DEE) CGY.

Right wing. Shoots right. 6'1", 206 lbs. Born, Calgary, Alta., May 25, 1987.
(Calgary's 4th choice, 111th overall, in 2005 Entry Draft).

			Regular Season					Playoffs				
Season	Club	League	GP	G	A	Pts	PIM	GP	G	A	Pts	PIM
2003-04	Drumheller	AJHL	59	20	17	37	245	....	....	....	....	....
	Vancouver Giants	WHL	3	1	0	1	0	10	0	3	3	14
2004-05	Vancouver Giants	WHL	66	6	7	13	213	....	....	....	....	....
2005-06	Vancouver Giants	WHL	58	8	29	37	199	18	4	3	7	42

WEBER, Mike (WEH-buhr, MIGHK) BUF.

Defense. Shoots left. 6'2", 199 lbs. Born, Pittsburgh, PA, December 16, 1987.
(Buffalo's 3rd choice, 57th overall, in 2006 Entry Draft).

			Regular Season					Playoffs				
Season	Club	League	GP	G	A	Pts	PIM	GP	G	A	Pts	PIM
2002-03	Jr. Penguins	EmJHL	28	4	11	15	109	3	0	0	0	20
2003-04	Windsor Spitfires	OHL	65	0	2	2	49	....	....	....	....	....
2004-05	Windsor Spitfires	OHL	68	2	6	8	132	11	0	1	1	18
2005-06	Windsor Spitfires	OHL	68	5	21	26	181	7	0	0	0	12

WELLAR, Patrick (WEHL-uhr, PAT-rihk) ST.L.

Defense. Shoots left. 6'3", 210 lbs. Born, Carrot River, Sask., December 4, 1983.
(Washington's 5th choice, 77th overall, in 2002 Entry Draft).

			Regular Season					Playoffs				
Season	Club	League	GP	G	A	Pts	PIM	GP	G	A	Pts	PIM
99-2000	Sask. Contacts	SMHL	44	5	15	20	120	....	....	....	....	....
	Portland	WHL	1	0	0	0	0	....	....	....	....	....
2000-01	Portland	WHL	57	2	7	9	65	10	0	1	1	13
2001-02	Portland	WHL	61	3	10	13	125	7	0	2	2	4
2002-03	Portland	WHL	11	1	4	5	31	....	....	....	....	....
	Calgary Hitmen	WHL	49	3	11	14	88	5	0	0	0	15
2003-04	Calgary Hitmen	WHL	68	7	10	17	132	7	1	1	2	10
2004-05	Worcester IceCats	AHL	2	0	1	1	0	....	....	....	....	....
	Peoria Rivermen	ECHL	62	2	10	12	91	....	....	....	....	....
2005-06	Peoria Rivermen	AHL	5	0	0	0	2	....	....	....	....	....
	Alaska Aces	ECHL	53	6	13	19	89	22	2	2	4	30

Signed as a free agent by **St. Louis**, June 30, 2004.

WELLER, Craig (WEHL-uhr, KRAIG) NYR

Right wing. Shoots right. 6'3", 195 lbs. Born, Calgary, Alta., January 17, 1981.
(St. Louis' 6th choice, 167th overall, in 2000 Entry Draft).

			Regular Season					Playoffs				
Season	Club	League	GP	G	A	Pts	PIM	GP	G	A	Pts	PIM
1997-98	Cgy. AAA Flames	AMHL	33	2	10	12	65	3	0	1	1	2
1998-99	Calgary Canucks	AJHL	49	4	14	18	80	13	0	1	1	10
99-2000	Calgary Canucks	AJHL	53	3	14	17	100	4	0	0	0	4
2000-01	U. Minn-Duluth	WCHA	6	0	1	1	0	....	....	....	....	....
	Kootenay Ice	WHL	30	1	5	6	40	11	0	2	2	26
2001-02	Kootenay Ice	WHL	69	5	13	18	127	22	3	7	10	27
2002-03	Charlotte	ECHL	48	3	11	14	84	....	....	....	....	....
	Hartford Wolf Pack	AHL	11	0	0	0	8	2	0	0	0	0
2003-04	Hartford Wolf Pack	AHL	68	5	9	14	86	16	2	2	4	30
2004-05	Hartford Wolf Pack	AHL	76	10	9	19	182	6	0	1	1	6
2005-06	Hartford Wolf Pack	AHL	80	12	21	33	152	13	2	3	5	44

WHL West Second All-Star Team (2002)

• Left **U. of Minnesota-Duluth** (WCHA) and signed as a free agent by **Kootenay** (WHL), January 7, 2001. Signed as a free agent by **NY Rangers**, July 11, 2002.

WELLER, Shawn (WEHL-uhr, SHAWN) OTT.

Left wing. Shoots left. 6'1", 188 lbs. Born, Glens Falls, NY, July 8, 1986.
(Ottawa's 3rd choice, 77th overall, in 2004 Entry Draft).

			Regular Season					Playoffs				
Season	Club	League	GP	G	A	Pts	PIM	GP	G	A	Pts	PIM
2001-02	South Glen Falls	High-NY	25	32	21	53	....	....	....	....	....	....
2002-03	Capital District	EJHL	STATISTICS NOT AVAILABLE									
2003-04	Capital District	EJHL	37	18	25	43	110	3	3	3	6	6
	Capital District	Exhib.	30	16	19	35	78	....	....	....	....	....
2004-05	Clarkson Knights	ECACHL	33	3	11	14	72	....	....	....	....	....
2005-06	Clarkson Knights	ECACHL	37	14	10	24	*103	....	....	....	....	....

WERNER, Steve (WUHR-nuhr, STEEV) WSH.

Right wing. Shoots right. 6', 197 lbs. Born, Washington, DC, August 8, 1984.
(Washington's 2nd choice, 83rd overall, in 2003 Entry Draft).

			Regular Season					Playoffs				
Season	Club	League	GP	G	A	Pts	PIM	GP	G	A	Pts	PIM
99-2000	Wsh. Jr. Capitals	MetroHL	42	32	45	77	....	....	....	....	....	....
2000-01	USNTDP	U-17	13	5	2	7	2	....	....	....	....	....
	USNTDP	NAHL	56	7	21	28	24	....	....	....	....	....
2001-02	USNTDP	U-18	34	10	16	26	10	....	....	....	....	....
	USNTDP	USHL	10	2	3	5	9	....	....	....	....	....
	USNTDP	NAHL	10	4	1	5	23	....	....	....	....	....
2002-03	Massachusetts	H-East	37	16	22	38	4	....	....	....	....	....
2003-04	Massachusetts	H-East	33	7	17	24	18	....	....	....	....	....
2004-05	Massachusetts	H-East	38	14	13	27	12	....	....	....	....	....
2005-06	Massachusetts	H-East	35	13	14	27	26	....	....	....	....	....
	Hershey Bears	AHL	4	0	3	3	2	....	....	....	....	....

Hockey East All-Rookie Team (2003)

WESSBECKER, John (WEHS-beh-kuhr, JAWN) T.B.

Defense. Shoots right. 6'1", 180 lbs. Born, Edina, MN, September 15, 1986.
(Tampa Bay's 9th choice, 225th overall, in 2005 Entry Draft).

			Regular Season					Playoffs				
Season	Club	League	GP	G	A	Pts	PIM	GP	G	A	Pts	PIM
2004-05	Blake Bears	High-MN	16	6	16	22	38	....	....	....	....	....
2005-06	Massachusetts	H-East	36	0	3	3	30	....	....	....	....	....

WHARTON, Kyle (WAWR-tuhn, KIGHL) CBJ

Defense. Shoots left. 6'3", 192 lbs. Born, Ottawa, Ont., March 3, 1986.
(Columbus' 3rd choice, 59th overall, in 2004 Entry Draft).

			Regular Season					Playoffs				
Season	Club	League	GP	G	A	Pts	PIM	GP	G	A	Pts	PIM
2001-02	Ottawa Valley	OMHA	34	18	24	42	....	....	....	....	....	....
2002-03	Ottawa 67's	OHL	39	3	5	8	16	....	....	....	....	....
2003-04	Ottawa 67's	OHL	43	4	10	14	50	7	2	3	5	4
2004-05	Ottawa 67's	OHL	29	1	12	13	23	....	....	....	....	....
	Sault Ste. Marie	OHL	28	4	12	16	22	7	1	5	6	4
2005-06	Sault Ste. Marie	OHL	34	6	16	22	62	....	....	....	....	....
	Guelph Storm	OHL	24	2	14	16	34	15	4	8	12	20

WHEELER, Blake (WEE-luhr, BLAYK) PHX.

Right wing. Shoots right. 6'5", 214 lbs. Born, Robbinsdale, MN, August 31, 1986.
(Phoenix's 1st choice, 5th overall, in 2004 Entry Draft).

			Regular Season					Playoffs				
Season	Club	League	GP	G	A	Pts	PIM	GP	G	A	Pts	PIM
2002-03	Breck Mustangs	High-MN	26	15	27	42	....	....	....	....	....	....
2003-04	Team Northwest	UMEHL	24	5	6	11	....	....	....	....	....	....
	Breck Mustangs	High-MN	27	39	50	89	34	3	6	5	11	0
2004-05	Green Bay	USHL	58	19	28	47	43	....	....	....	....	....
2005-06	U. of Minnesota	WCHA	39	9	14	23	41	....	....	....	....	....

USHL All-Rookie Team (2005)

WHITE, Ryan (WIGHT, RIGH-uhn) MTL.

Center. Shoots right. 6', 195 lbs. Born, Brandon, Man., March 17, 1988.
(Montreal's 4th choice, 66th overall, in 2006 Entry Draft).

			Regular Season					Playoffs				
Season	Club	League	GP	G	A	Pts	PIM	GP	G	A	Pts	PIM
2003-04	Brandon	MMHL	39	21	41	62	90	11	7	7	14	22
2004-05	Calgary Hitmen	WHL	63	9	14	23	95	12	2	1	3	26
2005-06	Calgary Hitmen	WHL	72	20	33	53	121	13	3	4	7	18

WICK, Roman (WIHK, ROH-muhn) OTT.

Right wing. Shoots left. 6'1", 187 lbs. Born, Kloten, Switz., December 30, 1985.
(Ottawa's 8th choice, 156th overall, in 2004 Entry Draft).

			Regular Season					Playoffs				
Season	Club	League	GP	G	A	Pts	PIM	GP	G	A	Pts	PIM
2000-01	Kloten Flyers Jr.	Swiss-Jr.	26	4	1	5	6	5	1	0	1	2
2001-02	Kloten Flyers Jr.	Swiss-Jr.	34	19	27	46	32	8	1	2	3	4
2002-03	Kloten Flyers Jr.	Swiss-Jr.	28	29	22	51	68	2	0	1	1	0
	Kloten Flyers	Swiss	9	1	0	1	4	1	0	0	0	0
2003-04	Kloten Flyers	Swiss	20	1	1	2	6	....	....	....	....	....
	Kloten Flyers	Swiss-Q	7	3	1	4	0	....	....	....	....	....
	GCK Lions Zurich	Swiss-2	6	4	0	4	6	....	....	....	....	....
2004-05	Red Deer Rebels	WHL	66	32	38	70	25	7	1	2	3	6
2005-06	Red Deer Rebels	WHL	23	7	10	17	8	....	....	....	....	....
	Lethbridge	WHL	38	14	17	31	20	6	4	3	7	6

WIDING, Daniel (VEE-dihng, DAN-yehl) NSH.

Right wing. Shoots right. 6'1", 202 lbs. Born, Gavle, Sweden, April 13, 1982.
(Nashville's 2nd choice, 36th overall, in 2000 Entry Draft).

			Regular Season					Playoffs				
Season	Club	League	GP	G	A	Pts	PIM	GP	G	A	Pts	PIM
99-2000	Leksands IF U18	Swe-U18	6	2	1	3	20	....	....	....	....	....
	Leksands IF Jr.	Swe-Jr.	34	15	12	27	65	2	1	0	1	4
	Leksands IF	Sweden	3	0	0	0	2	....	....	....	....	....
2000-01	Leksands IF Jr.	Swe-Jr.	6	2	3	5	31	....	....	....	....	....
	Leksands IF	Sweden	40	6	5	11	18	....	....	....	....	....
2001-02	Leksands IF Jr.	Swe-Jr.	3	2	6	8	2	....	....	....	....	....
	Leksands IF	Sweden-2	55	12	12	24	92	....	....	....	....	....
2002-03	Leksands IF	Sweden	47	2	2	4	8	5	0	0	0	2
	Leksands IF Jr.	Swe-Jr.	2	0	1	1	4	....	....	....	....	....
2003-04	Pelicans Lahti	Finland	54	6	7	13	62	....	....	....	....	....
2004-05	Pelicans Lahti	Finland	56	13	15	28	74	....	....	....	....	....
2005-06	TPS Turku	Finland	38	5	7	12	35	....	....	....	....	....
	Brynas IF Gavle	Sweden	11	1	1	2	2	4	1	0	1	33

WIKNER, Fred (WIHK-nuhr, FREHD) CGY.

Left wing. Shoots left. 6'1", 187 lbs. Born, Molndal, Sweden, January 1, 1986.
(Calgary's 7th choice, 182nd overall, in 2004 Entry Draft).

			Regular Season					Playoffs				
Season	Club	League	GP	G	A	Pts	PIM	GP	G	A	Pts	PIM
2002-03	V.Frolunda Jr.	Swe-Jr.	22	2	5	7	14	7	2	1	3	2
2003-04	V.Frolunda Jr.	Swe-Jr.	36	9	6	15	67	9	2	2	4	8
2004-05	IF Molndal Hockey	Sweden-3	5	1	1	2	10	....	....	....	....	....
	Frolunda Jr.	Swe-Jr.	28	8	11	19	36	6	1	3	4	4
2005-06	Prince George	WHL	66	10	8	18	32	1	0	0	0	2

WIKNER, John (WIHK-nuhr, JAWN) OTT.

Left wing. Shoots left. 6'1", 179 lbs. Born, Molndal, Sweden, January 1, 1986.
(Ottawa's 11th choice, 284th overall, in 2004 Entry Draft).

			Regular Season					Playoffs				
Season	Club	League	GP	G	A	Pts	PIM	GP	G	A	Pts	PIM
2002-03	V.Frolunda Jr.	Swe-Jr.	19	3	6	9	41	6	0	0	0	10
2003-04	V.Frolunda Jr.	Swe-Jr.	31	6	3	9	22	9	0	0	0	6
2004-05	IF Molndal Hockey	Sweden-3	5	2	2	4	6	....	....	....	....	....
	Frolunda Jr.	Swe-Jr.	32	10	14	24	56	6	0	2	2	0
2005-06	Brandon	WHL	60	9	13	22	32	6	0	0	0	4

WILD, Cody (WIGHLD, KOH-dee) EDM.

Defense. Shoots left. 6'1", 183 lbs. Born, Limestone, ME, June 5, 1987.
(Edmonton's 4th choice, 140th overall, in 2006 Entry Draft).

			Regular Season					Playoffs				
Season	Club	League	GP	G	A	Pts	PIM	GP	G	A	Pts	PIM
2003-04	Junior Bruins	EJHL	53	5	24	29	12	....	....	....	....	....
2004-05	Junior Bruins	EJHL	64	16	36	52	44	....	....	....	....	....
2005-06	Providence College	H-East	36	6	15	21	24	....	....	....	....	....

Hockey East All-Rookie Team (2006)

WILFORD, Marty (WIHL-fohrd, MAHR-tee)

Defense. Shoots left. 6'1", 212 lbs. Born, Cobourg, Ont., April 17, 1977.
(Chicago's 7th choice, 149th overall, in 1995 Entry Draft).

			Regular Season					Playoffs				
Season	Club	League	GP	G	A	Pts	PIM	GP	G	A	Pts	PIM
1993-94	Peterborough	OPJHL	40	3	19	22	*107	....	....	....	....	....
1994-95	Oshawa Generals	OHL	63	1	6	7	95	7	1	1	2	4
1995-96	Oshawa Generals	OHL	65	3	24	27	107	5	0	1	1	4
1996-97	Oshawa Generals	OHL	62	19	43	62	126	16	2	18	20	28
1997-98	Indianapolis Ice	IHL	26	0	4	4	16	....	....	....	....	....
	Columbus Chill	ECHL	46	8	27	35	123	....	....	....	....	....
1998-99	Indianapolis Ice	IHL	80	3	13	16	116	7	0	1	1	16
99-2000	Cleveland	IHL	7	0	3	3	24	....	....	....	....	....
	Houston Aeros	IHL	45	0	9	9	30	11	2	2	4	18
2000-01	Norfolk Admirals	AHL	80	7	41	48	102	9	1	5	6	8
2001-02	St. John's	AHL	60	4	21	25	70	....	....	....	....	....
	Milwaukee	AHL	8	1	3	4	12	....	....	....	....	....
	Hartford Wolf Pack	AHL	9	0	2	2	2	10	3	3	6	4
2002-03	Norfolk Admirals	AHL	80	13	35	48	87	9	0	3	3	16
2003-04	Norfolk Admirals	AHL	80	5	35	40	67	8	0	3	3	18
2004-05	Norfolk Admirals	AHL	78	7	30	37	80	6	0	4	4	15
2005-06	Manchester	AHL	79	5	36	41	81	7	0	3	3	19

OHL Second All-Star Team (1997)

Traded to **Toronto** by **Chicago** for Shawn Thornton, September 30, 2001. Traded to **Nashville** by **Toronto** with D.J. Smith for Marc Moro, March 1, 2002. Signed as a free agent by **Chicago**, July 8, 2003. Signed as a free agent by **Los Angeles**, August 10, 2005. Signed as a free agent by **Iowa** (AHL), July 25, 2006.

WILLIAMS, Nigel (WIHL-yuhms, NIGH-juhl) COL.

Defense. Shoots left. 6'4", 226 lbs. Born, Aurora, IL, April 18, 1988.
(Colorado's 2nd choice, 51st overall, in 2006 Entry Draft).

			Regular Season					Playoffs				
Season	Club	League	GP	G	A	Pts	PIM	GP	G	A	Pts	PIM
2004-05	Team Illinois	MWEHL	60	14	18	32	....	....	....	....	....	....
	USNTDP	U-17	3	2	1	3	4	....	....	....	....	....
2005-06	USNTDP	U-18	40	3	6	9	40	....	....	....	....	....
	USNTDP	NAHL	19	3	4	7	23	....	....	....	....	....

Signed Letter of Intent to attend **U. of Wisconsin** (WCHA) in fall of 2006.

WILSON, Clay (WIHL-suhn, KLAY) ANA.

Defense. Shoots left. 6', 195 lbs. Born, Sturgeon Lake, MN, April 5, 1983.

			Regular Season					Playoffs				
Season	Club	League	GP	G	A	Pts	PIM	GP	G	A	Pts	PIM
2001-02	Michigan Tech	WCHA	38	4	8	12	18	....	....	....	....	....
2002-03	Michigan Tech	WCHA	38	8	17	25	37	....	....	....	....	....
2003-04	Michigan Tech	WCHA	37	2	11	13	22	....	....	....	....	....
2004-05	Michigan Tech	WCHA	35	3	4	7	42	....	....	....	....	....
	Muskegon Fury	UHL	14	3	3	6	2	17	0	2	2	8
2005-06	Muskegon Fury	UHL	13	3	9	12	9	....	....	....	....	....
	Grand Rapids	AHL	60	10	27	37	40	16	0	3	3	8

Signed as a free agent by **Anaheim**, July 11, 2006.

WILSON, Kyle (WIHL-suhn, KIGHL) MIN.

Center. Shoots right. 6'1", 200 lbs. Born, Oakville, Ont., December 15, 1984.
(Minnesota's 12th choice, 272nd overall, in 2004 Entry Draft).

			Regular Season					Playoffs				
Season	Club	League	GP	G	A	Pts	PIM	GP	G	A	Pts	PIM
2000-01	Strathroy Rockets	OHA-B	33	12	17	29	15	5	2	2	4	2
2001-02	Strathroy Rockets	OHA-B	53	42	25	67	16	....	....	....	....	....
2002-03	Colgate	ECAC	33	4	2	6	15	....	....	....	....	....
2003-04	Colgate	ECAC	37	14	17	31	23	....	....	....	....	....
2004-05	Colgate	ECACHL	30	5	18	23	12	....	....	....	....	....
2005-06	Colgate	ECACHL	39	*23	18	41	22	....	....	....	....	....

ECACHL Second All-Star Team (2006)

WINNIK, Daniel (WIHN-ihk, DAN-yehl) PHX.

Center/Left wing. Shoots right. 6'2", 218 lbs. Born, Toronto, Ont., March 6, 1985.
(Phoenix's 10th choice, 265th overall, in 2004 Entry Draft).

			Regular Season					Playoffs				
Season	Club	League	GP	G	A	Pts	PIM	GP	G	A	Pts	PIM
2002-03	Wexford	OPJHL	47	20	33	53	70	18	11	11	22	24
2003-04	New Hampshire	H-East	38	4	10	14	12	....	....	....	....	....
2004-05	New Hampshire	H-East	42	18	22	40	26	....	....	....	....	....
2005-06	New Hampshire	H-East	39	15	26	41	44	....	....	....	....	....
	San Antonio	AHL	7	1	1	2	8	....	....	....	....	....

Hockey East Second All-Star Team (2006)

WIRTANEN, Petteri (WEER-tah-nehn, PEH-tur-ree) ANA.

Center. Shoots left. 6'1", 202 lbs. Born, Hyvinkaa, Finland, May 28, 1986.
(Anaheim's 5th choice, 172nd overall, in 2006 Entry Draft).

			Regular Season					Playoffs				
Season	Club	League	GP	G	A	Pts	PIM	GP	G	A	Pts	PIM
2001-02	Ahmat Jr.	Fin-Jr.	1	1	0	1	2	....	....	....	....	....
2002-03	HPK U18	Fin-U18	27	17	12	29	36	2	0	0	0	2
	HPK Jr.	Fin-Jr.	2	1	0	1	0	....	....	....	....	....
2003-04	HPK U18	Fin-U18	7	2	3	5	10	2	0	0	0	0
	HPK Jr.	Fin-Jr.	40	7	11	18	26	....	....	....	....	....
2004-05	HPK Jr.	Fin-Jr.	43	14	25	39	42	2	0	0	0	10
	HPK Hameenlinna	Finland	8	0	0	0	0	....	....	....	....	....
2005-06	Suomi U20	Finland-2	2	2	0	2	2	....	....	....	....	....
	HPK Jr.	Fin-Jr.	3	4	2	6	4	....	....	....	....	....
	HPK Hameenlinna	Finland	50	8	3	11	24	13	1	0	1	12

WISHART, Ty (wih-SHAHRT, TIGH) S.J.

Defense. Shoots left. 6'4", 205 lbs. Born, Belleville, Ont., May 19, 1988.
(San Jose's 1st choice, 16th overall, in 2006 Entry Draft).

			Regular Season					Playoffs				
Season	Club	League	GP	G	A	Pts	PIM	GP	G	A	Pts	PIM
2004-05	Prince George	WHL	58	1	7	8	41	....	....	....	....	....
2005-06	Prince George	WHL	70	5	32	37	68	5	0	0	0	4

WOOD, Dustin (WUD, DUHS-tihn)

Defense. Shoots left. 6'1", 208 lbs. Born, Scarborough, Ont., May 21, 1981.

			Regular Season					Playoffs				
Season	Club	League	GP	G	A	Pts	PIM	GP	G	A	Pts	PIM
1998-99	Peterborough	OHL	62	1	8	9	14	5	0	0	0	0
99-2000	Peterborough	OHL	66	2	13	15	29	5	0	1	1	0
2000-01	Peterborough	OHL	64	5	20	25	41	7	0	3	3	11
2001-02	Peterborough	OHL	68	13	38	51	57	6	2	1	3	4
2002-03	Bridgeport	AHL	6	0	0	0	2	....	....	....	....	....
	Trenton Titans	ECHL	63	4	23	27	28	3	0	1	1	2
2003-04	Adirondack	UHL	1	0	0	0	0	....	....	....	....	....
	Springfield Falcons	AHL	75	2	6	8	22	....	....	....	....	....
2004-05	Utah Grizzlies	AHL	80	2	8	10	39	....	....	....	....	....
2005-06	Houston Aeros	AHL	64	1	6	7	48	....	....	....	....	....
	Syracuse Crunch	AHL	14	0	3	3	14	6	0	0	0	8

Signed as a free agent by **Phoenix**, June 2, 2004. Traded to **Minnesota** by **Phoenix** with Erik Westrum for Zbynek Michalek, August 26, 2005.

WOOD, Stephen (WUD, STEE-vehn)

Defense. Shoots right. 6'3", 210 lbs. Born, Sudbury, MA, August 18, 1981.

			Regular Season					Playoffs				
Season	Club	League	GP	G	A	Pts	PIM	GP	G	A	Pts	PIM
2000-01	Providence College	H-East	36	3	4	7	68	....	....	....	....	....
2001-02	Providence College	H-East	36	5	18	23	78	....	....	....	....	....
2002-03	Providence College	H-East	34	9	20	29	48	....	....	....	....	....
2003-04	Providence College	H-East	37	11	18	29	66	....	....	....	....	....
	Philadelphia	AHL	4	0	0	0	0	....	....	....	....	....
2004-05	Trenton Titans	ECHL	42	4	13	17	83	20	4	6	10	39
	Philadelphia	AHL	24	0	2	2	14	....	....	....	....	....
2005-06	Philadelphia	AHL	28	2	9	11	22	....	....	....	....	....
	Trenton Titans	ECHL	38	7	21	28	67	2	2	0	2	2

Hockey East Second All-Star Team (2003) • Hockey East First All-Star Team (2004) • NCAA East Second All-American Team (2004)

Signed as a free agent by **Philadelphia**, March 21, 2004.

WRIGHT, Ben (RIGHT, BEHN) CBJ

Defense. Shoots right. 6'2", 189 lbs. Born, Foremost, Alta., March 18, 1988.
(Columbus' 4th choice, 113th overall, in 2006 Entry Draft).

			Regular Season					Playoffs				
Season	Club	League	GP	G	A	Pts	PIM	GP	G	A	Pts	PIM
2003-04	Lethbridge Y	AMHL	36	9	24	33	28	....	....	....	....	....
	Lethbridge	WHL	3	0	0	0	4	....	....	....	....	....
2004-05	Brooks Bandits	AJHL	38	8	13	21	78	11	0	2	2	6
	Lethbridge	WHL	4	0	0	0	0	....	....	....	....	....
2005-06	Lethbridge	WHL	55	5	13	18	79	6	3	5	8	12

WYMAN, James (WIGH-muhn, JAYMZ) MTL.

Right wing. Shoots right. 6'2", 206 lbs. Born, Edina, MN, February 27, 1986.
(Montreal's 3rd choice, 100th overall, in 2004 Entry Draft).

			Regular Season					Playoffs				
Season	Club	League	GP	G	A	Pts	PIM	GP	G	A	Pts	PIM
2001-02	Blake Bears	High-MN	26	7	5	12	....	....	....	....	....	....
2002-03	Blake Bears	High-MN	28	17	23	40	12	....	....	....	....	....
2003-04	Blake Bears	High-MN	27	31	24	55	4	....	....	....	....	....
	Team Southwest	UMEHL	24	8	8	16	....	....	....	....	....	....
2004-05	Dartmouth	ECACHL	33	5	6	11	4	....	....	....	....	....
2005-06	Dartmouth	ECACHL	28	8	12	20	6	....	....	....	....	....

YACHMENEV, Denis (YATCH-muh-nehv, DEH-nihs) FLA.

Left wing. Shoots left. 6'1", 185 lbs. Born, Chelyabinsk, USSR, June 4, 1984.
(Florida's 9th choice, 200th overall, in 2002 Entry Draft).

			Regular Season					Playoffs				
Season	Club	League	GP	G	A	Pts	PIM	GP	G	A	Pts	PIM
2000-01	Chelyabinsk 2	Russia-3	36	40	27	67	....	....	....	....	....	....
2001-02	North Bay	OHL	65	17	12	29	32	5	2	0	2	0
2002-03	Saginaw Spirit	OHL	68	17	28	45	69	....	....	....	....	....
2003-04	Omsk 2	Russia-3	13	12	4	16	10	....	....	....	....	....
	Amur Khabarovsk	Russia	25	0	1	1	4	....	....	....	....	....
2004-05	Amur Khabarovsk	Russia-2	42	7	14	21	28	13	3	1	4	8
2005-06	Amur Khabarovsk	Russia-2	46	9	14	23	43	11	2	3	5	6

YANDLE, Keith (Yan-duhl, KEETH) PHX.

Defense. Shoots left. 6'2", 195 lbs. Born, Boston, MA, September 9, 1986.
(Phoenix's 3rd choice, 105th overall, in 2005 Entry Draft).

			Regular Season					Playoffs				
Season	Club	League	GP	G	A	Pts	PIM	GP	G	A	Pts	PIM
2004-05	Cushing	High-MA	34	14	40	54	52	....	....	....	....	....
2005-06	Moncton Wildcats	QMJHL	66	25	59	84	109	21	6	14	20	36

QMJHL First All-Star Team (2006) • Canadian Major Junior Defenseman of the Year (2006)

YEMELIN, Alexei (yeh-MUH-lehn, al-EXH-ay) MTL.

Defense. Shoots left. 6', 187 lbs. Born, Togliatti, USSR, April 25, 1986.
(Montreal's 2nd choice, 84th overall, in 2004 Entry Draft).

			Regular Season					Playoffs				
Season	Club	League	GP	G	A	Pts	PIM	GP	G	A	Pts	PIM
2002-03	Lada Togliatti 2	Russia-3	31	1	1	2	20	....	....	....	....	....
2003-04	Lada Togliatti 2	Russia-3	2	0	0	0	10	....	....	....	....	....
	CSK VVS Samara	Russia-2	52	2	4	6	180	7	0	0	0	18
2004-05	Lada Togliatti	Russia	12	0	1	1	24	2	0	0	0	2
2005-06	Lada Togliatti	Russia	44	6	6	12	131	6	0	1	1	*47

YIP, Brandon (YIHP, BRAN-duhn) COL.

Right wing. Shoots right. 6'1", 170 lbs. Born, Vancouver, B.C., April 25, 1985.
(Colorado's 7th choice, 239th overall, in 2004 Entry Draft).

			Regular Season					Playoffs				
Season	Club	League	GP	G	A	Pts	PIM	GP	G	A	Pts	PIM
2003-04	Coquitlam Express	BCHL	56	31	38	69	87	4	1	2	3	14
2004-05	Coquitlam Express	BCHL	43	20	42	62	92	7	6	1	7	12
2005-06	Boston University	H-East	39	9	22	31	59	....	....	....	....	....

Hockey East All-Rookie Team (2006) • Hockey East Rookie of the Year (2006)

YOUNG, Bryan (YUHNG, BRIGH-uhn) EDM.

Defense. Shoots left. 6'1", 191 lbs. Born, Kitchener, Ont., August 6, 1986.
(Edmonton's 6th choice, 146th overall, in 2004 Entry Draft).

			Regular Season					Playoffs				
Season	Club	League	GP	G	A	Pts	PIM	GP	G	A	Pts	PIM
2002-03	Lindsay Muskies	OPJHL	47	1	9	10	56	....	....	....	....	....
	Peterborough	OHL	2	0	0	0	0	....	....	....	....	....
2003-04	Peterborough	OHL	60	0	8	8	63	....	....	....	....	....
2004-05	Peterborough	OHL	60	1	11	12	44	14	0	1	1	10
2005-06	Peterborough	OHL	64	0	10	10	113	19	0	0	0	37

YUNKOV , Mikhail (yuhn-KAWF, mih-kigh-EHL) WSH.

Center. Shoots left. 6', 180 lbs. Born, Voskresensk, USSR, February 16, 1986.
(Washington's 5th choice, 62nd overall, in 2004 Entry Draft).

			Regular Season					Playoffs				
Season	Club	League	GP	G	A	Pts	PIM	GP	G	A	Pts	PIM
2001-02	Krylja Sovetov 2	Russia-3	4	0	1	1	0	....	....	....	....	....
2002-03	Krylja Sovetov	Russia	7	1	0	1	2	....	....	....	....	....
	Krylja Sovetov 2	Russia-3	3	0	1	1	0	....	....	....	....	....
2003-04	Krylja Sovetov	Russia-2	38	5	10	15	12	4	0	1	1	0
	Krylja Sovetov 2	Russia-3	STATISTICS NOT AVAILABLE									
2004-05	Krylja Sovetov 2	Russia-3	1	0	0	0	0	....	....	....	....	....
	Krylja Sovetov	Russia-2	38	9	14	23	22	3	0	1	1	4
2005-06	Ak Bars Kazan	Russia	33	3	4	7	35	11	0	1	1	6

ZABORSKY, Tomas (za-BOHR-skee, TAW-mahsh) NYR

Wing. Shoots left. 5'11", 180 lbs. Born, Banska Bystrica, Slovakia, November 14, 1987.
(NY Rangers' 5th choice, 137th overall, in 2006 Entry Draft).

			Regular Season					Playoffs				
Season	Club	League	GP	G	A	Pts	PIM	GP	G	A	Pts	PIM
2003-04	Dukla Trencin U18	Slovak-U18	46	20	12	32	8	7	4	2	6	4
2004-05	Dukla Trencin U18	Slovak-U18	46	44	25	69	53	7	4	4	8	39
	Dukla Trencin Jr.	Slovak-Jr.	7	1	2	3	0	1	0	1	1	0
2005-06	Dukla Trencin Jr.	Slovak-Jr.	42	39	22	61	18	7	10	5	15	2
	Dukla Trencin	Slovakia	4	0	0	0	2	....	....	....	....	....
	P. Bystrica	Slovak-2	5	0	1	1	2	....	....	....	....	....

ZAGRAPAN, Marek (ZAG-rah-pahn, MAHR-ehk) BUF.

Center. Shoots left. 6'1", 195 lbs. Born, Presov, Czech., December 6, 1986.
(Buffalo's 1st choice, 13th overall, in 2005 Entry Draft).

			Regular Season					Playoffs				
Season	Club	League	GP	G	A	Pts	PIM	GP	G	A	Pts	PIM
2001-02	HC Zlin U17	CzR-U17	48	23	14	37	24	6	1	0	1	2
2002-03	HC Zlin U17	CzR-U17	15	18	16	34	14	3	1	0	1	6
	HC Zlin Jr.	CzRep-Jr.	25	9	13	22	10	....	....	....	....	....
	HC Hame Zlin	CzRep	13	1	1	2	10	....	....	....	....	....
2003-04	HC Zlin Jr.	CzRep-Jr.	42	23	12	35	40	7	1	3	4	4
	HC Hame Zlin	CzRep	5	0	0	0	0	....	....	....	....	....
	HC Kometa Brno	CzRep-2	5	0	1	1	0	....	....	....	....	....
2004-05	Chicoutimi	QMJHL	59	32	50	82	50	17	11	6	17	28
2005-06	Chicoutimi	QMJHL	59	35	52	87	63	8	4	6	10	4

ZAINULLIN, Ruslan (zihj-NOO-luhn, roos-LAHN) CGY.

Right wing. Shoots left. 6'2", 202 lbs. Born, Kazan, USSR, February 14, 1982.
(Tampa Bay's 2nd choice, 34th overall, in 2000 Entry Draft).

			Regular Season					Playoffs				
Season	Club	League	GP	G	A	Pts	PIM	GP	G	A	Pts	PIM
1997-98	Ak Bars Kazan 2	Russia-3	27	0	1	1	2	....	....	....	....	....
1998-99	Ak Bars Kazan 2	Russia-4	36	13	8	21	22	....	....	....	....	....
99-2000	Ak Bars Kazan 2	Russia-3	12	13	6	19	....	....	....	....	....	....
	Ak Bars Kazan	Russia	14	1	1	2	4	....	....	....	....	....
2000-01	Ak Bars Kazan	Russia	29	1	3	4	14	1	0	0	0	0
2001-02	Ak Bars Kazan	Russia	21	0	2	2	8	3	0	0	0	2
2002-03	Ak Bars Kazan	Russia	4	0	1	1	2	....	....	....	....	....
	Nizhnekamsk	Russia	13	1	1	2	8	....	....	....	....	....
2003-04	Dynamo Moscow	Russia	47	3	5	8	30	3	0	0	0	0
2004-05	Spartak Moscow	Russia	45	4	5	9	28	....	....	....	....	....
2005-06	Spartak Moscow	Russia	40	7	3	10	22	3	0	0	0	4
	Spartak Moscow 2	Russia-3	3	0	0	0	4	....	....	....	....	....

Traded to **Phoenix** by **Tampa Bay** with Mike Johnson, Paul Mara and NY Islanders' 2nd round choice (previously acquired, Phoenix selected Matthew Spiller) in 2001 Entry Draft for Nikolai Khabibulin and Stan Neckar, March 5, 2001. Rights traded to **Atlanta** by **Phoenix** with Kirill Safronov and Phoenix's 4th round choice (Patrick Dwyer) in 2002 Entry Draft for Darcy Hordichuk and Atlanta's 4th (Lance Monych) and 5th (John Zeiler) round choices in 2002 Entry Draft, March 19, 2002. Traded to **Calgary** by **Atlanta** for Marc Savard, November 15, 2002.

ZAJAC, Travis (ZAY-jak, TRA-vihs) N.J.

Center. Shoots right. 6'2", 205 lbs. Born, Winnipeg, Man., May 13, 1985.
(New Jersey's 1st choice, 20th overall, in 2004 Entry Draft).

			Regular Season					Playoffs				
Season	Club	League	GP	G	A	Pts	PIM	GP	G	A	Pts	PIM
2002-03	Salmon Arm	BCHL	59	16	36	52	27	11	2	4	6	6
2003-04	Salmon Arm	BCHL	59	43	69	112	110	14	10	13	23	10
2004-05	North Dakota	WCHA	45	20	19	39	16	....	....	....	....	....
2005-06	North Dakota	WCHA	46	18	29	47	20	....	....	....	....	....
	Albany River Rats	AHL	2	0	1	1	2	....	....	....	....	....

WCHA All-Rookie Team (2005) • NCAA Championship All-Tournament Team (2005)

ZAKHAROV, Konstantin (za-KHAHR-awv, kawn-stuhn-TIHN) ST.L.

Left wing. Shoots right. 6'1", 190 lbs. Born, Minsk, USSR, May 2, 1985.
(St. Louis' 5th choice, 101st overall, in 2003 Entry Draft).

			Regular Season					Playoffs				
Season	Club	League	GP	G	A	Pts	PIM	GP	G	A	Pts	PIM
2000-01	Yunost Minsk	Belarus	19	11	7	18	40	....	....	....	....	....
2001-02	Yunost Minsk	Belarus	16	7	5	12	39	....	....	....	....	....
2002-03	HK Gomel	Belarus	19	8	19	27	18	....	....	....	....	....
	HK Gomel	EEHL	14	2	4	6	10	....	....	....	....	....
	Yunost Minsk	Belarus	17	18	19	37	34	....	....	....	....	....
2003-04	Moncton Wildcats	QMJHL	55	33	16	49	63	20	7	9	16	18
2004-05	Worcester IceCats	AHL	59	4	10	14	26	....	....	....	....	....
2005-06	Yunost-Minsk	BelOpen	36	14	15	29	78	....	....	....	....	....
	Alaska Aces	ECHL	8	0	2	2	4	....	....	....	....	....

ZALEWSKI, Steven (zuh-LOO-skee, STEE-vehn) S.J.

Center. Shoots left. 6', 185 lbs. Born, Utica, NY, August 20, 1986.
(San Jose's 5th choice, 153rd overall, in 2004 Entry Draft).

			Regular Season					Playoffs				
Season	Club	League	GP	G	A	Pts	PIM	GP	G	A	Pts	PIM
2003-04	Northwood	High-NY	40	32	34	66	22	....	....	....	....	....
2004-05	Clarkson Knights	ECACHL	39	12	7	19	60	....	....	....	....	....
2005-06	Clarkson Knights	ECACHL	35	9	13	22	50	....	....	....	....	....

ZAPLETAL, Jan (ZAH-pleht-tuhl, YAHN) T.B.

Defense. Shoots right. 6'3", 190 lbs. Born, Brno, Czech., August 21, 1986.
(Tampa Bay's 6th choice, 188th overall, in 2004 Entry Draft).

			Regular Season					Playoffs				
Season	Club	League	GP	G	A	Pts	PIM	GP	G	A	Pts	PIM
2001-02	HC Ytong Brno Jr.	CzRep-Jr.	27	3	0	3	8	....	....	....	....	....
2002-03	HC Vsetin Jr.	CzRep-Jr.	27	4	3	7	8	10	0	0	0	2
2003-04	HC Vsetin Jr.	CzRep-Jr.	51	2	4	6	26	4	0	0	0	0
2004-05	Regina Pats	WHL	55	3	2	5	20	....	....	....	....	....
2005-06	HC Vsetin Jr.	CzRep-Jr.	9	0	3	3	2	....	....	....	....	....
	HC Vsetin	CzRep	16	0	0	0	10	....	....	....	....	....
	Jind. Hradec	CzRep-2	20	0	0	0	16	....	....	....	....	....

ZARB, Chris (ZAHRB, KRIHS) PHI.

Defense. Shoots right. 6'4", 176 lbs. Born, San Diego, CA, January 11, 1985.
(Philadelphia's 4th choice, 144th overall, in 2004 Entry Draft).

			Regular Season					Playoffs				
Season	Club	League	GP	G	A	Pts	PIM	GP	G	A	Pts	PIM
2002-03	Det. Ceasars	MWEHL	60	15	35	50	60	....	....	....	....	....
2003-04	Tri-City Storm	USHL	43	4	20	24	78	11	0	4	4	17
2004-05	Tri-City Storm	USHL	48	9	14	23	147	....	....	....	....	....
2005-06	Ferris State	CCHA	29	0	10	10	35	....	....	....	....	....

ZEILER, John (ZIGH-luhr, JAWN) PHX.

Right wing. Shoots right. 6', 207 lbs. Born, Pittsburgh, PA, November 21, 1982.
(Phoenix's 7th choice, 132nd overall, in 2002 Entry Draft).

			Regular Season					Playoffs				
Season	Club	League	GP	G	A	Pts	PIM	GP	G	A	Pts	PIM
99-2000	Pittsburgh Hornets	PAHA	27	17	15	32	94	....	....	....	....	....
2000-01	Sioux City	USHL	56	8	20	28	45	2	0	0	0	26
2001-02	Sioux City	USHL	60	23	27	50	116	12	2	3	5	25
2002-03	St. Lawrence	ECAC	37	10	17	27	28	....	....	....	....	....
2003-04	St. Lawrence	ECAC	41	8	*28	36	42	....	....	....	....	....
2004-05	St. Lawrence	ECACHL	38	9	23	32	42	....	....	....	....	....
2005-06	St. Lawrence	ECACHL	28	13	15	28	28	....	....	....	....	....
	San Antonio	AHL	8	0	1	1	10	....	....	....	....	....
	Lubbock	CHL	4	2	0	2	16	....	....	....	....	....

ECAC All-Rookie Team (2003)

ZELISKA, Lukas (ZEH-lihs-kah, LOO-kahsh) NYR

Center. Shoots right. 5'11", 176 lbs. Born, Martin, Slovakia, January 8, 1988.
(NY Rangers' 7th choice, 204th overall, in 2006 Entry Draft).

			Regular Season					Playoffs				
Season	Club	League	GP	G	A	Pts	PIM	GP	G	A	Pts	PIM
2003-04	HC Trinec U17	CzR-U17	48	39	41	80	166	5	2	2	4	4
	HC Trinec Jr.	CzRep-Jr.	7	1	1	2	2	....	....	....	....	....
2004-05	HC Trinec U17	CzR-U17	11	7	11	18	40	....	....	....	....	....
	HC Trinec Jr.	CzRep-Jr.	13	1	2	3	6	....	....	....	....	....
2005-06	HC Trinec Jr.	CzRep-Jr.	29	8	3	11	81	7	4	1	5	22
	HC Ocelari Trinec	CzRep	1	0	0	0	0	....	....	....	....	....

ZHARKOV, Vladimir (zhar-KAWV, vla-DIH-meer) N.J.

Right wing. Shoots left. 6', 187 lbs. Born, Elektrostal, Russia, January 10, 1988.
(New Jersey's 4th choice, 77th overall, in 2006 Entry Draft).

			Regular Season					Playoffs				
Season	Club	League	GP	G	A	Pts	PIM	GP	G	A	Pts	PIM
2004-05	CSKA Moscow 2	Russia-3	STATISTICS NOT AVAILABLE									
2005-06	CSKA Moscow	Russia	4	0	1	1	4	1	0	0	0	0
	CSKA Moscow 2	Russia-3	48	17	22	39	86	....	....	....	....	....

ZIB, Lukas (ZIHB, LOO-kahsh) EDM.

Defense. Shoots right. 6'1", 200 lbs. Born, Ceske Budejovice, Czech., February 24, 1977.
(Edmonton's 3rd choice, 57th overall, in 1995 Entry Draft).

			Regular Season					Playoffs				
Season	Club	League	GP	G	A	Pts	PIM	GP	G	A	Pts	PIM
1994-95	C. Budejovice	CzRep	13	2	0	2	16	9	1	0	1	6
1995-96	C. Budejovice Jr.	CzRep-Jr.	11	5	1	6	....	....	....	....	....	....
	C. Budejovice	CzRep	10	1	0	1	....	2	0	0	0	....
1996-97	C. Budejovice	CzRep	13	0	0	0	4	2	0	0	0	0
1997-98	C. Budejovice	CzRep	47	5	6	11	22	....	....	....	....	....
1998-99	C. Budejovice	CzRep	24	1	4	5	18	....	....	....	....	....
99-2000	C. Budejovice	CzRep	38	3	6	9	10	1	0	0	0	0
2000-01	C. Budejovice	CzRep	22	2	3	5	16	....	....	....	....	....
	Zlin	CzRep	19	4	3	7	8	....	....	....	....	....
2001-02	Karlovy Vary	CzRep	36	4	10	14	20	....	....	....	....	....
	Blues Espoo	Finland	5	0	0	0	2	....	....	....	....	....
2002-03	Schwenningen	Germany	49	3	11	14	52	6	1	2	3	6
2003-04	Nizhny Novgorod	Russia	47	8	5	13	44	....	....	....	....	....
	Perm	Russia-2	9	5	7	12	20	11	1	2	3	12
2004-05	Perm	Russia	57	0	5	5	36	....	....	....	....	....
2005-06	Vityaz Chekhov	Russia	36	2	2	4	67	....	....	....	....	....

ZIMAKOV, Sergei
(zih-MAH-kahv, SAIR-gay) **WSH.**

Defense. Shoots left. 6'1", 194 lbs.   Born, Moscow, USSR, January 15, 1978.
(Washington's 4th choice, 58th overall, in 1996 Entry Draft).

				Regular Season					Playoffs			
Season	Club	League	GP	G	A	Pts	PIM	GP	G	A	Pts	PIM
1994-95	Omaha Lancers	USHL	48	14	46	60	22	....	....	....	....	....
1995-96	Krylja Sovetov	CIS	49	2	7	9	36	....	....	....	....	....
1996-97	Krylja Sovetov	Russia	39	4	3	7	57	2	0	0	0	0
1997-98	Krylja Sovetov	Russia	42	4	1	5	48	....	....	....	....	....
1998-99	Ak Bars Kazan	Russia	28	1	0	1	6	8	0	1	1	6
99-2000	Perm	Russia	31	1	2	3	34	3	0	1	1	0
2000-01	CSKA Moscow 2	Russia-3	3	2	2	4	2	....	....	....	....	....
	CSKA Moscow	Russia	26	1	5	6	28	....	....	....	....	....
2001-02	CSKA Moscow	Russia	42	3	10	13	74	....	....	....	....	....
2002-03	Ufa	Russia	11	0	0	0	8	....	....	....	....	....
	Ufa 2	Russia-3			STATISTICS NOT AVAILABLE								
2003-04	Spartak Moscow	Russia-2	60	11	17	28	38	12	0	1	1	10
2004-05	Spartak Moscow	Russia	23	1	3	4	20	....	....	....	....	....
2005-06	Spartak Moscow	Russia	46	3	11	14	55	3	0	0	0	4

ZIMMERMAN, Sean
(ZIH-mehr-man, SHAWN) **N.J.**

Defense. Shoots right. 6'2", 200 lbs.   Born, Denver, CO, May 24, 1987.
(New Jersey's 6th choice, 170th overall, in 2005 Entry Draft).

				Regular Season					Playoffs			
Season	Club	League	GP	G	A	Pts	PIM	GP	G	A	Pts	PIM
2002-03	Spokane Braves	KIJHL	45	3	5	8	70	....	....	....	....	....
2003-04	Spokane Chiefs	WHL	67	4	4	8	16	4	0	0	0	0
2004-05	Spokane Chiefs	WHL	71	2	14	16	36	....	....	....	....	....
2005-06	Spokane Chiefs	WHL	72	2	19	21	44	....	....	....	....	....
	Albany River Rats	AHL	6	0	0	0	4	....	....	....	....	....

ZUBAREV, Andrei
(ZOO-bah-rehv, AWN-dray) **ATL.**

Defense. Shoots left. 6'1", 198 lbs.   Born, Ufa, USSR, March 3, 1987.
(Atlanta's 7th choice, 187th overall, in 2005 Entry Draft).

				Regular Season					Playoffs			
Season	Club	League	GP	G	A	Pts	PIM	GP	G	A	Pts	PIM
2003-04	Ufa 2	Russia-3			STATISTICS NOT AVAILABLE								
	Ufa	Russia	6	0	1	1	4	....	....	....	....	....
2004-05	Ufa 2	Russia-3	28	2	4	6	32	....	....	....	....	....
	Ufa	Russia	5	0	0	0	4	....	....	....	....	....
2005-06	Ak Bars Kazan	Russia	40	2	11	13	40	....	....	....	....	....

ZUBOV, Ilja
(ZOO-bahf, IHL-yah) **OTT.**

Center. Shoots left. 6', 176 lbs.   Born, Chelyabinsk, USSR, February 14, 1987.
(Ottawa's 4th choice, 98th overall, in 2005 Entry Draft).

				Regular Season					Playoffs			
Season	Club	League	GP	G	A	Pts	PIM	GP	G	A	Pts	PIM
2003-04	Chelyabinsk	Russia-2	33	7	7	14	16	8	2	1	3	2
2004-05	Chelyabinsk	Russia-2	40	9	8	17	36	....	....	....	....	....
	Chelyabinsk 2	Russia-3	1	0	0	0	0	....	....	....	....	....
2005-06	Spartak Moscow 2	Russia-3	1	0	1	1	4	....	....	....	....	....
	Spartak Moscow	Russia	43	4	8	12	12	3	2	2	4	0

Sidney Crosby, C, 2005 #1

Bobby Ryan, RW, 2005 #2

Jack Johnson, D, 2005 #3

Benoit Pouliot, LW, 2005 #4

Alex Ovechkin, LW, 2004, #1

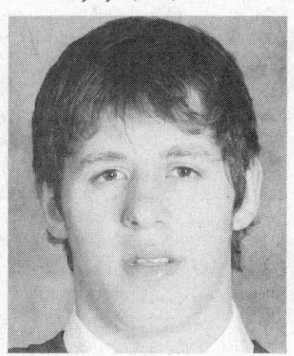

Evgeni Malkin, C, 2004 #2

Cam Barker, D, 2004 #3

Andrew Ladd, LW, 2004 #4

Marc-Andre Fleury, G, 2003 #1

Eric Staal, C, 2003 #2

Nathan Horton, C, 2003 #3

Nikolai Zherdev, D, 2003 #4

One...Two...Three...Four

Along with the top picks in the 2006 Entry Draft (found on page 218), the top four players selected in the last four Drafts break down as follows: by position: centers 7, defensemen 4, left wing 3, right wing 1, goaltenders 1; by country of birth: Canada 9, Russia 3, USA 3, Sweden 1; by source: Ontario Hockey League 5, Russia 3, Quebec Major Junior Hockey League 2, USA Hockey 2, Western Hockey League 2, NCAA 1, Sweden 1. Of these 16 players, eight have already reached the NHL, three recorded 100-point seasons in 2005-06, and two played on a Stanley Cup champion.

League Abbreviations

AAHA ....Alberta Amateur Hockey Association
AAHL ....Alaska Amateur Hockey League
AASHA..........Alaska All-Stars Hockey Association
ACHA...........American Collegiate Hockey Association
ACHL ....Atlantic Coast Hockey League
AFHL...........American Frontier Hockey League
AHL ....American Hockey League
AJHL ....Alberta Junior Hockey League
Alpenliga .....Alpenliga (Austria, Italy, Slovenia 1994-1999)
AMHA..........Alberta Minor Hockey Association
AMBHL ....Alberta Major Bantam Hockey League
AMHL ....Alberta Midget AAA Hockey League
AUAA...........Atlantic University Athletic Association
AtJHL ....Atlantic Junior Hockey League
AWHL ....American West Hockey League
BCAHA ....British Columbia Amateur Hockey Association
BCHL ....British Columbia (Junior) Hockey League (also BCJHL)
CABHL ....Central Alberta Bantam Hockey League
Cal-Am ....California Amateur Hockey Association
CBHL ....Calgary Bantam Hockey League
CCHA...........Central Collegiate Hockey Association
CEGEP ....Quebec College Prep
CHA.............College Hockey America
CHL..............Central Hockey League
CIS..............Commonwealth of Independent States
CIS..............Canadian Interuniversity Sport
CJHL ....Central Junior A Hockey League
CMHA..........Calgary Minor Hockey Association
ColHL...........Colonial Hockey League
CSHL ....Central States Hockey League
CSJHL ....Central States Junior Hockey League
CWUAA ....Canadian Western University Athletic Association
ECAC ....Eastern College Athletic Conference
ECHL ....East Coast Hockey League
EEHL............Eastern European Hockey League
EJHL............Eastern Junior Hockey League
EMHA ....Edmonton Minor Hockey Association
EmJHL..........Empire Junior B Hockey League
EuroHL.........European Hockey League
Exhib. ....Exhibition Games, Series or Season
GLHL...........Great Lakes Hockey League
GNML ....Greater North Midget League
GPAC ....Great Plains Athletic Conference
GTHL ....Greater Toronto Hockey League
H-East..........Hockey East
HJHL ....Heritage Junior Hockey League
High-(XX) .....High School (state/province)
IEHL............Internationale Eishockey Liga
IHL...............International Hockey League
KIJHL...........Kootenay International Junior B Hockey League
LCJHL..........Little Caesar's Junior Hockey League
MAAC.........Metro Atlantic Athletic Conference
MAHA.........Manitoba Amateur Hockey Association
MAHL ....Mid America Hockey League
MBAHL ....Metropolitan Boston Amateur Hockey League
MBHL ....Metropolitan Boston Hockey League
MEHL..........Midwest Elite Hockey League
Metro-HL .....Metro Hockey League
MIAC ....Minnesota Intercollegiate Athletic Conference
MJHL ....Manitoba Junior Hockey League
MJrHL ....Maritime Junior A Hockey League
MMBHL ......Manitoba Major Bantam Hockey League
MMHL.........Manitoba Midget AAA Hockey League
MMHL.........Michigan Minor Hockey League
MMMHL ......Manitoba Minor Midget Hockey League
MNHL ....Michigan National Hockey League
MtJHL ....Metropolitan Junior Hockey League (New York)
MTJHL....:....Metropolitan Toronto Junior Hockey League

MTHL..........Metro Toronto Hockey League
MWEHL ....Midwest Elite Hockey League
NAHL ....North American Hockey League (Tier I Junior)
NAJHL..........North American Junior Hockey League
Nat-Team......National Team (also Nt.-Team)
NBAHA ....New Brunswick Amateur Hockey Association
NBMHL ....New Brunswick Midget Hockey League
NCAA ....National Collegiate Athletic Association
NCHA ....Northern Collegiate Hockey Association
NEJHL ....New England Junior Hockey League
NFAHA ....Newfoundland Amateur Hockey Association
NHL..............National Hockey League
NJCAA ....National Junior Collegiate Athletic Association
NOBHL..........Northern Ontario Bantam Hockey League
NOHA...........Northern Ontario Hockey Association
NOJHA.........Northern Ontario Junior Hockey Association
NOJHL..........Northern Ontario Junior Hockey League
NSBHL ....Nova Scotia Bantam Hockey League
NSMHL ....Nova Scotia Midget AAA Hockey League
NWJHL..........Northwest Junior B Hockey League
NYJHL..........New York Junior Hockey League
OCJHL..........Ontario Central Junior A Hockey League
OHA.............Ontario Hockey Association
OHL..............Ontario Hockey League
OJHL-B..........Ontario Junior B Hockey Leagues
OMHA...........Ontario Minor Hockey Association
OMJHL.........Ontario Major Junior Hockey League
OPJHL..........Ontario Provincial Junior A Hockey League
OUAA ....Ontario Universities Athletic Association
PAHA ....Pennsylvania Amateur Hockey Association
PCJHL ....Pacific Coast Junior Hockey League
PEIHA ....Prince Edward Island Hockey Association
PIJHL...........Pacific International Junior Hockey League
QAAA ....Quebec Amateur Athletic Association
QAHA ....Quebec Amateur Hockey Association
QJHL ....Quebec Junior Hockey League
QMJHL ....Quebec Major Junior Hockey League
QNAHL ....(Quebec) North American Hockey League
Q-RHL..........(Quebec) Richelieu Elite Hockey League
QSPHL...........Quebec Semi-Pro Hockey League
RAMHL ....Rural Alberta Midget Hockey League
RMJHL ....Rocky Mountain Junior Hockey League
SAHA...........Saskatchewan Amateur Hockey Association
SBHL............Saskatchewan Bantam Hockey League
SCAHA.........Southern California Amateur Hockey Association
SIJHL ....Superior International Junior Hockey League
SJHL.............Saskatchewan Junior Hockey League
SMBHL.........Saskatchewan Major Bantam Hockey League
SMHL...........Saskatchewan Midget AAA Hockey League
SMMHL........Saskatchewan Minor Midget Hockey League
SPHL............Southern Professional Hockey League
SSJHL...........South Saskatchewan Junior B Hockey League
SSMHL ....South Saskatchewan Minor Hockey League
SunHL ....Sunshine Hockey League
TBAHA........Thunder Bay Amateur Hockey Association
TBJHL...........Thunder Bay Junior Hockey League
TBMHL.........Thunder Bay Midget Hockey League
UHL ....United Hockey League
UMEHL ....Upper Midwest Elite Hockey League
USAHA.........United States Amateur Hockey Association
USDP ....United States National Development Program
USHL............United States (Junior A) Hockey League
VIJHL ....Vancouver Island Junior Hockey League
WCHA..........Western Collegiate Hockey Association
WCHL ....West Coast Hockey League
WHA............World Hockey Association
WHL.............Western Hockey League
WNYHA ....Western New York Hockey Association
WPHL...........Western Professional Hockey League
WSJHL ....Western States Junior Hockey League
WMHA........Winnipeg Minor Hockey Association

2006-07 NHL Player Register

Note: The 2006-07 NHL Player Register lists forwards and defensemen only. Goaltenders are listed separately. The NHL Player Register lists every active skater who played in the NHL in 2005-06 plus additional players with NHL experience. Trades and roster changes are current as of August 15, 2006.

Abbreviations: A – assists; **F%** – faceoff winning percentage; **G** – goals; **GP** – games played; **GW** – game-winning goals scored; **Min** – average time on ice; **PIM** – penalties in minutes; **+/–** – plus/minus rating; **PP** – powerplay goals scored; **Pts** – points; **S** – shots on goal; **S%** – shooting percentage; **SH** – shorthand goal scored; **TF** – Total faceoffs taken; * – league-leading total; ♦ – member of Stanley Cup-winning team.

Prospect Register begins on page 273.
Goaltender Register begins on page 587.
League abbreviations are listed on page 346.

ABID, Ramzi
(a-BIHD, RAM-zee)   **NSH.**

Left wing. Shoots left. 6'2", 210 lbs.   Born, Montreal, Que., March 24, 1980. Phoenix's 3rd choice, 85th overall, in 2000 Entry Draft.

| | | | | | | | | | | | Regular Season | | | | | | | | | | Playoffs | | | | | |
Season	Club	League	GP	G	A	Pts	PIM	PP	SH	GW	S	%	+/-	TF	F%	Min	GP	G	A	Pts	PIM	PP	SH	GW	Min
1995-96	Richelieu Riverains	QAAA	42	10	14	24	18	....	....	....	....	....	....	....	....	....	4	1	2	3	2	....	....	....	....
1996-97	Chicoutimi	QMJHL	65	13	24	37	141	....	....	....	....	....	....	....	....	....	21	2	12	14	28	....	....	....	....
1997-98	Chicoutimi	QMJHL	68	50	*85	*135	266	....	....	....	....	....	....	....	....	....	6	3	4	7	10	....	....	....	....
1998-99	Chicoutimi	QMJHL	21	11	15	26	97	....	....	....	....	....	....	....	....	....									
	Acadie-Bathurst	QMJHL	24	14	22	36	102	....	....	....	....	....	....	....	....	....	23	14	20	34	*84	....	....	....	....
99-2000	Acadie-Bathurst	QMJHL	13	10	11	21	61	....	....	....	....	....	....	....	....	....									
	Halifax	QMJHL	59	57	80	137	148	....	....	....	....	....	....	....	....	....	10	10	13	23	18	....	....	....	....
2000-01	Springfield	AHL	17	6	4	10	38	....	....	....	....	....	....	....	....	....									
2001-02	Springfield	AHL	66	18	25	43	214	....	....	....	....	....	....	....	....	....									
2002-03	**Phoenix**	**NHL**	30	10	8	18	30	4	0	3	52	19.2	1	1100.0		12:30									
	Springfield	AHL	27	15	10	25	50	....	....	....	....	....	....	....	....	....									
	Pittsburgh	**NHL**	3	0	0	0	2	0	0	0	7	0.0	-5	1	0.0	17:33									
2003-04	**Pittsburgh**	**NHL**	16	3	2	5	27	2	0	1	35	8.6	-5	2	0.0	12:56									
2004-05	Wilkes-Barre	AHL	78	26	29	55	119	....	....	....	....	....	....	....	....	....	7	2	2	18					
2005-06	**Atlanta**	**NHL**	6	0	2	2	6	0	0	0	6	0.0	1	0	0.0	8:10									
	Chicago Wolves	AHL	75	34	42	76	165	....	....	....	....	....	....	....	....	....									
	NHL Totals		55	13	12	25	65	6	0	4	100	13.0		4	25.0	12:26									

• Re-entered NHL Entry Draft. Originally Colorado's 5th choice, 28th overall, in 1998 Entry Draft.
QMJHL First All-Star Team (1998, 2000) • Jean Beliveau Trophy (QMJHL Leading Scorer) (1998) • Michel Briere Trophy (QMJHL MVP) (1998) • Canadian Major Junior First All-Star Team (2000) • Ed Chynoweth Trophy (Memorial Cup Tournament Leading Scorer) (2000)
• Missed majority of 2000-01 season recovering from wrist injury suffered in game vs. Louisville (AHL), October 27, 2000. Traded to **Pittsburgh** by **Phoenix** with Dan Focht and Guillaume Lefebvre for Jan Hrdina and Francois Leroux, March 11, 2003. • Missed majority of 2003-04 season recovering from knee injury suffered in game vs. Edmonton, December 6, 2003. Signed as a free agent by **Atlanta**, August 8, 2005. Signed as a free agent by **Nashville**, July 21, 2006.

ADAMS, Craig
(A-duhms, KRAYG)   **CAR.**

Right wing. Shoots right. 6', 200 lbs.   Born, Seria, Brunei, April 26, 1977. Hartford's 9th choice, 223rd overall, in 1996 Entry Draft.

Season	Club	League	GP	G	A	Pts	PIM	PP	SH	GW	S	%	+/-	TF	F%	Min	GP	G	A	Pts	PIM	PP	SH	GW	Min
1995-96	Harvard Crimson	ECAC	34	8	9	17	56	....	....	....	....	....	....	....	....	....									
1996-97	Harvard Crimson	ECAC	32	6	4	10	36	....	....	....	....	....	....	....	....	....									
1997-98	Harvard Crimson	ECAC	12	6	6	12	12	....	....	....	....	....	....	....	....	....									
1998-99	Harvard Crimson	ECAC	31	9	14	23	53	....	....	....	....	....	....	....	....	....									
99-2000	Cincinnati	IHL	73	12	12	24	124	....	....	....	....	....	....	....	....	....	8	0	1	1	14				
2000-01	**Carolina**	**NHL**	44	1	0	1	20	0	0	0	15	6.7	-7	4	25.0	4:30	3	0	0	0	0	0	0	0	3:45
	Cincinnati	IHL	4	0	1	1	9	....	....	....	....	....	....	....	....	....	1	0	0	0	2				
2001-02	**Carolina**	**NHL**	33	0	1	1	38	0	0	0	17	0.0	2	9	33.3	5:54	1	0	0	0	0	0	0	0	7:41
	Lowell	AHL	22	5	4	9	51	....	....	....	....	....	....	....	....	....									
2002-03	**Carolina**	**NHL**	81	6	12	18	71	1	0	1	107	5.6	-11	20	35.0	12:12									
2003-04	**Carolina**	**NHL**	80	7	10	17	69	0	1	0	110	6.4	-5	20	45.0	13:41									
2004-05	Milano Vipers	Italy	30	15	14	29	57	....	....	....	....	....	....	....	....	....	15	4	7	11	26				
2005-06♦	**Carolina**	**NHL**	67	10	11	21	51	1	1	0	68	14.7	1	13	53.9	12:18	25	0	0	0	10	0	0	0	8:16
	Lowell	AHL	13	4	3	7	20	....	....	....	....	....	....	....	....	....									
	NHL Totals		305	24	34	58	249	2	2	3	317	7.6		66	40.9	10:49	29	0	0	0	10	0	0	0	7:46

Rights transferred to **Carolina** after **Hartford** franchise relocated, June 25, 1997. • Missed majority of 1997-98 season recovering from shoulder injury suffered in game vs. University of Wisconsin (WCHA), December 27, 1997. Signed as a free agent by **Milano**, (Italy), July 28, 2004. Signed as a free agent by **Anaheim**, August 25, 2005. Traded to **Carolina** by **Anaheim** for Bruno St. Jacques, October 3, 2005.

ADAMS, Kevyn
(A-duhms, KEH-vihn)   **CAR.**

Center. Shoots right. 6'1", 195 lbs.   Born, Washington, DC, October 8, 1974. Boston's 1st choice, 25th overall, in 1993 Entry Draft.

Season	Club	League	GP	G	A	Pts	PIM	PP	SH	GW	S	%	+/-	TF	F%	Min	GP	G	A	Pts	PIM	PP	SH	GW	Min
1990-91	Niagara Scenics	NAHL	55	17	20	37	24	....	....	....	....	....	....	....	....	....									
1991-92	Niagara Scenics	NAHL	40	25	33	58	51	....	....	....	....	....	....	....	....	....									
1992-93	Miami U.	CCHA	40	17	15	32	18	....	....	....	....	....	....	....	....	....									
1993-94	Miami U.	CCHA	36	15	28	43	24	....	....	....	....	....	....	....	....	....									
1994-95	Miami U.	CCHA	38	20	29	49	30	....	....	....	....	....	....	....	....	....									
1995-96	Miami U.	CCHA	36	17	30	47	30	....	....	....	....	....	....	....	....	....									
1996-97	Grand Rapids	IHL	82	22	25	47	47	....	....	....	....	....	....	....	....	....	5	1	1	2	4				
1997-98	**Toronto**	**NHL**	5	0	0	0	7	0	0	0	3	0.0	0												
	St. John's	AHL	59	17	20	37	99	....	....	....	....	....	....	....	....	....	4	0	0	0	4				
1998-99	**Toronto**	**NHL**	1	0	0	0	0	0	0	0	1	0.0	0	9	44.4	7:56	7	0	2	2	14	0	0	0	11:18
	St. John's	AHL	80	15	35	50	85	....	....	....	....	....	....	....	....	....	5	2	0	2	4				
99-2000	**Toronto**	**NHL**	52	5	8	13	39	0	0	0	70	7.1	-7	604	56.5	12:23	12	1	0	1	7	0	1	0	11:06
	St. John's	AHL	23	6	11	17	24	....	....	....	....	....	....	....	....	....									
2000-01	**Columbus**	**NHL**	66	8	12	20	52	0	0	1	84	9.5	-4	1152	57.4	15:18									
	Florida	**NHL**	12	3	6	9	2	0	0	2	21	14.3	7	198	47.5	17:25									
2001-02	**Florida**	**NHL**	44	4	8	12	28	0	0	1	71	5.6	-3	572	57.9	13:21									
	Carolina	**NHL**	33	2	3	5	15	0	0	0	37	5.4	-2	187	58.8	9:05	23	1	0	1					7:29
2002-03	**Carolina**	**NHL**	77	9	9	18	57	0	0	0	169	5.3	-8	1018	53.1	14:39									

			Regular Season														Playoffs								
Season	Club	League	GP	G	A	Pts	PIM	PP	SH	GW	S	%	+/-	TF	F%	Min	GP	G	A	Pts	PIM	PP	SH	GW	Min
2003-04	**Carolina**	**NHL**	**73**	**10**	**12**	**22**	**43**	**0**	**5**	**1**	**141**	**7.1**	**6**	**722**	**51.9**	**13:17**	....	....	....	....	....	....	....	....	....
2004-05	Dusseldorf	Germany	9	1	2	3	4	....	....	....	....	....	....	....	....	....	....	....	....	....	....	....	....	....	....
2005-06 ♦	**Carolina**	**NHL**	**82**	**15**	**8**	**23**	**36**	**0**	**2**	**2**	**160**	**9.4**	**0**	**633**	**49.1**	**12:53**	**25**	**0**	**0**	**0**	**14**	**0**	**0**	**0**	**11:44**
	NHL Totals		**445**	**56**	**66**	**122**	**279**	**0**	**7**	**8**	**757**	**7.4**		**5095**	**54.3**	**13:26**	**67**	**2**	**2**	**4**	**39**	**0**	**1**	**0**	**10:07**

CCHA Second All-Star Team (1995)

Signed as a free agent by **Toronto**, August 7, 1997. Claimed by **Columbus** from **Toronto** in Expansion Draft, June 23, 2000. Traded to **Florida** by **Columbus** with Columbus's 4th round choice (Mike Woodford) in 2001 Entry Draft for Ray Whitney and future considerations, March 13, 2001. Traded to **Carolina** by **Florida** with Bret Hedican and Tomas Malec for Sandis Ozolinsh and Byron Ritchie, January 16, 2002. Signed as a free agent by **Dusseldorf** (Germany), February 13, 2005.

AFANASENKOV, Dmitry

(a-fahn-A-sehn-kahv, dih-MEE-tree) **T.B.**

Left wing. Shoots right. 6'2", 209 lbs. Born, Arkhangelsk, USSR, May 12, 1980. Tampa Bay's 3rd choice, 72nd overall, in 1998 Entry Draft.

Season	Club	League	GP	G	A	Pts	PIM	PP	SH	GW	S	%	+/-	TF	F%	Min	GP	G	A	Pts	PIM	PP	SH	GW	Min
1995-96	Yaroslavl 2	CIS-2	25	10	5	15	10	....	....	....	....	....	....	....	....	....	....	....	....	....	....	....	....	....	....
1996-97	Yaroslavl 2	Russia-3	45	20	15	35	14	....	....	....	....	....	....	....	....	....	....	....	....	....	....	....	....	....	....
1997-98	Yaroslavl 2	Russia-2	48	14	7	21	20	....	....	....	....	....	....	....	....	....	....	....	....	....	....	....	....	....	....
1998-99	Moncton Wildcats	QMJHL	15	5	5	10	12	....	....	....	....	....	....	....	....	....	....	....	....	....	....	....	....	....	....
	Sherbrooke	QMJHL	51	23	30	53	22	....	....	....	....	....	....	....	....	....	13	10	6	16	6	....	....	....	....
99-2000	Sherbrooke	QMJHL	60	56	43	99	70	....	....	....	....	....	....	....	....	....	5	3	2	5	4	....	....	....	....
2000-01	**Tampa Bay**	**NHL**	**9**	**1**	**1**	**2**	**4**	**0**	**0**	**0**	**8**	**12.5**	**1**	**7**	**28.6**	**11:24**	....	....	....	....	....	....	....	....	....
	Detroit Vipers	IHL	65	15	22	37	26	....	....	....	....	....	....	....	....	....	....	....	....	....	....	....	....	....	....
2001-02	**Tampa Bay**	**NHL**	**5**	**0**	**0**	**0**	**0**	**0**	**0**	**0**	**1**	**0.0**	**–1**	**0**	**0.0**	**4:54**	....	....	....	....	....	....	....	....	....
	Springfield	AHL	28	4	5	9	4	....	....	....	....	....	....	....	....	....	....	....	....	....	....	....	....	....	....
	Grand Rapids	AHL	18	1	2	3	2	....	....	....	....	....	....	....	....	....	....	....	....	....	....	....	....	....	....
2002-03	Springfield	AHL	41	4	9	13	25	....	....	....	....	....	....	....	....	....	....	....	....	....	....	....	....	....	....
	Kloten Flyers	Swiss	....	....	....	....	....	....	....	....	....	....	....	....	....	....	5	1	1	2	0	....	....	....	....
2003-04 ♦	**Tampa Bay**	**NHL**	**71**	**6**	**10**	**16**	**12**	**0**	**0**	**1**	**98**	**6.1**	**–4**	**2**	**0.0**	**12:21**	**23**	**1**	**2**	**3**	**6**	**0**	**0**	**0**	**13:06**
2004-05	Lada Togliatti	Russia	30	2	9	11	12	....	....	....	....	....	....	....	....	....	9	0	0	0	4	....	....	....	....
2005-06	**Tampa Bay**	**NHL**	**68**	**9**	**6**	**15**	**16**	**1**	**0**	**0**	**78**	**11.5**	**–7**	**17**	**29.4**	**9:44**	**5**	**0**	**1**	**1**	**2**	**0**	**0**	**0**	**15:46**
	NHL Totals		**153**	**16**	**17**	**33**	**32**	**1**	**0**	**1**	**185**	**8.6**		**26**	**26.9**	**10:53**	**28**	**1**	**3**	**4**	**8**	**0**	**0**	**0**	**13:34**

• Assigned to **Kloten** (Swiss) by **Tampa Bay**, February 19, 2003. Signed as a free agent by **Togliatti** (Russia), September 28, 2004.

AFINOGENOV, Maxim

(ah-fihn-ah-GEHN-ahf, mahx-EEM) **BUF.**

Right wing. Shoots left. 6', 190 lbs. Born, Moscow, USSR, September 4, 1979. Buffalo's 3rd choice, 69th overall, in 1997 Entry Draft.

Season	Club	League	GP	G	A	Pts	PIM	PP	SH	GW	S	%	+/-	TF	F%	Min	GP	G	A	Pts	PIM	PP	SH	GW	Min
1996-97	Dynamo Moscow	Russia	29	6	5	11	10	....	....	....	....	....	....	....	....	....	4	0	2	2	0	....	....	....	....
	Dynamo Moscow	EuroHL	3	0	0	0	0	....	....	....	....	....	....	....	....	....	3	1	0	1	4	....	....	....	....
1997-98	Dynamo Moscow	Russia	35	10	5	15	53	....	....	....	....	....	....	....	....	....	....	....	....	....	....	....	....	....	....
	Dynamo Moscow	EuroHL	6	3	1	4	27	....	....	....	....	....	....	....	....	....	....	....	....	....	....	....	....	....	....
1998-99	Dynamo Moscow	Russia	38	8	13	21	24	....	....	....	....	....	....	....	....	....	16	*10	6	*16	14	....	....	....	....
	Dynamo Moscow	EuroHL	5	3	5	8	29	....	....	....	....	....	....	....	....	....	4	2	1	3	27	....	....	....	....
99-2000	**Buffalo**	**NHL**	**65**	**16**	**18**	**34**	**41**	**2**	**0**	**2**	**128**	**12.5**	**–4**	**0**	**0.0**	**13:09**	**5**	**0**	**1**	**1**	**2**	**0**	**0**	**0**	**12:53**
	Rochester	AHL	15	6	12	18	8	....	....	....	....	....	....	....	....	....	8	3	1	4	4	....	....	....	....
2000-01	**Buffalo**	**NHL**	**78**	**14**	**22**	**36**	**40**	**3**	**0**	**5**	**190**	**7.4**	**1**	**2**	**0.0**	**14:32**	**11**	**2**	**3**	**5**	**4**	**0**	**0**	**0**	**10:56**
2001-02	**Buffalo**	**NHL**	**81**	**21**	**19**	**40**	**69**	**3**	**1**	**0**	**234**	**9.0**	**–9**	**1**	**100.0**	**15:22**	....	....	....	....	....	....	....	....	....
	Russia	Olympics	6	2	2	4	4	....	....	....	....	....	....	....	....	....	....	....	....	....	....	....	....	....	....
2002-03	**Buffalo**	**NHL**	**35**	**5**	**6**	**11**	**21**	**2**	**0**	**2**	**77**	**6.5**	**–12**	**4**	**50.0**	**13:24**	....	....	....	....	....	....	....	....	....
2003-04	**Buffalo**	**NHL**	**73**	**17**	**14**	**31**	**57**	**3**	**0**	**4**	**148**	**11.5**	**–4**	**9**	**22.2**	**13:46**	....	....	....	....	....	....	....	....	....
2004-05	Dynamo Moscow	Russia	36	13	14	27	91	....	....	....	....	....	....	....	....	....	10	4	4	8	8	....	....	....	....
2005-06	**Buffalo**	**NHL**	**77**	**22**	**51**	**73**	**84**	**11**	**0**	**3**	**241**	**9.1**	**6**	**17**	**17.7**	**16:20**	**18**	**3**	**5**	**8**	**10**	**0**	**0**	**0**	**16:53**
	Russia	Olympics	8	0	1	1	10	....	....	....	....	....	....	....	....	....	....	....	....	....	....	....	....	....	....
	NHL Totals		**409**	**95**	**130**	**225**	**312**	**24**	**1**	**16**	**1018**	**9.3**		**33**	**24.2**	**14:35**	**34**	**5**	**9**	**14**	**16**	**0**	**0**	**0**	**14:22**

• Missed majority of 2002-03 season recovering from head injury suffered prior to training camp, August, 2002. Signed as a free agent by **Dynamo Moscow** (Russia), June 19, 2004.

AITKEN, Johnathan

(ATE-kin, JAWN-uh-thuhn)

Defense. Shoots left. 6'4", 230 lbs. Born, Edmonton, Alta., May 24, 1978. Boston's 1st choice, 8th overall, in 1996 Entry Draft.

Season	Club	League	GP	G	A	Pts	PIM	PP	SH	GW	S	%	+/-	TF	F%	Min	GP	G	A	Pts	PIM	PP	SH	GW	Min
1993-94	Sherwood Park	AMHL	31	4	9	13	54	....	....	....	....	....	....	....	....	....	....	....	....	....	....	....	....	....	....
1994-95	Medicine Hat	WHL	53	0	5	5	71	....	....	....	....	....	....	....	....	....	5	0	0	0	0	....	....	....	....
1995-96	Medicine Hat	WHL	71	6	14	20	131	....	....	....	....	....	....	....	....	....	5	1	0	1	6	....	....	....	....
1996-97	Brandon	WHL	65	4	18	22	211	....	....	....	....	....	....	....	....	....	6	0	0	0	4	....	....	....	....
1997-98	Brandon	WHL	69	9	25	34	183	....	....	....	....	....	....	....	....	....	18	0	8	8	67	....	....	....	....
1998-99	Providence Bruins	AHL	65	2	9	11	92	....	....	....	....	....	....	....	....	....	13	0	0	0	17	....	....	....	....
99-2000	**Boston**	**NHL**	**3**	**0**	**0**	**0**	**0**	**0**	**0**	**0**	**2**	**0.0**	**–3**	**0**	**0.0**	**18:57**	....	....	....	....	....	....	....	....	....
	Providence Bruins	AHL	70	2	12	14	121	....	....	....	....	....	....	....	....	....	11	1	0	1	26	....	....	....	....
2000-01	HC Sparta Praha	CzRep	24	0	3	3	62	....	....	....	....	....	....	....	....	....	....	....	....	....	....	....	....	....	....
2001-02	Norfolk Admirals	AHL	28	0	1	1	43	....	....	....	....	....	....	....	....	....	4	0	0	0	2	....	....	....	....
	Jackson Bandits	ECHL	43	1	9	10	141	....	....	....	....	....	....	....	....	....	....	....	....	....	....	....	....	....	....
2002-03	Norfolk Admirals	AHL	80	1	7	8	207	....	....	....	....	....	....	....	....	....	9	2	1	3	18	....	....	....	....
2003-04	**Chicago**	**NHL**	**41**	**0**	**1**	**1**	**70**	**0**	**0**	**0**	**37**	**0.0**	**–9**	**0**	**0.0**	**17:15**	....	....	....	....	....	....	....	....	....
	Norfolk Admirals	AHL	40	1	4	5	97	....	....	....	....	....	....	....	....	....	8	1	4	5	27	....	....	....	....
2004-05	Manitoba Moose	AHL	46	1	6	7	101	....	....	....	....	....	....	....	....	....	1	0	0	0	7	....	....	....	....
2005-06	Hamilton	AHL	47	1	2	3	81	....	....	....	....	....	....	....	....	....	....	....	....	....	....	....	....	....	....
	NHL Totals		**44**	**0**	**1**	**1**	**70**	**0**	**0**	**0**	**39**	**0.0**		**0**	**0.0**	**17:22**	....	....	....	....	....	....	....	....	....

WHL East Second All-Star Team (1998)

Signed as a free agent by **Norfolk** (AHL), September 6, 2001. Signed as a free agent by **Chicago**, May 22, 2002. Signed as a free agent by **Vancouver**, July 7, 2004. Signed as a free agent by **Montreal**, August 16, 2005.

ALBELIN, Tommy

(AHL-buh-leen,TAW-mee)

Defense. Shoots left. 6'2", 195 lbs. Born, Stockholm, Sweden, May 21, 1964. Quebec's 7th choice, 158th overall, in 1983 Entry Draft.

Season	Club	League	GP	G	A	Pts	PIM	PP	SH	GW	S	%	+/-	TF	F%	Min	GP	G	A	Pts	PIM	PP	SH	GW	Min
1980-81	Stocksunds IF	Sweden-3	18	6	1	7	....	....	....	....	....	....	....	....	....	....	....	....	....	....	....	....	....	....	....
1981-82	Stocksunds IF	Sweden-3	22	6	2	8	....	....	....	....	....	....	....	....	....	....	....	....	....	....	....	....	....	....	....
1982-83	Djurgarden	Sweden	19	2	5	7	4	....	....	....	....	....	....	....	....	....	6	1	0	1	2	....	....	....	....
1983-84	Djurgarden	Sweden	30	9	5	14	26	....	....	....	....	....	....	....	....	....	4	0	1	1	2	....	....	....	....
1984-85	Djurgarden	Sweden	32	9	8	17	22	....	....	....	....	....	....	....	....	....	8	2	1	3	4	....	....	....	....
1985-86	Djurgarden	Sweden	35	4	8	12	26	....	....	....	....	....	....	....	....	....	....	....	....	....	....	....	....	....	....
1986-87	Djurgarden	Sweden	33	7	5	12	49	....	....	....	....	....	....	....	....	....	2	0	0	0	0	....	....	....	....
1987-88	**Quebec**	**NHL**	**60**	**3**	**23**	**26**	**47**	**0**	**0**	**0**	**98**	**3.1**	**–7**	....	....	....	....	....	....	....	....	....	....	....	....
1988-89	**Quebec**	**NHL**	**14**	**2**	**4**	**6**	**27**	**1**	**0**	**1**	**16**	**12.5**	**–6**	....	....	....	....	....	....	....	....	....	....	....	....
	Halifax Citadels	AHL	8	2	5	7	4	....	....	....	....	....	....	....	....	....	....	....	....	....	....	....	....	....	....
	New Jersey	**NHL**	**46**	**7**	**24**	**31**	**40**	**1**	**1**	**1**	**82**	**8.5**	**18**	....	....	....	....	....	....	....	....	....	....	....	....
1989-90	**New Jersey**	**NHL**	**68**	**6**	**23**	**29**	**63**	**4**	**0**	**0**	**125**	**4.8**	**–1**	....	....	....	....	....	....	....	....	....	....	....	....
1990-91	**New Jersey**	**NHL**	**47**	**2**	**12**	**14**	**44**	**1**	**0**	**0**	**66**	**3.0**	**1**	....	....	....	**3**	**0**	**1**	**1**	**2**	**0**	**0**	**0**	....
	Utica Devils	AHL	14	4	2	6	10	....	....	....	....	....	....	....	....	....	....	....	....	....	....	....	....	....	....
1991-92	**New Jersey**	**NHL**	**19**	**0**	**4**	**4**	**4**	**0**	**0**	**0**	**18**	**0.0**	**7**	....	....	....	**1**	**1**	**1**	**2**	**0**	**0**	**0**	**0**	....
	Utica Devils	AHL	11	4	6	10	4	....	....	....	....	....	....	....	....	....	....	....	....	....	....	....	....	....	....
1992-93	**New Jersey**	**NHL**	**36**	**1**	**5**	**6**	**14**	**1**	**0**	**1**	**33**	**3.0**	**0**	....	....	....	**5**	**2**	**0**	**2**	**0**	**1**	**0**	**1**	....
1993-94	**New Jersey**	**NHL**	**62**	**2**	**17**	**19**	**36**	**1**	**0**	**1**	**62**	**3.2**	**20**	....	....	....	**20**	**2**	**5**	**7**	**14**	**1**	**0**	**1**	....
	Albany River Rats	AHL	4	0	2	2	17	....	....	....	....	....	....	....	....	....	....	....	....	....	....	....	....	....	....
1994-95 ♦	**New Jersey**	**NHL**	**48**	**5**	**10**	**15**	**20**	**2**	**0**	**0**	**60**	**8.3**	**9**	....	....	....	**20**	**1**	**7**	**8**	**2**	**0**	**0**	**0**	....
1995-96	**New Jersey**	**NHL**	**53**	**1**	**12**	**13**	**14**	**0**	**0**	**0**	**90**	**1.1**	**0**	....	....	....	....	....	....	....	....	....	....	....	....
	Calgary	**NHL**	**20**	**0**	**1**	**1**	**4**	**0**	**0**	**0**	**31**	**0.0**	**1**	....	....	....	**4**	**0**	**0**	**0**	**0**	**0**	**0**	**0**	....
1996-97	**Calgary**	**NHL**	**72**	**4**	**11**	**15**	**14**	**2**	**0**	**0**	**103**	**3.9**	**–8**	....	....	....	....	....	....	....	....	....	....	....	....
1997-98	**Calgary**	**NHL**	**69**	**2**	**17**	**19**	**32**	**1**	**0**	**2**	**88**	**2.3**	**9**	....	....	....	....	....	....	....	....	....	....	....	....
	Sweden	Olympics	3	0	0	0	4	....	....	....	....	....	....	....	....	....	....	....	....	....	....	....	....	....	....
1998-99	**Calgary**	**NHL**	**60**	**1**	**5**	**6**	**8**	**0**	**0**	**0**	**54**	**1.9**	**–11**	**1**	**0.0**	**19:08**	....	....	....	....	....	....	....	....	....
99-2000	**Calgary**	**NHL**	**41**	**4**	**6**	**10**	**12**	**1**	**1**	**1**	**37**	**10.8**	**–3**	**0**	**0.0**	**21:35**	....	....	....	....	....	....	....	....	....
2000-01	**Calgary**	**NHL**	**77**	**1**	**19**	**20**	**22**	**1**	**0**	**0**	**69**	**1.4**	**2**	**0**	**0.0**	**20:53**	....	....	....	....	....	....	....	....	....
2001-02	**New Jersey**	**NHL**	**42**	**1**	**3**	**4**	**4**	**0**	**0**	**1**	**33**	**3.0**	**0**	**0**	**0.0**	**13:20**	**6**	**0**	**0**	**0**	**0**	**0**	**0**	**0**	**14:11**

Season	Club	League	GP	G	A	Pts	PIM	PP	SH	GW	S	%	+/-	TF	F%	Min	GP	G	A	Pts	PIM	PP	SH	GW	Min
			Regular Season														Playoffs								
2002-03♦	**New Jersey**	**NHL**	**37**	**1**	**6**	**7**	**6**	**0**	**1**	**0**	**30**	**3.3**	**10**	**0**	**0.0**	**15:13**	**16**	**1**	**0**	**1**	**2**	**0**	**0**	**0**	**14:18**
	Albany River Rats	AHL	5	0	2	2	2																		
2003-04	**New Jersey**	**NHL**	**45**	**1**	**3**	**4**	**4**	**0**	**0**	**0**	**27**	**3.7**	**7**	**0**	**0.0**	**14:48**	**4**	**0**	**1**	**1**	**0**	**0**	**0**	**0**	**13:13**
2005-06	**New Jersey**	**NHL**	**36**	**0**	**6**	**6**	**2**	**0**	**0**	**0**	**15**	**0.0**	**4**	**0**	**0.0**	**13:59**	**2**	**0**	**0**	**0**	**2**	**0**	**0**	**0**	**10:38**
	NHL Totals		**952**	**44**	**211**	**255**	**417**	**16**	**3**	**8**	**1137**	**3.9**		**1**	**0.0**	**17:33**	**81**	**7**	**15**	**22**	**22**	**2**	**0**	**2**	**13:51**

Traded to **New Jersey** by **Quebec** for New Jersey's 4th round choice (Niklas Andersson) in 1989 Entry Draft, December 12, 1988. Traded to **Calgary** by **New Jersey** with Cale Hulse and Jocelyn Lemieux for Phil Housley and Dan Keczmer, February 26, 1996. Signed as a free agent by **New Jersey**, July 9, 2001. • Officially announced retirement, July 29, 2004. Signed as a free agent by **New Jersey**, December 20, 2005.

ALBERTS, Andrew

(AL-buhrts, AN-droo) **BOS.**

Defense. Shoots left. 6'4", 218 lbs. Born, Minneapolis, MN, June 30, 1981. Boston's 5th choice, 179th overall, in 2001 Entry Draft.

Season	Club	League	GP	G	A	Pts	PIM	PP	SH	GW	S	%	+/-	TF	F%	Min	GP	G	A	Pts	PIM	PP	SH	GW	Min
1998-99	Benide	High-MN	26	10	25	35																			
99-2000	Waterloo	USHL	49	2	2	4	55										4	0	0	0	12				
2000-01	Waterloo	USHL	54	4	10	14	128																		
2001-02	Boston College	H-East	38	2	10	12	52																		
2002-03	Boston College	H-East	39	6	16	22	60																		
2003-04	Boston College	H-East	42	4	12	16	64																		
2004-05	Boston College	H-East	30	4	12	16	67																		
	Providence Bruins	AHL	8	0	0	0	16										16	1	4	5	40				
2005-06	**Boston**	**NHL**	**73**	**1**	**6**	**7**	**68**	**0**	**1**	**0**	**30**	**3.3**	**3**	**2**	**50.0**	**12:50**									
	Providence Bruins	AHL	6	0	1	1	7																		
	NHL Totals		**73**	**1**	**6**	**7**	**68**	**0**	**1**	**0**	**30**	**3.3**		**2**	**50.0**	**12:50**									

Hockey East Second All-Star Team (2004) • NCAA East First All-American Team (2004, 2005) • Hockey East First All-Star Team (2005)

ALEXEEV, Nikita

(uh-LEHX-ee-ehv, nih-KEE-tuh) **T.B.**

Right wing. Shoots left. 6'5", 227 lbs. Born, Murmansk, USSR, December 27, 1981. Tampa Bay's 1st choice, 8th overall, in 2000 Entry Draft.

Season	Club	League	GP	G	A	Pts	PIM	PP	SH	GW	S	%	+/-	TF	F%	Min	GP	G	A	Pts	PIM	PP	SH	GW	Min
1996-97	Krylja Sovetov 2	Russia-3	45	4	6	10	8																		
1997-98	Krylja Sovetov 2	Russia-3	61	11	4	15	36																		
1998-99	Erie Otters	OHL	61	17	18	35	14										5	1	1	2	4				
99-2000	Erie Otters	OHL	64	24	29	53	42										13	4	3	7	6				
2000-01	Erie Otters	OHL	64	31	41	72	45										12	7	7	14	12				
2001-02	**Tampa Bay**	**NHL**	**44**	**4**	**4**	**8**	**8**	**1**	**0**	**1**	**47**	**8.5**	**-9**	**0**	**0.0**	**11:26**									
	Springfield	AHL	35	5	9	14	16																		
2002-03	**Tampa Bay**	**NHL**	**37**	**4**	**2**	**6**	**8**	**1**	**0**	**1**	**52**	**7.7**	**-6**	**3**	**33.3**	**11:31**	**11**	**1**	**0**	**1**	**0**	**0**	**0**	**0**	**10:12**
	Springfield	AHL	36	7	5	12	8																		
2003-04	Hershey Bears	AHL	14	0	1	1	8																		
2004-05	Springfield	AHL	72	13	9	22	16																		
2005-06	Avangard Omsk	Russia	40	6	3	9	14										5	0	0	0	2				
	NHL Totals		**81**	**8**	**6**	**14**	**16**	**2**	**0**	**2**	**99**	**8.1**		**3**	**33.3**	**11:28**	**11**	**1**	**0**	**1**	**0**	**0**	**0**	**0**	**10:12**

• Missed majority of 2003-04 season recovering from shoulder injury suffered in game vs. Philadelphia (AHL) on November 2, 2003.

ALFREDSSON, Daniel

(AHL-frehd-suhn, DAN-yehl) **OTT.**

Right wing. Shoots right. 5'11", 208 lbs. Born, Goteborg, Sweden, December 11, 1972. Ottawa's 5th choice, 133rd overall, in 1994 Entry Draft.

Season	Club	League	GP	G	A	Pts	PIM	PP	SH	GW	S	%	+/-	TF	F%	Min	GP	G	A	Pts	PIM	PP	SH	GW	Min
1990-91	Molndal Hockey	Sweden-2	3	0	0	0	2										8	4	4	8	4				
1991-92	Molndal	Sweden-2	32	12	8	20	43																		
1992-93	V.Frolunda	Sweden	20	1	5	6	8																		
1993-94	V.Frolunda	Sweden	39	20	10	30	18										4	1	1	2					
1994-95	V.Frolunda	Sweden	22	7	11	18	22																		
1995-96	**Ottawa**	**NHL**	**82**	**26**	**35**	**61**	**28**	**8**	**2**	**3**	**212**	**12.3**	**-18**												
1996-97	**Ottawa**	**NHL**	**76**	**24**	**47**	**71**	**30**	**11**	**1**	**1**	**247**	**9.7**	**5**				**7**	**5**	**2**	**7**	**6**	**3**	**0**	**2**	
1997-98	**Ottawa**	**NHL**	**55**	**17**	**28**	**45**	**18**	**7**	**0**	**7**	**149**	**11.4**	**7**				**11**	**7**	**2**	**9**	**20**	**2**	**1**	**1**	
	Sweden	Olympics	4	2	3	5	2																		
1998-99	**Ottawa**	**NHL**	**58**	**11**	**22**	**33**	**14**	**3**	**0**	**5**	**163**	**6.7**	**8**	**7**	**57.1**	**17:22**	**4**	**1**	**2**	**3**	**4**	**1**	**0**	**0**	**22:23**
99-2000	**Ottawa**	**NHL**	**57**	**21**	**38**	**59**	**28**	**4**	**2**	**0**	**164**	**12.8**	**11**	**3**	**66.7**	**18:45**	**6**	**1**	**3**	**4**	**2**	**1**	**0**	**0**	**20:22**
2000-01	**Ottawa**	**NHL**	**68**	**24**	**46**	**70**	**30**	**10**	**0**	**3**	**206**	**11.7**	**11**	**8**	**50.0**	**18:47**	**4**	**1**	**0**	**1**	**2**	**0**	**0**	**0**	**21:20**
2001-02	**Ottawa**	**NHL**	**78**	**37**	**34**	**71**	**45**	**9**	**1**	**4**	**243**	**15.2**	**3**	**30**	**30.0**	**20:19**	**12**	**7**	**6**	**13**	**4**	**3**	**0**	**3**	**21:43**
	Sweden	Olympics	4	1	4	5	2																		
2002-03	**Ottawa**	**NHL**	**78**	**27**	**51**	**78**	**42**	**9**	**0**	**6**	**240**	**11.3**	**15**	**40**	**40.0**	**19:32**	**18**	**4**	**4**	**8**	**12**	**4**	**0**	**1**	**18:00**
2003-04	**Ottawa**	**NHL**	**77**	**32**	**48**	**80**	**24**	**9**	**0**	**5**	**230**	**13.9**	**12**	**33**	**24.2**	**19:24**	**7**	**1**	**2**	**3**	**2**	**0**	**0**	**0**	**20:03**
2004-05	Frolunda	Sweden	15	8	9	17	10										14	*12	6	*18	8				
2005-06	**Ottawa**	**NHL**	**77**	**43**	**60**	**103**	**50**	**16**	**5**	**8**	**249**	**17.3**	**29**	**44**	**20.5**	**21:41**	**10**	**2**	**8**	**10**	**4**	**1**	**0**	**0**	**21:10**
	Sweden	Olympics	8	5	5	10	4																		
	NHL Totals		**706**	**262**	**409**	**671**	**309**	**86**	**11**	**42**	**2103**	**12.5**		**165**	**31.5**	**19:31**	**79**	**29**	**29**	**58**	**56**	**15**	**1**	**7**	**20:13**

NHL All-Rookie Team (1996) • Calder Memorial Trophy (1996) • NHL Second All-Star Team (2006)

Played in NHL All-Star Game (1996, 1997, 1998, 2004)

Signed as a free agent by **Frolunda** (Sweden), November 10, 2004.

ALLEN, Bobby

(AHL-lehn, BAW-bee) **BOS.**

Defense. Shoots left. 6', 200 lbs. Born, Braintree, MA, November 14, 1978. Boston's 2nd choice, 52nd overall, in 1998 Entry Draft.

Season	Club	League	GP	G	A	Pts	PIM	PP	SH	GW	S	%	+/-	TF	F%	Min	GP	G	A	Pts	PIM	PP	SH	GW	Min
1996-97	Cushing	High-MA	36	11	33	44	28																		
1997-98	Boston College	H-East	40	7	21	28	49																		
1998-99	Boston College	H-East	43	9	23	32	34																		
99-2000	Boston College	H-East	42	4	23	27	40																		
2000-01	Boston College	H-East	42	5	18	23	28																		
2001-02	Providence Bruins	AHL	49	5	10	15	18																		
	Hamilton	AHL	10	1	6	7	0										14	0	3	3	6				
2002-03	**Edmonton**	**NHL**	**1**	**0**	**0**	**0**	**0**	**0**	**0**	**0**	**0**	**0.0**	**0**	**0**	**0.0**	**2:53**									
	Hamilton	AHL	56	1	12	13	24										23	0	5	5	10				
2003-04	Toronto	AHL	56	5	10	15	18										3	0	2	2	4				
2004-05	Albany River Rats	AHL	66	5	11	16	20																		
2005-06	Albany River Rats	AHL	68	4	14	18	28																		
	NHL Totals		**1**	**0**	**0**	**0**	**0**	**0**	**0**	**0**	**0**	**0.0**		**0**	**0.0**	**2:53**									

Hockey East Second All-Star Team (2000) • Hockey East First All-Star Team (2001) • NCAA East First All-American Team (2001)

Traded to **Edmonton** by **Boston** for Sean Brown, March 19, 2002. Signed as a free agent by **New Jersey**, July 22, 2004. Signed as a free agent by **Boston**, July 17, 2006.

ALLEN, Bryan

(AHL-lehn, BRIGH-uhn) **FLA.**

Defense. Shoots left. 6'4", 220 lbs. Born, Kingston, Ont., August 21, 1980. Vancouver's 1st choice, 4th overall, in 1998 Entry Draft.

Season	Club	League	GP	G	A	Pts	PIM	PP	SH	GW	S	%	+/-	TF	F%	Min	GP	G	A	Pts	PIM	PP	SH	GW	Min
1995-96	Ernestown Jets	OHA-C	36	1	16	17	71																		
1996-97	Oshawa Generals	OHL	60	2	4	6	76										18	1	3	4	26				
1997-98	Oshawa Generals	OHL	48	6	13	19	126										5	0	5	5	18				
1998-99	Oshawa Generals	OHL	37	7	15	22	77										15	0	3	3	26				
99-2000	Oshawa Generals	OHL	3	0	2	2	12										3	0	0	0	13				
	Syracuse Crunch	AHL	9	1	1	2	11										2	0	0	0	2				
2000-01	**Vancouver**	**NHL**	**6**	**0**	**0**	**0**	**0**	**0**	**0**	**0**	**2**	**0.0**	**0**	**0**	**0.0**	**9:20**	**2**	**0**	**0**	**0**	**2**	**0**	**0**	**0**	**13:47**
	Kansas City	IHL	75	5	20	25	99																		
2001-02	**Vancouver**	**NHL**	**11**	**0**	**0**	**0**	**6**	**0**	**0**	**0**	**4**	**0.0**	**1**	**0**	**0.0**	**10:47**									
	Manitoba Moose	AHL	68	7	18	25	121										5	0	1	1	8				
2002-03	**Vancouver**	**NHL**	**48**	**5**	**3**	**8**	**73**	**0**	**0**	**1**	**43**	**11.6**	**8**	**0**	**0.0**	**12:56**	**1**	**0**	**0**	**0**	**2**	**0**	**0**	**0**	**10:35**
	Manitoba Moose	AHL	7	0	1	1	4																		
2003-04	**Vancouver**	**NHL**	**74**	**2**	**5**	**7**	**94**	**0**	**0**	**0**	**70**	**2.9**	**-10**	**0**	**0.0**	**16:51**	**4**	**0**	**0**	**0**	**2**	**0**	**0**	**0**	**14:37**

Season	Club	League	GP	G	A	Pts	PIM	PP	SH	GW	S	%	+/-	TF	F%	Min	GP	G	A	Pts	PIM	PP	SH	GW	Min
			Regular Season														Playoffs								
2004-05	Voskresensk	Russia	19	0	3	3	34																		
2005-06	**Vancouver**	**NHL**	**77**	**7**	**10**	**17**	**115**	**1**	**0**	**0**	**88**	**8.0**	**4**	**0**	**0.0**	**20:27**									
	NHL Totals		**216**	**14**	**18**	**32**	**288**	**1**	**0**	**1**	**207**	**6.8**		**0**	**0.0**	**16:45**	**7**	**0**	**0**	**0**	**6**	**0**	**0**	**0**	**13:48**

OHL First All-Star Team (1999)

• Missed majority of 1999-2000 season recovering from knee injury suffered in training camp, September 21, 1999. Signed as a free agent by **Voskresensk** (Russia), December 20, 2004. Traded to **Florida** by **Vancouver** with Todd Bertuzzi and Alex Auld for Roberto Luongo, Lukas Krajicek and Florida's 6th round choice (Sergei Shirokov) in 2006 Entry Draft, June 23, 2006.

ALLISON, Jamie

(AL-lih-suhn, JAY-mee) **OTT.**

Defense. Shoots left. 6'1", 210 lbs. Born, Lindsay, Ont., May 13, 1975. Calgary's 2nd choice, 44th overall, in 1993 Entry Draft.

Season	Club	League	GP	G	A	Pts	PIM	PP	SH	GW	S	%	+/-	TF	F%	Min	GP	G	A	Pts	PIM	PP	SH	GW	Min
1990-91	Waterloo Siskins	OHA-B	38	3	8	11	91																		
1991-92	Windsor Spitfires	OHL	59	4	8	12	70										4	1	1	2	2				
1992-93	Detroit	OHL	61	0	13	13	64										15	2	5	7	23				
1993-94	Detroit	OHL	40	2	22	24	69										17	2	9	11	35				
1994-95	Detroit	OHL	50	1	14	15	119										18	2	7	9	35				
	Calgary	**NHL**	**1**	**0**	**0**	**0**	**0**	**0**	**0**	**0**	**0**	**0.0**	**0**												
1995-96	Saint John Flames	AHL	71	3	16	19	223										14	0	2	2	16				
1996-97	**Calgary**	**NHL**	**20**	**0**	**0**	**0**	**35**	**0**	**0**	**0**	**8**	**0.0**	**-4**												
	Saint John Flames	AHL	46	3	6	9	139										5	0	1	1	4				
1997-98	**Calgary**	**NHL**	**43**	**3**	**8**	**11**	**104**	**0**	**0**	**1**	**27**	**11.1**	**3**												
	Saint John Flames	AHL	16	0	5	5	49																		
1998-99	Saint John Flames	AHL	5	0	0	0	23																		
	Chicago	**NHL**	**39**	**2**	**2**	**4**	**62**	**0**	**0**	**0**	**24**	**8.3**	**0**	**0**	**0.0**	**14:01**									
	Indianapolis Ice	IHL	3	1	0	1	10																		
99-2000	**Chicago**	**NHL**	**59**	**1**	**3**	**4**	**102**	**0**	**0**	**0**	**24**	**4.2**	**-5**	**0**	**0.0**	**14:14**									
2000-01	**Chicago**	**NHL**	**44**	**1**	**3**	**4**	**53**	**0**	**0**	**0**	**16**	**6.3**	**7**	**1**	**100.0**	**14:33**									
2001-02	**Calgary**	**NHL**	**37**	**0**	**2**	**2**	**24**	**0**	**0**	**0**	**14**	**0.0**	**-3**	**2**	**0.0**	**7:44**									
	Columbus	**NHL**	**7**	**0**	**0**	**0**	**28**	**0**	**0**	**0**	**2**	**0.0**	**-4**	**0**	**0.0**	**11:23**									
2002-03	**Columbus**	**NHL**	**48**	**0**	**1**	**1**	**99**	**0**	**0**	**0**	**23**	**0.0**	**-15**	**1**	**100.0**	**11:57**									
2003-04	**Nashville**	**NHL**	**47**	**0**	**3**	**3**	**76**	**0**	**0**	**0**	**19**	**0.0**	**-7**	**0**	**0.0**	**13:04**									
2004-05	Cambridge	OHA-Sr.	5	0	3	3	4																		
2005-06	**Nashville**	**NHL**	**20**	**0**	**1**	**1**	**45**	**0**	**0**	**0**	**3**	**0.0**	**-6**	**3**	**66.7**	**8:00**									
	Florida	**NHL**	**7**	**0**	**0**	**0**	**11**	**0**	**0**	**0**	**4**	**0.0**	**0**	**0**	**0.0**	**11:48**									
	NHL Totals		**372**	**7**	**23**	**30**	**639**	**0**	**0**	**1**	**164**	**4.3**		**7**	**57.1**	**12:25**									

Traded to **Chicago** by **Calgary** with Marty McInnis and Erik Andersson for Jeff Shantz and Steve Dubinsky, October 27, 1998. Claimed by **Calgary** from **Chicago** in Waiver Draft, September 28, 2001. Traded to **Columbus** by **Calgary** for Blake Sloan, March 19, 2002. Signed as a free agent by **Nashville**, September 10, 2003. Claimed on waivers by **Florida** from **Nashville**, February 13, 2006. Signed as a free agent by **Ottawa**, July 26, 2006.

ALLISON, Jason

(AL-lih-suhn, JAY-suhn)

Center. Shoots right. 6'3", 215 lbs. Born, North York, Ont., May 29, 1975. Washington's 2nd choice, 17th overall, in 1993 Entry Draft.

Season	Club	League	GP	G	A	Pts	PIM	PP	SH	GW	S	%	+/-	TF	F%	Min	GP	G	A	Pts	PIM	PP	SH	GW	Min
1990-91	North York	MTJHL	63	53	41	94																			
1991-92	London Knights	OHL	65	11	19	30	15										7	0	0	0	0				
1992-93	London Knights	OHL	66	42	76	118	50										12	7	13	20	8				
1993-94	London Knights	OHL	56	55	87	*142	68										5	2	13	15	13				
	Washington	**NHL**	**2**	**0**	**1**	**1**	**0**	**0**	**0**	**0**	**5**	**0.0**	**1**												
	Portland Pirates	AHL															6	2	1	3	0				
1994-95	London Knights	OHL	15	15	21	36	43																		
	Washington	**NHL**	**12**	**2**	**1**	**3**	**6**	**2**	**0**	**0**	**9**	**22.2**	**-3**												
	Portland Pirates	AHL	8	5	4	9	2										7	3	8	11	2				
1995-96	**Washington**	**NHL**	**19**	**0**	**3**	**3**	**2**	**0**	**0**	**0**	**18**	**0.0**	**-3**												
	Portland Pirates	AHL	57	28	41	69	42										6	1	6	7	9				
1996-97	**Washington**	**NHL**	**53**	**5**	**17**	**22**	**25**	**1**	**0**	**1**	**71**	**7.0**	**-3**												
	Boston	**NHL**	**19**	**3**	**9**	**12**	**9**	**1**	**0**	**0**	**28**	**10.7**	**-3**												
1997-98	**Boston**	**NHL**	**81**	**33**	**50**	**83**	**60**	**5**	**0**	**8**	**158**	**20.9**	**33**				**6**	**2**	**6**	**8**	**4**	**1**	**0**	**0**	
1998-99	**Boston**	**NHL**	**82**	**23**	**53**	**76**	**68**	**5**	**1**	**3**	**158**	**14.6**	**5**	**1760**	**52.2**	**22:23**	**12**	**2**	**9**	**11**	**6**	**1**	**0**	**0**	**25:36**
99-2000	**Boston**	**NHL**	**37**	**10**	**18**	**28**	**20**	**3**	**0**	**1**	**66**	**15.2**	**5**	**100**	**60.0**	**21:33**									
2000-01	**Boston**	**NHL**	**82**	**36**	**59**	**95**	**85**	**11**	**3**	**6**	**185**	**19.5**	**-8**	**1897**	**51.9**	**23:21**									
2001-02	**Los Angeles**	**NHL**	**73**	**19**	**55**	**74**	**68**	**5**	**0**	**2**	**139**	**13.7**	**2**	**1698**	**54.5**	**21:47**	**7**	**3**	**3**	**6**	**4**	**0**	**0**	**1**	**22:26**
2002-03	**Los Angeles**	**NHL**	**26**	**6**	**22**	**28**	**22**	**2**	**0**	**3**	**46**	**13.0**	**9**	**538**	**50.9**	**21:36**									
2003-04	**Los Angeles**	**NHL**	DID NOT PLAY – INJURED																						
2004-05			DID NOT PLAY																						
2005-06	**Toronto**	**NHL**	**66**	**17**	**43**	**60**	**76**	**9**	**0**	**2**	**111**	**15.3**	**-18**	**876**	**50.1**	**18:42**									
	NHL Totals		**552**	**154**	**331**	**485**	**441**	**44**	**4**	**26**	**994**	**15.5**		**6869**	**52.4**	**21:41**	**25**	**7**	**18**	**25**	**14**	**2**	**0**	**1**	**24:26**

OHL First All-Star Team (1994) • OHL MVP (1994) • Canadian Major Junior First All-Star Team (1994) • Canadian Major Junior Player of the Year (1994)

Played in NHL All-Star Game (2001)

Traded to **Boston** by **Washington** with Jim Carey, Anson Carter and Washington's 3rd round choice (Lee Goren) in 1997 Entry Draft for Bill Ranford, Adam Oates and Rick Tocchet, March 1, 1997. • Missed majority of 1999-2000 season recovering from thumb injury suffered in game vs. NY Islanders, January 8, 2000. Traded to **Los Angeles** by **Boston** with Mikko Eloranta for Jozef Stumpel and Glen Murray, October 24, 2001. • Missed majority of 2002-03 season and entire 2003-04 season recovering from knee (October 29, 2002 vs. Atlanta) and hip (January 25, 2003 vs. New Jersey) injuries. Signed as a free agent by **Toronto**, August 5, 2005.

AMONTE, Tony

(uh-MAHN-tee, TOH-nee) **CGY.**

Right wing. Shoots left. 6', 200 lbs. Born, Hingham, MA, August 2, 1970. NY Rangers' 3rd choice, 68th overall, in 1988 Entry Draft.

Season	Club	League	GP	G	A	Pts	PIM	PP	SH	GW	S	%	+/-	TF	F%	Min	GP	G	A	Pts	PIM	PP	SH	GW	Min
1985-86	Thayer Academy	High-MA	2	0	0	0	0																		
1986-87	Thayer Academy	High-MA	25	25	32	57																			
1987-88	Thayer Academy	High-MA	28	30	38	68																			
1988-89	Thayer Academy	High-MA	25	35	38	73																			
1989-90	Boston University	H-East	41	25	33	58	52																		
1990-91	Boston University	H-East	38	31	37	68	82																		
	NY Rangers	**NHL**															**2**	**0**	**2**	**2**	**2**	**0**	**0**	**0**	
1991-92	**NY Rangers**	**NHL**	**79**	**35**	**34**	**69**	**55**	**9**	**0**	**4**	**234**	**15.0**	**12**				**13**	**3**	**6**	**9**	**2**	**2**	**0**	**0**	
1992-93	**NY Rangers**	**NHL**	**83**	**33**	**43**	**76**	**49**	**13**	**0**	**4**	**270**	**12.2**	**0**												
1993-94	**NY Rangers**	**NHL**	**72**	**16**	**22**	**38**	**31**	**3**	**0**	**4**	**179**	**8.9**	**5**												
	Chicago	**NHL**	**7**	**1**	**3**	**4**	**6**	**1**	**0**	**0**	**16**	**6.3**	**-5**				**6**	**4**	**2**	**6**	**4**	**1**	**0**	**1**	
1994-95	HC Fassa	Euroliga	14	22	16	38	10																		
	HC Fassa	EuroHL	2	5	1	6	0																		
	Chicago	**NHL**	**48**	**15**	**20**	**35**	**41**	**6**	**1**	**3**	**105**	**14.3**	**7**				**16**	**3**	**3**	**6**	**10**	**0**	**0**	**0**	
1995-96	**Chicago**	**NHL**	**81**	**31**	**32**	**63**	**62**	**5**	**4**	**5**	**216**	**14.4**	**10**				**7**	**2**	**4**	**6**	**6**	**1**	**0**	**0**	
1996-97	**Chicago**	**NHL**	**81**	**41**	**36**	**77**	**64**	**9**	**2**	**4**	**266**	**15.4**	**35**				**6**	**4**	**2**	**6**	**8**	**0**	**0**	**0**	
1997-98	**Chicago**	**NHL**	**82**	**31**	**42**	**73**	**66**	**7**	**3**	**5**	**296**	**10.5**	**21**												
	United States	Olympics	4	0	1	1	4																		
1998-99	**Chicago**	**NHL**	**82**	**44**	**31**	**75**	**60**	**14**	**3**	**8**	**256**	**17.2**	**0**	**8**	**12.5**	**22:12**									
99-2000	**Chicago**	**NHL**	**82**	**43**	**41**	**84**	**48**	**11**	**5**	**2**	**260**	**16.5**	**10**	**22**	**22.7**	**21:54**									
2000-01	**Chicago**	**NHL**	**82**	**35**	**29**	**64**	**54**	**9**	**1**	**3**	**256**	**13.7**	**-22**	**27**	**40.7**	**22:09**									
2001-02	**Chicago**	**NHL**	**82**	**27**	**39**	**66**	**67**	**6**	**1**	**4**	**232**	**11.6**	**11**	**30**	**43.3**	**21:18**	**5**	**0**	**1**	**1**	**4**	**0**	**0**	**0**	**18:43**
	United States	Olympics	6	2	2	4	0																		
2002-03	**Phoenix**	**NHL**	**59**	**13**	**23**	**36**	**26**	**6**	**0**	**3**	**170**	**7.6**	**-12**	**53**	**35.9**	**19:27**									
	Philadelphia	**NHL**	**13**	**7**	**8**	**15**	**2**	**1**	**1**	**2**	**37**	**18.9**	**12**	**3**	**33.3**	**17:39**	**13**	**1**	**6**	**7**	**4**	**0**	**0**	**0**	**19:16**
2003-04	**Philadelphia**	**NHL**	**80**	**20**	**33**	**53**	**38**	**4**	**0**	**3**	**173**	**11.6**	**13**	**8**	**37.5**	**15:14**	**18**	**3**	**5**	**8**	**6**	**2**	**0**	**0**	**14:41**
2004-05			DID NOT PLAY																						
2005-06	**Calgary**	**NHL**	**80**	**14**	**28**	**42**	**43**	**3**	**1**	**3**	**155**	**9.0**	**3**	**66**	**31.8**	**17:07**	**7**	**2**	**1**	**3**	**10**	**0**	**1**	**0**	**17:28**
	NHL Totals		**1093**	**406**	**464**	**870**	**712**	**107**	**22**	**57**	**3121**	**13.0**		**217**	**34.1**	**19:54**	**93**	**22**	**32**	**54**	**56**	**6**	**1**	**1**	**16:59**

Hockey East Second All-Star Team (1991) • NCAA Championship All-Tournament Team (1991) • NHL All-Rookie Team (1992)

Played in NHL All-Star Game (1997, 1998, 1999, 2000, 2001)

• Missed majority of 1985-86 season recovering from knee injury, October, 1985. Traded to **Chicago** by **NY Rangers** with the rights to Matt Oates for Stephane Matteau and Brian Noonan, March 21, 1994. Signed as a free agent by **Phoenix**, July 12, 2002. Traded to **Philadelphia** by **Phoenix** for Guillaume Lefebvre, Atlanta's 3rd round choice (previously acquired, Phoenix selected Tyler Redenbach) in 2003 Entry Draft and Philadelphia's 2nd round choice (later traded to NY Rangers – NY Rangers selected Brandon Dubinsky) in 2004 Entry Draft, March 10, 2003. Signed as a free agent by **Calgary**, August 2, 2005.

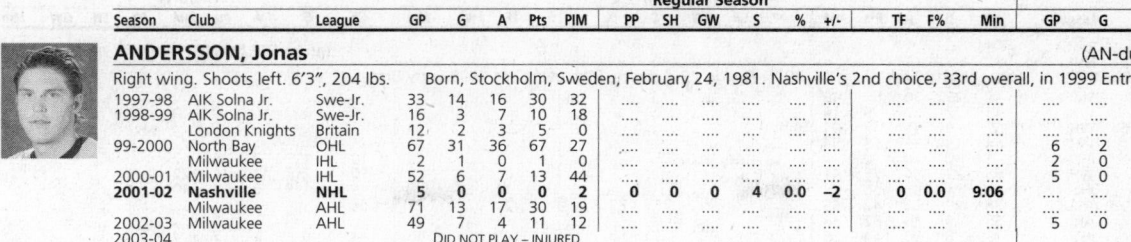

ANDERSSON, Jonas
(AN-duhr-suhn, JOH-nas) **NSH.**

Right wing. Shoots left. 6'3", 204 lbs. Born, Stockholm, Sweden, February 24, 1981. Nashville's 2nd choice, 33rd overall, in 1999 Entry Draft.

			Regular Season														Playoffs								
Season	Club	League	GP	G	A	Pts	PIM	PP	SH	GW	S	%	+/-	TF	F%	Min	GP	G	A	Pts	PIM	PP	SH	GW	Min
1997-98	AIK Solna Jr.	Swe-Jr.	33	14	16	30	32	....	....	....	....	....	....	....	....	....	....	....	....	....	....	....	....	....	....
1998-99	AIK Solna Jr.	Swe-Jr.	16	3	7	10	18	....	....	....	....	....	....	....	....	....	....	....	....	....	....	....	....	....	....
	London Knights	Britain	12	2	3	5	0	....	....	....	....	....	....	....	....	....	....	....	....	....	....	....	....	....	....
99-2000	North Bay	OHL	67	31	36	67	27	....	....	....	....	....	....	....	....	....	6	2	2	4	2	....	....	....	....
	Milwaukee	IHL	2	1	0	1	0	....	....	....	....	....	....	....	....	....	2	0	0	0	2	....	....	....	....
2000-01	Milwaukee	IHL	52	6	7	13	44	....	....	....	....	....	....	....	....	....	5	0	0	0	2	....	....	....	....
2001-02	**Nashville**	**NHL**	**5**	**0**	**0**	**0**	**2**	**0**	**0**	**0**	**4**	**0.0**	**–2**	**0**	**0.0**	**9:06**	....	....	....	....	....	....	....	....	....
	Milwaukee	AHL	71	13	17	30	19	....	....	....	....	....	....	....	....	....	....	....	....	....	....	....	....	....	....
2002-03	Milwaukee	AHL	49	7	4	11	12	....	....	....	....	....	....	....	....	....	5	0	1	1	4	....	....	....	....
2003-04			DID NOT PLAY – INJURED																						
2004-05	Sodertalje SK	Sweden	34	0	4	4	8	....	....	....	....	....	....	....	....	....	....	....	....	....	....	....	....	....	....
	Brynas IF Gavle	Sweden	7	2	0	2	2	....	....	....	....	....	....	....	....	....	....	....	....	....	....	....	....	....	....
2005-06	Ilves Tampere	Finland	48	8	10	18	26	....	....	....	....	....	....	....	....	....	4	2	0	2	0	....	....	....	....
	NHL Totals		**5**	**0**	**0**	**0**	**2**	**0**	**0**	**0**	**4**	**0.0**		**0**	**0.0**	**9:06**	....	....	....	....	....	....	....	....	....

• Missed entire 2003-04 season recovering from wrist injury suffered in training camp, September 30, 2003. Signed as a free agent by **Sodertalje** (Sweden), April 28, 2004. Signed as a free agent by **Gavle** (Sweden), January 22, 2005.

ANDREYCHUK, Dave
(AN-druh-chuhk, DAYV)

Left wing. Shoots right. 6'4", 220 lbs. Born, Hamilton, Ont., September 29, 1963. Buffalo's 3rd choice, 16th overall, in 1982 Entry Draft.

			Regular Season														Playoffs								
Season	Club	League	GP	G	A	Pts	PIM	PP	SH	GW	S	%	+/-	TF	F%	Min	GP	G	A	Pts	PIM	PP	SH	GW	Min
1979-80	Hamilton Hawks	OMHA	21	25	24	49		....	....	....	....	....	....	....	....	....	....	....	....	....	....	....	....	....	....
1980-81	Oshawa Generals	OMJHL	67	22	22	44	80	....	....	....	....	....	....	....	....	....	10	3	2	5	20	....	....	....	....
1981-82	Oshawa Generals	OHL	67	57	43	100	71	....	....	....	....	....	....	....	....	....	3	1	4	5	16	....	....	....	....
1982-83	Oshawa Generals	OHL	14	8	24	32	6	....	....	....	....	....	....	....	....	....	....	....	....	....	....	....	....	....	....
	Buffalo	**NHL**	**43**	**14**	**23**	**37**	**16**	**3**	**0**	**1**	**66**	**21.2**	**6**	....	....	....	**4**	**1**	**0**	**1**	**4**	**0**	**0**	**0**	....
1983-84	**Buffalo**	**NHL**	**78**	**38**	**42**	**80**	**42**	**10**	**0**	**7**	**178**	**21.3**	**20**	....	....	....	**2**	**0**	**1**	**1**	**2**	**0**	**0**	**0**	....
1984-85	**Buffalo**	**NHL**	**64**	**31**	**30**	**61**	**54**	**14**	**0**	**2**	**153**	**20.3**	**–4**	....	....	....	**5**	**4**	**2**	**6**	**4**	**0**	**0**	**2**	....
1985-86	**Buffalo**	**NHL**	**80**	**36**	**51**	**87**	**61**	**12**	**0**	**3**	**225**	**16.0**	**3**	....	....	....	....	....	....	....	....	....	....	....	....
1986-87	**Buffalo**	**NHL**	**77**	**25**	**48**	**73**	**46**	**13**	**0**	**2**	**255**	**9.8**	**2**	....	....	....	....	....	....	....	....	....	....	....	....
1987-88	**Buffalo**	**NHL**	**80**	**30**	**48**	**78**	**112**	**15**	**0**	**5**	**253**	**11.9**	**1**	....	....	....	**6**	**2**	**4**	**6**	**0**	**1**	**0**	**0**	....
1988-89	**Buffalo**	**NHL**	**56**	**28**	**24**	**52**	**40**	**7**	**0**	**3**	**145**	**19.3**	**0**	....	....	....	**5**	**0**	**3**	**3**	**0**	**0**	**0**	**0**	....
1989-90	**Buffalo**	**NHL**	**73**	**40**	**42**	**82**	**42**	**18**	**0**	**3**	**206**	**19.4**	**6**	....	....	....	**6**	**2**	**5**	**7**	**2**	**1**	**0**	**0**	....
1990-91	**Buffalo**	**NHL**	**80**	**36**	**33**	**69**	**32**	**13**	**0**	**4**	**234**	**15.4**	**11**	....	....	....	**6**	**2**	**2**	**4**	**8**	**1**	**0**	**0**	....
1991-92	**Buffalo**	**NHL**	**80**	**41**	**50**	**91**	**71**	**28**	**0**	**2**	**337**	**12.2**	**–9**	....	....	....	**7**	**1**	**3**	**4**	**12**	**0**	**0**	**0**	....
1992-93	**Buffalo**	**NHL**	**52**	**29**	**32**	**61**	**48**	**20**	**0**	**2**	**171**	**17.0**	**–8**	....	....	....	....	....	....	....	....	....	....	....	....
	Toronto	**NHL**	**31**	**25**	**13**	**38**	**8**	**12**	**0**	**2**	**139**	**18.0**	**12**	....	....	....	**21**	**12**	**7**	**19**	**35**	**4**	**0**	**3**	....
1993-94	**Toronto**	**NHL**	**83**	**53**	**46**	**99**	**98**	**21**	**5**	**8**	**333**	**15.9**	**22**	....	....	....	**18**	**5**	**5**	**10**	**16**	**3**	**1**	**0**	....
1994-95	**Toronto**	**NHL**	**48**	**22**	**16**	**38**	**34**	**8**	**0**	**2**	**168**	**13.1**	**–7**	....	....	....	**7**	**3**	**2**	**5**	**25**	**2**	**0**	**0**	....
1995-96	**Toronto**	**NHL**	**61**	**20**	**24**	**44**	**54**	**12**	**2**	**3**	**200**	**10.0**	**–11**	....	....	....	....	....	....	....	....	....	....	....	....
	New Jersey	**NHL**	**15**	**8**	**5**	**13**	**10**	**2**	**0**	**0**	**41**	**19.5**	**2**	....	....	....	....	....	....	....	....	....	....	....	....
1996-97	**New Jersey**	**NHL**	**82**	**27**	**34**	**61**	**48**	**4**	**1**	**2**	**233**	**11.6**	**38**	....	....	....	**1**	**0**	**0**	**0**	**0**	**0**	**0**	**0**	....
1997-98	**New Jersey**	**NHL**	**75**	**14**	**34**	**48**	**26**	**4**	**0**	**2**	**180**	**7.8**	**19**	....	....	....	**6**	**1**	**0**	**1**	**4**	**1**	**0**	**0**	....
1998-99	**New Jersey**	**NHL**	**52**	**15**	**13**	**28**	**20**	**4**	**0**	**3**	**110**	**13.6**	**1**	**9**	**44.4**	**15:32**	**4**	**2**	**0**	**2**	**4**	**0**	**0**	**0**	**10:40**
99-2000	**Boston**	**NHL**	**63**	**19**	**14**	**33**	**28**	**7**	**0**	**2**	**192**	**9.9**	**–11**	**446**	**52.0**	**19:50**	....	....	....	....	....	....	....	....	....
	Colorado	**NHL**	**14**	**1**	**2**	**3**	**2**	**1**	**0**	**1**	**41**	**2.4**	**–9**	**15**	**60.0**	**17:16**	**17**	**3**	**2**	**5**	**18**	**2**	**0**	**0**	**16:22**
2000-01	**Buffalo**	**NHL**	**74**	**20**	**13**	**33**	**32**	**8**	**0**	**4**	**119**	**16.8**	**0**	**187**	**49.7**	**12:00**	**13**	**1**	**2**	**3**	**4**	**1**	**0**	**0**	**11:04**
2001-02	**Tampa Bay**	**NHL**	**82**	**21**	**17**	**38**	**109**	**9**	**1**	**5**	**161**	**13.0**	**–12**	**1393**	**53.0**	**16:26**	....	....	....	....	....	....	....	....	....
2002-03	**Tampa Bay**	**NHL**	**72**	**20**	**14**	**34**	**34**	**15**	**0**	**3**	**170**	**11.8**	**–12**	**1117**	**58.4**	**16:27**	**11**	**3**	**3**	**6**	**10**	**1**	**0**	**1**	**21:23**
2003-04◆	**Tampa Bay**	**NHL**	**82**	**21**	**18**	**39**	**42**	**10**	**0**	**5**	**165**	**12.7**	**–9**	**1475**	**57.8**	**17:06**	**23**	**1**	**13**	**14**	**14**	**0**	**0**	**0**	**18:51**
2004-05			DID NOT PLAY																						
2005-06	**Tampa Bay**	**NHL**	**42**	**6**	**12**	**18**	**16**	**4**	**1**	**1**	**81**	**7.4**	**–13**	**474**	**54.4**	**13:26**	....	....	....	....	....	....	....	....	....
	NHL Totals		**1639**	**640**	**698**	**1338**	**1125**	**274**	**10**	**77**	**4556**	**14.0**		**5116**	**55.5**	**15:58**	**162**	**43**	**54**	**97**	**162**	**17**	**1**	**6**	**16:40**

Played in NHL All-Star Game (1990, 1994)

Traded to **Toronto** by **Buffalo** with Daren Puppa and Buffalo's 1st round choice (Kenny Jonsson) in 1993 Entry Draft for Grant Fuhr and Toronto's 5th round choice (Kevin Popp) in 1995 Entry Draft, February 2, 1993. Traded to **New Jersey** by **Toronto** for New Jersey's 2nd round choice (Marek Posmyk) in 1996 Entry Draft and New Jersey's 3rd round choice (later traded back to New Jersey – New Jersey selected Andre Lakos) in 1999 Entry Draft, March 13, 1996. Signed as a free agent by **Boston**, July 29, 1999. Traded to **Colorado** by **Boston** with Raymond Bourque for Brian Rolston, Martin Grenier, Samuel Pahlsson and New Jersey's 1st round choice (previously acquired, Boston selected Martin Samuelsson) in 2000 Entry Draft, March 6, 2000. Signed as a free agent by **Buffalo**, July 13, 2000. Signed as a free agent by **Tampa Bay**, July 13, 2001.

ANTROPOV, Nik
(an-TROH-pahv, NIHK) **TOR.**

Center. Shoots left. 6'6", 230 lbs. Born, Ust-Kamenogorsk, USSR, February 18, 1980. Toronto's 1st choice, 10th overall, in 1998 Entry Draft.

			Regular Season														Playoffs								
Season	Club	League	GP	G	A	Pts	PIM	PP	SH	GW	S	%	+/-	TF	F%	Min	GP	G	A	Pts	PIM	PP	SH	GW	Min
1996-97	Ust-Kamenogorsk	Russia-2	8	2	1	3	6	....	....	....	....	....	....	....	....	....	....	....	....	....	....	....	....	....	....
1997-98	Ust-Kamenogorsk	Russia-2	42	15	24	39	62	....	....	....	....	....	....	....	....	....	....	....	....	....	....	....	....	....	....
1998-99	Dynamo Moscow	Russia	30	5	9	14	30	....	....	....	....	....	....	....	....	....	11	0	1	1	4	....	....	....	....
99-2000	**Toronto**	**NHL**	**66**	**12**	**18**	**30**	**41**	**0**	**0**	**2**	**89**	**13.5**	**14**	**501**	**46.3**	**12:48**	**3**	**0**	**0**	**0**	**4**	**0**	**0**	**0**	**10:14**
	St. John's	AHL	2	0	0	0	4	....	....	....	....	....	....	....	....	....	....	....	....	....	....	....	....	....	....
2000-01	**Toronto**	**NHL**	**52**	**6**	**11**	**17**	**30**	**0**	**0**	**1**	**71**	**8.5**	**5**	**431**	**44.3**	**10:02**	**9**	**2**	**1**	**3**	**12**	**1**	**0**	**1**	**11:04**
2001-02	**Toronto**	**NHL**	**11**	**1**	**1**	**2**	**4**	**0**	**0**	**0**	**12**	**8.3**	**–1**	**31**	**38.7**	**8:57**	....	....	....	....	....	....	....	....	....
	St. John's	AHL	34	11	24	35	47	....	....	....	....	....	....	....	....	....	....	....	....	....	....	....	....	....	....
2002-03	**Toronto**	**NHL**	**72**	**16**	**29**	**45**	**124**	**2**	**1**	**6**	**102**	**15.7**	**11**	**621**	**40.1**	**15:00**	**3**	**0**	**0**	**0**	**0**	**0**	**0**	**0**	**19:17**
2003-04	**Toronto**	**NHL**	**62**	**13**	**18**	**31**	**62**	**1**	**1**	**2**	**89**	**14.6**	**7**	**309**	**40.8**	**15:18**	**13**	**0**	**2**	**2**	**18**	**0**	**0**	**0**	**15:56**
2004-05	Ak Bars Kazan	Russia	10	2	3	5	6	....	....	....	....	....	....	....	....	....	....	....	....	....	....	....	....	....	....
	Yaroslavl	Russia	26	4	15	19	44	....	....	....	....	....	....	....	....	....	9	3	4	7	18	....	....	....	....
2005-06	**Toronto**	**NHL**	**57**	**12**	**19**	**31**	**56**	**2**	**1**	**0**	**113**	**10.6**	**13**	**172**	**34.3**	**15:34**	....	....	....	....	....	....	....	....	....
	Kazakhstan	Olympics	5	1	0	1	4	....	....	....	....	....	....	....	....	....	....	....	....	....	....	....	....	....	....
	NHL Totals		**320**	**60**	**96**	**156**	**317**	**5**	**3**	**11**	**476**	**12.6**		**2065**	**42.1**	**13:41**	**28**	**2**	**3**	**5**	**34**	**1**	**0**	**1**	**14:07**

Signed as a free agent by **Kazan** (Russia), October 27, 2004. Signed as a free agent by **Yaroslavl** (Russia), December 20, 2004.

ARKHIPOV, Denis
(AHR-kih-pahv, DEH-nihs) **CHI.**

Center. Shoots left. 6'3", 214 lbs. Born, Kazan, USSR, May 19, 1979. Nashville's 2nd choice, 60th overall, in 1998 Entry Draft.

			Regular Season														Playoffs								
Season	Club	League	GP	G	A	Pts	PIM	PP	SH	GW	S	%	+/-	TF	F%	Min	GP	G	A	Pts	PIM	PP	SH	GW	Min
1994-95	Itil Kazan 2	CIS-2	40	20	12	32	10	....	....	....	....	....	....	....	....	....	....	....	....	....	....	....	....	....	....
1995-96	Ak Bars Kazan	CIS	15	10	8	18	10	....	....	....	....	....	....	....	....	....	....	....	....	....	....	....	....	....	....
1996-97	Ak Bars Kazan 2	Russia-3	50	17	23	40	20	....	....	....	....	....	....	....	....	....	....	....	....	....	....	....	....	....	....
	Ak Bars Kazan	Russia	1	1	0	1	0	....	....	....	....	....	....	....	....	....	....	....	....	....	....	....	....	....	....
1997-98	Ak Bars Kazan	Russia	29	2	2	4	2	....	....	....	....	....	....	....	....	....	....	....	....	....	....	....	....	....	....
1998-99	Ak Bars Kazan	Russia	34	12	1	13	22	....	....	....	....	....	....	....	....	....	9	2	3	5	6	....	....	....	....
	Ak Bars Kazan	EuroHL	4	0	0	0	0	....	....	....	....	....	....	....	....	....	1	0	0	0	0	....	....	....	....
99-2000	Ak Bars Kazan	Russia	32	7	9	16	14	....	....	....	....	....	....	....	....	....	18	5	5	10	6	....	....	....	....
2000-01	**Nashville**	**NHL**	**40**	**6**	**7**	**13**	**4**	**0**	**0**	**0**	**42**	**14.3**	**0**	**299**	**43.8**	**9:56**	....	....	....	....	....	....	....	....	....
	Milwaukee	IHL	40	9	8	17	11	....	....	....	....	....	....	....	....	....	....	....	....	....	....	....	....	....	....
2001-02	**Nashville**	**NHL**	**82**	**20**	**22**	**42**	**16**	**7**	**0**	**6**	**118**	**16.9**	**–18**	**1108**	**44.8**	**15:43**	....	....	....	....	....	....	....	....	....
2002-03	**Nashville**	**NHL**	**79**	**11**	**24**	**35**	**32**	**3**	**0**	**1**	**148**	**7.4**	**–18**	**1069**	**46.7**	**15:09**	....	....	....	....	....	....	....	....	....
2003-04	**Nashville**	**NHL**	**72**	**9**	**12**	**21**	**22**	**3**	**0**	**3**	**91**	**9.9**	**–2**	**926**	**44.7**	**13:58**	....	....	....	....	....	....	....	....	....
2004-05	Ak Bars Kazan	Russia	45	9	8	17	28	....	....	....	....	....	....	....	....	....	4	0	0	0	0	....	....	....	....
2005-06	Mytischi	Russia	50	8	8	16	28	....	....	....	....	....	....	....	....	....	9	2	1	3	0	....	....	....	....
	NHL Totals		**273**	**46**	**65**	**111**	**74**	**13**	**0**	**10**	**399**	**11.5**		**3402**	**45.3**	**14:15**	....	....	....	....	....	....	....	....	....

Signed as a free agent by **Kazan** (Russia), July 27, 2004. Signed as a free agent by **Chicago**, July 6, 2006.

ARMSTRONG, Chris

(ahrm-STRAWNG, KRIHS)

Defense. Shoots left. 6', 205 lbs. Born, Regina, Sask., June 26, 1975. Florida's 3rd choice, 57th overall, in 1993 Entry Draft.

			Regular Season														Playoffs								
Season	Club	League	GP	G	A	Pts	PIM	PP	SH	GW	S	%	+/-	TF	F%	Min	GP	G	A	Pts	PIM	PP	SH	GW	Min
1990-91	Whitewood	SMHL	40	25	30	55	40	....	....	....	....	....	....	....	....	....	....	....	....	....	....	....	....	....	....
1991-92	Moose Jaw	WHL	43	2	7	9	19	....	....	....	....	....	....	....	....	....	4	0	0	0	0	....	....	....	....
1992-93	Moose Jaw	WHL	67	9	35	44	104	....	....	....	....	....	....	....	....	....	....	....	....	....	....	....	....	....	....
1993-94	Moose Jaw	WHL	64	13	55	68	54	....	....	....	....	....	....	....	....	....	....	....	....	....	....	....	....	....	....
	Cincinnati	IHL	1	0	0	0	0	....	....	....	....	....	....	....	....	....	10	1	3	4	2	....	....	....	....
1994-95	Moose Jaw	WHL	66	17	54	71	61	....	....	....	....	....	....	....	....	....	10	2	12	14	22	....	....	....	....
	Cincinnati	IHL	....	....	....	....	....	....	....	....	....	....	....	....	....	....	9	1	3	4	10	....	....	....	....
1995-96	Carolina Panthers	AHL	78	9	33	42	65	....	....	....	....	....	....	....	....	....	....	....	....	....	....	....	....	....	....
1996-97	Carolina	AHL	66	9	23	32	38	....	....	....	....	....	....	....	....	....	....	....	....	....	....	....	....	....	....
1997-98	Fort Wayne	IHL	79	8	36	44	66	....	....	....	....	....	....	....	....	....	4	0	2	2	4	....	....	....	....
1998-99	Hershey Bears	AHL	65	12	32	44	30	....	....	....	....	....	....	....	....	....	5	0	1	1	0	....	....	....	....
	Milwaukee	IHL	5	0	3	3	4	....	....	....	....	....	....	....	....	....	....	....	....	....	....	....	....	....	....
99-2000	Kentucky	AHL	78	9	48	57	77	....	....	....	....	....	....	....	....	....	9	1	5	6	4	....	....	....	....
2000-01	**Minnesota**	**NHL**	**3**	**0**	**0**	**0**	**0**	**0**	**0**	**0**	**4**	**0.0**	**-3**	**0**	**0.0**	**18:06**	....	....	....	....	....	....	....	....	....
	Cleveland	IHL	77	9	32	41	42	....	....	....	....	....	....	....	....	....	4	0	2	2	2	....	....	....	....
2001-02	Bridgeport	AHL	80	10	38	48	49	....	....	....	....	....	....	....	....	....	20	3	8	11	4	....	....	....	....
2002-03	EV Zug	Swiss	21	0	7	7	45	....	....	....	....	....	....	....	....	....	....	....	....	....	....	....	....	....	....
	Augsburg	Germany	22	3	16	19	32	....	....	....	....	....	....	....	....	....	....	....	....	....	....	....	....	....	....
2003-04	**Anaheim**	**NHL**	**4**	**0**	**1**	**1**	**0**	**0**	**0**	**0**	**8**	**0.0**	**-1**	**0**	**0.0**	**12:32**	....	....	....	....	....	....	....	....	....
	Cincinnati	AHL	70	9	37	46	48	....	....	....	....	....	....	....	....	....	9	1	3	4	2	....	....	....	....
2004-05	ERC Ingolstadt	Germany	46	5	19	24	36	....	....	....	....	....	....	....	....	....	11	2	6	8	18	....	....	....	....
2005-06	ERC Ingolstadt	Germany	43	6	16	22	52	....	....	....	....	....	....	....	....	....	7	0	2	2	4	....	....	....	....
	NHL Totals		**7**	**0**	**1**	**1**	**0**	**0**	**0**	**0**	**12**	**0.0**		**0**	**0.0**	**14:55**	....	....	....	....	....	....	....	....	....

WHL East First All-Star Team (1994) • Canadian Major Junior Second All-Star Team (1994) • WHL East Second All-Star Team (1995)

Claimed by **Nashville** from **Florida** in Expansion Draft, June 26, 1998. Signed as a free agent by **San Jose**, September 2, 1999. Claimed by **Minnesota** from **San Jose** in Expansion Draft, June 23, 2000. Signed as a free agent by **NY Islanders**, August 8, 2001. Signed as a free agent by **Zug** (Swiss), June 14, 2002. Signed as a free agent by **Anaheim**, June 26, 2003. Signed as a free agent by **Ingolstadt** (Germany), April 4, 2004.

ARMSTRONG, Colby

(AHRM-stawng, KOHL-bee) **PIT.**

Right wing. Shoots right. 6'2", 195 lbs. Born, Lloydminster, Sask., November 23, 1982. Pittsburgh's 1st choice, 21st overall, in 2001 Entry Draft.

			Regular Season														Playoffs								
Season	Club	League	GP	G	A	Pts	PIM	PP	SH	GW	S	%	+/-	TF	F%	Min	GP	G	A	Pts	PIM	PP	SH	GW	Min
1998-99	Sask. Contacts	SMHL	33	21	19	40	103	....	....	....	....	....	....	....	....	....	....	....	....	....	....	....	....	....	....
	Red Deer Rebels	WHL	1	0	1	1	0	....	....	....	....	....	....	....	....	....	....	....	....	....	....	....	....	....	....
99-2000	Red Deer Rebels	WHL	68	13	25	38	122	....	....	....	....	....	....	....	....	....	2	0	1	1	11	....	....	....	....
2000-01	Red Deer Rebels	WHL	72	36	42	78	156	....	....	....	....	....	....	....	....	....	21	6	6	12	29	....	....	....	....
2001-02	Red Deer Rebels	WHL	64	27	41	68	115	....	....	....	....	....	....	....	....	....	23	6	10	16	32	....	....	....	....
2002-03	Wilkes-Barre	AHL	73	7	11	18	76	....	....	....	....	....	....	....	....	....	3	0	0	0	4	....	....	....	....
2003-04	Wilkes-Barre	AHL	67	10	17	27	71	....	....	....	....	....	....	....	....	....	24	3	1	4	45	....	....	....	....
2004-05	Wilkes-Barre	AHL	80	18	37	55	89	....	....	....	....	....	....	....	....	....	10	4	2	6	14	....	....	....	....
2005-06	**Pittsburgh**	**NHL**	**47**	**16**	**24**	**40**	**58**	**7**	**2**	**3**	**86**	**18.6**	**15**	**44**	**27.3**	**19:04**	....	....	....	....	....	....	....	....	....
	Wilkes-Barre	AHL	31	11	18	29	44	....	....	....	....	....	....	....	....	....	....	....	....	....	....	....	....	....	....
	NHL Totals		**47**	**16**	**24**	**40**	**58**	**7**	**2**	**3**	**86**	**18.6**		**44**	**27.3**	**19:04**	....	....	....	....	....	....	....	....	....

ARMSTRONG, Derek

(ahrm-STRAWNG, DAIR-ihk) **L.A.**

Center. Shoots right. 6', 195 lbs. Born, Ottawa, Ont., April 23, 1973. NY Islanders' 5th choice, 128th overall, in 1992 Entry Draft.

			Regular Season														Playoffs								
Season	Club	League	GP	G	A	Pts	PIM	PP	SH	GW	S	%	+/-	TF	F%	Min	GP	G	A	Pts	PIM	PP	SH	GW	Min
1989-90	Hawkesbury	CJHL	48	8	10	18	30	....	....	....	....	....	....	....	....	....	....	....	....	....	....	....	....	....	....
1990-91	Hawkesbury	CJHL	54	27	45	72	49	....	....	....	....	....	....	....	....	....	....	....	....	....	....	....	....	....	....
	Sudbury Wolves	OHL	2	0	2	2	0	....	....	....	....	....	....	....	....	....	....	....	....	....	....	....	....	....	....
1991-92	Sudbury Wolves	OHL	66	31	54	85	22	....	....	....	....	....	....	....	....	....	9	2	2	4	2	....	....	....	....
1992-93	Sudbury Wolves	OHL	66	44	62	106	56	....	....	....	....	....	....	....	....	....	14	9	10	19	26	....	....	....	....
1993-94	**NY Islanders**	**NHL**	**1**	**0**	**0**	**0**	**0**	**0**	**0**	**0**	**2**	**0.0**	**0**	....	....	....	....	....	....	....	....	....	....	....	....
	Salt Lake	IHL	76	23	35	58	61	....	....	....	....	....	....	....	....	....	....	....	....	....	....	....	....	....	....
1994-95	Denver Grizzlies	IHL	59	13	18	31	65	....	....	....	....	....	....	....	....	....	6	0	2	2	0	....	....	....	....
1995-96	**NY Islanders**	**NHL**	**19**	**1**	**3**	**4**	**14**	**0**	**0**	**0**	**23**	**4.3**	**-6**	....	....	....	....	....	....	....	....	....	....	....	....
	Worcester IceCats	AHL	51	11	15	26	33	....	....	....	....	....	....	....	....	....	4	2	1	3	0	....	....	....	....
1996-97	**NY Islanders**	**NHL**	**50**	**6**	**7**	**13**	**33**	**0**	**0**	**2**	**36**	**16.7**	**-8**	....	....	....	....	....	....	....	....	....	....	....	....
	Utah Grizzlies	IHL	17	4	8	12	10	....	....	....	....	....	....	....	....	....	6	0	4	4	4	....	....	....	....
1997-98	**Ottawa**	**NHL**	**9**	**2**	**0**	**2**	**9**	**0**	**0**	**1**	**8**	**25.0**	**1**	....	....	....	....	....	....	....	....	....	....	....	....
	Detroit Vipers	IHL	10	0	1	1	2	....	....	....	....	....	....	....	....	....	....	....	....	....	....	....	....	....	....
	Hartford	AHL	54	16	30	46	40	....	....	....	....	....	....	....	....	....	15	2	6	8	22	....	....	....	....
1998-99	**NY Rangers**	**NHL**	**3**	**0**	**0**	**0**	**0**	**0**	**0**	**0**	**1**	**0.0**	**0**	**0**	**0.0**	**2:50**	....	....	....	....	....	....	....	....	....
	Hartford	AHL	59	29	51	80	73	....	....	....	....	....	....	....	....	....	7	5	4	9	10	....	....	....	....
99-2000	**NY Rangers**	**NHL**	**1**	**0**	**0**	**0**	**0**	**0**	**0**	**0**	**1**	**0.0**	**0**	**3**	**33.3**	**3:10**	....	....	....	....	....	....	....	....	....
	Hartford	AHL	77	28	54	82	101	....	....	....	....	....	....	....	....	....	23	7	16	23	24	....	....	....	....
2000-01	**NY Rangers**	**NHL**	**3**	**0**	**0**	**0**	**0**	**0**	**0**	**0**	**6**	**0.0**	**0**	**30**	**50.0**	**11:22**	....	....	....	....	....	....	....	....	....
	Hartford	AHL	75	32	*69	*101	73	....	....	....	....	....	....	....	....	....	5	0	6	6	6	....	....	....	....
2001-02	SC Bern	Swiss	44	17	36	53	62	....	....	....	....	....	....	....	....	....	6	3	5	8	8	....	....	....	....
2002-03	**Los Angeles**	**NHL**	**66**	**12**	**26**	**38**	**30**	**2**	**0**	**1**	**106**	**11.3**	**5**	**708**	**50.0**	**15:40**	....	....	....	....	....	....	....	....	....
	Manchester	AHL	2	3	0	3	4	....	....	....	....	....	....	....	....	....	....	....	....	....	....	....	....	....	....
2003-04	**Los Angeles**	**NHL**	**57**	**14**	**21**	**35**	**33**	**5**	**0**	**1**	**101**	**13.9**	**4**	**912**	**52.0**	**17:00**	....	....	....	....	....	....	....	....	....
2004-05	Geneve	Swiss	9	6	7	13	18	....	....	....	....	....	....	....	....	....	....	....	....	....	....	....	....	....	....
	Rapperswil	Swiss	3	1	3	4	4	....	....	....	....	....	....	....	....	....	....	....	....	....	....	....	....	....	....
2005-06	**Los Angeles**	**NHL**	**62**	**13**	**28**	**41**	**46**	**7**	**0**	**1**	**100**	**13.0**	**-2**	**546**	**50.7**	**15:31**	....	....	....	....	....	....	....	....	....
	NHL Totals		**271**	**48**	**85**	**133**	**165**	**14**	**0**	**6**	**384**	**12.5**		**2199**	**51.0**	**15:41**	....	....	....	....	....	....	....	....	....

AHL Second All-Star Team (2000) • Jack A. Butterfield Trophy (Playoff MVP – AHL) (2000) • AHL First All-Star Team (2001) • John P. Sollenberger Trophy (Leading Scorer – AHL) (2001) • Les Cunningham Award (MVP – AHL) (2001)

Signed as a free agent by **Ottawa**, July 28, 1997. Loaned to **Hartford** (AHL) by **Ottawa**, October 28, 1997. Signed as a free agent by **NY Rangers**, August 10, 1998. Signed as a free agent by **Bern** (Swiss) with NY Rangers retaining NHL rights, July 18, 2001. Traded to **Los Angeles** by **NY Rangers** for Los Angeles' 6th round choice (Chris Holt) in 2003 Entry Draft, July 16, 2002. Signed as a free agent by **Geneve** (Swiss), October 12, 2004. Signed as a free agent by **Rapperswil** (Swiss), February 13, 2005.

ARNASON, Tyler

(AHR-na-suhn, TIGH-luhr) **COL.**

Center. Shoots left. 5'11", 204 lbs. Born, Oklahoma City, OK, March 16, 1979. Chicago's 6th choice, 183rd overall, in 1998 Entry Draft.

			Regular Season														Playoffs								
Season	Club	League	GP	G	A	Pts	PIM	PP	SH	GW	S	%	+/-	TF	F%	Min	GP	G	A	Pts	PIM	PP	SH	GW	Min
1996-97	Winnipeg South	MJHL	50	35	50	85	15	....	....	....	....	....	....	....	....	....	6	3	3	6	18	....	....	....	....
1997-98	Fargo-Moorhead	USHL	52	37	45	82	16	....	....	....	....	....	....	....	....	....	4	1	1	2	2	....	....	....	....
1998-99	St. Cloud State	WCHA	38	14	17	31	16	....	....	....	....	....	....	....	....	....	....	....	....	....	....	....	....	....	....
99-2000	St. Cloud State	WCHA	39	19	30	49	18	....	....	....	....	....	....	....	....	....	....	....	....	....	....	....	....	....	....
2000-01	St. Cloud State	WCHA	41	28	28	56	14	....	....	....	....	....	....	....	....	....	....	....	....	....	....	....	....	....	....
2001-02	**Chicago**	**NHL**	**21**	**3**	**1**	**4**	**4**	**0**	**0**	**0**	**19**	**15.8**	**-3**	**112**	**41.1**	**9:28**	**3**	**0**	**0**	**0**	**0**	**0**	**0**	**0**	**7:43**
	Norfolk Admirals	AHL	60	26	30	56	42	....	....	....	....	....	....	....	....	....	....	....	....	....	....	....	....	....	....
2002-03	**Chicago**	**NHL**	**82**	**19**	**20**	**39**	**20**	**3**	**0**	**6**	**178**	**10.7**	**7**	**626**	**40.3**	**14:30**	....	....	....	....	....	....	....	....	....
2003-04	**Chicago**	**NHL**	**82**	**22**	**33**	**55**	**16**	**6**	**0**	**2**	**222**	**9.9**	**-13**	**904**	**43.1**	**16:34**	....	....	....	....	....	....	....	....	....
2004-05	Brynas IF Gavle	Sweden	4	0	0	0	0	....	....	....	....	....	....	....	....	....	....	....	....	....	....	....	....	....	....
2005-06	**Chicago**	**NHL**	**60**	**13**	**28**	**41**	**40**	**5**	**0**	**1**	**161**	**8.1**	**5**	**492**	**44.7**	**14:58**	....	....	....	....	....	....	....	....	....
	Ottawa	**NHL**	**19**	**0**	**4**	**4**	**4**	**0**	**0**	**0**	**42**	**0.0**	**-4**	**172**	**51.7**	**12:19**	....	....	....	....	....	....	....	....	....
	NHL Totals		**264**	**57**	**86**	**143**	**84**	**14**	**0**	**9**	**622**	**9.2**		**2306**	**43.2**	**14:41**	**3**	**0**	**0**	**0**	**0**	**0**	**0**	**0**	**7:43**

USHL First All-Star Team (1998) • WCHA All-Rookie Team (1999) • WCHA Second All-Star Team (2000) • AHL All-Rookie Team (2002) • Dudley "Red" Garrett Memorial Award (Rookie of the Year – AHL) (2002) • NHL All-Rookie Team (2003)

Signed as a free agent by **Gavle** (Sweden), October 29, 2004. Traded to **Ottawa** by **Chicago** for Brandon Bochenski and Ottawa's 2nd round choice (Simon Danis-Pepin) in 2006 Entry Draft, March 9, 2006. Signed as a free agent by **Colorado**, July 1, 2006.

ARNOTT, Jason
(AHR-niht, JAY-suhn) **NSH.**

Center. Shoots right. 6'4", 220 lbs. Born, Collingwood, Ont., October 11, 1974. Edmonton's 1st choice, 7th overall, in 1993 Entry Draft.

			Regular Season														Playoffs								
Season	Club	League	GP	G	A	Pts	PIM	PP	SH	GW	S	%	+/-	TF	F%	Min	GP	G	A	Pts	PIM	PP	SH	GW	Min
1989-90	Stayner Siskins	OHA-C	34	21	31	52	12	....	....	....	....	....	....	....	....	....	....	....	....	....	....	....	....	....	....
1990-91	Lindsay Bears	OHA-B	42	17	44	61	10	....	....	....	....	....	....	....	....	....	8	9	8	17	6	....	....	....	....
1991-92	Oshawa Generals	OHL	57	9	15	24	12	....	....	....	....	....	....	....	....	....	....	....	....	....	....	....	....	....	....
1992-93	Oshawa Generals	OHL	56	41	57	98	74	....	....	....	....	....	....	....	....	....	13	9	9	18	20	....	....	....	....
1993-94	**Edmonton**	**NHL**	78	33	35	68	104	10	0	4	194	17.0	1	....	....	....	....	....	....	....	....	....	....	....	....
1994-95	**Edmonton**	**NHL**	42	15	22	37	128	7	0	1	156	9.6	–14	....	....	....	....	....	....	....	....	....	....	....	....
1995-96	**Edmonton**	**NHL**	64	28	31	59	87	8	0	5	244	11.5	–6	....	....	....	....	....	....	....	....	....	....	....	....
1996-97	**Edmonton**	**NHL**	67	19	38	57	92	10	1	2	248	7.7	–21	....	....	....	12	3	6	9	18	1	0	0	....
1997-98	**Edmonton**	**NHL**	35	5	13	18	78	1	0	0	100	5.0	–16	....	....	....	....	....	....	....	....	....	....	....	....
	New Jersey	**NHL**	35	5	10	15	21	3	0	2	99	5.1	–8	....	....	....	5	0	2	2	0	0	0	0	....
1998-99	**New Jersey**	**NHL**	74	27	27	54	79	8	0	3	200	13.5	10	872	49.3	15:24	7	2	2	4	4	1	0	0	16:48
99-2000 ◆	**New Jersey**	**NHL**	76	22	34	56	51	7	0	4	244	9.0	22	1172	46.9	17:05	23	8	12	20	18	3	0	1	16:29
2000-01	**New Jersey**	**NHL**	54	21	34	55	75	8	0	3	138	15.2	23	760	49.6	16:12	23	8	7	15	16	5	0	0	15:49
2001-02	**New Jersey**	**NHL**	63	22	19	41	59	8	0	1	169	13.0	3	934	47.8	17:13	....	....	....	....	....	....	....	....	....
	Dallas	**NHL**	10	3	1	4	6	2	0	2	28	10.7	–1	77	52.0	18:13	....	....	....	....	....	....	....	....	....
2002-03	**Dallas**	**NHL**	72	23	24	47	51	7	0	6	169	13.6	9	1130	53.3	16:12	11	3	2	5	6	1	0	0	15:35
2003-04	**Dallas**	**NHL**	73	21	36	57	66	5	0	5	143	14.7	23	1203	53.0	17:00	5	1	1	2	2	1	0	0	17:23
2004-05			DID NOT PLAY																						
2005-06	**Dallas**	**NHL**	81	32	44	76	102	11	1	5	167	19.2	13	1306	51.2	17:12	5	0	3	3	4	0	0	0	20:04
	NHL Totals		**824**	**276**	**368**	**644**	**999**	**95**	**2**	**43**	**2299**	**12.0**		**7454**	**50.3**	**16:40**	**91**	**25**	**35**	**60**	**68**	**12**	**0**	**1**	**16:29**

NHL All-Rookie Team (1994)

Played in NHL All-Star Game (1997)

Traded to **New Jersey** by **Edmonton** with Bryan Muir for Valeri Zelepukin and Bill Guerin, January 4, 1998. Traded to **Dallas** by **New Jersey** with Randy McKay and New Jersey's 1st round choice (later traded to Columbus – later traded to Buffalo – Buffalo selected Dan Paille) in 2002 Entry Draft for Joe Nieuwendyk and Jamie Langenbrunner, March 19, 2002. Signed as a free agent by **Nashville**, July 2, 2006.

ARTYUKHIN, Evgeny
(ahr-TYEW-khin, yehv-GEH-nee) **T.B.**

Right wing. Shoots left. 6'4", 254 lbs. Born, Moscow, USSR, April 4, 1983. Tampa Bay's 4th choice, 94th overall, in 2001 Entry Draft.

99-2000	Vityaz Podolsk 2	Russia-3	26	9	8	17	46	....	....	....	....	....	....	....	....	....	....	....	....	....	....	....	....	....	....
	Vityaz Podolsk	Russia-2	3	0	0	0	2	....	....	....	....	....	....	....	....	....	....	....	....	....	....	....	....	....	....
2000-01	Vityaz Podolsk	Russia	24	0	1	1	14	....	....	....	....	....	....	....	....	....	....	....	....	....	....	....	....	....	....
2001-02	Vityaz Podolsk 2	Russia-3	4	3	1	4	6	....	....	....	....	....	....	....	....	....	....	....	....	....	....	....	....	....	....
	Vityaz Podolsk	Russia-2	49	15	7	22	94	....	....	....	....	....	....	....	....	....	12	0	1	1	18	....	....	....	....
2002-03	Moncton Wildcats	QMJHL	53	13	27	40	204	....	....	....	....	....	....	....	....	....	6	1	2	3	29	....	....	....	....
2003-04	Hershey Bears	AHL	36	3	3	6	111	....	....	....	....	....	....	....	....	....	....	....	....	....	....	....	....	....	....
	Pensacola	ECHL	6	1	0	1	14	....	....	....	....	....	....	....	....	....	....	....	....	....	....	....	....	....	....
2004-05	Springfield	AHL	62	9	19	28	142	....	....	....	....	....	....	....	....	....	....	....	....	....	....	....	....	....	....
2005-06	**Tampa Bay**	**NHL**	72	4	13	17	90	1	0	0	79	5.1	–4	0	0.0	8:43	5	1	0	1	6	0	0	0	8:14
	NHL Totals		**72**	**4**	**13**	**17**	**90**	**1**	**0**	**0**	**79**	**5.1**		**0**	**0.0**	**8:43**	**5**	**1**	**0**	**1**	**6**	**0**	**0**	**0**	**8:14**

ASHAM, Arron
(ASH-uhm, AIR-ruhn) **NYI**

Right wing. Shoots right. 5'11", 209 lbs. Born, Portage La Prairie, Man., April 13, 1978. Montreal's 3rd choice, 71st overall, in 1996 Entry Draft.

1993-94	Portage	MAHA	21	18	19	37	82	....	....	....	....	....	....	....	....	....	....	....	....	....	....	....	....	....	....
1994-95	Red Deer Rebels	WHL	62	11	16	27	126	....	....	....	....	....	....	....	....	....	....	....	....	....	....	....	....	....	....
1995-96	Red Deer Rebels	WHL	70	32	45	77	174	....	....	....	....	....	....	....	....	....	10	6	3	9	20	....	....	....	....
1996-97	Red Deer Rebels	WHL	67	45	51	96	149	....	....	....	....	....	....	....	....	....	16	12	14	26	36	....	....	....	....
1997-98	Red Deer Rebels	WHL	67	43	49	92	153	....	....	....	....	....	....	....	....	....	5	0	2	2	8	....	....	....	....
	Fredericton	AHL	2	1	1	2	0	....	....	....	....	....	....	....	....	....	2	0	1	1	0	....	....	....	....
1998-99	**Montreal**	**NHL**	7	0	0	0	0	0	0	0	5	0.0	–4	0	0.0	7:27	....	....	....	....	....	....	....	....	....
	Fredericton	AHL	60	16	18	34	118	....	....	....	....	....	....	....	....	....	13	8	6	14	11	....	....	....	....
99-2000	**Montreal**	**NHL**	33	4	2	6	24	0	1	1	29	13.8	–7	1	0.0	10:14	....	....	....	....	....	....	....	....	....
	Quebec Citadelles	AHL	13	4	5	9	32	....	....	....	....	....	....	....	....	....	2	0	0	0	2	....	....	....	....
2000-01	**Montreal**	**NHL**	46	2	3	5	59	0	0	0	32	6.3	–9	3	100.0	8:28	....	....	....	....	....	....	....	....	....
	Quebec Citadelles	AHL	15	7	9	16	51	....	....	....	....	....	....	....	....	....	7	1	2	3	2	....	....	....	....
2001-02	**Montreal**	**NHL**	35	5	4	9	55	0	0	0	30	16.7	7	4	25.0	8:13	3	0	1	1	0	0	0	0	5:39
	Quebec Citadelles	AHL	24	9	14	23	35	....	....	....	....	....	....	....	....	....	....	....	....	....	....	....	....	....	....
2002-03	**NY Islanders**	**NHL**	78	15	19	34	57	4	0	1	114	13.2	1	17	41.2	12:13	5	0	0	0	16	0	0	0	15:09
2003-04	**NY Islanders**	**NHL**	79	12	12	24	92	1	0	0	108	11.1	–12	23	34.8	13:13	5	0	1	1	4	0	0	0	8:44
2004-05	EHC Visp	Swiss-2	5	2	4	6	6	....	....	....	....	....	....	....	....	....	4	1	1	2	8	....	....	....	....
2005-06	**NY Islanders**	**NHL**	63	9	15	24	103	2	1	0	99	9.1	–5	63	41.3	13:33	....	....	....	....	....	....	....	....	....
	NHL Totals		**341**	**47**	**55**	**102**	**390**	**7**	**2**	**2**	**417**	**11.3**		**111**	**40.5**	**11:29**	**13**	**0**	**2**	**2**	**20**	**0**	**0**	**0**	**10:29**

Traded to **NY Islanders** by **Montreal** with Montreal's 5th round choice (Marcus Paulsson) in 2002 Entry Draft for Mariusz Czerkawski, June 22, 2002. Signed as a free agent by **Visp** (Swiss-2), January 19, 2005.

AUBIN, Serge
(oh-BEHN, SAIRZH)

Left wing. Shoots left. 6'1", 200 lbs. Born, Val-d'Or, Que., February 15, 1975. Pittsburgh's 9th choice, 161st overall, in 1994 Entry Draft.

1990-91	Abitibi Forestiers	QAAA	27	2	4	6	10	....	....	....	....	....	....	....	....	....	....	....	....	....	....	....	....	....	....
1991-92	Abitibi Forestiers	QAAA	42	28	32	60	36	....	....	....	....	....	....	....	....	....	1	0	1	1	0	....	....	....	....
1992-93	Drummondville	QMJHL	65	16	34	50	30	....	....	....	....	....	....	....	....	....	8	0	1	1	16	....	....	....	....
1993-94	Granby Bisons	QMJHL	63	42	32	74	80	....	....	....	....	....	....	....	....	....	7	2	3	5	8	....	....	....	....
1994-95	Granby Bisons	QMJHL	60	37	73	110	55	....	....	....	....	....	....	....	....	....	11	8	15	23	4	....	....	....	....
1995-96	Hampton Roads	ECHL	62	24	62	86	74	....	....	....	....	....	....	....	....	....	3	1	4	5	10	....	....	....	....
	Cleveland	IHL	2	0	0	0	0	....	....	....	....	....	....	....	....	....	2	0	0	0	0	....	....	....	....
1996-97	Cleveland	IHL	57	9	16	25	38	....	....	....	....	....	....	....	....	....	2	0	0	0	0	....	....	....	....
1997-98	Syracuse Crunch	AHL	55	6	14	20	57	....	....	....	....	....	....	....	....	....	....	....	....	....	....	....	....	....	....
	Hershey Bears	AHL	5	2	1	3	0	....	....	....	....	....	....	....	....	....	7	1	3	4	6	....	....	....	....
1998-99	Hershey Bears	AHL	64	30	39	69	58	....	....	....	....	....	....	....	....	....	3	0	1	1	2	....	....	....	....
	Colorado	**NHL**	1	0	0	0	0	0	0	0	1	0.0	0	1	0.0	4:16	....	....	....	....	....	....	....	....	....
99-2000	**Colorado**	**NHL**	15	2	1	3	6	0	0	1	14	14.3	1	79	50.6	6:37	17	0	1	1	6	0	0	0	5:06
	Hershey Bears	AHL	58	42	38	80	56	....	....	....	....	....	....	....	....	....	....	....	....	....	....	....	....	....	....
2000-01	**Columbus**	**NHL**	81	13	17	30	107	0	0	2	110	11.8	–20	1346	51.3	16:20	....	....	....	....	....	....	....	....	....
2001-02	**Columbus**	**NHL**	71	8	8	16	32	1	0	1	86	9.3	–20	780	50.5	15:30	....	....	....	....	....	....	....	....	....
2002-03	**Colorado**	**NHL**	66	4	6	10	64	0	0	1	62	6.5	–2	613	50.2	11:58	5	0	0	0	4	0	0	0	5:25
2003-04	**Atlanta**	**NHL**	66	10	15	25	73	1	0	2	97	10.3	0	668	49.1	16:00	....	....	....	....	....	....	....	....	....
2004-05	Geneve	Swiss	6	2	1	3	8	....	....	....	....	....	....	....	....	....	3	1	2	3	2	....	....	....	....
2005-06	**Atlanta**	**NHL**	74	7	17	24	79	1	0	0	82	8.5	–4	468	45.9	11:06	....	....	....	....	....	....	....	....	....
	NHL Totals		**374**	**44**	**64**	**108**	**361**	**3**	**0**	**7**	**452**	**9.7**		**3955**	**50.0**	**13:53**	**22**	**0**	**1**	**1**	**10**	**0**	**0**	**0**	**5:10**

AHL First All-Star Team (2000)

Signed as a free agent by **Hershey** (AHL), July 24, 1998. Signed as a free agent by **Colorado**, December 22, 1998. Signed as a free agent by **Columbus**, July 11, 2000. Signed as a free agent by **Colorado**, August 27, 2002. Claimed by **Atlanta** from **Colorado** in Waiver Draft, October 3, 2003. Signed as a free agent by **Geneve** (Swiss), January 5, 2005.

AUCOIN, Adrian
(oh-KOIN, AY-dree-an) **CHI.**

Defense. Shoots right. 6'2", 214 lbs. Born, Ottawa, Ont., July 3, 1973. Vancouver's 7th choice, 117th overall, in 1992 Entry Draft.

1989-90	Nepean Raiders	CJHL	54	2	14	16	95	....	....	....	....	....	....	....	....	....	4	0	1	1	....	....	....	....	....
1990-91	Nepean Raiders	CJHL	56	17	33	50	125	....	....	....	....	....	....	....	....	....	....	....	....	....	....	....	....	....	....
1991-92	Boston University	H-East	32	2	10	12	60	....	....	....	....	....	....	....	....	....	....	....	....	....	....	....	....	....	....
1992-93	Canada	Nat-Tm	42	8	10	18	71	....	....	....	....	....	....	....	....	....	....	....	....	....	....	....	....	....	....
1993-94	Canada	Nat-Tm	59	5	12	17	80	....	....	....	....	....	....	....	....	....	....	....	....	....	....	....	....	....	....
	Canada	Olympics	4	0	0	0	2	....	....	....	....	....	....	....	....	....	....	....	....	....	....	....	....	....	....
	Hamilton	AHL	13	1	2	3	19	....	....	....	....	....	....	....	....	....	4	0	2	2	6	....	....	....	....
1994-95	Syracuse Crunch	AHL	71	13	18	31	52	....	....	....	....	....	....	....	....	....	....	....	....	....	....	....	....	....	....
	Vancouver	**NHL**	1	1	0	1	0	0	0	0	2	50.0	1	....	....	....	4	1	0	1	0	1	0	0	....

						Regular Season											Playoffs								
Season	Club	League	GP	G	A	Pts	PIM	PP	SH	GW	S	%	+/-	TF	F%	Min	GP	G	A	Pts	PIM	PP	SH	GW	Min
1995-96	Vancouver	NHL	49	4	14	18	34	2	0	0	85	4.7	8	....	....	....	6	0	0	0	2	0	0	0	....
	Syracuse Crunch	AHL	29	5	13	18	47	....	....	....	....	....	....	....	....	....	....	....	....	....	....	....	....	....	....
1996-97	Vancouver	NHL	70	5	16	21	63	1	0	0	116	4.3	0	....	....	....	....	....	....	....	....	....	....	....	....
1997-98	Vancouver	NHL	35	3	3	6	21	1	0	1	44	6.8	–4	....	....	....	....	....	....	....	....	....	....	....	....
1998-99	Vancouver	NHL	82	23	11	34	77	18	2	3	174	13.2	–14	1	100.0	23:52	....	....	....	....	....	....	....	....	....
99-2000	Vancouver	NHL	57	10	14	24	30	4	0	1	126	7.9	7	0	0.0	23:06	....	....	....	....	....	....	....	....	....
2000-01	Vancouver	NHL	47	3	13	16	20	1	0	0	99	3.0	13	0	0.0	18:21	....	....	....	....	....	....	....	....	....
	Tampa Bay	NHL	26	1	11	12	25	1	0	0	60	1.7	–8	0	0.0	23:34	....	....	....	....	....	....	....	....	....
2001-02	NY Islanders	NHL	81	12	22	34	62	7	0	1	232	5.2	23	0	0.0	28:54	7	2	5	7	4	2	0	0	32:19
2002-03	NY Islanders	NHL	73	8	27	35	70	5	0	1	175	4.6	–5	0	0.0	29:01	5	1	2	3	4	0	0	0	31:43
2003-04	NY Islanders	NHL	81	13	31	44	54	4	0	2	213	6.1	29	0	0.0	26:38	5	0	0	0	6	0	0	0	28:21
2004-05	MODO	Sweden	14	2	4	6	32	....	....	....	....	....	....	....	....	....	6	1	0	1	16	....	....	....	....
2005-06	Chicago	NHL	33	1	5	6	38	1	0	0	59	1.7	–13	0	0.0	22:58	....	....	....	....	....	....	....	....	....
	NHL Totals		635	84	167	251	494	45	2	9	1385	6.1		1	100.0	25:15	27	4	7	11	16	3	0	0	30:58

Played in NHL All-Star Game (2004)

• Missed majority of 1997-98 season recovering from ankle (October 4, 1997 vs. Anaheim) and groin (November 1, 1997 vs. Pittsburgh) injuries. Traded to **Tampa Bay** by **Vancouver** with Vancouver's 2nd round choice (Alexander Polushin) in 2001 Entry Draft for Dan Cloutier, February 7, 2001. Traded to **NY Islanders** by **Tampa Bay** with Alexander Kharitonov for Mathieu Biron and NY Islanders' 2nd round choice (later traded to Washington – later traded to Vancouver – Vancouver selected Denis Grot) in 2002 Entry Draft, June 22, 2001. Signed as a free agent by **MODO** (Sweden), December 21, 2004. Signed as a free agent by **Chicago**, August 2, 2005.

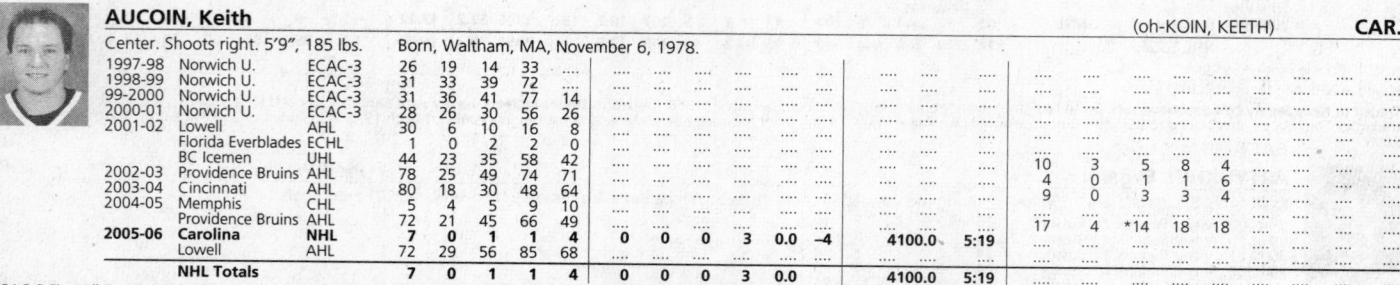

AUCOIN, Keith

(oh-KOIN, KEETH) **CAR.**

Center. Shoots right. 5'9", 185 lbs. Born, Waltham, MA, November 6, 1978.

1997-98	Norwich U.	ECAC-3	26	19	14	33	....	....	....	....	....	....	....	....	....	....	....	....	....	....	....	....	....	....	....
1998-99	Norwich U.	ECAC-3	31	33	39	72	....	....	....	....	....	....	....	....	....	....	....	....	....	....	....	....	....	....	....
99-2000	Norwich U.	ECAC-3	31	36	41	77	14	....	....	....	....	....	....	....	....	....	....	....	....	....	....	....	....	....	....
2000-01	Norwich U.	ECAC-3	28	26	30	56	26	....	....	....	....	....	....	....	....	....	....	....	....	....	....	....	....	....	....
2001-02	Lowell	AHL	30	6	10	16	8	....	....	....	....	....	....	....	....	....	....	....	....	....	....	....	....	....	....
	Florida Everblades	ECHL	1	0	2	2	0	....	....	....	....	....	....	....	....	....	....	....	....	....	....	....	....	....	....
	BC Icemen	UHL	44	23	35	58	42	....	....	....	....	....	....	....	....	....	10	3	5	8	4	....	....	....	....
2002-03	Providence Bruins	AHL	78	25	49	74	71	....	....	....	....	....	....	....	....	....	4	0	1	1	6	....	....	....	....
2003-04	Cincinnati	AHL	80	18	30	48	64	....	....	....	....	....	....	....	....	....	9	0	3	3	4	....	....	....	....
2004-05	Memphis	CHL	5	4	5	9	10	....	....	....	....	....	....	....	....	....	....	....	....	....	....	....	....	....	....
	Providence Bruins	AHL	72	21	45	66	49	....	....	....	....	....	....	....	....	....	17	4	*14	18	18	....	....	....	....
2005-06	Carolina	NHL	7	0	1	1	4	0	0	0	3	0.0	–4	4	100.0	5:19	....	....	....	....	....	....	....	....	....
	Lowell	AHL	72	29	56	85	68	....	....	....	....	....	....	....	....	....	....	....	....	....	....	....	....	....	....
	NHL Totals		7	0	1	1	4	0	0	0	3	0.0		4	100.0	5:19	....	....	....	....	....	....	....	....	....

ECAC-3 First All-Star Team (2000, 2001) • ECAC-3 Player of the Year (2000, 2001) • AHL Second All-Star Team (2006)

Signed as a free agent by **Lowell** (AHL), June 19, 2001. Signed as a free agent by **Providence** (AHL), August 2, 2002. Signed as a free agent by **Anaheim**, August 29, 2003. Signed to a PTO (tryout) contract by **Providence** (AHL), November 4, 2004, Signed as a free agent by **Providence** (AHL), December 9, 2004. Signed as a free agent by **Carolina**, August 4, 2005.

AULIN, Jared

(AW-lihn, JAIR-ehd)

Center/Right wing. Shoots right. 6', 192 lbs. Born, Calgary, Alta., March 15, 1982. Colorado's 2nd choice, 47th overall, in 2000 Entry Draft.

1997-98	Airdrie Xtreme	AAHA	55	42	61	103	60	....	....	....	....	....	....	....	....	....	....	....	....	....	....	....	....	....	....
	Kamloops Blazers	WHL	2	0	0	0	0	....	....	....	....	....	....	....	....	....	....	....	....	....	....	....	....	....	....
1998-99	Kamloops Blazers	WHL	55	7	19	26	23	....	....	....	....	....	....	....	....	....	13	1	3	4	2	....	....	....	....
99-2000	Kamloops Blazers	WHL	57	17	38	55	70	....	....	....	....	....	....	....	....	....	4	0	1	1	6	....	....	....	....
2000-01	Kamloops Blazers	WHL	70	31	*77	108	62	....	....	....	....	....	....	....	....	....	4	0	2	2	0	....	....	....	....
2001-02	Kamloops Blazers	WHL	46	33	34	67	80	....	....	....	....	....	....	....	....	....	4	1	2	3	2	....	....	....	....
2002-03	Los Angeles	NHL	17	2	2	4	0	1	0	0	21	9.5	–3	92	41.3	9:55	....	....	....	....	....	....	....	....	....
	Manchester	AHL	44	12	32	44	21	....	....	....	....	....	....	....	....	....	3	0	4	4	0	....	....	....	....
2003-04	Portland Pirates	AHL	10	2	1	3	4	....	....	....	....	....	....	....	....	....	6	1	1	2	4	....	....	....	....
2004-05	Portland Pirates	AHL	65	11	28	39	30	....	....	....	....	....	....	....	....	....	....	....	....	....	....	....	....	....	....
2005-06	Hershey Bears	AHL	61	11	28	39	38	....	....	....	....	....	....	....	....	....	5	0	0	0	6	....	....	....	....
	NHL Totals		17	2	2	4	0	1	0	0	21	9.5		92	41.3	9:55	....	....	....	....	....	....	....	....	....

WHL West First All-Star Team (2001, 2002)

Traded to **Los Angeles** by **Colorado** to complete transaction that sent Rob Blake and Steve Reinprecht to Colorado (February 21, 2001), March 22, 2001. • Missed majority of 2003-04 season recovering from shoulder injury suffered in training camp, September 4, 2003. Traded to **Washington** by **Los Angeles** for Anson Carter, March 8, 2004.

AVERY, Sean

(AY-vuhr-ee, SHAWN) **L.A.**

Center. Shoots left. 5'10", 185 lbs. Born, Pickering, Ont., April 10, 1980.

1995-96	Markham	OMHA	70	34	81	115	180	....	....	....	....	....	....	....	....	....	....	....	....	....	....	....	....	....	....
	Markham Waxers	MTJHL	1	0	0	0	4	....	....	....	....	....	....	....	....	....	....	....	....	....	....	....	....	....	....
1996-97	Owen Sound	OHL	58	10	21	31	86	....	....	....	....	....	....	....	....	....	4	1	0	1	4	....	....	....	....
1997-98	Owen Sound	OHL	47	13	41	54	105	....	....	....	....	....	....	....	....	....	....	....	....	....	....	....	....	....	....
1998-99	Owen Sound	OHL	28	22	23	45	70	....	....	....	....	....	....	....	....	....	....	....	....	....	....	....	....	....	....
	Kingston	OHL	33	14	25	39	88	....	....	....	....	....	....	....	....	....	5	1	3	4	13	....	....	....	....
99-2000	Kingston	OHL	55	28	56	84	215	....	....	....	....	....	....	....	....	....	5	2	2	4	26	....	....	....	....
2000-01	Cincinnati	AHL	58	8	15	23	304	....	....	....	....	....	....	....	....	....	4	1	0	1	19	....	....	....	....
2001-02	Detroit	NHL	36	2	2	4	68	0	0	1	30	6.7	1	299	51.8	7:51	....	....	....	....	....	....	....	....	....
	Cincinnati	AHL	36	14	7	21	106	....	....	....	....	....	....	....	....	....	....	....	....	....	....	....	....	....	....
2002-03	Detroit	NHL	39	5	6	11	120	0	0	2	40	12.5	7	224	58.0	7:03	....	....	....	....	....	....	....	....	....
	Grand Rapids	AHL	15	6	6	12	82	....	....	....	....	....	....	....	....	....	....	....	....	....	....	....	....	....	....
	Los Angeles	NHL	12	1	3	4	33	0	0	0	19	5.3	0	49	46.9	13:50	....	....	....	....	....	....	....	....	....
	Manchester	AHL	....	....	....	....	....	....	....	....	....	....	....	....	....	....	3	2	1	3	8	....	....	....	....
2003-04	Los Angeles	NHL	76	9	19	28	*261	0	0	2	125	7.2	2	124	54.8	11:41	....	....	....	....	....	....	....	....	....
2004-05	Pelicans Lahti	Finland	2	3	0	3	26	....	....	....	....	....	....	....	....	....	....	....	....	....	....	....	....	....	....
	Motor City	UHL	16	15	11	26	149	....	....	....	....	....	....	....	....	....	....	....	....	....	....	....	....	....	....
2005-06	Los Angeles	NHL	75	15	24	39	*257	1	3	1	189	7.9	–5	226	44.3	13:37	....	....	....	....	....	....	....	....	....
	NHL Totals		238	32	54	86	739	1	3	6	403	7.9		922	51.6	11:04	....	....	....	....	....	....	....	....	....

Signed as a free agent by **Detroit**, September 21, 1999. Traded to **Los Angeles** by **Detroit** with Maxim Kuznetsov, Detroit's 1st round choice (Jeff Tambellini) in 2003 Entry Draft and Detroit's 2nd round choice (later traded to Boston – Boston selected Martins Karsums) in 2004 Entry Draft for Mathieu Schneider, March 11, 2003. Signed as a free agent by **Lahti** (Finland), November 24, 2004. Signed as a free agent by **Motor City** (UHL), February 11, 2005.

AXELSSON, P.J.

(AHX-ehl-suhn, PEE-JAY) **BOS.**

Left wing. Shoots left. 6'1", 184 lbs. Born, Kungalv, Sweden, February 26, 1975. Boston's 7th choice, 177th overall, in 1995 Entry Draft.

1992-93	V.Frolunda Jr.	Swe-Jr.	16	9	5	14	12	....	....	....	....	....	....	....	....	....	....	....	....	....	....	....	....	....	....
	V.Frolunda	Sweden	1	0	0	0	0	....	....	....	....	....	....	....	....	....	....	....	....	....	....	....	....	....	....
1993-94	V.Frolunda	Sweden	11	0	0	0	4	....	....	....	....	....	....	....	....	....	4	0	0	0	0	....	....	....	....
1994-95	V.Frolunda Jr.	Swe-Jr.	19	16	9	25	22	....	....	....	....	....	....	....	....	....	....	....	....	....	....	....	....	....	....
	V.Frolunda	Sweden	11	2	1	3	6	....	....	....	....	....	....	....	....	....	5	0	0	0	0	....	....	....	....
1995-96	V.Frolunda	Sweden	36	15	5	20	10	....	....	....	....	....	....	....	....	....	13	3	0	3	10	....	....	....	....
1996-97	V.Frolunda	Sweden	50	19	15	34	34	....	....	....	....	....	....	....	....	....	3	0	2	2	0	....	....	....	....
	V.Frolunda	EuroHL	3	1	1	2	0	....	....	....	....	....	....	....	....	....	3	0	0	0	2	....	....	....	....
1997-98	Boston	NHL	82	8	19	27	38	2	0	1	144	5.6	–14	....	....	....	6	1	0	1	0	0	0	0	....
1998-99	Boston	NHL	77	7	10	17	18	0	0	2	146	4.8	–14	8	75.0	16:38	12	1	1	2	4	0	0	0	15:11
99-2000	Boston	NHL	81	10	16	26	24	0	0	4	186	5.4	1	22	27.3	16:43	....	....	....	....	....	....	....	....	....
2000-01	Boston	NHL	81	8	15	23	27	0	0	2	146	5.5	–12	41	36.6	12:30	....	....	....	....	....	....	....	....	....
2001-02	Boston	NHL	78	7	17	24	16	0	2	0	127	5.5	6	17	35.3	14:42	6	2	1	3	6	0	1	1	16:48
	Sweden	Olympics	4	0	0	0	2	....	....	....	....	....	....	....	....	....	....	....	....	....	....	....	....	....	....
2002-03	Boston	NHL	66	17	19	36	24	2	2	1	122	13.9	8	17	23.5	16:37	5	0	0	0	6	0	0	0	13:23
2003-04	Boston	NHL	68	6	14	20	42	0	0	1	107	5.6	2	13	15.4	16:19	7	0	0	0	4	0	0	0	14:43
2004-05	Frolunda	Sweden	45	8	9	17	95	....	....	....	....	....	....	....	....	....	14	1	*10	11	18	....	....	....	....

			Regular Season														Playoffs								
Season	Club	League	GP	G	A	Pts	PIM	PP	SH	GW	S	%	+/-	TF	F%	Min	GP	G	A	Pts	PIM	PP	SH	GW	Min
2005-06	**Boston**	**NHL**	**59**	**10**	**18**	**28**	**4**	**1**	**2**	**1**	**113**	**8.8**	**–3**	**27**	**40.7**	**17:36**	....	....	....	....	....	....	....	....	....
	Sweden	Olympics	8	3	3	6	0	....	....	....	....	....	....	....	....	....	....	....	....	....	....	....	....	....	....
	NHL Totals		**592**	**73**	**128**	**201**	**193**	**5**	**6**	**12**	**1091**	**6.7**		**145**	**34.5**	**15:46**	**36**	**4**	**2**	**6**	**20**	**0**	**1**	**1**	**15:06**

Signed as a free agent by **Frolunda** (Sweden), September 15, 2004.

BABCHUK, Anton

(bab-CHUHK, AN-tawn) **CAR.**

Defense. Shoots right. 6'5", 202 lbs. Born, Kiev, USSR, May 6, 1984. Chicago's 1st choice, 21st overall, in 2002 Entry Draft.

Season	Club	League	GP	G	A	Pts	PIM	PP	SH	GW	S	%	+/-	TF	F%	Min	GP	G	A	Pts	PIM	PP	SH	GW	Min
99-2000	Elektrostal 2	Russia-3	6	0	0	0	8	....	....	....	....	....	....	....	....	....	....	....	....	....	....	....	....	....	....
	Elektrostal 2	Russia-3	18	0	1	1	18	....	....	....	....	....	....	....	....	....	....	....	....	....	....	....	....	....	....
2000-01	Elektrostal	Russia-2	7	0	0	0	12	....	....	....	....	....	....	....	....	....	....	....	....	....	....	....	....	....	....
	Russia 17	Nat-Tm	15	1	3	4	12	....	....	....	....	....	....	....	....	....	....	....	....	....	....	....	....	....	....
2001-02	Elektrostal	Russia-2	40	7	8	15	90	....	....	....	....	....	....	....	....	....	....	....	....	....	....	....	....	....	....
	Elektrostal 2	Russia-3	3	0	0	0	8	....	....	....	....	....	....	....	....	....	....	....	....	....	....	....	....	....	....
2002-03	Ak Bars Kazan	Russia	10	0	0	0	4	....	....	....	....	....	....	....	....	....	....	....	....	....	....	....	....	....	....
	St. Petersburg	Russia	20	3	0	3	10	....	....	....	....	....	....	....	....	....	....	....	....	....	....	....	....	....	....
	Spartak St. Pet.	Russia-2	1	1	0	1	0	....	....	....	....	....	....	....	....	....	....	....	....	....	....	....	....	....	....
2003-04	**Chicago**	**NHL**	**5**	**0**	**2**	**2**	**2**	**0**	**0**	**0**	**11**	**0.0**	**–1**	**0**	**0.0**	**12:43**	....	....	....	....	....	....	....	....	....
	Norfolk Admirals	AHL	73	8	14	22	89	....	....	....	....	....	....	....	....	....	8	0	2	2	6	....	....	....	....
2004-05	Norfolk Admirals	AHL	66	8	16	24	88	....	....	....	....	....	....	....	....	....	2	0	0	0	2	....	....	....	....
2005-06	**Chicago**	**NHL**	**17**	**2**	**3**	**5**	**16**	**1**	**0**	**0**	**24**	**8.3**	**–5**	**0**	**0.0**	**16:38**	....	....	....	....	....	....	....	....	....
	Norfolk Admirals	AHL	24	5	7	12	22	....	....	....	....	....	....	....	....	....	....	....	....	....	....	....	....	....	....
	Carolina	**NHL**	**22**	**3**	**2**	**5**	**6**	**2**	**0**	**0**	**32**	**9.4**	**–2**	**0**	**0.0**	**13:22**	....	....	....	....	....	....	....	....	....
	Lowell	AHL	5	1	3	4	0	....	....	....	....	....	....	....	....	....	....	....	....	....	....	....	....	....	....
	NHL Totals		**44**	**5**	**7**	**12**	**24**	**3**	**0**	**0**	**67**	**7.5**		**0**	**0.0**	**14:33**	....	....	....	....	....	....	....	....	....

Traded to **Carolina** by **Chicago** for Danny Richmond and Columbus' 4th round choice (previously acquired, later traded to Toronto -Toronto selected James Reimer) in 2006 Entry Draft, January 20, 2006.

BACKMAN, Christian

(BAK-man, KRIH-stan) **ST.L.**

Defense. Shoots left. 6'4", 198 lbs. Born, Alingsas, Sweden, April 28, 1980. St. Louis' 1st choice, 24th overall, in 1998 Entry Draft.

Season	Club	League	GP	G	A	Pts	PIM	PP	SH	GW	S	%	+/-	TF	F%	Min	GP	G	A	Pts	PIM	PP	SH	GW	Min
1996-97	V.Frolunda Jr.	Swe-Jr.	26	2	5	7	16	....	....	....	....	....	....	....	....	....	....	....	....	....	....	....	....	....	....
1997-98	V.Frolunda U18	Swe-U18	4	4	1	5	2	....	....	....	....	....	....	....	....	....	5	2	2	4	2	....	....	....	....
	V.Frolunda Jr.	Swe-Jr.	28	5	14	19	12	....	....	....	....	....	....	....	....	....	2	0	1	1	4	....	....	....	....
1998-99	V.Frolunda Jr.	Swe-Jr.	4	0	2	2	4	....	....	....	....	....	....	....	....	....	....	....	....	....	....	....	....	....	....
	V.Frolunda	Sweden	49	0	4	4	4	....	....	....	....	....	....	....	....	....	4	0	0	0	0	....	....	....	....
99-2000	V.Frolunda Jr.	Swe-Jr.	5	1	1	2	0	....	....	....	....	....	....	....	....	....	3	1	1	2	0	....	....	....	....
	Gislaveds SK	Sweden-2	21	5	2	7	8	....	....	....	....	....	....	....	....	....	....	....	....	....	....	....	....	....	....
	V.Frolunda	Sweden	27	1	0	1	14	....	....	....	....	....	....	....	....	....	5	0	0	0	0	....	....	....	....
2000-01	V.Frolunda	Sweden	50	1	10	11	32	....	....	....	....	....	....	....	....	....	3	0	2	2	2	....	....	....	....
2001-02	V.Frolunda	Sweden	44	7	4	11	38	....	....	....	....	....	....	....	....	....	10	0	0	0	8	....	....	....	....
2002-03	**St. Louis**	**NHL**	**4**	**0**	**0**	**0**	**0**	**0**	**0**	**0**	**4**	**0.0**	**–3**	**0**	**0.0**	**12:22**	....	....	....	....	....	....	....	....	....
	Worcester IceCats	AHL	72	8	19	27	66	....	....	....	....	....	....	....	....	....	3	0	1	1	5	....	....	....	....
2003-04	**St. Louis**	**NHL**	**66**	**5**	**13**	**18**	**16**	**1**	**0**	**0**	**92**	**5.4**	**3**	**0**	**0.0**	**19:20**	**5**	**0**	**2**	**2**	**4**	**0**	**0**	**0**	**23:06**
	Worcester IceCats	AHL	4	1	2	3	2	....	....	....	....	....	....	....	....	....	....	....	....	....	....	....	....	....	....
2004-05	Frolunda	Sweden	50	4	15	19	40	....	....	....	....	....	....	....	....	....	14	2	7	9	10	....	....	....	....
2005-06	**St. Louis**	**NHL**	**52**	**6**	**12**	**18**	**48**	**3**	**0**	**1**	**70**	**8.6**	**–15**	**0**	**0.0**	**24:49**	....	....	....	....	....	....	....	....	....
	Sweden	Olympics	8	1	2	3	6	....	....	....	....	....	....	....	....	....	....	....	....	....	....	....	....	....	....
	NHL Totals		**122**	**11**	**25**	**36**	**64**	**4**	**0**	**1**	**166**	**6.6**		**0**	**0.0**	**21:27**	**5**	**0**	**2**	**2**	**4**	**0**	**0**	**0**	**23:06**

Signed as a free agent by **Frolunda** (Sweden), September 15, 2004.

BALASTIK, Jaroslav

(ba-LASH-tihk, YAHR-roh-slav) **CBJ**

Right wing. Shoots left. 6'2", 205 lbs. Born, Gottwaldov, Czech., November 28, 1979. Columbus' 9th choice, 184th overall, in 2002 Entry Draft.

Season	Club	League	GP	G	A	Pts	PIM	PP	SH	GW	S	%	+/-	TF	F%	Min	GP	G	A	Pts	PIM	PP	SH	GW	Min
1996-97	AC ZPS Zlin Jr.	CzRep-Jr.	45	27	24	51	....	....	....	....	....	....	....	....	....	....	....	....	....	....	....	....	....	....	....
1997-98	HC ZPS Zlin Jr.	CzRep-Jr.	36	21	35	56	....	....	....	....	....	....	....	....	....	....	7	2	3	5	....	....	....	....	....
	Zlin	CzRep	6	0	2	2	....	....	....	....	....	....	....	....	....	....	....	....	....	....	....	....	....	....	....
1998-99	HC ZPS Zlin Jr.	CzRep-Jr.	....	....	....	....	....	....	....	....	....	....	....	....	....	....	2	0	0	0	....	....	....	....	....
	Zlin	CzRep	41	4	8	12	12	....	....	....	....	....	....	....	....	....	9	1	0	1	27	....	....	....	....
99-2000	HC Zlin Jr.	CzRep-Jr.	4	5	5	10	2	....	....	....	....	....	....	....	....	....	....	....	....	....	....	....	....	....	....
	Zlin	CzRep	48	7	10	17	0	....	....	....	....	....	....	....	....	....	4	0	1	1	2	....	....	....	....
2000-01	Zlin	CzRep	52	8	17	25	32	....	....	....	....	....	....	....	....	....	6	1	1	2	6	....	....	....	....
2001-02	Zlin	CzRep	50	25	19	44	32	....	....	....	....	....	....	....	....	....	11	3	5	8	14	....	....	....	....
2002-03	HC Hame Zlin	CzRep	31	14	8	22	26	....	....	....	....	....	....	....	....	....	....	....	....	....	....	....	....	....	....
	HPK Hameenlinna	Finland	13	5	7	12	2	....	....	....	....	....	....	....	....	....	13	4	3	7	6	....	....	....	....
2003-04	HC Hame Zlin	CzRep	51	*29	18	47	54	....	....	....	....	....	....	....	....	....	17	*9	9	*18	32	....	....	....	....
2004-05	HC Hame Zlin	CzRep	52	*30	16	46	74	....	....	....	....	....	....	....	....	....	17	4	9	13	*52	....	....	....	....
2005-06	**Columbus**	**NHL**	**66**	**12**	**10**	**22**	**26**	**7**	**0**	**2**	**158**	**7.6**	**–1**	**5**	**20.0**	**12:50**	....	....	....	....	....	....	....	....	....
	Syracuse Crunch	AHL	14	3	3	6	6	....	....	....	....	....	....	....	....	....	....	....	....	....	....	....	....	....	....
	NHL Totals		**66**	**12**	**10**	**22**	**26**	**7**	**0**	**2**	**158**	**7.6**		**5**	**20.0**	**12:50**	....	....	....	....	....	....	....	....	....

BALEJ, Jozef

(BAH-lay, YOH-zehf) **VAN.**

Right wing. Shoots right. 6'1", 195 lbs. Born, Myjava, Czech., February 22, 1982. Montreal's 3rd choice, 78th overall, in 2000 Entry Draft.

Season	Club	League	GP	G	A	Pts	PIM	PP	SH	GW	S	%	+/-	TF	F%	Min	GP	G	A	Pts	PIM	PP	SH	GW	Min
1996-97	Dukla Trencin Jr.	Slovak-Jr.	51	31	25	56	36	....	....	....	....	....	....	....	....	....	....	....	....	....	....	....	....	....	....
1997-98	Dukla Trencin Jr.	Slovak-Jr.	52	57	40	97	60	....	....	....	....	....	....	....	....	....	....	....	....	....	....	....	....	....	....
1998-99	Thunder Bay	USHL	38	8	7	15	9	....	....	....	....	....	....	....	....	....	....	....	....	....	....	....	....	....	....
	Rochester	USHL	17	0	1	1	2	....	....	....	....	....	....	....	....	....	....	....	....	....	....	....	....	....	....
99-2000	Portland	WHL	65	22	23	45	33	....	....	....	....	....	....	....	....	....	....	....	....	....	....	....	....	....	....
2000-01	Portland	WHL	46	32	21	53	18	....	....	....	....	....	....	....	....	....	16	9	6	15	6	....	....	....	....
2001-02	Portland	WHL	65	51	41	92	52	....	....	....	....	....	....	....	....	....	7	0	2	2	6	....	....	....	....
2002-03	Hamilton	AHL	56	5	15	20	29	....	....	....	....	....	....	....	....	....	....	....	....	....	....	....	....	....	....
2003-04	**Montreal**	**NHL**	**4**	**0**	**0**	**0**	**0**	**0**	**0**	**0**	**4**	**0.0**	**–1**	**2**	**50.0**	**12:38**	....	....	....	....	....	....	....	....	....
	Hamilton	AHL	55	25	33	58	32	....	....	....	....	....	....	....	....	....	....	....	....	....	....	....	....	....	....
	NY Rangers	**NHL**	**13**	**1**	**4**	**5**	**4**	**0**	**0**	**0**	**25**	**4.0**	**0**	**1**	**0.0**	**13:06**	....	....	....	....	....	....	....	....	....
	Hartford	AHL	5	1	3	4	21	....	....	....	....	....	....	....	....	....	16	9	7	16	10	....	....	....	....
2004-05	Hartford	AHL	69	20	22	42	46	....	....	....	....	....	....	....	....	....	6	0	0	0	4	....	....	....	....
2005-06	**Vancouver**	**NHL**	**1**	**0**	**1**	**1**	**0**	**0**	**0**	**0**	**3**	**0.0**	**1**	**0**	**0.0**	**7:56**	....	....	....	....	....	....	....	....	....
	Manitoba Moose	AHL	39	14	15	29	20	....	....	....	....	....	....	....	....	....	4	1	0	1	4	....	....	....	....
	NHL Totals		**18**	**1**	**5**	**6**	**4**	**0**	**0**	**0**	**32**	**3.1**		**3**	**33.3**	**12:43**	....	....	....	....	....	....	....	....	....

WHL West First All-Star Team (2002)

Traded to **NY Rangers** by **Montreal** with Montreal's 2nd round choice (Bruce Graham) in 2004 Entry Draft for Alex Kovalev, March 2, 2004. Traded to **Vancouver** by **NY Rangers** with future consdierations for Fedor Fedorov, October 7, 2005.

BALLARD, Keith

(BAL-uhrd, KEETH) **PHX.**

Defense. Shoots left. 5'11", 208 lbs. Born, Baudette, MN, November 26, 1982. Buffalo's 1st choice, 11th overall, in 2002 Entry Draft.

Season	Club	League	GP	G	A	Pts	PIM	PP	SH	GW	S	%	+/-	TF	F%	Min	GP	G	A	Pts	PIM	PP	SH	GW	Min
99-2000	USNTDP	U-18	6	1	1	2	4	....	....	....	....	....	....	....	....	....	....	....	....	....	....	....	....	....	....
	USNTDP	USHL	58	12	21	33	119	....	....	....	....	....	....	....	....	....	....	....	....	....	....	....	....	....	....
2000-01	Omaha Lancers	USHL	56	22	29	51	168	....	....	....	....	....	....	....	....	....	10	1	6	7	8	....	....	....	....
2001-02	U. of Minnesota	WCHA	41	10	13	23	42	....	....	....	....	....	....	....	....	....	....	....	....	....	....	....	....	....	....
2002-03	U. of Minnesota	WCHA	41	12	29	41	78	....	....	....	....	....	....	....	....	....	....	....	....	....	....	....	....	....	....
2003-04	U. of Minnesota	WCHA	37	11	25	36	83	....	....	....	....	....	....	....	....	....	....	....	....	....	....	....	....	....	....
2004-05	Utah Grizzlies	AHL	60	2	18	20	88	....	....	....	....	....	....	....	....	....	....	....	....	....	....	....	....	....	....
2005-06	**Phoenix**	**NHL**	**82**	**8**	**31**	**39**	**99**	**1**	**3**	**1**	**102**	**7.8**	**–18**	**0**	**0.0**	**19:59**	....	....	....	....	....	....	....	....	....
	NHL Totals		**82**	**8**	**31**	**39**	**99**	**1**	**3**	**1**	**102**	**7.8**		**0**	**0.0**	**19:59**	....	....	....	....	....	....	....	....	....

USHL First All-Star Team (2001) • WCHA All-Rookie Team (2002) • WCHA First All-Star Team (2003, 2004) • NCAA West First All-American Team (2004)

Traded to **Colorado** by **Buffalo** for Steve Reinprecht, July 3, 2003. Traded to **Phoenix** by **Colorado** with Derek Morris for Ossi Vaananen, Chris Gratton and Phoenix's 2nd round choice (Paul Stastny) in 2005 Entry Draft, March 8, 2004.

BARINKA, Michal
(ba-RIHN-kuh, MIGH-kuhl) **OTT.**

Defense. Shoots left. 6'3", 217 lbs. Born, Vyskov, Czech., June 12, 1984. Chicago's 3rd choice, 59th overall, in 2003 Entry Draft.

			Regular Season														Playoffs								
Season	Club	League	GP	G	A	Pts	PIM	PP	SH	GW	S	%	+/-	TF	F%	Min	GP	G	A	Pts	PIM	PP	SH	GW	Min
99-2000	C. Budejovice U17	CzR-U17	48	1	12	13	26										6	0	2	2	4				
2000-01	C. Budejovice Jr.	CzRep-Jr.	26	1	8	9	14										3	0	0	0	0				
	C. Budejovice U17	CzR-U17	7	0	1	1	6																		
2001-02	C. Budejovice Jr.	CzRep-Jr.	31	3	13	16	60										7	3	4	7	35				
	C. Budejovice	CzRep	3	0	0	0	0																		
2002-03	C. Budejovice Jr.	CzRep-Jr.	14	1	5	6	34																		
	C. Budejovice	CzRep	31	0	1	1	14										4	0	0	0	2				
2003-04	**Chicago**	**NHL**	**9**	**0**	**1**	**1**	**6**	**0**	**0**	**0**	**15**	**0.0**	**–5**	**0**	**0.0**	**13:48**									
	Norfolk Admirals	AHL	40	4	2	6	80																		
2004-05	Norfolk Admirals	AHL	59	1	10	11	77																		
2005-06	**Chicago**	**NHL**	**25**	**0**	**1**	**1**	**20**	**0**	**0**	**0**	**19**	**0.0**	**–7**	**1**	**0.0**	**14:38**									
	Norfolk Admirals	AHL	54	1	11	12	86										4	0	0	0	11				
	NHL Totals		**34**	**0**	**2**	**2**	**26**	**0**	**0**	**0**	**34**	**0.0**		**1**	**0.0**	**14:25**									

Traded to **Ottawa** by **Chicago** with Tom Preissing, Josh Hennessy and a 2nd round choice in 2008 Entry Draft for Martin Havlat and Bryan Smolinski, July 10, 2006.

BARKER, Cam
(BAR-kuhr, KAM) **CHI.**

Defense. Shoots left. 6'3", 222 lbs. Born, Winnipeg, Man., April 4, 1986. Chicago's 1st choice, 3rd overall, in 2004 Entry Draft.

			Regular Season														Playoffs								
Season	Club	League	GP	G	A	Pts	PIM	PP	SH	GW	S	%	+/-	TF	F%	Min	GP	G	A	Pts	PIM	PP	SH	GW	Min
2001-02	Cornwall Colts	CJHL	72	6	23	29	132																		
	Medicine Hat	WHL	3	0	1	1	0																		
2002-03	Medicine Hat	WHL	64	10	37	47	79										11	3	4	7	17				
2003-04	Medicine Hat	WHL	69	21	44	65	105										20	3	9	12	18				
2004-05	Medicine Hat	WHL	52	15	33	48	99										12	3	3	6	16				
2005-06	Medicine Hat	WHL	26	5	13	18	63										13	4	8	12	*59				
	Chicago	**NHL**	**1**	**0**	**0**	**0**	**0**	**0**	**0**	**0**	**1**	**0.0**	**0**	**0**	**0.0**	**11:02**									
	NHL Totals		**1**	**0**	**0**	**0**	**0**	**0**	**0**	**0**	**1**	**0.0**		**0**	**0.0**	**11:02**									

BARNABY, Matthew
(BAHR-na-BEE, MA-thew) **DAL.**

Right wing. Shoots left. 6', 189 lbs. Born, Ottawa, Ont., May 4, 1973. Buffalo's 5th choice, 83rd overall, in 1992 Entry Draft.

			Regular Season														Playoffs								
Season	Club	League	GP	G	A	Pts	PIM	PP	SH	GW	S	%	+/-	TF	F%	Min	GP	G	A	Pts	PIM	PP	SH	GW	Min
1989-90	Hull Frontaliers	QAHA	50	43	50	93	149																		
	L'Outaouais	QAAA	2	0	0	0	0																		
1990-91	Beauport	QMJHL	52	9	5	14	262																		
1991-92	Beauport	QMJHL	63	29	37	66	*476																		
1992-93	Victoriaville Tigres	QMJHL	65	44	67	111	*448										6	2	4	6	44				
	Buffalo	**NHL**	**2**	**1**	**0**	**1**	**10**	**1**	**0**	**0**	**8**	**12.5**	**0**				**1**	**0**	**1**	**1**	**4**	**0**	**0**	**0**	
1993-94	**Buffalo**	**NHL**	**35**	**2**	**4**	**6**	**106**	**1**	**0**	**0**	**13**	**15.4**	**–7**				**3**	**0**	**0**	**0**	**17**	**0**	**0**	**0**	
	Rochester	AHL	42	10	32	42	153																		
1994-95	Rochester	AHL	56	21	29	50	274																		
	Buffalo	**NHL**	**23**	**1**	**1**	**2**	**116**	**0**	**0**	**0**	**27**	**3.7**	**–2**												
1995-96	**Buffalo**	**NHL**	**73**	**15**	**16**	**31**	***335**	**0**	**0**	**0**	**131**	**11.5**	**–2**												
1996-97	**Buffalo**	**NHL**	**68**	**19**	**24**	**43**	**249**	**2**	**0**	**1**	**121**	**15.7**	**16**				**8**	**0**	**4**	**4**	**36**	**0**	**0**	**0**	
1997-98	**Buffalo**	**NHL**	**72**	**5**	**20**	**25**	**289**	**0**	**0**	**2**	**96**	**5.2**	**8**				**15**	**7**	**6**	**13**	**22**	**3**	**0**	**1**	
1998-99	**Buffalo**	**NHL**	**44**	**4**	**14**	**18**	**143**	**0**	**0**	**3**	**52**	**7.7**	**–2**	**6**	**16.7**	**13:56**									
	Pittsburgh	**NHL**	**18**	**2**	**2**	**4**	**34**	**1**	**0**	**0**	**27**	**7.4**	**–10**	**3**	**66.7**	**13:33**	**13**	**0**	**0**	**0**	**35**	**0**	**0**	**0**	**10:27**
99-2000	**Pittsburgh**	**NHL**	**64**	**12**	**12**	**24**	**197**	**0**	**0**	**3**	**80**	**15.0**	**3**	**75**	**44.0**	**12:38**	**11**	**0**	**2**	**2**	**29**	**0**	**0**	**0**	**13:41**
2000-01	**Pittsburgh**	**NHL**	**47**	**1**	**4**	**5**	***168**	**0**	**0**	**0**	**38**	**2.6**	**–7**	**15**	**33.3**	**7:49**									
	Tampa Bay	**NHL**	**29**	**4**	**4**	**8**	***97**	**1**	**0**	**0**	**29**	**13.8**	**–3**	**1**	**100.0**	**12:34**									
2001-02	**Tampa Bay**	**NHL**	**29**	**0**	**0**	**0**	**70**	**0**	**0**	**0**	**13**	**0.0**	**–7**	**1**	**0.0**	**7:54**									
	NY Rangers	**NHL**	**48**	**8**	**13**	**21**	**144**	**0**	**0**	**1**	**56**	**14.3**	**–3**	**12**	**33.3**	**11:24**									
2002-03	**NY Rangers**	**NHL**	**79**	**14**	**22**	**36**	**142**	**1**	**0**	**1**	**104**	**13.5**	**9**	**5**	**40.0**	**13:00**									
2003-04	**NY Rangers**	**NHL**	**69**	**12**	**20**	**32**	**120**	**0**	**0**	**1**	**80**	**15.0**	**15**	**23**	**43.5**	**11:49**									
	Colorado	**NHL**	**13**	**4**	**5**	**9**	**37**	**1**	**0**	**2**	**24**	**16.7**	**3**	**1**	**100.0**	**15:25**	**11**	**0**	**2**	**2**	**27**	**0**	**0**	**0**	**12:22**
2004-05			DID NOT PLAY																						
2005-06	**Chicago**	**NHL**	**82**	**8**	**20**	**28**	**178**	**0**	**0**	**1**	**85**	**9.4**	**–11**	**11**	**45.5**	**13:26**									
	NHL Totals		**795**	**112**	**181**	**293**	**2435**	**8**	**0**	**15**	**984**	**11.4**		**153**	**41.8**	**12:06**	**62**	**7**	**15**	**22**	**170**	**3**	**0**	**1**	**12:04**

Traded to **Pittsburgh** by **Buffalo** for Stu Barnes, March 11, 1999. Traded to **Tampa Bay** by **Pittsburgh** for Wayne Primeau, February 1, 2001. Traded to **NY Rangers** by **Tampa Bay** for Zdeno Ciger, December 12, 2001. Traded to **Colorado** by **NY Rangers** with NY Rangers' 3rd round choice (Denis Parshin) in 2004 Entry Draft for Chris McAllister, David Liffiton and Florida's 2nd round choice (previously acquired, later traded back to Florida – Florida selected David Shantz) in 2004 Entry Draft, March 8, 2004. Signed as a free agent by **Chicago**, July 2, 2004. Signed as a free agent by **Dallas**, July 5, 2006.

BARNES, Stu
(BAHRNZ, STEW) **DAL.**

Center. Shoots right. 5'11", 180 lbs. Born, Spruce Grove, Alta., December 25, 1970. Winnipeg's 1st choice, 4th overall, in 1989 Entry Draft.

			Regular Season														Playoffs								
Season	Club	League	GP	G	A	Pts	PIM	PP	SH	GW	S	%	+/-	TF	F%	Min	GP	G	A	Pts	PIM	PP	SH	GW	Min
1986-87	St. Albert Saints	AJHL	53	41	34	*75	103										19	7	15	22					
1987-88	New Westminster	WHL	71	37	64	101	88										5	2	3	5	6				
1988-89	Tri-City	WHL	70	59	82	141	117										7	6	5	11	10				
1989-90	Tri-City	WHL	63	52	92	144	165										7	1	5	6	26				
1990-91	Canada	Nat-Tm	53	22	27	49	68																		
1991-92	**Winnipeg**	**NHL**	**46**	**8**	**9**	**17**	**26**	**4**	**0**	**0**	**75**	**10.7**	**–2**												
	Moncton Hawks	AHL	30	13	19	32	10										11	3	9	12	6				
1992-93	**Winnipeg**	**NHL**	**38**	**12**	**10**	**22**	**10**	**3**	**0**	**3**	**73**	**16.4**	**–3**				**6**	**1**	**3**	**4**	**2**	**0**	**0**	**0**	
	Moncton Hawks	AHL	42	23	31	54	58																		
1993-94	**Winnipeg**	**NHL**	**18**	**5**	**4**	**9**	**8**	**2**	**0**	**0**	**24**	**20.8**	**–1**												
	Florida	**NHL**	**59**	**18**	**20**	**38**	**30**	**6**	**1**	**3**	**148**	**12.2**	**5**												
1994-95	**Florida**	**NHL**	**41**	**10**	**19**	**29**	**8**	**1**	**0**	**2**	**93**	**10.8**	**7**												
1995-96	**Florida**	**NHL**	**72**	**19**	**25**	**44**	**46**	**8**	**0**	**5**	**158**	**12.0**	**–12**				**22**	**6**	**10**	**16**	**4**	**2**	**0**	**2**	
1996-97	**Florida**	**NHL**	**19**	**2**	**8**	**10**	**10**	**1**	**0**	**0**	**44**	**4.5**	**–3**												
	Pittsburgh	**NHL**	**62**	**17**	**22**	**39**	**16**	**4**	**0**	**3**	**132**	**12.9**	**–20**				**5**	**0**	**1**	**1**	**0**	**0**	**0**	**0**	
1997-98	**Pittsburgh**	**NHL**	**78**	**30**	**35**	**65**	**30**	**15**	**1**	**5**	**196**	**15.3**	**15**				**6**	**3**	**3**	**6**	**2**	**0**	**0**	**1**	
1998-99	**Pittsburgh**	**NHL**	**64**	**20**	**12**	**32**	**20**	**13**	**0**	**3**	**155**	**12.9**	**–12**	**720**	**51.9**	**17:52**									
	Buffalo	**NHL**	**17**	**0**	**4**	**4**	**10**	**0**	**0**	**0**	**25**	**0.0**	**1**	**236**	**51.3**	**18:20**	**21**	**7**	**3**	**10**	**6**	**4**	**0**	**1**	**14:40**
99-2000	**Buffalo**	**NHL**	**82**	**20**	**25**	**45**	**16**	**8**	**2**	**2**	**137**	**14.6**	**–3**	**778**	**48.5**	**17:23**	**5**	**3**	**0**	**3**	**2**	**2**	**0**	**1**	**17:02**
2000-01	**Buffalo**	**NHL**	**75**	**19**	**24**	**43**	**26**	**3**	**2**	**5**	**160**	**11.9**	**–2**	**1470**	**48.3**	**19:06**	**13**	**4**	**4**	**8**	**2**	**2**	**0**	**2**	**18:30**
2001-02	**Buffalo**	**NHL**	**68**	**17**	**31**	**48**	**26**	**5**	**0**	**4**	**127**	**13.4**	**6**	**984**	**47.2**	**18:35**									
2002-03	**Buffalo**	**NHL**	**68**	**11**	**21**	**32**	**20**	**2**	**1**	**2**	**124**	**8.9**	**–13**	**923**	**49.0**	**18:29**									
	Dallas	**NHL**	**13**	**2**	**5**	**7**	**8**	**2**	**0**	**1**	**25**	**8.0**	**2**	**76**	**44.7**	**17:23**	**12**	**2**	**3**	**5**	**0**	**0**	**0**	**2**	**19:06**
2003-04	**Dallas**	**NHL**	**77**	**11**	**18**	**29**	**18**	**0**	**1**	**4**	**135**	**8.1**	**7**	**879**	**52.9**	**18:05**	**5**	**0**	**0**	**0**	**0**	**0**	**0**	**0**	**14:59**
2004-05			DID NOT PLAY																						
2005-06	**Dallas**	**NHL**	**78**	**15**	**21**	**36**	**44**	**0**	**1**	**2**	**123**	**12.2**	**9**	**649**	**50.1**	**16:29**	**5**	**1**	**1**	**2**	**0**	**0**	**1**	**0**	**17:33**
	NHL Totals		**975**	**236**	**313**	**549**	**372**	**77**	**9**	**44**	**1954**	**12.1**		**6715**	**49.5**	**17:58**	**100**	**27**	**28**	**55**	**18**	**10**	**1**	**9**	**16:49**

WHL West Second All-Star Team (1988, 1989) • WHL Rookie of the Year (1988) • WHL Player of the Year (1989)

Traded to **Florida** by **Winnipeg** with St. Louis' 6th round choice (previously acquired, later traded to Edmonton – later traded back to Winnipeg – Winnipeg selected Chris Kibermanis) in 1994 Entry Draft for Randy Gilhen, November 25, 1993. Traded to **Pittsburgh** by **Florida** with Jason Woolley for Chris Wells, November 19, 1996. Traded to **Buffalo** by **Pittsburgh** for Matthew Barnaby, March 11, 1999. Traded to **Dallas** by **Buffalo** for Michael Ryan and Dallas's 2nd round choice (Branislav Fabry) in 2003 Entry Draft, March 10, 2003.

BARNEY, Scott
(BAHR-nee, SKAWT)

Center. Shoots right. 6'4", 210 lbs. Born, Oshawa, Ont., March 27, 1979. Los Angeles' 3rd choice, 29th overall, in 1997 Entry Draft.

			Regular Season														Playoffs								
Season	Club	League	GP	G	A	Pts	PIM	PP	SH	GW	S	%	+/-	TF	F%	Min	GP	G	A	Pts	PIM	PP	SH	GW	Min
1994-95	North York	MTJHL	41	16	19	35	88																		
1995-96	Peterborough	OHL	60	22	24	46	52										24	6	8	14	38				
1996-97	Peterborough	OHL	64	21	33	54	110										9	0	3	3	16				
1997-98	Peterborough	OHL	62	44	32	76	60										4	1	0	1	6				
1998-99	Peterborough	OHL	44	41	26	67	80										5	4	1	5	4				
	Springfield	AHL	5	0	0	0	2										1	0	0	0	2				

			Regular Season														Playoffs								
Season	Club	League	GP	G	A	Pts	PIM	PP	SH	GW	S	%	+/-	TF	F%	Min	GP	G	A	Pts	PIM	PP	SH	GW	Min
99-2000			Did not play – injured																						
2000-01			Did not play – injured																						
2001-02			Did not play – injured																						
2002-03	**Los Angeles**	**NHL**	**5**	**0**	**0**	**0**	**0**	**0**	**0**	**0**	**5**	**0.0**	**–1**	**0**	**0.0**	**9:04**	....	....	....	....	....	....	....	....	....
	Manchester	AHL	57	13	5	18	74	....	....	....	....	....	....	....	....	....	....	....	....	....	....	....	....	....	....
2003-04	**Los Angeles**	**NHL**	**19**	**5**	**6**	**11**	**4**	**2**	**0**	**0**	**31**	**16.1**	**3**	**7**	**14.3**	**11:12**	....	....	....	....	....	....	....	....	....
	Manchester	AHL	44	20	14	34	28	....	....	....	....	....	....	....	....	....	6	2	3	5	8	....	....	....	....
2004-05			Did not play																						
2005-06	**Atlanta**	**NHL**	**3**	**0**	**0**	**0**	**0**	**0**	**0**	**0**	**4**	**0.0**	**–1**	**0**	**0.0**	**6:45**	....	....	....	....	....	....	....	....	....
	Chicago Wolves	AHL	53	32	19	51	56	....	....	....	....	....	....	....	....	....	....	....	....	....	....	....	....	....	....
	NHL Totals		**27**	**5**	**6**	**11**	**4**	**2**	**0**	**0**	**40**	**12.5**		**7**	**14.3**	**10:19**	....	....	....	....	....	....	....	....	....

• Missed entire 1999-2000, 2000-01 and 2001-02 seasons recovering from back injury suffered in training camp, September 28, 1999. Signed as a free agent by **Atlanta**, August 8, 2005.

BARTECKO, Lubos

(bahr-TESHK-oh, LOO-bohsh)

Left wing. Shoots left. 5'11", 200 lbs. Born, Kezmarok, Czech., July 14, 1976.

1994-95	HC SKP PS Poprad	Slovakia	3	1	0	1	0	....	....	....	....	....	....	....	....	....	....	....	....	....	....	....	....	....	....
1995-96	Chicoutimi	QMJHL	70	32	41	73	50	....	....	....	....	....	....	....	....	....	17	8	15	23	10	....	....	....	....
1996-97	Drummondville	QMJHL	58	40	51	91	49	....	....	....	....	....	....	....	....	....	8	1	8	9	4	....	....	....	....
1997-98	Worcester IceCats	AHL	34	10	12	22	24	....	....	....	....	....	....	....	....	....	10	4	2	6	2	....	....	....	....
1998-99	HC SKP Poprad	Slovakia	1	1	0	1	0	....	....	....	....	....	....	....	....	....	....	....	....	....	....	....	....	....	....
	St. Louis	**NHL**	**32**	**5**	**11**	**16**	**6**	**0**	**0**	**1**	**37**	**13.5**	**4**	**0**	**0.0**	**13:13**	**5**	**0**	**0**	**0**	**2**	**0**	**0**	**0**	**13:29**
	Worcester IceCats	AHL	49	14	24	38	22	....	....	....	....	....	....	....	....	....	....	....	....	....	....	....	....	....	....
99-2000	**St. Louis**	**NHL**	**67**	**16**	**23**	**39**	**51**	**3**	**0**	**3**	**75**	**21.3**	**24**	**10**	**50.0**	**13:33**	**7**	**1**	**1**	**2**	**0**	**0**	**0**	**0**	**12:02**
	Worcester IceCats	AHL	12	4	7	11	4	....	....	....	....	....	....	....	....	....	....	....	....	....	....	....	....	....	....
2000-01	**St. Louis**	**NHL**	**50**	**5**	**8**	**13**	**12**	**0**	**0**	**3**	**51**	**9.8**	**–1**	**2**	**50.0**	**10:25**	....	....	....	....	....	....	....	....	....
2001-02	**Atlanta**	**NHL**	**71**	**13**	**14**	**27**	**30**	**1**	**0**	**0**	**96**	**13.5**	**–15**	**4**	**25.0**	**14:28**	....	....	....	....	....	....	....	....	....
	Slovakia	Olympics	4	0	1	1	0	....	....	....	....	....	....	....	....	....	....	....	....	....	....	....	....	....	....
2002-03	**Atlanta**	**NHL**	**37**	**7**	**9**	**16**	**8**	**0**	**0**	**1**	**54**	**13.0**	**3**	**6**	**100.0**	**12:31**	....	....	....	....	....	....	....	....	....
2003-04	HC Sparta Praha	CzRep	25	12	8	20	45	....	....	....	....	....	....	....	....	....	13	2	4	6	26	....	....	....	....
2004-05	Dynamo Moscow	Russia	40	6	10	16	28	....	....	....	....	....	....	....	....	....	7	0	1	1	2	....	....	....	....
2005-06	Poprad	Slovakia	7	4	1	5	36	....	....	....	....	....	....	....	....	....	....	....	....	....	....	....	....	....	....
	Lulea HF	Sweden	50	14	26	40	32	....	....	....	....	....	....	....	....	....	6	3	3	6	35	....	....	....	....
	Slovakia	Olympics	6	0	0	0	6	....	....	....	....	....	....	....	....	....	....	....	....	....	....	....	....	....	....
	NHL Totals		**257**	**46**	**65**	**111**	**107**	**4**	**0**	**8**	**313**	**14.7**		**22**	**59.1**	**13:00**	**12**	**1**	**1**	**2**	**2**	**0**	**0**	**0**	**12:39**

Signed as a free agent by **St. Louis**, October 3, 1997. Traded to **Atlanta** by **St. Louis** for Buffalo's 4th round choice (previously acquired, St. Louis selected Igor Valeyev) in 2001 Entry Draft, June 23, 2001. • Missed majority of 2002-03 season recovering from wrist (November 2, 2002 vs. Florida) and groin (January 13, 2003 vs. Philadelphia) injuries. Signed as a free agent by **Sparta Praha** (CzRep), November 2, 2003. Signed as a free agent by **Dynamo Moscow** (Russia), August 24, 2004. Signed as a free agent by **Poprad** (Slovakia), September 5, 2005.

BARTOVIC, Milan

(BAHR-tuh-vihch, MIH-lan)

Right wing. Shoots left. 5'11", 197 lbs. Born, Trencin, Czech., April 9, 1981. Buffalo's 2nd choice, 35th overall, in 1999 Entry Draft.

1997-98	Dukla Trencin Jr.	Slovak-Jr.	26	2	6	8	27	....	....	....	....	....	....	....	....	....	....	....	....	....	....	....	....	....	....
1998-99	Dukla Trencin Jr.	Slovak-Jr.	46	36	35	71	62	....	....	....	....	....	....	....	....	....	6	9	3	12	10	....	....	....	....
99-2000	Tri-City	WHL	18	8	9	17	12	....	....	....	....	....	....	....	....	....	....	....	....	....	....	....	....	....	....
	Brandon	WHL	38	18	22	40	28	....	....	....	....	....	....	....	....	....	....	....	....	....	....	....	....	....	....
2000-01	Brandon	WHL	34	15	25	40	40	....	....	....	....	....	....	....	....	....	6	1	2	3	8	....	....	....	....
	Rochester	AHL	2	1	1	2	0	....	....	....	....	....	....	....	....	....	4	0	1	1	2	....	....	....	....
2001-02	Rochester	AHL	73	15	11	26	56	....	....	....	....	....	....	....	....	....	2	0	0	0	0	....	....	....	....
2002-03	**Buffalo**	**NHL**	**3**	**1**	**0**	**1**	**0**	**0**	**0**	**0**	**5**	**20.0**	**0**	**1**	**100.0**	**9:52**	....	....	....	....	....	....	....	....	....
	Rochester	AHL	74	18	10	28	84	....	....	....	....	....	....	....	....	....	3	0	0	0	0	....	....	....	....
2003-04	**Buffalo**	**NHL**	**23**	**1**	**8**	**9**	**18**	**0**	**0**	**0**	**30**	**3.3**	**1**	**2**	**100.0**	**12:53**	....	....	....	....	....	....	....	....	....
	Rochester	AHL	52	18	11	29	52	....	....	....	....	....	....	....	....	....	2	0	0	0	2	....	....	....	....
2004-05	Rochester	AHL	69	10	18	28	83	....	....	....	....	....	....	....	....	....	9	0	3	3	22	....	....	....	....
2005-06	**Chicago**	**NHL**	**24**	**1**	**6**	**7**	**8**	**0**	**0**	**0**	**35**	**2.9**	**0**	**1**	**0.0**	**8:50**	....	....	....	....	....	....	....	....	....
	Norfolk Admirals	AHL	49	10	14	24	34	....	....	....	....	....	....	....	....	....	3	0	0	0	8	....	....	....	....
	NHL Totals		**50**	**3**	**14**	**17**	**26**	**0**	**0**	**0**	**70**	**4.3**		**4**	**75.0**	**10:45**	....	....	....	....	....	....	....	....	....

• Missed majority of 2000-01 season recovering from shoulder injury suffered in game vs. Red Deer (WHL), October 10, 2000. Traded to **Chicago** by **Buffalo** for Michael Leighton, October 4, 2005.

BATES, Shawn

(BAYTS, SHAWN) **NYI**

Center. Shoots right. 6', 205 lbs. Born, Melrose, MA, April 3, 1975. Boston's 4th choice, 103rd overall, in 1993 Entry Draft.

1990-91	Medford	High-MA	22	18	43	61	6	....	....	....	....	....	....	....	....	....	....	....	....	....	....	....	....	....	....
1991-92	Medford	High-MA	22	38	41	79	10	....	....	....	....	....	....	....	....	....	....	....	....	....	....	....	....	....	....
1992-93	Medford	High-MA	25	49	46	95	20	....	....	....	....	....	....	....	....	....	....	....	....	....	....	....	....	....	....
1993-94	Boston University	H-East	41	10	19	29	24	....	....	....	....	....	....	....	....	....	....	....	....	....	....	....	....	....	....
1994-95	Boston University	H-East	38	18	12	30	48	....	....	....	....	....	....	....	....	....	....	....	....	....	....	....	....	....	....
1995-96	Boston University	H-East	40	28	22	50	54	....	....	....	....	....	....	....	....	....	....	....	....	....	....	....	....	....	....
1996-97	Boston University	H-East	41	17	18	35	64	....	....	....	....	....	....	....	....	....	....	....	....	....	....	....	....	....	....
1997-98	**Boston**	**NHL**	**13**	**2**	**0**	**2**	**2**	**0**	**0**	**0**	**12**	**16.7**	**–3**	....	....	....	....	....	....	....	....	....	....	....	....
	Providence Bruins	AHL	50	15	19	34	22	....	....	....	....	....	....	....	....	....	....	....	....	....	....	....	....	....	....
1998-99	**Boston**	**NHL**	**33**	**5**	**4**	**9**	**2**	**0**	**0**	**0**	**30**	**16.7**	**3**	**178**	**51.1**	**8:35**	**12**	**0**	**0**	**0**	**4**	**0**	**0**	**0**	**5:12**
	Providence Bruins	AHL	37	25	21	46	39	....	....	....	....	....	....	....	....	....	....	....	....	....	....	....	....	....	....
99-2000	**Boston**	**NHL**	**44**	**5**	**7**	**12**	**14**	**0**	**0**	**1**	**65**	**7.7**	**–17**	**460**	**47.0**	**10:52**	....	....	....	....	....	....	....	....	....
2000-01	**Boston**	**NHL**	**45**	**2**	**3**	**5**	**26**	**0**	**0**	**0**	**59**	**3.4**	**–12**	**413**	**50.6**	**9:19**	....	....	....	....	....	....	....	....	....
	Providence Bruins	AHL	11	5	8	13	12	....	....	....	....	....	....	....	....	....	8	2	6	8	8	....	....	....	....
2001-02	**NY Islanders**	**NHL**	**71**	**17**	**35**	**52**	**30**	**1**	**4**	**4**	**150**	**11.3**	**18**	**306**	**49.4**	**18:45**	**7**	**2**	**4**	**6**	**11**	**1**	**0**	**1**	**20:27**
2002-03	**NY Islanders**	**NHL**	**74**	**13**	**29**	**42**	**52**	**1**	**6**	**1**	**126**	**10.3**	**–9**	**398**	**57.0**	**18:26**	**5**	**1**	**0**	**1**	**0**	**1**	**0**	**0**	**18:36**
2003-04	**NY Islanders**	**NHL**	**69**	**9**	**23**	**32**	**46**	**0**	**1**	**1**	**115**	**7.8**	**–8**	**603**	**55.9**	**18:26**	**5**	**0**	**0**	**0**	**4**	**0**	**0**	**0**	**17:14**
2004-05			Did not play																						
2005-06	**NY Islanders**	**NHL**	**66**	**15**	**19**	**34**	**60**	**1**	**1**	**4**	**95**	**15.8**	**–11**	**1063**	**51.3**	**17:12**	....	....	....	....	....	....	....	....	....
	NHL Totals		**415**	**68**	**120**	**188**	**232**	**3**	**12**	**11**	**652**	**10.4**		**3421**	**51.9**	**15:38**	**29**	**3**	**4**	**7**	**19**	**2**	**0**	**1**	**13:16**

NCAA Championship All-Tournament Team (1995)

Signed as a free agent by **NY Islanders**, July 8, 2001.

BATTAGLIA, Bates

(buh-TAG-lee-ah, BAYTS) **TOR.**

Left wing. Shoots left. 6'2", 205 lbs. Born, Chicago, IL, December 13, 1975. Anaheim's 6th choice, 132nd overall, in 1994 Entry Draft.

1992-93	Team Illinois	MEHL	60	42	42	84	68	....	....	....	....	....	....	....	....	....	....	....	....	....	....	....	....	....	....
1993-94	Caledon	MTJHL	44	15	33	48	104	....	....	....	....	....	....	....	....	....	....	....	....	....	....	....	....	....	....
1994-95	Lake Superior	CCHA	38	6	14	20	34	....	....	....	....	....	....	....	....	....	....	....	....	....	....	....	....	....	....
1995-96	Lake Superior	CCHA	40	13	22	35	48	....	....	....	....	....	....	....	....	....	....	....	....	....	....	....	....	....	....
1996-97	Lake Superior	CCHA	38	12	27	39	80	....	....	....	....	....	....	....	....	....	....	....	....	....	....	....	....	....	....
1997-98	**Carolina**	**NHL**	**33**	**2**	**4**	**6**	**10**	**0**	**0**	**1**	**21**	**9.5**	**–1**	....	....	....	....	....	....	....	....	....	....	....	....
	New Haven	AHL	48	15	21	36	48	....	....	....	....	....	....	....	....	....	1	0	0	0	0	....	....	....	....
1998-99	**Carolina**	**NHL**	**60**	**7**	**11**	**18**	**97**	**0**	**0**	**0**	**52**	**13.5**	**7**	**144**	**39.6**	**9:53**	**6**	**0**	**3**	**3**	**8**	**0**	**0**	**0**	**15:22**
99-2000	**Carolina**	**NHL**	**77**	**16**	**18**	**34**	**39**	**3**	**0**	**3**	**86**	**18.6**	**20**	**23**	**26.1**	**15:12**	....	....	....	....	....	....	....	....	....
2000-01	**Carolina**	**NHL**	**80**	**12**	**15**	**27**	**76**	**2**	**0**	**3**	**133**	**9.0**	**–14**	**5**	**60.0**	**14:28**	**6**	**0**	**2**	**2**	**2**	**0**	**0**	**0**	**11:25**
2001-02	**Carolina**	**NHL**	**82**	**21**	**25**	**46**	**44**	**5**	**1**	**2**	**167**	**12.6**	**–6**	**12**	**33.3**	**19:05**	**23**	**5**	**9**	**14**	**14**	**1**	**0**	**1**	**20:42**
2002-03	**Carolina**	**NHL**	**70**	**5**	**14**	**19**	**90**	**0**	**1**	**1**	**96**	**5.2**	**–17**	**16**	**25.0**	**18:39**	....	....	....	....	....	....	....	....	....
	Colorado	**NHL**	**13**	**1**	**5**	**6**	**10**	**1**	**0**	**1**	**27**	**3.7**	**–2**	**3**	**0.0**	**15:19**	**7**	**0**	**2**	**2**	**4**	**0**	**0**	**0**	**14:39**
2003-04	**Colorado**	**NHL**	**4**	**0**	**1**	**1**	**4**	**0**	**0**	**0**	**1**	**0.0**	**–1**	**1**	**100.0**	**11:04**	....	....	....	....	....	....	....	....	....
	Washington	**NHL**	**66**	**4**	**6**	**10**	**38**	**0**	**0**	**1**	**69**	**5.8**	**–23**	**116**	**32.8**	**13:37**	....	....	....	....	....	....	....	....	....
2004-05	Mississippi	ECHL	25	6	11	17	24	....	....	....	....	....	....	....	....	....	4	0	0	0	10	....	....	....	....
2005-06	Toronto Marlies	AHL	79	20	47	67	86	....	....	....	....	....	....	....	....	....	5	1	1	2	6	....	....	....	....
	NHL Totals		**485**	**68**	**99**	**167**	**408**	**11**	**2**	**12**	**652**	**10.4**		**320**	**35.3**	**15:20**	**42**	**5**	**16**	**21**	**28**	**1**	**0**	**1**	**17:36**

Traded to **Hartford** by **Anaheim** with Anaheim's 4th round choice (Josef Vasicek) in 1998 Entry Draft for Mark Janssens, March 18, 1997. Rights transferred to **Carolina** after **Hartford** franchise relocated, June 25, 1997. Traded to **Colorado** by **Carolina** for Radim Vrbata, March 11, 2003. Traded to **Washington** by **Colorado** with Jonas Johansson for Steve Konowalchuk and Washington's 3rd round choice (later traded to Carolina – Carolina selected Casey Borer) in 2004 Entry Draft, October 22, 2003. Signed as a free agent by **Mississippi** (ECHL), February 21, 2005. Signed to a PTO (tryout) contract by **Toronto** (AHL), October 2, 2005. Signed as a free agent by **Toronto**, July 8, 2006.

BAUMGARTNER, Nolan

(BAWM-gahrt-nuhr, NOH-lan) **PHI.**

Defense. Shoots right. 6'2", 205 lbs. Born, Calgary, Alta., March 23, 1976. Washington's 1st choice, 10th overall, in 1994 Entry Draft.

			Regular Season														Playoffs								
Season	Club	League	GP	G	A	Pts	PIM	PP	SH	GW	S	%	+/-	TF	F%	Min	GP	G	A	Pts	PIM	PP	SH	GW	Min
1991-92	Cgy. AAA Flames	AMHL	39	11	29	40	40																		
1992-93	Kamloops Blazers	WHL	43	0	5	5	30										11	1	1	2	0				
1993-94	Kamloops Blazers	WHL	69	13	42	55	109										19	3	14	17	33				
1994-95	Kamloops Blazers	WHL	62	8	36	44	71										21	4	13	17	16				
1995-96	Kamloops Blazers	WHL	28	13	15	28	45										16	1	9	10	26				
	Washington	**NHL**	**1**	**0**	**0**	**0**	**0**	**0**	**0**	**0**	**0**	**0.0**	**–1**				**1**	**0**	**0**	**0**	**10**	**0**	**0**	**0**	
1996-97	Portland Pirates	AHL	8	2	2	4	4																		
1997-98	**Washington**	**NHL**	**4**	**0**	**1**	**1**	**0**	**0**	**0**	**0**	**4**	**0.0**	**0**												
	Portland Pirates	AHL	70	2	24	26	70										10	1	4	5	10				
1998-99	**Washington**	**NHL**	**5**	**0**	**0**	**0**	**0**	**0**	**0**	**0**	**1**	**0.0**	**–3**	**0**	**0.0**	**8:41**									
	Portland Pirates	AHL	38	5	14	19	62																		
99-2000	**Washington**	**NHL**	**8**	**0**	**1**	**1**	**2**	**0**	**0**	**0**	**6**	**0.0**	**1**	**0**	**0.0**	**10:31**									
	Portland Pirates	AHL	71	5	18	23	56										4	1	2	3	10				
2000-01	**Chicago**	**NHL**	**8**	**0**	**0**	**0**	**6**	**0**	**0**	**0**	**7**	**0.0**	**–4**	**2**	**50.0**	**12:40**									
	Norfolk Admirals	AHL	63	5	28	33	75										9	2	3	5	11				
2001-02	Norfolk Admirals	AHL	76	10	24	34	72										4	0	1	1	2				
2002-03	**Vancouver**	**NHL**	**8**	**1**	**2**	**3**	**4**	**1**	**0**	**0**	**7**	**14.3**	**4**	**0**	**0.0**	**11:36**	**2**	**0**	**0**	**0**	**0**	**0**	**0**	**0**	**11:06**
	Manitoba Moose	AHL	59	8	31	39	82										1	0	0	0	4				
2003-04	**Pittsburgh**	**NHL**	**5**	**0**	**0**	**0**	**2**	**0**	**0**	**0**	**6**	**0.0**	**–7**	**0**	**0.0**	**19:20**									
	Vancouver	**NHL**	**9**	**0**	**3**	**3**	**2**	**0**	**0**	**0**	**9**	**0.0**	**3**	**0**	**0.0**	**11:52**									
	Manitoba Moose	AHL	55	6	21	27	101																		
2004-05	Manitoba Moose	AHL	78	9	30	39	51										14	0	4	4	10				
2005-06	**Vancouver**	**NHL**	**70**	**5**	**29**	**34**	**30**	**4**	**1**	**1**	**73**	**6.8**	**11**	**1**	**0.0**	**16:29**									
	NHL Totals		**118**	**6**	**36**	**42**	**46**	**5**	**1**	**1**	**113**	**5.3**		**3**	**33.3**	**14:52**	**3**	**0**	**0**	**0**	**10**	**0**	**0**	**0**	**11:06**

Memorial Cup Tournement All-Star Team (1994, 1995) • WHL West First All-Star Team (1995, 1996) • Canadian Major Junior First All-Star Team (1995) • Canadian Major Junior Defenseman of the Year (1995)

Traded to **Chicago** by **Washington** for Remi Royer, July 20, 2000. Signed as a free agent by **Vancouver**, July 11, 2002. Claimed by **Pittsburgh** from **Vancouver** in Waiver Draft, October 3, 2003. Claimed on waivers by **Vancouver** from **Pittsburgh**, November 1, 2003. Signed as a free agent by **Philadelphia**, July 1, 2006.

BAYDA, Ryan

(BAY-duh, RIGH-uhn) **CAR.**

Left wing. Shoots left. 5'11", 185 lbs. Born, Saskatoon, Sask., December 9, 1980. Carolina's 2nd choice, 80th overall, in 2000 Entry Draft.

Season	Club	League	GP	G	A	Pts	PIM	PP	SH	GW	S	%	+/-	TF	F%	Min	GP	G	A	Pts	PIM	PP	SH	GW	Min
1995-96	Saskatoon Flyers	SMHL	60	85	74	159	85																		
1996-97	Sask. Contacts	SMHL	44	22	23	45	18																		
1997-98	Sask. Contacts	SMHL	41	29	49	78	103																		
1998-99	Vernon Vipers	BCHL	45	24	58	82	15																		
99-2000	North Dakota	WCHA	44	17	23	40	30																		
2000-01	North Dakota	WCHA	46	25	34	59	48																		
2001-02	North Dakota	WCHA	37	19	28	47	52																		
	Lowell	AHL	3	1	1	2	0										5	3	0	3	0				
2002-03	**Carolina**	**NHL**	**25**	**4**	**10**	**14**	**16**	**0**	**0**	**1**	**49**	**8.2**	**–5**	**2**	**100.0**	**17:15**									
	Lowell	AHL	53	11	32	43	32																		
2003-04	**Carolina**	**NHL**	**44**	**3**	**3**	**6**	**22**	**0**	**0**	**1**	**65**	**4.6**	**–14**	**4**	**0.0**	**10:57**									
	Lowell	AHL	34	7	15	22	28																		
2004-05	Lowell	AHL	80	13	27	40	91										9	3	3	6	4				
2005-06	Manitoba Moose	AHL	59	13	25	38	52										13	1	6	7	27				
	NHL Totals		**69**	**7**	**13**	**20**	**38**	**0**	**0**	**2**	**114**	**6.1**		**6**	**33.3**	**13:14**									

BCHL Rookie of the Year (1999) • WCHA All-Rookie Team (2000) • WCHA Second All-Star Team (2001, 2002)

BEAUCHEMIN, Francois

(boh-sheh-MEH, frahn-SWUH) **ANA.**

Defense. Shoots left. 6', 214 lbs. Born, Sorel, Que., June 4, 1980. Montreal's 3rd choice, 75th overall, in 1998 Entry Draft.

Season	Club	League	GP	G	A	Pts	PIM	PP	SH	GW	S	%	+/-	TF	F%	Min	GP	G	A	Pts	PIM	PP	SH	GW	Min
1995-96	Richelieu Riverains	QAAA	40	9	23	32	59																		
1996-97	Laval Titan	QMJHL	66	7	21	28	132										3	0	0	0	2				
1997-98	Laval Titan	QMJHL	70	12	35	47	132										16	1	3	4	23				
1998-99	Acadie-Bathurst	QMJHL	31	4	17	21	53										23	2	16	18	55				
99-2000	Acadie-Bathurst	QMJHL	38	11	36	47	64																		
	Moncton Wildcats	QMJHL	33	8	31	39	35										16	2	11	13	14				
2000-01	Quebec Citadelles	AHL	56	3	6	9	44																		
2001-02	Quebec Citadelles	AHL	56	8	11	19	88										3	0	1	1	0				
	Mississippi	ECHL	7	1	3	4	2																		
2002-03	**Montreal**	**NHL**	**1**	**0**	**0**	**0**	**0**	**0**	**0**	**0**	**1**	**0.0**	**–1**	**0**	**0.0**	**17:11**									
	Hamilton	AHL	75	7	21	28	92										23	1	9	10	16				
2003-04	Hamilton	AHL	77	9	27	36	57										10	2	4	6	18				
2004-05	Syracuse Crunch	AHL	72	3	27	30	55																		
2005-06	**Columbus**	**NHL**	**11**	**0**	**2**	**2**	**11**	**0**	**0**	**0**	**16**	**0.0**	**–6**	**0**	**0.0**	**17:16**									
	Anaheim	**NHL**	**61**	**8**	**26**	**34**	**41**	**4**	**0**	**3**	**121**	**6.6**	**8**	**1**	**0.0**	**24:14**	**16**	**3**	**6**	**9**	**11**	**3**	**0**	**0**	**27:26**
	NHL Totals		**73**	**8**	**28**	**36**	**52**	**4**	**0**	**3**	**138**	**5.8**		**1**	**0.0**	**23:05**	**16**	**3**	**6**	**9**	**11**	**3**	**0**	**0**	**27:26**

QMJHL All-Rookie Team (1997) • QMJHL Second All-Star Team (2000)

Claimed on waivers by **Columbus** from **Montreal**, September 15, 2004. Traded to **Anaheim** by **Columbus** with Tyler Wright for Sergei Fedorov and Anaheim's 5th round choice (Maxime Frechette) in 2006 Entry Draft, November 15, 2005.

BEAUDOIN, Eric

(boh-DWEH, AIR-ihk)

Left wing. Shoots left. 6'5", 210 lbs. Born, Ottawa, Ont., May 3, 1980. Tampa Bay's 4th choice, 92nd overall, in 1998 Entry Draft.

Season	Club	League	GP	G	A	Pts	PIM	PP	SH	GW	S	%	+/-	TF	F%	Min	GP	G	A	Pts	PIM	PP	SH	GW	Min
1996-97	Ott. Jr. Senators	CJHL	54	12	19	31	55																		
1997-98	Guelph Storm	OHL	62	9	13	22	43										12	3	2	5	4				
1998-99	Guelph Storm	OHL	66	28	43	71	79										11	5	3	8	12				
99-2000	Guelph Storm	OHL	68	38	34	72	126										6	3	0	3	2				
2000-01	Louisville Panthers	AHL	71	15	10	25	78																		
2001-02	**Florida**	**NHL**	**8**	**1**	**3**	**4**	**4**	**0**	**0**	**1**	**11**	**9.1**	**–2**	**1**	**0.0**	**17:27**									
	Utah Grizzlies	AHL	44	5	16	21	83																		
2002-03	**Florida**	**NHL**	**15**	**0**	**1**	**1**	**25**	**0**	**0**	**0**	**11**	**0.0**	**–7**	**27**	**29.6**	**9:52**									
	San Antonio	AHL	41	14	23	37	36										3	1	0	1	0				
2003-04	**Florida**	**NHL**	**30**	**2**	**4**	**6**	**12**	**0**	**0**	**0**	**30**	**6.7**	**–6**	**13**	**30.8**	**10:19**									
	San Antonio	AHL	38	20	22	42	45																		
2004-05	San Antonio	AHL	32	6	4	10	21																		
	Edmonton	AHL	24	3	1	4	9																		
2005-06	Jokerit Helsinki	Finland	11	1	2	3	14																		
	HPK Hameenlinna	Finland	2	0	1	1	4																		
	Mora IK	Sweden	32	2	9	11	24										2	0	0	0	0				
	NHL Totals		**53**	**3**	**8**	**11**	**41**	**0**	**0**	**1**	**52**	**5.8**		**41**	**29.3**	**11:16**									

Traded to **Florida** by **Tampa Bay** for Florida's 7th round choice (Marek Priechodsky) in 2000 Entry Draft, June 1, 2000. • Loaned to **Edmonton** (AHL) by **Florida** (San Antonio-AHL), January 3, 2005. Signed as a free agent by **Jokerit Helsinki** (Finland), October 3, 2005. Signed as a free agent by **Mora** (Sweden), November 11, 2005.

BEECH, Kris

(BEECH, KRIHS) **WSH.**

Center. Shoots left. 6'2", 208 lbs. Born, Salmon Arm, B.C., February 5, 1981. Washington's 1st choice, 7th overall, in 1999 Entry Draft.

Season	Club	League	GP	G	A	Pts	PIM	PP	SH	GW	S	%	+/-	TF	F%	Min	GP	G	A	Pts	PIM	PP	SH	GW	Min
1996-97	Sicamous Eagles	KIJHL	49	34	36	70	80																		
	Calgary Hitmen	WHL	8	1	1	2	0																		
1997-98	Calgary Hitmen	WHL	58	10	25	35	24										12	4	5	9	32				
1998-99	Calgary Hitmen	WHL	68	26	41	67	103										6	1	4	5	8				
99-2000	Calgary Hitmen	WHL	66	32	54	86	99										5	3	5	8	16				
2000-01	**Washington**	**NHL**	**4**	**0**	**0**	**0**	**2**	**0**	**0**	**0**	**0**	**0.0**	**–2**	**25**	**36.0**	**7:29**									
	Calgary Hitmen	WHL	40	22	44	66	103										10	2	8	10	26				
2001-02	**Pittsburgh**	**NHL**	**79**	**10**	**15**	**25**	**45**	**2**	**0**	**0**	**126**	**7.9**	**–25**	**604**	**45.2**	**13:33**									

			Regular Season														Playoffs								
Season	Club	League	GP	G	A	Pts	PIM	PP	SH	GW	S	%	+/-	TF	F%	Min	GP	G	A	Pts	PIM	PP	SH	GW	Min
2002-03	Pittsburgh	NHL	12	0	1	1	6	0	0	0	6	0.0	–3	96	42.7	10:34									
	Wilkes-Barre	AHL	50	19	24	43	76										5	1	1	2	0				
2003-04	Pittsburgh	NHL	4	0	1	1	6	0	0	0	6	0.0	0	45	40.0	12:32									
	Wilkes-Barre	AHL	53	20	25	45	97										22	9	6	15	22				
2004-05	Wilkes-Barre	AHL	68	14	48	62	146										11	4	6	10	14				
2005-06	Nashville	NHL	5	1	2	3	0	0	0	0	6	16.7	1	81	54.3	14:40									
	Milwaukee	AHL	48	18	32	50	48																		
	Washington	NHL	5	0	0	0	4	0	0	0	6	0.0	0	36	50.0	9:24									
	Hershey Bears	AHL	10	8	6	14	6										21	14	14	28	30				
	NHL Totals		109	11	19	30	63	2	0	0	150	7.3		887	45.4	12:50									

Traded to **Pittsburgh** by **Washington** with Michal Sivek, Ross Lupaschuk and future considerations for Jaromir Jagr and Frantisek Kucera, July 11, 2001. Traded to **Nashville** by **Pittsburgh** for Nashville's 4th round choice (later traded to Florida - Florida selected Derrick Lapoint) in 2006 Entry Draft, September 9, 2005. Traded to **Washington** by **Nashville** with Nashville's 1st round choice (Simeon Varlamov) in 2006 Entry Draft for Brendan Witt, March 9, 2006.

BEGIN, Steve
(bay-ZHIN, STEEV) **MTL.**

Center. Shoots left. 6', 188 lbs. Born, Trois-Rivieres, Que., June 14, 1978. Calgary's 3rd choice, 40th overall, in 1996 Entry Draft.

Season	Club	League	GP	G	A	Pts	PIM	PP	SH	GW	S	%	+/-	TF	F%	Min	GP	G	A	Pts	PIM	PP	SH	GW	Min
1993-94	Cap-d-Madelaine	QAAA	8	0	1	1	6										2	0	0	0	0				
1994-95	Cap-d-Madelaine	QAAA	35	9	15	24	48										3	0	0	0	2				
1995-96	Val-d'Or Foreurs	QMJHL	64	13	23	36	218										13	1	3	4	33				
1996-97	Val-d'Or Foreurs	QMJHL	58	13	33	46	229										10	0	3	3	8				
	Saint John Flames	AHL															4	0	2	2	6				
1997-98	Calgary	NHL	5	0	0	0	23	0	0	0	2	0.0	0												
	Val-d'Or Foreurs	QMJHL	35	18	17	35	73										15	2	12	14	34				
1998-99	Saint John Flames	AHL	73	11	9	20	156										7	2	0	2	18				
99-2000	Calgary	NHL	13	1	1	2	18	0	0	0	3	33.3	–3	19	47.4	7:13									
	Saint John Flames	AHL	47	13	12	25	99																		
2000-01	Calgary	NHL	4	0	0	0	21	0	0	0	3	0.0	0	0	0.0	6:04									
	Saint John Flames	AHL	58	14	14	28	109										19	10	7	17	18				
2001-02	Calgary	NHL	51	7	5	12	79	1	0	0	65	10.8	–3	129	53.5	9:25									
2002-03	Calgary	NHL	50	3	1	4	51	0	0	1	59	5.1	–7	50	60.0	9:13									
2003-04	Montreal	NHL	52	10	5	15	41	0	1	1	91	11.0	6	436	48.6	12:32	9	0	1	1	10	0	0	0	12:26
2004-05	Hamilton	AHL	21	10	3	13	20										4	0	2	2	8				
2005-06	Montreal	NHL	76	11	12	23	113	1	2	2	134	8.2	9	573	50.1	14:19	2	0	0	0	2	0	0	0	13:42
	NHL Totals		251	32	24	56	346	2	3	4	357	9.0		1207	50.3	11:23	11	0	1	1	12	0	0	0	12:40

Jack A. Butterfield Trophy (Playoff MVP – AHL) (2001)
Traded to **Buffalo** by **Calgary** with Chris Drury for Steve Reinprecht and Rhett Warrener, July 3, 2003. Claimed by **Montreal** from **Buffalo** in Waiver Draft, October 3, 2003.

BELAK, Wade
(BEE-lak, WAYD) **TOR.**

Right wing. Shoots right. 6'5", 221 lbs. Born, Saskatoon, Sask., July 3, 1976. Quebec's 1st choice, 12th overall, in 1994 Entry Draft.

Season	Club	League	GP	G	A	Pts	PIM	PP	SH	GW	S	%	+/-	TF	F%	Min	GP	G	A	Pts	PIM	PP	SH	GW	Min
1991-92	North Battleford	SMBHL	57	6	20	26	186																		
1992-93	North Battleford	SJHL	50	5	15	20	146																		
	Saskatoon Blades	WHL	7	0	0	0	23										7	0	0	0	0				
1993-94	Saskatoon Blades	WHL	69	4	13	17	226										16	2	2	4	43				
1994-95	Saskatoon Blades	WHL	72	4	14	18	290										9	0	0	0	36				
	Cornwall Aces	AHL															11	1	2	3	40				
1995-96	Saskatoon Blades	WHL	63	3	15	18	207										4	0	0	0	9				
	Cornwall Aces	AHL	5	0	0	0	18										2	0	0	0	2				
1996-97	Colorado	NHL	5	0	0	0	11	0	0	0	1	0.0	–1												
	Hershey Bears	AHL	65	1	7	8	320										16	0	1	1	61				
1997-98	Colorado	NHL	8	1	1	2	27	0	0	1	2	50.0	–3												
	Hershey Bears	AHL	11	0	0	0	30																		
1998-99	Colorado	NHL	22	0	0	0	71	0	0	0	5	0.0	–2	0	0.0	6:48									
	Hershey Bears	AHL	17	0	1	1	49																		
	Calgary	NHL	9	0	1	1	23	0	0	0	2	0.0	3	0	0.0	10:46									
	Saint John Flames	AHL	12	0	2	2	43										6	0	1	1	23				
99-2000	Calgary	NHL	40	0	2	2	122	0	0	0	11	0.0	–4	1	0.0	7:33									
2000-01	Calgary	NHL	23	0	0	0	79	0	0	0	8	0.0	–2	0	0.0	6:54									
	Toronto	NHL	16	1	1	2	31	0	0	0	8	12.5	–4	0	0.0	13:38									
2001-02	Toronto	NHL	63	1	3	4	142	0	0	0	47	2.1	2	0	0.0	9:14	16	1	0	1	18	0	0	0	7:28
2002-03	Toronto	NHL	55	3	6	9	196	0	0	0	33	9.1	–2	0	0.0	10:50	2	0	0	0	4	0	0	0	8:22
2003-04	Toronto	NHL	34	1	1	2	109	0	0	0	15	6.7	0	0	0.0	7:00	4	0	0	0	14	0	0	0	9:59
2004-05	Coventry Blaze	Britain	20	3	5	8	109										8	1	1	2	16				
2005-06	Toronto	NHL	55	0	3	3	109	0	0	0	16	0.0	–13	0	0.0	9:59									
	NHL Totals		330	7	18	25	920	0	0	1	148	4.7		1	0.0	9:07	22	1	0	1	36	0	0	0	8:00

Rights transferred to **Colorado** after **Quebec** franchise relocated, June 21, 1995. Traded to **Calgary** by **Colorado** with Rene Corbet, Robyn Regehr and Colorado's 2nd round compensatory choice (Jarret Stoll) in 2000 Entry Draft for Theoren Fleury and Chris Dingman, February 28, 1999. • Missed majority of 1999-2000 and 2000-01 seasons recovering from shoulder injury suffered in game vs. Colorado, February 10, 2000. Claimed on waivers by **Toronto** from **Calgary**, February 16, 2001. • Missed majority of 2003-04 season recovering from abdomen (November 20, 2003 vs. Edmonton) and knee (January 6, 2004 vs. Nashville) injuries. Signed as a free agent by **Coventry** (Britain), November 8, 2004.

BELANGER, Eric
(buh-LAWN-zhay, AIR-ihk) **L.A.**

Center. Shoots left. 6', 185 lbs. Born, Sherbrooke, Que., December 16, 1977. Los Angeles' 5th choice, 96th overall, in 1996 Entry Draft.

Season	Club	League	GP	G	A	Pts	PIM	PP	SH	GW	S	%	+/-	TF	F%	Min	GP	G	A	Pts	PIM	PP	SH	GW	Min
1993-94	Magog	QAAA	32	19	24	43	24										13	5	6	11	36				
1994-95	Beauport	QMJHL	71	12	28	40	24										18	5	9	14	25				
1995-96	Beauport	QMJHL	59	35	48	83	18										20	13	14	27	6				
1996-97	Beauport	QMJHL	31	13	37	50	30																		
	Rimouski Oceanic	QMJHL	31	26	41	67	36										4	2	3	5	10				
1997-98	Fredericton	AHL	56	17	34	51	28										4	2	1	3	2				
1998-99	Springfield	AHL	33	8	18	26	10										3	0	1	1	2				
	Long Beach	IHL	1	0	0	0	0																		
99-2000	Lowell	AHL	65	15	25	40	20										7	3	3	6	2				
2000-01	Los Angeles	NHL	62	9	12	21	16	1	2	1	80	11.3	14	849	56.4	13:25	13	1	4	5	2	0	0	1	13:47
	Lowell	AHL	13	8	10	18	4																		
2001-02	Los Angeles	NHL	53	8	16	24	21	2	1	1	67	11.9	2	882	57.7	14:33	7	0	0	0	4	0	0	0	12:57
2002-03	Los Angeles	NHL	62	16	19	35	26	0	3	1	114	14.0	–5	1143	51.8	17:42									
2003-04	Los Angeles	NHL	81	13	20	33	44	0	1	2	132	9.8	–16	1418	53.7	17:01									
2004-05	HC Forst Bolzano	Italy	12	13	10	23	20										9	3	7	10	33				
2005-06	Los Angeles	NHL	65	17	20	37	62	5	0	1	119	14.3	–5	1179	49.0	17:33									
	NHL Totals		323	63	87	150	169	8	7	6	512	12.3		5471	53.4	16:10	20	1	4	5	6	0	0	1	13:30

Signed as a free agent by **Bolzano** (Italy), December 22, 2004.

BELANGER, Ken
(buh-LAWN-zhay, KEHN)

Left wing. Shoots left. 6'4", 225 lbs. Born, Sault Ste. Marie, Ont., May 14, 1974. Hartford's 7th choice, 153rd overall, in 1992 Entry Draft.

Season	Club	League	GP	G	A	Pts	PIM	PP	SH	GW	S	%	+/-	TF	F%	Min	GP	G	A	Pts	PIM	PP	SH	GW	Min
1990-91	Soo Legion	NOHA	43	24	29	53	169																		
1991-92	Ottawa 67's	OHL	51	4	4	8	174										11	0	0	0	24				
1992-93	Ottawa 67's	OHL	34	6	12	18	139																		
	Guelph Storm	OHL	29	10	14	24	86										5	2	1	3	14				
1993-94	Guelph Storm	OHL	55	11	22	33	185										9	2	3	5	30				
1994-95	St. John's	AHL	47	5	5	10	246										4	0	0	0	30				
	Toronto	NHL	3	0	0	0	9	0	0	0	1	0.0	0												
1995-96	St. John's	AHL	40	16	14	30	222																		
	NY Islanders	NHL	7	0	0	0	27	0	0	0	0	0.0	–2												
1996-97	NY Islanders	NHL	18	0	2	2	102	0	0	0	5	0.0	–1												
	Kentucky	AHL	38	10	12	22	164										4	0	1	1	27				
1997-98	NY Islanders	NHL	37	3	1	4	101	0	0	1	10	30.0	1												
1998-99	NY Islanders	NHL	9	1	1	2	30	0	0	0	3	33.3	1	0	0.0	5:05									
	Boston	NHL	45	1	4	5	152	0	0	0	16	6.3	–2	1	0.0	4:38	12	1	0	1	16	0	0	0	5:11

			Regular Season														Playoffs								
Season	Club	League	GP	G	A	Pts	PIM	PP	SH	GW	S	%	+/-	TF	F%	Min	GP	G	A	Pts	PIM	PP	SH	GW	Min
99-2000	**Boston**	**NHL**	**37**	**2**	**2**	**4**	**44**	**0**	**0**	**0**	**20**	**10.0**	**–4**	**1**	**0.0**	**5:17**	....	....	....	....	....	....	....	....	....
2000-01	**Boston**	**NHL**	**40**	**2**	**2**	**4**	**121**	**0**	**0**	**1**	**35**	**5.7**	**–6**	**1**	**100.0**	**7:06**	....	....	....	....	....	....	....	....	....
	Providence Bruins	AHL	10	1	4	5	47	....	....	....	....	....	....	....	....	....	2	0	0	0	4	....	....	....	....
2001-02	**Los Angeles**	**NHL**	**43**	**2**	**0**	**2**	**85**	**0**	**0**	**0**	**22**	**9.1**	**–5**	**0**	**0.0**	**4:22**	....	....	....	....	....	....	....	....	....
2002-03	**Los Angeles**	**NHL**	**4**	**0**	**0**	**0**	**17**	**0**	**0**	**0**	**0**	**0.0**	**0**	**0**	**0.0**	**4:03**	....	....	....	....	....	....	....	....	....
2003-04	**Los Angeles**	**NHL**	DID NOT PLAY – INJURED																						
2004-05	Adirondack	UHL	1	0	0	0	5	....	....	....	....	....	....	....	....	....	....	....	....	....	....	....	....	....	....
2005-06	**Los Angeles**	**NHL**	**5**	**0**	**0**	**0**	**7**	**0**	**0**	**0**	**0**	**0.0**	**–1**	**0**	**0.0**	**3:39**	....	....	....	....	....	....	....	....	....
	NHL Totals		**248**	**11**	**12**	**23**	**695**	**0**	**0**	**2**	**112**	**9.8**		**3**	**33.3**	**5:14**	**12**	**1**	**0**	**1**	**16**	**0**	**0**	**0**	**5:11**

Traded to **Toronto** by **Hartford** for Toronto's 9th round choice (Matt Ball) in 1994 Entry Draft, March 18, 1994. Traded to **NY Islanders** by **Toronto** with Damian Rhodes for future considerations (Kirk Muller and Don Beaupre, January 23, 1996), January 23, 1996. Traded to **Boston** by **NY Islanders** for Ted Donato, November 7, 1998. • Missed majority of 1999-2000 season recovering from head injury suffered in game vs. Toronto, November 11, 1999. Signed as a free agent by **Los Angeles**, July 2, 2001. • Missed majority of 2002-03 season and entire 2003-04 season recovering from head injury suffered in game vs. San Jose, November 5, 2002. Signed as a free agent by **Adirondack** (UHL), December 30, 2004. • Officially announced retirement, November 14, 2005.

BELL, Brendan

(BEHL, BREHN-duhn) **TOR.**

Defense. Shoots left. 6'1", 205 lbs. Born, Ottawa, Ont., March 31, 1983. Toronto's 3rd choice, 65th overall, in 2001 Entry Draft.

1998-99	Ott. Jr. Senators	CJHL	54	7	20	27	46	....	....	....	....	....	....	....	....	....	....	....	....	....	....	....	....	....	....
99-2000	Ottawa 67's	OHL	48	1	32	33	34	....	....	....	....	....	....	....	....	....	5	0	1	1	4	....	....	....	....
2000-01	Ottawa 67's	OHL	68	7	32	39	59	....	....	....	....	....	....	....	....	....	20	1	11	12	22	....	....	....	....
2001-02	Ottawa 67's	OHL	67	10	36	46	56	....	....	....	....	....	....	....	....	....	13	2	5	7	25	....	....	....	....
2002-03	Ottawa 67's	OHL	55	14	39	53	46	....	....	....	....	....	....	....	....	....	23	8	19	27	25	....	....	....	....
2003-04	St. John's	AHL	74	7	18	25	72	....	....	....	....	....	....	....	....	....	....	....	....	....	....	....	....	....	....
2004-05	St. John's	AHL	75	6	25	31	57	....	....	....	....	....	....	....	....	....	5	0	1	1	2	....	....	....	....
2005-06	**Toronto**	**NHL**	**1**	**0**	**0**	**0**	**0**	**0**	**0**	**0**	**2**	**0.0**	**0**	**0**	**0.0**	**14:00**	....	....	....	....	....	....	....	....	....
	Toronto Marlies	AHL	70	6	37	43	99	....	....	....	....	....	....	....	....	....	5	0	4	4	10	....	....	....	....
	NHL Totals		**1**	**0**	**0**	**0**	**0**	**0**	**0**	**0**	**2**	**0.0**		**0**	**0.0**	**14:00**	....	....	....	....	....	....	....	....	....

OHL First All-Star Team (2003) • Canadian Major Junior First All-Star Team (2003) • Canadian Major Junior Defenseman of the Year (2003)

BELL, Mark

(BEHL, MAHRK) **S.J.**

Center. Shoots left. 6'4", 205 lbs. Born, St. Paul's, Ont., August 5, 1980. Chicago's 1st choice, 8th overall, in 1998 Entry Draft.

1995-96	Stratford Cullitons	OHA-B	47	8	15	23	32	....	....	....	....	....	....	....	....	....	....	....	....	....	....	....	....	....	....
1996-97	Ottawa 67's	OHL	65	8	12	20	40	....	....	....	....	....	....	....	....	....	24	4	7	11	13	....	....	....	....
1997-98	Ottawa 67's	OHL	55	34	26	60	87	....	....	....	....	....	....	....	....	....	13	6	5	11	14	....	....	....	....
1998-99	Ottawa 67's	OHL	44	29	26	55	69	....	....	....	....	....	....	....	....	....	9	6	5	11	8	....	....	....	....
99-2000	Ottawa 67's	OHL	48	34	38	72	95	....	....	....	....	....	....	....	....	....	2	0	1	1	0	....	....	....	....
2000-01	**Chicago**	**NHL**	**13**	**0**	**1**	**1**	**4**	**0**	**0**	**0**	**14**	**0.0**	**0**	**141**	**48.9**	**12:00**	....	....	....	....	....	....	....	....	....
	Norfolk Admirals	AHL	61	15	27	42	126	....	....	....	....	....	....	....	....	....	9	4	3	7	10	....	....	....	....
2001-02	**Chicago**	**NHL**	**80**	**12**	**16**	**28**	**124**	**1**	**0**	**1**	**120**	**10.0**	**–6**	**47**	**42.6**	**12:39**	**5**	**0**	**0**	**0**	**8**	**0**	**0**	**0**	**9:18**
2002-03	**Chicago**	**NHL**	**82**	**14**	**15**	**29**	**113**	**0**	**2**	**0**	**127**	**11.0**	**0**	**377**	**52.5**	**14:04**	....	....	....	....	....	....	....	....	....
2003-04	**Chicago**	**NHL**	**82**	**21**	**24**	**45**	**106**	**2**	**0**	**1**	**202**	**10.4**	**–14**	**387**	**48.3**	**17:37**	....	....	....	....	....	....	....	....	....
2004-05	Trondheim IK	Norway	25	10	17	27	87	....	....	....	....	....	....	....	....	....	11	6	6	12	44	....	....	....	....
2005-06	**Chicago**	**NHL**	**82**	**25**	**23**	**48**	**107**	**11**	**1**	**1**	**227**	**11.0**	**–14**	**1034**	**48.5**	**17:37**	....	....	....	....	....	....	....	....	....
	NHL Totals		**339**	**72**	**79**	**151**	**454**	**14**	**3**	**3**	**690**	**10.4**		**1986**	**49.1**	**15:22**	**5**	**0**	**0**	**0**	**8**	**0**	**0**	**0**	**9:18**

Signed as a free agent by **Trondheim** (Norway), November 6, 2004. Traded to **San Jose** by **Chicago** for Tom Preissing and Josh Hennessy, July 10, 2006.

BERARD, Bryan

(buh-RAHRD, BRIGH-uhn) **CBJ**

Defense. Shoots left. 6'2", 220 lbs. Born, Woonsocket, RI, March 5, 1977. Ottawa's 1st choice, 1st overall, in 1995 Entry Draft.

1991-92	Mount St. Charles	High-RI	15	3	15	18	4	....	....	....	....	....	....	....	....	....	....	....	....	....	....	....	....	....	....
1992-93	Mount St. Charles	High-RI	15	8	12	20	18	....	....	....	....	....	....	....	....	....	....	....	....	....	....	....	....	....	....
1993-94	Mount St. Charles	High-RI	15	11	26	37	45	....	....	....	....	....	....	....	....	....	4	3	3	6	6	....	....	....	....
1994-95	Detroit	OHL	58	20	55	75	97	....	....	....	....	....	....	....	....	....	21	4	20	24	38	....	....	....	....
1995-96	Detroit	OHL	56	31	58	89	116	....	....	....	....	....	....	....	....	....	17	7	18	25	41	....	....	....	....
1996-97	**NY Islanders**	**NHL**	**82**	**8**	**40**	**48**	**86**	**3**	**0**	**1**	**172**	**4.7**	**1**	....	....	....	....	....	....	....	....	....	....	....	....
1997-98	**NY Islanders**	**NHL**	**75**	**14**	**32**	**46**	**59**	**8**	**1**	**2**	**192**	**7.3**	**–32**	....	....	....	....	....	....	....	....	....	....	....	....
	United States	Olympics	2	0	0	0	0	....	....	....	....	....	....	....	....	....	....	....	....	....	....	....	....	....	....
1998-99	**NY Islanders**	**NHL**	**31**	**4**	**11**	**15**	**26**	**2**	**0**	**3**	**72**	**5.6**	**–6**	**0**	**0.0**	**24:45**	....	....	....	....	....	....	....	....	....
	Toronto	**NHL**	**38**	**5**	**14**	**19**	**22**	**2**	**0**	**2**	**63**	**7.9**	**7**	**0**	**0.0**	**22:38**	**17**	**1**	**8**	**9**	**8**	**1**	**0**	**0**	**21:11**
99-2000	**Toronto**	**NHL**	**64**	**3**	**27**	**30**	**42**	**1**	**0**	**0**	**98**	**3.1**	**11**	**0**	**0.0**	**19:34**	....	....	....	....	....	....	....	....	....
2000-01	**Toronto**	**NHL**	DID NOT PLAY – INJURED																						
2001-02	**NY Rangers**	**NHL**	**82**	**2**	**21**	**23**	**60**	**0**	**0**	**0**	**132**	**1.5**	**–1**	**0**	**0.0**	**19:38**	....	....	....	....	....	....	....	....	....
2002-03	**Boston**	**NHL**	**80**	**10**	**28**	**38**	**64**	**4**	**0**	**1**	**205**	**4.9**	**–4**	**0**	**0.0**	**21:21**	**3**	**1**	**0**	**1**	**2**	**0**	**0**	**0**	**21:50**
2003-04	**Chicago**	**NHL**	**58**	**13**	**34**	**47**	**53**	**6**	**0**	**0**	**203**	**6.4**	**–24**	**0**	**0.0**	**21:46**	....	....	....	....	....	....	....	....	....
2004-05			DID NOT PLAY																						
2005-06	**Columbus**	**NHL**	**44**	**12**	**20**	**32**	**32**	**11**	**0**	**2**	**126**	**9.5**	**–29**	**0**	**0.0**	**22:40**	....	....	....	....	....	....	....	....	....
	NHL Totals		**554**	**71**	**227**	**298**	**444**	**37**	**1**	**11**	**1263**	**5.6**		**0**	**0.0**	**21:18**	**20**	**2**	**8**	**10**	**10**	**1**	**0**	**0**	**21:17**

OHL All-Rookie Team (1995) • OHL First All-Star Team (1995, 1996) • OHL Rookie of the Year (1995) • Canadian Major Junior First All-Star Team (1995, 1996) • Canadian Major Junior Rookie of the Year (1995) • Canadian Major Junior Defenseman of the Year (1996) • NHL All-Rookie Team (1997) • Calder Memorial Trophy (1997) • Bill Masterton Memorial Trophy (2004)

Traded to **NY Islanders** by **Ottawa** with Don Beaupre and Martin Straka for Damian Rhodes and Wade Redden, January 23, 1996. Traded to **Toronto** by **NY Islanders** with NY Islanders' 6th round choice (Jan Sochor) in 1999 Entry Draft for Felix Potvin and Toronto's 6th round choice (later traded to Tampa Bay – Tampa Bay selected Fedor Fedorov) in 1999 Entry Draft, January 9, 1999. • Missed remainder of 1999-2000 season and entire 2000-01 season recovering from eye injury suffered in game vs. Ottawa, March 11, 2000. Signed as a free agent by **NY Rangers**, October 5, 2001. Signed as a free agent by **Boston**, August 13, 2002. Signed as a free agent by **Chicago**, October 31, 2003. Signed as a free agent by **Columbus**, August 3, 2005.

BERG, Aki

(BUHRG, AH-kee)

Defense. Shoots left. 6'3", 213 lbs. Born, Turku, Finland, July 28, 1977. Los Angeles' 1st choice, 3rd overall, in 1995 Entry Draft.

1992-93	TPS Turku Jr.	Fin-Jr.	39	18	24	42	24	....	....	....	....	....	....	....	....	....	....	....	....	....	....	....	....	....	....
1993-94	TPS Turku U18	Fin-U18	3	2	1	3	6	....	....	....	....	....	....	....	....	....	....	....	....	....	....	....	....	....	....
	TPS Turku Jr.	Fin-Jr.	21	3	11	14	24	....	....	....	....	....	....	....	....	....	....	....	....	....	....	....	....	....	....
	TPS Turku	Finland	6	0	3	3	4	....	....	....	....	....	....	....	....	....	7	0	0	0	10	....	....	....	....
	Kiekko-67 Turku	Finland-2	12	1	1	2	16	....	....	....	....	....	....	....	....	....	....	....	....	....	....	....	....	....	....
1994-95	TPS Turku Jr.	Fin-Jr.	8	1	0	1	30	....	....	....	....	....	....	....	....	....	....	....	....	....	....	....	....	....	....
	Kiekko-67 Turku	Finland-2	20	3	9	12	34	....	....	....	....	....	....	....	....	....	....	....	....	....	....	....	....	....	....
	TPS Turku U18	Fin-U18	6	2	8	10	42	....	....	....	....	....	....	....	....	....	....	....	....	....	....	....	....	....	....
	TPS Turku	Finland	5	0	0	0	4	....	....	....	....	....	....	....	....	....	3	1	1	2	6	....	....	....	....
1995-96	**Los Angeles**	**NHL**	**51**	**0**	**7**	**7**	**29**	**0**	**0**	**0**	**56**	**0.0**	**–13**	....	....	....	....	....	....	....	....	....	....	....	....
	Phoenix	IHL	20	0	3	3	18	....	....	....	....	....	....	....	....	....	2	0	0	0	4	....	....	....	....
1996-97	**Los Angeles**	**NHL**	**41**	**2**	**6**	**8**	**24**	**2**	**0**	**0**	**65**	**3.1**	**–9**	....	....	....	....	....	....	....	....	....	....	....	....
	Phoenix	IHL	23	1	3	4	21	....	....	....	....	....	....	....	....	....	....	....	....	....	....	....	....	....	....
1997-98	**Los Angeles**	**NHL**	**72**	**0**	**8**	**8**	**61**	**0**	**0**	**0**	**58**	**0.0**	**3**	....	....	....	**4**	**0**	**3**	**3**	**0**	**0**	**0**	**0**	....
	Finland	Olympics	6	0	0	0	6	....	....	....	....	....	....	....	....	....	....	....	....	....	....	....	....	....	....
1998-99	TPS Turku	Finland	48	8	7	15	137	....	....	....	....	....	....	....	....	....	9	1	1	2	45	....	....	....	....
99-2000	**Los Angeles**	**NHL**	**70**	**3**	**13**	**16**	**45**	**0**	**0**	**0**	**70**	**4.3**	**–1**	**0**	**0.0**	**16:39**	**2**	**0**	**0**	**0**	**2**	**0**	**0**	**0**	**15:03**
2000-01	**Los Angeles**	**NHL**	**47**	**0**	**4**	**4**	**43**	**0**	**0**	**0**	**31**	**0.0**	**3**	**0**	**0.0**	**14:54**	....	....	....	....	....	....	....	....	....
	Toronto	**NHL**	**12**	**3**	**0**	**3**	**2**	**3**	**0**	**1**	**12**	**25.0**	**–6**	**0**	**0.0**	**18:13**	**11**	**0**	**2**	**2**	**4**	**0**	**0**	**0**	**16:31**
2001-02	**Toronto**	**NHL**	**81**	**1**	**10**	**11**	**46**	**0**	**0**	**0**	**66**	**1.5**	**14**	**1**	**100.0**	**18:43**	**20**	**0**	**1**	**1**	**37**	**0**	**0**	**0**	**18:25**
	Finland	Olympics	4	1	0	1	2	....	....	....	....	....	....	....	....	....	....	....	....	....	....	....	....	....	....
2002-03	**Toronto**	**NHL**	**78**	**4**	**7**	**11**	**28**	**0**	**0**	**2**	**49**	**8.2**	**3**	**0**	**0.0**	**15:02**	**7**	**1**	**1**	**2**	**2**	**0**	**0**	**0**	**19:45**
2003-04	**Toronto**	**NHL**	**79**	**2**	**7**	**9**	**40**	**0**	**0**	**0**	**69**	**2.9**	**–1**	**1**	**0.0**	**18:18**	**10**	**0**	**0**	**0**	**2**	**0**	**0**	**0**	**14:52**
2004-05	Timra IK	Sweden	47	6	14	20	46	....	....	....	....	....	....	....	....	....	7	0	0	0	6	....	....	....	....
2005-06	**Toronto**	**NHL**	**75**	**0**	**8**	**8**	**56**	**0**	**0**	**0**	**42**	**0.0**	**–5**	**1**	**100.0**	**15:58**	....	....	....	....	....	....	....	....	....
	Finland	Olympics	8	0	0	0	4	....	....	....	....	....	....	....	....	....	....	....	....	....	....	....	....	....	....
	NHL Totals		**606**	**15**	**70**	**85**	**374**	**5**	**0**	**3**	**518**	**2.9**		**3**	**66.7**	**16:47**	**54**	**1**	**7**	**8**	**47**	**0**	**0**	**0**	**17:20**

Traded to **Toronto** by **Los Angeles** for Adam Mair and Toronto's 2nd round choice (Mike Cammalleri) in 2001 Entry Draft, March 13, 2001. Signed as a free agent by **Timra** (Sweden), September 22, 2004.

BERGENHEIM, Sean

(BUHR-gehn-highm, SHAWN) **NYI**

Left wing. Shoots left. 5'11", 194 lbs. Born, Helsinki, Finland, February 8, 1984. NY Islanders' 1st choice, 22nd overall, in 2002 Entry Draft.

			Regular Season														Playoffs								
Season	Club	League	GP	G	A	Pts	PIM	PP	SH	GW	S	%	+/-	TF	F%	Min	GP	G	A	Pts	PIM	PP	SH	GW	Min
99-2000	Jokerit U18	Fin-U18	30	22	11	33	34	....	....	....	....	....	....	....	....	....	3	1	0	1	0	....	....	....	....
	Jokerit U18	Fin-U18	17	10	8	18	14	....	....	....	....	....	....	....	....	....	3	1	0	1	2	....	....	....	....
2000-01	Jokerit U18	Fin-U18	1	1	0	1	4	....	....	....	....	....	....	....	....	....	6	9	5	14	8	....	....	....	....
	Jokerit Helsinki Jr.	Fin-Jr.	18	6	4	10	26	....	....	....	....	....	....	....	....	....	2	0	0	0	4	....	....	....	....
2001-02	Jokerit U18	Fin-U18	....	....	....	....	....	....	....	....	....	....	....	....	....	....	5	6	2	8	18	....	....	....	....
	Jokerit Helsinki Jr.	Fin-Jr.	23	11	19	30	36	....	....	....	....	....	....	....	....	....	1	0	0	0	2	....	....	....	....
	Kiekko-Vantaa	Finland-2	4	0	0	0	52	....	....	....	....	....	....	....	....	....	....	....	....	....	....	....	....	....	....
	Jokerit Helsinki	Finland	28	2	2	4	4	....	....	....	....	....	....	....	....	....	....	....	....	....	....	....	....	....	....
2002-03	Jokerit Helsinki Jr.	Fin-Jr.	2	3	0	3	2	....	....	....	....	....	....	....	....	....	....	....	....	....	....	....	....	....	....
	Jokerit Helsinki	Finland	38	3	3	6	4	....	....	....	....	....	....	....	....	....	2	0	0	0	0	....	....	....	....
2003-04	**NY Islanders**	**NHL**	**18**	**1**	**1**	**2**	**4**	**0**	**1**	**0**	**12**	**8.3**	**-4**	**2**	**50.0**	**8:55**	....	....	....	....	....	....	....	....	....
	Jokerit Helsinki	Finland	20	2	2	4	18	....	....	....	....	....	....	....	....	....	3	1	1	2	0	....	....	....	....
	Bridgeport	AHL	....	....	....	....	....	....	....	....	....	....	....	....	....	....	7	2	3	5	10	....	....	....	....
2004-05	Bridgeport	AHL	61	15	14	29	69	....	....	....	....	....	....	....	....	....	....	....	....	....	....	....	....	....	....
2005-06	**NY Islanders**	**NHL**	**28**	**4**	**5**	**9**	**20**	**0**	**0**	**1**	**63**	**6.3**	**-11**	**14**	**28.6**	**13:17**	....	....	....	....	....	....	....	....	....
	Bridgeport	AHL	55	25	22	47	112	....	....	....	....	....	....	....	....	....	7	0	2	2	24	....	....	....	....
	NHL Totals		**46**	**5**	**6**	**11**	**24**	**0**	**1**	**1**	**75**	**6.7**		**16**	**31.3**	**11:34**	....	....	....	....	....	....	....	....	....

BERGERON, Marc-Andre

(BAIR-zhur-uhn, MAHRK-AWN-dray) **EDM.**

Defense. Shoots left. 5'10", 197 lbs. Born, St-Louis-de-France, Que., October 13, 1980.

Season	Club	League	GP	G	A	Pts	PIM	PP	SH	GW	S	%	+/-	TF	F%	Min	GP	G	A	Pts	PIM	PP	SH	GW	Min
1996-97	Cap-d-Madeleine	QAAA	4	0	1	1	0	....	....	....	....	....	....	....	....	....	2	0	0	0	0	....	....	....	....
1997-98	Baie-Comeau	QMJHL	40	6	14	20	48	....	....	....	....	....	....	....	....	....	....	....	....	....	....	....	....	....	....
1998-99	Baie-Comeau	QMJHL	46	8	14	22	57	....	....	....	....	....	....	....	....	....	....	....	....	....	....	....	....	....	....
	Shawinigan	QMJHL	24	6	7	13	66	....	....	....	....	....	....	....	....	....	5	2	2	4	24	....	....	....	....
99-2000	Shawinigan	QMJHL	70	24	50	74	173	....	....	....	....	....	....	....	....	....	13	4	7	11	45	....	....	....	....
2000-01	Shawinigan	QMJHL	69	42	59	101	185	....	....	....	....	....	....	....	....	....	10	4	11	15	24	....	....	....	....
2001-02	Hamilton	AHL	50	2	13	15	61	....	....	....	....	....	....	....	....	....	9	1	4	5	8	....	....	....	....
2002-03	**Edmonton**	**NHL**	**5**	**1**	**1**	**2**	**9**	**0**	**0**	**0**	**5**	**20.0**	**2**	**0**	**0.0**	**16:30**	**1**	**0**	**1**	**1**	**0**	**0**	**0**	**0**	**19:20**
	Hamilton	AHL	66	8	31	39	73	....	....	....	....	....	....	....	....	....	20	0	7	7	25	....	....	....	....
2003-04	**Edmonton**	**NHL**	**54**	**9**	**17**	**26**	**26**	**3**	**0**	**0**	**105**	**8.6**	**13**	**0**	**0.0**	**17:39**	....	....	....	....	....	....	....	....	....
	Toronto	AHL	17	4	3	7	23	....	....	....	....	....	....	....	....	....	....	....	....	....	....	....	....	....	....
2004-05	Brynas IF Gavle	Sweden	10	3	2	5	72	....	....	....	....	....	....	....	....	....	....	....	....	....	....	....	....	....	....
	Brynas IF Gavle	Sweden-Q	9	1	2	3	8	....	....	....	....	....	....	....	....	....	....	....	....	....	....	....	....	....	....
2005-06	**Edmonton**	**NHL**	**75**	**15**	**20**	**35**	**38**	**8**	**0**	**1**	**144**	**10.4**	**3**	**0**	**0.0**	**21:14**	**18**	**2**	**1**	**3**	**14**	**2**	**0**	**0**	**14:56**
	NHL Totals		**134**	**25**	**38**	**63**	**73**	**11**	**0**	**1**	**254**	**9.8**		**0**	**0.0**	**19:37**	**19**	**2**	**2**	**4**	**14**	**2**	**0**	**0**	**15:10**

QMJHL First All-Star Team (2001) • Canadian Major Junior First All-Star Team (2001) • Canadian Major Junior Defenseman of the Year (2001) • AHL Second All-Star Team (2003)

Signed as a free agent by **Edmonton**, July 20, 2001. Signed as a free agent by **Gavle** (Sweden), January 23, 2005.

BERGERON, Patrice

(BAIR-zhuhr-uhn, pa-TREEZ) **BOS.**

Center. Shoots right. 6', 197 lbs. Born, Ancienne-Lorette, Que., July 24, 1985. Boston's 2nd choice, 45th overall, in 2003 Entry Draft.

Season	Club	League	GP	G	A	Pts	PIM	PP	SH	GW	S	%	+/-	TF	F%	Min	GP	G	A	Pts	PIM	PP	SH	GW	Min
2000-01	Ste-Foy	QAAA	5	1	2	3	0	....	....	....	....	....	....	....	....	....	....	....	....	....	....	....	....	....	....
2001-02	St-Francois	QAAA	38	25	37	62	18	....	....	....	....	....	....	....	....	....	8	6	4	10	10	....	....	....	....
	Acadie-Bathurst	QMJHL	4	0	1	1	0	....	....	....	....	....	....	....	....	....	....	....	....	....	....	....	....	....	....
2002-03	Acadie-Bathurst	QMJHL	70	23	50	73	62	....	....	....	....	....	....	....	....	....	11	6	9	15	6	....	....	....	....
2003-04	**Boston**	**NHL**	**71**	**16**	**23**	**39**	**22**	**7**	**0**	**2**	**133**	**12.0**	**5**	**699**	**49.4**	**16:21**	**7**	**1**	**3**	**4**	**0**	**0**	**0**	**1**	**17:13**
2004-05	Providence Bruins	AHL	68	21	40	61	59	....	....	....	....	....	....	....	....	....	16	5	7	12	4	....	....	....	....
2005-06	**Boston**	**NHL**	**81**	**31**	**42**	**73**	**22**	**12**	**1**	**6**	**310**	**10.0**	**3**	**1447**	**54.7**	**20:36**	....	....	....	....	....	....	....	....	....
	NHL Totals		**152**	**47**	**65**	**112**	**44**	**19**	**1**	**8**	**443**	**10.6**		**2146**	**52.9**	**18:37**	**7**	**1**	**3**	**4**	**0**	**0**	**0**	**1**	**17:13**

BERGLUND, Christian

(BUHRG-luhnd, KRIH-stan) **FLA.**

Left wing. Shoots left. 5'11", 190 lbs. Born, Orebro, Sweden, March 12, 1980. New Jersey's 3rd choice, 37th overall, in 1998 Entry Draft.

Season	Club	League	GP	G	A	Pts	PIM	PP	SH	GW	S	%	+/-	TF	F%	Min	GP	G	A	Pts	PIM	PP	SH	GW	Min
1994-95	Kariskoga IK	Sweden-4	20	14	13	27	....	....	....	....	....	....	....	....	....	....	....	....	....	....	....	....	....	....	....
1995-96	Kristinehamn SK	Sweden-3	23	8	8	16	12	....	....	....	....	....	....	....	....	....	....	....	....	....	....	....	....	....	....
1996-97	Farjestad Jr.	Swe-Jr.	21	2	3	5	24	....	....	....	....	....	....	....	....	....	....	....	....	....	....	....	....	....	....
1997-98	Farjestad Jr.	Swe-Jr.	29	23	19	42	88	....	....	....	....	....	....	....	....	....	2	0	0	0	0	....	....	....	....
	Farjestad	Sweden	1	0	0	0	0	....	....	....	....	....	....	....	....	....	....	....	....	....	....	....	....	....	....
1998-99	Farjestad Jr.	Swe-Jr.	5	3	4	7	22	....	....	....	....	....	....	....	....	....	....	....	....	....	....	....	....	....	....
	Farjestad	Sweden	37	2	4	6	37	....	....	....	....	....	....	....	....	....	4	1	0	1	4	....	....	....	....
99-2000	Farjestad Jr.	Swe-Jr.	5	3	5	8	8	....	....	....	....	....	....	....	....	....	....	....	....	....	....	....	....	....	....
	Bofors	Sweden-2	6	2	0	2	12	....	....	....	....	....	....	....	....	....	....	....	....	....	....	....	....	....	....
	Farjestad	Sweden	43	8	6	14	44	....	....	....	....	....	....	....	....	....	7	2	1	3	10	....	....	....	....
2000-01	Farjestad	Sweden	49	17	20	37	*142	....	....	....	....	....	....	....	....	....	16	7	7	14	22	....	....	....	....
2001-02	**New Jersey**	**NHL**	**15**	**2**	**7**	**9**	**8**	**0**	**0**	**0**	**22**	**9.1**	**-3**	**2**	**50.0**	**12:26**	**3**	**0**	**0**	**0**	**2**	**0**	**0**	**0**	**11:31**
	Albany River Rats	AHL	60	21	26	47	69	....	....	....	....	....	....	....	....	....	....	....	....	....	....	....	....	....	....
2002-03	**New Jersey**	**NHL**	**38**	**4**	**5**	**9**	**20**	**0**	**0**	**0**	**50**	**8.0**	**3**	**11**	**9.1**	**10:11**	....	....	....	....	....	....	....	....	....
	Albany River Rats	AHL	26	6	14	20	57	....	....	....	....	....	....	....	....	....	....	....	....	....	....	....	....	....	....
2003-04	**New Jersey**	**NHL**	**23**	**2**	**3**	**5**	**4**	**0**	**0**	**0**	**33**	**6.1**	**-4**	**2**	**50.0**	**11:22**	....	....	....	....	....	....	....	....	....
	Florida	**NHL**	**10**	**3**	**1**	**4**	**10**	**0**	**0**	**0**	**17**	**17.6**	**-2**	**14**	**28.6**	**12:01**	....	....	....	....	....	....	....	....	....
2004-05	Farjestad	Sweden	48	7	13	20	97	....	....	....	....	....	....	....	....	....	14	2	3	5	56	....	....	....	....
2005-06	Rapperswil	Swiss	44	24	20	44	124	....	....	....	....	....	....	....	....	....	11	4	8	12	*63	....	....	....	....
	NHL Totals		**86**	**11**	**16**	**27**	**42**	**0**	**0**	**0**	**122**	**9.0**		**29**	**24.1**	**11:06**	**3**	**0**	**0**	**0**	**2**	**0**	**0**	**0**	**11:31**

• Missed majority of 2003-04 season recovering from hip injury suffered in game vs. Philadelphia, December 12, 2003. Traded to **Florida** by **New Jersey** with Victor Uchevatov for Viktor Kozlov, March 1, 2004. Signed as a free agent by **Farjestad** (Sweden), September, 2004. Signed as a free agent by **Rapperswil** (Swiss), August 26, 2005.

BERNIER, Steve

(BAIRN-yay, STÉEV) **S.J.**

Right wing. Shoots right. 6'2", 230 lbs. Born, Quebec City, Que., March 31, 1985. San Jose's 2nd choice, 16th overall, in 2003 Entry Draft.

Season	Club	League	GP	G	A	Pts	PIM	PP	SH	GW	S	%	+/-	TF	F%	Min	GP	G	A	Pts	PIM	PP	SH	GW	Min
1998-99	Quebec AA Aces	QAHA	28	33	23	56	24	....	....	....	....	....	....	....	....	....	....	....	....	....	....	....	....	....	....
99-2000	Quebec AA Aces	QAHA	26	12	23	35	42	....	....	....	....	....	....	....	....	....	....	....	....	....	....	....	....	....	....
2000-01	Ste-Foy	QAAA	39	17	35	52	48	....	....	....	....	....	....	....	....	....	16	9	17	26	8	....	....	....	....
2001-02	Moncton Wildcats	QMJHL	66	31	28	59	51	....	....	....	....	....	....	....	....	....	....	....	....	....	....	....	....	....	....
2002-03	Moncton Wildcats	QMJHL	71	49	52	101	90	....	....	....	....	....	....	....	....	....	2	1	0	1	2	....	....	....	....
2003-04	Moncton Wildcats	QMJHL	66	36	46	82	80	....	....	....	....	....	....	....	....	....	20	7	10	17	17	....	....	....	....
2004-05	Moncton Wildcats	QMJHL	68	35	36	71	114	....	....	....	....	....	....	....	....	....	12	6	13	19	22	....	....	....	....
2005-06	**San Jose**	**NHL**	**39**	**14**	**13**	**27**	**35**	**2**	**1**	**1**	**75**	**18.7**	**4**	**8**	**62.5**	**14:08**	**11**	**1**	**5**	**6**	**8**	**1**	**0**	**1**	**15:17**
	Cleveland Barons	AHL	49	20	23	43	33	....	....	....	....	....	....	....	....	....	....	....	....	....	....	....	....	....	....
	NHL Totals		**39**	**14**	**13**	**27**	**35**	**2**	**1**	**1**	**75**	**18.7**		**8**	**62.5**	**14:08**	**11**	**1**	**5**	**6**	**8**	**1**	**0**	**1**	**15:17**

QMJHL All-Rookie Team (2002) • QMJHL Second All-Star Team (2003, 2004)

BERRY, Rick

(BAIR-ree, RIHK) **NYI**

Defense. Shoots left. 6'2", 210 lbs. Born, Birtle, Man., November 4, 1978. Colorado's 3rd choice, 55th overall, in 1997 Entry Draft.

Season	Club	League	GP	G	A	Pts	PIM	PP	SH	GW	S	%	+/-	TF	F%	Min	GP	G	A	Pts	PIM	PP	SH	GW	Min
1994-95	Yellowhead	MMMHL	33	12	19	31	90	....	....	....	....	....	....	....	....	....	....	....	....	....	....	....	....	....	....
1995-96	Seattle	WHL	59	4	9	13	103	....	....	....	....	....	....	....	....	....	1	0	0	0	0	....	....	....	....
1996-97	Seattle	WHL	72	12	21	33	125	....	....	....	....	....	....	....	....	....	15	3	7	10	23	....	....	....	....
1997-98	Seattle	WHL	37	5	12	17	100	....	....	....	....	....	....	....	....	....	....	....	....	....	....	....	....	....	....
	Spokane Chiefs	WHL	22	4	9	13	31	....	....	....	....	....	....	....	....	....	17	1	4	5	26	....	....	....	....
1998-99	Hershey Bears	AHL	62	2	6	8	153	....	....	....	....	....	....	....	....	....	....	....	....	....	....	....	....	....	....
99-2000	Hershey Bears	AHL	64	9	16	25	148	....	....	....	....	....	....	....	....	....	13	2	3	5	24	....	....	....	....
2000-01	**Colorado**	**NHL**	**19**	**0**	**4**	**4**	**38**	**0**	**0**	**0**	**10**	**0.0**	**5**	**0**	**0.0**	**12:08**	....	....	....	....	....	....	....	....	....
	Hershey Bears	AHL	48	6	17	23	87	....	....	....	....	....	....	....	....	....	12	2	2	4	18	....	....	....	....
2001-02	**Colorado**	**NHL**	**57**	**0**	**0**	**0**	**60**	**0**	**0**	**0**	**29**	**0.0**	**1**	**0**	**0.0**	**9:29**	....	....	....	....	....	....	....	....	....
	Pittsburgh	**NHL**	**13**	**0**	**2**	**2**	**21**	**0**	**0**	**0**	**20**	**0.0**	**-4**	**0**	**0.0**	**19:39**	....	....	....	....	....	....	....	....	....
2002-03	**Washington**	**NHL**	**43**	**2**	**1**	**3**	**87**	**0**	**0**	**1**	**40**	**5.0**	**-3**	**0**	**0.0**	**12:58**	....	....	....	....	....	....	....	....	....

			Regular Season														Playoffs								
Season	Club	League	GP	G	A	Pts	PIM	PP	SH	GW	S	%	+/-	TF	F%	Min	GP	G	A	Pts	PIM	PP	SH	GW	Min
2003-04	**Washington**	**NHL**	**65**	**0**	**6**	**6**	**108**	**0**	**0**	**0**	**43**	**0.0**	**–5**	**2**	**50.0**	**12:11**	....	....	....	....	....	....	....	....	....
	Portland Pirates	AHL	10	2	1	3	12	....	....	....	....	....	....	....	....	....	....	....	....	....	....	....	....	....	....
2004-05	Utah Grizzlies	AHL	45	2	6	8	83	....	....	....	....	....	....	....	....	....	....	....	....	....	....	....	....	....	....
2005-06	San Antonio	AHL	5	0	0	0	4	....	....	....	....	....	....	....	....	....	....	....	....	....	....	....	....	....	....
	Milwaukee	AHL	64	1	11	12	121	....	....	....	....	....	....	....	....	....	7	0	0	0	15	....	....	....	....
	NHL Totals		**197**	**2**	**13**	**15**	**314**	**0**	**0**	**1**	**142**	**1.4**		**2**	**50.0**	**12:04**	....	....	....	....	....	....	....	....	....

Traded to **Pittsburgh** by **Colorado** with Ville Nieminen for Darius Kasparaitis, March 19, 2002. Claimed by **Washington** from **Pittsburgh** in Waiver Draft, October 4, 2002. Signed as a free agent by **Phoenix**, September 2, 2004. Traded to **Nashville** by **Phoenix** for future considerations, October 24, 2005. Signed as a free agent by **NY Islanders**, July 20, 2006.

BERTUZZI, Todd

(buhr-TOO-zee, TAWD) **FLA.**

Right wing. Shoots left. 6'3", 245 lbs. Born, Sudbury, Ont., February 2, 1975. NY Islanders' 1st choice, 23rd overall, in 1993 Entry Draft.

Season	Club	League	GP	G	A	Pts	PIM	PP	SH	GW	S	%	+/-	TF	F%	Min	GP	G	A	Pts	PIM	PP	SH	GW	Min
1990-91	Sudbury Legion	NOHA	48	25	46	71	247	....	....	....	....	....	....	....	....	....	....	....	....	....	....	....	....	....	....
	Sudbury Cubs	NOJHA	3	3	2	5	10	....	....	....	....	....	....	....	....	....	....	....	....	....	....	....	....	....	....
1991-92	Guelph Storm	OHL	47	7	14	21	145	....	....	....	....	....	....	....	....	....	....	....	....	....	....	....	....	....	....
1992-93	Guelph Storm	OHL	59	27	32	59	164	....	....	....	....	....	....	....	....	....	5	2	2	4	6	....	....	....	....
1993-94	Guelph Storm	OHL	61	28	54	82	165	....	....	....	....	....	....	....	....	....	9	2	6	8	30	....	....	....	....
1994-95	Guelph Storm	OHL	62	54	65	119	58	....	....	....	....	....	....	....	....	....	14	*15	18	33	41	....	....	....	....
1995-96	**NY Islanders**	**NHL**	**76**	**18**	**21**	**39**	**83**	**4**	**0**	**2**	**127**	**14.2**	**–14**	....	....	....	....	....	....	....	....	....	....	....	....
1996-97	**NY Islanders**	**NHL**	**64**	**10**	**13**	**23**	**68**	**3**	**0**	**1**	**79**	**12.7**	**–3**	....	....	....	....	....	....	....	....	....	....	....	....
	Utah Grizzlies	IHL	13	5	5	10	16	....	....	....	....	....	....	....	....	....	....	....	....	....	....	....	....	....	....
1997-98	**NY Islanders**	**NHL**	**52**	**7**	**11**	**18**	**58**	**1**	**0**	**1**	**63**	**11.1**	**–19**	....	....	....	....	....	....	....	....	....	....	....	....
	Vancouver	**NHL**	**22**	**6**	**9**	**15**	**63**	**1**	**1**	**1**	**39**	**15.4**	**2**	....	....	....	....	....	....	....	....	....	....	....	....
1998-99	**Vancouver**	**NHL**	**32**	**8**	**8**	**16**	**44**	**1**	**0**	**3**	**72**	**11.1**	**–6**	**191**	**43.5**	**18:28**	....	....	....	....	....	....	....	....	....
99-2000	**Vancouver**	**NHL**	**80**	**25**	**25**	**50**	**126**	**4**	**0**	**2**	**173**	**14.5**	**–2**	**476**	**46.6**	**15:24**	....	....	....	....	....	....	....	....	....
2000-01	**Vancouver**	**NHL**	**79**	**25**	**30**	**55**	**93**	**14**	**0**	**3**	**203**	**12.3**	**–18**	**84**	**45.2**	**17:13**	**4**	**2**	**2**	**4**	**8**	**0**	**0**	**0**	**19:01**
2001-02	**Vancouver**	**NHL**	**72**	**36**	**49**	**85**	**110**	**14**	**0**	**3**	**203**	**17.7**	**21**	**151**	**49.0**	**19:40**	**6**	**2**	**2**	**4**	**14**	**1**	**0**	**0**	**21:50**
2002-03	**Vancouver**	**NHL**	**82**	**46**	**51**	**97**	**144**	**25**	**0**	**7**	**243**	**18.9**	**2**	**208**	**47.1**	**20:34**	**14**	**2**	**4**	**6**	***60**	**0**	**0**	**0**	**21:05**
2003-04	**Vancouver**	**NHL**	**69**	**17**	**43**	**60**	**122**	**8**	**0**	**2**	**156**	**10.9**	**21**	**111**	**45.1**	**21:00**	....	....	....	....	....	....	....	....	....
2004-05			DID NOT PLAY – SUSPENDED																						
2005-06	**Vancouver**	**NHL**	**82**	**25**	**46**	**71**	**120**	**12**	**0**	**3**	**200**	**12.5**	**–17**	**363**	**43.8**	**19:08**	....	....	....	....	....	....	....	....	....
	Canada	Olympics	6	0	3	3	6	....	....	....	....	....	....	....	....	....	....	....	....	....	....	....	....	....	....
	NHL Totals		**710**	**223**	**306**	**529**	**1031**	**87**	**1**	**28**	**1558**	**14.3**		**1584**	**45.7**	**18:45**	**24**	**6**	**8**	**14**	**82**	**1**	**0**	**0**	**20:55**

OHL Second All-Star Team (1995) • NHL First All-Star Team (2003)

Played in NHL All-Star Game (2003, 2004)

Traded to **Vancouver** by **NY Islanders** with Bryan McCabe and NY Islanders' 3rd round choice (Jarkko Ruutu) in 1998 Entry Draft for Trevor Linden, February 6, 1998. • Missed majority of 1998-99 season recovering from leg injury suffered in game vs. Washington, November 1, 1998. • Suspended indefinitely by NHL for deliberate injury to Steve Moore in game vs. Colorado, March 8, 2004. Reinstated by NHL on August 8, 2005. Traded to **Florida** by **Vancouver** with Bryan Allen and Alex Auld for Roberto Luongo, Lukas Krajicek and Florida's 6th round choice (Sergei Shirokov) in 2006 Entry Draft, June 23, 2006.

BETTS, Blair

(BEHTS, BLAIR) **NYR**

Center. Shoots left. 6'3", 207 lbs. Born, Edmonton, Alta., February 16, 1980. Calgary's 2nd choice, 33rd overall, in 1998 Entry Draft.

Season	Club	League	GP	G	A	Pts	PIM	PP	SH	GW	S	%	+/-	TF	F%	Min	GP	G	A	Pts	PIM	PP	SH	GW	Min
1995-96	Sherwood Park	AMHL	34	22	19	41	69	....	....	....	....	....	....	....	....	....	....	....	....	....	....	....	....	....	....
1996-97	Prince George	WHL	58	12	18	30	19	....	....	....	....	....	....	....	....	....	15	2	2	4	6	....	....	....	....
1997-98	Prince George	WHL	71	35	41	76	38	....	....	....	....	....	....	....	....	....	11	4	6	10	8	....	....	....	....
1998-99	Prince George	WHL	42	20	22	42	39	....	....	....	....	....	....	....	....	....	7	3	2	5	8	....	....	....	....
99-2000	Prince George	WHL	44	24	35	59	38	....	....	....	....	....	....	....	....	....	13	11	11	22	6	....	....	....	....
2000-01	Saint John Flames	AHL	75	13	15	28	28	....	....	....	....	....	....	....	....	....	19	2	3	5	4	....	....	....	....
2001-02	**Calgary**	**NHL**	**6**	**1**	**0**	**1**	**2**	**0**	**0**	**1**	**4**	**25.0**	**–1**	**39**	**48.7**	**7:05**	....	....	....	....	....	....	....	....	....
	Saint John Flames	AHL	67	20	29	49	10	....	....	....	....	....	....	....	....	....	....	....	....	....	....	....	....	....	....
2002-03	**Calgary**	**NHL**	**9**	**1**	**3**	**4**	**0**	**0**	**0**	**0**	**16**	**6.3**	**3**	**71**	**53.5**	**11:33**	....	....	....	....	....	....	....	....	....
	Saint John Flames	AHL	19	6	7	13	6	....	....	....	....	....	....	....	....	....	....	....	....	....	....	....	....	....	....
2003-04	**Calgary**	**NHL**	**20**	**1**	**2**	**3**	**10**	**1**	**0**	**1**	**21**	**4.8**	**–1**	**248**	**54.0**	**12:46**	....	....	....	....	....	....	....	....	....
2004-05	Hartford	AHL	16	5	4	9	4	....	....	....	....	....	....	....	....	....	....	....	....	....	....	....	....	....	....
2005-06	**NY Rangers**	**NHL**	**66**	**8**	**2**	**10**	**24**	**0**	**1**	**0**	**94**	**8.5**	**–10**	**817**	**53.4**	**12:55**	**4**	**1**	**1**	**2**	**2**	**0**	**0**	**0**	**16:12**
	NHL Totals		**101**	**11**	**7**	**18**	**36**	**1**	**1**	**2**	**135**	**8.1**		**1175**	**53.4**	**12:25**	**4**	**1**	**1**	**2**	**2**	**0**	**0**	**0**	**16:12**

• Missed majority of 2002-03 season recovering from shoulder injury suffered in training camp, September 27, 2002. • Missed majority of 2003-04 season recovering from shoulder injury suffered in game vs. Chicago, November 22, 2003. • Missed majority of 2003-04 season revovering from shoulder injury suffered in game vs. Colorado, December 31, 2003. Traded to **NY Rangers** by **Calgary** with Jamie McLennan and Greg Moore for Chris Simon and NY Rangers' 7th round choice (Matt Schneider) in 2004 Entry Draft, March 6, 2004.

BICEK, Jiri

(bee-SEHK, YEH-ree)

Right wing. Shoots left. 5'10", 190 lbs. Born, Kosice, Czech., December 3, 1978. New Jersey's 4th choice, 131st overall, in 1997 Entry Draft.

Season	Club	League	GP	G	A	Pts	PIM	PP	SH	GW	S	%	+/-	TF	F%	Min	GP	G	A	Pts	PIM	PP	SH	GW	Min
1994-95	HC Kosice Jr.	Slovak-Jr.	42	38	36	74	18	....	....	....	....	....	....	....	....	....	....	....	....	....	....	....	....	....	....
1995-96	HC Kosice	Slovakia	30	10	15	25	16	....	....	....	....	....	....	....	....	....	9	2	4	6	0	....	....	....	....
1996-97	HC Kosice	Slovakia	44	11	14	25	20	....	....	....	....	....	....	....	....	....	7	1	3	4	....	....	....	....	....
1997-98	Albany River Rats	AHL	50	10	10	20	22	....	....	....	....	....	....	....	....	....	13	1	6	7	4	....	....	....	....
1998-99	Albany River Rats	AHL	79	15	45	60	102	....	....	....	....	....	....	....	....	....	5	2	2	4	2	....	....	....	....
99-2000	Albany River Rats	AHL	80	7	36	43	51	....	....	....	....	....	....	....	....	....	4	0	2	2	0	....	....	....	....
2000-01	**New Jersey**	**NHL**	**5**	**1**	**0**	**1**	**4**	**0**	**0**	**0**	**10**	**10.0**	**0**	**0**	**0.0**	**13:04**	....	....	....	....	....	....	....	....	....
	Albany River Rats	AHL	73	12	29	41	73	....	....	....	....	....	....	....	....	....	....	....	....	....	....	....	....	....	....
2001-02	**New Jersey**	**NHL**	**1**	**0**	**0**	**0**	**0**	**0**	**0**	**0**	**2**	**0.0**	**–1**	**0**	**0.0**	**13:10**	....	....	....	....	....	....	....	....	....
	Albany River Rats	AHL	62	15	19	34	45	....	....	....	....	....	....	....	....	....	....	....	....	....	....	....	....	....	....
2002-03 ♦	**New Jersey**	**NHL**	**44**	**5**	**6**	**11**	**25**	**1**	**0**	**1**	**63**	**7.9**	**7**	**3**	**0.0**	**11:48**	**5**	**0**	**0**	**0**	**0**	**0**	**0**	**0**	**8:10**
	Albany River Rats	AHL	24	4	10	14	28	....	....	....	....	....	....	....	....	....	....	....	....	....	....	....	....	....	....
2003-04	**New Jersey**	**NHL**	**12**	**0**	**1**	**1**	**0**	**0**	**0**	**0**	**10**	**0.0**	**0**	**1**	**0.0**	**9:55**	**2**	**0**	**0**	**0**	**0**	**0**	**0**	**0**	**12:26**
	Albany River Rats	AHL	55	12	18	30	37	....	....	....	....	....	....	....	....	....	....	....	....	....	....	....	....	....	....
2004-05	HC Kosice	Slovakia	54	18	23	41	69	....	....	....	....	....	....	....	....	....	10	6	8	14	4	....	....	....	....
2005-06	Leksands IF	Sweden	50	16	12	28	48	....	....	....	....	....	....	....	....	....	....	....	....	....	....	....	....	....	....
	Leksands IF	Sweden-Q	10	2	2	4	14	....	....	....	....	....	....	....	....	....	....	....	....	....	....	....	....	....	....
	NHL Totals		**62**	**6**	**7**	**13**	**29**	**1**	**0**	**1**	**85**	**7.1**		**4**	**0.0**	**11:34**	**7**	**0**	**0**	**0**	**0**	**0**	**0**	**0**	**9:23**

Signed as a free agent by **Kosice** (Slovakia), September 17, 2004.

BIEKSA, Kevin

(BEEKS-ah, KEH-vihn) **VAN.**

Defense. Shoots right. 6'1", 195 lbs. Born, Grimsby, Ont., June 16, 1981. Vancouver's 4th choice, 151st overall, in 2001 Entry Draft.

Season	Club	League	GP	G	A	Pts	PIM	PP	SH	GW	S	%	+/-	TF	F%	Min	GP	G	A	Pts	PIM	PP	SH	GW	Min
1997-98	Burlington	OPJHL	27	0	3	3	10	....	....	....	....	....	....	....	....	....	....	....	....	....	....	....	....	....	....
1998-99	Burlington	OPJHL	49	8	29	37	83	....	....	....	....	....	....	....	....	....	....	....	....	....	....	....	....	....	....
99-2000	Burlington	OPJHL	49	6	27	33	139	....	....	....	....	....	....	....	....	....	....	....	....	....	....	....	....	....	....
2000-01	Bowling Green	CCHA	35	4	9	13	90	....	....	....	....	....	....	....	....	....	....	....	....	....	....	....	....	....	....
2001-02	Bowling Green	CCHA	40	5	10	15	68	....	....	....	....	....	....	....	....	....	....	....	....	....	....	....	....	....	....
2002-03	Bowling Green	CCHA	34	8	17	25	92	....	....	....	....	....	....	....	....	....	....	....	....	....	....	....	....	....	....
2003-04	Bowling Green	CCHA	38	7	15	22	66	....	....	....	....	....	....	....	....	....	....	....	....	....	....	....	....	....	....
	Manitoba Moose	AHL	4	0	2	2	2	....	....	....	....	....	....	....	....	....	....	....	....	....	....	....	....	....	....
2004-05	Manitoba Moose	AHL	80	12	27	39	192	....	....	....	....	....	....	....	....	....	14	1	1	2	52	....	....	....	....
2005-06	**Vancouver**	**NHL**	**39**	**0**	**6**	**6**	**77**	**0**	**0**	**0**	**38**	**0.0**	**–1**	**0**	**0.0**	**16:06**	....	....	....	....	....	....	....	....	....
	Manitoba Moose	AHL	23	3	17	20	73	....	....	....	....	....	....	....	....	....	13	0	10	10	38	....	....	....	....
	NHL Totals		**39**	**0**	**6**	**6**	**77**	**0**	**0**	**0**	**38**	**0.0**		**0**	**0.0**	**16:06**	....	....	....	....	....	....	....	....	....

AHL All-Rookie Team (2005)

Season	Club	League	Regular Season GP	G	A	Pts	PIM	PP	SH	GW	S	%	+/-	TF	F%	Min	Playoffs GP	G	A	Pts	PIM	PP	SH	GW	Min

BIRON, Mathieu

(BEE-rawn, MA-tyew) **S.J.**

Defense. Shoots right. 6'6", 220 lbs. Born, Lac-St-Charles, Que., April 29, 1980. Los Angeles' 1st choice, 21st overall, in 1998 Entry Draft.

Season	Club	League	GP	G	A	Pts	PIM	PP	SH	GW	S	%	+/-	TF	F%	Min	GP	G	A	Pts	PIM	PP	SH	GW	Min
1996-97	Ste-Foy	QAAA	40	4	22	26	49	....	....	....	....	....	....	....	....	....	10	3	4	7	....	....	....	....	....
1997-98	Shawinigan	QMJHL	59	8	28	36	60	....	....	....	....	....	....	....	....	....	6	0	1	1	10	....	....	....	....
1998-99	Shawinigan	QMJHL	69	13	32	45	116	....	....	....	....	....	....	....	....	....	6	0	2	2	6	....	....	....	....
99-2000	**NY Islanders**	**NHL**	**60**	**4**	**4**	**8**	**38**	**2**	**0**	**2**	**70**	**5.7**	**–13**	**2**	**0.0**	**15:02**	....	....	....	....	....	....	....	....	....
2000-01	**NY Islanders**	**NHL**	**14**	**0**	**1**	**1**	**12**	**0**	**0**	**0**	**10**	**0.0**	**2**	**0**	**0.0**	**12:21**	....	....	....	....	....	....	....	....	....
	Lowell	AHL	22	1	3	4	17	....	....	....	....	....	....	....	....	....	....	....	....	....	....	....	....	....	....
	Springfield	AHL	34	0	6	6	18	....	....	....	....	....	....	....	....	....	....	....	....	....	....	....	....	....	....
2001-02	**Tampa Bay**	**NHL**	**36**	**0**	**0**	**0**	**12**	**0**	**0**	**0**	**35**	**0.0**	**–16**	**0**	**0.0**	**14:47**	....	....	....	....	....	....	....	....	....
	Springfield	AHL	35	4	9	13	16	....	....	....	....	....	....	....	....	....	....	....	....	....	....	....	....	....	....
2002-03	**Florida**	**NHL**	**34**	**1**	**8**	**9**	**14**	**0**	**1**	**0**	**52**	**1.9**	**–18**	**0**	**0.0**	**21:08**	....	....	....	....	....	....	....	....	....
	San Antonio	AHL	43	3	8	11	58	....	....	....	....	....	....	....	....	....	....	....	....	....	....	....	....	....	....
2003-04	**Florida**	**NHL**	**57**	**3**	**10**	**13**	**51**	**0**	**0**	**1**	**75**	**4.0**	**–13**	**0**	**0.0**	**18:13**	....	....	....	....	....	....	....	....	....
2004-05			DID NOT PLAY																						
2005-06	**Washington**	**NHL**	**52**	**4**	**9**	**13**	**50**	**3**	**0**	**0**	**61**	**6.6**	**–11**	**0**	**0.0**	**12:14**	....	....	....	....	....	....	....	....	....
	NHL Totals		**253**	**12**	**32**	**44**	**177**	**5**	**1**	**3**	**303**	**4.0**		**2**	**0.0**	**15:49**	....	....	....	....	....	....	....	....	....

Traded to **NY Islanders** by **Los Angeles** with Olli Jokinen, Josh Green and Los Angeles' 1st round choice (Taylor Pyatt) in 1999 Entry Draft for Ziggy Palffy, Brian Smolinski, Marcel Cousineau and New Jersey's 4th round choice (previously acquired, Los Angeles selected Daniel Johansson) in 1999 Entry Draft, June 20, 1999. Traded to **Tampa Bay** by **NY Islanders** with NY Islanders' 2nd round choice (later traded to Washington – later traded to Vancouver – Vancouver selected Denis Grot) in 2002 Entry Draft for Adrian Aucoin and Alexander Kharitonov, June 22, 2001. Claimed by **Columbus** from **Tampa Bay** in Waiver Draft, October 4, 2002. Traded to **Florida** by **Columbus** for Petr Tenkrat, October 4, 2002. Signed as a free agent by **Washington**, August 10, 2005. Signed as a free agent by **San Jose**, August 9, 2006.

BISHAI, Mike

(BIHSH-igh, MIGHK)

Center. Shoots left. 5'11", 185 lbs. Born, Edmonton, Alta., May 30, 1979.

Season	Club	League	GP	G	A	Pts	PIM	PP	SH	GW	S	%	+/-	TF	F%	Min	GP	G	A	Pts	PIM	PP	SH	GW	Min
1996-97	South Surrey	BCHL	38	6	13	19	10	....	....	....	....	....	....	....	....	....	....	....	....	....	....	....	....	....	....
1997-98	South Surrey	BCHL	47	48	52	100	36	....	....	....	....	....	....	....	....	....	....	....	....	....	....	....	....	....	....
1998-99	Western Mich.	CCHA	26	0	3	3	20	....	....	....	....	....	....	....	....	....	....	....	....	....	....	....	....	....	....
99-2000	Western Mich.	CCHA	35	18	19	37	52	....	....	....	....	....	....	....	....	....	....	....	....	....	....	....	....	....	....
2000-01	Western Mich.	CCHA	37	23	*45	*68	37	....	....	....	....	....	....	....	....	....	....	....	....	....	....	....	....	....	....
2001-02	Western Mich.	CCHA	34	10	27	37	28	....	....	....	....	....	....	....	....	....	....	....	....	....	....	....	....	....	....
	Hamilton	AHL	3	0	0	0	0	....	....	....	....	....	....	....	....	....	....	....	....	....	....	....	....	....	....
2002-03	Hamilton	AHL	27	7	5	12	11	....	....	....	....	....	....	....	....	....	6	2	1	3	2	....	....	....	....
	Columbus	ECHL	25	12	17	29	24	....	....	....	....	....	....	....	....	....	....	....	....	....	....	....	....	....	....
2003-04	**Edmonton**	**NHL**	**14**	**0**	**2**	**2**	**19**	**0**	**0**	**0**	**14**	**0.0**	**0**	**113**	**41.6**	**9:09**	....	....	....	....	....	....	....	....	....
	Toronto	AHL	48	11	22	33	18	....	....	....	....	....	....	....	....	....	3	0	0	0	4	....	....	....	....
2004-05	Edmonton	AHL	70	10	24	34	36	....	....	....	....	....	....	....	....	....	....	....	....	....	....	....	....	....	....
2005-06	San Antonio	AHL	66	13	18	31	40	....	....	....	....	....	....	....	....	....	....	....	....	....	....	....	....	....	....
	NHL Totals		**14**	**0**	**2**	**2**	**19**	**0**	**0**	**0**	**14**	**0.0**		**113**	**41.6**	**9:09**	....	....	....	....	....	....	....	....	....

CCHA Second All-Star Team (2001) • NCAA West Second All-American Team (2001)

Signed as a free agent by **Edmonton**, May 28, 2002.

BLAKE, Jason

(BLAYK, JAY-suhn) **NYI**

Center. Shoots left. 5'10", 180 lbs. Born, Moorhead, MN, September 2, 1973.

Season	Club	League	GP	G	A	Pts	PIM	PP	SH	GW	S	%	+/-	TF	F%	Min	GP	G	A	Pts	PIM	PP	SH	GW	Min
1991-92	Moorhead Spuds	High-MN	25	30	30	60	....	....	....	....	....	....	....	....	....	....	....	....	....	....	....	....	....	....	....
1992-93	Waterloo	USHL	45	24	27	51	107	....	....	....	....	....	....	....	....	....	....	....	....	....	....	....	....	....	....
1993-94	Waterloo	USHL	47	50	50	100	76	....	....	....	....	....	....	....	....	....	....	....	....	....	....	....	....	....	....
1994-95	Ferris State	CCHA	36	16	16	32	46	....	....	....	....	....	....	....	....	....	....	....	....	....	....	....	....	....	....
1995-96	North Dakota	WCHA	DID NOT PLAY – TRANSFERRED COLLEGES																						
1996-97	North Dakota	WCHA	43	19	32	51	44	....	....	....	....	....	....	....	....	....	....	....	....	....	....	....	....	....	....
1997-98	North Dakota	WCHA	38	24	27	51	62	....	....	....	....	....	....	....	....	....	....	....	....	....	....	....	....	....	....
1998-99	North Dakota	WCHA	38	*28	*41	*69	49	....	....	....	....	....	....	....	....	....	....	....	....	....	....	....	....	....	....
	Los Angeles	**NHL**	**1**	**1**	**0**	**1**	**0**	**0**	**0**	**0**	**5**	**20.0**	**1**	**14**	**35.7**	**17:13**	....	....	....	....	....	....	....	....	....
	Orlando	IHL	5	3	5	8	6	....	....	....	....	....	....	....	....	....	13	3	4	7	20	....	....	....	....
99-2000	**Los Angeles**	**NHL**	**64**	**5**	**18**	**23**	**26**	**0**	**0**	**1**	**131**	**3.8**	**4**	**269**	**43.9**	**11:17**	**3**	**0**	**0**	**0**	**0**	**0**	**0**	**0**	**9:35**
	Long Beach	IHL	7	3	6	9	2	....	....	....	....	....	....	....	....	....	....	....	....	....	....	....	....	....	....
2000-01	**Los Angeles**	**NHL**	**17**	**1**	**3**	**4**	**10**	**0**	**0**	**0**	**27**	**3.7**	**–8**	**13**	**61.5**	**10:03**	....	....	....	....	....	....	....	....	....
	Lowell	AHL	2	0	1	1	2	....	....	....	....	....	....	....	....	....	....	....	....	....	....	....	....	....	....
	NY Islanders	**NHL**	**30**	**4**	**8**	**12**	**24**	**1**	**1**	**0**	**73**	**5.5**	**–12**	**118**	**44.1**	**15:43**	....	....	....	....	....	....	....	....	....
2001-02	**NY Islanders**	**NHL**	**82**	**8**	**10**	**18**	**36**	**0**	**0**	**1**	**136**	**5.9**	**–11**	**23**	**43.5**	**12:54**	**7**	**0**	**1**	**1**	**13**	**0**	**0**	**0**	**12:13**
2002-03	**NY Islanders**	**NHL**	**81**	**25**	**30**	**55**	**58**	**3**	**1**	**4**	**253**	**9.9**	**16**	**22**	**18.2**	**17:38**	**5**	**0**	**1**	**1**	**2**	**0**	**0**	**0**	**19:39**
2003-04	**NY Islanders**	**NHL**	**75**	**22**	**25**	**47**	**56**	**1**	**4**	**3**	**243**	**9.1**	**11**	**70**	**41.4**	**18:49**	**4**	**2**	**0**	**2**	**2**	**0**	**0**	**0**	**18:09**
2004-05	HC Lugano	Swiss	7	2	2	4	4	....	....	....	....	....	....	....	....	....	....	....	....	....	....	....	....	....	....
2005-06	**NY Islanders**	**NHL**	**76**	**28**	**29**	**57**	**60**	**12**	**2**	**2**	**304**	**9.2**	**0**	**152**	**42.8**	**18:47**	....	....	....	....	....	....	....	....	....
	United States	Olympics	6	0	0	0	2	....	....	....	....	....	....	....	....	....	....	....	....	....	....	....	....	....	....
	NHL Totals		**426**	**94**	**123**	**217**	**270**	**17**	**8**	**11**	**1172**	**8.0**		**681**	**42.7**	**15:45**	**19**	**2**	**2**	**4**	**17**	**0**	**0**	**0**	**15:00**

WCHA First All-Star Team (1997, 1998, 1999) • NCAA West Second All-American Team (1998) • WCHA Player of the Year (1999) • NCAA West First All-American Team (1999)

Signed as a free agent by **Los Angeles**, April 20, 1999. Traded to **NY Islanders** by **Los Angeles** for NY Islanders' 5th round choice (Joel Andresen) in 2002 Entry Draft, January 3, 2001. Signed as a free agent by **Lugano** (Swiss), December 1, 2004.

BLAKE, Rob

(BLAYK, RAWB) **L.A.**

Defense. Shoots right. 6'4", 225 lbs. Born, Simcoe, Ont., December 10, 1969. Los Angeles' 4th choice, 70th overall, in 1988 Entry Draft.

Season	Club	League	GP	G	A	Pts	PIM	PP	SH	GW	S	%	+/-	TF	F%	Min	GP	G	A	Pts	PIM	PP	SH	GW	Min
1985-86	Brantford Classics	OHA-B	39	3	13	16	43	....	....	....	....	....	....	....	....	....	....	....	....	....	....	....	....	....	....
1986-87	Stratford Cullitons	OHA-B	31	11	20	31	115	....	....	....	....	....	....	....	....	....	....	....	....	....	....	....	....	....	....
1987-88	Bowling Green	CCHA	43	5	8	13	88	....	....	....	....	....	....	....	....	....	....	....	....	....	....	....	....	....	....
1988-89	Bowling Green	CCHA	46	11	21	32	140	....	....	....	....	....	....	....	....	....	....	....	....	....	....	....	....	....	....
1989-90	Bowling Green	CCHA	42	23	36	59	140	....	....	....	....	....	....	....	....	....	....	....	....	....	....	....	....	....	....
	Los Angeles	**NHL**	**4**	**0**	**0**	**0**	**4**	**0**	**0**	**0**	**3**	**0.0**	**0**	....	....	....	**8**	**1**	**3**	**4**	**4**	**1**	**0**	**0**	....
1990-91	**Los Angeles**	**NHL**	**75**	**12**	**34**	**46**	**125**	**9**	**0**	**2**	**150**	**8.0**	**3**	....	....	....	**12**	**1**	**4**	**5**	**26**	**1**	**0**	**0**	....
1991-92	**Los Angeles**	**NHL**	**57**	**7**	**13**	**20**	**102**	**5**	**0**	**0**	**131**	**5.3**	**–5**	....	....	....	**6**	**2**	**1**	**3**	**12**	**0**	**0**	**0**	....
1992-93	**Los Angeles**	**NHL**	**76**	**16**	**43**	**59**	**152**	**10**	**0**	**4**	**243**	**6.6**	**18**	....	....	....	**23**	**4**	**6**	**10**	**46**	**1**	**1**	**0**	....
1993-94	**Los Angeles**	**NHL**	**84**	**20**	**48**	**68**	**137**	**7**	**0**	**6**	**304**	**6.6**	**–7**	....	....	....	....	....	....	....	....	....	....	....	....
1994-95	**Los Angeles**	**NHL**	**24**	**4**	**7**	**11**	**38**	**4**	**0**	**1**	**76**	**5.3**	**–16**	....	....	....	....	....	....	....	....	....	....	....	....
1995-96	**Los Angeles**	**NHL**	**6**	**1**	**2**	**3**	**8**	**0**	**0**	**0**	**13**	**7.7**	**0**	....	....	....	....	....	....	....	....	....	....	....	....
1996-97	**Los Angeles**	**NHL**	**62**	**8**	**23**	**31**	**82**	**4**	**0**	**1**	**169**	**4.7**	**–28**	....	....	....	....	....	....	....	....	....	....	....	....
1997-98	**Los Angeles**	**NHL**	**81**	**23**	**27**	**50**	**94**	**11**	**0**	**4**	**261**	**8.8**	**–3**	....	....	....	**4**	**0**	**0**	**0**	**6**	**0**	**0**	**0**	....
	Canada	Olympics	6	1	1	2	2	....	....	....	....	....	....	....	....	....	....	....	....	....	....	....	....	....	....
1998-99	**Los Angeles**	**NHL**	**62**	**12**	**23**	**35**	**128**	**5**	**1**	**2**	**216**	**5.6**	**–7**	**0**	**0.0**	**24:52**	....	....	....	....	....	....	....	....	....
99-2000	**Los Angeles**	**NHL**	**77**	**18**	**39**	**57**	**112**	**12**	**0**	**5**	**327**	**5.5**	**10**	**0**	**0.0**	**28:30**	**4**	**0**	**2**	**2**	**4**	**0**	**0**	**0**	**30:10**
2000-01	**Los Angeles**	**NHL**	**54**	**17**	**32**	**49**	**69**	**9**	**0**	**1**	**223**	**7.6**	**–8**	**0**	**0.0**	**28:11**	....	....	....	....	....	....	....	....	....
	♦ Colorado	**NHL**	**13**	**2**	**8**	**10**	**8**	**1**	**0**	**1**	**44**	**4.5**	**11**	**0**	**0.0**	**26:03**	**23**	**6**	**13**	**19**	**16**	**3**	**0**	**0**	**29:26**
2001-02	**Colorado**	**NHL**	**75**	**16**	**40**	**56**	**58**	**10**	**0**	**2**	**229**	**7.0**	**16**	**0**	**0.0**	**27:35**	**20**	**6**	**6**	**12**	**16**	**1**	**0**	**0**	**26:38**
	Canada	Olympics	6	1	2	3	2	....	....	....	....	....	....	....	....	....	....	....	....	....	....	....	....	....	....
2002-03	**Colorado**	**NHL**	**79**	**17**	**28**	**45**	**57**	**8**	**2**	**3**	**269**	**6.3**	**20**	**0**	**0.0**	**26:21**	**7**	**1**	**2**	**3**	**8**	**0**	**0**	**0**	**27:28**
2003-04	**Colorado**	**NHL**	**74**	**13**	**33**	**46**	**61**	**8**	**0**	**3**	**242**	**5.4**	**6**	**1**	**0.0**	**24:23**	**9**	**0**	**5**	**5**	**6**	**0**	**0**	**0**	**20:17**

Season	Club	League	Regular Season GP	G	A	Pts	PIM	PP	SH	GW	S	%	+/-	TF	F%	Min	Playoffs GP	G	A	Pts	PIM	PP	SH	GW	Min
2004-05			DID NOT PLAY																						
2005-06	**Colorado**	**NHL**	**81**	**14**	**37**	**51**	**94**	**7**	**1**	**1**	**264**	**5.3**	**2**	**2**	**0.0**	**24:22**	**9**	**3**	**1**	**4**	**8**	**2**	**0**	**1**	**28:19**
	Canada	Olympics	6	0	1	1	2	....	....	....	....	....	....	....	....	....	....	....	....	....	....	....	....	....	....
	NHL Totals		**984**	**200**	**437**	**637**	**1329**	**110**	**4**	**36**	**3164**	**6.3**		**3**	**0.0**	**26:16**	**125**	**24**	**43**	**67**	**152**	**9**	**1**	**1**	**27:13**

CCHA Second All-Star Team (1989) • CCHA First All-Star Team (1990) • NCAA West First All-American Team (1990) • NHL All-Rookie Team (1991) • NHL First All-Star Team (1998) • James Norris Memorial Trophy (1998) • NHL Second All-Star Team (2000, 2001, 2002)

Played in NHL All-Star Game (1994, 1999, 2000, 2001, 2002, 2003, 2004)

• Missed majority of 1995-96 season recovering from knee injury suffered in game vs. Washington, October 20, 1995. Traded to **Colorado** by **Los Angeles** with Steve Reinprecht for Adam Deadmarsh, Aaron Miller, a player to be named later (Jared Aulin, March 22, 2001) and Colorado's 1st round choices in 2001 (Dave Steckel) and 2003 (Brian Boyle) Entry Drafts, February 21, 2001. Signed as a free agent by **Los Angeles**, July 1, 2006.

BLATNY, Zdenek

(BLAT-nee, z'DEHN-ehk)

Left wing. Shoots left. 6'1", 190 lbs. Born, Brno, Czech., January 14, 1981. Atlanta's 3rd choice, 68th overall, in 1999 Entry Draft.

Season	Club	League	GP	G	A	Pts	PIM	PP	SH	GW	S	%	+/-	TF	F%	Min	GP	G	A	Pts	PIM	PP	SH	GW	Min
1997-98	Brno Jr.	CzRep-Jr.	42	22	21	43	40	....	....	....	....	....	....	....	....	....	....	....	....	....	....	....	....	....	....
1998-99	Seattle	WHL	44	18	15	33	25	....	....	....	....	....	....	....	....	....	11	4	0	4	24	....	....	....	....
99-2000	Seattle	WHL	7	4	5	9	12	....	....	....	....	....	....	....	....	....	....	....	....	....	....	....	....	....	....
	Kootenay Ice	WHL	61	43	39	82	119	....	....	....	....	....	....	....	....	....	21	10	*17	27	46	....	....	....	....
2000-01	Kootenay Ice	WHL	58	37	48	85	120	....	....	....	....	....	....	....	....	....	11	8	10	18	24	....	....	....	....
2001-02	Chicago Wolves	AHL	41	4	3	7	30	....	....	....	....	....	....	....	....	....	3	2	0	2	0	....	....	....	....
	Greenville	ECHL	12	5	5	10	17	....	....	....	....	....	....	....	....	....	9	2	8	10	14	....	....	....	....
2002-03	**Atlanta**	**NHL**	**4**	**0**	**0**	**0**	**0**	**0**	**0**	**0**	**2**	**0.0**	**−1**	**0**	**0.0**	**10:31**	....	....	....	....	....	....	....	....	....
	Chicago Wolves	AHL	72	12	9	21	62	....	....	....	....	....	....	....	....	....	9	0	2	2	20	....	....	....	....
2003-04	**Atlanta**	**NHL**	**16**	**3**	**0**	**3**	**6**	**0**	**0**	**0**	**17**	**17.6**	**0**	**13**	**38.5**	**10:27**	....	....	....	....	....	....	....	....	....
	Chicago Wolves	AHL	61	11	23	34	115	....	....	....	....	....	....	....	....	....	10	0	4	4	24	....	....	....	....
2004-05	Znojmo	CzRep	15	3	4	7	28	....	....	....	....	....	....	....	....	....	....	....	....	....	....	....	....	....	....
	Pelicans Lahti	Finland	9	1	1	2	32	....	....	....	....	....	....	....	....	....	....	....	....	....	....	....	....	....	....
2005-06	**Boston**	**NHL**	**5**	**0**	**0**	**0**	**2**	**0**	**0**	**0**	**3**	**0.0**	**−2**	**0**	**0.0**	**5:08**	....	....	....	....	....	....	....	....	....
	Providence Bruins	AHL	35	8	22	30	21	....	....	....	....	....	....	....	....	....	....	....	....	....	....	....	....	....	....
	Springfield	AHL	31	14	15	29	20	....	....	....	....	....	....	....	....	....	....	....	....	....	....	....	....	....	....
	NHL Totals		**25**	**3**	**0**	**3**	**8**	**0**	**0**	**0**	**22**	**13.6**		**13**	**38.5**	**9:24**	....	....	....	....	....	....	....	....	....

WHL East Second All-Star Team (2000)

Signed as a free agent by **Lahti** (Finland), November 19, 2004. Signed as a free agent by **Znojmo** (CzRep), January 6, 2005. Signed as a free agent by **Boston**, September 29, 2005. Traded to **Tampa Bay** by **Boston** for Brian Eklund, February 8, 2006.

BOCHENSKI, Brandon

(boh-CHEHN-skee, BRAN-duhn) **CHI.**

Right wing. Shoots right. 6', 196 lbs. Born, Blaine, MN, April 4, 1982. Ottawa's 9th choice, 223rd overall, in 2001 Entry Draft.

Season	Club	League	GP	G	A	Pts	PIM	PP	SH	GW	S	%	+/-	TF	F%	Min	GP	G	A	Pts	PIM	PP	SH	GW	Min
99-2000	Blaine Bengals	High-MN	28	32	30	62	....	....	....	....	....	....	....	....	....	....	....	....	....	....	....	....	....	....	....
2000-01	Lincoln Stars	USHL	55	*47	33	80	22	....	....	....	....	....	....	....	....	....	11	5	7	12	4	....	....	....	....
2001-02	North Dakota	WCHA	36	17	15	32	36	....	....	....	....	....	....	....	....	....	....	....	....	....	....	....	....	....	....
2002-03	North Dakota	WCHA	43	35	27	62	42	....	....	....	....	....	....	....	....	....	....	....	....	....	....	....	....	....	....
2003-04	North Dakota	WCHA	41	27	33	60	40	....	....	....	....	....	....	....	....	....	....	....	....	....	....	....	....	....	....
2004-05	Binghamton	AHL	75	34	36	70	16	....	....	....	....	....	....	....	....	....	6	1	0	1	2	....	....	....	....
2005-06	**Ottawa**	**NHL**	**20**	**6**	**7**	**13**	**14**	**2**	**0**	**0**	**39**	**15.4**	**7**	**4**	**50.0**	**12:17**	....	....	....	....	....	....	....	....	....
	Binghamton	AHL	33	22	24	46	36	....	....	....	....	....	....	....	....	....	....	....	....	....	....	....	....	....	....
	Chicago	**NHL**	**20**	**2**	**2**	**4**	**8**	**0**	**0**	**0**	**23**	**8.7**	**−9**	**8**	**37.5**	**8:53**	....	....	....	....	....	....	....	....	....
	Norfolk Admirals	AHL	....	....	....	....	....	....	....	....	....	....	....	....	....	....	3	1	1	2	0	....	....	....	....
	NHL Totals		**40**	**8**	**9**	**17**	**22**	**2**	**0**	**0**	**62**	**12.9**		**12**	**41.7**	**10:35**	....	....	....	....	....	....	....	....	....

USHL First All-Star Team (2001) • USHL Rookie of the Year (2001) • WCHA All-Rookie Team (2002) • WCHA Rookie of the Year (2002) • WCHA Second All-Star Team (2003) • WCHA First All-Star Team (2004) • NCAA West First All-American Team (2004) • AHL All-Rookie Team (2005)

Traded to **Chicago** by **Ottawa** with Ottawa's 2nd round choice (Simon Danis-Pepin) in 2006 Entry Draft for Tyler Arnason, March 9, 2006.

BOGUNIECKI, Eric

(BOH-guhn-ih-kee, AIR-ihk)

Center. Shoots right. 5'8", 192 lbs. Born, New Haven, CT, May 6, 1975. St. Louis' 6th choice, 193rd overall, in 1993 Entry Draft.

Season	Club	League	GP	G	A	Pts	PIM	PP	SH	GW	S	%	+/-	TF	F%	Min	GP	G	A	Pts	PIM	PP	SH	GW	Min
1992-93	Westminster	High-CT	24	30	24	54	55	....	....	....	....	....	....	....	....	....	....	....	....	....	....	....	....	....	....
1993-94	New Hampshire	H-East	40	17	16	33	66	....	....	....	....	....	....	....	....	....	....	....	....	....	....	....	....	....	....
1994-95	New Hampshire	H-East	34	12	16	28	62	....	....	....	....	....	....	....	....	....	....	....	....	....	....	....	....	....	....
1995-96	New Hampshire	H-East	32	23	28	51	46	....	....	....	....	....	....	....	....	....	....	....	....	....	....	....	....	....	....
1996-97	New Hampshire	H-East	36	26	31	57	58	....	....	....	....	....	....	....	....	....	....	....	....	....	....	....	....	....	....
1997-98	Dayton Bombers	ECHL	26	19	18	37	36	....	....	....	....	....	....	....	....	....	....	....	....	....	....	....	....	....	....
	Fort Wayne	IHL	35	4	8	12	29	....	....	....	....	....	....	....	....	....	4	1	2	3	10	....	....	....	....
1998-99	Fort Wayne	IHL	72	32	34	66	100	....	....	....	....	....	....	....	....	....	2	0	1	1	2	....	....	....	....
99-2000	**Florida**	**NHL**	**4**	**0**	**0**	**0**	**2**	**0**	**0**	**0**	**5**	**0.0**	**−1**	**25**	**36.0**	**8:35**	....	....	....	....	....	....	....	....	....
	Louisville Panthers	AHL	57	33	42	75	148	....	....	....	....	....	....	....	....	....	4	3	2	5	20	....	....	....	....
2000-01	Louisville Panthers	AHL	28	13	12	25	56	....	....	....	....	....	....	....	....	....	....	....	....	....	....	....	....	....	....
	St. Louis	**NHL**	**1**	**0**	**0**	**0**	**0**	**0**	**0**	**0**	**1**	**0.0**	**−1**	**0**	**0.0**	**13:44**	....	....	....	....	....	....	....	....	....
	Worcester IceCats	AHL	45	17	28	45	100	....	....	....	....	....	....	....	....	....	9	3	2	5	10	....	....	....	....
2001-02	**St. Louis**	**NHL**	**8**	**0**	**1**	**1**	**4**	**0**	**0**	**0**	**10**	**0.0**	**−2**	**21**	**38.1**	**11:42**	**1**	**0**	**1**	**1**	**0**	**0**	**0**	**0**	**8:01**
	Worcester IceCats	AHL	63	*38	46	84	181	....	....	....	....	....	....	....	....	....	3	2	0	2	4	....	....	....	....
2002-03	**St. Louis**	**NHL**	**80**	**22**	**27**	**49**	**38**	**3**	**1**	**5**	**117**	**18.8**	**22**	**5**	**40.0**	**14:00**	**7**	**1**	**2**	**3**	**2**	**1**	**0**	**0**	**13:09**
2003-04	**St. Louis**	**NHL**	**27**	**6**	**4**	**10**	**20**	**2**	**0**	**2**	**40**	**15.0**	**−1**	**1**	**0.0**	**14:42**	**1**	**0**	**0**	**0**	**0**	**0**	**0**	**0**	**12:52**
	Worcester IceCats	AHL	3	0	1	1	0	....	....	....	....	....	....	....	....	....	....	....	....	....	....	....	....	....	....
2004-05	Worcester IceCats	AHL	30	14	11	25	46	....	....	....	....	....	....	....	....	....	....	....	....	....	....	....	....	....	....
	SC Langenthal	Swiss-2	10	5	3	8	47	....	....	....	....	....	....	....	....	....	....	....	....	....	....	....	....	....	....
2005-06	**St. Louis**	**NHL**	**9**	**1**	**4**	**5**	**4**	**1**	**0**	**0**	**12**	**8.3**	**−1**	**1**	**100.0**	**12:15**	....	....	....	....	....	....	....	....	....
	Peoria Rivermen	AHL	2	0	0	0	4	....	....	....	....	....	....	....	....	....	....	....	....	....	....	....	....	....	....
	Pittsburgh	**NHL**	**38**	**5**	**6**	**11**	**29**	**1**	**0**	**0**	**36**	**13.9**	**−2**	**74**	**48.7**	**10:50**	....	....	....	....	....	....	....	....	....
	NHL Totals		**167**	**34**	**42**	**76**	**97**	**7**	**1**	**7**	**221**	**15.4**		**127**	**44.1**	**13:04**	**9**	**1**	**3**	**4**	**2**	**1**	**0**	**0**	**12:33**

Hockey East Second All-Star Team (1997) • AHL First All-Star Team (2002) • Les Cunningham Award (MVP – AHL) (2002)

Signed as a free agent by **Florida**, July 7, 1999. Traded to **St. Louis** by **Florida** for Andrei Podkonicky, December 17, 2000. • Missed majority of 2003-04 season recovering from shoulder (September 23, 2003 in training camp) and head (February 28, 2004 vs. Vancouver) injuries. Signed as a free agent by **Langenthal** (Swiss-2), October 4, 2004. Traded to **Pittsburgh** by **St. Louis** for Steve Poapst, December 9, 2005.

BOILEAU, Patrick

(BWOI-loh, PAT-rihk)

Defense. Shoots right. 6', 202 lbs. Born, Montreal, Que., February 22, 1975. Washington's 3rd choice, 69th overall, in 1993 Entry Draft.

Season	Club	League	GP	G	A	Pts	PIM	PP	SH	GW	S	%	+/-	TF	F%	Min	GP	G	A	Pts	PIM	PP	SH	GW	Min
1990-91	Laval-Laurentides	QAAA	3	0	1	1	0	....	....	....	....	....	....	....	....	....	....	....	....	....	....	....	....	....	....
1991-92	Laval-Laurentides	QAAA	42	9	36	45	94	....	....	....	....	....	....	....	....	....	12	3	5	8	10	....	....	....	....
1992-93	Laval Titan	QMJHL	69	4	19	23	73	....	....	....	....	....	....	....	....	....	13	1	2	3	10	....	....	....	....
1993-94	Laval Titan	QMJHL	64	13	57	70	56	....	....	....	....	....	....	....	....	....	21	1	7	8	24	....	....	....	....
1994-95	Laval Titan	QMJHL	38	8	25	33	46	....	....	....	....	....	....	....	....	....	20	4	16	20	24	....	....	....	....
1995-96	Portland Pirates	AHL	78	10	28	38	41	....	....	....	....	....	....	....	....	....	19	1	3	4	12	....	....	....	....
1996-97	**Washington**	**NHL**	**1**	**0**	**0**	**0**	**0**	**0**	**0**	**0**	**0**	**0.0**	**0**	....	....	....	....	....	....	....	....	....	....	....	....
	Portland Pirates	AHL	67	16	28	44	63	....	....	....	....	....	....	....	....	....	5	1	1	2	4	....	....	....	....
1997-98	Portland Pirates	AHL	47	6	21	27	53	....	....	....	....	....	....	....	....	....	10	0	1	1	8	....	....	....	....
1998-99	**Washington**	**NHL**	**4**	**0**	**1**	**1**	**2**	**0**	**0**	**0**	**7**	**0.0**	**−4**	**0**	**0.0**	**15:56**	....	....	....	....	....	....	....	....	....
	Portland Pirates	AHL	52	6	18	24	52	....	....	....	....	....	....	....	....	....	....	....	....	....	....	....	....	....	....
	Indianapolis Ice	IHL	29	8	13	21	27	....	....	....	....	....	....	....	....	....	4	0	1	1	2	....	....	....	....
99-2000	Portland Pirates	AHL	63	2	15	17	61	....	....	....	....	....	....	....	....	....	4	0	0	0	4	....	....	....	....
2000-01	Portland Pirates	AHL	77	6	14	20	50	....	....	....	....	....	....	....	....	....	3	0	0	0	8	....	....	....	....
2001-02	**Washington**	**NHL**	**2**	**0**	**0**	**0**	**2**	**0**	**0**	**0**	**0**	**0.0**	**−1**	**0**	**0.0**	**11:52**	....	....	....	....	....	....	....	....	....
	Portland Pirates	AHL	75	17	19	36	43	....	....	....	....	....	....	....	....	....	....	....	....	....	....	....	....	....	....
2002-03	**Detroit**	**NHL**	**25**	**2**	**6**	**8**	**14**	**0**	**0**	**1**	**18**	**11.1**	**8**	**0**	**0.0**	**13:58**	....	....	....	....	....	....	....	....	....
	Grand Rapids	AHL	23	2	11	13	39	....	....	....	....	....	....	....	....	....	....	....	....	....	....	....	....	....	....
2003-04	**Pittsburgh**	**NHL**	**16**	**3**	**4**	**7**	**8**	**3**	**0**	**0**	**41**	**7.3**	**−16**	**0**	**0.0**	**19:52**	....	....	....	....	....	....	....	....	....
	Wilkes-Barre	AHL	51	6	29	35	43	....	....	....	....	....	....	....	....	....	24	3	9	12	24	....	....	....	....

			Regular Season														Playoffs								
Season	Club	League	GP	G	A	Pts	PIM	PP	SH	GW	S	%	+/-	TF	F%	Min	GP	G	A	Pts	PIM	PP	SH	GW	Min
2004-05	Lausanne HC	Swiss	29	7	12	19	34	....	....	....	....	....	....	....	....	....	8	4	4	8	20	....	....	....	....
	Lausanne HC	Swiss-Q	....	....	....	....	....	....	....	....	....	....	....	....	....	....	7	0	1	1	4	....	....	....	....
2005-06	Frankfurt Lions	Germany	52	7	21	28	52	....	....	....	....	....	....	....	....	....	....	....	....	....	....	....	....	....	....
	NHL Totals		**48**	**5**	**11**	**16**	**26**	**3**	**0**	**1**	**66**	**7.6**		**0**	**0.0**	**16:03**	....	....	....	....	....	....	....	....	....

Canadian Major Junior Scholastic Player of the Year (1994)

Loaned to **Indianapolis** (IHL) by **Washington** (Portland-AHL), February 4, 1999. Signed as a free agent by **Detroit**, August 5, 2002. Signed as a free agent by **Pittsburgh**, August 28, 2003. Signed as a free agent by **Lausanne** (Swiss), May 13, 2004.

BONDRA, Peter

(BAWN-druh, PEE-tuhr)

Right wing. Shoots left. 6', 200 lbs. Born, Luck, USSR, February 7, 1968. Washington's 9th choice, 156th overall, in 1990 Entry Draft.

1986-87	VSZ Kosice	Czech	32	4	5	9	24	....	....	....	....	....	....	....	....	....	....	....	....	....	....	....	....	....	....
1987-88	VSZ Kosice	Czech	45	27	11	38	20	....	....	....	....	....	....	....	....	....	....	....	....	....	....	....	....	....	....
1988-89	VSZ Kosice	Czech	40	30	10	40	20	....	....	....	....	....	....	....	....	....	....	....	....	....	....	....	....	....	....
1989-90	VSZ Kosice	Czech	44	29	17	46	....	....	....	....	....	....	....	....	....	....	5	7	2	9	....	....	....	....	....
1990-91	**Washington**	**NHL**	**54**	**12**	**16**	**28**	**47**	**4**	**0**	**1**	**95**	**12.6**	**–10**	....	....	....	**4**	**0**	**1**	**1**	**2**	**0**	**0**	**0**	....
1991-92	**Washington**	**NHL**	**71**	**28**	**28**	**56**	**42**	**4**	**0**	**3**	**158**	**17.7**	**16**	....	....	....	**7**	**6**	**2**	**8**	**4**	**1**	**0**	**0**	....
1992-93	**Washington**	**NHL**	**83**	**37**	**48**	**85**	**70**	**10**	**0**	**7**	**239**	**15.5**	**8**	....	....	....	**6**	**0**	**6**	**6**	**0**	**0**	**0**	**0**	....
1993-94	**Washington**	**NHL**	**69**	**24**	**19**	**43**	**40**	**4**	**0**	**2**	**200**	**12.0**	**22**	....	....	....	**9**	**2**	**4**	**6**	**4**	**0**	**0**	**1**	....
1994-95	HC Kosice	Slovakia	2	1	0	1	0	....	....	....	....	....	....	....	....	....	....	....	....	....	....	....	....	....	....
	Washington	**NHL**	**47**	***34**	**9**	**43**	**24**	**12**	**6**	**3**	**177**	**19.2**	**9**	....	....	....	**7**	**5**	**3**	**8**	**10**	**2**	**0**	**1**	....
1995-96	Detroit Vipers	IHL	7	8	1	9	0	....	....	....	....	....	....	....	....	....	....	....	....	....	....	....	....	....	....
	Washington	**NHL**	**67**	**52**	**28**	**80**	**40**	**11**	**4**	**7**	**322**	**16.1**	**18**	....	....	....	**6**	**3**	**2**	**5**	**8**	**2**	**0**	**1**	....
1996-97	**Washington**	**NHL**	**77**	**46**	**31**	**77**	**72**	**10**	**4**	**3**	**314**	**14.6**	**7**	....	....	....	....	....	....	....	....	....	....	....	....
1997-98	**Washington**	**NHL**	**76**	***52**	**26**	**78**	**44**	**11**	**5**	**13**	**284**	**18.3**	**14**	....	....	....	**17**	**7**	**5**	**12**	**12**	**3**	**0**	**2**	....
	Slovakia	Olympics	2	1	0	1	25	....	....	....	....	....	....	....	....	....	....	....	....	....	....	....	....	....	....
1998-99	**Washington**	**NHL**	**66**	**31**	**24**	**55**	**56**	**6**	**3**	**5**	**284**	**10.9**	**–1**	**1**	**0.0**	**20:35**	....	....	....	....	....	....	....	....	....
99-2000	**Washington**	**NHL**	**62**	**21**	**17**	**38**	**30**	**5**	**3**	**5**	**187**	**11.2**	**5**	**2**	**50.0**	**18:48**	**5**	**1**	**1**	**2**	**4**	**1**	**0**	**0**	**17:30**
2000-01	**Washington**	**NHL**	**82**	**45**	**36**	**81**	**60**	**22**	**4**	**8**	**305**	**14.8**	**8**	**2**	**50.0**	**20:48**	**6**	**2**	**0**	**2**	**2**	**2**	**0**	**1**	**24:55**
2001-02	**Washington**	**NHL**	**77**	**39**	**31**	**70**	**80**	**17**	**1**	**8**	**333**	**11.7**	**–2**	**2**	**50.0**	**21:43**	....	....	....	....	....	....	....	....	....
2002-03	**Washington**	**NHL**	**76**	**30**	**26**	**56**	**52**	**9**	**2**	**4**	**256**	**11.7**	**–3**	**13**	**30.8**	**18:53**	**6**	**4**	**2**	**6**	**8**	**2**	**0**	**0**	**22:39**
2003-04	**Washington**	**NHL**	**54**	**21**	**14**	**35**	**22**	**12**	**0**	**4**	**136**	**15.4**	**–17**	**2**	**50.0**	**18:43**	....	....	....	....	....	....	....	....	....
	Ottawa	**NHL**	**23**	**5**	**9**	**14**	**16**	**2**	**0**	**1**	**52**	**9.6**	**1**	**4**	**0.0**	**18:21**	**7**	**0**	**0**	**0**	**6**	**0**	**0**	**0**	**16:36**
2004-05	HK SKP Poprad	Slovakia	6	4	2	6	4	....	....	....	....	....	....	....	....	....	....	....	....	....	....	....	....	....	....
2005-06	**Atlanta**	**NHL**	**60**	**21**	**18**	**39**	**40**	**8**	**0**	**1**	**143**	**14.7**	**–3**	**5**	**20.0**	**15:56**	....	....	....	....	....	....	....	....	....
	Slovakia	Olympics	6	4	0	4	2	....	....	....	....	....	....	....	....	....	....	....	....	....	....	....	....	....	....
	NHL Totals		**1044**	**498**	**380**	**878**	**735**	**147**	**32**	**75**	**3485**	**14.3**		**31**	**29.0**	**19:27**	**80**	**30**	**26**	**56**	**60**	**13**	**0**	**6**	**20:23**

Played in NHL All-Star Game (1993, 1996, 1997, 1998, 1999)

Traded to **Ottawa** by **Washington** for Brooks Laich and Ottawa's 2nd round choice (later traded to Colorado - Colorado selected Chris Durand) in 2005 Entry Draft, February 18, 2004. Signed as a free agent by **Poprad** (Slovakia), January 17, 2005. Signed as a free agent by **Atlanta**, September 18, 2005.

BONK, Radek

(BOHNK, RA-dehk) **MTL.**

Center. Shoots left. 6'3", 213 lbs. Born, Krnov, Czech., January 9, 1976. Ottawa's 1st choice, 3rd overall, in 1994 Entry Draft.

1990-91	Opava Jr.	Czech-Jr.	35	47	42	89	25	....	....	....	....	....	....	....	....	....	....	....	....	....	....	....	....	....	....
1991-92	AC ZPS Zlin Jr.	Czech-Jr.	45	47	36	83	30	....	....	....	....	....	....	....	....	....	....	....	....	....	....	....	....	....	....
1992-93	AC ZPS Zlin	Czech	30	5	5	10	10	....	....	....	....	....	....	....	....	....	....	....	....	....	....	....	....	....	....
1993-94	Las Vegas	IHL	76	42	45	87	208	....	....	....	....	....	....	....	....	....	5	1	2	3	10	....	....	....	....
1994-95	Las Vegas	IHL	33	7	13	20	62	....	....	....	....	....	....	....	....	....	....	....	....	....	....	....	....	....	....
	Ottawa	**NHL**	**42**	**3**	**8**	**11**	**28**	**1**	**0**	**0**	**40**	**7.5**	**–5**	....	....	....	....	....	....	....	....	....	....	....	....
	P.E.I. Senators	AHL	....	....	....	....	....	....	....	....	....	....	....	....	....	....	1	0	0	0	0	....	....	....	....
1995-96	**Ottawa**	**NHL**	**76**	**16**	**19**	**35**	**36**	**5**	**0**	**1**	**161**	**9.9**	**–5**	....	....	....	....	....	....	....	....	....	....	....	....
1996-97	**Ottawa**	**NHL**	**53**	**5**	**13**	**18**	**14**	**0**	**1**	**0**	**82**	**6.1**	**–4**	....	....	....	**7**	**0**	**1**	**1**	**4**	**0**	**0**	**0**	....
1997-98	**Ottawa**	**NHL**	**65**	**7**	**9**	**16**	**16**	**1**	**0**	**0**	**93**	**7.5**	**–13**	....	....	....	**5**	**0**	**0**	**0**	**2**	**0**	**0**	**0**	....
1998-99	**Ottawa**	**NHL**	**81**	**16**	**16**	**32**	**48**	**0**	**1**	**6**	**110**	**14.5**	**15**	**1184**	**50.1**	**13:44**	**4**	**0**	**0**	**0**	**6**	**0**	**0**	**0**	**16:16**
99-2000	Pardubice	CzRep	3	1	0	1	4	....	....	....	....	....	....	....	....	....	....	....	....	....	....	....	....	....	....
	Ottawa	**NHL**	**80**	**23**	**37**	**60**	**53**	**10**	**0**	**5**	**167**	**13.8**	**–2**	**1654**	**52.0**	**18:14**	**6**	**0**	**0**	**0**	**8**	**0**	**0**	**0**	**15:37**
2000-01	**Ottawa**	**NHL**	**74**	**23**	**36**	**59**	**52**	**5**	**2**	**3**	**139**	**16.5**	**27**	**1506**	**51.2**	**18:16**	**2**	**0**	**0**	**0**	**2**	**0**	**0**	**0**	**14:32**
2001-02	**Ottawa**	**NHL**	**82**	**25**	**45**	**70**	**52**	**6**	**2**	**5**	**170**	**14.7**	**3**	**1530**	**51.0**	**17:57**	**12**	**3**	**7**	**10**	**6**	**2**	**0**	**1**	**18:53**
2002-03	**Ottawa**	**NHL**	**70**	**22**	**32**	**54**	**36**	**11**	**0**	**4**	**146**	**15.1**	**6**	**1218**	**46.2**	**17:32**	**18**	**6**	**5**	**11**	**10**	**2**	**0**	**0**	**17:43**
2003-04	**Ottawa**	**NHL**	**66**	**12**	**32**	**44**	**66**	**6**	**0**	**1**	**98**	**12.2**	**2**	**1184**	**44.9**	**17:38**	**7**	**0**	**2**	**2**	**0**	**0**	**0**	**0**	**18:29**
2004-05	HC Ocelari Trinec	CzRep	27	6	10	16	44	....	....	....	....	....	....	....	....	....	....	....	....	....	....	....	....	....	....
	HC Hame Zlin	CzRep	6	3	2	5	4	....	....	....	....	....	....	....	....	....	6	0	2	2	8	....	....	....	....
2005-06	**Montreal**	**NHL**	**61**	**6**	**15**	**21**	**52**	**0**	**2**	**1**	**76**	**7.9**	**–3**	**963**	**47.4**	**15:10**	**6**	**2**	**0**	**2**	**2**	**0**	**0**	**1**	**15:36**
	NHL Totals		**750**	**158**	**262**	**420**	**453**	**45**	**8**	**26**	**1282**	**12.3**		**9239**	**49.3**	**16:57**	**67**	**11**	**15**	**26**	**40**	**4**	**0**	**2**	**17:23**

Garry F. Longman Memorial Trophy (Rookie of the Year – IHL) (1994)

Played in NHL All-Star Game (2000, 2001)

Traded to **Los Angeles** by **Ottawa** for Los Angeles' 3rd round choice (Shawn Weller) in 2004 Entry Draft, June 26, 2004. Traded to **Montreal** by **Los Angeles** with Cristobal Huet for Mathieu Garon and San Jose's 3rd round choice (previously acquired, Los Angeles selected Paul Baier) in 2004 Entry Draft, June 26, 2004. Signed as a free agent by **Trinec** (CzRep), September 17, 2004. Signed as a free agent by **Zlin** (CzRep), January 31, 2005.

BONVIE, Dennis

(BOHN-vee, DEHN-his)

Right wing. Shoots right. 5'11", 205 lbs. Born, Antigonish, N.S., July 23, 1973.

1989-90	Antigonish	NSMHL	50	15	30	45	52	....	....	....	....	....	....	....	....	....	....	....	....	....	....	....	....	....	....
1990-91	Antigonish	MJrHL	40	1	8	9	347	....	....	....	....	....	....	....	....	....	....	....	....	....	....	....	....	....	....
1991-92	Kitchener Rangers	OHL	7	1	1	2	23	....	....	....	....	....	....	....	....	....	....	....	....	....	....	....	....	....	....
	North Bay	OHL	49	0	12	12	261	....	....	....	....	....	....	....	....	....	21	0	1	1	91	....	....	....	....
1992-93	North Bay	OHL	64	3	21	24	*316	....	....	....	....	....	....	....	....	....	5	0	0	0	34	....	....	....	....
1993-94	Cape Breton	AHL	63	1	10	11	278	....	....	....	....	....	....	....	....	....	4	0	0	0	11	....	....	....	....
1994-95	Cape Breton	AHL	74	5	15	20	422	....	....	....	....	....	....	....	....	....	....	....	....	....	....	....	....	....	....
	Edmonton	**NHL**	**2**	**0**	**0**	**0**	**0**	**0**	**0**	**0**	**0**	**0.0**	**0**	....	....	....	....	....	....	....	....	....	....	....	....
1995-96	**Edmonton**	**NHL**	**8**	**0**	**0**	**0**	**47**	**0**	**0**	**0**	**0**	**0.0**	**–3**	....	....	....	....	....	....	....	....	....	....	....	....
	Cape Breton	AHL	38	13	14	27	269	....	....	....	....	....	....	....	....	....	....	....	....	....	....	....	....	....	....
1996-97	Hamilton	AHL	73	9	20	29	*522	....	....	....	....	....	....	....	....	....	22	3	11	14	*91	....	....	....	....
1997-98	**Edmonton**	**NHL**	**4**	**0**	**0**	**0**	**27**	**0**	**0**	**0**	**0**	**0.0**	**0**	....	....	....	....	....	....	....	....	....	....	....	....
	Hamilton	AHL	57	11	19	30	295	....	....	....	....	....	....	....	....	....	9	0	5	5	18	....	....	....	....
1998-99	**Chicago**	**NHL**	**11**	**0**	**0**	**0**	**44**	**0**	**0**	**0**	**1**	**0.0**	**–4**	**0**	**0.0**	**3:59**	....	....	....	....	....	....	....	....	....
	Portland Pirates	AHL	3	1	0	1	16	....	....	....	....	....	....	....	....	....	....	....	....	....	....	....	....	....	....
	Philadelphia	AHL	37	4	10	14	158	....	....	....	....	....	....	....	....	....	14	3	3	6	26	....	....	....	....
99-2000	**Pittsburgh**	**NHL**	**28**	**0**	**0**	**0**	**80**	**0**	**0**	**0**	**6**	**0.0**	**–2**	**0**	**0.0**	**3:14**	....	....	....	....	....	....	....	....	....
	Wilkes-Barre	AHL	42	5	26	31	243	....	....	....	....	....	....	....	....	....	....	....	....	....	....	....	....	....	....
2000-01	**Pittsburgh**	**NHL**	**3**	**0**	**0**	**0**	**0**	**0**	**0**	**0**	**1**	**0.0**	**–1**	**0**	**0.0**	**3:30**	....	....	....	....	....	....	....	....	....
	Wilkes-Barre	AHL	65	5	18	23	221	....	....	....	....	....	....	....	....	....	21	0	4	4	35	....	....	....	....
2001-02	**Boston**	**NHL**	**23**	**1**	**2**	**3**	**84**	**0**	**0**	**0**	**5**	**20.0**	**3**	**0**	**0.0**	**5:05**	**1**	**0**	**0**	**0**	**0**	**0**	**0**	**0**	**3:07**
	Providence Bruins	AHL	55	8	8	16	290	....	....	....	....	....	....	....	....	....	....	....	....	....	....	....	....	....	....
2002-03	**Ottawa**	**NHL**	**12**	**0**	**0**	**0**	**29**	**0**	**0**	**0**	**3**	**0.0**	**–1**	**0**	**0.0**	**3:05**	....	....	....	....	....	....	....	....	....
	Binghamton	AHL	51	7	3	10	311	....	....	....	....	....	....	....	....	....	14	2	4	6	*85	....	....	....	....
2003-04	Binghamton	AHL	29	2	4	6	137	....	....	....	....	....	....	....	....	....	....	....	....	....	....	....	....	....	....
	Colorado	**NHL**	**1**	**0**	**0**	**0**	**0**	**0**	**0**	**0**	**1**	**0.0**	**0**	**0**	**0.0**	**7:01**	....	....	....	....	....	....	....	....	....
	Hershey Bears	AHL	30	3	6	9	154	....	....	....	....	....	....	....	....	....	....	....	....	....	....	....	....	....	....
2004-05	Hershey Bears	AHL	76	4	14	18	357	....	....	....	....	....	....	....	....	....	....	....	....	....	....	....	....	....	....
2005-06	Wilkes-Barre	AHL	70	2	13	15	*431	....	....	....	....	....	....	....	....	....	9	0	0	0	29	....	....	....	....
	NHL Totals		**92**	**1**	**2**	**3**	**311**	**0**	**0**	**0**	**17**	**5.9**		**0**	**0.0**	**3:55**	**1**	**0**	**0**	**0**	**0**	**0**	**0**	**0**	**3:07**

Signed as a free agent by **Edmonton**, August 25, 1994. Claimed by **Chicago** from **Edmonton** in Waiver Draft, October 5, 1998. Traded to **Philadelphia** by **Chicago** for Frank Bialowas, January 8, 1999. Signed as a free agent by **Pittsburgh**, September 20, 1999. Signed as a free agent by **Boston**, October 5, 2001. Signed as a free agent by **Ottawa**, August 26, 2002. Traded to **Colorado** by **Ottawa** for Charlie Stephens, January 23, 2004.

BOOGAARD, Derek

(BOO-gard, DAIR-ihk) **MIN.**

Left wing. Shoots right. 6'7", 250 lbs. Born, Saskatoon, Sask., June 23, 1982. Minnesota's 6th choice, 202nd overall, in 2001 Entry Draft.

			Regular Season														Playoffs								
Season	Club	League	GP	G	A	Pts	PIM	PP	SH	GW	S	%	+/-	TF	F%	Min	GP	G	A	Pts	PIM	PP	SH	GW	Min
1998-99	Regina Caps	SJHL	35	2	3	5	166	....	....	....	....	....	....	....	....	....	....	....	....	....	....	....	....	....	....
99-2000	Regina Pats	WHL	5	0	0	0	17	....	....	....	....	....	....	....	....	....	....	....	....	....	....	....	....	....	....
	Prince George	WHL	33	0	0	0	149	....	....	....	....	....	....	....	....	....	....	....	....	....	....	....	....	....	....
2000-01	Prince George	WHL	61	1	8	9	245	....	....	....	....	....	....	....	....	....	6	1	0	1	31	....	....	....	....
2001-02	Prince George	WHL	2	0	0	0	16	....	....	....	....	....	....	....	....	....	....	....	....	....	....	....	....	....	....
	Medicine Hat	WHL	46	1	8	9	178	....	....	....	....	....	....	....	....	....	....	....	....	....	....	....	....	....	....
2002-03	Medicine Hat	WHL	27	1	2	3	65	....	....	....	....	....	....	....	....	....	....	....	....	....	....	....	....	....	....
	Louisiana	ECHL	33	1	2	3	240	....	....	....	....	....	....	....	....	....	2	0	0	0	0	....	....	....	....
2003-04	Houston Aeros	AHL	53	0	4	4	207	....	....	....	....	....	....	....	....	....	2	0	1	1	16	....	....	....	....
2004-05	Houston Aeros	AHL	56	1	4	5	259	....	....	....	....	....	....	....	....	....	5	0	0	0	38	....	....	....	....
2005-06	**Minnesota**	**NHL**	**65**	**2**	**4**	**6**	**158**	**0**	**0**	**1**	**15**	**13.3**	**2**	**0**	**0.0**	**5:23**	....	....	....	....	....	....	....	....	....
	NHL Totals		**65**	**2**	**4**	**6**	**158**	**0**	**0**	**1**	**15**	**13.3**		**0**	**0.0**	**5:23**	....	....	....	....	....	....	....	....	....

BOOTLAND, Darryl

(BOOT-land, DAIR-ihl) **DET.**

Right wing. Shoots right. 6'1", 194 lbs. Born, Toronto, Ont., November 2, 1981. Colorado's 12th choice, 252nd overall, in 2000 Entry Draft.

Season	Club	League	GP	G	A	Pts	PIM	PP	SH	GW	S	%	+/-	TF	F%	Min	GP	G	A	Pts	PIM	PP	SH	GW	Min
1997-98	Orangeville	OHA-B	44	22	26	48	177	....	....	....	....	....	....	....	....	....	....	....	....	....	....	....	....	....	....
1998-99	Barrie Colts	OHL	38	18	11	29	89	....	....	....	....	....	....	....	....	....	....	....	....	....	....	....	....	....	....
	St. Michael's	OHL	28	12	6	18	80	....	....	....	....	....	....	....	....	....	....	....	....	....	....	....	....	....	....
99-2000	St. Michael's	OHL	65	24	30	54	166	....	....	....	....	....	....	....	....	....	....	....	....	....	....	....	....	....	....
2000-01	St. Michael's	OHL	56	32	33	65	136	....	....	....	....	....	....	....	....	....	11	3	1	4	20	....	....	....	....
2001-02	St. Michael's	OHL	61	41	56	97	137	....	....	....	....	....	....	....	....	....	15	8	10	18	50	....	....	....	....
2002-03	Toledo Storm	ECHL	54	17	19	36	322	....	....	....	....	....	....	....	....	....	....	....	....	....	....	....	....	....	....
	Grand Rapids	AHL	16	1	4	5	41	....	....	....	....	....	....	....	....	....	15	3	2	5	46	....	....	....	....
2003-04	**Detroit**	**NHL**	**22**	**1**	**1**	**2**	**74**	**0**	**0**	**1**	**13**	**7.7**	**–3**	**1**	**100.0**	**6:07**	....	....	....	....	....	....	....	....	....
	Grand Rapids	AHL	54	12	2	14	175	....	....	....	....	....	....	....	....	....	4	0	1	1	2	....	....	....	....
2004-05	Grand Rapids	AHL	78	14	20	34	336	....	....	....	....	....	....	....	....	....	....	....	....	....	....	....	....	....	....
2005-06	Grand Rapids	AHL	77	27	29	56	392	....	....	....	....	....	....	....	....	....	16	5	7	12	50	....	....	....	....
	NHL Totals		**22**	**1**	**1**	**2**	**74**	**0**	**0**	**1**	**13**	**7.7**		**1**	**100.0**	**6:07**	....	....	....	....	....	....	....	....	....

Signed as a free agent by **Detroit**, July 25, 2002.

BOUCHARD, Joel

(BOO-shahrd, JOHL) **NYI**

Defense. Shoots left. 6'1", 209 lbs. Born, Montreal, Que., January 23, 1974. Calgary's 7th choice, 129th overall, in 1992 Entry Draft.

Season	Club	League	GP	G	A	Pts	PIM	PP	SH	GW	S	%	+/-	TF	F%	Min	GP	G	A	Pts	PIM	PP	SH	GW	Min
1989-90	Mtl-Bourassa	QAAA	41	7	17	24	10	....	....	....	....	....	....	....	....	....	1	1	0	1	0	....	....	....	....
1990-91	Longueuil	QMJHL	53	3	19	22	34	....	....	....	....	....	....	....	....	....	8	1	0	1	11	....	....	....	....
1991-92	Verdun	QMJHL	70	9	20	29	55	....	....	....	....	....	....	....	....	....	19	1	7	8	20	....	....	....	....
1992-93	Verdun	QMJHL	60	10	49	59	126	....	....	....	....	....	....	....	....	....	4	0	2	2	4	....	....	....	....
1993-94	Verdun	QMJHL	60	15	55	70	62	....	....	....	....	....	....	....	....	....	4	1	0	1	6	....	....	....	....
	Saint John Flames	AHL	1	0	0	0	0	....	....	....	....	....	....	....	....	....	2	0	0	0	0	....	....	....	....
1994-95	Saint John Flames	AHL	77	6	25	31	63	....	....	....	....	....	....	....	....	....	5	1	0	1	4	....	....	....	....
	Calgary	**NHL**	**2**	**0**	**0**	**0**	**0**	**0**	**0**	**0**	**0**	**0.0**	**0**	....	....	....	....	....	....	....	....	....	....	....	....
1995-96	**Calgary**	**NHL**	**4**	**0**	**0**	**0**	**4**	**0**	**0**	**0**	**0**	**0.0**	**0**	....	....	....	....	....	....	....	....	....	....	....	....
	Saint John Flames	AHL	74	8	25	33	104	....	....	....	....	....	....	....	....	....	16	1	4	5	10	....	....	....	....
1996-97	**Calgary**	**NHL**	**76**	**4**	**5**	**9**	**49**	**0**	**1**	**0**	**61**	**6.6**	**–23**	....	....	....	....	....	....	....	....	....	....	....	....
1997-98	**Calgary**	**NHL**	**44**	**5**	**7**	**12**	**57**	**0**	**1**	**1**	**51**	**9.8**	**0**	....	....	....	....	....	....	....	....	....	....	....	....
	Saint John Flames	AHL	3	2	1	3	6	....	....	....	....	....	....	....	....	....	....	....	....	....	....	....	....	....	....
1998-99	**Nashville**	**NHL**	**64**	**4**	**11**	**15**	**60**	**0**	**0**	**0**	**78**	**5.1**	**–10**	**0**	**0.0**	**22:34**	....	....	....	....	....	....	....	....	....
99-2000	**Nashville**	**NHL**	**52**	**1**	**4**	**5**	**23**	**0**	**0**	**0**	**60**	**1.7**	**–11**	**0**	**0.0**	**18:41**	....	....	....	....	....	....	....	....	....
	Dallas	**NHL**	**2**	**0**	**0**	**0**	**2**	**0**	**0**	**0**	**1**	**0.0**	**1**	**0**	**0.0**	**9:45**	....	....	....	....	....	....	....	....	....
2000-01	Grand Rapids	IHL	19	3	9	12	8	....	....	....	....	....	....	....	....	....	....	....	....	....	....	....	....	....	....
	Phoenix	**NHL**	**32**	**1**	**2**	**3**	**22**	**0**	**0**	**0**	**26**	**3.8**	**–8**	**0**	**0.0**	**14:28**	....	....	....	....	....	....	....	....	....
2001-02	**New Jersey**	**NHL**	**1**	**0**	**1**	**1**	**0**	**0**	**0**	**0**	**0**	**0.0**	**1**	**0**	**0.0**	**19:26**	....	....	....	....	....	....	....	....	....
	Albany River Rats	AHL	70	9	22	31	28	....	....	....	....	....	....	....	....	....	....	....	....	....	....	....	....	....	....
2002-03	**NY Rangers**	**NHL**	**27**	**5**	**7**	**12**	**14**	**1**	**0**	**2**	**41**	**12.2**	**6**	**0**	**0.0**	**20:07**	....	....	....	....	....	....	....	....	....
	Hartford	AHL	22	6	14	20	22	....	....	....	....	....	....	....	....	....	....	....	....	....	....	....	....	....	....
	Pittsburgh	**NHL**	**7**	**0**	**1**	**1**	**0**	**0**	**0**	**0**	**6**	**0.0**	**–6**	**0**	**0.0**	**21:49**	....	....	....	....	....	....	....	....	....
2003-04	**NY Rangers**	**NHL**	**28**	**1**	**7**	**8**	**10**	**0**	**0**	**0**	**34**	**2.9**	**2**	**0**	**0.0**	**16:42**	....	....	....	....	....	....	....	....	....
2004-05	Hartford	AHL	7	1	2	3	6	....	....	....	....	....	....	....	....	....	6	0	2	2	20	....	....	....	....
2005-06	**NY Islanders**	**NHL**	**25**	**1**	**8**	**9**	**23**	**0**	**0**	**0**	**45**	**2.2**	**5**	**0**	**0.0**	**21:56**	....	....	....	....	....	....	....	....	....
	Bridgeport	AHL	15	4	9	13	10	....	....	....	....	....	....	....	....	....	....	....	....	....	....	....	....	....	....
	NHL Totals		**364**	**22**	**53**	**75**	**264**	**1**	**2**	**3**	**403**	**5.5**		**0**	**0.0**	**19:27**	....	....	....	....	....	....	....	....	....

QMJHL First All-Star Team (1994)

Claimed by **Nashville** from **Calgary** in Expansion Draft, June 26, 1998. Claimed on waivers by **Dallas** from **Nashville**, March 14, 2000. Signed as a free agent by **Phoenix**, August 31, 2000. Signed as a free agent by **New Jersey**, October 25, 2001. Signed as a free agent by **NY Rangers**, August 5, 2002. Traded to **Pittsburgh** by **NY Rangers** with Richard Lintner, Rico Fata , Mikael Samuelsson and future considerations for Mike Wilson, Alex Kovalev, Janne Laukkanen and Dan LaCouture, February 10, 2003. Signed as a free agent by **Buffalo**, July 14, 2003. Claimed by **NY Rangers** from **Buffalo** in Waiver Draft, October 3, 2003. • Spent majority of 2003-04 season as a healthy reserve. Signed as a free agent by **Hartford** (AHL), March 17, 2005. Signed as a free agent by **NY Islanders**, August 18, 2005.

BOUCHARD, Pierre-Marc

(BOO-shahrd, PEE-air- MAHRK) **MIN.**

Center. Shoots left. 5'10", 165 lbs. Born, Sherbrooke, Que., April 27, 1984. Minnesota's 1st choice, 8th overall, in 2002 Entry Draft.

Season	Club	League	GP	G	A	Pts	PIM	PP	SH	GW	S	%	+/-	TF	F%	Min	GP	G	A	Pts	PIM	PP	SH	GW	Min
1998-99	Mtl.-Bourassa	QAHA	28	23	41	64	....	....	....	....	....	....	....	....	....	....	....	....	....	....	....	....	....	....	....
99-2000	Charles-Lemoyne	QAAA	42	28	*45	*74	20	....	....	....	....	....	....	....	....	....	9	4	8	12	6	....	....	....	....
2000-01	Chicoutimi	QMJHL	67	38	57	95	20	....	....	....	....	....	....	....	....	....	6	5	8	13	0	....	....	....	....
2001-02	Chicoutimi	QMJHL	69	46	*94	*140	54	....	....	....	....	....	....	....	....	....	4	2	3	5	4	....	....	....	....
2002-03	**Minnesota**	**NHL**	**50**	**7**	**13**	**20**	**18**	**5**	**0**	**1**	**53**	**13.2**	**1**	**474**	**40.7**	**13:16**	**5**	**0**	**1**	**1**	**2**	**0**	**0**	**0**	**13:15**
2003-04	**Minnesota**	**NHL**	**61**	**4**	**18**	**22**	**22**	**2**	**0**	**0**	**60**	**6.7**	**–7**	**60**	**50.0**	**14:00**	....	....	....	....	....	....	....	....	....
2004-05	Houston Aeros	AHL	67	12	42	54	46	....	....	....	....	....	....	....	....	....	5	0	1	1	0	....	....	....	....
2005-06	**Minnesota**	**NHL**	**80**	**17**	**42**	**59**	**28**	**7**	**0**	**3**	**118**	**14.4**	**3**	**15**	**46.7**	**15:15**	....	....	....	....	....	....	....	....	....
	NHL Totals		**191**	**28**	**73**	**101**	**68**	**14**	**0**	**4**	**231**	**12.1**		**549**	**41.9**	**14:20**	**5**	**0**	**1**	**1**	**2**	**0**	**0**	**0**	**13:15**

QMJHL Rookie of the Year (2001) • QMJHL First All-Star Team (2002) • Canadian Major Junior First All-Star Team (2002) • Canadian Major Junior Player of the Year (2002)

BOUCHER, Philippe

(boo-SHAY, fihl-EEP) **DAL.**

Defense. Shoots right. 6'3", 221 lbs. Born, Ste-Apollinaire, Que., March 24, 1973. Buffalo's 1st choice, 13th overall, in 1991 Entry Draft.

Season	Club	League	GP	G	A	Pts	PIM	PP	SH	GW	S	%	+/-	TF	F%	Min	GP	G	A	Pts	PIM	PP	SH	GW	Min
1988-89	Ste-Foy	QAAA	5	0	0	0	2	....	....	....	....	....	....	....	....	....	....	....	....	....	....	....	....	....	....
1989-90	Ste-Foy	QAAA	42	26	60	86	76	....	....	....	....	....	....	....	....	....	12	6	*19	25	16	....	....	....	....
1990-91	Granby Bisons	QMJHL	69	21	46	67	92	....	....	....	....	....	....	....	....	....	....	....	....	....	....	....	....	....	....
1991-92	Granby Bisons	QMJHL	49	22	37	59	47	....	....	....	....	....	....	....	....	....	....	....	....	....	....	....	....	....	....
	Laval Titan	QMJHL	16	7	11	18	36	....	....	....	....	....	....	....	....	....	10	5	6	11	8	....	....	....	....
1992-93	Laval Titan	QMJHL	16	12	15	27	37	....	....	....	....	....	....	....	....	....	13	6	15	21	12	....	....	....	....
	Buffalo	**NHL**	**18**	**0**	**4**	**4**	**14**	**0**	**0**	**0**	**28**	**0.0**	**1**	....	....	....	....	....	....	....	....	....	....	....	....
	Rochester	AHL	5	4	3	7	8	....	....	....	....	....	....	....	....	....	3	0	1	1	2	....	....	....	....
1993-94	**Buffalo**	**NHL**	**38**	**6**	**8**	**14**	**29**	**4**	**0**	**1**	**67**	**9.0**	**–1**	....	....	....	**7**	**1**	**1**	**2**	**2**	**1**	**0**	**0**	....
	Rochester	AHL	31	10	22	32	51	....	....	....	....	....	....	....	....	....	....	....	....	....	....	....	....	....	....
1994-95	Rochester	AHL	43	14	27	41	26	....	....	....	....	....	....	....	....	....	....	....	....	....	....	....	....	....	....
	Buffalo	**NHL**	**9**	**1**	**4**	**5**	**0**	**0**	**0**	**0**	**15**	**6.7**	**6**	....	....	....	....	....	....	....	....	....	....	....	....
	Los Angeles	**NHL**	**6**	**1**	**0**	**1**	**4**	**0**	**0**	**0**	**15**	**6.7**	**–3**	....	....	....	....	....	....	....	....	....	....	....	....
1995-96	**Los Angeles**	**NHL**	**53**	**7**	**16**	**23**	**31**	**5**	**0**	**1**	**145**	**4.8**	**–26**	....	....	....	....	....	....	....	....	....	....	....	....
	Phoenix	IHL	10	4	3	7	4	....	....	....	....	....	....	....	....	....	....	....	....	....	....	....	....	....	....
1996-97	**Los Angeles**	**NHL**	**60**	**7**	**18**	**25**	**25**	**2**	**0**	**1**	**159**	**4.4**	**0**	....	....	....	....	....	....	....	....	....	....	....	....
1997-98	**Los Angeles**	**NHL**	**45**	**6**	**10**	**16**	**49**	**1**	**0**	**0**	**80**	**7.5**	**6**	....	....	....	....	....	....	....	....	....	....	....	....
	Long Beach	IHL	2	0	1	1	4	....	....	....	....	....	....	....	....	....	....	....	....	....	....	....	....	....	....
1998-99	**Los Angeles**	**NHL**	**45**	**2**	**6**	**8**	**32**	**1**	**0**	**0**	**87**	**2.3**	**–12**	**0**	**0.0**	**17:51**	....	....	....	....	....	....	....	....	....
99-2000	**Los Angeles**	**NHL**	**1**	**0**	**0**	**0**	**0**	**0**	**0**	**0**	**3**	**0.0**	**0**	**0**	**0.0**	**17:04**	....	....	....	....	....	....	....	....	....
	Long Beach	IHL	14	4	11	15	8	....	....	....	....	....	....	....	....	....	6	0	9	9	8	....	....	....	....

			Regular Season														Playoffs								
Season	Club	League	GP	G	A	Pts	PIM	PP	SH	GW	S	%	+/-	TF	F%	Min	GP	G	A	Pts	PIM	PP	SH	GW	Min
2000-01	**Los Angeles**	**NHL**	**22**	**2**	**4**	**6**	**20**	**2**	**0**	**0**	**40**	**5.0**	**4**	**0**	**0.0**	**18:25**	**13**	**0**	**1**	**1**	**2**	**0**	**0**	**0**	**15:48**
	Manitoba Moose	IHL	45	10	22	32	39	....	....	....	....	....	....	....	....	....	....	....	....	....	....	....	....	....	....
2001-02	**Los Angeles**	**NHL**	**80**	**7**	**23**	**30**	**94**	**4**	**0**	**2**	**198**	**3.5**	**0**	**0**	**0.0**	**21:36**	**5**	**0**	**1**	**1**	**2**	**0**	**0**	**0**	**19:31**
2002-03	**Dallas**	**NHL**	**80**	**7**	**20**	**27**	**94**	**1**	**1**	**3**	**137**	**5.1**	**28**	**1**	**0.0**	**20:29**	**11**	**1**	**2**	**3**	**11**	**0**	**0**	**0**	**21:28**
2003-04	**Dallas**	**NHL**	**70**	**8**	**16**	**24**	**64**	**2**	**0**	**2**	**134**	**6.0**	**15**	**0**	**0.0**	**22:24**	**5**	**1**	**0**	**1**	**6**	**0**	**0**	**0**	**23:57**
2004-05		DID NOT PLAY																							
2005-06	**Dallas**	**NHL**	**66**	**16**	**27**	**43**	**77**	**8**	**0**	**3**	**174**	**9.2**	**28**	**1**	**100.0**	**23:25**	**5**	**0**	**1**	**1**	**2**	**0**	**0**	**0**	**21:35**
	NHL Totals		**593**	**70**	**156**	**226**	**533**	**30**	**1**	**13**	**1282**	**5.5**		**2**	**50.0**	**21:10**	**46**	**3**	**6**	**9**	**25**	**1**	**0**	**0**	**19:40**

QMJHL Second All-Star Team (1991, 1992) • QMJHL Defensive Rookie of the Year (1991) • Canadian Major Junior Rookie of the Year (1991)

Traded to **Los Angeles** by **Buffalo** with Denis Tsygurov and Grant Fuhr for Alexei Zhitnik, Robb Stauber, Charlie Huddy and Los Angeles' 5th round choice (Marian Menhart) in 1995 Entry Draft, February 14, 1995. • Missed majority of 1999-2000 season recovering from foot injury suffered in training camp, September, 1999. Signed as a free agent by **Dallas**, July 2, 2002.

BOUCK, Tyler

(BOWK, TIGH-luhr) **VAN.**

Center. Shoots left. 6', 196 lbs. Born, Camrose, Alta., January 13, 1980. Dallas' 2nd choice, 57th overall, in 1998 Entry Draft.

Season	Club	League	GP	G	A	Pts	PIM	PP	SH	GW	S	%	+/-	TF	F%	Min	GP	G	A	Pts	PIM	PP	SH	GW	Min
1995-96	Sherwood Park	AMHL	22	10	21	31	58	....	....	....	....	....	....	....	....	....	....	....	....	....	....	....	....	....	....
1996-97	Prince George	WHL	12	0	2	2	11	....	....	....	....	....	....	....	....	....	....	....	....	....	....	....	....	....	....
1997-98	Prince George	WHL	65	11	26	37	90	....	....	....	....	....	....	....	....	....	11	1	0	1	21	....	....	....	....
1998-99	Prince George	WHL	56	22	25	47	178	....	....	....	....	....	....	....	....	....	2	0	2	2	10	....	....	....	....
99-2000	Prince George	WHL	57	30	33	63	183	....	....	....	....	....	....	....	....	....	13	6	13	19	36	....	....	....	....
2000-01	**Dallas**	**NHL**	**48**	**2**	**5**	**7**	**29**	**0**	**0**	**1**	**41**	**4.9**	**–3**	**1**	**0.0**	**8:59**	**1**	**0**	**0**	**0**	**0**	**0**	**0**	**0**	**9:02**
	Utah Grizzlies	IHL	24	2	6	8	39	....	....	....	....	....	....	....	....	....	....	....	....	....	....	....	....	....	....
2001-02	**Phoenix**	**NHL**	**7**	**0**	**0**	**0**	**4**	**0**	**0**	**0**	**3**	**0.0**	**–1**	**0**	**0.0**	**6:54**	....	....	....	....	....	....	....	....	....
	Springfield	AHL	21	1	2	3	33	....	....	....	....	....	....	....	....	....	....	....	....	....	....	....	....	....	....
	Manitoba Moose	AHL	20	4	4	8	25	....	....	....	....	....	....	....	....	....	....	....	....	....	....	....	....	....	....
2002-03	Manitoba Moose	AHL	76	10	28	38	103	....	....	....	....	....	....	....	....	....	14	2	2	4	10	....	....	....	....
2003-04	**Vancouver**	**NHL**	**18**	**1**	**2**	**3**	**23**	**0**	**1**	**0**	**12**	**8.3**	**–4**	**0**	**0.0**	**9:18**	**1**	**0**	**0**	**0**	**0**	**0**	**0**	**0**	**5:15**
	Manitoba Moose	AHL	49	11	14	25	100	....	....	....	....	....	....	....	....	....	....	....	....	....	....	....	....	....	....
2004-05	TPS Turku	Finland	40	3	7	10	100	....	....	....	....	....	....	....	....	....	6	1	0	1	12	....	....	....	....
2005-06	**Vancouver**	**NHL**	**12**	**1**	**1**	**2**	**21**	**0**	**0**	**0**	**6**	**16.7**	**0**	**0**	**0.0**	**6:22**	....	....	....	....	....	....	....	....	....
	Manitoba Moose	AHL	8	0	1	1	8	....	....	....	....	....	....	....	....	....	....	....	....	....	....	....	....	....	....
	NHL Totals		**85**	**4**	**8**	**12**	**77**	**0**	**1**	**1**	**62**	**6.5**		**1**	**0.0**	**8:31**	**2**	**0**	**0**	**0**	**0**	**0**	**0**	**0**	**7:08**

WHL West First All-Star Team (2000)

Traded to **Phoenix** by **Dallas** for Jyrki Lumme, June 23, 2001. Traded to **Vancouver** by **Phoenix** with Todd Warriner, Trevor Letowski and Phoenix's 3rd round choice (later traded back to Phoenix – Phoenix selected Dimitri Pestunov) in 2003 Entry Draft for Drake Berehowsky and Denis Pederson, December 28, 2001. Signed as a free agent by **Turku** (Finland), October 22, 2004. • Missed majority of 2005-06 season recovering from a groin injury suffered in training camp (October 4, 2005) and as a healthy reserve.

BOUGHNER, Bob

(BOOG-nuhr, BAWB)

Defense. Shoots right. 6', 203 lbs. Born, Windsor, Ont., March 8, 1971. Detroit's 2nd choice, 32nd overall, in 1989 Entry Draft.

Season	Club	League	GP	G	A	Pts	PIM	PP	SH	GW	S	%	+/-	TF	F%	Min	GP	G	A	Pts	PIM	PP	SH	GW	Min
1986-87	Belle River	OHA-C	37	3	11	14	88	....	....	....	....	....	....	....	....	....	....	....	....	....	....	....	....	....	....
1987-88	St. Mary's Lincolns	OHA-B	36	4	18	22	177	....	....	....	....	....	....	....	....	....	....	....	....	....	....	....	....	....	....
1988-89	Sault Ste. Marie	OHL	64	6	15	21	182	....	....	....	....	....	....	....	....	....	....	....	....	....	....	....	....	....	....
1989-90	Sault Ste. Marie	OHL	49	7	23	30	122	....	....	....	....	....	....	....	....	....	....	....	....	....	....	....	....	....	....
1990-91	Sault Ste. Marie	OHL	64	13	33	46	156	....	....	....	....	....	....	....	....	....	14	2	9	11	35	....	....	....	....
1991-92	Toledo Storm	ECHL	28	3	10	13	79	....	....	....	....	....	....	....	....	....	5	2	0	2	15	....	....	....	....
	Adirondack	AHL	1	0	0	0	7	....	....	....	....	....	....	....	....	....	....	....	....	....	....	....	....	....	....
1992-93	Adirondack	AHL	69	1	16	17	190	....	....	....	....	....	....	....	....	....	....	....	....	....	....	....	....	....	....
1993-94	Adirondack	AHL	72	8	14	22	292	....	....	....	....	....	....	....	....	....	10	1	1	2	18	....	....	....	....
1994-95	Cincinnati	IHL	81	2	14	16	192	....	....	....	....	....	....	....	....	....	10	0	0	0	18	....	....	....	....
1995-96	Carolina Panthers	AHL	46	2	15	17	127	....	....	....	....	....	....	....	....	....	....	....	....	....	....	....	....	....	....
	Buffalo	**NHL**	**31**	**0**	**1**	**1**	**104**	**0**	**0**	**0**	**14**	**0.0**	**3**	....	....	....	....	....	....	....	....	....	....	....	....
1996-97	**Buffalo**	**NHL**	**77**	**1**	**7**	**8**	**225**	**0**	**0**	**0**	**34**	**2.9**	**12**	....	....	....	**11**	**0**	**1**	**1**	**9**	**0**	**0**	**0**	....
1997-98	**Buffalo**	**NHL**	**69**	**1**	**3**	**4**	**165**	**0**	**0**	**0**	**26**	**3.8**	**5**	....	....	....	**14**	**0**	**4**	**4**	**15**	**0**	**0**	**0**	....
1998-99	**Nashville**	**NHL**	**79**	**3**	**10**	**13**	**137**	**0**	**0**	**1**	**59**	**5.1**	**–6**	**0**	**0.0**	**18:31**	....	....	....	....	....	....	....	....	....
99-2000	**Nashville**	**NHL**	**62**	**2**	**4**	**6**	**97**	**0**	**0**	**0**	**32**	**6.3**	**–13**	**0**	**0.0**	**17:20**	....	....	....	....	....	....	....	....	....
	Pittsburgh	**NHL**	**11**	**1**	**0**	**1**	**69**	**1**	**0**	**1**	**8**	**12.5**	**2**	**0**	**0.0**	**17:05**	**11**	**0**	**2**	**2**	**15**	**0**	**0**	**0**	**18:40**
2000-01	**Pittsburgh**	**NHL**	**58**	**1**	**3**	**4**	**147**	**0**	**0**	**0**	**46**	**2.2**	**18**	**0**	**0.0**	**16:30**	**18**	**0**	**1**	**1**	**22**	**0**	**0**	**0**	**17:08**
2001-02	**Calgary**	**NHL**	**79**	**2**	**4**	**6**	**170**	**0**	**0**	**0**	**58**	**3.4**	**9**	**0**	**0.0**	**18:43**	....	....	....	....	....	....	....	....	....
2002-03	**Calgary**	**NHL**	**69**	**3**	**14**	**17**	**126**	**0**	**0**	**1**	**62**	**4.8**	**5**	**0**	**0.0**	**19:51**	....	....	....	....	....	....	....	....	....
2003-04	**Carolina**	**NHL**	**43**	**0**	**5**	**5**	**80**	**0**	**0**	**0**	**26**	**0.0**	**–9**	**0**	**0.0**	**14:47**	....	....	....	....	....	....	....	....	....
	Colorado	**NHL**	**11**	**0**	**0**	**0**	**8**	**0**	**0**	**0**	**8**	**0.0**	**–1**	**0**	**0.0**	**13:26**	**11**	**0**	**4**	**4**	**6**	**0**	**0**	**0**	**15:39**
2004-05		DID NOT PLAY																							
2005-06	**Colorado**	**NHL**	**41**	**1**	**6**	**7**	**54**	**0**	**0**	**1**	**15**	**6.7**	**2**	**2**	**50.0**	**7:15**	....	....	....	....	....	....	....	....	....
	NHL Totals		**630**	**15**	**57**	**72**	**1382**	**1**	**0**	**4**	**388**	**3.9**		**2**	**50.0**	**16:48**	**65**	**0**	**12**	**12**	**67**	**0**	**0**	**0**	**17:09**

Signed as a free agent by **Florida**, July 25, 1994. Traded to **Buffalo** by **Florida** for Buffalo's 3rd round choice (Chris Allen) in 1996 Entry Draft, February 1, 1996. Claimed by **Nashville** from **Buffalo** in Expansion Draft, June 26, 1998. Traded to **Pittsburgh** by **Nashville** for Pavel Skrbek, March 13, 2000. Signed as a free agent by **Calgary**, July 2, 2001. Traded to **Carolina** by **Calgary** for New Jersey's 4th round choice (previously acquired, Calgary selected Kristopher Hogg) in 2004 Entry Draft and Carolina's 5th round choice (Kevin Lalande) in 2005 Entry Draft, July 16, 2003. Traded to **Colorado** by **Carolina** for Chris Bahen, Washington's 3rd round choice (previously acquired, Carolina selected Casey Borer) in 2004 Entry Draft and Colorado's 5th round choice (Risto Korhonen) in 2005 Entry Draft, February 20, 2004.

BOUILLON, Francis

(BOO-liawn, FRAN-sihs) **MTL.**

Defense. Shoots left. 5'8", 196 lbs. Born, New York, NY, October 17, 1975.

Season	Club	League	GP	G	A	Pts	PIM	PP	SH	GW	S	%	+/-	TF	F%	Min	GP	G	A	Pts	PIM	PP	SH	GW	Min
1991-92	Mtl-Bourassa	QAAA	42	2	5	7	28	....	....	....	....	....	....	....	....	....	9	1	0	1	6	....	....	....	....
1992-93	Laval Titan	QMJHL	46	0	7	7	45	....	....	....	....	....	....	....	....	....	....	....	....	....	....	....	....	....	....
1993-94	Laval Titan	QMJHL	68	3	15	18	129	....	....	....	....	....	....	....	....	....	19	2	9	11	48	....	....	....	....
1994-95	Laval Titan	QMJHL	72	8	25	33	115	....	....	....	....	....	....	....	....	....	20	3	11	14	21	....	....	....	....
1995-96	Granby	QMJHL	68	11	35	46	156	....	....	....	....	....	....	....	....	....	21	2	12	14	30	....	....	....	....
1996-97	Wheeling Nailers	ECHL	69	10	32	42	77	....	....	....	....	....	....	....	....	....	3	0	2	2	10	....	....	....	....
1997-98	Quebec Rafales	IHL	71	8	27	35	76	....	....	....	....	....	....	....	....	....	....	....	....	....	....	....	....	....	....
1998-99	Fredericton	AHL	79	19	36	55	174	....	....	....	....	....	....	....	....	....	5	2	1	3	0	....	....	....	....
99-2000	**Montreal**	**NHL**	**74**	**3**	**13**	**16**	**38**	**2**	**0**	**1**	**76**	**3.9**	**–7**	**1**	**0.0**	**15:52**	....	....	....	....	....	....	....	....	....
2000-01	**Montreal**	**NHL**	**29**	**0**	**6**	**6**	**26**	**0**	**0**	**0**	**24**	**0.0**	**3**	**0**	**0.0**	**13:24**	....	....	....	....	....	....	....	....	....
	Quebec Citadelles	AHL	4	0	0	0	0	....	....	....	....	....	....	....	....	....	....	....	....	....	....	....	....	....	....
2001-02	**Montreal**	**NHL**	**28**	**0**	**5**	**5**	**33**	**0**	**0**	**0**	**24**	**0.0**	**–5**	**0**	**0.0**	**18:47**	....	....	....	....	....	....	....	....	....
	Quebec Citadelles	AHL	38	8	14	22	30	....	....	....	....	....	....	....	....	....	....	....	....	....	....	....	....	....	....
2002-03	**Nashville**	**NHL**	**4**	**0**	**0**	**0**	**2**	**0**	**0**	**0**	**0**	**0.0**	**–1**	**0**	**0.0**	**12:52**	....	....	....	....	....	....	....	....	....
	Montreal	**NHL**	**20**	**3**	**1**	**4**	**2**	**0**	**1**	**0**	**30**	**10.0**	**–1**	**0**	**0.0**	**20:24**	....	....	....	....	....	....	....	....	....
	Hamilton	AHL	29	1	12	13	31	....	....	....	....	....	....	....	....	....	....	....	....	....	....	....	....	....	....
2003-04	**Montreal**	**NHL**	**73**	**2**	**16**	**18**	**70**	**0**	**0**	**0**	**86**	**2.3**	**1**	**0**	**0.0**	**19:39**	**11**	**0**	**0**	**0**	**7**	**0**	**0**	**0**	**18:00**
2004-05	Leksands IF	Sweden-2	31	10	21	31	46	....	....	....	....	....	....	....	....	....	....	....	....	....	....	....	....	....	....
2005-06	**Montreal**	**NHL**	**67**	**3**	**19**	**22**	**34**	**3**	**0**	**1**	**75**	**4.0**	**–6**	**0**	**0.0**	**20:47**	**6**	**1**	**2**	**3**	**10**	**1**	**0**	**0**	**22:24**
	NHL Totals		**295**	**11**	**60**	**71**	**205**	**5**	**1**	**2**	**315**	**3.5**		**1**	**0.0**	**18:13**	**17**	**1**	**2**	**3**	**17**	**1**	**0**	**0**	**19:33**

Signed as a free agent by **Montreal**, August 18, 1998. • Missed majority of 2000-01 season recovering from ankle injury suffered in game vs. Calgary, December 31, 2000. Claimed by **Nashville** from **Montreal** in Waiver Draft, October 4, 2002. Claimed on waivers by **Montreal** from **Nashville**, October 25, 2002. Signed as a free agent by **Leksands** (Sweden-2), November 15, 2004.

BOULERICE, Jesse

(BOO-luhr-ighs, JEHS-see) **CAR.**

Right wing. Shoots right. 6'2", 215 lbs. Born, Plattsburgh, NY, August 10, 1978. Philadelphia's 4th choice, 133rd overall, in 1996 Entry Draft.

Season	Club	League	GP	G	A	Pts	PIM	PP	SH	GW	S	%	+/-	TF	F%	Min	GP	G	A	Pts	PIM	PP	SH	GW	Min
1994-95	Hawkesbury	CJHL	46	1	8	9	160	....	....	....	....	....	....	....	....	....	....	....	....	....	....	....	....	....	....
1995-96	Detroit	OHL	64	2	5	7	150	....	....	....	....	....	....	....	....	....	16	0	0	0	12	....	....	....	....
1996-97	Detroit	OHL	33	10	14	24	209	....	....	....	....	....	....	....	....	....	....	....	....	....	....	....	....	....	....
1997-98	Plymouth Whalers	OHL	53	20	23	43	170	....	....	....	....	....	....	....	....	....	13	2	4	6	35	....	....	....	....
1998-99	Philadelphia	AHL	24	1	2	3	82	....	....	....	....	....	....	....	....	....	....	....	....	....	....	....	....	....	....
	New Orleans	ECHL	12	0	1	1	38	....	....	....	....	....	....	....	....	....	....	....	....	....	....	....	....	....	....
99-2000	Philadelphia	AHL	40	3	4	7	85	....	....	....	....	....	....	....	....	....	4	0	2	2	4	....	....	....	....
	Trenton Titans	ECHL	25	8	8	16	90	....	....	....	....	....	....	....	....	....	....	....	....	....	....	....	....	....	....
2000-01	Philadelphia	AHL	60	3	4	7	256	....	....	....	....	....	....	....	....	....	10	1	1	2	28	....	....	....	....

Season	Club	League	GP	G	A	Pts	PIM	PP	SH	GW	S	%	+/-	TF	F%	Min	GP	G	A	Pts	PIM	PP	SH	GW	Min
			Regular Season														Playoffs								
2001-02	Philadelphia	NHL	3	0	0	0	5	0	0	0	1	0.0	-1	0	0.0	4:18									
	Philadelphia	AHL	41	2	5	7	204																		
	Lowell	AHL	15	2	4	6	80										5	0	2	2	6				
2002-03	Carolina	NHL	48	2	1	3	108	0	0	0	12	16.7	-2	0	0.0	3:54									
2003-04	Carolina	NHL	76	6	1	7	127	0	0	0	46	13.0	-5	0	0.0	6:32									
2004-05			DID NOT PLAY																						
2005-06	Carolina	NHL	26	0	0	0	51	0	0	0	3	0.0	-3	0	0.0	2:30									
	St. Louis	NHL	12	0	0	0	13	0	0	0	2	0.0	-4	0	0.0	2:39									
	NHL Totals		165	8	2	10	304	0	0	0	64	12.5		0	0.0	4:49									

Traded to **Carolina** by **Philadelphia** for Greg Koehler, February 13, 2002. Traded to **St. Louis** by **Carolina** with Mike Zigomanis, Magnus Kahnberg, Carolina's 1st round choice (later traded to New Jersey - New Jersey selected Matthew Corrente) in 2006 Entry Draft, Toronto's 4th round choice (previously acquired, St. Louis selected Reto Berra) in 2006 Entry Draft and Chicago's 4th round choice (previously acquired) in 2007 Entry Draft for Doug Weight and Erkki Rajamaki, January 30, 2006. Signed as a free agent by **Carolina**, August 2, 2006.

BOULTON, Eric

(BOHL-tuhn, AIR-ihk) **ATL.**

Left wing. Shoots left. 6'1", 225 lbs. Born, Halifax, N.S., August 17, 1976. NY Rangers' 12th choice, 234th overall, in 1994 Entry Draft.

Season	Club	League	GP	G	A	Pts	PIM	PP	SH	GW	S	%	+/-	TF	F%	Min	GP	G	A	Pts	PIM	PP	SH	GW	Min
1992-93	Cole Harbour	MJrHL	44	12	15	27	212																		
1993-94	Oshawa Generals	OHL	45	4	3	7	149										5	0	0	0	16				
1994-95	Oshawa Generals	OHL	27	7	5	12	125																		
	Sarnia Sting	OHL	24	3	7	10	134										4	0	1	1	10				
1995-96	Sarnia Sting	OHL	66	14	29	43	243										9	0	3	3	29				
1996-97	Binghamton	AHL	23	2	3	5	67										3	0	0	0	4				
	Charlotte	ECHL	44	14	11	25	325										3	0	1	1	6				
1997-98	Charlotte	ECHL	53	11	16	27	202										4	1	0	1	0				
	Fort Wayne	IHL	8	0	2	2	42																		
1998-99	Kentucky	AHL	34	3	3	6	154										10	0	1	1	36				
	Florida Everblades	ECHL	26	9	13	22	143																		
	Houston Aeros	IHL	7	1	0	1	41																		
99-2000	Rochester	AHL	76	2	2	4	276										18	2	1	3	53				
2000-01	Buffalo	NHL	35	1	2	3	94	0	0	0	20	5.0	-1	2	0.0	5:42									
2001-02	Buffalo	NHL	35	2	3	5	129	0	0	1	21	9.5	-1	0	0.0	6:08									
2002-03	Buffalo	NHL	58	1	5	6	178	0	0	0	33	3.0	1	6	33.3	6:35									
2003-04	Buffalo	NHL	44	1	2	3	110	0	0	0	20	5.0	-2	1	0.0	4:52									
2004-05	Columbia Inferno	ECHL	48	23	16	39	124										4	2	3	5	8				
2005-06	Atlanta	NHL	51	4	5	9	87	0	0	0	28	14.3	-4	2	50.0	4:54									
	NHL Totals		223	9	17	26	598	0	0	1	122	7.4		11	27.3	5:39									

Signed as a free agent by **Buffalo**, September 14, 1999. Signed as a free agent by **Columbia** (ECHL), November 24, 2004. Signed as a free agent by **Atlanta**, August 8, 2005.

BOURQUE, Rene

(BOHRK, reh-NAY) **CHI.**

Left wing. Shoots left. 6'2", 205 lbs. Born, Lac La Biche, Alta., December 10, 1981.

Season	Club	League	GP	G	A	Pts	PIM	PP	SH	GW	S	%	+/-	TF	F%	Min	GP	G	A	Pts	PIM	PP	SH	GW	Min
2000-01	U. of Wisconsin	WCHA	32	10	5	15	18																		
2001-02	U. of Wisconsin	WCHA	38	12	7	19	26																		
2002-03	U. of Wisconsin	WCHA	40	19	8	27	54																		
2003-04	U. of Wisconsin	WCHA	42	16	20	36	74																		
2004-05	Norfolk Admirals	AHL	78	33	27	60	105										6	1	0	1	8				
2005-06	Chicago	NHL	77	16	18	34	56	4	0	2	180	8.9	3	11	36.4	15:20									
	NHL Totals		77	16	18	34	56	4	0	2	180	8.9		11	36.4	15:20									

AHL All-Rookie Team (2005) • Dudley "Red" Garrett Memorial Trophy (Top Rookie - AHL) (2005)

Signed as a free agent by **Chicago**, July 29, 2004.

BOUWMEESTER, Jay

(BOW-mee-stuhr, JAY) **FLA.**

Defense. Shoots left. 6'4", 210 lbs. Born, Edmonton, Alta., September 27, 1983. Florida's 1st choice, 3rd overall, in 2002 Entry Draft.

Season	Club	League	GP	G	A	Pts	PIM	PP	SH	GW	S	%	+/-	TF	F%	Min	GP	G	A	Pts	PIM	PP	SH	GW	Min
1998-99	Edmonton SSAC	AMHL	32	14	29	43	36																		
	Medicine Hat	WHL	8	2	1	3	2																		
99-2000	Medicine Hat	WHL	64	13	21	34	26																		
2000-01	Medicine Hat	WHL	61	14	39	53	44																		
2001-02	Medicine Hat	WHL	61	11	50	61	42																		
2002-03	Florida	NHL	82	4	12	16	14	2	0	0	110	3.6	-29	0	0.0	20:09									
2003-04	Florida	NHL	61	2	18	20	30	0	0	0	85	2.4	-15	0	0.0	23:02									
	San Antonio	AHL	2	0	1	1	2																		
2004-05	San Antonio	AHL	64	4	13	17	50																		
	Chicago Wolves	AHL	18	6	3	9	12										18	0	0	0	14				
2005-06	Florida	NHL	82	5	41	46	79	0	0	0	189	2.6	1	1	0.0	25:29									
	Canada	Olympics	6	0	0	0	0																		
	NHL Totals		225	11	71	82	123	2	0	0	384	2.9		1	0.0	22:53									

WHL East First All-Star Team (2002) • NHL All-Rookie Team (2003)

Loaned to **Chicago** (AHL) by **Florida** (San Antonio-AHL) for cash, March 8, 2005.

BOYES, Brad

(BOIZ, BRAD) **BOS.**

Center. Shoots right. 6'1", 195 lbs. Born, Mississauga, Ont., April 17, 1982. Toronto's 1st choice, 24th overall, in 2000 Entry Draft.

Season	Club	League	GP	G	A	Pts	PIM	PP	SH	GW	S	%	+/-	TF	F%	Min	GP	G	A	Pts	PIM	PP	SH	GW	Min
1997-98	Mississauga Reps	MTHL	44	27	50	77																			
1998-99	Erie Otters	OHL	59	24	36	60	30										5	1	2	3	10				
99-2000	Erie Otters	OHL	68	36	46	82	38										13	6	8	14	10				
2000-01	Erie Otters	OHL	59	45	45	90	42										15	10	13	23	8				
2001-02	Erie Otters	OHL	47	36	41	77	42										21	22	*19	41	27				
2002-03	St. John's	AHL	65	23	28	51	45																		
	Cleveland Barons	AHL	15	7	6	13	21																		
2003-04	San Jose	NHL	1	0	0	0	2	0	0	0	0	0.0	-2	0	0.0	13:03									
	Cleveland Barons	AHL	61	25	35	60	38																		
	Providence Bruins	AHL	17	6	6	12	13										2	1	0	1	0				
2004-05	Providence Bruins	AHL	80	33	42	75	58										16	8	7	15	23				
2005-06	Boston	NHL	82	26	43	69	30	8	0	3	203	12.8	11	265	53.6	15:46									
	NHL Totals		83	26	43	69	32	8	0	3	203	12.8		265	53.6	15:44									

Canadian Major Junior Scholastic Player of the Year (2000) • OHL Second All-Star Team (2001) • OHL First All-Star Team (2002) • Canadian Major Junior Sportsman of the Year (2002) • AHL All-Rookie Team (2003) • AHL Second All-Star Team (2004) • NHL All-Rookie Team (2006)

Traded to **San Jose** by **Toronto** with Alyn McCauley and Toronto's 1st round choice (later traded to Boston – Boston selected Mark Stuart) in 2003 Entry Draft for Owen Nolan, March 5, 2003. Traded to **Boston** by **San Jose** for Jeff Jillson, March 9, 2004.

BOYLE, Dan

(BOIL, DAN) **T.B.**

Defense. Shoots right. 5'11", 190 lbs. Born, Ottawa, Ont., July 12, 1976.

Season	Club	League	GP	G	A	Pts	PIM	PP	SH	GW	S	%	+/-	TF	F%	Min	GP	G	A	Pts	PIM	PP	SH	GW	Min
1992-93	Gloucester	CJHL	55	22	51	73	60																		
1993-94	Gloucester	CJHL	53	27	54	81	155																		
1994-95	Miami U.	CCHA	35	8	18	26	24																		
1995-96	Miami U.	CCHA	36	7	20	27	70																		
1996-97	Miami U.	CCHA	40	11	43	54	52																		
1997-98	Miami U.	CCHA	37	14	26	40	58																		
1998-99	Florida	NHL	22	3	5	8	6	1	0	1	31	9.7	0	1	100.0	18:50									
	Kentucky	AHL	53	8	34	42	87										12	3	5	8	16				
99-2000	Florida	NHL	13	0	3	3	4	0	0	0	9	0.0	-2	0	0.0	16:57									
	Louisville Panthers	AHL	58	14	38	52	75										4	0	2	2	8				
2000-01	Florida	NHL	69	4	18	22	28	1	0	0	83	4.8	-14	0	0.0	16:56									
	Louisville Panthers	AHL	6	0	5	5	12																		
2001-02	Florida	NHL	25	3	3	6	12	1	0	0	31	9.7	-1	2	50.0	15:40									
	Tampa Bay	NHL	41	5	15	20	27	2	0	1	68	7.4	-15	0	0.0	22:28									
2002-03	Tampa Bay	NHL	77	13	40	53	44	8	0	1	136	9.6	9	2	0.0	24:31	11	0	7	7	6	0	0	0	27:45

			Regular Season														Playoffs								
Season	Club	League	GP	G	A	Pts	PIM	PP	SH	GW	S	%	+/-	TF	F%	Min	GP	G	A	Pts	PIM	PP	SH	GW	Min
2003-04♦	**Tampa Bay**	**NHL**	**78**	**9**	**30**	**39**	**60**	**3**	**0**	**2**	**137**	**6.6**	**23**	**0**	**0.0**	**22:46**	**23**	**2**	**8**	**10**	**16**	**1**	**0**	**0**	**21:27**
2004-05	Djurgarden	Sweden	32	9	9	18	47	....	....	....	....	....	....	....	....	....	12	2	3	5	26	....	....	....	....
2005-06	**Tampa Bay**	**NHL**	**79**	**15**	**38**	**53**	**38**	**6**	**0**	**4**	**153**	**9.8**	**–8**	**1**	**0.0**	**23:26**	**5**	**1**	**3**	**4**	**6**	**0**	**0**	**0**	**25:54**
	Canada	Olympics	DID NOT PLAY																						
	NHL Totals		**404**	**52**	**152**	**204**	**219**	**22**	**0**	**9**	**648**	**8.0**		**6**	**33.3**	**21:22**	**39**	**3**	**18**	**21**	**28**	**1**	**0**	**0**	**23:48**

CCHA First All-Star Team (1997, 1998) • NCAA West First All-American Team (1997, 1998) • AHL All-Rookie Team (1999 • AHL Second All-Star Team (1999, 2000)

Signed as a free agent by **Florida**, March 30, 1998. Traded to **Tampa Bay** by **Florida** for Tampa Bay's 5th round choice (Martin Tuma) in 2003 Entry Draft, January 7, 2002. Signed as a free agent by **Djurgarden** (Sweden), November 14,, 2004.

BOYNTON, Nick

(BOIN-tuhn, NIHK) **PHX.**

Defense. Shoots right. 6'2", 211 lbs. Born, Nobleton, Ont., January 14, 1979. Boston's 1st choice, 21st overall, in 1999 Entry Draft.

Season	Club	League	GP	G	A	Pts	PIM	PP	SH	GW	S	%	+/-	TF	F%	Min	GP	G	A	Pts	PIM	PP	SH	GW	Min
1993-94	Caledon	MTJHL	4	0	1	1	0	....	....	....	....	....	....	....	....	....	....	....	....	....	....	....	....	....	....
1994-95	Caledon	MTJHL	44	10	35	45	139	....	....	....	....	....	....	....	....	....	....	....	....	....	....	....	....	....	....
1995-96	Ottawa 67's	OHL	64	10	14	24	90	....	....	....	....	....	....	....	....	....	4	0	3	3	10	....	....	....	....
1996-97	Ottawa 67's	OHL	63	13	51	64	143	....	....	....	....	....	....	....	....	....	24	4	*24	28	38	....	....	....	....
1997-98	Ottawa 67's	OHL	40	7	31	38	94	....	....	....	....	....	....	....	....	....	13	0	4	4	24	....	....	....	....
1998-99	Ottawa 67's	OHL	51	11	48	59	83	....	....	....	....	....	....	....	....	....	9	1	9	10	18	....	....	....	....
99-2000	**Boston**	**NHL**	**5**	**0**	**0**	**0**	**0**	**0**	**0**	**0**	**6**	**0.0**	**–5**	**0**	**0.0**	**21:21**	....	....	....	....	....	....	....	....	....
	Providence Bruins	AHL	53	5	14	19	66	....	....	....	....	....	....	....	....	....	12	1	0	1	6	....	....	....	....
2000-01	**Boston**	**NHL**	**1**	**0**	**0**	**0**	**0**	**0**	**0**	**0**	**1**	**0.0**	**–1**	**0**	**0.0**	**14:27**	....	....	....	....	....	....	....	....	....
	Providence Bruins	AHL	78	6	27	33	105	....	....	....	....	....	....	....	....	....	17	0	2	2	35	....	....	....	....
2001-02	**Boston**	**NHL**	**80**	**4**	**14**	**18**	**107**	**0**	**0**	**1**	**136**	**2.9**	**18**	**0**	**0.0**	**18:30**	**6**	**1**	**2**	**3**	**8**	**0**	**0**	**0**	**21:30**
2002-03	**Boston**	**NHL**	**78**	**7**	**17**	**24**	**99**	**0**	**1**	**2**	**160**	**4.4**	**8**	**1**	**0.0**	**22:41**	**5**	**0**	**1**	**1**	**4**	**0**	**0**	**0**	**23:22**
2003-04	**Boston**	**NHL**	**81**	**6**	**24**	**30**	**98**	**1**	**1**	**1**	**178**	**3.4**	**17**	**0**	**0.0**	**22:32**	**7**	**0**	**2**	**2**	**2**	**0**	**0**	**0**	**24:44**
2004-05	Nottingham	Britain	9	1	3	4	4	....	....	....	....	....	....	....	....	....	6	1	2	3	22	....	....	....	....
2005-06	**Boston**	**NHL**	**54**	**5**	**7**	**12**	**93**	**1**	**1**	**0**	**89**	**5.6**	**–7**	**1**	**100.0**	**20:39**	....	....	....	....	....	....	....	....	....
	NHL Totals		**299**	**22**	**62**	**84**	**397**	**2**	**3**	**4**	**570**	**3.9**		**2**	**50.0**	**21:06**	**18**	**1**	**5**	**6**	**14**	**0**	**0**	**0**	**23:16**

• Re-entered NHL Entry Draft. Originally Washington's 1st choice, 9th overall, in 1997 Entry Draft.

OHL All-Rookie Team (1996) • Memorial Cup Tournament All-Star Team (1999) • Stafford Smythe Memorial Trophy (Memorial Cup Tournament MVP) (1999) • NHL All-Rookie Team (2002)

Played in NHL All-Star Game (2004)

Signed as a free agent by **Nottingham** (Britain), January 26, 2005. Traded to **Phoenix** by **Boston** with Boston's 4th round choice in 2007 Entry Draft for Paul Mara and future considerations, June 26, 2006.

BRADLEY, Matt

(BRAD-lee, MAT) **WSH.**

Right wing. Shoots right. 6'3", 205 lbs. Born, Stittsville, Ont., June 13, 1978. San Jose's 4th choice, 102nd overall, in 1996 Entry Draft.

Season	Club	League	GP	G	A	Pts	PIM	PP	SH	GW	S	%	+/-	TF	F%	Min	GP	G	A	Pts	PIM	PP	SH	GW	Min
1994-95	Cumberland	CJHL	49	13	20	33	18	....	....	....	....	....	....	....	....	....	....	....	....	....	....	....	....	....	....
1995-96	Kingston	OHL	55	10	14	24	17	....	....	....	....	....	....	....	....	....	6	0	1	1	6	....	....	....	....
1996-97	Kingston	OHL	65	24	24	48	41	....	....	....	....	....	....	....	....	....	5	0	4	4	2	....	....	....	....
	Kentucky	AHL	1	0	1	1	0	....	....	....	....	....	....	....	....	....	....	....	....	....	....	....	....	....	....
1997-98	Kingston	OHL	55	33	50	83	24	....	....	....	....	....	....	....	....	....	8	3	4	7	7	....	....	....	....
1998-99	Kentucky	AHL	79	23	20	43	57	....	....	....	....	....	....	....	....	....	10	1	4	5	4	....	....	....	....
99-2000	Kentucky	AHL	80	22	19	41	81	....	....	....	....	....	....	....	....	....	9	6	3	9	9	....	....	....	....
2000-01	**San Jose**	**NHL**	**21**	**1**	**1**	**2**	**19**	**0**	**0**	**0**	**16**	**6.3**	**0**	**0**	**0.0**	**6:58**	....	....	....	....	....	....	....	....	....
	Kentucky	AHL	22	5	8	13	16	....	....	....	....	....	....	....	....	....	1	1	0	1	5	....	....	....	....
2001-02	**San Jose**	**NHL**	**54**	**9**	**13**	**22**	**43**	**0**	**0**	**2**	**63**	**14.3**	**22**	**2**	**0.0**	**8:27**	**10**	**0**	**0**	**0**	**0**	**0**	**0**	**0**	**5:16**
2002-03	**San Jose**	**NHL**	**46**	**2**	**3**	**5**	**37**	**0**	**0**	**0**	**21**	**9.5**	**–1**	**1**	**0.0**	**7:54**	....	....	....	....	....	....	....	....	....
2003-04	**Pittsburgh**	**NHL**	**82**	**7**	**9**	**16**	**65**	**0**	**0**	**1**	**85**	**8.2**	**–27**	**29**	**41.4**	**12:48**	....	....	....	....	....	....	....	....	....
2004-05	Bulldogs Dornbirn	Austria-2	6	5	2	7	18	....	....	....	....	....	....	....	....	....	....	....	....	....	....	....	....	....	....
2005-06	**Washington**	**NHL**	**74**	**7**	**12**	**19**	**72**	**0**	**0**	**1**	**87**	**8.0**	**–8**	**25**	**52.0**	**12:36**	....	....	....	....	....	....	....	....	....
	NHL Totals		**277**	**26**	**38**	**64**	**236**	**0**	**0**	**4**	**272**	**9.6**		**57**	**43.9**	**10:38**	**10**	**0**	**0**	**0**	**0**	**0**	**0**	**0**	**5:16**

Traded to **Pittsburgh** by **San Jose** for Wayne Primeau, March 11, 2003. Signed as a free agent by **Dornbirn** (Austria-2), November 14, 2004. Signed as a free agent by **Washington**, August 18, 2005.

BRANDNER, Christoph

(BRAND-nuhr, KRIH-stahf)

Left wing. Shoots left. 6'4", 224 lbs. Born, Bruck an der Mur, Austria, July 5, 1975. Minnesota's 8th choice, 237th overall, in 2002 Entry Draft.

Season	Club	League	GP	G	A	Pts	PIM	PP	SH	GW	S	%	+/-	TF	F%	Min	GP	G	A	Pts	PIM	PP	SH	GW	Min
1997-98	Klagenfurter AC	Austria	27	12	7	19	18	....	....	....	....	....	....	....	....	....	....	....	....	....	....	....	....	....	....
	Klagenfurter AC	Alpenliga	STATISTICS NOT AVAILABLE																						
1998-99	Klagenfurter AC	Austria	21	8	8	16	6	....	....	....	....	....	....	....	....	....	....	....	....	....	....	....	....	....	....
	Klagenfurter AC	Alpenliga	33	23	10	33	16	....	....	....	....	....	....	....	....	....	....	....	....	....	....	....	....	....	....
99-2000	Klagenfurter AC	IEHL	34	29	19	48	30	....	....	....	....	....	....	....	....	....	....	....	....	....	....	....	....	....	....
	Klagenfurter AC	Austria	16	8	3	11	20	....	....	....	....	....	....	....	....	....	....	....	....	....	....	....	....	....	....
2000-01	Klagenfurter AC	Austria	6	6	2	8	4	....	....	....	....	....	....	....	....	....	....	....	....	....	....	....	....	....	....
	Krefeld Pinguine	Germany	59	24	24	48	34	....	....	....	....	....	....	....	....	....	....	....	....	....	....	....	....	....	....
2001-02	Krefeld Pinguine	Germany	50	30	25	55	20	....	....	....	....	....	....	....	....	....	3	1	0	1	4	....	....	....	....
	Austria	Olympics	4	0	1	1	2	....	....	....	....	....	....	....	....	....	....	....	....	....	....	....	....	....	....
2002-03	Krefeld Pinguine	Germany	49	*28	17	45	26	....	....	....	....	....	....	....	....	....	14	9	9	18	8	....	....	....	....
2003-04	**Minnesota**	**NHL**	**35**	**4**	**5**	**9**	**8**	**1**	**0**	**0**	**50**	**8.0**	**–2**	**4**	**50.0**	**13:20**	....	....	....	....	....	....	....	....	....
	Houston Aeros	AHL	37	7	7	14	18	....	....	....	....	....	....	....	....	....	2	1	0	1	0	....	....	....	....
2004-05	Houston Aeros	AHL	26	5	3	8	15	....	....	....	....	....	....	....	....	....	....	....	....	....	....	....	....	....	....
2005-06	Sodertalje SK	Sweden	25	3	2	5	10	....	....	....	....	....	....	....	....	....	....	....	....	....	....	....	....	....	....
	NHL Totals		**35**	**4**	**5**	**9**	**8**	**1**	**0**	**0**	**50**	**8.0**		**4**	**50.0**	**13:20**	....	....	....	....	....	....	....	....	....

Signed as a free agent by **Sodertalje** (Sweden), April 12, 2005.

BRASHEAR, Donald

(bra-SHEER, DAWN-ohld) **WSH.**

Left wing. Shoots left. 6'2", 235 lbs. Born, Bedford, IN, January 7, 1972.

Season	Club	League	GP	G	A	Pts	PIM	PP	SH	GW	S	%	+/-	TF	F%	Min	GP	G	A	Pts	PIM	PP	SH	GW	Min
1988-89	Ste-Foy	QAAA	10	1	2	3	10	....	....	....	....	....	....	....	....	....	....	....	....	....	....	....	....	....	....
1989-90	Longueuil	QMJHL	64	12	14	26	169	....	....	....	....	....	....	....	....	....	7	0	0	0	11	....	....	....	....
1990-91	Longueuil	QMJHL	68	12	26	38	195	....	....	....	....	....	....	....	....	....	8	0	3	3	33	....	....	....	....
1991-92	Verdun	QMJHL	65	18	24	42	283	....	....	....	....	....	....	....	....	....	18	4	2	6	98	....	....	....	....
1992-93	Fredericton	AHL	76	11	3	14	261	....	....	....	....	....	....	....	....	....	5	0	0	0	8	....	....	....	....
1993-94	**Montreal**	**NHL**	**14**	**2**	**2**	**4**	**34**	**0**	**0**	**0**	**15**	**13.3**	**0**	....	....	....	**2**	**0**	**0**	**0**	**0**	**0**	**0**	**0**	....
	Fredericton	AHL	62	38	28	66	250	....	....	....	....	....	....	....	....	....	....	....	....	....	....	....	....	....	....
1994-95	Fredericton	AHL	29	10	9	19	182	....	....	....	....	....	....	....	....	....	17	7	5	12	77	....	....	....	....
	Montreal	**NHL**	**20**	**1**	**1**	**2**	**63**	**0**	**0**	**1**	**10**	**10.0**	**–5**	....	....	....	....	....	....	....	....	....	....	....	....
1995-96	**Montreal**	**NHL**	**67**	**0**	**4**	**4**	**223**	**0**	**0**	**0**	**25**	**0.0**	**–10**	....	....	....	**6**	**0**	**0**	**0**	**2**	**0**	**0**	**0**	....
1996-97	**Montreal**	**NHL**	**10**	**0**	**0**	**0**	**38**	**0**	**0**	**0**	**6**	**0.0**	**–2**	....	....	....	....	....	....	....	....	....	....	....	....
	Vancouver	**NHL**	**59**	**8**	**5**	**13**	**207**	**0**	**0**	**2**	**55**	**14.5**	**–6**	....	....	....	....	....	....	....	....	....	....	....	....
1997-98	**Vancouver**	**NHL**	**77**	**9**	**9**	**18**	***372**	**0**	**0**	**1**	**64**	**14.1**	**–9**	....	....	....	....	....	....	....	....	....	....	....	....
1998-99	**Vancouver**	**NHL**	**82**	**8**	**10**	**18**	**209**	**2**	**0**	**1**	**112**	**7.1**	**–25**	**6**	**16.7**	**13:25**	....	....	....	....	....	....	....	....	....
99-2000	**Vancouver**	**NHL**	**60**	**11**	**2**	**13**	**136**	**1**	**0**	**3**	**83**	**13.3**	**–9**	**11**	**36.4**	**13:07**	....	....	....	....	....	....	....	....	....
2000-01	**Vancouver**	**NHL**	**79**	**9**	**19**	**28**	**145**	**0**	**0**	**1**	**127**	**7.1**	**0**	**6**	**16.7**	**13:27**	**4**	**0**	**0**	**0**	**0**	**0**	**0**	**0**	**14:47**
2001-02	**Vancouver**	**NHL**	**31**	**5**	**8**	**13**	**90**	**1**	**0**	**0**	**45**	**11.1**	**–8**	**4**	**25.0**	**13:58**	....	....	....	....	....	....	....	....	....
	Philadelphia	**NHL**	**50**	**4**	**15**	**19**	**109**	**0**	**0**	**2**	**62**	**6.5**	**0**	**1**	**0.0**	**13:00**	**5**	**0**	**0**	**0**	**19**	**0**	**0**	**0**	**9:55**
2002-03	**Philadelphia**	**NHL**	**80**	**8**	**17**	**25**	**161**	**0**	**0**	**1**	**99**	**8.1**	**5**	**27**	**33.3**	**13:23**	**13**	**1**	**2**	**3**	**21**	**0**	**0**	**0**	**11:09**
2003-04	**Philadelphia**	**NHL**	**64**	**6**	**7**	**13**	**212**	**0**	**0**	**0**	**72**	**8.3**	**–1**	**18**	**38.9**	**11:02**	**18**	**1**	**3**	**4**	**61**	**1**	**0**	**0**	**8:56**
2004-05	Quebec RadioX	QNAHL	47	18	32	50	260	....	....	....	....	....	....	....	....	....	8	4	6	10	42	....	....	....	....
2005-06	**Philadelphia**	**NHL**	**76**	**4**	**5**	**9**	**166**	**0**	**0**	**0**	**73**	**5.5**	**–2**	**7**	**28.6**	**8:36**	**1**	**0**	**0**	**0**	**0**	**0**	**0**	**0**	**4:20**
	NHL Totals		**769**	**75**	**104**	**179**	**2165**	**4**	**0**	**12**	**848**	**8.8**		**80**	**31.3**	**12:23**	**49**	**2**	**5**	**7**	**103**	**1**	**0**	**0**	**10:13**

Signed as a free agent by **Montreal**, July 28, 1992. Traded to **Vancouver** by **Montreal** for Jassen Cullimore, November 13, 1996. Traded to **Philadelphia** by **Vancouver** with Vancouver's 6th round choice (later traded to Columbus – Columbus selected Jaroslav Balastik) in 2002 Entry Draft for Jan Hlavac and Tampa Bay's 3rd round choice (previously acquired, Vancouver selected Brett Skinner) in 2002 Entry Draft, December 17, 2001. Signed as a free agent by **Quebec** (QNAHL), September 21, 2004. Signed as a free agent by **Washington**, July 14, 2006.

BRENDL, Pavel

(BREHN-duhl, PAH-vehl)

Right wing. Shoots right. 6'1", 204 lbs. Born, Opocno, Czech., March 23, 1981. NY Rangers' 1st choice, 4th overall, in 1999 Entry Draft.

			Regular Season														Playoffs								
Season	Club	League	GP	G	A	Pts	PIM	PP	SH	GW	S	%	+/-	TF	F%	Min	GP	G	A	Pts	PIM	PP	SH	GW	Min
1996-97	HC Olomouc Jr.	CzRep-Jr.	40	35	17	52	....	....	....	....	....	....	....	....	....	....	....	....	....	....	....	....	....	....	....
1997-98	HC Olomouc Jr.	CzRep-Jr.	38	29	23	52	....	....	....	....	....	....	....	....	....	....	....	....	....	....	....	....	....	....	....
	HC Olomouc	CzRep-2	12	1	1	2	....	....	....	....	....	....	....	....	....	....	....	....	....	....	....	....	....	....	....
1998-99	Calgary Hitmen	WHL	68	*73	61	*134	40	....	....	....	....	....	....	....	....	....	20	*21	*25	*46	18	....	....	....	....
99-2000	Calgary Hitmen	WHL	61	*59	52	111	94	....	....	....	....	....	....	....	....	....	10	7	12	19	8	....	....	....	....
	Hartford	AHL	....	....	....	....	....	....	....	....	....	....	....	....	....	....	2	0	0	0	0	....	....	....	....
2000-01	Calgary Hitmen	WHL	49	40	35	75	66	....	....	....	....	....	....	....	....	....	10	7	6	13	6	....	....	....	....
2001-02	**Philadelphia**	**NHL**	**8**	**1**	**0**	**1**	**2**	**0**	**0**	**0**	**6**	**16.7**	**–1**	**21**	**19.1**	**8:59**	**2**	**0**	**0**	**0**	**0**	**0**	**0**	**0**	**11:28**
	Philadelphia	AHL	64	15	22	37	22	....	....	....	....	....	....	....	....	....	5	4	1	5	0	....	....	....	....
2002-03	**Philadelphia**	**NHL**	**42**	**5**	**7**	**12**	**4**	**1**	**0**	**1**	**80**	**6.3**	**8**	**9**	**22.2**	**10:19**	....	....	....	....	....	....	....	....	....
	Carolina	**NHL**	**8**	**0**	**1**	**1**	**2**	**0**	**0**	**1**	**14**	**0.0**	**–3**	**2**	**50.0**	**15:05**	....	....	....	....	....	....	....	....	....
2003-04	**Carolina**	**NHL**	**18**	**5**	**3**	**8**	**8**	**1**	**0**	**1**	**27**	**18.5**	**0**	**1**	**0.0**	**14:48**	....	....	....	....	....	....	....	....	....
	Lowell	AHL	33	17	16	33	34	....	....	....	....	....	....	....	....	....	....	....	....	....	....	....	....	....	....
2004-05	HC Ocelari Trinec	CzRep	2	0	0	0	0	....	....	....	....	....	....	....	....	....	....	....	....	....	....	....	....	....	....
	HC Olomouc	CzRep-2	3	0	0	0	12	....	....	....	....	....	....	....	....	....	....	....	....	....	....	....	....	....	....
	Jokipojat Joensuu	Finland-2	21	9	10	19	48	....	....	....	....	....	....	....	....	....	....	....	....	....	....	....	....	....	....
	HC Thurgau	Swiss-2	4	3	0	3	4	....	....	....	....	....	....	....	....	....	....	....	....	....	....	....	....	....	....
2005-06	Lowell	AHL	25	6	7	13	10	....	....	....	....	....	....	....	....	....	....	....	....	....	....	....	....	....	....
	Phoenix	**NHL**	**2**	**0**	**0**	**0**	**0**	**0**	**0**	**0**	**3**	**0.0**	**–3**	**1**	**0.0**	**8:54**	....	....	....	....	....	....	....	....	....
	San Antonio	AHL	38	13	11	24	8	....	....	....	....	....	....	....	....	....	....	....	....	....	....	....	....	....	....
	NHL Totals		**78**	**11**	**11**	**22**	**16**	**2**	**0**	**2**	**130**	**8.5**		**34**	**20.6**	**11:40**	**2**	**0**	**0**	**0**	**0**	**0**	**0**	**0**	**11:28**

WHL East First All-Star Team (1999) • WHL Rookie of the Year (1999) • Canadian Major Junior First All-Star Team (1999) • Canadian Major Junior Rookie of the Year (1999) • Memorial Cup Tournament All-Star Team (1999) • WHL East Second All-Star Team (2000)

Traded to **Philadelphia** by **NY Rangers** with Jan Hlavac, Kim Johnsson and NY Rangers' 3rd round choice (Stefan Ruzicka) in 2003 Entry Draft for Eric Lindros, August 20, 2001. Traded to **Carolina** by **Philadelphia** with Bruno St. Jacques for Sami Kapanen and Ryan Bast, February 7, 2003. Signed as a free agent by **Trinec** (CzRep), September 17, 2004. Signed as a free agent by **Olomouc** (CzRep-2), October 14, 2004. Signed as a free agent by **Joensuu** (Finland-2), November 15, 2004. Signed as a free agent by **Thurgau** (Swiss-2), December 21, 2004. Signed as a free agent by **Joensuu** (Finland-2), January 13, 2005. Traded to **Phoenix** by **Carolina** for Krys Kolanos, December 28, 2005.

BRENNAN, Kip

(BREHN-nan, KIHP)

Left wing. Shoots left. 6'4", 230 lbs. Born, Kingston, Ont., August 27, 1980. Los Angeles' 4th choice, 103rd overall, in 1998 Entry Draft.

			Regular Season														Playoffs								
Season	Club	League	GP	G	A	Pts	PIM	PP	SH	GW	S	%	+/-	TF	F%	Min	GP	G	A	Pts	PIM	PP	SH	GW	Min
1995-96	St. Mike's B's	OPJHL	40	0	11	11	155	....	....	....	....	....	....	....	....	....	7	0	1	1	20	....	....	....	....
1996-97	Windsor Spitfires	OHL	42	0	10	10	156	....	....	....	....	....	....	....	....	....	5	0	1	1	16	....	....	....	....
1997-98	Windsor Spitfires	OHL	24	0	7	7	103	....	....	....	....	....	....	....	....	....	....	....	....	....	....	....	....	....	....
	Sudbury Wolves	OHL	24	0	3	3	85	....	....	....	....	....	....	....	....	....	....	....	....	....	....	....	....	....	....
1998-99	Sudbury Wolves	OHL	38	9	12	21	160	....	....	....	....	....	....	....	....	....	....	....	....	....	....	....	....	....	....
99-2000	Sudbury Wolves	OHL	55	16	16	32	228	....	....	....	....	....	....	....	....	....	12	3	3	6	67	....	....	....	....
2000-01	Lowell	AHL	23	2	3	5	117	....	....	....	....	....	....	....	....	....	....	....	....	....	....	....	....	....	....
	Sudbury Wolves	OHL	27	7	14	21	94	....	....	....	....	....	....	....	....	....	12	5	6	11	*92	....	....	....	....
2001-02	Manchester	AHL	44	4	1	5	269	....	....	....	....	....	....	....	....	....	4	0	1	1	26	....	....	....	....
	Los Angeles	**NHL**	**4**	**0**	**0**	**0**	**22**	**0**	**0**	**0**	**0**	**0.0**	**1**	**0**	**0.0**	**4:40**	....	....	....	....	....	....	....	....	....
2002-03	Manchester	AHL	35	3	2	5	195	....	....	....	....	....	....	....	....	....	3	0	0	0	0	....	....	....	....
	Los Angeles	**NHL**	**19**	**0**	**0**	**0**	**57**	**0**	**0**	**0**	**6**	**0.0**	**0**	**2**	**0.0**	**4:52**	....	....	....	....	....	....	....	....	....
2003-04	**Los Angeles**	**NHL**	**18**	**1**	**0**	**1**	**79**	**0**	**0**	**0**	**6**	**16.7**	**–1**	**0**	**0.0**	**5:01**	....	....	....	....	....	....	....	....	....
	Manchester	AHL	2	0	0	0	6	....	....	....	....	....	....	....	....	....	....	....	....	....	....	....	....	....	....
	Atlanta	**NHL**	**5**	**0**	**0**	**0**	**17**	**0**	**0**	**0**	**2**	**0.0**	**0**	**0**	**0.0**	**3:37**	....	....	....	....	....	....	....	....	....
2004-05	Chicago Wolves	AHL	48	7	6	13	267	....	....	....	....	....	....	....	....	....	18	1	1	2	*105	....	....	....	....
2005-06	**Anaheim**	**NHL**	**12**	**0**	**1**	**1**	**35**	**0**	**0**	**0**	**5**	**0.0**	**–2**	**1**	**0.0**	**4:16**	....	....	....	....	....	....	....	....	....
	Portland Pirates	AHL	9	2	1	3	22	....	....	....	....	....	....	....	....	....	....	....	....	....	....	....	....	....	....
	NHL Totals		**58**	**1**	**1**	**2**	**210**	**0**	**0**	**0**	**19**	**5.3**		**3**	**0.0**	**4:40**	....	....	....	....	....	....	....	....	....

Traded to **Atlanta** by **Los Angeles** for Jeff Cowan, March 9, 2004. • Spent the majority of the 2003-04 season as a healthy reserve. Signed as a free agent by **Chicago** (AHL), September 27, 2004. Traded to **Anaheim** by **Atlanta** for Mark Popovic, August 23, 2005.

BREWER, Eric

(BREW-uhr, AIR-ihk) **ST.L.**

Defense. Shoots left. 6'3", 225 lbs. Born, Vernon, B.C., April 17, 1979. NY Islanders' 2nd choice, 5th overall, in 1997 Entry Draft.

			Regular Season														Playoffs								
Season	Club	League	GP	G	A	Pts	PIM	PP	SH	GW	S	%	+/-	TF	F%	Min	GP	G	A	Pts	PIM	PP	SH	GW	Min
1994-95	Kamloops	BCAHA	40	19	19	38	62	....	....	....	....	....	....	....	....	....	....	....	....	....	....	....	....	....	....
1995-96	Prince George	WHL	63	4	10	14	25	....	....	....	....	....	....	....	....	....	....	....	....	....	....	....	....	....	....
1996-97	Prince George	WHL	71	5	24	29	81	....	....	....	....	....	....	....	....	....	15	2	4	6	16	....	....	....	....
1997-98	Prince George	WHL	34	5	28	33	45	....	....	....	....	....	....	....	....	....	11	4	2	6	19	....	....	....	....
1998-99	**NY Islanders**	**NHL**	**63**	**5**	**6**	**11**	**32**	**2**	**0**	**0**	**63**	**7.9**	**–14**	**0**	**0.0**	**15:28**	....	....	....	....	....	....	....	....	....
99-2000	**NY Islanders**	**NHL**	**26**	**0**	**2**	**2**	**20**	**0**	**0**	**0**	**30**	**0.0**	**–11**	**0**	**0.0**	**18:33**	....	....	....	....	....	....	....	....	....
	Lowell	AHL	25	2	2	4	26	....	....	....	....	....	....	....	....	....	7	0	0	0	0	....	....	....	....
2000-01	**Edmonton**	**NHL**	**77**	**7**	**14**	**21**	**53**	**2**	**0**	**2**	**91**	**7.7**	**15**	**0**	**0.0**	**18:31**	**6**	**1**	**5**	**6**	**2**	**1**	**0**	**0**	**28:12**
2001-02	**Edmonton**	**NHL**	**81**	**7**	**18**	**25**	**45**	**6**	**0**	**2**	**165**	**4.2**	**–5**	**0**	**0.0**	**23:56**	....	....	....	....	....	....	....	....	....
	Canada	Olympics	6	2	0	2	0	....	....	....	....	....	....	....	....	....	....	....	....	....	....	....	....	....	....
2002-03	**Edmonton**	**NHL**	**80**	**8**	**21**	**29**	**45**	**1**	**0**	**1**	**147**	**5.4**	**–11**	**1**	**100.0**	**24:56**	**6**	**1**	**3**	**4**	**6**	**0**	**0**	**0**	**25:31**
2003-04	**Edmonton**	**NHL**	**77**	**7**	**18**	**25**	**67**	**3**	**0**	**1**	**135**	**5.2**	**–6**	**0**	**0.0**	**24:40**	....	....	....	....	....	....	....	....	....
2004-05			DID NOT PLAY																						
2005-06	**St. Louis**	**NHL**	**32**	**6**	**3**	**9**	**45**	**1**	**0**	**1**	**64**	**9.4**	**–17**	**0**	**0.0**	**23:28**	....	....	....	....	....	....	....	....	....
	NHL Totals		**436**	**40**	**82**	**122**	**307**	**15**	**0**	**7**	**695**	**5.8**		**1**	**100.0**	**21:42**	**12**	**2**	**8**	**10**	**8**	**1**	**0**	**0**	**26:51**

WHL West Second All-Star Team (1998)

Played in NHL All-Star Game (2003)

Traded to **Edmonton** by **NY Islanders** with Josh Green and NY Islanders' 2nd round choice (Brad Winchester) in 2000 Entry Draft for Roman Hamrlik, June 24, 2000. Traded to **St. Louis** by **Edmonton** with Doug Lynch and Jeff Woywitka for Chris Pronger, August 2, 2005. • Missed majority of 2005-06 season recovering from shoulder injuries suffered in games at Columbus (November 16, 2005) and Atlanta (January 13, 2006).

BRIERE, Daniel

(bree-AIR, DAN-yehl) **BUF.**

Center. Shoots right. 5'10", 178 lbs. Born, Gatineau, Que., October 6, 1977. Phoenix's 2nd choice, 24th overall, in 1996 Entry Draft.

			Regular Season														Playoffs								
Season	Club	League	GP	G	A	Pts	PIM	PP	SH	GW	S	%	+/-	TF	F%	Min	GP	G	A	Pts	PIM	PP	SH	GW	Min
1992-93	Abitibi Regents	QAAA	42	24	30	54	28	....	....	....	....	....	....	....	....	....	3	0	3	3	8	....	....	....	....
1993-94	Gatineau	QAAA	44	56	47	103	56	....	....	....	....	....	....	....	....	....	....	....	....	....	....	....	....	....	....
1994-95	Drummondville	QMJHL	72	51	72	123	54	....	....	....	....	....	....	....	....	....	4	2	3	5	2	....	....	....	....
1995-96	Drummondville	QMJHL	67	*67	*96	*163	84	....	....	....	....	....	....	....	....	....	6	6	12	18	8	....	....	....	....
1996-97	Drummondville	QMJHL	59	52	78	130	94	....	....	....	....	....	....	....	....	....	8	7	7	14	14	....	....	....	....
1997-98	**Phoenix**	**NHL**	**5**	**1**	**0**	**1**	**2**	**0**	**0**	**0**	**4**	**25.0**	**1**	....	....	....	....	....	....	....	....	....	....	....	....
	Springfield	AHL	68	36	56	92	42	....	....	....	....	....	....	....	....	....	4	1	2	3	4	....	....	....	....
1998-99	**Phoenix**	**NHL**	**64**	**8**	**14**	**22**	**30**	**2**	**0**	**2**	**90**	**8.9**	**–3**	**484**	**47.5**	**11:13**	....	....	....	....	....	....	....	....	....
	Las Vegas	IHL	1	1	1	2	0	....	....	....	....	....	....	....	....	....	....	....	....	....	....	....	....	....	....
	Springfield	AHL	13	2	6	8	20	....	....	....	....	....	....	....	....	....	3	0	1	1	2	....	....	....	....
99-2000	**Phoenix**	**NHL**	**13**	**1**	**1**	**2**	**0**	**0**	**0**	**0**	**9**	**11.1**	**0**	**65**	**49.2**	**7:41**	**1**	**0**	**0**	**0**	**0**	**0**	**0**	**0**	**6:16**
	Springfield	AHL	58	29	42	71	56	....	....	....	....	....	....	....	....	....	....	....	....	....	....	....	....	....	....
2000-01	**Phoenix**	**NHL**	**30**	**11**	**4**	**15**	**12**	**9**	**0**	**1**	**43**	**25.6**	**–2**	**210**	**50.0**	**10:50**	....	....	....	....	....	....	....	....	....
	Springfield	AHL	30	21	25	46	30	....	....	....	....	....	....	....	....	....	....	....	....	....	....	....	....	....	....
2001-02	**Phoenix**	**NHL**	**78**	**32**	**28**	**60**	**52**	**12**	**0**	**5**	**149**	**21.5**	**6**	**951**	**51.8**	**15:44**	**5**	**2**	**1**	**3**	**2**	**1**	**0**	**1**	**16:25**
2002-03	**Phoenix**	**NHL**	**68**	**17**	**29**	**46**	**50**	**4**	**0**	**3**	**142**	**12.0**	**–21**	**1108**	**52.5**	**17:02**	....	....	....	....	....	....	....	....	....
	Buffalo	**NHL**	**14**	**7**	**5**	**12**	**12**	**5**	**0**	**1**	**39**	**17.9**	**1**	**206**	**50.0**	**17:49**	....	....	....	....	....	....	....	....	....
2003-04	**Buffalo**	**NHL**	**82**	**28**	**37**	**65**	**70**	**11**	**0**	**3**	**194**	**14.4**	**–7**	**1066**	**47.1**	**18:20**	....	....	....	....	....	....	....	....	....
2004-05	SC Bern	Swiss	36	16	29	45	26	....	....	....	....	....	....	....	....	....	11	1	6	7	2	....	....	....	....
2005-06	**Buffalo**	**NHL**	**48**	**25**	**33**	**58**	**48**	**11**	**0**	**4**	**147**	**17.0**	**3**	**517**	**50.7**	**19:04**	**18**	**8**	**11**	**19**	**12**	**3**	**0**	**2**	**18:48**
	NHL Totals		**402**	**130**	**151**	**281**	**276**	**54**	**0**	**19**	**817**	**15.9**		**4607**	**50.1**	**15:37**	**24**	**10**	**12**	**22**	**14**	**4**	**0**	**3**	**17:46**

QMJHL All-Rookie Team (1995) • QMJHL Offensive Rookie of the Year (1995) • QMJHL Second All-Star Team (1996, 1997) • AHL All-Rookie Team (1998) • AHL First All-Star Team (1998) • Dudley "Red" Garrett Memorial Award (Rookie of the Year – AHL) (1998)

Traded to **Buffalo** by **Phoenix** with Phoenix's 3rd round choice (Andrej Sekera) in 2004 Entry Draft for Chris Gratton and Buffalo's 4th round choice (later traded to Edmonton – Edmonton selected Liam Reddox) in 2004 Entry Draft, March 10, 2003. Signed as a free agent by **Bern** (Swiss), September 28, 2004.

Season	Club	League	Regular Season														Playoffs								
Season	Club	League	GP	G	A	Pts	PIM	PP	SH	GW	S	%	+/-	TF	F%	Min	GP	G	A	Pts	PIM	PP	SH	GW	Min

BRIGLEY, Travis

(BRIH-glee, TRA-vihs)

Left wing. Shoots left. 6', 205 lbs. Born, Coronation, Alta., June 16, 1977. Calgary's 2nd choice, 39th overall, in 1996 Entry Draft.

Season	Club	League	GP	G	A	Pts	PIM	PP	SH	GW	S	%	+/-	TF	F%	Min	GP	G	A	Pts	PIM	PP	SH	GW	Min
1992-93	Leduc Oil Barons	AMHL	32	36	24	60	56	....	....	....	....	....	....	....	....	....	....	....	....	....	....	....	....	....	....
1993-94	Leduc Oil Barons	AMHL	34	29	44	73	141	....	....	....	....	....	....	....	....	....	....	....	....	....	....	....	....	....	....
	Lethbridge	WHL	1	0	0	0	0	....	....	....	....	....	....	....	....	....	....	....	....	....	....	....	....	....	....
1994-95	Lethbridge	WHL	64	14	18	32	14	....	....	....	....	....	....	....	....	....	....	....	....	....	....	....	....	....	....
1995-96	Lethbridge	WHL	69	34	43	77	94	....	....	....	....	....	....	....	....	....	4	2	3	5	8	....	....	....	....
1996-97	Lethbridge	WHL	71	43	47	90	56	....	....	....	....	....	....	....	....	....	19	9	9	18	31	....	....	....	....
1997-98	**Calgary**	**NHL**	**2**	**0**	**0**	**0**	**2**	**0**	**0**	**0**	**1**	**0.0**	**0**	....	....	....	....	....	....	....	....	....	....	....	....
	Saint John Flames	AHL	79	17	15	32	28	....	....	....	....	....	....	....	....	....	8	0	0	0	0	....	....	....	....
1998-99	Saint John Flames	AHL	74	15	35	50	48	....	....	....	....	....	....	....	....	....	7	3	1	4	2	....	....	....	....
99-2000	**Calgary**	**NHL**	**17**	**0**	**2**	**2**	**4**	**0**	**0**	**0**	**17**	**0.0**	**–6**	**2**	**0.0**	**14:14**	....	....	....	....	....	....	....	....	....
	Saint John Flames	AHL	9	3	1	4	4	....	....	....	....	....	....	....	....	....	....	....	....	....	....	....	....	....	....
	Detroit Vipers	IHL	29	6	10	16	24	....	....	....	....	....	....	....	....	....	....	....	....	....	....	....	....	....	....
	Philadelphia	AHL	15	2	2	4	15	....	....	....	....	....	....	....	....	....	5	1	0	1	4	....	....	....	....
2000-01	Knoxville Speed	UHL	4	2	4	6	4	....	....	....	....	....	....	....	....	....	....	....	....	....	....	....	....	....	....
	Cardiff Devils	Britain-2	12	5	9	14	6	....	....	....	....	....	....	....	....	....	....	....	....	....	....	....	....	....	....
	Louisville Panthers	AHL	49	14	21	35	34	....	....	....	....	....	....	....	....	....	....	....	....	....	....	....	....	....	....
2001-02	Macon Whoopee	ECHL	8	4	3	7	2	....	....	....	....	....	....	....	....	....	....	....	....	....	....	....	....	....	....
	Cincinnati	AHL	70	22	21	43	40	....	....	....	....	....	....	....	....	....	3	2	0	2	0	....	....	....	....
2002-03	Cincinnati	AHL	64	18	27	45	58	....	....	....	....	....	....	....	....	....	....	....	....	....	....	....	....	....	....
	Hershey Bears	AHL	13	3	5	8	4	....	....	....	....	....	....	....	....	....	5	1	2	3	2	....	....	....	....
2003-04	**Colorado**	**NHL**	**36**	**3**	**4**	**7**	**10**	**1**	**0**	**0**	**39**	**7.7**	**0**	**198**	**43.4**	**11:52**	....	....	....	....	....	....	....	....	....
	Hershey Bears	AHL	18	6	6	12	8	....	....	....	....	....	....	....	....	....	....	....	....	....	....	....	....	....	....
2004-05	Valerengen IF Oslo	Norway	21	8	11	19	43	....	....	....	....	....	....	....	....	....	10	3	4	7	18	....	....	....	....
2005-06	Bridgeport	AHL	39	7	10	17	28	....	....	....	....	....	....	....	....	....	....	....	....	....	....	....	....	....	....
	Springfield	AHL	18	3	3	6	6	....	....	....	....	....	....	....	....	....	....	....	....	....	....	....	....	....	....
	NHL Totals		**55**	**3**	**6**	**9**	**16**	**1**	**0**	**0**	**57**	**5.3**		**200**	**43.0**	**12:38**	....	....	....	....	....	....	....	....	....

Traded to **Philadelphia** by **Calgary** with Calgary's 6th round choice (Andrei Razin) in 2001 Entry Draft for Marc Bureau, March 6, 2000. Signed as a free agent by **Cardiff** (Britain-2), November 3, 2000. Signed as a free agent by **Florida**, December 16, 2000. Signed as a free agent by **Anaheim**, January 22, 2002. Traded to **Colorado** by **Anaheim** for future considerations, August 12, 2003. Signed as a free agent by **Oslo** (Norway), October 21, 2004.

BRIND'AMOUR, Rod

(BRIHND-uh-MOHR, RAWD) **CAR.**

Center. Shoots left. 6'1", 200 lbs. Born, Ottawa, Ont., August 9, 1970. St. Louis' 1st choice, 9th overall, in 1988 Entry Draft.

Season	Club	League	GP	G	A	Pts	PIM	PP	SH	GW	S	%	+/-	TF	F%	Min	GP	G	A	Pts	PIM	PP	SH	GW	Min
1986-87	Notre Dame	SMHL	33	38	50	88	66	....	....	....	....	....	....	....	....	....	....	....	....	....	....	....	....	....	....
1987-88	Notre Dame	SJHL	56	46	61	107	136	....	....	....	....	....	....	....	....	....	....	....	....	....	....	....	....	....	....
1988-89	Michigan State	CCHA	42	27	32	59	63	....	....	....	....	....	....	....	....	....	....	....	....	....	....	....	....	....	....
	St. Louis	**NHL**	....	....	....	....	....	....	....	....	....	....	....	....	....	....	**5**	**2**	**0**	**2**	**4**	**0**	**0**	**0**	....
1989-90	**St. Louis**	**NHL**	**79**	**26**	**35**	**61**	**46**	**10**	**0**	**1**	**160**	**16.3**	**23**	....	....	....	**12**	**5**	**8**	**13**	**6**	**1**	**0**	**0**	....
1990-91	**St. Louis**	**NHL**	**78**	**17**	**32**	**49**	**93**	**4**	**0**	**3**	**169**	**10.1**	**2**	....	....	....	**13**	**2**	**5**	**7**	**10**	**1**	**0**	**0**	....
1991-92	**Philadelphia**	**NHL**	**80**	**33**	**44**	**77**	**100**	**8**	**4**	**5**	**202**	**16.3**	**–3**	....	....	....	....	....	....	....	....	....	....	....	....
1992-93	**Philadelphia**	**NHL**	**81**	**37**	**49**	**86**	**89**	**13**	**4**	**4**	**206**	**18.0**	**–8**	....	....	....	....	....	....	....	....	....	....	....	....
1993-94	**Philadelphia**	**NHL**	**84**	**35**	**62**	**97**	**85**	**14**	**1**	**4**	**230**	**15.2**	**–9**	....	....	....	....	....	....	....	....	....	....	....	....
1994-95	**Philadelphia**	**NHL**	**48**	**12**	**27**	**39**	**33**	**4**	**1**	**2**	**86**	**14.0**	**–4**	....	....	....	**15**	**6**	**9**	**15**	**8**	**2**	**1**	**1**	....
1995-96	**Philadelphia**	**NHL**	**82**	**26**	**61**	**87**	**110**	**4**	**4**	**5**	**213**	**12.2**	**20**	....	....	....	**12**	**2**	**5**	**7**	**6**	**1**	**0**	**0**	....
1996-97	**Philadelphia**	**NHL**	**82**	**27**	**32**	**59**	**41**	**8**	**2**	**3**	**205**	**13.2**	**2**	....	....	....	**19**	***13**	**8**	**21**	**10**	**4**	**2**	**1**	....
1997-98	**Philadelphia**	**NHL**	**82**	**36**	**38**	**74**	**54**	**10**	**2**	**8**	**205**	**17.6**	**–2**	....	....	....	**5**	**2**	**2**	**4**	**7**	**0**	**0**	**0**	....
	Canada	Olympics	6	1	2	3	0	....	....	....	....	....	....	....	....	....	....	....	....	....	....	....	....	....	....
1998-99	**Philadelphia**	**NHL**	**82**	**24**	**50**	**74**	**47**	**10**	**0**	**3**	**191**	**12.6**	**3**	**1773**	**56.5**	**21:29**	**6**	**1**	**3**	**4**	**0**	**0**	**0**	**0**	**25:08**
99-2000	**Philadelphia**	**NHL**	**12**	**5**	**3**	**8**	**4**	**4**	**0**	**0**	**26**	**19.2**	**–1**	**291**	**60.5**	**20:50**	....	....	....	....	....	....	....	....	....
	Carolina	**NHL**	**33**	**4**	**10**	**14**	**22**	**0**	**1**	**1**	**61**	**6.6**	**–12**	**704**	**55.5**	**20:35**	....	....	....	....	....	....	....	....	....
2000-01	**Carolina**	**NHL**	**79**	**20**	**36**	**56**	**47**	**5**	**1**	**5**	**163**	**12.3**	**–7**	**1907**	**60.4**	**22:07**	**6**	**1**	**3**	**4**	**6**	**0**	**0**	**1**	**23:27**
2001-02	**Carolina**	**NHL**	**81**	**23**	**32**	**55**	**40**	**5**	**2**	**5**	**162**	**14.2**	**3**	**2058**	**59.2**	**22:07**	**23**	**4**	**8**	**12**	**16**	**2**	**1**	**1**	**24:52**
2002-03	**Carolina**	**NHL**	**48**	**14**	**23**	**37**	**37**	**7**	**1**	**0**	**110**	**12.7**	**–9**	**1242**	**56.5**	**23:46**	....	....	....	....	....	....	....	....	....
2003-04	**Carolina**	**NHL**	**78**	**12**	**26**	**38**	**28**	**1**	**0**	**1**	**141**	**8.5**	**0**	**1817**	**61.1**	**21:23**	....	....	....	....	....	....	....	....	....
2004-05	Kloten Flyers	Swiss	2	2	1	3	0	....	....	....	....	....	....	....	....	....	5	2	4	6	6	....	....	....	....
2005-06♦	**Carolina**	**NHL**	**78**	**31**	**39**	**70**	**68**	**19**	**2**	**5**	**198**	**15.7**	**8**	**2145**	**59.1**	**24:18**	**25**	**12**	**6**	**18**	**16**	**6**	**0**	**4**	**23:52**
	NHL Totals		**1187**	**382**	**599**	**981**	**944**	**126**	**25**	**55**	**2728**	**14.0**		**11937**	**58.8**	**22:16**	**141**	**50**	**57**	**107**	**89**	**17**	**4**	**8**	**24:20**

CCHA Rookie of the Year (1989) • NHL All-Rookie Team (1990) • Frank J. Selke Trophy (2006)

Played in NHL All-Star Game (1992)

Traded to **Philadelphia** by **St. Louis** with Dan Quinn for Ron Sutter and Murray Baron, September 22, 1991. Traded to **Carolina** by **Philadelphia** with Jean-Marc Pelletier and Philadelphia's 2nd round choice (later traded to Colorado – Colorado selected Agris Saviels) in 2000 Entry Draft for Keith Primeau and Carolina's 5th round choice (later traded to NY Islanders – NY Islanders selected Kristofer Ottosson) in 2000 Entry Draft, January 23, 2000. Signed as a free agent by **Kloten** (Swiss), February 16, 2005.

BRISEBOIS, Patrice

(BREES-bwah, pa-TREEZ) **COL.**

Defense. Shoots right. 6'2", 203 lbs. Born, Montreal, Que., January 27, 1971. Montreal's 2nd choice, 30th overall, in 1989 Entry Draft.

Season	Club	League	GP	G	A	Pts	PIM	PP	SH	GW	S	%	+/-	TF	F%	Min	GP	G	A	Pts	PIM	PP	SH	GW	Min
1986-87	Mtl-Bourassa	QAAA	39	15	19	34	66	....	....	....	....	....	....	....	....	....	....	....	....	....	....	....	....	....	....
1987-88	Laval Titan	QMJHL	48	10	34	44	95	....	....	....	....	....	....	....	....	....	6	0	2	2	2	....	....	....	....
1988-89	Laval Titan	QMJHL	50	20	45	65	95	....	....	....	....	....	....	....	....	....	17	8	14	22	45	....	....	....	....
1989-90	Laval Titan	QMJHL	56	18	70	88	108	....	....	....	....	....	....	....	....	....	13	7	9	16	26	....	....	....	....
1990-91	Drummondville	QMJHL	54	17	44	61	72	....	....	....	....	....	....	....	....	....	14	6	18	24	49	....	....	....	....
	Montreal	**NHL**	**10**	**0**	**2**	**2**	**4**	**0**	**0**	**0**	**11**	**0.0**	**1**	....	....	....	....	....	....	....	....	....	....	....	....
1991-92	**Montreal**	**NHL**	**26**	**2**	**8**	**10**	**20**	**0**	**0**	**1**	**37**	**5.4**	**9**	....	....	....	**11**	**2**	**4**	**6**	**6**	**1**	**0**	**1**	....
	Fredericton	AHL	53	12	27	39	51	....	....	....	....	....	....	....	....	....	....	....	....	....	....	....	....	....	....
1992-93♦	**Montreal**	**NHL**	**70**	**10**	**21**	**31**	**79**	**4**	**0**	**2**	**123**	**8.1**	**6**	....	....	....	**20**	**0**	**4**	**4**	**18**	**0**	**0**	**0**	....
1993-94	**Montreal**	**NHL**	**53**	**2**	**21**	**23**	**63**	**1**	**0**	**0**	**71**	**2.8**	**5**	....	....	....	**7**	**0**	**4**	**4**	**6**	**0**	**0**	**0**	....
1994-95	**Montreal**	**NHL**	**35**	**4**	**8**	**12**	**26**	**0**	**0**	**2**	**67**	**6.0**	**–2**	....	....	....	....	....	....	....	....	....	....	....	....
1995-96	**Montreal**	**NHL**	**69**	**9**	**27**	**36**	**65**	**3**	**0**	**1**	**127**	**7.1**	**10**	....	....	....	**6**	**1**	**2**	**3**	**6**	**0**	**0**	**0**	....
1996-97	**Montreal**	**NHL**	**49**	**2**	**13**	**15**	**24**	**0**	**0**	**1**	**72**	**2.8**	**–7**	....	....	....	**3**	**1**	**1**	**2**	**24**	**0**	**0**	**1**	....
1997-98	**Montreal**	**NHL**	**79**	**10**	**27**	**37**	**67**	**5**	**0**	**1**	**125**	**8.0**	**16**	....	....	....	**10**	**1**	**0**	**1**	**0**	**0**	**0**	**0**	....
1998-99	**Montreal**	**NHL**	**54**	**3**	**9**	**12**	**28**	**1**	**0**	**1**	**90**	**3.3**	**–8**	**0**	**0.0**	**22:26**	....	....	....	....	....	....	....	....	....
99-2000	**Montreal**	**NHL**	**54**	**10**	**25**	**35**	**18**	**5**	**0**	**2**	**88**	**11.4**	**–1**	**0**	**0.0**	**23:14**	....	....	....	....	....	....	....	....	....
2000-01	**Montreal**	**NHL**	**77**	**15**	**21**	**36**	**28**	**11**	**0**	**4**	**178**	**8.4**	**–31**	**1**	**100.0**	**24:43**	....	....	....	....	....	....	....	....	....
2001-02	**Montreal**	**NHL**	**71**	**4**	**29**	**33**	**25**	**2**	**1**	**1**	**95**	**4.2**	**9**	**0**	**0.0**	**23:53**	**10**	**1**	**1**	**2**	**2**	**0**	**0**	**0**	**22:05**
2002-03	**Montreal**	**NHL**	**73**	**4**	**25**	**29**	**32**	**1**	**0**	**1**	**105**	**3.8**	**–14**	**0**	**0.0**	**23:23**	....	....	....	....	....	....	....	....	....
2003-04	**Montreal**	**NHL**	**71**	**4**	**27**	**31**	**22**	**2**	**0**	**0**	**96**	**4.2**	**17**	**0**	**0.0**	**21:20**	**11**	**2**	**1**	**3**	**4**	**1**	**0**	**0**	**22:30**
2004-05	Kloten Flyers	Swiss	10	3	1	4	2	....	....	....	....	....	....	....	....	....	....	....	....	....	....	....	....	....	....
2005-06	**Colorado**	**NHL**	**80**	**10**	**28**	**38**	**55**	**4**	**0**	**2**	**107**	**9.3**	**1**	**2**	**0.0**	**22:19**	**9**	**0**	**1**	**1**	**4**	**0**	**0**	**0**	**22:19**
	NHL Totals		**871**	**89**	**291**	**380**	**556**	**39**	**1**	**19**	**1392**	**6.4**		**3**	**33.3**	**23:04**	**87**	**8**	**18**	**26**	**70**	**2**	**0**	**2**	**22:18**

QMJHL Second All-Star Team (1990) • QMJHL First All-Star Team (1991) • Canadian Major Junior Defenseman of the Year (1991) • Memorial Cup Tournament All-Star Team (1991)

Signed as a free agent by **Kloten** (Swiss), October 13, 2004. Signed as a free agent by **Colorado**, August 3, 2005.

BRODZIAK, Kyle

(brohd-ZEE-ak, KIGHL) **EDM.**

Center. Shoots right. 6'2", 198 lbs. Born, St. Paul, Alta., May 25, 1984. Edmonton's 9th choice, 214th overall, in 2003 Entry Draft.

Season	Club	League	GP	G	A	Pts	PIM	PP	SH	GW	S	%	+/-	TF	F%	Min	GP	G	A	Pts	PIM	PP	SH	GW	Min
99-2000	Ft. Saskatchewan	AMBHL	36	23	33	56	57	....	....	....	....	....	....	....	....	....	....	....	....	....	....	....	....	....	....
	Moose Jaw	WHL	2	0	0	0	0	....	....	....	....	....	....	....	....	....	....	....	....	....	....	....	....	....	....
2000-01	Moose Jaw	WHL	57	2	8	10	49	....	....	....	....	....	....	....	....	....	3	0	0	0	0	....	....	....	....
2001-02	Moose Jaw	WHL	72	8	12	20	56	....	....	....	....	....	....	....	....	....	12	0	3	3	11	....	....	....	....
2002-03	Moose Jaw	WHL	72	32	30	62	84	....	....	....	....	....	....	....	....	....	13	5	3	8	16	....	....	....	....
2003-04	Moose Jaw	WHL	70	39	54	93	58	....	....	....	....	....	....	....	....	....	10	5	4	9	10	....	....	....	....
2004-05	Edmonton	AHL	56	6	26	32	49	....	....	....	....	....	....	....	....	....	....	....	....	....	....	....	....	....	....
2005-06	**Edmonton**	**NHL**	**10**	**0**	**0**	**0**	**4**	**0**	**0**	**0**	**7**	**0.0**	**–4**	**75**	**52.0**	**11:02**	....	....	....	....	....	....	....	....	....
	Iowa Stars	AHL	55	12	19	31	41	....	....	....	....	....	....	....	....	....	7	1	3	4	2	....	....	....	....
	NHL Totals		**10**	**0**	**0**	**0**	**4**	**0**	**0**	**0**	**7**	**0.0**		**75**	**52.0**	**11:02**	....	....	....	....	....	....	....	....	....

WHL East First All-Star Team (2004)

			Regular Season														Playoffs								
Season	Club	League	GP	G	A	Pts	PIM	PP	SH	GW	S	%	+/-	TF	F%	Min	GP	G	A	Pts	PIM	PP	SH	GW	Min

BROOKBANK, Wade

(BRUK-bank, WAYD) **BOS.**

Defense. Shoots left. 6'4", 225 lbs. Born, Lanigan, Sask., September 29, 1977.

Season	Club	League	GP	G	A	Pts	PIM	PP	SH	GW	S	%	+/-	TF	F%	Min	GP	G	A	Pts	PIM	PP	SH	GW	Min
1997-98	Melville	SJHL	58	8	21	29	330	....	....	....	....	....	....	....	....	....	....	....	....	....	....	....	....	....	....
	Anchorage Aces	WCHL	7	0	0	0	46	....	....	....	....	....	....	....	....	....	4	0	0	0	20	....	....	....	....
1998-99	Anchorage Aces	WCHL	56	0	4	4	337	....	....	....	....	....	....	....	....	....	....	....	....	....	....	....	....	....	....
99-2000	Oklahoma City	CHL	68	3	9	12	354	....	....	....	....	....	....	....	....	....	7	1	1	2	29	....	....	....	....
2000-01	Orlando	IHL	29	0	1	1	122	....	....	....	....	....	....	....	....	....	4	0	0	0	6	....	....	....	....
	Oklahoma City	CHL	46	1	13	14	267	....	....	....	....	....	....	....	....	....	5	0	0	0	24	....	....	....	....
2001-02	Grand Rapids	AHL	73	1	6	7	337	....	....	....	....	....	....	....	....	....	3	0	1	1	14	....	....	....	....
2002-03	Binghamton	AHL	8	0	0	0	28	....	....	....	....	....	....	....	....	....	....	....	....	....	....	....	....	....	....
2003-04	**Nashville**	**NHL**	**9**	**0**	**0**	**0**	**38**	**0**	**0**	**0**	**1**	**0.0**	**–4**	**0**	**0.0**	**3:28**	....	....	....	....	....	....	....	....	....
	Milwaukee	AHL	6	0	0	0	6	....	....	....	....	....	....	....	....	....	....	....	....	....	....	....	....	....	....
	Binghamton	AHL	4	0	0	0	31	....	....	....	....	....	....	....	....	....	....	....	....	....	....	....	....	....	....
	Vancouver	**NHL**	**20**	**2**	**0**	**2**	**95**	**0**	**0**	**1**	**6**	**33.3**	**3**	**0**	**0.0**	**3:50**	....	....	....	....	....	....	....	....	....
	Manitoba Moose	AHL	4	0	0	0	12	....	....	....	....	....	....	....	....	....	....	....	....	....	....	....	....	....	....
2004-05	Manitoba Moose	AHL	68	0	10	10	285	....	....	....	....	....	....	....	....	....	9	0	0	0	10	....	....	....	....
2005-06	**Vancouver**	**NHL**	**32**	**1**	**2**	**3**	**81**	**0**	**0**	**0**	**10**	**10.0**	**3**	**0**	**0.0**	**4:56**	....	....	....	....	....	....	....	....	....
	NHL Totals		**61**	**3**	**2**	**5**	**214**	**0**	**0**	**1**	**17**	**17.6**		**0**	**0.0**	**4:22**	....	....	....	....	....	....	....	....	....

Signed as a free agent by **Orlando** (IHL), September 1, 2000. Signed as a free agent by **Ottawa**, July 27, 2001. • Missed majority of 2002-03 season recovering from knee injury suffered in game vs. Wilkes-Barre (AHL), November 2, 2002. Claimed by **Nashville** from **Ottawa** in Waiver Draft, October 3, 2003. Traded to **Vancouver** by **Nashville** for future considerations, December 17, 2003. Claimed on waivers by **Ottawa** from **Vancouver**, December 19, 2003. Traded to **Florida** by **Ottawa** for future considerations, December 29, 2003. Claimed on waivers by **Vancouver** from **Florida**, January 3, 2004. • Missed majority of 2005-06 season recovering from two head injuries suffered during the season and as a healthy reserve. Signed as a free agent by **Boston**, July 21, 2006.

BROWN, Brad

(BROWN, BRAD) **TOR.**

Defense. Shoots right. 6'4", 220 lbs. Born, Baie Verte, Nfld., December 27, 1975. Montreal's 1st choice, 18th overall, in 1994 Entry Draft.

Season	Club	League	GP	G	A	Pts	PIM	PP	SH	GW	S	%	+/-	TF	F%	Min	GP	G	A	Pts	PIM	PP	SH	GW	Min
1990-91	Tor. Red Wings	MTHL	80	15	45	60	105	....	....	....	....	....	....	....	....	....	....	....	....	....	....	....	....	....	....
	St. Mike's B's	OHA-B	2	0	0	0	0	....	....	....	....	....	....	....	....	....	....	....	....	....	....	....	....	....	....
1991-92	North Bay	OHL	49	2	9	11	170	....	....	....	....	....	....	....	....	....	18	0	6	6	43	....	....	....	....
1992-93	North Bay	OHL	61	4	9	13	228	....	....	....	....	....	....	....	....	....	2	0	2	2	13	....	....	....	....
1993-94	North Bay	OHL	66	8	24	32	196	....	....	....	....	....	....	....	....	....	18	3	12	15	33	....	....	....	....
1994-95	North Bay	OHL	64	8	38	46	172	....	....	....	....	....	....	....	....	....	6	1	4	5	8	....	....	....	....
1995-96	Barrie Colts	OHL	27	3	13	16	82	....	....	....	....	....	....	....	....	....	....	....	....	....	....	....	....	....	....
	Fredericton	AHL	38	0	3	3	148	....	....	....	....	....	....	....	....	....	10	2	1	3	6	....	....	....	....
1996-97	**Montreal**	**NHL**	**8**	**0**	**0**	**0**	**22**	**0**	**0**	**0**	**0**	**0.0**	**–1**	....	....	....	....	....	....	....	....	....	....	....	....
	Fredericton	AHL	64	3	7	10	368	....	....	....	....	....	....	....	....	....	....	....	....	....	....	....	....	....	....
1997-98	Fredericton	AHL	64	1	8	9	297	....	....	....	....	....	....	....	....	....	4	0	0	0	29	....	....	....	....
1998-99	**Montreal**	**NHL**	**5**	**0**	**0**	**0**	**21**	**0**	**0**	**0**	**0**	**0.0**	**0**	**0**	**0.0**	**6:02**	....	....	....	....	....	....	....	....	....
	Chicago	**NHL**	**61**	**1**	**7**	**8**	**184**	**0**	**0**	**0**	**26**	**3.8**	**–4**	**0**	**0.0**	**15:08**	....	....	....	....	....	....	....	....	....
99-2000	**Chicago**	**NHL**	**57**	**0**	**9**	**9**	**134**	**0**	**0**	**0**	**15**	**0.0**	**–1**	**0**	**0.0**	**14:12**	....	....	....	....	....	....	....	....	....
2000-01	**NY Rangers**	**NHL**	**48**	**1**	**3**	**4**	**107**	**0**	**0**	**0**	**14**	**7.1**	**0**	**0**	**0.0**	**14:31**	....	....	....	....	....	....	....	....	....
2001-02	**Minnesota**	**NHL**	**51**	**0**	**4**	**4**	**123**	**0**	**0**	**0**	**23**	**0.0**	**–11**	**0**	**0.0**	**15:54**	....	....	....	....	....	....	....	....	....
2002-03	**Minnesota**	**NHL**	**57**	**0**	**1**	**1**	**90**	**0**	**0**	**0**	**10**	**0.0**	**–1**	**0**	**0.0**	**9:14**	**11**	**0**	**0**	**0**	**16**	**0**	**0**	**0**	**8:23**
2003-04	**Minnesota**	**NHL**	**30**	**0**	**1**	**1**	**54**	**0**	**0**	**0**	**14**	**0.0**	**–1**	**0**	**0.0**	**9:41**	....	....	....	....	....	....	....	....	....
	Buffalo	**NHL**	**13**	**0**	**2**	**2**	**12**	**0**	**0**	**0**	**6**	**0.0**	**3**	**0**	**0.0**	**16:33**	....	....	....	....	....	....	....	....	....
2004-05			DID NOT PLAY																						
2005-06	Toronto Marlies	AHL	38	2	2	4	93	....	....	....	....	....	....	....	....	....	2	0	0	0	0	....	....	....	....
	NHL Totals		**330**	**2**	**27**	**29**	**747**	**0**	**0**	**0**	**108**	**1.9**		**0**	**0.0**	**13:22**	**11**	**0**	**0**	**0**	**16**	**0**	**0**	**0**	**8:23**

OHL All-Rookie Team (1992)

Traded to **Chicago** by **Montreal** with Jocelyn Thibault and Dave Manson for Jeff Hackett, Eric Weinrich, Alain Nasreddine and Tampa Bay's 4th round choice (previously acquired, Montreal selected Chris Dyment) in 1999 Entry Draft, November 16, 1998. Traded to **NY Rangers** by **Chicago** with Michal Grosek for future considerations, October 5, 2000. Signed as a free agent by **Minnesota**, July 31, 2001. Traded to **Buffalo** by **Minnesota** with Minnesota's 6th round choice (Vjateslav Buravchikov) in 2005 Entry Draft for Buffalo's 4th round choice (Kyle Bailey) in 2005 Entry Draft, March 8, 2004. Signed as a free agent by **Toronto**, September 10, 2005.

BROWN, Curtis

(BROWN, KUHR-tihs) **S.J.**

Center/Left wing. Shoots left. 6', 196 lbs. Born, Unity, Sask., February 12, 1976. Buffalo's 2nd choice, 43rd overall, in 1994 Entry Draft.

Season	Club	League	GP	G	A	Pts	PIM	PP	SH	GW	S	%	+/-	TF	F%	Min	GP	G	A	Pts	PIM	PP	SH	GW	Min
1990-91	Unity Bantams	SBHL	60	93	104	197	55	....	....	....	....	....	....	....	....	....	....	....	....	....	....	....	....	....	....
1991-92	Moose Jaw	SMHL	36	35	30	65	44	....	....	....	....	....	....	....	....	....	....	....	....	....	....	....	....	....	....
1992-93	Moose Jaw	WHL	71	13	16	29	30	....	....	....	....	....	....	....	....	....	....	....	....	....	....	....	....	....	....
1993-94	Moose Jaw	WHL	72	27	38	65	82	....	....	....	....	....	....	....	....	....	....	....	....	....	....	....	....	....	....
1994-95	Moose Jaw	WHL	70	51	53	104	63	....	....	....	....	....	....	....	....	....	10	8	7	15	20	....	....	....	....
	Buffalo	**NHL**	**1**	**1**	**1**	**2**	**2**	**0**	**0**	**0**	**4**	**25.0**	**2**	....	....	....	....	....	....	....	....	....	....	....	....
1995-96	Moose Jaw	WHL	25	20	18	38	30	....	....	....	....	....	....	....	....	....	....	....	....	....	....	....	....	....	....
	Prince Albert	WHL	19	12	21	33	8	....	....	....	....	....	....	....	....	....	18	10	15	25	18	....	....	....	....
	Buffalo	**NHL**	**4**	**0**	**0**	**0**	**0**	**0**	**0**	**0**	**1**	**0.0**	**0**	....	....	....	....	....	....	....	....	....	....	....	....
	Rochester	AHL	....	....	....	....	....	....	....	....	....	....	....	....	....	....	12	0	1	1	2	....	....	....	....
1996-97	**Buffalo**	**NHL**	**28**	**4**	**3**	**7**	**18**	**0**	**0**	**1**	**31**	**12.9**	**4**	....	....	....	....	....	....	....	....	....	....	....	....
	Rochester	AHL	51	22	21	43	30	....	....	....	....	....	....	....	....	....	10	4	6	10	4	....	....	....	....
1997-98	**Buffalo**	**NHL**	**63**	**12**	**12**	**24**	**34**	**1**	**1**	**2**	**91**	**13.2**	**11**	....	....	....	**13**	**1**	**2**	**3**	**10**	**1**	**0**	**0**	....
1998-99	**Buffalo**	**NHL**	**78**	**16**	**31**	**47**	**56**	**5**	**1**	**3**	**128**	**12.5**	**23**	**1198**	**45.0**	**17:30**	**21**	**7**	**6**	**13**	**10**	**3**	**0**	**3**	**18:51**
99-2000	**Buffalo**	**NHL**	**74**	**22**	**29**	**51**	**42**	**5**	**0**	**4**	**149**	**14.8**	**19**	**1318**	**48.6**	**18:11**	**5**	**1**	**3**	**4**	**6**	**1**	**0**	**0**	**17:11**
2000-01	**Buffalo**	**NHL**	**70**	**10**	**22**	**32**	**34**	**2**	**1**	**0**	**105**	**9.5**	**15**	**1159**	**50.4**	**16:34**	**13**	**5**	**0**	**5**	**8**	**0**	**2**	**1**	**18:14**
2001-02	**Buffalo**	**NHL**	**82**	**20**	**17**	**37**	**32**	**4**	**1**	**5**	**171**	**11.7**	**–4**	**1608**	**49.0**	**17:48**	....	....	....	....	....	....	....	....	....
2002-03	**Buffalo**	**NHL**	**74**	**15**	**16**	**31**	**40**	**3**	**4**	**4**	**144**	**10.4**	**4**	**1387**	**49.5**	**16:53**	....	....	....	....	....	....	....	....	....
2003-04	**Buffalo**	**NHL**	**68**	**9**	**12**	**21**	**30**	**2**	**1**	**2**	**117**	**7.7**	**2**	**1182**	**51.5**	**16:36**	....	....	....	....	....	....	....	....	....
	San Jose	**NHL**	**12**	**2**	**2**	**4**	**6**	**0**	**0**	**0**	**21**	**9.5**	**1**	**105**	**47.6**	**16:26**	**17**	**0**	**2**	**2**	**18**	**0**	**0**	**0**	**14:37**
2004-05	San Diego Gulls	ECHL	47	9	29	38	24	....	....	....	....	....	....	....	....	....	....	....	....	....	....	....	....	....	....
2005-06	**Chicago**	**NHL**	**71**	**5**	**10**	**15**	**38**	**0**	**1**	**0**	**84**	**6.0**	**–9**	**881**	**50.6**	**13:39**	....	....	....	....	....	....	....	....	....
	NHL Totals		**625**	**116**	**155**	**271**	**332**	**22**	**10**	**21**	**1046**	**11.1**		**8838**	**49.1**	**16:47**	**69**	**14**	**13**	**27**	**52**	**5**	**2**	**4**	**17:16**

WHL East First All-Star Team (1995) • WHL East Second All-Star Team (1996)

Traded to **San Jose** by **Buffalo** with Andy Delmore for Jeff Jillson and a compensatory 7th round choice (Andrew Orpik) in 2005 Entry Draft, March 9, 2004. Signed as a free agent by **Chicago**, July 2, 2004. Signed as a free agent by **San Diego** (ECHL), November 16, 2004. Signed as a free agent by **San Jose**, July 3, 2006.

BROWN, Dustin

(BROWN, DUHS-tihn) **L.A.**

Right wing. Shoots right. 6', 195 lbs. Born, Ithaca, NY, November 4, 1984. Los Angeles' 1st choice, 13th overall, in 2003 Entry Draft.

Season	Club	League	GP	G	A	Pts	PIM	PP	SH	GW	S	%	+/-	TF	F%	Min	GP	G	A	Pts	PIM	PP	SH	GW	Min
1998-99	Ithaca	High-NY	18	4	13	17	....	....	....	....	....	....	....	....	....	....	....	....	....	....	....	....	....	....	....
99-2000	Ithaca	High-NY	24	33	21	53	....	....	....	....	....	....	....	....	....	....	....	....	....	....	....	....	....	....	....
2000-01	Guelph Storm	OHL	53	23	22	45	45	....	....	....	....	....	....	....	....	....	4	0	0	0	10	....	....	....	....
2001-02	Guelph Storm	OHL	63	41	32	73	56	....	....	....	....	....	....	....	....	....	9	8	5	13	14	....	....	....	....
2002-03	Guelph Storm	OHL	58	34	42	76	89	....	....	....	....	....	....	....	....	....	11	7	8	15	6	....	....	....	....
2003-04	**Los Angeles**	**NHL**	**31**	**1**	**4**	**5**	**16**	**0**	**0**	**0**	**40**	**2.5**	**0**	**1**	**0.0**	**10:29**	....	....	....	....	....	....	....	....	....
2004-05	Manchester	AHL	79	29	45	74	96	....	....	....	....	....	....	....	....	....	6	5	2	7	10	....	....	....	....
2005-06	**Los Angeles**	**NHL**	**79**	**14**	**14**	**28**	**80**	**6**	**0**	**2**	**159**	**8.8**	**–10**	**15**	**66.7**	**13:59**	....	....	....	....	....	....	....	....	....
	NHL Totals		**110**	**15**	**18**	**33**	**96**	**6**	**0**	**2**	**199**	**7.5**		**16**	**62.5**	**13:00**	....	....	....	....	....	....	....	....	....

OHL All-Rookie Team (2001) • Canadian Major Junior Scholastic Player of the Year (2003)

• Missed majority of 2003-04 season recovering from ankle injury suffered in game vs. Chicago, November 29, 2003.

BROWN, Mike

(BROWN, MIGHK)

Left wing. Shoots left. 6'5", 185 lbs. Born, Surrey, B.C., April 27, 1979. Florida's 1st choice, 20th overall, in 1997 Entry Draft.

Season	Club	League	GP	G	A	Pts	PIM	PP	SH	GW	S	%	+/-	TF	F%	Min	GP	G	A	Pts	PIM	PP	SH	GW	Min
1993-94	Penticton	BCJHL	50	52	48	100	100	....	....	....	....	....	....	....	....	....	....	....	....	....	....	....	....	....	....
1994-95	Merritt	BCJHL	45	3	4	7	145	....	....	....	....	....	....	....	....	....	....	....	....	....	....	....	....	....	....
	Red Deer Rebels	WHL	1	0	0	0	0	....	....	....	....	....	....	....	....	....	....	....	....	....	....	....	....	....	....
1995-96	Red Deer Rebels	WHL	62	4	5	9	125	....	....	....	....	....	....	....	....	....	10	0	0	0	18	....	....	....	....
1996-97	Red Deer Rebels	WHL	70	19	13	32	243	....	....	....	....	....	....	....	....	....	16	1	2	3	47	....	....	....	....
1997-98	Kamloops Blazers	WHL	72	23	33	56	305	....	....	....	....	....	....	....	....	....	7	2	1	3	22	....	....	....	....

			Regular Season														Playoffs								
Season	**Club**	**League**	**GP**	**G**	**A**	**Pts**	**PIM**	**PP**	**SH**	**GW**	**S**	**%**	**+/-**	**TF**	**F%**	**Min**	**GP**	**G**	**A**	**Pts**	**PIM**	**PP**	**SH**	**GW**	**Min**
1998-99	Kamloops Blazers	WHL	69	28	16	44	*285	....	....	....	....	....	....	....	....	....	15	3	7	10	*68	....	....	....	....
99-2000	Syracuse Crunch	AHL	71	13	18	31	284	....	....	....	....	....	....	....	....	....	4	0	0	0	0	....	....	....	....
2000-01	**Vancouver**	**NHL**	**1**	**0**	**0**	**0**	**5**	**0**	**0**	**0**	**1**	**0.0**	**0**	**0**	**0.0**	**4:48**	....	....	....	....	....	....	....	....	....
	Kansas City	IHL	78	14	13	27	214	....	....	....	....	....	....	....	....	....	....	....	....	....	....	....	....	....	....
2001-02	**Vancouver**	**NHL**	**15**	**0**	**0**	**0**	**72**	**0**	**0**	**0**	**2**	**0.0**	**1**	**0**	**0.0**	**3:29**	....	....	....	....	....	....	....	....	....
	Manitoba Moose	AHL	31	7	9	16	155	....	....	....	....	....	....	....	....	....	6	0	1	1	16	....	....	....	....
2002-03	**Anaheim**	**NHL**	**16**	**1**	**1**	**2**	**44**	**0**	**0**	**1**	**8**	**12.5**	**0**	**0**	**0.0**	**4:58**	....	....	....	....	....	....	....	....	....
	Cincinnati	AHL	27	3	3	6	85	....	....	....	....	....	....	....	....	....	....	....	....	....	....	....	....	....	....
2003-04	St. John's	AHL	21	3	3	6	74	....	....	....	....	....	....	....	....	....	....	....	....	....	....	....	....	....	....
	Binghamton	AHL	38	4	7	11	131	....	....	....	....	....	....	....	....	....	....	....	....	....	....	....	....	....	....
2004-05	Norfolk Admirals	AHL	68	7	8	15	284	....	....	....	....	....	....	....	....	....	....	....	....	....	....	....	....	....	....
2005-06	**Chicago**	**NHL**	**2**	**0**	**1**	**1**	**9**	**0**	**0**	**0**	**1**	**0.0**	**0**	**0**	**0.0**	**5:52**	....	....	....	....	....	....	....	....	....
	Norfolk Admirals	AHL	53	2	13	15	146	....	....	....	....	....	....	....	....	....	1	0	0	0	17	....	....	....	....
	NHL Totals		**34**	**1**	**2**	**3**	**130**	**0**	**0**	**1**	**12**	**8.3**		**0**	**0.0**	**4:16**	....	....	....	....	....	....	....	....	....

Traded to **Vancouver** by **Florida** with Ed Jovanovski, Dave Gagner, Kevin Weekes and Florida's 1st round choice (Nathan Smith) in 2000 Entry Draft for Pavel Bure, Bret Hedican, Brad Ference and Vancouver's 3rd round choice (Robert Fried) in 2000 Entry Draft, January 17, 1999. Claimed on waivers by **Anaheim** from **Vancouver**, October 11, 2002. Signed as a free agent by **St. John's** (AHL), October 11, 2003. Signed as a free agent by **Binghamton** (AHL), January 8, 2004. Signed to a PTO (tryout) contract by **Norfolk** (AHL), December 6, 2004.

BROWN, Sean

(BROWN, SHAWN)

Defense. Shoots left. 6'3", 215 lbs. Born, Oshawa, Ont., November 5, 1976. Boston's 2nd choice, 21st overall, in 1995 Entry Draft.

Season	**Club**	**League**	**GP**	**G**	**A**	**Pts**	**PIM**	**PP**	**SH**	**GW**	**S**	**%**	**+/-**	**TF**	**F%**	**Min**	**GP**	**G**	**A**	**Pts**	**PIM**	**PP**	**SH**	**GW**	**Min**
1992-93	Oshawa	MTJHL	15	0	1	1	9	....	....	....	....	....	....	....	....	....	....	....	....	....	....	....	....	....	....
1993-94	Wellington Dukes	MTJHL	32	5	14	19	165	....	....	....	....	....	....	....	....	....	....	....	....	....	....	....	....	....	....
	Belleville Bulls	OHL	28	1	2	3	53	....	....	....	....	....	....	....	....	....	8	0	0	0	17	....	....	....	....
1994-95	Belleville Bulls	OHL	58	2	16	18	200	....	....	....	....	....	....	....	....	....	16	4	2	6	*67	....	....	....	....
1995-96	Belleville Bulls	OHL	37	10	23	33	150	....	....	....	....	....	....	....	....	....	....	....	....	....	....	....	....	....	....
	Sarnia Sting	OHL	26	8	17	25	112	....	....	....	....	....	....	....	....	....	10	1	0	1	38	....	....	....	....
1996-97	**Edmonton**	**NHL**	**5**	**0**	**0**	**0**	**4**	**0**	**0**	**0**	**2**	**0.0**	**-1**	....	....	....	....	....	....	....	....	....	....	....	....
	Hamilton	AHL	61	1	7	8	238	....	....	....	....	....	....	....	....	....	19	1	0	1	47	....	....	....	....
1997-98	**Edmonton**	**NHL**	**18**	**0**	**1**	**1**	**43**	**0**	**0**	**0**	**9**	**0.0**	**-1**	....	....	....	....	....	....	....	....	....	....	....	....
	Hamilton	AHL	43	4	6	10	166	....	....	....	....	....	....	....	....	....	6	0	2	2	38	....	....	....	....
1998-99	**Edmonton**	**NHL**	**51**	**0**	**7**	**7**	**188**	**0**	**0**	**0**	**27**	**0.0**	**1**	**0**	**0.0**	**12:14**	**1**	**0**	**0**	**0**	**10**	**0**	**0**	**0**	**7:33**
99-2000	**Edmonton**	**NHL**	**72**	**4**	**8**	**12**	**192**	**0**	**0**	**2**	**36**	**11.1**	**1**	**0**	**0.0**	**12:41**	**3**	**0**	**0**	**0**	**23**	**0**	**0**	**0**	**6:12**
2000-01	**Edmonton**	**NHL**	**62**	**2**	**3**	**5**	**110**	**0**	**0**	**0**	**30**	**6.7**	**2**	**0**	**0.0**	**11:07**	....	....	....	....	....	....	....	....	....
2001-02	**Edmonton**	**NHL**	**61**	**6**	**4**	**10**	**127**	**3**	**0**	**1**	**58**	**10.3**	**8**	**0**	**0.0**	**12:36**	....	....	....	....	....	....	....	....	....
	Boston	**NHL**	**12**	**0**	**1**	**1**	**47**	**0**	**0**	**0**	**6**	**0.0**	**-1**	**0**	**0.0**	**16:22**	**4**	**0**	**0**	**0**	**2**	**0**	**0**	**0**	**5:49**
2002-03	**Boston**	**NHL**	**69**	**1**	**5**	**6**	**117**	**0**	**0**	**0**	**39**	**2.6**	**-6**	**2**	**50.0**	**6:26**	....	....	....	....	....	....	....	....	....
2003-04	**New Jersey**	**NHL**	**39**	**0**	**3**	**3**	**44**	**0**	**0**	**0**	**25**	**0.0**	**5**	**0**	**0.0**	**13:56**	**1**	**0**	**0**	**0**	**2**	**0**	**0**	**0**	**11:20**
	Albany River Rats	AHL	21	1	6	7	56	....	....	....	....	....	....	....	....	....	....	....	....	....	....	....	....	....	....
2004-05			DID NOT PLAY																						
2005-06	**New Jersey**	**NHL**	**35**	**1**	**11**	**12**	**27**	**0**	**0**	**0**	**37**	**2.7**	**-14**	**1**	**0.0**	**15:22**	....	....	....	....	....	....	....	....	....
	Vancouver	**NHL**	**12**	**0**	**0**	**0**	**8**	**0**	**0**	**0**	**12**	**0.0**	**-3**	**1**	**0.0**	**14:15**	....	....	....	....	....	....	....	....	....
	NHL Totals		**436**	**14**	**43**	**57**	**907**	**3**	**0**	**3**	**281**	**5.0**		**4**	**25.0**	**11:50**	**9**	**0**	**0**	**0**	**37**	**0**	**0**	**0**	**6:45**

OHL Second All-Star Team (1996)

Rights traded to **Edmonton** by **Boston** with Mariusz Czerkawski and Boston's 1st round choice (Matthieu Descoteaux) in 1996 Entry Draft for Bill Ranford, January 11, 1996. Traded to **Boston** by **Edmonton** for Bobby Allen, March 19, 2002. Signed as a free agent by **New Jersey**, July 24, 2003. Traded to **Vancouver** by **New Jersey** for Vancouver's 4th round choice (T. J. Miller) in 2006 Entry Draft, March 9, 2006. Signed as a free agent by **Dusseldorf** (Germany), July 28, 2006.

BRULE, Gilbert

(broo-LAY, zhihl-BAIR) **CBJ**

Center. Shoots right. 5'10", 180 lbs. Born, Edmonton, Alta., January 1, 1987. Columbus' 1st choice, 6th overall, in 2005 Entry Draft.

Season	**Club**	**League**	**GP**	**G**	**A**	**Pts**	**PIM**	**PP**	**SH**	**GW**	**S**	**%**	**+/-**	**TF**	**F%**	**Min**	**GP**	**G**	**A**	**Pts**	**PIM**	**PP**	**SH**	**GW**	**Min**
2002-03	Quesnel	BCHL	48	32	25	57	71	....	....	....	....	....	....	....	....	....	....	....	....	....	....	....	....	....	....
	Vancouver Giants	WHL	1	0	0	0	0	....	....	....	....	....	....	....	....	....	4	1	0	1	0	....	....	....	....
2003-04	Vancouver Giants	WHL	67	25	35	60	100	....	....	....	....	....	....	....	....	....	11	4	5	9	10	....	....	....	....
2004-05	Vancouver Giants	WHL	70	39	48	87	169	....	....	....	....	....	....	....	....	....	6	1	3	4	8	....	....	....	....
2005-06	**Columbus**	**NHL**	**7**	**2**	**2**	**4**	**0**	**0**	**0**	**0**	**11**	**18.2**	**-2**	**60**	**43.3**	**13:11**	....	....	....	....	....	....	....	....	....
	Vancouver Giants	WHL	27	23	15	38	40	....	....	....	....	....	....	....	....	....	18	*16	14	*30	44	....	....	....	....
	NHL Totals		**7**	**2**	**2**	**4**	**0**	**0**	**0**	**0**	**11**	**18.2**		**60**	**43.3**	**13:11**	....	....	....	....	....	....	....	....	....

WHL West First All-Star Team (2005) • Canadian Major Junior Scholastic Player of the Year (2005) • WHL West Second All-Star Team (2006)
• Missed majority of 2005-06 season recovering from sternum (October 7, 2005 vs. Calgary) and leg (November 30, 2005 at Minnesota) injuries.

BRUNETTE, Andrew

(broo-NEHT, AN-droo) **COL.**

Left wing. Shoots left. 6'1", 210 lbs. Born, Sudbury, Ont., August 24, 1973. Washington's 6th choice, 174th overall, in 1993 Entry Draft.

Season	**Club**	**League**	**GP**	**G**	**A**	**Pts**	**PIM**	**PP**	**SH**	**GW**	**S**	**%**	**+/-**	**TF**	**F%**	**Min**	**GP**	**G**	**A**	**Pts**	**PIM**	**PP**	**SH**	**GW**	**Min**
1989-90	Rayside-Balfour	NOHA	32	38	*65	*103	....	....	....	....	....	....	....	....	....	....	....	....	....	....	....	....	....	....	....
	Rayside-Balfour	NOJHA	4	1	1	2	0	....	....	....	....	....	....	....	....	....	....	....	....	....	....	....	....	....	....
1990-91	Owen Sound	OHL	63	15	20	35	15	....	....	....	....	....	....	....	....	....	....	....	....	....	....	....	....	....	....
1991-92	Owen Sound	OHL	66	51	47	98	42	....	....	....	....	....	....	....	....	....	5	5	0	5	8	....	....	....	....
1992-93	Owen Sound	OHL	66	*62	*100	*162	91	....	....	....	....	....	....	....	....	....	8	8	6	14	16	....	....	....	....
1993-94	Portland Pirates	AHL	23	9	11	20	10	....	....	....	....	....	....	....	....	....	2	0	1	1	0	....	....	....	....
	Providence Bruins	AHL	3	0	0	0	0	....	....	....	....	....	....	....	....	....	....	....	....	....	....	....	....	....	....
	Hampton Roads	ECHL	20	12	18	30	32	....	....	....	....	....	....	....	....	....	7	7	6	13	18	....	....	....	....
1994-95	Portland Pirates	AHL	79	30	50	80	53	....	....	....	....	....	....	....	....	....	7	3	3	6	10	....	....	....	....
1995-96	**Washington**	**NHL**	**11**	**3**	**3**	**6**	**0**	**0**	**0**	**1**	**16**	**18.8**	**5**	....	....	....	**6**	**1**	**3**	**4**	**0**	**0**	**0**	**0**	....
	Portland Pirates	AHL	69	28	66	94	125	....	....	....	....	....	....	....	....	....	20	11	18	29	15	....	....	....	....
1996-97	**Washington**	**NHL**	**23**	**4**	**7**	**11**	**12**	**2**	**0**	**0**	**23**	**17.4**	**-3**	....	....	....	....	....	....	....	....	....	....	....	....
	Portland Pirates	AHL	50	22	51	73	48	....	....	....	....	....	....	....	....	....	5	1	2	3	0	....	....	....	....
1997-98	**Washington**	**NHL**	**28**	**11**	**12**	**23**	**12**	**4**	**0**	**2**	**42**	**26.2**	**2**	....	....	....	....	....	....	....	....	....	....	....	....
	Portland Pirates	AHL	43	21	46	67	64	....	....	....	....	....	....	....	....	....	10	1	11	12	12	....	....	....	....
1998-99	**Nashville**	**NHL**	**77**	**11**	**20**	**31**	**26**	**7**	**0**	**1**	**65**	**16.9**	**-10**	**8**	**50.0**	**13:13**	....	....	....	....	....	....	....	....	....
99-2000	**Atlanta**	**NHL**	**81**	**23**	**27**	**50**	**30**	**9**	**0**	**2**	**107**	**21.5**	**-32**	**8**	**25.0**	**15:42**	....	....	....	....	....	....	....	....	....
2000-01	**Atlanta**	**NHL**	**77**	**15**	**44**	**59**	**26**	**6**	**0**	**4**	**104**	**14.4**	**-5**	**11**	**54.6**	**16:58**	....	....	....	....	....	....	....	....	....
2001-02	**Minnesota**	**NHL**	**81**	**21**	**48**	**69**	**18**	**10**	**0**	**2**	**106**	**19.8**	**-4**	**111**	**58.6**	**16:02**	....	....	....	....	....	....	....	....	....
2002-03	**Minnesota**	**NHL**	**82**	**18**	**28**	**46**	**30**	**9**	**0**	**2**	**97**	**18.6**	**-10**	**59**	**44.1**	**14:29**	**18**	**7**	**6**	**13**	**4**	**4**	**0**	**1**	**15:00**
2003-04	**Minnesota**	**NHL**	**82**	**15**	**34**	**49**	**12**	**7**	**0**	**3**	**90**	**16.7**	**3**	**49**	**46.9**	**15:32**	....	....	....	....	....	....	....	....	....
2004-05			DID NOT PLAY																						
2005-06	**Colorado**	**NHL**	**82**	**24**	**39**	**63**	**48**	**11**	**0**	**2**	**129**	**18.6**	**9**	**18**	**33.3**	**15:01**	**9**	**3**	**6**	**9**	**8**	**1**	**0**	**1**	**17:47**
	NHL Totals		**624**	**145**	**262**	**407**	**214**	**65**	**0**	**19**	**779**	**18.6**		**264**	**50.0**	**15:17**	**33**	**11**	**15**	**26**	**12**	**5**	**0**	**2**	**15:55**

OHL First All-Star Team (1993) • Canadian Major Junior Second All-Star Team (1993) • AHL Second All-Star Team (1995)

Claimed by **Nashville** from **Washington** in Expansion Draft, June 26, 1998. Traded to **Atlanta** by **Nashville** for Atlanta's 5th round choice (Matt Hendricks) in 2000 Entry Draft, June 21, 1999. Signed as a free agent by **Minnesota**, July 17, 2001. Signed as a free agent by **Colorado**, August 6, 2005.

BRYLIN, Sergei

(BRIH-lin, SAIR-gay) **N.J.**

Left wing. Shoots left. 5'10", 190 lbs. Born, Moscow, USSR, January 13, 1974. New Jersey's 2nd choice, 42nd overall, in 1992 Entry Draft.

Season	**Club**	**League**	**GP**	**G**	**A**	**Pts**	**PIM**	**PP**	**SH**	**GW**	**S**	**%**	**+/-**	**TF**	**F%**	**Min**	**GP**	**G**	**A**	**Pts**	**PIM**	**PP**	**SH**	**GW**	**Min**
1991-92	CSKA Moscow	CIS	44	1	6	7	4	....	....	....	....	....	....	....	....	....	....	....	....	....	....	....	....	....	....
1992-93	CSKA Moscow	CIS	42	5	4	9	36	....	....	....	....	....	....	....	....	....	....	....	....	....	....	....	....	....	....
1993-94	CSKA Moscow	CIS	39	4	6	10	36	....	....	....	....	....	....	....	....	....	3	1	0	1	2	....	....	....	....
	Russian Penguins	IHL	13	4	5	9	18	....	....	....	....	....	....	....	....	....	....	....	....	....	....	....	....	....	....
1994-95	Albany River Rats	AHL	63	19	35	54	78	....	....	....	....	....	....	....	....	....	....	....	....	....	....	....	....	....	....
	◆ New Jersey	**NHL**	**26**	**6**	**8**	**14**	**8**	**0**	**0**	**0**	**41**	**14.6**	**12**	....	....	....	**12**	**1**	**2**	**3**	**4**	**0**	**0**	**0**	....
1995-96	**New Jersey**	**NHL**	**50**	**4**	**5**	**9**	**26**	**0**	**0**	**1**	**51**	**7.8**	**-2**	....	....	....	....	....	....	....	....	....	....	....	....
1996-97	**New Jersey**	**NHL**	**29**	**2**	**2**	**4**	**20**	**0**	**0**	**0**	**34**	**5.9**	**-13**	....	....	....	....	....	....	....	....	....	....	....	....
	Albany River Rats	AHL	43	17	24	41	38	....	....	....	....	....	....	....	....	....	16	4	8	12	12	....	....	....	....
1997-98	**New Jersey**	**NHL**	**18**	**2**	**3**	**5**	**0**	**0**	**0**	**0**	**20**	**10.0**	**4**	....	....	....	....	....	....	....	....	....	....	....	....
	Albany River Rats	AHL	44	21	22	43	60	....	....	....	....	....	....	....	....	....	....	....	....	....	....	....	....	....	....
1998-99	**New Jersey**	**NHL**	**47**	**5**	**10**	**15**	**28**	**3**	**0**	**1**	**51**	**9.8**	**8**	**184**	**50.5**	**12:55**	**5**	**3**	**1**	**4**	**4**	**1**	**0**	**1**	**18:21**
99-2000	**◆ New Jersey**	**NHL**	**64**	**9**	**11**	**20**	**20**	**1**	**0**	**1**	**84**	**10.7**	**0**	**72**	**41.7**	**13:23**	**17**	**3**	**5**	**8**	**0**	**0**	**0**	**0**	**13:02**
2000-01	**New Jersey**	**NHL**	**75**	**23**	**29**	**52**	**24**	**3**	**1**	**0**	**130**	**17.7**	**25**	**43**	**44.2**	**15:31**	**20**	**3**	**4**	**7**	**6**	**1**	**0**	**1**	**13:07**
2001-02	**New Jersey**	**NHL**	**76**	**16**	**28**	**44**	**10**	**5**	**0**	**3**	**133**	**12.0**	**21**	**17**	**47.1**	**17:11**	**6**	**0**	**2**	**2**	**2**	**0**	**0**	**0**	**19:05**

			Regular Season														Playoffs								
Season	Club	League	GP	G	A	Pts	PIM	PP	SH	GW	S	%	+/-	TF	F%	Min	GP	G	A	Pts	PIM	PP	SH	GW	Min
2002-03♦	New Jersey	NHL	52	11	8	19	16	3	1	1	86	12.8	-2	90	32.2	16:11	19	1	3	4	8	0	0	1	17:03
2003-04	New Jersey	NHL	82	14	19	33	20	7	0	1	98	14.3	10	695	46.6	16:25	5	0	0	0	0	0	0	0	15:02
2004-05	Voskresensk	Russia	35	8	19	27	40	....	....	....	....	....	....	....	....	....	....	....	....	....	....	....	....	....	....
2005-06	New Jersey	NHL	82	15	22	37	46	4	0	3	126	11.9	-4	807	48.7	15:44	9	2	0	2	2	0	0	0	16:34
	NHL Totals		601	107	145	252	218	26	2	11	854	12.5		1908	47.0	15:30	93	13	17	30	26	2	0	3	15:17

Signed as a free agent by **Voskresensk** (Russia), November 4, 2004.

BULIS, Jan

(BOO-lihs, YAHN) **VAN.**

Center. Shoots left. 6'1", 208 lbs. Born, Pardubice, Czech., March 18, 1978. Washington's 3rd choice, 43rd overall, in 1996 Entry Draft.

1993-94	HC Pardubice Jr.	CzRep-Jr.	25	16	11	27	....	....	....	....	....	....	....	....	....	....	....	....	....	....	....	....	....	....	....
1994-95	Kelowna Spartans	BCJHL	51	23	25	48	36	....	....	....	....	....	....	....	....	....	17	7	9	16	0	....	....	....	....
1995-96	Barrie Colts	OHL	59	29	30	59	22	....	....	....	....	....	....	....	....	....	7	2	3	5	2	....	....	....	....
1996-97	Barrie Colts	OHL	64	42	61	103	42	....	....	....	....	....	....	....	....	....	9	3	7	10	10	....	....	....	....
1997-98	Kingston	OHL	2	0	1	1	0	....	....	....	....	....	....	....	....	....	12	8	10	18	12	....	....	....	....
	Washington	NHL	48	5	11	16	18	0	0	0	37	13.5	-5	....	....	....	....	....	....	....	....	....	....	....	....
	Portland Pirates	AHL	3	1	4	5	12	....	....	....	....	....	....	....	....	....	....	....	....	....	....	....	....	....	....
1998-99	Washington	NHL	38	7	16	23	6	3	0	3	57	12.3	3	599	48.9	14:27	....	....	....	....	....	....	....	....	....
	Cincinnati	IHL	10	2	2	4	14	....	....	....	....	....	....	....	....	....	....	....	....	....	....	....	....	....	....
99-2000	Washington	NHL	56	9	22	31	30	0	0	1	92	9.8	7	609	45.5	13:55	....	....	....	....	....	....	....	....	....
2000-01	Washington	NHL	39	5	13	18	26	1	0	0	41	12.2	0	224	46.9	11:53	....	....	....	....	....	....	....	....	....
	Portland Pirates	AHL	4	0	2	2	0	....	....	....	....	....	....	....	....	....	....	....	....	....	....	....	....	....	....
	Montreal	NHL	12	0	5	5	0	0	0	0	20	0.0	-1	230	48.3	18:25	....	....	....	....	....	....	....	....	....
2001-02	Montreal	NHL	53	9	10	19	8	1	0	3	87	10.3	-2	156	43.0	13:34	6	0	0	0	6	0	0	0	12:25
2002-03	Montreal	NHL	82	16	24	40	30	0	0	2	160	10.0	9	153	42.5	15:42	....	....	....	....	....	....	....	....	....
2003-04	Montreal	NHL	72	13	17	30	30	1	1	4	147	8.8	-8	103	46.6	17:07	11	1	1	2	4	0	0	0	17:23
2004-05	Pardubice	CzRep	45	24	25	49	113	....	....	....	....	....	....	....	....	....	16	7	4	11	43	....	....	....	....
2005-06	Montreal	NHL	73	20	20	40	50	6	1	3	131	15.3	2	129	44.2	15:37	6	1	1	2	2	0	0	0	16:42
	Czech Republic	Olympics	8	0	0	0	10	....	....	....	....	....	....	....	....	....	....	....	....	....	....	....	....	....	....
	NHL Totals		473	84	138	222	198	12	2	16	772	10.9		2203	46.4	15:03	23	2	2	4	12	0	0	0	15:54

Traded to **Montreal** by **Washington** with Richard Zednik and Washington's 1st round choice (Alexander Perezhogin) in 2001 Entry Draft for Trevor Linden, Dainius Zubrus and New Jersey's 2nd round choice (previously acquired, later traded to Tampa Bay – Tampa Bay selected Andreas Holmqvist) in 2001 Entry Draft, March 13, 2001. Signed as a free agent by **Pardubice** (CzRep), September 17, 2004. Signed as a free agent by **Vancouver**, July 25, 2006.

BURNETT, Garrett

(buhr-NEHT, GAIR-eht)

Left wing. Shoots left. 6'3", 225 lbs. Born, Coquitlam, B.C., September 23, 1975.

1993-94	Trail	RIJHL	26	2	1	3	248	....	....	....	....	....	....	....	....	....	....	....	....	....	....	....	....	....	....
1994-95	Sault Ste. Marie	OHL	14	0	1	1	78	....	....	....	....	....	....	....	....	....	....	....	....	....	....	....	....	....	....
	Kitchener Rangers	OHL	22	0	1	1	74	....	....	....	....	....	....	....	....	....	3	0	1	1	23	....	....	....	....
1995-96	Utica Blizzard	ColHL	15	0	1	1	78	....	....	....	....	....	....	....	....	....	....	....	....	....	....	....	....	....	....
	Oklahoma City	CHL	3	0	0	0	20	....	....	....	....	....	....	....	....	....	....	....	....	....	....	....	....	....	....
	Tulsa Oilers	CHL	6	1	0	1	94	....	....	....	....	....	....	....	....	....	....	....	....	....	....	....	....	....	....
	Nashville Knights	ECHL	3	0	0	0	22	....	....	....	....	....	....	....	....	....	....	....	....	....	....	....	....	....	....
	Jacksonville	ECHL	8	0	1	1	38	....	....	....	....	....	....	....	....	....	1	0	0	0	0	....	....	....	....
1996-97	Knoxville	ECHL	50	5	11	16	321	....	....	....	....	....	....	....	....	....	....	....	....	....	....	....	....	....	....
1997-98	Johnstown Chiefs	ECHL	34	1	1	2	331	....	....	....	....	....	....	....	....	....	....	....	....	....	....	....	....	....	....
	Philadelphia	AHL	14	1	2	3	129	....	....	....	....	....	....	....	....	....	....	....	....	....	....	....	....	....	....
1998-99	Kentucky	AHL	31	1	0	1	186	....	....	....	....	....	....	....	....	....	....	....	....	....	....	....	....	....	....
99-2000	Kentucky	AHL	58	3	3	6	*506	....	....	....	....	....	....	....	....	....	4	0	0	0	31	....	....	....	....
2000-01	Cleveland	IHL	54	2	4	6	250	....	....	....	....	....	....	....	....	....	....	....	....	....	....	....	....	....	....
2001-02	New Haven	UHL	4	1	0	1	40	....	....	....	....	....	....	....	....	....	....	....	....	....	....	....	....	....	....
	Cincinnati	AHL	32	1	0	1	175	....	....	....	....	....	....	....	....	....	....	....	....	....	....	....	....	....	....
2002-03	Hartford	AHL	62	6	1	7	*346	....	....	....	....	....	....	....	....	....	1	0	0	0	2	....	....	....	....
2003-04	Anaheim	NHL	39	1	2	3	184	0	0	0	24	4.2	0	1	0.0	3:36	....	....	....	....	....	....	....	....	....
2004-05	Danbury Trashers	UHL	7	0	1	1	48	....	....	....	....	....	....	....	....	....	....	....	....	....	....	....	....	....	....
2005-06	Phoenix	ECHL	29	1	2	3	74	....	....	....	....	....	....	....	....	....	....	....	....	....	....	....	....	....	....
	Iowa Stars	AHL	10	0	1	1	104	....	....	....	....	....	....	....	....	....	....	....	....	....	....	....	....	....	....
	NHL Totals		39	1	2	3	184	0	0	0	24	4.2		1	0.0	3:36	....	....	....	....	....	....	....	....	....

Signed as a free agent by **San Jose**, July 2, 1998. • Missed majority of 2001-02 season recovering from knee injury suffered in game vs. New Haven (AHL), January 15, 2002. Signed as a free agent by **Hartford** (AHL), August 22, 2002. Signed as a free agent by **Anaheim**, July 25, 2003. • Spent majority of 2003-04 season as a healthy reserve. Signed as a free agent by **Danbury** (UHL), October 8, 2004. Signed as a free agent by **Dallas**, August 15, 2005.

BURNS, Brent

(BUHRNZ, BREHNT) **MIN.**

Defense. Shoots right. 6'4", 200 lbs. Born, Ajax, Ont., March 9, 1985. Minnesota's 1st choice, 20th overall, in 2003 Entry Draft.

2000-01	North York	MTHL	46	4	7	11	16	....	....	....	....	....	....	....	....	....	....	....	....	....	....	....	....	....	....
2001-02	Couchiching	OPJHL	68	15	25	40	14	....	....	....	....	....	....	....	....	....	....	....	....	....	....	....	....	....	....
2002-03	Brampton	OHL	68	15	25	40	14	....	....	....	....	....	....	....	....	....	11	5	6	11	6	....	....	....	....
2003-04	Minnesota	NHL	36	1	5	6	12	0	0	0	34	2.9	-10	7	28.6	13:29	....	....	....	....	....	....	....	....	....
	Houston Aeros	AHL	1	0	1	1	2	....	....	....	....	....	....	....	....	....	....	....	....	....	....	....	....	....	....
2004-05	Houston Aeros	AHL	73	11	16	27	57	....	....	....	....	....	....	....	....	....	5	0	0	0	4	....	....	....	....
2005-06	Minnesota	NHL	72	4	12	16	32	1	0	1	73	5.5	-7	11	54.6	14:07	....	....	....	....	....	....	....	....	....
	NHL Totals		108	5	17	22	44	1	0	1	107	4.7		18	44.4	13:54	....	....	....	....	....	....	....	....	....

• Spent majority of 2003-04 season on assignment to Team Canada and as a healthy reserve.

BURROWS, Alexandre

(BUHR-ohz, ahl-ehx-AHN-drah) **VAN.**

Left wing. Shoots left. 6'1", 190 lbs. Born, Pincourt, Que., April 11, 1981.

2000-01	Shawinigan	QMJHL	63	16	14	30	105	....	....	....	....	....	....	....	....	....	10	2	1	3	8	....	....	....	....
2001-02	Shawinigan	QMJHL	64	35	35	70	184	....	....	....	....	....	....	....	....	....	10	9	10	19	20	....	....	....	....
2002-03	Greenville	ECHL	53	9	17	26	201	....	....	....	....	....	....	....	....	....	....	....	....	....	....	....	....	....	....
	Baton Rouge	ECHL	13	4	2	6	64	....	....	....	....	....	....	....	....	....	....	....	....	....	....	....	....	....	....
2003-04	Manitoba Moose	AHL	2	0	0	0	0	....	....	....	....	....	....	....	....	....	....	....	....	....	....	....	....	....	....
	Columbia Inferno	ECHL	64	29	44	73	194	....	....	....	....	....	....	....	....	....	4	2	0	2	28	....	....	....	....
2004-05	Manitoba Moose	AHL	72	9	17	26	107	....	....	....	....	....	....	....	....	....	14	0	3	3	37	....	....	....	....
	Columbia Inferno	ECHL	4	5	1	6	4	....	....	....	....	....	....	....	....	....	....	....	....	....	....	....	....	....	....
2005-06	Vancouver	NHL	43	7	5	12	61	0	1	1	49	14.3	5	19	47.4	10:24	....	....	....	....	....	....	....	....	....
	Manitoba Moose	AHL	33	12	18	30	57	....	....	....	....	....	....	....	....	....	13	6	7	13	27	....	....	....	....
	NHL Totals		43	7	5	12	61	0	1	1	49	14.3		19	47.4	10:24	....	....	....	....	....	....	....	....	....

Signed as a free agent by **Manitoba** (AHL), October 21, 2003. Signed as a free agent by **Vancouver**, November 8, 2005.

BUTENSCHON, Sven

(BUH-tehn-shohn, SVEHN)

Defense. Shoots left. 6'4", 215 lbs. Born, Itzehoe, West Germany, March 22, 1976. Pittsburgh's 3rd choice, 57th overall, in 1994 Entry Draft.

1991-92	Eastman Selects	MMMHL	36	2	10	12	110	....	....	....	....	....	....	....	....	....	....	....	....	....	....	....	....	....	....
1992-93	Eastman Selects	MMMHL	35	14	22	36	101	....	....	....	....	....	....	....	....	....	....	....	....	....	....	....	....	....	....
1993-94	Brandon	WHL	70	3	19	22	51	....	....	....	....	....	....	....	....	....	4	0	0	0	6	....	....	....	....
1994-95	Brandon	WHL	21	1	5	6	44	....	....	....	....	....	....	....	....	....	18	1	2	3	11	....	....	....	....
1995-96	Brandon	WHL	70	4	37	41	99	....	....	....	....	....	....	....	....	....	19	1	12	13	18	....	....	....	....
1996-97	Cleveland	IHL	75	3	12	15	68	....	....	....	....	....	....	....	....	....	10	0	1	1	4	....	....	....	....
1997-98	Pittsburgh	NHL	8	0	0	0	6	0	0	0	4	0.0	-1	....	....	....	....	....	....	....	....	....	....	....	....
	Syracuse Crunch	AHL	65	14	23	37	66	....	....	....	....	....	....	....	....	....	5	1	2	3	0	....	....	....	....
1998-99	Pittsburgh	NHL	17	0	0	0	6	0	0	0	8	0.0	-7	0	0.0	13:08	....	....	....	....	....	....	....	....	....
	Houston Aeros	IHL	57	1	4	5	81	....	....	....	....	....	....	....	....	....	....	....	....	....	....	....	....	....	....
99-2000	Pittsburgh	NHL	3	0	0	0	0	0	0	0	2	0.0	3	0	0.0	16:25	....	....	....	....	....	....	....	....	....
	Wilkes-Barre	AHL	75	19	21	40	101	....	....	....	....	....	....	....	....	....	....	....	....	....	....	....	....	....	....
2000-01	Pittsburgh	NHL	5	0	1	1	2	0	0	0	6	0.0	1	0	0.0	17:51	....	....	....	....	....	....	....	....	....
	Wilkes-Barre	AHL	55	7	28	35	85	....	....	....	....	....	....	....	....	....	....	....	....	....	....	....	....	....	....
	Edmonton	NHL	7	1	1	2	2	0	0	0	3	33.3	2	0	0.0	11:07	....	....	....	....	....	....	....	....	....

			Regular Season														Playoffs								
Season	Club	League	GP	G	A	Pts	PIM	PP	SH	GW	S	%	+/-	TF	F%	Min	GP	G	A	Pts	PIM	PP	SH	GW	Min
2001-02	Edmonton	NHL	14	0	0	0	4	0	0	0	8	0.0	0	0	0.0	9:39	....	....	....	....	....	....	....	....	....
	Hamilton	AHL	61	9	35	44	88	....	....	....	....	....	....	....	....	....	....	....	....	....	....	....	....	....	....
2002-03	NY Islanders	NHL	37	0	4	4	26	0	0	0	19	0.0	−6	0	0.0	12:26	....	....	....	....	....	....	....	....	....
	Bridgeport	AHL	36	3	13	16	58	....	....	....	....	....	....	....	....	....	9	3	6	9	6	....	....	....	....
2003-04	NY Islanders	NHL	41	1	6	7	30	0	0	0	17	5.9	−3	0	0.0	11:15	4	0	0	0	0	0	0	0	7:42
	Bridgeport	AHL	5	0	1	1	4	....	....	....	....	....	....	....	....	....	....	....	....	....	....	....	....	....	....
2004-05	Adler Mannheim	Germany	50	1	5	6	54	....	....	....	....	....	....	....	....	....	14	0	1	1	16	....	....	....	....
2005-06	Vancouver	NHL	8	0	0	0	10	0	0	0	4	0.0	1	1	0.0	14:05	....	....	....	....	....	....	....	....	....
	Manitoba Moose	AHL	60	15	22	37	30	....	....	....	....	....	....	....	....	....	13	0	6	6	12	....	....	....	....
	NHL Totals		**140**	**2**	**12**	**14**	**86**	**0**	**0**	**0**	**71**	**2.8**		**1**	**0.0**	**12:11**	**4**	**0**	**0**	**0**	**0**	**0**	**0**	**0**	**7:42**

Traded to **Edmonton** by **Pittsburgh** for Dan LaCouture, March 13, 2001. Signed as a free agent by **Florida**, July 9, 2002. Traded to **NY Islanders** by **Florida** for Juraj Kolnik and NY Islanders' 9th round choice (later traded to San Jose – San Jose selected Carter Lee) in 2003 Entry Draft, October 11, 2003. Signed as a free agent by **Mannheim** (Germany), August 2, 2004. Signed as a free agent by **Vancouver**, August 22, 2005.

BUTSAYEV, Yuri

(buht-SIGH-ehv, YOO-ree) **ATL.**

Left wing. Shoots left. 6', 195 lbs. Born, Togliatti, USSR, October 11, 1978. Detroit's 1st choice, 49th overall, in 1997 Entry Draft.

Season	Club	League	GP	G	A	Pts	PIM	PP	SH	GW	S	%	+/-	TF	F%	Min	GP	G	A	Pts	PIM	PP	SH	GW	Min
1995-96	Lada Togliatti 2	CIS-2	35	19	7	26	....	....	....	....	....	....	....	....	....	....	....	....	....	....	....	....	....	....	....
	Lada Togliatti	CIS	1	0	0	0	0	....	....	....	....	....	....	....	....	....	....	....	....	....	....	....	....	....	....
1996-97	Lada Togliatti	Russia	42	13	11	24	38	....	....	....	....	....	....	....	....	....	11	2	2	4	8	....	....	....	....
1997-98	Lada Togliatti	Russia	44	8	9	17	63	....	....	....	....	....	....	....	....	....	....	....	....	....	....	....	....	....	....
	Lada Togliatti	EuroHL	6	2	0	2	8	....	....	....	....	....	....	....	....	....	....	....	....	....	....	....	....	....	....
1998-99	Dynamo Moscow	Russia	1	0	1	1	0	....	....	....	....	....	....	....	....	....	....	....	....	....	....	....	....	....	....
	Lada Togliatti	Russia	39	10	7	17	55	....	....	....	....	....	....	....	....	....	7	1	2	3	14	....	....	....	....
99-2000	Detroit	NHL	57	5	3	8	12	0	0	0	46	10.9	−6	22	40.9	9:36	....	....	....	....	....	....	....	....	....
	Cincinnati	AHL	9	0	1	1	0	....	....	....	....	....	....	....	....	....	....	....	....	....	....	....	....	....	....
2000-01	Detroit	NHL	15	1	1	2	4	0	0	0	18	5.6	−2	6	33.3	9:09	....	....	....	....	....	....	....	....	....
	Cincinnati	AHL	54	29	17	46	26	....	....	....	....	....	....	....	....	....	4	0	2	2	2	....	....	....	....
2001-02	Detroit	NHL	3	0	0	0	0	0	0	0	4	0.0	−1	0	0.0	9:44	....	....	....	....	....	....	....	....	....
	Cincinnati	AHL	61	21	23	44	44	....	....	....	....	....	....	....	....	....	....	....	....	....	....	....	....	....	....
	Atlanta	NHL	8	2	0	2	4	0	0	0	6	33.3	1	1	100.0	13:28	....	....	....	....	....	....	....	....	....
	Chicago Wolves	AHL	4	1	1	2	0	....	....	....	....	....	....	....	....	....	22	7	4	11	20	....	....	....	....
2002-03	Atlanta	NHL	16	2	0	2	8	0	0	0	21	9.5	−5	26	30.8	12:05	....	....	....	....	....	....	....	....	....
	Chicago Wolves	AHL	7	6	3	9	0	....	....	....	....	....	....	....	....	....	....	....	....	....	....	....	....	....	....
	Yaroslavl	Russia	19	2	5	7	37	....	....	....	....	....	....	....	....	....	10	2	3	5	4	....	....	....	....
2003-04	CSKA Moscow	Russia	18	1	3	4	6	....	....	....	....	....	....	....	....	....	....	....	....	....	....	....	....	....	....
	Lada Togliatti	Russia	28	7	3	10	30	....	....	....	....	....	....	....	....	....	6	1	0	1	0	....	....	....	....
2004-05	Lada Togliatti	Russia	42	6	6	12	32	....	....	....	....	....	....	....	....	....	9	2	2	4	6	....	....	....	....
2005-06	MVD	Russia	38	2	7	9	37	....	....	....	....	....	....	....	....	....	....	....	....	....	....	....	....	....	....
	NHL Totals		**99**	**10**	**4**	**14**	**28**	**0**	**0**	**0**	**95**	**10.5**		**55**	**36.4**	**10:15**	....	....	....	....	....	....	....	....	....

Traded to **Atlanta** by **Detroit** with Detroit's 3rd round choice (later traded to Columbus – Columbus selected Jeff Genovy) in 2002 Entry Draft for Jiri Slegr, March 19, 2002. • Assigned to **Yaroslavl** (Russia) by **Atlanta**, November 22, 2002. Signed as a free agent by **CSKA Moscow** (Russia), July 1, 2003. Signed as a free agent by **Togliatti**, December, 2003.

BYFUGLIEN, Dustin

(bigh-FEWG-lehn, DUHS-tihn) **CHI.**

Defense. Shoots right. 6'3", 246 lbs. Born, Minneapolis, MN, March 27, 1985. Chicago's 8th choice, 245th overall, in 2003 Entry Draft.

Season	Club	League	GP	G	A	Pts	PIM	PP	SH	GW	S	%	+/-	TF	F%	Min	GP	G	A	Pts	PIM	PP	SH	GW	Min
2001-02	Chicago Mission	MAHL	52	32	30	62	40	....	....	....	....	....	....	....	....	....	....	....	....	....	....	....	....	....	....
	Brandon	WHL	3	0	0	0	0	....	....	....	....	....	....	....	....	....	....	....	....	....	....	....	....	....	....
2002-03	Brandon	WHL	8	1	1	2	4	....	....	....	....	....	....	....	....	....	....	....	....	....	....	....	....	....	....
	Prince George	WHL	48	9	28	37	74	....	....	....	....	....	....	....	....	....	5	1	3	4	12	....	....	....	....
2003-04	Prince George	WHL	66	16	29	45	137	....	....	....	....	....	....	....	....	....	....	....	....	....	....	....	....	....	....
2004-05	Prince George	WHL	64	22	36	58	184	....	....	....	....	....	....	....	....	....	....	....	....	....	....	....	....	....	....
2005-06	Chicago	NHL	25	3	2	5	24	0	0	1	45	6.7	−6	0	0.0	17:19	....	....	....	....	....	....	....	....	....
	Norfolk Admirals	AHL	53	8	15	23	75	....	....	....	....	....	....	....	....	....	4	1	2	3	4	....	....	....	....
	NHL Totals		**25**	**3**	**2**	**5**	**24**	**0**	**0**	**1**	**45**	**6.7**		**0**	**0.0**	**17:19**	....	....	....	....	....	....	....	....	....

BYKOV, Dmitri

(BEE-kawv, dih-MEE-tree)

Defense. Shoots left. 5'10", 169 lbs. Born, Izhevsk, USSR, May 5, 1977. Detroit's 6th choice, 258th overall, in 2001 Entry Draft.

Season	Club	League	GP	G	A	Pts	PIM	PP	SH	GW	S	%	+/-	TF	F%	Min	GP	G	A	Pts	PIM	PP	SH	GW	Min
1995-96	CSK VVS Samara	CIS	50	1	2	3	39	....	....	....	....	....	....	....	....	....	....	....	....	....	....	....	....	....	....
1996-97	CSK VVS Samara	Russia	44	1	6	7	20	....	....	....	....	....	....	....	....	....	2	0	0	0	2	....	....	....	....
1997-98	Lada Togliatti	Russia	9	0	1	1	4	....	....	....	....	....	....	....	....	....	....	....	....	....	....	....	....	....	....
	CSK VVS Samara	Russia	27	0	5	5	14	....	....	....	....	....	....	....	....	....	....	....	....	....	....	....	....	....	....
	Yaroslavl	Russia	10	1	2	3	6	....	....	....	....	....	....	....	....	....	7	0	1	1	10	....	....	....	....
1998-99	Lada Togliatti	Russia	39	0	6	6	24	....	....	....	....	....	....	....	....	....	7	1	0	1	8	....	....	....	....
	CSK VVS Samara	Russia	2	0	0	0	0	....	....	....	....	....	....	....	....	....	....	....	....	....	....	....	....	....	....
99-2000	Ak Bars Kazan	Russia	35	3	8	11	18	....	....	....	....	....	....	....	....	....	18	0	2	2	8	....	....	....	....
	Ak Bars Kazan 2	Russia-3	3	0	1	1	4	....	....	....	....	....	....	....	....	....	....	....	....	....	....	....	....	....	....
2000-01	Ak Bars Kazan	Russia	39	3	8	11	28	....	....	....	....	....	....	....	....	....	4	0	1	1	4	....	....	....	....
2001-02	Ak Bars Kazan	Russia	44	1	1	2	38	....	....	....	....	....	....	....	....	....	11	0	0	0	4	....	....	....	....
2002-03	Detroit	NHL	71	2	10	12	43	1	0	0	58	3.4	1	2	100.0	18:22	4	0	0	0	0	0	0	0	11:14
2003-04	Ak Bars Kazan	Russia	55	5	11	16	46	....	....	....	....	....	....	....	....	....	8	2	1	3	10	....	....	....	....
2004-05	Ak Bars Kazan	Russia	31	2	2	4	22	....	....	....	....	....	....	....	....	....	4	0	0	0	0	....	....	....	....
2005-06	Dynamo Moscow	Russia	26	3	3	6	16	....	....	....	....	....	....	....	....	....	4	0	1	1	4	....	....	....	....
	NHL Totals		**71**	**2**	**10**	**12**	**43**	**1**	**0**	**0**	**58**	**3.4**		**2**	**100.0**	**18:22**	**4**	**0**	**0**	**0**	**0**	**0**	**0**	**0**	**11:14**

Signed as a free agent by **Kazan** (Russia), June 18, 2003.

CAIRNS, Eric

(KAIRNZ, AIR-ihk) **PIT.**

Defense. Shoots left. 6'6", 230 lbs. Born, Oakville, Ont., June 27, 1974. NY Rangers' 3rd choice, 72nd overall, in 1992 Entry Draft.

Season	Club	League	GP	G	A	Pts	PIM	PP	SH	GW	S	%	+/-	TF	F%	Min	GP	G	A	Pts	PIM	PP	SH	GW	Min
1990-91	Burlington	OHA-B	37	5	16	21	120	....	....	....	....	....	....	....	....	....	....	....	....	....	....	....	....	....	....
1991-92	Detroit	OHL	64	1	11	12	237	....	....	....	....	....	....	....	....	....	7	0	0	0	31	....	....	....	....
1992-93	Detroit	OHL	64	3	13	16	194	....	....	....	....	....	....	....	....	....	15	0	3	3	24	....	....	....	....
1993-94	Detroit	OHL	59	7	35	42	204	....	....	....	....	....	....	....	....	....	17	0	4	4	46	....	....	....	....
1994-95	Birmingham Bulls	ECHL	11	1	3	4	49	....	....	....	....	....	....	....	....	....	....	....	....	....	....	....	....	....	....
	Binghamton	AHL	27	0	3	3	134	....	....	....	....	....	....	....	....	....	9	1	1	2	28	....	....	....	....
1995-96	Binghamton	AHL	46	1	13	14	192	....	....	....	....	....	....	....	....	....	4	0	0	0	37	....	....	....	....
	Charlotte	ECHL	6	0	1	1	34	....	....	....	....	....	....	....	....	....	....	....	....	....	....	....	....	....	....
1996-97	NY Rangers	NHL	40	0	1	1	147	0	0	0	17	0.0	−7	....	....	....	3	0	0	0	0	0	0	0	....
	Binghamton	AHL	10	1	1	2	96	....	....	....	....	....	....	....	....	....	....	....	....	....	....	....	....	....	....
1997-98	NY Rangers	NHL	39	0	3	3	92	0	0	0	17	0.0	−3	....	....	....	....	....	....	....	....	....	....	....	....
	Hartford	AHL	7	1	2	3	43	....	....	....	....	....	....	....	....	....	....	....	....	....	....	....	....	....	....
1998-99	Hartford	AHL	11	0	2	2	49	....	....	....	....	....	....	....	....	....	....	....	....	....	....	....	....	....	....
	NY Islanders	NHL	9	0	3	3	23	0	0	0	2	0.0	1	0	0.0	10:15	....	....	....	....	....	....	....	....	....
	Lowell	AHL	24	0	0	0	91	....	....	....	....	....	....	....	....	....	3	1	0	1	32	....	....	....	....
99-2000	NY Islanders	NHL	67	2	7	9	196	0	0	0	55	3.6	−5	0	0.0	17:43	....	....	....	....	....	....	....	....	....
	Providence Bruins	AHL	4	1	1	2	14	....	....	....	....	....	....	....	....	....	....	....	....	....	....	....	....	....	....
2000-01	NY Islanders	NHL	45	2	2	4	106	0	0	0	21	9.5	−18	1	0.0	16:24	....	....	....	....	....	....	....	....	....
2001-02	NY Islanders	NHL	74	2	5	7	176	0	0	1	34	5.9	−2	0	0.0	11:09	7	0	0	0	15	0	0	0	13:54
2002-03	NY Islanders	NHL	60	1	4	5	124	0	0	0	31	3.2	−7	0	0.0	11:50	5	0	0	0	13	0	0	0	6:02
2003-04	NY Islanders	NHL	72	2	6	8	189	0	0	0	24	8.3	−5	0	0.0	11:44	1	0	0	0	0	0	0	0	3:53
2004-05	London Racers	Britain	22	2	6	8	85	....	....	....	....	....	....	....	....	....	....	....	....	....	....	....	....	....	....
2005-06	Florida	NHL	23	0	1	1	37	0	0	0	11	0.0	1	0	0.0	7:48	....	....	....	....	....	....	....	....	....
	Pittsburgh	NHL	27	1	0	1	87	0	0	0	8	12.5	0	0	0.0	5:28	....	....	....	....	....	....	....	....	....
	NHL Totals		**456**	**10**	**32**	**42**	**1177**	**0**	**0**	**1**	**220**	**4.5**		**1**	**0.0**	**12:32**	**16**	**0**	**0**	**0**	**28**	**0**	**0**	**0**	**10:06**

Claimed on waivers by **NY Islanders** from **NY Rangers**, December 22, 1998. Signed as a free agent by **Florida**, July 5, 2004. Signed as a free agent by **London** (Britain), November 1, 2004. Traded to **Pittsburgh** by **Florida** for Pittsburgh's 6th round choice (Peter Aston) in 2006 Entry Draft, January 18, 2006.

CAJANEK, Petr
(chuh-YA-nihk, PEE-tuhr) **ST.L.**

Right wing. Shoots left. 5'11", 176 lbs. Born, Gottwaldov/Zlin, Czech., August 18, 1975. St. Louis' 6th choice, 253rd overall, in 2001 Entry Draft.

			Regular Season														Playoffs								
Season	Club	League	GP	G	A	Pts	PIM	PP	SH	GW	S	%	+/-	TF	F%	Min	GP	G	A	Pts	PIM	PP	SH	GW	Min
1993-94	AC ZPS Zlin	CzRep	34	5	4	9											3	0	0	0					
1994-95	AC ZPS Zlin	CzRep	35	7	9	16	8										12	2	6	8	4				
1995-96	AC ZPS Zlin	CzRep	36	8	11	19	32										8	2	6	8	8				
1996-97	AC ZPS Zlin	CzRep	50	9	30	39	46																		
1997-98	Zlin	CzRep	46	19	27	46	117																		
1998-99	Zlin	CzRep	49	15	33	48	123										11	5	7	12	12				
99-2000	Zlin	CzRep	50	23	34	57	66										4	1	0	1	0				
2000-01	Zlin	CzRep	52	18	31	49	105										6	0	4	4	22				
2001-02	Zlin	CzRep	49	20	44	64	64										11	5	7	12	10				
	Czech Republic	Olympics	4	0	0	0	0																		
2002-03	**St. Louis**	**NHL**	**51**	**9**	**29**	**38**	**20**	**2**	**2**	**1**	**90**	**10.0**	**16**	**793**	**48.4**	**15:56**	**2**	**0**	**0**	**0**	**2**	**0**	**0**	**0**	**11:07**
2003-04	**St. Louis**	**NHL**	**70**	**12**	**14**	**26**	**16**	**3**	**0**	**4**	**126**	**9.5**	**12**	**1000**	**47.6**	**17:48**	**5**	**0**	**2**	**2**	**2**	**0**	**0**	**0**	**19:27**
2004-05	HC Hame Zlin	CzRep	49	10	15	25	91										17	5	4	9	24				
2005-06	**St. Louis**	**NHL**	**71**	**10**	**31**	**41**	**54**	**3**	**0**	**0**	**150**	**6.7**	**–22**	**888**	**49.7**	**18:53**									
	Czech Republic	Olympics	7	1	0	1	4																		
	NHL Totals		**192**	**31**	**74**	**105**	**90**	**8**	**2**	**5**	**366**	**8.5**		**2681**	**48.5**	**17:42**	**7**	**0**	**2**	**2**	**4**	**0**	**0**	**0**	**17:04**

Signed as a free agent by **Zlin** (CzRep), September 5, 2004.

CALDER, Kyle
(KAWL-dehr, KIGHL) **PHI.**

Left wing. Shoots left. 5'11", 176 lbs. Born, Mannville, Alta., January 5, 1979. Chicago's 7th choice, 130th overall, in 1997 Entry Draft.

			Regular Season														Playoffs								
Season	Club	League	GP	G	A	Pts	PIM	PP	SH	GW	S	%	+/-	TF	F%	Min	GP	G	A	Pts	PIM	PP	SH	GW	Min
1994-95	Leduc Oil Barons	AMHL	27	25	32	57	22																		
1995-96	Regina Pats	WHL	27	1	7	8	10										11	0	0	0	0				
1996-97	Regina Pats	WHL	62	25	34	59	17										5	3	0	3	6				
1997-98	Regina Pats	WHL	62	27	50	77	58										2	0	1	1	0				
1998-99	Regina Pats	WHL	34	23	28	51	29																		
	Kamloops Blazers	WHL	27	19	18	37	30										15	6	10	16	6				
99-2000	**Chicago**	**NHL**	**8**	**1**	**1**	**2**	**2**	**0**	**0**	**0**	**5**	**20.0**	**–3**	**2**	**0.0**	**9:59**									
	Cleveland	IHL	74	14	22	36	43										9	2	2	4	14				
2000-01	**Chicago**	**NHL**	**43**	**5**	**10**	**15**	**14**	**0**	**0**	**1**	**63**	**7.9**	**–4**	**2**	**0.0**	**12:43**									
	Norfolk Admirals	AHL	37	12	15	27	21										9	2	6	8	2				
2001-02	**Chicago**	**NHL**	**81**	**17**	**36**	**53**	**47**	**6**	**0**	**3**	**133**	**12.8**	**8**	**0**	**0.0**	**16:33**	**5**	**2**	**0**	**2**	**2**	**1**	**0**	**0**	**16:45**
2002-03	**Chicago**	**NHL**	**82**	**15**	**27**	**42**	**40**	**7**	**0**	**2**	**164**	**9.1**	**–6**	**4**	**25.0**	**16:43**									
2003-04	**Chicago**	**NHL**	**66**	**21**	**18**	**39**	**29**	**10**	**0**	**1**	**144**	**14.6**	**–18**	**13**	**30.8**	**17:08**									
2004-05	Sodertalje SK	Sweden	12	5	1	6	6										10	5	1	6	2				
2005-06	**Chicago**	**NHL**	**79**	**26**	**33**	**59**	**52**	**6**	**2**	**6**	**183**	**14.2**	**–4**	**13**	**46.2**	**18:23**									
	NHL Totals		**359**	**85**	**125**	**210**	**184**	**29**	**2**	**13**	**692**	**12.3**		**34**	**32.4**	**16:30**	**5**	**2**	**0**	**2**	**2**	**1**	**0**	**0**	**16:45**

Signed as a free agent by **Sodertalje** (Sweden), January 20, 2005. Traded to **Philadelphia** by **Chicago** for Michael Handzus, August 4, 2006.

CALDWELL, Ryan
(KAWLD-wehl, RIGH-uhn) **NYI**

Defense. Shoots left. 6'2", 174 lbs. Born, Deloraine, Man., June 15, 1981. NY Islanders' 7th choice, 202nd overall, in 2000 Entry Draft.

			Regular Season														Playoffs								
Season	Club	League	GP	G	A	Pts	PIM	PP	SH	GW	S	%	+/-	TF	F%	Min	GP	G	A	Pts	PIM	PP	SH	GW	Min
1998-99	Shat.-St. Mary's	High-MN	29	24	55	79	22																		
99-2000	Thunder Bay	USHL	46	3	20	23	152																		
2000-01	U. of Denver	WCHA	36	3	20	23	76																		
2001-02	U. of Denver	WCHA	40	3	16	19	76																		
2002-03	U. of Denver	WCHA	38	5	14	19	58																		
2003-04	U. of Denver	WCHA	42	15	12	27	96																		
2004-05	Bridgeport	AHL	73	2	19	21	65																		
2005-06	**NY Islanders**	**NHL**	**2**	**0**	**0**	**0**	**2**	**0**	**0**	**0**	**2**	**0.0**	**–2**	**0**	**0.0**	**16:33**									
	Bridgeport	AHL	61	2	13	15	38										7	1	1	2	2				
	NHL Totals		**2**	**0**	**0**	**0**	**2**	**0**	**0**	**0**	**2**	**0.0**		**0**	**0.0**	**16:33**									

WCHA All-Rookie Team (2001) • WCHA Second All-Star Team (2004) • NCAA West First All-American Team (2004) • NCAA Championship All-Tournament Team (2004)

CAMMALLERI, Michael
(kam-UH-LAIR-ee, MIGH-kuhl) **L.A.**

Center. Shoots left. 5'9", 180 lbs. Born, Richmond Hill, Ont., June 8, 1982. Los Angeles' 3rd choice, 49th overall, in 2001 Entry Draft.

			Regular Season														Playoffs								
Season	Club	League	GP	G	A	Pts	PIM	PP	SH	GW	S	%	+/-	TF	F%	Min	GP	G	A	Pts	PIM	PP	SH	GW	Min
1997-98	Bramalea Blues	OPJHL	46	36	52	88	30																		
1998-99	Bramalea Blues	OPJHL	41	31	72	103	51																		
99-2000	U. of Michigan	CCHA	39	13	13	26	32																		
2000-01	U. of Michigan	CCHA	42	*29	32	61	24																		
2001-02	U. of Michigan	CCHA	29	23	21	44	28																		
2002-03	**Los Angeles**	**NHL**	**28**	**5**	**3**	**8**	**22**	**2**	**0**	**2**	**40**	**12.5**	**–4**	**253**	**51.4**	**14:05**									
	Manchester	AHL	13	5	15	20	12																		
2003-04	**Los Angeles**	**NHL**	**31**	**9**	**6**	**15**	**20**	**2**	**0**	**2**	**53**	**17.0**	**1**	**280**	**53.6**	**13:18**									
	Manchester	AHL	41	20	19	39	28										1	0	1	1	0				
2004-05	Manchester	AHL	79	*46	63	109	60										6	1	5	6	0				
2005-06	**Los Angeles**	**NHL**	**80**	**26**	**29**	**55**	**50**	**15**	**0**	**4**	**206**	**12.6**	**–14**	**578**	**53.5**	**16:45**									
	NHL Totals		**139**	**40**	**38**	**78**	**92**	**19**	**0**	**8**	**299**	**13.4**		**1111**	**53.0**	**15:27**									

CCHA First All-Star Team (2001) • NCAA West Second All-American Team (2001) • CCHA Second All-Star Team (2002) • NCAA West First All-American Team (2002) • AHL Second All-Star Team (2005) • Willie Marshall Award (Top Goal-scorer - AHL) (2005)

• Missed majority of 2002-03 season recovering from head injury suffered in game vs. San Jose, January 28, 2003.

CAMPBELL, Brian
(KAM-behl, BRIGH-uhn) **BUF.**

Defense. Shoots left. 6', 190 lbs. Born, Strathroy, Ont., May 23, 1979. Buffalo's 7th choice, 156th overall, in 1997 Entry Draft.

			Regular Season														Playoffs								
Season	Club	League	GP	G	A	Pts	PIM	PP	SH	GW	S	%	+/-	TF	F%	Min	GP	G	A	Pts	PIM	PP	SH	GW	Min
1994-95	Petrolia Oil Barons	OHA-B	49	11	27	38	43																		
1995-96	Ottawa 67's	OHL	66	5	22	27	23										4	0	1	1	2				
1996-97	Ottawa 67's	OHL	66	7	36	43	12										24	2	11	13	8				
1997-98	Ottawa 67's	OHL	66	14	39	53	31										13	1	14	15	0				
1998-99	Ottawa 67's	OHL	62	12	75	87	27										9	2	10	12	6				
	Rochester	AHL															2	0	0	0	0				
99-2000	**Buffalo**	**NHL**	**12**	**1**	**4**	**5**	**4**	**0**	**0**	**0**	**10**	**10.0**	**–2**	**0**	**0.0**	**15:48**									
	Rochester	AHL	67	2	24	26	22										21	0	3	3	0				
2000-01	**Buffalo**	**NHL**	**8**	**0**	**0**	**0**	**2**	**0**	**0**	**0**	**7**	**0.0**	**–2**	**0**	**0.0**	**15:40**									
	Rochester	AHL	65	7	25	32	24										4	0	1	1	0				
2001-02	**Buffalo**	**NHL**	**29**	**3**	**3**	**6**	**12**	**0**	**0**	**0**	**30**	**10.0**	**0**	**1**	**0.0**	**15:18**									
	Rochester	AHL	45	2	35	37	13																		
2002-03	**Buffalo**	**NHL**	**65**	**2**	**17**	**19**	**20**	**0**	**0**	**1**	**90**	**2.2**	**–8**	**1**	**0.0**	**18:40**									
2003-04	**Buffalo**	**NHL**	**53**	**3**	**8**	**11**	**12**	**0**	**0**	**0**	**45**	**6.7**	**–8**	**0**	**0.0**	**16:02**									
2004-05	Jokerit Helsinki	Finland	44	12	13	25	12										12	3	4	7	6				
2005-06	**Buffalo**	**NHL**	**79**	**12**	**32**	**44**	**16**	**5**	**0**	**5**	**105**	**11.4**	**–14**	**0**	**0.0**	**17:43**	**18**	**0**	**6**	**6**	**12**	**0**	**0**	**0**	**20:29**
	NHL Totals		**246**	**21**	**64**	**85**	**66**	**5**	**0**	**6**	**287**	**7.3**		**2**	**0.0**	**17:10**	**18**	**0**	**6**	**6**	**12**	**0**	**0**	**0**	**20:29**

OHL First All-Star Team (1999) • OHL MVP (1999) • Canadian Major Junior First All-Star Team (1999) • Canadian Major Junior Player of the Year (1999) • George Parsons Trophy (Memorial Cup Tournament Most Sportsmanlike Player) (1999)

Signed as a free agent by **Jokerit Helsinki** (Finland), October 19, 2004.

CAMPBELL, Gregory
(KAM-behl, GREH-goh-ree) **FLA.**

Left wing. Shoots left. 6', 191 lbs. Born, London, Ont., December 17, 1983. Florida's 4th choice, 67th overall, in 2002 Entry Draft.

			Regular Season														Playoffs								
Season	Club	League	GP	G	A	Pts	PIM	PP	SH	GW	S	%	+/-	TF	F%	Min	GP	G	A	Pts	PIM	PP	SH	GW	Min
1998-99	Aylmer Aces	OHA-B	49	5	9	14	44																		
99-2000	St. Thomas Stars	OHA-B	51	12	8	20	51																		
2000-01	Plymouth Whalers	OHL	65	2	12	14	40										10	0	0	0	7				
2001-02	Plymouth Whalers	OHL	65	17	36	53	105										6	0	2	2	13				
2002-03	Kitchener Rangers	OHL	55	23	33	56	116										21	15	4	19	34				

			Regular Season														Playoffs								
Season	Club	League	GP	G	A	Pts	PIM	PP	SH	GW	S	%	+/-	TF	F%	Min	GP	G	A	Pts	PIM	PP	SH	GW	Min
2003-04	**Florida**	**NHL**	**2**	**0**	**0**	**0**	**5**	**0**	**0**	**0**	**0**	**0.0**	**–1**	**1**	**0.0**	**9:09**	....	....	....	....	....	....	....	....	....
	San Antonio	AHL	76	13	16	29	73	....	....	....	....	....	....	....	....	....	....	....	....	....	....	....	....	....	....
2004-05	San Antonio	AHL	70	12	16	28	113	....	....	....	....	....	....	....	....	....	....	....	....	....	....	....	....	....	....
2005-06	**Florida**	**NHL**	**64**	**3**	**6**	**9**	**40**	**0**	**0**	**0**	**59**	**5.1**	**–11**	**38**	**34.2**	**8:38**	....	....	....	....	....	....	....	....	....
	Rochester	AHL	11	3	3	6	30	....	....	....	....	....	....	....	....	....	....	....	....	....	....	....	....	....	....
	NHL Totals		**66**	**3**	**6**	**9**	**45**	**0**	**0**	**0**	**59**	**5.1**		**39**	**33.3**	**8:39**	....	....	....	....	....	....	....	....	....

Memorial Cup Tournament All-Star Team (2003) • George Parsons Trophy (Memorial Cup Tournament Most Sportsmanlike Player) (2003) • Ed Chynoweth Trophy (Memorial Cup Tournament Leading Scorer) (2003)

CAMPBELL, Jim

(KAM-behl, JIHM)

Right wing. Shoots right. 6'2", 205 lbs. Born, Worcester, MA, April 3, 1973. Montreal's 2nd choice, 28th overall, in 1991 Entry Draft.

Season	Club	League	GP	G	A	Pts	PIM	PP	SH	GW	S	%	+/-	TF	F%	Min	GP	G	A	Pts	PIM	PP	SH	GW	Min
1988-89	Northwood	High-NY	12	12	8	20	6	....	....	....	....	....	....	....	....	....	....	....	....	....	....	....	....	....	....
1989-90	Northwood	High-NY	8	14	7	21	8	....	....	....	....	....	....	....	....	....	....	....	....	....	....	....	....	....	....
1990-91	Lawrence	High-MA	26	36	47	83	26	....	....	....	....	....	....	....	....	....	....	....	....	....	....	....	....	....	....
1991-92	Hull Olympiques	QMJHL	64	41	44	85	51	....	....	....	....	....	....	....	....	....	6	7	3	10	8	....	....	....	....
1992-93	Hull Olympiques	QMJHL	50	42	29	71	66	....	....	....	....	....	....	....	....	....	8	11	4	15	43	....	....	....	....
1993-94	United States	Nat-Tm	56	24	33	57	59	....	....	....	....	....	....	....	....	....	....	....	....	....	....	....	....	....	....
	United States	Olympics	8	0	0	0	6	....	....	....	....	....	....	....	....	....	....	....	....	....	....	....	....	....	....
	Fredericton	AHL	19	6	17	23	6	....	....	....	....	....	....	....	....	....	....	....	....	....	....	....	....	....	....
1994-95	Fredericton	AHL	77	27	24	51	103	....	....	....	....	....	....	....	....	....	12	0	7	7	8	....	....	....	....
1995-96	Fredericton	AHL	44	28	23	51	24	....	....	....	....	....	....	....	....	....	....	....	....	....	....	....	....	....	....
	Anaheim	**NHL**	**16**	**2**	**3**	**5**	**36**	**1**	**0**	**0**	**25**	**8.0**	**0**	....	....	....	....	....	....	....	....	....	....	....	....
	Baltimore Bandits	AHL	16	13	7	20	8	....	....	....	....	....	....	....	....	....	12	7	5	12	10	....	....	....	....
1996-97	**St. Louis**	**NHL**	**68**	**23**	**20**	**43**	**68**	**5**	**0**	**6**	**169**	**13.6**	**3**	....	....	....	**4**	**1**	**0**	**1**	**6**	**1**	**0**	**0**	....
1997-98	**St. Louis**	**NHL**	**76**	**22**	**19**	**41**	**55**	**7**	**0**	**6**	**147**	**15.0**	**0**	....	....	....	**10**	**7**	**3**	**10**	**12**	**4**	**0**	**2**	....
1998-99	**St. Louis**	**NHL**	**55**	**4**	**21**	**25**	**41**	**1**	**0**	**0**	**99**	**4.0**	**–8**	**7**	**42.9**	**13:34**	....	....	....	....	....	....	....	....	....
99-2000	Manitoba Moose	IHL	10	1	3	4	10	....	....	....	....	....	....	....	....	....	....	....	....	....	....	....	....	....	....
	St. Louis	**NHL**	**2**	**0**	**0**	**0**	**9**	**0**	**0**	**0**	**6**	**0.0**	**0**	**0**	**0.0**	**15:17**	....	....	....	....	....	....	....	....	....
	Worcester IceCats	AHL	66	31	34	65	88	....	....	....	....	....	....	....	....	....	9	1	2	3	6	....	....	....	....
2000-01	**Montreal**	**NHL**	**57**	**9**	**11**	**20**	**53**	**6**	**0**	**1**	**81**	**11.1**	**–3**	**14**	**42.9**	**10:19**	....	....	....	....	....	....	....	....	....
	Quebec Citadelles	AHL	3	5	0	5	6	....	....	....	....	....	....	....	....	....	....	....	....	....	....	....	....	....	....
2001-02	**Chicago**	**NHL**	**9**	**1**	**1**	**2**	**4**	**0**	**0**	**0**	**12**	**8.3**	**–3**	**1**	**0.0**	**13:21**	....	....	....	....	....	....	....	....	....
	Norfolk Admirals	AHL	44	11	14	25	26	....	....	....	....	....	....	....	....	....	4	3	1	4	2	....	....	....	....
2002-03	**Florida**	**NHL**	**1**	**0**	**0**	**0**	**0**	**0**	**0**	**0**	**3**	**0.0**	**0**	**1**	**0.0**	**8:56**	....	....	....	....	....	....	....	....	....
	San Antonio	AHL	64	16	37	53	55	....	....	....	....	....	....	....	....	....	1	0	0	0	0	....	....	....	....
2003-04	Chicago Wolves	AHL	41	10	13	23	41	....	....	....	....	....	....	....	....	....	....	....	....	....	....	....	....	....	....
	Nizhnekamsk	Russia	2	0	0	0	2	....	....	....	....	....	....	....	....	....	....	....	....	....	....	....	....	....	....
2004-05	Bridgeport	AHL	46	8	12	20	64	....	....	....	....	....	....	....	....	....	....	....	....	....	....	....	....	....	....
	Springfield	AHL	13	2	5	7	8	....	....	....	....	....	....	....	....	....	....	....	....	....	....	....	....	....	....
2005-06	**Tampa Bay**	**NHL**	**1**	**0**	**0**	**0**	**2**	**0**	**0**	**0**	**0**	**0.0**	**0**	**0**	**0.0**	**8:47**	....	....	....	....	....	....	....	....	....
	Philadelphia	AHL	35	12	17	29	46	....	....	....	....	....	....	....	....	....	....	....	....	....	....	....	....	....	....
	Springfield	AHL	32	12	12	24	24	....	....	....	....	....	....	....	....	....	....	....	....	....	....	....	....	....	....
	NHL Totals		**285**	**61**	**75**	**136**	**268**	**20**	**0**	**13**	**542**	**11.3**		**23**	**39.1**	**12:01**	**14**	**8**	**3**	**11**	**18**	**5**	**0**	**2**	....

NHL All-Rookie Team (1997)

Traded to **Anaheim** by **Montreal** for Robert Dirk, January 21, 1996. Signed as a free agent by **St. Louis**, July 11, 1996. Loaned to **Manitoba** (IHL) by **St. Louis**, October 4, 1999 and recalled November 1, 1999. Signed as a free agent by **Montreal**, August 21, 2000. Signed as a free agent by **Chicago**, November 19, 2001. Signed as a free agent by **Florida**, July 19, 2002. Signed as a free agent by **Chicago** (AHL), December 10, 2003. Signed as a free agent by **NY Islanders**, August 11, 2004. Signed as a free agent by **Tampa Bay**, August 18, 2005.

CAMPOLI, Chris

(kam-POH-lee, KRIHS) **NYI**

Defense. Shoots left. 6', 190 lbs. Born, North York, Ont., July 9, 1984. NY Islanders' 8th choice, 227th overall, in 2004 Entry Draft.

Season	Club	League	GP	G	A	Pts	PIM	PP	SH	GW	S	%	+/-	TF	F%	Min	GP	G	A	Pts	PIM	PP	SH	GW	Min
2001-02	Erie Otters	OHL	68	2	24	26	117	....	....	....	....	....	....	....	....	....	20	0	5	5	18	....	....	....	....
2002-03	Erie Otters	OHL	60	8	40	48	82	....	....	....	....	....	....	....	....	....	....	....	....	....	....	....	....	....	....
2003-04	Erie Otters	OHL	67	20	46	66	66	....	....	....	....	....	....	....	....	....	8	0	6	6	16	....	....	....	....
2004-05	Bridgeport	AHL	79	15	34	49	78	....	....	....	....	....	....	....	....	....	....	....	....	....	....	....	....	....	....
2005-06	**NY Islanders**	**NHL**	**80**	**9**	**25**	**34**	**46**	**2**	**0**	**2**	**123**	**7.3**	**–16**	**0**	**0.0**	**18:32**	....	....	....	....	....	....	....	....	....
	NHL Totals		**80**	**9**	**25**	**34**	**46**	**2**	**0**	**2**	**123**	**7.3**		**0**	**0.0**	**18:32**	....	....	....	....	....	....	....	....	....

OHL Humanitarian Player of the Year (2004) • Canadian Major Junior Humanitarian Player of the Year (2004) • AHL All-Rookie Team (2005)

CARKNER, Matt

(KARK-nehr, MAT) **PIT.**

Defense. Shoots right. 6'4", 235 lbs. Born, Winchester, Ont., November 3, 1980. Montreal's 2nd choice, 58th overall, in 1999 Entry Draft.

Season	Club	League	GP	G	A	Pts	PIM	PP	SH	GW	S	%	+/-	TF	F%	Min	GP	G	A	Pts	PIM	PP	SH	GW	Min
1996-97	Winchester	OHA-B	29	1	18	19	....	....	....	....	....	....	....	....	....	....	....	....	....	....	....	....	....	....	....
1997-98	Peterborough	OHL	57	0	6	6	121	....	....	....	....	....	....	....	....	....	4	0	0	0	2	....	....	....	....
1998-99	Peterborough	OHL	60	2	16	18	173	....	....	....	....	....	....	....	....	....	5	0	0	0	20	....	....	....	....
99-2000	Peterborough	OHL	62	3	13	16	177	....	....	....	....	....	....	....	....	....	5	0	1	1	6	....	....	....	....
2000-01	Peterborough	OHL	53	8	8	16	128	....	....	....	....	....	....	....	....	....	7	0	3	3	25	....	....	....	....
2001-02	Cleveland Barons	AHL	74	0	3	3	335	....	....	....	....	....	....	....	....	....	....	....	....	....	....	....	....	....	....
2002-03	Cleveland Barons	AHL	39	1	4	5	104	....	....	....	....	....	....	....	....	....	....	....	....	....	....	....	....	....	....
2003-04	Cleveland Barons	AHL	60	2	11	13	115	....	....	....	....	....	....	....	....	....	9	0	3	3	39	....	....	....	....
2004-05	Cleveland Barons	AHL	73	0	10	10	192	....	....	....	....	....	....	....	....	....	....	....	....	....	....	....	....	....	....
2005-06	**San Jose**	**NHL**	**1**	**0**	**1**	**1**	**2**	**0**	**0**	**0**	**0**	**0.0**	**0**	**0**	**0.0**	**6:01**	....	....	....	....	....	....	....	....	....
	Cleveland Barons	AHL	69	10	21	31	202	....	....	....	....	....	....	....	....	....	....	....	....	....	....	....	....	....	....
	NHL Totals		**1**	**0**	**1**	**1**	**2**	**0**	**0**	**0**	**0**	**0.0**		**0**	**0.0**	**6:01**	....	....	....	....	....	....	....	....	....

Signed as a free agent by **San Jose**, June 6, 2001. • Missed majority of 2002-03 season recovering from knee injury suffered in game vs. Utah (AHL), January 4, 2003. Signed as a free agent by **Pittsburgh**, July 23, 2006.

CARLE, Matthew

(KARL, MA-thew) **S.J.**

Defense. Shoots left. 6', 182 lbs. Born, Anchorage, AK, September 25, 1984. San Jose's 4th choice, 47th overall, in 2003 Entry Draft.

Season	Club	League	GP	G	A	Pts	PIM	PP	SH	GW	S	%	+/-	TF	F%	Min	GP	G	A	Pts	PIM	PP	SH	GW	Min
99-2000	Alaska All-Stars	AASHA	42	14	28	42	....	....	....	....	....	....	....	....	....	....	....	....	....	....	....	....	....	....	....
2000-01	USNTDP	U-17	13	0	1	1	....	....	....	....	....	....	....	....	....	....	....	....	....	....	....	....	....	....	....
	USNTDP	NAHL	55	1	4	5	33	....	....	....	....	....	....	....	....	....	....	....	....	....	....	....	....	....	....
2001-02	USNTDP	U-18	45	3	13	16	30	....	....	....	....	....	....	....	....	....	....	....	....	....	....	....	....	....	....
	USNTDP	USHL	12	0	0	0	21	....	....	....	....	....	....	....	....	....	....	....	....	....	....	....	....	....	....
	USNTDP	NAHL	7	1	2	3	0	....	....	....	....	....	....	....	....	....	....	....	....	....	....	....	....	....	....
2002-03	River City Lancers	USHL	59	12	30	42	98	....	....	....	....	....	....	....	....	....	11	2	2	4	20	....	....	....	....
2003-04	U. of Denver	WCHA	30	5	20	25	33	....	....	....	....	....	....	....	....	....	....	....	....	....	....	....	....	....	....
2004-05	U. of Denver	WCHA	43	13	31	44	68	....	....	....	....	....	....	....	....	....	....	....	....	....	....	....	....	....	....
2005-06	U. of Denver	WCHA	39	11	*42	53	58	....	....	....	....	....	....	....	....	....	....	....	....	....	....	....	....	....	....
	San Jose	**NHL**	**12**	**3**	**3**	**6**	**14**	**2**	**0**	**1**	**11**	**27.3**	**–2**	**0**	**0.0**	**16:07**	**11**	**0**	**3**	**3**	**4**	**0**	**0**	**0**	**15:17**
	NHL Totals		**12**	**3**	**3**	**6**	**14**	**2**	**0**	**1**	**11**	**27.3**		**0**	**0.0**	**16:07**	**11**	**0**	**3**	**3**	**4**	**0**	**0**	**0**	**15:17**

USHL First All-Star Team (2003) • USHL Defenseman of the Year (2003) • WCHA All-Rookie Team (2004) • WCHA First All-Star Team (2005, 2006) • NCAA West First All-American Team (2005, 2006) • NCAA Championship All-Tournament Team (2005) • WCHA Player of the Year (2006) • Hobey Baker Memorial Award (Top U.S. Collegiate Player) (2006)

CARNEY, Keith

(KAHRN-nee, KEETH) **MIN.**

Defense. Shoots left. 6'1", 216 lbs. Born, Providence, RI, February 3, 1970. Buffalo's 3rd choice, 76th overall, in 1988 Entry Draft.

Season	Club	League	GP	G	A	Pts	PIM	PP	SH	GW	S	%	+/-	TF	F%	Min	GP	G	A	Pts	PIM	PP	SH	GW	Min
1987-88	Mount St. Charles	High-RI	23	12	43	55	....	....	....	....	....	....	....	....	....	....	....	....	....	....	....	....	....	....	....
1988-89	U. of Maine	H-East	40	4	22	26	24	....	....	....	....	....	....	....	....	....	....	....	....	....	....	....	....	....	....
1989-90	U. of Maine	H-East	41	3	41	44	43	....	....	....	....	....	....	....	....	....	....	....	....	....	....	....	....	....	....
1990-91	U. of Maine	H-East	40	7	49	56	38	....	....	....	....	....	....	....	....	....	....	....	....	....	....	....	....	....	....
1991-92	United States	Nat-Tm	49	2	17	19	16	....	....	....	....	....	....	....	....	....	....	....	....	....	....	....	....	....	....
	Buffalo	**NHL**	**14**	**1**	**2**	**3**	**18**	**1**	**0**	**0**	**17**	**5.9**	**–3**	....	....	....	**7**	**0**	**3**	**3**	**0**	**0**	**0**	**0**	....
	Rochester	AHL	24	1	10	11	2	....	....	....	....	....	....	....	....	....	2	0	2	2	0	....	....	....	....
1992-93	**Buffalo**	**NHL**	**30**	**2**	**4**	**6**	**55**	**0**	**0**	**1**	**26**	**7.7**	**3**	....	....	....	**8**	**0**	**3**	**3**	**6**	**0**	**0**	**0**	....
	Rochester	AHL	41	5	21	26	32	....	....	....	....	....	....	....	....	....	....	....	....	....	....	....	....	....	....

Season	Club	League	Regular Season GP	G	A	Pts	PIM	PP	SH	GW	S	%	+/-	TF	F%	Min	Playoffs GP	G	A	Pts	PIM	PP	SH	GW	Min
1993-94	**Buffalo**	**NHL**	**7**	**1**	**3**	**4**	**4**	**0**	**0**	**0**	**6**	**16.7**	**–1**	....	....	....	....	....	....	....	....	....	....	....	....
	Chicago	**NHL**	**30**	**3**	**5**	**8**	**35**	**0**	**0**	**0**	**31**	**9.7**	**15**	....	....	....	**6**	**0**	**1**	**1**	**4**	**0**	**0**	**0**	....
	Indianapolis Ice	IHL	28	0	14	14	20	....	....	....	....	....	....	....	....	....	....	....	....	....	....	....	....	....	....
1994-95	**Chicago**	**NHL**	**18**	**1**	**0**	**1**	**11**	**0**	**0**	**1**	**14**	**7.1**	**–1**	....	....	....	**4**	**0**	**1**	**1**	**0**	**0**	**0**	**0**	....
1995-96	**Chicago**	**NHL**	**82**	**5**	**14**	**19**	**94**	**1**	**0**	**1**	**69**	**7.2**	**31**	....	....	....	**10**	**0**	**3**	**3**	**4**	**0**	**0**	**0**	....
1996-97	**Chicago**	**NHL**	**81**	**3**	**15**	**18**	**62**	**0**	**0**	**1**	**77**	**3.9**	**26**	....	....	....	**6**	**1**	**1**	**2**	**2**	**0**	**0**	**0**	....
1997-98	**Chicago**	**NHL**	**60**	**2**	**13**	**15**	**73**	**0**	**1**	**0**	**53**	**3.8**	**–7**	....	....	....	....	....	....	....	....	....	....	....	....
	United States	Olympics	4	0	0	0	2	....	....	....	....	....	....	....	....	....	....	....	....	....	....	....	....	....	....
	Phoenix	**NHL**	**20**	**1**	**6**	**7**	**18**	**1**	**0**	**0**	**18**	**5.6**	**5**	....	....	....	**6**	**0**	**0**	**0**	**4**	**0**	**0**	**0**	....
1998-99	**Phoenix**	**NHL**	**82**	**2**	**14**	**16**	**62**	**0**	**2**	**0**	**62**	**3.2**	**15**	**0**	**0.0**	**22:46**	**7**	**1**	**2**	**3**	**10**	**0**	**0**	**0**	**23:59**
99-2000	**Phoenix**	**NHL**	**82**	**4**	**20**	**24**	**87**	**0**	**0**	**1**	**73**	**5.5**	**11**	**0**	**0.0**	**21:12**	**5**	**0**	**0**	**0**	**17**	**0**	**0**	**0**	**22:38**
2000-01	**Phoenix**	**NHL**	**82**	**2**	**14**	**16**	**86**	**0**	**0**	**0**	**65**	**3.1**	**15**	**0**	**0.0**	**20:53**	....	....	....	....	....	....	....	....	....
2001-02	**Anaheim**	**NHL**	**60**	**5**	**9**	**14**	**30**	**0**	**0**	**1**	**66**	**7.6**	**14**	**0**	**0.0**	**20:47**	....	....	....	....	....	....	....	....	....
2002-03	**Anaheim**	**NHL**	**81**	**4**	**18**	**22**	**65**	**0**	**0**	**1**	**87**	**4.6**	**8**	**0**	**0.0**	**22:34**	**21**	**0**	**4**	**4**	**16**	**0**	**0**	**0**	**26:40**
2003-04	**Anaheim**	**NHL**	**69**	**2**	**5**	**7**	**42**	**1**	**0**	**0**	**58**	**3.4**	**–5**	**0**	**0.0**	**21:43**	....	....	....	....	....	....	....	....	....
2004-05			DID NOT PLAY																						
2005-06	**Anaheim**	**NHL**	**61**	**2**	**16**	**18**	**48**	**1**	**0**	**1**	**71**	**2.8**	**13**	**1**	**0.0**	**19:18**	....	....	....	....	....	....	....	....	....
	Vancouver	**NHL**	**18**	**0**	**2**	**2**	**14**	**0**	**0**	**0**	**14**	**0.0**	**–5**	**0**	**0.0**	**24:30**	....	....	....	....	....	....	....	....	....
	NHL Totals		**877**	**40**	**160**	**200**	**804**	**5**	**3**	**8**	**807**	**5.0**		**1**	**0.0**	**21:41**	**80**	**2**	**18**	**20**	**63**	**0**	**0**	**0**	**70:05**

Hockey East Second All-Star Team (1990) • NCAA East Second All-American Team (1990) • Hockey East First All-Star Team (1991) • NCAA East First All-American Team (1991)

Traded to **Chicago** by **Buffalo** with Buffalo's 6th round choice (Marc Magliarditi) in 1995 Entry Draft for Craig Muni and Chicago's 5th round choice (Daniel Bienvenue) in 1995 Entry Draft, October 26, 1993. Traded to **Phoenix** by **Chicago** with Jim Cummins for Chad Kilger and Jayson More, March 4, 1998. Traded to **Anaheim** by **Phoenix** for Calgary's 2nd round choice (previously acquired, later traded back to Calgary – Calgary selected Andrei Taratukhin) in 2001 Entry Draft, June 19, 2001. Traded to **Vancouver** by **Anaheim** with Juha Alen for Brett Skinner and NY Islanders' 2nd round choice (previously acquired, Anaheim selected Bryce Swan) in 2006 Entry Draft, March 9, 2006. Signed as a free agent by **Minnesota**, July 1, 2006.

CARTER, Anson

(KAHR-tuhr, AN-sohn)

Right wing. Shoots right. 6'1", 210 lbs. Born, Toronto, Ont., June 6, 1974. Quebec's 11th choice, 220th overall, in 1992 Entry Draft.

1989-90	Don Mills Flyers	MTHL	40	15	47	62	105	....	....	....	....	....	....	....	....	....	....	....	....	....	....	....	....	....	....
1990-91	Don Mills Flyers	MTHL	67	69	73	142	43	....	....	....	....	....	....	....	....	....	....	....	....	....	....	....	....	....	....
1991-92	Wexford Raiders	MTJHL	42	18	22	40	24	....	....	....	....	....	....	....	....	....	....	....	....	....	....	....	....	....	....
1992-93	Michigan State	CCHA	34	15	7	22	20	....	....	....	....	....	....	....	....	....	....	....	....	....	....	....	....	....	....
1993-94	Michigan State	CCHA	39	30	24	54	36	....	....	....	....	....	....	....	....	....	....	....	....	....	....	....	....	....	....
1994-95	Michigan State	CCHA	39	34	17	51	40	....	....	....	....	....	....	....	....	....	....	....	....	....	....	....	....	....	....
1995-96	Michigan State	CCHA	42	23	20	43	36	....	....	....	....	....	....	....	....	....	....	....	....	....	....	....	....	....	....
1996-97	**Washington**	**NHL**	**19**	**3**	**2**	**5**	**7**	**1**	**0**	**1**	**28**	**10.7**	**0**	....	....	....	....	....	....	....	....	....	....	....	....
	Portland Pirates	AHL	27	19	19	38	11	....	....	....	....	....	....	....	....	....	....	....	....	....	....	....	....	....	....
	Boston	**NHL**	**19**	**8**	**5**	**13**	**2**	**1**	**1**	**1**	**51**	**15.7**	**–7**	....	....	....	....	....	....	....	....	....	....	....	....
1997-98	**Boston**	**NHL**	**78**	**16**	**27**	**43**	**31**	**6**	**0**	**4**	**179**	**8.9**	**7**	....	....	....	**6**	**1**	**1**	**2**	**0**	**0**	**0**	**0**	....
1998-99	Utah Grizzlies	IHL	6	1	1	2	0	....	....	....	....	....	....	....	....	....	....	....	....	....	....	....	....	....	....
	Boston	**NHL**	**55**	**24**	**16**	**40**	**22**	**6**	**0**	**6**	**123**	**19.5**	**7**	**172**	**43.0**	**18:44**	**12**	**4**	**3**	**7**	**0**	**1**	**0**	**1**	**21:31**
99-2000	**Boston**	**NHL**	**59**	**22**	**25**	**47**	**14**	**4**	**0**	**1**	**144**	**15.3**	**8**	**793**	**48.2**	**20:31**	....	....	....	....	....	....	....	....	....
2000-01	**Edmonton**	**NHL**	**61**	**16**	**26**	**42**	**23**	**7**	**1**	**4**	**102**	**15.7**	**1**	**80**	**47.5**	**18:13**	**6**	**3**	**1**	**4**	**4**	**1**	**0**	**1**	**19:42**
2001-02	**Edmonton**	**NHL**	**82**	**28**	**32**	**60**	**25**	**12**	**0**	**6**	**181**	**15.5**	**3**	**316**	**46.5**	**19:18**	....	....	....	....	....	....	....	....	....
2002-03	**Edmonton**	**NHL**	**68**	**25**	**30**	**55**	**20**	**10**	**0**	**1**	**176**	**14.2**	**–11**	**217**	**43.8**	**19:39**	....	....	....	....	....	....	....	....	....
	NY Rangers	**NHL**	**11**	**1**	**4**	**5**	**6**	**0**	**0**	**0**	**17**	**5.9**	**0**	**5**	**20.0**	**17:49**	....	....	....	....	....	....	....	....	....
2003-04	**NY Rangers**	**NHL**	**43**	**10**	**7**	**17**	**14**	**4**	**1**	**2**	**63**	**15.9**	**–12**	**21**	**28.6**	**15:35**	....	....	....	....	....	....	....	....	....
	Washington	**NHL**	**19**	**5**	**5**	**10**	**6**	**2**	**0**	**2**	**33**	**15.2**	**2**	**9**	**44.4**	**19:33**	....	....	....	....	....	....	....	....	....
	Los Angeles	**NHL**	**15**	**0**	**1**	**1**	**0**	**0**	**0**	**0**	**18**	**0.0**	**–5**	**58**	**29.3**	**16:43**	....	....	....	....	....	....	....	....	....
2004-05			DID NOT PLAY																						
2005-06	**Vancouver**	**NHL**	**81**	**33**	**22**	**55**	**41**	**15**	**0**	**7**	**146**	**22.6**	**–1**	**28**	**39.3**	**14:34**	....	....	....	....	....	....	....	....	....
	NHL Totals		**610**	**191**	**202**	**393**	**211**	**68**	**3**	**35**	**1261**	**15.1**		**1699**	**45.6**	**18:06**	**24**	**8**	**5**	**13**	**4**	**2**	**0**	**2**	**20:54**

CCHA First All-Star Team (1994, 1995) • NCAA West Second All-American Team (1995) • CCHA Second All-Star Team (1996)

Rights transferred to **Colorado** after **Quebec** franchise relocated, June 21, 1995. Traded to **Washington** by **Colorado** for Washington's 4th round choice (Ben Storey) in 1996 Entry Draft, April 3, 1996. Traded to **Boston** by **Washington** with Jim Carey, Jason Allison and Washington's 3rd round choice (Lee Goren) in 1997 Entry Draft for Bill Ranford, Adam Oates and Rick Tocchet, March 1, 1997. Signed as a free agent by **Utah** (IHL) with Boston retaining NHL rights, October 20, 1998. Traded to **Edmonton** by **Boston** with Boston's 1st (Ales Hemsky) and 2nd (Doug Lynch) round choices in 2001 Entry Draft for Bill Guerin and future considerations, November 15, 2000. Traded to **NY Rangers** by **Edmonton** with Ales Pisa for Radek Dvorak and Cory Cross, March 11, 2003. Traded to **Washington** by **NY Rangers** for Jaromir Jagr, January 23, 2004. Traded to **Los Angeles** by **Washington** for Jared Aulin, March 8, 2004. Signed as a free agent by **Vancouver**, August 17, 2005.

CARTER, Jeff

(KAR-tuhr, JEHF) **PHI.**

Center. Shoots right. 6'3", 200 lbs. Born, London, Ont., January 1, 1985. Philadelphia's 1st choice, 11th overall, in 2003 Entry Draft.

2000-01	Strathroy Rockets	OHA-B	49	27	20	47	10	....	....	....	....	....	....	....	....	....	....	....	....	....	....	....	....	....	....
2001-02	Sault Ste. Marie	OHL	63	18	17	35	12	....	....	....	....	....	....	....	....	....	4	0	0	0	2	....	....	....	....
2002-03	Sault Ste. Marie	OHL	61	35	36	71	55	....	....	....	....	....	....	....	....	....	4	0	2	2	2	....	....	....	....
2003-04	Sault Ste. Marie	OHL	57	36	30	66	26	....	....	....	....	....	....	....	....	....	....	....	....	....	....	....	....	....	....
	Philadelphia	AHL	....	....	....	....	....	....	....	....	....	....	....	....	....	....	12	4	1	5	0	....	....	....	....
2004-05	Sault Ste. Marie	OHL	55	34	40	74	40	....	....	....	....	....	....	....	....	....	7	5	5	10	6	....	....	....	....
	Philadelphia	AHL	3	0	1	1	4	....	....	....	....	....	....	....	....	....	21	12	11	23	12	....	....	....	....
2005-06	**Philadelphia**	**NHL**	**81**	**23**	**19**	**42**	**40**	**6**	**2**	**7**	**189**	**12.2**	**10**	**683**	**48.2**	**12:04**	**6**	**0**	**0**	**0**	**10**	**0**	**0**	**0**	**13:04**
	NHL Totals		**81**	**23**	**19**	**42**	**40**	**6**	**2**	**7**	**189**	**12.2**		**683**	**48.2**	**12:04**	**6**	**0**	**0**	**0**	**10**	**0**	**0**	**0**	**13:04**

OHL Second All-Star Team (2004) • OHL First All-Star Team (2005) • Canadian Major Junior Sportsman of the Year (2005) • Canadian Major Junior First All-Star Team (2005)

CASSELS, Andrew

(KAS-uhls, AN-droo)

Center. Shoots left. 6'1", 185 lbs. Born, Bramalea, Ont., July 23, 1969. Montreal's 1st choice, 17th overall, in 1987 Entry Draft.

1985-86	Bramalea Blues	OJHL	33	18	25	43	26	....	....	....	....	....	....	....	....	....	....	....	....	....	....	....	....	....	....
1986-87	Ottawa 67's	OHL	66	26	66	92	28	....	....	....	....	....	....	....	....	....	11	5	9	14	7	....	....	....	....
1987-88	Ottawa 67's	OHL	61	48	*103	*151	39	....	....	....	....	....	....	....	....	....	16	8	*24	*32	13	....	....	....	....
1988-89	Ottawa 67's	OHL	56	37	97	134	66	....	....	....	....	....	....	....	....	....	12	5	10	15	10	....	....	....	....
1989-90	**Montreal**	**NHL**	**6**	**2**	**0**	**2**	**2**	**0**	**0**	**1**	**5**	**40.0**	**1**	....	....	....	....	....	....	....	....	....	....	....	....
	Sherbrooke	AHL	55	22	45	67	25	....	....	....	....	....	....	....	....	....	12	2	11	13	6	....	....	....	....
1990-91	**Montreal**	**NHL**	**54**	**6**	**19**	**25**	**20**	**1**	**0**	**3**	**55**	**10.9**	**2**	....	....	....	**8**	**0**	**2**	**2**	**2**	**0**	**0**	**0**	....
1991-92	**Hartford**	**NHL**	**67**	**11**	**30**	**41**	**18**	**2**	**2**	**3**	**99**	**11.1**	**3**	....	....	....	**7**	**2**	**4**	**6**	**6**	**1**	**0**	**0**	....
1992-93	**Hartford**	**NHL**	**84**	**21**	**64**	**85**	**62**	**8**	**3**	**1**	**134**	**15.7**	**–11**	....	....	....	....	....	....	....	....	....	....	....	....
1993-94	**Hartford**	**NHL**	**79**	**16**	**42**	**58**	**37**	**8**	**1**	**3**	**126**	**12.7**	**–21**	....	....	....	....	....	....	....	....	....	....	....	....
1994-95	**Hartford**	**NHL**	**46**	**7**	**30**	**37**	**18**	**1**	**0**	**1**	**74**	**9.5**	**–3**	....	....	....	....	....	....	....	....	....	....	....	....
1995-96	**Hartford**	**NHL**	**81**	**20**	**43**	**63**	**39**	**6**	**0**	**1**	**135**	**14.8**	**8**	....	....	....	....	....	....	....	....	....	....	....	....
1996-97	**Hartford**	**NHL**	**81**	**22**	**44**	**66**	**46**	**8**	**0**	**2**	**142**	**15.5**	**–16**	....	....	....	....	....	....	....	....	....	....	....	....
1997-98	**Calgary**	**NHL**	**81**	**17**	**27**	**44**	**32**	**6**	**1**	**2**	**138**	**12.3**	**–7**	....	....	....	....	....	....	....	....	....	....	....	....
1998-99	**Calgary**	**NHL**	**70**	**12**	**25**	**37**	**18**	**4**	**1**	**3**	**97**	**12.4**	**–12**	**1322**	**51.1**	**18:58**	....	....	....	....	....	....	....	....	....
99-2000	**Vancouver**	**NHL**	**79**	**17**	**45**	**62**	**16**	**6**	**0**	**1**	**109**	**15.6**	**8**	**1127**	**48.3**	**19:19**	....	....	....	....	....	....	....	....	....
2000-01	**Vancouver**	**NHL**	**66**	**12**	**44**	**56**	**10**	**2**	**0**	**1**	**104**	**11.5**	**1**	**1164**	**49.9**	**19:22**	....	....	....	....	....	....	....	....	....
2001-02	**Vancouver**	**NHL**	**53**	**11**	**39**	**50**	**22**	**7**	**0**	**1**	**64**	**17.2**	**5**	**866**	**50.4**	**17:27**	**6**	**2**	**1**	**3**	**0**	**1**	**0**	**0**	**16:55**
2002-03	**Columbus**	**NHL**	**79**	**20**	**48**	**68**	**30**	**9**	**1**	**5**	**113**	**17.7**	**–4**	**1649**	**48.8**	**19:52**	....	....	....	....	....	....	....	....	....
2003-04	**Columbus**	**NHL**	**58**	**6**	**20**	**26**	**26**	**2**	**0**	**0**	**91**	**6.6**	**–24**	**1205**	**45.1**	**19:18**	....	....	....	....	....	....	....	....	....
2004-05			DID NOT PLAY																						
2005-06	**Washington**	**NHL**	**31**	**4**	**8**	**12**	**14**	**2**	**0**	**0**	**29**	**13.8**	**–3**	**315**	**49.8**	**13:13**	....	....	....	....	....	....	....	....	....
	NHL Totals		**1015**	**204**	**528**	**732**	**410**	**72**	**9**	**28**	**1515**	**13.5**		**7648**	**48.9**	**18:42**	**21**	**4**	**7**	**11**	**8**	**2**	**0**	**0**	**16:55**

OHL Rookie of the Year (1987) • OHL First All-Star Team (1988,1989) • OHL MVP (1988)

Traded to **Hartford** by **Montreal** for Hartford's 2nd round choice (Valeri Bure) in 1992 Entry Draft, September 17, 1991. Transferred to **Carolina** after **Hartford** franchise relocated, June 25, 1997. Traded to **Calgary** by **Carolina** with Jean-Sebastien Giguere for Gary Roberts and Trevor Kidd, August 25, 1997. Signed as a free agent by **Vancouver**, August 19, 1999. Signed as a free agent by **Columbus**, August 15, 2002. Signed as a free agent by **Washington**, August 9, 2005. • Missed remainder of 2005-06 season after being released by Washington, January 28, 2006.

						Regular Season											Playoffs						
Season	Club	League	GP	G	A	Pts	PIM	PP	SH	GW	S	%	+/-	TF	F%	Min	GP	G	A	Pts	PIM	PP	SH	GW	Min

CHARA, Zdeno — (CHAH-rah, ZDEH-noh) — **BOS.**

Defense. Shoots left. 6'9", 260 lbs.　Born, Trencin, Czech., March 18, 1977. NY Islanders' 3rd choice, 56th overall, in 1996 Entry Draft.

Season	Club	League	GP	G	A	Pts	PIM	PP	SH	GW	S	%	+/-	TF	F%	Min	GP	G	A	Pts	PIM	PP	SH	GW	Min
1994-95	Dukla Trencin U18	Svk-U18	30	22	22	44	113	....	....	....	....	....	....				....	....	....	....	....				....
	Dukla Trencin Jr.	Slovak-Jr.	2	0	0	0	0	....	....	....	....	....	....				....	....	....	....	....				....
1995-96	Dukla Trencin Jr.	Slovak-Jr.	22	1	13	14	80	....	....	....	....	....	....				....	....	....	....	....				....
	HK VTJ Piestany	Slovak-2	10	1	3	4	10	....	....	....	....	....	....				....	....	....	....	....				....
	Sparta Jr.	CzRep-Jr.	15	1	2	3	42	....	....	....	....	....	....				....	....	....	....	....				....
	HC Sparta Praha	CzRep	0	0	0	0	0	....	....	....	....	....	....				15	1	7	8	45				....
1996-97	Prince George	WHL	49	3	19	22	120	....	....	....	....	....	....				15	1	7	8	45				....
1997-98	**NY Islanders**	**NHL**	25	0	1	1	50	0	0	0	10	0.0	1				1	0	0	0	4				....
	Kentucky	AHL	48	4	9	13	125	....	....	....	....	....	....				....	....	....	....	....				....
1998-99	**NY Islanders**	**NHL**	59	2	6	8	83	0	1	0	56	3.6	–8	0	0.0	18:54	....	....	....	....	....				....
	Lowell	AHL	23	2	2	4	47	....	....	....	....	....	....				....	....	....	....	....				....
99-2000	**NY Islanders**	**NHL**	65	2	9	11	57	0	0	1	47	4.3	–27	0	0.0	22:52	....	....	....	....	....				....
2000-01	**NY Islanders**	**NHL**	82	2	7	9	157	0	1	0	83	2.4	–27	0	0.0	22:20	....	....	....	....	....				....
2001-02	Dukla Trencin	Slovakia	8	2	2	4	32	....	....	....	....	....	....				....	....	....	....	....				....
	Ottawa	**NHL**	75	10	13	23	156	4	1	2	105	9.5	30	0	0.0	22:16	10	1	11	12	0	0	0	0	26:07
2002-03	**Ottawa**	**NHL**	74	9	30	39	116	3	0	2	168	5.4	29	0	0.0	24:57	18	1	6	7	14	0	0	0	25:07
2003-04	**Ottawa**	**NHL**	79	16	25	41	147	7	0	3	185	8.6	33	0	0.0	24:38	7	1	1	2	8	0	0	0	24:38
2004-05	Farjestad	Sweden	33	10	15	25	132	....	....	....	....	....	....				13	3	5	8	82				....
2005-06	**Ottawa**	**NHL**	71	16	27	43	135	10	1	3	212	7.5	17	24	41.7	27:11	10	1	3	4	23	0	0	0	27:32
	Slovakia	Olympics	6	1	1	2	2	....	....	....	....	....	....				....	....	....	....	....				....
	NHL Totals		530	57	118	175	901	24	4	11	866	6.6		24	41.7	23:25	45	3	11	14	57	1	0	0	25:48

AHL All-Rookie Team (1998) • NHL First All-Star Team (2004) • NHL Second All-Star Team (2006)
Played in NHL All-Star Game (2003)
Traded to **Ottawa** by NY Islanders with Bill Muckalt and NY Islanders' 1st round choice (Jason Spezza) in 2001 Entry Draft for Alexei Yashin, June 23, 2001. Signed as a free agent by **Farjestad** (Sweden), September 24, 2004. Signed as a free agent by **Boston**, July 1, 2006.

CHEECHOO, Jonathan — (CHEE-choo, JAWN-ah-thuhn) — **S.J.**

Right wing. Shoots right. 6'1", 190 lbs.　Born, Moose Factory, Ont., July 15, 1980. San Jose's 2nd choice, 29th overall, in 1998 Entry Draft.

Season	Club	League	GP	G	A	Pts	PIM	PP	SH	GW	S	%	+/-	TF	F%	Min	GP	G	A	Pts	PIM	PP	SH	GW	Min
1996-97	Kitchener	OHA-B	43	35	41	76	33	....	....	....	....	....	....				10	4	2	6	10				....
1997-98	Belleville Bulls	OHL	64	31	45	76	62	....	....	....	....	....	....				21	15	15	30	27				....
1998-99	Belleville Bulls	OHL	63	35	47	82	74	....	....	....	....	....	....				16	5	12	17	16				....
99-2000	Belleville Bulls	OHL	66	45	46	91	102	....	....	....	....	....	....				3	0	0	0	0				....
2000-01	Kentucky	AHL	75	32	34	66	63	....	....	....	....	....	....				....	....	....	....	....				....
2001-02	Cleveland Barons	AHL	53	21	25	46	54	....	....	....	....	....	....				....	....	....	....	....				....
2002-03	**San Jose**	**NHL**	66	9	7	16	39	0	0	3	94	9.6	–5	8	37.5	10:43	....	....	....	....	....				....
	Cleveland Barons	AHL	9	3	4	7	16	....	....	....	....	....	....				....	....	....	....	....				....
2003-04	**San Jose**	**NHL**	81	28	19	47	33	8	0	9	175	16.0	5	7	14.3	16:12	17	4	6	10	1	1	0	0	17:37
2004-05	HV 71 Jonkoping	Sweden	20	5	5	10	5	....	....	....	....	....	....				11	4	5	9	1				....
2005-06	**San Jose**	**NHL**	82	*56	37	93	58	24	2	11	317	17.7	23	20	20.0	19:57	11	4	5	9	8	1	0	1	24:00
	NHL Totals		229	93	63	156	130	32	2	23	586	15.9		35	22.9	15:58	28	8	11	19	18	2	0	1	20:08

OHL All-Rookie Team (1998) • AHL All-Rookie Team (2001) • Maurice "Rocket" Richard Trophy (2006)
Signed as a free agent by **Jonkoping** (Sweden), December 21, 2004.

CHELIOS, Chris — (CHELL-EE-ohs, KRIHS) — **DET.**

Defense. Shoots right. 6'1", 190 lbs.　Born, Chicago, IL, January 25, 1962. Montreal's 5th choice, 40th overall, in 1981 Entry Draft.

Season	Club	League	GP	G	A	Pts	PIM	PP	SH	GW	S	%	+/-	TF	F%	Min	GP	G	A	Pts	PIM	PP	SH	GW	Min
1979-80	Moose Jaw	SJHL	53	12	31	43	118	....	....	....	....	....	....				....	....	....	....	....				....
1980-81	Moose Jaw	SJHL	54	23	64	87	175	....	....	....	....	....	....				....	....	....	....	....				....
1981-82	U. of Wisconsin	WCHA	43	6	43	49	50	....	....	....	....	....	....				....	....	....	....	....				....
1982-83	U. of Wisconsin	WCHA	26	9	17	26	50	....	....	....	....	....	....				....	....	....	....	....				....
1983-84	United States	Nat-Tm	60	14	35	49	58	....	....	....	....	....	....				....	....	....	....	....				....
	United States	Olympics	6	0	4	4	8	....	....	....	....	....	....				....	....	....	....	....				....
	Montreal	**NHL**	12	0	2	2	12	0	0	0	23	0.0	–5				15	1	9	10	17	1	0	0	....
1984-85	**Montreal**	**NHL**	74	9	55	64	87	2	1	0	199	4.5	11				9	2	8	10	17	2	0	0	....
1985-86 ♦	**Montreal**	**NHL**	41	8	26	34	67	2	0	0	101	7.9	4				20	2	9	11	49	1	0	0	....
1986-87	**Montreal**	**NHL**	71	11	33	44	124	6	0	2	141	7.8	–5				17	4	9	13	38	2	1	0	....
1987-88	**Montreal**	**NHL**	71	20	41	61	172	10	1	5	199	10.1	14				11	3	1	4	29	1	0	0	....
1988-89	**Montreal**	**NHL**	80	15	58	73	185	8	0	6	206	7.3	35				21	4	15	19	28	1	0	2	....
1989-90	**Montreal**	**NHL**	53	9	22	31	136	1	2	1	123	7.3	20				5	0	1	1	8	0	0	0	....
1990-91	**Chicago**	**NHL**	77	12	52	64	192	5	2	2	187	6.4	23				6	1	7	8	46	1	0	0	....
1991-92	**Chicago**	**NHL**	80	9	47	56	245	2	2	2	239	3.8	24				18	6	15	21	37	3	0	1	....
1992-93	**Chicago**	**NHL**	84	15	58	73	282	8	0	2	290	5.2	14				4	1	2	3	14	0	0	0	....
1993-94	**Chicago**	**NHL**	76	16	44	60	212	7	1	2	219	7.3	12				6	1	1	2	8	1	0	0	....
1994-95	EHC Biel-Bienne	Swiss	3	0	3	3	4	....	....	....	....	....	....				16	4	7	11	12	0	1	3	....
	Chicago	**NHL**	48	5	33	38	72	3	1	0	166	3.0	17				16	4	7	11	12	0	1	3	....
1995-96	**Chicago**	**NHL**	81	14	58	72	140	7	0	3	219	6.4	25				9	0	3	3	8	0	0	0	....
1996-97	**Chicago**	**NHL**	72	10	38	48	112	2	0	2	194	5.2	16				6	0	1	1	4	0	0	0	....
1997-98	**Chicago**	**NHL**	81	3	39	42	151	1	0	0	205	1.5	–7				....	....	....	....	....				....
	United States	Olympics	4	0	2	2	2	....	....	....	....	....	....				....	....	....	....	....				....
1998-99	**Chicago**	**NHL**	65	8	26	34	89	2	1	0	172	4.7	–4	4	25.0	27:19	....	....	....	....	....				....
	Detroit	**NHL**	10	1	1	2	4	1	0	1	15	6.7	5	0	0.0	22:21	10	0	4	4	14	0	0	0	27:15
99-2000	**Detroit**	**NHL**	81	3	31	34	103	0	0	0	135	2.2	48	0	0.0	25:16	9	0	1	1	8	0	0	0	24:06
2000-01	**Detroit**	**NHL**	24	0	3	3	45	0	0	0	26	0.0	4	0	0.0	22:51	5	1	0	1	8	0	0	0	19:41
2001-02 ♦	**Detroit**	**NHL**	79	6	33	39	126	1	0	1	128	4.7	40	0	0.0	25:18	23	1	13	14	44	1	0	0	26:22
	United States	Olympics	6	1	0	1	4	....	....	....	....	....	....				....	....	....	....	....				....
2002-03	**Detroit**	**NHL**	66	2	17	19	78	0	1	0	92	2.2	4	0	0.0	24:15	4	0	2	2	4	0	0	0	25:43
2003-04	**Detroit**	**NHL**	69	2	19	21	61	0	0	0	113	1.8	12	0	0.0	21:21	8	0	1	1	4	0	0	0	21:13
2004-05	Motor City	UHL	23	5	19	24	25	....	....	....	....	....	....				....	....	....	....	....				....
2005-06	**Detroit**	**NHL**	81	4	7	11	108	1	1	0	83	4.8	22	4	25.0	18:29	6	0	0	0	6	0	0	0	19:25
	United States	Olympics	6	0	1	1	4	....	....	....	....	....	....				....	....	....	....	....				....
	NHL Totals		1476	182	743	925	2803	69	13	30	3475	5.2		8	25.0	23:30	228	30	107	137	399	14	2	6	24:22

WCHA Second All-Star Team (1983) • NCAA Championship All-Tournament Team (1983) • NHL All-Rookie Team (1985) • NHL First All-Star Team (1989, 1993, 1995, 1996, 2002) • James Norris Memorial Trophy (1989, 1993, 1996) • NHL Second All-Star Team (1991, 1997) • Bud Light Plus/Minus Award (2002)
Played in NHL All-Star Game (1985, 1990, 1991, 1992, 1993, 1994, 1996, 1997, 1998, 2000, 2002)
Traded to **Chicago** by Montreal with Montreal's 2nd round choice (Michael Pomichter) in 1991 Entry Draft for Denis Savard, June 29, 1990. Traded to **Detroit** by **Chicago** for Anders Eriksson and Detroit's 1st round choices in 1999 (Steve McCarthy) and 2001 (Adam Munro) Entry Drafts, March 23, 1999. • Missed majority of 2000-01 season recovering from knee injury suffered in game vs. Dallas, November 17, 2000. Signed as a free agent by **Motor City** (UHL), February 1, 2005.

CHIMERA, Jason — (chihm-AIR-a, JAY-suhn) — **CBJ**

Left wing. Shoots left. 6'2", 206 lbs.　Born, Edmonton, Alta., May 2, 1979. Edmonton's 5th choice, 121st overall, in 1997 Entry Draft.

Season	Club	League	GP	G	A	Pts	PIM	PP	SH	GW	S	%	+/-	TF	F%	Min	GP	G	A	Pts	PIM	PP	SH	GW	Min
1994-95	Edmonton Pats	AMHL	33	27	31	58	42	....	....	....	....	....	....				....	....	....	....	....				....
1995-96	Edmonton Pats	AMHL	34	23	24	47	44	....	....	....	....	....	....				4	0	1	1	4				....
1996-97	Medicine Hat	WHL	71	16	23	39	64	....	....	....	....	....	....				....	....	....	....	....				....
1997-98	Medicine Hat	WHL	72	34	32	66	93	....	....	....	....	....	....				....	....	....	....	....				....
	Hamilton	AHL	4	0	0	0	8	....	....	....	....	....	....				....	....	....	....	....				....
1998-99	Medicine Hat	WHL	37	18	22	40	84	....	....	....	....	....	....				5	1	4	5	8				....
	Brandon	WHL	21	14	12	26	32	....	....	....	....	....	....				10	4	2	6	12				....
99-2000	Hamilton	AHL	78	15	13	28	77	....	....	....	....	....	....				....	....	....	....	....				....
2000-01	**Edmonton**	**NHL**	1	0	0	0	0	0	0	0	0	0.0	0	0	0.0	6:58	....	....	....	....	....				....
	Hamilton	AHL	78	29	25	54	93	....	....	....	....	....	....				15	2	5	7	8				....
2001-02	**Edmonton**	**NHL**	3	1	0	1	0	0	0	0	3	33.3	–3	0	0.0	12:44	....	....	....	....	....				....
	Hamilton	AHL	77	26	51	77	158	....	....	....	....	....	....				15	6	4	10	6				....
2002-03	**Edmonton**	**NHL**	66	14	9	23	36	0	1	4	90	15.6	–2	11	54.6	10:46	2	0	2	2	0	0	0	0	10:55
2003-04	**Edmonton**	**NHL**	60	4	8	12	57	0	0	1	79	5.1	–1	22	31.8	10:07	....	....	....	....	....				....

Season	Club	League	Regular Season GP	G	A	Pts	PIM	PP	SH	GW	S	%	+/-	TF	F%	Min	Playoffs GP	G	A	Pts	PIM	PP	SH	GW	Min
2004-05	AS Varese Hockey	Italy	15	7	3	10	34	....	....	....	....	....	....	....	....	....	5	2	1	3	31	....	....	....	....
2005-06	**Columbus**	**NHL**	**80**	**17**	**13**	**30**	**95**	**1**	**1**	**5**	**127**	**13.4**	**–10**	**16**	**50.0**	**12:41**	....	....	....	....	....	....	....	....	....
	NHL Totals		**210**	**36**	**30**	**66**	**188**	**1**	**2**	**10**	**299**	**12.0**		**49**	**42.9**	**11:19**	**2**	**0**	**2**	**2**	**0**	**0**	**0**	**0**	**10:54**

AHL First All-Star Team (2002)

Traded to **Phoenix** by **Edmonton** with Edmonton's 3rd round choice (later transferred to Carolina – later traded to NY Rangers – NY Rangers selected Billy Ryan) in 2004 Entry Draft for New Jersey's 2nd round choice (previously acquired, Edmonton selected Geoff Paukovich) in 2004 Entry Draft and Buffalo's 4th round choice (previously acquired, Edmonton selected Liam Reddox) in 2004 Entry Draft, June 26, 2004. Signed as a free agent by **Varese** (Italy), December 15, 2004. Traded to **Columbus** by **Phoenix** with Cale Hulse and Mike Rupp for Geoff Sanderson and Tim Jackman, October 8, 2005.

CHISTOV, Stanislav

(chihs-TAHV, STAHN-ihs-lahv) **ANA.**

Left wing. Shoots right. 5'10", 193 lbs. Born, Chelyabinsk, USSR, April 17, 1983. Anaheim's 1st choice, 5th overall, in 2001 Entry Draft.

Season	Club	League	GP	G	A	Pts	PIM	PP	SH	GW	S	%	+/-	TF	F%	Min	GP	G	A	Pts	PIM	PP	SH	GW	Min
1998-99	Chelyabinsk 2	Russia-4	1	0	0	0	0	....	....	....	....	....	....	....	....	....	....	....	....	....	....	....	....	....	....
	Georgetown	OPJHL	14	10	7	17	21	....	....	....	....	....	....	....	....	....	....	....	....	....	....	....	....	....	....
99-2000	Omsk 2	Russia-3	5	4	3	7	8	....	....	....	....	....	....	....	....	....	....	....	....	....	....	....	....	....	....
	Omsk 2	Russia-3	18	12	4	16	24	....	....	....	....	....	....	....	....	....	....	....	....	....	....	....	....	....	....
	Novokuznetsk	Russia	9	7	4	11	18	....	....	....	....	....	....	....	....	....	....	....	....	....	....	....	....	....	....
	Avangard Omsk	Russia	3	1	0	1	2	....	....	....	....	....	....	....	....	....	....	....	....	....	....	....	....	....	....
2000-01	Omsk 2	Russia-3	8	5	4	9	2	....	....	....	....	....	....	....	....	....	....	....	....	....	....	....	....	....	....
	Avangard Omsk	Russia	24	4	8	12	12	....	....	....	....	....	....	....	....	....	5	0	0	0	2	....	....	....	....
2001-02	Avangard Omsk	Russia	9	0	0	0	4	....	....	....	....	....	....	....	....	....	....	....	....	....	....	....	....	....	....
	CSKA Moscow 2	Russia-3	1	1	2	3	0	....	....	....	....	....	....	....	....	....	....	....	....	....	....	....	....	....	....
2002-03	**Anaheim**	**NHL**	**79**	**12**	**18**	**30**	**54**	**3**	**0**	**2**	**114**	**10.5**	**4**	**3**	**0.0**	**13:35**	**21**	**4**	**2**	**6**	**8**	**0**	**0**	**1**	**13:22**
2003-04	**Anaheim**	**NHL**	**56**	**2**	**16**	**18**	**26**	**2**	**0**	**0**	**70**	**2.9**	**–16**	**4**	**0.0**	**12:20**	....	....	....	....	....	....	....	....	....
	Cincinnati	AHL	23	5	8	13	45	....	....	....	....	....	....	....	....	....	9	6	2	8	4	....	....	....	....
2004-05	Cincinnati	AHL	79	15	23	38	141	....	....	....	....	....	....	....	....	....	9	2	1	3	6	....	....	....	....
2005-06	Magnitogorsk	Russia	47	11	21	32	97	....	....	....	....	....	....	....	....	....	11	4	4	8	14	....	....	....	....
	NHL Totals		**135**	**14**	**34**	**48**	**80**	**5**	**0**	**2**	**184**	**7.6**		**7**	**0.0**	**13:04**	**21**	**4**	**2**	**6**	**8**	**0**	**0**	**1**	**13:22**

CHOUINARD, Eric

(shwee-NAHR, AIR-ihk)

Left wing. Shoots left. 6'3", 215 lbs. Born, Atlanta, GA, July 8, 1980. Montreal's 1st choice, 16th overall, in 1998 Entry Draft.

Season	Club	League	GP	G	A	Pts	PIM	PP	SH	GW	S	%	+/-	TF	F%	Min	GP	G	A	Pts	PIM	PP	SH	GW	Min
1995-96	Magog	QAHA	22	12	14	26	12	....	....	....	....	....	....	....	....	....	....	....	....	....	....	....	....	....	....
	Ste-Foy	QAAA	17	2	5	7	....	....	....	....	....	....	....	....	....	....	15	7	12	19	12	....	....	....	....
1996-97	Ste-Foy	QAAA	40	29	41	70	40	....	....	....	....	....	....	....	....	....	10	14	9	23	....	....	....	....	....
1997-98	Quebec Remparts	QMJHL	68	41	42	83	18	....	....	....	....	....	....	....	....	....	14	7	10	17	6	....	....	....	....
1998-99	Quebec Remparts	QMJHL	62	50	59	109	56	....	....	....	....	....	....	....	....	....	13	8	10	18	8	....	....	....	....
	Fredericton	AHL	....	....	....	....	....	....	....	....	....	....	....	....	....	....	6	3	2	5	0	....	....	....	....
99-2000	Quebec Remparts	QMJHL	50	57	47	104	105	....	....	....	....	....	....	....	....	....	11	14	4	18	8	....	....	....	....
2000-01	**Montreal**	**NHL**	**13**	**1**	**3**	**4**	**0**	**1**	**0**	**0**	**11**	**9.1**	**0**	**31**	**54.8**	**10:59**	....	....	....	....	....	....	....	....	....
	Quebec Citadelles	AHL	48	12	21	33	6	....	....	....	....	....	....	....	....	....	9	2	0	2	2	....	....	....	....
2001-02	Quebec Citadelles	AHL	65	19	23	42	18	....	....	....	....	....	....	....	....	....	2	0	0	0	0	....	....	....	....
2002-03	Utah Grizzlies	AHL	32	12	12	24	16	....	....	....	....	....	....	....	....	....	....	....	....	....	....	....	....	....	....
	Philadelphia	**NHL**	**28**	**4**	**4**	**8**	**8**	**1**	**0**	**0**	**45**	**8.9**	**2**	**12**	**33.3**	**9:38**	....	....	....	....	....	....	....	....	....
2003-04	**Philadelphia**	**NHL**	**17**	**3**	**0**	**3**	**0**	**0**	**0**	**0**	**15**	**20.0**	**–3**	**24**	**50.0**	**7:59**	....	....	....	....	....	....	....	....	....
	Minnesota	**NHL**	**31**	**3**	**4**	**7**	**6**	**0**	**0**	**1**	**45**	**6.7**	**–7**	**261**	**44.8**	**13:36**	....	....	....	....	....	....	....	....	....
	Philadelphia	AHL	1	0	0	0	0	....	....	....	....	....	....	....	....	....	....	....	....	....	....	....	....	....	....
2004-05	Salzburg	Austria	16	5	5	10	42	....	....	....	....	....	....	....	....	....	....	....	....	....	....	....	....	....	....
2005-06	**Philadelphia**	**NHL**	**1**	**0**	**0**	**0**	**2**	**0**	**0**	**0**	**0**	**0.0**	**0**	**2**	**50.0**	**4:30**	....	....	....	....	....	....	....	....	....
	Philadelphia	AHL	24	7	7	14	4	....	....	....	....	....	....	....	....	....	....	....	....	....	....	....	....	....	....
	San Antonio	AHL	47	8	12	20	22	....	....	....	....	....	....	....	....	....	....	....	....	....	....	....	....	....	....
	NHL Totals		**90**	**11**	**11**	**22**	**16**	**2**	**0**	**1**	**116**	**9.5**		**330**	**45.8**	**10:49**	....	....	....	....	....	....	....	....	....

Traded to **Philadelphia** by **Montreal** for Philadelphia's 2nd round choice (Maxim Lapierre) in 2003 Entry Draft, January 29, 2003. Traded to **Minnesota** by **Philadelphia** for Minnesota's 5th round choice (Chris Zarb) in 2004 Entry Draft, December 17, 2003. Signed as a free agent by **Salzburg** (Austria), October 14, 2004. Signed as a free agent by **Philadelphia**, August 22, 2005. Traded to **Phoenix** by **Philadelphia** for Kiel McLeod, December 28, 2005.

CHOUINARD, Marc

(shwee-NAHR, MAHRK) **VAN.**

Center. Shoots right. 6'5", 218 lbs. Born, Charlesbourg, Que., May 6, 1977. Winnipeg's 2nd choice, 32nd overall, in 1995 Entry Draft.

Season	Club	League	GP	G	A	Pts	PIM	PP	SH	GW	S	%	+/-	TF	F%	Min	GP	G	A	Pts	PIM	PP	SH	GW	Min
1992-93	Ste-Foy	QAAA	3	1	1	2	2	....	....	....	....	....	....	....	....	....	....	....	....	....	....	....	....	....	....
	Beauboury Selects	QAHA	28	26	45	71	42	....	....	....	....	....	....	....	....	....	....	....	....	....	....	....	....	....	....
1993-94	Beauport	QMJHL	62	11	19	30	23	....	....	....	....	....	....	....	....	....	13	2	5	7	2	....	....	....	....
1994-95	Beauport	QMJHL	68	24	40	64	32	....	....	....	....	....	....	....	....	....	18	1	6	7	4	....	....	....	....
1995-96	Beauport	QMJHL	30	14	21	35	19	....	....	....	....	....	....	....	....	....	....	....	....	....	....	....	....	....	....
	Halifax	QMJHL	24	6	12	18	17	....	....	....	....	....	....	....	....	....	6	2	1	3	2	....	....	....	....
1996-97	Halifax	QMJHL	63	24	49	73	74	....	....	....	....	....	....	....	....	....	18	9	16	25	12	....	....	....	....
1997-98	Cincinnati	AHL	8	1	2	3	4	....	....	....	....	....	....	....	....	....	....	....	....	....	....	....	....	....	....
1998-99	Cincinnati	AHL	69	7	8	15	20	....	....	....	....	....	....	....	....	....	3	0	0	0	4	....	....	....	....
99-2000	Cincinnati	AHL	70	17	16	33	29	....	....	....	....	....	....	....	....	....	....	....	....	....	....	....	....	....	....
2000-01	**Anaheim**	**NHL**	**44**	**3**	**4**	**7**	**12**	**0**	**0**	**1**	**26**	**11.5**	**–5**	**414**	**60.9**	**7:50**	....	....	....	....	....	....	....	....	....
	Cincinnati	AHL	32	10	9	19	4	....	....	....	....	....	....	....	....	....	....	....	....	....	....	....	....	....	....
2001-02	**Anaheim**	**NHL**	**45**	**4**	**5**	**9**	**10**	**0**	**0**	**0**	**40**	**10.0**	**2**	**581**	**54.9**	**10:36**	....	....	....	....	....	....	....	....	....
2002-03	**Anaheim**	**NHL**	**70**	**3**	**4**	**7**	**40**	**0**	**1**	**0**	**52**	**5.8**	**–9**	**662**	**54.5**	**9:25**	**15**	**1**	**0**	**1**	**0**	**0**	**0**	**0**	**7:16**
2003-04	**Minnesota**	**NHL**	**45**	**11**	**10**	**21**	**17**	**3**	**1**	**2**	**70**	**15.7**	**4**	**809**	**53.7**	**15:58**	....	....	....	....	....	....	....	....	....
2004-05	Frisk-Asker IF	Norway	16	9	8	17	26	....	....	....	....	....	....	....	....	....	3	5	2	7	29	....	....	....	....
2005-06	**Minnesota**	**NHL**	**74**	**14**	**16**	**30**	**34**	**6**	**2**	**3**	**112**	**12.5**	**1**	**1089**	**52.7**	**16:29**	....	....	....	....	....	....	....	....	....
	NHL Totals		**278**	**35**	**39**	**74**	**113**	**9**	**4**	**6**	**300**	**11.7**		**3555**	**54.6**	**12:18**	**15**	**1**	**0**	**1**	**0**	**0**	**0**	**0**	**7:16**

Traded to **Anaheim** by **Winnipeg** with Teemu Selanne and Winnipeg's 4th round choice (later traded to Toronto – later traded to Montreal – Montreal selected Kim Staal) in 1996 Entry Draft for Chad Kilger, Oleg Tverdovsky and Anaheim's 3rd round choice (Per-Anton Lundstrom) in 1996 Entry Draft, February 7, 1996. Signed as a free agent by **Minnesota**, July 28, 2003. Signed as a free agent by **Frisk-Asker** (Norway), January 1, 2005. Signed as a free agent by **Vancouver**, July 20, 2006.

CHRISTENSEN, Erik

(KRIHS-tehn-suhn, AIR-ihk) **PIT.**

Center. Shoots left. 6'1", 196 lbs. Born, Edmonton, Alta., December 17, 1983. Pittsburgh's 3rd choice, 69th overall, in 2002 Entry Draft.

Season	Club	League	GP	G	A	Pts	PIM	PP	SH	GW	S	%	+/-	TF	F%	Min	GP	G	A	Pts	PIM	PP	SH	GW	Min
1998-99	Leduc Oil Kings	AMBHL	36	34	42	76	70	....	....	....	....	....	....	....	....	....	....	....	....	....	....	....	....	....	....
99-2000	Kamloops Blazers	WHL	66	9	5	14	41	....	....	....	....	....	....	....	....	....	4	0	0	0	2	....	....	....	....
2000-01	Kamloops Blazers	WHL	72	21	23	44	36	....	....	....	....	....	....	....	....	....	4	1	1	2	0	....	....	....	....
2001-02	Kamloops Blazers	WHL	70	22	36	58	68	....	....	....	....	....	....	....	....	....	4	0	0	0	4	....	....	....	....
2002-03	Kamloops Blazers	WHL	67	*54	54	*108	60	....	....	....	....	....	....	....	....	....	6	1	7	8	14	....	....	....	....
2003-04	Kamloops Blazers	WHL	29	10	14	24	40	....	....	....	....	....	....	....	....	....	....	....	....	....	....	....	....	....	....
	Brandon	WHL	34	17	21	38	20	....	....	....	....	....	....	....	....	....	11	8	4	12	8	....	....	....	....
2004-05	Wilkes-Barre	AHL	77	14	13	27	33	....	....	....	....	....	....	....	....	....	11	1	6	7	4	....	....	....	....
2005-06	**Pittsburgh**	**NHL**	**33**	**6**	**7**	**13**	**34**	**2**	**0**	**0**	**85**	**7.1**	**–3**	**381**	**53.0**	**14:17**	....	....	....	....	....	....	....	....	....
	Wilkes-Barre	AHL	48	24	22	46	50	....	....	....	....	....	....	....	....	....	11	2	2	4	2	....	....	....	....
	NHL Totals		**33**	**6**	**7**	**13**	**34**	**2**	**0**	**0**	**85**	**7.1**		**381**	**53.0**	**14:17**	....	....	....	....	....	....	....	....	....

WHL West First All-Star Team (2003)

CHUBAROV, Artem

(choo-BAH-rahf, AHR-tehm) **VAN.**

Center. Shoots left. 6'1", 189 lbs. Born, Gorky, USSR, December 12, 1979. Vancouver's 2nd choice, 31st overall, in 1998 Entry Draft.

Season	Club	League	GP	G	A	Pts	PIM	PP	SH	GW	S	%	+/-	TF	F%	Min	GP	G	A	Pts	PIM	PP	SH	GW	Min
1994-95	Nizh. Novgorod 2	CIS-2	60	20	30	50	20	....	....	....	....	....	....	....	....	....	....	....	....	....	....	....	....	....	....
1995-96	Niz. Novgorod Jr.	CIS-Jr.	60	22	25	47	20	....	....	....	....	....	....	....	....	....	....	....	....	....	....	....	....	....	....
1996-97	Nizhny Novgorod	Russia	15	1	1	2	8	....	....	....	....	....	....	....	....	....	....	....	....	....	....	....	....	....	....
1997-98	Dynamo Moscow	Russia	30	1	4	5	4	....	....	....	....	....	....	....	....	....	....	....	....	....	....	....	....	....	....
1998-99	Dynamo Moscow	Russia	34	8	2	10	10	....	....	....	....	....	....	....	....	....	12	0	0	0	4	....	....	....	....
99-2000	**Vancouver**	**NHL**	**49**	**1**	**8**	**9**	**10**	**0**	**0**	**1**	**53**	**1.9**	**–4**	**488**	**48.0**	**11:43**	....	....	....	....	....	....	....	....	....
	Syracuse Crunch	AHL	14	7	6	13	4	....	....	....	....	....	....	....	....	....	1	0	0	0	0	....	....	....	....
2000-01	**Vancouver**	**NHL**	**1**	**0**	**0**	**0**	**0**	**0**	**0**	**0**	**0**	**0.0**	**–1**	**17**	**52.9**	**15:08**	....	....	....	....	....	....	....	....	....
	Kansas City	IHL	10	7	4	11	12	....	....	....	....	....	....	....	....	....	....	....	....	....	....	....	....	....	....
2001-02	**Vancouver**	**NHL**	**51**	**5**	**5**	**10**	**10**	**0**	**0**	**3**	**73**	**6.8**	**–3**	**517**	**53.6**	**12:37**	**6**	**0**	**1**	**1**	**0**	**0**	**0**	**0**	**14:44**
	Manitoba Moose	AHL	19	7	12	19	4	....	....	....	....	....	....	....	....	....	....	....	....	....	....	....	....	....	....

			Regular Season														Playoffs								
Season	Club	League	GP	G	A	Pts	PIM	PP	SH	GW	S	%	+/-	TF	F%	Min	GP	G	A	Pts	PIM	PP	SH	GW	Min
2002-03	**Vancouver**	**NHL**	**62**	**7**	**13**	**20**	**6**	**1**	**0**	**1**	**78**	**9.0**	**4**	**862**	**50.8**	**14:21**	**14**	**0**	**2**	**2**	**4**	**0**	**0**	**0**	**14:56**
2003-04	**Vancouver**	**NHL**	**65**	**12**	**7**	**19**	**14**	**1**	**1**	**3**	**93**	**12.9**	**1**	**963**	**53.3**	**14:05**	**7**	**0**	**1**	**1**	**0**	**0**	**0**	**0**	**19:07**
2004-05	Dynamo Moscow	Russia	27	4	9	13	10	....	....	....	....	....	....	....	....	....	....	....	....	....	....	....	....	....	....
2005-06	Avangard Omsk	Russia	47	10	15	25	36	....	....	....	....	....	....	....	....	....	11	5	3	8	10	....	....	....	....
	NHL Totals		**228**	**25**	**33**	**58**	**40**	**2**	**1**	**8**	**297**	**8.4**		**2847**	**51.7**	**13:19**	**27**	**0**	**4**	**4**	**4**	**0**	**0**	**0**	**15:59**

• Missed majority of 2000-01 season recovering from shoulder injury suffered in game vs. Manitoba (IHL), November 15, 2000. Signed as a free agent by **Dynamo Moscow** (Russia), June 19, 2004. Signed as a free agent by **Omsk** (Russia), August 22, 2005.

CIBAK, Martin

(TSEE-bak, MAHR-tihn)

Center. Shoots left. 6'1", 196 lbs. Born, Liptovsky Mikulas, Czech., May 17, 1980. Tampa Bay's 11th choice, 252nd overall, in 1998 Entry Draft.

1995-96	L. Mikulas Jr.	Slovak-Jr.	48	38	35	73	....	....	....	....	....	....	....	....	....	....	....	....	....	....	....	....	....	....	....
1996-97	L. Mikulas Jr.	Slovak-Jr.	45	22	18	40	....	....	....	....	....	....	....	....	....	....	....	....	....	....	....	....	....	....	....
1997-98	L. Mikulas Jr.	Slovak-Jr.	42	31	21	52	....	....	....	....	....	....	....	....	....	....	....	....	....	....	....	....	....	....	....
	L. Mikulas	Slovakia	28	1	3	4	10	....	....	....	....	....	....	....	....	....	....	....	....	....	....	....	....	....	....
1998-99	Medicine Hat	WHL	66	21	26	47	72	....	....	....	....	....	....	....	....	....	....	....	....	....	....	....	....	....	....
99-2000	Medicine Hat	WHL	58	16	29	45	77	....	....	....	....	....	....	....	....	....	....	....	....	....	....	....	....	....	....
2000-01	Detroit Vipers	IHL	79	10	28	38	88	....	....	....	....	....	....	....	....	....	....	....	....	....	....	....	....	....	....
2001-02	**Tampa Bay**	**NHL**	**26**	**1**	**5**	**6**	**8**	**0**	**0**	**0**	**22**	**4.5**	**-6**	**85**	**34.1**	**11:08**	....	....	....	....	....	....	....	....	....
	Springfield	AHL	52	5	9	14	44	....	....	....	....	....	....	....	....	....	....	....	....	....	....	....	....	....	....
2002-03	Springfield	AHL	62	5	15	20	78	....	....	....	....	....	....	....	....	....	6	1	2	3	4	....	....	....	....
2003-04♦	**Tampa Bay**	**NHL**	**63**	**2**	**7**	**9**	**30**	**0**	**0**	**0**	**44**	**4.5**	**-1**	**321**	**45.2**	**7:35**	**6**	**0**	**1**	**1**	**0**	**0**	**0**	**0**	**7:35**
	Hershey Bears	AHL	1	0	0	0	2	....	....	....	....	....	....	....	....	....	....	....	....	....	....	....	....	....	....
2004-05	L. Mikulas	Slovakia	4	0	0	0	6	....	....	....	....	....	....	....	....	....	....	....	....	....	....	....	....	....	....
	Plzen	CzRep	30	4	11	15	52	....	....	....	....	....	....	....	....	....	....	....	....	....	....	....	....	....	....
	HC Kosice	Slovakia	6	1	3	4	8	....	....	....	....	....	....	....	....	....	10	2	5	7	36	....	....	....	....
2005-06	**Tampa Bay**	**NHL**	**65**	**2**	**6**	**8**	**22**	**0**	**0**	**0**	**50**	**4.0**	**-9**	**175**	**32.6**	**6:36**	**5**	**0**	**0**	**0**	**0**	**0**	**0**	**0**	**3:56**
	NHL Totals		**154**	**5**	**18**	**23**	**60**	**0**	**0**	**0**	**116**	**4.3**		**581**	**39.8**	**7:46**	**11**	**0**	**1**	**1**	**0**	**0**	**0**	**0**	**5:56**

Signed as a free agent by **Libtovsky Mikulas** (Slovakia), September 17, 2004. Signed as a free agent by **Plzen** (CzRep), October 18, 2004. Signed as a free agent by **Kosice** (Slovakia), January 31, 2005. Signed as a free agent by **Frolunda** (Sweden), August 16, 2006.

CIERNIK, Ivan

(CHAIR-nihk, ee-VAHN)

Right wing. Shoots left. 6'1", 234 lbs. Born, Levice, Czech., October 30, 1977. Ottawa's 6th choice, 216th overall, in 1996 Entry Draft.

1994-95	HC Nitra Jr.	Slovak-Jr.	30	22	15	37	36	....	....	....	....	....	....	....	....	....	....	....	....	....	....	....	....	....	....
	HC Nitra	Slovakia	7	1	0	1	2	....	....	....	....	....	....	....	....	....	....	....	....	....	....	....	....	....	....
1995-96	HC Nitra	Slovakia	35	9	7	16	36	....	....	....	....	....	....	....	....	....	8	3	3	6	....	....	....	....	....
1996-97	HC Corgon Nitra	Slovakia	41	11	19	30	....	....	....	....	....	....	....	....	....	....	....	....	....	....	....	....	....	....	....
1997-98	**Ottawa**	**NHL**	**2**	**0**	**0**	**0**	**0**	**0**	**0**	**0**	**0**	**0.0**	**0**	....	....	....	....	....	....	....	....	....	....	....	....
	Worcester IceCats	AHL	53	9	12	21	38	....	....	....	....	....	....	....	....	....	1	0	0	0	2	....	....	....	....
1998-99	Adirondack	AHL	21	1	4	5	4	....	....	....	....	....	....	....	....	....	....	....	....	....	....	....	....	....	....
	Cincinnati	AHL	32	10	3	13	10	....	....	....	....	....	....	....	....	....	2	0	0	0	2	....	....	....	....
99-2000	Grand Rapids	IHL	66	13	12	25	64	....	....	....	....	....	....	....	....	....	6	0	6	6	2	....	....	....	....
2000-01	**Ottawa**	**NHL**	**4**	**2**	**0**	**2**	**2**	**0**	**0**	**0**	**7**	**28.6**	**2**	**0**	**0.0**	**7:41**	....	....	....	....	....	....	....	....	....
	Grand Rapids	IHL	66	27	38	65	53	....	....	....	....	....	....	....	....	....	10	5	6	11	26	....	....	....	....
2001-02	**Ottawa**	**NHL**	**23**	**1**	**2**	**3**	**4**	**0**	**0**	**0**	**18**	**5.6**	**0**	**7**	**71.4**	**7:51**	....	....	....	....	....	....	....	....	....
	Grand Rapids	AHL	2	2	1	3	0	....	....	....	....	....	....	....	....	....	....	....	....	....	....	....	....	....	....
	Washington	**NHL**	**6**	**0**	**1**	**1**	**2**	**0**	**0**	**0**	**5**	**0.0**	**0**	**0**	**0.0**	**9:15**	....	....	....	....	....	....	....	....	....
	Portland Pirates	AHL	26	10	5	15	28	....	....	....	....	....	....	....	....	....	....	....	....	....	....	....	....	....	....
2002-03	**Washington**	**NHL**	**47**	**8**	**10**	**18**	**24**	**0**	**0**	**2**	**61**	**13.1**	**6**	**9**	**33.3**	**11:48**	**2**	**0**	**1**	**1**	**6**	**0**	**0**	**0**	**9:09**
	Portland Pirates	AHL	13	4	6	10	6	....	....	....	....	....	....	....	....	....	....	....	....	....	....	....	....	....	....
2003-04	**Washington**	**NHL**	**7**	**1**	**1**	**2**	**0**	**0**	**0**	**0**	**8**	**12.5**	**1**	**0**	**0.0**	**9:38**	....	....	....	....	....	....	....	....	....
	Portland Pirates	AHL	54	10	21	31	43	....	....	....	....	....	....	....	....	....	7	2	1	3	10	....	....	....	....
2004-05	Wolfsburg	Germany	50	26	22	48	91	....	....	....	....	....	....	....	....	....	7	4	2	6	22	....	....	....	....
2005-06	Kolner Haie	Germany	51	29	31	60	86	....	....	....	....	....	....	....	....	....	9	4	2	6	30	....	....	....	....
	NHL Totals		**89**	**12**	**14**	**26**	**32**	**0**	**0**	**2**	**99**	**12.1**		**16**	**50.0**	**10:13**	**2**	**0**	**1**	**1**	**6**	**0**	**0**	**0**	**9:09**

Loaned to **Cincinnati** (AHL) by **Ottawa** with Ratislav Pavlikovsky and Erich Goldmann, January 12, 1999. Claimed on waivers by **Washington** from **Ottawa**, January 19, 2002. Signed as a free agent by **Wolfsburg** (Germany), May 4, 2004.

CISAR, Marian

(SIH-sahr, MAIR-ee-uhn) **NSH.**

Right wing. Shoots right. 6', 197 lbs. Born, Bratislava, Czech., February 25, 1978. Los Angeles' 2nd choice, 37th overall, in 1996 Entry Draft.

1994-95	Bratislava Jr.	Slovak-Jr.	38	42	28	70	16	....	....	....	....	....	....	....	....	....	....	....	....	....	....	....	....	....	....
1995-96	Bratislava Jr.	Slovak-Jr.	16	26	17	43	2	....	....	....	....	....	....	....	....	....	....	....	....	....	....	....	....	....	....
	Bratislava	Slovakia	13	3	3	6	0	....	....	....	....	....	....	....	....	....	6	3	0	3	0	....	....	....	....
1996-97	Spokane Chiefs	WHL	70	31	35	66	52	....	....	....	....	....	....	....	....	....	9	6	2	8	4	....	....	....	....
1997-98	Spokane Chiefs	WHL	52	33	40	73	34	....	....	....	....	....	....	....	....	....	18	8	5	13	8	....	....	....	....
1998-99	Milwaukee	IHL	51	11	17	28	31	....	....	....	....	....	....	....	....	....	2	0	0	0	12	....	....	....	....
99-2000	**Nashville**	**NHL**	**3**	**0**	**0**	**0**	**4**	**0**	**0**	**0**	**2**	**0.0**	**-2**	**0**	**0.0**	**8:18**	....	....	....	....	....	....	....	....	....
	Milwaukee	IHL	78	20	32	52	82	....	....	....	....	....	....	....	....	....	1	0	0	0	0	....	....	....	....
2000-01	**Nashville**	**NHL**	**60**	**12**	**15**	**27**	**45**	**5**	**0**	**1**	**97**	**12.4**	**-7**	**0**	**0.0**	**13:10**	....	....	....	....	....	....	....	....	....
	Milwaukee	IHL	15	4	7	11	4	....	....	....	....	....	....	....	....	....	....	....	....	....	....	....	....	....	....
2001-02	**Nashville**	**NHL**	**10**	**1**	**2**	**3**	**8**	**1**	**0**	**0**	**16**	**6.3**	**-3**	**1**	**100.0**	**12:55**	....	....	....	....	....	....	....	....	....
	Milwaukee	AHL	2	1	0	1	2	....	....	....	....	....	....	....	....	....	....	....	....	....	....	....	....	....	....
2002-03	Znojmo	CzRep	9	2	0	2	4	....	....	....	....	....	....	....	....	....	....	....	....	....	....	....	....	....	....
	Lukko Rauma	Finland	26	6	8	14	6	....	....	....	....	....	....	....	....	....	....	....	....	....	....	....	....	....	....
2003-04	Nurnberg	Germany	43	23	13	36	26	....	....	....	....	....	....	....	....	....	2	0	0	0	2	....	....	....	....
2004-05	Hannover	Germany	14	4	6	10	8	....	....	....	....	....	....	....	....	....	....	....	....	....	....	....	....	....	....
2005-06			DID NOT PLAY – INJURED																						
	NHL Totals		**73**	**13**	**17**	**30**	**57**	**6**	**0**	**1**	**115**	**11.3**		**1**	**100.0**	**12:56**	....	....	....	....	....	....	....	....	....

Traded to **Nashville** by **Los Angeles** for future considerations, June 1, 1998. • Missed remainder of 2001-02 season after suffering head iinjury in game vs. Milwaukee (AHL), November 23, 2001. Signed as a free agent by **Znojmo** (CzRep) with Nashville retaining NHL rights, July 22, 2002. Signed as a free agent by **Nurnberg** (Germany), May 21, 2003.

CLARK, Brett

(KLAHRK, BREHT) **COL.**

Defense. Shoots left. 6'1", 195 lbs. Born, Wapella, Sask., December 23, 1976. Montreal's 7th choice, 154th overall, in 1996 Entry Draft.

1994-95	Melville	SJHL	62	19	32	51	77	....	....	....	....	....	....	....	....	....	....	....	....	....	....	....	....	....	....
1995-96	U. of Maine	H-East	39	7	31	38	22	....	....	....	....	....	....	....	....	....	....	....	....	....	....	....	....	....	....
1996-97	Canada	Nat-Tm	57	6	21	27	52	....	....	....	....	....	....	....	....	....	....	....	....	....	....	....	....	....	....
1997-98	**Montreal**	**NHL**	**41**	**1**	**0**	**1**	**20**	**0**	**0**	**0**	**26**	**3.8**	**-3**	....	....	....	....	....	....	....	....	....	....	....	....
	Fredericton	AHL	20	0	6	6	6	....	....	....	....	....	....	....	....	....	4	0	1	1	17	....	....	....	....
1998-99	**Montreal**	**NHL**	**61**	**2**	**2**	**4**	**16**	**0**	**0**	**0**	**36**	**5.6**	**-3**	**0**	**0.0**	**13:11**	....	....	....	....	....	....	....	....	....
	Fredericton	AHL	3	1	0	1	0	....	....	....	....	....	....	....	....	....	....	....	....	....	....	....	....	....	....
99-2000	**Atlanta**	**NHL**	**14**	**0**	**1**	**1**	**4**	**0**	**0**	**0**	**13**	**0.0**	**-12**	**0**	**0.0**	**16:51**	....	....	....	....	....	....	....	....	....
	Orlando	IHL	63	9	17	26	31	....	....	....	....	....	....	....	....	....	6	0	1	1	0	....	....	....	....
2000-01	**Atlanta**	**NHL**	**28**	**1**	**2**	**3**	**14**	**0**	**0**	**0**	**35**	**2.9**	**-12**	**0**	**0.0**	**18:02**	....	....	....	....	....	....	....	....	....
	Orlando	IHL	43	2	9	11	32	....	....	....	....	....	....	....	....	....	15	1	6	7	2	....	....	....	....
2001-02	**Atlanta**	**NHL**	**2**	**0**	**0**	**0**	**0**	**0**	**0**	**0**	**0**	**0.0**	**-3**	**1**	**100.0**	**15:32**	....	....	....	....	....	....	....	....	....
	Chicago Wolves	AHL	42	3	17	20	18	....	....	....	....	....	....	....	....	....	....	....	....	....	....	....	....	....	....
	Hershey Bears	AHL	32	7	9	16	12	....	....	....	....	....	....	....	....	....	8	0	2	2	6	....	....	....	....
2002-03	Hershey Bears	AHL	80	8	27	35	26	....	....	....	....	....	....	....	....	....	5	0	4	4	4	....	....	....	....
2003-04	**Colorado**	**NHL**	**12**	**1**	**1**	**2**	**6**	**0**	**0**	**0**	**14**	**7.1**	**3**	**0**	**0.0**	**10:26**	....	....	....	....	....	....	....	....	....
	Hershey Bears	AHL	64	11	21	32	37	....	....	....	....	....	....	....	....	....	....	....	....	....	....	....	....	....	....
2004-05	Hershey Bears	AHL	67	7	37	44	54	....	....	....	....	....	....	....	....	....	....	....	....	....	....	....	....	....	....
2005-06	**Colorado**	**NHL**	**80**	**9**	**27**	**36**	**56**	**4**	**0**	**1**	**148**	**6.1**	**3**	**1**	**0.0**	**19:39**	**9**	**2**	**2**	**4**	**2**	**0**	**1**	**0**	**24:17**
	NHL Totals		**238**	**14**	**33**	**47**	**116**	**4**	**0**	**1**	**272**	**5.1**		**2**	**50.0**	**16:37**	**9**	**2**	**2**	**4**	**2**	**0**	**1**	**0**	**24:17**

Claimed by **Atlanta** from **Montreal** in Expansion Draft, June 25, 1999. Traded to **Colorado** by **Atlanta** for Frederic Cassivi, January 24, 2002.

CLARK, Chris
(KLAHRK, KRIHS) **WSH.**

Right wing. Shoots right. 6', 200 lbs. Born, South Windsor, CT, March 8, 1976. Calgary's 3rd choice, 77th overall, in 1994 Entry Draft.

			Regular Season														Playoffs								
Season	Club	League	GP	G	A	Pts	PIM	PP	SH	GW	S	%	+/-	TF	F%	Min	GP	G	A	Pts	PIM	PP	SH	GW	Min
1990-91	South Windsor	High-CT	23	16	15	31	24	....	....	....	....	....	....	....	....	....	....	....	....	....	....	....	....	....	....
1991-92	Spring. Olympics	NEJHL	49	21	29	50	56	....	....	....	....	....	....	....	....	....	....	....	....	....	....	....	....	....	....
1992-93	Spring. Olympics	NEJHL	43	17	60	77	120	....	....	....	....	....	....	....	....	....	....	....	....	....	....	....	....	....	....
1993-94	Spring. Olympics	NEJHL	35	31	26	57	185	....	....	....	....	....	....	....	....	....	....	....	....	....	....	....	....	....	....
1994-95	Clarkson Knights	ECAC	32	12	11	23	92	....	....	....	....	....	....	....	....	....	....	....	....	....	....	....	....	....	....
1995-96	Clarkson Knights	ECAC	38	10	8	18	108	....	....	....	....	....	....	....	....	....	....	....	....	....	....	....	....	....	....
1996-97	Clarkson Knights	ECAC	37	23	25	48	*86	....	....	....	....	....	....	....	....	....	....	....	....	....	....	....	....	....	....
1997-98	Clarkson Knights	ECAC	35	18	21	39	*106	....	....	....	....	....	....	....	....	....	....	....	....	....	....	....	....	....	....
1998-99	Saint John Flames	AHL	73	13	27	40	123	....	....	....	....	....	....	....	....	....	7	2	4	6	15	....	....	....	....
99-2000	**Calgary**	**NHL**	**22**	**0**	**1**	**1**	**14**	**0**	**0**	**0**	**17**	**0.0**	**-3**	**0**	**0.0**	**9:02**	....	....	....	....	....	....	....	....	....
	Saint John Flames	AHL	48	16	17	33	134	....	....	....	....	....	....	....	....	....	....	....	....	....	....	....	....	....	....
2000-01	**Calgary**	**NHL**	**29**	**5**	**1**	**6**	**38**	**1**	**0**	**0**	**43**	**11.6**	**0**	**3**	**33.3**	**11:56**	....	....	....	....	....	....	....	....	....
	Saint John Flames	AHL	48	18	17	35	131	....	....	....	....	....	....	....	....	....	18	4	10	14	49	....	....	....	....
2001-02	**Calgary**	**NHL**	**64**	**10**	**7**	**17**	**79**	**2**	**1**	**4**	**109**	**9.2**	**-12**	**21**	**33.3**	**13:57**	....	....	....	....	....	....	....	....	....
2002-03	**Calgary**	**NHL**	**81**	**10**	**12**	**22**	**126**	**2**	**0**	**2**	**156**	**6.4**	**-11**	**40**	**32.5**	**14:24**	....	....	....	....	....	....	....	....	....
2003-04	**Calgary**	**NHL**	**82**	**10**	**15**	**25**	**106**	**4**	**0**	**2**	**137**	**7.3**	**-3**	**97**	**36.1**	**14:05**	**26**	**3**	**3**	**6**	**30**	**1**	**0**	**0**	**14:34**
2004-05	SC Bern	Swiss	3	0	0	0	6	....	....	....	....	....	....	....	....	....	....	....	....	....	....	....	....	....	....
	Storhamar	Norway	15	10	4	14	86	....	....	....	....	....	....	....	....	....	7	4	4	8	14	....	....	....	....
2005-06	**Washington**	**NHL**	**78**	**20**	**19**	**39**	**110**	**1**	**3**	**0**	**144**	**13.9**	**9**	**209**	**49.3**	**15:24**	....	....	....	....	....	....	....	....	....
	NHL Totals		**356**	**55**	**55**	**110**	**473**	**10**	**4**	**8**	**606**	**9.1**		**370**	**43.0**	**13:56**	**26**	**3**	**3**	**6**	**30**	**1**	**0**	**0**	**14:34**

ECAC Second All-Star Team (1998)

Signed as a free agent by **Bern** (Swiss), October 3, 2004. Signed as a free agent by **Storhamar** (Norway), December 29, 2004. Traded to **Washington** by **Calgary** with Calgary's 7th round choice in 2007 Entry Draft for Washington's 7th round choice (Devin Didiomete) in 2006 Entry Draft and Washington's 6th round choice in 2007 Entry Draft, August 4, 2005.

CLARKE, Noah
(KLAHRK, NOH-uh) **L.A.**

Left wing. Shoots left. 5'9", 185 lbs. Born, La Verne, CA, June 11, 1979. Los Angeles' 10th choice, 250th overall, in 1999 Entry Draft.

			Regular Season														Playoffs								
Season	Club	League	GP	G	A	Pts	PIM	PP	SH	GW	S	%	+/-	TF	F%	Min	GP	G	A	Pts	PIM	PP	SH	GW	Min
1996-97	Shat.-St. Mary's	High-MN	30	33	44	77	....	....	....	....	....	....	....	....	....	....	....	....	....	....	....	....	....	....	....
1997-98	Des Moines	USHL	54	19	30	49	29	....	....	....	....	....	....	....	....	....	12	2	9	11	23	....	....	....	....
1998-99	Des Moines	USHL	52	31	32	63	47	....	....	....	....	....	....	....	....	....	13	8	2	10	16	....	....	....	....
99-2000	Colorado College	WCHA	39	17	20	37	30	....	....	....	....	....	....	....	....	....	....	....	....	....	....	....	....	....	....
2000-01	Colorado College	WCHA	41	12	20	32	22	....	....	....	....	....	....	....	....	....	....	....	....	....	....	....	....	....	....
2001-02	Colorado College	WCHA	42	13	24	37	32	....	....	....	....	....	....	....	....	....	....	....	....	....	....	....	....	....	....
2002-03	Colorado College	WCHA	42	21	*49	70	15	....	....	....	....	....	....	....	....	....	....	....	....	....	....	....	....	....	....
	Manchester	AHL	3	1	1	2	0	....	....	....	....	....	....	....	....	....	....	....	....	....	....	....	....	....	....
2003-04	**Los Angeles**	**NHL**	**2**	**0**	**1**	**1**	**0**	**0**	**0**	**0**	**3**	**0.0**	**1**	**0**	**0.0**	**9:39**	....	....	....	....	....	....	....	....	....
	Manchester	AHL	71	25	26	51	24	....	....	....	....	....	....	....	....	....	6	3	1	4	4	....	....	....	....
2004-05	Manchester	AHL	61	21	24	45	24	....	....	....	....	....	....	....	....	....	6	1	0	1	4	....	....	....	....
2005-06	**Los Angeles**	**NHL**	**5**	**0**	**0**	**0**	**0**	**0**	**0**	**0**	**3**	**0.0**	**0**	**3**	**33.3**	**7:23**	....	....	....	....	....	....	....	....	....
	Manchester	AHL	69	14	30	44	33	....	....	....	....	....	....	....	....	....	7	4	4	8	2	....	....	....	....
	NHL Totals		**7**	**0**	**1**	**1**	**0**	**0**	**0**	**0**	**6**	**0.0**		**3**	**33.3**	**8:02**									

USHL All-Rookie Team (1998) • USHL First All-Star Team (1999) • Curt Hammer Award (Most Gentlemanly Player – USHL) (1999) • WCHA All-Rookie Team (2000) • WCHA Second All-Star Team (2003) • NCAA West First All-American Team (2003) • AHL All-Rookie Team (2004)

CLASSEN, Greg
(KLAW-sihn, GREHG)

Center. Shoots left. 6'1", 200 lbs. Born, Aylsham, Sask., August 24, 1977.

			Regular Season														Playoffs								
Season	Club	League	GP	G	A	Pts	PIM	PP	SH	GW	S	%	+/-	TF	F%	Min	GP	G	A	Pts	PIM	PP	SH	GW	Min
1997-98	Nipawin Hawks	SJHL	59	32	50	82	50	....	....	....	....	....	....	....	....	....	14	8	13	21	6	....	....	....	....
1998-99	Merrimack	H-East	36	14	11	25	28	....	....	....	....	....	....	....	....	....	....	....	....	....	....	....	....	....	....
99-2000	Merrimack	H-East	36	14	16	30	16	....	....	....	....	....	....	....	....	....	....	....	....	....	....	....	....	....	....
	Milwaukee	IHL	11	1	0	1	2	....	....	....	....	....	....	....	....	....	2	0	0	0	2	....	....	....	....
2000-01	**Nashville**	**NHL**	**27**	**2**	**4**	**6**	**14**	**1**	**0**	**0**	**18**	**11.1**	**-4**	**195**	**42.1**	**10:16**	....	....	....	....	....	....	....	....	....
	Milwaukee	IHL	23	5	10	15	31	....	....	....	....	....	....	....	....	....	5	0	0	0	0	....	....	....	....
2001-02	**Nashville**	**NHL**	**55**	**5**	**6**	**11**	**30**	**0**	**1**	**0**	**32**	**15.6**	**1**	**389**	**43.2**	**10:09**	....	....	....	....	....	....	....	....	....
	Milwaukee	AHL	8	2	4	6	12	....	....	....	....	....	....	....	....	....	....	....	....	....	....	....	....	....	....
2002-03	**Nashville**	**NHL**	**8**	**0**	**0**	**0**	**4**	**0**	**0**	**0**	**2**	**0.0**	**-3**	**65**	**52.3**	**10:02**	....	....	....	....	....	....	....	....	....
	Milwaukee	AHL	72	20	28	48	61	....	....	....	....	....	....	....	....	....	6	1	1	2	4	....	....	....	....
2003-04	Milwaukee	AHL	68	18	29	47	95	....	....	....	....	....	....	....	....	....	20	4	3	7	12	....	....	....	....
2004-05	Assat Pori	Finland	42	8	10	18	74	....	....	....	....	....	....	....	....	....	2	0	0	0	0	....	....	....	....
2005-06	Milwaukee	AHL	76	24	26	50	67	....	....	....	....	....	....	....	....	....	21	1	15	16	18	....	....	....	....
	NHL Totals		**90**	**7**	**10**	**17**	**48**	**1**	**1**	**0**	**52**	**13.5**		**649**	**43.8**	**10:10**	....	....	....	....	....	....	....	....	....

Hockey East All-Rookie Team (1999)

Signed as a free agent by **Nashville**, March 27, 2000. Signed as a free agent by **Pori** (Finland), July 25, 2004.

CLEARY, Daniel
(KLIH-ree, DAN-yehl) **DET.**

Right wing. Shoots left. 6', 211 lbs. Born, Carbonear, Nfld., December 18, 1978. Chicago's 1st choice, 13th overall, in 1997 Entry Draft.

			Regular Season														Playoffs								
Season	Club	League	GP	G	A	Pts	PIM	PP	SH	GW	S	%	+/-	TF	F%	Min	GP	G	A	Pts	PIM	PP	SH	GW	Min
1993-94	Kingston	MTJHL	41	18	28	46	33	....	....	....	....	....	....	....	....	....	2	0	1	1	0	....	....	....	....
1994-95	Belleville Bulls	OHL	62	26	55	81	62	....	....	....	....	....	....	....	....	....	16	7	10	17	23	....	....	....	....
1995-96	Belleville Bulls	OHL	64	53	62	115	74	....	....	....	....	....	....	....	....	....	14	10	17	27	40	....	....	....	....
1996-97	Belleville Bulls	OHL	64	32	48	80	88	....	....	....	....	....	....	....	....	....	6	3	4	7	6	....	....	....	....
1997-98	**Chicago**	**NHL**	**6**	**0**	**0**	**0**	**0**	**0**	**0**	**0**	**4**	**0.0**	**-2**	....	....	....	....	....	....	....	....	....	....	....	....
	Belleville Bulls	OHL	30	16	31	47	14	....	....	....	....	....	....	....	....	....	10	6	*17	*23	10	....	....	....	....
	Indianapolis Ice	IHL	4	2	1	3	6	....	....	....	....	....	....	....	....	....	....	....	....	....	....	....	....	....	....
1998-99	**Chicago**	**NHL**	**35**	**4**	**5**	**9**	**24**	**0**	**0**	**0**	**49**	**8.2**	**-1**	**13**	**46.2**	**14:21**	....	....	....	....	....	....	....	....	....
	Portland Pirates	AHL	30	9	17	26	74	....	....	....	....	....	....	....	....	....	....	....	....	....	....	....	....	....	....
	Hamilton	AHL	9	0	1	1	7	....	....	....	....	....	....	....	....	....	3	0	0	0	0	....	....	....	....
99-2000	**Edmonton**	**NHL**	**17**	**3**	**2**	**5**	**8**	**0**	**0**	**1**	**18**	**16.7**	**-1**	**1**	**100.0**	**9:44**	**4**	**0**	**1**	**1**	**2**	**0**	**0**	**0**	**8:40**
	Hamilton	AHL	58	22	52	74	108	....	....	....	....	....	....	....	....	....	5	2	3	5	18	....	....	....	....
2000-01	**Edmonton**	**NHL**	**81**	**14**	**21**	**35**	**37**	**2**	**0**	**2**	**107**	**13.1**	**5**	**13**	**23.1**	**12:58**	**6**	**1**	**1**	**2**	**8**	**1**	**0**	**0**	**14:09**
2001-02	**Edmonton**	**NHL**	**65**	**10**	**19**	**29**	**51**	**2**	**1**	**1**	**75**	**13.3**	**-1**	**5**	**60.0**	**12:43**	....	....	....	....	....	....	....	....	....
2002-03	**Edmonton**	**NHL**	**57**	**4**	**13**	**17**	**31**	**0**	**0**	**1**	**89**	**4.5**	**5**	**5**	**40.0**	**11:58**	....	....	....	....	....	....	....	....	....
2003-04	**Phoenix**	**NHL**	**68**	**6**	**11**	**17**	**42**	**0**	**3**	**0**	**83**	**7.2**	**-8**	**51**	**39.2**	**13:12**	....	....	....	....	....	....	....	....	....
2004-05	Mora IK	Sweden	47	11	26	37	138	....	....	....	....	....	....	....	....	....	....	....	....	....	....	....	....	....	....
2005-06	**Detroit**	**NHL**	**77**	**3**	**12**	**15**	**40**	**0**	**0**	**1**	**106**	**2.8**	**5**	**286**	**45.8**	**10:30**	**6**	**0**	**1**	**1**	**6**	**0**	**0**	**0**	**10:44**
	NHL Totals		**406**	**44**	**83**	**127**	**233**	**4**	**4**	**6**	**531**	**8.3**		**374**	**44.4**	**12:20**	**16**	**1**	**3**	**4**	**16**	**1**	**0**	**0**	**11:30**

OHL All-Rookie Team (1995) • OHL First All-Star Team (1996, 1997) • AHL Second All-Star Team (2000)

Traded to **Edmonton** by **Chicago** with Chad Kilger, Ethan Moreau and Christian Laflamme for Boris Mironov, Dean McAmmond and Jonas Elofsson, March 20, 1999. Signed as a free agent by **Phoenix**, July 15, 2003. Signed as a free agent by **Mora** (Sweden), September 6, 2004. Signed as a free agent by **Detroit**, October 4, 2005.

CLOWE, Ryane
(KLOH, RIGH-uhn) **S.J.**

Right wing. Shoots right. 6'2", 215 lbs. Born, St. John's, Nfld., September 30, 1982. San Jose's 5th choice, 175th overall, in 2001 Entry Draft.

			Regular Season														Playoffs								
Season	Club	League	GP	G	A	Pts	PIM	PP	SH	GW	S	%	+/-	TF	F%	Min	GP	G	A	Pts	PIM	PP	SH	GW	Min
2000-01	Rimouski Oceanic	QMJHL	32	15	10	25	43	....	....	....	....	....	....	....	....	....	11	8	1	9	12	....	....	....	....
2001-02	Rimouski Oceanic	QMJHL	53	28	45	73	120	....	....	....	....	....	....	....	....	....	7	1	6	7	2	....	....	....	....
2002-03	Rimouski Oceanic	QMJHL	17	8	19	27	44	....	....	....	....	....	....	....	....	....	....	....	....	....	....	....	....	....	....
	Montreal Rocket	QMJHL	43	18	30	48	60	....	....	....	....	....	....	....	....	....	7	3	7	10	6	....	....	....	....
2003-04	Cleveland Barons	AHL	72	11	29	40	97	....	....	....	....	....	....	....	....	....	8	3	1	4	9	....	....	....	....
2004-05	Cleveland Barons	AHL	74	27	35	62	101	....	....	....	....	....	....	....	....	....	....	....	....	....	....	....	....	....	....
2005-06	**San Jose**	**NHL**	**18**	**0**	**2**	**2**	**9**	**0**	**0**	**0**	**14**	**0.0**	**-2**	**2**	**0.0**	**9:40**	**1**	**0**	**0**	**0**	**0**	**0**	**0**	**0**	**5:06**
	Cleveland Barons	AHL	35	13	21	34	35	....	....	....	....	....	....	....	....	....	....	....	....	....	....	....	....	....	....
	NHL Totals		**18**	**0**	**2**	**2**	**9**	**0**	**0**	**0**	**14**	**0.0**		**2**	**0.0**	**9:40**	**1**	**0**	**0**	**0**	**0**	**0**	**0**	**0**	**5:06**

			Regular Season														Playoffs								
Season	Club	League	GP	G	A	Pts	PIM	PP	SH	GW	S	%	+/-	TF	F%	Min	GP	G	A	Pts	PIM	PP	SH	GW	Min

CLYMER, Ben (KLIH-mehr, BEHN) WSH.

Left wing. Shoots right. 6'1", 201 lbs. Born, Bloomington, MN, April 11, 1978. Boston's 3rd choice, 27th overall, in 1997 Entry Draft.

Season	Club	League	GP	G	A	Pts	PIM	PP	SH	GW	S	%	+/-	TF	F%	Min	GP	G	A	Pts	PIM	PP	SH	GW	Min
1993-94	Jefferson Jaguars	High-MN	23	3	7	10	20	....	....	....	....	....	....	....	....	....	....	....	....	....	....	....	....	....	....
1994-95	Jefferson Jaguars	High-MN	28	11	22	33	36	....	....	....	....	....	....	....	....	....	....	....	....	....	....	....	....	....	....
1995-96	Jefferson Jaguars	High-MN	18	12	34	46	34	....	....	....	....	....	....	....	....	....	5	0	6	6	6	....	....	....	....
1996-97	U. of Minnesota	WCHA	29	7	13	20	64	....	....	....	....	....	....	....	....	....	....	....	....	....	....	....	....	....	....
1997-98	U. of Minnesota	WCHA	1	0	0	0	2	....	....	....	....	....	....	....	....	....	....	....	....	....	....	....	....	....	....
1998-99	Seattle	WHL	70	12	44	56	93	....	....	....	....	....	....	....	....	....	11	1	5	6	12	....	....	....	....
99-2000	**Tampa Bay**	**NHL**	**60**	**2**	**6**	**8**	**87**	**2**	**0**	**0**	**98**	**2.0**	**-26**	**3**	**66.7**	**19:37**	....	....	....	....	....	....	....	....	....
	Detroit Vipers	IHL	19	1	9	10	30	....	....	....	....	....	....	....	....	....	....	....	....	....	....	....	....	....	....
2000-01	**Tampa Bay**	**NHL**	**23**	**5**	**1**	**6**	**21**	**3**	**0**	**0**	**25**	**20.0**	**-7**	**8**	**25.0**	**13:03**	....	....	....	....	....	....	....	....	....
	Detroit Vipers	IHL	53	5	8	13	88	....	....	....	....	....	....	....	....	....	....	....	....	....	....	....	....	....	....
2001-02	**Tampa Bay**	**NHL**	**81**	**14**	**20**	**34**	**36**	**4**	**0**	**2**	**151**	**9.3**	**-10**	**14**	**28.6**	**17:26**	....	....	....	....	....	....	....	....	....
2002-03	**Tampa Bay**	**NHL**	**65**	**6**	**12**	**18**	**57**	**1**	**0**	**1**	**103**	**5.8**	**-2**	**15**	**0.0**	**13:39**	**11**	**0**	**2**	**2**	**6**	**0**	**0**	**0**	**13:30**
2003-04♦	**Tampa Bay**	**NHL**	**66**	**2**	**8**	**10**	**50**	**0**	**0**	**0**	**96**	**2.1**	**5**	**25**	**28.0**	**9:48**	**5**	**0**	**0**	**0**	**0**	**0**	**0**	**0**	**7:46**
2004-05	EHC Biel-Bienne	Swiss-2	19	11	12	23	30	....	....	....	....	....	....	....	....	....	11	6	11	17	24	....	....	....	....
2005-06	**Washington**	**NHL**	**77**	**16**	**17**	**33**	**72**	**3**	**0**	**3**	**149**	**10.7**	**-7**	**11**	**45.5**	**14:10**	....	....	....	....	....	....	....	....	....
	NHL Totals		**372**	**45**	**64**	**109**	**323**	**13**	**0**	**6**	**622**	**7.2**		**76**	**26.3**	**14:49**	**16**	**0**	**2**	**2**	**6**	**0**	**0**	**0**	**11:42**

• Missed majority of 1997-98 season recovering from shoulder injury suffered in game vs. U. of Michigan (CCHA), October 10, 1997. Signed as a free agent by **Tampa Bay**, October 2, 1999. Signed as a free agent by **Biel-Bienne** (Swiss-2), December 2, 2004. Signed as a free agent by **Washington**, August 8, 2005.

COBURN, Braydon (KOH-buhrn, BRAY-duhn) ATL.

Defense. Shoots left. 6'5", 220 lbs. Born, Calgary, Alta., February 27, 1985. Atlanta's 1st choice, 8th overall, in 2003 Entry Draft.

Season	Club	League	GP	G	A	Pts	PIM	PP	SH	GW	S	%	+/-	TF	F%	Min	GP	G	A	Pts	PIM	PP	SH	GW	Min
2000-01	Notre Dame	SMHL	32	3	19	22	70	....	....	....	....	....	....	....	....	....	....	....	....	....	....	....	....	....	....
	Portland	WHL	2	0	1	1	0	....	....	....	....	....	....	....	....	....	14	0	4	4	2	....	....	....	....
2001-02	Portland	WHL	68	4	33	37	100	....	....	....	....	....	....	....	....	....	7	1	1	2	9	....	....	....	....
2002-03	Portland	WHL	53	3	16	19	147	....	....	....	....	....	....	....	....	....	7	0	1	1	8	....	....	....	....
2003-04	Portland	WHL	55	10	20	30	92	....	....	....	....	....	....	....	....	....	5	0	1	1	10	....	....	....	....
2004-05	Portland	WHL	60	12	32	44	144	....	....	....	....	....	....	....	....	....	7	1	5	6	6	....	....	....	....
	Chicago Wolves	AHL	3	0	1	1	5	....	....	....	....	....	....	....	....	....	18	0	1	1	36	....	....	....	....
2005-06	**Atlanta**	**NHL**	**9**	**0**	**1**	**1**	**4**	**0**	**0**	**0**	**4**	**0.0**	**-2**	**0**	**0.0**	**7:43**	....	....	....	....	....	....	....	....	....
	Chicago Wolves	AHL	73	6	20	26	134	....	....	....	....	....	....	....	....	....	....	....	....	....	....	....	....	....	....
	NHL Totals		**9**	**0**	**1**	**1**	**4**	**0**	**0**	**0**	**4**	**0.0**		**0**	**0.0**	**7:43**	....	....	....	....	....	....	....	....	....

WHL Rookie of the Year (2002) • WHL West First All-Star Team (2004, 2005)

COLAIACOVO, Carlo (koh-lee-A-KOH-voh, KAR-loh) TOR.

Defense. Shoots left. 6'1", 200 lbs. Born, Toronto, Ont., January 27, 1983. Toronto's 1st choice, 17th overall, in 2001 Entry Draft.

Season	Club	League	GP	G	A	Pts	PIM	PP	SH	GW	S	%	+/-	TF	F%	Min	GP	G	A	Pts	PIM	PP	SH	GW	Min
1998-99	Mississauga Reps	GTHL	44	10	12	23	28	....	....	....	....	....	....	....	....	....	....	....	....	....	....	....	....	....	....
99-2000	Erie Otters	OHL	52	4	18	22	12	....	....	....	....	....	....	....	....	....	13	2	4	6	9	....	....	....	....
2000-01	Erie Otters	OHL	62	12	27	39	59	....	....	....	....	....	....	....	....	....	14	4	7	11	16	....	....	....	....
2001-02	Erie Otters	OHL	60	13	27	40	49	....	....	....	....	....	....	....	....	....	21	7	10	17	20	....	....	....	....
2002-03	**Toronto**	**NHL**	**2**	**0**	**1**	**1**	**0**	**0**	**0**	**0**	**1**	**0.0**	**0**	**0**	**0.0**	**13:43**	....	....	....	....	....	....	....	....	....
	Erie Otters	OHL	35	14	21	35	12	....	....	....	....	....	....	....	....	....	....	....	....	....	....	....	....	....	....
2003-04	**Toronto**	**NHL**	**2**	**0**	**1**	**1**	**2**	**0**	**0**	**0**	**0**	**0.0**	**1**	**0**	**0.0**	**13:56**	....	....	....	....	....	....	....	....	....
	St. John's	AHL	62	6	25	31	50	....	....	....	....	....	....	....	....	....	....	....	....	....	....	....	....	....	....
2004-05	St. John's	AHL	49	4	20	24	59	....	....	....	....	....	....	....	....	....	5	0	1	1	2	....	....	....	....
2005-06	**Toronto**	**NHL**	**21**	**2**	**5**	**7**	**17**	**1**	**0**	**0**	**21**	**9.5**	**0**	**1**	**0.0**	**15:26**	....	....	....	....	....	....	....	....	....
	Toronto Marlies	AHL	14	5	6	11	14	....	....	....	....	....	....	....	....	....	....	....	....	....	....	....	....	....	....
	NHL Totals		**25**	**2**	**7**	**9**	**19**	**1**	**0**	**0**	**22**	**9.1**		**1**	**0.0**	**15:11**	....	....	....	....	....	....	....	....	....

OHL Second All-Star Team (2002, 2003)

• Missed remainder of 2005-06 season recovering from head injury suffered in game at Ottawa, January 23, 2006.

COLE, Erik (KOHL, AIR-ihk) CAR.

Left wing. Shoots left. 6'2", 200 lbs. Born, Oswego, NY, November 6, 1978. Carolina's 3rd choice, 71st overall, in 1998 Entry Draft.

Season	Club	League	GP	G	A	Pts	PIM	PP	SH	GW	S	%	+/-	TF	F%	Min	GP	G	A	Pts	PIM	PP	SH	GW	Min
1995-96	Oswego	High-NY	40	49	41	90	....	....	....	....	....	....	....	....	....	....	....	....	....	....	....	....	....	....	....
1996-97	Des Moines	USHL	48	30	34	64	140	....	....	....	....	....	....	....	....	....	5	2	0	2	6	....	....	....	....
1997-98	Clarkson Knights	ECAC	34	11	20	31	55	....	....	....	....	....	....	....	....	....	....	....	....	....	....	....	....	....	....
1998-99	Clarkson Knights	ECAC	36	*22	20	42	50	....	....	....	....	....	....	....	....	....	....	....	....	....	....	....	....	....	....
99-2000	Clarkson Knights	ECAC	33	19	11	30	46	....	....	....	....	....	....	....	....	....	....	....	....	....	....	....	....	....	....
	Cincinnati	IHL	9	4	3	7	2	....	....	....	....	....	....	....	....	....	7	1	1	2	2	....	....	....	....
2000-01	Cincinnati	IHL	69	23	20	43	28	....	....	....	....	....	....	....	....	....	5	1	0	1	2	....	....	....	....
2001-02	**Carolina**	**NHL**	**81**	**16**	**24**	**40**	**35**	**3**	**0**	**2**	**159**	**10.1**	**-10**	**17**	**47.1**	**16:04**	**23**	**6**	**3**	**9**	**30**	**1**	**0**	**1**	**18:27**
2002-03	**Carolina**	**NHL**	**53**	**14**	**13**	**27**	**72**	**6**	**2**	**3**	**125**	**11.2**	**1**	**56**	**39.3**	**17:08**	....	....	....	....	....	....	....	....	....
2003-04	**Carolina**	**NHL**	**80**	**18**	**24**	**42**	**93**	**2**	**2**	**3**	**172**	**10.5**	**-4**	**15**	**46.7**	**18:06**	....	....	....	....	....	....	....	....	....
2004-05	Eisbaren Berlin	Germany	39	6	21	27	76	....	....	....	....	....	....	....	....	....	8	5	1	6	37	....	....	....	....
2005-06♦	**Carolina**	**NHL**	**60**	**30**	**29**	**59**	**54**	**3**	**3**	**8**	**164**	**18.3**	**19**	**19**	**36.8**	**19:18**	**2**	**0**	**0**	**0**	**0**	**0**	**0**	**0**	**15:29**
	United States	Olympics	6	1	2	3	0	....	....	....	....	....	....	....	....	....	....	....	....	....	....	....	....	....	....
	NHL Totals		**274**	**78**	**90**	**168**	**254**	**14**	**7**	**16**	**620**	**12.6**		**107**	**41.1**	**17:34**	**25**	**6**	**3**	**9**	**30**	**1**	**0**	**1**	**18:13**

ECAC Rookie of the Year (1998) (co-winner - Willie Mitchell) • ECAC First All-Star Team (1999) • NCAA East Second All-American Team (1999) • ECAC Second All-Star Team (2000)
Signed as a free agent by **Berlin** (Germany), October 24, 2004.

COLLEY, Kevin (KAW-lee, KEH-vihn)

Center. Shoots right. 5'10", 175 lbs. Born, New Haven, CT, January 4, 1979.

Season	Club	League	GP	G	A	Pts	PIM	PP	SH	GW	S	%	+/-	TF	F%	Min	GP	G	A	Pts	PIM	PP	SH	GW	Min
1996-97	Oshawa Generals	OHL	64	19	17	36	46	....	....	....	....	....	....	....	....	....	16	2	4	6	25	....	....	....	....
1997-98	Oshawa Generals	OHL	57	27	41	68	107	....	....	....	....	....	....	....	....	....	7	1	5	6	14	....	....	....	....
1998-99	Oshawa Generals	OHL	63	39	62	101	68	....	....	....	....	....	....	....	....	....	14	7	13	20	32	....	....	....	....
99-2000	Hartford	AHL	5	0	0	0	2	....	....	....	....	....	....	....	....	....	....	....	....	....	....	....	....	....	....
	Charlotte	ECHL	5	2	1	3	10	....	....	....	....	....	....	....	....	....	....	....	....	....	....	....	....	....	....
	Dayton Bombers	ECHL	24	8	6	14	111	....	....	....	....	....	....	....	....	....	2	1	0	1	4	....	....	....	....
2000-01	Pensacola	ECHL	23	6	11	17	44	....	....	....	....	....	....	....	....	....	....	....	....	....	....	....	....	....	....
	New Orleans	ECHL	23	11	8	19	27	....	....	....	....	....	....	....	....	....	8	1	1	2	12	....	....	....	....
2001-02	Providence Bruins	AHL	4	0	1	1	27	....	....	....	....	....	....	....	....	....	....	....	....	....	....	....	....	....	....
	Atlantic City	ECHL	41	23	30	53	90	....	....	....	....	....	....	....	....	....	....	....	....	....	....	....	....	....	....
	Rochester	AHL	25	3	4	7	70	....	....	....	....	....	....	....	....	....	2	0	1	1	0	....	....	....	....
2002-03	Syracuse Crunch	AHL	16	2	3	5	6	....	....	....	....	....	....	....	....	....	....	....	....	....	....	....	....	....	....
	Atlantic City	ECHL	50	33	38	71	190	....	....	....	....	....	....	....	....	....	17	*13	7	20	27	....	....	....	....
	Worcester IceCats	AHL	6	1	1	2	27	....	....	....	....	....	....	....	....	....	....	....	....	....	....	....	....	....	....
2003-04	Bridgeport	AHL	78	12	19	31	122	....	....	....	....	....	....	....	....	....	3	1	0	1	12	....	....	....	....
2004-05	Bridgeport	AHL	59	11	13	24	212	....	....	....	....	....	....	....	....	....	....	....	....	....	....	....	....	....	....
2005-06	**NY Islanders**	**NHL**	**16**	**0**	**0**	**0**	**52**	**0**	**0**	**0**	**4**	**0.0**	**-2**	**55**	**63.6**	**4:44**	....	....	....	....	....	....	....	....	....
	Bridgeport	AHL	21	5	5	10	60	....	....	....	....	....	....	....	....	....	....	....	....	....	....	....	....	....	....
	NHL Totals		**16**	**0**	**0**	**0**	**52**	**0**	**0**	**0**	**4**	**0.0**		**55**	**63.6**	**4:44**	....	....	....	....	....	....	....	....	....

Signed as a free agent by **NY Islanders**, June 10, 2004.

COLLINS, Rob (KAW-lihns, RAWB)

Center. Shoots right. 5'10", 174 lbs. Born, Kitchener, Ont., March 15, 1978.

Season	Club	League	GP	G	A	Pts	PIM	PP	SH	GW	S	%	+/-	TF	F%	Min	GP	G	A	Pts	PIM	PP	SH	GW	Min
1998-99	Ferris State	CCHA	36	3	9	12	14	....	....	....	....	....	....	....	....	....	....	....	....	....	....	....	....	....	....
99-2000	Ferris State	CCHA	38	11	20	31	39	....	....	....	....	....	....	....	....	....	....	....	....	....	....	....	....	....	....
2000-01	Ferris State	CCHA	35	15	17	32	23	....	....	....	....	....	....	....	....	....	....	....	....	....	....	....	....	....	....
2001-02	Ferris State	CCHA	36	15	33	48	30	....	....	....	....	....	....	....	....	....	....	....	....	....	....	....	....	....	....
	Grand Rapids	AHL	5	0	2	2	0	....	....	....	....	....	....	....	....	....	....	....	....	....	....	....	....	....	....
2002-03	Grand Rapids	AHL	73	11	20	31	16	....	....	....	....	....	....	....	....	....	15	3	8	11	10	....	....	....	....

Season	Club	League	GP	G	A	Pts	PIM	PP	SH	GW	S	%	+/-	TF	F%	Min	GP	G	A	Pts	PIM	PP	SH	GW	Min
										Regular Season										Playoffs					
2003-04	Bridgeport	AHL	75	9	23	32	42	....	....	....	....	....	....	....	....	....	7	3	5	8	10	....	....	....	....
2004-05	Bridgeport	AHL	78	23	39	62	67	....	....	....	....	....	....	....	....	....	....	....	....	....	....	....	....	....	....
2005-06	NY Islanders	NHL	8	1	1	2	0	1	0	0	8	12.5	1	2	0.0	6:27	....	....	....	....	....	....	....	....	....
	Bridgeport	AHL	67	21	48	69	54	....	....	....	....	....	....	....	....	....	7	4	2	6	10	....	....	....	....
	NHL Totals		8	1	1	2	0	1	0	0	8	12.5		2	0.0	6:27	....	....	....	....	....	....	....	....	....

CCHA First All-Star Team (2002) • NCAA West Second All-American Team (2002)
Signed as a free agent by **NY Islanders**, July 22, 2002. Signed as a free agent with **Dusseldorf** (Germany), July 12, 2006.

COLLITON, Jeremy
(KAW-lih-tuhn, JAIR-eh-mee)   **NYI**

Center. Shoots right. 6'2", 195 lbs.   Born, Blackie, Alta., January 13, 1985. NY Islanders' 4th choice, 58th overall, in 2003 Entry Draft.

Season	Club	League	GP	G	A	Pts	PIM	PP	SH	GW	S	%	+/-	TF	F%	Min	GP	G	A	Pts	PIM	PP	SH	GW	Min
99-2000	Airdrie Express	AMHL	33	16	25	41	28																		
2000-01	Crowsnest Pass	AJHL	63	18	30	48	98																		
2001-02	Prince Albert	WHL	68	11	21	32	53																		
2002-03	Prince Albert	WHL	58	20	28	48	76																		
2003-04	Prince Albert	WHL	62	24	26	50	73										6	5	5	10	8				
2004-05	Prince Albert	WHL	41	16	30	46	25										17	3	4	7	21				
2005-06	**NY Islanders**	NHL	19	1	1	2	6	0	0	0	9	11.1	2	76	40.8	6:18	....	....	....	....	....				
	Bridgeport	AHL	66	20	32	52	44										6	0	1	1	2				
	NHL Totals		19	1	1	2	6	0	0	0	9	11.1		76	40.8	6:18									

COMMODORE, Mike
(KAWM-uh-dohr, MIGHK)   **CAR.**

Defense. Shoots right. 6'4", 230 lbs.   Born, Fort Saskatchewan, Alta., November 7, 1979. New Jersey's 2nd choice, 42nd overall, in 1999 Entry Draft.

Season	Club	League	GP	G	A	Pts	PIM	PP	SH	GW	S	%	+/-	TF	F%	Min	GP	G	A	Pts	PIM	PP	SH	GW	Min
1996-97	Ft. Saskatchewan	AJHL	51	3	8	11	244																		
1997-98	North Dakota	WCHA	29	0	5	5	74																		
1998-99	North Dakota	WCHA	39	5	8	13	154																		
99-2000	North Dakota	WCHA	38	5	7	12	*154																		
2000-01	**New Jersey**	NHL	20	1	4	5	14	0	0	0	11	9.1	5	0	0.0	12:46	....	....	....	....	....				
	Albany River Rats	AHL	41	2	5	7	59																		
2001-02	**New Jersey**	NHL	37	0	1	1	30	0	0	0	22	0.0	−12	0	0.0	12:37	....	....	....	....	....				
	Albany River Rats	AHL	14	0	3	3	31																		
2002-03	Cincinnati	AHL	61	2	9	11	210																		
	Calgary	NHL	6	0	1	1	19	0	0	0	5	0.0	2	0	0.0	11:35	....	....	....	....	....				
	Saint John Flames	AHL	7	0	3	3	18																		
2003-04	**Calgary**	NHL	12	0	0	0	25	0	0	0	10	0.0	−4	0	0.0	15:17	20	0	2	2	19	0	0	0	11:34
	Lowell	AHL	37	5	11	16	75										11	1	2	3	18				
2004-05	Lowell	AHL	73	6	29	35	175																		
2005-06♦	**Carolina**	NHL	72	3	10	13	138	0	0	2	72	4.2	12	1	0.0	15:30	25	2	2	4	33	0	1	0	19:27
	NHL Totals		147	4	16	20	226	0	0	2	120	3.3		1	0.0	14:14	45	2	4	6	52	0	1	0	15:57

NCAA Championship All-Tournament Team (2000)
Traded to **Anaheim** by **New Jersey** with Petr Sykora, Jean-Francois Damphousse and Igor Pohanka for Jeff Friesen, Oleg Tverdovsky and Maxim Balmochnykh, July 6, 2002. Traded to **Calgary** by **Anaheim** with Jean-Francois Damphousse for Rob Niedermayer, March 11, 2003. Traded to **Carolina** by **Calgary** for Atlanta's 3rd round choice (previously acquired - Calgary selected Gord Baldwin) in 2005 Entry Draft, July 29, 2005.

COMRIE, Mike
(KAWM-ree, MIGHK)   **PHX.**

Center. Shoots left. 5'10", 185 lbs.   Born, Edmonton, Alta., September 11, 1980. Edmonton's 5th choice, 91st overall, in 1999 Entry Draft.

Season	Club	League	GP	G	A	Pts	PIM	PP	SH	GW	S	%	+/-	TF	F%	Min	GP	G	A	Pts	PIM	PP	SH	GW	Min
1995-96	Edmonton SSAC	AMHL	33	51	52	103	....																		
1996-97	St. Albert Saints	AJHL	63	37	41	78	44																		
1997-98	St. Albert Saints	AJHL	58	*60	*78	*138	134										19	*24	*24	*48	51				
1998-99	U. of Michigan	CCHA	42	19	25	44	38																		
99-2000	U. of Michigan	CCHA	40	24	35	59	95																		
2000-01	Kootenay Ice	WHL	37	39	40	79	79																		
	Edmonton	NHL	41	8	14	22	14	3	0	1	62	12.9	6	372	43.3	11:23	6	1	2	3	0	1	0	1	15:00
2001-02	**Edmonton**	NHL	82	33	27	60	45	8	0	5	170	19.4	16	1198	47.3	17:32	....	....	....	....	....				
2002-03	**Edmonton**	NHL	69	20	31	51	90	8	0	6	170	11.8	−18	1069	47.1	17:51	6	1	0	1	10	0	0	0	13:07
2003-04	**Philadelphia**	NHL	21	4	5	9	12	0	0	1	36	11.1	2	165	50.9	12:51	....	....	....	....	....				
	Phoenix	NHL	28	8	7	15	16	1	1	1	65	12.3	−8	304	50.7	17:50	....	....	....	....	....				
2004-05	Farjestad	Sweden	10	1	6	7	10																		
2005-06	**Phoenix**	NHL	80	30	30	60	55	10	0	4	190	15.8	2	781	52.8	16:01	....	....	....	....	....				
	NHL Totals		321	103	114	217	232	30	1	18	693	14.9		3889	48.3	16:10	12	2	2	4	10	1	0	1	14:03

CCHA All-Rookie Team (1999) • CCHA First All-Star Team (1999) • CCHA Rookie of the Year (1999) • CCHA First All-Star Team (2000) • NCAA West Second All-American Team (2000)
• Left **University of Michigan** (CCHA) and signed as a free agent by **Kootenay** (WHL), August 23, 2000. • Left **Kootenay** (WHL) and signed with **Edmonton**, December 30, 2000. Traded to **Philadelphia** by **Edmonton** for Jeff Woywitka, Philadelphia's 1st round choice (Rob Schremp) in 2004 Entry Draft and Philadelphia's 3rd round choice (Danny Syvret) in 2005 Entry Draft, December 16, 2003. Traded to **Phoenix** by **Philadelphia** for Sean Burke, Branko Radivojevic and Ben Eager, February 9, 2004. Signed as a free agent by **Farjestad** (Sweden), October 30, 2004.

CONNOLLY, Tim
(KAHN-noh-lee, TIHM)   **BUF.**

Center. Shoots right. 6'1", 190 lbs.   Born, Syracuse, NY, May 7, 1981. NY Islanders' 1st choice, 5th overall, in 1999 Entry Draft.

Season	Club	League	GP	G	A	Pts	PIM	PP	SH	GW	S	%	+/-	TF	F%	Min	GP	G	A	Pts	PIM	PP	SH	GW	Min
1996-97	Syracuse	MTJHL	50	42	62	104	34	....	....	....	....	....	....												
1997-98	Erie Otters	OHL	59	30	32	62	32	....	....	....	....	....	....				7	1	6	7	6				
1998-99	Erie Otters	OHL	46	34	34	68	50	....	....	....	....	....	....												
1999-2000	**NY Islanders**	NHL	81	14	20	34	44	2	1	1	114	12.3	−25	786	36.3	16:18	....	....	....	....	....				
2000-01	**NY Islanders**	NHL	82	10	31	41	42	5	0	0	171	5.8	−14	989	41.7	20:02	....	....	....	....	....				
2001-02	**Buffalo**	NHL	82	10	35	45	34	3	0	3	126	7.9	4	1074	39.6	16:58	....	....	....	....	....				
2002-03	**Buffalo**	NHL	80	12	13	25	32	6	0	2	159	7.5	−28	845	42.8	16:00	....	....	....	....	....				
2003-04	**Buffalo**	NHL				DID NOT PLAY – INJURED																			
2004-05	Langnau	Swiss	16	7	3	10	14																		
2005-06	**Buffalo**	NHL	63	16	39	55	28	7	0	3	99	16.2	5	844	42.5	18:00	8	5	6	11	0	1	1	1	17:29
	NHL Totals		388	62	138	200	180	23	1	9	669	9.3		4538	40.6	17:27	8	5	6	11	0	1	1	1	17:29

Traded to **Buffalo** by **NY Islanders** with Taylor Pyatt for Michael Peca, June 24, 2001. • Missed entire 2003-04 season recovering from head injury suffered in pre-season game vs. Chicago, October 2, 2003. Signed as a free agent by **Langnau** (Swiss), October 10, 2004.

CONROY, Craig
(KAWN-roi, KRAYG)   **L.A.**

Center. Shoots right. 6'2", 197 lbs.   Born, Potsdam, NY, September 4, 1971. Montreal's 7th choice, 123rd overall, in 1990 Entry Draft.

Season	Club	League	GP	G	A	Pts	PIM	PP	SH	GW	S	%	+/-	TF	F%	Min	GP	G	A	Pts	PIM	PP	SH	GW	Min
1989-90	Northwood	High-NY	31	33	43	76	....																		
1990-91	Clarkson Knights	ECAC	40	8	21	29	24																		
1991-92	Clarkson Knights	ECAC	31	19	17	36	36																		
1992-93	Clarkson Knights	ECAC	35	10	23	33	26																		
1993-94	Clarkson Knights	ECAC	34	26	*40	*66	46																		
1994-95	Fredericton	AHL	55	26	18	44	29										11	7	3	10	6				
	Montreal	NHL	6	1	0	1	0	0	0	0	4	25.0	−1				....	....	....	....	....				
1995-96	**Montreal**	NHL	7	0	0	0	2	0	0	0	1	0.0	−4				....	....	....	....	....				
	Fredericton	AHL	67	31	38	69	65										10	5	7	12	6				
1996-97	Fredericton	AHL	9	10	6	16	10																		
	St. Louis	NHL	61	6	11	17	43	0	0	1	74	8.1	0				6	0	0	0	8	0	0	0	
	Worcester IceCats	AHL	5	5	6	11	2																		
1997-98	**St. Louis**	NHL	81	14	29	43	46	0	3	1	118	11.9	20				10	1	2	3	8	0	1	0	
1998-99	**St. Louis**	NHL	69	14	25	39	38	0	1	1	134	10.4	14	1190	54.6	16:39	13	2	1	3	6	0	0	0	15:09
99-2000	**St. Louis**	NHL	79	12	15	27	36	1	2	3	98	12.2	5	1339	53.6	14:48	7	0	2	2	0	0	0	0	13:13
2000-01	**St. Louis**	NHL	69	11	14	25	46	0	1	2	101	10.9	2	729	55.1	14:01	....	....	....	....	....				
	Calgary	NHL	14	3	4	7	14	0	1	0	32	9.4	0	264	52.7	18:08	....	....	....	....	....				
2001-02	**Calgary**	NHL	81	27	48	75	32	7	2	4	146	18.5	14	1654	54.3	20:56	....	....	....	....	....				
2002-03	**Calgary**	NHL	79	22	37	59	36	5	2	3	143	15.4	−4	1579	57.0	19:47	....	....	....	....	....				
2003-04	**Calgary**	NHL	63	8	39	47	44	2	0	0	112	7.1	13	1402	53.9	19:13	26	6	11	17	12	2	0	1	20:23

			Regular Season														Playoffs								
Season	Club	League	GP	G	A	Pts	PIM	PP	SH	GW	S	%	+/-	TF	F%	Min	GP	G	A	Pts	PIM	PP	SH	GW	Min
2004-05			DID NOT PLAY																						
2005-06	**Los Angeles**	**NHL**	**78**	**22**	**44**	**66**	**78**	**5**	**3**	**3**	**154**	**14.3**	**13**	**1429**	**51.2**	**19:13**	....	....	....	....	....	....	....	....	....
	United States	Olympics	6	1	4	5	2	....	....	....	....	....	....	....	....	....	....	....	....	....	....	....	....	....	....
	NHL Totals		**687**	**140**	**266**	**406**	**415**	**20**	**15**	**17**	**1117**	**12.5**		**9586**	**54.2**	**17:52**	**62**	**9**	**16**	**25**	**36**	**2**	**0**	**2**	**17:48**

ECAC First All-Star Team (1994) • NCAA East First All-American Team (1994) • NCAA Final Four All-Tournament Team (1994)

Traded to **St. Louis** by **Montreal** with Pierre Turgeon and Rory Fitzpatrick for Murray Baron, Shayne Corson and St. Louis' 5th round choice (Gennady Razin) in 1997 Entry Draft, October 29, 1996. Traded to **Calgary** by **St. Louis** with St. Louis' 7th round choice (David Moss) in 2001 Entry Draft for Cory Stillman, March 13, 2001. Signed as a free agent by **Los Angeles**, July 6, 2004.

COOKE, Matt

(KUK, MAT) **VAN.**

Center. Shoots left. 6', 205 lbs. Born, Belleville, Ont., September 7, 1978. Vancouver's 8th choice, 144th overall, in 1997 Entry Draft.

Season	Club	League	GP	G	A	Pts	PIM	PP	SH	GW	S	%	+/-	TF	F%	Min	GP	G	A	Pts	PIM	PP	SH	GW	Min
1994-95	Wellington Dukes	MTJHL	46	9	23	32	62	....	....	....	....	....	....	....	....	....	....	....	....	....	....	....	....	....	....
1995-96	Windsor Spitfires	OHL	61	8	11	19	102	....	....	....	....	....	....	....	....	....	7	1	3	4	6	....	....	....	....
1996-97	Windsor Spitfires	OHL	65	45	50	95	146	....	....	....	....	....	....	....	....	....	5	5	5	10	10	....	....	....	....
1997-98	Windsor Spitfires	OHL	23	14	19	33	50	....	....	....	....	....	....	....	....	....	....	....	....	....	....	....	....	....	....
	Kingston	OHL	25	8	13	21	49	....	....	....	....	....	....	....	....	....	12	8	8	16	20	....	....	....	....
1998-99	**Vancouver**	**NHL**	**30**	**0**	**2**	**2**	**27**	**0**	**0**	**0**	**22**	**0.0**	**–12**	**189**	**40.2**	**8:07**	....	....	....	....	....	....	....	....	....
	Syracuse Crunch	AHL	37	15	18	33	119	....	....	....	....	....	....	....	....	....	....	....	....	....	....	....	....	....	....
99-2000	**Vancouver**	**NHL**	**51**	**5**	**7**	**12**	**39**	**0**	**1**	**1**	**58**	**8.6**	**3**	**71**	**39.4**	**11:48**	....	....	....	....	....	....	....	....	....
	Syracuse Crunch	AHL	18	5	8	13	27	....	....	....	....	....	....	....	....	....	....	....	....	....	....	....	....	....	....
2000-01	**Vancouver**	**NHL**	**81**	**14**	**13**	**27**	**94**	**0**	**2**	**0**	**121**	**11.6**	**5**	**321**	**43.0**	**14:35**	**4**	**0**	**0**	**0**	**4**	**0**	**0**	**0**	**12:04**
2001-02	**Vancouver**	**NHL**	**82**	**13**	**20**	**33**	**111**	**1**	**0**	**2**	**103**	**12.6**	**4**	**28**	**32.1**	**14:03**	**6**	**3**	**2**	**5**	**0**	**1**	**0**	**0**	**15:09**
2002-03	**Vancouver**	**NHL**	**82**	**15**	**27**	**42**	**82**	**1**	**4**	**0**	**118**	**12.7**	**21**	**31**	**35.5**	**13:24**	**14**	**2**	**1**	**3**	**12**	**0**	**0**	**0**	**14:06**
2003-04	**Vancouver**	**NHL**	**53**	**11**	**12**	**23**	**73**	**1**	**1**	**4**	**79**	**13.9**	**5**	**34**	**52.9**	**14:06**	**7**	**3**	**1**	**4**	**12**	**0**	**0**	**1**	**18:23**
2004-05			DID NOT PLAY																						
2005-06	**Vancouver**	**NHL**	**45**	**8**	**10**	**18**	**71**	**0**	**0**	**2**	**67**	**11.9**	**–8**	**25**	**24.0**	**13:57**	....	....	....	....	....	....	....	....	....
	NHL Totals		**424**	**66**	**91**	**157**	**497**	**3**	**8**	**9**	**568**	**11.6**		**699**	**40.9**	**13:20**	**31**	**8**	**4**	**12**	**28**	**1**	**0**	**1**	**15:01**

CORAZZINI, Carl

(koh-ra-ZEE-nee, KAHRL) **CHI.**

Center. Shoots right. 5'10", 182 lbs. Born, Framingham, MA, April 21, 1979.

Season	Club	League	GP	G	A	Pts	PIM	PP	SH	GW	S	%	+/-	TF	F%	Min	GP	G	A	Pts	PIM	PP	SH	GW	Min
1996-97	St. Sebastian's	High-MA	25	29	31	60	....	....	....	....	....	....	....	....	....	....	....	....	....	....	....	....	....	....	....
1997-98	Boston University	H-East	36	9	6	15	4	....	....	....	....	....	....	....	....	....	....	....	....	....	....	....	....	....	....
1998-99	Boston University	H-East	37	15	9	24	12	....	....	....	....	....	....	....	....	....	....	....	....	....	....	....	....	....	....
99-2000	Boston University	H-East	42	22	20	42	44	....	....	....	....	....	....	....	....	....	....	....	....	....	....	....	....	....	....
2000-01	Boston University	H-East	35	16	20	36	48	....	....	....	....	....	....	....	....	....	....	....	....	....	....	....	....	....	....
2001-02	Providence Bruins	AHL	61	7	8	15	10	....	....	....	....	....	....	....	....	....	....	....	....	....	....	....	....	....	....
2002-03	Providence Bruins	AHL	33	7	6	13	4	....	....	....	....	....	....	....	....	....	4	0	0	0	0	....	....	....	....
	Atlantic City	ECHL	27	13	8	21	14	....	....	....	....	....	....	....	....	....	....	....	....	....	....	....	....	....	....
2003-04	**Boston**	**NHL**	**12**	**2**	**0**	**2**	**0**	**0**	**1**	**0**	**16**	**12.5**	**2**	**6**	**33.3**	**10:41**	....	....	....	....	....	....	....	....	....
	Providence Bruins	AHL	62	16	9	25	6	....	....	....	....	....	....	....	....	....	2	1	0	1	2	....	....	....	....
2004-05	Providence Bruins	AHL	8	0	0	0	0	....	....	....	....	....	....	....	....	....	....	....	....	....	....	....	....	....	....
	Hershey Bears	AHL	52	10	13	23	6	....	....	....	....	....	....	....	....	....	....	....	....	....	....	....	....	....	....
2005-06	Norfolk Admirals	AHL	75	26	29	55	16	....	....	....	....	....	....	....	....	....	4	2	2	4	0	....	....	....	....
	NHL Totals		**12**	**2**	**0**	**2**	**0**	**0**	**1**	**0**	**16**	**12.5**		**6**	**33.3**	**10:41**	....	....	....	....	....	....	....	....	....

Hockey East All-Rookie Team (1998) • Hockey East First All-Star Team (2001) • NCAA East Second All-American Team (2001)

Signed as a free agent by **Boston**, August 8, 2001. Signed as a free agent by **Providence** (AHL), October 1. 2004. Traded to **Hershey** (AHL) by **Providence** (AHL) for Darrel Scoville, November 15, 2004. Signed as a free agent by **Norfolk** (AHL), October 18, 2005. Signed as a free agent by **Chicago**, July 17, 2006.

CORSO, Daniel

(KOHR-soh, DAN-yehl) **PHI.**

Center. Shoots left. 5'10", 187 lbs. Born, Montreal, Que., April 3, 1978. St. Louis' 6th choice, 169th overall, in 1996 Entry Draft.

Season	Club	League	GP	G	A	Pts	PIM	PP	SH	GW	S	%	+/-	TF	F%	Min	GP	G	A	Pts	PIM	PP	SH	GW	Min
1993-94	Magog	QAAA	36	17	22	39	....	....	....	....	....	....	....	....	....	....	12	10	12	22	....	....	....	....	....
1994-95	Victoriaville Tigres	QMJHL	65	27	26	53	6	....	....	....	....	....	....	....	....	....	4	2	5	7	2	....	....	....	....
1995-96	Victoriaville Tigres	QMJHL	65	49	65	114	77	....	....	....	....	....	....	....	....	....	12	6	7	13	4	....	....	....	....
1996-97	Victoriaville Tigres	QMJHL	54	51	68	119	50	....	....	....	....	....	....	....	....	....	....	....	....	....	....	....	....	....	....
1997-98	Victoriaville Tigres	QMJHL	35	24	51	75	20	....	....	....	....	....	....	....	....	....	3	1	1	2	2	....	....	....	....
1998-99	Worcester IceCats	AHL	63	14	14	28	26	....	....	....	....	....	....	....	....	....	....	....	....	....	....	....	....	....	....
99-2000	Worcester IceCats	AHL	71	21	34	55	19	....	....	....	....	....	....	....	....	....	9	2	3	5	10	....	....	....	....
2000-01	**St. Louis**	**NHL**	**28**	**10**	**3**	**13**	**14**	**5**	**0**	**4**	**42**	**23.8**	**0**	**296**	**56.1**	**13:56**	**12**	**0**	**1**	**1**	**0**	**0**	**0**	**0**	**8:52**
	Worcester IceCats	AHL	52	19	37	56	47	....	....	....	....	....	....	....	....	....	....	....	....	....	....	....	....	....	....
2001-02	**St. Louis**	**NHL**	**41**	**4**	**7**	**11**	**6**	**1**	**0**	**2**	**25**	**16.0**	**3**	**423**	**54.9**	**11:13**	**2**	**0**	**0**	**0**	**0**	**0**	**0**	**0**	**8:51**
2002-03	**St. Louis**	**NHL**	**1**	**0**	**0**	**0**	**0**	**0**	**0**	**0**	**0**	**0.0**	**–1**	**8**	**50.0**	**7:44**	....	....	....	....	....	....	....	....	....
	Worcester IceCats	AHL	1	0	0	0	0	....	....	....	....	....	....	....	....	....	....	....	....	....	....	....	....	....	....
2003-04	Binghamton	AHL	32	7	11	18	16	....	....	....	....	....	....	....	....	....	....	....	....	....	....	....	....	....	....
	Atlanta	**NHL**	**7**	**0**	**1**	**1**	**0**	**0**	**0**	**0**	**2**	**0.0**	**–2**	**105**	**47.6**	**12:59**	....	....	....	....	....	....	....	....	....
	Chicago Wolves	AHL	29	8	18	26	15	....	....	....	....	....	....	....	....	....	10	1	5	6	0	....	....	....	....
2004-05	Kassel Huskies	Germany	45	8	30	38	32	....	....	....	....	....	....	....	....	....	7	1	5	6	20	....	....	....	....
2005-06	Frankfurt Lions	Germany	29	11	17	28	57	....	....	....	....	....	....	....	....	....	....	....	....	....	....	....	....	....	....
	NHL Totals		**77**	**14**	**11**	**25**	**20**	**6**	**0**	**6**	**69**	**20.3**		**832**	**54.3**	**12:19**	**14**	**0**	**1**	**1**	**0**	**0**	**0**	**0**	**8:52**

QMJHL All-Rookie Team (1995) • QMJHL First All-Star Team (1997) • QMJHL MVP (1997)

• Spent majority of 2001-02 season on practice roster, October 22, 2001. • Missed majority of 2002-03 season recovering from shoulder injury suffered in game vs. Anaheim, October 10, 2003. Signed as a free agent by **Ottawa**, September 2, 2003. Traded to **Atlanta** by **Ottawa** for Brad Tapper, January 6, 2004. Signed as a free agent by **Kassel** (Germany), August 7, 2004. Signed as a free agent by **Frankfurt** (Germany), June 9, 2005. Signed as a free agent by **Philadelphia**, July 13, 2006.

CORVO, Joe

(KOHR-voh, JOH-sehf) **OTT.**

Defense. Shoots right. 6'1", 205 lbs. Born, Oak Park, IL, June 20, 1977. Los Angeles' 4th choice, 83rd overall, in 1997 Entry Draft.

Season	Club	League	GP	G	A	Pts	PIM	PP	SH	GW	S	%	+/-	TF	F%	Min	GP	G	A	Pts	PIM	PP	SH	GW	Min
1995-96	Western Mich.	CCHA	41	5	25	30	38	....	....	....	....	....	....	....	....	....	....	....	....	....	....	....	....	....	....
1996-97	Western Mich.	CCHA	32	12	21	33	85	....	....	....	....	....	....	....	....	....	....	....	....	....	....	....	....	....	....
1997-98	Western Mich.	CCHA	32	5	12	17	93	....	....	....	....	....	....	....	....	....	....	....	....	....	....	....	....	....	....
1998-99	Springfield	AHL	50	5	15	20	32	....	....	....	....	....	....	....	....	....	....	....	....	....	....	....	....	....	....
	Hampton Roads	ECHL	5	0	0	0	15	....	....	....	....	....	....	....	....	....	4	0	1	1	0	....	....	....	....
99-2000			DID NOT PLAY																						
2000-01	Lowell	AHL	77	10	23	33	31	....	....	....	....	....	....	....	....	....	4	3	1	4	0	....	....	....	....
2001-02	Manchester	AHL	80	13	37	50	30	....	....	....	....	....	....	....	....	....	5	0	5	5	0	....	....	....	....
2002-03	**Los Angeles**	**NHL**	**50**	**5**	**7**	**12**	**14**	**2**	**0**	**0**	**84**	**6.0**	**2**	**0**	**0.0**	**18:37**	....	....	....	....	....	....	....	....	....
	Manchester	AHL	26	8	18	26	8	....	....	....	....	....	....	....	....	....	3	0	0	0	0	....	....	....	....
2003-04	**Los Angeles**	**NHL**	**72**	**8**	**17**	**25**	**36**	**0**	**0**	**3**	**150**	**5.3**	**7**	**1**	**0.0**	**21:08**	....	....	....	....	....	....	....	....	....
2004-05	Chicago Wolves	AHL	23	7	7	14	14	....	....	....	....	....	....	....	....	....	18	4	5	9	12	....	....	....	....
2005-06	**Los Angeles**	**NHL**	**81**	**14**	**26**	**40**	**38**	**7**	**0**	**3**	**190**	**7.4**	**16**	**0**	**0.0**	**19:59**	....	....	....	....	....	....	....	....	....
	NHL Totals		**203**	**27**	**50**	**77**	**88**	**9**	**0**	**6**	**424**	**6.4**		**1**	**0.0**	**20:04**	....	....	....	....	....	....	....	....	....

CCHA All-Rookie Team (1996) • CCHA Second All-Star Team (1997)

• Missed entire 1999-2000 season after failing to come to contract terms with **Los Angeles.** Signed as a free agent by **Chicago** (AHL), February 24, 2005. Signed as a free agent by **Ottawa**, July 1, 2006.

COTE, Jean-Philippe

(KOH-tay, zhawn-fihl-EEP) **MTL.**

Defense. Shoots left. 6'2", 216 lbs. Born, Charlesbourg, Que., April 22, 1982. Toronto's 10th choice, 265th overall, in 2000 Entry Draft.

Season	Club	League	GP	G	A	Pts	PIM	PP	SH	GW	S	%	+/-	TF	F%	Min	GP	G	A	Pts	PIM	PP	SH	GW	Min
1998-99	Ste-Foy	QAAA	38	10	24	34	34	....	....	....	....	....	....	....	....	....	17	1	8	9	17	....	....	....	....
	Quebec Remparts	QMJHL	8	0	0	0	2	....	....	....	....	....	....	....	....	....	....	....	....	....	....	....	....	....	....
99-2000	Quebec Remparts	QMJHL	34	0	10	10	15	....	....	....	....	....	....	....	....	....	....	....	....	....	....	....	....	....	....
	Cape Breton	QMJHL	28	0	4	4	21	....	....	....	....	....	....	....	....	....	4	0	1	1	4	....	....	....	....
2000-01	Cape Breton	QMJHL	71	6	29	35	90	....	....	....	....	....	....	....	....	....	12	0	0	0	18	....	....	....	....
2001-02	Cape Breton	QMJHL	61	4	20	24	72	....	....	....	....	....	....	....	....	....	16	1	6	7	38	....	....	....	....
2002-03	Cape Breton	QMJHL	16	1	3	4	12	....	....	....	....	....	....	....	....	....	....	....	....	....	....	....	....	....	....
	Acadie-Bathurst	QMJHL	48	8	18	26	87	....	....	....	....	....	....	....	....	....	11	2	3	5	20	....	....	....	....
2003-04	Hamilton	AHL	75	2	7	9	79	....	....	....	....	....	....	....	....	....	10	0	4	4	24	....	....	....	....
2004-05	Hamilton	AHL	51	1	8	9	58	....	....	....	....	....	....	....	....	....	4	0	1	1	0	....	....	....	....

Season	Club	League	GP	G	A	Pts	PIM	PP	SH	GW	S	%	+/-	TF	F%	Min	GP	G	A	Pts	PIM	PP	SH	GW	Min
			Regular Season														Playoffs								
2005-06	**Montreal**	**NHL**	**8**	**0**	**0**	**0**	**4**	**0**	**0**	**0**	**2**	**0.0**	**2**	**0**	**0.0**	**11:02**									
	Hamilton	AHL	61	3	8	11	113																		
	NHL Totals		**8**	**0**	**0**	**0**	**4**	**0**	**0**	**0**	**2**	**0.0**		**0**	**0.0**	**11:02**									

Signed as a free agent by **Montreal**, August 19, 2004.

COWAN, Jeff

(KOW-an, JEHF) **L.A.**

Left wing. Shoots left. 6'2", 210 lbs. Born, Scarborough, Ont., September 27, 1976.

Season	Club	League	GP	G	A	Pts	PIM	PP	SH	GW	S	%	+/-	TF	F%	Min	GP	G	A	Pts	PIM	PP	SH	GW	Min
1992-93	Guelph Platers	OHA-B	45	8	8	16	22																		
1993-94	Guelph Platers	OHA-B	43	30	26	56	96																		
	Guelph Storm	OHL	17	1	0	1	5																		
1994-95	Guelph Storm	OHL	51	10	7	17	14										14	1	1	2	0				
1995-96	Barrie Colts	OHL	66	38	14	52	29										5	1	2	3	6				
1996-97	Saint John Flames	AHL	22	5	5	10	8																		
	Roanoke Express	ECHL	47	21	13	34	42																		
1997-98	Saint John Flames	AHL	69	15	13	28	23										13	4	1	5	14				
1998-99	Saint John Flames	AHL	71	7	12	19	117										4	0	1	1	10				
99-2000	**Calgary**	**NHL**	**13**	**4**	**1**	**5**	**16**	**0**	**0**	**0**	**26**	**15.4**	**2**	**0**	**0.0**	**10:22**									
	Saint John Flames	AHL	47	15	10	25	77																		
2000-01	**Calgary**	**NHL**	**51**	**9**	**4**	**13**	**74**	**2**	**0**	**1**	**48**	**18.8**	**–8**	**5**	**20.0**	**9:06**									
2001-02	**Calgary**	**NHL**	**19**	**1**	**0**	**1**	**40**	**0**	**0**	**1**	**13**	**7.7**	**–3**	**2**	**50.0**	**7:44**									
	Atlanta	**NHL**	**38**	**4**	**1**	**5**	**50**	**0**	**0**	**1**	**51**	**7.8**	**–11**	**5**	**20.0**	**12:27**									
2002-03	**Atlanta**	**NHL**	**66**	**3**	**5**	**8**	**115**	**0**	**0**	**0**	**52**	**5.8**	**–15**	**10**	**30.0**	**8:24**									
2003-04	**Atlanta**	**NHL**	**58**	**9**	**15**	**24**	**68**	**1**	**0**	**1**	**74**	**12.2**	**2**	**9**	**22.2**	**10:04**									
	Los Angeles	**NHL**	**13**	**2**	**1**	**3**	**24**	**1**	**0**	**0**	**15**	**13.3**	**–1**	**2**	**50.0**	**11:43**									
2004-05			DID NOT PLAY																						
2005-06	**Los Angeles**	**NHL**	**46**	**8**	**1**	**9**	**73**	**0**	**0**	**0**	**53**	**15.1**	**–8**	**4**	**25.0**	**8:26**									
	NHL Totals		**304**	**40**	**28**	**68**	**460**	**4**	**0**	**4**	**332**	**12.0**		**37**	**27.0**	**9:32**									

Signed as a free agent by **Calgary**, October 2, 1995. Traded to **Atlanta** by **Calgary** with the rights to Kurtis Foster for Petr Buzek and Atlanta's 6th round choice (Adam Pardy) in 2004 Entry Draft, December 18, 2001. Traded to **Los Angeles** by **Atlanta** for Kip Brennan, March 9, 2004.

CRAIG, Ryan

(KRAIG, RIGH-uhn) **T.B.**

Center. Shoots left. 6'2", 220 lbs. Born, Abbotsford, B.C., January 6, 1982. Tampa Bay's 10th choice, 255th overall, in 2002 Entry Draft.

Season	Club	League	GP	G	A	Pts	PIM	PP	SH	GW	S	%	+/-	TF	F%	Min	GP	G	A	Pts	PIM	PP	SH	GW	Min
1997-98	Abbotsford	BCAHA	80	118	120	238	110																		
	Brandon	WHL	1	0	0	0	0																		
1998-99	Brandon	WHL	54	11	12	23	46										5	0	0	0	4				
99-2000	Brandon	WHL	65	17	19	36	40																		
2000-01	Brandon	WHL	70	38	33	71	49										6	3	0	3	7				
2001-02	Brandon	WHL	52	29	35	64	52										19	11	10	21	13				
2002-03	Brandon	WHL	60	42	32	74	69										17	5	8	13	29				
2003-04	Hershey Bears	AHL	61	4	8	12	24																		
	Pensacola	ECHL	5	3	5	8	0										2	0	1	1	0				
2004-05	Springfield	AHL	80	27	14	41	50																		
2005-06	**Tampa Bay**	**NHL**	**48**	**15**	**13**	**28**	**6**	**6**	**0**	**0**	**81**	**18.5**	**–4**	**95**	**46.3**	**15:21**	**5**	**0**	**0**	**0**	**10**	**0**	**0**	**0**	**12:59**
	Springfield	AHL	28	12	10	22	14																		
	NHL Totals		**48**	**15**	**13**	**28**	**6**	**6**	**0**	**0**	**81**	**18.5**		**95**	**46.3**	**15:21**	**5**	**0**	**0**	**0**	**10**	**0**	**0**	**0**	**12:59**

WHL East First All-Star Team (2003) • Canadian Major Junior Humanitarian Player of the Year (2003)

CROSBY, Sidney

(KRAWZ-bee, SIHD-nee) **PIT.**

Center. Shoots left. 5'11", 193 lbs. Born, Cole Harbour, N.S., August 7, 1987. Pittsburgh's 1st choice, 1st overall, in 2005 Entry Draft.

Season	Club	League	GP	G	A	Pts	PIM	PP	SH	GW	S	%	+/-	TF	F%	Min	GP	G	A	Pts	PIM	PP	SH	GW	Min
2002-03	Shat.-St. Mary's	High-MN	57	72	90	162																			
2003-04	Rimouski Oceanic	QMJHL	59	54	*81	*135	74										9	7	9	16	10				
2004-05	Rimouski Oceanic	QMJHL	62	*66	*102	*168	84										13	*14	*17	*31	16				
2005-06	**Pittsburgh**	**NHL**	**81**	**39**	**63**	**102**	**110**	**16**	**0**	**5**	**278**	**14.0**	**–1**	**1174**	**45.5**	**20:08**									
	NHL Totals		**81**	**39**	**63**	**102**	**110**	**16**	**0**	**5**	**278**	**14.0**		**1174**	**45.5**	**20:08**									

QMJHL All-Rookie Team (2004) • QMJHL First All-Star Team (2004, 2005) • QMJHL Player of the Year (2004, 2005) • Canadian Major Junior First All-Star Team (2004, 2005) • Canadian Major Junior Rookie of the Year (2004) • Canadian Major Junior Player of the Year (2004, 2005) • Memorial Cup All-Star Team (2005) • Ed Chynoweth Trophy (Memorial Cup Tournament Leading Scorer) (2005) • NHL All-Rookie Team (2006)

CROSS, Cory

(KRAWS, KOHR-ee)

Defense. Shoots left. 6'5", 225 lbs. Born, Lloydminster, Alta., January 3, 1971. Tampa Bay's 1st choice, 1st overall, in 1992 Supplemental Draft.

Season	Club	League	GP	G	A	Pts	PIM	PP	SH	GW	S	%	+/-	TF	F%	Min	GP	G	A	Pts	PIM	PP	SH	GW	Min
1990-91	U. of Alberta	CWUAA	20	2	5	7	16																		
1991-92	U. of Alberta	CWUAA	41	4	11	15	82																		
1992-93	U. of Alberta	CWUAA	43	11	28	39	107																		
	Atlanta Knights	IHL	7	0	1	1	2										4	0	0	0	6				
1993-94	**Tampa Bay**	**NHL**	**5**	**0**	**0**	**0**	**6**	**0**	**0**	**0**	**5**	**0.0**	**–3**												
	Atlanta Knights	IHL	70	4	14	18	72										9	1	2	3	14				
1994-95	Atlanta Knights	IHL	41	5	10	15	67																		
	Tampa Bay	**NHL**	**43**	**1**	**5**	**6**	**41**	**0**	**0**	**1**	**35**	**2.9**	**–6**												
1995-96	**Tampa Bay**	**NHL**	**75**	**2**	**14**	**16**	**66**	**0**	**0**	**0**	**57**	**3.5**	**4**				**6**	**0**	**0**	**0**	**22**	**0**	**0**	**0**	
1996-97	**Tampa Bay**	**NHL**	**72**	**4**	**5**	**9**	**95**	**0**	**0**	**2**	**75**	**5.3**	**6**												
1997-98	**Tampa Bay**	**NHL**	**74**	**3**	**6**	**9**	**77**	**0**	**1**	**0**	**72**	**4.2**	**–24**												
1998-99	**Tampa Bay**	**NHL**	**67**	**2**	**16**	**18**	**92**	**0**	**0**	**0**	**96**	**2.1**	**–25**	**0**	**0.0**	**22:38**									
99-2000	**Toronto**	**NHL**	**71**	**4**	**11**	**15**	**64**	**0**	**0**	**1**	**60**	**6.7**	**13**	**0**	**0.0**	**15:59**	**12**	**0**	**2**	**2**	**2**	**0**	**0**	**0**	**15:21**
2000-01	**Toronto**	**NHL**	**41**	**3**	**5**	**8**	**50**	**1**	**0**	**1**	**34**	**8.8**	**7**	**0**	**0.0**	**18:00**	**11**	**2**	**1**	**3**	**10**	**0**	**0**	**1**	**16:05**
2001-02	**Toronto**	**NHL**	**50**	**3**	**9**	**12**	**54**	**0**	**0**	**1**	**39**	**7.7**	**11**	**0**	**0.0**	**15:18**	**12**	**0**	**0**	**0**	**8**	**0**	**0**	**0**	**17:00**
2002-03	**NY Rangers**	**NHL**	**26**	**0**	**4**	**4**	**16**	**0**	**0**	**0**	**18**	**0.0**	**13**	**1**	**0.0**	**17:12**									
	Hartford	AHL	2	0	0	0	2																		
	Edmonton	**NHL**	**11**	**2**	**3**	**5**	**8**	**1**	**0**	**1**	**11**	**18.2**	**3**	**0**	**0.0**	**17:51**	**6**	**0**	**1**	**1**	**20**	**0**	**0**	**0**	**20:37**
2003-04	**Edmonton**	**NHL**	**68**	**7**	**14**	**21**	**56**	**1**	**0**	**1**	**83**	**8.4**	**9**	**0**	**0.0**	**19:14**									
2004-05			DID NOT PLAY																						
2005-06	**Edmonton**	**NHL**	**34**	**2**	**3**	**5**	**38**	**0**	**1**	**0**	**20**	**10.0**	**–5**	**0**	**0.0**	**12:46**									
	Pittsburgh	**NHL**	**6**	**0**	**1**	**1**	**6**	**0**	**0**	**0**	**1**	**0.0**	**–1**	**0**	**0.0**	**13:13**									
	Detroit	**NHL**	**16**	**1**	**1**	**2**	**15**	**0**	**0**	**0**	**11**	**9.1**	**3**	**0**	**0.0**	**12:44**									
	NHL Totals		**659**	**34**	**97**	**131**	**684**	**3**	**2**	**8**	**617**	**5.5**		**1**	**0.0**	**17:30**	**47**	**2**	**4**	**6**	**62**	**0**	**0**	**1**	**16:48**

Traded to **Toronto** by **Tampa Bay** with Tampa Bay's 7th round choice (Ivan Kolozvary) in 2001 Entry Draft for Fredrik Modin, October 1, 1999. Signed as a free agent by **NY Rangers**, December 17, 2002. Traded to **Edmonton** by **NY Rangers** with Radek Dvorak for Anson Carter and Ales Pisa, March 11, 2003. Traded to **Pittsburgh** by **Edmonton** with Jani Rita for Dick Tarnstrom, January 26, 2006. Traded to **Detroit** by **Pittsburgh** for a 4th round choice in 2007 Entry Draft, March 8, 2006. Signed as a free agent by **Hamburg** (Germany), July 25, 2006.

CULLEN, David

(KUH-lehn, DAY-vihd)

Defense. Shoots right. 6'2", 209 lbs. Born, St. Catharines, Ont., December 30, 1976.

Season	Club	League	GP	G	A	Pts	PIM	PP	SH	GW	S	%	+/-	TF	F%	Min	GP	G	A	Pts	PIM	PP	SH	GW	Min
1992-93	Thorold Eagles	OHA-B	34	4	6	10	28																		
1993-94	Thorold	OHA-B	40	10	35	45	26																		
1994-95	Thorold	OHA-B	36	16	30	46	12																		
1995-96	U. of Maine	H-East	34	2	4	6	22																		
1996-97	U. of Maine	H-East	35	5	25	30	8																		
1997-98	U. of Maine	H-East	36	10	27	37	24																		
1998-99	U. of Maine	H-East	41	11	33	44	24																		
99-2000	Springfield	AHL	78	10	21	31	57										2	0	0	0	2				
2000-01	**Phoenix**	**NHL**	**2**	**0**	**0**	**0**	**0**	**0**	**0**	**0**	**0**	**0.0**	**1**	**0**	**0.0**	**12:25**									
	Springfield	AHL	69	13	29	42	40																		
2001-02	**Phoenix**	**NHL**	**14**	**0**	**0**	**0**	**6**	**0**	**0**	**0**	**3**	**0.0**	**–5**	**0**	**0.0**	**12:21**									
	Springfield	AHL	15	1	4	5	4																		
	Minnesota	**NHL**	**3**	**0**	**0**	**0**	**0**	**0**	**0**	**0**	**0**	**0.0**	**–3**	**0**	**0.0**	**14:02**									
	Houston Aeros	AHL	38	5	15	20	4										13	0	6	6	6				
2002-03	Houston Aeros	AHL	72	2	27	29	42										23	3	4	7	14				

Season	Club	League	Regular Season														Playoffs								
			GP	G	A	Pts	PIM	PP	SH	GW	S	%	+/-	TF	F%	Min	GP	G	A	Pts	PIM	PP	SH	GW	Min
2003-04	Rochester	AHL	75	12	35	47	26										16	1	4	5	6				
2004-05	Rochester	AHL	43	2	19	21	25										9	2	3	5	4				
2005-06	Rochester	AHL	68	5	28	33	72																		
	NHL Totals		**19**	**0**	**0**	**0**	**6**	**0**	**0**	**0**	**3**	**0.0**		**0**	**0.0**	**12:37**									

Hockey East First All-Star Team (1999) • NCAA East First All-American Team (1999) • NCAA Championship All-Tournament Team (1999)

Signed as a free agent by **Phoenix**, April 16, 1999. Traded to **Minnesota** by **Phoenix** for Sebastien Bordeleau, January 4, 2002. Signed as a free agent by **Buffalo**, July 28, 2003. Signed as a free agent by **Dusseldorf** (Germany), July 17, 2006.

CULLEN, Mark

(KUH-lehn, MAHRK) **PHI.**

Center. Shoots left. 5'11", 175 lbs. Born, Moorhead, MN, October 28, 1978.

Season	Club	League	GP	G	A	Pts	PIM	PP	SH	GW	S	%	+/-	TF	F%	Min	GP	G	A	Pts	PIM	PP	SH	GW	Min
1996-97	Fargo High	High-ND	30	20	45	65																			
1997-98	Fargo-Moorhead	USHL	30	17	37	54	16										4	3	0	3	25				
1998-99	Colorado College	WCHA	42	8	25	33	22																		
99-2000	Colorado College	WCHA	37	11	20	31	22																		
2000-01	Colorado College	WCHA	31	20	33	53	26																		
2001-02	Colorado College	WCHA	43	14	36	50	14																		
2002-03	Houston Aeros	AHL	72	22	25	47	20										15	3	7	10	4				
2003-04	Houston Aeros	AHL	53	10	28	38	28										2	0	0	0	0				
2004-05	Houston Aeros	AHL	64	10	24	34	26										5	1	1	2	0				
2005-06	**Chicago**	**NHL**	**29**	**7**	**9**	**16**	**2**	**0**	**0**	**0**	**45**	**15.6**	**7**	**281**	**48.8**	**13:15**									
	Norfolk Admirals	AHL	54	29	39	68	48										4	2	2	4	0				
	NHL Totals		**29**	**7**	**9**	**16**	**2**	**0**	**0**	**0**	**45**	**15.6**		**281**	**48.8**	**13:15**									

USHL All-Rookie Team (1998) • USHL Rookie of the Year (1998) • WCHA First All-Star Team (2001, 2002) • NCAA West Second All-American Team (2001) • Fred Hunt Memorial Trophy (Sportsmanship - AHL) (2006)

Signed as a free agent by **Minnesota**, April 8, 2002. Signed as a free agent by **Chicago**, August 4, 2005. Signed as a free agent by **Philadelphia**, July 5, 2006.

CULLEN, Matt

(KUH-lehn, MAT) **NYR**

Center. Shoots left. 6'1", 205 lbs. Born, Virginia, MN, November 2, 1976. Anaheim's 2nd choice, 35th overall, in 1996 Entry Draft.

Season	Club	League	GP	G	A	Pts	PIM	PP	SH	GW	S	%	+/-	TF	F%	Min	GP	G	A	Pts	PIM	PP	SH	GW	Min
1994-95	Moorhead Spuds	High-MN	28	47	42	89	78																		
1995-96	St. Cloud State	WCHA	39	12	29	41	28																		
1996-97	St. Cloud State	WCHA	36	15	30	45	70																		
	Baltimore Bandits	AHL	6	3	3	6	7										3	0	2	2	0				
1997-98	**Anaheim**	**NHL**	**61**	**6**	**21**	**27**	**23**	**2**	**0**	**0**	**75**	**8.0**	**–4**												
	Cincinnati	AHL	18	15	12	27	2																		
1998-99	**Anaheim**	**NHL**	**75**	**11**	**14**	**25**	**47**	**5**	**1**	**1**	**112**	**9.8**	**–12**	**1047**	**47.7**	**15:31**	**4**	**0**	**0**	**0**	**0**	**0**	**0**	**0**	**15:30**
	Cincinnati	AHL	3	1	2	3	8																		
99-2000	**Anaheim**	**NHL**	**80**	**13**	**26**	**39**	**24**	**1**	**0**	**1**	**137**	**9.5**	**5**	**1247**	**44.6**	**16:54**									
2000-01	**Anaheim**	**NHL**	**82**	**10**	**30**	**40**	**38**	**4**	**0**	**1**	**159**	**6.3**	**–23**	**1478**	**48.0**	**18:15**									
2001-02	**Anaheim**	**NHL**	**79**	**18**	**30**	**48**	**24**	**3**	**1**	**4**	**164**	**11.0**	**–1**	**1283**	**51.4**	**17:01**									
2002-03	**Anaheim**	**NHL**	**50**	**7**	**14**	**21**	**12**	**1**	**0**	**1**	**77**	**9.1**	**–4**	**271**	**50.6**	**14:18**									
	Florida	**NHL**	**30**	**6**	**6**	**12**	**22**	**2**	**1**	**1**	**54**	**11.1**	**–4**	**423**	**47.3**	**14:43**									
2003-04	**Florida**	**NHL**	**56**	**6**	**13**	**19**	**24**	**1**	**0**	**2**	**75**	**8.0**	**–2**	**735**	**50.6**	**14:12**									
2004-05	SG Cortina	Italy	36	*27	33	60	64										18	8	14	22	32				
2005-06 ♦	**Carolina**	**NHL**	**78**	**25**	**24**	**49**	**40**	**8**	**0**	**5**	**214**	**11.7**	**4**	**583**	**52.1**	**16:26**	**25**	**4**	**14**	**18**	**12**	**2**	**0**	**1**	**15:37**
	NHL Totals		**591**	**102**	**178**	**280**	**254**	**27**	**3**	**16**	**1067**	**9.6**		**7067**	**48.6**	**16:13**	**29**	**4**	**14**	**18**	**12**	**2**	**0**	**1**	**15:36**

WCHA Second All-Star Team (1997)

Traded to **Florida** by **Anaheim** with Pavel Trnka and Anaheim's 4th round choice (James Pemberton) in 2003 Entry Draft for Sandis Ozolinsh and Lance Ward, January 30, 2003. Signed as a free agent by **Carolina**, August 5, 2004. Signed as a free agent by **Cortina** (Italy), September 18, 2004. Signed as a free agent by **NY Rangers**, July 1, 2006.

CULLIMORE, Jassen

(KUHL-ih-mohr, JAY-sehn) **CHI.**

Defense. Shoots left. 6'5", 244 lbs. Born, Simcoe, Ont., December 4, 1972. Vancouver's 2nd choice, 29th overall, in 1991 Entry Draft.

Season	Club	League	GP	G	A	Pts	PIM	PP	SH	GW	S	%	+/-	TF	F%	Min	GP	G	A	Pts	PIM	PP	SH	GW	Min
1986-87	Caledonia	OHA-C	18	2	0	2	9																		
1987-88	Simcoe Rams	OHA-C	35	11	14	25	92																		
1988-89	Peterborough	OHA-B	29	11	17	28	88																		
	Peterborough	OHL	20	2	1	3	6																		
1989-90	Peterborough	OHL	59	2	6	8	61										11	0	2	2	8				
1990-91	Peterborough	OHL	62	8	16	24	74										4	1	0	1	7				
1991-92	Peterborough	OHL	54	9	37	46	65										10	3	6	9	8				
1992-93	Hamilton	AHL	56	5	7	12	60																		
1993-94	Hamilton	AHL	71	8	20	28	86										3	0	1	1	2				
1994-95	Syracuse Crunch	AHL	33	2	7	9	66																		
	Vancouver	**NHL**	**34**	**1**	**2**	**3**	**39**	**0**	**0**	**0**	**30**	**3.3**	**–2**				**11**	**0**	**0**	**0**	**12**	**0**	**0**	**0**	
1995-96	**Vancouver**	**NHL**	**27**	**1**	**1**	**2**	**21**	**0**	**0**	**1**	**12**	**8.3**	**4**												
1996-97	**Vancouver**	**NHL**	**3**	**0**	**0**	**0**	**2**	**0**	**0**	**0**	**2**	**0.0**	**–2**												
	Montreal	**NHL**	**49**	**2**	**6**	**8**	**42**	**0**	**1**	**1**	**52**	**3.8**	**4**				**2**	**0**	**0**	**0**	**2**	**0**	**0**	**0**	
1997-98	**Montreal**	**NHL**	**3**	**0**	**0**	**0**	**4**	**0**	**0**	**0**	**1**	**0.0**	**0**												
	Fredericton	AHL	5	1	0	1	8																		
	Tampa Bay	**NHL**	**25**	**1**	**2**	**3**	**22**	**1**	**0**	**0**	**17**	**5.9**	**–4**												
1998-99	**Tampa Bay**	**NHL**	**78**	**5**	**12**	**17**	**81**	**1**	**1**	**1**	**73**	**6.8**	**–22**	**0**	**0.0**	**20:14**									
99-2000	Providence Bruins	AHL	16	5	10	15	31																		
	Tampa Bay	**NHL**	**46**	**1**	**1**	**2**	**66**	**0**	**0**	**0**	**23**	**4.3**	**–12**	**2**	**0.0**	**15:38**									
2000-01	**Tampa Bay**	**NHL**	**74**	**1**	**6**	**7**	**80**	**0**	**0**	**0**	**56**	**1.8**	**–6**	**0**	**0.0**	**19:43**									
2001-02	**Tampa Bay**	**NHL**	**78**	**4**	**9**	**13**	**58**	**0**	**0**	**1**	**84**	**4.8**	**–1**	**0**	**0.0**	**20:07**									
2002-03	**Tampa Bay**	**NHL**	**28**	**1**	**3**	**4**	**31**	**0**	**0**	**0**	**23**	**4.3**	**3**	**0**	**0.0**	**18:25**	**11**	**1**	**1**	**2**	**4**	**0**	**0**	**0**	**22:11**
2003-04 ♦	**Tampa Bay**	**NHL**	**79**	**2**	**5**	**7**	**58**	**0**	**0**	**1**	**78**	**2.6**	**8**	**0**	**0.0**	**19:02**	**11**	**0**	**2**	**2**	**6**	**0**	**0**	**0**	**15:15**
2004-05			DID NOT PLAY																						
2005-06	**Chicago**	**NHL**	**54**	**1**	**6**	**7**	**53**	**1**	**0**	**1**	**23**	**4.3**	**–24**	**0**	**0.0**	**16:58**									
	NHL Totals		**578**	**20**	**53**	**73**	**557**	**3**	**2**	**6**	**474**	**4.2**		**2**	**0.0**	**18:54**	**35**	**1**	**3**	**4**	**24**	**0**	**0**	**0**	**18:43**

OHL Second All-Star Team (1992)

Traded to **Montreal** by **Vancouver** for Donald Brashear, November 13, 1996. Claimed on waivers by **Tampa Bay** from **Montreal**, January 22, 1998. Loaned to **Providence** (AHL) by **Tampa Bay**, October 1, 1999. • Missed majority of 2002-03 season recovering from elbow injury suffered in game vs. Vancouver, November 29, 2002. Signed as a free agent by **Chicago**, July 22, 2004.

CUTTA, Jakub

(KOO-tuh, YA-kuhb) **WSH.**

Defense. Shoots left. 6'3", 210 lbs. Born, Jablonec nad Nisou, Czech., December 29, 1981. Washington's 3rd choice, 61st overall, in 2000 Entry Draft.

Season	Club	League	GP	G	A	Pts	PIM	PP	SH	GW	S	%	+/-	TF	F%	Min	GP	G	A	Pts	PIM	PP	SH	GW	Min
1997-98	Liberec Jr.	CzRep-Jr.	29	3	13	16	70																		
1998-99	Swift Current	WHL	59	3	3	6	63																		
99-2000	Swift Current	WHL	71	2	12	14	114										12	0	2	2	24				
2000-01	**Washington**	**NHL**	**3**	**0**	**0**	**0**	**0**	**0**	**0**	**0**	**1**	**0.0**	**–1**	**0**	**0.0**	**11:33**									
	Swift Current	WHL	47	5	8	13	102										16	1	3	4	32				
2001-02	**Washington**	**NHL**	**2**	**0**	**0**	**0**	**0**	**0**	**0**	**0**	**2**	**0.0**	**–3**	**0**	**0.0**	**16:02**									
	Portland Pirates	AHL	56	1	3	4	69																		
2002-03	Portland Pirates	AHL	66	3	12	15	106										3	0	0	0	2				
2003-04	**Washington**	**NHL**	**3**	**0**	**0**	**0**	**0**	**0**	**0**	**0**	**1**	**0.0**	**–1**	**0**	**0.0**	**13:54**									
	Portland Pirates	AHL	59	1	5	6	58										7	2	0	2	7				
2004-05	Portland Pirates	AHL	63	0	5	5	100																		
2005-06	Hershey Bears	AHL	51	1	2	3	84										21	2	3	5	38				
	NHL Totals		**8**	**0**	**0**	**0**	**0**	**0**	**0**	**0**	**4**	**0.0**		**0**	**0.0**	**13:33**									

CZERKAWSKI, Mariusz

(chehr-KAWV-skee, MAIR-ee-UHZ)

Right wing. Shoots left. 6', 200 lbs. Born, Radomsko, Poland, April 13, 1972. Boston's 5th choice, 106th overall, in 1991 Entry Draft.

			Regular Season														Playoffs								
Season	Club	League	GP	G	A	Pts	PIM	PP	SH	GW	S	%	+/-	TF	F%	Min	GP	G	A	Pts	PIM	PP	SH	GW	Min
1990-91	GKS Tychy	Poland	24	25	15	40	....	....	....	....	....	....	....	....	....	....	....	....	....	....	....	....	....	....	....
1991-92	Djurgarden	Sweden	39	8	5	13	4	....	....	....	....	....	....	....	....	....	3	0	0	0	2	....	....	....	....
	Poland	Olympics	5	0	1	1	4	....	....	....	....	....	....	....	....	....	....	....	....	....	....	....	....	....	....
1992-93	Hammarby	Sweden-2	32	*39	30	*69	74	....	....	....	....	....	....	....	....	....	13	*16	7	*23	34	....	....	....	....
1993-94	Djurgarden	Sweden	39	13	21	34	20	....	....	....	....	....	....	....	....	....	6	3	1	4	2	....	....	....	....
	Boston	**NHL**	**4**	**2**	**1**	**3**	**0**	**1**	**0**	**0**	**11**	**18.2**	**−2**	....	....	....	**13**	**3**	**3**	**6**	**4**	**1**	**0**	**0**	....
1994-95	Kiekko-Espoo	Finland	7	9	3	12	10	....	....	....	....	....	....	....	....	....	....	....	....	....	....	....	....	....	....
	Boston	**NHL**	**47**	**12**	**14**	**26**	**31**	**1**	**0**	**2**	**126**	**9.5**	**4**	....	....	....	**5**	**1**	**0**	**1**	**0**	**0**	**0**	**0**	....
1995-96	**Boston**	**NHL**	**33**	**5**	**6**	**11**	**10**	**1**	**0**	**0**	**63**	**7.9**	**−11**	....	....	....	....	....	....	....	....	....	....	....	....
	Edmonton	**NHL**	**37**	**12**	**17**	**29**	**8**	**2**	**0**	**1**	**79**	**15.2**	**7**	....	....	....	....	....	....	....	....	....	....	....	....
1996-97	**Edmonton**	**NHL**	**76**	**26**	**21**	**47**	**16**	**4**	**0**	**3**	**182**	**14.3**	**0**	....	....	....	**12**	**2**	**1**	**3**	**10**	**0**	**0**	**0**	....
1997-98	**NY Islanders**	**NHL**	**68**	**12**	**13**	**25**	**23**	**2**	**0**	**1**	**136**	**8.8**	**11**	....	....	....	....	....	....	....	....	....	....	....	....
1998-99	**NY Islanders**	**NHL**	**78**	**21**	**17**	**38**	**14**	**4**	**0**	**1**	**205**	**10.2**	**−10**	**2**	**0.0**	**14:18**	....	....	....	....	....	....	....	....	....
99-2000	**NY Islanders**	**NHL**	**79**	**35**	**35**	**70**	**34**	**16**	**0**	**4**	**276**	**12.7**	**−16**	**4**	**25.0**	**17:45**	....	....	....	....	....	....	....	....	....
2000-01	**NY Islanders**	**NHL**	**82**	**30**	**32**	**62**	**48**	**10**	**1**	**0**	**287**	**10.5**	**−24**	**8**	**50.0**	**18:44**	....	....	....	....	....	....	....	....	....
2001-02	**NY Islanders**	**NHL**	**82**	**22**	**29**	**51**	**48**	**6**	**0**	**6**	**169**	**13.0**	**−8**	**10**	**10.0**	**15:58**	**7**	**2**	**2**	**4**	**4**	**1**	**0**	**0**	**12:58**
2002-03	**Montreal**	**NHL**	**43**	**5**	**9**	**14**	**16**	**1**	**0**	**0**	**77**	**6.5**	**−7**	**2**	**0.0**	**13:10**	....	....	....	....	....	....	....	....	....
	Hamilton	AHL	20	8	12	20	12	....	....	....	....	....	....	....	....	....	6	1	3	4	6	....	....	....	....
2003-04	**NY Islanders**	**NHL**	**81**	**25**	**24**	**49**	**16**	**9**	**0**	**2**	**157**	**15.9**	**8**	**6**	**16.7**	**13:02**	**5**	**0**	**1**	**1**	**0**	**0**	**0**	**0**	**10:43**
2004-05	Djurgarden	Sweden	46	15	9	24	20	....	....	....	....	....	....	....	....	....	5	1	0	1	2	....	....	....	....
2005-06	**Toronto**	**NHL**	**19**	**4**	**1**	**5**	**6**	**1**	**0**	**0**	**41**	**9.8**	**−2**	**0**	**0.0**	**13:30**	....	....	....	....	....	....	....	....	....
	Boston	**NHL**	**16**	**4**	**1**	**5**	**4**	**0**	**0**	**0**	**31**	**12.9**	**−4**	**0**	**0.0**	**12:01**	....	....	....	....	....	....	....	....	....
	NHL Totals		**745**	**215**	**220**	**435**	**274**	**58**	**1**	**20**	**1840**	**11.7**		**32**	**21.9**	**15:29**	**42**	**8**	**7**	**15**	**18**	**2**	**0**	**0**	**12:02**

Played in NHL All-Star Game (2000)

Traded to **Edmonton** by **Boston** with Sean Brown and Boston's 1st round choice (Matthieu Descoteaux) in 1996 Entry Draft for Bill Ranford, January 11, 1996. Traded to **NY Islanders** by **Edmonton** for Dan LaCouture, August 25, 1997. Traded to **Montreal** by **NY Islanders** for Arron Asham and Montreal's 5th round choice (Marcus Paulsson) in 2002 Entry Draft, June 22, 2002. Signed as a free agent by **NY Islanders**, July 17, 2003. Signed as a free agent by **Djurgarden** (Sweden), September 9, 2004. Signed as a free agent by **Toronto**, September 10, 2005. Claimed on waivers by **Boston** from **Toronto**, March 8, 2006. Signed as a free agent by **Rapperswil** (Swiss), July 21, 2006.

DAGENAIS, Pierre

(da-ZHUH-nay, PEE-air)

Right wing. Shoots left. 6'4", 217 lbs. Born, Blainville, Que., March 4, 1978. New Jersey's 6th choice, 105th overall, in 1998 Entry Draft.

Season	Club	League	GP	G	A	Pts	PIM	PP	SH	GW	S	%	+/-	TF	F%	Min	GP	G	A	Pts	PIM	PP	SH	GW	Min
1994-95	Laval-Laurentides	QAAA	34	28	14	42	68	....	....	....	....	....	....	....	....	....	13	10	9	19	32	....	....	....	....
1995-96	Moncton Alpines	QMJHL	67	43	25	68	59	....	....	....	....	....	....	....	....	....	....	....	....	....	....	....	....	....	....
1996-97	Moncton Wildcats	QMJHL	6	4	2	6	0	....	....	....	....	....	....	....	....	....	....	....	....	....	....	....	....	....	....
	Laval Titan	QMJHL	37	16	14	30	40	....	....	....	....	....	....	....	....	....	....	....	....	....	....	....	....	....	....
	Rouyn-Noranda	QMJHL	27	21	8	29	22	....	....	....	....	....	....	....	....	....	....	....	....	....	....	....	....	....	....
1997-98	Rouyn-Noranda	QMJHL	60	*66	67	133	50	....	....	....	....	....	....	....	....	....	6	6	2	8	2	....	....	....	....
1998-99	Albany River Rats	AHL	69	17	13	30	37	....	....	....	....	....	....	....	....	....	4	0	0	0	0	....	....	....	....
99-2000	Albany River Rats	AHL	80	35	30	65	47	....	....	....	....	....	....	....	....	....	5	1	0	1	14	....	....	....	....
2000-01	**New Jersey**	**NHL**	**9**	**3**	**2**	**5**	**6**	**1**	**0**	**1**	**20**	**15.0**	**1**	**8**	**37.5**	**12:22**	....	....	....	....	....	....	....	....	....
	Albany River Rats	AHL	69	34	28	62	52	....	....	....	....	....	....	....	....	....	....	....	....	....	....	....	....	....	....
2001-02	**New Jersey**	**NHL**	**16**	**3**	**3**	**6**	**4**	**1**	**0**	**1**	**30**	**10.0**	**−5**	**5**	**40.0**	**10:54**	....	....	....	....	....	....	....	....	....
	Albany River Rats	AHL	6	0	2	2	2	....	....	....	....	....	....	....	....	....	....	....	....	....	....	....	....	....	....
	Florida	**NHL**	**26**	**7**	**1**	**8**	**4**	**2**	**0**	**0**	**47**	**14.9**	**−5**	**4**	**75.0**	**11:04**	....	....	....	....	....	....	....	....	....
	Utah Grizzlies	AHL	4	1	1	2	2	....	....	....	....	....	....	....	....	....	....	....	....	....	....	....	....	....	....
2002-03	**Florida**	**NHL**	**9**	**0**	**0**	**0**	**4**	**0**	**0**	**0**	**5**	**0.0**	**−1**	**0**	**0.0**	**6:01**	....	....	....	....	....	....	....	....	....
	San Antonio	AHL	49	21	14	35	28	....	....	....	....	....	....	....	....	....	3	2	0	2	2	....	....	....	....
2003-04	**Montreal**	**NHL**	**50**	**17**	**10**	**27**	**24**	**4**	**0**	**3**	**149**	**11.4**	**15**	**121**	**42.2**	**13:53**	**8**	**0**	**1**	**1**	**6**	**0**	**0**	**0**	**12:06**
	Hamilton	AHL	20	12	9	21	19	....	....	....	....	....	....	....	....	....	....	....	....	....	....	....	....	....	....
2004-05	HC Ajoie	Swiss-2	7	5	5	10	12	....	....	....	....	....	....	....	....	....	6	7	7	14	6	....	....	....	....
2005-06	**Montreal**	**NHL**	**32**	**5**	**7**	**12**	**16**	**2**	**0**	**1**	**74**	**6.8**	**−5**	**81**	**53.1**	**9:55**	....	....	....	....	....	....	....	....	....
	Hamilton	AHL	38	12	13	25	23	....	....	....	....	....	....	....	....	....	....	....	....	....	....	....	....	....	....
	NHL Totals		**142**	**35**	**23**	**58**	**58**	**10**	**0**	**6**	**325**	**10.8**		**219**	**46.6**	**11:33**	**8**	**0**	**1**	**1**	**6**	**0**	**0**	**0**	**12:06**

• Re-entered NHL Entry Draft. Originally New Jersey's 4th choice, 47th overall, in 1996 Entry Draft.

QMJHL All-Rookie Team (1996) • QMJHL Second All-Star Team (1998) • AHL Second All-Star Team (2001)

Claimed on waivers by **Florida** from **New Jersey**, January 12, 2002. Signed as a free agent by **Montreal**, July 4, 2003. Signed as a free agent by **Ajoie** (Swiss-2), January 10, 2005.

DAIGLE, Alexandre

(DAYG, al-ehx-AHN-druh)

Center. Shoots left. 6', 195 lbs. Born, Montreal, Que., February 7, 1975. Ottawa's 1st choice, 1st overall, in 1993 Entry Draft.

Season	Club	League	GP	G	A	Pts	PIM	PP	SH	GW	S	%	+/-	TF	F%	Min	GP	G	A	Pts	PIM	PP	SH	GW	Min
1990-91	Laval-Laurentides	QAAA	42	*50	*60	*110	98	....	....	....	....	....	....	....	....	....	13	5	9	14	23	....	....	....	....
1991-92	Victoriaville Tigres	QMJHL	66	35	75	110	63	....	....	....	....	....	....	....	....	....	....	....	....	....	....	....	....	....	....
1992-93	Victoriaville Tigres	QMJHL	53	45	92	137	85	....	....	....	....	....	....	....	....	....	6	5	6	11	4	....	....	....	....
1993-94	**Ottawa**	**NHL**	**84**	**20**	**31**	**51**	**40**	**4**	**0**	**2**	**168**	**11.9**	**−45**	....	....	....	....	....	....	....	....	....	....	....	....
1994-95	Victoriaville Tigres	QMJHL	18	14	20	34	16	....	....	....	....	....	....	....	....	....	....	....	....	....	....	....	....	....	....
	Ottawa	**NHL**	**47**	**16**	**21**	**37**	**14**	**4**	**1**	**2**	**105**	**15.2**	**−22**	....	....	....	....	....	....	....	....	....	....	....	....
1995-96	**Ottawa**	**NHL**	**50**	**5**	**12**	**17**	**24**	**1**	**0**	**0**	**77**	**6.5**	**−30**	....	....	....	....	....	....	....	....	....	....	....	....
1996-97	**Ottawa**	**NHL**	**82**	**26**	**25**	**51**	**33**	**4**	**0**	**5**	**203**	**12.8**	**−33**	....	....	....	**7**	**0**	**0**	**0**	**2**	**0**	**0**	**0**	....
1997-98	**Ottawa**	**NHL**	**38**	**7**	**9**	**16**	**8**	**4**	**0**	**2**	**68**	**10.3**	**−7**	....	....	....	....	....	....	....	....	....	....	....	....
	Philadelphia	**NHL**	**37**	**9**	**17**	**26**	**6**	**4**	**0**	**3**	**78**	**11.5**	**−1**	....	....	....	**5**	**0**	**2**	**2**	**0**	**0**	**0**	**0**	....
1998-99	**Philadelphia**	**NHL**	**31**	**3**	**2**	**5**	**2**	**1**	**0**	**1**	**26**	**11.5**	**−1**	**53**	**39.6**	**7:59**	....	....	....	....	....	....	....	....	....
	Tampa Bay	**NHL**	**32**	**6**	**6**	**12**	**2**	**3**	**0**	**0**	**56**	**10.7**	**−12**	**4**	**50.0**	**13:59**	....	....	....	....	....	....	....	....	....
99-2000	**NY Rangers**	**NHL**	**58**	**8**	**18**	**26**	**23**	**1**	**0**	**1**	**52**	**15.4**	**−5**	**339**	**53.1**	**10:59**	....	....	....	....	....	....	....	....	....
	Hartford	AHL	16	6	13	19	4	....	....	....	....	....	....	....	....	....	....	....	....	....	....	....	....	....	....
2000-01			OUT OF HOCKEY – RETIRED																						
2001-02			OUT OF HOCKEY – RETIRED																						
2002-03	**Pittsburgh**	**NHL**	**33**	**4**	**3**	**7**	**8**	**1**	**0**	**0**	**48**	**8.3**	**−10**	**24**	**33.3**	**10:57**									
	Wilkes-Barre	AHL	40	9	29	38	18	....	....	....	....	....	....	....	....	....	4	0	1	1	0	....	....	....	....
2003-04	**Minnesota**	**NHL**	**78**	**20**	**31**	**51**	**14**	**6**	**0**	**3**	**145**	**13.8**	**−4**	**72**	**51.4**	**15:10**	....	....	....	....	....	....	....	....	....
2004-05	Morges	Swiss-2	....	....	....	....	....	....	....	....	....	....	....	....	....	....	2	1	1	2	0	....	....	....	....
2005-06	**Minnesota**	**NHL**	**46**	**5**	**23**	**28**	**12**	**2**	**0**	**1**	**59**	**8.5**	**−6**	**12**	**41.7**	**13:00**	....	....	....	....	....	....	....	....	....
	Manchester	AHL	16	6	8	14	4	....	....	....	....	....	....	....	....	....	7	4	7	11	6	....	....	....	....
	NHL Totals		**616**	**129**	**198**	**327**	**186**	**35**	**1**	**20**	**1085**	**11.9**		**504**	**50.2**	**12:30**	**12**	**0**	**2**	**2**	**2**	**0**	**0**	**0**	....

QMJHL Second All-Star Team (1992) • QMJHL Offensive Rookie of the Year (1992) • Canadian Major Junior Rookie of the Year (1992) • QMJHL First All-Star Team (1993)

Traded to **Philadelphia** by **Ottawa** for Vaclav Prospal, Pat Falloon and Dallas' 2nd round choice (previously acquired, Ottawa selected Chris Bala) in 1998 Entry Draft, January 17, 1998. Traded to **Edmonton** by **Philadelphia** for Andrei Kovalenko, January 29, 1999. Traded to **Tampa Bay** by **Edmonton** for Alexander Selivanov, January 29, 1999. Traded to **NY Rangers** by **Tampa Bay** for cash, October 3, 1999. Signed as a free agent by **Pittsburgh**, August 13, 2002. Signed as a free agent by **Minnesota**, September 30, 2003. Signed as a free agent by **Morges** (Swiss-2), February 5, 2005.

DALEY, Trevor

(DAY-lee, TREH-vuhr) **DAL.**

Defense. Shoots left. 5'9", 197 lbs. Born, Toronto, Ont., October 9, 1983. Dallas' 5th choice, 43rd overall, in 2002 Entry Draft.

Season	Club	League	GP	G	A	Pts	PIM	PP	SH	GW	S	%	+/-	TF	F%	Min	GP	G	A	Pts	PIM	PP	SH	GW	Min
1998-99	Vaughan Vipers	OPJHL	44	10	36	46	79	....	....	....	....	....	....	....	....	....	....	....	....	....	....	....	....	....	....
99-2000	Sault Ste. Marie	OHL	54	16	30	46	77	....	....	....	....	....	....	....	....	....	15	3	7	10	12	....	....	....	....
2000-01	Sault Ste. Marie	OHL	58	14	27	41	105	....	....	....	....	....	....	....	....	....	....	....	....	....	....	....	....	....	....
2001-02	Sault Ste. Marie	OHL	47	9	39	48	38	....	....	....	....	....	....	....	....	....	6	2	2	4	4	....	....	....	....
2002-03	Sault Ste. Marie	OHL	57	20	33	53	128	....	....	....	....	....	....	....	....	....	1	0	0	0	2	....	....	....	....
2003-04	**Dallas**	**NHL**	**27**	**1**	**5**	**6**	**14**	**1**	**0**	**0**	**34**	**2.9**	**−6**	**0**	**0.0**	**16:02**	**1**	**0**	**0**	**0**	**0**	**0**	**0**	**0**	**10:21**
	Utah Grizzlies	AHL	40	8	6	14	76	....	....	....	....	....	....	....	....	....	....	....	....	....	....	....	....	....	....
2004-05	Hamilton	AHL	78	7	27	34	109	....	....	....	....	....	....	....	....	....	4	0	1	1	2	....	....	....	....
2005-06	**Dallas**	**NHL**	**81**	**3**	**11**	**14**	**87**	**0**	**0**	**1**	**91**	**3.3**	**−2**	**0**	**0.0**	**18:40**	**3**	**0**	**0**	**0**	**0**	**0**	**0**	**0**	**11:30**
	NHL Totals		**108**	**4**	**16**	**20**	**101**	**1**	**0**	**1**	**125**	**3.2**		**0**	**0.0**	**18:01**	**4**	**0**	**0**	**0**	**0**	**0**	**0**	**0**	**11:13**

DALLMAN, Kevin

(DAL-mahn, KEH-vihn) **L.A.**

Defense. Shoots right. 5'11", 195 lbs. Born, Niagara Falls, Ont., February 26, 1981.

			Regular Season														Playoffs								
Season	Club	League	GP	G	A	Pts	PIM	PP	SH	GW	S	%	+/-	TF	F%	Min	GP	G	A	Pts	PIM	PP	SH	GW	Min
1996-97	Niagara Falls	OHA-B	3	0	1	1	2	....	....	....	....	....	....	....	....	....	....	....	....	....	....	....	....	....	....
1997-98	Niagara Falls	OHA-B	47	13	25	38	42	....	....	....	....	....	....	....	....	....	....	....	....	....	....	....	....	....	....
1998-99	Guelph Storm	OHL	68	8	30	38	52	....	....	....	....	....	....	....	....	....	11	1	4	5	2	....	....	....	....
99-2000	Guelph Storm	OHL	67	13	46	59	38	....	....	....	....	....	....	....	....	....	6	0	2	2	11	....	....	....	....
2000-01	Guelph Storm	OHL	66	25	52	77	88	....	....	....	....	....	....	....	....	....	1	0	0	0	0	....	....	....	....
2001-02	Guelph Storm	OHL	67	23	63	86	68	....	....	....	....	....	....	....	....	....	9	8	8	16	22	....	....	....	....
2002-03	Providence Bruins	AHL	72	2	19	21	53	....	....	....	....	....	....	....	....	....	....	....	....	....	....	....	....	....	....
2003-04	Providence Bruins	AHL	65	6	23	29	44	....	....	....	....	....	....	....	....	....	2	0	0	0	0	....	....	....	....
2004-05	Providence Bruins	AHL	71	8	26	34	48	....	....	....	....	....	....	....	....	....	17	4	6	10	20	....	....	....	....
2005-06	**Boston**	**NHL**	**21**	**0**	**1**	**1**	**8**	**0**	**0**	**0**	**42**	**0.0**	**1**	**0**	**0.0**	**19:24**	....	....	....	....	....	....	....	....	....
	St. Louis	**NHL**	**46**	**4**	**9**	**13**	**21**	**3**	**0**	**0**	**89**	**4.5**	**–15**	**11**	**18.2**	**18:49**	....	....	....	....	....	....	....	....	....
	NHL Totals		**67**	**4**	**10**	**14**	**29**	**3**	**0**	**0**	**131**	**3.1**		**11**	**18.2**	**19:00**	....	....	....	....	....	....	....	....	....

Memorial Cup Tournament All-Star Team (2002)

Signed as a free agent by **Boston**, July 18, 2002. Claimed on waivers by **St. Louis** from **Boston**, December 3, 2005. Signed as a free agent by **Los Angeles**, July 10, 2006.

DANDENAULT, Mathieu

(DAHN-deh-noh, MA-tyew) **MTL.**

Defense. Shoots right. 6'1", 205 lbs. Born, Sherbrooke, Que., February 3, 1976. Detroit's 2nd choice, 49th overall, in 1994 Entry Draft.

Season	Club	League	GP	G	A	Pts	PIM	PP	SH	GW	S	%	+/-	TF	F%	Min	GP	G	A	Pts	PIM	PP	SH	GW	Min
1990-91	Gloucester	OMHA	44	52	50	102	30	....	....	....	....	....	....	....	....	....	....	....	....	....	....	....	....	....	....
1991-92	Vanier Voyageurs	OHA-B	33	27	31	58	20	....	....	....	....	....	....	....	....	....	....	....	....	....	....	....	....	....	....
	Gloucester	CJHL	6	3	4	7	0	....	....	....	....	....	....	....	....	....	....	....	....	....	....	....	....	....	....
1992-93	Gloucester	CJHL	55	11	26	37	64	....	....	....	....	....	....	....	....	....	....	....	....	....	....	....	....	....	....
1993-94	Sherbrooke	QMJHL	67	17	36	53	67	....	....	....	....	....	....	....	....	....	12	4	10	14	12	....	....	....	....
1994-95	Sherbrooke	QMJHL	67	37	70	107	76	....	....	....	....	....	....	....	....	....	7	1	7	8	10	....	....	....	....
1995-96	**Detroit**	**NHL**	**34**	**5**	**7**	**12**	**6**	**1**	**0**	**0**	**32**	**15.6**	**6**	....	....	....	....	....	....	....	....	....	....	....	....
	Adirondack	AHL	4	0	0	0	0	....	....	....	....	....	....	....	....	....	....	....	....	....	....	....	....	....	....
1996-97♦	**Detroit**	**NHL**	**65**	**3**	**9**	**12**	**28**	**0**	**0**	**0**	**81**	**3.7**	**–10**	....	....	....	....	....	....	....	....	....	....	....	....
1997-98♦	**Detroit**	**NHL**	**68**	**5**	**12**	**17**	**43**	**0**	**0**	**0**	**75**	**6.7**	**5**	....	....	....	**3**	**1**	**0**	**1**	**0**	**1**	**0**	**0**	....
1998-99	**Detroit**	**NHL**	**75**	**4**	**10**	**14**	**59**	**0**	**0**	**0**	**94**	**4.3**	**17**	**3**	**0.0**	**15:10**	**10**	**0**	**1**	**1**	**0**	**0**	**0**	**0**	**11:51**
99-2000	**Detroit**	**NHL**	**81**	**6**	**12**	**18**	**20**	**0**	**0**	**0**	**98**	**6.1**	**–12**	**1**	**100.0**	**12:10**	**6**	**0**	**0**	**0**	**2**	**0**	**0**	**0**	**8:31**
2000-01	**Detroit**	**NHL**	**73**	**10**	**15**	**25**	**38**	**2**	**0**	**2**	**95**	**10.5**	**11**	**0**	**0.0**	**16:06**	**6**	**0**	**1**	**1**	**0**	**0**	**0**	**0**	**14:11**
2001-02♦	**Detroit**	**NHL**	**81**	**8**	**12**	**20**	**44**	**2**	**0**	**3**	**97**	**8.2**	**–5**	**1**	**0.0**	**16:43**	**23**	**1**	**2**	**3**	**8**	**0**	**1**	**0**	**13:29**
2002-03	**Detroit**	**NHL**	**74**	**4**	**15**	**19**	**64**	**1**	**0**	**0**	**74**	**5.4**	**25**	**0**	**0.0**	**19:08**	**4**	**0**	**0**	**0**	**2**	**0**	**0**	**0**	**25:51**
2003-04	**Detroit**	**NHL**	**65**	**3**	**9**	**12**	**40**	**0**	**1**	**0**	**68**	**4.4**	**9**	**1**	**0.0**	**13:47**	**12**	**1**	**1**	**2**	**6**	**0**	**0**	**1**	**13:33**
2004-05	Asiago	Italy	10	0	2	2	2	....	....	....	....	....	....	....	....	....	9	1	6	7	4	....	....	....	....
2005-06	**Montreal**	**NHL**	**82**	**5**	**15**	**20**	**83**	**0**	**0**	**1**	**101**	**5.0**	**8**	**0**	**0.0**	**18:38**	**6**	**0**	**3**	**3**	**4**	**0**	**0**	**0**	**19:48**
	NHL Totals		**698**	**53**	**116**	**169**	**425**	**6**	**1**	**6**	**815**	**6.5**		**6**	**16.7**	**16:00**	**70**	**3**	**8**	**11**	**22**	**1**	**1**	**1**	**14:10**

Signed as a free agent by **Asiago** (Italy), December 27, 2004. Signed as a free agent by **Montreal**, August 3, 2005.

DARBY, Craig

(DAHR-bee, KRAYG)

Center. Shoots right. 6'4", 200 lbs. Born, Oneida, NY, September 26, 1972. Montreal's 3rd choice, 43rd overall, in 1991 Entry Draft.

Season	Club	League	GP	G	A	Pts	PIM	PP	SH	GW	S	%	+/-	TF	F%	Min	GP	G	A	Pts	PIM	PP	SH	GW	Min
1987-88	Albany	High-NY	29	11	27	38	....	....	....	....	....	....	....	....	....	....	....	....	....	....	....	....	....	....	....
1988-89	Albany	High-NY	29	36	40	*76	....	....	....	....	....	....	....	....	....	....	....	....	....	....	....	....	....	....	....
1989-90	Albany	High-NY	29	32	53	85	....	....	....	....	....	....	....	....	....	....	....	....	....	....	....	....	....	....	....
1990-91	Albany	High-NY	29	33	61	*94	....	....	....	....	....	....	....	....	....	....	4	8	1	9	....	....	....	....	....
1991-92	Providence	H-East	35	17	24	41	47	....	....	....	....	....	....	....	....	....	....	....	....	....	....	....	....	....	....
1992-93	Providence	H-East	35	11	21	32	62	....	....	....	....	....	....	....	....	....	....	....	....	....	....	....	....	....	....
1993-94	Fredericton	AHL	66	23	33	56	51	....	....	....	....	....	....	....	....	....	....	....	....	....	....	....	....	....	....
1994-95	Fredericton	AHL	64	21	47	68	82	....	....	....	....	....	....	....	....	....	....	....	....	....	....	....	....	....	....
	Montreal	**NHL**	**10**	**0**	**2**	**2**	**0**	**0**	**0**	**0**	**4**	**0.0**	**–5**	....	....	....	....	....	....	....	....	....	....	....	....
	NY Islanders	**NHL**	**3**	**0**	**0**	**0**	**0**	**0**	**0**	**0**	**1**	**0.0**	**–1**	....	....	....	....	....	....	....	....	....	....	....	....
1995-96	**NY Islanders**	**NHL**	**10**	**0**	**2**	**2**	**0**	**0**	**0**	**0**	**1**	**0.0**	**–1**	....	....	....	....	....	....	....	....	....	....	....	....
	Worcester IceCats	AHL	68	22	28	50	47	....	....	....	....	....	....	....	....	....	4	1	1	2	2	....	....	....	....
1996-97	**Philadelphia**	**NHL**	**9**	**1**	**4**	**5**	**2**	**0**	**1**	**0**	**13**	**7.7**	**2**	....	....	....	....	....	....	....	....	....	....	....	....
	Philadelphia	AHL	59	26	33	59	24	....	....	....	....	....	....	....	....	....	10	3	6	9	0	....	....	....	....
1997-98	**Philadelphia**	**NHL**	**3**	**1**	**0**	**1**	**0**	**0**	**0**	**0**	**3**	**33.3**	**0**	....	....	....	....	....	....	....	....	....	....	....	....
	Philadelphia	AHL	77	*42	45	87	34	....	....	....	....	....	....	....	....	....	20	5	9	14	4	....	....	....	....
1998-99	Milwaukee	IHL	81	32	22	54	33	....	....	....	....	....	....	....	....	....	2	3	0	3	0	....	....	....	....
99-2000	**Montreal**	**NHL**	**76**	**7**	**10**	**17**	**14**	**0**	**1**	**2**	**90**	**7.8**	**–14**	**1068**	**48.3**	**13:45**	....	....	....	....	....	....	....	....	....
2000-01	**Montreal**	**NHL**	**78**	**12**	**16**	**28**	**16**	**0**	**1**	**0**	**97**	**12.4**	**–17**	**1214**	**46.9**	**15:53**	....	....	....	....	....	....	....	....	....
2001-02	**Montreal**	**NHL**	**2**	**0**	**0**	**0**	**0**	**0**	**0**	**0**	**0**	**0.0**	**0**	**10**	**30.0**	**5:20**	....	....	....	....	....	....	....	....	....
	Quebec Citadelles	AHL	66	16	55	71	18	....	....	....	....	....	....	....	....	....	3	2	1	3	0	....	....	....	....
2002-03	**New Jersey**	**NHL**	**3**	**0**	**1**	**1**	**0**	**0**	**0**	**0**	**1**	**0.0**	**–1**	**21**	**47.6**	**10:36**	....	....	....	....	....	....	....	....	....
	Albany River Rats	AHL	76	23	51	74	42	....	....	....	....	....	....	....	....	....	....	....	....	....	....	....	....	....	....
2003-04	**New Jersey**	**NHL**	**2**	**0**	**0**	**0**	**0**	**0**	**0**	**0**	**0**	**0.0**	**–1**	**17**	**58.8**	**7:06**	....	....	....	....	....	....	....	....	....
	Albany River Rats	AHL	77	21	48	69	44	....	....	....	....	....	....	....	....	....	....	....	....	....	....	....	....	....	....
2004-05	Springfield	AHL	70	8	26	34	28	....	....	....	....	....	....	....	....	....	....	....	....	....	....	....	....	....	....
2005-06	Manitoba Moose	AHL	80	15	36	51	44	....	....	....	....	....	....	....	....	....	13	3	7	10	2	....	....	....	....
	NHL Totals		**196**	**21**	**35**	**56**	**32**	**0**	**3**	**2**	**210**	**10.0**		**2330**	**47.6**	**14:32**	....	....	....	....	....	....	....	....	....

Hockey East Rookie of the Year (1992) (co-winner - Ian Moran) • AHL First All-Star Team (1998) • AHL Second All-Star Team (2003)

Traded to **NY Islanders** by **Montreal** with Kirk Muller and Mathieu Schneider for Pierre Turgeon and Vladimir Malakhov, April 5, 1995. Claimed on waivers by **Philadelphia** from **NY Islanders**, June 4, 1996. Claimed by **Nashville** from **Philadelphia** in Expansion Draft, June 26, 1998. Signed as a free agent by **Montreal**, August 4, 1999. Signed as a free agent by **New Jersey**, July 12, 2002. Signed as a free agent by **Tampa Bay**, July 19, 2004. Traded to **Vancouver** from **Tampa Bay**, September 9, 2005.

DARCHE, Mathieu

(DAHRSH, MA-thew) **S.J.**

Left wing. Shoots left. 6'1", 210 lbs. Born, St. Laurent, Que., November 26, 1976.

Season	Club	League	GP	G	A	Pts	PIM	PP	SH	GW	S	%	+/-	TF	F%	Min	GP	G	A	Pts	PIM	PP	SH	GW	Min
1995-96	Choate-Rosemary	High-CT	STATISTICS NOT AVAILABLE																						
1996-97	McGill Redmen	OUAA	23	1	2	3	27	....	....	....	....	....	....	....	....	....	....	....	....	....	....	....	....	....	....
1997-98	McGill Redmen	OUAA	40	28	17	45	69	....	....	....	....	....	....	....	....	....	....	....	....	....	....	....	....	....	....
1998-99	McGill Redmen	OUAA	32	16	24	40	60	....	....	....	....	....	....	....	....	....	....	....	....	....	....	....	....	....	....
99-2000	McGill Redmen	OUAA	33	31	41	*72	38	....	....	....	....	....	....	....	....	....	5	2	8	10	16	....	....	....	....
2000-01	**Columbus**	**NHL**	**9**	**0**	**0**	**0**	**0**	**0**	**0**	**0**	**9**	**0.0**	**–4**	**1**	**0.0**	**10:07**	....	....	....	....	....	....	....	....	....
	Syracuse Crunch	AHL	66	16	24	40	21	....	....	....	....	....	....	....	....	....	5	0	1	1	4	....	....	....	....
2001-02	**Columbus**	**NHL**	**14**	**1**	**1**	**2**	**6**	**0**	**0**	**0**	**15**	**6.7**	**–5**	**3**	**33.3**	**9:49**	....	....	....	....	....	....	....	....	....
	Syracuse Crunch	AHL	63	22	23	45	26	....	....	....	....	....	....	....	....	....	10	2	5	7	2	....	....	....	....
2002-03	**Columbus**	**NHL**	**1**	**0**	**0**	**0**	**0**	**0**	**0**	**0**	**0**	**0.0**	**–1**	**0**	**0.0**	**6:57**	....	....	....	....	....	....	....	....	....
	Syracuse Crunch	AHL	76	32	32	64	38	....	....	....	....	....	....	....	....	....	....	....	....	....	....	....	....	....	....
2003-04	**Nashville**	**NHL**	**2**	**0**	**0**	**0**	**0**	**0**	**0**	**0**	**1**	**0.0**	**–1**	**0**	**0.0**	**6:39**	....	....	....	....	....	....	....	....	....
	Milwaukee	AHL	76	28	31	59	41	....	....	....	....	....	....	....	....	....	22	6	8	14	8	....	....	....	....
2004-05	Hershey Bears	AHL	79	29	25	54	49	....	....	....	....	....	....	....	....	....	....	....	....	....	....	....	....	....	....
2005-06	Duisburg	Germany	52	12	13	25	88	....	....	....	....	....	....	....	....	....	5	1	3	4	4	....	....	....	....
	NHL Totals		**26**	**1**	**1**	**2**	**6**	**0**	**0**	**0**	**25**	**4.0**		**4**	**25.0**	**9:34**	....	....	....	....	....	....	....	....	....

OUAA East Second All-Star Team (1998) • OUAA East First All-Star Team (1999) • OUAA First All-Star Team (2000) • CIAU All-Canadian Team (2000)

• Played CIAU Football (1996-97). Signed as a free agent by **Columbus**, May 16, 2000. Signed as a free agent by **Nashville**, September 10, 2003. Signed as a free agent by **Colorado**, July 26, 2004. Signed as a free agent by **San Jose**, July 10, 2006.

DATSYUK, Pavel

(daht-SOOK, PAH-vehl) **DET.**

Center. Shoots left. 5'11", 180 lbs. Born, Sverdlovsk, USSR, July 20, 1978. Detroit's 8th choice, 171st overall, in 1998 Entry Draft.

			Regular Season														Playoffs								
Season	Club	League	GP	G	A	Pts	PIM	PP	SH	GW	S	%	+/-	TF	F%	Min	GP	G	A	Pts	PIM	PP	SH	GW	Min
1996-97	Yekaterinburg 2	Russia-3	18	2	2	4	4																		
	Yekaterinburg	Russia	36	12	10	22	12	....	....	....	....	....	....	....	....	....	....	....	....	....	....	....	....	....	....
1997-98	Yekaterinburg	Russia	24	3	5	8	4	....	....	....	....	....	....	....	....	....	....	....	....	....	....	....	....	....	....
	Yekaterinburg	Russia	22	7	8	15	4	....	....	....	....	....	....	....	....	....	....	....	....	....	....	....	....	....	....
1998-99	Yekaterinburg 2	Russia-4	10	14	14	28	4	....	....	....	....	....	....	....	....	....	....	....	....	....	....	....	....	....	....
	Yekaterinburg	Russia-2	35	21	23	44	14	....	....	....	....	....	....	....	....	....	9	3	7	10	10	....	....	....	....
99-2000	Yekaterinburg	Russia	15	1	3	4	4	....	....	....	....	....	....	....	....	....	....	....	....	....	....	....	....	....	....
2000-01	Ak Bars Kazan	Russia	42	9	18	27	10	....	....	....	....	....	....	....	....	....	4	0	1	1	2	....	....	....	....
2001-02 ◆	**Detroit**	**NHL**	**70**	**11**	**24**	**35**	**4**	**2**	**0**	**1**	**79**	**13.9**	**4**	**794**	**47.7**	**13:39**	**21**	**3**	**3**	**6**	**2**	**1**	**0**	**1**	**10:40**
	Russia	Olympics	6	1	2	3	0	....	....	....	....	....	....	....	....	....	....	....	....	....	....	....	....	....	....
2002-03	**Detroit**	**NHL**	**64**	**12**	**39**	**51**	**16**	**1**	**0**	**1**	**82**	**14.6**	**20**	**778**	**48.2**	**15:28**	**4**	**0**	**0**	**0**	**0**	**0**	**0**	**0**	**18:48**
2003-04	**Detroit**	**NHL**	**75**	**30**	**38**	**68**	**35**	**8**	**1**	**4**	**136**	**22.1**	**–2**	**1314**	**54.0**	**18:16**	**12**	**0**	**6**	**6**	**2**	**0**	**0**	**0**	**17:23**
2004-05	Dynamo Moscow	Russia	47	15	17	32	16	....	....	....	....	....	....	....	....	....	10	*6	3	9	4	....	....	....	....
2005-06	**Detroit**	**NHL**	**75**	**28**	**59**	**87**	**22**	**11**	**0**	**4**	**145**	**19.3**	**26**	**1059**	**53.1**	**17:53**	**5**	**0**	**3**	**3**	**0**	**0**	**0**	**0**	**20:05**
	Russia	Olympics	8	1	7	8	10	....	....	....	....	....	....	....	....	....	....	....	....	....	....	....	....	....	....
	NHL Totals		**284**	**81**	**160**	**241**	**77**	**22**	**1**	**10**	**442**	**18.3**		**3945**	**51.3**	**16:24**	**42**	**3**	**12**	**15**	**4**	**1**	**0**	**1**	**14:29**

Played in NHL All-Star Game (2004) • Lady Byng Trophy (2006)

• Spent majority of 1999-2000 season on **Kazan** (Russia) reserve squad. Signed as a free agent by **Dynamo Moscow** (Russia), June 19, 2004. Signed as a free agent by **Omsk**, September 5, 2005.

DAVISON, Rob

(DAY-vihs-ohn, RAWB) **S.J.**

Defense. Shoots left. 6'2", 225 lbs. Born, St. Catharines, Ont., May 1, 1980. San Jose's 4th choice, 98th overall, in 1998 Entry Draft.

Season	Club	League	GP	G	A	Pts	PIM	PP	SH	GW	S	%	+/-	TF	F%	Min	GP	G	A	Pts	PIM	PP	SH	GW	Min
1996-97	St. Mike's B's	OPJHL	45	2	6	8	93										6	0	0	0	9	....	....	....	....
1997-98	North Bay	OHL	59	0	11	11	200	....	....	....	....	....	....	....	....	....	....	....	....	....	....	....	....	....	....
1998-99	North Bay	OHL	59	2	17	19	150	....	....	....	....	....	....	....	....	....	4	0	1	1	12	....	....	....	....
99-2000	North Bay	OHL	67	4	6	10	194	....	....	....	....	....	....	....	....	....	6	0	1	1	8	....	....	....	....
2000-01	Kentucky	AHL	72	0	4	4	230	....	....	....	....	....	....	....	....	....	3	0	0	0	0	....	....	....	....
2001-02	Cleveland Barons	AHL	70	1	3	4	206	....	....	....	....	....	....	....	....	....	....	....	....	....	....	....	....	....	....
2002-03	**San Jose**	**NHL**	**15**	**1**	**2**	**3**	**22**	**0**	**0**	**0**	**15**	**6.7**	**4**	**0**	**0.0**	**17:53**	....	....	....	....	....	....	....	....	....
	Cleveland Barons	AHL	42	1	3	4	82	....	....	....	....	....	....	....	....	....	....	....	....	....	....	....	....	....	....
2003-04	**San Jose**	**NHL**	**55**	**0**	**3**	**3**	**92**	**0**	**0**	**0**	**33**	**0.0**	**–3**	**0**	**0.0**	**14:22**	**5**	**0**	**2**	**2**	**4**	**0**	**0**	**0**	**9:01**
2004-05	Cardiff Devils	Britain	24	2	3	5	114	....	....	....	....	....	....	....	....	....	8	0	1	1	12	....	....	....	....
2005-06	**San Jose**	**NHL**	**69**	**1**	**5**	**6**	**76**	**0**	**0**	**0**	**36**	**2.8**	**6**	**0**	**0.0**	**13:50**	**1**	**0**	**0**	**0**	**0**	**0**	**0**	**0**	**8:00**
	NHL Totals		**139**	**2**	**10**	**12**	**190**	**0**	**0**	**0**	**84**	**2.4**		**0**	**0.0**	**14:29**	**6**	**0**	**2**	**2**	**4**	**0**	**0**	**0**	**8:51**

Signed as a free agent by **Cardiff** (Britain), October 5, 2004.

DAZE, Eric

(dah-ZAY, AIR-ihk)

Right wing. Shoots left. 6'6", 235 lbs. Born, Montreal, Que., July 2, 1975. Chicago's 5th choice, 90th overall, in 1993 Entry Draft.

Season	Club	League	GP	G	A	Pts	PIM	PP	SH	GW	S	%	+/-	TF	F%	Min	GP	G	A	Pts	PIM	PP	SH	GW	Min
1990-91	Laval-Laurentides	QAHA	30	25	20	45	30																		
1991-92	Laval-Laurentides	QAAA	35	30	29	59	40	....	....	....	....	....	....	....	....	....	12	8	10	18	8	....	....	....	....
1992-93	Beauport	QMJHL	68	19	36	55	24	....	....	....	....	....	....	....	....	....	....	....	....	....	....	....	....	....	....
1993-94	Beauport	QMJHL	66	59	48	107	31	....	....	....	....	....	....	....	....	....	15	16	8	24	2	....	....	....	....
1994-95	Beauport	QMJHL	57	54	45	99	20	....	....	....	....	....	....	....	....	....	16	9	12	21	23	....	....	....	....
	Chicago	**NHL**	**4**	**1**	**1**	**2**	**2**	**0**	**0**	**0**	**1**	**100.0**	**2**	....	....	....	**16**	**0**	**1**	**1**	**4**	**0**	**0**	**0**	....
1995-96	**Chicago**	**NHL**	**80**	**30**	**23**	**53**	**18**	**2**	**0**	**2**	**167**	**18.0**	**16**	....	....	....	**10**	**3**	**5**	**8**	**0**	**0**	**0**	**1**	....
1996-97	**Chicago**	**NHL**	**71**	**22**	**19**	**41**	**16**	**11**	**0**	**4**	**176**	**12.5**	**–4**	....	....	....	**6**	**2**	**1**	**3**	**2**	**0**	**0**	**0**	....
1997-98	**Chicago**	**NHL**	**80**	**31**	**11**	**42**	**22**	**10**	**0**	**7**	**216**	**14.4**	**4**	....	....	....	....	....	....	....	....	....	....	....	....
1998-99	**Chicago**	**NHL**	**72**	**22**	**20**	**42**	**22**	**8**	**0**	**2**	**189**	**11.6**	**–13**	**4**	**0.0**	**16:16**	....	....	....	....	....	....	....	....	....
99-2000	**Chicago**	**NHL**	**59**	**23**	**13**	**36**	**28**	**6**	**0**	**1**	**143**	**16.1**	**–16**	**9**	**22.2**	**16:15**	....	....	....	....	....	....	....	....	....
2000-01	**Chicago**	**NHL**	**79**	**33**	**24**	**57**	**16**	**9**	**1**	**8**	**205**	**16.1**	**1**	**3**	**33.3**	**17:45**	....	....	....	....	....	....	....	....	....
2001-02	**Chicago**	**NHL**	**82**	**38**	**32**	**70**	**36**	**12**	**0**	**5**	**264**	**14.4**	**17**	**5**	**0.0**	**17:07**	**5**	**0**	**0**	**0**	**2**	**0**	**0**	**0**	**17:12**
2002-03	**Chicago**	**NHL**	**54**	**22**	**22**	**44**	**14**	**3**	**0**	**5**	**170**	**12.9**	**10**	**4**	**25.0**	**16:17**	....	....	....	....	....	....	....	....	....
2003-04	**Chicago**	**NHL**	**19**	**4**	**7**	**11**	**0**	**1**	**0**	**0**	**76**	**5.3**	**–7**	**1**	**0.0**	**18:56**	....	....	....	....	....	....	....	....	....
2004-05			DID NOT PLAY																						
2005-06	**Chicago**	**NHL**	**1**	**0**	**0**	**0**	**2**	**0**	**0**	**0**	**0**	**0.0**	**–2**	**0**	**0.0**	**11:56**	....	....	....	....	....	....	....	....	....
	NHL Totals		**601**	**226**	**172**	**398**	**176**	**62**	**1**	**34**	**1607**	**14.1**		**26**	**15.4**	**16:54**	**37**	**5**	**7**	**12**	**8**	**0**	**0**	**1**	**17:12**

QMJHL First All-Star Team (1994, 1995) • Canadian Major Junior Most Sportsmanlike Player of the Year (1995) • NHL All-Rookie Team (1996)

Played in NHL All-Star Game (2002)

• Missed majority of 2003-04 and 2005-06 seasons recovering from back injury suffered in game vs. Los Angeles, October 16, 2003.

DELMORE, Andy

(DEHL-mohr, AN-dee) **T.B.**

Defense. Shoots right. 6', 200 lbs. Born, LaSalle, Ont., December 26, 1976.

Season	Club	League	GP	G	A	Pts	PIM	PP	SH	GW	S	%	+/-	TF	F%	Min	GP	G	A	Pts	PIM	PP	SH	GW	Min
1992-93	Chatham	OHA-B	47	4	21	25	38																		
1993-94	North Bay	OHL	45	2	7	9	33	....	....	....	....	....	....	....	....	....	17	0	0	0	2	....	....	....	....
1994-95	North Bay	OHL	40	2	14	16	21	....	....	....	....	....	....	....	....	....	....	....	....	....	....	....	....	....	....
	Sarnia Sting	OHL	27	5	13	18	27	....	....	....	....	....	....	....	....	....	3	0	0	0	2	....	....	....	....
1995-96	Sarnia Sting	OHL	64	21	38	59	45	....	....	....	....	....	....	....	....	....	10	3	7	10	2	....	....	....	....
1996-97	Sarnia Sting	OHL	64	18	60	78	39	....	....	....	....	....	....	....	....	....	12	2	10	12	10	....	....	....	....
	Fredericton	AHL	4	0	1	1	0	....	....	....	....	....	....	....	....	....	....	....	....	....	....	....	....	....	....
1997-98	Philadelphia	AHL	73	9	30	39	46	....	....	....	....	....	....	....	....	....	18	4	4	8	21	....	....	....	....
1998-99	**Philadelphia**	**NHL**	**2**	**0**	**1**	**1**	**0**	**0**	**0**	**0**	**2**	**0.0**	**–1**	**0**	**0.0**	**20:42**	....	....	....	....	....	....	....	....	....
	Philadelphia	AHL	70	5	18	23	51	....	....	....	....	....	....	....	....	....	15	1	4	5	6	....	....	....	....
99-2000	**Philadelphia**	**NHL**	**27**	**2**	**5**	**7**	**8**	**0**	**0**	**1**	**55**	**3.6**	**–1**	**0**	**0.0**	**17:17**	**18**	**5**	**2**	**7**	**14**	**1**	**0**	**1**	**17:33**
	Philadelphia	AHL	39	12	14	26	31	....	....	....	....	....	....	....	....	....	....	....	....	....	....	....	....	....	....
2000-01	**Philadelphia**	**NHL**	**66**	**5**	**9**	**14**	**16**	**2**	**0**	**0**	**119**	**4.2**	**2**	**0**	**0.0**	**17:39**	**2**	**1**	**0**	**1**	**2**	**0**	**0**	**1**	**15:20**
2001-02	**Nashville**	**NHL**	**73**	**16**	**22**	**38**	**22**	**11**	**0**	**3**	**175**	**9.1**	**–13**	**0**	**0.0**	**19:40**	....	....	....	....	....	....	....	....	....
2002-03	**Nashville**	**NHL**	**71**	**18**	**16**	**34**	**28**	**14**	**0**	**6**	**149**	**12.1**	**–17**	**0**	**0.0**	**17:05**	....	....	....	....	....	....	....	....	....
2003-04	**Buffalo**	**NHL**	**37**	**2**	**5**	**7**	**29**	**2**	**0**	**0**	**40**	**5.0**	**–5**	**0**	**0.0**	**15:11**	....	....	....	....	....	....	....	....	....
	Rochester	AHL	8	0	2	2	2	....	....	....	....	....	....	....	....	....	....	....	....	....	....	....	....	....	....
2004-05	Adler Mannheim	Germany	50	7	16	23	59	....	....	....	....	....	....	....	....	....	14	1	6	7	12	....	....	....	....
2005-06	**Columbus**	**NHL**	**7**	**0**	**0**	**0**	**2**	**0**	**0**	**0**	**7**	**0.0**	**–1**	**0**	**0.0**	**15:24**	....	....	....	....	....	....	....	....	....
	Syracuse Crunch	AHL	66	17	55	72	46	....	....	....	....	....	....	....	....	....	6	0	1	1	19	....	....	....	....
	NHL Totals		**283**	**43**	**58**	**101**	**105**	**29**	**0**	**10**	**547**	**7.9**		**0**	**0.0**	**17:38**	**20**	**6**	**2**	**8**	**16**	**1**	**0**	**2**	**17:19**

OHL First All-Star Team (1997) • AHL First All-Star Team (2006) • Eddie Shore Award (Outstanding Defenseman - AHL) (2006)

Signed as a free agent by **Philadelphia**, June 9, 1997. Traded to **Nashville** by **Philadelphia** for Nashville's 3rd round choice (later traded to Phoenix – Phoenix selected Joe Callahan) in 2002 Entry Draft, July 31, 2001. Traded to **Buffalo** by **Nashville** for Buffalo's 3rd round choice (later traded to Minnesota – Minnesota selected Clayton Stoner) in 2004 Entry Draft, June 27, 2003. Traded to **San Jose** by **Buffalo** with Curtis Brown for Jeff Jillson and a compensatory 7th round choice (Andrew Orpik) in 2005 Entry Draft, March 9, 2004. Traded to **Boston** by **San Jose** for future considerations, March 9, 2004. Signed as a free agent by **Mannheim** (Germany), July 21, 2004. Signed as a free agent by **Detroit**, August 16, 2005. Claimed on waivers by **Columbus** from **Detroit**, October 4, 2005. Signed as a free agent by **Tampa Bay**, July 1, 2006.

DEMITRA, Pavol

(deh-MEET-rah, PAH-vohl) **MIN.**

Left wing. Shoots left. 6', 206 lbs. Born, Dubnica, Czech., November 29, 1974. Ottawa's 9th choice, 227th overall, in 1993 Entry Draft.

Season	Club	League	GP	G	A	Pts	PIM	PP	SH	GW	S	%	+/-	TF	F%	Min	GP	G	A	Pts	PIM	PP	SH	GW	Min
1991-92	Dubnica	Czech-2	28	13	10	23	12																		
1992-93	Dubnica	Czech-2	4	3	0	3	....	....	....	....	....	....	....	....	....	....	....	....	....	....	....	....	....	....	....
	Dukla Trencin	Czech	46	11	17	28	0	....	....	....	....	....	....	....	....	....	....	....	....	....	....	....	....	....	....
1993-94	**Ottawa**	**NHL**	**12**	**1**	**1**	**2**	**4**	**1**	**0**	**0**	**10**	**10.0**	**–7**	....	....	....	....	....	....	....	....	....	....	....	....
	P.E.I. Senators	AHL	41	18	23	41	8	....	....	....	....	....	....	....	....	....	....	....	....	....	....	....	....	....	....
1994-95	P.E.I. Senators	AHL	61	26	48	74	23	....	....	....	....	....	....	....	....	....	5	0	7	7	0	....	....	....	....
	Ottawa	**NHL**	**16**	**4**	**3**	**7**	**0**	**1**	**0**	**0**	**21**	**19.0**	**–4**	....	....	....	....	....	....	....	....	....	....	....	....
1995-96	**Ottawa**	**NHL**	**31**	**7**	**10**	**17**	**6**	**2**	**0**	**1**	**66**	**10.6**	**–3**	....	....	....	....	....	....	....	....	....	....	....	....
	P.E.I. Senators	AHL	48	28	53	81	44	....	....	....	....	....	....	....	....	....	....	....	....	....	....	....	....	....	....

			Regular Season														Playoffs								
Season	Club	League	GP	G	A	Pts	PIM	PP	SH	GW	S	%	+/-	TF	F%	Min	GP	G	A	Pts	PIM	PP	SH	GW	Min
1996-97	Dukla Trencin	Slovakia	1	1	1	2	....	....	....	....	....	....	....	....	....	....	....	....	....	....	....	....	....	....	....
	Las Vegas	IHL	22	8	13	21	10	....	....	....	....	....	....	....	....	....	....	....	....	....	....	....	....	....	....
	St. Louis	NHL	8	3	0	3	2	2	0	1	15	20.0	0	....	....	....	6	1	3	4	6	0	0	0	....
	Grand Rapids	IHL	42	20	30	50	24	....	....	....	....	....	....	....	....	....	....	....	....	....	....	....	....	....	....
1997-98	St. Louis	NHL	61	22	30	52	22	4	4	6	147	15.0	11	....	....	....	10	3	3	6	2	0	0	0	....
1998-99	St. Louis	NHL	82	37	52	89	16	14	0	10	259	14.3	13	250	44.0	20:10	13	5	4	9	4	3	0	1	19:10
99-2000	St. Louis	NHL	71	28	47	75	8	8	0	4	241	11.6	34	41	39.0	19:13	....	....	....	....	....	....	....	....	....
2000-01	St. Louis	NHL	44	20	25	45	16	5	0	5	124	16.1	27	8	37.5	18:03	15	2	4	6	2	0	0	1	18:13
2001-02	St. Louis	NHL	82	35	43	78	46	11	0	10	212	16.5	13	1224	48.1	19:11	10	4	7	11	6	2	1	1	19:45
	Slovakia	Olympics	2	1	2	3	2	....	....	....	....	....	....	....	....	....	....	....	....	....	....	....	....	....	....
2002-03	St. Louis	NHL	78	36	57	93	32	11	0	4	205	17.6	0	1253	46.1	19:47	7	2	4	6	2	1	0	0	18:20
2003-04	St. Louis	NHL	68	23	35	58	18	8	0	5	179	12.8	1	770	47.3	20:30	5	1	0	1	4	0	0	0	18:07
2004-05	Dukla Trencin	Slovakia	54	*28	*54	*82	39	....	....	....	....	....	....	....	....	....	12	4	13	17	14	....	....	....	....
2005-06	Los Angeles	NHL	58	25	37	62	42	7	5	7	184	13.6	21	114	49.1	21:04	....	....	....	....	....	....	....	....	....
	Slovakia	Olympics	6	2	5	7	2	....	....	....	....	....	....	....	....	....	....	....	....	....	....	....	....	....	....
	NHL Totals		611	241	340	581	212	74	9	53	1663	14.5		3660	46.9	19:46	66	18	25	43	26	6	1	3	18:47

Lady Byng Trophy (2000)

Played in NHL All-Star Game (1999, 2000, 2002)

Traded to **St. Louis** by **Ottawa** for Christer Olsson, November 27, 1996. Signed as a free agent by **Trencin** (Slovakia), September 17, 2004. Signed as a free agent by **Los Angeles**, August 2, 2005. Traded to **Minnesota** by **Los Angeles** for Patrick O'Sullivan and Edmonton's 1st round choice (previously acquired, Los Angeles selected Trevor Lewis) in 2006 Entry Draft, June 24, 2006.

DEMPSEY, Nathan

(DEHMP-see, NAY-thun) **BOS.**

Defense. Shoots right. 6', 190 lbs. Born, Spruce Grove, Alta., July 14, 1974. Toronto's 12th choice, 245th overall, in 1992 Entry Draft.

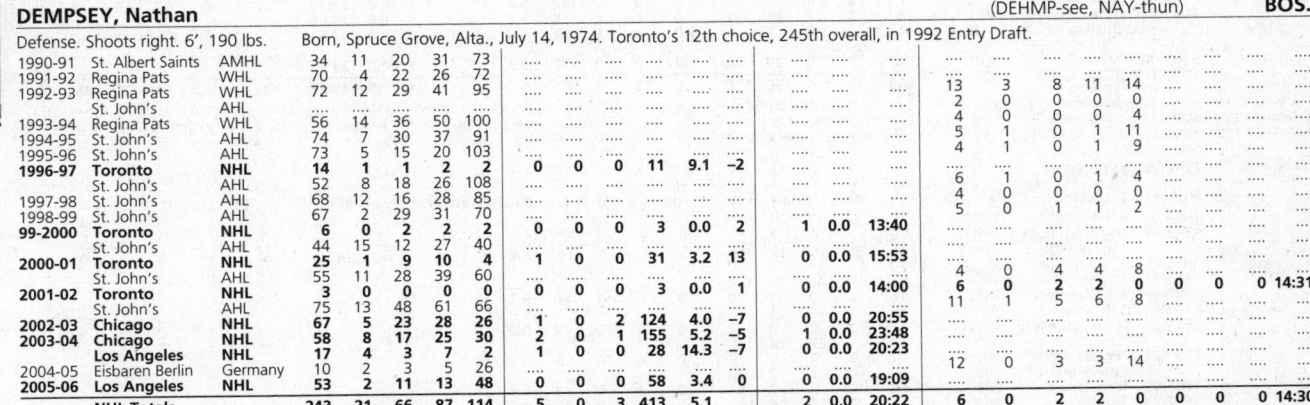

Season	Club	League	GP	G	A	Pts	PIM	PP	SH	GW	S	%	+/-	TF	F%	Min	GP	G	A	Pts	PIM	PP	SH	GW	Min
1990-91	St. Albert Saints	AMHL	34	11	20	31	73	....	....	....	....	....	....	....	....	....	....	....	....	....	....	....	....	....	....
1991-92	Regina Pats	WHL	70	4	22	26	72	....	....	....	....	....	....	....	....	....	....	....	....	....	....	....	....	....	....
1992-93	Regina Pats	WHL	72	12	29	41	95	....	....	....	....	....	....	....	....	....	13	3	8	11	14	....	....	....	....
	St. John's	AHL	....	....	....	....	....	....	....	....	....	....	....	....	....	....	2	0	0	0	0	....	....	....	....
1993-94	Regina Pats	WHL	56	14	36	50	100	....	....	....	....	....	....	....	....	....	4	0	0	0	4	....	....	....	....
1994-95	St. John's	AHL	74	7	30	37	91	....	....	....	....	....	....	....	....	....	5	1	0	1	11	....	....	....	....
1995-96	St. John's	AHL	73	5	15	20	103	....	....	....	....	....	....	....	....	....	4	1	0	1	9	....	....	....	....
1996-97	Toronto	NHL	14	1	1	2	2	0	0	0	11	9.1	–2	....	....	....	....	....	....	....	....	....	....	....	....
	St. John's	AHL	52	8	18	26	108	....	....	....	....	....	....	....	....	....	6	1	0	1	4	....	....	....	....
1997-98	St. John's	AHL	68	12	16	28	85	....	....	....	....	....	....	....	....	....	4	0	0	0	0	....	....	....	....
1998-99	St. John's	AHL	67	2	29	31	70	....	....	....	....	....	....	....	....	....	5	0	1	1	2	....	....	....	....
99-2000	Toronto	NHL	6	0	2	2	2	0	0	0	3	0.0	2	1	0.0	13:40	....	....	....	....	....	....	....	....	....
	St. John's	AHL	44	15	12	27	40	....	....	....	....	....	....	....	....	....	....	....	....	....	....	....	....	....	....
2000-01	Toronto	NHL	25	1	9	10	4	1	0	0	31	3.2	13	0	0.0	15:53	....	....	....	....	....	....	....	....	....
	St. John's	AHL	55	11	28	39	60	....	....	....	....	....	....	....	....	....	4	0	4	4	8	....	....	....	....
2001-02	Toronto	NHL	3	0	0	0	0	0	0	0	3	0.0	1	0	0.0	14:00	6	0	2	2	0	0	0	0	14:31
	St. John's	AHL	75	13	48	61	66	....	....	....	....	....	....	....	....	....	11	1	5	6	8	....	....	....	....
2002-03	Chicago	NHL	67	5	23	28	26	1	0	2	124	4.0	–7	0	0.0	20:55	....	....	....	....	....	....	....	....	....
2003-04	Chicago	NHL	58	8	17	25	30	2	0	1	155	5.2	–5	1	0.0	23:48	....	....	....	....	....	....	....	....	....
	Los Angeles	NHL	17	4	3	7	2	1	0	0	28	14.3	–7	0	0.0	20:23	....	....	....	....	....	....	....	....	....
2004-05	Eisbaren Berlin	Germany	10	2	3	5	26	....	....	....	....	....	....	....	....	....	12	0	3	3	14	....	....	....	....
2005-06	Los Angeles	NHL	53	2	11	13	48	0	0	0	58	3.4	0	0	0.0	19:09	....	....	....	....	....	....	....	....	....
	NHL Totals		243	21	66	87	114	5	0	3	413	5.1		2	0.0	20:22	6	0	2	2	0	0	0	0	14:30

WHL East Second All-Star Team (1994) • AHL Second All-Star Team (2002) • Fred T. Hunt Memorial Award (Sportsmanship – AHL) (2002)

Signed as a free agent by **Chicago**, July 12, 2002. Traded to **Los Angeles** by **Chicago** for Los Angeles' 4th round choice (Nathan Davis) in 2005 Entry Draft, March 2, 2004. Signed as a free agent by **Berlin** (Germany), February 9, 2005. Signed as a free agent by **Boston**, August 7, 2006.

DESJARDINS, Eric

(deh-ZHAHR-dai, AIR-ihk)

Defense. Shoots right. 6'1", 205 lbs. Born, Rouyn, Que., June 14, 1969. Montreal's 3rd choice, 38th overall, in 1987 Entry Draft.

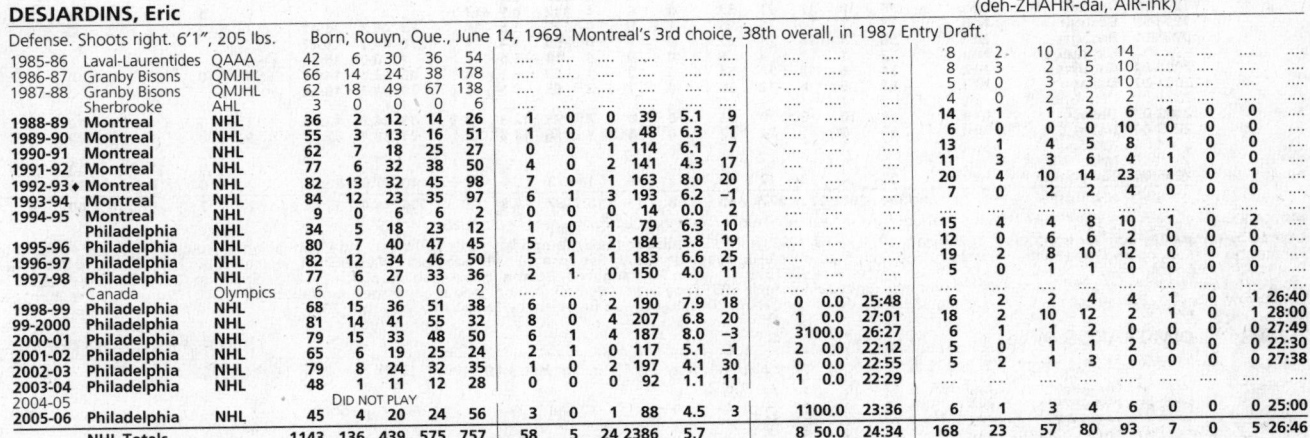

Season	Club	League	GP	G	A	Pts	PIM	PP	SH	GW	S	%	+/-	TF	F%	Min	GP	G	A	Pts	PIM	PP	SH	GW	Min
1985-86	Laval-Laurentides	QAAA	42	6	30	36	54	....	....	....	....	....	....	....	....	....	8	2	10	12	14	....	....	....	....
1986-87	Granby Bisons	QMJHL	66	14	24	38	178	....	....	....	....	....	....	....	....	....	8	3	2	5	10	....	....	....	....
1987-88	Granby Bisons	QMJHL	62	18	49	67	138	....	....	....	....	....	....	....	....	....	5	0	3	3	10	....	....	....	....
	Sherbrooke	AHL	3	0	0	0	6	....	....	....	....	....	....	....	....	....	4	0	2	2	2	....	....	....	....
1988-89	Montreal	NHL	36	2	12	14	26	1	0	0	39	5.1	9	....	....	....	14	1	1	2	6	1	0	0	....
1989-90	Montreal	NHL	55	3	13	16	51	1	0	0	48	6.3	1	....	....	....	6	0	0	0	10	0	0	0	....
1990-91	Montreal	NHL	62	7	18	25	27	0	0	1	114	6.1	7	....	....	....	13	1	4	5	8	1	0	0	....
1991-92	Montreal	NHL	77	6	32	38	50	4	0	2	141	4.3	17	....	....	....	11	3	3	6	4	1	0	0	....
1992-93 ♦	Montreal	NHL	82	13	32	45	98	7	0	1	163	8.0	20	....	....	....	20	4	10	14	23	1	0	1	....
1993-94	Montreal	NHL	84	12	23	35	97	6	1	3	193	6.2	–1	....	....	....	7	0	2	2	4	0	0	0	....
1994-95	Montreal	NHL	9	0	6	6	2	0	0	0	14	0.0	2	....	....	....	....	....	....	....	....	....	....	....	....
	Philadelphia	NHL	34	5	18	23	12	1	0	1	79	6.3	10	....	....	....	15	4	4	8	10	1	0	2	....
1995-96	Philadelphia	NHL	80	7	40	47	45	5	0	2	184	3.8	19	....	....	....	12	0	6	6	2	0	0	0	....
1996-97	Philadelphia	NHL	82	12	34	46	50	5	1	1	183	6.6	25	....	....	....	19	2	8	10	12	0	0	0	....
1997-98	Philadelphia	NHL	77	6	27	33	36	2	1	0	150	4.0	11	....	....	....	5	0	1	1	0	0	0	0	....
	Canada	Olympics	6	0	0	0	2	....	....	....	....	....	....	....	....	....	....	....	....	....	....	....	....	....	....
1998-99	Philadelphia	NHL	68	15	36	51	38	6	0	2	190	7.9	18	0	0.0	25:48	6	2	2	4	4	1	0	1	26:40
99-2000	Philadelphia	NHL	81	14	41	55	32	8	0	4	207	6.8	20	1	0.0	27:01	18	2	10	12	2	1	0	1	28:00
2000-01	Philadelphia	NHL	79	15	33	48	50	6	1	4	187	8.0	–3	3	100.0	26:27	6	1	1	2	0	0	0	0	27:49
2001-02	Philadelphia	NHL	65	6	19	25	24	2	1	0	117	5.1	–1	2	0.0	22:12	5	0	1	1	2	0	0	0	22:30
2002-03	Philadelphia	NHL	79	8	24	32	35	1	0	2	197	4.1	30	0	0.0	22:55	5	2	1	3	0	0	0	0	27:38
2003-04	Philadelphia	NHL	48	1	11	12	28	0	0	0	92	1.1	11	1	0.0	22:29	....	....	....	....	....	....	....	....	....
2004-05			DID NOT PLAY																						
2005-06	Philadelphia	NHL	45	4	20	24	56	3	0	1	88	4.5	3	1	100.0	23:36	6	1	3	4	6	0	0	0	25:00
	NHL Totals		1143	136	439	575	757	58	5	24	2386	5.7		8	50.0	24:34	168	23	57	80	93	7	0	5	26:46

QMJHL Second All-Star Team (1987) • QMJHL First All-Star Team (1988) • NHL Second All-Star Team (1999, 2000)

Played in NHL All-Star Game (1992, 1996, 2000)

Traded to **Philadelphia** by **Montreal** with Gilbert Dionne and John LeClair for Mark Recchi and Philadelphia's 3rd round choice (Martin Hohenberger) in 1995 Entry Draft, February 9, 1995. • Officially announced retirement, August 10, 2006.

DEVEREAUX, Boyd

(DEH-vuhr-oh, BOID)

Center. Shoots left. 6'2", 195 lbs. Born, Seaforth, Ont., April 16, 1978. Edmonton's 1st choice, 6th overall, in 1996 Entry Draft.

Season	Club	League	GP	G	A	Pts	PIM	PP	SH	GW	S	%	+/-	TF	F%	Min	GP	G	A	Pts	PIM	PP	SH	GW	Min
1992-93	Seaforth Sailors	OHA-D	34	7	20	27	13	....	....	....	....	....	....	....	....	....	....	....	....	....	....	....	....	....	....
1993-94	Stratford Cullitons	OHA-B	46	12	27	39	8	....	....	....	....	....	....	....	....	....	....	....	....	....	....	....	....	....	....
1994-95	Stratford Cullitons	OHA-B	45	31	74	105	21	....	....	....	....	....	....	....	....	....	....	....	....	....	....	....	....	....	....
1995-96	Kitchener Rangers	OHL	66	20	38	58	35	....	....	....	....	....	....	....	....	....	12	3	7	10	4	....	....	....	....
1996-97	Kitchener Rangers	OHL	54	28	41	69	37	....	....	....	....	....	....	....	....	....	13	4	11	15	8	....	....	....	....
	Hamilton	AHL	....	....	....	....	....	....	....	....	....	....	....	....	....	....	1	0	1	1	0	....	....	....	....
1997-98	Edmonton	NHL	38	1	4	5	6	0	0	0	27	3.7	–5	....	....	....	....	....	....	....	....	....	....	....	....
	Hamilton	AHL	14	5	6	11	6	....	....	....	....	....	....	....	....	....	9	1	1	2	8	....	....	....	....
1998-99	Edmonton	NHL	61	6	8	14	23	0	1	4	39	15.4	2	409	42.8	10:09	1	0	0	0	0	0	0	0	32:46
	Hamilton	AHL	7	4	6	10	2	....	....	....	....	....	....	....	....	....	8	0	3	3	4	....	....	....	....
99-2000	Edmonton	NHL	76	8	19	27	20	0	1	2	108	7.4	7	241	34.9	12:36	....	....	....	....	....	....	....	....	....
2000-01	Detroit	NHL	55	5	6	11	14	0	0	0	66	7.6	1	124	37.1	10:08	2	0	0	0	0	0	0	0	10:39
2001-02 ♦	Detroit	NHL	79	9	16	25	24	0	0	2	116	7.8	9	12	33.3	11:30	21	2	4	6	4	0	0	0	10:58
2002-03	Detroit	NHL	61	3	9	12	16	0	0	1	72	4.2	4	7	42.9	9:26	....	....	....	....	....	....	....	....	....
2003-04	Detroit	NHL	61	6	9	15	20	0	0	2	62	9.7	–1	14	50.0	9:58	3	1	0	1	0	0	0	0	6:36
2004-05			DID NOT PLAY																						
2005-06	Phoenix	NHL	78	8	14	22	44	1	0	1	76	10.5	–13	281	36.7	12:47	....	....	....	....	....	....	....	....	....
	NHL Totals		509	46	85	131	167	1	2	12	566	8.1		1088	38.8	11:05	27	3	4	7	4	0	0	0	11:16

Canadian Major Junior Scholastic Player of the Year (1996)

Signed as a free agent by **Detroit**, August 23, 2000. Signed as a free agent by **Phoenix**, July 5, 2004.

			Regular Season														Playoffs							
Season	Club	League	GP	G	A	Pts	PIM	PP	SH	GW	S	%	+/-	TF	F%	Min	GP	G	A	Pts	PIM	PP	SH	GW	Min

de VRIES, Greg

(deh-VREES, GREHG)   ATL.

Defense. Shoots left. 6'2", 220 lbs.   Born, Sundridge, Ont., January 4, 1973.

Season	Club	League	GP	G	A	Pts	PIM	PP	SH	GW	S	%	+/-	TF	F%	Min	GP	G	A	Pts	PIM	PP	SH	GW	Min
1988-89	Cortina Astros	OMHA	35	28	40	68		...	...	...	...	...	...				...	...	...	...	...	...	...	...	
1989-90	Aurora Eagles	OHA-B	42	1	16	17	32	...	...	...	...	...	...				...	...	...	...	...	...	...	...	
1990-91	Stratford Cullitons	OHA-B	40	8	32	40	120	...	...	...	...	...	...				...	...	...	...	...	...	...	...	
1991-92	Thorold	OHA-B	3	0	0	0	0	...	...	...	...	...	...				3	2	1	3	20				
	Bowling Green	CCHA	24	0	3	3	20	...	...	...	...	...	...				...	...	...	...	...	...	...	...	
1992-93	Niagara Falls	OHL	62	3	23	26	86	...	...	...	...	...	...				4	0	1	1	6				
1993-94	Niagara Falls	OHL	64	5	40	45	135	...	...	...	...	...	...				...	...	...	...	...	...	...	...	
	Cape Breton	AHL	9	0	0	0	11	...	...	...	...	...	...				1	0	0	0	0				
1994-95	Cape Breton	AHL	77	5	19	24	68	...	...	...	...	...	...				...	...	...	...	...	...	...	...	
1995-96	**Edmonton**	**NHL**	13	1	1	2	12	0	0	0	8	12.5	-2				...	...	...	...	...	...	...	...	
	Cape Breton	AHL	58	9	30	39	174	...	...	...	...	...	...				...	...	...	...	...	...	...	...	
1996-97	**Edmonton**	**NHL**	37	0	4	4	52	0	0	0	31	0.0	-2				12	0	1	1	8	0	0	0	
	Hamilton	AHL	34	4	14	18	26	...	...	...	...	...	...				...	...	...	...	...	...	...	...	
1997-98	**Edmonton**	**NHL**	65	7	4	11	80	1	0	0	53	13.2	-17				7	0	0	0	21	0	0	0	
1998-99	**Nashville**	**NHL**	6	0	0	0	4	0	0	0	1	1.0	-4	0	0.0	18:11	...	...	...	...	...	...	...	...	
	Colorado	NHL	67	1	3	4	60	0	0	0	56	56.0	-3	1000.0	16:23		19	0	2	2	22	0	0	0	12:09
99-2000	**Colorado**	**NHL**	69	2	7	9	73	0	0	0	40	5.0	-7	0	0.0	14:59	5	0	0	0	4	0	0	0	8:09
2000-01♦	**Colorado**	**NHL**	79	5	12	17	51	0	0	0	76	6.6	23	0	0.0	17:06	23	0	1	1	20	0	0	0	14:17
2001-02	**Colorado**	**NHL**	82	8	12	20	57	1	1	3	148	5.4	18	1	0.0	23:03	21	4	9	13	2	0	0	1	24:12
2002-03	**Colorado**	**NHL**	82	6	26	32	70	0	0	2	112	5.4	15	1000.0	22:15	7	2	0	2	0	0	0	0	22:11
2003-04	**NY Rangers**	**NHL**	53	3	12	15	37	0	0	0	58	5.2	12	0	0.0	19:01	...	...	...	...	...	...	...	...	
	Ottawa	NHL	13	0	1	1	6	0	0	0	12	0.0	0	0	0.0	17:51	7	0	1	1	0	0	0	0	17:51
2004-05						DID NOT PLAY																			
2005-06	**Atlanta**	**NHL**	82	7	28	35	76	3	0	2	111	6.3	1		1000.0	22:01									
	NHL Totals		648	40	110	150	578	5	1	7	706	5.7		4	75.0	19:25	101	6	14	20	85	0	0	1	16:56

Signed as a free agent by **Edmonton**, March 20, 1994. Traded to **Nashville** by **Edmonton** with Eric Fichaud and Drake Berehowsky for Mikhail Shtalenkov and Jim Dowd, October 1, 1998. Traded to **Colorado** by **Nashville** for Colorado's 2nd round choice (Ed Hill) in 1999 Entry Draft, October 24, 1998. Signed as a free agent by **NY Rangers**, July 14, 2003. Traded to **Ottawa** by **NY Rangers** for Karel Rachunek and Alexandre Giroux, March 9, 2004. Traded to **Atlanta** by **Ottawa** with Marian Hossa for Dany Heatley, August 23, 2005.

DiMAIO, Rob

(duh-MIGH-oh, RAWB)   T.B.

Right wing. Shoots right. 5'10", 190 lbs.   Born, Calgary, Alta., February 19, 1968. NY Islanders' 6th choice, 118th overall, in 1987 Entry Draft.

Season	Club	League	GP	G	A	Pts	PIM	PP	SH	GW	S	%	+/-	TF	F%	Min	GP	G	A	Pts	PIM	PP	SH	GW	Min
1984-85	Kamloops Blazers	WHL	55	9	18	27	29	...	...	...	...	...	...				7	1	3	4	2				
1985-86	Kamloops Blazers	WHL	6	1	0	1	0	...	...	...	...	...	...				...	...	...	...	...	...	...	...	
	Medicine Hat	WHL	55	20	30	50	82	...	...	...	...	...	...				22	6	6	12	39				
1986-87	Medicine Hat	WHL	70	27	43	70	130	...	...	...	...	...	...				20	7	11	18	46				
1987-88	Medicine Hat	WHL	54	47	43	90	120	...	...	...	...	...	...				14	12	19	*31	59				
1988-89	**NY Islanders**	**NHL**	16	1	0	1	30	0	0	1	16	6.3	-6				...	...	...	...	...	...	...	...	
	Springfield	AHL	40	13	18	31	67	...	...	...	...	...	...				...	...	...	...	...	...	...	...	
1989-90	**NY Islanders**	**NHL**	7	0	0	0	2	0	0	0	2	0.0	0				1	1	0	1	4	0	0	0	
	Springfield	AHL	54	25	27	52	69	...	...	...	...	...	...				16	4	7	11	45				
1990-91	**NY Islanders**	**NHL**	1	0	0	0	0	0	0	0	0	0.0	0				...	...	...	...	...	...	...	...	
	Capital District	AHL	12	3	4	7	22	...	...	...	...	...	...				...	...	...	...	...	...	...	...	
1991-92	**NY Islanders**	**NHL**	50	5	2	7	43	0	2	0	43	11.6	-23				...	...	...	...	...	...	...	...	
1992-93	**Tampa Bay**	**NHL**	54	9	15	24	62	2	0	0	75	12.0	0				...	...	...	...	...	...	...	...	
1993-94	**Tampa Bay**	**NHL**	39	8	7	15	40	2	0	1	51	15.7	-5				...	...	...	...	...	...	...	...	
	Philadelphia	NHL	14	3	5	8	6	0	0	1	30	10.0	1				...	...	...	...	...	...	...	...	
1994-95	**Philadelphia**	**NHL**	36	3	1	4	53	0	0	0	34	8.8	8				15	2	4	6	4	0	1	1	
1995-96	**Philadelphia**	**NHL**	59	6	15	21	58	1	1	0	49	12.2	0				3	0	0	0	0	0	0	0	
1996-97	**Boston**	**NHL**	72	13	15	28	82	0	3	2	152	8.6	-21				...	...	...	...	...	...	...	...	
1997-98	**Boston**	**NHL**	79	10	17	27	82	0	0	4	112	8.9	-13				6	1	0	1	8	0	0	0	
1998-99	**Boston**	**NHL**	71	7	14	21	95	1	0	0	121	5.8	-14	83	45.8	16:41	12	2	0	2	8	0	0	1	16:50
99-2000	**Boston**	**NHL**	50	5	16	21	42	0	0	0	93	5.4	-1	278	44.2	16:47	...	...	...	...	...	...	...	...	
	NY Rangers	NHL	12	1	3	4	8	0	0	0	18	5.6	-8	1	0.0	15:30	...	...	...	...	...	...	...	...	
2000-01	**Carolina**	**NHL**	74	6	18	24	54	0	2	1	99	6.1	-14	46	43.5	14:58	6	0	0	0	4	0	0	0	14:30
2001-02	**Dallas**	**NHL**	61	6	6	12	25	0	2	2	63	9.5	-2	76	44.7	10:52	...	...	...	...	...	...	...	...	
	Utah Grizzlies	AHL	3	1	1	2	0	...	...	...	...	...	...				...	...	...	...	...	...	...	...	
2002-03	**Dallas**	**NHL**	69	10	9	19	76	0	0	2	81	12.3	18	49	44.9	12:58	12	1	4	5	10	0	0	0	15:50
2003-04	**Dallas**	**NHL**	69	9	15	24	52	0	1	1	76	11.8	0	21	38.1	12:58	5	0	1	1	2	0	0	0	10:28
2004-05	Langnau	Swiss	9	2	3	5	8	...	...	...	...	...	...				...	...	...	...	...	...	...	...	
	Milano Vipers	Italy	9	4	8	12	4	...	...	...	...	...	...				15	9	11	20	20				
2005-06	**Tampa Bay**	**NHL**	61	4	13	17	30	2	0	1	72	5.6	-7	40	47.5	11:41	2	0	0	0	0	0	0	0	2:12
	NHL Totals		894	106	171	277	840	8	11	16	1187	8.9		594	44.4	13:53	62	7	9	16	40	0	1	2	14:29

Memorial Cup Tournament All-Star Team (1988) • Stafford Smythe Memorial Trophy (Memorial Cup Tournament MVP) (1988)

Claimed by **Tampa Bay** from **NY Islanders** in Expansion Draft, June 18, 1992. Traded to **Philadelphia** by **Tampa Bay** for Jim Cummins and Philadelphia's 4th round choice (later traded back to Philadelphia – Philadelphia selected Radovan Somik) in 1995 Entry Draft, March 18, 1994. Claimed by **San Jose** from **Philadelphia** in Waiver Draft, September 30, 1996. Traded to **Boston** by **San Jose** for Boston's 5th round choice (Adam Nittel) in 1997 Entry Draft, September 30, 1996. Traded to **NY Rangers** by **Boston** for Mike Knuble, March 10, 2000. Traded to **Carolina** by **NY Rangers** with Darren Langdon for Sandy McCarthy and Carolina's 4th round choice (Bryce Lampman) in 2001 Entry Draft, August 4, 2000. Signed as a free agent by **Dallas**, July 1, 2001. Signed as a free agent by **Langnau** (Swiss), November 2, 2004. Signed as a free agent by **Milano** (Italy), December 20, 2004. Signed as a free agent by **Tampa Bay**, August 9, 2005.

DIMITRAKOS, Niko

(DIH-mih-tra-kohs, NEEK-oh)   PHI.

Right wing. Shoots right. 5'10", 205 lbs.   Born, Somerville, MA, May 21, 1979. San Jose's 4th choice, 155th overall, in 1999 Entry Draft.

Season	Club	League	GP	G	A	Pts	PIM	PP	SH	GW	S	%	+/-	TF	F%	Min	GP	G	A	Pts	PIM	PP	SH	GW	Min
1994-95	Matignon	High-MA	23	10	12	22		...	...	...	...	...	...				...	...	...	...	...	...	...	...	
1995-96	Matignon	High-MA	25	12	28	40		...	...	...	...	...	...				...	...	...	...	...	...	...	...	
1996-97	Matignon	High-MA	25	23	32	55		...	...	...	...	...	...				...	...	...	...	...	...	...	...	
1997-98	Avon Old Farms	High-CT	26	27	28	55		...	...	...	...	...	...				...	...	...	...	...	...	...	...	
1998-99	U. of Maine	H-East	35	8	19	27	33	...	...	...	...	...	...				...	...	...	...	...	...	...	...	
99-2000	U. of Maine	H-East	32	11	16	27	16	...	...	...	...	...	...				...	...	...	...	...	...	...	...	
2000-01	U. of Maine	H-East	29	11	14	25	43	...	...	...	...	...	...				...	...	...	...	...	...	...	...	
2001-02	U. of Maine	H-East	43	20	31	51	44	...	...	...	...	...	...	•			...	...	...	...	...	...	...	...	
2002-03	**San Jose**	**NHL**	21	6	7	13	8	3	0	0	34	17.6	-7	2	50.0	14:15	...	...	...	...	...	...	...	...	
	Cleveland Barons	AHL	55	15	29	44	30	...	...	...	...	...	...				...	...	...	...	...	...	...	...	
2003-04	**San Jose**	**NHL**	68	9	15	24	49	2	0	4	116	7.8	6	4	50.0	13:20	15	1	8	9	8	0	0	1	14:31
	Cleveland Barons	AHL	7	4	4	8	4	...	...	...	...	...	...				...	...	...	...	...	...	...	...	
2004-05	Langnau	Swiss	3	0	1	1	2	...	...	...	...	...	...				6	3	3	6	16				
2005-06	**San Jose**	**NHL**	45	4	12	16	26	0	0	1	66	6.1	0	8	25.0	11:54	...	...	...	...	...	...	...	...	
	Philadelphia	**NHL**	19	5	4	9	6	1	0	1	27	18.5	4	2	50.0	10:52	5	0	0	0	0	0	0	0	10:07
	NHL Totals		153	24	38	62	89	6	0	5	243	9.9		16	37.5	12:44	20	1	8	9	10	0	0	1	13:25

NCAA Championship All-Tournament Team (1999) • Hockey East Second All-Star Team (2002)

Signed as a free agent by **Langnau** (Swiss), February 2, 2005. Traded to **Philadelphia** by **San Jose** for Philadelphia's 3rd round choice (later traded to Columbus - Columbus selected Tommy Sestito) in 2006 Entry Draft, March 9, 2006.

DINGMAN, Chris

(DIHNG-man, KRIHS)

Left wing. Shoots left. 6'4", 235 lbs.   Born, Edmonton, Alta., July 6, 1976. Calgary's 1st choice, 19th overall, in 1994 Entry Draft.

Season	Club	League	GP	G	A	Pts	PIM	PP	SH	GW	S	%	+/-	TF	F%	Min	GP	G	A	Pts	PIM	PP	SH	GW	Min
1991-92	Edm. Mercurys	AMHL	36	23	18	41	72	...	...	...	...	...	...				...	...	...	...	...	...	...	...	
1992-93	Brandon	WHL	50	10	17	27	64	...	...	...	...	...	...				4	0	0	0	0				
1993-94	Brandon	WHL	45	21	20	41	77	...	...	...	...	...	...				13	1	7	8	39				
1994-95	Brandon	WHL	66	40	43	83	201	...	...	...	...	...	...				3	1	0	1	9				
1995-96	Brandon	WHL	40	16	29	45	109	...	...	...	...	...	...				19	12	11	23	60				
	Saint John Flames	AHL	...	...	...	...	...	...	...	...	...	...	...				1	0	0	0	0				
1996-97	Saint John Flames	AHL	71	5	6	11	195	...	...	...	...	...	...				...	...	...	...	...	...	...	...	
1997-98	**Calgary**	**NHL**	70	3	3	6	149	1	0	0	47	6.4	-11				...	...	...	...	...	...	...	...	
1998-99	**Calgary**	**NHL**	2	0	0	0	17	0	0	0	1	0.0	-2	0	0.0	8:11	...	...	...	...	...	...	...	...	
	Saint John Flames	AHL	50	5	7	12	140	...	...	...	...	...	...				...	...	...	...	...	...	...	...	
	Colorado	NHL	1	0	0	0	7	0	0	0	0	0.0	0	0	0.0	0:30	...	...	...	...	...	...	...	...	
	Hershey Bears	AHL	17	1	3	4	102	...	...	...	...	...	...				5	0	2	2	6				

			Regular Season														Playoffs								
Season	Club	League	GP	G	A	Pts	PIM	PP	SH	GW	S	%	+/-	TF	F%	Min	GP	G	A	Pts	PIM	PP	SH	GW	Min
99-2000	Colorado	NHL	68	8	3	11	132	2	0	1	54	14.8	−2	2	0.0	6:29	....	....	....	....	....	....	....	....	....
2000-01 ◆	Colorado	NHL	41	1	1	2	108	0	0	0	33	3.0	−3	0	0.0	6:26	16	0	4	4	14	0	0	0	6:18
2001-02	Carolina	NHL	30	0	1	1	77	0	0	0	17	0.0	−2	2	100.0	6:54	....	....	....	....	....	....	....	....	....
	Tampa Bay	NHL	14	0	4	4	26	0	0	0	24	0.0	−8	0	0.0	10:43	....	....	....	....	....	....	....	....	....
2002-03	Tampa Bay	NHL	51	2	1	3	91	0	0	0	41	4.9	−11	3	33.3	9:34	10	1	0	1	4	0	0	0	12:45
2003-04 ◆	Tampa Bay	NHL	74	1	5	6	140	0	0	0	65	1.5	−9	20	30.0	8:16	23	1	1	2	63	0	0	0	5:58
2004-05			DID NOT PLAY																						
2005-06	Tampa Bay	NHL	34	0	1	1	22	0	0	0	24	0.0	−10	3	0.0	5:29	3	0	0	0	19	0	0	0	2:23
	NHL Totals		385	15	19	34	769	3	0	1	306	4.9		30	30.0	7:31	52	2	5	7	100	0	0	0	7:10

Traded to **Colorado** by **Calgary** with Theoren Fleury for Rene Corbet, Wade Belak, Robyn Regehr and Colorado's 2nd round compensatory choice (Jarret Stoll) in 2000 Entry Draft, February 28, 1999. • Missed majority of 2000-01 season recovering from knee injury suffered in game vs. Ottawa, November 15, 2000. Traded to **Carolina** by **Colorado** for Carolina's 5th round choice (Mikko Viitanen) in 2001 Entry Draft, June 24, 2001. Traded to **Tampa Bay** by **Carolina** with Shane Willis for Kevin Weekes, March 5, 2002.

DiPENTA, Joe

(DIH-pehn-tah, JOH) **ANA.**

Defense. Shoots left. 6'2", 205 lbs. Born, Barrie, Ont., February 25, 1979. Florida's 2nd choice, 61st overall, in 1998 Entry Draft.

Season	Club	League	GP	G	A	Pts	PIM	PP	SH	GW	S	%	+/-	TF	F%	Min	GP	G	A	Pts	PIM	PP	SH	GW	Min
1996-97	Smiths Falls Bears	CJHL	54	13	22	35	92	....	....	....	....	....	....	....	....	....	....	....	....	....	....	....	....	....	....
1997-98	Boston University	H-East	38	2	16	18	50	....	....	....	....	....	....	....	....	....	....	....	....	....	....	....	....	....	....
1998-99	Boston University	H-East	36	2	15	17	72	....	....	....	....	....	....	....	....	....	....	....	....	....	....	....	....	....	....
99-2000	Halifax	QMJHL	63	13	43	56	83	....	....	....	....	....	....	....	....	....	10	3	4	7	26	....	....	....	....
2000-01	Philadelphia	AHL	71	3	5	8	65	....	....	....	....	....	....	....	....	....	10	1	2	3	15	....	....	....	....
2001-02	Philadelphia	AHL	61	2	4	6	71	....	....	....	....	....	....	....	....	....	....	....	....	....	....	....	....	....	....
	Chicago Wolves	AHL	15	0	2	2	15	....	....	....	....	....	....	....	....	....	25	1	3	4	22	....	....	....	....
2002-03	Atlanta	NHL	3	1	1	2	0	0	0	0	2	50.0	3	0	0.0	15:47	....	....	....	....	....	....	....	....	....
	Chicago Wolves	AHL	76	2	17	19	107	....	....	....	....	....	....	....	....	....	9	0	1	1	7	....	....	....	....
2003-04	Chicago Wolves	AHL	73	0	6	6	105	....	....	....	....	....	....	....	....	....	10	1	0	1	13	....	....	....	....
2004-05	Manitoba Moose	AHL	73	2	10	12	48	....	....	....	....	....	....	....	....	....	14	0	5	5	2	....	....	....	....
2005-06	Anaheim	NHL	72	2	6	8	46	0	0	0	27	7.4	8	0	0.0	13:31	16	0	0	0	13	0	0	0	11:34
	NHL Totals		75	3	7	10	46	0	0	0	29	10.3		0	0.0	13:36	16	0	0	0	13	0	0	0	11:34

• Left **Boston U.** (H-East) and signed with **Halifax** (QMJHL), May 2, 1999. Signed as a free agent by **Philadelphia**, July 12, 2000. Traded to **Atlanta** by **Philadelphia** for Jarrod Skalde, March 5, 2002. Signed as a free agent by **Vancouver**, August 19, 2004. Signed as a free agent by **Anaheim**, August 11, 2005.

DISALVATORE, Jon

(dih-sal-vuh-TOH-ray, JAWN) **ST.L.**

Right wing. Shoots right. 6'1", 200 lbs. Born, Bangor, ME, March 30, 1981. San Jose's 2nd choice, 104th overall, in 2000 Entry Draft.

Season	Club	League	GP	G	A	Pts	PIM	PP	SH	GW	S	%	+/-	TF	F%	Min	GP	G	A	Pts	PIM	PP	SH	GW	Min
1997-98	N.E. Jr. Coyotes	EJHL	38	24	41	65	....	....	....	....	....	....	....	....	....	....	....	....	....	....	....	....	....	....	....
1998-99	N.E. Jr. Coyotes	EJHL	48	44	76	*120	38	....	....	....	....	....	....	....	....	....	....	....	....	....	....	....	....	....	....
99-2000	Providence	H-East	38	15	12	27	12	....	....	....	....	....	....	....	....	....	....	....	....	....	....	....	....	....	....
2000-01	Providence	H-East	36	9	16	25	29	....	....	....	....	....	....	....	....	....	....	....	....	....	....	....	....	....	....
2001-02	Providence	H-East	38	16	26	42	6	....	....	....	....	....	....	....	....	....	....	....	....	....	....	....	....	....	....
2002-03	Providence	H-East	36	19	29	48	12	....	....	....	....	....	....	....	....	....	....	....	....	....	....	....	....	....	....
2003-04	Cleveland Barons	AHL	74	22	24	46	30	....	....	....	....	....	....	....	....	....	8	1	1	2	2	....	....	....	....
2004-05	Worcester IceCats	AHL	79	22	23	45	42	....	....	....	....	....	....	....	....	....	....	....	....	....	....	....	....	....	....
2005-06	St. Louis	NHL	5	0	0	0	2	0	0	0	3	0.0	−1	0	0.0	8:27	....	....	....	....	....	....	....	....	....
	Peoria Rivermen	AHL	72	22	45	67	42	....	....	....	....	....	....	....	....	....	4	0	0	0	0	....	....	....	....
	NHL Totals		5	0	0	0	2	0	0	0	3	0.0		0	0.0	8:27	....	....	....	....	....	....	....	....	....

Signed as a free agent by **St. Louis**, June 30, 2004.

DOAN, Shane

(DOHN, SHAYN) **PHX.**

Right wing. Shoots right. 6'2", 216 lbs. Born, Halkirk, Alta., October 10, 1976. Winnipeg's 1st choice, 7th overall, in 1995 Entry Draft.

Season	Club	League	GP	G	A	Pts	PIM	PP	SH	GW	S	%	+/-	TF	F%	Min	GP	G	A	Pts	PIM	PP	SH	GW	Min
1991-92	Killam Selects	AAHA	56	80	84	164	74	....	....	....	....	....	....	....	....	....	....	....	....	....	....	....	....	....	....
1992-93	Kamloops Blazers	WHL	51	7	12	19	65	....	....	....	....	....	....	....	....	....	13	0	1	1	8	....	....	....	....
1993-94	Kamloops Blazers	WHL	52	24	24	48	88	....	....	....	....	....	....	....	....	....	....	....	....	....	....	....	....	....	....
1994-95	Kamloops Blazers	WHL	71	37	57	94	106	....	....	....	....	....	....	....	....	....	21	6	10	16	16	....	....	....	....
1995-96	Winnipeg	NHL	74	7	10	17	101	1	0	3	106	6.6	−9	....	....	....	6	0	0	0	6	0	0	0	....
1996-97	Phoenix	NHL	63	4	8	12	49	0	0	0	100	4.0	−3	....	....	....	4	0	0	0	2	0	0	0	....
1997-98	Phoenix	NHL	33	5	6	11	35	0	0	3	42	11.9	−3	....	....	....	6	1	0	1	6	0	0	0	....
	Springfield	AHL	39	21	21	42	64	....	....	....	....	....	....	....	....	....	....	....	....	....	....	....	....	....	....
1998-99	Phoenix	NHL	79	6	16	22	54	0	0	0	156	3.8	−5	6	16.7	12:42	7	2	2	4	6	0	0	2	17:58
99-2000	Phoenix	NHL	81	26	25	51	66	1	1	4	221	11.8	6	25	36.0	16:51	4	1	2	3	8	1	0	0	18:11
2000-01	Phoenix	NHL	76	26	37	63	89	6	1	6	220	11.8	0	15	40.0	19:32	....	....	....	....	....	....	....	....	....
2001-02	Phoenix	NHL	81	20	29	49	61	6	0	2	205	9.8	11	52	44.2	18:10	5	2	2	4	6	0	0	0	17:21
2002-03	Phoenix	NHL	82	21	37	58	86	7	0	2	225	9.3	3	623	39.8	18:47	....	....	....	....	....	....	....	....	....
2003-04	Phoenix	NHL	79	27	41	68	47	9	2	1	254	10.6	−11	55	40.0	21:46	....	....	....	....	....	....	....	....	....
2004-05			DID NOT PLAY																						
2005-06	Phoenix	NHL	82	30	36	66	123	17	0	7	254	11.8	−9	126	43.7	19:08	....	....	....	....	....	....	....	....	....
	Canada	Olympics	6	2	1	3	2	....	....	....	....	....	....	....	....	....	....	....	....	....	....	....	....	....	....
	NHL Totals		730	172	245	417	711	47	4	28	1783	9.6		902	40.4	18:08	32	6	6	12	34	1	0	2	17:49

Memorial Cup Tournament All-Star Team (1995) • Stafford Smythe Memorial Trophy (Memorial Cup Tournament MVP) (1995)

Played in NHL All-Star Game (2004)

Transferred to **Phoenix** after **Winnipeg** franchise relocated, July 1, 1996.

DOIG, Jason

(DOIG, JAY-suhn)

Defense. Shoots right. 6'3", 230 lbs. Born, Montreal, Que., January 29, 1977. Winnipeg's 3rd choice, 34th overall, in 1995 Entry Draft.

Season	Club	League	GP	G	A	Pts	PIM	PP	SH	GW	S	%	+/-	TF	F%	Min	GP	G	A	Pts	PIM	PP	SH	GW	Min
1990-91	North Shore	QAHA	31	30	33	63	53	....	....	....	....	....	....	....	....	....	....	....	....	....	....	....	....	....	....
1991-92	North Shore	QAHA	29	11	11	22	20	....	....	....	....	....	....	....	....	....	....	....	....	....	....	....	....	....	....
1992-93	Lac St-Louis Lions	QAAA	35	11	16	27	40	....	....	....	....	....	....	....	....	....	7	5	5	10	16	....	....	....	....
1993-94	St-Jean Lynx	QMJHL	63	8	17	25	65	....	....	....	....	....	....	....	....	....	5	0	2	2	2	....	....	....	....
1994-95	Laval Titan	QMJHL	55	13	42	55	259	....	....	....	....	....	....	....	....	....	20	4	13	17	39	....	....	....	....
1995-96	Laval Titan	QMJHL	5	3	6	9	20	....	....	....	....	....	....	....	....	....	....	....	....	....	....	....	....	....	....
	Granby	QMJHL	24	4	30	34	91	....	....	....	....	....	....	....	....	....	20	10	22	32	*110	....	....	....	....
	Winnipeg	NHL	15	1	1	2	28	0	0	0	7	14.3	−2	....	....	....	....	....	....	....	....	....	....	....	....
	Springfield	AHL	5	0	0	0	28	....	....	....	....	....	....	....	....	....	....	....	....	....	....	....	....	....	....
1996-97	Granby	QMJHL	39	14	33	47	211	....	....	....	....	....	....	....	....	....	5	0	4	4	27	....	....	....	....
	Las Vegas	IHL	6	0	1	1	19	....	....	....	....	....	....	....	....	....	....	....	....	....	....	....	....	....	....
	Springfield	AHL	5	0	3	3	2	....	....	....	....	....	....	....	....	....	17	1	4	5	37	....	....	....	....
1997-98	Phoenix	NHL	4	0	1	1	12	0	0	0	1	0.0	−4	....	....	....	....	....	....	....	....	....	....	....	....
	Springfield	AHL	46	2	25	27	153	....	....	....	....	....	....	....	....	....	3	0	0	0	2	....	....	....	....
1998-99	Phoenix	NHL	9	0	1	1	10	0	0	0	0	0.0	2	0	0.0	5:08	....	....	....	....	....	....	....	....	....
	Springfield	AHL	32	3	5	8	67	....	....	....	....	....	....	....	....	....	....	....	....	....	....	....	....	....	....
	Hartford	AHL	8	1	4	5	40	....	....	....	....	....	....	....	....	....	7	1	1	2	39	....	....	....	....
99-2000	NY Rangers	NHL	7	0	1	1	22	0	0	0	3	0.0	−2	0	0.0	8:50	....	....	....	....	....	....	....	....	....
	Hartford	AHL	27	3	11	14	70	....	....	....	....	....	....	....	....	....	21	1	5	6	20	....	....	....	....
2000-01	NY Rangers	NHL	3	0	0	0	0	0	0	0	1	0.0	0	0	0.0	6:35	....	....	....	....	....	....	....	....	....
	Hartford	AHL	52	4	20	24	178	....	....	....	....	....	....	....	....	....	5	0	1	1	4	....	....	....	....
2001-02	Grand Rapids	AHL	57	1	17	18	103	....	....	....	....	....	....	....	....	....	5	0	0	0	18	....	....	....	....
2002-03	Washington	NHL	55	3	5	8	108	0	0	1	41	7.3	−3	1	0.0	14:11	6	0	1	1	6	0	0	0	16:52
	Portland Pirates	AHL	21	1	4	5	66	....	....	....	....	....	....	....	....	....	....	....	....	....	....	....	....	....	....
2003-04	Washington	NHL	65	2	9	11	105	0	0	0	59	3.4	−12	0	0.0	19:09	....	....	....	....	....	....	....	....	....
2004-05			DID NOT PLAY																						
2005-06	Manitoba Moose	AHL	18	0	4	4	24	....	....	....	....	....	....	....	....	....	....	....	....	....	....	....	....	....	....
	NHL Totals		158	6	18	24	285	0	0	1	112	5.4		1	0.0	15:29	6	0	1	1	6	0	0	0	16:52

QMJHL All-Rookie Team (1994) • Memorial Cup Tournament All-Star Team (1996)

Transferred to **Phoenix** after **Winnipeg** franchise relocated, July 1, 1996. Traded to **NY Rangers** by **Phoenix** with Phoenix's 6th round choice (Jay Dardis) in 1999 Entry Draft for Stan Neckar, March 23, 1999. Traded to **Ottawa** by **NY Rangers** with Jeff Ulmer for Sean Gagnon, June 29, 2001. Signed as free agent by **Washington**, September 12, 2002. Signed as a free agent by **Vancouver**, October 26, 2005. • Missed majority of 2005-06 season recovering from shoulder injury suffered in game at Grand Rapids (AHL), November 15, 2005.

DOMI, Tie

(DOH-mee, TIGH)

Right wing. Shoots right. 5'10", 213 lbs. Born, Windsor, Ont., November 1, 1969. Toronto's 2nd choice, 27th overall, in 1988 Entry Draft.

			Regular Season														Playoffs								
Season	Club	League	GP	G	A	Pts	PIM	PP	SH	GW	S	%	+/-	TF	F%	Min	GP	G	A	Pts	PIM	PP	SH	GW	Min
1984-85	Belle River	OHA-C	28	7	5	12	98	....	....	....	....	....	....	....	....	....	....	....	....	....	....	....	....	....	....
1985-86	Windsor Bulldogs	OHA-B	42	8	17	25	*346	....	....	....	....	....	....	....	....	....	....	....	....	....	....	....	....	....	....
1986-87	Peterborough	OHA-B	2	0	0	0	10	....	....	....	....	....	....	....	....	....	....	....	....	....	....	....	....	....	....
	Peterborough	OHL	18	1	1	2	79	....	....	....	....	....	....	....	....	....	....	....	....	....	....	....	....	....	....
1987-88	Peterborough	OHL	60	22	21	43	*292	....	....	....	....	....	....	....	....	....	12	3	9	12	24	....	....	....	....
1988-89	Peterborough	OHL	43	14	16	30	175	....	....	....	....	....	....	....	....	....	17	10	9	19	*70	....	....	....	....
1989-90	Toronto	NHL	2	0	0	0	42	0	0	0	0	0.0	0	....	....	....	....	....	....	....	....	....	....	....	....
	Newmarket Saints	AHL	57	14	11	25	285	....	....	....	....	....	....	....	....	....	....	....	....	....	....	....	....	....	....
1990-91	NY Rangers	NHL	28	1	0	1	185	0	0	0	5	20.0	–5	....	....	....	....	....	....	....	....	....	....	....	....
	Binghamton	AHL	25	11	6	17	219	....	....	....	....	....	....	....	....	....	7	3	2	5	16	....	....	....	....
1991-92	NY Rangers	NHL	42	2	4	6	246	0	0	1	20	10.0	–4	....	....	....	6	1	1	2	32	0	0	0	....
1992-93	NY Rangers	NHL	12	2	0	2	95	0	0	0	11	18.2	–1	....	....	....	....	....	....	....	....	....	....	....	....
	Winnipeg	NHL	49	3	10	13	249	0	0	0	29	10.3	2	....	....	....	6	1	0	1	23	0	0	0	....
1993-94	Winnipeg	NHL	81	8	11	19	*347	0	0	1	98	8.2	–8	....	....	....	....	....	....	....	....	....	....	....	....
1994-95	Winnipeg	NHL	31	4	4	8	128	0	0	0	34	11.8	–6	....	....	....	....	....	....	....	....	....	....	....	....
	Toronto	NHL	9	0	1	1	31	0	0	0	12	0.0	1	....	....	....	7	1	0	1	0	0	0	0	....
1995-96	Toronto	NHL	72	7	6	13	297	0	0	1	61	11.5	–3	....	....	....	6	0	2	2	4	0	0	0	....
1996-97	Toronto	NHL	80	11	17	28	275	2	0	1	98	11.2	–17	....	....	....	....	....	....	....	....	....	....	....	....
1997-98	Toronto	NHL	80	4	10	14	365	0	0	0	72	5.6	–5	....	....	....	....	....	....	....	....	....	....	....	....
1998-99	Toronto	NHL	72	8	14	22	198	0	0	1	65	12.3	5	9	44.4	9:42	14	0	2	2	24	0	0	0	6:58
99-2000	Toronto	NHL	70	5	9	14	198	0	0	2	64	7.8	–5	4	25.0	9:58	12	0	1	1	20	0	0	0	6:40
2000-01	Toronto	NHL	82	13	7	20	214	1	0	1	60	21.7	2	5	80.0	8:23	8	0	1	1	20	0	0	0	8:27
2001-02	Toronto	NHL	74	9	10	19	157	0	0	2	93	9.7	3	22	45.5	10:20	19	1	3	4	*61	0	0	1	11:15
2002-03	Toronto	NHL	79	15	14	29	171	4	0	0	91	16.5	–1	21	19.1	10:56	7	1	0	1	13	0	0	0	14:47
2003-04	Toronto	NHL	80	7	13	20	208	1	0	0	84	8.3	–2	7	0.0	11:12	13	2	2	4	41	0	0	1	11:49
2004-05			DID NOT PLAY																						
2005-06	Toronto	NHL	77	5	11	16	109	1	0	0	67	7.5	–10	5	40.0	9:43	....	....	....	....	....	....	....	....	....
	NHL Totals		1020	104	141	245	3515	9	0	10	964	10.8		73	34.2	10:02	98	7	12	19	238	0	0	2	9:49

Traded to **NY Rangers** by **Toronto** with Mark LaForest for Greg Johnston, June 28, 1990. Traded to **Winnipeg** by **NY Rangers** with Kris King for Ed Olczyk, December 28, 1992. Traded to **Toronto** by **Winnipeg** for Mike Eastwood and Toronto's 3rd round choice (Brad Isbister) in 1995 Entry Draft, April 7, 1995. Traded to **Nashville** by **Toronto** for Nashville's 8th round choice (Shaun Landolt) in 2003 Entry Draft, June 30, 2002. Signed as a free agent by **Toronto**, July 14, 2002.

DONOVAN, Shean

(DAW-nuh-vuhn, SHAWN) **BOS.**

Right wing. Shoots right. 6'2", 209 lbs. Born, Timmins, Ont., January 22, 1975. San Jose's 2nd choice, 28th overall, in 1993 Entry Draft.

1990-91	Kanata Valley	CJHL	44	8	5	13	8	....	....	....	....	....	....	....	....	....	....	....	....	....	....	....	....	....	....
1991-92	Ottawa 67's	OHL	58	11	8	19	14	....	....	....	....	....	....	....	....	....	11	1	0	1	5	....	....	....	....
1992-93	Ottawa 67's	OHL	66	29	23	52	33	....	....	....	....	....	....	....	....	....	....	....	....	....	....	....	....	....	....
1993-94	Ottawa 67's	OHL	62	35	49	84	63	....	....	....	....	....	....	....	....	....	17	10	11	21	14	....	....	....	....
1994-95	Ottawa 67's	OHL	29	22	19	41	41	....	....	....	....	....	....	....	....	....	....	....	....	....	....	....	....	....	....
	San Jose	NHL	14	0	0	0	6	0	0	0	13	0.0	–6	....	....	....	7	0	1	1	6	0	0	0	....
	Kansas City	IHL	5	0	2	2	7	....	....	....	....	....	....	....	....	....	14	5	3	8	23	....	....	....	....
1995-96	San Jose	NHL	74	13	8	21	39	0	1	2	73	17.8	–17	....	....	....	....	....	....	....	....	....	....	....	....
	Kansas City	IHL	4	0	0	0	8	....	....	....	....	....	....	....	....	....	5	0	0	0	8	....	....	....	....
1996-97	San Jose	NHL	73	9	6	15	42	0	1	0	115	7.8	–18	....	....	....	....	....	....	....	....	....	....	....	....
	Kentucky	AHL	3	1	3	4	18	....	....	....	....	....	....	....	....	....	....	....	....	....	....	....	....	....	....
1997-98	San Jose	NHL	20	3	3	6	22	0	0	0	24	12.5	3	....	....	....	....	....	....	....	....	....	....	....	....
	Colorado	NHL	47	5	7	12	48	0	0	0	57	8.8	3	....	....	....	....	....	....	....	....	....	....	....	....
1998-99	Colorado	NHL	68	7	12	19	37	1	0	1	81	8.6	4	9	22.2	8:46	5	0	0	0	2	0	0	0	4:55
99-2000	Colorado	NHL	18	1	0	1	8	0	0	0	13	7.7	–4	1	0.0	5:20	....	....	....	....	....	....	....	....	....
	Atlanta	NHL	33	4	7	11	18	1	0	1	53	7.5	–13	22	31.8	14:19	....	....	....	....	....	....	....	....	....
2000-01	Atlanta	NHL	63	12	11	23	47	1	3	1	93	12.9	–14	218	45.9	14:03	....	....	....	....	....	....	....	....	....
2001-02	Atlanta	NHL	48	6	6	12	40	1	0	2	64	9.4	–16	12	50.0	13:30	....	....	....	....	....	....	....	....	....
	Pittsburgh	NHL	13	2	1	3	4	0	0	0	18	11.1	–5	4	0.0	14:34	....	....	....	....	....	....	....	....	....
2002-03	Pittsburgh	NHL	52	4	5	9	30	0	1	0	66	6.1	–6	37	24.3	13:01	....	....	....	....	....	....	....	....	....
	Calgary	NHL	13	1	2	3	7	0	0	1	22	4.5	–2	3	66.7	15:39	....	....	....	....	....	....	....	....	....
2003-04	Calgary	NHL	82	18	24	42	72	3	3	8	138	13.0	14	53	39.6	14:55	24	5	5	10	23	0	0	2	15:27
2004-05	Geneve	Swiss	12	5	3	8	30	....	....	....	....	....	....	....	....	....	....	....	....	....	....	....	....	....	....
2005-06	Calgary	NHL	80	9	11	20	82	0	1	0	132	6.8	9	26	30.8	11:47	7	0	0	0	6	0	0	0	11:24
	NHL Totals		698	94	103	197	502	7	10	16	962	9.8		385	40.3	12:38	43	5	6	11	37	0	0	2	13:12

Traded to **Colorado** by **San Jose** with San Jose's 1st round choice (Alex Tanguay) in 1998 Entry Draft for Mike Ricci and Colorado's 2nd round choice (later traded to Buffalo – Buffalo selected Jaroslav Kristek), in 1998 Entry Draft, November 21, 1997. Traded to **Atlanta** by **Colorado** for Rick Tabaracci, December 8, 1999. Claimed on waivers by **Pittsburgh** from **Atlanta**, March 15, 2002. Traded to **Calgary** by **Pittsburgh** for Micki Dupont and Mathias Johansson, March 11, 2003. Signed as a free agent by **Geneve** (Swiss), November 13, 2004. Signed as a free agent by **Boston**, July 2, 2006.

DOULL, Doug

(DOOL, DUHG)

Left wing. Shoots left. 6'2", 216 lbs. Born, Green Bay, N.S., May 31, 1974.

1990-91	Wexford Raiders	MTHL	39	22	36	58	141	....	....	....	....	....	....	....	....	....	....	....	....	....	....	....	....	....	....
1991-92	Belleville Bulls	OHL	62	6	11	17	123	....	....	....	....	....	....	....	....	....	....	....	....	....	....	....	....	....	....
1992-93	Belleville Bulls	OHL	65	19	37	56	143	....	....	....	....	....	....	....	....	....	....	....	....	....	....	....	....	....	....
1993-94	Belleville Bulls	OHL	62	13	24	37	143	....	....	....	....	....	....	....	....	....	....	....	....	....	....	....	....	....	....
1994-95	Belleville Bulls	OHL	29	7	12	19	71	....	....	....	....	....	....	....	....	....	16	2	13	15	39	....	....	....	....
1995-96	St. Mary's Huskies	AUAA	11	4	4	8	54	....	....	....	....	....	....	....	....	....	....	....	....	....	....	....	....	....	....
1996-97	St. Mary's Huskies	AUAA	18	3	10	13	138	....	....	....	....	....	....	....	....	....	....	....	....	....	....	....	....	....	....
1997-98	St. Mary's Huskies	AUAA	25	4	11	15	227	....	....	....	....	....	....	....	....	....	....	....	....	....	....	....	....	....	....
1998-99	Michigan	IHL	55	4	11	15	227	....	....	....	....	....	....	....	....	....	3	1	1	2	4	....	....	....	....
99-2000	Detroit Vipers	IHL	17	0	2	2	69	....	....	....	....	....	....	....	....	....	....	....	....	....	....	....	....	....	....
	Manitoba Moose	IHL	45	4	4	8	184	....	....	....	....	....	....	....	....	....	2	0	0	0	2	....	....	....	....
2000-01	Manchester Storm	Britain	15	1	6	7	51	....	....	....	....	....	....	....	....	....	....	....	....	....	....	....	....	....	....
	Saint John Flames	AHL	49	3	10	13	167	....	....	....	....	....	....	....	....	....	16	0	1	1	32	....	....	....	....
2001-02	St. John's	AHL	36	5	8	13	166	....	....	....	....	....	....	....	....	....	9	0	1	1	17	....	....	....	....
2002-03	St. John's	AHL	70	15	10	25	257	....	....	....	....	....	....	....	....	....	....	....	....	....	....	....	....	....	....
2003-04	Boston	NHL	35	0	1	1	132	0	0	0	4	0.0	2	0	0.0	2:50	....	....	....	....	....	....	....	....	....
	Providence Bruins	AHL	22	1	0	1	98	....	....	....	....	....	....	....	....	....	....	....	....	....	....	....	....	....	....
2004-05	Utah Grizzlies	AHL	40	1	1	2	232	....	....	....	....	....	....	....	....	....	....	....	....	....	....	....	....	....	....
2005-06	San Antonio	AHL	26	1	2	3	84	....	....	....	....	....	....	....	....	....	....	....	....	....	....	....	....	....	....
	Washington	NHL	2	0	0	0	19	0	0	0	0	0.0	–1	0	0.0	3:57	....	....	....	....	....	....	....	....	....
	Hershey Bears	AHL	21	1	2	3	117	....	....	....	....	....	....	....	....	....	1	0	0	0	4	....	....	....	....
	NHL Totals		37	0	1	1	151	0	0	0	4	0.0		0	0.0	2:53	....	....	....	....	....	....	....	....	....

Signed as a free agent by **Manchester** (Britain), August 15, 2000. Signed to a 25-game tryout contract by **Saint John** (AHL) after securing release from **Manchester** (Britain), December 19, 2000. Signed as a free agent by **Saint John** (AHL), February 18, 2001. Signed as a free agent by **Toronto**, July 25, 2001. • Missed majority of 2001-02 season recovering from ankle injury suffered in game vs. Manitoba (AHL), October 19, 2001. Signed as a free agent by **Boston**, July 28, 2003. Signed as a free agent by **Phoenix**, September 2, 2004. Traded to **Washington** by **Phoenix** for Dwayne Zinger, February 3, 2006.

DOWD, Jim

(DOWD, JIHM)

Center. Shoots right. 6'1", 190 lbs. Born, Brick, NJ, December 25, 1968. New Jersey's 7th choice, 149th overall, in 1987 Entry Draft.

1983-84	Brick	High-NJ	20	19	30	49	....	....	....	....	....	....	....	....	....	....	....	....	....	....	....	....	....	....	....
1984-85	Brick	High-NJ	24	58	55	113	....	....	....	....	....	....	....	....	....	....	....	....	....	....	....	....	....	....	....
1985-86	Brick	High-NJ	24	47	51	98	....	....	....	....	....	....	....	....	....	....	....	....	....	....	....	....	....	....	....
1986-87	Brick	High-NJ	24	22	33	55	....	....	....	....	....	....	....	....	....	....	....	....	....	....	....	....	....	....	....
1987-88	Lake Superior	CCHA	45	18	27	45	16	....	....	....	....	....	....	....	....	....	....	....	....	....	....	....	....	....	....
1988-89	Lake Superior	CCHA	46	24	35	59	40	....	....	....	....	....	....	....	....	....	....	....	....	....	....	....	....	....	....
1989-90	Lake Superior	CCHA	46	25	*67	92	30	....	....	....	....	....	....	....	....	....	....	....	....	....	....	....	....	....	....
1990-91	Lake Superior	CCHA	44	24	*54	*78	53	....	....	....	....	....	....	....	....	....	....	....	....	....	....	....	....	....	....
1991-92	New Jersey	NHL	1	0	0	0	0	0	0	0	0	0.0	0	....	....	....	....	....	....	....	....	....	....	....	....
	Utica Devils	AHL	78	17	42	59	47	....	....	....	....	....	....	....	....	....	4	2	2	4	4	....	....	....	....
1992-93	New Jersey	NHL	1	0	0	0	0	0	0	0	1	0.0	–1	....	....	....	....	....	....	....	....	....	....	....	....
	Utica Devils	AHL	78	27	45	72	62	....	....	....	....	....	....	....	....	....	5	1	7	8	10	....	....	....	....

			Regular Season														Playoffs								
Season	Club	League	GP	G	A	Pts	PIM	PP	SH	GW	S	%	+/-	TF	F%	Min	GP	G	A	Pts	PIM	PP	SH	GW	Min
1993-94	**New Jersey**	**NHL**	**15**	**5**	**10**	**15**	**0**	**2**	**0**	**0**	**26**	**19.2**	**8**	....	....	....	**19**	**2**	**6**	**8**	**8**	**0**	**0**	**0**	....
	Albany River Rats	AHL	58	26	37	63	76	....	....	....	....	....	....	....	....	....	....	....	....	....	....	....	....	....	....
1994-95 ♦	**New Jersey**	**NHL**	**10**	**1**	**4**	**5**	**0**	**1**	**0**	**0**	**14**	**7.1**	**–5**	....	....	....	**11**	**2**	**1**	**3**	**8**	**0**	**0**	**1**	....
1995-96	**New Jersey**	**NHL**	**28**	**4**	**9**	**13**	**17**	**0**	**0**	**0**	**41**	**9.8**	**–1**	....	....	....	....	....	....	....	....	....	....	....	....
	Vancouver	**NHL**	**38**	**1**	**6**	**7**	**6**	**0**	**0**	**0**	**35**	**2.9**	**–8**	....	....	....	**1**	**0**	**0**	**0**	**0**	**0**	**0**	**0**	....
1996-97	**NY Islanders**	**NHL**	**3**	**0**	**0**	**0**	**0**	**0**	**0**	**0**	**0**	**0.0**	**–1**	....	....	....	....	....	....	....	....	....	....	....	....
	Utah Grizzlies	IHL	48	10	21	31	27	....	....	....	....	....	....	....	....	....	....	....	....	....	....	....	....	....	....
	Saint John Flames	AHL	24	5	11	16	18	....	....	....	....	....	....	....	....	....	5	1	2	3	0	....	....	....	....
1997-98	**Calgary**	**NHL**	**48**	**6**	**8**	**14**	**12**	**0**	**1**	**0**	**58**	**10.3**	**10**	....	....	....	....	....	....	....	....	....	....	....	....
	Saint John Flames	AHL	35	8	30	38	20	....	....	....	....	....	....	....	....	....	19	3	13	16	10	....	....	....	....
1998-99	**Edmonton**	**NHL**	**1**	**0**	**0**	**0**	**0**	**0**	**0**	**0**	**1**	**0.0**	**0**	**7**	**14.3**	**9:47**	....	....	....	....	....	....	....	....	....
	Hamilton	AHL	51	15	29	44	82	....	....	....	....	....	....	....	....	....	11	3	6	9	8	....	....	....	....
99-2000	**Edmonton**	**NHL**	**69**	**5**	**18**	**23**	**45**	**2**	**0**	**1**	**103**	**4.9**	**10**	**720**	**54.0**	**13:08**	**5**	**2**	**1**	**3**	**4**	**0**	**0**	**0**	**15:22**
2000-01	**Minnesota**	**NHL**	**68**	**7**	**22**	**29**	**80**	**0**	**0**	**0**	**92**	**7.6**	**–6**	**1154**	**50.7**	**17:50**	....	....	....	....	....	....	....	....	....
2001-02	**Minnesota**	**NHL**	**82**	**13**	**30**	**43**	**54**	**5**	**0**	**1**	**111**	**11.7**	**–14**	**1243**	**52.9**	**15:34**	....	....	....	....	....	....	....	....	....
2002-03	**Minnesota**	**NHL**	**78**	**8**	**17**	**25**	**31**	**3**	**1**	**2**	**78**	**10.3**	**–1**	**930**	**47.9**	**13:03**	**15**	**0**	**2**	**2**	**0**	**0**	**0**	**0**	**12:58**
2003-04	**Minnesota**	**NHL**	**55**	**4**	**20**	**24**	**38**	**2**	**0**	**2**	**41**	**9.8**	**6**	**712**	**48.5**	**14:07**	....	....	....	....	....	....	....	....	....
	Montreal	**NHL**	**14**	**3**	**2**	**5**	**6**	**0**	**1**	**0**	**13**	**23.1**	**6**	**167**	**47.3**	**13:30**	**11**	**0**	**2**	**2**	**2**	**0**	**0**	**0**	**15:34**
2004-05	Hamburg Freezers	Germany	20	4	9	13	12	....	....	....	....	....	....	....	....	....	....	....	....	....	....	....	....	....	....
2005-06	**Chicago**	**NHL**	**60**	**3**	**12**	**15**	**38**	**0**	**0**	**0**	**55**	**5.5**	**–5**	**664**	**51.7**	**12:43**	....	....	....	....	....	....	....	....	....
	Colorado	**NHL**	**18**	**2**	**1**	**3**	**2**	**0**	**1**	**0**	**12**	**16.7**	**–6**	**180**	**51.7**	**12:04**	**9**	**2**	**3**	**5**	**20**	**0**	**1**	**0**	**14:11**
	NHL Totals		**589**	**62**	**159**	**221**	**329**	**15**	**4**	**6**	**681**	**9.1**		**5777**	**50.9**	**14:19**	**71**	**8**	**15**	**23**	**42**	**0**	**1**	**1**	**14:15**

CCHA Second All-Star Team (1990) • NCAA West Second All-American Team (1990) • CCHA First All-Star Team (1991) • CCHA Player of the Year (1991) • NCAA West First All-American Team (1991)

• Missed majority of 1994-95 season recovering from shoulder injury suffered in game vs. Quebec, February 2, 1995. Traded to **Hartford** by **New Jersey** with New Jersey's 2nd round choice (later traded to Calgary – Calgary selected Dmitri Kokorev) in 1997 Entry Draft for Jocelyn Lemieux and Hartford's 2nd round choice (later traded to Dallas – Dallas selected John Erskine) in 1998 Entry Draft, December 19, 1995. Traded to **Vancouver** by **Hartford** with Frantisek Kucera and Hartford's 2nd round choice (Ryan Bonni) in 1997 Entry Draft for Jeff Brown and Vancouver's 3rd round choice (later traded to Calgary – Calgary selected Paul Manning) in 1998 Entry Draft, December 19, 1995. Claimed by **NY Islanders** from **Vancouver** in Waiver Draft, September 30, 1996. Signed as a free agent by **Calgary**, August, 1997. Traded to **Nashville** by **Calgary** for future considerations, June 26, 1998. Traded to **Edmonton** by **Nashville** with Mikhail Shtalenkov for Eric Fichaud, Drake Berehowsky and Greg de Vries, October 1, 1998. Claimed by **Minnesota** from **Edmonton** in Expansion Draft, June 23, 2000. Traded to **Montreal** by **Minnesota** for Montreal's 4th round choice (Julien Sprunger) in 2004 Entry Draft, March 4, 2004. Signed as a free agent by **Hamburg** (Germany), October 1, 2004. Signed as a free agent by **Chicago**, August 5, 2005. Traded to **Colorado** by **Chicago** for Colorado's 4th round choice (later traded to Toronto - Toronto selected James Reimer) in 2006 Entry Draft, March 9, 2006.

DOWNEY, Aaron

(DOW-nee, AIR-ruhn) **MTL.**

Right wing. Shoots right. 6'1", 220 lbs. Born, Shelburne, Ont., August 27, 1974.

Season	Club	League	GP	G	A	Pts	PIM	PP	SH	GW	S	%	+/-	TF	F%	Min	GP	G	A	Pts	PIM	PP	SH	GW	Min
1990-91	Grand Valley	OHA-C	27	6	8	14	57	....	....	....	....	....	....	....	....	....	....	....	....	....	....	....	....	....	....
1991-92	Collingwood	OHA-B	40	9	8	17	111	....	....	....	....	....	....	....	....	....	....	....	....	....	....	....	....	....	....
1992-93	Guelph Storm	OHL	53	3	3	6	88	....	....	....	....	....	....	....	....	....	5	1	0	1	0	....	....	....	....
1993-94	Cole Harbour	NSMHL	35	8	20	28	210	....	....	....	....	....	....	....	....	....	....	....	....	....	....	....	....	....	....
1994-95	Cole Harbour	NSMHL	40	10	31	41	320	....	....	....	....	....	....	....	....	....	....	....	....	....	....	....	....	....	....
1995-96	Hampton Roads	ECHL	65	12	11	23	354	....	....	....	....	....	....	....	....	....	....	....	....	....	....	....	....	....	....
1996-97	Manitoba Moose	IHL	2	0	0	0	17	....	....	....	....	....	....	....	....	....	....	....	....	....	....	....	....	....	....
	Portland Pirates	AHL	3	0	0	0	19	....	....	....	....	....	....	....	....	....	....	....	....	....	....	....	....	....	....
	Hampton Roads	ECHL	64	8	8	16	338	....	....	....	....	....	....	....	....	....	9	0	3	3	26	....	....	....	....
1997-98	Providence Bruins	AHL	78	5	10	15	*407	....	....	....	....	....	....	....	....	....	....	....	....	....	....	....	....	....	....
1998-99	Providence Bruins	AHL	75	10	12	22	*401	....	....	....	....	....	....	....	....	....	19	1	1	2	46	....	....	....	....
99-2000	**Boston**	**NHL**	**1**	**0**	**0**	**0**	**0**	**0**	**0**	**0**	**0**	**0.0**	**0**	**0**	**0.0**	**8:31**	....	....	....	....	....	....	....	....	....
	Providence Bruins	AHL	47	6	4	10	221	....	....	....	....	....	....	....	....	....	14	1	0	1	24	....	....	....	....
2000-01	**Chicago**	**NHL**	**3**	**0**	**0**	**0**	**6**	**0**	**0**	**0**	**2**	**0.0**	**–1**	**0**	**0.0**	**5:30**	....	....	....	....	....	....	....	....	....
	Norfolk Admirals	AHL	67	6	15	21	234	....	....	....	....	....	....	....	....	....	9	0	0	0	4	....	....	....	....
2001-02	**Chicago**	**NHL**	**36**	**1**	**0**	**1**	**76**	**0**	**0**	**1**	**10**	**10.0**	**–2**	**0**	**0.0**	**5:06**	**4**	**0**	**0**	**0**	**8**	**0**	**0**	**0**	**6:29**
	Norfolk Admirals	AHL	12	0	2	2	21	....	....	....	....	....	....	....	....	....	....	....	....	....	....	....	....	....	....
2002-03	**Dallas**	**NHL**	**43**	**1**	**1**	**2**	**69**	**0**	**0**	**0**	**14**	**7.1**	**1**	**0**	**0.0**	**4:47**	....	....	....	....	....	....	....	....	....
2003-04	**Dallas**	**NHL**	**37**	**1**	**1**	**2**	**77**	**0**	**0**	**1**	**11**	**9.1**	**2**	**0**	**0.0**	**4:30**	....	....	....	....	....	....	....	....	....
2004-05			DID NOT PLAY																						
2005-06	**St. Louis**	**NHL**	**17**	**2**	**0**	**2**	**45**	**0**	**0**	**0**	**11**	**18.2**	**0**	**0**	**0.0**	**3:56**	....	....	....	....	....	....	....	....	....
	Montreal	**NHL**	**25**	**1**	**4**	**5**	**50**	**0**	**0**	**0**	**10**	**10.0**	**2**	**1**	**0.0**	**6:43**	**1**	**0**	**0**	**0**	**0**	**0**	**0**	**0**	**6:17**
	NHL Totals		**162**	**6**	**6**	**12**	**323**	**0**	**0**	**2**	**58**	**10.3**		**1**	**0.0**	**5:02**	**5**	**0**	**0**	**0**	**8**	**0**	**0**	**0**	**6:27**

Signed as a free agent by **Boston**, January 20, 1998. Signed as a free agent by **Chicago**, August 13, 2000. Signed as a free agent by **Dallas**, July 3, 2002. • Spent majority of 2003-04 season as a healthy reserve. Signed as a free agent by **St. Louis**, August 1, 2005. Claimed on waivers by **Montreal** from **St. Louis**, January 23, 2006.

DRAKE, Dallas

(DRAYK, DAL-uhs) **ST.L.**

Right wing. Shoots left. 6'1", 195 lbs. Born, Trail, B.C., February 4, 1969. Detroit's 6th choice, 116th overall, in 1989 Entry Draft.

Season	Club	League	GP	G	A	Pts	PIM	PP	SH	GW	S	%	+/-	TF	F%	Min	GP	G	A	Pts	PIM	PP	SH	GW	Min
1984-85	Rossland	KIJHL	30	13	37	50	....	....	....	....	....	....	....	....	....	....	....	....	....	....	....	....	....	....	....
1985-86	Rossland	KIJHL	41	53	73	126	....	....	....	....	....	....	....	....	....	....	....	....	....	....	....	....	....	....	....
1986-87	Rossland	KIJHL	40	55	80	135	....	....	....	....	....	....	....	....	....	....	....	....	....	....	....	....	....	....	....
1987-88	Vernon Lakers	BCJHL	47	39	85	124	50	....	....	....	....	....	....	....	....	....	11	9	17	26	30	....	....	....	....
1988-89	Northern Mich.	WCHA	38	17	22	39	22	....	....	....	....	....	....	....	....	....	7	1	2	3	4	....	....	....	....
1989-90	Northern Mich.	WCHA	36	13	24	37	42	....	....	....	....	....	....	....	....	....	....	....	....	....	....	....	....	....	....
1990-91	Northern Mich.	WCHA	44	22	36	58	89	....	....	....	....	....	....	....	....	....	....	....	....	....	....	....	....	....	....
1991-92	Northern Mich.	WCHA	38	*39	41	*80	46	....	....	....	....	....	....	....	....	....	....	....	....	....	....	....	....	....	....
1992-93	**Detroit**	**NHL**	**72**	**18**	**26**	**44**	**93**	**3**	**2**	**5**	**89**	**20.2**	**15**	....	....	....	**7**	**3**	**3**	**6**	**6**	**1**	**0**	**0**	....
1993-94	**Detroit**	**NHL**	**47**	**10**	**22**	**32**	**37**	**0**	**1**	**2**	**78**	**12.8**	**5**	....	....	....	....	....	....	....	....	....	....	....	....
	Adirondack	AHL	1	2	0	2	0	....	....	....	....	....	....	....	....	....	....	....	....	....	....	....	....	....	....
	Winnipeg	**NHL**	**15**	**3**	**5**	**8**	**12**	**1**	**1**	**1**	**34**	**8.8**	**–6**	....	....	....	....	....	....	....	....	....	....	....	....
1994-95	**Winnipeg**	**NHL**	**43**	**8**	**18**	**26**	**30**	**0**	**0**	**1**	**66**	**12.1**	**–6**	....	....	....	....	....	....	....	....	....	....	....	....
1995-96	**Winnipeg**	**NHL**	**69**	**19**	**20**	**39**	**36**	**4**	**4**	**2**	**121**	**15.7**	**–7**	....	....	....	**3**	**0**	**0**	**0**	**0**	**0**	**0**	**0**	....
1996-97	**Phoenix**	**NHL**	**63**	**17**	**19**	**36**	**52**	**5**	**1**	**1**	**113**	**15.0**	**–11**	....	....	....	**7**	**0**	**1**	**1**	**2**	**0**	**0**	**0**	....
1997-98	**Phoenix**	**NHL**	**60**	**11**	**29**	**40**	**71**	**3**	**0**	**2**	**112**	**9.8**	**17**	....	....	....	**4**	**0**	**1**	**1**	**2**	**0**	**0**	**0**	....
1998-99	**Phoenix**	**NHL**	**53**	**9**	**22**	**31**	**65**	**0**	**0**	**3**	**105**	**8.6**	**17**	**5**	**60.0**	**15:38**	**7**	**4**	**3**	**7**	**4**	**2**	**0**	**1**	**19:51**
99-2000	**Phoenix**	**NHL**	**79**	**15**	**30**	**45**	**62**	**0**	**2**	**5**	**127**	**11.8**	**11**	**4**	**25.0**	**15:48**	**5**	**0**	**1**	**1**	**4**	**0**	**0**	**0**	**15:30**
2000-01	**St. Louis**	**NHL**	**82**	**12**	**29**	**41**	**71**	**2**	**0**	**3**	**142**	**8.5**	**18**	**11**	**45.5**	**14:44**	**15**	**4**	**2**	**6**	**16**	**0**	**1**	**1**	**14:08**
2001-02	**St. Louis**	**NHL**	**80**	**11**	**15**	**26**	**87**	**1**	**3**	**2**	**116**	**9.5**	**8**	**92**	**32.6**	**13:26**	**8**	**0**	**0**	**0**	**8**	**0**	**0**	**0**	**11:59**
2002-03	**St. Louis**	**NHL**	**80**	**20**	**10**	**30**	**66**	**4**	**1**	**2**	**113**	**17.7**	**–7**	**56**	**39.3**	**14:48**	**7**	**1**	**4**	**5**	**23**	**0**	**0**	**1**	**13:04**
2003-04	**St. Louis**	**NHL**	**79**	**13**	**22**	**35**	**65**	**3**	**2**	**1**	**121**	**10.7**	**10**	**92**	**45.7**	**16:57**	**5**	**1**	**1**	**2**	**2**	**0**	**0**	**1**	**16:45**
2004-05			DID NOT PLAY																						
2005-06	**St. Louis**	**NHL**	**62**	**2**	**24**	**26**	**59**	**1**	**0**	**1**	**88**	**2.3**	**–13**	**122**	**45.9**	**16:55**	....	....	....	....	....	....	....	....	....
	NHL Totals		**884**	**168**	**291**	**459**	**806**	**27**	**17**	**31**	**1425**	**11.8**		**382**	**41.6**	**15:24**	**68**	**13**	**16**	**29**	**67**	**3**	**1**	**4**	**14:53**

WCHA First All-Star Team (1992) • NCAA West First All-American Team (1992)

Traded to **Winnipeg** by **Detroit** with Tim Cheveldae for Bob Essensa and Sergei Bautin, March 8, 1994. Transferred to **Phoenix** after **Winnipeg** franchise relocated, July 1, 1996. Claimed by **Minnesota** from **Phoenix** in Expansion Draft, June 23, 2000. Signed as a free agent by **St. Louis**, July 1, 2000.

DRAPER, Kris

(DRAY-puhr, KRIHS) **DET.**

Center. Shoots left. 5'11", 190 lbs. Born, Toronto, Ont., May 24, 1971. Winnipeg's 4th choice, 62nd overall, in 1989 Entry Draft.

Season	Club	League	GP	G	A	Pts	PIM	PP	SH	GW	S	%	+/-	TF	F%	Min	GP	G	A	Pts	PIM	PP	SH	GW	Min
1987-88	Don Mills Flyers	MTHL	40	35	32	67	46	....	....	....	....	....	....	....	....	....	....	....	....	....	....	....	....	....	....
1988-89	Canada	Nat-Tm	60	11	15	26	16	....	....	....	....	....	....	....	....	....	....	....	....	....	....	....	....	....	....
1989-90	Canada	Nat-Tm	61	12	22	34	44	....	....	....	....	....	....	....	....	....	....	....	....	....	....	....	....	....	....
1990-91	Ottawa 67's	OHL	39	19	42	61	35	....	....	....	....	....	....	....	....	....	17	8	11	19	20	....	....	....	....
	Winnipeg	**NHL**	**3**	**1**	**0**	**1**	**5**	**0**	**0**	**0**	**1**	**100.0**	**0**	....	....	....	....	....	....	....	....	....	....	....	....
	Moncton Hawks	AHL	7	2	1	3	2	....	....	....	....	....	....	....	....	....	....	....	....	....	....	....	....	....	....
1991-92	**Winnipeg**	**NHL**	**10**	**2**	**0**	**2**	**2**	**0**	**0**	**0**	**19**	**10.5**	**0**	....	....	....	**2**	**0**	**0**	**0**	**0**	**0**	**0**	**0**	....
	Moncton Hawks	AHL	61	11	18	29	113	....	....	....	....	....	....	....	....	....	4	0	1	1	6	....	....	....	....
1992-93	**Winnipeg**	**NHL**	**7**	**0**	**0**	**0**	**2**	**0**	**0**	**0**	**5**	**0.0**	**–6**	....	....	....	....	....	....	....	....	....	....	....	....
	Moncton Hawks	AHL	67	12	23	35	40	....	....	....	....	....	....	....	....	....	5	2	2	4	18	....	....	....	....
1993-94	**Detroit**	**NHL**	**39**	**5**	**8**	**13**	**31**	**0**	**1**	**0**	**55**	**9.1**	**11**	....	....	....	**7**	**2**	**2**	**4**	**4**	**0**	**1**	**0**	....
	Adirondack	AHL	46	20	23	43	49	....	....	....	....	....	....	....	....	....	....	....	....	....	....	....	....	....	....
1994-95	**Detroit**	**NHL**	**36**	**2**	**6**	**8**	**22**	**0**	**0**	**0**	**44**	**4.5**	**1**	....	....	....	**18**	**4**	**1**	**5**	**12**	**0**	**1**	**1**	....
1995-96	**Detroit**	**NHL**	**52**	**7**	**9**	**16**	**32**	**0**	**1**	**0**	**51**	**13.7**	**2**	....	....	....	**18**	**4**	**2**	**6**	**18**	**0**	**1**	**0**	....
1996-97 ♦	**Detroit**	**NHL**	**76**	**8**	**5**	**13**	**73**	**1**	**0**	**1**	**85**	**9.4**	**–11**	....	....	....	**20**	**2**	**4**	**6**	**12**	**0**	**1**	**0**	....

Season	Club	League	GP	G	A	Pts	PIM	PP	SH	GW	S	%	+/-	TF	F%	Min	GP	G	A	Pts	PIM	PP	SH	GW	Min
			Regular Season														Playoffs								
1997-98♦	**Detroit**	**NHL**	**64**	**13**	**10**	**23**	**45**	**1**	**0**	**4**	**96**	**13.5**	**5**	....	....	....	**19**	**1**	**3**	**4**	**12**	**0**	**0**	**1**	....
1998-99	**Detroit**	**NHL**	**80**	**4**	**14**	**18**	**79**	**0**	**1**	**1**	**78**	**5.1**	**2**	**887**	**54.6**	**12:43**	**10**	**0**	**1**	**1**	**6**	**0**	**0**	**0**	**11:35**
99-2000	**Detroit**	**NHL**	**51**	**5**	**7**	**12**	**28**	**0**	**0**	**3**	**76**	**6.6**	**3**	**380**	**57.6**	**13:33**	**9**	**2**	**0**	**2**	**6**	**0**	**0**	**0**	**12:26**
2000-01	**Detroit**	**NHL**	**75**	**8**	**17**	**25**	**38**	**0**	**1**	**1**	**123**	**6.5**	**17**	**997**	**56.5**	**13:26**	**6**	**0**	**1**	**1**	**2**	**0**	**0**	**0**	**16:08**
2001-02♦	**Detroit**	**NHL**	**82**	**15**	**15**	**30**	**56**	**0**	**2**	**3**	**137**	**10.9**	**26**	**756**	**53.2**	**15:35**	**23**	**2**	**3**	**5**	**20**	**0**	**0**	**0**	**17:00**
2002-03	**Detroit**	**NHL**	**82**	**14**	**21**	**35**	**82**	**0**	**1**	**2**	**142**	**9.9**	**6**	**1059**	**56.9**	**16:12**	**4**	**0**	**0**	**0**	**4**	**0**	**0**	**0**	**17:29**
2003-04	**Detroit**	**NHL**	**67**	**24**	**16**	**40**	**31**	**2**	**5**	**1**	**149**	**16.1**	**22**	**1058**	**56.9**	**17:44**	**12**	**1**	**3**	**4**	**6**	**0**	**0**	**0**	**18:29**
2004-05		DID NOT PLAY																							
2005-06	**Detroit**	**NHL**	**80**	**10**	**22**	**32**	**58**	**0**	**1**	**1**	**153**	**6.5**	**3**	**1287**	**57.7**	**17:46**	**6**	**0**	**0**	**0**	**6**	**0**	**0**	**0**	**19:58**
	Canada	Olympics	6	0	0	0	0	....	....	....	....	....	....	....	....	....	....	....	....	....	....	....	....	....	....
	NHL Totals		**804**	**118**	**150**	**268**	**584**	**4**	**13**	**17**	**1214**	**9.7**		**6424**	**56.3**	**15:20**	**154**	**18**	**20**	**38**	**108**	**0**	**4**	**2**	**16:06**

Frank J. Selke Trophy (2004)

Traded to **Detroit** by **Winnipeg** for future considerations, June 30, 1993.

DRURY, Chris

(DROO-ree, KRIHS) **BUF.**

Center. Shoots right. 5'10", 200 lbs. Born, Trumbull, CT, August 20, 1976. Quebec's 5th choice, 72nd overall, in 1994 Entry Draft.

Season	Club	League	GP	G	A	Pts	PIM	PP	SH	GW	S	%	+/-	TF	F%	Min	GP	G	A	Pts	PIM	PP	SH	GW	Min
1991-92	Fairfield Prep	High-CT	25	22	27	49	....	....	....	....	....	....	....	....	....	....	....	....	....	....	....	....	....	....	....
1992-93	Fairfield Prep	High-CT	24	25	32	57	15	....	....	....	....	....	....	....	....	....	....	....	....	....	....	....	....	....	....
1993-94	Fairfield Prep	High-CT	24	37	18	55	....	....	....	....	....	....	....	....	....	....	....	....	....	....	....	....	....	....	....
1994-95	Boston University	H-East	39	12	15	27	38	....	....	....	....	....	....	....	....	....	....	....	....	....	....	....	....	....	....
1995-96	Boston University	H-East	37	35	33	*68	46	....	....	....	....	....	....	....	....	....	....	....	....	....	....	....	....	....	....
1996-97	Boston University	H-East	41	*38	24	62	64	....	....	....	....	....	....	....	....	....	....	....	....	....	....	....	....	....	....
1997-98	Boston University	H-East	38	28	29	57	88	....	....	....	....	....	....	....	....	....	....	....	....	....	....	....	....	....	....
1998-99	**Colorado**	**NHL**	**79**	**20**	**24**	**44**	**62**	**6**	**0**	**3**	**138**	**14.5**	**9**	**418**	**46.9**	**13:15**	**19**	**6**	**2**	**8**	**4**	**0**	**0**	**4**	**11:28**
99-2000	**Colorado**	**NHL**	**82**	**20**	**47**	**67**	**42**	**7**	**0**	**2**	**213**	**9.4**	**8**	**1321**	**53.1**	**18:33**	**17**	**4**	**10**	**14**	**4**	**1**	**0**	**2**	**18:30**
2000-01♦	**Colorado**	**NHL**	**71**	**24**	**41**	**65**	**47**	**11**	**0**	**5**	**204**	**11.8**	**6**	**552**	**55.1**	**18:03**	**23**	**11**	**5**	**16**	**4**	**2**	**0**	**2**	**19:06**
2001-02	**Colorado**	**NHL**	**82**	**21**	**25**	**46**	**38**	**5**	**0**	**6**	**236**	**8.9**	**1**	**1139**	**53.2**	**17:57**	**21**	**5**	**7**	**12**	**10**	**1**	**0**	**3**	**17:01**
	United States	Olympics	6	0	0	0	0	....	....	....	....	....	....	....	....	....	....	....	....	....	....	....	....	....	....
2002-03	**Calgary**	**NHL**	**80**	**23**	**30**	**53**	**33**	**5**	**1**	**5**	**224**	**10.3**	**–9**	**942**	**53.8**	**18:33**	....	....	....	....	....	....	....	....	....
2003-04	**Buffalo**	**NHL**	**76**	**18**	**35**	**53**	**68**	**5**	**1**	**2**	**152**	**11.8**	**8**	**1491**	**54.9**	**18:04**	....	....	....	....	....	....	....	....	....
2004-05		DID NOT PLAY																							
2005-06	**Buffalo**	**NHL**	**81**	**30**	**37**	**67**	**32**	**16**	**2**	**5**	**172**	**17.4**	**–11**	**1641**	**55.5**	**18:06**	**18**	**9**	**9**	**18**	**10**	**5**	**1**	**1**	**19:20**
	United States	Olympics	6	0	3	3	2	....	....	....	....	....	....	....	....	....	....	....	....	....	....	....	....	....	....
	NHL Totals		**551**	**156**	**239**	**395**	**322**	**55**	**4**	**28**	**1339**	**11.7**		**7504**	**53.9**	**17:30**	**98**	**35**	**33**	**68**	**32**	**9**	**1**	**12**	**17:07**

Hockey East Second All-Star Team (1996, 1997) • NCAA East Second All-American Team (1996) • Hockey East Player of the Year (1997, 1998) • NCAA East First All-American Team (1997, 1998) • NCAA Championship All-Tournament Team (1997) • Hockey East First All-Star Team (1998) • Hobey Baker Memorial Award (Top U.S. Collegiate Player) (1998) • NHL All-Rookie Team (1999) • Calder Memorial Trophy (1999)

Rights transferred to **Colorado** after **Quebec** franchise relocated, June 21, 1995. Traded to **Calgary** by **Colorado** with Stephane Yelle for Derek Morris, Jeff Shantz and Dean McAmmond, October 1, 2002. Traded to **Buffalo** by **Calgary** with Steve Begin for Steve Reinprecht and Rhett Warrener, July 3, 2003.

DUMONT, J.P.

(DOO-mawnt, JAY-pee)

Right wing. Shoots left. 6'1", 205 lbs. Born, Montreal, Que., April 1, 1978. NY Islanders' 1st choice, 3rd overall, in 1996 Entry Draft.

Season	Club	League	GP	G	A	Pts	PIM	PP	SH	GW	S	%	+/-	TF	F%	Min	GP	G	A	Pts	PIM	PP	SH	GW	Min
1993-94	Mtl-Bourassa	QAAA	44	27	20	47	44	....	....	....	....	....	....	....	....	....	4	2	3	5	4	....	....	....	....
1994-95	Mtl-Bourassa	QAAA	10	2	7	9	12	....	....	....	....	....	....	....	....	....	....	....	....	....	....	....	....	....	....
	Val-d'Or Foreurs	QMJHL	48	5	14	19	24	....	....	....	....	....	....	....	....	....	....	....	....	....	....	....	....	....	....
1995-96	Val-d'Or Foreurs	QMJHL	66	48	57	105	109	....	....	....	....	....	....	....	....	....	13	12	8	20	22	....	....	....	....
1996-97	Val-d'Or Foreurs	QMJHL	62	44	64	108	86	....	....	....	....	....	....	....	....	....	13	9	7	16	12	....	....	....	....
1997-98	Val-d'Or Foreurs	QMJHL	55	57	42	99	63	....	....	....	....	....	....	....	....	....	19	31	15	46	18	....	....	....	....
1998-99	**Chicago**	**NHL**	**25**	**9**	**6**	**15**	**10**	**0**	**0**	**2**	**42**	**21.4**	**7**	**10**	**50.0**	**14:14**	....	....	....	....	....	....	....	....	....
	Portland Pirates	AHL	50	32	14	46	39	....	....	....	....	....	....	....	....	....	....	....	....	....	....	....	....	....	....
	Chicago Wolves	IHL	....	....	....	....	....	....	....	....	....	....	....	....	....	....	10	4	1	5	6	....	....	....	....
99-2000	**Chicago**	**NHL**	**47**	**10**	**8**	**18**	**18**	**0**	**0**	**1**	**86**	**11.6**	**–6**	**12**	**33.3**	**12:54**	....	....	....	....	....	....	....	....	....
	Cleveland	IHL	7	5	2	7	8	....	....	....	....	....	....	....	....	....	....	....	....	....	....	....	....	....	....
	Rochester	AHL	13	7	10	17	18	....	....	....	....	....	....	....	....	....	21	14	7	21	32	....	....	....	....
2000-01	**Buffalo**	**NHL**	**79**	**23**	**28**	**51**	**54**	**9**	**0**	**5**	**156**	**14.7**	**1**	**3**	**33.3**	**15:01**	**13**	**4**	**3**	**7**	**8**	**0**	**0**	**0**	**14:32**
2001-02	**Buffalo**	**NHL**	**76**	**23**	**21**	**44**	**42**	**7**	**0**	**3**	**154**	**14.9**	**–10**	**4**	**50.0**	**15:14**	....	....	....	....	....	....	....	....	....
2002-03	**Buffalo**	**NHL**	**76**	**14**	**21**	**35**	**44**	**2**	**0**	**2**	**135**	**10.4**	**–14**	**15**	**20.0**	**15:04**	....	....	....	....	....	....	....	....	....
2003-04	**Buffalo**	**NHL**	**77**	**22**	**31**	**53**	**40**	**10**	**0**	**1**	**156**	**14.1**	**–9**	**32**	**43.8**	**17:00**	....	....	....	....	....	....	....	....	....
2004-05	SC Bern	Swiss	3	2	2	4	6	....	....	....	....	....	....	....	....	....	10	4	1	5	16	....	....	....	....
2005-06	**Buffalo**	**NHL**	**54**	**20**	**20**	**40**	**38**	**9**	**0**	**4**	**116**	**17.2**	**–1**	**9**	**11.1**	**16:00**	**18**	**7**	**7**	**14**	**14**	**3**	**0**	**1**	**16:39**
	NHL Totals		**434**	**121**	**135**	**256**	**246**	**37**	**0**	**18**	**845**	**14.3**		**85**	**35.3**	**15:16**	**31**	**11**	**10**	**21**	**22**	**3**	**0**	**1**	**15:46**

QMJHL Second All-Star Team (1997) • AHL All-Rookie Team (1999)

Rights traded to **Chicago** by **NY Islanders** with NY Islanders' 5th round choice (later traded to Philadelphia – Philadelphia selected Francis Belanger) in 1998 Entry Draft for Dmitri Nabokov, May 30, 1998. Traded to **Buffalo** by **Chicago** with Doug Gilmour for Michal Grosek, March 10, 2000. Signed as a free agent by **Bern** (Swiss), February 9, 2005.

DuPONT, Micki

(DOO-pawnt, MIH-kee) **PIT.**

Defense. Shoots right. 5'10", 186 lbs. Born, Calgary, Alta., April 15, 1980. Calgary's 9th choice, 270th overall, in 2000 Entry Draft.

Season	Club	League	GP	G	A	Pts	PIM	PP	SH	GW	S	%	+/-	TF	F%	Min	GP	G	A	Pts	PIM	PP	SH	GW	Min
1995-96	Calgary Blazers	AMHL	35	10	35	45	68	....	....	....	....	....	....	....	....	....	....	....	....	....	....	....	....	....	....
1996-97	Kamloops Blazers	WHL	59	8	27	35	39	....	....	....	....	....	....	....	....	....	5	0	4	4	8	....	....	....	....
1997-98	Kamloops Blazers	WHL	71	13	41	54	91	....	....	....	....	....	....	....	....	....	7	0	1	1	10	....	....	....	....
1998-99	Kamloops Blazers	WHL	59	8	27	35	110	....	....	....	....	....	....	....	....	....	15	2	8	10	22	....	....	....	....
99-2000	Kamloops Blazers	WHL	70	26	62	88	156	....	....	....	....	....	....	....	....	....	4	0	2	2	17	....	....	....	....
	Long Beach	IHL	1	0	0	0	0	....	....	....	....	....	....	....	....	....	....	....	....	....	....	....	....	....	....
	San Diego Gulls	WCHL	....	....	....	....	....	....	....	....	....	....	....	....	....	....	7	2	2	4	0	....	....	....	....
2000-01	Saint John Flames	AHL	67	8	21	29	28	....	....	....	....	....	....	....	....	....	19	1	9	10	14	....	....	....	....
2001-02	**Calgary**	**NHL**	**2**	**0**	**0**	**0**	**2**	**0**	**0**	**0**	**2**	**0.0**	**0**	**0**	**0.0**	**14:44**	....	....	....	....	....	....	....	....	....
	Saint John Flames	AHL	77	7	33	40	77	....	....	....	....	....	....	....	....	....	....	....	....	....	....	....	....	....	....
2002-03	**Calgary**	**NHL**	**16**	**1**	**2**	**3**	**4**	**0**	**0**	**0**	**27**	**3.7**	**–5**	**0**	**0.0**	**16:45**	....	....	....	....	....	....	....	....	....
	Saint John Flames	AHL	44	12	21	33	73	....	....	....	....	....	....	....	....	....	....	....	....	....	....	....	....	....	....
	Wilkes-Barre	AHL	14	1	4	5	16	....	....	....	....	....	....	....	....	....	6	3	0	3	21	....	....	....	....
2003-04	Eisbaren Berlin	Germany	45	10	22	32	76	....	....	....	....	....	....	....	....	....	10	3	6	9	35	....	....	....	....
2004-05	Eisbaren Berlin	Germany	51	11	22	33	93	....	....	....	....	....	....	....	....	....	11	2	5	7	41	....	....	....	....
2005-06	Eisbaren Berlin	Germany	52	11	21	32	78	....	....	....	....	....	....	....	....	....	11	4	10	*14	10	....	....	....	....
	NHL Totals		**18**	**1**	**2**	**3**	**6**	**0**	**0**	**0**	**29**	**3.4**		**0**	**0.0**	**16:31**	....	....	....	....	....	....	....	....	....

AHL All-Rookie Team (2001)

Traded to **Pittsburgh** by **Calgary** with Mathias Johansson for Shean Donovan, March 11, 2003. Signed as a free agent by **Berlin** (Germany), August 6, 2003.

DUPUIS, Pascal

(doo-PWEE, pas-KAL) **MIN.**

Left wing. Shoots left. 6', 196 lbs. Born, Laval, Que., April 7, 1979.

Season	Club	League	GP	G	A	Pts	PIM	PP	SH	GW	S	%	+/-	TF	F%	Min	GP	G	A	Pts	PIM	PP	SH	GW	Min
1995-96	Laval-Laurentides	QAAA	41	10	15	25	....	....	....	....	....	....	....	....	....	....	14	11	11	22	....	....	....	....	....
1996-97	Rouyn-Noranda	QMJHL	44	9	15	24	20	....	....	....	....	....	....	....	....	....	....	....	....	....	....	....	....	....	....
1997-98	Rouyn-Noranda	QMJHL	39	9	17	26	36	....	....	....	....	....	....	....	....	....	....	....	....	....	....	....	....	....	....
	Shawinigan	QMJHL	28	7	13	20	10	....	....	....	....	....	....	....	....	....	6	2	0	2	4	....	....	....	....
1998-99	Shawinigan	QMJHL	57	30	42	72	118	....	....	....	....	....	....	....	....	....	6	1	8	9	18	....	....	....	....
99-2000	Shawinigan	QMJHL	61	50	55	105	99	....	....	....	....	....	....	....	....	....	13	*15	7	22	4	....	....	....	....
2000-01	**Minnesota**	**NHL**	**4**	**1**	**0**	**1**	**4**	**1**	**0**	**0**	**8**	**12.5**	**0**	**0**	**0.0**	**15:36**	....	....	....	....	....	....	....	....	....
	Cleveland	IHL	70	19	24	43	37	....	....	....	....	....	....	....	....	....	4	0	0	0	0	....	....	....	....
2001-02	**Minnesota**	**NHL**	**76**	**15**	**12**	**27**	**16**	**3**	**2**	**0**	**154**	**9.7**	**–10**	**40**	**32.5**	**15:08**	....	....	....	....	....	....	....	....	....
2002-03	**Minnesota**	**NHL**	**80**	**20**	**28**	**48**	**44**	**6**	**0**	**4**	**183**	**10.9**	**17**	**186**	**40.9**	**17:30**	**16**	**4**	**4**	**8**	**8**	**2**	**0**	**1**	**16:58**
2003-04	**Minnesota**	**NHL**	**59**	**11**	**15**	**26**	**20**	**2**	**0**	**1**	**127**	**8.7**	**5**	**129**	**45.7**	**15:48**	....	....	....	....	....	....	....	....	....
2004-05	HC Ajoie	Swiss-2	8	5	5	10	26	....	....	....	....	....	....	....	....	....	6	6	8	14	8	....	....	....	....
2005-06	**Minnesota**	**NHL**	**67**	**10**	**16**	**26**	**40**	**4**	**0**	**2**	**151**	**6.6**	**–10**	**93**	**29.0**	**16:30**	....	....	....	....	....	....	....	....	....
	NHL Totals		**286**	**57**	**71**	**128**	**124**	**16**	**2**	**7**	**623**	**9.1**		**448**	**39.1**	**16:16**	**16**	**4**	**4**	**8**	**8**	**2**	**0**	**1**	**16:58**

Signed as a free agent by **Minnesota**, August 18, 2000. Signed as a free agent by **Ajoie** (Swiss-2), January 14, 2005.

			Regular Season														Playoffs								
Season	Club	League	GP	G	A	Pts	PIM	PP	SH	GW	S	%	+/-	TF	F%	Min	GP	G	A	Pts	PIM	PP	SH	GW	Min

DVORAK, Radek (duh-VOHR-ak, RA-dehk)

Right wing. Shoots right. 6'2", 200 lbs. Born, Tabor, Czech., March 9, 1977. Florida's 1st choice, 10th overall, in 1995 Entry Draft.

Season	Club	League	GP	G	A	Pts	PIM	PP	SH	GW	S	%	+/-	TF	F%	Min	GP	G	A	Pts	PIM	PP	SH	GW	Min
1992-93	C. Budejovice Jr.	Czech-Jr.	35	44	46	90	....	....	....	....	....	....	....	....	....	....	....	....	....	....	....	....	....	....	....
1993-94	C. Budejovice Jr.	CzRep-Jr.	20	17	18	35	....	....	....	....	....	....	....	....	....	....	....	....	....	....	....	....	....	....	....
	C. Budejovice	CzRep	8	0	0	0	0	....	....	....	....	....	....	....	....	....	....	....	....	....	....	....	....	....	....
1994-95	C. Budejovice	CzRep	10	3	5	8	2	....	....	....	....	....	....	....	....	....	9	5	1	6	....	....	....	....	....
1995-96	**Florida**	**NHL**	**77**	**13**	**14**	**27**	**20**	**0**	**0**	**4**	**126**	**10.3**	**5**	....	....	....	**16**	**1**	**3**	**4**	**0**	**0**	**0**	**0**	....
1996-97	**Florida**	**NHL**	**78**	**18**	**21**	**39**	**30**	**2**	**0**	**1**	**139**	**12.9**	**–2**	....	....	....	**3**	**0**	**0**	**0**	**0**	**0**	**0**	**0**	....
1997-98	**Florida**	**NHL**	**64**	**12**	**24**	**36**	**33**	**2**	**3**	**0**	**112**	**10.7**	**–1**	....	....	....	....	....	....	....	....	....	....	....	....
1998-99	**Florida**	**NHL**	**82**	**19**	**24**	**43**	**29**	**0**	**4**	**0**	**182**	**10.4**	**7**	**98**	**46.9**	**16:13**	....	....	....	....	....	....	....	....	....
99-2000	**Florida**	**NHL**	**35**	**7**	**10**	**17**	**6**	**0**	**0**	**1**	**67**	**10.4**	**5**	**16**	**37.5**	**15:25**	....	....	....	....	....	....	....	....	....
	NY Rangers	**NHL**	**46**	**11**	**22**	**33**	**10**	**2**	**1**	**0**	**90**	**12.2**	**0**	**34**	**35.3**	**18:24**	....	....	....	....	....	....	....	....	....
2000-01	**NY Rangers**	**NHL**	**82**	**31**	**36**	**67**	**20**	**5**	**2**	**3**	**230**	**13.5**	**9**	**20**	**30.0**	**19:04**	....	....	....	....	....	....	....	....	....
2001-02	**NY Rangers**	**NHL**	**65**	**17**	**20**	**37**	**14**	**3**	**3**	**1**	**210**	**8.1**	**–20**	**5**	**0.0**	**19:44**	....	....	....	....	....	....	....	....	....
	Czech Republic	Olympics	4	0	0	0	0	....	....	....	....	....	....	....	....	....	....	....	....	....	....	....	....	....	....
2002-03	**NY Rangers**	**NHL**	**63**	**6**	**21**	**27**	**16**	**2**	**0**	**0**	**134**	**4.5**	**–3**	**9**	**44.4**	**15:42**	....	....	....	....	....	....	....	....	....
	Edmonton	**NHL**	**12**	**4**	**4**	**8**	**14**	**1**	**0**	**0**	**32**	**12.5**	**–3**	**1**	**0.0**	**16:07**	**4**	**1**	**0**	**1**	**0**	**0**	**0**	**1**	**15:05**
2003-04	**Edmonton**	**NHL**	**78**	**15**	**35**	**50**	**26**	**6**	**0**	**0**	**188**	**8.0**	**18**	**24**	**29.2**	**16:56**	....	....	....	....	....	....	....	....	....
2004-05	C. Budejovice	CzRep-2	32	23	35	58	18	....	....	....	....	....	....	....	....	....	16	5	13	18	20	....	....	....	....
2005-06	**Edmonton**	**NHL**	**64**	**8**	**20**	**28**	**26**	**2**	**0**	**2**	**131**	**6.1**	**–2**	**14**	**28.6**	**16:34**	**16**	**0**	**2**	**2**	**4**	**0**	**0**	**0**	**13:29**
	NHL Totals		**746**	**161**	**251**	**412**	**244**	**25**	**13**	**12**	**1641**	**9.8**		**221**	**38.5**	**17:19**	**39**	**2**	**5**	**7**	**4**	**0**	**0**	**1**	**13:48**

Traded to **San Jose** by **Florida** for Mike Vernon and San Jose's 3rd round choice (Sean O'Connor) in 2000 Entry Draft, December 30, 1999. Traded to **NY Rangers** by **San Jose** for Todd Harvey and NY Rangers' 4th round choice (Dimitri Patzold) in 2001 Entry Draft, December 30, 1999. Traded to **Edmonton** by **NY Rangers** with Cory Cross for Anson Carter and Ales Pisa, March 11, 2003. Signed as a free agent by **Ceske Budejovice** (CzRep-2), September 15, 2004.

EAGER, Ben (EE-guhr, BEHN) **PHI.**

Left wing. Shoots left. 6'2", 225 lbs. Born, Ottawa, Ont., January 22, 1984. Phoenix's 2nd choice, 23rd overall, in 2002 Entry Draft. •

Season	Club	League	GP	G	A	Pts	PIM	PP	SH	GW	S	%	+/-	TF	F%	Min	GP	G	A	Pts	PIM	PP	SH	GW	Min
99-2000	Ott. Jr. Senators	CJHL	50	8	11	19	119	....	....	....	....	....	....	....	....	....	....	....	....	....	....	....	....	....	....
2000-01	Oshawa Generals	OHL	61	4	6	10	120	....	....	....	....	....	....	....	....	....	....	....	....	....	....	....	....	....	....
2001-02	Oshawa Generals	OHL	63	14	23	37	255	....	....	....	....	....	....	....	....	....	5	0	1	1	13	....	....	....	....
2002-03	Oshawa Generals	OHL	58	16	24	40	216	....	....	....	....	....	....	....	....	....	8	0	4	4	8	....	....	....	....
2003-04	Oshawa Generals	OHL	61	25	27	52	204	....	....	....	....	....	....	....	....	....	7	2	3	5	31	....	....	....	....
	Philadelphia	AHL	5	0	0	0	0	....	....	....	....	....	....	....	....	....	3	0	1	1	8	....	....	....	....
2004-05	Philadelphia	AHL	66	7	10	17	232	....	....	....	....	....	....	....	....	....	16	1	1	2	71	....	....	....	....
2005-06	**Philadelphia**	**NHL**	**25**	**3**	**5**	**8**	**18**	**0**	**0**	**0**	**21**	**14.3**	**0**	**0**	**0.0**	**7:24**	**2**	**0**	**0**	**0**	**26**	**0**	**0**	**0**	**7:06**
	Philadelphia	AHL	49	6	12	18	251	....	....	....	....	....	....	....	....	....	....	....	....	....	....	....	....	....	....
	NHL Totals		**25**	**3**	**5**	**8**	**18**	**0**	**0**	**0**	**21**	**14.3**		**0**	**0.0**	**7:24**	**2**	**0**	**0**	**0**	**26**	**0**	**0**	**0**	**7:06**

Traded to **Philadelphia** by **Phoenix** with Sean Burke and Branko Radivojevic for Mike Comrie, February 9, 2004.

EATON, Mark (EE-tohn, MAHRK) **PIT.**

Defense. Shoots left. 6'2", 212 lbs. Born, Wilmington, DE, May 6, 1977.

Season	Club	League	GP	G	A	Pts	PIM	PP	SH	GW	S	%	+/-	TF	F%	Min	GP	G	A	Pts	PIM	PP	SH	GW	Min
1995-96	Waterloo	USHL	50	4	21	25	....	....	....	....	....	....	....	....	....	....	....	....	....	....	....	....	....	....	....
1996-97	Waterloo	USHL	50	6	32	38	62	....	....	....	....	....	....	....	....	....	....	....	....	....	....	....	....	....	....
1997-98	U. of Notre Dame	CCHA	41	12	17	29	32	....	....	....	....	....	....	....	....	....	....	....	....	....	....	....	....	....	....
1998-99	Philadelphia	AHL	74	9	27	36	38	....	....	....	....	....	....	....	....	....	16	4	8	12	0	....	....	....	....
99-2000	**Philadelphia**	**NHL**	**27**	**1**	**1**	**2**	**8**	**0**	**0**	**1**	**25**	**4.0**	**1**	**0**	**0.0**	**18:17**	**7**	**0**	**0**	**0**	**0**	**0**	**0**	**0**	**13:36**
	Philadelphia	AHL	47	9	17	26	6	....	....	....	....	....	....	....	....	....	....	....	....	....	....	....	....	....	....
2000-01	**Nashville**	**NHL**	**34**	**3**	**8**	**11**	**14**	**1**	**0**	**1**	**32**	**9.4**	**7**	**0**	**0.0**	**17:13**	....	....	....	....	....	....	....	....	....
	Milwaukee	IHL	34	3	12	15	27	....	....	....	....	....	....	....	....	....	....	....	....	....	....	....	....	....	....
2001-02	**Nashville**	**NHL**	**58**	**3**	**5**	**8**	**24**	**0**	**0**	**0**	**52**	**5.8**	**–12**	**0**	**0.0**	**17:12**	....	....	....	....	....	....	....	....	....
2002-03	**Nashville**	**NHL**	**50**	**2**	**7**	**9**	**22**	**0**	**0**	**0**	**52**	**3.8**	**1**	**0**	**0.0**	**15:45**	....	....	....	....	....	....	....	....	....
	Milwaukee	AHL	3	1	0	1	2	....	....	....	....	....	....	....	....	....	....	....	....	....	....	....	....	....	....
2003-04	**Nashville**	**NHL**	**75**	**4**	**9**	**13**	**26**	**0**	**0**	**1**	**82**	**4.9**	**16**	**0**	**0.0**	**20:56**	**6**	**0**	**0**	**0**	**2**	**0**	**0**	**0**	**19:51**
2004-05	Grand Rapids	AHL	29	3	3	6	21	....	....	....	....	....	....	....	....	....	....	....	....	....	....	....	....	....	....
2005-06	**Nashville**	**NHL**	**69**	**3**	**1**	**4**	**44**	**0**	**0**	**0**	**28**	**10.7**	**–2**	**0**	**0.0**	**19:43**	**5**	**0**	**0**	**0**	**8**	**0**	**0**	**0**	**17:49**
	NHL Totals		**313**	**16**	**31**	**47**	**138**	**1**	**0**	**3**	**271**	**5.9**		**0**	**0.0**	**18:31**	**18**	**0**	**0**	**0**	**10**	**0**	**0**	**0**	**16:51**

USHL Second All-Star Team (1997) • Curt Hammer Award (Most Gentlemanly Player – USHL) (1997) • CCHA Rookie of the Year (1998)

Signed as a free agent by **Philadelphia**, August 4, 1998. Traded to **Nashville** by **Philadelphia** for Detroit's 3rd round choice (previously acquired, Philadelphia selected Patrick Sharp) in 2001 Entry Draft, September 29, 2000. Signed as a free agent by **Grand Rapids** (AHL), February 16, 2005. Signed as a free agent by **Pittsburgh**, July 3, 2006.

EAVES, Patrick (EEVZ, PAT-rihk) **OTT.**

Right wing. Shoots right. 6', 192 lbs. Born, Calgary, Alta., May 1, 1984. Ottawa's 1st choice, 29th overall, in 2003 Entry Draft.

Season	Club	League	GP	G	A	Pts	PIM	PP	SH	GW	S	%	+/-	TF	F%	Min	GP	G	A	Pts	PIM	PP	SH	GW	Min
99-2000	Shat.-St. Mary's	High-MN	50	23	24	47	....	....	....	....	....	....	....	....	....	....	....	....	....	....	....	....	....	....	....
2000-01	USNTDP	U-17	13	7	8	15	3	....	....	....	....	....	....	....	....	....	....	....	....	....	....	....	....	....	....
	USNTDP	NAHL	34	12	11	23	75	....	....	....	....	....	....	....	....	....	....	....	....	....	....	....	....	....	....
2001-02	USNTDP	U-18	32	19	21	40	87	....	....	....	....	....	....	....	....	....	....	....	....	....	....	....	....	....	....
	USNTDP	USHL	9	1	4	5	18	....	....	....	....	....	....	....	....	....	....	....	....	....	....	....	....	....	....
	USNTDP	NAHL	8	5	3	8	37	....	....	....	....	....	....	....	....	....	....	....	....	....	....	....	....	....	....
2002-03	Boston College	H-East	14	10	8	18	61	....	....	....	....	....	....	....	....	....	....	....	....	....	....	....	....	....	....
2003-04	Boston College	H-East	34	18	23	41	66	....	....	....	....	....	....	....	....	....	....	....	....	....	....	....	....	....	....
2004-05	Boston College	H-East	36	19	29	48	36	....	....	....	....	....	....	....	....	....	....	....	....	....	....	....	....	....	....
2005-06	**Ottawa**	**NHL**	**58**	**20**	**9**	**29**	**22**	**5**	**1**	**4**	**100**	**20.0**	**7**	**14**	**21.4**	**12:29**	**10**	**1**	**0**	**1**	**10**	**0**	**0**	**0**	**11:40**
	Binghamton	AHL	18	5	8	13	10	....	....	....	....	....	....	....	....	....	....	....	....	....	....	....	....	....	....
	NHL Totals		**58**	**20**	**9**	**29**	**22**	**5**	**1**	**4**	**100**	**20.0**		**14**	**21.4**	**12:29**	**10**	**1**	**0**	**1**	**10**	**0**	**0**	**0**	**11:40**

Hockey East Second All-Star Team (2004) • NCAA East Second All-American Team (2004) • Hockey East First All-Star Team (2005) • NCAA East First All-American Team (2005)

• Missed majority of 2002-03 season recovering from neck injury suffered in game vs. Maine (H-East), December 7, 2002.

EHRHOFF, Christian (AIR-hawf, KRIHS-tyehn) **S.J.**

Defense. Shoots left. 6'2", 195 lbs. Born, Moers, West Germany, July 6, 1982. San Jose's 2nd choice, 106th overall, in 2001 Entry Draft.

Season	Club	League	GP	G	A	Pts	PIM	PP	SH	GW	S	%	+/-	TF	F%	Min	GP	G	A	Pts	PIM	PP	SH	GW	Min
1998-99	Krefelder EV Jr.	Ger-Jr.	22	10	14	24	46	....	....	....	....	....	....	....	....	....	....	....	....	....	....	....	....	....	....
99-2000	EV Duisburg	German-3	41	3	12	15	50	....	....	....	....	....	....	....	....	....	....	....	....	....	....	....	....	....	....
	Krefeld Pinguine	Germany	9	1	0	1	6	....	....	....	....	....	....	....	....	....	3	0	0	0	0	....	....	....	....
2000-01	EV Duisburg	German-3	6	1	2	3	12	....	....	....	....	....	....	....	....	....	....	....	....	....	....	....	....	....	....
	Krefeld Pinguine	Germany	58	3	11	14	73	....	....	....	....	....	....	....	....	....	....	....	....	....	....	....	....	....	....
2001-02	Krefeld Pinguine	Germany	46	7	17	24	81	....	....	....	....	....	....	....	....	....	3	0	0	0	2	....	....	....	....
	Germany	Olympics	7	0	0	0	8	....	....	....	....	....	....	....	....	....	....	....	....	....	....	....	....	....	....
2002-03	Krefeld Pinguine	Germany	48	10	17	27	54	....	....	....	....	....	....	....	....	....	14	3	6	9	24	....	....	....	....
2003-04	**San Jose**	**NHL**	**41**	**1**	**11**	**12**	**14**	**0**	**0**	**1**	**58**	**1.7**	**4**	**0**	**0.0**	**15:23**	....	....	....	....	....	....	....	....	....
	Cleveland Barons	AHL	27	4	10	14	43	....	....	....	....	....	....	....	....	....	9	2	6	8	11	....	....	....	....
2004-05	Cleveland Barons	AHL	79	12	23	35	103	....	....	....	....	....	....	....	....	....	....	....	....	....	....	....	....	....	....
2005-06	**San Jose**	**NHL**	**64**	**5**	**18**	**23**	**32**	**2**	**0**	**2**	**124**	**4.0**	**10**	**0**	**0.0**	**17:48**	**11**	**2**	**6**	**8**	**18**	**1**	**0**	**1**	**19:47**
	Germany	Olympics	5	1	1	2	4	....	....	....	....	....	....	....	....	....	....	....	....	....	....	....	....	....	....
	NHL Totals		**105**	**6**	**29**	**35**	**46**	**2**	**0**	**3**	**182**	**3.3**		**0**	**0.0**	**16:51**	**11**	**2**	**6**	**8**	**18**	**1**	**0**	**1**	**19:47**

EKMAN, Nils (EHK-mahn, NIHLS) **PIT.**

Left wing. Shoots left. 6', 185 lbs. Born, Stockholm, Sweden, March 11, 1976. Calgary's 6th choice, 107th overall, in 1994 Entry Draft.

Season	Club	League	GP	G	A	Pts	PIM	PP	SH	GW	S	%	+/-	TF	F%	Min	GP	G	A	Pts	PIM	PP	SH	GW	Min
1993-94	Hammarby Jr.	Swe-Jr.	11	4	5	9	14	....	....	....	....	....	....	....	....	....	....	....	....	....	....	....	....	....	....
	Hammarby	Sweden-2	18	7	2	9	4	....	....	....	....	....	....	....	....	....	....	....	....	....	....	....	....	....	....
1994-95	Hammarby Jr.	Swe-Jr.	2	2	1	3	0	....	....	....	....	....	....	....	....	....	....	....	....	....	....	....	....	....	....
	Hammarby	Sweden-2	32	10	8	18	18	....	....	....	....	....	....	....	....	....	....	....	....	....	....	....	....	....	....
1995-96	Hammarby	Sweden-2	26	9	7	16	53	....	....	....	....	....	....	....	....	....	1	0	0	0	0	....	....	....	....
1996-97	Kiekko-Espoo	Finland	50	24	19	43	60	....	....	....	....	....	....	....	....	....	4	2	0	2	4	....	....	....	....

			Regular Season														Playoffs								
Season	Club	League	GP	G	A	Pts	PIM	PP	SH	GW	S	%	+/-	TF	F%	Min	GP	G	A	Pts	PIM	PP	SH	GW	Min
1997-98	Kiekko-Espoo	Finland	43	14	14	28	86										7	2	2	4	27				
	Saint John Flames	AHL															1	0	0	0	2				
1998-99	Blues Espoo	Finland	52	20	14	34	96										3	1	1	2	6				
99-2000	Detroit Vipers	IHL	10	7	2	9	8																		
	Tampa Bay	**NHL**	**28**	**2**	**2**	**4**	**36**	**1**	**0**	**0**	**42**	**4.8**	**–8**	**3**	**0.0**	**11:12**									
	Long Beach	IHL	27	11	12	23	26										5	3	3	6	4				
2000-01	**Tampa Bay**	**NHL**	**43**	**9**	**11**	**20**	**40**	**2**	**1**	**1**	**72**	**12.5**	**–15**	**16**	**37.5**	**15:45**									
	Detroit Vipers	IHL	33	22	14	36	63																		
2001-02	Djurgarden	Sweden	38	16	15	31	57										4	1	0	1	32				
2002-03	Hartford	AHL	57	30	36	66	73										2	0	2	2	4				
2003-04	**San Jose**	**NHL**	**82**	**22**	**33**	**55**	**34**	**1**	**4**	**5**	**147**	**15.0**	**30**	**23**	**21.7**	**14:54**	**16**	**0**	**3**	**3**	**8**	**0**	**0**	**0**	**13:02**
2004-05	Djurgarden	Sweden	44	18	27	45	106										12	4	5	9	20				
2005-06	**San Jose**	**NHL**	**77**	**21**	**36**	**57**	**54**	**5**	**0**	**2**	**176**	**11.9**	**20**	**39**	**46.2**	**15:12**	**11**	**2**	**2**	**4**	**8**	**1**	**0**	**0**	**15:14**
	NHL Totals		**230**	**54**	**82**	**136**	**164**	**9**	**5**	**8**	**437**	**12.4**		**81**	**35.8**	**14:43**	**27**	**2**	**5**	**7**	**16**	**1**	**0**	**0**	**13:56**

Garry F. Longman Memorial Trophy (Rookie of the Year – IHL) (2000)

Traded to **Tampa Bay** by **Calgary** with Calgary's 4th round choice (later traded to NY Islanders – NY Islanders selected Vladimir Gorbunov) in 2000 Entry Draft for Andreas Johansson, November 20, 1999. Traded to **NY Rangers** by **Tampa Bay** with Kyle Freadrich for Tim Taylor, June 30, 2001. Traded to **San Jose** by **NY Rangers** for Chad Wiseman, August 12, 2003. Signed as a free agent by **Djurgarden** (Sweden), September 16, 2004. Traded to **Pittsburgh** by **San Jose** with Patrick Ehelechner for Carolina's 2nd round choice (previously acquired) in 2007 Entry Draft, July 20, 2006.

ELIAS, Patrik

(ehl-EE-ahsh, PA-trihk) **N.J.**

Left wing. Shoots left. 6'1", 195 lbs. Born, Trebic, Czech., April 13, 1976. New Jersey's 2nd choice, 51st overall, in 1994 Entry Draft.

Season	Club	League	GP	G	A	Pts	PIM	PP	SH	GW	S	%	+/-	TF	F%	Min	GP	G	A	Pts	PIM	PP	SH	GW	Min
1992-93	Poldi Kladno	Czech	2	0	0	0																			
1993-94	HC Kladno	CzRep	15	1	2	3											11	2	2	4					
1994-95	HC Kladno	CzRep	28	4	3	7	37										7	1	2	3	12				
1995-96	**New Jersey**	**NHL**	**1**	**0**	**0**	**0**	**0**	**0**	**0**	**0**	**2**	**0.0**	**–1**												
	Albany River Rats	AHL	74	27	36	63	83										4	1	1	2	2				
1996-97	**New Jersey**	**NHL**	**17**	**2**	**3**	**5**	**2**	**0**	**0**	**0**	**23**	**8.7**	**–4**				**8**	**2**	**3**	**5**	**4**	**1**	**0**	**0**	
	Albany River Rats	AHL	57	24	43	67	76										6	1	2	3	8				
1997-98	**New Jersey**	**NHL**	**74**	**18**	**19**	**37**	**28**	**5**	**0**	**6**	**147**	**12.2**	**18**				**4**	**0**	**1**	**1**	**0**	**0**	**0**	**0**	
	Albany River Rats	AHL	3	3	0	3	2																		
1998-99	**New Jersey**	**NHL**	**74**	**17**	**33**	**50**	**34**	**3**	**0**	**2**	**157**	**10.8**	**19**	**99**	**38.4**	**15:50**	**7**	**0**	**5**	**5**	**6**	**0**	**0**	**0**	**18:07**
99-2000	Trebic	CzRep-2	2	2	1	3	2																		
	Pardubice	CzRep	5	1	4	5	31																		
	♦ **New Jersey**	**NHL**	**72**	**35**	**37**	**72**	**58**	**9**	**0**	**9**	**183**	**19.1**	**16**	**134**	**45.5**	**17:28**	**23**	**7**	***13**	**20**	**9**	**2**	**1**	**1**	**17:44**
2000-01	**New Jersey**	**NHL**	**82**	**40**	**56**	**96**	**51**	**8**	**3**	**6**	**220**	**18.2**	**45**	**155**	**41.3**	**18:44**	**25**	**9**	**14**	**23**	**10**	**3**	**1**	**2**	**18:14**
2001-02	**New Jersey**	**NHL**	**75**	**29**	**32**	**61**	**36**	**8**	**1**	**8**	**199**	**14.6**	**4**	**128**	**45.3**	**18:57**	**6**	**2**	**4**	**6**	**6**	**2**	**0**	**0**	**20:33**
	Czech Republic	Olympics	4	1	1	2	0																		
2002-03 ♦	**New Jersey**	**NHL**	**81**	**28**	**29**	**57**	**22**	**6**	**0**	**4**	**255**	**11.0**	**17**	**427**	**43.8**	**18:05**	**24**	**5**	**8**	**13**	**26**	**2**	**0**	**2**	**17:14**
2003-04	**New Jersey**	**NHL**	**82**	**38**	**43**	**81**	**44**	**9**	**3**	**9**	**300**	**12.7**	**26**	**49**	**36.7**	**18:46**	**5**	**3**	**2**	**5**	**2**	**1**	**0**	**1**	**18:59**
2004-05	Znojmo	CzRep	28	8	20	28	65																		
	Magnitogorsk	Russia	17	5	9	14	28																		
2005-06	**New Jersey**	**NHL**	**38**	**16**	**29**	**45**	**20**	**6**	**0**	**3**	**142**	**11.3**	**11**	**10**	**20.0**	**18:34**	**9**	**6**	**10**	**16**	**4**	**4**	**0**	**0**	**18:43**
	Czech Republic	Olympics	1	0	0	0	2																		
	NHL Totals		**596**	**223**	**281**	**504**	**295**	**54**	**7**	**47**	**1628**	**13.7**		**1002**	**42.7**	**18:03**	**111**	**34**	**60**	**94**	**67**	**15**	**2**	**6**	**18:05**

NHL All-Rookie Team (1998) • NHL First All-Star Team (2001) • Bud Light Plus/Minus Award (2001) (tied with Joe Sakic)

Played in NHL All-Star Game (2000, 2002)

Signed as a free agent by **Znojmo** (CzRep), September 6, 2004. Signed as a free agent by **Magnitogorsk** (Russia), December 9, 2004. • Missed majority of 2005-06 season recovering from hepatitis-A.

ELLISON, Matt

(EHL-ih-suhn, MAT) **PHI.**

Right wing. Shoots right. 6', 192 lbs. Born, Duncan, B.C., December 8, 1983. Chicago's 4th choice, 128th overall, in 2002 Entry Draft.

Season	Club	League	GP	G	A	Pts	PIM	PP	SH	GW	S	%	+/-	TF	F%	Min	GP	G	A	Pts	PIM	PP	SH	GW	Min
1997-98	Cowichan Valley	BCAHA	24	27	31	58	10																		
1998-99	Kerry Park	VIJHL	38	40	47	87	110																		
99-2000	Cowichan Valley	BCHL	60	11	23	34	95																		
2000-01	Cowichan Valley	BCHL	60	22	44	66	102																		
2001-02	Cowichan Valley	BCHL	60	42	*75	*117	76										10	5	6	11	8				
2002-03	Red Deer Rebels	WHL	72	40	56	96	80										22	7	13	20	28				
2003-04	**Chicago**	**NHL**	**10**	**0**	**1**	**1**	**0**	**0**	**0**	**0**	**4**	**0.0**	**–3**	**46**	**39.1**	**12:40**									
	Norfolk Admirals	AHL	71	14	21	35	115										7	0	1	1	4				
2004-05	Norfolk Admirals	AHL	71	14	37	51	44										5	0	1	1	2				
2005-06	**Chicago**	**NHL**	**26**	**3**	**9**	**12**	**17**	**1**	**0**	**0**	**47**	**6.4**	**–4**	**76**	**43.4**	**14:45**									
	Philadelphia	**NHL**	**5**	**0**	**1**	**1**	**2**	**0**	**0**	**0**	**2**	**0.0**	**2**	**10**	**50.0**	**6:28**									
	Philadelphia	AHL	48	12	13	25	35																		
	NHL Totals		**41**	**3**	**11**	**14**	**19**	**1**	**0**	**0**	**53**	**5.7**		**132**	**42.4**	**13:14**									

WHL East Second All-Star Team (2003) • WHL Rookie of the Year (2003) • Canadian Major Junior Rookie of the Year (2003)

Traded to **Philadelphia** by **Chicago** with Chicago's 3rd round choice (later traded to Montreal - Montreal selected Ryan White) in 2006 Entry Draft for Patrick Sharp and Eric Meloche, December 5, 2005.

EMINGER, Steve

(EH-mihn-juhr, STEEV) **WSH.**

Defense. Shoots right. 6'2", 217 lbs. Born, Woodbridge, Ont., October 31, 1983. Washington's 1st choice, 12th overall, in 2002 Entry Draft.

Season	Club	League	GP	G	A	Pts	PIM	PP	SH	GW	S	%	+/-	TF	F%	Min	GP	G	A	Pts	PIM	PP	SH	GW	Min
1998-99	Bramalea Blues	OPJHL	47	6	9	15	81																		
99-2000	Kitchener Rangers	OHL	50	2	14	16	74										5	0	0	0	0				
2000-01	Kitchener Rangers	OHL	54	6	26	32	66																		
2001-02	Kitchener Rangers	OHL	64	19	39	58	93										4	0	2	2	10				
2002-03	**Washington**	**NHL**	**17**	**0**	**2**	**2**	**24**	**0**	**0**	**0**	**6**	**0.0**	**–3**	**0**	**0.0**	**10:08**									
	Kitchener Rangers	OHL	23	2	27	29	40										21	3	8	11	44				
2003-04	**Washington**	**NHL**	**41**	**0**	**4**	**4**	**45**	**0**	**0**	**0**	**12**	**0.0**	**–11**	**0**	**0.0**	**17:32**									
	Portland Pirates	AHL	41	0	4	4	40																		
2004-05	Portland Pirates	AHL	62	3	17	20	40										7	0	1	1	2				
2005-06	**Washington**	**NHL**	**66**	**5**	**13**	**18**	**81**	**1**	**0**	**0**	**50**	**10.0**	**–12**	**1**	**100.0**	**21:21**									
	NHL Totals		**124**	**5**	**19**	**24**	**150**	**1**	**0**	**0**	**68**	**7.4**		**1**	**100.0**	**18:33**									

OHL Second All-Star Team (2002, 2003) • Memorial Cup Tournament All-Star Team (2003)

ENDICOTT, Shane

(ehn-DIH-kawt, SHAYN) **NSH.**

Center. Shoots left. 6'3", 214 lbs. Born, Saskatoon, Sask., December 21, 1981. Pittsburgh's 2nd choice, 52nd overall, in 2000 Entry Draft.

Season	Club	League	GP	G	A	Pts	PIM	PP	SH	GW	S	%	+/-	TF	F%	Min	GP	G	A	Pts	PIM	PP	SH	GW	Min
1997-98	Sask. Contacts	SMHL	43	31	32	63	42																		
	Seattle	WHL															5	0	0	0	0				
1998-99	Seattle	WHL	72	13	26	39	27										11	0	1	1	0				
99-2000	Seattle	WHL	70	23	32	55	62										7	1	6	7	6				
2000-01	Seattle	WHL	72	36	43	79	86										9	4	5	9	12				
2001-02	**Pittsburgh**	**NHL**	**4**	**0**	**1**	**1**	**4**	**0**	**0**	**0**	**2**	**0.0**	**–1**	**18**	**33.3**	**8:28**									
	Wilkes-Barre	AHL	63	19	20	39	46																		
2002-03	Wilkes-Barre	AHL	74	13	26	39	68										6	0	2	2	4				
2003-04	Wilkes-Barre	AHL	79	17	22	39	68										24	8	4	12	26				
2004-05	Wilkes-Barre	AHL	68	24	23	47	89										11	2	2	4	31				
2005-06	**Pittsburgh**	**NHL**	**41**	**1**	**1**	**2**	**43**	**0**	**1**	**0**	**44**	**2.3**	**–9**	**422**	**51.7**	**11:43**									
	Wilkes-Barre	AHL	8	0	2	2	4										10	1	3	4	2				
	NHL Totals		**45**	**1**	**2**	**3**	**47**	**0**	**1**	**0**	**46**	**2.2**		**440**	**50.9**	**11:26**									

Signed as a free agent by **Nashville**, July 17, 2006.

								Regular Season									Playoffs								
Season	Club	League	GP	G	A	Pts	PIM	PP	SH	GW	S	%	+/-	TF	F%	Min	GP	G	A	Pts	PIM	PP	SH	GW	Min

ERAT, Martin (EE-rat, mahr-TIHN) NSH.

Left wing. Shoots left. 6', 195 lbs. Born, Trebic, Czech., August 29, 1981. Nashville's 12th choice, 191st overall, in 1999 Entry Draft.

Season	Club	League	GP	G	A	Pts	PIM	PP	SH	GW	S	%	+/-	TF	F%	Min	GP	G	A	Pts	PIM	PP	SH	GW	Min
1997-98	HC ZPS Zlin Jr.	CzRep-Jr.	46	35	30	65	....																		
1998-99	HC ZPS Zlin Jr.	CzRep-Jr.	35	21	23	44	....																		
	Zlin	CzRep	5	0	0	0	2																		
99-2000	Saskatoon Blades	WHL	66	27	26	53	82										11	4	8	12	16				
2000-01	Saskatoon Blades	WHL	31	19	35	54	48																		
	Red Deer Rebels	WHL	17	4	24	28	24										22	*15	*21	*36	32				
2001-02	Nashville	NHL	80	9	24	33	32	2	0	2	84	10.7	-11	3	66.7	13:10									
2002-03	Nashville	NHL	27	1	7	8	14	1	0	0	39	2.6	-9	1	0.0	12:47									
	Milwaukee	AHL	45	10	22	32	41										6	5	4	9	4				
2003-04	Nashville	NHL	76	16	33	49	38	4	0	2	137	11.7	10	31	29.0	15:00	6	0	1	1	6	0	0	0	14:09
2004-05	HC Hame Zlin	CzRep	48	20	23	43	129										16	*7	5	12	12				
2005-06	Nashville	NHL	80	20	29	49	76	5	0	1	143	14.0	0	25	16.0	14:45	5	1	1	2	6	1	0	0	19:31
	Czech Republic	Olympics	8	1	1	2	4																		
	NHL Totals		263	46	93	139	160	12	0	5	403	11.4		60	25.0	14:08	11	1	2	3	12	1	0	0	16:35

Signed as a free agent by **Zlin** (CzRep), September 5, 2004.

ERIKSSON, Anders (AIR-ihk-suhn, AND-uhrs) CBJ

Defense. Shoots left. 6'2", 220 lbs. Born, Bollnas, Sweden, January 9, 1975. Detroit's 1st choice, 22nd overall, in 1993 Entry Draft.

Season	Club	League	GP	G	A	Pts	PIM	PP	SH	GW	S	%	+/-	TF	F%	Min	GP	G	A	Pts	PIM	PP	SH	GW	Min
1992-93	MoDo Jr.	Swe-Jr.	10	5	3	8	14										1	0	0	0	0				
	MoDo	Sweden	20	0	2	2	0																		
1993-94	MoDo Jr.	Swe-Jr.	3	1	2	3	34										11	0	0	0	8				
	MoDo	Sweden	38	2	8	10	42																		
1994-95	MoDo	Sweden	39	3	6	9	54																		
1995-96	**Detroit**	NHL	1	0	0	0	2	0	0	0	0	0.0	1				3	0	0	0	0	0	0	0	
	Adirondack	AHL	75	6	36	42	64										3	0	0	0	0				
1996-97	**Detroit**	NHL	23	0	6	6	10	0	0	0	27	0.0	5				4	0	1	1	4				
	Adirondack	AHL	44	3	25	28	36										18	0	5	5	16	0	0	0	
1997-98♦	**Detroit**	NHL	66	7	14	21	32	1	0	2	91	7.7	21												
1998-99	**Detroit**	NHL	61	2	10	12	34	0	0	0	67	3.0	5	0	0.0	15:54									
	Chicago	NHL	11	0	8	8	0	0	0	0	12	0.0	6	0	0.0	22:51									
99-2000	**Chicago**	NHL	73	3	25	28	20	0	0	1	86	3.5	4	1	100.0	21:03									
2000-01	**Chicago**	NHL	13	2	3	5	2	1	0	0	19	10.5	-4	0	0.0	21:20									
	Florida	NHL	60	0	21	21	28	0	0	0	80	0.0	2	1	0.0	21:02									
2001-02	**Toronto**	NHL	34	0	2	2	12	0	0	0	31	0.0	-1	0	0.0	15:55	10	0	0	0	0	0	0	0	17:24
	St. John's	AHL	25	4	6	10	14										11	0	5	5	6				
2002-03	**Toronto**	NHL	4	0	0	0	0	0	0	0	7	0.0	1	0	0.0	19:02									
	St. John's	AHL	72	5	34	39	133																		
2003-04	**Columbus**	NHL	66	7	20	27	18	2	0	1	84	8.3	-6	0	0.0	20:42									
	Syracuse Crunch	AHL	9	1	3	4	12																		
2004-05	HV 71 Jonkoping	Sweden	32	1	9	10	54										11	3	2	5	16				
2005-06	Magnitogorsk	Russia	17	2	7	9	10																		
	Springfield	AHL	12	1	8	9	10																		
	NHL Totals		412	21	109	130	158	4	0	5	504	4.2		2	50.0	19:30	31	0	5	5	16	0	0	0	17:24

Traded to **Chicago** by **Detroit** with Detroit's 1st round choices in 1999 (Steve McCarthy) and 2001 (Adam Munro) Entry Drafts for Chris Chelios, March 23, 1999. Traded to **Florida** by **Chicago** for Jaroslav Spacek, November 6, 2000. Signed as a free agent by **Toronto**, July 9, 2001. Signed as a free agent by **Columbus**, October 10, 2003. Signed as a free agent by **Calgary**, September 16, 2004. Signed as a free agent by **Jonkoping** (Sweden), October 29, 2004. Signed as a fee agent by **Columbus**, July 1, 2006.

ERSKINE, John (AIR-skign, JAWN)

Defense. Shoots left. 6'4", 215 lbs. Born, Kingston, Ont., June 26, 1980. Dallas' 1st choice, 39th overall, in 1998 Entry Draft.

Season	Club	League	GP	G	A	Pts	PIM	PP	SH	GW	S	%	+/-	TF	F%	Min	GP	G	A	Pts	PIM	PP	SH	GW	Min
1996-97	Quinte Hawks	MTJHL	48	4	16	20	241										16	0	5	5	25				
1997-98	London Knights	OHL	55	0	9	9	205										25	5	10	15	38				
1998-99	London Knights	OHL	57	8	12	20	208																		
99-2000	London Knights	OHL	58	12	31	43	177																		
2000-01	Utah Grizzlies	IHL	77	1	8	9	284																		
2001-02	**Dallas**	NHL	33	0	1	1	62	0	0	0	16	0.0	-8	0	0.0	10:44	3	0	0	0	10				
	Utah Grizzlies	AHL	39	2	6	8	118																		
2002-03	**Dallas**	NHL	16	2	0	2	29	0	0	0	12	16.7	1	0	0.0	10:45	1	0	1	1	15				
	Utah Grizzlies	AHL	52	2	8	10	274																		
2003-04	**Dallas**	NHL	32	0	1	1	84	0	0	0	23	0.0	-9	0	0.0	12:36	5	0	1	1	20				
	Utah Grizzlies	AHL	5	0	0	0	18																		
2004-05	Houston Aeros	AHL	61	3	7	10	238																		
2005-06	**Dallas**	NHL	26	0	0	0	62	0	0	0	9	0.0	-3	0	0.0	11:00									
	NY Islanders	NHL	34	1	0	1	99	0	0	0	23	4.3	-12	0	0.0	14:37									
	NHL Totals		141	3	2	5	336	0	0	0	83	3.6		0	0.0	12:09									

OHL First All-Star Team (2000)

• Missed majority of 2003-04 season recovering from ankle (December 27, 2003 vs. Columbus) and hernia (January 24, 2004 vs. St. Louis) injuries. Traded to **NY Islanders** by **Dallas** with Dallas' 2nd round choice (Jesse Joensuu) in 2006 Entry Draft for Janne Niinimaa and NY Islanders' 5th round choice in 2007 Entry Draft, January 10, 2005.

EVANS, Brennan (EH-vans, BREHN-nan)

Defense. Shoots left. 6'3", 205 lbs. Born, North Battleford, Sask., January 6, 1982.

Season	Club	League	GP	G	A	Pts	PIM	PP	SH	GW	S	%	+/-	TF	F%	Min	GP	G	A	Pts	PIM	PP	SH	GW	Min
1998-99	Camrose Kodiaks	AJHL	47	1	6	7	98										5	0	2	2	0				
	Seattle	WHL															1	0	0	0	0				
99-2000	Seattle	WHL	52	1	2	3	40										1	0	0	0	0				
2000-01	Seattle	WHL	11	1	0	1	25																		
	Kootenay Ice	WHL	55	2	7	9	105										11	0	0	0	25				
2001-02	Kootenay Ice	WHL	72	2	3	5	121										22	0	6	6	38				
2002-03	Kootenay Ice	WHL	67	6	17	23	182										11	1	1	2	24				
2003-04	Lowell	AHL	64	1	9	10	65										5	0	0	0	0				
	Calgary	NHL															2	0	0	0	0	0	0	0	2:52
2004-05	Lowell	AHL	51	0	7	7	79																		
2005-06	Binghamton	AHL	70	3	6	9	198																		
	NHL Totals																2	0	0	0	0	0	0	0	2:52

Signed as a free agent by **Calgary**, September 30, 2003.

EXELBY, Garnet (EHX-uhl-bee, GAHR-neht) ATL.

Defense. Shoots left. 6'1", 215 lbs. Born, Ste. Anne, Man., August 16, 1981. Atlanta's 9th choice, 217th overall, in 1999 Entry Draft.

Season	Club	League	GP	G	A	Pts	PIM	PP	SH	GW	S	%	+/-	TF	F%	Min	GP	G	A	Pts	PIM	PP	SH	GW	Min
1997-98	Winnipeg South	MJHL	46	5	11	16	110																		
1998-99	Saskatoon Blades	WHL	61	5	3	8	91																		
99-2000	Saskatoon Blades	WHL	63	1	8	9	79										11	0	2	2	21				
2000-01	Saskatoon Blades	WHL	43	5	10	15	110										6	0	2	2	4				
	Regina Pats	WHL	22	2	8	10	51										25	0	4	4	49				
2001-02	Chicago Wolves	AHL	75	3	4	7	257																		
2002-03	**Atlanta**	NHL	15	0	2	2	41	0	0	0	9	0.0	0	0	0.0	18:04	9	0	1	1	27				
	Chicago Wolves	AHL	53	3	6	9	140																		
2003-04	**Atlanta**	NHL	71	1	9	10	134	0	0	0	42	2.4	-10	0	0.0	19:32									
2004-05				DID NOT PLAY																					
2005-06	**Atlanta**	NHL	75	1	9	10	75	0	0	0	44	2.3	11	0	0.0	15:41									
	NHL Totals		161	2	20	22	250	0	0	0	95	2.1		0	0.0	17:36									

FAHEY, Jim
(FA-hee, JIHM) **S.J.**

Defense. Shoots right. 6', 205 lbs. Born, Boston, MA, May 11, 1979. San Jose's 9th choice, 212th overall, in 1998 Entry Draft.

			Regular Season														Playoffs								
Season	Club	League	GP	G	A	Pts	PIM	PP	SH	GW	S	%	+/-	TF	F%	Min	GP	G	A	Pts	PIM	PP	SH	GW	Min
1997-98	Catholic Memorial	High-MA	24	12	32	44	28	....	....	....	....	....	....	....	....	....	....	....	....	....	....	....	....	....	....
1998-99	Northeastern	H-East	32	5	13	18	34	....	....	....	....	....	....	....	....	....	....	....	....	....	....	....	....	....	....
99-2000	Northeastern	H-East	36	3	17	20	62	....	....	....	....	....	....	....	....	....	....	....	....	....	....	....	....	....	....
2000-01	Northeastern	H-East	36	4	23	27	48	....	....	....	....	....	....	....	....	....	....	....	....	....	....	....	....	....	....
2001-02	Northeastern	H-East	39	14	32	46	50	....	....	....	....	....	....	....	....	....	....	....	....	....	....	....	....	....	....
2002-03	**San Jose**	**NHL**	**43**	**1**	**19**	**20**	**33**	**0**	**0**	**0**	**66**	**1.5**	**–3**	**1**	**100.0**	**18:20**	....	....	....	....	....	....	....	....	....
	Cleveland Barons	AHL	25	3	14	17	42	....	....	....	....	....	....	....	....	....	....	....	....	....	....	....	....	....	....
2003-04	**San Jose**	**NHL**	**15**	**0**	**2**	**2**	**18**	**0**	**0**	**0**	**19**	**0.0**	**–2**	**0**	**0.0**	**16:54**	**2**	**0**	**0**	**0**	**0**	**0**	**0**	**0**	**4:41**
	Cleveland Barons	AHL	32	1	18	19	64	....	....	....	....	....	....	....	....	....	....	....	....	....	....	....	....	....	....
2004-05	Cleveland Barons	AHL	69	4	22	26	146	....	....	....	....	....	....	....	....	....	....	....	....	....	....	....	....	....	....
2005-06	**San Jose**	**NHL**	**21**	**0**	**2**	**2**	**14**	**0**	**0**	**0**	**22**	**0.0**	**–11**	**0**	**0.0**	**12:39**	....	....	....	....	....	....	....	....	....
	NHL Totals		**79**	**1**	**23**	**24**	**65**	**0**	**0**	**0**	**107**	**0.9**		**1**	**100.0**	**16:33**	**2**	**0**	**0**	**0**	**0**	**0**	**0**	**0**	**4:41**

Hockey East Second All-Star Team (2001) • Hockey East First All-Star Team (2002)

• Spent majority of the 2005-06 season as a healthy reserve.

FAST, Brad
(FAST, BRAD)

Defense. Shoots left. 6', 195 lbs. Born, Fort St. John, B.C., February 21, 1980. Carolina's 2nd choice, 84th overall, in 1999 Entry Draft.

Season	Club	League	GP	G	A	Pts	PIM	PP	SH	GW	S	%	+/-	TF	F%	Min	GP	G	A	Pts	PIM	PP	SH	GW	Min
1994-95	Fort St. John	BCAHA	40	9	26	35	40	....	....	....	....	....	....	....	....	....	....	....	....	....	....	....	....	....	....
1995-96	Fort St. John	BCAHA	60	53	52	105	70	....	....	....	....	....	....	....	....	....	....	....	....	....	....	....	....	....	....
1996-97	Prince George	BCHL	49	3	7	10	19	....	....	....	....	....	....	....	....	....	....	....	....	....	....	....	....	....	....
1997-98	Prince George	BCJHL	59	10	33	43	22	....	....	....	....	....	....	....	....	....	....	....	....	....	....	....	....	....	....
1998-99	Prince George	BCHL	59	27	46	73	....	....	....	....	....	....	....	....	....	....	....	....	....	....	....	....	....	....	....
99-2000	Michigan State	CCHA	42	5	9	14	20	....	....	....	....	....	....	....	....	....	....	....	....	....	....	....	....	....	....
2000-01	Michigan State	CCHA	42	4	24	28	16	....	....	....	....	....	....	....	....	....	....	....	....	....	....	....	....	....	....
2001-02	Michigan State	CCHA	41	10	16	26	26	....	....	....	....	....	....	....	....	....	....	....	....	....	....	....	....	....	....
2002-03	Michigan State	CCHA	39	11	35	46	28	....	....	....	....	....	....	....	....	....	....	....	....	....	....	....	....	....	....
	Lowell	AHL	7	0	1	1	12	....	....	....	....	....	....	....	....	....	....	....	....	....	....	....	....	....	....
2003-04	**Carolina**	**NHL**	**1**	**1**	**0**	**1**	**0**	**0**	**0**	**0**	**4**	**25.0**	**1**	**0**	**0.0**	**21:24**	....	....	....	....	....	....	....	....	....
	Lowell	AHL	79	10	25	35	35	....	....	....	....	....	....	....	....	....	....	....	....	....	....	....	....	....	....
2004-05	Lowell	AHL	32	1	5	6	23	....	....	....	....	....	....	....	....	....	....	....	....	....	....	....	....	....	....
	Florida Everblades	ECHL	14	2	5	7	0	....	....	....	....	....	....	....	....	....	18	1	3	4	6	....	....	....	....
2005-06	Manchester	AHL	62	5	13	18	38	....	....	....	....	....	....	....	....	....	7	0	2	2	8	....	....	....	....
	NHL Totals		**1**	**1**	**0**	**1**	**0**	**0**	**0**	**0**	**4**	**25.0**		**0**	**0.0**	**21:24**	....	....	....	....	....	....	....	....	....

CCHA First All-Star Team (2003) • NCAA West Second All-American Team (2003)

• One of only three players (Rolly Huard, Dean Morton) to score a goal in his only NHL game. Signed as a free agent by **Los Angeles**, August 15, 2005. Signed as a free agent by **Langnau** (Swiss), August 16, 2006.

FATA, Rico
(FA-tuh, REE-koh) **WSH.**

Right wing. Shoots left. 6', 205 lbs. Born, Sault Ste. Marie, Ont., February 12, 1980. Calgary's 1st choice, 6th overall, in 1998 Entry Draft.

Season	Club	League	GP	G	A	Pts	PIM	PP	SH	GW	S	%	+/-	TF	F%	Min	GP	G	A	Pts	PIM	PP	SH	GW	Min
1994-95	Soo Legion	NOHA	51	52	51	103	....	....	....	....	....	....	....	....	....	....	....	....	....	....	....	....	....	....	....
1995-96	Sault Ste. Marie	OHL	62	11	15	26	52	....	....	....	....	....	....	....	....	....	4	0	0	0	0	....	....	....	....
1996-97	London Knights	OHL	59	19	34	53	76	....	....	....	....	....	....	....	....	....	....	....	....	....	....	....	....	....	....
1997-98	London Knights	OHL	64	43	33	76	110	....	....	....	....	....	....	....	....	....	16	9	5	14	*49	....	....	....	....
1998-99	**Calgary**	**NHL**	**20**	**0**	**1**	**1**	**4**	**0**	**0**	**0**	**13**	**0.0**	**0**	**2**	**50.0**	**7:36**	....	....	....	....	....	....	....	....	....
	London Knights	OHL	23	15	18	33	41	....	....	....	....	....	....	....	....	....	25	10	12	22	42	....	....	....	....
99-2000	**Calgary**	**NHL**	**2**	**0**	**0**	**0**	**0**	**0**	**0**	**0**	**0**	**0.0**	**–1**	**0**	**0.0**	**10:06**	....	....	....	....	....	....	....	....	....
	Saint John Flames	AHL	76	29	29	58	65	....	....	....	....	....	....	....	....	....	3	0	0	0	4	....	....	....	....
2000-01	**Calgary**	**NHL**	**5**	**0**	**0**	**0**	**6**	**0**	**0**	**0**	**6**	**0.0**	**–3**	**0**	**0.0**	**9:25**	....	....	....	....	....	....	....	....	....
	Saint John Flames	AHL	70	23	29	52	129	....	....	....	....	....	....	....	....	....	19	2	3	5	22	....	....	....	....
2001-02	**NY Rangers**	**NHL**	**10**	**0**	**0**	**0**	**0**	**0**	**0**	**0**	**8**	**0.0**	**–2**	**55**	**47.3**	**8:31**	....	....	....	....	....	....	....	....	....
	Hartford	AHL	61	35	36	71	36	....	....	....	....	....	....	....	....	....	10	2	5	7	4	....	....	....	....
2002-03	Hartford	AHL	9	8	6	14	6	....	....	....	....	....	....	....	....	....	....	....	....	....	....	....	....	....	....
	NY Rangers	**NHL**	**36**	**2**	**4**	**6**	**6**	**0**	**0**	**0**	**30**	**6.7**	**–1**	**30**	**50.0**	**7:16**	....	....	....	....	....	....	....	....	....
	Pittsburgh	**NHL**	**27**	**5**	**8**	**13**	**10**	**0**	**0**	**0**	**49**	**10.2**	**–6**	**87**	**49.4**	**17:46**	....	....	....	....	....	....	....	....	....
2003-04	**Pittsburgh**	**NHL**	**73**	**16**	**18**	**34**	**54**	**6**	**2**	**1**	**163**	**9.8**	**–46**	**1205**	**47.1**	**17:58**	....	....	....	....	....	....	....	....	....
2004-05	Asiago	Italy	35	18	20	38	36	....	....	....	....	....	....	....	....	....	9	7	5	12	10	....	....	....	....
2005-06	**Pittsburgh**	**NHL**	**20**	**0**	**0**	**0**	**10**	**0**	**0**	**0**	**18**	**0.0**	**–5**	**204**	**41.7**	**13:06**	....	....	....	....	....	....	....	....	....
	Wilkes-Barre	AHL	25	8	10	18	39	....	....	....	....	....	....	....	....	....	....	....	....	....	....	....	....	....	....
	Atlanta	**NHL**	**6**	**0**	**1**	**1**	**4**	**0**	**0**	**0**	**1**	**0.0**	**–2**	**20**	**55.0**	**7:18**	....	....	....	....	....	....	....	....	....
	Washington	**NHL**	**21**	**3**	**3**	**6**	**8**	**1**	**0**	**0**	**31**	**9.7**	**3**	**3**	**33.3**	**8:11**	....	....	....	....	....	....	....	....	....
	NHL Totals		**220**	**26**	**35**	**61**	**102**	**7**	**2**	**1**	**319**	**8.2**		**1606**	**46.7**	**12:53**	....	....	....	....	....	....	....	....	....

AHL All-Rookie Team (2000) • AHL Second All-Star Team (2002)

Claimed on waivers by **NY Rangers** from **Calgary**, October 3, 2001. Traded to **Pittsburgh** by **NY Rangers** with Joel Bouchard, Richard Lintner, Mikael Samuelsson and future considerations for Mike Wilson, Alex Kovalev, Janne Laukkanen and Dan LaCouture, February 10, 2003. Signed as a free agent by **Asiago** (Italy), August 15, 2004. Claimed on waivers by **Atlanta** from **Pittsburgh**, January 31, 2006. Claimed on waivers by **Washington** from **Atlanta**, March 9, 2006.

FEDOROV, Fedor
(FEH-duh-rahf, feh-DUHR)

Center. Shoots left. 6'3", 230 lbs. Born, Appatity, USSR, June 11, 1981. Vancouver's 2nd choice, 66th overall, in 2001 Entry Draft.

Season	Club	League	GP	G	A	Pts	PIM	PP	SH	GW	S	%	+/-	TF	F%	Min	GP	G	A	Pts	PIM	PP	SH	GW	Min
1997-98	Det. Caesars	MNHL	13	3	7	10	18	....	....	....	....	....	....	....	....	....	....	....	....	....	....	....	....	....	....
1998-99	Port Huron	UHL	42	2	5	7	20	....	....	....	....	....	....	....	....	....	....	....	....	....	....	....	....	....	....
99-2000	Windsor Spitfires	OHL	60	7	10	17	115	....	....	....	....	....	....	....	....	....	12	1	0	1	4	....	....	....	....
2000-01	Sudbury Wolves	OHL	67	33	45	78	88	....	....	....	....	....	....	....	....	....	12	4	6	10	36	....	....	....	....
2001-02	Manitoba Moose	AHL	8	2	1	3	6	....	....	....	....	....	....	....	....	....	....	....	....	....	....	....	....	....	....
	Columbia Inferno	ECHL	2	0	2	2	0	....	....	....	....	....	....	....	....	....	....	....	....	....	....	....	....	....	....
2002-03	**Vancouver**	**NHL**	**7**	**0**	**1**	**1**	**4**	**0**	**0**	**0**	**2**	**0.0**	**0**	**26**	**46.2**	**9:10**	....	....	....	....	....	....	....	....	....
	Manitoba Moose	AHL	50	10	13	23	61	....	....	....	....	....	....	....	....	....	3	1	2	3	0	....	....	....	....
2003-04	**Vancouver**	**NHL**	**8**	**0**	**1**	**1**	**4**	**0**	**0**	**0**	**10**	**0.0**	**0**	**4**	**50.0**	**10:59**	....	....	....	....	....	....	....	....	....
	Manitoba Moose	AHL	58	23	16	39	52	....	....	....	....	....	....	....	....	....	....	....	....	....	....	....	....	....	....
2004-05	Spartak Moscow	Russia	19	4	7	11	52	....	....	....	....	....	....	....	....	....	....	....	....	....	....	....	....	....	....
	Magnitogorsk	Russia	10	3	0	3	22	....	....	....	....	....	....	....	....	....	5	2	0	2	30	....	....	....	....
2005-06	**NY Rangers**	**NHL**	**3**	**0**	**0**	**0**	**6**	**0**	**0**	**0**	**2**	**0.0**	**0**	**1**	**0.0**	**9:49**	....	....	....	....	....	....	....	....	....
	Hartford	AHL	38	2	15	17	80	....	....	....	....	....	....	....	....	....	....	....	....	....	....	....	....	....	....
	Syracuse Crunch	AHL	12	2	3	5	22	....	....	....	....	....	....	....	....	....	3	0	0	0	2	....	....	....	....
	NHL Totals		**18**	**0**	**2**	**2**	**14**	**0**	**0**	**0**	**14**	**0.0**		**31**	**45.2**	**10:05**	....	....	....	....	....	....	....	....	....

• Re-entered NHL Entry Draft. Originally Tampa Bay's 7th choice, 182nd overall, in 1999 Entry Draft.

Signed as an underage free agent by **Detroit** (IHL), August 5, 1998. Released by **Detroit** (IHL), September 30, 1998. Signed as an underage free agent by **Port Huron** (UHL), October 1, 1998. • Missed majority of 2001-02 season recovering from eye injury suffered in game vs. Macon (ECHL), November 17, 2001. Signed as a free agent by **Spartak Moscow** (Russia), November 15, 2004. Signed as a free agent by **Magnitogorsk** (Russia), February 16, 2005. Traded to **NY Rangers** by **Vancouver** for Jozef Balej and future considerations, October 7, 2005. Loaned to **Syracuse** (AHL) by **NY Rangers** (Hartford-AHL) for cash, March 11, 2006. Signed as a free agent by **Yaroslavl** (Russia), July 25, 2006.

FEDOROV, Sergei
(FEH-duh-rahf, SAIR-gay) **CBJ**

Center. Shoots left. 6'2", 205 lbs. Born, Pskov, USSR, December 13, 1969. Detroit's 4th choice, 74th overall, in 1989 Entry Draft.

Season	Club	League	GP	G	A	Pts	PIM	PP	SH	GW	S	%	+/-	TF	F%	Min	GP	G	A	Pts	PIM	PP	SH	GW	Min
1985-86	Dynamo Minsk	USSR-2	15	6	1	7	10	....	....	....	....	....	....	....	....	....	....	....	....	....	....	....	....	....	....
1986-87	CSKA Moscow	USSR	29	6	6	12	12	....	....	....	....	....	....	....	....	....	....	....	....	....	....	....	....	....	....
1987-88	CSKA Moscow	USSR	48	7	9	16	20	....	....	....	....	....	....	....	....	....	....	....	....	....	....	....	....	....	....
1988-89	CSKA Moscow	USSR	44	9	8	17	35	....	....	....	....	....	....	....	....	....	....	....	....	....	....	....	....	....	....
1989-90	CSKA Moscow	USSR	48	19	10	29	22	....	....	....	....	....	....	....	....	....	....	....	....	....	....	....	....	....	....
1990-91	**Detroit**	**NHL**	**77**	**31**	**48**	**79**	**66**	**11**	**3**	**5**	**259**	**12.0**	**11**	....	....	....	**7**	**1**	**5**	**6**	**4**	**0**	**0**	**1**	....
1991-92	**Detroit**	**NHL**	**80**	**32**	**54**	**86**	**72**	**7**	**2**	**5**	**249**	**12.9**	**26**	....	....	....	**11**	**5**	**5**	**10**	**8**	**1**	**2**	**1**	....
1992-93	**Detroit**	**NHL**	**73**	**34**	**53**	**87**	**72**	**13**	**4**	**3**	**217**	**15.7**	**33**	....	....	....	**7**	**3**	**6**	**9**	**23**	**1**	**1**	**0**	....
1993-94	**Detroit**	**NHL**	**82**	**56**	**64**	**120**	**34**	**13**	**4**	**10**	**337**	**16.6**	**48**	....	....	....	**7**	**1**	**7**	**8**	**6**	**0**	**0**	**0**	....
1994-95	**Detroit**	**NHL**	**42**	**20**	**30**	**50**	**24**	**7**	**3**	**5**	**147**	**13.6**	**6**	....	....	....	**17**	**7**	***17**	***24**	**6**	**3**	**0**	**0**	....

			Regular Season														Playoffs								
Season	Club	League	GP	G	A	Pts	PIM	PP	SH	GW	S	%	+/-	TF	F%	Min	GP	G	A	Pts	PIM	PP	SH	GW	Min
1995-96	Detroit	NHL	78	39	68	107	48	11	3	11	306	12.7	49	....	....	....	19	2	*18	20	10	0	0	2	....
1996-97 ◆	Detroit	NHL	74	30	33	63	30	9	2	4	273	11.0	29	....	....	....	20	8	12	20	12	3	0	4	....
1997-98	Russia	Olympics	6	1	5	6	8	....	....	....	....	....	....	....	....	....	....	....	....	....	....	....	....	....	....
◆	Detroit	NHL	21	6	11	17	25	2	0	2	68	8.8	10	....	....	....	22	*10	10	20	12	2	1	1	....
1998-99	Detroit	NHL	77	26	37	63	66	6	2	3	224	11.6	9	1414	51.7	19:21	10	1	8	9	8	0	0	0	19:54
99-2000	Detroit	NHL	68	27	35	62	22	4	4	7	263	10.3	8	1274	53.8	20:05	9	4	4	8	4	2	0	1	20:48
2000-01	Detroit	NHL	75	32	37	69	40	14	2	7	268	11.9	12	1601	55.8	21:05	6	2	5	7	0	1	0	1	22:19
2001-02 ◆	Detroit	NHL	81	31	37	68	36	10	0	6	256	12.1	20	1160	51.7	19:33	23	5	14	19	20	2	1	0	22:20
	Russia	Olympics	6	2	2	4	4	....	....	....	....	....	....	....	....	....	....	....	....	....	....	....	....	....	....
2002-03	Detroit	NHL	80	36	47	83	52	10	2	11	281	12.8	15	1580	53.4	21:11	4	1	2	3	0	0	0	0	22:07
2003-04	Anaheim	NHL	80	31	34	65	42	9	2	6	268	11.6	–5	1558	56.6	21:05	....	....	....	....	....	....	....	....	....
2004-05		DID NOT PLAY																							
2005-06	Anaheim	NHL	5	0	1	1	2	0	0	0	18	0.0	–1	80	55.0	20:17	....	....	....	....	....	....	....	....	....
	Columbus	NHL	62	12	31	43	64	3	1	2	142	8.5	–1	1169	51.8	21:06	....	....	....	....	....	....	....	....	....
	NHL Totals		1055	443	620	1063	695	129	34	87	3576	12.4		9836	53.7	20:28	162	50	113	163	113	15	5	11	21:35

NHL All-Rookie Team (1991) • NHL First All-Star Team (1994) • Frank J. Selke Trophy (1994, 1996) • Lester B. Pearson Award (1994) • Hart Trophy (1994)

Played in NHL All-Star Game (1992, 1994, 1996, 2001, 2002, 2003)

• Missed majority of 1997-98 season after failing to come to contract terms with **Detroit**. Signed as a free agent by **Anaheim**, July 19, 2003. Traded to **Columbus** by **Anaheim** with Anaheim's 5th round choice (Maxime Frechette) in 2006 Entry Draft for Tyler Wright and Francois Beauchemin, November 15, 2005.

FEDORUK, Todd

(FEH-duh-ruhk, TAWD) **ANA.**

Left wing. Shoots left. 6'2", 235 lbs. Born, Redwater, Alta., February 13, 1979. Philadelphia's 6th choice, 164th overall, in 1997 Entry Draft.

1994-95	Ft. Saskatchewan	AMHL	STATISTICS NOT AVAILABLE																						
1995-96	Kelowna Rockets	WHL	44	1	1	2	83	....	....	....	....	....	....	....	....	....	4	0	0	0	6	....	....	....	....
1996-97	Kelowna Rockets	WHL	31	1	5	6	87	....	....	....	....	....	....	....	....	....	6	0	0	0	13	....	....	....	....
1997-98	Kelowna Rockets	WHL	31	3	5	8	120	....	....	....	....	....	....	....	....	....	....	....	....	....	....	....	....	....	....
	Regina Pats	WHL	21	4	3	7	80	....	....	....	....	....	....	....	....	....	9	1	2	3	23	....	....	....	....
1998-99	Regina Pats	WHL	39	12	12	24	107	....	....	....	....	....	....	....	....	....	....	....	....	....	....	....	....	....	....
	Prince Albert	WHL	28	6	4	10	75	....	....	....	....	....	....	....	....	....	13	1	6	7	49	....	....	....	....
99-2000	Trenton Titans	ECHL	18	2	5	7	118	....	....	....	....	....	....	....	....	....	....	....	....	....	....	....	....	....	....
	Philadelphia	AHL	19	1	2	3	40	....	....	....	....	....	....	....	....	....	5	0	1	1	2	....	....	....	....
2000-01	Philadelphia	NHL	53	5	5	10	109	0	0	0	28	17.9	0	0	0.0	7:02	2	0	0	0	20	0	0	0	5:57
	Philadelphia	AHL	14	0	1	1	49	....	....	....	....	....	....	....	....	....	....	....	....	....	....	....	....	....	....
2001-02	Philadelphia	NHL	55	3	4	7	141	0	0	0	21	14.3	–2	5	0.0	6:21	3	0	0	0	0	0	0	0	2:46
	Philadelphia	AHL	7	0	1	1	54	....	....	....	....	....	....	....	....	....	....	....	....	....	....	....	....	....	....
2002-03	Philadelphia	NHL	63	1	5	6	105	0	0	0	33	3.0	1	1	0.0	6:30	1	0	0	0	0	0	0	0	4:52
2003-04	Philadelphia	NHL	49	1	4	5	136	0	0	1	33	3.0	–4	0	0.0	6:47	1	0	0	0	2	0	0	0	6:42
	Philadelphia	AHL	2	0	2	2	2	....	....	....	....	....	....	....	....	....	....	....	....	....	....	....	....	....	....
2004-05	Philadelphia	AHL	42	4	12	16	142	....	....	....	....	....	....	....	....	....	16	2	2	4	33	....	....	....	....
2005-06	Anaheim	NHL	76	4	19	23	174	0	0	1	69	5.8	6	8	37.5	8:24	12	0	0	0	16	0	0	0	8:19
	NHL Totals		296	14	37	51	665	0	0	2	184	7.6		14	21.4	7:06	19	0	0	0	38	0	0	0	6:56

Traded to **Anaheim** by **Philadelphia** for Anaheim's 2nd round choice (later traded to Phoenix - Phoenix selected Pier-Olivier Pelletier) in 2005 Entry Draft, July 29, 2005.

FEDOTENKO, Ruslan

(feh-doh-TEHN-koh, roos-LAHN) **T.B.**

Left wing. Shoots left. 6'2", 195 lbs. Born, Kiev, Ukraine, January 18, 1979.

1995-96	Kiev 2	EEHL	33	9	11	20	12	....	....	....	....	....	....	....	....	....	....	....	....	....	....	....	....	....	....
	Sokol Kiev	CIS	2	0	0	0	0	....	....	....	....	....	....	....	....	....	....	....	....	....	....	....	....	....	....
1996-97	TPS Turku U18	Fin-U18	3	3	2	5	2	....	....	....	....	....	....	....	....	....	....	....	....	....	....	....	....	....	....
	TPS Turku Jr.	Fin-Jr.	11	1	1	2	2	....	....	....	....	....	....	....	....	....	....	....	....	....	....	....	....	....	....
	Kiekko-67 Turku	Finland-2	22	4	3	7	16	....	....	....	....	....	....	....	....	....	....	....	....	....	....	....	....	....	....
	Kiekko Turku	Finland-3	....	....	....	....	....	....	....	....	....	....	....	....	....	....	3	1	0	1	2	....	....	....	....
1997-98	Melfort Mustangs	SJHL	68	35	31	66	55	....	....	....	....	....	....	....	....	....	....	....	....	....	....	....	....	....	....
1998-99	Sioux City	USHL	55	43	34	77	139	....	....	....	....	....	....	....	....	....	5	5	1	6	9	....	....	....	....
99-2000	Trenton Titans	ECHL	8	5	3	8	9	....	....	....	....	....	....	....	....	....	....	....	....	....	....	....	....	....	....
	Philadelphia	AHL	67	16	34	50	42	....	....	....	....	....	....	....	....	....	2	0	0	0	0	....	....	....	....
2000-01	Philadelphia	NHL	74	16	20	36	72	3	0	4	119	13.4	8	7	71.4	14:38	6	0	1	1	4	0	0	0	11:18
	Philadelphia	AHL	8	1	0	1	8	....	....	....	....	....	....	....	....	....	....	....	....	....	....	....	....	....	....
2001-02	Philadelphia	NHL	78	17	9	26	43	0	1	3	121	14.0	15	41	43.9	13:56	5	1	0	1	2	0	0	1	14:11
	Ukraine	Olympics	1	1	0	1	4	....	....	....	....	....	....	....	....	....	....	....	....	....	....	....	....	....	....
2002-03	Tampa Bay	NHL	76	19	13	32	44	6	0	6	114	16.7	–7	90	48.9	16:01	11	0	1	1	2	0	0	0	13:58
2003-04 ◆	Tampa Bay	NHL	77	17	22	39	30	0	0	3	116	14.7	14	58	55.2	14:39	22	12	2	14	14	5	0	3	16:40
2004-05		DID NOT PLAY																							
2005-06	Tampa Bay	NHL	80	26	15	41	44	4	0	6	164	15.9	–4	28	42.9	15:21	5	0	0	0	20	0	0	0	14:38
	NHL Totals		385	95	79	174	233	13	1	22	634	15.0		224	49.6	14:55	49	13	4	17	42	5	0	4	14:57

Signed as a free agent by **Philadelphia**, August 3, 1999. Traded to **Tampa Bay** by **Philadelphia** with Tampa Bay's 2nd round choice (previously acquired, later traded to Dallas – Dallas selected Tobias Stephan) in 2002 Entry Draft and Phoenix's 2nd round choice (previously acquired, later traded to San Jose – San Jose selected Dan Spang) in 2002 Entry Draft for Tampa Bay's 1st round choice (Joni Pitkanen) in 2002 Entry Draft, June 21, 2002.

FEHR, Eric

(FAIR, AIR-ihk) **WSH.**

Right wing. Shoots right. 6'4", 204 lbs. Born, Winkler, Man., September 7, 1985. Washington's 1st choice, 18th overall, in 2003 Entry Draft.

2000-01	Pembina Valley	MMMHL	36	45	13	58	30	....	....	....	....	....	....	....	....	....	....	....	....	....	....	....	....	....	....
	Brandon	WHL	4	0	0	0	0	....	....	....	....	....	....	....	....	....	....	....	....	....	....	....	....	....	....
2001-02	Brandon	WHL	63	11	16	27	29	....	....	....	....	....	....	....	....	....	12	1	1	2	0	....	....	....	....
2002-03	Brandon	WHL	70	26	29	55	76	....	....	....	....	....	....	....	....	....	17	4	8	12	26	....	....	....	....
2003-04	Brandon	WHL	71	50	34	84	129	....	....	....	....	....	....	....	....	....	7	5	0	5	16	....	....	....	....
2004-05	Brandon	WHL	71	*59	52	*111	91	....	....	....	....	....	....	....	....	....	24	16	16	*32	47	....	....	....	....
2005-06	Washington	NHL	11	0	0	0	2	0	0	0	10	0.0	0	4	25.0	5:45	....	....	....	....	....	....	....	....	....
	Hershey Bears	AHL	70	25	28	53	70	....	....	....	....	....	....	....	....	....	19	8	3	11	8	....	....	....	....
	NHL Totals		11	0	0	0	2	0	0	0	10	0.0		4	25.0	5:45	....	....	....	....	....	....	....	....	....

WHL East First All-Star Team (2005) • WHL Player of the Year (2005)

FERENCE, Andrew

(FAIR-ehns, AN-droo) **CGY.**

Defense. Shoots left. 5'10", 196 lbs. Born, Edmonton, Alta., March 17, 1979. Pittsburgh's 8th choice, 208th overall, in 1997 Entry Draft.

1994-95	Sherwood Park	AMHL	31	4	14	18	74	....	....	....	....	....	....	....	....	....	....	....	....	....	....	....	....	....	....
	Portland	WHL	2	0	0	0	4	....	....	....	....	....	....	....	....	....	....	....	....	....	....	....	....	....	....
1995-96	Portland	WHL	72	9	31	40	159	....	....	....	....	....	....	....	....	....	7	1	3	4	12	....	....	....	....
1996-97	Portland	WHL	72	12	32	44	163	....	....	....	....	....	....	....	....	....	6	1	2	3	12	....	....	....	....
1997-98	Portland	WHL	72	11	57	68	142	....	....	....	....	....	....	....	....	....	16	2	18	20	28	....	....	....	....
1998-99	Portland	WHL	40	11	21	32	104	....	....	....	....	....	....	....	....	....	4	1	4	5	10	....	....	....	....
	Kansas City	IHL	5	1	2	3	4	....	....	....	....	....	....	....	....	....	3	0	0	0	9	....	....	....	....
99-2000	Pittsburgh	NHL	30	2	4	6	20	0	0	1	26	7.7	3	0	0.0	16:19	....	....	....	....	....	....	....	....	....
	Wilkes-Barre	AHL	44	8	20	28	58	....	....	....	....	....	....	....	....	....	....	....	....	....	....	....	....	....	....
2000-01	Pittsburgh	NHL	36	4	11	15	28	1	0	1	47	8.5	6	0	0.0	18:51	18	3	7	10	16	1	0	1	22:02
	Wilkes-Barre	AHL	43	6	18	24	95	....	....	....	....	....	....	....	....	....	3	1	0	1	12	....	....	....	....
2001-02	Pittsburgh	NHL	75	4	7	11	73	1	0	0	82	4.9	–12	2	0.0	18:34	....	....	....	....	....	....	....	....	....
2002-03	Pittsburgh	NHL	22	1	3	4	36	1	0	0	22	4.5	–16	1	100.0	19:33	....	....	....	....	....	....	....	....	....
	Wilkes-Barre	AHL	1	0	0	0	2	....	....	....	....	....	....	....	....	....	....	....	....	....	....	....	....	....	....
	Calgary	NHL	16	0	4	4	6	0	0	0	17	0.0	1	0	0.0	17:38	....	....	....	....	....	....	....	....	....
2003-04	Calgary	NHL	72	4	12	16	53	1	0	0	86	4.7	5	0	0.0	18:40	26	0	3	3	25	0	0	0	24:13
2004-05	C. Budejovice	CzRep-2	19	5	6	11	45	....	....	....	....	....	....	....	....	....	12	2	7	9	10	....	....	....	....
2005-06	Calgary	NHL	82	4	27	31	85	2	0	0	111	3.6	–12	1	0.0	20:08	7	0	4	4	12	0	0	0	23:09
	NHL Totals		333	19	68	87	301	6	0	2	391	4.9		4	25.0	18:49	51	3	14	17	53	1	0	1	23:18

WHL West First All-Star Team (1998) • WHL West Second All-Star Team (1999)

• Missed majority of 2002-03 season recovering from groin (November 18, 2002 vs. Montreal) and ankle (March 20, 2003 vs. Los Angeles) injuries. Traded to **Calgary** by **Pittsburgh** for Calgary's 3rd round choice (Brian Gifford) in 2004 Entry Draft, February 9, 2003. Signed as a free agent by **Ceske Budejovice** (CzRep-2), December 1, 2004.

FERENCE, Brad

(FAIR-ehns, BRAD) **CGY.**

Defense. Shoots right. 6'3", 218 lbs. Born, Calgary, Alta., April 2, 1979. Vancouver's 1st choice, 10th overall, in 1997 Entry Draft.

			Regular Season														Playoffs								
Season	Club	League	GP	G	A	Pts	PIM	PP	SH	GW	S	%	+/-	TF	F%	Min	GP	G	A	Pts	PIM	PP	SH	GW	Min
1994-95	Calgary Royals	ABHL	60	19	47	66	220	....	....	....	....	....	....	....	....	....	....	....	....	....	....	....	....	....	....
1995-96	Calgary Royals	ABHL	22	7	21	28	140	....	....	....	....	....	....	....	....	....	....	....	....	....	....	....	....	....	....
	Spokane Chiefs	WHL	5	0	2	2	18	....	....	....	....	....	....	....	....	....	....	....	....	....	....	....	....	....	....
1996-97	Spokane Chiefs	WHL	67	6	20	26	324	....	....	....	....	....	....	....	....	....	9	0	4	4	21	....	....	....	....
1997-98	Spokane Chiefs	WHL	54	9	30	39	213	....	....	....	....	....	....	....	....	....	18	0	7	7	59	....	....	....	....
1998-99	Spokane Chiefs	WHL	31	3	22	25	125	....	....	....	....	....	....	....	....	....	....	....	....	....	....	....	....	....	....
	Tri-City	WHL	20	6	15	21	116	....	....	....	....	....	....	....	....	....	12	1	9	10	63	....	....	....	....
99-2000	**Florida**	**NHL**	**13**	**0**	**2**	**2**	**46**	**0**	**0**	**0**	**10**	**0.0**	**2**	**0**	**0.0**	**13:40**	....	....	....	....	....	....	....	....	....
	Louisville Panthers	AHL	58	2	7	9	231	....	....	....	....	....	....	....	....	....	2	0	0	0	2	....	....	....	....
2000-01	**Florida**	**NHL**	**14**	**0**	**1**	**1**	**14**	**0**	**0**	**0**	**5**	**0.0**	**–10**	**0**	**0.0**	**13:03**	....	....	....	....	....	....	....	....	....
	Louisville Panthers	AHL	52	3	21	24	200	....	....	....	....	....	....	....	....	....	....	....	....	....	....	....	....	....	....
2001-02	**Florida**	**NHL**	**80**	**2**	**15**	**17**	**254**	**0**	**0**	**0**	**65**	**3.1**	**–13**	**1**	**0.0**	**19:44**	....	....	....	....	....	....	....	....	....
2002-03	**Florida**	**NHL**	**60**	**2**	**6**	**8**	**118**	**0**	**0**	**0**	**41**	**4.9**	**2**	**0**	**0.0**	**15:58**	....	....	....	....	....	....	....	....	....
	Phoenix	**NHL**	**15**	**0**	**1**	**1**	**28**	**0**	**0**	**0**	**8**	**0.0**	**–5**	**0**	**0.0**	**16:33**	....	....	....	....	....	....	....	....	....
2003-04	**Phoenix**	**NHL**	**63**	**0**	**5**	**5**	**103**	**0**	**0**	**0**	**39**	**0.0**	**–19**	**0**	**0.0**	**14:03**	....	....	....	....	....	....	....	....	....
2004-05	Morzine-Avoriaz	France	17	2	10	12	138	....	....	....	....	....	....	....	....	....	4	1	4	5	10	....	....	....	....
2005-06	San Antonio	AHL	19	2	9	11	39	....	....	....	....	....	....	....	....	....	....	....	....	....	....	....	....	....	....
	Albany River Rats	AHL	43	3	8	11	96	....	....	....	....	....	....	....	....	....	....	....	....	....	....	....	....	....	....
	NHL Totals		**245**	**4**	**30**	**34**	**563**	**0**	**0**	**0**	**168**	**2.4**		**1**	**0.0**	**16:27**	....	....	....	....	....	....	....	....	....

Memorial Cup Tournament All-Star Team (1998)

Traded to **Florida** by **Vancouver** with Pavel Bure, Bret Hedican and Vancouver's 3rd round choice (Robert Fried) in 2000 Entry Draft for Ed Jovanovski, Dave Gagner, Mike Brown, Kevin Weekes and Florida's 1st round choice (Nathan Smith) in 2000 Entry Draft, January 17, 1999. Traded to **Phoenix** by **Florida** for Darcy Hordichuk and Phoenix's 2nd round choice (later traded to Tampa Bay – Tampa Bay selected Matt Smaby) in 2003 Entry Draft, March 8, 2003. Signed as a free agent by **Morzine-Avoriaz** (France), October 28, 2004. Traded to **New Jersey** by **Phoenix** for Pascal Rheaume, Ray Schultz and Steven Spencer, November 25, 2005. Signed as a free agent by **Calgary**, July 27, 2006.

FERGUSON, Scott

(fuhr-GUH-sohn, SKAWT) **S.J.**

Defense. Shoots left. 6'1", 195 lbs. Born, Camrose, Alta., January 6, 1973.

Season	Club	League	GP	G	A	Pts	PIM	PP	SH	GW	S	%	+/-	TF	F%	Min	GP	G	A	Pts	PIM	PP	SH	GW	Min
1990-91	Sherwood Park	AJHL	32	2	9	11	91	....	....	....	....	....	....	....	....	....	....	....	....	....	....	....	....	....	....
	Kamloops Blazers	WHL	4	0	0	0	0	....	....	....	....	....	....	....	....	....	....	....	....	....	....	....	....	....	....
1991-92	Kamloops Blazers	WHL	62	4	10	14	138	....	....	....	....	....	....	....	....	....	12	0	2	2	21	....	....	....	....
1992-93	Kamloops Blazers	WHL	71	4	19	23	206	....	....	....	....	....	....	....	....	....	13	0	2	2	24	....	....	....	....
1993-94	Kamloops Blazers	WHL	68	5	49	54	180	....	....	....	....	....	....	....	....	....	19	5	11	16	48	....	....	....	....
1994-95	Cape Breton	AHL	58	4	6	10	103	....	....	....	....	....	....	....	....	....	....	....	....	....	....	....	....	....	....
	Wheeling	ECHL	5	1	5	6	16	....	....	....	....	....	....	....	....	....	....	....	....	....	....	....	....	....	....
1995-96	Cape Breton	AHL	80	5	16	21	196	....	....	....	....	....	....	....	....	....	....	....	....	....	....	....	....	....	....
1996-97	Hamilton	AHL	74	6	14	20	115	....	....	....	....	....	....	....	....	....	21	5	7	12	59	....	....	....	....
1997-98	**Edmonton**	**NHL**	**1**	**0**	**0**	**0**	**0**	**0**	**0**	**0**	**0**	**0.0**	**1**	....	....	....	....	....	....	....	....	....	....	....	....
	Hamilton	AHL	77	7	17	24	150	....	....	....	....	....	....	....	....	....	9	0	3	3	16	....	....	....	....
1998-99	**Anaheim**	**NHL**	**2**	**0**	**1**	**1**	**0**	**0**	**0**	**0**	**1**	**0.0**	**0**	**0**	**0.0**	**15:09**	....	....	....	....	....	....	....	....	....
	Cincinnati	AHL	78	4	31	35	59	....	....	....	....	....	....	....	....	....	3	0	0	0	4	....	....	....	....
99-2000	Cincinnati	AHL	77	7	25	32	166	....	....	....	....	....	....	....	....	....	....	....	....	....	....	....	....	....	....
2000-01	**Edmonton**	**NHL**	**20**	**0**	**1**	**1**	**13**	**0**	**0**	**0**	**8**	**0.0**	**2**	**0**	**0.0**	**10:55**	**6**	**0**	**0**	**0**	**0**	**0**	**0**	**0**	**8:21**
	Hamilton	AHL	42	3	18	21	79	....	....	....	....	....	....	....	....	....	....	....	....	....	....	....	....	....	....
2001-02	**Edmonton**	**NHL**	**50**	**3**	**2**	**5**	**75**	**0**	**0**	**0**	**27**	**11.1**	**11**	**0**	**0.0**	**13:40**	....	....	....	....	....	....	....	....	....
2002-03	**Edmonton**	**NHL**	**78**	**3**	**5**	**8**	**120**	**0**	**0**	**0**	**45**	**6.7**	**11**	**1**	**100.0**	**12:18**	**5**	**0**	**0**	**0**	**8**	**0**	**0**	**0**	**11:44**
2003-04	**Edmonton**	**NHL**	**52**	**1**	**5**	**6**	**80**	**0**	**0**	**1**	**38**	**2.6**	**–5**	**0**	**0.0**	**13:21**	....	....	....	....	....	....	....	....	....
2004-05			DID NOT PLAY																						
2005-06	**Minnesota**	**NHL**	**15**	**0**	**0**	**0**	**22**	**0**	**0**	**0**	**6**	**0.0**	**–3**	**1**	**100.0**	**9:10**	....	....	....	....	....	....	....	....	....
	Houston Aeros	AHL	46	5	8	13	105	....	....	....	....	....	....	....	....	....	8	0	2	2	21	....	....	....	....
	NHL Totals		**218**	**7**	**14**	**21**	**310**	**0**	**0**	**1**	**125**	**5.6**		**2**	**50.0**	**12:48**	**11**	**0**	**0**	**0**	**8**	**0**	**0**	**0**	**18:07**

WHL West Second All-Star Team (1994)

Signed as a free agent by **Edmonton**, June 2, 1994. Traded to **Ottawa** by **Edmonton** for Frantisek Musil, March 9, 1998. Signed as a free agent by **Anaheim**, July 27, 1998. Signed as a free agent by **Edmonton**, July 5, 2000. Signed as a free agent by **Minnesota**, August 4, 2005. Signed as a free agent by **San Jose**, July 14, 2006.

FERLAND, Jonathan

(fair-LAWN, JAWN-ah-thun) **MTL.**

Right wing. Shoots right. 6'2", 208 lbs. Born, Quebec City, Que., February 9, 1983. Montreal's 5th choice, 212th overall, in 2002 Entry Draft.

Season	Club	League	GP	G	A	Pts	PIM	PP	SH	GW	S	%	+/-	TF	F%	Min	GP	G	A	Pts	PIM	PP	SH	GW	Min
1998-99	Laval-Laurentides	QAAA	42	18	17	35	50	....	....	....	....	....	....	....	....	....	....	....	....	....	....	....	....	....	....
99-2000	Moncton Wildcats	QMJHL	52	3	6	9	21	....	....	....	....	....	....	....	....	....	11	0	1	1	0	....	....	....	....
2000-01	Acadie-Bathurst	QMJHL	70	17	11	28	135	....	....	....	....	....	....	....	....	....	13	0	4	4	47	....	....	....	....
2001-02	Acadie-Bathurst	QMJHL	55	28	46	74	104	....	....	....	....	....	....	....	....	....	16	5	12	17	16	....	....	....	....
2002-03	Acadie-Bathurst	QMJHL	68	45	44	89	94	....	....	....	....	....	....	....	....	....	11	4	5	9	16	....	....	....	....
2003-04	Hamilton	AHL	70	5	10	15	43	....	....	....	....	....	....	....	....	....	10	0	0	0	6	....	....	....	....
2004-05	Hamilton	AHL	62	6	8	14	24	....	....	....	....	....	....	....	....	....	4	0	0	0	4	....	....	....	....
2005-06	**Montreal**	**NHL**	**7**	**1**	**0**	**1**	**2**	**0**	**0**	**0**	**9**	**11.1**	**–2**	**2**	**0.0**	**6:37**	....	....	....	....	....	....	....	....	....
	Hamilton	AHL	39	7	8	15	65	....	....	....	....	....	....	....	....	....	....	....	....	....	....	....	....	....	....
	NHL Totals		**7**	**1**	**0**	**1**	**2**	**0**	**0**	**0**	**9**	**11.1**		**2**	**0.0**	**6:37**	....	....	....	....	....	....	....	....	....

FIBIGER, Jesse

(feh-BEH-gehr, JEH-see)

Defense. Shoots left. 6'3", 210 lbs. Born, Victoria, B.C., April 4, 1978. Anaheim's 5th choice, 178th overall, in 1998 Entry Draft.

Season	Club	League	GP	G	A	Pts	PIM	PP	SH	GW	S	%	+/-	TF	F%	Min	GP	G	A	Pts	PIM	PP	SH	GW	Min
1996-97	Victoria Salsa	BCHL	53	6	18	24	88	....	....	....	....	....	....	....	....	....	....	....	....	....	....	....	....	....	....
1997-98	U. Minn-Duluth	WCHA	40	3	6	9	82	....	....	....	....	....	....	....	....	....	....	....	....	....	....	....	....	....	....
1998-99	U. Minn-Duluth	WCHA	36	4	16	20	61	....	....	....	....	....	....	....	....	....	....	....	....	....	....	....	....	....	....
99-2000	U. Minn-Duluth	WCHA	37	4	6	10	83	....	....	....	....	....	....	....	....	....	....	....	....	....	....	....	....	....	....
2000-01	U. Minn-Duluth	WCHA	37	0	8	8	56	....	....	....	....	....	....	....	....	....	....	....	....	....	....	....	....	....	....
2001-02	Cleveland Barons	AHL	79	6	12	18	94	....	....	....	....	....	....	....	....	....	....	....	....	....	....	....	....	....	....
2002-03	**San Jose**	**NHL**	**16**	**0**	**0**	**0**	**2**	**0**	**0**	**0**	**2**	**0.0**	**–5**	**0**	**0.0**	**6:05**	....	....	....	....	....	....	....	....	....
	Cleveland Barons	AHL	59	3	11	14	63	....	....	....	....	....	....	....	....	....	....	....	....	....	....	....	....	....	....
2003-04	Cleveland Barons	AHL	55	5	12	17	39	....	....	....	....	....	....	....	....	....	9	0	2	2	8	....	....	....	....
2004-05	Binghamton	AHL	79	3	19	22	79	....	....	....	....	....	....	....	....	....	6	1	0	1	6	....	....	....	....
2005-06	EHC Wolfsburg	German-2	44	9	22	31	146	....	....	....	....	....	....	....	....	....	4	0	0	0	33	....	....	....	....
	NHL Totals		**16**	**0**	**0**	**0**	**2**	**0**	**0**	**0**	**2**	**0.0**		**0**	**0.0**	**6:05**	....	....	....	....	....	....	....	....	....

Signed as a free agent by **San Jose**, August 15, 2001. Signed as a free agent by **Ottawa**, August 11, 2004.

FIDDLER, Vern

(FIHD-luhr, VUHRN) **NSH.**

Center. Shoots left. 5'11", 204 lbs. Born, Edmonton, Alta., May 9, 1980.

Season	Club	League	GP	G	A	Pts	PIM	PP	SH	GW	S	%	+/-	TF	F%	Min	GP	G	A	Pts	PIM	PP	SH	GW	Min
1997-98	Kelowna Rockets	WHL	65	10	11	21	31	....	....	....	....	....	....	....	....	....	7	0	1	1	4	....	....	....	....
1998-99	Kelowna Rockets	WHL	68	22	21	43	82	....	....	....	....	....	....	....	....	....	6	2	0	2	8	....	....	....	....
99-2000	Kelowna Rockets	WHL	64	20	28	48	60	....	....	....	....	....	....	....	....	....	5	1	3	4	4	....	....	....	....
2000-01	Kelowna Rockets	WHL	3	0	2	2	0	....	....	....	....	....	....	....	....	....	....	....	....	....	....	....	....	....	....
	Medicine Hat	WHL	67	33	38	71	100	....	....	....	....	....	....	....	....	....	....	....	....	....	....	....	....	....	....
	Arkansas	ECHL	3	0	1	1	2	....	....	....	....	....	....	....	....	....	....	....	....	....	....	....	....	....	....
2001-02	Roanoke Express	ECHL	44	27	28	55	71	....	....	....	....	....	....	....	....	....	5	3	0	3	5	....	....	....	....
	Norfolk Admirals	AHL	38	8	5	13	28	....	....	....	....	....	....	....	....	....	4	1	3	4	2	....	....	....	....
2002-03	**Nashville**	**NHL**	**19**	**4**	**2**	**6**	**14**	**0**	**0**	**1**	**20**	**20.0**	**2**	**171**	**53.8**	**9:40**	....	....	....	....	....	....	....	....	....
	Milwaukee	AHL	54	8	16	24	70	....	....	....	....	....	....	....	....	....	6	1	2	3	14	....	....	....	....
2003-04	**Nashville**	**NHL**	**17**	**0**	**0**	**0**	**23**	**0**	**0**	**0**	**8**	**0.0**	**–6**	**123**	**49.6**	**8:06**	....	....	....	....	....	....	....	....	....
	Milwaukee	AHL	47	9	15	24	72	....	....	....	....	....	....	....	....	....	22	5	3	8	36	....	....	....	....
2004-05	Milwaukee	AHL	73	20	22	42	70	....	....	....	....	....	....	....	....	....	7	0	0	0	18	....	....	....	....

Season	Club	League	GP	G	A	Pts	PIM	PP	SH	GW	S	%	+/-	TF	F%	Min	GP	G	A	Pts	PIM	PP	SH	GW	Min
			Regular Season														Playoffs								
2005-06	**Nashville**	**NHL**	**40**	**8**	**4**	**12**	**42**	**3**	**0**	**2**	**46**	**17.4**	**–2**	**464**	**52.6**	**13:49**	**2**	**0**	**1**	**1**	**0**	**0**	**0**	**0**	**8:48**
	Milwaukee	AHL	11	1	6	7	20	....	....	....	....	....	....	....	....	....	....	....	....	....	....	....	....	....	....
	NHL Totals		**76**	**12**	**6**	**18**	**79**	**3**	**0**	**3**	**74**	**16.2**		**758**	**52.4**	**11:30**	**2**	**0**	**1**	**1**	**0**	**0**	**0**	**0**	**8:48**

ECHL All-Rookie Team (2002)

Signed as a free agent by **Arkansas** (ECHL), March 31, 2001. Traded to **Roanoke** (ECHL) by **Arkansas** (ECHL) for Calvin Elfring, August 11, 2001. Signed as a free agent by **Nashville**, May 6, 2002.

FILPPULA, Valtteri
(FIHL-poo-luh, VAL-tuhr-ee) **DET.**

Center. Shoots left. 5'11", 185 lbs. Born, Vantaa, Finland, March 20, 1984. Detroit's 3rd choice, 95th overall, in 2002 Entry Draft.

Season	Club	League	GP	G	A	Pts	PIM	PP	SH	GW	S	%	+/-	TF	F%	Min	GP	G	A	Pts	PIM	PP	SH	GW	Min
2000-01	Jokerit U18	Fin-U18	31	18	29	47	4	....	....	....	....	....	....	....	....	....	6	4	4	8	0	....	....	....	....
	Jokerit Helsinki Jr.	Fin-Jr.	1	0	1	1	0	....	....	....	....	....	....	....	....	....	....	....	....	....	....	....	....	....	....
2001-02	Jokerit U18	Fin-U18	1	0	1	1	0	....	....	....	....	....	....	....	....	....	8	4	9	13	2	....	....	....	....
	Jokerit Helsinki Jr.	Fin-Jr.	40	8	15	23	14	....	....	....	....	....	....	....	....	....	1	0	0	0	0	....	....	....	....
2002-03	Jokerit Helsinki Jr.	Fin-Jr.	35	16	37	53	14	....	....	....	....	....	....	....	....	....	11	4	10	14	4	....	....	....	....
2003-04	Suomi U20	Finland-2	1	0	0	0	2	....	....	....	....	....	....	....	....	....	....	....	....	....	....	....	....	....	....
	Jokerit Helsinki	Finland	49	5	13	18	6	....	....	....	....	....	....	....	....	....	....	....	....	....	....	....	....	....	....
2004-05	Jokerit Helsinki	Finland	55	10	20	30	20	....	....	....	....	....	....	....	....	....	12	5	6	11	2	....	....	....	....
2005-06	**Detroit**	**NHL**	**4**	**0**	**1**	**1**	**2**	**0**	**0**	**0**	**1**	**0.0**	**1**	**21**	**47.6**	**7:19**	....	....	....	....	....	....	....	....	....
	Grand Rapids	AHL	74	20	51	71	30	....	....	....	....	....	....	....	....	....	16	7	9	16	4	....	....	....	....
	NHL Totals		**4**	**0**	**1**	**1**	**2**	**0**	**0**	**0**	**1**	**0.0**		**21**	**47.6**	**7:19**	....	....	....	....	....	....	....	....	....

FISCHER, Jiri
(FIH-shuhr, YIH-ree) **DET.**

Defense. Shoots left. 6'5", 225 lbs. Born, Horovice, Czech., July 31, 1980. Detroit's 1st choice, 25th overall, in 1998 Entry Draft.

Season	Club	League	GP	G	A	Pts	PIM	PP	SH	GW	S	%	+/-	TF	F%	Min	GP	G	A	Pts	PIM	PP	SH	GW	Min
1995-96	Kladno Jr.	CzRep-Jr.	39	6	10	16	....	....	....	....	....	....	....	....	....	....	....	....	....	....	....	....	....	....	....
1996-97	Kladno Jr.	CzRep-Jr.	38	7	21	28	....	....	....	....	....	....	....	....	....	....	....	....	....	....	....	....	....	....	....
1997-98	Hull Olympiques	QMJHL	70	3	19	22	112	....	....	....	....	....	....	....	....	....	11	1	4	5	16	....	....	....	....
1998-99	Hull Olympiques	QMJHL	65	22	56	78	141	....	....	....	....	....	....	....	....	....	23	6	17	23	44	....	....	....	....
99-2000	**Detroit**	**NHL**	**52**	**0**	**8**	**8**	**45**	**0**	**0**	**0**	**41**	**0.0**	**1**	**0**	**0.0**	**10:51**	....	....	....	....	....	....	....	....	....
	Cincinnati	AHL	7	0	2	2	10	....	....	....	....	....	....	....	....	....	....	....	....	....	....	....	....	....	....
2000-01	**Detroit**	**NHL**	**55**	**1**	**8**	**9**	**59**	**0**	**0**	**0**	**64**	**1.6**	**3**	**0**	**0.0**	**16:46**	**5**	**0**	**0**	**0**	**9**	**0**	**0**	**0**	**16:25**
	Cincinnati	AHL	18	2	6	8	22	....	....	....	....	....	....	....	....	....	....	....	....	....	....	....	....	....	....
2001-02♦	**Detroit**	**NHL**	**80**	**2**	**8**	**10**	**67**	**0**	**0**	**1**	**103**	**1.9**	**17**	**0**	**0.0**	**17:10**	**22**	**3**	**3**	**6**	**30**	**0**	**0**	**1**	**19:41**
2002-03	**Detroit**	**NHL**	**15**	**1**	**5**	**6**	**16**	**0**	**0**	**0**	**19**	**5.3**	**0**	**0**	**0.0**	**21:24**	....	....	....	....	....	....	....	....	....
2003-04	**Detroit**	**NHL**	**81**	**4**	**15**	**19**	**75**	**1**	**0**	**0**	**115**	**3.5**	**0**	**0**	**0.0**	**18:30**	**11**	**1**	**0**	**1**	**16**	**0**	**0**	**0**	**11:29**
2004-05	Liberec	CzRep	27	6	12	18	52	....	....	....	....	....	....	....	....	....	11	1	4	5	22	....	....	....	....
	Beroun	CzRep-2	1	0	1	1	25	....	....	....	....	....	....	....	....	....	....	....	....	....	....	....	....	....	....
2005-06	**Detroit**	**NHL**	**22**	**3**	**5**	**8**	**33**	**0**	**1**	**1**	**36**	**8.3**	**8**	**0**	**0.0**	**20:43**	....	....	....	....	....	....	....	....	....
	NHL Totals		**305**	**11**	**49**	**60**	**295**	**1**	**1**	**2**	**378**	**2.9**		**0**	**0.0**	**16:50**	**38**	**4**	**3**	**7**	**55**	**0**	**0**	**1**	**16:53**

QMJHL First All-Star Team (1999)

• Missed majority of 2002-03 season recovering from knee injury suffered in game vs. Nashville, November 12, 2002. Signed as a free agent by **Liberec** (CzRep), September 4, 2004. • Missed majority of 2005-06 season after collapsing on the bench due to a heart seizure in a game vs. Nashville, November 21, 2005.

FISHER, Mike
(FIH-shuhr, MIGHK) **OTT.**

Center. Shoots right. 6'1", 211 lbs. Born, Peterborough, Ont., June 5, 1980. Ottawa's 2nd choice, 44th overall, in 1998 Entry Draft.

Season	Club	League	GP	G	A	Pts	PIM	PP	SH	GW	S	%	+/-	TF	F%	Min	GP	G	A	Pts	PIM	PP	SH	GW	Min
1996-97	Peterborough	OPJHL	51	26	30	56	35	....	....	....	....	....	....	....	....	....	....	....	....	....	....	....	....	....	....
1997-98	Sudbury Wolves	OHL	66	24	25	49	65	....	....	....	....	....	....	....	....	....	9	2	2	4	13	....	....	....	....
1998-99	Sudbury Wolves	OHL	68	41	65	106	55	....	....	....	....	....	....	....	....	....	4	2	1	3	4	....	....	....	....
99-2000	**Ottawa**	**NHL**	**32**	**4**	**5**	**9**	**15**	**0**	**0**	**1**	**49**	**8.2**	**–6**	**356**	**47.8**	**12:57**	....	....	....	....	....	....	....	....	....
2000-01	**Ottawa**	**NHL**	**60**	**7**	**12**	**19**	**46**	**0**	**0**	**3**	**83**	**8.4**	**–1**	**709**	**50.2**	**11:38**	**4**	**0**	**1**	**1**	**4**	**0**	**0**	**0**	**13:41**
2001-02	**Ottawa**	**NHL**	**58**	**15**	**9**	**24**	**55**	**0**	**3**	**4**	**123**	**12.2**	**8**	**848**	**48.7**	**14:05**	**10**	**2**	**1**	**3**	**0**	**0**	**0**	**0**	**16:17**
2002-03	**Ottawa**	**NHL**	**74**	**18**	**20**	**38**	**54**	**5**	**1**	**3**	**142**	**12.7**	**13**	**1077**	**48.1**	**15:59**	**18**	**2**	**2**	**4**	**16**	**0**	**1**	**1**	**16:58**
2003-04	**Ottawa**	**NHL**	**24**	**4**	**6**	**10**	**39**	**1**	**0**	**0**	**47**	**8.5**	**–3**	**357**	**42.0**	**17:26**	**7**	**1**	**0**	**1**	**4**	**0**	**0**	**1**	**16:11**
2004-05	EV Zug	Swiss	21	9	18	27	34	....	....	....	....	....	....	....	....	....	9	2	3	5	10	....	....	....	....
2005-06	**Ottawa**	**NHL**	**68**	**22**	**22**	**44**	**64**	**2**	**4**	**3**	**150**	**14.7**	**23**	**883**	**50.3**	**17:09**	**10**	**2**	**2**	**4**	**12**	**0**	**1**	**0**	**18:50**
	NHL Totals		**316**	**70**	**74**	**144**	**273**	**8**	**8**	**14**	**594**	**11.8**		**4230**	**48.5**	**14:52**	**49**	**7**	**6**	**13**	**36**	**0**	**2**	**2**	**16:50**

• Missed majority of 1999-2000 season recovering from knee injury suffered in game vs. Boston, December 30, 1999. • Missed majority of 2003-04 season recovering from elbow injury suffered in practice, October 4, 2003. Signed as a free agent by **Zug** (Swiss), November 1, 2004.

FITZGERALD, Tom
(fihtz-JAIR-uhld, TAWM)

Right wing. Shoots right. 6', 190 lbs. Born, Billerica, MA, August 28, 1968. NY Islanders' 1st choice, 17th overall, in 1986 Entry Draft.

Season	Club	League	GP	G	A	Pts	PIM	PP	SH	GW	S	%	+/-	TF	F%	Min	GP	G	A	Pts	PIM	PP	SH	GW	Min
1984-85	Austin Mustangs	High-MA	18	20	21	41	....	....	....	....	....	....	....	....	....	....	....	....	....	....	....	....	....	....	....
1985-86	Austin Mustangs	High-MA	24	35	38	73	....	....	....	....	....	....	....	....	....	....	....	....	....	....	....	....	....	....	....
1986-87	Providence	H-East	27	8	14	22	22	....	....	....	....	....	....	....	....	....	....	....	....	....	....	....	....	....	....
1987-88	Providence	H-East	36	19	15	34	50	....	....	....	....	....	....	....	....	....	....	....	....	....	....	....	....	....	....
1988-89	**NY Islanders**	**NHL**	**23**	**3**	**5**	**8**	**10**	**0**	**0**	**1**	**24**	**12.5**	**1**	....	....	....	....	....	....	....	....	....	....	....	....
	Springfield	AHL	61	24	18	42	43	....	....	....	....	....	....	....	....	....	....	....	....	....	....	....	....	....	....
1989-90	**NY Islanders**	**NHL**	**19**	**2**	**5**	**7**	**4**	**0**	**0**	**1**	**24**	**8.3**	**–3**	....	....	....	**4**	**1**	**0**	**1**	**4**	**0**	**0**	**0**	....
	Springfield	AHL	53	30	23	53	32	....	....	....	....	....	....	....	....	....	14	2	9	11	13	....	....	....	....
1990-91	**NY Islanders**	**NHL**	**41**	**5**	**5**	**10**	**24**	**0**	**0**	**2**	**60**	**8.3**	**–9**	....	....	....	....	....	....	....	....	....	....	....	....
	Capital District	AHL	27	7	7	14	50	....	....	....	....	....	....	....	....	....	....	....	....	....	....	....	....	....	....
1991-92	**NY Islanders**	**NHL**	**45**	**6**	**11**	**17**	**28**	**0**	**2**	**2**	**71**	**8.5**	**–3**	....	....	....	....	....	....	....	....	....	....	....	....
	Capital District	AHL	4	1	1	2	4	....	....	....	....	....	....	....	....	....	....	....	....	....	....	....	....	....	....
1992-93	**NY Islanders**	**NHL**	**77**	**9**	**18**	**27**	**34**	**0**	**3**	**1**	**83**	**10.8**	**–2**	....	....	....	**18**	**2**	**5**	**7**	**18**	**0**	**0**	**0**	....
1993-94	**Florida**	**NHL**	**83**	**18**	**14**	**32**	**54**	**0**	**3**	**1**	**144**	**12.5**	**–3**	....	....	....	....	....	....	....	....	....	....	....	....
1994-95	**Florida**	**NHL**	**48**	**3**	**13**	**16**	**31**	**0**	**0**	**0**	**78**	**3.8**	**–3**	....	....	....	....	....	....	....	....	....	....	....	....
1995-96	**Florida**	**NHL**	**82**	**13**	**21**	**34**	**75**	**1**	**6**	**2**	**141**	**9.2**	**–3**	....	....	....	**22**	**4**	**4**	**8**	**34**	**0**	**0**	**2**	....
1996-97	**Florida**	**NHL**	**71**	**10**	**14**	**24**	**64**	**0**	**2**	**1**	**135**	**7.4**	**7**	....	....	....	**5**	**0**	**1**	**1**	**0**	**0**	**0**	**0**	....
1997-98	**Florida**	**NHL**	**69**	**10**	**5**	**15**	**57**	**0**	**1**	**1**	**105**	**9.5**	**–4**	....	....	....	....	....	....	....	....	....	....	....	....
	Colorado	**NHL**	**11**	**2**	**1**	**3**	**22**	**0**	**1**	**0**	**14**	**14.3**	**0**	....	....	....	**7**	**0**	**1**	**1**	**20**	**0**	**0**	**0**	....
1998-99	**Nashville**	**NHL**	**80**	**13**	**19**	**32**	**48**	**0**	**0**	**1**	**180**	**7.2**	**–18**	**155**	**52.3**	**17:17**	....	....	....	....	....	....	....	....	....
99-2000	**Nashville**	**NHL**	**82**	**13**	**9**	**22**	**66**	**0**	**3**	**1**	**119**	**10.9**	**–18**	**264**	**51.9**	**13:57**	....	....	....	....	....	....	....	....	....
2000-01	**Nashville**	**NHL**	**82**	**9**	**9**	**18**	**71**	**0**	**2**	**2**	**135**	**6.7**	**–5**	**458**	**54.6**	**14:58**	....	....	....	....	....	....	....	....	....
2001-02	**Nashville**	**NHL**	**63**	**7**	**9**	**16**	**33**	**0**	**1**	**0**	**101**	**6.9**	**–4**	**525**	**48.4**	**14:15**	....	....	....	....	....	....	....	....	....
	Chicago	**NHL**	**15**	**1**	**3**	**4**	**6**	**0**	**1**	**0**	**24**	**4.2**	**–3**	**110**	**50.0**	**16:16**	**5**	**0**	**0**	**0**	**4**	**0**	**0**	**0**	**15:15**
2002-03	**Toronto**	**NHL**	**66**	**4**	**13**	**17**	**57**	**0**	**0**	**0**	**89**	**4.5**	**10**	**90**	**50.0**	**12:07**	**7**	**0**	**1**	**1**	**4**	**0**	**0**	**0**	**18:11**
2003-04	**Toronto**	**NHL**	**69**	**7**	**10**	**17**	**52**	**1**	**0**	**1**	**81**	**8.6**	**–2**	**300**	**53.0**	**12:23**	**10**	**0**	**0**	**0**	**6**	**0**	**0**	**0**	**13:26**
2004-05			DID NOT PLAY																						
2005-06	**Boston**	**NHL**	**71**	**4**	**6**	**10**	**40**	**0**	**0**	**0**	**50**	**8.0**	**–10**	**123**	**44.7**	**9:27**	....	....	....	....	....	....	....	....	....
	NHL Totals		**1097**	**139**	**190**	**329**	**776**	**2**	**25**	**17**	**1658**	**8.4**		**2025**	**51.2**	**13:41**	**78**	**7**	**12**	**19**	**90**	**0**	**0**	**2**	**15:22**

Claimed by **Florida** from **NY Islanders** in Expansion Draft, June 24, 1993. Traded to **Colorado** by **Florida** for the rights to Mark Parrish and Anaheim's 3rd round choice (previously acquired, Florida selected Lance Ward) in 1998 Entry Draft, March 24, 1998. Signed as a free agent by **Nashville**, July 6, 1998. Traded to **Chicago** by **Nashville** for Chicago's 4th round choice (later traded to Anaheim – Anaheim selected Nathan Saunders) in 2003 Entry Draft and future considerations, March 13, 2002. Signed as a free agent by **Toronto**, July 17, 2002. Signed as a free agent by **Boston**, July 28, 2004.

FITZPATRICK, Rory
(FIHTZ-pa-trihk, ROHR-ee)

Defense. Shoots right. 6'2", 208 lbs. Born, Rochester, NY, January 11, 1975. Montreal's 2nd choice, 47th overall, in 1993 Entry Draft.

Season	Club	League	GP	G	A	Pts	PIM	PP	SH	GW	S	%	+/-	TF	F%	Min	GP	G	A	Pts	PIM	PP	SH	GW	Min
1990-91	Rochester	EmJHL	40	0	5	5	....	....	....	....	....	....	....	....	....	....	....	....	....	....	....	....	....	....	....
1991-92	Rochester	EmJHL	28	8	28	36	141	....	....	....	....	....	....	....	....	....	....	....	....	....	....	....	....	....	....
1992-93	Sudbury Wolves	OHL	58	4	20	24	68	....	....	....	....	....	....	....	....	....	14	0	0	0	17	....	....	....	....
1993-94	Sudbury Wolves	OHL	65	12	34	46	112	....	....	....	....	....	....	....	....	....	10	2	5	7	10	....	....	....	....
1994-95	Sudbury Wolves	OHL	56	12	36	48	72	....	....	....	....	....	....	....	....	....	18	3	15	18	21	....	....	....	....
	Fredericton	AHL	....	....	....	....	....	....	....	....	....	....	....	....	....	....	10	1	2	3	5	....	....	....	....
1995-96	**Montreal**	**NHL**	**42**	**0**	**2**	**2**	**18**	**0**	**0**	**0**	**31**	**0.0**	**–7**	....	....	....	**6**	**1**	**1**	**2**	**0**	**0**	**0**	**0**	....
	Fredericton	AHL	18	4	6	10	36	....	....	....	....	....	....	....	....	....	....	....	....	....	....	....	....	....	....

			Regular Season															Playoffs							
Season	Club	League	GP	G	A	Pts	PIM	PP	SH	GW	S	%	+/-	TF	F%	Min	GP	G	A	Pts	PIM	PP	SH	GW	Min
1996-97	Montreal	NHL	6	0	1	1	6	0	0	0	5	0.0	-2	....	....	....	....	....	....	....	....	....	....	....	....
	St. Louis	NHL	2	0	0	0	2	0	0	0	1	0.0	-2	....	....	....	....	....	....	....	....	....	....	....	....
	Worcester IceCats	AHL	49	4	13	17	78										5	1	2	-3	0				
1997-98	Worcester IceCats	AHL	62	8	22	30	111										11	0	3	3	26				
1998-99	St. Louis	NHL	1	0	0	0	2	0	0	0	0	0.0	-3	0	0.0	4:49	....	....	....	....	....				
	Worcester IceCats	AHL	53	5	16	21	82										4	0	1	1	17				
99-2000	Worcester IceCats	AHL	28	0	5	5	48																		
	Milwaukee	IHL	27	2	1	3	27										3	2	2	2					
2000-01	Nashville	NHL	2	0	0	0	2	0	0	0	0	0.0	-2	0	0.0	9:47	....	....	....	....	....				
	Milwaukee	IHL	22	0	2	2	32																		
	Hamilton	AHL	34	3	17	20	29																		
2001-02	Buffalo	NHL	5	0	0	0	4	0	0	0	2	0.0	-2	0	0.0	11:54	....	....	....	....	....				
	Rochester	AHL	60	4	8	12	83										2	0	1	1	0				
2002-03	Buffalo	NHL	36	1	3	4	16	0	0	0	29	3.4	-7	0	0.0	17:02	....	....	....	....	....				
	Rochester	AHL	41	5	11	16	65																		
2003-04	Buffalo	NHL	60	4	7	11	44	2	0	0	78	5.1	-5	1	100.0	19:02	....	....	....	....	....				
2004-05	Rochester	AHL	20	1	1	2	18										9	0	1	1	12				
2005-06	Buffalo	NHL	56	4	5	9	50	0	0	1	45	8.9	-18	1	0.0	16:22	11	0	4	4	16	0	0	0	17:12
	NHL Totals		210	9	18	27	144	4	0	3	191	4.7		2	50.0	17:13	17	1	5	6	16	0	0	0	17:12

OHL All-Rookie Team (1993)

Traded to **St. Louis** by **Montreal** with Pierre Turgeon and Craig Conroy for Murray Baron, Shayne Corson and St. Louis' 5th round choice (Gennady Razin) in 1997 Entry Draft, October 29, 1996. Claimed by **Boston** from **St. Louis** in Waiver Draft, October 5, 1998. Claimed on waivers by **St. Louis** from **Boston**, October 7, 1998. Traded to **Nashville** by **St. Louis** for Dan Keczmer, February 9, 2000. Traded to **Edmonton** by **Nashville** for future considerations, January 12, 2001. Signed as a free agent by **Buffalo**, August 14, 2001. Signed as a free agent by **Rochester** (AHL), March 2, 2005.

FLEISCHMANN, Tomas
(FLIGHSH-muhn, TAW-mash) **WSH.**

Left wing. Shoots left. 6'1", 188 lbs. Born, Koprivnice, Czech., May 16, 1984. Detroit's 2nd choice, 63rd overall, in 2002 Entry Draft.

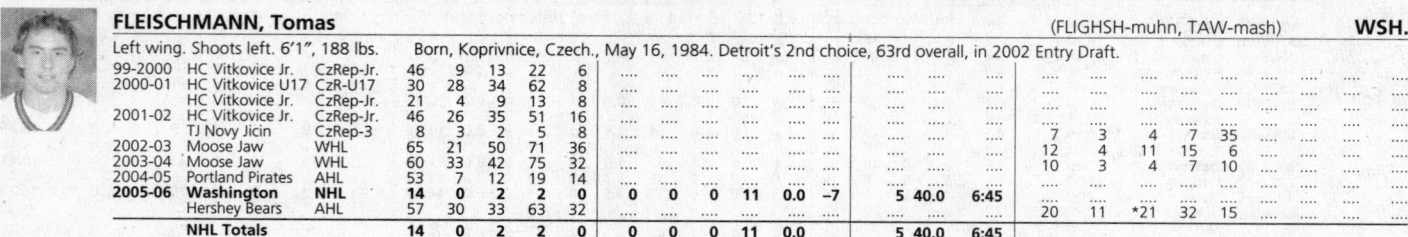

Season	Club	League	GP	G	A	Pts	PIM	PP	SH	GW	S	%	+/-	TF	F%	Min	GP	G	A	Pts	PIM	PP	SH	GW	Min
99-2000	HC Vitkovice Jr.	CzRep-Jr.	46	9	13	22	6																		
2000-01	HC Vitkovice U17	CzR-U17	30	28	34	62	8																		
	HC Vitkovice Jr.	CzRep-Jr.	21	4	9	13	8																		
2001-02	HC Vitkovice Jr.	CzRep-Jr.	46	26	35	51	16																		
	TJ Novy Jicin	CzRep-3	8	3	2	5	8										7	3	4	7	35				
2002-03	Moose Jaw	WHL	65	21	50	71	36										12	4	11	15	6				
2003-04	Moose Jaw	WHL	60	33	42	75	32										10	3	4	7	10				
2004-05	Portland Pirates	AHL	53	7	12	19	14																		
2005-06	Washington	NHL	14	0	2	2	0	0	0	0	11	0.0	-7	5	40.0	6:45	....	....	....	....	....				
	Hershey Bears	AHL	57	30	33	63	32										20	11	*21	32	15				
	NHL Totals		14	0	2	2	0	0	0	0	11	0.0		5	40.0	6:45	....	....	....	....	....				

WHL East Second All-Star Team (2004)

Traded to **Washington** by **Detroit** with Detroit's 1st round choice (Mike Green) in 2004 Entry Draft and Detroit's 4th round choice (Luke Lynes) in 2006 Entry Draft for Robert Lang, February 27, 2004.

FLINN, Ryan
(FLIHN, RIGH-yan)

Left wing. Shoots left. 6'5", 248 lbs. Born, Halifax, N.S., April 20, 1980. New Jersey's 8th choice, 143rd overall, in 1998 Entry Draft.

Season	Club	League	GP	G	A	Pts	PIM	PP	SH	GW	S	%	+/-	TF	F%	Min	GP	G	A	Pts	PIM	PP	SH	GW	Min
1996-97	Laval Titan	QMJHL	23	3	2	5	56										0	0	0	0	0				
1997-98	Laval Titan	QMJHL	59	4	12	16	217										15	1	0	1	63				
1998-99	Acadie-Bathurst	QMJHL	44	3	4	7	195										23	2	0	2	37				
99-2000	Halifax	QMJHL	67	14	19	33	365										9	1	1	2	43				
2000-01	Cape Breton	QMJHL	57	16	17	33	280																		
2001-02	Reading Royals	ECHL	20	1	3	4	130																		
	Los Angeles	NHL	10	0	0	0	51	0	0	0	2	0.0	0	0	0.0	3:29	1	0	0	0	0				
	Manchester	AHL	37	0	1	1	113																		
2002-03	Los Angeles	NHL	19	1	0	1	28	0	0	0	13	7.7	0	0	0.0	5:28	....	....	....	....	....				
	Manchester	AHL	27	2	2	4	95																		
2003-04	Manchester	AHL	59	3	5	8	164										6	0	0	0	4				
2004-05	Manchester	AHL	14	1	1	2	112																		
2005-06	Los Angeles	NHL	2	0	0	0	5	0	0	0	0	0.0	0	0	0.0	0:25	....	....	....	....	....				
	Manchester	AHL	14	0	1	1	38																		
	NHL Totals		31	1	0	1	84	0	0	0	15	6.7		0	0.0	4:30	....	....	....	....	....				

Signed as a free agent by **Los Angeles**, January 8, 2002. • Missed majority of 2004-05 season recovering from foot and leg injuries. • Missed majority of 2005-06 season recovering from head injury suffered in game vs. Chicago, November 26, 2005.

FOCHT, Dan
(FOHKT, DAN)

Defense. Shoots left. 6'6", 234 lbs. Born, Regina, Sask., December 31, 1977. Phoenix's 1st choice, 11th overall, in 1996 Entry Draft.

Season	Club	League	GP	G	A	Pts	PIM	PP	SH	GW	S	%	+/-	TF	F%	Min	GP	G	A	Pts	PIM	PP	SH	GW	Min
1994-95	Saskatoon Blazers	SMHL	65	6	12	18	98																		
1995-96	Tri-City	WHL	63	6	12	18	161										11	1	1	2	23				
1996-97	Tri-City	WHL	28	0	5	5	92																		
	Regina Pats	WHL	22	2	2	4	59										5	0	2	2	8				
	Springfield	AHL	1	0	0	0	2																		
1997-98	Springfield	AHL	61	2	5	7	125										3	0	0	0	4				
1998-99	Mississippi	ECHL	2	0	0	0	6																		
	Springfield	AHL	30	0	2	2	58										3	1	0	1	10				
99-2000	Jokerit Helsinki	Finland	2	0	0	0	0																		
	Mississippi	ECHL	4	0	1	1	0																		
	Springfield	AHL	44	2	9	11	86										5	0	1	1	2				
2000-01	Springfield	AHL	69	0	6	6	156																		
2001-02	Phoenix	NHL	8	0	0	0	11	0	0	0	5	0.0	0	0	0.0	12:25	1	0	1	1	0	0	0	0	8:20
	Springfield	AHL	56	2	8	10	134																		
2002-03	Phoenix	NHL	10	0	0	0	10	0	0	0	1	0.0	-2	0	0.0	8:40	....	....	....	....	....				
	Springfield	AHL	37	2	7	9	80																		
	Pittsburgh	NHL	12	0	3	3	19	0	0	0	11	0.0	-7	1	0.0	18:14	....	....	....	....	....				
2003-04	Pittsburgh	NHL	52	2	3	5	105	0	0	0	56	3.6	-23	0	0.0	16:36	....	....	....	....	....				
2004-05	Hamilton	AHL	26	2	3	5	84																		
2005-06	Rochester	AHL	54	2	5	7	146																		
	NHL Totals		82	2	6	8	145	0	0	0	73	2.7		1	0.0	15:28	1	0	1	1	0	0	0	0	8:20

Traded to **Pittsburgh** by **Phoenix** with Ramzi Abid and Guillaume Lefebvre for Jan Hrdina and Francois Leroux, March 11, 2003. Signed as a free agent by **Hamilton** (AHL), October 25, 2004. Signed as a free agent by **Florida**, August 26, 2005.

FOOTE, Adam
(FUT, A-duhm) **CBJ**

Defense. Shoots right. 6'2", 224 lbs. Born, Toronto, Ont., July 10, 1971. Quebec's 2nd choice, 22nd overall, in 1989 Entry Draft.

Season	Club	League	GP	G	A	Pts	PIM	PP	SH	GW	S	%	+/-	TF	F%	Min	GP	G	A	Pts	PIM	PP	SH	GW	Min
1987-88	Whitby Midgets	OMHA	65	25	43	68	108																		
1988-89	Sault Ste. Marie	OHL	66	7	32	39	120																		
1989-90	Sault Ste. Marie	OHL	61	12	43	55	199																		
1990-91	Sault Ste. Marie	OHL	59	18	51	69	93										14	5	12	17	28				
1991-92	Quebec	NHL	46	2	5	7	44	0	0	0	55	3.6	-4				....	....	....	....	....				
	Halifax Citadels	AHL	6	0	1	1	2																		
1992-93	Quebec	NHL	81	4	12	16	168	0	1	0	54	7.4	6				6	0	1	1	2	0	0	0	
1993-94	Quebec	NHL	45	2	6	8	67	0	0	0	42	4.8	3				....	....	....	....	....				
1994-95	Quebec	NHL	35	0	7	7	52	0	0	0	17	0.0	17				6	0	1	1	14	0	0	0	
1995-96♦	Colorado	NHL	73	5	11	16	88	1	0	1	49	10.2	27				22	1	3	4	36	0	0	0	
1996-97	Colorado	NHL	78	2	19	21	135	0	0	0	60	3.3	16				17	0	4	4	62	0	0	0	
1997-98	Colorado	NHL	77	3	14	17	124	0	0	1	64	4.7	-3				7	0	0	0	23	0	0	0	
	Canada	Olympics	6	0	1	1	4																		
1998-99	Colorado	NHL	64	5	16	21	92	3	0	0	83	6.0	20	0	0.0	24:50	19	2	3	5	18	0	0	0	28:34
99-2000	Colorado	NHL	59	5	13	18	98	1	0	2	63	7.9	5	0	0.0	25:51	16	0	7	7	28	0	0	0	26:05
2000-01•	Colorado	NHL	35	3	12	15	64	1	0	0	59	5.1	6	0	0.0	25:22	23	3	4	7	*47	0	0	1	28:22
2001-02	Colorado	NHL	55	5	22	27	55	1	1	0	85	5.9	7	0	0.0	25:59	21	1	6	7	28	0	0	0	27:46
	Canada	Olympics	6	1	0	1	2																		

			Regular Season														Playoffs								
Season	Club	League	GP	G	A	Pts	PIM	PP	SH	GW	S	%	+/-	TF	F%	Min	GP	G	A	Pts	PIM	PP	SH	GW	Min
2002-03	Colorado	NHL	78	11	20	31	88	3	0	2	106	10.4	30	0	0.0	25:43	6	0	1	1	8	0	0	0	24:12
2003-04	Colorado	NHL	73	8	22	30	87	5	0	1	105	7.6	13	0	0.0	24:03	11	0	4	4	10	0	0	0	25:06
2004-05		DID NOT PLAY																							
2005-06	Columbus	NHL	65	6	16	22	89	2	2	1	67	9.0	–16	0	0.0	24:34	....	....	....	....	....	....	....	....	....
	Canada	Olympics	6	0	1	1	6	....	....	....	....	....	....	....	....	....	....	....	....	....	....	....	....	....	....
	NHL Totals		864	61	195	256	1229	17	5	9	916	6.7		0	0.0	25:09	154	7	34	41	282	2	0	1	27:15

OHL First All-Star Team (1991)

Transferred to **Colorado** after **Quebec** franchise relocated, June 21, 1995. • Missed majority of 2000-01 season recovering from shoulder injury suffered in game vs. Carolina, January 6, 2001. Signed as a free agent by **Columbus**, August 2, 2005.

FORBES, Colin

(FOHRBS, COHL-ihn)

Center. Shoots left. 6'3", 215 lbs. Born, New Westminster, B.C., February 16, 1976. Philadelphia's 5th choice, 166th overall, in 1994 Entry Draft.

Season	Club	League	GP	G	A	Pts	PIM	PP	SH	GW	S	%	+/-	TF	F%	Min	GP	G	A	Pts	PIM	PP	SH	GW	Min
1993-94	Sherwood Park	AJHL	47	18	22	40	76	....	....	....	....	....	....	....	....	....	....	....	....	....	....	....	....	....	....
1994-95	Portland	WHL	72	24	31	55	108	....	....	....	....	....	....	....	....	....	9	1	3	4	10	....	....	....	....
1995-96	Portland	WHL	72	33	44	77	137	....	....	....	....	....	....	....	....	....	7	2	5	7	14	....	....	....	....
	Hershey Bears	AHL	2	1	0	1	2	....	....	....	....	....	....	....	....	....	4	0	2	2	2	....	....	....	....
1996-97	Philadelphia	NHL	3	1	0	1	0	0	0	0	3	33.3	0	....	....	....	3	0	0	0	0	0	0	0	....
	Philadelphia	AHL	74	21	28	49	108	....	....	....	....	....	....	....	....	....	10	5	5	10	33	....	....	....	....
1997-98	Philadelphia	NHL	63	12	7	19	59	2	0	2	93	12.9	2	....	....	....	5	0	0	0	2	0	0	0	....
	Philadelphia	AHL	13	7	4	11	22	....	....	....	....	....	....	....	....	....	....	....	....	....	....	....	....	....	....
1998-99	Philadelphia	NHL	66	9	7	16	51	0	0	4	92	9.8	0	2	50.0	12:35	....	....	....	....	....	....	....	....	....
	Tampa Bay	NHL	14	3	1	4	10	0	1	0	25	12.0	–5	0	0.0	17:30	....	....	....	....	....	....	....	....	....
99-2000	Tampa Bay	NHL	8	0	0	0	18	0	0	0	3	0.0	–4	1	0.0	8:53	....	....	....	....	....	....	....	....	....
	Ottawa	NHL	45	2	5	7	12	0	0	0	54	3.7	–1	82	47.6	8:34	5	1	0	1	14	0	0	0	6:48
2000-01	Ottawa	NHL	39	0	1	1	31	0	0	0	26	0.0	–3	10	40.0	6:10	....	....	....	....	....	....	....	....	....
	NY Rangers	NHL	19	1	4	5	15	0	0	0	20	5.0	–3	1	0.0	7:52	....	....	....	....	....	....	....	....	....
2001-02	Utah Grizzlies	AHL	4	0	0	0	21	....	....	....	....	....	....	....	....	....	....	....	....	....	....	....	....	....	....
	Washington	NHL	38	5	3	8	15	0	1	1	49	10.2	–2	253	44.7	11:01	....	....	....	....	....	....	....	....	....
	Portland Pirates	AHL	14	4	5	9	18	....	....	....	....	....	....	....	....	....	....	....	....	....	....	....	....	....	....
2002-03	Washington	NHL	5	0	0	0	0	0	0	0	3	0.0	–2	12	50.0	9:38	....	....	....	....	....	....	....	....	....
	Portland Pirates	AHL	69	22	38	60	73	....	....	....	....	....	....	....	....	....	3	2	2	4	4	....	....	....	....
2003-04	Washington	NHL	2	0	0	0	0	0	0	0	2	0.0	0	3	33.3	8:53	....	....	....	....	....	....	....	....	....
	Portland Pirates	AHL	69	16	32	48	59	....	....	....	....	....	....	....	....	....	7	0	6	6	16	....	....	....	....
2004-05	Lowell	AHL	76	27	37	64	80	....	....	....	....	....	....	....	....	....	11	3	1	4	20	....	....	....	....
2005-06	Lowell	AHL	34	10	18	28	24	....	....	....	....	....	....	....	....	....	....	....	....	....	....	....	....	....	....
	Washington	NHL	9	0	0	0	2	0	0	0	10	0.0	–2	7	42.9	8:16	....	....	....	....	....	....	....	....	....
	Hershey Bears	AHL	36	11	12	23	16	....	....	....	....	....	....	....	....	....	21	5	9	14	16	....	....	....	....
	NHL Totals		311	33	28	61	213	2	2	7	380	8.7		371	45.0	10:08	13	1	0	1	16	0	0	0	6:48

Traded to **Tampa Bay** by **Philadelphia** with Philadelphia's 4th round choice (Michal Lanicek) in 1999 Entry Draft for Mikael Andersson and Sandy McCarthy, March 20, 1999. Traded to **Ottawa** by **Tampa Bay** for Bruce Gardiner, November 11, 1999. Traded to **NY Rangers** by **Ottawa** for Eric Lacroix, March 1, 2001. Signed as a free agent by **Washington**, January 8, 2002. Signed as a free agent by **Hershey** (AHL), September 11, 2003. Signed as a free agent by **Portland** (AHL), October 14, 2003. Signed as a free agent by **Washington**, November 4, 2003. Signed as a free agent by **Carolina**, August 11, 2004. Traded to **Washington** by **Carolina** for Stephen Peat, December 28, 2005.

FORSBERG, Peter

(FOHRS-buhrg, PEE-tuhr) **PHI.**

Center. Shoots left. 6', 205 lbs. Born, Ornskoldsvik, Sweden, July 20, 1973. Philadelphia's 1st choice, 6th overall, in 1991 Entry Draft.

Season	Club	League	GP	G	A	Pts	PIM	PP	SH	GW	S	%	+/-	TF	F%	Min	GP	G	A	Pts	PIM	PP	SH	GW	Min
1989-90	MoDo Jr.	Swe-Jr.	30	15	12	27	42	....	....	....	....	....	....	....	....	....	....	....	....	....	....	....	....	....	....
	MoDo	Sweden	1	0	1	1	4	....	....	....	....	....	....	....	....	....	....	....	....	....	....	....	....	....	....
1990-91	MoDo Jr.	Swe-Jr.	39	38	64	102	56	....	....	....	....	....	....	....	....	....	....	....	....	....	....	....	....	....	....
	MoDo	Sweden	23	7	10	17	22	....	....	....	....	....	....	....	....	....	....	....	....	....	....	....	....	....	....
1991-92	MoDo	Sweden	39	9	18	27	78	....	....	....	....	....	....	....	....	....	....	....	....	....	....	....	....	....	....
1992-93	MoDo Jr.	Swe-Jr.	2	0	3	3	4	....	....	....	....	....	....	....	....	....	....	....	....	....	....	....	....	....	....
	MoDo	Sweden	39	23	24	47	92	....	....	....	....	....	....	....	....	....	3	4	1	5	0	....	....	....	....
1993-94	MoDo	Sweden	39	18	26	44	82	....	....	....	....	....	....	....	....	....	11	9	7	16	14	....	....	....	....
	Sweden	Olympics	8	2	6	8	6	....	....	....	....	....	....	....	....	....	....	....	....	....	....	....	....	....	....
1994-95	MoDo	Sweden	11	5	9	14	20	....	....	....	....	....	....	....	....	....	....	....	....	....	....	....	....	....	....
	Quebec	NHL	47	15	35	50	16	3	0	3	86	17.4	17	....	....	....	6	2	4	6	4	1	0	0	....
1995-96 ◆	Colorado	NHL	82	30	86	116	47	7	3	3	217	13.8	26	....	....	....	22	10	11	21	18	3	0	1	....
1996-97	Colorado	NHL	65	28	58	86	73	5	4	4	188	14.9	31	....	....	....	14	5	12	17	10	3	0	0	....
1997-98	Colorado	NHL	72	25	66	91	94	7	3	7	202	12.4	6	....	....	....	7	6	5	11	12	2	0	0	....
	Sweden	Olympics	4	1	4	5	6	....	....	....	....	....	....	....	....	....	....	....	....	....	....	....	....	....	....
1998-99	Colorado	NHL	78	30	67	97	108	9	2	7	217	13.8	27	895	54.4	23:29	19	8	16	*24	31	1	1	0	21:39
99-2000	Colorado	NHL	49	14	37	51	52	3	0	2	105	13.3	9	519	46.6	20:55	16	7	8	15	12	2	1	4	20:59
2000-01 ◆	Colorado	NHL	73	27	62	89	54	12	2	5	178	15.2	23	755	46.6	20:48	11	4	10	14	6	1	0	2	21:55
2001-02	Colorado	NHL	....	....	....	....	....	....	....	....	....	....	....	....	....	....	20	9	*18	*27	20	0	0	4	18:10
2002-03	Colorado	NHL	75	29	*77	*106	70	8	0	2	166	17.5	52	709	47.0	19:20	7	2	6	8	6	1	0	0	20:01
2003-04	Colorado	NHL	39	18	37	55	30	3	1	5	85	21.2	16	549	42.3	19:12	11	4	7	11	12	1	0	1	19:02
2004-05	MODO	Sweden	33	13	26	39	88	....	....	....	....	....	....	....	....	....	1	0	0	0	2	....	....	....	....
2005-06	Philadelphia	NHL	60	19	56	75	46	8	1	2	132	14.4	21	941	50.6	18:47	6	4	4	8	6	1	0	2	18:55
	Sweden	Olympics	6	0	6	6	0	....	....	....	....	....	....	....	....	....	....	....	....	....	....	....	....	....	....
	NHL Totals		640	235	581	816	590	65	16	40	1576	14.9		4368	48.6	20:35	139	61	101	162	137	16	2	14	20:10

NHL All-Rookie Team (1995) • Calder Memorial Trophy (1995) • NHL First All-Star Team (1998, 1999, 2003) • Bud Light Plus/Minus Award (2003) (tied with Milan Hejduk) • Art Ross Trophy (2003) • Hart Trophy (2003)

Played in NHL All-Star Game (1996, 1998, 1999, 2001, 2003)

Traded to **Quebec** by **Philadelphia** with Steve Duchesne, Kerry Huffman, Mike Ricci, Ron Hextall, Philadelphia's 1st round choice (Jocelyn Thibault) in 1993 Entry Draft, $15,000,000 and future considerations (Chris Simon and Philadelphia's 1st round choice (later traded to Toronto – later traded to Washington – Washington selected Nolan Baumgartner) in 1994 Entry Draft, July 21, 1992) for Eric Lindros, June 30, 1992. Transferred to **Colorado** after **Quebec** franchise relocated, June 21, 1995. • Missed entire 2001-02 regular season recovering from spleen injury suffered in game vs. Los Angeles, May 9, 2001 and ankle injury suffered in practice, January 10, 2002. • Missed majority of 2003-04 season recovering from groin (October 28, 2003 vs. Calgary) and hip (February 16, 2004 vs. Vancouver) injuries. Signed as a free agent by **MODO** (Sweden), September 18, 2004. Signed as a free agent by **Philadelphia**, August 3, 2005.

FORTIN, Jean-Francois

(fohr-TEHN, ZHAWN-fran-SWUH)

Defense. Shoots right. 6'2", 205 lbs. Born, Laval, Que., March 15, 1979. Washington's 2nd choice, 35th overall, in 1997 Entry Draft.

Season	Club	League	GP	G	A	Pts	PIM	PP	SH	GW	S	%	+/-	TF	F%	Min	GP	G	A	Pts	PIM	PP	SH	GW	Min
1993-94	Laval-Laurentides	QAHA	31	8	20	28	32	....	....	....	....	....	....	....	....	....	....	....	....	....	....	....	....	....	....
1994-95	Abitibi Forestiers	QAAA	44	2	14	16	34	....	....	....	....	....	....	....	....	....	10	2	2	4	....	....	....	....	....
1995-96	Sherbrooke	QMJHL	69	7	15	22	40	....	....	....	....	....	....	....	....	....	7	2	6	8	2	....	....	....	....
1996-97	Sherbrooke	QMJHL	59	7	30	37	89	....	....	....	....	....	....	....	....	....	2	0	1	1	14	....	....	....	....
1997-98	Sherbrooke	QMJHL	55	12	25	37	37	....	....	....	....	....	....	....	....	....	....	....	....	....	....	....	....	....	....
1998-99	Sherbrooke	QMJHL	64	17	33	50	78	....	....	....	....	....	....	....	....	....	12	5	13	18	20	....	....	....	....
99-2000	Portland Pirates	AHL	43	3	5	8	44	....	....	....	....	....	....	....	....	....	2	0	0	0	0	....	....	....	....
	Hampton Roads	ECHL	7	0	2	2	0	....	....	....	....	....	....	....	....	....	....	....	....	....	....	....	....	....	....
2000-01	Richmond	ECHL	15	0	4	4	2	....	....	....	....	....	....	....	....	....	....	....	....	....	....	....	....	....	....
	Portland Pirates	AHL	32	1	7	8	22	....	....	....	....	....	....	....	....	....	1	0	0	0	0	....	....	....	....
2001-02	Washington	NHL	36	1	3	4	20	0	0	0	24	4.2	–1	1	100.0	19:25	....	....	....	....	....	....	....	....	....
	Portland Pirates	AHL	44	4	9	13	20	....	....	....	....	....	....	....	....	....	....	....	....	....	....	....	....	....	....
2002-03	Washington	NHL	33	0	1	1	22	0	0	0	20	0.0	–3	0	0.0	15:14	....	....	....	....	....	....	....	....	....
	Portland Pirates	AHL	10	2	1	3	17	....	....	....	....	....	....	....	....	....	....	....	....	....	....	....	....	....	....
2003-04	Washington	NHL	2	0	0	0	0	0	0	0	0	0.0	0	0	0.0	7:57	....	....	....	....	....	....	....	....	....
	Portland Pirates	AHL	4	0	1	1	6	....	....	....	....	....	....	....	....	....	....	....	....	....	....	....	....	....	....
2004-05	Portland Pirates	AHL	39	1	8	9	50	....	....	....	....	....	....	....	....	....	....	....	....	....	....	....	....	....	....
2005-06	Hershey Bears	AHL	37	6	12	18	90	....	....	....	....	....	....	....	....	....	5	0	1	1	4	....	....	....	....
	NHL Totals		71	1	4	5	42	0	0	0	44	2.3		1	100.0	17:09	....	....	....	....	....	....	....	....	....

• Missed majority of 2003-04 season recovering from back injury suffered in game vs.St. John's (AHL), October 24, 2003. Signed as a free agent by **Portland** (AHL), February 3, 2005.

FOSTER, Kurtis
(FAW-stuhr, KUHR-this) **MIN.**

Defense. Shoots right. 6'5", 235 lbs. Born, Carp, Ont., November 24, 1981. Calgary's 2nd choice, 40th overall, in 2000 Entry Draft.

			Regular Season														Playoffs								
Season	Club	League	GP	G	A	Pts	PIM	PP	SH	GW	S	%	+/-	TF	F%	Min	GP	G	A	Pts	PIM	PP	SH	GW	Min
1996-97	Ottawa Valley	ODMHA	36	7	18	25	88	....	....	....	....	....	....	....	....	....	....	....	....	....	....	....	....	....	....
1997-98	Peterborough	OHL	39	1	1	2	45	....	....	....	....	....	....	....	....	....	4	0	0	0	2	....	....	....	....
1998-99	Peterborough	OHL	54	2	13	15	59	....	....	....	....	....	....	....	....	....	5	0	0	0	6	....	....	....	....
99-2000	Peterborough	OHL	68	6	18	24	116	....	....	....	....	....	....	....	....	....	5	1	2	3	4	....	....	....	....
2000-01	Peterborough	OHL	62	17	24	41	78	....	....	....	....	....	....	....	....	....	7	1	1	2	10	....	....	....	....
2001-02	Peterborough	OHL	33	10	4	14	58	....	....	....	....	....	....	....	....	....	....	....	....	....	....	....	....	....	....
	Chicago Wolves	AHL	39	6	9	15	59	....	....	....	....	....	....	....	....	....	14	1	1	2	21	....	....	....	....
2002-03	**Atlanta**	**NHL**	**2**	**0**	**0**	**0**	**0**	**0**	**0**	**0**	**1**	**0.0**	**–2**	**0**	**0.0**	**11:06**	....	....	....	....	....	....	....	....	....
	Chicago Wolves	AHL	75	15	27	42	159	....	....	....	....	....	....	....	....	....	9	1	3	4	14	....	....	....	....
2003-04	**Atlanta**	**NHL**	**3**	**0**	**1**	**1**	**0**	**0**	**0**	**0**	**1**	**0.0**	**0**	**0**	**0.0**	**6:58**	....	....	....	....	....	....	....	....	....
	Chicago Wolves	AHL	67	11	19	30	95	....	....	....	....	....	....	....	....	....	10	0	3	3	12	....	....	....	....
2004-05	Cincinnati	AHL	78	17	25	42	71	....	....	....	....	....	....	....	....	....	9	2	3	5	28	....	....	....	....
2005-06	**Minnesota**	**NHL**	**58**	**10**	**18**	**28**	**60**	**6**	**0**	**2**	**124**	**8.1**	**–3**	**0**	**0.0**	**19:13**	....	....	....	....	....	....	....	....	....
	Houston Aeros	AHL	19	4	11	15	32	....	....	....	....	....	....	....	....	....	....	....	....	....	....	....	....	....	....
	NHL Totals		**63**	**10**	**19**	**29**	**60**	**6**	**0**	**2**	**126**	**7.9**		**0**	**0.0**	**18:23**	....	....	....	....	....	....	....	....	....

Rights traded to **Atlanta** by **Calgary** with Jeff Cowan for Petr Buzek and Atlanta's 6th round choice (Adam Pardy) in 2004 Entry Draft, December 18, 2001. Traded to **Anaheim** by **Atlanta** for Niclas Havelid, June 26, 2004. Signed as a free agent by **Minnesota**, August 4, 2005.

FOY, Matt
(FOI, MAT) **MIN.**

Right wing. Shoots right. 6'2", 219 lbs. Born, Oakville, Ont., May 18, 1983. Minnesota's 6th choice, 175th overall, in 2002 Entry Draft.

Season	Club	League	GP	G	A	Pts	PIM	PP	SH	GW	S	%	+/-	TF	F%	Min	GP	G	A	Pts	PIM	PP	SH	GW	Min
2000-01	Wexford Raiders	OPJHL	47	43	49	92	30	....	....	....	....	....	....	....	....	....	....	....	....	....	....	....	....	....	....
2001-02	Merrimack	H-East	31	7	17	24	48	....	....	....	....	....	....	....	....	....	....	....	....	....	....	....	....	....	....
2002-03	Ottawa 67's	OHL	68	61	71	132	112	....	....	....	....	....	....	....	....	....	21	11	20	31	47	....	....	....	....
2003-04	Houston Aeros	AHL	51	11	13	24	74	....	....	....	....	....	....	....	....	....	1	0	0	0	0	....	....	....	....
2004-05	Houston Aeros	AHL	69	12	13	25	78	....	....	....	....	....	....	....	....	....	5	1	2	3	6	....	....	....	....
2005-06	**Minnesota**	**NHL**	**19**	**2**	**3**	**5**	**16**	**1**	**0**	**0**	**21**	**9.5**	**–4**	**1**	**0.0**	**10:59**	....	....	....	....	....	....	....	....	....
	Houston Aeros	AHL	51	15	25	40	122	....	....	....	....	....	....	....	....	....	8	5	3	8	29	....	....	....	....
	NHL Totals		**19**	**2**	**3**	**5**	**16**	**1**	**0**	**0**	**21**	**9.5**		**1**	**0.0**	**10:59**	....	....	....	....	....	....	....	....	....

OHL First All-Star Team (2003)

• Officially announced intention to withdraw from **Merrimack College** (H-East) for academic reasons, May 30, 2002.

FRANZEN, Johan
(FRAN-zehn, YOH-hahn) **DET.**

Left wing. Shoots left. 6'2", 207 lbs. Born, Landsbro, Sweden, December 23, 1979. Detroit's 1st choice, 97th overall, in 2004 Entry Draft.

Season	Club	League	GP	G	A	Pts	PIM	PP	SH	GW	S	%	+/-	TF	F%	Min	GP	G	A	Pts	PIM	PP	SH	GW	Min
2001-02	Linkopings HC	Sweden	36	2	6	8	64	....	....	....	....	....	....	....	....	....	....	....	....	....	....	....	....	....	....
2002-03	Linkopings HC	Sweden	37	2	4	6	14	....	....	....	....	....	....	....	....	....	....	....	....	....	....	....	....	....	....
2003-04	Linkopings HC	Sweden	49	12	18	30	26	....	....	....	....	....	....	....	....	....	5	0	1	1	8	....	....	....	....
2004-05	Linkopings HC	Sweden	43	7	7	14	45	....	....	....	....	....	....	....	....	....	6	2	0	2	16	....	....	....	....
2005-06	**Detroit**	**NHL**	**80**	**12**	**4**	**16**	**36**	**0**	**2**	**2**	**119**	**10.1**	**4**	**171**	**41.5**	**12:27**	**6**	**1**	**2**	**3**	**4**	**0**	**0**	**0**	**12:00**
	NHL Totals		**80**	**12**	**4**	**16**	**36**	**0**	**2**	**2**	**119**	**10.1**		**171**	**41.5**	**12:27**	**6**	**1**	**2**	**3**	**4**	**0**	**0**	**0**	**12:00**

FRIESEN, Jeff
(FREE-zuhn, JEHF) **CGY.**

Left wing. Shoots left. 6'1", 205 lbs. Born, Meadow Lake, Sask., August 5, 1976. San Jose's 1st choice, 11th overall, in 1994 Entry Draft.

Season	Club	League	GP	G	A	Pts	PIM	PP	SH	GW	S	%	+/-	TF	F%	Min	GP	G	A	Pts	PIM	PP	SH	GW	Min
1991-92	Sask. Contacts	SMHL	35	37	51	88	75	....	....	....	....	....	....	....	....	....	....	....	....	....	....	....	....	....	....
	Regina Pats	WHL	4	3	1	4	2	....	....	....	....	....	....	....	....	....	....	....	....	....	....	....	....	....	....
1992-93	Regina Pats	WHL	70	45	38	83	23	....	....	....	....	....	....	....	....	....	13	7	10	17	8	....	....	....	....
1993-94	Regina Pats	WHL	66	51	67	118	48	....	....	....	....	....	....	....	....	....	4	3	2	5	2	....	....	....	....
1994-95	Regina Pats	WHL	25	21	23	44	22	....	....	....	....	....	....	....	....	....	....	....	....	....	....	....	....	....	....
	San Jose	**NHL**	**48**	**15**	**10**	**25**	**14**	**5**	**1**	**2**	**86**	**17.4**	**–8**	....	....	....	**11**	**1**	**5**	**6**	**4**	**0**	**0**	**0**	....
1995-96	**San Jose**	**NHL**	**79**	**15**	**31**	**46**	**42**	**2**	**0**	**0**	**123**	**12.2**	**–19**	....	....	....	....	....	....	....	....	....	....	....	....
1996-97	**San Jose**	**NHL**	**82**	**28**	**34**	**62**	**75**	**6**	**2**	**5**	**200**	**14.0**	**–8**	....	....	....	....	....	....	....	....	....	....	....	....
1997-98	**San Jose**	**NHL**	**79**	**31**	**32**	**63**	**40**	**7**	**6**	**7**	**186**	**16.7**	**8**	....	....	....	**6**	**0**	**1**	**1**	**2**	**0**	**0**	**0**	....
1998-99	**San Jose**	**NHL**	**78**	**22**	**35**	**57**	**42**	**10**	**1**	**3**	**215**	**10.2**	**3**	**24**	**33.3**	**19:25**	**6**	**2**	**2**	**4**	**14**	**1**	**0**	**0**	**22:22**
99-2000	**San Jose**	**NHL**	**82**	**26**	**35**	**61**	**47**	**11**	**3**	**7**	**191**	**13.6**	**–2**	**3**	**66.7**	**19:48**	**11**	**2**	**2**	**4**	**10**	**0**	**0**	**0**	**17:21**
2000-01	**San Jose**	**NHL**	**64**	**12**	**24**	**36**	**56**	**2**	**0**	**1**	**120**	**10.0**	**7**	**7**	**28.6**	**18:51**	....	....	....	....	....	....	....	....	....
	Anaheim	**NHL**	**15**	**2**	**10**	**12**	**10**	**2**	**0**	**0**	**29**	**6.9**	**–2**	**43**	**55.8**	**21:28**	....	....	....	....	....	....	....	....	....
2001-02	**Anaheim**	**NHL**	**81**	**17**	**26**	**43**	**44**	**1**	**1**	**0**	**161**	**10.6**	**–1**	**45**	**48.9**	**17:59**	....	....	....	....	....	....	....	....	....
2002-03 ♦	**New Jersey**	**NHL**	**81**	**23**	**28**	**51**	**26**	**3**	**0**	**4**	**179**	**12.8**	**23**	**11**	**45.5**	**15:33**	**24**	**10**	**4**	**14**	**6**	**1**	**0**	**4**	**16:02**
2003-04	**New Jersey**	**NHL**	**81**	**17**	**20**	**37**	**26**	**5**	**0**	**4**	**177**	**9.6**	**8**	**31**	**45.2**	**15:08**	**5**	**0**	**0**	**0**	**4**	**0**	**0**	**0**	**12:55**
2004-05			DID NOT PLAY																						
2005-06	**Washington**	**NHL**	**33**	**3**	**4**	**7**	**24**	**0**	**0**	**0**	**64**	**4.7**	**–11**	**13**	**46.2**	**14:45**	....	....	....	....	....	....	....	....	....
	Anaheim	**NHL**	**18**	**1**	**3**	**4**	**8**	**0**	**0**	**1**	**11**	**9.1**	**–4**	**0**	**0.0**	**10:53**	**16**	**3**	**1**	**4**	**6**	**0**	**0**	**0**	**11:14**
	NHL Totals		**821**	**212**	**292**	**504**	**454**	**54**	**14**	**34**	**1742**	**12.2**		**177**	**46.9**	**17:26**	**79**	**18**	**15**	**33**	**46**	**2**	**0**	**4**	**15:23**

WHL Rookie of the Year (1993) • Canadian Major Junior Rookie of the Year (1993) • NHL All-Rookie Team (1995)

Traded to **Anaheim** by **San Jose** with Steve Shields and San Jose's 2nd round choice (later traded to Dallas – Dallas selected Vojtech Polak) in 2003 Entry Draft for Teemu Selanne, March 5, 2001. Traded to **New Jersey** by **Anaheim** with Oleg Tverdovsky and Maxim Balmochnykh for Petr Sykora, Mike Commodore, Jean-Francois Damphousse and Igor Pohanka, July 6, 2002. Traded to **Washington** by **New Jersey** for Washington's 3rd round choice (Kirill Tulupov) in 2006 Entry Draft, September 26, 2005. Traded to **Anaheim** by **Washington** for Anaheim's 2nd round choice (Keith Seabrook) in 2006 Entry Draft, March 9, 2006. Signed as a free agent by **Calgary**, July 5, 2006.

FRITSCHE, Dan
(FRIHCH, DAN) **CBJ**

Center. Shoots right. 6'1", 202 lbs. Born, Parma, OH, July 13, 1985. Columbus' 2nd choice, 46th overall, in 2003 Entry Draft.

Season	Club	League	GP	G	A	Pts	PIM	PP	SH	GW	S	%	+/-	TF	F%	Min	GP	G	A	Pts	PIM	PP	SH	GW	Min
2000-01	Cleveland Barons	NAHL	49	23	29	52	47	....	....	....	....	....	....	....	....	....	1	1	1	2	0	....	....	....	....
2001-02	Sarnia Sting	OHL	17	5	13	18	20	....	....	....	....	....	....	....	....	....	....	....	....	....	....	....	....	....	....
2002-03	Sarnia Sting	OHL	61	32	39	71	79	....	....	....	....	....	....	....	....	....	5	2	2	4	4	....	....	....	....
2003-04	**Columbus**	**NHL**	**19**	**1**	**0**	**1**	**12**	**0**	**0**	**0**	**19**	**5.3**	**–5**	**139**	**38.1**	**8:24**	....	....	....	....	....	....	....	....	....
	Sarnia Sting	OHL	27	16	13	29	26	....	....	....	....	....	....	....	....	....	5	1	5	6	0	....	....	....	....
	Syracuse Crunch	AHL	4	2	0	2	0	....	....	....	....	....	....	....	....	....	4	0	1	1	4	....	....	....	....
2004-05	Sarnia Sting	OHL	2	1	1	2	0	....	....	....	....	....	....	....	....	....	....	....	....	....	....	....	....	....	....
	London Knights	OHL	28	17	18	35	18	....	....	....	....	....	....	....	....	....	17	9	13	22	12	....	....	....	....
2005-06	**Columbus**	**NHL**	**59**	**6**	**7**	**13**	**22**	**0**	**0**	**0**	**93**	**6.5**	**–14**	**270**	**48.9**	**10:17**	....	....	....	....	....	....	....	....	....
	Syracuse Crunch	AHL	19	5	4	9	12	....	....	....	....	....	....	....	....	....	6	2	2	4	8	....	....	....	....
	NHL Totals		**78**	**7**	**7**	**14**	**34**	**0**	**0**	**0**	**112**	**6.3**		**409**	**45.2**	**9:50**	....	....	....	....	....	....	....	....	....

Memorial Cup Tournament All-Star Team (2005)

• Missed majority of 2001-02 season recovering from shoulder surgery, December 12, 2001. • Returned to **Sarnia** (OHL) by **Columbus**, January 7, 2004.

FROLOV, Alexander
(froh-LAHF, al-ehx-AN-duhr) **L.A.**

Left wing. Shoots right. 6'3", 210 lbs. Born, Moscow, USSR, June 19, 1982. Los Angeles' 1st choice, 20th overall, in 2000 Entry Draft.

Season	Club	League	GP	G	A	Pts	PIM	PP	SH	GW	S	%	+/-	TF	F%	Min	GP	G	A	Pts	PIM	PP	SH	GW	Min
1998-99	Spartak Moscow	Russia	1	0	0	0	0	....	....	....	....	....	....	....	....	....	....	....	....	....	....	....	....	....	....
99-2000	Yaroslavl 2	Russia-3	36	27	13	40	30	....	....	....	....	....	....	....	....	....	....	....	....	....	....	....	....	....	....
2001-02	Spartak Moscow	Russia	44	20	19	39	8	....	....	....	....	....	....	....	....	....	....	....	....	....	....	....	....	....	....
	Krylja Sovetov 2	Russia-3	2	0	0	0	4	....	....	....	....	....	....	....	....	....	....	....	....	....	....	....	....	....	....
	Krylja Sovetov	Russia	43	18	12	30	16	....	....	....	....	....	....	....	....	....	3	1	0	1	0	....	....	....	....
2002-03	**Los Angeles**	**NHL**	**79**	**14**	**17**	**31**	**34**	**1**	**0**	**3**	**141**	**9.9**	**12**	**9**	**22.2**	**14:23**	....	....	....	....	....	....	....	....	....
2003-04	**Los Angeles**	**NHL**	**77**	**24**	**24**	**48**	**24**	**5**	**2**	**3**	**168**	**14.3**	**8**	**34**	**32.4**	**17:13**	....	....	....	....	....	....	....	....	....
	Nizhny Novgorod	Russia	1	0	0	0	0	....	....	....	....	....	....	....	....	....	....	....	....	....	....	....	....	....	....
2004-05	CSKA Moscow	Russia	42	20	17	37	10	....	....	....	....	....	....	....	....	....	....	....	....	....	....	....	....	....	....
	Dynamo Moscow	Russia	6	2	1	3	2	....	....	....	....	....	....	....	....	....	6	2	1	3	0	....	....	....	....
2005-06	**Los Angeles**	**NHL**	**69**	**21**	**33**	**54**	**40**	**4**	**3**	**4**	**174**	**12.1**	**17**	**4**	**50.0**	**19:18**	....	....	....	....	....	....	....	....	....
	Russia	Olympics	3	0	1	1	0	....	....	....	....	....	....	....	....	....	....	....	....	....	....	....	....	....	....
	NHL Totals		**225**	**59**	**74**	**133**	**98**	**10**	**5**	**10**	**483**	**12.2**		**47**	**31.9**	**16:52**	....	....	....	....	....	....	....	....	....

Signed as a free agent by **CSKA Moscow** (Russia), July 14, 2004. Signed as a free agent by **Dynamo Moscow** (Russia), February 17, 2005.

FUSSEY, Owen
(FOO-see, OH-when)

Right wing. Shoots left. 6', 195 lbs. Born, Winnipeg, Man., April 2, 1983. Washington's 2nd choice, 90th overall, in 2001 Entry Draft.

			Regular Season														Playoffs								
Season	Club	League	GP	G	A	Pts	PIM	PP	SH	GW	S	%	+/-	TF	F%	Min	GP	G	A	Pts	PIM	PP	SH	GW	Min
1998-99	Wpg. Warriors	MMMHL	40	38	33	71	24	....	....	....	....	....	....	....	....	....	....	....	....	....	....	....	....	....	....
99-2000	Calgary Hitmen	WHL	51	7	6	13	35	....	....	....	....	....	....	....	....	....	12	3	4	7	2	....	....	....	....
2000-01	Calgary Hitmen	WHL	48	15	10	25	33	....	....	....	....	....	....	....	....	....	12	2	1	3	6	....	....	....	....
2001-02	Calgary Hitmen	WHL	72	43	27	70	61	....	....	....	....	....	....	....	....	....	7	3	1	4	4	....	....	....	....
2002-03	Calgary Hitmen	WHL	39	17	18	35	31	....	....	....	....	....	....	....	....	....	....	....	....	....	....	....	....	....	....
	Moose Jaw	WHL	27	24	12	36	20	....	....	....	....	....	....	....	....	....	13	6	6	12	10	....	....	....	....
2003-04	**Washington**	**NHL**	**4**	**0**	**1**	**1**	**0**	**0**	**0**	**0**	**6**	**0.0**	**–1**	**0**	**0.0**	**8:16**	....	....	....	....	....	....	....	....	....
	Portland Pirates	AHL	69	6	7	13	23	....	....	....	....	....	....	....	....	....	7	0	0	0	5	....	....	....	....
2004-05	Portland Pirates	AHL	71	14	12	26	26	....	....	....	....	....	....	....	....	....	....	....	....	....	....	....	....	....	....
2005-06	Hershey Bears	AHL	50	2	10	12	38	....	....	....	....	....	....	....	....	....	1	0	0	0	0	....	....	....	....
	NHL Totals		**4**	**0**	**1**	**1**	**0**	**0**	**0**	**0**	**6**	**0.0**		**0**	**0.0**	**8:16**	....	....	....	....	....	....	....	....	....

GABORIK, Marian
(GA-bohr-ihk, MAIR-ee-uhn) **MIN.**

Right wing. Shoots left. 6'1", 190 lbs. Born, Trencin, Czech., February 14, 1982. Minnesota's 1st choice, 3rd overall, in 2000 Entry Draft.

			Regular Season														Playoffs								
Season	Club	League	GP	G	A	Pts	PIM	PP	SH	GW	S	%	+/-	TF	F%	Min	GP	G	A	Pts	PIM	PP	SH	GW	Min
1997-98	Dukla Trencin Jr.	Slovak-Jr.	36	37	22	59	28	....	....	....	....	....	....	....	....	....	....	....	....	....	....	....	....	....	....
	Dukla Trencin	Slovakia	1	1	0	1	0	....	....	....	....	....	....	....	....	....	....	....	....	....	....	....	....	....	....
1998-99	Dukla Trencin	Slovakia	33	11	9	20	6	....	....	....	....	....	....	....	....	....	3	1	0	1	2	....	....	....	....
99-2000	Dukla Trencin	Slovakia	50	25	21	46	34	....	....	....	....	....	....	....	....	....	5	1	2	3	2	....	....	....	....
2000-01	**Minnesota**	**NHL**	**71**	**18**	**18**	**36**	**32**	**6**	**0**	**3**	**179**	**10.1**	**–6**	**3**	**33.3**	**15:26**	....	....	....	....	....	....	....	....	....
2001-02	**Minnesota**	**NHL**	**78**	**30**	**37**	**67**	**34**	**10**	**0**	**4**	**221**	**13.6**	**0**	**4**	**25.0**	**16:47**	....	....	....	....	....	....	....	....	....
2002-03	**Minnesota**	**NHL**	**81**	**30**	**35**	**65**	**46**	**5**	**1**	**8**	**280**	**10.7**	**12**	**16**	**25.0**	**17:24**	**18**	**9**	**8**	**17**	**6**	**4**	**0**	**0**	**18:12**
2003-04	Dukla Trencin	Slovakia	9	10	3	13	10	....	....	....	....	....	....	....	....	....	....	....	....	....	....	....	....	....	....
	Minnesota	**NHL**	**65**	**18**	**22**	**40**	**20**	**3**	**0**	**4**	**220**	**8.2**	**10**	**11**	**45.5**	**18:17**	....	....	....	....	....	....	....	....	....
2004-05	Dukla Trencin	Slovakia	29	25	27	52	46	....	....	....	....	....	....	....	....	....	....	....	....	....	....	....	....	....	....
	Farjestad	Sweden	12	6	4	10	45	....	....	....	....	....	....	....	....	....	12	8	9	17	26	....	....	....	....
2005-06	**Minnesota**	**NHL**	**65**	**38**	**28**	**66**	**64**	**10**	**2**	**7**	**252**	**15.1**	**6**	**11**	**27.3**	**18:26**	....	....	....	....	....	....	....	....	....
	Slovakia	Olympics	6	3	4	7	4	....	....	....	....	....	....	....	....	....	....	....	....	....	....	....	....	....	....
	NHL Totals		**360**	**134**	**140**	**274**	**196**	**34**	**3**	**26**	**1152**	**11.6**		**45**	**31.1**	**17:13**	**18**	**9**	**8**	**17**	**6**	**4**	**0**	**0**	**18:12**

Played in NHL All-Star Game (2003)

Signed as a free agent by **Trencin** (Slovakia), July 5, 2004. Signed as a free agent by **Farjestad** (Sweden), December 21, 2004. Signed as a free agent by **Trencin** (Slovakia), January 31, 2005.

GAGNE, Simon
(GAH-nyay, see-MOHN) **PHI.**

Left wing. Shoots left. 6', 190 lbs. Born, Ste-Foy, Que., February 29, 1980. Philadelphia's 1st choice, 22nd overall, in 1998 Entry Draft.

			Regular Season														Playoffs								
Season	Club	League	GP	G	A	Pts	PIM	PP	SH	GW	S	%	+/-	TF	F%	Min	GP	G	A	Pts	PIM	PP	SH	GW	Min
1995-96	Ste-Foy	QAAA	27	13	9	22	18	....	....	....	....	....	....	....	....	....	15	7	8	15	8	....	....	....	....
1996-97	Beauport	QMJHL	51	9	22	31	49	....	....	....	....	....	....	....	....	....	....	....	....	....	....	....	....	....	....
1997-98	Quebec Remparts	QMJHL	53	30	39	69	26	....	....	....	....	....	....	....	....	....	12	11	5	16	23	....	....	....	....
1998-99	Quebec Remparts	QMJHL	61	50	*70	*120	42	....	....	....	....	....	....	....	....	....	13	9	8	17	4	....	....	....	....
99-2000	**Philadelphia**	**NHL**	**80**	**20**	**28**	**48**	**22**	**8**	**1**	**4**	**159**	**12.6**	**11**	**443**	**42.2**	**14:59**	**17**	**5**	**5**	**10**	**2**	**2**	**0**	**1**	**16:46**
2000-01	**Philadelphia**	**NHL**	**69**	**27**	**32**	**59**	**18**	**6**	**0**	**7**	**191**	**14.1**	**24**	**21**	**28.6**	**18:05**	**6**	**3**	**0**	**3**	**0**	**2**	**0**	**0**	**19:09**
2001-02	**Philadelphia**	**NHL**	**79**	**33**	**33**	**66**	**32**	**4**	**1**	**7**	**199**	**16.6**	**31**	**6**	**83.3**	**18:09**	**5**	**0**	**0**	**0**	**2**	**0**	**0**	**0**	**19:16**
	Canada	Olympics	6	1	3	4	0	....	....	....	....	....	....	....	....	....	....	....	....	....	....	....	....	....	....
2002-03	**Philadelphia**	**NHL**	**46**	**9**	**18**	**27**	**16**	**1**	**1**	**3**	**115**	**7.8**	**20**	**70**	**42.9**	**17:24**	**13**	**4**	**1**	**5**	**6**	**0**	**1**	**1**	**18:13**
2003-04	**Philadelphia**	**NHL**	**80**	**24**	**21**	**45**	**29**	**6**	**0**	**6**	**211**	**11.4**	**12**	**104**	**39.4**	**16:27**	**18**	**5**	**4**	**9**	**12**	**0**	**0**	**1**	**16:48**
2004-05				DID NOT PLAY																					
2005-06	**Philadelphia**	**NHL**	**72**	**47**	**32**	**79**	**38**	**12**	**2**	**7**	**334**	**14.1**	**31**	**18**	**38.9**	**20:46**	**6**	**3**	**1**	**4**	**2**	**1**	**0**	**0**	**21:45**
	Canada	Olympics	6	1	2	3	6	....	....	....	....	....	....	....	....	....	....	....	....	....	....	....	....	....	....
	NHL Totals		**426**	**160**	**164**	**324**	**155**	**37**	**5**	**34**	**1209**	**13.2**		**662**	**41.7**	**17:35**	**65**	**20**	**11**	**31**	**24**	**5**	**1**	**3**	**19:46**

QMJHL Second All-Star Team (1999) • NHL All-Rookie Team (2000)
Played in NHL ALL-Star Game (2001)

GAINEY, Steve
(GAY-nee, STEEV)

Left wing. Shoots left. 6'1", 192 lbs. Born, Montreal, Que., January 26, 1979. Dallas' 3rd choice, 77th overall, in 1997 Entry Draft.

			Regular Season														Playoffs								
Season	Club	League	GP	G	A	Pts	PIM	PP	SH	GW	S	%	+/-	TF	F%	Min	GP	G	A	Pts	PIM	PP	SH	GW	Min
1995-96	Kamloops Blazers	WHL	49	1	4	5	40	....	....	....	....	....	....	....	....	....	3	0	0	0	0	....	....	....	....
1996-97	Kamloops Blazers	WHL	60	9	18	27	60	....	....	....	....	....	....	....	....	....	2	0	0	0	9	....	....	....	....
1997-98	Kamloops Blazers	WHL	68	21	34	55	93	....	....	....	....	....	....	....	....	....	7	1	7	8	15	....	....	....	....
1998-99	Kamloops Blazers	WHL	68	30	34	64	155	....	....	....	....	....	....	....	....	....	15	5	4	9	38	....	....	....	....
99-2000	Fort Wayne	UHL	1	0	0	0	0	....	....	....	....	....	....	....	....	....	....	....	....	....	....	....	....	....	....
	Michigan	IHL	58	8	10	18	41	....	....	....	....	....	....	....	....	....	....	....	....	....	....	....	....	....	....
2000-01	**Dallas**	**NHL**	**1**	**0**	**0**	**0**	**0**	**0**	**0**	**0**	**0**	**0.0**	**0**	**0**	**0.0**	**2:21**	....	....	....	....	....	....	....	....	....
	Utah Grizzlies	IHL	61	7	7	14	167	....	....	....	....	....	....	....	....	....	....	....	....	....	....	....	....	....	....
2001-02	**Dallas**	**NHL**	**5**	**0**	**1**	**1**	**7**	**0**	**0**	**0**	**1**	**0.0**	**–1**	**0**	**0.0**	**7:24**	....	....	....	....	....	....	....	....	....
	Utah Grizzlies	AHL	58	16	18	34	87	....	....	....	....	....	....	....	....	....	....	....	....	....	....	....	....	....	....
2002-03	Utah Grizzlies	AHL	68	9	17	26	106	....	....	....	....	....	....	....	....	....	2	0	0	0	11	....	....	....	....
2003-04	**Dallas**	**NHL**	**7**	**0**	**0**	**0**	**7**	**0**	**0**	**0**	**0**	**0.0**	**1**	**0**	**0.0**	**5:27**	....	....	....	....	....	....	....	....	....
	Utah Grizzlies	AHL	45	7	8	15	74	....	....	....	....	....	....	....	....	....	....	....	....	....	....	....	....	....	....
	Philadelphia	AHL	27	2	7	9	27	....	....	....	....	....	....	....	....	....	11	0	1	1	14	....	....	....	....
2004-05	HC d'Epinal	France	30	10	13	23	97	....	....	....	....	....	....	....	....	....	....	....	....	....	....	....	....	....	....
2005-06	**Phoenix**	**NHL**	**20**	**0**	**1**	**1**	**20**	**0**	**0**	**0**	**11**	**0.0**	**–3**	**4**	**0.0**	**8:14**	....	....	....	....	....	....	....	....	....
	San Antonio	AHL	56	10	20	30	85	....	....	....	....	....	....	....	....	....	....	....	....	....	....	....	....	....	....
	NHL Totals		**33**	**0**	**2**	**2**	**34**	**0**	**0**	**0**	**12**	**0.0**		**4**	**0.0**	**7:20**	....	....	....	....	....	....	....	....	....

Traded to **Philadelphia** by **Dallas** for Mike Siklenka, February 16, 2004. Signed as a free agent by **Epinal** (France), September 17, 2004. Signed as a free agent by **Phoenix**, November 4, 2005.

GAMACHE, Simon
(ga-MOHSH, see-MOHN)

Center. Shoots left. 5'10", 186 lbs. Born, Thetford Mines, Que., January 3, 1981. Atlanta's 14th choice, 290th overall, in 2000 Entry Draft.

			Regular Season														Playoffs								
Season	Club	League	GP	G	A	Pts	PIM	PP	SH	GW	S	%	+/-	TF	F%	Min	GP	G	A	Pts	PIM	PP	SH	GW	Min
1997-98	Levis-Lauzon	QAAA	42	28	26	54	....	....	....	....	....	....	....	....	....	....	4	1	1	2	....	....	....	....	....
1998-99	Val-d'Or Foreurs	QMJHL	70	19	43	62	54	....	....	....	....	....	....	....	....	....	6	1	2	3	4	....	....	....	....
99-2000	Val-d'Or Foreurs	QMJHL	72	64	79	143	74	....	....	....	....	....	....	....	....	....	....	....	....	....	....	....	....	....	....
2000-01	Val-d'Or Foreurs	QMJHL	72	*74	*110	*184	70	....	....	....	....	....	....	....	....	....	21	*22	*35	*57	18	....	....	....	....
2001-02	Chicago Wolves	AHL	26	2	4	6	11	....	....	....	....	....	....	....	....	....	....	....	....	....	....	....	....	....	....
	Greenville	ECHL	31	19	19	38	35	....	....	....	....	....	....	....	....	....	17	*15	9	*24	22	....	....	....	....
2002-03	**Atlanta**	**NHL**	**2**	**0**	**0**	**0**	**2**	**0**	**0**	**0**	**3**	**0.0**	**–1**	**0**	**0.0**	**12:37**	....	....	....	....	....	....	....	....	....
	Chicago Wolves	AHL	76	35	42	77	37	....	....	....	....	....	....	....	....	....	9	7	2	9	4	....	....	....	....
2003-04	**Atlanta**	**NHL**	**2**	**0**	**1**	**1**	**0**	**0**	**0**	**0**	**1**	**0.0**	**0**	**0**	**0.0**	**6:39**	....	....	....	....	....	....	....	....	....
	Chicago Wolves	AHL	16	5	6	11	4	....	....	....	....	....	....	....	....	....	....	....	....	....	....	....	....	....	....
	Nashville	**NHL**	**7**	**1**	**0**	**1**	**0**	**1**	**0**	**0**	**4**	**25.0**	**–3**	**18**	**55.6**	**7:35**	....	....	....	....	....	....	....	....	....
	Milwaukee	AHL	52	18	27	45	26	....	....	....	....	....	....	....	....	....	22	6	*18	24	14	....	....	....	....
2004-05	Milwaukee	AHL	80	29	57	86	93	....	....	....	....	....	....	....	....	....	7	6	4	10	18	....	....	....	....
2005-06	**Nashville**	**NHL**	**11**	**0**	**0**	**0**	**0**	**0**	**0**	**0**	**4**	**0.0**	**–6**	**2**	**50.0**	**8:16**	....	....	....	....	....	....	....	....	....
	Milwaukee	AHL	39	18	19	37	46	....	....	....	....	....	....	....	....	....	21	12	16	28	22	....	....	....	....
	St. Louis	**NHL**	**15**	**3**	**4**	**7**	**10**	**0**	**0**	**0**	**32**	**9.4**	**1**	**4**	**50.0**	**13:53**	....	....	....	....	....	....	....	....	....
	NHL Totals		**37**	**4**	**5**	**9**	**12**	**1**	**0**	**0**	**44**	**9.1**		**24**	**54.2**	**10:34**	....	....	....	....	....	....	....	....	....

Canadian Major Junior Second All-Star Team (2000) • QMJHL First All-Star Team (2001) • Michel Briere Trophy (MVP – QMJHL) (2001) • Canadian Major Junior First All-Star Team (2001) • Canadian Major Junior Player of the Year (2001) • Memorial Cup Tournament All-Star Team (2001) • Ed Chynoweth Trophy (Memorial Cup Tournament Leading Scorer) (2001) • ECHL All-Rookie Team (2002) • ECHL Playoff MVP (2002) (co-winner - Tyrone Garner) • AHL First All-Star Team (2005)

Traded to **Nashville** by **Atlanta** with Kirill Safronov for Ben Simon and Tomas Kloucek, December 2, 2003. Claimed on waivers by **St. Louis** from **Nashville**, November 29, 2005.

GAUSTAD, Paul

(GAW-stad, PAWL) **BUF.**

Center. Shoots left. 6'4", 220 lbs. Born, Fargo, ND, February 3, 1982. Buffalo's 6th choice, 220th overall, in 2000 Entry Draft.

			Regular Season														Playoffs								
Season	Club	League	GP	G	A	Pts	PIM	PP	SH	GW	S	%	+/-	TF	F%	Min	GP	G	A	Pts	PIM	PP	SH	GW	Min
1998-99	Portland Hawks	USAHA	45	47	53	100	81																		
99-2000	Portland	WHL	56	6	8	14	110																		
2000-01	Portland	WHL	70	11	30	41	168										16	10	6	16	59				
2001-02	Portland	WHL	72	36	44	80	202										6	3	1	4	16				
2002-03	**Buffalo**	**NHL**	**1**	**0**	**0**	**0**	**0**	**0**	**0**	**0**	**0**	**0.0**	**0**	**7**	**42.9**	**5:48**									
	Rochester	AHL	80	14	39	53	137										3	0	0	0	4				
2003-04	Rochester	AHL	78	9	22	31	169										16	3	10	13	30				
2004-05	Rochester	AHL	76	18	25	43	192										9	6	5	11	16				
2005-06	**Buffalo**	**NHL**	**78**	**9**	**15**	**24**	**65**	**0**	**0**	**0**	**113**	**8.0**	**4**	**829**	**52.2**	**12:08**	**18**	**0**	**4**	**4**	**14**	**0**	**0**	**0**	**12:21**
	NHL Totals		**79**	**9**	**15**	**24**	**65**	**0**	**0**	**0**	**113**	**8.0**		**836**	**52.2**	**12:03**	**18**	**0**	**4**	**4**	**14**	**0**	**0**	**0**	**12:21**

GAUTHIER, Denis

(GOH-tyay, DEH-nihs) **PHI.**

Defense. Shoots left. 6'3", 224 lbs. Born, Montreal, Que., October 1, 1976. Calgary's 1st choice, 20th overall, in 1995 Entry Draft.

			Regular Season														Playoffs								
Season	Club	League	GP	G	A	Pts	PIM	PP	SH	GW	S	%	+/-	TF	F%	Min	GP	G	A	Pts	PIM	PP	SH	GW	Min
1991-92	Richelieu AA	QAHA	STATISTICS NOT AVAILABLE																						
1992-93	Drummondville	QMJHL	61	1	7	8	136										10	0	5	5	40				
1993-94	Drummondville	QMJHL	60	0	7	7	176										9	2	0	2	41				
1994-95	Drummondville	QMJHL	64	9	31	40	190										4	0	5	5	12				
1995-96	Drummondville	QMJHL	53	25	49	74	140										6	4	4	8	32				
	Saint John Flames	AHL	5	2	0	2	8										16	1	6	7	20				
1996-97	Saint John Flames	AHL	73	3	28	31	74										5	0	0	0	6				
1997-98	**Calgary**	**NHL**	**10**	**0**	**0**	**0**	**16**	**0**	**0**	**0**	**3**	**0.0**	**-5**												
	Saint John Flames	AHL	68	4	20	24	154										21	0	4	4	83				
1998-99	**Calgary**	**NHL**	**55**	**3**	**4**	**7**	**68**	**0**	**0**	**0**	**40**	**7.5**	**3**	**0**	**0.0**	**12:41**									
	Saint John Flames	AHL	16	0	3	3	31																		
99-2000	**Calgary**	**NHL**	**39**	**1**	**1**	**2**	**50**	**0**	**0**	**0**	**29**	**3.4**	**-4**	**0**	**0.0**	**19:21**									
2000-01	**Calgary**	**NHL**	**62**	**2**	**6**	**8**	**78**	**0**	**0**	**0**	**33**	**6.1**	**3**	**0**	**0.0**	**16:37**									
2001-02	**Calgary**	**NHL**	**66**	**5**	**8**	**13**	**91**	**0**	**1**	**2**	**76**	**6.6**	**9**	**0**	**0.0**	**19:19**									
2002-03	**Calgary**	**NHL**	**72**	**1**	**11**	**12**	**99**	**0**	**0**	**1**	**50**	**2.0**	**5**	**0**	**0.0**	**19:52**									
2003-04	**Calgary**	**NHL**	**80**	**1**	**15**	**16**	**113**	**0**	**0**	**0**	**90**	**1.1**	**4**	**0**	**0.0**	**18:43**	**6**	**0**	**1**	**1**	**4**	**0**	**0**	**0**	**18:33**
2004-05			DID NOT PLAY																						
2005-06	**Phoenix**	**NHL**	**45**	**2**	**9**	**11**	**61**	**0**	**0**	**0**	**43**	**4.7**	**-4**	**0**	**0.0**	**16:58**									
	Philadelphia	**NHL**	**17**	**0**	**0**	**0**	**37**	**0**	**0**	**0**	**13**	**0.0**	**6**	**0**	**0.0**	**15:21**	**6**	**0**	**1**	**1**	**19**	**0**	**0**	**0**	**18:21**
	NHL Totals		**446**	**15**	**54**	**69**	**613**	**0**	**1**	**3**	**377**	**4.0**		**0**	**0.0**	**17:41**	**12**	**0**	**2**	**2**	**23**	**0**	**0**	**0**	**18:27**

QMJHL First All-Star Team (1996) • Canadian Major Junior First All-Star Team (1996)

• Missed majority of 1999-2000 season recovering from hip injury suffered in game vs. St. Louis, February 1, 2000. Traded to **Phoenix** by **Calgary** with Oleg Saprykin for Daymond Langkow, August 26, 2004. Traded to **Philadelphia** by **Phoenix** for Josh Gratton, Florida's 2nd round choice (previously acquired, later traded to Detroit - Detroit selected Cory Emerton) in 2006 Entry Draft, Tampa Bay's 2nd round choice (previously acquired, later traded to Detroit - Detroit selected Shawn Matthias) in 2006 Entry Draft, March 9, 2006.

GAVEY, Aaron

(GAY-vee, AIR-ruhn)

Center. Shoots left. 6'2", 189 lbs. Born, Sudbury, Ont., February 22, 1974. Tampa Bay's 4th choice, 74th overall, in 1992 Entry Draft.

			Regular Season														Playoffs								
Season	Club	League	GP	G	A	Pts	PIM	PP	SH	GW	S	%	+/-	TF	F%	Min	GP	G	A	Pts	PIM	PP	SH	GW	Min
1990-91	Peterborough	OHA-B	42	26	30	56	68																		
1991-92	Sault Ste. Marie	OHL	48	7	11	18	27										19	5	1	6	10				
1992-93	Sault Ste. Marie	OHL	62	45	39	84	116										18	5	9	14	36				
1993-94	Sault Ste. Marie	OHL	60	42	60	102	116										14	11	10	21	22				
1994-95	Atlanta Knights	IHL	66	18	17	35	85										5	0	1	1	9				
1995-96	**Tampa Bay**	**NHL**	**73**	**8**	**4**	**12**	**56**	**1**	**1**	**2**	**65**	**12.3**	**-6**				**6**	**0**	**0**	**0**	**4**	**0**	**0**	**0**	
1996-97	**Tampa Bay**	**NHL**	**16**	**1**	**2**	**3**	**12**	**0**	**0**	**0**	**8**	**12.5**	**-1**												
	Calgary	**NHL**	**41**	**7**	**9**	**16**	**34**	**3**	**0**	**1**	**54**	**13.0**	**-11**												
1997-98	**Calgary**	**NHL**	**26**	**2**	**3**	**5**	**24**	**0**	**0**	**1**	**27**	**7.4**	**-5**												
	Saint John Flames	AHL	8	4	3	7	28																		
1998-99	**Dallas**	**NHL**	**7**	**0**	**0**	**0**	**10**	**0**	**0**	**0**	**4**	**0.0**	**-1**	**43**	**48.8**	**8:09**									
	Michigan	IHL	67	24	33	57	128										5	2	3	5	4				
99-2000	**Dallas**	**NHL**	**41**	**7**	**6**	**13**	**44**	**1**	**0**	**2**	**39**	**17.9**	**0**	**263**	**51.7**	**9:55**	**13**	**1**	**2**	**3**	**10**	**0**	**0**	**1**	**6:09**
	Michigan	IHL	28	14	15	29	73																		
2000-01	**Minnesota**	**NHL**	**75**	**10**	**14**	**24**	**52**	**1**	**0**	**2**	**100**	**10.0**	**-8**	**584**	**43.5**	**14:00**									
2001-02	**Minnesota**	**NHL**	**71**	**6**	**11**	**17**	**38**	**1**	**0**	**0**	**75**	**8.0**	**-21**	**254**	**42.5**	**11:55**									
2002-03	**Toronto**	**NHL**	**5**	**0**	**1**	**1**	**0**	**0**	**0**	**0**	**8**	**0.0**	**1**	**31**	**48.4**	**11:19**									
	St. John's	AHL	70	14	29	43	83																		
2003-04	St. John's	AHL	75	22	45	67	100																		
2004-05	Storhamar	Norway	1	0	0	0	0																		
	Utah Grizzlies	AHL	60	5	14	19	58																		
2005-06	**Anaheim**	**NHL**	**5**	**0**	**0**	**0**	**2**	**0**	**0**	**0**	**2**	**0.0**	**0**	**12**	**50.0**	**4:03**									
	Portland Pirates	AHL	72	16	31	47	106										19	1	3	4	43				
	NHL Totals		**360**	**41**	**50**	**91**	**272**	**7**	**1**	**8**	**382**	**10.7**		**1187**	**45.5**	**11:57**	**19**	**1**	**2**	**3**	**14**	**0**	**0**	**1**	**6:09**

Traded to **Calgary** by **Tampa Bay** for Rick Tabaracci, November 19, 1996. Traded to **Dallas** by **Calgary** for Bob Bassen, July 14, 1998. Traded to **Minnesota** by **Dallas** with Pavel Patera, Dallas' 8th round choice (Eric Johansson) in 2000 Entry Draft and Minnesota's 4th round choice (previously acquired, later traded to Los Angeles – Los Angeles selected Aaron Rome) in 2002 Entry Draft for Brad Lukowich and Minnesota's 3rd (Yared Hagos) and 9th (Dale Sullivan) round choices in 2001 Entry Draft, June 25, 2000. Signed as a free agent by **Toronto**, July 24, 2002. Signed as a free agent by **Storhamar** (Norway), November 2, 2004. Signed as a free agent by **Phoenix**, November 29, 2004. Signed as a free agent by **Anaheim**, September 12, 2005.

GELINAS, Martin

(ZHEHL-in-nuh, MAHR-tihn) **FLA.**

Left wing. Shoots left. 5'11", 195 lbs. Born, Shawinigan, Que., June 5, 1970. Los Angeles' 1st choice, 7th overall, in 1988 Entry Draft.

			Regular Season														Playoffs								
Season	Club	League	GP	G	A	Pts	PIM	PP	SH	GW	S	%	+/-	TF	F%	Min	GP	G	A	Pts	PIM	PP	SH	GW	Min
1985-86	Noranda Aces	NOHA	5	1	1	2	0																		
1986-87	Montreal L'est	QAAA	41	36	42	78	36										7	7	5	12	2				
1987-88	Hull Olympiques	QMJHL	65	63	68	131	74										17	15	18	33	32				
1988-89	Hull Olympiques	QMJHL	41	38	39	77	31										9	5	4	9	14				
	Edmonton	**NHL**	**6**	**1**	**2**	**3**	**0**	**0**	**0**	**0**	**14**	**7.1**	**-1**												
1989-90♦	**Edmonton**	**NHL**	**46**	**17**	**8**	**25**	**30**	**5**	**0**	**2**	**71**	**23.9**	**0**				**20**	**2**	**3**	**5**	**6**	**0**	**0**	**0**	
1990-91	**Edmonton**	**NHL**	**73**	**20**	**20**	**40**	**34**	**4**	**0**	**2**	**124**	**16.1**	**-7**				**18**	**3**	**6**	**9**	**25**	**0**	**0**	**1**	
1991-92	**Edmonton**	**NHL**	**68**	**11**	**18**	**29**	**62**	**1**	**0**	**0**	**94**	**11.7**	**14**				**15**	**1**	**3**	**4**	**10**	**0**	**0**	**0**	
1992-93	**Edmonton**	**NHL**	**65**	**11**	**12**	**23**	**30**	**0**	**0**	**1**	**93**	**11.8**	**3**												
1993-94	**Quebec**	**NHL**	**31**	**6**	**6**	**12**	**8**	**0**	**0**	**0**	**53**	**11.3**	**-2**												
	Vancouver	**NHL**	**33**	**8**	**8**	**16**	**26**	**3**	**0**	**1**	**54**	**14.8**	**-6**				**24**	**5**	**4**	**9**	**14**	**2**	**0**	**1**	
1994-95	**Vancouver**	**NHL**	**46**	**13**	**10**	**23**	**36**	**1**	**0**	**4**	**75**	**17.3**	**8**				**3**	**0**	**1**	**1**	**0**	**0**	**0**	**0**	
1995-96	**Vancouver**	**NHL**	**81**	**30**	**26**	**56**	**59**	**3**	**4**	**5**	**181**	**16.6**	**8**				**6**	**1**	**1**	**2**	**12**	**1**	**0**	**0**	
1996-97	**Vancouver**	**NHL**	**74**	**35**	**33**	**68**	**42**	**6**	**1**	**3**	**177**	**19.8**	**6**												
1997-98	**Vancouver**	**NHL**	**24**	**4**	**4**	**8**	**10**	**1**	**1**	**1**	**49**	**8.2**	**-6**												
	Carolina	**NHL**	**40**	**12**	**14**	**26**	**30**	**2**	**1**	**4**	**98**	**12.2**	**1**												
1998-99	**Carolina**	**NHL**	**76**	**13**	**15**	**28**	**67**	**0**	**0**	**2**	**111**	**11.7**	**3**	**6**	**50.0**	**13:13**	**6**	**0**	**3**	**3**	**2**	**0**	**0**	**0**	**19:33**
99-2000	**Carolina**	**NHL**	**81**	**14**	**16**	**30**	**40**	**3**	**0**	**0**	**139**	**10.1**	**-10**	**5**	**40.0**	**13:39**									
2000-01	**Carolina**	**NHL**	**79**	**23**	**29**	**52**	**59**	**6**	**1**	**4**	**170**	**13.5**	**-4**	**6**	**0.0**	**17:54**	**6**	**0**	**1**	**1**	**6**	**0**	**0**	**0**	**17:51**
2001-02	**Carolina**	**NHL**	**72**	**13**	**16**	**29**	**30**	**3**	**0**	**1**	**121**	**10.7**	**-1**	**13**	**23.1**	**16:05**	**23**	**3**	**4**	**7**	**10**	**0**	**0**	**1**	**14:16**
2002-03	**Calgary**	**NHL**	**81**	**21**	**31**	**52**	**51**	**6**	**0**	**3**	**152**	**13.8**	**-3**	**96**	**51.0**	**16:33**									
2003-04	**Calgary**	**NHL**	**76**	**17**	**18**	**35**	**70**	**5**	**0**	**3**	**139**	**12.2**	**10**	**27**	**48.2**	**14:50**	**26**	**8**	**7**	**15**	**35**	**2**	**0**	**3**	**15:58**
2004-05	HC Lugano	Swiss	1	0	0	0	0										5	0	1	1	2				
	Morges	Swiss-2	41	37	21	58	81										4	2	2	4	24				
2005-06	**Florida**	**NHL**	**82**	**17**	**24**	**41**	**80**	**4**	**0**	**3**	**186**	**9.1**	**27**	**24**	**41.7**	**15:59**									
	NHL Totals		**1134**	**286**	**310**	**596**	**764**	**53**	**8**	**39**	**2101**	**13.6**		**177**	**45.2**	**15:28**	**147**	**23**	**33**	**56**	**120**	**5**	**0**	**6**	**15:51**

QMJHL First All-Star Team (1988) • QMJHL Offensive Rookie of the Year (1988) • Canadian Major Junior Rookie of the Year (1988) • George Parsons Trophy (Memorial Cup Tournament Most Sportsmanlike Player) (1988)

Traded to **Edmonton** by **Los Angeles** with Jimmy Carson and Los Angeles' 1st round choices in 1989 (later traded to New Jersey – New Jersey selected Jason Miller), 1991 (Martin Rucinsky) and 1993 (Nick Stajduhar) Entry Drafts and cash for Wayne Gretzky, Mike Krushelnyski and Marty McSorley, August 9, 1988. Traded to **Quebec** by **Edmonton** with Edmonton's 6th round choice (Nicholas Checco) in 1993 Entry Draft for Scott Pearson, June 20, 1993. Claimed on waivers by **Vancouver** from **Quebec**, January 15, 1994. Traded to **Carolina** by **Vancouver** with Kirk McLean for Sean Burke, Geoff Sanderson and Enrico Ciccone, January 3, 1998. Signed as a free agent by **Calgary**, July 2, 2002. Signed as a free agent by **Morges** (Swiss-2), September 23, 2004. Signed as a free agent by **Lugano** (Swiss), February 17, 2005. Signed as a free agent by **Florida**, August 2, 2005.

					Regular Season													Playoffs							
Season	Club	League	GP	G	A	Pts	PIM	PP	SH	GW	S	%	+/-	TF	F%	Min	GP	G	A	Pts	PIM	PP	SH	GW	Min

GERMYN, Carsen (JUHR-mihn, KAHR-sehn) **CGY.**

Right wing. Shoots right. 5'10", 185 lbs. Born, Campbell River, B.C., February 22, 1982.

Season	Club	League	GP	G	A	Pts	PIM	PP	SH	GW	S	%	+/-	TF	F%	Min	GP	G	A	Pts	PIM	PP	SH	GW	Min
1998-99	Kelowna Rockets	WHL	59	6	10	16	61	....	....	....	....	....	....	....	....	....	5	0	0	0	2				
99-2000	Kelowna Rockets	WHL	71	16	29	45	111	....	....	....	....	....	....	....	....	....	5	3	3	6	4				
2000-01	Kelowna Rockets	WHL	71	35	52	87	102	....	....	....	....	....	....	....	....	....	6	2	6	8	10				
2001-02	Kelowna Rockets	WHL	23	10	18	28	43	....	....	....	....	....	....	....	....	....	....	....	....	....	....				
	Red Deer Rebels	WHL	37	23	25	48	83	....	....	....	....	....	....	....	....	....	23	4	12	16	24				
2002-03	Red Deer Rebels	WHL	63	26	33	59	108	....	....	....	....	....	....	....	....	....	23	4	9	13	25				
2003-04	Norfolk Admirals	AHL	77	11	16	27	104	....	....	....	....	....	....	....	....	....	6	1	0	1	2				
2004-05	Lowell	AHL	60	9	11	20	115	....	....	....	....	....	....	....	....	....	10	0	0	0	25				
2005-06	**Calgary**	**NHL**	**2**	**0**	**0**	**0**	**0**	0	0	0	2	0.0	–1	0	0.0	5:00	....	....	....	....	....				
	Omaha	AHL	77	24	31	55	127	....	....	....	....	....	....	....	....	....	....	....	....	....	....				
	NHL Totals		**2**	**0**	**0**	**0**	**0**	**0**	**0**	**0**	**2**	**0.0**		**0**	**0.0**	**5:00**	....	....	....	....	....				

Signed as a free agent by **Calgary**, July 6, 2004.

GERVAIS, Bruno (ZHUR-vay, BROO-noh) **NYI**

Defense. Shoots right. 6', 188 lbs. Born, Longueuil, Que., October 3, 1984. NY Islanders' 6th choice, 182nd overall, in 2003 Entry Draft.

Season	Club	League	GP	G	A	Pts	PIM	PP	SH	GW	S	%	+/-	TF	F%	Min	GP	G	A	Pts	PIM	PP	SH	GW	Min
99-2000	Antoine-Girouard	QAAA	6	4	9	13		....	....	....	....	....	....	....	....	....	4	0	0	0	0				
2000-01	Antoine-Girouard	QAAA	40	8	27	35	46	....	....	....	....	....	....	....	....	....	7	4	2	6	8				
2001-02	Acadie-Bathurst	QMJHL	65	4	12	16	42	....	....	....	....	....	....	....	....	....	16	3	1	4	8				
2002-03	Acadie-Bathurst	QMJHL	72	22	28	50	73	....	....	....	....	....	....	....	....	....	11	3	5	8	14				
2003-04	Acadie-Bathurst	QMJHL	23	4	6	10	28	....	....	....	....	....	....	....	....	....	....	....	....	....	....				
2004-05	Bridgeport	AHL	76	8	22	30	58	....	....	....	....	....	....	....	....	....	....	....	....	....	....				
2005-06	**NY Islanders**	**NHL**	**27**	**3**	**4**	**7**	**8**	1	0	0	21	14.3	–1	0	0.0	16:47	....	....	....	....	....				
	Bridgeport	AHL	55	17	25	42	70	....	....	....	....	....	....	....	....	....	7	1	2	3	0				
	NHL Totals		**27**	**3**	**4**	**7**	**8**	**1**	**0**	**0**	**21**	**14.3**		**0**	**0.0**	**16:47**	....	....	....	....	....				

QMJHL Second All-Star Team (2003)
• Missed majority of 2003-04 season recovering from knee injury suffered during Team Canada Jr. training camp, December 12, 2003.

GETZLAF, Ryan (GEHTZ-laf, RIGH-uhn) **ANA.**

Center. Shoots right. 6'3", 210 lbs. Born, Regina, Sask., May 10, 1985. Anaheim's 1st choice, 19th overall, in 2003 Entry Draft.

Season	Club	League	GP	G	A	Pts	PIM	PP	SH	GW	S	%	+/-	TF	F%	Min	GP	G	A	Pts	PIM	PP	SH	GW	Min
2000-01	Regina Rangers	SBHL	41	33	41	74	189	....	....	....	....	....	....	....	....	....	....	....	....	....	....				
	Reg. Pat Cdns.	SMHL	8	4	3	7	8	....	....	....	....	....	....	....	....	....	....	....	....	....	....				
2001-02	Calgary Hitmen	WHL	63	9	9	18	34	....	....	....	....	....	....	....	....	....	7	2	1	3	4				
2002-03	Calgary Hitmen	WHL	70	29	39	68	121	....	....	....	....	....	....	....	....	....	5	1	1	2	6				
2003-04	Calgary Hitmen	WHL	49	28	47	75	97	....	....	....	....	....	....	....	....	....	7	5	1	6	12				
2004-05	Calgary Hitmen	WHL	51	29	25	54	102	....	....	....	....	....	....	....	....	....	12	4	13	17	18				
	Cincinnati	AHL	....	....	....	....	....	....	....	....	....	....	....	....	....	....	....	10	1	4	5	4				
2005-06	**Anaheim**	**NHL**	**57**	**14**	**25**	**39**	**22**	10	0	1	116	12.1	6	534	44.0	12:35	16	3	4	7	13	2	0	1	15:49
	Portland Pirates	AHL	17	8	25	33	36	....	....	....	....	....	....	....	....	....	1	0	0	0	4				
	NHL Totals		**57**	**14**	**25**	**39**	**22**	**10**	**0**	**1**	**116**	**12.1**		**534**	**44.0**	**12:35**	**16**	**3**	**4**	**7**	**13**	**2**	**0**	**1**	**15:49**

WHL East First All-Star Team (2004) • WHL East Second All-Star Team (2005)

GILL, Hal (GIHL, HAL) **TOR.**

Defense. Shoots left. 6'7", 250 lbs. Born, Concord, MA, April 6, 1975. Boston's 8th choice, 207th overall, in 1993 Entry Draft.

Season	Club	League	GP	G	A	Pts	PIM	PP	SH	GW	S	%	+/-	TF	F%	Min	GP	G	A	Pts	PIM	PP	SH	GW	Min
1992-93	Nashoba	High-MA	20	25	25	50		....	....	....	....	....	....	....	....	....	....	....	....	....	....				
1993-94	Providence	H-East	31	1	2	3	26	....	....	....	....	....	....	....	....	....	....	....	....	....	....				
1994-95	Providence	H-East	26	1	3	4	22	....	....	....	....	....	....	....	....	....	....	....	....	....	....				
1995-96	Providence	H-East	39	5	12	17	54	....	....	....	....	....	....	....	....	....	....	....	....	....	....				
1996-97	Providence	H-East	35	5	16	21	52	....	....	....	....	....	....	....	....	....	....	....	....	....	....				
1997-98	**Boston**	**NHL**	**68**	**2**	**4**	**6**	**47**	0	0	0	56	3.6	4	....	....	....	6	0	0	0	4	0	0	0	
	Providence Bruins	AHL	4	1	0	1	23	....	....	....	....	....	....	....	....	....	....	....	....	....	....				
1998-99	**Boston**	**NHL**	**80**	**3**	**7**	**10**	**63**	0	0	2	102	2.9	–10	1100.0		20:54	12	0	0	0	14	0	0	0	20:41
99-2000	**Boston**	**NHL**	**81**	**3**	**9**	**12**	**51**	0	0	0	120	2.5	0	0	0.0	17:15	....	....	....	....	....				
2000-01	**Boston**	**NHL**	**80**	**1**	**10**	**11**	**71**	0	0	0	79	1.3	–2	0	0.0	18:21	....	....	....	....	....				
2001-02	**Boston**	**NHL**	**79**	**4**	**18**	**22**	**77**	0	0	0	137	2.9	16	0	0.0	24:13	6	0	1	1	2	0	0	0	23:04
2002-03	**Boston**	**NHL**	**76**	**4**	**13**	**17**	**56**	0	0	0	114	3.5	21	0	0.0	20:42	5	0	0	0	4	0	0	0	20:19
2003-04	**Boston**	**NHL**	**82**	**2**	**7**	**9**	**99**	0	0	0	104	1.9	16	0	0.0	18:24	7	0	1	1	4	0	0	0	19:03
2004-05	Lukko Rauma	Finland	31	2	8	10	110	....	....	....	....	....	....	....	....	....	8	0	0	0	*57				
2005-06	**Boston**	**NHL**	**80**	**1**	**9**	**10**	**124**	0	0	0	68	1.5	–4	0	0.0	18:37	....	....	....	....	....				
	NHL Totals		**626**	**20**	**77**	**97**	**588**	**0**	**0**	**2**	**780**	**2.6**		**1100.0**		**19:45**	**36**	**0**	**2**	**2**	**28**	**0**	**0**	**0**	**20:43**

Signed as a free agent by **Rauma** (Finland), November 25, 2004. Signed as a free agent by **Toronto**, July 1, 2006.

GILLIES, Trevor (GIHL-ees, TREH-vuhr) **ANA.**

Left wing. Shoots left. 6'3", 210 lbs. Born, Cambridge, Ont., January 30, 1979.

Season	Club	League	GP	G	A	Pts	PIM	PP	SH	GW	S	%	+/-	TF	F%	Min	GP	G	A	Pts	PIM	PP	SH	GW	Min
1996-97	North Bay	OHL	26	0	3	3	72	....	....	....	....	....	....	....	....	....	....	....	....	....	....				
1997-98	North Bay	OHL	2	0	0	0	4	....	....	....	....	....	....	....	....	....	....	....	....	....	....				
	Sarnia Sting	OHL	17	0	1	1	33	....	....	....	....	....	....	....	....	....	....	....	....	....	....				
	Oshawa Generals	OHL	45	1	2	3	184	....	....	....	....	....	....	....	....	....	7	0	1	1	12				
1998-99	Oshawa Generals	OHL	66	6	9	15	270	....	....	....	....	....	....	....	....	....	11	0	2	2	28				
99-2000	Lowell	AHL	8	0	0	0	38	....	....	....	....	....	....	....	....	....	....	....	....	....	....				
	Mississippi	ECHL	53	0	6	6	202	....	....	....	....	....	....	....	....	....	....	....	....	....	....				
2000-01	Greensboro	ECHL	63	1	6	7	303	....	....	....	....	....	....	....	....	....	....	....	....	....	....				
	Worcester IceCats	AHL	....	....	....	....	....	....	....	....	....	....	....	....	....	....	....	6	0	0	0	24				
2001-02	Providence Bruins	AHL	5	0	0	0	21	....	....	....	....	....	....	....	....	....	....	....	....	....	....				
	Augusta Lynx	ECHL	46	0	1	1	*269	....	....	....	....	....	....	....	....	....	....	....	....	....	....				
	Richmond	ECHL	18	0	1	1	*51	....	....	....	....	....	....	....	....	....	....	....	....	....	....				
2002-03	Lowell	AHL	25	0	1	1	132	....	....	....	....	....	....	....	....	....	....	....	....	....	....				
	Richmond	ECHL	6	0	0	0	20	....	....	....	....	....	....	....	....	....	....	....	....	....	....				
	Peoria Rivermen	ECHL	24	0	1	1	180	....	....	....	....	....	....	....	....	....	....	....	....	....	....				
2003-04	Springfield	AHL	61	2	1	3	277	....	....	....	....	....	....	....	....	....	....	....	....	....	....				
2004-05	Hartford	AHL	49	0	2	2	277	....	....	....	....	....	....	....	....	....	....	....	....	....	....				
2005-06	**Anaheim**	**NHL**	**1**	**0**	**0**	**0**	**21**	0	0	0	1	0.0	0	0	0.0	2:40	....	....	....	....	....				
	Portland Pirates	AHL	50	2	3	5	169	....	....	....	....	....	....	....	....	....	4	0	0	0	6				
	NHL Totals		**1**	**0**	**0**	**0**	**21**	**0**	**0**	**0**	**1**	**0.0**		**0**	**0.0**	**2:40**	....	....	....	....	....				

Signed as a free agent by **NY Rangers**, July 20, 2004. Traded to **Anaheim** by **NY Rangers** with a conditional choice in 2007 Entry Draft for Steve Rucchin, August 23, 2005.

GIONTA, Brian (jee-OHN-tuh, BRIGH-uhn) **N.J.**

Right wing. Shoots right. 5'7", 175 lbs. Born, Rochester, NY, January 18, 1979. New Jersey's 4th choice, 82nd overall, in 1998 Entry Draft.

Season	Club	League	GP	G	A	Pts	PIM	PP	SH	GW	S	%	+/-	TF	F%	Min	GP	G	A	Pts	PIM	PP	SH	GW	Min
1994-95	Rochester	EmJHL	28	*52	37	*89	....	....	....	....	....	....	....	....	....	....	....	....	....	....	....				
1995-96	Niagara Scenic	MTJHL	51	47	44	91	59	....	....	....	....	....	....	....	....	....	....	....	....	....	....				
1996-97	Niagara Scenic	MTJHL	50	57	70	127	101	....	....	....	....	....	....	....	....	....	6	6*	11	17	21				
1997-98	Boston College	H-East	40	30	32	62	44	....	....	....	....	....	....	....	....	....	....	....	....	....	....				
1998-99	Boston College	H-East	39	27	33	60	46	....	....	....	....	....	....	....	....	....	....	....	....	....	....				
99-2000	Boston College	H-East	42	*33	23	56	66	....	....	....	....	....	....	....	....	....	....	....	....	....	....				
2000-01	Boston College	H-East	43	*33	21	*54	47	....	....	....	....	....	....	....	....	....	....	....	....	....	....				
2001-02	**New Jersey**	**NHL**	**33**	**4**	**7**	**11**	**8**	0	0	0	58	6.9	10	36	44.4	13:25	6	2	2	4	0	1	0	0	2 17:08
	Albany River Rats	AHL	37	9	16	25	18	....	....	....	....	....	....	....	....	....	....	....	....	....	....				
2002-03 ♦	**New Jersey**	**NHL**	**58**	**12**	**13**	**25**	**23**	2	0	3	129	9.3	5	14	57.1	14:48	24	1	8	9	6	0	0	0	14:31
2003-04	**New Jersey**	**NHL**	**75**	**21**	**8**	**29**	**36**	0	0	8	174	12.1	19	60	58.3	14:44	5	2	3	5	0	1	0	0	15:41
2004-05	Albany River Rats	AHL	15	5	7	12	10	....	....	....	....	....	....	....	....	....	....	....	....	....	....				

			Regular Season														Playoffs								
Season	Club	League	GP	G	A	Pts	PIM	PP	SH	GW	S	%	+/-	TF	F%	Min	GP	G	A	Pts	PIM	PP	SH	GW	Min
2005-06	**New Jersey**	**NHL**	**82**	**48**	**41**	**89**	**46**	**24**	**1**	**10**	**291**	**16.5**	**18**	**73**	**38.4**	**19:49**	**9**	**3**	**4**	**7**	**2**	**1**	**1**	**2**	**20:06**
	United States	Olympics	6	4	0	4	2																		
	NHL Totals		**248**	**85**	**69**	**154**	**113**	**26**	**1**	**21**	**652**	**13.0**		**183**	**47.5**	**16:15**	**44**	**8**	**17**	**25**	**8**	**2**	**2**	**4**	**16:09**

Hockey East Rookie of the Year (1998) • Hockey East Second All-Star Team (1998) • NCAA East Second All-American Team (1998) • Hockey East First All-Star Team (1999, 2000, 2001) • NCAA East First All-American Team (1999, 2000, 2001) • Hockey East Player of the Year (2001) • Walter Brown Award (New England's Outstanding American-born College player) (2001) (co-winner - Ty Conklin)

GIORDANO, Mark
(jee-ohr-DAN-oh, MAHRK) **CGY.**

Defense. Shoots left. 6', 203 lbs. Born, Toronto, Ont., May 10, 1983.

Season	Club	League	GP	G	A	Pts	PIM	PP	SH	GW	S	%	+/-	TF	F%	Min	GP	G	A	Pts	PIM	PP	SH	GW	Min
2002-03	Owen Sound	OHL	68	18	30	48	109										4	1	3	4	2				
2003-04	Owen Sound	OHL	65	14	35	49	72										7	1	3	4	5				
2004-05	Lowell	AHL	66	6	10	16	85										11	0	1	1	41				
2005-06	**Calgary**	**NHL**	**7**	**0**	**1**	**1**	**8**	**0**	**0**	**0**	**5**	**0.0**	**2**	**0**	**0.0**	**12:05**									
	Omaha	AHL	73	16	42	58	141																		
	NHL Totals		**7**	**0**	**1**	**1**	**8**	**0**	**0**	**0**	**5**	**0.0**		**0**	**0.0**	**12:05**									

Signed as a free agent by **Calgary**, July 6, 2004.

GIROUX, Alexandre
(ZHIH-roo, al-ehx-AN-dreh) **WSH.**

Center/Left wing. Shoots left. 6'3", 190 lbs. Born, Quebec City, Que., June 16, 1981. Ottawa's 9th choice, 213th overall, in 1999 Entry Draft.

Season	Club	League	GP	G	A	Pts	PIM	PP	SH	GW	S	%	+/-	TF	F%	Min	GP	G	A	Pts	PIM	PP	SH	GW	Min
1997-98	Ste-Foy	QAAA	42	28	30	58	96																		
1998-99	Hull Olympiques	QMJHL	67	15	22	37	124										22	2	2	4	8				
99-2000	Hull Olympiques	QMJHL	72	52	47	99	117										15	12	6	18	30				
2000-01	Hull Olympiques	QMJHL	38	31	32	63	62																		
	Rouyn-Noranda	QMJHL	25	13	14	27	56										9	2	6	8	22				
2001-02	Grand Rapids	AHL	70	11	16	27	74																		
2002-03	Binghamton	AHL	67	19	16	35	101										10	1	0	1	10				
2003-04	Binghamton	AHL	59	19	23	42	79																		
	Hartford	AHL	16	6	3	9	13										16	3	4	7	28				
2004-05	Hartford	AHL	78	32	22	54	128										6	3	3	6	23				
2005-06	**NY Rangers**	**NHL**	**1**	**0**	**0**	**0**	**0**	**0**	**0**	**0**	**0**	**0.0**	**–1**	**0**	**0.0**	**2:50**									
	Hartford	AHL	73	36	31	67	102										13	7	9	16	17				
	NHL Totals		**1**	**0**	**0**	**0**	**0**	**0**	**0**	**0**	**0**	**0.0**		**0**	**0.0**	**2:50**									

Traded to **NY Rangers** by **Ottawa** with Karel Rachunek for Greg De Vries, March 9, 2004. Signed as a free agent by **Washington**, July 14, 2006.

GIROUX, Raymond
(zhih-ROO, ray-MAWN)

Defense. Shoots left. 6'1", 190 lbs. Born, North Bay, Ont., July 20, 1976. Philadelphia's 7th choice, 202nd overall, in 1994 Entry Draft.

Season	Club	League	GP	G	A	Pts	PIM	PP	SH	GW	S	%	+/-	TF	F%	Min	GP	G	A	Pts	PIM	PP	SH	GW	Min
1992-93	Powassan Hawks	NOHA	45	8	18	26	117																		
1993-94	Powassan Hawks	NOJHA	36	10	40	50	42																		
1994-95	Yale	ECAC	27	1	3	4	8																		
1995-96	Yale	ECAC	30	3	16	19	36																		
1996-97	Yale	ECAC	32	9	12	21	38																		
1997-98	Yale	ECAC	35	9	*30	39	62																		
1998-99	Lowell	AHL	59	13	19	32	92										3	1	1	2	0				
99-2000	**NY Islanders**	**NHL**	**14**	**0**	**9**	**9**	**10**	**0**	**0**	**0**	**24**	**0.0**	**0**	**9**	**22.2**	**14:40**									
	Lowell	AHL	49	12	21	33	34										7	0	0	0	2				
2000-01	HIFK Helsinki	Finland	22	3	9	12	34																		
	AIK Solna	Sweden	9	0	1	1	16																		
	Jokerit Helsinki	Finland	24	4	9	13	16										5	0	0	0	0				
2001-02	**NY Islanders**	**NHL**	**2**	**0**	**0**	**0**	**2**	**0**	**0**	**0**	**2**	**0.0**	**–1**	**0**	**0.0**	**12:18**									
	Bridgeport	AHL	79	13	40	53	73										19	1	7	8	20				
2002-03	**New Jersey**	**NHL**	**11**	**0**	**1**	**1**	**6**	**0**	**0**	**0**	**20**	**0.0**	**–2**	**0**	**0.0**	**18:18**									
	Albany River Rats	AHL	67	11	38	49	49																		
2003-04	**New Jersey**	**NHL**	**11**	**0**	**3**	**3**	**4**	**0**	**0**	**0**	**17**	**0.0**	**–3**	**0**	**0.0**	**20:55**	**4**	**0**	**0**	**0**	**0**	**0**	**0**	**0**	**15:15**
	Albany River Rats	AHL	65	11	17	28	34																		
2004-05	Houston Aeros	AHL	70	13	20	33	54										5	0	0	0	13				
2005-06	Ak Bars Kazan	Russia	46	9	11	20	56										13	3	8	11	14				
	NHL Totals		**38**	**0**	**13**	**13**	**22**	**0**	**0**	**0**	**63**	**0.0**		**9**	**22.2**	**17:24**	**4**	**0**	**0**	**0**	**0**	**0**	**0**	**0**	**15:15**

ECAC First All-Star Team (1998) • ECAC Player of the Year (1998) • NCAA East First All-American Team (1998) • AHL First All-Star Team (2003)

Rights traded to **NY Islanders** by **Philadelphia** for NY Islanders' 6th round choice (later traded to Montreal – Montreal selected Scott Selig) in 2000 Entry Draft, August 25, 1998. Signed as a free agent by **New Jersey**, July 12, 2002. Signed as a free agent by **Minnesota**, July 7, 2004. Signed as a free agent by **Kazan** (Russia), September 11, 2005.

GIULIANO, Jeff
(JOO-lee-A-noh, JEHF) **L.A.**

Left wing. Shoots left. 5'9", 205 lbs. Born, Nashua, NH, June 20, 1979.

Season	Club	League	GP	G	A	Pts	PIM	PP	SH	GW	S	%	+/-	TF	F%	Min	GP	G	A	Pts	PIM	PP	SH	GW	Min
1998-99	Boston College	H-East	43	5	15	20	10																		
99-2000	Boston College	H-East	42	10	13	23	16																		
2000-01	Boston College	H-East	43	14	22	36	28																		
2001-02	Boston College	H-East	38	11	24	35	14																		
2002-03	Manchester	AHL	47	4	11	15	8										3	1	0	1	0				
	Reading Royals	ECHL	38	7	23	30	6																		
2003-04	Manchester	AHL	80	6	14	20	16										1	0	0	0	0				
2004-05	Manchester	AHL	69	8	16	24	21										2	0	0	0	0				
2005-06	**Los Angeles**	**NHL**	**48**	**3**	**4**	**7**	**26**	**0**	**0**	**2**	**32**	**9.4**	**0**	**252**	**46.0**	**9:45**									
	Manchester	AHL	19	5	6	11	17										7	3	1	4	2				
	NHL Totals		**48**	**3**	**4**	**7**	**26**	**0**	**0**	**2**	**32**	**9.4**		**252**	**46.0**	**9:45**									

Signed as a free agent by **Los Angeles**, August 12, 2005.

GLEASON, Tim
(GLEE-suhn, TIHM) **L.A.**

Defense. Shoots left. 6'1", 202 lbs. Born, Clawson, MI, January 29, 1983. Ottawa's 2nd choice, 23rd overall, in 2001 Entry Draft.

Season	Club	League	GP	G	A	Pts	PIM	PP	SH	GW	S	%	+/-	TF	F%	Min	GP	G	A	Pts	PIM	PP	SH	GW	Min
1998-99	Leamington Flyers	OHA-B	52	5	26	31	76																		
99-2000	Windsor Spitfires	OHL	55	5	13	18	101										12	2	4	6	14				
2000-01	Windsor Spitfires	OHL	47	8	28	36	124										9	1	2	3	23				
2001-02	Windsor Spitfires	OHL	67	17	42	59	109										16	7	13	20	40				
2002-03	Windsor Spitfires	OHL	45	7	31	38	75										7	5	2	7	17				
2003-04	**Los Angeles**	**NHL**	**47**	**0**	**7**	**7**	**21**	**0**	**0**	**0**	**45**	**0.0**	**1**	**0**	**0.0**	**14:59**									
	Manchester	AHL	22	0	8	8	19										6	0	1	1	4				
2004-05	Manchester	AHL	67	10	14	24	112										5	0	0	0	4				
2005-06	**Los Angeles**	**NHL**	**78**	**2**	**19**	**21**	**77**	**0**	**0**	**0**	**72**	**2.8**	**0**	**0**	**0.0**	**17:41**									
	NHL Totals		**125**	**2**	**26**	**28**	**98**	**0**	**0**	**0**	**117**	**1.7**		**0**	**0.0**	**16:40**									

Rights traded to **Los Angeles** by **Ottawa** with future considerations for Bryan Smolinski, March 11, 2003.

GLOBKE, Rob
(GLAWB-kee, RAWB) **FLA.**

Center. Shoots right. 6'2", 200 lbs. Born, Farmington, MI, October 24, 1982. Florida's 3rd choice, 40th overall, in 2002 Entry Draft.

Season	Club	League	GP	G	A	Pts	PIM	PP	SH	GW	S	%	+/-	TF	F%	Min	GP	G	A	Pts	PIM	PP	SH	GW	Min
1998-99	Det. Compuware	NAHL	55	8	14	22	111										7	1	2	3	2				
99-2000	USNTDP	U-18	6	4	2	6	6																		
	USNTDP	USHL	54	15	21	36	68																		
2000-01	U. of Notre Dame	CCHA	33	17	9	26	74																		
2001-02	U. of Notre Dame	CCHA	33	11	11	22	79																		
2002-03	U. of Notre Dame	CCHA	40	21	15	36	44																		
2003-04	U. of Notre Dame	CCHA	39	19	21	40	42																		
2004-05	San Antonio	AHL	63	6	6	12	21																		
	Texas Wildcatters	ECHL	10	8	4	12	13																		

Season	Club	League	GP	G	A	Pts	PIM	Regular Season PP	SH	GW	S	%	+/-	TF	F%	Min	Playoffs GP	G	A	Pts	PIM	PP	SH	GW	Min
2005-06	Florida	NHL	18	1	0	1	6	0	0	0	18	5.6	0	1	0.0	7:17	....	....	....	....	....				
	Rochester	AHL	52	6	9	15	54	....	....	....	....	....	....				....	....	....	....	....				
	NHL Totals		18	1	0	1	6	0	0	0	18	5.6		1	0.0	7:17	....	....	....	....	....				

CCHA Second All-Star Team (2004)

GLUMAC, Mike (GLOO-kmak, MIGHK) ST.L.

Right wing. Shoots right. 6'2", 205 lbs. Born, Niagara Falls, Ont., April 5, 1980.

Season	Club	League	GP	G	A	Pts	PIM	PP	SH	GW	S	%	+/-	TF	F%	Min	GP	G	A	Pts	PIM	PP	SH	GW	Min
1996-97	St. Mike's B's	OPJHL	50	13	25	38	33										6	1	0	1	2				
1997-98	Newmarket	OPJHL	36	16	16	32	57																		
1998-99	Miami U.	CCHA	35	2	0	2	44																		
99-2000	Miami U.	CCHA	36	8	5	13	52																		
2000-01	Miami U.	CCHA	37	9	10	19	46																		
2001-02	Miami U.	CCHA	36	15	8	23	28																		
2002-03	Pee Dee Pride	ECHL	69	37	32	69	49																		
	Cleveland Barons	AHL	2	0	0	0	0																		
2003-04	Worcester IceCats	AHL	80	28	24	52	74										10	3	3	6	11				
2004-05	Worcester IceCats	AHL	45	12	17	29	27																		
2005-06	**St. Louis**	NHL	33	7	5	12	33	5	0	0	55	12.7	−8	5	40.0	12:25									
	Peoria Rivermen	AHL	49	25	32	57	64										4	1	1	2	5				
	NHL Totals		33	7	5	12	33	5	0	0	55	12.7		5	40.0	12:25									

ECHL All-Rookie Team (2003)
Signed as a free agent by **Pee Dee** (ECHL), August 28, 2002. Signed as a free agent by **Worcester** (AHL), October 6, 2003. Signed as a free agent by **St. Louis**, June 29, 2004.

GOC, Marcel (GAWCH, mahr-SEHL) S.J.

Center. Shoots left. 6', 195 lbs. Born, Calw, West Germany, August 24, 1983. San Jose's 1st choice, 20th overall, in 2001 Entry Draft.

Season	Club	League	GP	G	A	Pts	PIM	PP	SH	GW	S	%	+/-	TF	F%	Min	GP	G	A	Pts	PIM	PP	SH	GW	Min
1998-99	Schwenningen Jr.	Ger-Jr.	12	23	10	33	12																		
99-2000	Schwenningen	Germany	51	0	3	3	4										11	1	1	2	2				
2000-01	Schwenningen	Germany	58	13	28	41	12																		
2001-02	Schwenningen	Germany	45	8	9	17	24																		
	Adler Mannheim	Germany	8	0	2	2	0																		
2002-03	Adler Mannheim	Germany	36	6	14	20	16										8	1	2	3	0				
2003-04	Cleveland Barons	AHL	78	16	21	37	24										5	1	1	2	0	0	0	1	7:08
	San Jose	NHL	....	....	....	....	....																		
2004-05	Cleveland Barons	AHL	76	16	34	50	28																		
2005-06	**San Jose**	NHL	81	8	14	22	22	2	0	2	96	8.3	−7	808	47.9	11:42	11	0	3	3	0	0	0	0	12:38
	Germany	Olympics	5	1	0	1	0																		
	NHL Totals		81	8	14	22	22	2	0	2	96	8.3		808	47.9	11:42	16	1	4	5	0	0	0	1	10:55

GOC, Sascha (GAWCH, SA-shah) T.B.

Defense. Shoots right. 6'6", 220 lbs. Born, Calw, West Germany, April 14, 1979. New Jersey's 5th choice, 159th overall, in 1997 Entry Draft.

Season	Club	League	GP	G	A	Pts	PIM	PP	SH	GW	S	%	+/-	TF	F%	Min	GP	G	A	Pts	PIM	PP	SH	GW	Min
1994-95	Schwenningen	Germany	14	5	1	6	10																		
1995-96	Schwenningen Jr.	Ger-Jr.	11	3	6	9	77																		
	Schwenningen	Germany	1	0	0	0	0																		
1996-97	Schwenningen Jr.	Ger-Jr.	1	1	1	2	2																		
	Schwenningen	Germany	41	3	1	4	28										5	0	0	0	0				
1997-98	Schwenningen	Germany	49	5	5	10	45																		
	Schwenningen Jr.	Ger-Jr.	4	1	3	4	8																		
1998-99	Albany River Rats	AHL	55	1	12	13	24										2	0	0	0	0				
99-2000	Albany River Rats	AHL	64	9	22	31	35										5	2	0	2	6				
2000-01	**New Jersey**	NHL	11	0	0	0	4	0	0	0	7	0.0	7	0	0.0	13:37									
	Albany River Rats	AHL	55	10	29	39	49																		
2001-02	**New Jersey**	NHL	2	0	0	0	0	0	0	0	2	0.0	−2	0	0.0	19:21									
	Albany River Rats	AHL	10	0	5	5	12																		
	Tampa Bay	NHL	9	0	0	0	0	0	0	0	2	0.0	0	0	0.0	5:32									
	Springfield	AHL	36	3	9	12	30										7	1	0	1	*41				
2002-03	Adler Mannheim	Germany	49	1	3	4	87										3	0	0	0	0				
2003-04	Adler Mannheim	Germany	46	5	12	17	58										4	0	0	0	0				
2004-05	Adler Mannheim	Germany	39	1	4	5	67										10	2	4	6	*64				
2005-06	Hannover	Germany	50	17	13	30	164																		
	Germany	Olympics	5	0	0	0	10																		
	NHL Totals		22	0	0	0	4	0	0	0	11	0.0		0	0.0	10:50									

Traded to **Tampa Bay** by **New Jersey** with Josef Boumedienne and the rights to Anton But for Andrei Zyuzin, November 9, 2001. Signed as a free agent by **Mannheim** (Germany), April 23, 2002.

GODARD, Eric (GAW-duhrd, AIR-ihk) CGY

Right wing. Shoots right. 6'4", 220 lbs. Born, Vernon, B.C., March 7, 1980.

Season	Club	League	GP	G	A	Pts	PIM	PP	SH	GW	S	%	+/-	TF	F%	Min	GP	G	A	Pts	PIM	PP	SH	GW	Min
1997-98	Lethbridge	WHL	7	0	0	0	26										2	0	0	0	0				
1998-99	Lethbridge	WHL	66	2	5	7	213										4	0	0	0	14				
99-2000	Lethbridge	WHL	60	3	5	8	*310																		
	Louisville Panthers	AHL	4	0	1	1	16																		
2000-01	Louisville Panthers	AHL	45	0	0	0	132																		
2001-02	Bridgeport	AHL	67	1	4	5	198										20	0	4	4	30				
2002-03	**NY Islanders**	NHL	19	0	0	0	48	0	0	0	6	0.0	−3	0	0.0	4:32	2	0	1	1	4				
	Bridgeport	AHL	46	2	2	4	199										6	0	0	0	1				
2003-04	**NY Islanders**	NHL	31	0	1	1	97	0	0	0	5	0.0	−2	1	0.0	3:46									
	Bridgeport	AHL	7	0	0	0	13																		
2004-05	Bridgeport	AHL	75	7	11	18	295																		
2005-06	**NY Islanders**	NHL	57	2	2	4	115	0	0	0	17	11.8	−2	1	0.0	3:34									
	NHL Totals		107	2	3	5	260	0	0	0	28	7.1		2	0.0	3:48	2	0							

Signed as a free agent by **Florida**, September 24, 1999. Traded to **NY Islanders** by **Florida** for Florida's 3rd round choice (previously acquired, Florida selected Gr... 22, 2002. • Spent majority of 2003-04 season as a healthy reserve. Signed as a free agent by **Calgary**, August 14, 2006.

GOERTZEN, Steven

Right wing. Shoots right. 6'1", 216 lbs. Born, Stony Plain, Alta., May 26, 1984. Columbus' 11th choice, 225th overall, i...

Season	Club	League	GP	G	A	Pts	PIM	PP	SH	GW	S	%	+/-	TF	F%	Min	GP	G	A	Pts	PIM	PP	SH	GW	Min
99-2000	Spruce Grove	AMBHL	36	16	17	33	30																		
2000-01	St. Albert Raiders	AMHL	34	11	19	30	70																		
	St. Albert Saints	AJHL	1	0	0	0	0																		
2001-02	Seattle	WHL	66	6	9	15	45																		
2002-03	Seattle	WHL	71	12	19	31	95																		
2003-04	Seattle	WHL	69	15	18	33	115																		
	Syracuse Crunch	AHL	8	0	3	3	4																		
2004-05	Syracuse Crunch	AHL	57	2	7	9	100																		
2005-06	**Columbus**	NHL	39	0	0	0	44	0	0	0	23	0.0	−17	11	54.6	8:32									
	Syracuse Crunch	AHL	40	7	8	15	55																		
	NHL Totals		39	0	0	0	44	0	0	0	23	0.0		11	54.5	8:32									

GOMEZ, Scott

Center. Shoots left. 5'11", 200 lbs. Born, Anchorage, AK, December 23, 1979. New Jersey's 2nd choice, 27th overall, in...

Season	Club	League	GP	G	A	Pts	PIM	PP	SH	GW	S	%	+/-	TF	F%	Min	GP	G	A	Pts	PIM	PP	SH	GW	Min
1994-95	East	High-AK	28	30	48	78	....																		
1995-96	East	High-AK	27	*56	49	*101	....																		
	Anchorage	AAHL	40	*70	*67	*137	44																		
1996-97	South Surrey	BCHL	56	48	76	124	94																		
1997-98	Tri-City	WHL	45	12	37	49	57																		
1998-99	Tri-City	WHL	58	30	*78	108	55																		

Season	Club	League	GP	G	A	Pts	PIM	PP	SH	GW	S	%	+/-	TF	F%	Min	GP	G	A	Pts	PIM	PP	SH	GW	Min
												Regular Season										**Playoffs**			
99-2000♦	New Jersey	NHL	82	19	51	70	78	7	0	1	204	9.3	14	341	44.6	16:21	23	4	6	10	4	1	0	2	14:08
2000-01	New Jersey	NHL	76	14	49	63	46	2	0	4	155	9.0	-1	1010	44.6	15:46	25	5	9	14	24	0	0	0	16:06
2001-02	New Jersey	NHL	76	10	38	48	36	1	0	1	156	6.4	-4	628	48.7	16:46									
2002-03♦	New Jersey	NHL	80	13	42	55	48	2	0	4	205	6.3	17	864	47.5	16:01	24	3	9	12	2	0	0	0	13:45
2003-04	New Jersey	NHL	80	14	*56	70	70	3	0	1	189	7.4	18	1129	46.2	16:00	5	0	6	6	0	0	0	0	17:14
2004-05	Alaska Aces	ECHL	61	13	*73	*86	69										4	1	3	4	4				
2005-06	New Jersey	NHL	82	33	51	84	42	9	0	5	244	13.5	8	1434	52.6	18:47	9	5	4	9	6	4	0	1	18:14
	United States	Olympics	6	1	4	5	10																		
	NHL Totals		476	103	287	390	320	24	0	16	1153	8.9		5406	48.0	16:38	86	17	34	51	36	5	0	3	15:12

WHL West First All-Star Team (1999) • NHL All-Rookie Team (2000) • Calder Memorial Trophy (2000) • ECHL First All-Star Team (2005) • ECHL MVP (2005)
Played in NHL All-Star Game (2000)
Signed as a free agent by **Alaska** (ECHL), October 25, 2004.

GONCHAR, Sergei
(gohn-CHAR, SAIR-gay) **PIT.**

Defense. Shoots left. 6'2", 215 lbs. Born, Chelyabinsk, USSR, April 13, 1974. Washington's 1st choice, 14th overall, in 1992 Entry Draft.

Season	Club	League	GP	G	A	Pts	PIM	PP	SH	GW	S	%	+/-	TF	F%	Min	GP	G	A	Pts	PIM	PP	SH	GW	Min
1991-92	Chelyabinsk	CIS	31	1	0	1	6																		
1992-93	Dynamo Moscow	CIS	31	1	3	4	70										10	0	0	0	12				
1993-94	Dynamo Moscow	CIS	44	4	5	9	36										10	0	3	3	14				
	Portland Pirates	AHL															2	0	0	0	0				
1994-95	Portland Pirates	AHL	61	10	32	42	67																		
	Washington	NHL	31	2	5	7	22	0	0	0	38	5.3	4				7	2	2	4	2	0	0	1	
1995-96	**Washington**	NHL	78	15	26	41	60	4	0	4	139	10.8	25				6	2	4	6	4	1	0	0	
1996-97	**Washington**	NHL	57	13	17	30	36	3	0	3	129	10.1	-11												
1997-98	Lada Togliatti	Russia	7	3	2	5	4																		
	Lada Togliatti	EuroHL	1	1	0	1	2																		
	Washington	NHL	72	5	16	21	66	2	0	0	134	3.7	2				21	7	4	11	30	3	1	2	
	Russia	Olympics	6	0	2	2	0																		
1998-99	**Washington**	NHL	53	21	10	31	57	13	1	3	180	11.7	1												
99-2000	**Washington**	NHL	73	18	36	54	52	5	0	3	181	9.9	26	0	0.0	23:55	5	1	0	1	6	0	0	0	19:58
2000-01	**Washington**	NHL	76	19	38	57	70	8	0	2	241	7.9	12	1100		22:26	6	1	3	4	2	1	0	0	19:45
2001-02	**Washington**	NHL	76	26	33	59	58	7	0	2	216	12.0	-1	1100		23:51									
	Russia	Olympics	6	0	0	0	2																		
2002-03	**Washington**	NHL	82	18	49	67	52	7	0	2	224	8.0	13	0	0.0	26:35	6	0	5	5	4	0	0	0	29:00
2003-04	**Washington**	NHL	56	7	42	49	44	4	0	0	127	5.5	-20	0	0.0	27:57									
	Boston	NHL	15	4	5	9	12	2	0	0	34	11.8	6	0	0.0	25:32	7	1	4	5	4	1	0	1	27:51
2004-05	Magnitogorsk	Russia	40	2	17	19	54										4	1	1	2	6				
2005-06	**Pittsburgh**	NHL	75	12	46	58	100	8	0	2	192	6.3	-13	0	0.0	24:40									
	Russia	Olympics	8	0	2	2	8																		
	NHL Totals		744	160	323	483	629	63	1	21	1835	8.7		2100.0		24:25	58	14	22	36	52	6	1	4	24:28

NHL Second All-Star Team (2002, 2003)
Played in NHL All-Star Game (2001, 2002, 2003)
Traded to **Boston** by **Washington** for Shaonne Morrisonn and Boston's 1st (Jeff Schultz) and 2nd (Michail Yunkov) round choices in 2004 Entry Draft, March 3, 2004. Signed as a free agent by **Magnitogorsk** (Russia), September 21, 2004. Signed as a free agent by **Pittsburgh**, August 3, 2005.

GORDON, Boyd
(GOHR-duhn, BOYD) **WSH.**

Right wing. Shoots right. 6'1", 201 lbs. Born, Unity, Sask., October 19, 1983. Washington's 3rd choice, 17th overall, in 2002 Entry Draft.

Season	Club	League	GP	G	A	Pts	PIM	PP	SH	GW	S	%	+/-	TF	F%	Min	GP	G	A	Pts	PIM	PP	SH	GW	Min
1997-98	Regina Flyers	SMHA	60	70	102	172	53																		
1998-99	Regina Rangers	SMBHL	60	70	102	172	53																		
99-2000	Red Deer Rebels	WHL	66	10	26	36	24										4	0	1	1	16				
2000-01	Red Deer Rebels	WHL	72	12	27	39	39										22	3	6	9	2				
2001-02	Red Deer Rebels	WHL	66	22	29	51	19										23	10	12	22	8				
2002-03	Red Deer Rebels	WHL	56	33	48	81	28										23	8	12	20	14				
2003-04	**Washington**	NHL	41	1	5	6	8	0	0	0	42	2.4	-9	328	43.0	13:11									
	Portland Pirates	AHL	43	5	17	22	16										7	2	1	3	7				
2004-05	Portland Pirates	AHL	80	17	22	39	35																		
2005-06	**Washington**	NHL	25	0	1	1	4	0	0	0	12	0.0	-4	216	46.3	11:40									
	Hershey Bears	AHL	58	16	22	38	23										21	3	5	8	10				
	NHL Totals		66	1	6	7	12	0	0	0	54	1.9		544	44.3	12:37									

WHL East First All-Star Team (2003)

GOREN, Lee
(GOH-rehn, LEE) **VAN.**

Right wing. Shoots right. 6'3", 205 lbs. Born, Winnipeg, Man., December 26, 1977. Boston's 5th choice, 63rd overall, in 1997 Entry Draft.

Season	Club	League	GP	G	A	Pts	PIM	PP	SH	GW	S	%	+/-	TF	F%	Min	GP	G	A	Pts	PIM	PP	SH	GW	Min
1994-95	Wpg. Warriors	MMMHL	31	19	31	50	50																		
1995-96	Minot Top Guns	SJHL	56	25	35	61												12	5	20	25					
	Saskatoon Blades	WHL	2	0	0	0	2																		
1996-97	North Dakota	WCHA		DID NOT PLAY																					
1997-98	North Dakota	WCHA	29	3	13	16	26																		
1998-99	North Dakota	WCHA	38	26	19	45	20																		
99-2000	North Dakota	WCHA	44	*34	29	63	42																		
2000-01	**Boston**	NHL	21	2	0	2	7	1	0	0	9	22.2	-3	21	38.1	4:24									
	Providence Bruins	AHL	54	15	18	33	72										17	5	2	7	11				
2001-02	Providence Bruins	AHL	71	11	26	37	121										2	0	0	0	0				
2002-03	**Boston**	NHL	14	2	1	3	7	2	0	0	15	13.3	-2	0	0.0	8:15	5	0	0	0	5	0	0	0	6:29
	Providence Bruins	AHL	65	32	37	69	106										3	0	1	1	0				
2003-04	**Florida**	NHL	2	0	1	1	0	0	0	0	1	0.0	-4	1100.0		13:20									
	San Antonio	AHL	65	27	22	49	72																		
2004-05	Manitoba Moose	AHL	79	32	30	62	117										14	*10	3	13	23				
2005-06	**Vancouver**	NHL	28	1	2	3	30	0	0	1	37	2.7	-6	9	22.2	7:25									
	Manitoba Moose	AHL	42	22	19	41	84										13	3	7	10	27				
	NHL Totals		65	5	4	9	44	3	0	1	62	8.1		31	35.5	6:48	5	0	0	0	5	0	0	0	6:29

...nd All-Star Team (2000) • NCAA West Second All-American Team (2000) • NCAA Championship All-Tournament Team (2000) • NCAA Championship Tournament MVP (2000)
...ble to play during 1996-97 season by NCAA due to appearance with **Saskatoon** (WHL) in 1995-96 season. Signed as a free agent by **Florida**, July 24, 2003. Signed as a free agent by ...ly 7, 2004.

GORGES, Josh
(GOHR-juhz, JAWSH) **S.J.**

...fense. Shoots left. 6'1", 190 lbs. Born, Kelowna, B.C., August 14, 1984.

Season	Club	League	GP	G	A	Pts	PIM	PP	SH	GW	S	%	+/-	TF	F%	Min	GP	G	A	Pts	PIM	PP	SH	GW	Min
...0-01	Kelowna Rockets	WHL	57	4	6	10	24										6	1	1	2	4				
...-02	Kelowna Rockets	WHL	72	7	34	41	74										15	1	7	8	8				
...03	Kelowna Rockets	WHL	54	11	48	59	76										19	3	17	20	16				
...4	Kelowna Rockets	WHL	62	11	31	42	38										17	2	13	15	6				
	Cleveland Barons	AHL	74	4	8	12	37																		
	San Jose	NHL	49	0	6	6	31	0	0	0	25	0.0	5	0	0.0	17:38	11	0	1	1	4	0	0	0	18:56
	Cleveland Barons	AHL	18	2	3	5	12																		
	NHL Totals		49	0	6	6	31	0	0	0	25	0.0		0	0.0	17:38	11	0	1	1	4	0	0	0	18:56

...am (2003) • WHL West First All-Star Team (2004) • George Parsons Trophy (Memorial Cup Tournament Most Sportsmanlike Player) (2004)
...Jose, September 20, 2002.

GOVE, David — (GOHV, DAYV) — CAR.

Center. Shoots left. 5'9", 190 lbs. Born, Centerville, MA, May 4, 1978.

							Regular Season												Playoffs						
Season	Club	League	GP	G	A	Pts	PIM	PP	SH	GW	S	%	+/-	TF	F%	Min	GP	G	A	Pts	PIM	PP	SH	GW	Min
1997-98	Western Mich.	CCHA	36	8	7	15	8																		
1998-99	Western Mich.	CCHA	33	9	14	23	12																		
99-2000	Western Mich.	CCHA	36	18	28	46	22																		
2000-01	Western Mich.	CCHA	39	22	37	59	16																		
	Orlando	IHL	9	1	1	2	2										1	0	0	0	0				
2001-02	Grand Rapids	AHL	17	2	4	6	8																		
	Johnstown Chiefs	ECHL	54	17	32	49	32										8	1	3	4	4				
2002-03	San Antonio	AHL	72	15	20	35	30										3	0	1	1	4				
	Laredo Bucks	CHL	8	4	12	16	15																		
2003-04	Utah Grizzlies	AHL	75	14	22	36	28																		
2004-05	Providence Bruins	AHL	70	13	18	31	30										17	3	3	6	14				
2005-06	**Carolina**	**NHL**	1	0	1	1	0	0	0	0	0	0.0	2	0	0.0	7:12									
	Lowell	AHL	65	20	26	46	50																		
	NHL Totals		1	0	1	1	0	0	0	0	0	0.0		0	0.0	7:12									

Signed as a free agent by **Carolina**, August 4, 2005.

GRAND-PIERRE, Jean-Luc — (GRAHN pee-AIR, ZHAHN-LOOK)

Defense. Shoots right. 6'3", 223 lbs. Born, Montreal, Que., February 2, 1977. St. Louis' 6th choice, 179th overall, in 1995 Entry Draft.

							Regular Season												Playoffs						
Season	Club	League	GP	G	A	Pts	PIM	PP	SH	GW	S	%	+/-	TF	F%	Min	GP	G	A	Pts	PIM	PP	SH	GW	Min
1992-93	Lac St-Louis Lions	QAAA	1	0	0	0	2																		
1993-94	Beauport	QMJHL	46	1	4	5	27										1	0	0	0	0				
1994-95	Val-d'Or Foreurs	QMJHL	59	10	13	23	126																		
1995-96	Val-d'Or Foreurs	QMJHL	67	13	21	34	209										13	1	4	5	47				
1996-97	Val-d'Or Foreurs	QMJHL	58	9	24	33	186										13	5	8	13	46				
1997-98	Rochester	AHL	75	4	6	10	211										4	0	0	0	2				
1998-99	**Buffalo**	**NHL**	16	0	1	1	17	0	0	0	11	0.0	0	0	0.0	13:36									
	Rochester	AHL	55	5	4	9	90																		
99-2000	**Buffalo**	**NHL**	11	0	0	0	15	0	0	0	11	0.0	-1	0	0.0	15:11	4	0	0	0	.0			0	17:34
	Rochester	AHL	62	5	8	13	124										17	0	1	1	40				
2000-01	**Columbus**	**NHL**	64	1	4	5	73	0	0	0	33	3.0	-6	0	0.0	12:51									
2001-02	**Columbus**	**NHL**	81	2	6	8	90	0	0	0	62	3.2	-28	3	0.0	15:20									
2002-03	**Columbus**	**NHL**	41	1	0	1	64	0	0	0	32	3.1	-6	0	0.0	13:38									
	Syracuse Crunch	AHL	2	1	0	1	6																		
2003-04	**Columbus**	**NHL**	16	0	0	0	12	0	0	0	15	0.0	-3	2	100.0	7:25									
	Atlanta	**NHL**	27	2	2	4	26	0	1	0	19	10.5	-7	1	0.0	15:25									
	Washington	**NHL**	13	1	0	1	14	0	0	0	19	5.3	-2	2	0.0	11:34									
2004-05	IF Troja-Ljungby	Sweden-2	21	2	3	5	69																		
2005-06	Duisburg	Germany	45	10	9	19	176										5	2	2	4	8				
	NHL Totals		269	7	13	20	311	0	1	0	202	3.5		8	25.0	13:44	4	0	0	0		4		0	17:34

Traded to **Buffalo** by **St. Louis** with Ottawa's 2nd round choice (previously acquired, Buffalo selected Cory Sarich) in 1996 Entry Draft and St. Louis' 3rd round choice (Maxim Afinogenov) in 1997 Entry Draft for Yuri Khmylev and Buffalo's 8th round choice (Andrei Podkonicky) in 1996 Entry Draft, March 20, 1996. Traded to **Columbus** by **Buffalo** with Matt Davidson, San Jose's 5th round choice (previously acquired, Columbus selected Tyler Kolarik) in 2000 Entry Draft and Buffalo's 5th round choice (later traded to Calgary – later traded to Detroit – Detroit selected Andreas Jamtin) in 2001 Entry Draft to complete Expansion Draft agreement which had Columbus select Geoff Sanderson and Dwayne Roloson from Buffalo, June 23, 2000. Traded to **Atlanta** by **Columbus** for future considerations, December 31, 2003. Claimed on waivers by **Washington** from **Atlanta**, March 9, 2004. Signed as a free agent by **Troja-Ljungby** (Sweden-2), December 10, 2004. Signed as a free agent by **Duisburg** (Germany), September 2, 2005. Signed as a free agent by **Dusseldorf** (Germany), July 28, 2006.

GRATTON, Chris — (grah-TOHN, KRIHS) — FLA.

Center. Shoots left. 6'4", 220 lbs. Born, Brantford, Ont., July 5, 1975. Tampa Bay's 1st choice, 3rd overall, in 1993 Entry Draft.

							Regular Season												Playoffs						
Season	Club	League	GP	G	A	Pts	PIM	PP	SH	GW	S	%	+/-	TF	F%	Min	GP	G	A	Pts	PIM	PP	SH	GW	Min
1989-90	Brantford Classics	OHA-B	1	0	2	2	2																		
1990-91	Brantford Classics	OHA-B	31	30	30	60	28																		
1991-92	Kingston	OHL	62	27	39	66	37																		
1992-93	Kingston	OHL	58	55	54	109	125										16	11	18	29	42				
1993-94	**Tampa Bay**	**NHL**	84	13	29	42	123	5	1	2	161	8.1	-25												
1994-95	**Tampa Bay**	**NHL**	46	7	20	27	89	2	0	0	91	7.7	-2												
1995-96	**Tampa Bay**	**NHL**	82	17	21	38	105	7	0	5	183	9.3	-13				6	0	2	2	27	0	0	0	
1996-97	**Tampa Bay**	**NHL**	82	30	32	62	201	9	0	4	230	13.0	-28												
1997-98	**Philadelphia**	**NHL**	82	22	40	62	159	5	0	2	182	12.1	11				5	2	0	2	10	0	0		
1998-99	**Philadelphia**	**NHL**	26	1	7	8	41	0	0	0	54	1.9	-8	38	42.1	14:25									
	Tampa Bay	**NHL**	52	7	19	26	102	1	0	1	127	5.5	-20	1032	53.9	18:20									
99-2000	**Tampa Bay**	**NHL**	58	14	27	41	121	4	0	0	168	8.3	-24	1341	55.9	20:03									
	Buffalo	**NHL**	14	1	7	8	15	0	0	0	34	2.9	1	256	54.3	16:40	5	0	1	1	4	0	0		14:56
2000-01	**Buffalo**	**NHL**	82	19	21	40	102	5	0	0	156	12.2	0	1161	57.3	14:37	13	6	4	10	14	2	0	1	12:33
2001-02	**Buffalo**	**NHL**	82	15	24	39	75	1	0	5	139	10.8	0	1297	53.8	14:57									
2002-03	**Buffalo**	**NHL**	66	15	29	44	86	4	0	2	187	8.0	-5	1099	58.9	16:26									
	Phoenix	**NHL**	14	0	1	1	21	0	0	0	28	0.0	-11	231	57.1	17:12									
2003-04	**Phoenix**	**NHL**	68	11	18	29	93	3	0	1	122	9.0	-19	1090	54.4	14:40									
	Colorado	**NHL**	13	2	1	3	18	0	0	0	28	7.1	1	252	57.5	16:55	11	0	0	0	27	0	0	0	12:14
2004-05								DID NOT PLAY																	
2005-06	**Florida**	**NHL**	76	17	22	39	104	4	1	2	135	12.6	6	960	51.3	15:43									
	NHL Totals		927	191	318	509	1455	50	2	28	2025	9.4		8757	55.3	16:08	40	8	7	15	82	2	0	1	12:50

OHL All-Rookie Team (1992) • OHL Rookie of the Year (1992)

Signed as a free agent by **Philadelphia**, August 14, 1997. Traded to **Tampa Bay** by **Philadelphia** with Mike Sillinger for Mikael Renberg and Daymond Langkow, December 12, 1998. Traded to **Buffalo** by **Tampa Bay** with Tampa Bay's 2nd round choice (Derek Roy) in 2001 Entry Draft for Cory Sarich, Wayne Primeau, Brian Holzinger and Buffalo's 3rd round choice (Alexander Kharitonov) in 2000 Entry Draft, March 9, 2000. Traded to **Phoenix** by **Buffalo** with Buffalo's 4th round choice (later traded to Edmonton – Edmonton selected Liam Reddox) in 2004 Entry Draft for Daniel Briere and Phoenix's 3rd round choice (Andrej Sekera) in 2004 Entry Draft, March 10, 2003. Traded to **Colorado** by **Phoenix** with Ossi Vaananen and Phoenix's 2nd round choice (Paul Stastny) in 2005 Entry Draft for Derek Morris and Keith Ballard, March 8, 2004. Signed as a free agent by **Florida**, August 12, 2005.

GRATTON, Josh — (grah-TOHN, JAWSH) — PHX.

Left wing. Shoots left. 6'2", 214 lbs. Born, Brantford, Ont., September 9, 1982.

							Regular Season												Playoffs						
Season	Club	League	GP	G	A	Pts	PIM	PP	SH	GW	S	%	+/-	TF	F%	Min	GP	G	A	Pts	PIM	PP	SH	GW	Min
2000-01	Sudbury Wolves	OHL	44	5	13	18	110										9	1	1	2	25				
2001-02	Sudbury Wolves	OHL	14	5	4	9	47										1	0	1	1	7				
	Kingston	OHL	46	14	14	28	140										6	2	1	3	8				
2002-03	Windsor Spitfires	OHL	62	26	30	56	192										6	1	2	3	8				
2003-04	Cincinnati	AHL	21	2	2	4	69										8	0	0	0	35				
	San Diego Gulls	ECHL	30	4	6	10	239																		
2004-05	Philadelphia	AHL	57	9	5	14	246										21	3	3	6	78				
	Trenton Titans	ECHL	1	0	0	0	0																		
2005-06	**Philadelphia**	**NHL**	3	0	0	0	14	0	0	0	3	0.0	0	0	0.0	5:00									
	Philadelphia	AHL	53	9	10	19	265																		
	Phoenix	**NHL**	11	1	0	1	30	0	0	0	14	7.1	-3	0	0.0	8:00									
	NHL Totals		14	1	0	1	44	0	0	0	17	5.9		0	0.0	7:21									

Signed as a free agent by **Philadelphia**, July 27, 2004. Traded to **Phoenix** by **Philadelphia** with Florida's 2nd round choice (previously acquired, later traded to Detroit - Detroit selected Cory Emerton) in 2006 Entry Draft, Tampa Bay's 2nd round choice (previously acquired, later traded to Detroit - Detroit selected Shawn Matthias) in 2006 Entry Draft for Denis Gauthier, March 9, 2006.

GREBESHKOV, Denis — (greh-behsh-KAHV, DEH-nihs)

Defense. Shoots left. 6'1", 200 lbs. Born, Yaroslavl, USSR, October 11, 1983. Los Angeles' 1st choice, 18th overall, in 2002 Entry Draft.

							Regular Season												Playoffs						
Season	Club	League	GP	G	A	Pts	PIM	PP	SH	GW	S	%	+/-	TF	F%	Min	GP	G	A	Pts	PIM	PP	SH	GW	Min
99-2000	Yaroslavl 2	Russia-3	42	1	2	3	12										6	0	0	0	2				
2000-01	Yaroslavl 2	Russia-3	34	7	2	9	20																		
2001-02	Yaroslavl 2	Russia-3	7	1	1	2	2																		
	Yaroslavl	Russia	27	1	2	3	10																		
2002-03	Yaroslavl	Russia	48	0	7	7	26										10	0	1	1	2				
2003-04	**Los Angeles**	**NHL**	4	0	1	1	0	0	0	0	5	0.0	-4	0	0.0	18:29									
	Manchester	AHL	43	2	7	9	34										6	1	5	6	6				
2004-05	Manchester	AHL	75	5	44	49	87										6	0	4	4	2				

Season	Club	League	GP	G	A	Pts	PIM	PP	SH	GW	S	%	+/-	TF	F%	Min	GP	G	A	Pts	PIM	PP	SH	GW	Min
			Regular Season														Playoffs								
2005-06	Los Angeles	NHL	8	0	2	2	12	0	0	0	10	0.0	-4	0	0.0	15:16	....	....	....	....	....	....	....	....	....
	Manchester	AHL	48	2	25	27	59	....	....	....	....	....	....	....	....	....	....	....	....	....	....	....	....	....	....
	NY Islanders	NHL	21	0	3	3	8	0	0	0	14	0.0	-8	0	0.0	17:11	....	....	....	....	....	....	....	....	....
	Bridgeport	AHL	....	....	....	....	....	....	....	....	....	....	....	....	....	....	7	1	1	2	8	....	....	....	....
	NHL Totals		33	0	6	6	20	0	0	0	29	0.0		0	0.0	16:53	....	....	....	....	....	....	....	....	....

Traded to **NY Islanders** by **Los Angeles** with Jeff Tambellini for Mark Parrish and Brent Sopel, March 8, 2006. Signed as a free agent by **Yaroslavl** (Russia), July 10, 2006.

GREEN, Josh

(GREEN, JAWSH) **VAN.**

Left wing. Shoots left. 6'3", 215 lbs. Born, Camrose, Alta., November 16, 1977. Los Angeles' 1st choice, 30th overall, in 1996 Entry Draft.

Season	Club	League	GP	G	A	Pts	PIM	PP	SH	GW	S	%	+/-	TF	F%	Min	GP	G	A	Pts	PIM	PP	SH	GW	Min
1992-93	Camrose Kodiaks	ABHL	60	55	45	100	80	....	....	....	....	....	....	....	....	....	....	....	....	....	....	....	....	....	....
1993-94	Medicine Hat	WHL	63	22	22	44	43	....	....	....	....	....	....	....	....	....	3	0	0	0	4	....	....	....	....
1994-95	Medicine Hat	WHL	68	32	23	55	64	....	....	....	....	....	....	....	....	....	5	5	1	6	2	....	....	....	....
1995-96	Medicine Hat	WHL	46	18	25	43	55	....	....	....	....	....	....	....	....	....	5	2	2	4	4	....	....	....	....
1996-97	Medicine Hat	WHL	51	25	32	57	61	....	....	....	....	....	....	....	....	....	....	....	....	....	....	....	....	....	....
	Swift Current	WHL	23	10	15	25	33	....	....	....	....	....	....	....	....	....	10	9	7	16	19	....	....	....	....
1997-98	Swift Current	WHL	5	9	1	10	9	....	....	....	....	....	....	....	....	....	....	....	....	....	....	....	....	....	....
	Portland	WHL	26	26	18	44	27	....	....	....	....	....	....	....	....	....	....	....	....	....	....	....	....	....	....
	Fredericton	AHL	43	16	15	31	14	....	....	....	....	....	....	....	....	....	4	1	3	4	6	....	....	....	....
1998-99	Los Angeles	NHL	27	1	3	4	8	1	0	0	35	2.9	-5	2	50.0	11:44	....	....	....	....	....	....	....	....	....
	Springfield	AHL	41	15	15	30	29	....	....	....	....	....	....	....	....	....	....	....	....	....	....	....	....	....	....
99-2000	NY Islanders	NHL	49	12	14	26	41	2	0	3	109	11.0	-7	12	50.0	13:36	....	....	....	....	....	....	....	....	....
	Lowell	AHL	17	6	2	8	19	....	....	....	....	....	....	....	....	....	....	....	....	....	....	....	....	....	....
2000-01	Hamilton	AHL	2	2	0	2	2	....	....	....	....	....	....	....	....	....	....	....	....	....	....	....	....	....	....
	Edmonton	NHL	....	....	....	....	....	....	....	....	....	....	....	....	....	....	3	0	0	0	0	0	0	0	7:55
2001-02	Edmonton	NHL	61	10	5	15	52	1	0	1	78	12.8	9	18	38.9	10:05	....	....	....	....	....	....	....	....	....
2002-03	Edmonton	NHL	20	0	2	2	12	0	0	0	20	0.0	-3	5	0.0	10:22	....	....	....	....	....	....	....	....	....
	NY Rangers	NHL	4	0	0	0	2	0	0	0	3	0.0	-1	0	0.0	9:06	....	....	....	....	....	....	....	....	....
	Washington	NHL	21	1	2	3	7	0	0	0	20	5.0	1	3	0.0	8:07	....	....	....	....	....	....	....	....	....
2003-04	Calgary	NHL	36	2	4	6	24	0	0	0	47	4.3	-3	39	30.8	11:18	....	....	....	....	....	....	....	....	....
	Lowell	AHL	22	6	9	15	46	....	....	....	....	....	....	....	....	....	....	....	....	....	....	....	....	....	....
	NY Rangers	NHL	14	3	2	5	8	0	0	1	29	10.3	0	9	55.6	14:16	....	....	....	....	....	....	....	....	....
2004-05	Manitoba Moose	AHL	67	21	19	40	72	....	....	....	....	....	....	....	....	....	14	9	5	14	26	....	....	....	....
2005-06	Vancouver	NHL	33	4	2	6	14	0	0	0	35	11.4	2	146	40.4	8:35	....	....	....	....	....	....	....	....	....
	Manitoba Moose	AHL	35	7	24	31	33	....	....	....	....	....	....	....	....	....	10	5	5	10	23	....	....	....	....
	NHL Totals		265	33	34	67	168	4	0	5	376	8.8		234	38.5	10:57	3	0	0	0	0	0	0	0	7:55

Traded to **NY Islanders** by **Los Angeles** with Olli Jokinen, Mathieu Biron and Los Angeles' 1st round choice (Taylor Pyatt) in 1999 Entry Draft for Ziggy Palffy, Brian Smolinski, Marcel Cousineau and New Jersey's 4th round choice (previously acquired, Los Angeles selected Daniel Johansson) in 1999 Entry Draft, June 20, 1999. Traded to **Edmonton** by **NY Islanders** with Eric Brewer and NY Islanders' 2nd round choice (Brad Winchester) in 2000 Entry Draft for Roman Hamrlik, June 24, 2000. • Missed majority of 2000-01 season recovering from shoulder injury suffered in game vs. Detroit, October 10, 2000. Traded to **NY Rangers** by **Edmonton** for future considerations, December 12, 2002. Claimed on waivers by **Washington** from **NY Rangers**, January 15, 2003. Signed as a free agent by **Calgary**, July 17, 2003. Claimed on waivers by **NY Rangers** from **Calgary**, March 6, 2004. Signed to a PTO (tryout) contract by **Manitoba** (AHL), September 27, 2004. Signed as a free agent by **Vancouver**, August 23, 2005.

GREEN, Mike

(GREEN, MIGHK) **DAL.**

Center. Shoots right. 5'11", 192 lbs. Born, Calgary, Alta., August 23, 1979.

Season	Club	League	GP	G	A	Pts	PIM	PP	SH	GW	S	%	+/-	TF	F%	Min	GP	G	A	Pts	PIM	PP	SH	GW	Min
1996-97	Cgy. North Stars	AMHL	35	34	27	61	78	....	....	....	....	....	....	....	....	....	....	....	....	....	....	....	....	....	....
	Edmonton Ice	WHL	7	0	2	2	0	....	....	....	....	....	....	....	....	....	....	....	....	....	....	....	....	....	....
1997-98	Edmonton Ice	WHL	71	15	26	41	16	....	....	....	....	....	....	....	....	....	....	....	....	....	....	....	....	....	....
1998-99	Kootenay Ice	WHL	71	35	45	80	37	....	....	....	....	....	....	....	....	....	7	2	2	4	4	....	....	....	....
99-2000	Kootenay Ice	WHL	69	43	49	92	63	....	....	....	....	....	....	....	....	....	21	9	16	25	20	....	....	....	....
2000-01	Port Huron	UHL	11	1	5	6	6	....	....	....	....	....	....	....	....	....	....	....	....	....	....	....	....	....	....
	Louisville Panthers	AHL	24	2	1	3	4	....	....	....	....	....	....	....	....	....	....	....	....	....	....	....	....	....	....
	Knoxville Speed	UHL	48	18	24	42	35	....	....	....	....	....	....	....	....	....	1	0	0	0	0	....	....	....	....
2001-02	Macon Whoopee	ECHL	54	27	35	62	18	....	....	....	....	....	....	....	....	....	....	....	....	....	....	....	....	....	....
	Cincinnati	AHL	22	2	9	11	4	....	....	....	....	....	....	....	....	....	3	0	0	0	0	....	....	....	....
2002-03	San Antonio	AHL	80	26	34	60	25	....	....	....	....	....	....	....	....	....	3	0	2	2	0	....	....	....	....
2003-04	Florida	NHL	11	0	1	1	2	0	0	0	7	0.0	0	42	47.6	8:16	....	....	....	....	....	....	....	....	....
	San Antonio	AHL	45	12	23	35	16	....	....	....	....	....	....	....	....	....	....	....	....	....	....	....	....	....	....
	NY Rangers	NHL	13	1	2	3	2	0	0	0	13	7.7	0	98	39.8	9:53	....	....	....	....	....	....	....	....	....
2004-05	Nurnberg	Germany	44	11	17	28	38	....	....	....	....	....	....	....	....	....	6	1	3	4	0	....	....	....	....
2005-06	Hannover	Germany	50	17	26	43	122	....	....	....	....	....	....	....	....	....	9	3	0	3	14	....	....	....	....
	NHL Totals		24	1	3	4	4	0	0	0	20	5.0		140	42.1	9:08	....	....	....	....	....	....	....	....	....

WHL East Second All-Star Team (2000)

Signed as a free agent by **Florida**, April 7, 2000. Claimed on waivers by **NY Rangers** from **Florida**, March 9, 2004. Signed as a free agent by **Nurnberg** (Germany), August 2, 2004. Traded to **Dallas** by **NY Rangers** for a conditional choice in 2008 Entry Draft, June 14, 2006.

GREEN, Mike

(GREEN, MIGHK) **WSH.**

Defense. Shoots right. 6'1", 200 lbs. Born, Calgary, Alta., October 12, 1985. Washington's 3rd choice, 29th overall, in 2004 Entry Draft.

Season	Club	League	GP	G	A	Pts	PIM	PP	SH	GW	S	%	+/-	TF	F%	Min	GP	G	A	Pts	PIM	PP	SH	GW	Min
2000-01	Cgy. North Stars	AMHL	36	4	23	27	34	....	....	....	....	....	....	....	....	....	....	....	....	....	....	....	....	....	....
	Saskatoon Blades	WHL	7	0	2	2	0	....	....	....	....	....	....	....	....	....	....	....	....	....	....	....	....	....	....
2001-02	Saskatoon Blades	WHL	62	3	20	23	57	....	....	....	....	....	....	....	....	....	7	0	1	1	2	....	....	....	....
2002-03	Saskatoon Blades	WHL	72	6	36	42	70	....	....	....	....	....	....	....	....	....	6	0	2	2	6	....	....	....	....
2003-04	Saskatoon Blades	WHL	59	14	25	39	92	....	....	....	....	....	....	....	....	....	....	....	....	....	....	....	....	....	....
2004-05	Saskatoon Blades	WHL	67	14	52	66	105	....	....	....	....	....	....	....	....	....	4	0	0	0	6	....	....	....	....
2005-06	Washington	NHL	22	1	2	3	18	0	0	0	13	7.7	-8	0	0.0	14:54	....	....	....	....	....	....	....	....	....
	Hershey Bears	AHL	56	9	34	43	79	....	....	....	....	....	....	....	....	....	21	3	15	18	30	....	....	....	....
	NHL Totals		22	1	2	3	18	0	0	0	13	7.7		0	0.0	14:54	....	....	....	....	....	....	....	....	....

WHL East First All-Star Team (2005) • AHL All-Rookie Team (2006)

GREEN, Travis

(GREEN, TRA-vihs) **ANA.**

Center. Shoots right. 6'2", 200 lbs. Born, Castlegar, B.C., December 20, 1970. NY Islanders' 2nd choice, 23rd overall, in 1989 Entry Draft.

Season	Club	League	GP	G	A	Pts	PIM	PP	SH	GW	S	%	+/-	TF	F%	Min	GP	G	A	Pts	PIM	PP	SH	GW	Min
1985-86	Castlegar Rebels	KIJHL	35	30	40	70	41	....	....	....	....	....	....	....	....	....	....	....	....	....	....	....	....	....	....
1986-87	Spokane Chiefs	WHL	64	8	17	25	27	....	....	....	....	....	....	....	....	....	3	0	0	0	0	....	....	....	....
1987-88	Spokane Chiefs	WHL	72	33	54	87	42	....	....	....	....	....	....	....	....	....	15	10	10	20	13	....	....	....	....
1988-89	Spokane Chiefs	WHL	75	51	51	102	79	....	....	....	....	....	....	....	....	....	....	....	....	....	....	....	....	....	....
1989-90	Spokane Chiefs	WHL	50	45	44	89	80	....	....	....	....	....	....	....	....	....	....	....	....	....	....	....	....	....	....
	Medicine Hat	WHL	25	15	24	39	19	....	....	....	....	....	....	....	....	....	3	0	0	0	2	....	....	....	....
1990-91	Capital District	AHL	73	21	34	55	26	....	....	....	....	....	....	....	....	....	....	....	....	....	....	....	....	....	....
1991-92	Capital District	AHL	71	23	27	50	10	....	....	....	....	....	....	....	....	....	7	0	4	4	21	....	....	....	....
1992-93	NY Islanders	NHL	61	7	18	25	43	1	0	0	115	6.1	4	....	....	....	12	3	1	4	6	0	0	0	....
	Capital District	AHL	20	12	11	23	39	....	....	....	....	....	....	....	....	....	....	....	....	....	....	....	....	....	....
1993-94	NY Islanders	NHL	83	18	22	40	44	1	0	2	164	11.0	16	....	....	....	4	0	0	0	2	0	0	0	....
1994-95	NY Islanders	NHL	42	5	7	12	25	0	0	0	59	8.5	-10	....	....	....	....	....	....	....	....	....	....	....	....
1995-96	NY Islanders	NHL	69	25	45	70	42	14	1	2	186	13.4	-20	....	....	....	....	....	....	....	....	....	....	....	....
1996-97	NY Islanders	NHL	79	23	41	64	38	10	0	3	177	13.0	-5	....	....	....	....	....	....	....	....	....	....	....	....
1997-98	NY Islanders	NHL	54	14	12	26	66	8	0	2	99	14.1	-19	....	....	....	....	....	....	....	....	....	....	....	....
	Anaheim	NHL	22	5	11	16	16	1	0	0	42	11.9	-10	....	....	....	....	....	....	....	....	....	....	....	....
1998-99	Anaheim	NHL	79	13	17	30	81	3	1	2	165	7.9	-7	1325	52.8	17:17	4	0	1	1	4	0	0	0	15:02
99-2000	Phoenix	NHL	78	25	21	46	45	6	0	2	157	15.9	-4	1322	55.6	16:36	5	2	1	3	2	0	0	0	17:23
2000-01	Phoenix	NHL	69	13	15	28	63	3	0	0	113	11.5	-11	1135	54.9	16:45	....	....	....	....	....	....	....	....	....
2001-02	Toronto	NHL	82	11	23	34	61	3	0	2	119	9.2	13	647	54.1	14:32	20	3	6	9	34	0	0	1	20:34
2002-03	Toronto	NHL	75	12	12	24	67	2	1	3	86	14.0	2	802	53.5	12:57	4	2	1	3	4	0	1	1	18:08
2003-04	Boston	NHL	64	11	5	16	67	2	0	2	104	10.6	-6	845	55.6	15:17	7	0	1	1	8	0	0	0	15:37

			Regular Season														Playoffs								
Season	Club	League	GP	G	A	Pts	PIM	PP	SH	GW	S	%	+/-	TF	F%	Min	GP	G	A	Pts	PIM	PP	SH	GW	Min
2004-05		DID NOT PLAY																							
2005-06	**Boston**	**NHL**	**82**	**10**	**12**	**22**	**79**	**0**	**2**	**1**	**118**	**8.5**	**–2**	**976**	**54.4**	**15:04**	....	....	....	....	....	....	....	....	....
	NHL Totals		**939**	**192**	**261**	**453**	**737**	**54**	**5**	**21**	**1704**	**11.3**		**7052**	**54.4**	**15:24**	**56**	**10**	**11**	**21**	**60**	**0**	**1**	**2**	**18:30**

Traded to **Anaheim** by **NY Islanders** with Doug Houda and Tony Tuzzolino for Joe Sacco, J.J. Daigneault and Mark Janssens, February 6, 1998. Traded to **Phoenix** by **Anaheim** with Anaheim's 1st round choice (Scott Kelman) in 1999 Entry Draft for Oleg Tverdovsky, June 26, 1999. Traded to **Toronto** by **Phoenix** with Robert Reichel and Craig Mills for Danny Markov, June 12, 2001. Claimed by **Columbus** from **Toronto** in Waiver Draft, October 3, 2003. Traded to **Boston** by **Columbus** for Boston's 6th round choice (Lennart Petrell) in 2004 Entry Draft, October 3, 2003. Signed as a free agent by **Anaheim**, August 10, 2006.

GREENE, Matt
(GREEN, MAT) **EDM.**

Defense. Shoots right. 6'3", 223 lbs. Born, Grand Ledge, MI, May 13, 1983. Edmonton's 4th choice, 44th overall, in 2002 Entry Draft.

Season	Club	League	GP	G	A	Pts	PIM	PP	SH	GW	S	%	+/-	TF	F%	Min	GP	G	A	Pts	PIM	PP	SH	GW	Min
2000-01	USNTDP	U-18	34	0	9	9	8	....	....	....	....	....	....	....	....	....	....	....	....	....	....	....	....	....	....
	USNTDP	USHL	20	0	1	1	51	....	....	....	....	....	....	....	....	....	....	....	....	....	....	....	....	....	....
2001-02	Green Bay	USHL	55	4	20	24	150	....	....	....	....	....	....	....	....	....	7	0	1	1	31	....	....	....	....
2002-03	North Dakota	WCHA	39	0	4	4	*135	....	....	....	....	....	....	....	....	....	....	....	....	....	....	....	....	....	....
2003-04	North Dakota	WCHA	40	1	16	17	86	....	....	....	....	....	....	....	....	....	....	....	....	....	....	....	....	....	....
2004-05	North Dakota	WCHA	43	2	8	10	*126	....	....	....	....	....	....	....	....	....	....	....	....	....	....	....	....	....	....
2005-06	**Edmonton**	**NHL**	**27**	**0**	**2**	**2**	**43**	**0**	**0**	**0**	**10**	**0.0**	**–6**	**0**	**0.0**	**11:13**	**18**	**0**	**1**	**1**	**34**	**0**	**0**	**0**	**10:03**
	Iowa Stars	AHL	26	2	5	7	47	....	....	....	....	....	....	....	....	....	....	....	....	....	....	....	....	....	....
	NHL Totals		**27**	**0**	**2**	**2**	**43**	**0**	**0**	**0**	**10**	**0.0**		**0**	**0.0**	**11:13**	**18**	**0**	**1**	**1**	**34**	**0**	**0**	**0**	**10:03**

USHL Second All-Star Team (2002)

GRENIER, Martin
(GREH-nyay, MAHR-tihn) **PHI.**

Defense. Shoots left. 6'5", 255 lbs. Born, Laval, Que., November 2, 1980. Colorado's 2nd choice, 45th overall, in 1999 Entry Draft.

Season	Club	League	GP	G	A	Pts	PIM	PP	SH	GW	S	%	+/-	TF	F%	Min	GP	G	A	Pts	PIM	PP	SH	GW	Min
1996-97	Laval-Laurentides	QAAA	34	3	16	19	117	....	....	....	....	....	....	....	....	....	13	0	4	4	....	....	....	....	....
1997-98	Quebec Remparts	QMJHL	61	4	11	15	202	....	....	....	....	....	....	....	....	....	14	0	2	2	36	....	....	....	....
1998-99	Quebec Remparts	QMJHL	60	7	18	25	*479	....	....	....	....	....	....	....	....	....	13	0	4	4	29	....	....	....	....
99-2000	Quebec Remparts	QMJHL	67	11	35	46	302	....	....	....	....	....	....	....	....	....	7	1	4	5	27	....	....	....	....
2000-01	Quebec Remparts	QMJHL	26	5	16	21	82	....	....	....	....	....	....	....	....	....	....	....	....	....	....	....	....	....	....
	Victoriaville Tigres	QMJHL	28	9	19	28	108	....	....	....	....	....	....	....	....	....	13	2	8	10	51	....	....	....	....
2001-02	**Phoenix**	**NHL**	**5**	**0**	**0**	**0**	**5**	**0**	**0**	**0**	**1**	**0.0**	**0**	**1**	**100.0**	**5:56**	....	....	....	....	....	....	....	....	....
	Springfield	AHL	69	2	6	8	241	....	....	....	....	....	....	....	....	....	....	....	....	....	....	....	....	....	....
2002-03	**Phoenix**	**NHL**	**3**	**0**	**0**	**0**	**0**	**0**	**0**	**0**	**0**	**0.0**	**–1**	**0**	**0.0**	**6:11**	....	....	....	....	....	....	....	....	....
	Springfield	AHL	73	2	10	12	232	....	....	....	....	....	....	....	....	....	6	0	1	1	12	....	....	....	....
2003-04	**Vancouver**	**NHL**	**7**	**1**	**0**	**1**	**9**	**0**	**0**	**0**	**6**	**16.7**	**3**	**0**	**0.0**	**6:50**	....	....	....	....	....	....	....	....	....
	Manitoba Moose	AHL	38	5	4	9	145	....	....	....	....	....	....	....	....	....	....	....	....	....	....	....	....	....	....
	Hartford	AHL	12	0	2	2	105	....	....	....	....	....	....	....	....	....	9	0	1	1	32	....	....	....	....
2004-05	Charlotte	ECHL	4	0	2	2	10	....	....	....	....	....	....	....	....	....	....	....	....	....	....	....	....	....	....
	Hartford	AHL	23	2	5	7	136	....	....	....	....	....	....	....	....	....	5	0	0	0	32	....	....	....	....
2005-06	Hartford	AHL	76	4	8	12	278	....	....	....	....	....	....	....	....	....	11	0	0	0	33	....	....	....	....
	NHL Totals		**15**	**1**	**0**	**1**	**14**	**0**	**0**	**0**	**7**	**14.3**		**1**	**100.0**	**6:24**	....	....	....	....	....	....	....	....	....

Traded to **Boston** by **Colorado** with Brian Rolston, Samuel Pahlsson and New Jersey's 1st round choice (previously acquired, Boston selected Martin Samuelsson) in 2000 Entry Draft for Raymond Bourque and Dave Andreychuk, March 6, 2000. Signed as a free agent by **Phoenix**, June 27, 2001. Traded to **Vancouver** by **Phoenix** for Bryan Helmer, July 25, 2003. Traded to **NY Rangers** by **Vancouver** with R.J. Umberger for Martin Rucinsky, March 9, 2004. Signed as a free agent by **Philadelphia**, July 13, 2006.

GRIER, Mike
(GREER, MIGHK) **S.J.**

Right wing. Shoots right. 6'1", 227 lbs. Born, Detroit, MI, January 5, 1975. St. Louis' 7th choice, 219th overall, in 1993 Entry Draft.

Season	Club	League	GP	G	A	Pts	PIM	PP	SH	GW	S	%	+/-	TF	F%	Min	GP	G	A	Pts	PIM	PP	SH	GW	Min
1992-93	St. Sebastian's	High-MA	22	16	27	43	32	....	....	....	....	....	....	....	....	....	....	....	....	....	....	....	....	....	....
1993-94	Boston University	H-East	39	9	9	18	56	....	....	....	....	....	....	....	....	....	....	....	....	....	....	....	....	....	....
1994-95	Boston University	H-East	37	*29	26	55	85	....	....	....	....	....	....	....	....	....	....	....	....	....	....	....	....	....	....
1995-96	Boston University	H-East	38	21	25	46	82	....	....	....	....	....	....	....	....	....	....	....	....	....	....	....	....	....	....
1996-97	**Edmonton**	**NHL**	**79**	**15**	**17**	**32**	**45**	**4**	**0**	**2**	**89**	**16.9**	**7**	....	....	....	**12**	**3**	**1**	**4**	**4**	**1**	**0**	**1**	....
1997-98	**Edmonton**	**NHL**	**66**	**9**	**6**	**15**	**73**	**1**	**0**	**1**	**90**	**10.0**	**–3**	....	....	....	**12**	**2**	**2**	**4**	**13**	**0**	**0**	**1**	....
1998-99	**Edmonton**	**NHL**	**82**	**20**	**24**	**44**	**54**	**3**	**2**	**1**	**143**	**14.0**	**5**	**34**	**20.6**	**15:57**	**4**	**1**	**1**	**2**	**6**	**0**	**0**	**0**	**23:26**
99-2000	**Edmonton**	**NHL**	**65**	**9**	**22**	**31**	**68**	**0**	**3**	**2**	**115**	**7.8**	**9**	**32**	**46.8**	**15:45**	....	....	....	....	....	....	....	....	....
2000-01	**Edmonton**	**NHL**	**74**	**20**	**16**	**36**	**20**	**2**	**3**	**2**	**124**	**16.1**	**11**	**36**	**38.9**	**16:44**	**6**	**0**	**0**	**0**	**8**	**0**	**0**	**0**	**21:23**
2001-02	**Edmonton**	**NHL**	**82**	**8**	**17**	**25**	**32**	**0**	**2**	**3**	**112**	**7.1**	**1**	**38**	**47.4**	**15:01**	....	....	....	....	....	....	....	....	....
2002-03	**Washington**	**NHL**	**82**	**15**	**17**	**32**	**36**	**2**	**2**	**2**	**133**	**11.3**	**–14**	**98**	**43.9**	**17:48**	**6**	**1**	**1**	**2**	**2**	**0**	**0**	**0**	**17:59**
2003-04	**Washington**	**NHL**	**68**	**8**	**12**	**20**	**32**	**1**	**1**	**0**	**115**	**7.0**	**–19**	**54**	**44.4**	**17:25**	....	....	....	....	....	....	....	....	....
	Buffalo	**NHL**	**14**	**1**	**8**	**9**	**4**	**0**	**0**	**0**	**18**	**5.6**	**10**	**11**	**63.6**	**17:29**	....	....	....	....	....	....	....	....	....
2004-05		DID NOT PLAY																							
2005-06	**Buffalo**	**NHL**	**81**	**7**	**16**	**23**	**28**	**0**	**0**	**4**	**109**	**6.4**	**–7**	**9**	**22.2**	**14:22**	**18**	**3**	**5**	**8**	**2**	**0**	**1**	**0**	**16:17**
	NHL Totals		**693**	**112**	**155**	**267**	**392**	**13**	**13**	**17**	**1048**	**10.7**		**312**	**41.7**	**16:09**	**58**	**10**	**10**	**20**	**35**	**1**	**1**	**2**	**18:19**

Hockey East First All-Star Team (1995) • NCAA East First All-American Team (1995)

Rights traded to **Edmonton** by **St. Louis** with Curtis Joseph for St. Louis' 1st round choices in 1996 (previously acquired, St. Louis selected Marty Reasoner) and 1997 (previously acquired, later traded to Los Angeles – Los Angeles selected Matt Zultek) Entry Drafts, August 4, 1995. Traded to **Washington** by **Edmonton** for Washington's 2nd round choice (later traded to NY Islanders – NY Islanders selected Evgeni Tunik) in 2003 Entry Draft and Vancouver's 3rd round choice (previously acquired, Edmonton selected Zachery Stortini) in 2003 Entry Draft, October 7, 2002. Traded to **Buffalo** by **Washington** for Jakub Klepis, March 9, 2004. Signed as a free agent by **San Jose**, July 3, 2006.

GUERIN, Bill
(GAIR-ihn, BIHL) **ST.L.**

Right wing. Shoots right. 6'2", 210 lbs. Born, Worcester, MA, November 9, 1970. New Jersey's 1st choice, 5th overall, in 1989 Entry Draft.

Season	Club	League	GP	G	A	Pts	PIM	PP	SH	GW	S	%	+/-	TF	F%	Min	GP	G	A	Pts	PIM	PP	SH	GW	Min
1985-86	Spring. Olympics	NEJHL	48	26	19	45	71	....	....	....	....	....	....	....	....	....	....	....	....	....	....	....	....	....	....
1986-87	Spring. Olympics	NEJHL	32	34	20	54	40	....	....	....	....	....	....	....	....	....	....	....	....	....	....	....	....	....	....
1987-88	Spring. Olympics	NEJHL	38	31	44	75	146	....	....	....	....	....	....	....	....	....	....	....	....	....	....	....	....	....	....
1988-89	Spring. Olympics	NEJHL	31	32	35	67	90	....	....	....	....	....	....	....	....	....	....	....	....	....	....	....	....	....	....
1989-90	Boston College	H-East	39	14	11	25	54	....	....	....	....	....	....	....	....	....	....	....	....	....	....	....	....	....	....
1990-91	Boston College	H-East	38	26	19	45	102	....	....	....	....	....	....	....	....	....	....	....	....	....	....	....	....	....	....
1991-92	United States	Nat-Tm	46	12	15	27	67	....	....	....	....	....	....	....	....	....	....	....	....	....	....	....	....	....	....
	New Jersey	**NHL**	**5**	**0**	**1**	**1**	**9**	**0**	**0**	**0**	**8**	**0.0**	**1**	....	....	....	**6**	**3**	**0**	**3**	**4**	**0**	**0**	**0**	....
	Utica Devils	AHL	22	13	10	23	6	....	....	....	....	....	....	....	....	....	4	1	3	4	14	....	....	....	....
1992-93	**New Jersey**	**NHL**	**65**	**14**	**20**	**34**	**63**	**0**	**0**	**2**	**123**	**11.4**	**14**	....	....	....	**5**	**1**	**1**	**2**	**4**	**0**	**0**	**0**	....
	Utica Devils	AHL	18	10	7	17	47	....	....	....	....	....	....	....	....	....	....	....	....	....	....	....	....	....	....
1993-94	**New Jersey**	**NHL**	**81**	**25**	**19**	**44**	**101**	**2**	**0**	**3**	**195**	**12.8**	**14**	....	....	....	**17**	**2**	**1**	**3**	**35**	**0**	**0**	**1**	....
1994-95♦	**New Jersey**	**NHL**	**48**	**12**	**13**	**25**	**72**	**4**	**0**	**3**	**96**	**12.5**	**6**	....	....	....	**20**	**3**	**8**	**11**	**30**	**1**	**0**	**0**	....
1995-96	**New Jersey**	**NHL**	**80**	**23**	**30**	**53**	**116**	**8**	**0**	**6**	**216**	**10.6**	**7**	....	....	....	....	....	....	....	....	....	....	....	....
1996-97	**New Jersey**	**NHL**	**82**	**29**	**18**	**47**	**95**	**7**	**0**	**9**	**177**	**16.4**	**–2**	....	....	....	**8**	**2**	**1**	**3**	**18**	**1**	**0**	**1**	....
1997-98	**New Jersey**	**NHL**	**19**	**5**	**5**	**10**	**13**	**1**	**0**	**2**	**48**	**10.4**	**0**	....	....	....	....	....	....	....	....	....	....	....	....
	Edmonton	**NHL**	**40**	**13**	**16**	**29**	**80**	**8**	**0**	**2**	**130**	**10.0**	**1**	....	....	....	**12**	**7**	**1**	**8**	**17**	**4**	**0**	**0**	....
	United States	Olympics	4	0	3	3	2	....	....	....	....	....	....	....	....	....	....	....	....	....	....	....	....	....	....
1998-99	**Edmonton**	**NHL**	**80**	**30**	**34**	**64**	**133**	**13**	**0**	**2**	**261**	**11.5**	**7**	**74**	**40.5**	**19:42**	**3**	**0**	**2**	**2**	**2**	**0**	**0**	**0**	**26:14**
99-2000	**Edmonton**	**NHL**	**70**	**24**	**22**	**46**	**123**	**11**	**0**	**2**	**188**	**12.8**	**4**	**13**	**46.2**	**18:01**	**5**	**3**	**2**	**5**	**9**	**1**	**0**	**0**	**17:55**
2000-01	**Edmonton**	**NHL**	**21**	**12**	**10**	**22**	**18**	**4**	**0**	**1**	**64**	**18.8**	**11**	**0**	**0.0**	**19:49**	....	....	....	....	....	....	....	....	....
	Boston	**NHL**	**64**	**28**	**35**	**63**	**122**	**7**	**1**	**4**	**225**	**12.4**	**–4**	**36**	**41.7**	**22:43**	....	....	....	....	....	....	....	....	....
2001-02	**Boston**	**NHL**	**78**	**41**	**25**	**66**	**91**	**10**	**1**	**7**	**355**	**11.5**	**–1**	**17**	**52.9**	**20:45**	**6**	**4**	**2**	**6**	**6**	**3**	**0**	**0**	**21:17**
	United States	Olympics	6	4	0	4	4	....	....	....	....	....	....	....	....	....	....	....	....	....	....	....	....	....	....
2002-03	**Dallas**	**NHL**	**64**	**25**	**25**	**50**	**113**	**11**	**0**	**2**	**229**	**10.9**	**5**	**20**	**25.0**	**18:33**	**4**	**0**	**0**	**0**	**4**	**0**	**0**	**0**	**8:34**
2003-04	**Dallas**	**NHL**	**82**	**34**	**35**	**69**	**109**	**9**	**0**	**10**	**263**	**12.9**	**14**	**16**	**18.8**	**18:42**	**5**	**0**	**1**	**1**	**4**	**0**	**0**	**0**	**20:09**
2004-05		DID NOT PLAY																							
2005-06	**Dallas**	**NHL**	**70**	**13**	**27**	**40**	**115**	**3**	**0**	**2**	**210**	**6.2**	**0**	**16**	**50.0**	**16:25**	**5**	**3**	**1**	**4**	**0**	**1**	**0**	**0**	**16:14**
	United States	Olympics	6	1	0	1	0	....	....	....	....	....	....	....	....	....	....	....	....	....	....	....	....	....	....
	NHL Totals		**949**	**328**	**335**	**663**	**1373**	**98**	**2**	**57**	**2788**	**11.8**		**192**	**39.6**	**19:16**	**96**	**28**	**20**	**48**	**133**	**11**	**0**	**2**	**18:17**

NHL Second All-Star Team (2002)

Played in NHL All-Star Game (2001, 2003, 2004)

Traded to **Edmonton** by **New Jersey** with Valeri Zelepukin for Jason Arnott and Bryan Muir, January 4, 1998. Traded to **Boston** by **Edmonton** for Anson Carter, Boston's 1st (Ales Hemsky) and 2nd (Doug Lynch) round choices in 2001 Entry Draft and future considerations, November 15, 2000. Signed as a free agent by **Dallas**, July 3, 2002. Signed as a free agent by **St. Louis**, July 3, 2006.

GUITE, Ben
(GEE-tay, BEHN) **COL.**

Right wing. Shoots right. 6'1", 211 lbs. Born, Montreal, Que., July 17, 1978. Montreal's 8th choice, 172nd overall, in 1997 Entry Draft.

			Regular Season														Playoffs								
Season	Club	League	GP	G	A	Pts	PIM	PP	SH	GW	S	%	+/-	TF	F%	Min	GP	G	A	Pts	PIM	PP	SH	GW	Min
1994-95	Lac St-Louis Lions	QAAA	40	9	12	21											4	0	0	0	0				
1995-96	Capital District	Exhib.	STATISTICS NOT AVAILABLE																						
1996-97	U. of Maine	H-East	34	7	7	14	21																		
1997-98	U. of Maine	H-East	32	6	12	18	20																		
1998-99	U. of Maine	H-East	40	12	16	28	30																		
99-2000	U. of Maine	H-East	40	22	14	36	36																		
2000-01	Tallahassee	ECHL	68	11	18	29	34																		
2001-02	Bridgeport	AHL	68	12	18	30	39																		
	Cincinnati	AHL	10	2	5	7	4										3	0	0	0	2				
2002-03	Cincinnati	AHL	80	13	16	29	44																		
2003-04	Bridgeport	AHL	79	6	18	24	73										7	0	0	0	6				
2004-05	Providence Bruins	AHL	77	9	15	24	69										17	3	4	7	34				
2005-06	**Boston**	**NHL**	**1**	**0**	**0**	**0**	**0**	0	0	0	2	0.0	0	11	18.2	8:53									
	Providence Bruins	AHL	73	22	30	52	87										6	1	3	4	14				
	NHL Totals		**1**	**0**	**0**	**0**	**0**	0	0	0	2	0.0		11	18.2	8:53									

Signed as a free agent by **NY Islanders**, August, 2001. Traded to **Anaheim** by **NY Islanders** with the rights to Bjorn Mellin for Dave Roche, March 19, 2002. Signed as a free agent by **NY Rangers**, September 16, 2003. Signed as a free agent by **Bridgeport** (AHL), October 10, 2003. Signed to a PTO (tryout) contract by **Providence** (AHL), September 28, 2004. Signed as a free agent by **Boston**, August 15, 2005. Signed as a free agent by **Colorado**, July 12, 2006.

HAGMAN, Niklas
(HAG-muhn, NIHK-las) **DAL.**

Left wing. Shoots left. 6', 200 lbs. Born, Espoo, Finland, December 5, 1979. Florida's 3rd choice, 70th overall, in 1999 Entry Draft.

1995-96	HIFK Helsinki U18	Fin-U18	26	12	21	33	32										4	3	0	3	2				
	HIFK Helsinki Jr.	Fin-Jr.	12	3	1	4	0																		
1996-97	HIFK Helsinki Jr.	Fin-Jr.	30	13	12	25	30																		
	HIFK Helsinki U18	Fin-U18	21	19	12	31	46										4	1	1	2	0				
1997-98	HIFK Helsinki U18	Fin-U18	1	0	1	1	0																		
	HIFK Helsinki Jr.	Fin-Jr.	26	9	5	14	16																		
	HIFK Helsinki	Finland	8	1	0	1	0																		
1998-99	HIFK Helsinki Jr.	Fin-Jr.	15	4	10	14	43																		
	HIFK Helsinki	Finland	17	1	1	2	14																		
	HIFK Helsinki	EuroHL	1	0	1	1	0																		
	Blues Espoo	Finland	14	1	1	2	2										4	1	0	1	0				
99-2000	Karpat Oulu Jr.	Fin-Jr.	4	7	3	10	0																		
	Karpat Oulu	Finland-2	41	17	18	35	12										7	4	2	6	0				
2000-01	Karpat Oulu	Finland	56	28	18	46	32										8	3	1	4	0				
2001-02	**Florida**	**NHL**	**78**	**10**	**18**	**28**	**8**	0	1	2	134	7.5	-6	32	28.1	13:50									
	Finland	Olympics	4	1	2	3	0																		
2002-03	**Florida**	**NHL**	**80**	**8**	**15**	**23**	**20**	2	0	0	132	6.1	-8	17	11.8	13:31									
2003-04	**Florida**	**NHL**	**75**	**10**	**13**	**23**	**22**	0	1	2	122	8.2	-5	19	21.1	14:47									
2004-05	HC Davos	Swiss	44	17	22	39	20										15	10	7	17	6				
2005-06	**Florida**	**NHL**	**30**	**2**	**4**	**6**	**2**	0	0	0	52	3.8	-8	10	10.0	14:00									
	Dallas	**NHL**	**54**	**6**	**9**	**15**	**16**	0	1	0	74	8.1	-2	6	66.7	11:17	**5**	**2**	**1**	**3**	**4**	0	0	1	10:50
	Finland	Olympics	8	0	1	1	2																		
	NHL Totals		**317**	**36**	**59**	**95**	**68**	2	3	4	514	7.0		84	23.8	13:33	**5**	**2**	**1**	**3**	**4**	0	0	1	10:50

Signed as a free agent by **Davos** (Swiss), July 23, 2004. Traded to **Dallas** by **Florida** for Dallas' 7th round choice in 2007 Entry Draft, December 12, 2005.

HAHL, Riku
(HAHL, REE-koo) **COL.**

Center. Shoots left. 6'1", 205 lbs. Born, Hameenlinna, Finland, November 1, 1980. Colorado's 9th choice, 183rd overall, in 1999 Entry Draft.

1996-97	HPK U18	Fin-U18	32	19	24	43	22																		
	HPK Jr.	Fin-Jr.	2	0	1	1	2										6	2	0	2	2				
1997-98	HPK U18	Fin-U18	10	5	14	19	6																		
	HPK Jr.	Fin-Jr.	35	13	6	19	12																		
1998-99	HPK Jr.	Fin-Jr.	7	0	2	2	6										2	0	3	3	0				
	HPK Hameenlinna	Finland	28	0	1	1	0										8	0	0	0	2				
99-2000	HPK Jr.	Fin-Jr.	19	6	10	16	24																		
	HPK Hameenlinna	Finland	50	4	3	7	18										8	0	0	0	2				
2000-01	HPK Jr.	Fin-Jr.	2	1	3	4	0																		
	HPK Hameenlinna	Finland	55	3	9	12	32																		
2001-02	**Colorado**	**NHL**	**22**	**2**	**3**	**5**	**14**	0	0	1	17	11.8	1	94	35.1	9:26	**21**	**1**	**2**	**3**	**0**	0	0	0	7:31
	Hershey Bears	AHL	52	6	17	23	16																		
2002-03	**Colorado**	**NHL**	**42**	**3**	**4**	**7**	**12**	0	0	0	61	4.9	3	69	37.7	11:03	**6**	**0**	**2**	**2**	**2**	0	0	0	13:49
	Hershey Bears	AHL	28	7	7	14	17																		
2003-04	**Colorado**	**NHL**	**28**	**0**	**1**	**1**	**12**	0	0	0	40	0.0	-7	107	41.1	12:17	**7**	**1**	**0**	**1**	**2**	0	0	0	12:08
2004-05	HPK Hameenlinna	Finland	44	8	13	21	12										10	2	6	8	2				
2005-06	HC Davos	Swiss	41	8	17	25	22										14	2	9	11	20				
	NHL Totals		**92**	**5**	**8**	**13**	**38**	0	0	1	118	4.2		270	38.1	11:02	**34**	**2**	**4**	**6**	**4**	0	0	0	9:35

• Missed majority of 2003-04 season recovering from shoulder injury suffered in game vs. Edmonton, October 23, 2003. Signed as a free agent by **Hameenlinna** (Finland), September 15, 2004. Signed as a free agent by **Davos** (Swiss), September 5, 2005.

HAINSEY, Ron
(HAYN-zee, RAWN) **CBJ**

Defense. Shoots left. 6'3", 211 lbs. Born, Bolton, CT, March 24, 1981. Montreal's 1st choice, 13th overall, in 2000 Entry Draft.

1997-98	USNTDP	U-17	18	2	7	9	28																		
	USNTDP	USHL	3	0	0	0	0																		
	USNTDP	NAHL	40	4	7	11	16										5	0	1	1	0				
1998-99	USNTDP	U-18	6	2	1	3	8																		
	USNTDP	USHL	48	5	12	17	45																		
99-2000	U. Mass-Lowell	H-East	30	3	8	11	20																		
2000-01	U. Mass-Lowell	H-East	33	10	26	36	51																		
	Quebec Citadelles	AHL	4	1	0	1	0										1	0	0	0	0				
2001-02	Quebec Citadelles	AHL	63	7	24	31	26										3	0	0	0	0				
2002-03	**Montreal**	**NHL**	**21**	**0**	**0**	**0**	**2**	0	0	0	12	0.0	-1	0	0.0	12:25									
	Hamilton	AHL	33	2	11	13	26										23	1	10	11	20				
2003-04	**Montreal**	**NHL**	**11**	**1**	**1**	**2**	**4**	0	0	0	11	9.1	3	0	0.0	13:15									
	Hamilton	AHL	54	7	24	31	35										10	0	5	5	6				
2004-05	Hamilton	AHL	68	9	14	23	45										4	1	1	2	0				
2005-06	Hamilton	AHL	22	3	14	17	19																		
	Columbus	**NHL**	**55**	**2**	**15**	**17**	**43**	1	0	0	81	2.5	13	1	0.0	17:47									
	NHL Totals		**87**	**3**	**16**	**19**	**49**	1	0	0	104	2.9		1	0.0	15:55									

Hockey East First All-Star Team (2001) • NCAA East Second All-American Team (2001) • AHL All-Rookie Team (2002)

Claimed on waivers by **Columbus** from **Montreal**, November 29, 2005.

HAJT, Chris
(HIGHT, KRIHS)

Defense. Shoots left. 6'3", 206 lbs. Born, Saskatoon, Sask., July 5, 1978. Edmonton's 3rd choice, 32nd overall, in 1996 Entry Draft.

1993-94	Amherst Knights	WNYHA	38	8	20	28	16																		
1994-95	Guelph Storm	OHL	57	1	7	8	35										14	0	2	2	9				
1995-96	Guelph Storm	OHL	63	8	27	35	69										16	0	6	6	13				
1996-97	Guelph Storm	OHL	58	11	15	26	62										18	0	8	8	25				
1997-98	Guelph Storm	OHL	44	2	21	23	46										12	1	5	6	11				
1998-99	Hamilton	AHL	64	0	4	4	36																		
99-2000	Hamilton	AHL	54	0	8	8	30										10	0	2	2	0				
2000-01	**Edmonton**	**NHL**	**1**	**0**	**0**	**0**	**0**	0	0	0	0	0.0	-1	0	0.0	7:38									
	Hamilton	AHL	70	0	10	10	48																		
2001-02	Hamilton	AHL	39	2	3	5	34										15	1	2	3	8				

			Regular Season														Playoffs								
Season	Club	League	GP	G	A	Pts	PIM	PP	SH	GW	S	%	+/-	TF	F%	Min	GP	G	A	Pts	PIM	PP	SH	GW	Min
2002-03	Portland Pirates	AHL	71	11	15	26	61	....	....	....	....	....	....	....	....	....	1	0	0	0	2	....	....	....	....
2003-04	**Washington**	**NHL**	**5**	**0**	**0**	**0**	**2**	**0**	**0**	**0**	**1**	**0.0**	**0**	**0**	**0.0**	**10:44**	....	....	....	....	....	....	....	....	....
	Portland Pirates	AHL	66	3	13	16	53	....	....	....	....	....	....	....	....	....	7	1	2	3	8	....	....	....	....
2004-05	Portland Pirates	AHL	53	3	6	9	16	....	....	....	....	....	....	....	....	....	....	....	....	....	....	....	....	....	....
	Augusta Lynx	ECHL	13	1	4	5	8	....	....	....	....	....	....	....	....	....	....	....	....	....	....	....	....	....	....
2005-06	Lowell	AHL	60	1	12	13	59	....	....	....	....	....	....	....	....	....	....	....	....	....	....	....	....	....	....
	NHL Totals		**6**	**0**	**0**	**0**	**2**	**0**	**0**	**0**	**1**	**0.0**		**0**	**0.0**	**10:13**	....	....	....	....	....	....	....	....	....

OHL Second All-Star Team (1998)

Signed as a free agent by **Washington**, July 23, 2002. Signed as a free agent by **Carolina**, August 16, 2005.

HALE, David

(HAYL, DAY-vihd) **N.J.**

Defense. Shoots left. 6'2", 215 lbs. Born, Colorado Springs, CO, June 18, 1981. New Jersey's 1st choice, 22nd overall, in 2000 Entry Draft.

1997-98	Colorado North	High-CO	25	11	33	44	154	....	....	....	....	....	....	....	....	....	....	....	....	....	....	....	....	....	....
1998-99	Sioux City	USHL	56	3	15	18	127	....	....	....	....	....	....	....	....	....	5	0	0	0	18	....	....	....	....
99-2000	Sioux City	USHL	54	6	18	24	187	....	....	....	....	....	....	....	....	....	5	0	2	2	6	....	....	....	....
2000-01	North Dakota	WCHA	44	4	5	9	79	....	....	....	....	....	....	....	....	....	....	....	....	....	....	....	....	....	....
2001-02	North Dakota	WCHA	34	4	5	9	63	....	....	....	....	....	....	....	....	....	....	....	....	....	....	....	....	....	....
2002-03	North Dakota	WCHA	26	2	6	8	49	....	....	....	....	....	....	....	....	....	....	....	....	....	....	....	....	....	....
2003-04	**New Jersey**	**NHL**	**65**	**0**	**4**	**4**	**72**	**0**	**0**	**0**	**45**	**0.0**	**12**	**0**	**0.0**	**15:01**	**1**	**0**	**0**	**0**	**0**	**0**	**0**	**0**	**8:59**
2004-05	Albany River Rats	AHL	30	2	3	5	39	....	....	....	....	....	....	....	....	....	....	....	....	....	....	....	....	....	....
2005-06	**New Jersey**	**NHL**	**38**	**0**	**4**	**4**	**21**	**0**	**0**	**0**	**19**	**0.0**	**5**	**0**	**0.0**	**12:03**	**8**	**0**	**2**	**2**	**12**	**0**	**0**	**0**	**12:06**
	Albany River Rats	AHL	30	2	5	7	64	....	....	....	....	....	....	....	....	....	....	....	....	....	....	....	....	....	....
	NHL Totals		**103**	**0**	**8**	**8**	**93**	**0**	**0**	**0**	**64**	**0.0**		**0**	**0.0**	**13:55**	**9**	**0**	**2**	**2**	**12**	**0**	**0**	**0**	**11:45**

USHL First All-Star Team (2000)

HALL, Adam

(HAWL, A-duhm) **NYR**

Right wing. Shoots right. 6'3", 210 lbs. Born, Kalamazoo, MI, August 14, 1980. Nashville's 3rd choice, 52nd overall, in 1999 Entry Draft.

1996-97	Bramalea Blues	OPJHL	43	9	14	23	92	....	....	....	....	....	....	....	....	....	....	....	....	....	....	....	....	....	....
1997-98	USNTDP	U-18	29	18	9	27	19	....	....	....	....	....	....	....	....	....	....	....	....	....	....	....	....	....	....
	USNTDP	USHL	21	9	11	20	20	....	....	....	....	....	....	....	....	....	....	....	....	....	....	....	....	....	....
	USNTDP	NAHL	15	12	1	13	20	....	....	....	....	....	....	....	....	....	6	3	2	5	4	....	....	....	....
1998-99	Michigan State	CCHA	36	16	7	23	74	....	....	....	....	....	....	....	....	....	....	....	....	....	....	....	....	....	....
99-2000	Michigan State	CCHA	40	*26	13	39	38	....	....	....	....	....	....	....	....	....	....	....	....	....	....	....	....	....	....
2000-01	Michigan State	CCHA	42	18	12	30	42	....	....	....	....	....	....	....	....	....	....	....	....	....	....	....	....	....	....
2001-02	Michigan State	CCHA	41	19	15	34	36	....	....	....	....	....	....	....	....	....	....	....	....	....	....	....	....	....	....
	Nashville	**NHL**	**1**	**0**	**1**	**1**	**0**	**0**	**0**	**0**	**2**	**0.0**	**0**	**0**	**0.0**	**14:04**	....	....	....	....	....	....	....	....	....
	Milwaukee	AHL	6	2	2	4	4	....	....	....	....	....	....	....	....	....	....	....	....	....	....	....	....	....	....
2002-03	**Nashville**	**NHL**	**79**	**16**	**12**	**28**	**31**	**8**	**0**	**2**	**146**	**11.0**	**-8**	**17**	**52.9**	**14:09**	....	....	....	....	....	....	....	....	....
	Milwaukee	AHL	1	0	0	0	2	....	....	....	....	....	....	....	....	....	....	....	....	....	....	....	....	....	....
2003-04	**Nashville**	**NHL**	**79**	**13**	**14**	**27**	**37**	**6**	**0**	**1**	**151**	**8.6**	**-8**	**348**	**56.3**	**16:14**	**6**	**2**	**1**	**3**	**2**	**0**	**0**	**1**	**18:29**
2004-05	KalPa Kuopio	Finland-2	36	23	17	40	28	....	....	....	....	....	....	....	....	....	9	2	3	5	4	....	....	....	....
2005-06	**Nashville**	**NHL**	**75**	**14**	**15**	**29**	**40**	**10**	**0**	**5**	**122**	**11.5**	**0**	**470**	**48.9**	**16:47**	**5**	**1**	**0**	**1**	**0**	**1**	**0**	**1**	**12:10**
	NHL Totals		**234**	**43**	**42**	**85**	**108**	**24**	**0**	**8**	**421**	**10.2**		**835**	**52.1**	**15:42**	**11**	**3**	**1**	**4**	**2**	**1**	**0**	**2**	**15:37**

CCHA Second All-Star Team (2000)

Signed as a free agent by **Kuopio** (Finland-2), October 11, 2004. Traded to **NY Rangers** by **Nashville** for Dominic Moore, July 19, 2006.

HALPERN, Jeff

(HAL-pehrn, JEHF) **DAL.**

Center. Shoots right. 6', 198 lbs. Born, Potomac, MD, May 3, 1976.

1994-95	Stratford Cullitons	OHA-B	44	29	54	83	43	....	....	....	....	....	....	....	....	....	....	....	....	....	....	....	....	....	....
1995-96	Princeton	ECAC	29	3	11	14	30	....	....	....	....	....	....	....	....	....	....	....	....	....	....	....	....	....	....
1996-97	Princeton	ECAC	33	7	24	31	35	....	....	....	....	....	....	....	....	....	....	....	....	....	....	....	....	....	....
1997-98	Princeton	ECAC	36	*28	25	*53	46	....	....	....	....	....	....	....	....	....	....	....	....	....	....	....	....	....	....
1998-99	Princeton	ECAC	33	*22	22	44	32	....	....	....	....	....	....	....	....	....	....	....	....	....	....	....	....	....	....
	Portland Pirates	AHL	6	2	1	3	4	....	....	....	....	....	....	....	....	....	....	....	....	....	....	....	....	....	....
99-2000	**Washington**	**NHL**	**79**	**18**	**11**	**29**	**39**	**4**	**4**	**1**	**108**	**16.7**	**21**	**812**	**51.1**	**13:14**	**5**	**2**	**1**	**3**	**0**	**1**	**0**	**1**	**15:16**
2000-01	**Washington**	**NHL**	**80**	**21**	**21**	**42**	**60**	**2**	**1**	**5**	**110**	**19.1**	**13**	**1293**	**52.4**	**16:08**	**6**	**2**	**3**	**5**	**17**	**1**	**0**	**1**	**20:01**
2001-02	**Washington**	**NHL**	**48**	**5**	**14**	**19**	**29**	**0**	**0**	**4**	**74**	**6.8**	**-9**	**661**	**56.0**	**15:19**	....	....	....	....	....	....	....	....	....
2002-03	**Washington**	**NHL**	**82**	**13**	**21**	**34**	**88**	**1**	**2**	**2**	**126**	**10.3**	**6**	**1492**	**54.1**	**17:25**	**6**	**0**	**1**	**1**	**2**	**0**	**0**	**0**	**19:59**
2003-04	**Washington**	**NHL**	**79**	**19**	**27**	**46**	**56**	**7**	**0**	**2**	**114**	**16.7**	**-21**	**1509**	**54.3**	**19:03**	....	....	....	....	....	....	....	....	....
2004-05	HC Ajoie	Swiss-2	15	5	12	17	52	....	....	....	....	....	....	....	....	....	....	....	....	....	....	....	....	....	....
	Kloten Flyers	Swiss	9	7	4	11	6	....	....	....	....	....	....	....	....	....	....	....	....	....	....	....	....	....	....
2005-06	**Washington**	**NHL**	**70**	**11**	**33**	**44**	**79**	**6**	**0**	**1**	**151**	**7.3**	**-8**	**1454**	**55.2**	**20:00**	....	....	....	....	....	....	....	....	....
	NHL Totals		**438**	**87**	**127**	**214**	**351**	**20**	**7**	**15**	**683**	**12.7**		**7221**	**53.9**	**16:54**	**17**	**4**	**5**	**9**	**19**	**2**	**0**	**2**	**18:37**

ECAC Second All-Star Team (1998, 1999)

Signed as a free agent by **Washington**, March 29, 1999. Signed as a free agent by **Ajoie** (Swiss-2), October 8, 2004. Signed as a free agent by **Kloten** (Swiss), December 30, 2004. Signed as a free agent by **Dallas**, July 5, 2006.

HAMEL, Denis

(ha-MEHL, deh-NEE) **OTT.**

Left wing. Shoots left. 6'1", 201 lbs. Born, Lachute, Que., May 10, 1977. St. Louis' 5th choice, 153rd overall, in 1995 Entry Draft.

1992-93	Lachute Regents	QAAA	32	18	24	42	....	....	....	....	....	....	....	....	....	....	....	....	....	....	....	....	....	....	....
1993-94	Lac St-Louis Lions	QAAA	28	10	11	21	50	....	....	....	....	....	....	....	....	....	....	....	....	....	....	....	....	....	....
	Abitibi Forestiers	QAAA	15	5	7	12	29	....	....	....	....	....	....	....	....	....	5	0	3	3	16	....	....	....	....
1994-95	Chicoutimi	QMJHL	66	15	12	27	155	....	....	....	....	....	....	....	....	....	12	2	0	2	27	....	....	....	....
1995-96	Chicoutimi	QMJHL	65	40	49	89	199	....	....	....	....	....	....	....	....	....	17	10	14	24	64	....	....	....	....
1996-97	Chicoutimi	QMJHL	70	50	50	100	357	....	....	....	....	....	....	....	....	....	20	15	10	25	58	....	....	....	....
1997-98	Rochester	AHL	74	10	15	25	98	....	....	....	....	....	....	....	....	....	4	1	2	3	0	....	....	....	....
1998-99	Rochester	AHL	74	16	17	33	121	....	....	....	....	....	....	....	....	....	20	3	4	7	10	....	....	....	....
99-2000	**Buffalo**	**NHL**	**3**	**1**	**0**	**1**	**0**	**0**	**0**	**0**	**3**	**33.3**	**-1**	**0**	**0.0**	**9:45**	....	....	....	....	....	....	....	....	....
	Rochester	AHL	76	34	24	58	122	....	....	....	....	....	....	....	....	....	21	6	7	13	49	....	....	....	....
2000-01	**Buffalo**	**NHL**	**41**	**8**	**3**	**11**	**22**	**1**	**1**	**3**	**55**	**14.5**	**-2**	**171**	**33.9**	**10:58**	....	....	....	....	....	....	....	....	....
2001-02	**Buffalo**	**NHL**	**61**	**2**	**6**	**8**	**28**	**0**	**0**	**0**	**80**	**2.5**	**-1**	**94**	**39.4**	**11:00**	....	....	....	....	....	....	....	....	....
2002-03	**Buffalo**	**NHL**	**25**	**2**	**0**	**2**	**17**	**0**	**0**	**1**	**41**	**4.9**	**-4**	**4**	**25.0**	**12:40**	....	....	....	....	....	....	....	....	....
	Rochester	AHL	48	27	20	47	64	....	....	....	....	....	....	....	....	....	3	3	2	5	4	....	....	....	....
2003-04	**Ottawa**	**NHL**	**5**	**0**	**0**	**0**	**0**	**0**	**0**	**0**	**6**	**0.0**	**-3**	**1**	**100.0**	**6:16**	....	....	....	....	....	....	....	....	....
	Binghamton	AHL	78	29	38	67	116	....	....	....	....	....	....	....	....	....	2	0	0	0	2	....	....	....	....
2004-05	Binghamton	AHL	80	39	39	78	75	....	....	....	....	....	....	....	....	....	5	1	0	1	4	....	....	....	....
2005-06	**Ottawa**	**NHL**	**4**	**1**	**0**	**1**	**0**	**0**	**0**	**0**	**9**	**11.1**	**1**	**1**	**0.0**	**9:10**	....	....	....	....	....	....	....	....	....
	Binghamton	AHL	77	*56	35	91	65	....	....	....	....	....	....	....	....	....	....	....	....	....	....	....	....	....	....
	NHL Totals		**139**	**14**	**9**	**23**	**67**	**1**	**1**	**4**	**194**	**7.2**		**271**	**35.8**	**11:02**	....	....	....	....	....	....	....	....	....

QMJHL All-Rookie Team (1995) • AHL First All-Star Team (2004) • Willie Marshall Award (Top Goal-scorer - AHL) (2006) (tied with Don MacLean)

Traded to **Buffalo** by **St. Louis** for Charlie Huddy and Buffalo's 7th round choice (Daniel Corso) in 1996 Entry Draft, March 19, 1996. • Missed majority of 2000-01 season recovering from knee injury suffered in game vs. NY Islanders, January 27, 2001. Signed as a free agent by **Ottawa**, July 5, 2003. Claimed by **Washington** from **Ottawa** in Waiver Draft, October 3, 2003. Traded to **Ottawa** by **Washington** for future considerations, October 5, 2003.

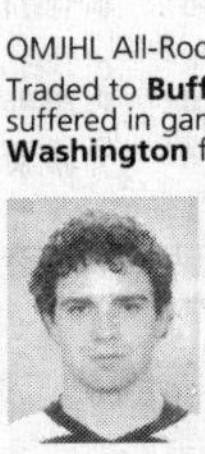

HAMHUIS, Dan

(HAM-yoos, DAN) **NSH.**

Defense. Shoots left. 6'1", 200 lbs. Born, Smithers, B.C., December 13, 1982. Nashville's 1st choice, 12th overall, in 2001 Entry Draft.

1997-98	Smithers A's	BCAHA	59	59	72	131	59	....	....	....	....	....	....	....	....	....	....	....	....	....	....	....	....	....	....
1998-99	Prince George	WHL	56	1	3	4	45	....	....	....	....	....	....	....	....	....	7	1	2	3	8	....	....	....	....
99-2000	Prince George	WHL	70	10	23	33	140	....	....	....	....	....	....	....	....	....	13	2	3	5	35	....	....	....	....
2000-01	Prince George	WHL	62	13	47	60	125	....	....	....	....	....	....	....	....	....	6	2	3	5	15	....	....	....	....
2001-02	Prince George	WHL	59	10	50	60	135	....	....	....	....	....	....	....	....	....	7	0	5	5	16	....	....	....	....
2002-03	Milwaukee	AHL	68	6	21	27	81	....	....	....	....	....	....	....	....	....	6	0	3	3	2	....	....	....	....
2003-04	**Nashville**	**NHL**	**80**	**7**	**19**	**26**	**57**	**2**	**0**	**4**	**115**	**6.1**	**-12**	**0**	**0.0**	**22:08**	**6**	**0**	**2**	**2**	**6**	**0**	**0**	**0**	**20:29**

			Regular Season														Playoffs								
Season	**Club**	**League**	**GP**	**G**	**A**	**Pts**	**PIM**	**PP**	**SH**	**GW**	**S**	**%**	**+/-**	**TF**	**F%**	**Min**	**GP**	**G**	**A**	**Pts**	**PIM**	**PP**	**SH**	**GW**	**Min**
2004-05	Milwaukee	AHL	76	13	38	51	85	....	....	....	....	....	....	....	....	....	7	0	2	2	10	....	....	....	....
2005-06	**Nashville**	**NHL**	82	7	31	38	70	4	1	1	135	5.2	11	0	0.0	22:34	5	0	2	2	2	0	0	0	19:41
	NHL Totals		162	14	50	64	127	6	1	5	250	5.6		0	0.0	22:21	11	0	4	4	8	0	0	0	20:07

WHL West First All-Star Team (2001, 2002) • WHL Player of the Year (2002) • Canadian Major Junior First All-Star Team (2002) • Canadian Major Junior Defenseman of the Year (2002) • AHL Second All-Star Team (2005)

HAMILTON, Jeff

(HAM-ihl-tuhn, JEHF)

Center. Shoots right. 5'10", 180 lbs. Born, Englewood, OH, September 4, 1977.

1995-96	Avon Old Farms	High-CT	24	29	23	52	....	....	....	....	....	....	....	....	....	....	....	....	....	....	....	....	....	....	....
1996-97	Yale	ECAC	31	10	13	23	26	....	....	....	....	....	....	....	....	....	....	....	....	....	....	....	....	....	....
1997-98	Yale	ECAC	33	27	20	47	28	....	....	....	....	....	....	....	....	....	....	....	....	....	....	....	....	....	....
1998-99	Yale	ECAC	30	20	28	48	51	....	....	....	....	....	....	....	....	....	....	....	....	....	....	....	....	....	....
99-2000	Yale	ECAC	2	0	1	1	0	....	....	....	....	....	....	....	....	....	....	....	....	....	....	....	....	....	....
2000-01	Yale	ECAC	31	23	32	55	39	....	....	....	....	....	....	....	....	....	....	....	....	....	....	....	....	....	....
2001-02	Karpat Oulu	Finland	39	18	15	33	16	....	....	....	....	....	....	....	....	....	3	0	0	0	0	....	....	....	....
2002-03	Bridgeport	AHL	67	22	16	38	35	....	....	....	....	....	....	....	....	....	9	3	3	6	0	....	....	....	....
2003-04	**NY Islanders**	**NHL**	1	0	0	0	0	0	0	0	1	0.0	0	0	0.0	10:00	....	....	....	....	....	....	....	....	....
	Bridgeport	AHL	67	*43	25	68	26	....	....	....	....	....	....	....	....	....	7	4	0	4	4	....	....	....	....
2004-05	Hartford	AHL	60	23	30	53	32	....	....	....	....	....	....	....	....	....	6	4	3	7	0	....	....	....	....
2005-06	Ak Bars Kazan	Russia	8	0	1	1	16	....	....	....	....	....	....	....	....	....	....	....	....	....	....	....	....	....	....
	Bridgeport	AHL	39	24	26	50	28	....	....	....	....	....	....	....	....	....	....	....	....	....	....	....	....	....	....
	NHL Totals		1	0	0	0	0	0	0	0	1	0.0		0	0.0	10:00	....	....	....	....	....	....	....	....	....

ECAC All-Rookie Team (1997) • ECAC First All-Star Team (1998, 1999, 2001) • NCAA East Second All-American Team (1998, 1999) • NCAA East First All-American Team (2001) • AHL First All-Star Team (2004) • Willie Marshall Award (Top Goal-scorer - AHL) (2004)

• Missed majority of 1999-2000 season recovering from abdominal injury originally suffered in game vs. U. of Michigan (CCHA), October 30, 1999. Signed as a free agent by **Oulu** (Finland), October 4, 2001. Signed as a free agent by **NY Islanders**, August 6, 2002. Signed as a free agent by **Hartford** (AHL), October 10, 2004.

HAMRLIK, Roman

(HAHM-reh-lik, ROH-muhn) **CGY.**

Defense. Shoots left. 6'2", 210 lbs. Born, Gottwaldov/Zlin, Czech., April 12, 1974. Tampa Bay's 1st choice, 1st overall, in 1992 Entry Draft.

1990-91	AC ZPS Zlin	Czech	14	2	2	4	18	....	....	....	....	....	....	....	....	....	....	....	....	....	....	....	....	....	....
1991-92	AC ZPS Zlin	Czech	34	5	5	10	50	....	....	....	....	....	....	....	....	....	....	....	....	....	....	....	....	....	....
1992-93	**Tampa Bay**	**NHL**	67	6	15	21	71	1	0	1	113	5.3	-21	....	....	....	....	....	....	....	....	....	....	....	....
	Atlanta Knights	IHL	2	1	1	2	2	....	....	....	....	....	....	....	....	....	....	....	....	....	....	....	....	....	....
1993-94	**Tampa Bay**	**NHL**	64	3	18	21	135	0	0	0	158	1.9	-14	....	....	....	....	....	....	....	....	....	....	....	....
1994-95	AC ZPS Zlin	CzRep	2	1	0	1	10	....	....	....	....	....	....	....	....	....	....	....	....	....	....	....	....	....	....
	Tampa Bay	**NHL**	48	12	11	23	86	7	1	2	134	9.0	-18	....	....	....	....	....	....	....	....	....	....	....	....
1995-96	**Tampa Bay**	**NHL**	82	16	49	65	103	12	0	2	281	5.7	-24	....	....	....	5	0	1	1	4	0	0	0	....
1996-97	**Tampa Bay**	**NHL**	79	12	28	40	57	6	0	0	238	5.0	-29	....	....	....	....	....	....	....	....	....	....	....	....
1997-98	**Tampa Bay**	**NHL**	37	3	12	15	22	1	0	0	86	3.5	-18	....	....	....	....	....	....	....	....	....	....	....	....
	Edmonton	**NHL**	41	6	20	26	48	4	1	3	112	5.4	3	....	....	....	12	0	6	6	12	0	0	0	....
	Czech Republic	Olympics	6	1	0	1	2	....	....	....	....	....	....	....	....	....	....	....	....	....	....	....	....	....	....
1998-99	**Edmonton**	**NHL**	75	8	24	32	70	3	0	0	172	4.7	9	0	0.0	23:49	3	0	0	0	2	0	0	0	16:23
99-2000	Zlin	CzRep	6	0	3	3	4	....	....	....	....	....	....	....	....	....	....	....	....	....	....	....	....	....	....
	Edmonton	**NHL**	80	8	37	45	68	5	0	0	180	4.4	1	0	0.0	25:18	5	0	1	1	4	0	0	0	24:44
2000-01	**NY Islanders**	**NHL**	76	16	30	46	92	5	1	4	232	6.9	-20	1	100.0	25:12	....	....	....	....	....	....	....	....	....
2001-02	**NY Islanders**	**NHL**	70	11	26	37	78	4	1	1	169	6.5	7	1	0.0	25:32	7	1	6	7	6	0	0	0	29:09
	Czech Republic	Olympics	4	0	1	1	2	....	....	....	....	....	....	....	....	....	....	....	....	....	....	....	....	....	....
2002-03	**NY Islanders**	**NHL**	73	9	32	41	87	3	0	2	151	6.0	21	0	0.0	26:34	5	0	2	2	2	0	0	0	29:24
2003-04	**NY Islanders**	**NHL**	81	7	22	29	68	2	0	2	182	3.8	2	0	0.0	24:35	5	0	1	1	2	0	0	0	25:30
2004-05	HC Hame Zlin	CzRep	45	2	14	16	70	....	....	....	....	....	....	....	....	....	17	1	3	4	24	....	....	....	....
2005-06	**Calgary**	**NHL**	51	7	19	26	56	1	1	0	89	7.9	8	0	0.0	21:51	7	0	2	2	2	0	0	0	19:44
	NHL Totals		924	124	343	467	1041	54	5	17	2297	5.4		2	50.0	24:49	49	1	19	20	34	0	0	0	24:40

Played in NHL All-Star Game (1996, 1999, 2003)

Traded to **Edmonton** by **Tampa Bay** with Paul Comrie for Bryan Marchment, Steve Kelly and Jason Bonsignore, December 30, 1997. Traded to **NY Islanders** by **Edmonton** for Eric Brewer, Josh Green and NY Islanders' 2nd round choice (Brad Winchester) in 2000 Entry Draft, June 24, 2000. Signed as a free agent by **Zlin** (CzRep), August 4, 2004. Signed as a free agent by **Calgary**, August 14, 2005.

HANDZUS, Michal

(HAHND-zuhs, MIGH-kuhl) **CHI.**

Center. Shoots left. 6'5", 217 lbs. Born, Banska Bystrica, Czech., March 11, 1977. St. Louis' 3rd choice, 101st overall, in 1995 Entry Draft.

1993-94	B. Bystrica Jr.	Slovak-Jr.	40	23	36	59	....	....	....	....	....	....	....	....	....	....	....	....	....	....	....	....	....	....	....
1994-95	B. Bystrica	Slovak-2	22	15	14	29	10	....	....	....	....	....	....	....	....	....	....	....	....	....	....	....	....	....	....
1995-96	B. Bystrica	Slovakia	19	3	1	4	8	....	....	....	....	....	....	....	....	....	....	....	....	....	....	....	....	....	....
1996-97	HC SKP PS Poprad	Slovakia	44	15	18	33	....	....	....	....	....	....	....	....	....	....	....	....	....	....	....	....	....	....	....
1997-98	Worcester IceCats	AHL	69	27	36	63	54	....	....	....	....	....	....	....	....	....	11	2	6	8	10	....	....	....	....
1998-99	**St. Louis**	**NHL**	66	4	12	16	30	0	0	0	78	5.1	-9	794	49.9	14:48	11	0	2	2	8	0	0	0	16:52
99-2000	**St. Louis**	**NHL**	81	25	28	53	44	3	4	5	166	15.1	19	1243	51.5	17:43	7	0	3	3	6	0	0	0	16:35
2000-01	**St. Louis**	**NHL**	36	10	14	24	12	3	2	2	58	17.2	11	581	50.6	18:00	....	....	....	....	....	....	....	....	....
	Phoenix	**NHL**	10	4	4	8	21	0	1	0	14	28.6	5	111	60.4	15:26	....	....	....	....	....	....	....	....	....
2001-02	**Phoenix**	**NHL**	79	15	30	45	34	3	1	1	94	16.0	-8	1227	48.7	16:09	5	0	0	0	2	0	0	0	15:01
	Slovakia	Olympics	2	1	0	1	6	....	....	....	....	....	....	....	....	....	....	....	....	....	....	....	....	....	....
2002-03	**Philadelphia**	**NHL**	82	23	21	44	46	1	1	9	133	17.3	13	1350	52.3	17:33	13	2	6	8	6	0	0	1	18:23
2003-04	**Philadelphia**	**NHL**	82	20	38	58	82	7	1	2	135	14.8	18	1457	49.9	18:43	18	5	5	10	10	0	0	0	18:33
2004-05	HKm Zvolen	Slovakia	33	14	24	38	34	....	....	....	....	....	....	....	....	....	17	5	10	15	6	....	....	....	....
2005-06	**Philadelphia**	**NHL**	73	11	33	44	38	2	1	1	113	9.7	-2	1143	53.2	18:28	6	0	2	2	2	0	0	0	15:56
	Slovakia	Olympics	DID NOT PLAY – INJURED																						
	NHL Totals		509	112	180	292	307	19	11	20	791	14.2		7906	51.0	17:19	60	7	18	25	34	0	0	1	17:25

Traded to **Phoenix** by **St. Louis** with Ladislav Nagy, the rights to Jeff Taffe and St. Louis' 1st round choice (Ben Eager) in 2002 Entry Draft for Keith Tkachuk, March 13, 2001. Traded to **Philadelphia** by **Phoenix** with Robert Esche for Brian Boucher and Nashville's 3rd round choice (previously acquired, Phoenix selected Joe Callahan) in 2002 Entry Draft, June 12, 2002. Signed as a free agent by **Zvolen** (Slovakia), October 27, 2004. Traded to **Chicago** by **Philadelphia** for Kyle Calder, August 4, 2006.

HANNAN, Scott

(HAN-nan, SKAWT) **S.J.**

Defense. Shoots left. 6'1", 220 lbs. Born, Richmond, B.C., January 23, 1979. San Jose's 2nd choice, 23rd overall, in 1997 Entry Draft.

1994-95	Surrey Wolves	BCAHA	70	54	54	108	200	....	....	....	....	....	....	....	....	....	....	....	....	....	....	....	....	....	....
	Tacoma Rockets	WHL	2	0	0	0	0	....	....	....	....	....	....	....	....	....	....	....	....	....	....	....	....	....	....
1995-96	Kelowna Rockets	WHL	69	4	5	9	76	....	....	....	....	....	....	....	....	....	6	0	1	1	4	....	....	....	....
1996-97	Kelowna Rockets	WHL	70	17	26	43	101	....	....	....	....	....	....	....	....	....	6	0	0	0	8	....	....	....	....
1997-98	Kelowna Rockets	WHL	47	10	30	40	70	....	....	....	....	....	....	....	....	....	7	2	7	9	14	....	....	....	....
1998-99	**San Jose**	**NHL**	5	0	2	2	6	0	0	0	4	0.0	0	0	0.0	7:15	....	....	....	....	....	....	....	....	....
	Kelowna Rockets	WHL	47	15	30	45	92	....	....	....	....	....	....	....	....	....	6	1	2	3	14	....	....	....	....
	Kentucky	AHL	2	0	0	0	2	....	....	....	....	....	....	....	....	....	12	0	2	2	10	....	....	....	....
99-2000	**San Jose**	**NHL**	30	1	2	3	10	0	0	0	28	3.6	7	1	0.0	17:09	1	0	1	1	0	0	0	0	18:14
	Kentucky	AHL	41	5	12	17	40	....	....	....	....	....	....	....	....	....	....	....	....	....	....	....	....	....	....
2000-01	**San Jose**	**NHL**	75	3	14	17	51	0	0	1	96	3.1	10	0	0.0	19:02	6	0	1	1	6	0	0	0	25:10
2001-02	**San Jose**	**NHL**	75	2	12	14	57	0	0	1	68	2.9	10	1	100.0	20:19	12	0	2	2	12	0	0	0	20:46
2002-03	**San Jose**	**NHL**	81	3	19	22	61	1	0	0	103	2.9	0	3	33.3	24:16	....	....	....	....	....	....	....	....	....
2003-04	**San Jose**	**NHL**	82	6	15	21	48	0	0	0	114	5.3	10	0	0.0	23:41	17	1	5	6	22	1	0	1	26:38
2004-05			DID NOT PLAY																						
2005-06	**San Jose**	**NHL**	81	6	18	24	58	2	0	1	104	5.8	7	0	0.0	24:34	11	0	1	1	6	0	0	0	25:16
	NHL Totals		429	21	82	103	291	3	0	3	517	4.1		5	40.0	21:55	47	1	10	11	46	1	0	1	24:27

WHL West First All-Star Team (1999)

HARRISON, Jay

(HAIR-ih-suhn, JAY) **TOR.**

Defense. Shoots left. 6'4", 211 lbs. Born, Oshawa, Ont., November 3, 1982. Toronto's 4th choice, 82nd overall, in 2001 Entry Draft.

			Regular Season														Playoffs								
Season	Club	League	GP	G	A	Pts	PIM	PP	SH	GW	S	%	+/-	TF	F%	Min	GP	G	A	Pts	PIM	PP	SH	GW	Min
1997-98	Oshawa	OHA-B	42	1	11	12	143	....	....	....	....	....	....	....	....	....	....	....	....	....	....	....	....	....	....
1998-99	Brampton	OHL	63	1	14	15	108	....	....	....	....	....	....	....	....	....	....	....	....	....	....	....	....	....	....
99-2000	Brampton	OHL	68	2	18	20	139	....	....	....	....	....	....	....	....	....	6	0	2	2	15	....	....	....	....
2000-01	Brampton	OHL	53	4	15	19	112	....	....	....	....	....	....	....	....	....	9	1	1	2	17	....	....	....	....
2001-02	Brampton	OHL	61	12	31	43	116	....	....	....	....	....	....	....	....	....	....	....	....	....	....	....	....	....	....
	St. John's	AHL	7	0	1	1	2	....	....	....	....	....	....	....	....	....	10	0	0	0	4	....	....	....	....
	Memphis	CHL	....	....	....	....	....	....	....	....	....	....	....	....	....	....	1	0	0	0	2	....	....	....	....
2002-03	St. John's	AHL	72	2	8	10	72	....	....	....	....	....	....	....	....	....	....	....	....	....	....	....	....	....	....
2003-04	St. John's	AHL	70	4	5	9	141	....	....	....	....	....	....	....	....	....	....	....	....	....	....	....	....	....	....
2004-05	St. John's	AHL	60	0	4	4	108	....	....	....	....	....	....	....	....	....	4	0	1	1	14	....	....	....	....
2005-06	**Toronto**	**NHL**	**8**	**0**	**1**	**1**	**2**	**0**	**0**	**0**	**7**	**0.0**	**5**	**0**	**0.0**	**18:50**	....	....	....	....	....	....	....	....	....
	Toronto Marlies	AHL	57	9	20	29	100	....	....	....	....	....	....	....	....	....	5	1	3	4	8	....	....	....	....
	NHL Totals		**8**	**0**	**1**	**1**	**2**	**0**	**0**	**0**	**7**	**0.0**		**0**	**0.0**	**18:50**	....	....	....	....	....	....	....	....	....

OHL All-Rookie Team (1999)

HARTIGAN, Mark

(HAHR-tih-guhn, MAHRK) **CBJ**

Center. Shoots left. 6', 200 lbs. Born, Fort St. John, B.C., October 15, 1977.

Season	Club	League	GP	G	A	Pts	PIM	PP	SH	GW	S	%	+/-	TF	F%	Min	GP	G	A	Pts	PIM	PP	SH	GW	Min
1996-97	Weyburn	SJHL	52	44	32	76	....	....	....	....	....	....	....	....	....	....	....	....	....	....	....	....	....	....	....
1997-98	Weyburn	SJHL	62	*59	46	*105	81	....	....	....	....	....	....	....	....	....	23	17	21	38	10	....	....	....	....
1998-99	St. Cloud State	WCHA	DID NOT PLAY – FRESHMAN																						
99-2000	St. Cloud State	WCHA	37	22	20	42	24	....	....	....	....	....	....	....	....	....	....	....	....	....	....	....	....	....	....
2000-01	St. Cloud State	WCHA	40	27	21	48	20	....	....	....	....	....	....	....	....	....	....	....	....	....	....	....	....	....	....
2001-02	St. Cloud State	WCHA	42	*37	38	75	42	....	....	....	....	....	....	....	....	....	....	....	....	....	....	....	....	....	....
	Atlanta	**NHL**	**2**	**0**	**0**	**0**	**2**	**0**	**0**	**0**	**3**	**0.0**	**–2**	**18**	**38.9**	**13:16**	....	....	....	....	....	....	....	....	....
2002-03	Chicago Wolves	AHL	55	15	31	46	43	....	....	....	....	....	....	....	....	....	9	1	2	3	10	....	....	....	....
	Atlanta	**NHL**	**23**	**5**	**2**	**7**	**6**	**1**	**0**	**0**	**25**	**20.0**	**–8**	**220**	**47.3**	**10:52**	....	....	....	....	....	....	....	....	....
2003-04	**Columbus**	**NHL**	**9**	**1**	**3**	**4**	**6**	**1**	**0**	**0**	**15**	**6.7**	**–2**	**138**	**40.6**	**16:19**	....	....	....	....	....	....	....	....	....
	Syracuse Crunch	AHL	69	23	23	46	86	....	....	....	....	....	....	....	....	....	7	1	4	5	8	....	....	....	....
2004-05	Syracuse Crunch	AHL	69	31	28	59	105	....	....	....	....	....	....	....	....	....	....	....	....	....	....	....	....	....	....
2005-06	**Columbus**	**NHL**	**33**	**9**	**3**	**12**	**22**	**3**	**0**	**1**	**54**	**16.7**	**–1**	**194**	**44.9**	**11:39**	....	....	....	....	....	....	....	....	....
	Syracuse Crunch	AHL	49	34	41	75	48	....	....	....	....	....	....	....	....	....	6	1	2	3	33	....	....	....	....
	NHL Totals		**67**	**15**	**8**	**23**	**36**	**5**	**0**	**1**	**97**	**15.5**		**570**	**44.6**	**12:03**	....	....	....	....	....	....	....	....	....

WCHA First All-Star Team (2002) • WCHA Player of the Year (2002)

Signed as a free agent by **Atlanta**, March 27, 2002. Signed as a free agent by **Columbus**, July 15, 2003.

HARTNELL, Scott

(HAHRT-nuhl, SKAWT) **NSH.**

Left wing. Shoots left. 6'2", 210 lbs. Born, Regina, Sask., April 18, 1982. Nashville's 1st choice, 6th overall, in 2000 Entry Draft.

Season	Club	League	GP	G	A	Pts	PIM	PP	SH	GW	S	%	+/-	TF	F%	Min	GP	G	A	Pts	PIM	PP	SH	GW	Min
1997-98	Lloydminster	AJHL	56	9	25	34	82	....	....	....	....	....	....	....	....	....	4	2	1	3	8	....	....	....	....
	Prince Albert	WHL	1	0	1	1	2	....	....	....	....	....	....	....	....	....	....	....	....	....	....	....	....	....	....
1998-99	Prince Albert	WHL	65	10	34	44	104	....	....	....	....	....	....	....	....	....	14	0	5	5	22	....	....	....	....
99-2000	Prince Albert	WHL	62	27	55	82	124	....	....	....	....	....	....	....	....	....	6	3	2	5	6	....	....	....	....
2000-01	**Nashville**	**NHL**	**75**	**2**	**14**	**16**	**48**	**0**	**0**	**0**	**92**	**2.2**	**–8**	**3**	**33.3**	**10:54**	....	....	....	....	....	....	....	....	....
2001-02	**Nashville**	**NHL**	**75**	**14**	**27**	**41**	**111**	**3**	**0**	**4**	**162**	**8.6**	**5**	**12**	**25.0**	**16:58**	....	....	....	....	....	....	....	....	....
2002-03	**Nashville**	**NHL**	**82**	**12**	**22**	**34**	**101**	**2**	**0**	**2**	**221**	**5.4**	**–3**	**23**	**30.4**	**15:17**	....	....	....	....	....	....	....	....	....
2003-04	**Nashville**	**NHL**	**59**	**18**	**15**	**33**	**87**	**5**	**0**	**3**	**154**	**11.7**	**–5**	**48**	**37.5**	**16:16**	**6**	**1**	**2**	**3**	**2**	**0**	**0**	**0**	**15:37**
2004-05	Valerengen IF Oslo	Norway	28	17	12	29	103	....	....	....	....	....	....	....	....	....	11	12	7	19	24	....	....	....	....
2005-06	**Nashville**	**NHL**	**81**	**25**	**23**	**48**	**101**	**10**	**2**	**8**	**211**	**11.8**	**8**	**58**	**37.9**	**16:05**	**5**	**1**	**0**	**1**	**4**	**0**	**0**	**0**	**12:12**
	NHL Totals		**372**	**71**	**101**	**172**	**448**	**20**	**2**	**17**	**840**	**8.5**		**144**	**35.4**	**15:04**	**11**	**2**	**2**	**4**	**6**	**0**	**0**	**0**	**14:04**

Signed as a free agent by **Oslo** (Norway), October 21, 2004.

HARVEY, Todd

(HAHR-vee, TAWD)

Right wing/Center. Shoots right. 6', 210 lbs. Born, Hamilton, Ont., February 17, 1975. Dallas' 1st choice, 9th overall, in 1993 Entry Draft.

Season	Club	League	GP	G	A	Pts	PIM	PP	SH	GW	S	%	+/-	TF	F%	Min	GP	G	A	Pts	PIM	PP	SH	GW	Min
1989-90	Cambridge	OHA-B	41	35	27	62	213	....	....	....	....	....	....	....	....	....	....	....	....	....	....	....	....	....	....
1990-91	Cambridge	OHA-B	35	32	39	71	174	....	....	....	....	....	....	....	....	....	....	....	....	....	....	....	....	....	....
1991-92	Detroit	OHL	58	21	43	64	141	....	....	....	....	....	....	....	....	....	7	3	5	8	30	....	....	....	....
1992-93	Detroit	OHL	55	50	50	100	83	....	....	....	....	....	....	....	....	....	15	9	12	21	39	....	....	....	....
1993-94	Detroit	OHL	49	34	51	85	75	....	....	....	....	....	....	....	....	....	17	10	12	22	26	....	....	....	....
1994-95	Detroit	OHL	11	8	14	22	12	....	....	....	....	....	....	....	....	....	....	....	....	....	....	....	....	....	....
	Dallas	**NHL**	**40**	**11**	**9**	**20**	**67**	**2**	**0**	**1**	**64**	**17.2**	**–3**	....	....	....	**5**	**0**	**0**	**0**	**8**	**0**	**0**	**0**	....
1995-96	**Dallas**	**NHL**	**69**	**9**	**20**	**29**	**136**	**3**	**0**	**1**	**101**	**8.9**	**–13**	....	....	....	....	....	....	....	....	....	....	....	....
	Michigan	IHL	5	1	3	4	8	....	....	....	....	....	....	....	....	....	....	....	....	....	....	....	....	....	....
1996-97	**Dallas**	**NHL**	**71**	**9**	**22**	**31**	**142**	**1**	**0**	**2**	**99**	**9.1**	**19**	....	....	....	**7**	**0**	**1**	**1**	**10**	**0**	**0**	**0**	....
1997-98	**Dallas**	**NHL**	**59**	**9**	**10**	**19**	**104**	**0**	**0**	**1**	**88**	**10.2**	**5**	....	....	....	....	....	....	....	....	....	....	....	....
1998-99	**NY Rangers**	**NHL**	**37**	**11**	**17**	**28**	**72**	**6**	**0**	**2**	**58**	**19.0**	**–1**	**175**	**50.3**	**17:19**	....	....	....	....	....	....	....	....	....
99-2000	**NY Rangers**	**NHL**	**31**	**3**	**3**	**6**	**62**	**0**	**0**	**0**	**31**	**9.7**	**–9**	**173**	**49.1**	**12:21**	....	....	....	....	....	....	....	....	....
	San Jose	**NHL**	**40**	**8**	**4**	**12**	**78**	**2**	**0**	**0**	**59**	**13.6**	**–2**	**44**	**43.2**	**12:55**	**12**	**1**	**0**	**1**	**8**	**1**	**0**	**0**	**10:47**
2000-01	**San Jose**	**NHL**	**69**	**10**	**11**	**21**	**72**	**1**	**0**	**2**	**66**	**15.2**	**6**	**98**	**40.8**	**11:05**	**6**	**0**	**0**	**0**	**8**	**0**	**0**	**0**	**6:59**
2001-02	**San Jose**	**NHL**	**69**	**9**	**13**	**22**	**73**	**0**	**0**	**1**	**66**	**13.6**	**16**	**223**	**48.4**	**9:47**	**12**	**0**	**2**	**2**	**12**	**0**	**0**	**0**	**7:32**
2002-03	**San Jose**	**NHL**	**76**	**3**	**16**	**19**	**74**	**0**	**0**	**0**	**64**	**4.7**	**5**	**119**	**44.5**	**9:57**	....	....	....	....	....	....	....	....	....
2003-04	**San Jose**	**NHL**	**47**	**4**	**5**	**9**	**38**	**0**	**0**	**0**	**51**	**7.8**	**3**	**29**	**44.8**	**9:46**	**16**	**1**	**2**	**3**	**2**	**0**	**0**	**0**	**10:30**
	Cleveland Barons	AHL	13	6	1	7	29	....	....	....	....	....	....	....	....	....	....	....	....	....	....	....	....	....	....
2004-05	Cambridge	OHA-Sr.	16	9	15	24	31	....	....	....	....	....	....	....	....	....	....	....	....	....	....	....	....	....	....
2005-06	**Edmonton**	**NHL**	**63**	**5**	**2**	**7**	**32**	**0**	**0**	**0**	**45**	**11.1**	**–7**	**41**	**34.2**	**7:33**	**10**	**1**	**1**	**2**	**4**	**0**	**0**	**0**	**7:57**
	NHL Totals		**671**	**91**	**132**	**223**	**950**	**15**	**0**	**10**	**792**	**11.5**		**902**	**46.6**	**10:49**	**68**	**3**	**6**	**9**	**52**	**1**	**0**	**0**	**9:06**

OHL All-Rookie Team (1992)

Traded to **NY Rangers** by **Dallas** with Bob Errey and Dallas' 4th round choice (Boyd Kane) in 1998 Entry Draft for Brian Skrudland, Mike Keane and NY Rangers' 6th round choice (Pavel Patera) in 1998 Entry Draft, March 24, 1998. Traded to **San Jose** by **NY Rangers** with NY Rangers' 4th round choice (Dimitri Patzold) in 2001 Entry Draft for Radek Dvorak, December 30, 1999. Signed as a free agent by **Edmonton**, September 15, 2004. Signed as a free agent by **Cambridge** (OHA-Sr.), October 21, 2004.

HATCHER, Derian

(HAT-chuhr, DAIR-ee-an) **PHI.**

Defense. Shoots left. 6'5", 235 lbs. Born, Sterling Hts., MI, June 4, 1972. Minnesota's 1st choice, 8th overall, in 1990 Entry Draft.

Season	Club	League	GP	G	A	Pts	PIM	PP	SH	GW	S	%	+/-	TF	F%	Min	GP	G	A	Pts	PIM	PP	SH	GW	Min
1987-88	Detroit GPD	MNHL	25	5	13	18	52	....	....	....	....	....	....	....	....	....	....	....	....	....	....	....	....	....	....
1988-89	Detroit GPD	MNHL	51	19	35	54	100	....	....	....	....	....	....	....	....	....	....	....	....	....	....	....	....	....	....
1989-90	North Bay	OHL	64	14	38	52	81	....	....	....	....	....	....	....	....	....	5	2	3	5	8	....	....	....	....
1990-91	North Bay	OHL	64	13	49	62	163	....	....	....	....	....	....	....	....	....	10	2	10	12	28	....	....	....	....
1991-92	**Minnesota**	**NHL**	**43**	**8**	**4**	**12**	**88**	**0**	**0**	**2**	**51**	**15.7**	**7**	....	....	....	**5**	**0**	**2**	**2**	**8**	**0**	**0**	**0**	....
1992-93	**Minnesota**	**NHL**	**67**	**4**	**15**	**19**	**178**	**0**	**0**	**1**	**73**	**5.5**	**–27**	....	....	....	....	....	....	....	....	....	....	....	....
	Kalamazoo Wings	IHL	2	1	2	3	21	....	....	....	....	....	....	....	....	....	....	....	....	....	....	....	....	....	....
1993-94	**Dallas**	**NHL**	**83**	**12**	**19**	**31**	**211**	**2**	**1**	**2**	**132**	**9.1**	**19**	....	....	....	**9**	**0**	**2**	**2**	**14**	**0**	**0**	**0**	....
1994-95	**Dallas**	**NHL**	**43**	**5**	**11**	**16**	**105**	**2**	**0**	**2**	**74**	**6.8**	**3**	....	....	....	....	....	....	....	....	....	....	....	....
1995-96	**Dallas**	**NHL**	**79**	**8**	**23**	**31**	**129**	**2**	**0**	**1**	**125**	**6.4**	**–12**	....	....	....	....	....	....	....	....	....	....	....	....
1996-97	**Dallas**	**NHL**	**63**	**3**	**19**	**22**	**97**	**0**	**0**	**0**	**96**	**3.1**	**8**	....	....	....	**7**	**0**	**2**	**2**	**20**	**0**	**0**	**0**	....
1997-98	**Dallas**	**NHL**	**70**	**6**	**25**	**31**	**132**	**3**	**0**	**2**	**74**	**8.1**	**9**	....	....	....	**17**	**3**	**3**	**6**	**39**	**2**	**0**	**0**	....
	United States	Olympics	4	0	0	0	0	....	....	....	....	....	....	....	....	....	....	....	....	....	....	....	....	....	....
1998-99♦	**Dallas**	**NHL**	**80**	**9**	**21**	**30**	**102**	**3**	**0**	**2**	**125**	**7.2**	**21**	**0**	**0.0**	**24:44**	**18**	**1**	**6**	**7**	**24**	**0**	**0**	**0**	**29:06**
99-2000	**Dallas**	**NHL**	**57**	**2**	**22**	**24**	**68**	**0**	**0**	**0**	**90**	**2.2**	**6**	**0**	**0.0**	**27:33**	**23**	**1**	**3**	**4**	**29**	**0**	**0**	**0**	**27:40**
2000-01	**Dallas**	**NHL**	**80**	**2**	**21**	**23**	**77**	**1**	**0**	**2**	**97**	**2.1**	**5**	**0**	**0.0**	**25:53**	**10**	**0**	**1**	**1**	**16**	**0**	**0**	**0**	**28:53**
2001-02	**Dallas**	**NHL**	**80**	**4**	**21**	**25**	**87**	**1**	**0**	**0**	**111**	**3.6**	**12**	**0**	**0.0**	**26:40**	....	....	....	....	....	....	....	....	....
2002-03	**Dallas**	**NHL**	**82**	**8**	**22**	**30**	**106**	**1**	**1**	**2**	**159**	**5.0**	**37**	**0**	**0.0**	**25:51**	**11**	**1**	**2**	**3**	**33**	**0**	**0**	**0**	**30:02**
2003-04	**Detroit**	**NHL**	**15**	**0**	**4**	**4**	**8**	**0**	**0**	**0**	**18**	**0.0**	**4**	**0**	**0.0**	**19:38**	**12**	**0**	**1**	**1**	**15**	**0**	**0**	**0**	**22:54**
2004-05	Motor City	UHL	24	5	12	17	27	....	....	....	....	....	....	....	....	....	....	....	....	....	....	....	....	....	....

			Regular Season														Playoffs								
Season	Club	League	GP	G	A	Pts	PIM	PP	SH	GW	S	%	+/-	TF	F%	Min	GP	G	A	Pts	PIM	PP	SH	GW	Min
2005-06	**Philadelphia**	**NHL**	77	4	13	17	93	1	1	0	98	4.1	2	0	0.0	23:30	6	0	2	2	10	0	0	0	21:36
	United States	Olympics	6	0	0	0	12	....	....	....	....	....	....	....	....	....	....	....	....	....	....	....	....	....	....
	NHL Totals		919	75	240	315	1481	16	3	16	1323	5.7		0	0.0	25:26	118	6	24	30	208	2	0	0	27:18

NHL Second All-Star Team (2003)

Played in NHL All-Star Game (1997)

Transferred to **Dallas** after **Minnesota** franchise relocated, June 9, 1993. Signed as a free agent by **Detroit**, July 3, 2003. • Missed majority of 2003-04 season recovering from knee injury suffered in game vs. Vancouver, October 16, 2003. Signed as a free agent by **Motor City** (UHL), February 1, 2005. Signed as a free agent by **Philadelphia**, August 2, 2005.

HAVELID, Niclas

(HAHV-lihd, NIHK-lahs) **ATL.**

Defense. Shoots left. 6', 200 lbs. Born, Stockholm, Sweden, April 12, 1973. Anaheim's 2nd choice, 83rd overall, in 1999 Entry Draft.

Season	Club	League	GP	G	A	Pts	PIM	PP	SH	GW	S	%	+/-	TF	F%	Min	GP	G	A	Pts	PIM	PP	SH	GW	Min
1988-89	Enkopings SK	Sweden-3	7	0	1	1	0	....	....	....	....	....	....	....	....	....	....	....	....	....	....	....	....	....	....
1989-90	Enkopings SK	Sweden-3	24	1	2	3	28	....	....	....	....	....	....	....	....	....	....	....	....	....	....	....	....	....	....
1990-91	Arlanda	Sweden-2	30	2	3	5	22	....	....	....	....	....	....	....	....	....	....	....	....	....	....	....	....	....	....
1991-92	AIK Solna	Sweden	10	0	0	0	2	....	....	....	....	....	....	....	....	....	....	....	....	....	....	....	....	....	....
1992-93	AIK Solna	Sweden	30	1	2	3	22	....	....	....	....	....	....	....	....	....	3	0	0	0	2	....	....	....	....
1993-94	AIK Solna	Sweden-2	22	3	9	12	14	....	....	....	....	....	....	....	....	....	....	....	....	....	....	....	....	....	....
1994-95	AIK Solna	Sweden	40	3	7	10	38	....	....	....	....	....	....	....	....	....	....	....	....	....	....	....	....	....	....
1995-96	AIK Solna	Sweden	40	5	6	11	30	....	....	....	....	....	....	....	....	....	....	....	....	....	....	....	....	....	....
1996-97	AIK Solna	Sweden	49	3	6	9	42	....	....	....	....	....	....	....	....	....	7	1	2	3	8	....	....	....	....
1997-98	AIK Solna	Sweden	43	8	4	12	42	....	....	....	....	....	....	....	....	....	10	1	3	4	39	....	....	....	....
1998-99	Malmo	Sweden	50	10	12	22	42	....	....	....	....	....	....	....	....	....	8	0	4	4	10	....	....	....	....
99-2000	**Anaheim**	**NHL**	50	2	7	9	20	0	0	2	70	2.9	0	1	0.0	19:10	....	....	....	....	....	....	....	....	....
	Cincinnati	AHL	2	0	0	0	0	....	....	....	....	....	....	....	....	....	....	....	....	....	....	....	....	....	....
2000-01	**Anaheim**	**NHL**	47	4	10	14	34	2	0	1	69	5.8	−6	4	0.0	21:51	....	....	....	....	....	....	....	....	....
2001-02	**Anaheim**	**NHL**	52	1	2	3	40	0	0	0	45	2.2	−13	1	0.0	17:01	....	....	....	....	....	....	....	....	....
2002-03	**Anaheim**	**NHL**	82	11	22	33	30	4	0	5	169	6.5	5	3	0.0	22:30	21	0	4	4	2	0	0	0	25:41
2003-04	**Anaheim**	**NHL**	79	6	20	26	28	5	0	3	122	4.9	−28	0	0.0	22:39	....	....	....	....	....	....	....	....	....
2004-05	Sodertalje SK	Sweden	46	2	2	4	60	....	....	....	....	....	....	....	....	....	10	1	1	2	18	....	....	....	....
2005-06	**Atlanta**	**NHL**	82	4	28	32	48	2	0	0	84	4.8	9	0	0.0	24:25	....	....	....	....	....	....	....	....	....
	Sweden	Olympics	7	0	0	0	4	....	....	....	....	....	....	....	....	....	....	....	....	....	....	....	....	....	....
	NHL Totals		392	28	89	117	200	13	0	11	559	5.0		9	0.0	21:42	21	0	4	4	2	0	0	0	25:41

Traded to **Atlanta** by **Anaheim** for Kurtis Foster, June 26, 2004. Signed as a free agent by **Sodertalje** (Sweden), August 9, 2004.

HAVLAT, Martin

(HAHV-lat, MAHR-tihn) **CHI.**

Left wing. Shoots left. 6'1", 190 lbs. Born, Mlada Boleslav, Czech., April 19, 1981. Ottawa's 1st choice, 26th overall, in 1999 Entry Draft.

Season	Club	League	GP	G	A	Pts	PIM	PP	SH	GW	S	%	+/-	TF	F%	Min	GP	G	A	Pts	PIM	PP	SH	GW	Min
1997-98	Ytong Brno Jr.	CzRep-Jr.	32	38	29	67	....	....	....	....	....	....	....	....	....	....	....	....	....	....	....	....	....	....	....
1998-99	HC Trinec Jr.	CzRep-Jr.	31	28	23	51	....	....	....	....	....	....	....	....	....	....	....	....	....	....	....	....	....	....	....
	Trinec	CzRep	24	2	3	5	4	....	....	....	....	....	....	....	....	....	8	0	0	0	....	....	....	....	....
99-2000	HC Ocelari Trinec	CzRep	46	13	29	42	42	....	....	....	....	....	....	....	....	....	4	0	2	2	8	....	....	....	....
2000-01	**Ottawa**	**NHL**	73	19	23	42	20	7	0	5	133	14.3	8	40	30.0	13:47	4	0	0	0	2	0	0	0	14:04
2001-02	**Ottawa**	**NHL**	72	22	28	50	66	9	0	6	145	15.2	−7	15	40.0	14:46	12	2	5	7	14	2	0	2	16:19
	Czech Republic	Olympics	4	3	1	4	27	....	....	....	....	....	....	....	....	....	....	....	....	....	....	....	....	....	....
2002-03	**Ottawa**	**NHL**	67	24	35	59	30	9	0	4	179	13.4	20	7	14.3	16:27	18	5	6	11	14	1	0	2	16:27
2003-04	HC Sparta Praha	CzRep	5	1	3	4	8	....	....	....	....	....	....	....	....	....	....	....	....	....	....	....	....	....	....
	Ottawa	**NHL**	68	31	37	68	46	13	0	7	175	17.7	12	11	36.4	16:44	7	0	3	3	2	0	0	0	16:10
2004-05	Znojmo	CzRep	12	10	4	14	16	....	....	....	....	....	....	....	....	....	....	....	....	....	....	....	....	....	....
	Dynamo Moscow	Russia	10	2	0	2	14	....	....	....	....	....	....	....	....	....	....	....	....	....	....	....	....	....	....
	HC Sparta Praha	CzRep	9	5	4	9	37	....	....	....	....	....	....	....	....	....	5	0	0	0	20	....	....	....	....
2005-06	**Ottawa**	**NHL**	18	9	7	16	4	2	1	1	57	15.8	6	25	36.0	18:11	10	7	6	13	4	3	0	1	17:13
	NHL Totals		298	105	130	235	166	40	1	23	689	15.2		98	32.7	15:33	51	14	20	34	36	6	0	5	16:21

NHL All-Rookie Team (2001)

Signed as a free agent by **Znojmo** (CzRep), September 24, 2004. Signed as a free agent by **Dynamo Moscow** (Russia), November 10, 2004. Signed as a free agent by **Znojmo** (CzRep), January 18, 2005. Signed as a free agent by **Sparta Praha** (CzRep), January 31, 2005. • Missed majority of 2005-06 season recovering from shoulder injury suffered in game vs. Montreal, November 29, 2005. Traded to **Chicago** by **Ottawa** with Bryan Smolinski for Tom Preissing, Josh Hennessy, Michal Barinka and Chicago's 2nd round choice in 2008 Entry Draft, July 10, 2006.

HAYDAR, Darren

(HAY-duhr, DAIR-ehn) **ATL.**

Right wing. Shoots left. 5'9", 166 lbs. Born, Toronto, Ont., October 22, 1979. Nashville's 14th choice, 248th overall, in 1999 Entry Draft.

Season	Club	League	GP	G	A	Pts	PIM	PP	SH	GW	S	%	+/-	TF	F%	Min	GP	G	A	Pts	PIM	PP	SH	GW	Min
1995-96	Milton Merchants	OPJHL	6	1	2	3	4	....	....	....	....	....	....	....	....	....	....	....	....	....	....	....	....	....	....
1996-97	Milton Merchants	OPJHL	51	32	68	100	68	....	....	....	....	....	....	....	....	....	....	....	....	....	....	....	....	....	....
1997-98	Milton Merchants	OPJHL	51	*71	*69	*140	65	....	....	....	....	....	....	....	....	....	....	....	....	....	....	....	....	....	....
1998-99	New Hampshire	H-East	41	31	30	61	34	....	....	....	....	....	....	....	....	....	....	....	....	....	....	....	....	....	....
99-2000	New Hampshire	H-East	38	22	19	41	42	....	....	....	....	....	....	....	....	....	....	....	....	....	....	....	....	....	....
2000-01	New Hampshire	H-East	39	18	23	41	38	....	....	....	....	....	....	....	....	....	....	....	....	....	....	....	....	....	....
2001-02	New Hampshire	H-East	40	31	*45	*76	28	....	....	....	....	....	....	....	....	....	....	....	....	....	....	....	....	....	....
2002-03	**Nashville**	**NHL**	2	0	0	0	0	0	0	0	1	0.0	−1	0	0.0	8:54	....	....	....	....	....	....	....	....	....
	Milwaukee	AHL	75	29	46	75	36	....	....	....	....	....	....	....	....	....	6	1	4	5	2	....	....	....	....
2003-04	Milwaukee	AHL	79	22	37	59	35	....	....	....	....	....	....	....	....	....	22	11	15	26	10	....	....	....	....
2004-05	Milwaukee	AHL	59	24	26	50	42	....	....	....	....	....	....	....	....	....	7	3	4	7	14	....	....	....	....
2005-06	Milwaukee	AHL	80	35	57	92	50	....	....	....	....	....	....	....	....	....	21	18	17	35	18	....	....	....	....
	NHL Totals		2	0	0	0	0	0	0	0	1	0.0		0	0.0	8:54	....	....	....	....	....	....	....	....	....

Hockey East Second All-Star Team (1999, 2000) • Hockey East Rookie of the Year (1999) • Hockey East First All-Star Team (2002) • Hockey East Player of the Year (2002) • AHL All-Rookie Team (2003) • Dudley "Red" Garrett Memorial Award (Rookie of the Year – AHL) (2003)

Signed as a free agent by **Atlanta**, July 4, 2006.

HEALEY, Eric

(HEE-lee, AIR-ihk) **T.B.**

Left wing. Shoots left. 6', 196 lbs. Born, Hull, MA, January 20, 1975.

Season	Club	League	GP	G	A	Pts	PIM	PP	SH	GW	S	%	+/-	TF	F%	Min	GP	G	A	Pts	PIM	PP	SH	GW	Min
1993-94	New England	NEJHL	37	61	76	137	....	....	....	....	....	....	....	....	....	....	....	....	....	....	....	....	....	....	....
1994-95	RPI Engineers	ECAC	37	13	11	24	35	....	....	....	....	....	....	....	....	....	....	....	....	....	....	....	....	....	....
1995-96	RPI Engineers	ECAC	35	18	22	40	57	....	....	....	....	....	....	....	....	....	....	....	....	....	....	....	....	....	....
1996-97	RPI Engineers	ECAC	36	30	26	56	63	....	....	....	....	....	....	....	....	....	....	....	....	....	....	....	....	....	....
1997-98	RPI Engineers	ECAC	35	21	27	48	42	....	....	....	....	....	....	....	....	....	....	....	....	....	....	....	....	....	....
1998-99	Saint John Flames	AHL	64	14	24	38	77	....	....	....	....	....	....	....	....	....	....	....	....	....	....	....	....	....	....
	Orlando	IHL	13	5	4	9	13	....	....	....	....	....	....	....	....	....	8	1	0	1	12	....	....	....	....
99-2000	Springfield	AHL	32	14	15	29	51	....	....	....	....	....	....	....	....	....	1	0	0	0	2	....	....	....	....
2000-01	Springfield	AHL	66	16	17	33	53	....	....	....	....	....	....	....	....	....	....	....	....	....	....	....	....	....	....
2001-02	Jackson Bandits	ECHL	2	1	1	2	0	....	....	....	....	....	....	....	....	....	....	....	....	....	....	....	....	....	....
	Manchester	AHL	65	24	34	58	45	....	....	....	....	....	....	....	....	....	5	2	2	4	8	....	....	....	....
2002-03	Manchester	AHL	75	*42	31	73	47	....	....	....	....	....	....	....	....	....	3	1	0	1	2	....	....	....	....
2003-04	Chicago Wolves	AHL	71	31	20	51	52	....	....	....	....	....	....	....	....	....	10	3	6	9	10	....	....	....	....
2004-05	Adler Mannheim	Germany	50	16	13	29	54	....	....	....	....	....	....	....	....	....	13	2	4	6	12	....	....	....	....
2005-06	**Boston**	**NHL**	2	0	0	0	2	0	0	0	1	0.0	0	0	0.0	8:28	....	....	....	....	....	....	....	....	....
	Providence Bruins	AHL	66	29	42	71	49	....	....	....	....	....	....	....	....	....	5	2	3	5	0	....	....	....	....
	NHL Totals		2	0	0	0	2	0	0	0	1	0.0		0	0.0	8:28	....	....	....	....	....	....	....	....	....

ECAC Second All-Star Team (1997) • NCAA East Second All-American Team (1997, 1998) • ECAC First All-Star Team (1998) • Fred T. Hunt Memorial Award (Sportsmanship – AHL) (2003) (co-winner - Chris Ferraro)

Signed as a free agent by **Calgary**, September 22, 1998. Signed as a free agent by **Phoenix**, July 26, 1999. Signed to a PTO (try-out) contract by **Manchester** (AHL), September 30, 2001. Signed as a free agent by **Atlanta**, August 12, 2003. Signed as a free agent by **Mannheim** (Germany), July 9, 2004. Signed as a free agent by **Boston**, August 15, 2005. Signed as a free agent by **Tampa Bay**, July 15, 2006.

HEALEY, Paul

(HEE-lee, PAWL)

Left wing. Shoots right. 6'2", 198 lbs. Born, Edmonton, Alta., March 20, 1975. Philadelphia's 7th choice, 192nd overall, in 1993 Entry Draft.

			Regular Season														Playoffs								
Season	Club	League	GP	G	A	Pts	PIM	PP	SH	GW	S	%	+/-	TF	F%	Min	GP	G	A	Pts	PIM	PP	SH	GW	Min
1991-92	Ft. Saskatchewan	AJHL	52	11	19	30	40	....	....	....	....	....	....	....	....	....	....	....	....	....	....	....	....	....	....
1992-93	Prince Albert	WHL	72	12	20	32	66	....	....	....	....	....	....	....	....	....	....	....	....	....	....	....	....	....	....
1993-94	Prince Albert	WHL	63	23	26	49	70	....	....	....	....	....	....	....	....	....	....	....	....	....	....	....	....	....	....
1994-95	Prince Albert	WHL	71	43	50	93	67	....	....	....	....	....	....	....	....	....	12	3	4	7	2	....	....	....	....
1995-96	Hershey Bears	AHL	60	7	15	22	35	....	....	....	....	....	....	....	....	....	....	....	....	....	....	....	....	....	....
1996-97	**Philadelphia**	**NHL**	**2**	**0**	**0**	**0**	**0**	**0**	**0**	**0**	**0**	**0.0**	**0**	....	....	....	....	....	....	....	....	....	....	....	....
	Philadelphia	AHL	64	21	19	40	56	....	....	....	....	....	....	....	....	....	10	4	1	5	10	....	....	....	....
1997-98	**Philadelphia**	**NHL**	**4**	**0**	**0**	**0**	**12**	**0**	**0**	**0**	**0**	**0.0**	**0**	....	....	....	....	....	....	....	....	....	....	....	....
	Philadelphia	AHL	71	34	18	52	48	....	....	....	....	....	....	....	....	....	20	6	2	8	4	....	....	....	....
1998-99	Philadelphia	AHL	72	26	20	46	39	....	....	....	....	....	....	....	....	....	15	4	6	10	11	....	....	....	....
99-2000	Milwaukee	IHL	76	21	18	39	28	....	....	....	....	....	....	....	....	....	3	1	2	3	0	....	....	....	....
2000-01	Hamilton	AHL	79	39	32	71	34	....	....	....	....	....	....	....	....	....	....	....	....	....	....	....	....	....	....
2001-02	**Toronto**	**NHL**	**21**	**3**	**7**	**10**	**2**	**0**	**0**	**0**	**29**	**10.3**	**7**	**5**	**60.0**	**11:03**	**18**	**0**	**1**	**1**	**2**	**0**	**0**	**0**	**9:01**
	St. John's	AHL	58	27	29	56	30	....	....	....	....	....	....	....	....	....	2	1	1	2	8	....	....	....	....
2002-03	**Toronto**	**NHL**	**44**	**3**	**7**	**10**	**16**	**1**	**0**	**0**	**43**	**7.0**	**8**	**13**	**38.5**	**12:00**	**4**	**0**	**1**	**1**	**2**	**0**	**0**	**0**	**9:14**
	St. John's	AHL	17	6	10	16	12	....	....	....	....	....	....	....	....	....	....	....	....	....	....	....	....	....	....
2003-04	**NY Rangers**	**NHL**	**4**	**0**	**0**	**0**	**0**	**0**	**0**	**0**	**0**	**0.0**	**0**	**1**	**0.0**	**4:50**	....	....	....	....	....	....	....	....	....
	Hartford	AHL	50	11	10	21	37	....	....	....	....	....	....	....	....	....	....	....	....	....	....	....	....	....	....
	San Antonio	AHL	18	5	5	10	20	....	....	....	....	....	....	....	....	....	....	....	....	....	....	....	....	....	....
2004-05	San Antonio	AHL	62	6	17	23	50	....	....	....	....	....	....	....	....	....	....	....	....	....	....	....	....	....	....
	Edmonton	AHL	17	3	6	9	29	....	....	....	....	....	....	....	....	....	....	....	....	....	....	....	....	....	....
2005-06	**Colorado**	**NHL**	**2**	**0**	**0**	**0**	**14**	**0**	**0**	**0**	**0**	**0.0**	**0**	**0**	**0.0**	**5:33**	....	....	....	....	....	....	....	....	....
	Lowell	AHL	59	19	21	40	51	....	....	....	....	....	....	....	....	....	....	....	....	....	....	....	....	....	....
	NHL Totals		**77**	**6**	**14**	**20**	**44**	**1**	**0**	**0**	**72**	**8.3**		**19**	**42.1**	**11:08**	**22**	**0**	**2**	**2**	**4**	**0**	**0**	**0**	**9:03**

WHL East Second All-Star Team (1995)

Traded to **Nashville** by **Philadelphia** for Matt Henderson, September 27, 1999. Signed as a free agent by **Edmonton**, August 31, 2000. Signed as a free agent by **Toronto**, July 24, 2001. Signed as a free agent by **NY Rangers**, July 28, 2003. Traded to **Florida** by **NY Rangers** for Jeff Paul, March 9, 2004. Loaned to **Edmonton** (AHL) by **Florida** (San Antonio-AHL) for cash, March 12, 2005. Signed as a free agent by **Colorado**, August 16, 2005.

HEATLEY, Dany

(HEET-lee, DA-nee) **OTT.**

Right wing. Shoots left. 6'3", 215 lbs. Born, Freiburg, West Germany, January 21, 1981. Atlanta's 1st choice, 2nd overall, in 2000 Entry Draft.

			Regular Season														Playoffs								
Season	Club	League	GP	G	A	Pts	PIM	PP	SH	GW	S	%	+/-	TF	F%	Min	GP	G	A	Pts	PIM	PP	SH	GW	Min
1996-97	Calgary Blazers	AMHL	25	30	42	72	26	....	....	....	....	....	....	....	....	....	....	....	....	....	....	....	....	....	....
1997-98	Calgary Buffaloes	AMHL	36	39	42	*81	34	....	....	....	....	....	....	....	....	....	10	10	12	*22	30	....	....	....	....
1998-99	Calgary Canucks	AJHL	60	*70	56	*126	91	....	....	....	....	....	....	....	....	....	13	*22	13	*35	6	....	....	....	....
99-2000	U. of Wisconsin	WCHA	38	28	28	56	32	....	....	....	....	....	....	....	....	....	....	....	....	....	....	....	....	....	....
2000-01	U. of Wisconsin	WCHA	39	24	33	57	74	....	....	....	....	....	....	....	....	....	....	....	....	....	....	....	....	....	....
2001-02	**Atlanta**	**NHL**	**82**	**26**	**41**	**67**	**56**	**7**	**0**	**4**	**202**	**12.9**	**–19**	**116**	**32.8**	**19:53**	....	....	....	....	....	....	....	....	....
2002-03	**Atlanta**	**NHL**	**77**	**41**	**48**	**89**	**58**	**19**	**1**	**6**	**252**	**16.3**	**–8**	**49**	**36.7**	**21:57**	....	....	....	....	....	....	....	....	....
2003-04	**Atlanta**	**NHL**	**31**	**13**	**12**	**25**	**18**	**5**	**0**	**3**	**83**	**15.7**	**–8**	**41**	**24.4**	**19:53**	....	....	....	....	....	....	....	....	....
2004-05	SC Bern	Swiss	16	14	10	24	58	....	....	....	....	....	....	....	....	....	....	....	....	....	....	....	....	....	....
	Ak Bars Kazan	Russia	11	3	1	4	22	....	....	....	....	....	....	....	....	....	4	2	1	3	4	....	....	....	....
2005-06	**Ottawa**	**NHL**	**82**	**50**	**53**	**103**	**86**	**23**	**2**	**7**	**300**	**16.7**	**29**	**166**	**53.6**	**21:09**	**10**	**3**	**9**	**12**	**11**	**3**	**0**	**1**	**18:56**
	Canada	Olympics	6	2	1	3	8	....	....	....	....	....	....	....	....	....	....	....	....	....	....	....	....	....	....
	NHL Totals		**272**	**130**	**154**	**284**	**218**	**54**	**3**	**20**	**837**	**15.5**		**372**	**41.7**	**20:51**	**10**	**3**	**9**	**12**	**11**	**3**	**0**	**1**	**18:56**

WCHA First All-Star Team (2000) • WCHA Rookie of the Year (2000) • NCAA West Second All-American Team (2000) • WCHA Second All-Star Team (2001) • NCAA West First All-American Team (2001) • NHL All-Rookie Team (2002) • Calder Memorial Trophy (2002) • NHL Second All-Star Team (2006)

Played in NHL All-Star Game (2003)

• Missed majority of 2003-04 season recovering from injuries suffered in automobile accident, September 29, 2003. Signed as a free agent by **Bern** (Swiss), October 13, 2004. Signed as a free agent by **Kazan** (Russia), February 9, 2005. Traded to **Ottawa** by **Atlanta** for Marian Hossa and Greg de Vries, August 23, 2005.

HECHT, Jochen

(HEHKHT, YOH-khehn) **BUF.**

Left wing. Shoots left. 6'1", 200 lbs. Born, Mannheim, West Germany, June 21, 1977. St. Louis' 1st choice, 49th overall, in 1995 Entry Draft.

			Regular Season														Playoffs								
Season	Club	League	GP	G	A	Pts	PIM	PP	SH	GW	S	%	+/-	TF	F%	Min	GP	G	A	Pts	PIM	PP	SH	GW	Min
1993-94	Mannheim Jr.	Ger-Jr.	28	27	13	40	103	....	....	....	....	....	....	....	....	....	....	....	....	....	....	....	....	....	....
1994-95	Adler Mannheim	Germany	43	11	12	23	68	....	....	....	....	....	....	....	....	....	10	5	4	9	12	....	....	....	....
1995-96	Adler Mannheim	Germany	44	12	16	28	68	....	....	....	....	....	....	....	....	....	8	3	2	5	6	....	....	....	....
1996-97	Adler Mannheim	Germany	46	21	21	42	36	....	....	....	....	....	....	....	....	....	9	3	3	6	4	....	....	....	....
1997-98	Adler Mannheim	Germany	44	7	19	26	42	....	....	....	....	....	....	....	....	....	10	1	1	2	14	....	....	....	....
	Adler Mannheim	EuroHL	5	0	4	4	8	....	....	....	....	....	....	....	....	....	....	....	....	....	....	....	....	....	....
	Germany	Olympics	4	1	0	1	6	....	....	....	....	....	....	....	....	....	....	....	....	....	....	....	....	....	....
1998-99	**St. Louis**	**NHL**	**3**	**0**	**0**	**0**	**0**	**0**	**0**	**0**	**4**	**0.0**	**–2**	**19**	**21.1**	**13:16**	**5**	**2**	**0**	**2**	**0**	**0**	**0**	**0**	**16:40**
	Worcester IceCats	AHL	74	21	35	56	48	....	....	....	....	....	....	....	....	....	4	1	1	2	2	....	....	....	....
99-2000	**St. Louis**	**NHL**	**63**	**13**	**21**	**34**	**28**	**5**	**0**	**1**	**140**	**9.3**	**20**	**75**	**49.3**	**15:25**	**7**	**4**	**6**	**10**	**2**	**1**	**0**	**1**	**17:02**
2000-01	**St. Louis**	**NHL**	**72**	**19**	**25**	**44**	**48**	**8**	**3**	**1**	**208**	**9.1**	**11**	**160**	**43.8**	**17:56**	**15**	**2**	**4**	**6**	**4**	**0**	**0**	**0**	**17:19**
2001-02	**Edmonton**	**NHL**	**82**	**16**	**24**	**40**	**60**	**5**	**0**	**3**	**211**	**7.6**	**4**	**26**	**53.9**	**15:00**	....	....	....	....	....	....	....	....	....
	Germany	Olympics	4	1	1	2	2	....	....	....	....	....	....	....	....	....	....	....	....	....	....	....	....	....	....
2002-03	**Buffalo**	**NHL**	**49**	**10**	**16**	**26**	**30**	**2**	**0**	**2**	**145**	**6.9**	**4**	**33**	**30.3**	**17:55**	....	....	....	....	....	....	....	....	....
2003-04	**Buffalo**	**NHL**	**64**	**15**	**37**	**52**	**49**	**2**	**1**	**0**	**174**	**8.6**	**17**	**141**	**43.3**	**19:00**	....	....	....	....	....	....	....	....	....
2004-05	Adler Mannheim	Germany	48	16	34	50	151	....	....	....	....	....	....	....	....	....	14	10	10	*20	14	....	....	....	....
2005-06	**Buffalo**	**NHL**	**64**	**18**	**24**	**42**	**34**	**4**	**2**	**4**	**179**	**10.1**	**10**	**156**	**39.7**	**18:07**	**15**	**2**	**6**	**8**	**8**	**0**	**0**	**1**	**17:29**
	NHL Totals		**397**	**91**	**147**	**238**	**249**	**26**	**6**	**11**	**1061**	**8.6**		**610**	**42.3**	**17:05**	**42**	**10**	**16**	**26**	**14**	**1**	**0**	**2**	**17:15**

Traded to **Edmonton** by **St. Louis** with Marty Reasoner and Jan Horacek for Doug Weight and Michel Riesen, July 1, 2001. Traded to **Buffalo** by **Edmonton** for Atlanta's 2nd round choice (previously acquired, Edmonton selected Jeff Deslauriers) in 2002 Entry Draft and Nashville's 2nd round choice (previously acquired, Edmonton selected Jarret Stoll) in 2002 Entry Draft, June 22, 2002. Signed as a free agent by **Mannheim** (Germany), August 2, 2004.

HEDICAN, Bret

(HEH-dih-kan, BREHT) **CAR.**

Defense. Shoots left. 6'2", 205 lbs. Born, St. Paul, MN, August 10, 1970. St. Louis' 10th choice, 198th overall, in 1988 Entry Draft.

			Regular Season														Playoffs								
Season	Club	League	GP	G	A	Pts	PIM	PP	SH	GW	S	%	+/-	TF	F%	Min	GP	G	A	Pts	PIM	PP	SH	GW	Min
1987-88	North St. Paul	High-MN	23	15	19	34	16	....	....	....	....	....	....	....	....	....	....	....	....	....	....	....	....	....	....
1988-89	St. Cloud State	NCAA-3	28	5	3	8	28	....	....	....	....	....	....	....	....	....	....	....	....	....	....	....	....	....	....
1989-90	St. Cloud State	NCAA-3	36	4	17	21	37	....	....	....	....	....	....	....	....	....	....	....	....	....	....	....	....	....	....
1990-91	St. Cloud State	WCHA	41	21	26	47	26	....	....	....	....	....	....	....	....	....	....	....	....	....	....	....	....	....	....
1991-92	United States	Nat-Tm	54	1	8	9	59	....	....	....	....	....	....	....	....	....	....	....	....	....	....	....	....	....	....
	United States	Olympics	8	0	0	0	4	....	....	....	....	....	....	....	....	....	....	....	....	....	....	....	....	....	....
	St. Louis	**NHL**	**4**	**1**	**0**	**1**	**0**	**0**	**0**	**0**	**1**	**100.0**	**1**	....	....	....	**5**	**0**	**0**	**0**	**0**	**0**	**0**	**0**	....
1992-93	**St. Louis**	**NHL**	**42**	**0**	**8**	**8**	**30**	**0**	**0**	**0**	**40**	**0.0**	**–2**	....	....	....	**10**	**0**	**0**	**0**	**14**	**0**	**0**	**0**	....
	Peoria Rivermen	IHL	19	0	8	8	10	....	....	....	....	....	....	....	....	....	....	....	....	....	....	....	....	....	....
1993-94	**St. Louis**	**NHL**	**61**	**0**	**11**	**11**	**64**	**0**	**0**	**0**	**78**	**0.0**	**–8**	....	....	....	....	....	....	....	....	....	....	....	....
	Vancouver	**NHL**	**8**	**0**	**1**	**1**	**0**	**0**	**0**	**0**	**10**	**0.0**	**1**	....	....	....	**24**	**1**	**6**	**7**	**16**	**0**	**0**	**0**	....
1994-95	**Vancouver**	**NHL**	**45**	**2**	**11**	**13**	**34**	**0**	**0**	**0**	**56**	**3.6**	**–3**	....	....	....	**11**	**0**	**2**	**2**	**6**	**0**	**0**	**0**	....
1995-96	**Vancouver**	**NHL**	**77**	**6**	**23**	**29**	**83**	**1**	**0**	**0**	**113**	**5.3**	**8**	....	....	....	**6**	**0**	**1**	**1**	**10**	**0**	**0**	**0**	....
1996-97	**Vancouver**	**NHL**	**67**	**4**	**15**	**19**	**51**	**2**	**0**	**1**	**93**	**4.3**	**–3**	....	....	....	....	....	....	....	....	....	....	....	....
1997-98	**Vancouver**	**NHL**	**71**	**3**	**24**	**27**	**79**	**1**	**0**	**0**	**84**	**3.6**	**3**	....	....	....	....	....	....	....	....	....	....	....	....
1998-99	**Vancouver**	**NHL**	**42**	**2**	**11**	**13**	**34**	**0**	**2**	**0**	**52**	**3.8**	**7**	**0**	**0.0**	**18:40**	....	....	....	....	....	....	....	....	....
	Florida	**NHL**	**25**	**3**	**7**	**10**	**17**	**0**	**0**	**1**	**38**	**7.9**	**–2**	**0**	**0.0**	**22:24**	....	....	....	....	....	....	....	....	....
99-2000	**Florida**	**NHL**	**76**	**6**	**19**	**25**	**68**	**2**	**0**	**1**	**58**	**10.3**	**4**	**0**	**0.0**	**19:36**	**4**	**0**	**0**	**0**	**0**	**0**	**0**	**0**	**20:42**
2000-01	**Florida**	**NHL**	**70**	**5**	**15**	**20**	**72**	**4**	**0**	**1**	**104**	**4.8**	**–7**	**0**	**0.0**	**21:49**	....	....	....	....	....	....	....	....	....
2001-02	**Florida**	**NHL**	**31**	**3**	**7**	**10**	**12**	**0**	**0**	**0**	**46**	**6.5**	**–4**	**0**	**0.0**	**24:27**	....	....	....	....	....	....	....	....	....
	Carolina	**NHL**	**26**	**2**	**4**	**6**	**10**	**0**	**0**	**1**	**39**	**5.1**	**3**	**0**	**0.0**	**22:56**	**23**	**1**	**4**	**5**	**20**	**0**	**0**	**0**	**23:52**
2002-03	**Carolina**	**NHL**	**72**	**3**	**14**	**17**	**75**	**1**	**0**	**1**	**113**	**2.7**	**–24**	**0**	**0.0**	**23:02**	....	....	....	....	....	....	....	....	....
2003-04	**Carolina**	**NHL**	**81**	**7**	**17**	**24**	**64**	**2**	**0**	**3**	**112**	**6.3**	**–10**	**0**	**0.0**	**22:35**	....	....	....	....	....	....	....	....	....

			Regular Season														Playoffs								
Season	Club	League	GP	G	A	Pts	PIM	PP	SH	GW	S	%	+/-	TF	F%	Min	GP	G	A	Pts	PIM	PP	SH	GW	Min
2004-05			DID NOT PLAY																						
2005-06♦	**Carolina**	**NHL**	**74**	**5**	**22**	**27**	**58**	**2**	**1**	**1**	**73**	**6.8**	**11**	**0**	**0.0**	**20:19**	**25**	**2**	**9**	**11**	**42**	**0**	**0**	**0**	**22:40**
	United States	Olympics	6	0	1	1	6	....	....	....	....	....	....	....	....	....	....	....	....	....	....	....	....	....	....
	NHL Totals		**872**	**52**	**209**	**261**	**751**	**15**	**3**	**10**	**1110**	**4.7**		**0**	**0.0**	**21:32**	**108**	**4**	**22**	**26**	**108**	**0**	**0**	**0**	**23:03**

WCHA First All-Star Team (1991)

Traded to **Vancouver** by **St. Louis** with Jeff Brown and Nathan LaFayette for Craig Janney, March 21, 1994. Traded to **Florida** by **Vancouver** with Pavel Bure, Brad Ference and Vancouver's 3rd round choice (Robert Fried) in 2000 Entry Draft for Ed Jovanovski, Dave Gagner, Mike Brown, Kevin Weekes and Florida's 1st round choice (Nathan Smith) in 2000 Entry Draft, January 17, 1999. Traded to **Carolina** by **Florida** with Kevyn Adams, Tomas Malec for Sandis Ozolinsh and Byron Ritchie, January 16, 2002.

HEDIN, Pierre

(heh-DEEN, PEE-air) **TOR.**

Defense. Shoots left. 6'2", 200 lbs. Born, Ornskoldsvik, Sweden, February 19, 1978. Toronto's 8th choice, 239th overall, in 1999 Entry Draft.

Season	Club	League	GP	G	A	Pts	PIM	PP	SH	GW	S	%	+/-	TF	F%	Min	GP	G	A	Pts	PIM	PP	SH	GW	Min
1995-96	MoDo Jr.	Swe-Jr.	21	0	3	3	20																		
1996-97	MoDo Jr.	Swe-Jr.	29	6	8	14	34	....	....	....	....	....	....	....	....	....	....	....	....	....	....	....	....	....	....
	MoDo	Sweden	19	1	2	3	6	....	....	....	....	....	....	....	....	....	....	....	....	....	....	....	....	....	....
1997-98	Malmo Jr.	Swe-Jr.	7	1	6	7	10	....	....	....	....	....	....	....	....	....	....	....	....	....	....	....	....	....	....
	MoDo	Sweden	29	2	1	3	26	....	....	....	....	....	....	....	....	....	9	1	1	2	4	....	....	....	....
1998-99	MoDo	Sweden	41	6	5	11	28	....	....	....	....	....	....	....	....	....	13	1	1	2	12	....	....	....	....
99-2000	MoDo	Sweden	48	9	5	14	36	....	....	....	....	....	....	....	....	....	13	0	2	2	8	....	....	....	....
2000-01	MoDo	Sweden	46	5	8	13	59	....	....	....	....	....	....	....	....	....	7	3	0	3	4	....	....	....	....
2001-02	MODO	Sweden	39	7	9	16	20	....	....	....	....	....	....	....	....	....	14	*8	2	10	10	....	....	....	....
2002-03	MODO	Sweden	46	8	14	22	32	....	....	....	....	....	....	....	....	....	6	0	1	1	4	....	....	....	....
2003-04	**Toronto**	**NHL**	**3**	**0**	**1**	**1**	**0**	**0**	**0**	**0**	**4**	**0.0**	**–1**	**0**	**0.0**	**19:20**	....	....	....	....	....	....	....	....	....
	St. John's	AHL	62	5	19	24	52	....	....	....	....	....	....	....	....	....	....	....	....	....	....	....	....	....	....
2004-05	MODO	Sweden	31	3	4	7	28	....	....	....	....	....	....	....	....	....	6	1	0	1	6	....	....	....	....
2005-06	Adler Mannheim	Germany	50	8	13	21	52	....	....	....	....	....	....	....	....	....	....	....	....	....	....	....	....	....	....
	NHL Totals		**3**	**0**	**1**	**1**	**0**	**0**	**0**	**0**	**4**	**0.0**		**0**	**0.0**	**19:20**	....	....	....	....	....	....	....	....	....

Signed as a free agent by **MODO** (Sweden), September 18, 2004. Signed as a free agent by **Mannheim** (Germany), August 25, 2005.

HEDSTROM, Jonathan

(HEHD-struhm, JAWN-ah-thuhn)

Right wing. Shoots left. 6', 200 lbs. Born, Skelleftea, Sweden, December 27, 1977. Toronto's 8th choice, 221st overall, in 1997 Entry Draft.

Season	Club	League	GP	G	A	Pts	PIM	PP	SH	GW	S	%	+/-	TF	F%	Min	GP	G	A	Pts	PIM	PP	SH	GW	Min
1995-96	Skelleftea AIK HK	Sweden-2	7	0	0	0	0	....	....	....	....	....	....	....	....	....	....	....	....	....	....	....	....	....	....
1996-97	Skelleftea Jr.	Swe-Jr.	9	4	4	8	....	....	....	....	....	....	....	....	....	....	....	....	....	....	....	....	....	....	....
	Skelleftea AIK HK	Sweden-2	12	1	1	2	10	....	....	....	....	....	....	....	....	....	6	0	0	0	2	....	....	....	....
1997-98	Skelleftea Jr.	Swe-Jr.	1	0	0	0	2	....	....	....	....	....	....	....	....	....	....	....	....	....	....	....	....	....	....
	Skelleftea AIK HK	Sweden-2	16	2	3	5	....	....	....	....	....	....	....	....	....	....	....	....	....	....	....	....	....	....	....
1998-99	Skelleftea AIK HK	Sweden-2	36	15	28	43	74	....	....	....	....	....	....	....	....	....	....	....	....	....	....	....	....	....	....
99-2000	Lulea HF	Sweden	48	9	17	26	46	....	....	....	....	....	....	....	....	....	9	2	1	3	12	....	....	....	....
2000-01	Lulea HF	Sweden	46	9	19	28	68	....	....	....	....	....	....	....	....	....	12	1	6	7	16	....	....	....	....
2001-02	Lulea HF	Sweden	47	11	7	18	38	....	....	....	....	....	....	....	....	....	4	2	1	3	6	....	....	....	....
2002-03	**Anaheim**	**NHL**	**4**	**0**	**0**	**0**	**0**	**0**	**0**	**0**	**3**	**0.0**	**–1**	**1**	**0.0**	**7:51**	....	....	....	....	....	....	....	....	....
	Cincinnati	AHL	50	14	21	35	62	....	....	....	....	....	....	....	....	....	....	....	....	....	....	....	....	....	....
2003-04	Djurgarden	Sweden	48	12	22	34	94	....	....	....	....	....	....	....	....	....	3	0	2	2	12	....	....	....	....
2004-05	Timra IK	Sweden	46	14	21	35	92	....	....	....	....	....	....	....	....	....	7	3	5	8	16	....	....	....	....
2005-06	**Anaheim**	**NHL**	**79**	**13**	**14**	**27**	**48**	**2**	**2**	**5**	**99**	**13.1**	**2**	**26**	**26.9**	**16:17**	**3**	**0**	**1**	**1**	**2**	**0**	**0**	**0**	**16:58**
	NHL Totals		**83**	**13**	**14**	**27**	**48**	**2**	**2**	**5**	**102**	**12.7**		**27**	**25.9**	**15:52**	**3**	**0**	**1**	**1**	**2**	**0**	**0**	**0**	**16:58**

Rights traded to **Anaheim** by **Toronto** for Anaheim's 6th (Vadim Sozinov) and 7th (Markus Seikola) round choices in 2000 Entry Draft, June 25, 2000. Signed as a free agent by **Djurgarden** (Sweden), September 1, 2003. Signed as a free agent by **Timra** (Sweden), September, 2004.

HEEREMA, Jeff

(HEER-eh-muh, JEHF) **OTT.**

Right wing. Shoots right. 6'2", 212 lbs. Born, Thunder Bay, Ont., January 17, 1980. Carolina's 1st choice, 11th overall, in 1998 Entry Draft.

Season	Club	League	GP	G	A	Pts	PIM	PP	SH	GW	S	%	+/-	TF	F%	Min	GP	G	A	Pts	PIM	PP	SH	GW	Min
1996-97	T. Bay Kings	TBMHL	54	42	29	71	112	....	....	....	....	....	....	....	....	....	....	....	....	....	....	....	....	....	....
1997-98	Sarnia Sting	OHL	63	32	40	72	88	....	....	....	....	....	....	....	....	....	5	4	1	5	10	....	....	....	....
1998-99	Sarnia Sting	OHL	62	31	39	70	113	....	....	....	....	....	....	....	....	....	6	5	1	6	0	....	....	....	....
99-2000	Sarnia Sting	OHL	67	36	41	77	62	....	....	....	....	....	....	....	....	....	7	4	2	6	10	....	....	....	....
2000-01	Cincinnati	IHL	73	17	16	33	42	....	....	....	....	....	....	....	....	....	4	0	0	0	0	....	....	....	....
2001-02	Lowell	AHL	76	33	37	70	90	....	....	....	....	....	....	....	....	....	5	2	3	5	2	....	....	....	....
2002-03	**Carolina**	**NHL**	**10**	**3**	**0**	**3**	**2**	**1**	**0**	**0**	**16**	**18.8**	**–2**	**0**	**0.0**	**9:37**	....	....	....	....	....	....	....	....	....
	Lowell	AHL	36	15	17	32	25	....	....	....	....	....	....	....	....	....	....	....	....	....	....	....	....	....	....
2003-04	**St. Louis**	**NHL**	**22**	**1**	**2**	**3**	**4**	**0**	**0**	**1**	**28**	**3.6**	**–5**	**2**	**50.0**	**10:26**	....	....	....	....	....	....	....	....	....
	Worcester IceCats	AHL	1	0	0	0	2	....	....	....	....	....	....	....	....	....	....	....	....	....	....	....	....	....	....
	Hartford	AHL	41	12	15	27	25	....	....	....	....	....	....	....	....	....	4	0	0	0	9	....	....	....	....
2004-05	Manitoba Moose	AHL	80	14	31	45	67	....	....	....	....	....	....	....	....	....	14	4	6	10	12	....	....	....	....
2005-06	Binghamton	AHL	77	27	47	74	69	....	....	....	....	....	....	....	....	....	....	....	....	....	....	....	....	....	....
	NHL Totals		**32**	**4**	**2**	**6**	**6**	**1**	**0**	**1**	**44**	**9.1**		**2**	**50.0**	**10:11**	....	....	....	....	....	....	....	....	....

Claimed on waivers by **NY Rangers** from **Carolina**, September 30, 2003. Claimed by **St. Louis** from **NY Rangers** in Waiver Draft, October 3, 2003. Claimed on waivers by **NY Rangers** from **St. Louis**, January 10, 2004. Signed as a free agent by **Vancouver**, August 19, 2004. Signed as a free agent by **Ottawa**, August 26, 2005.

HEJDUK, Milan

(HAY-dook, MEE-lan) **COL.**

Right wing. Shoots right. 6', 190 lbs. Born, Usti nad Labem, Czech., February 14, 1976. Quebec's 6th choice, 87th overall, in 1994 Entry Draft.

Season	Club	League	GP	G	A	Pts	PIM	PP	SH	GW	S	%	+/-	TF	F%	Min	GP	G	A	Pts	PIM	PP	SH	GW	Min
1993-94	HC Pardubice	CzRep	22	6	3	9	....	....	....	....	....	....	....	....	....	....	10	5	1	6	....	....	....	....	....
1994-95	HC Pardubice	CzRep	43	11	13	24	6	....	....	....	....	....	....	....	....	....	6	3	1	4	0	....	....	....	....
1995-96	Pardubice	CzRep	37	13	7	20	....	....	....	....	....	....	....	....	....	....	....	....	....	....	....	....	....	....	....
1996-97	Pardubice	CzRep	51	27	11	38	10	....	....	....	....	....	....	....	....	....	10	6	0	6	27	....	....	....	....
1997-98	Pardubice	CzRep	48	26	19	45	20	....	....	....	....	....	....	....	....	....	3	0	0	0	2	....	....	....	....
	Czech Republic	Olympics	4	0	0	0	2	....	....	....	....	....	....	....	....	....	....	....	....	....	....	....	....	....	....
1998-99	**Colorado**	**NHL**	**82**	**14**	**34**	**48**	**26**	**4**	**0**	**5**	**178**	**7.9**	**8**	**2**	**50.0**	**15:45**	**16**	**6**	**6**	**12**	**4**	**1**	**0**	**3**	**15:53**
99-2000	**Colorado**	**NHL**	**82**	**36**	**36**	**72**	**16**	**13**	**0**	**9**	**228**	**15.8**	**14**	**3**	**100.0**	**19:58**	**17**	**5**	**4**	**9**	**6**	**3**	**0**	**1**	**19:56**
2000-01♦	**Colorado**	**NHL**	**80**	**41**	**38**	**79**	**36**	**12**	**1**	**9**	**213**	**19.2**	**32**	**3**	**33.3**	**19:52**	**23**	**7**	***16**	**23**	**6**	**4**	**0**	**1**	**21:33**
2001-02	**Colorado**	**NHL**	**62**	**21**	**23**	**44**	**24**	**7**	**1**	**5**	**139**	**15.1**	**0**	**5**	**40.0**	**20:11**	**16**	**3**	**3**	**6**	**4**	**1**	**0**	**0**	**18:24**
	Czech Republic	Olympics	4	1	0	1	0	....	....	....	....	....	....	....	....	....	....	....	....	....	....	....	....	....	....
2002-03	**Colorado**	**NHL**	**82**	***50**	**48**	**98**	**32**	**18**	**0**	**4**	**244**	**20.5**	**52**	**43**	**44.2**	**19:50**	**7**	**2**	**2**	**4**	**2**	**1**	**0**	**0**	**20:42**
2003-04	**Colorado**	**NHL**	**82**	**35**	**40**	**75**	**20**	**16**	**0**	**6**	**237**	**14.8**	**19**	**69**	**47.8**	**18:46**	**11**	**5**	**2**	**7**	**0**	**2**	**0**	**0**	**18:40**
2004-05	Pardubice	CzRep	48	25	26	51	14	....	....	....	....	....	....	....	....	....	16	6	2	8	6	....	....	....	....
2005-06	**Colorado**	**NHL**	**74**	**24**	**34**	**58**	**24**	**14**	**1**	**2**	**221**	**10.9**	**13**	**23**	**17.4**	**18:33**	**9**	**2**	**6**	**8**	**2**	**0**	**0**	**0**	**20:56**
	Czech Republic	Olympics	8	2	1	3	2	....	....	....	....	....	....	....	....	....	....	....	....	....	....	....	....	....	....
	NHL Totals		**544**	**221**	**253**	**474**	**178**	**84**	**3**	**40**	**1460**	**15.1**		**148**	**42.6**	**18:57**	**99**	**30**	**39**	**69**	**24**	**12**	**0**	**5**	**19:25**

NHL All-Rookie Team (1999) • NHL Second All-Star Team (2003) • Bud Light Plus/Minus Award (2003) (tied with Peter Forsberg) • Maurice "Rocket" Richard Trophy (2003)

Played in NHL All-Star Game (2000, 2001)

Rights transferred to **Colorado** after **Quebec** franchise relocated, June 21, 1995. Signed as a free agent by **Pardubice** (CzRep), September 18, 2004.

HELBLING, Timo

(HEHL-blihng, TEE-moh) **WSH.**

Defense. Shoots right. 6'3", 209 lbs. Born, Basel, Switz., July 21, 1981. Nashville's 11th choice, 162nd overall, in 1999 Entry Draft.

Season	Club	League	GP	G	A	Pts	PIM	PP	SH	GW	S	%	+/-	TF	F%	Min	GP	G	A	Pts	PIM	PP	SH	GW	Min
1997-98	HC Davos Jr.	Swiss-Jr.	34	6	6	12	38	....	....	....	....	....	....	....	....	....	....	....	....	....	....	....	....	....	....
1998-99	HC Davos Jr.	Swiss-Jr.	28	5	10	15	116	....	....	....	....	....	....	....	....	....	2	1	3	4	35	....	....	....	....
	HC Davos	Swiss	44	0	0	0	8	....	....	....	....	....	....	....	....	....	4	0	0	0	0	....	....	....	....
99-2000	HC Davos	Swiss	44	0	0	0	49	....	....	....	....	....	....	....	....	....	5	0	0	0	0	....	....	....	....
2000-01	Windsor Spitfires	OHL	54	7	14	21	90	....	....	....	....	....	....	....	....	....	7	0	2	2	11	....	....	....	....
	Milwaukee	IHL	....	....	....	....	....	....	....	....	....	....	....	....	....	....	1	0	0	0	0	....	....	....	....
2001-02	Milwaukee	AHL	67	2	6	8	59	....	....	....	....	....	....	....	....	....	....	....	....	....	....	....	....	....	....
2002-03	Milwaukee	AHL	23	0	1	1	37	....	....	....	....	....	....	....	....	....	....	....	....	....	....	....	....	....	....
	Toledo Storm	ECHL	35	3	8	11	75	....	....	....	....	....	....	....	....	....	....	....	....	....	....	....	....	....	....
2003-04	Milwaukee	AHL	37	0	2	2	46	....	....	....	....	....	....	....	....	....	7	0	1	1	2	....	....	....	....
	Utah Grizzlies	AHL	23	3	2	5	47	....	....	....	....	....	....	....	....	....	....	....	....	....	....	....	....	....	....
2004-05	Kloten Flyers	Swiss	44	2	9	11	120	....	....	....	....	....	....	....	....	....	5	1	3	4	8	....	....	....	....

			Regular Season														Playoffs								
Season	Club	League	GP	G	A	Pts	PIM	PP	SH	GW	S	%	+/-	TF	F%	Min	GP	G	A	Pts	PIM	PP	SH	GW	Min
2005-06	**Tampa Bay**	**NHL**	**9**	**0**	**1**	**1**	**6**	**0**	**0**	**0**	**2**	**0.0**	**–3**	**0**	**0.0**	**10:19**									
	Springfield	AHL	60	7	14	21	56																		
	NHL Totals		**9**	**0**	**1**	**1**	**6**	**0**	**0**	**0**	**2**	**0.0**		**0**	**0.0**	**10:19**									

Traded to **Tampa Bay** by **Nashville** for Tampa Bay's 8th round choice (Pekka Rinne) in 2004 Entry Draft, February 25, 2004. Signed as a free agent by **Kloten** (Swiss), June 17, 2004. Signed as a free agent by **Washington**, August 9, 2006.

HELMER, Bryan

(HEHL-muhr, BRIGH-uhn) **PHX.**

Defense. Shoots right. 6'1", 200 lbs. Born, Sault Ste. Marie, Ont., July 15, 1972.

Season	Club	League	GP	G	A	Pts	PIM	PP	SH	GW	S	%	+/-	TF	F%	Min	GP	G	A	Pts	PIM	PP	SH	GW	Min
1989-90	Wellington Dukes	OHA-B	44	4	20	24	204																		
	Belleville Bulls	OHL	6	0	1	1	0																		
1990-91	Wellington Dukes	OHA-B	50	11	14	25	109																		
1991-92	Wellington Dukes	MTJHL	42	17	31	48	66										3	2	1	3	0				
1992-93	Wellington Dukes	MTJHL	48	21	54	75	84										9	4	8	12	22				
1993-94	Albany River Rats	AHL	65	4	19	23	79										5	0	0	0	9				
1994-95	Albany River Rats	AHL	77	7	36	43	101										7	1	0	1	0				
1995-96	Albany River Rats	AHL	80	14	30	44	107										4	2	0	2	6				
1996-97	Albany River Rats	AHL	77	12	27	39	113										16	1	7	8	10				
1997-98	Albany River Rats	AHL	80	14	49	63	101										13	4	9	13	18				
1998-99	**Phoenix**	**NHL**	**11**	**0**	**0**	**0**	**23**	**0**	**0**	**0**	**11**	**0.0**	**2**	**0**	**0.0**	**7:43**									
	Las Vegas	IHL	8	1	3	4	28																		
	St. Louis	**NHL**	**29**	**0**	**4**	**4**	**19**	**0**	**0**	**0**	**38**	**0.0**	**3**	**1**	**100.0**	**19:08**									
	Worcester IceCats	AHL	16	7	8	15	18										4	0	0	0	12				
99-2000	**St. Louis**	**NHL**	**15**	**1**	**1**	**2**	**10**	**1**	**0**	**1**	**19**	**5.3**	**–3**	**0**	**0.0**	**16:15**									
	Worcester IceCats	AHL	54	10	25	35	124										9	1	4	5	10				
2000-01	**Vancouver**	**NHL**	**20**	**2**	**4**	**6**	**18**	**0**	**0**	**0**	**28**	**7.1**	**0**	**0**	**0.0**	**16:51**									
	Kansas City	IHL	42	4	15	19	76																		
2001-02	**Vancouver**	**NHL**	**40**	**5**	**5**	**10**	**53**	**2**	**0**	**1**	**43**	**11.6**	**10**	**0**	**0.0**	**12:04**	**6**	**0**	**0**	**0**	**0**	**0**	**0**	**0**	**9:09**
	Manitoba Moose	AHL	34	6	18	24	69																		
2002-03	Manitoba Moose	AHL	60	7	24	31	82										14	0	4	4	20				
	Vancouver	**NHL**	**2**	**0**	**0**	**0**	**0**	**0**	**0**	**0**	**2**	**0.0**	**1**	**0**	**0.0**	**13:24**									
2003-04	**Phoenix**	**NHL**	**17**	**0**	**1**	**1**	**10**	**0**	**0**	**0**	**10**	**0.0**	**–5**	**0**	**0.0**	**12:46**									
	Springfield	AHL	9	1	6	7	6																		
2004-05	Grand Rapids	AHL	80	7	18	25	64																		
2005-06	Grand Rapids	AHL	80	12	44	56	138										16	1	8	9	24				
	NHL Totals		**134**	**8**	**15**	**23**	**133**	**3**	**0**	**2**	**151**	**5.3**		**1**	**100.0**	**14:32**	**6**	**0**	**0**	**0**	**0**	**0**	**0**	**0**	**9:09**

AHL First All-Star Team (1998) • AHL Second All-Star Team (2006)

Signed as a free agent by **New Jersey**, July 10, 1994. Signed as a free agent by **Phoenix**, July 17, 1998. Claimed on waivers by **St. Louis** from **Phoenix**, December 19, 1998. Signed as a free agent by **Vancouver**, August 21, 2000. Traded to **Phoenix** by **Vancouver** for Martin Grenier, July 25, 2003. • Missed majority of 2003-04 season recovering from shoulder injury suffered in training camp, September 29, 2003. Signed as a free agent by **Detroit**, July 21, 2004. Signed as a free agent by **Phoenix**, July 19, 2006.

HEMINGWAY, Colin

(HEH-mihng-way, CAW-lihn)

Right wing. Shoots right. 6', 194 lbs. Born, Surrey, B.C., August 12, 1980. St. Louis' 7th choice, 221st overall, in 1999 Entry Draft.

Season	Club	League	GP	G	A	Pts	PIM	PP	SH	GW	S	%	+/-	TF	F%	Min	GP	G	A	Pts	PIM	PP	SH	GW	Min
1996-97	Port Coquitlam	PIJHL	34	23	24	47	52																		
1997-98	South Surrey	BCHL	58	12	16	28	46																		
1998-99	South Surrey	BCHL	59	40	64	104	52																		
99-2000	New Hampshire	H-East	22	3	5	8	6																		
2000-01	New Hampshire	H-East	37	9	18	27	16																		
2001-02	New Hampshire	H-East	40	*33	33	66	30																		
2002-03	New Hampshire	H-East	40	22	25	47	51																		
2003-04	Worcester IceCats	AHL	13	2	0	2	11																		
	Peoria Rivermen	ECHL	36	20	24	44	34										2	0	0	0	0				
2004-05	Worcester IceCats	AHL	24	5	2	7	6																		
	Peoria Rivermen	ECHL	20	8	10	18	6																		
2005-06	**St. Louis**	**NHL**	**3**	**0**	**0**	**0**	**0**	**0**	**0**	**0**	**2**	**0.0**	**–2**	**1**	**0.0**	**7:18**									
	Peoria Rivermen	AHL	29	7	9	16	19																		
	Alaska Aces	ECHL	5	1	2	3	2																		
	NHL Totals		**3**	**0**	**0**	**0**	**0**	**0**	**0**	**0**	**2**	**0.0**		**1**	**0.0**	**7:18**									

Hockey East First All-Star Team (2002) • Hockey East Second All-Star Team (2003) • NCAA East Second All-American Team (2003)

HEMSKY, Ales

(HEHM-skee, ahl-EHSH) **EDM.**

Right wing. Shoots right. 6', 192 lbs. Born, Pardubice, Czech., August 13, 1983. Edmonton's 1st choice, 13th overall, in 2001 Entry Draft.

Season	Club	League	GP	G	A	Pts	PIM	PP	SH	GW	S	%	+/-	TF	F%	Min	GP	G	A	Pts	PIM	PP	SH	GW	Min
99-2000	HC Pardubice Jr.	CzRep-Jr.	45	20	36	56	54										7	4	14	18	36				
	Pardubice	CzRep	4	0	1	1	0																		
2000-01	Hull Olympiques	QMJHL	68	36	64	100	67										5	2	3	5	2				
2001-02	Hull Olympiques	QMJHL	53	27	70	97	86										10	6	10	16	6				
2002-03	**Edmonton**	**NHL**	**59**	**6**	**24**	**30**	**14**	**0**	**0**	**1**	**50**	**12.0**	**5**	**3**	**33.3**	**12:04**	**6**	**0**	**0**	**0**	**0**	**0**	**0**	**0**	**12:46**
2003-04	**Edmonton**	**NHL**	**71**	**12**	**22**	**34**	**14**	**4**	**0**	**3**	**87**	**13.8**	**–7**	**3**	**33.3**	**14:26**									
2004-05	Pardubice	CzRep	47	13	18	31	28										16	4	*10	*14	26				
2005-06	**Edmonton**	**NHL**	**81**	**19**	**58**	**77**	**64**	**7**	**1**	**4**	**178**	**10.7**	**–5**	**7**	**42.9**	**16:59**	**24**	**6**	**11**	**17**	**14**	**4**	**0**	**2**	**16:06**
	Czech Republic	Olympics	8	1	2	3	2																		
	NHL Totals		**211**	**37**	**104**	**141**	**92**	**11**	**1**	**8**	**315**	**11.7**		**13**	**38.5**	**14:45**	**30**	**6**	**11**	**17**	**14**	**4**	**0**	**2**	**15:26**

QMJHL Second All-Star Team (2002)
Signed as a free agent by **Pardubice** (CzRep), September 18, 2004.

HENRY, Alex

(HEHN-ree, AL-ehx)

Defense. Shoots left. 6'5", 220 lbs. Born, Elliot Lake, Ont., October 18, 1979. Edmonton's 2nd choice, 67th overall, in 1998 Entry Draft.

Season	Club	League	GP	G	A	Pts	PIM	PP	SH	GW	S	%	+/-	TF	F%	Min	GP	G	A	Pts	PIM	PP	SH	GW	Min
1995-96	Timmins Majors	NOHA	30	4	11	15	6																		
	Timmins	NOJHA	2	0	0	0	0																		
1996-97	London Knights	OHL	61	1	10	11	65																		
1997-98	London Knights	OHL	62	5	9	14	97										16	0	3	3	14				
1998-99	London Knights	OHL	68	5	23	28	105										25	3	10	13	22				
99-2000	Hamilton	AHL	60	1	0	1	69																		
2000-01	Hamilton	AHL	56	2	3	5	87																		
2001-02	Hamilton	AHL	69	4	8	12	143										15	1	2	3	16				
2002-03	**Edmonton**	**NHL**	**3**	**0**	**0**	**0**	**0**	**0**	**0**	**0**	**0**	**0.0**	**–1**	**0**	**0.0**	**7:02**									
	Washington	**NHL**	**38**	**0**	**0**	**0**	**80**	**0**	**0**	**0**	**8**	**0.0**	**–4**	**1**	**0.0**	**3:39**									
	Portland Pirates	AHL	3	0	1	1	0																		
2003-04	**Minnesota**	**NHL**	**71**	**2**	**4**	**6**	**106**	**0**	**0**	**0**	**37**	**5.4**	**4**	**2**	**0.0**	**14:53**									
2004-05	ESV Kaufbeuren	German-2	26	6	6	12	32																		
2005-06	**Minnesota**	**NHL**	**63**	**0**	**5**	**5**	**73**	**0**	**0**	**0**	**41**	**0.0**	**–4**	**2**	**50.0**	**11:26**									
	NHL Totals		**175**	**2**	**9**	**11**	**259**	**0**	**0**	**0**	**86**	**2.3**		**5**	**20.0**	**11:04**									

Claimed on waivers by **Washington** from **Edmonton**, October 24, 2002. Claimed on waivers by **Minnesota** from **Washington**, October 9, 2003. Signed as a free agent by **Kaufbeuren** (German-2), January 15, 2005.

HEWARD, Jamie

(HEW-uhrd, JAY-mee) **WSH.**

Defense. Shoots right. 6'2", 215 lbs. Born, Regina, Sask., March 30, 1971. Pittsburgh's 1st choice, 16th overall, in 1989 Entry Draft.

Season	Club	League	GP	G	A	Pts	PIM	PP	SH	GW	S	%	+/-	TF	F%	Min	GP	G	A	Pts	PIM	PP	SH	GW	Min
1987-88	Regina Pats	WHL	68	10	17	27	17										4	1	1	2	2				
1988-89	Regina Pats	WHL	52	31	28	59	29																		
1989-90	Regina Pats	WHL	72	14	44	58	42										11	2	2	4	10				
1990-91	Regina Pats	WHL	71	23	61	84	41										8	2	9	11	6				
1991-92	Muskegon	IHL	54	6	21	27	37										14	1	4	5	4				
1992-93	Cleveland	IHL	58	9	18	27	64																		
1993-94	Cleveland	IHL	73	8	16	24	72																		
1994-95	Canada	Nat-Tm	51	11	35	46	32																		

Season	Club	League	GP	G	A	Pts	PIM	PP	SH	GW	S	%	+/-	TF	F%	Min	GP	G	A	Pts	PIM	PP	SH	GW	Min
			Regular Season														Playoffs								
1995-96	**Toronto**	**NHL**	**5**	**0**	**0**	**0**	**0**	**0**	**0**	**0**	**8**	**0.0**	**–1**	....	....	....	....	....	....	....	....	....	....	....	....
	St. John's	AHL	73	22	34	56	33	....	....	....	....	....	....	....	....	....	3	1	1	2	6	....	....	....	....
1996-97	**Toronto**	**NHL**	**20**	**1**	**4**	**5**	**6**	**0**	**0**	**0**	**23**	**4.3**	**–6**	....	....	....	....	....	....	....	....	....	....	....	....
	St. John's	AHL	27	8	19	27	26	....	....	....	....	....	....	....	....	....	9	1	3	4	6	....	....	....	....
1997-98	Philadelphia	AHL	72	17	48	65	54	....	....	....	....	....	....	....	....	....	20	3	16	19	10	....	....	....	....
1998-99	**Nashville**	**NHL**	**63**	**6**	**12**	**18**	**44**	**4**	**0**	**1**	**124**	**4.8**	**–24**	**0**	**0.0**	**16:12**	....	....	....	....	....	....	....	....	....
99-2000	**NY Islanders**	**NHL**	**54**	**6**	**11**	**17**	**26**	**2**	**0**	**1**	**92**	**6.5**	**–9**	**0**	**0.0**	**19:58**	....	....	....	....	....	....	....	....	....
2000-01	**Columbus**	**NHL**	**69**	**11**	**16**	**27**	**33**	**9**	**0**	**1**	**108**	**10.2**	**3**	**0**	**0.0**	**14:21**	....	....	....	....	....	....	....	....	....
2001-02	**Columbus**	**NHL**	**28**	**1**	**2**	**3**	**7**	**0**	**0**	**0**	**38**	**2.6**	**–9**	**1**	**100.0**	**14:04**	....	....	....	....	....	....	....	....	....
	Syracuse Crunch	AHL	14	3	10	13	6	....	....	....	....	....	....	....	....	....	10	0	4	4	6	....	....	....	....
2002-03	Geneve	Swiss	40	8	23	31	60	....	....	....	....	....	....	....	....	....	6	1	1	2	22	....	....	....	....
2003-04	ZSC Lions Zurich	Swiss	25	5	9	14	57	....	....	....	....	....	....	....	....	....	6	0	1	1	24	....	....	....	....
2004-05	Langnau	Swiss	44	3	14	17	91	....	....	....	....	....	....	....	....	....	5	0	0	0	40	....	....	....	....
2005-06	**Washington**	**NHL**	**71**	**7**	**21**	**28**	**54**	**4**	**0**	**2**	**140**	**5.0**	**–5**	**1**	**0.0**	**21:52**	....	....	....	....	....	....	....	....	....
	NHL Totals		**310**	**32**	**66**	**98**	**170**	**19**	**0**	**5**	**533**	**6.0**		**2**	**50.0**	**17:40**	....	....	....	....	....	....	....	....	....

WHL East First All-Star Team (1991) • AHL First All-Star Team (1996, 1998) • Eddie Shore Award (Outstanding Defenseman – AHL) (1998)

Signed as a free agent by **Toronto**, May 4, 1995. Signed as a free agent by **Philadelphia**, July 31, 1997. Signed as a free agent by **Nashville**, August 10, 1998. Signed as a free agent by **NY Islanders**, July 27, 1999. Claimed on waivers by **Columbus** from **NY Islanders**, May 26, 2000. Signed as a free agent by **Geneve** (Swiss), April 17, 2002. Signed as a free agent by **Washington**, August 12, 2005.

HIGGINS, Christopher

(HIH-gihns, KRIHS-toh-fuhr) **MTL.**

Center. Shoots left. 6', 192 lbs. Born, Smithtown, NY, June 2, 1983. Montreal's 1st choice, 14th overall, in 2002 Entry Draft.

Season	Club	League	GP	G	A	Pts	PIM	PP	SH	GW	S	%	+/-	TF	F%	Min	GP	G	A	Pts	PIM	PP	SH	GW	Min
99-2000	Avon Old Farms	High-CT	27	19	20	39	10	....	....	....	....	....	....	....	....	....	....	....	....	....	....	....	....	....	....
2000-01	Avon Old Farms	High-CT	24	22	14	36	29	....	....	....	....	....	....	....	....	....	....	....	....	....	....	....	....	....	....
2001-02	Yale	ECAC	27	14	17	31	32	....	....	....	....	....	....	....	....	....	....	....	....	....	....	....	....	....	....
2002-03	Yale	ECAC	28	20	21	41	41	....	....	....	....	....	....	....	....	....	....	....	....	....	....	....	....	....	....
2003-04	**Montreal**	**NHL**	**2**	**0**	**0**	**0**	**0**	**0**	**0**	**0**	**0**	**0.0**	**0**	**9**	**22.2**	**6:18**	....	....	....	....	....	....	....	....	....
	Hamilton	AHL	67	21	27	48	18	....	....	....	....	....	....	....	....	....	10	3	2	5	0	....	....	....	....
2004-05	Hamilton	AHL	76	28	23	51	33	....	....	....	....	....	....	....	....	....	4	3	3	6	4	....	....	....	....
2005-06	**Montreal**	**NHL**	**80**	**23**	**15**	**38**	**26**	**7**	**3**	**3**	**148**	**15.5**	**–1**	**45**	**51.1**	**14:25**	**6**	**1**	**3**	**4**	**0**	**0**	**0**	**0**	**17:04**
	NHL Totals		**82**	**23**	**15**	**38**	**26**	**7**	**3**	**3**	**148**	**15.5**		**54**	**46.3**	**14:13**	**6**	**1**	**3**	**4**	**0**	**0**	**0**	**0**	**17:04**

ECAC All-Rookie Team (2002) • ECAC Second All-Star Team (2002) • ECAC Rookie of the Year (2002) • ECAC First All-Star Team (2003) • ECAC Player of the Year (2003) (co-winner - David LeNeveu) • NCAA East First All-American Team (2003)

HILBERT, Andy

(HIHL-buhrt, AN-dee) **NYI**

Center/Left wing. Shoots left. 5'11", 194 lbs. Born, Lansing, MI, February 6, 1981. Boston's 3rd choice, 37th overall, in 2000 Entry Draft.

Season	Club	League	GP	G	A	Pts	PIM	PP	SH	GW	S	%	+/-	TF	F%	Min	GP	G	A	Pts	PIM	PP	SH	GW	Min
1997-98	USNTDP	U-17	29	14	10	24	34	....	....	....	....	....	....	....	....	....	....	....	....	....	....	....	....	....	....
	USNTDP	NAHL	39	19	16	35	102	....	....	....	....	....	....	....	....	....	7	1	4	5	12	....	....	....	....
1998-99	USNTDP	U-18	6	6	1	7	4	....	....	....	....	....	....	....	....	....	....	....	....	....	....	....	....	....	....
	USNTDP	USHL	46	23	35	58	140	....	....	....	....	....	....	....	....	....	....	....	....	....	....	....	....	....	....
99-2000	U. of Michigan	CCHA	35	17	15	32	39	....	....	....	....	....	....	....	....	....	....	....	....	....	....	....	....	....	....
2000-01	U. of Michigan	CCHA	42	26	38	64	72	....	....	....	....	....	....	....	....	....	....	....	....	....	....	....	....	....	....
2001-02	**Boston**	**NHL**	**6**	**1**	**0**	**1**	**2**	**0**	**0**	**0**	**11**	**9.1**	**–2**	**4**	**50.0**	**11:34**	....	....	....	....	....	....	....	....	....
	Providence Bruins	AHL	72	26	27	53	74	....	....	....	....	....	....	....	....	....	2	0	0	0	2	....	....	....	....
2002-03	Providence Bruins	AHL	64	35	35	70	119	....	....	....	....	....	....	....	....	....	4	0	1	1	4	....	....	....	....
	Boston	**NHL**	**14**	**0**	**3**	**3**	**7**	**0**	**0**	**0**	**22**	**0.0**	**–1**	**34**	**44.1**	**11:30**	....	....	....	....	....	....	....	....	....
2003-04	**Boston**	**NHL**	**18**	**2**	**0**	**2**	**9**	**0**	**0**	**0**	**27**	**7.4**	**1**	**11**	**54.6**	**8:57**	**5**	**1**	**0**	**1**	**0**	**0**	**0**	**0**	**5:32**
	Providence Bruins	AHL	19	3	5	8	20	....	....	....	....	....	....	....	....	....	....	....	....	....	....	....	....	....	....
2004-05	Providence Bruins	AHL	79	37	42	79	83	....	....	....	....	....	....	....	....	....	17	7	*14	*21	27	....	....	....	....
2005-06	**Chicago**	**NHL**	**28**	**5**	**4**	**9**	**22**	**0**	**0**	**1**	**50**	**10.0**	**–4**	**21**	**38.1**	**10:05**	....	....	....	....	....	....	....	....	....
	Norfolk Admirals	AHL	5	3	4	7	2	....	....	....	....	....	....	....	....	....	....	....	....	....	....	....	....	....	....
	Pittsburgh	**NHL**	**19**	**7**	**11**	**18**	**16**	**3**	**0**	**1**	**51**	**13.7**	**8**	**146**	**38.4**	**17:27**	....	....	....	....	....	....	....	....	....
	NHL Totals		**85**	**15**	**18**	**33**	**56**	**3**	**0**	**2**	**161**	**9.3**		**216**	**40.3**	**11:50**	**5**	**1**	**0**	**1**	**0**	**0**	**0**	**0**	**5:32**

CCHA First All-Star Team (2001) • NCAA West First All-American Team (2001) • AHL All-Rookie Team (2002) • AHL Second All-Star Team (2005)

• Missed majority of 2003-04 season recovering from groin injury suffered in pre-season game vs. Detroit, September 15, 2003. Traded to **Chicago** by **Boston** for Chicago's 5th round choice (later traded to NY Islanders - NY Islanders selected Shane Sims) in 2006 Entry Draft, November 6, 2005. Claimed on waivers by **Pittsburgh** from **Chicago**, March 9, 2006. Signed as a free agent by **NY Islanders**, July 4, 2006.

HILL, Sean

(HIHL, SHAWN) **NYI**

Defense. Shoots right. 6', 205 lbs. Born, Duluth, MN, February 14, 1970. Montreal's 9th choice, 167th overall, in 1988 Entry Draft.

Season	Club	League	GP	G	A	Pts	PIM	PP	SH	GW	S	%	+/-	TF	F%	Min	GP	G	A	Pts	PIM	PP	SH	GW	Min
1986-87	Lakefield Chiefs	OHA-C	3	1	1	2	14	....	....	....	....	....	....	....	....	....	....	....	....	....	....	....	....	....	....
1987-88	Duluth East	High-MN	24	10	17	27	....	....	....	....	....	....	....	....	....	....	....	....	....	....	....	....	....	....	....
1988-89	U. of Wisconsin	WCHA	45	2	23	25	69	....	....	....	....	....	....	....	....	....	....	....	....	....	....	....	....	....	....
1989-90	U. of Wisconsin	WCHA	42	14	39	53	78	....	....	....	....	....	....	....	....	....	....	....	....	....	....	....	....	....	....
1990-91	U. of Wisconsin	WCHA	37	19	32	51	122	....	....	....	....	....	....	....	....	....	....	....	....	....	....	....	....	....	....
	Montreal	**NHL**	....	....	....	....	....	....	....	....	....	....	....	....	....	....	**1**	**0**	**0**	**0**	**0**	**0**	**0**	**0**	....
	Fredericton	AHL	....	....	....	....	....	....	....	....	....	....	....	....	....	....	3	0	2	2	2	....	....	....	....
1991-92	Fredericton	AHL	42	7	20	27	65	....	....	....	....	....	....	....	....	....	7	1	3	4	6	....	....	....	....
	United States	Nat-Tm	12	4	3	7	16	....	....	....	....	....	....	....	....	....	....	....	....	....	....	....	....	....	....
	United States	Olympics	8	2	0	2	6	....	....	....	....	....	....	....	....	....	....	....	....	....	....	....	....	....	....
	Montreal	**NHL**	....	....	....	....	....	....	....	....	....	....	....	....	....	....	**4**	**1**	**0**	**1**	**2**	**0**	**0**	**0**	....
1992-93 ♦	**Montreal**	**NHL**	**31**	**2**	**6**	**8**	**54**	**1**	**0**	**1**	**37**	**5.4**	**–5**	....	....	....	**3**	**0**	**0**	**0**	**4**	**0**	**0**	**0**	....
	Fredericton	AHL	6	1	3	4	10	....	....	....	....	....	....	....	....	....	....	....	....	....	....	....	....	....	....
1993-94	**Anaheim**	**NHL**	**68**	**7**	**20**	**27**	**78**	**2**	**1**	**1**	**165**	**4.2**	**–12**	....	....	....	....	....	....	....	....	....	....	....	....
1994-95	**Ottawa**	**NHL**	**45**	**1**	**14**	**15**	**30**	**0**	**0**	**0**	**107**	**0.9**	**–11**	....	....	....	....	....	....	....	....	....	....	....	....
1995-96	**Ottawa**	**NHL**	**80**	**7**	**14**	**21**	**94**	**2**	**0**	**2**	**157**	**4.5**	**–26**	....	....	....	....	....	....	....	....	....	....	....	....
1996-97	**Ottawa**	**NHL**	**5**	**0**	**0**	**0**	**4**	**0**	**0**	**0**	**9**	**0.0**	**1**	....	....	....	....	....	....	....	....	....	....	....	....
1997-98	**Ottawa**	**NHL**	**13**	**1**	**1**	**2**	**6**	**0**	**0**	**0**	**16**	**6.3**	**–3**	....	....	....	....	....	....	....	....	....	....	....	....
	Carolina	**NHL**	**42**	**0**	**5**	**5**	**48**	**0**	**0**	**0**	**37**	**0.0**	**–2**	....	....	....	....	....	....	....	....	....	....	....	....
1998-99	**Carolina**	**NHL**	**54**	**0**	**10**	**10**	**48**	**0**	**0**	**0**	**44**	**0.0**	**9**	**0**	**0.0**	**19:02**	....	....	....	....	....	....	....	....	....
99-2000	**Carolina**	**NHL**	**62**	**13**	**31**	**44**	**59**	**8**	**0**	**2**	**150**	**8.7**	**3**	**1**	**0.0**	**24:31**	....	....	....	....	....	....	....	....	....
2000-01	**St. Louis**	**NHL**	**48**	**1**	**10**	**11**	**51**	**0**	**0**	**0**	**47**	**2.1**	**5**	**1**	**0.0**	**17:23**	**15**	**0**	**1**	**1**	**12**	**0**	**0**	**0**	**13:46**
2001-02	**St. Louis**	**NHL**	**23**	**0**	**3**	**3**	**28**	**0**	**0**	**0**	**29**	**0.0**	**1**	**0**	**0.0**	**15:56**	....	....	....	....	....	....	....	....	....
	Carolina	**NHL**	**49**	**7**	**23**	**30**	**61**	**4**	**0**	**2**	**116**	**6.0**	**–1**	**1**	**0.0**	**23:58**	**23**	**4**	**4**	**8**	**20**	**4**	**0**	**1**	**25:55**
2002-03	**Carolina**	**NHL**	**82**	**5**	**24**	**29**	**141**	**1**	**0**	**0**	**188**	**2.7**	**4**	**1**	**0.0**	**24:21**	....	....	....	....	....	....	....	....	....
2003-04	**Carolina**	**NHL**	**80**	**13**	**26**	**39**	**84**	**6**	**0**	**1**	**228**	**5.7**	**–2**	**2**	**50.0**	**25:24**	....	....	....	....	....	....	....	....	....
2004-05			DID NOT PLAY																						
2005-06	**Florida**	**NHL**	**78**	**2**	**18**	**20**	**80**	**1**	**0**	**0**	**110**	**1.8**	**3**	**0**	**0.0**	**20:09**	....	....	....	....	....	....	....	....	....
	NHL Totals		**760**	**59**	**205**	**264**	**866**	**25**	**1**	**9**	**1440**	**4.1**		**6**	**16.7**	**22:07**	**46**	**5**	**5**	**10**	**38**	**4**	**0**	**1**	**21:07**

WCHA Second All-Star Team (1990, 1991) • NCAA West Second All-American Team (1991)

Claimed by **Anaheim** from **Montreal** in Expansion Draft, June 24, 1993. Traded to **Ottawa** by **Anaheim** with Anaheim's 9th round choice (Frederic Cassivi) in 1994 Entry Draft for Ottawa's 3rd round choice (later traded to Tampa Bay – Tampa Bay selected Vadim Epanchintsev) in 1994 Entry Draft, June 29, 1994. • Missed remainder of 1996-97 season recovering from knee injury suffered in game vs. New Jersey, October 18, 1996. Traded to **Carolina** by **Ottawa** for Chris Murray, November 18, 1997. Signed as a free agent by **St. Louis**, July 1, 2000. Traded to **Carolina** by **St. Louis** for Steve Halko and Carolina's 4th round choice (later traded to Atlanta – Atlanta selected Lane Manson) in 2002 Entry Draft, December 5, 2001. Signed as a free agent by **Florida**, July 15, 2004. Signed as a free agent by **NY Islanders**, August 15, 2006.

HINOTE, Dan

(HIGH-noht, DAN) **ST.L.**

Right wing. Shoots right. 6', 190 lbs. Born, Leesburg, FL, January 30, 1977. Colorado's 9th choice, 167th overall, in 1996 Entry Draft.

Season	Club	League	GP	G	A	Pts	PIM	PP	SH	GW	S	%	+/-	TF	F%	Min	GP	G	A	Pts	PIM	PP	SH	GW	Min
1993-94	Elk River Elks	High-MN	STATISTICS NOT AVAILABLE																						
1994-95	Army	NCAA	33	20	24	44	20	....	....	....	....	....	....	....	....	....	....	....	....	....	....	....	....	....	....
1995-96	Army	NCAA	34	21	24	45	22	....	....	....	....	....	....	....	....	....	....	....	....	....	....	....	....	....	....
1996-97	Oshawa Generals	OHL	60	15	13	28	58	....	....	....	....	....	....	....	....	....	18	4	5	9	8	....	....	....	....
1997-98	Oshawa Generals	OHL	35	12	15	27	39	....	....	....	....	....	....	....	....	....	5	2	2	4	7	....	....	....	....
	Hershey Bears	AHL	24	1	4	5	25	....	....	....	....	....	....	....	....	....	....	....	....	....	....	....	....	....	....
1998-99	Hershey Bears	AHL	65	4	16	20	95	....	....	....	....	....	....	....	....	....	5	3	1	4	6	....	....	....	....
99-2000	**Colorado**	**NHL**	**27**	**1**	**3**	**4**	**10**	**0**	**0**	**0**	**14**	**7.1**	**0**	**132**	**51.5**	**7:51**	....	....	....	....	....	....	....	....	....
	Hershey Bears	AHL	55	28	31	59	96	....	....	....	....	....	....	....	....	....	14	4	5	9	19	....	....	....	....

			Regular Season														Playoffs								
Season	Club	League	GP	G	A	Pts	PIM	PP	SH	GW	S	%	+/-	TF	F%	Min	GP	G	A	Pts	PIM	PP	SH	GW	Min
2000-01 ♦	**Colorado**	**NHL**	76	5	10	15	51	1	0	1	69	7.2	1	506	49.8	10:21	23	2	4	6	21	0	0	0	8:22
2001-02	**Colorado**	**NHL**	58	6	6	12	39	0	1	3	75	8.0	8	267	51.3	12:27	19	1	2	3	9	0	0	0	10:46
2002-03	**Colorado**	**NHL**	60	6	4	10	49	0	0	3	65	9.2	4	218	46.8	10:36	7	1	2	3	2	0	0	0	14:19
2003-04	**Colorado**	**NHL**	59	4	7	11	57	0	2	0	53	7.5	−6	151	48.3	12:42	11	1	0	1	0	0	1	0	13:04
2004-05	MODO	Sweden	18	2	1	3	106	....	....	....	....	....	....	....	....	....	5	0	0	0	56	....	....	....	....
2005-06	**Colorado**	**NHL**	73	5	8	13	48	0	1	2	70	7.1	−5	335	42.1	10:41	9	1	1	2	31	0	0	0	13:27
	NHL Totals		353	27	38	65	254	1	4	9	346	7.8		1609	48.0	11:01	69	6	9	15	63	0	1	0	11:02

Signed as a free agent by **MODO** (Sweden), December 22, 2004. Signed as a free agent by **St. Louis**, July 3, 2006.

HLAVAC, Jan

(huh-LAH-vahch, YAHN)

Left wing. Shoots left. 6', 185 lbs. Born, Prague, Czech., September 20, 1976. NY Islanders' 2nd choice, 28th overall, in 1995 Entry Draft.

Season	Club	League	GP	G	A	Pts	PIM	PP	SH	GW	S	%	+/-	TF	F%	Min	GP	G	A	Pts	PIM	PP	SH	GW	Min
1993-94	Sparta Jr.	CzRep-Jr.	27	12	15	27	....	....	....	....	....	....	....	....	....	....	....	....	....	....	....	....	....	....	....
	HC Sparta Praha	CzRep	9	1	1	2	....	....	....	....	....	....	....	....	....	....	....	....	....	....	....	....	....	....	....
1994-95	HC Sparta Praha	CzRep	38	7	6	13	18	....	....	....	....	....	....	....	....	....	5	0	2	2	0	....	....	....	....
1995-96	HC Sparta Praha	CzRep	34	8	5	13	....	....	....	....	....	....	....	....	....	....	12	1	2	3	....	....	....	....	....
1996-97	HC Sparta Praha	CzRep	38	8	13	21	24	....	....	....	....	....	....	....	....	....	10	5	2	7	2	....	....	....	....
	HC Sparta Praha	EuroHL	3	4	0	4	6	....	....	....	....	....	....	....	....	....	....	....	....	....	....	....	....	....	....
1997-98	HC Sparta Praha	CzRep	48	17	30	47	40	....	....	....	....	....	....	....	....	....	5	1	0	1	2	....	....	....	....
	HC Sparta Praha	EuroHL	5	0	3	3	4	....	....	....	....	....	....	....	....	....	....	....	....	....	....	....	....	....	....
1998-99	HC Sparta Praha	CzRep	49	*33	20	53	52	....	....	....	....	....	....	....	....	....	6	1	3	4	....	....	....	....	....
	HC Sparta Praha	EuroHL	5	4	2	6	0	....	....	....	....	....	....	....	....	....	1	1	1	2	0	....	....	....	....
99-2000	**NY Rangers**	**NHL**	67	19	23	42	16	6	0	2	134	14.2	3	6	33.3	15:09	....	....	....	....	....	....	....	....	....
	Hartford	AHL	3	1	0	1	0	....	....	....	....	....	....	....	....	....	....	....	....	....	....	....	....	....	....
2000-01	**NY Rangers**	**NHL**	79	28	36	64	20	5	0	6	195	14.4	3	0	0.0	16:38	....	....	....	....	....	....	....	....	....
2001-02	**Philadelphia**	**NHL**	31	7	3	10	8	0	0	1	62	11.3	5	0	0.0	12:36	....	....	....	....	....	....	....	....	....
	Vancouver	**NHL**	46	9	12	21	10	1	0	2	70	12.9	4	2	100.0	14:46	5	0	1	1	0	0	0	0	9:38
2002-03	**Vancouver**	**NHL**	9	1	1	2	6	0	0	0	7	14.3	−1	0	0.0	10:51	....	....	....	....	....	....	....	....	....
	Carolina	**NHL**	52	9	15	24	22	6	0	1	116	7.8	−9	21	38.1	17:10	....	....	....	....	....	....	....	....	....
2003-04	**NY Rangers**	**NHL**	72	5	21	26	16	2	0	0	125	4.0	−8	7	42.9	13:52	....	....	....	....	....	....	....	....	....
2004-05	HC Sparta Praha	CzRep	48	10	28	38	34	....	....	....	....	....	....	....	....	....	5	2	0	2	6	....	....	....	....
2005-06	Geneve	Swiss	42	12	22	34	28	....	....	....	....	....	....	....	....	....	4	1	0	1	2	....	....	....	....
	NHL Totals		356	78	111	189	98	20	0	12	709	11.0		36	41.7	15:08	5	0	1	1	0	0	0	0	9:38

Traded to **Calgary** by **NY Islanders** for Jorgen Jonsson, July 14, 1998. Rights traded to **NY Rangers** by **Calgary** with Calgary's 1st (Jamie Lundmark) and 3rd (later traded back to Calgary – Calgary selected Craig Andersson) round choices in 1999 Entry Draft for Marc Savard and NY Rangers' 1st round choice (Oleg Saprykin) in 1999 Entry Draft, June 26, 1999. Traded to **Philadelphia** by **NY Rangers** with Kim Johnsson, Pavel Brendl and NY Rangers' 3rd round choice (Stefan Ruzicka) in 2003 Entry Draft for Eric Lindros, August 20, 2001. Traded to **Vancouver** by **Philadelphia** with Tampa Bay's 3rd round choice (previously acquired, Vancouver selected Brett Skinner) in 2002 Entry Draft for Donald Brashear and Vancouver's 6th round choice (later traded to Columbus – Columbus selected Jaroslav Balastik) in 2002 Entry Draft, December 17, 2001. Traded to **Carolina** by **Vancouver** with Harold Druken for Darren Langdon and Marek Malik, November 1, 2002. Signed as a free agent by **NY Rangers**, August 28, 2003. Signed as a free agent by **Sparta Praha** (CzRep), August 9, 2004. Signed as a free agent by **Geneve** (Swiss), September, 2005. Signed as a free agent by **Sparta Praha** (CzRep), May 24, 2006.

HNIDY, Shane

(NIGH-dee, SHAYN) **ATL.**

Defense. Shoots right. 6'2", 205 lbs. Born, Neepawa, Man., November 8, 1975. Buffalo's 7th choice, 173rd overall, in 1994 Entry Draft.

Season	Club	League	GP	G	A	Pts	PIM	PP	SH	GW	S	%	+/-	TF	F%	Min	GP	G	A	Pts	PIM	PP	SH	GW	Min
1990-91	Yellowhead	MMMHL	36	9	11	20	92	....	....	....	....	....	....	....	....	....	....	....	....	....	....	....	....	....	....
1991-92	Swift Current	WHL	56	1	3	4	11	....	....	....	....	....	....	....	....	....	4	0	0	0	0	....	....	....	....
1992-93	Swift Current	WHL	45	5	12	17	62	....	....	....	....	....	....	....	....	....	....	....	....	....	....	....	....	....	....
	Prince Albert	WHL	27	2	10	12	43	....	....	....	....	....	....	....	....	....	....	....	....	....	....	....	....	....	....
1993-94	Prince Albert	WHL	69	7	26	33	113	....	....	....	....	....	....	....	....	....	....	....	....	....	....	....	....	....	....
1994-95	Prince Albert	WHL	72	5	29	34	169	....	....	....	....	....	....	....	....	....	15	4	7	11	29	....	....	....	....
1995-96	Prince Albert	WHL	58	11	42	53	100	....	....	....	....	....	....	....	....	....	18	4	11	15	34	....	....	....	....
1996-97	Baton Rouge	ECHL	21	3	10	13	50	....	....	....	....	....	....	....	....	....	....	....	....	....	....	....	....	....	....
	Saint John Flames	AHL	44	2	12	14	112	....	....	....	....	....	....	....	....	....	....	....	....	....	....	....	....	....	....
1997-98	Grand Rapids	IHL	77	6	12	18	210	....	....	....	....	....	....	....	....	....	3	0	2	2	23	....	....	....	....
1998-99	Adirondack	AHL	68	9	20	29	121	....	....	....	....	....	....	....	....	....	3	0	1	1	0	....	....	....	....
99-2000	Cincinnati	AHL	68	9	19	28	153	....	....	....	....	....	....	....	....	....	....	....	....	....	....	....	....	....	....
2000-01	**Ottawa**	**NHL**	52	3	2	5	84	0	0	1	47	6.4	8	0	0.0	13:05	1	0	0	0	0	0	0	0	13:23
	Grand Rapids	IHL	2	0	0	0	2	....	....	....	....	....	....	....	....	....	....	....	....	....	....	....	....	....	....
2001-02	**Ottawa**	**NHL**	33	1	1	2	57	0	0	0	34	2.9	−10	0	0.0	16:56	12	1	1	2	12	0	0	0	16:00
2002-03	**Ottawa**	**NHL**	67	0	8	8	130	0	0	0	58	0.0	−1	1	0.0	13:55	1	0	0	0	0	0	0	0	9:38
2003-04	**Ottawa**	**NHL**	37	0	5	5	72	0	0	0	16	0.0	2	0	0.0	11:19	....	....	....	....	....	....	....	....	....
	Nashville	**NHL**	9	0	2	2	10	0	0	0	12	0.0	3	0	0.0	18:11	5	0	0	0	6	0	0	0	12:31
2004-05	Florida Everblades	ECHL	19	1	4	5	56	....	....	....	....	....	....	....	....	....	17	0	4	4	6	....	....	....	....
2005-06	**Atlanta**	**NHL**	66	0	3	3	33	0	0	0	50	0.0	1	0	0.0	10:14	....	....	....	....	....	....	....	....	....
	NHL Totals		264	4	21	25	386	0	0	1	217	1.8		1	0.0	12:59	19	1	1	2	18	0	0	0	14:37

Signed as a free agent by **Detroit**, August 6, 1998. Traded to **Ottawa** by **Detroit** for Ottawa's 8th round choice (Todd Jackson) in 2000 Entry Draft, June 25, 2000. • Missed majority of 2001-02 season recovering from ankle injury suffered in game vs. Boston, December 26, 2001. Traded to **Nashville** by **Ottawa** for Colorado's 3rd round choice (previously acquired, Ottawa selected Peter Regin) in 2004 Entry Draft, March 9, 2004. Signed as a free agent by **Florida** (ECHL), December 6, 2004. Traded to **Atlanta** by **Nashville** for Atlanta's 4th round choice (Niko Snellman) in 2006 Entry Draft, July 30, 2005.

HOGGAN, Jeff

(HOH-guhn, JEHF) **BOS.**

Right wing. Shoots left. 6'1", 195 lbs. Born, Hope, B.C., February 1, 1978.

Season	Club	League	GP	G	A	Pts	PIM	PP	SH	GW	S	%	+/-	TF	F%	Min	GP	G	A	Pts	PIM	PP	SH	GW	Min
1998-99	Powell River Kings	BCHL	STATISTICS NOT AVAILABLE																						
99-2000	Nebraska-Omaha	CCHA	34	16	9	25	82	....	....	....	....	....	....	....	....	....	....	....	....	....	....	....	....	....	....
2000-01	Nebraska-Omaha	CCHA	42	12	17	29	78	....	....	....	....	....	....	....	....	....	....	....	....	....	....	....	....	....	....
2001-02	Nebraska-Omaha	CCHA	41	24	21	45	92	....	....	....	....	....	....	....	....	....	....	....	....	....	....	....	....	....	....
	Houston Aeros	AHL	....	....	....	....	....	....	....	....	....	....	....	....	....	....	4	0	0	0	2	....	....	....	....
2002-03	Houston Aeros	AHL	65	6	5	11	45	....	....	....	....	....	....	....	....	....	14	1	2	3	23	....	....	....	....
2003-04	Houston Aeros	AHL	77	21	15	36	88	....	....	....	....	....	....	....	....	....	2	0	1	1	4	....	....	....	....
2004-05	Worcester IceCats	AHL	47	16	9	25	55	....	....	....	....	....	....	....	....	....	....	....	....	....	....	....	....	....	....
2005-06	**St. Louis**	**NHL**	52	2	6	8	34	0	0	0	60	3.3	−16	4	25.0	8:47	....	....	....	....	....	....	....	....	....
	NHL Totals		52	2	6	8	34	0	0	0	60	3.3		4	25.0	8:47									

CCHA First All-Star Team (2002) • NCAA West Second All-American Team (2002)

Signed to a try-out contract by **Houston** (AHL), April 4, 2002. Signed as a free agent by **Minnesota**, August 20, 2002. Signed as a free agent by **Worcester** (AHL), September, 2004. Signed as a free agent by **St. Louis**, August 2, 2005. Signed as a free agent by **Boston**, July 21, 2006.

HOLIK, Bobby

(HOH-leek, BAWB-ee) **ATL.**

Center. Shoots right. 6'4", 240 lbs. Born, Jihlava, Czech., January 1, 1971. Hartford's 1st choice, 10th overall, in 1989 Entry Draft.

Season	Club	League	GP	G	A	Pts	PIM	PP	SH	GW	S	%	+/-	TF	F%	Min	GP	G	A	Pts	PIM	PP	SH	GW	Min
1987-88	Dukla Jihlava	Czech	31	5	9	14	16	....	....	....	....	....	....	....	....	....	....	....	....	....	....	....	....	....	....
1988-89	Dukla Jihlava	Czech	24	7	10	17	32	....	....	....	....	....	....	....	....	....	....	....	....	....	....	....	....	....	....
1989-90	Dukla Jihlava	Czech	42	15	26	41	....	....	....	....	....	....	....	....	....	....	....	....	....	....	....	....	....	....	....
1990-91	**Hartford**	**NHL**	78	21	22	43	113	8	0	3	173	12.1	−3	....	....	....	6	0	0	0	7	0	0	0	....
1991-92	**Hartford**	**NHL**	76	21	24	45	44	1	0	2	207	10.1	4	....	....	....	7	0	1	1	6	0	0	0	....
1992-93	**New Jersey**	**NHL**	61	20	19	39	76	7	0	4	180	11.1	−6	....	....	....	5	1	1	2	6	0	0	0	....
	Utica Devils	AHL	1	0	0	0	2	....	....	....	....	....	....	....	....	....	....	....	....	....	....	....	....	....	....
1993-94	**New Jersey**	**NHL**	70	13	20	33	72	2	0	3	130	10.0	28	....	....	....	20	0	3	3	6	0	0	0	....
1994-95 ♦	**New Jersey**	**NHL**	48	10	10	20	18	0	0	2	84	11.9	9	....	....	....	20	4	4	8	22	2	0	1	....
1995-96	**New Jersey**	**NHL**	63	13	17	30	58	1	0	1	157	8.3	9	....	....	....	....	....	....	....	....	....	....	....	....
1996-97	**New Jersey**	**NHL**	82	23	39	62	54	5	0	6	192	12.0	24	....	....	....	10	2	3	5	4	1	0	0	....
1997-98	**New Jersey**	**NHL**	82	29	36	65	100	8	0	8	238	12.2	23	....	....	....	5	0	0	0	8	0	0	0	....
1998-99	**New Jersey**	**NHL**	78	27	37	64	119	5	0	8	253	10.7	16	1350	53.6	17:34	7	0	7	7	6	0	0	0	18:14
99-2000 ♦	**New Jersey**	**NHL**	79	23	23	46	106	7	0	4	257	8.9	7	1390	55.6	16:53	23	3	7	10	14	0	0	1	17:29
2000-01	**New Jersey**	**NHL**	80	15	35	50	97	3	0	3	206	7.3	19	1365	56.0	15:49	25	6	10	16	37	1	0	3	16:05
2001-02	**New Jersey**	**NHL**	81	25	29	54	97	6	0	3	270	9.3	7	1594	54.5	17:42	6	4	1	5	2	1	0	0	17:53
2002-03	**NY Rangers**	**NHL**	64	16	19	35	52	3	0	2	213	7.5	−1	1390	58.2	18:07	....	....	....	....	....	....	....	....	....
2003-04	**NY Rangers**	**NHL**	82	25	31	56	96	8	0	4	225	11.1	4	1664	54.2	18:34	....	....	....	....	....	....	....	....	....

			Regular Season														Playoffs								
Season	Club	League	GP	G	A	Pts	PIM	PP	SH	GW	S	%	+/-	TF	F%	Min	GP	G	A	Pts	PIM	PP	SH	GW	Min
2004-05			Did not play																						
2005-06	**Atlanta**	**NHL**	**64**	**15**	**18**	**33**	**79**	**5**	**0**	**0**	**151**	**9.9**	**–6**	**1385**	**55.7**	**17:31**									
	NHL Totals		**1088**	**296**	**379**	**675**	**1181**	**69**	**0**	**53**	**2936**	**10.1**		**10138**	**55.4**	**17:26**	**134**	**20**	**37**	**57**	**118**	**5**	**0**	**5**	**17:02**

Played in NHL All-Star Game (1998, 1999)

Traded to **New Jersey** by **Hartford** with Hartford's 2nd round choice (Jay Pandolfo) in 1993 Entry Draft for Sean Burke and Eric Weinrich, August 28, 1992. Signed as a free agent by **NY Rangers**, July 1, 2002. Signed as a free agent by **Atlanta**, August 2, 2005.

HOLLWEG, Ryan

(HOHL-wehg, RIGH-uhn) **NYR**

Center. Shoots left. 5'11", 213 lbs. Born, Downey, CA, April 23, 1983. NY Rangers' 10th choice, 238th overall, in 2001 Entry Draft.

1998-99	Grandview	PIJHL	41	23	27	50	135																		
	Langley Hornets	BCHL	58	14	40	54	187																		
99-2000	Medicine Hat	WHL	54	19	27	46	107																		
2000-01	Medicine Hat	WHL	65	19	39	58	125																		
2001-02	Medicine Hat	WHL	58	30	40	70	121																		
	Hartford	AHL	8	1	1	2	2										9	0	2	2	19				
2002-03	Medicine Hat	WHL	4	1	1	2	8																		
2003-04	Medicine Hat	WHL	52	25	32	57	117										20	6	9	15	22				
2004-05	Hartford	AHL	73	8	6	14	239										6	1	0	1	9				
2005-06	**NY Rangers**	**NHL**	**52**	**2**	**3**	**5**	**84**	**0**	**0**	**0**	**32**	**6.3**	**–3**	**19**	**57.9**	**7:15**	**4**	**0**	**1**	**1**	**19**	**0**	**0**	**0**	**10:26**
	Hartford	AHL	7	2	1	3	11																		
	NHL Totals		**52**	**2**	**3**	**5**	**84**	**0**	**0**	**0**	**32**	**6.3**		**19**	**57.9**	**7:15**	**4**	**0**	**1**	**1**	**19**	**0**	**0**	**0**	**10:26**

• Missed majority of 2002-03 season recovering from head injury suffered in game vs. Vancouver (WHL), October 8, 2002.

HOLMQVIST, Michael

(HOHLM-kvihst, MIGH-kuhl) **CHI.**

Center. Shoots left. 6'3", 205 lbs. Born, Stockholm, Sweden, June 8, 1979. Anaheim's 1st choice, 18th overall, in 1997 Entry Draft.

1995-96	Djurgarden Jr.	Swe-Jr.	24	7	2	9	4																		
1996-97	Djurgarden Jr.	Swe-Jr.	39	29	35	64	110																		
	Djurgarden	Sweden	9	0	0	0	0																		
1997-98	Farjestad	Sweden	41	2	3	5	6										7	0	0	0	0				
	Farjestad	EuroHL	5	2	2	4	2																		
1998-99	Farjestad Jr.	Swe-Jr.	2	2	2	4	2																		
	Farjestad	EuroHL	3	0	0	0	0										1	0	0	0	0				
	Farjestad	Sweden	15	0	0	0	6																		
	Hammarby	Sweden-2	3	2	0	2	0																		
99-2000	TPS Turku	Finland	54	12	3	15	14										11	2	3	5	4				
2000-01	TPS Turku	Finland	46	4	5	9	8										10	1	3	4	2				
2001-02	TPS Turku	Finland	56	9	13	22	16										8	1	0	1	12				
2002-03	TPS Turku	Finland	56	15	25	40	36										7	0	0	0	4				
2003-04	**Anaheim**	**NHL**	**21**	**2**	**0**	**2**	**25**	**0**	**0**	**0**	**18**	**11.1**	**–6**	**16**	**31.3**	**8:24**									
	Cincinnati	AHL	24	7	7	14	20																		
2004-05	Cincinnati	AHL	79	14	32	46	111										11	2	2	4	10				
2005-06	**Chicago**	**NHL**	**72**	**10**	**10**	**20**	**16**	**2**	**0**	**1**	**106**	**9.4**	**–14**	**85**	**36.5**	**13:32**									
	NHL Totals		**93**	**12**	**10**	**22**	**41**	**2**	**0**	**1**	**124**	**9.7**		**101**	**35.6**	**12:23**									

Traded to **Chicago** by **Anaheim** for Travis Moen, July 30, 2005.

HOLMSTROM, Tomas

(HOHLM-struhm, TAW-mas) **DET.**

Left wing. Shoots left. 6', 200 lbs. Born, Pitea, Sweden, January 23, 1973. Detroit's 9th choice, 257th overall, in 1994 Entry Draft.

1989-90	Pitea HC	Sweden-2	9	1	0	1	4																		
1990-91	Pitea HC	Sweden-2	26	5	4	9	16																		
1991-92	Pitea HC	Sweden-2	31	15	12	27	44																		
1992-93	Pitea HC	Sweden-2	32	17	15	32	30																		
1993-94	Bodens IK	Sweden-2	34	23	16	39	86										9	3	3	6	24				
1994-95	Lulea HF	Sweden	40	14	14	28	56										8	1	2	3	20				
1995-96	Lulea HF	Sweden	34	12	11	23	78										11	6	2	8	22				
1996-97 ♦	**Detroit**	**NHL**	**47**	**6**	**3**	**9**	**33**	**3**	**0**	**0**	**53**	**11.3**	**–10**				**1**	**0**	**0**	**0**	**0**	**0**	**0**	**0**	
	Adirondack	AHL	6	3	1	4	7																		
1997-98 ♦	**Detroit**	**NHL**	**57**	**5**	**17**	**22**	**44**	**1**	**0**	**1**	**48**	**10.4**	**6**				**22**	**7**	**12**	**19**	**16**	**2**	**0**	**0**	
1998-99	**Detroit**	**NHL**	**82**	**13**	**21**	**34**	**69**	**5**	**0**	**4**	**100**	**13.0**	**–11**	**0**	**0.0**	**12:22**	**10**	**4**	**3**	**7**	**4**	**2**	**0**	**1**	**12:32**
99-2000	**Detroit**	**NHL**	**72**	**13**	**22**	**35**	**43**	**4**	**0**	**1**	**71**	**18.3**	**4**	**0**	**0.0**	**12:06**	**9**	**3**	**1**	**4**	**16**	**1**	**0**	**1**	**11:42**
2000-01	**Detroit**	**NHL**	**73**	**16**	**24**	**40**	**40**	**9**	**0**	**2**	**74**	**21.6**	**–12**	**2**	**50.0**	**11:41**	**6**	**1**	**3**	**4**	**8**	**1**	**0**	**0**	**14:23**
2001-02 ♦	**Detroit**	**NHL**	**69**	**8**	**18**	**26**	**58**	**6**	**0**	**1**	**79**	**10.1**	**–12**	**2**	**0.0**	**12:23**	**23**	**8**	**3**	**11**	**8**	**3**	**0**	**2**	**11:31**
	Sweden	Olympics	4	1	0	1	0																		
2002-03	**Detroit**	**NHL**	**74**	**20**	**20**	**40**	**62**	**12**	**0**	**2**	**109**	**18.3**	**11**	**2**	**0.0**	**12:28**	**4**	**1**	**1**	**2**	**4**	**1**	**0**	**0**	**14:37**
2003-04	**Detroit**	**NHL**	**67**	**15**	**15**	**30**	**38**	**6**	**0**	**0**	**74**	**20.3**	**8**	**3**	**0.0**	**12:23**	**12**	**2**	**2**	**4**	**10**	**1**	**0**	**1**	**11:27**
2004-05	Lulea HF	Sweden	47	14	16	30	50										4	0	0	0	18				
2005-06	**Detroit**	**NHL**	**81**	**29**	**30**	**59**	**66**	**11**	**0**	**8**	**140**	**20.7**	**14**	**0**	**0.0**	**13:59**	**6**	**1**	**2**	**3**	**12**	**1**	**0**	**0**	**17:04**
	Sweden	Olympics	8	1	3	4	10																		
	NHL Totals		**622**	**125**	**170**	**295**	**453**	**57**	**0**	**19**	**748**	**16.7**		**9**	**11.1**	**12:30**	**93**	**27**	**27**	**54**	**78**	**12**	**0**	**5**	**12:34**

Signed as a free agent by **Lulea** (Sweden), September 16, 2004.

HORCOFF, Shawn

(HOHR-cuhf, SHAWN) **EDM.**

Center. Shoots left. 6'1", 204 lbs. Born, Trail, B.C., September 17, 1978. Edmonton's 3rd choice, 99th overall, in 1998 Entry Draft.

1994-95	Trail Smokies	RMJHL	47	50	46	96	26																		
1995-96	Chilliwack Chiefs	BCHL	58	49	96	*145	44										9	5	19	24	12				
1996-97	Michigan State	CCHA	40	10	13	23	20																		
1997-98	Michigan State	CCHA	34	14	13	27	50																		
1998-99	Michigan State	CCHA	39	12	25	37	70																		
99-2000	Michigan State	CCHA	42	14	*51	*65	50																		
2000-01	**Edmonton**	**NHL**	**49**	**9**	**7**	**16**	**10**	**0**	**0**	**2**	**42**	**21.4**	**8**	**122**	**41.8**	**9:14**	**5**	**0**	**0**	**0**	**0**	**0**	**0**	**0**	**6:31**
	Hamilton	AHL	24	10	18	28	19																		
2001-02	**Edmonton**	**NHL**	**61**	**8**	**14**	**22**	**18**	**0**	**0**	**0**	**57**	**14.0**	**3**	**454**	**46.3**	**11:20**									
	Hamilton	AHL	2	1	2	3	6																		
2002-03	**Edmonton**	**NHL**	**78**	**12**	**21**	**33**	**55**	**2**	**0**	**3**	**98**	**12.2**	**10**	**301**	**42.9**	**13:30**	**6**	**3**	**1**	**4**	**6**	**0**	**0**	**1**	**15:27**
2003-04	**Edmonton**	**NHL**	**80**	**15**	**25**	**40**	**73**	**0**	**2**	**3**	**110**	**13.6**	**0**	**1378**	**50.7**	**17:31**									
2004-05	Mora IK	Sweden	50	19	27	46	117																		
2005-06	**Edmonton**	**NHL**	**79**	**22**	**51**	**73**	**85**	**3**	**3**	**5**	**167**	**13.2**	**0**	**1421**	**52.7**	**19:59**	**24**	**7**	**12**	**19**	**12**	**1**	**1**	**2**	**21:37**
	NHL Totals		**347**	**66**	**118**	**184**	**241**	**5**	**5**	**13**	**474**	**13.9**		**3676**	**50.0**	**14:55**	**35**	**10**	**13**	**23**	**18**	**1**	**1**	**3**	**18:24**

CCHA First All-Star Team (2000) • CCHA Player of the Year (2000) • NCAA West First All-American Team (2000)

Signed as a free agent by **Mora** (Sweden), September 6, 2004.

HORDICHUK, Darcy

(HOHR-dih-chuhk, DAHR-see) **NSH.**

Left wing. Shoots left. 6'1", 215 lbs. Born, Kamsack, Sask., August 10, 1980. Atlanta's 9th choice, 180th overall, in 2000 Entry Draft.

1996-97	Yorkton Mallers	SMHL	57	6	15	21	230																		
	Calgary Hitmen	WHL	3	0	0	0	2																		
1997-98	Dauphin Kings	MJHL	58	12	21	33	279																		
1998-99	Saskatoon Blades	WHL	66	3	2	5	246																		
99-2000	Saskatoon Blades	WHL	63	6	8	14	269										11	4	2	6	43				
2000-01	**Atlanta**	**NHL**	**11**	**0**	**0**	**0**	**38**	**0**	**0**	**0**	**6**	**0.0**	**–3**	**0**	**0.0**	**7:18**									
	Orlando	IHL	69	7	3	10	*369										16	3	3	6	*41				
2001-02	**Atlanta**	**NHL**	**33**	**1**	**1**	**2**	**127**	**0**	**0**	**0**	**8**	**12.5**	**–5**	**4**	**25.0**	**6:03**									
	Chicago Wolves	AHL	34	5	4	9	127																		
	Phoenix	**NHL**	**1**	**0**	**0**	**0**	**14**	**0**	**0**	**0**	**0**	**0.0**	**0**	**0**	**0.0**	**7:18**									

			Regular Season														Playoffs								
Season	Club	League	GP	G	A	Pts	PIM	PP	SH	GW	S	%	+/-	TF	F%	Min	GP	G	A	Pts	PIM	PP	SH	GW	Min
2002-03	**Phoenix**	**NHL**	**25**	**0**	**0**	**0**	**82**	**0**	**0**	**0**	**5**	**0.0**	**–1**	**0**	**0.0**	**4:47**	....	....	....	....	....	....	....	....	....
	Springfield	AHL	22	1	3	4	38	....	....	....	....	....	....	....	....	....	....	....	....	....	....	....	....	....	....
	Florida	**NHL**	**3**	**0**	**0**	**0**	**15**	**0**	**0**	**0**	**2**	**0.0**	**–1**	**0**	**0.0**	**9:45**	....	....	....	....	....	....	....	....	....
2003-04	**Florida**	**NHL**	**57**	**3**	**1**	**4**	**158**	**0**	**0**	**1**	**27**	**11.1**	**–10**	**4**	**50.0**	**6:46**	....	....	....	....	....	....	....	....	....
2004-05			DID NOT PLAY																						
2005-06	**Nashville**	**NHL**	**74**	**7**	**6**	**13**	**163**	**0**	**0**	**1**	**52**	**13.5**	**9**	**1**	**0.0**	**6:09**	....	....	....	....	....	....	....	....	....
	NHL Totals		**204**	**11**	**8**	**19**	**597**	**0**	**0**	**2**	**100**	**11.0**		**9**	**33.3**	**6:15**	....	....	....	....	....	....	....	....	....

Traded to **Phoenix** by **Atlanta** with Atlanta's 4th (Lance Monych) and 5th (John Zeiler) round choices in 2002 Entry Draft for Kiril Safronov, the rights to Ruslan Zainullin and Phoenix's 4th round choice (Patrick Dwyer) in 2002 Entry Draft, March 19, 2002. Traded to **Florida** by **Phoenix** with Phoenix's 2nd round choice (later traded to Tampa Bay – Tampa Bay selected Matt Smaby) in 2003 Entry Draft for Brad Ference, March 8, 2003. Traded to **Nashville** by **Florida** for Nashville's 4th round choice (Matt Duffy) in 2005 Entry Draft, July 27, 2005.

HORTON, Nathan

(HOHR-tohn, NAY-thun) **FLA.**

Center. Shoots right. 6'2", 201 lbs. Born, Welland, Ont., May 29, 1985. Florida's 1st choice, 3rd overall, in 2003 Entry Draft.

Season	Club	League	GP	G	A	Pts	PIM	PP	SH	GW	S	%	+/-	TF	F%	Min	GP	G	A	Pts	PIM	PP	SH	GW	Min
2000-01	Thorold	OHA-B	41	16	31	47	75	....	....	....	....	....	....	....	....	....	....	....	....	....	....	....	....	....	....
2001-02	Oshawa Generals	OHL	64	31	36	67	84	....	....	....	....	....	....	....	....	....	5	1	2	3	10	....	....	....	....
2002-03	Oshawa Generals	OHL	54	33	35	68	111	....	....	....	....	....	....	....	....	....	13	9	6	15	10	....	....	....	....
2003-04	**Florida**	**NHL**	**55**	**14**	**8**	**22**	**57**	**6**	**1**	**0**	**81**	**17.3**	**–5**	**270**	**41.9**	**13:20**	....	....	....	....	....	....	....	....	....
2004-05	San Antonio	AHL	21	5	4	9	21	....	....	....	....	....	....	....	....	....	....	....	....	....	....	....	....	....	....
2005-06	**Florida**	**NHL**	**71**	**28**	**19**	**47**	**89**	**3**	**0**	**1**	**162**	**17.3**	**8**	**24**	**45.8**	**16:53**	....	....	....	....	....	....	....	....	....
	NHL Totals		**126**	**42**	**27**	**69**	**146**	**9**	**1**	**1**	**243**	**17.3**		**294**	**42.2**	**15:20**	....	....	....	....	....	....	....	....	....

OHL All-Rookie Team (2002)

Signed as a free agent by **San Antonio** (AHL), October 28, 2004.

HOSSA, Marcel

(HOH-sah, MAHR-sehl) **NYR**

Left wing. Shoots left. 6'3", 220 lbs. Born, Ilava, Czech., October 12, 1981. Montreal's 2nd choice, 16th overall, in 2000 Entry Draft.

Season	Club	League	GP	G	A	Pts	PIM	PP	SH	GW	S	%	+/-	TF	F%	Min	GP	G	A	Pts	PIM	PP	SH	GW	Min
1996-97	Dukla Trencin Jr.	Slovak-Jr.	45	30	21	51	30	....	....	....	....	....	....	....	....	....	....	....	....	....	....	....	....	....	....
1997-98	Dukla Trencin Jr.	Slovak-Jr.	39	11	38	49	44	....	....	....	....	....	....	....	....	....	....	....	....	....	....	....	....	....	....
1998-99	Portland	WHL	70	7	14	21	66	....	....	....	....	....	....	....	....	....	2	0	0	0	2	....	....	....	....
99-2000	Portland	WHL	60	24	29	53	58	....	....	....	....	....	....	....	....	....	....	....	....	....	....	....	....	....	....
2000-01	Portland	WHL	58	34	56	90	58	....	....	....	....	....	....	....	....	....	16	5	7	12	14	....	....	....	....
2001-02	**Montreal**	**NHL**	**10**	**3**	**1**	**4**	**2**	**0**	**0**	**0**	**20**	**15.0**	**2**	**0**	**0.0**	**11:09**	....	....	....	....	....	....	....	....	....
	Quebec Citadelles	AHL	50	17	15	32	24	....	....	....	....	....	....	....	....	....	3	0	0	0	4	....	....	....	....
2002-03	**Montreal**	**NHL**	**34**	**6**	**7**	**13**	**14**	**2**	**0**	**1**	**51**	**11.8**	**3**	**4**	**50.0**	**13:58**	....	....	....	....	....	....	....	....	....
	Hamilton	AHL	37	19	13	32	18	....	....	....	....	....	....	....	....	....	21	4	7	11	12	....	....	....	....
2003-04	**Montreal**	**NHL**	**15**	**1**	**1**	**2**	**8**	**0**	**0**	**0**	**19**	**5.3**	**–3**	**5**	**40.0**	**14:50**	....	....	....	....	....	....	....	....	....
	Hamilton	AHL	57	18	22	40	45	....	....	....	....	....	....	....	....	....	10	2	3	5	8	....	....	....	....
2004-05	Mora IK	Sweden	48	18	6	24	69	....	....	....	....	....	....	....	....	....	....	....	....	....	....	....	....	....	....
2005-06	**NY Rangers**	**NHL**	**64**	**10**	**6**	**16**	**28**	**3**	**0**	**0**	**105**	**9.5**	**–6**	**7**	**28.6**	**10:45**	**4**	**0**	**0**	**0**	**6**	**0**	**0**	**0**	**13:18**
	Slovakia	Olympics	6	0	0	0	0	....	....	....	....	....	....	....	....	....	....	....	....	....	....	....	....	....	....
	NHL Totals		**123**	**20**	**15**	**35**	**52**	**5**	**0**	**1**	**195**	**10.3**		**16**	**37.5**	**12:10**	**4**	**0**	**0**	**0**	**6**	**0**	**0**	**0**	**13:18**

WHL West Second All-Star Team (2001)

Signed as a free agent by **Mora** (Sweden), September 25, 2004. Traded to **NY Rangers** by **Montreal** for Garth Murray, September 30, 2005.

HOSSA, Marian

(HOH-sah, MAIR-ee-uhn) **ATL.**

Right wing. Shoots left. 6'1", 210 lbs. Born, Stara Lubovna, Czech., January 12, 1979. Ottawa's 1st choice, 12th overall, in 1997 Entry Draft.

Season	Club	League	GP	G	A	Pts	PIM	PP	SH	GW	S	%	+/-	TF	F%	Min	GP	G	A	Pts	PIM	PP	SH	GW	Min
1995-96	Dukla Trencin Jr.	Slovak-Jr.	53	42	49	91	26	....	....	....	....	....	....	....	....	....	....	....	....	....	....	....	....	....	....
1996-97	Dukla Trencin	Slovakia	46	25	19	44	33	....	....	....	....	....	....	....	....	....	7	5	5	10	....	....	....	....	....
1997-98	Portland	WHL	53	45	40	85	50	....	....	....	....	....	....	....	....	....	16	13	6	19	6	....	....	....	....
	Ottawa	**NHL**	**7**	**0**	**1**	**1**	**0**	**0**	**0**	**0**	**10**	**0.0**	**–1**	....	....	....	....	....	....	....	....	....	....	....	....
1998-99	**Ottawa**	**NHL**	**60**	**15**	**15**	**30**	**37**	**1**	**0**	**2**	**124**	**12.1**	**18**	**4**	**25.0**	**13:59**	**4**	**0**	**2**	**2**	**4**	**0**	**0**	**0**	**16:46**
99-2000	**Ottawa**	**NHL**	**78**	**29**	**27**	**56**	**32**	**5**	**0**	**4**	**240**	**12.1**	**5**	**7**	**57.1**	**17:12**	**6**	**0**	**0**	**0**	**2**	**0**	**0**	**0**	**15:22**
2000-01	**Ottawa**	**NHL**	**81**	**32**	**43**	**75**	**44**	**11**	**2**	**7**	**249**	**12.9**	**19**	**14**	**42.9**	**18:01**	**4**	**1**	**1**	**2**	**4**	**0**	**0**	**0**	**19:01**
2001-02	Dukla Trencin	Slovakia	8	3	4	7	16	....	....	....	....	....	....	....	....	....	....	....	....	....	....	....	....	....	....
	Ottawa	**NHL**	**80**	**31**	**35**	**66**	**50**	**9**	**1**	**4**	**278**	**11.2**	**11**	**12**	**33.3**	**18:29**	**12**	**4**	**6**	**10**	**2**	**1**	**0**	**0**	**19:04**
	Slovakia	Olympics	2	4	2	6	0	....	....	....	....	....	....	....	....	....	....	....	....	....	....	....	....	....	....
2002-03	**Ottawa**	**NHL**	**80**	**45**	**35**	**80**	**34**	**14**	**0**	**10**	**229**	**19.7**	**8**	**19**	**36.8**	**18:31**	**18**	**5**	**11**	**16**	**6**	**3**	**0**	**1**	**18:41**
2003-04	**Ottawa**	**NHL**	**81**	**36**	**46**	**82**	**46**	**14**	**1**	**5**	**233**	**15.5**	**4**	**25**	**40.0**	**18:37**	**7**	**3**	**1**	**4**	**0**	**1**	**0**	**2**	**21:24**
2004-05	Dukla Trencin	Slovakia	25	22	20	42	38	....	....	....	....	....	....	....	....	....	5	4	5	9	14	....	....	....	....
	Mora IK	Sweden	24	18	14	32	22	....	....	....	....	....	....	....	....	....	....	....	....	....	....	....	....	....	....
2005-06	**Atlanta**	**NHL**	**80**	**39**	**53**	**92**	**67**	**14**	**7**	**7**	**341**	**11.4**	**17**	**15**	**26.7**	**21:41**	....	....	....	....	....	....	....	....	....
	Slovakia	Olympics	6	5	5	10	4	....	....	....	....	....	....	....	....	....	....	....	....	....	....	....	....	....	....
	NHL Totals		**547**	**227**	**255**	**482**	**310**	**68**	**11**	**39**	**1704**	**13.3**		**96**	**37.5**	**18:14**	**51**	**13**	**21**	**34**	**18**	**5**	**0**	**3**	**18:38**

WHL West First All-Star Team (1998) • WHL Rookie of the Year (1998) • Canadian Major Junior First All-Star Team (1998) • Memorial Cup Tournament All-Star Team (1998) • NHL All-Rookie Team (1999)

Played in NHL All-Star Game (2001, 2003)

Signed as a free agent by **Trencin** (Slovakia), September 16, 2004. Signed as a free agent by **Mora** (Sweden), November 11, 2004. Signed as a free agent by **Trencin** (Slovakia), January 31, 2005. Traded to **Atlanta** by **Ottawa** with Greg de Vries for Dany Heatley, August 23, 2005.

HRDINA, Jan

(huhr-DEE-nah, YAN)

Center. Shoots right. 6', 205 lbs. Born, Hradec Kralove, Czech., February 5, 1976. Pittsburgh's 4th choice, 128th overall, in 1995 Entry Draft.

Season	Club	League	GP	G	A	Pts	PIM	PP	SH	GW	S	%	+/-	TF	F%	Min	GP	G	A	Pts	PIM	PP	SH	GW	Min
1993-94	Hr. Kralove Jr.	CzRep-Jr.	10	1	6	7	0	....	....	....	....	....	....	....	....	....	....	....	....	....	....	....	....	....	....
	Hr. Kralove	CzRep	23	1	5	6	....	....	....	....	....	....	....	....	....	....	4	0	1	1	....	....	....	....	....
1994-95	Seattle	WHL	69	41	59	100	79	....	....	....	....	....	....	....	....	....	4	0	1	1	8	....	....	....	....
1995-96	Seattle	WHL	30	19	28	47	37	....	....	....	....	....	....	....	....	....	....	....	....	....	....	....	....	....	....
	Spokane Chiefs	WHL	18	10	16	26	25	....	....	....	....	....	....	....	....	....	18	5	14	19	49	....	....	....	....
1996-97	Cleveland	IHL	68	23	31	54	82	....	....	....	....	....	....	....	....	....	13	1	2	3	8	....	....	....	....
1997-98	Syracuse Crunch	AHL	72	20	24	44	82	....	....	....	....	....	....	....	....	....	5	1	3	4	10	....	....	....	....
1998-99	**Pittsburgh**	**NHL**	**82**	**13**	**29**	**42**	**40**	**3**	**0**	**2**	**94**	**13.8**	**–2**	**1461**	**56.7**	**16:26**	**13**	**4**	**1**	**5**	**12**	**1**	**0**	**1**	**21:03**
99-2000	**Pittsburgh**	**NHL**	**70**	**13**	**33**	**46**	**43**	**3**	**0**	**1**	**84**	**15.5**	**13**	**1392**	**53.7**	**18:47**	**9**	**4**	**8**	**12**	**2**	**1**	**0**	**0**	**22:04**
2000-01	**Pittsburgh**	**NHL**	**78**	**15**	**28**	**43**	**48**	**3**	**0**	**1**	**89**	**16.9**	**19**	**1067**	**53.8**	**15:56**	**18**	**2**	**5**	**7**	**8**	**0**	**0**	**0**	**15:04**
2001-02	**Pittsburgh**	**NHL**	**79**	**24**	**33**	**57**	**50**	**6**	**0**	**6**	**115**	**20.9**	**–7**	**667**	**50.4**	**19:51**	....	....	....	....	....	....	....	....	....
	Czech Republic	Olympics	4	0	0	0	0	....	....	....	....	....	....	....	....	....	....	....	....	....	....	....	....	....	....
2002-03	**Pittsburgh**	**NHL**	**57**	**14**	**25**	**39**	**34**	**11**	**0**	**4**	**84**	**16.7**	**1**	**984**	**56.0**	**19:45**	....	....	....	....	....	....	....	....	....
	Phoenix	**NHL**	**4**	**0**	**4**	**4**	**8**	**0**	**0**	**0**	**2**	**0.0**	**3**	**70**	**60.0**	**18:12**	....	....	....	....	....	....	....	....	....
2003-04	**Phoenix**	**NHL**	**55**	**11**	**15**	**26**	**30**	**5**	**0**	**1**	**62**	**17.7**	**–10**	**677**	**50.7**	**17:57**	....	....	....	....	....	....	....	....	....
	New Jersey	**NHL**	**13**	**1**	**6**	**7**	**10**	**0**	**0**	**0**	**11**	**9.1**	**4**	**148**	**55.4**	**12:51**	**5**	**2**	**0**	**2**	**2**	**0**	**0**	**0**	**13:22**
2004-05	HC Rabat Kladno	CzRep	23	4	3	7	38	....	....	....	....	....	....	....	....	....	7	3	3	6	4	....	....	....	....
2005-06	**Columbus**	**NHL**	**75**	**10**	**23**	**33**	**78**	**4**	**1**	**0**	**78**	**12.8**	**–8**	**1086**	**51.9**	**16:58**	....	....	....	....	....	....	....	....	....
	NHL Totals		**513**	**101**	**196**	**297**	**341**	**35**	**1**	**15**	**619**	**16.3**		**7552**	**53.9**	**17:44**	**45**	**12**	**14**	**26**	**24**	**2**	**0**	**1**	**18:00**

Traded to **Phoenix** by **Pittsburgh** with Francois Leroux for Ramzi Abid, Dan Focht and Guillaume Lefebvre, March 11, 2003. Traded to **New Jersey** by **Phoenix** for Mike Rupp and New Jersey's 2nd round choice (later traded to Edmonton – Edmonton selected Geoff Paukovich) in 2004 Entry Draft, March 5, 2004. Signed as a free agent by **Kladno** (CzRep), October 4, 2004. Signed as a free agent by **Columbus**, August 10, 2005.

HUBACEK, Petr

(HOO-buh-chehk, PEE-tuhr) **NSH.**

Center. Shoots right. 6'2", 183 lbs. Born, Brno, Czech., September 2, 1979. Philadelphia's 11th choice, 243rd overall, in 1998 Entry Draft.

Season	Club	League	GP	G	A	Pts	PIM	PP	SH	GW	S	%	+/-	TF	F%	Min	GP	G	A	Pts	PIM	PP	SH	GW	Min
1997-98	Brno Jr.	CzRep-Jr.	17	9	5	14	....	....	....	....	....	....	....	....	....	....	....	....	....	....	....	....	....	....	....
	Brno	CzRep-2	48	6	10	16	....	....	....	....	....	....	....	....	....	....	....	....	....	....	....	....	....	....	....
1998-99	HC Vitkovice	CzRep	25	0	4	4	2	....	....	....	....	....	....	....	....	....	4	0	0	0	....	....	....	....	....
99-2000	HC Vitkovice	CzRep	48	11	12	23	81	....	....	....	....	....	....	....	....	....	....	....	....	....	....	....	....	....	....
2000-01	**Philadelphia**	**NHL**	**6**	**1**	**0**	**1**	**2**	**0**	**0**	**0**	**5**	**20.0**	**–1**	**39**	**25.6**	**11:20**	....	....	....	....	....	....	....	....	....
	Philadelphia	AHL	62	3	9	12	29	....	....	....	....	....	....	....	....	....	9	0	1	1	6	....	....	....	....
2001-02	Philadelphia	AHL	22	1	6	7	8	....	....	....	....	....	....	....	....	....	....	....	....	....	....	....	....	....	....
	Milwaukee	AHL	14	2	0	2	0	....	....	....	....	....	....	....	....	....	....	....	....	....	....	....	....	....	....

			Regular Season														Playoffs								
Season	Club	League	GP	G	A	Pts	PIM	PP	SH	GW	S	%	+/-	TF	F%	Min	GP	G	A	Pts	PIM	PP	SH	GW	Min
2002-03	HC Hame Zlin	CzRep	44	4	15	19	14	....	....	....	....	....	....	....	....	....	....	....	....	....	....	....	....	....	....
	HC Vitkovice	CzRep	7	1	4	5	10	....	....	....	....	....	....	....	....	....	6	1	0	1	16	....	....	....	....
2003-04	HC Vitkovice	CzRep	46	7	14	21	26	....	....	....	....	....	....	....	....	....	6	1	0	1	*53	....	....	....	....
2004-05	Vitkovice	CzRep	51	13	11	24	38	....	....	....	....	....	....	....	....	....	9	0	1	1	33	....	....	....	....
2005-06	Vitkovice	CzRep	52	17	23	40	46	....	....	....	....	....	....	....	....	....	6	1	0	1	2	....	....	....	....
	NHL Totals		**6**	**1**	**0**	**1**	**2**	**0**	**0**	**0**	**5**	**20.0**		**39**	**25.6**	**11:20**	....	....	....	....	....	....	....	....	....

Traded to **Nashville** by **Philadelphia** with Jason Beckett for Yves Sarault, January 11, 2002. Signed as a free agent by **Zlin** (CzRep) with Nashville retaining NHL rights, August 4, 2002.

HUDLER, Jiri

(HUHD-luhr, YIH-ree) **DET.**

Center. Shoots left. 5'9", 178 lbs. Born, Olomouc, Czech., January 4, 1984. Detroit's 1st choice, 58th overall, in 2002 Entry Draft.

1998-99	HC Vsetin U17	CzR-U17	46	57	57	114	....	....	....	....	....	....	....	....	....	....	....	....	....	....	....	....	....	....	....
99-2000	HC Vsetin Jr.	CzRep-Jr.	53	29	31	60	75	....	....	....	....	....	....	....	....	....	....	....	....	....	....	....	....	....	....
	Vsetin	CzRep	2	0	1	1	0	....	....	....	....	....	....	....	....	....	....	....	....	....	....	....	....	....	....
2000-01	HC Vsetin Jr.	CzRep-Jr.	16	8	14	22	16	....	....	....	....	....	....	....	....	....	....	....	....	....	....	....	....	....	....
	HC Slovnaft Vsetin	CzRep	22	1	4	5	10	....	....	....	....	....	....	....	....	....	....	....	....	....	....	....	....	....	....
	HC Femax Havirov	CzRep	15	5	1	6	12	....	....	....	....	....	....	....	....	....	....	....	....	....	....	....	....	....	....
2001-02	HC Vsetin	CzRep	46	15	31	46	54	....	....	....	....	....	....	....	....	....	....	....	....	....	....	....	....	....	....
	Liberec	CzRep-2	13	9	7	16	10	....	....	....	....	....	....	....	....	....	....	....	....	....	....	....	....	....	....
	HC Olomouc	CzRep-3	1	0	2	2	4	....	....	....	....	....	....	....	....	....	....	....	....	....	....	....	....	....	....
2002-03	HC Vsetin	CzRep	30	19	27	46	22	....	....	....	....	....	....	....	....	....	....	....	....	....	....	....	....	....	....
	Ak Bars Kazan	Russia	11	1	5	6	12	....	....	....	....	....	....	....	....	....	1	0	0	0	0	....	....	....	....
2003-04	**Detroit**	**NHL**	**12**	**1**	**2**	**3**	**10**	**1**	**0**	**0**	**8**	**12.5**	**−1**	**50**	**30.0**	**8:09**	....	....	....	....	....	....	....	....	....
	Grand Rapids	AHL	57	17	32	49	46	....	....	....	....	....	....	....	....	....	4	1	5	6	2	....	....	....	....
2004-05	Grand Rapids	AHL	52	12	22	34	10	....	....	....	....	....	....	....	....	....	....	....	....	....	....	....	....	....	....
	HC Vsetin	CzRep	7	5	2	7	10	....	....	....	....	....	....	....	....	....	....	....	....	....	....	....	....	....	....
2005-06	**Detroit**	**NHL**	**4**	**0**	**0**	**0**	**2**	**0**	**0**	**0**	**3**	**0.0**	**0**	**0**	**0.0**	**7:13**	....	....	....	....	....	....	....	....	....
	Grand Rapids	AHL	76	36	61	97	56	....	....	....	....	....	....	....	....	....	16	6	16	22	20	....	....	....	....
	NHL Totals		**16**	**1**	**2**	**3**	**12**	**1**	**0**	**0**	**11**	**9.1**		**50**	**30.0**	**7:55**	....	....	....	....	....	....	....	....	....

AHL Second All-Star Team (2006)

Signed as a free agent by **Vsetin** (CzRep), December 2, 2004.

HULL, Brett

(HUHL, BREHT)

Right wing. Shoots right. 5'11", 203 lbs. Born, Belleville, Ont., August 9, 1964. Calgary's 6th choice, 117th overall, in 1984 Entry Draft.

1982-83	Penticton Knights	BCJHL	50	48	56	104	27	....	....	....	....	....	....	....	....	....	....	....	....	....	....	....	....	....	....
1983-84	Penticton Knights	BCJHL	56	*105	83	*188	20	....	....	....	....	....	....	....	....	....	....	....	....	....	....	....	....	....	....
1984-85	U. Minn-Duluth	WCHA	48	32	28	60	24	....	....	....	....	....	....	....	....	....	....	....	....	....	....	....	....	....	....
1985-86	U. Minn-Duluth	WCHA	42	52	32	84	46	....	....	....	....	....	....	....	....	....	....	....	....	....	....	....	....	....	....
	Calgary	**NHL**	....	....	....	....	....	....	....	....	....	....	....	....	....	....	**2**	**0**	**0**	**0**	**0**	**0**	**0**	**0**	....
1986-87	**Calgary**	**NHL**	**5**	**1**	**0**	**1**	**0**	**0**	**0**	**1**	**5**	**20.0**	**−1**	....	....	....	**4**	**2**	**1**	**3**	**0**	**0**	**0**	**0**	....
	Moncton	AHL	67	50	42	92	16	....	....	....	....	....	....	....	....	....	3	2	2	4	2	....	....	....	....
1987-88	**Calgary**	**NHL**	**52**	**26**	**24**	**50**	**12**	**4**	**0**	**3**	**153**	**17.0**	**10**	....	....	....	....	....	....	....	....	....	....	....	....
	St. Louis	**NHL**	**13**	**6**	**8**	**14**	**4**	**2**	**0**	**0**	**58**	**10.3**	**4**	....	....	....	**10**	**7**	**2**	**9**	**4**	**4**	**0**	**3**	....
1988-89	**St. Louis**	**NHL**	**78**	**41**	**43**	**84**	**33**	**16**	**0**	**6**	**305**	**13.4**	**−17**	....	....	....	**10**	**5**	**5**	**10**	**6**	**1**	**0**	**2**	....
1989-90	**St. Louis**	**NHL**	**80**	***72**	**41**	**113**	**24**	**27**	**0**	**12**	**385**	**18.7**	**−1**	....	....	....	**12**	**13**	**8**	**21**	**17**	**7**	**0**	**3**	....
1990-91	**St. Louis**	**NHL**	**78**	***86**	**45**	**131**	**22**	**29**	**0**	**11**	**389**	**22.1**	**23**	....	....	....	**13**	**11**	**8**	**19**	**4**	**3**	**0**	**2**	....
1991-92	**St. Louis**	**NHL**	**73**	***70**	**39**	**109**	**48**	**20**	**5**	**9**	**408**	**17.2**	**−2**	....	....	....	**6**	**4**	**4**	**8**	**4**	**1**	**1**	**1**	....
1992-93	**St. Louis**	**NHL**	**80**	**54**	**47**	**101**	**41**	**29**	**0**	**2**	**390**	**13.8**	**−27**	....	....	....	**11**	**8**	**5**	**13**	**2**	**5**	**0**	**2**	....
1993-94	**St. Louis**	**NHL**	**81**	**57**	**40**	**97**	**38**	**25**	**3**	**6**	**392**	**14.5**	**−3**	....	....	....	**4**	**2**	**1**	**3**	**0**	**1**	**0**	**0**	....
1994-95	**St. Louis**	**NHL**	**48**	**29**	**21**	**50**	**10**	**9**	**3**	**6**	**200**	**14.5**	**13**	....	....	....	**7**	**6**	**2**	**8**	**0**	**2**	**0**	**0**	....
1995-96	**St. Louis**	**NHL**	**70**	**43**	**40**	**83**	**30**	**16**	**5**	**6**	**327**	**13.1**	**4**	....	....	....	**13**	**6**	**5**	**11**	**10**	**2**	**1**	**1**	....
1996-97	**St. Louis**	**NHL**	**77**	**42**	**40**	**82**	**10**	**12**	**2**	**6**	**302**	**13.9**	**−9**	....	....	....	**6**	**2**	**7**	**9**	**2**	**0**	**0**	**0**	....
1997-98	**St. Louis**	**NHL**	**66**	**27**	**45**	**72**	**26**	**10**	**0**	**6**	**211**	**12.8**	**−1**	....	....	....	**10**	**3**	**3**	**6**	**2**	**1**	**0**	**1**	....
	United States	Olympics	4	2	1	3	0	....	....	....	....	....	....	....	....	....	....	....	....	....	....	....	....	....	....
1998-99 ♦	**Dallas**	**NHL**	**60**	**32**	**26**	**58**	**30**	**15**	**0**	**11**	**192**	**16.7**	**19**	**12**	**50.0**	**17:24**	**22**	**8**	**7**	**15**	**4**	**3**	**0**	**2**	**18:29**
99-2000	**Dallas**	**NHL**	**79**	**24**	**35**	**59**	**43**	**11**	**0**	**3**	**223**	**10.8**	**−21**	**10**	**40.0**	**18:37**	**23**	***11**	***13**	***24**	**4**	**3**	**0**	**4**	**19:59**
2000-01	**Dallas**	**NHL**	**79**	**39**	**40**	**79**	**18**	**11**	**0**	**8**	**219**	**17.8**	**10**	**10**	**30.0**	**17:53**	**10**	**2**	**5**	**7**	**6**	**1**	**0**	**0**	**20:10**
2001-02 ♦	**Detroit**	**NHL**	**82**	**30**	**33**	**63**	**35**	**7**	**1**	**4**	**247**	**12.1**	**18**	**5**	**20.0**	**18:49**	**23**	***10**	**8**	**18**	**4**	**3**	**2**	**2**	**17:54**
	United States	Olympics	6	3	5	8	6	....	....	....	....	....	....	....	....	....	....	....	....	....	....	....	....	....	....
2002-03	**Detroit**	**NHL**	**82**	**37**	**39**	**76**	**22**	**12**	**1**	**4**	**262**	**14.1**	**11**	**18**	**38.9**	**18:07**	**4**	**0**	**1**	**1**	**0**	**0**	**0**	**0**	**20:17**
2003-04	**Detroit**	**NHL**	**81**	**25**	**43**	**68**	**12**	**10**	**0**	**6**	**200**	**12.5**	**−4**	**7**	**42.9**	**16:54**	**12**	**3**	**2**	**5**	**4**	**1**	**0**	**1**	**15:15**
2004-05			Did not play																						
2005-06	**Phoenix**	**NHL**	**5**	**0**	**1**	**1**	**0**	**0**	**0**	**0**	**8**	**0.0**	**−3**	**0**	**0.0**	**13:45**	....	....	....	....	....	....	....	....	....
	NHL Totals		**1269**	**741**	**650**	**1391**	**458**	**265**	**20**	**110**	**4876**	**15.2**		**62**	**38.7**	**17:56**	**202**	**103**	**87**	**190**	**73**	**38**	**4**	**24**	**18:33**

WCHA Freshman of the Year (1985) • WCHA First All-Star Team (1986) • AHL First All-Star Team (1987) • Dudley "Red" Garrett Memorial Award (Rookie of the Year – AHL) (1987) • NHL First All-Star Team (1990, 1991, 1992) • Dodge Ram Tough Award (1990, 1991) • Lady Byng Trophy (1990) • ProSet/NHL Player of the Year Award (1991) • Lester B. Pearson Award (1991) • Hart Memorial Trophy (1991)

Played in NHL All-Star Game (1989, 1990, 1992, 1993, 1994, 1996, 1997, 2001)

Traded to **St. Louis** by **Calgary** with Steve Bozek for Rob Ramage and Rick Wamsley, March 7, 1988. Signed as a free agent by **Dallas**, July 3, 1998. Signed as a free agent by **Detroit**, August 22, 2001. Signed as a free agent by **Phoenix**, August 6, 2004. • Officially announced retirement, October 15, 2005.

HULSE, Cale

(HUHLS, KAYL)

Defense. Shoots right. 6'3", 220 lbs. Born, Edmonton, Alta., November 10, 1973. New Jersey's 3rd choice, 66th overall, in 1992 Entry Draft.

1990-91	Calgary Royals	AJHL	49	3	23	26	220	....	....	....	....	....	....	....	....	....	....	....	....	....	....	....	....	....	....
1991-92	Portland	WHL	70	4	18	22	230	....	....	....	....	....	....	....	....	....	6	0	2	2	27	....	....	....	....
1992-93	Portland	WHL	72	10	26	36	284	....	....	....	....	....	....	....	....	....	16	4	4	8	65	....	....	....	....
1993-94	Albany River Rats	AHL	79	7	14	21	186	....	....	....	....	....	....	....	....	....	5	0	3	3	11	....	....	....	....
1994-95	Albany River Rats	AHL	77	5	13	18	215	....	....	....	....	....	....	....	....	....	12	1	1	2	17	....	....	....	....
1995-96	**New Jersey**	**NHL**	**8**	**0**	**0**	**0**	**15**	**0**	**0**	**0**	**5**	**0.0**	**−2**	....	....	....	....	....	....	....	....	....	....	....	....
	Albany River Rats	AHL	42	4	23	27	107	....	....	....	....	....	....	....	....	....	....	....	....	....	....	....	....	....	....
	Calgary	**NHL**	**3**	**0**	**0**	**0**	**5**	**0**	**0**	**0**	**4**	**0.0**	**3**	....	....	....	**1**	**0**	**0**	**0**	**0**	**0**	**0**	**0**	....
	Saint John Flames	AHL	13	2	7	9	39	....	....	....	....	....	....	....	....	....	....	....	....	....	....	....	....	....	....
1996-97	**Calgary**	**NHL**	**63**	**1**	**6**	**7**	**91**	**0**	**1**	**0**	**58**	**1.7**	**−2**	....	....	....	....	....	....	....	....	....	....	....	....
1997-98	**Calgary**	**NHL**	**79**	**5**	**22**	**27**	**169**	**1**	**1**	**0**	**117**	**4.3**	**1**	....	....	....	....	....	....	....	....	....	....	....	....
1998-99	**Calgary**	**NHL**	**73**	**3**	**9**	**12**	**117**	**0**	**0**	**0**	**83**	**3.6**	**−8**	**1**	**0.0**	**16:38**	....	....	....	....	....	....	....	....	....
99-2000	**Calgary**	**NHL**	**47**	**1**	**6**	**7**	**47**	**0**	**0**	**0**	**41**	**2.4**	**−11**	**1**	**100.0**	**12:38**	....	....	....	....	....	....	....	....	....
2000-01	**Nashville**	**NHL**	**82**	**1**	**7**	**8**	**128**	**0**	**0**	**1**	**93**	**1.1**	**−5**	**0**	**0.0**	**20:05**	....	....	....	....	....	....	....	....	....
2001-02	**Nashville**	**NHL**	**63**	**0**	**2**	**2**	**121**	**0**	**0**	**0**	**70**	**0.0**	**−18**	**0**	**0.0**	**18:51**	....	....	....	....	....	....	....	....	....
2002-03	**Nashville**	**NHL**	**80**	**2**	**6**	**8**	**121**	**0**	**0**	**1**	**82**	**2.4**	**−11**	**0**	**0.0**	**19:05**	....	....	....	....	....	....	....	....	....
2003-04	**Phoenix**	**NHL**	**82**	**3**	**17**	**20**	**123**	**1**	**0**	**0**	**115**	**2.6**	**−4**	**0**	**0.0**	**21:28**	....	....	....	....	....	....	....	....	....
2004-05			Did not play																						
2005-06	**Columbus**	**NHL**	**27**	**0**	**3**	**3**	**43**	**0**	**0**	**0**	**27**	**0.0**	**−9**	**0**	**0.0**	**15:04**	....	....	....	....	....	....	....	....	....
	Calgary	**NHL**	**12**	**0**	**1**	**1**	**20**	**0**	**0**	**0**	**7**	**0.0**	**1**	**0**	**0.0**	**15:47**	....	....	....	....	....	....	....	....	....
	NHL Totals		**619**	**16**	**79**	**95**	**1000**	**2**	**2**	**2**	**702**	**2.3**		**2**	**50.0**	**18:18**	**1**	**0**	**0**	**0**	**0**	**0**	**0**	**0**	....

Traded to **Calgary** by **New Jersey** with Tommy Albelin and Jocelyn Lemieux for Phil Housley and Dan Keczmer, February 26, 1996. Traded to **Nashville** by **Calgary** with Calgary's 3rd round choice (Denis Platonov) in 2001 Entry Draft for Sergei Krivokrasov, March 14, 2000. Signed as a free agent by **Phoenix**, July 10, 2003. Traded to **Columbus** by **Phoenix** with Mike Rupp and Jason Chimera for Geoff Sanderson and Tim Jackman, October 8, 2005. Traded to **Calgary** by **Columbus** for Cam Severson, February 28, 2006.

HUNTER, Trent

(HUHN-tuhr, TREHNT) **NYI**

Right wing. Shoots right. 6'3", 191 lbs. Born, Red Deer, Alta., July 5, 1980. Anaheim's 4th choice, 150th overall, in 1998 Entry Draft.

1996-97	Red Deer	AMHL	42	30	25	55	50	....	....	....	....	....	....	....	....	....	....	....	....	....	....	....	....	....	....
1997-98	Prince George	WHL	60	13	14	27	34	....	....	....	....	....	....	....	....	....	8	1	0	1	4	....	....	....	....
1998-99	Prince George	WHL	50	18	20	38	34	....	....	....	....	....	....	....	....	....	7	2	5	7	2	....	....	....	....
99-2000	Prince George	WHL	67	46	49	95	47	....	....	....	....	....	....	....	....	....	13	7	15	22	6	....	....	....	....
2000-01	Springfield	AHL	57	18	17	35	14	....	....	....	....	....	....	....	....	....	....	....	....	....	....	....	....	....	....
2001-02	Bridgeport	AHL	80	30	35	65	30	....	....	....	....	....	....	....	....	....	17	8	11	19	6	....	....	....	....
	NY Islanders	**NHL**	....	....	....	....	....	....	....	....	....	....	....	....	....	....	**4**	**1**	**1**	**2**	**2**	**0**	**0**	**0**	**11:13**

									Regular Season										Playoffs							
Season	Club	League	GP	G	A	Pts	PIM	PP	SH	GW	S	%	+/-	TF	F%	Min	GP	G	A	Pts	PIM	PP	SH	GW	Min
2002-03	Bridgeport	AHL	70	30	41	71	39										9	7	4	11	10				
	NY Islanders	NHL	8	0	4	4	4	0	0	0	19	0.0	5	1	0.0	12:13									
2003-04	NY Islanders	NHL	77	25	26	51	16	4	0	7	187	13.4	23	19	36.8	15:39	5	0	0	0	4	0	0	0	11:38
2004-05	Nykoping	Sweden-2	33	13	12	25	73										4	5	3	8	2				
2005-06	NY Islanders	NHL	82	16	19	35	34	5	0	3	221	7.2	−9	32	28.1	17:50									
	NHL Totals		167	41	49	90	54	9	0	10	427	9.6		52	30.8	16:33	9	1	1	2	6	0	0	0	11:27

WHL West First All-Star Team (2000) • NHL All-Rookie Team (2004)
Traded to **NY Islanders** by **Anaheim** for Columbus' 4th round choice (previously acquired, Anaheim selected Jonas Ronnqvist) in 2000 Entry Draft, May 23, 2000. Signed as a free agent by **Nykoping** (Sweden-2), November 8, 2004.

HUSELIUS, Kristian
(hoo-SAY-lee-oos, KRIHST-yan)   **CGY.**

Left wing. Shoots left. 6'1", 190 lbs.   Born, Osterhaninge, Sweden, November 10, 1978. Florida's 2nd choice, 47th overall, in 1997 Entry Draft.

1994-95	Hammarby Jr.	Swe-Jr.	17	6	2	8	2																	
1995-96	Hammarby Jr.	Swe-Jr.	25	13	8	21	14																	
	Hammarby	Sweden-2	6	1	0	1	0																	
1996-97	Farjestad	Sweden	13	2	0	2	4										5	1	0	1	0			
1997-98	Farjestad	Sweden	34	2	1	3	2										11	0	0	0	0			
	Farjestad	EuroHL	5	2	3	5	0																	
1998-99	Farjestad	Sweden	28	4	4	8	4										1	0	0	0	0			
	Farjestad	EuroHL	6	2	2	4	8										4	1	0	1	0			
99-2000	V.Frolunda	Sweden	50	21	23	44	20										5	2	2	4	8			
2000-01	V.Frolunda	Sweden	49	*32	*35	*67	26										5	4	5	9	14			
2001-02	**Florida**	**NHL**	79	23	22	45	14	6	1	3	169	13.6	−4	14	21.4	16:55								
2002-03	**Florida**	**NHL**	78	20	23	43	20	3	0	3	187	10.7	−6	6	33.3	17:20								
2003-04	**Florida**	**NHL**	76	10	21	31	24	2	0	2	168	6.0	−6	185	37.8	14:14								
2004-05	Rapperswil	Swiss															4	1	3	4	2			
	Linkopings HC	Sweden	34	14	*35	49	10																	
2005-06	**Florida**	**NHL**	24	5	3	8	4	2	0	0	57	8.8	−11	3	66.7	14:44								
	Calgary	**NHL**	54	15	24	39	36	6	0	4	107	14.0	2	3	33.3	14:55	7	2	4	6	4	2	0	0	15:35
	NHL Totals		311	73	93	166	98	19	1	12	688	10.6		211	37.0	15:51	7	2	4	6	4	2	0	0	15:35

NHL All-Rookie Team (2002)
Signed as a free agent by **Linkopings** (Sweden), July 29, 2004. Signed as a free agent by **Rapperswil** (Swiss), February 23, 2005. Traded to **Calgary** by **Florida** for Steve Montador and Dustin Johner, December 2, 2005.

HUSSEY, Matt
(HUH-see, MAT)   **DET.**

Center. Shoots left. 6'2", 215 lbs.   Born, New Haven, CT, May 28, 1979. Pittsburgh's 10th choice, 254th overall, in 1998 Entry Draft.

1996-97	Wayzata	High-MN	48	34	31	65																
1997-98	Avon Old Farms	High-CT	26	26	23	49	20																
1998-99	U. of Wisconsin	WCHA	37	10	5	15	18																
99-2000	U. of Wisconsin	WCHA	35	5	11	16	8																
2000-01	U. of Wisconsin	WCHA	40	9	11	20	24																
2001-02	U. of Wisconsin	WCHA	39	18	15	33	16										2	0	0	0	0		
2002-03	Wilkes-Barre	AHL	69	12	11	23	28																
2003-04	**Pittsburgh**	**NHL**	3	2	1	3	0	2	0	0	8	25.0	−1	0	0.0	13:35	6	2	2	4	0		
	Wilkes-Barre	AHL	55	6	3	6	6										10	1	2	3	2		
2004-05	Wilkes-Barre	AHL	80	16	14	30	19																
2005-06	**Pittsburgh**	**NHL**	13	0	1	1	0	0	0	0	17	0.0	−5	63	38.1	10:17	9	0	1	1	0		
	Wilkes-Barre	AHL	65	21	30	51	34																
	NHL Totals		16	2	2	4	0	2	0	0	25	8.0		63	38.1	10:54							

Signed as a free agent by **Detroit**, July 13, 2006.

HUTCHINSON, Andrew
(HUHT-chihn-suhn, AN-droo)   **CAR.**

Defense. Shoots right. 6'2", 204 lbs.   Born, Evanston, IL, March 24, 1980. Nashville's 4th choice, 54th overall, in 1999 Entry Draft.

1996-97	Det. Caesars	MNHL	82	15	41	56																	
1997-98	USNTDP	U-18	27	3	11	14	35																
	USNTDP	USHL	15	0	7	7	8										5	2	3	5	2		
	USNTDP	NAHL	12	2	0	2	8																
1998-99	Michigan State	CCHA	37	3	12	15	26																
99-2000	Michigan State	CCHA	42	5	12	17	64																
2000-01	Michigan State	CCHA	42	5	19	24	46																
2001-02	Milwaukee	AHL	5	0	1	1	0																
	Michigan State	CCHA	39	6	16	22	24																
2002-03	Toledo Storm	ECHL	10	2	5	7	4										3	1	0	1	0		
	Milwaukee	AHL	63	9	17	26	40																
2003-04	**Nashville**	**NHL**	18	4	4	8	4	2	0	1	24	16.7	1	0	0.0	16:43	22	5	11	16	33		
	Milwaukee	AHL	46	12	12	24	39										7	1	3	4	8		
2004-05	Milwaukee	AHL	76	10	35	45	79																
2005-06◆	**Carolina**	**NHL**	36	3	8	11	18	2	0	0	33	9.1	−2	0	0.0	10:22							
	NHL Totals		54	7	12	19	22	4	0	1	57	12.3		0	0.0	12:29							

CCHA Second All-Star Team (2001, 2002) • NCAA West Second All-American Team (2002)
Traded to **Carolina** by **Nashville** for Phoenix's 3rd round choice (previously acquired, Nashville selected Teemu Laakso) in 2005 Entry Draft, July 29, 2005.

IGINLA, Jarome
(ih-GIHN-lah, jah-ROHM)   **CGY.**

Right wing. Shoots right. 6'1", 208 lbs.   Born, Edmonton, Alta., July 1, 1977. Dallas' 1st choice, 11th overall, in 1995 Entry Draft.

1991-92	St. Albert Raiders	AMHL	36	26	30	56	22																		
1992-93	St. Albert Raiders	AMHL	36	34	53	*87	20										19	3	6	9	10				
1993-94	Kamloops Blazers	WHL	48	6	23	29	33										21	7	11	18	34				
1994-95	Kamloops Blazers	WHL	72	33	38	71	111										16	16	13	29	44				
1995-96	Kamloops Blazers	WHL	63	63	73	136	120										2	1	1	2	0	0	0	0	0
	Calgary	**NHL**																							
1996-97	**Calgary**	**NHL**	82	21	29	50	37	8	1	3	169	12.4	−4												
1997-98	**Calgary**	**NHL**	70	13	19	32	29	0	2	1	154	8.4	−10												
1998-99	**Calgary**	**NHL**	82	28	23	51	58	7	0	4	211	13.3	1	111	51.4	16:30									
99-2000	**Calgary**	**NHL**	77	29	34	63	26	12	0	4	256	11.3	0	278	52.9	18:24									
2000-01	**Calgary**	**NHL**	77	31	40	71	62	10	0	4	229	13.5	−2	638	51.7	19:58									
2001-02	**Calgary**	**NHL**	82	*52	44	*96	77	16	1	7	311	16.7	27	308	55.2	22:22									
	Canada	Olympics	6	3	1	4	0																		
2002-03	**Calgary**	**NHL**	75	35	32	67	49	11	3	6	316	11.1	−10	90	43.3	21:26									
2003-04	**Calgary**	**NHL**	81	*41	32	73	84	8	4	10	265	15.5	21	305	54.4	21:18	26	*13	9	22	45	4	2	3	23:18
2004-05			DID NOT PLAY																						
2005-06	**Calgary**	**NHL**	82	35	32	67	86	17	1	6	293	11.9	5	541	54.2	21:42	7	5	3	8	11	1	1	1	24:14
	Canada	Olympics	6	2	1	3	4																		
	NHL Totals		708	285	285	570	508	89	12	45	2204	12.9		2271	52.9	20:14	35	19	13	32	56	5	3	4	23:30

George Parsons Trophy (Memorial Cup Tournament Most Sportsmanlike Player) (1995) • WHL West First All-Star Team (1996) • WHL Player of the Year (1996) • Canadian Major Junior First All-Star Team (1996) • NHL All-Rookie Team (1997) • NHL First All-Star Team (2002) • Maurice "Rocket" Richard Trophy (2002) • Art Ross Trophy (2002) • Lester B. Pearson Award (2002) • NHL Second All-Star Team (2004) • King Clancy Memorial Trophy (2004) • Maurice "Rocket" Richard Trophy (2004) (tied with Ilya Kovalchuk and Rick Nash)
Played in NHL All-Star Game (2002, 2003, 2004)
Traded to **Calgary** by **Dallas** with Corey Millen for Joe Nieuwendyk, December 19, 1995.

IMMONEN, Jarkko

(IH-moh-nihn, YAHR-koh) **NYR**

Center. Shoots right. 5'11", 202 lbs. Born, Rantasalmi, Finland, April 19, 1982. Toronto's 8th choice, 254th overall, in 2002 Entry Draft.

			Regular Season														Playoffs								
Season	Club	League	GP	G	A	Pts	PIM	PP	SH	GW	S	%	+/-	TF	F%	Min	GP	G	A	Pts	PIM	PP	SH	GW	Min
1997-98	SaPKo Jr.	Fin-Jr.	14	8	12	20	0	....	....	....	....	....	....	....	....	....	....	....	....	....	....	....	....	....	....
1998-99	SaPKo Jr.	Fin-Jr.	12	6	10	16	14	....	....	....	....	....	....	....	....	....	....	....	....	....	....	....	....	....	....
	SaPKo Savonlinna	Finland-2	36	2	2	4	6	....	....	....	....	....	....	....	....	....	....	....	....	....	....	....	....	....	....
99-2000	SaPKo Jr.	Fin-Jr.	....	....	....	....	....	....	....	....	....	....	....	....	....	....	2	0	4	4	4	....	....	....	....
	SaPKo Savonlinna	Finland-2	42	18	16	34	34	....	....	....	....	....	....	....	....	....	....	....	....	....	....	....	....	....	....
2000-01	TuTo Turku Jr.	Fin-Jr.	1	0	1	1	0	....	....	....	....	....	....	....	....	....	1	0	0	0	2	....	....	....	....
	TuTo Turku	Finland-2	41	20	20	40	22	....	....	....	....	....	....	....	....	....	11	5	7	12	10	....	....	....	....
2001-02	Assat Pori	Finland	44	0	2	2	6	....	....	....	....	....	....	....	....	....	....	....	....	....	....	....	....	....	....
	Assat Pori Jr.	Fin-Jr.	....	....	....	....	....	....	....	....	....	....	....	....	....	....	8	5	1	6	10	....	....	....	....
2002-03	JYP Jyvaskyla	Finland	56	10	23	33	34	....	....	....	....	....	....	....	....	....	7	1	1	2	8	....	....	....	....
2003-04	JYP Jyvaskyla	Finland	52	23	26	49	28	....	....	....	....	....	....	....	....	....	2	0	0	0	0	....	....	....	....
2004-05	JYP Jyvaskyla	Finland	54	19	28	47	24	....	....	....	....	....	....	....	....	....	3	0	2	2	2	....	....	....	....
2005-06	**NY Rangers**	**NHL**	**6**	**2**	**0**	**2**	**0**	**1**	**0**	**0**	**8**	**25.0**	**–1**	**51**	**56.9**	**10:15**	....	....	....	....	....	....	....	....	....
	Hartford	AHL	74	30	40	70	34	....	....	....	....	....	....	....	....	....	6	2	3	5	2	....	....	....	....
	NHL Totals		**6**	**2**	**0**	**2**	**0**	**1**	**0**	**0**	**8**	**25.0**		**51**	**56.9**	**10:15**	....	....	....	....	....	....	....	....	....

Traded to **NY Rangers** by **Toronto** with Maxim Kondratiev, Toronto's 1st round choice (later traded to Calgary - Calgary selected Kris Chucko) in 2004 Entry Draft and Toronto's 2nd round choice (Michael Sauer) in 2005 Entry Draft for Brian Leetch and Edmonton's 4th round choice (previously acquired, Toronto selected Roman Kukumberg) in 2004 Entry Draft, March 3, 2004.

ISBISTER, Brad

(IHZ-bihs-tuhr, BRAD)

Left wing. Shoots right. 6'4", 231 lbs. Born, Edmonton, Alta., May 7, 1977. Winnipeg's 4th choice, 67th overall, in 1995 Entry Draft.

			Regular Season														Playoffs								
Season	Club	League	GP	G	A	Pts	PIM	PP	SH	GW	S	%	+/-	TF	F%	Min	GP	G	A	Pts	PIM	PP	SH	GW	Min
1992-93	Calgary Canucks	ABHL	35	24	25	49	74	....	....	....	....	....	....	....	....	....	....	....	....	....	....	....	....	....	....
1993-94	Portland	WHL	64	7	10	17	45	....	....	....	....	....	....	....	....	....	10	0	2	2	0	....	....	....	....
1994-95	Portland	WHL	67	16	20	36	123	....	....	....	....	....	....	....	....	....	....	....	....	....	....	....	....	....	....
1995-96	Portland	WHL	71	45	44	89	184	....	....	....	....	....	....	....	....	....	7	2	4	6	20	....	....	....	....
1996-97	Portland	WHL	24	15	18	33	45	....	....	....	....	....	....	....	....	....	6	2	1	3	16	....	....	....	....
	Springfield	AHL	7	3	1	4	14	....	....	....	....	....	....	....	....	....	9	1	2	3	10	....	....	....	....
1997-98	**Phoenix**	**NHL**	**66**	**9**	**8**	**17**	**102**	**1**	**0**	**1**	**115**	**7.8**	**4**	....	....	....	**5**	**0**	**0**	**0**	**2**	**0**	**0**	**0**	....
	Springfield	AHL	9	8	2	10	36	....	....	....	....	....	....	....	....	....	....	....	....	....	....	....	....	....	....
1998-99	**Phoenix**	**NHL**	**32**	**4**	**4**	**8**	**46**	**0**	**0**	**2**	**48**	**8.3**	**1**	**3**	**0.0**	**11:33**	....	....	....	....	....	....	....	....	....
	Springfield	AHL	4	1	1	2	12	....	....	....	....	....	....	....	....	....	....	....	....	....	....	....	....	....	....
	Las Vegas	IHL	2	0	0	0	9	....	....	....	....	....	....	....	....	....	....	....	....	....	....	....	....	....	....
99-2000	**NY Islanders**	**NHL**	**64**	**22**	**20**	**42**	**100**	**9**	**0**	**1**	**135**	**16.3**	**–18**	**55**	**54.6**	**16:58**	....	....	....	....	....	....	....	....	....
2000-01	**NY Islanders**	**NHL**	**51**	**18**	**14**	**32**	**59**	**7**	**1**	**4**	**129**	**14.0**	**–19**	**255**	**45.9**	**19:26**	....	....	....	....	....	....	....	....	....
2001-02	**NY Islanders**	**NHL**	**79**	**17**	**21**	**38**	**113**	**4**	**0**	**2**	**142**	**12.0**	**1**	**71**	**45.1**	**15:18**	**3**	**1**	**1**	**2**	**17**	**1**	**0**	**1**	**12:33**
2002-03	**NY Islanders**	**NHL**	**53**	**10**	**13**	**23**	**34**	**2**	**0**	**2**	**90**	**11.1**	**–9**	**13**	**46.2**	**13:54**	....	....	....	....	....	....	....	....	....
	Edmonton	**NHL**	**13**	**3**	**2**	**5**	**9**	**0**	**0**	**1**	**29**	**10.3**	**0**	**10**	**50.0**	**13:14**	**6**	**0**	**1**	**1**	**12**	**0**	**0**	**0**	**10:04**
2003-04	**Edmonton**	**NHL**	**51**	**10**	**8**	**18**	**54**	**1**	**0**	**2**	**80**	**12.5**	**–2**	**55**	**56.4**	**12:46**	....	....	....	....	....	....	....	....	....
2004-05	Innsbruck	Austria	11	7	4	11	41	....	....	....	....	....	....	....	....	....	5	3	1	4	6	....	....	....	....
2005-06	**Boston**	**NHL**	**58**	**6**	**17**	**23**	**46**	**1**	**0**	**0**	**112**	**5.4**	**–2**	**10**	**60.0**	**13:55**	....	....	....	....	....	....	....	....	....
	NHL Totals		**467**	**99**	**107**	**206**	**563**	**25**	**1**	**15**	**880**	**11.3**		**472**	**48.1**	**15:01**	**14**	**1**	**2**	**3**	**31**	**1**	**0**	**1**	**10:54**

WHL West Second All-Star Team (1997)

Rights transferred to **Phoenix** after **Winnipeg** franchise relocated, July 1, 1996. Traded to **NY Islanders** by **Phoenix** with Phoenix's 3rd round choice (Brian Collins) in 1999 Entry Draft for Robert Reichel, NY Islanders' 3rd round choice (Jason Jaspers) in 1999 Entry Draft and Ottawa's 4th round choice (previously acquired, Phoenix selected Preston Mizzi) in 1999 Entry Draft, March 20, 1999. Traded to **Edmonton** by **NY Islanders** with Raffi Torres for Janne Niinimaa and Washington's 2nd round choice (previously acquired, NY Islanders selected Evgeni Tunik) in 2003 Entry Draft , March 11, 2003. Signed as a free agent by **Innsbuck** (Austria), February 12, 2005. Traded to **Boston** by **Edmonton** for Boston's 4th round choice (later traded back to Boston - later traded to San Jose - San Jose selected James Delory) in 2006 Entry Draft, August 1, 2005.

IVANANS, Raitis

(ih-VAH-nehns, RIGH-this) **L.A.**

Left wing. Shoots left. 6'3", 263 lbs. Born, Riga, Latvia, January 1, 1979.

			Regular Season														Playoffs								
Season	Club	League	GP	G	A	Pts	PIM	PP	SH	GW	S	%	+/-	TF	F%	Min	GP	G	A	Pts	PIM	PP	SH	GW	Min
1997-98	Flint Generals	UHL	18	0	1	1	20	....	....	....	....	....	....	....	....	....	....	....	....	....	....	....	....	....	....
1998-99	Macon Whoopee	CHL	16	1	1	2	20	....	....	....	....	....	....	....	....	....	....	....	....	....	....	....	....	....	....
	Tulsa Oilers	CHL	32	2	7	9	39	....	....	....	....	....	....	....	....	....	....	....	....	....	....	....	....	....	....
99-2000	Pensacola	ECHL	59	3	7	10	146	....	....	....	....	....	....	....	....	....	2	0	0	0	0	....	....	....	....
2000-01	Hershey Bears	AHL	2	0	0	0	0	....	....	....	....	....	....	....	....	....	....	....	....	....	....	....	....	....	....
	New Haven	UHL	66	4	10	14	270	....	....	....	....	....	....	....	....	....	8	1	0	1	4	....	....	....	....
2001-02	Toledo Storm	ECHL	16	2	2	4	59	....	....	....	....	....	....	....	....	....	....	....	....	....	....	....	....	....	....
	Baton Rouge	ECHL	40	4	5	9	180	....	....	....	....	....	....	....	....	....	....	....	....	....	....	....	....	....	....
2002-03	Milwaukee	AHL	17	0	0	0	38	....	....	....	....	....	....	....	....	....	1	0	0	0	15	....	....	....	....
	Rockford IceHogs	UHL	50	4	2	6	208	....	....	....	....	....	....	....	....	....	....	....	....	....	....	....	....	....	....
2003-04	Milwaukee	AHL	54	1	7	8	166	....	....	....	....	....	....	....	....	....	7	0	1	1	17	....	....	....	....
	Rockford IceHogs	UHL	1	0	0	0	0	....	....	....	....	....	....	....	....	....	....	....	....	....	....	....	....	....	....
2004-05	Hamilton	AHL	75	2	5	7	259	....	....	....	....	....	....	....	....	....	2	0	1	1	0	....	....	....	....
2005-06	**Montreal**	**NHL**	**4**	**0**	**0**	**0**	**9**	**0**	**0**	**0**	**0**	**0.0**	**–1**	**0**	**0.0**	**2:58**	....	....	....	....	....	....	....	....	....
	Hamilton	AHL	43	2	0	2	120	....	....	....	....	....	....	....	....	....	....	....	....	....	....	....	....	....	....
	NHL Totals		**4**	**0**	**0**	**0**	**9**	**0**	**0**	**0**	**0**	**0.0**		**0**	**0.0**	**2:58**	....	....	....	....	....	....	....	....	....

Signed as a free agent by **Montreal**, July 16, 2004 Signed as a free agent by **Los Angeles**, July 13, 2006.

JACINA, Greg

(ja-SEE-nah, GREHG) **FLA.**

Left wing. Shoots right. 6', 203 lbs. Born, Guelph, Ont., May 22, 1982.

			Regular Season														Playoffs								
Season	Club	League	GP	G	A	Pts	PIM	PP	SH	GW	S	%	+/-	TF	F%	Min	GP	G	A	Pts	PIM	PP	SH	GW	Min
99-2000	Owen Sound	OHL	66	12	29	41	62	....	....	....	....	....	....	....	....	....	....	....	....	....	....	....	....	....	....
2000-01	Owen Sound	OHL	57	25	26	51	101	....	....	....	....	....	....	....	....	....	4	0	1	1	15	....	....	....	....
2001-02	Owen Sound	OHL	33	15	20	35	64	....	....	....	....	....	....	....	....	....	....	....	....	....	....	....	....	....	....
	Mississauga	OHL	28	14	26	40	43	....	....	....	....	....	....	....	....	....	....	....	....	....	....	....	....	....	....
2002-03	Mississauga	OHL	56	19	47	66	114	....	....	....	....	....	....	....	....	....	5	6	5	11	17	....	....	....	....
2003-04	San Antonio	AHL	13	0	4	4	22	....	....	....	....	....	....	....	....	....	....	....	....	....	....	....	....	....	....
	Augusta Lynx	ECHL	58	15	23	38	170	....	....	....	....	....	....	....	....	....	....	....	....	....	....	....	....	....	....
2004-05	San Antonio	AHL	78	11	20	31	150	....	....	....	....	....	....	....	....	....	....	....	....	....	....	....	....	....	....
2005-06	**Florida**	**NHL**	**11**	**0**	**1**	**1**	**4**	**0**	**0**	**0**	**10**	**0.0**	**–1**	**2**	**0.0**	**5:50**	....	....	....	....	....	....	....	....	....
	Rochester	AHL	35	7	4	11	152	....	....	....	....	....	....	....	....	....	....	....	....	....	....	....	....	....	....
	NHL Totals		**11**	**0**	**1**	**1**	**4**	**0**	**0**	**0**	**10**	**0.0**		**2**	**0.0**	**5:50**	....	....	....	....	....	....	....	....	....

Signed as a free agent by **Florida**, August 12, 2003.

JACKMAN, Barret

(JAK-man, BAIR-reht) **ST.L.**

Defense. Shoots left. 6', 200 lbs. Born, Trail, B.C., March 5, 1981. St. Louis' 1st choice, 17th overall, in 1999 Entry Draft.

			Regular Season														Playoffs								
Season	Club	League	GP	G	A	Pts	PIM	PP	SH	GW	S	%	+/-	TF	F%	Min	GP	G	A	Pts	PIM	PP	SH	GW	Min
1996-97	Beaver Valley	VIJHL	32	22	25	47	180	....	....	....	....	....	....	....	....	....	....	....	....	....	....	....	....	....	....
1997-98	Regina Pats	WHL	68	2	11	13	224	....	....	....	....	....	....	....	....	....	9	0	3	3	32	....	....	....	....
1998-99	Regina Pats	WHL	70	8	36	44	259	....	....	....	....	....	....	....	....	....	....	....	....	....	....	....	....	....	....
99-2000	Regina Pats	WHL	53	9	37	46	175	....	....	....	....	....	....	....	....	....	6	1	1	2	19	....	....	....	....
	Worcester IceCats	AHL	....	....	....	....	....	....	....	....	....	....	....	....	....	....	2	0	0	0	13	....	....	....	....
2000-01	Regina Pats	WHL	43	9	27	36	138	....	....	....	....	....	....	....	....	....	6	0	3	3	8	....	....	....	....
2001-02	**St. Louis**	**NHL**	**1**	**0**	**0**	**0**	**0**	**0**	**0**	**0**	**1**	**0.0**	**0**	**0**	**0.0**	**18:56**	**1**	**0**	**0**	**0**	**2**	**0**	**0**	**0**	**18:24**
	Worcester IceCats	AHL	75	2	12	14	266	....	....	....	....	....	....	....	....	....	3	0	1	1	4	....	....	....	....
2002-03	**St. Louis**	**NHL**	**82**	**3**	**16**	**19**	**190**	**0**	**0**	**0**	**66**	**4.5**	**23**	**0**	**0.0**	**20:03**	**7**	**0**	**0**	**0**	**14**	**0**	**0**	**0**	**21:59**
2003-04	**St. Louis**	**NHL**	**15**	**1**	**2**	**3**	**41**	**0**	**0**	**0**	**11**	**9.1**	**–1**	**0**	**0.0**	**18:16**	....	....	....	....	....	....	....	....	....
2004-05	Missouri	UHL	28	3	17	20	61	....	....	....	....	....	....	....	....	....	3	0	0	0	4	....	....	....	....
2005-06	**St. Louis**	**NHL**	**63**	**4**	**6**	**10**	**156**	**0**	**0**	**2**	**56**	**7.1**	**–6**	**0**	**0.0**	**18:46**	....	....	....	....	....	....	....	....	....
	NHL Totals		**161**	**8**	**24**	**32**	**387**	**0**	**0**	**2**	**134**	**6.0**		**0**	**0.0**	**19:22**	**8**	**0**	**0**	**0**	**16**	**0**	**0**	**0**	**21:32**

WHL East Second All-Star Team (2000) • AHL All-Rookie Team (2002) • NHL All-Rookie Team (2003) • Calder Memorial Trophy (2003)

• Missed majority of 2003-04 season recovering from shoulder injury suffered in game vs. Vancouver, October 22, 2003. Signed as a free agent by **Missouri** (UHL), February 3, 2005.

			Regular Season														Playoffs								
Season	Club	League	GP	G	A	Pts	PIM	PP	SH	GW	S	%	+/-	TF	F%	Min	GP	G	A	Pts	PIM	PP	SH	GW	Min

JACKMAN, Ric

(JAK-man, RIHK) **FLA.**

Defense. Shoots right. 6'2", 197 lbs. Born, Toronto, Ont., June 28, 1978. Dallas' 1st choice, 5th overall, in 1996 Entry Draft.

Season	Club	League	GP	G	A	Pts	PIM	PP	SH	GW	S	%	+/-	TF	F%	Min	GP	G	A	Pts	PIM	PP	SH	GW	Min
1993-94	Miss. Sens	MTHL	81	35	53	88	156																		
1994-95	Miss. Sens	MTHL	53	20	37	57	120																		
	Richmond Hill	MTJHL	10	2	9	11	16																		
1995-96	Sault Ste. Marie	OHL	66	13	29	42	97										4	1	0	1	15				
1996-97	Sault Ste. Marie	OHL	53	13	34	47	116										10	2	6	8	24				
1997-98	Sault Ste. Marie	OHL	60	33	40	73	111																		
	Michigan	IHL	14	1	5	6	10										4	0	0	0	10				
1998-99	Michigan	IHL	71	13	17	30	106										5	0	4	4	6				
99-2000	**Dallas**	**NHL**	**22**	**1**	**2**	**3**	**6**	**1**	**0**	**0**	**16**	**6.3**	**–1**	**0**	**0.0**	**8:06**									
	Michigan	IHL	50	3	16	19	51																		
2000-01	**Dallas**	**NHL**	**16**	**0**	**0**	**0**	**18**	**0**	**0**	**0**	**10**	**0.0**	**–6**	**0**	**0.0**	**8:51**									
	Utah Grizzlies	IHL	57	9	19	28	24																		
2001-02	**Boston**	**NHL**	**2**	**0**	**0**	**0**	**2**	**0**	**0**	**0**	**4**	**0.0**	**–1**	**0**	**0.0**	**13:26**									
	Providence Bruins	AHL	9	0	1	1	8										2	0	0	0	2				
2002-03	**Toronto**	**NHL**	**42**	**0**	**2**	**2**	**41**	**0**	**0**	**0**	**35**	**0.0**	**–10**	**0**	**0.0**	**13:59**									
	St. John's	AHL	8	2	6	8	24																		
2003-04	**Toronto**	**NHL**	**29**	**2**	**4**	**6**	**13**	**1**	**0**	**1**	**35**	**5.7**	**–11**	**0**	**0.0**	**18:00**									
	Pittsburgh	**NHL**	**25**	**7**	**17**	**24**	**14**	**6**	**0**	**1**	**56**	**12.5**	**–5**	**0**	**0.0**	**24:14**									
2004-05	Bjorkloven	Sweden-2	46	13	26	39	209																		
2005-06	**Pittsburgh**	**NHL**	**49**	**6**	**22**	**28**	**46**	**3**	**0**	**1**	**95**	**6.3**	**–20**	**0**	**0.0**	**18:21**									
	Florida	**NHL**	**15**	**1**	**1**	**2**	**6**	**0**	**0**	**0**	**25**	**4.0**	**0**	**0**	**0.0**	**14:04**									
	NHL Totals		**200**	**17**	**48**	**65**	**146**	**11**	**0**	**3**	**276**	**6.2**		**0**	**0.0**	**15:52**									

OHL All-Rookie Team (1996) • OHL Second All-Star Team (1998)

Traded to **Boston** by **Dallas** for Cameron Mann, June 23, 2001. • Missed majority of 2001-02 season recovering from shoulder injury suffered in game vs. St. Louis, October 21, 2001. Traded to **Toronto** by **Boston** for the rights to Kris Vernarsky, May 13, 2002. Traded to **Pittsburgh** by **Toronto** for Drake Berehowsky, February 11, 2004. Signed as a free agent by **Bjorkloven** (Sweden-2), September 17, 2004. Traded to **Florida** by **Pittsburgh** for Petr Taticek, March 9, 2006.

JACKMAN, Tim

(JAK-man, TIHM) **L.A.**

Right wing. Shoots right. 6'4", 210 lbs. Born, Minot, ND, November 14, 1981. Columbus' 2nd choice, 38th overall, in 2001 Entry Draft.

Season	Club	League	GP	G	A	Pts	PIM	PP	SH	GW	S	%	+/-	TF	F%	Min	GP	G	A	Pts	PIM	PP	SH	GW	Min
1998-99	Park Center	High-MN	22	22	22	44																			
99-2000	Park Center	High-MN	19	34	22	56																			
	Twin Cities	USHL	25	11	9	20	58										13	8	5	13	12				
2000-01	Minnesota State	WCHA	37	11	14	25	92																		
2001-02	Minnesota State	WCHA	36	14	14	28	86																		
2002-03	Syracuse Crunch	AHL	77	9	7	16	48																		
2003-04	**Columbus**	**NHL**	**19**	**1**	**2**	**3**	**16**	**0**	**0**	**0**	**18**	**5.6**	**–7**	**1**	**100.0**	**9:56**									
	Syracuse Crunch	AHL	64	23	13	36	61										7	2	3	5	12				
2004-05	Syracuse Crunch	AHL	73	14	21	35	98																		
2005-06	**Phoenix**	**NHL**	**8**	**0**	**0**	**0**	**21**	**0**	**0**	**0**	**4**	**0.0**	**1**	**1**	**0.0**	**7:13**									
	San Antonio	AHL	50	7	13	20	127																		
	Manchester	AHL	18	2	3	5	33										7	0	3	3	20				
	NHL Totals		**27**	**1**	**2**	**3**	**37**	**0**	**0**	**0**	**22**	**4.5**		**2**	**50.0**	**9:07**									

Traded to **Phoenix** by **Columbus** with Geoff Sanderson for Cale Hulse, Mike Rupp and Jason Chimera, October 8, 2005. Traded to **Los Angeles** by **Phoenix** for Yanick Lehoux, March 9, 2006.

JACQUES, Jean-Francois

(ZHAWK, ZHAWN-fran-SWUH) **EDM.**

Left wing. Shoots left. 6'4", 217 lbs. Born, Montreal, Que., April 29, 1985. Edmonton's 3rd choice, 68th overall, in 2003 Entry Draft.

Season	Club	League	GP	G	A	Pts	PIM	PP	SH	GW	S	%	+/-	TF	F%	Min	GP	G	A	Pts	PIM	PP	SH	GW	Min
2000-01	Cap-d-Madeleine	QAAA	39	22	13	35	28										10	5	8	13	14				
2001-02	Baie-Comeau	QMJHL	66	10	14	24	136										5	1	0	1	2				
2002-03	Baie-Comeau	QMJHL	67	12	21	33	123										12	4	2	6	13				
2003-04	Baie-Comeau	QMJHL	59	20	24	44	70										4	1	0	1	4				
2004-05	Baie-Comeau	QMJHL	69	36	42	78	56										6	3	5	8	6				
	Edmonton	AHL	6	0	0	0	5																		
2005-06	**Edmonton**	**NHL**	**7**	**0**	**0**	**0**	**0**	**0**	**0**	**0**	**8**	**0.0**	**–3**	**0**	**0.0**	**6:43**									
	Hamilton	AHL	65	24	19	43	131																		
	NHL Totals		**7**	**0**	**0**	**0**	**0**	**0**	**0**	**0**	**8**	**0.0**		**0**	**0.0**	**6:43**									

JAGR, Jaromir

(YAH-guhr, YAIR-oh-MEER) **NYR**

Right wing. Shoots left. 6'3", 245 lbs. Born, Kladno, Czech., February 15, 1972. Pittsburgh's 1st choice, 5th overall, in 1990 Entry Draft.

Season	Club	League	GP	G	A	Pts	PIM	PP	SH	GW	S	%	+/-	TF	F%	Min	GP	G	A	Pts	PIM	PP	SH	GW	Min
1984-85	Kladno Jr.	Czech-Jr.	34	24	17	41																			
1985-86	Kladno Jr.	Czech-Jr.	36	41	29	70																			
1986-87	Kladno Jr.	Czech-Jr.	30	35	35	70																			
1987-88	Kladno Jr.	Czech-Jr.	35	57	27	84																			
1988-89	Kladno	Czech	29	3	3	6	4										10	5	7	12	0				
1989-90	Poldi Kladno	Czech	42	22	28	50											9	*8	2	10					
1990-91 ♦	**Pittsburgh**	**NHL**	**80**	**27**	**30**	**57**	**42**	**7**	**0**	**4**	**136**	**19.9**	**–4**				**24**	**3**	**10**	**13**	**6**	**1**	**0**	**1**	
1991-92 ♦	**Pittsburgh**	**NHL**	**70**	**32**	**37**	**69**	**34**	**4**	**0**	**4**	**194**	**16.5**	**12**				**21**	**11**	**13**	**24**	**6**	**2**	**0**	**4**	
1992-93	**Pittsburgh**	**NHL**	**81**	**34**	**60**	**94**	**61**	**10**	**1**	**9**	**242**	**14.0**	**30**				**12**	**5**	**4**	**9**	**23**	**1**	**0**	**1**	
1993-94	**Pittsburgh**	**NHL**	**80**	**32**	**67**	**99**	**61**	**9**	**0**	**6**	**298**	**10.7**	**15**				**6**	**2**	**4**	**6**	**16**	**0**	**0**	**1**	
1994-95	HC Kladno	CzRep	11	8	14	22	10																		
	HC Bolzano	Euroliga	5	8	8	16	4																		
	HC Bolzano	Italy	1	0	0	0	0																		
	Schalke	German-2	1	1	10	11	0																		
	Pittsburgh	**NHL**	**48**	**32**	**38**	***70**	**37**	**8**	**3**	**7**	**192**	**16.7**	**23**				**12**	**10**	**5**	**15**	**6**	**2**	**1**	**1**	
1995-96	**Pittsburgh**	**NHL**	**82**	**62**	**87**	**149**	**96**	**20**	**1**	**12**	**403**	**15.4**	**31**				**18**	**11**	**12**	**23**	**18**	**5**	**1**	**1**	
1996-97	**Pittsburgh**	**NHL**	**63**	**47**	**48**	**95**	**40**	**11**	**2**	**6**	**234**	**20.1**	**22**				**5**	**4**	**4**	**8**	**4**	**2**	**0**	**0**	
1997-98	**Pittsburgh**	**NHL**	**77**	**35**	***67**	***102**	**64**	**7**	**0**	**8**	**262**	**13.4**	**17**				**6**	**4**	**5**	**9**	**2**	**1**	**0**	**0**	
	Czech Republic	Olympics	6	1	4	5	2																		
1998-99	**Pittsburgh**	**NHL**	**81**	**44**	***83**	***127**	**66**	**10**	**1**	**7**	**343**	**12.8**	**17**	**4**	**50.0**	**25:51**	**9**	**5**	**7**	**12**	**16**	**1**	**0**	**1**	**25:32**
99-2000	**Pittsburgh**	**NHL**	**63**	**42**	**54**	***96**	**50**	**10**	**0**	**5**	**290**	**14.5**	**25**	**9**	**22.2**	**23:12**	**11**	**8**	**8**	**16**	**6**	**2**	**0**	**4**	**24:32**
2000-01	**Pittsburgh**	**NHL**	**81**	**52**	***69**	***121**	**42**	**14**	**1**	**10**	**317**	**16.4**	**19**	**2**	**0.0**	**23:19**	**16**	**2**	**10**	**12**	**18**	**2**	**0**	**0**	**22:15**
2001-02	**Washington**	**NHL**	**69**	**31**	**48**	**79**	**30**	**10**	**0**	**3**	**197**	**15.7**	**0**	**2**	**50.0**	**21:43**									
	Czech Republic	Olympics	4	2	3	5	4																		
2002-03	**Washington**	**NHL**	**75**	**36**	**41**	**77**	**38**	**13**	**2**	**9**	**290**	**12.4**	**5**	**5**	**20.0**	**21:18**	**6**	**2**	**5**	**7**	**2**	**1**	**0**	**0**	**25:13**
2003-04	**Washington**	**NHL**	**46**	**16**	**29**	**45**	**26**	**6**	**0**	**1**	**159**	**10.1**	**–4**	**1**	**0.0**	**21:05**									
	NY Rangers	**NHL**	**31**	**15**	**14**	**29**	**12**	**4**	**0**	**2**	**98**	**15.3**	**–1**	**0**	**0.0**	**20:45**									
2004-05	HC Rabat Kladno	CzRep	17	11	17	28	16																		
	Avangard Omsk	Russia	32	16	22	38	63										11	4	*10	*14	22				
2005-06	**NY Rangers**	**NHL**	**82**	**54**	**69**	**123**	**72**	**24**	**0**	**9**	**368**	**14.7**	**34**	**6**	**16.7**	**22:05**	**3**	**0**	**1**	**1**	**2**	**0**	**0**	**0**	**13:47**
	Czech Republic	Olympics	8	2	5	7	6																		
	NHL Totals		**1109**	**591**	**841**	**1432**	**771**	**167**	**11**	**102**	**4023**	**14.7**		**29**	**24.1**	**22:39**	**149**	**67**	**88**	**155**	**125**	**20**	**2**	**14**	**23:18**

NHL All-Rookie Team (1991) • NHL First All-Star Team (1995, 1996, 1998, 1999, 2000, 2001, 2006) • Art Ross Trophy (1995, 1998, 1999, 2000, 2001) • NHL Second All-Star Team (1997) • Lester B. Pearson Award (1999, 2000, 2006) • Hart Trophy (1999)

Played in NHL All-Star Game (1992, 1993, 1996, 1998, 1999, 2000, 2002, 2003, 2004)

Traded to **Washington** by **Pittsburgh** with Frantisek Kucera for Kris Beech, Michal Sivek, Ross Lupaschuk and future considerations, July 11, 2001. Traded to **NY Rangers** by **Washington** for Anson Carter, January 23, 2004. Signed as a free agent by **Kladno** (CzRep), September 17, 2004. Signed as a free agent by **Omsk** (Russia), November 7, 2004.

			Regular Season														Playoffs								
Season	Club	League	GP	G	A	Pts	PIM	PP	SH	GW	S	%	+/-	TF	F%	Min	GP	G	A	Pts	PIM	PP	SH	GW	Min

JAMES, Connor

(JAYMZ, KAW-nuhr) **PIT.**

Right wing. Shoots right. 5'10", 168 lbs. Born, Calgary, Alta., August 25, 1982. Los Angeles' 11th choice, 279th overall, in 2002 Entry Draft.

1998-99	Calgary Buffaloes	AMHL	36	33	53	86	20	....	....	....	....	....	....	....	....	....	....	....	....	....	....	....	....	....	....
99-2000	Calgary Royals	AJHL	64	36	57	93	41	....	....	....	....	....	....	....	....	....	....	....	....	....	....	....	....	....	....
2000-01	U. of Denver	WCHA	38	8	19	27	14	....	....	....	....	....	....	....	....	....	....	....	....	....	....	....	....	....	....
2001-02	U. of Denver	WCHA	41	16	26	42	18	....	....	....	....	....	....	....	....	....	....	....	....	....	....	....	....	....	....
2002-03	U. of Denver	WCHA	41	20	23	43	12	....	....	....	....	....	....	....	....	....	....	....	....	....	....	....	....	....	....
2003-04	U. of Denver	WCHA	40	13	25	38	16	....	....	....	....	....	....	....	....	....	....	....	....	....	....	....	....	....	....
2004-05	Bakersfield	ECHL	51	21	25	46	34	....	....	....	....	....	....	....	....	....	5	3	1	4	0	....	....	....	....
	Manchester	AHL	14	2	1	3	10	....	....	....	....	....	....	....	....	....	3	0	0	0	0	....	....	....	....
2005-06	**Los Angeles**	**NHL**	**2**	**0**	**0**	**0**	**0**	**0**	**0**	**0**	**1**	**0.0**	**–1**	**6**	**33.3**	**7:19**	....	....	....	....	....	....	....	....	....
	Manchester	AHL	77	17	25	42	43	....	....	....	....	....	....	....	....	....	7	0	0	0	2	....	....	....	....
	NHL Totals		**2**	**0**	**0**	**0**	**0**	**0**	**0**	**0**	**1**	**0.0**		**6**	**33.3**	**7:19**	....	....	....	....	....	....	....	....	....

NCAA Championship All-Tournament Team (2004)

Signed as a free agent by **Pittsburgh**, August 9, 2006.

JANCEVSKI, Dan

(jan-SEHV-skee, DAN) **MTL.**

Defense. Shoots left. 6'3", 220 lbs. Born, Windsor, Ont., June 15, 1981. Dallas' 2nd choice, 66th overall, in 1999 Entry Draft.

1995-96	Riverside Selects	OMHA	59	9	22	31	67	....	....	....	....	....	....	....	....	....	....	....	....	....	....	....	....	....	....
1996-97	Windsor Lions	OMHA	47	6	20	26	99	....	....	....	....	....	....	....	....	....	....	....	....	....	....	....	....	....	....
1997-98	Tecumseh	OHA-B	49	3	11	14	145	....	....	....	....	....	....	....	....	....	....	....	....	....	....	....	....	....	....
1998-99	London Knights	OHL	68	2	12	14	115	....	....	....	....	....	....	....	....	....	25	1	7	8	24	....	....	....	....
99-2000	London Knights	OHL	59	8	15	23	138	....	....	....	....	....	....	....	....	....	....	....	....	....	....	....	....	....	....
2000-01	London Knights	OHL	39	4	23	27	95	....	....	....	....	....	....	....	....	....	....	....	....	....	....	....	....	....	....
	Sudbury Wolves	OHL	31	3	14	17	42	....	....	....	....	....	....	....	....	....	12	0	9	9	17	....	....	....	....
2001-02	Utah Grizzlies	AHL	77	0	13	13	147	....	....	....	....	....	....	....	....	....	5	0	0	0	4	....	....	....	....
2002-03	Utah Grizzlies	AHL	76	1	10	11	172	....	....	....	....	....	....	....	....	....	2	0	1	1	12	....	....	....	....
2003-04	Utah Grizzlies	AHL	80	5	17	22	171	....	....	....	....	....	....	....	....	....	....	....	....	....	....	....	....	....	....
2004-05	Hamilton	AHL	80	6	20	26	163	....	....	....	....	....	....	....	....	....	4	0	0	0	2	....	....	....	....
2005-06	**Dallas**	**NHL**	**2**	**0**	**0**	**0**	**0**	**0**	**0**	**0**	**0**	**0.0**	**1**	**0**	**0.0**	**9:13**	....	....	....	....	....	....	....	....	....
	Iowa Stars	AHL	77	9	29	38	91	....	....	....	....	....	....	....	....	....	7	1	1	2	6	....	....	....	....
	NHL Totals		**2**	**0**	**0**	**0**	**0**	**0**	**0**	**0**	**0**	**0.0**		**0**	**0.0**	**9:13**	....	....	....	....	....	....	....	....	....

Signed as a free agent by **Montreal**, July 13, 2006.

JANIK, Doug

(JAN-nihk, DUHG) **T.B.**

Defense. Shoots left. 6'2", 209 lbs. Born, Agawam, MA, March 26, 1980. Buffalo's 3rd choice, 55th overall, in 1999 Entry Draft.

1995-96	N.E. Jr. Whalers	EJHL	48	16	38	54	....	....	....	....	....	....	....	....	....	....	....	....	....	....	....	....	....	....	....
1996-97	N.E. Jr. Whalers	EJHL	39	12	24	36	22	....	....	....	....	....	....	....	....	....	11	5	9	14	10	....	....	....	....
1997-98	USNTDP	U-18	29	6	13	19	43	....	....	....	....	....	....	....	....	....	....	....	....	....	....	....	....	....	....
	USNTDP	USHL	19	1	6	7	34	....	....	....	....	....	....	....	....	....	....	....	....	....	....	....	....	....	....
	USNTDP	NAHL	10	0	4	4	10	....	....	....	....	....	....	....	....	....	7	1	3	4	18	....	....	....	....
1998-99	U. of Maine	H-East	35	3	13	16	44	....	....	....	....	....	....	....	....	....	....	....	....	....	....	....	....	....	....
99-2000	U. of Maine	H-East	36	6	14	20	54	....	....	....	....	....	....	....	....	....	....	....	....	....	....	....	....	....	....
2000-01	U. of Maine	H-East	39	3	15	18	52	....	....	....	....	....	....	....	....	....	....	....	....	....	....	....	....	....	....
2001-02	Rochester	AHL	80	6	17	23	100	....	....	....	....	....	....	....	....	....	2	0	0	0	0	....	....	....	....
2002-03	**Buffalo**	**NHL**	**6**	**0**	**0**	**0**	**2**	**0**	**0**	**0**	**1**	**0.0**	**1**	**0**	**0.0**	**7:42**	....	....	....	....	....	....	....	....	....
	Rochester	AHL	75	3	13	16	120	....	....	....	....	....	....	....	....	....	3	0	0	0	6	....	....	....	....
2003-04	**Buffalo**	**NHL**	**4**	**0**	**0**	**0**	**19**	**0**	**0**	**0**	**3**	**0.0**	**0**	**0**	**0.0**	**8:26**	....	....	....	....	....	....	....	....	....
	Rochester	AHL	74	2	14	16	109	....	....	....	....	....	....	....	....	....	16	1	2	3	22	....	....	....	....
2004-05	Rochester	AHL	76	2	10	12	196	....	....	....	....	....	....	....	....	....	9	0	2	2	10	....	....	....	....
2005-06	**Buffalo**	**NHL**	....	....	....	....	....	....	....	....	....	....	....	....	....	....	**5**	**1**	**0**	**1**	**2**	**0**	**0**	**0**	**10:30**
	Rochester	AHL	71	5	19	24	161	....	....	....	....	....	....	....	....	....	....	....	....	....	....	....	....	....	....
	NHL Totals		**10**	**0**	**0**	**0**	**21**	**0**	**0**	**0**	**4**	**0.0**		**0**	**0.0**	**8:00**	**5**	**1**	**0**	**1**	**2**	**0**	**0**	**0**	**10:30**

Signed as a free agent by **Tampa Bay**, July 6, 2006.

JANSSEN, Cam

(JAN-suhn, KAM) **N.J.**

Right wing. Shoots right. 6', 205 lbs. Born, St. Louis, MO, April 15, 1984. New Jersey's 6th choice, 117th overall, in 2002 Entry Draft.

2000-01	St. Louis Jr. Blues	CSJHL	45	1	2	3	244	....	....	....	....	....	....	....	....	....	....	....	....	....	....	....	....	....	....
2001-02	Windsor Spitfires	OHL	64	5	17	22	*268	....	....	....	....	....	....	....	....	....	10	0	0	0	13	....	....	....	....
2002-03	Windsor Spitfires	OHL	50	1	12	13	211	....	....	....	....	....	....	....	....	....	7	0	1	1	22	....	....	....	....
2003-04	Windsor Spitfires	OHL	35	4	9	13	144	....	....	....	....	....	....	....	....	....	....	....	....	....	....	....	....	....	....
	Guelph Storm	OHL	29	7	4	11	125	....	....	....	....	....	....	....	....	....	22	3	3	6	49	....	....	....	....
2004-05	Albany River Rats	AHL	70	1	3	4	337	....	....	....	....	....	....	....	....	....	....	....	....	....	....	....	....	....	....
2005-06	**New Jersey**	**NHL**	**47**	**0**	**0**	**0**	**91**	**0**	**0**	**0**	**10**	**0.0**	**–3**	**2**	**100.0**	**4:44**	**9**	**0**	**0**	**0**	**26**	**0**	**0**	**0**	**3:43**
	Albany River Rats	AHL	26	1	3	4	117	....	....	....	....	....	....	....	....	....	....	....	....	....	....	....	....	....	....
	NHL Totals		**47**	**0**	**0**	**0**	**91**	**0**	**0**	**0**	**10**	**0.0**		**2**	**100.0**	**4:44**	**9**	**0**	**0**	**0**	**26**	**0**	**0**	**0**	**3:43**

JARDINE, Ryan

(JAHR-dighn, RIGH-yan)

Left wing. Shoots left. 6', 210 lbs. Born, Ottawa, Ont., March 15, 1980. Florida's 4th choice, 89th overall, in 1998 Entry Draft.

1996-97	Kanata Valley	CJHL	52	30	27	57	76	....	....	....	....	....	....	....	....	....	....	....	....	....	....	....	....	....	....
1997-98	Sault Ste. Marie	OHL	65	28	32	60	16	....	....	....	....	....	....	....	....	....	....	....	....	....	....	....	....	....	....
1998-99	Sault Ste. Marie	OHL	68	27	34	61	56	....	....	....	....	....	....	....	....	....	5	0	1	1	6	....	....	....	....
99-2000	Sault Ste. Marie	OHL	65	43	34	77	58	....	....	....	....	....	....	....	....	....	17	11	8	19	16	....	....	....	....
2000-01	Louisville Panthers	AHL	77	12	14	26	38	....	....	....	....	....	....	....	....	....	....	....	....	....	....	....	....	....	....
2001-02	**Florida**	**NHL**	**8**	**0**	**2**	**2**	**2**	**0**	**0**	**0**	**6**	**0.0**	**0**	**2**	**100.0**	**8:55**	....	....	....	....	....	....	....	....	....
	Utah Grizzlies	AHL	64	16	16	32	56	....	....	....	....	....	....	....	....	....	4	1	1	2	0	....	....	....	....
2002-03	San Antonio	AHL	64	14	17	31	37	....	....	....	....	....	....	....	....	....	3	1	0	1	0	....	....	....	....
2003-04	San Antonio	AHL	22	6	1	7	12	....	....	....	....	....	....	....	....	....	....	....	....	....	....	....	....	....	....
2004-05	San Antonio	AHL	77	14	20	34	72	....	....	....	....	....	....	....	....	....	....	....	....	....	....	....	....	....	....
2005-06	Hamburg Freezers	Germany	31	5	6	11	22	....	....	....	....	....	....	....	....	....	6	0	0	0	2	....	....	....	....
	NHL Totals		**8**	**0**	**2**	**2**	**2**	**0**	**0**	**0**	**6**	**0.0**		**2**	**100.0**	**8:55**	....	....	....	....	....	....	....	....	....

OHL All-Rookie Team (1998)

• Missed majority of 2003-04 season recovering from knee injury suffered in game vs. Milwaukee (AHL), November 7, 2003. Signed as a free agent by **Hamburg** (Germany), October 2, 2005. Signed as a free agent by **Mora** (Sweden), August 16, 2006.

JARRETT, Cole

(JAIR-reht, KOHL)

Wing. Shoots left. 6', 195 lbs. Born, Sault Ste. Marie, Ont., January 4, 1983. Columbus' 6th choice, 141st overall, in 2001 Entry Draft.

1998-99	Waterloo Siskins	OHA-B	44	6	10	16	43	....	....	....	....	....	....	....	....	....	4	2	2	4	5	....	....	....	....
99-2000	Plymouth Whalers	OHL	57	3	7	10	47	....	....	....	....	....	....	....	....	....	23	3	7	10	19	....	....	....	....
2000-01	Plymouth Whalers	OHL	60	12	36	48	98	....	....	....	....	....	....	....	....	....	19	6	12	18	29	....	....	....	....
2001-02	Plymouth Whalers	OHL	51	14	24	38	92	....	....	....	....	....	....	....	....	....	6	1	1	2	18	....	....	....	....
2002-03	Plymouth Whalers	OHL	58	14	41	55	138	....	....	....	....	....	....	....	....	....	14	5	6	11	29	....	....	....	....
2003-04	Bridgeport	AHL	59	2	14	16	38	....	....	....	....	....	....	....	....	....	....	....	....	....	....	....	....	....	....
2004-05	Bridgeport	AHL	61	7	13	20	65	....	....	....	....	....	....	....	....	....	....	....	....	....	....	....	....	....	....
2005-06	**NY Islanders**	**NHL**	**1**	**0**	**0**	**0**	**0**	**0**	**0**	**0**	**1**	**0.0**	**1**	**0**	**0.0**	**13:48**	....	....	....	....	....	....	....	....	....
	Bridgeport	AHL	78	3	20	23	88	....	....	....	....	....	....	....	....	....	7	0	0	0	13	....	....	....	....
	NHL Totals		**1**	**0**	**0**	**0**	**0**	**0**	**0**	**0**	**1**	**0.0**		**0**	**0.0**	**13:48**	....	....	....	....	....	....	....	....	....

Signed as a free agent by **NY Islanders**, September 9, 2003.

JASPERS, Jason
(JAS-puhrs, JAY-suhn)

Center. Shoots left. 5'11", 207 lbs. Born, Thunder Bay, Ont., April 8, 1981. Phoenix's 4th choice, 71st overall, in 1999 Entry Draft.

			Regular Season														Playoffs								
Season	Club	League	GP	G	A	Pts	PIM	PP	SH	GW	S	%	+/-	TF	F%	Min	GP	G	A	Pts	PIM	PP	SH	GW	Min
1996-97	Thunder Bay	TBAHA	70	51	69	120	67	....	....	....	....	....	....	....	....	....	....	....	....	....	....	....	....	....	....
1997-98	Thunder Bay	TBAHA	72	45	75	120	90	....	....	....	....	....	....	....	....	....	....	....	....	....	....	....	....	....	....
1998-99	Sudbury Wolves	OHL	68	28	33	61	81	....	....	....	....	....	....	....	....	....	4	2	1	3	13	....	....	....	....
99-2000	Sudbury Wolves	OHL	68	46	61	107	107	....	....	....	....	....	....	....	....	....	12	4	6	10	27	....	....	....	....
2000-01	Sudbury Wolves	OHL	63	42	42	84	77	....	....	....	....	....	....	....	....	....	12	3	16	19	18	....	....	....	....
2001-02	**Phoenix**	**NHL**	**4**	**0**	**1**	**1**	**4**	**0**	**0**	**0**	**1**	**0.0**	**–1**	**14**	**35.7**	**8:07**	....	....	....	....	....	....	....	....	....
	Springfield	AHL	71	25	23	48	55	....	....	....	....	....	....	....	....	....	....	....	....	....	....	....	....	....	....
2002-03	Springfield	AHL	63	4	15	19	57	....	....	....	....	....	....	....	....	....	6	0	0	0	4	....	....	....	....
	Phoenix	**NHL**	**2**	**0**	**0**	**0**	**0**	**0**	**0**	**0**	**0**	**0.0**	**–1**	**14**	**57.1**	**7:17**	....	....	....	....	....	....	....	....	....
2003-04	**Phoenix**	**NHL**	**3**	**0**	**0**	**0**	**2**	**0**	**0**	**0**	**3**	**0.0**	**–1**	**19**	**57.9**	**11:24**	....	....	....	....	....	....	....	....	....
	Springfield	AHL	58	16	22	38	56	....	....	....	....	....	....	....	....	....	....	....	....	....	....	....	....	....	....
2004-05	Utah Grizzlies	AHL	11	0	3	3	6	....	....	....	....	....	....	....	....	....	....	....	....	....	....	....	....	....	....
	Springfield	AHL	48	12	17	29	45	....	....	....	....	....	....	....	....	....	....	....	....	....	....	....	....	....	....
2005-06	Springfield	AHL	77	29	37	66	86	....	....	....	....	....	....	....	....	....	....	....	....	....	....	....	....	....	....
	NHL Totals		**9**	**0**	**1**	**1**	**6**	**0**	**0**	**0**	**4**	**0.0**		**47**	**51.1**	**9:01**	....	....	....	....	....	....	....	....	....

OHL Second All-Star Team (2000)

Loaned to **Springfield** (AHL) by **Utah** (AHL) for cash, November 20, 2004. Signed as a free agent by **Tampa Bay**, August 18, 2005. Signed as a free agent by **Mannheim** (Germany), July 18, 2006.

JILLSON, Jeff
(JIHL-sohn, JEHF) **BUF.**

Defense. Shoots right. 6'3", 215 lbs. Born, North Smithfield, RI, July 24, 1980. San Jose's 1st choice, 14th overall, in 1999 Entry Draft.

			Regular Season														Playoffs								
Season	Club	League	GP	G	A	Pts	PIM	PP	SH	GW	S	%	+/-	TF	F%	Min	GP	G	A	Pts	PIM	PP	SH	GW	Min
1995-96	Mount St. Charles	High-RI	15	8	7	15	15	....	....	....	....	....	....	....	....	....	5	1	1	2	4	....	....	....	....
1996-97	Mount St. Charles	High-RI	15	16	14	30	20	....	....	....	....	....	....	....	....	....	4	0	4	4	6	....	....	....	....
1997-98	Mount St. Charles	High-RI	15	10	13	23	32	....	....	....	....	....	....	....	....	....	5	4	5	9	6	....	....	....	....
1998-99	U. of Michigan	CCHA	38	5	19	24	71	....	....	....	....	....	....	....	....	....	....	....	....	....	....	....	....	....	....
99-2000	U. of Michigan	CCHA	38	8	26	34	115	....	....	....	....	....	....	....	....	....	....	....	....	....	....	....	....	....	....
2000-01	U. of Michigan	CCHA	43	10	20	30	74	....	....	....	....	....	....	....	....	....	....	....	....	....	....	....	....	....	....
2001-02	**San Jose**	**NHL**	**48**	**5**	**13**	**18**	**29**	**3**	**0**	**2**	**47**	**10.6**	**2**	**0**	**0.0**	**14:36**	**4**	**0**	**0**	**0**	**0**	**0**	**0**	**0**	**5:45**
	Cleveland Barons	AHL	27	2	13	15	45	....	....	....	....	....	....	....	....	....	....	....	....	....	....	....	....	....	....
2002-03	**San Jose**	**NHL**	**26**	**0**	**6**	**6**	**9**	**0**	**0**	**0**	**22**	**0.0**	**–7**	**0**	**0.0**	**13:45**	....	....	....	....	....	....	....	....	....
	Cleveland Barons	AHL	19	3	5	8	12	....	....	....	....	....	....	....	....	....	....	....	....	....	....	....	....	....	....
	Providence Bruins	AHL	30	4	11	15	26	....	....	....	....	....	....	....	....	....	4	0	2	2	8	....	....	....	....
2003-04	**Boston**	**NHL**	**50**	**4**	**10**	**14**	**35**	**1**	**0**	**1**	**80**	**5.0**	**–1**	**0**	**0.0**	**17:53**	....	....	....	....	....	....	....	....	....
	Buffalo	**NHL**	**14**	**0**	**3**	**3**	**19**	**0**	**0**	**0**	**35**	**0.0**	**–3**	**0**	**0.0**	**18:21**	....	....	....	....	....	....	....	....	....
2004-05	Rochester	AHL	78	12	17	29	46	....	....	....	....	....	....	....	....	....	9	1	1	2	12	....	....	....	....
2005-06	**Buffalo**	**NHL**	**2**	**0**	**0**	**0**	**4**	**0**	**0**	**0**	**1**	**0.0**	**0**	**0**	**0.0**	**14:40**	**4**	**0**	**0**	**0**	**0**	**0**	**0**	**0**	**11:41**
	Rochester	AHL	73	10	20	30	94	....	....	....	....	....	....	....	....	....	....	....	....	....	....	....	....	....	....
	NHL Totals		**140**	**9**	**32**	**41**	**96**	**4**	**0**	**3**	**185**	**4.9**		**0**	**0.0**	**15:59**	**8**	**0**	**0**	**0**	**0**	**0**	**0**	**0**	**8:43**

CCHA All-Rookie Team (1999) • CCHA First All-Star Team (2000, 2001) • NCAA West First All-American Team (2000) • NCAA West Second All-American Team (2001)

Traded to **Boston** by **San Jose** with Jeff Hackett for Kyle McLaren and Boston's 4th round choice (Torrey Mitchell) in 2004 Entry Draft, January 23, 2003. Traded to **San Jose** by **Boston** for Brad Boyes, March 9, 2004. Traded to **Buffalo** by **San Jose** with a compensatory 7th round choice (Andrew Orpik) in 2005 Entry Draft for Curtis Brown and Andy Delmore, March 9, 2004.

JOHANSSON, Jonas
(yoh-HAHN-suhn, YOH-nuhs) **WSH.**

Right wing. Shoots right. 6'3", 215 lbs. Born, Jonkoping, Sweden, March 18, 1984. Colorado's 1st choice, 28th overall, in 2002 Entry Draft.

			Regular Season														Playoffs								
Season	Club	League	GP	G	A	Pts	PIM	PP	SH	GW	S	%	+/-	TF	F%	Min	GP	G	A	Pts	PIM	PP	SH	GW	Min
99-2000	HV 71 Jr.	Swe-Jr.	9	6	3	9	2	....	....	....	....	....	....	....	....	....	2	0	0	0	4	....	....	....	....
2000-01	HV 71 Jr.	Swe-Jr.	27	13	8	21	14	....	....	....	....	....	....	....	....	....	2	1	0	1	0	....	....	....	....
2001-02	HV 71 Jr.	Swe-Jr.	26	15	19	34	20	....	....	....	....	....	....	....	....	....	....	....	....	....	....	....	....	....	....
	HV 71 Jonkoping	Sweden	5	0	0	0	0	....	....	....	....	....	....	....	....	....	2	0	0	0	0	....	....	....	....
2002-03	Kamloops Blazers	WHL	26	10	25	35	8	....	....	....	....	....	....	....	....	....	6	1	2	3	4	....	....	....	....
2003-04	Kamloops Blazers	WHL	72	18	19	37	70	....	....	....	....	....	....	....	....	....	5	2	2	4	4	....	....	....	....
2004-05	Portland Pirates	AHL	50	3	6	9	8	....	....	....	....	....	....	....	....	....	....	....	....	....	....	....	....	....	....
	South Carolina	ECHL	5	4	2	6	10	....	....	....	....	....	....	....	....	....	....	....	....	....	....	....	....	....	....
2005-06	Lulea HF	Sweden	10	0	0	0	0	....	....	....	....	....	....	....	....	....	....	....	....	....	....	....	....	....	....
	Washington	**NHL**	**1**	**0**	**0**	**0**	**2**	**0**	**0**	**0**	**0**	**0.0**	**0**	**0**	**0.0**	**4:14**	....	....	....	....	....	....	....	....	....
	Hershey Bears	AHL	37	5	5	10	24	....	....	....	....	....	....	....	....	....	2	1	0	1	4	....	....	....	....
	South Carolina	ECHL	5	5	3	8	2	....	....	....	....	....	....	....	....	....	....	....	....	....	....	....	....	....	....
	NHL Totals		**1**	**0**	**0**	**0**	**2**	**0**	**0**	**0**	**0**	**0.0**		**0**	**0.0**	**4:14**	....	....	....	....	....	....	....	....	....

Traded to **Washington** by **Colorado** with Bates Battaglia for Steve Konowalchuk and Washington's 3rd round choice (later traded to Carolina – Carolina selected Casey Borer) in 2004 Entry Draft, October 22, 2003.

JOHNSON, Aaron
(JAWN-suhn, AIR-ruhn) **CBJ**

Defense. Shoots left. 6'2", 211 lbs. Born, Port Hawkesbury, N.S., April 30, 1983. Columbus' 4th choice, 85th overall, in 2001 Entry Draft.

			Regular Season														Playoffs								
Season	Club	League	GP	G	A	Pts	PIM	PP	SH	GW	S	%	+/-	TF	F%	Min	GP	G	A	Pts	PIM	PP	SH	GW	Min
1998-99	Cape Breton	NSAHA	56	28	42	70	98	....	....	....	....	....	....	....	....	....	....	....	....	....	....	....	....	....	....
99-2000	Rimouski Oceanic	QMJHL	63	1	14	15	57	....	....	....	....	....	....	....	....	....	8	0	0	0	0	....	....	....	....
2000-01	Rimouski Oceanic	QMJHL	64	12	41	53	128	....	....	....	....	....	....	....	....	....	11	2	4	6	35	....	....	....	....
2001-02	Rimouski Oceanic	QMJHL	68	17	49	66	172	....	....	....	....	....	....	....	....	....	7	1	2	3	12	....	....	....	....
2002-03	Rimouski Oceanic	QMJHL	25	4	20	24	41	....	....	....	....	....	....	....	....	....	....	....	....	....	....	....	....	....	....
	Quebec Remparts	QMJHL	32	6	31	37	41	....	....	....	....	....	....	....	....	....	11	4	4	8	25	....	....	....	....
2003-04	**Columbus**	**NHL**	**29**	**2**	**6**	**8**	**32**	**0**	**0**	**1**	**33**	**6.1**	**–2**	**0**	**0.0**	**15:02**	....	....	....	....	....	....	....	....	....
	Syracuse Crunch	AHL	49	6	15	21	83	....	....	....	....	....	....	....	....	....	7	2	3	5	27	....	....	....	....
2004-05	Syracuse Crunch	AHL	77	6	17	23	140	....	....	....	....	....	....	....	....	....	....	....	....	....	....	....	....	....	....
2005-06	**Columbus**	**NHL**	**26**	**2**	**6**	**8**	**23**	**1**	**0**	**1**	**28**	**7.1**	**9**	**0**	**0.0**	**14:12**	....	....	....	....	....	....	....	....	....
	Syracuse Crunch	AHL	49	5	24	29	122	....	....	....	....	....	....	....	....	....	6	1	3	4	19	....	....	....	....
	NHL Totals		**55**	**4**	**12**	**16**	**55**	**1**	**0**	**2**	**61**	**6.6**		**0**	**0.0**	**14:38**	....	....	....	....	....	....	....	....	....

JOHNSON, Greg
(JAWN-suhn, GREHG) **DET.**

Center. Shoots left. 5'11", 200 lbs. Born, Thunder Bay, Ont., March 16, 1971. Philadelphia's 1st choice, 33rd overall, in 1989 Entry Draft.

			Regular Season														Playoffs								
Season	Club	League	GP	G	A	Pts	PIM	PP	SH	GW	S	%	+/-	TF	F%	Min	GP	G	A	Pts	PIM	PP	SH	GW	Min
1988-89	Thunder Bay	USHL	47	32	64	96	4	....	....	....	....	....	....	....	....	....	12	5	13	18	0	....	....	....	....
1989-90	North Dakota	WCHA	44	17	38	55	11	....	....	....	....	....	....	....	....	....	....	....	....	....	....	....	....	....	....
1990-91	North Dakota	WCHA	38	18	*61	79	6	....	....	....	....	....	....	....	....	....	....	....	....	....	....	....	....	....	....
1991-92	North Dakota	WCHA	39	20	*54	74	8	....	....	....	....	....	....	....	....	....	....	....	....	....	....	....	....	....	....
1992-93	North Dakota	WCHA	34	19	45	64	18	....	....	....	....	....	....	....	....	....	....	....	....	....	....	....	....	....	....
	Canada	Nat-Tm	23	6	14	20	2	....	....	....	....	....	....	....	....	....	....	....	....	....	....	....	....	....	....
1993-94	**Detroit**	**NHL**	**52**	**6**	**11**	**17**	**22**	**1**	**1**	**0**	**48**	**12.5**	**–7**	....	....	....	**7**	**2**	**2**	**4**	**2**	**1**	**0**	**0**	....
	Adirondack	AHL	3	2	4	6	0	....	....	....	....	....	....	....	....	....	4	0	4	4	2	....	....	....	....
	Canada	Olympics	8	0	3	3	0	....	....	....	....	....	....	....	....	....	....	....	....	....	....	....	....	....	....
1994-95	**Detroit**	**NHL**	**22**	**3**	**5**	**8**	**14**	**2**	**0**	**0**	**32**	**9.4**	**1**	....	....	....	**1**	**0**	**0**	**0**	**0**	**0**	**0**	**0**	....
1995-96	**Detroit**	**NHL**	**60**	**18**	**22**	**40**	**30**	**5**	**0**	**2**	**87**	**20.7**	**6**	....	....	....	**13**	**3**	**1**	**4**	**8**	**0**	**0**	**0**	....
1996-97	**Detroit**	**NHL**	**43**	**6**	**10**	**16**	**12**	**0**	**0**	**0**	**56**	**10.7**	**–5**	....	....	....	....	....	....	....	....	....	....	....	....
	Pittsburgh	**NHL**	**32**	**7**	**9**	**16**	**14**	**1**	**0**	**0**	**52**	**13.5**	**–13**	....	....	....	**5**	**1**	**0**	**1**	**2**	**0**	**0**	**0**	....
1997-98	**Pittsburgh**	**NHL**	**5**	**1**	**0**	**1**	**2**	**0**	**0**	**0**	**4**	**25.0**	**0**	....	....	....	....	....	....	....	....	....	....	....	....
	Chicago	**NHL**	**69**	**11**	**22**	**33**	**38**	**4**	**0**	**3**	**85**	**12.9**	**–2**	....	....	....	....	....	....	....	....	....	....	....	....
1998-99	**Nashville**	**NHL**	**68**	**16**	**34**	**50**	**24**	**2**	**3**	**0**	**120**	**13.3**	**–8**	**1441**	**53.6**	**19:26**	....	....	....	....	....	....	....	....	....
99-2000	**Nashville**	**NHL**	**82**	**11**	**33**	**44**	**40**	**2**	**0**	**1**	**133**	**8.3**	**–15**	**1684**	**50.8**	**19:13**	....	....	....	....	....	....	....	....	....
2000-01	**Nashville**	**NHL**	**82**	**15**	**17**	**32**	**46**	**1**	**0**	**4**	**97**	**15.5**	**–6**	**1583**	**51.8**	**17:49**	....	....	....	....	....	....	....	....	....
2001-02	**Nashville**	**NHL**	**82**	**18**	**26**	**44**	**38**	**3**	**0**	**2**	**145**	**12.4**	**–14**	**1764**	**51.8**	**19:34**	....	....	....	....	....	....	....	....	....
2002-03	**Nashville**	**NHL**	**38**	**8**	**9**	**17**	**22**	**0**	**0**	**0**	**55**	**14.5**	**7**	**753**	**52.1**	**17:11**	....	....	....	....	....	....	....	....	....
2003-04	**Nashville**	**NHL**	**82**	**14**	**18**	**32**	**33**	**1**	**4**	**4**	**100**	**14.0**	**–21**	**1607**	**55.1**	**17:38**	**6**	**1**	**2**	**3**	**0**	**0**	**0**	**0**	**17:48**

			Regular Season														Playoffs								
Season	Club	League	GP	G	A	Pts	PIM	PP	SH	GW	S	%	+/-	TF	F%	Min	GP	G	A	Pts	PIM	PP	SH	GW	Min
2004-05			DID NOT PLAY																						
2005-06	**Nashville**	**NHL**	68	11	8	19	10	0	4	3	76	14.5	5	1016	54.9	16:36	5	0	1	1	2	0	0	0	14:43
	NHL Totals		785	145	224	369	345	22	12	19	1090	13.3		9848	52.8	18:19	37	7	6	13	14	1	0	0	16:24

WCHA First All-Star Team (1991, 1992, 1993) • NCAA West First All-American Team (1991, 1993) • NCAA West Second All-American Team (1992)

Traded to **Detroit** by **Philadelphia** with Philadelphia's 5th round choice (Frederic Deschenes) in 1994 Entry Draft for Jim Cummins and Philadelphia's 4th round choice (previously acquired, later traded to Boston – Boston selected Charles Paquette) in 1993 Entry Draft, June 20, 1993. Traded to **Pittsburgh** by **Detroit** for Tomas Sandstrom, January 27, 1997. Traded to **Chicago** by **Pittsburgh** for Tuomas Gronman, October 27, 1997. Claimed by **Nashville** from **Chicago** in Expansion Draft, June 26, 1998. • Missed majority of 2002-03 season recovering from head injury suffered in game vs. Vancouver, October 21, 2002. Signed as a free agent by **Detroit**, August 14, 2006..

JOHNSON, Mike

(JAWN-suhn, MIGHK) **MTL.**

Right wing. Shoots right. 6'2", 201 lbs. Born, Scarborough, Ont., October 3, 1974.

1991-92	Hillcrest Summits	MTHL	45	43	66	109											20	10	19	29					
1992-93	Aurora Eagles	MTJHL	48	25	40	65	18										7	7	15	22					
1993-94	Bowling Green	CCHA	38	6	14	20	18																		
1994-95	Bowling Green	CCHA	37	16	33	49	35																		
1995-96	Bowling Green	CCHA	30	12	19	31	22																		
1996-97	Bowling Green	CCHA	38	30	32	62	46																		
	Toronto	**NHL**	13	2	2	4	4	0	1	1	27	7.4	–2												
1997-98	**Toronto**	**NHL**	82	15	32	47	24	5	0	0	143	10.5	–4												
1998-99	**Toronto**	**NHL**	79	20	24	44	35	5	3	2	149	13.4	13	15	53.3	16:16	17	3	2	5	4	0	0	1	16:28
99-2000	**Toronto**	**NHL**	52	11	14	25	23	2	1	3	89	12.4	8	2	50.0	15:22									
	Tampa Bay	**NHL**	28	10	12	22	4	4	0	0	43	23.3	–2	5	60.0	20:33									
2000-01	**Tampa Bay**	**NHL**	64	11	27	38	38	3	1	0	107	10.3	–10	2	0.0	18:13									
	Phoenix	**NHL**	12	2	3	5	4	1	0	0	17	11.8	0	0	0.0	12:12									
2001-02	**Phoenix**	**NHL**	57	5	22	27	28	1	2	0	73	6.8	14	13	30.8	15:49	5	1	1	2	6	0	0	0	14:45
2002-03	**Phoenix**	**NHL**	82	23	40	63	47	8	0	3	178	12.9	9	34	50.0	19:39									
2003-04	**Phoenix**	**NHL**	11	1	9	10	10	1	0	0	17	5.9	–1	2	50.0	19:50									
2004-05	Farjestad	Sweden	8	1	2	3	4										6	0	2	2	4				
2005-06	**Phoenix**	**NHL**	80	16	38	54	50	6	1	3	145	11.0	7	234	44.4	16:34									
	NHL Totals		560	116	223	339	267	36	9	12	988	11.7		307	45.0	17:16	22	4	3	7	10	0	0	1	16:05

NHL All-Rookie Team (1998)

Signed as a free agent by **Toronto**, March 16, 1997. Traded to **Tampa Bay** by **Toronto** with Marek Posmyk and Toronto's 5th (Pavel Sedov) and 6th (Aaron Gionet) round choices in 2000 Entry Draft for Darcy Tucker and Tampa Bay's 4th round choice (Miguel Delisle) in 2000 Entry Draft, February 9, 2000. Traded to **Phoenix** by **Tampa Bay** with Paul Mara, Ruslan Zainullin and NY Islanders' 2nd round choice (previously acquired, Phoenix selected Matthew Spiller) in 2001 Entry Draft for Nikolai Khabibulin and Stan Neckar, March 5, 2001. • Missed majority of 2003-04 season recovering from shoulder injury suffered in game vs. Los Angeles, Novembeer 1, 2003. Signed as a free agent by **Farjestad** (Sweden), January 31, 2005. Traded to **Montreal** by **Phoenix** for a 4th round choice in 2007 Entry Draft, July 12, 2006.

JOHNSON, Ryan

(JAWN-suhn, RIGH-yuhn) **ST.L.**

Center. Shoots left. 6'1", 205 lbs. Born, Thunder Bay, Ont., June 14, 1976. Florida's 4th choice, 36th overall, in 1994 Entry Draft.

1992-93	Thunder Bay	TBAHA	60	25	33	58																			
1993-94	Thunder Bay	USHL	48	14	36	50	28																		
1994-95	North Dakota	WCHA	38	6	22	28	39																		
1995-96	North Dakota	WCHA	21	2	17	19	14																		
	Canada	Nat-Tm	28	5	12	17	14																		
1996-97	Carolina	AHL	79	18	24	42	28																		
1997-98	**Florida**	**NHL**	10	0	2	2	0	0	0	0	6	0.0	–4												
	New Haven	AHL	64	19	48	67	12										3	0	1	1	0				
1998-99	**Florida**	**NHL**	1	1	0	1	0	0	0	0	1	100.0	0	16	37.5	15:26									
	New Haven	AHL	37	8	19	27	18																		
99-2000	**Florida**	**NHL**	66	4	12	16	14	0	0	0	44	9.1	1	684	51.8	11:47									
	Tampa Bay	**NHL**	14	0	2	2	2	0	0	0	5	0.0	–9	117	53.0	11:02									
2000-01	**Tampa Bay**	**NHL**	80	7	14	21	44	1	0	0	71	9.9	–20	951	48.9	15:47									
2001-02	**Florida**	**NHL**	29	1	3	4	10	0	0	0	24	4.2	–5	336	47.9	13:00									
2002-03	**Florida**	**NHL**	58	2	5	7	26	0	0	0	54	3.7	–13	689	48.0	10:40									
	St. Louis	**NHL**	17	0	0	0	12	0	0	0	13	0.0	0	180	51.7	10:34	6	0	2	2	6	0	0	0	8:14
2003-04	**St. Louis**	**NHL**	69	4	7	11	8	0	1	1	36	11.1	–2	537	53.6	9:54	3	0	0	0	0	0	0	0	6:11
2004-05	Missouri	UHL	29	7	14	21	12										6	1	0	1	13				
2005-06	**St. Louis**	**NHL**	65	3	6	9	33	1	1	0	57	5.3	–21	569	55.9	11:24									
	NHL Totals		409	22	51	73	149	2	2	1	311	7.1		4079	50.9	12:03	9	0	2	2	6	0	0	0	7:33

Traded to **Tampa Bay** by **Florida** with Dwayne Hay for Mike Sillinger, March 14, 2000. Traded to **Florida** by **Tampa Bay** with Tampa Bay's 6th round choice (later traded back to Tampa Bay – Tampa Bay selected Doug O'Brien) in 2003 Entry Draft for Vaclav Prospal, July 10, 2001. • Missed majority of 2001-02 season recovering from head injury suffered in game vs. St. Louis, December 22, 2001. Claimed on waivers by **St. Louis** from **Florida**, February 19, 2003. Signed as a free agent by **Missouri** (UHL), February 3, 2005.

JOHNSSON, Kim

(YAWN-suhn, KIHM) **MIN.**

Defense. Shoots left. 6'1", 205 lbs. Born, Malmo, Sweden, March 16, 1976. NY Rangers' 15th choice, 286th overall, in 1994 Entry Draft.

1993-94	Malmo IF Jr.	Swe-Jr.	14	5	3	8	14																		
	Malmo IF	Sweden	2	0	0	0	0																		
1994-95	Malmo IF Jr.	Swe-Jr.	29	6	15	21	40																		
	Malmo IF	Sweden	13	0	0	0	4										1	0	0	0	0				
1995-96	Malmo IF	Sweden	38	2	0	2	30										4	0	1	1	8				
1996-97	Malmo	Sweden	49	4	9	13	42										4	0	0	0	2				
1997-98	Malmo	Sweden	45	5	9	14	29																		
1998-99	Malmo	Sweden	49	9	8	17	76										8	2	3	5	12				
99-2000	**NY Rangers**	**NHL**	76	6	15	21	46	1	0	1	101	5.9	–13	0	0.0	18:06									
2000-01	**NY Rangers**	**NHL**	75	5	21	26	40	4	0	0	104	4.8	–3	0	0.0	21:16									
2001-02	**Philadelphia**	**NHL**	82	11	30	41	42	5	0	1	150	7.3	12	0	0.0	23:02	5	0	0	0	2	0	0	0	22:48
	Sweden	Olympics	4	1	1	2	0																		
2002-03	**Philadelphia**	**NHL**	82	10	29	39	38	5	0	2	159	6.3	11	0	0.0	24:05	13	0	3	3	8	0	0	0	26:07
2003-04	**Philadelphia**	**NHL**	80	13	29	42	26	4	0	3	189	6.9	16	0	0.0	24:27	15	2	6	8	8	0	0	1	26:11
2004-05	HC Ambri-Piotta	Swiss	24	4	10	14	61																		
2005-06	**Philadelphia**	**NHL**	47	6	19	25	34	3	0	0	97	6.2	5	0	0.0	23:17									
	Sweden	Olympics	DID NOT PLAY																						
	NHL Totals		442	51	143	194	226	22	0	7	800	6.4		0	0.0	22:22	33	2	9	11	18	0	0	1	25:39

Traded to **Philadelphia** by **NY Rangers** with Jan Hlavac, Pavel Brendl and NY Rangers' 3rd round choice (Stefan Ruzicka) in 2003 Entry Draft for Eric Lindros, August 20, 2001. Signed as a free agent by **Ambri-Piotta** (Swiss), September 18, 2004. Signed as a free agent by **Minnesota**, July 1, 2006.

JOKELA, Mikko

(YOH-kih-lah, MIH-koh) **VAN.**

Defense. Shoots right. 6'1", 210 lbs. Born, Lappeenranta, Finland, March 4, 1980. New Jersey's 5th choice, 96th overall, in 1998 Entry Draft.

1995-96	KalPa Kuopio U18	Fin-U18	9	2	1	3	20																		
	KalPa Kuopio Jr.	Fin-Jr.	2	0	0	0	0																		
1996-97	KalPa Kuopio U18	Fin-U18	11	3	2	5	8																		
	KalPa Kuopio Jr.	Fin-Jr.	34	2	5	7	18										5	1	1	2	4				
1997-98	HIFK Helsinki U18	Fin-U18	4	5	1	6	2																		
	HIFK Helsinki Jr.	Fin-Jr.	22	2	5	7	14																		
	HIFK Helsinki	Finland	16	0	0	0	0																		
	Hermes Kokkola	Finland-2	6	0	1	1	2																		
1998-99	HIFK Helsinki	Finland	3	0	0	0	2																		
	KalPa Kuopio Jr.	Fin-Jr.	8	7	4	11	8																		
	KalPa Kuopio	Finland	42	1	2	3	18																		
	KalPa Kuopio	Finland-Q																							
99-2000	SaiPa Jr.	Fin-Jr.	1	0	0	0	0										6	0	0	0	2				
	SaiPa	Finland	48	0	5	5	50																		
2000-01	SaiPa Jr.	Fin-Jr.	4	2	2	4	2																		
	KooKoo Kouvola	Finland-2	5	3	0	3	0										2	0	0	0	2				
	SaiPa	Finland	50	1	0	1	26																		
2001-02	Albany River Rats	AHL	56	5	13	18	28																		

Season	Club	League	GP	G	A	Pts	PIM	PP	SH	GW	S	%	+/-	TF	F%	Min	GP	G	A	Pts	PIM	PP	SH	GW	Min
										Regular Season									Playoffs					
2002-03	Albany River Rats	AHL	44	8	11	19	35										....								
	Vancouver	NHL	1	0	0	0	0	0	0	0	3	0.0	0	0	0.0	5:09	14	1	4	5	2				
	Manitoba Moose	AHL	32	3	7	10	17									....	10	2	1	3	12				
2003-04	Manitoba Moose	AHL	78	5	10	15	52									....	11	2	3	5	43				
2004-05	HPK Hameenlinna	Finland	55	4	12	16	102									....									
2005-06	HPK Hameenlinna	Finland	25	6	2	8	65									....									
	NHL Totals		1	0	0	0	0	0	0	0	3	0.0		0	0.0	5:09									

Traded to **Vancouver** by **New Jersey** for Steve Kariya, January 24, 2003. Signed as a free agent by **Hameenlinna** (Finland), April 17, 2004.

JOKINEN, Jussi
(YOH-kih-nihn, YOO-see)   **DAL.**

Center. Shoots left. 5'11", 189 lbs.   Born, Kalajoki, Finland, April 1, 1983. Dallas' 7th choice, 192nd overall, in 2001 Entry Draft.

Season	Club	League	GP	G	A	Pts	PIM	PP	SH	GW	S	%	+/-	TF	F%	Min	GP	G	A	Pts	PIM	PP	SH	GW	Min
99-2000	Karpat Oulu U18	Fin-U18	15	6	25	31	14										6	2	3	5	0				
	Karpat Oulu Jr.	Fin-Jr.	28	4	7	11	14																		
2000-01	Karpat Oulu U18	Fin-U18	1	2	1	3	0										6	2	1	3	0				
	Karpat Oulu Jr.	Fin-Jr.	41	18	31	49	69										1	1	1	2	0				
2001-02	Karpat Oulu Jr.	Fin-Jr.	2	4	1	5	2										4	1	0	1	0				
	Karpat Oulu	Finland	54	10	6	16	38										15	2	1	3	33				
2002-03	Karpat Oulu	Finland	51	14	23	37	10										15	3	4	7	6				
2003-04	Karpat Oulu	Finland	55	15	23	38	20										12	3	4	7	2				
2004-05	Karpat Oulu	Finland	56	23	24	47	24										5	2	1	3	0	1	0	0	13:40
2005-06	**Dallas**	**NHL**	81	17	38	55	30	8	0	2	107	15.9	2	23	30.4	13:34	5	2	1	3	0	1	0	0	13:40
	Finland	Olympics	8	1	3	4	2																		
	NHL Totals		81	17	38	55	30	8	0	2	107	15.9		23	30.4	13:34	5	2	1	3	0	1	0	0	13:40

JOKINEN, Olli
(YOH-kih-nihn, OH-lee)   **FLA.**

Center. Shoots left. 6'3", 205 lbs.   Born, Kuopio, Finland, December 5, 1978. Los Angeles' 1st choice, 3rd overall, in 1997 Entry Draft.

Season	Club	League	GP	G	A	Pts	PIM	PP	SH	GW	S	%	+/-	TF	F%	Min	GP	G	A	Pts	PIM	PP	SH	GW	Min
1994-95	KalPa Kuopio U18	Fin-U18	30	22	28	50	92																		
	KalPa Kuopio Jr.	Fin-Jr.	6	0	1	1	6																		
1995-96	KalPa Kuopio U18	Fin-U18	9	9	13	22	4										7	4	4	8	20				
	KalPa Kuopio Jr.	Fin-Jr.	25	20	14	34	47																		
	KalPa Kuopio	Finland	15	1	1	2	2																		
1996-97	HIFK Helsinki Jr.	Fin-Jr.	2	1	0	1	6																		
	HIFK Helsinki	Finland	50	14	27	41	88																		
1997-98	**Los Angeles**	**NHL**	8	0	0	0	6	0	0	0	12	0.0	−5				9	7	2	9	2				
	HIFK Helsinki	Finland	30	11	28	39	32																		
1998-99	**Los Angeles**	**NHL**	66	9	12	21	44	3	1	1	87	10.3	−10	779	43.9	14:42									
	Springfield	AHL	9	3	6	9	6																		
99-2000	**NY Islanders**	**NHL**	82	11	10	21	80	1	2	3	138	8.0	0	841	46.1	16:15									
2000-01	**Florida**	**NHL**	78	6	10	16	106	0	0	0	121	5.0	−22	638	42.3	13:23									
2001-02	**Florida**	**NHL**	80	9	20	29	98	3	1	0	153	5.9	−16	1222	45.2	18:05									
	Finland	Olympics	4	2	1	3	0																		
2002-03	**Florida**	**NHL**	81	36	29	65	79	13	3	6	240	15.0	−17	1925	46.7	22:02									
2003-04	**Florida**	**NHL**	82	26	32	58	81	8	2	8	280	9.3	−16	1986	47.1	22:35									
2004-05	Kloten Flyers	Swiss	8	6	1	7	14																		
	Sodertalje SK	Sweden	23	13	9	22	52										5	2	0	2	24				
	HIFK Helsinki	Finland	14	9	8	17	10																		
2005-06	**Florida**	**NHL**	82	38	51	89	88	14	1	9	351	10.8	14	955	46.9	20:29									
	Finland	Olympics	8	6	2	8	2																		
	NHL Totals		559	135	164	299	582	42	10	27	1382	9.8		8346	45.9	18:21									

Played in NHL All-Star Game (2003)

Traded to **NY Islanders** by **Los Angeles** with Josh Green, Mathieu Biron and Los Angeles' 1st round choice (Taylor Pyatt) in 1999 Entry Draft for Ziggy Palffy, Bryan Smolinski, Marcel Cousineau and New Jersey's 4th round choice (previously acquired, Los Angeles selected Daniel Johansson) in 1999 Entry Draft, June 20, 1999. Traded to **Florida** by **NY Islanders** with Roberto Luongo for Mark Parrish and Oleg Kvasha, June 24, 2000. Signed as a free agent by **Kloten** (Swiss), September 15, 2004. Signed as a free agent by **Sodertalje** (Sweden), November, 2004. Signed as a free agent by **HIFK Helsinki** (Finland), January 30, 2005.

JONES, Matt
(JOHNZ, MAT)   **PHX.**

Defense. Shoots left. 6', 215 lbs.   Born, Downers Grove, IL, August 8, 1983. Phoenix's 5th choice, 80th overall, in 2002 Entry Draft.

Season	Club	League	GP	G	A	Pts	PIM	PP	SH	GW	S	%	+/-	TF	F%	Min	GP	G	A	Pts	PIM	PP	SH	GW	Min
99-2000	Green Bay	USHL	54	1	4	5	59										13	0	0	0	2				
2000-01	Green Bay	USHL	52	3	10	13	58										4	0	0	0	2				
2001-02	North Dakota	WCHA	37	2	5	7	20																		
2002-03	North Dakota	WCHA	39	1	6	7	26																		
2003-04	North Dakota	WCHA	41	7	14	21	40																		
2004-05	North Dakota	WCHA	45	6	11	17	66																		
2005-06	**Phoenix**	**NHL**	16	0	2	2	14	0	0	0	10	0.0	−2	0	0.0	11:35									
	San Antonio	AHL	59	2	11	13	46																		
	NHL Totals		16	0	2	2	14	0	0	0	10	0.0		0	0.0	11:35									

WCHA Second All-Star Team (2004)

JONES, Randy
(JOHNZ, RAN-dee)   **PHI.**

Defense. Shoots left. 6'2", 200 lbs.   Born, Quispamsis, N.B., July 23, 1981.

Season	Club	League	GP	G	A	Pts	PIM	PP	SH	GW	S	%	+/-	TF	F%	Min	GP	G	A	Pts	PIM	PP	SH	GW	Min
99-2000	Cobourg Cougars	OPJHL	44	20	36	56	51																		
2000-01	Cobourg Cougars	OPJHL	28	15	21	36	46																		
2001-02	Clarkson Knights	ECAC	34	9	11	20	32																		
2002-03	Clarkson Knights	ECAC	33	13	20	33	65																		
2003-04	**Philadelphia**	**NHL**	5	0	0	0	0	0	0	0	5	0.0	1	0	0.0	12:00									
	Philadelphia	AHL	55	8	24	32	63										18	0	5	5	10				
2004-05	Philadelphia	AHL	69	5	19	24	32																		
2005-06	**Philadelphia**	**NHL**	28	0	8	8	16	0	0	0	21	0.0	−6		1100.0	14:58									
	Philadelphia	AHL	21	2	3	5	53																		
	NHL Totals		33	0	8	8	16	0	0	0	26	0.0			1100.0	14:31									

ECAC First All-Star Team (2003)

Signed as a free agent by **Philadelphia**, July 24, 2003.

JONSSON, Kenny
(YAWN-suhn, KEHN-nee)   **PHI.**

Defense. Shoots left. 6'3", 217 lbs.   Born, Angelholm, Sweden, October 6, 1974. Toronto's 1st choice, 12th overall, in 1993 Entry Draft.

Season	Club	League	GP	G	A	Pts	PIM	PP	SH	GW	S	%	+/-	TF	F%	Min	GP	G	A	Pts	PIM	PP	SH	GW	Min
1991-92	Rogle	Swe-2	30	4	11	15	24										5	0	0	0	0				
1992-93	Rogle Jr.	Swe-Jr.	2	1	2	3	25																		
	Rogle	Sweden	39	3	10	13	42										3	1	1	2	2				
1993-94	Rogle	Sweden	36	4	13	17	40																		
	Sweden	Olympics	3	1	0	1	0																		
1994-95	Rogle	Sweden	8	3	1	4	20																		
	St. John's	AHL	10	2	5	7	2										4	0	0	0	0	0	0	0	....
	Toronto	**NHL**	39	2	7	9	16	0	0	1	50	4.0	−8												
1995-96	**Toronto**	**NHL**	50	4	22	26	22	3	0	0	90	4.4	12												
	NY Islanders	**NHL**	16	0	4	4	4	0	0	0	40	0.0	−5												
1996-97	**NY Islanders**	**NHL**	81	3	18	21	24	1	0	0	92	3.3	10												
1997-98	**NY Islanders**	**NHL**	81	14	26	40	58	6	0	2	108	13.0	−2	0	0.0	24:59									
1998-99	**NY Islanders**	**NHL**	63	8	18	26	34	6	0	0	91	8.8	−18	0	0.0	24:29									
99-2000	**NY Islanders**	**NHL**	65	1	24	25	32	1	0	0	84	1.2	−15	0	0.0	24:04									
2000-01	**NY Islanders**	**NHL**	65	8	21	29	30	5	0	0	91	8.8	−22	0	0.0	25:34	5	1	2	3	0			0	23:48
2001-02	**NY Islanders**	**NHL**	76	10	22	32	26	2	1	0	107	9.3	15												
	Sweden	Olympics	3	1	0	1	0										5	0	0	0	0			0	28:46
2002-03	**NY Islanders**	**NHL**	71	8	18	26	24	3	1	0	108	7.4	−8	6	50.0	23:12	5	0	1	1	0			0	21:58
2003-04	**NY Islanders**	**NHL**	79	5	24	29	22	3	0	0	106	4.7	25	0	0.0	22:56	5	0	0	0	0				

Season	Club	League	GP	G	A	Pts	PIM	PP	SH	GW	S	%	+/-	TF	F%	Min	GP	G	A	Pts	PIM	PP	SH	GW	Min
2004-05	Rogle	Sweden-2	11	3	7	10	12	….	….	….	….	….	….	….	….	….	2	0	0	0	2	….	….	….	….
2005-06	Rogle	Sweden-2	37	8	15	23	73	….	….	….	….	….	….	….	….	….									
	Sweden	Olympics	8	0	4	4	4	….	….	….	….	….	….	….	….	….									
	NHL Totals		**686**	**63**	**204**	**267**	**298**	**30**	**2**	**6**	**967**	**6.5**		**8**	**37.5**	**24:11**	**19**	**1**	**3**	**4**	**6**	**1**	**0**	**0**	**24:51**

NHL All-Rookie Team (1995) • Olympic Tournament All-Star Team (2006) • Named Best Defenseman at Olympics (2006)
Traded to **NY Islanders** by **Toronto** with Sean Haggerty, Darby Hendrickson and Toronto's 1st round choice (Roberto Luongo) in 1997 Entry Draft for Wendel Clark, Mathieu Schneider and D.J. Smith, March 13, 1996. Signed as a free agent by **Rogle** (Sweden-2), December 20, 2004.

JOVANOVSKI, Ed

(joh-van-OHV-skee, EHD) **PHX.**

Defense. Shoots left. 6'2", 210 lbs.   Born, Windsor, Ont., June 26, 1976. Florida's 1st choice, 1st overall, in 1994 Entry Draft.

Season	Club	League	GP	G	A	Pts	PIM	PP	SH	GW	S	%	+/-	TF	F%	Min	GP	G	A	Pts	PIM	PP	SH	GW	Min
1991-92	Windsor	OMHA	50	25	40	65	88																		
1992-93	Windsor Bulldogs	OHA-B	48	7	46	53	88																		
1993-94	Windsor Spitfires	OHL	62	15	36	51	221										4	0	0	0	15				
1994-95	Windsor Spitfires	OHL	50	23	42	65	198										9	2	7	9	39				
1995-96	**Florida**	**NHL**	70	10	11	21	137	2	0	2	116	8.6	-3				22	1	8	9	52	0	0	0	
1996-97	**Florida**	**NHL**	61	7	16	23	172	3	0	1	80	8.8	-1				5	0	0	0	4	0	0	0	
1997-98	**Florida**	**NHL**	81	9	14	23	158	2	1	3	142	6.3	-12												
1998-99	**Florida**	**NHL**	41	3	13	16	82	1	0	1	68	4.4	-4	0	0.0	22:35									
	Vancouver	**NHL**	31	2	9	11	44	0	0	0	41	4.9	-5	0	0.0	21:16									
99-2000	**Vancouver**	**NHL**	75	5	21	26	54	1	0	1	109	4.6	-3	0	0.0	24:03									
2000-01	**Vancouver**	**NHL**	79	12	35	47	102	4	0	2	193	6.2	-1	0	0.0	24:57	4	1	1	2	0	0	0	0	25:54
2001-02	**Vancouver**	**NHL**	82	17	31	48	101	7	1	3	202	8.4	-7	0	0.0	25:11	6	1	4	5	8	1	0	0	25:48
	Canada	Olympics	6	0	3	3	4																		
2002-03	**Vancouver**	**NHL**	67	6	40	46	113	2	0	1	145	4.1	19	0	0.0	24:15	14	7	1	8	22	4	1	2	23:40
2003-04	**Vancouver**	**NHL**	56	7	16	23	64	2	0	1	143	4.9	2	0	0.0	23:11	7	0	4	4	6	0	0	0	26:36
2004-05				DID NOT PLAY																				
2005-06	**Vancouver**	**NHL**	44	8	25	33	58	6	0	2	87	9.2	-8	0	0.0	24:26									
	Canada	Olympics			DID NOT PLAY – INJURED																				
	NHL Totals		**687**	**86**	**231**	**317**	**1085**	**30**	**2**	**17**	**1326**	**6.5**		**0**	**0.0**	**24:03**	**58**	**10**	**18**	**28**	**92**	**5**	**1**	**2**	**25:02**

OHL All-Rookie Team (1994) • OHL Second All-Star Team (1994) • OHL First All-Star Team (1995) • NHL All-Rookie Team (1996)
Played in NHL All-Star Game (2001, 2002, 2003)
Traded to **Vancouver** by **Florida** with Dave Gagner, Mike Brown, Kevin Weekes and Florida's 1st round choice (Nathan Smith) in 2000 Entry Draft for Pavel Bure, Bret Hedican, Brad Ference and Vancouver's 3rd round choice (Robert Fried) in 2000 Entry Draft, January 17, 1999. Signed as a free agent by **Phoenix**, July 1, 2006.

JURCINA, Milan

(YEWR-chee-nah, MEE-lan) **BOS.**

Defense. Shoots right. 6'4", 233 lbs.   Born, Liptovsky Mikulas, Czech., June 7, 1983. Boston's 7th choice, 241st overall, in 2001 Entry Draft.

Season	Club	League	GP	G	A	Pts	PIM	PP	SH	GW	S	%	+/-	TF	F%	Min	GP	G	A	Pts	PIM	PP	SH	GW	Min
99-2000	L. Mikulas Jr.	Slovak-Jr.		STATISTICS NOT AVAILABLE																					
2000-01	Halifax	QMJHL	68	0	5	5	56										6	0	2	2	12				
2001-02	Halifax	QMJHL	61	4	16	20	58										13	5	3	8	10				
2002-03	Halifax	QMJHL	51	15	13	28	102										25	6	6	12	40				
2003-04	Providence Bruins	AHL	73	5	12	17	52										2	0	1	1	2				
2004-05	Providence Bruins	AHL	79	6	17	23	92										17	1	3	4	30				
2005-06	**Boston**	**NHL**	51	6	5	11	54	2	0	0	64	9.4	-9	1	0.0	16:28									
	Providence Bruins	AHL	7	0	3	3	8																		
	Slovakia	Olympics	6	0	1	1	8																		
	NHL Totals		**51**	**6**	**5**	**11**	**54**	**2**	**0**	**0**	**64**	**9.4**		**1**	**0.0**	**16:28**									

KABERLE, Frantisek

(KA-buhr-lay, FRAN-tih-sehk) **CAR.**

Defense. Shoots left. 6'1", 190 lbs.   Born, Kladno, Czech., November 8, 1973. Los Angeles' 3rd choice, 76th overall, in 1999 Entry Draft.

Season	Club	League	GP	G	A	Pts	PIM	PP	SH	GW	S	%	+/-	TF	F%	Min	GP	G	A	Pts	PIM	PP	SH	GW	Min
1991-92	Poldi Kladno	Czech	37	1	4	5	8										8	0	1	1	0				
1992-93	Poldi Kladno	Czech	40	4	5	9												9	2	4	6					
1993-94	HC Kladno	CzRep	41	4	16	20												11	1	1	2					
1994-95	HC Kladno	CzRep	40	7	17	24	20										8	0	3	3	12				
1995-96	MoDo	Sweden	40	5	7	12	34										8	0	1	1	0				
1996-97	MoDo	Sweden	50	3	11	14	28																		
1997-98	MoDo	Sweden	46	5	4	9	22										9	1	1	2	4				
1998-99	MoDo	Sweden	45	15	18	33	4										13	2	5	7	8				
99-2000	**Los Angeles**	**NHL**	37	0	9	9	4	0	0	0	41	0.0	3	0	0.0	17:04									
	Long Beach	IHL	18	2	8	10	8																		
	Atlanta	**NHL**	14	1	6	7	6	0	1	0	35	2.9	-13	0	0.0	24:39									
	Lowell	AHL	4	0	4	4	4																		
2000-01	**Atlanta**	**NHL**	51	4	11	15	18	1	0	1	99	4.0	11	1	0.0	22:17									
2001-02	**Atlanta**	**NHL**	61	5	20	25	24	1	0	0	82	6.1	-11	0	0.0	21:35									
2002-03	**Atlanta**	**NHL**	79	7	19	26	32	3	1	0	105	6.7	-19	0	0.0	21:57									
2003-04	**Atlanta**	**NHL**	67	3	26	29	30	2	0	1	94	3.2	2	2	50.0	23:20									
2004-05	HC Rabat Kladno	CzRep	22	5	11	16	34										6	1	0	1	27				
	MODO	Sweden	8	2	2	4	0																		
2005-06♦	**Carolina**	**NHL**	77	6	38	44	46	1	0	3	126	4.8	8	0	0.0	19:37	25	4	9	13	8	3	0	1	18:25
	Czech Republic	Olympics	8	0	1	1	6																		
	NHL Totals		**386**	**26**	**129**	**155**	**160**							**3**	**33.3**	**21:20**	**25**	**4**	**9**	**13**	**8**	**3**	**0**	**1**	**18:25**

Traded to **Atlanta** by **Los Angeles** with Donald Audette for Kelly Buchberger and Nelson Emerson, March 13, 2000. Signed as a free agent by **Carolina**, July 15, 2004. Signed as a free agent by **Kladno** (CzRep), September 17, 2004. Signed as a free agent by **MODO** (Sweden), January 31, 2005.

KABERLE, Tomas

(KA-buhr-lay, TAW-mas) **TOR.**

Defense. Shoots left. 6'1", 198 lbs.   Born, Rakovnik, Czech., March 2, 1978. Toronto's 13th choice, 204th overall, in 1996 Entry Draft.

Season	Club	League	GP	G	A	Pts	PIM	PP	SH	GW	S	%	+/-	TF	F%	Min	GP	G	A	Pts	PIM	PP	SH	GW	Min
1994-95	HC Kladno Jr.	CzRep-Jr.	37	7	10	17																				
	HC Kladno	CzRep	4	0	1	1	0																		
1995-96	Kladno Jr.	CzRep-Jr.	23	6	13	19																				
	HC Poldi Kladno	CzRep	23	0	1	1	2										2	0	0	0	0				
1996-97	HC Poldi Kladno	CzRep	49	0	5	5	26										3	0	0	0	0				
1997-98	Kladno	CzRep	47	4	19	23	12																		
	St. John's	AHL	2	0	0	0	0																		
1998-99	**Toronto**	**NHL**	57	4	18	22	12	0	0	2	71	5.6	3	0	0.0	18:42	14	0	3	3	2	0	0	0	17:10
99-2000	**Toronto**	**NHL**	82	7	33	40	24	2	0	0	82	8.5	9	0	0.0	22:55	12	1	4	5	0	0	0	1	23:01
2000-01	**Toronto**	**NHL**	82	6	39	45	24	0	0	1	96	6.3	10	2	0.0	22:41	11	1	3	4	0	0	0	1	21:33
2001-02	Kladno	CzRep	9	1	7	8	4																		
	Toronto	**NHL**	69	10	29	39	2	5	0	3	85	11.8	5				20	2	8	10	16	0	0	0	28:40
	Czech Republic	Olympics	4	0	1	1	2							2	100.0	25:00									
2002-03	**Toronto**	**NHL**	82	11	36	47	30	4	1	2	119	9.2	20	3	66.7	24:50	7	2	1	3	0	0	0	1	30:04
2003-04	**Toronto**	**NHL**	71	3	28	31	18	0	0	1	88	3.4	16	2	0.0	23:12	13	0	3	3	6	0	0	0	20:16
2004-05	HC Rabat Kladno	CzRep	49	8	31	39	38																		
2005-06	**Toronto**	**NHL**	82	9	58	67	46	6	0	2	163	5.5	-1	0	0.0	28:10									
	Czech Republic	Olympics	8	2	2	4	2																		
	NHL Totals		**525**	**50**	**241**	**291**	**156**	**17**	**1**	**11**	**704**	**7.1**		**9**	**44.4**	**23:51**	**77**	**6**	**22**	**28**	**24**	**1**	**0**	**3**	**23:23**

Played in NHL All-Star Game (2002)
Signed as a restricted free agent by **Kladno** (CzRep) with **Toronto** retaining NHL rights, September 29, 2001. Signed as a free agent by **Kladno** (CzRep), September 17, 2004.

			Regular Season														Playoffs								
Season	Club	League	GP	G	A	Pts	PIM	PP	SH	GW	S	%	+/-	TF	F%	Min	GP	G	A	Pts	PIM	PP	SH	GW	Min

KALININ, Dmitri
(kah-LIHN-ihn, DIH-mih-TREE) **BUF.**

Defense. Shoots left. 6'3", 206 lbs. Born, Chelyabinsk, USSR, July 22, 1980. Buffalo's 1st choice, 18th overall, in 1998 Entry Draft.

Season	Club	League	GP	G	A	Pts	PIM	PP	SH	GW	S	%	+/-	TF	F%	Min	GP	G	A	Pts	PIM	PP	SH	GW	Min
1995-96	Chelyabinsk	CIS	20	0	3	3	10	....	....	....	....	....	....	....	....	....	....	....	....	....	....	....	....	....	....
1996-97	Yunior-T Kurgan	Russia-3	20	0	0	0	10	....	....	....	....	....	....	....	....	....	....	....	....	....	....	....	....	....	....
	Chelyabinsk	Russia	2	0	0	0	0	....	....	....	....	....	....	....	....	....	2	0	0	0	0	....	....	....	....
1997-98	Chelyabinsk	Russia	26	0	2	2	24	....	....	....	....	....	....	....	....	....	....	....	....	....	....	....	....	....	....
1998-99	Moncton Wildcats	QMJHL	39	7	18	25	44	....	....	....	....	....	....	....	....	....	4	1	1	2	0	....	....	....	....
	Rochester	AHL	3	0	1	1	14	....	....	....	....	....	....	....	....	....	7	0	0	0	6	....	....	....	....
99-2000	**Buffalo**	**NHL**	**4**	**0**	**0**	**0**	**4**	**0**	**0**	**0**	**3**	**0.0**	**0**	**0**	**0.0**	**16:53**	....	....	....	....	....	....	....	....	....
	Rochester	AHL	75	2	19	21	52	....	....	....	....	....	....	....	....	....	21	2	9	11	8	....	....	....	....
2000-01	**Buffalo**	**NHL**	**79**	**4**	**18**	**22**	**38**	**2**	**0**	**0**	**88**	**4.5**	**–2**	**1**	**100.0**	**19:50**	**13**	**0**	**2**	**2**	**4**	**0**	**0**	**0**	**20:05**
2001-02	**Buffalo**	**NHL**	**58**	**2**	**11**	**13**	**26**	**0**	**0**	**0**	**67**	**3.0**	**–6**	**0**	**0.0**	**18:03**	....	....	....	....	....	....	....	....	....
2002-03	**Buffalo**	**NHL**	**65**	**8**	**13**	**21**	**57**	**3**	**1**	**0**	**83**	**9.6**	**–7**	**0**	**0.0**	**21:41**	....	....	....	....	....	....	....	....	....
	Rochester	AHL	1	0	0	0	0	....	....	....	....	....	....	....	....	....	....	....	....	....	....	....	....	....	....
2003-04	**Buffalo**	**NHL**	**77**	**10**	**24**	**34**	**42**	**2**	**1**	**4**	**118**	**8.5**	**0**	**0**	**0.0**	**23:06**	....	....	....	....	....	....	....	....	....
2004-05	Magnitogorsk	Russia	48	2	8	10	14	....	....	....	....	....	....	....	....	....	5	0	0	0	2	....	....	....	....
2005-06	**Buffalo**	**NHL**	**55**	**2**	**16**	**18**	**54**	**0**	**0**	**0**	**47**	**4.3**	**14**	**0**	**0.0**	**16:45**	**8**	**0**	**2**	**2**	**2**	**0**	**0**	**0**	**16:53**
	NHL Totals		**338**	**26**	**82**	**108**	**221**	**7**	**2**	**4**	**406**	**6.4**		**1**	**100.0**	**20:05**	**21**	**0**	**4**	**4**	**6**	**0**	**0**	**0**	**18:52**

AHL All-Rookie Team (2000)

Signed as a free agent by **Magnitogorsk** (Russia), September 25, 2004.

KANE, Boyd
(KAYN, BOIYD) **PHI.**

Left wing. Shoots left. 6'2", 218 lbs. Born, Swift Current, Sask., April 18, 1978. NY Rangers' 4th choice, 114th overall, in 1998 Entry Draft.

Season	Club	League	GP	G	A	Pts	PIM	PP	SH	GW	S	%	+/-	TF	F%	Min	GP	G	A	Pts	PIM	PP	SH	GW	Min
1994-95	Regina Pats	WHL	25	6	5	11	6	....	....	....	....	....	....	....	....	....	4	0	0	0	0	....	....	....	....
1995-96	Regina Pats	WHL	72	21	42	63	155	....	....	....	....	....	....	....	....	....	11	5	7	12	12	....	....	....	....
1996-97	Regina Pats	WHL	66	25	50	75	154	....	....	....	....	....	....	....	....	....	5	1	1	2	15	....	....	....	....
1997-98	Regina Pats	WHL	68	48	45	93	133	....	....	....	....	....	....	....	....	....	9	5	7	12	29	....	....	....	....
1998-99	Hartford	AHL	56	3	5	8	23	....	....	....	....	....	....	....	....	....	....	....	....	....	....	....	....	....	....
	Charlotte	ECHL	12	5	6	11	14	....	....	....	....	....	....	....	....	....	....	....	....	....	....	....	....	....	....
99-2000	Charlotte	ECHL	47	10	19	29	110	....	....	....	....	....	....	....	....	....	....	....	....	....	....	....	....	....	....
	Hartford	AHL	8	0	0	0	9	....	....	....	....	....	....	....	....	....	....	....	....	....	....	....	....	....	....
	Binghamton	UHL	3	0	2	2	4	....	....	....	....	....	....	....	....	....	1	0	0	0	0	....	....	....	....
2000-01	Charlotte	ECHL	12	9	8	17	6	....	....	....	....	....	....	....	....	....	....	....	....	....	....	....	....	....	....
	Hartford	AHL	56	11	17	28	81	....	....	....	....	....	....	....	....	....	5	2	0	2	2	....	....	....	....
2001-02	Hartford	AHL	78	17	22	39	193	....	....	....	....	....	....	....	....	....	10	1	2	3	50	....	....	....	....
2002-03	Springfield	AHL	72	15	22	37	121	....	....	....	....	....	....	....	....	....	6	3	1	4	8	....	....	....	....
2003-04	**Philadelphia**	**NHL**	**7**	**0**	**0**	**0**	**7**	**0**	**0**	**0**	**6**	**0.0**	**–4**	**3**	**33.3**	**9:56**	....	....	....	....	....	....	....	....	....
	Philadelphia	AHL	73	13	22	35	177	....	....	....	....	....	....	....	....	....	12	0	1	1	39	....	....	....	....
2004-05	Philadelphia	AHL	58	9	15	24	112	....	....	....	....	....	....	....	....	....	21	0	7	7	28	....	....	....	....
2005-06	**Washington**	**NHL**	**5**	**0**	**1**	**1**	**2**	**0**	**0**	**0**	**1**	**0.0**	**1**	**0**	**0.0**	**4:04**	....	....	....	....	....	....	....	....	....
	Hershey Bears	AHL	74	20	29	49	185	....	....	....	....	....	....	....	....	....	21	4	9	13	14	....	....	....	....
	NHL Totals		**12**	**0**	**1**	**1**	**9**	**0**	**0**	**0**	**7**	**0.0**		**3**	**33.3**	**7:30**	....	....	....	....	....	....	....	....	....

• Re-entered NHL Entry Draft. Originally Pittsburgh's 3rd choice, 72nd overall, in 1996 Entry Draft.

Traded to **Tampa Bay** by **NY Rangers** for Gordie Dwyer, October 10, 2002. Signed as a free agent by **Philadelphia**, July 14, 2003. Signed as a free agent by **Washington**, August 12, 2005. Signed as a free agent by **Philadelphia**, July 13, 2006.

KANKO, Petr
(KAN-koh, PEE-tuhr) **L.A.**

Right wing. Shoots left. 5'9", 195 lbs. Born, Pribram, Czech., February 7, 1984. Los Angeles' 3rd choice, 66th overall, in 2002 Entry Draft.

Season	Club	League	GP	G	A	Pts	PIM	PP	SH	GW	S	%	+/-	TF	F%	Min	GP	G	A	Pts	PIM	PP	SH	GW	Min
2000-01	Sparta Jr.	CzRep-Jr.	43	27	10	37	80	....	....	....	....	....	....	....	....	....	....	....	....	....	....	....	....	....	....
	HC Sparta Praha	CzRep	6	1	0	1	0	....	....	....	....	....	....	....	....	....	....	....	....	....	....	....	....	....	....
2001-02	Kitchener Rangers	OHL	61	28	32	60	54	....	....	....	....	....	....	....	....	....	4	0	2	2	0	....	....	....	....
2002-03	Kitchener Rangers	OHL	60	33	34	67	123	....	....	....	....	....	....	....	....	....	20	11	16	27	17	....	....	....	....
2003-04	Kitchener Rangers	OHL	55	26	42	68	97	....	....	....	....	....	....	....	....	....	5	2	2	4	10	....	....	....	....
	Manchester	AHL	6	1	3	4	0	....	....	....	....	....	....	....	....	....	6	1	3	4	2	....	....	....	....
2004-05	Manchester	AHL	60	4	14	18	118	....	....	....	....	....	....	....	....	....	6	0	0	0	18	....	....	....	....
2005-06	**Los Angeles**	**NHL**	**10**	**1**	**0**	**1**	**0**	**0**	**0**	**0**	**7**	**14.3**	**1**	**0**	**0.0**	**4:42**	....	....	....	....	....	....	....	....	....
	Manchester	AHL	60	15	12	27	52	....	....	....	....	....	....	....	....	....	7	1	1	2	5	....	....	....	....
	NHL Totals		**10**	**1**	**0**	**1**	**0**	**0**	**0**	**0**	**7**	**14.3**		**0**	**0.0**	**4:42**	....	....	....	....	....	....	....	....	....

KAPANEN, Niko
(KA-pah-nehn, NEE-KOH) **ATL.**

Center. Shoots left. 5'9", 180 lbs. Born, Hameenlinna, Finland, April 29, 1978. Dallas' 5th choice, 173rd overall, in 1998 Entry Draft.

Season	Club	League	GP	G	A	Pts	PIM	PP	SH	GW	S	%	+/-	TF	F%	Min	GP	G	A	Pts	PIM	PP	SH	GW	Min
1993-94	HPK U18	Fin-U18	31	17	33	50	34	....	....	....	....	....	....	....	....	....	....	....	....	....	....	....	....	....	....
1994-95	HPK U18	Fin-U18	31	16	39	55	40	....	....	....	....	....	....	....	....	....	....	....	....	....	....	....	....	....	....
	HPK Jr.	Fin-Jr.	6	3	5	8	0	....	....	....	....	....	....	....	....	....	....	....	....	....	....	....	....	....	....
1995-96	HPK U18	Fin-U18	10	6	6	12	8	....	....	....	....	....	....	....	....	....	....	....	....	....	....	....	....	....	....
	HPK Jr.	Fin-Jr.	26	15	22	37	34	....	....	....	....	....	....	....	....	....	....	....	....	....	....	....	....	....	....
	HPK Hameenlinna	Finland	7	1	0	1	0	....	....	....	....	....	....	....	....	....	....	....	....	....	....	....	....	....	....
1996-97	HPK Jr.	Fin-Jr.	5	1	7	8	2	....	....	....	....	....	....	....	....	....	2	0	1	1	2	....	....	....	....
	HPK Hameenlinna	Finland	41	6	9	15	12	....	....	....	....	....	....	....	....	....	10	4	5	9	2	....	....	....	....
	HPK Hameenlinna	EuroHL	6	3	0	3	4	....	....	....	....	....	....	....	....	....	1	0	0	0	0	....	....	....	....
1997-98	HPK Jr.	Fin-Jr.	2	1	1	2	0	....	....	....	....	....	....	....	....	....	....	....	....	....	....	....	....	....	....
	HPK Hameenlinna	Finland	48	8	18	26	44	....	....	....	....	....	....	....	....	....	....	....	....	....	....	....	....	....	....
1998-99	HPK Jr.	Fin-Jr.	5	3	1	4	0	....	....	....	....	....	....	....	....	....	1	0	2	2	0	....	....	....	....
	HPK Hameenlinna	Finland	53	14	29	43	49	....	....	....	....	....	....	....	....	....	8	3	4	7	4	....	....	....	....
99-2000	HPK Hameenlinna	Finland	53	20	28	48	38	....	....	....	....	....	....	....	....	....	8	1	9	10	4	....	....	....	....
2000-01	TPS Turku	Finland	56	11	22	33	20	....	....	....	....	....	....	....	....	....	10	2	1	3	4	....	....	....	....
2001-02	**Dallas**	**NHL**	**9**	**0**	**1**	**1**	**2**	**0**	**0**	**0**	**3**	**0.0**	**–1**	**59**	**40.7**	**9:44**	....	....	....	....	....	....	....	....	....
	Utah Grizzlies	AHL	59	13	28	41	40	....	....	....	....	....	....	....	....	....	5	2	1	3	0	....	....	....	....
2002-03	**Dallas**	**NHL**	**82**	**5**	**29**	**34**	**44**	**0**	**1**	**1**	**80**	**6.3**	**25**	**1111**	**47.5**	**14:39**	**12**	**4**	**3**	**7**	**12**	**0**	**1**	**0**	**16:03**
2003-04	**Dallas**	**NHL**	**67**	**1**	**5**	**6**	**16**	**0**	**0**	**0**	**57**	**1.8**	**–15**	**619**	**47.7**	**11:30**	**1**	**0**	**0**	**1**	**0**	**0**	**0**	**0**	**6:51**
2004-05	EV Zug	Swiss	44	10	33	43	24	....	....	....	....	....	....	....	....	....	9	2	5	7	35	....	....	....	....
2005-06	**Dallas**	**NHL**	**81**	**14**	**21**	**35**	**36**	**5**	**2**	**4**	**97**	**14.4**	**–10**	**798**	**49.9**	**14:13**	**5**	**0**	**1**	**1**	**10**	**0**	**0**	**0**	**14:52**
	Finland	Olympics	8	2	1	3	2	....	....	....	....	....	....	....	....	....	....	....	....	....	....	....	....	....	....
	NHL Totals		**239**	**20**	**56**	**76**	**98**	**5**	**3**	**5**	**237**	**8.4**		**2587**	**48.1**	**13:26**	**18**	**5**	**4**	**9**	**22**	**0**	**1**	**0**	**15:13**

Signed as a free agent by **Zug** (Swiss), June 9, 2004. Traded to **Atlanta** by **Dallas** with Dallas' 7th round choice (Will O'Neill) in 2006 Entry Draft for Patrik Stefan and Jaroslav Modry, June 24, 2006.

KAPANEN, Sami
(KA-pah-nehn, SA-mee) **PHI.**

Right wing. Shoots left. 5'10", 185 lbs. Born, Vantaa, Finland, June 14, 1973. Hartford's 4th choice, 87th overall, in 1995 Entry Draft.

Season	Club	League	GP	G	A	Pts	PIM	PP	SH	GW	S	%	+/-	TF	F%	Min	GP	G	A	Pts	PIM	PP	SH	GW	Min
1989-90	KalPa Kuopio Jr.	Fin-Jr.	30	14	13	27	4	....	....	....	....	....	....	....	....	....	....	....	....	....	....	....	....	....	....
1990-91	KalPa Kuopio Jr.	Fin-Jr.	31	9	27	36	10	....	....	....	....	....	....	....	....	....	....	....	....	....	....	....	....	....	....
	KalPa Kuopio	Finland	14	1	2	3	2	....	....	....	....	....	....	....	....	....	8	2	1	3	2	....	....	....	....
1991-92	KalPa Kuopio Jr.	Fin-Jr.	8	1	3	4	12	....	....	....	....	....	....	....	....	....	....	....	....	....	....	....	....	....	....
	KalPa Kuopio	Finland	42	15	10	25	8	....	....	....	....	....	....	....	....	....	....	....	....	....	....	....	....	....	....
1992-93	KalPa Kuopio Jr.	Fin-Jr.	8	11	16	27	2	....	....	....	....	....	....	....	....	....	....	....	....	....	....	....	....	....	....
	KalPa Kuopio	Finland	37	4	17	21	12	....	....	....	....	....	....	....	....	....	....	....	....	....	....	....	....	....	....
1993-94	KalPa Kuopio	Finland	48	23	32	55	16	....	....	....	....	....	....	....	....	....	....	....	....	....	....	....	....	....	....
	Finland	Olympics	8	1	0	1	2	....	....	....	....	....	....	....	....	....	....	....	....	....	....	....	....	....	....
1994-95	HIFK Helsinki	Finland	49	14	28	42	42	....	....	....	....	....	....	....	....	....	3	0	0	0	0	....	....	....	....
1995-96	**Hartford**	**NHL**	**35**	**5**	**4**	**9**	**6**	**0**	**0**	**0**	**46**	**10.9**	**0**				....	....	....	....	....	....	....	....	....
	Springfield	AHL	28	14	17	31	4	....	....	....	....	....	....	....	....	....	3	1	2	3	0	....	....	....	....
1996-97	**Hartford**	**NHL**	**45**	**13**	**12**	**25**	**2**	**3**	**0**	**2**	**82**	**15.9**	**6**				....	....	....	....	....	....	....	....	....
1997-98	**Carolina**	**NHL**	**81**	**26**	**37**	**63**	**16**	**4**	**0**	**5**	**190**	**13.7**	**9**				....	....	....	....	....	....	....	....	....
	Finland	Olympics	6	0	1	1	0	....	....	....	....	....	....	....	....	....	....	....	....	....	....	....	....	....	....
1998-99	**Carolina**	**NHL**	**81**	**24**	**35**	**59**	**10**	**5**	**0**	**7**	**254**	**9.4**	**–1**	**10**	**50.0**	**19:25**	**5**	**1**	**1**	**2**	**0**	**0**	**0**	**0**	**19:09**
99-2000	**Carolina**	**NHL**	**76**	**24**	**24**	**48**	**12**	**7**	**0**	**5**	**229**	**10.5**	**10**	**2**	**50.0**	**19:53**	....	....	....	....	....	....	....	....	....

Season	Club	League	GP	G	A	Pts	PIM	PP	SH	GW	S	%	+/-	TF	F%	Min	GP	G	A	Pts	PIM	PP	SH	GW	Min
			Regular Season														Playoffs								
2000-01	**Carolina**	**NHL**	**82**	**20**	**37**	**57**	**24**	**7**	**0**	**4**	**223**	**9.0**	**−12**	**6**	**16.7**	**18:56**	**6**	**2**	**3**	**5**	**0**	**1**	**0**	**0**	**20:13**
2001-02	**Carolina**	**NHL**	**77**	**27**	**42**	**69**	**23**	**11**	**0**	**4**	**248**	**10.9**	**9**	**7**	**14.3**	**20:38**	**23**	**1**	**8**	**9**	**6**	**0**	**0**	**0**	**20:03**
	Finland	Olympics	4	1	2	3	4	....	....	....	....	....	....	....	....	....	....	....	....	....	....	....	....	....	....
2002-03	**Carolina**	**NHL**	**43**	**6**	**12**	**18**	**12**	**3**	**0**	**1**	**108**	**5.6**	**−17**	**16**	**31.3**	**18:37**	....	....	....	....	....	....	....	....	....
	Philadelphia	**NHL**	**28**	**4**	**9**	**13**	**6**	**2**	**0**	**1**	**81**	**4.9**	**−1**	**5**	**40.0**	**19:21**	**13**	**4**	**3**	**7**	**6**	**2**	**0**	**0**	**20:12**
2003-04	**Philadelphia**	**NHL**	**74**	**12**	**18**	**30**	**14**	**0**	**1**	**2**	**149**	**8.1**	**9**	**18**	**44.4**	**16:31**	**18**	**3**	**7**	**10**	**6**	**0**	**1**	**1**	**17:41**
2004-05	KalPa Kuopio	Finland-2	10	6	3	9	2	....	....	....	....	....	....	....	....	....	9	5	3	8	4	....	....	....	....
2005-06	**Philadelphia**	**NHL**	**58**	**12**	**22**	**34**	**12**	**3**	**4**	**2**	**123**	**9.8**	**−9**	**43**	**39.5**	**18:04**	**6**	**0**	**0**	**0**	**2**	**0**	**0**	**0**	**20:19**
	NHL Totals		**680**	**173**	**252**	**425**	**137**	**45**	**5**	**33**	**1733**	**10.0**		**107**	**37.4**	**18:57**	**71**	**11**	**22**	**33**	**20**	**3**	**1**	**1**	**19:27**

Played in NHL All-Star Game (2000, 2002)

Transferred to **Carolina** after **Hartford** franchise relocated, June 25, 1997. Traded to **Philadelphia** by **Carolina** with Ryan Bast for Pavel Brendl and Bruno St. Jacques, February 7, 2003. Signed as a free agent by **Kuopio** (Finland-2), November 17, 2004.

KARIYA, Paul

(kah-REE-ah, PAWL) **NSH.**

Left wing. Shoots left. 5'10", 176 lbs. Born, Vancouver, B.C., October 16, 1974. Anaheim's 1st choice, 4th overall, in 1993 Entry Draft.

Season	Club	League	GP	G	A	Pts	PIM	PP	SH	GW	S	%	+/-	TF	F%	Min	GP	G	A	Pts	PIM	PP	SH	GW	Min
1990-91	Penticton	BCJHL	54	45	67	112	8	....	....	....	....	....	....	....	....	....	....	....	....	....	....	....	....	....	....
1991-92	Penticton	BCJHL	40	46	86	132	18	....	....	....	....	....	....	....	....	....	....	....	....	....	....	....	....	....	....
1992-93	U. of Maine	H-East	39	25	*75	*100	12	....	....	....	....	....	....	....	....	....	....	....	....	....	....	....	....	....	....
1993-94	U. of Maine	H-East	12	8	16	24	4	....	....	....	....	....	....	....	....	....	....	....	....	....	....	....	....	....	....
	Canada	Nat-Tm	23	7	34	41	2	....	....	....	....	....	....	....	....	....	....	....	....	....	....	....	....	....	....
	Canada	Olympics	8	3	4	7	2	....	....	....	....	....	....	....	....	....	....	....	....	....	....	....	....	....	....
1994-95	**Anaheim**	**NHL**	**47**	**18**	**21**	**39**	**4**	**7**	**1**	**3**	**134**	**13.4**	**−17**	....	....	....	....	....	....	....	....	....	....	....	....
1995-96	**Anaheim**	**NHL**	**82**	**50**	**58**	**108**	**20**	**20**	**3**	**9**	**349**	**14.3**	**9**	....	....	....	....	....	....	....	....	....	....	....	....
1996-97	**Anaheim**	**NHL**	**69**	**44**	**55**	**99**	**6**	**15**	**3**	**10**	**340**	**12.9**	**36**	....	....	....	**11**	**7**	**6**	**13**	**4**	**4**	**0**	**1**	....
1997-98	**Anaheim**	**NHL**	**22**	**17**	**14**	**31**	**23**	**3**	**0**	**2**	**103**	**16.5**	**12**	....	....	....	....	....	....	....	....	....	....	....	....
1998-99	**Anaheim**	**NHL**	**82**	**39**	**62**	**101**	**40**	**11**	**2**	**4**	**429**	**9.1**	**17**	**91**	**48.4**	**25:32**	**3**	**1**	**3**	**4**	**0**	**0**	**0**	**0**	**26:03**
99-2000	**Anaheim**	**NHL**	**74**	**42**	**44**	**86**	**24**	**11**	**3**	**3**	**324**	**13.0**	**22**	**99**	**39.4**	**24:22**	....	....	....	....	....	....	....	....	....
2000-01	**Anaheim**	**NHL**	**66**	**33**	**34**	**67**	**20**	**18**	**3**	**3**	**230**	**14.3**	**−9**	**149**	**44.3**	**23:02**	....	....	....	....	....	....	....	....	....
2001-02	**Anaheim**	**NHL**	**82**	**32**	**25**	**57**	**28**	**11**	**0**	**8**	**289**	**11.1**	**−15**	**94**	**41.5**	**22:13**	....	....	....	....	....	....	....	....	....
	Canada	Olympics	6	3	1	4	0	....	....	....	....	....	....	....	....	....	....	....	....	....	....	....	....	....	....
2002-03	**Anaheim**	**NHL**	**82**	**25**	**56**	**81**	**48**	**11**	**1**	**2**	**257**	**9.7**	**−3**	**39**	**30.8**	**20:17**	**21**	**6**	**6**	**12**	**6**	**0**	**0**	**1**	**21:15**
2003-04	**Colorado**	**NHL**	**51**	**11**	**25**	**36**	**22**	**5**	**1**	**1**	**110**	**10.0**	**−5**	**18**	**27.8**	**18:37**	**1**	**0**	**1**	**1**	**0**	**0**	**0**	**0**	**16:00**
2004-05			DID NOT PLAY																						
2005-06	**Nashville**	**NHL**	**82**	**31**	**54**	**85**	**40**	**14**	**0**	**3**	**245**	**12.7**	**−6**	**9**	**11.1**	**19:05**	**5**	**2**	**5**	**7**	**0**	**2**	**0**	**0**	**20:47**
	NHL Totals		**739**	**342**	**448**	**790**	**275**	**126**	**17**	**48**	**2810**	**12.2**		**499**	**41.3**	**22:00**	**41**	**16**	**21**	**37**	**10**	**6**	**0**	**2**	**21:28**

Hockey East First All-Star Team (1993) • Hockey East Rookie of the Year (1993) • Hockey East Player of the Year (1993) • NCAA East First All-American Team (1993) • NCAA Championship All-Tournament Team (1993) • Hobey Baker Memorial Award (Top U.S. Collegiate Player) (1993) • NHL All-Rookie Team (1995) • Lady Byng Trophy (1996, 1997) • NHL First All-Star Team (1996, 1997, 1999) • NHL Second All-Star Team (2000, 2003)

Played in NHL All-Star Game (1996, 1997, 1999, 2000, 2001, 2002, 2003)

• Missed majority of 1997-98 season after failing to come to contract terms with **Anaheim** and recovering from head injury suffered in game vs. San Jose, February 1, 1998. Signed as a free agent by **Colorado**, July 3, 2003. Signed as a free agent by **Nashville**, August 5, 2005.

KARLSSON, Andreas

(KARLS-uhn, AN-dray-uhs) **T.B.**

Center. Shoots left. 6'4", 205 lbs. Born, Ludvika, Sweden, August 19, 1975. Calgary's 8th choice, 148th overall, in 1993 Entry Draft.

Season	Club	League	GP	G	A	Pts	PIM	PP	SH	GW	S	%	+/-	TF	F%	Min	GP	G	A	Pts	PIM	PP	SH	GW	Min
1992-93	Leksands IF	Sweden	13	0	0	0	6	....	....	....	....	....	....	....	....	....	....	....	....	....	....	....	....	....	....
1993-94	Leksands IF	Sweden	21	0	0	0	10	....	....	....	....	....	....	....	....	....	3	0	0	0	0	....	....	....	....
1994-95	Leksands IF Jr.	Swe-Jr.	3	3	3	6	0	....	....	....	....	....	....	....	....	....	....	....	....	....	....	....	....	....	....
	Leksands IF	Sweden	24	7	8	15	0	....	....	....	....	....	....	....	....	....	4	0	1	1	0	....	....	....	....
1995-96	Leksands IF Jr.	Swe-Jr.	2	4	1	5	6	....	....	....	....	....	....	....	....	....	....	....	....	....	....	....	....	....	....
	Leksands IF	Sweden	40	10	13	23	10	....	....	....	....	....	....	....	....	....	....	....	....	....	....	....	....	....	....
1996-97	Leksands IF	Sweden	49	13	11	24	39	....	....	....	....	....	....	....	....	....	9	2	0	2	2	....	....	....	....
1997-98	Leksands IF	Sweden	33	9	14	23	20	....	....	....	....	....	....	....	....	....	4	1	0	1	0	....	....	....	....
	Leksands IF	EuroHL	6	2	3	5	2	....	....	....	....	....	....	....	....	....	....	....	....	....	....	....	....	....	....
1998-99	Leksands IF	Sweden	49	18	15	33	18	....	....	....	....	....	....	....	....	....	4	1	0	1	6	....	....	....	....
	Leksands IF	EuroHL	6	1	3	4	2	....	....	....	....	....	....	....	....	....	2	1	1	2	2	....	....	....	....
99-2000	**Atlanta**	**NHL**	**51**	**5**	**9**	**14**	**14**	**1**	**0**	**0**	**74**	**6.8**	**−17**	**552**	**46.7**	**13:00**	....	....	....	....	....	....	....	....	....
	Orlando	IHL	18	5	5	10	6	....	....	....	....	....	....	....	....	....	....	....	....	....	....	....	....	....	....
2000-01	**Atlanta**	**NHL**	**60**	**5**	**11**	**16**	**16**	**0**	**1**	**0**	**83**	**6.0**	**−2**	**743**	**48.6**	**12:54**	....	....	....	....	....	....	....	....	....
2001-02	**Atlanta**	**NHL**	**42**	**1**	**7**	**8**	**20**	**0**	**0**	**0**	**41**	**2.4**	**−8**	**386**	**45.1**	**12:30**	....	....	....	....	....	....	....	....	....
	Chicago Wolves	AHL	16	6	14	20	11	....	....	....	....	....	....	....	....	....	23	7	14	21	6	....	....	....	....
2002-03	Chicago Wolves	AHL	41	12	20	32	16	....	....	....	....	....	....	....	....	....	9	1	3	4	4	....	....	....	....
2003-04	EHC Basel	Swiss	40	7	21	28	30	....	....	....	....	....	....	....	....	....	....	....	....	....	....	....	....	....	....
2004-05	HV 71 Jonkoping	Sweden	39	11	13	24	12	....	....	....	....	....	....	....	....	....	....	....	....	....	....	....	....	....	....
2005-06	HV 71 Jonkoping	Sweden	50	*26	29	*55	30	....	....	....	....	....	....	....	....	....	12	5	8	13	8	....	....	....	....
	NHL Totals		**153**	**11**	**27**	**38**	**50**	**1**	**1**	**0**	**198**	**5.6**		**1681**	**47.2**	**12:49**	....	....	....	....	....	....	....	....	....

Traded to **Atlanta** by **Calgary** for future considerations, June 25, 1999. Signed as a free agent by **Basel** (Swiss), July 18, 2003. Signed as a free agent by **Tampa Bay**, July 1, 2006.

KARPOVTSEV, Alexander

(kar-POHV-tzehv, al-ehx-AN-duhr)

Defense. Shoots right. 6'3", 221 lbs. Born, Moscow, USSR, April 7, 1970. Quebec's 7th choice, 158th overall, in 1990 Entry Draft.

Season	Club	League	GP	G	A	Pts	PIM	PP	SH	GW	S	%	+/-	TF	F%	Min	GP	G	A	Pts	PIM	PP	SH	GW	Min
1989-90	Dynamo Moscow	USSR	35	1	1	2	27	....	....	....	....	....	....	....	....	....	....	....	....	....	....	....	....	....	....
1990-91	Dynamo Moscow	USSR	40	0	5	5	15	....	....	....	....	....	....	....	....	....	....	....	....	....	....	....	....	....	....
1991-92	Dynamo Moscow	CIS	35	4	2	6	26	....	....	....	....	....	....	....	....	....	....	....	....	....	....	....	....	....	....
1992-93	Dynamo Moscow	CIS	36	3	11	14	100	....	....	....	....	....	....	....	....	....	7	2	1	3	0	....	....	....	....
1993-94 ◆	**NY Rangers**	**NHL**	**67**	**3**	**15**	**18**	**58**	**1**	**0**	**1**	**78**	**3.8**	**12**	....	....	....	**17**	**0**	**4**	**4**	**12**	**0**	**0**	**0**	....
1994-95	Dynamo Moscow	CIS	13	0	2	2	10	....	....	....	....	....	....	....	....	....	....	....	....	....	....	....	....	....	....
	NY Rangers	**NHL**	**47**	**4**	**8**	**12**	**30**	**1**	**0**	**1**	**82**	**4.9**	**−4**	....	....	....	**8**	**1**	**0**	**1**	**0**	**0**	**0**	**0**	....
1995-96	**NY Rangers**	**NHL**	**40**	**2**	**16**	**18**	**26**	**1**	**0**	**1**	**71**	**2.8**	**12**	....	....	....	**6**	**0**	**1**	**1**	**4**	**0**	**0**	**0**	....
1996-97	**NY Rangers**	**NHL**	**77**	**9**	**29**	**38**	**59**	**6**	**1**	**0**	**84**	**10.7**	**1**	....	....	....	**13**	**1**	**3**	**4**	**20**	**1**	**0**	**0**	....
1997-98	**NY Rangers**	**NHL**	**47**	**3**	**7**	**10**	**38**	**1**	**0**	**1**	**46**	**6.5**	**−1**	....	....	....	....	....	....	....	....	....	....	....	....
1998-99	**NY Rangers**	**NHL**	**2**	**1**	**0**	**1**	**0**	**0**	**0**	**0**	**4**	**25.0**	**1**	**0**	**0.0**	**22:38**	....	....	....	....	....	....	....	....	....
	Toronto	**NHL**	**56**	**2**	**25**	**27**	**52**	**1**	**0**	**1**	**61**	**3.3**	**38**	**0**	**0.0**	**20:58**	**14**	**1**	**3**	**4**	**12**	**1**	**0**	**0**	**19:44**
99-2000	**Toronto**	**NHL**	**69**	**3**	**14**	**17**	**54**	**3**	**0**	**0**	**51**	**5.9**	**9**	**2**	**0.0**	**20:14**	**11**	**0**	**3**	**3**	**4**	**0**	**0**	**0**	**21:04**
2000-01	Dynamo Moscow	Russia	5	0	1	1	0	....	....	....	....	....	....	....	....	....	....	....	....	....	....	....	....	....	....
	Chicago	**NHL**	**53**	**2**	**13**	**15**	**39**	**1**	**0**	**0**	**52**	**3.8**	**−4**	**0**	**0.0**	**20:28**	....	....	....	....	....	....	....	....	....
2001-02	**Chicago**	**NHL**	**65**	**1**	**9**	**10**	**40**	**0**	**1**	**0**	**40**	**2.5**	**10**	**3**	**33.3**	**20:40**	**5**	**1**	**0**	**1**	**0**	**0**	**0**	**1**	**20:53**
2002-03	**Chicago**	**NHL**	**40**	**4**	**10**	**14**	**12**	**3**	**0**	**1**	**36**	**11.1**	**−8**	**0**	**0.0**	**21:40**	....	....	....	....	....	....	....	....	....
2003-04	**Chicago**	**NHL**	**24**	**0**	**7**	**7**	**14**	**0**	**0**	**0**	**31**	**0.0**	**−17**	**0**	**0.0**	**19:56**	....	....	....	....	....	....	....	....	....
	NY Islanders	**NHL**	**3**	**0**	**1**	**1**	**4**	**0**	**0**	**0**	**3**	**0.0**	**1**	**0**	**0.0**	**10:54**	....	....	....	....	....	....	....	....	....
2004-05	Sibir Novosibirsk	Russia	5	0	1	1	16	....	....	....	....	....	....	....	....	....	....	....	....	....	....	....	....	....	....
	Yaroslavl	Russia	33	2	5	7	45	....	....	....	....	....	....	....	....	....	9	0	0	0	0	....	....	....	....
2005-06	**Florida**	**NHL**	**6**	**0**	**0**	**0**	**4**	**0**	**0**	**0**	**4**	**0.0**	**−3**	**0**	**0.0**	**11:05**	....	....	....	....	....	....	....	....	....
	Sibir Novosibirsk	Russia	18	2	1	3	39	....	....	....	....	....	....	....	....	....	3	0	0	0	4	....	....	....	....
	NHL Totals		**596**	**34**	**154**	**188**	**430**	**18**	**2**	**6**	**643**	**5.3**		**5**	**20.0**	**20:24**	**74**	**4**	**14**	**18**	**52**	**2**	**0**	**1**	**20:25**

Traded to **NY Rangers** by **Quebec** for Mike Hurlbut, September 7, 1993. Traded to **Toronto** by **NY Rangers** with NY Rangers' 4th round choice (Mirko Murovic) in 1999 Entry Draft for Mathieu Schneider, October 14, 1998. Traded to **Chicago** by **Toronto** with Toronto's 4th round choice (Vladimir Gusev) in 2001 Entry Draft for Bryan McCabe, October 2, 2000. • Missed majority of 2002-03 season recovering from ankle (November 5, 2002 vs. Detroit) and cheekbone (February 20, 2003 vs. Phoenix) injuries. • Missed majority of 2003-04 season recovering from ankle injury suffered in game vs. San Jose, November 26, 2003. Traded to **NY Islanders** by **Chicago** for NY Islanders' 4th round choice (Niklas Hjalmarsson) in 2005 Entry Draft, March 9, 2004. Signed as a free agent by **Florida**, July 14, 2004. Signed as a free agent by **Novosibirsk** (Russia), August 21, 2004. Signed as a free agent by **Yaroslavl** (Russia), November, 2004. Loaned to **Novosibirsk** (Russia) by **Florida**, December 8, 2005.

			Regular Season														Playoffs								
Season	Club	League	GP	G	A	Pts	PIM	PP	SH	GW	S	%	+/-	TF	F%	Min	GP	G	A	Pts	PIM	PP	SH	GW	Min

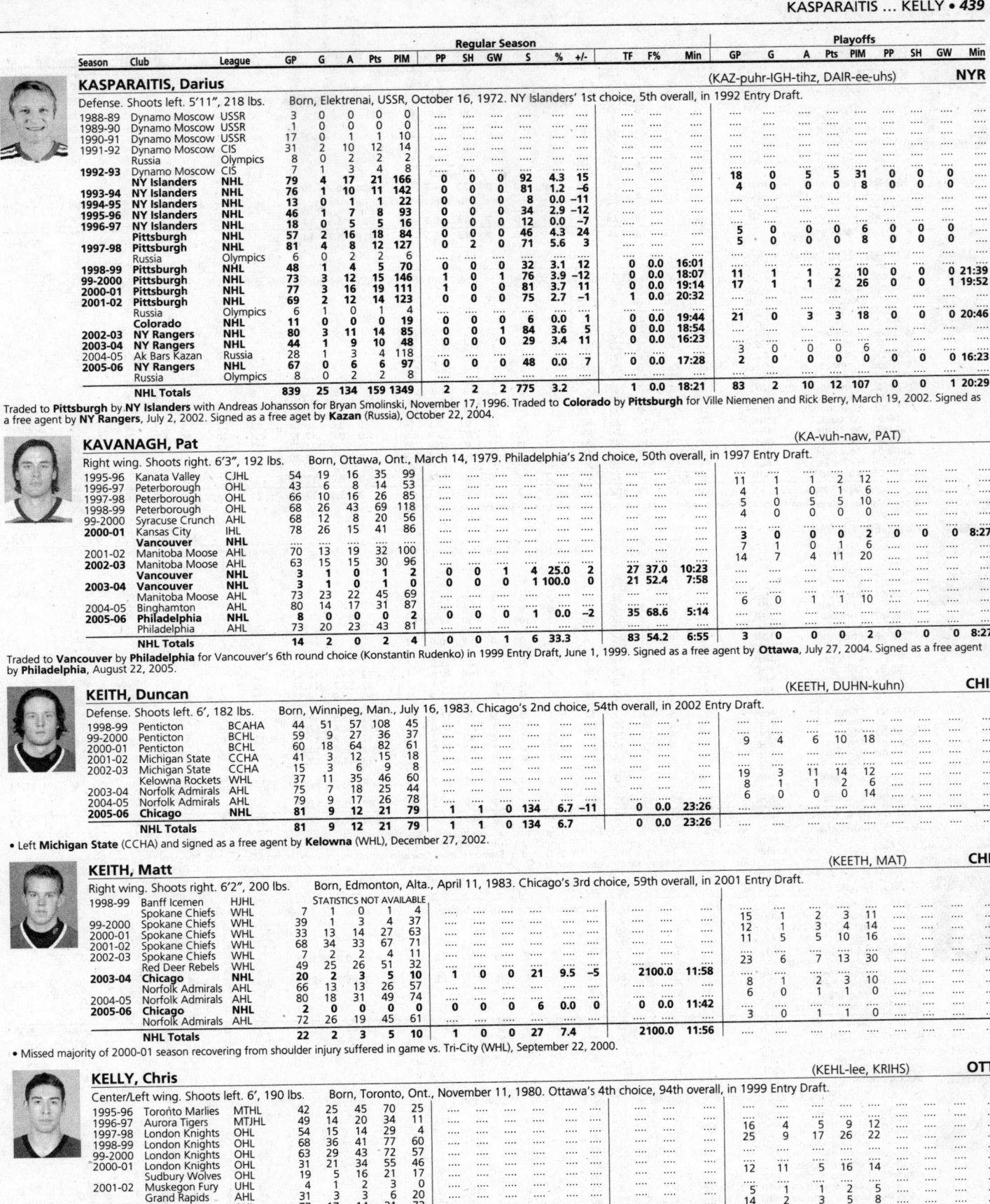

KASPARAITIS, Darius (KAZ-puhr-IGH-tihz, DAIR-ee-uhs) **NYR**

Defense. Shoots left. 5'11", 218 lbs.   Born, Elektrenai, USSR, October 16, 1972. NY Islanders' 1st choice, 5th overall, in 1992 Entry Draft.

Season	Club	League	GP	G	A	Pts	PIM	PP	SH	GW	S	%	+/-	TF	F%	Min	GP	G	A	Pts	PIM	PP	SH	GW	Min
1988-89	Dynamo Moscow	USSR	3	0	0	0	0																		
1989-90	Dynamo Moscow	USSR	1	0	0	0	0																		
1990-91	Dynamo Moscow	USSR	17	0	1	1	10																		
1991-92	Dynamo Moscow	CIS	31	2	10	12	14																		
	Russia	Olympics	8	0	2	2	2																		
1992-93	Dynamo Moscow	CIS	7	1	3	4	8																		
	NY Islanders	NHL	79	4	17	21	166	0	0	0	92	4.3	15				18	0	5	5	31	0	0	0	
1993-94	NY Islanders	NHL	76	1	10	11	142	0	0	0	81	1.2	-6				4	0	0	0	0	0	0	0	
1994-95	NY Islanders	NHL	13	0	1	1	22	0	0	0	8	0.0	-11												
1995-96	NY Islanders	NHL	46	1	7	8	93	0	0	0	34	2.9	-12												
1996-97	NY Islanders	NHL	18	0	5	5	16	0	0	0	12	0.0	-7												
	Pittsburgh	NHL	57	2	16	18	84	0	0	0	46	4.3	24				5	0	0	0	0	0	0	0	
1997-98	Pittsburgh	NHL	81	4	8	12	127	0	0	0	71	5.6	3				5	0	0	0	0	0	0	0	
	Russia	Olympics	6	0	2	2	6																		
1998-99	Pittsburgh	NHL	48	1	4	5	70	0	0	0	32	3.1	12	0	0.0	16:01	11	1	1	2	10	0	0	0	21:39
99-2000	Pittsburgh	NHL	73	3	12	15	146	1	0	1	76	3.9	-12	0	0.0	18:07	17	1	1	2	26	0	0	1	19:52
2000-01	Pittsburgh	NHL	77	3	16	19	111	1	0	0	81	3.7	-1	0	0.0	19:14									
2001-02	Pittsburgh	NHL	69	2	12	14	123	0	0	0	75	2.7	-1	1	0.0	20:32									
	Russia	Olympics	6	1	0	1	4																		
	Colorado	NHL	11	0	0	0	19	0	0	0	6	0.0	0	0	0.0	19:44	21	0	3	3	18	0	0	0	20:46
2002-03	NY Rangers	NHL	80	3	11	14	85	0	0	1	84	3.6	5	0	0.0	18:54									
2003-04	NY Rangers	NHL	44	1	9	10	48	0	0	0	29	3.4	11	0	0.0	16:23	3	0	0	0	0	0	0	0	
2004-05	Ak Bars Kazan	Russia	28	1	3	4	118																		
2005-06	NY Rangers	NHL	67	0	6	6	97	0	0	0	48	0.0	7	0	0.0	17:28	2	0	0	0	0	0	0	0	16:23
	Russia	Olympics	8	0	2	2	8																		
NHL Totals			839	25	134	159	1349	2	2	2	775	3.2		1	0.0	18:21	83	2	10	12	107	0	0	1	20:29

Traded to **Pittsburgh** by **NY Islanders** with Andreas Johansson for Bryan Smolinski, November 17, 1996. Traded to **Colorado** by Pittsburgh for Ville Niemenen and Rick Berry, March 19, 2002. Signed as a free agent by **NY Rangers**, July 2, 2002. Signed as a free aget by **Kazan** (Russia), October 22, 2004.

KAVANAGH, Pat (KA-vuh-naw, PAT)

Right wing. Shoots right. 6'3", 192 lbs.   Born, Ottawa, Ont., March 14, 1979. Philadelphia's 2nd choice, 50th overall, in 1997 Entry Draft.

Season	Club	League	GP	G	A	Pts	PIM	PP	SH	GW	S	%	+/-	TF	F%	Min	GP	G	A	Pts	PIM	PP	SH	GW	Min
1995-96	Kanata Valley	CJHL	54	19	16	35	99										11	1	1	2	12				
1996-97	Peterborough	OHL	43	6	8	14	53										4	1	0	1	6				
1997-98	Peterborough	OHL	66	10	16	26	85										5	0	5	5	10				
1998-99	Peterborough	OHL	68	26	43	69	118										4	0	0	0	0				
99-2000	Syracuse Crunch	AHL	68	12	8	20	56																		
2000-01	Kansas City	IHL	78	26	15	41	86										3	0	0	0	0	0	0	0	8:27
	Vancouver	NHL															7	1	0	1	6				
2001-02	Manitoba Moose	AHL	70	13	19	32	100										14	4	11	20	0				
2002-03	Manitoba Moose	AHL	63	15	15	30	96																		
	Vancouver	NHL	3	1	0	1	2	0	0	1	4	25.0	2	27	37.0	10:23									
2003-04	Vancouver	NHL	3	1	0	1	1	0	0	0	1	100.0	0	21	52.4	7:58									
	Manitoba Moose	AHL	73	23	22	45	69										6	0	1	1	10				
2004-05	Binghamton	AHL	80	14	17	31	87																		
2005-06	Philadelphia	NHL	8	0	0	0	2	0	0	0	1	0.0	-2	35	68.6	5:14									
	Philadelphia	AHL	73	20	23	43	81																		
NHL Totals			14	2	0	2	4	0	0	1	6	33.3		83	54.2	6:55	3	0	0	0	0	0	0	0	8:27

Traded to **Vancouver** by **Philadelphia** for Vancouver's 6th round choice (Konstantin Rudenko) in 1999 Entry Draft, June 1, 1999. Signed as a free agent by **Ottawa**, July 27, 2004. Signed as a free agent by **Philadelphia**, August 22, 2005.

KEITH, Duncan (KEETH, DUHN-kuhn) **CHI.**

Defense. Shoots left. 6', 182 lbs.   Born, Winnipeg, Man., July 16, 1983. Chicago's 2nd choice, 54th overall, in 2002 Entry Draft.

Season	Club	League	GP	G	A	Pts	PIM	PP	SH	GW	S	%	+/-	TF	F%	Min	GP	G	A	Pts	PIM	PP	SH	GW	Min
1998-99	Penticton	BCAHA	44	51	57	108	45																		
99-2000	Penticton	BCHL	59	9	27	36	37																		
2000-01	Penticton	BCHL	60	18	64	82	61										9	4	6	10	18				
2001-02	Michigan State	CCHA	41	3	12	15	18																		
2002-03	Michigan State	CCHA	15	3	6	9	8										19	3	11	14	12				
	Kelowna Rockets	WHL	37	11	35	46	60										8	1	1	2	6				
2003-04	Norfolk Admirals	AHL	75	7	18	25	44										6	0	0	0	14				
2004-05	Norfolk Admirals	AHL	79	9	17	26	78																		
2005-06	Chicago	NHL	81	9	12	21	79	1	1	0	134	6.7	-11	0	0.0	23:26									
NHL Totals			81	9	12	21	79	1	1	0	134	6.7		0	0.0	23:26									

• Left **Michigan State** (CCHA) and signed as a free agent by **Kelowna** (WHL), December 27, 2002.

KEITH, Matt (KEETH, MAT) **CHI.**

Right wing. Shoots right. 6'2", 200 lbs.   Born, Edmonton, Alta., April 11, 1983. Chicago's 3rd choice, 59th overall, in 2001 Entry Draft.

Season	Club	League	GP	G	A	Pts	PIM	PP	SH	GW	S	%	+/-	TF	F%	Min	GP	G	A	Pts	PIM	PP	SH	GW	Min
1998-99	Banff Icemen	HJHL	STATISTICS NOT AVAILABLE																						
	Spokane Chiefs	WHL	7	1	0	1	4										15	1	2	3	11				
99-2000	Spokane Chiefs	WHL	39	1	3	4	37										12	1	3	4	14				
2000-01	Spokane Chiefs	WHL	33	13	14	27	63										11	5	5	10	16				
2001-02	Spokane Chiefs	WHL	68	34	33	67	71																		
2002-03	Spokane Chiefs	WHL	7	2	2	4	11										23	6	7	13	30				
	Red Deer Rebels	WHL	49	25	26	51	32																		
2003-04	Chicago	NHL	20	2	3	5	10	1	0	0	21	9.5	-5	2	100.0	11:58	8	1	2	3	10				
	Norfolk Admirals	AHL	66	13	13	26	57										6	0	1	1	0				
2004-05	Norfolk Admirals	AHL	80	18	31	49	74																		
2005-06	Chicago	NHL	2	0	0	0	0	0	0	0	6	0.0	0	0	0.0	11:42	3	0	1	1	0				
	Norfolk Admirals	AHL	72	26	19	45	61																		
NHL Totals			22	2	3	5	10	1	0	0	27	7.4		2	100.0	11:56									

• Missed majority of 2000-01 season recovering from shoulder injury suffered in game vs. Tri-City (WHL), September 22, 2000.

KELLY, Chris (KEHL-lee, KRIHS) **OTT.**

Center/Left wing. Shoots left. 6', 190 lbs.   Born, Toronto, Ont., November 11, 1980. Ottawa's 4th choice, 94th overall, in 1999 Entry Draft.

Season	Club	League	GP	G	A	Pts	PIM	PP	SH	GW	S	%	+/-	TF	F%	Min	GP	G	A	Pts	PIM	PP	SH	GW	Min
1995-96	Toronto Marlies	MTHL	42	25	45	70	25																		
1996-97	Aurora Tigers	MTJHL	49	14	20	34	11										16	4	5	9	12				
1997-98	London Knights	OHL	54	15	14	29	4										25	9	17	26	22				
1998-99	London Knights	OHL	68	36	41	77	60																		
99-2000	London Knights	OHL	63	29	43	72	57																		
2000-01	London Knights	OHL	31	21	34	55	46										12	11	16	14	0				
	Sudbury Wolves	OHL	19	5	16	21	17																		
2001-02	Muskegon Fury	UHL	4	1	2	3	0										5	1	1	2	5				
	Grand Rapids	AHL	31	3	3	6	20										14	2	3	5	8				
2002-03	Binghamton	AHL	77	17	14	31	73																		
2003-04	Ottawa	NHL	4	0	0	0	0	0	0	0	4	0.0	-2	5	40.0	9:29	2	0	0	0	0				
	Binghamton	AHL	54	15	19	34	40										6	1	2	3	11				
2004-05	Binghamton	AHL	77	24	36	60	57										10	0	0	0	2	0	0	0	11:49
2005-06	Ottawa	NHL	82	10	20	30	76	1	0	2	112	8.9	21	808	45.8	12:20									
NHL Totals			86	10	20	30	76	1	0	2	116	8.6		813	45.8	12:12	10	0	0	0	2	0	0	0	11:49

KESLER, Ryan — (KEHZ-luhr, RIGH-uhn) — VAN.

Center. Shoots right. 6'2", 195 lbs. Born, Detroit, MI, August 31, 1984. Vancouver's 1st choice, 23rd overall, in 2003 Entry Draft.

Season	Club	League	GP	G	A	Pts	PIM	PP	SH	GW	S	%	+/-	TF	F%	Min	GP	G	A	Pts	PIM	PP	SH	GW	Min
99-2000	Det. Honeybaked	MWEHL	72	44	73	117	....																		
2000-01	USNTDP	U-18	26	8	20	28	24																		
	USNTDP	NAHL	56	7	21	28	40																		
2001-02	USNTDP	U-18	46	11	33	44	23																		
	USNTDP	USHL	13	5	5	10	10																		
	USNTDP	NAHL	10	5	6	11	4																		
2002-03	Ohio State	CCHA	40	11	20	31	44																		
2003-04	**Vancouver**	**NHL**	28	2	3	5	16	0	0	0	23	8.7	-2	194	40.2	10:42									
	Manitoba Moose	AHL	33	3	8	11	29																		
2004-05	Manitoba Moose	AHL	78	30	27	57	105										14	4	5	9	8				
2005-06	**Vancouver**	**NHL**	82	10	13	23	79	1	0	2	119	8.4	1	984	46.8	14:03									
	NHL Totals		110	12	16	28	95	1	0	2	142	8.5		1178	45.7	13:12									

KHAVANOV, Alexander — (khuh-VAN-ahf, al-ehx-AN-duhr)

Defense. Shoots left. 6'2", 205 lbs. Born, Moscow, USSR, January 30, 1972. St. Louis' 8th choice, 232nd overall, in 1999 Entry Draft.

Season	Club	League	GP	G	A	Pts	PIM	PP	SH	GW	S	%	+/-	TF	F%	Min	GP	G	A	Pts	PIM	PP	SH	GW	Min
1992-93	Birmingham Bulls	ECHL	19	0	3	3	14																		
	Raleigh IceCaps	ECHL	17	0	6	6	8																		
1993-94	St. Petersburg	CIS	41	1	2	3	24																		
1994-95	St. Petersburg	CIS	49	7	0	7	32																		
1995-96	St. Petersburg	CIS	32	1	5	6	41										3	0	0	0	0				
	HPK Hameenlinna	Finland	16	0	2	2	4										9	0	1	1	4				
1996-97	Cherepovets	Russia	39	3	8	11	56										3	1	0	1	4				
1997-98	Cherepovets	Russia	44	3	5	8	46																		
1998-99	Dynamo Moscow	Russia	40	2	7	9	14										16	1	5	6	35				
	Dynamo Moscow	EuroHL	5	0	1	1	2										6	0	0	0	4				
99-2000	Dynamo Moscow	Russia	38	5	12	17	49										17	0	3	3	4				
	Dynamo Moscow	EuroHL	6	2	0	2	0																		
2000-01	**St. Louis**	**NHL**	74	7	16	23	52	2	0	0	92	7.6	16	0	0.0	20:54	15	3	2	5	14	1	0	0	21:16
2001-02	**St. Louis**	**NHL**	81	3	21	24	55	0	0	0	87	3.4	9	0	0.0	17:13	4	0	0	2	0	0	0	0	15:08
2002-03	**St. Louis**	**NHL**	81	8	25	33	48	2	1	0	90	8.9	-1	2	50.0	21:57	7	2	3	5	2	1	0	0	19:05
2003-04	**St. Louis**	**NHL**	48	3	7	10	18	2	0	0	62	4.8	2	1	0.0	19:20									
2004-05	St. Petersburg	Russia	3	0	0	0	27																		
2005-06	**Toronto**	**NHL**	64	6	9	15	60	2	1	0	44	13.6	-11	0	0.0	17:08									
	NHL Totals		348	27	75	102	233	8	2	2	375	7.2		3	33.3	19:23	26	5	5	10	18	2	0	0	19:44

Signed as a free agent by **St. Petersburg** (Russia), September 25, 2004. Signed as a free agent by **Toronto**, August 9, 2005.

KILGER, Chad — (KIHL-guhr, CHAD) — TOR.

Left wing. Shoots left. 6'4", 224 lbs. Born, Cornwall, Ont., November 27, 1976. Anaheim's 1st choice, 4th overall, in 1995 Entry Draft.

Season	Club	League	GP	G	A	Pts	PIM	PP	SH	GW	S	%	+/-	TF	F%	Min	GP	G	A	Pts	PIM	PP	SH	GW	Min
1992-93	Cornwall Colts	CJHL	55	30	36	66	26										6	0	0	0	0				
1993-94	Kingston	OHL	66	17	35	52	23										6	7	2	9	8				
1994-95	Kingston	OHL	65	42	53	95	95										6	5	2	7	10				
1995-96	**Anaheim**	**NHL**	45	5	7	12	22	0	0	1	38	13.2	-2												
	Winnipeg	**NHL**	29	2	3	5	12	0	0	0	19	10.5	-2												
1996-97	**Phoenix**	**NHL**	24	4	3	7	13	1	0	0	30	13.3	-5				4	1	0	1	0	0	0	1	
	Springfield	AHL	52	17	28	45	36																		
1997-98	**Phoenix**	**NHL**	10	0	1	1	4	0	0	0	9	0.0	-2				16	5	7	12	56				
	Springfield	AHL	35	14	14	28	33																		
	Chicago	**NHL**	22	3	8	11	6	2	0	1	23	13.0	2												
1998-99	**Chicago**	**NHL**	64	14	11	25	30	2	1	1	68	20.6	1	488	56.6	14:03									
99-2000	**Edmonton**	**NHL**	13	1	1	2	4	0	0	0	13	7.7	-3	82	53.7	11:22	4	0	0	0	4	0	0	0	12:59
	Edmonton	**NHL**	40	3	2	5	18	0	0	0	32	9.4	-6	269	48.0	8:33	3	0	0	0	0	0	0	0	8:01
	Hamilton	AHL	7	4	2	6	4																		
2000-01	**Edmonton**	**NHL**	34	5	2	7	17	1	0	0	28	17.9	-7	391	53.5	8:18									
	Montreal	**NHL**	43	9	16	25	34	0	1	1	75	12.0	-1	319	52.4	17:57									
2001-02	**Montreal**	**NHL**	75	8	15	23	27	0	1	2	87	9.2	-7	357	53.8	13:14	12	0	1	1	9	0	0	0	14:00
2002-03	**Montreal**	**NHL**	60	9	7	16	21	0	0	1	60	15.0	-4	208	46.6	10:42									
2003-04	**Montreal**	**NHL**	36	2	2	4	14	0	0	0	29	6.9	2	95	48.4	10:26									
	Hamilton	AHL	2	1	0	1	0																		
	Toronto	**NHL**	5	1	1	2	2	0	0	1	6	16.7	2	2	0.0	12:14	13	2	1	3	0	0	0	0	11:41
2004-05				DID NOT PLAY																					
2005-06	**Toronto**	**NHL**	79	17	11	28	63	1	1	2	103	16.5	-6	89	51.7	12:25									
	NHL Totals		579	83	90	173	287	8	4	10	620	13.4		2300	52.4	12:14	36	3	2	5	13	0	0	1	12:22

Traded to **Winnipeg** by **Anaheim** with Oleg Tverdovsky and Anaheim's 3rd round choice (Per-Anton Lundstrom) in 1996 Entry Draft for Teemu Selanne, Marc Chouinard and Winnipeg's 4th round choice (later traded to Toronto – later traded to Montreal – Montreal selected Kim Staal) in 1996 Entry Draft, February 7, 1996. Transferred to **Phoenix** after **Winnipeg** franchise relocated, July 1, 1996. Traded to **Chicago** by **Phoenix** with Jayson More for Keith Carney and Jim Cummins, March 4, 1998. Traded to **Edmonton** by **Chicago** with Daniel Cleary, Ethan Moreau and Christian Laflamme for Boris Mironov, Dean McAmmond and Jonas Elofsson, March 20, 1999. Traded to **Montreal** by **Edmonton** for Sergei Zholtok, December 18, 2000. Claimed on waivers by **Toronto** from **Montreal**, March 9, 2004.

KING, Jason — (KIHNG, JAY-suhn) — VAN.

Center. Shoots left. 6'1", 195 lbs. Born, Corner Brook, Nfld., September 14, 1981. Vancouver's 5th choice, 212th overall, in 2001 Entry Draft.

Season	Club	League	GP	G	A	Pts	PIM	PP	SH	GW	S	%	+/-	TF	F%	Min	GP	G	A	Pts	PIM	PP	SH	GW	Min
99-2000	Halifax	QMJHL	53	3	7	10	8										10	0	0	0	2				
2000-01	Halifax	QMJHL	72	48	41	89	78										6	3	2	5	16				
2001-02	Halifax	QMJHL	61	*63	36	99	39										13	9	8	17	13				
2002-03	**Vancouver**	**NHL**	8	0	2	2	0	0	0	0	12	0.0	0	0	0.0	11:17									
	Manitoba Moose	AHL	67	26	20	40	15										14	4	3	7	14				
2003-04	**Vancouver**	**NHL**	47	12	9	21	8	6	0	1	107	11.2	0	3	66.7	12:43	1	0	0	0	0	0	0	0	6:21
	Manitoba Moose	AHL	29	12	11	23	6																		
2004-05	Manitoba Moose	AHL	59	26	27	53	22																		
2005-06	Manitoba Moose	AHL	36	20	14	34	34										13	3	4	7	8				
	NHL Totals		55	12	11	23	8	6	0	1	119	10.1		3	66.7	12:30	1	0	0	0	0	0	0	0	6:21

QMJHL Second All-Star Team (2001)

• Missed majority of 2005-06 season recovering from head injury suffered near the end of the 2004-05 season.

KLEE, Ken — (KLEE, KEHN) — COL.

Defense. Shoots right. 6', 210 lbs. Born, Indianapolis, IN, April 24, 1971. Washington's 11th choice, 177th overall, in 1990 Entry Draft.

Season	Club	League	GP	G	A	Pts	PIM	PP	SH	GW	S	%	+/-	TF	F%	Min	GP	G	A	Pts	PIM	PP	SH	GW	Min
1988-89	St. Mike's B's	OHA-B	40	9	23	32	64										27	5	12	17	54				
1989-90	Bowling Green	CCHA	39	0	5	5	52																		
1990-91	Bowling Green	CCHA	37	7	28	35	50																		
1991-92	Bowling Green	CCHA	10	0	1	1	14																		
1992-93	Baltimore	AHL	77	4	14	18	93										7	0	1	1	15				
1993-94	Portland Pirates	AHL	65	2	9	11	87										17	1	2	3	14				
1994-95	Portland Pirates	AHL	49	5	7	12	89																		
	Washington	**NHL**	23	3	1	4	41	0	0	0	18	16.7	2				7	0	1	1	6				
1995-96	**Washington**	**NHL**	66	8	3	11	60	0	1	2	76	10.5	-1				1	0	0	0	0				
1996-97	**Washington**	**NHL**	80	3	8	11	115	0	0	2	108	2.8	-5												
1997-98	**Washington**	**NHL**	51	4	2	6	46	0	0	1	44	9.1	-3				9	1	0	1	10	0	0	0	
1998-99	**Washington**	**NHL**	78	7	13	20	80	0	0	1	132	5.3	-9												
99-2000	**Washington**	**NHL**	80	7	13	20	79	0	0	2	113	6.2	8	0	0.0	19:07									
2000-01	**Washington**	**NHL**	54	2	4	6	60	0	0	0	58	3.4	-5	0	0.0	20:29	5	0	1	1	0	0	0	0	21:49
2001-02	**Washington**	**NHL**	68	6	8	14	68	2	0	3	85	9.4	4	0	0.0	17:15	6	0	1	1	0	0	0	0	21:38
2002-03	**Washington**	**NHL**	70	1	16	17	89	0	0	1	67	1.5	-5	0	0.0	19:24								0	13:47
2003-04	**Toronto**	**NHL**	66	4	25	29	36	3	0	1	85	4.7	-1	1	100.0	22:08	11	0	0	0	6	0	0	0	23:11

Season	Club	League	Regular Season GP	G	A	Pts	PIM	PP	SH	GW	S	%	+/-	TF	F%	Min	Playoffs GP	G	A	Pts	PIM	PP	SH	GW	Min
2004-05			DID NOT PLAY																						
2005-06	**Toronto**	**NHL**	**56**	**3**	**12**	**15**	**66**	**1**	**0**	**1**	**65**	**4.6**	**–1**	**0**	**0.0**	**20:02**									
	New Jersey	**NHL**	**18**	**0**	**0**	**0**	**14**	**0**	**0**	**0**	**5**	**0.0**	**–3**	**0**	**0.0**	**15:03**	**6**	**1**	**0**	**1**	**6**	**0**	**0**	**0**	**12:05**
	NHL Totals		**710**	**50**	**105**	**155**	**724**	**6**	**1**	**13**	**856**	**5.8**		**3**	**33.3**	**19:55**	**51**	**2**	**2**	**4**	**50**	**0**	**0**	**0**	**17:54**

Signed as a free agent by **Toronto**, September 27, 2003. Traded to **New Jersey** by **Toronto** for Aleksander Suglobov, March 8, 2006. Signed as a free agent by **Colorado**, July 24, 2006.

KLEIN, Kevin

(KLIGHN, KEH-vihn) **NSH.**

Defense. Shoots right. 6'1", 195 lbs. Born, Kitchener, Ont., December 13, 1984. Nashville's 3rd choice, 37th overall, in 2003 Entry Draft.

Season	Club	League	GP	G	A	Pts	PIM	PP	SH	GW	S	%	+/-	TF	F%	Min	GP	G	A	Pts	PIM	PP	SH	GW	Min
99-2000	Kitchener Midgets	OMHA	54	12	29	41	40																		
2000-01	St. Michael's	OHL	58	3	16	19	21										18	0	5	5	17				
2001-02	St. Michael's	OHL	68	5	22	27	35										15	2	7	9	12				
2002-03	St. Michael's	OHL	67	11	33	44	88										17	1	9	10	8				
2003-04	St. Michael's	OHL	5	0	1	1	2																		
	Guelph Storm	OHL	46	6	23	29	40										22	10	11	21	12				
2004-05	Milwaukee	AHL	65	4	12	16	22										7	0	0	0	11				
	Rockford IceHogs	UHL	3	2	1	3	0																		
2005-06	**Nashville**	**NHL**	**2**	**0**	**0**	**0**	**0**	**0**	**0**	**0**	**0**	**0.0**	**–1**	**0**	**0.0**	**13:40**									
	Milwaukee	AHL	76	10	33	43	31										21	3	7	10	31				
	NHL Totals		**2**	**0**	**0**	**0**	**0**	**0**	**0**	**0**	**0**	**0.0**		**0**	**0.0**	**13:40**									

KLEMM, Jon

(KLEHM, JAWN) **DAL.**

Defense. Shoots right. 6'2", 200 lbs. Born, Cranbrook, B.C., January 8, 1970.

Season	Club	League	GP	G	A	Pts	PIM	PP	SH	GW	S	%	+/-	TF	F%	Min	GP	G	A	Pts	PIM	PP	SH	GW	Min
1986-87	Cranbrook Colts	KIJHL	59	20	51	71	54																		
1987-88	Seattle	WHL	68	6	7	13	24																		
1988-89	Seattle	WHL	2	1	1	2	0																		
	Spokane Chiefs	WHL	66	6	34	40	42																		
1989-90	Spokane Chiefs	WHL	66	3	28	31	100										6	1	1	2	5				
1990-91	Spokane Chiefs	WHL	72	7	58	65	65										15	3	6	9	8				
1991-92	**Quebec**	**NHL**	**4**	**0**	**1**	**1**	**0**	**0**	**0**	**0**	**2**	**0.0**	**2**												
	Halifax Citadels	AHL	70	6	13	19	40																		
1992-93	Halifax Citadels	AHL	80	3	20	23	32																		
1993-94	**Quebec**	**NHL**	**7**	**0**	**0**	**0**	**4**	**0**	**0**	**0**	**11**	**0.0**	**–1**												
	Cornwall Aces	AHL	66	4	26	30	78										13	1	2	3	6				
1994-95	Cornwall Aces	AHL	65	6	13	19	84																		
	Quebec	**NHL**	**4**	**1**	**0**	**1**	**2**	**0**	**0**	**0**	**5**	**20.0**	**3**												
1995-96 ♦	**Colorado**	**NHL**	**56**	**3**	**12**	**15**	**20**	**0**	**1**	**1**	**61**	**4.9**	**12**				**15**	**2**	**1**	**3**	**0**	**1**	**0**	**0**	
1996-97	**Colorado**	**NHL**	**80**	**9**	**15**	**24**	**37**	**1**	**2**	**1**	**103**	**8.7**	**12**				**17**	**1**	**1**	**2**	**6**	**0**	**0**	**0**	
1997-98	**Colorado**	**NHL**	**67**	**6**	**8**	**14**	**30**	**0**	**0**	**0**	**60**	**10.0**	**–3**				**4**	**0**	**0**	**0**	**0**	**0**	**0**	**0**	
1998-99	**Colorado**	**NHL**	**39**	**1**	**2**	**3**	**31**	**0**	**0**	**0**	**28**	**3.6**	**4**	**14**	**35.7**	**13:43**	**19**	**0**	**1**	**1**	**10**	**0**	**0**	**0**	**8:32**
99-2000	**Colorado**	**NHL**	**73**	**5**	**7**	**12**	**34**	**0**	**0**	**0**	**64**	**7.8**	**26**	**17**	**47.1**	**17:22**	**17**	**2**	**1**	**3**	**9**	**0**	**0**	**0**	**14:25**
2000-01 ♦	**Colorado**	**NHL**	**78**	**4**	**11**	**15**	**54**	**2**	**0**	**2**	**97**	**4.1**	**22**	**1**	**100.0**	**19:56**	**22**	**1**	**2**	**3**	**16**	**0**	**0**	**1**	**16:15**
2001-02	**Chicago**	**NHL**	**82**	**4**	**16**	**20**	**42**	**2**	**0**	**1**	**111**	**3.6**	**–3**	**1**	**0.0**	**23:50**	**5**	**0**	**1**	**1**	**4**	**0**	**0**	**0**	**21:58**
2002-03	**Chicago**	**NHL**	**70**	**2**	**14**	**16**	**44**	**1**	**0**	**1**	**74**	**2.7**	**–9**	**2**	**0.0**	**21:57**									
2003-04	**Chicago**	**NHL**	**19**	**0**	**1**	**1**	**20**	**0**	**0**	**0**	**19**	**0.0**	**6**	**0**	**0.0**	**21:21**									
	Dallas	**NHL**	**58**	**2**	**4**	**6**	**24**	**0**	**0**	**1**	**52**	**3.8**	**10**	**1**	**0.0**	**16:00**									
2004-05			DID NOT PLAY																						
2005-06	**Dallas**	**NHL**	**76**	**4**	**7**	**11**	**60**	**1**	**0**	**1**	**57**	**7.0**	**–3**	**2**	**50.0**	**16:56**	**5**	**1**	**0**	**1**	**0**	**0**	**0**	**0**	**15:44**
	NHL Totals		**713**	**41**	**98**	**139**	**402**	**7**	**3**	**8**	**744**	**5.5**		**38**	**39.5**	**19:08**	**104**	**7**	**7**	**14**	**45**	**1**	**0**	**1**	**14:01**

WHL West Second All-Star Team (1991)

Signed as a free agent by **Quebec**, May 14, 1991. Transferred to **Colorado** after **Quebec** franchise relocated, June 21, 1995. • Missed majority of 1998-99 season recovering from knee injury suffered in game vs. Phoenix, November 10, 1998. Signed as a free agent by **Chicago**, July 1, 2001. Traded to **Dallas** by **Chicago** with NY Rangers' 4th round choice (previously acquired, Dallas selected Fredrik Naslund) in 2004 Entry Draft for Stephane Robidas and Dallas' 2nd round choice (Jakub Sindel) in 2004 Entry Draft, November 17, 2003.

KLEPIS, Jakub

(KLEH-pihsh, YA-kuhb) **WSH.**

Center. Shoots right. 6', 200 lbs. Born, Prague, Czech., June 5, 1984. Ottawa's 1st choice, 16th overall, in 2002 Entry Draft.

Season	Club	League	GP	G	A	Pts	PIM	PP	SH	GW	S	%	+/-	TF	F%	Min	GP	G	A	Pts	PIM	PP	SH	GW	Min
99-2000	Slavia Jr.	CzRep-Jr.	48	14	26	40	30																		
2000-01	Slavia Jr.	CzRep-Jr.	52	21	25	46	82																		
2001-02	Portland	WHL	70	14	50	64	111										7	0	3	3	22				
2002-03	HC Slavia Praha	CzRep	38	2	6	8	22										4	0	0	0	6				
	Slavia Jr.	CzRep-Jr.	11	4	5	9	59										3	0	3	3	4				
2003-04	HC Slavia Praha	CzRep	44	4	9	13	43										17	5	3	8	10				
2004-05	Portland Pirates	AHL	78	13	14	27	76																		
2005-06	**Washington**	**NHL**	**25**	**1**	**3**	**4**	**8**	**0**	**0**	**0**	**26**	**3.8**	**–11**	**22**	**40.9**	**7:25**									
	Hershey Bears	AHL	54	11	20	31	49										15	2	6	8	4				
	NHL Totals		**25**	**1**	**3**	**4**	**8**	**0**	**0**	**0**	**26**	**3.8**		**22**	**40.9**	**7:25**									

Traded to **Buffalo** by **Ottawa** for Vaclav Varada and Buffalo's 5th round choice (Tim Cook) in 2003 Entry Draft, February 25, 2003. Traded to **Washington** by **Buffalo** for Mike Grier, March 9, 2004.

KLESLA, Rostislav

(KLEHS-luh, RAHS-tih-slav) **CBJ**

Defense. Shoots left. 6'3", 216 lbs. Born, Novy Jicin, Czech., March 21, 1982. Columbus' 1st choice, 4th overall, in 2000 Entry Draft.

Season	Club	League	GP	G	A	Pts	PIM	PP	SH	GW	S	%	+/-	TF	F%	Min	GP	G	A	Pts	PIM	PP	SH	GW	Min
1997-98	HC Opava Jr.	CzRep-Jr.	38	11	18	29	87										8	2	2	4	0				
1998-99	Sioux City	USHL	54	4	12	16	100										5	2	0	2	2				
99-2000	Brampton	OHL	67	16	29	45	174										6	1	1	2	21				
2000-01	**Columbus**	**NHL**	**8**	**2**	**0**	**2**	**6**	**0**	**0**	**0**	**10**	**20.0**	**–1**	**0**	**0.0**	**18:25**									
	Brampton	OHL	45	18	36	54	59										9	2	9	11	26				
2001-02	**Columbus**	**NHL**	**75**	**8**	**8**	**16**	**74**	**1**	**0**	**0**	**102**	**7.8**	**–6**	**0**	**0.0**	**18:52**									
2002-03	**Columbus**	**NHL**	**72**	**2**	**14**	**16**	**71**	**0**	**0**	**0**	**89**	**2.2**	**–22**	**0**	**0.0**	**18:45**									
2003-04	**Columbus**	**NHL**	**47**	**2**	**11**	**13**	**27**	**0**	**0**	**1**	**74**	**2.7**	**–16**	**0**	**0.0**	**18:19**									
2004-05	HC Vsetin	CzRep	41	7	17	24	136																		
	HPK Hameenlinna	Finland	9	1	2	3	12										10	0	2	2	12				
2005-06	**Columbus**	**NHL**	**51**	**6**	**13**	**19**	**75**	**2**	**0**	**1**	**84**	**7.1**	**–4**	**2**	**100.0**	**21:27**									
	NHL Totals		**253**	**20**	**46**	**66**	**253**	**3**	**0**	**2**	**359**	**5.6**		**2**	**100.0**	**19:14**									

OHL All-Rookie Team (2000) • Canadian Major Junior All-Rookie Team (2000) • OHL First All-Star Team (2001) • NHL All-Rookie Team (2002)

Returned to **Brampton** (OHL) by **Columbus**, October 28, 2000. Signed as a free agent by **Vsetin** (CzRep), September 17, 2004. Signed as a free agent by **Hameenlinna** (Finland), January 29, 2005.

KLOUCEK, Tomas

(KLOH-chehk, TAW-mahsh) **CBJ**

Defense. Shoots left. 6'3", 235 lbs. Born, Prague, Czech., March 7, 1980. NY Rangers' 6th choice, 131st overall, in 1998 Entry Draft.

Season	Club	League	GP	G	A	Pts	PIM	PP	SH	GW	S	%	+/-	TF	F%	Min	GP	G	A	Pts	PIM	PP	SH	GW	Min
1995-96	Slavia Jr.	CzRep-Jr.	40	2	8	10	....																		
1996-97	Slavia Jr.	CzRep-Jr.	43	4	14	18	44																		
1997-98	Slavia Jr.	CzRep-Jr.	43	1	9	10	....																		
1998-99	Cape Breton	QMJHL	59	4	17	21	162										2	0	0	0	4				
99-2000	Hartford	AHL	73	2	8	10	113										23	0	4	4	18				
2000-01	**NY Rangers**	**NHL**	**43**	**1**	**4**	**5**	**74**	**0**	**0**	**0**	**22**	**4.5**	**–3**	**0**	**0.0**	**16:43**									
	Hartford	AHL	21	0	2	2	44																		
2001-02	**NY Rangers**	**NHL**	**52**	**1**	**3**	**4**	**137**	**0**	**0**	**0**	**21**	**4.8**	**–2**	**1**	**0.0**	**11:58**									
	Hartford	AHL	9	0	2	2	27										10	1	1	2	8				
2002-03	Hartford	AHL	20	3	4	7	102																		
	Nashville	**NHL**	**3**	**0**	**0**	**0**	**2**	**0**	**0**	**0**	**1**	**0.0**	**1**	**0**	**0.0**	**9:45**									
	Milwaukee	AHL	34	0	6	6	80																		
2003-04	**Nashville**	**NHL**	**5**	**0**	**1**	**1**	**10**	**0**	**0**	**0**	**0**	**0.0**	**3**	**0**	**0.0**	**11:34**									
	Atlanta	**NHL**	**37**	**0**	**0**	**0**	**25**	**0**	**0**	**0**	**12**	**0.0**	**–8**	**0**	**0.0**	**8:00**									
2004-05	HC Slavia Praha	CzRep	29	1	1	2	28																		
	HC Ocelari Trinec	CzRep	11	1	2	3	24																		
	Liberec	CzRep	8	1	0	1	12										9	0	1	1	35				

			Regular Season														Playoffs								
Season	Club	League	GP	G	A	Pts	PIM	PP	SH	GW	S	%	+/-	TF	F%	Min	GP	G	A	Pts	PIM	PP	SH	GW	Min
2005-06	**Atlanta**	**NHL**	**1**	**0**	**0**	**0**	**2**	**0**	**0**	**0**	**0**	**0.0**	**0**	**0**	**0.0**	**3:14**									
	Chicago Wolves	AHL	33	0	1	1	94																		
	NHL Totals		**141**	**2**	**8**	**10**	**250**	**0**	**0**	**0**	**56**	**3.6**		**1**	**0.0**	**12:15**									

AHL All-Rookie Team (2000)

Traded to **Nashville** by **NY Rangers** with Rem Murray and Marek Zidlicky for Mike Dunham, December 12, 2002. Traded to **Atlanta** by **Nashville** with Ben Simon for Simon Gamache and Kirill Safronov, December 2, 2003. Signed as a free agent by **Slavia Praha** (CzRep), September 17, 2004. Signed as a free agent by **Trinec** (CzRep), December, 2004. Signed as a free agent by **Liberec** (CzRep), January 31, 2005. • Missed majority of 2005-06 season recovering from ankle injury suffered in game vs. Cleveland (AHL), January 15, 2006. Signed as a free agent by **Columbus**, July 6, 2006.

KNUBLE, Mike

(kuh-NOO-buhl, MIGHK) **PHI.**

Right wing. Shoots right. 6'3", 228 lbs. Born, Toronto, Ont., July 4, 1972. Detroit's 4th choice, 76th overall, in 1991 Entry Draft.

Season	Club	League	GP	G	A	Pts	PIM	PP	SH	GW	S	%	+/-	TF	F%	Min	GP	G	A	Pts	PIM	PP	SH	GW	Min
1988-89	East Kentwood	High-MI	28	52	37	89	60																		
1989-90	East Kentwood	High-MI	29	63	40	103	40																		
1990-91	Kalamazoo	NAHL	36	18	24	42	30																		
1991-92	U. of Michigan	CCHA	43	7	8	15	48																		
1992-93	U. of Michigan	CCHA	39	26	16	42	57																		
1993-94	U. of Michigan	CCHA	41	32	26	58	71																		
1994-95	U. of Michigan	CCHA	34	*38	22	60	62																		
	Adirondack	AHL															3	0	0	0	0				
1995-96	Adirondack	AHL	80	22	23	45	59										3	1	0	1	0				
1996-97	**Detroit**	**NHL**	**9**	**1**	**0**	**1**	**0**	**0**	**0**	**0**	**10**	**10.0**	**-1**												
	Adirondack	AHL	68	28	35	63	54																		
1997-98 ♦	**Detroit**	**NHL**	**53**	**7**	**6**	**13**	**16**	**0**	**0**	**0**	**54**	**13.0**	**2**				**3**	**0**	**1**	**1**	**0**	**0**	**0**	**0**	
1998-99	**NY Rangers**	**NHL**	**82**	**15**	**20**	**35**	**26**	**3**	**0**	**1**	**113**	**13.3**	**-7**	**1**	**100.0**	**14:52**									
99-2000	**NY Rangers**	**NHL**	**59**	**9**	**5**	**14**	**18**	**1**	**0**	**1**	**50**	**18.0**	**-5**	**9**	**55.6**	**10:39**									
	Boston	**NHL**	**14**	**3**	**3**	**6**	**8**	**1**	**0**	**1**	**28**	**10.7**	**-2**	**3**	**0.0**	**19:29**									
2000-01	**Boston**	**NHL**	**82**	**7**	**13**	**20**	**37**	**0**	**1**	**1**	**92**	**7.6**	**0**	**115**	**31.3**	**10:34**									
2001-02	**Boston**	**NHL**	**54**	**8**	**6**	**14**	**42**	**0**	**0**	**2**	**77**	**10.4**	**9**	**27**	**44.4**	**9:45**	**2**	**0**	**0**	**0**	**0**	**0**	**0**	**0**	**3:30**
2002-03	**Boston**	**NHL**	**75**	**30**	**29**	**59**	**45**	**9**	**0**	**4**	**185**	**16.2**	**18**	**34**	**44.1**	**17:24**	**5**	**0**	**2**	**2**	**2**	**0**	**0**	**0**	**17:35**
2003-04	**Boston**	**NHL**	**82**	**21**	**25**	**46**	**32**	**4**	**0**	**3**	**192**	**10.9**	**19**	**54**	**31.5**	**18:47**	**7**	**2**	**0**	**2**	**0**	**1**	**0**	**0**	**19:45**
2004-05	Linkopings HC	Sweden	49	*26	13	39	40										6	0	1	1	2				
2005-06	**Philadelphia**	**NHL**	**82**	**34**	**31**	**65**	**80**	**13**	**2**	**6**	**217**	**15.7**	**25**	**161**	**32.3**	**20:21**	**6**	**1**	**3**	**4**	**8**	**0**	**0**	**0**	**19:17**
	United States	Olympics	6	1	1	2	4																		
	NHL Totals		**592**	**135**	**138**	**273**	**304**	**31**	**3**	**19**	**1018**	**13.3**		**404**	**34.2**	**15:09**	**23**	**3**	**6**	**9**	**10**	**1**	**0**	**0**	**17:26**

CCHA Second All-Star Team (1994, 1995) • NCAA West Second All-American Team (1995)

Traded to **NY Rangers** by **Detroit** for NY Rangers' 2nd round choice (Tomas Kopecky) in 2000 Entry Draft, October 1, 1998. Traded to **Boston** by **NY Rangers** for Rob DiMaio, March 10, 2000. Signed as a free agent by **Philadelphia**, July 3, 2004. Signed as a free agent by **Linkopings** (Sweden), August 2, 2004.

KOALSKA, Matt

(KOHL-skuh, MAT) **NYI**

Center. Shoots left. 6'1", 196 lbs. Born, St. Paul, MN, May 16, 1980. Nashville's 7th choice, 154th overall, in 2000 Entry Draft.

Season	Club	League	GP	G	A	Pts	PIM	PP	SH	GW	S	%	+/-	TF	F%	Min	GP	G	A	Pts	PIM	PP	SH	GW	Min
1998-99	Hill-Murray	High-MN	26	20	50	70	18																		
99-2000	Twin Cities	USHL	57	24	34	58	19										13	5	5	10	4				
2000-01	U. of Minnesota	WCHA	42	10	24	34	36																		
2001-02	U. of Minnesota	WCHA	44	10	23	33	34																		
2002-03	U. of Minnesota	WCHA	41	9	31	40	26																		
2003-04	U. of Minnesota	WCHA	44	13	26	39	44																		
2004-05	Bridgeport	AHL	60	7	8	15	22																		
2005-06	**NY Islanders**	**NHL**	**3**	**0**	**0**	**0**	**2**	**0**	**0**	**0**	**3**	**0.0**	**-1**	**13**	**53.9**	**5:44**									
	Bridgeport	AHL	75	19	30	49	82										7	2	1	3	0				
	NHL Totals		**3**	**0**	**0**	**0**	**2**	**0**	**0**	**0**	**3**	**0.0**		**13**	**53.8**	**5:44**									

Signed as a free agent by **NY Islanders**, August 11, 2004.

KOBASEW, Chuck

(KOH-buh-soo, CHUK) **CGY.**

Center. Shoots left. 6'1", 195 lbs. Born, Osoyoos, B.C., April 17, 1982. Calgary's 1st choice, 14th overall, in 2001 Entry Draft.

Season	Club	League	GP	G	A	Pts	PIM	PP	SH	GW	S	%	+/-	TF	F%	Min	GP	G	A	Pts	PIM	PP	SH	GW	Min
1997-98	Osoyoos Heat	KIJHL	6	2	2	4	2																		
1998-99	Osoyoos Heat	KIJHL	23	25	24	49																			
	Penticton	BCHL	30	11	17	28	18																		
99-2000	Penticton	BCHL	58	*54	52	106	83																		
2000-01	Boston College	H-East	43	27	22	49	38																		
2001-02	Kelowna Rockets	WHL	55	41	21	62	114										15	10	5	15	22				
2002-03	**Calgary**	**NHL**	**23**	**4**	**2**	**6**	**8**	**1**	**0**	**1**	**29**	**13.8**	**-3**	**5**	**0.0**	**11:48**									
	Saint John Flames	AHL	48	21	12	33	61																		
2003-04	**Calgary**	**NHL**	**70**	**6**	**11**	**17**	**51**	**3**	**0**	**0**	**78**	**7.7**	**-12**	**91**	**42.9**	**10:22**	**26**	**0**	**1**	**1**	**24**	**0**	**0**	**0**	**9:02**
2004-05	Lowell	AHL	79	38	37	75	110										11	6	3	9	27				
2005-06	**Calgary**	**NHL**	**77**	**20**	**11**	**31**	**64**	**10**	**0**	**4**	**143**	**14.0**	**-10**	**47**	**25.5**	**12:16**	**7**	**1**	**0**	**1**	**0**	**0**	**0**	**1**	**12:29**
	NHL Totals		**170**	**30**	**24**	**54**	**123**	**14**	**0**	**5**	**250**	**12.0**		**143**	**35.7**	**11:25**	**33**	**1**	**1**	**2**	**24**	**0**	**0**	**1**	**9:45**

Hockey East Second All-Star Team (2001) • Hockey East Rookie of the Year (2001) • NCAA Championship All-Tournament Team (2001) • NCAA Championship Tournament MVP (2001) • AHL First All-Star Team (2005)

• Left **Boston College** (H-East) and signed with **Kelowna** (WHL), August 13, 2001.

KOIVU, Mikko

(KOI-voo, MEE-koh) **MIN.**

Center. Shoots left. 6'2", 205 lbs. Born, Turku, Finland, March 12, 1983. Minnesota's 1st choice, 6th overall, in 2001 Entry Draft.

Season	Club	League	GP	G	A	Pts	PIM	PP	SH	GW	S	%	+/-	TF	F%	Min	GP	G	A	Pts	PIM	PP	SH	GW	Min
99-2000	TPS Turku U18	Fin-U18	11	4	9	13	18																		
	TPS Turku Jr.	Fin-Jr.	30	4	8	12	22										13	1	4	5	8				
2000-01	TPS Turku U18	Fin-U18															7	2	10	12	2				
	TPS Turku Jr.	Fin-Jr.	26	9	36	45	26										3	1	1	2	6				
	TPS Turku	Finland	21	0	1	1	2																		
2001-02	TPS Turku Jr.	Fin-Jr.	2	0	1	1	12																		
	TPS Turku	Finland	48	4	3	7	34										8	0	3	3	4				
2002-03	TPS Turku	Finland	37	7	13	20	20										7	2	2	4	6				
2003-04	TPS Turku	Finland	45	6	24	30	36										13	1	7	8	8				
2004-05	Houston Aeros	AHL	67	20	28	48	47										5	1	0	1	2				
2005-06	**Minnesota**	**NHL**	**64**	**6**	**15**	**21**	**40**	**3**	**0**	**0**	**96**	**6.3**	**-9**	**724**	**47.4**	**13:17**									
	Finland	Olympics	8	0	0	0	6																		
	NHL Totals		**64**	**6**	**15**	**21**	**40**	**3**	**0**	**0**	**96**	**6.3**		**724**	**47.4**	**13:17**									

KOIVU, Saku

(KOI-voo, SA-koo) **MTL.**

Center. Shoots left. 5'10", 184 lbs. Born, Turku, Finland, November 23, 1974. Montreal's 1st choice, 21st overall, in 1993 Entry Draft.

Season	Club	League	GP	G	A	Pts	PIM	PP	SH	GW	S	%	+/-	TF	F%	Min	GP	G	A	Pts	PIM	PP	SH	GW	Min
1990-91	TPS Turku U18	Fin-U18	24	20	28	48	26																		
	TPS Turku Jr.	Fin-Jr.	13	3	7	10	6																		
1991-92	TPS Turku U18	Fin-U18	12	3	7	10	6																		
	TPS Turku Jr.	Fin-Jr.	34	25	28	53	57										8	5	9	14	6				
1992-93	TPS Turku	Finland	46	3	7	10	28										11	3	2	5	2				
1993-94	TPS Turku	Finland	47	23	30	53	42										11	4	8	12	16				
	Finland	Olympics	8	4	3	7	12																		
1994-95	TPS Turku	Finland	45	27	47	74	73										13	7	10	17	16				
1995-96	**Montreal**	**NHL**	**82**	**20**	**25**	**45**	**40**	**8**	**3**	**2**	**136**	**14.7**	**-7**				**6**	**3**	**1**	**4**	**8**	**0**	**0**	**0**	
1996-97	**Montreal**	**NHL**	**50**	**17**	**39**	**56**	**38**	**5**	**0**	**3**	**135**	**12.6**	**7**				**5**	**1**	**3**	**4**	**10**	**0**	**0**	**0**	
1997-98	**Montreal**	**NHL**	**69**	**14**	**43**	**57**	**48**	**2**	**2**	**3**	**145**	**9.7**	**8**				**6**	**2**	**3**	**5**	**2**	**1**	**0**	**0**	
	Finland	Olympics	6	2	8	10	4																		
1998-99	**Montreal**	**NHL**	**65**	**14**	**30**	**44**	**38**	**4**	**2**	**0**	**145**	**9.7**	**-7**	**1427**	**52.6**	**20:02**									
99-2000	**Montreal**	**NHL**	**24**	**3**	**18**	**21**	**14**	**1**	**0**	**0**	**53**	**5.7**	**7**	**495**	**52.9**	**19:13**									
2000-01	**Montreal**	**NHL**	**54**	**17**	**30**	**47**	**40**	**7**	**0**	**3**	**113**	**15.0**	**2**	**1092**	**47.6**	**21:23**									
2001-02	**Montreal**	**NHL**	**3**	**0**	**2**	**2**	**0**	**0**	**0**	**0**	**2**	**0.0**	**0**	**13**	**61.5**	**13:57**	**12**	**4**	**6**	**10**	**4**	**1**	**0**	**1**	**15:54**
2002-03	**Montreal**	**NHL**	**82**	**21**	**50**	**71**	**72**	**5**	**1**	**5**	**147**	**14.3**	**5**	**1566**	**49.6**	**19:14**									

Season	Club	League	GP	G	A	Pts	PIM	PP	SH	GW	S	%	+/-	TF	F%	Min	GP	G	A	Pts	PIM	PP	SH	GW	Min
			Regular Season														Playoffs								
2003-04	**Montreal**	**NHL**	**68**	**14**	**41**	**55**	**52**	**5**	**0**	**3**	**112**	**12.5**	**–5**	**1194**	**53.9**	**19:18**	**11**	**3**	**8**	**11**	**10**	**2**	**0**	**0**	**20:34**
2004-05	TPS Turku	Finland	20	8	8	16	28										6	3	2	5	30				
2005-06	**Montreal**	**NHL**	**72**	**17**	**45**	**62**	**70**	**5**	**0**	**4**	**138**	**12.3**	**1**	**1412**	**53.8**	**18:31**	**3**	**0**	**2**	**2**	**2**	**0**	**0**	**0**	**14:24**
	Finland	Olympics	8	3	8	11	12																		
	NHL Totals		**569**	**137**	**323**	**460**	**412**	**42**	**8**	**23**	**1126**	**12.2**		**7199**	**51.7**	**19:31**	**43**	**13**	**23**	**36**	**36**	**4**	**0**	**1**	**17:42**

Bill Masterton Memorial Trophy (2002) • Olympic Tournament All-Star Team (2006)

Played in NHL All-Star Game (1998)

Missed majority of 1999-2000 season recovering from shoulder injury suffered in game vs. NY Rangers, October 30, 1999. • Missed majority of 2001-02 season recovering from non-Hodgkin's lymphoma, September 6, 2001. Signed as a free agent by **Turku** (Finland), October 21, 2004.

KOLANOS, Krys

(koh-LA-nohs, KRIHS) **DET.**

Center. Shoots right. 6'3", 206 lbs. Born, Calgary, Alta., July 27, 1981. Phoenix's 1st choice, 19th overall, in 2000 Entry Draft.

Season	Club	League	GP	G	A	Pts	PIM	PP	SH	GW	S	%	+/-	TF	F%	Min	GP	G	A	Pts	PIM	PP	SH	GW	Min
1996-97	Calgary Flames	AAHA	24	24	35	59	....																		
1997-98	Calgary Buffaloes	AMHL	34	34	43	77	29																		
1998-99	Calgary Royals	AJHL	58	43	67	110	98																		
99-2000	Boston College	H-East	42	16	16	32	48																		
2000-01	Boston College	H-East	41	25	25	50	54																		
2001-02	**Phoenix**	**NHL**	**57**	**11**	**11**	**22**	**48**	**0**	**0**	**5**	**81**	**13.6**	**6**	**703**	**46.4**	**13:05**	**2**	**0**	**0**	**0**	**6**	**0**	**0**	**0**	**11:12**
2002-03	**Phoenix**	**NHL**	**2**	**0**	**0**	**0**	**0**	**0**	**0**	**0**	**8**	**0.0**	**0**	**16**	**31.3**	**14:06**									
2003-04	**Phoenix**	**NHL**	**41**	**4**	**6**	**10**	**24**	**1**	**0**	**1**	**61**	**6.6**	**–9**	**283**	**43.8**	**13:31**									
	Springfield	AHL	32	10	11	21	38																		
2004-05	Blues Espoo	Finland	15	7	9	16	40																		
	Krefeld Pinguine	Germany	7	3	2	5	16																		
2005-06	**Phoenix**	**NHL**	**9**	**2**	**1**	**3**	**2**	**1**	**0**	**0**	**15**	**13.3**	**2**	**75**	**53.3**	**11:30**									
	San Antonio	AHL	3	0	1	1	0																		
	Edmonton	**NHL**	**6**	**0**	**0**	**0**	**2**	**0**	**0**	**0**	**7**	**0.0**	**–1**	**32**	**50.0**	**7:39**									
	Lowell	AHL	19	10	11	21	40																		
	Wilkes-Barre	AHL	18	10	8	18	19										11	2	0	2	16				
	NHL Totals		**115**	**17**	**18**	**35**	**76**	**2**	**0**	**6**	**172**	**9.9**		**1109**	**46.1**	**12:51**	**2**	**0**	**0**	**0**	**6**	**0**	**0**	**0**	**11:12**

Hockey East All-Rookie Team (2000) • Hockey East Second All-Star Team (2001) • NCAA East Second All-American Team (2001) • NCAA Championship All-Tournament Team (2001)

• Missed majority of 2002-03 season recovering from head injury suffered in game vs. Pittsburgh, March 20, 2002. Signed as a free agent by **Blues** (Finland), October 25, 2004. Signed as a free agent by **Krefeld** (Germany), February 16, 2005. Claimed on waivers by **Edmonton** from **Phoenix**, November 11, 2005. Claimed on waivers by **Phoenix** from **Edmonton**, December 19, 2005. Traded to **Carolina** by **Phoenix** for Pavel Brendl, December 28, 2005. Traded to **Pittsburgh** by **Carolina** with Niklas Nordgren and Carolina's 2nd round choice (later traded to San Jose) in 2007 Entry Draft for Mark Recchi, March 9, 2006. Signed as a free agent by **Detroit**, July, 2006.

KOLNIK, Juraj

(KOHL-nihk, YEW-igh) **FLA.**

Right wing. Shoots right. 5'10", 190 lbs. Born, Nitra, Czech., November 13, 1980. NY Islanders' 7th choice, 101st overall, in 1999 Entry Draft.

Season	Club	League	GP	G	A	Pts	PIM	PP	SH	GW	S	%	+/-	TF	F%	Min	GP	G	A	Pts	PIM	PP	SH	GW	Min
1997-98	Nitra Jr.	Slovak-Jr.	26	28	16	44	50																		
	Nitra	Slovakia	28	1	3	4	6																		
1998-99	Quebec Remparts	QMJHL	12	6	5	11	6																		
	Rimouski Oceanic	QMJHL	50	36	37	73	34										11	9	6	15	6				
99-2000	Rimouski Oceanic	QMJHL	47	53	53	106	53										14	10	17	27	16				
2000-01	**NY Islanders**	**NHL**	**29**	**4**	**3**	**7**	**12**	**0**	**0**	**0**	**38**	**10.5**	**–8**	**1**	**100.0**	**10:28**									
	Lowell	AHL	25	2	6	8	18																		
	Springfield	AHL	29	15	20	35	20																		
2001-02	**NY Islanders**	**NHL**	**7**	**2**	**0**	**2**	**0**	**1**	**0**	**0**	**10**	**20.0**	**–2**	**1**	**0.0**	**7:57**									
	Bridgeport	AHL	67	18	30	48	40										20	7	14	21	17				
2002-03	**Florida**	**NHL**	**10**	**0**	**1**	**1**	**0**	**0**	**0**	**0**	**14**	**0.0**	**1**	**1**	**0.0**	**10:33**									
	San Antonio	AHL	65	25	15	40	36										3	0	1	1	4				
2003-04	**Florida**	**NHL**	**53**	**14**	**11**	**25**	**14**	**2**	**0**	**1**	**100**	**14.0**	**–7**	**25**	**64.0**	**16:05**									
	San Antonio	AHL	15	2	14	16	21																		
2004-05	San Antonio	AHL	74	13	16	29	24																		
2005-06	**Florida**	**NHL**	**77**	**15**	**20**	**35**	**40**	**4**	**1**	**3**	**145**	**10.3**	**1**	**28**	**28.6**	**14:19**									
	NHL Totals		**176**	**35**	**35**	**70**	**66**	**7**	**1**	**4**	**307**	**11.4**		**56**	**44.6**	**13:45**									

Memorial Cup Tournament All-Star Team (2000)

Traded to **Florida** by **NY Islanders** with NY Islanders' 9th round choice (later traded to San Jose – San Jose selected Carter Lee) in 2003 Entry Draft for Sven Butenschon, October 11, 2002.

KOLTSOV, Konstantin

(kohlt-SAHV, kawn-stuhn-TEEN)

Right wing. Shoots left. 6', 206 lbs. Born, Minsk, USSR, April 17, 1981. Pittsburgh's 1st choice, 18th overall, in 1999 Entry Draft.

Season	Club	League	GP	G	A	Pts	PIM	PP	SH	GW	S	%	+/-	TF	F%	Min	GP	G	A	Pts	PIM	PP	SH	GW	Min
1997-98	Cherepovets 2	Russia-3	44	11	12	23	16																		
	Cherepovets	Russia	2	0	0	0	2																		
1998-99	Cherepovets 3	Russia-4	2	0	1	1	2																		
	Cherepovets 2	Russia-3	11	1	4	5	18																		
	Cherepovets	Russia	33	3	0	3	8										1	0	0	0	2				
99-2000	Magnitogorsk	Russia	30	3	4	7	12										11	1	1	2	6				
2000-01	Ak Bars Kazan	Russia	24	7	8	15	10										2	0	0	0	4				
	Spartak 2	Russia-3	2	0	1	1	0																		
2001-02	Ak Bars Kazan	Russia	10	1	2	3	2																		
	Spartak Moscow	Russia	23	1	0	1	12																		
	Belarus	Olympics	2	0	0	0	0																		
2002-03	**Pittsburgh**	**NHL**	**2**	**0**	**0**	**0**	**0**	**0**	**0**	**0**	**4**	**0.0**	**–2**	**0**	**0.0**	**13:06**									
	Wilkes-Barre	AHL	65	9	21	30	41										6	2	4	6	4				
2003-04	**Pittsburgh**	**NHL**	**82**	**9**	**20**	**29**	**30**	**2**	**0**	**3**	**123**	**7.3**	**–30**	**12**	**33.3**	**15:21**									
	Wilkes-Barre	AHL															24	6	11	17	18				
2004-05	Dynamo Minsk	BelOpen	11	6	2	8	38																		
	Spartak Moscow	Russia	31	6	10	16	48																		
2005-06	**Pittsburgh**	**NHL**	**60**	**3**	**6**	**9**	**20**	**0**	**1**	**0**	**72**	**4.2**	**–10**	**14**	**21.4**	**13:15**									
	Wilkes-Barre	AHL	18	7	5	12	13																		
	NHL Totals		**144**	**12**	**26**	**38**	**50**	**2**	**1**	**3**	**199**	**6.0**		**26**	**26.9**	**14:27**									

Signed as a free agent by **Minsk** (BelOpen), September 15, 2004. Signed as a free agent by **Spartak Moscow** (Russia), November, 2004. Signed as a free agent by **Kazan** (Russia), July 1, 2006.

KOMARNISKI, Zenith

(KOH-mahr-NIHS-kee, ZEE-nihth)

Defense. Shoots left. 6', 200 lbs. Born, Edmonton, Alta., August 13, 1978. Vancouver's 2nd choice, 75th overall, in 1996 Entry Draft.

Season	Club	League	GP	G	A	Pts	PIM	PP	SH	GW	S	%	+/-	TF	F%	Min	GP	G	A	Pts	PIM	PP	SH	GW	Min
1993-94	Ft. Saskatchewan	AMHL	32	14	32	46	42																		
1994-95	Tri-City	WHL	66	5	19	24	110										17	1	2	3	47				
1995-96	Tri-City	WHL	42	5	21	26	85																		
1996-97	Tri-City	WHL	58	12	44	56	112																		
1997-98	Tri-City	WHL	3	0	4	4	18																		
	Spokane Chiefs	WHL	43	7	20	27	90										18	4	6	10	49				
1998-99	Syracuse Crunch	AHL	58	9	19	28	89																		
99-2000	**Vancouver**	**NHL**	**18**	**1**	**1**	**2**	**8**	**0**	**0**	**0**	**21**	**4.8**	**–1**	**0**	**0.0**	**16:11**									
	Syracuse Crunch	AHL	42	4	12	16	130										4	2	0	2	6				
2000-01	Kansas City	IHL	70	7	22	29	191																		
2001-02	Manitoba Moose	AHL	77	5	20	25	153										7	0	2	2	13				
2002-03	**Vancouver**	**NHL**	**1**	**0**	**0**	**0**	**2**	**0**	**0**	**0**	**0**	**0.0**	**0**	**0**	**0.0**	**6:25**									
	Manitoba Moose	AHL	53	15	8	23	94										13	2	2	4	30				
2003-04	Manitoba Moose	AHL	10	0	0	0	35																		
	Columbus	**NHL**	**2**	**0**	**0**	**0**	**0**	**0**	**0**	**0**	**1**	**0.0**	**0**	**0**	**0.0**	**14:48**									
	Syracuse Crunch	AHL	54	2	22	24	84										7	0	1	1	4				
2004-05	Syracuse Crunch	AHL	62	3	11	14	99																		
2005-06	Omaha	AHL	68	6	15	21	99																		
	NHL Totals		**21**	**1**	**1**	**2**	**10**	**0**	**0**	**0**	**22**	**4.5**		**0**	**0.0**	**15:35**									

WHL West First All-Star Team (1997)

Traded to **Columbus** by **Vancouver** for Sean Pronger, October 30, 2003. Signed as a free agent by **Calgary**, August 11, 2005.

Season	Club	League	GP	G	A	Pts	PIM	PP	SH	GW	S	%	+/-	TP	F%	Min	GP	G	A	Pts	PIM	PP	SH	GW	Min
										Regular Season										Playoffs					

KOMISAREK, Mike (koh-mih-SAIR-ehk, MIGHK) MTL.

Defense. Shoots right. 6'4", 241 lbs.   Born, Islip Terrace, NY, January 19, 1982. Montreal's 1st choice, 7th overall, in 2001 Entry Draft.

Season	Club	League	GP	G	A	Pts	PIM	PP	SH	GW	S	%	+/-	TP	F%	Min	GP	G	A	Pts	PIM	PP	SH	GW	Min
1998-99	N.E. Jr. Coyotes	EJHL	53	17	24	51		….	….	….	….	….	….	….	….	….	….	….	….	….	….	….	….	….	….
99-2000	USNTDP	U-18	6	0	0	0	12	….	….	….	….	….	….	….	….	….	….	….	….	….	….	….	….	….	….
	USNTDP	USHL	51	5	8	13	124	….	….	….	….	….	….	….	….	….	….	….	….	….	….	….	….	….	….
	USNTDP	NAHL	1	0	0	0	16	….	….	….	….	….	….	….	….	….	….	….	….	….	….	….	….	….	….
2000-01	U. of Michigan	CCHA	41	4	12	16	77	….	….	….	….	….	….	….	….	….	….	….	….	….	….	….	….	….	….
2001-02	U. of Michigan	CCHA	40	11	19	30	70	….	….	….	….	….	….	….	….	….	….	….	….	….	….	….	….	….	….
2002-03	**Montreal**	**NHL**	**21**	**0**	**1**	**1**	**28**	0	0	0	26	0.0	-6	0	0.0	16:42	….	….	….	….	….	….	….	….	….
	Hamilton	AHL	56	5	25	30	79	….	….	….	….	….	….	….	….	….	23	1	5	6	60	….	….	….	….
2003-04	**Montreal**	**NHL**	**46**	**0**	**4**	**4**	**34**	0	0	0	40	0.0	4	0	0.0	12:00	7	0	0	0	8	0	0	0	14:09
	Hamilton	AHL	18	2	7	9	47	….	….	….	….	….	….	….	….	….	….	….	….	….	….	….	….	….	….
2004-05	Hamilton	AHL	20	1	4	5	49	….	….	….	….	….	….	….	….	….	4	0	1	1	8	….	….	….	….
2005-06	**Montreal**	**NHL**	**71**	**2**	**4**	**6**	**116**	0	0	0	66	3.0	-1	0	0.0	14:40	6	0	0	0	10	0	0	0	18:35
	NHL Totals		**138**	**2**	**9**	**11**	**178**	0	0	0	132	1.5		0	0.0	14:05	13	0	0	0	18	0	0	0	16:11

CCHA First All-Star Team (2002) • NCAA West First All-American Team (2002) • AHL All-Rookie Team (2003)

KONDRATIEV, Maxim (kohn-DRAT-yehv, mahx-EEM) ANA.

Defense. Shoots left. 6'1", 192 lbs.   Born, Togliatti, USSR, January 20, 1983. Toronto's 7th choice, 168th overall, in 2001 Entry Draft.

Season	Club	League	GP	G	A	Pts	PIM	PP	SH	GW	S	%	+/-	TP	F%	Min	GP	G	A	Pts	PIM	PP	SH	GW	Min
99-2000	Lada Togliatti 2	Russia-3	16	0	2	2	6	….	….	….	….	….	….	….	….	….	….	….	….	….	….	….	….	….	….
	Lada Togliatti	Russia	20	1	1	2	…	….	….	….	….	….	….	….	….	….	….	….	….	….	….	….	….	….	….
2000-01	Lada Togliatti 2	Russia-3	STATISTICS NOT AVAILABLE														….	….	….	….	….	….	….	….	….
	CSK VVS Samara	Russia-2	18	2	1	3	24	….	….	….	….	….	….	….	….	….	….	….	….	….	….	….	….	….	….
2001-02	Lada Togliatti	Russia	43	3	3	6	32	….	….	….	….	….	….	….	….	….	4	0	0	0	0	….	….	….	….
2002-03	Lada Togliatti	Russia	47	2	3	5	56	….	….	….	….	….	….	….	….	….	10	0	0	0	6	….	….	….	….
2003-04	**Toronto**	**NHL**	**7**	**0**	**0**	**0**	**2**	0	0	0	6	0.0	0	0	0.0	15:36	….	….	….	….	….	….	….	….	….
	St. John's	AHL	18	3	5	8	10	….	….	….	….	….	….	….	….	….	….	….	….	….	….	….	….	….	….
	Lada Togliatti	Russia	29	2	3	5	85	….	….	….	….	….	….	….	….	….	6	0	0	0	16	….	….	….	….
2004-05	Hartford	AHL	13	1	4	5	8	….	….	….	….	….	….	….	….	….	….	….	….	….	….	….	….	….	….
	Lada Togliatti	Russia	32	4	2	6	65	….	….	….	….	….	….	….	….	….	5	0	2	2	0	….	….	….	….
2005-06	**NY Rangers**	**NHL**	**29**	**1**	**2**	**3**	**22**	1	0	0	16	6.3	-2	0	0.0	16:17	….	….	….	….	….	….	….	….	….
	Hartford	AHL	4	0	0	0	0	….	….	….	….	….	….	….	….	….	….	….	….	….	….	….	….	….	….
	Portland Pirates	AHL	37	4	13	17	19	….	….	….	….	….	….	….	….	….	13	5	9	14	12	….	….	….	….
	NHL Totals		**36**	**1**	**2**	**3**	**24**	1	0	0	22	4.5		0	0.0	16:09	….	….	….	….	….	….	….	….	….

Assigned to **Togliatti** (Russia) by **Toronto**, December 16, 2003. Traded to **NY Rangers** by **Toronto** with Jarkko Immonen, Toronto's 1st round choice (later traded to Calgary - Calgary selected Kris Chucko) in 2004 Entry Draft and Toronto's 2nd round choice (Michael Sauer) in 2005 Entry Draft for Brian Leetch and Edmonton's 4th round choice (previously acquired, Toronto selected Roman Kukumberg) in 2004 Entry Draft, March 3, 2004. Signed as a free agent by **Togliatti** (Russia), November 11, 2004. Traded to **Anaheim** by **NY Rangers** for Petr Sykora and NY Rangers' 4th round choice (previously acquired) in 2007 Entry Draft, January 8, 2006.

KONOPKA, Zenon (kuh-NOHP-kah, ZEH-nohn) ANA.

Center. Shoots left. 6', 206 lbs.   Born, Niagara Falls, Ont., January 2, 1981.

Season	Club	League	GP	G	A	Pts	PIM	PP	SH	GW	S	%	+/-	TP	F%	Min	GP	G	A	Pts	PIM	PP	SH	GW	Min
1998-99	Ottawa 67's	OHL	56	7	8	15	62	….	….	….	….	….	….	….	….	….	7	0	0	0	2	….	….	….	….
99-2000	Ottawa 67's	OHL	59	8	11	19	107	….	….	….	….	….	….	….	….	….	11	1	2	3	8	….	….	….	….
2000-01	Ottawa 67's	OHL	66	20	45	65	120	….	….	….	….	….	….	….	….	….	20	7	13	20	47	….	….	….	….
2001-02	Ottawa 67's	OHL	61	18	68	86	100	….	….	….	….	….	….	….	….	….	13	8	6	14	49	….	….	….	….
2002-03	Wilkes-Barre	AHL	4	0	1	1	9	….	….	….	….	….	….	….	….	….	….	….	….	….	….	….	….	….	….
	Wheeling Nailers	ECHL	68	22	48	70	231	….	….	….	….	….	….	….	….	….	….	….	….	….	….	….	….	….	….
2003-04	Utah Grizzlies	AHL	43	7	4	11	198	….	….	….	….	….	….	….	….	….	….	….	….	….	….	….	….	….	….
	Idaho Steelheads	ECHL	23	6	22	28	82	….	….	….	….	….	….	….	….	….	17	9	8	17	30	….	….	….	….
2004-05	Cincinnati	AHL	75	17	29	46	212	….	….	….	….	….	….	….	….	….	12	3	3	6	26	….	….	….	….
2005-06	**Anaheim**	**NHL**	**23**	**4**	**3**	**7**	**48**	2	0	0	18	22.2	-4	142	53.5	7:19	….	….	….	….	….	….	….	….	….
	Portland Pirates	AHL	34	18	26	44	57	….	….	….	….	….	….	….	….	….	19	11	18	29	46	….	….	….	….
	NHL Totals		**23**	**4**	**3**	**7**	**48**	2	0	0	18	22.2		142	53.5	7:19	….	….	….	….	….	….	….	….	….

ECHL All-Rookie Team (2003)
Signed as a free agent by **Utah** (AHL), September 10, 2003. Signed as a free agent by **Anaheim**, September 1, 2004.

KONOWALCHUK, Steve (kahn-uh-WAHL-chuk, STEEV) COL.

Left wing. Shoots left. 6'1", 207 lbs.   Born, Salt Lake City, UT, November 11, 1972. Washington's 5th choice, 58th overall, in 1991 Entry Draft.

Season	Club	League	GP	G	A	Pts	PIM	PP	SH	GW	S	%	+/-	TP	F%	Min	GP	G	A	Pts	PIM	PP	SH	GW	Min
1989-90	Prince Albert	SMHL	36	30	28	58	22	….	….	….	….	….	….	….	….	….	….	….	….	….	….	….	….	….	….
1990-91	Portland	WHL	72	43	49	92	78	….	….	….	….	….	….	….	….	….	….	….	….	….	….	….	….	….	….
1991-92	Portland	WHL	64	51	53	104	95	….	….	….	….	….	….	….	….	….	6	3	6	9	12	….	….	….	….
	Washington	**NHL**	1	0	0	0	0	0	0	0	1	0.0	0	….	….	….	….	….	….	….	….	….	….	….	….
	Baltimore	AHL	3	1	1	2	0	….	….	….	….	….	….	….	….	….	….	….	….	….	….	….	….	….	….
1992-93	**Washington**	**NHL**	**36**	**4**	**7**	**11**	**16**	1	0	1	34	11.8	4	….	….	….	2	0	1	1	0	0	0	0	….
	Baltimore	AHL	37	18	28	46	74	….	….	….	….	….	….	….	….	….	….	….	….	….	….	….	….	….	….
1993-94	**Washington**	**NHL**	**62**	**12**	**14**	**26**	**33**	0	0	0	63	19.0	9	….	….	….	11	0	1	1	10	0	0	0	….
	Portland Pirates	AHL	8	1	4	15	4	….	….	….	….	….	….	….	….	….	….	….	….	….	….	….	….	….	….
1994-95	**Washington**	**NHL**	**46**	**11**	**14**	**25**	**44**	3	3	3	88	12.5	7	….	….	….	7	2	5	7	12	0	1	0	….
1995-96	**Washington**	**NHL**	**70**	**23**	**22**	**45**	**92**	7	1	3	197	11.7	13	….	….	….	2	0	2	2	0	0	0	0	….
1996-97	**Washington**	**NHL**	**78**	**17**	**25**	**42**	**67**	2	1	3	155	11.0	-3	….	….	….	….	….	….	….	….	….	….	….	….
1997-98	**Washington**	**NHL**	**80**	**10**	**24**	**34**	**80**	2	0	2	131	7.6	9	….	….	….	….	….	….	….	….	….	….	….	….
1998-99	**Washington**	**NHL**	**45**	**12**	**12**	**24**	**26**	4	1	2	98	12.2	0	….	….	….	….	….	….	….	….	….	….	….	….
99-2000	**Washington**	**NHL**	**82**	**16**	**27**	**43**	**80**	3	0	1	146	11.0	19	124	51.6	17:50	5	1	0	1	2	0	1	0	17:25
2000-01	**Washington**	**NHL**	**82**	**24**	**23**	**47**	**87**	6	0	5	163	14.7	5	147	49.7	17:36	6	2	3	5	14	2	0	0	19:39
2001-02	**Washington**	**NHL**	**28**	**2**	**12**	**14**	**23**	0	0	0	36	5.6	-2	91	55.0	17:04	….	….	….	….	….	….	….	….	….
2002-03	**Washington**	**NHL**	**77**	**15**	**15**	**30**	**71**	2	0	3	119	12.6	3	92	44.6	16:42	6	0	0	0	6	0	0	0	16:07
2003-04	**Washington**	**NHL**	**6**	**0**	**1**	**1**	**0**	0	0	0	7	0.0	-5	7	57.1	14:38	….	….	….	….	….	….	….	….	….
	Colorado	**NHL**	**76**	**19**	**20**	**39**	**70**	3	0	3	145	13.1	2	338	47.0	18:20	11	4	0	4	12	4	0	1	18:15
2004-05			DID NOT PLAY														….	….	….	….	….	….	….	….	….
2005-06	**Colorado**	**NHL**	**21**	**6**	**9**	**15**	**14**	1	2	0	39	15.4	5	35	28.6	16:33	2	0	0	0	4	0	0	0	14:10
	NHL Totals		**790**	**171**	**225**	**396**	**703**	34	8	26	1422	12.0		898	48.7	17:19	52	9	12	21	60	6	2	1	17:42

WHL West First All-Star Team (1992) • WHL Player of the Year (1992)
• Missed majority of 2001-02 season recovering from shoulder injury suffered in game vs. Los Angeles, October 16, 2001. Traded to **Colorado** by **Washington** with Washington's 3rd round choice (later traded to Carolina – Carolina selected Casey Borer) in 2004 Entry Draft for Bates Battaglia and Jonas Johansson, October 22, 2003. • Missed majority of 2005-06 regular season recovering from wrist injury suffered in game at Calgary, November 21, 2005.

KOPECKY, Tomas (koh-PEHTS-kee, TAW-mahsh) DET.

Center. Shoots left. 6'3", 187 lbs.   Born, Ilava, Czech., February 5, 1982. Detroit's 2nd choice, 38th overall, in 2000 Entry Draft.

Season	Club	League	GP	G	A	Pts	PIM	PP	SH	GW	S	%	+/-	TP	F%	Min	GP	G	A	Pts	PIM	PP	SH	GW	Min
1997-98	Dukla Trencin Jr.	Slovak-Jr.	41	19	22	41	…	….	….	….	….	….	….	….	….	….	….	….	….	….	….	….	….	….	….
1998-99	Dukla Trencin Jr.	Slovak-Jr.	44	13	16	29	18	….	….	….	….	….	….	….	….	….	….	….	….	….	….	….	….	….	….
99-2000	Dukla Trencin Jr.	Slovak-Jr.	14	8	9	17	36	….	….	….	….	….	….	….	….	….	….	….	….	….	….	….	….	….	….
	Dukla Trencin	Slovakia	52	3	4	7	24	….	….	….	….	….	….	….	….	….	5	0	0	0	0	….	….	….	….
2000-01	Lethbridge	WHL	49	22	28	50	52	….	….	….	….	….	….	….	….	….	5	1	1	2	6	….	….	….	….
	Cincinnati	AHL	1	0	0	0	0	….	….	….	….	….	….	….	….	….	….	….	….	….	….	….	….	….	….
2001-02	Lethbridge	WHL	60	34	42	76	94	….	….	….	….	….	….	….	….	….	4	2	1	3	15	….	….	….	….
	Cincinnati	AHL	2	1	1	2	6	….	….	….	….	….	….	….	….	….	2	0	0	0	0	….	….	….	….
2002-03	Grand Rapids	AHL	70	17	21	38	32	….	….	….	….	….	….	….	….	….	14	0	0	0	6	….	….	….	….
2003-04	Grand Rapids	AHL	48	6	6	12	28	….	….	….	….	….	….	….	….	….	….	….	….	….	….	….	….	….	….
2004-05	Grand Rapids	AHL	48	8	8	16	35	….	….	….	….	….	….	….	….	….	….	….	….	….	….	….	….	….	….
2005-06	**Detroit**	**NHL**	**1**	**0**	**0**	**0**	**2**	0	0	0	1	0.0	0	0	0.0	9:41	….	….	….	….	….	….	….	….	….
	Grand Rapids	AHL	77	32	37	69	108	….	….	….	….	….	….	….	….	….	16	3	4	7	25	….	….	….	….
	NHL Totals		**1**	**0**	**0**	**0**	**2**	0	0	0	1	0.0		0	0.0	9:41	….	….	….	….	….	….	….	….	….

KOROLEV, Evgeny

(KOH-roh-lehv, ehv-GEHN-ee) **NYI**

Defense. Shoots left. 6'1", 214 lbs. Born, Moscow, USSR, July 24, 1978. NY Islanders' 6th choice, 182nd overall, in 1998 Entry Draft.

			Regular Season														Playoffs								
Season	Club	League	GP	G	A	Pts	PIM	PP	SH	GW	S	%	+/-	TF	F%	Min	GP	G	A	Pts	PIM	PP	SH	GW	Min
1995-96	Peterborough	OHL	60	2	12	14	60	....	....	....	....	....	....	....	....	....	6	0	0	0	2	....	....	....	....
1996-97	Peterborough	OHL	64	5	17	22	60	....	....	....	....	....	....	....	....	....	11	1	1	2	8	....	....	....	....
1997-98	Peterborough	OHL	37	5	21	26	39	....	....	....	....	....	....	....	....	....	....	....	....	....	....	....	....	....	....
	London Knights	OHL	27	4	10	14	36	....	....	....	....	....	....	....	....	....	15	2	7	9	29	....	....	....	....
1998-99	Roanoke Express	ECHL	2	0	1	1	0	....	....	....	....	....	....	....	....	....	....	....	....	....	....	....	....	....	....
	Lowell	AHL	54	2	6	8	48	....	....	....	....	....	....	....	....	....	2	0	1	1	0	....	....	....	....
99-2000	**NY Islanders**	**NHL**	**17**	**1**	**2**	**3**	**8**	**0**	**0**	**0**	**7**	**14.3**	**–10**	**0**	**0.0**	**16:12**	....	....	....	....	....	....	....	....	....
	Lowell	AHL	57	1	10	11	61	....	....	....	....	....	....	....	....	....	6	0	0	0	4	....	....	....	....
2000-01	**NY Islanders**	**NHL**	**8**	**0**	**0**	**0**	**6**	**0**	**0**	**0**	**11**	**0.0**	**0**	**0**	**0.0**	**16:40**	....	....	....	....	....	....	....	....	....
	Chicago Wolves	IHL	4	0	1	1	0	....	....	....	....	....	....	....	....	....	....	....	....	....	....	....	....	....	....
	Louisville Panthers	AHL	36	2	14	16	68	....	....	....	....	....	....	....	....	....	....	....	....	....	....	....	....	....	....
2001-02	**NY Islanders**	**NHL**	**17**	**0**	**2**	**2**	**6**	**0**	**0**	**0**	**9**	**0.0**	**0**	**0**	**0.0**	**10:22**	**2**	**0**	**0**	**0**	**0**	**0**	**0**	**0**	**5:35**
	Bridgeport	AHL	53	5	8	13	30	....	....	....	....	....	....	....	....	....	....	....	....	....	....	....	....	....	....
2002-03	Yaroslavl	Russia	16	1	2	3	22	....	....	....	....	....	....	....	....	....	8	0	0	0	6	....	....	....	....
2003-04	Yaroslavl 2	Russia-3	3	0	1	1	0	....	....	....	....	....	....	....	....	....	....	....	....	....	....	....	....	....	....
	Yaroslavl	Russia	25	1	1	2	39	....	....	....	....	....	....	....	....	....	....	....	....	....	....	....	....	....	....
	Cherepovets	Russia	22	1	5	6	20	....	....	....	....	....	....	....	....	....	....	....	....	....	....	....	....	....	....
2004-05	Cherepovets	Russia	58	5	14	19	72	....	....	....	....	....	....	....	....	....	....	....	....	....	....	....	....	....	....
2005-06	Dynamo Moscow	Russia	45	7	6	13	86	....	....	....	....	....	....	....	....	....	1	0	0	0	0	....	....	....	....
	NHL Totals		**42**	**1**	**4**	**5**	**20**	**0**	**0**	**0**	**27**	**3.7**		**0**	**0.0**	**13:56**	**2**	**0**	**0**	**0**	**0**	**0**	**0**	**0**	**5:35**

• Re-entered NHL Entry Draft. Originally NY Islanders' 9th choice, 192nd overall, in 1996 Entry Draft.
Signed as a free agent by **Yaroslavl** (Russia), October 14, 2002. Signed as a free agent by **Dynamo Moscow** (Russia), May 30, 2005.

KOROLYUK, Alexander

(koh-roh-LYUHK, al-ehx-AN-duhr) **S.J.**

Left wing. Shoots left. 5'9", 190 lbs. Born, Moscow, USSR, January 15, 1976. San Jose's 6th choice, 141st overall, in 1994 Entry Draft.

Season	Club	League	GP	G	A	Pts	PIM	PP	SH	GW	S	%	+/-	TF	F%	Min	GP	G	A	Pts	PIM	PP	SH	GW	Min
1993-94	Krylja Sovetov	CIS	22	4	4	8	20	....	....	....	....	....	....	....	....	....	3	1	0	1	4	....	....	....	....
1994-95	Krylja Sovetov	CIS	52	16	13	29	62	....	....	....	....	....	....	....	....	....	4	1	2	3	4	....	....	....	....
1995-96	Krylja Sovetov	CIS	50	30	19	49	77	....	....	....	....	....	....	....	....	....	....	....	....	....	....	....	....	....	....
1996-97	Krylja Sovetov	Russia	17	8	5	13	46	....	....	....	....	....	....	....	....	....	....	....	....	....	....	....	....	....	....
	Manitoba Moose	IHL	42	20	16	36	71	....	....	....	....	....	....	....	....	....	....	....	....	....	....	....	....	....	....
1997-98	**San Jose**	**NHL**	**19**	**2**	**3**	**5**	**6**	**1**	**0**	**0**	**23**	**8.7**	**–5**	....	....	....	....	....	....	....	....	....	....	....	....
	Kentucky	AHL	44	16	23	39	96	....	....	....	....	....	....	....	....	....	3	0	0	0	0	....	....	....	....
1998-99	**San Jose**	**NHL**	**55**	**12**	**18**	**30**	**26**	**2**	**0**	**0**	**96**	**12.5**	**3**	**4**	**50.0**	**13:53**	**6**	**1**	**3**	**4**	**2**	**0**	**0**	**1**	**11:01**
	Kentucky	AHL	23	9	13	22	16	....	....	....	....	....	....	....	....	....	....	....	....	....	....	....	....	....	....
99-2000	**San Jose**	**NHL**	**57**	**14**	**21**	**35**	**35**	**3**	**0**	**1**	**124**	**11.3**	**4**	**1**	**100.0**	**13:36**	**9**	**0**	**3**	**3**	**6**	**0**	**0**	**0**	**11:37**
2000-01	Ak Bars Kazan	Russia	6	0	5	5	4	....	....	....	....	....	....	....	....	....	....	....	....	....	....	....	....	....	....
	San Jose	**NHL**	**70**	**12**	**13**	**25**	**41**	**3**	**0**	**1**	**140**	**8.6**	**2**	**30**	**33.3**	**11:56**	**2**	**0**	**0**	**0**	**0**	**0**	**0**	**0**	**8:11**
2001-02	**San Jose**	**NHL**	**32**	**3**	**7**	**10**	**14**	**0**	**0**	**1**	**49**	**6.1**	**2**	**10**	**30.0**	**12:16**	....	....	....	....	....	....	....	....	....
2002-03	Ak Bars Kazan	Russia	45	14	17	31	46	....	....	....	....	....	....	....	....	....	4	0	0	0	0	....	....	....	....
2003-04	**San Jose**	**NHL**	**63**	**19**	**18**	**37**	**18**	**4**	**0**	**2**	**108**	**17.6**	**20**	**14**	**50.0**	**14:55**	**17**	**5**	**2**	**7**	**10**	**2**	**0**	**1**	**16:40**
2004-05	Vityaz Chekhov	Russia-2	42	24	28	52	54	....	....	....	....	....	....	....	....	....	....	....	....	....	....	....	....	....	....
	Voskresensk	Russia	10	4	3	7	14	....	....	....	....	....	....	....	....	....	....	....	....	....	....	....	....	....	....
2005-06	Vityaz Chekhov	Russia	45	19	15	34	86	....	....	....	....	....	....	....	....	....	....	....	....	....	....	....	....	....	....
	Russia	Olympics	6	1	1	2	6	....	....	....	....	....	....	....	....	....	....	....	....	....	....	....	....	....	....
	NHL Totals		**296**	**62**	**80**	**142**	**140**	**13**	**0**	**5**	**540**	**11.5**		**59**	**39.0**	**13:23**	**34**	**6**	**8**	**14**	**18**	**2**	**0**	**2**	**13:50**

• Spent majority of 2001-02 season on practice roster. Signed as a free agent by **Kazan** (Russia), July 9, 2002. Signed as a free agent by **Chekhov** (Russia-2), September 25, 2004. Signed as a free agent by **Voskresensk** (Russia), February 14, 2005.

KOSTITSYN, Andrei

(kaws-TIHT-sihn, AWN-dray) **MTL.**

Wing. Shoots left. 6', 200 lbs. Born, Novopolosk, USSR, February 3, 1985. Montreal's 1st choice, 10th overall, in 2003 Entry Draft.

Season	Club	League	GP	G	A	Pts	PIM	PP	SH	GW	S	%	+/-	TF	F%	Min	GP	G	A	Pts	PIM	PP	SH	GW	Min
2000-01	Novopolotsk	Belarus	1	2	1	3	2	....	....	....	....	....	....	....	....	....	....	....	....	....	....	....	....	....	....
	Novopolotsk	EEHL	5	1	0	1	0	....	....	....	....	....	....	....	....	....	....	....	....	....	....	....	....	....	....
	Yunost Minsk	Belarus	3	1	4	5	8	....	....	....	....	....	....	....	....	....	....	....	....	....	....	....	....	....	....
	HC Vitebsk	Belarus	17	17	6	23	42	....	....	....	....	....	....	....	....	....	....	....	....	....	....	....	....	....	....
2001-02	Novopolotsk	Belarus	17	9	6	15	28	....	....	....	....	....	....	....	....	....	....	....	....	....	....	....	....	....	....
	Novopolotsk	EEHL	29	9	8	17	16	....	....	....	....	....	....	....	....	....	....	....	....	....	....	....	....	....	....
	Yunost Minsk	Belarus	6	2	0	2	8	....	....	....	....	....	....	....	....	....	....	....	....	....	....	....	....	....	....
2002-03	CSKA Moscow	Russia	6	0	0	0	2	....	....	....	....	....	....	....	....	....	....	....	....	....	....	....	....	....	....
	Voskresensk	Russia-2	2	1	1	2	0	....	....	....	....	....	....	....	....	....	....	....	....	....	....	....	....	....	....
	Yunost Minsk	Belarus	4	6	4	10	43	....	....	....	....	....	....	....	....	....	....	....	....	....	....	....	....	....	....
	CSKA Moscow 2	Russia-3	3	2	2	4	25	....	....	....	....	....	....	....	....	....	....	....	....	....	....	....	....	....	....
2003-04	CSKA Moscow 2	Russia-3	STATISTICS NOT AVAILABLE																						
	CSKA Moscow	Russia	12	0	1	1	2	....	....	....	....	....	....	....	....	....	....	....	....	....	....	....	....	....	....
	Yunost Minsk	Belarus	STATISTICS NOT AVAILABLE																						
2004-05	Hamilton	AHL	66	12	11	23	24	....	....	....	....	....	....	....	....	....	3	0	0	0	0	....	....	....	....
2005-06	**Montreal**	**NHL**	**12**	**2**	**1**	**3**	**2**	**0**	**0**	**0**	**9**	**22.2**	**1**	**1**	**0.0**	**7:32**	....	....	....	....	....	....	....	....	....
	Hamilton	AHL	64	18	29	47	76	....	....	....	....	....	....	....	....	....	....	....	....	....	....	....	....	....	....
	NHL Totals		**12**	**2**	**1**	**3**	**2**	**0**	**0**	**0**	**9**	**22.2**		**1**	**0.0**	**7:32**	....	....	....	....	....	....	....	....	....

KOSTOPOULOS, Tom

(kaw-STAWP-oh-lihs, TAWM) **L.A.**

Right wing. Shoots right. 6', 200 lbs. Born, Mississauga, Ont., January 24, 1979. Pittsburgh's 9th choice, 204th overall, in 1999 Entry Draft.

Season	Club	League	GP	G	A	Pts	PIM	PP	SH	GW	S	%	+/-	TF	F%	Min	GP	G	A	Pts	PIM	PP	SH	GW	Min
1995-96	Brampton	OPJHL	24	9	9	18	28	....	....	....	....	....	....	....	....	....	....	....	....	....	....	....	....	....	....
1996-97	London Knights	OHL	64	13	12	25	67	....	....	....	....	....	....	....	....	....	....	....	....	....	....	....	....	....	....
1997-98	London Knights	OHL	66	24	26	50	108	....	....	....	....	....	....	....	....	....	16	6	4	10	26	....	....	....	....
1998-99	London Knights	OHL	66	27	60	87	114	....	....	....	....	....	....	....	....	....	25	19	16	35	32	....	....	....	....
99-2000	Wilkes-Barre	AHL	76	26	32	58	121	....	....	....	....	....	....	....	....	....	....	....	....	....	....	....	....	....	....
2000-01	Wilkes-Barre	AHL	80	16	36	52	120	....	....	....	....	....	....	....	....	....	21	3	9	12	6	....	....	....	....
2001-02	**Pittsburgh**	**NHL**	**11**	**1**	**2**	**3**	**9**	**0**	**0**	**0**	**8**	**12.5**	**–1**	**0**	**0.0**	**12:03**	....	....	....	....	....	....	....	....	....
	Wilkes-Barre	AHL	70	27	26	53	112	....	....	....	....	....	....	....	....	....	....	....	....	....	....	....	....	....	....
2002-03	**Pittsburgh**	**NHL**	**8**	**0**	**1**	**1**	**0**	**0**	**0**	**0**	**6**	**0.0**	**–4**	**2**	**0.0**	**4:33**	....	....	....	....	....	....	....	....	....
	Wilkes-Barre	AHL	71	21	42	63	131	....	....	....	....	....	....	....	....	....	6	1	2	3	7	....	....	....	....
2003-04	**Pittsburgh**	**NHL**	**60**	**9**	**13**	**22**	**67**	**2**	**1**	**1**	**101**	**8.9**	**–14**	**10**	**30.0**	**14:26**	....	....	....	....	....	....	....	....	....
	Wilkes-Barre	AHL	21	7	13	20	43	....	....	....	....	....	....	....	....	....	24	7	16	23	32	....	....	....	....
2004-05	Manchester	AHL	64	25	46	71	99	....	....	....	....	....	....	....	....	....	6	0	7	7	10	....	....	....	....
2005-06	**Los Angeles**	**NHL**	**76**	**8**	**14**	**22**	**100**	**0**	**0**	**1**	**74**	**10.8**	**–8**	**30**	**36.7**	**12:56**	....	....	....	....	....	....	....	....	....
	NHL Totals		**155**	**18**	**30**	**48**	**176**	**2**	**1**	**2**	**189**	**9.5**		**42**	**33.3**	**13:01**	....	....	....	....	....	....	....	....	....

Signed as a free agent by **Manchester** (AHL), July 12, 2004. Signed as a free agent by **Los Angeles**, August 1, 2005.

KOTALIK, Ales

(KOH-tahl-eek, al-EHSH) **BUF.**

Right wing. Shoots right. 6'1", 227 lbs. Born, Jindrichuv Hradec, Czech., December 23, 1978. Buffalo's 7th choice, 164th overall, in 1998 Entry Draft.

Season	Club	League	GP	G	A	Pts	PIM	PP	SH	GW	S	%	+/-	TF	F%	Min	GP	G	A	Pts	PIM	PP	SH	GW	Min
1993-94	C. Budejovice Jr.	CzRep-Jr.	28	12	12	24	....	....	....	....	....	....	....	....	....	....	....	....	....	....	....	....	....	....	....
1994-95	C. Budejovice Jr.	CzRep-Jr.	36	26	17	43	....	....	....	....	....	....	....	....	....	....	....	....	....	....	....	....	....	....	....
1995-96	C. Budejovice Jr.	CzRep-Jr.	28	6	7	13	....	....	....	....	....	....	....	....	....	....	....	....	....	....	....	....	....	....	....
1996-97	C. Budejovice Jr.	CzRep-Jr.	36	15	16	31	24	....	....	....	....	....	....	....	....	....	....	....	....	....	....	....	....	....	....
1997-98	C. Budejovice	CzRep	47	9	7	16	14	....	....	....	....	....	....	....	....	....	....	....	....	....	....	....	....	....	....
1998-99	C. Budejovice	CzRep	41	8	13	21	16	....	....	....	....	....	....	....	....	....	3	0	0	0	....	....	....	....	....
99-2000	C. Budejovice	CzRep	43	7	12	19	34	....	....	....	....	....	....	....	....	....	3	0	1	1	6	....	....	....	....
2000-01	C. Budejovice	CzRep	52	19	29	48	54	....	....	....	....	....	....	....	....	....	....	....	....	....	....	....	....	....	....
2001-02	Rochester	AHL	68	18	25	43	55	....	....	....	....	....	....	....	....	....	1	0	0	0	0	....	....	....	....
	Buffalo	**NHL**	**13**	**1**	**3**	**4**	**2**	**0**	**0**	**0**	**21**	**4.8**	**–1**	**11**	**27.3**	**12:35**	....	....	....	....	....	....	....	....	....
2002-03	**Buffalo**	**NHL**	**68**	**21**	**14**	**35**	**30**	**4**	**0**	**2**	**138**	**15.2**	**–2**	**37**	**51.4**	**15:15**	....	....	....	....	....	....	....	....	....
	Rochester	AHL	8	0	2	2	4	....	....	....	....	....	....	....	....	....	....	....	....	....	....	....	....	....	....
2003-04	**Buffalo**	**NHL**	**62**	**15**	**11**	**26**	**41**	**2**	**0**	**3**	**142**	**10.6**	**–1**	**14**	**50.0**	**15:11**	....	....	....	....	....	....	....	....	....

Season	Club	League	GP	G	A	Pts	PIM	PP	SH	GW	S	%	+/-	TF	F%	Min	GP	G	A	Pts	PIM	PP	SH	GW	Min
			Regular Season														Playoffs								
2004-05	Liberec	CzRep	25	8	8	16	46	....	....	....	....	....	....	....	....	....	12	2	5	7	12	....	....	....	....
2005-06	**Buffalo**	**NHL**	**82**	**25**	**37**	**62**	**62**	**10**	**0**	**5**	**261**	**9.6**	**-3**	**29**	**41.4**	**15:34**	**18**	**4**	**7**	**11**	**8**	**0**	**0**	**3**	**15:15**
	Czech Republic	Olympics	4	0	0	0	0	....	....	....	....	....	....	....	....	....	....	....	....	....	....	....	....	....	....
	NHL Totals		**225**	**62**	**65**	**127**	**135**	**16**	**0**	**10**	**562**	**11.0**		**91**	**45.1**	**15:11**	**18**	**4**	**7**	**11**	**8**	**0**	**0**	**3**	**15:15**

Signed as a free agent by **Liberec** (CzRep), September 6, 2004.

KOVALCHUK, Ilya

(koh-vuhl-CHUHK, IHL-yah) **ATL.**

Left wing. Shoots right. 6'1", 225 lbs. Born, Tver, USSR, April 15, 1983. Atlanta's 1st choice, 1st overall, in 2001 Entry Draft.

Season	Club	League	GP	G	A	Pts	PIM	PP	SH	GW	S	%	+/-	TF	F%	Min	GP	G	A	Pts	PIM	PP	SH	GW	Min
99-2000	Spartak Moscow	Russia-2	49	12	5	17	75	....	....	....	....	....	....	....	....	....	....	....	....	....	....	....	....	....	....
	Spartak 2	Russia-3	2	2	1	3	14	....	....	....	....	....	....	....	....	....	....	....	....	....	....	....	....	....	....
2000-01	Spartak Moscow	Russia	40	28	18	46	78	....	....	....	....	....	....	....	....	....	12	14	4	18	38	....	....	....	....
2001-02	**Atlanta**	**NHL**	**65**	**29**	**22**	**51**	**28**	**7**	**0**	**4**	**184**	**15.8**	**-19**	**6**	**16.7**	**18:32**	....	....	....	....	....	....	....	....	....
	Russia	Olympics	6	1	2	3	14	....	....	....	....	....	....	....	....	....	....	....	....	....	....	....	....	....	....
2002-03	**Atlanta**	**NHL**	**81**	**38**	**29**	**67**	**57**	**9**	**0**	**3**	**257**	**14.8**	**-24**	**15**	**40.0**	**19:27**	....	....	....	....	....	....	....	....	....
2003-04	**Atlanta**	**NHL**	**81**	***41**	**46**	**87**	**63**	**16**	**1**	**6**	**341**	**12.0**	**-10**	**28**	**32.1**	**23:41**	....	....	....	....	....	....	....	....	....
2004-05	Ak Bars Kazan	Russia	53	19	23	42	72	....	....	....	....	....	....	....	....	....	4	0	1	1	0	....	....	....	....
2005-06	**Atlanta**	**NHL**	**78**	**52**	**46**	**98**	**68**	**27**	**0**	**7**	**323**	**16.1**	**-6**	**47**	**40.4**	**22:23**	....	....	....	....	....	....	....	....	....
	Russia	Olympics	8	4	1	5	31	....	....	....	....	....	....	....	....	....	....	....	....	....	....	....	....	....	....
	NHL Totals		**305**	**160**	**143**	**303**	**216**	**59**	**1**	**20**	**1105**	**14.5**		**96**	**36.5**	**21:08**	....	....	....	....	....	....	....	....	....

NHL All-Rookie Team (2002) • NHL Second All-Star Team (2004) • Maurice "Rocket" Richard Trophy (2004) (tied with Jarome Iginla and Rick Nash)
Played in NHL All-Star Game (2004)
Signed as a free agent by **Kazan** (Russia) August 22, 2004. Signed as a free agent by **Khimik** (Russia), September 1, 2005.

KOVALEV, Alex

(koh-VAH-lehv, al-EHX) **MTL.**

Right wing. Shoots left. 6'2", 229 lbs. Born, Togliatti, USSR, February 24, 1973. NY Rangers' 1st choice, 15th overall, in 1991 Entry Draft.

Season	Club	League	GP	G	A	Pts	PIM	PP	SH	GW	S	%	+/-	TF	F%	Min	GP	G	A	Pts	PIM	PP	SH	GW	Min
1989-90	Dynamo Moscow	USSR	1	0	0	0	0	....	....	....	....	....	....	....	....	....	....	....	....	....	....	....	....	....	....
1990-91	Dynamo Moscow	USSR	18	1	2	3	4	....	....	....	....	....	....	....	....	....	....	....	....	....	....	....	....	....	....
1991-92	Dynamo Moscow	CIS	33	16	9	25	20	....	....	....	....	....	....	....	....	....	....	....	....	....	....	....	....	....	....
	Russia	Olympics	8	1	2	3	14	....	....	....	....	....	....	....	....	....	....	....	....	....	....	....	....	....	....
1992-93	**NY Rangers**	**NHL**	**65**	**20**	**18**	**38**	**79**	**3**	**0**	**3**	**134**	**14.9**	**-10**	....	....	....	....	....	....	....	....	....	....	....	....
	Binghamton	AHL	13	13	11	24	35	....	....	....	....	....	....	....	....	....	9	3	5	8	14	....	....	....	....
1993-94♦	**NY Rangers**	**NHL**	**76**	**23**	**33**	**56**	**154**	**7**	**0**	**3**	**184**	**12.5**	**18**	....	....	....	**23**	**9**	**12**	**21**	**18**	**5**	**0**	**2**	....
1994-95	Lada Togliatti	CIS	12	8	8	16	49	....	....	....	....	....	....	....	....	....	....	....	....	....	....	....	....	....	....
	NY Rangers	**NHL**	**48**	**13**	**15**	**28**	**30**	**1**	**1**	**1**	**103**	**12.6**	**-6**	....	....	....	**10**	**4**	**7**	**11**	**10**	**0**	**0**	**0**	....
1995-96	**NY Rangers**	**NHL**	**81**	**24**	**34**	**58**	**98**	**8**	**1**	**7**	**206**	**11.7**	**5**	....	....	....	**11**	**3**	**4**	**7**	**14**	**0**	**0**	**1**	....
1996-97	**NY Rangers**	**NHL**	**45**	**13**	**22**	**35**	**42**	**1**	**0**	**0**	**110**	**11.8**	**11**	....	....	....	....	....	....	....	....	....	....	....	....
1997-98	**NY Rangers**	**NHL**	**73**	**23**	**30**	**53**	**44**	**8**	**0**	**3**	**173**	**13.3**	**-22**	....	....	....	....	....	....	....	....	....	....	....	....
1998-99	**NY Rangers**	**NHL**	**14**	**3**	**4**	**7**	**12**	**1**	**0**	**1**	**35**	**8.6**	**-6**	**18**	**44.4**	**19:53**	....	....	....	....	....	....	....	....	....
	Pittsburgh	**NHL**	**63**	**20**	**26**	**46**	**37**	**5**	**1**	**4**	**156**	**12.8**	**8**	**226**	**43.4**	**20:30**	**10**	**5**	**7**	**12**	**14**	**0**	**0**	**1**	**20:24**
99-2000	**Pittsburgh**	**NHL**	**82**	**26**	**40**	**66**	**94**	**9**	**2**	**4**	**254**	**10.2**	**-3**	**306**	**47.4**	**22:53**	**11**	**1**	**5**	**6**	**10**	**0**	**0**	**0**	**26:35**
2000-01	**Pittsburgh**	**NHL**	**79**	**44**	**51**	**95**	**96**	**12**	**2**	**9**	**307**	**14.3**	**12**	**255**	**40.0**	**23:35**	**18**	**5**	**5**	**10**	**16**	**1**	**0**	**0**	**20:57**
2001-02	**Pittsburgh**	**NHL**	**67**	**32**	**44**	**76**	**80**	**8**	**1**	**3**	**266**	**12.0**	**2**	**179**	**45.3**	**24:03**	....	....	....	....	....	....	....	....	....
	Russia	Olympics	6	3	1	4	4	....	....	....	....	....	....	....	....	....	....	....	....	....	....	....	....	....	....
2002-03	**Pittsburgh**	**NHL**	**54**	**27**	**37**	**64**	**50**	**8**	**0**	**1**	**212**	**12.7**	**-11**	**19**	**31.6**	**24:03**	....	....	....	....	....	....	....	....	....
	NY Rangers	**NHL**	**24**	**10**	**3**	**13**	**20**	**3**	**0**	**2**	**59**	**16.9**	**2**	**19**	**42.1**	**20:09**	....	....	....	....	....	....	....	....	....
2003-04	**NY Rangers**	**NHL**	**66**	**13**	**29**	**42**	**54**	**3**	**0**	**0**	**178**	**7.3**	**-5**	**29**	**48.3**	**19:37**	....	....	....	....	....	....	....	....	....
	Montreal	**NHL**	**12**	**1**	**2**	**3**	**12**	**0**	**0**	**1**	**29**	**3.4**	**-4**	**2**	**50.0**	**15:36**	**11**	**6**	**4**	**10**	**8**	**1**	**0**	**1**	**20:11**
2004-05	Ak Bars Kazan	Russia	35	10	12	22	80	....	....	....	....	....	....	....	....	....	4	0	0	0	8	....	....	....	....
2005-06	**Montreal**	**NHL**	**69**	**23**	**42**	**65**	**76**	**9**	**0**	**5**	**206**	**11.2**	**-1**	**47**	**48.9**	**19:28**	**6**	**4**	**3**	**7**	**4**	**1**	**0**	**0**	**19:21**
	Russia	Olympics	8	4	2	6	4	....	....	....	....	....	....	....	....	....	....	....	....	....	....	....	....	....	....
	NHL Totals		**918**	**315**	**430**	**745**	**978**	**86**	**8**	**47**	**2612**	**12.1**		**1100**	**44.2**	**21:45**	**100**	**37**	**47**	**84**	**94**	**8**	**0**	**5**	**21:38**

Played in NHL All-Star Game (2001, 2003)
Traded to **Pittsburgh** by **NY Rangers** with Harry York for Petr Nedved, Chris Tamer and Sean Pronger, November 25, 1998. Traded to **NY Rangers** by **Pittsburgh** with Mike Wilson, Janne Laukkanen and Dan LaCouture for Joel Bouchard, Richard Lintner, Rico Fata, Mikael Samuelsson and future considerations, February 10, 2003. Traded to **Montreal** by **NY Rangers** for Jozef Balej and Montreal's 2nd round choice (Bruce Graham) in 2004 Entry Draft, March 2, 2004. Signed as a free agent by **Kazan** (Russia), November 3, 2004.

KOZLOV, Viktor

(KAHS-lahf, VIHK-tohr)

Center. Shoots right. 6'5", 235 lbs. Born, Togliatti, USSR, February 14, 1975. San Jose's 1st choice, 6th overall, in 1993 Entry Draft.

Season	Club	League	GP	G	A	Pts	PIM	PP	SH	GW	S	%	+/-	TF	F%	Min	GP	G	A	Pts	PIM	PP	SH	GW	Min
1990-91	Lada Togliatti	USSR-2	2	2	0	2	0	....	....	....	....	....	....	....	....	....	....	....	....	....	....	....	....	....	....
1991-92	Lada Togliatti	CIS	3	0	0	0	0	....	....	....	....	....	....	....	....	....	....	....	....	....	....	....	....	....	....
1992-93	Dynamo Moscow	CIS	30	6	5	11	4	....	....	....	....	....	....	....	....	....	10	3	0	3	0	....	....	....	....
1993-94	Dynamo Moscow	CIS	42	16	9	25	14	....	....	....	....	....	....	....	....	....	7	3	2	5	0	....	....	....	....
1994-95	Dynamo Moscow	CIS	3	1	1	2	2	....	....	....	....	....	....	....	....	....	....	....	....	....	....	....	....	....	....
	San Jose	**NHL**	**16**	**2**	**0**	**2**	**2**	**0**	**0**	**0**	**23**	**8.7**	**-5**	....	....	....	....	....	....	....	....	....	....	....	....
	Kansas City	IHL	4	1	1	2	0	....	....	....	....	....	....	....	....	....	13	4	5	9	12	....	....	....	....
1995-96	**San Jose**	**NHL**	**62**	**6**	**13**	**19**	**6**	**1**	**0**	**0**	**107**	**5.6**	**-15**	....	....	....	....	....	....	....	....	....	....	....	....
	Kansas City	IHL	15	4	7	11	12	....	....	....	....	....	....	....	....	....	....	....	....	....	....	....	....	....	....
1996-97	**San Jose**	**NHL**	**78**	**16**	**25**	**41**	**40**	**4**	**0**	**4**	**184**	**8.7**	**-16**	....	....	....	....	....	....	....	....	....	....	....	....
1997-98	**San Jose**	**NHL**	**18**	**5**	**2**	**7**	**2**	**2**	**0**	**0**	**51**	**9.8**	**-2**	....	....	....	....	....	....	....	....	....	....	....	....
	Florida	**NHL**	**46**	**12**	**11**	**23**	**14**	**3**	**2**	**0**	**114**	**10.5**	**-1**	....	....	....	....	....	....	....	....	....	....	....	....
1998-99	**Florida**	**NHL**	**65**	**16**	**35**	**51**	**24**	**5**	**1**	**1**	**209**	**7.7**	**13**	**985**	**41.2**	**19:03**	....	....	....	....	....	....	....	....	....
99-2000	**Florida**	**NHL**	**80**	**17**	**53**	**70**	**16**	**6**	**0**	**2**	**223**	**7.6**	**24**	**1616**	**42.9**	**19:27**	**4**	**0**	**1**	**1**	**0**	**0**	**0**	**0**	**16:05**
2000-01	**Florida**	**NHL**	**51**	**14**	**23**	**37**	**10**	**6**	**0**	**2**	**139**	**10.1**	**-4**	**817**	**41.6**	**18:23**	....	....	....	....	....	....	....	....	....
2001-02	**Florida**	**NHL**	**50**	**9**	**18**	**27**	**20**	**6**	**0**	**1**	**143**	**6.3**	**-16**	**840**	**43.1**	**19:54**	....	....	....	....	....	....	....	....	....
2002-03	**Florida**	**NHL**	**74**	**22**	**34**	**56**	**18**	**7**	**1**	**1**	**232**	**9.5**	**-8**	**404**	**42.8**	**22:35**	....	....	....	....	....	....	....	....	....
2003-04	**Florida**	**NHL**	**48**	**11**	**16**	**27**	**16**	**3**	**1**	**1**	**117**	**9.4**	**-4**	**200**	**49.0**	**19:30**	....	....	....	....	....	....	....	....	....
	New Jersey	**NHL**	**11**	**2**	**4**	**6**	**2**	**0**	**0**	**0**	**26**	**7.7**	**0**	**112**	**56.3**	**13:26**	**2**	**0**	**0**	**0**	**0**	**0**	**0**	**0**	**8:55**
2004-05	Lada Togliatti	Russia	52	15	22	37	22	....	....	....	....	....	....	....	....	....	10	3	3	6	6	....	....	....	....
2005-06	**New Jersey**	**NHL**	**69**	**12**	**13**	**25**	**16**	**2**	**0**	**1**	**122**	**9.8**	**0**	**185**	**47.0**	**13:32**	**3**	**0**	**0**	**0**	**0**	**0**	**0**	**0**	**14:05**
	Russia	Olympics	8	2	3	5	2	....	....	....	....	....	....	....	....	....	....	....	....	....	....	....	....	....	....
	NHL Totals		**668**	**144**	**247**	**391**	**186**	**45**	**5**	**13**	**1690**	**8.5**		**5159**	**43.1**	**18:47**	**9**	**0**	**1**	**1**	**0**	**0**	**0**	**0**	**13:49**

Played in NHL All-Star Game (2000)
Traded to **Florida** by **San Jose** with Florida's 5th round choice (previously acquired, Florida selected Jaroslav Spacek) in 1998 Entry Draft for Dave Lowry and Florida's 1st round choice (later traded to Tampa Bay – Tampa Bay selected Vincent Lecavalier) in 1998 Entry Draft, November 13, 1997. Traded to **New Jersey** by **Florida** for Christian Berglund and Victor Uchevatov, March 1, 2004. Signed as a free agent by **Togliatti** (Russia), July 11, 2004.

KOZLOV, Vyacheslav

(KAHS-lahf, vee-YATCH-ih-slav) **ATL.**

Left wing. Shoots left. 5'10", 190 lbs. Born, Voskresensk, USSR, May 3, 1972. Detroit's 2nd choice, 45th overall, in 1990 Entry Draft.

Season	Club	League	GP	G	A	Pts	PIM	PP	SH	GW	S	%	+/-	TF	F%	Min	GP	G	A	Pts	PIM	PP	SH	GW	Min
1987-88	Voskresensk	USSR	2	0	0	0	0	....	....	....	....	....	....	....	....	....	....	....	....	....	....	....	....	....	....
1988-89	Voskresensk	USSR	14	0	1	1	2	....	....	....	....	....	....	....	....	....	....	....	....	....	....	....	....	....	....
1989-90	Voskresensk	USSR	45	14	12	26	38	....	....	....	....	....	....	....	....	....	....	....	....	....	....	....	....	....	....
1990-91	Voskresensk	USSR	45	11	13	24	46	....	....	....	....	....	....	....	....	....	....	....	....	....	....	....	....	....	....
1991-92	CSKA Moscow	CIS	11	6	5	11	12	....	....	....	....	....	....	....	....	....	....	....	....	....	....	....	....	....	....
	Detroit	**NHL**	**7**	**0**	**2**	**2**	**2**	**0**	**0**	**0**	**9**	**0.0**	**-2**	....	....	....	....	....	....	....	....	....	....	....	....
1992-93	**Detroit**	**NHL**	**17**	**4**	**1**	**5**	**14**	**0**	**0**	**0**	**26**	**15.4**	**-1**	....	....	....	**4**	**0**	**2**	**2**	**2**	**0**	**0**	**0**	....
	Adirondack	AHL	45	23	36	59	54	....	....	....	....	....	....	....	....	....	4	1	1	2	4	....	....	....	....
1993-94	**Detroit**	**NHL**	**77**	**34**	**39**	**73**	**50**	**8**	**2**	**6**	**202**	**16.8**	**27**	....	....	....	**7**	**2**	**5**	**7**	**12**	**0**	**0**	**0**	....
	Adirondack	AHL	3	0	1	1	15	....	....	....	....	....	....	....	....	....	....	....	....	....	....	....	....	....	....
1994-95	CSKA Moscow	CIS	10	3	4	7	14	....	....	....	....	....	....	....	....	....	....	....	....	....	....	....	....	....	....
	Detroit	**NHL**	**46**	**13**	**20**	**33**	**45**	**5**	**0**	**3**	**97**	**13.4**	**12**	....	....	....	**18**	**9**	**7**	**16**	**10**	**1**	**0**	**4**	....
1995-96	**Detroit**	**NHL**	**82**	**36**	**37**	**73**	**70**	**9**	**0**	**7**	**237**	**15.2**	**33**	....	....	....	**19**	**5**	**7**	**12**	**10**	**2**	**0**	**1**	....
1996-97♦	**Detroit**	**NHL**	**75**	**23**	**22**	**45**	**46**	**3**	**0**	**6**	**211**	**10.9**	**21**	....	....	....	**20**	**8**	**5**	**13**	**14**	**4**	**0**	**2**	....
1997-98♦	**Detroit**	**NHL**	**80**	**25**	**27**	**52**	**46**	**6**	**0**	**1**	**221**	**11.3**	**14**	....	....	....	**22**	**6**	**8**	**14**	**10**	**1**	**0**	**4**	....
1998-99	**Detroit**	**NHL**	**79**	**29**	**29**	**58**	**45**	**6**	**1**	**4**	**209**	**13.9**	**10**	**38**	**36.8**	**16:02**	**10**	**6**	**1**	**7**	**4**	**3**	**0**	**0**	**14:44**
99-2000	**Detroit**	**NHL**	**72**	**18**	**18**	**36**	**28**	**4**	**0**	**3**	**165**	**10.9**	**11**	**28**	**35.7**	**15:30**	**8**	**2**	**1**	**3**	**12**	**1**	**0**	**1**	**12:20**

			Regular Season														Playoffs								
Season	Club	League	GP	G	A	Pts	PIM	PP	SH	GW	S	%	+/-	TF	F%	Min	GP	G	A	Pts	PIM	PP	SH	GW	Min
2000-01	**Detroit**	**NHL**	**72**	**20**	**18**	**38**	**30**	**4**	**0**	**5**	**187**	**10.7**	**9**	**51**	**47.1**	**14:43**	**6**	**4**	**1**	**5**	**2**	**2**	**0**	**0**	**16:27**
2001-02	**Buffalo**	**NHL**	**38**	**9**	**13**	**22**	**16**	**3**	**0**	**1**	**68**	**13.2**	**0**	**24**	**41.7**	**16:31**	....	....	....	....	....	....	....	....	....
2002-03	**Atlanta**	**NHL**	**79**	**21**	**49**	**70**	**66**	**9**	**1**	**2**	**185**	**11.4**	**–10**	**67**	**34.3**	**20:01**	....	....	....	....	....	....	....	....	....
2003-04	**Atlanta**	**NHL**	**76**	**20**	**32**	**52**	**74**	**6**	**0**	**1**	**191**	**10.5**	**–12**	**164**	**32.3**	**20:20**	....	....	....	....	....	....	....	....	....
2004-05	Voskresensk	Russia	38	12	18	30	69	....	....	....	....	....	....	....	....	....	....	....	....	....	....	....	....	....	....
	Ak Bars Kazan	Russia	8	2	4	6	0	....	....	....	....	....	....	....	....	....	4	1	0	1	8	....	....	....	....
2005-06	**Atlanta**	**NHL**	**82**	**25**	**46**	**71**	**33**	**8**	**0**	**1**	**206**	**12.1**	**14**	**317**	**39.8**	**17:47**	....	....	....	....	....	....	....	....	....
	NHL Totals		**882**	**277**	**353**	**630**	**565**	**71**	**4**	**40**	**2214**	**12.5**		**689**	**37.7**	**17:23**	**114**	**42**	**37**	**79**	**76**	**14**	**0**	**12**	**14:22**

Traded to **Buffalo** by **Detroit** with Detroit's 1st round choice (later traded to Columbus – later traded to Atlanta – Atlanta selected Jim Slater) in 2002 Entry Draft and future considerations for Dominik Hasek, July 1, 2001. • Missed majority of 2001-02 season recovering from Achilles tendon injury suffered in game vs. Columbus, December 31, 2001. Traded to **Atlanta** by **Buffalo** with Buffalo's 2nd round choice (later traded to Columbus – Columbus selected Joakim Lindstrom) in 2003 Entry Draft for Atlanta's 2nd round choice (later traded to Edmonton – Edmonton selected Jeff Deslauriers) in 2003 Entry Draft and Vancouver's 3rd round choice (previously acquired by Atlanta via Florida - Buffalo selected John Adams) in 2003 Entry Draft, June 22, 2002. Signed as a free agent by **Voskresensk** (Russia), September 15, 2004. Signed as a free agent by **Kazan** (Russia), February 17, 2005.

KRAFT, Milan

(KRAFT, MIH-lan) **PIT.**

Center. Shoots right. 6'4", 212 lbs. Born, Plzen, Czech., January 17, 1980. Pittsburgh's 1st choice, 23rd overall, in 1998 Entry Draft.

1995-96	HC Plzen Jr.	CzRep-Jr.	49	54	41	95	....	....	....	....	....	....	....	....	....	....	....	....	....	....	....	....	....	....	....
1996-97	HC Plzen Jr.	CzRep-Jr.	29	24	12	36	....	....	....	....	....	....	....	....	....	....	....	....	....	....	....	....	....	....	....
	HC ZKZ Plzen	CzRep	9	0	1	1	2	....	....	....	....	....	....	....	....	....	....	....	....	....	....	....	....	....	....
1997-98	HC Plzen Jr.	CzRep-Jr.	24	22	21	43	12	....	....	....	....	....	....	....	....	....	....	....	....	....	....	....	....	....	....
	Plzen	CzRep	16	0	5	5	0	....	....	....	....	....	....	....	....	....	1	0	0	0	0	....	....	....	....
1998-99	Prince Albert	WHL	68	40	46	86	32	....	....	....	....	....	....	....	....	....	14	7	13	20	6	....	....	....	....
99-2000	Prince Albert	WHL	56	34	35	69	42	....	....	....	....	....	....	....	....	....	6	4	1	5	4	....	....	....	....
2000-01	**Pittsburgh**	**NHL**	**42**	**7**	**7**	**14**	**8**	**1**	**1**	**1**	**63**	**11.1**	**–6**	**427**	**37.9**	**11:41**	**8**	**0**	**0**	**0**	**2**	**0**	**0**	**0**	**12:13**
	Wilkes-Barre	AHL	40	21	23	44	27	....	....	....	....	....	....	....	....	....	14	12	7	19	6	....	....	....	....
2001-02	**Pittsburgh**	**NHL**	**68**	**8**	**8**	**16**	**16**	**1**	**0**	**2**	**103**	**7.8**	**–9**	**766**	**44.7**	**12:29**	....	....	....	....	....	....	....	....	....
	Wilkes-Barre	AHL	8	4	4	8	10	....	....	....	....	....	....	....	....	....	....	....	....	....	....	....	....	....	....
2002-03	**Pittsburgh**	**NHL**	**31**	**7**	**5**	**12**	**10**	**0**	**0**	**1**	**50**	**14.0**	**–8**	**392**	**43.1**	**13:56**	....	....	....	....	....	....	....	....	....
	Wilkes-Barre	AHL	40	13	24	37	28	....	....	....	....	....	....	....	....	....	6	2	4	6	4	....	....	....	....
2003-04	**Pittsburgh**	**NHL**	**66**	**19**	**21**	**40**	**18**	**6**	**0**	**1**	**134**	**14.2**	**–22**	**970**	**47.4**	**15:16**	....	....	....	....	....	....	....	....	....
2004-05	Plzen	CzRep	17	2	4	6	6	....	....	....	....	....	....	....	....	....	....	....	....	....	....	....	....	....	....
	Karlovy Vary	CzRep	35	9	10	19	20	....	....	....	....	....	....	....	....	....	....	....	....	....	....	....	....	....	....
2005-06	Avangard Omsk	Russia	28	2	5	7	14	....	....	....	....	....	....	....	....	....	....	....	....	....	....	....	....	....	....
	Karlovy Vary	CzRep	19	7	5	12	16	....	....	....	....	....	....	....	....	....	....	....	....	....	....	....	....	....	....
	NHL Totals		**207**	**41**	**41**	**82**	**52**	**8**	**1**	**5**	**350**	**11.7**		**2555**	**44.3**	**13:26**	**8**	**0**	**0**	**0**	**2**	**0**	**0**	**0**	**12:13**

Signed as a free agent by **Plzen** (CzRep), September 17, 2004. Signed as a free agent by **Karlovy Vary** (CzRep), October 27, 2004. Signed as a free agent by **Omsk** (Russia), August 26, 2005.

KRAFT, Ryan

(KRAFT, RIGH-uhn)

Center. Shoots left. 5'9", 181 lbs. Born, Bottineau, ND, November 7, 1975. San Jose's 11th choice, 194th overall, in 1995 Entry Draft.

1993-94	Moorhead Spuds	High-MN	25	40	45	85	....	....	....	....	....	....	....	....	....	....	....	....	....	....	....	....	....	....	....
1994-95	U. of Minnesota	WCHA	44	13	33	46	44	....	....	....	....	....	....	....	....	....	....	....	....	....	....	....	....	....	....
1995-96	U. of Minnesota	WCHA	41	13	24	37	24	....	....	....	....	....	....	....	....	....	....	....	....	....	....	....	....	....	....
1996-97	U. of Minnesota	WCHA	42	25	21	46	37	....	....	....	....	....	....	....	....	....	....	....	....	....	....	....	....	....	....
1997-98	U. of Minnesota	WCHA	32	11	26	37	16	....	....	....	....	....	....	....	....	....	....	....	....	....	....	....	....	....	....
1998-99	Richmond	ECHL	63	28	36	64	35	....	....	....	....	....	....	....	....	....	18	10	10	20	4	....	....	....	....
99-2000	Richmond	ECHL	44	32	35	67	32	....	....	....	....	....	....	....	....	....	....	....	....	....	....	....	....	....	....
	Cleveland	IHL	1	0	1	1	0	....	....	....	....	....	....	....	....	....	....	....	....	....	....	....	....	....	....
	Kentucky	AHL	15	7	6	13	2	....	....	....	....	....	....	....	....	....	5	3	1	4	0	....	....	....	....
2000-01	Kentucky	AHL	77	38	50	88	36	....	....	....	....	....	....	....	....	....	3	2	0	2	0	....	....	....	....
2001-02	Cleveland Barons	AHL	63	19	41	60	42	....	....	....	....	....	....	....	....	....	....	....	....	....	....	....	....	....	....
2002-03	**San Jose**	**NHL**	**7**	**0**	**1**	**1**	**0**	**0**	**0**	**0**	**1**	**0.0**	**2**	**41**	**34.2**	**8:33**	....	....	....	....	....	....	....	....	....
	Cleveland Barons	AHL	53	14	27	41	12	....	....	....	....	....	....	....	....	....	....	....	....	....	....	....	....	....	....
2003-04	Bridgeport	AHL	74	15	21	36	20	....	....	....	....	....	....	....	....	....	6	2	2	4	0	....	....	....	....
2004-05	Bridgeport	AHL	38	9	9	18	12	....	....	....	....	....	....	....	....	....	....	....	....	....	....	....	....	....	....
2005-06	Kassel Huskies	Germany	49	17	31	48	34	....	....	....	....	....	....	....	....	....	5	1	5	6	0	....	....	....	....
	NHL Totals		**7**	**0**	**1**	**1**	**0**	**0**	**0**	**0**	**1**	**0.0**		**41**	**34.1**	**8:33**	....	....	....	....	....	....	....	....	....

WCHA All-Rookie Team (1995) • WCHA All-Academic Team (1996) • AHL All-Rookie Team (2001) • AHL Second All-Star Team (2001) • Dudley "Red" Garrett Memorial Award (Rookie of the Year – AHL) (2001)

Signed as a free agent by **NY Islanders**, July 8, 2003. Signed as a free agent by **Kassel** (Germany), August 12, 2005.

KRAJICEK, Lukas

(KRIGH-ee-chehk, LOO-kahsh) **VAN.**

Defense. Shoots left. 6'2", 185 lbs. Born, Prostejov, Czech., March 11, 1983. Florida's 2nd choice, 24th overall, in 2001 Entry Draft.

1998-99	HC ZPS Zlin Jr.	CzRep-Jr.	48	8	18	26	40	....	....	....	....	....	....	....	....	....	....	....	....	....	....	....	....	....	....
99-2000	Det. Compuware	NAHL	53	5	22	27	61	....	....	....	....	....	....	....	....	....	5	0	1	1	18	....	....	....	....
2000-01	Peterborough	OHL	61	8	27	35	53	....	....	....	....	....	....	....	....	....	7	0	5	5	0	....	....	....	....
2001-02	**Florida**	**NHL**	**5**	**0**	**0**	**0**	**0**	**0**	**0**	**0**	**3**	**0.0**	**0**	**0**	**0.0**	**13:23**	....	....	....	....	....	....	....	....	....
	Peterborough	OHL	55	10	32	42	56	....	....	....	....	....	....	....	....	....	6	0	5	5	6	....	....	....	....
2002-03	Peterborough	OHL	52	11	42	53	42	....	....	....	....	....	....	....	....	....	7	0	3	3	0	....	....	....	....
	San Antonio	AHL	3	0	1	1	0	....	....	....	....	....	....	....	....	....	3	0	0	0	0	....	....	....	....
2003-04	**Florida**	**NHL**	**18**	**1**	**6**	**7**	**12**	**1**	**0**	**0**	**16**	**6.3**	**–2**	**0**	**0.0**	**13:32**	....	....	....	....	....	....	....	....	....
	San Antonio	AHL	54	5	12	17	24	....	....	....	....	....	....	....	....	....	....	....	....	....	....	....	....	....	....
2004-05	San Antonio	AHL	78	2	22	24	57	....	....	....	....	....	....	....	....	....	....	....	....	....	....	....	....	....	....
2005-06	**Florida**	**NHL**	**67**	**2**	**14**	**16**	**50**	**2**	**0**	**0**	**89**	**2.2**	**1**	**0**	**0.0**	**18:30**	....	....	....	....	....	....	....	....	....
	NHL Totals		**90**	**3**	**20**	**23**	**62**	**3**	**0**	**0**	**108**	**2.8**		**0**	**0.0**	**17:13**	....	....	....	....	....	....	....	....	....

OHL All-Rookie Team (2001) • OHL First All-Star Team (2003)

• Returned to **Peterborough** (OHL) by **Florida**, October 28, 2001. Traded to **Vancouver** by **Florida** with Roberto Luongo and Florida's 6th round choice (Sergei Shirokov) in 2006 Entry Draft for Todd Bertuzzi, Bryan Allen and Alex Auld, June 23, 2006.

KROG, Jason

(KROHG, JAY-suhn) **ATL.**

Center. Shoots right. 5'11", 191 lbs. Born, Fernie, B.C., October 9, 1975.

1992-93	Chilliwack Chiefs	BCJHL	52	30	27	57	52	....	....	....	....	....	....	....	....	....	....	....	....	....	....	....	....	....	....
1993-94	Chilliwack Chiefs	BCJHL	42	19	36	55	20	....	....	....	....	....	....	....	....	....	....	....	....	....	....	....	....	....	....
1994-95	Chilliwack Chiefs	BCJHL	60	47	81	128	36	....	....	....	....	....	....	....	....	....	....	....	....	....	....	....	....	....	....
1995-96	New Hampshire	H-East	34	4	16	20	20	....	....	....	....	....	....	....	....	....	....	....	....	....	....	....	....	....	....
1996-97	New Hampshire	H-East	39	23	*44	*67	28	....	....	....	....	....	....	....	....	....	....	....	....	....	....	....	....	....	....
1997-98	New Hampshire	H-East	38	*33	33	66	44	....	....	....	....	....	....	....	....	....	....	....	....	....	....	....	....	....	....
1998-99	New Hampshire	H-East	41	*34	*51	*85	38	....	....	....	....	....	....	....	....	....	....	....	....	....	....	....	....	....	....
99-2000	**NY Islanders**	**NHL**	**17**	**2**	**4**	**6**	**6**	**1**	**0**	**0**	**22**	**9.1**	**–1**	**81**	**53.1**	**10:03**	....	....	....	....	....	....	....	....	....
	Lowell	AHL	45	6	21	27	22	....	....	....	....	....	....	....	....	....	....	....	....	....	....	....	....	....	....
	Providence Bruins	AHL	11	9	8	17	4	....	....	....	....	....	....	....	....	....	6	2	2	4	0	....	....	....	....
2000-01	**NY Islanders**	**NHL**	**9**	**0**	**3**	**3**	**0**	**0**	**0**	**0**	**7**	**0.0**	**4**	**60**	**48.3**	**10:32**	....	....	....	....	....	....	....	....	....
	Lowell	AHL	26	11	16	27	6	....	....	....	....	....	....	....	....	....	....	....	....	....	....	....	....	....	....
	Springfield	AHL	24	7	23	30	4	....	....	....	....	....	....	....	....	....	....	....	....	....	....	....	....	....	....
2001-02	**NY Islanders**	**NHL**	**2**	**0**	**0**	**0**	**0**	**0**	**0**	**0**	**0**	**0.0**	**0**	**13**	**46.2**	**6:40**	....	....	....	....	....	....	....	....	....
	Bridgeport	AHL	64	26	36	62	13	....	....	....	....	....	....	....	....	....	20	10	13	23	8	....	....	....	....
2002-03	**Anaheim**	**NHL**	**67**	**10**	**15**	**25**	**12**	**0**	**1**	**1**	**92**	**10.9**	**1**	**634**	**60.4**	**13:47**	**21**	**3**	**1**	**4**	**4**	**0**	**0**	**0**	**12:10**
	Cincinnati	AHL	9	3	4	7	6	....	....	....	....	....	....	....	....	....	....	....	....	....	....	....	....	....	....
2003-04	**Anaheim**	**NHL**	**80**	**6**	**12**	**18**	**16**	**1**	**0**	**1**	**111**	**5.4**	**–4**	**769**	**58.5**	**11:58**	....	....	....	....	....	....	....	....	....
2004-05	EC Villacher SV	Austria	48	27	33	60	38	....	....	....	....	....	....	....	....	....	3	0	1	1	4	....	....	....	....

			Regular Season														Playoffs								
Season	Club	League	GP	G	A	Pts	PIM	PP	SH	GW	S	%	+/-	TF	F%	Min	GP	G	A	Pts	PIM	PP	SH	GW	Min
2005-06	Geneve	Swiss	29	15	14	29	32	....	....	....	....	....	....	....	....	....	....	....	....	....	....	....	....	....	....
	Frolunda	Sweden	7	5	1	6	6	....	....	....	....	....	....	....	....	....	17	5	3	8	10	....	....	....	....
	NHL Totals		**175**	**18**	**34**	**52**	**34**	**2**	**1**	**2**	**232**	**7.8**		**1557**	**58.5**	**12:21**	**21**	**3**	**1**	**4**	**4**	**0**	**0**	**0**	**12:10**

Hockey East First All-Star Team (1997, 1998, 1999) • NCAA East Second All-American Team (1997) • Hockey East Player of the Year (1999) • NCAA East First All-American Team (1999) • NCAA Championship All-Tournament Team (1999) • Hobey Baker Memorial Award (Top U.S. Collegiate Player) (1999)

Signed as a free agent by **NY Islanders**, May 14, 1999. Loaned to **Providence** (AHL) by **NY Islanders**, March 1, 2000. Signed as a free agent by **Anaheim**, July 17, 2002. Signed as a free agent by **Villacher** (Austria), August 24, 2004. Signed as a free agent by **Geneve** (Swiss), May 19, 2005. Signed as a free agent by **Frolunda** (Sweden), January 31, 2006. Signed as a free agent by **Atlanta**, July 4, 2006.

KRONWALL, Niklas

(KRAWN-wahl, NIHK-las) **DET.**

Defense. Shoots left. 5'11", 165 lbs. Born, Stockholm, Sweden, January 12, 1981. Detroit's 1st choice, 29th overall, in 2000 Entry Draft.

Season	Club	League	GP	G	A	Pts	PIM	PP	SH	GW	S	%	+/-	TF	F%	Min	GP	G	A	Pts	PIM	PP	SH	GW	Min
1996-97	Djurgarden Jr.	Swe-Jr.	1	0	0	0	0	....	....	....	....	....	....	....	....	....	....	....	....	....	....	....	....	....	....
1997-98	Djurgarden Jr.	Swe-Jr.	27	4	3	7	71	....	....	....	....	....	....	....	....	....	2	0	0	0	2	....	....	....	....
1998-99	Huddinge IK	Sweden-2	14	0	1	1	10	....	....	....	....	....	....	....	....	....	....	....	....	....	....	....	....	....	....
	Huddinge IK Jr.	Swe-Jr.	2	0	0	0	6	....	....	....	....	....	....	....	....	....	....	....	....	....	....	....	....	....	....
99-2000	Djurgarden	Sweden	37	1	4	5	16	....	....	....	....	....	....	....	....	....	8	0	0	0	8	....	....	....	....
2000-01	Djurgarden	Sweden	31	1	9	10	32	....	....	....	....	....	....	....	....	....	15	0	1	1	8	....	....	....	....
2001-02	Djurgarden	Sweden	48	5	7	12	34	....	....	....	....	....	....	....	....	....	5	0	0	0	0	....	....	....	....
2002-03	Djurgarden	Sweden	50	5	13	18	46	....	....	....	....	....	....	....	....	....	12	3	2	5	18	....	....	....	....
2003-04	**Detroit**	**NHL**	**20**	**1**	**4**	**5**	**16**	**0**	**0**	**1**	**18**	**5.6**	**5**	**0**	**0.0**	**13:51**	....	....	....	....	....	....	....	....	....
	Grand Rapids	AHL	25	2	11	13	20	....	....	....	....	....	....	....	....	....	....	....	....	....	....	....	....	....	....
2004-05	Grand Rapids	AHL	76	13	40	53	53	....	....	....	....	....	....	....	....	....	....	....	....	....	....	....	....	....	....
2005-06	**Detroit**	**NHL**	**27**	**1**	**8**	**9**	**28**	**1**	**0**	**0**	**28**	**3.6**	**11**	**0**	**0.0**	**20:31**	**6**	**0**	**3**	**3**	**2**	**0**	**0**	**0**	**22:43**
	Grand Rapids	AHL	1	0	0	0	0	....	....	....	....	....	....	....	....	....	....	....	....	....	....	....	....	....	....
	Sweden	Olympics	2	1	1	2	8	....	....	....	....	....	....	....	....	....	....	....	....	....	....	....	....	....	....
	NHL Totals		**47**	**2**	**12**	**14**	**44**	**1**	**0**	**1**	**46**	**4.3**		**0**	**0.0**	**17:41**	**6**	**0**	**3**	**3**	**2**	**0**	**0**	**0**	**22:43**

AHL First All-Star Team (2005) • Eddie Shore Award (Outstanding Defenseman – AHL) (2005)

• Missed majority of 2005-06 season recovering from knee surgery.

KRONWALL, Staffan

(KRAWN-wahl, STAH-fuhn) **TOR.**

Defense. Shoots left. 6'3", 209 lbs. Born, Jarfalla, Sweden, September 10, 1982. Toronto's 9th choice, 285th overall, in 2002 Entry Draft.

Season	Club	League	GP	G	A	Pts	PIM	PP	SH	GW	S	%	+/-	TF	F%	Min	GP	G	A	Pts	PIM	PP	SH	GW	Min
99-2000	Huddinge IK Jr.	Swe-Jr.	34	2	0	2	38	....	....	....	....	....	....	....	....	....	....	....	....	....	....	....	....	....	....
	Huddinge IK U18	Swe-U18	7	0	3	3	0	....	....	....	....	....	....	....	....	....	....	....	....	....	....	....	....	....	....
2000-01	Huddinge IK Jr.	Swe-Jr.	23	6	1	7	16	....	....	....	....	....	....	....	....	....	....	....	....	....	....	....	....	....	....
	Huddinge IK	Sweden-3	1	0	0	0	0	....	....	....	....	....	....	....	....	....	....	....	....	....	....	....	....	....	....
2001-02	Huddinge IK	Sweden-2	42	4	7	11	30	....	....	....	....	....	....	....	....	....	....	....	....	....	....	....	....	....	....
	Huddinge IK Jr.	Swe-Jr.	1	0	0	0	0	....	....	....	....	....	....	....	....	....	4	2	1	3	27	....	....	....	....
2002-03	Djurgarden	Sweden	48	4	6	10	65	....	....	....	....	....	....	....	....	....	12	1	1	2	8	....	....	....	....
2003-04	Djurgarden	Sweden	44	1	5	6	54	....	....	....	....	....	....	....	....	....	4	0	1	1	2	....	....	....	....
2004-05	Brynas IF Gavle	Sweden	3	0	1	1	4	....	....	....	....	....	....	....	....	....	....	....	....	....	....	....	....	....	....
	Djurgarden Jr.	Swe-Jr.	5	2	4	6	0	....	....	....	....	....	....	....	....	....	....	....	....	....	....	....	....	....	....
	Djurgarden	Sweden	35	1	4	5	43	....	....	....	....	....	....	....	....	....	12	2	0	2	10	....	....	....	....
2005-06	**Toronto**	**NHL**	**34**	**0**	**1**	**1**	**14**	**0**	**0**	**0**	**18**	**0.0**	**–3**	**0**	**0.0**	**12:57**	....	....	....	....	....	....	....	....	....
	Toronto Marlies	AHL	16	1	10	11	12	....	....	....	....	....	....	....	....	....	4	0	2	2	2	....	....	....	....
	NHL Totals		**34**	**0**	**1**	**1**	**14**	**0**	**0**	**0**	**18**	**0.0**		**0**	**0.0**	**12:57**	....	....	....	....	....	....	....	....	....

KUBA, Filip

(KOO-bah, FIHL-ihp) **T.B.**

Defense. Shoots left. 6'3", 205 lbs. Born, Ostrava, Czech., December 29, 1976. Florida's 8th choice, 192nd overall, in 1995 Entry Draft.

Season	Club	League	GP	G	A	Pts	PIM	PP	SH	GW	S	%	+/-	TF	F%	Min	GP	G	A	Pts	PIM	PP	SH	GW	Min
1994-95	HC Vitkovice Jr.	CzRep-Jr.	35	10	15	25	....	....	....	....	....	....	....	....	....	....	....	....	....	....	....	....	....	....	....
	HC Vitkovice	CzRep	....	....	....	....	....	....	....	....	....	....	....	....	....	....	4	0	0	0	2	....	....	....	....
1995-96	HC Vitkovice	CzRep	19	0	1	1	....	....	....	....	....	....	....	....	....	....	....	....	....	....	....	....	....	....	....
1996-97	Carolina	AHL	51	0	12	12	38	....	....	....	....	....	....	....	....	....	....	....	....	....	....	....	....	....	....
1997-98	New Haven	AHL	77	4	13	17	58	....	....	....	....	....	....	....	....	....	3	1	1	2	0	....	....	....	....
1998-99	**Florida**	**NHL**	**5**	**0**	**1**	**1**	**0**	**0**	**0**	**0**	**5**	**0.0**	**2**	**0**	**0.0**	**22:29**	....	....	....	....	....	....	....	....	....
	Kentucky	AHL	45	2	8	10	33	....	....	....	....	....	....	....	....	....	10	0	1	1	4	....	....	....	....
99-2000	**Florida**	**NHL**	**13**	**1**	**5**	**6**	**2**	**1**	**0**	**1**	**16**	**6.3**	**–3**	**0**	**0.0**	**13:52**	....	....	....	....	....	....	....	....	....
	Houston Aeros	IHL	27	3	6	9	13	....	....	....	....	....	....	....	....	....	11	1	2	3	4	....	....	....	....
2000-01	**Minnesota**	**NHL**	**75**	**9**	**21**	**30**	**28**	**4**	**0**	**4**	**141**	**6.4**	**–6**	**1**	**0.0**	**24:16**	....	....	....	....	....	....	....	....	....
2001-02	**Minnesota**	**NHL**	**62**	**5**	**19**	**24**	**32**	**3**	**0**	**1**	**101**	**5.0**	**–6**	**0**	**0.0**	**25:30**	....	....	....	....	....	....	....	....	....
2002-03	**Minnesota**	**NHL**	**78**	**8**	**21**	**29**	**29**	**4**	**2**	**1**	**129**	**6.2**	**0**	**1**	**0.0**	**23:56**	**18**	**3**	**5**	**8**	**24**	**3**	**0**	**0**	**26:46**
2003-04	**Minnesota**	**NHL**	**77**	**5**	**19**	**24**	**28**	**2**	**1**	**2**	**114**	**4.4**	**–7**	**2**	**0.0**	**24:06**	....	....	....	....	....	....	....	....	....
2004-05			DID NOT PLAY																						
2005-06	**Minnesota**	**NHL**	**65**	**6**	**19**	**25**	**44**	**1**	**1**	**1**	**69**	**8.7**	**0**	**2**	**0.0**	**21:46**	....	....	....	....	....	....	....	....	....
	Czech Republic	Olympics	8	1	0	1	0	....	....	....	....	....	....	....	....	....	....	....	....	....	....	....	....	....	....
	NHL Totals		**375**	**34**	**105**	**139**	**163**	**15**	**4**	**10**	**575**	**5.9**		**6**	**0.0**	**23:33**	**18**	**3**	**5**	**8**	**24**	**3**	**0**	**0**	**26:46**

Played in NHL All-Star Game (2004)

Traded to **Calgary** by **Florida** for Rocky Thompson, March 16, 2000. Claimed by **Minnesota** from **Calgary** in Expansion Draft, June 23, 2000. Signed as a free agent by **Tampa Bay**, July 1, 2006.

KUBINA, Pavel

(koo-BEE-nuh, PAH-vehl) **TOR.**

Defense. Shoots right. 6'4", 244 lbs. Born, Celadna, Czech., April 15, 1977. Tampa Bay's 6th choice, 179th overall, in 1996 Entry Draft.

Season	Club	League	GP	G	A	Pts	PIM	PP	SH	GW	S	%	+/-	TF	F%	Min	GP	G	A	Pts	PIM	PP	SH	GW	Min
1993-94	HC Vitkovice Jr.	CzRep-Jr.	35	4	3	7	....	....	....	....	....	....	....	....	....	....	....	....	....	....	....	....	....	....	....
	HC Vitkovice	CzRep	1	0	0	0	....	....	....	....	....	....	....	....	....	....	....	....	....	....	....	....	....	....	....
1994-95	HC Vitkovice Jr.	CzRep-Jr.	20	6	10	16	....	....	....	....	....	....	....	....	....	....	....	....	....	....	....	....	....	....	....
	HC Vitkovice	CzRep	8	2	0	2	10	....	....	....	....	....	....	....	....	....	4	0	0	0	0	....	....	....	....
1995-96	HC Vitkovice Jr.	CzRep-Jr.	16	5	10	15	....	....	....	....	....	....	....	....	....	....	....	....	....	....	....	....	....	....	....
	HC Vitkovice	CzRep	33	3	4	7	32	....	....	....	....	....	....	....	....	....	4	0	0	0	0	....	....	....	....
1996-97	HC Vitkovice	CzRep	1	0	0	0	0	....	....	....	....	....	....	....	....	....	....	....	....	....	....	....	....	....	....
	Moose Jaw	WHL	61	12	32	44	116	....	....	....	....	....	....	....	....	....	11	2	5	7	27	....	....	....	....
1997-98	**Tampa Bay**	**NHL**	**10**	**1**	**2**	**3**	**22**	**0**	**0**	**0**	**8**	**12.5**	**–1**	....	....	....	....	....	....	....	....	....	....	....	....
	Adirondack	AHL	55	4	8	12	86	....	....	....	....	....	....	....	....	....	1	1	0	1	14	....	....	....	....
1998-99	**Tampa Bay**	**NHL**	**68**	**9**	**12**	**21**	**80**	**3**	**1**	**1**	**119**	**7.6**	**–33**	**2**	**0.0**	**22:47**	....	....	....	....	....	....	....	....	....
	Cleveland	IHL	6	2	2	4	16	....	....	....	....	....	....	....	....	....	....	....	....	....	....	....	....	....	....
99-2000	**Tampa Bay**	**NHL**	**69**	**8**	**18**	**26**	**93**	**6**	**0**	**3**	**128**	**6.3**	**–19**	**0**	**0.0**	**22:32**	....	....	....	....	....	....	....	....	....
2000-01	**Tampa Bay**	**NHL**	**70**	**11**	**19**	**30**	**103**	**6**	**1**	**1**	**128**	**8.6**	**–14**	**2**	**0.0**	**24:06**	....	....	....	....	....	....	....	....	....
2001-02	**Tampa Bay**	**NHL**	**82**	**11**	**23**	**34**	**106**	**5**	**2**	**3**	**189**	**5.8**	**–22**	**1**	**100.0**	**23:39**	....	....	....	....	....	....	....	....	....
	Czech Republic	Olympics	4	0	1	1	0	....	....	....	....	....	....	....	....	....	....	....	....	....	....	....	....	....	....
2002-03	**Tampa Bay**	**NHL**	**75**	**3**	**19**	**22**	**78**	**0**	**0**	**0**	**139**	**2.2**	**–7**	**1**	**0.0**	**21:24**	**11**	**0**	**0**	**0**	**12**	**0**	**0**	**0**	**24:52**
2003-04♦	**Tampa Bay**	**NHL**	**81**	**17**	**18**	**35**	**85**	**8**	**1**	**4**	**153**	**11.1**	**9**	**1**	**0.0**	**21:09**	**22**	**0**	**4**	**4**	**50**	**0**	**0**	**0**	**22:54**
2004-05	Vitkovice	CzRep	28	6	5	11	46	....	....	....	....	....	....	....	....	....	12	4	6	10	34	....	....	....	....
2005-06	**Tampa Bay**	**NHL**	**76**	**5**	**33**	**38**	**96**	**4**	**0**	**3**	**155**	**3.2**	**–12**	**2**	**0.0**	**22:25**	**5**	**1**	**1**	**2**	**26**	**1**	**0**	**0**	**20:09**
	Czech Republic	Olympics	8	1	1	2	12	....	....	....	....	....	....	....	....	....	....	....	....	....	....	....	....	....	....
	NHL Totals		**531**	**65**	**144**	**209**	**663**	**32**	**5**	**15**	**1019**	**6.4**		**9**	**11.1**	**22:33**	**38**	**1**	**5**	**6**	**88**	**1**	**0**	**0**	**23:06**

Played in NHL All-Star Game (2004)

Signed as a free agent by **Vitkovice** (CzRep), September 17, 2004. Signed as a free agent by **Toronto**, July 1, 2006.

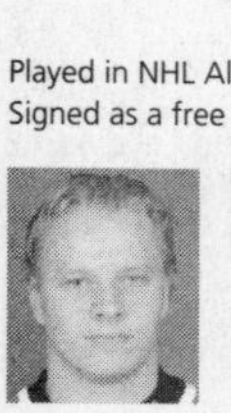

KUKKONEN, Lasse

(koo-KOH-nuhn, LA-she) **CHI.**

Defense. Shoots left. 6', 187 lbs. Born, Oulu, Finland, September 18, 1981. Chicago's 4th choice, 151st overall, in 2003 Entry Draft.

Season	Club	League	GP	G	A	Pts	PIM	PP	SH	GW	S	%	+/-	TF	F%	Min	GP	G	A	Pts	PIM	PP	SH	GW	Min
1997-98	Karpat Oulu U18	Fin-U18	36	5	16	21	46	....	....	....	....	....	....	....	....	....	....	....	....	....	....	....	....	....	....
1998-99	Karpat Oulu U18	Fin-U18	2	1	2	3	0	....	....	....	....	....	....	....	....	....	....	....	....	....	....	....	....	....	....
	Karpat Oulu Jr.	Fin-Jr.	34	2	13	15	24	....	....	....	....	....	....	....	....	....	....	....	....	....	....	....	....	....	....
99-2000	Karpat Oulu Jr.	Fin-Jr.	27	9	11	20	26	....	....	....	....	....	....	....	....	....	....	....	....	....	....	....	....	....	....
	Karpat Oulu	Finland-2	22	0	4	4	14	....	....	....	....	....	....	....	....	....	....	....	....	....	....	....	....	....	....
2000-01	Karpat Oulu	Finland	47	1	5	6	46	....	....	....	....	....	....	....	....	....	9	0	2	2	4	....	....	....	....

			Regular Season														Playoffs								
Season	Club	League	GP	G	A	Pts	PIM	PP	SH	GW	S	%	+/-	TF	F%	Min	GP	G	A	Pts	PIM	PP	SH	GW	Min
2001-02	Karpat Oulu	Finland	55	2	6	8	42	....	....	....	....	....	....	....	....	....	4	0	3	3	4	....	....	....	....
	Karpat Oulu Jr.	Fin-Jr.	....	....	....	....	....	....	....	....	....	....	....	....	....	....	1	1	0	1	0	....	....	....	....
2002-03	Karpat Oulu	Finland	56	6	12	18	67	....	....	....	....	....	....	....	....	....	15	1	4	5	16	....	....	....	....
2003-04	**Chicago**	**NHL**	**10**	**0**	**1**	**1**	**4**	**0**	**0**	**0**	**9**	**0.0**	**–2**	**0**	**0.0**	**13:37**	....	....	....	....	....	....	....	....	....
	Norfolk Admirals	AHL	59	3	11	14	58	....	....	....	....	....	....	....	....	....	8	0	0	0	8	....	....	....	....
2004-05	Karpat Oulu	Finland	55	5	13	18	68	....	....	....	....	....	....	....	....	....	12	0	2	2	6	....	....	....	....
2005-06	Karpat Oulu	Finland	56	11	16	27	38	....	....	....	....	....	....	....	....	....	11	5	7	12	8	....	....	....	....
	Finland	Olympics	2	0	0	0	0	....	....	....	....	....	....	....	....	....	....	....	....	....	....	....	....	....	....
	NHL Totals		**10**	**0**	**1**	**1**	**4**	**0**	**0**	**0**	**9**	**0.0**		**0**	**0.0**	**13:37**	....	....	....	....	....	....	....	....	....

Signed as a free agent by **Oulu** (Finland), September 11, 2004.

KUNITZ, Chris

(KOO-hihtz, KRIHS) **ANA.**

Left wing. Shoots left. 6', 194 lbs. Born, Regina, Sask., September 26, 1979.

1996-97	Yorkton Mallers	SMHL	64	38	38	76	233	....	....	....	....	....	....	....	....	....	....	....	....	....	....	....	....	....	....
1997-98	Melville	SJHL	STATISTICS NOT AVAILABLE																						
1998-99	Melville	SJHL	63	57	32	89	222	....	....	....	....	....	....	....	....	....	....	....	....	....	....	....	....	....	....
99-2000	Ferris State	CCHA	38	20	9	29	70	....	....	....	....	....	....	....	....	....	....	....	....	....	....	....	....	....	....
2000-01	Ferris State	CCHA	37	16	13	29	81	....	....	....	....	....	....	....	....	....	....	....	....	....	....	....	....	....	....
2001-02	Ferris State	CCHA	35	*28	10	38	68	....	....	....	....	....	....	....	....	....	....	....	....	....	....	....	....	....	....
2002-03	Ferris State	CCHA	42	*35	*44	*79	56	....	....	....	....	....	....	....	....	....	....	....	....	....	....	....	....	....	....
2003-04	**Anaheim**	**NHL**	**21**	**0**	**6**	**6**	**12**	**0**	**0**	**0**	**31**	**0.0**	**1**	**7**	**14.3**	**9:07**	....	....	....	....	....	....	....	....	....
	Cincinnati	AHL	59	19	25	44	101	....	....	....	....	....	....	....	....	....	9	3	2	5	24	....	....	....	....
2004-05	Cincinnati	AHL	54	22	17	39	71	....	....	....	....	....	....	....	....	....	12	1	7	8	20	....	....	....	....
2005-06	**Atlanta**	**NHL**	**2**	**0**	**0**	**0**	**2**	**0**	**0**	**0**	**0**	**0.0**	**–3**	**0**	**0.0**	**5:43**	....	....	....	....	....	....	....	....	....
	Anaheim	**NHL**	**67**	**19**	**22**	**41**	**69**	**5**	**1**	**2**	**149**	**12.8**	**19**	**15**	**46.7**	**14:08**	**16**	**3**	**5**	**8**	**8**	**0**	**0**	**0**	**12:30**
	Portland Pirates	AHL	5	0	4	4	12	....	....	....	....	....	....	....	....	....	....	....	....	....	....	....	....	....	....
	NHL Totals		**90**	**19**	**28**	**47**	**83**	**5**	**1**	**2**	**180**	**10.6**		**22**	**36.4**	**12:47**	**16**	**3**	**5**	**8**	**8**	**0**	**0**	**0**	**12:30**

CCHA First All-Star Team (2002, 2003) • CCHA Player of the Year (2003) • NCAA West First All-American Team (2003)

Signed as a free agent by **Anaheim**, April 1, 2003. Claimed on waivers by **Atlanta** from **Anaheim**, October 4, 2005. Claimed on waivers by **Anaheim** from **Atlanta**, October 18, 2005.

KUTLAK, Zdenek

(KUHT-lak, z'DEHN-ehk) **BOS.**

Defense. Shoots left. 6'3", 221 lbs. Born, Ceske Budejovice, Czech., February 13, 1980. Boston's 10th choice, 237th overall, in 2000 Entry Draft.

1996-97	C. Budejovice Jr.	CzRep-Jr.	45	8	11	19	20	....	....	....	....	....	....	....	....	....	....	....	....	....	....	....	....	....	....
1997-98	C. Budejovice Jr.	CzRep-Jr.	43	1	6	7	30	....	....	....	....	....	....	....	....	....	....	....	....	....	....	....	....	....	....
1998-99	C. Budejovice Jr.	CzRep-Jr.	31	6	14	20	20	....	....	....	....	....	....	....	....	....	....	....	....	....	....	....	....	....	....
	C. Budejovice	CzRep	22	1	3	4	4	....	....	....	....	....	....	....	....	....	3	0	0	0	0	....	....	....	....
99-2000	C. Budejovice Jr.	CzRep-Jr.	8	4	2	6	26	....	....	....	....	....	....	....	....	....	....	....	....	....	....	....	....	....	....
	Jind. Hradec	CzRep-3	4	1	1	2	0	....	....	....	....	....	....	....	....	....	....	....	....	....	....	....	....	....	....
	IHC Pisek	CzRep-2	3	1	0	1	0	....	....	....	....	....	....	....	....	....	2	0	0	0	2	....	....	....	....
	C. Budejovice	CzRep	28	1	0	1	2	....	....	....	....	....	....	....	....	....	1	0	0	0	0	....	....	....	....
2000-01	**Boston**	**NHL**	**10**	**0**	**2**	**2**	**4**	**0**	**0**	**0**	**7**	**0.0**	**–3**	**0**	**0.0**	**16:05**	....	....	....	....	....	....	....	....	....
	Providence Bruins	AHL	62	4	5	9	16	....	....	....	....	....	....	....	....	....	....	....	....	....	....	....	....	....	....
2001-02	Providence Bruins	AHL	80	5	15	20	73	....	....	....	....	....	....	....	....	....	2	0	0	0	0	....	....	....	....
2002-03	**Boston**	**NHL**	**4**	**1**	**0**	**1**	**0**	**0**	**0**	**0**	**1**	**100.0**	**0**	**0**	**0.0**	**5:16**	....	....	....	....	....	....	....	....	....
	Providence Bruins	AHL	68	4	12	16	52	....	....	....	....	....	....	....	....	....	4	1	0	1	2	....	....	....	....
2003-04	**Boston**	**NHL**	**2**	**0**	**0**	**0**	**0**	**0**	**0**	**0**	**0**	**0.0**	**–1**	**0**	**0.0**	**11:33**	....	....	....	....	....	....	....	....	....
	Providence Bruins	AHL	47	7	12	19	22	....	....	....	....	....	....	....	....	....	2	0	0	0	2	....	....	....	....
2004-05	Karlovy Vary	CzRep	52	5	9	14	26	....	....	....	....	....	....	....	....	....	....	....	....	....	....	....	....	....	....
2005-06	C. Budejovice	CzRep	49	6	9	15	32	....	....	....	....	....	....	....	....	....	10	2	2	4	12	....	....	....	....
	NHL Totals		**16**	**1**	**2**	**3**	**4**	**0**	**0**	**0**	**8**	**12.5**		**0**	**0.0**	**12:49**	....	....	....	....	....	....	....	....	....

Signed as a free agent by **Karlovy Vary** (CzRep), May 16, 2004.

KVASHA, Oleg

(kuh-VAH-shah, OH-lehg)

Left wing/Center. Shoots right. 6'5", 230 lbs. Born, Moscow, USSR, July 26, 1978. Florida's 3rd choice, 65th overall, in 1996 Entry Draft.

1995-96	CSKA Moscow	CIS	38	2	3	5	14	....	....	....	....	....	....	....	....	....	2	0	0	0	0	....	....	....	....
1996-97	CSKA Moscow	Russia-2	44	20	22	42	115	....	....	....	....	....	....	....	....	....	....	....	....	....	....	....	....	....	....
1997-98	New Haven	AHL	57	13	16	29	46	....	....	....	....	....	....	....	....	....	3	2	1	3	0	....	....	....	....
1998-99	**Florida**	**NHL**	**68**	**12**	**13**	**25**	**45**	**4**	**0**	**2**	**138**	**8.7**	**5**	**373**	**28.4**	**12:48**	....	....	....	....	....	....	....	....	....
99-2000	**Florida**	**NHL**	**78**	**5**	**20**	**25**	**34**	**2**	**0**	**0**	**110**	**4.5**	**3**	**553**	**34.9**	**11:24**	**4**	**0**	**0**	**0**	**0**	**0**	**0**	**0**	**10:18**
2000-01	**NY Islanders**	**NHL**	**62**	**11**	**9**	**20**	**46**	**0**	**0**	**0**	**118**	**9.3**	**–15**	**627**	**43.7**	**14:56**	....	....	....	....	....	....	....	....	....
2001-02	**NY Islanders**	**NHL**	**71**	**13**	**25**	**38**	**80**	**2**	**0**	**3**	**119**	**10.9**	**–4**	**456**	**47.4**	**14:12**	**7**	**0**	**1**	**1**	**6**	**0**	**0**	**0**	**15:17**
	Russia	Olympics	5	0	0	0	0	....	....	....	....	....	....	....	....	....	....	....	....	....	....	....	....	....	....
2002-03	**NY Islanders**	**NHL**	**69**	**12**	**14**	**26**	**44**	**0**	**1**	**2**	**121**	**9.9**	**4**	**256**	**43.0**	**13:03**	**5**	**0**	**1**	**1**	**2**	**0**	**0**	**0**	**16:26**
2003-04	**NY Islanders**	**NHL**	**81**	**15**	**36**	**51**	**48**	**5**	**3**	**3**	**147**	**10.2**	**4**	**656**	**38.3**	**17:52**	**5**	**1**	**0**	**1**	**0**	**1**	**0**	**0**	**16:05**
2004-05	Cherepovets	Russia	22	6	5	11	24	....	....	....	....	....	....	....	....	....	....	....	....	....	....	....	....	....	....
	CSKA Moscow	Russia	26	3	6	9	20	....	....	....	....	....	....	....	....	....	....	....	....	....	....	....	....	....	....
2005-06	**NY Islanders**	**NHL**	**49**	**9**	**12**	**21**	**32**	**1**	**0**	**1**	**104**	**8.7**	**–2**	**238**	**52.9**	**14:26**	....	....	....	....	....	....	....	....	....
	Phoenix	**NHL**	**15**	**4**	**7**	**11**	**6**	**0**	**0**	**0**	**32**	**12.5**	**5**	**16**	**43.8**	**13:32**	....	....	....	....	....	....	....	....	....
	NHL Totals		**493**	**81**	**136**	**217**	**335**	**14**	**4**	**11**	**889**	**9.1**		**3175**	**40.4**	**14:06**	**21**	**1**	**2**	**3**	**8**	**1**	**0**	**0**	**14:48**

Traded to **NY Islanders** by **Florida** with Mark Parrish for Roberto Luongo and Olli Jokinen, June 24, 2000. Signed as a free agent by **Cherepovets** (Russia), September 25, 2004. Loaned to **CSKA Moscow** (Russia), December 20, 2004. Traded to **Phoenix** by **NY Islanders** for Phoenix's 3rd round choice (later traded to Boston - Boston selected Brad Marchand) in 2006 Entry Draft, March 9, 2006.

KWIATKOWSKI, Joel

(KWEE-at-KOW-skee, JOHL) **FLA.**

Defense. Shoots left. 6'2", 210 lbs. Born, Kindersley, Sask., March 22, 1977. Dallas' 7th choice, 194th overall, in 1996 Entry Draft.

1994-95	Tacoma Rockets	WHL	70	4	13	17	66	....	....	....	....	....	....	....	....	....	4	0	0	0	2	....	....	....	....
1995-96	Kelowna Rockets	WHL	40	6	17	23	85	....	....	....	....	....	....	....	....	....	....	....	....	....	....	....	....	....	....
	Prince George	WHL	32	6	11	17	48	....	....	....	....	....	....	....	....	....	....	....	....	....	....	....	....	....	....
1996-97	Prince George	WHL	72	15	37	52	94	....	....	....	....	....	....	....	....	....	15	4	2	6	24	....	....	....	....
1997-98	Prince George	WHL	62	21	43	64	65	....	....	....	....	....	....	....	....	....	11	3	6	9	6	....	....	....	....
1998-99	Cincinnati	AHL	80	12	21	33	48	....	....	....	....	....	....	....	....	....	3	2	0	2	0	....	....	....	....
99-2000	Cincinnati	AHL	70	4	22	26	28	....	....	....	....	....	....	....	....	....	....	....	....	....	....	....	....	....	....
2000-01	**Ottawa**	**NHL**	**4**	**1**	**0**	**1**	**0**	**0**	**0**	**0**	**2**	**50.0**	**1**	**0**	**0.0**	**12:04**	....	....	....	....	....	....	....	....	....
	Grand Rapids	IHL	77	4	17	21	58	....	....	....	....	....	....	....	....	....	10	1	0	1	4	....	....	....	....
2001-02	**Ottawa**	**NHL**	**11**	**0**	**0**	**0**	**12**	**0**	**0**	**0**	**9**	**0.0**	**5**	**0**	**0.0**	**13:41**	....	....	....	....	....	....	....	....	....
	Grand Rapids	AHL	65	8	21	29	94	....	....	....	....	....	....	....	....	....	5	1	2	3	12	....	....	....	....
2002-03	**Ottawa**	**NHL**	**20**	**0**	**2**	**2**	**6**	**0**	**0**	**0**	**28**	**0.0**	**2**	**2**	**0.0**	**12:13**	....	....	....	....	....	....	....	....	....
	Binghamton	AHL	1	0	0	0	2	....	....	....	....	....	....	....	....	....	....	....	....	....	....	....	....	....	....
	Washington	**NHL**	**34**	**0**	**3**	**3**	**12**	**0**	**0**	**0**	**28**	**0.0**	**1**	**2**	**0.0**	**15:32**	**6**	**0**	**0**	**0**	**2**	**0**	**0**	**0**	**17:48**
2003-04	**Washington**	**NHL**	**80**	**6**	**6**	**12**	**89**	**2**	**0**	**0**	**90**	**6.7**	**–28**	**0**	**0.0**	**21:16**	....	....	....	....	....	....	....	....	....
2004-05	San Antonio	AHL	64	13	19	32	76	....	....	....	....	....	....	....	....	....	....	....	....	....	....	....	....	....	....
	St. John's	AHL	17	7	6	13	16	....	....	....	....	....	....	....	....	....	5	0	4	4	23	....	....	....	....
2005-06	**Florida**	**NHL**	**73**	**4**	**8**	**12**	**86**	**1**	**0**	**1**	**87**	**4.6**	**3**	**0**	**0.0**	**16:21**	....	....	....	....	....	....	....	....	....
	NHL Totals		**222**	**11**	**19**	**30**	**205**	**3**	**0**	**1**	**244**	**4.5**		**4**	**0.0**	**17:25**	**6**	**0**	**0**	**0**	**2**	**0**	**0**	**0**	**17:48**

WHL West Second All-Star Team (1997) • WHL West First All-Star Team (1998)

Signed as a free agent by **Anaheim**, June 18, 1998. Traded to **Ottawa** by **Anaheim** for Patrick Traverse, June 12, 2000. Traded to **Washington** by **Ottawa** for Washington's 9th round choice (later traded back to Washington – Washington selected Mark Olafson) in 2003 Entry Draft, January 15, 2003. Signed as a free agent by **Florida**, July 16, 2004. Loaned to **St. John's** by **Florida** (San Antonio-AHL) for cash, March 11, 2005.

LAAKSONEN, Antti (lah-AHK-soh-nehn, AHN-tee) **COL.**

Left wing. Shoots left. 6', 187 lbs. Born, Tammela, Finland, October 3, 1973. Boston's 10th choice, 191st overall, in 1997 Entry Draft.

			Regular Season														Playoffs								
Season	Club	League	GP	G	A	Pts	PIM	PP	SH	GW	S	%	+/-	TF	F%	Min	GP	G	A	Pts	PIM	PP	SH	GW	Min
1989-90	FoPS Forssa Jr.	Fin-Jr.	3	0	0	0	0																		
1990-91	FoPS Forssa Jr.	Fin-Jr.	STATISTICS NOT AVAILABLE																						
	FoPS Forssa	Finland-2	2	0	0	0	0																		
1991-92	FoPS Forssa Jr.	Fin-Jr.	24	19	23	42	22																		
	FoPS Forssa	Finland-2	41	16	15	31	8																		
1992-93	FoPS Forssa Jr.	Fin-Jr.	12	7	7	14	14																		
	FoPS Forssa	Finland-2	34	11	19	30	36																		
	HPK Jr.	Fin-Jr.	1	1	1	2	0																		
	HPK Hameenlinna	Finland	2	0	0	0	0																		
1993-94	U. of Denver	WCHA	36	12	9	21	38																		
1994-95	U. of Denver	WCHA	40	17	18	35	42																		
1995-96	U. of Denver	WCHA	39	25	28	53	71																		
1996-97	U. of Denver	WCHA	39	21	17	38	63																		
1997-98	Providence Bruins	AHL	38	3	2	5	14																		
	Charlotte	ECHL	15	4	3	7	12										6	0	3	3	0				
1998-99	**Boston**	**NHL**	**11**	**1**	**2**	**3**	**2**	**0**	**0**	**0**	**8**	**12.5**	**–1**	**0**	**0.0**	**9:20**									
	Providence Bruins	AHL	66	25	33	58	52										19	7	2	9	28				
99-2000	**Boston**	**NHL**	**27**	**6**	**3**	**9**	**2**	**0**	**0**	**1**	**23**	**26.1**	**3**	**3**	**66.7**	**7:50**									
	Providence Bruins	AHL	40	10	12	22	57										14	5	4	9	4				
2000-01	**Minnesota**	**NHL**	**82**	**12**	**16**	**28**	**24**	**0**	**2**	**1**	**129**	**9.3**	**–7**	**15**	**26.7**	**16:27**									
2001-02	**Minnesota**	**NHL**	**82**	**16**	**17**	**33**	**22**	**0**	**0**	**1**	**104**	**15.4**	**–5**	**19**	**42.1**	**16:20**									
2002-03	**Minnesota**	**NHL**	**82**	**15**	**16**	**31**	**26**	**1**	**2**	**4**	**106**	**14.2**	**4**	**51**	**29.4**	**15:55**	**16**	**1**	**3**	**4**	**4**	**0**	**0**	**0**	**16:34**
2003-04	**Minnesota**	**NHL**	**77**	**12**	**14**	**26**	**20**	**0**	**1**	**1**	**100**	**12.0**	**0**	**144**	**36.1**	**16:03**									
2004-05			DID NOT PLAY																						
2005-06	**Colorado**	**NHL**	**81**	**16**	**18**	**34**	**40**	**0**	**2**	**4**	**141**	**11.3**	**–2**	**46**	**28.3**	**16:00**	**9**	**0**	**2**	**2**	**2**	**0**	**0**	**0**	**15:23**
	Finland	Olympics	8	0	0	0	6																		
	NHL Totals		**442**	**78**	**86**	**164**	**136**	**1**	**7**	**12**	**611**	**12.8**		**278**	**33.8**	**15:28**	**25**	**1**	**5**	**6**	**6**	**0**	**0**	**0**	**16:09**

WCHA Second All-Star Team (1996)

Signed as a free agent by **Minnesota**, July 14, 2000. Signed as a free agent by **Colorado**, July 2, 2004.

LaCOUTURE, Dan (LA-koo-TUHR, DAN) **N.J.**

Left wing. Shoots left. 6'3", 215 lbs. Born, Hyannis, MA, April 18, 1977. NY Islanders' 2nd choice, 29th overall, in 1996 Entry Draft.

Season	Club	League	GP	G	A	Pts	PIM	PP	SH	GW	S	%	+/-	TF	F%	Min	GP	G	A	Pts	PIM	PP	SH	GW	Min
1992-93	Natick Redmen	High-MA	20	38	34	72	46																		
1993-94	Natick Redmen	High-MA	21	52	49	101	58																		
1994-95	Spring. Olympics	NEJHL	52	44	56	100	98																		
1995-96	Spring. Olympics	NEJHL	29	24	35	59	79										13	12	13	25	23				
1996-97	Boston University	H-East	31	13	12	25	18																		
1997-98	Hamilton	AHL	77	15	10	25	31										5	1	0	1	0				
1998-99	**Edmonton**	**NHL**	**3**	**0**	**0**	**0**	**0**	**0**	**0**	**0**	**0**	**0.0**	**1**	**0**	**0.0**	**6:30**									
	Hamilton	AHL	72	17	14	31	73										9	2	1	3	2				
99-2000	**Edmonton**	**NHL**	**5**	**0**	**0**	**0**	**10**	**0**	**0**	**0**	**2**	**0.0**	**0**	**0**	**0.0**	**7:02**	**1**	**0**	**0**	**0**	**0**	**0**	**0**	**0**	**2:05**
	Hamilton	AHL	70	23	17	40	85										6	2	1	3	0				
2000-01	**Edmonton**	**NHL**	**37**	**2**	**4**	**6**	**29**	**0**	**0**	**1**	**22**	**9.1**	**–2**	**5**	**20.0**	**7:06**									
	Pittsburgh	**NHL**	**11**	**0**	**0**	**0**	**14**	**0**	**0**	**0**	**1**	**0.0**	**0**	**1**	**100.0**	**5:57**	**5**	**0**	**0**	**0**	**2**	**0**	**0**	**0**	**5:46**
2001-02	**Pittsburgh**	**NHL**	**82**	**6**	**11**	**17**	**71**	**0**	**1**	**0**	**77**	**7.8**	**–19**	**21**	**38.1**	**13:16**									
2002-03	**Pittsburgh**	**NHL**	**44**	**2**	**2**	**4**	**72**	**0**	**0**	**0**	**30**	**6.7**	**–8**	**5**	**80.0**	**9:13**									
	NY Rangers	**NHL**	**24**	**1**	**4**	**5**	**0**	**0**	**0**	**0**	**17**	**5.9**	**4**	**1**	**0.0**	**10:18**									
2003-04	**NY Rangers**	**NHL**	**59**	**5**	**2**	**7**	**82**	**1**	**0**	**1**	**39**	**12.8**	**–13**	**8**	**50.0**	**9:29**									
2004-05	Providence Bruins	AHL	64	12	15	27	52										6	1	1	2	4				
2005-06	HC Davos	Swiss	4	2	1	3	4																		
	Boston	**NHL**	**55**	**2**	**2**	**4**	**53**	**0**	**1**	**0**	**37**	**5.4**	**–6**	**0**	**0.0**	**6:15**									
	NHL Totals		**320**	**18**	**25**	**43**	**331**	**1**	**2**	**2**	**225**	**8.0**		**41**	**43.9**	**9:28**	**6**	**0**	**0**	**0**	**2**	**0**	**0**	**0**	**5:09**

Traded to **Edmonton** by **NY Islanders** for Mariusz Czerkawski, August 25, 1997. Traded to **Pittsburgh** by **Edmonton** for Sven Butenschon, March 13, 2001. Traded to **NY Rangers** by **Pittsburgh** with Mike Wilson, Alex Kovalev and Janne Laukkanen for Joel Bouchard, Richard Lintner, Rico Fata, Mikael Samuelsson and future considerations, February 10, 2003. Signed to a PTO (tryout) contract by **Providence** (AHL), November 2, 2004, Signed as a free agent by **New Jersey**, August, 2006.

LADD, Andrew (LAD, AN-droo) **CAR.**

Left wing. Shoots left. 6'2", 200 lbs. Born, Maple Ridge, B.C., December 12, 1985. Carolina's 1st choice, 4th overall, in 2004 Entry Draft.

Season	Club	League	GP	G	A	Pts	PIM	PP	SH	GW	S	%	+/-	TF	F%	Min	GP	G	A	Pts	PIM	PP	SH	GW	Min
2000-01	Okanagan Chiefs	BCAHA	6	4	8	12	10																		
2001-02	Port Coquitlam	BCAHA	50	50	41	91	49																		
	Vancouver Giants	WHL	1	0	0	0	0																		
2002-03	Coquitlam	BCHL	58	15	40	55	61																		
2003-04	Calgary Hitmen	WHL	71	30	45	75	119										7	1	6	7	10				
2004-05	Calgary Hitmen	WHL	65	19	26	45	167										12	7	4	11	18				
2005-06♦	**Carolina**	**NHL**	**29**	**6**	**5**	**11**	**4**	**3**	**0**	**0**	**43**	**14.0**	**0**	**0**	**0.0**	**11:10**	**17**	**2**	**3**	**5**	**4**	**0**	**0**	**1**	**9:27**
	Lowell	AHL	25	11	8	19	28																		
	NHL Totals		**29**	**6**	**5**	**11**	**4**	**3**	**0**	**0**	**43**	**14.0**		**0**	**0.0**	**11:10**	**17**	**2**	**3**	**5**	**4**	**0**	**0**	**1**	**9:27**

LAICH, Brooks (LAYCH, BROOKS) **WSH.**

Center. Shoots left. 6'2", 208 lbs. Born, Wawota, Sask., June 23, 1983. Ottawa's 7th choice, 193rd overall, in 2001 Entry Draft.

Season	Club	League	GP	G	A	Pts	PIM	PP	SH	GW	S	%	+/-	TF	F%	Min	GP	G	A	Pts	PIM	PP	SH	GW	Min
99-2000	Tisdale Trojans	SMHL	57	51	52	103																			
2000-01	Moose Jaw	WHL	71	9	21	30	28										4	0	0	0	5				
2001-02	Moose Jaw	WHL	28	6	14	20	12																		
	Seattle	WHL	47	22	36	58	42										11	5	3	8	11				
2002-03	Seattle	WHL	60	41	53	94	65										15	5	14	19	24				
2003-04	**Ottawa**	**NHL**	**1**	**0**	**0**	**0**	**2**	**0**	**0**	**0**	**1**	**0.0**	**0**	**7**	**42.9**	**9:34**									
	Binghamton	AHL	44	15	18	33	16																		
	Washington	**NHL**	**4**	**0**	**1**	**1**	**0**	**0**	**0**	**0**	**2**	**0.0**	**–1**	**49**	**51.0**	**10:50**									
	Portland Pirates	AHL	22	1	3	4	12										6	0	0	0	0				
2004-05	Portland Pirates	AHL	68	16	10	26	33																		
2005-06	**Washington**	**NHL**	**73**	**7**	**14**	**21**	**26**	**1**	**0**	**1**	**118**	**5.9**	**–9**	**666**	**49.7**	**11:13**									
	Hershey Bears	AHL	10	7	6	13	8										21	8	7	15	29				
	NHL Totals		**78**	**7**	**15**	**22**	**28**	**1**	**0**	**1**	**121**	**5.8**		**722**	**49.7**	**11:11**									

WHL West First All-Star Team (2003)

Traded to **Washington** by **Ottawa** with Ottawa's 2nd round choice (later traded to Colorado - Colorado selected Chris Durand) in 2005 Entry Draft for Peter Bondra, February 18, 2004.

LAING, Quintin (LAY-ihng, QUIHN-tihn) **WSH.**

Left wing. Shoots left. 6'2", 175 lbs. Born, Rosetown, Sask., June 8, 1979. Detroit's 3rd choice, 102nd overall, in 1997 Entry Draft.

Season	Club	League	GP	G	A	Pts	PIM	PP	SH	GW	S	%	+/-	TF	F%	Min	GP	G	A	Pts	PIM	PP	SH	GW	Min
1993-94	Delisle Contacts	SAHA	30	25	50	75	25																		
1994-95	Delisle Contacts	SAHA	30	30	45	75	15																		
1995-96	Sask. Contacts	SMHL	44	18	12	30	20																		
1996-97	Kelowna Rockets	WHL	63	13	24	37	54										1	0	0	0	0				
1997-98	Kelowna Rockets	WHL	59	11	24	35	47										7	0	1	1	8				
1998-99	Kelowna Rockets	WHL	70	11	10	21	107										6	3	0	3	0				
99-2000	Kelowna Rockets	WHL	68	22	30	52	61										5	1	1	2	8				
2000-01	Norfolk Admirals	AHL	10	0	1	1	10																		
	Jackson Bandits	ECHL	60	13	24	37	39										5	0	0	0	0				
2001-02	Jackson Bandits	ECHL	16	4	6	10	12																		
	Norfolk Admirals	AHL	61	6	15	21	32										4	0	0	0	2				
2002-03	Norfolk Admirals	AHL	69	5	12	17	33										8	2	2	4	0				
2003-04	**Chicago**	**NHL**	**3**	**0**	**1**	**1**	**0**	**0**	**0**	**0**	**3**	**0.0**	**1**	**0**	**0.0**	**11:57**									
	Norfolk Admirals	AHL	78	12	10	22	74										8	5	1	6	4				

Season	Club	League	GP	G	A	Pts	PIM	PP	SH	GW	S	%	+/-	TF	F%	Min	GP	G	A	Pts	PIM	PP	SH	GW	Min
			Regular Season														Playoffs								
2004-05	Norfolk Admirals	AHL	66	10	13	23	54	....	....	....	....	....	....	....	....	....	4	0	0	0	0	....	....	....	....
2005-06	Norfolk Admirals	AHL	73	14	31	45	70	....	....	....	....	....	....	....	....	....	4	0	0	0	0	....	....	....	....
	NHL Totals		**3**	**0**	**1**	**1**	**0**	**0**	**0**	**0**	**3**	**0.0**		**0**	**0.0**	**11:57**	....	....	....	....	....	....	....	....	....

Signed as a free agent by **Chicago**, June 4, 2003. Signed as a free agent by **Washington**, July 18, 2006.

LAMPMAN, Bryce

(LAMP-man, BRIGHS) **NYR**

Defense. Shoots left. 6'1", 199 lbs. Born, Rochester, MN, August 31, 1982. NY Rangers' 4th choice, 113th overall, in 2001 Entry Draft.

Season	Club	League	GP	G	A	Pts	PIM	PP	SH	GW	S	%	+/-	TF	F%	Min	GP	G	A	Pts	PIM	PP	SH	GW	Min
1998-99	Rochester	USHL	53	3	8	11	33	....	....	....	....	....	....	....	....	....	....	....	....	....	....	....	....	....	....
99-2000	Rochester	USHL	10	0	0	0	14	....	....	....	....	....	....	....	....	....	....	....	....	....	....	....	....	....	....
	Omaha Lancers	USHL	11	1	2	3	38	....	....	....	....	....	....	....	....	....	4	0	0	0	0	....	....	....	....
2000-01	Omaha Lancers	USHL	55	10	11	21	77	....	....	....	....	....	....	....	....	....	12	1	4	5	12	....	....	....	....
2001-02	Nebraska-Omaha	CCHA	26	0	4	4	28	....	....	....	....	....	....	....	....	....	....	....	....	....	....	....	....	....	....
2002-03	Kamloops Blazers	WHL	29	1	17	18	32	....	....	....	....	....	....	....	....	....	....	....	....	....	....	....	....	....	....
	Hartford	AHL	45	0	6	6	32	....	....	....	....	....	....	....	....	....	2	0	1	1	0	....	....	....	....
2003-04	**NY Rangers**	**NHL**	**8**	**0**	**0**	**0**	**0**	**0**	**0**	**0**	**7**	**0.0**	**–4**	**0**	**0.0**	**19:34**	....	....	....	....	....	....	....	....	....
	Hartford	AHL	68	4	11	15	50	....	....	....	....	....	....	....	....	....	16	1	3	4	14	....	....	....	....
2004-05	Hartford	AHL	74	7	18	25	74	....	....	....	....	....	....	....	....	....	4	0	0	0	4	....	....	....	....
2005-06	**NY Rangers**	**NHL**	**1**	**0**	**0**	**0**	**2**	**0**	**0**	**0**	**1**	**0.0**	**–1**	**0**	**0.0**	**13:40**	....	....	....	....	....	....	....	....	....
	Hartford	AHL	11	2	3	5	16	....	....	....	....	....	....	....	....	....	....	....	....	....	....	....	....	....	....
	NHL Totals		**9**	**0**	**0**	**0**	**2**	**0**	**0**	**0**	**8**	**0.0**		**0**	**0.0**	**18:54**	....	....	....	....	....	....	....	....	....

• Left **U. of Nebraska-Omaha** (CCHA) and signed as a free agent by **Kamloops** (WHL), August 1, 2002. • Missed majority of 2005-06 season recovering from a shoulder injury.

LANG, Robert

(LANG, RAW-buhrt) **DET.**

Center. Shoots right. 6'2", 216 lbs. Born, Teplice, Czech., December 19, 1970. Los Angeles' 6th choice, 133rd overall, in 1990 Entry Draft.

Season	Club	League	GP	G	A	Pts	PIM	PP	SH	GW	S	%	+/-	TF	F%	Min	GP	G	A	Pts	PIM	PP	SH	GW	Min
1988-89	CHZ Litvinov	Czech	7	3	2	5	0	....	....	....	....	....	....	....	....	....	....	....	....	....	....	....	....	....	....
1989-90	CHZ Litvinov	Czech	32	8	7	15	....	....	....	....	....	....	....	....	....	....	8	3	3	6	....	....	....	....	....
1990-91	HC CHZ Litvinov	Czech	56	26	26	52	38	....	....	....	....	....	....	....	....	....	....	....	....	....	....	....	....	....	....
1991-92	Litvinov	Czech	43	12	31	43	34	....	....	....	....	....	....	....	....	....	....	....	....	....	....	....	....	....	....
	Czechoslovakia	Olympics	8	5	8	13	8	....	....	....	....	....	....	....	....	....	....	....	....	....	....	....	....	....	....
1992-93	**Los Angeles**	**NHL**	**11**	**0**	**5**	**5**	**2**	**0**	**0**	**0**	**3**	**0.0**	**–3**	....	....	....	....	....	....	....	....	....	....	....	....
	Phoenix	IHL	38	9	21	30	20	....	....	....	....	....	....	....	....	....	....	....	....	....	....	....	....	....	....
1993-94	**Los Angeles**	**NHL**	**32**	**9**	**10**	**19**	**10**	**0**	**0**	**0**	**41**	**22.0**	**7**	....	....	....	....	....	....	....	....	....	....	....	....
	Phoenix	IHL	44	11	24	35	34	....	....	....	....	....	....	....	....	....	....	....	....	....	....	....	....	....	....
1994-95	Litvinov	CzRep	16	4	19	23	28	....	....	....	....	....	....	....	....	....	....	....	....	....	....	....	....	....	....
	Los Angeles	**NHL**	**36**	**4**	**8**	**12**	**4**	**0**	**0**	**0**	**38**	**10.5**	**–7**	....	....	....	....	....	....	....	....	....	....	....	....
1995-96	**Los Angeles**	**NHL**	**68**	**6**	**16**	**22**	**10**	**0**	**2**	**0**	**71**	**8.5**	**–15**	....	....	....	....	....	....	....	....	....	....	....	....
1996-97	HC Sparta Praha	CzRep	38	14	27	41	30	....	....	....	....	....	....	....	....	....	5	1	2	3	4	....	....	....	....
	HC Sparta Praha	EuroHL	4	2	2	4	0	....	....	....	....	....	....	....	....	....	4	2	1	3	2	....	....	....	....
1997-98	**Boston**	**NHL**	**3**	**0**	**0**	**0**	**2**	**0**	**0**	**0**	**2**	**0.0**	**1**	....	....	....	....	....	....	....	....	....	....	....	....
	Pittsburgh	**NHL**	**51**	**9**	**13**	**22**	**14**	**1**	**1**	**2**	**64**	**14.1**	**6**	....	....	....	**6**	**0**	**3**	**3**	**2**	**0**	**0**	**0**	....
	Czech Republic	Olympics	6	0	3	3	0	....	....	....	....	....	....	....	....	....	....	....	....	....	....	....	....	....	....
	Houston Aeros	IHL	9	1	7	8	4	....	....	....	....	....	....	....	....	....	....	....	....	....	....	....	....	....	....
1998-99	**Pittsburgh**	**NHL**	**72**	**21**	**23**	**44**	**24**	**7**	**0**	**3**	**137**	**15.3**	**–10**	**964**	**44.8**	**16:24**	**12**	**0**	**2**	**2**	**0**	**0**	**0**	**0**	**13:58**
99-2000	**Pittsburgh**	**NHL**	**78**	**23**	**42**	**65**	**14**	**13**	**0**	**5**	**142**	**16.2**	**–9**	**1433**	**50.7**	**19:22**	**11**	**3**	**3**	**6**	**0**	**2**	**0**	**0**	**21:42**
2000-01	**Pittsburgh**	**NHL**	**82**	**32**	**48**	**80**	**28**	**10**	**0**	**2**	**177**	**18.1**	**20**	**1348**	**43.9**	**20:24**	**16**	**4**	**4**	**8**	**4**	**0**	**0**	**0**	**19:21**
2001-02	**Pittsburgh**	**NHL**	**62**	**18**	**32**	**50**	**16**	**5**	**1**	**3**	**175**	**10.3**	**9**	**1172**	**46.3**	**22:56**	....	....	....	....	....	....	....	....	....
	Czech Republic	Olympics	4	1	2	3	2	....	....	....	....	....	....	....	....	....	....	....	....	....	....	....	....	....	....
2002-03	**Washington**	**NHL**	**82**	**22**	**47**	**69**	**22**	**10**	**0**	**2**	**146**	**15.1**	**12**	**1069**	**45.9**	**18:47**	**6**	**2**	**1**	**3**	**2**	**0**	**0**	**1**	**21:55**
2003-04	**Washington**	**NHL**	**63**	**29**	**45**	**74**	**24**	**10**	**0**	**2**	**149**	**19.5**	**2**	**744**	**44.1**	**21:46**	....	....	....	....	....	....	....	....	....
	Detroit	**NHL**	**6**	**1**	**4**	**5**	**0**	**0**	**0**	**1**	**14**	**7.1**	**2**	**96**	**57.3**	**16:20**	**12**	**4**	**5**	**9**	**6**	**0**	**0**	**0**	**18:10**
2004-05			DID NOT PLAY																						
2005-06	**Detroit**	**NHL**	**72**	**20**	**42**	**62**	**72**	**8**	**0**	**3**	**171**	**11.7**	**17**	**861**	**50.3**	**16:15**	**6**	**3**	**3**	**6**	**2**	**2**	**0**	**0**	**19:12**
	Czech Republic	Olympics	8	0	4	4	4	....	....	....	....	....	....	....	....	....	....	....	....	....	....	....	....	....	....
	NHL Totals		**718**	**194**	**335**	**529**	**242**	**64**	**4**	**23**	**1330**	**14.6**		**7687**	**46.8**	**19:16**	**69**	**16**	**21**	**37**	**16**	**4**	**0**	**1**	**18:44**

Played in NHL All-Star Game (2004)

Signed as a free agent by **Pittsburgh**, September 2, 1997. Claimed by **Boston** from **Pittsburgh** in Waiver Draft, September 28, 1997. Claimed on waivers by **Pittsburgh** from **Boston**, October 25, 1997. Signed as a free agent by **Washington**, July 1, 2002. Traded to **Detroit** by **Washington** for Tomas Fleischmann, Detroit's 1st round choice (Mike Green) in 2004 Entry Draft and Detroit's 4th round choice (Luke Lynes) in 2006 Entry Draft, February 27, 2004.

LANGDON, Darren

(LAING-duhn, DAIR-uhn)

Left wing. Shoots left. 6'1", 205 lbs. Born, Deer Lake, Nfld., January 8, 1971.

Season	Club	League	GP	G	A	Pts	PIM	PP	SH	GW	S	%	+/-	TF	F%	Min	GP	G	A	Pts	PIM	PP	SH	GW	Min
1991-92	Summerside	MJrHL	44	34	49	83	441	....	....	....	....	....	....	....	....	....	....	....	....	....	....	....	....	....	....
1992-93	Binghamton	AHL	18	3	4	7	115	....	....	....	....	....	....	....	....	....	8	0	1	1	14	....	....	....	....
	Dayton Bombers	ECHL	54	23	22	45	429	....	....	....	....	....	....	....	....	....	3	0	1	1	40	....	....	....	....
1993-94	Binghamton	AHL	54	2	7	9	327	....	....	....	....	....	....	....	....	....	....	....	....	....	....	....	....	....	....
1994-95	Binghamton	AHL	55	6	14	20	296	....	....	....	....	....	....	....	....	....	11	1	3	4	*84	....	....	....	....
	NY Rangers	**NHL**	**18**	**1**	**1**	**2**	**62**	**0**	**0**	**0**	**6**	**16.7**	**0**	....	....	....	....	....	....	....	....	....	....	....	....
1995-96	**NY Rangers**	**NHL**	**64**	**7**	**4**	**11**	**175**	**0**	**0**	**1**	**29**	**24.1**	**2**	....	....	....	**2**	**0**	**0**	**0**	**0**	**0**	**0**	**0**	....
	Binghamton	AHL	1	0	0	0	12	....	....	....	....	....	....	....	....	....	....	....	....	....	....	....	....	....	....
1996-97	**NY Rangers**	**NHL**	**60**	**3**	**6**	**9**	**195**	**0**	**0**	**1**	**24**	**12.5**	**–1**	....	....	....	**10**	**0**	**0**	**0**	**2**	**0**	**0**	**0**	....
1997-98	**NY Rangers**	**NHL**	**70**	**3**	**3**	**6**	**197**	**0**	**0**	**0**	**15**	**20.0**	**0**	....	....	....	....	....	....	....	....	....	....	....	....
1998-99	**NY Rangers**	**NHL**	**44**	**0**	**0**	**0**	**80**	**0**	**0**	**0**	**8**	**0.0**	**–3**	**0**	**0.0**	**3:33**	....	....	....	....	....	....	....	....	....
99-2000	**NY Rangers**	**NHL**	**21**	**0**	**1**	**1**	**26**	**0**	**0**	**0**	**13**	**0.0**	**–2**	**0**	**0.0**	**5:36**	....	....	....	....	....	....	....	....	....
2000-01	**Carolina**	**NHL**	**54**	**0**	**2**	**2**	**94**	**0**	**0**	**0**	**6**	**0.0**	**–4**	**2**	**100.0**	**3:21**	**4**	**0**	**0**	**0**	**12**	**0**	**0**	**0**	**3:32**
2001-02	**Carolina**	**NHL**	**58**	**2**	**1**	**3**	**106**	**0**	**0**	**1**	**12**	**16.7**	**2**	**1**	**100.0**	**4:11**	....	....	....	....	....	....	....	....	....
2002-03	**Carolina**	**NHL**	**9**	**0**	**0**	**0**	**16**	**0**	**0**	**0**	**4**	**0.0**	**0**	**0**	**0.0**	**2:45**	....	....	....	....	....	....	....	....	....
	Vancouver	**NHL**	**45**	**0**	**1**	**1**	**143**	**0**	**0**	**0**	**15**	**0.0**	**–2**	**1**	**0.0**	**5:26**	....	....	....	....	....	....	....	....	....
2003-04	**Montreal**	**NHL**	**64**	**0**	**3**	**3**	**135**	**0**	**0**	**0**	**22**	**0.0**	**–2**	**1**	**0.0**	**6:16**	**9**	**1**	**0**	**1**	**6**	**0**	**0**	**0**	**3:15**
2004-05			DID NOT PLAY																						
2005-06	**New Jersey**	**NHL**	**14**	**0**	**1**	**1**	**22**	**0**	**0**	**0**	**2**	**0.0**	**–3**	**0**	**0.0**	**3:17**	....	....	....	....	....	....	....	....	....
	NHL Totals		**521**	**16**	**23**	**39**	**1251**	**0**	**0**	**3**	**156**	**10.3**		**5**	**60.0**	**4:34**	**25**	**1**	**0**	**1**	**20**	**0**	**0**	**0**	**3:20**

Signed as a free agent by **NY Rangers**, August 16, 1993. • Missed majority of 1999-2000 season recovering from hernia injury suffered in game vs. New Jersey, December 1, 1999. Traded to **Carolina** by **NY Rangers** with Rob DiMaio for Sandy McCarthy and Carolina's 4th round choice (Bryce Lampman) in 2001 Entry Draft, August 4, 2000. Traded to **Vancouver** by **Carolina** with Marek Malik for Jan Hlavac and Harold Druken, November 1, 2002. Claimed by **Montreal** from **Vancouver** in Waiver Draft, October 3, 2003. Signed as a free agent by **New Jersey**, July 3, 2004. • Missed majority of 2005-06 season as a healthy reserve and recovering from a groin injury.

LANGENBRUNNER, Jamie

(lan-gehn-BRUH-nuhr, JAY-mee) **N.J.**

Right wing. Shoots right. 6'1", 200 lbs. Born, Cloquet, MN, July 24, 1975. Dallas' 2nd choice, 35th overall, in 1993 Entry Draft.

Season	Club	League	GP	G	A	Pts	PIM	PP	SH	GW	S	%	+/-	TF	F%	Min	GP	G	A	Pts	PIM	PP	SH	GW	Min
1990-91	Cloquet	High-MN	20	6	16	22	8	....	....	....	....	....	....	....	....	....	....	....	....	....	....	....	....	....	....
1991-92	Cloquet	High-MN	23	16	23	39	24	....	....	....	....	....	....	....	....	....	....	....	....	....	....	....	....	....	....
1992-93	Cloquet	High-MN	27	27	62	89	18	....	....	....	....	....	....	....	....	....	....	....	....	....	....	....	....	....	....
1993-94	Peterborough	OHL	62	33	58	91	53	....	....	....	....	....	....	....	....	....	7	4	6	10	2	....	....	....	....
1994-95	Peterborough	OHL	62	42	57	99	84	....	....	....	....	....	....	....	....	....	11	8	14	22	12	....	....	....	....
	Dallas	**NHL**	**2**	**0**	**0**	**0**	**2**	**0**	**0**	**0**	**1**	**0.0**	**0**	....	....	....	....	....	....	....	....	....	....	....	....
	Kalamazoo Wings	IHL	....	....	....	....	....	....	....	....	....	....	....	....	....	....	11	1	3	4	2	....	....	....	....
1995-96	**Dallas**	**NHL**	**12**	**2**	**2**	**4**	**6**	**1**	**0**	**0**	**15**	**13.3**	**–2**	....	....	....	....	....	....	....	....	....	....	....	....
	Michigan	IHL	59	25	40	65	129	....	....	....	....	....	....	....	....	....	10	3	10	13	8	....	....	....	....
1996-97	**Dallas**	**NHL**	**76**	**13**	**26**	**39**	**51**	**3**	**0**	**3**	**112**	**11.6**	**–2**	....	....	....	**5**	**1**	**1**	**2**	**14**	**0**	**0**	**1**	....
1997-98	**Dallas**	**NHL**	**81**	**23**	**29**	**52**	**61**	**8**	**0**	**6**	**159**	**14.5**	**9**	....	....	....	**16**	**1**	**4**	**5**	**14**	**0**	**0**	**1**	....
	United States	Olympics	3	0	0	0	4	....	....	....	....	....	....	....	....	....	....	....	....	....	....	....	....	....	....
1998-99♦	**Dallas**	**NHL**	**75**	**12**	**33**	**45**	**62**	**4**	**0**	**1**	**145**	**8.3**	**10**	**217**	**46.1**	**15:51**	**23**	**10**	**7**	**17**	**16**	**4**	**0**	**3**	**17:43**
99-2000	**Dallas**	**NHL**	**65**	**18**	**21**	**39**	**68**	**4**	**2**	**6**	**153**	**11.8**	**16**	**40**	**50.0**	**17:33**	**15**	**1**	**7**	**8**	**18**	**1**	**0**	**0**	**15:28**
2000-01	**Dallas**	**NHL**	**53**	**12**	**18**	**30**	**57**	**3**	**2**	**4**	**104**	**11.5**	**4**	**316**	**45.3**	**16:30**	**10**	**2**	**2**	**4**	**6**	**0**	**0**	**1**	**19:26**
2001-02	**Dallas**	**NHL**	**68**	**10**	**16**	**26**	**54**	**0**	**1**	**2**	**132**	**7.6**	**–11**	**120**	**45.0**	**15:45**	....	....	....	....	....	....	....	....	....
	New Jersey	**NHL**	**14**	**3**	**3**	**6**	**23**	**0**	**0**	**2**	**31**	**9.7**	**2**	**2**	**50.0**	**15:27**	**5**	**0**	**1**	**1**	**8**	**0**	**0**	**0**	**14:57**
2002-03♦	**New Jersey**	**NHL**	**78**	**22**	**33**	**55**	**65**	**5**	**1**	**5**	**197**	**11.2**	**17**	**72**	**47.2**	**17:48**	**24**	***11**	**7**	***18**	**16**	**1**	**0**	**4**	**17:34**

Season	Club	League	GP	G	A	Pts	PIM	PP	SH	GW	S	%	+/-	TF	F%	Min	GP	G	A	Pts	PIM	PP	SH	GW	Min
			Regular Season														Playoffs								
2003-04	New Jersey	NHL	53	10	16	26	43	1	2	2	130	7.7	9	31	51.6	16:01	5	0	2	2	2	0	0	0	15:04
2004-05	ERC Ingolstadt	Germany	11	2	2	4	22	....	....	....	....	....	....	....	....	....	11	1	6	7	6	....	....	....	....
2005-06	New Jersey	NHL	80	19	34	53	74	8	1	1	243	7.8	–1	41	43.9	18:36	9	3	10	13	16	1	0	1	19:46
	NHL Totals		657	144	231	375	566	37	9	32	1422	10.1		839	46.0	16:55	112	29	41	70	110	7	0	11	17:24

Traded to **New Jersey** by **Dallas** with Joe Nieuwendyk for Jason Arnott, Randy McKay and New Jersey's 1st round choice (later traded to Columbus – later traded to Buffalo – Buffalo selected Dan Paille) in 2002 Entry Draft, March 19, 2002. Signed as a free agent by **Ingolstadt** (Germany), January 24, 2005.

LANGFELD, Josh (LANG-fehld, JAWSH) DET.

Right wing. Shoots right. 6'3", 216 lbs. Born, Fridley, MN, July 17, 1977. Ottawa's 3rd choice, 66th overall, in 1997 Entry Draft.

Season	Club	League	GP	G	A	Pts	PIM	PP	SH	GW	S	%	+/-	TF	F%	Min	GP	G	A	Pts	PIM	PP	SH	GW	Min
1995-96	Great Falls	AFHL	45	45	40	85	105	....	....	....	....	....	....	....	....	....	....	....	....	....	....	....	....	....	....
1996-97	Lincoln Stars	USHL	38	35	23	58	100	....	....	....	....	....	....	....	....	....	14	8	*13	*21	42	....	....	....	....
1997-98	U. of Michigan	CCHA	46	19	17	36	66	....	....	....	....	....	....	....	....	....	....	....	....	....	....	....	....	....	....
1998-99	U. of Michigan	CCHA	41	21	14	35	84	....	....	....	....	....	....	....	....	....	....	....	....	....	....	....	....	....	....
99-2000	U. of Michigan	CCHA	39	9	21	30	56	....	....	....	....	....	....	....	....	....	....	....	....	....	....	....	....	....	....
2000-01	U. of Michigan	CCHA	42	16	12	28	44	....	....	....	....	....	....	....	....	....	....	....	....	....	....	....	....	....	....
2001-02	**Ottawa**	**NHL**	**1**	**0**	**0**	**0**	**2**	**0**	**0**	**0**	**5**	**0.0**	**0**	**0**	**0.0**	**8:15**	....	....	....	....	....	....	....	....	....
	Grand Rapids	AHL	68	21	16	37	29	....	....	....	....	....	....	....	....	....	5	2	0	2	0	....	....	....	....
2002-03	**Ottawa**	**NHL**	**12**	**0**	**1**	**1**	**4**	**0**	**0**	**0**	**16**	**0.0**	**2**	**0**	**0.0**	**11:11**	....	....	....	....	....	....	....	....	....
	Binghamton	AHL	59	14	21	35	38	....	....	....	....	....	....	....	....	....	13	5	3	8	8	....	....	....	....
2003-04	**Ottawa**	**NHL**	**38**	**7**	**10**	**17**	**16**	**2**	**0**	**2**	**59**	**11.9**	**6**	**5**	**80.0**	**10:53**	....	....	....	....	....	....	....	....	....
	Binghamton	AHL	30	13	14	27	25	....	....	....	....	....	....	....	....	....	2	0	0	0	0	....	....	....	....
2004-05	Binghamton	AHL	74	32	25	57	75	....	....	....	....	....	....	....	....	....	6	2	2	4	2	....	....	....	....
2005-06	**San Jose**	**NHL**	**39**	**2**	**9**	**11**	**16**	**0**	**1**	**0**	**53**	**3.8**	**4**	**8**	**12.5**	**11:46**	....	....	....	....	....	....	....	....	....
	Boston	**NHL**	**18**	**0**	**1**	**1**	**10**	**0**	**0**	**0**	**32**	**0.0**	**–6**	**6**	**16.7**	**9:24**	....	....	....	....	....	....	....	....	....
	NHL Totals		**108**	**9**	**21**	**30**	**48**	**2**	**1**	**2**	**165**	**5.5**		**19**	**31.6**	**10:58**	....	....	....	....	....	....	....	....	....

NCAA Championship All-Tournament Team (1998)

Signed as a free agent by **San Jose**, September 12, 2005. Claimed on waivers by **Boston** from **San Jose**, January 31, 2006. Signed as a free agent by **Detroit**, August, 2006.

LANGKOW, Daymond (LAING-kow, DAY-muhn) CGY.

Center. Shoots left. 5'11", 192 lbs. Born, Edmonton, Alta., September 27, 1976. Tampa Bay's 1st choice, 5th overall, in 1995 Entry Draft.

Season	Club	League	GP	G	A	Pts	PIM	PP	SH	GW	S	%	+/-	TF	F%	Min	GP	G	A	Pts	PIM	PP	SH	GW	Min
1991-92	Edmonton Pats	AMHL	35	36	45	81	100	....	....	....	....	....	....	....	....	....	....	....	....	....	....	....	....	....	....
	Tri-City	WHL	1	0	0	0	0	....	....	....	....	....	....	....	....	....	....	....	....	....	....	....	....	....	....
1992-93	Tri-City	WHL	64	22	42	64	100	....	....	....	....	....	....	....	....	....	4	1	0	1	4	....	....	....	....
1993-94	Tri-City	WHL	61	40	43	83	174	....	....	....	....	....	....	....	....	....	4	2	2	4	15	....	....	....	....
1994-95	Tri-City	WHL	72	*67	73	*140	142	....	....	....	....	....	....	....	....	....	17	12	15	27	52	....	....	....	....
1995-96	Tri-City	WHL	48	30	61	91	103	....	....	....	....	....	....	....	....	....	11	14	13	27	20	....	....	....	....
	Tampa Bay	**NHL**	**4**	**0**	**1**	**1**	**0**	**0**	**0**	**0**	**4**	**0.0**	**–1**	....	....	....	....	....	....	....	....	....	....	....	....
1996-97	**Tampa Bay**	**NHL**	**79**	**15**	**13**	**28**	**35**	**3**	**1**	**1**	**170**	**8.8**	**1**	....	....	....	....	....	....	....	....	....	....	....	....
	Adirondack	AHL	2	1	1	2	0	....	....	....	....	....	....	....	....	....	....	....	....	....	....	....	....	....	....
1997-98	**Tampa Bay**	**NHL**	**68**	**8**	**14**	**22**	**62**	**2**	**0**	**1**	**156**	**5.1**	**–9**	....	....	....	....	....	....	....	....	....	....	....	....
1998-99	**Tampa Bay**	**NHL**	**22**	**4**	**6**	**10**	**15**	**1**	**0**	**1**	**40**	**10.0**	**0**	**399**	**48.4**	**17:10**	....	....	....	....	....	....	....	....	....
	Cleveland	IHL	4	1	1	2	18	....	....	....	....	....	....	....	....	....	....	....	....	....	....	....	....	....	....
	Philadelphia	**NHL**	**56**	**10**	**13**	**23**	**24**	**3**	**1**	**1**	**109**	**9.2**	**–8**	**738**	**48.0**	**15:12**	**6**	**0**	**2**	**2**	**2**	**0**	**0**	**0**	**16:50**
99-2000	**Philadelphia**	**NHL**	**82**	**18**	**32**	**50**	**56**	**5**	**0**	**7**	**222**	**8.1**	**1**	**1263**	**45.1**	**16:57**	**16**	**5**	**5**	**10**	**23**	**1**	**1**	**2**	**20:03**
2000-01	**Philadelphia**	**NHL**	**71**	**13**	**41**	**54**	**50**	**3**	**0**	**2**	**190**	**6.8**	**12**	**1181**	**47.2**	**18:38**	**6**	**2**	**4**	**6**	**2**	**1**	**0**	**0**	**20:17**
2001-02	**Phoenix**	**NHL**	**80**	**27**	**35**	**62**	**36**	**6**	**3**	**2**	**171**	**15.8**	**18**	**1379**	**46.2**	**19:11**	**5**	**1**	**0**	**1**	**0**	**0**	**0**	**0**	**21:06**
2002-03	**Phoenix**	**NHL**	**82**	**20**	**32**	**52**	**56**	**4**	**2**	**2**	**196**	**10.2**	**20**	**1972**	**46.5**	**21:00**	....	....	....	....	....	....	....	....	....
2003-04	**Phoenix**	**NHL**	**81**	**21**	**31**	**52**	**40**	**4**	**1**	**2**	**174**	**12.1**	**4**	**1472**	**43.1**	**21:07**	....	....	....	....	....	....	....	....	....
2004-05			DID NOT PLAY																						
2005-06	**Calgary**	**NHL**	**82**	**25**	**34**	**59**	**46**	**11**	**0**	**7**	**171**	**14.6**	**2**	**1130**	**47.4**	**18:07**	**7**	**1**	**5**	**6**	**6**	**1**	**0**	**0**	**19:42**
	NHL Totals		**707**	**161**	**252**	**413**	**420**	**42**	**8**	**26**	**1603**	**10.0**		**9534**	**46.1**	**18:42**	**40**	**9**	**16**	**25**	**33**	**3**	**1**	**2**	**19:40**

WHL West First All-Star Team (1995) • Canadian Major Junior First All-Star Team (1995) • WHL West Second All-Star Team (1996)

Traded to **Philadelphia** by **Tampa Bay** with Mikael Renberg for Chris Gratton and Mike Sillinger, December 12, 1998. Traded to **Phoenix** by **Philadelphia** for Phoenix's 2nd round choice (later traded to Tampa Bay – later traded to San Jose – San Jose selected Dan Spang) in 2002 Entry Draft and Phoenix's 1st round choice (Jeff Carter) in 2003 Entry Draft, July 2, 2001. Traded to **Calgary** by **Phoenix** for Denis Gauthier and Oleg Saprykin, August 26, 2004.

LAPERRIERE, Ian (luh-PAIR-ee-YAIR, EE-an) COL.

Right wing. Shoots right. 6'1", 201 lbs. Born, Montreal, Que., January 19, 1974. St. Louis' 6th choice, 158th overall, in 1992 Entry Draft.

Season	Club	League	GP	G	A	Pts	PIM	PP	SH	GW	S	%	+/-	TF	F%	Min	GP	G	A	Pts	PIM	PP	SH	GW	Min
1989-90	Mtl-Bourassa	QAAA	22	4	10	14	10	....	....	....	....	....	....	....	....	....	3	0	1	1	6	....	....	....	....
1990-91	Drummondville	QMJHL	65	19	29	48	117	....	....	....	....	....	....	....	....	....	14	2	9	11	48	....	....	....	....
1991-92	Drummondville	QMJHL	70	28	49	77	160	....	....	....	....	....	....	....	....	....	4	2	2	4	9	....	....	....	....
1992-93	Drummondville	QMJHL	60	44	*96	140	188	....	....	....	....	....	....	....	....	....	10	6	13	19	20	....	....	....	....
1993-94	Drummondville	QMJHL	62	41	72	113	150	....	....	....	....	....	....	....	....	....	9	4	6	10	35	....	....	....	....
	St. Louis	**NHL**	**1**	**0**	**0**	**0**	**0**	**0**	**0**	**0**	**1**	**0.0**	**0**	....	....	....	....	....	....	....	....	....	....	....	....
	Peoria Rivermen	IHL	....	....	....	....	....	....	....	....	....	....	....	....	....	....	5	1	3	4	2	....	....	....	....
1994-95	Peoria Rivermen	IHL	51	16	32	48	111	....	....	....	....	....	....	....	....	....	....	....	....	....	....	....	....	....	....
	St. Louis	**NHL**	**37**	**13**	**14**	**27**	**85**	**1**	**0**	**1**	**53**	**24.5**	**12**	....	....	....	**7**	**0**	**4**	**4**	**21**	**0**	**0**	**0**	....
1995-96	**St. Louis**	**NHL**	**33**	**3**	**6**	**9**	**87**	**1**	**0**	**1**	**31**	**9.7**	**–4**	....	....	....	....	....	....	....	....	....	....	....	....
	Worcester IceCats	AHL	3	2	1	3	22	....	....	....	....	....	....	....	....	....	....	....	....	....	....	....	....	....	....
	NY Rangers	**NHL**	**28**	**1**	**2**	**3**	**53**	**0**	**0**	**0**	**21**	**4.8**	**–5**	....	....	....	....	....	....	....	....	....	....	....	....
	Los Angeles	**NHL**	**10**	**2**	**3**	**5**	**15**	**0**	**0**	**0**	**18**	**11.1**	**–2**	....	....	....	....	....	....	....	....	....	....	....	....
1996-97	**Los Angeles**	**NHL**	**62**	**8**	**15**	**23**	**102**	**0**	**1**	**2**	**84**	**9.5**	**–25**	....	....	....	....	....	....	....	....	....	....	....	....
1997-98	**Los Angeles**	**NHL**	**77**	**6**	**15**	**21**	**131**	**0**	**1**	**1**	**74**	**8.1**	**0**	....	....	....	**4**	**1**	**0**	**1**	**6**	**0**	**0**	**0**	....
1998-99	**Los Angeles**	**NHL**	**72**	**3**	**10**	**13**	**138**	**0**	**0**	**1**	**62**	**4.8**	**–5**	**643**	**47.3**	**11:47**	....	....	....	....	....	....	....	....	....
99-2000	**Los Angeles**	**NHL**	**79**	**9**	**13**	**22**	**185**	**0**	**0**	**1**	**87**	**10.3**	**–14**	**1111**	**53.7**	**13:15**	**4**	**0**	**0**	**0**	**2**	**0**	**0**	**0**	**10:22**
2000-01	**Los Angeles**	**NHL**	**79**	**8**	**10**	**18**	**141**	**0**	**0**	**0**	**60**	**13.3**	**5**	**297**	**51.9**	**12:02**	**13**	**1**	**2**	**3**	**12**	**0**	**0**	**0**	**14:01**
2001-02	**Los Angeles**	**NHL**	**81**	**8**	**14**	**22**	**125**	**0**	**0**	**3**	**89**	**9.0**	**5**	**134**	**49.3**	**13:45**	**7**	**0**	**1**	**1**	**9**	**0**	**0**	**0**	**14:18**
2002-03	**Los Angeles**	**NHL**	**73**	**7**	**12**	**19**	**122**	**1**	**1**	**1**	**85**	**8.2**	**–9**	**317**	**49.2**	**15:46**	....	....	....	....	....	....	....	....	....
2003-04	**Los Angeles**	**NHL**	**62**	**10**	**12**	**22**	**58**	**1**	**0**	**3**	**59**	**16.9**	**–4**	**446**	**54.0**	**15:50**	....	....	....	....	....	....	....	....	....
2004-05			DID NOT PLAY																						
2005-06	**Colorado**	**NHL**	**82**	**21**	**24**	**45**	**116**	**1**	**1**	**3**	**133**	**15.8**	**3**	**963**	**45.9**	**17:10**	**9**	**0**	**1**	**1**	**27**	**0**	**0**	**0**	**13:40**
	NHL Totals		**776**	**99**	**150**	**249**	**1358**	**5**	**4**	**17**	**857**	**11.6**		**3911**	**50.1**	**14:12**	**44**	**2**	**8**	**10**	**77**	**0**	**0**	**0**	**13:32**

QMJHL Second All-Star Team (1993)

Traded to **NY Rangers** by **St. Louis** for Stephane Matteau, December 28, 1995. Traded to **Los Angeles** by **NY Rangers** with Ray Ferraro, Mattias Norstrom, Nathan LaFayette and NY Rangers' 4th round choice (Sean Blanchard) in 1997 Entry Draft for Marty McSorley, Jari Kurri and Shane Churla, March 14, 1996. Signed as a free agent by **Colorado**, July 2, 2004.

LAPIERRE, Maxim (la-PEE-air, MAX-ihm) MTL.

Center. Shoots right. 6'2", 197 lbs. Born, St. Leonard, Que., March 29, 1985. Montreal's 3rd choice, 61st overall, in 2003 Entry Draft.

Season	Club	League	GP	G	A	Pts	PIM	PP	SH	GW	S	%	+/-	TF	F%	Min	GP	G	A	Pts	PIM	PP	SH	GW	Min
2001-02	Cap-d-Madeleine	QAAA	42	14	27	41	44	....	....	....	....	....	....	....	....	....	10	3	5	8	16	....	....	....	....
	Montreal Rocket	QMJHL	9	2	0	2	2	....	....	....	....	....	....	....	....	....	....	....	....	....	....	....	....	....	....
2002-03	Montreal Rocket	QMJHL	72	22	21	43	55	....	....	....	....	....	....	....	....	....	7	1	3	4	6	....	....	....	....
2003-04	PEI Rocket	QMJHL	67	25	36	61	138	....	....	....	....	....	....	....	....	....	11	7	2	9	14	....	....	....	....
2004-05	PEI Rocket	QMJHL	69	25	27	52	139	....	....	....	....	....	....	....	....	....	....	....	....	....	....	....	....	....	....
2005-06	**Montreal**	**NHL**	**1**	**0**	**0**	**0**	**0**	**0**	**0**	**0**	**0**	**0.0**	**–1**	**2**	**50.0**	**3:04**	....	....	....	....	....	....	....	....	....
	Hamilton	AHL	73	13	23	36	214	....	....	....	....	....	....	....	....	....	....	....	....	....	....	....	....	....	....
	NHL Totals		**1**	**0**	**0**	**0**	**0**	**0**	**0**	**0**	**0**	**0.0**		**2**	**50.0**	**3:04**	....	....	....	....	....	....	....	....	....

LAPOINTE, Martin

(luh-POYNT, MAHR-tihn) **CHI.**

Right wing. Shoots right. 5'11", 215 lbs. Born, Ville St-Pierre, Que., September 12, 1973. Detroit's 1st choice, 10th overall, in 1991 Entry Draft.

			Regular Season														Playoffs								
Season	Club	League	GP	G	A	Pts	PIM	PP	SH	GW	S	%	+/-	TF	F%	Min	GP	G	A	Pts	PIM	PP	SH	GW	Min
1988-89	Lac St-Louis Lions	QAAA	42	39	45	84	46										3	6	2	8	4				
1989-90	Laval Titan	QMJHL	65	42	54	96	77										14	8	17	25	54				
1990-91	Laval Titan	QMJHL	64	44	54	98	66										13	7	14	21	26				
1991-92	Laval Titan	QMJHL	31	25	30	55	84										10	4	10	14	32				
	Detroit	**NHL**	**4**	**0**	**1**	**1**	**5**	**0**	**0**	**0**	**2**	**0.0**	**2**				**3**	**0**	**1**	**1**	**4**	**0**	**0**	**0**	
	Adirondack	AHL															8	2	2	4	4				
1992-93	Laval Titan	QMJHL	35	38	51	89	41										13	*13	*17	*30	22				
	Detroit	**NHL**	**3**	**0**	**0**	**0**	**0**	**0**	**0**	**0**	**2**	**0.0**	**−2**												
	Adirondack	AHL	8	1	2	3	9																		
1993-94	**Detroit**	**NHL**	**50**	**8**	**8**	**16**	**55**	**2**	**0**	**0**	**45**	**17.8**	**7**				**4**	**0**	**0**	**0**	**6**	**0**	**0**	**0**	
	Adirondack	AHL	28	25	21	46	47										4	1	1	2	8				
1994-95	Adirondack	AHL	39	29	16	45	80																		
	Detroit	**NHL**	**39**	**4**	**6**	**10**	**73**	**0**	**0**	**1**	**46**	**8.7**	**1**				**2**	**0**	**1**	**1**	**8**	**0**	**0**	**0**	
1995-96	**Detroit**	**NHL**	**58**	**6**	**3**	**9**	**93**	**1**	**0**	**0**	**76**	**7.9**	**0**				**11**	**1**	**2**	**3**	**12**	**0**	**0**	**0**	
1996-97♦	**Detroit**	**NHL**	**78**	**16**	**17**	**33**	**167**	**5**	**1**	**1**	**149**	**10.7**	**−14**				**20**	**4**	**8**	**12**	**60**	**1**	**0**	**1**	
1997-98♦	**Detroit**	**NHL**	**79**	**15**	**19**	**34**	**106**	**4**	**0**	**3**	**154**	**9.7**	**0**				**21**	**9**	**6**	**15**	**20**	**2**	**1**	**1**	
1998-99	**Detroit**	**NHL**	**77**	**16**	**13**	**29**	**141**	**7**	**1**	**4**	**153**	**10.5**	**7**	**217**	**47.9**	**15:06**	**10**	**0**	**2**	**2**	**20**	**0**	**0**	**0**	**11:43**
99-2000	**Detroit**	**NHL**	**82**	**16**	**25**	**41**	**121**	**1**	**1**	**2**	**127**	**12.6**	**17**	**287**	**54.4**	**14:43**	**9**	**3**	**1**	**4**	**20**	**2**	**0**	**1**	**14:28**
2000-01	**Detroit**	**NHL**	**82**	**27**	**30**	**57**	**127**	**13**	**0**	**8**	**181**	**14.9**	**3**	**461**	**53.2**	**16:06**	**6**	**0**	**1**	**1**	**8**	**0**	**0**	**0**	**16:53**
2001-02	**Boston**	**NHL**	**68**	**17**	**23**	**40**	**101**	**4**	**0**	**2**	**141**	**12.1**	**12**	**222**	**53.6**	**17:22**	**6**	**1**	**2**	**3**	**12**	**1**	**0**	**1**	**16:58**
2002-03	**Boston**	**NHL**	**59**	**8**	**10**	**18**	**87**	**1**	**0**	**1**	**110**	**7.3**	**−19**	**52**	**48.1**	**15:22**	**5**	**1**	**0**	**1**	**14**	**0**	**0**	**0**	**14:39**
2003-04	**Boston**	**NHL**	**78**	**15**	**10**	**25**	**67**	**9**	**0**	**2**	**136**	**11.0**	**−5**	**101**	**51.5**	**14:26**	**7**	**0**	**0**	**0**	**14**	**0**	**0**	**0**	**15:21**
2004-05			DID NOT PLAY																						
2005-06	**Chicago**	**NHL**	**82**	**14**	**17**	**31**	**106**	**6**	**0**	**3**	**135**	**10.4**	**−30**	**354**	**56.5**	**14:46**									
	NHL Totals		**839**	**162**	**182**	**344**	**1249**	**53**	**3**	**27**	**1457**	**11.1**		**1694**	**53.2**	**15:22**	**104**	**19**	**24**	**43**	**198**	**6**	**1**	**4**	**14:41**

QMJHL First All-Star Team (1990, 1993) • QMJHL Offensive Rookie of the Year (1990) • QMJHL Second All-Star Team (1991) • Memorial Cup Tournament All-Star Team (1993)

Signed as a free agent by **Boston**, July 2, 2001. Signed as a free agent by **Chicago**, August 3, 2005.

LARAQUE, Georges

(luh-RAK, zhawrzh) **PHX.**

Right wing. Shoots right. 6'3", 243 lbs. Born, Montreal, Que., December 7, 1976. Edmonton's 2nd choice, 31st overall, in 1995 Entry Draft.

Season	Club	League	GP	G	A	Pts	PIM	PP	SH	GW	S	%	+/-	TF	F%	Min	GP	G	A	Pts	PIM	PP	SH	GW	Min
1991-92	Mtl-Bourassa	QAHA	28	20	20	40	30																		
1992-93	Mtl-Bourassa	QAAA	37	8	20	28	50										3	1	2	3	2				
1993-94	St-Jean Lynx	QMJHL	70	11	11	22	142										4	0	0	0	7				
1994-95	St-Jean Lynx	QMJHL	62	19	22	41	259										7	1	1	2	42				
1995-96	Laval Titan	QMJHL	11	8	13	21	76																		
	St-Hyacinthe	QMJHL	8	3	4	7	59																		
	Granby	QMJHL	22	9	7	16	125										18	7	6	13	104				
1996-97	Hamilton	AHL	73	14	20	34	179										15	1	3	4	12				
1997-98	**Edmonton**	**NHL**	**11**	**0**	**0**	**0**	**59**	**0**	**0**	**0**	**4**	**0.0**	**−4**												
	Hamilton	AHL	46	10	20	30	154										3	0	0	0	11				
1998-99	**Edmonton**	**NHL**	**39**	**3**	**2**	**5**	**57**	**0**	**0**	**0**	**17**	**17.6**	**−1**	**0**	**0.0**	**5:31**	**4**	**0**	**0**	**0**	**2**	**0**	**0**	**0**	**7:35**
	Hamilton	AHL	25	6	8	14	93																		
99-2000	**Edmonton**	**NHL**	**76**	**8**	**8**	**16**	**123**	**0**	**0**	**0**	**56**	**14.3**	**5**	**0**	**0.0**	**8:28**	**5**	**0**	**1**	**1**	**6**	**0**	**0**	**0**	**9:14**
2000-01	**Edmonton**	**NHL**	**82**	**13**	**16**	**29**	**148**	**1**	**0**	**1**	**73**	**17.8**	**5**	**0**	**0.0**	**9:03**	**6**	**1**	**1**	**2**	**8**	**0**	**0**	**0**	**9:54**
2001-02	**Edmonton**	**NHL**	**80**	**5**	**14**	**19**	**157**	**1**	**0**	**1**	**95**	**5.3**	**6**	**0**	**0.0**	**9:48**									
2002-03	**Edmonton**	**NHL**	**64**	**6**	**7**	**13**	**110**	**0**	**0**	**2**	**46**	**13.0**	**−4**	**0**	**0.0**	**9:15**	**6**	**1**	**3**	**4**	**4**	**0**	**0**	**0**	**12:11**
2003-04	**Edmonton**	**NHL**	**66**	**6**	**11**	**17**	**99**	**1**	**0**	**1**	**54**	**11.1**	**7**	**0**	**0.0**	**9:22**									
2004-05	AIK Solna	Sweden-3	16	11	5	16	24																		
2005-06	**Edmonton**	**NHL**	**72**	**2**	**10**	**12**	**73**	**0**	**0**	**0**	**50**	**4.0**	**−5**	**3**	**33.3**	**6:35**	**15**	**1**	**1**	**2**	***44**	**0**	**0**	**0**	**5:31**
	NHL Totals		**490**	**43**	**68**	**111**	**826**	**3**	**0**	**5**	**395**	**10.9**		**3**	**33.3**	**8:30**	**36**	**3**	**6**	**9**	**64**	**0**	**0**	**0**	**8:06**

Signed as a free agent by **Solna** (Sweden-3), January 31, 2005. Signed as a free agent by **Phoenix**, July 5, 2006.

LaROSE, Chad

(lah-ROHZ, CHAD) **CAR.**

Right wing. Shoots right. 5'10", 173 lbs. Born, Fraser, MI, March 27, 1982.

Season	Club	League	GP	G	A	Pts	PIM	PP	SH	GW	S	%	+/-	TF	F%	Min	GP	G	A	Pts	PIM	PP	SH	GW	Min
99-2000	Sioux Falls	USHL	54	29	26	55	28										3	0	1	1	0				
2000-01	Sioux Falls	USHL	24	11	22	33	50																		
	Plymouth Whalers	OHL	32	18	7	25	24										19	10	10	20	22				
2001-02	Plymouth Whalers	OHL	53	32	27	59	40										6	3	4	7	16				
2002-03	Plymouth Whalers	OHL	67	61	56	117	52										15	9	8	17	25				
2003-04	Lowell	AHL	36	7	9	16	29																		
	Florida Everblades	ECHL	41	16	19	35	16										14	3	4	7	20				
2004-05	Lowell	AHL	66	20	22	42	32										11	3	5	8	10				
2005-06♦	**Carolina**	**NHL**	**49**	**1**	**12**	**13**	**35**	**0**	**0**	**1**	**62**	**1.6**	**7**	**5**	**40.0**	**10:35**	**21**	**0**	**1**	**1**	**10**	**0**	**0**	**0**	**8:58**
	Lowell	AHL	23	14	11	25	10																		
	NHL Totals		**49**	**1**	**12**	**13**	**35**	**0**	**0**	**1**	**62**	**1.6**		**5**	**40.0**	**10:35**	**21**	**0**	**1**	**1**	**10**	**0**	**0**	**0**	**8:58**

OHL Second All-Star Team (2003)

Signed as a free agent by **Carolina**, August 6, 2003.

LAROSE, Cory

(la-ROHZ, KOH-ree) **ATL.**

Center. Shoots left. 6', 191 lbs. Born, Campbellton, N.B., May 14, 1975.

Season	Club	League	GP	G	A	Pts	PIM	PP	SH	GW	S	%	+/-	TF	F%	Min	GP	G	A	Pts	PIM	PP	SH	GW	Min
1993-94	Kimball Union	High-NH	21	18	11	29	14																		
1994-95	Langley Thunder	BCJHL	STATISTICS NOT AVAILABLE																						
1995-96	Langley Thunder	BCJHL	54	28	46	74	61																		
1996-97	U. of Maine	H-East	35	10	27	37	32																		
1997-98	U. of Maine	H-East	34	15	25	40	22																		
1998-99	U. of Maine	H-East	38	21	31	52	34																		
99-2000	U. of Maine	H-East	39	15	*36	51	45																		
2000-01	Cleveland	IHL	4	1	1	2	6																		
	Jackson Bandits	ECHL	63	21	32	53	73										5	2	2	4	12				
2001-02	Houston Aeros	AHL	78	32	32	64	73										14	6	8	14	15				
2002-03	Houston Aeros	AHL	58	18	38	56	57																		
	Hartford	AHL	24	9	10	19	20										2	0	1	1	0				
2003-04	**NY Rangers**	**NHL**	**7**	**0**	**1**	**1**	**4**	**0**	**0**	**0**	**10**	**0.0**	**−2**	**40**	**47.5**	**11:27**									
	Hartford	AHL	69	13	36	49	66										14	4	6	10	24				
2004-05	Chicago Wolves	AHL	80	26	37	63	44										18	6	6	12	29				
2005-06	Langnau	Swiss	42	17	14	31	76										6	4	3	7	6				
	NHL Totals		**7**	**0**	**1**	**1**	**4**	**0**	**0**	**0**	**10**	**0.0**		**40**	**47.5**	**11:27**									

Hockey East First All-Star Team (2000) • NCAA East Second All-American Team (2000) • AHL All-Rookie Team (2002)

Signed as a free agent by **Minnesota**, May 10, 2000. Traded to **NY Rangers** by **Minnesota** for Jay Henderson, February 20, 2003. Signed as a free agent by **Atlanta**, July 14, 2004. Signed as a free agent by **Langnau** (Swiss), May 5, 2005.

LARSEN, Brad

(LARH-sehn, BRAD) **ATL.**

Left wing. Shoots left. 6', 210 lbs. Born, Nakusp, B.C., June 28, 1977. Colorado's 5th choice, 87th overall, in 1997 Entry Draft.

Season	Club	League	GP	G	A	Pts	PIM	PP	SH	GW	S	%	+/-	TF	F%	Min	GP	G	A	Pts	PIM	PP	SH	GW	Min
1992-93	Nelson	RMJHL	42	31	37	68	164																		
1993-94	Swift Current	WHL	64	15	18	33	32										7	1	2	3	4				
1994-95	Swift Current	WHL	62	24	33	57	73										6	0	1	1	2				
1995-96	Swift Current	WHL	51	30	47	77	67										6	3	2	5	13				
1996-97	Swift Current	WHL	61	36	46	82	61																		
1997-98	**Colorado**	**NHL**	**1**	**0**	**0**	**0**	**0**	**0**	**0**	**0**	**0**	**0.0**	**0**												
	Hershey Bears	AHL	65	12	10	22	80										7	3	2	5	2				
1998-99	Hershey Bears	AHL	18	3	4	7	11										5	0	1	1	6				
99-2000	Hershey Bears	AHL	52	13	26	39	66										14	5	2	7	29				

Season	Club	League	GP	G	A	Pts	PIM	PP	SH	GW	S	%	+/-	TF	F%	Min	GP	G	A	Pts	PIM	PP	SH	GW	Min
																	Regular Season					Playoffs			
2000-01	Colorado	NHL	9	0	0	0	0	0	0	0	3	0.0	1	14	57.1	9:17	....								....
	Hershey Bears	AHL	67	21	25	46	93										10	1	3	4	6				....
2001-02	Colorado	NHL	50	2	7	9	47	1	0	0	38	5.3	4	71	54.9	8:07	21	1	1	2	13	0	0	0	7:07
2002-03	Colorado	NHL	6	0	3	3	2	0	0	0	6	0.0	3	31	41.9	8:17									
	Hershey Bears	AHL	25	3	6	9	25										4	1	1	2	8				....
2003-04	Colorado	NHL	26	2	2	4	11	0	0	0	17	11.8	2	9	44.4	7:41									
	Hershey Bears	AHL	21	4	13	17	40																		
	Atlanta	NHL	6	0	0	0	2	0	0	0	6	0.0	-2	6	66.7	13:39	18	4	7	11	22				....
2004-05	Chicago Wolves	AHL	75	26	23	49	112																		
2005-06	Atlanta	NHL	62	7	8	15	21	0	3	1	48	14.6	-3	81	34.6	10:59									
	Chicago Wolves	AHL	6	1	0	1	8																		
	NHL Totals		160	11	20	31	83	1	3	1	118	9.3		212	45.3	9:27	21	1	1	2	13	0	0	0	7:07

• Re-entered NHL Entry Draft. Originally Ottawa's 3rd choice, 53rd overall, in 1995 Entry Draft.
WHL East Second All-Star Team (1997)
Rights traded to **Colorado** by **Ottawa** for Janne Laukkanen, January 26, 1996. • Missed majority of 1998-99 season recovering from abdominal injury suffered in game vs. Albany (AHL), November 20, 1998. • Missed majority of 2002-03 season recovering from groin (October 27, 2002 vs. Minnesota) and back (December 11, 2002 vs. Vancouver) injuries. Claimed on waivers by **Atlanta** from **Colorado**, February 25, 2004.

LAW, Kirby
(LAW, KUHR-bee)

Right wing. Shoots right. 6'1", 185 lbs. Born, McCreary, Man., March 11, 1977.

Season	Club	League	GP	G	A	Pts	PIM	PP	SH	GW	S	%	+/-	TF	F%	Min	GP	G	A	Pts	PIM
1991-92	McCreary	MAHA	60	89	103	192	60														
1992-93	Dauphin Kings	MJHL	48	20	15	35	8														
1993-94	Saskatoon Blades	WHL	66	9	11	20	39										16	0	0	0	6
1994-95	Saskatoon Blades	WHL	46	10	15	25	44														
	Lethbridge	WHL	24	4	10	14	38														
1995-96	Lethbridge	WHL	71	17	45	62	133										4	0	0	0	12
1996-97	Lethbridge	WHL	72	39	52	91	200										19	4	14	18	60
1997-98	Brandon	WHL	49	34	44	78	153										9	3	3	6	41
1998-99	Orlando	IHL	67	18	13	31	136														
	Adirondack	AHL	11	2	3	5	40										3	1	0	1	2
99-2000	Louisville Panthers	AHL	66	31	21	52	173														
	Orlando	IHL	1	1	0	1	0														
	Philadelphia	AHL	12	1	4	5	6										5	2	0	2	0
2000-01	**Philadelphia**	**NHL**	1	0	0	0	0	0	0	0	0	0.0	-1	0	0.0	3:23	10	1	6	7	16
	Philadelphia	AHL	78	27	34	61	150														
2001-02	Philadelphia	AHL	71	18	24	42	102										5	0	0	0	0
2002-03	**Philadelphia**	**NHL**	2	0	0	0	2	0	0	0	0	0.0	0	0	0.0	1:41					
	Philadelphia	AHL	74	22	19	41	166														
2003-04	**Philadelphia**	**NHL**	6	0	1	1	2	0	0	0	1	0.0	0	0	0.0	8:09					
	Philadelphia	AHL	74	32	41	73	139										12	0	5	5	12
2004-05	Houston Aeros	AHL	80	25	24	49	134										5	0	1	1	4
2005-06	Houston Aeros	AHL	80	43	*67	*110	95										8	4	5	9	4
	NHL Totals		9	0	1	1	4	0	0	0	1	0.0		0	0.0	6:11					

AHL First All-Star Team (2006)
Signed as a free agent by **Atlanta**, July 27, 1999. Traded to **Philadelphia** by **Atlanta** for Vancouver's 6th round choice (previously acquired, Atlanta selected Jeff Dwyer) in 2000 Entry Draft and Philadelphia's 6th round choice (Pasi Nurminen) in 2001 Entry Draft, March 14, 2000. Signed as a free agent by **Minnesota**, July 6, 2004.

LEACH, Jay
(LEECH, JAY) **BOS.**

Defense. Shoots left. 6'4", 220 lbs. Born, Syracuse, NY, September 2, 1979. Phoenix's 5th choice, 115th overall, in 1998 Entry Draft.

Season	Club	League	GP	G	A	Pts	PIM	PP	SH	GW	S	%	+/-	TF	F%	Min	GP	G	A	Pts	PIM
1994-95	John Marshall	High-MN	10	0	0	0	14														
1995-96	John Marshall	High-MN	11	1	2	3	8										4	0	0	0	0
	Capital District	Exhib.	53	3	8	11	33														
1996-97	Capital District	Exhib.	57	8	50	58	140														
1997-98	Providence	H-East	32	0	8	8	29														
1998-99	Providence	H-East	33	1	8	9	42														
99-2000	Providence	H-East	37	1	9	10	101														
2000-01	Providence	H-East	40	4	21	25	104														
2001-02	Mississippi	ECHL	70	3	13	16	116										10	1	1	2	8
2002-03	Springfield	AHL	9	0	0	0	0														
	Augusta Lynx	ECHL	65	8	11	19	162														
2003-04	Providence Bruins	AHL	3	0	0	0	4														
	Long Beach	ECHL	3	0	1	1	4														
	Bridgeport	AHL	23	1	1	1	33										7	0	1	1	10
	Trenton Titans	ECHL	31	2	11	13	45														
2004-05	Providence Bruins	AHL	62	4	5	9	92										17	0	0	0	28
	Trenton Titans	ECHL	11	0	2	2	17														
2005-06	**Boston**	**NHL**	2	0	0	0	7	0	0	0	0	0.0	1	0	0.0	6:20					
	Providence Bruins	AHL	72	5	11	16	100										6	0	1	1	15
	NHL Totals		2	0	0	0	7	0	0	0	0	0.0		0	0.0	6:20					

Hockey East All-Academic Team (2000)
Signed as a free agent by **Boston**, September 26, 2003.

LEAHY, Patrick
(LEH-hey, PAT-rihk) **NSH.**

Right wing. Shoots right. 6'3", 200 lbs. Born, Brighton, MA, June 9, 1979. NY Rangers' 5th choice, 122nd overall, in 1998 Entry Draft.

Season	Club	League	GP	G	A	Pts	PIM	PP	SH	GW	S	%	+/-	TF	F%	Min	GP	G	A	Pts	PIM
1996-97	Bos. College High	High-MA	25	24	24	48															
1997-98	Miami U.	CCHA	28	0	1	1	24														
1998-99	Miami U.	CCHA	34	10	20	30	40														
99-2000	Miami U.	CCHA	36	16	22	38	89														
2000-01	Miami U.	CCHA	37	13	19	32	14														
2001-02	Trenton Titans	ECHL	41	20	21	41	64														
	Hershey Bears	AHL	9	1	2	3	8														
	Portland Pirates	AHL	9	1	1	2	8														
	Bridgeport	AHL	14	2	2	4	2										20	3	4	7	4
2002-03	Providence Bruins	AHL	66	20	23	43	63										4	1	0	1	18
2003-04	**Boston**	**NHL**	6	0	0	0	0	0	0	0	2	0.0	1	0	0.0	5:27					
	Providence Bruins	AHL	55	14	16	30	37										2	0	0	0	0
2004-05	Providence Bruins	AHL	38	1	14	15	18										17	4	6	10	20
2005-06	**Boston**	**NHL**	43	4	4	8	19	0	0	0	46	8.7	-2	12	58.3	9:06					
	Providence Bruins	AHL	4	1	2	3	4														
	NHL Totals		49	4	4	8	19	0	0	0	48	8.3		12	58.3	8:39					

Signed as a free agent by **Boston**, July 28, 2003. Signed as a free agent by **Nashville**, July 17, 2006.

LEBDA, Brett
(LEHB-dah, BREHT) **DET.**

Defense. Shoots left. 5'11", 194 lbs. Born, Buffalo Grove, IL, January 15, 1982.

Season	Club	League	GP	G	A	Pts	PIM	PP	SH	GW	S	%	+/-	TF	F%	Min	GP	G	A	Pts	PIM
1998-99	USNTDP	U-17	11	1	7	8	4														
	USNTDP	USHL	3	0	0	0	0														
	USNTDP	NAHL	52	11	17	28	56														
99-2000	USNTDP	U-18	4	0	0	0	6														
	USNTDP	USHL	22	6	7	13	28														
2000-01	U. of Notre Dame	CCHA	39	7	19	26	109														
2001-02	U. of Notre Dame	CCHA	34	6	8	14	54														
2002-03	U. of Notre Dame	CCHA	40	7	14	21	48														
2003-04	U. of Notre Dame	CCHA	39	6	18	24	42														
	Grand Rapids	AHL	6	0	1	1	0										4	0	0	0	2
2004-05	Grand Rapids	AHL	80	2	10	12	34														

			Regular Season														Playoffs								
Season	Club	League	GP	G	A	Pts	PIM	PP	SH	GW	S	%	+/-	TF	F%	Min	GP	G	A	Pts	PIM	PP	SH	GW	Min
2005-06	Detroit	NHL	46	3	9	12	20	1	0	1	50	6.0	9	2	0.0	12:38	6	0	0	0	4	0	0	0	13:09
	Grand Rapids	AHL	25	4	14	18	42	....	....	....	....	....	....	....	....	....	11	1	4	5	8	....	....	....	....
	NHL Totals		46	3	9	12	20	1	0	1	50	6.0		2	0.0	12:38	6	0	0	0	4	0	0	0	13:09

CCHA All-Rookie Team (2001) • CCHA Second All-Star Team (2004)

Signed as a free agent by **Detroit**, April 1, 2004.

LECAVALIER, Vincent

(luh-KAV-uhl-YAY, VIHN-sihnt) **T.B.**

Center. Shoots left. 6'4", 223 lbs. Born, Ile Bizard, Que., April 21, 1980. Tampa Bay's 1st choice, 1st overall, in 1998 Entry Draft.

Season	Club	League	GP	G	A	Pts	PIM	PP	SH	GW	S	%	+/-	TF	F%	Min	GP	G	A	Pts	PIM	PP	SH	GW	Min
1995-96	Notre Dame	SMHL	22	52	52	104	....	....	....	....	....	....	....	....	....	....	....	....	....	....	....	....	....	....	....
1996-97	Rimouski Oceanic	QMJHL	64	42	61	103	38	....	....	....	....	....	....	....	....	....	4	4	3	7	2	....	....	....	....
1997-98	Rimouski Oceanic	QMJHL	58	44	71	115	117	....	....	....	....	....	....	....	....	....	18	*15	*26	*41	46	....	....	....	....
1998-99	Tampa Bay	NHL	82	13	15	28	23	2	0	2	125	10.4	–19	953	40.3	13:40	....	....	....	....	....	....	....	....	....
99-2000	Tampa Bay	NHL	80	25	42	67	43	6	0	3	166	15.1	–25	1288	44.4	19:18	....	....	....	....	....	....	....	....	....
2000-01	Tampa Bay	NHL	68	23	28	51	66	7	0	3	165	13.9	–26	1278	44.9	19:57	....	....	....	....	....	....	....	....	....
2001-02	Tampa Bay	NHL	76	20	17	37	61	5	0	3	164	12.2	–18	931	41.5	17:09	....	....	....	....	....	....	....	....	....
2002-03	Tampa Bay	NHL	80	33	45	78	39	11	2	3	274	12.0	0	1200	43.9	19:33	11	3	3	6	22	1	0	1	22:36
2003-04♦	Tampa Bay	NHL	81	32	34	66	52	5	2	6	242	13.2	23	1119	41.4	18:04	23	9	7	16	25	2	0	0	19:39
2004-05	Ak Bars Kazan	Russia	30	7	9	16	78	....	....	....	....	....	....	....	....	....	4	1	0	1	6	....	....	....	....
2005-06	Tampa Bay	NHL	80	35	40	75	90	13	2	7	309	11.3	0	1366	51.2	20:08	5	1	3	4	7	1	0	0	22:17
	Canada	Olympics	6	0	3	3	16	....	....	....	....	....	....	....	....	....	....	....	....	....	....	....	....	....	....
	NHL Totals		547	181	221	402	374	49	6	27	1445	12.5		8135	44.3	18:13	39	13	13	26	54	4	0	1	20:49

QMJHL All-Rookie Team (1997) • QMJHL Offensive Rookie of the Year (1997) • Canadian Major Junior Rookie of the Year (1997) • QMJHL First All-Star Team (1998) • Canadian Major Junior First All-Star Team (1998)

Played in NHL All-Star Game (2003)

Signed as a free agent by **Kazan** (Russia), November 4, 2004.

LeCLAIR, John

(luh-KLAIR, JAWN) **PIT.**

Left wing. Shoots left. 6'3", 226 lbs. Born, St. Albans, VT, July 5, 1969. Montreal's 2nd choice, 33rd overall, in 1987 Entry Draft.

Season	Club	League	GP	G	A	Pts	PIM	PP	SH	GW	S	%	+/-	TF	F%	Min	GP	G	A	Pts	PIM	PP	SH	GW	Min
1985-86	Bellows	High-VT	22	41	28	69	14	....	....	....	....	....	....	....	....	....	....	....	....	....	....	....	....	....	....
1986-87	Bellows	High-VT	23	44	40	84	14	....	....	....	....	....	....	....	....	....	....	....	....	....	....	....	....	....	....
1987-88	U. of Vermont	ECAC	31	12	22	34	62	....	....	....	....	....	....	....	....	....	....	....	....	....	....	....	....	....	....
1988-89	U. of Vermont	ECAC	18	9	12	21	40	....	....	....	....	....	....	....	....	....	....	....	....	....	....	....	....	....	....
1989-90	U. of Vermont	ECAC	10	10	6	16	38	....	....	....	....	....	....	....	....	....	....	....	....	....	....	....	....	....	....
1990-91	U. of Vermont	ECAC	33	25	20	45	58	....	....	....	....	....	....	....	....	....	....	....	....	....	....	....	....	....	....
	Montreal	NHL	10	2	5	7	2	0	0	1	12	16.7	1	....	....	....	3	0	0	0	0	0	0	0	....
1991-92	Montreal	NHL	59	8	11	19	14	3	0	0	73	11.0	5	....	....	....	8	1	1	2	4	0	0	0	....
	Fredericton	AHL	8	7	7	14	10	....	....	....	....	....	....	....	....	....	2	0	0	0	4	....	....	....	....
1992-93♦	Montreal	NHL	72	19	25	44	33	2	0	2	139	13.7	11	....	....	....	20	4	6	10	14	0	0	3	....
1993-94	Montreal	NHL	74	19	24	43	32	1	0	1	153	12.4	17	....	....	....	7	2	1	3	8	1	0	0	....
1994-95	Montreal	NHL	9	1	4	5	10	1	0	0	18	5.6	–1	....	....	....	....	....	....	....	....	....	....	....	....
	Philadelphia	NHL	37	25	24	49	20	5	0	7	113	22.1	21	....	....	....	15	5	7	12	4	1	0	1	....
1995-96	Philadelphia	NHL	82	51	46	97	64	19	0	10	270	18.9	21	....	....	....	11	6	5	11	6	4	0	1	....
1996-97	Philadelphia	NHL	82	50	47	97	58	10	0	5	324	15.4	44	....	....	....	19	9	12	21	10	4	0	3	....
1997-98	Philadelphia	NHL	82	51	36	87	32	16	0	9	303	16.8	30	....	....	....	5	1	1	2	8	1	0	1	....
	United States	Olympics	4	0	1	1	0	....	....	....	....	....	....	....	....	....	....	....	....	....	....	....	....	....	....
1998-99	Philadelphia	NHL	76	43	47	90	30	16	0	7	246	17.5	36	7	14.3	21:03	6	3	0	3	12	2	0	0	20:14
99-2000	Philadelphia	NHL	82	40	37	77	36	13	0	7	249	16.1	8	7	28.6	20:18	18	6	7	13	6	4	0	2	21:16
2000-01	Philadelphia	NHL	16	7	5	12	0	3	0	2	48	14.6	2	0	0.0	19:06	6	1	2	3	2	0	0	0	19:34
2001-02	Philadelphia	NHL	82	25	26	51	30	4	0	6	220	11.4	5	4	75.0	17:30	5	0	0	0	2	0	0	0	17:18
	United States	Olympics	6	*6	1	7	2	....	....	....	....	....	....	....	....	....	....	....	....	....	....	....	....	....	....
2002-03	Philadelphia	NHL	35	18	10	28	16	8	0	4	99	18.2	10	3	66.7	16:09	13	2	3	5	10	1	0	0	17:09
2003-04	Philadelphia	NHL	75	23	32	55	51	8	0	4	182	12.6	20	9	33.3	16:06	18	2	2	4	8	0	0	0	15:57
2004-05			DID NOT PLAY																						
2005-06	Pittsburgh	NHL	73	22	29	51	61	8	1	0	135	16.3	–24	13	46.2	15:45	....	....	....	....	....	....	....	....	....
	NHL Totals		946	404	408	812	489	117	1	65	2584	15.6		43	39.5	18:03	154	42	47	89	94	18	0	11	18:28

ECAC Second All-Star Team (1991) • NHL First All-Star Team (1995, 1998) • NHL Second All-Star Team (1996, 1997, 1999) • Bud Ice Plus/Minus Award (1997) • Bud Light Plus/Minus Award (1999)

Played in NHL All-Star Game (1996, 1997, 1998, 1999, 2000)

• Missed majority of 1989-90 season recovering from knee surgery, January 20, 1990. Traded to **Philadelphia** by **Montreal** with Eric Desjardins and Gilbert Dionne for Mark Recchi and Philadelphia's 3rd round choice (Martin Hohenberger) in 1995 Entry Draft, February 9, 1995. • Missed majority of 2000-01 season recovering from back injury suffered in game vs. Boston, October 7, 2000. • Missed majority of 2002-03 season recovering from shoulder injury suffered in game vs. St. Louis, November 27, 2002. Signed as a free agent by **Pittsburgh**, August 15, 2005.

LECLERC, Mike

(luh-KLAIR, MIGHK)

Left wing. Shoots left. 6'2", 208 lbs. Born, Winnipeg, Man., November 10, 1976. Anaheim's 3rd choice, 55th overall, in 1995 Entry Draft.

Season	Club	League	GP	G	A	Pts	PIM	PP	SH	GW	S	%	+/-	TF	F%	Min	GP	G	A	Pts	PIM	PP	SH	GW	Min
1991-92	St. Boniface	MJHL	43	16	12	28	25	....	....	....	....	....	....	....	....	....	....	....	....	....	....	....	....	....	....
	Victoria Cougars	WHL	2	0	0	0	0	....	....	....	....	....	....	....	....	....	....	....	....	....	....	....	....	....	....
1992-93	Victoria Cougars	WHL	70	4	11	15	118	....	....	....	....	....	....	....	....	....	....	....	....	....	....	....	....	....	....
1993-94	Victoria Cougars	WHL	68	29	11	40	112	....	....	....	....	....	....	....	....	....	....	....	....	....	....	....	....	....	....
1994-95	Prince George	WHL	43	20	36	56	78	....	....	....	....	....	....	....	....	....	....	....	....	....	....	....	....	....	....
	Brandon	WHL	23	5	8	13	50	....	....	....	....	....	....	....	....	....	18	10	6	16	33	....	....	....	....
1995-96	Brandon	WHL	71	58	53	111	161	....	....	....	....	....	....	....	....	....	19	6	19	25	25	....	....	....	....
1996-97	Anaheim	NHL	5	1	1	2	0	0	0	1	3	33.3	2	....	....	....	1	0	0	0	0	0	0	0	....
	Baltimore Bandits	AHL	71	29	27	56	134	....	....	....	....	....	....	....	....	....	....	....	....	....	....	....	....	....	....
1997-98	Anaheim	NHL	7	0	0	0	6	0	0	0	11	0.0	–6	....	....	....	....	....	....	....	....	....	....	....	....
	Cincinnati	AHL	48	18	22	40	83	....	....	....	....	....	....	....	....	....	....	....	....	....	....	....	....	....	....
1998-99	Anaheim	NHL	7	0	0	0	4	0	0	0	1	0.0	–2	0	0.0	5:52	1	0	0	0	0	0	0	0	15:02
	Cincinnati	AHL	65	25	28	53	153	....	....	....	....	....	....	....	....	....	3	0	1	1	19	....	....	....	....
99-2000	Anaheim	NHL	69	8	11	19	70	0	0	2	105	7.6	–15	1	0.0	12:08	....	....	....	....	....	....	....	....	....
2000-01	Anaheim	NHL	54	15	20	35	26	3	0	3	130	11.5	–1	5	20.0	17:35	....	....	....	....	....	....	....	....	....
2001-02	Anaheim	NHL	82	20	24	44	107	8	0	4	178	11.2	–12	10	50.0	17:23	....	....	....	....	....	....	....	....	....
2002-03	Anaheim	NHL	57	9	19	28	34	1	0	4	122	7.4	–8	17	29.4	16:56	21	2	9	11	12	1	0	2	19:02
2003-04	Anaheim	NHL	10	1	3	4	4	0	0	0	19	5.3	–1	4	75.0	15:37	....	....	....	....	....	....	....	....	....
2004-05			DID NOT PLAY																						
2005-06	Phoenix	NHL	35	9	12	21	29	4	0	0	44	20.5	0	20	25.0	13:50	....	....	....	....	....	....	....	....	....
	Calgary	NHL	15	1	4	5	8	0	0	0	21	4.8	0	2	0.0	12:14	3	0	0	0	2	0	0	0	10:29
	NHL Totals		341	64	94	158	288	16	0	14	634	10.1		59	32.2	15:20	26	2	9	11	14	1	0	2	17:50

WHL East Second All-Star Team (1996) • AHL All-Rookie Team (1997)

• Missed majority of 2003-04 season recovering from knee surgery, July 15, 2003. Traded to **Phoenix** by **Anaheim** for a conditional choice in 2007 Entry Draft, August 23, 2005. Traded to **Calgary** by **Phoenix** with Brian Boucher for Steve Reinprecht and Philippe Sauve, February 2, 2006.

LEEB, Brad

(LEEB, BRAD) **TOR.**

Right wing. Shoots right. 5'11", 187 lbs. Born, Red Deer, Alta., August 27, 1979.

Season	Club	League	GP	G	A	Pts	PIM	PP	SH	GW	S	%	+/-	TF	F%	Min	GP	G	A	Pts	PIM	PP	SH	GW	Min
1994-95	Red Deer Vipers	AMHL	36	31	14	45	93	....	....	....	....	....	....	....	....	....	....	....	....	....	....	....	....	....	....
	Red Deer Rebels	WHL	3	0	0	0	4	....	....	....	....	....	....	....	....	....	....	....	....	....	....	....	....	....	....
1995-96	Red Deer Rebels	WHL	38	3	6	9	30	....	....	....	....	....	....	....	....	....	10	2	0	2	11	....	....	....	....
1996-97	Red Deer Rebels	WHL	70	15	20	35	76	....	....	....	....	....	....	....	....	....	16	3	3	6	6	....	....	....	....
1997-98	Red Deer Rebels	WHL	63	23	23	46	88	....	....	....	....	....	....	....	....	....	3	2	0	2	2	....	....	....	....
1998-99	Red Deer Rebels	WHL	64	32	47	79	84	....	....	....	....	....	....	....	....	....	9	5	9	14	10	....	....	....	....
99-2000	Vancouver	NHL	2	0	0	0	2	0	0	0	3	0.0	–2	0	0.0	12:07	....	....	....	....	....	....	....	....	....
	Syracuse Crunch	AHL	61	19	18	37	50	....	....	....	....	....	....	....	....	....	4	0	0	0	6	....	....	....	....
2000-01	Kansas City	IHL	53	18	16	34	53	....	....	....	....	....	....	....	....	....	....	....	....	....	....	....	....	....	....
2001-02	Vancouver	NHL	2	0	0	0	0	0	0	0	1	0.0	1	0	0.0	9:35	....	....	....	....	....	....	....	....	....
	Manitoba Moose	AHL	60	17	15	32	45	....	....	....	....	....	....	....	....	....	....	....	....	....	....	....	....	....	....
2002-03	St. John's	AHL	79	35	26	61	78	....	....	....	....	....	....	....	....	....	....	....	....	....	....	....	....	....	....
2003-04	Toronto	NHL	1	0	0	0	0	0	0	0	1	0.0	–1	0	0.0	10:31	....	....	....	....	....	....	....	....	....
	St. John's	AHL	77	24	25	49	116	....	....	....	....	....	....	....	....	....	....	....	....	....	....	....	....	....	....

			Regular Season														Playoffs								
Season	Club	League	GP	G	A	Pts	PIM	PP	SH	GW	S	%	+/-	TF	F%	Min	GP	G	A	Pts	PIM	PP	SH	GW	Min
2004-05	St. John's	AHL	48	16	13	29	43	....	....	....	....	....	....	....	....	....	3	2	1	3	0	....	....	....	....
2005-06	Toronto Marlies	AHL	79	34	24	58	91	....	....	....	....	....	....	....	....	....	5	3	0	3	6	....	....	....	....
	NHL Totals		**5**	**0**	**0**	**0**	**2**	**0**	**0**	**0**	**5**	**0.0**		**0**	**0.0**	**10:47**	....	....	....	....	....	....	....	....	....

WHL East Second All-Star Team (1999)

Signed as a free agent by **Vancouver**, October 8, 1999. Traded to **Toronto** by **Vancouver** for Tomas Mojzis, September 4, 2002.

LEETCH, Brian

(LEECH, BRIGH-uhn)

Defense. Shoots left. 6', 185 lbs. Born, Corpus Christi, TX, March 3, 1968. NY Rangers' 1st choice, 9th overall, in 1986 Entry Draft.

Season	Club	League	GP	G	A	Pts	PIM	PP	SH	GW	S	%	+/-	TF	F%	Min	GP	G	A	Pts	PIM	PP	SH	GW	Min
1983-84	Cheshire	High-CT	28	52	49	101	24	....	....	....	....	....	....	....	....	....	....	....	....	....	....	....	....	....	....
1984-85	Avon Old Farms	High-CT	26	30	46	76	15	....	....	....	....	....	....	....	....	....	....	....	....	....	....	....	....	....	....
1985-86	Avon Old Farms	High-CT	28	40	44	84	18	....	....	....	....	....	....	....	....	....	....	....	....	....	....	....	....	....	....
1986-87	Boston College	H-East	37	9	38	47	10	....	....	....	....	....	....	....	....	....	....	....	....	....	....	....	....	....	....
1987-88	United States	Nat-Tm	50	13	61	74	38	....	....	....	....	....	....	....	....	....	....	....	....	....	....	....	....	....	....
	United States	Olympics	6	1	5	6	4	....	....	....	....	....	....	....	....	....	....	....	....	....	....	....	....	....	....
	NY Rangers	**NHL**	**17**	**2**	**12**	**14**	**0**	**1**	**0**	**1**	**40**	**5.0**	**5**	....	....	....	....	....	....	....	....	....	....	....	....
1988-89	**NY Rangers**	**NHL**	**68**	**23**	**48**	**71**	**50**	**8**	**3**	**1**	**268**	**8.6**	**8**	....	....	....	**4**	**3**	**2**	**5**	**2**	**2**	**0**	**0**	....
1989-90	**NY Rangers**	**NHL**	**72**	**11**	**45**	**56**	**26**	**5**	**0**	**2**	**222**	**5.0**	**–18**	....	....	....	....	....	....	....	....	....	....	....	....
1990-91	**NY Rangers**	**NHL**	**80**	**16**	**72**	**88**	**42**	**6**	**0**	**4**	**206**	**7.8**	**2**	....	....	....	**6**	**1**	**3**	**4**	**0**	**0**	**0**	**0**	....
1991-92	**NY Rangers**	**NHL**	**80**	**22**	**80**	**102**	**26**	**10**	**1**	**3**	**245**	**9.0**	**25**	....	....	....	**13**	**4**	**11**	**15**	**4**	**1**	**1**	**0**	....
1992-93	**NY Rangers**	**NHL**	**36**	**6**	**30**	**36**	**26**	**2**	**1**	**1**	**150**	**4.0**	**2**	....	....	....	....	....	....	....	....	....	....	....	....
1993-94♦	**NY Rangers**	**NHL**	**84**	**23**	**56**	**79**	**67**	**17**	**1**	**4**	**328**	**7.0**	**28**	....	....	....	**23**	**11**	***23**	***34**	**6**	**4**	**0**	**4**	....
1994-95	**NY Rangers**	**NHL**	**48**	**9**	**32**	**41**	**18**	**3**	**0**	**2**	**182**	**4.9**	**0**	....	....	....	**10**	**6**	**8**	**14**	**8**	**3**	**0**	**1**	....
1995-96	**NY Rangers**	**NHL**	**82**	**15**	**70**	**85**	**30**	**7**	**0**	**3**	**276**	**5.4**	**12**	....	....	....	**11**	**1**	**6**	**7**	**4**	**1**	**0**	**0**	....
1996-97	**NY Rangers**	**NHL**	**82**	**20**	**58**	**78**	**40**	**9**	**0**	**2**	**256**	**7.8**	**31**	....	....	....	**15**	**2**	**8**	**10**	**6**	**1**	**0**	**1**	....
1997-98	**NY Rangers**	**NHL**	**76**	**17**	**33**	**50**	**32**	**11**	**0**	**2**	**230**	**7.4**	**–36**	....	....	....	....	....	....	....	....	....	....	....	....
	United States	Olympics	4	1	1	2	0	....	....	....	....	....	....	....	....	....	....	....	....	....	....	....	....	....	....
1998-99	**NY Rangers**	**NHL**	**82**	**13**	**42**	**55**	**42**	**4**	**0**	**1**	**184**	**7.1**	**–7**	**0**	**0.0**	**29:52**	....	....	....	....	....	....	....	....	....
99-2000	**NY Rangers**	**NHL**	**50**	**7**	**19**	**26**	**20**	**3**	**0**	**2**	**124**	**5.6**	**–16**	**0**	**0.0**	**26:57**	....	....	....	....	....	....	....	....	....
2000-01	**NY Rangers**	**NHL**	**82**	**21**	**58**	**79**	**34**	**10**	**1**	**3**	**241**	**8.7**	**–18**	**0**	**0.0**	**29:21**	....	....	....	....	....	....	....	....	....
2001-02	**NY Rangers**	**NHL**	**82**	**10**	**45**	**55**	**28**	**1**	**0**	**3**	**202**	**5.0**	**14**	**0**	**0.0**	**25:52**	....	....	....	....	....	....	....	....	....
	United States	Olympics	6	0	5	5	0	....	....	....	....	....	....	....	....	....	....	....	....	....	....	....	....	....	....
2002-03	**NY Rangers**	**NHL**	**51**	**12**	**18**	**30**	**20**	**5**	**0**	**2**	**150**	**8.0**	**–3**	**0**	**0.0**	**26:06**	....	....	....	....	....	....	....	....	....
2003-04	**NY Rangers**	**NHL**	**57**	**13**	**23**	**36**	**24**	**4**	**1**	**1**	**165**	**7.9**	**–5**	**0**	**0.0**	**26:15**	....	....	....	....	....	....	....	....	....
	Toronto	**NHL**	**15**	**2**	**13**	**15**	**10**	**1**	**0**	**1**	**41**	**4.9**	**11**	**0**	**0.0**	**26:26**	**13**	**0**	**8**	**8**	**6**	**0**	**0**	**0**	**28:29**
2004-05			DID NOT PLAY																						
2005-06	**Boston**	**NHL**	**61**	**5**	**27**	**32**	**36**	**4**	**0**	**0**	**130**	**3.8**	**–10**	**1**	**0.0**	**23:31**	....	....	....	....	....	....	....	....	....
	NHL Totals		**1205**	**247**	**781**	**1028**	**571**	**111**	**8**	**38**	**3640**	**6.8**		**1**	**0.0**	**27:03**	**95**	**28**	**69**	**97**	**36**	**12**	**1**	**6**	**28:29**

Hockey East First All-Star Team (1987) • Hockey East Rookie of the Year (1987) • Hockey East Player of the Year (1987) • NCAA East First All-American Team (1987) • NHL All-Rookie Team (1989) • Calder Memorial Trophy (1989) • NHL Second All-Star Team (1991, 1994, 1996) • NHL First All-Star Team (1992, 1997) • James Norris Memorial Trophy (1992, 1997) • Conn Smythe Trophy (1994)

Played in NHL All-Star Game (1990, 1991, 1992, 1994, 1996, 1997, 1998, 2001, 2002)

Traded to **Edmonton** by **NY Rangers** for Jussi Markkanen and Edmonton's 4th round choice (later traded to Toronto – Toronto selected Roman Kukumberg), June 30, 2003. Signed as a free agent by **NY Rangers**, July 30, 2003. Traded to **Toronto** by **NY Rangers** with Edmonton's 4th round choice (previously acquired, Toronto selected Roman Kukumberg) in 2004 Entry Draft for Maxim Kondratiev, Jarkko Immonen, Toronto's 1st round choice (later traded to Calgary – Calgary selected Kris Chucko) in 2004 Entry Draft and Toronto's 2nd round choice (Michael Sauer) in 2005 Entry Draft, March 3, 2004. Signed as a free agent by **Boston**, August 3, 2005.

LEFEBVRE, Guillaume

(luh-FAYV, GEE-ohm)

Left wing. Shoots left. 6'1", 202 lbs. Born, Amos, Que., May 7, 1981. Philadelphia's 6th choice, 227th overall, in 2000 Entry Draft.

Season	Club	League	GP	G	A	Pts	PIM	PP	SH	GW	S	%	+/-	TF	F%	Min	GP	G	A	Pts	PIM	PP	SH	GW	Min
1996-97	Amos Foresters	QAAA	40	7	12	19	14	....	....	....	....	....	....	....	....	....	....	....	....	....	....	....	....	....	....
1997-98	Amos Foresters	QAAA	42	12	16	28	100	....	....	....	....	....	....	....	....	....	6	4	5	9	....	....	....	....	....
1998-99	Shawinigan	QMJHL	40	3	1	4	49	....	....	....	....	....	....	....	....	....	....	....	....	....	....	....	....	....	....
	Cape Breton	QMJHL	24	2	7	9	13	....	....	....	....	....	....	....	....	....	5	0	1	1	0	....	....	....	....
99-2000	Cape Breton	QMJHL	44	26	28	54	82	....	....	....	....	....	....	....	....	....	....	....	....	....	....	....	....	....	....
	Quebec Remparts	QMJHL	2	3	1	4	0	....	....	....	....	....	....	....	....	....	....	....	....	....	....	....	....	....	....
	Rouyn-Noranda	QMJHL	25	4	11	15	39	....	....	....	....	....	....	....	....	....	11	4	0	4	25	....	....	....	....
2000-01	Rouyn-Noranda	QMJHL	61	24	43	67	160	....	....	....	....	....	....	....	....	....	9	3	1	4	22	....	....	....	....
	Philadelphia	AHL	....	....	....	....	....	....	....	....	....	....	....	....	....	....	9	0	1	1	2	....	....	....	....
2001-02	**Philadelphia**	**NHL**	**3**	**0**	**0**	**0**	**0**	**0**	**0**	**0**	**3**	**0.0**	**–1**	**0**	**0.0**	**5:55**	....	....	....	....	....	....	....	....	....
	Philadelphia	AHL	78	19	15	34	111	....	....	....	....	....	....	....	....	....	5	0	0	0	4	....	....	....	....
2002-03	**Philadelphia**	**NHL**	**14**	**0**	**0**	**0**	**4**	**0**	**0**	**0**	**5**	**0.0**	**1**	**0**	**0.0**	**7:27**	....	....	....	....	....	....	....	....	....
	Philadelphia	AHL	47	7	6	13	113	....	....	....	....	....	....	....	....	....	....	....	....	....	....	....	....	....	....
	Pittsburgh	**NHL**	**12**	**2**	**4**	**6**	**0**	**0**	**0**	**0**	**14**	**14.3**	**1**	**1**	**100.0**	**17:30**	....	....	....	....	....	....	....	....	....
	Wilkes-Barre	AHL	1	1	0	1	0	....	....	....	....	....	....	....	....	....	5	0	0	0	6	....	....	....	....
2003-04	Wilkes-Barre	AHL	64	4	12	16	78	....	....	....	....	....	....	....	....	....	14	1	0	1	19	....	....	....	....
2004-05	Wilkes-Barre	AHL	34	3	3	6	76	....	....	....	....	....	....	....	....	....	11	1	0	1	23	....	....	....	....
2005-06	**Pittsburgh**	**NHL**	**9**	**0**	**0**	**0**	**9**	**0**	**0**	**0**	**3**	**0.0**	**–3**	**1**	**0.0**	**12:21**	....	....	....	....	....	....	....	....	....
	Wilkes-Barre	AHL	66	16	19	35	113	....	....	....	....	....	....	....	....	....	8	0	2	2	14	....	....	....	....
	NHL Totals		**38**	**2**	**4**	**6**	**13**	**0**	**0**	**0**	**25**	**8.0**		**2**	**50.0**	**11:40**	....	....	....	....	....	....	....	....	....

Traded to **Phoenix** by **Philadelphia** with Atlanta's 3rd round choice (previously acquired, Phoenix selected Tyler Redenbach) in 2003 Entry Draft and Philadelphia's 2nd round choice (later traded to NY Rangers – NY Rangers selected Brandon Dubinsky) in 2004 Entry Draft for Tony Amonte, March 10, 2003. Traded to **Pittsburgh** by **Phoenix** with Ramzi Abid and Dan Focht for Jan Hrdina and Francois Leroux, March 11, 2003.

LEGWAND, David

(LEHG-wuhnd, DAY-vihd) **NSH.**

Center. Shoots left. 6'2", 190 lbs. Born, Detroit, MI, August 17, 1980. Nashville's 1st choice, 2nd overall, in 1998 Entry Draft.

Season	Club	League	GP	G	A	Pts	PIM	PP	SH	GW	S	%	+/-	TF	F%	Min	GP	G	A	Pts	PIM	PP	SH	GW	Min
1996-97	Det. Compuware	MNHL	44	21	41	62	58	....	....	....	....	....	....	....	....	....	....	....	....	....	....	....	....	....	....
1997-98	Plymouth Whalers	OHL	59	54	51	105	56	....	....	....	....	....	....	....	....	....	15	8	12	20	24	....	....	....	....
1998-99	Plymouth Whalers	OHL	55	31	49	80	65	....	....	....	....	....	....	....	....	....	11	3	8	11	8	....	....	....	....
	Nashville	**NHL**	**1**	**0**	**0**	**0**	**0**	**0**	**0**	**0**	**2**	**0.0**	**0**	**9**	**55.6**	**12:50**	....	....	....	....	....	....	....	....	....
99-2000	**Nashville**	**NHL**	**71**	**13**	**15**	**28**	**30**	**4**	**0**	**2**	**111**	**11.7**	**–6**	**637**	**41.6**	**14:43**	....	....	....	....	....	....	....	....	....
2000-01	**Nashville**	**NHL**	**81**	**13**	**28**	**41**	**38**	**3**	**0**	**3**	**172**	**7.6**	**1**	**888**	**40.3**	**15:14**	....	....	....	....	....	....	....	....	....
2001-02	**Nashville**	**NHL**	**63**	**11**	**19**	**30**	**54**	**1**	**1**	**1**	**121**	**9.1**	**1**	**843**	**40.5**	**16:25**	....	....	....	....	....	....	....	....	....
2002-03	**Nashville**	**NHL**	**64**	**17**	**31**	**48**	**34**	**3**	**1**	**4**	**167**	**10.2**	**–2**	**1095**	**46.6**	**19:14**	....	....	....	....	....	....	....	....	....
2003-04	**Nashville**	**NHL**	**82**	**18**	**29**	**47**	**46**	**5**	**1**	**5**	**165**	**10.9**	**9**	**1109**	**45.1**	**17:16**	**6**	**1**	**0**	**1**	**8**	**0**	**1**	**0**	**15:41**
2004-05	EHC Basel	Swiss-2	3	6	2	8	2	....	....	....	....	....	....	....	....	....	19	16	23	39	20	....	....	....	....
2005-06	**Nashville**	**NHL**	**44**	**7**	**19**	**26**	**34**	**0**	**0**	**5**	**109**	**6.4**	**3**	**580**	**44.7**	**16:50**	**5**	**0**	**1**	**1**	**8**	**0**	**0**	**0**	**17:21**
	Milwaukee	AHL	3	0	0	0	0	....	....	....	....	....	....	....	....	....	....	....	....	....	....	....	....	....	....
	NHL Totals		**406**	**79**	**141**	**220**	**236**	**16**	**3**	**20**	**847**	**9.3**		**5161**	**43.4**	**16:32**	**11**	**1**	**1**	**2**	**16**	**0**	**1**	**0**	**16:27**

OHL All-Rookie Team (1998) • OHL First All-Star Team (1998) • OHL Rookie of the Year (1998) • OHL MVP (1998) • Canadian Major Junior Rookie of the Year (1998)

Signed as a free agent by **Basel** (Swiss-2), January 27, 2005.

LEHOUX, Yanick

(luh-HOO, YAH-nihk) **PHX.**

Center. Shoots right. 6'1", 200 lbs. Born, Montreal, Que., April 8, 1982. Los Angeles' 3rd choice, 86th overall, in 2000 Entry Draft.

Season	Club	League	GP	G	A	Pts	PIM	PP	SH	GW	S	%	+/-	TF	F%	Min	GP	G	A	Pts	PIM	PP	SH	GW	Min
1997-98	Cap-d-Madeleine	QAAA	42	29	50	79	26	....	....	....	....	....	....	....	....	....	....	....	....	....	....	....	....	....	....
1998-99	Baie-Comeau	QMJHL	63	10	20	30	31	....	....	....	....	....	....	....	....	....	....	....	....	....	....	....	....	....	....
99-2000	Baie-Comeau	QMJHL	67	31	61	92	14	....	....	....	....	....	....	....	....	....	6	1	2	3	2	....	....	....	....
2000-01	Baie-Comeau	QMJHL	70	67	68	135	62	....	....	....	....	....	....	....	....	....	11	8	16	24	0	....	....	....	....
2001-02	Baie-Comeau	QMJHL	66	56	69	125	63	....	....	....	....	....	....	....	....	....	5	5	4	9	0	....	....	....	....
	Manchester	AHL	....	....	....	....	....	....	....	....	....	....	....	....	....	....	1	0	0	0	0	....	....	....	....
2002-03	Manchester	AHL	78	16	21	37	26	....	....	....	....	....	....	....	....	....	1	0	0	0	0	....	....	....	....
2003-04	Manchester	AHL	66	14	28	42	22	....	....	....	....	....	....	....	....	....	5	2	3	5	16	....	....	....	....
2004-05	Manchester	AHL	38	23	31	54	16	....	....	....	....	....	....	....	....	....	....	....	....	....	....	....	....	....	....

			Regular Season														Playoffs								
Season	Club	League	GP	G	A	Pts	PIM	PP	SH	GW	S	%	+/-	TF	F%	Min	GP	G	A	Pts	PIM	PP	SH	GW	Min
2005-06	Geneve	Swiss	7	5	2	7	6	....	....	....	....	....	....	....	....	....	....	....	....	....	....	....	....	....	....
	EHC Basel	Swiss	4	0	2	2	4	....	....	....	....	....	....	....	....	....	....	....	....	....	....	....	....	....	....
	Phoenix	**NHL**	**3**	**1**	**0**	**1**	**2**	**0**	**0**	**0**	**5**	**20.0**	**1**	**24**	**33.3**	**9:50**	....	....	....	....	....	....	....	....	....
	Manchester	AHL	31	10	6	16	23	....	....	....	....	....	....	....	....	....	....	....	....	....	....	....	....	....	....
	San Antonio	AHL	23	8	6	14	13	....	....	....	....	....	....	....	....	....	....	....	....	....	....	....	....	....	....
	NHL Totals		**3**	**1**	**0**	**1**	**2**	**0**	**0**	**0**	**5**	**20.0**		**24**	**33.3**	**9:50**	....	....	....	....	....	....	....	....	....

QMJHL Second All-Star Team (2002)

Claimed on waivers by **Phoenix** from **Los Angeles**, November 5, 2005. Claimed on waivers by **Los Angeles** from **Phoenix**, November 25, 2005. Traded to **Phoenix** by **Los Angeles** for Tim Jackman, March 9, 2006.

LEHTINEN, Jere

(LEH-tih-nehn, YUH-ree) **DAL.**

Right wing. Shoots right. 6', 200 lbs. Born, Espoo, Finland, June 24, 1973. Minnesota's 3rd choice, 88th overall, in 1992 Entry Draft.

Season	Club	League	GP	G	A	Pts	PIM	PP	SH	GW	S	%	+/-	TF	F%	Min	GP	G	A	Pts	PIM	PP	SH	GW	Min
1989-90	Kiekko-Espoo Jr.	Fin-Jr.	32	23	23	46	6	....	....	....	....	....	....	....	....	....	5	0	3	3	0	....	....	....	....
1990-91	K-Espoo U18	Fin-U18	11	18	14	32	0	....	....	....	....	....	....	....	....	....	....	....	....	....	....	....	....	....	....
	Kiekko-Espoo Jr.	Fin-Jr.	10	8	6	14	4	....	....	....	....	....	....	....	....	....	....	....	....	....	....	....	....	....	....
	Kiekko-Espoo	Finland-2	32	15	9	24	12	....	....	....	....	....	....	....	....	....	....	....	....	....	....	....	....	....	....
1991-92	Kiekko-67 Jr.	Fin-Jr.	8	5	4	9	2	....	....	....	....	....	....	....	....	....	....	....	....	....	....	....	....	....	....
	Kiekko-Espoo Jr.	Fin-Jr.	8	5	4	9	2	....	....	....	....	....	....	....	....	....	....	....	....	....	....	....	....	....	....
	Kiekko-Espoo	Finland-2	43	32	17	49	6	....	....	....	....	....	....	....	....	....	5	2	4	6	2	....	....	....	....
1992-93	Kiekko-67 Jr.	Fin-Jr.	4	5	3	8	8	....	....	....	....	....	....	....	....	....	....	....	....	....	....	....	....	....	....
	Kiekko-Espoo Jr.	Fin-Jr.	4	5	3	8	8	....	....	....	....	....	....	....	....	....	....	....	....	....	....	....	....	....	....
	Kiekko-Espoo	Finland	45	13	14	27	6	....	....	....	....	....	....	....	....	....	....	....	....	....	....	....	....	....	....
1993-94	TPS Turku	Finland	42	19	20	39	6	....	....	....	....	....	....	....	....	....	11	11	2	13	2	....	....	....	....
	Finland	Olympics	8	3	0	3	0	....	....	....	....	....	....	....	....	....	....	....	....	....	....	....	....	....	....
1994-95	TPS Turku	Finland	39	19	23	42	33	....	....	....	....	....	....	....	....	....	13	8	6	14	4	....	....	....	....
1995-96	**Dallas**	**NHL**	**57**	**6**	**22**	**28**	**16**	**0**	**0**	**1**	**109**	**5.5**	**5**	....	....	....	....	....	....	....	....	....	....	....	....
	Michigan	IHL	1	1	0	1	0	....	....	....	....	....	....	....	....	....	....	....	....	....	....	....	....	....	....
1996-97	**Dallas**	**NHL**	**63**	**16**	**27**	**43**	**2**	**3**	**1**	**2**	**134**	**11.9**	**26**	....	....	....	**7**	**2**	**2**	**4**	**0**	**0**	**0**	**0**	....
1997-98	**Dallas**	**NHL**	**72**	**23**	**19**	**42**	**20**	**7**	**2**	**6**	**201**	**11.4**	**19**	....	....	....	**12**	**3**	**5**	**8**	**2**	**1**	**0**	**0**	....
	Finland	Olympics	6	4	2	6	2	....	....	....	....	....	....	....	....	....	....	....	....	....	....	....	....	....	....
1998-99♦	**Dallas**	**NHL**	**74**	**20**	**32**	**52**	**18**	**7**	**1**	**2**	**173**	**11.6**	**29**	**9**	**33.3**	**19:36**	**23**	**10**	**3**	**13**	**2**	**1**	**1**	**0**	**21:09**
99-2000	**Dallas**	**NHL**	**17**	**3**	**5**	**8**	**0**	**0**	**0**	**1**	**29**	**10.3**	**1**	**0**	**0.0**	**17:31**	**13**	**1**	**5**	**6**	**2**	**0**	**0**	**0**	**21:15**
2000-01	**Dallas**	**NHL**	**74**	**20**	**25**	**45**	**24**	**7**	**0**	**1**	**148**	**13.5**	**14**	**7**	**28.6**	**19:17**	**10**	**1**	**0**	**1**	**2**	**0**	**0**	**0**	**20:13**
2001-02	**Dallas**	**NHL**	**73**	**25**	**24**	**49**	**14**	**7**	**1**	**4**	**198**	**12.6**	**27**	**18**	**22.2**	**19:50**	....	....	....	....	....	....	....	....	....
	Finland	Olympics	4	1	2	3	2	....	....	....	....	....	....	....	....	....	....	....	....	....	....	....	....	....	....
2002-03	**Dallas**	**NHL**	**80**	**31**	**17**	**48**	**20**	**5**	**0**	**3**	**238**	**13.0**	**39**	**36**	**22.2**	**18:47**	**12**	**3**	**2**	**5**	**0**	**1**	**0**	**1**	**21:12**
2003-04	**Dallas**	**NHL**	**58**	**13**	**13**	**26**	**20**	**4**	**1**	**4**	**138**	**9.4**	**0**	**10**	**40.0**	**19:27**	**5**	**0**	**0**	**0**	**0**	**0**	**0**	**0**	**19:19**
2004-05			DID NOT PLAY																						
2005-06	**Dallas**	**NHL**	**80**	**33**	**19**	**52**	**30**	**14**	**1**	**6**	**216**	**15.3**	**9**	**28**	**21.4**	**18:42**	**5**	**3**	**1**	**4**	**0**	**1**	**0**	**0**	**22:10**
	Finland	Olympics	8	3	5	8	0	....	....	....	....	....	....	....	....	....	....	....	....	....	....	....	....	....	....
	NHL Totals		**648**	**190**	**203**	**393**	**164**	**54**	**7**	**30**	**1584**	**12.0**		**108**	**25.0**	**19:11**	**87**	**23**	**18**	**41**	**8**	**4**	**1**	**1**	**20:59**

Frank J. Selke Trophy (1998, 1999, 2003)

Played in NHL All-Star Game (1998)

Rights transferred to **Dallas** after **Minnesota** franchise relocated, June 9, 1993. • Missed majority of 1999-2000 season recovering from leg injury suffered in game vs. Nashville, October 16, 1999.

LEMIEUX, Mario

(lehm-YOO, MAHR-ee-oh)

Center. Shoots right. 6'4", 230 lbs. Born, Montreal, Que., October 5, 1965. Pittsburgh's 1st choice, 1st overall, in 1984 Entry Draft.

Season	Club	League	GP	G	A	Pts	PIM	PP	SH	GW	S	%	+/-	TF	F%	Min	GP	G	A	Pts	PIM	PP	SH	GW	Min
1980-81	Mtl-Concordia	QAAA	47	62	62	124	127	....	....	....	....	....	....	....	....	....	3	2	5	7	8	....	....	....	....
1981-82	Laval Voisins	QMJHL	64	30	66	96	22	....	....	....	....	....	....	....	....	....	18	5	9	14	31	....	....	....	....
1982-83	Laval Voisins	QMJHL	66	84	100	184	76	....	....	....	....	....	....	....	....	....	12	14	18	32	18	....	....	....	....
1983-84	Laval Voisins	QMJHL	70	*133	*149	*282	92	....	....	....	....	....	....	....	....	....	14	*29	*23	*52	29	....	....	....	....
1984-85	**Pittsburgh**	**NHL**	**73**	**43**	**57**	**100**	**54**	**11**	**0**	**2**	**209**	**20.6**	**–35**	....	....	....	....	....	....	....	....	....	....	....	....
1985-86	**Pittsburgh**	**NHL**	**79**	**48**	**93**	**141**	**43**	**17**	**0**	**4**	**276**	**17.4**	**–6**	....	....	....	....	....	....	....	....	....	....	....	....
1986-87	**Pittsburgh**	**NHL**	**63**	**54**	**53**	**107**	**57**	**19**	**0**	**4**	**267**	**20.2**	**13**	....	....	....	....	....	....	....	....	....	....	....	....
1987-88	**Pittsburgh**	**NHL**	**77**	***70**	**98**	***168**	**92**	**22**	**10**	**7**	**382**	**18.3**	**23**	....	....	....	....	....	....	....	....	....	....	....	....
1988-89	**Pittsburgh**	**NHL**	**76**	***85**	***114**	***199**	**100**	**31**	**13**	**8**	**313**	**27.2**	**41**	....	....	....	**11**	**12**	**7**	**19**	**16**	**7**	**1**	**0**	....
1989-90	**Pittsburgh**	**NHL**	**59**	**45**	**78**	**123**	**78**	**14**	**3**	**4**	**226**	**19.9**	**–18**	....	....	....	....	....	....	....	....	....	....	....	....
1990-91♦	**Pittsburgh**	**NHL**	**26**	**19**	**26**	**45**	**30**	**6**	**1**	**2**	**89**	**21.3**	**8**	....	....	....	**23**	**16**	***28**	***44**	**16**	**6**	**2**	**0**	....
1991-92♦	**Pittsburgh**	**NHL**	**64**	**44**	**87**	***131**	**94**	**12**	**4**	**5**	**249**	**17.7**	**27**	....	....	....	**15**	***16**	**18**	***34**	**2**	**8**	**2**	**5**	....
1992-93	**Pittsburgh**	**NHL**	**60**	**69**	**91**	***160**	**38**	**16**	**6**	**10**	**286**	**24.1**	**55**	....	....	....	**11**	**8**	**10**	**18**	**10**	**3**	**1**	**1**	....
1993-94	**Pittsburgh**	**NHL**	**22**	**17**	**20**	**37**	**32**	**7**	**0**	**4**	**92**	**18.5**	**–2**	....	....	....	**6**	**4**	**3**	**7**	**2**	**1**	**0**	**0**	....
1994-95	**Pittsburgh**	**NHL**	DID NOT PLAY																						
1995-96	**Pittsburgh**	**NHL**	**70**	***69**	***92**	***161**	**54**	**31**	**8**	**8**	**338**	**20.4**	**10**	....	....	....	**18**	**11**	**16**	**27**	**33**	**3**	**1**	**2**	....
1996-97	**Pittsburgh**	**NHL**	**76**	**50**	***72**	***122**	**65**	**15**	**3**	**7**	**327**	**15.3**	**27**	....	....	....	**5**	**3**	**3**	**6**	**4**	**0**	**0**	**0**	....
1997-98			OUT OF HOCKEY – RETIRED																						
1998-99			OUT OF HOCKEY – RETIRED																						
99-2000			OUT OF HOCKEY – RETIRED																						
2000-01	**Pittsburgh**	**NHL**	**43**	**35**	**41**	**76**	**18**	**16**	**1**	**5**	**171**	**20.5**	**15**	**852**	**52.1**	**24:20**	**18**	**6**	**11**	**17**	**4**	**1**	**0**	**3**	**24:35**
2001-02	**Pittsburgh**	**NHL**	**24**	**6**	**25**	**31**	**14**	**2**	**0**	**0**	**75**	**8.0**	**0**	**354**	**44.6**	**22:16**	....	....	....	....	....	....	....	....	....
	Canada	Olympics	5	2	4	6	0	....	....	....	....	....	....	....	....	....	....	....	....	....	....	....	....	....	....
2002-03	**Pittsburgh**	**NHL**	**67**	**28**	**63**	**91**	**43**	**14**	**0**	**4**	**235**	**11.9**	**–25**	**1029**	**46.1**	**23:05**	....	....	....	....	....	....	....	....	....
2003-04	**Pittsburgh**	**NHL**	**10**	**1**	**8**	**9**	**6**	**0**	**0**	**0**	**21**	**4.8**	**–2**	**173**	**49.1**	**22:24**	....	....	....	....	....	....	....	....	....
2004-05			DID NOT PLAY																						
2005-06	**Pittsburgh**	**NHL**	**26**	**7**	**15**	**22**	**16**	**3**	**0**	**0**	**77**	**9.1**	**–16**	**457**	**55.4**	**19:22**	....	....	....	....	....	....	....	....	....
	NHL Totals		**915**	**690**	**1033**	**1723**	**834**	**236**	**49**	**74**	**3633**	**19.0**		**2865**	**49.4**	**22:40**	**107**	**76**	**96**	**172**	**87**	**29**	**7**	**11**	**24:35**

QMJHL Second All-Star Team (1983) • QMJHL First All-Star Team (1984) • QMJHL MVP (1984) • Canadian Major Junior Player of the Year (1984) • NHL All-Rookie Team (1985) • Calder Memorial Trophy (1985) • NHL Second All-Star Team (1986, 1987, 1992, 2001) • Lester B. Pearson Award (1986, 1988, 1993, 1996) • Canada Cup All-Star Team (1987) • NHL First All-Star Team (1988, 1989, 1993, 1996, 1997) • Dodge Performance of the Year Award (1988) • Dodge Performer of the Year Award (1988, 1989) • Art Ross Trophy (1988, 1989, 1992, 1993, 1996, 1997) • Hart Trophy (1988, 1993, 1996) • Dodge Ram Tough Award (1989) • Conn Smythe Trophy (1991, 1992) • ProSet/NHL Player of the Year Award (1992) • Alka-Seltzer Plus Award (1993) • Bill Masterton Memorial Trophy (1993) • Lester Patrick Trophy (2000)

Played in NHL All-Star Game (1985, 1986, 1988, 1989, 1990, 1992, 1996, 1997, 2001, 2002)

• Missed remainder of 1989-90 and majority of 1990-91 seasons recovering from back injury suffered in game vs. NY Rangers, February 14, 1989. • Missed remainder of 1992-93 season after being diagnosed with Hodgkin's Disease, January 12, 1993. • Missed majority of 1993-94 season recovering from back injury suffered in game vs. Chicago, November 11, 1993. • Missed entire 1994-95 season recovering from effects of treatment for Hodgkin's Disease and back injury suffered in game vs. NY Rangers, March 12, 1994. • Became third player (Gordie Howe, Guy Lafleur) to appear in NHL game after being inducted into Hockey Hall of Fame, December 27, 2000. • Missed majority of 2001-02 season recovering from hip injury suffered in game vs. Anaheim, October 6, 2001. • Missed majority of 2003-04 season recovering from hip injury suffered in game vs. Boston, November 1, 2003. • Officially announced retirement, January 24, 2006.

LEOPOLD, Jordan

(LEE-oh-pohld, JOHR-dan) **COL.**

Defense. Shoots left. 6'1", 200 lbs. Born, Golden Valley, MN, August 3, 1980. Anaheim's 1st choice, 44th overall, in 1999 Entry Draft.

Season	Club	League	GP	G	A	Pts	PIM	PP	SH	GW	S	%	+/-	TF	F%	Min	GP	G	A	Pts	PIM	PP	SH	GW	Min
1995-96	Armstrong	High-MN	19	11	14	25	30	....	....	....	....	....	....	....	....	....	....	....	....	....	....	....	....	....	....
1996-97	Armstrong	High-MN	30	24	36	60	....	....	....	....	....	....	....	....	....	....	....	....	....	....	....	....	....	....	....
1997-98	USNTDP	U-18	25	7	3	10	2	....	....	....	....	....	....	....	....	....	....	....	....	....	....	....	....	....	....
	USNTDP	USHL	19	2	4	6	6	....	....	....	....	....	....	....	....	....	....	....	....	....	....	....	....	....	....
	USNTDP	NAHL	16	2	5	7	8	....	....	....	....	....	....	....	....	....	....	....	....	....	....	....	....	....	....
1998-99	U. of Minnesota	WCHA	39	7	16	23	20	....	....	....	....	....	....	....	....	....	....	....	....	....	....	....	....	....	....
99-2000	U. of Minnesota	WCHA	39	6	18	24	20	....	....	....	....	....	....	....	....	....	....	....	....	....	....	....	....	....	....
2000-01	U. of Minnesota	WCHA	42	12	37	49	38	....	....	....	....	....	....	....	....	....	....	....	....	....	....	....	....	....	....
2001-02	U. of Minnesota	WCHA	44	20	28	48	28	....	....	....	....	....	....	....	....	....	....	....	....	....	....	....	....	....	....
2002-03	**Calgary**	**NHL**	**58**	**4**	**10**	**14**	**12**	**3**	**0**	**0**	**78**	**5.1**	**–15**	**0**	**0.0**	**20:36**	....	....	....	....	....	....	....	....	....
	Saint John Flames	AHL	3	1	2	3	0	....	....	....	....	....	....	....	....	....	....	....	....	....	....	....	....	....	....
2003-04	**Calgary**	**NHL**	**82**	**9**	**24**	**33**	**24**	**6**	**0**	**1**	**138**	**6.5**	**8**	**0**	**0.0**	**22:14**	**26**	**0**	**10**	**10**	**6**	**0**	**0**	**0**	**25:41**

Season	Club	League	GP	G	A	Pts	PIM	PP	SH	GW	S	%	+/-	TF	F%	Min	GP	G	A	Pts	PIM	PP	SH	GW	Min
																						Regular Season			

(Column groups: Regular Season — GP G A Pts PIM | PP SH GW S % +/- | TF F% Min; Playoffs — GP G A Pts PIM PP SH GW Min)

Season	Club	League	GP	G	A	Pts	PIM	PP	SH	GW	S	%	+/-	TF	F%	Min	GP	G	A	Pts	PIM	PP	SH	GW	Min
2004-05			*DID NOT PLAY*																						
2005-06	Calgary	NHL	74	2	18	20	68	2	0	1	87	2.3	6	0	0.0	22:20	7	0	1	1	4	0	0	0	19:13
	United States	Olympics	6	1	0	1	4																		
	NHL Totals		214	15	52	67	104	11	0	2	303	5.0		0	0.0	21:49	33	0	11	11	10	0	0	0	24:19

WCHA All-Rookie Team (1999) • WCHA Second All-Star Team (2000) • WCHA First All-Star Team (2001, 2002) • NCAA West First All-American Team (2001) • Hobey Baker Memorial Award (Top U.S. Collegiate Player) (2002)

Traded to **Calgary** by **Anaheim** for Andrei Nazarov and Calgary's 2nd round choice (later traded to Phoenix – later traded back to Calgary – Calgary selected Andrei Taratukhin) in 2001 Entry Draft, September 26, 2000. Traded to **Colorado** by **Calgary** with Calgary's 2nd round choice (Codey Burki) in 2006 Entry Draft and future considerations for Alex Tanguay, June 24, 2006.

LESSARD, Francis

Right wing. Shoots right. 6'3", 225 lbs. Born, Montreal, Que., May 30, 1979. Carolina's 3rd choice, 80th overall, in 1997 Entry Draft.   (leh-SAHR, FRAN-sihs)

Season	Club	League	GP	G	A	Pts	PIM	PP	SH	GW	S	%	+/-	TF	F%	Min	GP	G	A	Pts	PIM	PP	SH	GW	Min
1994-95	Laval-Laurentides	QAAA	1	0	0	0	0																		
1995-96	Laval-Laurentides	QAAA	41	5	7	12	73										13	1	3	4					
1996-97	Val-d'Or Foreurs	QMJHL	66	1	9	10	287																		
1997-98	Val-d'Or Foreurs	QMJHL	63	3	20	23	338										19	1	6	7	*101				
1998-99	Drummondville	QMJHL	53	12	36	48	295																		
99-2000	Philadelphia	AHL	78	4	8	12	416										5	0	1	1	7				
2000-01	Philadelphia	AHL	64	3	7	10	330										10	0	0	0	33				
2001-02	Philadelphia	AHL	60	0	6	6	251																		
	Atlanta	NHL	5	0	0	0	26	0	0	0	2	0.0	0	0	0.0	12:45									
	Chicago Wolves	AHL	7	1	2	3	34										15	0	1	1	40				
2002-03	Atlanta	NHL	18	0	2	2	61	0	0	0	7	0.0	1	0	0.0	5:40									
	Chicago Wolves	AHL	50	2	5	7	194										1	0	0	0	0				
2003-04	Atlanta	NHL	62	1	1	2	181	0	0	0	19	5.3	-5	1	0.0	4:28									
2004-05			*DID NOT PLAY*																						
2005-06	Atlanta	NHL	6	0	0	0	0	0	0	0	0	0.0	-2	0	0.0	2:33									
	Chicago Wolves	AHL	36	2	3	5	163																		
	NHL Totals		91	1	3	4	268	0	0	0	28	3.6		1	0.0	5:02									

Memorial Cup Tournament All-Star Team (1998)

Traded to **Philadelphia** by **Carolina** for Philadelphia's 8th round choice (Antti Jokella) in 1999 Entry Draft, May 25, 1999. Traded to **Atlanta** by **Philadelphia** for David Harlock and Atlanta's 3rd (later traded to Phoenix – Phoenix selected Tyler Redenbach) and 7th (later traded to San Jose – San Jose selected Joe Pavelski) round choices in 2003 Entry Draft, March 15, 2002.

LESSARD, Junior   **DAL.**

Right wing/Center. Shoots right. 6', 195 lbs. Born, St-Joseph-de-Beauce, Que., May 26, 1980.   (leh-SAHRD, JOO-nyuhr)

Season	Club	League	GP	G	A	Pts	PIM	PP	SH	GW	S	%	+/-	TF	F%	Min	GP	G	A	Pts	PIM	PP	SH	GW	Min
99-2000	Portage Terriers	MJHL	60	60	48	108	61																		
2000-01	U. Minn-Duluth	WCHA	36	4	8	12	12																		
2001-02	U. Minn-Duluth	WCHA	39	17	13	30	50																		
2002-03	U. Minn-Duluth	WCHA	40	21	16	37	20																		
2003-04	U. Minn-Duluth	WCHA	45	*32	31	*63	34																		
2004-05	Houston Aeros	AHL	71	11	11	22	25										5	1	0	1	0				
2005-06	Dallas	NHL	5	1	0	1	12	0	0	0	6	16.7	0	0	0.0	7:23									
	Iowa Stars	AHL	66	26	31	57	30										7	3	4	7	4				
	NHL Totals		5	1	0	1	12	0	0	0	6	16.7		0	0.0	7:23									

WCHA First All-Star Team (2004) • WCHA Player of the Year (2004) • NCAA West First All-American Team (2004) • NCAA Championship All-Tournament Team (2004) • Hobey Baker Memorial Award (Top U.S. Collegiate Player) (2004)

Signed as a free agent by **Dallas**, April 15, 2004.

LETOWSKI, Trevor   **CAR.**

Right wing. Shoots right. 5'10", 180 lbs. Born, Thunder Bay, Ont., April 5, 1977. Phoenix's 6th choice, 174th overall, in 1996 Entry Draft.   (leh-TOW-skee, TREH-vuhr)

Season	Club	League	GP	G	A	Pts	PIM	PP	SH	GW	S	%	+/-	TF	F%	Min	GP	G	A	Pts	PIM	PP	SH	GW	Min
1993-94	T. Bay Kings	TBMHL	64	41	60	101	48																		
1994-95	Sarnia Sting	OHL	66	22	19	41	33										4	0	1	1	9				
1995-96	Sarnia Sting	OHL	66	36	63	99	66										10	9	5	14	10				
1996-97	Sarnia Sting	OHL	55	35	73	108	51										12	9	12	21	20				
1997-98	Springfield	AHL	75	11	20	31	26										4	1	0	1	2				
1998-99	Phoenix	NHL	14	2	2	4	2	0	0	0	8	25.0	1	49	55.1	6:01									
	Springfield	AHL	67	32	35	67	46										3	1	0	1	2				
99-2000	Phoenix	NHL	82	19	20	39	20	3	4	3	125	15.2	2	692	47.7	16:03	5	1	1	2	4	0	0	0	15:52
2000-01	Phoenix	NHL	77	7	15	22	32	0	1	3	110	6.4	-2	726	46.1	16:20									
2001-02	Phoenix	NHL	33	2	6	8	4	0	0	0	43	4.7	2	250	52.4	14:27									
	Vancouver	NHL	42	7	10	17	15	1	0	0	65	10.8	2	111	44.1	12:47	6	0	1	1	8	0	0	0	11:50
2002-03	Vancouver	NHL	78	11	14	25	36	1	1	2	136	8.1	8	70	41.4	12:26	6	0	1	1	0	0	0	0	9:40
2003-04	Columbus	NHL	73	15	17	32	16	4	0	1	126	11.9	-12	146	43.8	16:19									
2004-05	Fribourg	Swiss	9	4	5	9	6										11	7	9	16	8				
2005-06	Columbus	NHL	81	10	18	28	36	1	1	1	135	7.4	-2	284	45.8	16:32									
	NHL Totals		480	73	102	175	161	10	7	10	748	9.8		2328	47.0	14:57	17	1	3	4	12	0	0	0	12:15

Traded to **Vancouver** by **Phoenix** with Todd Warriner, Tyler Bouck and Phoenix's 3rd round choice (later traded back to Phoenix – Phoenix selected Dimitri Pestunov) in 2003 Entry Draft for Drake Berehowsky and Denis Pederson, December 28, 2001. Signed as a free agent by **Columbus**, July 3, 2003. Signed as a free agent by **Fribourg** (Swiss), January 7, 2005. Signed as a free agent by **Carolina**, July 6, 2006.

LIDSTROM, Nicklas   **DET.**

Defense. Shoots left. 6'2", 185 lbs. Born, Vasteras, Sweden, April 28, 1970. Detroit's 3rd choice, 53rd overall, in 1989 Entry Draft.   (LID-struhm, NIHK-las)

Season	Club	League	GP	G	A	Pts	PIM	PP	SH	GW	S	%	+/-	TF	F%	Min	GP	G	A	Pts	PIM	PP	SH	GW	Min
1987-88	Vasteras	Sweden-2	3	0	0	0	0										5	0	0	0	6				
1988-89	Vasteras IK	Sweden	34	1	6	7	4										5	0	2	2	0				
1989-90	Vasteras IK	Sweden	39	8	8	16	14										2	0	1	1	2				
1990-91	Vasteras IK	Sweden	38	4	19	23	2										4	0	0	0	4				
1991-92	Detroit	NHL	80	11	49	60	22	5	0	1	168	6.5	36				11	1	2	3	0	1	0	0	
1992-93	Detroit	NHL	84	7	34	41	28	3	0	2	156	4.5	7				7	1	0	1	0	1	0	0	
1993-94	Detroit	NHL	84	10	46	56	26	4	0	3	200	5.0	43				7	3	2	5	0	1	1	0	
1994-95	Vasteras IK	Sweden	13	2	10	12	4																		
	Detroit	NHL	43	10	16	26	6	7	0	0	90	11.1	15				18	4	12	16	8	3	0	2	
1995-96	Detroit	NHL	81	17	50	67	20	8	1	1	211	8.1	29				19	5	9	14	10	1	0	0	
1996-97 ♦	Detroit	NHL	79	15	42	57	30	8	0	1	214	7.0	11				20	2	6	8	2	0	0	0	
1997-98 ♦	Detroit	NHL	80	17	42	59	18	7	1	1	205	8.3	22				22	6	13	19	8	2	0	2	
	Sweden	Olympics	4	1	1	2	2																		
1998-99	Detroit	NHL	81	14	43	57	14	6	2	3	205	6.8	14	0	0.0	26:31	10	2	9	11	4	1	0	0	30:21
99-2000	Detroit	NHL	81	20	53	73	18	9	4	3	218	9.2	19	0	0.0	28:45	9	2	4	6	4	1	0	0	30:28
2000-01	Detroit	NHL	82	15	56	71	18	8	0	0	272	5.5	9	0	0.0	28:27	6	1	7	8	0	0	0	0	29:17
2001-02 ♦	Detroit	NHL	78	9	50	59	20	6	0	0	215	4.2	13	0	0.0	28:49	23	5	11	16	2	2	1	2	31:10
	Sweden	Olympics	4	1	5	6	0																		
2002-03	Detroit	NHL	82	18	44	62	38	8	1	4	175	10.3	40	0	0.0	29:20	4	0	3	3	0	0	0	0	33:35
2003-04	Detroit	NHL	81	10	28	38	18	3	1	3	194	5.2	19	0	0.0	27:39	12	2	5	7	4	2	0	0	27:01
2004-05			*DID NOT PLAY*																						
2005-06	Detroit	NHL	80	16	64	80	50	9	0	2	243	6.6	21	0	0.0	28:07	6	1	1	2	2	1	0	1	31:55
	Sweden	Olympics	8	2	4	6	2																		
	NHL Totals		1096	189	617	806	326	91	10	24	2766	6.8		0	0.0	28:14	174	35	83	118	44	17	2	7	30:18

NHL All-Rookie Team (1992) • NHL First All-Star Team (1998, 1999, 2000, 2001, 2002, 2003, 2006) • James Norris Memorial Trophy (2001, 2002, 2003, 2006) • Conn Smythe Trophy (2002) • Olympic Tournament All-Star Team (2006)

Played in NHL All-Star Game (1996, 1998, 1999, 2000, 2001, 2002, 2003, 2004)

LIFFITON, David
(LIH-fih-tuhn, DAY-vihd) **NYR**

Defense. Shoots left. 6'2", 210 lbs. Born, Windsor, Ont., October 18, 1984. Colorado's 1st choice, 63rd overall, in 2003 Entry Draft.

			Regular Season														Playoffs								
Season	Club	League	GP	G	A	Pts	PIM	PP	SH	GW	S	%	+/-	TF	F%	Min	GP	G	A	Pts	PIM	PP	SH	GW	Min
2000-01	Aylmer Aces	OHA-B	51	1	9	10	51	....	....	....	....	....	....	....	....	....	....	....	....	....	....	....	....	....	....
2001-02	Plymouth Whalers	OHL	62	3	9	12	65	....	....	....	....	....	....	....	....	....	6	0	0	0	0	....	....	....	....
2002-03	Plymouth Whalers	OHL	64	5	11	16	139	....	....	....	....	....	....	....	....	....	18	1	3	4	29	....	....	....	....
2003-04	Plymouth Whalers	OHL	44	2	9	11	85	....	....	....	....	....	....	....	....	....	9	0	0	0	12	....	....	....	....
2004-05	Hartford	AHL	33	0	1	1	74	....	....	....	....	....	....	....	....	....	....	....	....	....	....	....	....	....	....
	Charlotte	ECHL	16	0	2	2	18	....	....	....	....	....	....	....	....	....	15	1	4	5	27	....	....	....	....
2005-06	**NY Rangers**	**NHL**	**1**	**0**	**0**	**0**	**2**	**0**	**0**	**0**	**0**	**0.0**	**0**	**0**	**0.0**	**8:42**	....	....	....	....	....	....	....	....	....
	Hartford	AHL	50	2	7	9	158	....	....	....	....	....	....	....	....	....	....	....	....	....	....	....	....	....	....
	NHL Totals		**1**	**0**	**0**	**0**	**2**	**0**	**0**	**0**	**0**	**0.0**		**0**	**0.0**	**8:42**	....	....	....	....	....	....	....	....	....

Traded to **NY Rangers** by **Colorado** with Chris McAllister and Florida's 2nd round choice (previously acquired, later traded back to Florida – Florida selected David Shantz) in 2004 Entry Draft for Matthew Barnaby and NY Rangers' 3rd round choice (Denis Parshin) in 2004 Entry Draft, March 8, 2004.

LILES, John-Michael
(LIGH-uhls, JAWN-MIGHK-uhl) **COL.**

Defense. Shoots left. 5'10", 185 lbs. Born, Zionsville, IN, November 25, 1980. Colorado's 8th choice, 159th overall, in 2000 Entry Draft.

			Regular Season														Playoffs								
Season	Club	League	GP	G	A	Pts	PIM	PP	SH	GW	S	%	+/-	TF	F%	Min	GP	G	A	Pts	PIM	PP	SH	GW	Min
1997-98	USNTDP	U-17	15	0	6	6	4	....	....	....	....	....	....	....	....	....	....	....	....	....	....	....	....	....	....
	USNTDP	USHL	5	0	1	1	0	....	....	....	....	....	....	....	....	....	....	....	....	....	....	....	....	....	....
	USNTDP	NAHL	42	4	7	11	40	....	....	....	....	....	....	....	....	....	5	2	0	2	0	....	....	....	....
1998-99	USNTDP	USHL	46	4	14	18	47	....	....	....	....	....	....	....	....	....	....	....	....	....	....	....	....	....	....
	USNTDP	NAHL	13	2	5	7	6	....	....	....	....	....	....	....	....	....	....	....	....	....	....	....	....	....	....
99-2000	Michigan State	CCHA	40	8	20	28	26	....	....	....	....	....	....	....	....	....	....	....	....	....	....	....	....	....	....
2000-01	Michigan State	CCHA	42	7	18	25	28	....	....	....	....	....	....	....	....	....	....	....	....	....	....	....	....	....	....
2001-02	Michigan State	CCHA	41	13	22	35	18	....	....	....	....	....	....	....	....	....	....	....	....	....	....	....	....	....	....
2002-03	Michigan State	CCHA	39	16	34	50	46	....	....	....	....	....	....	....	....	....	....	....	....	....	....	....	....	....	....
	Hershey Bears	AHL	5	0	1	1	4	....	....	....	....	....	....	....	....	....	5	0	0	0	2	....	....	....	....
2003-04	**Colorado**	**NHL**	**79**	**10**	**24**	**34**	**28**	**2**	**0**	**1**	**115**	**8.7**	**7**	**0**	**0.0**	**16:14**	**11**	**0**	**1**	**1**	**4**	**0**	**0**	**0**	**16:41**
2004-05	Iserlohn Roosters	Germany	17	5	6	11	24	....	....	....	....	....	....	....	....	....	....	....	....	....	....	....	....	....	....
2005-06	**Colorado**	**NHL**	**82**	**14**	**35**	**49**	**44**	**6**	**0**	**1**	**154**	**9.1**	**5**	**1**	**100.0**	**18:31**	**9**	**1**	**2**	**3**	**6**	**1**	**0**	**0**	**17:35**
	United States	Olympics	6	0	2	2	2	....	....	....	....	....	....	....	....	....	....	....	....	....	....	....	....	....	....
	NHL Totals		**161**	**24**	**59**	**83**	**72**	**8**	**0**	**2**	**269**	**8.9**		**1**	**100.0**	**17:24**	**20**	**1**	**3**	**4**	**10**	**1**	**0**	**0**	**17:05**

CCHA Second All-Star Team (2001) • CCHA First All-Star Team (2002, 2003) • NCAA West Second All-American Team (2002) • NCAA West First All-American Team (2003) • NHL All-Rookie Team (2004)

Signed as a free agent by **Iserlohn** (Germany), December 29, 2004.

LILJA, Andreas
(LIHL-yuh, an-DRAY-uhs) **DET.**

Defense. Shoots left. 6'3", 228 lbs. Born, Helsingborg, Sweden, July 13, 1975. Los Angeles' 2nd choice, 54th overall, in 2000 Entry Draft.

			Regular Season														Playoffs								
Season	Club	League	GP	G	A	Pts	PIM	PP	SH	GW	S	%	+/-	TF	F%	Min	GP	G	A	Pts	PIM	PP	SH	GW	Min
1993-94	Malmo IF Jr.	Swe-Jr.	14	3	7	10	38	....	....	....	....	....	....	....	....	....	....	....	....	....	....	....	....	....	....
1994-95	Malmo IF Jr.	Swe-Jr.	30	7	13	20	82	....	....	....	....	....	....	....	....	....	....	....	....	....	....	....	....	....	....
	Malmo IF	Sweden	3	0	0	0	2	....	....	....	....	....	....	....	....	....	....	....	....	....	....	....	....	....	....
1995-96	Malmo IF Jr.	Swe-Jr.	3	0	1	1	6	....	....	....	....	....	....	....	....	....	....	....	....	....	....	....	....	....	....
	Malmo IF	Sweden	40	1	5	6	63	....	....	....	....	....	....	....	....	....	5	0	1	1	2	....	....	....	....
1996-97	Malmo	Sweden	47	1	0	1	22	....	....	....	....	....	....	....	....	....	4	0	0	0	10	....	....	....	....
1997-98	Malmo	Sweden	10	0	0	0	0	....	....	....	....	....	....	....	....	....	....	....	....	....	....	....	....	....	....
	Mora IK	Sweden-2	13	1	4	5	30	....	....	....	....	....	....	....	....	....	4	1	0	1	14	....	....	....	....
1998-99	Malmo	Sweden	41	0	3	3	44	....	....	....	....	....	....	....	....	....	1	0	0	0	4	....	....	....	....
99-2000	Malmo	Sweden	49	8	11	19	88	....	....	....	....	....	....	....	....	....	6	0	0	0	8	....	....	....	....
2000-01	**Los Angeles**	**NHL**	**2**	**0**	**0**	**0**	**4**	**0**	**0**	**0**	**1**	**0.0**	**–2**	**0**	**0.0**	**12:22**	**1**	**0**	**0**	**0**	**0**	**0**	**0**	**0**	**6:56**
	Lowell	AHL	61	7	29	36	149	....	....	....	....	....	....	....	....	....	4	0	6	6	6	....	....	....	....
2001-02	**Los Angeles**	**NHL**	**26**	**1**	**4**	**5**	**22**	**1**	**0**	**0**	**12**	**8.3**	**3**	**0**	**0.0**	**11:27**	**5**	**0**	**0**	**0**	**6**	**0**	**0**	**0**	**10:26**
	Manchester	AHL	4	0	1	1	4	....	....	....	....	....	....	....	....	....	....	....	....	....	....	....	....	....	....
2002-03	**Los Angeles**	**NHL**	**17**	**0**	**3**	**3**	**14**	**0**	**0**	**0**	**13**	**0.0**	**5**	**0**	**0.0**	**20:04**	....	....	....	....	....	....	....	....	....
	Florida	**NHL**	**56**	**4**	**8**	**12**	**56**	**0**	**0**	**0**	**59**	**6.8**	**8**	**0**	**0.0**	**19:11**	....	....	....	....	....	....	....	....	....
2003-04	**Florida**	**NHL**	**79**	**3**	**4**	**7**	**90**	**0**	**0**	**0**	**79**	**3.8**	**–8**	**1**	**0.0**	**19:34**	....	....	....	....	....	....	....	....	....
2004-05	Mora IK	Sweden	44	3	8	11	67	....	....	....	....	....	....	....	....	....	....	....	....	....	....	....	....	....	....
	HC Ambri-Piotta	Swiss	....	....	....	....	....	....	....	....	....	....	....	....	....	....	5	0	2	2	6	....	....	....	....
2005-06	**Detroit**	**NHL**	**82**	**2**	**13**	**15**	**98**	**0**	**0**	**1**	**78**	**2.6**	**18**	**1**	**0.0**	**19:01**	**6**	**0**	**1**	**1**	**6**	**0**	**0**	**0**	**19:21**
	NHL Totals		**262**	**10**	**32**	**42**	**284**	**1**	**0**	**1**	**242**	**4.1**		**2**	**0.0**	**18:29**	**12**	**0**	**1**	**1**	**12**	**0**	**0**	**0**	**14:36**

• Spent majority of 2001-02 season as a healthy reserve. Traded to **Florida** by **Los Angeles** with Jaroslav Bednar for Dmitry Yushkevich and Florida's 5th round choice (previously acquired, Los Angeles selected Brady Murray) in 2003 Entry Draft, Novermber 26, 2002. Signed as a free agent by **Nashville**, July 26, 2004. Signed as a free agent by **Mora** (Sweden), September 15, 2004. Signed as a free agent by **Ambri-Piotta** (Swiss), February 25, 2005. Signed as a free agent by **Detroit**, August 24, 2005.

LINDEN, Trevor
(LIHND-dehn, TREH-vuhr)

Right wing. Shoots right. 6'4", 215 lbs. Born, Medicine Hat, Alta., April 11, 1970. Vancouver's 1st choice, 2nd overall, in 1988 Entry Draft.

			Regular Season														Playoffs								
Season	Club	League	GP	G	A	Pts	PIM	PP	SH	GW	S	%	+/-	TF	F%	Min	GP	G	A	Pts	PIM	PP	SH	GW	Min
1985-86	Medicine Hat	AMHL	40	14	22	36	14	....	....	....	....	....	....	....	....	....	....	....	....	....	....	....	....	....	....
	Medicine Hat	WHL	5	2	0	2	0	....	....	....	....	....	....	....	....	....	....	....	....	....	....	....	....	....	....
1986-87	Medicine Hat	WHL	72	14	22	36	59	....	....	....	....	....	....	....	....	....	20	5	4	9	17	....	....	....	....
1987-88	Medicine Hat	WHL	67	46	64	110	76	....	....	....	....	....	....	....	....	....	16	*13	12	25	19	....	....	....	....
1988-89	**Vancouver**	**NHL**	**80**	**30**	**29**	**59**	**41**	**10**	**1**	**2**	**186**	**16.1**	**–10**	....	....	....	**7**	**3**	**4**	**7**	**8**	**2**	**1**	**0**	....
1989-90	**Vancouver**	**NHL**	**73**	**21**	**30**	**51**	**43**	**6**	**2**	**3**	**171**	**12.3**	**–17**	....	....	....	....	....	....	....	....	....	....	....	....
1990-91	**Vancouver**	**NHL**	**80**	**33**	**37**	**70**	**65**	**16**	**2**	**4**	**229**	**14.4**	**–25**	....	....	....	**6**	**0**	**7**	**7**	**2**	**0**	**0**	**0**	....
1991-92	**Vancouver**	**NHL**	**80**	**31**	**44**	**75**	**101**	**6**	**1**	**6**	**201**	**15.4**	**3**	....	....	....	**13**	**4**	**8**	**12**	**6**	**2**	**0**	**1**	....
1992-93	**Vancouver**	**NHL**	**84**	**33**	**39**	**72**	**64**	**8**	**0**	**3**	**209**	**15.8**	**19**	....	....	....	**12**	**5**	**8**	**13**	**16**	**2**	**0**	**1**	....
1993-94	**Vancouver**	**NHL**	**84**	**32**	**29**	**61**	**73**	**10**	**2**	**3**	**234**	**13.7**	**6**	....	....	....	**24**	**12**	**13**	**25**	**18**	**5**	**1**	**1**	....
1994-95	**Vancouver**	**NHL**	**48**	**18**	**22**	**40**	**40**	**9**	**0**	**1**	**129**	**14.0**	**–5**	....	....	....	**11**	**2**	**6**	**8**	**12**	**1**	**0**	**0**	....
1995-96	**Vancouver**	**NHL**	**82**	**33**	**47**	**80**	**42**	**12**	**1**	**2**	**202**	**16.3**	**6**	....	....	....	**6**	**4**	**4**	**8**	**6**	**2**	**0**	**0**	....
1996-97	**Vancouver**	**NHL**	**49**	**9**	**31**	**40**	**27**	**2**	**2**	**2**	**84**	**10.7**	**5**	....	....	....	....	....	....	....	....	....	....	....	....
1997-98	**Vancouver**	**NHL**	**42**	**7**	**14**	**21**	**49**	**2**	**0**	**1**	**74**	**9.5**	**–13**	....	....	....	....	....	....	....	....	....	....	....	....
	NY Islanders	**NHL**	**25**	**10**	**7**	**17**	**33**	**3**	**2**	**1**	**59**	**16.9**	**–1**	....	....	....	....	....	....	....	....	....	....	....	....
	Canada	Olympics	6	1	0	1	10	....	....	....	....	....	....	....	....	....	....	....	....	....	....	....	....	....	....
1998-99	**NY Islanders**	**NHL**	**82**	**18**	**29**	**47**	**32**	**8**	**1**	**1**	**167**	**10.8**	**–14**	**261**	**50.2**	**21:29**	....	....	....	....	....	....	....	....	....
99-2000	**Montreal**	**NHL**	**50**	**13**	**17**	**30**	**34**	**4**	**0**	**3**	**87**	**14.9**	**–3**	**860**	**56.3**	**17:51**	....	....	....	....	....	....	....	....	....
2000-01	**Montreal**	**NHL**	**57**	**12**	**21**	**33**	**52**	**6**	**0**	**3**	**96**	**12.5**	**–2**	**1142**	**52.7**	**20:47**	....	....	....	....	....	....	....	....	....
	Washington	**NHL**	**12**	**3**	**1**	**4**	**8**	**0**	**0**	**0**	**30**	**10.0**	**2**	**75**	**60.0**	**18:03**	**6**	**0**	**4**	**4**	**14**	**0**	**0**	**0**	**22:41**
2001-02	**Washington**	**NHL**	**16**	**1**	**2**	**3**	**6**	**1**	**0**	**0**	**19**	**5.3**	**–2**	**71**	**49.3**	**16:06**	....	....	....	....	....	....	....	....	....
	Vancouver	**NHL**	**64**	**12**	**22**	**34**	**65**	**2**	**0**	**2**	**122**	**9.8**	**–3**	**1190**	**53.4**	**19:23**	**6**	**1**	**4**	**5**	**0**	**0**	**0**	**0**	**19:36**
2002-03	**Vancouver**	**NHL**	**71**	**19**	**22**	**41**	**30**	**4**	**1**	**1**	**116**	**16.4**	**–1**	**568**	**54.4**	**15:52**	**14**	**1**	**2**	**3**	**10**	**0**	**1**	**0**	**17:38**
2003-04	**Vancouver**	**NHL**	**82**	**14**	**22**	**36**	**26**	**4**	**0**	**1**	**97**	**14.4**	**–6**	**1285**	**55.8**	**16:17**	**7**	**0**	**0**	**0**	**6**	**0**	**0**	**0**	**18:29**
2004-05		DID NOT PLAY																							
2005-06	**Vancouver**	**NHL**	**82**	**7**	**9**	**16**	**15**	**1**	**1**	**0**	**55**	**12.7**	**3**	**668**	**49.6**	**11:20**	....	....	....	....	....	....	....	....	....
	NHL Totals		**1243**	**356**	**474**	**830**	**846**	**114**	**16**	**39**	**2567**	**13.9**		**6120**	**53.7**	**17:20**	**112**	**32**	**60**	**92**	**98**	**14**	**3**	**3**	**19:05**

WHL East Second All-Star Team (1988) • Memorial Cup Tournament All-Star Team (1988) • NHL All-Rookie Team (1989) • King Clancy Memorial Trophy (1997)

Played in NHL All-Star Game (1991, 1992)

Traded to **NY Islanders** by **Vancouver** for Todd Bertuzzi, Bryan McCabe and NY Islanders' 3rd round choice (Jarkko Ruutu) in 1998 Entry Draft, February 6, 1998. Traded to **Montreal** by **NY Islanders** for Montreal's 1st round choice (Branislav Mezei) in 1999 Entry Draft, May 29, 1999. Traded to **Washington** by **Montreal** with Dainius Zubrus and New Jersey's 2nd round choice (previously acquired, later traded to Tampa Bay – Tampa Bay selected Andreas Holmqvist) in 2001 Entry Draft for Richard Zednik, Jan Bulis and Washington's 1st round choice (Alexander Perezhogin) in 2001 Entry Draft, March 13, 2001. Traded to **Vancouver** by **Washington** with NY Islanders' 2nd round choice (previously acquired, Vancouver selected Denis Grot) in 2002 Entry Draft for Vancouver's 1st round choice (Boyd Gordon) in 2002 Entry Draft and Vancouver's 3rd round choice (later traded to Edmonton – Edmonton selected Zachery Stortini) in 2003 Entry Draft, November 10, 2001.

LINDROS, Eric — (LIHND-rahz, AIR-ihk) — DAL.

Center. Shoots right. 6'4", 240 lbs. Born, London, Ont., February 28, 1973. Quebec's 1st choice, 1st overall, in 1991 Entry Draft.

			Regular Season														Playoffs								
Season	Club	League	GP	G	A	Pts	PIM	PP	SH	GW	S	%	+/-	TF	F%	Min	GP	G	A	Pts	PIM	PP	SH	GW	Min
1988-89	St. Mike's B's	OHA-B	37	24	43	67	193	....	....	....	....	....	....	....	....	....	27	23	25	48	155	....	....	....	....
1989-90	Det. Compuware	NAHL	14	23	29	52	123	....	....	....	....	....	....	....	....	....	....	....	....	....	....	....	....	....	....
	Oshawa Generals	OHL	25	17	19	36	61	....	....	....	....	....	....	....	....	....	17	18	18	36	76	....	....	....	....
1990-91	Oshawa Generals	OHL	57	*71	78	*149	189	....	....	....	....	....	....	....	....	....	16	*18	20	*38	*93	....	....	....	....
1991-92	Oshawa Generals	OHL	13	9	22	31	54	....	....	....	....	....	....	....	....	....	....	....	....	....	....	....	....	....	....
	Canada	Nat-Tm	24	19	16	35	34	....	....	....	....	....	....	....	....	....	....	....	....	....	....	....	....	....	....
	Canada	Olympics	8	5	6	11	5	....	....	....	....	....	....	....	....	....	....	....	....	....	....	....	....	....	....
1992-93	**Philadelphia**	**NHL**	**61**	**41**	**34**	**75**	**147**	**8**	**1**	**5**	**180**	**22.8**	**28**	....	....	....	....	....	....	....	....	....	....	....	....
1993-94	**Philadelphia**	**NHL**	**65**	**44**	**53**	**97**	**103**	**13**	**2**	**9**	**197**	**22.3**	**16**	....	....	....	....	....	....	....	....	....	....	....	....
1994-95	**Philadelphia**	**NHL**	**46**	**29**	**41**	***70**	**60**	**7**	**0**	**4**	**144**	**20.1**	**27**	....	....	....	**12**	**4**	**11**	**15**	**18**	**0**	**0**	**1**	....
1995-96	**Philadelphia**	**NHL**	**73**	**47**	**68**	**115**	**163**	**15**	**0**	**4**	**294**	**16.0**	**26**	....	....	....	**12**	**6**	**6**	**12**	**43**	**3**	**0**	**2**	....
1996-97	**Philadelphia**	**NHL**	**52**	**32**	**47**	**79**	**136**	**9**	**0**	**7**	**198**	**16.2**	**31**	....	....	....	**19**	**12**	**14**	***26**	**40**	**4**	**0**	**1**	....
1997-98	**Philadelphia**	**NHL**	**63**	**30**	**41**	**71**	**134**	**10**	**1**	**4**	**202**	**14.9**	**14**	....	....	....	**5**	**1**	**2**	**3**	**17**	**0**	**0**	**0**	....
	Canada	Olympics	6	2	3	5	2	....	....	....	....	....	....	....	....	....	....	....	....	....	....	....	....	....	....
1998-99	**Philadelphia**	**NHL**	**71**	**40**	**53**	**93**	**120**	**10**	**1**	**2**	**242**	**16.5**	**35**	**1529**	**60.0**	**22:56**	....	....	....	....	....	....	....	....	....
99-2000	**Philadelphia**	**NHL**	**55**	**27**	**32**	**59**	**83**	**10**	**1**	**2**	**187**	**14.4**	**11**	**1318**	**57.8**	**22:02**	**2**	**1**	**0**	**1**	**0**	**0**	**0**	**0**	**8:26**
2000-01	**Philadelphia**	**NHL**	DID NOT PLAY – INJURED																						
2001-02	**NY Rangers**	**NHL**	**72**	**37**	**36**	**73**	**138**	**12**	**1**	**4**	**196**	**18.9**	**19**	**1707**	**54.4**	**21:03**	....	....	....	....	....	....	....	....	....
	Canada	Olympics	6	1	0	1	8	....	....	....	....	....	....	....	....	....	....	....	....	....	....	....	....	....	....
2002-03	**NY Rangers**	**NHL**	**81**	**19**	**34**	**53**	**141**	**9**	**0**	**3**	**235**	**8.1**	**5**	**778**	**53.0**	**20:15**	....	....	....	....	....	....	....	....	....
2003-04	**NY Rangers**	**NHL**	**39**	**10**	**22**	**32**	**60**	**3**	**0**	**0**	**83**	**12.0**	**7**	**492**	**54.5**	**15:59**	....	....	....	....	....	....	....	....	....
2004-05			DID NOT PLAY																						
2005-06	**Toronto**	**NHL**	**33**	**11**	**11**	**22**	**43**	**4**	**0**	**2**	**59**	**18.6**	**–3**	**480**	**53.5**	**17:24**	....	....	....	....	....	....	....	....	....
	NHL Totals		**711**	**367**	**472**	**839**	**1328**	**110**	**7**	**46**	**2217**	**16.6**		**6304**	**56.2**	**20:30**	**50**	**24**	**33**	**57**	**118**	**7**	**0**	**4**	**8:26**

Memorial Cup Tournament All-Star Team (1990) • OHL First All-Star Team (1991) • OHL MVP (1991) • Canadian Major Junior Player of the Year (1991) • NHL All-Rookie Team (1993) • NHL First All-Star Team (1995) • Lester B. Pearson Award (1995) • Hart Trophy (1995) • NHL Second All-Star Team (1996)

Played in NHL All-Star Game (1994, 1996, 1997, 1998, 1999, 2000)

Traded to **Philadelphia** by **Quebec** for Peter Forsberg, Steve Duchesne, Kerry Huffman, Mike Ricci, Ron Hextall, Philadelphia's 1st round choice (Jocelyn Thibault) in 1993 Entry Draft, $15,000,000 and future considerations (Chris Simon and Philadelphia's 1st round choice (later traded to Toronto – later traded to Washington – Washington selected Nolan Baumgartner) in 1994 Entry Draft, July 21, 1992), June 30, 1992. • Missed entire 2000-01 season recovering from head injury suffered in game vs. New Jersey, May 26, 2000 and due to contract dispute with Philadelphia Flyers. Traded to **NY Rangers** by **Philadelphia** for Kim Johnsson, Jan Havac, Pavel Brendl and NY Rangers' 3rd round choice (Stefan Ruzicka) in 2003 Entry Draft, August 20, 2001. • Missed majority of 2003-04 season recovering from shoulder (October 23, 2003 vs. Florida) and head (January 28, 2004 vs. Washington) injuries. Signed as a free agent by **Toronto**, August 11, 2005. Signed as a free agent by **Dallas**, July 17, 2006.

LINDSTROM, Joakim — (LIHND-struhm, YOH-ah-kihm) — CBJ

Center. Shoots left. 6', 187 lbs. Born, Skelleftea, Sweden, December 5, 1983. Columbus' 2nd choice, 41st overall, in 2002 Entry Draft.

			Regular Season														Playoffs								
Season	Club	League	GP	G	A	Pts	PIM	PP	SH	GW	S	%	+/-	TF	F%	Min	GP	G	A	Pts	PIM	PP	SH	GW	Min
99-2000	MoDo U18	Swe-U18	17	6	*14	20	32	....	....	....	....	....	....	....	....	....	....	....	....	....	....	....	....	....	....
	Malmo Jr.	Swe-Jr.	10	4	4	8	2	....	....	....	....	....	....	....	....	....	....	....	....	....	....	....	....	....	....
2000-01	Malmo Jr.	Swe-Jr.	12	7	14	21	46	....	....	....	....	....	....	....	....	....	4	2	3	5	24	....	....	....	....
	MoDo	Sweden	10	2	3	5	2	....	....	....	....	....	....	....	....	....	7	0	1	1	0	....	....	....	....
2001-02	Malmo Jr.	Swe-Jr.	10	9	6	15	67	....	....	....	....	....	....	....	....	....	....	....	....	....	....	....	....	....	....
	IF Troja-Ljungby	Sweden-2	3	0	0	0	12	....	....	....	....	....	....	....	....	....	....	....	....	....	....	....	....	....	....
	MODO	Sweden	42	4	3	7	20	....	....	....	....	....	....	....	....	....	14	3	5	8	8	....	....	....	....
2002-03	MODO	Sweden	29	4	2	6	14	....	....	....	....	....	....	....	....	....	6	1	1	2	2	....	....	....	....
	Malmo Jr.	Swe-Jr.	2	5	1	6	8	....	....	....	....	....	....	....	....	....	....	....	....	....	....	....	....	....	....
	Ornskoldsviks SK	Sweden-2	2	1	1	2	4	....	....	....	....	....	....	....	....	....	....	....	....	....	....	....	....	....	....
2003-04	MODO	Sweden	15	0	2	2	0	....	....	....	....	....	....	....	....	....	....	....	....	....	....	....	....	....	....
	Sundsvall	Sweden-2	2	0	5	5	0	....	....	....	....	....	....	....	....	....	....	....	....	....	....	....	....	....	....
2004-05	MODO Jr.	Swe-Jr.	2	4	1	5	0	....	....	....	....	....	....	....	....	....	....	....	....	....	....	....	....	....	....
	MODO	Sweden	37	2	3	5	24	....	....	....	....	....	....	....	....	....	....	....	....	....	....	....	....	....	....
	Syracuse Crunch	AHL	13	4	4	8	0	....	....	....	....	....	....	....	....	....	....	....	....	....	....	....	....	....	....
2005-06	**Columbus**	**NHL**	**3**	**0**	**0**	**0**	**0**	**0**	**0**	**0**	**4**	**0.0**	**0**	**0**	**0.0**	**5:11**	....	....	....	....	....	....	....	....	....
	Syracuse Crunch	AHL	64	14	29	43	52	....	....	....	....	....	....	....	....	....	6	1	1	2	0	....	....	....	....
	NHL Totals		**3**	**0**	**0**	**0**	**0**	**0**	**0**	**0**	**4**	**0.0**		**0**	**0.0**	**5:11**	....	....	....	....	....	....	....	....	....

LOMBARDI, Matthew — (lawm-BAHR-dee, MA-thew) — CGY.

Center. Shoots left. 6', 195 lbs. Born, Montreal, Que., March 18, 1982. Calgary's 3rd choice, 90th overall, in 2002 Entry Draft.

			Regular Season														Playoffs								
Season	Club	League	GP	G	A	Pts	PIM	PP	SH	GW	S	%	+/-	TF	F%	Min	GP	G	A	Pts	PIM	PP	SH	GW	Min
1997-98	Gatineau	QAAA	42	10	13	23	....	....	....	....	....	....	....	....	....	....	13	4	7	11	....	....	....	....	....
1998-99	Victoriaville Tigres	QMJHL	47	6	10	16	8	....	....	....	....	....	....	....	....	....	5	0	0	0	0	....	....	....	....
99-2000	Victoriaville Tigres	QMJHL	65	18	26	44	28	....	....	....	....	....	....	....	....	....	6	0	0	0	6	....	....	....	....
2000-01	Victoriaville Tigres	QMJHL	72	28	39	67	66	....	....	....	....	....	....	....	....	....	13	12	6	18	10	....	....	....	....
2001-02	Victoriaville Tigres	QMJHL	66	57	73	130	70	....	....	....	....	....	....	....	....	....	22	*17	18	35	18	....	....	....	....
2002-03	Saint John Flames	AHL	76	25	21	46	41	....	....	....	....	....	....	....	....	....	....	....	....	....	....	....	....	....	....
2003-04	**Calgary**	**NHL**	**79**	**16**	**13**	**29**	**32**	**3**	**2**	**4**	**130**	**12.3**	**4**	**992**	**47.9**	**14:26**	**13**	**1**	**5**	**6**	**4**	**0**	**0**	**1**	**14:46**
2004-05	Lowell	AHL	9	3	1	4	9	....	....	....	....	....	....	....	....	....	11	0	3	3	16	....	....	....	....
2005-06	**Calgary**	**NHL**	**55**	**6**	**20**	**26**	**48**	**1**	**2**	**2**	**72**	**8.3**	**–1**	**499**	**52.9**	**14:09**	**7**	**0**	**2**	**2**	**2**	**0**	**0**	**0**	**15:51**
	Omaha	AHL	1	1	1	2	0	....	....	....	....	....	....	....	....	....	....	....	....	....	....	....	....	....	....
	NHL Totals		**134**	**22**	**33**	**55**	**80**	**4**	**4**	**6**	**202**	**10.9**		**1491**	**49.6**	**14:19**	**20**	**1**	**7**	**8**	**6**	**0**	**0**	**1**	**15:09**

• Re-entered NHL Entry Draft. Originally Edmonton's 7th choice, 215th overall, in 2000 Entry Draft.

Memorial Cup Tournament All-Star Team (2002) • Ed Chynoweth Trophy (Memorial Cup Tournament Leading Scorer) (2002)

LOW, Reed — (LOH, REED) — CHI.

Right wing. Shoots right. 6'4", 220 lbs. Born, Moose Jaw, Sask., June 21, 1976. St. Louis' 7th choice, 177th overall, in 1996 Entry Draft.

			Regular Season														Playoffs								
Season	Club	League	GP	G	A	Pts	PIM	PP	SH	GW	S	%	+/-	TF	F%	Min	GP	G	A	Pts	PIM	PP	SH	GW	Min
1994-95	Minot Top Guns	SJHL	STATISTICS NOT AVAILABLE																						
	Regina Pats	WHL	2	0	0	0	5	....	....	....	....	....	....	....	....	....	....	....	....	....	....	....	....	....	....
1995-96	Moose Jaw	WHL	61	12	7	19	221	....	....	....	....	....	....	....	....	....	....	....	....	....	....	....	....	....	....
1996-97	Moose Jaw	WHL	62	16	11	27	228	....	....	....	....	....	....	....	....	....	12	2	1	3	50	....	....	....	....
1997-98	Worcester IceCats	AHL	17	1	1	2	75	....	....	....	....	....	....	....	....	....	3	0	0	0	0	....	....	....	....
	Baton Rouge	ECHL	39	4	2	6	145	....	....	....	....	....	....	....	....	....	....	....	....	....	....	....	....	....	....
1998-99	Worcester IceCats	AHL	77	5	6	11	239	....	....	....	....	....	....	....	....	....	4	0	0	0	2	....	....	....	....
99-2000	Worcester IceCats	AHL	80	12	16	28	203	....	....	....	....	....	....	....	....	....	9	1	3	4	16	....	....	....	....
2000-01	**St. Louis**	**NHL**	**56**	**1**	**5**	**6**	**159**	**0**	**0**	**0**	**31**	**3.2**	**4**	**2**	**50.0**	**6:17**	....	....	....	....	....	....	....	....	....
2001-02	**St. Louis**	**NHL**	**58**	**0**	**5**	**5**	**160**	**0**	**0**	**0**	**25**	**0.0**	**–3**	**0**	**0.0**	**5:22**	....	....	....	....	....	....	....	....	....
2002-03	**St. Louis**	**NHL**	**79**	**2**	**4**	**6**	**234**	**0**	**0**	**1**	**48**	**4.2**	**3**	**14**	**71.4**	**6:19**	....	....	....	....	....	....	....	....	....
2003-04	**St. Louis**	**NHL**	**57**	**0**	**2**	**2**	**141**	**0**	**0**	**0**	**28**	**0.0**	**–6**	**0**	**0.0**	**5:42**	....	....	....	....	....	....	....	....	....
2004-05			DID NOT PLAY																						
2005-06	Peoria Rivermen	AHL	20	3	5	8	40	....	....	....	....	....	....	....	....	....	....	....	....	....	....	....	....	....	....
	Missouri	UHL	4	2	1	3	13	....	....	....	....	....	....	....	....	....	....	....	....	....	....	....	....	....	....
	NHL Totals		**250**	**3**	**16**	**19**	**694**	**0**	**0**	**1**	**132**	**2.3**		**16**	**68.8**	**5:57**	....	....	....	....	....	....	....	....	....

Signed as a free agent by **Chicago**, July 27, 2006.

LOYNS, Lynn — (LOINZ, LIHN)

Left wing. Shoots left. 5'11", 205 lbs. Born, Naicam, Sask., February 21, 1981.

			Regular Season														Playoffs								
Season	Club	League	GP	G	A	Pts	PIM	PP	SH	GW	S	%	+/-	TF	F%	Min	GP	G	A	Pts	PIM	PP	SH	GW	Min
1996-97	Naicam Vikings	SAHA	41	90	70	160	58	....	....	....	....	....	....	....	....	....	....	....	....	....	....	....	....	....	....
1997-98	Spokane Chiefs	WHL	49	1	12	13	8	....	....	....	....	....	....	....	....	....	13	1	4	5	2	....	....	....	....
1998-99	Spokane Chiefs	WHL	72	20	30	50	43	....	....	....	....	....	....	....	....	....	....	....	....	....	....	....	....	....	....
99-2000	Spokane Chiefs	WHL	71	20	29	49	47	....	....	....	....	....	....	....	....	....	14	3	2	5	12	....	....	....	....
2000-01	Spokane Chiefs	WHL	66	31	42	73	81	....	....	....	....	....	....	....	....	....	....	....	....	....	....	....	....	....	....
2001-02	Cleveland Barons	AHL	76	9	9	18	81	....	....	....	....	....	....	....	....	....	....	....	....	....	....	....	....	....	....
2002-03	**San Jose**	**NHL**	**19**	**3**	**0**	**3**	**19**	**0**	**0**	**0**	**12**	**25.0**	**–4**	**1**	**0.0**	**7:50**	....	....	....	....	....	....	....	....	....
	Cleveland Barons	AHL	36	7	8	15	39	....	....	....	....	....	....	....	....	....	....	....	....	....	....	....	....	....	....

Season	Club	League	GP	G	A	Pts	PIM	PP	SH	GW	S	%	+/-	TF	F%	Min	GP	G	A	Pts	PIM	PP	SH	GW	Min
								Regular Season									Playoffs								
2003-04	**San Jose**	**NHL**	**2**	**0**	**0**	**0**	**0**	**0**	**0**	**0**	**0**	**0.0**	**–1**	**0**	**0.0**	**7:33**									
	Cleveland Barons	AHL	30	5	9	14	40																		
	Calgary	**NHL**	**12**	**0**	**2**	**2**	**2**	**0**	**0**	**0**	**6**	**0.0**	**–2**	**86**	**44.2**	**11:13**									
	Lowell	AHL	18	6	6	12	9																		
2004-05	Lowell	AHL	77	7	8	15	42										11	0	0	0	0				
2005-06	**Calgary**	**NHL**	**1**	**0**	**0**	**0**	**0**	**0**	**0**	**0**	**0**	**0.0**	**0**	**0**	**0.0**	**6:15**									
	Omaha	AHL	68	9	8	17	50																		
	NHL Totals		**34**	**3**	**2**	**5**	**21**	**0**	**0**	**0**	**18**	**16.7**		**87**	**43.7**	**8:58**									

Signed as a free agent by **San Jose**, October 3, 2001. Traded to **Calgary** by **San Jose** for Calgary's 5th round choice (later traded to Florida – Florida selected Bret Nasby) in 2004 Entry Draft, January 9, 2004.

LUKOWICH, Brad

(loo-KUH-which, BRAD) **N.J.**

Defense. Shoots left. 6'1", 205 lbs. Born, Cranbrook, B.C., August 12, 1976. NY Islanders' 4th choice, 90th overall, in 1994 Entry Draft.

Season	Club	League	GP	G	A	Pts	PIM	PP	SH	GW	S	%	+/-	TF	F%	Min	GP	G	A	Pts	PIM	PP	SH	GW	Min
1992-93	Cranbrook Colts	RMJHL	54	21	41	62	162																		
	Kamloops Blazers	WHL	1	0	0	0	0																		
1993-94	Kamloops Blazers	WHL	42	5	11	16	166										16	0	1	1	35				
1994-95	Kamloops Blazers	WHL	63	10	35	45	125										18	0	7	7	21				
1995-96	Kamloops Blazers	WHL	65	14	55	69	114										13	2	10	12	29				
1996-97	Michigan	IHL	69	2	6	8	77										4	0	1	1	2				
1997-98	**Dallas**	**NHL**	**4**	**0**	**1**	**1**	**2**	**0**	**0**	**0**	**2**	**0.0**	**–2**												
	Michigan	IHL	60	6	27	33	104										4	0	4	4	14				
1998-99	**Dallas**	**NHL**	**14**	**1**	**2**	**3**	**19**	**0**	**0**	**0**	**8**	**12.5**	**3**	**0**	**0.0**	**16:18**	**8**	**0**	**1**	**1**	**4**	**0**	**0**	**0**	**10:00**
	Michigan	IHL	67	8	21	29	95																		
99-2000	**Dallas**	**NHL**	**60**	**3**	**1**	**4**	**50**	**0**	**0**	**1**	**33**	**9.1**	**–14**	**1**	**0.0**	**11:44**									
2000-01	**Dallas**	**NHL**	**80**	**4**	**10**	**14**	**76**	**0**	**0**	**2**	**43**	**9.3**	**28**	**1**	**100.0**	**14:48**	**10**	**1**	**0**	**1**	**4**	**0**	**0**	**0**	**17:28**
2001-02	**Dallas**	**NHL**	**66**	**1**	**6**	**7**	**40**	**0**	**0**	**0**	**56**	**1.8**	**–1**	**0**	**0.0**	**13:14**									
2002-03	**Tampa Bay**	**NHL**	**70**	**1**	**14**	**15**	**46**	**0**	**0**	**0**	**52**	**1.9**	**4**	**1**	**0.0**	**17:34**	**9**	**0**	**1**	**1**	**2**	**0**	**0**	**0**	**17:48**
2003-04 ♦	**Tampa Bay**	**NHL**	**79**	**5**	**14**	**19**	**24**	**0**	**0**	**1**	**86**	**5.8**	**29**	**3**	**0.0**	**18:45**	**18**	**0**	**2**	**2**	**6**	**0**	**0**	**0**	**15:51**
2004-05	Fort Worth	CHL	16	3	5	8	33																		
2005-06	**NY Islanders**	**NHL**	**57**	**1**	**12**	**13**	**32**	**0**	**0**	**1**	**36**	**2.8**	**–3**	**0**	**0.0**	**19:15**									
	New Jersey	**NHL**	**18**	**1**	**7**	**8**	**8**	**0**	**0**	**0**	**13**	**7.7**	**3**	**0**	**0.0**	**19:11**	**9**	**0**	**0**	**0**	**4**	**0**	**0**	**0**	**21:28**
	NHL Totals		**448**	**17**	**67**	**84**	**297**	**0**	**0**	**5**	**329**	**5.2**		**6**	**16.7**	**16:05**	**54**	**1**	**4**	**5**	**20**	**0**	**0**	**0**	**16:33**

Traded to **Dallas** by **NY Islanders** for Dallas' 3rd round choice (Robert Schnabel) in 1997 Entry Draft, June 1, 1996. Traded to **Minnesota** by **Dallas** with Manny Fernandez for Minnesota's 3rd round choice (Joel Lundqvist) in 2000 Entry Draft and Minnesota's 4th round choice (later traded back to Minnesota – later traded to Los Angeles – Los Angeles selected Aaron Rome) in 2002 Entry Draft, June 12, 2000. Traded to **Dallas** by **Minnesota** with Minnesota's 3rd (Yared Hagos) and 9th (Dale Sullivan) round choices in 2001 Entry Draft for Aaron Gavey, Pavel Patera, Dallas' 8th round choice (Eric Johansson) in 2000 Entry Draft and Minnesota's 4th round choice (previously acquired, later traded to Los Angeles – Los Angeles selected Aaron Rome) in 2002 Entry Draft, June 25, 2000. Traded to **Tampa Bay** by **Dallas** with Dallas' 7th round choice (Jay Rosehill) in 2003 Entry Draft for Tampa Bay's 2nd round choice (previously acquired, later traded back to Tampa Bay – later traded to Dallas – Dallas selected Tobias Stephan) in 2002 Entry Draft, June 22, 2002. Signed as a free agent by **Fort Worth** (CHL), September 21, 2004. Signed as a free agent by **NY Islanders**, August 11, 2005. Traded to **New Jersey** by **NY Islanders** for New Jersey's 3rd round choice (later traded to Phoenix - Phoenix selected Jonas Ahnelov) in 2006 Entry Draft, March 9, 2006.

LUNDMARK, Jamie

(LUHND-mahrk, JAY-mee) **CGY.**

Center. Shoots right. 6', 200 lbs. Born, Edmonton, Alta., January 16, 1981. NY Rangers' 2nd choice, 9th overall, in 1999 Entry Draft.

Season	Club	League	GP	G	A	Pts	PIM	PP	SH	GW	S	%	+/-	TF	F%	Min	GP	G	A	Pts	PIM	PP	SH	GW	Min
1996-97	St. Albert Saints	AJHL	35	10	9	19	8																		
1997-98	St. Albert Saints	AJHL	57	33	58	91	171										19	13	18	31	5				
1998-99	Moose Jaw	WHL	70	40	51	91	121										11	5	4	9	24				
99-2000	Moose Jaw	WHL	37	21	27	48	33																		
2000-01	Seattle	WHL	52	35	42	77	49										9	4	4	8	16				
2001-02	Hartford	AHL	79	27	32	59	56										10	3	4	7	16				
2002-03	**NY Rangers**	**NHL**	**55**	**8**	**11**	**19**	**16**	**0**	**0**	**0**	**78**	**10.3**	**–3**	**62**	**43.6**	**12:04**									
	Hartford	AHL	22	9	9	18	18										2	0	0	0	0				
2003-04	**NY Rangers**	**NHL**	**56**	**2**	**8**	**10**	**33**	**0**	**0**	**1**	**68**	**2.9**	**–8**	**379**	**40.4**	**12:46**									
2004-05	HC Forst Bolzano	Italy	14	9	9	18	22																		
	Hartford	AHL	64	14	27	41	146										6	2	4	6	8				
2005-06	**NY Rangers**	**NHL**	**3**	**1**	**0**	**1**	**6**	**0**	**0**	**0**	**1**	**100.0**	**–2**	**2**	**0.0**	**9:49**									
	Phoenix	**NHL**	**38**	**5**	**13**	**18**	**36**	**1**	**0**	**0**	**61**	**8.2**	**–1**	**366**	**58.7**	**12:37**									
	San Antonio	AHL	4	1	2	3	2																		
	Calgary	**NHL**	**12**	**4**	**6**	**10**	**20**	**1**	**0**	**1**	**16**	**25.0**	**2**	**103**	**53.4**	**12:32**	**4**	**0**	**1**	**1**	**7**	**0**	**0**	**0**	**9:44**
	NHL Totals		**164**	**20**	**38**	**58**	**111**	**2**	**0**	**2**	**224**	**8.9**		**912**	**49.3**	**12:25**	**4**	**0**	**1**	**1**	**7**	**0**	**0**	**0**	**9:44**

WHL All-Rookie Team (1999) • WHL East Second All-Star Team (1999) • WHL West First All-Star Team (2001)

Signed as a free agent by **Bolzano** (Italy), September 21, 2004. Signed as a free agent by **Hartford** (AHL), November 16, 2004. Traded to **Phoenix** by **NY Rangers** for Jeff Taffe, October 18. 2005. Traded to **Calgary** by **Phoenix** for Calgary's 4th round choice (later traded to NY Islanders - NY Islanders selected Doug Rogers) in 2006 Entry Draft, March 9, 2006.

LUPASCHUK, Ross

(LOO-puhs-chuhk, RAWS) **PIT.**

Defense. Shoots right. 6'1", 210 lbs. Born, Edmonton, Alta., January 19, 1981. Washington's 4th choice, 34th overall, in 1999 Entry Draft.

Season	Club	League	GP	G	A	Pts	PIM	PP	SH	GW	S	%	+/-	TF	F%	Min	GP	G	A	Pts	PIM	PP	SH	GW	Min
1996-97	Edmonton Mets	AJHL	65	5	22	27	87																		
1997-98	Prince Albert	WHL	67	6	12	18	170																		
1998-99	Prince Albert	WHL	67	8	20	28	127										14	4	9	13	16				
99-2000	Prince Albert	WHL	22	8	8	16	42																		
	Red Deer Rebels	WHL	46	13	27	40	116										4	0	1	1	10				
2000-01	Red Deer Rebels	WHL	65	28	37	65	135										22	5	10	15	54				
2001-02	Wilkes-Barre	AHL	72	9	20	29	91																		
2002-03	**Pittsburgh**	**NHL**	**3**	**0**	**0**	**0**	**4**	**0**	**0**	**0**	**3**	**0.0**	**–3**	**0**	**0.0**	**16:20**									
	Wilkes-Barre	AHL	74	18	18	36	101										4	0	2	2	20				
2003-04	Wilkes-Barre	AHL	58	4	17	21	96										8	0	2	2	37				
2004-05	Wilkes-Barre	AHL	67	11	19	30	145										5	0	0	0	2				
2005-06	Mora IK	Sweden	49	13	18	31	*168										5	2	2	4	18				
	NHL Totals		**3**	**0**	**0**	**0**	**4**	**0**	**0**	**0**	**3**	**0.0**		**0**	**0.0**	**16:20**									

WHL East Second All-Star Team (2001) • Memorial Cup Tournament All-Star Team (2001)

Traded to **Pittsburgh** by **Washington** with Kris Beech, Michal Sivek and future considerations for Jaromir Jagr and Frantisek Kucera, July 11, 2001.

LUPUL, Joffrey

(LOO-puhl, JAWF-ree) **EDM.**

Center. Shoots right. 6'1", 205 lbs. Born, Fort Saskatchewan, Alta., September 23, 1983. Anaheim's 1st choice, 7th overall, in 2002 Entry Draft.

Season	Club	League	GP	G	A	Pts	PIM	PP	SH	GW	S	%	+/-	TF	F%	Min	GP	G	A	Pts	PIM	PP	SH	GW	Min
1998-99	Ft. Saskatchewan	ABHL	36	40	50	90	40																		
99-2000	Ft. Saskatchewan	AMHL	34	43	30	*73	47										4	0	1	1	2				
2000-01	Medicine Hat	WHL	69	30	26	56	39										22	3	6	9	2				
2001-02	Medicine Hat	WHL	72	*56	50	106	95																		
2002-03	Medicine Hat	WHL	50	41	37	78	82										11	4	11	15	20				
2003-04	**Anaheim**	**NHL**	**75**	**13**	**21**	**34**	**28**	**4**	**0**	**2**	**137**	**9.5**	**–6**	**11**	**9.1**	**13:37**									
	Cincinnati	AHL	3	3	2	5	2																		
2004-05	Cincinnati	AHL	65	30	26	56	58										12	3	9	12	27				
2005-06	**Anaheim**	**NHL**	**81**	**28**	**25**	**53**	**48**	**12**	**2**	**2**	**296**	**9.5**	**–13**	**101**	**37.6**	**16:38**	**16**	**9**	**2**	**11**	**31**	**1**	**0**	**1**	**16:43**
	NHL Totals		**156**	**41**	**46**	**87**	**76**	**16**	**2**	**4**	**433**	**9.5**		**112**	**34.8**	**15:11**	**16**	**9**	**2**	**11**	**31**	**1**	**0**	**1**	**16:43**

WHL East First All-Star Team (2002) • Canadian Major Junior First All-Star Team (2002)

Traded to **Edmonton** by **Anaheim** with Ladislav Smid, a 1st round choice in 2007 Entry Draft, a 2nd round choice in 2008 Entry Draft and future considerations for Chris Pronger, July 3, 2006.

LYDMAN, Toni

(LEWD-man, TOH-nee) **BUF.**

Defense. Shoots left. 6'1", 202 lbs. Born, Lahti, Finland, September 25, 1977. Calgary's 5th choice, 89th overall, in 1996 Entry Draft.

Season	Club	League	GP	G	A	Pts	PIM	PP	SH	GW	S	%	+/-	TF	F%	Min	GP	G	A	Pts	PIM	PP	SH	GW	Min
1993-94	K-Reipas U18	Fin-U18	9	3	1	4	4																		
	K-Reipas Jr.	Fin-Jr.	1	0	0	0	0																		
1994-95	K-Reipas U18	Fin-U18	9	7	4	11	12																		
	K-Reipas Jr.	Fin-Jr.	26	6	4	10	10																		
1995-96	Reipas Lahti Jr.	Fin-Jr.	9	2	2	4	6																		
	Reipas Lahti	Finland-2	39	5	2	7	30										3	0	1	1	0				
1996-97	Tappara Tampere	Finland	49	1	2	3	65										3	0	0	0	6				

			Regular Season														Playoffs								
Season	Club	League	GP	G	A	Pts	PIM	PP	SH	GW	S	%	+/-	TF	F%	Min	GP	G	A	Pts	PIM	PP	SH	GW	Min
1997-98	Tappara Tampere	Finland	48	4	10	14	48	....	....	....	....	....	....	....	....	....	4	0	2	2	0	....	....	....	....
1998-99	HIFK Helsinki	Finland	42	4	7	11	36	....	....	....	....	....	....	....	....	....	11	0	3	3	2	....	....	....	....
	HIFK Helsinki	EuroHL	6	0	2	2	29	....	....	....	....	....	....	....	....	....	4	1	....	....	....	....	....	....	....
99-2000	HIFK Helsinki	Finland	46	4	18	22	36	....	....	....	....	....	....	....	....	....	9	0	4	4	6	....	....	....	....
2000-01	**Calgary**	**NHL**	62	3	16	19	30	1	0	0	80	3.8	–7	0	0.0	20:36	....	....	....	....	....	....	....	....	....
2001-02	**Calgary**	**NHL**	79	6	22	28	52	1	0	0	126	4.8	–8	0	0.0	21:10	....	....	....	....	....	....	....	....	....
2002-03	**Calgary**	**NHL**	81	6	20	26	28	3	0	0	143	4.2	–7	0	0.0	25:47	....	....	....	....	....	....	....	....	....
2003-04	**Calgary**	**NHL**	67	4	16	20	30	2	0	1	93	4.3	6	0	0.0	21:13	6	0	1	1	2	0	0	0	14:30
2004-05	HIFK Helsinki	Finland	8	1	2	3	2	....	....	....	....	....	....	....	....	....	5	0	3	3	0	....	....	....	....
2005-06	**Buffalo**	**NHL**	75	1	16	17	82	0	0	0	68	1.5	9	0	0.0	21:38	18	1	4	5	18	0	0	0	23:03
	Finland	Olympics	8	1	0	1	10	....	....	....	....	....	....	....	....	....	....	....	....	....	....	....	....	....	....
	NHL Totals		**364**	**20**	**90**	**110**	**222**	**7**	**0**	**1**	**510**	**3.9**		**0**	**0.0**	**22:12**	**24**	**1**	**5**	**6**	**20**	**0**	**0**	**0**	**20:55**

Signed as a free agent by **HIFK Helsinki** (Finland), January 31, 2005. Traded to **Buffalo** by **Calgary** for Buffalo's 3rd round choice (John Armstrong) in 2006 Entry Draft, August 25, 2005.

LYNCH, Doug

(LIHNCH, DUHG) **ST.L.**

Defense. Shoots left. 6'3", 214 lbs. Born, North Vancouver, B.C., April 4, 1983. Edmonton's 2nd choice, 43rd overall, in 2001 Entry Draft.

Season	Club	League	GP	G	A	Pts	PIM	PP	SH	GW	S	%	+/-	TF	F%	Min	GP	G	A	Pts	PIM	PP	SH	GW	Min
1998-99	Port Coquitlam	BCAHA	45	47	48	95	120	....	....	....	....	....	....	....	....	....	....	....	....	....	....	....	....	....	....
	Red Deer Rebels	WHL	2	0	1	1	2	....	....	....	....	....	....	....	....	....	....	....	....	....	....	....	....	....	....
99-2000	Red Deer Rebels	WHL	65	9	5	14	57	....	....	....	....	....	....	....	....	....	4	0	0	0	5	....	....	....	....
2000-01	Red Deer Rebels	WHL	72	12	37	49	181	....	....	....	....	....	....	....	....	....	21	1	9	10	30	....	....	....	....
2001-02	Red Deer Rebels	WHL	71	21	27	48	202	....	....	....	....	....	....	....	....	....	22	5	4	9	12	....	....	....	....
2002-03	Red Deer Rebels	WHL	13	7	5	12	27	....	....	....	....	....	....	....	....	....	....	....	....	....	....	....	....	....	....
	Spokane Chiefs	WHL	42	6	12	18	129	....	....	....	....	....	....	....	....	....	4	1	0	1	16	....	....	....	....
2003-04	**Edmonton**	**NHL**	2	0	0	0	0	0	0	0	2	0.0	0	0	0.0	10:16	....	....	....	....	....	....	....	....	....
	Toronto	AHL	74	11	25	36	77	....	....	....	....	....	....	....	....	....	3	0	1	1	2	....	....	....	....
2004-05	Edmonton	AHL	74	1	13	14	109	....	....	....	....	....	....	....	....	....	....	....	....	....	....	....	....	....	....
2005-06	Alaska Aces	ECHL	8	1	1	2	2	....	....	....	....	....	....	....	....	....	22	0	4	4	10	....	....	....	....
	Peoria Rivermen	AHL	29	0	2	2	57	....	....	....	....	....	....	....	....	....	....	....	....	....	....	....	....	....	....
	NHL Totals		**2**	**0**	**0**	**0**	**0**	**0**	**0**	**0**	**2**	**0.0**		**0**	**0.0**	**10:16**	....	....	....	....	....	....	....	....	....

AHL All-Rookie Team (2004)

Traded to **St. Louis** by **Edmonton** with Eric Brewer and Jeff Woywitka for Chris Pronger, August 2, 2005.

LYSAK, Brett

(LIGH-sak, BREHT)

Center. Shoots left. 6', 190 lbs. Born, Edmonton, Alta., December 30, 1980. Carolina's 2nd choice, 49th overall, in 1999 Entry Draft.

Season	Club	League	GP	G	A	Pts	PIM	PP	SH	GW	S	%	+/-	TF	F%	Min	GP	G	A	Pts	PIM	PP	SH	GW	Min
1994-95	St. Albert Sabres	AMBHL	STATISTICS NOT AVAILABLE																						
1995-96	St. Albert Raiders	AMHL	35	20	23	43	68	....	....	....	....	....	....	....	....	....	....	....	....	....	....	....	....	....	....
1996-97	Regina Pats	WHL	66	11	14	25	41	....	....	....	....	....	....	....	....	....	5	0	1	1	5	....	....	....	....
1997-98	Regina Pats	WHL	70	22	38	60	82	....	....	....	....	....	....	....	....	....	9	6	2	8	8	....	....	....	....
1998-99	Regina Pats	WHL	61	39	49	88	84	....	....	....	....	....	....	....	....	....	....	....	....	....	....	....	....	....	....
99-2000	Regina Pats	WHL	70	38	40	78	24	....	....	....	....	....	....	....	....	....	7	5	4	9	2	....	....	....	....
2000-01	Regina Pats	WHL	64	35	48	83	44	....	....	....	....	....	....	....	....	....	6	5	1	6	4	....	....	....	....
2001-02	Florida Everblades	ECHL	16	2	7	9	14	....	....	....	....	....	....	....	....	....	6	3	1	4	6	....	....	....	....
	Lowell	AHL	53	6	8	14	26	....	....	....	....	....	....	....	....	....	3	0	0	0	0	....	....	....	....
2002-03	Lowell	AHL	49	6	9	15	59	....	....	....	....	....	....	....	....	....	....	....	....	....	....	....	....	....	....
2003-04	**Carolina**	**NHL**	2	0	0	0	2	0	0	0	0	0.0	0	1	0.0	3:24	....	....	....	....	....	....	....	....	....
	Lowell	AHL	71	17	18	35	104	....	....	....	....	....	....	....	....	....	....	....	....	....	....	....	....	....	....
2004-05	Iserlohn Roosters	Germany	49	9	9	18	151	....	....	....	....	....	....	....	....	....	....	....	....	....	....	....	....	....	....
2005-06	Manitoba Moose	AHL	4	0	0	0	0	....	....	....	....	....	....	....	....	....	....	....	....	....	....	....	....	....	....
	NHL Totals		**2**	**0**	**0**	**0**	**2**	**0**	**0**	**0**	**0**	**0.0**		**1**	**0.0**	**3:24**	....	....	....	....	....	....	....	....	....

WHL East Second All-Star Team (1999) • Memorial Cup Tournament All-Star Team (2001)

Signed as a free agent by **Iserlohn** (Germany), September, 2004.

MacDONALD, Craig

(MAK-DAWN-uhld, KRAYG) **CHI.**

Left wing. Shoots left. 6'1", 195 lbs. Born, Antigonish, N.S., April 7, 1977. Hartford's 3rd choice, 88th overall, in 1996 Entry Draft.

Season	Club	League	GP	G	A	Pts	PIM	PP	SH	GW	S	%	+/-	TF	F%	Min	GP	G	A	Pts	PIM	PP	SH	GW	Min
1994-95	Lawrence	High-MA	30	25	52	77	10	....	....	....	....	....	....	....	....	....	....	....	....	....	....	....	....	....	....
1995-96	Harvard Crimson	ECAC	34	7	10	17	10	....	....	....	....	....	....	....	....	....	....	....	....	....	....	....	....	....	....
1996-97	Harvard Crimson	ECAC	32	6	10	16	20	....	....	....	....	....	....	....	....	....	....	....	....	....	....	....	....	....	....
1997-98	Canada	Nat-Tm	58	18	29	47	38	....	....	....	....	....	....	....	....	....	....	....	....	....	....	....	....	....	....
1998-99	**Carolina**	**NHL**	11	0	0	0	0	0	0	0	5	0.0	0	2	100.0	2:29	1	0	0	0	0	0	0	0	2:46
	New Haven	AHL	62	17	31	48	77	....	....	....	....	....	....	....	....	....	....	....	....	....	....	....	....	....	....
99-2000	Cincinnati	IHL	78	12	24	36	76	....	....	....	....	....	....	....	....	....	11	4	1	5	8	....	....	....	....
2000-01	Cincinnati	IHL	82	20	28	48	104	....	....	....	....	....	....	....	....	....	5	0	1	1	6	....	....	....	....
2001-02	**Carolina**	**NHL**	12	1	1	2	0	0	0	0	15	6.7	–1	19	47.4	10:11	4	0	0	0	2	0	0	0	4:42
	Lowell	AHL	64	19	22	41	61	....	....	....	....	....	....	....	....	....	....	....	....	....	....	....	....	....	....
2002-03	**Carolina**	**NHL**	35	1	3	4	20	0	0	0	43	2.3	–3	72	55.6	9:21	....	....	....	....	....	....	....	....	....
	Lowell	AHL	27	7	20	27	38	....	....	....	....	....	....	....	....	....	....	....	....	....	....	....	....	....	....
2003-04	**Florida**	**NHL**	34	0	3	3	25	0	0	0	42	0.0	–5	398	45.7	12:31	....	....	....	....	....	....	....	....	....
	San Antonio	AHL	2	0	0	0	4	....	....	....	....	....	....	....	....	....	....	....	....	....	....	....	....	....	....
	Boston	**NHL**	18	0	3	3	8	0	0	0	17	0.0	0	155	47.1	8:42	1	0	0	0	0	0	0	0	2:11
2004-05	Lowell	AHL	71	10	18	28	104	....	....	....	....	....	....	....	....	....	2	0	0	0	0	....	....	....	....
2005-06	**Calgary**	**NHL**	25	3	2	5	8	1	0	0	27	11.1	5	33	45.5	10:16	1	0	0	0	0	0	0	0	7:50
	Omaha	AHL	37	8	19	27	57	....	....	....	....	....	....	....	....	....	....	....	....	....	....	....	....	....	....
	NHL Totals		**135**	**5**	**12**	**17**	**61**	**1**	**0**	**0**	**149**	**3.4**		**679**	**47.3**	**9:45**	**7**	**0**	**0**	**0**	**2**	**0**	**0**	**0**	**4:31**

Rights transferred to **Carolina** after **Hartford** franchise relocated, June 25, 1997. Signed as a free agent by **Florida**, August 14, 2003. Claimed on waivers by **Boston** from **Florida**, January 20, 2004. Signed as a free agent by **Calgary**, August 11, 2005. Signed as a free agent by **Chicago**, August 1, 2006.

MacDONALD, Jason

(MAK-DAWN-uhld, JAY-suhn)

Right wing. Shoots right. 5'11", 210 lbs. Born, Charlottetown, P.E.I., April 1, 1974. Detroit's 5th choice, 142nd overall, in 1992 Entry Draft.

Season	Club	League	GP	G	A	Pts	PIM	PP	SH	GW	S	%	+/-	TF	F%	Min	GP	G	A	Pts	PIM	PP	SH	GW	Min
1989-90	Charlotwn Abbies	MJrHL	29	11	29	40	206	....	....	....	....	....	....	....	....	....	....	....	....	....	....	....	....	....	....
1990-91	North Bay	OHL	57	12	15	27	126	....	....	....	....	....	....	....	....	....	10	3	3	6	15	....	....	....	....
1991-92	North Bay	OHL	17	5	8	13	50	....	....	....	....	....	....	....	....	....	....	....	....	....	....	....	....	....	....
	Owen Sound	OHL	42	17	19	36	129	....	....	....	....	....	....	....	....	....	5	0	3	3	16	....	....	....	....
1992-93	Owen Sound	OHL	56	46	43	89	197	....	....	....	....	....	....	....	....	....	8	6	5	11	28	....	....	....	....
1993-94	Owen Sound	OHL	66	55	61	116	177	....	....	....	....	....	....	....	....	....	9	7	11	18	36	....	....	....	....
	Adirondack	AHL	....	....	....	....	....	....	....	....	....	....	....	....	....	....	1	0	0	0	0	....	....	....	....
1994-95	Adirondack	AHL	68	14	21	35	238	....	....	....	....	....	....	....	....	....	4	0	0	0	2	....	....	....	....
1995-96	Adirondack	AHL	43	9	13	22	99	....	....	....	....	....	....	....	....	....	....	....	....	....	....	....	....	....	....
	Toledo Storm	ECHL	9	5	5	10	26	....	....	....	....	....	....	....	....	....	9	3	1	4	39	....	....	....	....
1996-97	Adirondack	AHL	1	0	0	0	2	....	....	....	....	....	....	....	....	....	....	....	....	....	....	....	....	....	....
	Fredericton	AHL	63	22	25	47	189	....	....	....	....	....	....	....	....	....	....	....	....	....	....	....	....	....	....
1997-98	Canada	Nat-Tm	51	15	20	35	133	....	....	....	....	....	....	....	....	....	....	....	....	....	....	....	....	....	....
	Saint John Flames	AHL	6	2	0	2	27	....	....	....	....	....	....	....	....	....	11	1	3	4	17	....	....	....	....
1998-99	Manitoba Moose	IHL	82	25	27	52	283	....	....	....	....	....	....	....	....	....	5	2	2	4	13	....	....	....	....
99-2000	Manitoba Moose	IHL	30	5	10	15	77	....	....	....	....	....	....	....	....	....	....	....	....	....	....	....	....	....	....
	Orlando	IHL	29	7	7	14	113	....	....	....	....	....	....	....	....	....	4	0	0	0	19	....	....	....	....
2000-01	Wilkes-Barre	AHL	74	17	16	33	290	....	....	....	....	....	....	....	....	....	17	1	3	4	*66	....	....	....	....
2001-02	Wilkes-Barre	AHL	57	8	13	21	330	....	....	....	....	....	....	....	....	....	....	....	....	....	....	....	....	....	....
2002-03	Wilkes-Barre	AHL	56	4	7	11	137	....	....	....	....	....	....	....	....	....	1	0	0	0	0	....	....	....	....
2003-04	Hartford	AHL	41	11	11	22	101	....	....	....	....	....	....	....	....	....	10	4	0	4	50	....	....	....	....
	NY Rangers	**NHL**	4	0	0	0	19	0	0	0	3	0.0	–1	0	0.0	8:11	....	....	....	....	....	....	....	....	....

			Regular Season														Playoffs								
Season	**Club**	**League**	**GP**	**G**	**A**	**Pts**	**PIM**	**PP**	**SH**	**GW**	**S**	**%**	**+/-**	**TF**	**F%**	**Min**	**GP**	**G**	**A**	**Pts**	**PIM**	**PP**	**SH**	**GW**	**Min**
2004-05	St. John's	AHL	29	4	8	12	152	....	....	....	....	....	....	....	....	....	5	2	0	2	27	....	....	....	....
2005-06	Providence Bruins	AHL	74	13	14	27	132	....	....	....	....	....	....	....	....	....	5	2	0	2	38	....	....	....	....
	NHL Totals		**4**	**0**	**0**	**0**	**19**	**0**	**0**	**0**	**3**	**0.0**		**0**	**0.0**	**8:11**	....	....	....	....	....	....	....	....	....

OHL Second All-Star Team (1994)

Traded to **Montreal** by **Detroit** for cash, November 8, 1996. Signed as a free agent by **Pittsburgh**, July 18, 2001. Signed as a free agent by **Hartford** (AHL), September 9, 2003. Signed as a free agent by **NY Rangers**, December 11, 2003. Signed as a free agent by **Toronto**, July 29, 2004. Signed as a free agent by **Boston**, August 15, 2005.

MacKENZIE, Derek

(muh-KEHN-zee, DAIR-ihk) **ATL.**

Center. Shoots left. 5'11", 180 lbs. Born, Sudbury, Ont., June 11, 1981. Atlanta's 6th choice, 128th overall, in 1999 Entry Draft.

Season	Club	League	GP	G	A	Pts	PIM	PP	SH	GW	S	%	+/-	TF	F%	Min	GP	G	A	Pts	PIM	PP	SH	GW	Min
1996-97	Rayside-Balfour	NOJHA	40	23	32	55	40	....	....	....	....	....	....	....	....	....	....	....	....	....	....	....	....	....	....
1997-98	Sudbury Wolves	OHL	59	9	11	20	26	....	....	....	....	....	....	....	....	....	....	....	....	....	....	....	....	....	....
1998-99	Sudbury Wolves	OHL	68	22	65	87	74	....	....	....	....	....	....	....	....	....	4	2	4	6	2	....	....	....	....
99-2000	Sudbury Wolves	OHL	68	24	33	57	110	....	....	....	....	....	....	....	....	....	12	5	9	14	16	....	....	....	....
2000-01	Sudbury Wolves	OHL	62	40	49	89	89	....	....	....	....	....	....	....	....	....	12	6	8	14	16	....	....	....	....
2001-02	**Atlanta**	**NHL**	**1**	**0**	**0**	**0**	**2**	**0**	**0**	**0**	**1**	**0.0**	**–1**	**16**	**56.3**	**13:51**	....	....	....	....	....	....	....	....	....
	Chicago Wolves	AHL	68	13	12	25	80	....	....	....	....	....	....	....	....	....	25	4	2	6	20	....	....	....	....
2002-03	Chicago Wolves	AHL	80	14	18	32	97	....	....	....	....	....	....	....	....	....	9	0	0	0	4	....	....	....	....
2003-04	**Atlanta**	**NHL**	**12**	**0**	**1**	**1**	**10**	**0**	**0**	**0**	**7**	**0.0**	**0**	**63**	**46.0**	**6:38**	....	....	....	....	....	....	....	....	....
	Chicago Wolves	AHL	63	19	16	35	67	....	....	....	....	....	....	....	....	....	10	7	1	8	13	....	....	....	....
2004-05	Chicago Wolves	AHL	78	13	20	33	87	....	....	....	....	....	....	....	....	....	18	5	6	11	33	....	....	....	....
2005-06	**Atlanta**	**NHL**	**11**	**0**	**1**	**1**	**8**	**0**	**0**	**0**	**11**	**0.0**	**0**	**59**	**55.9**	**6:33**	....	....	....	....	....	....	....	....	....
	Chicago Wolves	AHL	36	10	12	22	48	....	....	....	....	....	....	....	....	....	....	....	....	....	....	....	....	....	....
	NHL Totals		**24**	**0**	**2**	**2**	**20**	**0**	**0**	**0**	**19**	**0.0**		**138**	**51.4**	**6:54**	....	....	....	....	....	....	....	....	....

MacLEAN, Don

(mihk-LAYN, DAWN) **PHX.**

Center. Shoots left. 6'2", 199 lbs. Born, Sydney, N.S., January 14, 1977. Los Angeles' 2nd choice, 33rd overall, in 1995 Entry Draft.

Season	Club	League	GP	G	A	Pts	PIM	PP	SH	GW	S	%	+/-	TF	F%	Min	GP	G	A	Pts	PIM	PP	SH	GW	Min
1992-93	Halifax Hawks	NSMHL	27	15	25	40	34	....	....	....	....	....	....	....	....	....	....	....	....	....	....	....	....	....	....
1993-94	Halifax Hawks	NSMHL	25	35	35	70	151	....	....	....	....	....	....	....	....	....	....	....	....	....	....	....	....	....	....
1994-95	Beauport	QMJHL	64	15	27	42	37	....	....	....	....	....	....	....	....	....	17	4	4	8	6	....	....	....	....
1995-96	Beauport	QMJHL	1	0	1	1	0	....	....	....	....	....	....	....	....	....	....	....	....	....	....	....	....	....	....
	Laval Titan	QMJHL	21	17	11	28	29	....	....	....	....	....	....	....	....	....	....	....	....	....	....	....	....	....	....
	Hull Olympiques	QMJHL	39	26	34	60	44	....	....	....	....	....	....	....	....	....	17	6	7	13	14	....	....	....	....
1996-97	Hull Olympiques	QMJHL	69	34	47	81	67	....	....	....	....	....	....	....	....	....	14	11	10	21	39	....	....	....	....
1997-98	**Los Angeles**	**NHL**	**22**	**5**	**2**	**7**	**4**	**2**	**0**	**0**	**25**	**20.0**	**–1**	....	....	....	....	....	....	....	....	....	....	....	....
	Fredericton	AHL	39	9	5	14	32	....	....	....	....	....	....	....	....	....	4	1	3	4	2	....	....	....	....
1998-99	Springfield	AHL	41	5	14	19	31	....	....	....	....	....	....	....	....	....	....	....	....	....	....	....	....	....	....
	Grand Rapids	IHL	28	6	13	19	8	....	....	....	....	....	....	....	....	....	....	....	....	....	....	....	....	....	....
99-2000	Lowell	AHL	40	11	17	28	18	....	....	....	....	....	....	....	....	....	....	....	....	....	....	....	....	....	....
	St. John's	AHL	21	14	12	26	8	....	....	....	....	....	....	....	....	....	....	....	....	....	....	....	....	....	....
2000-01	**Toronto**	**NHL**	**3**	**0**	**1**	**1**	**2**	**0**	**0**	**0**	**2**	**0.0**	**–2**	**33**	**54.6**	**9:48**	....	....	....	....	....	....	....	....	....
	St. John's	AHL	61	26	34	60	48	....	....	....	....	....	....	....	....	....	4	2	1	3	2	....	....	....	....
2001-02	St. John's	AHL	75	33	*54	*87	49	....	....	....	....	....	....	....	....	....	9	5	5	10	6	....	....	....	....
	Toronto	**NHL**	....	....	....	....	....	....	....	....	....	....	....	....	....	....	**3**	**0**	**0**	**0**	**0**	**0**	**0**	**0**	**1:39**
2002-03	Syracuse Crunch	AHL	17	9	9	18	6	....	....	....	....	....	....	....	....	....	....	....	....	....	....	....	....	....	....
2003-04	**Columbus**	**NHL**	**4**	**1**	**0**	**1**	**0**	**0**	**0**	**0**	**10**	**10.0**	**–1**	**31**	**58.1**	**11:41**	....	....	....	....	....	....	....	....	....
	Syracuse Crunch	AHL	77	27	41	68	45	....	....	....	....	....	....	....	....	....	7	0	3	3	4	....	....	....	....
2004-05	Blues Espoo	Finland	51	22	21	43	46	....	....	....	....	....	....	....	....	....	....	....	....	....	....	....	....	....	....
2005-06	**Detroit**	**NHL**	**3**	**1**	**1**	**2**	**0**	**1**	**0**	**1**	**3**	**33.3**	**2**	**13**	**61.5**	**12:45**	....	....	....	....	....	....	....	....	....
	Grand Rapids	AHL	76	*56	32	88	63	....	....	....	....	....	....	....	....	....	14	6	2	8	8	....	....	....	....
	NHL Totals		**32**	**7**	**4**	**11**	**6**	**3**	**0**	**1**	**40**	**17.5**		**77**	**57.1**	**11:26**	**3**	**0**	**0**	**0**	**0**	**0**	**0**	**0**	**1:39**

John P. Sollenberger Trophy (Leading Scorer – AHL) (2002) • AHL First All-Star Team (2006) • Willie Marshall Award (Top Goal-scorer - AHL) (2006) (tied with Denis Hamel) • Les Cunningham Plaque (MVP-AHL) (2006)

Traded to **Toronto** by **Los Angeles** for Craig Charron, February 23, 2000. Signed as a free agent by **Columbus**, July 17, 2002. • Missed majority of 2002-03 season recovering from neck surgery, September 16, 2002. Signed as a free agent by **Espoo** (Finland), July 2, 2004. Signed as a free agent by **Detroit**, August 24, 2005. Signed as a free agent by **Phoenix**, July 17, 2006.

MacMILLAN, Jeff

(muhk-MIHL-uhn, JEHF)

Defense. Shoots left. 6'3", 210 lbs. Born, Durham, Ont., March 30, 1979. Dallas' 8th choice, 215th overall, in 1999 Entry Draft.

Season	Club	League	GP	G	A	Pts	PIM	PP	SH	GW	S	%	+/-	TF	F%	Min	GP	G	A	Pts	PIM	PP	SH	GW	Min
1995-96	Hanover Barons	OHA-C	29	7	13	20	26	....	....	....	....	....	....	....	....	....	....	....	....	....	....	....	....	....	....
1996-97	Oshawa Generals	OHL	39	0	4	4	15	....	....	....	....	....	....	....	....	....	15	0	0	0	4	....	....	....	....
1997-98	Oshawa Generals	OHL	64	3	12	15	72	....	....	....	....	....	....	....	....	....	7	0	3	3	11	....	....	....	....
1998-99	Oshawa Generals	OHL	65	3	18	21	109	....	....	....	....	....	....	....	....	....	15	3	6	9	28	....	....	....	....
99-2000	Michigan	IHL	53	0	3	3	54	....	....	....	....	....	....	....	....	....	....	....	....	....	....	....	....	....	....
	Fort Wayne	UHL	7	1	1	2	25	....	....	....	....	....	....	....	....	....	9	0	2	2	10	....	....	....	....
2000-01	Utah Grizzlies	IHL	81	5	15	20	105	....	....	....	....	....	....	....	....	....	....	....	....	....	....	....	....	....	....
2001-02	Utah Grizzlies	AHL	77	6	9	15	146	....	....	....	....	....	....	....	....	....	5	1	0	1	17	....	....	....	....
2002-03	Utah Grizzlies	AHL	78	8	7	15	132	....	....	....	....	....	....	....	....	....	2	0	0	0	6	....	....	....	....
2003-04	**Dallas**	**NHL**	**4**	**0**	**0**	**0**	**0**	**0**	**0**	**0**	**3**	**0.0**	**–2**	**0**	**0.0**	**8:19**	....	....	....	....	....	....	....	....	....
	Utah Grizzlies	AHL	73	4	6	10	108	....	....	....	....	....	....	....	....	....	....	....	....	....	....	....	....	....	....
2004-05	Hartford	AHL	71	2	5	7	136	....	....	....	....	....	....	....	....	....	6	0	0	0	4	....	....	....	....
2005-06	Syracuse Crunch	AHL	78	1	9	10	143	....	....	....	....	....	....	....	....	....	5	0	0	0	23	....	....	....	....
	NHL Totals		**4**	**0**	**0**	**0**	**0**	**0**	**0**	**0**	**3**	**0.0**		**0**	**0.0**	**8:19**	....	....	....	....	....	....	....	....	....

Signed as a free agent by **NY Rangers**, July 22, 2004. Signed as a free agent by **Columbus**, August 12, 2005.

MADDEN, John

(MA-dehn, JAWN) **N.J.**

Center. Shoots left. 5'11", 190 lbs. Born, Barrie, Ont., May 4, 1973.

Season	Club	League	GP	G	A	Pts	PIM	PP	SH	GW	S	%	+/-	TF	F%	Min	GP	G	A	Pts	PIM	PP	SH	GW	Min
1989-90	Alliston Hornets	OHA-C	31	24	25	49	26	....	....	....	....	....	....	....	....	....	....	....	....	....	....	....	....	....	....
1990-91	Alliston Hornets	OHA-C	14	15	21	36	10	....	....	....	....	....	....	....	....	....	....	....	....	....	....	....	....	....	....
	Barrie Colts	OHA-B	1	0	0	0	0	....	....	....	....	....	....	....	....	....	....	....	....	....	....	....	....	....	....
1991-92	Barrie Colts	OHA-B	42	50	54	104	46	....	....	....	....	....	....	....	....	....	13	10	9	19	14	....	....	....	....
1992-93	Barrie Colts	COJHL	43	49	75	124	62	....	....	....	....	....	....	....	....	....	....	....	....	....	....	....	....	....	....
1993-94	U. of Michigan	CCHA	36	6	11	17	14	....	....	....	....	....	....	....	....	....	....	....	....	....	....	....	....	....	....
1994-95	U. of Michigan	CCHA	39	21	22	43	8	....	....	....	....	....	....	....	....	....	....	....	....	....	....	....	....	....	....
1995-96	U. of Michigan	CCHA	43	27	30	57	45	....	....	....	....	....	....	....	....	....	....	....	....	....	....	....	....	....	....
1996-97	U. of Michigan	CCHA	42	26	37	63	56	....	....	....	....	....	....	....	....	....	....	....	....	....	....	....	....	....	....
1997-98	Albany River Rats	AHL	74	20	36	56	40	....	....	....	....	....	....	....	....	....	13	3	13	16	14	....	....	....	....
1998-99	**New Jersey**	**NHL**	**4**	**0**	**1**	**1**	**0**	**0**	**0**	**0**	**4**	**0.0**	**–2**	**0**	**0.0**	**9:13**	....	....	....	....	....	....	....	....	....
	Albany River Rats	AHL	75	38	60	98	44	....	....	....	....	....	....	....	....	....	5	2	2	4	6	....	....	....	....
99-2000 ♦	**New Jersey**	**NHL**	**74**	**16**	**9**	**25**	**6**	**0**	**6**	**3**	**115**	**13.9**	**7**	**770**	**47.5**	**11:40**	**20**	**3**	**4**	**7**	**0**	**0**	**1**	**2**	**15:30**
2000-01	**New Jersey**	**NHL**	**80**	**23**	**15**	**38**	**12**	**0**	**3**	**4**	**163**	**14.1**	**24**	**974**	**46.6**	**15:35**	**25**	**4**	**3**	**7**	**6**	**0**	**0**	**0**	**15:15**
2001-02	**New Jersey**	**NHL**	**82**	**15**	**8**	**23**	**25**	**0**	**0**	**2**	**170**	**8.8**	**6**	**1001**	**47.0**	**15:36**	**6**	**0**	**0**	**0**	**0**	**0**	**0**	**0**	**17:25**
2002-03 ♦	**New Jersey**	**NHL**	**80**	**19**	**22**	**41**	**26**	**2**	**2**	**3**	**207**	**9.2**	**13**	**1502**	**50.9**	**18:18**	**24**	**6**	**10**	**16**	**2**	**2**	**1**	**1**	**19:38**
2003-04	**New Jersey**	**NHL**	**80**	**12**	**23**	**35**	**22**	**1**	**1**	**1**	**210**	**5.7**	**7**	**1377**	**53.3**	**17:17**	**5**	**0**	**0**	**0**	**0**	**0**	**0**	**0**	**14:51**
2004-05	HIFK Helsinki	Finland	3	0	0	0	0	....	....	....	....	....	....	....	....	....	....	....	....	....	....	....	....	....	....
2005-06	**New Jersey**	**NHL**	**82**	**16**	**20**	**36**	**36**	**0**	**1**	**0**	**194**	**8.2**	**–7**	**1613**	**51.5**	**18:59**	**9**	**4**	**1**	**5**	**8**	**0**	**2**	**0**	**18:56**
	NHL Totals		**482**	**101**	**98**	**199**	**127**	**3**	**13**	**13**	**1063**	**9.5**		**7237**	**50.0**	**16:15**	**89**	**17**	**18**	**35**	**16**	**2**	**4**	**3**	**16:59**

CCHA First All-Star Team (1997) • NCAA West First All-American Team (1997) • Frank J. Selke Trophy (2001)

Signed as a free agent by **New Jersey**, June 26, 1997. Signed as a free agent by **HIFK Helsinki** (Finland), November 29, 2004.

MAIR, Adam

(MAIR, A-duhm) **BUF.**

Center. Shoots right. 6'2", 208 lbs. Born, Hamilton, Ont., February 15, 1979. Toronto's 2nd choice, 84th overall, in 1997 Entry Draft.

			Regular Season														Playoffs								
Season	Club	League	GP	G	A	Pts	PIM	PP	SH	GW	S	%	+/-	TF	F%	Min	GP	G	A	Pts	PIM	PP	SH	GW	Min
1994-95	Ohsweken	OHA-B	39	21	23	44	91	....	....	....	....	....	....	....	....	....	....	....	....	....	....	....	....	....	....
1995-96	Owen Sound	OHL	62	12	15	27	63	....	....	....	....	....	....	....	....	....	6	0	0	0	2	....	....	....	....
1996-97	Owen Sound	OHL	65	16	35	51	113	....	....	....	....	....	....	....	....	....	4	1	0	1	2	....	....	....	....
1997-98	Owen Sound	OHL	56	25	27	52	179	....	....	....	....	....	....	....	....	....	11	6	3	9	31	....	....	....	....
1998-99	Owen Sound	OHL	43	23	41	64	109	....	....	....	....	....	....	....	....	....	16	10	10	20	*47	....	....	....	....
	Toronto	**NHL**	....	....	....	....	....	....	....	....	....	....	....	....	....	....	**5**	**1**	**0**	**1**	**14**	**0**	**0**	**0**	**5:37**
	St. John's	AHL	....	....	....	....	....	....	....	....	....	....	....	....	....	....	3	1	0	1	6	....	....	....	....
99-2000	**Toronto**	**NHL**	**8**	**1**	**0**	**1**	**6**	**0**	**0**	**0**	**7**	**14.3**	**–1**	**9**	**33.3**	**11:33**	**5**	**0**	**0**	**0**	**8**	**0**	**0**	**0**	**10:15**
	St. John's	AHL	66	22	27	49	124	....	....	....	....	....	....	....	....	....	....	....	....	....	....	....	....	....	....
2000-01	**Toronto**	**NHL**	**16**	**0**	**2**	**2**	**14**	**0**	**0**	**0**	**17**	**0.0**	**3**	**56**	**51.8**	**9:00**	....	....	....	....	....	....	....	....	....
	St. John's	AHL	47	18	27	45	69	....	....	....	....	....	....	....	....	....	....	....	....	....	....	....	....	....	....
	Los Angeles	**NHL**	**10**	**0**	**0**	**0**	**6**	**0**	**0**	**0**	**5**	**0.0**	**–3**	**21**	**61.9**	**6:14**	....	....	....	....	....	....	....	....	....
2001-02	**Los Angeles**	**NHL**	**18**	**1**	**1**	**2**	**57**	**0**	**0**	**0**	**10**	**10.0**	**1**	**31**	**58.1**	**7:11**	....	....	....	....	....	....	....	....	....
	Manchester	AHL	27	10	9	19	48	....	....	....	....	....	....	....	....	....	5	5	1	6	10	....	....	....	....
2002-03	**Buffalo**	**NHL**	**79**	**6**	**11**	**17**	**146**	**0**	**1**	**1**	**83**	**7.2**	**–4**	**572**	**51.2**	**10:37**	....	....	....	....	....	....	....	....	....
2003-04	**Buffalo**	**NHL**	**81**	**6**	**14**	**20**	**146**	**1**	**0**	**1**	**82**	**7.3**	**–3**	**340**	**45.9**	**9:38**	....	....	....	....	....	....	....	....	....
2004-05			DID NOT PLAY																						
2005-06	**Buffalo**	**NHL**	**40**	**2**	**5**	**7**	**47**	**0**	**0**	**0**	**40**	**5.0**	**–2**	**12**	**41.7**	**7:59**	**3**	**0**	**0**	**0**	**0**	**0**	**0**	**0**	**9:17**
	NHL Totals		**252**	**16**	**33**	**49**	**422**	**1**	**1**	**2**	**244**	**6.6**		**1041**	**49.7**	**9:24**	**13**	**1**	**0**	**1**	**22**	**0**	**0**	**0**	**8:14**

Traded to **Los Angeles** by **Toronto** with Toronto's 2nd round choice (Mike Cammalleri) in 2001 Entry Draft for Aki Berg, March 13, 2001. Traded to **Buffalo** by **Los Angeles** with Los Angeles' 5th round choice (Thomas Morrow) in 2003 Entry Draft for Erik Rasmussen, July 24, 2002. • Missed majority of 2005-06 season recovering from groin injury suffered in training camp (September, 2005) and head injury suffered in game vs. Phoenix (January 12, 2006).

MAJESKY, Ivan

(migh-EHV-skee, ee-VAHN)

Defense. Shoots right. 6'5", 230 lbs. Born, Banska Bystrica, Czech., September 2, 1976. Florida's 12th choice, 267th overall, in 2001 Entry Draft.

Season	Club	League	GP	G	A	Pts	PIM	PP	SH	GW	S	%	+/-	TF	F%	Min	GP	G	A	Pts	PIM	PP	SH	GW	Min
1995-96	B. Bystrica	Slovakia	17	0	0	0	18	....	....	....	....	....	....	....	....	....	....	....	....	....	....	....	....	....	....
1996-97	B. Bystrica	Slovakia	49	2	4	6	....	....	....	....	....	....	....	....	....	....	....	....	....	....	....	....	....	....	....
1997-98	B. Bystrica	Slovak-2	43	6	7	13	50	....	....	....	....	....	....	....	....	....	....	....	....	....	....	....	....	....	....
1998-99	B. Bystrica	Slovakia	48	7	7	14	68	....	....	....	....	....	....	....	....	....	....	....	....	....	....	....	....	....	....
	HKm Zvolen	Slovakia	....	....	....	....	....	....	....	....	....	....	....	....	....	....	6	0	2	2	2	....	....	....	....
99-2000	HKm Zvolen	Slovakia	51	7	9	16	68	....	....	....	....	....	....	....	....	....	10	0	4	4	2	....	....	....	....
2000-01	Ilves Tampere	Finland	54	2	14	16	99	....	....	....	....	....	....	....	....	....	9	0	1	1	6	....	....	....	....
2001-02	Ilves Tampere	Finland	44	6	6	12	84	....	....	....	....	....	....	....	....	....	....	....	....	....	....	....	....	....	....
	Slovakia	Olympics	4	0	1	1	4	....	....	....	....	....	....	....	....	....	....	....	....	....	....	....	....	....	....
2002-03	**Florida**	**NHL**	**82**	**4**	**8**	**12**	**92**	**0**	**0**	**2**	**52**	**7.7**	**–18**	**0**	**0.0**	**20:53**	....	....	....	....	....	....	....	....	....
2003-04	**Atlanta**	**NHL**	**63**	**3**	**7**	**10**	**76**	**0**	**0**	**0**	**35**	**8.6**	**–7**	**2**	**50.0**	**14:28**	....	....	....	....	....	....	....	....	....
2004-05	HC Sparta Praha	CzRep	28	2	6	8	40	....	....	....	....	....	....	....	....	....	5	2	1	3	6	....	....	....	....
2005-06	**Washington**	**NHL**	**57**	**1**	**8**	**9**	**66**	**0**	**1**	**0**	**35**	**2.9**	**–2**	**0**	**0.0**	**17:19**	....	....	....	....	....	....	....	....	....
	Slovakia	Olympics	6	0	0	0	4	....	....	....	....	....	....	....	....	....	....	....	....	....	....	....	....	....	....
	NHL Totals		**202**	**8**	**23**	**31**	**234**	**0**	**1**	**2**	**122**	**6.6**		**2**	**50.0**	**17:53**	....	....	....	....	....	....	....	....	....

Traded to **Atlanta** by **Florida** for Atlanta's 2nd round choice (Kamil Kreps) in 2003 Entry Draft, June 21, 2003. Signed as a free agent by **Sparta Praha** (CzRep), November 12, 2004. Signed as a free agent by **Washington**, August 10, 2005.

MALAKHOV, Vladimir

(mah-LAH-kahf, vla-DIH-meer) **N.J.**

Defense. Shoots left. 6'4", 230 lbs. Born, Sverdlovsk, USSR, August 30, 1968. NY Islanders' 12th choice, 191st overall, in 1989 Entry Draft.

Season	Club	League	GP	G	A	Pts	PIM	PP	SH	GW	S	%	+/-	TF	F%	Min	GP	G	A	Pts	PIM	PP	SH	GW	Min
1986-87	Spartak Moscow	USSR	22	0	1	1	12	....	....	....	....	....	....	....	....	....	....	....	....	....	....	....	....	....	....
1987-88	Spartak Moscow	USSR	28	2	2	4	26	....	....	....	....	....	....	....	....	....	....	....	....	....	....	....	....	....	....
1988-89	CSKA Moscow	USSR	34	6	2	8	16	....	....	....	....	....	....	....	....	....	....	....	....	....	....	....	....	....	....
1989-90	CSKA Moscow	USSR	48	2	10	12	34	....	....	....	....	....	....	....	....	....	....	....	....	....	....	....	....	....	....
1990-91	CSKA Moscow	USSR	46	5	13	18	22	....	....	....	....	....	....	....	....	....	....	....	....	....	....	....	....	....	....
1991-92	CSKA Moscow	CIS	40	1	9	10	12	....	....	....	....	....	....	....	....	....	....	....	....	....	....	....	....	....	....
	Russia	Olympics	8	3	0	3	4	....	....	....	....	....	....	....	....	....	....	....	....	....	....	....	....	....	....
1992-93	**NY Islanders**	**NHL**	**64**	**14**	**38**	**52**	**59**	**7**	**0**	**0**	**178**	**7.9**	**14**				**17**	**3**	**6**	**9**	**12**	**0**	**0**	**0**	
	Capital District	AHL	3	2	1	3	11	....	....	....	....	....	....	....	....	....	....	....	....	....	....	....	....	....	....
1993-94	**NY Islanders**	**NHL**	**76**	**10**	**47**	**57**	**80**	**4**	**0**	**2**	**235**	**4.3**	**29**				**4**	**0**	**0**	**0**	**6**	**0**	**0**	**0**	
1994-95	**NY Islanders**	**NHL**	**26**	**3**	**13**	**16**	**32**	**1**	**0**	**0**	**61**	**4.9**	**–1**				....	....	....	....	....	....	....	....	....
	Montreal	**NHL**	**14**	**1**	**4**	**5**	**14**	**0**	**0**	**0**	**30**	**3.3**	**–2**				....	....	....	....	....	....	....	....	....
1995-96	**Montreal**	**NHL**	**61**	**5**	**23**	**28**	**79**	**2**	**0**	**0**	**122**	**4.1**	**7**				....	....	....	....	....	....	....	....	....
1996-97	**Montreal**	**NHL**	**65**	**10**	**20**	**30**	**43**	**5**	**0**	**1**	**177**	**5.6**	**3**				**5**	**0**	**0**	**0**	**6**	**0**	**0**	**0**	
1997-98	**Montreal**	**NHL**	**74**	**13**	**31**	**44**	**70**	**8**	**0**	**2**	**166**	**7.8**	**16**				**9**	**3**	**4**	**7**	**10**	**2**	**0**	**0**	
1998-99	**Montreal**	**NHL**	**62**	**13**	**21**	**34**	**77**	**8**	**0**	**3**	**143**	**9.1**	**–7**	**0**	**0.0**	**23:29**	....	....	....	....	....	....	....	....	....
99-2000	**Montreal**	**NHL**	**7**	**0**	**0**	**0**	**4**	**0**	**0**	**0**	**7**	**0.0**	**0**	**0**	**0.0**	**21:20**	....	....	....	....	....	....	....	....	....
	♦ **New Jersey**	**NHL**	**17**	**1**	**4**	**5**	**19**	**1**	**0**	**1**	**11**	**9.1**	**1**	**0**	**0.0**	**20:18**	**23**	**1**	**4**	**5**	**18**	**1**	**0**	**0**	**19:31**
2000-01	**NY Rangers**	**NHL**	**3**	**0**	**2**	**2**	**4**	**0**	**0**	**0**	**6**	**0.0**	**0**	**0**	**0.0**	**19:07**	....	....	....	....	....	....	....	....	....
2001-02	**NY Rangers**	**NHL**	**81**	**6**	**22**	**28**	**83**	**1**	**0**	**0**	**145**	**4.1**	**10**	**1**	**100.0**	**22:48**	....	....	....	....	....	....	....	....	....
	Russia	Olympics	6	1	3	4	4	....	....	....	....	....	....	....	....	....	....	....	....	....	....	....	....	....	....
2002-03	**NY Rangers**	**NHL**	**71**	**3**	**14**	**17**	**52**	**1**	**0**	**0**	**131**	**2.3**	**–7**	**0**	**0.0**	**21:24**	....	....	....	....	....	....	....	....	....
2003-04	**NY Rangers**	**NHL**	**56**	**3**	**15**	**18**	**53**	**1**	**0**	**0**	**83**	**3.6**	**–5**	**1**	**100.0**	**19:37**	....	....	....	....	....	....	....	....	....
	Philadelphia	**NHL**	**6**	**0**	**1**	**1**	**2**	**0**	**0**	**0**	**12**	**0.0**	**–1**	**0**	**0.0**	**22:57**	**17**	**1**	**5**	**6**	**12**	**0**	**0**	**0**	**24:56**
2004-05			DID NOT PLAY																						
2005-06	**New Jersey**	**NHL**	**29**	**4**	**5**	**9**	**26**	**3**	**0**	**0**	**43**	**9.3**	**–9**	**0**	**0.0**	**20:44**	....	....	....	....	....	....	....	....	....
	NHL Totals		**712**	**86**	**260**	**346**	**697**	**42**	**0**	**9**	**1550**	**5.5**		**2**	**100.0**	**21:43**	**75**	**8**	**19**	**27**	**64**	**3**	**0**	**0**	**21:49**

NHL All-Rookie Team (1993)

Traded to **Montreal** by **NY Islanders** with Pierre Turgeon for Kirk Muller, Mathieu Schneider and Craig Darby, April 5, 1995. • Missed majority of 1999-2000 season recovering from knee injury suffered in exhibition game vs. Boston, September 27, 1999. Traded to **New Jersey** by **Montreal** for Sheldon Souray, Josh DeWolf and New Jersey's 2nd round choice (later traded to Washington – later traded to Tampa Bay – Tampa Bay selected Andreas Holmqvist) in 2001 Entry Draft, March 1, 2000. Signed as a free agent by **NY Rangers**, July 10, 2000. • Missed majority of 2000-01 season recovering from knee injury suffered in game vs. Montreal, November 11, 2000. Traded to **Philadelphia** by **NY Rangers** for Rick Kozak and Philadelphia's 2nd round choice (later traded to Atlanta - Atlanta selected Ondrej Pavelec) in 2005 Entry Draft, March 8, 2004. Signed as a free agent by **New Jersey**, August 4, 2005. • Missed remainder of 2005-06 season after being suspended by New Jersey, December 19, 2005.

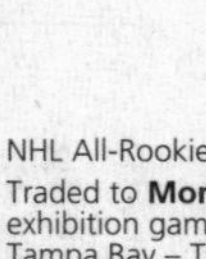

MALEC, Tomas

(MA-lehts, TAW-mahsh) **OTT.**

Defense. Shoots left. 6'2", 193 lbs. Born, Skalica, Czech., May 13, 1982. Florida's 4th choice, 64th overall, in 2001 Entry Draft.

Season	Club	League	GP	G	A	Pts	PIM	PP	SH	GW	S	%	+/-	TF	F%	Min	GP	G	A	Pts	PIM	PP	SH	GW	Min
99-2000	HK 36 Skalica Jr.	Slovak-Jr.	46	6	5	11	150	....	....	....	....	....	....	....	....	....	....	....	....	....	....	....	....	....	....
2000-01	Rimouski Oceanic	QMJHL	64	13	50	63	198	....	....	....	....	....	....	....	....	....	11	0	11	11	26	....	....	....	....
2001-02	Rimouski Oceanic	QMJHL	51	14	32	46	164	....	....	....	....	....	....	....	....	....	7	3	1	4	10	....	....	....	....
	Lowell	AHL	....	....	....	....	....	....	....	....	....	....	....	....	....	....	4	0	0	0	4	....	....	....	....
2002-03	**Carolina**	**NHL**	**41**	**0**	**2**	**2**	**43**	**0**	**0**	**0**	**30**	**0.0**	**–5**	**1**	**100.0**	**11:13**	....	....	....	....	....	....	....	....	....
	Lowell	AHL	30	0	4	4	50	....	....	....	....	....	....	....	....	....	....	....	....	....	....	....	....	....	....
2003-04	**Carolina**	**NHL**	**2**	**0**	**0**	**0**	**2**	**0**	**0**	**0**	**1**	**0.0**	**–1**	**0**	**0.0**	**9:32**	....	....	....	....	....	....	....	....	....
	Lowell	AHL	74	7	13	20	101	....	....	....	....	....	....	....	....	....	....	....	....	....	....	....	....	....	....
2004-05	Cincinnati	AHL	66	4	14	18	104	....	....	....	....	....	....	....	....	....	6	0	2	2	10	....	....	....	....
2005-06	**Ottawa**	**NHL**	**2**	**0**	**0**	**0**	**2**	**0**	**0**	**0**	**1**	**0.0**	**4**	**0**	**0.0**	**11:44**	....	....	....	....	....	....	....	....	....
	Binghamton	AHL	79	1	27	28	118	....	....	....	....	....	....	....	....	....	....	....	....	....	....	....	....	....	....
	NHL Totals		**45**	**0**	**2**	**2**	**47**	**0**	**0**	**0**	**32**	**0.0**		**1**	**100.0**	**11:10**	....	....	....	....	....	....	....	....	....

Traded to **Carolina** by **Florida** with Bret Hedican and Kevyn Adams for Sandis Ozolinsh and Byron Ritchie, January 16, 2002. Traded to **Anaheim** by **Carolina** with Carolina's 3rd round choice (Kyle Klubertanz) in 2004 Entry Draft for Martin Gerber, June 18, 2004. Signed as a free agent by **Ottawa**, August 19, 2005.

							Regular Season												Playoffs						
Season	Club	League	GP	G	A	Pts	PIM	PP	SH	GW	S	%	+/-	TF	F%	Min	GP	G	A	Pts	PIM	PP	SH	GW	Min

MALHOTRA, Manny (mal-HOH-truh, MAHN-ee) **CBJ**

Center. Shoots left. 6'2", 215 lbs. Born, Mississauga, Ont., May 18, 1980. NY Rangers' 1st choice, 7th overall, in 1998 Entry Draft.

Season	Club	League	GP	G	A	Pts	PIM	PP	SH	GW	S	%	+/-	TF	F%	Min	GP	G	A	Pts	PIM	PP	SH	GW	Min
1995-96	Mississauga Reps	MTHL	54	27	44	71	62	....	....	....	....	....	....	....	....	....	....	....	....	....	....	....	....	....	....
1996-97	Guelph Storm	OHL	61	16	28	44	26	....	....	....	....	....	....	....	....	....	18	7	7	14	11	....	....	....	....
1997-98	Guelph Storm	OHL	57	16	35	51	29	....	....	....	....	....	....	....	....	....	12	7	6	13	8	....	....	....	....
1998-99	**NY Rangers**	**NHL**	73	8	8	16	13	1	0	2	61	13.1	–2	588	43.9	8:36	....	....	....	....	....	....	....	....	....
99-2000	**NY Rangers**	**NHL**	27	0	0	0	4	0	0	0	18	0.0	–6	132	44.7	6:42	....	....	....	....	....	....	....	....	....
	Guelph Storm	OHL	5	2	2	4	4	....	....	....	....	....	....	....	....	....	6	0	2	2	4	....	....	....	....
	Hartford	AHL	12	1	5	6	2	....	....	....	....	....	....	....	....	....	23	1	2	3	10	....	....	....	....
2000-01	Hartford	AHL	28	5	6	11	69	....	....	....	....	....	....	....	....	....	5	0	0	0	0	....	....	....	....
	NY Rangers	**NHL**	50	4	8	12	31	0	0	2	46	8.7	–10	248	44.4	9:03	....	....	....	....	....	....	....	....	....
2001-02	**NY Rangers**	**NHL**	56	7	6	13	42	0	1	1	41	17.1	–1	310	42.9	10:14	....	....	....	....	....	....	....	....	....
	Dallas	**NHL**	16	1	0	1	5	0	0	0	19	5.3	–3	121	48.8	10:37	....	....	....	....	....	....	....	....	....
2002-03	**Dallas**	**NHL**	59	3	7	10	42	0	0	1	62	4.8	–2	447	47.0	9:22	5	1	0	1	0	0	0	0	8:13
2003-04	**Dallas**	**NHL**	9	0	0	0	4	0	0	0	4	0.0	–2	13	61.5	7:48	....	....	....	....	....	....	....	....	....
	Columbus	**NHL**	56	12	13	25	24	1	0	2	103	11.7	–5	840	53.8	14:47	....	....	....	....	....	....	....	....	....
2004-05	Ljubljana	Slovenia	13	6	7	13	20	....	....	....	....	....	....	....	....	....	....	....	....	....	....	....	....	....	....
	Ljubljana	Interliga	13	7	7	14	16	....	....	....	....	....	....	....	....	....	....	....	....	....	....	....	....	....	....
	HV 71 Jonkoping	Sweden	20	5	2	7	16	....	....	....	....	....	....	....	....	....	....	....	....	....	....	....	....	....	....
2005-06	**Columbus**	**NHL**	58	10	21	31	41	1	1	0	102	9.8	1	827	56.4	16:21	....	....	....	....	....	....	....	....	....
	NHL Totals		404	45	63	108	206	3	2	8	456	9.9		3526	49.8	10:54	5	1	0	1	0	0	0	0	8:13

Memorial Cup Tournament All-Star Team (1998) • George Parsons Trophy (Memorial Cup Tournament Most Sportsmanlike Player) (1998)

Traded to **Dallas** by **NY Rangers** with Barrett Heisten for Martin Rucinsky and Roman Lyashenko, March 12, 2002. Claimed on waivers by **Columbus** from **Dallas**, November 21, 2003. Signed as a free agent by **Ljubljana** (Slovenia), October 8, 2004. Signed as a free agent by **Jonkoping** (Sweden), December 20, 2004.

MALIK, Marek (MAW-leck, MAIR-ehk) **NYR**

Defense. Shoots left. 6'6", 238 lbs. Born, Ostrava, Czech., June 24, 1975. Hartford's 2nd choice, 72nd overall, in 1993 Entry Draft.

Season	Club	League	GP	G	A	Pts	PIM	PP	SH	GW	S	%	+/-	TF	F%	Min	GP	G	A	Pts	PIM	PP	SH	GW	Min
1992-93	TJ Vitkovice Jr.	Czech-Jr.	20	5	10	15	16	....	....	....	....	....	....	....	....	....	3	0	1	1	0	....	....	....	....
1993-94	HC Vitkovice	CzRep	38	3	3	6	0	....	....	....	....	....	....	....	....	....	....	....	....	....	....	....	....	....	....
1994-95	Springfield	AHL	58	11	30	41	91	....	....	....	....	....	....	....	....	....	....	....	....	....	....	....	....	....	....
	Hartford	**NHL**	1	0	1	1	0	0	0	0	0	0.0	1	....	....	....	....	....	....	....	....	....	....	....	....
1995-96	**Hartford**	**NHL**	7	0	0	0	4	0	0	0	2	0.0	–3	....	....	....	8	1	3	4	20	....	....	....	....
	Springfield	AHL	68	8	14	22	135	....	....	....	....	....	....	....	....	....	....	....	....	....	....	....	....	....	....
1996-97	**Hartford**	**NHL**	47	1	5	6	50	0	0	1	33	3.0	5	....	....	....	....	....	....	....	....	....	....	....	....
	Springfield	AHL	3	0	3	3	4	....	....	....	....	....	....	....	....	....	....	....	....	....	....	....	....	....	....
1997-98	Malmo	Sweden	37	1	5	6	21	....	....	....	....	....	....	....	....	....	....	....	....	....	....	....	....	....	....
1998-99	HC Vitkovice	CzRep	1	1	0	1	6	....	....	....	....	....	....	....	....	....	....	....	....	....	....	....	....	....	....
	Carolina	**NHL**	52	2	9	11	36	1	0	0	36	5.6	–6	0	0.0	21:14	4	0	0	0	4	0	0	0	11:26
	New Haven	AHL	21	2	8	10	28	....	....	....	....	....	....	....	....	....	....	....	....	....	....	....	....	....	....
99-2000	**Carolina**	**NHL**	57	4	10	14	63	0	0	1	57	7.0	13	0	0.0	18:00	....	....	....	....	....	....	....	....	....
2000-01	**Carolina**	**NHL**	61	6	14	20	34	1	0	1	72	8.3	–4	0	0.0	19:36	3	0	0	0	6	0	0	0	19:37
2001-02	**Carolina**	**NHL**	82	4	19	23	88	0	0	0	91	4.4	8	0	0.0	20:29	23	1	3	18	0	0	0	0	18:09
2002-03	**Carolina**	**NHL**	10	0	2	2	16	0	0	0	9	0.0	–3	0	0.0	17:02	....	....	....	....	....	....	....	....	....
	Vancouver	**NHL**	69	7	11	18	52	1	1	2	68	10.3	23	1	0.0	18:06	14	1	1	2	10	1	0	0	16:06
2003-04	**Vancouver**	**NHL**	78	3	16	19	45	0	0	0	61	4.9	35	1	0.0	18:05	7	0	0	0	10	0	0	0	20:03
2004-05	Vitkovice	CzRep	42	1	9	10	50	....	....	....	....	....	....	....	....	....	7	0	0	0	37	....	....	....	....
2005-06	**NY Rangers**	**NHL**	74	2	16	18	78	0	0	2	70	2.9	28	0	0.0	20:26	4	0	1	1	6	0	0	0	20:43
	Czech Republic	Olympics	8	0	0	0	8	....	....	....	....	....	....	....	....	....	....	....	....	....	....	....	....	....	....
	NHL Totals		538	29	103	132	466	3	1	7	499	5.8		2	0.0	19:21	55	1	5	6	54	1	0	0	17:39

Transferred to **Carolina** after **Hartford** franchise relocated, June 25, 1997. Traded to **Vancouver** by **Carolina** with Darren Langdon for Jan Hlavac and Harold Druken, November 1, 2002. Signed as a free agent by **Vitkovice** (CzRep), September 17, 2004. Signed as a free agent by **NY Rangers**, August 2, 2005.

MALONE, Ryan (MA-lohn, RIGH-yan) **PIT.**

Left wing. Shoots left. 6'4", 216 lbs. Born, Pittsburgh, PA, December 1, 1979. Pittsburgh's 5th choice, 115th overall, in 1999 Entry Draft.

Season	Club	League	GP	G	A	Pts	PIM	PP	SH	GW	S	%	+/-	TF	F%	Min	GP	G	A	Pts	PIM	PP	SH	GW	Min
1997-98	Shat.-St. Mary's	High-MN	50	41	44	85	69	....	....	....	....	....	....	....	....	....	....	....	....	....	....	....	....	....	....
1998-99	Omaha Lancers	USHL	51	14	22	36	81	....	....	....	....	....	....	....	....	....	12	2	4	6	23	....	....	....	....
99-2000	St. Cloud State	WCHA	38	9	21	30	68	....	....	....	....	....	....	....	....	....	....	....	....	....	....	....	....	....	....
2000-01	St. Cloud State	WCHA	36	7	18	25	52	....	....	....	....	....	....	....	....	....	....	....	....	....	....	....	....	....	....
2001-02	St. Cloud State	WCHA	41	24	25	49	76	....	....	....	....	....	....	....	....	....	....	....	....	....	....	....	....	....	....
2002-03	St. Cloud State	WCHA	27	16	20	36	85	....	....	....	....	....	....	....	....	....	....	....	....	....	....	....	....	....	....
	Wilkes-Barre	AHL	3	0	1	1	2	....	....	....	....	....	....	....	....	....	....	....	....	....	....	....	....	....	....
2003-04	**Pittsburgh**	**NHL**	81	22	21	43	64	5	3	4	139	15.8	–23	230	27.4	18:54	....	....	....	....	....	....	....	....	....
2004-05	Blues Espoo	Finland	9	2	1	3	36	....	....	....	....	....	....	....	....	....	6	4	4	8	36	....	....	....	....
	SV Renon	Italy	10	6	2	8	20	....	....	....	....	....	....	....	....	....	1	0	0	0	2	....	....	....	....
	HC Ambri-Piotta	Swiss	....	....	....	....	....	....	....	....	....	....	....	....	....	....	....	....	....	....	....	....	....	....	....
2005-06	**Pittsburgh**	**NHL**	77	22	22	44	63	10	5	1	153	14.4	–22	728	39.6	18:06	....	....	....	....	....	....	....	....	....
	NHL Totals		158	44	43	87	127	15	8	5	292	15.1		958	36.6	18:30	....	....	....	....	....	....	....	....	....

NHL All-Rookie Team (2004)

Signed as a free agent by **Espoo** (Finland), September 29, 2004. Signed as a free agent by **Renon** (Italy), January 3, 2005. Signed as a free agent by **Ambri-Piotta** (Swiss), February 25, 2005.

MALTBY, Kirk (MAHLT-bee, KUHRK) **DET.**

Right wing. Shoots right. 6', 180 lbs. Born, Guelph, Ont., December 22, 1972. Edmonton's 4th choice, 65th overall, in 1992 Entry Draft.

Season	Club	League	GP	G	A	Pts	PIM	PP	SH	GW	S	%	+/-	TF	F%	Min	GP	G	A	Pts	PIM	PP	SH	GW	Min
1988-89	Cambridge	OHA-B	48	28	18	46	138	....	....	....	....	....	....	....	....	....	....	....	....	....	....	....	....	....	....
1989-90	Owen Sound	OHL	61	12	15	27	90	....	....	....	....	....	....	....	....	....	12	1	6	7	15	....	....	....	....
1990-91	Owen Sound	OHL	66	34	32	66	100	....	....	....	....	....	....	....	....	....	5	3	3	6	18	....	....	....	....
1991-92	Owen Sound	OHL	66	50	41	91	99	....	....	....	....	....	....	....	....	....	16	3	3	6	45	....	....	....	....
1992-93	Cape Breton	AHL	73	22	23	45	130	....	....	....	....	....	....	....	....	....	....	....	....	....	....	....	....	....	....
1993-94	**Edmonton**	**NHL**	68	11	8	19	74	0	1	1	89	12.4	–2	....	....	....	....	....	....	....	....	....	....	....	....
1994-95	**Edmonton**	**NHL**	47	8	3	11	49	0	2	1	73	11.0	–11	....	....	....	....	....	....	....	....	....	....	....	....
1995-96	**Edmonton**	**NHL**	49	2	6	8	61	0	0	1	51	3.9	–16	....	....	....	....	....	....	....	....	....	....	....	....
	Cape Breton	AHL	4	1	2	3	6	....	....	....	....	....	....	....	....	....	....	....	....	....	....	....	....	....	....
	Detroit	**NHL**	6	1	0	1	6	0	0	0	4	25.0	0	....	....	....	8	0	1	1	4	0	0	0	....
1996-97 ◆	**Detroit**	**NHL**	66	3	5	8	75	0	0	0	62	4.8	3	....	....	....	20	5	2	7	24	0	1	1	....
1997-98 ◆	**Detroit**	**NHL**	65	14	9	23	89	2	1	3	106	13.2	11	....	....	....	22	3	1	4	30	0	1	0	....
1998-99	**Detroit**	**NHL**	53	8	6	14	34	0	1	2	76	10.5	–6	10	40.0	13:13	10	1	0	1	8	0	0	1	11:32
99-2000	**Detroit**	**NHL**	41	6	8	14	24	0	2	1	71	8.5	1	2	50.0	13:30	8	0	1	1	4	0	0	0	13:45
2000-01	**Detroit**	**NHL**	79	12	7	19	22	1	3	3	119	10.1	16	14	35.7	14:17	6	0	0	0	2	0	0	0	15:23
2001-02 ◆	**Detroit**	**NHL**	82	9	15	24	40	0	1	5	108	8.3	15	38	47.4	13:23	23	3	3	6	32	0	2	0	16:34
2002-03	**Detroit**	**NHL**	82	14	23	37	91	0	4	1	116	12.1	17	43	37.2	16:10	4	0	0	4	0	0	0	0	17:18
2003-04	**Detroit**	**NHL**	79	14	19	33	80	1	4	4	123	11.4	24	30	43.3	16:16	12	1	3	4	11	0	0	0	17:34
2004-05			DID NOT PLAY																						
2005-06	**Detroit**	**NHL**	82	5	6	11	80	0	1	0	115	4.3	–9	22	50.0	13:44	6	1	2	3	4	0	0	1	13:02
	NHL Totals		799	107	115	222	725	4	20	22	1113	9.6		159	42.8	14:29	119	15	12	27	127	0	4	3	15:19

Traded to **Detroit** by **Edmonton** for Dan McGillis, March 20, 1996. • Missed majority of 1999-2000 season recovering from hernia injury suffered in game vs. Dallas, October 5, 1999.

MANLOW, Eric (MAN-low, AIR-ihk)

Center. Shoots left. 6', 180 lbs. Born, Belleville, Ont., April 7, 1975. Chicago's 2nd choice, 50th overall, in 1993 Entry Draft.

Season	Club	League	GP	G	A	Pts	PIM	PP	SH	GW	S	%	+/-	TF	F%	Min	GP	G	A	Pts	PIM	PP	SH	GW	Min
1990-91	Peterborough	OMHA	59	67	51	118	90	....	....	....	....	....	....	....	....	....	....	....	....	....	....	....	....	....	....
	Peterborough	OHA-B	1	0	0	0	0	....	....	....	....	....	....	....	....	....	....	....	....	....	....	....	....	....	....
1991-92	Kitchener Rangers	OHL	59	12	20	32	17	....	....	....	....	....	....	....	....	....	14	2	5	7	10	....	....	....	....
1992-93	Kitchener Rangers	OHL	53	26	21	47	31	....	....	....	....	....	....	....	....	....	4	0	1	1	2	....	....	....	....
1993-94	Kitchener Rangers	OHL	49	28	32	60	25	....	....	....	....	....	....	....	....	....	3	0	1	1	4	....	....	....	....
1994-95	Kitchener Rangers	OHL	44	25	29	54	26	....	....	....	....	....	....	....	....	....	....	....	....	....	....	....	....	....	....
	Detroit	OHL	16	4	16	20	11	....	....	....	....	....	....	....	....	....	21	11	10	21	18	....	....	....	....

			Regular Season														Playoffs								
Season	Club	League	GP	G	A	Pts	PIM	PP	SH	GW	S	%	+/-	TF	F%	Min	GP	G	A	Pts	PIM	PP	SH	GW	Min
1995-96	Indianapolis Ice	IHL	75	6	11	17	32	....	....	....	....	....	....	....	....	....	4	0	1	1	4	....	....	....	....
1996-97	Baltimore Bandits	AHL	36	6	6	12	13	....	....	....	....	....	....	....	....	....	3	0	0	0	0	....	....	....	....
	Columbus Chill	ECHL	32	18	18	36	20	....	....	....	....	....	....	....	....	....	....	....	....	....	....	....	....	....	....
1997-98	Indianapolis Ice	IHL	60	8	11	19	25	....	....	....	....	....	....	....	....	....	3	1	0	1	0	....	....	....	....
1998-99	Long Beach	IHL	51	9	19	28	30	....	....	....	....	....	....	....	....	....	8	0	0	0	8	....	....	....	....
	Florida Everblades	ECHL	18	8	15	23	11	....	....	....	....	....	....	....	....	....	....	....	....	....	....	....	....	....	....
99-2000	Florida Everblades	ECHL	26	14	24	38	24	....	....	....	....	....	....	....	....	....	....	....	....	....	....	....	....	....	....
	Providence Bruins	AHL	46	17	16	33	14	....	....	....	....	....	....	....	....	....	14	6	8	14	8	....	....	....	....
2000-01	**Boston**	**NHL**	**8**	**0**	**1**	**1**	**2**	**0**	**0**	**0**	**3**	**0.0**	**0**	**61**	**50.8**	**7:26**	....	....	....	....	....	....	....	....	....
	Providence Bruins	AHL	60	16	51	67	18	....	....	....	....	....	....	....	....	....	17	6	7	13	6	....	....	....	....
2001-02	**Boston**	**NHL**	**3**	**0**	**0**	**0**	**0**	**0**	**0**	**0**	**2**	**0.0**	**0**	**16**	**31.3**	**6:05**	....	....	....	....	....	....	....	....	....
	Providence Bruins	AHL	70	13	35	48	30	....	....	....	....	....	....	....	....	....	2	0	0	0	2	....	....	....	....
2002-03	**NY Islanders**	**NHL**	**8**	**2**	**1**	**3**	**4**	**1**	**0**	**0**	**7**	**28.6**	**2**	**84**	**54.8**	**12:27**	....	....	....	....	....	....	....	....	....
	Bridgeport	AHL	62	19	40	59	58	....	....	....	....	....	....	....	....	....	9	0	6	6	2	....	....	....	....
2003-04	**NY Islanders**	**NHL**	**18**	**0**	**2**	**2**	**2**	**0**	**0**	**0**	**10**	**0.0**	**–2**	**178**	**53.9**	**10:13**	....	....	....	....	....	....	....	....	....
	Bridgeport	AHL	40	8	27	35	16	....	....	....	....	....	....	....	....	....	1	0	0	0	2	....	....	....	....
2004-05	Grand Rapids	AHL	61	21	20	41	24	....	....	....	....	....	....	....	....	....	....	....	....	....	....	....	....	....	....
2005-06	Grand Rapids	AHL	80	25	47	72	44	....	....	....	....	....	....	....	....	....	16	3	3	6	12	....	....	....	....
	NHL Totals		**37**	**2**	**4**	**6**	**8**	**1**	**0**	**0**	**22**	**9.1**		**339**	**52.5**	**9:46**	....	....	....	....	....	....	....	....	....

Signed as a free agent by **Providence** (AHL), January 24, 2000. Signed as a free agent by **Boston**, July 11, 2000. Signed as a free agent by **NY Islanders**, July 21, 2002. Signed as a free agent by **Detroit**, July 21, 2004. Signed as a free agent by **Hamilton** (AHL), July 10, 2006.

MANNING, Paul

(MAN-nihng, PAWL) **CBJ**

Defense. Shoots left. 6'4", 205 lbs. Born, Red Deer, Alta., April 15, 1979. Calgary's 3rd choice, 62nd overall, in 1998 Entry Draft.

1995-96	Red Deer	AMHL	32	8	32	40	....	....	....	....	....	....	....	....	....	....	....	....	....	....	....	....	....	....	....
1996-97	Red Deer Vipers	HJHL	36	9	33	42	....	....	....	....	....	....	....	....	....	....	....	....	....	....	....	....	....	....	....
1997-98	Colorado College	WCHA	30	1	5	6	16	....	....	....	....	....	....	....	....	....	....	....	....	....	....	....	....	....	....
1998-99	Colorado College	WCHA	41	3	10	13	75	....	....	....	....	....	....	....	....	....	....	....	....	....	....	....	....	....	....
99-2000	Colorado College	WCHA	39	6	17	23	26	....	....	....	....	....	....	....	....	....	....	....	....	....	....	....	....	....	....
2000-01	Colorado College	WCHA	34	2	28	30	48	....	....	....	....	....	....	....	....	....	....	....	....	....	....	....	....	....	....
2001-02	Syracuse Crunch	AHL	35	1	4	5	16	....	....	....	....	....	....	....	....	....	....	....	....	....	....	....	....	....	....
	Elmira Jackals	UHL	1	1	0	1	0	....	....	....	....	....	....	....	....	....	....	....	....	....	....	....	....	....	....
2002-03	**Columbus**	**NHL**	**8**	**0**	**0**	**0**	**2**	**0**	**0**	**0**	**4**	**0.0**	**0**	**0**	**0.0**	**13:02**	....	....	....	....	....	....	....	....	....
	Syracuse Crunch	AHL	52	2	5	7	37	....	....	....	....	....	....	....	....	....	....	....	....	....	....	....	....	....	....
2003-04	Hamburg Freezers	Germany	50	2	2	4	67	....	....	....	....	....	....	....	....	....	11	0	3	3	6	....	....	....	....
2004-05	Hamburg Freezers	Germany	36	4	6	10	90	....	....	....	....	....	....	....	....	....	6	1	0	1	10	....	....	....	....
2005-06	Hamburg Freezers	Germany	49	4	11	15	56	....	....	....	....	....	....	....	....	....	5	0	0	0	35	....	....	....	....
	NHL Totals		**8**	**0**	**0**	**0**	**2**	**0**	**0**	**0**	**4**	**0.0**		**0**	**0.0**	**13:02**	....	....	....	....	....	....	....	....	....

WCHA Second All-Star Team (2001)

Rights traded to **Columbus** by **Calgary** for Buffalo's 5th round choice (previously acquired, later traded to Detroit – Detroit selected Andreas Jamtin) in 2001 Entry Draft, June 24, 2001. Signed as a free agent by **Hamburg** (Germany), August 9, 2003.

MAPLETOFT, Justin

(MAPLE-tawft, JUHS-tihn) **NYI**

Center. Shoots left. 6'1", 180 lbs. Born, Lloydminster, Sask., January 11, 1981. NY Islanders' 9th choice, 130th overall, in 1999 Entry Draft.

1996-97	Calgary Royals	AMHL	36	25	36	51	....	....	....	....	....	....	....	....	....	....	....	....	....	....	....	....	....	....	....
	Red Deer Rebels	WHL	2	0	0	0	0	....	....	....	....	....	....	....	....	....	....	....	....	....	....	....	....	....	....
1997-98	Red Deer Rebels	WHL	65	9	4	13	41	....	....	....	....	....	....	....	....	....	....	....	....	....	....	....	....	....	....
1998-99	Red Deer Rebels	WHL	72	24	22	46	81	....	....	....	....	....	....	....	....	....	....	....	....	....	....	....	....	....	....
99-2000	Red Deer Rebels	WHL	72	39	57	96	135	....	....	....	....	....	....	....	....	....	4	2	1	3	28	....	....	....	....
2000-01	Red Deer Rebels	WHL	70	43	*77	*120	111	....	....	....	....	....	....	....	....	....	22	13	*21	34	59	....	....	....	....
2001-02	Bridgeport	AHL	80	13	20	33	60	....	....	....	....	....	....	....	....	....	20	7	10	17	23	....	....	....	....
2002-03	**NY Islanders**	**NHL**	**11**	**2**	**2**	**4**	**2**	**1**	**0**	**0**	**12**	**16.7**	**–1**	**138**	**41.3**	**12:17**	**2**	**0**	**0**	**0**	**0**	**0**	**0**	**0**	**7:23**
	Bridgeport	AHL	63	13	26	39	47	....	....	....	....	....	....	....	....	....	7	1	2	3	6	....	....	....	....
2003-04	**NY Islanders**	**NHL**	**27**	**1**	**4**	**5**	**6**	**0**	**0**	**0**	**15**	**6.7**	**–1**	**134**	**48.5**	**6:09**	....	....	....	....	....	....	....	....	....
	Bridgeport	AHL	36	10	13	23	59	....	....	....	....	....	....	....	....	....	....	....	....	....	....	....	....	....	....
2004-05	Bridgeport	AHL	61	11	24	35	51	....	....	....	....	....	....	....	....	....	....	....	....	....	....	....	....	....	....
2005-06	Sodertalje SK	Sweden	31	14	7	21	34	....	....	....	....	....	....	....	....	....	....	....	....	....	....	....	....	....	....
	Jokerit Helsinki	Finland	18	1	3	4	8	....	....	....	....	....	....	....	....	....	....	....	....	....	....	....	....	....	....
	Sodertalje SK	Sweden-Q	10	1	5	6	8	....	....	....	....	....	....	....	....	....	....	....	....	....	....	....	....	....	....
	NHL Totals		**38**	**3**	**6**	**9**	**8**	**1**	**0**	**0**	**27**	**11.1**		**272**	**44.9**	**7:56**	**2**	**0**	**0**	**0**	**0**	**0**	**0**	**0**	**7:23**

WHL East First All-Star Team (2000, 2001) • WHL Player of the Year (2001) • Canadian Major Junior First All-Star Team (2001)

Signed as a free agent by **Jokerit Helsinki** (Finland), September 6, 2005. Signed as a free agent by **Sodertalje** (Sweden), November 8, 2005.

MARA, Paul

(MAIR-uh, PAWL) **BOS.**

Defense. Shoots left. 6'4", 219 lbs. Born, Ridgewood, NJ, September 7, 1979. Tampa Bay's 1st choice, 7th overall, in 1997 Entry Draft.

1994-95	Belmont Hill	High-MA	28	5	17	22	28	....	....	....	....	....	....	....	....	....	....	....	....	....	....	....	....	....	....
1995-96	Belmont Hill	High-MA	28	18	20	38	40	....	....	....	....	....	....	....	....	....	....	....	....	....	....	....	....	....	....
1996-97	Sudbury Wolves	OHL	44	9	34	43	61	....	....	....	....	....	....	....	....	....	....	....	....	....	....	....	....	....	....
1997-98	Sudbury Wolves	OHL	25	8	18	26	79	....	....	....	....	....	....	....	....	....	....	....	....	....	....	....	....	....	....
	Plymouth Whalers	OHL	25	8	15	23	30	....	....	....	....	....	....	....	....	....	15	3	14	17	30	....	....	....	....
1998-99	Plymouth Whalers	OHL	52	13	41	54	95	....	....	....	....	....	....	....	....	....	11	5	7	12	28	....	....	....	....
	Tampa Bay	**NHL**	**1**	**1**	**1**	**2**	**0**	**1**	**0**	**0**	**1**	**100.0**	**–3**	**0**	**0.0**	**19:34**	....	....	....	....	....	....	....	....	....
99-2000	**Tampa Bay**	**NHL**	**54**	**7**	**11**	**18**	**73**	**4**	**0**	**1**	**78**	**9.0**	**–27**	**0**	**0.0**	**22:13**	....	....	....	....	....	....	....	....	....
	Detroit Vipers	IHL	15	3	5	8	22	....	....	....	....	....	....	....	....	....	....	....	....	....	....	....	....	....	....
2000-01	**Tampa Bay**	**NHL**	**46**	**6**	**10**	**16**	**40**	**2**	**0**	**1**	**58**	**10.3**	**–17**	**0**	**0.0**	**23:06**	....	....	....	....	....	....	....	....	....
	Detroit Vipers	IHL	10	3	3	6	22	....	....	....	....	....	....	....	....	....	....	....	....	....	....	....	....	....	....
	Phoenix	**NHL**	**16**	**0**	**4**	**4**	**14**	**0**	**0**	**0**	**20**	**0.0**	**1**	**0**	**0.0**	**19:22**	....	....	....	....	....	....	....	....	....
2001-02	**Phoenix**	**NHL**	**75**	**7**	**17**	**24**	**58**	**2**	**0**	**0**	**112**	**6.3**	**–6**	**2**	**100.0**	**21:34**	**5**	**0**	**0**	**0**	**4**	**0**	**0**	**0**	**22:57**
2002-03	**Phoenix**	**NHL**	**73**	**10**	**15**	**25**	**78**	**1**	**0**	**0**	**95**	**10.5**	**–7**	**1**	**0.0**	**21:06**	....	....	....	....	....	....	....	....	....
2003-04	**Phoenix**	**NHL**	**81**	**6**	**36**	**42**	**48**	**1**	**0**	**0**	**140**	**4.3**	**–11**	**2**	**0.0**	**23:37**	....	....	....	....	....	....	....	....	....
2004-05	Hannover	Germany	35	5	13	18	89	....	....	....	....	....	....	....	....	....	....	....	....	....	....	....	....	....	....
2005-06	**Phoenix**	**NHL**	**78**	**15**	**32**	**47**	**70**	**8**	**0**	**0**	**157**	**9.6**	**–12**	**1**	**0.0**	**21:29**	....	....	....	....	....	....	....	....	....
	NHL Totals		**424**	**52**	**126**	**178**	**381**	**19**	**0**	**2**	**661**	**7.9**		**6**	**33.3**	**22:02**	**5**	**0**	**0**	**0**	**4**	**0**	**0**	**0**	**22:57**

Traded to **Phoenix** by **Tampa Bay** with Mike Johnson, Ruslan Zainullin and NY Islanders' 2nd round choice (previously acquired, Phoenix selected Matthew Spiller) in 2001 Entry Draft for Nikolai Khabibulin and Stan Neckar, March 5, 2001. Signed as a free agent by **Hannover** (Germany), October 29, 2004. Traded to **Boston** by **Phoenix** with future considerations for Nick Boynton and Boston's 4th round choice in 2007 Entry Draft, June 26, 2006.

MARCHANT, Todd

(mahr-SHAHNT, TAWD) **ANA.**

Center. Shoots left. 5'10", 180 lbs. Born, Buffalo, NY, August 12, 1973. NY Rangers' 8th choice, 164th overall, in 1993 Entry Draft.

1990-91	Niagara Scenics	NAHL	37	31	47	78	....	....	....	....	....	....	....	....	....	....	....	....	....	....	....	....	....	....	....
1991-92	Clarkson Knights	ECAC	32	20	12	32	32	....	....	....	....	....	....	....	....	....	....	....	....	....	....	....	....	....	....
1992-93	Clarkson Knights	ECAC	33	18	28	46	38	....	....	....	....	....	....	....	....	....	....	....	....	....	....	....	....	....	....
1993-94	United States	Nat-Tm	59	28	39	67	48	....	....	....	....	....	....	....	....	....	....	....	....	....	....	....	....	....	....
	United States	Olympics	8	1	1	2	6	....	....	....	....	....	....	....	....	....	....	....	....	....	....	....	....	....	....
	NY Rangers	**NHL**	**1**	**0**	**0**	**0**	**0**	**0**	**0**	**0**	**1**	**0.0**	**–1**	....	....	....	....	....	....	....	....	....	....	....	....
	Binghamton	AHL	8	2	7	9	6	....	....	....	....	....	....	....	....	....	....	....	....	....	....	....	....	....	....
	Edmonton	**NHL**	**3**	**0**	**1**	**1**	**2**	**0**	**0**	**0**	**5**	**0.0**	**–1**	....	....	....	....	....	....	....	....	....	....	....	....
	Cape Breton	AHL	3	1	4	5	2	....	....	....	....	....	....	....	....	....	5	1	1	2	0	....	....	....	....
1994-95	Cape Breton	AHL	38	22	25	47	25	....	....	....	....	....	....	....	....	....	....	....	....	....	....	....	....	....	....
	Edmonton	**NHL**	**45**	**13**	**14**	**27**	**32**	**3**	**2**	**2**	**95**	**13.7**	**–3**	....	....	....	....	....	....	....	....	....	....	....	....
1995-96	**Edmonton**	**NHL**	**81**	**19**	**19**	**38**	**66**	**2**	**3**	**2**	**221**	**8.6**	**–19**	....	....	....	....	....	....	....	....	....	....	....	....
1996-97	**Edmonton**	**NHL**	**79**	**14**	**19**	**33**	**44**	**0**	**4**	**3**	**202**	**6.9**	**11**	....	....	....	**12**	**4**	**2**	**6**	**12**	**0**	**3**	**1**	....
1997-98	**Edmonton**	**NHL**	**76**	**14**	**21**	**35**	**71**	**2**	**1**	**3**	**194**	**7.2**	**9**	....	....	....	**12**	**1**	**1**	**2**	**10**	**0**	**0**	**0**	....
1998-99	**Edmonton**	**NHL**	**82**	**14**	**22**	**36**	**65**	**3**	**1**	**2**	**183**	**7.7**	**3**	**1449**	**50.0**	**16:47**	**4**	**1**	**1**	**2**	**12**	**0**	**0**	**0**	**24:21**
99-2000	**Edmonton**	**NHL**	**82**	**17**	**23**	**40**	**70**	**0**	**1**	**0**	**170**	**10.0**	**7**	**1593**	**52.9**	**17:08**	**3**	**1**	**0**	**1**	**2**	**0**	**0**	**0**	**18:07**
2000-01	**Edmonton**	**NHL**	**71**	**13**	**26**	**39**	**51**	**0**	**4**	**2**	**113**	**11.5**	**1**	**1549**	**53.8**	**17:54**	**6**	**0**	**0**	**0**	**4**	**0**	**0**	**0**	**22:57**

			Regular Season														Playoffs								
Season	Club	League	GP	G	A	Pts	PIM	PP	SH	GW	S	%	+/-	TF	F%	Min	GP	G	A	Pts	PIM	PP	SH	GW	Min
2001-02	Edmonton	NHL	82	12	22	34	41	0	3	1	124	9.7	7	1523	52.4	16:58	....	....	....	....	....	....	....	....	....
2002-03	Edmonton	NHL	77	20	40	60	48	7	1	3	146	13.7	13	1336	58.0	19:54	6	0	2	2	2	0	0	0	20:03
2003-04	Columbus	NHL	77	9	25	34	34	4	0	2	163	5.5	–17	1412	50.9	20:39	....	....	....	....	....	....	....	....	....
2004-05			DID NOT PLAY																						
2005-06	Columbus	NHL	18	3	6	9	20	0	0	0	42	7.1	–1	289	50.2	20:05	....	....	....	....	....	....	....	....	....
	Anaheim	NHL	61	6	19	25	46	0	0	0	90	6.7	3	743	51.7	16:25	16	3	10	13	14	0	0	0	17:34
	NHL Totals		835	154	257	411	590	21	20	20	1749	8.8		9894	52.8	18:03	59	10	16	26	56	0	3	1	19:44

ECAC Second All-Star Team (1993)

Traded to **Edmonton** by **NY Rangers** for Craig MacTavish, March 21, 1994. Signed as a free agent by **Columbus**, July 3, 2003. Claimed on waivers by **Anaheim** from **Columbus**, November 21, 2005.

MARCHMENT, Bryan

(MAHRCH-mehnt, BRIGH-uhn)

Defense. Shoots left. 6'1", 200 lbs. Born, Scarborough, Ont., May 1, 1969. Winnipeg's 1st choice, 16th overall, in 1987 Entry Draft.

Season	Club	League	GP	G	A	Pts	PIM	PP	SH	GW	S	%	+/-	TF	F%	Min	GP	G	A	Pts	PIM	PP	SH	GW	Min
1984-85	Tor. Young Nats	MTHL	69	14	35	49	229	....	....	....	....	....	....	....	....	....	....	....	....	....	....	....	....	....	....
1985-86	Belleville Bulls	OHL	57	5	15	20	225	....	....	....	....	....	....	....	....	....	21	0	7	7	83	....	....	....	....
1986-87	Belleville Bulls	OHL	52	6	38	44	238	....	....	....	....	....	....	....	....	....	6	0	4	4	17	....	....	....	....
1987-88	Belleville Bulls	OHL	56	7	51	58	200	....	....	....	....	....	....	....	....	....	6	1	3	4	19	....	....	....	....
1988-89	Belleville Bulls	OHL	43	14	36	50	118	....	....	....	....	....	....	....	....	....	5	0	1	1	12	....	....	....	....
	Winnipeg	NHL	2	0	0	0	2	0	0	0	1	0.0	0	....	....	....	....	....	....	....	....	....	....	....	....
1989-90	Winnipeg	NHL	7	0	2	2	28	0	0	0	5	0.0	0	....	....	....	....	....	....	....	....	....	....	....	....
	Moncton Hawks	AHL	56	4	19	23	217	....	....	....	....	....	....	....	....	....	....	....	....	....	....	....	....	....	....
1990-91	Winnipeg	NHL	28	2	2	4	91	0	0	0	24	8.3	–5	....	....	....	....	....	....	....	....	....	....	....	....
	Moncton Hawks	AHL	33	2	11	13	101	....	....	....	....	....	....	....	....	....	....	....	....	....	....	....	....	....	....
1991-92	Chicago	NHL	58	5	10	15	168	2	0	0	55	9.1	–4	....	....	....	16	1	0	1	36	0	0	0	....
1992-93	Chicago	NHL	78	5	15	20	313	1	0	1	75	6.7	15	....	....	....	4	0	0	0	12	0	0	0	....
1993-94	Chicago	NHL	13	1	4	5	42	0	0	0	18	5.6	–2	....	....	....	....	....	....	....	....	....	....	....	....
	Hartford	NHL	42	3	7	10	124	0	1	1	74	4.1	–12	....	....	....	....	....	....	....	....	....	....	....	....
1994-95	Edmonton	NHL	40	1	5	6	184	0	0	0	57	1.8	–11	....	....	....	....	....	....	....	....	....	....	....	....
1995-96	Edmonton	NHL	78	3	15	18	202	0	0	0	96	3.1	–7	....	....	....	....	....	....	....	....	....	....	....	....
1996-97	Edmonton	NHL	71	3	13	16	132	1	0	0	89	3.4	13	....	....	....	3	0	0	0	4	0	0	0	....
1997-98	Edmonton	NHL	27	0	4	4	58	0	0	0	23	0.0	–2	....	....	....	....	....	....	....	....	....	....	....	....
	Tampa Bay	NHL	22	2	4	6	43	0	0	0	20	10.0	–3	....	....	....	....	....	....	....	....	....	....	....	....
	San Jose	NHL	12	0	3	3	43	0	0	0	13	0.0	2	....	....	....	6	0	0	0	10	0	0	0	....
1998-99	San Jose	NHL	59	2	6	8	101	0	0	0	49	4.1	–7	0	0.0	17:43	6	0	0	0	4	0	0	0	16:41
99-2000	San Jose	NHL	49	0	4	4	72	0	0	0	51	0.0	3	0	0.0	18:55	11	2	1	3	12	0	0	0	18:40
2000-01	San Jose	NHL	75	7	11	18	204	0	1	3	73	9.6	15	1	100.0	18:12	5	0	1	1	2	0	0	0	17:00
2001-02	San Jose	NHL	72	2	20	22	178	0	0	0	68	2.9	22	0	0.0	18:47	12	1	1	2	10	0	0	0	15:29
2002-03	San Jose	NHL	67	2	9	11	108	0	0	0	66	3.0	–2	0	0.0	19:19	....	....	....	....	....	....	....	....	....
	Colorado	NHL	14	0	3	3	33	0	0	0	18	0.0	4	0	0.0	16:42	7	0	0	0	4	0	0	0	16:02
2003-04	Toronto	NHL	75	1	3	4	106	0	0	0	56	1.8	4	0	0.0	15:13	13	0	0	0	8	0	0	0	14:31
2004-05			DID NOT PLAY																						
2005-06	Calgary	NHL	37	1	2	3	75	0	0	0	16	6.3	8	1	0.0	13:07	....	....	....	....	....	....	....	....	....
	NHL Totals		926	40	142	182	2307	4	2	5	947	4.2		2	50.0	17:31	83	4	3	7	102	0	0	0	16:15

OHL Second All-Star Team (1989)

Traded to **Chicago** by **Winnipeg** with Chris Norton for Troy Murray and Warren Rychel, July 22, 1991. Traded to **Hartford** by **Chicago** with Steve Larmer for Eric Weinrich and Patrick Poulin, November 2, 1993. Transferred to **Edmonton** from **Hartford** as compensation for Hartford's signing of free agent Steven Rice, August 30, 1994. Traded to **Tampa Bay** by **Edmonton** with Steve Kelly and Jason Bonsignore for Roman Hamrlik and Paul Comrie, December 30, 1997. Traded to **San Jose** by **Tampa Bay** with David Shaw and Tampa Bay's 1st round choice (later traded to Nashville – Nashville selected David Legwand) in 1998 Entry Draft for Andrei Nazarov and Florida's 1st round choice (previously acquired, Tampa Bay selected Vincent Lecavallier) in 1998 Entry Draft, March 24, 1998. Traded to **Colorado** by **San Jose** for Colorado's 3rd (later traded to Calgary – Calgary selected Ryan Donally) and 5th (later traded back to Colorado – Colorado selected Brad Richardson) round choices in 2003 Entry Draft, March 8, 2003. Signed as a free agent by **Toronto**, July 11, 2003. Signed as a free agent by **Calgary**, October 11, 2005.

MARJAMAKI, Masi

(mahr-juh-MA-kee, MAH-see) **NYI**

Right wing. Shoots left. 6'2", 202 lbs. Born, Pori, Finland, January 16, 1985. NY Islanders' 4th choice, 144th overall, in 2005 Entry Draft.

Season	Club	League	GP	G	A	Pts	PIM	PP	SH	GW	S	%	+/-	TF	F%	Min	GP	G	A	Pts	PIM	PP	SH	GW	Min
2001-02	Assat Pori U18	Fin-U18	24	6	16	22	93	....	....	....	....	....	....	....	....	....	1	0	1	1	2	....	....	....	....
	Assat Pori Jr.	Fin-Jr.	1	0	0	0	0	....	....	....	....	....	....	....	....	....	6	3	2	5	2	....	....	....	....
2002-03	Red Deer Rebels	WHL	65	15	20	35	56	....	....	....	....	....	....	....	....	....	23	1	2	3	20	....	....	....	....
2003-04	Red Deer Rebels	WHL	28	6	8	14	46	....	....	....	....	....	....	....	....	....	....	....	....	....	....	....	....	....	....
	Moose Jaw	WHL	35	15	10	25	57	....	....	....	....	....	....	....	....	....	10	1	3	4	15	....	....	....	....
2004-05	Moose Jaw	WHL	51	14	32	46	49	....	....	....	....	....	....	....	....	....	5	1	2	3	5	....	....	....	....
2005-06	NY Islanders	NHL	1	0	0	0	0	0	0	0	0	0.0	0	0	0.0	5:17	....	....	....	....	....	....	....	....	....
	Bridgeport	AHL	75	9	22	31	77	....	....	....	....	....	....	....	....	....	7	3	0	3	4	....	....	....	....
	NHL Totals		1	0	0	0	0	0	0	0	0	0.0		0	0.0	5:17	....	....	....	....	....	....	....	....	....

• Re-entered NHL Entry Draft. Originally Boston's 3rd choice, 66th overall, in 2003 Entry Draft.

MARKOV, Andrei

(MAHR-kahf, AHN-dray) **MTL.**

Defense. Shoots left. 6', 200 lbs. Born, Voskresensk, USSR, December 20, 1978. Montreal's 6th choice, 162nd overall, in 1998 Entry Draft.

Season	Club	League	GP	G	A	Pts	PIM	PP	SH	GW	S	%	+/-	TF	F%	Min	GP	G	A	Pts	PIM	PP	SH	GW	Min
1995-96	Voskresensk	CIS	38	0	0	0	14	....	....	....	....	....	....	....	....	....	....	....	....	....	....	....	....	....	....
1996-97	Voskresensk	Russia	43	8	4	12	32	....	....	....	....	....	....	....	....	....	2	1	1	2	0	....	....	....	....
1997-98	Voskresensk	Russia	43	10	5	15	83	....	....	....	....	....	....	....	....	....	....	....	....	....	....	....	....	....	....
1998-99	Dynamo Moscow	Russia	38	10	11	21	32	....	....	....	....	....	....	....	....	....	16	3	6	9	6	....	....	....	....
	Dynamo Moscow	EuroHL	12	7	5	12	12	....	....	....	....	....	....	....	....	....	6	2	2	4	4	....	....	....	....
99-2000	Dynamo Moscow	Russia	29	11	12	23	28	....	....	....	....	....	....	....	....	....	17	4	3	7	8	....	....	....	....
2000-01	Montreal	NHL	63	6	17	23	18	2	0	0	82	7.3	–6	2	50.0	16:53	....	....	....	....	....	....	....	....	....
	Quebec Citadelles	AHL	14	0	5	5	4	....	....	....	....	....	....	....	....	....	7	1	1	2	2	....	....	....	....
2001-02	Montreal	NHL	56	5	19	24	24	2	0	1	73	6.8	–1	0	0.0	17:15	12	1	3	4	8	0	0	1	15:53
	Quebec Citadelles	AHL	12	4	6	10	7	....	....	....	....	....	....	....	....	....	....	....	....	....	....	....	....	....	....
2002-03	Montreal	NHL	79	13	24	37	34	3	0	2	159	8.2	13	1	0.0	23:17	....	....	....	....	....	....	....	....	....
2003-04	Montreal	NHL	69	6	22	28	20	2	0	0	105	5.7	–2	2	50.0	21:29	11	1	4	5	8	0	0	1	22:52
2004-05	Dynamo Moscow	Russia	42	7	16	23	76	....	....	....	....	....	....	....	....	....	10	2	0	2	22	....	....	....	....
2005-06	Montreal	NHL	67	10	36	46	74	6	1	1	88	11.4	13	1	0.0	23:33	6	0	1	1	4	0	0	0	25:29
	Russia	Olympics	8	1	2	3	6	....	....	....	....	....	....	....	....	....	....	....	....	....	....	....	....	....	....
	NHL Totals		334	40	118	158	170	15	1	4	507	7.9		6	33.3	20:45	29	2	8	10	20	0	0	2	20:31

Signed as a free agent by **Dynamo Moscow** (Russia), June 19, 2004.

MARKOV, Danny

(MAHR-kahf, DA-nee) **DET.**

Defense. Shoots left. 6'1", 190 lbs. Born, Moscow, USSR, July 30, 1976. Toronto's 7th choice, 223rd overall, in 1995 Entry Draft.

Season	Club	League	GP	G	A	Pts	PIM	PP	SH	GW	S	%	+/-	TF	F%	Min	GP	G	A	Pts	PIM	PP	SH	GW	Min
1993-94	Spartak Moscow	CIS	13	1	0	1	6	....	....	....	....	....	....	....	....	....	1	0	0	0	0	....	....	....	....
1994-95	Spartak Moscow	CIS	39	0	1	1	36	....	....	....	....	....	....	....	....	....	....	....	....	....	....	....	....	....	....
1995-96	Spartak Moscow	CIS	38	2	0	2	12	....	....	....	....	....	....	....	....	....	2	0	0	0	2	....	....	....	....
1996-97	Spartak Moscow	Russia	39	3	6	9	41	....	....	....	....	....	....	....	....	....	....	....	....	....	....	....	....	....	....
	St. John's	AHL	10	2	4	6	18	....	....	....	....	....	....	....	....	....	11	2	6	8	14	....	....	....	....
1997-98	Toronto	NHL	25	2	5	7	28	1	0	0	15	13.3	0	....	....	....	....	....	....	....	....	....	....	....	....
	St. John's	AHL	52	3	23	26	124	....	....	....	....	....	....	....	....	....	2	0	1	1	0	....	....	....	....
1998-99	Toronto	NHL	57	4	8	12	47	0	0	0	34	11.8	5	0	0.0	18:41	17	0	6	6	18	0	0	0	22:24
99-2000	Toronto	NHL	59	0	10	10	28	0	0	0	38	0.0	13	1	0.0	20:08	12	0	3	3	10	0	0	0	21:05
2000-01	Toronto	NHL	59	3	13	16	34	1	0	2	49	6.1	6	0	0.0	19:02	11	1	1	2	12	0	0	0	21:30
2001-02	Phoenix	NHL	72	6	30	36	67	4	0	1	103	5.8	–7	0	0.0	22:55	....	....	....	....	....	....	....	....	....
	Russia	Olympics	5	0	1	1	0	....	....	....	....	....	....	....	....	....	....	....	....	....	....	....	....	....	....
2002-03	Phoenix	NHL	64	4	16	20	36	2	0	0	105	3.8	2	0	0.0	23:16	....	....	....	....	....	....	....	....	....
2003-04	Carolina	NHL	44	4	10	14	37	2	0	1	73	5.5	–6	0	0.0	23:39	....	....	....	....	....	....	....	....	....
	Philadelphia	NHL	34	2	3	5	58	1	0	1	27	7.4	0	0	0.0	21:16	18	1	2	3	25	0	0	1	23:03
2004-05	Vityaz Chekhov	Russia-2	26	5	7	12	16	....	....	....	....	....	....	....	....	....	12	0	3	3	6	....	....	....	....

			Regular Season														Playoffs								
Season	Club	League	GP	G	A	Pts	PIM	PP	SH	GW	S	%	+/-	TF	F%	Min	GP	G	A	Pts	PIM	PP	SH	GW	Min
2005-06	**Nashville**	**NHL**	**58**	**0**	**11**	**11**	**62**	**0**	**0**	**0**	**59**	**0.0**	**9**	**0**	**0.0**	**19:33**	**5**	**0**	**0**	**0**	**6**	**0**	**0**	**0**	**19:22**
	Russia	Olympics	8	0	2	2	4	....	....	....	....	....	....	....	....	....	....	....	....	....	....	....	....	....	....
	NHL Totals		**472**	**25**	**106**	**131**	**397**	**11**	**0**	**5**	**503**	**5.0**		**1**	**0.0**	**21:03**	**63**	**2**	**12**	**14**	**71**	**0**	**0**	**1**	**21:56**

Traded to **Phoenix** by **Toronto** for Robert Reichel, Travis Green and Craig Mills, June 12, 2001. Traded to **Carolina** by **Phoenix** with future considerations (Edmonton's 3rd round choice (previously acquired, later traded to NY Rangers - NY Rangers selected Billy Ryan) in 2004 Entry Draft, June 26, 2004) for David Tanabe and Igor Knyazev, June 21, 2003. Traded to **Philadelphia** by **Carolina** for Justin Williams, January 20, 2004. Signed as a free agent by **Chekhov** (Russia-2), November 15, 2004. Traded to **Nashville** by **Philadelphia** for Nashville's 3rd round choice (later traded to Los Angeles - Los Angeles selected Bud Holloway) in 2006 Entry Draft, August 2, 2005. Signed as a free agent by **Detroit**, July 26, 2006.

MARLEAU, Patrick (mahr-LOH, PAT-rihk) S.J.

Center. Shoots left. 6'2", 220 lbs. Born, Aneroid, Sask., September 15, 1979. San Jose's 1st choice, 2nd overall, in 1997 Entry Draft.

1993-94	Swift Current	SMHL	53	72	95	167	....	....	....	....	....	....	....	....	....	....	....	....	....	....	....	....	....	....	....
1994-95	Swift Current	SMHL	31	30	22	52	18	....	....	....	....	....	....	....	....	....	....	....	....	....	....	....	....	....	....
1995-96	Seattle	WHL	72	32	42	74	22	....	....	....	....	....	....	....	....	....	5	3	4	7	4	....	....	....	....
1996-97	Seattle	WHL	71	51	74	125	37	....	....	....	....	....	....	....	....	....	15	7	16	23	12	....	....	....	....
1997-98	**San Jose**	**NHL**	**74**	**13**	**19**	**32**	**14**	**1**	**0**	**2**	**90**	**14.4**	**5**	....	....	....	**5**	**0**	**1**	**1**	**0**	**0**	**0**	**0**	....
1998-99	**San Jose**	**NHL**	**81**	**21**	**24**	**45**	**24**	**4**	**0**	**4**	**134**	**15.7**	**10**	**1121**	**43.4**	**15:11**	**6**	**2**	**1**	**3**	**4**	**2**	**0**	**0**	**11:08**
99-2000	**San Jose**	**NHL**	**81**	**17**	**23**	**40**	**36**	**3**	**0**	**3**	**161**	**10.6**	**-9**	**851**	**42.0**	**14:11**	**5**	**1**	**1**	**2**	**2**	**1**	**0**	**0**	**11:51**
2000-01	**San Jose**	**NHL**	**81**	**25**	**27**	**52**	**22**	**5**	**0**	**6**	**146**	**17.1**	**7**	**1088**	**44.8**	**16:17**	**6**	**2**	**0**	**2**	**4**	**0**	**0**	**0**	**14:50**
2001-02	**San Jose**	**NHL**	**79**	**21**	**23**	**44**	**40**	**3**	**0**	**5**	**121**	**17.4**	**9**	**897**	**47.3**	**14:04**	**12**	**6**	**5**	**11**	**6**	**1**	**0**	**3**	**15:50**
2002-03	**San Jose**	**NHL**	**82**	**28**	**29**	**57**	**33**	**8**	**1**	**3**	**172**	**16.3**	**-10**	**1403**	**47.3**	**18:31**	....	....	....	....	....	....	....	....	....
2003-04	**San Jose**	**NHL**	**80**	**28**	**29**	**57**	**24**	**9**	**0**	**5**	**220**	**12.7**	**-5**	**1014**	**41.6**	**18:12**	**17**	**8**	**4**	**12**	**6**	**4**	**1**	**2**	**19:16**
2004-05		DID NOT PLAY																							
2005-06	**San Jose**	**NHL**	**82**	**34**	**52**	**86**	**26**	**20**	**1**	**4**	**260**	**13.1**	**-12**	**1216**	**46.8**	**19:56**	**11**	**9**	**5**	**14**	**8**	**4**	**0**	**2**	**21:07**
	NHL Totals		**640**	**187**	**226**	**413**	**219**	**53**	**2**	**32**	**1304**	**14.3**		**7590**	**44.9**	**16:38**	**62**	**28**	**17**	**45**	**30**	**12**	**1**	**7**	**16:56**

WHL West First All-Star Team (1997)
Played in NHL All-Star Game (2004)

MARSHALL, Grant (MAHR-shahl, GRANT) N.J.

Right wing. Shoots right. 6'1", 200 lbs. Born, Mississauga, Ont., June 9, 1973. Toronto's 2nd choice, 23rd overall, in 1992 Entry Draft.

1989-90	Tor. Young Nats	MTHL	39	15	28	43	56	....	....	....	....	....	....	....	....	....	....	....	....	....	....	....	....	....	....
1990-91	Ottawa 67's	OHL	26	6	11	17	25	....	....	....	....	....	....	....	....	....	1	0	0	0	0	....	....	....	....
1991-92	Ottawa 67's	OHL	61	32	51	83	132	....	....	....	....	....	....	....	....	....	11	6	11	17	11	....	....	....	....
1992-93	Ottawa 67's	OHL	30	14	29	43	83	....	....	....	....	....	....	....	....	....	....	....	....	....	....	....	....	....	....
	Newmarket	OHL	31	11	25	36	89	....	....	....	....	....	....	....	....	....	7	4	7	11	20	....	....	....	....
	St. John's	AHL	2	0	0	0	0	....	....	....	....	....	....	....	....	....	2	0	0	0	2	....	....	....	....
1993-94	St. John's	AHL	67	11	29	40	155	....	....	....	....	....	....	....	....	....	11	1	5	6	17	....	....	....	....
1994-95	Kalamazoo Wings	IHL	61	17	29	46	96	....	....	....	....	....	....	....	....	....	16	9	3	12	27	....	....	....	....
	Dallas	**NHL**	**2**	**0**	**1**	**1**	**0**	**0**	**0**	**0**	**0**	**0.0**	**1**	....	....	....	....	....	....	....	....	....	....	....	....
1995-96	**Dallas**	**NHL**	**70**	**9**	**19**	**28**	**111**	**0**	**0**	**0**	**62**	**14.5**	**0**	....	....	....	....	....	....	....	....	....	....	....	....
1996-97	**Dallas**	**NHL**	**56**	**6**	**4**	**10**	**98**	**0**	**0**	**0**	**0**	**0.0**	**5**	....	....	....	**5**	**0**	**2**	**2**	**8**	**0**	**0**	**0**	....
1997-98	**Dallas**	**NHL**	**72**	**9**	**10**	**19**	**96**	**3**	**0**	**1**	**91**	**9.9**	**-2**	....	....	....	**17**	**0**	**2**	**2**	***47**	**0**	**0**	**0**	....
1998-99♦	**Dallas**	**NHL**	**82**	**13**	**18**	**31**	**85**	**2**	**0**	**4**	**112**	**11.6**	**1**	**2**	**50.0**	**12:39**	**14**	**0**	**3**	**3**	**20**	**0**	**0**	**0**	**11:42**
99-2000	**Dallas**	**NHL**	**45**	**2**	**6**	**8**	**38**	**1**	**0**	**0**	**43**	**4.7**	**-5**	**3**	**0.0**	**11:19**	**14**	**0**	**1**	**1**	**4**	**0**	**0**	**0**	**10:08**
2000-01	**Dallas**	**NHL**	**75**	**13**	**24**	**37**	**64**	**4**	**0**	**1**	**93**	**14.0**	**1**	**16**	**56.3**	**11:05**	**9**	**0**	**0**	**0**	**0**	**0**	**0**	**0**	**11:15**
2001-02	**Columbus**	**NHL**	**81**	**15**	**18**	**33**	**86**	**6**	**0**	**4**	**152**	**9.9**	**-20**	**28**	**39.3**	**15:27**	....	....	....	....	....	....	....	....	....
2002-03	**Columbus**	**NHL**	**66**	**8**	**20**	**28**	**71**	**3**	**0**	**2**	**96**	**8.3**	**-8**	**26**	**46.2**	**13:56**	....	....	....	....	....	....	....	....	....
	♦ New Jersey	**NHL**	**10**	**1**	**3**	**4**	**7**	**0**	**0**	**0**	**17**	**5.9**	**-3**	**1**	**100.0**	**11:38**	**24**	**6**	**2**	**8**	**8**	**2**	**0**	**1**	**14:30**
2003-04	**New Jersey**	**NHL**	**65**	**8**	**7**	**15**	**67**	**5**	**0**	**2**	**76**	**10.5**	**-9**	**5**	**40.0**	**12:53**	....	....	....	....	....	....	....	....	....
2004-05		DID NOT PLAY																							
2005-06	**New Jersey**	**NHL**	**76**	**8**	**17**	**25**	**70**	**4**	**0**	**3**	**89**	**9.0**	**-18**	**4**	**25.0**	**12:38**	**7**	**0**	**1**	**1**	**8**	**0**	**0**	**0**	**14:07**
	NHL Totals		**700**	**92**	**147**	**239**	**793**	**28**	**0**	**17**	**831**	**11.1**		**85**	**43.5**	**12:56**	**90**	**6**	**11**	**17**	**95**	**2**	**0**	**1**	**12:33**

• Missed majority of 1990-91 season recovering from neck injury suffered in game vs. Sudbury (OHL), December 4, 1990. Awarded to **Dallas** from **Toronto** with Peter Zezel as compensation for Toronto's signing of free agent Mike Craig, August 10, 1994. Traded to **Columbus** by **Dallas** for Columbus' 2nd round choice (Loui Eriksson) in 2003 Entry Draft, August 29, 2001. Traded to **New Jersey** by **Columbus** for New Jersey's 4th round choice (later traded to Carolina – later traded to Calgary – Calgary selected Kristopher Hogg) in 2004 Entry Draft, March 10, 2003.

MARSHALL, Jason (MAHR-shahl, JAY-suhn)

Defense. Shoots right. 6'2", 200 lbs. Born, Cranbrook, B.C., February 22, 1971. St. Louis' 1st choice, 9th overall, in 1989 Entry Draft.

1987-88	Columbia Valley	RMJHL	40	4	28	32	150	....	....	....	....	....	....	....	....	....	....	....	....	....	....	....	....	....	....
1988-89	Vernon Lakers	BCJHL	48	10	30	40	197	....	....	....	....	....	....	....	....	....	31	6	6	12	14	....	....	....	....
1989-90	Canada	Nat-Tm	73	1	11	12	57	....	....	....	....	....	....	....	....	....	....	....	....	....	....	....	....	....	....
1990-91	Tri-City	WHL	59	10	34	44	236	....	....	....	....	....	....	....	....	....	7	1	2	3	20	....	....	....	....
	Peoria Rivermen	IHL	....	....	....	....	....	....	....	....	....	....	....	....	....	....	18	0	1	1	48	....	....	....	....
1991-92	**St. Louis**	**NHL**	**2**	**1**	**0**	**1**	**4**	**0**	**0**	**0**	**2**	**50.0**	**0**	....	....	....	....	....	....	....	....	....	....	....	....
	Peoria Rivermen	IHL	78	4	18	22	178	....	....	....	....	....	....	....	....	....	10	0	1	1	16	....	....	....	....
1992-93	Peoria Rivermen	IHL	77	4	16	20	229	....	....	....	....	....	....	....	....	....	4	0	0	0	20	....	....	....	....
1993-94	Canada	Nat-Tm	41	3	10	13	60	....	....	....	....	....	....	....	....	....	....	....	....	....	....	....	....	....	....
	Peoria Rivermen	IHL	20	1	1	2	72	....	....	....	....	....	....	....	....	....	3	2	0	2	2	....	....	....	....
1994-95	San Diego Gulls	IHL	80	7	18	25	218	....	....	....	....	....	....	....	....	....	5	0	1	1	8	....	....	....	....
	Anaheim	**NHL**	**1**	**0**	**0**	**0**	**0**	**0**	**0**	**0**	**1**	**0.0**	**-2**	....	....	....	....	....	....	....	....	....	....	....	....
1995-96	**Anaheim**	**NHL**	**24**	**0**	**1**	**1**	**42**	**0**	**0**	**0**	**9**	**0.0**	**3**	....	....	....	....	....	....	....	....	....	....	....	....
	Baltimore Bandits	AHL	57	1	13	14	150	....	....	....	....	....	....	....	....	....	....	....	....	....	....	....	....	....	....
1996-97	**Anaheim**	**NHL**	**73**	**1**	**9**	**10**	**140**	**0**	**0**	**0**	**34**	**2.9**	**6**	....	....	....	**7**	**0**	**1**	**1**	**4**	**0**	**0**	**0**	....
1997-98	**Anaheim**	**NHL**	**72**	**3**	**6**	**9**	**189**	**1**	**0**	**0**	**68**	**4.4**	**-8**	....	....	....	....	....	....	....	....	....	....	....	....
1998-99	**Anaheim**	**NHL**	**72**	**1**	**7**	**8**	**142**	**1**	**0**	**0**	**63**	**1.6**	**-5**	**0**	**0.0**	**19:06**	**4**	**1**	**0**	**1**	**10**	**1**	**0**	**0**	**21:29**
99-2000	**Anaheim**	**NHL**	**55**	**0**	**3**	**3**	**88**	**0**	**0**	**0**	**41**	**0.0**	**-10**	**2**	**50.0**	**16:33**	....	....	....	....	....	....	....	....	....
2000-01	**Anaheim**	**NHL**	**50**	**3**	**4**	**7**	**105**	**2**	**1**	**1**	**38**	**7.9**	**-12**	**1**	**0.0**	**14:36**	....	....	....	....	....	....	....	....	....
	Washington	**NHL**	**5**	**0**	**0**	**0**	**17**	**0**	**0**	**0**	**5**	**0.0**	**-1**	**0**	**0.0**	**11:48**	....	....	....	....	....	....	....	....	....
2001-02	**Minnesota**	**NHL**	**80**	**5**	**6**	**11**	**148**	**1**	**0**	**0**	**73**	**6.8**	**-8**	**0**	**0.0**	**16:18**	....	....	....	....	....	....	....	....	....
2002-03	**Minnesota**	**NHL**	**45**	**1**	**5**	**6**	**69**	**1**	**0**	**0**	**40**	**2.5**	**4**	**7**	**28.6**	**11:24**	**15**	**1**	**1**	**2**	**16**	**0**	**0**	**1**	**10:50**
2003-04	**Minnesota**	**NHL**	**12**	**1**	**4**	**5**	**18**	**1**	**0**	**0**	**16**	**6.3**	**-1**	**0**	**0.0**	**15:36**	....	....	....	....	....	....	....	....	....
	Houston Aeros	AHL	49	7	12	19	87	....	....	....	....	....	....	....	....	....	....	....	....	....	....	....	....	....	....
	San Jose	**NHL**	**12**	**0**	**2**	**2**	**8**	**0**	**0**	**0**	**14**	**0.0**	**-2**	**0**	**0.0**	**16:00**	**17**	**0**	**1**	**1**	**25**	**0**	**0**	**0**	**14:44**
2004-05	Plzen	CzRep	11	1	3	4	53	....	....	....	....	....	....	....	....	....	....	....	....	....	....	....	....	....	....
2005-06	**Anaheim**	**NHL**	**23**	**0**	**4**	**4**	**34**	**0**	**0**	**0**	**25**	**0.0**	**2**	**0**	**0.0**	**11:46**	....	....	....	....	....	....	....	....	....
	Portland Pirates	AHL	2	0	0	0	4	....	....	....	....	....	....	....	....	....	....	....	....	....	....	....	....	....	....
	NHL Totals		**526**	**16**	**51**	**67**	**1004**	**5**	**1**	**1**	**429**	**3.7**		**10**	**30.0**	**15:39**	**43**	**2**	**3**	**5**	**55**	**1**	**0**	**1**	**13:52**

Traded to **Anaheim** by **St. Louis** for Bill Houlder, August 29, 1994. Traded to **Washington** by **Anaheim** for Alexei Tezikov and Edmonton's 4th round choice (previously acquired, Anaheim selected Brandon Rogers) in 2001 Entry Draft, March 13, 2001. Signed as a free agent by **Minnesota**, July 2, 2001. Traded to **San Jose** by **Minnesota** for San Jose's 5th round choice (Jean-Claude Sawyer) in 2004 Entry Draft, March 3, 2004. Signed as a free agent by **NY Rangers**, August 25, 2004. Signed as a free agent by **Plzen** (CzRep), January 22, 2005. Signed as a free agent by **Anaheim**, August 8, 2005. Signed as a free agent by **Kolner** (Germany), June 7, 2006.

MARTENSSON, Tony (MOHR-tehn-suhn, TOH-nee) ANA.

Center. Shoots left. 6', 189 lbs. Born, Upplands Vasby, Sweden, June 23, 1980. Anaheim's 9th choice, 224th overall, in 2001 Entry Draft.

1997-98	Arlanda	Sweden-2	12	2	4	6	0	....	....	....	....	....	....	....	....	....	2	0	0	0	0	....	....	....	....
1998-99	Arlanda	Sweden-2	37	8	22	30	8	....	....	....	....	....	....	....	....	....	2	0	0	0	0	....	....	....	....
99-2000	Arlanda	Sweden-2	44	21	28	49	14	....	....	....	....	....	....	....	....	....	....	....	....	....	....	....	....	....	....
2000-01	Brynas IF Gavle	Sweden	50	15	11	26	20	....	....	....	....	....	....	....	....	....	4	0	1	1	2	....	....	....	....
	Brynas IF Gavle Jr.	Swe-Jr.	1	1	0	1	0	....	....	....	....	....	....	....	....	....	....	....	....	....	....	....	....	....	....
2001-02	Brynas IF Gavle	Sweden	50	9	17	26	14	....	....	....	....	....	....	....	....	....	4	1	3	4	0	....	....	....	....
2002-03	Cincinnati	AHL	79	17	36	53	20	....	....	....	....	....	....	....	....	....	....	....	....	....	....	....	....	....	....
2003-04	**Anaheim**	**NHL**	**6**	**1**	**1**	**2**	**0**	**0**	**0**	**0**	**4**	**25.0**	**-2**	**18**	**44.4**	**6:58**	....	....	....	....	....	....	....	....	....
	Cincinnati	AHL	67	16	34	50	20	....	....	....	....	....	....	....	....	....	9	3	10	13	4	....	....	....	....
2004-05	Linkopings HC	Sweden	50	13	21	34	12	....	....	....	....	....	....	....	....	....	5	0	1	1	0	....	....	....	....
2005-06	Linkopings HC	Sweden	49	16	30	46	32	....	....	....	....	....	....	....	....	....	13	2	6	8	2	....	....	....	....
	NHL Totals		**6**	**1**	**1**	**2**	**0**	**0**	**0**	**0**	**4**	**25.0**		**18**	**44.4**	**6:58**									

Signed as a free agent by **Linkopings** (Sweden), May 17, 2004.

MARTIN, Paul

(MAHR-tihn, PAWL) **N.J.**

Defense. Shoots left. 6'1", 190 lbs. Born, Minneapolis, MN, March 5, 1981. New Jersey's 5th choice, 62nd overall, in 2000 Entry Draft.

			Regular Season														Playoffs								
Season	Club	League	GP	G	A	Pts	PIM	PP	SH	GW	S	%	+/-	TF	F%	Min	GP	G	A	Pts	PIM	PP	SH	GW	Min
1998-99	Elk River Elks	High-MN	24	9	11	20	....	....	....	....	....	....	....	....	....	....	....	....	....	....	....	....	....	....	....
99-2000	Elk River Elks	High-MN	24	15	35	50	26	....	....	....	....	....	....	....	....	....	....	....	....	....	....	....	....	....	....
2000-01	U. of Minnesota	WCHA	38	3	17	20	8	....	....	....	....	....	....	....	....	....	....	....	....	....	....	....	....	....	....
2001-02	U. of Minnesota	WCHA	44	8	30	38	22	....	....	....	....	....	....	....	....	....	....	....	....	....	....	....	....	....	....
2002-03	U. of Minnesota	WCHA	45	9	30	39	32	....	....	....	....	....	....	....	....	....	....	....	....	....	....	....	....	....	....
2003-04	**New Jersey**	**NHL**	**70**	**6**	**18**	**24**	**4**	**2**	**0**	**2**	**82**	**7.3**	**12**	**0**	**0.0**	**20:08**	**5**	**1**	**1**	**2**	**4**	**1**	**0**	**0**	**23:40**
2004-05	Fribourg	Swiss	11	3	4	7	2	....	....	....	....	....	....	....	....	....	....	....	....	....	....	....	....	....	....
2005-06	**New Jersey**	**NHL**	**80**	**5**	**32**	**37**	**32**	**3**	**0**	**0**	**97**	**5.2**	**1**	**0**	**0.0**	**23:37**	**9**	**0**	**3**	**3**	**4**	**0**	**0**	**0**	**24:17**
	United States	Olympics	DID NOT PLAY																						
	NHL Totals		**150**	**11**	**50**	**61**	**36**	**5**	**0**	**2**	**179**	**6.1**		**0**	**0.0**	**21:59**	**14**	**1**	**4**	**5**	**8**	**1**	**0**	**0**	**24:04**

Minnesota High School Player of the Year (1999) • WCHA All-Rookie Team (2001) • WCHA Second All-Star Team (2002, 2003) • NCAA West Second All-American Team (2003) • NCAA Championship All-Tournament Team (2003)

Signed as a free agent by **Fribourg** (Swiss), November 4, 2004.

MARTINEK, Radek

(MAHR-tih-nehk, RA-dehk) **NYI**

Defense. Shoots right. 6'1", 200 lbs. Born, Havlickuv Brod, Czech., August 31, 1976. NY Islanders' 12th choice, 228th overall, in 1999 Entry Draft.

			Regular Season														Playoffs								
Season	Club	League	GP	G	A	Pts	PIM	PP	SH	GW	S	%	+/-	TF	F%	Min	GP	G	A	Pts	PIM	PP	SH	GW	Min
1996-97	C. Budejovice	CzRep	52	3	5	8	40	....	....	....	....	....	....	....	....	....	5	0	1	1	2	....	....	....	....
	C. Budejovice	EuroHL	6	0	0	0	0	....	....	....	....	....	....	....	....	....	2	0	0	0	0	....	....	....	....
1997-98	C. Budejovice	CzRep	42	2	7	9	36	....	....	....	....	....	....	....	....	....	....	....	....	....	....	....	....	....	....
1998-99	C. Budejovice	CzRep	52	12	13	25	50	....	....	....	....	....	....	....	....	....	3	0	2	2		....	....	....	....
99-2000	C. Budejovice	CzRep	45	5	18	23	24	....	....	....	....	....	....	....	....	....	3	0	0	0	6	....	....	....	....
2000-01	C. Budejovice	CzRep	44	8	10	18	45	....	....	....	....	....	....	....	....	....	....	....	....	....	....	....	....	....	....
2001-02	**NY Islanders**	**NHL**	**23**	**1**	**4**	**5**	**16**	**0**	**0**	**1**	**25**	**4.0**	**5**	**0**	**0.0**	**21:07**	....	....	....	....	....	....	....	....	....
2002-03	**NY Islanders**	**NHL**	**66**	**2**	**11**	**13**	**26**	**0**	**0**	**1**	**67**	**3.0**	**15**	**0**	**0.0**	**17:15**	**4**	**0**	**0**	**0**	**4**	**0**	**0**	**0**	**10:16**
	Bridgeport	AHL	3	0	3	3	2	....	....	....	....	....	....	....	....	....	....	....	....	....	....	....	....	....	....
2003-04	**NY Islanders**	**NHL**	**47**	**4**	**3**	**7**	**43**	**0**	**0**	**1**	**48**	**8.3**	**–9**	**0**	**0.0**	**13:03**	**5**	**0**	**1**	**1**	**0**	**0**	**0**	**0**	**12:12**
2004-05	C. Budejovice	CzRep-2	30	12	18	30	80	....	....	....	....	....	....	....	....	....	12	2	3	5	6	....	....	....	....
2005-06	**NY Islanders**	**NHL**	**74**	**1**	**16**	**17**	**32**	**0**	**0**	**0**	**79**	**1.3**	**–9**	**1**	**0.0**	**18:16**	....	....	....	....	....	....	....	....	....
	NHL Totals		**210**	**8**	**34**	**42**	**117**	**0**	**0**	**3**	**219**	**3.7**		**1**	**0.0**	**17:05**	**9**	**0**	**1**	**1**	**4**	**0**	**0**	**0**	**11:20**

• Missed majority of 2001-02 season recovering from knee injury suffered in game vs. NY Rangers, November 11, 2001. Signed as a free agent by **Ceske Budejovice** (CzRep-2), September 17, 2004.

MARTINS, Steve

(MAHR-tihns, STEEV)

Center. Shoots left. 5'9", 185 lbs. Born, Gatineau, Que., April 13, 1972. Hartford's 1st choice, 5th overall, in 1994 Supplemental Draft.

			Regular Season														Playoffs								
Season	Club	League	GP	G	A	Pts	PIM	PP	SH	GW	S	%	+/-	TF	F%	Min	GP	G	A	Pts	PIM	PP	SH	GW	Min
1988-89	L'Outaouais	QAAA	38	18	33	51	70	....	....	....	....	....	....	....	....	....	....	....	....	....	....	....	....	....	....
1989-90	Choate-Rosemary	High-CT	STATISTICS NOT AVAILABLE																						
1990-91	Choate-Rosemary	High-CT	STATISTICS NOT AVAILABLE																						
1991-92	Harvard Crimson	ECAC	20	13	14	27	26	....	....	....	....	....	....	....	....	....	....	....	....	....	....	....	....	....	....
1992-93	Harvard Crimson	ECAC	18	6	8	14	40	....	....	....	....	....	....	....	....	....	....	....	....	....	....	....	....	....	....
1993-94	Harvard Crimson	ECAC	32	25	35	60	*93	....	....	....	....	....	....	....	....	....	....	....	....	....	....	....	....	....	....
1994-95	Harvard Crimson	ECAC	28	15	23	38	93	....	....	....	....	....	....	....	....	....	....	....	....	....	....	....	....	....	....
1995-96	**Hartford**	**NHL**	**23**	**1**	**3**	**4**	**8**	**0**	**0**	**0**	**27**	**3.7**	**–3**	....	....	....	....	....	....	....	....	....	....	....	....
	Springfield	AHL	30	9	20	29	10	....	....	....	....	....	....	....	....	....	....	....	....	....	....	....	....	....	....
1996-97	**Hartford**	**NHL**	**2**	**0**	**1**	**1**	**0**	**0**	**0**	**0**	**2**	**0.0**	**0**	....	....	....	....	....	....	....	....	....	....	....	....
	Springfield	AHL	63	12	31	43	78	....	....	....	....	....	....	....	....	....	17	1	3	4	26	....	....	....	....
1997-98	**Carolina**	**NHL**	**3**	**0**	**0**	**0**	**0**	**0**	**0**	**0**	**0**	**0.0**	**0**	....	....	....	....	....	....	....	....	....	....	....	....
	Chicago Wolves	IHL	78	20	41	61	122	....	....	....	....	....	....	....	....	....	21	6	14	20	28	....	....	....	....
1998-99	**Ottawa**	**NHL**	**36**	**4**	**3**	**7**	**10**	**1**	**0**	**1**	**27**	**14.8**	**4**	**191**	**56.0**	**8:28**	....	....	....	....	....	....	....	....	....
	Detroit Vipers	IHL	4	1	6	7	16	....	....	....	....	....	....	....	....	....	....	....	....	....	....	....	....	....	....
99-2000	**Ottawa**	**NHL**	**2**	**1**	**0**	**1**	**0**	**0**	**0**	**0**	**3**	**33.3**	**–1**	**3**	**0.0**	**11:10**	....	....	....	....	....	....	....	....	....
	Tampa Bay	**NHL**	**57**	**5**	**7**	**12**	**37**	**0**	**1**	**1**	**62**	**8.1**	**–11**	**806**	**50.9**	**13:27**	....	....	....	....	....	....	....	....	....
2000-01	**Tampa Bay**	**NHL**	**20**	**1**	**1**	**2**	**13**	**0**	**0**	**0**	**18**	**5.6**	**–9**	**184**	**52.2**	**9:35**	....	....	....	....	....	....	....	....	....
	Detroit Vipers	IHL	8	5	4	9	4	....	....	....	....	....	....	....	....	....	....	....	....	....	....	....	....	....	....
	NY Islanders	**NHL**	**39**	**1**	**3**	**4**	**20**	**0**	**1**	**0**	**28**	**3.6**	**–7**	**302**	**58.0**	**9:41**	....	....	....	....	....	....	....	....	....
	Chicago Wolves	IHL	5	1	2	3	0	....	....	....	....	....	....	....	....	....	16	1	6	7	22	....	....	....	....
2001-02	**Ottawa**	**NHL**	**14**	**1**	**0**	**1**	**4**	**0**	**0**	**0**	**11**	**9.1**	**1**	**121**	**55.4**	**9:33**	**2**	**0**	**0**	**0**	**0**	**0**	**0**	**0**	**7:13**
	Grand Rapids	AHL	51	10	21	31	66	....	....	....	....	....	....	....	....	....	3	0	0	0	0	....	....	....	....
2002-03	**Ottawa**	**NHL**	**14**	**2**	**3**	**5**	**10**	**0**	**0**	**0**	**13**	**15.4**	**3**	**111**	**55.9**	**9:45**	....	....	....	....	....	....	....	....	....
	Binghamton	AHL	26	5	11	16	31	....	....	....	....	....	....	....	....	....	....	....	....	....	....	....	....	....	....
	St. Louis	**NHL**	**28**	**3**	**3**	**6**	**18**	**0**	**1**	**0**	**25**	**12.0**	**–8**	**369**	**54.7**	**13:38**	**2**	**0**	**1**	**1**	**0**	**0**	**0**	**0**	**9:23**
2003-04	**St. Louis**	**NHL**	**25**	**1**	**0**	**1**	**22**	**0**	**1**	**0**	**27**	**3.7**	**–7**	**172**	**61.1**	**10:29**	**1**	**0**	**0**	**0**	**0**	**0**	**0**	**0**	**5:29**
	Worcester IceCats	AHL	22	4	9	13	16	....	....	....	....	....	....	....	....	....	....	....	....	....	....	....	....	....	....
2004-05	JYP Jyvaskyla	Finland	54	13	12	25	66	....	....	....	....	....	....	....	....	....	3	0	0	0	4	....	....	....	....
2005-06	**Ottawa**	**NHL**	**4**	**1**	**1**	**2**	**0**	**0**	**0**	**0**	**6**	**16.7**	**2**	**23**	**47.8**	**7:50**	....	....	....	....	....	....	....	....	....
	Binghamton	AHL	76	22	58	80	80	....	....	....	....	....	....	....	....	....	....	....	....	....	....	....	....	....	....
	NHL Totals		**267**	**21**	**25**	**46**	**142**	**1**	**4**	**2**	**249**	**8.4**		**2282**	**54.1**	**10:55**	**5**	**0**	**1**	**1**	**0**	**0**	**0**	**0**	**7:44**

ECAC First All-Star Team (1994) • ECAC Player of the Year (1994) • NCAA East First All-American Team (1994) • NCAA Final Four All-Tournament Team (1994)

Transferred to **Carolina** after **Hartford** franchise relocated, June 25, 1997. Signed as a free agent by **Ottawa**, July 20, 1998. Claimed on waivers by **Tampa Bay** from **Ottawa**, October 29, 1999. Traded to **NY Islanders** by **Tampa Bay** for future considerations, January 3, 2001. Signed as a free agent by **Ottawa**, August 30, 2001. Claimed on waivers by **St. Louis** from **Ottawa**, January 15, 2003. Signed as a free agent by **Jyvaskyla** (Finland), September 7, 2004. Signed as a free agent by **Ottawa**, August 19, 2005.

MATVICHUK, Richard

(MAT-vih-chuhk, RIH-chuhrd) **N.J.**

Defense. Shoots left. 6'3", 215 lbs. Born, Edmonton, Alta., February 5, 1973. Minnesota's 1st choice, 8th overall, in 1991 Entry Draft.

			Regular Season														Playoffs								
Season	Club	League	GP	G	A	Pts	PIM	PP	SH	GW	S	%	+/-	TF	F%	Min	GP	G	A	Pts	PIM	PP	SH	GW	Min
1988-89	Ft. Saskatchewan	AJHL	58	7	36	43	147	....	....	....	....	....	....	....	....	....	....	....	....	....	....	....	....	....	....
1989-90	Saskatoon Blades	WHL	56	8	24	32	126	....	....	....	....	....	....	....	....	....	10	2	8	10	16	....	....	....	....
1990-91	Saskatoon Blades	WHL	68	13	36	49	117	....	....	....	....	....	....	....	....	....	....	....	....	....	....	....	....	....	....
1991-92	Saskatoon Blades	WHL	58	14	40	54	126	....	....	....	....	....	....	....	....	....	22	1	9	10	61	....	....	....	....
1992-93	**Minnesota**	**NHL**	**53**	**2**	**3**	**5**	**26**	**1**	**0**	**0**	**51**	**3.9**	**–8**	....	....	....	....	....	....	....	....	....	....	....	....
	Kalamazoo Wings	IHL	3	0	1	1	6	....	....	....	....	....	....	....	....	....	....	....	....	....	....	....	....	....	....
1993-94	**Dallas**	**NHL**	**25**	**0**	**3**	**3**	**22**	**0**	**0**	**0**	**18**	**0.0**	**1**	....	....	....	**7**	**1**	**1**	**2**	**12**	**1**	**0**	**0**	....
	Kalamazoo Wings	IHL	43	8	17	25	84	....	....	....	....	....	....	....	....	....	....	....	....	....	....	....	....	....	....
1994-95	**Dallas**	**NHL**	**14**	**0**	**2**	**2**	**14**	**0**	**0**	**0**	**21**	**0.0**	**–7**	....	....	....	**5**	**0**	**2**	**2**	**4**	**0**	**0**	**0**	....
	Kalamazoo Wings	IHL	17	0	6	6	16	....	....	....	....	....	....	....	....	....	....	....	....	....	....	....	....	....	....
1995-96	**Dallas**	**NHL**	**73**	**6**	**16**	**22**	**71**	**0**	**0**	**1**	**81**	**7.4**	**4**	....	....	....	....	....	....	....	....	....	....	....	....
1996-97	**Dallas**	**NHL**	**57**	**5**	**7**	**12**	**87**	**0**	**2**	**0**	**83**	**6.0**	**1**	....	....	....	**7**	**0**	**1**	**1**	**20**	**0**	**0**	**0**	....
1997-98	**Dallas**	**NHL**	**74**	**3**	**15**	**18**	**63**	**0**	**0**	**0**	**71**	**4.2**	**7**	....	....	....	**16**	**1**	**1**	**2**	**14**	**0**	**0**	**0**	....
1998-99 ♦	**Dallas**	**NHL**	**64**	**3**	**9**	**12**	**51**	**1**	**0**	**0**	**54**	**5.6**	**23**	**0**	**0.0**	**21:19**	**22**	**1**	**5**	**6**	**20**	**0**	**0**	**0**	**22:40**
99-2000	**Dallas**	**NHL**	**70**	**4**	**21**	**25**	**42**	**0**	**0**	**1**	**73**	**5.5**	**7**	**0**	**0.0**	**24:27**	**23**	**2**	**5**	**7**	**14**	**0**	**0**	**0**	**25:51**
2000-01	**Dallas**	**NHL**	**78**	**4**	**16**	**20**	**62**	**2**	**0**	**1**	**85**	**4.7**	**5**	**1**	**100.0**	**22:53**	**10**	**0**	**0**	**0**	**14**	**0**	**0**	**0**	**22:43**
2001-02	**Dallas**	**NHL**	**82**	**9**	**12**	**21**	**52**	**4**	**0**	**2**	**109**	**8.3**	**11**	**1**	**0.0**	**23:47**	....	....	....	....	....	....	....	....	....
2002-03	**Dallas**	**NHL**	**68**	**1**	**5**	**6**	**58**	**0**	**0**	**1**	**59**	**1.7**	**1**	**3**	**0.0**	**19:23**	**12**	**0**	**3**	**3**	**8**	**0**	**0**	**0**	**19:55**
2003-04	**Dallas**	**NHL**	**75**	**1**	**20**	**21**	**36**	**0**	**0**	**1**	**85**	**1.2**	**0**	**2**	**50.0**	**21:50**	**5**	**0**	**1**	**1**	**8**	**0**	**0**	**0**	**22:15**
2004-05			DID NOT PLAY																						
2005-06	**New Jersey**	**NHL**	**62**	**1**	**10**	**11**	**40**	**0**	**0**	**0**	**43**	**2.3**	**2**	**0**	**0.0**	**18:13**	**7**	**0**	**0**	**0**	**4**	**0**	**0**	**0**	**16:41**
	NHL Totals		**795**	**39**	**139**	**178**	**624**	**8**	**2**	**7**	**833**	**4.7**		**7**	**28.6**	**21:50**	**114**	**5**	**19**	**24**	**118**	**1**	**0**	**0**	**22:38**

WHL East First All-Star Team (1992)

Transferred to **Dallas** after **Minnesota** franchise relocated, June 9, 1993. Signed as a free agent by **New Jersey**, July 12, 2004.

MAULDIN, Greg

(MAWL-dihn, GREHG)

Center. Shoots right. 5'11", 180 lbs. Born, Boston, MA, June 10, 1982. Columbus' 10th choice, 199th overall, in 2002 Entry Draft.

			Regular Season														Playoffs								
Season	Club	League	GP	G	A	Pts	PIM	PP	SH	GW	S	%	+/-	TF	F%	Min	GP	G	A	Pts	PIM	PP	SH	GW	Min
99-2000	Junior Bruins	EJHL	58	45	42	87	14																		
2000-01	Junior Bruins	EJHL	53	48	58	106	73																		
2001-02	Massachusetts	H-East	33	12	12	24	10																		
2002-03	Massachusetts	H-East	36	21	20	41	26																		
2003-04	Massachusetts	H-East	29	15	14	29	15																		
	Columbus	NHL	6	0	0	0	4	0	0	0	6	0.0	–2	0	0.0	8:47									
	Syracuse Crunch	AHL	2	0	0	0	0																		
2004-05	Syracuse Crunch	AHL	66	7	20	27	49										1	0	0	0	0				
2005-06	Syracuse Crunch	AHL	56	12	17	29	53																		
	Houston Aeros	AHL	11	1	3	4	0										8	1	1	2	2				
	NHL Totals		6	0	0	0	4	0	0	0	6	0.0		0	0.0	8:47									

EJHL First All-Star Team (2000, 2001) • EJHL MVP (2000)

MAY, Brad

(MAY, BRAD) **COL.**

Left wing. Shoots left. 6'1", 217 lbs. Born, Toronto, Ont., November 29, 1971. Buffalo's 1st choice, 14th overall, in 1990 Entry Draft.

Season	Club	League	GP	G	A	Pts	PIM	PP	SH	GW	S	%	+/-	TF	F%	Min	GP	G	A	Pts	PIM	PP	SH	GW	Min
1987-88	Markham	OMHA	31	22	37	59	58																		
	Markham	OHA-B	6	1	1	2	21																		
1988-89	Niagara Falls	OHL	65	8	14	22	304										17	0	1	1	55				
1989-90	Niagara Falls	OHL	61	32	58	90	223										16	9	13	22	64				
1990-91	Niagara Falls	OHL	34	37	32	69	93										14	11	14	25	53				
1991-92	Buffalo	NHL	69	11	6	17	309	1	0	3	82	13.4	–12				7	1	4	5	2	0	0	1	
1992-93	Buffalo	NHL	82	13	13	26	242	0	0	1	114	11.4	3				8	1	1	2	14	0	0	1	
1993-94	Buffalo	NHL	84	18	27	45	171	3	0	3	166	10.8	–6				7	0	2	2	9	0	0	0	
1994-95	Buffalo	NHL	33	3	3	6	87	1	0	0	42	7.1	5				4	0	0	0	2	0	0	0	
1995-96	Buffalo	NHL	79	15	29	44	295	3	0	4	168	8.9	6												
1996-97	Buffalo	NHL	42	3	4	7	106	1	0	1	75	4.0	–8				10	1	1	2	32	0	0	0	
1997-98	Buffalo	NHL	36	4	7	11	113	0	0	0	41	9.8	2												
	Vancouver	NHL	27	9	3	12	41	4	0	2	56	16.1	0												
1998-99	Vancouver	NHL	66	6	11	17	102	1	0	1	91	6.6	–14	8	12.5	13:04									
99-2000	Vancouver	NHL	59	9	7	16	90	0	0	3	66	13.6	–2	3	0.0	10:24									
2000-01	Phoenix	NHL	62	11	14	25	107	0	0	0	83	13.3	10	3	33.3	11:11									
2001-02	Phoenix	NHL	72	10	12	22	95	1	0	3	105	9.5	11	3	0.0	12:04	5	0	0	0	0	0	0	0	10:19
2002-03	Phoenix	NHL	20	3	4	7	32	0	0	0	24	12.5	3	0	0.0	9:56									
	Vancouver	NHL	3	0	0	0	10	0	0	0	1	0.0	1	0	0.0	7:48	14	0	0	0	15	0	0	0	7:25
2003-04	Vancouver	NHL	70	5	6	11	137	0	0	0	75	6.7	–2	8	50.0	8:56	6	1	0	1	6	0	0	0	7:07
2004-05			DID NOT PLAY																						
2005-06	Colorado	NHL	54	3	3	6	82	0	0	0	55	5.5	–14	6	33.3	8:23	3	0	0	0	0	0	0	0	9:21
	NHL Totals		858	123	149	272	2019	15	0	21	1244	9.9		31	25.8	10:41	64	4	8	12	80	0	0	2	8:04

OHL Second All-Star Team (1990, 1991)

• Missed majority of 1990-91 season recovering from knee injury suffered at Team Canada Juniors evaluation camp, August 21, 1990. Traded to **Vancouver** by **Buffalo** with Buffalo's 3rd round choice (later traded to Tampa Bay – Tampa Bay selected Jimmie Olvestad) in 1999 Entry Draft for Geoff Sanderson, February 4, 1998. Traded to **Phoenix** by **Vancouver** for future considerations, June 24, 2000. • Missed majority of 2002-03 season recovering from shoulder injury suffered in pre-season game vs. Detroit, October 6, 2002. Traded to **Vancouver** by **Phoenix** for Phoenix's 3rd round choice (previously acquired, Phoenix selected Dimitri Pestunov) in 2003 Entry Draft, March 11, 2003. Signed as a free agent by **Colorado**, August 5, 2005.

MAYERS, Jamal

(MAI-uhrz, JUH-MAHL) **ST.L.**

Right wing. Shoots right. 6'1", 212 lbs. Born, Toronto, Ont., October 24, 1974. St. Louis' 3rd choice, 89th overall, in 1993 Entry Draft.

Season	Club	League	GP	G	A	Pts	PIM	PP	SH	GW	S	%	+/-	TF	F%	Min	GP	G	A	Pts	PIM	PP	SH	GW	Min
1990-91	Thornhill	MTJHL	44	12	24	36	78																		
1991-92	Thornhill	MTJHL	56	38	69	107	36																		
1992-93	Western Mich.	CCHA	38	8	17	25	26																		
1993-94	Western Mich.	CCHA	40	17	32	49	40																		
1994-95	Western Mich.	CCHA	39	13	32	45	40																		
1995-96	Western Mich.	CCHA	38	17	22	39	75																		
1996-97	St. Louis	NHL	6	0	1	1	2	0	0	0	7	0.0	–3												
	Worcester IceCats	AHL	62	12	14	26	104										5	4	5	9	4				
1997-98	Worcester IceCats	AHL	61	19	24	43	117										11	3	4	7	10				
1998-99	St. Louis	NHL	34	4	5	9	40	0	0	0	48	8.3	–3	2	50.0	8:08	11	0	1	1	8	0	0	0	8:34
	Worcester IceCats	AHL	20	9	7	16	34																		
99-2000	St. Louis	NHL	79	7	10	17	90	0	0	0	99	7.1	0	77	52.0	9:46	7	0	4	4	2	0	0	0	10:42
2000-01	St. Louis	NHL	77	8	13	21	117	0	0	0	132	6.1	–3	273	51.3	11:04	15	2	3	5	8	0	0	0	11:28
2001-02	St. Louis	NHL	77	9	8	17	99	0	1	0	105	8.6	9	761	52.6	11:36	10	3	0	3	2	0	0	2	11:14
2002-03	St. Louis	NHL	15	2	5	7	8	0	0	0	26	7.7	1	111	51.4	14:21									
2003-04	St. Louis	NHL	80	6	5	11	91	0	1	3	130	4.6	–19	681	48.6	13:01	5	0	0	0	0	0	0	0	12:55
2004-05	Hammarby	Sweden-2	19	9	13	22	36																		
	Missouri	UHL	13	5	2	7	68																		
2005-06	St. Louis	NHL	67	15	11	26	129	0	2	1	111	13.5	–22	363	48.5	15:07									
	NHL Totals		435	51	58	109	576	0	4	4	658	7.8		2268	50.5	11:48	48	5	8	13	20	0	0	2	10:47

• Missed majority of 2002-03 season recovering from knee injury suffered in game vs. Calgary, November 16, 2002. Signed as a free agent by **Hammarby** (Sweden-2), November 16, 2004. Signed as a free agent by **Missouri** (UHL), March 11, 2005.

McALLISTER, Chris

(mih-KAL-ihs-tuhr, KRIHS)

Defense. Shoots left. 6'8", 250 lbs. Born, Saskatoon, Sask., June 16, 1975. Vancouver's 1st choice, 40th overall, in 1995 Entry Draft.

Season	Club	League	GP	G	A	Pts	PIM	PP	SH	GW	S	%	+/-	TF	F%	Min	GP	G	A	Pts	PIM	PP	SH	GW	Min
1992-93	Saskatoon Royals	NSJHL	40	14	14	28	224																		
	Saskatoon Blades	WHL	4	0	0	0	2																		
1993-94	Humboldt	SJHL	50	3	5	8	150																		
	Saskatoon Blades	WHL	2	0	0	0	5																		
1994-95	Saskatoon Blades	WHL	65	2	8	10	134										10	0	0	0	28				
1995-96	Syracuse Crunch	AHL	68	0	2	2	142										16	0	0	0	34				
1996-97	Syracuse Crunch	AHL	43	3	1	4	108										3	0	0	0	6				
1997-98	Vancouver	NHL	36	1	2	3	106	0	0	0	15	6.7	–12												
	Syracuse Crunch	AHL	23	0	1	1	71										5	0	0	0	21				
1998-99	Vancouver	NHL	28	1	1	2	63	0	0	0	6	16.7	–7	0	0.0	5:53									
	Syracuse Crunch	AHL	5	0	0	0	24																		
	Toronto	NHL	20	0	2	2	39	0	0	0	12	0.0	4	0	0.0	13:59	6	0	1	1	4	0	0	0	13:00
99-2000	Toronto	NHL	36	0	3	3	68	0	0	0	12	0.0	–4	0	0.0	12:02									
2000-01	Philadelphia	NHL	60	2	2	4	124	0	0	0	33	6.1	1	0	0.0	11:36	2	0	0	0	0	0	0	0	8:00
2001-02	Philadelphia	NHL	42	0	5	5	113	0	0	0	26	0.0	–7	0	0.0	9:12									
2002-03	Philadelphia	NHL	19	0	0	0	21	0	0	0	9	0.0	–2	0	0.0	9:32									
	Philadelphia	AHL	4	0	0	0	12																		
	Colorado	NHL	14	0	1	1	26	0	0	0	4	0.0	6	0	0.0	8:02	1	0	0	0	0	0	0	0	2:34
2003-04	Colorado	NHL	34	0	0	0	62	0	0	0	11	0.0	–2	0	0.0	5:34									
	NY Rangers	NHL	12	0	1	1	12	0	0	0	8	0.0	–4	4	50.0	12:49									
2004-05	Newcastle Vipers	Britain-2	14	0	4	4	30																		
2005-06	San Antonio	AHL	59	3	6	9	171																		
	NHL Totals		301	4	17	21	634	0	0	0	136	2.9		4	50.0	9:48	9	0	1	1	4	0	0	0	10:43

Traded to **Toronto** by **Vancouver** for Darby Hendrickson, February 16, 1999. Traded to **Philadelphia** by **Toronto** for the rights to Regan Kelly, September 26, 2000. Traded to **Colorado** by **Philadelphia** for Colorado's 6th round choice (Ville Hostikka) in 2003 Entry Draft, February 5, 2003. Traded to **NY Rangers** by **Colorado** with David Liffiton and Florida's 2nd round choice (previously acquired, later traded back to Florida – Florida selected David Shantz) in 2004 Entry Draft for Matthew Barnaby and NY Rangers' 3rd round choice (Denis Parshin) in 2004 Entry Draft, March 8, 2004. Signed as a free agent by **Newcastle** (Britain-2), January 7, 2005. Signed as a free agent by **Phoenix**, August 11, 2005.

			Regular Season														Playoffs								
Season	Club	League	GP	G	A	Pts	PIM	PP	SH	GW	S	%	+/-	TF	F%	Min	GP	G	A	Pts	PIM	PP	SH	GW	Min

McAMMOND, Dean

(MIHK-AM-uhnd, DEEN) **OTT.**

Center. Shoots left. 5'11", 200 lbs. Born, Grand Cache, Alta., June 15, 1973. Chicago's 1st choice, 22nd overall, in 1991 Entry Draft.

Season	Club	League	GP	G	A	Pts	PIM	PP	SH	GW	S	%	+/-	TF	F%	Min	GP	G	A	Pts	PIM	PP	SH	GW	Min
1988-89	St. Albert Raiders	AMHL	36	33	44	77	132	....	....	....	....	....	....	....	....	....	....	....	....	....	....	....	....	....	....
1989-90	Prince Albert	WHL	53	11	11	22	49	....	....	....	....	....	....	....	....	....	14	2	3	5	18	....	....	....	....
1990-91	Prince Albert	WHL	71	33	35	68	108	....	....	....	....	....	....	....	....	....	2	0	1	1	6	....	....	....	....
1991-92	Prince Albert	WHL	63	37	54	91	189	....	....	....	....	....	....	....	....	....	10	12	11	23	26	....	....	....	....
	Chicago	**NHL**	5	0	2	2	0	0	0	0	4	0.0	−2	....	....	....	3	0	0	0	2	0	0	0	....
1992-93	Prince Albert	WHL	30	19	29	48	44	....	....	....	....	....	....	....	....	....	....	....	....	....	....	....	....	....	....
	Swift Current	WHL	18	10	13	23	24	....	....	....	....	....	....	....	....	....	17	*16	19	35	20	....	....	....	....
1993-94	**Edmonton**	**NHL**	45	6	21	27	16	2	0	0	52	11.5	12	....	....	....	....	....	....	....	....	....	....	....	....
	Cape Breton	AHL	28	9	12	21	38	....	....	....	....	....	....	....	....	....	....	....	....	....	....	....	....	....	....
1994-95	**Edmonton**	**NHL**	6	0	0	0	0	0	0	0	3	0.0	−1	....	....	....	....	....	....	....	....	....	....	....	....
1995-96	**Edmonton**	**NHL**	53	15	15	30	23	4	0	0	79	19.0	6	....	....	....	....	....	....	....	....	....	....	....	....
	Cape Breton	AHL	22	9	15	24	55	....	....	....	....	....	....	....	....	....	....	....	....	....	....	....	....	....	....
1996-97	**Edmonton**	**NHL**	57	12	17	29	28	4	0	6	106	11.3	−15	....	....	....	....	....	....	....	....	....	....	....	....
1997-98	**Edmonton**	**NHL**	77	19	31	50	46	8	0	3	128	14.8	9	....	....	....	12	1	4	5	12	0	0	0	....
1998-99	**Edmonton**	**NHL**	65	9	16	25	36	1	0	0	122	7.4	5	26	38.5	14:15	....	....	....	....	....	....	....	....	....
	Chicago	**NHL**	12	1	4	5	2	0	0	1	16	6.3	3	37	48.6	15:43	....	....	....	....	....	....	....	....	....
99-2000	**Chicago**	**NHL**	76	14	18	32	72	1	0	1	118	11.9	11	257	39.7	16:25	....	....	....	....	....	....	....	....	....
2000-01	**Chicago**	**NHL**	61	10	16	26	43	1	0	1	95	10.5	4	23	43.5	15:30	....	....	....	....	....	....	....	....	....
	Philadelphia	**NHL**	10	1	1	2	0	1	0	0	17	5.9	−1	65	46.2	12:00	4	0	0	0	2	0	0	0	9:25
2001-02	**Calgary**	**NHL**	73	21	30	51	60	7	0	4	152	13.8	2	143	55.2	18:56	....	....	....	....	....	....	....	....	....
2002-03	**Colorado**	**NHL**	41	10	8	18	10	2	0	2	72	13.9	1	9	55.6	14:24	....	....	....	....	....	....	....	....	....
2003-04	**Calgary**	**NHL**	64	17	13	30	18	4	1	5	101	16.8	9	768	49.1	16:52	....	....	....	....	....	....	....	....	....
2004-05	Albany River Rats	AHL	79	19	42	61	72	....	....	....	....	....	....	....	....	....	....	....	....	....	....	....	....	....	....
2005-06	**St. Louis**	**NHL**	78	15	22	37	32	4	0	0	116	12.9	−25	289	47.4	16:02	....	....	....	....	....	....	....	....	....
	NHL Totals		**723**	**150**	**214**	**364**	**386**	**39**	**1**	**23**	**1181**	**12.7**		**1617**	**47.5**	**16:06**	**19**	**1**	**4**	**5**	**16**	**0**	**0**	**0**	**9:25**

Traded to **Edmonton** by **Chicago** with Igor Kravchuk for Joe Murphy, February 24, 1993. Traded to **Chicago** by **Edmonton** with Boris Mironov and Jonas Elofsson for Chad Kilger, Daniel Cleary, Ethan Moreau and Christian Laflamme, March 20, 1999. Traded to **Philadelphia** by **Chicago** for Philadelphia's 3rd round choice (later traded to Toronto – Toronto selected Nicolas Corbeil) in 2001 Entry Draft, March 13, 2001. Traded to **Calgary** by **Philadelphia** for Calgary's 4th round choice (Rosario Ruggeri) in 2002 Entry Draft, June 24, 2001. Traded to **Colorado** by **Calgary** with Derek Morris and Jeff Shantz for Chris Drury and Stephane Yelle, October 1, 2002. Traded to **Calgary** by **Colorado** for Calgary's 5th round choice (Mark McCutcheon) in 2003 Entry Draft, March 11, 2003. • Ruled ineligible to play remainder of 2002-03 season by NHL due to transaction violation by Calgary, March 15, 2003. Signed as a free agent by **New Jersey**, October 5, 2004. Signed as a free agent by **St. Louis**, August 9, 2005. Signed as a free agent by **Ottawa**, August 2, 2006.

McCABE, Bryan

(mih-KAYB, BRIGH-uhn) **TOR.**

Defense. Shoots left. 6'2", 220 lbs. Born, St. Catharines, Ont., June 8, 1975. NY Islanders' 2nd choice, 40th overall, in 1993 Entry Draft.

Season	Club	League	GP	G	A	Pts	PIM	PP	SH	GW	S	%	+/-	TF	F%	Min	GP	G	A	Pts	PIM	PP	SH	GW	Min
1990-91	Calgary Canucks	AMHL	33	14	34	48	55	....	....	....	....	....	....	....	....	....	....	....	....	....	....	....	....	....	....
1991-92	Medicine Hat	WHL	68	6	24	30	157	....	....	....	....	....	....	....	....	....	4	0	0	0	6	....	....	....	....
1992-93	Medicine Hat	WHL	14	0	13	13	83	....	....	....	....	....	....	....	....	....	....	....	....	....	....	....	....	....	....
	Spokane Chiefs	WHL	46	3	44	47	134	....	....	....	....	....	....	....	....	....	6	1	5	6	28	....	....	....	....
1993-94	Spokane Chiefs	WHL	64	22	62	84	218	....	....	....	....	....	....	....	....	....	3	0	4	4	4	....	....	....	....
1994-95	Spokane Chiefs	WHL	42	14	39	53	115	....	....	....	....	....	....	....	....	....	....	....	....	....	....	....	....	....	....
	Brandon	WHL	20	6	10	16	38	....	....	....	....	....	....	....	....	....	18	4	13	17	59	....	....	....	....
1995-96	**NY Islanders**	**NHL**	82	7	16	23	156	3	0	1	130	5.4	−24	....	....	....	....	....	....	....	....	....	....	....	....
1996-97	**NY Islanders**	**NHL**	82	8	20	28	165	2	1	2	117	6.8	−2	....	....	....	....	....	....	....	....	....	....	....	....
1997-98	**NY Islanders**	**NHL**	56	3	9	12	145	1	0	0	81	3.7	9	....	....	....	....	....	....	....	....	....	....	....	....
	Vancouver	**NHL**	26	1	11	12	64	0	1	0	42	2.4	10	....	....	....	....	....	....	....	....	....	....	....	....
1998-99	**Vancouver**	**NHL**	69	7	14	21	120	1	2	0	98	7.1	−11	1	0.0	24:13	....	....	....	....	....	....	....	....	....
99-2000	**Chicago**	**NHL**	79	6	19	25	139	2	0	2	119	5.0	−8	1	0.0	23:23	....	....	....	....	....	....	....	....	....
2000-01	**Toronto**	**NHL**	82	5	24	29	123	3	0	2	159	3.1	16	0	0.0	23:49	11	2	3	5	16	1	0	0	23:56
2001-02	**Toronto**	**NHL**	82	17	26	43	129	8	0	1	157	10.8	16	1	0.0	24:34	20	5	5	10	30	3	0	1	29:33
2002-03	**Toronto**	**NHL**	75	6	18	24	135	3	0	1	149	4.0	9	1	0.0	23:39	7	0	3	3	10	0	0	0	27:28
2003-04	**Toronto**	**NHL**	75	16	37	53	86	8	0	2	168	9.5	22	2	50.0	25:44	13	3	5	8	14	2	0	0	28:47
2004-05	HV 71 Jonkoping	Sweden	10	1	0	1	30	....	....	....	....	....	....	....	....	....	....	....	....	....	....	....	....	....	....
2005-06	**Toronto**	**NHL**	73	19	49	68	116	13	0	6	207	9.2	−1	1	0.0	28:18	....	....	....	....	....	....	....	....	....
	Canada	Olympics	6	0	0	0	18	....	....	....	....	....	....	....	....	....	....	....	....	....	....	....	....	....	....
	NHL Totals		**781**	**95**	**243**	**338**	**1378**	**44**	**4**	**17**	**1427**	**6.7**		**7**	**14.3**	**24:47**	**51**	**10**	**16**	**26**	**70**	**6**	**0**	**1**	**27:51**

WHL West Second All-Star Team (1993) • WHL West First All-Star Team (1994) • WHL East First All-Star Team (1995) • Memorial Cup Tournament All-Star Team (1995) • NHL Second All-Star Team (2004)

Traded to **Vancouver** by **NY Islanders** with Todd Bertuzzi and NY Islanders' 3rd round choice (Jarkko Ruutu) in 1998 Entry Draft for Trevor Linden, February 6, 1998. Traded to **Chicago** by **Vancouver** with Vancouver's 1st round choice (Pavel Vorobiev) in 2000 Entry Draft for Chicago's 1st round choice (later traded to Tampa Bay – later traded to NY Rangers – NY Rangers selected Pavel Brendl) in 1999 Entry Draft, June 25, 1999. Traded to **Toronto** by **Chicago** for Alexander Karpovtsev and Toronto's 4th round choice (Vladimir Gusev) in 2001 Entry Draft, October 2, 2000. Signed as a free agent by **Jonkoping** (Sweden), October 29, 2004.

McCARTHY, Steve

(mih-KAHR-thee, STEEV) **ATL.**

Defense. Shoots left. 6'1", 198 lbs. Born, Trail, B.C., February 3, 1981. Chicago's 1st choice, 23rd overall, in 1999 Entry Draft.

Season	Club	League	GP	G	A	Pts	PIM	PP	SH	GW	S	%	+/-	TF	F%	Min	GP	G	A	Pts	PIM	PP	SH	GW	Min
1996-97	Trail	BCHL	57	25	52	77	81	....	....	....	....	....	....	....	....	....	....	....	....	....	....	....	....	....	....
	Edmonton Ice	WHL	2	0	0	0	0	....	....	....	....	....	....	....	....	....	....	....	....	....	....	....	....	....	....
1997-98	Edmonton Ice	WHL	58	11	29	40	59	....	....	....	....	....	....	....	....	....	....	....	....	....	....	....	....	....	....
1998-99	Kootenay Ice	WHL	57	19	33	52	79	....	....	....	....	....	....	....	....	....	6	0	5	5	8	....	....	....	....
99-2000	**Chicago**	**NHL**	5	1	1	2	4	1	0	0	4	25.0	0	0	0.0	15:09	....	....	....	....	....	....	....	....	....
	Kootenay Ice	WHL	37	13	23	36	36	....	....	....	....	....	....	....	....	....	....	....	....	....	....	....	....	....	....
2000-01	**Chicago**	**NHL**	44	0	5	5	8	0	0	0	32	0.0	−7	0	0.0	14:47	....	....	....	....	....	....	....	....	....
	Norfolk Admirals	AHL	7	0	4	4	2	....	....	....	....	....	....	....	....	....	....	....	....	....	....	....	....	....	....
2001-02	**Chicago**	**NHL**	3	0	0	0	2	0	0	0	2	0.0	−1	0	0.0	11:48	....	....	....	....	....	....	....	....	....
	Norfolk Admirals	AHL	77	7	21	28	37	....	....	....	....	....	....	....	....	....	2	0	3	3	2	....	....	....	....
2002-03	Norfolk Admirals	AHL	19	1	6	7	14	....	....	....	....	....	....	....	....	....	9	0	4	4	0	....	....	....	....
	Chicago	**NHL**	57	1	4	5	23	0	0	0	55	1.8	−1	0	0.0	16:25	....	....	....	....	....	....	....	....	....
2003-04	**Chicago**	**NHL**	25	1	3	4	8	0	0	0	29	3.4	−9	0	0.0	19:21	....	....	....	....	....	....	....	....	....
2004-05			DID NOT PLAY																						
2005-06	**Vancouver**	**NHL**	51	2	4	6	43	0	0	0	46	4.3	3	0	0.0	13:17	....	....	....	....	....	....	....	....	....
	Atlanta	**NHL**	16	7	3	10	8	2	0	0	20	35.0	0	0	0.0	16:44	....	....	....	....	....	....	....	....	....
	NHL Totals		**201**	**12**	**20**	**32**	**96**	**3**	**0**	**0**	**188**	**6.4**		**0**	**0.0**	**15:33**	....	....	....	....	....	....	....	....	....

• Missed majority of 2003-04 season recovering from groin injury suffered in game vs. Calgary, November 22, 2003. Traded to **Vancouver** by **Chicago** for Vancouver's 3rd round choice in 2007 Entry Draft, August 22, 2005. Traded to **Atlanta** by **Vancouver** for a conditional choice in 2007 Entry Draft, March 9, 2006.

McCARTY, Darren

(mih-KAHR-tee, DAIR-ehn) **CGY.**

Right wing. Shoots right. 6'1", 210 lbs. Born, Burnaby, B.C., April 1, 1972. Detroit's 2nd choice, 46th overall, in 1992 Entry Draft.

Season	Club	League	GP	G	A	Pts	PIM	PP	SH	GW	S	%	+/-	TF	F%	Min	GP	G	A	Pts	PIM	PP	SH	GW	Min
1988-89	Peterborough	OHA-B	34	18	17	35	135	....	....	....	....	....	....	....	....	....	....	....	....	....	....	....	....	....	....
1989-90	Belleville Bulls	OHL	63	12	15	27	142	....	....	....	....	....	....	....	....	....	11	1	1	2	21	....	....	....	....
1990-91	Belleville Bulls	OHL	60	30	37	67	151	....	....	....	....	....	....	....	....	....	6	2	2	4	13	....	....	....	....
1991-92	Belleville Bulls	OHL	65	*55	72	127	177	....	....	....	....	....	....	....	....	....	5	1	4	5	13	....	....	....	....
1992-93	Adirondack	AHL	73	17	19	36	278	....	....	....	....	....	....	....	....	....	11	0	1	1	33	....	....	....	....
1993-94	**Detroit**	**NHL**	67	9	17	26	181	0	0	2	81	11.1	12	....	....	....	7	2	2	4	8	0	0	0	....
1994-95	**Detroit**	**NHL**	31	5	8	13	88	1	0	2	27	18.5	5	....	....	....	18	3	2	5	14	0	0	0	....
1995-96	**Detroit**	**NHL**	63	15	14	29	158	8	0	1	102	14.7	14	....	....	....	19	3	2	5	20	0	0	1	....
1996-97◆	**Detroit**	**NHL**	68	19	30	49	126	5	0	6	171	11.1	14	....	....	....	20	3	4	7	34	0	0	2	....
1997-98◆	**Detroit**	**NHL**	71	15	22	37	157	5	1	2	166	9.0	0	....	....	....	22	3	8	11	34	0	0	1	....
1998-99	**Detroit**	**NHL**	69	14	26	40	108	6	0	1	140	10.0	10	15	33.3	17:04	10	1	1	2	23	0	0	0	13:04
99-2000	**Detroit**	**NHL**	24	6	6	12	48	0	0	1	40	15.0	1	1	0.0	13:40	9	0	1	1	12	0	0	0	14:09
2000-01	**Detroit**	**NHL**	72	12	10	22	123	1	1	3	118	10.2	−5	26	53.9	13:26	6	1	0	1	2	0	0	0	13:11
2001-02◆	**Detroit**	**NHL**	62	5	7	12	98	0	0	1	74	6.8	2	26	38.5	11:47	23	4	4	8	34	0	0	1	13:33
2002-03	**Detroit**	**NHL**	73	13	9	22	138	1	0	2	129	10.1	10	320	57.8	13:18	4	0	0	0	6	0	0	0	15:45
2003-04	**Detroit**	**NHL**	43	6	5	11	50	1	0	0	61	9.8	2	141	50.4	12:20	12	0	1	1	7	0	0	0	11:30

			Regular Season														Playoffs								
Season	Club	League	GP	G	A	Pts	PIM	PP	SH	GW	S	%	+/-	TF	F%	Min	GP	G	A	Pts	PIM	PP	SH	GW	Min
2004-05			Did not play																						
2005-06	**Calgary**	**NHL**	67	7	6	13	117	1	0	0	67	10.4	–1	234	50.0	11:43	7	2	0	2	15	0	0	1	9:50
	NHL Totals		710	126	160	286	1392	29	2	21	1176	10.7		763	52.7	13:23	157	22	25	47	209	0	0	6	12:56

OHL First All-Star Team (1992)

• Missed majority of 1999-2000 season recovering from hernia injury suffered in game vs. Dallas, November 10, 1999. Signed as a free agent by **Calgary**, August 2, 2005.

McCAULEY, Alyn

(mih-KAW-lee, AL-ihn) **L.A.**

Center. Shoots left. 5'11", 200 lbs. Born, Brockville, Ont., May 29, 1977. New Jersey's 5th choice, 79th overall, in 1995 Entry Draft.

1991-92	Kingston	MTJHL	37	5	17	22	6	....	....	....	....	....	....	....	....	....	....	....	....	....	....	....	....	....	....
1992-93	Kingston	MTJHL	38	31	29	60	18	....	....	....	....	....	....	....	....	....	....	....	....	....	....	....	....	....	....
1993-94	Ottawa 67's	OHL	38	13	23	36	10	....	....	....	....	....	....	....	....	....	13	5	14	19	4	....	....	....	....
1994-95	Ottawa 67's	OHL	65	16	38	54	20	....	....	....	....	....	....	....	....	....	....	....	....	....	....	....	....	....	....
1995-96	Ottawa 67's	OHL	55	34	48	82	24	....	....	....	....	....	....	....	....	....	2	0	0	0	0	....	....	....	....
1996-97	Ottawa 67's	OHL	50	*56	56	112	16	....	....	....	....	....	....	....	....	....	22	14	22	36	14	....	....	....	....
	St. John's	AHL	....	....	....	....	....	....	....	....	....	....	....	....	....	....	3	0	1	1	0	....	....	....	....
1997-98	**Toronto**	**NHL**	60	6	10	16	6	0	0	1	77	7.8	–7	....	....	....	....	....	....	....	....	....	....	....	....
1998-99	**Toronto**	**NHL**	39	9	15	24	2	1	0	1	76	11.8	7	591	46.4	15:10	....	....	....	....	....	....	....	....	....
99-2000	**Toronto**	**NHL**	45	5	5	10	10	1	0	0	41	12.2	–6	450	47.8	10:46	5	0	0	0	6	0	0	0	7:51
	St. John's	AHL	5	1	1	2	0	....	....	....	....	....	....	....	....	....	....	....	....	....	....	....	....	....	....
2000-01	**Toronto**	**NHL**	14	1	0	1	0	0	0	0	13	7.7	0	139	46.8	10:28	10	0	0	0	2	0	0	0	9:34
	St. John's	AHL	47	16	28	44	12	....	....	....	....	....	....	....	....	....	....	....	....	....	....	....	....	....	....
2001-02	**Toronto**	**NHL**	82	6	10	16	18	0	1	1	95	6.3	10	951	48.1	11:24	20	5	10	15	4	1	0	2	19:12
2002-03	**Toronto**	**NHL**	64	6	9	15	16	0	0	0	79	7.6	3	515	44.5	12:54	....	....	....	....	....	....	....	....	....
	San Jose	**NHL**	16	3	7	10	4	3	0	0	29	10.3	–2	81	50.6	17:29	....	....	....	....	....	....	....	....	....
2003-04	**San Jose**	**NHL**	82	20	27	47	28	5	0	4	146	13.7	23	1216	47.7	16:51	11	2	1	3	2	0	0	0	14:17
2004-05			Did not play																						
2005-06	**San Jose**	**NHL**	76	12	14	26	30	4	2	3	105	11.4	–3	692	49.1	14:14	6	0	1	1	4	0	0	0	11:17
	NHL Totals		478	68	97	165	114	14	3	10	661	10.3		4635	47.5	13:42	52	7	12	19	18	1	0	2	14:18

OHL First All-Star Team (1996, 1997) • OHL MVP (1996, 1997) • Canadian Major Junior First All-Star Team (1997) • Canadian Major Junior Player of the Year (1997)

Rights traded to **Toronto** by **New Jersey** with Jason Smith and Steve Sullivan for Doug Gilmour, Dave Ellett and New Jersey's 3rd round choice (previously acquired, New Jersey selected Andre Lakos) in 1999 Entry Draft, February 25, 1997. Traded to **San Jose** by **Toronto** with Brad Boyes and Toronto's 1st round choice (later traded to Boston – Boston selected Mark Stuart) in 2003 Entry Draft for Owen Nolan, March 5, 2003. Signed as a free agent by **Los Angeles**, July 2, 2006.

McCLEMENT, Jay

(muh-KLEHM-ehnt, JAY) **ST.L.**

Center. Shoots left. 6'1", 199 lbs. Born, Kingston, Ont., March 2, 1983. St. Louis' 1st choice, 57th overall, in 2001 Entry Draft.

1997-98	Kingston	OPJHL	48	3	8	11	15	....	....	....	....	....	....	....	....	....	....	....	....	....	....	....	....	....	....
1998-99	Kingston	OPJHL	51	25	28	53	34	....	....	....	....	....	....	....	....	....	....	....	....	....	....	....	....	....	....
99-2000	Brampton	OHL	63	13	16	29	34	....	....	....	....	....	....	....	....	....	6	0	4	4	8	....	....	....	....
2000-01	Brampton	OHL	66	30	19	49	61	....	....	....	....	....	....	....	....	....	9	4	2	6	10	....	....	....	....
2001-02	Brampton	OHL	61	26	29	55	43	....	....	....	....	....	....	....	....	....	....	....	....	....	....	....	....	....	....
2002-03	Brampton	OHL	45	22	27	49	37	....	....	....	....	....	....	....	....	....	11	3	4	7	11	....	....	....	....
	Worcester IceCats	AHL	....	....	....	....	....	....	....	....	....	....	....	....	....	....	1	0	0	0	0	....	....	....	....
2003-04	Worcester IceCats	AHL	69	12	13	25	20	....	....	....	....	....	....	....	....	....	10	0	3	3	0	....	....	....	....
2004-05	Worcester IceCats	AHL	79	17	34	51	45	....	....	....	....	....	....	....	....	....	....	....	....	....	....	....	....	....	....
2005-06	**St. Louis**	**NHL**	67	6	21	27	30	1	0	2	76	7.9	–23	691	46.9	13:56	....	....	....	....	....	....	....	....	....
	Peoria Rivermen	AHL	11	4	5	9	4	....	....	....	....	....	....	....	....	....	4	0	2	2	2	....	....	....	....
	NHL Totals		67	6	21	27	30	1	0	2	76	7.9		691	46.9	13:56	....	....	....	....	....	....	....	....	....

McCORMICK, Cody

(muh-KOHR-mihk, KOH-dee) **COL.**

Center/Right wing. Shoots right. 6'3", 215 lbs. Born, London, Ont., April 18, 1983. Colorado's 5th choice, 144th overall, in 2001 Entry Draft.

1998-99	Elgin-Middlesex	MHAO	58	22	40	62	81	....	....	....	....	....	....	....	....	....	....	....	....	....	....	....	....	....	....
99-2000	Belleville Bulls	OHL	45	3	4	7	42	....	....	....	....	....	....	....	....	....	9	1	0	1	10	....	....	....	....
2000-01	Belleville Bulls	OHL	66	7	16	23	135	....	....	....	....	....	....	....	....	....	10	1	1	2	23	....	....	....	....
2001-02	Belleville Bulls	OHL	63	10	17	27	118	....	....	....	....	....	....	....	....	....	11	2	4	6	24	....	....	....	....
2002-03	Belleville Bulls	OHL	61	36	33	69	166	....	....	....	....	....	....	....	....	....	7	4	7	11	11	....	....	....	....
2003-04	**Colorado**	**NHL**	44	2	3	5	73	0	0	1	33	6.1	–4	110	32.7	8:07	....	....	....	....	....	....	....	....	....
	Hershey Bears	AHL	32	3	6	9	60	....	....	....	....	....	....	....	....	....	....	....	....	....	....	....	....	....	....
2004-05	Hershey Bears	AHL	40	5	6	11	68	....	....	....	....	....	....	....	....	....	....	....	....	....	....	....	....	....	....
2005-06	**Colorado**	**NHL**	45	4	4	8	29	0	0	1	43	9.3	1	16	25.0	7:42	....	....	....	....	....	....	....	....	....
	Lowell	AHL	13	1	6	7	34	....	....	....	....	....	....	....	....	....	....	....	....	....	....	....	....	....	....
	NHL Totals		89	6	7	13	102	0	0	2	76	7.9		126	31.7	7:54	....	....	....	....	....	....	....	....	....

OHL First All-Star Team (2003)

McDONALD, Andy

(mihk-DAW-nuhld, AN-dee) **ANA.**

Center. Shoots left. 5'10", 186 lbs. Born, Strathroy, Ont., August 25, 1977.

1993-94	Strathroy Rockets	OHA-B	7	2	2	4	0	....	....	....	....	....	....	....	....	....	....	....	....	....	....	....	....	....	....
1994-95	Strathroy Rockets	OHA-B	50	32	41	73	24	....	....	....	....	....	....	....	....	....	....	....	....	....	....	....	....	....	....
1995-96	Strathroy Rockets	OHA-B	52	31	56	87	103	....	....	....	....	....	....	....	....	....	....	....	....	....	....	....	....	....	....
1996-97	Colgate	ECAC	33	9	10	19	16	....	....	....	....	....	....	....	....	....	....	....	....	....	....	....	....	....	....
1997-98	Colgate	ECAC	35	13	19	32	26	....	....	....	....	....	....	....	....	....	....	....	....	....	....	....	....	....	....
1998-99	Colgate	ECAC	35	20	26	46	42	....	....	....	....	....	....	....	....	....	....	....	....	....	....	....	....	....	....
99-2000	Colgate	ECAC	34	25	*33	*58	49	....	....	....	....	....	....	....	....	....	....	....	....	....	....	....	....	....	....
2000-01	**Anaheim**	**NHL**	16	1	0	1	6	0	0	0	21	4.8	0	139	48.9	11:11	....	....	....	....	....	....	....	....	....
	Cincinnati	AHL	46	15	25	40	21	....	....	....	....	....	....	....	....	....	3	0	1	1	2	....	....	....	....
2001-02	**Anaheim**	**NHL**	53	7	21	28	10	2	0	3	79	8.9	2	818	53.7	15:59	....	....	....	....	....	....	....	....	....
	Cincinnati	AHL	21	7	25	32	6	....	....	....	....	....	....	....	....	....	....	....	....	....	....	....	....	....	....
2002-03	**Anaheim**	**NHL**	46	10	11	21	14	3	0	1	92	10.9	–1	604	56.0	18:31	....	....	....	....	....	....	....	....	....
2003-04	**Anaheim**	**NHL**	79	9	21	30	24	2	1	1	162	5.6	–13	282	54.3	16:34	....	....	....	....	....	....	....	....	....
2004-05	ERC Ingolstadt	Germany	36	13	17	30	26	....	....	....	....	....	....	....	....	....	10	5	2	7	35	....	....	....	....
2005-06	**Anaheim**	**NHL**	82	34	51	85	32	13	0	7	229	14.8	24	1095	56.3	16:48	16	2	7	9	10	2	0	0	16:33
	NHL Totals		276	61	104	165	86	20	1	12	583	10.5		2938	54.9	16:32	16	2	7	9	10	2	0	0	16:33

ECAC Second All-Star Team (1999) • ECAC First All-Star Team (2000) • ECAC Player of the Year (2000) • NCAA East First All-American Team (2000)

Signed as a free agent by **Anaheim**, April 3, 2000. Signed as a free agent by **Ingolstadt** (Germany), September 17, 2004.

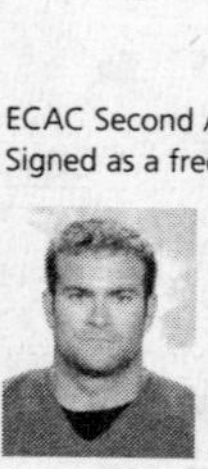

McDONELL, Kent

(MAHK-dah-NEHL, KEHNT)

Right wing. Shoots right. 6'2", 205 lbs. Born, Williamstown, Ont., March 1, 1979. Detroit's 3rd choice, 181st overall, in 1999 Entry Draft.

1995-96	Cornwall Colts	CJHL	33	21	14	35	64	....	....	....	....	....	....	....	....	....	....	....	....	....	....	....	....	....	....
1996-97	Guelph Storm	OHL	56	7	5	12	57	....	....	....	....	....	....	....	....	....	16	0	2	2	4	....	....	....	....
1997-98	Guelph Storm	OHL	64	28	23	51	76	....	....	....	....	....	....	....	....	....	12	7	4	11	18	....	....	....	....
1998-99	Guelph Storm	OHL	60	31	38	69	110	....	....	....	....	....	....	....	....	....	11	4	3	7	36	....	....	....	....
99-2000	Guelph Storm	OHL	56	35	35	70	100	....	....	....	....	....	....	....	....	....	6	1	4	5	6	....	....	....	....
2000-01	Dayton Bombers	ECHL	28	16	9	25	94	....	....	....	....	....	....	....	....	....	3	0	0	0	4	....	....	....	....
	Syracuse Crunch	AHL	32	3	3	6	36	....	....	....	....	....	....	....	....	....	3	1	0	1	0	....	....	....	....
2001-02	Syracuse Crunch	AHL	72	18	13	31	122	....	....	....	....	....	....	....	....	....	3	0	2	2	0	....	....	....	....
2002-03	**Columbus**	**NHL**	3	0	0	0	0	0	0	0	4	0.0	–1	0	0.0	8:40	....	....	....	....	....	....	....	....	....
	Syracuse Crunch	AHL	72	14	24	38	93	....	....	....	....	....	....	....	....	....	....	....	....	....	....	....	....	....	....
2003-04	**Columbus**	**NHL**	29	1	2	3	36	0	0	0	23	4.3	–7	5	60.0	10:18	....	....	....	....	....	....	....	....	....
	Syracuse Crunch	AHL	51	17	31	48	102	....	....	....	....	....	....	....	....	....	5	0	1	1	10	....	....	....	....

			Regular Season														Playoffs								
Season	Club	League	GP	G	A	Pts	PIM	PP	SH	GW	S	%	+/-	TF	F%	Min	GP	G	A	Pts	PIM	PP	SH	GW	Min
2004-05	Aylmer Blues	OHA-Sr.	5	2	4	6	21																		
	Bergen Flyers	Norway	11	12	3	15	75																		
	EV Duisburg	German-2	19	4	9	13	57										10	3	3	6	37				
2005-06	Grand Rapids	AHL	77	21	37	58	171										16	5	4	9	20				
	NHL Totals		**32**	**1**	**2**	**3**	**36**	**0**	**0**	**0**	**27**	**3.7**		**5**	**60.0**	**10:09**									

• Re-entered NHL Entry Draft. Originally Carolina's 9th choice, 225th overall, in 1997 Entry Draft.

Traded to **Columbus** by **Detroit** for Columbus's 6th round choice (Andreas Sundin) in 2003 Entry Draft, August 14, 2000. Signed as a free agent by **Aylmer** (OHA-Sr.), October, 2004. Signed as a free agent by **Bergen** (Norway), October 22, 2004. Signed as a free agent by **Duisburg** (German-2), December 30, 2004. Signed as a free agent by **Detroit**, August 12, 2005.

McEACHERN, Shawn

(muh-GEH-kruhn, SHAWN)

Right wing. Shoots left. 5'11", 200 lbs. Born, Waltham, MA, February 28, 1969. Pittsburgh's 6th choice, 110th overall, in 1987 Entry Draft.

1985-86	Matignon	High-MA	20	32	20	52																			
1986-87	Matignon	High-MA	16	29	28	57																			
1987-88	Matignon	High-MA	22	52	40	92																			
1988-89	Boston University	H-East	36	20	28	48	32																		
1989-90	Boston University	H-East	43	25	31	56	78																		
1990-91	Boston University	H-East	41	34	48	82	43																		
1991-92	United States	Nat-Tm	57	26	23	49	38																		
	United States	Olympics	8	1	0	1	10																		
	♦ **Pittsburgh**	**NHL**	15	0	4	4	0	0	0	0	14	0.0	1				19	2	7	9	4	0	0	0	
1992-93	**Pittsburgh**	**NHL**	84	28	33	61	46	7	0	6	196	14.3	21				12	3	2	5	10	0	0	1	
1993-94	**Los Angeles**	**NHL**	49	8	13	21	24	0	3	0	81	9.9	1												
	Pittsburgh	**NHL**	27	12	9	21	10	0	2	1	78	15.4	13				6	1	0	1	2	0	0	0	
1994-95	Kiekko-Espoo	Finland	8	1	3	4	6																		
	Pittsburgh	**NHL**	44	13	13	26	22	1	2	1	97	13.4	4				11	0	2	2	8	0	0	0	
1995-96	**Boston**	**NHL**	82	24	29	53	34	3	2	3	238	10.1	–5				5	2	1	3	8	0	0	0	
1996-97	**Ottawa**	**NHL**	65	11	20	31	18	0	1	2	150	7.3	–5				7	2	0	2	8	1	0	0	
1997-98	**Ottawa**	**NHL**	81	24	24	48	42	8	2	4	229	10.5	1				11	0	4	4	8	0	0	0	
1998-99	**Ottawa**	**NHL**	77	31	25	56	46	7	0	4	223	13.9	8	441	48.5	18:45	4	2	0	2	6	1	0	0	21:51
99-2000	**Ottawa**	**NHL**	69	29	22	51	24	10	0	4	219	13.2	2	54	50.0	17:50	6	0	3	3	4	0	0	0	18:08
2000-01	**Ottawa**	**NHL**	82	32	40	72	62	9	0	1	231	13.9	10	420	48.8	18:25	4	0	2	2	2	0	0	0	20:49
2001-02	**Ottawa**	**NHL**	80	15	31	46	52	5	0	3	196	7.7	9	210	52.4	17:40	12	0	4	4	2	0	0	0	16:59
2002-03	**Atlanta**	**NHL**	46	10	16	26	28	4	1	1	120	8.3	–27	154	43.5	19:18									
2003-04	**Atlanta**	**NHL**	82	17	38	55	76	5	1	3	176	9.7	5	181	44.2	20:14									
2004-05	Malmo	Sweden	6	0	1	1	14																		
	Malmo	Sweden-Q	10	1	1	2	12																		
2005-06	**Boston**	**NHL**	28	2	6	8	22	1	0	0	40	5.0	–12	21	42.9	14:20									
	Providence Bruins	AHL	10	2	4	6	6																		
	NHL Totals		**911**	**256**	**323**	**579**	**506**	**60**	**14**	**33**	**2288**	**11.2**		**1481**	**48.1**	**18:25**	**97**	**12**	**25**	**37**	**62**	**2**	**0**	**1**	**18:35**

Hockey East Second All-Star Team (1990) • Hockey East First All-Star Team (1991) • NCAA East First All-American Team (1991)

Traded to **Los Angeles** by **Pittsburgh** for Marty McSorley, August 27, 1993. Traded to **Pittsburgh** by **Los Angeles** with Tomas Sandstrom for Marty McSorley and Jim Paek, February 16, 1994. Traded to **Boston** by **Pittsburgh** with Kevin Stevens for Glen Murray, Bryan Smolinski and Boston's 3rd round choice (Boyd Kane) in 1996 Entry Draft, August 2, 1995. Traded to **Ottawa** by **Boston** for Trent McCleary and Ottawa's 3rd round choice (Eric Naud) in 1996 Entry Draft, June 22, 1996. Traded to **Atlanta** by **Ottawa** with Ottawa's 6th round choice (Dan Turple) in 2004 Entry Draft for Brian Pothier, June 29, 2002. Signed as a free agent by **Malmo** (Sweden), January 24, 2005. Signed as a free agent by **Boston**, August 2, 2005.

McGILLIS, Dan

(MIHK-gihl-his, DAN) **N.J.**

Defense. Shoots left. 6'3", 220 lbs. Born, Hawkesbury, Ont., July 1, 1972. Detroit's 10th choice, 238th overall, in 1992 Entry Draft.

1989-90	Hawkesbury	CJHL	55	2	1	3	52																		
1990-91	Hawkesbury	CJHL	56	8	22	30	92																		
1991-92	Hawkesbury	CJHL	36	5	19	24	106																		
1992-93	Northeastern	H-East	35	5	12	17	42																		
1993-94	Northeastern	H-East	38	4	25	29	82																		
1994-95	Northeastern	H-East	34	9	22	31	70																		
1995-96	Northeastern	H-East	34	12	24	36	50																		
1996-97	**Edmonton**	**NHL**	73	6	16	22	52	2	1	2	139	4.3	2				12	0	5	5	24	0	0	0	
1997-98	**Edmonton**	**NHL**	67	10	15	25	74	5	0	3	119	8.4	–17												
	Philadelphia	**NHL**	13	1	5	6	35	1	0	0	18	5.6	–4				5	1	2	3	10	1	0	0	
1998-99	**Philadelphia**	**NHL**	78	8	37	45	61	6	0	4	164	4.9	16	0	0.0	21:41	6	0	1	1	12	0	0	0	19:36
99-2000	**Philadelphia**	**NHL**	68	4	14	18	55	3	0	1	128	3.1	16	0	0.0	20:04	18	2	6	8	12	0	0	0	24:42
2000-01	**Philadelphia**	**NHL**	82	14	35	49	86	4	0	4	207	6.8	13	1	0.0	23:23	6	1	0	1	6	0	1	0	24:12
2001-02	**Philadelphia**	**NHL**	75	5	14	19	46	2	0	1	147	3.4	17	0	0.0	21:04	5	1	0	1	8	1	0	0	20:27
2002-03	**Philadelphia**	**NHL**	24	0	3	3	20	0	0	0	41	0.0	7	0	0.0	18:13									
	San Jose	**NHL**	37	3	13	16	30	2	0	0	71	4.2	–6	0	0.0	21:54									
	Boston	**NHL**	10	0	1	1	10	0	0	0	18	0.0	2	0	0.0	21:15	5	3	0	3	2	2	0	1	18:54
2003-04	**Boston**	**NHL**	80	5	23	28	65	1	0	2	117	4.3	–1	1	0.0	19:43	7	0	0	0	2	0	0	0	18:38
2004-05			DID NOT PLAY																						
2005-06	**New Jersey**	**NHL**	27	0	6	6	36	0	0	0	32	0.0	–5	0	0.0	14:14									
	Albany River Rats	AHL	40	7	18	25	57																		
	NHL Totals		**634**	**56**	**182**	**238**	**570**	**26**	**1**	**17**	**1201**	**4.7**		**2**	**0.0**	**20:44**	**64**	**8**	**14**	**22**	**76**	**4**	**1**	**1**	**22:01**

Hockey East First All-Star Team (1995, 1996) • NCAA East First All-American Team (1996)

Traded to **Edmonton** by **Detroit** for Kirk Maltby, March 20, 1996. Traded to **Philadelphia** by **Edmonton** with Edmonton's 2nd round choice (Jason Beckett) in 1998 Entry Draft for Janne Niinimaa, March 24, 1998. Traded to **San Jose** by **Philadelphia** for Marcus Ragnarsson, December 6, 2002. Traded to **Boston** by **San Jose** for Boston's 2nd round choice (later traded to NY Rangers – NY Rangers selected Ivan Baranka) in 2003 Entry Draft, March 11, 2003. Signed as a free agent by **New Jersey**, August 4, 2005.

McGRATTAN, Brian

(muhk-GRA-tuhn, BRIGH-uhn) **OTT.**

Right wing. Shoots right. 6'5", 238 lbs. Born, Hamilton, Ont., September 2, 1981. Los Angeles' 5th choice, 104th overall, in 1999 Entry Draft.

1997-98	Guelph Fire	OHA-B	15	4	3	7	94																		
	Guelph Storm	OHL	25	3	2	5	11																		
1998-99	Guelph Storm	OHL	6	1	3	4	15																		
	Sudbury Wolves	OHL	53	7	10	17	153										4	0	0	0	8				
99-2000	Sudbury Wolves	OHL	25	2	8	10	79																		
	Mississauga	OHL	42	9	13	22	166																		
2000-01	Mississauga	OHL	31	20	9	29	83																		
2001-02	Mississauga	OHL	7	2	3	5	16																		
	Owen Sound	OHL	2	0	0	0	0																		
	Oshawa Generals	OHL	25	10	5	15	72																		
	Sault Ste. Marie	OHL	26	8	7	15	71										6	2	0	2	20				
2002-03	Binghamton	AHL	59	9	10	19	173										1	0	0	0	0				
2003-04	Binghamton	AHL	66	9	11	20	327										1	0	0	0	0				
2004-05	Binghamton	AHL	71	7	1	8	*551										6	0	2	2	28				
2005-06	**Ottawa**	**NHL**	60	2	3	5	141	0	0	0	36	5.6	0	0	0.0	4:14									
	NHL Totals		**60**	**2**	**3**	**5**	**141**	**0**	**0**	**0**	**36**	**5.6**		**0**	**0.0**	**4:14**									

Signed as a free agent by **Ottawa**, June 2, 2002.

McKEE, Jay

(mih-KEE, JAY) **ST.L.**

Defense. Shoots left. 6'4", 200 lbs. Born, Kingston, Ont., September 8, 1977. Buffalo's 1st choice, 14th overall, in 1995 Entry Draft.

1992-93	Ernestown Jets	OHA-C	36	0	17	17	37																		
	Kingston	MTJHL	2	0	0	0	0																		
1993-94	Sudbury Wolves	OHL	51	0	1	1	51										3	0	0	0	0				
1994-95	Sudbury Wolves	OHL	39	6	6	12	91																		
	Niagara Falls	OHL	26	3	13	16	60										6	2	3	5	10				
1995-96	Niagara Falls	OHL	64	5	41	46	129										10	1	5	6	16				
	Buffalo	**NHL**	1	0	1	1	2	0	0	0	2	0.0	1												
	Rochester	AHL	4	0	1	1	15																		
1996-97	**Buffalo**	**NHL**	43	1	9	10	35	0	0	0	29	3.4	3				3	0	0	0	0	0	0	0	
	Rochester	AHL	7	2	5	7	4																		

			Regular Season														Playoffs								
Season	Club	League	GP	G	A	Pts	PIM	PP	SH	GW	S	%	+/-	TF	F%	Min	GP	G	A	Pts	PIM	PP	SH	GW	Min
1997-98	**Buffalo**	**NHL**	**56**	**1**	**13**	**14**	**42**	**0**	**0**	**0**	**55**	**1.8**	**-1**	....	....	....	**1**	**0**	**0**	**0**	**0**	**0**	**0**	**0**	....
	Rochester	AHL	13	1	7	8	11	....	....	....	....	....	....	....	....	....	....	....	....	....	....	....	....	....	....
1998-99	**Buffalo**	**NHL**	**72**	**0**	**6**	**6**	**75**	**0**	**0**	**0**	**57**	**0.0**	**20**	**0**	**0.0**	**20:28**	**21**	**0**	**3**	**3**	**24**	**0**	**0**	**0**	**22:31**
99-2000	**Buffalo**	**NHL**	**78**	**5**	**12**	**17**	**50**	**1**	**0**	**1**	**84**	**6.0**	**5**	**0**	**0.0**	**20:58**	**1**	**0**	**0**	**0**	**0**	**0**	**0**	**0**	**17:57**
2000-01	**Buffalo**	**NHL**	**74**	**1**	**10**	**11**	**76**	**0**	**0**	**0**	**62**	**1.6**	**9**	**2**	**0.0**	**19:24**	**8**	**1**	**0**	**1**	**6**	**0**	**0**	**1**	**19:23**
2001-02	**Buffalo**	**NHL**	**81**	**2**	**11**	**13**	**43**	**0**	**0**	**1**	**50**	**4.0**	**18**	**0**	**0.0**	**19:26**	....	....	....	....	....	....	....	....	....
2002-03	**Buffalo**	**NHL**	**59**	**0**	**5**	**5**	**49**	**0**	**0**	**0**	**44**	**0.0**	**-16**	**0**	**0.0**	**18:45**	....	....	....	....	....	....	....	....	....
2003-04	**Buffalo**	**NHL**	**43**	**2**	**3**	**5**	**41**	**0**	**0**	**1**	**29**	**6.9**	**6**	**0**	**0.0**	**17:44**	....	....	....	....	....	....	....	....	....
2004-05			DID NOT PLAY																						
2005-06	**Buffalo**	**NHL**	**75**	**5**	**11**	**16**	**57**	**0**	**1**	**0**	**50**	**10.0**	**0**	**1**	**0.0**	**18:03**	**17**	**2**	**3**	**5**	**30**	**0**	**0**	**1**	**20:17**
	NHL Totals		**582**	**17**	**81**	**98**	**470**	**1**	**1**	**3**	**462**	**3.7**		**3**	**0.0**	**19:23**	**51**	**3**	**6**	**9**	**60**	**0**	**0**	**2**	**21:05**

OHL Second All-Star Team (1996)
Signed as a free agent by **St. Louis**, July 1, 2006.

McLAREN, Kyle
(mih-KLAIR-uhn, KIGHL) **S.J.**

Defense. Shoots left. 6'4", 225 lbs. Born, Humboldt, Sask., June 18, 1977. Boston's 1st choice, 9th overall, in 1995 Entry Draft.

Season	Club	League	GP	G	A	Pts	PIM	PP	SH	GW	S	%	+/-	TF	F%	Min	GP	G	A	Pts	PIM	PP	SH	GW	Min
1992-93	Lethbridge	AMHL	60	28	28	56	84	....	....	....	....	....	....	....	....	....	....	....	....	....	....	....	....	....	....
1993-94	Tacoma Rockets	WHL	62	1	9	10	53	....	....	....	....	....	....	....	....	....	6	1	4	5	6	....	....	....	....
1994-95	Tacoma Rockets	WHL	47	13	19	32	68	....	....	....	....	....	....	....	....	....	4	1	1	2	4	....	....	....	....
1995-96	**Boston**	**NHL**	**74**	**5**	**12**	**17**	**73**	**0**	**0**	**0**	**74**	**6.8**	**16**	....	....	....	**5**	**0**	**0**	**0**	**14**	**0**	**0**	**0**	....
1996-97	**Boston**	**NHL**	**58**	**5**	**9**	**14**	**54**	**0**	**0**	**1**	**68**	**7.4**	**-9**	....	....	....	....	....	....	....	....	....	....	....	....
1997-98	**Boston**	**NHL**	**66**	**5**	**20**	**25**	**56**	**2**	**0**	**0**	**101**	**5.0**	**13**	....	....	....	**6**	**1**	**0**	**1**	**4**	**1**	**0**	**0**	....
1998-99	**Boston**	**NHL**	**52**	**6**	**18**	**24**	**48**	**3**	**0**	**0**	**97**	**6.2**	**1**	**0**	**0.0**	**23:25**	**12**	**0**	**3**	**3**	**10**	**0**	**0**	**0**	**26:45**
99-2000	**Boston**	**NHL**	**71**	**8**	**11**	**19**	**67**	**2**	**0**	**3**	**142**	**5.6**	**-4**	**5**	**40.0**	**23:18**	....	....	....	....	....	....	....	....	....
2000-01	**Boston**	**NHL**	**58**	**5**	**12**	**17**	**53**	**2**	**0**	**0**	**91**	**5.5**	**-5**	**4**	**50.0**	**24:14**	....	....	....	....	....	....	....	....	....
2001-02	**Boston**	**NHL**	**38**	**0**	**8**	**8**	**19**	**0**	**0**	**0**	**57**	**0.0**	**-4**	**1**	**0.0**	**19:21**	**4**	**0**	**0**	**0**	**20**	**0**	**0**	**0**	**18:37**
2002-03	**San Jose**	**NHL**	**33**	**0**	**8**	**8**	**30**	**0**	**0**	**0**	**43**	**0.0**	**-10**	**0**	**0.0**	**22:40**	....	....	....	....	....	....	....	....	....
2003-04	**San Jose**	**NHL**	**64**	**2**	**22**	**24**	**60**	**0**	**1**	**0**	**67**	**3.0**	**10**	**1**	**0.0**	**21:01**	**16**	**0**	**3**	**3**	**10**	**0**	**0**	**0**	**24:09**
2004-05			DID NOT PLAY																						
2005-06	**San Jose**	**NHL**	**77**	**2**	**21**	**23**	**66**	**0**	**0**	**1**	**67**	**3.0**	**6**	**0**	**0.0**	**22:52**	**11**	**0**	**3**	**3**	**4**	**0**	**0**	**0**	**20:42**
	NHL Totals		**591**	**38**	**141**	**179**	**526**	**9**	**1**	**5**	**807**	**4.7**		**11**	**36.4**	**22:34**	**54**	**1**	**9**	**10**	**62**	**1**	**0**	**0**	**23:28**

NHL All-Rookie Team (1996)
• Missed majority of 2001-02 season recovering from chest (October 10, 2001 vs. Minnesota) and wrist (December 26, 2001 vs. Ottawa) injuries. • Missed majority of 2002-03 season in contract dispute with Boston. Traded to **San Jose** by **Boston** with Boston's 4th round choice (Torrey Mitchell) in 2004 Entry Draft for Jeff Hackett and Jeff Jillson, January 23, 2003.

McLEAN, Brett
(mihk-LAYN, BREHT) **COL.**

Center. Shoots left. 5'11", 194 lbs. Born, Comox, B.C., August 14, 1978. Dallas' 9th choice, 242nd overall, in 1997 Entry Draft.

Season	Club	League	GP	G	A	Pts	PIM	PP	SH	GW	S	%	+/-	TF	F%	Min	GP	G	A	Pts	PIM	PP	SH	GW	Min
1993-94	Notre Dame	SMBHL	71	109	124	233	70	....	....	....	....	....	....	....	....	....	....	....	....	....	....	....	....	....	....
1994-95	Tacoma Rockets	WHL	67	11	23	34	33	....	....	....	....	....	....	....	....	....	4	0	1	1	0	....	....	....	....
1995-96	Kelowna Rockets	WHL	71	37	42	79	60	....	....	....	....	....	....	....	....	....	6	2	2	4	6	....	....	....	....
1996-97	Kelowna Rockets	WHL	72	44	60	104	98	....	....	....	....	....	....	....	....	....	6	4	2	6	12	....	....	....	....
1997-98	Kelowna Rockets	WHL	54	42	45	87	91	....	....	....	....	....	....	....	....	....	7	4	5	9	17	....	....	....	....
1998-99	Kelowna Rockets	WHL	44	32	38	70	46	....	....	....	....	....	....	....	....	....	....	....	....	....	....	....	....	....	....
	Brandon	WHL	21	15	16	31	20	....	....	....	....	....	....	....	....	....	5	1	6	7	8	....	....	....	....
	Cincinnati	AHL	7	0	3	3	6	....	....	....	....	....	....	....	....	....	....	....	....	....	....	....	....	....	....
99-2000	Johnstown Chiefs	ECHL	8	4	7	11	6	....	....	....	....	....	....	....	....	....	....	....	....	....	....	....	....	....	....
	Saint John Flames	AHL	72	15	23	38	115	....	....	....	....	....	....	....	....	....	3	0	1	1	2	....	....	....	....
2000-01	Cleveland	IHL	74	20	24	44	54	....	....	....	....	....	....	....	....	....	4	0	0	0	18	....	....	....	....
2001-02	Houston Aeros	AHL	78	24	21	45	71	....	....	....	....	....	....	....	....	....	14	1	6	7	12	....	....	....	....
2002-03	**Chicago**	**NHL**	**2**	**0**	**0**	**0**	**0**	**0**	**0**	**0**	**1**	**0.0**	**-1**	**19**	**26.3**	**10:47**	....	....	....	....	....	....	....	....	....
	Norfolk Admirals	AHL	77	23	38	61	60	....	....	....	....	....	....	....	....	....	9	2	6	8	9	....	....	....	....
2003-04	**Chicago**	**NHL**	**76**	**11**	**20**	**31**	**54**	**5**	**1**	**0**	**125**	**8.8**	**-11**	**1135**	**51.1**	**17:33**	....	....	....	....	....	....	....	....	....
	Norfolk Admirals	AHL	4	3	3	6	6	....	....	....	....	....	....	....	....	....	....	....	....	....	....	....	....	....	....
2004-05	Malmo	Sweden	38	7	6	13	102	....	....	....	....	....	....	....	....	....	....	....	....	....	....	....	....	....	....
	Malmo	Sweden-Q	9	1	1	2	16	....	....	....	....	....	....	....	....	....	....	....	....	....	....	....	....	....	....
2005-06	**Colorado**	**NHL**	**82**	**9**	**31**	**40**	**51**	**1**	**0**	**0**	**115**	**7.8**	**-7**	**770**	**50.7**	**12:12**	**8**	**0**	**1**	**1**	**4**	**0**	**0**	**0**	**10:40**
	NHL Totals		**160**	**20**	**51**	**71**	**105**	**6**	**1**	**0**	**241**	**8.3**		**1924**	**50.7**	**14:44**	**8**	**0**	**1**	**1**	**4**	**0**	**0**	**0**	**10:40**

WHL West Second All-Star Team (1998)
Signed as a free agent by **Calgary**, September, 1999. Signed as a free agent by **Minnesota**, July 13, 2000. Signed as a free agent by **Chicago**, July 23, 2002. Signed as a free agent by **Colorado**, July 22, 2004. Signed as a free agent by **Malmo** (Sweden), September 24, 2004.

McMORROW, Sean
(muhk-MOHR-roh, SHAWN)

Left wing. Shoots right. 6'4", 235 lbs. Born, Vancouver, B.C., January 19, 1982. Buffalo's 7th choice, 258th overall, in 2000 Entry Draft.

Season	Club	League	GP	G	A	Pts	PIM	PP	SH	GW	S	%	+/-	TF	F%	Min	GP	G	A	Pts	PIM	PP	SH	GW	Min
1998-99	Pickering Panthers	OPJHL	35	2	10	12	175	....	....	....	....	....	....	....	....	....	....	....	....	....	....	....	....	....	....
99-2000	Sarnia Sting	OHL	31	0	1	1	75	....	....	....	....	....	....	....	....	....	....	....	....	....	....	....	....	....	....
	Kitchener Rangers	OHL	31	0	1	1	67	....	....	....	....	....	....	....	....	....	4	0	0	0	12	....	....	....	....
2000-01	Mississauga	OHL	13	0	0	0	34	....	....	....	....	....	....	....	....	....	....	....	....	....	....	....	....	....	....
	Kingston	OHL	7	0	1	1	22	....	....	....	....	....	....	....	....	....	....	....	....	....	....	....	....	....	....
	London Knights	OHL	29	0	3	3	75	....	....	....	....	....	....	....	....	....	5	0	0	0	0	....	....	....	....
2001-02	London Knights	OHL	38	0	1	1	107	....	....	....	....	....	....	....	....	....	....	....	....	....	....	....	....	....	....
	Oshawa Generals	OHL	27	6	1	7	63	....	....	....	....	....	....	....	....	....	5	1	0	1	12	....	....	....	....
2002-03	**Buffalo**	**NHL**	**1**	**0**	**0**	**0**	**0**	**0**	**0**	**0**	**0**	**0.0**	**0**	**0**	**0.0**	**1:27**	....	....	....	....	....	....	....	....	....
	Rochester	AHL	64	0	1	1	315	....	....	....	....	....	....	....	....	....	3	0	0	0	17	....	....	....	....
2003-04	Rochester	AHL	57	0	0	0	287	....	....	....	....	....	....	....	....	....	14	1	0	1	15	....	....	....	....
2004-05	Rochester	AHL	59	3	3	6	288	....	....	....	....	....	....	....	....	....	4	0	0	0	16	....	....	....	....
2005-06	Rochester	AHL	40	1	1	2	130	....	....	....	....	....	....	....	....	....	....	....	....	....	....	....	....	....	....
	NHL Totals		**1**	**0**	**0**	**0**	**0**	**0**	**0**	**0**	**0**	**0.0**		**0**	**0.0**	**1:27**	....	....	....	....	....	....	....	....	....

MELICHAR, Josef
(mehl-ee-KHAHR, YOH-sehf) **PIT.**

Defense. Shoots left. 6'2", 220 lbs. Born, Ceske Budejovice, Czech., January 20, 1979. Pittsburgh's 3rd choice, 71st overall, in 1997 Entry Draft.

Season	Club	League	GP	G	A	Pts	PIM	PP	SH	GW	S	%	+/-	TF	F%	Min	GP	G	A	Pts	PIM	PP	SH	GW	Min
1995-96	C. Budejovice Jr.	CzRep-Jr.	38	3	4	7	....	....	....	....	....	....	....	....	....	....	....	....	....	....	....	....	....	....	....
1996-97	C. Budejovice Jr.	CzRep-Jr.	41	2	3	5	10	....	....	....	....	....	....	....	....	....	....	....	....	....	....	....	....	....	....
1997-98	Tri-City	WHL	67	9	24	33	154	....	....	....	....	....	....	....	....	....	....	....	....	....	....	....	....	....	....
1998-99	Tri-City	WHL	65	8	28	36	125	....	....	....	....	....	....	....	....	....	11	1	0	1	15	....	....	....	....
99-2000	Wilkes-Barre	AHL	80	3	9	12	126	....	....	....	....	....	....	....	....	....	....	....	....	....	....	....	....	....	....
2000-01	**Pittsburgh**	**NHL**	**18**	**0**	**2**	**2**	**21**	**0**	**0**	**0**	**9**	**0.0**	**-5**	**0**	**0.0**	**14:54**	....	....	....	....	....	....	....	....	....
	Wilkes-Barre	AHL	46	2	5	7	69	....	....	....	....	....	....	....	....	....	21	0	5	5	6	....	....	....	....
2001-02	**Pittsburgh**	**NHL**	**60**	**0**	**3**	**3**	**68**	**0**	**0**	**0**	**46**	**0.0**	**-1**	**0**	**0.0**	**16:46**	....	....	....	....	....	....	....	....	....
2002-03	**Pittsburgh**	**NHL**	**8**	**0**	**0**	**0**	**2**	**0**	**0**	**0**	**6**	**0.0**	**-2**	**0**	**0.0**	**15:19**	....	....	....	....	....	....	....	....	....
2003-04	**Pittsburgh**	**NHL**	**82**	**3**	**5**	**8**	**62**	**0**	**0**	**0**	**78**	**3.8**	**-17**	**0**	**0.0**	**19:01**	....	....	....	....	....	....	....	....	....
2004-05	HC Sparta Praha	CzRep	13	0	4	4	8	....	....	....	....	....	....	....	....	....	5	0	0	0	6	....	....	....	....
2005-06	**Pittsburgh**	**NHL**	**72**	**3**	**12**	**15**	**66**	**0**	**1**	**0**	**53**	**5.7**	**-2**	**0**	**0.0**	**17:26**	....	....	....	....	....	....	....	....	....
	NHL Totals		**240**	**6**	**22**	**28**	**219**	**0**	**1**	**0**	**192**	**3.1**		**0**	**0.0**	**17:33**	....	....	....	....	....	....	....	....	....

• Missed majority of 2002-03 season recovering from shoulder injury suffered in game vs. Boston, October 13, 2002. Signed as a free agent by **Sparta Praha** (CzRep), September 17, 2004.

MELLANBY, Scott
(MEH-lihn-bee, SKAWT) **ATL.**

Right wing. Shoots right. 6'1", 210 lbs. Born, Montreal, Que., June 11, 1966. Philadelphia's 2nd choice, 27th overall, in 1984 Entry Draft.

Season	Club	League	GP	G	A	Pts	PIM	PP	SH	GW	S	%	+/-	TF	F%	Min	GP	G	A	Pts	PIM	PP	SH	GW	Min
1982-83	Don Mills Flyers	MTHL	72	66	52	118	38	....	....	....	....	....	....	....	....	....	....	....	....	....	....	....	....	....	....
1983-84	Henry Carr	OHA-B	39	37	37	74	97	....	....	....	....	....	....	....	....	....	....	....	....	....	....	....	....	....	....
1984-85	U. of Wisconsin	WCHA	40	14	24	38	60	....	....	....	....	....	....	....	....	....	....	....	....	....	....	....	....	....	....
1985-86	U. of Wisconsin	WCHA	32	21	23	44	89	....	....	....	....	....	....	....	....	....	....	....	....	....	....	....	....	....	....
	Philadelphia	**NHL**	**2**	**0**	**0**	**0**	**0**	**0**	**0**	**0**	**0**	**0.0**	**-1**	....	....	....	....	....	....	....	....	....	....	....	....
1986-87	**Philadelphia**	**NHL**	**71**	**11**	**21**	**32**	**94**	**1**	**0**	**0**	**118**	**9.3**	**8**	....	....	....	**24**	**5**	**5**	**10**	**46**	**0**	**0**	**1**	....
1987-88	**Philadelphia**	**NHL**	**75**	**25**	**26**	**51**	**185**	**7**	**0**	**2**	**190**	**13.2**	**-7**	....	....	....	**7**	**0**	**1**	**1**	**16**	**0**	**0**	**0**	....

			Regular Season														Playoffs								
Season	Club	League	GP	G	A	Pts	PIM	PP	SH	GW	S	%	+/-	TF	F%	Min	GP	G	A	Pts	PIM	PP	SH	GW	Min
1988-89	Philadelphia	NHL	76	21	29	50	183	11	0	3	202	10.4	–13	....	....	....	19	4	5	9	28	0	0	0	....
1989-90	Philadelphia	NHL	57	6	17	23	77	0	0	1	104	5.8	–4	....	....	....	....	....	....	....	....	....	....	....	....
1990-91	Philadelphia	NHL	74	20	21	41	155	5	0	6	165	12.1	8	....	....	....	....	....	....	....	....	....	....	....	....
1991-92	Edmonton	NHL	80	23	27	50	197	7	0	5	159	14.5	5	....	....	....	16	2	1	3	29	1	0	1	....
1992-93	Edmonton	NHL	69	15	17	32	147	6	0	3	114	13.2	–4	....	....	....	....	....	....	....	....	....	....	....	....
1993-94	Florida	NHL	80	30	30	60	149	17	0	4	204	14.7	0	....	....	....	....	....	....	....	....	....	....	....	....
1994-95	Florida	NHL	48	13	12	25	90	4	0	5	130	10.0	–16	....	....	....	....	....	....	....	....	....	....	....	....
1995-96	Florida	NHL	79	32	38	70	160	19	0	3	225	14.2	4	....	....	....	22	3	6	9	44	2	0	0	....
1996-97	Florida	NHL	82	27	29	56	170	9	1	4	221	12.2	7	....	....	....	5	0	2	2	4	0	0	0	....
1997-98	Florida	NHL	79	15	24	39	127	6	0	1	188	8.0	–14	....	....	....	....	....	....	....	....	....	....	....	....
1998-99	Florida	NHL	67	18	27	45	85	4	0	3	136	13.2	5	11	27.3	16:14	....	....	....	....	....	....	....	....	....
99-2000	Florida	NHL	77	18	28	46	126	6	0	2	134	13.4	14	20	60.0	14:51	4	0	1	1	2	0	0	0	13:09
2000-01	Florida	NHL	40	4	9	13	46	1	0	0	58	6.9	–13	4	50.0	14:59	....	....	....	....	....	....	....	....	....
	St. Louis	NHL	23	7	1	8	25	2	0	0	37	18.9	0	1	0.0	15:00	15	3	3	6	17	2	0	0	14:43
2001-02	St. Louis	NHL	64	15	26	41	93	8	0	2	137	10.9	–5	3	0.0	15:40	10	7	3	10	18	4	0	1	17:54
2002-03	St. Louis	NHL	80	26	31	57	176	13	0	4	132	19.7	1	11	45.5	16:39	6	0	1	1	10	0	0	0	16:18
2003-04	St. Louis	NHL	68	14	17	31	76	6	0	3	103	13.6	–7	4	50.0	15:29	4	0	1	1	2	0	0	0	14:16
2004-05			DID NOT PLAY																						
2005-06	Atlanta	NHL	71	12	22	34	55	3	0	3	100	12.0	5	37	43.2	13:25	....	....	....	....	....	....	....	....	....
	NHL Totals		1362	352	452	804	2416	135	1	54	2857	12.3		91	44.0	15:20	132	24	29	53	216	9	0	3	15:34

Played in NHL All-Star Game (1996)

Traded to **Edmonton** by **Philadelphia** with Craig Fisher and Craig Berube for Dave Brown, Corey Foster and Jari Kurri, May 30, 1991. Claimed by **Florida** from **Edmonton** in Expansion Draft, June 24, 1993. Traded to **St. Louis** by **Florida** for the rights to Dave Morisset and St. Louis' 5th round choice (Vince Bellissimo) in 2002 Entry Draft, February 9, 2001. Signed as a free agent by **Atlanta**, July 26, 2004.

MELOCHE, Eric

(muh-LAWSH, AIR-ihk) **PHI.**

Right wing. Shoots right. 5'10", 202 lbs. Born, Montreal, Que., May 1, 1976. Pittsburgh's 7th choice, 186th overall, in 1996 Entry Draft.

Season	Club	League	GP	G	A	Pts	PIM	PP	SH	GW	S	%	+/-	TF	F%	Min	GP	G	A	Pts	PIM	PP	SH	GW	Min
1994-95	Cornwall Colts	CJHL	40	7	15	22	51	....	....	....	....	....	....	....	....	....	....	....	....	....	....	....	....	....	....
1995-96	Cornwall Colts	CJHL	64	68	53	121	162	....	....	....	....	....	....	....	....	....	....	....	....	....	....	....	....	....	....
1996-97	Ohio State	CCHA	39	12	11	23	78	....	....	....	....	....	....	....	....	....	....	....	....	....	....	....	....	....	....
1997-98	Ohio State	CCHA	42	26	22	48	86	....	....	....	....	....	....	....	....	....	....	....	....	....	....	....	....	....	....
1998-99	Ohio State	CCHA	35	11	16	27	87	....	....	....	....	....	....	....	....	....	....	....	....	....	....	....	....	....	....
99-2000	Ohio State	CCHA	36	20	11	31	*138	....	....	....	....	....	....	....	....	....	....	....	....	....	....	....	....	....	....
2000-01	Wilkes-Barre	AHL	79	20	20	40	72	....	....	....	....	....	....	....	....	....	21	6	10	16	17	....	....	....	....
2001-02	Pittsburgh	NHL	23	0	1	1	8	0	0	0	29	0.0	–7	4	0.0	10:10	....	....	....	....	....	....	....	....	....
	Wilkes-Barre	AHL	55	13	14	27	91	....	....	....	....	....	....	....	....	....	....	....	....	....	....	....	....	....	....
2002-03	Pittsburgh	NHL	13	5	1	6	4	2	0	1	34	14.7	–2	27	55.6	16:52	....	....	....	....	....	....	....	....	....
	Wilkes-Barre	AHL	59	12	17	29	95	....	....	....	....	....	....	....	....	....	6	1	0	1	20	....	....	....	....
2003-04	Pittsburgh	NHL	25	3	7	10	20	0	0	0	28	10.7	–6	92	39.1	14:47	....	....	....	....	....	....	....	....	....
	Wilkes-Barre	AHL	56	16	26	42	49	....	....	....	....	....	....	....	....	....	23	9	6	15	14	....	....	....	....
2004-05	Philadelphia	AHL	63	6	11	17	102	....	....	....	....	....	....	....	....	....	17	3	2	5	18	....	....	....	....
2005-06	Philadelphia	AHL	10	1	2	3	16	....	....	....	....	....	....	....	....	....	....	....	....	....	....	....	....	....	....
	Norfolk Admirals	AHL	47	7	14	21	81	....	....	....	....	....	....	....	....	....	4	0	0	0	11	....	....	....	....
	NHL Totals		61	8	9	17	32	2	0	1	91	8.8		123	41.5	13:29	....	....	....	....	....	....	....	....	....

Signed as a free agent by **Philadelphia**, July 14, 2004. Traded to **Chicago** by **Philadelphia** with Patrick Sharp for Matt Ellison and Chicago's 3rd round choice (later traded to Montreal.- Montereal selected Ryan White) in 2006 Entry Draft, December 5, 2005. Traded to **Philadelphia** by **Chicago** for Vaclav Pletka, August 2, 2006.

MESZAROS, Andrej

(MEHT-zahr-ohsh, AWN-dray) **OTT.**

Defense. Shoots left. 6'2", 215 lbs. Born, Povazska Bystrica, Czech., October 13, 1985. Ottawa's 1st choice, 23rd overall, in 2004 Entry Draft.

Season	Club	League	GP	G	A	Pts	PIM	PP	SH	GW	S	%	+/-	TF	F%	Min	GP	G	A	Pts	PIM	PP	SH	GW	Min
2002-03	Dukla Trencin Jr.	Slovak-Jr.	33	6	10	16	12	....	....	....	....	....	....	....	....	....	....	....	....	....	....	....	....	....	....
	Dukla Trencin	Slovakia	23	0	1	1	4	....	....	....	....	....	....	....	....	....	....	....	....	....	....	....	....	....	....
2003-04	Dukla Trencin Jr.	Slovak-Jr.	5	2	2	4	0	....	....	....	....	....	....	....	....	....	....	....	....	....	....	....	....	....	....
	Dukla Trencin	Slovakia	44	3	3	6	8	....	....	....	....	....	....	....	....	....	14	3	1	4	2	....	....	....	....
2004-05	Vancouver Giants	WHL	59	11	30	41	94	....	....	....	....	....	....	....	....	....	6	1	3	4	14	....	....	....	....
2005-06	Ottawa	NHL	82	10	29	39	61	5	0	2	137	7.3	34	1	0.0	18:11	10	1	0	1	18	0	0	0	17:50
	Slovakia	Olympics	6	0	2	2	4	....	....	....	....	....	....	....	....	....	....	....	....	....	....	....	....	....	....
	NHL Totals		82	10	29	39	61	5	0	2	137	7.3		1	0.0	18:11	10	1	0	1	18	0	0	0	17:50

WHL West Second All-Star Team (2005) • NHL All-Rookie Team (2006)

METROPOLIT, Glen

(MEH-troh-poh-LIHT, GLEHN) **ATL.**

Center. Shoots right. 5'10", 195 lbs. Born, Toronto, Ont., June 25, 1974.

Season	Club	League	GP	G	A	Pts	PIM	PP	SH	GW	S	%	+/-	TF	F%	Min	GP	G	A	Pts	PIM	PP	SH	GW	Min
1992-93	Richmond Hill	MTJHL	43	27	36	63	36	....	....	....	....	....	....	....	....	....	....	....	....	....	....	....	....	....	....
1993-94	Richmond Hill	MTJHL	49	38	62	100	83	....	....	....	....	....	....	....	....	....	....	....	....	....	....	....	....	....	....
1994-95	Vernon Vipers	BCJHL	60	43	74	117	92	....	....	....	....	....	....	....	....	....	....	....	....	....	....	....	....	....	....
1995-96	Nashville Knights	ECHL	58	30	31	61	62	....	....	....	....	....	....	....	....	....	5	3	8	11	2	....	....	....	....
	Atlanta Knights	IHL	1	0	0	0	0	....	....	....	....	....	....	....	....	....	....	....	....	....	....	....	....	....	....
1996-97	Pensacola	ECHL	54	35	47	82	45	....	....	....	....	....	....	....	....	....	12	9	16	25	28	....	....	....	....
	Quebec Rafales	IHL	22	5	4	9	14	....	....	....	....	....	....	....	....	....	5	0	0	0	2	....	....	....	....
1997-98	Grand Rapids	IHL	79	20	35	55	90	....	....	....	....	....	....	....	....	....	3	1	1	2	0	....	....	....	....
1998-99	Grand Rapids	IHL	77	28	53	81	92	....	....	....	....	....	....	....	....	....	....	....	....	....	....	....	....	....	....
99-2000	Washington	NHL	30	6	13	19	4	1	0	1	57	10.5	5	37	46.0	13:17	2	0	0	0	2	0	0	0	7:07
	Portland Pirates	AHL	48	18	42	60	73	....	....	....	....	....	....	....	....	....	1	1	0	1	0	....	....	....	....
2000-01	Washington	NHL	15	1	5	6	10	0	0	0	20	5.0	–2	3	33.3	11:50	1	0	0	0	0	0	0	0	7:03
	Portland Pirates	AHL	51	25	42	67	59	....	....	....	....	....	....	....	....	....	....	....	....	....	....	....	....	....	....
2001-02	Tampa Bay	NHL	2	0	0	0	0	0	0	0	1	0.0	–2	2	50.0	10:26	....	....	....	....	....	....	....	....	....
	Washington	NHL	33	1	16	17	6	0	0	0	51	2.0	3	145	49.7	14:24	....	....	....	....	....	....	....	....	....
	Portland Pirates	AHL	32	17	22	39	20	....	....	....	....	....	....	....	....	....	....	....	....	....	....	....	....	....	....
2002-03	Washington	NHL	23	2	3	5	6	0	0	1	22	9.1	4	99	49.5	10:07	....	....	....	....	....	....	....	....	....
	Portland Pirates	AHL	33	7	23	30	23	....	....	....	....	....	....	....	....	....	3	1	1	2	0	....	....	....	....
2003-04	Jokerit Helsinki	Finland	55	15	35	50	77	....	....	....	....	....	....	....	....	....	7	6	1	7	33	....	....	....	....
2004-05	Jokerit Helsinki	Finland	51	16	31	47	42	....	....	....	....	....	....	....	....	....	12	5	6	11	20	....	....	....	....
2005-06	HC Lugano	Swiss	44	24	*39	*63	60	....	....	....	....	....	....	....	....	....	17	9	18	27	8	....	....	....	....
	NHL Totals		103	10	37	47	26	1	0	2	151	6.6		286	49.0	12:40	3	0	0	0	2	0	0	0	7:05

Signed as a free agent by **Washington**, July 19, 1999. Claimed by **Tampa Bay** from **Washington** in Waiver Draft, September 28, 2001. Claimed on waivers by **Washington** from **Tampa Bay**, October 20, 2001. Signed as a free agent by **Jokerit Helsinki** (Finland), April 22, 2003. Claimed by **Ottawa** from **Washington** in Waiver Draft, October 3, 2003. Signed as a free agent by **Atlanta**, July 3, 2006.

MEYER, Freddy

(MAY-uhr, FREHD) **PHI.**

Defense. Shoots left. 5'10", 192 lbs. Born, Sanbornville, NH, January 4, 1981.

Season	Club	League	GP	G	A	Pts	PIM	PP	SH	GW	S	%	+/-	TF	F%	Min	GP	G	A	Pts	PIM	PP	SH	GW	Min
1996-97	Cardigan Mtn.	High-NH	STATISTICS NOT AVAILABLE														2	1	0	1	37	....	....	....	....
1997-98	USNTDP	NAHL	....	....	....	....	....	....	....	....	....	....	....	....	....	....	....	....	....	....	....	....	....	....	....
1998-99	USNTDP	U-18	6	1	4	5	8	....	....	....	....	....	....	....	....	....	....	....	....	....	....	....	....	....	....
	USNTDP	USHL	54	10	23	33	151	....	....	....	....	....	....	....	....	....	....	....	....	....	....	....	....	....	....
99-2000	USNTDP	USHL	28	3	8	11	60	....	....	....	....	....	....	....	....	....	....	....	....	....	....	....	....	....	....
	USNTDP	NAHL	3	0	2	2	0	....	....	....	....	....	....	....	....	....	....	....	....	....	....	....	....	....	....
	Boston University	H-East	25	1	11	12	52	....	....	....	....	....	....	....	....	....	....	....	....	....	....	....	....	....	....
2000-01	Boston University	H-East	28	6	13	19	82	....	....	....	....	....	....	....	....	....	....	....	....	....	....	....	....	....	....
2001-02	Boston University	H-East	37	5	15	20	78	....	....	....	....	....	....	....	....	....	....	....	....	....	....	....	....	....	....
2002-03	Boston University	H-East	36	5	16	21	76	....	....	....	....	....	....	....	....	....	....	....	....	....	....	....	....	....	....
2003-04	Philadelphia	NHL	1	0	0	0	0	0	0	0	1	0.0	0	0	0.0	15:24	....	....	....	....	....	....	....	....	....
	Philadelphia	AHL	59	14	14	28	50	....	....	....	....	....	....	....	....	....	12	0	3	3	8	....	....	....	....
2004-05	Philadelphia	AHL	59	6	9	15	71	....	....	....	....	....	....	....	....	....	21	3	9	12	34	....	....	....	....

Season	Club	League	Regular Season GP	G	A	Pts	PIM	PP	SH	GW	S	%	+/-	TF	F%	Min	Playoffs GP	G	A	Pts	PIM	PP	SH	GW	Min
2005-06	Philadelphia	NHL	57	6	21	27	33	2	0	0	68	8.8	10	0	0.0	17:56	6	0	1	1	8	0	0	0	18:23
	Philadelphia	AHL	11	3	3	6	22																		
	NHL Totals		58	6	21	27	33	2	0	0	69	8.7		0	0.0	17:54	6	0	1	1	8	0	0	0	18:23

Hockey East All-Rookie Team (2000) • Hockey East First All-Star Team (2003) • NCAA East First All-American Team (2003)

Signed as a free agent by **Philadelphia**, May 21, 2003.

MEZEI, Branislav
(MEH-tzay, BRAN-ih-slav) **FLA.**

Defense. Shoots left. 6'5", 236 lbs. Born, Nitra, Czech., October 8, 1980. NY Islanders' 3rd choice, 10th overall, in 1999 Entry Draft.

Season	Club	League	GP	G	A	Pts	PIM	PP	SH	GW	S	%	+/-	TF	F%	Min	GP	G	A	Pts	PIM	PP	SH	GW	Min
1996-97	Nitra Jr.	Slovak-Jr.	40	8	17	25	42																		
1997-98	Belleville Bulls	OHL	53	3	5	8	58										8	0	2	2	8				
1998-99	Belleville Bulls	OHL	60	5	18	23	90										18	0	4	4	29				
99-2000	Belleville Bulls	OHL	58	7	21	28	99										6	0	3	3	10				
2000-01	**NY Islanders**	**NHL**	**42**	**1**	**4**	**5**	**53**	**0**	**0**	**0**	**29**	**3.4**	**–5**	**0**	**0.0**	**14:48**									
	Lowell	AHL	20	0	3	3	28																		
2001-02	**NY Islanders**	**NHL**	**24**	**0**	**2**	**2**	**12**	**0**	**0**	**0**	**4**	**0.0**	**2**	**0**	**0.0**	**8:28**									
	Bridgeport	AHL	59	1	9	10	137										20	0	1	1	48				
2002-03	**Florida**	**NHL**	**11**	**2**	**0**	**2**	**10**	**0**	**0**	**1**	**10**	**20.0**	**–2**	**0**	**0.0**	**18:22**									
	San Antonio	AHL	1	0	0	0	0										3	0	0	0	0				
2003-04	**Florida**	**NHL**	**45**	**0**	**7**	**7**	**80**	**0**	**0**	**0**	**26**	**0.0**	**–4**	**0**	**0.0**	**17:43**									
2004-05	HC Ocelari Trinec	CzRep	41	1	2	3	68																		
	Dukla Trencin	Slovakia	10	1	1	2	16										12	1	2	3	38				
2005-06	**Florida**	**NHL**	**16**	**0**	**1**	**1**	**37**	**0**	**0**	**0**	**13**	**0.0**	**3**	**0**	**0.0**	**19:17**									
	NHL Totals		**138**	**3**	**14**	**17**	**192**	**0**	**0**	**1**	**82**	**3.7**		**0**	**0.0**	**15:27**									

OHL First All-Star Team (2000)

Traded to **Florida** by **NY Islanders** for Jason Wiemer, July 3, 2002. • Missed majority of 2002-03 season recovering from ankle (October 12, 2002 vs. Atlanta) and foot (January 1, 2003 vs. New Jersey) injuries. Signed as a free agent by **Trinec** (CzRep), September 25, 2004. Signed as a free agent by **Trencin** (Slovakia), January 30, 2005. • Missed remainder of 2005-06 season recovering from knee injury sufferd in game vs. NY Rangers, November 9, 2005.

MICHALEK, Milan
(mih-KHAL-ihk, MEE-lahn) **S.J.**

Right wing. Shoots left. 6'2", 220 lbs. Born, Jindrichuv Hradec, Czech., December 7, 1984. San Jose's 1st choice, 6th overall, in 2003 Entry Draft.

Season	Club	League	GP	G	A	Pts	PIM	PP	SH	GW	S	%	+/-	TF	F%	Min	GP	G	A	Pts	PIM	PP	SH	GW	Min
99-2000	C. Budejovice Jr.	CzRep-Jr.	48	16	26	42	42										6	3	1	4	4				
2000-01	C. Budejovice Jr.	CzRep-Jr.	30	10	13	23	30										4	1	3	4	2				
	C. Budejovice	CzRep	5	0	0	0	0																		
2001-02	C. Budejovice	CzRep	47	6	11	17	12																		
	C. Budejovice Jr.	CzRep-Jr.	5	3	2	5	4										7	5	4	9	14				
2002-03	C. Budejovice	CzRep	46	3	5	8	14										4	1	0	1	2				
	Kladno	CzRep-2															6	2	2	4	16				
2003-04	**San Jose**	**NHL**	**2**	**1**	**0**	**1**	**4**	**0**	**0**	**0**	**1**	**100.0**	**1**	**0**	**0.0**	**9:05**									
	Cleveland Barons	AHL	7	2	2	4	4																		
2004-05			DID NOT PLAY																						
2005-06	**San Jose**	**NHL**	**81**	**17**	**18**	**35**	**45**	**4**	**0**	**2**	**159**	**10.7**	**1**	**4**	**0.0**	**15:46**	**9**	**1**	**4**	**5**	**8**	**1**	**0**	**0**	**15:11**
	NHL Totals		**83**	**18**	**18**	**36**	**49**	**4**	**0**	**2**	**160**	**11.3**		**4**	**0.0**	**15:36**	**9**	**1**	**4**	**5**	**8**	**1**	**0**	**0**	**15:11**

• Missed majority of 2003-04 season recovering from knee injury suffered in game vs. Calgary, October 11, 2003.

MICHALEK, Zbynek
(mih-KHAL-ihk, ZBIGH-nehk) **PHX.**

Defense. Shoots right. 6'1", 200 lbs. Born, Jindrichuv Hradec, Czech., December 23, 1982.

Season	Club	League	GP	G	A	Pts	PIM	PP	SH	GW	S	%	+/-	TF	F%	Min	GP	G	A	Pts	PIM	PP	SH	GW	Min
99-2000	Karlovy Vary Jr.	CzRep-Jr.	40	2	10	12	20																		
2000-01	Shawinigan	QMJHL	69	10	29	39	52										3	0	0	0	0				
2001-02	Shawinigan	QMJHL	68	16	35	51	54										12	8	9	17	17				
2002-03	Houston Aeros	AHL	62	4	10	14	26										23	1	1	2	6				
2003-04	**Minnesota**	**NHL**	**22**	**1**	**1**	**2**	**4**	**0**	**0**	**0**	**17**	**5.9**	**–7**	**0**	**0.0**	**14:13**									
	Houston Aeros	AHL	55	5	16	21	32										2	1	0	1	0				
2004-05	Houston Aeros	AHL	76	7	17	24	48										5	1	2	3	4				
2005-06	**Phoenix**	**NHL**	**82**	**9**	**15**	**24**	**62**	**5**	**0**	**2**	**105**	**8.6**	**4**	**0**	**0.0**	**22:50**									
	NHL Totals		**104**	**10**	**16**	**26**	**66**	**5**	**0**	**2**	**122**	**8.2**		**0**	**0.0**	**21:00**									

Signed as a free agent by **Minnesota**, September 29, 2001. Traded to **Phoenix** by **Minnesota** for Erik Westrum and Dustin Wood, August 26, 2005.

MIETTINEN, Antti
(mih-EHT-tih-nehn, AN-tee) **DAL.**

Center. Shoots right. 5'11", 185 lbs. Born, Hameenlinna, Finland, July 3, 1980. Dallas' 10th choice, 224th overall, in 2000 Entry Draft.

Season	Club	League	GP	G	A	Pts	PIM	PP	SH	GW	S	%	+/-	TF	F%	Min	GP	G	A	Pts	PIM	PP	SH	GW	Min
1996-97	HPK U18	Fin-U18	36	24	29	53	34																		
1997-98	HPK U18	Fin-U18	34	13	28	41	63																		
	HPK Jr.	Fin-Jr.	8	1	0	1	2																		
1998-99	HPK Jr.	Fin-Jr.	35	17	22	39	28																		
	FPS Forssa	Finland-2	4	3	1	4	6										3	2	3	5	2				
	HPK Hameenlinna	Finland	13	0	0	0	2										4	0	0	0	0				
99-2000	HPK Jr.	Fin-Jr.	31	24	53	77	28										2	1	6	7	2				
	HPK Hameenlinna	Finland	39	2	1	3	8										7	1	0	1	0				
2000-01	HPK Jr.	Fin-Jr.	4	3	10	13	2																		
	HPK Hameenlinna	Finland	55	13	11	24	20																		
2001-02	HPK Hameenlinna	Finland	56	19	37	56	50										8	2	4	6	8				
2002-03	HPK Hameenlinna	Finland	53	25	25	50	54										10	1	7	8	29				
2003-04	**Dallas**	**NHL**	**16**	**1**	**0**	**1**	**0**	**0**	**0**	**1**	**17**	**5.9**	**–9**	**1**	**0.0**	**9:51**									
	Utah Grizzlies	AHL	48	7	23	30	20																		
2004-05	Hamilton	AHL	35	8	20	28	21										4	1	1	2	6				
2005-06	**Dallas**	**NHL**	**79**	**11**	**20**	**31**	**46**	**4**	**0**	**1**	**107**	**10.3**	**0**	**1**	**100.0**	**12:06**	**5**	**0**	**1**	**1**	**8**	**0**	**0**	**0**	**12:10**
	NHL Totals		**95**	**12**	**20**	**32**	**46**	**4**	**0**	**2**	**124**	**9.7**		**2**	**50.0**	**11:43**	**5**	**0**	**1**	**1**	**8**	**0**	**0**	**0**	**12:10**

MILLER, Aaron
(MIHL-luhr, AIR-ruhn) **L.A.**

Defense. Shoots right. 6'4", 200 lbs. Born, Buffalo, NY, August 11, 1971. NY Rangers' 6th choice, 88th overall, in 1989 Entry Draft.

Season	Club	League	GP	G	A	Pts	PIM	PP	SH	GW	S	%	+/-	TF	F%	Min	GP	G	A	Pts	PIM	PP	SH	GW	Min
1987-88	Niagara Scenics	NAHL	30	4	9	13	2																		
1988-89	Niagara Scenics	NAHL	59	24	38	62	60																		
1989-90	U. of Vermont	ECAC	31	1	15	16	24																		
1990-91	U. of Vermont	ECAC	30	3	7	10	22																		
1991-92	U. of Vermont	ECAC	31	3	16	19	28																		
1992-93	U. of Vermont	ECAC	30	4	13	17	16																		
1993-94	**Quebec**	**NHL**	**1**	**0**	**0**	**0**	**0**	**0**	**0**	**0**	**0**	**0.0**	**–1**												
	Cornwall Aces	AHL	64	4	10	14	49										13	0	2	2	10				
1994-95	Cornwall Aces	AHL	76	4	18	22	69																		
	Quebec	**NHL**	**9**	**0**	**3**	**3**	**6**	**0**	**0**	**0**	**12**	**0.0**	**2**												
1995-96	**Colorado**	**NHL**	**5**	**0**	**0**	**0**	**0**	**0**	**0**	**0**	**2**	**0.0**	**0**												
	Cornwall Aces	AHL	62	4	23	27	77										8	0	1	1	6				
1996-97	**Colorado**	**NHL**	**56**	**5**	**12**	**17**	**15**	**0**	**0**	**3**	**47**	**10.6**	**15**				**17**	**1**	**2**	**3**	**10**	**0**	**0**	**0**	
1997-98	**Colorado**	**NHL**	**55**	**2**	**2**	**4**	**51**	**0**	**0**	**0**	**29**	**6.9**	**0**				**7**	**0**	**0**	**0**	**8**	**0**	**0**	**0**	
1998-99	**Colorado**	**NHL**	**76**	**5**	**13**	**18**	**42**	**1**	**0**	**2**	**87**	**5.7**	**3**	**0**	**0.0**	**21:49**	**19**	**1**	**5**	**6**	**10**	**0**	**0**	**0**	**21:13**
99-2000	**Colorado**	**NHL**	**53**	**1**	**7**	**8**	**36**	**0**	**0**	**0**	**44**	**2.3**	**3**	**0**	**0.0**	**19:05**	**17**	**1**	**1**	**2**	**6**	**0**	**0**	**0**	**19:12**
2000-01	**Colorado**	**NHL**	**56**	**4**	**9**	**13**	**29**	**0**	**0**	**0**	**49**	**8.2**	**19**	**0**	**0.0**	**18:25**									
	Los Angeles	**NHL**	**13**	**0**	**5**	**5**	**14**	**0**	**0**	**0**	**10**	**0.0**	**3**	**1**	**0.0**	**22:44**	**13**	**0**	**1**	**1**	**6**	**0**	**0**	**0**	**22:02**
2001-02	**Los Angeles**	**NHL**	**74**	**5**	**12**	**17**	**54**	**0**	**1**	**3**	**75**	**6.7**	**14**	**0**	**0.0**	**22:21**	**7**	**0**	**0**	**0**	**0**	**0**	**0**	**0**	**26:28**
	United States	Olympics	6	0	0	0	4																		
2002-03	**Los Angeles**	**NHL**	**49**	**1**	**5**	**6**	**24**	**0**	**0**	**0**	**34**	**2.9**	**–7**	**1**	**100.0**	**21:30**									
2003-04	**Los Angeles**	**NHL**	**35**	**1**	**2**	**3**	**32**	**0**	**0**	**0**	**26**	**3.8**	**–3**	**0**	**0.0**	**19:00**									

Season	Club	League	GP	G	A	Pts	PIM	PP	SH	GW	S	%	+/-	TF	F%	Min	GP	G	A	Pts	PIM	PP	SH	GW	Min
								Regular Season									Playoffs								
2004-05			DID NOT PLAY																						
2005-06	**Los Angeles**	**NHL**	**56**	**0**	**8**	**8**	**27**	**0**	**0**	**0**	**32**	**0.0**	**–6**	**1**	**100.0**	**18:26**									
	NHL Totals		**538**	**24**	**78**	**102**	**330**	**1**	**1**	**8**	**447**	**5.4**		**3**	**66.7**	**20:23**	**80**	**3**	**9**	**12**	**40**	**0**	**0**	**0**	**21:27**

ECAC First All-Star Team (1993) • NCAA East Second All-American Team (1993)

Traded to **Quebec** by **NY Rangers** with NY Rangers' 5th round choice (Bill Lindsay) in 1991 Entry Draft for Joe Cirella, January 17, 1991. Transferred to **Colorado** after **Quebec** franchise relocated, June 21, 1995. Traded to **Los Angeles** by **Colorado** with Adam Deadmarsh, a player to be named later (Jared Aulin, March 22, 2001) and Colorado's 1st round choices in 2001 (Dave Steckel) and 2003 (Brian Boyle) Entry Drafts for Rob Blake and Steve Reinprecht, February 21, 2001. • Missed majority of 2003-04 season recovering from cervical injury suffered in game vs. Atlanta, December 10, 2003.

MILLER, Kip

(MIHL-luhr, KIHP)

Center. Shoots left. 5'10", 190 lbs. Born, Lansing, MI, June 11, 1969. Quebec's 4th choice, 72nd overall, in 1987 Entry Draft.

Season	Club	League	GP	G	A	Pts	PIM	PP	SH	GW	S	%	+/-	TF	F%	Min	GP	G	A	Pts	PIM	PP	SH	GW	Min
1984-85	Det. Compuware	MNHL	65	69	63	132																			
1985-86	Det. Compuware	GLJHL	30	25	28	53																			
1986-87	Michigan State	CCHA	41	20	19	39	92																		
1987-88	Michigan State	CCHA	39	16	25	41	51																		
1988-89	Michigan State	CCHA	47	32	45	77	94																		
1989-90	Michigan State	CCHA	45	*48	53	*101	60																		
1990-91	**Quebec**	**NHL**	**13**	**4**	**3**	**7**	**7**	**0**	**0**	**0**	**16**	**25.0**	**–1**												
	Halifax Citadels	AHL	66	36	33	69	40																		
1991-92	**Quebec**	**NHL**	**36**	**5**	**10**	**15**	**12**	**1**	**0**	**2**	**46**	**10.9**	**–21**												
	Halifax Citadels	AHL	24	9	17	26	8																		
	Minnesota	**NHL**	**3**	**1**	**2**	**3**	**2**	**1**	**0**	**0**	**3**	**33.3**	**–1**												
	Kalamazoo Wings	IHL	6	1	8	9	4										12	3	9	12	12				
1992-93	Kalamazoo Wings	IHL	61	17	39	56	59																		
1993-94	**San Jose**	**NHL**	**11**	**2**	**2**	**4**	**6**	**0**	**0**	**0**	**21**	**9.5**	**–1**												
	Kansas City	IHL	71	38	54	92	51																		
1994-95	Denver Grizzlies	IHL	71	46	60	106	54										17	*15	14	29	8				
	NY Islanders	**NHL**	**8**	**0**	**1**	**1**	**0**	**0**	**0**	**0**	**11**	**0.0**	**1**												
1995-96	**Chicago**	**NHL**	**10**	**1**	**4**	**5**	**2**	**0**	**0**	**0**	**12**	**8.3**	**1**												
	Indianapolis Ice	IHL	73	32	59	91	46										5	2	6	8	2				
1996-97	Chicago Wolves	IHL	43	11	41	52	32																		
	Indianapolis Ice	IHL	37	17	24	41	18										4	2	2	4	2				
1997-98	Utah Grizzlies	IHL	72	38	59	97	30										4	3	2	5	10				
	NY Islanders	**NHL**	**9**	**1**	**3**	**4**	**2**	**0**	**0**	**0**	**11**	**9.1**	**–2**												
1998-99	**Pittsburgh**	**NHL**	**77**	**19**	**23**	**42**	**22**	**1**	**0**	**4**	**125**	**15.2**	**1**	**150**	**44.7**	**16:55**	**13**	**2**	**7**	**9**	**19**	**1**	**0**	**0**	**18:56**
99-2000	**Pittsburgh**	**NHL**	**44**	**4**	**15**	**19**	**10**	**0**	**0**	**1**	**50**	**8.0**	**–1**	**132**	**40.2**	**14:18**									
	Anaheim	**NHL**	**30**	**6**	**17**	**23**	**4**	**2**	**0**	**1**	**32**	**18.8**	**1**	**7**	**42.9**	**13:44**									
2000-01	**Pittsburgh**	**NHL**	**33**	**3**	**8**	**11**	**6**	**1**	**0**	**0**	**38**	**7.9**	**0**	**61**	**50.8**	**9:46**									
	Grand Rapids	IHL	34	16	19	35	12										10	5	8	13	2				
2001-02	Grand Rapids	AHL	41	21	35	56	27																		
	NY Islanders	**NHL**	**37**	**7**	**17**	**24**	**6**	**2**	**0**	**1**	**52**	**13.5**	**2**	**119**	**58.8**	**14:07**	**7**	**4**	**2**	**6**	**2**	**2**	**0**	**1**	**11:14**
2002-03	**Washington**	**NHL**	**72**	**12**	**38**	**50**	**18**	**3**	**0**	**4**	**89**	**13.5**	**–1**	**171**	**49.7**	**14:58**	**5**	**0**	**2**	**2**	**2**	**0**	**0**	**0**	**10:36**
2003-04	**Washington**	**NHL**	**66**	**9**	**22**	**31**	**8**	**6**	**0**	**2**	**74**	**12.2**	**–10**	**297**	**47.5**	**14:03**									
2004-05	Grand Rapids	AHL	50	13	32	45	17																		
2005-06	Chicago Wolves	AHL	67	19	40	59	48																		
	NHL Totals		**449**	**74**	**165**	**239**	**105**	**17**	**0**	**15**	**580**	**12.8**		**937**	**48.0**	**14:28**	**25**	**6**	**11**	**17**	**23**	**3**	**0**	**1**	**15:07**

CCHA First All-Star Team (1989, 1990) • CCHA Player of the Year (1990) • NCAA West First All-American Team (1989, 1990) • Hobey Baker Memorial Award (Top U.S. Collegiate Player) (1990) • N.R. "Bud" Poile Trophy (Playoff MVP – IHL) (1995)

Traded to **Minnesota** by **Quebec** for Steve Maltais, March 8, 1992. Signed as a free agent by **San Jose**, August 10, 1993. Signed as a free agent by **NY Islanders**, July 7, 1994. Signed as a free agent by **Chicago**, July 21, 1995. Signed as a free agent by **NY Islanders**, November 26, 1997. Claimed by **Pittsburgh** from **NY Islanders** in Waiver Draft, October 5, 1998. Traded to **Anaheim** by **Pittsburgh** for Anaheim's 9th round choice (Roman Simicek) in 2000 Entry Draft, January 29, 2000. Signed as a free agent by **Pittsburgh**, September 24, 2000. Signed as a free agent by **Grand Rapids** (AHL), May 31, 2001. Signed as a free agent by **NY Islanders**, January 16, 2002. Signed as a free agent by **Washington**, July 9, 2002. Signed as a free agent by **Grand Rapids** (AHL), December 26, 2004.

MILLEY, Norm

(MIHL-lee, NOHR-man) **T.B.**

Right wing. Shoots right. 6', 211 lbs. Born, Toronto, Ont., February 14, 1980. Buffalo's 3rd choice, 47th overall, in 1998 Entry Draft.

Season	Club	League	GP	G	A	Pts	PIM	PP	SH	GW	S	%	+/-	TF	F%	Min	GP	G	A	Pts	PIM	PP	SH	GW	Min
1995-96	Tor. Red Wings	MTHL	42	42	36	78																			
	St. Mike's B's	OPJHL	5	2	1	3	0																		
1996-97	Sudbury Wolves	OHL	61	30	32	62	15																		
1997-98	Sudbury Wolves	OHL	62	33	41	74	48										10	0	1	1	4				
1998-99	Sudbury Wolves	OHL	68	52	68	120	47										4	2	3	5	4				
99-2000	Sudbury Wolves	OHL	68	*52	60	112	47										12	8	11	19	6				
2000-01	Rochester	AHL	77	20	27	47	56										4	0	0	0	2				
2001-02	**Buffalo**	**NHL**	**5**	**0**	**1**	**1**	**0**	**0**	**0**	**0**	**10**	**0.0**	**0**	**1**	**0.0**	**13:12**									
	Rochester	AHL	74	20	18	38	20										2	0	3	3	6				
2002-03	**Buffalo**	**NHL**	**8**	**0**	**2**	**2**	**6**	**0**	**0**	**0**	**8**	**0.0**	**–2**	**2**	**50.0**	**10:41**									
	Rochester	AHL	67	16	32	48	39										3	2	0	2	2				
2003-04	**Buffalo**	**NHL**	**2**	**0**	**0**	**0**	**2**	**0**	**0**	**0**	**2**	**0.0**	**0**	**0**	**0.0**	**8:20**									
	Rochester	AHL	77	18	19	37	60										16	7	6	13	10				
2004-05	Rochester	AHL	72	12	21	33	46										9	1	2	3	4				
2005-06	**Tampa Bay**	**NHL**	**14**	**2**	**1**	**3**	**4**	**1**	**0**	**0**	**12**	**16.7**	**–2**	**0**	**0.0**	**7:09**									
	Springfield	AHL	53	19	29	48	34																		
	NHL Totals		**29**	**2**	**4**	**6**	**12**	**1**	**0**	**0**	**32**	**6.3**		**3**	**33.3**	**9:15**									

OHL All-Rookie Team (1997) • OHL Second All-Star Team (1999) • OHL First All-Star Team (2000) • Canadian Major Junior First All-Star Team (2000)

Signed as a free agent by **Tampa Bay**, August 18, 2005.

MINK, Graham

(MIHNK, GRAY-uhm) **S.J.**

Center. Shoots right. 6'3", 217 lbs. Born, Stowe, VT, May 21, 1979.

Season	Club	League	GP	G	A	Pts	PIM	PP	SH	GW	S	%	+/-	TF	F%	Min	GP	G	A	Pts	PIM	PP	SH	GW	Min
1997-98	Northfield Mt.H.	High-MA	25	17	25	42																			
1998-99	U. of Vermont	ECAC	27	4	2	6	34																		
99-2000	U. of Vermont	ECAC	17	7	4	11	14																		
2000-01	U. of Vermont	ECAC	32	17	12	29	52																		
2001-02	Richmond	ECHL	29	8	9	17	78																		
	Portland Pirates	AHL	56	17	17	34	50																		
2002-03	Portland Pirates	AHL	71	22	15	37	115																		
2003-04	**Washington**	**NHL**	**2**	**0**	**0**	**0**	**2**	**0**	**0**	**0**	**0**	**0.0**	**–1**	**1**	**0.0**	**5:32**									
	Portland Pirates	AHL	68	18	19	37	74										3	0	1	1	4				
2004-05	Portland Pirates	AHL	63	18	21	39	86																		
2005-06	**Washington**	**NHL**	**3**	**0**	**0**	**0**	**0**	**0**	**0**	**0**	**1**	**0.0**	**0**	**0**	**0.0**	**5:32**									
	Hershey Bears	AHL	43	21	19	40	50										21	8	13	21	29				
	NHL Totals		**5**	**0**	**0**	**0**	**2**	**0**	**0**	**0**	**1**	**0.0**		**1**	**0.0**	**5:32**									

Signed as a free agent by **Portland** (AHL), September 30, 2001. Signed as a free agent by **Washington**, April 9, 2002. Signed as a free agent by **San Jose**, July 14, 2006.

MITCHELL, Willie

(MIH-chuhl, WIHL-lee) **VAN.**

Defense. Shoots left. 6'3", 205 lbs. Born, Port McNeill, B.C., April 23, 1977. New Jersey's 12th choice, 199th overall, in 1996 Entry Draft.

Season	Club	League	GP	G	A	Pts	PIM	PP	SH	GW	S	%	+/-	TF	F%	Min	GP	G	A	Pts	PIM	PP	SH	GW	Min
1993-94	Notre Dame	SMHL	31	4	11	15	81																		
1994-95	Kelowna Spartans	BCHL	42	3	8	11	71																		
1995-96	Melfort Mustangs	SJHL	19	2	6	8											14	0	2	2	12				
1996-97	Melfort Mustangs	SJHL	64	14	42	56	227										4	0	1	1	23				
1997-98	Clarkson Knights	ECAC	34	9	17	26	105																		
1998-99	Clarkson Knights	ECAC	34	10	19	29	40																		
	Albany River Rats	AHL	6	1	3	4	29																		
99-2000	**New Jersey**	**NHL**	**2**	**0**	**0**	**0**	**0**	**0**	**0**	**0**	**2**	**0.0**	**1**	**0**	**0.0**	**16:04**									
	Albany River Rats	AHL	63	5	14	19	71										5	1	2	3	4				
2000-01	**New Jersey**	**NHL**	**16**	**0**	**2**	**2**	**29**	**0**	**0**	**0**	**14**	**0.0**	**0**	**0**	**0.0**	**14:52**									
	Albany River Rats	AHL	41	3	13	16	94																		
	Minnesota	**NHL**	**17**	**1**	**7**	**8**	**11**	**0**	**0**	**0**	**16**	**6.3**	**4**	**0**	**0.0**	**20:49**									
2001-02	**Minnesota**	**NHL**	**68**	**3**	**10**	**13**	**68**	**0**	**0**	**1**	**67**	**4.5**	**–16**	**0**	**0.0**	**21:25**									

Season	Club	League	GP	G	A	Pts	PIM	PP	SH	GW	S	%	+/-	TF	F%	Min	Playoffs GP	G	A	Pts	PIM	PP	SH	GW	Min
2002-03	Minnesota	NHL	69	2	12	14	84	0	1	1	67	3.0	13	0	0.0	21:28	18	1	3	4	14	0	0	0	24:48
2003-04	Minnesota	NHL	70	1	13	14	83	0	0	0	58	1.7	12	2	50.0	22:36	....	....	....	....	....	....	....	....	....
2004-05			DID NOT PLAY																						
2005-06	Minnesota	NHL	64	2	6	8	87	0	0	0	48	4.2	15	0	0.0	20:52	....	....	....	....	....	....	....	....	....
	Dallas	NHL	16	0	2	2	26	0	0	0	10	0.0	4	0	0.0	20:46	5	0	0	0	2	0	0	0	23:21
	NHL Totals		322	9	52	61	388	0	1	2	282	3.2		2	50.0	21:09	23	1	3	4	16	0	0	0	24:29

SJHL First All-Star Team (1997) • SJHL Top Defenseman Award (1997) • ECAC Second All-Star Team (1998) • ECAC Rookie of the Year (1998) (co-winner - Erik Cole) • ECAC First All-Star Team (1999) • NCAA East Second All-American Team (1999)

Traded to **Minnesota** by **New Jersey** for Sean O'Donnell, March 4, 2001. Traded to **Dallas** by **Minnesota** with a 2nd round choice in 2007 Entry Draft for Martin Skoula and Shawn Belle, March 9, 2006. Signed as a free agent by **Vancouver**, July 1, 2006.

MODANO, Mike

(moh-DA-noh, MIGHK) **DAL.**

Center. Shoots left. 6'3", 205 lbs. Born, Livonia, MI, June 7, 1970. Minnesota's 1st choice, 1st overall, in 1988 Entry Draft.

Season	Club	League	GP	G	A	Pts	PIM	PP	SH	GW	S	%	+/-	TF	F%	Min	Playoffs GP	G	A	Pts	PIM	PP	SH	GW	Min
1985-86	Det. Compuware	MNHL	69	66	65	131	32	....	....	....	....	....	....	....	....	....	....	....	....	....	....	....	....	....	....
1986-87	Prince Albert	WHL	70	32	30	62	96	....	....	....	....	....	....	....	....	....	8	1	4	5	4	....	....	....	....
1987-88	Prince Albert	WHL	65	47	80	127	80	....	....	....	....	....	....	....	....	....	9	7	11	18	18	....	....	....	....
1988-89	Prince Albert	WHL	41	39	66	105	74	....	....	....	....	....	....	....	....	....	....	....	....	....	....	....	....	....	....
	Minnesota	NHL	....	....	....	....	....	....	....	....	....	....	....	....	....	....	2	0	0	0	0	0	0	0	....
1989-90	Minnesota	NHL	80	29	46	75	63	12	0	2	172	16.9	-7	....	....	....	7	1	1	2	12	0	0	0	....
1990-91	Minnesota	NHL	79	28	36	64	65	9	0	2	232	12.1	2	....	....	....	23	8	12	20	16	3	0	1	....
1991-92	Minnesota	NHL	76	33	44	77	46	5	0	8	256	12.9	-9	....	....	....	7	3	2	5	4	1	0	0	....
1992-93	Minnesota	NHL	82	33	60	93	83	9	0	7	307	10.7	-7	....	....	....	....	....	....	....	....	....	....	....	....
1993-94	Dallas	NHL	76	50	43	93	54	18	0	4	281	17.8	-8	....	....	....	9	7	3	10	16	2	0	2	....
1994-95	Dallas	NHL	30	12	17	29	8	4	1	0	100	12.0	7	....	....	....	....	....	....	....	....	....	....	....	....
1995-96	Dallas	NHL	78	36	45	81	63	8	4	4	320	11.3	-12	....	....	....	....	....	....	....	....	....	....	....	....
1996-97	Dallas	NHL	80	35	48	83	42	9	5	9	291	12.0	43	....	....	....	7	4	1	5	0	1	1	2	....
1997-98	Dallas	NHL	52	21	38	59	32	7	5	2	191	11.0	25	....	....	....	17	4	10	14	12	1	0	1	....
	United States	Olympics	4	2	0	2	0	....	....	....	....	....	....	....	....	....	....	....	....	....	....	....	....	....	....
1998-99 ♦	Dallas	NHL	77	34	47	81	44	6	4	7	224	15.2	29	1572	51.1	20:50	23	5	*18	23	16	1	1	1	24:40
99-2000	Dallas	NHL	77	38	43	81	48	11	1	8	188	20.2	0	1763	51.4	22:55	23	10	*13	23	10	4	0	2	25:26
2000-01	Dallas	NHL	81	33	51	84	52	8	3	7	208	15.9	26	1791	52.0	22:24	9	3	4	7	0	2	0	0	25:43
2001-02	Dallas	NHL	78	34	43	77	38	6	2	5	219	15.5	14	1710	53.7	22:27	....	....	....	....	....	....	....	....	....
	United States	Olympics	6	0	*6	6	4	....	....	....	....	....	....	....	....	....	....	....	....	....	....	....	....	....	....
2002-03	Dallas	NHL	79	28	57	85	30	5	2	6	193	14.5	34	1808	51.4	20:53	12	5	10	15	4	1	0	2	23:53
2003-04	Dallas	NHL	76	14	30	44	46	6	0	0	152	9.2	-21	1523	52.6	20:27	5	1	2	3	8	1	0	0	23:17
2004-05			DID NOT PLAY																						
2005-06	Dallas	NHL	78	27	50	77	58	12	1	4	207	13.0	23	1421	51.1	19:34	5	1	3	4	4	1	0	0	22:14
	United States	Olympics	6	2	0	2	6	....	....	....	....	....	....	....	....	....	....	....	....	....	....	....	....	....	....
	NHL Totals		1179	485	698	1183	772	135	28	75	3541	13.7		11588	51.9	21:22	149	52	79	131	102	18	2	11	24:39

WHL East First All-Star Team (1989) • NHL All-Rookie Team (1990) • NHL Second All-Star Team (2000)

Played in NHL All-Star Game (1993, 1998, 1999, 2000, 2003, 2004)

Transferred to **Dallas** after **Minnesota** franchise relocated, June 9, 1993.

MODIN, Fredrik

(moh-DEEN, FREHD-rihk) **CBJ**

Left wing. Shoots left. 6'4", 220 lbs. Born, Sundsvall, Sweden, October 8, 1974. Toronto's 3rd choice, 64th overall, in 1994 Entry Draft.

Season	Club	League	GP	G	A	Pts	PIM	PP	SH	GW	S	%	+/-	TF	F%	Min	Playoffs GP	G	A	Pts	PIM	PP	SH	GW	Min
1991-92	Sundsvall/Timra	Sweden-2	11	1	0	1	0	....	....	....	....	....	....	....	....	....	....	....	....	....	....	....	....	....	....
1992-93	Sundsvall/Timra	Sweden-2	30	5	7	12	12	....	....	....	....	....	....	....	....	....	5	1	0	1	0	....	....	....	....
1993-94	Sundsvall/Timra	Sweden-2	30	16	15	31	36	....	....	....	....	....	....	....	....	....	2	0	1	1	6	....	....	....	....
1994-95	Brynas IF Gavle	Sweden	38	9	10	19	33	....	....	....	....	....	....	....	....	....	14	4	4	8	6	....	....	....	....
1995-96	Brynas IF Gavle	Sweden	22	4	8	12	22	....	....	....	....	....	....	....	....	....	....	....	....	....	....	....	....	....	....
1996-97	Toronto	NHL	76	6	7	13	24	0	0	0	85	7.1	-14	....	....	....	....	....	....	....	....	....	....	....	....
1997-98	Toronto	NHL	74	16	16	32	32	1	0	4	137	11.7	-5	....	....	....	....	....	....	....	....	....	....	....	....
1998-99	Toronto	NHL	67	16	15	31	35	1	0	3	108	14.8	14	2	50.0	13:34	8	0	0	0	6	0	0	0	9:50
99-2000	Tampa Bay	NHL	80	22	26	48	18	3	0	5	167	13.2	-26	6	50.0	15:32	....	....	....	....	....	....	....	....	....
2000-01	Tampa Bay	NHL	76	32	24	56	48	8	0	4	217	14.7	-1	21	42.9	17:15	....	....	....	....	....	....	....	....	....
2001-02	Tampa Bay	NHL	54	14	17	31	27	2	0	4	141	9.9	0	25	40.0	19:05	....	....	....	....	....	....	....	....	....
2002-03	Tampa Bay	NHL	76	17	23	40	43	2	1	4	179	9.5	7	35	28.6	17:35	11	2	0	2	18	0	0	0	19:18
2003-04 ♦	Tampa Bay	NHL	82	29	28	57	32	5	1	2	206	14.1	31	138	38.4	18:12	23	8	11	19	10	3	0	2	20:47
2004-05	Timra IK	Sweden	43	12	24	36	58	....	....	....	....	....	....	....	....	....	7	1	1	2	8	....	....	....	....
2005-06	Tampa Bay	NHL	77	31	23	54	56	12	1	4	221	14.0	5	171	51.5	19:35	5	0	0	0	6	0	0	0	18:46
	Sweden	Olympics	8	2	1	3	6	....	....	....	....	....	....	....	....	....	....	....	....	....	....	....	....	....	....
	NHL Totals		662	183	179	362	315	34	3	30	1461	12.5		398	43.7	17:15	47	10	11	21	40	3	0	2	18:21

Played in NHL All-Star Game (2001)

Traded to **Tampa Bay** by **Toronto** for Cory Cross and Tampa Bay's 7th round choice (Ivan Kolozvary) in 2001 Entry Draft, October 1, 1999. Signed as a free agent by **Timra** (Sweden), October 5, 2004. Traded to **Columbus** by **Tampa Bay** with Fredrik Norrena for Marc Denis, June 30, 2006.

MODRY, Jaroslav

(MOH-dree, YAHRO-slahv) **DAL.**

Defense. Shoots left. 6'2", 225 lbs. Born, Ceske Budejovice, Czech., February 27, 1971. New Jersey's 11th choice, 179th overall, in 1990 Entry Draft.

Season	Club	League	GP	G	A	Pts	PIM	PP	SH	GW	S	%	+/-	TF	F%	Min	Playoffs GP	G	A	Pts	PIM	PP	SH	GW	Min
1987-88	C. Budejovice	Czech	3	0	0	0	0	....	....	....	....	....	....	....	....	....	....	....	....	....	....	....	....	....	....
1988-89	C. Budejovice	Czech	28	0	1	1	8	....	....	....	....	....	....	....	....	....	....	....	....	....	....	....	....	....	....
1989-90	C. Budejovice	Czech	41	2	2	4	....	....	....	....	....	....	....	....	....	....	....	....	....	....	....	....	....	....	....
1990-91	Dukla Trencin	Czech	33	1	9	10	6	....	....	....	....	....	....	....	....	....	....	....	....	....	....	....	....	....	....
1991-92	C. Budejovice	Czech-2	14	4	10	14	....	....	....	....	....	....	....	....	....	....	....	....	....	....	....	....	....	....	....
	Dukla Trencin	Czech	18	0	4	4	6	....	....	....	....	....	....	....	....	....	....	....	....	....	....	....	....	....	....
1992-93	Utica Devils	AHL	80	7	35	42	62	....	....	....	....	....	....	....	....	....	5	0	2	2	2	....	....	....	....
1993-94	New Jersey	NHL	41	2	15	17	18	2	0	0	35	5.7	10	....	....	....	....	....	....	....	....	....	....	....	....
	Albany River Rats	AHL	19	1	5	6	25	....	....	....	....	....	....	....	....	....	....	....	....	....	....	....	....	....	....
1994-95	C. Budejovice	CzRep	19	1	3	4	30	....	....	....	....	....	....	....	....	....	....	....	....	....	....	....	....	....	....
	New Jersey	NHL	11	0	0	0	0	0	0	0	10	0.0	-1	....	....	....	....	....	....	....	....	....	....	....	....
	Albany River Rats	AHL	18	5	6	11	14	....	....	....	....	....	....	....	....	....	14	3	3	6	4	....	....	....	....
1995-96	Ottawa	NHL	64	4	14	18	38	1	0	1	89	4.5	-17	....	....	....	....	....	....	....	....	....	....	....	....
	Los Angeles	NHL	9	0	3	3	6	0	0	0	17	0.0	-4	....	....	....	....	....	....	....	....	....	....	....	....
1996-97	Los Angeles	NHL	30	3	3	6	25	1	1	0	32	9.4	-13	....	....	....	....	....	....	....	....	....	....	....	....
	Phoenix	IHL	23	3	12	15	17	....	....	....	....	....	....	....	....	....	....	....	....	....	....	....	....	....	....
	Utah Grizzlies	IHL	11	1	4	5	20	....	....	....	....	....	....	....	....	....	7	0	1	1	6	....	....	....	....
1997-98	Utah Grizzlies	IHL	74	12	21	33	72	....	....	....	....	....	....	....	....	....	4	0	2	2	6	....	....	....	....
1998-99	Los Angeles	NHL	5	0	1	1	0	0	0	0	11	0.0	1	0	0.0	26:00	....	....	....	....	....	....	....	....	....
	Long Beach	IHL	64	6	29	35	44	....	....	....	....	....	....	....	....	....	8	4	2	6	4	....	....	....	....
99-2000	Los Angeles	NHL	26	5	4	9	18	5	0	1	32	15.6	-2	0	0.0	19:13	2	0	0	0	2	0	0	0	16:48
	Long Beach	IHL	11	2	4	6	8	....	....	....	....	....	....	....	....	....	....	....	....	....	....	....	....	....	....
2000-01	Los Angeles	NHL	63	4	15	19	48	0	0	0	72	5.6	16	0	0.0	18:22	10	1	0	1	4	1	0	1	16:08
2001-02	Los Angeles	NHL	80	4	38	42	65	4	0	0	119	3.4	-4	0	0.0	19:31	7	0	2	2	0	0	0	0	21:26
2002-03	Los Angeles	NHL	82	13	25	38	68	8	0	1	205	6.3	-13	1	0.0	22:39	....	....	....	....	....	....	....	....	....
2003-04	Los Angeles	NHL	79	5	27	32	44	1	0	1	196	2.6	11	1	0.0	24:24	....	....	....	....	....	....	....	....	....
2004-05	Liberec	CzRep	19	3	7	10	24	....	....	....	....	....	....	....	....	....	12	0	4	4	22	....	....	....	....
2005-06	Atlanta	NHL	79	7	31	38	76	5	0	2	143	4.9	-9	0	0.0	20:48	....	....	....	....	....	....	....	....	....
	NHL Totals		569	47	176	223	406	27	1	6	961	4.9		2	0.0	21:12	19	1	2	3	6	1	0	1	18:09

Played in NHL All-Star Game (2002)

Traded to **Ottawa** by **New Jersey** for Ottawa's 4th round choice (Alyn McCauley) in 1995 Entry Draft, July 8, 1995. Traded to **Los Angeles** by **Ottawa** with Ottawa's 8th round choice (Stephen Valiquette) in 1996 Entry Draft for Kevin Brown, March 20, 1996. Signed as a free agent by **Atlanta**, July 1, 2004. Signed as a free agent by **Liberec** (CzRep), October 20, 2004. Traded to **Dallas** by **Atlanta** with Patrik Stefan for Niko Kapanen and Dallas's 7th round choice (Will O'Neill) in 2006 Entry Draft, June 24, 2006.

MOEN, Travis
(MOH-ehn, TRA-vihs) **ANA.**

Left wing. Shoots left. 6'2", 210 lbs. Born, Stewart Valley, Sask., April 6, 1982. Calgary's 6th choice, 155th overall, in 2000 Entry Draft.

Season	Club	League	Regular Season GP	G	A	Pts	PIM	PP	SH	GW	S	%	+/-	TF	F%	Min	Playoffs GP	G	A	Pts	PIM	PP	SH	GW	Min
1998-99	Swift Current	SMHL	STATISTICS NOT AVAILABLE																						
	Kelowna Rockets	WHL	4	0	0	0	0	....	....	....	....	....	....	....	....	....	....	....	....	....	....	....	....	....	....
99-2000	Kelowna Rockets	WHL	66	9	6	15	96	....	....	....	....	....	....	....	....	....	5	1	1	2	2	....	....	....	....
2000-01	Kelowna Rockets	WHL	40	8	8	16	106	....	....	....	....	....	....	....	....	....	....	....	....	....	....	....	....	....	....
2001-02	Kelowna Rockets	WHL	71	10	17	27	197	....	....	....	....	....	....	....	....	....	13	1	0	1	28	....	....	....	....
2002-03	Norfolk Admirals	AHL	42	1	2	3	62	....	....	....	....	....	....	....	....	....	9	0	0	0	20	....	....	....	....
2003-04	**Chicago**	**NHL**	**82**	**4**	**2**	**6**	**142**	**0**	**0**	**2**	**51**	**7.8**	**–17**	**19**	**15.8**	**10:57**	....	....	....	....	....	....	....	....	....
2004-05	Norfolk Admirals	AHL	79	8	12	20	187	....	....	....	....	....	....	....	....	....	6	0	1	1	6	....	....	....	....
2005-06	**Anaheim**	**NHL**	**39**	**4**	**1**	**5**	**72**	**0**	**0**	**0**	**28**	**14.3**	**–3**	**8**	**12.5**	**11:03**	**9**	**1**	**0**	**1**	**10**	**0**	**0**	**0**	**8:25**
	NHL Totals		**121**	**8**	**3**	**11**	**214**	**0**	**0**	**2**	**79**	**10.1**		**27**	**14.8**	**10:59**	**9**	**1**	**0**	**1**	**10**	**0**	**0**	**0**	**8:25**

Signed as a free agent by **Chicago**, October 21, 2002. Traded to **Anaheim** by **Chicago** for Michael Holmqvist, July 30, 2005. • Missed the majority of the 2005-06 season as a healthy reserve as well as recovering from minor injuries to his shoulder and knee.

MOGILNY, Alexander
(moh-GIHL-nee, al-ehx-AN-duhr) **N.J.**

Right wing. Shoots left. 6', 210 lbs. Born, Khabarovsk, USSR, February 18, 1969. Buffalo's 4th choice, 89th overall, in 1988 Entry Draft.

Season	Club	League	Regular Season GP	G	A	Pts	PIM	PP	SH	GW	S	%	+/-	TF	F%	Min	Playoffs GP	G	A	Pts	PIM	PP	SH	GW	Min
1986-87	CSKA Moscow	USSR	28	15	1	16	4	....	....	....	....	....	....	....	....	....	....	....	....	....	....	....	....	....	....
1987-88	CSKA Moscow	USSR	39	12	8	20	14	....	....	....	....	....	....	....	....	....	....	....	....	....	....	....	....	....	....
	Soviet Union	Olympics	6	3	2	5	2	....	....	....	....	....	....	....	....	....	....	....	....	....	....	....	....	....	....
1988-89	CSKA Moscow	USSR	31	11	11	22	24	....	....	....	....	....	....	....	....	....	....	....	....	....	....	....	....	....	....
1989-90	**Buffalo**	**NHL**	**65**	**15**	**28**	**43**	**16**	**4**	**0**	**2**	**130**	**11.5**	**8**	....	....	....	**4**	**0**	**1**	**1**	**2**	**0**	**0**	**0**	....
1990-91	**Buffalo**	**NHL**	**62**	**30**	**34**	**64**	**16**	**3**	**3**	**5**	**201**	**14.9**	**14**	....	....	....	**6**	**0**	**6**	**6**	**2**	**0**	**0**	**0**	....
1991-92	**Buffalo**	**NHL**	**67**	**39**	**45**	**84**	**73**	**15**	**0**	**2**	**236**	**16.5**	**7**	....	....	....	**2**	**0**	**2**	**2**	**0**	**0**	**0**	**0**	....
1992-93	**Buffalo**	**NHL**	**77**	***76**	**51**	**127**	**40**	**27**	**0**	**11**	**360**	**21.1**	**7**	....	....	....	**7**	**7**	**3**	**10**	**6**	**2**	**0**	**0**	....
1993-94	**Buffalo**	**NHL**	**66**	**32**	**47**	**79**	**22**	**17**	**0**	**7**	**258**	**12.4**	**8**	....	....	....	**7**	**4**	**2**	**6**	**6**	**1**	**0**	**0**	....
1994-95	Spartak Moscow	CIS	1	0	1	1	0	....	....	....	....	....	....	....	....	....	....	....	....	....	....	....	....	....	....
	Buffalo	**NHL**	**44**	**19**	**28**	**47**	**36**	**12**	**0**	**2**	**148**	**12.8**	**0**	....	....	....	**5**	**3**	**2**	**5**	**2**	**0**	**0**	**0**	....
1995-96	**Vancouver**	**NHL**	**79**	**55**	**52**	**107**	**16**	**10**	**5**	**6**	**292**	**18.8**	**14**	....	....	....	**6**	**1**	**8**	**9**	**8**	**0**	**0**	**0**	....
1996-97	**Vancouver**	**NHL**	**76**	**31**	**42**	**73**	**18**	**7**	**1**	**4**	**174**	**17.8**	**9**	....	....	....	....	....	....	....	....	....	....	....	....
1997-98	**Vancouver**	**NHL**	**51**	**18**	**27**	**45**	**36**	**5**	**4**	**1**	**118**	**15.3**	**–6**	....	....	....	....	....	....	....	....	....	....	....	....
1998-99	**Vancouver**	**NHL**	**59**	**14**	**31**	**45**	**58**	**3**	**2**	**1**	**110**	**12.7**	**0**	**47**	**23.4**	**20:35**	....	....	....	....	....	....	....	....	....
99-2000	**Vancouver**	**NHL**	**47**	**21**	**17**	**38**	**16**	**3**	**1**	**1**	**126**	**16.7**	**7**	**9**	**11.1**	**19:34**	....	....	....	....	....	....	....	....	....
	♦ New Jersey	**NHL**	**12**	**3**	**3**	**6**	**4**	**2**	**0**	**0**	**35**	**8.6**	**–4**	**0**	**0.0**	**17:04**	**23**	**4**	**3**	**7**	**4**	**2**	**0**	**1**	**16:06**
2000-01	**New Jersey**	**NHL**	**75**	**43**	**40**	**83**	**43**	**12**	**0**	**7**	**240**	**17.9**	**10**	**11**	**36.4**	**16:53**	**25**	**5**	**11**	**16**	**8**	**1**	**0**	**2**	**16:42**
2001-02	**Toronto**	**NHL**	**66**	**24**	**33**	**57**	**8**	**5**	**0**	**4**	**188**	**12.8**	**1**	**5**	**40.0**	**17:38**	**20**	**8**	**3**	**11**	**8**	**2**	**0**	**2**	**19:23**
2002-03	**Toronto**	**NHL**	**73**	**33**	**46**	**79**	**12**	**5**	**3**	**9**	**165**	**20.0**	**4**	**18**	**33.3**	**20:03**	**6**	**5**	**2**	**7**	**4**	**0**	**1**	**0**	**21:43**
2003-04	**Toronto**	**NHL**	**37**	**8**	**22**	**30**	**12**	**4**	**1**	**1**	**92**	**8.7**	**9**	**10**	**60.0**	**18:29**	**13**	**2**	**4**	**6**	**8**	**0**	**0**	**0**	**16:28**
2004-05			DID NOT PLAY																						
2005-06	**New Jersey**	**NHL**	**34**	**12**	**13**	**25**	**6**	**7**	**0**	**3**	**93**	**12.9**	**–7**	**5**	**40.0**	**16:09**	....	....	....	....	....	....	....	....	....
	Albany River Rats	AHL	19	4	10	14	17	....	....	....	....	....	....	....	....	....	....	....	....	....	....	....	....	....	....
	NHL Totals		**990**	**473**	**559**	**1032**	**432**	**141**	**20**	**66**	**2966**	**15.9**		**105**	**30.5**	**18:32**	**124**	**39**	**47**	**86**	**58**	**8**	**1**	**5**	**17:28**

NHL Second All-Star Team (1993, 1996) • Lady Byng Trophy (2003)

Played in NHL All-Star Game (1992, 1993, 1994, 1996)

Traded to **Vancouver** by **Buffalo** with Buffalo's 5th round choice (Todd Norman) in 1995 Entry Draft for Michael Peca, Mike Wilson and Vancouver's 1st round choice (Jay McKee) in 1995 Entry Draft, July 8, 1995. Traded to **New Jersey** by **Vancouver** for Brendan Morrison and Denis Pederson, March 14, 2000. Signed as a free agent by **Toronto**, July 3, 2001. • Missed majority of 2003-04 season recovering from hip injury suffered in game vs. Edmonton, November 20, 2003. Signed as a free agent by **New Jersey**, August 17, 2005.

MOJZIS, Tomas
(MOI-shihsh, TAW-mash) **ST.L.**

Defense. Shoots left. 6'1", 192 lbs. Born, Kolin, Czech., May 2, 1982. Toronto's 11th choice, 246th overall, in 2001 Entry Draft.

Season	Club	League	Regular Season GP	G	A	Pts	PIM	PP	SH	GW	S	%	+/-	TF	F%	Min	Playoffs GP	G	A	Pts	PIM	PP	SH	GW	Min
99-2000	HC Pardubice Jr.	CzRep-Jr.	40	7	1	8	....	....	....	....	....	....	....	....	....	....	....	....	....	....	....	....	....	....	....
2000-01	Moose Jaw	WHL	72	11	25	36	115	....	....	....	....	....	....	....	....	....	4	0	1	1	8	....	....	....	....
2001-02	Moose Jaw	WHL	28	2	11	13	43	....	....	....	....	....	....	....	....	....	....	....	....	....	....	....	....	....	....
	Seattle	WHL	36	8	15	23	66	....	....	....	....	....	....	....	....	....	11	1	3	4	20	....	....	....	....
2002-03	Seattle	WHL	62	21	49	70	126	....	....	....	....	....	....	....	....	....	15	1	6	7	36	....	....	....	....
2003-04	Manitoba Moose	AHL	63	5	13	18	50	....	....	....	....	....	....	....	....	....	....	....	....	....	....	....	....	....	....
2004-05	Manitoba Moose	AHL	80	7	23	30	62	....	....	....	....	....	....	....	....	....	14	0	2	2	28	....	....	....	....
2005-06	**Vancouver**	**NHL**	**7**	**0**	**1**	**1**	**12**	**0**	**0**	**0**	**7**	**0.0**	**2**	**0**	**0.0**	**13:57**	....	....	....	....	....	....	....	....	....
	Manitoba Moose	AHL	37	5	13	18	52	....	....	....	....	....	....	....	....	....	....	....	....	....	....	....	....	....	....
	Peoria Rivermen	AHL	12	3	4	7	14	....	....	....	....	....	....	....	....	....	1	0	0	0	0	....	....	....	....
	NHL Totals		**7**	**0**	**1**	**1**	**12**	**0**	**0**	**0**	**7**	**0.0**		**0**	**0.0**	**13:57**	....	....	....	....	....	....	....	....	....

WHL West First All-Star Team (2003) • Canadian Major Junior First All-Star Team (2003)

Traded to **Vancouver** by **Toronto** for Brad Leeb, September 4, 2002. Traded to **St. Louis** by **Vancouver** with Vancouver's 3rd round choice (later traded to New Jersey - New Jersey selected Vladimir Zharkov) in 2006 Entry Draft for Eric Weinrich, March 9, 2006.

MONTADOR, Steve
(MAWN-tuh-dohr, STEEV) **FLA.**

Defense. Shoots right. 6', 210 lbs. Born, Vancouver, B.C., December 21, 1979.

Season	Club	League	Regular Season GP	G	A	Pts	PIM	PP	SH	GW	S	%	+/-	TF	F%	Min	Playoffs GP	G	A	Pts	PIM	PP	SH	GW	Min
1995-96	St. Mike's B's	OPJHL	46	3	16	19	145	....	....	....	....	....	....	....	....	....	7	1	2	3	10	....	....	....	....
1996-97	North Bay	OHL	63	7	28	35	129	....	....	....	....	....	....	....	....	....	....	....	....	....	....	....	....	....	....
1997-98	North Bay	OHL	37	5	16	21	54	....	....	....	....	....	....	....	....	....	....	....	....	....	....	....	....	....	....
	Erie Otters	OHL	26	3	17	20	35	....	....	....	....	....	....	....	....	....	7	1	1	2	9	....	....	....	....
1998-99	Erie Otters	OHL	61	9	33	42	114	....	....	....	....	....	....	....	....	....	5	0	2	2	4	....	....	....	....
99-2000	Peterborough	OHL	64	14	42	56	97	....	....	....	....	....	....	....	....	....	5	0	2	2	4	....	....	....	....
	Saint John Flames	AHL	....	....	....	....	....	....	....	....	....	....	....	....	....	....	2	0	0	0	0	....	....	....	....
2000-01	Saint John Flames	AHL	58	1	6	7	95	....	....	....	....	....	....	....	....	....	19	0	8	8	13	....	....	....	....
2001-02	**Calgary**	**NHL**	**11**	**1**	**2**	**3**	**26**	**0**	**0**	**0**	**10**	**10.0**	**–2**	**0**	**0.0**	**12:12**	....	....	....	....	....	....	....	....	....
	Saint John Flames	AHL	67	9	16	25	107	....	....	....	....	....	....	....	....	....	....	....	....	....	....	....	....	....	....
2002-03	Saint John Flames	AHL	11	1	7	8	20	....	....	....	....	....	....	....	....	....	....	....	....	....	....	....	....	....	....
	Calgary	**NHL**	**50**	**1**	**1**	**2**	**114**	**0**	**0**	**0**	**64**	**1.6**	**–9**	**0**	**0.0**	**15:11**	....	....	....	....	....	....	....	....	....
2003-04	**Calgary**	**NHL**	**26**	**1**	**2**	**3**	**50**	**0**	**0**	**1**	**31**	**3.2**	**–1**	**1**	**0.0**	**11:46**	**20**	**1**	**2**	**3**	**6**	**0**	**0**	**1**	**17:43**
2004-05	HC Mulhouse	France	15	1	7	8	69	....	....	....	....	....	....	....	....	....	....	....	....	....	....	....	....	....	....
2005-06	**Calgary**	**NHL**	**7**	**1**	**0**	**1**	**11**	**0**	**0**	**0**	**13**	**7.7**	**0**	**0**	**0.0**	**11:49**	....	....	....	....	....	....	....	....	....
	Florida	**NHL**	**51**	**1**	**5**	**6**	**68**	**0**	**0**	**0**	**42**	**2.4**	**4**	**0**	**0.0**	**14:04**	....	....	....	....	....	....	....	....	....
	NHL Totals		**145**	**5**	**10**	**15**	**269**	**0**	**0**	**1**	**160**	**3.1**		**1**	**0.0**	**13:48**	**20**	**1**	**2**	**3**	**6**	**0**	**0**	**1**	**17:43**

Signed as a free agent by **Calgary**, April 10, 2000. • Spent majority of 2003-04 season as a healthy reserve. Signed as a free agent by **Mulhouse** (France), September 17, 2004. Traded to **Florida** by **Calgary** with Dustin Johner for Kristian Huselius, December 2, 2005.

MOORE, Dominic
(MOOR, DOHM-ih-nihk) **PIT.**

Center. Shoots left. 6', 195 lbs. Born, Thornhill, Ont., August 3, 1980. NY Rangers' 2nd choice, 95th overall, in 2000 Entry Draft.

Season	Club	League	Regular Season GP	G	A	Pts	PIM	PP	SH	GW	S	%	+/-	TF	F%	Min	Playoffs GP	G	A	Pts	PIM	PP	SH	GW	Min
1996-97	Thornhill Islanders	MTJHL	29	4	6	10	48	....	....	....	....	....	....	....	....	....	1	0	1	1	0	....	....	....	....
1997-98	Aurora Tigers	OPJHL	51	10	15	25	16	....	....	....	....	....	....	....	....	....	....	....	....	....	....	....	....	....	....
1998-99	Aurora Tigers	OPJHL	51	34	53	87	70	....	....	....	....	....	....	....	....	....	....	....	....	....	....	....	....	....	....
99-2000	Harvard Crimson	ECAC	30	12	24	28	16	....	....	....	....	....	....	....	....	....	....	....	....	....	....	....	....	....	....
2000-01	Harvard Crimson	ECAC	32	15	28	43	40	....	....	....	....	....	....	....	....	....	....	....	....	....	....	....	....	....	....
2001-02	Harvard Crimson	ECAC	32	13	16	29	37	....	....	....	....	....	....	....	....	....	....	....	....	....	....	....	....	....	....
2002-03	Harvard Crimson	ECAC	34	*24	27	*51	30	....	....	....	....	....	....	....	....	....	....	....	....	....	....	....	....	....	....
2003-04	**NY Rangers**	**NHL**	**5**	**0**	**3**	**3**	**0**	**0**	**0**	**0**	**3**	**0.0**	**0**	**36**	**30.6**	**9:18**	....	....	....	....	....	....	....	....	....
	Hartford	AHL	70	14	25	39	60	....	....	....	....	....	....	....	....	....	16	3	3	6	8	....	....	....	....
2004-05	Hartford	AHL	78	19	31	50	78	....	....	....	....	....	....	....	....	....	6	1	1	2	4	....	....	....	....
2005-06	**NY Rangers**	**NHL**	**82**	**9**	**9**	**18**	**28**	**2**	**0**	**1**	**139**	**6.5**	**4**	**814**	**46.3**	**12:28**	**4**	**0**	**0**	**0**	**2**	**0**	**0**	**0**	**11:21**
	NHL Totals		**87**	**9**	**12**	**21**	**28**	**2**	**0**	**1**	**142**	**6.3**		**850**	**45.6**	**12:17**	**4**	**0**	**0**	**0**	**2**	**0**	**0**	**0**	**11:21**

ECAC All-Rookie Team (2000) • ECAC Second All-Star Team (2001) • ECAC First All-Star Team (2003) • NCAA East First All-American Team (2003)

Traded to **Nashville** by **NY Rangers** for Adam Hall, July 19, 2006. Traded to **Pittsburgh** by **Nashville** with Libor Pivko for Pittsburgh's 3rd round choice in 2007 Entry Draft, July 19, 2006.

			Regular Season														Playoffs								
Season	Club	League	GP	G	A	Pts	PIM	PP	SH	GW	S	%	+/-	TF	F%	Min	GP	G	A	Pts	PIM	PP	SH	GW	Min

MORAN, Brad

Center. Shoots left. 5'11", 187 lbs. Born, Abbotsford, B.C., March 20, 1979. Buffalo's 8th choice, 191st overall, in 1998 Entry Draft.   (moh-RAN, BRAD)   **VAN.**

Season	Club	League	GP	G	A	Pts	PIM	PP	SH	GW	S	%	+/-	TF	F%	Min	GP	G	A	Pts	PIM	PP	SH	GW	Min
1994-95	Abbotsford	BCAHA	56	66	93	159	40																		
1995-96	Calgary Hitmen	WHL	70	13	31	44	28																		
1996-97	Calgary Hitmen	WHL	72	30	36	66	61																		
1997-98	Calgary Hitmen	WHL	72	53	49	102	64																		
1998-99	Calgary Hitmen	WHL	71	60	58	118	96										18	10	8	18	20				
99-2000	Calgary Hitmen	WHL	72	48	*72	*120	84										21	17	*25	42	26				
2000-01	Syracuse Crunch	AHL	71	11	19	30	30										13	7	15	22	18				
2001-02	**Columbus**	**NHL**	3	0	0	0	0	0	0	0	2	0.0	0	22	40.9	7:39									
	Syracuse Crunch	AHL	64	25	24	49	51										10	5	8	13	2				
2002-03	Syracuse Crunch	AHL	47	12	19	31	22																		
2003-04	**Columbus**	**NHL**	2	1	1	2	2	0	0	0	4	25.0	-1	25	64.0	10:03									
	Syracuse Crunch	AHL	72	24	35	59	44										7	5	3	8	2				
2004-05	Syracuse Crunch	AHL	80	26	46	72	70																		
2005-06	Langnau	Swiss	18	4	4	8	18										6	4	6	10	10				
	NHL Totals		5	1	1	2	2	0	0	0	6	16.7		47	53.2	8:36									

WHL East First All-Star Team (1999, 2000) • WHL Player of the Year (2000)
Signed as a free agent by **Columbus**, June 5, 2000. Signed as a free agent by **Vancouver**, June 19, 2006.

MORAN, Ian

Defense. Shoots right. 6', 200 lbs. Born, Cleveland, OH, August 24, 1972. Pittsburgh's 5th choice, 107th overall, in 1990 Entry Draft.   (moh-RAN, EE-an)   **ANA.**

Season	Club	League	GP	G	A	Pts	PIM	PP	SH	GW	S	%	+/-	TF	F%	Min	GP	G	A	Pts	PIM	PP	SH	GW	Min
1987-88	Belmont Hill	High-MA	25	3	13	16	15																		
1988-89	Belmont Hill	High-MA	23	7	25	32	8																		
1989-90	Belmont Hill	High-MA	23	10	36	46	....																		
1990-91	Belmont Hill	High-MA	23	7	44	51	12																		
1991-92	Boston College	H-East	30	2	16	18	44																		
1992-93	Boston College	H-East	31	8	12	20	32																		
1993-94	United States	Nat-Tm	50	8	15	23	69																		
	Cleveland	IHL	33	5	13	18	39																		
1994-95	Cleveland	IHL	64	7	31	38	94										4	0	1	1	2				
	Pittsburgh	**NHL**															8	0	0	0	0	0	0	0	
1995-96	**Pittsburgh**	**NHL**	51	1	1	2	47	0	0	0	44	2.3	-1				5	1	2	3	4	0	0	0	
1996-97	**Pittsburgh**	**NHL**	36	4	5	9	22	0	0	0	50	8.0	-11												
	Cleveland	IHL	36	6	23	29	26																		
1997-98	**Pittsburgh**	**NHL**	37	1	6	7	19	0	0	1	33	3.0	0				6	0	0	0	0	0	0	0	
1998-99	**Pittsburgh**	**NHL**	62	4	5	9	37	0	1	0	65	6.2	1	32	34.4	16:34	13	0	2	2	8	0	0	0	21:10
99-2000	**Pittsburgh**	**NHL**	73	4	8	12	28	0	0	0	58	6.9	-10	210	33.8	11:21	11	0	1	1	2	0	0	0	8:52
2000-01	**Pittsburgh**	**NHL**	40	3	4	7	28	0	0	0	73	4.1	5	4	25.0	17:42	18	0	1	1	4	0	0	0	15:54
2001-02	**Pittsburgh**	**NHL**	64	2	8	10	54	0	0	1	94	2.1	-11	2	100.0	20:00									
2002-03	**Pittsburgh**	**NHL**	70	0	7	7	46	0	0	0	85	0.0	-17	4	75.0	18:37									
	Boston	**NHL**	8	0	1	1	2	0	0	0	11	0.0	-1	1	100.0	16:22	5	0	1	1	4				18:24
2003-04	**Boston**	**NHL**	35	1	4	5	28	0	0	0	54	1.9	3	1	100.0	18:45									
2004-05	Bofors	Sweden-2	7	0	4	4	12																		
	Nottingham	Britain	9	0	4	4	8										5	0	1	1	2				
2005-06	**Boston**	**NHL**	12	1	1	2	10	0	0	0	14	14.3	0	1	0.0	14:25									
	NHL Totals		488	21	50	71	321	0	1	3	574	3.7		255	35.3	16:47	66	1	7	8	24	0	0	0	15:59

Hockey East All-Rookie Team (1992) • Hockey East Rookie of the Year (1992) (co-winner - Craig Darby)
• Missed majority of 1997-98 season recovering from knee injury suffered in training camp, September 30, 1997. • Missed majority of 2000-01 season recovering from hand injury suffered in game vs. Edmonton, November 11, 2000. Traded to **Boston** by **Pittsburgh** for Boston's 4th round choice (Paul Bissonnette) in 2003 Entry Draft, March 11, 2003. • Missed majority of 2003-04 season recovering from ankle injury suffered in game vs. Tampa Bay, December 23, 2003. Signed as a free agent by **Bofors** (Sweden-2), November 3, 2004. Signed as a free agent by **Nottingham** (Britain), January 22, 2005. • Missed remainder of 2005-06 season after suffering knee injury in game vs. Toronto (October 27, 2005) and recovering from resulting knee surgery (November 3, 2005). Signed as a free agent by **Anaheim**, August 15, 2006.

MOREAU, Ethan

Left wing. Shoots left. 6'2", 220 lbs. Born, Huntsville, Ont., September 22, 1975. Chicago's 1st choice, 14th overall, in 1994 Entry Draft.   (moh-ROH, EE-than)   **EDM.**

Season	Club	League	GP	G	A	Pts	PIM	PP	SH	GW	S	%	+/-	TF	F%	Min	GP	G	A	Pts	PIM	PP	SH	GW	Min
1990-91	Orillia Terriers	OHA-B	42	17	22	39	26										12	6	6	12	18				
1991-92	Niagara Falls	OHL	62	20	35	55	39										17	4	6	10	4				
1992-93	Niagara Falls	OHL	65	32	41	73	69										4	0	3	3	4				
1993-94	Niagara Falls	OHL	59	44	54	98	100																		
1994-95	Niagara Falls	OHL	39	25	41	66	69																		
	Sudbury Wolves	OHL	23	13	17	30	22										18	6	12	18	26				
1995-96	**Chicago**	**NHL**	8	0	1	1	4	0	0	0	1	0.0	1												
	Indianapolis Ice	IHL	71	21	20	41	126										5	4	0	4	8				
1996-97	**Chicago**	**NHL**	82	15	16	31	123	0	0	1	114	13.2	13				6	1	0	1	4	0	0	0	
1997-98	**Chicago**	**NHL**	54	9	9	18	73	2	0	0	87	10.3	0												
1998-99	**Chicago**	**NHL**	66	9	6	15	84	0	0	1	80	11.3	-5	3	33.3	12:30									
	Edmonton	**NHL**	14	1	5	6	8	0	0	1	16	6.3	2	1	0.0	11:47	4	0	3	3	6	0	0	0	17:26
99-2000	**Edmonton**	**NHL**	73	17	10	27	62	1	0	3	106	16.0	0	8	62.5	15:07	5	0	1	1	0	0	0	0	15:46
2000-01	**Edmonton**	**NHL**	68	9	10	19	90	0	1	3	97	9.3	-6	2	0.0	14:11	4	0	0	0	0	0	0	0	10:35
2001-02	**Edmonton**	**NHL**	80	11	5	16	81	0	0	1	129	8.5	4	11	54.6	12:43									
2002-03	**Edmonton**	**NHL**	78	14	17	31	112	2	0	1	137	10.2	-7	25	12.0	13:30	6	0	1	1	16	0	0	0	12:23
2003-04	**Edmonton**	**NHL**	81	20	12	32	96	0	3	5	180	11.1	7	59	44.1	15:04									
2004-05	EC Villacher SV	Austria	16	10	6	16	73										3	4	0	4	0				
2005-06	**Edmonton**	**NHL**	74	11	16	27	87	2	4	4	151	7.3	6	29	48.3	15:59	21	2	1	3	19	0	0	0	14:35
	NHL Totals		678	116	107	223	820	7	13	21	1098	10.6		138	39.9	14:06	46	3	6	9	52	0	0	0	14:17

OHL All-Rookie Team (1992)
Traded to **Edmonton** by **Chicago** with Daniel Cleary, Chad Kilger and Christian Laflamme for Boris Mironov, Dean McAmmond and Jonas Elofsson, March 20, 1999. Signed as a free agent by **Villacher** (Austria), December 20, 2004.

MORGAN, Gavin

Center. Shoots right. 5'11", 191 lbs. Born, Scarborough, Ont., July 9, 1976.   (MOHR-guhn, GA-vign)

Season	Club	League	GP	G	A	Pts	PIM	PP	SH	GW	S	%	+/-	TF	F%	Min	GP	G	A	Pts	PIM	PP	SH	GW	Min
1992-93	Wexford Raiders	MTJHL	3	0	1	1	0																		
1993-94	Wexford Raiders	MTJHL	49	18	32	50	91																		
1994-95	Wexford Raiders	MTJHL	49	26	39	65	170																		
1995-96	U. of Denver	WCHA	28	2	9	11	47																		
1996-97	U. of Denver	WCHA	41	8	15	23	46																		
1997-98	U. of Denver	WCHA	37	9	8	17	42																		
1998-99	U. of Denver	WCHA	40	13	16	29	85																		
99-2000	Idaho Steelheads	WCHL	54	17	33	50	150										3	0	3	3	4				
	Long Beach	IHL	7	0	1	1	10																		
	Utah Grizzlies	IHL	10	0	2	2	4										2	1	0	1	2				
2000-01	Utah Grizzlies	IHL	79	7	14	21	187																		
2001-02	Utah Grizzlies	AHL	76	8	24	32	249										5	0	1	1	2				
2002-03	Utah Grizzlies	AHL	73	15	24	39	244										2	0	1	1	17				
2003-04	**Dallas**	**NHL**	6	0	0	0	21	0	0		7	0.0	0	20	70.0	5:49									
	Hershey Bears	AHL	67	10	23	33	152										2	0	1	1	4				
2004-05	Hamilton	AHL	76	10	23	33	147										4	0	0	0	6				
2005-06	Peoria Rivermen	AHL	73	18	22	40	116										4	0	1	1	6				
	EHC Basel	Swiss	10	1	3	4	38																		
	NHL Totals		6	0	0	0	21	0	0		7	0.0		20	70.0	5:49									

Signed as a free agent by **Idaho** (WCHL), August 25, 1999. Signed as a free agent by **Utah** (IHL), June 26, 2000. Signed as a free agent by **Dallas**, July 17, 2001. Signed as a free agent by **Montreal**, July 26, 2004. Signed as a free agent by **Basel** (Swiss), August 29, 2005.

MORGAN, Jason

(MOHR-gan, JAY-son) **MIN.**

Center. Shoots left. 6'1", 200 lbs. Born, St. John's, Nfld., October 9, 1976. Los Angeles' 5th choice, 118th overall, in 1995 Entry Draft.

			Regular Season														Playoffs								
Season	Club	League	GP	G	A	Pts	PIM	PP	SH	GW	S	%	+/-	TF	F%	Min	GP	G	A	Pts	PIM	PP	SH	GW	Min
1992-93	Kitchener AA	OMHA	69	44	40	84	85																		
1993-94	Kitchener Rangers	OHL	65	6	15	21	16										5	1	0	1	0				
1994-95	Kitchener Rangers	OHL	35	3	15	18	25																		
	Kingston	OHL	20	0	3	3	14										6	0	2	2	0				
1995-96	Kingston	OHL	66	16	38	54	50										6	1	2	3	0				
1996-97	**Los Angeles**	**NHL**	**3**	**0**	**0**	**0**	**0**	**0**	**0**	**0**	**4**	**0.0**	**-3**												
	Phoenix	IHL	57	3	6	9	29																		
	Mississippi	ECHL	6	3	0	3	0										3	1	1	2	6				
1997-98	**Los Angeles**	**NHL**	**11**	**1**	**0**	**1**	**4**	**0**	**0**	**0**	**5**	**20.0**	**-7**												
	Springfield	AHL	58	13	22	35	66										3	1	0	1	18				
1998-99	Long Beach	IHL	13	4	6	10	18																		
	Springfield	AHL	46	6	16	22	51										3	0	0	0	6				
99-2000	Cincinnati	IHL	15	1	3	4	14																		
	Florida Everblades	ECHL	48	14	25	39	79										5	2	2	4	16				
2000-01	Florida Everblades	ECHL	37	15	22	37	41										5	2	3	5	17				
	Hamilton	AHL	11	2	0	2	10																		
	Springfield	AHL	16	1	4	5	19																		
	Saint John Flames	AHL															6	0	1	1	2				
2001-02	Saint John Flames	AHL	76	17	20	37	69																		
2002-03	Saint John Flames	AHL	80	13	40	53	63																		
2003-04	**Calgary**	**NHL**	**13**	**0**	**2**	**2**	**2**	**0**	**0**	**0**	**14**	**0.0**	**1**	**98**	**44.9**	**9:45**									
	Lowell	AHL	21	6	13	19	16																		
	Nashville	**NHL**	**6**	**0**	**2**	**2**	**2**	**0**	**0**	**0**	**6**	**0.0**	**0**	**15**	**73.3**	**10:06**									
	Norfolk Admirals	AHL	19	6	8	14	16										8	0	1	1	10				
2004-05	Norfolk Admirals	AHL	71	9	20	29	116										6	2	2	4	8				
2005-06	**Chicago**	**NHL**	**7**	**1**	**1**	**2**	**6**	**0**	**0**	**0**	**6**	**16.7**	**1**	**52**	**55.8**	**10:06**									
	Norfolk Admirals	AHL	51	8	31	39	58																		
	NHL Totals		**40**	**2**	**5**	**7**	**14**	**0**	**0**	**0**	**35**	**5.7**		**165**	**50.9**	**9:55**									

Signed to a PTO (tryout) contract by **Saint John** (AHL), April 22, 2001. Signed as a free agent by **Saint John** (AHL), August 28, 2001. Signed as a free agent by **Calgary**, July 11, 2002. Claimed on waivers by **Nashville** from **Calgary**, December 31, 2003. Claimed on waivers by **Calgary** from **Nashville**, February 19, 2004. Traded to **Chicago** by **Calgary** with Calgary's 6th round choice (Joseph Fallon) in 2005 Entry Draft for Ville Nieminen, February 24, 2004. Signed as a free agent by **Minnesota**, July 17, 2006.

MORO, Marc

(MOH-roh, MAHRK)

Defense. Shoots left. 6'1", 218 lbs. Born, Toronto, Ont., July 17, 1977. Ottawa's 2nd choice, 27th overall, in 1995 Entry Draft.

Season	Club	League	GP	G	A	Pts	PIM	PP	SH	GW	S	%	+/-	TF	F%	Min	GP	G	A	Pts	PIM	PP	SH	GW	Min
1992-93	Miss. Sens	MTHL	42	9	18	27	56																		
	Miss. Sens	MTJHL	2	0	0	0	0																		
1993-94	Kingston	MTJHL	12	0	2	2	10																		
	Kingston	OHL	43	0	3	3	81																		
1994-95	Kingston	OHL	64	4	12	16	255										6	0	0	0	23				
1995-96	Kingston	OHL	66	4	17	21	261										6	0	0	0	12				
	P.E.I. Senators	AHL	2	0	0	0	7										2	0	0	0	4				
1996-97	Kingston	OHL	37	4	8	12	97																		
	Sault Ste. Marie	OHL	26	0	5	5	74										11	1	6	7	38				
1997-98	**Anaheim**	**NHL**	**1**	**0**	**0**	**0**	**0**	**0**	**0**	**0**	**0**	**0.0**	**0**												
	Cincinnati	AHL	74	1	6	7	181																		
1998-99	Milwaukee	IHL	80	0	5	5	264										2	0	0	0	4				
99-2000	**Nashville**	**NHL**	**8**	**0**	**0**	**0**	**40**	**0**	**0**	**0**	**3**	**0.0**	**-3**	**0**	**0.0**	**10:55**									
	Milwaukee	IHL	64	5	5	10	203																		
2000-01	**Nashville**	**NHL**	**6**	**0**	**0**	**0**	**12**	**0**	**0**	**0**	**1**	**0.0**	**1**	**0**	**0.0**	**3:34**									
	Milwaukee	IHL	68	2	9	11	190										5	1	0	1	10				
2001-02	**Nashville**	**NHL**	**13**	**0**	**0**	**0**	**23**	**0**	**0**	**0**	**7**	**0.0**	**-3**	**0**	**0.0**	**12:02**									
	Milwaukee	AHL	41	1	8	9	81																		
	Toronto	**NHL**	**2**	**0**	**0**	**0**	**2**	**0**	**0**	**0**	**0**	**0.0**	**0**	**0**	**0.0**	**11:23**									
	St. John's	AHL	7	1	0	1	21																		
2002-03	St. John's	AHL	68	3	8	11	128																		
2003-04	St. John's	AHL	76	1	9	10	144																		
2004-05	St. John's	AHL	78	2	6	8	202										5	0	1	1	4				
2005-06	Toronto Marlies	AHL	73	1	8	9	149										5	0	0	0	11				
	NHL Totals		**30**	**0**	**0**	**0**	**77**	**0**	**0**	**0**	**11**	**0.0**		**0**	**0.0**	**9:56**									

Rights traded to **Anaheim** by **Ottawa** with Ted Drury for Jason York and Shaun Van Allen, October 1, 1996. Traded to **Nashville** by **Anaheim** with Chris Mason for Dominic Roussel, October 5, 1998. Traded to **Toronto** by **Nashville** for D.J. Smith and Marty Wilford, March 1, 2002.

MOROZOV, Aleksey

(moh-ROH-zohv, ah-LEHK-see)

Right wing. Shoots left. 6'1", 204 lbs. Born, Moscow, USSR, February 16, 1977. Pittsburgh's 1st choice, 24th overall, in 1995 Entry Draft.

Season	Club	League	GP	G	A	Pts	PIM	PP	SH	GW	S	%	+/-	TF	F%	Min	GP	G	A	Pts	PIM	PP	SH	GW	Min
1993-94	Krylja Sovetov	CIS	7	0	0	0	0										3	0	0	0	2				
1994-95	Krylja Sovetov	CIS	48	15	12	27	53										4	0	3	3	0				
1995-96	Krylja Sovetov	CIS	47	13	9	22	26																		
1996-97	Krylja Sovetov	Russia	44	21	11	32	32										2	0	1	1	2				
1997-98	Krylja Sovetov	Russia	6	2	1	3	4																		
	Pittsburgh	**NHL**	**76**	**13**	**13**	**26**	**8**	**2**	**0**	**3**	**80**	**16.3**	**-4**				**6**	**0**	**1**	**1**	**2**	**0**	**0**	**0**	
	Russia	Olympics	6	2	2	4	0																		
1998-99	**Pittsburgh**	**NHL**	**67**	**9**	**10**	**19**	**14**	**0**	**0**	**0**	**75**	**12.0**	**5**	**7**	**42.9**	**11:50**	**10**	**1**	**1**	**2**	**0**	**0**	**0**	**0**	**12:01**
99-2000	**Pittsburgh**	**NHL**	**68**	**12**	**19**	**31**	**14**	**0**	**1**	**0**	**101**	**11.9**	**12**	**27**	**33.3**	**13:51**	**5**	**0**	**0**	**0**	**0**	**0**	**0**	**0**	**11:48**
2000-01	**Pittsburgh**	**NHL**	**66**	**5**	**14**	**19**	**6**	**0**	**0**	**1**	**72**	**6.9**	**-8**	**19**	**42.1**	**10:41**	**18**	**3**	**3**	**6**	**6**	**0**	**1**	**0**	**14:59**
2001-02	**Pittsburgh**	**NHL**	**72**	**20**	**29**	**49**	**16**	**7**	**0**	**3**	**162**	**12.3**	**-7**	**1**	**100.0**	**16:42**									
2002-03	**Pittsburgh**	**NHL**	**27**	**9**	**16**	**25**	**16**	**6**	**0**	**2**	**46**	**19.6**	**-3**	**0**	**0.0**	**18:42**									
2003-04	**Pittsburgh**	**NHL**	**75**	**16**	**34**	**50**	**24**	**8**	**0**	**5**	**132**	**12.1**	**-24**	**0**	**0.0**	**16:34**									
2004-05	Ak Bars Kazan	Russia	58	20	27	47	30										4	0	1	1	2				
2005-06	Ak Bars Kazan	Russia	51	*23	25	48	69										13	*13	*13	*26	8				
	NHL Totals		**451**	**84**	**135**	**219**	**98**	**23**	**1**	**14**	**668**	**12.6**		**54**	**38.9**	**14:22**	**39**	**4**	**5**	**9**	**8**	**0**	**1**	**0**	**13:36**

• Missed majority of 2002-03 season recovering from wrist injury suffered in game vs. Toronto, December 10, 2002. Signed as a free agent by **Kazan** (Russia), September 25, 2004.

MORRIS, Derek

(MOH-rihs, DAIR-ihk) **PHX.**

Defense. Shoots right. 6', 220 lbs. Born, Edmonton, Alta., August 24, 1978. Calgary's 1st choice, 13th overall, in 1996 Entry Draft.

Season	Club	League	GP	G	A	Pts	PIM	PP	SH	GW	S	%	+/-	TF	F%	Min	GP	G	A	Pts	PIM	PP	SH	GW	Min
1994-95	Red Deer Vipers	AMHL	31	6	35	41	74																		
1995-96	Regina Pats	WHL	67	8	44	52	70										11	1	7	8	26				
1996-97	Regina Pats	WHL	67	18	57	75	180										5	0	3	3	9				
	Saint John Flames	AHL	7	0	3	3	7										5	0	3	3	7				
1997-98	**Calgary**	**NHL**	**82**	**9**	**20**	**29**	**88**	**5**	**1**	**1**	**120**	**7.5**	**1**												
1998-99	**Calgary**	**NHL**	**71**	**7**	**27**	**34**	**73**	**3**	**0**	**2**	**150**	**4.7**	**4**	**0**	**0.0**	**20:44**									
99-2000	**Calgary**	**NHL**	**78**	**9**	**29**	**38**	**80**	**3**	**0**	**2**	**193**	**4.7**	**2**	**0**	**0.0**	**24:51**									
2000-01	**Calgary**	**NHL**	**51**	**5**	**23**	**28**	**56**	**3**	**1**	**4**	**142**	**3.5**	**-15**	**0**	**0.0**	**25:51**									
	Saint John Flames	AHL	3	1	2	3	2																		
2001-02	**Calgary**	**NHL**	**61**	**4**	**30**	**34**	**88**	**2**	**0**	**1**	**166**	**2.4**	**-4**	**1**	**100.0**	**24:40**									
2002-03	**Colorado**	**NHL**	**75**	**11**	**37**	**48**	**68**	**9**	**0**	**7**	**191**	**5.8**	**16**	**0**	**0.0**	**23:49**	**7**	**0**	**3**	**3**	**6**	**0**	**0**	**0**	**22:44**
2003-04	**Colorado**	**NHL**	**69**	**6**	**22**	**28**	**47**	**2**	**0**	**1**	**139**	**4.3**	**4**	**0**	**0.0**	**20:53**									
	Phoenix	**NHL**	**14**	**0**	**4**	**4**	**2**	**0**	**0**	**0**	**28**	**0.0**	**-5**	**0**	**0.0**	**25:02**									
2004-05			DID NOT PLAY																						
2005-06	**Phoenix**	**NHL**	**53**	**6**	**21**	**27**	**54**	**4**	**1**	**2**	**91**	**6.6**	**-7**	**1**	**0.0**	**20:52**									
	NHL Totals		**554**	**57**	**213**	**270**	**556**	**31**	**3**	**20**	**1220**	**4.7**		**2**	**50.0**	**23:08**	**7**	**0**	**3**	**3**	**6**	**0**	**0**	**0**	**22:44**

WHL East First All-Star Team (1997) • NHL All-Rookie Team (1998)

Traded to **Colorado** by **Calgary** with Jeff Shantz and Dean McAmmond for Chris Drury and Stephane Yelle, October 1, 2002. Traded to **Phoenix** by **Colorado** with Keith Ballard for Ossi Vaananen, Chris Gratton and Phoenix's 2nd round choice (Paul Stastny) in 2005 Entry Draft, March 8, 2004.

MORRISON, Brendan

(MOHR-ih-suhn, BREHN-duhn) **VAN.**

Center. Shoots left. 5'11", 190 lbs. Born, Pitt Meadows, B.C., August 15, 1975. New Jersey's 3rd choice, 39th overall, in 1993 Entry Draft.

Season	Club	League	GP	G	A	Pts	PIM	PP	SH	GW	S	%	+/-	TF	F%	Min	GP	G	A	Pts	PIM	PP	SH	GW	Min
			Regular Season														Playoffs								
1990-91	Ridge Meadows	BCAHA	77	126	127	253	88	....	....	....	....	....	....	....	....	....	....	....	....	....	....	....	....	....	....
1991-92	Ridge Meadows	BCAHA	55	56	111	167	56	....	....	....	....	....	....	....	....	....	....	....	....	....	....	....	....	....	....
1992-93	Penticton	BCJHL	56	35	59	94	45	....	....	....	....	....	....	....	....	....	....	....	....	....	....	....	....	....	....
1993-94	U. of Michigan	CCHA	38	20	28	48	24	....	....	....	....	....	....	....	....	....	5	2	7	9	2	....	....	....	....
1994-95	U. of Michigan	CCHA	39	23	*53	*76	42	....	....	....	....	....	....	....	....	....	5	1	11	12	6	....	....	....	....
1995-96	U. of Michigan	CCHA	35	28	44	*72	41	....	....	....	....	....	....	....	....	....	7	6	9	15	4	....	....	....	....
1996-97	U. of Michigan	CCHA	43	31	*57	*88	52	....	....	....	....	....	....	....	....	....	6	6	8	14	8	....	....	....	....
1997-98	New Jersey	NHL	11	5	4	9	0	0	0	1	19	26.3	3	....	....	....	3	0	1	1	0	0	0	0	....
	Albany River Rats	AHL	72	35	49	84	44	....	....	....	....	....	....	....	....	....	8	3	4	7	19	....	....	....	....
1998-99	New Jersey	NHL	76	13	33	46	18	5	0	2	111	11.7	–4	920	51.1	13:55	7	0	2	2	0	0	0	0	13:04
99-2000	Trebic	CzRep-2	2	0	0	0	0	....	....	....	....	....	....	....	....	....	....	....	....	....	....	....	....	....	....
	Pardubice	CzRep	6	5	2	7	2	....	....	....	....	....	....	....	....	....	....	....	....	....	....	....	....	....	....
	New Jersey	NHL	44	5	21	26	8	2	0	1	79	6.3	8	572	51.1	16:09	....	....	....	....	....	....	....	....	....
	Vancouver	NHL	12	2	7	9	10	0	0	0	17	11.8	4	48	54.2	14:41	....	....	....	....	....	....	....	....	....
2000-01	Vancouver	NHL	82	16	38	54	42	3	2	3	179	8.9	2	1685	50.1	18:22	4	1	2	3	0	1	0	0	20:50
2001-02	Vancouver	NHL	82	23	44	67	26	6	0	4	183	12.6	18	1307	49.9	19:21	6	0	2	2	6	0	0	0	19:44
2002-03	Vancouver	NHL	82	25	46	71	36	6	2	8	167	15.0	18	1585	48.3	21:13	14	4	7	11	18	1	0	1	20:18
2003-04	Vancouver	NHL	82	22	38	60	50	5	1	4	161	13.7	16	1486	51.0	20:08	7	2	3	5	8	1	0	1	22:00
2004-05	Linkopings HC	Sweden	45	16	28	44	50	....	....	....	....	....	....	....	....	....	6	0	2	2	10	....	....	....	....
2005-06	Vancouver	NHL	82	19	37	56	84	8	0	5	156	12.2	–1	1328	50.5	19:31	....	....	....	....	....	....	....	....	....
	NHL Totals		553	130	268	398	274	35	5	28	1072	12.1		8931	50.1	18:30	41	7	17	24	32	3	0	2	19:15

CCHA Rookie of the Year (1994) • CCHA First All-Star Team (1995, 1996, 1997) • NCAA West First All-American Team (1995, 1996, 1997) • CCHA Player of the Year (1996, 1997) • NCAA Championship All-Tournament Team (1996) • NCAA Championship Tournament MVP (1996) • Hobey Baker Memorial Award (Top U.S. Collegiate Player) (1997) • AHL All-Rookie Team (1998)

Traded to **Vancouver** by **New Jersey** with Denis Pederson for Alexander Mogilny, March 14, 2000. Signed as a free agent by **Linkopings** (Sweden), September, 2004.

MORRISONN, Shaone

(MOHR-ih-suhn, SHAWN) **WSH.**

Defense. Shoots left. 6'4", 210 lbs. Born, Vancouver, B.C., December 23, 1982. Boston's 1st choice, 19th overall, in 2001 Entry Draft.

Season	Club	League	GP	G	A	Pts	PIM	PP	SH	GW	S	%	+/-	TF	F%	Min	GP	G	A	Pts	PIM	PP	SH	GW	Min
1997-98	Vancouver T-Birds	BCAHA	45	16	44	60	75	....	....	....	....	....	....	....	....	....	....	....	....	....	....	....	....	....	....
1998-99	South Surrey	BCHL	19	0	2	2	13	....	....	....	....	....	....	....	....	....	....	....	....	....	....	....	....	....	....
99-2000	Kamloops Blazers	WHL	57	1	6	7	80	....	....	....	....	....	....	....	....	....	4	0	0	0	6	....	....	....	....
2000-01	Kamloops Blazers	WHL	61	13	25	38	132	....	....	....	....	....	....	....	....	....	4	0	0	0	6	....	....	....	....
2001-02	Kamloops Blazers	WHL	61	11	26	37	106	....	....	....	....	....	....	....	....	....	4	0	2	2	2	....	....	....	....
2002-03	Boston	NHL	11	0	0	0	8	0	0	0	4	0.0	0	0	0.0	8:57	....	....	....	....	....	....	....	....	....
	Providence Bruins	AHL	60	5	16	21	103	....	....	....	....	....	....	....	....	....	4	0	0	0	6	....	....	....	....
2003-04	Boston	NHL	30	1	7	8	10	0	0	0	13	7.7	10	0	0.0	18:11	....	....	....	....	....	....	....	....	....
	Providence Bruins	AHL	18	0	2	2	16	....	....	....	....	....	....	....	....	....	....	....	....	....	....	....	....	....	....
	Washington	NHL	3	0	0	0	0	0	0	0	1	0.0	0	0	0.0	18:52	....	....	....	....	....	....	....	....	....
	Portland Pirates	AHL	13	1	4	5	10	....	....	....	....	....	....	....	....	....	7	0	1	1	4	....	....	....	....
2004-05	Portland Pirates	AHL	71	4	14	18	63	....	....	....	....	....	....	....	....	....	....	....	....	....	....	....	....	....	....
2005-06	Washington	NHL	80	1	13	14	91	0	0	0	56	1.8	7	4	0.0	20:44	....	....	....	....	....	....	....	....	....
	NHL Totals		124	2	20	22	109	0	0	0	74	2.7		4	0.0	19:01	....	....	....	....	....	....	....	....	....

Traded to **Washington** by **Boston** with Boston's 1st (Jeff Schultz) and 2nd (Michail Yunkov) round choices in 2004 Entry Draft for Sergei Gonchar, March 3, 2004.

MORROW, Brenden

(MOHR-roh, BREHN-duhn) **DAL.**

Left wing. Shoots left. 5'11", 210 lbs. Born, Carlyle, Sask., January 16, 1979. Dallas' 1st choice, 25th overall, in 1997 Entry Draft.

Season	Club	League	GP	G	A	Pts	PIM	PP	SH	GW	S	%	+/-	TF	F%	Min	GP	G	A	Pts	PIM	PP	SH	GW	Min
1994-95	Estevan	SMBHL	60	117	72	189	45	....	....	....	....	....	....	....	....	....	....	....	....	....	....	....	....	....	....
1995-96	Portland	WHL	65	13	12	25	61	....	....	....	....	....	....	....	....	....	7	0	0	0	8	....	....	....	....
1996-97	Portland	WHL	71	39	49	88	178	....	....	....	....	....	....	....	....	....	6	2	1	3	4	....	....	....	....
1997-98	Portland	WHL	68	34	52	86	184	....	....	....	....	....	....	....	....	....	16	10	8	18	65	....	....	....	....
1998-99	Portland	WHL	61	41	44	85	248	....	....	....	....	....	....	....	....	....	4	0	4	4	18	....	....	....	....
99-2000	Dallas	NHL	64	14	19	33	81	3	0	3	113	12.4	8	25	48.0	15:51	21	2	4	6	22	1	0	0	15:04
	Michigan	IHL	9	2	0	2	18	....	....	....	....	....	....	....	....	....	....	....	....	....	....	....	....	....	....
2000-01	Dallas	NHL	82	20	24	44	128	7	0	6	121	16.5	18	22	45.5	15:29	10	0	3	3	12	0	0	0	17:00
2001-02	Dallas	NHL	72	17	18	35	109	4	0	3	102	16.7	12	39	41.0	16:52	....	....	....	....	....	....	....	....	....
2002-03	Dallas	NHL	71	21	22	43	134	2	3	4	105	20.0	20	29	27.6	15:43	12	3	5	8	16	2	0	0	21:03
2003-04	Dallas	NHL	81	25	24	49	121	9	0	3	132	18.9	10	38	47.4	19:24	5	0	1	1	4	0	0	0	21:29
2004-05	Oklahoma City	CHL	19	8	14	22	31	....	....	....	....	....	....	....	....	....	....	....	....	....	....	....	....	....	....
2005-06	Dallas	NHL	81	23	42	65	183	8	1	4	146	15.8	30	32	37.5	19:15	5	1	5	6	6	0	0	0	21:57
	NHL Totals		451	120	149	269	756	33	4	23	719	16.7		185	41.1	17:10	53	6	18	24	60	3	0	0	18:02

WHL West First All-Star Team (1999)

Signed as a free agent by **Oklahoma City** (CHL), October 19, 2004.

MOTTAU, Mike

(MAW-tuh, MIGHK) **N.J.**

Defense. Shoots left. 6', 195 lbs. Born, Quincy, MA, March 19, 1978. NY Rangers' 10th choice, 182nd overall, in 1997 Entry Draft.

Season	Club	League	GP	G	A	Pts	PIM	PP	SH	GW	S	%	+/-	TF	F%	Min	GP	G	A	Pts	PIM	PP	SH	GW	Min
1994-95	Thayer Academy	High-MA	29	7	19	26	....	....	....	....	....	....	....	....	....	....	....	....	....	....	....	....	....	....	....
1995-96	Thayer Academy	High-MA	31	6	20	26	14	....	....	....	....	....	....	....	....	....	....	....	....	....	....	....	....	....	....
1996-97	Boston College	H-East	38	5	18	23	77	....	....	....	....	....	....	....	....	....	....	....	....	....	....	....	....	....	....
1997-98	Boston College	H-East	40	13	36	49	50	....	....	....	....	....	....	....	....	....	....	....	....	....	....	....	....	....	....
1998-99	Boston College	H-East	43	3	39	42	44	....	....	....	....	....	....	....	....	....	....	....	....	....	....	....	....	....	....
99-2000	Boston College	H-East	42	6	37	43	61	....	....	....	....	....	....	....	....	....	....	....	....	....	....	....	....	....	....
2000-01	NY Rangers	NHL	18	0	3	3	13	0	0	0	17	0.0	–6	0	0.0	15:18	....	....	....	....	....	....	....	....	....
	Hartford	AHL	61	10	33	43	45	....	....	....	....	....	....	....	....	....	5	0	1	1	19	....	....	....	....
2001-02	NY Rangers	NHL	1	0	0	0	0	0	0	0	0	0.0	0	0	0.0	6:20	....	....	....	....	....	....	....	....	....
	Hartford	AHL	80	9	42	51	56	....	....	....	....	....	....	....	....	....	10	0	5	5	4	....	....	....	....
2002-03	Hartford	AHL	29	1	18	19	24	....	....	....	....	....	....	....	....	....	....	....	....	....	....	....	....	....	....
	Calgary	NHL	4	0	0	0	0	0	0	0	0	0.0	–1	0	0.0	9:50	....	....	....	....	....	....	....	....	....
	Saint John Flames	AHL	32	5	12	17	14	....	....	....	....	....	....	....	....	....	....	....	....	....	....	....	....	....	....
2003-04	Cincinnati	AHL	69	9	22	31	79	....	....	....	....	....	....	....	....	....	9	1	2	3	8	....	....	....	....
2004-05	Worcester IceCats	AHL	73	4	31	35	23	....	....	....	....	....	....	....	....	....	....	....	....	....	....	....	....	....	....
2005-06	Peoria Rivermen	AHL	76	8	48	56	81	....	....	....	....	....	....	....	....	....	4	0	1	1	6	....	....	....	....
	NHL Totals		23	0	3	3	13	0	0	0	17	0.0		0	0.0	13:57	....	....	....	....	....	....	....	....	....

Hockey East First All-Star Team (1998, 2000) • NCAA East Second All-American Team (1998) • NCAA Championship All-Tournament Team (1998, 2000) • Hockey East Second All-Star Team (1999) • NCAA East First All-American Team (1999, 2000) • Hockey East Player of the Year (2000) (co-winner - Ty Conklin) • Hobey Baker Memorial Award (Top U.S. Collegiate Player) (2000) • AHL All-Rookie Team (2001)

Traded to **Calgary** by **NY Rangers** for Calgary's 6th round choice (Ivan Dornic) in 2003 Entry Draft and future considerations, January 22, 2003. Signed as a free agent by **Anaheim**, July 25, 2003. Signed as a free agent by **Worcester** (AHL), September 30, 2004. Signed as a free agent by **New Jersey**, July 17, 2006.

MOTZKO, Joe

(MAWTS-koh, JOH) **CBJ**

Right wing. Shoots right. 6', 196 lbs. Born, Bemidji, MN, March 14, 1980.

Season	Club	League	GP	G	A	Pts	PIM	PP	SH	GW	S	%	+/-	TF	F%	Min	GP	G	A	Pts	PIM	PP	SH	GW	Min
1997-98	Bemidji Jacks	High-MN	25	24	28	52	....	....	....	....	....	....	....	....	....	....	....	....	....	....	....	....	....	....	....
1998-99	Omaha Lancers	USHL	51	15	21	36	60	....	....	....	....	....	....	....	....	....	12	7	3	10	12	....	....	....	....
99-2000	St. Cloud State	WCHA	36	9	15	24	52	....	....	....	....	....	....	....	....	....	....	....	....	....	....	....	....	....	....
2000-01	St. Cloud State	WCHA	41	17	20	37	54	....	....	....	....	....	....	....	....	....	....	....	....	....	....	....	....	....	....
2001-02	St. Cloud State	WCHA	39	9	30	39	34	....	....	....	....	....	....	....	....	....	....	....	....	....	....	....	....	....	....
2002-03	St. Cloud State	WCHA	38	17	25	42	59	....	....	....	....	....	....	....	....	....	....	....	....	....	....	....	....	....	....
	Syracuse Crunch	AHL	2	0	0	0	0	....	....	....	....	....	....	....	....	....	....	....	....	....	....	....	....	....	....
2003-04	Columbus	NHL	2	0	0	0	0	0	0	0	1	0.0	0	0	0.0	7:16	....	....	....	....	....	....	....	....	....
	Syracuse Crunch	AHL	70	17	24	41	38	....	....	....	....	....	....	....	....	....	....	....	....	....	....	....	....	....	....
2004-05	Syracuse Crunch	AHL	79	28	38	66	72	....	....	....	....	....	....	....	....	....	7	2	2	4	6	....	....	....	....
2005-06	Columbus	NHL	2	0	0	0	0	0	0	0	3	0.0	–2	1	0.0	10:35	....	....	....	....	....	....	....	....	....
	Syracuse Crunch	AHL	61	27	34	61	54	....	....	....	....	....	....	....	....	....	3	0	0	0	0	....	....	....	....
	NHL Totals		4	0	0	0	0	0	0	0	4	0.0		1	0.0	8:55	....	....	....	....	....	....	....	....	....

Signed as a free agent by **Columbus**, May 15, 2003.

MOWERS, Mark

(MAHW-uhrs, MAHRK) **BOS.**

Center. Shoots right. 5'11", 185 lbs. Born, Decatur, GA, February 16, 1974.

Season	Club	League	Regular Season GP	G	A	Pts	PIM	PP	SH	GW	S	%	+/-	TF	F%	Min	Playoffs GP	G	A	Pts	PIM	PP	SH	GW	Min
1992-93	Saginaw Jr. Gears	NAHL	39	31	39	70	....																		
1993-94	Dubuque	USHL	47	51	31	82	80																		
1994-95	New Hampshire	H-East	36	13	23	36	16																		
1995-96	New Hampshire	H-East	34	21	26	47	18																		
1996-97	New Hampshire	H-East	39	26	32	58	52																		
1997-98	New Hampshire	H-East	35	25	31	56	32																		
1998-99	**Nashville**	**NHL**	**30**	**0**	**6**	**6**	**4**	**0**	**0**	**0**	**24**	**0.0**	**–4**	**241**	**49.0**	**9:22**									
	Milwaukee	IHL	51	14	22	36	24										1	0	0	0	0				
99-2000	**Nashville**	**NHL**	**41**	**4**	**5**	**9**	**10**	**0**	**0**	**0**	**50**	**8.0**	**0**	**312**	**45.2**	**10:58**									
	Milwaukee	IHL	23	11	15	26	34																		
2000-01	Milwaukee	IHL	63	25	25	50	54										5	1	2	3	2				
2001-02	**Nashville**	**NHL**	**14**	**1**	**2**	**3**	**2**	**0**	**0**	**0**	**5**	**20.0**	**–2**	**24**	**33.3**	**8:31**									
	Milwaukee	AHL	45	19	20	39	34																		
2002-03	Grand Rapids	AHL	78	34	47	81	47										15	3	4	7	4				
2003-04	**Detroit**	**NHL**	**52**	**3**	**8**	**11**	**4**	**1**	**0**	**1**	**48**	**6.3**	**3**	**400**	**47.8**	**10:27**									
	Grand Rapids	AHL	16	8	6	14	4																		
2004-05	Malmo	Sweden	9	2	0	2	0																		
	Fribourg	Swiss	3	2	0	2	0										9	9	8	17	12				
2005-06	**Detroit**	**NHL**	**46**	**4**	**11**	**15**	**16**	**0**	**0**	**0**	**65**	**6.2**	**13**	**100**	**52.0**	**8:18**	**3**	**0**	**0**	**0**	**0**	**0**	**0**	**0**	**9:27**
	NHL Totals		**183**	**12**	**32**	**44**	**36**	**1**	**0**	**1**	**192**	**6.3**		**1077**	**47.4**	**9:42**	**3**	**0**	**0**	**0**	**0**	**0**	**0**	**0**	**9:27**

Hockey East Rookie of the Year (1995) • Hockey East Second All-Star Team (1998) • NCAA East First All-American Team (1998) • Ken McKenzie Trophy (U.S. - Born Rookie of the Year – IHL) (1999) • AHL Second All-Star Team (2003)

Signed as a free agent by **Nashville**, June 11, 1998. Signed as a free agent by **Detroit**, August 5, 2002. Signed as a free agent by **Malmo** (Sweden), December 21, 2004. Signed as a free agent by **Fribourg** (Swiss), February 4, 2005. Signed as a free agent by **Boston**, July 6, 2006.

MUIR, Bryan

(MEWR, BRIGH-uhn) **WSH.**

Defense. Shoots left. 6'3", 224 lbs. Born, Winnipeg, Man., June 8, 1973.

Season	Club	League	Regular Season GP	G	A	Pts	PIM	PP	SH	GW	S	%	+/-	TF	F%	Min	Playoffs GP	G	A	Pts	PIM	PP	SH	GW	Min
1991-92	Wexford Raiders	MTJHL	44	3	19	22	35																		
1992-93	New Hampshire	H-East	26	1	2	3	24																		
1993-94	New Hampshire	H-East	40	0	4	4	48																		
1994-95	New Hampshire	H-East	28	9	9	18	46																		
1995-96	Canada	Nat-Tm	42	6	12	18	38																		
	Edmonton	**NHL**	**5**	**0**	**0**	**0**	**6**	**0**	**0**	**0**	**4**	**0.0**	**–4**												
1996-97	Hamilton	AHL	75	8	16	24	80										14	0	5	5	12				
	Edmonton	**NHL**	....	....	....	....	....										**5**	**0**	**0**	**0**	**4**	**0**	**0**	**0**	
1997-98	**Edmonton**	**NHL**	**7**	**0**	**0**	**0**	**17**	**0**	**0**	**0**	**6**	**0.0**	**0**												
	Hamilton	AHL	28	3	10	13	62																		
	Albany River Rats	AHL	41	3	10	13	67										13	3	0	3	12				
1998-99	**New Jersey**	**NHL**	**1**	**0**	**0**	**0**	**0**	**0**	**0**	**0**	**4**	**0.0**	**0**	**0**	**0.0**	**9:54**									
	Albany River Rats	AHL	10	0	0	0	29																		
	Chicago	**NHL**	**53**	**1**	**4**	**5**	**50**	**0**	**0**	**0**	**78**	**1.3**	**1**	**0**	**0.0**	**18:49**									
	Portland Pirates	AHL	2	1	1	2	2																		
99-2000	**Chicago**	**NHL**	**11**	**2**	**3**	**5**	**13**	**0**	**1**	**0**	**19**	**10.5**	**–1**	**0**	**0.0**	**17:54**									
	Tampa Bay	**NHL**	**30**	**1**	**1**	**2**	**32**	**0**	**0**	**0**	**32**	**3.1**	**–8**	**1**	**100.0**	**19:29**									
2000-01	**Tampa Bay**	**NHL**	**10**	**0**	**3**	**3**	**15**	**0**	**0**	**0**	**14**	**0.0**	**–7**	**1**	**0.0**	**18:34**									
	Detroit Vipers	IHL	21	5	7	12	36																		
	Colorado	**NHL**	**8**	**0**	**0**	**0**	**4**	**0**	**0**	**0**	**3**	**0.0**	**0**	**0**	**0.0**	**8:14**	**3**	**0**	**0**	**0**	**0**	**0**	**0**	**0**	**3:15**
	Hershey Bears	AHL	26	5	8	13	50																		
2001-02	**Colorado**	**NHL**	**22**	**1**	**1**	**2**	**9**	**0**	**0**	**0**	**26**	**3.8**	**1**	**0**	**0.0**	**10:20**	**21**	**0**	**0**	**0**	**2**	**0**	**0**	**0**	**5:39**
	Hershey Bears	AHL	59	10	16	26	133																		
2002-03	**Colorado**	**NHL**	**32**	**0**	**2**	**2**	**19**	**0**	**0**	**0**	**9**	**0.0**	**3**	**0**	**0.0**	**6:33**									
	Hershey Bears	AHL	36	9	12	21	75										5	2	6	8	6				
2003-04	**Los Angeles**	**NHL**	**2**	**0**	**1**	**1**	**2**	**0**	**0**	**0**	**2**	**0.0**	**1**	**0**	**0.0**	**17:56**									
	Manchester	AHL	73	13	37	50	141										6	2	3	5	12				
2004-05	MODO	Sweden	26	1	5	6	36																		
	Blues Espoo	Finland	11	1	0	1	30																		
2005-06	**Washington**	**NHL**	**72**	**8**	**18**	**26**	**72**	**4**	**0**	**0**	**136**	**5.9**	**–9**	**1**	**100.0**	**21:10**									
	NHL Totals		**253**	**13**	**33**	**46**	**239**	**4**	**1**	**0**	**333**	**3.9**		**3**	**66.7**	**16:45**	**29**	**0**	**0**	**0**	**6**	**0**	**0**	**0**	**5:21**

AHL First All-Star Team (2004)

Signed to five-game amateur tryout contract by **Edmonton**, February 29, 1996. Signed as a free agent by **Edmonton**, April 30, 1996. Traded to **New Jersey** by **Edmonton** with Jason Arnott for Valeri Zelepukin and Bill Guerin, January 4, 1998. Traded to **Chicago** by **New Jersey** for Chicago's 3rd round choice (Mike Rupp) in 2000 Entry Draft. November 13, 1998. Traded to **Tampa Bay** by **Chicago** with Reid Simpson for Michael Nylander, November 12, 1999. • Missed majority of 1999-2000 season recovering from leg injury suffered in game vs. Atlanta, November 17, 1999. Traded to **Colorado** by **Tampa Bay** for Colorado's 8th round choice (Dmitri Bezrukov) in 2001 Entry Draft, January 23, 2001. Signed as a free agent by **Los Angeles**, July 31, 2003. Signed as a free agent by **MODO** (Sweden), July 26, 2004. Signed as a free agent by **Blues Espoo** (Finland), January 31, 2005. Signed as a free agent by **Washington**, August 30, 2005.

MURLEY, Matt

(MUHR-lee, MAT) **COL.**

Left wing. Shoots left. 6'1", 206 lbs. Born, Troy, NY, December 17, 1979. Pittsburgh's 2nd choice, 51st overall, in 1999 Entry Draft.

Season	Club	League	Regular Season GP	G	A	Pts	PIM	PP	SH	GW	S	%	+/-	TF	F%	Min	Playoffs GP	G	A	Pts	PIM	PP	SH	GW	Min
1996-97	Syracuse	MTJHL	48	52	58	110	111																		
1997-98	Syracuse	MTJHL	49	56	70	126	103																		
1998-99	RPI Engineers	ECAC	36	17	32	49	32																		
99-2000	RPI Engineers	ECAC	35	9	29	38	42																		
2000-01	RPI Engineers	ECAC	34	*24	18	42	34																		
2001-02	RPI Engineers	ECAC	32	*24	22	46	26																		
2002-03	Wilkes-Barre	AHL	73	21	37	58	45										6	0	2	2	15				
2003-04	**Pittsburgh**	**NHL**	**18**	**1**	**1**	**2**	**14**	**0**	**0**	**0**	**20**	**5.0**	**–6**	**2**	**50.0**	**11:49**									
	Wilkes-Barre	AHL	63	10	26	36	69										24	7	6	13	17				
2004-05	Wilkes-Barre	AHL	80	17	24	41	55										11	3	0	3	0				
2005-06	**Pittsburgh**	**NHL**	**41**	**1**	**5**	**6**	**24**	**0**	**0**	**0**	**48**	**2.1**	**–9**	**11**	**36.4**	**11:29**									
	NHL Totals		**59**	**2**	**6**	**8**	**38**	**0**	**0**	**0**	**68**	**2.9**		**13**	**38.5**	**11:35**									

ECAC First All-Star Team (2002)

Signed as a free agent by **Colorado**, July 12, 2006.

MURPHY, Curtis

(MUHR-fee, KUHR-this)

Defense. Shoots right. 5'8", 185 lbs. Born, Kerrobert, Sask., December 3, 1975.

Season	Club	League	Regular Season GP	G	A	Pts	PIM	PP	SH	GW	S	%	+/-	TF	F%	Min	Playoffs GP	G	A	Pts	PIM	PP	SH	GW	Min
1993-94	Nipawin Hawks	SJHL	60	21	33	54	....																		
1994-95	North Dakota	WCHA	33	6	10	16	28																		
1995-96	North Dakota	WCHA	38	6	12	18	58																		
1996-97	North Dakota	WCHA	43	12	30	42	36																		
1997-98	North Dakota	WCHA	39	8	34	42	78																		
1998-99	Orlando	IHL	80	22	35	57	60										17	4	5	9	16				
99-2000	Orlando	IHL	81	8	43	51	59										6	0	2	2	6				
2000-01	Orlando	IHL	51	19	30	49	55										10	2	9	11	12				
2001-02	Houston Aeros	AHL	80	12	35	47	75										14	2	4	6	10				
2002-03	**Minnesota**	**NHL**	**1**	**0**	**0**	**0**	**0**	**0**	**0**	**0**	**0**	**0.0**	**0**	**0**	**0.0**	**8:56**									
	Houston Aeros	AHL	80	23	31	54	63										23	2	7	9	22				
2003-04	Milwaukee	AHL	79	17	36	53	51										22	4	8	12	12				
2004-05	Yaroslavl	Russia	60	6	6	12	50										9	1	1	2	6				
2005-06	Houston Aeros	AHL	80	14	53	67	76										8	0	4	4	4				
	NHL Totals		**1**	**0**	**0**	**0**	**0**	**0**	**0**	**0**	**0**	**0.0**		**0**	**0.0**	**8:56**									

WCHA First All-Star Team (1997, 1998) • NCAA West Second All-American Team (1997) • WCHA Player of the Year (1998) • NCAA West First All-American Team (1998) • IHL First All-Star Team (2001) • AHL First All-Star Team (2003, 2004, 2006) • Eddie Shore Award (Outstanding Defenseman – AHL) (2003, 2004)

Signed as a free agent by **Minnesota**, June 18, 2001. Traded to **Nashville** by **Minnesota** for Chris Bala, June 26, 2003. Signed as a free agent by **Yaroslavl** (Russia), May 28, 2004.

			Regular Season														Playoffs								
Season	Club	League	GP	G	A	Pts	PIM	PP	SH	GW	S	%	+/-	TF	F%	Min	GP	G	A	Pts	PIM	PP	SH	GW	Min

MURRAY, Doug

(MUHR-ree, DUHG) **S.J.**

Defense. Shoots left. 6'3", 245 lbs. Born, Bromma, Sweden, March 12, 1980. San Jose's 6th choice, 241st overall, in 1999 Entry Draft.

Season	Club	League	GP	G	A	Pts	PIM	PP	SH	GW	S	%	+/-	TF	F%	Min	GP	G	A	Pts	PIM	PP	SH	GW	Min
1998-99	NY Apple Core	EJHL	60	17	47	64	62	....	....	....	....	....	....	....	....	....	....	....	....	....	....	....	....	....	....
99-2000	Cornell Big Red	ECAC	32	3	6	9	38	....	....	....	....	....	....	....	....	....	....	....	....	....	....	....	....	....	....
2000-01	Cornell Big Red	ECAC	25	5	13	18	39	....	....	....	....	....	....	....	....	....	....	....	....	....	....	....	....	....	....
2001-02	Cornell Big Red	ECAC	35	11	21	32	67	....	....	....	....	....	....	....	....	....	....	....	....	....	....	....	....	....	....
2002-03	Cornell Big Red	ECAC	35	5	20	25	30	....	....	....	....	....	....	....	....	....	....	....	....	....	....	....	....	....	....
2003-04	Cleveland Barons	AHL	72	10	12	22	75	....	....	....	....	....	....	....	....	....	9	3	0	3	37	....	....	....	....
2004-05	Cleveland Barons	AHL	54	6	17	23	56	....	....	....	....	....	....	....	....	....	....	....	....	....	....	....	....	....	....
2005-06	**San Jose**	**NHL**	**34**	**0**	**1**	**1**	**27**	**0**	**0**	**0**	**21**	**0.0**	**3**	**0**	**0.0**	**13:53**	....	....	....	....	....	....	....	....	....
	Cleveland Barons	AHL	20	1	7	8	37	....	....	....	....	....	....	....	....	....	....	....	....	....	....	....	....	....	....
	NHL Totals		**34**	**0**	**1**	**1**	**27**	**0**	**0**	**0**	**21**	**0.0**		**0**	**0.0**	**13:53**	....	....	....	....	....	....	....	....	....

ECAC First All-Star Team (2002, 2003) • NCAA East First All-American Team (2003)

MURRAY, Garth

(MUHR-ree, GARTH) **MTL.**

Center. Shoots left. 6'1", 213 lbs. Born, Regina, Sask., September 17, 1982. NY Rangers' 3rd choice, 79th overall, in 2001 Entry Draft.

Season	Club	League	GP	G	A	Pts	PIM	PP	SH	GW	S	%	+/-	TF	F%	Min	GP	G	A	Pts	PIM	PP	SH	GW	Min
1997-98	Calgary Buffaloes	AMHL	56	26	34	60	110	....	....	....	....	....	....	....	....	....	....	....	....	....	....	....	....	....	....
	Regina Pats	WHL	4	0	0	0	2	....	....	....	....	....	....	....	....	....	2	0	0	0	0	....	....	....	....
1998-99	Regina Pats	WHL	60	3	5	8	101	....	....	....	....	....	....	....	....	....	....	....	....	....	....	....	....	....	....
99-2000	Regina Pats	WHL	68	14	26	40	155	....	....	....	....	....	....	....	....	....	7	1	1	2	7	....	....	....	....
2000-01	Regina Pats	WHL	72	28	16	44	183	....	....	....	....	....	....	....	....	....	6	1	1	2	10	....	....	....	....
2001-02	Regina Pats	WHL	62	33	30	63	154	....	....	....	....	....	....	....	....	....	6	2	3	5	9	....	....	....	....
	Hartford	AHL	4	0	0	0	0	....	....	....	....	....	....	....	....	....	9	1	3	4	6	....	....	....	....
2002-03	Hartford	AHL	64	10	14	24	121	....	....	....	....	....	....	....	....	....	2	0	0	0	6	....	....	....	....
2003-04	**NY Rangers**	**NHL**	**20**	**1**	**0**	**1**	**24**	**0**	**0**	**0**	**18**	**5.6**	**–5**	**5**	**20.0**	**9:16**	....	....	....	....	....	....	....	....	....
	Hartford	AHL	63	11	11	22	159	....	....	....	....	....	....	....	....	....	16	0	4	4	29	....	....	....	....
2004-05	Hartford	AHL	55	4	5	9	182	....	....	....	....	....	....	....	....	....	5	1	0	1	8	....	....	....	....
2005-06	**Montreal**	**NHL**	**36**	**5**	**1**	**6**	**44**	**0**	**0**	**1**	**25**	**20.0**	**–2**	**99**	**46.5**	**9:15**	**6**	**0**	**0**	**0**	**0**	**0**	**0**	**0**	**12:39**
	Hamilton	AHL	26	1	1	2	46	....	....	....	....	....	....	....	....	....	....	....	....	....	....	....	....	....	....
	NHL Totals		**56**	**6**	**1**	**7**	**68**	**0**	**0**	**1**	**43**	**14.0**		**104**	**45.2**	**9:15**	**6**	**0**	**0**	**0**	**0**	**0**	**0**	**0**	**12:39**

Traded to **Montreal** by **NY Rangers** for Marcel Hossa, September 30, 2005.

MURRAY, Glen

(MUHR-ree, GLEHN) **BOS.**

Right wing. Shoots right. 6'3", 225 lbs. Born, Halifax, N.S., November 1, 1972. Boston's 1st choice, 18th overall, in 1991 Entry Draft.

Season	Club	League	GP	G	A	Pts	PIM	PP	SH	GW	S	%	+/-	TF	F%	Min	GP	G	A	Pts	PIM	PP	SH	GW	Min
1988-89	Bridgewater	NSMHL	45	50	56	106	62	....	....	....	....	....	....	....	....	....	....	....	....	....	....	....	....	....	....
1989-90	Sudbury Wolves	OHL	62	8	28	36	17	....	....	....	....	....	....	....	....	....	7	0	0	0	4	....	....	....	....
1990-91	Sudbury Wolves	OHL	66	27	38	65	82	....	....	....	....	....	....	....	....	....	5	8	4	12	10	....	....	....	....
1991-92	Sudbury Wolves	OHL	54	37	47	84	93	....	....	....	....	....	....	....	....	....	11	7	4	11	18	....	....	....	....
	Boston	**NHL**	**5**	**3**	**1**	**4**	**0**	**1**	**0**	**0**	**20**	**15.0**	**2**	....	....	....	**15**	**4**	**2**	**6**	**10**	**1**	**0**	**0**	....
1992-93	**Boston**	**NHL**	**27**	**3**	**4**	**7**	**8**	**2**	**0**	**1**	**28**	**10.7**	**–6**	....	....	....	....	....	....	....	....	....	....	....	....
	Providence Bruins	AHL	48	30	26	56	42	....	....	....	....	....	....	....	....	....	6	1	4	5	4	....	....	....	....
1993-94	**Boston**	**NHL**	**81**	**18**	**13**	**31**	**48**	**0**	**0**	**4**	**114**	**15.8**	**–1**	....	....	....	**13**	**4**	**5**	**9**	**14**	**0**	**0**	**0**	....
1994-95	**Boston**	**NHL**	**35**	**5**	**2**	**7**	**46**	**0**	**0**	**2**	**64**	**7.8**	**–11**	....	....	....	**2**	**0**	**0**	**0**	**2**	**0**	**0**	**0**	....
1995-96	**Pittsburgh**	**NHL**	**69**	**14**	**15**	**29**	**57**	**0**	**0**	**2**	**100**	**14.0**	**4**	....	....	....	**18**	**2**	**6**	**8**	**10**	**0**	**0**	**1**	....
1996-97	**Pittsburgh**	**NHL**	**66**	**11**	**11**	**22**	**24**	**3**	**0**	**1**	**127**	**8.7**	**–19**	....	....	....	....	....	....	....	....	....	....	....	....
	Los Angeles	**NHL**	**11**	**5**	**3**	**8**	**8**	**0**	**0**	**0**	**26**	**19.2**	**–2**	....	....	....	....	....	....	....	....	....	....	....	....
1997-98	**Los Angeles**	**NHL**	**81**	**29**	**31**	**60**	**54**	**7**	**3**	**7**	**193**	**15.0**	**6**	....	....	....	**4**	**2**	**0**	**2**	**6**	**0**	**0**	**0**	....
1998-99	**Los Angeles**	**NHL**	**61**	**16**	**15**	**31**	**36**	**3**	**3**	**3**	**173**	**9.2**	**–14**	**12**	**25.0**	**20:33**	....	....	....	....	....	....	....	....	....
99-2000	**Los Angeles**	**NHL**	**78**	**29**	**33**	**62**	**60**	**10**	**1**	**2**	**202**	**14.4**	**13**	**15**	**80.0**	**18:30**	**4**	**0**	**0**	**0**	**2**	**0**	**0**	**0**	**19:04**
2000-01	**Los Angeles**	**NHL**	**64**	**18**	**21**	**39**	**32**	**3**	**1**	**1**	**138**	**13.0**	**9**	**7**	**42.9**	**18:12**	**13**	**4**	**3**	**7**	**4**	**1**	**0**	**1**	**19:51**
2001-02	**Los Angeles**	**NHL**	**9**	**6**	**5**	**11**	**0**	**4**	**0**	**2**	**34**	**17.6**	**5**	**1**	**100.0**	**19:08**	....	....	....	....	....	....	....	....	....
	Boston	**NHL**	**73**	**35**	**25**	**60**	**40**	**5**	**0**	**7**	**212**	**16.5**	**26**	**39**	**23.1**	**19:50**	**6**	**1**	**4**	**5**	**4**	**0**	**0**	**0**	**18:02**
2002-03	**Boston**	**NHL**	**82**	**44**	**48**	**92**	**64**	**12**	**0**	**5**	**331**	**13.3**	**9**	**32**	**37.5**	**22:36**	**5**	**1**	**1**	**2**	**4**	**0**	**0**	**0**	**19:36**
2003-04	**Boston**	**NHL**	**81**	**32**	**28**	**60**	**56**	**11**	**0**	**9**	**260**	**12.3**	**17**	**53**	**35.9**	**20:56**	**7**	**2**	**1**	**3**	**8**	**0**	**0**	**1**	**19:57**
2004-05			Did not play																						
2005-06	**Boston**	**NHL**	**64**	**24**	**29**	**53**	**52**	**6**	**1**	**3**	**195**	**12.3**	**–8**	**14**	**28.6**	**20:12**	....	....	....	....	....	....	....	....	....
	NHL Totals		**887**	**292**	**284**	**576**	**585**	**67**	**9**	**49**	**2217**	**13.2**		**173**	**36.4**	**20:10**	**87**	**20**	**22**	**42**	**64**	**2**	**0**	**3**	**19:26**

Played in NHL All-Star Game (2003, 2004)

Traded to **Pittsburgh** by **Boston** with Bryan Smolinski and Boston's 3rd round choice (Boyd Kane) in 1996 Entry Draft for Kevin Stevens and Shawn McEachern, August 2, 1995. Traded to **Los Angeles** by **Pittsburgh** for Ed Olczyk, March 18, 1997. Traded to **Boston** by **Los Angeles** with Jozef Stumpel for Jason Allison and Mikko Eloranta, October 24, 2001.

MURRAY, Marty

(MUHR-ree, MAHR-tee) **PHI.**

Center. Shoots left. 5'9", 180 lbs. Born, Deloraine, Man., February 16, 1975. Calgary's 5th choice, 96th overall, in 1993 Entry Draft.

Season	Club	League	GP	G	A	Pts	PIM	PP	SH	GW	S	%	+/-	TF	F%	Min	GP	G	A	Pts	PIM	PP	SH	GW	Min
1990-91	S-W Cougars	MMMHL	36	46	47	93	50	....	....	....	....	....	....	....	....	....	....	....	....	....	....	....	....	....	....
1991-92	Brandon	WHL	68	20	36	56	22	....	....	....	....	....	....	....	....	....	....	....	....	....	....	....	....	....	....
1992-93	Brandon	WHL	67	29	65	94	50	....	....	....	....	....	....	....	....	....	4	1	3	4	0	....	....	....	....
1993-94	Brandon	WHL	64	43	71	114	33	....	....	....	....	....	....	....	....	....	14	6	14	20	14	....	....	....	....
1994-95	Brandon	WHL	65	40	*88	128	53	....	....	....	....	....	....	....	....	....	18	9	*20	29	16	....	....	....	....
1995-96	**Calgary**	**NHL**	**15**	**3**	**3**	**6**	**0**	**2**	**0**	**0**	**22**	**13.6**	**–4**	....	....	....	....	....	....	....	....	....	....	....	....
	Saint John Flames	AHL	58	25	31	56	20	....	....	....	....	....	....	....	....	....	14	2	4	6	4	....	....	....	....
1996-97	**Calgary**	**NHL**	**2**	**0**	**0**	**0**	**4**	**0**	**0**	**0**	**2**	**0.0**	**0**	....	....	....	....	....	....	....	....	....	....	....	....
	Saint John Flames	AHL	67	19	39	58	40	....	....	....	....	....	....	....	....	....	5	2	3	5	4	....	....	....	....
1997-98	**Calgary**	**NHL**	**2**	**0**	**0**	**0**	**2**	**0**	**0**	**0**	**2**	**0.0**	**1**	....	....	....	....	....	....	....	....	....	....	....	....
	Saint John Flames	AHL	41	10	30	40	16	....	....	....	....	....	....	....	....	....	21	10	10	20	12	....	....	....	....
1998-99	EC Villacher SV	Alpenliga	33	26	41	67	12	....	....	....	....	....	....	....	....	....	....	....	....	....	....	....	....	....	....
	EC Villacher SV	Austria	17	13	17	30	6	....	....	....	....	....	....	....	....	....	6	1	4	5	0	....	....	....	....
99-2000	Kolner Haie	Germany	56	12	47	59	28	....	....	....	....	....	....	....	....	....	10	4	3	7	2	....	....	....	....
2000-01	**Calgary**	**NHL**	**7**	**0**	**0**	**0**	**0**	**0**	**0**	**0**	**6**	**0.0**	**–2**	**88**	**55.7**	**14:28**	....	....	....	....	....	....	....	....	....
	Saint John Flames	AHL	56	24	52	76	36	....	....	....	....	....	....	....	....	....	19	4	16	20	18	....	....	....	....
2001-02	**Philadelphia**	**NHL**	**74**	**12**	**15**	**27**	**10**	**1**	**1**	**2**	**109**	**11.0**	**10**	**913**	**50.7**	**13:56**	**5**	**0**	**1**	**1**	**0**	**0**	**0**	**0**	**13:14**
	Philadelphia	AHL	3	0	3	3	2	....	....	....	....	....	....	....	....	....	....	....	....	....	....	....	....	....	....
2002-03	**Philadelphia**	**NHL**	**76**	**11**	**15**	**26**	**13**	**1**	**1**	**0**	**105**	**10.5**	**–1**	**472**	**55.1**	**12:22**	**4**	**0**	**0**	**0**	**4**	**0**	**0**	**0**	**11:00**
2003-04	**Carolina**	**NHL**	**66**	**5**	**7**	**12**	**8**	**0**	**0**	**0**	**56**	**8.9**	**6**	**229**	**52.8**	**11:49**	....	....	....	....	....	....	....	....	....
2004-05			Did not play																						
2005-06	Hannover	Germany	24	7	15	22	16	....	....	....	....	....	....	....	....	....	9	4	3	7	35	....	....	....	....
	NHL Totals		**242**	**31**	**40**	**71**	**37**	**4**	**2**	**2**	**302**	**10.3**		**1702**	**52.5**	**12:47**	**9**	**0**	**1**	**1**	**4**	**0**	**0**	**0**	**12:15**

WHL East First All-Star Team (1994, 1995) • Canadian Major Junior Second All-Star Team (1994) • WHL Player of the Year (1995)

Signed as a free agent by **Philadelphia**, July 9, 2001. Traded to **Carolina** by **Philadelphia** for Carolina's 6th round choice (Frederik Cabana) in 2004 Entry Draft, June 22, 2003. Signed as a free agent by **Hannover** (Germany), August 16, 2005. Signed as a free agent by **Philadelphia**, June 15, 2006.

MURRAY, Rem

(MUHR-ree, REHM)

Center/left wing. Shoots left. 6'2", 200 lbs. Born, Stratford, Ont., October 9, 1972. Los Angeles' 5th choice, 135th overall, in 1992 Entry Draft.

Season	Club	League	GP	G	A	Pts	PIM	PP	SH	GW	S	%	+/-	TF	F%	Min	GP	G	A	Pts	PIM	PP	SH	GW	Min
1989-90	Stratford Cullitons	OHA-B	46	19	32	51	48	....	....	....	....	....	....	....	....	....	....	....	....	....	....	....	....	....	....
1990-91	Stratford Cullitons	OHA-B	48	39	59	98	39	....	....	....	....	....	....	....	....	....	....	....	....	....	....	....	....	....	....
1991-92	Michigan State	CCHA	41	12	36	48	16	....	....	....	....	....	....	....	....	....	....	....	....	....	....	....	....	....	....
1992-93	Michigan State	CCHA	40	22	35	57	24	....	....	....	....	....	....	....	....	....	....	....	....	....	....	....	....	....	....
1993-94	Michigan State	CCHA	41	16	38	54	18	....	....	....	....	....	....	....	....	....	....	....	....	....	....	....	....	....	....
1994-95	Michigan State	CCHA	40	20	36	56	21	....	....	....	....	....	....	....	....	....	....	....	....	....	....	....	....	....	....
1995-96	Cape Breton	AHL	79	31	59	90	40	....	....	....	....	....	....	....	....	....	....	....	....	....	....	....	....	....	....
1996-97	**Edmonton**	**NHL**	**82**	**11**	**20**	**31**	**16**	**1**	**0**	**2**	**85**	**12.9**	**9**	....	....	....	**12**	**1**	**2**	**3**	**4**	**0**	**0**	**0**	....
1997-98	**Edmonton**	**NHL**	**61**	**9**	**9**	**18**	**39**	**2**	**2**	**0**	**59**	**15.3**	**–9**	....	....	....	**11**	**1**	**4**	**5**	**2**	**0**	**0**	**0**	....
1998-99	**Edmonton**	**NHL**	**78**	**21**	**18**	**39**	**20**	**4**	**1**	**4**	**116**	**18.1**	**4**	**1013**	**48.1**	**15:50**	**4**	**1**	**1**	**2**	**2**	**0**	**0**	**0**	**22:40**
99-2000	**Edmonton**	**NHL**	**44**	**9**	**5**	**14**	**8**	**2**	**0**	**3**	**65**	**13.8**	**–2**	**303**	**50.5**	**14:16**	**5**	**0**	**1**	**1**	**2**	**0**	**0**	**0**	**15:19**
2000-01	**Edmonton**	**NHL**	**82**	**15**	**21**	**36**	**24**	**1**	**3**	**3**	**122**	**12.3**	**5**	**694**	**49.3**	**15:21**	**6**	**2**	**0**	**2**	**6**	**1**	**0**	**0**	**18:10**

Season	Club	League	Regular Season GP	G	A	Pts	PIM	PP	SH	GW	S	%	+/-	TF	F%	Min	Playoffs GP	G	A	Pts	PIM	PP	SH	GW	Min
2001-02	Edmonton	NHL	69	7	17	24	14	0	2	1	84	8.3	5	825	50.9	14:27	....	....	....	....	....	....	....	....	....
	NY Rangers	NHL	11	1	2	3	4	0	0	0	14	7.1	–9	151	51.7	15:51	....	....	....	....	....	....	....	....	....
2002-03	NY Rangers	NHL	32	6	6	12	4	1	1	1	62	9.7	–3	118	53.4	15:39	....	....	....	....	....	....	....	....	....
	Nashville	NHL	53	6	13	19	18	1	0	0	81	7.4	1	720	49.2	17:16	....	....	....	....	....	....	....	....	....
2003-04	Nashville	NHL	39	8	9	17	12	0	2	1	58	13.8	–1	169	46.2	16:37	....	....	....	....	....	....	....	....	....
2004-05			DID NOT PLAY																						
2005-06	Edmonton	NHL	9	1	1	2	2	0	0	0	6	16.7	1	40	50.0	7:49	24	0	4	4	2	0	0	0	8:37
	Houston Aeros	AHL	54	11	24	35	8	....	....	....	....	....	....	....	....	....	....	....	....	....	....	....	....	....	....
	NHL Totals		560	94	121	215	161	12	11	15	752	12.5		4033	49.5	15:25	62	5	12	17	18	1	0	0	12:24

CCHA Second All-Star Team (1995)

Signed as a free agent by **Edmonton**, September 19, 1995. Traded to **NY Rangers** by **Edmonton** with Tom Poti for Mike York and NY Rangers' 4th round choice (Ivan Koltsov) in 2002 Entry Draft, March 19, 2002. Traded to **Nashville** by **NY Rangers** with Tomas Kloucek and Marek Zidlicky for Mike Dunham, December 12, 2002. • Missed majority of 2003-04 season recovering from neck injury suffered in game vs. Detroit, January 5, 2004.

MYHRES, Brantt

(MIGH-uhrs, BRANT)

Right wing. Shoots right. 6'3", 220 lbs. Born, Edmonton, Alta., March 18, 1974. Tampa Bay's 5th choice, 97th overall, in 1992 Entry Draft.

Season	Club	League	GP	G	A	Pts	PIM	PP	SH	GW	S	%	+/-	TF	F%	Min	GP	G	A	Pts	PIM	PP	SH	GW	Min
1989-90	Bonnyville Barons	AAHA	60	40	62	102	195	....	....	....	....	....	....	....	....	....	....	....	....	....	....	....	....	....	....
1990-91	Portland	WHL	59	2	7	9	125	....	....	....	....	....	....	....	....	....	....	....	....	....	....	....	....	....	....
1991-92	Portland	WHL	4	0	2	2	22	....	....	....	....	....	....	....	....	....	....	....	....	....	....	....	....	....	....
	Lethbridge	WHL	53	4	11	15	359	....	....	....	....	....	....	....	....	....	5	0	0	0	36	....	....	....	....
1992-93	Lethbridge	WHL	64	13	35	48	277	....	....	....	....	....	....	....	....	....	3	0	0	0	11	....	....	....	....
1993-94	Lethbridge	WHL	34	10	21	31	103	....	....	....	....	....	....	....	....	....	....	....	....	....	....	....	....	....	....
	Spokane Chiefs	WHL	27	10	22	32	139	....	....	....	....	....	....	....	....	....	3	1	4	5	7	....	....	....	....
	Atlanta Knights	IHL	2	0	0	0	17	....	....	....	....	....	....	....	....	....	....	....	....	....	....	....	....	....	....
1994-95	Atlanta Knights	IHL	40	5	5	10	213	....	....	....	....	....	....	....	....	....	....	....	....	....	....	....	....	....	....
	Tampa Bay	NHL	15	2	0	2	81	0	0	1	4	50.0	–2	....	....	....	....	....	....	....	....	....	....	....	....
1995-96	Atlanta Knights	IHL	12	0	2	2	58	....	....	....	....	....	....	....	....	....	....	....	....	....	....	....	....	....	....
1996-97	Tampa Bay	NHL	47	3	1	4	136	0	0	1	13	23.1	1	....	....	....	....	....	....	....	....	....	....	....	....
	San Antonio	IHL	12	0	0	0	98	....	....	....	....	....	....	....	....	....	....	....	....	....	....	....	....	....	....
1997-98	Philadelphia	NHL	23	0	0	0	169	0	0	0	0	0.0	–1	....	....	....	....	....	....	....	....	....	....	....	....
	Philadelphia	AHL	18	4	4	8	67	....	....	....	....	....	....	....	....	....	....	....	....	....	....	....	....	....	....
1998-99	San Jose	NHL	30	1	0	1	116	0	0	0	7	14.3	–2	1	0.0	4:47	....	....	....	....	....	....	....	....	....
	Kentucky	AHL	4	0	0	0	16	....	....	....	....	....	....	....	....	....	....	....	....	....	....	....	....	....	....
99-2000	San Jose	NHL	13	0	1	1	97	0	0	0	2	0.0	0	1	0.0	3:03	....	....	....	....	....	....	....	....	....
	Kentucky	AHL	10	1	5	6	18	....	....	....	....	....	....	....	....	....	7	0	1	1	21	....	....	....	....
2000-01	Nashville	NHL	20	0	0	0	28	0	0	0	1	0.0	–5	0	0.0	3:48	....	....	....	....	....	....	....	....	....
	Milwaukee	IHL	6	0	1	1	10	....	....	....	....	....	....	....	....	....	....	....	....	....	....	....	....	....	....
	Washington	NHL	5	0	0	0	29	0	0	0	0	0.0	0	0	0.0	3:36	....	....	....	....	....	....	....	....	....
	Portland Pirates	AHL	9	1	0	1	53	....	....	....	....	....	....	....	....	....	....	....	....	....	....	....	....	....	....
2001-02			DID NOT PLAY																						
2002-03	Boston	NHL	1	0	0	0	31	0	0	0	0	0.0	0	0	0.0	5:26	....	....	....	....	....	....	....	....	....
	Providence Bruins	AHL	63	3	10	13	185	....	....	....	....	....	....	....	....	....	4	0	0	0	2	....	....	....	....
2003-04			DID NOT PLAY																						
2004-05	Lowell	AHL	29	1	1	2	77	....	....	....	....	....	....	....	....	....	4	0	0	0	9	....	....	....	....
2005-06	Omaha	AHL	34	4	2	6	78	....	....	....	....	....	....	....	....	....	....	....	....	....	....	....	....	....	....
	NHL Totals		154	6	2	8	687	0	0	2	27	22.2		2	0.0	4:06	....	....	....	....	....	....	....	....	....

Traded to **Edmonton** by **Tampa Bay** with Toronto's 3rd round choice (previously acquired, Edmonton selected Alex Henry) in 1998 Entry Draft for Vladimir Vujtek and Edmonton's 3rd round choice (Dmitry Afanasenkov) in 1998 Entry Draft, July 16, 1997. Traded to **Philadelphia** by **Edmonton** for Jason Bowen, October 15, 1997. Signed as a free agent by **San Jose**, September 11, 1998. Signed as a free agent by **Nashville**, August 15, 2000. Traded to **Washington** by **Nashville** for future considerations, February 1, 2001. Signed as a free agent by **Boston**, September 19, 2002. Signed as a free agent by **Lowell** (AHL), October 3, 2004. Signed as a free agent by **Calgary**, August 11, 2005.

NAGY, Ladislav

(NA-gee, LA-dih-slahv) **PHX.**

Left wing. Shoots left. 5'11", 192 lbs. Born, Saca, Czech., June 1, 1979. St. Louis' 6th choice, 177th overall, in 1997 Entry Draft.

Season	Club	League	GP	G	A	Pts	PIM	PP	SH	GW	S	%	+/-	TF	F%	Min	GP	G	A	Pts	PIM	PP	SH	GW	Min
1995-96	HK Dragon Presov	Slovakia	11	6	5	11	....	....	....	....	....	....	....	....	....	....	....	....	....	....	....	....	....	....	....
1996-97	HC Kosice Jr.	Slovak-Jr.	45	29	30	59	105	....	....	....	....	....	....	....	....	....	....	....	....	....	....	....	....	....	....
1997-98	HC Kosice	Slovakia	29	19	15	34	41	....	....	....	....	....	....	....	....	....	11	2	4	6	6	....	....	....	....
1998-99	Halifax	QMJHL	63	71	55	126	148	....	....	....	....	....	....	....	....	....	5	3	3	6	18	....	....	....	....
	Worcester IceCats	AHL	....	....	....	....	....	....	....	....	....	....	....	....	....	....	3	2	2	4	0	....	....	....	....
99-2000	St. Louis	NHL	11	2	4	6	2	1	0	0	15	13.3	2	6	33.3	12:19	6	1	1	2	0	0	0	0	13:29
	Worcester IceCats	AHL	69	23	28	51	67	....	....	....	....	....	....	....	....	....	2	1	0	1	0	....	....	....	....
2000-01	St. Louis	NHL	40	8	8	16	20	2	0	2	59	13.6	–2	28	50.0	13:03	....	....	....	....	....	....	....	....	....
	Worcester IceCats	AHL	20	6	14	20	36	....	....	....	....	....	....	....	....	....	....	....	....	....	....	....	....	....	....
	Phoenix	NHL	6	0	1	1	2	0	0	0	5	0.0	0	0	0.0	12:38	....	....	....	....	....	....	....	....	....
2001-02	Phoenix	NHL	74	23	19	42	50	5	0	5	187	12.3	6	17	47.1	15:04	5	0	0	0	21	0	0	0	15:45
2002-03	HC Kosice	Slovakia	1	2	1	3	0	....	....	....	....	....	....	....	....	....	....	....	....	....	....	....	....	....	....
	Phoenix	NHL	80	22	35	57	92	8	0	6	209	10.5	17	41	34.2	17:28	....	....	....	....	....	....	....	....	....
2003-04	Phoenix	NHL	55	24	28	52	46	11	0	6	160	15.0	11	33	42.4	18:10	....	....	....	....	....	....	....	....	....
2004-05	HC Kosice	Slovakia	18	9	7	16	40	....	....	....	....	....	....	....	....	....	....	....	....	....	....	....	....	....	....
	Mora IK	Sweden	19	4	4	8	22	....	....	....	....	....	....	....	....	....	....	....	....	....	....	....	....	....	....
2005-06	Phoenix	NHL	51	15	41	56	74	7	1	4	132	11.4	8	72	40.3	18:53	....	....	....	....	....	....	....	....	....
	NHL Totals		317	94	136	230	286	34	1	23	767	12.3		197	41.1	16:26	11	1	1	2	21	0	0	0	14:30

Traded to **Phoenix** by **St. Louis** with Michal Handzus, the rights to Jeff Taffe and St. Louis' 1st round choice (Ben Eager) in 2002 Entry Draft for Keith Tkachuk, March 13, 2001. Signed as a free agent by **Kosice** (Slovakia), September 17, 2004. Signed as a free agent by **Mora** (Sweden), December 17, 2004.

NASH, Rick

(NASH, RIHK) **CBJ**

Left wing. Shoots left. 6'4", 215 lbs. Born, Brampton, Ont., June 16, 1984. Columbus' 1st choice, 1st overall, in 2002 Entry Draft.

Season	Club	League	GP	G	A	Pts	PIM	PP	SH	GW	S	%	+/-	TF	F%	Min	GP	G	A	Pts	PIM	PP	SH	GW	Min
99-2000	Tor. Marlboros	GTHL	34	61	54	115	34	....	....	....	....	....	....	....	....	....	....	....	....	....	....	....	....	....	....
2000-01	London Knights	OHL	58	31	35	66	56	....	....	....	....	....	....	....	....	....	4	3	3	6	8	....	....	....	....
2001-02	London Knights	OHL	54	32	40	72	88	....	....	....	....	....	....	....	....	....	12	10	9	19	21	....	....	....	....
2002-03	Columbus	NHL	74	17	22	39	78	6	0	2	154	11.0	–27	14	35.7	13:57	....	....	....	....	....	....	....	....	....
2003-04	Columbus	NHL	80	*41	16	57	87	19	0	7	269	15.2	–35	21	28.6	17:38	....	....	....	....	....	....	....	....	....
2004-05	HC Davos	Swiss	44	26	20	46	83	....	....	....	....	....	....	....	....	....	15	9	2	11	26	....	....	....	....
2005-06	Columbus	NHL	54	31	23	54	51	11	0	4	170	18.2	5	38	50.0	18:16	....	....	....	....	....	....	....	....	....
	Canada	Olympics	6	0	1	1	10	....	....	....	....	....	....	....	....	....	....	....	....	....	....	....	....	....	....
	NHL Totals		208	89	61	150	216	36	0	13	593	15.0		73	41.1	16:29	....	....	....	....	....	....	....	....	....

OHL All-Rookie Team (2001) • OHL Rookie of the Year (2001) • CHL All-Rookie Team (2001) • NHL All-Rookie Team (2003) • Maurice "Rocket" Richard Trophy (2004) (tied with Jarome Iginla and Ilya Kovalchuk)

Played in NHL All-Star Game (2004)

Signed as a free agent by **Davos** (Swiss), August 3, 2004.

NASH, Tyson

(NASH, TIGH-sohn) **PHX.**

Left wing. Shoots left. 5'11", 191 lbs. Born, Edmonton, Alta., March 11, 1975. Vancouver's 10th choice, 247th overall, in 1994 Entry Draft.

Season	Club	League	GP	G	A	Pts	PIM	PP	SH	GW	S	%	+/-	TF	F%	Min	GP	G	A	Pts	PIM	PP	SH	GW	Min
1990-91	Sherwood Park	AMHL	40	17	28	43	63	....	....	....	....	....	....	....	....	....	....	....	....	....	....	....	....	....	....
1991-92	Kamloops Blazers	WHL	33	1	6	7	62	....	....	....	....	....	....	....	....	....	4	0	0	0	0	....	....	....	....
1992-93	Kamloops Blazers	WHL	61	10	16	26	78	....	....	....	....	....	....	....	....	....	13	3	2	5	32	....	....	....	....
1993-94	Kamloops Blazers	WHL	65	20	36	56	135	....	....	....	....	....	....	....	....	....	16	3	4	7	12	....	....	....	....
1994-95	Kamloops Blazers	WHL	63	34	41	75	70	....	....	....	....	....	....	....	....	....	21	10	7	17	30	....	....	....	....
1995-96	Syracuse Crunch	AHL	50	4	7	11	58	....	....	....	....	....	....	....	....	....	4	0	0	0	11	....	....	....	....
	Raleigh IceCaps	ECHL	6	1	1	2	8	....	....	....	....	....	....	....	....	....	....	....	....	....	....	....	....	....	....
1996-97	Syracuse Crunch	AHL	77	17	17	34	105	....	....	....	....	....	....	....	....	....	3	0	2	2	0	....	....	....	....
1997-98	Syracuse Crunch	AHL	74	20	20	40	184	....	....	....	....	....	....	....	....	....	5	0	2	2	28	....	....	....	....
1998-99	St. Louis	NHL	2	0	0	0	5	0	0	0	1	0.0	–1	0	0.0	7:44	1	0	0	0	2	0	0	0	6:25
	Worcester IceCats	AHL	55	14	22	36	143	....	....	....	....	....	....	....	....	....	4	4	1	5	27	....	....	....	....
99-2000	St. Louis	NHL	66	4	9	13	150	0	1	1	68	5.9	6	0	0.0	8:35	6	1	0	1	24	0	0	0	8:36
2000-01	St. Louis	NHL	57	8	7	15	110	0	1	0	113	7.1	8	2	50.0	12:29	....	....	....	....	....	....	....	....	....
2001-02	St. Louis	NHL	64	6	7	13	100	0	0	1	66	9.1	2	14	35.7	10:02	9	0	1	1	20	0	0	0	8:03

Season	Club	League	GP	G	A	Pts	PIM	PP	SH	GW	S	%	+/-	TF	F%	Min	GP	G	A	Pts	PIM	PP	SH	GW	Min
			Regular Season														Playoffs								
2002-03	**St. Louis**	**NHL**	**66**	**6**	**3**	**9**	**114**	**1**	**0**	**2**	**77**	**7.8**	**0**	**9**	**11.1**	**9:53**	**7**	**2**	**1**	**3**	**6**	**0**	**0**	**0**	**9:05**
2003-04	**Phoenix**	**NHL**	**69**	**3**	**5**	**8**	**110**	**0**	**0**	**0**	**83**	**3.6**	**–6**	**13**	**38.5**	**11:53**									
2004-05			DID NOT PLAY																						
2005-06	**Phoenix**	**NHL**	**50**	**0**	**6**	**6**	**84**	**0**	**0**	**0**	**44**	**0.0**	**–7**	**20**	**55.0**	**10:03**									
	NHL Totals		**374**	**27**	**37**	**64**	**673**	**1**	**2**	**4**	**452**	**6.0**		**58**	**39.7**	**10:27**	**23**	**3**	**2**	**5**	**52**	**0**	**0**	**0**	**8:26**

Signed as a free agent by **St. Louis**, July 14, 1998. Traded to **Phoenix** by **St. Louis** for Phoenix's 5th round choice (Lee Stempniak) in 2003 Enrey Draft, June 21, 2003.

NASLUND, Markus

(NAZ-luhnd, MAHR-kuhs) **VAN.**

Left wing. Shoots left. 5'11", 195 lbs. Born, Ornskoldsvik, Sweden, July 30, 1973. Pittsburgh's 1st choice, 16th overall, in 1991 Entry Draft.

Season	Club	League	GP	G	A	Pts	PIM	PP	SH	GW	S	%	+/-	TF	F%	Min	GP	G	A	Pts	PIM	PP	SH	GW	Min
1988-89	Ornskoldsviks IF	Sweden-3	14	7	6	13																			
1989-90	MoDo Jr.	Swe-Jr.	33	43	35	78	20																		
1990-91	MoDo	Sweden	32	10	9	19	14																		
1991-92	MoDo	Sweden	39	22	18	40	54																		
1992-93	MoDo Jr.	Swe-Jr.	2	4	1	5	2																		
	MoDo	Sweden	39	22	17	39	67										3	3	2	5	0				
1993-94	**Pittsburgh**	**NHL**	**71**	**4**	**7**	**11**	**27**	**1**	**0**	**0**	**80**	**5.0**	**–3**												
	Cleveland	IHL	5	1	6	7	4																		
1994-95	**Pittsburgh**	**NHL**	**14**	**2**	**2**	**4**	**2**	**0**	**0**	**0**	**13**	**15.4**	**0**												
	Cleveland	IHL	7	3	4	7	6										4	1	3	4	8				
1995-96	**Pittsburgh**	**NHL**	**66**	**19**	**33**	**52**	**36**	**3**	**0**	**4**	**125**	**15.2**	**17**												
	Vancouver	**NHL**	**10**	**3**	**0**	**3**	**6**	**1**	**0**	**1**	**19**	**15.8**	**3**				**6**	**1**	**2**	**3**	**8**	**1**	**0**	**0**	
1996-97	**Vancouver**	**NHL**	**78**	**21**	**20**	**41**	**30**	**4**	**0**	**4**	**120**	**17.5**	**–15**												
1997-98	**Vancouver**	**NHL**	**76**	**14**	**20**	**34**	**56**	**2**	**1**	**0**	**106**	**13.2**	**5**												
1998-99	**Vancouver**	**NHL**	**80**	**36**	**30**	**66**	**74**	**15**	**2**	**3**	**205**	**17.6**	**–13**	**14**	**57.1**	**19:57**									
99-2000	**Vancouver**	**NHL**	**82**	**27**	**38**	**65**	**64**	**6**	**2**	**3**	**271**	**10.0**	**–5**	**13**	**46.2**	**20:13**									
2000-01	**Vancouver**	**NHL**	**72**	**41**	**34**	**75**	**58**	**18**	**1**	**5**	**277**	**14.8**	**–2**	**6**	**50.0**	**19:03**									
2001-02	**Vancouver**	**NHL**	**81**	**40**	**50**	**90**	**50**	**8**	**0**	**6**	**302**	**13.2**	**22**	**5**	**20.0**	**19:31**	**6**	**1**	**1**	**2**	**2**	**0**	**0**	**0**	**18:54**
	Sweden	Olympics	4	2	1	3	0																		
2002-03	**Vancouver**	**NHL**	**82**	**48**	**56**	**104**	**52**	**24**	**0**	**12**	**294**	**16.3**	**6**	**6**	**33.3**	**19:54**	**14**	**5**	**9**	**14**	**18**	**2**	**0**	**1**	**18:14**
2003-04	**Vancouver**	**NHL**	**78**	**35**	**49**	**84**	**58**	**5**	**0**	**6**	**296**	**11.8**	**24**	**14**	**35.7**	**19:23**	**7**	**2**	**7**	**9**	**2**	**2**	**0**	**0**	**19:21**
2004-05	MODO	Sweden	13	8	9	17	8										6	0	1	1	10				
2005-06	**Vancouver**	**NHL**	**81**	**32**	**47**	**79**	**66**	**13**	**0**	**2**	**264**	**12.1**	**–19**	**7**	**28.6**	**18:28**									
	Sweden	Olympics	DID NOT PLAY – INJURED																						
	NHL Totals		**871**	**322**	**386**	**708**	**579**	**100**	**6**	**46**	**2372**	**13.6**		**65**	**41.5**	**19:30**	**33**	**9**	**19**	**28**	**30**	**5**	**0**	**1**	**18:40**

NHL First All-Star Team (2002, 2003, 2004) • Lester B. Pearson Award (2003)

Played in NHL All-Star Game (1999, 2001, 2002, 2003, 2004)

Traded to **Vancouver** by **Pittsburgh** for Alek Stojanov, March 20, 1996. Signed as a free agent by **MODO** (Sweden), December 20, 2004.

NASREDDINE, Alain

(NAS-ruh-deen, AL-eh) **PIT.**

Defense. Shoots left. 6'1", 201 lbs. Born, Montreal, Que., July 10, 1975. Florida's 8th choice, 135th overall, in 1993 Entry Draft.

Season	Club	League	GP	G	A	Pts	PIM	PP	SH	GW	S	%	+/-	TF	F%	Min	GP	G	A	Pts	PIM	PP	SH	GW	Min
1990-91	Mtl-Bourassa	QAAA	35	10	25	35	50																		
1991-92	Drummondville	QMJHL	61	1	9	10	78										4	0	0	0	17				
1992-93	Drummondville	QMJHL	64	0	14	14	137										10	0	1	1	36				
1993-94	Chicoutimi	QMJHL	60	3	24	27	218										26	2	10	12	118				
1994-95	Chicoutimi	QMJHL	67	8	31	39	342										13	3	5	8	40				
1995-96	Carolina Panthers	AHL	63	0	5	5	245																		
1996-97	Carolina	AHL	26	0	4	4	109																		
	Indianapolis Ice	IHL	49	0	2	2	248										4	1	1	2	27				
1997-98	Indianapolis Ice	IHL	75	1	12	13	258										5	0	2	2	12				
1998-99	**Chicago**	**NHL**	**7**	**0**	**0**	**0**	**19**	**0**	**0**	**0**	**2**	**0.0**	**–2**	**0**	**0.0**	**12:11**									
	Portland Pirates	AHL	7	0	1	1	36																		
	Montreal	**NHL**	**8**	**0**	**0**	**0**	**33**	**0**	**0**	**0**	**1**	**0.0**	**1**	**0**	**0.0**	**8:12**									
	Fredericton	AHL	38	0	10	10	108										15	0	3	3	39				
99-2000	Quebec Citadelles	AHL	59	1	6	7	178																		
	Hamilton	AHL	11	0	0	0	12										10	1	1	2	14				
2000-01	Hamilton	AHL	74	4	14	18	164																		
2001-02	Hamilton	AHL	79	7	10	17	154										12	1	3	4	22				
2002-03	Bridgeport	AHL	67	3	9	12	114										9	0	0	0	27				
	NY Islanders	**NHL**	**3**	**0**	**0**	**0**	**2**	**0**	**0**	**0**	**0**	**0.0**	**0**	**0**	**0.0**	**12:11**									
2003-04	Bridgeport	AHL	53	1	6	7	70																		
	Wilkes-Barre	AHL	17	1	1	2	16										24	1	0	1	48				
2004-05	Wilkes-Barre	AHL	75	3	15	18	129										11	0	1	1	18				
2005-06	**Pittsburgh**	**NHL**	**6**	**0**	**0**	**0**	**8**	**0**	**0**	**0**	**3**	**0.0**	**2**	**0**	**0.0**	**15:11**									
	Wilkes-Barre	AHL	71	0	12	12	71																		
	NHL Totals		**24**	**0**	**0**	**0**	**62**	**0**	**0**	**0**	**6**	**0.0**		**0**	**0.0**	**11:36**									

QMJHL Second All-Star Team (1995)

Traded to **Chicago** by **Florida** for Ivan Droppa, December 18, 1996. Traded to **Montreal** by **Chicago** with Jeff Hackett, Eric Weinrich and Tampa Bay's 4th round choice (previously acquired, Montreal selected Chris Dyment) in 1999 Entry Draft for Jocelyn Thibault, Dave Manson and Brad Brown, November 16, 1998. Traded to **Edmonton** by **Montreal** with Igor Ulanov for Christian Laflamme and Matthieu Descoteaux, March 9, 2000. Signed as a free agent by **NY Islanders**, September 6, 2002. Traded to **Pittsburgh** by **NY Islanders** for Steve Webb, March 8, 2004.

NAZAROV, Andrei

(nah-ZAH-rohv, AWN-dray)

Left wing. Shoots right. 6'5", 242 lbs. Born, Chelyabinsk, USSR, May 22, 1974. San Jose's 2nd choice, 10th overall, in 1992 Entry Draft.

Season	Club	League	GP	G	A	Pts	PIM	PP	SH	GW	S	%	+/-	TF	F%	Min	GP	G	A	Pts	PIM	PP	SH	GW	Min
1991-92	Dynamo Moscow	CIS	2	1	0	1	2																		
1992-93	Dynamo Moscow	CIS	42	8	2	10	79										10	1	1	2	8				
1993-94	Dynamo Moscow	CIS	6	2	2	4	0																		
	San Jose	**NHL**	**1**	**0**	**0**	**0**	**0**	**0**	**0**	**0**	**0**	**0.0**	**0**												
	Kansas City	IHL	71	15	18	33	64																		
1994-95	Kansas City	IHL	43	15	10	25	55																		
	San Jose	**NHL**	**26**	**3**	**5**	**8**	**94**	**0**	**0**	**0**	**19**	**15.8**	**–1**				**6**	**0**	**0**	**0**	**9**	**0**	**0**	**0**	
1995-96	**San Jose**	**NHL**	**42**	**7**	**7**	**14**	**62**	**2**	**0**	**1**	**55**	**12.7**	**–15**												
	Kansas City	IHL	27	4	6	10	118										2	0	0	0	2				
1996-97	**San Jose**	**NHL**	**60**	**12**	**15**	**27**	**222**	**1**	**0**	**1**	**116**	**10.3**	**–4**												
	Kentucky	AHL	3	1	2	3	4																		
1997-98	**San Jose**	**NHL**	**40**	**1**	**1**	**2**	**112**	**0**	**0**	**0**	**31**	**3.2**	**–4**												
	Tampa Bay	**NHL**	**14**	**1**	**1**	**2**	**58**	**0**	**0**	**0**	**19**	**5.3**	**–9**												
1998-99	**Tampa Bay**	**NHL**	**26**	**2**	**0**	**2**	**43**	**0**	**0**	**0**	**18**	**11.1**	**–5**	**4**	**50.0**	**8:13**									
	Calgary	**NHL**	**36**	**5**	**9**	**14**	**30**	**0**	**0**	**2**	**53**	**9.4**	**1**	**0**	**0.0**	**14:31**									
99-2000	**Calgary**	**NHL**	**76**	**10**	**22**	**32**	**78**	**1**	**0**	**1**	**110**	**9.1**	**3**	**2**	**100.0**	**11:44**									
2000-01	**Anaheim**	**NHL**	**16**	**1**	**0**	**1**	**29**	**0**	**0**	**0**	**13**	**7.7**	**–9**	**2**	**50.0**	**8:42**									
	Boston	**NHL**	**63**	**1**	**4**	**5**	**200**	**0**	**0**	**0**	**50**	**2.0**	**–14**	**14**	**21.4**	**8:12**									
2001-02	**Boston**	**NHL**	**47**	**0**	**2**	**2**	**164**	**0**	**0**	**0**	**18**	**0.0**	**–2**	**1**	**100.0**	**3:10**									
	Phoenix	**NHL**	**30**	**6**	**3**	**9**	**51**	**0**	**0**	**0**	**38**	**15.8**	**7**	**1**	**100.0**	**7:35**	**3**	**0**	**0**	**0**	**2**	**0**	**0**	**0**	**9:34**
2002-03	**Phoenix**	**NHL**	**59**	**3**	**0**	**3**	**135**	**2**	**0**	**0**	**35**	**8.6**	**–9**	**6**	**33.3**	**6:34**									
2003-04	**Phoenix**	**NHL**	**33**	**1**	**2**	**3**	**125**	**0**	**0**	**0**	**17**	**5.9**	**–7**	**0**	**0.0**	**5:28**									
2004-05	Novokuznetsk	Russia	9	0	0	0	*20																		
	Avangard Omsk	Russia	23	0	2	2	*153										7	0	0	0	6				
2005-06	**Minnesota**	**NHL**	**2**	**0**	**0**	**0**	**6**	**0**	**0**	**0**	**0**	**0.0**	**–1**	**0**	**0.0**	**4:48**									
	Houston Aeros	AHL	1	0	0	0	0																		
	NHL Totals		**571**	**53**	**71**	**124**	**1409**	**6**	**0**	**5**	**592**	**9.0**		**30**	**40.0**	**8:21**	**9**	**0**	**0**	**0**	**11**	**0**	**0**	**0**	**9:34**

Traded to **Tampa Bay** by **San Jose** with Florida's 1st round choice (previously acquired, Tampa Bay selected Vincent Lecavalier) in 1998 Entry Draft for Bryan Marchment, David Shaw and Tampa Bay's 1st round choice (later traded to Nashville – Nashville selected David Legwand) in 1998 Entry Draft, March 24, 1998. Traded to **Calgary** by **Tampa Bay** for Michael Nylander, January 19, 1999. Traded to **Anaheim** by **Calgary** with Calgary's 2nd round choice (later traded to Phoenix – later traded back to Calgary – Calgary selected Andrei Taratukhin) in 2001 Entry Draft for Jordan Leopold, September 26, 2000. Traded to **Boston** by **Anaheim** with Patrick Traverse for Samuel Pahlsson, November 18, 2000. Traded to **Phoenix** by **Boston** for Phoenix's 5th round choice (Peter Hamerlik) in 2002 Entry Draft, January 25, 2002. • Spent majority of 2003-04 season as a healthy reserve. Signed as a free agent by **Novokuznetsk** (Russia), September 25, 2004. Signed as a free agent by **Omsk** (Russia), November, 2004. Signed as a free agent by **Minnesota**, August 1, 2005. • Spent the majority of the 2005-06 season as a healthy reserve. • Officially announced retirement, July 14, 2006.

NEDOROST, Andrej

(NEHD-ohr-ohst, AWN-dray) **CBJ**

Left wing. Shoots left. 6'1", 198 lbs. Born, Trencin, Czech., April 30, 1980. Columbus' 10th choice, 286th overall, in 2000 Entry Draft.

			Regular Season														Playoffs								
Season	Club	League	GP	G	A	Pts	PIM	PP	SH	GW	S	%	+/-	TF	F%	Min	GP	G	A	Pts	PIM	PP	SH	GW	Min
1995-96	Dukla Trencin Jr.	Slovak-Jr.	40	50	35	85																			
1996-97	Dukla Trencin Jr.	Slovak-Jr.	45	15	16	31																			
1997-98	Dukla Trencin Jr.	Slovak-Jr.	45	27	22	49	61																		
	Dukla Trencin	Slovakia	1	0	0	0	0																		
1998-99	Essen Jr.	Ger-Jr.	17	37	18	55	43																		
	Essen	German-2	30	3	5	8	22																		
99-2000	Essen	Germany	66	7	5	12	44																		
2000-01	Plzen	CzRep	33	10	8	18	22																		
2001-02	**Columbus**	**NHL**	**7**	**0**	**2**	**2**	**2**	**0**	**0**	**0**	**12**	**0.0**	**–3**	**1**	**100.0**	**12:56**									
	Syracuse Crunch	AHL	37	5	13	18	28										10	1	3	4	4				
2002-03	Syracuse Crunch	AHL	63	14	19	33	85																		
	Columbus	**NHL**	**12**	**0**	**1**	**1**	**4**	**0**	**0**	**0**	**10**	**0.0**	**–6**	**30**	**36.7**	**9:15**									
2003-04	**Columbus**	**NHL**	**9**	**2**	**0**	**2**	**6**	**0**	**0**	**0**	**16**	**12.5**	**0**	**13**	**69.2**	**13:02**									
	Syracuse Crunch	AHL	8	0	2	2	6																		
	Magnitogorsk	Russia	16	3	4	7	12										7	0	3	3	4				
2004-05	Magnitogorsk	Russia	12	1	0	1	4																		
	Nizhnekamsk	Russia	7	0	0	0	4																		
	Karlovy Vary	CzRep	20	6	5	11	16																		
2005-06	Karlovy Vary	CzRep	36	7	11	18	26																		
	Hamburg Freezers	Germany	5	0	2	2	4										6	1	0	1	2				
	NHL Totals		**28**	**2**	**3**	**5**	**12**	**0**	**0**	**0**	**38**	**5.3**		**44**	**47.7**	**11:23**									

Assigned to **Magnitogorsk** (Russia) by **Columbus**, December 17, 2003. Signed as a free agent by **Karlovy Vary** (CzRep), January 22, 2005. Signed as a free agent by **Hamburg** (Germany), February 17, 2006. Signed as a free agent by **Malmo** (Sweden), August 16, 2006.

NEDOROST, Vaclav

(neh-DOHR-uhst, VAT-slav) **FLA.**

Center. Shoots left. 6'1", 190 lbs. Born, Ceske Budejovice, Czech., March 16, 1982. Colorado's 1st choice, 14th overall, in 2000 Entry Draft.

Season	Club	League	GP	G	A	Pts	PIM	PP	SH	GW	S	%	+/-	TF	F%	Min	GP	G	A	Pts	PIM	PP	SH	GW	Min
1997-98	C. Budejovice Jr.	CzRep-Jr.	43	30	23	53	20																		
1998-99	C. Budejovice Jr.	CzRep-Jr.	39	6	15	21	20																		
	C. Budejovice	CzRep	7	0	2	2	0																		
99-2000	C. Budejovice Jr.	CzRep-Jr.	14	4	7	11	4																		
	C. Budejovice	CzRep	38	8	6	14	6										3	0	0	0	0				
2000-01	C. Budejovice	CzRep	36	3	12	15	14																		
2001-02	**Colorado**	**NHL**	**25**	**2**	**2**	**4**	**2**	**1**	**0**	**0**	**22**	**9.1**	**–4**	**62**	**45.2**	**10:15**									
	Hershey Bears	AHL	49	12	22	34	16										7	2	3	5	2				
2002-03	**Colorado**	**NHL**	**42**	**4**	**5**	**9**	**20**	**1**	**0**	**0**	**35**	**11.4**	**8**	**151**	**44.4**	**10:29**									
	Hershey Bears	AHL	5	3	2	5	0										5	2	2	4	0				
2003-04	**Florida**	**NHL**	**32**	**4**	**3**	**7**	**12**	**2**	**0**	**0**	**38**	**10.5**	**–6**	**121**	**42.2**	**11:32**									
	San Antonio	AHL	21	9	6	15	2																		
2004-05	Liberec	CzRep	48	15	18	33	20										6	0	1	1	12				
2005-06			DID NOT PLAY																						
	NHL Totals		**99**	**10**	**10**	**20**	**34**	**4**	**0**	**0**	**95**	**10.5**		**334**	**43.7**	**10:46**									

Traded to **Florida** by **Colorado** with Eric Messier for Peter Worrell and Florida's 2nd round choice (later traded to NY Rangers – later traded back to Florida – Florida selected David Shantz) in 2004 Entry Draft, July 18, 2003. Signed as a free agent by **Liberec** (CzRep), September 4, 2004. Signed as a free agent by **Ceske Budejovice** (CzRep), April 28, 2005. • Missed entire 2005-06 season recovering from knee surgery.

NEDVED, Petr

(NEHD-VEHD, PEE-tuhr) **PHI.**

Center. Shoots left. 6'3", 196 lbs. Born, Liberec, Czech., December 9, 1971. Vancouver's 1st choice, 2nd overall, in 1990 Entry Draft.

Season	Club	League	GP	G	A	Pts	PIM	PP	SH	GW	S	%	+/-	TF	F%	Min	GP	G	A	Pts	PIM	PP	SH	GW	Min
1988-89	CHZ Litvinov Jr.	Czech-Jr.	20	32	19	51	12																		
1989-90	Seattle	WHL	71	65	80	145	80										11	4	9	13	2				
1990-91	**Vancouver**	**NHL**	**61**	**10**	**6**	**16**	**20**	**1**	**0**	**0**	**97**	**10.3**	**–21**				**6**	**0**	**1**	**1**	**0**	**0**	**0**	**0**	
1991-92	**Vancouver**	**NHL**	**77**	**15**	**22**	**37**	**36**	**5**	**0**	**1**	**99**	**15.2**	**–3**				**10**	**1**	**4**	**5**	**16**	**0**	**0**	**0**	
1992-93	**Vancouver**	**NHL**	**84**	**38**	**33**	**71**	**96**	**2**	**1**	**3**	**149**	**25.5**	**20**				**12**	**2**	**3**	**5**	**2**	**0**	**0**	**0**	
1993-94	Canada	Nat-Tm	17	19	12	31	16																		
	Canada	Olympics	8	5	1	6	6																		
	St. Louis	**NHL**	**19**	**6**	**14**	**20**	**8**	**2**	**0**	**0**	**63**	**9.5**	**2**				**4**	**0**	**1**	**1**	**4**	**0**	**0**	**0**	
1994-95	**NY Rangers**	**NHL**	**46**	**11**	**12**	**23**	**26**	**1**	**0**	**3**	**123**	**8.9**	**–1**				**10**	**3**	**2**	**5**	**6**	**2**	**0**	**0**	
1995-96	**Pittsburgh**	**NHL**	**80**	**45**	**54**	**99**	**68**	**8**	**1**	**5**	**204**	**22.1**	**37**				**18**	**10**	**10**	**20**	**16**	**4**	**0**	**2**	
1996-97	**Pittsburgh**	**NHL**	**74**	**33**	**38**	**71**	**66**	**12**	**3**	**4**	**189**	**17.5**	**–2**				**5**	**1**	**2**	**3**	**12**	**0**	**1**	**0**	
1997-98	Stadion Liberec	CzRep-2	2	0	3	3																			
	TJ Novy Jicin	CzRep-3	7	9	16	25																			
	HC Sparta Praha	CzRep	5	2	3	5	8										6	0	2	2	52				
	Las Vegas	IHL	3	3	3	6	4																		
1998-99	Las Vegas	IHL	13	8	10	18	32																		
	NY Rangers	**NHL**	**56**	**20**	**27**	**47**	**50**	**9**	**1**	**3**	**153**	**13.1**	**–6**	**1069**	**52.5**	**20:31**									
99-2000	**NY Rangers**	**NHL**	**76**	**24**	**44**	**68**	**40**	**6**	**2**	**4**	**201**	**11.9**	**2**	**1354**	**54.0**	**19:54**									
2000-01	**NY Rangers**	**NHL**	**79**	**32**	**46**	**78**	**54**	**9**	**1**	**5**	**230**	**13.9**	**10**	**1349**	**49.7**	**20:16**									
2001-02	Liberec	CzRep-2	1	3	0	3	2																		
	NY Rangers	**NHL**	**78**	**21**	**25**	**46**	**36**	**6**	**1**	**3**	**175**	**12.0**	**–8**	**1402**	**52.1**	**19:22**									
2002-03	**NY Rangers**	**NHL**	**78**	**27**	**31**	**58**	**64**	**8**	**3**	**4**	**205**	**13.2**	**–4**	**1142**	**53.0**	**20:21**									
2003-04	**NY Rangers**	**NHL**	**65**	**14**	**17**	**31**	**42**	**5**	**0**	**3**	**153**	**9.2**	**–9**	**929**	**48.6**	**18:51**									
	Edmonton	**NHL**	**16**	**5**	**10**	**15**	**4**	**2**	**0**	**0**	**37**	**13.5**	**1**	**226**	**46.9**	**18:11**									
2004-05	HC Sparta Praha	CzRep	46	22	13	35	44										5	2	3	5	10				
2005-06	**Phoenix**	**NHL**	**25**	**2**	**9**	**11**	**34**	**1**	**0**	**1**	**43**	**4.7**	**–6**	**299**	**48.2**	**16:29**									
	Philadelphia	**NHL**	**28**	**5**	**9**	**14**	**36**	**2**	**0**	**0**	**47**	**10.6**	**–8**	**416**	**53.4**	**17:05**	**6**	**2**	**0**	**2**	**8**	**1**	**0**	**0**	**17:28**
	NHL Totals		**942**	**308**	**397**	**705**	**680**	**79**	**13**	**39**	**2168**	**14.2**		**8186**	**51.6**	**19:30**	**71**	**19**	**23**	**42**	**64**	**7**	**1**	**2**	**17:28**

WHL Rookie of the Year (1990) • Canadian Major Junior Rookie of the Year (1990)

Signed as a free agent by **St. Louis**, March 5, 1994. Traded to **NY Rangers** by **St. Louis** for Esa Tikkanen and Doug Lidster, July 24, 1994. Traded to **Pittsburgh** by **NY Rangers** with Sergei Zubov for Luc Robitaille and Ulf Samuelsson, August 31, 1995. Traded to **NY Rangers** by **Pittsburgh** with Chris Tamer and Sean Pronger for Alex Kovalev and Harry York, November 25, 1998. Traded to **Edmonton** by **NY Rangers** with Jussi Markkanen for Stephen Valiquette, Dwight Helminen, Edmonton's 2nd round compensatory choice (Dane Byers) in 2004 Entry Draft and future considerations, March 3, 2004. Signed as a free agent by **Phoenix**, August 26, 2004. Signed as a free agent by **Sparta Praha** (CzRep), September 17, 2004. Traded to **Philadelphia** by **Phoenix** with Phoenix's 4th round choice (Joonas Lehtivuori) in 2006 Entry Draft for Dennis Seidenberg and Philadelphia's 4th round choice (later traded to NY Islanders - NY Islanders selected Tomas Marcinko) in 2006 Entry Draft, January 20, 2006.

NEIL, Chris

(NEEL, KRIHS) **OTT.**

Right wing. Shoots right. 6', 213 lbs. Born, Markdale, Ont., June 18, 1979. Ottawa's 7th choice, 161st overall, in 1998 Entry Draft.

Season	Club	League	GP	G	A	Pts	PIM	PP	SH	GW	S	%	+/-	TF	F%	Min	GP	G	A	Pts	PIM	PP	SH	GW	Min
1995-96	Orangeville	OHA-B	43	15	15	30	50																		
1996-97	North Bay	OHL	65	13	16	29	150																		
1997-98	North Bay	OHL	59	26	29	55	231																		
1998-99	North Bay	OHL	66	26	46	72	215										4	1	0	1	15				
99-2000	Mobile Mysticks	ECHL	4	0	2	2	39																		
	Grand Rapids	IHL	51	9	10	19	301										8	0	2	2	24				
2000-01	Grand Rapids	IHL	78	15	21	36	354										10	2	2	4	22				
2001-02	**Ottawa**	**NHL**	**72**	**10**	**7**	**17**	**231**	**1**	**0**	**0**	**56**	**17.9**	**5**	**0**	**0.0**	**8:22**	**12**	**0**	**0**	**0**	**12**	**0**	**0**	**0**	**7:12**
2002-03	**Ottawa**	**NHL**	**68**	**6**	**4**	**10**	**147**	**0**	**0**	**0**	**62**	**9.7**	**8**	**5**	**60.0**	**7:40**	**15**	**1**	**0**	**1**	**24**	**0**	**0**	**0**	**7:57**
2003-04	**Ottawa**	**NHL**	**82**	**8**	**8**	**16**	**194**	**0**	**0**	**1**	**76**	**10.5**	**13**	**14**	**42.9**	**8:51**	**7**	**0**	**1**	**1**	**19**	**0**	**0**	**0**	**6:45**
2004-05	Binghamton	AHL	22	4	6	10	132										6	1	1	2	26				
2005-06	**Ottawa**	**NHL**	**79**	**16**	**17**	**33**	**204**	**8**	**0**	**0**	**126**	**12.7**	**9**	**9**	**22.2**	**12:18**	**10**	**1**	**0**	**1**	**14**	**0**	**0**	**0**	**6:58**
	NHL Totals		**301**	**40**	**36**	**76**	**776**	**9**	**0**	**1**	**320**	**12.5**		**28**	**39.3**	**9:22**	**44**	**2**	**1**	**3**	**69**	**0**	**0**	**0**	**7:20**

Signed as a free agent by **Binghamton** (AHL), March 2, 2005.

NICHOL, Scott

(NIH-KOHL, SKAWT) **NSH.**

Center. Shoots right. 5'8", 173 lbs. Born, Edmonton, Alta., December 31, 1974. Buffalo's 9th choice, 272nd overall, in 1993 Entry Draft.

			Regular Season														Playoffs								
Season	Club	League	GP	G	A	Pts	PIM	PP	SH	GW	S	%	+/-	TF	F%	Min	GP	G	A	Pts	PIM	PP	SH	GW	Min
1991-92	Cgy. AAA Flames	AMHL	23	26	16	42	132	....	....	....	....	....	....	....	....	....	....	....	....	....	....	....	....	....	....
1992-93	Portland	WHL	67	31	33	64	146	....	....	....	....	....	....	....	....	....	16	8	8	16	41	....	....	....	....
1993-94	Portland	WHL	65	40	53	93	144	....	....	....	....	....	....	....	....	....	10	3	8	11	16	....	....	....	....
1994-95	Rochester	AHL	71	11	16	27	136	....	....	....	....	....	....	....	....	....	5	0	3	3	14	....	....	....	....
1995-96	**Buffalo**	**NHL**	**2**	**0**	**0**	**0**	**10**	**0**	**0**	**0**	**4**	**0.0**	**0**	....	....	....	....	....	....	....	....	....	....	....	....
	Rochester	AHL	62	14	18	32	170	....	....	....	....	....	....	....	....	....	19	7	6	13	36	....	....	....	....
1996-97	Rochester	AHL	68	22	21	43	133	....	....	....	....	....	....	....	....	....	10	2	1	3	26	....	....	....	....
1997-98	**Buffalo**	**NHL**	**3**	**0**	**0**	**0**	**4**	**0**	**0**	**0**	**5**	**0.0**	**0**	....	....	....	....	....	....	....	....	....	....	....	....
	Rochester	AHL	35	13	7	20	113	....	....	....	....	....	....	....	....	....	17	0	6	6	18	....	....	....	....
1998-99	Rochester	AHL	52	13	20	33	120	....	....	....	....	....	....	....	....	....	....	....	....	....	....	....	....	....	....
99-2000	Rochester	AHL	37	7	11	18	141	....	....	....	....	....	....	....	....	....	12	0	3	3	10	....	....	....	....
2000-01	Detroit Vipers	IHL	67	7	24	31	198	....	....	....	....	....	....	....	....	....	11	1	1	2	12	....	....	....	....
2001-02	**Calgary**	**NHL**	**60**	**8**	**9**	**17**	**107**	**2**	**1**	**0**	**49**	**16.3**	**–9**	**458**	**53.1**	**12:41**	....	....	....	....	....	....	....	....	....
2002-03	**Calgary**	**NHL**	**68**	**5**	**5**	**10**	**149**	**0**	**1**	**0**	**66**	**7.6**	**–7**	**357**	**58.3**	**10:47**	....	....	....	....	....	....	....	....	....
2003-04	**Chicago**	**NHL**	**75**	**7**	**11**	**18**	**145**	**0**	**0**	**1**	**112**	**6.3**	**–16**	**1178**	**57.4**	**15:46**	....	....	....	....	....	....	....	....	....
2004-05	London Racers	Britain	10	1	7	8	70	....	....	....	....	....	....	....	....	....	....	....	....	....	....	....	....	....	....
2005-06	**Nashville**	**NHL**	**34**	**3**	**3**	**6**	**79**	**0**	**1**	**0**	**32**	**9.4**	**3**	**242**	**58.3**	**10:30**	**3**	**0**	**0**	**0**	**2**	**0**	**0**	**0**	**7:45**
	Milwaukee	AHL	6	3	5	8	18	....	....	....	....	....	....	....	....	....	....	....	....	....	....	....	....	....	....
	NHL Totals		**242**	**23**	**28**	**51**	**494**	**2**	**3**	**1**	**268**	**8.6**		**2235**	**56.7**	**12:48**	**3**	**0**	**0**	**0**	**2**	**0**	**0**	**0**	**7:45**

• Missed majority of 1999-2000 season recovering from knee injury suffered in game vs. Saint John (AHL), February 16, 2000. Signed as a free agent by **Calgary**, July 1, 2001. Signed as a free agent by **Chicago**, July 1, 2003. Signed as a free agent by **London** (Britain), October 26, 2004. Signed as a free agent by **Nashville**, August 6, 2005.

NICKULAS, Eric

(NICK-luhs, AIR-ihk)

Right wing. Shoots right. 5'11", 206 lbs. Born, Hyannis, MA, March 25, 1975. Boston's 3rd choice, 99th overall, in 1994 Entry Draft.

			Regular Season														Playoffs								
Season	Club	League	GP	G	A	Pts	PIM	PP	SH	GW	S	%	+/-	TF	F%	Min	GP	G	A	Pts	PIM	PP	SH	GW	Min
1991-92	Barnstable	High-MA	24	30	25	55	....	....	....	....	....	....	....	....	....	....	....	....	....	....	....	....	....	....	....
1992-93	Tabor Academy	High-MA	28	25	25	50	....	....	....	....	....	....	....	....	....	....	....	....	....	....	....	....	....	....	....
1993-94	Cushing	High-MA	25	46	36	82	....	....	....	....	....	....	....	....	....	....	....	....	....	....	....	....	....	....	....
1994-95	New Hampshire	H-East	33	15	9	24	32	....	....	....	....	....	....	....	....	....	....	....	....	....	....	....	....	....	....
1995-96	New Hampshire	H-East	34	26	12	38	66	....	....	....	....	....	....	....	....	....	....	....	....	....	....	....	....	....	....
1996-97	New Hampshire	H-East	39	29	22	51	80	....	....	....	....	....	....	....	....	....	....	....	....	....	....	....	....	....	....
1997-98	Orlando	IHL	76	22	9	31	77	....	....	....	....	....	....	....	....	....	6	0	0	0	10	....	....	....	....
1998-99	**Boston**	**NHL**	**2**	**0**	**0**	**0**	**0**	**0**	**0**	**0**	**0**	**0.0**	**0**	**0**	**0.0**	**3:27**	**1**	**0**	**0**	**0**	**2**	**0**	**0**	**0**	**4:35**
	Providence Bruins	AHL	75	31	27	58	83	....	....	....	....	....	....	....	....	....	18	8	12	20	33	....	....	....	....
99-2000	**Boston**	**NHL**	**20**	**5**	**6**	**11**	**12**	**1**	**0**	**0**	**28**	**17.9**	**–1**	**4**	**50.0**	**11:13**	....	....	....	....	....	....	....	....	....
	Providence Bruins	AHL	40	6	6	12	37	....	....	....	....	....	....	....	....	....	12	2	3	5	20	....	....	....	....
2000-01	**Boston**	**NHL**	**7**	**0**	**0**	**0**	**4**	**0**	**0**	**0**	**6**	**0.0**	**–2**	**1**	**100.0**	**7:07**	....	....	....	....	....	....	....	....	....
	Providence Bruins	AHL	62	20	23	43	100	....	....	....	....	....	....	....	....	....	12	4	4	8	24	....	....	....	....
2001-02	Worcester IceCats	AHL	54	11	25	36	48	....	....	....	....	....	....	....	....	....	3	0	1	1	2	....	....	....	....
2002-03	**St. Louis**	**NHL**	**8**	**0**	**1**	**1**	**6**	**0**	**0**	**0**	**3**	**0.0**	**–2**	**0**	**0.0**	**9:31**	....	....	....	....	....	....	....	....	....
	Worcester IceCats	AHL	39	17	16	33	40	....	....	....	....	....	....	....	....	....	3	0	0	0	2	....	....	....	....
2003-04	**St. Louis**	**NHL**	**44**	**7**	**11**	**18**	**44**	**1**	**0**	**1**	**80**	**8.8**	**–2**	**10**	**30.0**	**12:50**	....	....	....	....	....	....	....	....	....
	Chicago	**NHL**	**21**	**1**	**1**	**2**	**8**	**0**	**0**	**0**	**41**	**2.4**	**–6**	**11**	**45.5**	**13:46**	....	....	....	....	....	....	....	....	....
2004-05	Norfolk Admirals	AHL	53	11	11	22	32	....	....	....	....	....	....	....	....	....	6	0	3	3	8	....	....	....	....
2005-06	**Boston**	**NHL**	**16**	**2**	**4**	**6**	**8**	**0**	**0**	**0**	**14**	**14.3**	**2**	**8**	**25.0**	**8:08**	....	....	....	....	....	....	....	....	....
	Providence Bruins	AHL	38	10	16	26	46	....	....	....	....	....	....	....	....	....	5	1	1	2	4	....	....	....	....
	NHL Totals		**118**	**15**	**23**	**38**	**82**	**2**	**0**	**1**	**172**	**8.7**		**34**	**38.2**	**11:22**	**1**	**0**	**0**	**0**	**2**	**0**	**0**	**0**	**4:35**

Ken McKenzie Trophy (U.S.- Born Rookie of the Year – IHL) (1998)

Signed as a free agent by **Worcester** (AHL), November 10, 2001. Signed as a free agent by **St. Louis**, July 16, 2002. Claimed on waivers by **Chicago** from **St. Louis**, February 24, 2004. Signed as a free agent by **Boston**, August 23, 2005.

NIEDERMAYER, Rob

(NEE-duhr-MIGH-uhr, RAWB) **ANA.**

Center. Shoots left. 6'2", 204 lbs. Born, Cassiar, B.C., December 28, 1974. Florida's 1st choice, 5th overall, in 1993 Entry Draft.

			Regular Season														Playoffs								
Season	Club	League	GP	G	A	Pts	PIM	PP	SH	GW	S	%	+/-	TF	F%	Min	GP	G	A	Pts	PIM	PP	SH	GW	Min
1989-90	Cranbrook Blazers	BCAHA	35	42	40	82	30	....	....	....	....	....	....	....	....	....	....	....	....	....	....	....	....	....	....
1990-91	Medicine Hat	WHL	71	24	26	50	8	....	....	....	....	....	....	....	....	....	12	3	7	10	2	....	....	....	....
1991-92	Medicine Hat	WHL	71	32	46	78	77	....	....	....	....	....	....	....	....	....	4	2	3	5	2	....	....	....	....
1992-93	Medicine Hat	WHL	52	43	34	77	67	....	....	....	....	....	....	....	....	....	....	....	....	....	....	....	....	....	....
1993-94	**Florida**	**NHL**	**65**	**9**	**17**	**26**	**51**	**3**	**0**	**2**	**67**	**13.4**	**–11**	....	....	....	....	....	....	....	....	....	....	....	....
1994-95	Medicine Hat	WHL	13	9	15	24	14	....	....	....	....	....	....	....	....	....	....	....	....	....	....	....	....	....	....
	Florida	**NHL**	**48**	**4**	**6**	**10**	**36**	**1**	**0**	**0**	**58**	**6.9**	**–13**	....	....	....	....	....	....	....	....	....	....	....	....
1995-96	**Florida**	**NHL**	**82**	**26**	**35**	**61**	**107**	**11**	**0**	**6**	**155**	**16.8**	**1**	....	....	....	**22**	**5**	**3**	**8**	**12**	**2**	**0**	**2**	....
1996-97	**Florida**	**NHL**	**60**	**14**	**24**	**38**	**54**	**3**	**0**	**2**	**136**	**10.3**	**4**	....	....	....	**5**	**2**	**1**	**3**	**6**	**1**	**0**	**0**	....
1997-98	**Florida**	**NHL**	**33**	**8**	**7**	**15**	**41**	**5**	**0**	**2**	**64**	**12.5**	**–9**	....	....	....	....	....	....	....	....	....	....	....	....
1998-99	**Florida**	**NHL**	**82**	**18**	**33**	**51**	**50**	**6**	**1**	**3**	**142**	**12.7**	**–13**	**1895**	**47.1**	**21:17**	....	....	....	....	....	....	....	....	....
99-2000	**Florida**	**NHL**	**81**	**10**	**23**	**33**	**46**	**1**	**0**	**4**	**135**	**7.4**	**–5**	**1632**	**47.9**	**19:04**	**4**	**1**	**0**	**1**	**6**	**0**	**0**	**0**	**15:55**
2000-01	**Florida**	**NHL**	**67**	**12**	**20**	**32**	**50**	**3**	**1**	**0**	**115**	**10.4**	**–12**	**997**	**45.0**	**20:30**	....	....	....	....	....	....	....	....	....
2001-02	**Calgary**	**NHL**	**57**	**6**	**14**	**20**	**49**	**1**	**2**	**1**	**87**	**6.9**	**–15**	**777**	**48.4**	**18:01**	....	....	....	....	....	....	....	....	....
2002-03	**Calgary**	**NHL**	**54**	**8**	**10**	**18**	**42**	**2**	**0**	**1**	**104**	**7.7**	**–13**	**139**	**48.9**	**17:29**	....	....	....	....	....	....	....	....	....
	Anaheim	**NHL**	**12**	**2**	**2**	**4**	**15**	**1**	**0**	**0**	**21**	**9.5**	**3**	**14**	**42.9**	**15:21**	**21**	**3**	**7**	**10**	**18**	**0**	**2**	**0**	**23:35**
2003-04	**Anaheim**	**NHL**	**55**	**12**	**16**	**28**	**34**	**6**	**0**	**2**	**111**	**10.8**	**–6**	**45**	**64.4**	**19:28**	....	....	....	....	....	....	....	....	....
2004-05	Ferencvaros	Hungary	5	2	1	3	14	....	....	....	....	....	....	....	....	....	....	....	....	....	....	....	....	....	....
2005-06	**Anaheim**	**NHL**	**76**	**15**	**24**	**39**	**89**	**4**	**1**	**2**	**140**	**10.7**	**–5**	**447**	**45.6**	**17:52**	**16**	**1**	**3**	**4**	**10**	**1**	**0**	**0**	**19:36**
	NHL Totals		**772**	**144**	**231**	**375**	**664**	**47**	**5**	**25**	**1335**	**10.8**		**5946**	**47.2**	**19:06**	**68**	**12**	**14**	**26**	**52**	**4**	**2**	**2**	**21:17**

WHL East First All-Star Team (1993)

• Missed majority of 1997-98 season recovering from thumb (November 26, 1997 vs. Boston) and head (March 19, 1998 vs. Buffalo) injuries. Traded to **Calgary** by **Florida** with Philadelphia's 2nd round choice (previously acquired, Calgary selected Andrei Medvedev) in 2001 Entry Draft for Valeri Bure and Jason Wiemer, June 23, 2001. Traded to **Anaheim** by **Calgary** for Mike Commodore and Jean-Francois Damphousse, March 11, 2003. Signed as a free agent by **Ferencvaros** (Hungary), January 17, 2005.

NIEDERMAYER, Scott

(NEE-duhr-MIGH-uhr, SKAWT) **ANA.**

Defense. Shoots left. 6'1", 200 lbs. Born, Edmonton, Alta., August 31, 1973. New Jersey's 1st choice, 3rd overall, in 1991 Entry Draft.

			Regular Season														Playoffs								
Season	Club	League	GP	G	A	Pts	PIM	PP	SH	GW	S	%	+/-	TF	F%	Min	GP	G	A	Pts	PIM	PP	SH	GW	Min
1988-89	Cranbrook Blazers	BCAHA	62	55	37	92	100	....	....	....	....	....	....	....	....	....	....	....	....	....	....	....	....	....	....
1989-90	Kamloops Blazers	WHL	64	14	55	69	64	....	....	....	....	....	....	....	....	....	17	2	14	16	35	....	....	....	....
1990-91	Kamloops Blazers	WHL	57	26	56	82	52	....	....	....	....	....	....	....	....	....	....	....	....	....	....	....	....	....	....
1991-92	Kamloops Blazers	WHL	35	7	32	39	61	....	....	....	....	....	....	....	....	....	17	9	14	23	28	....	....	....	....
	New Jersey	**NHL**	**4**	**0**	**1**	**1**	**2**	**0**	**0**	**0**	**4**	**0.0**	**1**	....	....	....	....	....	....	....	....	....	....	....	....
1992-93	**New Jersey**	**NHL**	**80**	**11**	**29**	**40**	**47**	**5**	**0**	**0**	**131**	**8.4**	**8**	....	....	....	**5**	**0**	**3**	**3**	**2**	**0**	**0**	**0**	....
1993-94	**New Jersey**	**NHL**	**81**	**10**	**36**	**46**	**42**	**5**	**0**	**2**	**135**	**7.4**	**34**	....	....	....	**20**	**2**	**2**	**4**	**8**	**1**	**0**	**0**	....
1994-95 ♦	**New Jersey**	**NHL**	**48**	**4**	**15**	**19**	**18**	**4**	**0**	**0**	**52**	**7.7**	**19**	....	....	....	**20**	**4**	**7**	**11**	**10**	**2**	**0**	**1**	....
1995-96	**New Jersey**	**NHL**	**79**	**8**	**25**	**33**	**46**	**6**	**0**	**0**	**179**	**4.5**	**5**	....	....	....	....	....	....	....	....	....	....	....	....
1996-97	**New Jersey**	**NHL**	**81**	**5**	**30**	**35**	**64**	**3**	**0**	**3**	**159**	**3.1**	**–4**	....	....	....	**10**	**2**	**4**	**6**	**6**	**2**	**0**	**1**	....
1997-98	**New Jersey**	**NHL**	**81**	**14**	**43**	**57**	**27**	**11**	**0**	**1**	**175**	**8.0**	**5**	....	....	....	**6**	**0**	**2**	**2**	**4**	**0**	**0**	**0**	....
1998-99	Utah Grizzlies	IHL	5	0	2	2	0	....	....	....	....	....	....	....	....	....	....	....	....	....	....	....	....	....	....
	New Jersey	**NHL**	**72**	**11**	**35**	**46**	**26**	**1**	**1**	**3**	**161**	**6.8**	**16**	**13**	**15.4**	**24:40**	**7**	**1**	**3**	**4**	**18**	**1**	**0**	**0**	**25:30**
99-2000 ♦	**New Jersey**	**NHL**	**71**	**7**	**31**	**38**	**48**	**1**	**0**	**0**	**109**	**6.4**	**19**	**8**	**37.5**	**24:21**	**22**	**5**	**2**	**7**	**10**	**0**	**2**	**1**	**25:28**
2000-01	**New Jersey**	**NHL**	**57**	**6**	**29**	**35**	**22**	**1**	**0**	**5**	**87**	**6.9**	**14**	**5**	**0.0**	**23:19**	**21**	**0**	**6**	**6**	**14**	**0**	**0**	**0**	**23:53**
2001-02	**New Jersey**	**NHL**	**76**	**11**	**22**	**33**	**30**	**2**	**0**	**6**	**129**	**8.5**	**12**	**1**	**100.0**	**24:17**	**6**	**0**	**2**	**2**	**6**	**0**	**0**	**0**	**26:37**
	Canada	Olympics	6	1	1	2	4	....	....	....	....	....	....	....	....	....	....	....	....	....	....	....	....	....	....
2002-03 ♦	**New Jersey**	**NHL**	**81**	**11**	**28**	**39**	**62**	**3**	**0**	**3**	**164**	**6.7**	**23**	**1**	**0.0**	**24:30**	**24**	**2**	***16**	***18**	**16**	**1**	**0**	**0**	**26:07**
2003-04	**New Jersey**	**NHL**	**81**	**14**	**40**	**54**	**44**	**9**	**0**	**3**	**165**	**8.5**	**20**	**1**	**0.0**	**25:56**	**5**	**1**	**0**	**1**	**6**	**0**	**0**	**0**	**27:21**
2004-05			DID NOT PLAY																						
2005-06	**Anaheim**	**NHL**	**82**	**13**	**50**	**63**	**96**	**9**	**0**	**3**	**181**	**7.2**	**8**	**7**	**28.6**	**25:30**	**16**	**2**	**9**	**11**	**14**	**1**	**1**	**1**	**28:54**

Season	Club	League	GP	G	A	Pts	PIM	PP	SH	GW	S	%	+/-	TF	F%	Min	GP	G	A	Pts	PIM	PP	SH	GW	Min
			Regular Season														Playoffs								
	Canada	Olympics	DID NOT PLAY – INJURED																						
	NHL Totals		974	125	414	539	574	60	1	29	1831	6.8		36	22.2	24:43	162	19	56	75	114	8	3	4	26:00

WHL West First All-Star Team (1991, 1992) • Canadian Major Junior Scholastic Player of the Year (1991) • Memorial Cup Tournament All-Star Team (1992) • Stafford Smythe Memorial Trophy (Memorial Cup Tournament MVP) (1992) • NHL All-Rookie Team (1993) • NHL Second All-Star Team (1998) • NHL First All-Star Team (2004, 2006) • James Norris Trophy (2004)

Played in NHL All-Star Game (1998, 2001, 2004)

Signed to tryout (PTO) contract by **Utah** (IHL) with **New Jersey** retaining NHL rights, October 19, 1998. Signed as a free agent by **Anaheim**, August 4, 2005.

NIEMINEN, Ville

(nee-EHM-ih-nehn, VIHL-ee) **S.J.**

Left wing. Shoots left. 5'11", 200 lbs. Born, Tampere, Finland, April 6, 1977. Colorado's 4th choice, 78th overall, in 1997 Entry Draft.

Season	Club	League	GP	G	A	Pts	PIM	PP	SH	GW	S	%	+/-	TF	F%	Min	GP	G	A	Pts	PIM	PP	SH	GW	Min
1993-94	Tappara U18	Fin-U18	29	13	20	33	66	....	....	....	....	....	....	....	....	....	5	1	2	3	0	....	....	....	....
1994-95	Tappara U18	Fin-U18	15	14	18	32	68	....	....	....	....	....	....	....	....	....	7	2	16	18	22	....	....	....	....
	Tappara Jr.	Fin-Jr.	16	11	21	32	47	....	....	....	....	....	....	....	....	....	....	....	....	....	....	....	....	....	....
	Tappara Tampere	Finland	16	0	0	0	0	....	....	....	....	....	....	....	....	....	....	....	....	....	....	....	....	....	....
1995-96	Tappara Jr.	Fin-Jr.	20	20	23	43	63	....	....	....	....	....	....	....	....	....	....	....	....	....	....	....	....	....	....
	Tappara Tampere	Finland	4	0	1	1	8	....	....	....	....	....	....	....	....	....	....	....	....	....	....	....	....	....	....
	KooVee Tampere	Finland-2	7	2	1	3	4	....	....	....	....	....	....	....	....	....	....	....	....	....	....	....	....	....	....
1996-97	Tappara Jr.	Fin-Jr.	2	2	7	9	2	....	....	....	....	....	....	....	....	....	....	....	....	....	....	....	....	....	....
	Tappara Tampere	Finland	49	10	13	23	120	....	....	....	....	....	....	....	....	....	3	1	0	1	8	....	....	....	....
1997-98	Hershey Bears	AHL	74	14	22	36	85	....	....	....	....	....	....	....	....	....	....	....	....	....	....	....	....	....	....
1998-99	Hershey Bears	AHL	67	24	19	43	127	....	....	....	....	....	....	....	....	....	3	0	1	1	0	....	....	....	....
99-2000	**Colorado**	**NHL**	**1**	**0**	**0**	**0**	**0**	**0**	**0**	**0**	**2**	**0.0**	**0**	**0**	**0.0**	**10:12**	....	....	....	....	....	....	....	....	....
	Hershey Bears	AHL	74	21	30	51	54	....	....	....	....	....	....	....	....	....	9	2	4	6	6	....	....	....	....
2000-01 ♦	**Colorado**	**NHL**	**50**	**14**	**8**	**22**	**38**	**2**	**0**	**3**	**68**	**20.6**	**8**	**3**	**33.3**	**12:26**	**23**	**4**	**6**	**10**	**20**	**3**	**0**	**1**	**14:10**
	Hershey Bears	AHL	28	10	11	21	48	....	....	....	....	....	....	....	....	....	....	....	....	....	....	....	....	....	....
2001-02	**Colorado**	**NHL**	**53**	**10**	**14**	**24**	**30**	**1**	**0**	**5**	**72**	**13.9**	**1**	**8**	**62.5**	**12:41**	....	....	....	....	....	....	....	....	....
	Finland	Olympics	4	0	1	1	2	....	....	....	....	....	....	....	....	....	....	....	....	....	....	....	....	....	....
	Pittsburgh	**NHL**	**13**	**1**	**2**	**3**	**8**	**0**	**0**	**0**	**11**	**9.1**	**–2**	**0**	**0.0**	**16:10**	....	....	....	....	....	....	....	....	....
2002-03	**Pittsburgh**	**NHL**	**75**	**9**	**12**	**21**	**93**	**0**	**2**	**1**	**86**	**10.5**	**–25**	**46**	**52.2**	**14:08**	....	....	....	....	....	....	....	....	....
2003-04	**Chicago**	**NHL**	**60**	**2**	**11**	**13**	**40**	**1**	**0**	**0**	**56**	**3.6**	**–15**	**4**	**25.0**	**11:46**	....	....	....	....	....	....	....	....	....
	Calgary	**NHL**	**19**	**3**	**5**	**8**	**18**	**0**	**0**	**1**	**27**	**11.1**	**6**	**5**	**0.0**	**14:36**	**24**	**4**	**4**	**8**	**55**	**1**	**0**	**0**	**16:17**
2004-05	Tappara Tampere	Finland	26	14	13	27	32	....	....	....	....	....	....	....	....	....	8	2	4	6	12	....	....	....	....
2005-06	**NY Rangers**	**NHL**	**48**	**5**	**12**	**17**	**53**	**0**	**0**	**2**	**73**	**6.8**	**10**	**6**	**33.3**	**11:38**	....	....	....	....	....	....	....	....	....
	Finland	Olympics	8	0	1	1	4	....	....	....	....	....	....	....	....	....	....	....	....	....	....	....	....	....	....
	San Jose	**NHL**	**22**	**3**	**4**	**7**	**10**	**0**	**1**	**0**	**41**	**7.3**	**–3**	**3**	**33.3**	**15:23**	**11**	**0**	**2**	**2**	**24**	**0**	**0**	**0**	**15:39**
	NHL Totals		**341**	**47**	**68**	**115**	**290**	**4**	**3**	**12**	**436**	**10.8**		**75**	**45.3**	**13:04**	**58**	**8**	**12**	**20**	**99**	**4**	**0**	**1**	**15:19**

Traded to **Pittsburgh** by **Colorado** with Rick Berry for Darius Kasparaitis, March 19, 2002. Signed as a free agent by **Chicago**, July 29, 2003. Traded to **Calgary** by **Chicago** for Jason Morgan and Calgary's 6th round choice (Joseph Fallon) in 2005 Entry Draft, February 24, 2004. Signed as a free agent by **Tappara Tampere** (Finland), July 22, 2004. Signed as a free agent by **NY Rangers**, August 4, 2005. Traded to **San Jose** by **NY Rangers** for San Jose's 3rd round choice (later traded to Anaheim - Anaheim selected John DeGray) in 2006 Entry Draft, March 8, 2006.

NIEUWENDYK, Joe

(NOO-ihn-DIGHK, JOH) **FLA.**

Center. Shoots left. 6'2", 205 lbs. Born, Oshawa, Ont., September 10, 1966. Calgary's 2nd choice, 27th overall, in 1985 Entry Draft.

Season	Club	League	GP	G	A	Pts	PIM	PP	SH	GW	S	%	+/-	TF	F%	Min	GP	G	A	Pts	PIM	PP	SH	GW	Min
1983-84	Pickering Panthers	OHA-B	38	30	28	58	35	....	....	....	....	....	....	....	....	....	....	....	....	....	....	....	....	....	....
1984-85	Cornell Big Red	ECAC	29	21	24	45	30	....	....	....	....	....	....	....	....	....	....	....	....	....	....	....	....	....	....
1985-86	Cornell Big Red	ECAC	29	26	28	54	67	....	....	....	....	....	....	....	....	....	....	....	....	....	....	....	....	....	....
1986-87	Cornell Big Red	ECAC	23	26	26	52	26	....	....	....	....	....	....	....	....	....	....	....	....	....	....	....	....	....	....
	Calgary	**NHL**	**9**	**5**	**1**	**6**	**0**	**2**	**0**	**1**	**16**	**31.3**	**0**	....	....	....	**6**	**2**	**2**	**4**	**0**	**0**	**0**	**0**	....
1987-88	**Calgary**	**NHL**	**75**	**51**	**41**	**92**	**23**	**31**	**3**	**8**	**212**	**24.1**	**20**	....	....	....	**8**	**3**	**4**	**7**	**2**	**1**	**0**	**0**	....
1988-89 ♦	**Calgary**	**NHL**	**77**	**51**	**31**	**82**	**40**	**19**	**3**	**11**	**215**	**23.7**	**26**	....	....	....	**22**	**10**	**4**	**14**	**10**	**6**	**0**	**1**	....
1989-90	**Calgary**	**NHL**	**79**	**45**	**50**	**95**	**40**	**18**	**0**	**3**	**226**	**19.9**	**32**	....	....	....	**6**	**4**	**6**	**10**	**4**	**1**	**0**	**0**	....
1990-91	**Calgary**	**NHL**	**79**	**45**	**40**	**85**	**36**	**22**	**4**	**1**	**222**	**20.3**	**19**	....	....	....	**7**	**4**	**1**	**5**	**10**	**2**	**0**	**0**	....
1991-92	**Calgary**	**NHL**	**69**	**22**	**34**	**56**	**55**	**7**	**0**	**2**	**137**	**16.1**	**–1**	....	....	....	....	....	....	....	....	....	....	....	....
1992-93	**Calgary**	**NHL**	**79**	**38**	**37**	**75**	**52**	**14**	**0**	**6**	**208**	**18.3**	**9**	....	....	....	**6**	**3**	**6**	**9**	**10**	**1**	**0**	**0**	....
1993-94	**Calgary**	**NHL**	**64**	**36**	**39**	**75**	**51**	**14**	**1**	**7**	**191**	**18.8**	**19**	....	....	....	**6**	**2**	**2**	**4**	**0**	**1**	**0**	**0**	....
1994-95	**Calgary**	**NHL**	**46**	**21**	**29**	**50**	**33**	**3**	**0**	**4**	**122**	**17.2**	**11**	....	....	....	**5**	**4**	**3**	**7**	**0**	**2**	**0**	**1**	....
1995-96	**Dallas**	**NHL**	**52**	**14**	**18**	**32**	**41**	**8**	**0**	**3**	**138**	**10.1**	**–17**	....	....	....	....	....	....	....	....	....	....	....	....
1996-97	**Dallas**	**NHL**	**66**	**30**	**21**	**51**	**32**	**8**	**0**	**2**	**173**	**17.3**	**–5**	....	....	....	**7**	**2**	**2**	**4**	**6**	**0**	**0**	**0**	....
1997-98	**Dallas**	**NHL**	**73**	**39**	**30**	**69**	**30**	**14**	**0**	**11**	**203**	**19.2**	**16**	....	....	....	**1**	**1**	**0**	**1**	**0**	**0**	**0**	**0**	....
	Canada	Olympics	6	2	3	5	2	....	....	....	....	....	....	....	....	....	....	....	....	....	....	....	....	....	....
1998-99 ♦	**Dallas**	**NHL**	**67**	**28**	**27**	**55**	**34**	**8**	**0**	**8**	**157**	**17.8**	**11**	**1170**	**63.2**	**15:33**	**23**	***11**	**10**	**21**	**19**	**3**	**0**	**6**	**18:27**
99-2000	**Dallas**	**NHL**	**48**	**15**	**19**	**34**	**26**	**7**	**0**	**2**	**110**	**13.6**	**–1**	**924**	**59.1**	**16:15**	**23**	**7**	**3**	**10**	**18**	**3**	**0**	**2**	**16:41**
2000-01	**Dallas**	**NHL**	**69**	**29**	**23**	**52**	**30**	**12**	**0**	**4**	**166**	**17.5**	**5**	**1262**	**57.2**	**16:11**	**7**	**4**	**0**	**4**	**4**	**1**	**0**	**1**	**15:50**
2001-02	**Dallas**	**NHL**	**67**	**23**	**24**	**47**	**18**	**6**	**0**	**5**	**157**	**14.6**	**–2**	**1345**	**59.6**	**16:59**	....	....	....	....	....	....	....	....	....
	Canada	Olympics	6	1	1	2	0	....	....	....	....	....	....	....	....	....	....	....	....	....	....	....	....	....	....
	New Jersey	**NHL**	**14**	**2**	**9**	**11**	**4**	**0**	**0**	**1**	**32**	**6.3**	**2**	**275**	**55.3**	**16:22**	**5**	**0**	**1**	**1**	**0**	**0**	**0**	**0**	**19:22**
2002-03 ♦	**New Jersey**	**NHL**	**80**	**17**	**28**	**45**	**56**	**3**	**0**	**4**	**201**	**8.5**	**10**	**1383**	**58.5**	**16:45**	**17**	**3**	**6**	**9**	**4**	**1**	**0**	**0**	**15:03**
2003-04	**Toronto**	**NHL**	**64**	**22**	**28**	**50**	**26**	**10**	**1**	**5**	**131**	**16.8**	**7**	**970**	**60.4**	**15:38**	**9**	**6**	**0**	**6**	**4**	**1**	**0**	**2**	**15:24**
2004-05			DID NOT PLAY																						
2005-06	**Florida**	**NHL**	**65**	**26**	**30**	**56**	**46**	**7**	**0**	**3**	**195**	**13.3**	**–2**	**1224**	**59.4**	**16:23**	....	....	....	....	....	....	....	....	....
	NHL Totals		**1242**	**559**	**559**	**1118**	**673**	**213**	**12**	**91**	**3212**	**17.4**		**8553**	**59.4**	**16:16**	**158**	**66**	**50**	**116**	**91**	**23**	**0**	**13**	**16:47**

ECAC Rookie of the Year (1985) • ECAC First All-Star Team (1986, 1987) • NCAA East First All-American Team (1986, 1987) • ECAC Player of the Year (1987) • Calder Memorial Trophy (1988) • NHL All-Rookie Team (1988) • Dodge Ram Tough Award (1988) • King Clancy Memorial Trophy (1995) • Conn Smythe Trophy (1999)

Played in NHL All-Star Game (1988, 1989, 1990, 1994)

Traded to **Dallas** by **Calgary** for Corey Millen and Jarome Iginla, December 19, 1995. Traded to **New Jersey** by **Dallas** with Jamie Langenbrunner for Jason Arnott, Randy McKay and New Jersey's 1st round choice (later traded to Columbus – later traded to Buffalo – Buffalo selected Dan Paille) in 2002 Entry Draft, March 19, 2002. Signed as a free agent by **Toronto**, September 9, 2003. Signed as a free agent by **Florida**, August 1, 2005.

NIINIMAA, Janne

(nihn-EE-mah, YAH-nee) **DAL.**

Defense. Shoots left. 6'1", 220 lbs. Born, Raahe, Finland, May 22, 1975. Philadelphia's 1st choice, 36th overall, in 1993 Entry Draft.

Season	Club	League	GP	G	A	Pts	PIM	PP	SH	GW	S	%	+/-	TF	F%	Min	GP	G	A	Pts	PIM	PP	SH	GW	Min
1990-91	Karpat Oulu Jr.	Fin-Jr.	7	1	1	2	4	....	....	....	....	....	....	....	....	....	....	....	....	....	....	....	....	....	....
1991-92	Karpat Oulu Jr.	Fin-Jr.	3	0	0	0	4	....	....	....	....	....	....	....	....	....	....	....	....	....	....	....	....	....	....
	Karpat Oulu	Finland-2	41	2	11	13	49	....	....	....	....	....	....	....	....	....	4	0	0	0	0	....	....	....	....
1992-93	Karpat Oulu U18	Fin-U18	....	....	....	....	....	....	....	....	....	....	....	....	....	....	6	2	5	7	6	....	....	....	....
	Karpat Oulu Jr.	Fin-Jr.	10	3	9	12	16	....	....	....	....	....	....	....	....	....	....	....	....	....	....	....	....	....	....
	Karpat Oulu	Finland-2	29	2	3	5	14	....	....	....	....	....	....	....	....	....	....	....	....	....	....	....	....	....	....
	KKP Kiiminki	Finland-3	1	0	2	2	2	....	....	....	....	....	....	....	....	....	....	....	....	....	....	....	....	....	....
1993-94	Jokerit Helsinki Jr.	Fin-Jr.	10	2	6	8	41	....	....	....	....	....	....	....	....	....	....	....	....	....	....	....	....	....	....
	Jokerit Helsinki	Finland	45	3	8	11	24	....	....	....	....	....	....	....	....	....	12	1	1	2	4	....	....	....	....
1994-95	Jokerit Helsinki Jr.	Fin-Jr.	6	6	3	9	39	....	....	....	....	....	....	....	....	....	....	....	....	....	....	....	....	....	....
	Jokerit Helsinki	Finland	42	7	10	17	36	....	....	....	....	....	....	....	....	....	10	1	4	5	35	....	....	....	....
1995-96	Jokerit Helsinki Jr.	Fin-Jr.	....	....	....	....	....	....	....	....	....	....	....	....	....	....	2	3	4	7	6	....	....	....	....
	Jokerit Helsinki	Finland	49	5	15	20	79	....	....	....	....	....	....	....	....	....	11	0	2	2	12	....	....	....	....
1996-97	**Philadelphia**	**NHL**	**77**	**4**	**40**	**44**	**58**	**1**	**0**	**2**	**141**	**2.8**	**12**	....	....	....	**19**	**1**	**12**	**13**	**16**	**1**	**0**	**1**	....
1997-98	**Philadelphia**	**NHL**	**66**	**3**	**31**	**34**	**56**	**2**	**0**	**1**	**115**	**2.6**	**6**	....	....	....	....	....	....	....	....	....	....	....	....
	Edmonton	**NHL**	**11**	**1**	**8**	**9**	**6**	**1**	**0**	**0**	**19**	**5.3**	**7**	....	....	....	**11**	**1**	**1**	**2**	**12**	**0**	**0**	**1**	....
	Finland	Olympics	6	0	3	3	8	....	....	....	....	....	....	....	....	....	....	....	....	....	....	....	....	....	....
1998-99	**Edmonton**	**NHL**	**81**	**4**	**24**	**28**	**88**	**2**	**0**	**1**	**142**	**2.8**	**7**	**1**	**0.0**	**23:54**	**4**	**0**	**0**	**0**	**2**	**0**	**0**	**0**	**28:16**
99-2000	**Edmonton**	**NHL**	**81**	**8**	**25**	**33**	**89**	**2**	**2**	**0**	**133**	**6.0**	**14**	**0**	**0.0**	**24:28**	**5**	**0**	**2**	**2**	**2**	**0**	**0**	**0**	**21:39**
2000-01	**Edmonton**	**NHL**	**82**	**12**	**34**	**46**	**90**	**8**	**0**	**1**	**122**	**9.8**	**6**	**0**	**0.0**	**25:20**	**6**	**0**	**2**	**2**	**6**	**0**	**0**	**0**	**28:33**
2001-02	**Edmonton**	**NHL**	**81**	**5**	**39**	**44**	**80**	**1**	**0**	**2**	**119**	**4.2**	**13**	**0**	**0.0**	**26:02**	....	....	....	....	....	....	....	....	....
	Finland	Olympics	4	0	3	3	2	....	....	....	....	....	....	....	....	....	....	....	....	....	....	....	....	....	....
2002-03	**Edmonton**	**NHL**	**63**	**4**	**24**	**28**	**66**	**2**	**0**	**0**	**90**	**4.4**	**–7**	**1**	**0.0**	**26:48**	....	....	....	....	....	....	....	....	....
	NY Islanders	**NHL**	**13**	**1**	**5**	**6**	**14**	**1**	**0**	**0**	**11**	**9.1**	**–2**	**0**	**0.0**	**23:02**	**5**	**0**	**1**	**1**	**12**	**0**	**0**	**0**	**23:32**
2003-04	**NY Islanders**	**NHL**	**82**	**9**	**19**	**28**	**64**	**4**	**0**	**2**	**97**	**9.3**	**12**	**0**	**0.0**	**23:15**	**5**	**1**	**2**	**3**	**2**	**1**	**0**	**1**	**24:31**
2004-05	Malmo	Sweden	10	0	3	3	34	....	....	....	....	....	....	....	....	....	....	....	....	....	....	....	....	....	....
	Karpat Oulu	Finland	26	3	10	13	30	....	....	....	....	....	....	....	....	....	12	0	5	5	8	....	....	....	....

Season	Club	League	GP	G	A	Pts	PIM	PP	SH	GW	S	%	+/-	TF	F%	Min	GP	G	A	Pts	PIM	PP	SH	GW	Min
								Regular Season									**Playoffs**								
2005-06	NY Islanders	NHL	41	1	9	10	62	0	0	0	23	4.3	-7	1	0.0	20:30									
	Dallas	NHL	22	2	4	6	24	1	1	1	26	7.7	-5	0	0.0	18:25	4	0	1	1	8	0	0	0	14:07
	NHL Totals		700	54	262	316	697	25	3	10	1038	5.2		3	0.0	24:15	59	3	21	24	60	2	0	3	23:46

NHL All-Rookie Team (1997)
Played in NHL All-Star Game (2001)

Traded to **Edmonton** by **Philadelphia** for Dan McGillis and Edmonton's 2nd round choice (Jason Beckett) in 1998 Entry Draft, March 24, 1998. Traded to **NY Islanders** by **Edmonton** with Washington's 2nd round choice (previously acquired, NY Islanders selected Evgeni Tunik) in 2003 Entry Draft for Brad Isbister and Raffi Torres, March 11, 2003. Signed as a free agent by **Oulu** (Finland), October 6, 2004. Signed as a free agent by **Malmo** (Sweden), November 17, 2004. Signed as a free agent by **Oulu** (Finland), January 3, 2005. Traded to **Dallas** by **NY Islanders** with NY Islanders' 5th round choice in 2007 Entry Draft for John Erskine and Dallas' 2nd round choice (Jesse Joensuu) in 2006 Entry Draft, January 10, 2005.

NILSON, Marcus
(NIHL-suhn, MAHR-kuhs)   **CGY.**

Left wing. Shoots right. 6'2", 195 lbs.   Born, Balsta, Sweden, March 1, 1978. Florida's 1st choice, 20th overall, in 1996 Entry Draft.

Season	Club	League	GP	G	A	Pts	PIM	PP	SH	GW	S	%	+/-	TF	F%	Min	GP	G	A	Pts	PIM	PP	SH	GW	Min
1994-95	Djurgarden Jr.	Swe-Jr.	24	7	8	15	22																		
1995-96	Djurgarden Jr.	Swe-Jr.	25	19	17	36	46										2	1	1	2	12				
	Djurgarden	Sweden	12	0	0	0	0										1	0	0	0	0				
1996-97	Djurgarden	Sweden	37	0	3	3	33										4	0	0	0	0				
1997-98	Djurgarden	Sweden	41	4	7	11	18										15	2	1	3	16				
1998-99	**Florida**	**NHL**	8	1	1	2	5	0	0	1	7	14.3	2	6	50.0	12:24									
	New Haven	AHL	69	8	25	33	10																		
99-2000	**Florida**	**NHL**	9	0	2	2	2	0	0	0	6	0.0	2	14	64.3	7:56									
	Louisville Panthers	AHL	64	9	23	32	52										4	0	0	0	0				
2000-01	**Florida**	**NHL**	78	12	24	36	74	0	0	2	141	8.5	-3	169	40.8	15:46									
2001-02	**Florida**	**NHL**	81	14	19	33	55	6	1	2	147	9.5	-14	539	43.8	16:31									
2002-03	**Florida**	**NHL**	82	15	19	34	31	7	1	0	187	8.0	-2	469	46.7	15:31									
2003-04	**Florida**	**NHL**	69	6	13	19	26	1	1	1	110	5.5	-9	151	44.4	15:30									
	Calgary	**NHL**	14	5	0	5	14	1	0	2	23	21.7	3	173	45.1	16:43	26	4	7	11	12	0	0	1	19:25
2004-05	Djurgarden	Sweden	48	17	22	39	110										7	1	2	3	10				
2005-06	**Calgary**	**NHL**	70	6	11	17	32	2	0	2	83	7.2	13	392	45.4	14:50									
	NHL Totals		411	59	89	148	239	17	3	10	704	8.4		1913	44.9	15:28	26	4	7	11	12	0	0	1	19:25

Traded to **Calgary** by **Florida** for Calgary's 2nd round choice (David Booth) in 2004 Entry Draft, March 8, 2004. Signed as a free agent by **Djurgarden** (Sweden), September 16, 2004.

NILSSON, Robert
(NIHL-suhn, RAW-buhrt)   **NYI**

Center. Shoots left. 5'11", 176 lbs.   Born, Calgary, Alta., January 10, 1985. NY Islanders' 1st choice, 15th overall, in 2003 Entry Draft.

Season	Club	League	GP	G	A	Pts	PIM	PP	SH	GW	S	%	+/-	TF	F%	Min	GP	G	A	Pts	PIM	PP	SH	GW	Min
2000-01	Leksands IF Jr.	Swe-Jr.	23	14	28	42	26										2	0	0	0	2				
	Leksands IF U18	Swe-U18	4	6	3	9	6										2	0	2	2	2				
2001-02	Leksands IF Jr.	Swe-Jr.	21	13	18	31	24										5	0	5	5	8				
	Leksands IF	Sweden-2	14	1	4	5	8																		
2002-03	Leksands IF	Sweden	41	8	13	21	10										5	0	1	1	2				
	Leksands IF Jr.	Swe-Jr.															2	1	1	2	2				
2003-04	Leksands IF Jr.	Swe-Jr.	4	2	8	10	4																		
	Leksands IF	Sweden	34	2	4	6	6																		
	Fribourg	Swiss	7	1	3	4	2										4	1	0	1	2				
2004-05	Almtuna	Sweden-2	3	0	1	1	2																		
	Hammarby	Sweden-2	7	0	4	4	4																		
	Djurgarden Jr.	Swe-Jr.	8	8	4	12	12																		
	Djurgarden	Sweden	23	2	4	6	6										3	0	0	0	0				
2005-06	**NY Islanders**	**NHL**	53	6	14	20	26	1	0	1	70	8.6	-6	31	29.0	11:52									
	Bridgeport	AHL	29	8	20	28	12										7	1	4	5	0				
	NHL Totals		53	6	14	20	26	1	0	1	70	8.6		31	29.0	11:52									

NOKELAINEN, Petteri
(noh-kuh-LAY-nehn, PEH-tuh-ree)   **NYI**

Center. Shoots right. 6'1", 187 lbs.   Born, Imatra, Finland, January 16, 1986. NY Islanders' 1st choice, 16th overall, in 2004 Entry Draft.

Season	Club	League	GP	G	A	Pts	PIM	PP	SH	GW	S	%	+/-	TF	F%	Min	GP	G	A	Pts	PIM	PP	SH	GW	Min
2001-02	SaiPa U18	Fin-U18	6	2	1	3	14																		
2002-03	SaiPa U18	Fin-U18	10	3	8	11	18																		
	SaiPa Jr.	Fin-Jr.	28	7	4	11	28										3	1	0	1	4				
	SaiPa	Finland	2	1	0	1	2																		
2003-04	Suomi U20	Finland-2	3	0	1	1	0																		
	SaiPa Jr.	Fin-Jr.	10	5	3	8	4																		
	SaiPa	Finland	40	4	4	8	16										4	0	1	1	0				
2004-05	SaiPa	Finland	52	15	5	20	34																		
2005-06	**NY Islanders**	**NHL**	15	1	1	2	4	0	0	1	13	7.7	-1	82	48.8	7:47									
	NHL Totals		15	1	1	2	4	0	0	1	13	7.7		82	48.8	7:47									

• Missed majority of 2005-06 season recovering from knee injury suffered in game vs. Pittsburgh, November 3, 2005.

NORDGREN, Niklas
(NORHD-grehn, NIHK-las)   **PIT.**

Left wing. Shoots right. 5'11", 185 lbs.   Born, Ornskoldsvik, Sweden, June 28, 1979. Carolina's 7th choice, 195th overall, in 1997 Entry Draft.

Season	Club	League	GP	G	A	Pts	PIM	PP	SH	GW	S	%	+/-	TF	F%	Min	GP	G	A	Pts	PIM	PP	SH	GW	Min
1996-97	MoDo	Sweden	5	0	0	0	0																		
1997-98	MoDo Jr.	Swe-Jr.	22	14	6	20																			
	Malmo Jr.	Swe-Jr.	28	15	15	30	52																		
1998-99	MoDo	Sweden	7	0	0	0	2																		
	Malmo Jr.	Swe-Jr.	22	7	4	11	22										3	2	1	3	0				
99-2000	Sundsvall	Sweden-2	27	21	11	32	58																		
	MoDo	EuroHL	1	0	0	0	0										1	0	0	0	0				
2000-01	Sundsvall	Sweden-2	35	22	19	41	45																		
2001-02	Timra IK Jr.	Swe-Jr.	1	1	1	2	0																		
	Timra IK	Sweden	49	8	6	14	16																		
	Timra IK	Sweden-Q	10	3	3	5	4																		
2002-03	Timra IK	Sweden	47	20	23	43	40										10	1	4	5	4				
2003-04	Timra IK	Sweden	46	13	15	28	44										10	4	1	5	32				
2004-05	Timra IK	Sweden	46	19	17	36	71										7	0	2	2	6				
2005-06	**Carolina**	**NHL**	43	4	2	6	30	0	0	0	32	12.5	-4	4	25.0	7:28									
	Lowell	AHL	8	6	4	10	10																		
	Pittsburgh	**NHL**	15	0	0	0	4	0	0	0	6	0.0	-4	1	0.0	5:59									
	NHL Totals		58	4	2	6	34	0	0	0	38	10.5		5	20.0	7:05									

Traded to **Pittsburgh** by **Carolina** with Krys Kolanos and Carolina's 2nd round choice (later traded to San Jose) in 2007 Entry Draft for Mark Recchi, March 9, 2006.

NORSTROM, Mattias
(NOHR-struhm, MAT-tee-ahs)   **L.A.**

Defense. Shoots left. 6'2", 210 lbs.   Born, Stockholm, Sweden, January 2, 1972. NY Rangers' 2nd choice, 48th overall, in 1992 Entry Draft.

Season	Club	League	GP	G	A	Pts	PIM	PP	SH	GW	S	%	+/-	TF	F%	Min	GP	G	A	Pts	PIM	PP	SH	GW	Min
1990-91	Mora IK	Sweden-2	1	1	1	2	6										1	0	0	0	2				
1991-92	AIK Solna	Sweden	39	4	3	7	28										3	0	2	2	2				
1992-93	AIK Solna	Sweden	22	0	1	1	16																		
1993-94	**NY Rangers**	**NHL**	9	0	2	2	6	0	0	0	3	0.0	0												
	Binghamton	AHL	55	1	9	10	70																		
1994-95	Binghamton	AHL	63	9	10	19	91																		
	NY Rangers	**NHL**	9	0	3	3	2	0	0	0	4	0.0	2				3	0	0	0	0				
1995-96	**NY Rangers**	**NHL**	25	2	1	3	22	0	0	0	17	11.8	5												
	Los Angeles	**NHL**	11	0	1	1	18	0	0	0	17	0.0	-8												
1996-97	**Los Angeles**	**NHL**	80	1	21	22	84	0	0	0	106	0.9	-4												
1997-98	**Los Angeles**	**NHL**	73	1	12	13	90	0	0	0	61	1.6	14				4	0	0	0	4				
	Sweden	Olympics	4	0	1	1	2																		
1998-99	**Los Angeles**	**NHL**	78	2	5	7	36	0	0	0	61	3.3	-10	1	0.0	20:20									
99-2000	**Los Angeles**	**NHL**	82	1	13	14	66	0	0	0	62	1.6	22	0	0.0	21:49	4	0	0	0	6			0	21:35
2000-01	**Los Angeles**	**NHL**	82	0	18	18	60	0	0	0	59	0.0	10	0	0.0	21:50	13	0	2	2	18	0	0	0	23:16

			Regular Season														Playoffs								
Season	Club	League	GP	G	A	Pts	PIM	PP	SH	GW	S	%	+/-	TF	F%	Min	GP	G	A	Pts	PIM	PP	SH	GW	Min
2001-02	**Los Angeles**	**NHL**	**79**	**2**	**9**	**11**	**38**	**0**	**0**	**0**	**42**	**4.8**	**−2**	**0**	**0.0**	**23:01**	**7**	**0**	**0**	**0**	**4**	**0**	**0**	**0**	**23:24**
	Sweden	Olympics	4	0	0	0	0																		
2002-03	**Los Angeles**	**NHL**	**82**	**0**	**6**	**6**	**49**	**0**	**0**	**0**	**63**	**0.0**	**0**	**1**	**100.0**	**21:30**									
2003-04	**Los Angeles**	**NHL**	**74**	**1**	**13**	**14**	**44**	**0**	**0**	**0**	**65**	**1.5**	**−3**	**1**	**100.0**	**22:26**									
2004-05	AIK Solna	Sweden-3	8	1	0	1	4																		
2005-06	**Los Angeles**	**NHL**	**77**	**4**	**23**	**27**	**58**	**2**	**1**	**1**	**83**	**4.8**	**−3**	**0**	**0.0**	**21:07**									
	NHL Totals		**761**	**14**	**127**	**141**	**573**	**2**	**2**	**1**	**643**	**2.2**		**5**	**40.0**	**21:43**	**31**	**0**	**2**	**2**	**30**	**0**	**0**	**0**	**23:02**

Played in NHL All-Star Game (1999, 2004)

Traded to **Los Angeles** by **NY Rangers** with Ray Ferraro, Ian Laperriere, Nathan Lafayette and NY Rangers' 4th round choice (Sean Blanchard) in 1997 Entry Draft for Marty McSorley, Jari Kurri and Shane Churla, March 14, 1996. Signed as a free agent by **Solna** (Sweden-3), January 11, 2005.

NORTON, Brad

(NOHR-tuhn, BRAD) **DET.**

Defense. Shoots left. 6'4", 235 lbs. Born, Cambridge, MA, February 13, 1975. Edmonton's 9th choice, 215th overall, in 1993 Entry Draft.

1992-93	Cushing	High-MA	31	10	26	36	....																		
1993-94	Cushing	High-MA	STATISTICS NOT AVAILABLE																						
1994-95	U. Mass-Amherst	H-East	30	0	6	6	89																		
1995-96	U. Mass-Amherst	H-East	34	4	12	16	99																		
1996-97	U. Mass-Amherst	H-East	35	2	16	18	88																		
1997-98	U. Mass-Amherst	H-East	20	2	13	15	28																		
	Detroit Vipers	IHL	33	1	4	5	56										22	0	2	2	87				
1998-99	Hamilton	AHL	58	1	8	9	134										11	0	1	1	6				
99-2000	Hamilton	AHL	40	5	12	17	104										10	1	4	5	26				
2000-01	Hamilton	AHL	46	3	15	18	114																		
2001-02	**Florida**	**NHL**	**22**	**0**	**2**	**2**	**45**	**0**	**0**	**0**	**6**	**0.0**	**−2**	**1**	**0.0**	**9:15**									
	Hershey Bears	AHL	40	0	10	10	62										2	0	0	0	6				
2002-03	**Los Angeles**	**NHL**	**53**	**3**	**3**	**6**	**97**	**0**	**0**	**0**	**19**	**15.8**	**1**	**2**	**0.0**	**6:04**									
2003-04	**Los Angeles**	**NHL**	**20**	**0**	**1**	**1**	**77**	**0**	**0**	**0**	**10**	**0.0**	**−1**	**0**	**0.0**	**8:34**									
	Washington	**NHL**	**16**	**0**	**1**	**1**	**17**	**0**	**0**	**0**	**6**	**0.0**	**−4**	**0**	**0.0**	**12:50**									
2004-05			DID NOT PLAY																						
2005-06	Jokerit Helsinki	Finland	20	2	2	4	91																		
	Ottawa	**NHL**	**7**	**0**	**0**	**0**	**31**	**0**	**0**	**0**	**3**	**0.0**	**1**	**0**	**0.0**	**10:10**									
	Binghamton	AHL	36	0	4	4	102																		
	NHL Totals		**118**	**3**	**7**	**10**	**267**	**0**	**0**	**0**	**44**	**6.8**		**3**	**0.0**	**8:15**									

Signed as a free agent by **Florida**, July 27, 2001. Signed as a free agent by **Los Angeles**, October, 8, 2002. Claimed on waivers by **Washington** from **Los Angeles**, March 4, 2004. • Missed majority of 2003-04 season recovering from arm injury suffered in pre-season game vs. Phoenix, September 20, 2003. Signed as a free agent by **Jokerit Helsinki** (Finland), October 11, 2005. Signed as a free agent by **Ottawa**, March 8, 2006. Signed as a free agent by **Detroit**, July 24, 2006.

NOVAK, Filip

(NOH-vak, FIH-lihp) **CBJ**

Defense. Shoots left. 6'1", 198 lbs. Born, Ceske Budejovice, Czech., May 7, 1982. NY Rangers' 1st choice, 64th overall, in 2000 Entry Draft.

1998-99	C. Budejovice Jr.	CzRep-Jr.	68	8	10	18	34																		
99-2000	Regina Pats	WHL	47	7	32	39	70										7	1	4	5	5				
2000-01	Regina Pats	WHL	64	17	50	67	75										6	1	4	5	6				
2001-02	Regina Pats	WHL	60	12	46	58	125										6	2	2	4	19				
2002-03	San Antonio	AHL	57	10	17	27	79										1	0	0	0	0				
2003-04			DID NOT PLAY – INJURED																						
2004-05	San Antonio	AHL	71	1	12	13	84																		
2005-06	**Ottawa**	**NHL**	**11**	**0**	**0**	**0**	**4**	**0**	**0**	**0**	**5**	**0.0**	**−2**	**0**	**0.0**	**9:26**									
	Binghamton	AHL	64	8	44	52	58																		
	NHL Totals		**11**	**0**	**0**	**0**	**4**	**0**	**0**	**0**	**5**	**0.0**		**0**	**0.0**	**9:26**									

WHL East Second All-Star Team (2001) • WHL East First All-Star Team (2002) • AHL All-Rookie Team (2003)

Traded to **Florida** by **NY Rangers** with Igor Ulanov, NY Rangers' 1st (later traded to Calgary – Calgary selected Eric Nystrom) and 2nd (Rob Globke) round choices in 2002 Entry Draft and NY Rangers' 4th round choice (later traded to Atlanta – Atlanta selected Guillaume Desbiens) in 2003 Entry Draft for Pavel Bure and Florida's 2nd round choice (Lee Falardeau) in 2002 Entry Draft, March 18, 2002. • Missed entire 2003-04 season recovering from ankle injury suffered in training camp, September 17, 2003. Traded to **Ottawa** by **Florida** for a 6th round choice in 2007 Entry Draft, October 5, 2005. Signed as a free agent by **Columbus**, August 13, 2006.

NOVOTNY, Jiri

(NOH-vaht-nee, YOO-ree) **BUF.**

Center. Shoots right. 6'2", 204 lbs. Born, Pelhrimov, Czech., August 12, 1983. Buffalo's 1st choice, 22nd overall, in 2001 Entry Draft.

99-2000	C. Budejovice Jr.	CzRep-Jr.	36	11	10	21	6																		
	C. Budejovice U17	CzR-U17	11	5	7	12	4																		
	HC Slezan Opava	CzRep-2	17	2	2	4	6																		
2000-01	C. Budejovice Jr.	CzRep-Jr.	33	10	10	20	....																		
	Havl. Brod	CzRep-3	1	0	0	0	0																		
2001-02	C. Budejovice Jr.	CzRep-Jr.	7	4	4	8	4																		
	Jind. Hradec	CzRep-3	3	1	3	4	0																		
	C. Budejovice	CzRep	41	8	6	14	6																		
2002-03	Rochester	AHL	43	2	9	11	14										3	0	1	1	10				
2003-04	Rochester	AHL	48	1	14	15	16										13	0	1	1	10				
2004-05	Rochester	AHL	61	5	20	25	36										9	2	2	4	4				
2005-06	**Buffalo**	**NHL**	**14**	**2**	**1**	**3**	**0**	**0**	**1**	**0**	**15**	**13.3**	**−5**	**139**	**45.3**	**12:15**	**4**	**0**	**0**	**0**	**0**	**0**	**0**	**0**	**10:27**
	Rochester	AHL	66	17	37	54	40																		
	NHL Totals		**14**	**2**	**1**	**3**	**0**	**0**	**1**	**0**	**15**	**13.3**		**139**	**45.3**	**12:15**	**4**	**0**	**0**	**0**	**0**	**0**	**0**	**0**	**10:27**

NUMMELIN, Petteri

(NOO-muh-lihn, PEH-tuh-ree) **MIN.**

Defense. Shoots left. 5'10", 187 lbs. Born, Turku, Finland, November 25, 1972. Columbus' 3rd choice, 133rd overall, in 2000 Entry Draft.

1988-89	TPS Turku U18	Fin-U18	9	4	10	14	12																		
	TPS Turku Jr.	Fin-Jr.	11	2	3	5	2																		
1989-90	TPS Turku Jr.	Fin-Jr.	33	6	14	20	45																		
1990-91	TPS Turku Jr.	Fin-Jr.	35	20	16	36	28																		
	Kiekko-67 Turku	Finland-2	2	0	2	2	4																		
1991-92	Kiekko-67 Jr.	Fin-Jr.	13	16	15	31	28																		
	Kiekko-67 Turku	Finland-2	41	12	24	36	36																		
1992-93	TPS Turku Jr.	Fin-Jr.	1	1	0	1	0																		
	TPS Turku	Finland	3	0	0	0	8																		
	Kiekko-67 Turku	Finland-2	28	14	15	29	18																		
	Reipas Lahti	Finland	14	3	4	7	18																		
	Reipas Lahti	Finland-Q	6	2	4	6	2																		
1993-94	TPS Turku	Finland	44	14	24	38	20										11	0	3	3	4				
1994-95	TPS Turku	Finland	48	10	17	27	32										11	4	3	7	0				
1995-96	V.Frolunda	Sweden	32	7	11	18	26										12	2	7	9	4				
1996-97	V.Frolunda	Sweden	44	20	14	34	39										2	0	1	1	0				
1997-98	HC Davos	Swiss	33	13	17	30	24										17	8	14	22	2				
1998-99	HC Davos	Swiss	44	11	42	53	22										4	0	2	2	2				
99-2000	HC Davos	Swiss	40	15	23	38	20										5	0	3	3	0				
2000-01	**Columbus**	**NHL**	**61**	**4**	**12**	**16**	**10**	**2**	**0**	**0**	**99**	**4.0**	**−11**	**1**	**0.0**	**17:14**									
2001-02	HC Lugano	Swiss	35	4	18	22	6										13	6	9	15	2				
2002-03	HC Lugano	Swiss	43	18	39	57	12										8	3	6	9	2				
2003-04	HC Lugano	Swiss	48	20	39	59	59										16	6	19	25	4				
2004-05	HC Lugano	Swiss	36	13	34	47	18										3	1	0	1	2				
2005-06	HC Lugano	Swiss	38	13	30	43	22										17	9	*20	*29	10				
	Finland	Olympics	8	0	2	2	2																		
	NHL Totals		**61**	**4**	**12**	**16**	**10**	**2**	**0**	**0**	**99**	**4.0**		**1**	**0.0**	**17:14**									

Traded to **Atlanta** by **Columbus** with Chris Nielsen for Tomi Kallio and Pauli Levokari, December 2, 2002. Traded to **Minnesota** by **Atlanta** for Minnesota's 3rd round choice in 2007 Entry Draft, June 14, 2006.

NUMMINEN, Teppo

(NOO-mih-nehn, TEH-poh) **BUF.**

Defense. Shoots right. 6'1", 198 lbs. Born, Tampere, Finland, July 3, 1968. Winnipeg's 2nd choice, 29th overall, in 1986 Entry Draft.

			Regular Season														Playoffs								
Season	Club	League	GP	G	A	Pts	PIM	PP	SH	GW	S	%	+/-	TF	F%	Min	GP	G	A	Pts	PIM	PP	SH	GW	Min
1984-85	Whitby Lawmen	OJHL	16	3	9	12	0																		
1985-86	Tappara Jr.	Fin-Jr.	2	0	0	0	0										3	0	1	1	2				
	Tappara Tampere	Finland	31	2	4	6	6										8	0	0	0	0				
1986-87	Tappara Tampere	Finland	44	9	9	18	16										9	4	1	5	4				
1987-88	Tappara Tampere	Finland	40	10	10	20	29										10	6	6	12	6				
	Finland	Olympics	6	1	4	5	0																		
1988-89	**Winnipeg**	**NHL**	69	1	14	15	36	0	1	0	85	1.2	–11												
1989-90	**Winnipeg**	**NHL**	79	11	32	43	20	1	0	1	105	10.5	–4				7	1	2	3	10	0	0	0	
1990-91	**Winnipeg**	**NHL**	80	8	25	33	28	3	0	0	151	5.3	–15												
1991-92	**Winnipeg**	**NHL**	80	5	34	39	32	4	0	1	143	3.5	15				7	0	0	0	0	0	0	0	
1992-93	**Winnipeg**	**NHL**	66	7	30	37	33	3	1	0	103	6.8	4				6	1	1	2	2	1	0	0	
1993-94	**Winnipeg**	**NHL**	57	5	18	23	28	4	0	1	89	5.6	–23												
1994-95	TuTo Turku	Finland	12	3	8	11	4																		
	Winnipeg	**NHL**	42	5	16	21	16	2	0	0	86	5.8	12												
1995-96	**Winnipeg**	**NHL**	74	11	43	54	22	6	0	3	165	6.7	–4				6	0	0	0	2	0	0	0	
1996-97	**Phoenix**	**NHL**	82	2	25	27	28	0	0	0	135	1.5	–3				7	3	3	6	0	1	0	1	
1997-98	**Phoenix**	**NHL**	82	11	40	51	30	6	0	2	126	8.7	25				1	0	0	0	0	0	0	0	
	Finland	Olympics	6	1	1	2	2																		
1998-99	**Phoenix**	**NHL**	82	10	30	40	30	1	0	0	156	6.4	3	2	0.0	24:26	7	2	1	3	4	2	0	0	26:09
99-2000	**Phoenix**	**NHL**	79	8	34	42	16	2	0	2	126	6.3	21	1	0.0	23:37	5	1	1	2	0	0	0	0	23:11
2000-01	**Phoenix**	**NHL**	72	5	26	31	36	1	0	2	109	4.6	9	0	0.0	24:28									
2001-02	**Phoenix**	**NHL**	76	13	35	48	20	4	0	6	117	11.1	13	0	0.0	23:51	4	0	0	0	2	0	0	0	25:33
	Finland	Olympics	4	0	1	1	0																		
2002-03	**Phoenix**	**NHL**	78	6	24	30	30	2	0	1	108	5.6	0	0	0.0	23:51									
2003-04	**Dallas**	**NHL**	62	3	14	17	18	0	0	0	83	3.6	–5	1	100.0	21:40	4	0	1	1	0	0	0	0	19:12
2004-05		DID NOT PLAY																							
2005-06	**Buffalo**	**NHL**	75	2	38	40	36	0	0	0	60	3.3	6	1	100.0	19:30	12	1	1	2	4	1	0	0	18:45
	Finland	Olympics	8	1	2	3	2																		
	NHL Totals		1235	113	478	591	459	39	2	19	1947	5.8		5	40.0	23:07	66	9	10	19	24	5	0	1	21:58

Played in NHL All-Star Game (1999, 2000, 2001)

Transferred to **Phoenix** after **Winnipeg** franchise relocated, July 1, 1996. Traded to **Dallas** by **Phoenix** for Mike Sillinger, July 22, 2003. Signed as a free agent by **Buffalo**, August 4, 2005.

NYCHOLAT, Lawrence

(NIH-coh-lat, LAW-rehnts) **WSH.**

Defense. Shoots left. 6', 192 lbs. Born, Calgary, Alta., May 7, 1979.

			Regular Season														Playoffs								
Season	Club	League	GP	G	A	Pts	PIM	PP	SH	GW	S	%	+/-	TF	F%	Min	GP	G	A	Pts	PIM	PP	SH	GW	Min
1995-96	Notre Dame	SMHL	42	10	36	46	66																		
1996-97	Swift Current	WHL	67	8	13	21	82										10	0	0	0	24				
1997-98	Swift Current	WHL	71	13	35	48	108										1	0	0	0	0				
1998-99	Swift Current	WHL	72	16	44	60	125										6	2	2	4	12				
99-2000	Swift Current	WHL	70	22	58	80	92										2	0	0	0	0				
2000-01	Jackson Bandits	ECHL	5	1	2	3	5																		
	Cleveland	IHL	42	3	7	10	69										4	0	0	0	2				
2001-02	Houston Aeros	AHL	72	3	11	14	92										14	1	0	1	23				
2002-03	Houston Aeros	AHL	66	11	28	39	155																		
	Hartford	AHL	15	2	9	11	6										2	2	0	2	0				
2003-04	**NY Rangers**	**NHL**	9	0	0	0	6	0	0	0	6	0.0	–2	0	0.0	17:09									
	Hartford	AHL	72	6	26	32	130										16	0	5	5	28				
2004-05	Hartford	AHL	79	5	38	43	132										6	0	3	3	11				
2005-06	Hershey Bears	AHL	73	13	44	57	94										16	2	12	14	12				
	NHL Totals		9	0	0	0	6	0	0	0	6	0.0		0	0.0	17:09									

Signed as a free agent by **Minnesota**, August 31, 2000. Traded to **NY Rangers** by **Minnesota** for Johan Holmqvist, March 11, 2003. Signed as a free agent by **Washington**, August 9, 2005.

NYLANDER, Michael

(NEE-lan-duhr, MIGH-kuhl) **NYR**

Center. Shoots left. 6'1", 193 lbs. Born, Stockholm, Sweden, October 3, 1972. Hartford's 4th choice, 59th overall, in 1991 Entry Draft.

			Regular Season														Playoffs								
Season	Club	League	GP	G	A	Pts	PIM	PP	SH	GW	S	%	+/-	TF	F%	Min	GP	G	A	Pts	PIM	PP	SH	GW	Min
1989-90	Huddinge IK	Sweden-2	31	7	15	22	4										5	3	0	3	0				
1990-91	Huddinge IK	Sweden-2	33	14	20	34	10										2	0	0	0	0				
1991-92	AIK Solna	Sweden	40	11	17	28	30										3	1	4	5	4				
1992-93	**Hartford**	**NHL**	59	11	22	33	36	3	0	1	85	12.9	–7												
	Springfield	AHL															3	3	3	6	2				
1993-94	**Hartford**	**NHL**	58	11	33	44	24	4	0	1	74	14.9	–2												
	Springfield	AHL	4	0	9	9	0																		
	Calgary	**NHL**	15	2	9	11	6	0	0	0	21	9.5	10				3	0	0	0	0	0	0	0	
1994-95	JYP HT Jyvaskyla	Finland	16	11	19	30	63																		
	Calgary	**NHL**	6	0	1	1	2	0	0	0	2	0.0	1				6	0	6	6	2	0	0	0	
1995-96	**Calgary**	**NHL**	73	17	38	55	20	4	0	6	163	10.4	0				4	0	0	0	0	0	0	0	
1996-97	HC Lugano	Swiss	36	12	43	55	28										8	3	8	11	8				
1997-98	**Calgary**	**NHL**	65	13	23	36	24	0	0	2	117	11.1	10												
	Sweden	Olympics	4	0	0	0	6																		
1998-99	**Calgary**	**NHL**	9	2	3	5	2	1	0	0	7	28.6	1	25	60.0	11:10									
	Tampa Bay	**NHL**	24	2	7	9	6	0	0	0	26	7.7	–10	75	44.0	13:29									
99-2000	**Tampa Bay**	**NHL**	11	1	2	3	4	1	0	0	10	10.0	–3	35	57.1	10:32									
	Chicago	**NHL**	66	23	28	51	26	4	0	2	112	20.5	9	561	46.9	16:39									
2000-01	**Chicago**	**NHL**	82	25	39	64	32	4	0	5	176	14.2	7	1036	48.3	18:52									
2001-02	**Chicago**	**NHL**	82	15	46	61	50	6	0	2	158	9.5	28	974	50.2	15:33	5	0	3	3	2	0	0	0	15:20
	Sweden	Olympics	4	1	2	3	0																		
2002-03	**Chicago**	**NHL**	9	0	4	4	4	0	0	0	20	0.0	0	86	48.8	15:19									
	Washington	**NHL**	71	17	39	56	36	7	0	2	141	12.1	3	1005	47.4	18:41	6	3	2	5	8	1	0	1	16:45
2003-04	**Washington**	**NHL**	3	0	2	2	8	0	0	0	1	0.0	1	22	54.6	14:57									
	Boston	**NHL**	15	1	11	12	14	0	0	1	29	3.4	3	128	46.1	15:43	6	3	3	6	0	0	0	0	18:57
2004-05	Karpat Oulu	Finland	23	5	15	20	22																		
	St. Petersburg	Russia	8	2	5	7	0																		
	Ak Bars Kazan	Russia	5	0	1	1	2																		
2005-06	**NY Rangers**	**NHL**	81	23	56	79	76	6	0	4	172	13.4	31	1143	46.5	19:20	4	0	1	1	0	0	0	0	20:33
	NHL Totals		729	163	363	526	370	40	0	26	1314	12.4		5090	48.0	17:09	34	6	15	21	12	1	0	1	17:46

Traded to **Calgary** by **Hartford** with James Patrick and Zarley Zalapski for Gary Suter, Paul Ranheim and Ted Drury, March 10, 1994. • Missed majority of 1994-95 season recovering from wrist injury suffered in game vs. St. Louis, January 24, 1995. Traded to **Tampa Bay** by **Calgary** for Andrei Nazarov, January 19, 1999. Traded to **Chicago** by **Tampa Bay** for Bryan Muir and Reid Simpson, November 12, 1999. Traded to **Washington** by **Chicago** with Chicago's 3rd round choice (Stephen Werner) in 2003 Entry Draft and future considerations for Chris Simon and Andrei Nikolishin, November 1, 2002. • Missed majority of 2003-04 season recovering from leg injury suffered in practice, October 2, 2003. Traded to **Boston** by **Washington** for Boston's 4th round compensatory choice (Patrick McNeill) in 2005 Entry Draft and Boston's 2nd round choice (Francois Bouchard) in 2006 Entry Draft, March 4, 2004. Signed as a free agent by **NY Rangers**, August 10, 2004. Signed as a free agent by **Oulu** (Finland), September 25, 2004. Signed as a free agent by **St. Petersburg** (Russia), December 20, 2004. Signed as a free agent by **Kazan** (Russia), February 14, 2005.

NYSTROM, Eric

(NIGH-stuhm, AIR-ihk) **CGY.**

Left wing. Shoots left. 6'1", 205 lbs. Born, Syosset, NY, February 14, 1983. Calgary's 1st choice, 10th overall, in 2002 Entry Draft.

			Regular Season														Playoffs								
Season	Club	League	GP	G	A	Pts	PIM	PP	SH	GW	S	%	+/-	TF	F%	Min	GP	G	A	Pts	PIM	PP	SH	GW	Min
99-2000	USNTDP	NAHL	55	7	16	23	57										3	0	0	0	0				
2000-01	USNTDP	U-18	43	10	12	22	52																		
	USNTDP	USHL	23	5	5	10	50																		
2001-02	U. of Michigan	CCHA	40	18	13	31	42																		
2002-03	U. of Michigan	CCHA	39	15	11	26	24																		
2003-04	U. of Michigan	CCHA	43	10	12	22	50																		
2004-05	U. of Michigan	CCHA	38	13	19	32	33																		
2005-06	**Calgary**	**NHL**	2	0	0	0	0	0	0	0	0	0.0	–1	5	60.0	12:01									
	Omaha	AHL	78	15	18	33	37																		
	NHL Totals		2	0	0	0	0	0	0	0	0	0.0		5	60.0	12:00									

CCHA All-Rookie Team (2002)

O'BRIEN, Doug

(oh-BRIGH-uhn, DUHG) **T.B.**

Defense. Shoots left. 6'1", 200 lbs. Born, St. John's, Nfld., February 16, 1984. Tampa Bay's 4th choice, 192nd overall, in 2003 Entry Draft.

			Regular Season														Playoffs								
Season	Club	League	GP	G	A	Pts	PIM	PP	SH	GW	S	%	+/-	TF	F%	Min	GP	G	A	Pts	PIM	PP	SH	GW	Min
2000-01	Hull Olympiques	QMJHL	47	1	6	7	16	....	....	....	....	....	....	....	....	....	5	0	1	1	0	....	....	....	....
2001-02	Hull Olympiques	QMJHL	46	1	5	6	36	....	....	....	....	....	....	....	....	....	12	0	0	0	14	....	....	....	....
2002-03	Hull Olympiques	QMJHL	71	10	34	44	102	....	....	....	....	....	....	....	....	....	19	3	12	15	18	....	....	....	....
2003-04	Gatineau	QMJHL	66	17	46	63	146	....	....	....	....	....	....	....	....	....	15	1	8	9	16	....	....	....	....
2004-05	Springfield	AHL	74	4	13	17	76	....	....	....	....	....	....	....	....	....	....	....	....	....	....	....	....	....	....
	Johnstown Chiefs	ECHL	3	0	0	0	2	....	....	....	....	....	....	....	....	....	....	....	....	....	....	....	....	....	....
2005-06	**Tampa Bay**	**NHL**	**5**	**0**	**0**	**0**	**2**	**0**	**0**	**0**	**2**	**0.0**	**0**	**0**	**0.0**	**7:44**	....	....	....	....	....	....	....	....	....
	Springfield	AHL	74	7	25	32	70	....	....	....	....	....	....	....	....	....	....	....	....	....	....	....	....	....	....
	NHL Totals		**5**	**0**	**0**	**0**	**2**	**0**	**0**	**0**	**2**	**0.0**		**0**	**0.0**	**7:44**	....	....	....	....	....	....	....	....	....

QMJHL First All-Star Team (2004) • Memorial Cup Tournament All-Star Team (2003, 2004) • Ed Chynoweth Trophy (Memorial Cup Tournament Leading Scorer) (2004)

ODELEIN, Lyle

(OH-duh-LIGHN, LIGHL)

Defense. Shoots right. 6', 210 lbs. Born, Quill Lake, Sask., July 21, 1968. Montreal's 8th choice, 141st overall, in 1986 Entry Draft.

Season	Club	League	GP	G	A	Pts	PIM	PP	SH	GW	S	%	+/-	TF	F%	Min	GP	G	A	Pts	PIM	PP	SH	GW	Min
1984-85	Reg. Pat Cdns.	SMHL	26	12	13	25	30	....	....	....	....	....	....	....	....	....	....	....	....	....	....	....	....	....	....
1985-86	Moose Jaw	WHL	67	9	37	46	117	....	....	....	....	....	....	....	....	....	13	1	6	7	34	....	....	....	....
1986-87	Moose Jaw	WHL	59	9	50	59	70	....	....	....	....	....	....	....	....	....	9	2	5	7	26	....	....	....	....
1987-88	Moose Jaw	WHL	63	15	43	58	166	....	....	....	....	....	....	....	....	....	....	....	....	....	....	....	....	....	....
1988-89	Sherbrooke	AHL	33	3	4	7	120	....	....	....	....	....	....	....	....	....	3	0	2	2	5	....	....	....	....
	Peoria Rivermen	IHL	36	2	8	10	116	....	....	....	....	....	....	....	....	....	....	....	....	....	....	....	....	....	....
1989-90	**Montreal**	**NHL**	**8**	**0**	**2**	**2**	**33**	**0**	**0**	**0**	**1**	**0.0**	**-1**	....	....	....	....	....	....	....	....	....	....	....	....
	Sherbrooke	AHL	68	7	24	31	265	....	....	....	....	....	....	....	....	....	12	6	5	11	79	....	....	....	....
1990-91	**Montreal**	**NHL**	**52**	**0**	**2**	**2**	**259**	**0**	**0**	**0**	**25**	**0.0**	**7**	....	....	....	**12**	**0**	**0**	**0**	**54**	**0**	**0**	**0**	....
1991-92	**Montreal**	**NHL**	**71**	**1**	**7**	**8**	**212**	**0**	**0**	**0**	**43**	**2.3**	**15**	....	....	....	**7**	**0**	**0**	**0**	**11**	**0**	**0**	**0**	....
1992-93 ♦	**Montreal**	**NHL**	**83**	**2**	**14**	**16**	**205**	**0**	**0**	**0**	**79**	**2.5**	**35**	....	....	....	**20**	**1**	**5**	**6**	**30**	**0**	**0**	**0**	....
1993-94	**Montreal**	**NHL**	**79**	**11**	**29**	**40**	**276**	**6**	**0**	**2**	**116**	**9.5**	**8**	....	....	....	**7**	**0**	**0**	**0**	**17**	**0**	**0**	**0**	....
1994-95	**Montreal**	**NHL**	**48**	**3**	**7**	**10**	**152**	**0**	**0**	**0**	**74**	**4.1**	**-13**	....	....	....	....	....	....	....	....	....	....	....	....
1995-96	**Montreal**	**NHL**	**79**	**3**	**14**	**17**	**230**	**0**	**1**	**0**	**74**	**4.1**	**8**	....	....	....	**6**	**1**	**1**	**2**	**6**	**0**	**1**	**0**	....
1996-97	**New Jersey**	**NHL**	**79**	**3**	**13**	**16**	**110**	**1**	**0**	**2**	**93**	**3.2**	**16**	....	....	....	**10**	**2**	**2**	**4**	**19**	**1**	**0**	**0**	....
1997-98	**New Jersey**	**NHL**	**79**	**4**	**19**	**23**	**171**	**1**	**0**	**0**	**76**	**5.3**	**11**	....	....	....	**6**	**1**	**1**	**2**	**21**	**1**	**0**	**1**	....
1998-99	**New Jersey**	**NHL**	**70**	**5**	**26**	**31**	**114**	**1**	**0**	**0**	**101**	**5.0**	**6**	**0**	**0.0**	**19:53**	**7**	**0**	**3**	**3**	**10**	**0**	**0**	**0**	**18:28**
99-2000	**New Jersey**	**NHL**	**57**	**1**	**15**	**16**	**104**	**0**	**0**	**1**	**59**	**1.7**	**-10**	**0**	**0.0**	**16:42**	....	....	....	....	....	....	....	....	....
	Phoenix	**NHL**	**16**	**1**	**7**	**8**	**19**	**1**	**0**	**0**	**30**	**3.3**	**1**	**0**	**0.0**	**21:45**	**5**	**0**	**0**	**0**	**16**	**0**	**0**	**0**	**16:38**
2000-01	**Columbus**	**NHL**	**81**	**3**	**14**	**17**	**118**	**1**	**0**	**0**	**104**	**2.9**	**-16**	**0**	**0.0**	**21:31**	....	....	....	....	....	....	....	....	....
2001-02	**Columbus**	**NHL**	**65**	**2**	**14**	**16**	**89**	**0**	**0**	**0**	**76**	**2.6**	**-28**	**0**	**0.0**	**22:12**	....	....	....	....	....	....	....	....	....
	Chicago	**NHL**	**12**	**0**	**2**	**2**	**4**	**0**	**0**	**0**	**10**	**0.0**	**0**	**0**	**0.0**	**24:23**	**4**	**0**	**1**	**1**	**25**	**0**	**0**	**0**	**24:08**
2002-03	**Chicago**	**NHL**	**65**	**7**	**4**	**11**	**76**	**0**	**0**	**0**	**77**	**9.1**	**7**	**1**	**100.0**	**19:05**	....	....	....	....	....	....	....	....	....
	Dallas	**NHL**	**3**	**0**	**0**	**0**	**6**	**0**	**0**	**0**	**1**	**0.0**	**0**	**0**	**0.0**	**17:49**	**2**	**0**	**0**	**0**	**0**	**0**	**0**	**0**	**12:52**
2003-04	**Florida**	**NHL**	**82**	**4**	**12**	**16**	**88**	**2**	**0**	**0**	**67**	**6.0**	**-7**	**1**	**100.0**	**18:53**	....	....	....	....	....	....	....	....	....
2004-05			DID NOT PLAY																						
2005-06	**Pittsburgh**	**NHL**	**27**	**0**	**1**	**1**	**50**	**0**	**0**	**0**	**17**	**0.0**	**-10**	**0**	**0.0**	**16:13**	....	....	....	....	....	....	....	....	....
	NHL Totals		**1056**	**50**	**202**	**252**	**2316**	**13**	**1**	**5**	**1123**	**4.5**		**2**	**100.0**	**19:46**	**86**	**5**	**13**	**18**	**209**	**2**	**1**	**1**	**18:36**

Traded to **New Jersey** by **Montreal** for Stephane Richer, August 22, 1996. Traded to **Phoenix** by **New Jersey** for Deron Quint and Phoenix's 3rd round choice (later traded back to Phoenix – Phoenix selected Beat Forster) in 2001 Entry Draft, March 7, 2000. Claimed by **Columbus** from **Phoenix** in Expansion Draft, June 23, 2000. Traded to **Chicago** by **Columbus** for Jaroslav Spacek and Chicago's 2nd round choice (Dan Fritsche) in 2003 Entry Draft, March 19, 2002. Traded to **Dallas** by **Chicago** for Sami Helenius and Dallas's 7th round choice (Troy Brouwer) in 2004 Entry Draft, March 10, 2003. Signed as a free agent by **Florida**, September 9, 2003. Signed as a free agent by **Pittsburgh**, September 2, 2005.

O'DONNELL, Sean

(oh-DOHN-ehl, SHAWN) **ANA.**

Defense. Shoots left. 6'3", 227 lbs. Born, Ottawa, Ont., October 13, 1971. Buffalo's 6th choice, 123rd overall, in 1991 Entry Draft.

Season	Club	League	GP	G	A	Pts	PIM	PP	SH	GW	S	%	+/-	TF	F%	Min	GP	G	A	Pts	PIM	PP	SH	GW	Min
1987-88	Kanata Valley	CJHL	54	4	25	29	96	....	....	....	....	....	....	....	....	....	....	....	....	....	....	....	....	....	....
1988-89	Sudbury Wolves	OHL	56	1	9	10	49	....	....	....	....	....	....	....	....	....	....	....	....	....	....	....	....	....	....
1989-90	Sudbury Wolves	OHL	64	7	19	26	84	....	....	....	....	....	....	....	....	....	7	1	2	3	8	....	....	....	....
1990-91	Sudbury Wolves	OHL	66	8	23	31	114	....	....	....	....	....	....	....	....	....	5	1	4	5	10	....	....	....	....
1991-92	Rochester	AHL	73	4	9	13	193	....	....	....	....	....	....	....	....	....	16	1	2	3	21	....	....	....	....
1992-93	Rochester	AHL	74	3	18	21	203	....	....	....	....	....	....	....	....	....	17	1	6	7	38	....	....	....	....
1993-94	Rochester	AHL	64	2	10	12	242	....	....	....	....	....	....	....	....	....	4	0	1	1	21	....	....	....	....
1994-95	Phoenix	IHL	61	2	18	20	132	....	....	....	....	....	....	....	....	....	9	0	1	1	21	....	....	....	....
	Los Angeles	**NHL**	**15**	**0**	**2**	**2**	**49**	**0**	**0**	**0**	**12**	**0.0**	**-2**	....	....	....	....	....	....	....	....	....	....	....	....
1995-96	**Los Angeles**	**NHL**	**71**	**2**	**5**	**7**	**127**	**0**	**0**	**0**	**65**	**3.1**	**3**	....	....	....	....	....	....	....	....	....	....	....	....
1996-97	**Los Angeles**	**NHL**	**55**	**5**	**12**	**17**	**144**	**2**	**0**	**0**	**68**	**7.4**	**-13**	....	....	....	....	....	....	....	....	....	....	....	....
1997-98	**Los Angeles**	**NHL**	**80**	**2**	**15**	**17**	**179**	**0**	**0**	**1**	**71**	**2.8**	**7**	....	....	....	**4**	**1**	**0**	**1**	**36**	**0**	**0**	**0**	....
1998-99	**Los Angeles**	**NHL**	**80**	**1**	**13**	**14**	**186**	**0**	**0**	**0**	**64**	**1.6**	**1**	**0**	**0.0**	**19:10**	....	....	....	....	....	....	....	....	....
99-2000	**Los Angeles**	**NHL**	**80**	**2**	**12**	**14**	**114**	**0**	**0**	**1**	**51**	**3.9**	**4**	**0**	**0.0**	**17:41**	**4**	**1**	**0**	**1**	**4**	**0**	**0**	**0**	**16:26**
2000-01	**Minnesota**	**NHL**	**63**	**4**	**12**	**16**	**128**	**1**	**0**	**2**	**58**	**6.9**	**-2**	**12**	**50.0**	**23:00**	....	....	....	....	....	....	....	....	....
	New Jersey	**NHL**	**17**	**0**	**1**	**1**	**33**	**0**	**0**	**0**	**9**	**0.0**	**2**	**0**	**0.0**	**16:27**	**23**	**1**	**2**	**3**	**41**	**0**	**0**	**0**	**16:21**
2001-02	**Boston**	**NHL**	**80**	**3**	**22**	**25**	**89**	**1**	**0**	**2**	**112**	**2.7**	**27**	**0**	**0.0**	**24:50**	**6**	**0**	**2**	**2**	**4**	**0**	**0**	**0**	**24:57**
2002-03	**Boston**	**NHL**	**70**	**1**	**15**	**16**	**76**	**0**	**0**	**1**	**61**	**1.6**	**8**	**1**	**0.0**	**22:05**	....	....	....	....	....	....	....	....	....
2003-04	**Boston**	**NHL**	**82**	**1**	**10**	**11**	**110**	**0**	**0**	**0**	**72**	**1.4**	**10**	**3**	**33.3**	**20:36**	**7**	**0**	**0**	**0**	**0**	**0**	**0**	**0**	**19:53**
2004-05			DID NOT PLAY																						
2005-06	**Phoenix**	**NHL**	**57**	**1**	**7**	**8**	**121**	**0**	**0**	**0**	**23**	**4.3**	**3**	**0**	**0.0**	**16:18**	....	....	....	....	....	....	....	....	....
	Anaheim	**NHL**	**21**	**1**	**2**	**3**	**26**	**0**	**0**	**0**	**10**	**10.0**	**3**	**0**	**0.0**	**17:13**	**16**	**2**	**3**	**5**	**23**	**0**	**0**	**1**	**16:44**
	NHL Totals		**771**	**23**	**128**	**151**	**1382**	**4**	**0**	**7**	**676**	**3.4**		**16**	**43.8**	**20:21**	**60**	**5**	**7**	**12**	**108**	**0**	**0**	**1**	**17:50**

Traded to **Los Angeles** by **Buffalo** for Doug Houda, July 26, 1994. Claimed by **Minnesota** from **Los Angeles** in Expansion Draft, June 23, 2000. Traded to **New Jersey** by **Minnesota** for Willie Mitchell, March 4, 2001. Signed as a free agent by **Boston**, July 2, 2001. Signed as a free agent by **Phoenix**, July 6, 2004. Traded to **Anaheim** by **Phoenix** for Joel Perreault, March 9, 2006.

OHLUND, Mattias

(OH-luhnd, MAT-tee-ahs) **VAN.**

Defense. Shoots left. 6'2", 220 lbs. Born, Pitea, Sweden, September 9, 1976. Vancouver's 1st choice, 13th overall, in 1994 Entry Draft.

Season	Club	League	GP	G	A	Pts	PIM	PP	SH	GW	S	%	+/-	TF	F%	Min	GP	G	A	Pts	PIM	PP	SH	GW	Min
1992-93	Pitea HC	Sweden-2	22	0	6	6	16	....	....	....	....	....	....	....	....	....	....	....	....	....	....	....	....	....	....
1993-94	Pitea HC	Sweden-2	28	7	10	17	62	....	....	....	....	....	....	....	....	....	....	....	....	....	....	....	....	....	....
1994-95	Lulea HF	Sweden	34	6	10	16	34	....	....	....	....	....	....	....	....	....	9	4	0	4	16	....	....	....	....
1995-96	Lulea HF	Sweden	38	4	10	14	26	....	....	....	....	....	....	....	....	....	13	1	0	1	47	....	....	....	....
1996-97	Lulea HF	Sweden	47	7	9	16	38	....	....	....	....	....	....	....	....	....	10	1	2	3	8	....	....	....	....
	Lulea HF	EuroHL	6	0	3	3	0	....	....	....	....	....	....	....	....	....	....	....	....	....	....	....	....	....	....
1997-98	**Vancouver**	**NHL**	**77**	**7**	**23**	**30**	**76**	**1**	**0**	**0**	**172**	**4.1**	**3**	....	....	....	....	....	....	....	....	....	....	....	....
	Sweden	Olympics	4	0	1	1	4	....	....	....	....	....	....	....	....	....	....	....	....	....	....	....	....	....	....
1998-99	**Vancouver**	**NHL**	**74**	**9**	**26**	**35**	**83**	**2**	**1**	**1**	**129**	**7.0**	**-19**	**0**	**0.0**	**26:04**	....	....	....	....	....	....	....	....	....
99-2000	**Vancouver**	**NHL**	**42**	**4**	**16**	**20**	**24**	**2**	**1**	**1**	**63**	**6.3**	**6**	**0**	**0.0**	**27:41**	....	....	....	....	....	....	....	....	....
2000-01	**Vancouver**	**NHL**	**65**	**8**	**20**	**28**	**46**	**1**	**1**	**4**	**136**	**5.9**	**-16**	**0**	**0.0**	**25:00**	**4**	**1**	**3**	**4**	**6**	**1**	**0**	**0**	**26:32**
2001-02	**Vancouver**	**NHL**	**81**	**10**	**26**	**36**	**56**	**4**	**1**	**3**	**193**	**5.2**	**16**	**0**	**0.0**	**25:17**	**6**	**1**	**1**	**2**	**6**	**0**	**0**	**0**	**28:48**
	Sweden	Olympics	4	0	2	2	2	....	....	....	....	....	....	....	....	....	....	....	....	....	....	....	....	....	....
2002-03	**Vancouver**	**NHL**	**59**	**2**	**27**	**29**	**42**	**0**	**0**	**0**	**100**	**2.0**	**1**	**0**	**0.0**	**25:23**	**13**	**3**	**4**	**7**	**12**	**0**	**0**	**0**	**24:01**
2003-04	**Vancouver**	**NHL**	**82**	**14**	**20**	**34**	**73**	**5**	**0**	**3**	**129**	**10.9**	**14**	**0**	**0.0**	**25:47**	**7**	**1**	**4**	**5**	**13**	**0**	**0**	**1**	**27:25**
2004-05	Lulea HF	Sweden	2	1	0	1	4	....	....	....	....	....	....	....	....	....	....	....	....	....	....	....	....	....	....
2005-06	**Vancouver**	**NHL**	**78**	**13**	**20**	**33**	**92**	**8**	**1**	**2**	**183**	**7.1**	**-6**	**1**	**0.0**	**25:40**	....	....	....	....	....	....	....	....	....
	Sweden	Olympics	6	0	2	2	2	....	....	....	....	....	....	....	....	....	....	....	....	....	....	....	....	....	....
	NHL Totals		**558**	**67**	**178**	**245**	**492**	**23**	**5**	**14**	**1105**	**6.1**		**1**	**0.0**	**25:44**	**30**	**6**	**12**	**18**	**37**	**1**	**0**	**1**	**26:06**

NHL All-Rookie Team (1998)
Played in NHL All-Star Game (1999)
Signed as a free agent by **Lulea** (Sweden), December 21, 2004.

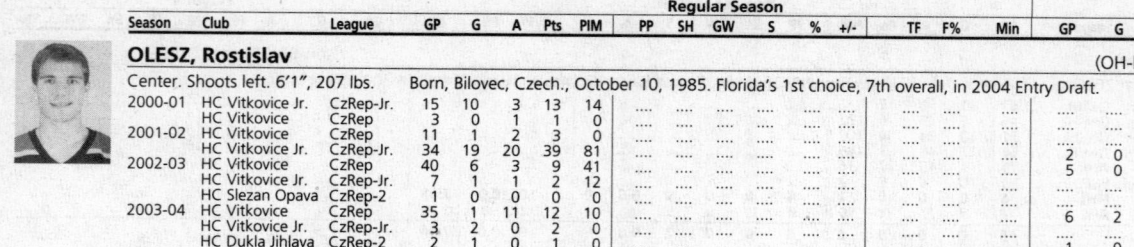

OLESZ, Rostislav

(OH-lehsh, RAHS-tih-slav) **FLA.**

Center. Shoots left. 6'1", 207 lbs. Born, Bilovec, Czech., October 10, 1985. Florida's 1st choice, 7th overall, in 2004 Entry Draft.

			Regular Season														Playoffs								
Season	Club	League	GP	G	A	Pts	PIM	PP	SH	GW	S	%	+/-	TF	F%	Min	GP	G	A	Pts	PIM	PP	SH	GW	Min
2000-01	HC Vitkovice Jr.	CzRep-Jr.	15	10	3	13	14																		
	HC Vitkovice	CzRep	3	0	1	1	0																		
2001-02	HC Vitkovice	CzRep	11	1	2	3	0																		
	HC Vitkovice Jr.	CzRep-Jr.	34	19	20	39	81										2	0	0	0	2				
2002-03	HC Vitkovice	CzRep	40	6	3	9	41										5	0	0	0	2				
	HC Vitkovice Jr.	CzRep-Jr.	7	1	1	2	12																		
	HC Slezan Opava	CzRep-2	1	0	0	0	0																		
2003-04	HC Vitkovice	CzRep	35	1	11	12	10										6	2	1	3	4				
	HC Vitkovice Jr.	CzRep-Jr.	3	2	0	2	0																		
	HC Dukla Jihlava	CzRep-2	2	1	0	1	0										1	0	0	0	0				
2004-05	HC Sparta Praha	CzRep	47	6	7	13	12										5	0	2	2	0				
	Sparta Jr.	CzRep-Jr.															1	0	1	1	0				
2005-06	**Florida**	**NHL**	**59**	**8**	**13**	**21**	**24**	**0**	**1**	**3**	**105**	**7.6**	**–4**	**10**	**30.0**	**14:52**									
	Czech Republic	Olympics	8	0	0	0	2																		
	NHL Totals		**59**	**8**	**13**	**21**	**24**	**0**	**1**	**3**	**105**	**7.6**		**10**	**30.0**	**14:52**									

OLIVER, David

(AWL-ih-vuhr, DAY-vihd)

Right wing. Shoots right. 6', 190 lbs. Born, Sechelt, B.C., April 17, 1971. Edmonton's 7th choice, 144th overall, in 1991 Entry Draft.

			Regular Season														Playoffs								
Season	Club	League	GP	G	A	Pts	PIM	PP	SH	GW	S	%	+/-	TF	F%	Min	GP	G	A	Pts	PIM	PP	SH	GW	Min
1988-89	Vernon Lakers	BCJHL	58	41	38	79	38																		
1989-90	Vernon Lakers	BCJHL	58	51	48	99	22																		
1990-91	U. of Michigan	CCHA	27	13	11	24	34																		
1991-92	U. of Michigan	CCHA	44	31	27	58	32																		
1992-93	U. of Michigan	CCHA	40	35	20	55	18																		
1993-94	U. of Michigan	CCHA	41	28	40	68	16																		
1994-95	Cape Breton	AHL	32	11	18	29	8																		
	Edmonton	**NHL**	**44**	**16**	**14**	**30**	**20**	**10**	**0**	**0**	**79**	**20.3**	**–11**												
1995-96	**Edmonton**	**NHL**	**80**	**20**	**19**	**39**	**34**	**14**	**0**	**0**	**131**	**15.3**	**–22**												
1996-97	**Edmonton**	**NHL**	**17**	**1**	**2**	**3**	**4**	**0**	**0**	**0**	**22**	**4.5**	**–8**												
	NY Rangers	**NHL**	**14**	**2**	**1**	**3**	**4**	**0**	**0**	**0**	**13**	**15.4**	**3**				**3**	**0**	**0**	**0**	**0**	**0**	**0**	**0**	
1997-98	Houston Aeros	IHL	78	38	27	65	60										4	3	0	3	4				
1998-99	**Ottawa**	**NHL**	**17**	**2**	**5**	**7**	**4**	**0**	**0**	**0**	**18**	**11.1**	**1**	**3**	**33.3**	**10:34**									
	Houston Aeros	IHL	37	18	17	35	30										19	10	6	16	22				
99-2000	**Phoenix**	**NHL**	**9**	**1**	**0**	**1**	**2**	**1**	**0**	**0**	**6**	**16.7**	**0**	**0**	**0.0**	**7:38**									
	Houston Aeros	IHL	45	16	11	27	40										11	3	4	7	8				
2000-01	**Ottawa**	**NHL**	**7**	**0**	**0**	**0**	**2**	**0**	**0**	**0**	**2**	**0.0**	**0**	**0**	**0.0**	**5:37**									
	Grand Rapids	IHL	51	14	17	31	35										10	6	2	8	8				
2001-02	Munchen Barons	Germany	59	20	14	34	30										9	2	2	4	6				
2002-03	**Dallas**	**NHL**	**6**	**0**	**3**	**3**	**2**	**0**	**0**	**0**	**5**	**0.0**	**1**	**0**	**0.0**	**9:13**	**6**	**0**	**0**	**0**	**2**	**0**	**0**	**0**	**6:33**
	Utah Grizzlies	AHL	37	11	14	25	14																		
2003-04	**Dallas**	**NHL**	**36**	**7**	**5**	**12**	**12**	**3**	**0**	**1**	**30**	**23.3**	**6**	**1**	**100.0**	**9:51**	**1**	**0**	**0**	**0**	**0**	**0**	**0**	**0**	**7:31**
	Utah Grizzlies	AHL	31	5	12	17	12																		
2004-05	Guildford Flames	Britain-2	16	8	14	22	4										15	3	5	8	31				
2005-06	**Dallas**	**NHL**	**3**	**0**	**0**	**0**	**0**	**0**	**0**	**0**	**1**	**0.0**	**–1**	**0**	**0.0**	**7:37**									
	Iowa Stars	AHL	54	21	13	34	26										5	3	0	3	4				
	NHL Totals		**233**	**49**	**49**	**98**	**84**	**28**	**0**	**1**	**307**	**16.0**		**4**	**50.0**	**9:14**	**10**	**0**	**0**	**0**	**2**	**0**	**0**	**0**	**6:41**

CCHA Second All-Star Team (1993) • CCHA First All-Star Team (1994) • CCHA Player of the Year (1994) • NCAA West First All-American Team (1994)

Claimed on waivers by **NY Rangers** from **Edmonton**, February 21, 1997. Signed as a free agent by **Ottawa**, July 2, 1998. Signed as a free agent by **Phoenix**, July 20, 1999. Signed as a free agent by **Ottawa**, August 2, 2000. Signed as a free agent by **Dallas**, July 30, 2002. Signed as a free agent by **Guildford** (Britain-2), January 13, 2005.

OLIWA, Krzysztof

(oh-LEE-vuh, KHRIH-stahf)

Left wing. Shoots left. 6'5", 245 lbs. Born, Tychy, Poland, April 12, 1973. New Jersey's 4th choice, 65th overall, in 1993 Entry Draft.

			Regular Season														Playoffs								
Season	Club	League	GP	G	A	Pts	PIM	PP	SH	GW	S	%	+/-	TF	F%	Min	GP	G	A	Pts	PIM	PP	SH	GW	Min
1990-91	GKS Katowski Jr.	Poland-Jr.	5	4	4	8	10																		
1991-92	GKS Tychy	Poland	10	3	7	10	6																		
1992-93	Welland Cougars	OHA-B	30	13	21	34	127																		
1993-94	Albany River Rats	AHL	33	2	4	6	151																		
	Raleigh IceCaps	ECHL	15	0	2	2	65																		
1994-95	Albany River Rats	AHL	20	1	1	2	77										9	0	0	0	35				
	Saint John Flames	AHL	14	1	4	5	79																		
	Raleigh IceCaps	ECHL	5	0	2	2	32																		
	Detroit Vipers	IHL	4	0	1	1	24																		
1995-96	Albany River Rats	AHL	51	5	11	16	217																		
	Raleigh IceCaps	ECHL	9	1	0	1	53																		
1996-97	**New Jersey**	**NHL**	**1**	**0**	**0**	**0**	**5**	**0**	**0**	**0**	**0**	**0.0**	**–1**												
	Albany River Rats	AHL	60	13	14	27	322										15	7	1	8	49				
1997-98	**New Jersey**	**NHL**	**73**	**2**	**3**	**5**	**295**	**0**	**0**	**2**	**53**	**3.8**	**3**				**6**	**0**	**0**	**0**	**23**	**0**	**0**	**0**	
1998-99	**New Jersey**	**NHL**	**64**	**5**	**7**	**12**	**240**	**0**	**0**	**1**	**59**	**8.5**	**4**	**1**	**0.0**	**7:02**	**1**	**0**	**0**	**0**	**2**	**0**	**0**	**0**	**2:35**
99-2000♦	**New Jersey**	**NHL**	**69**	**6**	**10**	**16**	**184**	**1**	**0**	**2**	**61**	**9.8**	**–2**	**3**	**66.7**	**6:45**									
2000-01	**Columbus**	**NHL**	**10**	**0**	**2**	**2**	**34**	**0**	**0**	**0**	**5**	**0.0**	**1**	**0**	**0.0**	**5:17**									
	Pittsburgh	**NHL**	**26**	**1**	**2**	**3**	**131**	**0**	**0**	**0**	**17**	**5.9**	**–4**	**1**	**100.0**	**4:58**	**5**	**0**	**0**	**0**	**16**	**0**	**0**	**0**	**2:14**
2001-02	**Pittsburgh**	**NHL**	**57**	**0**	**2**	**2**	**150**	**0**	**0**	**0**	**31**	**0.0**	**–5**	**0**	**0.0**	**5:35**									
2002-03	**NY Rangers**	**NHL**	**9**	**0**	**0**	**0**	**51**	**0**	**0**	**0**	**3**	**0.0**	**1**	**1**	**0.0**	**3:45**									
	Hartford	AHL	15	0	1	1	30																		
	Boston	**NHL**	**33**	**0**	**0**	**0**	**110**	**0**	**0**	**0**	**11**	**0.0**	**–4**	**1**	**0.0**	**3:58**									
2003-04	**Calgary**	**NHL**	**65**	**3**	**2**	**5**	**247**	**0**	**0**	**0**	**32**	**9.4**	**–8**	**5**	**20.0**	**4:56**	**20**	**2**	**0**	**2**	**6**	**0**	**0**	**0**	**3:44**
2004-05	Nowy Targ	Poland															2	0	0	0	12				
2005-06	**New Jersey**	**NHL**	**3**	**0**	**0**	**0**	**0**	**0**	**0**	**0**	**1**	**0.0**	**–2**	**1**	**0.0**	**6:18**									
	NHL Totals		**410**	**17**	**28**	**45**	**1447**	**1**	**0**	**5**	**273**	**6.2**		**13**	**30.8**	**5:43**	**32**	**2**	**0**	**2**	**47**	**0**	**0**	**0**	**3:24**

Traded to **Columbus** by **New Jersey** with future considerations (Deron Quint, June 23, 2000) for Columbus' 3rd round choice (Brandon Nolan) in 2001 Entry Draft and future considerations (Turner Stevenson, June 23, 2000), June 12, 2000. • Missed majority of 2000-01 season recovering from arm injury suffered in game vs. Detroit, October 28, 2000. Traded to **Pittsburgh** by **Columbus** for San Jose's 3rd round choice (previously acquired, Columbus selected Aaron Johnson) in 2001 Entry Draft, January 14, 2001. Traded to **NY Rangers** by **Pittsburgh** for NY Rangers' 9th round choice (later traded to Tampa Bay – Tampa Bay selected Albert Vishnyakov) in 2003 Entry Draft, June 23, 2002. Traded to **Boston** by **NY Rangers** for Boston's 9th round choice (later traded to San Jose - San Jose selected Brian Mahoney-Wilson) in 2004 Entry Draft, January 6, 2003. Signed as a free agent by **Calgary**, July 30, 2003. Signed as a free agent by **New Jersey**, July 15, 2004. Signed as a free agent by **Nowy Targ** (Poland), October 1, 2004.

OLSON, Josh

(OHL-suhn, JAWSH)

Left wing. Shoots left. 6'5", 225 lbs. Born, Grand Forks, ND, July 13, 1981. Florida's 6th choice, 190th overall, in 2000 Entry Draft.

			Regular Season														Playoffs								
Season	Club	League	GP	G	A	Pts	PIM	PP	SH	GW	S	%	+/-	TF	F%	Min	GP	G	A	Pts	PIM	PP	SH	GW	Min
1998-99	Fargo-Moorhead	USHL	11	2	2	4	8																		
99-2000	Fargo-Moorhead	USHL	18	2	5	7	37																		
	Omaha Lancers	USHL	43	6	7	13	44										4	0	0	0	4				
2000-01	Portland	WHL	72	22	38	60	86										16	5	4	9	17				
2001-02	Utah Grizzlies	AHL	1	0	0	0	0										1	0	0	0	0				
	Portland	WHL	72	40	48	88	85										7	4	3	7	8				
2002-03	Jackson Bandits	ECHL	39	10	17	27	13										1	0	1	1	0				
	San Antonio	AHL	23	0	1	1	14																		
2003-04	**Florida**	**NHL**	**5**	**1**	**0**	**1**	**0**	**0**	**0**	**0**	**6**	**16.7**	**1**	**0**	**0.0**	**8:17**									
	San Antonio	AHL	73	22	16	38	33																		
2004-05	San Antonio	AHL	53	9	7	16	17																		
	Hershey Bears	AHL	23	1	2	3	4																		
2005-06	Houston Aeros	AHL	75	12	12	24	75										8	2	3	5	6				
	NHL Totals		**5**	**1**	**0**	**1**	**0**	**0**	**0**	**0**	**6**	**16.7**		**0**	**0.0**	**8:17**									

Loaned to **Hershey** (AHL) by **San Antonio** (AHL) for the loan of Andre Savage, February 25, 2005.

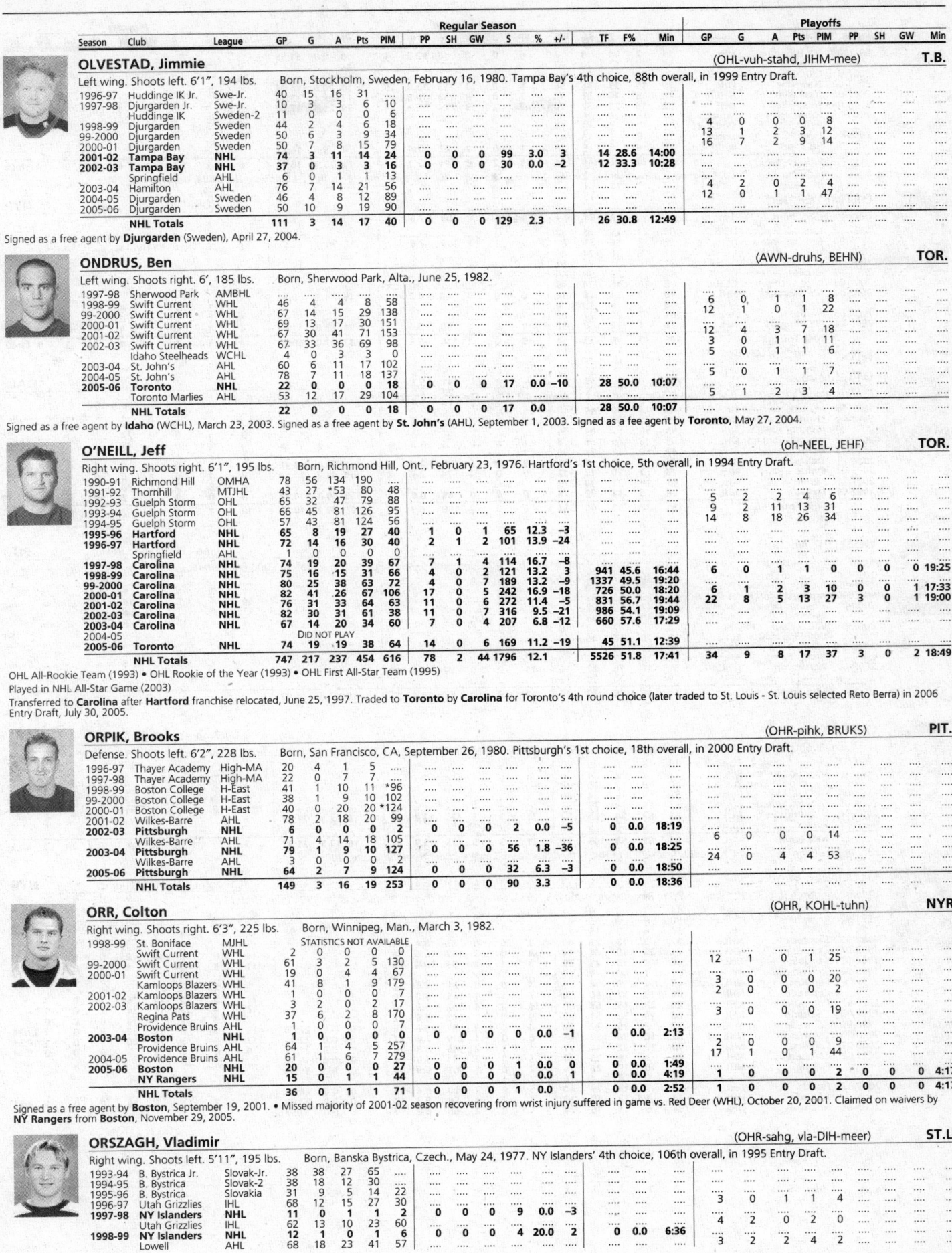

OLVESTAD, Jimmie
(OHL-vuh-stahd, JIHM-mee) **T.B.**

Left wing. Shoots left. 6'1", 194 lbs. Born, Stockholm, Sweden, February 16, 1980. Tampa Bay's 4th choice, 88th overall, in 1999 Entry Draft.

			Regular Season														Playoffs								
Season	Club	League	GP	G	A	Pts	PIM	PP	SH	GW	S	%	+/-	TF	F%	Min	GP	G	A	Pts	PIM	PP	SH	GW	Min
1996-97	Huddinge IK Jr.	Swe-Jr.	40	15	16	31	....	....	....	....	....	....	....	....	....	....	....	....	....	....	....	....	....	....	....
1997-98	Djurgarden Jr.	Swe-Jr.	10	3	3	6	10	....	....	....	....	....	....	....	....	....	....	....	....	....	....	....	....	....	....
	Huddinge IK	Sweden-2	11	0	0	0	6	....	....	....	....	....	....	....	....	....	....	....	....	....	....	....	....	....	....
1998-99	Djurgarden	Sweden	44	2	4	6	18	....	....	....	....	....	....	....	....	....	4	0	0	0	8	....	....	....	....
99-2000	Djurgarden	Sweden	50	6	3	9	34	....	....	....	....	....	....	....	....	....	13	1	2	3	12	....	....	....	....
2000-01	Djurgarden	Sweden	50	7	8	15	79	....	....	....	....	....	....	....	....	....	16	7	2	9	14	....	....	....	....
2001-02	**Tampa Bay**	**NHL**	**74**	**3**	**11**	**14**	**24**	**0**	**0**	**0**	**99**	**3.0**	**3**	**14**	**28.6**	**14:00**	....	....	....	....	....	....	....	....	....
2002-03	**Tampa Bay**	**NHL**	**37**	**0**	**3**	**3**	**16**	**0**	**0**	**0**	**30**	**0.0**	**–2**	**12**	**33.3**	**10:28**	....	....	....	....	....	....	....	....	....
	Springfield	AHL	6	0	1	1	13	....	....	....	....	....	....	....	....	....	....	....	....	....	....	....	....	....	....
2003-04	Hamilton	AHL	76	7	14	21	56	....	....	....	....	....	....	....	....	....	4	2	0	2	4	....	....	....	....
2004-05	Djurgarden	Sweden	46	4	8	12	89	....	....	....	....	....	....	....	....	....	12	0	1	1	47	....	....	....	....
2005-06	Djurgarden	Sweden	50	10	9	19	90	....	....	....	....	....	....	....	....	....	....	....	....	....	....	....	....	....	....
	NHL Totals		**111**	**3**	**14**	**17**	**40**	**0**	**0**	**0**	**129**	**2.3**		**26**	**30.8**	**12:49**	....	....	....	....	....	....	....	....	....

Signed as a free agent by **Djurgarden** (Sweden), April 27, 2004.

ONDRUS, Ben
(AWN-druhs, BEHN) **TOR.**

Left wing. Shoots right. 6', 185 lbs. Born, Sherwood Park, Alta., June 25, 1982.

			Regular Season														Playoffs								
Season	Club	League	GP	G	A	Pts	PIM	PP	SH	GW	S	%	+/-	TF	F%	Min	GP	G	A	Pts	PIM	PP	SH	GW	Min
1997-98	Sherwood Park	AMBHL	....	....	....	....	....	....	....	....	....	....	....	....	....	....	....	....	....	....	....	....	....	....	....
1998-99	Swift Current	WHL	46	4	4	8	58	....	....	....	....	....	....	....	....	....	6	0	1	1	8	....	....	....	....
99-2000	Swift Current	WHL	67	14	15	29	138	....	....	....	....	....	....	....	....	....	12	1	0	1	22	....	....	....	....
2000-01	Swift Current	WHL	69	13	17	30	151	....	....	....	....	....	....	....	....	....	....	....	....	....	....	....	....	....	....
2001-02	Swift Current	WHL	67	30	41	71	153	....	....	....	....	....	....	....	....	....	12	4	3	7	18	....	....	....	....
2002-03	Swift Current	WHL	67	33	36	69	98	....	....	....	....	....	....	....	....	....	3	0	1	1	11	....	....	....	....
	Idaho Steelheads	WCHL	4	0	3	3	0	....	....	....	....	....	....	....	....	....	5	0	1	1	6	....	....	....	....
2003-04	St. John's	AHL	60	6	11	17	102	....	....	....	....	....	....	....	....	....	....	....	....	....	....	....	....	....	....
2004-05	St. John's	AHL	78	7	11	18	137	....	....	....	....	....	....	....	....	....	5	0	1	1	7	....	....	....	....
2005-06	**Toronto**	**NHL**	**22**	**0**	**0**	**0**	**18**	**0**	**0**	**0**	**17**	**0.0**	**–10**	**28**	**50.0**	**10:07**	....	....	....	....	....	....	....	....	....
	Toronto Marlies	AHL	53	12	17	29	104	....	....	....	....	....	....	....	....	....	5	1	2	3	4	....	....	....	....
	NHL Totals		**22**	**0**	**0**	**0**	**18**	**0**	**0**	**0**	**17**	**0.0**		**28**	**50.0**	**10:07**	....	....	....	....	....	....	....	....	....

Signed as a free agent by **Idaho** (WCHL), March 23, 2003. Signed as a free agent by **St. John's** (AHL), September 1, 2003. Signed as a fee agent by **Toronto**, May 27, 2004.

O'NEILL, Jeff
(oh-NEEL, JEHF) **TOR.**

Right wing. Shoots right. 6'1", 195 lbs. Born, Richmond Hill, Ont., February 23, 1976. Hartford's 1st choice, 5th overall, in 1994 Entry Draft.

			Regular Season														Playoffs								
Season	Club	League	GP	G	A	Pts	PIM	PP	SH	GW	S	%	+/-	TF	F%	Min	GP	G	A	Pts	PIM	PP	SH	GW	Min
1990-91	Richmond Hill	OMHA	78	56	134	190	....	....	....	....	....	....	....	....	....	....	....	....	....	....	....	....	....	....	....
1991-92	Thornhill	MTJHL	43	27	*53	80	48	....	....	....	....	....	....	....	....	....	....	....	....	....	....	....	....	....	....
1992-93	Guelph Storm	OHL	65	32	47	79	88	....	....	....	....	....	....	....	....	....	5	2	2	4	6	....	....	....	....
1993-94	Guelph Storm	OHL	66	45	81	126	95	....	....	....	....	....	....	....	....	....	9	2	11	13	31	....	....	....	....
1994-95	Guelph Storm	OHL	57	43	81	124	56	....	....	....	....	....	....	....	....	....	14	8	18	26	34	....	....	....	....
1995-96	**Hartford**	**NHL**	**65**	**8**	**19**	**27**	**40**	**1**	**0**	**1**	**65**	**12.3**	**–3**	....	....	....	....	....	....	....	....	....	....	....	....
1996-97	**Hartford**	**NHL**	**72**	**14**	**16**	**30**	**40**	**2**	**1**	**2**	**101**	**13.9**	**–24**	....	....	....	....	....	....	....	....	....	....	....	....
	Springfield	AHL	1	0	0	0	0	....	....	....	....	....	....	....	....	....	....	....	....	....	....	....	....	....	....
1997-98	**Carolina**	**NHL**	**74**	**19**	**20**	**39**	**67**	**7**	**1**	**4**	**114**	**16.7**	**–8**	....	....	....	....	....	....	....	....	....	....	....	....
1998-99	**Carolina**	**NHL**	**75**	**16**	**15**	**31**	**66**	**4**	**0**	**2**	**121**	**13.2**	**3**	**941**	**45.6**	**16:44**	**6**	**0**	**1**	**1**	**0**	**0**	**0**	**0**	**19:25**
99-2000	**Carolina**	**NHL**	**80**	**25**	**38**	**63**	**72**	**4**	**0**	**7**	**189**	**13.2**	**–9**	**1337**	**49.5**	**19:20**	....	....	....	....	....	....	....	....	....
2000-01	**Carolina**	**NHL**	**82**	**41**	**26**	**67**	**106**	**17**	**0**	**5**	**242**	**16.9**	**–18**	**726**	**50.0**	**18:20**	**6**	**1**	**2**	**3**	**10**	**0**	**0**	**1**	**17:33**
2001-02	**Carolina**	**NHL**	**76**	**31**	**33**	**64**	**63**	**11**	**0**	**6**	**272**	**11.4**	**–5**	**831**	**56.7**	**19:44**	**22**	**8**	**5**	**13**	**27**	**3**	**0**	**1**	**19:00**
2002-03	**Carolina**	**NHL**	**82**	**30**	**31**	**61**	**38**	**11**	**0**	**7**	**316**	**9.5**	**–21**	**986**	**54.1**	**19:09**	....	....	....	....	....	....	....	....	....
2003-04	**Carolina**	**NHL**	**67**	**14**	**20**	**34**	**60**	**7**	**0**	**4**	**207**	**6.8**	**–12**	**660**	**57.6**	**17:29**	....	....	....	....	....	....	....	....	....
2004-05				Did not play																					
2005-06	**Toronto**	**NHL**	**74**	**19**	**19**	**38**	**64**	**14**	**0**	**6**	**169**	**11.2**	**–19**	**45**	**51.1**	**12:39**	....	....	....	....	....	....	....	....	....
	NHL Totals		**747**	**217**	**237**	**454**	**616**	**78**	**2**	**44**	**1796**	**12.1**		**5526**	**51.8**	**17:41**	**34**	**9**	**8**	**17**	**37**	**3**	**0**	**2**	**18:49**

OHL All-Rookie Team (1993) • OHL Rookie of the Year (1993) • OHL First All-Star Team (1995)

Played in NHL All-Star Game (2003)

Transferred to **Carolina** after **Hartford** franchise relocated, June 25, 1997. Traded to **Toronto** by **Carolina** for Toronto's 4th round choice (later traded to St. Louis - St. Louis selected Reto Berra) in 2006 Entry Draft, July 30, 2005.

ORPIK, Brooks
(OHR-pihk, BRUKS) **PIT.**

Defense. Shoots left. 6'2", 228 lbs. Born, San Francisco, CA, September 26, 1980. Pittsburgh's 1st choice, 18th overall, in 2000 Entry Draft.

			Regular Season														Playoffs								
Season	Club	League	GP	G	A	Pts	PIM	PP	SH	GW	S	%	+/-	TF	F%	Min	GP	G	A	Pts	PIM	PP	SH	GW	Min
1996-97	Thayer Academy	High-MA	20	4	1	5	....	....	....	....	....	....	....	....	....	....	....	....	....	....	....	....	....	....	....
1997-98	Thayer Academy	High-MA	22	0	7	7	....	....	....	....	....	....	....	....	....	....	....	....	....	....	....	....	....	....	....
1998-99	Boston College	H-East	41	1	10	11	*96	....	....	....	....	....	....	....	....	....	....	....	....	....	....	....	....	....	....
99-2000	Boston College	H-East	38	1	9	10	102	....	....	....	....	....	....	....	....	....	....	....	....	....	....	....	....	....	....
2000-01	Boston College	H-East	40	0	20	20	*124	....	....	....	....	....	....	....	....	....	....	....	....	....	....	....	....	....	....
2001-02	Wilkes-Barre	AHL	78	2	18	20	99	....	....	....	....	....	....	....	....	....	....	....	....	....	....	....	....	....	....
2002-03	**Pittsburgh**	**NHL**	**6**	**0**	**0**	**0**	**2**	**0**	**0**	**0**	**2**	**0.0**	**–5**	**0**	**0.0**	**18:19**	....	....	....	....	....	....	....	....	....
	Wilkes-Barre	AHL	71	4	14	18	105	....	....	....	....	....	....	....	....	....	6	0	0	0	14	....	....	....	....
2003-04	**Pittsburgh**	**NHL**	**79**	**1**	**9**	**10**	**127**	**0**	**0**	**0**	**56**	**1.8**	**–36**	**0**	**0.0**	**18:25**	....	....	....	....	....	....	....	....	....
	Wilkes-Barre	AHL	3	0	0	0	2	....	....	....	....	....	....	....	....	....	24	0	4	4	53	....	....	....	....
2005-06	**Pittsburgh**	**NHL**	**64**	**2**	**7**	**9**	**124**	**0**	**0**	**0**	**32**	**6.3**	**–3**	**0**	**0.0**	**18:50**	....	....	....	....	....	....	....	....	....
	NHL Totals		**149**	**3**	**16**	**19**	**253**	**0**	**0**	**0**	**90**	**3.3**		**0**	**0.0**	**18:36**	....	....	....	....	....	....	....	....	....

ORR, Colton
(OHR, KOHL-tuhn) **NYR**

Right wing. Shoots right. 6'3", 225 lbs. Born, Winnipeg, Man., March 3, 1982.

			Regular Season														Playoffs								
Season	Club	League	GP	G	A	Pts	PIM	PP	SH	GW	S	%	+/-	TF	F%	Min	GP	G	A	Pts	PIM	PP	SH	GW	Min
1998-99	St. Boniface	MJHL	Statistics not available																						
	Swift Current	WHL	2	0	0	0	0	....	....	....	....	....	....	....	....	....	....	....	....	....	....	....	....	....	....
99-2000	Swift Current	WHL	61	3	2	5	130	....	....	....	....	....	....	....	....	....	12	1	0	1	25	....	....	....	....
2000-01	Swift Current	WHL	19	0	4	4	67	....	....	....	....	....	....	....	....	....	....	....	....	....	....	....	....	....	....
	Kamloops Blazers	WHL	41	8	1	9	179	....	....	....	....	....	....	....	....	....	3	0	0	0	20	....	....	....	....
2001-02	Kamloops Blazers	WHL	1	0	0	0	7	....	....	....	....	....	....	....	....	....	2	0	0	0	2	....	....	....	....
2002-03	Kamloops Blazers	WHL	3	2	0	2	17	....	....	....	....	....	....	....	....	....	....	....	....	....	....	....	....	....	....
	Regina Pats	WHL	37	6	2	8	170	....	....	....	....	....	....	....	....	....	3	0	0	0	19	....	....	....	....
	Providence Bruins	AHL	1	0	0	0	7	....	....	....	....	....	....	....	....	....	....	....	....	....	....	....	....	....	....
2003-04	**Boston**	**NHL**	**1**	**0**	**0**	**0**	**0**	**0**	**0**	**0**	**0**	**0.0**	**–1**	**0**	**0.0**	**2:13**	....	....	....	....	....	....	....	....	....
	Providence Bruins	AHL	64	1	4	5	257	....	....	....	....	....	....	....	....	....	2	0	0	0	9	....	....	....	....
2004-05	Providence Bruins	AHL	61	1	6	7	279	....	....	....	....	....	....	....	....	....	17	1	0	1	44	....	....	....	....
2005-06	**Boston**	**NHL**	**20**	**0**	**0**	**0**	**27**	**0**	**0**	**0**	**1**	**0.0**	**0**	**0**	**0.0**	**1:49**	....	....	....	....	....	....	....	....	....
	NY Rangers	**NHL**	**15**	**0**	**1**	**1**	**44**	**0**	**0**	**0**	**0**	**0.0**	**1**	**0**	**0.0**	**4:19**	**1**	**0**	**0**	**0**	**2**	**0**	**0**	**0**	**4:17**
	NHL Totals		**36**	**0**	**1**	**1**	**71**	**0**	**0**	**0**	**1**	**0.0**		**0**	**0.0**	**2:52**	**1**	**0**	**0**	**0**	**2**	**0**	**0**	**0**	**4:17**

Signed as a free agent by **Boston**, September 19, 2001. • Missed majority of 2001-02 season recovering from wrist injury suffered in game vs. Red Deer (WHL), October 20, 2001. Claimed on waivers by **NY Rangers** from **Boston**, November 29, 2005.

ORSZAGH, Vladimir
(OHR-sahg, vla-DIH-meer) **ST.L.**

Right wing. Shoots left. 5'11", 195 lbs. Born, Banska Bystrica, Czech., May 24, 1977. NY Islanders' 4th choice, 106th overall, in 1995 Entry Draft.

			Regular Season														Playoffs								
Season	Club	League	GP	G	A	Pts	PIM	PP	SH	GW	S	%	+/-	TF	F%	Min	GP	G	A	Pts	PIM	PP	SH	GW	Min
1993-94	B. Bystrica Jr.	Slovak-Jr.	38	38	27	65	....	....	....	....	....	....	....	....	....	....	....	....	....	....	....	....	....	....	....
1994-95	B. Bystrica	Slovak-2	38	18	12	30	....	....	....	....	....	....	....	....	....	....	....	....	....	....	....	....	....	....	....
1995-96	B. Bystrica	Slovakia	31	9	5	14	22	....	....	....	....	....	....	....	....	....	....	....	....	....	....	....	....	....	....
1996-97	Utah Grizzlies	IHL	68	12	15	27	30	....	....	....	....	....	....	....	....	....	3	0	1	1	4	....	....	....	....
1997-98	**NY Islanders**	**NHL**	**11**	**0**	**1**	**1**	**2**	**0**	**0**	**0**	**9**	**0.0**	**–3**	....	....	....	....	....	....	....	....	....	....	....	....
	Utah Grizzlies	IHL	62	13	10	23	60	....	....	....	....	....	....	....	....	....	4	2	0	2	0	....	....	....	....
1998-99	**NY Islanders**	**NHL**	**12**	**1**	**0**	**1**	**6**	**0**	**0**	**0**	**4**	**20.0**	**2**	**0**	**0.0**	**6:36**	....	....	....	....	....	....	....	....	....
	Lowell	AHL	68	18	23	41	57	....	....	....	....	....	....	....	....	....	3	2	2	4	2	....	....	....	....

Season	Club	League	GP	G	A	Pts	PIM	PP	SH	GW	S	%	+/-	TF	F%	Min	GP	G	A	Pts	PIM	PP	SH	GW	Min
								Regular Season									Playoffs								
99-2000	NY Islanders	NHL	11	2	1	3	4	0	0	0	16	12.5	1	0	0.0	11:55	....	....	....	....	....	....	....	....	....
	Lowell	AHL	55	8	12	20	22	....	....	....	....	....	....	....	....	....	7	3	3	6	2	....	....	....	....
2000-01	Djurgarden	Sweden	50	23	13	36	62	....	....	....	....	....	....	....	....	....	16	*7	3	10	20	....	....	....	....
2001-02	Nashville	NHL	79	15	21	36	56	5	0	3	113	13.3	–15	10	20.0	16:04	....	....	....	....	....	....	....	....	....
2002-03	Nashville	NHL	78	16	16	32	38	3	0	3	152	10.5	–1	17	29.4	17:34	....	....	....	....	....	....	....	....	....
2003-04	Nashville	NHL	82	16	21	37	74	2	2	3	124	12.9	–4	39	25.6	17:00	6	2	0	2	4	0	0	0	16:08
2004-05	HKm Zvolen	Slovakia	37	16	14	30	50	....	....	....	....	....	....	....	....	....	17	5	2	7	24	....	....	....	....
	B. Bystrica	Slovak-2	2	2	0	2	4	....	....	....	....	....	....	....	....	....	....	....	....	....	....	....	....	....	....
2005-06	Lulea HF	Sweden	19	8	5	13	42	....	....	....	....	....	....	....	....	....	....	....	....	....	....	....	....	....	....
	St. Louis	NHL	16	4	5	9	14	1	0	0	23	17.4	–2	4	25.0	16:52	....	....	....	....	....	....	....	....	....
	NHL Totals		289	54	65	119	194	11	2	9	441	12.2		70	25.7	16:14	6	2	0	2	4	0	0	0	16:08

Signed as a free agent by **Nashville**, May 30, 2001. Signed as a free agent by **Zvolen** (Slovakia), October 6, 2004. Claimed on waivers by **St. Louis** from **Nashville**, December 30, 2005.

ORTMEYER, Jed

(OHRT-migh-uhr, JEHD) **NYR**

Center. Shoots right. 6', 193 lbs. Born, Omaha, NE, September 3, 1978.

Season	Club	League	GP	G	A	Pts	PIM	PP	SH	GW	S	%	+/-	TF	F%	Min	GP	G	A	Pts	PIM	PP	SH	GW	Min
1997-98	Omaha Lancers	USHL	54	23	25	48	52	....	....	....	....	....	....	....	....	....	14	3	4	7	31	....	....	....	....
1998-99	Omaha Lancers	USHL	52	23	36	59	81	....	....	....	....	....	....	....	....	....	12	5	6	11	16	....	....	....	....
99-2000	U. of Michigan	CCHA	41	8	16	24	40	....	....	....	....	....	....	....	....	....	....	....	....	....	....	....	....	....	....
2000-01	U. of Michigan	CCHA	27	10	11	21	52	....	....	....	....	....	....	....	....	....	....	....	....	....	....	....	....	....	....
2001-02	U. of Michigan	CCHA	41	15	23	38	40	....	....	....	....	....	....	....	....	....	....	....	....	....	....	....	....	....	....
2002-03	U. of Michigan	CCHA	36	18	16	34	48	....	....	....	....	....	....	....	....	....	....	....	....	....	....	....	....	....	....
2003-04	NY Rangers	NHL	58	2	4	6	16	0	0	0	48	4.2	–10	16	31.3	9:52	....	....	....	....	....	....	....	....	....
	Hartford	AHL	13	2	8	10	4	....	....	....	....	....	....	....	....	....	16	5	2	7	6	....	....	....	....
2004-05	Hartford	AHL	61	7	20	27	63	....	....	....	....	....	....	....	....	....	6	0	1	1	4	....	....	....	....
2005-06	NY Rangers	NHL	78	5	2	7	38	0	0	1	90	5.6	2	21	23.8	11:06	4	1	0	1	4	0	0	0	11:40
	NHL Totals		136	7	6	13	54	0	0	1	138	5.1		37	27.0	10:34	4	1	0	1	4	0	0	0	11:40

Signed as a free agent by **NY Rangers**, May 10, 2003.

OTT, Steve

(AWT, STEEV) **DAL.**

Center. Shoots left. 6', 185 lbs. Born, Summerside, P.E.I., August 19, 1982. Dallas' 1st choice, 25th overall, in 2000 Entry Draft.

Season	Club	League	GP	G	A	Pts	PIM	PP	SH	GW	S	%	+/-	TF	F%	Min	GP	G	A	Pts	PIM	PP	SH	GW	Min
1998-99	Leamington Flyers	OHA-B	48	14	30	44	110	....	....	....	....	....	....	....	....	....	....	....	....	....	....	....	....	....	....
99-2000	Windsor Spitfires	OHL	66	23	39	62	131	....	....	....	....	....	....	....	....	....	12	3	5	8	21	....	....	....	....
2000-01	Windsor Spitfires	OHL	55	50	37	87	164	....	....	....	....	....	....	....	....	....	9	3	8	11	27	....	....	....	....
2001-02	Windsor Spitfires	OHL	53	43	45	88	178	....	....	....	....	....	....	....	....	....	14	6	10	16	49	....	....	....	....
2002-03	Utah Grizzlies	AHL	40	9	11	20	98	....	....	....	....	....	....	....	....	....	....	....	....	....	....	....	....	....	....
	Dallas	NHL	26	3	4	7	31	0	0	0	25	12.0	6	4	50.0	8:46	1	0	0	0	0	0	0	0	6:57
2003-04	Dallas	NHL	73	2	10	12	152	0	0	1	74	2.7	–2	59	49.2	10:14	4	1	0	1	0	0	0	1	6:55
2004-05	Hamilton	AHL	67	18	21	39	279	....	....	....	....	....	....	....	....	....	4	0	0	0	20	....	....	....	....
2005-06	Dallas	NHL	82	5	17	22	178	0	0	1	89	5.6	1	535	49.2	11:54	5	0	1	1	2	0	0	0	7:41
	NHL Totals		181	10	31	41	361	0	0	2	188	5.3		598	49.2	10:47	10	1	1	2	2	0	0	1	7:18

OHL Second All-Star Team (2002)

OUELLET, Michel

(oo-LEHT, mee-SHEHL) **PIT.**

Right wing. Shoots right. 6', 201 lbs. Born, Rimouski, Que., March 5, 1982. Pittsburgh's 4th choice, 124th overall, in 2000 Entry Draft.

Season	Club	League	GP	G	A	Pts	PIM	PP	SH	GW	S	%	+/-	TF	F%	Min	GP	G	A	Pts	PIM	PP	SH	GW	Min
1997-98	Jonquiere Elites	QAAA	33	20	32	52	52	....	....	....	....	....	....	....	....	....	....	....	....	....	....	....	....	....	....
1998-99	Rimouski Oceanic	QMJHL	28	7	13	20	10	....	....	....	....	....	....	....	....	....	11	0	1	1	6	....	....	....	....
99-2000	Rimouski Oceanic	QMJHL	72	36	53	89	38	....	....	....	....	....	....	....	....	....	14	4	5	9	14	....	....	....	....
2000-01	Rimouski Oceanic	QMJHL	63	42	50	92	50	....	....	....	....	....	....	....	....	....	11	6	7	13	8	....	....	....	....
2001-02	Rimouski Oceanic	QMJHL	61	40	58	98	66	....	....	....	....	....	....	....	....	....	7	3	6	9	4	....	....	....	....
2002-03	Wilkes-Barre	AHL	4	0	2	2	0	....	....	....	....	....	....	....	....	....	....	....	....	....	....	....	....	....	....
	Wheeling Nailers	ECHL	55	20	26	46	40	....	....	....	....	....	....	....	....	....	....	....	....	....	....	....	....	....	....
2003-04	Wilkes-Barre	AHL	79	30	19	49	34	....	....	....	....	....	....	....	....	....	22	2	10	12	6	....	....	....	....
2004-05	Wilkes-Barre	AHL	80	31	32	63	56	....	....	....	....	....	....	....	....	....	11	2	3	5	6	....	....	....	....
2005-06	Pittsburgh	NHL	50	16	16	32	16	11	0	0	87	18.4	–13	16	37.5	14:02	....	....	....	....	....	....	....	....	....
	Wilkes-Barre	AHL	19	10	20	30	12	....	....	....	....	....	....	....	....	....	....	....	....	....	....	....	....	....	....
	NHL Totals		50	16	16	32	16	11	0	0	87	18.4		16	37.5	14:02	....	....	....	....	....	....	....	....	....

AHL All-Rookie Team (2004)

OVECHKIN, Alex

(oh-VEHCH-kihn, al-EHX) **WSH.**

Left wing. Shoots right. 6'2", 212 lbs. Born, Moscow, USSR, September 17, 1985. Washington's 1st choice, 1st overall, in 2004 Entry Draft.

Season	Club	League	GP	G	A	Pts	PIM	PP	SH	GW	S	%	+/-	TF	F%	Min	GP	G	A	Pts	PIM	PP	SH	GW	Min
2001-02	Dyn'o Moscow 2	Russia-3	19	18	8	26	20	....	....	....	....	....	....	....	....	....	....	....	....	....	....	....	....	....	....
	Dynamo Moscow	Russia	22	2	2	4	4	....	....	....	....	....	....	....	....	....	3	0	0	0	0	....	....	....	....
2002-03	Dynamo Moscow	Russia	40	8	7	15	28	....	....	....	....	....	....	....	....	....	5	0	0	0	2	....	....	....	....
2003-04	Dynamo Moscow	Russia	53	13	11	24	40	....	....	....	....	....	....	....	....	....	3	0	0	0	2	....	....	....	....
2004-05	Dynamo Moscow	Russia	37	13	13	26	32	....	....	....	....	....	....	....	....	....	10	2	4	6	31	....	....	....	....
2005-06	Washington	NHL	81	52	54	106	52	21	3	5	425	12.2	2	16	12.5	21:37	....	....	....	....	....	....	....	....	....
	Russia	Olympics	8	5	0	5	8	....	....	....	....	....	....	....	....	....	....	....	....	....	....	....	....	....	....
	NHL Totals		81	52	54	106	52	21	3	5	425	12.2		16	12.5	21:37	....	....	....	....	....	....	....	....	....

Olympic Tournament All-Star Team (2006) • NHL All-Rookie Team (2006) • NHL First All-Star Team (2006) • Calder Memorial Trophy (2006)

OZOLINSH, Sandis

(OH-zoh-LIHNCH, SAN-dihz) **NYR**

Defense. Shoots left. 6'3", 220 lbs. Born, Riga, Latvia, August 3, 1972. San Jose's 3rd choice, 30th overall, in 1991 Entry Draft.

Season	Club	League	GP	G	A	Pts	PIM	PP	SH	GW	S	%	+/-	TF	F%	Min	GP	G	A	Pts	PIM	PP	SH	GW	Min
1990-91	Dynamo Riga	USSR	44	0	3	3	51	....	....	....	....	....	....	....	....	....	....	....	....	....	....	....	....	....	....
1991-92	Rigas Stars	CIS	30	6	0	6	42	....	....	....	....	....	....	....	....	....	....	....	....	....	....	....	....	....	....
	Kansas City	IHL	34	6	9	15	20	....	....	....	....	....	....	....	....	....	15	2	5	7	22	....	....	....	....
1992-93	San Jose	NHL	37	7	16	23	40	2	0	0	83	8.4	–9	....	....	....	....	....	....	....	....	....	....	....	....
1993-94	San Jose	NHL	81	26	38	64	24	4	0	3	157	16.6	16	....	....	....	14	0	10	10	8	0	0	0	....
1994-95	San Jose	NHL	48	9	16	25	30	3	1	2	83	10.8	–6	....	....	....	11	3	2	5	6	1	0	0	....
1995-96	San Francisco	IHL	2	1	0	1	0	....	....	....	....	....	....	....	....	....	....	....	....	....	....	....	....	....	....
	San Jose	NHL	7	1	3	4	4	1	0	0	21	4.8	2	....	....	....	....	....	....	....	....	....	....	....	....
	♦ Colorado	NHL	66	13	37	50	50	7	1	1	145	9.0	0	....	....	....	22	5	14	19	16	2	0	1	....
1996-97	Colorado	NHL	80	23	45	68	88	13	0	4	232	9.9	4	....	....	....	17	4	13	17	24	2	0	1	....
1997-98	Colorado	NHL	66	13	38	51	65	9	0	2	135	9.6	–12	....	....	....	7	0	7	7	14	0	0	0	....
1998-99	Colorado	NHL	39	7	25	32	22	4	0	3	81	8.6	10	0	0.0	22:06	19	4	8	12	22	3	0	1	22:24
99-2000	Colorado	NHL	82	16	36	52	46	6	0	1	210	7.6	17	0	0.0	22:41	17	5	5	10	20	3	0	1	18:35
2000-01	Carolina	NHL	72	12	32	44	71	4	2	2	145	8.3	–25	0	0.0	22:12	6	0	2	2	5	0	0	0	19:04
2001-02	Carolina	NHL	46	4	19	23	34	1	0	0	71	5.6	–4	0	0.0	19:30	....	....	....	....	....	....	....	....	....
	Florida	NHL	37	10	19	29	24	2	0	1	101	9.9	–3	0	0.0	30:30	....	....	....	....	....	....	....	....	....
	Latvia	Olympics	1	0	4	4	0	....	....	....	....	....	....	....	....	....	....	....	....	....	....	....	....	....	....
2002-03	Florida	NHL	51	7	19	26	40	5	0	2	83	8.4	–16	0	0.0	28:23	....	....	....	....	....	....	....	....	....
	Anaheim	NHL	31	5	13	18	16	1	0	1	54	9.3	10	0	0.0	22:08	21	2	6	8	10	0	0	1	23:37
2003-04	Anaheim	NHL	36	5	11	16	24	1	0	2	58	8.6	–7	0	0.0	19:57	....	....	....	....	....	....	....	....	....

			Regular Season														Playoffs								
Season	Club	League	GP	G	A	Pts	PIM	PP	SH	GW	S	%	+/-	TF	F%	Min	GP	G	A	Pts	PIM	PP	SH	GW	Min
2004-05			DID NOT PLAY																						
2005-06	**Anaheim**	**NHL**	**17**	**3**	**3**	**6**	**8**	**0**	**0**	**2**	**17**	**17.6**	**–4**	**0**	**0.0**	**17:45**	....	....	....	....	....	....	....	....	....
	NY Rangers	**NHL**	**19**	**3**	**11**	**14**	**20**	**2**	**0**	**0**	**41**	**7.3**	**2**	**0**	**0.0**	**23:48**	**3**	**0**	**0**	**0**	**6**	**0**	**0**	**0**	**21:27**
	Latvia	Olympics	5	1	3	4	0	....	....	....	....	....	....	....	....	....	....	....	....	....	....	....	....	....	....
	NHL Totals		**815**	**164**	**381**	**545**	**606**	**65**	**4**	**26**	**1717**	**9.6**		**0**	**0.0**	**23:09**	**137**	**23**	**67**	**90**	**131**	**11**	**0**	**5**	**21:28**

NHL First All-Star Team (1997)

Played in NHL All-Star Game (1994, 1997, 1998, 2000, 2001, 2002, 2003)

• Missed majority of 1992-93 season recovering from knee injury suffered in game vs. Philadelphia, December 30, 1992. Traded to **Colorado** by **San Jose** for Owen Nolan, October 26, 1995. Traded to **Carolina** by **Colorado** with Columbus' 2nd round choice (previously acquired, Carolina selected Tomas Kurka) in 2000 Entry Draft for Nolan Pratt, Carolina's 1st (Vaclav Nedorost) and 2nd (Jared Aulin) round choices in 2000 Entry Draft and Philadelphia's 2nd round choice (previously acquired, Colorado selected Agris Saviels) in 2000 Entry Draft, June 24, 2000. Traded to **Florida** by **Carolina** with Byron Ritchie for Bret Hedican, Kevyn Adams and Tomas Malec, January 16, 2002. Traded to **Anaheim** by **Florida** with Lance Ward for Pavel Trnka, Matt Cullen and Anaheim's 4th round choice (James Pemberton) in 2003 Entry Draft, January 30, 2003. • Missed majority of 2003-04 season recovering from shoulder injury suffered in game vs. Colorado, December 19, 2003. Traded to **NY Rangers** by **Anaheim** for San Jose's 3rd round choice (previously acquired, Anaheim selected John DeGray) in 2006 Entry Draft, March 9, 2006.

PAETSCH, Nathan (PASH, NAY-thuhn) BUF.

Defense. Shoots left. 6', 198 lbs. Born, Humboldt, Sask., March 30, 1983. Buffalo's 8th choice, 202nd overall, in 2003 Entry Draft.

Season	Club	League	GP	G	A	Pts	PIM	PP	SH	GW	S	%	+/-	TF	F%	Min	GP	G	A	Pts	PIM	PP	SH	GW	Min
1998-99	Tisdale Trojans	SMHL	74	20	55	75	120	....	....	....	....	....	....	....	....	....	....	....	....	....	....	....	....	....	....
	Moose Jaw	WHL	2	0	0	0	0	....	....	....	....	....	....	....	....	....	....	....	....	....	....	....	....	....	....
99-2000	Moose Jaw	WHL	68	9	35	44	49	....	....	....	....	....	....	....	....	....	4	0	1	1	0	....	....	....	....
2000-01	Moose Jaw	WHL	70	8	54	62	118	....	....	....	....	....	....	....	....	....	4	1	2	3	6	....	....	....	....
2001-02	Moose Jaw	WHL	59	16	36	52	86	....	....	....	....	....	....	....	....	....	12	0	4	4	16	....	....	....	....
2002-03	Moose Jaw	WHL	59	15	39	54	81	....	....	....	....	....	....	....	....	....	13	3	10	13	6	....	....	....	....
2003-04	Rochester	AHL	54	5	5	10	49	....	....	....	....	....	....	....	....	....	16	1	1	2	28	....	....	....	....
2004-05	Rochester	AHL	80	4	19	23	150	....	....	....	....	....	....	....	....	....	9	1	1	2	16	....	....	....	....
2005-06	**Buffalo**	**NHL**	**1**	**0**	**1**	**1**	**0**	**0**	**0**	**0**	**0**	**0.0**	**–1**	**0**	**0.0**	**15:38**	**1**	**0**	**0**	**0**	**0**	**0**	**0**	**0**	**12:06**
	Rochester	AHL	72	11	39	50	90	....	....	....	....	....	....	....	....	....	....	....	....	....	....	....	....	....	....
	NHL Totals		**1**	**0**	**1**	**1**	**0**	**0**	**0**	**0**	**0**	**0.0**		**0**	**0.0**	**15:38**	**1**	**0**	**0**	**0**	**0**	**0**	**0**	**0**	**12:06**

• Re-entered NHL Entry Draft. Originally Washington's 1st choice, 58th overall, in 2001 Entry Draft.

WHL East Second All-Star Team (2003)

PAHLSSON, Samuel (PAWL-suhn, SAM-ew-l) ANA.

Center. Shoots left. 5'11", 212 lbs. Born, Ornskoldsvik, Sweden, December 17, 1977. Colorado's 10th choice, 176th overall, in 1996 Entry Draft.

Season	Club	League	GP	G	A	Pts	PIM	PP	SH	GW	S	%	+/-	TF	F%	Min	GP	G	A	Pts	PIM	PP	SH	GW	Min
1992-93	Ange IK	Sweden-4	9	0	0	0	0	....	....	....	....	....	....	....	....	....	....	....	....	....	....	....	....	....	....
1993-94	Ange IK	Sweden-4	STATISTICS NOT AVAILABLE																						
1994-95	MoDo	Sweden	1	0	0	0	0	....	....	....	....	....	....	....	....	....	....	....	....	....	....	....	....	....	....
1995-96	MoDo Jr.	Swe-Jr.	30	10	11	21	26	....	....	....	....	....	....	....	....	....	....	....	....	....	....	....	....	....	....
	MoDo	Sweden	36	1	3	4	8	....	....	....	....	....	....	....	....	....	4	0	0	0	0	....	....	....	....
1996-97	MoDo	Sweden	49	8	9	17	83	....	....	....	....	....	....	....	....	....	....	....	....	....	....	....	....	....	....
	MoDo Jr.	Swe-Jr.	5	2	6	8	2	....	....	....	....	....	....	....	....	....	....	....	....	....	....	....	....	....	....
1997-98	MoDo	Sweden	23	6	11	17	24	....	....	....	....	....	....	....	....	....	9	3	0	3	6	....	....	....	....
1998-99	MoDo	Sweden	50	17	17	34	44	....	....	....	....	....	....	....	....	....	13	3	3	6	10	....	....	....	....
99-2000	MoDo	Sweden	47	16	11	27	67	....	....	....	....	....	....	....	....	....	13	3	3	6	8	....	....	....	....
	MoDo	EuroHL	4	1	0	1	0	....	....	....	....	....	....	....	....	....	3	1	1	2	2	....	....	....	....
2000-01	**Boston**	**NHL**	**17**	**1**	**1**	**2**	**6**	**0**	**0**	**0**	**13**	**7.7**	**–5**	**239**	**40.2**	**14:19**	....	....	....	....	....	....	....	....	....
	Anaheim	**NHL**	**59**	**3**	**4**	**7**	**14**	**1**	**1**	**1**	**46**	**6.5**	**–9**	**867**	**45.1**	**14:14**	....	....	....	....	....	....	....	....	....
2001-02	**Anaheim**	**NHL**	**80**	**6**	**14**	**20**	**26**	**1**	**1**	**0**	**99**	**6.1**	**–16**	**1201**	**49.8**	**16:24**	....	....	....	....	....	....	....	....	....
2002-03	**Anaheim**	**NHL**	**34**	**4**	**11**	**15**	**18**	**0**	**1**	**2**	**28**	**14.3**	**10**	**118**	**52.5**	**13:20**	**21**	**2**	**4**	**6**	**12**	**0**	**0**	**0**	**16:41**
	Cincinnati	AHL	13	1	7	8	24	....	....	....	....	....	....	....	....	....	....	....	....	....	....	....	....	....	....
2003-04	**Anaheim**	**NHL**	**82**	**8**	**14**	**22**	**52**	**1**	**0**	**2**	**134**	**6.0**	**–2**	**908**	**55.3**	**16:51**	....	....	....	....	....	....	....	....	....
2004-05	Frolunda	Sweden	48	6	18	24	56	....	....	....	....	....	....	....	....	....	14	4	7	11	24	....	....	....	....
2005-06	**Anaheim**	**NHL**	**82**	**11**	**10**	**21**	**34**	**0**	**3**	**1**	**116**	**9.5**	**–1**	**1517**	**52.8**	**16:30**	**16**	**2**	**3**	**5**	**18**	**0**	**0**	**2**	**17:06**
	Sweden	Olympics	8	2	2	4	8	....	....	....	....	....	....	....	....	....	....	....	....	....	....	....	....	....	....
	NHL Totals		**354**	**33**	**54**	**87**	**150**	**3**	**6**	**6**	**436**	**7.6**		**4850**	**50.5**	**15:46**	**37**	**4**	**7**	**11**	**30**	**0**	**0**	**2**	**16:52**

Traded to **Boston** by **Colorado** with Brian Rolston, Martin Grenier and New Jersey's 1st round choice (previously acquired, Boston selected Martin Samuelsson) in 2000 Entry Draft for Raymond Bourque and Dave Andreychuk, March 6, 2000. Traded to **Anaheim** by **Boston** for Patrick Traverse and Andrei Nazarov, November 18, 2000. Signed as a free agent by **Frolunda** (Sweden), September, 2004.

PAILLE, Dan (PIGH-yay, DAN) BUF.

Left wing. Shoots left. 6', 200 lbs. Born, Welland, Ont., April 15, 1984. Buffalo's 2nd choice, 20th overall, in 2002 Entry Draft.

Season	Club	League	GP	G	A	Pts	PIM	PP	SH	GW	S	%	+/-	TF	F%	Min	GP	G	A	Pts	PIM	PP	SH	GW	Min
99-2000	Welland Cougars	OHA-B	42	14	17	31	19	....	....	....	....	....	....	....	....	....	16	16	16	32	....	....	....	....	....
2000-01	Guelph Storm	OHL	64	22	31	53	57	....	....	....	....	....	....	....	....	....	4	2	0	2	2	....	....	....	....
2001-02	Guelph Storm	OHL	62	27	30	57	54	....	....	....	....	....	....	....	....	....	9	5	2	7	9	....	....	....	....
2002-03	Guelph Storm	OHL	54	30	27	57	28	....	....	....	....	....	....	....	....	....	11	8	6	14	6	....	....	....	....
2003-04	Guelph Storm	OHL	59	37	43	80	63	....	....	....	....	....	....	....	....	....	22	9	9	18	14	....	....	....	....
2004-05	Rochester	AHL	79	14	15	29	54	....	....	....	....	....	....	....	....	....	9	2	2	4	6	....	....	....	....
2005-06	**Buffalo**	**NHL**	**14**	**1**	**2**	**3**	**2**	**0**	**0**	**0**	**15**	**6.7**	**5**	**4**	**25.0**	**10:24**	....	....	....	....	....	....	....	....	....
	Rochester	AHL	45	14	13	27	29	....	....	....	....	....	....	....	....	....	....	....	....	....	....	....	....	....	....
	NHL Totals		**14**	**1**	**2**	**3**	**2**	**0**	**0**	**0**	**15**	**6.7**		**4**	**25.0**	**10:24**	....	....	....	....	....	....	....	....	....

PALFFY, Ziggy (PAHL-fee, ZIHG-gee)

Right wing. Shoots left. 5'10", 183 lbs. Born, Skalica, Czech., May 5, 1972. NY Islanders' 2nd choice, 26th overall, in 1991 Entry Draft.

Season	Club	League	GP	G	A	Pts	PIM	PP	SH	GW	S	%	+/-	TF	F%	Min	GP	G	A	Pts	PIM	PP	SH	GW	Min
1990-91	AC Nitra	Czech	50	34	16	50	18	....	....	....	....	....	....	....	....	....	....	....	....	....	....	....	....	....	....
1991-92	Dukla Trencin	Czech	45	41	33	74	36	....	....	....	....	....	....	....	....	....	....	....	....	....	....	....	....	....	....
1992-93	Dukla Trencin	Czech	43	38	41	79	....	....	....	....	....	....	....	....	....	....	....	....	....	....	....	....	....	....	....
1993-94	**NY Islanders**	**NHL**	**5**	**0**	**0**	**0**	**0**	**0**	**0**	**0**	**5**	**0.0**	**–6**	....	....	....	....	....	....	....	....	....	....	....	....
	Salt Lake	IHL	57	25	32	57	83	....	....	....	....	....	....	....	....	....	....	....	....	....	....	....	....	....	....
	Slovakia	Olympics	8	3	*7	*10	8	....	....	....	....	....	....	....	....	....	....	....	....	....	....	....	....	....	....
1994-95	Denver Grizzlies	IHL	33	20	23	43	40	....	....	....	....	....	....	....	....	....	....	....	....	....	....	....	....	....	....
	NY Islanders	**NHL**	**33**	**10**	**7**	**17**	**6**	**1**	**0**	**1**	**75**	**13.3**	**3**	....	....	....	....	....	....	....	....	....	....	....	....
1995-96	**NY Islanders**	**NHL**	**81**	**43**	**44**	**87**	**56**	**17**	**1**	**6**	**257**	**16.7**	**–17**	....	....	....	....	....	....	....	....	....	....	....	....
1996-97	Dukla Trencin	Slovakia	1	0	0	0	....	....	....	....	....	....	....	....	....	....	....	....	....	....	....	....	....	....	....
	NY Islanders	**NHL**	**80**	**48**	**42**	**90**	**43**	**6**	**4**	**6**	**292**	**16.4**	**21**	....	....	....	....	....	....	....	....	....	....	....	....
1997-98	**NY Islanders**	**NHL**	**82**	**45**	**42**	**87**	**34**	**17**	**2**	**5**	**277**	**16.2**	**–2**	....	....	....	....	....	....	....	....	....	....	....	....
1998-99	HK 36 Skalica	Slovakia	9	11	8	19	6	....	....	....	....	....	....	....	....	....	....	....	....	....	....	....	....	....	....
	NY Islanders	**NHL**	**50**	**22**	**28**	**50**	**34**	**5**	**2**	**1**	**168**	**13.1**	**–6**	**1**	**100.0**	**22:04**	....	....	....	....	....	....	....	....	....
99-2000	**Los Angeles**	**NHL**	**64**	**27**	**39**	**66**	**32**	**4**	**0**	**3**	**186**	**14.5**	**18**	**7**	**42.9**	**19:39**	**4**	**2**	**0**	**2**	**0**	**0**	**0**	**0**	**21:21**
2000-01	**Los Angeles**	**NHL**	**73**	**38**	**51**	**89**	**20**	**12**	**4**	**8**	**217**	**17.5**	**22**	**5**	**80.0**	**19:46**	**13**	**3**	**5**	**8**	**8**	**0**	**0**	**0**	**22:27**
2001-02	**Los Angeles**	**NHL**	**63**	**32**	**27**	**59**	**26**	**15**	**1**	**6**	**161**	**19.9**	**5**	**3**	**66.7**	**20:18**	**7**	**4**	**5**	**9**	**0**	**0**	**0**	**0**	**22:23**
	Slovakia	Olympics	1	0	0	0	0	....	....	....	....	....	....	....	....	....	....	....	....	....	....	....	....	....	....
2002-03	**Los Angeles**	**NHL**	**76**	**37**	**48**	**85**	**47**	**10**	**2**	**5**	**277**	**13.4**	**22**	**10**	**30.0**	**22:27**	....	....	....	....	....	....	....	....	....
2003-04	**Los Angeles**	**NHL**	**35**	**16**	**25**	**41**	**12**	**3**	**3**	**2**	**109**	**14.7**	**18**	**7**	**0.0**	**21:32**	....	....	....	....	....	....	....	....	....
2004-05	HK 36 Skalica	Slovakia	8	10	3	13	6	....	....	....	....	....	....	....	....	....	....	....	....	....	....	....	....	....	....
	HC Slavia Praha	CzRep	41	21	19	40	30	....	....	....	....	....	....	....	....	....	7	5	2	7	2	....	....	....	....
2005-06	**Pittsburgh**	**NHL**	**42**	**11**	**31**	**42**	**12**	**2**	**0**	**2**	**112**	**9.8**	**5**	**4**	**50.0**	**19:19**	....	....	....	....	....	....	....	....	....
	NHL Totals		**684**	**329**	**384**	**713**	**322**	**92**	**19**	**45**	**2136**	**15.4**		**37**	**40.5**	**20:44**	**24**	**9**	**10**	**19**	**8**	**0**	**0**	**0**	**22:15**

Played in NHL All-Star Game (1998, 2001, 2002)

Traded to **Los Angeles** by **NY Islanders** with Brian Smolinski, Marcel Cousineau and New Jersey's 4th round choice (previously acquired, Los Angeles selected Daniel Johansson) in 1999 Entry Draft for Olli Jokinen, Josh Green, Mathieu Biron and Los Angeles' 1st round choice (Taylor Pyatt) in 1999 Entry Draft, June 20, 1999. • Missed majority of 2003-04 season recovering from shoulder injury suffered in game vs. Anaheim, January 7, 2004. Signed as a free agent by **Slavia Praha** (CzRep), September 15, 2004. Signed as a free agent by **Skalica** (Slovakia), October 7, 2004. Signed as a free agent by **Slavia Praha** (CzRep), November 16, 2004. Signed as a free agent by **Pittsburgh**, August 6, 2005. • Officially announced retirement January 18, 2006.

PANDOLFO, Jay

(pan-DAHL-foh, JAY) **N.J.**

Left wing. Shoots left. 6'1", 190 lbs. Born, Winchester, MA, December 27, 1974. New Jersey's 2nd choice, 32nd overall, in 1993 Entry Draft.

			Regular Season														Playoffs								
Season	Club	League	GP	G	A	Pts	PIM	PP	SH	GW	S	%	+/-	TF	F%	Min	GP	G	A	Pts	PIM	PP	SH	GW	Min
1989-90	Burlington	High-MA	23	33	30	63	18	....	....	....	....	....	....	....	....	....	....	....	....	....	....	....	....	....	....
1990-91	Burlington	High-MA	20	19	27	46	10	....	....	....	....	....	....	....	....	....	....	....	....	....	....	....	....	....	....
1991-92	Burlington	High-MA	20	35	34	69	14	....	....	....	....	....	....	....	....	....	....	....	....	....	....	....	....	....	....
1992-93	Boston University	H-East	37	16	22	38	16	....	....	....	....	....	....	....	....	....	....	....	....	....	....	....	....	....	....
1993-94	Boston University	H-East	37	17	25	42	27	....	....	....	....	....	....	....	....	....	....	....	....	....	....	....	....	....	....
1994-95	Boston University	H-East	20	7	13	20	6	....	....	....	....	....	....	....	....	....	....	....	....	....	....	....	....	....	....
1995-96	Boston University	H-East	39	*38	29	67	6	....	....	....	....	....	....	....	....	....	....	....	....	....	....	....	....	....	....
	Albany River Rats	AHL	5	3	1	4	0	....	....	....	....	....	....	....	....	....	3	0	0	0	0	....	....	....	....
1996-97	**New Jersey**	**NHL**	**46**	**6**	**8**	**14**	**6**	**0**	**0**	**1**	**61**	**9.8**	**–1**	....	....	....	**6**	**0**	**1**	**1**	**0**	**0**	**0**	**0**	....
	Albany River Rats	AHL	12	3	9	12	0	....	....	....	....	....	....	....	....	....	....	....	....	....	....	....	....	....	....
1997-98	**New Jersey**	**NHL**	**23**	**1**	**3**	**4**	**4**	**0**	**0**	**0**	**23**	**4.3**	**–4**	....	....	....	**3**	**0**	**2**	**2**	**0**	**0**	**0**	**0**	....
	Albany River Rats	AHL	51	18	19	37	24	....	....	....	....	....	....	....	....	....	....	....	....	....	....	....	....	....	....
1998-99	**New Jersey**	**NHL**	**70**	**14**	**13**	**27**	**10**	**1**	**1**	**4**	**100**	**14.0**	**3**	**10**	**40.0**	**15:13**	**7**	**1**	**0**	**1**	**0**	**0**	**0**	**0**	**13:19**
99-2000 ♦	**New Jersey**	**NHL**	**71**	**7**	**8**	**15**	**4**	**0**	**0**	**0**	**86**	**8.1**	**0**	**19**	**47.4**	**13:25**	**23**	**0**	**5**	**5**	**0**	**0**	**0**	**0**	**15:35**
2000-01	**New Jersey**	**NHL**	**63**	**4**	**12**	**16**	**16**	**0**	**0**	**0**	**57**	**7.0**	**3**	**15**	**53.3**	**14:05**	**25**	**1**	**4**	**5**	**4**	**0**	**0**	**0**	**12:38**
2001-02	**New Jersey**	**NHL**	**65**	**4**	**10**	**14**	**15**	**0**	**1**	**0**	**72**	**5.6**	**12**	**12**	**41.7**	**13:59**	**6**	**0**	**0**	**0**	**0**	**0**	**0**	**0**	**16:11**
2002-03 ♦	**New Jersey**	**NHL**	**68**	**6**	**11**	**17**	**23**	**0**	**1**	**4**	**92**	**6.5**	**12**	**13**	**23.1**	**16:08**	**24**	**6**	**6**	**12**	**2**	**0**	**0**	**1**	**16:34**
2003-04	**New Jersey**	**NHL**	**82**	**13**	**13**	**26**	**14**	**1**	**2**	**4**	**140**	**9.3**	**5**	**25**	**44.0**	**16:00**	**5**	**0**	**0**	**0**	**0**	**0**	**0**	**0**	**13:41**
2004-05	Salzburg	Austria	19	5	7	12	0	....	....	....	....	....	....	....	....	....	....	....	....	....	....	....	....	....	....
2005-06	**New Jersey**	**NHL**	**82**	**10**	**10**	**20**	**16**	**0**	**0**	**0**	**116**	**8.6**	**2**	**13**	**30.8**	**18:03**	**9**	**1**	**4**	**5**	**0**	**0**	**1**	**1**	**18:37**
	NHL Totals		**570**	**65**	**88**	**153**	**108**	**2**	**5**	**13**	**747**	**8.7**		**107**	**41.1**	**15:23**	**108**	**9**	**22**	**31**	**6**	**0**	**1**	**2**	**15:08**

Hockey East First All-Star Team (1996) • Hockey East Player of the Year (1996) • NCAA East First All-American Team (1996)
Signed as a free agent by **Salzburg** (Austria), December 27, 2004.

PANDOLFO, Mike

(pan-DAHL-foh, MIGHK)

Left wing. Shoots left. 6'3", 221 lbs. Born, Winchester, MA, September 15, 1979. Buffalo's 5th choice, 77th overall, in 1998 Entry Draft.

1996-97	St. Sebastian's	High-MA	32	27	28	55	30	....	....	....	....	....	....	....	....	....	....	....	....	....	....	....	....	....	....
1997-98	St. Sebastian's	High-MA	28	29	23	52	18	....	....	....	....	....	....	....	....	....	....	....	....	....	....	....	....	....	....
1998-99	Boston University	H-East	34	13	4	17	26	....	....	....	....	....	....	....	....	....	....	....	....	....	....	....	....	....	....
99-2000	Boston University	H-East	41	13	10	23	37	....	....	....	....	....	....	....	....	....	....	....	....	....	....	....	....	....	....
2000-01	Boston University	H-East	37	16	13	29	30	....	....	....	....	....	....	....	....	....	....	....	....	....	....	....	....	....	....
2001-02	Boston University	H-East	38	22	18	40	22	....	....	....	....	....	....	....	....	....	....	....	....	....	....	....	....	....	....
2002-03	Syracuse Crunch	AHL	74	9	9	18	31	....	....	....	....	....	....	....	....	....	....	....	....	....	....	....	....	....	....
2003-04	**Columbus**	**NHL**	**3**	**0**	**0**	**0**	**0**	**0**	**0**	**0**	**3**	**0.0**	**–2**	**0**	**0.0**	**8:18**	....	....	....	....	....	....	....	....	....
	Syracuse Crunch	AHL	77	18	19	37	29	....	....	....	....	....	....	....	....	....	7	1	0	1	2	....	....	....	....
2004-05	Syracuse Crunch	AHL	62	8	8	16	18	....	....	....	....	....	....	....	....	....	....	....	....	....	....	....	....	....	....
2005-06	Reading Royals	ECHL	23	14	11	25	8	....	....	....	....	....	....	....	....	....	....	....	....	....	....	....	....	....	....
	Binghamton	AHL	1	0	0	0	4	....	....	....	....	....	....	....	....	....	....	....	....	....	....	....	....	....	....
	NHL Totals		**3**	**0**	**0**	**0**	**0**	**0**	**0**	**0**	**3**	**0.0**		**0**	**0.0**	**8:18**	....	....	....	....	....	....	....	....	....

Rights traded to **Columbus** by **Buffalo** with Detroit's 1st round choice (previously acquired, later traded to Atlanta – Atlanta selected Jim Slater) in 2002 Entry Draft for New Jersey's 1st round choice (previously acquired, Buffalo selected Dan Paille) in 2002 Entry Draft, June 22, 2002.

PAPINEAU, Justin

(PA-pee-noh, JUHS-tihn) **N.J.**

Center. Shoots left. 5'11", 205 lbs. Born, Ottawa, Ont., January 15, 1980. St. Louis' 3rd choice, 75th overall, in 2000 Entry Draft.

1995-96	Ott. Jr. Senators	CJHL	52	31	19	50	51	....	....	....	....	....	....	....	....	....	....	....	....	....	....	....	....	....	....
1996-97	Belleville Bulls	OHL	50	10	32	42	32	....	....	....	....	....	....	....	....	....	....	....	....	....	....	....	....	....	....
1997-98	Belleville Bulls	OHL	66	41	53	94	34	....	....	....	....	....	....	....	....	....	10	5	9	14	6	....	....	....	....
1998-99	Belleville Bulls	OHL	68	52	47	99	28	....	....	....	....	....	....	....	....	....	21	*21	*30	*51	20	....	....	....	....
99-2000	Belleville Bulls	OHL	60	40	36	76	52	....	....	....	....	....	....	....	....	....	16	4	12	16	16	....	....	....	....
2000-01	Worcester IceCats	AHL	43	7	22	29	33	....	....	....	....	....	....	....	....	....	11	7	3	10	8	....	....	....	....
2001-02	**St. Louis**	**NHL**	**1**	**0**	**0**	**0**	**0**	**0**	**0**	**0**	**0**	**0.0**	**–2**	**7**	**42.9**	**8:40**	....	....	....	....	....	....	....	....	....
	Worcester IceCats	AHL	75	*38	38	76	86	....	....	....	....	....	....	....	....	....	3	1	2	3	4	....	....	....	....
2002-03	**St. Louis**	**NHL**	**11**	**2**	**1**	**3**	**0**	**0**	**0**	**1**	**15**	**13.3**	**–1**	**99**	**44.4**	**10:59**	....	....	....	....	....	....	....	....	....
	Worcester IceCats	AHL	44	21	17	38	42	....	....	....	....	....	....	....	....	....	....	....	....	....	....	....	....	....	....
	NY Islanders	**NHL**	**5**	**1**	**2**	**3**	**4**	**0**	**0**	**1**	**8**	**12.5**	**1**	**15**	**53.3**	**14:50**	**1**	**0**	**0**	**0**	**0**	**0**	**0**	**0**	**5:12**
	Bridgeport	AHL	5	7	1	8	4	....	....	....	....	....	....	....	....	....	7	1	3	4	7	....	....	....	....
2003-04	**NY Islanders**	**NHL**	**64**	**8**	**5**	**13**	**8**	**5**	**0**	**2**	**44**	**18.2**	**4**	**49**	**38.8**	**7:42**	....	....	....	....	....	....	....	....	....
2004-05	Bridgeport	AHL	59	18	15	33	52	....	....	....	....	....	....	....	....	....	....	....	....	....	....	....	....	....	....
2005-06	Bridgeport	AHL	12	6	6	12	12	....	....	....	....	....	....	....	....	....	5	1	3	4	4	....	....	....	....
	NHL Totals		**81**	**11**	**8**	**19**	**12**	**5**	**0**	**4**	**67**	**16.4**		**170**	**43.5**	**8:36**	**1**	**0**	**0**	**0**	**0**	**0**	**0**	**0**	**5:12**

• Re-entered NHL Entry Draft. Originally Los Angeles' 2nd choice, 46th overall, in 1998 Entry Draft.
Traded to **NY Islanders** by **St. Louis** with St. Louis' 2nd round choice (Jeremy Colliton) in 2003 Entry Draft for Chris Osgood and NY Islanders' 3rd round choice (Konstantin Barulin) in 2003 Entry Draft, March 11, 2003. Signed as a free agent by **New Jersey**, August, 2006.

PARISE, Zach

(pah-REE-say, ZAK) **N.J.**

Center. Shoots left. 5'11", 185 lbs. Born, Minneapolis, MN, July 28, 1984. New Jersey's 1st choice, 17th overall, in 2003 Entry Draft.

2000-01	Shat.-St. Mary's	High-MN	58	69	93	162																			
2001-02	Shat.-St. Mary's	High-MN	67	77	101	178	58	....	....	....	....	....	....	....	....	....	....	....	....	....	....	....	....	....	....
	USNTDP	U-18	12	7	7	14	6	....	....	....	....	....	....	....	....	....	....	....	....	....	....	....	....	....	....
2002-03	North Dakota	WCHA	39	26	35	61	34	....	....	....	....	....	....	....	....	....	....	....	....	....	....	....	....	....	....
2003-04	North Dakota	WCHA	37	23	32	55	24	....	....	....	....	....	....	....	....	....	....	....	....	....	....	....	....	....	....
2004-05	Albany River Rats	AHL	73	18	40	58	56	....	....	....	....	....	....	....	....	....	....	....	....	....	....	....	....	....	....
2005-06	**New Jersey**	**NHL**	**81**	**14**	**18**	**32**	**28**	**2**	**0**	**5**	**133**	**10.5**	**–1**	**162**	**42.6**	**13:08**	**9**	**1**	**2**	**3**	**2**	**0**	**0**	**0**	**15:03**
	NHL Totals		**81**	**14**	**18**	**32**	**28**	**2**	**0**	**5**	**133**	**10.5**		**162**	**42.6**	**13:08**	**9**	**1**	**2**	**3**	**2**	**0**	**0**	**0**	**15:03**

WCHA All-Rookie Team (2003) • WCHA First All-Star Team (2004) • NCAA West First All-American Team (2004)

PARK, Richard

(PAHRK, RIH-chuhrd)

Right wing. Shoots right. 5'11", 190 lbs. Born, Seoul, South Korea, May 27, 1976. Pittsburgh's 2nd choice, 50th overall, in 1994 Entry Draft.

1991-92	Tor. Young Nats	MTHL	76	49	58	107	91	....	....	....	....	....	....	....	....	....	....	....	....	....	....	....	....	....	....
1992-93	Belleville Bulls	OHL	66	23	38	61	38	....	....	....	....	....	....	....	....	....	5	0	0	0	14	....	....	....	....
1993-94	Belleville Bulls	OHL	59	27	49	76	70	....	....	....	....	....	....	....	....	....	12	3	5	8	18	....	....	....	....
1994-95	Belleville Bulls	OHL	45	28	51	79	35	....	....	....	....	....	....	....	....	....	16	9	18	27	12	....	....	....	....
	Pittsburgh	**NHL**	**1**	**0**	**1**	**1**	**2**	**0**	**0**	**0**	**4**	**0.0**	**1**	....	....	....	**3**	**0**	**0**	**0**	**2**	**0**	**0**	**0**	....
1995-96	Belleville Bulls	OHL	6	7	6	13	2	....	....	....	....	....	....	....	....	....	14	18	12	30	10	....	....	....	....
	Pittsburgh	**NHL**	**56**	**4**	**6**	**10**	**36**	**0**	**1**	**1**	**62**	**6.5**	**3**	....	....	....	**1**	**0**	**0**	**0**	**0**	**0**	**0**	**0**	....
1996-97	**Pittsburgh**	**NHL**	**1**	**0**	**0**	**0**	**0**	**0**	**0**	**0**	**1**	**0.0**	**–1**	....	....	....	....	....	....	....	....	....	....	....	....
	Cleveland	IHL	50	12	15	27	30	....	....	....	....	....	....	....	....	....	....	....	....	....	....	....	....	....	....
	Anaheim	**NHL**	**11**	**1**	**1**	**2**	**10**	**0**	**0**	**0**	**9**	**11.1**	**0**	....	....	....	**11**	**0**	**1**	**1**	**2**	**0**	**0**	**0**	....
1997-98	**Anaheim**	**NHL**	**15**	**0**	**2**	**2**	**8**	**0**	**0**	**0**	**14**	**0.0**	**–3**	....	....	....	....	....	....	....	....	....	....	....	....
	Cincinnati	AHL	56	17	26	43	36	....	....	....	....	....	....	....	....	....	....	....	....	....	....	....	....	....	....
1998-99	**Philadelphia**	**NHL**	**7**	**0**	**0**	**0**	**0**	**0**	**0**	**0**	**5**	**0.0**	**–1**	**15**	**53.3**	**9:21**	....	....	....	....	....	....	....	....	....
	Philadelphia	AHL	75	41	42	83	33	....	....	....	....	....	....	....	....	....	16	9	6	15	4	....	....	....	....
99-2000	Utah Grizzlies	IHL	82	28	32	60	36	....	....	....	....	....	....	....	....	....	5	1	0	1	0	....	....	....	....
2000-01	Cleveland	IHL	75	27	21	48	29	....	....	....	....	....	....	....	....	....	4	0	2	2	4	....	....	....	....
2001-02	**Minnesota**	**NHL**	**63**	**10**	**15**	**25**	**10**	**2**	**1**	**2**	**115**	**8.7**	**–1**	**79**	**41.8**	**16:28**	....	....	....	....	....	....	....	....	....
	Houston Aeros	AHL	13	4	10	14	6	....	....	....	....	....	....	....	....	....	....	....	....	....	....	....	....	....	....
2002-03	**Minnesota**	**NHL**	**81**	**14**	**10**	**24**	**16**	**2**	**2**	**3**	**149**	**9.4**	**–3**	**178**	**48.9**	**16:36**	**18**	**3**	**3**	**6**	**4**	**0**	**0**	**1**	**17:03**
2003-04	**Minnesota**	**NHL**	**73**	**13**	**12**	**25**	**28**	**4**	**0**	**1**	**142**	**9.2**	**0**	**379**	**40.1**	**16:30**	....	....	....	....	....	....	....	....	....

								Regular Season									Playoffs								
Season	Club	League	GP	G	A	Pts	PIM	PP	SH	GW	S	%	+/-	TF	F%	Min	GP	G	A	Pts	PIM	PP	SH	GW	Min
2004-05	Malmo	Sweden	9	1	3	4	4	....	....	....	....	....	....	....	....	....	....	....	....	....	....	....	....	....	....
	Langnau	Swiss	10	3	0	3	8	....	....	....	....	....	....	....	....	....	6	4	1	5	6	....	....	....	....
2005-06	**Vancouver**	**NHL**	**60**	**8**	**10**	**18**	**29**	**0**	**1**	**2**	**97**	**8.2**	**−2**	**26**	**26.9**	**11:00**	....	....	....	....	....	....	....	....	....
	NHL Totals		**368**	**50**	**57**	**107**	**139**	**8**	**5**	**9**	**598**	**8.4**		**677**	**42.4**	**15:11**	**33**	**3**	**4**	**7**	**8**	**0**	**0**	**1**	**17:03**

OHL All-Rookie Team (1993) • AHL Second All-Star Team (1999)

Traded to **Anaheim** by **Pittsburgh** for Roman Oksiuta, March 18, 1997. Signed as a free agent by **Philadelphia**, August 24, 1998. Signed as a free agent by **Utah** (IHL), September 22, 1999. Signed as a free agent by **Minnesota**, June 6, 2000. Signed as a free agent by **Malmo** (Sweden), November 8, 2004. Signed as a free agent by **Langnau** (Swiss), January 4, 2005. Signed as a free agent by **Vancouver**, August 8, 2005.

PARKER, Scott

(PAR-kuhr, SKAWT) **S.J.**

Right wing. Shoots right. 6'5", 230 lbs. Born, Hanford, CA, January 29, 1978. Colorado's 4th choice, 20th overall, in 1998 Entry Draft.

1993-94	Alaska Arctic Ice	AAHL	34	8	12	20	86	....	....	....	....	....	....	....	....	....	....	....	....	....	....	....	....	....	....
1994-95	Spokane Braves	KIJHL	43	7	21	28	128	....	....	....	....	....	....	....	....	....	....	....	....	....	....	....	....	....	....
1995-96	Kelowna Rockets	WHL	64	3	4	7	159	....	....	....	....	....	....	....	....	....	6	0	0	0	12	....	....	....	....
1996-97	Kelowna Rockets	WHL	68	18	8	26	*330	....	....	....	....	....	....	....	....	....	6	0	2	2	4	....	....	....	....
1997-98	Kelowna Rockets	WHL	71	30	22	52	243	....	....	....	....	....	....	....	....	....	7	6	0	6	23	....	....	....	....
1998-99	**Colorado**	**NHL**	**27**	**0**	**0**	**0**	**71**	**0**	**0**	**0**	**3**	**0.0**	**−3**	**1**	**0.0**	**1:37**	....	....	....	....	....	....	....	....	....
	Hershey Bears	AHL	32	4	3	7	143	....	....	....	....	....	....	....	....	....	4	0	0	0	6	....	....	....	....
99-2000	Hershey Bears	AHL	68	12	7	19	206	....	....	....	....	....	....	....	....	....	11	1	1	2	56	....	....	....	....
2000-01 ◆	**Colorado**	**NHL**	**69**	**2**	**3**	**5**	**155**	**0**	**0**	**1**	**35**	**5.7**	**−2**	**2**	**0.0**	**5:42**	**4**	**0**	**0**	**0**	**2**	**0**	**0**	**0**	**2:12**
2001-02	**Colorado**	**NHL**	**63**	**1**	**4**	**5**	**154**	**0**	**0**	**0**	**32**	**3.1**	**0**	**0**	**0.0**	**5:50**	....	....	....	....	....	....	....	....	....
2002-03	**Colorado**	**NHL**	**43**	**1**	**3**	**4**	**82**	**0**	**0**	**0**	**20**	**5.0**	**6**	**0**	**0.0**	**6:15**	**1**	**0**	**0**	**0**	**2**	**0**	**0**	**0**	**1:44**
2003-04	**San Jose**	**NHL**	**50**	**1**	**3**	**4**	**101**	**0**	**0**	**0**	**20**	**5.0**	**0**	**5**	**40.0**	**6:37**	....	....	....	....	....	....	....	....	....
2004-05			DID NOT PLAY																						
2005-06	**San Jose**	**NHL**	**10**	**1**	**0**	**1**	**38**	**0**	**0**	**0**	**6**	**16.7**	**3**	**0**	**0.0**	**5:39**	....	....	....	....	....	....	....	....	....
	NHL Totals		**262**	**6**	**13**	**19**	**601**	**0**	**0**	**1**	**116**	**5.2**		**8**	**25.0**	**5:35**	**5**	**0**	**0**	**0**	**4**	**0**	**0**	**0**	**2:06**

• Re-entered NHL Entry Draft. Originally New Jersey's 6th choice, 63rd overall, in 1996 Entry Draft.

Traded to **San Jose** by **Colorado** for Colorado's 5th round choice (previously acquired, Colorado selected Brad Richardson) in 2003 Entry Draft, June 21, 2003. • Missed majority of 2005-06 season due to a pre-season facial injury and a head injury sustained during game at Edmonton, November 21, 2005.

PARRISH, Mark

(PAIR-ihsh, MAHRK) **MIN.**

Right wing. Shoots right. 5'11", 200 lbs. Born, Bloomington, MN, February 2, 1977. Colorado's 3rd choice, 79th overall, in 1996 Entry Draft.

1994-95	Jefferson Jaguars	High-MN	27	40	20	60	42	....	....	....	....	....	....	....	....	....	....	....	....	....	....	....	....	....	....
1995-96	St. Cloud State	WCHA	39	15	13	28	30	....	....	....	....	....	....	....	....	....	....	....	....	....	....	....	....	....	....
1996-97	St. Cloud State	WCHA	35	*27	15	42	60	....	....	....	....	....	....	....	....	....	....	....	....	....	....	....	....	....	....
1997-98	Seattle	WHL	54	54	38	92	29	....	....	....	....	....	....	....	....	....	5	2	3	5	2	....	....	....	....
	New Haven	AHL	1	1	0	1	2	....	....	....	....	....	....	....	....	....	....	....	....	....	....	....	....	....	....
1998-99	**Florida**	**NHL**	**73**	**24**	**13**	**37**	**25**	**5**	**0**	**5**	**129**	**18.6**	**−6**	**1**	**0.0**	**13:59**	....	....	....	....	....	....	....	....	....
	New Haven	AHL	2	1	0	1	0	....	....	....	....	....	....	....	....	....	....	....	....	....	....	....	....	....	....
99-2000	**Florida**	**NHL**	**81**	**26**	**18**	**44**	**39**	**6**	**0**	**3**	**152**	**17.1**	**1**	**8**	**75.0**	**14:04**	**4**	**0**	**1**	**1**	**0**	**0**	**0**	**0**	**12:37**
2000-01	**NY Islanders**	**NHL**	**70**	**17**	**13**	**30**	**28**	**6**	**0**	**3**	**123**	**13.8**	**−27**	**3**	**33.3**	**15:27**	....	....	....	....	....	....	....	....	....
2001-02	**NY Islanders**	**NHL**	**78**	**30**	**30**	**60**	**32**	**9**	**1**	**6**	**162**	**18.5**	**10**	**10**	**40.0**	**16:48**	**7**	**2**	**1**	**3**	**6**	**2**	**0**	**0**	**17:27**
2002-03	**NY Islanders**	**NHL**	**81**	**23**	**25**	**48**	**28**	**9**	**0**	**5**	**147**	**15.6**	**−11**	**9**	**44.4**	**16:12**	**5**	**1**	**0**	**1**	**4**	**1**	**0**	**0**	**16:02**
2003-04	**NY Islanders**	**NHL**	**59**	**24**	**11**	**35**	**18**	**6**	**0**	**6**	**105**	**22.9**	**8**	**5**	**20.0**	**17:20**	**5**	**1**	**2**	**3**	**0**	**0**	**0**	**0**	**20:35**
2004-05			DID NOT PLAY																						
2005-06	**NY Islanders**	**NHL**	**57**	**24**	**17**	**41**	**16**	**13**	**0**	**5**	**102**	**23.5**	**−14**	**12**	**16.7**	**19:34**	....	....	....	....	....	....	....	....	....
	Los Angeles	**NHL**	**19**	**5**	**3**	**8**	**4**	**3**	**0**	**0**	**35**	**14.3**	**−9**	**0**	**0.0**	**15:29**	....	....	....	....	....	....	....	....	....
	United States	Olympics	6	0	0	0	4	....	....	....	....	....	....	....	....	....	....	....	....	....	....	....	....	....	....
	NHL Totals		**518**	**173**	**130**	**303**	**190**	**57**	**1**	**33**	**955**	**18.1**		**48**	**37.5**	**16:01**	**21**	**4**	**4**	**8**	**10**	**3**	**0**	**0**	**16:56**

NCAA West Second All-American Team (1997) • WHL West First All-Star Team (1998)

Played in NHL All-Star Game (2002)

Rights traded to **Florida** by **Colorado** with Anaheim's 3rd round choice (previously acquired, Florida selected Lance Ward) in 1998 Entry Draft for Tom Fitzgerald, March 24, 1998. Traded to **NY Islanders** by **Florida** with Oleg Kvasha for Roberto Luongo and Olli Jokinen, June 24, 2000. Traded to **Los Angeles** by **NY Islanders** with Brent Sopel for Denis Grebeshkov and Jeff Tambellini, March 8, 2006. Signed as a free agent by **Minnesota**, July 1, 2006.

PARROS, George

(PAIR-ohs, JOHRJ) **L.A.**

Right wing. Shoots right. 6'4", 232 lbs. Born, Washington, PA, December 29, 1979. Los Angeles' 9th choice, 222nd overall, in 1999 Entry Draft.

1996-97	Delbarton	High-NJ	14	15	8	23	....	....	....	....	....	....	....	....	....	....	....	....	....	....	....	....	....	....	....
1997-98	Delbarton	High-NJ	15	22	17	39	....	....	....	....	....	....	....	....	....	....	....	....	....	....	....	....	....	....	....
1998-99	Chicago Freeze	NAHL	54	30	20	50	126	....	....	....	....	....	....	....	....	....	....	....	....	....	....	....	....	....	....
99-2000	Princeton	ECAC	27	4	2	6	14	....	....	....	....	....	....	....	....	....	....	....	....	....	....	....	....	....	....
2000-01	Princeton	ECAC	31	7	10	17	38	....	....	....	....	....	....	....	....	....	....	....	....	....	....	....	....	....	....
2001-02	Princeton	ECAC	31	9	13	22	36	....	....	....	....	....	....	....	....	....	....	....	....	....	....	....	....	....	....
2002-03	Princeton	ECAC	22	0	7	7	29	....	....	....	....	....	....	....	....	....	....	....	....	....	....	....	....	....	....
	Manchester	AHL	9	0	1	1	7	....	....	....	....	....	....	....	....	....	....	....	....	....	....	....	....	....	....
2003-04	Manchester	AHL	57	3	6	9	126	....	....	....	....	....	....	....	....	....	5	0	0	0	4	....	....	....	....
2004-05	Reading Royals	ECHL	3	0	0	0	9	....	....	....	....	....	....	....	....	....	....	....	....	....	....	....	....	....	....
	Manchester	AHL	67	14	8	22	247	....	....	....	....	....	....	....	....	....	6	1	1	2	27	....	....	....	....
2005-06	**Los Angeles**	**NHL**	**55**	**2**	**3**	**5**	**138**	**0**	**0**	**0**	**23**	**8.7**	**1**	**1**	**0.0**	**4:56**	....	....	....	....	....	....	....	....	....
	NHL Totals		**55**	**2**	**3**	**5**	**138**	**0**	**0**	**0**	**23**	**8.7**		**1**	**0.0**	**4:56**	....	....	....	....	....	....	....	....	....

PAUL, Jeff

(PAWL, JEHF)

Defense. Shoots right. 6'4", 225 lbs. Born, London, Ont., March 1, 1978. Chicago's 2nd choice, 42nd overall, in 1996 Entry Draft.

1993-94	Woodstock	OHA-C	36	1	6	7	73	....	....	....	....	....	....	....	....	....	....	....	....	....	....	....	....	....	....
1994-95	Niagara Falls	OHL	57	3	10	13	64	....	....	....	....	....	....	....	....	....	6	0	2	2	0	....	....	....	....
1995-96	Niagara Falls	OHL	48	1	7	8	81	....	....	....	....	....	....	....	....	....	10	0	4	4	37	....	....	....	....
1996-97	Erie Otters	OHL	60	4	23	27	152	....	....	....	....	....	....	....	....	....	5	2	0	2	12	....	....	....	....
1997-98	Erie Otters	OHL	48	3	17	20	108	....	....	....	....	....	....	....	....	....	7	0	2	2	13	....	....	....	....
1998-99	Portland Pirates	AHL	6	0	0	0	4	....	....	....	....	....	....	....	....	....	....	....	....	....	....	....	....	....	....
	Indianapolis Ice	IHL	55	0	7	7	120	....	....	....	....	....	....	....	....	....	7	0	2	2	12	....	....	....	....
99-2000	Cleveland	IHL	69	6	6	12	210	....	....	....	....	....	....	....	....	....	9	1	0	1	12	....	....	....	....
2000-01	Norfolk Admirals	AHL	59	5	6	11	171	....	....	....	....	....	....	....	....	....	9	0	2	2	12	....	....	....	....
2001-02	Hershey Bears	AHL	58	1	13	14	201	....	....	....	....	....	....	....	....	....	7	0	1	1	6	....	....	....	....
2002-03	**Colorado**	**NHL**	**2**	**0**	**0**	**0**	**7**	**0**	**0**	**0**	**0**	**0.0**	**0**	**0**	**0.0**	**3:32**	....	....	....	....	....	....	....	....	....
	Hershey Bears	AHL	50	2	3	5	123	....	....	....	....	....	....	....	....	....	....	....	....	....	....	....	....	....	....
2003-04	San Antonio	AHL	57	2	6	8	174	....	....	....	....	....	....	....	....	....	....	....	....	....	....	....	....	....	....
	Hartford	AHL	17	0	5	5	38	....	....	....	....	....	....	....	....	....	15	1	2	3	31	....	....	....	....
2004-05	Portland Pirates	AHL	54	1	2	3	137	....	....	....	....	....	....	....	....	....	....	....	....	....	....	....	....	....	....
2005-06	Hamilton	AHL	27	0	4	4	68	....	....	....	....	....	....	....	....	....	....	....	....	....	....	....	....	....	....
	NHL Totals		**2**	**0**	**0**	**0**	**7**	**0**	**0**	**0**	**0**	**0.0**		**0**	**0.0**	**3:32**	....	....	....	....	....	....	....	....	....

Signed as a free agent by **Colorado**, August 8, 2001. Signed as a free agent by **Florida**, August 19, 2003. Traded to **NY Rangers** by **Florida** for Paul Healey, March 9, 2004. Signed as a free agent by **Washington**, August 2, 2004. Signed as a free agent by **Montreal**, September 1, 2005. • Spent majority of 2005-06 season as a healthy reserve.

PAYER, Serge

(pie-YAY, SAIRZH) **OTT.**

Center. Shoots left. 6', 191 lbs. Born, Rockland, Ont., May 7, 1979.

1994-95	Cumberland Colts	ODMHA	42	37	46	83	55	....	....	....	....	....	....	....	....	....	....	....	....	....	....	....	....	....	....
1995-96	Kitchener Rangers	OHL	66	8	16	24	18	....	....	....	....	....	....	....	....	....	12	0	2	2	2	....	....	....	....
1996-97	Kitchener Rangers	OHL	63	7	16	23	27	....	....	....	....	....	....	....	....	....	13	1	3	4	2	....	....	....	....
1997-98	Kitchener Rangers	OHL	44	20	21	41	51	....	....	....	....	....	....	....	....	....	6	3	0	3	7	....	....	....	....
1998-99	Kitchener Rangers	OHL	40	18	19	37	22	....	....	....	....	....	....	....	....	....	....	....	....	....	....	....	....	....	....
99-2000	Kitchener Rangers	OHL	44	10	26	36	53	....	....	....	....	....	....	....	....	....	5	0	3	3	6	....	....	....	....
2000-01	**Florida**	**NHL**	**43**	**5**	**1**	**6**	**21**	**0**	**1**	**0**	**34**	**14.7**	**0**	**97**	**42.3**	**7:27**	....	....	....	....	....	....	....	....	....
	Louisville Panthers	AHL	32	6	6	12	15	....	....	....	....	....	....	....	....	....	....	....	....	....	....	....	....	....	....
2001-02	Utah Grizzlies	AHL	20	6	2	8	9	....	....	....	....	....	....	....	....	....	....	....	....	....	....	....	....	....	....

Season	Club	League	Regular Season														Playoffs								
			GP	G	A	Pts	PIM	PP	SH	GW	S	%	+/-	TF	F%	Min	GP	G	A	Pts	PIM	PP	SH	GW	Min
2002-03	San Antonio	AHL	78	10	31	41	30	....	....	....	....	....	....	....	....	....	1	0	0	0	2	....	....	....	....
2003-04	**Ottawa**	**NHL**	**5**	**0**	**1**	**1**	**2**	**0**	**0**	**0**	**2**	**0.0**	**1**	**43**	**46.5**	**10:30**	....	....	....	....	....	....	....	....	....
	Binghamton	AHL	67	14	20	34	91	....	....	....	....	....	....	....	....	....	2	0	0	0	0	....	....	....	....
2004-05	San Antonio	AHL	3	1	1	2	4	....	....	....	....	....	....	....	....	....	....	....	....	....	....	....	....	....	....
2005-06	**Florida**	**NHL**	**71**	**2**	**4**	**6**	**26**	**0**	**0**	**0**	**70**	**2.9**	**–7**	**543**	**47.5**	**9:53**	....	....	....	....	....	....	....	....	....
	NHL Totals		**119**	**7**	**6**	**13**	**49**	**0**	**1**	**0**	**106**	**6.6**		**683**	**46.7**	**9:02**	....	....	....	....	....	....	....	....	....

Signed as a free agent by **Florida**, September 30, 1997. • Missed majority of 2001-02 season recovering from back injury suffered in training camp, September, 2001. Traded to **Ottawa** by **Florida** for Ottawa's 9th round choice (Luke Beaverson) in 2004 Entry Draft, September 10, 2003. Signed as a free agent by **Florida**, July 23, 2004. Signed as a free agent by **Ottawa**, August 2, 2006.

PEAT, Stephen

(PEET, STEE-vehn) **CAR.**

Right wing. Shoots right. 6'3", 230 lbs. Born, Princeton, B.C., March 10, 1980. Anaheim's 2nd choice, 32nd overall, in 1998 Entry Draft.

Season	Club	League	GP	G	A	Pts	PIM	PP	SH	GW	S	%	+/-	TF	F%	Min	GP	G	A	Pts	PIM	PP	SH	GW	Min
1995-96	Langley Thunder	BCJHL	59	5	15	20	112	....	....	....	....	....	....	....	....	....	....	....	....	....	....	....	....	....	....
	Red Deer Rebels	WHL	1	0	0	0	0	....	....	....	....	....	....	....	....	....	....	....	....	....	....	....	....	....	....
1996-97	Red Deer Rebels	WHL	68	3	14	17	161	....	....	....	....	....	....	....	....	....	16	0	2	2	22	....	....	....	....
1997-98	Red Deer Rebels	WHL	63	6	12	18	189	....	....	....	....	....	....	....	....	....	5	0	0	0	8	....	....	....	....
1998-99	Red Deer Rebels	WHL	31	2	6	8	98	....	....	....	....	....	....	....	....	....	....	....	....	....	....	....	....	....	....
	Tri-City	WHL	5	0	0	0	19	....	....	....	....	....	....	....	....	....	....	....	....	....	....	....	....	....	....
99-2000	Tri-City	WHL	12	0	2	2	48	....	....	....	....	....	....	....	....	....	....	....	....	....	....	....	....	....	....
	Calgary Hitmen	WHL	23	0	8	8	100	....	....	....	....	....	....	....	....	....	13	0	1	1	33	....	....	....	....
2000-01	Portland Pirates	AHL	6	0	0	0	16	....	....	....	....	....	....	....	....	....	....	....	....	....	....	....	....	....	....
2001-02	**Washington**	**NHL**	**38**	**2**	**2**	**4**	**85**	**0**	**0**	**0**	**11**	**18.2**	**–1**	**0**	**0.0**	**5:04**	....	....	....	....	....	....	....	....	....
	Portland Pirates	AHL	17	2	2	4	57	....	....	....	....	....	....	....	....	....	....	....	....	....	....	....	....	....	....
2002-03	**Washington**	**NHL**	**27**	**1**	**0**	**1**	**57**	**0**	**0**	**0**	**7**	**14.3**	**–3**	**0**	**0.0**	**4:09**	....	....	....	....	....	....	....	....	....
	Portland Pirates	AHL	18	0	0	0	52	....	....	....	....	....	....	....	....	....	....	....	....	....	....	....	....	....	....
2003-04	**Washington**	**NHL**	**64**	**5**	**0**	**5**	**90**	**0**	**0**	**0**	**21**	**23.8**	**–10**	**4**	**0.0**	**6:38**	....	....	....	....	....	....	....	....	....
2004-05	Danbury Trashers	UHL	7	0	1	1	45	....	....	....	....	....	....	....	....	....	....	....	....	....	....	....	....	....	....
2005-06	**Washington**	**NHL**	**1**	**0**	**0**	**0**	**2**	**0**	**0**	**0**	**2**	**0.0**	**–2**	**0**	**0.0**	**4:47**	....	....	....	....	....	....	....	....	....
	Hershey Bears	AHL	5	0	1	1	7	....	....	....	....	....	....	....	....	....	....	....	....	....	....	....	....	....	....
	Lowell	AHL	3	1	1	2	23	....	....	....	....	....	....	....	....	....	....	....	....	....	....	....	....	....	....
	NHL Totals		**130**	**8**	**2**	**10**	**234**	**0**	**0**	**0**	**41**	**19.5**		**4**	**0.0**	**5:38**	....	....	....	....	....	....	....	....	....

• Missed majority of 1999-2000 season recovering from injuries sustained off-ice, February 8, 2000. Rights traded to **Washington** by **Anaheim** for Washington's 4th round choice (later traded to Montreal – later traded to Pittsburgh – Pittsburgh selected Michel Ouellet) in 2000 Entry Draft, June 1, 2000. • Missed majority of 2000-01 season recovering from groin injury suffered in training camp, September, 29, 2000. Signed as a free agent by **Danbury** (UHL), December 16, 2004. Traded to **Carolina** by **Washington** for Colin Forbes, December 28, 2005. • Missed majority of 2005-06 season recovering from a groin/abdominal injury.

PECA, Michael

(PEH-kuh, MIGH-kuhl) **TOR.**

Center. Shoots right. 5'11", 190 lbs. Born, Toronto, Ont., March 26, 1974. Vancouver's 2nd choice, 40th overall, in 1992 Entry Draft.

Season	Club	League	GP	G	A	Pts	PIM	PP	SH	GW	S	%	+/-	TF	F%	Min	GP	G	A	Pts	PIM	PP	SH	GW	Min
1989-90	Tor. Red Wings	MTHL	39	42	53	95	40	....	....	....	....	....	....	....	....	....	....	....	....	....	....	....	....	....	....
1990-91	Sudbury Wolves	OHL	62	14	27	41	24	....	....	....	....	....	....	....	....	....	5	1	0	1	7	....	....	....	....
1991-92	Sudbury Wolves	OHL	39	16	34	50	61	....	....	....	....	....	....	....	....	....	....	....	....	....	....	....	....	....	....
	Ottawa 67's	OHL	27	8	17	25	32	....	....	....	....	....	....	....	....	....	11	6	10	16	6	....	....	....	....
1992-93	Ottawa 67's	OHL	55	38	64	102	80	....	....	....	....	....	....	....	....	....	....	....	....	....	....	....	....	....	....
	Hamilton	AHL	9	6	3	9	11	....	....	....	....	....	....	....	....	....	....	....	....	....	....	....	....	....	....
1993-94	Ottawa 67's	OHL	55	50	63	113	101	....	....	....	....	....	....	....	....	....	17	7	22	29	30	....	....	....	....
	Vancouver	**NHL**	**4**	**0**	**0**	**0**	**2**	**0**	**0**	**0**	**5**	**0.0**	**–1**	....	....	....	....	....	....	....	....	....	....	....	....
1994-95	Syracuse Crunch	AHL	35	10	24	34	75	....	....	....	....	....	....	....	....	....	....	....	....	....	....	....	....	....	....
	Vancouver	**NHL**	**33**	**6**	**6**	**12**	**30**	**2**	**0**	**1**	**46**	**13.0**	**–6**	....	....	....	**5**	**0**	**1**	**1**	**8**	**0**	**0**	**0**	....
1995-96	**Buffalo**	**NHL**	**68**	**11**	**20**	**31**	**67**	**4**	**3**	**1**	**109**	**10.1**	**–1**	....	....	....	....	....	....	....	....	....	....	....	....
1996-97	**Buffalo**	**NHL**	**79**	**20**	**29**	**49**	**80**	**5**	**6**	**4**	**137**	**14.6**	**26**	....	....	....	**10**	**0**	**2**	**2**	**8**	**0**	**0**	**0**	....
1997-98	**Buffalo**	**NHL**	**61**	**18**	**22**	**40**	**57**	**6**	**5**	**1**	**132**	**13.6**	**12**	....	....	....	**13**	**3**	**2**	**5**	**8**	**0**	**0**	**1**	....
1998-99	**Buffalo**	**NHL**	**82**	**27**	**29**	**56**	**81**	**10**	**0**	**8**	**199**	**13.6**	**7**	**1855**	**49.4**	**20:44**	**21**	**5**	**8**	**13**	**18**	**2**	**1**	**0**	**22:28**
99-2000	**Buffalo**	**NHL**	**73**	**20**	**21**	**41**	**67**	**2**	**0**	**3**	**144**	**13.9**	**6**	**1604**	**48.6**	**19:57**	**5**	**0**	**1**	**1**	**4**	**0**	**0**	**0**	**18:42**
2000-01			DID NOT PLAY																						
2001-02	**NY Islanders**	**NHL**	**80**	**25**	**35**	**60**	**62**	**3**	**6**	**5**	**168**	**14.9**	**19**	**1804**	**52.4**	**20:14**	**5**	**1**	**0**	**1**	**2**	**0**	**0**	**0**	**16:15**
	Canada	Olympics	6	0	2	2	2	....	....	....	....	....	....	....	....	....	....	....	....	....	....	....	....	....	....
2002-03	**NY Islanders**	**NHL**	**66**	**13**	**29**	**42**	**43**	**4**	**2**	**2**	**117**	**11.1**	**–4**	**1315**	**53.0**	**18:57**	**5**	**0**	**0**	**0**	**4**	**0**	**0**	**0**	**20:10**
2003-04	**NY Islanders**	**NHL**	**76**	**11**	**29**	**40**	**71**	**0**	**1**	**0**	**117**	**9.4**	**17**	**1674**	**53.1**	**19:02**	**5**	**0**	**0**	**0**	**6**	**0**	**0**	**0**	**23:01**
2004-05			DID NOT PLAY																						
2005-06	**Edmonton**	**NHL**	**71**	**9**	**14**	**23**	**56**	**2**	**2**	**1**	**108**	**8.3**	**–4**	**1048**	**54.9**	**16:39**	**24**	**6**	**5**	**11**	**20**	**0**	**1**	**1**	**19:06**
	NHL Totals		**693**	**160**	**234**	**394**	**616**	**38**	**25**	**26**	**1282**	**12.5**		**9300**	**51.6**	**19:19**	**93**	**15**	**19**	**34**	**78**	**2**	**2**	**2**	**20:19**

Frank J. Selke Trophy (1997, 2002)

Traded to **Buffalo** by **Vancouver** with Mike Wilson and Vancouver's 1st round choice (Jay McKee) in 1995 Entry Draft for Alexander Mogilny and Buffalo's 5th round choice (Todd Norman) in 1995 Entry Draft, July 8, 1995. • Missed entire 2000-01 season after failing to come to contract terms with **Buffalo**. Rights traded to **NY Islanders** by **Buffalo** for Tim Connolly and Taylor Pyatt, June 24, 2001. Traded to **Edmonton** by **NY Islanders** for Mike York and Edmonton's 4th round choice (later traded to Colorado - Colorado selected Kevin Montgomery) in 2006 Entry Draft, August 3, 2005. Signed as a free agent by **Toronto**, July 18, 2006.

PELTONEN, Ville

(PEHL-TOH-nen, VIHL-ee) **FLA.**

Left wing. Shoots left. 5'9", 185 lbs. Born, Vantaa, Finland, May 24, 1973. San Jose's 4th choice, 58th overall, in 1993 Entry Draft.

Season	Club	League	GP	G	A	Pts	PIM	PP	SH	GW	S	%	+/-	TF	F%	Min	GP	G	A	Pts	PIM	PP	SH	GW	Min
1989-90	HIFK Helsinki U18	Fin-U18	24	21	24	45	14	....	....	....	....	....	....	....	....	....	....	....	....	....	....	....	....	....	....
1990-91	HIFK Helsinki Jr.	Fin-Jr.	36	21	16	37	16	....	....	....	....	....	....	....	....	....	7	2	3	5	10	....	....	....	....
1991-92	HIFK Helsinki Jr.	Fin-Jr.	37	28	23	51	28	....	....	....	....	....	....	....	....	....	4	0	2	2	0	....	....	....	....
	HIFK Helsinki	Finland	6	0	0	0	0	....	....	....	....	....	....	....	....	....	....	....	....	....	....	....	....	....	....
1992-93	HIFK Helsinki Jr.	Fin-Jr.	2	4	2	6	4	....	....	....	....	....	....	....	....	....	....	....	....	....	....	....	....	....	....
	HIFK Helsinki	Finland	46	13	24	37	16	....	....	....	....	....	....	....	....	....	4	0	2	2	2	....	....	....	....
1993-94	HIFK Helsinki	Finland	43	16	22	38	14	....	....	....	....	....	....	....	....	....	3	0	0	0	2	....	....	....	....
	Finland	Olympics	8	4	3	7	0	....	....	....	....	....	....	....	....	....	....	....	....	....	....	....	....	....	....
1994-95	HIFK Helsinki	Finland	45	20	16	36	16	....	....	....	....	....	....	....	....	....	3	0	0	0	0	....	....	....	....
1995-96	**San Jose**	**NHL**	**31**	**2**	**11**	**13**	**14**	**0**	**0**	**0**	**58**	**3.4**	**–7**	....	....	....	....	....	....	....	....	....	....	....	....
	Kansas City	IHL	29	5	13	18	8	....	....	....	....	....	....	....	....	....	....	....	....	....	....	....	....	....	....
1996-97	**San Jose**	**NHL**	**28**	**2**	**3**	**5**	**0**	**1**	**0**	**0**	**35**	**5.7**	**–8**	....	....	....	....	....	....	....	....	....	....	....	....
	Kentucky	AHL	40	22	30	52	21	....	....	....	....	....	....	....	....	....	....	....	....	....	....	....	....	....	....
1997-98	V.Frolunda	Sweden	45	22	29	51	44	....	....	....	....	....	....	....	....	....	7	4	2	6	0	....	....	....	....
	Finland	Olympics	6	2	1	3	6	....	....	....	....	....	....	....	....	....	....	....	....	....	....	....	....	....	....
1998-99	**Nashville**	**NHL**	**14**	**5**	**5**	**10**	**2**	**1**	**0**	**0**	**31**	**16.1**	**1**	**0**	**0.0**	**15:54**	....	....	....	....	....	....	....	....	....
99-2000	**Nashville**	**NHL**	**79**	**6**	**22**	**28**	**22**	**2**	**0**	**2**	**125**	**4.8**	**–1**	**1**	**100.0**	**14:41**	....	....	....	....	....	....	....	....	....
2000-01	**Nashville**	**NHL**	**23**	**3**	**1**	**4**	**2**	**0**	**0**	**0**	**38**	**7.9**	**–7**	**2**	**0.0**	**11:40**	....	....	....	....	....	....	....	....	....
	Milwaukee	IHL	53	27	33	60	26	....	....	....	....	....	....	....	....	....	5	2	1	3	6	....	....	....	....
2001-02	Jokerit Helsinki	Finland	30	11	18	29	8	....	....	....	....	....	....	....	....	....	....	....	....	....	....	....	....	....	....
2002-03	Jokerit Helsinki	Finland	49	23	19	42	14	....	....	....	....	....	....	....	....	....	10	4	6	10	0	....	....	....	....
2003-04	HC Lugano	Swiss	48	28	44	72	14	....	....	....	....	....	....	....	....	....	16	4	7	11	8	....	....	....	....
2004-05	HC Lugano	Swiss	44	24	33	57	16	....	....	....	....	....	....	....	....	....	5	0	3	3	2	....	....	....	....
2005-06	HC Lugano	Swiss	39	22	25	47	22	....	....	....	....	....	....	....	....	....	17	*12	12	24	8	....	....	....	....
	Finland	Olympics	8	4	5	9	6	....	....	....	....	....	....	....	....	....	....	....	....	....	....	....	....	....	....
	NHL Totals		**175**	**18**	**42**	**60**	**40**	**4**	**0**	**2**	**287**	**6.3**		**3**	**33.3**	**14:14**	....	....	....	....	....	....	....	....	....

IHL Second All-Star Team (2001)

Traded to **Nashville** by **San Jose** for Nashville's 5th round choice (later traded to Phoenix – Phoenix selected Josh Blackburn) in 1998 Entry Draft, June 26, 1998. • Missed majority of 1998-99 season recovering from shoulder surgery, December 10, 1998. Signed as a free agent by **Jokerit Helsinki** (Finland), April 26, 2001. Signed as a free agent by **Lugano** (Swiss), April 9, 2003. Signed as a free agent by **Florida**, June 15, 2006.

PENNER, Dustin
(PEH-nuhr, DUHS-tihn) **ANA.**

Left wing. Shoots left. 6'4", 245 lbs. Born, Winkler, Man., September 28, 1982.

			Regular Season														Playoffs								
Season	Club	League	GP	G	A	Pts	PIM	PP	SH	GW	S	%	+/-	TF	F%	Min	GP	G	A	Pts	PIM	PP	SH	GW	Min
2001-02	MSU - Bottineau	NJCAA	23	20	12	32	30	....	....	....	....	....	....	....	....	....	....	....	....	....	....	....	....	....	....
2002-03	U. of Maine	H-East	DID NOT PLAY – FRESHMAN																						
2003-04	U. of Maine	H-East	43	11	12	23	52	....	....	....	....	....	....	....	....	....	....	....	....	....	....	....	....	....	....
2004-05	Cincinnati	AHL	77	10	18	28	82	....	....	....	....	....	....	....	....	....	9	2	3	5	13	....	....	....	....
2005-06	**Anaheim**	**NHL**	**19**	**4**	**3**	**7**	**14**	**2**	**0**	**1**	**46**	**8.7**	**3**	**1**	**0.0**	**11:58**	**13**	**3**	**6**	**9**	**12**	**0**	**0**	**0**	**13:16**
	Portland Pirates	AHL	57	39	45	84	68	....	....	....	....	....	....	....	....	....	5	4	3	7	0	....	....	....	....
	NHL Totals		**19**	**4**	**3**	**7**	**14**	**2**	**0**	**1**	**46**	**8.7**		**1**	**0.0**	**11:58**	**13**	**3**	**6**	**9**	**12**	**0**	**0**	**0**	**13:16**

NCAA Championship All-Tournament Team (2004) • AHL Second All-Star Team (2006)

Signed as a free agent by **Anaheim**, May 12, 2004.

PEREZHOGIN, Alexander
(pehr-eh-ZHO-ghin, al-ehx-AN-duhr) **MTL.**

Left wing. Shoots left. 6', 205 lbs. Born, Ust-Kamenogorsk, USSR, August 10, 1983. Montreal's 2nd choice, 25th overall, in 2001 Entry Draft.

Season	Club	League	GP	G	A	Pts	PIM	PP	SH	GW	S	%	+/-	TF	F%	Min	GP	G	A	Pts	PIM	PP	SH	GW	Min
1998-99	Omsk 2	Russia-4	10	3	4	7	0	....	....	....	....	....	....	....	....	....	....	....	....	....	....	....	....	....	....
99-2000	Omsk 2	Russia-3	22	12	11	23	12	....	....	....	....	....	....	....	....	....	....	....	....	....	....	....	....	....	....
	Avangard Omsk	Russia	1	0	0	0	0	....	....	....	....	....	....	....	....	....	....	....	....	....	....	....	....	....	....
2000-01	Omsk 2	Russia-3	41	47	24	71	40	....	....	....	....	....	....	....	....	....	....	....	....	....	....	....	....	....	....
	Avangard Omsk	Russia	....	....	....	....	....	....	....	....	....	....	....	....	....	....	1	0	0	0	0	....	....	....	....
2001-02	Avangard Omsk	Russia	4	1	0	1	4	....	....	....	....	....	....	....	....	....	....	....	....	....	....	....	....	....	....
	Mostovik Kurgan	Russia-2	19	14	10	24	10	....	....	....	....	....	....	....	....	....	....	....	....	....	....	....	....	....	....
2002-03	Avangard Omsk	Russia	48	15	6	21	28	....	....	....	....	....	....	....	....	....	8	0	2	2	4	....	....	....	....
2003-04	Hamilton	AHL	77	23	27	50	52	....	....	....	....	....	....	....	....	....	5	3	3	6	16	....	....	....	....
2004-05	Avangard Omsk	Russia	43	15	18	33	18	....	....	....	....	....	....	....	....	....	11	3	2	5	8	....	....	....	....
2005-06	**Montreal**	**NHL**	**67**	**9**	**10**	**19**	**38**	**3**	**0**	**2**	**109**	**8.3**	**5**	**6**	**33.3**	**10:08**	**6**	**1**	**1**	**2**	**4**	**0**	**0**	**0**	**13:42**
	Hamilton	AHL	11	0	2	2	8	....	....	....	....	....	....	....	....	....	....	....	....	....	....	....	....	....	....
	NHL Totals		**67**	**9**	**10**	**19**	**38**	**3**	**0**	**2**	**109**	**8.3**		**6**	**33.3**	**10:08**	**6**	**1**	**1**	**2**	**4**	**0**	**0**	**0**	**13:42**

PERREAULT, Joel
(PAIR-oh, JOHL) **PHX.**

Right wing. Shoots right. 6'1", 197 lbs. Born, Montreal, Que., April 6, 1983. Anaheim's 7th choice, 137th overall, in 2001 Entry Draft.

Season	Club	League	GP	G	A	Pts	PIM	PP	SH	GW	S	%	+/-	TF	F%	Min	GP	G	A	Pts	PIM	PP	SH	GW	Min
99-2000	Antoine-Girouard	QAAA	19	4	7	11	6	....	....	....	....	....	....	....	....	....	....	....	....	....	....	....	....	....	....
2000-01	Baie-Comeau	QMJHL	68	10	14	24	46	....	....	....	....	....	....	....	....	....	11	1	1	2	10	....	....	....	....
2001-02	Baie-Comeau	QMJHL	57	18	44	62	96	....	....	....	....	....	....	....	....	....	5	2	0	2	6	....	....	....	....
2002-03	Baie-Comeau	QMJHL	70	51	65	*116	93	....	....	....	....	....	....	....	....	....	12	3	7	10	14	....	....	....	....
2003-04	Cincinnati	AHL	65	14	14	28	38	....	....	....	....	....	....	....	....	....	9	1	1	2	2	....	....	....	....
2004-05	Cincinnati	AHL	51	9	19	28	40	....	....	....	....	....	....	....	....	....	....	....	....	....	....	....	....	....	....
2005-06	Portland Pirates	AHL	25	12	12	24	20	....	....	....	....	....	....	....	....	....	....	....	....	....	....	....	....	....	....
	Phoenix	**NHL**	**5**	**1**	**1**	**2**	**2**	**0**	**0**	**0**	**7**	**14.3**	**0**	**47**	**34.0**	**11:29**	....	....	....	....	....	....	....	....	....
	San Antonio	AHL	12	1	6	7	4	....	....	....	....	....	....	....	....	....	....	....	....	....	....	....	....	....	....
	NHL Totals		**5**	**1**	**1**	**2**	**2**	**0**	**0**	**0**	**7**	**14.3**		**47**	**34.0**	**11:29**	....	....	....	....	....	....	....	....	....

QMJHL First All-Star Team (2003) • Canadian Major Junior First All-Star Team (2003)

Traded to **Phoenix** by **Anaheim** for Sean O'Donnell, March 9, 2006.

PERREAULT, Yanic
(puh-ROH, YAH-nihk)

Center. Shoots left. 5'11", 185 lbs. Born, Sherbrooke, Que., April 4, 1971. Toronto's 1st choice, 47th overall, in 1991 Entry Draft.

Season	Club	League	GP	G	A	Pts	PIM	PP	SH	GW	S	%	+/-	TF	F%	Min	GP	G	A	Pts	PIM	PP	SH	GW	Min
1987-88	Montreal L'est	QAAA	42	*70	57	*127	14	....	....	....	....	....	....	....	....	....	8	12	10	22	6	....	....	....	....
1988-89	Trois-Rivieres	QMJHL	70	53	55	108	48	....	....	....	....	....	....	....	....	....	....	....	....	....	....	....	....	....	....
1989-90	Trois-Rivieres	QMJHL	63	51	63	114	75	....	....	....	....	....	....	....	....	....	7	6	5	11	19	....	....	....	....
1990-91	Trois-Rivieres	QMJHL	67	*87	98	*185	103	....	....	....	....	....	....	....	....	....	6	4	7	11	6	....	....	....	....
1991-92	St. John's	AHL	62	38	38	76	19	....	....	....	....	....	....	....	....	....	16	7	8	15	4	....	....	....	....
1992-93	St. John's	AHL	79	49	46	95	56	....	....	....	....	....	....	....	....	....	9	4	5	9	2	....	....	....	....
1993-94	**Toronto**	**NHL**	**13**	**3**	**3**	**6**	**0**	**2**	**0**	**0**	**24**	**12.5**	**1**	....	....	....	....	....	....	....	....	....	....	....	....
	St. John's	AHL	62	45	60	105	38	....	....	....	....	....	....	....	....	....	11	*12	6	18	14	....	....	....	....
1994-95	Phoenix	IHL	68	51	48	99	52	....	....	....	....	....	....	....	....	....	....	....	....	....	....	....	....	....	....
	Los Angeles	**NHL**	**26**	**2**	**5**	**7**	**20**	**0**	**0**	**1**	**43**	**4.7**	**3**	....	....	....	....	....	....	....	....	....	....	....	....
1995-96	**Los Angeles**	**NHL**	**78**	**25**	**24**	**49**	**16**	**8**	**3**	**7**	**175**	**14.3**	**–11**	....	....	....	....	....	....	....	....	....	....	....	....
1996-97	**Los Angeles**	**NHL**	**41**	**11**	**14**	**25**	**20**	**1**	**1**	**0**	**98**	**11.2**	**0**	....	....	....	....	....	....	....	....	....	....	....	....
1997-98	**Los Angeles**	**NHL**	**79**	**28**	**20**	**48**	**32**	**3**	**2**	**3**	**206**	**13.6**	**6**	....	....	....	**4**	**1**	**2**	**3**	**6**	**1**	**0**	**0**	....
1998-99	**Los Angeles**	**NHL**	**64**	**10**	**17**	**27**	**30**	**2**	**2**	**1**	**113**	**8.8**	**–3**	**1024**	**56.5**	**15:24**	....	....	....	....	....	....	....	....	....
	Toronto	**NHL**	**12**	**7**	**8**	**15**	**12**	**2**	**1**	**2**	**28**	**25.0**	**10**	**164**	**62.8**	**13:20**	**17**	**3**	**6**	**9**	**6**	**0**	**0**	**2**	**15:55**
99-2000	**Toronto**	**NHL**	**58**	**18**	**27**	**45**	**22**	**5**	**0**	**4**	**114**	**15.8**	**3**	**987**	**61.8**	**15:18**	**1**	**0**	**1**	**1**	**0**	**0**	**0**	**0**	**12:56**
2000-01	**Toronto**	**NHL**	**76**	**24**	**28**	**52**	**52**	**5**	**0**	**2**	**134**	**17.9**	**0**	**1055**	**62.7**	**14:01**	**11**	**2**	**3**	**5**	**4**	**1**	**0**	**1**	**12:20**
2001-02	**Montreal**	**NHL**	**82**	**27**	**29**	**56**	**40**	**6**	**0**	**7**	**156**	**17.3**	**–3**	**1485**	**61.3**	**16:47**	**11**	**3**	**5**	**8**	**0**	**2**	**0**	**1**	**13:05**
2002-03	**Montreal**	**NHL**	**73**	**24**	**22**	**46**	**30**	**7**	**0**	**4**	**145**	**16.6**	**–11**	**1156**	**62.9**	**16:05**	....	....	....	....	....	....	....	....	....
2003-04	**Montreal**	**NHL**	**69**	**16**	**15**	**31**	**40**	**5**	**0**	**3**	**114**	**14.0**	**–10**	**861**	**65.2**	**13:46**	**9**	**2**	**2**	**4**	**0**	**0**	**0**	**1**	**12:29**
2004-05			DID NOT PLAY																						
2005-06	**Nashville**	**NHL**	**69**	**22**	**35**	**57**	**30**	**10**	**0**	**2**	**145**	**15.2**	**–3**	**899**	**62.2**	**14:57**	**1**	**0**	**0**	**0**	**2**	**0**	**0**	**0**	**10:09**
	NHL Totals		**740**	**217**	**247**	**464**	**344**	**56**	**9**	**36**	**1495**	**14.5**		**7631**	**61.7**	**15:10**	**54**	**11**	**19**	**30**	**18**	**4**	**0**	**5**	**13:43**

QMJHL All-Rookie Team (1989) • QMJHL Offensive Rookie of the Year (1989) • Canadian Major Junior Rookie of the Year (1989) • QMJHL First All-Star Team (1991) • QMJHL MVP (1991)

Traded to **Los Angeles** by **Toronto** for Los Angeles' 4th round choice (later traded to Philadelphia – later traded back to Los Angeles – Los Angeles selected Mikael Simons) in 1996 Entry Draft, July 11, 1994. Traded to **Toronto** by **Los Angeles** for Jason Podollan and Toronto's 3rd round choice (Cory Campbell) in 1999 Entry Draft, March 23, 1999. Signed as a free agent by **Montreal**, July 4, 2001. Signed as a free agent by **Nashville**, October 3, 2005.

PERRIN, Eric
(peh-REHN, AIR-ihk) **T.B.**

Center. Shoots left. 5'9", 176 lbs. Born, Laval, Que., November 1, 1975.

Season	Club	League	GP	G	A	Pts	PIM	PP	SH	GW	S	%	+/-	TF	F%	Min	GP	G	A	Pts	PIM	PP	SH	GW	Min
1991-92	Laval-Laurentides	QAAA	42	41	50	91	....	....	....	....	....	....	....	....	....	....	12	7	16	23	....	....	....	....	....
1992-93	Laval College	CEGEP	STATISTICS NOT AVAILABLE																						
1993-94	U. of Vermont	ECAC	32	24	21	45	34	....	....	....	....	....	....	....	....	....	....	....	....	....	....	....	....	....	....
1994-95	U. of Vermont	ECAC	35	28	39	67	38	....	....	....	....	....	....	....	....	....	....	....	....	....	....	....	....	....	....
1995-96	U. of Vermont	ECAC	38	29	56	85	38	....	....	....	....	....	....	....	....	....	....	....	....	....	....	....	....	....	....
1996-97	U. of Vermont	ECAC	36	26	33	59	40	....	....	....	....	....	....	....	....	....	....	....	....	....	....	....	....	....	....
1997-98	Cleveland	IHL	69	12	31	43	34	....	....	....	....	....	....	....	....	....	....	....	....	....	....	....	....	....	....
	Quebec Rafales	IHL	13	2	12	14	4	....	....	....	....	....	....	....	....	....	....	....	....	....	....	....	....	....	....
1998-99	Kansas City	IHL	82	24	37	61	71	....	....	....	....	....	....	....	....	....	3	0	0	0	0	....	....	....	....
99-2000	Kansas City	IHL	21	3	15	18	16	....	....	....	....	....	....	....	....	....	....	....	....	....	....	....	....	....	....
2000-01	Jokerit Helsinki	Finland	6	1	1	2	4	....	....	....	....	....	....	....	....	....	....	....	....	....	....	....	....	....	....
	Assat Pori	Finland	43	15	23	38	70	....	....	....	....	....	....	....	....	....	....	....	....	....	....	....	....	....	....
2001-02	Assat Pori	Finland	45	13	13	26	16	....	....	....	....	....	....	....	....	....	....	....	....	....	....	....	....	....	....
	HPK Hameenlinna	Finland	12	5	10	15	4	....	....	....	....	....	....	....	....	....	8	2	4	6	6	....	....	....	....
2002-03	JYP Jyvaskyla	Finland	56	18	28	46	36	....	....	....	....	....	....	....	....	....	7	4	6	10	8	....	....	....	....
2003-04♦	**Tampa Bay**	**NHL**	**4**	**0**	**0**	**0**	**0**	**0**	**0**	**0**	**3**	**0.0**	**–1**	**30**	**60.0**	**8:32**	**12**	**0**	**1**	**1**	**6**	**0**	**0**	**0**	**5:20**
	Hershey Bears	AHL	71	21	54	75	49	....	....	....	....	....	....	....	....	....	....	....	....	....	....	....	....	....	....
2004-05	Hershey Bears	AHL	80	24	49	73	46	....	....	....	....	....	....	....	....	....	....	....	....	....	....	....	....	....	....
2005-06	SC Bern	Swiss	44	13	25	38	28	....	....	....	....	....	....	....	....	....	6	2	4	6	8	....	....	....	....
	NHL Totals		**4**	**0**	**0**	**0**	**0**	**0**	**0**	**0**	**3**	**0.0**		**30**	**60.0**	**8:32**	**12**	**0**	**1**	**1**	**6**	**0**	**0**	**0**	**5:20**

ECAC All-Rookie Team (1994) • ECAC Rookie of the Year (1994) • ECAC First All-Star Team (1995, 1996) • ECAC Player of the Year (1996) • NCAA East First All-American Team (1996) • AHL First All-Star Team (2004)

Signed as a free agent by **Tampa Bay**, June 19, 2003. Signed as a free agent by **Bern** (Swiss), August 22, 2005. Signed as a free agent by **Tampa Bay**, June 14, 2006.

PERROTT, Nathan

(PEHR-roht, NAY-than)

Right wing. Shoots right. 6', 225 lbs. Born, Owen Sound, Ont., December 8, 1976. New Jersey's 2nd choice, 44th overall, in 1995 Entry Draft.

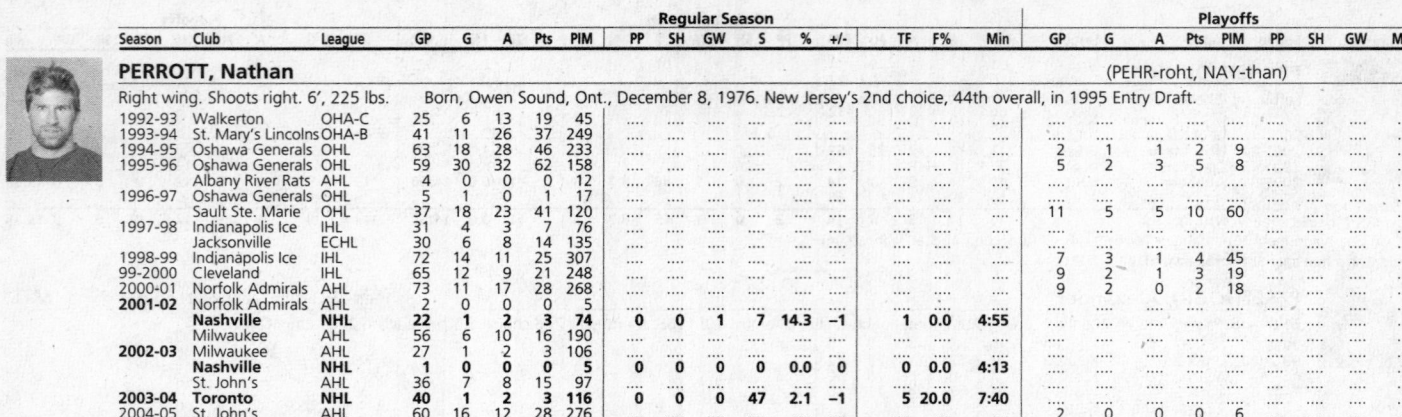

			Regular Season														Playoffs								
Season	Club	League	GP	G	A	Pts	PIM	PP	SH	GW	S	%	+/-	TF	F%	Min	GP	G	A	Pts	PIM	PP	SH	GW	Min
1992-93	Walkerton	OHA-C	25	6	13	19	45	....	....	....	....	....	....	....	....	....	....	....	....	....	....	....	....	....	....
1993-94	St. Mary's Lincolns	OHA-B	41	11	26	37	249	....	....	....	....	....	....	....	....	....	....	....	....	....	....	....	....	....	....
1994-95	Oshawa Generals	OHL	63	18	28	46	233	....	....	....	....	....	....	....	....	....	2	1	1	2	9	....	....	....	....
1995-96	Oshawa Generals	OHL	59	30	32	62	158	....	....	....	....	....	....	....	....	....	5	2	3	5	8	....	....	....	....
	Albany River Rats	AHL	4	0	0	0	12	....	....	....	....	....	....	....	....	....	....	....	....	....	....	....	....	....	....
1996-97	Oshawa Generals	OHL	5	1	0	1	17	....	....	....	....	....	....	....	....	....	....	....	....	....	....	....	....	....	....
	Sault Ste. Marie	OHL	37	18	23	41	120	....	....	....	....	....	....	....	....	....	11	5	5	10	60	....	....	....	....
1997-98	Indianapolis Ice	IHL	31	4	3	7	76	....	....	....	....	....	....	....	....	....	....	....	....	....	....	....	....	....	....
	Jacksonville	ECHL	30	6	8	14	135	....	....	....	....	....	....	....	....	....	....	....	....	....	....	....	....	....	....
1998-99	Indianapolis Ice	IHL	72	14	11	25	307	....	....	....	....	....	....	....	....	....	7	3	1	4	45	....	....	....	....
99-2000	Cleveland	IHL	65	12	9	21	248	....	....	....	....	....	....	....	....	....	9	2	1	3	19	....	....	....	....
2000-01	Norfolk Admirals	AHL	73	11	17	28	268	....	....	....	....	....	....	....	....	....	9	2	0	2	18	....	....	....	....
2001-02	Norfolk Admirals	AHL	2	0	0	0	5	....	....	....	....	....	....	....	....	....	....	....	....	....	....	....	....	....	....
	Nashville	**NHL**	**22**	**1**	**2**	**3**	**74**	**0**	**0**	**1**	**7**	**14.3**	**–1**	**1**	**0.0**	**4:55**	....	....	....	....	....	....	....	....	....
	Milwaukee	AHL	56	6	10	16	190	....	....	....	....	....	....	....	....	....	....	....	....	....	....	....	....	....	....
2002-03	Milwaukee	AHL	27	1	2	3	106	....	....	....	....	....	....	....	....	....	....	....	....	....	....	....	....	....	....
	Nashville	**NHL**	**1**	**0**	**0**	**0**	**5**	**0**	**0**	**0**	**0**	**0.0**	**0**	**0**	**0.0**	**4:13**	....	....	....	....	....	....	....	....	....
	St. John's	AHL	36	7	8	15	97	....	....	....	....	....	....	....	....	....	....	....	....	....	....	....	....	....	....
2003-04	**Toronto**	**NHL**	**40**	**1**	**2**	**3**	**116**	**0**	**0**	**0**	**47**	**2.1**	**–1**	**5**	**20.0**	**7:40**	....	....	....	....	....	....	....	....	....
2004-05	St. John's	AHL	60	16	12	28	276	....	....	....	....	....	....	....	....	....	2	0	0	0	6	....	....	....	....
2005-06	**Toronto**	**NHL**	**3**	**0**	**0**	**0**	**2**	**0**	**0**	**0**	**2**	**0.0**	**–5**	**0**	**0.0**	**9:07**	....	....	....	....	....	....	....	....	....
	Dallas	**NHL**	**23**	**2**	**1**	**3**	**54**	**0**	**0**	**1**	**17**	**11.8**	**2**	**3**	**33.3**	**5:02**	....	....	....	....	....	....	....	....	....
	NHL Totals		**89**	**4**	**5**	**9**	**251**	**0**	**0**	**2**	**73**	**5.5**		**9**	**22.2**	**6:19**	....	....	....	....	....	....	....	....	....

Signed as a free agent by **Chicago**, August 27, 1997. Traded to **Nashville** by **Chicago** for future considerations, October 9, 2001. Traded to **Toronto** by **Nashville** for Bob Wren, Deceber 31, 2002. • Spent majority of 2003-04 season as a healthy reserve. Traded to **Dallas** by **Toronto** for Dallas' 6th round choice (Leo Komarov) in 2006 Entry Draft, November 6, 2005.

PERRY, Corey

(PAIR-ee, KOHR-ee) **ANA.**

Right wing. Shoots right. 6'2", 202 lbs. Born, Peterborough, Ont., May 16, 1985. Anaheim's 2nd choice, 28th overall, in 2003 Entry Draft.

Season	Club	League	GP	G	A	Pts	PIM	PP	SH	GW	S	%	+/-	TF	F%	Min	GP	G	A	Pts	PIM	PP	SH	GW	Min
2000-01	Peterborough	OMHA	64	69	46	115	20	....	....	....	....	....	....	....	....	....	3	3	0	3	0	....	....	....	....
2001-02	London Knights	OHL	67	28	31	59	56	....	....	....	....	....	....	....	....	....	12	2	3	5	30	....	....	....	....
2002-03	London Knights	OHL	67	25	53	78	145	....	....	....	....	....	....	....	....	....	14	7	16	23	27	....	....	....	....
2003-04	London Knights	OHL	66	40	*73	113	98	....	....	....	....	....	....	....	....	....	15	7	15	22	20	....	....	....	....
	Cincinnati	AHL	....	....	....	....	....	....	....	....	....	....	....	....	....	....	3	1	1	2	4	....	....	....	....
2004-05	London Knights	OHL	60	*47	*83	*130	117	....	....	....	....	....	....	....	....	....	18	11	*27	*38	46	....	....	....	....
2005-06	**Anaheim**	**NHL**	**56**	**13**	**12**	**25**	**50**	**4**	**0**	**2**	**98**	**13.3**	**1**	**11**	**27.3**	**11:34**	**11**	**0**	**3**	**3**	**16**	**0**	**0**	**0**	**9:33**
	Portland Pirates	AHL	19	16	18	34	32	....	....	....	....	....	....	....	....	....	1	1	0	1	0	....	....	....	....
	NHL Totals		**56**	**13**	**12**	**25**	**50**	**4**	**0**	**2**	**98**	**13.3**		**11**	**27.3**	**11:34**	**11**	**0**	**3**	**3**	**16**	**0**	**0**	**0**	**9:33**

OHL First All-Star Team (2004, 2005) • Canadian Major Junior First All-Star Team (2005) • Memorial Cup Tournament All-Star Team (2005) • Stafford Smythe Memorial Trophy (Memorial Cup Tournament MVP) (2005)

PETERS, Andrew

(PEE-tuhrs, AN-droo) **BUF.**

Left wing. Shoots left. 6'4", 240 lbs. Born, St. Catharines, Ont., May 5, 1980. Buffalo's 2nd choice, 34th overall, in 1998 Entry Draft.

Season	Club	League	GP	G	A	Pts	PIM	PP	SH	GW	S	%	+/-	TF	F%	Min	GP	G	A	Pts	PIM	PP	SH	GW	Min
1996-97	Georgetown	OPJHL	46	11	16	27	65	....	....	....	....	....	....	....	....	....	....	....	....	....	....	....	....	....	....
1997-98	Oshawa Generals	OHL	60	11	7	18	220	....	....	....	....	....	....	....	....	....	7	2	0	2	19	....	....	....	....
1998-99	Oshawa Generals	OHL	54	14	10	24	137	....	....	....	....	....	....	....	....	....	15	2	7	9	36	....	....	....	....
99-2000	Kitchener Rangers	OHL	42	6	13	19	95	....	....	....	....	....	....	....	....	....	4	0	1	1	14	....	....	....	....
2000-01	Rochester	AHL	49	0	4	4	118	....	....	....	....	....	....	....	....	....	....	....	....	....	....	....	....	....	....
2001-02	Rochester	AHL	67	4	1	5	*388	....	....	....	....	....	....	....	....	....	....	....	....	....	....	....	....	....	....
2002-03	Rochester	AHL	57	3	0	3	223	....	....	....	....	....	....	....	....	....	3	0	0	0	24	....	....	....	....
2003-04	**Buffalo**	**NHL**	**42**	**2**	**0**	**2**	**151**	**0**	**0**	**0**	**19**	**10.5**	**–3**	**2**	**0.0**	**4:10**	....	....	....	....	....	....	....	....	....
2004-05	Bodens IK	Sweden-2	22	2	4	6	195	....	....	....	....	....	....	....	....	....	....	....	....	....	....	....	....	....	....
2005-06	**Buffalo**	**NHL**	**28**	**0**	**0**	**0**	**100**	**0**	**0**	**0**	**6**	**0.0**	**–2**	**2**	**100.0**	**3:16**	....	....	....	....	....	....	....	....	....
	NHL Totals		**70**	**2**	**0**	**2**	**251**	**0**	**0**	**0**	**25**	**8.0**		**4**	**50.0**	**3:48**	....	....	....	....	....	....	....	....	....

Signed as a free agent by **Bodens** (Sweden-2), August 20, 2004.

PETERSEN, Toby

(PEE-tuhr-sohn, TOH-bee) **EDM.**

Center. Shoots left. 5'10", 197 lbs. Born, Minneapolis, MN, October 27, 1978. Pittsburgh's 9th choice, 244th overall, in 1998 Entry Draft.

Season	Club	League	GP	G	A	Pts	PIM	PP	SH	GW	S	%	+/-	TF	F%	Min	GP	G	A	Pts	PIM	PP	SH	GW	Min
1995-96	Jefferson Jaguars	High-MN	25	29	30	59		....	....	....	....	....	....	....	....	....	....	....	....	....	....	....	....	....	....
1996-97	Colorado College	WCHA	40	17	21	38	18	....	....	....	....	....	....	....	....	....	....	....	....	....	....	....	....	....	....
1997-98	Colorado College	WCHA	40	16	17	33	34	....	....	....	....	....	....	....	....	....	....	....	....	....	....	....	....	....	....
1998-99	Colorado College	WCHA	21	12	12	24	2	....	....	....	....	....	....	....	....	....	....	....	....	....	....	....	....	....	....
99-2000	Colorado College	WCHA	37	14	19	33	8	....	....	....	....	....	....	....	....	....	....	....	....	....	....	....	....	....	....
2000-01	**Pittsburgh**	**NHL**	**12**	**2**	**6**	**8**	**4**	**0**	**0**	**1**	**25**	**8.0**	**3**	**39**	**35.9**	**13:22**	....	....	....	....	....	....	....	....	....
	Wilkes-Barre	AHL	73	26	41	67	22	....	....	....	....	....	....	....	....	....	21	7	6	13	4	....	....	....	....
2001-02	**Pittsburgh**	**NHL**	**79**	**8**	**10**	**18**	**4**	**1**	**1**	**0**	**116**	**6.9**	**–15**	**338**	**45.6**	**12:16**	....	....	....	....	....	....	....	....	....
2002-03	Wilkes-Barre	AHL	80	31	35	66	24	....	....	....	....	....	....	....	....	....	6	1	3	4	4	....	....	....	....
2003-04	Wilkes-Barre	AHL	62	15	29	44	4	....	....	....	....	....	....	....	....	....	21	2	10	12	12	....	....	....	....
2004-05	Edmonton	AHL	78	14	15	29	21	....	....	....	....	....	....	....	....	....	....	....	....	....	....	....	....	....	....
2005-06	**Edmonton**	**NHL**	....	....	....	....	....	....	....	....	....	....	....	....	....	....	**2**	**1**	**0**	**1**	**0**	**0**	**0**	**0**	**6:23**
	Iowa Stars	AHL	79	26	47	73	48	....	....	....	....	....	....	....	....	....	7	2	4	6	2	....	....	....	....
	NHL Totals		**91**	**10**	**16**	**26**	**8**	**1**	**1**	**1**	**141**	**7.1**		**377**	**44.6**	**12:25**	**2**	**1**	**0**	**1**	**0**	**0**	**0**	**0**	**6:22**

WCHA All-Rookie Team (1997) • AHL All-Rookie Team (2001)

Signed as a free agent by **Edmonton**, July 30, 2004.

PETIOT, Richard

(PEH-tee-awt, RIH-chuhrd) **L.A.**

Defense. Shoots left. 6'2", 190 lbs. Born, Daysland, Alta., August 20, 1982. Los Angeles' 6th choice, 116th overall, in 2001 Entry Draft.

Season	Club	League	GP	G	A	Pts	PIM	PP	SH	GW	S	%	+/-	TF	F%	Min	GP	G	A	Pts	PIM	PP	SH	GW	Min
2000-01	Camrose Kodiaks	AJHL	55	8	16	24	81	....	....	....	....	....	....	....	....	....	8	2	1	3	8	....	....	....	....
2001-02	Colorado College	WCHA	39	4	6	10	35	....	....	....	....	....	....	....	....	....	....	....	....	....	....	....	....	....	....
2002-03	Colorado College	WCHA	38	1	6	7	86	....	....	....	....	....	....	....	....	....	....	....	....	....	....	....	....	....	....
2003-04	Colorado College	WCHA	39	3	5	8	61	....	....	....	....	....	....	....	....	....	....	....	....	....	....	....	....	....	....
2004-05	Colorado College	WCHA	26	3	5	8	42	....	....	....	....	....	....	....	....	....	....	....	....	....	....	....	....	....	....
2005-06	**Los Angeles**	**NHL**	**2**	**0**	**0**	**0**	**2**	**0**	**0**	**0**	**1**	**0.0**	**–2**	**0**	**0.0**	**4:47**	....	....	....	....	....	....	....	....	....
	Manchester	AHL	63	4	10	14	52	....	....	....	....	....	....	....	....	....	7	1	0	1	6	....	....	....	....
	NHL Totals		**2**	**0**	**0**	**0**	**2**	**0**	**0**	**0**	**1**	**0.0**		**0**	**0.0**	**4:47**	....	....	....	....	....	....	....	....	....

AJHL All-Rookie Team (2001) • AJHL South Second All-Star Team (2001)

PETROVICKY, Ronald

(PEHT-roh-vih-kee, RAW-nohld) **PIT.**

Right wing. Shoots right. 5'11", 190 lbs. Born, Zilina, Czechoslovakia, February 15, 1977. Calgary's 9th choice, 228th overall, in 1996 Entry Draft.

Season	Club	League	GP	G	A	Pts	PIM	PP	SH	GW	S	%	+/-	TF	F%	Min	GP	G	A	Pts	PIM	PP	SH	GW	Min
1993-94	Dukla Trencin Jr.	Slovak-Jr.	36	28	27	55	42	....	....	....	....	....	....	....	....	....	....	....	....	....	....	....	....	....	....
	Dukla Trencin	Slovakia	1	0	0	0	0	....	....	....	....	....	....	....	....	....	....	....	....	....	....	....	....	....	....
1994-95	Tri-City	WHL	39	4	11	15	86	....	....	....	....	....	....	....	....	....	....	....	....	....	....	....	....	....	....
	Prince George	WHL	21	4	6	10	37	....	....	....	....	....	....	....	....	....	....	....	....	....	....	....	....	....	....
1995-96	Prince George	WHL	39	19	21	40	61	....	....	....	....	....	....	....	....	....	....	....	....	....	....	....	....	....	....
1996-97	Prince George	WHL	72	32	37	69	119	....	....	....	....	....	....	....	....	....	15	4	9	13	31	....	....	....	....
1997-98	Regina Pats	WHL	71	64	49	113	168	....	....	....	....	....	....	....	....	....	9	2	4	6	11	....	....	....	....
1998-99	Saint John Flames	AHL	78	12	21	33	114	....	....	....	....	....	....	....	....	....	7	1	2	3	19	....	....	....	....
99-2000	Saint John Flames	AHL	67	23	33	56	131	....	....	....	....	....	....	....	....	....	3	1	1	2	6	....	....	....	....
2000-01	**Calgary**	**NHL**	**30**	**4**	**5**	**9**	**54**	**1**	**0**	**1**	**30**	**13.3**	**0**	**7**	**42.9**	**11:33**	....	....	....	....	....	....	....	....	....
2001-02	**Calgary**	**NHL**	**77**	**5**	**7**	**12**	**85**	**1**	**0**	**1**	**78**	**6.4**	**0**	**28**	**46.4**	**11:42**	....	....	....	....	....	....	....	....	....
2002-03	**NY Rangers**	**NHL**	**66**	**5**	**9**	**14**	**77**	**2**	**1**	**1**	**65**	**7.7**	**–12**	**52**	**42.3**	**12:25**	....	....	....	....	....	....	....	....	....
2003-04	**Atlanta**	**NHL**	**78**	**16**	**15**	**31**	**123**	**0**	**0**	**1**	**102**	**15.7**	**–9**	**27**	**40.7**	**14:16**	....	....	....	....	....	....	....	....	....

Season	Club	League	GP	G	A	Pts	PIM	PP	SH	GW	S	%	+/-	TF	F%	Min	GP	G	A	Pts	PIM	PP	SH	GW	Min
			Regular Season														Playoffs								
2004-05	MsHK SKP Zilina	Slovakia	34	10	9	19	34	....	....	....	....	....	....	....	....	....	....	....	....	....	....	....	....	....	....
	Brynas IF Gavle	Sweden	10	0	5	5	27	....	....	....	....	....	....	....	....	....	....	....	....	....	....	....	....	....	....
	Brynas IF Gavle	Sweden-Q	9	0	2	2	0	....	....	....	....	....	....	....	....	....	....	....	....	....	....	....	....	....	....
2005-06	**Atlanta**	**NHL**	**60**	**8**	**12**	**20**	**62**	**2**	**0**	**2**	**70**	**11.4**	**–8**	**25**	**52.0**	**11:53**	....	....	....	....	....	....	....	....	....
	Slovakia	Olympics	6	1	0	1	2	....	....	....	....	....	....	....	....	....	....	....	....	....	....	....	....	....	....
	NHL Totals		**311**	**38**	**48**	**86**	**401**	**6**	**1**	**6**	**345**	**11.0**		**139**	**44.6**	**12:31**	....	....	....	....	....	....	....	....	....

WHL East Second All-Star Team (1998)

• Missed majority of 2000-01 season recovering from wrist injury suffered in game vs. Detroit, October 5, 2000. Claimed by **NY Rangers** from **Calgary** in Waiver Draft, October 4, 2002. Claimed by **Atlanta** from **NY Rangers** in Waiver Draft, October 3, 2003. Signed as a free agent by **Zilina** (Slovakia), September 17, 2004. Signed as a free agent by **Gavle** (Sweden), January 23, 2005. Signed as a free agent by **Pittsburgh**, July 24, 2006.

PETTINEN, Tomi
(peh-TIHN-ehn, TAW-mee)

Defense. Shoots left. 6'3", 220 lbs. Born, Ylojarvi, Finland, June 17, 1977. NY Islanders' 9th choice, 267th overall, in 2000 Entry Draft.

Season	Club	League	GP	G	A	Pts	PIM	PP	SH	GW	S	%	+/-	TF	F%	Min	GP	G	A	Pts	PIM	PP	SH	GW	Min
1994-95	Ilves Tampere U18	Fin-U18	31	1	6	7	46	....	....	....	....	....	....	....	....	....	4	0	0	0	2	....	....	....	....
	Ilves Tampere Jr.	Fin-Jr.	1	0	0	0	0	....	....	....	....	....	....	....	....	....	....	....	....	....	....	....	....	....	....
1995-96	Ilves Tampere Jr.	Fin-Jr.	12	1	1	2	18	....	....	....	....	....	....	....	....	....	....	....	....	....	....	....	....	....	....
	KooVee Jr.	Fin-Jr.	21	0	0	0	64	....	....	....	....	....	....	....	....	....	....	....	....	....	....	....	....	....	....
1996-97	Ilves Tampere	Finland	16	1	0	1	12	....	....	....	....	....	....	....	....	....	....	....	....	....	....	....	....	....	....
	Ilves Tampere Jr.	Fin-Jr.	26	3	8	11	44	....	....	....	....	....	....	....	....	....	....	....	....	....	....	....	....	....	....
1997-98	Ilves Tampere Jr.	Fin-Jr.	14	1	4	5	24	....	....	....	....	....	....	....	....	....	....	....	....	....	....	....	....	....	....
	Ilves Tampere	Finland	3	0	0	0	0	....	....	....	....	....	....	....	....	....	....	....	....	....	....	....	....	....	....
	Lukko Rauma	Finland	27	0	2	2	16	....	....	....	....	....	....	....	....	....	....	....	....	....	....	....	....	....	....
	Lukko Rauma Jr.	Fin-Jr.	11	2	6	8	14	....	....	....	....	....	....	....	....	....	....	....	....	....	....	....	....	....	....
1998-99	HIFK Helsinki	Finland	4	0	0	0	2	....	....	....	....	....	....	....	....	....	....	....	....	....	....	....	....	....	....
	Hermes Kokkola	Finland-2	42	8	6	14	76	....	....	....	....	....	....	....	....	....	3	0	0	0	6	....	....	....	....
99-2000	Ilves Tampere	Finland	51	1	6	7	84	....	....	....	....	....	....	....	....	....	3	1	2	3	2	....	....	....	....
2000-01	Ilves Tampere	Finland	56	2	2	4	86	....	....	....	....	....	....	....	....	....	9	0	0	0	4	....	....	....	....
2001-02	Ilves Tampere	Finland	48	5	4	9	51	....	....	....	....	....	....	....	....	....	3	0	0	0	4	....	....	....	....
	Bridgeport	AHL	....	....	....	....	....	....	....	....	....	....	....	....	....	....	9	0	1	1	0	....	....	....	....
2002-03	**NY Islanders**	**NHL**	**2**	**0**	**0**	**0**	**0**	**0**	**0**	**0**	**0**	**0.0**	**1**	**0**	**0.0**	**11:34**	....	....	....	....	....	....	....	....	....
	Bridgeport	AHL	75	1	8	9	56	....	....	....	....	....	....	....	....	....	9	0	0	0	17	....	....	....	....
2003-04	**NY Islanders**	**NHL**	**4**	**0**	**0**	**0**	**2**	**0**	**0**	**0**	**2**	**0.0**	**–2**	**0**	**0.0**	**10:24**	....	....	....	....	....	....	....	....	....
	Bridgeport	AHL	71	1	8	9	37	....	....	....	....	....	....	....	....	....	7	1	0	1	0	....	....	....	....
2004-05	Lukko Rauma	Finland	56	6	14	20	49	....	....	....	....	....	....	....	....	....	9	0	2	2	33	....	....	....	....
2005-06	**NY Islanders**	**NHL**	**18**	**0**	**0**	**0**	**16**	**0**	**0**	**0**	**7**	**0.0**	**–2**	**0**	**0.0**	**14:40**	....	....	....	....	....	....	....	....	....
	Bridgeport	AHL	29	0	6	6	38	....	....	....	....	....	....	....	....	....	7	0	1	1	14	....	....	....	....
	NHL Totals		**24**	**0**	**0**	**0**	**18**	**0**	**0**	**0**	**9**	**0.0**		**0**	**0.0**	**13:41**	....	....	....	....	....	....	....	....	....

Signed as a free agent by **Rauma** (Finland), June 7, 2004.

PETTINGER, Matt
(PEH-tihn-juhr, MAT) **WSH.**

Left wing. Shoots left. 6'1", 210 lbs. Born, Edmonton, Alta., October 22, 1980. Washington's 2nd choice, 43rd overall, in 2000 Entry Draft.

Season	Club	League	GP	G	A	Pts	PIM	PP	SH	GW	S	%	+/-	TF	F%	Min	GP	G	A	Pts	PIM	PP	SH	GW	Min
1994-95	Victoria Racquet	BCAHA	55	52	48	100	41	....	....	....	....	....	....	....	....	....	....	....	....	....	....	....	....	....	....
1995-96	Victoria Racquet	BCAHA	60	80	65	145	45	....	....	....	....	....	....	....	....	....	....	....	....	....	....	....	....	....	....
1996-97	Victoria Salsa	BCHL	49	22	14	36	31	....	....	....	....	....	....	....	....	....	....	....	....	....	....	....	....	....	....
1997-98	Victoria Salsa	BCHL	55	22	20	42	56	....	....	....	....	....	....	....	....	....	7	5	1	6	8	....	....	....	....
1998-99	U. of Denver	WCHA	33	6	14	20	44	....	....	....	....	....	....	....	....	....	....	....	....	....	....	....	....	....	....
99-2000	U. of Denver	WCHA	19	2	6	8	49	....	....	....	....	....	....	....	....	....	....	....	....	....	....	....	....	....	....
	Calgary Hitmen	WHL	27	14	6	20	41	....	....	....	....	....	....	....	....	....	11	2	6	8	30	....	....	....	....
2000-01	**Washington**	**NHL**	**10**	**0**	**0**	**0**	**2**	**0**	**0**	**0**	**6**	**0.0**	**–1**	**2**	**50.0**	**7:47**	....	....	....	....	....	....	....	....	....
	Portland Pirates	AHL	64	19	17	36	92	....	....	....	....	....	....	....	....	....	2	0	0	0	4	....	....	....	....
2001-02	**Washington**	**NHL**	**61**	**7**	**3**	**10**	**44**	**1**	**0**	**1**	**73**	**9.6**	**–8**	**5**	**20.0**	**9:39**	....	....	....	....	....	....	....	....	....
	Portland Pirates	AHL	9	3	3	6	24	....	....	....	....	....	....	....	....	....	....	....	....	....	....	....	....	....	....
2002-03	**Washington**	**NHL**	**1**	**0**	**0**	**0**	**0**	**0**	**0**	**0**	**0**	**0.0**	**0**	**1**	**0.0**	**3:30**	....	....	....	....	....	....	....	....	....
	Portland Pirates	AHL	69	14	13	27	72	....	....	....	....	....	....	....	....	....	3	0	2	2	2	....	....	....	....
2003-04	**Washington**	**NHL**	**71**	**7**	**5**	**12**	**37**	**1**	**0**	**1**	**92**	**7.6**	**–9**	**18**	**44.4**	**11:25**	....	....	....	....	....	....	....	....	....
2004-05	Ljubljana	Slovenia	1	0	1	1	0	....	....	....	....	....	....	....	....	....	....	....	....	....	....	....	....	....	....
	Ljubljana	Interliga	7	2	4	6	41	....	....	....	....	....	....	....	....	....	....	....	....	....	....	....	....	....	....
2005-06	**Washington**	**NHL**	**71**	**20**	**18**	**38**	**39**	**4**	**5**	**2**	**134**	**14.9**	**–2**	**39**	**12.8**	**15:29**	....	....	....	....	....	....	....	....	....
	NHL Totals		**214**	**34**	**26**	**60**	**122**	**6**	**5**	**4**	**305**	**11.1**		**65**	**23.1**	**12:03**	....	....	....	....	....	....	....	....	....

Left **U. of Denver** (WCHA) and signed as a free agent with **Calgary** (WHL), January 10, 2000. Signed as a free agent by **Ljubljana** (Slovenia), December 6, 2004.

PHANEUF, Dion
(fah-NOOF, DEE-awn) **CGY.**

Defense. Shoots left. 6'3", 213 lbs. Born, Edmonton, Alta., April 10, 1985. Calgary's 1st choice, 9th overall, in 2003 Entry Draft.

Season	Club	League	GP	G	A	Pts	PIM	PP	SH	GW	S	%	+/-	TF	F%	Min	GP	G	A	Pts	PIM	PP	SH	GW	Min
2000-01	Southgate Lions	AMBHL	35	15	50	65	208	....	....	....	....	....	....	....	....	....	4	3	4	7	15	....	....	....	....
2001-02	Red Deer Rebels	WHL	67	5	12	17	170	....	....	....	....	....	....	....	....	....	21	0	2	2	14	....	....	....	....
2002-03	Red Deer Rebels	WHL	71	16	14	30	185	....	....	....	....	....	....	....	....	....	23	7	7	14	34	....	....	....	....
2003-04	Red Deer Rebels	WHL	62	19	24	43	126	....	....	....	....	....	....	....	....	....	19	2	9	11	30	....	....	....	....
2004-05	Red Deer Rebels	WHL	55	24	32	56	73	....	....	....	....	....	....	....	....	....	7	1	4	5	12	....	....	....	....
2005-06	**Calgary**	**NHL**	**82**	**20**	**29**	**49**	**93**	**16**	**0**	**7**	**242**	**8.3**	**5**	**0**	**0.0**	**21:44**	**7**	**1**	**0**	**1**	**7**	**1**	**0**	**0**	**18:37**
	NHL Totals		**82**	**20**	**29**	**49**	**93**	**16**	**0**	**7**	**242**	**8.3**		**0**	**0.0**	**21:44**	**7**	**1**	**0**	**1**	**7**	**1**	**0**	**0**	**18:37**

WHL East First All-Star Team (2004, 2005) • WHL Defenseman of the Year (2004, 2005) • Canadian Major Junior First All-Star Team (2004, 2005) • NHL All-Rookie Team (2006)

PHILLIPS, Chris
(FIHL-ihps, KRIHS) **OTT.**

Defense. Shoots left. 6'3", 215 lbs. Born, Calgary, Alta., March 9, 1978. Ottawa's 1st choice, 1st overall, in 1996 Entry Draft.

Season	Club	League	GP	G	A	Pts	PIM	PP	SH	GW	S	%	+/-	TF	F%	Min	GP	G	A	Pts	PIM	PP	SH	GW	Min
1993-94	Fort McMurray	AJHL	56	6	16	22	72	....	....	....	....	....	....	....	....	....	10	0	3	3	16	....	....	....	....
1994-95	Fort McMurray	AJHL	48	16	32	48	127	....	....	....	....	....	....	....	....	....	11	4	2	6	10	....	....	....	....
1995-96	Prince Albert	WHL	61	10	30	40	97	....	....	....	....	....	....	....	....	....	18	2	12	14	30	....	....	....	....
1996-97	Prince Albert	WHL	32	3	23	26	58	....	....	....	....	....	....	....	....	....	....	....	....	....	....	....	....	....	....
	Lethbridge	WHL	26	4	18	22	28	....	....	....	....	....	....	....	....	....	19	4	*21	25	20	....	....	....	....
1997-98	**Ottawa**	**NHL**	**72**	**5**	**11**	**16**	**38**	**2**	**0**	**2**	**107**	**4.7**	**2**	....	....	....	**11**	**0**	**2**	**2**	**2**	**0**	**0**	**0**	....
1998-99	**Ottawa**	**NHL**	**34**	**3**	**3**	**6**	**32**	**2**	**0**	**0**	**51**	**5.9**	**–5**	**0**	**0.0**	**18:06**	**3**	**0**	**0**	**0**	**0**	**0**	**0**	**0**	**13:50**
99-2000	**Ottawa**	**NHL**	**65**	**5**	**14**	**19**	**39**	**0**	**0**	**1**	**96**	**5.2**	**12**	**0**	**0.0**	**16:50**	**6**	**0**	**1**	**1**	**4**	**0**	**0**	**0**	**18:17**
2000-01	**Ottawa**	**NHL**	**73**	**2**	**12**	**14**	**31**	**2**	**0**	**0**	**77**	**2.6**	**8**	**1**	**0.0**	**21:28**	**1**	**1**	**0**	**1**	**0**	**0**	**0**	**0**	**20:52**
2001-02	**Ottawa**	**NHL**	**63**	**6**	**16**	**22**	**29**	**1**	**0**	**1**	**103**	**5.8**	**5**	**0**	**0.0**	**19:31**	**12**	**0**	**0**	**0**	**12**	**0**	**0**	**0**	**21:44**
2002-03	**Ottawa**	**NHL**	**78**	**3**	**16**	**19**	**71**	**2**	**0**	**1**	**97**	**3.1**	**7**	**0**	**0.0**	**20:13**	**18**	**2**	**4**	**6**	**12**	**0**	**0**	**1**	**21:36**
2003-04	**Ottawa**	**NHL**	**82**	**7**	**16**	**23**	**46**	**0**	**0**	**1**	**93**	**7.5**	**15**	**1**	**100.0**	**20:50**	**7**	**1**	**0**	**1**	**12**	**1**	**0**	**0**	**20:26**
2004-05	Brynas IF Gavle	Sweden	27	5	3	8	45	....	....	....	....	....	....	....	....	....	....	....	....	....	....	....	....	....	....
	Brynas IF Gavle	Sweden-Q	9	1	2	3	2	....	....	....	....	....	....	....	....	....	....	....	....	....	....	....	....	....	....
2005-06	**Ottawa**	**NHL**	**69**	**1**	**18**	**19**	**90**	**0**	**0**	**0**	**79**	**1.3**	**19**	**0**	**0.0**	**20:52**	**9**	**2**	**0**	**2**	**6**	**0**	**0**	**0**	**21:41**
	NHL Totals		**536**	**32**	**106**	**138**	**376**	**9**	**0**	**6**	**703**	**4.6**		**2**	**50.0**	**19:54**	**67**	**6**	**7**	**13**	**48**	**1**	**0**	**1**	**20:43**

WHL Rookie of the Year (1996) • WHL East First All-Star Team (1997) • Canadian Major Junior First All-Star Team (1997) • Memorial Cup Tournament All-Star Team (1997)

• Missed majority of 1998-99 season recovering from ankle injury suffered in game vs. Buffalo, December 30, 1998. Signed as a free agent by **Gavle** (Sweden), November 2, 2004.

PICARD, Alexandre
(pee-KAR, ahl-ehx-AHN-druh) **CBJ**

Left wing. Shoots left. 6'2", 190 lbs. Born, Les Saules, Que., October 9, 1985. Columbus' 1st choice, 8th overall, in 2004 Entry Draft.

Season	Club	League	GP	G	A	Pts	PIM	PP	SH	GW	S	%	+/-	TF	F%	Min	GP	G	A	Pts	PIM	PP	SH	GW	Min
2000-01	St-Francois	QAAA	5	1	1	2	0	....	....	....	....	....	....	....	....	....	....	....	....	....	....	....	....	....	....
2001-02	St-Francois	QAAA	41	21	30	51	48	....	....	....	....	....	....	....	....	....	8	2	7	9	8	....	....	....	....
	Sherbrooke	QMJHL	6	0	3	3	0	....	....	....	....	....	....	....	....	....	....	....	....	....	....	....	....	....	....
2002-03	Sherbrooke	QMJHL	66	14	15	29	41	....	....	....	....	....	....	....	....	....	12	4	0	4	10	....	....	....	....
2003-04	Lewiston	QMJHL	69	39	41	80	88	....	....	....	....	....	....	....	....	....	7	7	4	11	6	....	....	....	....
2004-05	Lewiston	QMJHL	65	40	45	85	160	....	....	....	....	....	....	....	....	....	8	5	2	7	18	....	....	....	....

			Regular Season														Playoffs								
Season	Club	League	GP	G	A	Pts	PIM	PP	SH	GW	S	%	+/-	TF	F%	Min	GP	G	A	Pts	PIM	PP	SH	GW	Min
2005-06	**Columbus**	**NHL**	**17**	**0**	**0**	**0**	**14**	**0**	**0**	**0**	**10**	**0.0**	**−2**	**3**	**33.3**	**9:09**	....	....	....	....	....	....	....	....	....
	Syracuse Crunch	AHL	45	15	15	30	54	....	....	....	....	....	....	....	....	....	6	1	0	1	19	....	....	....	....
	NHL Totals		**17**	**0**	**0**	**0**	**14**	**0**	**0**	**0**	**10**	**0.0**		**3**	**33.3**	**9:09**	....	....	....	....	....	....	....	....	....

QMJHL Second All-Star Team (2004)

PICARD, Alexandre

(pee-KAR, ahl-ehx-AHN-druh) **PHI.**

Defense. Shoots left. 6'2", 214 lbs. Born, Gatineau, Que., July 5, 1985. Philadelphia's 5th choice, 85th overall, in 2003 Entry Draft.

2000-01	Gatineau	QAAA	42	6	15	21	38	....	....	....	....	....	....	....	....	....	11	0	1	1	8	....	....	....	....
2001-02	Halifax	QMJHL	59	2	12	14	28	....	....	....	....	....	....	....	....	....	13	2	3	5	6	....	....	....	....
2002-03	Halifax	QMJHL	71	4	30	34	64	....	....	....	....	....	....	....	....	....	25	1	5	6	14	....	....	....	....
2003-04	Cape Breton	QMJHL	57	10	26	36	44	....	....	....	....	....	....	....	....	....	5	0	0	0	0	....	....	....	....
2004-05	Halifax	QMJHL	68	15	23	38	46	....	....	....	....	....	....	....	....	....	13	1	5	6	14	....	....	....	....
	Philadelphia	AHL	....	....	....	....	....	....	....	....	....	....	....	....	....	....	2	0	0	0	0	....	....	....	....
2005-06	**Philadelphia**	**NHL**	**6**	**0**	**0**	**0**	**4**	**0**	**0**	**0**	**9**	**0.0**	**−2**	**0**	**0.0**	**9:33**	....	....	....	....	....	....	....	....	....
	Philadelphia	AHL	75	7	26	33	82	....	....	....	....	....	....	....	....	....	....	....	....	....	....	....	....	....	....
	NHL Totals		**6**	**0**	**0**	**0**	**4**	**0**	**0**	**0**	**9**	**0.0**		**0**	**0.0**	**9:33**	....	....	....	....	....	....	....	....	....

QMJHL Second All-Star Team (2005)

PIHLMAN, Tuomas

(PIHL-mahn, TAWH-muhs) **N.J.**

Left wing. Shoots left. 6'2", 210 lbs. Born, Espoo, Finland, November 13, 1982. New Jersey's 3rd choice, 48th overall, in 2001 Entry Draft.

1997-98	JYP Jyvaskyla U18	Fin-U18	30	2	5	7	18	....	....	....	....	....	....	....	....	....	4	1	3	4	6	....	....	....	....
1998-99	JYP Jyvaskyla U18	Fin-U18	35	21	20	41	64	....	....	....	....	....	....	....	....	....	6	1	1	2	12	....	....	....	....
99-2000	JYP Jyvaskyla U18	Fin-U18	3	3	0	3	0	....	....	....	....	....	....	....	....	....	....	....	....	....	....	....	....	....	....
	JYP Jyvaskyla Jr.	Fin-Jr.	20	4	4	8	54	....	....	....	....	....	....	....	....	....	4	0	0	0	8	....	....	....	....
	JYP Jyvaskyla	Finland	17	0	0	0	18	....	....	....	....	....	....	....	....	....	....	....	....	....	....	....	....	....	....
2000-01	JYP Jyvaskyla Jr.	Fin-Jr.	1	1	0	1	2	....	....	....	....	....	....	....	....	....	6	2	4	6	4	....	....	....	....
	JYP Jyvaskyla	Finland	47	3	6	9	59	....	....	....	....	....	....	....	....	....	....	....	....	....	....	....	....	....	....
2001-02	JYP Jyvaskyla Jr.	Fin-Jr.	3	1	1	2	4	....	....	....	....	....	....	....	....	....	....	....	....	....	....	....	....	....	....
	JYP Jyvaskyla	Finland	44	9	2	11	95	....	....	....	....	....	....	....	....	....	....	....	....	....	....	....	....	....	....
2002-03	JYP Jyvaskyla	Finland	53	19	15	34	58	....	....	....	....	....	....	....	....	....	1	0	0	0	0	....	....	....	....
2003-04	**New Jersey**	**NHL**	**2**	**0**	**0**	**0**	**2**	**0**	**0**	**0**	**1**	**0.0**	**0**	**0**	**0.0**	**6:56**	....	....	....	....	....	....	....	....	....
	Albany River Rats	AHL	73	10	19	29	59	....	....	....	....	....	....	....	....	....	....	....	....	....	....	....	....	....	....
2004-05	Albany River Rats	AHL	68	9	13	22	48	....	....	....	....	....	....	....	....	....	....	....	....	....	....	....	....	....	....
2005-06	**New Jersey**	**NHL**	**11**	**1**	**1**	**2**	**10**	**0**	**0**	**0**	**14**	**7.1**	**−1**	**22**	**40.9**	**10:04**	....	....	....	....	....	....	....	....	....
	Albany River Rats	AHL	63	12	15	27	64	....	....	....	....	....	....	....	....	....	....	....	....	....	....	....	....	....	....
	NHL Totals		**13**	**1**	**1**	**2**	**12**	**0**	**0**	**0**	**15**	**6.7**		**22**	**40.9**	**9:35**	....	....	....	....	....	....	....	....	....

PIRJETA, Lasse

(PEER-yeh-tuh, LAH-see)

Center. Shoots left. 6'4", 225 lbs. Born, Haukipudas, Finland, April 4, 1974. Columbus' 7th choice, 133rd overall, in 2002 Entry Draft.

1989-90	Karpat Oulu Jr.	Fin-Jr.	2	0	0	0	0	....	....	....	....	....	....	....	....	....	....	....	....	....	....	....	....	....	....
1990-91	Karpat Oulu Jr.	Fin-Jr.	28	6	7	13	12	....	....	....	....	....	....	....	....	....	....	....	....	....	....	....	....	....	....
1991-92	Karpat Oulu Jr.	Fin-Jr.	7	1	4	5	8	....	....	....	....	....	....	....	....	....	....	....	....	....	....	....	....	....	....
	Tacoma Rockets	WHL	16	5	2	7	4	....	....	....	....	....	....	....	....	....	....	....	....	....	....	....	....	....	....
	Karpat Oulu	Finland-2	2	0	0	0	0	....	....	....	....	....	....	....	....	....	....	....	....	....	....	....	....	....	....
1992-93	Karpat Oulu Jr.	Fin-Jr.	24	13	19	32	34	....	....	....	....	....	....	....	....	....	....	....	....	....	....	....	....	....	....
	Karpat Oulu	Finland-2	20	4	3	7	6	....	....	....	....	....	....	....	....	....	....	....	....	....	....	....	....	....	....
1993-94	TPS Turku Jr.	Fin-Jr.	6	2	2	4	2	....	....	....	....	....	....	....	....	....	4	6	2	8	2	....	....	....	....
	Kiekko-67 Turku	Finland-2	2	2	1	3	0	....	....	....	....	....	....	....	....	....	....	....	....	....	....	....	....	....	....
	TPS Turku	Finland	43	9	9	18	14	....	....	....	....	....	....	....	....	....	11	4	0	4	2	....	....	....	....
1994-95	TPS Turku Jr.	Fin-Jr.	1	0	0	0	0	....	....	....	....	....	....	....	....	....	....	....	....	....	....	....	....	....	....
	TPS Turku	Finland	49	7	13	20	64	....	....	....	....	....	....	....	....	....	8	0	1	1	29	....	....	....	....
1995-96	TPS Turku	Finland	45	13	14	27	34	....	....	....	....	....	....	....	....	....	11	6	3	9	4	....	....	....	....
1996-97	V.Frolunda	Sweden	50	14	8	22	36	....	....	....	....	....	....	....	....	....	3	0	1	1	4	....	....	....	....
	V.Frolunda	EuroHL	5	2	6	8	4	....	....	....	....	....	....	....	....	....	....	....	....	....	....	....	....	....	....
1997-98	Tappara Tampere	Finland	48	24	22	46	20	....	....	....	....	....	....	....	....	....	4	1	1	2	2	....	....	....	....
1998-99	Tappara Tampere	Finland	54	22	19	41	32	....	....	....	....	....	....	....	....	....	....	....	....	....	....	....	....	....	....
99-2000	HIFK Helsinki	Finland	54	18	25	43	24	....	....	....	....	....	....	....	....	....	9	2	3	5	10	....	....	....	....
	HIFK Helsinki	EuroHL	6	1	3	4	6	....	....	....	....	....	....	....	....	....	2	1	1	2	0	....	....	....	....
2000-01	HIFK Helsinki	Finland	56	15	18	33	20	....	....	....	....	....	....	....	....	....	....	....	....	....	....	....	....	....	....
2001-02	Karpat Oulu	Finland	55	15	26	41	24	....	....	....	....	....	....	....	....	....	4	2	2	4	2	....	....	....	....
2002-03	**Columbus**	**NHL**	**51**	**11**	**10**	**21**	**12**	**2**	**0**	**2**	**80**	**13.8**	**−4**	**327**	**43.1**	**11:28**	....	....	....	....	....	....	....	....	....
2003-04	**Columbus**	**NHL**	**57**	**2**	**8**	**10**	**20**	**0**	**0**	**0**	**78**	**2.6**	**−6**	**465**	**49.5**	**10:46**	....	....	....	....	....	....	....	....	....
	Syracuse Crunch	AHL	5	1	2	3	2	....	....	....	....	....	....	....	....	....	....	....	....	....	....	....	....	....	....
	Pittsburgh	**NHL**	**13**	**6**	**6**	**12**	**0**	**1**	**0**	**1**	**33**	**18.2**	**3**	**187**	**51.9**	**14:22**	....	....	....	....	....	....	....	....	....
2004-05	HIFK Helsinki	Finland	45	16	20	36	26	....	....	....	....	....	....	....	....	....	5	2	0	2	2	....	....	....	....
2005-06	**Pittsburgh**	**NHL**	**25**	**4**	**3**	**7**	**18**	**0**	**0**	**0**	**30**	**13.3**	**4**	**220**	**46.4**	**9:15**	....	....	....	....	....	....	....	....	....
	Wilkes-Barre	AHL	8	1	4	5	6	....	....	....	....	....	....	....	....	....	....	....	....	....	....	....	....	....	....
	Kloten Flyers	Swiss	6	0	2	2	2	....	....	....	....	....	....	....	....	....	9	0	2	2	2	....	....	....	....
	NHL Totals		**146**	**23**	**27**	**50**	**50**	**3**	**0**	**3**	**221**	**10.4**		**1199**	**47.5**	**11:04**	....	....	....	....	....	....	....	....	....

Traded to **Pittsburgh** by **Columbus** for Brian Holzinger, March 9, 2004. Signed as a free agent by **HIFK Helsinki** (Finland), September 30, 2004. Assigned to **Kloten** (Swiss) by **Pittsburgh**. January 20, 2006. Signed as a free agent by **Malmo** (Sweden), June 17, 2006.

PIRNES, Esa

(PEER-nehz, EH-sah)

Center. Shoots left. 6', 189 lbs. Born, Oulu, Finland, April 1, 1977. Los Angeles' 7th choice, 174th overall, in 2003 Entry Draft.

1993-94	Karpat Oulu U18	Fin-U18	31	15	15	30	24	....	....	....	....	....	....	....	....	....	4	1	0	1	2	....	....	....	....
1994-95	Karpat Oulu U18	Fin-U18	6	6	3	9	8	....	....	....	....	....	....	....	....	....	....	....	....	....	....	....	....	....	....
	Karpat Oulu Jr.	Fin-Jr.	32	8	9	17	16	....	....	....	....	....	....	....	....	....	....	....	....	....	....	....	....	....	....
1995-96	Karpat Oulu Jr.	Fin-Jr.	24	19	13	32	8	....	....	....	....	....	....	....	....	....	....	....	....	....	....	....	....	....	....
	Karpat Oulu	Finland-2	20	8	4	12	12	....	....	....	....	....	....	....	....	....	3	0	0	0	0	....	....	....	....
1996-97	Karpat Oulu Jr.	Fin-Jr.	3	5	3	8	2	....	....	....	....	....	....	....	....	....	....	....	....	....	....	....	....	....	....
	Karpat Oulu Jr.	Fin-Jr.	9	5	5	10	6	....	....	....	....	....	....	....	....	....	....	....	....	....	....	....	....	....	....
	Karpat Oulu	Finland-2	36	17	16	33	20	....	....	....	....	....	....	....	....	....	9	0	2	2	16	....	....	....	....
1997-98	Karpat Oulu Jr.	Fin-Jr.	15	9	23	32	4	....	....	....	....	....	....	....	....	....	....	....	....	....	....	....	....	....	....
	Karpat Oulu	Finland-2	32	6	15	21	12	....	....	....	....	....	....	....	....	....	....	....	....	....	....	....	....	....	....
1998-99	Karpat Oulu	Finland-2	47	26	26	52	16	....	....	....	....	....	....	....	....	....	5	0	3	3	2	....	....	....	....
99-2000	Blues Espoo	Finland	51	15	24	39	12	....	....	....	....	....	....	....	....	....	4	0	1	1	2	....	....	....	....
2000-01	Blues Espoo	Finland	54	10	8	18	51	....	....	....	....	....	....	....	....	....	....	....	....	....	....	....	....	....	....
2001-02	Tappara Tampere	Finland	49	8	16	24	30	....	....	....	....	....	....	....	....	....	10	0	1	1	2	....	....	....	....
2002-03	Tappara Tampere	Finland	56	23	14	37	6	....	....	....	....	....	....	....	....	....	15	5	9	14	2	....	....	....	....
2003-04	**Los Angeles**	**NHL**	**57**	**3**	**8**	**11**	**12**	**0**	**1**	**0**	**57**	**5.3**	**−9**	**549**	**45.4**	**11:45**	....	....	....	....	....	....	....	....	....
	Manchester	AHL	4	3	1	4	2	....	....	....	....	....	....	....	....	....	....	....	....	....	....	....	....	....	....
2004-05	Lukko Rauma	Finland	47	9	29	38	31	....	....	....	....	....	....	....	....	....	9	1	3	4	2	....	....	....	....
2005-06	Blues Espoo	Finland	44	10	23	33	24	....	....	....	....	....	....	....	....	....	9	5	3	8	2	....	....	....	....
	NHL Totals		**57**	**3**	**8**	**11**	**12**	**0**	**1**	**0**	**57**	**5.3**		**549**	**45.4**	**11:45**	....	....	....	....	....	....	....	....	....

Signed as a free agent by **Rauma** (Finland), July 30, 2004. Signed as a free agent by **Espoo** (Finland), April 28, 2005.

PIROS, Kamil

(PIH-ruhsh, KA-mihl)

Center. Shoots left. 6', 200 lbs. Born, Most, Czech., November 20, 1978. Buffalo's 9th choice, 212th overall, in 1997 Entry Draft.

1993-94	Banik Most Jr.	CzRep-Jr.	16	12	10	22	....	....	....	....	....	....	....	....	....	....	....	....	....	....	....	....	....	....	....
	Litvinov Jr.	CzRep-Jr.	22	6	13	19	....	....	....	....	....	....	....	....	....	....	....	....	....	....	....	....	....	....	....
1994-95	Litvinov Jr.	CzRep-Jr.	40	27	16	43	....	....	....	....	....	....	....	....	....	....	....	....	....	....	....	....	....	....	....
1995-96	Litvinov Jr.	CzRep-Jr.	42	16	13	29	....	....	....	....	....	....	....	....	....	....	....	....	....	....	....	....	....	....	....
1996-97	Litvinov Jr.	CzRep-Jr.	3	2	1	3	....	....	....	....	....	....	....	....	....	....	....	....	....	....	....	....	....	....	....
	Litvinov	CzRep	38	4	9	13	10	....	....	....	....	....	....	....	....	....	....	....	....	....	....	....	....	....	....

			Regular Season														Playoffs								
Season	Club	League	GP	G	A	Pts	PIM	PP	SH	GW	S	%	+/-	TF	F%	Min	GP	G	A	Pts	PIM	PP	SH	GW	Min
1997-98	Litvinov	CzRep	14	0	1	1	2	....	....	....	....	....	....	....	....	....	....	....	....	....	....	....	....	....	....
	HC Vitkovice	CzRep	26	2	9	11	14	....	....	....	....	....	....	....	....	....	....	....	....	....	....	....	....	....	....
1998-99	Litvinov	CzRep	41	7	9	16	10	....	....	....	....	....	....	....	....	....	....	....	....	....	....	....	....	....	....
99-2000	Litvinov	CzRep	40	8	8	16	18	....	....	....	....	....	....	....	....	....	7	0	3	3	2	....	....	....	....
2000-01	Litvinov	CzRep	48	11	13	24	28	....	....	....	....	....	....	....	....	....	6	1	1	2	2	....	....	....	....
2001-02	**Atlanta**	**NHL**	**8**	**0**	**1**	**1**	**4**	**0**	**0**	**0**	**4**	**0.0**	**–2**	**81**	**32.1**	**12:12**	....	....	....	....	....	....	....	....	....
	Chicago Wolves	AHL	64	19	30	49	16	....	....	....	....	....	....	....	....	....	25	6	11	17	6	....	....	....	....
2002-03	**Atlanta**	**NHL**	**3**	**3**	**2**	**5**	**2**	**0**	**0**	**1**	**8**	**37.5**	**4**	**47**	**40.4**	**17:05**	....	....	....	....	....	....	....	....	....
	Chicago Wolves	AHL	51	10	9	19	16	....	....	....	....	....	....	....	....	....	9	1	0	1	4	....	....	....	....
2003-04	**Atlanta**	**NHL**	**14**	**0**	**1**	**1**	**4**	**0**	**0**	**0**	**10**	**0.0**	**–3**	**3**	**33.3**	**9:57**	....	....	....	....	....	....	....	....	....
	Chicago Wolves	AHL	50	10	20	30	20	....	....	....	....	....	....	....	....	....	....	....	....	....	....	....	....	....	....
	Florida	**NHL**	**3**	**1**	**0**	**1**	**0**	**1**	**0**	**0**	**1**	**100.0**	**–1**	**19**	**26.3**	**6:59**	....	....	....	....	....	....	....	....	....
	San Antonio	AHL	14	2	5	7	6	....	....	....	....	....	....	....	....	....	....	....	....	....	....	....	....	....	....
2004-05	Voskresensk	Russia	27	2	6	8	8	....	....	....	....	....	....	....	....	....	....	....	....	....	....	....	....	....	....
2005-06	Nizhnekamsk	Russia	33	6	5	11	32	....	....	....	....	....	....	....	....	....	5	1	0	1	2	....	....	....	....
	NHL Totals		**28**	**4**	**4**	**8**	**10**	**1**	**0**	**1**	**23**	**17.4**		**150**	**34.0**	**11:02**	....	....	....	....	....	....	....	....	....

Rights traded to **Atlanta** by **Buffalo** with Buffalo's 4th round choice (later traded to St. Louis – St. Louis selected Igor Valeyev) in 2001 Entry Draft for Donald Audette, March 13, 2001. Traded to **Florida** by **Atlanta** for Kyle Rossiter, March 8, 2004. Signed as a free agent by **Voskresensk** (Russia), November 15, 2004.

PISANI, Fernando

(pih-ZAN-ee, FUHR-nan-DOH) **EDM.**

Right wing. Shoots left. 6'1", 205 lbs. Born, Edmonton, Alta., December 27, 1976. Edmonton's 9th choice, 195th overall, in 1996 Entry Draft.

1993-94	St. Albert Saints	AJHL	50	6	21	27	24	....	....	....	....	....	....	....	....	....	....	....	....	....	....	....	....	....	....
1994-95	Bonnyville	AJHL	16	4	34	37	97	....	....	....	....	....	....	....	....	....	....	....	....	....	....	....	....	....	....
	St. Albert Saints	AJHL	40	26	21	47	16	....	....	....	....	....	....	....	....	....	....	....	....	....	....	....	....	....	....
1995-96	St. Albert Saints	AJHL	58	40	63	103	134	....	....	....	....	....	....	....	....	....	18	7	22	29	28	....	....	....	....
1996-97	Providence	H-East	35	12	18	30	36	....	....	....	....	....	....	....	....	....	....	....	....	....	....	....	....	....	....
1997-98	Providence	H-East	36	16	18	34	20	....	....	....	....	....	....	....	....	....	....	....	....	....	....	....	....	....	....
1998-99	Providence	H-East	38	14	37	51	42	....	....	....	....	....	....	....	....	....	....	....	....	....	....	....	....	....	....
99-2000	Providence	H-East	38	14	24	38	56	....	....	....	....	....	....	....	....	....	....	....	....	....	....	....	....	....	....
2000-01	Hamilton	AHL	52	12	13	25	28	....	....	....	....	....	....	....	....	....	....	....	....	....	....	....	....	....	....
2001-02	Hamilton	AHL	79	26	34	60	60	....	....	....	....	....	....	....	....	....	15	4	6	10	4	....	....	....	....
2002-03	**Edmonton**	**NHL**	**35**	**8**	**5**	**13**	**10**	**0**	**1**	**0**	**32**	**25.0**	**9**	**1**	**100.0**	**10:43**	**6**	**1**	**0**	**1**	**2**	**0**	**0**	**0**	**13:48**
	Hamilton	AHL	41	17	15	32	24	....	....	....	....	....	....	....	....	....	....	....	....	....	....	....	....	....	....
2003-04	**Edmonton**	**NHL**	**76**	**16**	**14**	**30**	**46**	**4**	**1**	**1**	**99**	**16.2**	**14**	**10**	**20.0**	**12:46**	....	....	....	....	....	....	....	....	....
2004-05	Langnau	Swiss	7	1	3	4	0	....	....	....	....	....	....	....	....	....	....	....	....	....	....	....	....	....	....
	Asiago	Italy	12	1	5	6	6	....	....	....	....	....	....	....	....	....	9	4	6	10	0	....	....	....	....
2005-06	**Edmonton**	**NHL**	**80**	**18**	**19**	**37**	**42**	**4**	**1**	**2**	**131**	**13.7**	**5**	**35**	**22.9**	**13:51**	**24**	***14**	**4**	**18**	**10**	**3**	**1**	**5**	**17:12**
	NHL Totals		**191**	**42**	**38**	**80**	**98**	**8**	**3**	**3**	**262**	**16.0**		**46**	**23.9**	**12:51**	**30**	**15**	**4**	**19**	**12**	**3**	**1**	**5**	**16:31**

Signed as a free agent by **Langnau** (Swiss), October 24, 2004. Signed as a free agent by **Asiago** (Italy), December 23, 2004.

PITKANEN, Joni

(PIHT-ka-nuhn, YOH-nee) **PHI.**

Defense. Shoots left. 6'3", 200 lbs. Born, Oulu, Finland, September 19, 1983. Philadelphia's 1st choice, 4th overall, in 2002 Entry Draft.

1998-99	Karpat Oulu U18	Fin-U18	30	1	5	6	12	....	....	....	....	....	....	....	....	....	....	....	....	....	....	....	....	....	....
99-2000	Karpat Oulu U18	Fin-U18	36	12	14	26	26	....	....	....	....	....	....	....	....	....	6	1	4	5	2	....	....	....	....
	Karpat Oulu Jr.	Fin-Jr.	2	0	0	0	0	....	....	....	....	....	....	....	....	....	....	....	....	....	....	....	....	....	....
2000-01	Karpat Oulu Jr.	Fin-Jr.	24	6	11	17	77	....	....	....	....	....	....	....	....	....	....	....	....	....	....	....	....	....	....
	Karpat Oulu	Finland	21	0	0	0	10	....	....	....	....	....	....	....	....	....	2	0	0	0	2	....	....	....	....
2001-02	Karpat Oulu Jr.	Fin-Jr.	....	....	....	....	....	....	....	....	....	....	....	....	....	....	1	0	0	0	0	....	....	....	....
	Karpat Oulu	Finland	49	4	15	19	65	....	....	....	....	....	....	....	....	....	4	0	0	0	12	....	....	....	....
2002-03	Karpat Oulu	Finland	35	5	15	20	38	....	....	....	....	....	....	....	....	....	....	....	....	....	....	....	....	....	....
2003-04	**Philadelphia**	**NHL**	**71**	**8**	**19**	**27**	**44**	**5**	**0**	**2**	**133**	**6.0**	**15**	**0**	**0.0**	**16:35**	**15**	**0**	**3**	**3**	**6**	**0**	**0**	**0**	**12:13**
2004-05	Philadelphia	AHL	76	6	35	41	105	....	....	....	....	....	....	....	....	....	21	3	4	7	16	....	....	....	....
2005-06	**Philadelphia**	**NHL**	**58**	**13**	**33**	**46**	**78**	**5**	**0**	**3**	**118**	**11.0**	**22**	**0**	**0.0**	**23:43**	**6**	**0**	**2**	**2**	**2**	**0**	**0**	**0**	**24:12**
	Finland	Olympics	DID NOT PLAY – INJURED																						
	NHL Totals		**129**	**21**	**52**	**73**	**122**	**10**	**0**	**5**	**251**	**8.4**		**0**	**0.0**	**19:47**	**21**	**0**	**5**	**5**	**8**	**0**	**0**	**0**	**15:39**

NHL All-Rookie Team (2004)

PITTIS, Domenic

(PIH-THIS, DOHM-ihn-ihk)

Center. Shoots left. 5'11", 190 lbs. Born, Calgary, Alta., October 1, 1974. Pittsburgh's 2nd choice, 52nd overall, in 1993 Entry Draft.

1990-91	Cgy. AAA Flames	AMHL	35	23	54	77	43	....	....	....	....	....	....	....	....	....	....	....	....	....	....	....	....	....	....
1991-92	Lethbridge	WHL	65	6	17	23	18	....	....	....	....	....	....	....	....	....	5	0	2	2	4	....	....	....	....
1992-93	Lethbridge	WHL	66	46	73	119	69	....	....	....	....	....	....	....	....	....	4	3	3	6	8	....	....	....	....
1993-94	Lethbridge	WHL	72	58	69	127	93	....	....	....	....	....	....	....	....	....	8	4	11	15	16	....	....	....	....
1994-95	Cleveland	IHL	62	18	32	50	66	....	....	....	....	....	....	....	....	....	3	0	2	2	2	....	....	....	....
1995-96	Cleveland	IHL	74	10	28	38	100	....	....	....	....	....	....	....	....	....	3	0	0	0	2	....	....	....	....
1996-97	**Pittsburgh**	**NHL**	**1**	**0**	**0**	**0**	**0**	**0**	**0**	**0**	**0**	**0.0**	**–1**	....	....	....	....	....	....	....	....	....	....	....	....
	Long Beach	IHL	65	23	43	66	91	....	....	....	....	....	....	....	....	....	18	5	9	14	26	....	....	....	....
1997-98	Syracuse Crunch	AHL	75	23	41	64	90	....	....	....	....	....	....	....	....	....	5	1	3	4	4	....	....	....	....
1998-99	**Buffalo**	**NHL**	**3**	**0**	**0**	**0**	**2**	**0**	**0**	**0**	**1**	**0.0**	**0**	**19**	**42.1**	**8:35**	....	....	....	....	....	....	....	....	....
	Rochester	AHL	76	38	66	*104	108	....	....	....	....	....	....	....	....	....	20	7	*14	*21	40	....	....	....	....
99-2000	**Buffalo**	**NHL**	**7**	**1**	**0**	**1**	**6**	**0**	**0**	**0**	**6**	**16.7**	**1**	**65**	**44.6**	**11:27**	....	....	....	....	....	....	....	....	....
	Rochester	AHL	53	17	48	65	85	....	....	....	....	....	....	....	....	....	21	4	*26	*30	28	....	....	....	....
2000-01	**Edmonton**	**NHL**	**47**	**4**	**5**	**9**	**49**	**0**	**0**	**2**	**42**	**9.5**	**–5**	**367**	**54.8**	**10:46**	**3**	**0**	**0**	**0**	**2**	**0**	**0**	**0**	**8:00**
2001-02	**Edmonton**	**NHL**	**22**	**0**	**6**	**6**	**8**	**0**	**0**	**0**	**18**	**0.0**	**–2**	**52**	**55.8**	**11:23**	....	....	....	....	....	....	....	....	....
2002-03	Milwaukee	AHL	30	11	21	32	65	....	....	....	....	....	....	....	....	....	6	2	4	6	8	....	....	....	....
	Nashville	**NHL**	**2**	**0**	**0**	**0**	**2**	**0**	**0**	**0**	**1**	**0.0**	**0**	**6**	**16.7**	**5:00**	....	....	....	....	....	....	....	....	....
2003-04	**Buffalo**	**NHL**	**4**	**0**	**0**	**0**	**4**	**0**	**0**	**0**	**3**	**0.0**	**–1**	**47**	**53.2**	**11:37**	....	....	....	....	....	....	....	....	....
	Rochester	AHL	75	20	*57	77	137	....	....	....	....	....	....	....	....	....	16	5	14	19	30	....	....	....	....
2004-05	Kloten Flyers	Swiss	43	17	29	46	110	....	....	....	....	....	....	....	....	....	3	2	2	4	4	....	....	....	....
2005-06	Kloten Flyers	Swiss	39	13	19	32	66	....	....	....	....	....	....	....	....	....	11	3	7	....	....	....	....	....	....
	NHL Totals		**86**	**5**	**11**	**16**	**71**	**0**	**0**	**2**	**71**	**7.0**		**556**	**52.7**	**10:49**	**3**	**0**	**0**	**0**	**2**	**0**	**0**	**0**	**8:00**

WHL East Second All-Star Team (1994) • John P. Sollenberger Trophy (Leading Scorer – AHL) (1999)

Signed as a free agent by **Buffalo**, August 10, 1998. Signed as a free agent by **Edmonton**, July 25, 2000. • Missed majority of 2001-02 season recovering from head injury suffered in game vs. Nashvile, February 28, 2002. Signed as a free agent by **Nashville**, July 24, 2002. • Missed majority of 2002-03 season recovering from head injury suffered in game vs. San Jose, November 7, 2002. Signed as a free agent by **Buffalo**, July 26, 2003. Signed as a free agent by **Kloten** (Swiss), April 4, 2004.

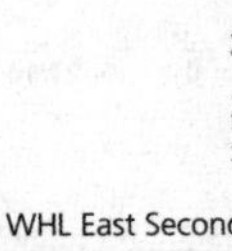

PIVKO, Libor

(PIHV-koh, LEE-bohr) **PIT.**

Left wing. Shoots left. 6'3", 214 lbs. Born, Novy Vicin, Czech., March 29, 1980. Nashville's 4th choice, 89th overall, in 2000 Entry Draft.

1995-96	Opava Jr.	CzRep-Jr.	37	19	14	33	30	....	....	....	....	....	....	....	....	....	....	....	....	....	....	....	....	....	....
1996-97	Opava Jr.	CzRep-Jr.	16	12	9	21	22	....	....	....	....	....	....	....	....	....	....	....	....	....	....	....	....	....	....
1997-98	HC Opava Jr.	CzRep-Jr.	37	15	11	26	36	....	....	....	....	....	....	....	....	....	....	....	....	....	....	....	....	....	....
1998-99	HC Opava Jr.	CzRep-Jr.	38	21	14	35	....	....	....	....	....	....	....	....	....	....	....	....	....	....	....	....	....	....	....
	Opava	CzRep	5	0	1	1	0	....	....	....	....	....	....	....	....	....	....	....	....	....	....	....	....	....	....
99-2000	HC Havirov Jr.	CzRep-Jr.	5	1	3	4	4	....	....	....	....	....	....	....	....	....	....	....	....	....	....	....	....	....	....
	HC Femax Havirov	CzRep	40	11	11	22	41	....	....	....	....	....	....	....	....	....	....	....	....	....	....	....	....	....	....
	HC Ytong Brno	CzRep-3	....	....	....	....	....	....	....	....	....	....	....	....	....	....	4	3	4	7	0	....	....	....	....
2000-01	HC Femax Havirov	CzRep	45	7	12	19	58	....	....	....	....	....	....	....	....	....	....	....	....	....	....	....	....	....	....
2001-02	Zlin	CzRep	46	8	20	28	36	....	....	....	....	....	....	....	....	....	9	5	3	8	8	....	....	....	....
2002-03	HC Hame Zlin	CzRep	52	13	12	25	60	....	....	....	....	....	....	....	....	....	....	....	....	....	....	....	....	....	....
2003-04	**Nashville**	**NHL**	**1**	**0**	**0**	**0**	**0**	**0**	**0**	**0**	**2**	**0.0**	**0**	**0**	**0.0**	**6:50**	....	....	....	....	....	....	....	....	....
	Milwaukee	AHL	67	11	20	31	50	....	....	....	....	....	....	....	....	....	21	7	6	13	22	....	....	....	....
2004-05	Milwaukee	AHL	56	5	15	20	59	....	....	....	....	....	....	....	....	....	6	0	1	1	2	....	....	....	....
2005-06	Milwaukee	AHL	69	12	57	69	63	....	....	....	....	....	....	....	....	....	12	3	5	8	16	....	....	....	....
	NHL Totals		**1**	**0**	**0**	**0**	**0**	**0**	**0**	**0**	**2**	**0.0**		**0**	**0.0**	**6:50**	....	....	....	....	....	....	....	....	....

Traded to **Pittsburgh** by **Nashville** with Dominic Moore for Pittsburgh's 3rd round choice in 2007 Entry Draft, July 19, 2006.

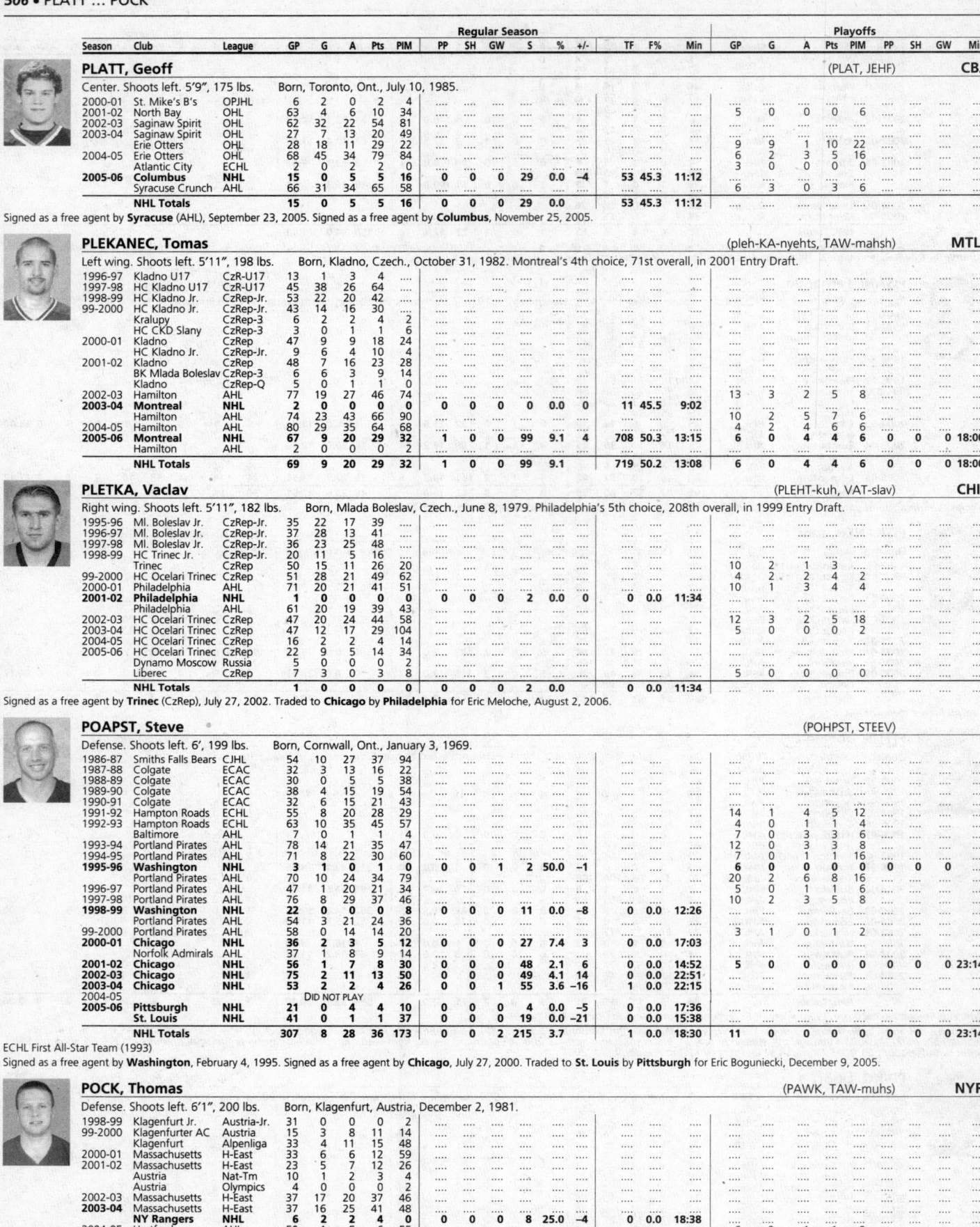

					Regular Season														Playoffs						
Season	Club	League	GP	G	A	Pts	PIM	PP	SH	GW	S	%	+/-	TF	F%	Min	GP	G	A	Pts	PIM	PP	SH	GW	Min

PLATT, Geoff (PLAT, JEHF) CBJ

Center. Shoots left. 5'9", 175 lbs.   Born, Toronto, Ont., July 10, 1985.

Season	Club	League	GP	G	A	Pts	PIM	PP	SH	GW	S	%	+/-	TF	F%	Min	GP	G	A	Pts	PIM	PP	SH	GW	Min
2000-01	St. Mike's B's	OPJHL	6	2	0	2	4	....	....	....	....	....	....	....	....	....	....	....	....	....	....				
2001-02	North Bay	OHL	63	4	6	10	34	....	....	....	....	....	....	....	....	....	5	0	0	0	6				
2002-03	Saginaw Spirit	OHL	62	32	22	54	81	....	....	....	....	....	....	....	....	....	....	....	....	....	....				
2003-04	Saginaw Spirit	OHL	27	7	13	20	49	....	....	....	....	....	....	....	....	....	....	....	....	....	....				
	Erie Otters	OHL	28	18	11	29	22	....	....	....	....	....	....	....	....	....	9	9	1	10	22				
2004-05	Erie Otters	OHL	68	45	34	79	84	....	....	....	....	....	....	....	....	....	6	2	3	5	16				
	Atlantic City	ECHL	2	0	2	2	0	....	....	....	....	....	....	....	....	....	3	0	0	0	0				
2005-06	**Columbus**	**NHL**	**15**	**0**	**5**	**5**	**16**	**0**	**0**	**0**	**29**	**0.0**	**−4**	**53**	**45.3**	**11:12**	....	....	....	....	....				
	Syracuse Crunch	AHL	66	31	34	65	58	....	....	....	....	....	....	....	....	....	6	3	0	3	6				
	NHL Totals		**15**	**0**	**5**	**5**	**16**	**0**	**0**	**0**	**29**	**0.0**		**53**	**45.3**	**11:12**	....	....	....	....	....				

Signed as a free agent by **Syracuse** (AHL), September 23, 2005. Signed as a free agent by **Columbus**, November 25, 2005.

PLEKANEC, Tomas (pleh-KA-nyehts, TAW-mahsh) MTL.

Left wing. Shoots left. 5'11", 198 lbs.   Born, Kladno, Czech., October 31, 1982. Montreal's 4th choice, 71st overall, in 2001 Entry Draft.

Season	Club	League	GP	G	A	Pts	PIM	PP	SH	GW	S	%	+/-	TF	F%	Min	GP	G	A	Pts	PIM	PP	SH	GW	Min
1996-97	Kladno U17	CzR-U17	13	1	3	4	....											....	....	....	....				
1997-98	HC Kladno U17	CzR-U17	45	38	26	64	....								....			....	....	....	....				
1998-99	HC Kladno Jr.	CzRep-Jr.	53	22	20	42	....											....	....	....	....				
99-2000	HC Kladno Jr.	CzRep-Jr.	43	14	16	30	....											....	....	....	....				
	Kralupy	CzRep-3	6	2	2	4	2											....	....	....	....				
	HC CKD Slany	CzRep-3	3	0	1	1	6											....	....	....	....				
2000-01	Kladno	CzRep	47	9	9	18	24											....	....	....	....				
	HC Kladno Jr.	CzRep-Jr.	9	6	4	10	4											....	....	....	....				
2001-02	Kladno	CzRep	48	7	16	23	28											....	....	....	....				
	BK Mlada Boleslav	CzRep-3	6	6	3	9	14											....	....	....	....				
	Kladno	CzRep-Q	5	0	1	1	0											....	....	....	....				
2002-03	Hamilton	AHL	77	19	27	46	74											13	3	2	5	8				
2003-04	**Montreal**	**NHL**	**2**	**0**	**0**	**0**	**0**	**0**	**0**	**0**	**0**	**0.0**	**0**	**11**	**45.5**	**9:02**	....	....	....	....	....				
	Hamilton	AHL	74	23	43	66	90											10	2	5	7	6				
2004-05	Hamilton	AHL	80	29	35	64	68											4	2	4	6	6				
2005-06	**Montreal**	**NHL**	**67**	**9**	**20**	**29**	**32**	**1**	**0**	**0**	**99**	**9.1**	**4**	**708**	**50.3**	**13:15**	**6**	**0**	**4**	**4**	**6**	**0**	**0**	**0**	**18:00**
	Hamilton	AHL	2	0	0	0	2											....	....	....	....	....				
	NHL Totals		**69**	**9**	**20**	**29**	**32**	**1**	**0**	**0**	**99**	**9.1**		**719**	**50.2**	**13:08**	**6**	**0**	**4**	**4**	**6**	**0**	**0**	**0**	**18:00**

PLETKA, Vaclav (PLEHT-kuh, VAT-slav) CHI.

Right wing. Shoots left. 5'11", 182 lbs.   Born, Mlada Boleslav, Czech., June 8, 1979. Philadelphia's 5th choice, 208th overall, in 1999 Entry Draft.

Season	Club	League	GP	G	A	Pts	PIM	PP	SH	GW	S	%	+/-	TF	F%	Min	GP	G	A	Pts	PIM	PP	SH	GW	Min
1995-96	Ml. Boleslav Jr.	CzRep-Jr.	35	22	17	39	....											....	....	....	....				
1996-97	Ml. Boleslav Jr.	CzRep-Jr.	37	28	13	41	....											....	....	....	....				
1997-98	Ml. Boleslav Jr.	CzRep-Jr.	36	23	25	48	....											....	....	....	....				
1998-99	HC Trinec Jr.	CzRep-Jr.	20	11	5	16	....											....	....	....	....				
	Trinec	CzRep	50	15	11	26	20											10	2	1	3					
99-2000	HC Ocelari Trinec	CzRep	51	28	21	49	62											4	2	2	4	2				
2000-01	Philadelphia	AHL	71	20	21	41	51											10	1	3	4	4				
2001-02	**Philadelphia**	**NHL**	**1**	**0**	**0**	**0**	**0**	**0**	**0**	**0**	**2**	**0.0**	**0**	**0**	**0.0**	**11:34**	....	....	....	....	....				
	Philadelphia	AHL	61	20	19	39	43											....	....	....	....	....				
2002-03	HC Ocelari Trinec	CzRep	47	20	24	44	58											12	3	2	5	18				
2003-04	HC Ocelari Trinec	CzRep	47	12	17	29	104											5	0	0	0	2				
2004-05	HC Ocelari Trinec	CzRep	16	2	2	4	14											....	....	....	....	....				
2005-06	HC Ocelari Trinec	CzRep	22	9	5	14	34											....	....	....	....	....				
	Dynamo Moscow	Russia	5	0	0	0	2											....	....	....	....	....				
	Liberec	CzRep	7	3	0	3	8											5	0	0	0	0				
	NHL Totals		**1**	**0**	**0**	**0**	**0**	**0**	**0**	**0**	**2**	**0.0**		**0**	**0.0**	**11:34**	....	....	....	....	....				

Signed as a free agent by **Trinec** (CzRep), July 27, 2002. Traded to **Chicago** by **Philadelphia** for Eric Meloche, August 2, 2006.

POAPST, Steve (POHPST, STEEV)

Defense. Shoots left. 6', 199 lbs.   Born, Cornwall, Ont., January 3, 1969.

Season	Club	League	GP	G	A	Pts	PIM	PP	SH	GW	S	%	+/-	TF	F%	Min	GP	G	A	Pts	PIM	PP	SH	GW	Min
1986-87	Smiths Falls Bears	CJHL	54	10	27	37	94											....	....	....	....	....				
1987-88	Colgate	ECAC	32	3	13	16	22											....	....	....	....	....				
1988-89	Colgate	ECAC	30	0	5	5	38											....	....	....	....	....				
1989-90	Colgate	ECAC	38	4	15	19	54											....	....	....	....	....				
1990-91	Colgate	ECAC	32	6	15	21	43											....	....	....	....	....				
1991-92	Hampton Roads	ECHL	55	8	20	28	29											14	1	4	5	12				
1992-93	Hampton Roads	ECHL	63	10	35	45	57											4	0	1	1	4				
	Baltimore	AHL	7	0	1	1	4											7	0	3	3	6				
1993-94	Portland Pirates	AHL	78	14	21	35	47											12	0	3	3	8				
1994-95	Portland Pirates	AHL	71	8	22	30	60											7	0	1	1	16				
1995-96	**Washington**	**NHL**	**3**	**1**	**0**	**1**	**0**	**0**	**0**	**1**	**2**	**50.0**	**−1**				**6**	**0**	**0**	**0**	**0**	**0**	**0**	**0**	
	Portland Pirates	AHL	70	10	24	34	79											20	2	6	8	16				
1996-97	Portland Pirates	AHL	47	1	20	21	34											5	0	1	1	6				
1997-98	Portland Pirates	AHL	76	8	29	37	46											10	2	3	5	8				
1998-99	**Washington**	**NHL**	**22**	**0**	**0**	**0**	**8**	**0**	**0**	**0**	**11**	**0.0**	**−8**	**0**	**0.0**	**12:26**	....	....	....	....	....				
	Portland Pirates	AHL	54	3	21	24	36											....	....	....	....	....				
99-2000	Portland Pirates	AHL	58	0	14	14	40											3	1	0	1	2				
2000-01	**Chicago**	**NHL**	**36**	**2**	**3**	**5**	**12**	**0**	**0**	**0**	**27**	**7.4**	**3**	**0**	**0.0**	**17:03**	....	....	....	....	....				
	Norfolk Admirals	AHL	37	1	8	9	14											....	....	....	....	....				
2001-02	**Chicago**	**NHL**	**56**	**1**	**7**	**8**	**30**	**0**	**0**	**0**	**48**	**2.1**	**6**	**0**	**0.0**	**14:52**	**5**	**0**	**0**	**0**	**0**	**0**	**0**	**0**	**23:14**
2002-03	**Chicago**	**NHL**	**75**	**2**	**11**	**13**	**50**	**0**	**0**	**0**	**49**	**4.1**	**14**	**0**	**0.0**	**22:51**	....	....	....	....	....				
2003-04	**Chicago**	**NHL**	**53**	**2**	**2**	**4**	**26**	**0**	**0**	**1**	**55**	**3.6**	**−16**	**1**	**0.0**	**22:15**	....	....	....	....	....				
2004-05			DID NOT PLAY																						
2005-06	**Pittsburgh**	**NHL**	**21**	**0**	**4**	**4**	**10**	**0**	**0**	**0**	**4**	**0.0**	**−5**	**0**	**0.0**	**17:36**	....	....	....	....	....				
	St. Louis	**NHL**	**41**	**0**	**1**	**1**	**37**	**0**	**0**	**0**	**19**	**0.0**	**−21**	**0**	**0.0**	**15:38**	....	....	....	....	....				
	NHL Totals		**307**	**8**	**28**	**36**	**173**	**0**	**0**	**2**	**215**	**3.7**		**1**	**0.0**	**18:30**	**11**	**0**	**0**	**0**	**0**	**0**	**0**	**0**	**23:14**

ECHL First All-Star Team (1993)
Signed as a free agent by **Washington**, February 4, 1995. Signed as a free agent by **Chicago**, July 27, 2000. Traded to **St. Louis** by **Pittsburgh** for Eric Boguniecki, December 9, 2005.

POCK, Thomas (PAWK, TAW-muhs) NYR

Defense. Shoots left. 6'1", 200 lbs.   Born, Klagenfurt, Austria, December 2, 1981.

Season	Club	League	GP	G	A	Pts	PIM	PP	SH	GW	S	%	+/-	TF	F%	Min	GP	G	A	Pts	PIM	PP	SH	GW	Min
1998-99	Klagenfurt Jr.	Austria-Jr.	31	0	0	0	2											....	....	....	....	....				
99-2000	Klagenfurter AC	Austria	15	3	8	11	14											....	....	....	....	....				
	Klagenfurt	Alpenliga	33	4	11	15	48											....	....	....	....	....				
2000-01	Massachusetts	H-East	33	6	6	12	59											....	....	....	....	....				
2001-02	Massachusetts	H-East	23	5	7	12	26											....	....	....	....	....				
	Austria	Nat-Tm	10	1	2	3	4											....	....	....	....	....				
	Austria	Olympics	4	0	0	0	2											....	....	....	....	....				
2002-03	Massachusetts	H-East	37	17	20	37	46											....	....	....	....	....				
2003-04	Massachusetts	H-East	37	16	25	41	48											....	....	....	....	....				
	NY Rangers	**NHL**	**6**	**2**	**2**	**4**	**0**	**0**	**0**	**0**	**8**	**25.0**	**−4**	**0**	**0.0**	**18:38**	....	....	....	....	....				
2004-05	Hartford	AHL	50	1	5	6	55											6	0	1	1	8				
	Charlotte	ECHL	3	0	2	2	2											....	....	....	....	....				

			Regular Season														Playoffs								
Season	Club	League	GP	G	A	Pts	PIM	PP	SH	GW	S	%	+/-	TF	F%	Min	GP	G	A	Pts	PIM	PP	SH	GW	Min
2005-06	**NY Rangers**	**NHL**	**8**	**1**	**1**	**2**	**4**	**0**	**0**	**0**	**15**	**6.7**	**-3**	**0**	**0.0**	**15:10**	....	....	....	....	....	....	....	....	....
	Hartford	AHL	67	15	46	61	99	....	....	....	....	....	....	....	....	....	6	0	3	3	15	....	....	....	....
	NHL Totals		**14**	**3**	**3**	**6**	**4**	**0**	**0**	**0**	**23**	**13.0**		**0**	**0.0**	**16:39**	....	....	....	....	....	....	....	....	....

Hockey East Second All-Star Team (2003) • Hockey East First All-Star Team (2004) • NCAA East First All-American Team (2004) • AHL Second All-Star Team (2006)
Signed as a free agent by **NY Rangers**, March 23, 2004.

POHL, John

(PAWL, JAWN) **TOR.**

Center. Shoots right. 6'1", 196 lbs. Born, Rochester, MN, June 29, 1979. St. Louis' 8th choice, 255th overall, in 1998 Entry Draft.

Season	Club	League	GP	G	A	Pts	PIM	PP	SH	GW	S	%	+/-	TF	F%	Min	GP	G	A	Pts	PIM	PP	SH	GW	Min
1997-98	Red Wing	High-MN	28	30	77	107	18	....	....	....	....	....	....	....	....	....	....	....	....	....	....	....	....	....	....
	Twin Cities	USHL	10	5	3	8	10	....	....	....	....	....	....	....	....	....	....	....	....	....	....	....	....	....	....
1998-99	U. of Minnesota	WCHA	42	7	10	17	18	....	....	....	....	....	....	....	....	....	....	....	....	....	....	....	....	....	....
99-2000	U. of Minnesota	WCHA	41	18	41	59	26	....	....	....	....	....	....	....	....	....	....	....	....	....	....	....	....	....	....
2000-01	U. of Minnesota	WCHA	38	19	26	45	24	....	....	....	....	....	....	....	....	....	....	....	....	....	....	....	....	....	....
2001-02	U. of Minnesota	WCHA	44	27	*52	*79	26	....	....	....	....	....	....	....	....	....	....	....	....	....	....	....	....	....	....
2002-03	Worcester IceCats	AHL	58	26	32	58	34	....	....	....	....	....	....	....	....	....	3	0	1	1	6	....	....	....	....
2003-04	**St. Louis**	**NHL**	**1**	**0**	**0**	**0**	**0**	**0**	**0**	**0**	**1**	**0.0**	**-2**	**9**	**55.6**	**8:18**	....	....	....	....	....	....	....	....	....
	Worcester IceCats	AHL	65	16	25	41	65	....	....	....	....	....	....	....	....	....	3	0	1	1	2	....	....	....	....
2004-05	Worcester IceCats	AHL	13	3	6	9	2	....	....	....	....	....	....	....	....	....	....	....	....	....	....	....	....	....	....
2005-06	**Toronto**	**NHL**	**7**	**3**	**1**	**4**	**4**	**1**	**0**	**0**	**17**	**17.6**	**2**	**41**	**53.7**	**12:47**	....	....	....	....	....	....	....	....	....
	Toronto Marlies	AHL	60	36	39	75	42	....	....	....	....	....	....	....	....	....	5	1	5	6	10	....	....	....	....
	NHL Totals		**8**	**3**	**1**	**4**	**4**	**1**	**0**	**0**	**18**	**16.7**		**50**	**54.0**	**12:13**	....	....	....	....	....	....	....	....	....

WCHA Second All-Star Team (2000) • WCHA First All-Star Team (2002) • NCAA Championship All-Tournament Team (2002)
Traded to **Toronto** by **St. Louis** for future considerations, August 24, 2005.

POLAK, Vojtech

(POH-lahk, VOI-tehk) **DAL.**

Left wing. Shoots left. 5'11", 180 lbs. Born, Ostrov nad Ohri, Czech., June 27, 1985. Dallas' 2nd choice, 36th overall, in 2003 Entry Draft.

Season	Club	League	GP	G	A	Pts	PIM	PP	SH	GW	S	%	+/-	TF	F%	Min	GP	G	A	Pts	PIM	PP	SH	GW	Min
99-2000	Karlovy Vary Jr.	CzRep-Jr.	49	17	23	40	48	....	....	....	....	....	....	....	....	....	....	....	....	....	....	....	....	....	....
2000-01	Karlovy Vary Jr.	CzRep-Jr.	47	36	33	69	38	....	....	....	....	....	....	....	....	....	....	....	....	....	....	....	....	....	....
	Karlovy Vary	CzRep	2	0	0	0	0	....	....	....	....	....	....	....	....	....	....	....	....	....	....	....	....	....	....
2001-02	Karlovy Vary Jr.	CzRep-Jr.	37	11	14	25	26	....	....	....	....	....	....	....	....	....	....	....	....	....	....	....	....	....	....
	Karlovy Vary	CzRep	9	1	1	2	2	....	....	....	....	....	....	....	....	....	....	....	....	....	....	....	....	....	....
2002-03	Karlovy Vary	CzRep	41	7	9	16	51	....	....	....	....	....	....	....	....	....	....	....	....	....	....	....	....	....	....
	Karlovy Vary Jr.	CzRep-Jr.	6	3	7	10	18	....	....	....	....	....	....	....	....	....	....	....	....	....	....	....	....	....	....
2003-04	HC Sparta Praha	CzRep	1	1	0	1	0	....	....	....	....	....	....	....	....	....	....	....	....	....	....	....	....	....	....
	Karlovy Vary	CzRep	44	0	8	8	42	....	....	....	....	....	....	....	....	....	....	....	....	....	....	....	....	....	....
	Karlovy Vary Jr.	CzRep-Jr.	5	8	4	12	2	....	....	....	....	....	....	....	....	....	....	....	....	....	....	....	....	....	....
2004-05	Jihlava Jr.	CzRep-Jr.	5	4	1	5	6	....	....	....	....	....	....	....	....	....	....	....	....	....	....	....	....	....	....
	HC Dukla Jihlava	CzRep	16	1	2	3	12	....	....	....	....	....	....	....	....	....	....	....	....	....	....	....	....	....	....
	Karlovy Vary Jr.	CzRep-Jr.	3	5	5	10	6	....	....	....	....	....	....	....	....	....	....	....	....	....	....	....	....	....	....
	SK Kadan	CzRep-2	7	1	2	3	39	....	....	....	....	....	....	....	....	....	....	....	....	....	....	....	....	....	....
	Karlovy Vary	CzRep	26	1	5	6	4	....	....	....	....	....	....	....	....	....	....	....	....	....	....	....	....	....	....
2005-06	**Dallas**	**NHL**	**3**	**0**	**0**	**0**	**0**	**0**	**0**	**0**	**3**	**0.0**	**-1**	**2**	**50.0**	**6:31**	....	....	....	....	....	....	....	....	....
	Iowa Stars	AHL	60	12	22	34	41	....	....	....	....	....	....	....	....	....	3	0	1	1	0	....	....	....	....
	NHL Totals		**3**	**0**	**0**	**0**	**0**	**0**	**0**	**0**	**3**	**0.0**		**2**	**50.0**	**6:31**	....	....	....	....	....	....	....	....	....

POLLOCK, Jame

(PAWL-lawk, JAYM)

Defense. Shoots right. 6'1", 210 lbs. Born, Quebec City, Que., June 16, 1979. St. Louis' 4th choice, 106th overall, in 1997 Entry Draft.

Season	Club	League	GP	G	A	Pts	PIM	PP	SH	GW	S	%	+/-	TF	F%	Min	GP	G	A	Pts	PIM	PP	SH	GW	Min
1994-95	Victoria Legion	BCAHA	43	22	56	78	96	....	....	....	....	....	....	....	....	....	....	....	....	....	....	....	....	....	....
1995-96	Seattle	WHL	32	0	1	1	15	....	....	....	....	....	....	....	....	....	....	....	....	....	....	....	....	....	....
1996-97	Seattle	WHL	66	15	19	34	94	....	....	....	....	....	....	....	....	....	15	3	5	8	16	....	....	....	....
1997-98	Seattle	WHL	66	11	36	47	78	....	....	....	....	....	....	....	....	....	5	0	1	1	17	....	....	....	....
1998-99	Seattle	WHL	59	10	32	42	78	....	....	....	....	....	....	....	....	....	11	3	4	7	8	....	....	....	....
99-2000	Worcester IceCats	AHL	56	12	12	24	50	....	....	....	....	....	....	....	....	....	9	5	3	8	6	....	....	....	....
2000-01	Worcester IceCats	AHL	55	15	8	23	36	....	....	....	....	....	....	....	....	....	11	1	7	8	10	....	....	....	....
2001-02	Worcester IceCats	AHL	71	23	43	66	89	....	....	....	....	....	....	....	....	....	3	1	0	1	2	....	....	....	....
2002-03	Worcester IceCats	AHL	44	5	17	22	50	....	....	....	....	....	....	....	....	....	3	1	0	1	2	....	....	....	....
2003-04	**St. Louis**	**NHL**	**9**	**0**	**0**	**0**	**6**	**0**	**0**	**0**	**19**	**0.0**	**-1**	**0**	**0.0**	**15:25**	....	....	....	....	....	....	....	....	....
	Worcester IceCats	AHL	44	8	24	32	52	....	....	....	....	....	....	....	....	....	7	1	4	5	14	....	....	....	....
2004-05	Kloten Flyers	Swiss	26	4	8	12	34	....	....	....	....	....	....	....	....	....	....	....	....	....	....	....	....	....	....
	HC Lugano	Swiss	....	....	....	....	....	....	....	....	....	....	....	....	....	....	2	0	1	1	8	....	....	....	....
2005-06	Nurnberg	Germany	52	8	11	19	130	....	....	....	....	....	....	....	....	....	4	1	0	1	10	....	....	....	....
	NHL Totals		**9**	**0**	**0**	**0**	**6**	**0**	**0**	**0**	**19**	**0.0**		**0**	**0.0**	**15:25**	....	....	....	....	....	....	....	....	....

Signed as a free agent by **Kloten** (Swiss), April 6, 2004. Signed as a free agent by **Lugano** (Swiss), February 22, 2005.

POMINVILLE, Jason

(paw-MIHN-vihl, JAY-suhn) **BUF.**

Right wing. Shoots right. 6', 186 lbs. Born, Repentigny, Que., November 30, 1982. Buffalo's 4th choice, 55th overall, in 2001 Entry Draft.

Season	Club	League	GP	G	A	Pts	PIM	PP	SH	GW	S	%	+/-	TF	F%	Min	GP	G	A	Pts	PIM	PP	SH	GW	Min
1997-98	Cap-d-Madeleine	QAAA	13	3	7	10	....	....	....	....	....	....	....	....	....	....	....	....	....	....	....	....	....	....	....
1998-99	Cap-d-Madeleine	QAAA	41	18	38	56	16	....	....	....	....	....	....	....	....	....	7	2	7	9	0	....	....	....	....
	Shawinigan	QMJHL	2	0	0	0	0	....	....	....	....	....	....	....	....	....	....	....	....	....	....	....	....	....	....
99-2000	Shawinigan	QMJHL	60	4	17	21	12	....	....	....	....	....	....	....	....	....	13	2	3	5	0	....	....	....	....
2000-01	Shawinigan	QMJHL	71	46	67	113	24	....	....	....	....	....	....	....	....	....	10	6	6	12	0	....	....	....	....
2001-02	Shawinigan	QMJHL	66	57	64	121	32	....	....	....	....	....	....	....	....	....	2	0	0	0	0	....	....	....	....
2002-03	Rochester	AHL	73	13	21	34	16	....	....	....	....	....	....	....	....	....	3	1	1	2	0	....	....	....	....
2003-04	**Buffalo**	**NHL**	**1**	**0**	**0**	**0**	**0**	**0**	**0**	**0**	**3**	**0.0**	**0**	**0**	**0.0**	**14:22**	....	....	....	....	....	....	....	....	....
	Rochester	AHL	66	34	30	64	30	....	....	....	....	....	....	....	....	....	16	9	10	19	6	....	....	....	....
2004-05	Rochester	AHL	78	30	38	68	43	....	....	....	....	....	....	....	....	....	....	....	....	....	....	....	....	....	....
2005-06	**Buffalo**	**NHL**	**57**	**18**	**12**	**30**	**22**	**10**	**2**	**2**	**124**	**14.5**	**-4**	**5**	**20.0**	**14:07**	**18**	**5**	**5**	**10**	**8**	**0**	**1**	**1**	**12:11**
	Rochester	AHL	18	19	7	26	11	....	....	....	....	....	....	....	....	....	....	....	....	....	....	....	....	....	....
	NHL Totals		**58**	**18**	**12**	**30**	**22**	**10**	**2**	**2**	**127**	**14.2**		**5**	**20.0**	**14:07**	**18**	**5**	**5**	**10**	**8**	**0**	**1**	**1**	**12:11**

QMJHL First All-Star Team (2002)

PONIKAROVSKY, Alexei

(poh-NIH-kahr-ohv-skee, al-EHX-ay) **TOR.**

Left wing. Shoots left. 6'4", 220 lbs. Born, Kiev, USSR, April 9, 1980. Toronto's 4th choice, 87th overall, in 1998 Entry Draft.

Season	Club	League	GP	G	A	Pts	PIM	PP	SH	GW	S	%	+/-	TF	F%	Min	GP	G	A	Pts	PIM	PP	SH	GW	Min
1996-97	Dyn'o Moscow 2	Russia-3	60	12	15	27	30	....	....	....	....	....	....	....	....	....	....	....	....	....	....	....	....	....	....
	Dyn'o Moscow 2	Russia-3	2	0	0	0	2	....	....	....	....	....	....	....	....	....	....	....	....	....	....	....	....	....	....
1997-98	Dynamo Moscow	Russia	24	1	2	3	30	....	....	....	....	....	....	....	....	....	....	....	....	....	....	....	....	....	....
1998-99	Krylja Sovetov	Russia	13	2	1	3	2	....	....	....	....	....	....	....	....	....	....	....	....	....	....	....	....	....	....
	Dynamo Moscow	Russia	....	....	....	....	....	....	....	....	....	....	....	....	....	....	3	0	0	0	2	....	....	....	....
99-2000	THK Tver	Russia-2	29	8	14	22	26	....	....	....	....	....	....	....	....	....	....	....	....	....	....	....	....	....	....
	Dynamo Moscow	Russia	19	1	0	1	8	....	....	....	....	....	....	....	....	....	1	0	0	0	0	....	....	....	....
	Dynamo Moscow	EuroHL	2	0	2	2	0	....	....	....	....	....	....	....	....	....	....	....	....	....	....	....	....	....	....
2000-01	**Toronto**	**NHL**	**22**	**1**	**3**	**4**	**14**	**0**	**0**	**0**	**21**	**4.8**	**-1**	**7**	**28.6**	**8:32**	....	....	....	....	....	....	....	....	....
	St. John's	AHL	49	12	24	36	44	....	....	....	....	....	....	....	....	....	4	0	0	0	4	....	....	....	....
2001-02	**Toronto**	**NHL**	**8**	**2**	**0**	**2**	**0**	**0**	**0**	**1**	**8**	**25.0**	**2**	**2**	**50.0**	**8:03**	**10**	**0**	**0**	**0**	**4**	**0**	**0**	**0**	**8:15**
	St. John's	AHL	72	21	27	48	74	....	....	....	....	....	....	....	....	....	5	2	1	3	8	....	....	....	....
	Ukraine	Olympics	4	1	1	2	6	....	....	....	....	....	....	....	....	....	....	....	....	....	....	....	....	....	....
2002-03	**Toronto**	**NHL**	**13**	**0**	**3**	**3**	**11**	**0**	**0**	**0**	**13**	**0.0**	**4**	**4**	**25.0**	**10:43**	....	....	....	....	....	....	....	....	....
	St. John's	AHL	63	24	22	46	68	....	....	....	....	....	....	....	....	....	....	....	....	....	....	....	....	....	....
2003-04	**Toronto**	**NHL**	**73**	**9**	**19**	**28**	**44**	**1**	**0**	**2**	**110**	**8.2**	**14**	**20**	**30.0**	**11:36**	**13**	**1**	**3**	**4**	**8**	**0**	**0**	**1**	**14:20**
2004-05	Voskresensk	Russia	19	1	5	6	16	....	....	....	....	....	....	....	....	....	....	....	....	....	....	....	....	....	....
2005-06	**Toronto**	**NHL**	**81**	**21**	**17**	**38**	**68**	**2**	**4**	**3**	**157**	**13.4**	**15**	**13**	**30.8**	**14:06**	....	....	....	....	....	....	....	....	....
	NHL Totals		**197**	**33**	**42**	**75**	**137**	**3**	**4**	**6**	**309**	**10.7**		**46**	**30.4**	**12:05**	**23**	**1**	**3**	**4**	**12**	**0**	**0**	**1**	**11:42**

Signed as a free agent by **Voskresensk** (Russia), November 13, 2004.

POPOVIC, Mark
(poh-PUH-vihk, MAHRK) **ATL.**

Defense. Shoots left. 6'1", 210 lbs. Born, Stoney Creek, Ont., October 11, 1982. Anaheim's 2nd choice, 35th overall, in 2001 Entry Draft.

Season	Club	League	GP	G	A	Pts	PIM	PP	SH	GW	S	%	+/-	TF	F%	Min	GP	G	A	Pts	PIM	PP	SH	GW	Min
			Regular Season														**Playoffs**								
1997-98	Mississauga	OPJHL	51	10	16	26	32	....	....	....	....	....	....	....	....	....	....	....	....	....	....	....	....	....	....
1998-99	St. Michael's	OHL	60	6	26	32	46	....	....	....	....	....	....	....	....	....	....	....	....	....	....	....	....	....	....
99-2000	St. Michael's	OHL	68	11	29	40	68	....	....	....	....	....	....	....	....	....	....	....	....	....	....	....	....	....	....
2000-01	St. Michael's	OHL	61	7	35	42	54	....	....	....	....	....	....	....	....	....	18	3	5	8	22	....	....	....	....
2001-02	St. Michael's	OHL	58	12	29	41	42	....	....	....	....	....	....	....	....	....	15	1	11	12	10	....	....	....	....
2002-03	Cincinnati	AHL	73	3	21	24	46	....	....	....	....	....	....	....	....	....	....	....	....	....	....	....	....	....	....
2003-04	**Anaheim**	**NHL**	**1**	**0**	**0**	**0**	**0**	**0**	**0**	**0**	**1**	**0.0**	**0**	**0**	**0.0**	**13:48**	....	....	....	....	....	....	....	....	....
	Cincinnati	AHL	74	4	10	14	63	....	....	....	....	....	....	....	....	....	9	1	2	3	4	....	....	....	....
2004-05	Cincinnati	AHL	74	1	17	18	47	....	....	....	....	....	....	....	....	....	11	2	3	5	6	....	....	....	....
2005-06	**Atlanta**	**NHL**	**7**	**0**	**0**	**0**	**0**	**0**	**0**	**0**	**6**	**0.0**	**–5**	**0**	**0.0**	**11:04**	....	....	....	....	....	....	....	....	....
	Chicago Wolves	AHL	73	12	26	38	51	....	....	....	....	....	....	....	....	....	....	....	....	....	....	....	....	....	....
	NHL Totals		**8**	**0**	**0**	**0**	**0**	**0**	**0**	**0**	**7**	**0.0**		**0**	**0.0**	**11:25**	....	....	....	....	....	....	....	....	....

OHL First All-Star Team (2002)

Traded to **Atlanta** by **Anaheim** for Kip Brennan, August 23, 2005.

POTHIER, Brian
(POH-thee-uhr, BRIGH-uhn) **WSH.**

Defense. Shoots right. 6', 195 lbs. Born, New Bedford, MA, April 15, 1977.

Season	Club	League	GP	G	A	Pts	PIM	PP	SH	GW	S	%	+/-	TF	F%	Min	GP	G	A	Pts	PIM	PP	SH	GW	Min
1995-96	Northfield Mt.H.	High-MA	27	11	22	33	36	....	....	....	....	....	....	....	....	....	....	....	....	....	....	....	....	....	....
1996-97	RPI Engineers	ECAC	34	1	11	12	42	....	....	....	....	....	....	....	....	....	....	....	....	....	....	....	....	....	....
1997-98	RPI Engineers	ECAC	35	2	9	11	28	....	....	....	....	....	....	....	....	....	....	....	....	....	....	....	....	....	....
1998-99	RPI Engineers	ECAC	37	5	13	18	36	....	....	....	....	....	....	....	....	....	....	....	....	....	....	....	....	....	....
99-2000	RPI Engineers	ECAC	36	9	24	33	44	....	....	....	....	....	....	....	....	....	....	....	....	....	....	....	....	....	....
2000-01	**Atlanta**	**NHL**	**3**	**0**	**0**	**0**	**2**	**0**	**0**	**0**	**0**	**0.0**	**4**	**0**	**0.0**	**20:38**	....	....	....	....	....	....	....	....	....
	Orlando	IHL	76	12	29	41	69	....	....	....	....	....	....	....	....	....	16	3	5	8	11	....	....	....	....
2001-02	**Atlanta**	**NHL**	**33**	**3**	**6**	**9**	**22**	**1**	**0**	**1**	**65**	**4.6**	**–19**	**0**	**0.0**	**21:41**	....	....	....	....	....	....	....	....	....
	Chicago Wolves	AHL	39	6	13	19	30	....	....	....	....	....	....	....	....	....	....	....	....	....	....	....	....	....	....
2002-03	**Ottawa**	**NHL**	**14**	**2**	**4**	**6**	**6**	**0**	**0**	**1**	**23**	**8.7**	**11**	**0**	**0.0**	**15:23**	**1**	**0**	**0**	**0**	**2**	**0**	**0**	**0**	**13:11**
	Binghamton	AHL	68	7	40	47	58	....	....	....	....	....	....	....	....	....	8	2	8	10	4	....	....	....	....
2003-04	**Ottawa**	**NHL**	**55**	**2**	**6**	**8**	**24**	**1**	**0**	**1**	**78**	**2.6**	**6**	**0**	**0.0**	**16:43**	**7**	**0**	**0**	**0**	**6**	**0**	**0**	**0**	**17:15**
2004-05	Binghamton	AHL	77	12	36	48	64	....	....	....	....	....	....	....	....	....	6	0	1	1	6	....	....	....	....
2005-06	**Ottawa**	**NHL**	**77**	**5**	**30**	**35**	**59**	**3**	**0**	**0**	**133**	**3.8**	**29**	**0**	**0.0**	**16:46**	**8**	**2**	**1**	**3**	**2**	**0**	**0**	**0**	**15:02**
	NHL Totals		**182**	**12**	**46**	**58**	**113**	**5**	**0**	**3**	**299**	**4.0**		**0**	**0.0**	**17:36**	**16**	**2**	**1**	**3**	**10**	**0**	**0**	**0**	**15:53**

ECAC Second All-Star Team (2000) • ECAC All-Tournament Team (2000) • NCAA East Second All-American Team (2000) • Ken McKenzie Trophy (U.S. - Born Rookie of the Year – IHL) (2001) • Garry F. Longman Memorial Trophy (Rookie of the Year – IHL) (2001) • AHL Second All-Star Team (2003, 2005)

Signed as a free agent by **Atlanta**, March 27, 2000. Traded to **Ottawa** by **Atlanta** for Shawn McEachern and Ottawa's 6th round choice (Dan Turple) in 2004 Entry Draft, June 29, 2002. Signed as a free agent by **Washington**, July 1, 2006.

POTI, Tom
(POH-tee, TAWM) **NYI**

Defense. Shoots left. 6'3", 210 lbs. Born, Worcester, MA, March 22, 1977. Edmonton's 4th choice, 59th overall, in 1996 Entry Draft.

Season	Club	League	GP	G	A	Pts	PIM	PP	SH	GW	S	%	+/-	TF	F%	Min	GP	G	A	Pts	PIM	PP	SH	GW	Min
1992-93	St. Peter's Marian	High-MA	55	25	46	71	....	....	....	....	....	....	....	....	....	....	....	....	....	....	....	....	....	....	....
1993-94	Cushing	High-MA	30	10	35	45	....	....	....	....	....	....	....	....	....	....	....	....	....	....	....	....	....	....	....
1994-95	Cushing	High-MA	36	17	54	71	35	....	....	....	....	....	....	....	....	....	....	....	....	....	....	....	....	....	....
	Central-Mass	MBAHL	8	8	10	18	....	....	....	....	....	....	....	....	....	....	....	....	....	....	....	....	....	....	....
1995-96	Cushing	High-MA	29	14	59	73	18	....	....	....	....	....	....	....	....	....	....	....	....	....	....	....	....	....	....
1996-97	Boston University	H-East	38	4	17	21	54	....	....	....	....	....	....	....	....	....	....	....	....	....	....	....	....	....	....
1997-98	Boston University	H-East	38	13	29	42	60	....	....	....	....	....	....	....	....	....	....	....	....	....	....	....	....	....	....
1998-99	**Edmonton**	**NHL**	**73**	**5**	**16**	**21**	**42**	**2**	**0**	**3**	**94**	**5.3**	**10**	**0**	**0.0**	**19:33**	**4**	**0**	**1**	**1**	**2**	**0**	**0**	**0**	**28:02**
99-2000	**Edmonton**	**NHL**	**76**	**9**	**26**	**35**	**65**	**2**	**1**	**1**	**125**	**7.2**	**8**	**0**	**0.0**	**24:10**	**5**	**0**	**1**	**1**	**0**	**0**	**0**	**0**	**23:53**
2000-01	**Edmonton**	**NHL**	**81**	**12**	**20**	**32**	**60**	**6**	**0**	**3**	**161**	**7.5**	**–4**	**0**	**0.0**	**22:44**	**6**	**0**	**2**	**2**	**2**	**0**	**0**	**0**	**20:25**
2001-02	**Edmonton**	**NHL**	**55**	**1**	**16**	**17**	**42**	**1**	**0**	**0**	**100**	**1.0**	**–6**	**0**	**0.0**	**24:32**	....	....	....	....	....	....	....	....	....
	United States	Olympics	6	0	1	1	4	....	....	....	....	....	....	....	....	....	....	....	....	....	....	....	....	....	....
	NY Rangers	**NHL**	**11**	**1**	**7**	**8**	**2**	**1**	**0**	**1**	**9**	**11.1**	**–4**	**0**	**0.0**	**21:45**	....	....	....	....	....	....	....	....	....
2002-03	**NY Rangers**	**NHL**	**80**	**11**	**37**	**48**	**58**	**3**	**0**	**2**	**148**	**7.4**	**–6**	**0**	**0.0**	**24:43**	....	....	....	....	....	....	....	....	....
2003-04	**NY Rangers**	**NHL**	**67**	**10**	**14**	**24**	**47**	**4**	**0**	**5**	**124**	**8.1**	**–1**	**0**	**0.0**	**22:28**	....	....	....	....	....	....	....	....	....
2004-05			DID NOT PLAY																						
2005-06	**NY Rangers**	**NHL**	**73**	**3**	**20**	**23**	**70**	**2**	**0**	**2**	**122**	**2.5**	**16**	**4**	**25.0**	**20:46**	**4**	**0**	**0**	**0**	**2**	**0**	**0**	**0**	**19:39**
	NHL Totals		**516**	**52**	**156**	**208**	**386**	**21**	**1**	**17**	**883**	**5.9**		**4**	**25.0**	**22:40**	**19**	**0**	**4**	**4**	**6**	**0**	**0**	**0**	**22:46**

NCAA Championship All-Tournament Team (1997) • Hockey East First All-Star Team (1998) • NCAA East First All-American Team (1998) • NHL All-Rookie Team (1999)

Played in NHL All-Star Game (2003)

Traded to **NY Rangers** by **Edmonton** with Rem Murray for Mike York and NY Rangers' 4th round choice (Ivan Koltsov) in 2002 Entry Draft, March 19, 2002. Signed as a free agent by **NY Islanders**, July 8, 2006.

POTULNY, Ryan
(poh-TUHL-nee, RIGH-uhn) **PHI.**

Center. Shoots left. 6', 190 lbs. Born, Grand Forks, ND, September 5, 1984. Philadelphia's 6th choice, 87th overall, in 2003 Entry Draft.

Season	Club	League	GP	G	A	Pts	PIM	PP	SH	GW	S	%	+/-	TF	F%	Min	GP	G	A	Pts	PIM	PP	SH	GW	Min
2001-02	Lincoln Stars	USHL	60	23	34	57	65	....	....	....	....	....	....	....	....	....	4	0	1	1	2	....	....	....	....
2002-03	Lincoln Stars	USHL	54	35	*43	*78	18	....	....	....	....	....	....	....	....	....	10	6	*11	*17	8	....	....	....	....
2003-04	U. of Minnesota	WCHA	15	6	8	14	10	....	....	....	....	....	....	....	....	....	....	....	....	....	....	....	....	....	....
2004-05	U. of Minnesota	WCHA	44	24	17	41	20	....	....	....	....	....	....	....	....	....	....	....	....	....	....	....	....	....	....
2005-06	U. of Minnesota	WCHA	41	*38	25	*63	31	....	....	....	....	....	....	....	....	....	....	....	....	....	....	....	....	....	....
	Philadelphia	**NHL**	**2**	**0**	**1**	**1**	**0**	**0**	**0**	**0**	**0**	**0.0**	**1**	**9**	**44.4**	**6:09**	....	....	....	....	....	....	....	....	....
	NHL Totals		**2**	**0**	**1**	**1**	**0**	**0**	**0**	**0**	**0**	**0.0**		**9**	**44.4**	**6:09**	....	....	....	....	....	....	....	....	....

USHL First All-Star Team (2003) • USHL Player of the Year (2003) • USA Junior Player of the Year (2003) • WCHA First All-Star Team (2006) • NCAA West First All-American Team (2006)

• Missed majority of 2003-04 season recovering from knee injury suffered in game vs. North Dakota (WCHA), November 7, 2003.

POULIOT, Marc-Antoine
(poo-YOH, MAHRK-AN-twahn) **EDM.**

Center. Shoots right. 6'1", 195 lbs. Born, Quebec City, Que., May 22, 1985. Edmonton's 1st choice, 22nd overall, in 2003 Entry Draft.

Season	Club	League	GP	G	A	Pts	PIM	PP	SH	GW	S	%	+/-	TF	F%	Min	GP	G	A	Pts	PIM	PP	SH	GW	Min
2000-01	Ste-Foy	QAAA	38	16	39	55	52	....	....	....	....	....	....	....	....	....	16	8	12	20	16	....	....	....	....
2001-02	Rimouski Oceanic	QMJHL	28	9	14	23	32	....	....	....	....	....	....	....	....	....	5	0	0	0	4	....	....	....	....
2002-03	Rimouski Oceanic	QMJHL	65	32	41	73	100	....	....	....	....	....	....	....	....	....	....	....	....	....	....	....	....	....	....
2003-04	Rimouski Oceanic	QMJHL	42	25	33	58	62	....	....	....	....	....	....	....	....	....	9	5	7	12	12	....	....	....	....
2004-05	Rimouski Oceanic	QMJHL	70	45	69	114	83	....	....	....	....	....	....	....	....	....	13	4	15	19	8	....	....	....	....
2005-06	**Edmonton**	**NHL**	**8**	**1**	**0**	**1**	**0**	**0**	**0**	**0**	**5**	**20.0**	**1**	**56**	**55.4**	**8:30**	....	....	....	....	....	....	....	....	....
	Hamilton	AHL	65	15	31	46	63	....	....	....	....	....	....	....	....	....	....	....	....	....	....	....	....	....	....
	NHL Totals		**8**	**1**	**0**	**1**	**0**	**0**	**0**	**0**	**5**	**20.0**		**56**	**55.4**	**8:30**	....	....	....	....	....	....	....	....	....

QMJHL First All-Star Team (2005) • George Parsons Trophy (Memorial Cup Tournament Most Sportsmanlike Player) (2005)

PRATT, Nolan
(PRAT, NOH-lan) **T.B.**

Defense. Shoots left. 6'3", 207 lbs. Born, Fort McMurray, Alta., August 14, 1975. Hartford's 4th choice, 115th overall, in 1993 Entry Draft.

Season	Club	League	GP	G	A	Pts	PIM	PP	SH	GW	S	%	+/-	TF	F%	Min	GP	G	A	Pts	PIM	PP	SH	GW	Min
1991-92	Bonnyville	AJHL	33	3	7	10	57	....	....	....	....	....	....	....	....	....	....	....	....	....	....	....	....	....	....
	Portland	WHL	22	2	9	11	13	....	....	....	....	....	....	....	....	....	6	1	3	4	12	....	....	....	....
1992-93	Portland	WHL	70	4	19	23	97	....	....	....	....	....	....	....	....	....	16	2	7	9	31	....	....	....	....
1993-94	Portland	WHL	72	4	32	36	105	....	....	....	....	....	....	....	....	....	10	1	2	3	14	....	....	....	....
1994-95	Portland	WHL	72	6	37	43	196	....	....	....	....	....	....	....	....	....	9	1	6	7	10	....	....	....	....
1995-96	Springfield	AHL	62	2	6	8	72	....	....	....	....	....	....	....	....	....	2	0	0	0	0	....	....	....	....
	Richmond	ECHL	4	1	0	1	2	....	....	....	....	....	....	....	....	....	....	....	....	....	....	....	....	....	....
1996-97	**Hartford**	**NHL**	**9**	**0**	**2**	**2**	**6**	**0**	**0**	**0**	**4**	**0.0**	**0**	....	....	....	....	....	....	....	....	....	....	....	....
	Springfield	AHL	66	1	18	19	127	....	....	....	....	....	....	....	....	....	17	0	3	3	18	....	....	....	....
1997-98	**Carolina**	**NHL**	**23**	**0**	**2**	**2**	**44**	**0**	**0**	**0**	**11**	**0.0**	**–2**	....	....	....	....	....	....	....	....	....	....	....	....
	New Haven	AHL	54	3	15	18	135	....	....	....	....	....	....	....	....	....	....	....	....	....	....	....	....	....	....
1998-99	**Carolina**	**NHL**	**61**	**1**	**14**	**15**	**95**	**0**	**0**	**1**	**46**	**2.2**	**15**	**0**	**0.0**	**16:45**	**3**	**0**	**0**	**0**	**2**	**0**	**0**	**0**	**19:58**

			Regular Season														Playoffs								
Season	**Club**	**League**	**GP**	**G**	**A**	**Pts**	**PIM**	**PP**	**SH**	**GW**	**S**	**%**	**+/-**	**TF**	**F%**	**Min**	**GP**	**G**	**A**	**Pts**	**PIM**	**PP**	**SH**	**GW**	**Min**
99-2000	**Carolina**	**NHL**	**64**	**3**	**1**	**4**	**90**	**0**	**0**	**1**	**47**	**6.4**	**–22**	**0**	**0.0**	**19:10**	....	....	....	....	....	....	....	....	....
2000-01	**Colorado**	**NHL**	**46**	**1**	**2**	**3**	**40**	**0**	**0**	**1**	**26**	**3.8**	**2**	**1**	**0.0**	**9:50**	....	....	....	....	....	....	....	....	....
2001-02	**Tampa Bay**	**NHL**	**46**	**0**	**3**	**3**	**51**	**0**	**0**	**0**	**38**	**0.0**	**–4**	**1**	**0.0**	**18:25**	....	....	....	....	....	....	....	....	....
2002-03	**Tampa Bay**	**NHL**	**67**	**1**	**7**	**8**	**35**	**0**	**0**	**0**	**38**	**2.6**	**–6**	**0**	**0.0**	**17:34**	**4**	**0**	**1**	**1**	**0**	**0**	**0**	**0**	**21:01**
2003-04 ♦	**Tampa Bay**	**NHL**	**58**	**1**	**3**	**4**	**42**	**0**	**0**	**0**	**35**	**2.9**	**11**	**0**	**0.0**	**16:25**	**20**	**0**	**0**	**0**	**8**	**0**	**0**	**0**	**18:06**
2004-05	EV Duisburg	German-2	10	2	2	4	14	....	....	....	....	....	....	....	....	....	12	0	3	3	10	....	....	....	....
2005-06	**Tampa Bay**	**NHL**	**82**	**0**	**9**	**9**	**60**	**0**	**0**	**0**	**26**	**0.0**	**7**	**0**	**0.0**	**17:59**	**5**	**0**	**0**	**0**	**7**	**0**	**0**	**0**	**15:30**
	NHL Totals		**456**	**7**	**43**	**50**	**463**	**0**	**0**	**3**	**271**	**2.6**		**2**	**0.0**	**16:52**	**32**	**0**	**1**	**1**	**17**	**0**	**0**	**0**	**18:14**

Transferred to **Carolina** after **Hartford** franchise relocated, June 25, 1997. Traded to **Colorado** by **Carolina** with Carolina's 1st (Vaclav Nedorost) and 2nd (Jared Aulin) round choices in 2000 Entry Draft and Philadelphia's 2nd round choice (previously acquired, Colorado selected Agris Saviels) in 2000 Entry Draft for Sandis Ozolinsh and Columbus' 2nd round choice (previously acquired, Carolina selected Tomas Kurka) in 2000 Entry Draft, June 24, 2000. Traded to **Tampa Bay** by **Colorado** for Los Angeles' 6th round choice (previously acquired, Colorado selected Scott Horvath) in 2001 Entry Draft, June 24, 2001. Signed as a free agent by **Duisburg** (German-2), January 15, 2005.

PREISSING, Tom

(PREH-sihng, TAWM) **OTT.**

Defense. Shoots right. 6', 205 lbs. Born, Arlington Heights, IL, December 3, 1978.

Season	Club	League	GP	G	A	Pts	PIM	PP	SH	GW	S	%	+/-	TF	F%	Min	GP	G	A	Pts	PIM	PP	SH	GW	Min
1997-98	Green Bay	USHL	56	8	13	21	30	....	....	....	....	....	....	....	....	....	4	0	2	2	2	....	....	....	....
1998-99	Green Bay	USHL	53	18	37	55	40	....	....	....	....	....	....	....	....	....	6	3	6	9	2	....	....	....	....
99-2000	Colorado College	WCHA	36	4	14	18	20	....	....	....	....	....	....	....	....	....	....	....	....	....	....	....	....	....	....
2000-01	Colorado College	WCHA	33	6	18	24	26	....	....	....	....	....	....	....	....	....	....	....	....	....	....	....	....	....	....
2001-02	Colorado College	WCHA	43	6	26	32	42	....	....	....	....	....	....	....	....	....	....	....	....	....	....	....	....	....	....
2002-03	Colorado College	WCHA	42	23	29	52	16	....	....	....	....	....	....	....	....	....	....	....	....	....	....	....	....	....	....
2003-04	**San Jose**	**NHL**	**69**	**2**	**17**	**19**	**12**	**2**	**0**	**1**	**89**	**2.2**	**8**	**0**	**0.0**	**18:12**	**11**	**0**	**1**	**1**	**0**	**0**	**0**	**0**	**12:49**
2004-05	Krefeld Pinguine	Germany	33	1	6	7	32	....	....	....	....	....	....	....	....	....	....	....	....	....	....	....	....	....	....
2005-06	**San Jose**	**NHL**	**74**	**11**	**32**	**43**	**26**	**2**	**0**	**2**	**131**	**8.4**	**17**	**1**	**0.0**	**20:30**	**11**	**1**	**6**	**7**	**4**	**0**	**0**	**0**	**23:50**
	NHL Totals		**143**	**13**	**49**	**62**	**38**	**4**	**0**	**3**	**220**	**5.9**		**1**	**0.0**	**19:23**	**22**	**1**	**7**	**8**	**4**	**0**	**0**	**0**	**18:19**

WCHA First All-Star Team (2003) • NCAA West First All-American Team (2003)

Signed as a free agent by **San Jose**, April 4, 2003. Signed as a free agent by **Krefeld** (Germany), November 15, 2004. Traded to **Chicago** by **San Jose** with Josh Hennessy for Mark Bell, July 9, 2006. Traded to **Ottawa** by **Chicago** with Josh Hennessy, Michal Barinka and a 2nd round choice in 2008 Entry Draft for Martin Havlat and Bryan Smolinski, July 10, 2006.

PRIMEAU, Keith

(PREE-moh, KEETH) **PHI.**

Center. Shoots left. 6'5", 220 lbs. Born, Toronto, Ont., November 24, 1971. Detroit's 1st choice, 3rd overall, in 1990 Entry Draft.

Season	Club	League	GP	G	A	Pts	PIM	PP	SH	GW	S	%	+/-	TF	F%	Min	GP	G	A	Pts	PIM	PP	SH	GW	Min
1986-87	Whitby Flyers	OMHA	65	69	80	149	116	....	....	....	....	....	....	....	....	....	....	....	....	....	....	....	....	....	....
1987-88	Hamilton Kilty B's	OHA-B	19	19	17	36	16	....	....	....	....	....	....	....	....	....	....	....	....	....	....	....	....	....	....
	Hamilton	OHL	47	6	6	12	69	....	....	....	....	....	....	....	....	....	11	0	2	2	2	....	....	....	....
1988-89	Niagara Falls	OHL	48	20	35	55	56	....	....	....	....	....	....	....	....	....	17	9	16	25	12	....	....	....	....
1989-90	Niagara Falls	OHL	65	*57	70	*127	97	....	....	....	....	....	....	....	....	....	16	*16	17	*33	49	....	....	....	....
1990-91	**Detroit**	**NHL**	**58**	**3**	**12**	**15**	**106**	**0**	**0**	**1**	**33**	**9.1**	**–12**	....	....	....	**5**	**1**	**1**	**2**	**25**	**0**	**0**	**0**	....
	Adirondack	AHL	6	3	5	8	8	....	....	....	....	....	....	....	....	....	....	....	....	....	....	....	....	....	....
1991-92	**Detroit**	**NHL**	**35**	**6**	**10**	**16**	**83**	**0**	**0**	**0**	**27**	**22.2**	**9**	....	....	....	**11**	**0**	**0**	**0**	**14**	**0**	**0**	**0**	....
	Adirondack	AHL	42	21	24	45	89	....	....	....	....	....	....	....	....	....	9	1	7	8	27	....	....	....	....
1992-93	**Detroit**	**NHL**	**73**	**15**	**17**	**32**	**152**	**4**	**1**	**2**	**75**	**20.0**	**–6**	....	....	....	**7**	**0**	**2**	**2**	**26**	**0**	**0**	**0**	....
1993-94	**Detroit**	**NHL**	**78**	**31**	**42**	**73**	**173**	**7**	**3**	**4**	**155**	**20.0**	**34**	....	....	....	**7**	**0**	**2**	**2**	**6**	**0**	**0**	**0**	....
1994-95	**Detroit**	**NHL**	**45**	**15**	**27**	**42**	**99**	**1**	**0**	**3**	**96**	**15.6**	**17**	....	....	....	**17**	**4**	**5**	**9**	**45**	**2**	**0**	**0**	....
1995-96	**Detroit**	**NHL**	**74**	**27**	**25**	**52**	**168**	**6**	**2**	**7**	**150**	**18.0**	**19**	....	....	....	**17**	**1**	**4**	**5**	**28**	**0**	**0**	**0**	....
1996-97	**Hartford**	**NHL**	**75**	**26**	**25**	**51**	**161**	**6**	**3**	**2**	**169**	**15.4**	**–3**	....	....	....	....	....	....	....	....	....	....	....	....
1997-98	**Carolina**	**NHL**	**81**	**26**	**37**	**63**	**110**	**7**	**3**	**2**	**180**	**14.4**	**19**	....	....	....	....	....	....	....	....	....	....	....	....
	Canada	Olympics	6	2	1	3	4	....	....	....	....	....	....	....	....	....	....	....	....	....	....	....	....	....	....
1998-99	**Carolina**	**NHL**	**78**	**30**	**32**	**62**	**75**	**9**	**1**	**5**	**178**	**16.9**	**8**	**1823**	**53.5**	**21:21**	**6**	**0**	**3**	**3**	**6**	**0**	**0**	**0**	**24:35**
99-2000	**Philadelphia**	**NHL**	**23**	**7**	**10**	**17**	**31**	**1**	**0**	**1**	**51**	**13.7**	**10**	**478**	**54.2**	**17:38**	**18**	**2**	**11**	**13**	**13**	**0**	**0**	**1**	**20:25**
2000-01	**Philadelphia**	**NHL**	**71**	**34**	**39**	**73**	**76**	**11**	**0**	**4**	**165**	**20.6**	**17**	**1811**	**53.5**	**19:58**	**4**	**0**	**3**	**3**	**8**	**0**	**0**	**0**	**19:44**
2001-02	**Philadelphia**	**NHL**	**75**	**19**	**29**	**48**	**128**	**5**	**0**	**3**	**151**	**12.6**	**–3**	**1595**	**51.3**	**18:00**	**5**	**0**	**0**	**0**	**6**	**0**	**0**	**0**	**17:20**
2002-03	**Philadelphia**	**NHL**	**80**	**19**	**27**	**46**	**93**	**6**	**0**	**4**	**171**	**11.1**	**4**	**1613**	**51.4**	**19:16**	**13**	**1**	**1**	**2**	**14**	**0**	**0**	**0**	**20:21**
2003-04	**Philadelphia**	**NHL**	**54**	**7**	**15**	**22**	**80**	**0**	**1**	**2**	**86**	**8.1**	**11**	**1010**	**53.3**	**16:36**	**18**	**9**	**7**	**16**	**22**	**0**	**2**	**3**	**18:58**
2004-05			DID NOT PLAY																						
2005-06	**Philadelphia**	**NHL**	**9**	**1**	**6**	**7**	**6**	**1**	**0**	**0**	**12**	**8.3**	**0**	**174**	**54.6**	**15:56**	....	....	....	....	....	....	....	....	....
	NHL Totals		**909**	**266**	**353**	**619**	**1541**	**64**	**14**	**40**	**1699**	**15.7**		**8504**	**52.7**	**19:02**	**128**	**18**	**39**	**57**	**213**	**2**	**2**	**4**	**20:06**

OHL Second All-Star Team (1990)

Played in NHL All-Star Game (1999, 2004)

Traded to **Hartford** by **Detroit** with Paul Coffey and Detroit's 1st round choice (Nikos Tselios) in 1997 Entry Draft for Brendan Shanahan and Brian Glynn, October 9, 1996. Transferred to **Carolina** after **Hartford** franchise relocated, June 25, 1997. • Missed majority of 1999-2000 season after failing to come to contract terms with **Carolina**. Traded to **Philadelphia** by **Carolina** with Carolina's 5th round choice (later traded to NY Islanders – NY Islanders selected Kristofer Ottosson) in 2000 Entry Draft for Rod Brind'Amour, Jean-Marc Pelletier and Philadelphia's 2nd round choice (later traded to Colorado – Colorado selected Agris Saviels) in 2000 Entry Draft, January 23, 2000. • Missed majority of 2005-06 season recovering from head injury sufferd in game at Montreal, October 25, 2005.

PRIMEAU, Wayne

(PREE-moh, WAYN) **BOS.**

Center. Shoots left. 6'4", 230 lbs. Born, Scarborough, Ont., June 4, 1976. Buffalo's 1st choice, 17th overall, in 1994 Entry Draft.

Season	Club	League	GP	G	A	Pts	PIM	PP	SH	GW	S	%	+/-	TF	F%	Min	GP	G	A	Pts	PIM	PP	SH	GW	Min
1991-92	Whitby Flyers	OMHA	63	36	50	86	96	....	....	....	....	....	....	....	....	....	....	....	....	....	....	....	....	....	....
1992-93	Owen Sound	OHL	66	10	27	37	108	....	....	....	....	....	....	....	....	....	8	1	4	5	0	....	....	....	....
1993-94	Owen Sound	OHL	65	25	50	75	75	....	....	....	....	....	....	....	....	....	9	1	6	7	8	....	....	....	....
1994-95	Owen Sound	OHL	66	34	62	96	84	....	....	....	....	....	....	....	....	....	10	4	9	13	15	....	....	....	....
	Buffalo	**NHL**	**1**	**1**	**0**	**1**	**0**	**0**	**0**	**1**	**2**	**50.0**	**–2**	....	....	....	....	....	....	....	....	....	....	....	....
1995-96	Owen Sound	OHL	28	15	29	44	52	....	....	....	....	....	....	....	....	....	....	....	....	....	....	....	....	....	....
	Oshawa Generals	OHL	24	12	13	25	33	....	....	....	....	....	....	....	....	....	3	2	3	5	2	....	....	....	....
	Buffalo	**NHL**	**2**	**0**	**0**	**0**	**0**	**0**	**0**	**0**	**0**	**0.0**	**0**	....	....	....	....	....	....	....	....	....	....	....	....
	Rochester	AHL	8	2	3	5	6	....	....	....	....	....	....	....	....	....	17	3	1	4	11	....	....	....	....
1996-97	**Buffalo**	**NHL**	**45**	**2**	**4**	**6**	**64**	**1**	**0**	**0**	**25**	**8.0**	**–2**	....	....	....	**9**	**0**	**0**	**0**	**6**	**0**	**0**	**0**	....
	Rochester	AHL	24	9	5	14	27	....	....	....	....	....	....	....	....	....	1	0	0	0	0	....	....	....	....
1997-98	**Buffalo**	**NHL**	**69**	**6**	**6**	**12**	**87**	**2**	**0**	**1**	**51**	**11.8**	**9**	....	....	....	**14**	**1**	**3**	**4**	**6**	**0**	**0**	**0**	....
1998-99	**Buffalo**	**NHL**	**67**	**5**	**8**	**13**	**38**	**0**	**0**	**0**	**55**	**9.1**	**–6**	**529**	**48.6**	**10:19**	**19**	**3**	**4**	**7**	**6**	**1**	**0**	**0**	**13:29**
99-2000	**Buffalo**	**NHL**	**41**	**5**	**7**	**12**	**38**	**2**	**0**	**1**	**40**	**12.5**	**–8**	**430**	**45.6**	**11:03**	....	....	....	....	....	....	....	....	....
	Tampa Bay	**NHL**	**17**	**2**	**3**	**5**	**25**	**0**	**0**	**0**	**35**	**5.7**	**–4**	**290**	**45.5**	**14:21**	....	....	....	....	....	....	....	....	....
2000-01	**Tampa Bay**	**NHL**	**47**	**2**	**13**	**15**	**77**	**0**	**0**	**0**	**47**	**4.3**	**–17**	**630**	**52.2**	**14:11**	....	....	....	....	....	....	....	....	....
	Pittsburgh	**NHL**	**28**	**1**	**6**	**7**	**54**	**0**	**0**	**0**	**30**	**3.3**	**0**	**318**	**51.3**	**12:45**	**18**	**1**	**3**	**4**	**2**	**0**	**0**	**0**	**15:06**
2001-02	**Pittsburgh**	**NHL**	**33**	**3**	**7**	**10**	**18**	**0**	**1**	**0**	**28**	**10.7**	**–1**	**519**	**53.2**	**12:38**	....	....	....	....	....	....	....	....	....
2002-03	**Pittsburgh**	**NHL**	**70**	**5**	**11**	**16**	**55**	**1**	**0**	**0**	**101**	**5.0**	**–30**	**1240**	**50.4**	**16:17**	....	....	....	....	....	....	....	....	....
	San Jose	**NHL**	**7**	**1**	**1**	**2**	**0**	**0**	**0**	**0**	**13**	**7.7**	**2**	**98**	**45.9**	**15:59**	....	....	....	....	....	....	....	....	....
2003-04	**San Jose**	**NHL**	**72**	**9**	**20**	**29**	**90**	**0**	**1**	**1**	**142**	**6.3**	**4**	**867**	**46.6**	**15:28**	**17**	**1**	**2**	**3**	**4**	**0**	**0**	**0**	**15:41**
2004-05			DID NOT PLAY																						
2005-06	**San Jose**	**NHL**	**21**	**5**	**3**	**8**	**17**	**1**	**1**	**1**	**35**	**14.3**	**–6**	**194**	**41.8**	**13:55**	....	....	....	....	....	....	....	....	....
	Boston	**NHL**	**50**	**6**	**8**	**14**	**40**	**0**	**0**	**0**	**66**	**9.1**	**–10**	**749**	**49.8**	**17:16**	....	....	....	....	....	....	....	....	....
	NHL Totals		**570**	**53**	**97**	**150**	**603**	**7**	**3**	**5**	**670**	**7.9**		**5864**	**49.1**	**14:01**	**77**	**6**	**12**	**18**	**24**	**1**	**0**	**0**	**14:43**

Traded to **Tampa Bay** by **Buffalo** with Cory Sarich, Brian Holzinger and Buffalo's 3rd round choice (Alexander Kharitonov) in 2000 Entry Draft for Chris Gratton and Tampa Bay's 2nd round choice (Derek Roy) in 2001 Entry Draft, March 9, 2000. Traded to **Pittsburgh** by **Tampa Bay** for Matthew Barnaby, February 1, 2001. • Missed majority of 2001-02 season recovering from knee injury suffered in game vs. Buffalo, January 8, 2002. Traded to **San Jose** by **Pittsburgh** for Matt Bradley, March 11, 2003. Traded to **Boston** by **San Jose** with Brad Stuart and Marco Sturm for Joe Thornton, November 30, 2005.

PRINTZ, David

(PRIHNTS, DAY-vihd) **PHI.**

Defense. Shoots left. 6'5", 220 lbs. Born, Stockholm, Sweden, July 24, 1980. Philadelphia's 9th choice, 225th overall, in 2001 Entry Draft.

Season	Club	League	GP	G	A	Pts	PIM	PP	SH	GW	S	%	+/-	TF	F%	Min	GP	G	A	Pts	PIM	PP	SH	GW	Min
1996-97	AIK Solna Jr.	Swe-Jr.	1	0	0	0	0	....	....	....	....	....	....	....	....	....	....	....	....	....	....	....	....	....	....
1997-98	AIK Solna Jr.	Swe-Jr.	8	0	0	0	6	....	....	....	....	....	....	....	....	....	....	....	....	....	....	....	....	....	....
1998-99	AIK Solna Jr.	Swe-Jr.	23	1	0	1	14	....	....	....	....	....	....	....	....	....	....	....	....	....	....	....	....	....	....
99-2000	AIK Solna Jr.	Swe-Jr.	36	8	4	12	53	....	....	....	....	....	....	....	....	....	....	....	....	....	....	....	....	....	....
2000-01	Great Falls	AWHL	54	13	23	36	93	....	....	....	....	....	....	....	....	....	13	3	5	8	16	....	....	....	....
2001-02	AIK Solna Jr.	Swe-Jr.	8	2	3	5	20	....	....	....	....	....	....	....	....	....	....	....	....	....	....	....	....	....	....
	AIK Solna	Sweden	37	3	2	5	59	....	....	....	....	....	....	....	....	....	....	....	....	....	....	....	....	....	....
	AIK Solna	Sweden-Q	10	0	0	0	12	....	....	....	....	....	....	....	....	....	....	....	....	....	....	....	....	....	....
2002-03	HPK Hameenlinna	Finland	17	1	0	1	10	....	....	....	....	....	....	....	....	....	....	....	....	....	....	....	....	....	....
	Ilves Tampere	Finland	25	1	2	3	10	....	....	....	....	....	....	....	....	....	....	....	....	....	....	....	....	....	....

			Regular Season														Playoffs								
Season	Club	League	GP	G	A	Pts	PIM	PP	SH	GW	S	%	+/-	TF	F%	Min	GP	G	A	Pts	PIM	PP	SH	GW	Min
2003-04	AIK Solna	Sweden-2	51	2	9	11	60	....	....	....	....	....	....	....	....	....	5	2	0	2	4	....	....	....	....
2004-05	Philadelphia	AHL	50	1	5	6	66	....	....	....	....	....	....	....	....	....	1	0	0	0	0	....	....	....	....
	Trenton Titans	ECHL	2	0	1	1	0	....	....	....	....	....	....	....	....	....	....	....	....	....	....	....	....	....	....
2005-06	**Philadelphia**	**NHL**	**1**	**0**	**0**	**0**	**0**	**0**	**0**	**0**	**0**	**0.0**	**0**	**0**	**0.0**	**5:45**	....	....	....	....	....	....	....	....	....
	Philadelphia	AHL	80	6	14	20	135	....	....	....	....	....	....	....	....	....	....	....	....	....	....	....	....	....	....
	NHL Totals		**1**	**0**	**0**	**0**	**0**	**0**	**0**	**0**	**0**	**0.0**		**0**	**0.0**	**5:45**	....	....	....	....	....	....	....	....	....

PRONGER, Chris

(PRAHN-guhr, KRIHS) **ANA.**

Defense. Shoots left. 6'6", 220 lbs. Born, Dryden, Ont., October 10, 1974. Hartford's 1st choice, 2nd overall, in 1993 Entry Draft.

Season	Club	League	GP	G	A	Pts	PIM	PP	SH	GW	S	%	+/-	TF	F%	Min	GP	G	A	Pts	PIM	PP	SH	GW	Min
1990-91	Stratford Cullitons	OHA-B	48	15	37	52	132	....	....	....	....	....	....	....	....	....	....	....	....	....	....	....	....	....	....
1991-92	Peterborough	OHL	63	17	45	62	90	....	....	....	....	....	....	....	....	....	10	1	8	9	28	....	....	....	....
1992-93	Peterborough	OHL	61	15	62	77	108	....	....	....	....	....	....	....	....	....	21	15	25	40	51	....	....	....	....
1993-94	**Hartford**	**NHL**	**81**	**5**	**25**	**30**	**113**	**2**	**0**	**0**	**174**	**2.9**	**−3**	....	....	....	....	....	....	....	....	....	....	....	....
1994-95	**Hartford**	**NHL**	**43**	**5**	**9**	**14**	**54**	**3**	**0**	**1**	**94**	**5.3**	**−12**	....	....	....	....	....	....	....	....	....	....	....	....
1995-96	**St. Louis**	**NHL**	**78**	**7**	**18**	**25**	**110**	**3**	**1**	**1**	**138**	**5.1**	**−18**	....	....	....	**13**	**1**	**5**	**6**	**16**	**0**	**0**	**0**	....
1996-97	**St. Louis**	**NHL**	**79**	**11**	**24**	**35**	**143**	**4**	**0**	**0**	**147**	**7.5**	**15**	....	....	....	**6**	**1**	**1**	**2**	**22**	**0**	**0**	**0**	....
1997-98	**St. Louis**	**NHL**	**81**	**9**	**27**	**36**	**180**	**1**	**0**	**2**	**145**	**6.2**	**47**	....	....	....	**10**	**1**	**9**	**10**	**26**	**0**	**0**	**0**	....
	Canada	Olympics	6	0	0	0	4	....	....	....	....	....	....	....	....	....	....	....	....	....	....	....	....	....	....
1998-99	**St. Louis**	**NHL**	**67**	**13**	**33**	**46**	**113**	**8**	**0**	**0**	**172**	**7.6**	**3**	**0**	**0.0**	**30:36**	**13**	**1**	**4**	**5**	**28**	**1**	**0**	**0**	**35:53**
99-2000	**St. Louis**	**NHL**	**79**	**14**	**48**	**62**	**92**	**8**	**0**	**3**	**192**	**7.3**	**52**	**1**	**0.0**	**30:14**	**7**	**3**	**4**	**7**	**32**	**2**	**0**	**2**	**30:14**
2000-01	**St. Louis**	**NHL**	**51**	**8**	**39**	**47**	**75**	**4**	**0**	**0**	**121**	**6.6**	**21**	**0**	**0.0**	**27:45**	**15**	**1**	**7**	**8**	**32**	**0**	**0**	**0**	**33:50**
2001-02	**St. Louis**	**NHL**	**78**	**7**	**40**	**47**	**120**	**4**	**1**	**3**	**204**	**3.4**	**23**	**0**	**0.0**	**29:28**	**9**	**1**	**7**	**8**	**24**	**0**	**0**	**0**	**27:51**
	Canada	Olympics	6	0	1	1	2	....	....	....	....	....	....	....	....	....	....	....	....	....	....	....	....	....	....
2002-03	**St. Louis**	**NHL**	**5**	**1**	**3**	**4**	**10**	**0**	**0**	**0**	**11**	**9.1**	**−2**	**1**	**0.0**	**21:39**	**7**	**1**	**3**	**4**	**14**	**0**	**0**	**0**	**24:36**
2003-04	**St. Louis**	**NHL**	**80**	**14**	**40**	**54**	**88**	**7**	**0**	**3**	**203**	**6.9**	**−1**	**2**	**0.0**	**27:28**	**5**	**0**	**1**	**1**	**16**	**0**	**0**	**0**	**27:54**
2004-05			DID NOT PLAY																						
2005-06	**Edmonton**	**NHL**	**80**	**12**	**44**	**56**	**74**	**10**	**0**	**3**	**155**	**7.7**	**2**	**1**	**0.0**	**27:59**	**24**	**5**	**16**	**21**	**26**	**3**	**0**	**0**	**30:57**
	Canada	Olympics	6	1	2	3	16	....	....	....	....	....	....	....	....	....	....	....	....	....	....	....	....	....	....
	NHL Totals		**802**	**106**	**350**	**456**	**1172**	**54**	**2**	**16**	**1756**	**6.0**		**5**	**0.0**	**28:52**	**109**	**15**	**57**	**72**	**236**	**6**	**0**	**2**	**31:08**

OHL All-Rookie Team (1992) • OHL First All-Star Team (1993) • Canadian Major Junior First All-Star Team (1993) • Canadian Major Junior Defenseman of the Year (1993) • NHL All-Rookie Team (1994) • NHL Second All-Star Team (1998, 2004) • Bud Ice Plus/Minus Award (1998) • NHL First All-Star Team (2000) • Bud Light Plus/Minus Award (2000) • James Norris Memorial Trophy (2000) • Hart Trophy (2000)

Played in NHL All-Star Game (1999, 2000, 2002, 2004)

Traded to **St. Louis** by **Hartford** for Brendan Shanahan, July 27, 1995. • Missed majority of 2002-03 season recovering from wrist and knee surgery, September 10, 2002. Traded to **Edmonton** by **St. Louis** for Eric Brewer, Doug Lynch and Jeff Woywitka, August 2, 2005. Traded to **Anaheim** by **Edmonton** for Joffrey Lupul, Ladislav Smid, a 1st round choice in 2007 Entry Draft, a 2nd round choice in 2008 Entry Draft and future considerations, July 3, 2006.

PROSPAL, Vaclav

(PRAWS-pahl, VAT-slav) **T.B.**

Center. Shoots left. 6'1", 195 lbs. Born, Ceske Budejovice, Czech., February 17, 1975. Philadelphia's 2nd choice, 71st overall, in 1993 Entry Draft.

Season	Club	League	GP	G	A	Pts	PIM	PP	SH	GW	S	%	+/-	TF	F%	Min	GP	G	A	Pts	PIM	PP	SH	GW	Min
1991-92	C. Budejovice Jr.	Czech-Jr.	36	16	16	32	12	....	....	....	....	....	....	....	....	....	....	....	....	....	....	....	....	....	....
1992-93	C. Budejovice Jr.	Czech-Jr.	32	26	31	57	24	....	....	....	....	....	....	....	....	....	....	....	....	....	....	....	....	....	....
1993-94	Hershey Bears	AHL	55	14	21	35	38	....	....	....	....	....	....	....	....	....	2	0	0	0	2	....	....	....	....
1994-95	Hershey Bears	AHL	69	13	32	45	36	....	....	....	....	....	....	....	....	....	2	1	0	1	4	....	....	....	....
1995-96	Hershey Bears	AHL	68	15	36	51	59	....	....	....	....	....	....	....	....	....	5	2	4	6	2	....	....	....	....
1996-97	**Philadelphia**	**NHL**	**18**	**5**	**10**	**15**	**4**	**0**	**0**	**0**	**35**	**14.3**	**3**	....	....	....	**5**	**1**	**3**	**4**	**4**	**0**	**0**	**0**	....
	Philadelphia	AHL	63	32	63	95	70	....	....	....	....	....	....	....	....	....	....	....	....	....	....	....	....	....	....
1997-98	**Philadelphia**	**NHL**	**41**	**5**	**13**	**18**	**17**	**4**	**0**	**0**	**60**	**8.3**	**−10**	....	....	....	....	....	....	....	....	....	....	....	....
	Ottawa	**NHL**	**15**	**1**	**6**	**7**	**4**	**0**	**0**	**0**	**28**	**3.6**	**−1**	....	....	....	**6**	**0**	**0**	**0**	**0**	**0**	**0**	**0**	....
1998-99	**Ottawa**	**NHL**	**79**	**10**	**26**	**36**	**58**	**2**	**0**	**3**	**114**	**8.8**	**8**	**997**	**56.2**	**13:03**	**4**	**0**	**0**	**0**	**0**	**0**	**0**	**0**	**12:37**
99-2000	**Ottawa**	**NHL**	**79**	**22**	**33**	**55**	**40**	**5**	**0**	**4**	**204**	**10.8**	**−2**	**1331**	**49.6**	**16:26**	**6**	**0**	**4**	**4**	**4**	**0**	**0**	**0**	**17:40**
2000-01	**Ottawa**	**NHL**	**40**	**1**	**12**	**13**	**12**	**0**	**0**	**0**	**68**	**1.5**	**1**	**501**	**50.1**	**12:57**	....	....	....	....	....	....	....	....	....
	Florida	**NHL**	**34**	**4**	**12**	**16**	**10**	**1**	**0**	**0**	**68**	**5.9**	**−2**	**487**	**54.6**	**16:36**	....	....	....	....	....	....	....	....	....
2001-02	**Tampa Bay**	**NHL**	**81**	**18**	**37**	**55**	**38**	**7**	**0**	**2**	**166**	**10.8**	**−11**	**555**	**52.8**	**17:31**	....	....	....	....	....	....	....	....	....
2002-03	**Tampa Bay**	**NHL**	**80**	**22**	**57**	**79**	**53**	**9**	**0**	**4**	**134**	**16.4**	**9**	**161**	**51.6**	**18:39**	**11**	**4**	**2**	**6**	**8**	**2**	**0**	**0**	**21:15**
2003-04	**Anaheim**	**NHL**	**82**	**19**	**35**	**54**	**54**	**7**	**0**	**4**	**185**	**10.3**	**−9**	**45**	**46.7**	**18:37**	....	....	....	....	....	....	....	....	....
2004-05	C. Budejovice	CzRep-2	39	28	60	88	82	....	....	....	....	....	....	....	....	....	16	15	15	30	32	....	....	....	....
2005-06	**Tampa Bay**	**NHL**	**81**	**25**	**55**	**80**	**50**	**10**	**0**	**3**	**236**	**10.6**	**−3**	**267**	**45.3**	**19:10**	**5**	**0**	**2**	**2**	**0**	**0**	**0**	**0**	**15:56**
	Czech Republic	Olympics	8	4	2	6	2	....	....	....	....	....	....	....	....	....	....	....	....	....	....	....	....	....	....
	NHL Totals		**630**	**132**	**296**	**428**	**340**	**45**	**0**	**20**	**1298**	**10.2**		**4344**	**51.9**	**16:55**	**37**	**5**	**11**	**16**	**16**	**2**	**0**	**0**	**18:04**

AHL First All-Star Team (1997)

Traded to **Ottawa** by **Philadelphia** with Pat Falloon and Dallas' 2nd round choice (previously acquired, Ottawa selected Chris Bala) in 1998 Entry Draft for Alexandre Daigle, January 17, 1998. Traded to **Florida** by **Ottawa** for future considerations, January 20, 2001. Traded to **Tampa Bay** by **Florida** for Ryan Johnson and Tampa Bay's 6th round choice (later traded back to Tampa Bay – Tampa Bay selected Doug O'Brien) in 2003 Entry Draft, July 10, 2001. Signed as a free agent by **Anaheim**, July 17, 2003. Traded to **Tampa Bay** by **Anaheim** for Tampa Bay's 2nd round choice (Brendan Mikkelson) in 2005 Entry Draft, August 16, 2004. Signed as a free agent by **Ceske Budejovice** (CzRep-2), September 17, 2004.

PRUCHA, Petr

(PROO-khah, PEE-tuhr) **NYR**

Right wing. Shoots right. 6', 170 lbs. Born, Chrudim, Czech., September 14, 1982. NY Rangers' 8th choice, 240th overall, in 2002 Entry Draft.

Season	Club	League	GP	G	A	Pts	PIM	PP	SH	GW	S	%	+/-	TF	F%	Min	GP	G	A	Pts	PIM	PP	SH	GW	Min
99-2000	HC Chrudim Jr.	CzRep-Jr.	43	35	27	62	62	....	....	....	....	....	....	....	....	....	....	....	....	....	....	....	....	....	....
2000-01	HC Pardubice Jr.	CzRep-Jr.	54	39	22	61	18	....	....	....	....	....	....	....	....	....	....	....	....	....	....	....	....	....	....
2001-02	HC Pardubice Jr.	CzRep-Jr.	28	38	28	66	18	....	....	....	....	....	....	....	....	....	3	2	6	8	0	....	....	....	....
	Sumperk	CzRep-2	8	6	4	10	0	....	....	....	....	....	....	....	....	....	....	....	....	....	....	....	....	....	....
	Sumperk	CzRep-Q	5	5	3	8	0	....	....	....	....	....	....	....	....	....	....	....	....	....	....	....	....	....	....
	Pardubice	CzRep	20	1	1	2	2	....	....	....	....	....	....	....	....	....	5	0	0	0	0	....	....	....	....
2002-03	Pardubice	CzRep	49	7	9	16	12	....	....	....	....	....	....	....	....	....	17	2	6	8	8	....	....	....	....
	HC Pardubice Jr.	CzRep-Jr.	4	5	4	9	25	....	....	....	....	....	....	....	....	....	....	....	....	....	....	....	....	....	....
	Hr. Kralove	CzRep-2	11	3	5	8	35	....	....	....	....	....	....	....	....	....	....	....	....	....	....	....	....	....	....
2003-04	Hr. Kralove	CzRep-2	3	1	0	1	25	....	....	....	....	....	....	....	....	....	....	....	....	....	....	....	....	....	....
	Pardubice	CzRep	48	11	13	24	24	....	....	....	....	....	....	....	....	....	7	4	3	7	2	....	....	....	....
2004-05	Pardubice	CzRep	47	7	10	17	24	....	....	....	....	....	....	....	....	....	16	6	7	13	2	....	....	....	....
2005-06	**NY Rangers**	**NHL**	**68**	**30**	**17**	**47**	**32**	**16**	**0**	**2**	**130**	**23.1**	**3**	**150**	**52.0**	**13:42**	**4**	**1**	**0**	**1**	**0**	**1**	**0**	**0**	**14:13**
	Hartford	AHL	2	2	1	3	0	....	....	....	....	....	....	....	....	....	....	....	....	....	....	....	....	....	....
	Czech Republic	Olympics	DID NOT PLAY – INJURED																						
	NHL Totals		**68**	**30**	**17**	**47**	**32**	**16**	**0**	**2**	**130**	**23.1**		**150**	**52.0**	**13:42**	**4**	**1**	**0**	**1**	**0**	**1**	**0**	**0**	**14:13**

PURINTON, Dale

(PUHR-ihn-TOHN, DAYL)

Defense. Shoots left. 6'3", 228 lbs. Born, Fort Wayne, IN, October 11, 1976. NY Rangers' 5th choice, 117th overall, in 1995 Entry Draft.

Season	Club	League	GP	G	A	Pts	PIM	PP	SH	GW	S	%	+/-	TF	F%	Min	GP	G	A	Pts	PIM	PP	SH	GW	Min
1992-93	Moose Jaw	SMHL	34	1	16	17	107	....	....	....	....	....	....	....	....	....	....	....	....	....	....	....	....	....	....
	Moose Jaw	WHL	2	0	0	0	2	....	....	....	....	....	....	....	....	....	....	....	....	....	....	....	....	....	....
1993-94	Vernon Vipers	BCJHL	42	1	6	7	194	....	....	....	....	....	....	....	....	....	....	....	....	....	....	....	....	....	....
1994-95	Tacoma Rockets	WHL	65	0	8	8	291	....	....	....	....	....	....	....	....	....	3	0	0	0	13	....	....	....	....
1995-96	Kelowna Rockets	WHL	22	1	4	5	88	....	....	....	....	....	....	....	....	....	....	....	....	....	....	....	....	....	....
	Lethbridge	WHL	37	3	6	9	144	....	....	....	....	....	....	....	....	....	4	1	1	2	25	....	....	....	....
1996-97	Lethbridge	WHL	51	6	26	32	254	....	....	....	....	....	....	....	....	....	18	3	5	8	*88	....	....	....	....
1997-98	Hartford	AHL	17	0	0	0	95	....	....	....	....	....	....	....	....	....	....	....	....	....	....	....	....	....	....
	Charlotte	ECHL	34	3	5	8	186	....	....	....	....	....	....	....	....	....	....	....	....	....	....	....	....	....	....
1998-99	Hartford	AHL	45	1	3	4	306	....	....	....	....	....	....	....	....	....	7	0	2	2	24	....	....	....	....
99-2000	**NY Rangers**	**NHL**	**1**	**0**	**0**	**0**	**7**	**0**	**0**	**0**	**1**	**0.0**	**−1**	**0**	**0.0**	**12:45**	....	....	....	....	....	....	....	....	....
	Hartford	AHL	62	4	4	8	415	....	....	....	....	....	....	....	....	....	23	0	3	3	*87	....	....	....	....
2000-01	**NY Rangers**	**NHL**	**42**	**0**	**2**	**2**	**180**	**0**	**0**	**0**	**13**	**0.0**	**5**	**0**	**0.0**	**9:33**	....	....	....	....	....	....	....	....	....
	Hartford	AHL	11	0	1	1	75	....	....	....	....	....	....	....	....	....	....	....	....	....	....	....	....	....	....
2001-02	**NY Rangers**	**NHL**	**40**	**0**	**4**	**4**	**113**	**0**	**0**	**0**	**11**	**0.0**	**4**	**0**	**0.0**	**7:37**	....	....	....	....	....	....	....	....	....
2002-03	**NY Rangers**	**NHL**	**58**	**3**	**9**	**12**	**161**	**0**	**0**	**0**	**50**	**6.0**	**−2**	**0**	**0.0**	**15:02**	....	....	....	....	....	....	....	....	....
2003-04	**NY Rangers**	**NHL**	**40**	**1**	**1**	**2**	**117**	**0**	**0**	**0**	**31**	**3.2**	**−9**	**0**	**0.0**	**12:47**	....	....	....	....	....	....	....	....	....

			Regular Season														Playoffs								
Season	Club	League	GP	G	A	Pts	PIM	PP	SH	GW	S	%	+/-	TF	F%	Min	GP	G	A	Pts	PIM	PP	SH	GW	Min
2004-05	Victoria	ECHL	25	3	9	12	192	....	....	....	....	....	....	....	....	....	....	....	....	....	....	....	....	....	....
2005-06	Hartford	AHL	25	3	3	6	109	....	....	....	....	....	....	....	....	....	10	0	2	2	45	....	....	....	....
	NHL Totals		**181**	**4**	**16**	**20**	**578**	**0**	**0**	**0**	**106**	**3.8**		**0**	**0.0**	**11:37**	....	....	....	....	....	....	....	....	....

• Spent majority of 2003-04 season as a healthy reserve. Signed as a free agent by **Victoria** (ECHL), December 3, 2004. • Missed majority of 2005-06 season recovering from a knee injury suffered in a game at Springfield (AHL) (November 6, 2005) and a finger injury suffered in practice (January 3, 2006).

PUSHKAREV, Konstantin

(puhsh-kar-EHV, kawn-stuhn-TIHN) **L.A.**

Right wing. Shoots left. 6', 180 lbs. Born, Ust-Kamenogorsk, USSR, February 12, 1985. Los Angeles' 4th choice, 44th overall, in 2003 Entry Draft.

2002-03	Ust-Kam'gorsk 2	Russia-3	STATISTICS NOT AVAILABLE																						
	Ust-Kamenogorsk	Russia-2	4	0	0	0	4	....	....	....	....	....	....	....	....	....	....	....	....	....	....	....	....	....	....
2003-04	Omsk 2	Russia-3	34	17	11	28	64	....	....	....	....	....	....	....	....	....	....	....	....	....	....	....	....	....	....
	Avangard Omsk	Russia	5	1	0	1	0	....	....	....	....	....	....	....	....	....	....	....	....	....	....	....	....	....	....
2004-05	Avangard Omsk	Russia	1	0	0	0	0	....	....	....	....	....	....	....	....	....	....	....	....	....	....	....	....	....	....
	Calgary Hitmen	WHL	69	22	30	52	50	....	....	....	....	....	....	....	....	....	12	2	5	7	4	....	....	....	....
2005-06	**Los Angeles**	**NHL**	**1**	**0**	**1**	**1**	**0**	**0**	**0**	**0**	**0**	**0.0**	**0**	**0**	**0.0**	**9:33**	....	....	....	....	....	....	....	....	....
	Manchester	AHL	77	19	19	38	95	....	....	....	....	....	....	....	....	....	7	1	1	2	4	....	....	....	....
	NHL Totals		**1**	**0**	**1**	**1**	**0**	**0**	**0**	**0**	**0**	**0.0**		**0**	**0.0**	**9:33**	....	....	....	....	....	....	....	....	....

PUSHOR, Jamie

(PUH-shohr, JAY-mee) **CBJ**

Defense. Shoots right. 6'3", 218 lbs. Born, Lethbridge, Alta., February 11, 1973. Detroit's 2nd choice, 32nd overall, in 1991 Entry Draft.

1988-89	Lethbridge	AMHL	37	1	8	9	20	....	....	....	....	....	....	....	....	....	....	....	....	....	....	....	....	....	....
	Lethbridge	WHL	2	0	0	0	0	....	....	....	....	....	....	....	....	....	....	....	....	....	....	....	....	....	....
1989-90	Lethbridge	AMHL	35	6	27	33	92	....	....	....	....	....	....	....	....	....	....	....	....	....	....	....	....	....	....
	Lethbridge	WHL	10	0	2	2	2	....	....	....	....	....	....	....	....	....	16	0	0	0	63	....	....	....	....
1990-91	Lethbridge	WHL	71	1	13	14	202	....	....	....	....	....	....	....	....	....	....	....	....	....	....	....	....	....	....
1991-92	Lethbridge	WHL	49	2	15	17	232	....	....	....	....	....	....	....	....	....	5	0	0	0	33	....	....	....	....
1992-93	Lethbridge	WHL	72	6	22	28	200	....	....	....	....	....	....	....	....	....	4	0	1	1	9	....	....	....	....
1993-94	Adirondack	AHL	73	1	17	18	124	....	....	....	....	....	....	....	....	....	12	0	0	0	22	....	....	....	....
1994-95	Adirondack	AHL	58	2	11	13	129	....	....	....	....	....	....	....	....	....	4	0	1	1	0	....	....	....	....
1995-96	**Detroit**	**NHL**	**5**	**0**	**1**	**1**	**17**	**0**	**0**	**0**	**6**	**0.0**	**2**	....	....	....	....	....	....	....	....	....	....	....	....
	Adirondack	AHL	65	2	16	18	126	....	....	....	....	....	....	....	....	....	3	0	0	0	5	....	....	....	....
1996-97 ♦	**Detroit**	**NHL**	**75**	**4**	**7**	**11**	**129**	**0**	**0**	**0**	**63**	**6.3**	**1**	....	....	....	**5**	**0**	**1**	**1**	**5**	**0**	**0**	**0**	....
1997-98	**Detroit**	**NHL**	**54**	**2**	**5**	**7**	**71**	**0**	**0**	**0**	**43**	**4.7**	**2**	....	....	....	....	....	....	....	....	....	....	....	....
	Anaheim	**NHL**	**10**	**0**	**2**	**2**	**10**	**0**	**0**	**0**	**8**	**0.0**	**1**	....	....	....	....	....	....	....	....	....	....	....	....
1998-99	**Anaheim**	**NHL**	**70**	**1**	**2**	**3**	**112**	**0**	**0**	**0**	**75**	**1.3**	**-20**	**0**	**0.0**	**19:16**	**4**	**0**	**0**	**0**	**6**	**0**	**0**	**0**	**14:08**
99-2000	**Dallas**	**NHL**	**62**	**0**	**8**	**8**	**53**	**0**	**0**	**0**	**27**	**0.0**	**0**	**0**	**0.0**	**11:36**	**5**	**0**	**0**	**0**	**5**	**0**	**0**	**0**	**10:06**
2000-01	**Columbus**	**NHL**	**75**	**3**	**10**	**13**	**94**	**0**	**1**	**0**	**64**	**4.7**	**7**	**0**	**0.0**	**20:48**	....	....	....	....	....	....	....	....	....
2001-02	**Columbus**	**NHL**	**61**	**0**	**6**	**6**	**54**	**0**	**0**	**0**	**46**	**0.0**	**-10**	**0**	**0.0**	**17:06**	....	....	....	....	....	....	....	....	....
	Pittsburgh	**NHL**	**15**	**0**	**2**	**2**	**30**	**0**	**0**	**0**	**14**	**0.0**	**-3**	**0**	**0.0**	**19:03**	....	....	....	....	....	....	....	....	....
2002-03	**Pittsburgh**	**NHL**	**76**	**3**	**1**	**4**	**76**	**0**	**0**	**0**	**54**	**5.6**	**-28**	**0**	**0.0**	**16:58**	....	....	....	....	....	....	....	....	....
2003-04	Syracuse Crunch	AHL	17	1	4	5	24	....	....	....	....	....	....	....	....	....	....	....	....	....	....	....	....	....	....
	Columbus	**NHL**	**7**	**0**	**0**	**0**	**2**	**0**	**0**	**0**	**6**	**0.0**	**-2**	**0**	**0.0**	**13:12**	....	....	....	....	....	....	....	....	....
	NY Rangers	**NHL**	**7**	**0**	**0**	**0**	**0**	**0**	**0**	**0**	**4**	**0.0**	**-3**	**0**	**0.0**	**13:08**	....	....	....	....	....	....	....	....	....
	Hartford	AHL	14	0	2	2	21	....	....	....	....	....	....	....	....	....	16	1	1	2	18	....	....	....	....
2004-05	Syracuse Crunch	AHL	68	1	9	10	85	....	....	....	....	....	....	....	....	....	....	....	....	....	....	....	....	....	....
2005-06	**Columbus**	**NHL**	**4**	**1**	**2**	**3**	**0**	**0**	**0**	**0**	**2**	**50.0**	**1**	**0**	**0.0**	**18:13**	....	....	....	....	....	....	....	....	....
	Syracuse Crunch	AHL	72	5	17	22	132	....	....	....	....	....	....	....	....	....	6	0	1	1	9	....	....	....	....
	NHL Totals		**521**	**14**	**46**	**60**	**648**	**0**	**1**	**0**	**412**	**3.4**		**0**	**0.0**	**17:15**	**14**	**0**	**1**	**1**	**16**	**0**	**0**	**0**	**11:53**

Traded to **Anaheim** by **Detroit** with Detroit's 4th round choice (Viktor Wallin) in 1998 Entry Draft for Dmitri Mironov, March 24, 1998. Claimed by **Atlanta** from **Anaheim** in Expansion Draft, June 25, 1999. Traded to **Dallas** by **Atlanta** for Jason Botterill, July 15, 1999. Claimed by **Columbus** from **Dallas** in Expansion Draft, June 23, 2000. Traded to **Pittsburgh** by **Columbus** for Pittsburgh's 4th round choice (Kevin Jarman) in 2003 Entry Draft, March 15, 2002. Signed as a free agent by **Syracuse** (AHL), November 18, 2003. Signed as a free agent by **Columbus**, December 10, 2003. Traded to **NY Rangers** by **Columbus** for NY Rangers' 8th round choice (Matt Greer) in 2004 Entry Draft, January 23, 2004. Signed as a free agent by **Syracuse** (AHL), August 9, 2004. Traded to **Phoenix** by **Detroit** for Phoenix's 7th round choice (Nick Oslund) in 2006 Entry Draft, March 9, 2006. Signed as a free agent by **Columbus**, July 21, 2006.

PYATT, Taylor

(PIGH-at, TAY-luhr) **VAN.**

Left wing. Shoots left. 6'4", 227 lbs. Born, Thunder Bay, Ont., August 19, 1981. NY Islanders' 2nd choice, 8th overall, in 1999 Entry Draft.

1996-97	Thunder Bay	TBAHA	60	52	61	113	72	....	....	....	....	....	....	....	....	....	....	....	....	....	....	....	....	....	....
1997-98	Sudbury Wolves	OHL	58	14	17	31	104	....	....	....	....	....	....	....	....	....	10	3	1	4	8	....	....	....	....
1998-99	Sudbury Wolves	OHL	68	37	38	75	95	....	....	....	....	....	....	....	....	....	4	0	4	4	6	....	....	....	....
99-2000	Sudbury Wolves	OHL	68	40	49	89	98	....	....	....	....	....	....	....	....	....	12	8	7	15	25	....	....	....	....
2000-01	**NY Islanders**	**NHL**	**78**	**4**	**14**	**18**	**39**	**1**	**0**	**2**	**86**	**4.7**	**-17**	**1**	**0.0**	**12:14**	....	....	....	....	....	....	....	....	....
2001-02	**Buffalo**	**NHL**	**48**	**10**	**10**	**20**	**35**	**0**	**0**	**0**	**61**	**16.4**	**4**	**0**	**0.0**	**13:30**	....	....	....	....	....	....	....	....	....
	Rochester	AHL	27	6	4	10	36	....	....	....	....	....	....	....	....	....	....	....	....	....	....	....	....	....	....
2002-03	**Buffalo**	**NHL**	**78**	**14**	**14**	**28**	**38**	**2**	**0**	**0**	**110**	**12.7**	**-8**	**8**	**25.0**	**14:06**	....	....	....	....	....	....	....	....	....
2003-04	**Buffalo**	**NHL**	**63**	**8**	**12**	**20**	**25**	**1**	**2**	**4**	**98**	**8.2**	**-7**	**19**	**26.3**	**15:36**	....	....	....	....	....	....	....	....	....
2004-05	Hammarby	Sweden-2	24	11	9	20	20	....	....	....	....	....	....	....	....	....	....	....	....	....	....	....	....	....	....
2005-06	**Buffalo**	**NHL**	**41**	**6**	**6**	**12**	**33**	**0**	**0**	**1**	**62**	**9.7**	**-1**	**11**	**18.2**	**11:14**	**14**	**0**	**5**	**5**	**10**	**0**	**0**	**0**	**11:08**
	NHL Totals		**308**	**42**	**56**	**98**	**170**	**4**	**2**	**7**	**417**	**10.1**		**39**	**23.1**	**13:27**	**14**	**0**	**5**	**5**	**10**	**0**	**0**	**0**	**11:08**

OHL First All-Star Team (2000)

Traded to **Buffalo** by **NY Islanders** with Tim Connolly for Michael Peca, June 24, 2001. Signed as a free agent by **Hammarby** (Sweden-2), November 16, 2004. Traded to **Vancouver** by **Buffalo** for a 4th round choice in 2007 Entry Draft, July 14, 2006.

QUINCEY, Kyle

(KWIHN-see, KIGHL) **DET.**

Defense. Shoots left. 6'1", 194 lbs. Born, Kitchener, Ont., August 12, 1985. Detroit's 2nd choice, 132nd overall, in 2003 Entry Draft.

2001-02	Mississauga	OPJHL	27	5	14	19	31	....	....	....	....	....	....	....	....	....	....	....	....	....	....	....	....	....	....
2002-03	London Knights	OHL	66	6	12	18	77	....	....	....	....	....	....	....	....	....	14	3	4	7	11	....	....	....	....
2003-04	London Knights	OHL	3	0	2	2	4	....	....	....	....	....	....	....	....	....	....	....	....	....	....	....	....	....	....
	Mississauga	OHL	61	14	23	37	135	....	....	....	....	....	....	....	....	....	24	3	13	16	32	....	....	....	....
2004-05	Mississauga	OHL	59	15	31	46	111	....	....	....	....	....	....	....	....	....	5	0	3	3	4	....	....	....	....
2005-06	**Detroit**	**NHL**	**1**	**0**	**0**	**0**	**0**	**0**	**0**	**0**	**1**	**0.0**	**0**	**0**	**0.0**	**11:37**	....	....	....	....	....	....	....	....	....
	Grand Rapids	AHL	70	7	26	33	107	....	....	....	....	....	....	....	....	....	16	0	1	1	27	....	....	....	....
	NHL Totals		**1**	**0**	**0**	**0**	**0**	**0**	**0**	**0**	**1**	**0.0**		**0**	**0.0**	**11:37**	....	....	....	....	....	....	....	....	....

OHL Second All-Star Team (2005)

QUINT, Deron

(KWIHNT, DAIR-ohn)

Defense. Shoots left. 6'2", 219 lbs. Born, Durham, NH, March 12, 1976. Winnipeg's 1st choice, 30th overall, in 1994 Entry Draft.

1990-91	Cardigan Mtn.	High-NH	31	67	54	121	....	....	....	....	....	....	....	....	....	....	....	....	....	....	....	....	....	....	....
1991-92	Cardigan Mtn.	High-NH	21	111	58	169	....	....	....	....	....	....	....	....	....	....	....	....	....	....	....	....	....	....	....
1992-93	Tabor Academy	High-MA	28	15	26	41	30	....	....	....	....	....	....	....	....	....	1	0	2	2	0	....	....	....	....
1993-94	Seattle	WHL	63	15	29	44	47	....	....	....	....	....	....	....	....	....	9	4	12	16	8	....	....	....	....
1994-95	Seattle	WHL	65	29	60	89	82	....	....	....	....	....	....	....	....	....	3	1	2	3	6	....	....	....	....
1995-96	**Winnipeg**	**NHL**	**51**	**5**	**13**	**18**	**22**	**2**	**0**	**0**	**97**	**5.2**	**-2**	....	....	....	....	....	....	....	....	....	....	....	....
	Springfield	AHL	11	2	3	5	4	....	....	....	....	....	....	....	....	....	10	2	3	5	6	....	....	....	....
	Seattle	WHL	....	....	....	....	....	....	....	....	....	....	....	....	....	....	5	4	1	5	6	....	....	....	....
1996-97	**Phoenix**	**NHL**	**27**	**3**	**11**	**14**	**4**	**1**	**0**	**0**	**63**	**4.8**	**-4**	....	....	....	**7**	**0**	**2**	**2**	**0**	**0**	**0**	**0**	....
	Springfield	AHL	43	6	18	24	20	....	....	....	....	....	....	....	....	....	12	2	7	9	4	....	....	....	....
1997-98	**Phoenix**	**NHL**	**32**	**4**	**7**	**11**	**16**	**1**	**0**	**1**	**61**	**6.6**	**-6**	....	....	....	....	....	....	....	....	....	....	....	....
	Springfield	AHL	8	1	7	8	10	....	....	....	....	....	....	....	....	....	1	0	0	0	0	....	....	....	....
1998-99	**Phoenix**	**NHL**	**60**	**5**	**8**	**13**	**20**	**2**	**0**	**0**	**94**	**5.3**	**-10**	**0**	**0.0**	**16:12**	....	....	....	....	....	....	....	....	....
99-2000	**Phoenix**	**NHL**	**50**	**3**	**7**	**10**	**22**	**0**	**0**	**1**	**88**	**3.4**	**0**	**0**	**0.0**	**16:39**	....	....	....	....	....	....	....	....	....
	New Jersey	**NHL**	**4**	**1**	**0**	**1**	**2**	**0**	**0**	**0**	**6**	**16.7**	**-2**	**0**	**0.0**	**16:26**	....	....	....	....	....	....	....	....	....
2000-01	**Columbus**	**NHL**	**57**	**7**	**16**	**23**	**16**	**3**	**0**	**0**	**148**	**4.7**	**-19**	**1**	**100.0**	**24:06**	....	....	....	....	....	....	....	....	....
	Syracuse Crunch	AHL	21	5	15	20	30	....	....	....	....	....	....	....	....	....	....	....	....	....	....	....	....	....	....
2001-02	**Columbus**	**NHL**	**75**	**7**	**18**	**25**	**26**	**3**	**0**	**1**	**169**	**4.1**	**-34**	**0**	**0.0**	**22:01**	....	....	....	....	....	....	....	....	....

			Regular Season														Playoffs								
Season	Club	League	GP	G	A	Pts	PIM	PP	SH	GW	S	%	+/-	TF	F%	Min	GP	G	A	Pts	PIM	PP	SH	GW	Min
2002-03	Springfield	AHL	4	1	2	3	4																		
	Phoenix	**NHL**	**51**	**7**	**10**	**17**	**20**	**2**	**0**	**0**	**85**	**8.2**	**–5**	**0**	**0.0**	**15:51**									
2003-04	**Chicago**	**NHL**	**51**	**4**	**7**	**11**	**18**	**2**	**0**	**0**	**72**	**5.6**	**–26**	**0**	**0.0**	**18:08**									
2004-05	HC Forst Bolzano	Italy	14	5	11	16	10										9	4	5	9	12				
2005-06	Kloten Flyers	Swiss	16	5	10	15	6																		
	Eisbaren Berlin	Germany	31	5	7	12	26										11	4	7	11	6				
	NHL Totals		**458**	**46**	**97**	**143**	**166**	**16**	**0**	**3**	**883**	**5.2**		**1**	**100.0**	**19:03**	**7**	**0**	**2**	**2**	**0**	**0**	**0**	**0**	

WHL West First All-Star Team (1995)

Transferred to **Phoenix** after **Winnipeg** franchise relocated, July 1, 1996. Traded to **New Jersey** by **Phoenix** with Phoenix's 3rd round choice (later traded back to Phoenix – Phoenix selected Beat Forster) in 2001 Entry Draft for Lyle Odelein, March 7, 2000. Traded to **Columbus** by **New Jersey** to complete transaction that sent Krzysztof Oliwa to Columbus (June 12, 2000) and Turner Stevenson to New Jersey (June 23, 2000), June 23, 2000. Signed to a PTO (tryout) contract by **Springfield** (AHL), October 16, 2002. Signed as a free agent by **Phoenix**, October 26, 2002. Signed as a free agent by **Chicago**, August 5, 2003. Signed as a free agent by **Bolzano** (Italy), December 20, 2004. Signed as a free agent by **Kloten** (Swiss), May 21, 2005. Signed as a free agent by **Berlin** (Germany), November 11, 2005.

RACHUNEK, Karel

(ra-KHOO-nehk, KAH-rehl) **NYR**

Defense. Shoots right. 6'2", 212 lbs. Born, Gottwaldov/Zlin, Czech., August 27, 1979. Ottawa's 8th choice, 229th overall, in 1997 Entry Draft.

Season	Club	League	GP	G	A	Pts	PIM	PP	SH	GW	S	%	+/-	TF	F%	Min	GP	G	A	Pts	PIM	PP	SH	GW	Min
1995-96	AC ZPS Zlin Jr.	CzRep-Jr.	38	8	11	19																			
1996-97	AC ZPS Zlin Jr.	CzRep-Jr.	27	2	11	13																			
1997-98	Zlin	CzRep	27	1	2	3	16																		
1998-99	Zlin	CzRep	39	3	9	12	88										6	0	0	0					
99-2000	**Ottawa**	**NHL**	**6**	**0**	**0**	**0**	**2**	**0**	**0**	**0**	**3**	**0.0**	**0**	**0**	**0.0**	**8:03**									
	Grand Rapids	IHL	62	6	20	26	64										9	0	5	5	6				
2000-01	**Ottawa**	**NHL**	**71**	**3**	**30**	**33**	**60**	**3**	**0**	**0**	**77**	**3.9**	**17**	**0**	**0.0**	**20:54**	**3**	**0**	**0**	**0**	**0**	**0**	**0**	**0**	**22:38**
2001-02	**Ottawa**	**NHL**	**51**	**3**	**15**	**18**	**24**	**1**	**0**	**2**	**55**	**5.5**	**7**	**2**	**0.0**	**19:19**									
2002-03	Yaroslavl	Russia	9	3	0	3	8																		
	Ottawa	**NHL**	**58**	**4**	**25**	**29**	**30**	**3**	**0**	**1**	**110**	**3.6**	**23**	**3**	**33.3**	**21:46**	**17**	**1**	**3**	**4**	**14**	**0**	**0**	**0**	**23:14**
	Binghamton	AHL	6	0	2	2	10																		
2003-04	**Ottawa**	**NHL**	**60**	**1**	**16**	**17**	**29**	**0**	**0**	**0**	**99**	**1.0**	**17**	**0**	**0.0**	**19:43**									
	NY Rangers	**NHL**	**12**	**1**	**3**	**4**	**4**	**1**	**0**	**0**	**21**	**4.8**	**–9**	**0**	**0.0**	**19:04**									
2004-05	Znojmo	CzRep	21	5	6	11	55																		
	Yaroslavl	Russia	27	6	8	14	69										9	2	0	2	6				
2005-06	Yaroslavl	Russia	45	11	16	27	73										2	0	0	0	29				
	NHL Totals		**258**	**12**	**89**	**101**	**149**	**8**	**0**	**3**	**365**	**3.3**		**5**	**20.0**	**20:07**	**20**	**1**	**3**	**4**	**14**	**0**	**0**	**0**	**23:09**

Traded to **NY Rangers** by **Ottawa** with Alexandre Giroux for Greg De Vries, March 9, 2004. Signed as a free agent by **Znojmo** (CzRep), September 6, 2004. Signed as a free agent by **Yaroslavl** (Russia), November 1, 2004.

RADIVOJEVIC, Branko

(ra-dih-VOI-uh-vihch, BRAN-koh) **MIN.**

Right wing. Shoots right. 6'1", 209 lbs. Born, Piestany, Czech., November 24, 1980. Colorado's 3rd choice, 93rd overall, in 1999 Entry Draft.

Season	Club	League	GP	G	A	Pts	PIM	PP	SH	GW	S	%	+/-	TF	F%	Min	GP	G	A	Pts	PIM	PP	SH	GW	Min
1997-98	Dukla Trencin Jr.	Slovak-Jr.	52	30	31	61	50																		
	Dukla Trencin	Slovakia	1	0	0	0	2																		
1998-99	Belleville Bulls	OHL	68	20	38	58	61										21	7	17	24	18				
99-2000	Belleville Bulls	OHL	59	23	49	72	86										16	5	8	13	32				
2000-01	Belleville Bulls	OHL	61	34	70	104	77										10	6	10	16	18				
2001-02	**Phoenix**	**NHL**	**18**	**4**	**2**	**6**	**4**	**0**	**0**	**1**	**19**	**21.1**	**1**	**0**	**0.0**	**9:22**	**1**	**0**	**0**	**0**	**2**	**0**	**0**	**0**	**8:07**
	Springfield	AHL	62	18	21	39	64																		
2002-03	**Phoenix**	**NHL**	**79**	**12**	**15**	**27**	**63**	**1**	**0**	**3**	**109**	**11.0**	**–2**	**20**	**40.0**	**13:18**									
2003-04	**Phoenix**	**NHL**	**53**	**9**	**14**	**23**	**36**	**2**	**1**	**2**	**83**	**10.8**	**–5**	**30**	**30.0**	**16:27**									
	Philadelphia	**NHL**	**24**	**1**	**8**	**9**	**36**	**0**	**0**	**0**	**24**	**4.2**	**0**	**11**	**54.6**	**10:28**	**18**	**1**	**1**	**2**	**32**	**0**	**0**	**0**	**9:56**
2004-05	HC Vsetin	CzRep	31	7	11	18	114																		
	Lulea HF	Sweden	10	6	5	11	8										4	0	0	0	44				
2005-06	**Philadelphia**	**NHL**	**64**	**8**	**6**	**14**	**44**	**1**	**0**	**1**	**84**	**9.5**	**–6**	**14**	**42.9**	**12:46**	**5**	**1**	**0**	**1**	**0**	**0**	**0**	**0**	**10:34**
	NHL Totals		**238**	**34**	**45**	**79**	**183**	**4**	**1**	**7**	**319**	**10.7**		**75**	**38.7**	**13:17**	**24**	**2**	**1**	**3**	**34**	**0**	**0**	**0**	**10:00**

OHL First All-Star Team (2001)

Signed as a free agent by **Phoenix**, June 19, 2001. Traded to **Philadelphia** by **Phoenix** with Sean Burke and Ben Eager for Mike Comrie, February 9, 2004. Signed as a free agent by **Vsetin** (CzRep), September 17, 2004. Signed as a free agent by **Lulea** (Sweden), January 27, 2005. Signed as a free agent by **Minnesota**, July 6, 2006.

RADULOV, Igor

(rah-DOO-lahf, EE-gohr)

Left wing. Shoots left. 6'1", 186 lbs. Born, Nizhny Tagil, USSR, August 23, 1982. Chicago's 4th choice, 74th overall, in 2000 Entry Draft.

Season	Club	League	GP	G	A	Pts	PIM	PP	SH	GW	S	%	+/-	TF	F%	Min	GP	G	A	Pts	PIM	PP	SH	GW	Min
1997-98	Yaroslavl	Russia	5	0	2	2	4																		
1998-99	Yaroslavl 2	Russia-3	21	2	3	5	4																		
99-2000	Yaroslavl 2	Russia-3	31	17	16	33																			
2000-01	Kristall Saratov	Russia-2	4	0	2	2	2																		
	St. Petersburg	Russia	8	1	0	1	6																		
2001-02	Mississauga	OHL	62	33	30	63	30																		
2002-03	**Chicago**	**NHL**	**7**	**5**	**0**	**5**	**4**	**3**	**0**	**0**	**14**	**35.7**	**–3**	**0**	**0.0**	**15:06**									
	Norfolk Admirals	AHL	62	18	9	27	26										9	2	2	4	8				
2003-04	**Chicago**	**NHL**	**36**	**4**	**7**	**11**	**18**	**0**	**0**	**0**	**47**	**8.5**	**–2**	**0**	**0.0**	**12:15**									
	Norfolk Admirals	AHL	38	9	14	23	26										8	0	1	1	4				
2004-05	Norfolk Admirals	AHL	16	0	0	0	16																		
	Spartak Moscow	Russia	25	2	2	4	22																		
2005-06	Spartak Moscow	Russia	42	4	6	10	54										3	0	0	0	4				
	NHL Totals		**43**	**9**	**7**	**16**	**22**	**3**	**0**	**0**	**61**	**14.8**		**0**	**0.0**	**12:43**									

Assigned to **Spartak Moscow** (Russia) by **Chicago** (Norfolk-AHL), December 20, 2004.

RAFALSKI, Brian

(ra-FAWL-skee, BRIGH-uhn) **N.J.**

Defense. Shoots right. 5'10", 190 lbs. Born, Dearborn, MI, September 28, 1973.

Season	Club	League	GP	G	A	Pts	PIM	PP	SH	GW	S	%	+/-	TF	F%	Min	GP	G	A	Pts	PIM	PP	SH	GW	Min
1990-91	Madison Capitols	USHL	47	12	11	23	28																		
1991-92	U. of Wisconsin	WCHA	34	3	14	17	34																		
1992-93	U. of Wisconsin	WCHA	32	0	13	13	10																		
1993-94	U. of Wisconsin	WCHA	37	6	17	23	26																		
1994-95	U. of Wisconsin	WCHA	43	11	34	45	48																		
1995-96	Brynas IF Gavle	Sweden	40	4	14	18	26										9	0	1	1	2				
1996-97	HPK Hameenlinna	Finland	49	11	24	35	26										10	6	5	11	4				
1997-98	HIFK Helsinki	Finland	40	13	10	23	20										9	5	6	11	0				
1998-99	HIFK Helsinki	Finland	53	19	34	53	18										11	5	*9	*14	4				
	HIFK Helsinki	EuroHL	6	4	6	10	10										4	1	0	1	2				
99-2000♦	**New Jersey**	**NHL**	**75**	**5**	**27**	**32**	**28**	**1**	**0**	**1**	**128**	**3.9**	**21**	**1**	**0.0**	**18:51**	**23**	**2**	**6**	**8**	**8**	**0**	**0**	**1**	**21:25**
2000-01	**New Jersey**	**NHL**	**78**	**9**	**43**	**52**	**26**	**6**	**0**	**1**	**142**	**6.3**	**36**	**2**	**100.0**	**21:41**	**25**	**7**	**11**	**18**	**7**	**1**	**0**	**3**	**22:08**
2001-02	**New Jersey**	**NHL**	**76**	**7**	**40**	**47**	**18**	**2**	**0**	**4**	**125**	**5.6**	**15**	**0**	**0.0**	**22:08**	**6**	**3**	**2**	**5**	**4**	**3**	**0**	**0**	**21:45**
	United States	Olympics	6	1	2	3	2																		
2002-03♦	**New Jersey**	**NHL**	**79**	**3**	**37**	**40**	**14**	**2**	**0**	**0**	**178**	**1.7**	**18**	**1**	**0.0**	**23:09**	**23**	**2**	**9**	**11**	**8**	**2**	**0**	**0**	**25:46**
2003-04	**New Jersey**	**NHL**	**69**	**6**	**30**	**36**	**24**	**2**	**0**	**1**	**130**	**4.6**	**6**	**0**	**0.0**	**22:48**	**5**	**0**	**1**	**1**	**0**	**0**	**0**	**0**	**22:22**
2004-05			DID NOT PLAY																						
2005-06	**New Jersey**	**NHL**	**82**	**6**	**43**	**49**	**36**	**3**	**0**	**2**	**126**	**4.8**	**0**	**1**	**0.0**	**25:32**	**9**	**1**	**8**	**9**	**2**	**1**	**0**	**0**	**27:26**
	United States	Olympics	5	0	2	2	0																		
	NHL Totals		**459**	**36**	**220**	**256**	**146**	**16**	**0**	**9**	**829**	**4.3**		**5**	**40.0**	**22:24**	**91**	**15**	**37**	**52**	**29**	**7**	**0**	**4**	**23:23**

WCHA First All-Star Team (1995) • NCAA West First All-American Team (1995) • NHL All-Rookie Team (2000)

Played in NHL All-Star Game (2004)

Signed as a free agent by **New Jersey**, June 18, 1999.

RANGER, Paul

(RAIN-juhr, PAWL) **T.B.**

Defense. Shoots left. 6'2", 215 lbs. Born, Whitby, Ont., September 12, 1984. Tampa Bay's 7th choice, 183rd overall, in 2002 Entry Draft.

			Regular Season														Playoffs								
Season	Club	League	GP	G	A	Pts	PIM	PP	SH	GW	S	%	+/-	TF	F%	Min	GP	G	A	Pts	PIM	PP	SH	GW	Min
2000-01	Oshawa Generals	OHL	32	0	1	1	2	....	....	....	....	....	....	....	....	....	....	....	....	....	....	....	....	....	....
2001-02	Oshawa Generals	OHL	62	0	9	9	49	....	....	....	....	....	....	....	....	....	5	0	0	0	4	....	....	....	....
2002-03	Oshawa Generals	OHL	68	10	28	38	70	....	....	....	....	....	....	....	....	....	13	0	3	3	10	....	....	....	....
2003-04	Oshawa Generals	OHL	62	12	31	43	72	....	....	....	....	....	....	....	....	....	7	0	1	1	10	....	....	....	....
2004-05	Springfield	AHL	69	3	8	11	46	....	....	....	....	....	....	....	....	....	....	....	....	....	....	....	....	....	....
2005-06	**Tampa Bay**	**NHL**	**76**	**1**	**17**	**18**	**58**	**0**	**0**	**1**	**73**	**1.4**	**5**	**0**	**0.0**	**17:07**	**5**	**2**	**4**	**6**	**0**	**1**	**0**	**0**	**21:43**
	Springfield	AHL	1	1	2	3	0	....	....	....	....	....	....	....	....	....	....	....	....	....	....	....	....	....	....
	NHL Totals		**76**	**1**	**17**	**18**	**58**	**0**	**0**	**1**	**73**	**1.4**		**0**	**0.0**	**17:07**	**5**	**2**	**4**	**6**	**0**	**1**	**0**	**0**	**21:43**

RASMUSSEN, Erik

(RAS-moo-suhn, AIR-ihk) **N.J.**

Left wing/Center. Shoots left. 6'1", 215 lbs. Born, Minneapolis, MN, March 28, 1977. Buffalo's 1st choice, 7th overall, in 1996 Entry Draft.

Season	Club	League	GP	G	A	Pts	PIM	PP	SH	GW	S	%	+/-	TF	F%	Min	GP	G	A	Pts	PIM	PP	SH	GW	Min
1992-93	St. Louis Park	High-MN	23	16	24	40	50	....	....	....	....	....	....	....	....	....	....	....	....	....	....	....	....	....	....
1993-94	St. Louis Park	High-MN	18	25	18	43	80	....	....	....	....	....	....	....	....	....	....	....	....	....	....	....	....	....	....
1994-95	St. Louis Park	High-MN	23	19	33	52	80	....	....	....	....	....	....	....	....	....	....	....	....	....	....	....	....	....	....
1995-96	U. of Minnesota	WCHA	40	16	32	48	55	....	....	....	....	....	....	....	....	....	....	....	....	....	....	....	....	....	....
1996-97	U. of Minnesota	WCHA	34	15	12	27	*123	....	....	....	....	....	....	....	....	....	....	....	....	....	....	....	....	....	....
1997-98	**Buffalo**	**NHL**	**21**	**2**	**3**	**5**	**14**	**0**	**0**	**0**	**28**	**7.1**	**2**	....	....	....	....	....	....	....	....	....	....	....	....
	Rochester	AHL	53	9	14	23	83	....	....	....	....	....	....	....	....	....	1	0	0	0	5	....	....	....	....
1998-99	**Buffalo**	**NHL**	**42**	**3**	**7**	**10**	**37**	**0**	**0**	**0**	**40**	**7.5**	**6**	**67**	**40.3**	**12:22**	**21**	**2**	**4**	**6**	**18**	**0**	**0**	**1**	**12:51**
	Rochester	AHL	37	12	14	26	47	....	....	....	....	....	....	....	....	....	....	....	....	....	....	....	....	....	....
99-2000	**Buffalo**	**NHL**	**67**	**8**	**6**	**14**	**43**	**0**	**0**	**2**	**76**	**10.5**	**1**	**130**	**44.6**	**11:27**	**3**	**0**	**0**	**0**	**4**	**0**	**0**	**0**	**8:59**
2000-01	**Buffalo**	**NHL**	**82**	**12**	**19**	**31**	**51**	**1**	**0**	**3**	**95**	**12.6**	**0**	**565**	**43.7**	**13:47**	**3**	**0**	**1**	**1**	**0**	**0**	**0**	**0**	**16:26**
2001-02	**Buffalo**	**NHL**	**69**	**8**	**11**	**19**	**34**	**0**	**0**	**2**	**89**	**9.0**	**−1**	**236**	**39.8**	**13:03**	....	....	....	....	....	....	....	....	....
2002-03	**Los Angeles**	**NHL**	**57**	**4**	**12**	**16**	**28**	**0**	**0**	**1**	**75**	**5.3**	**−1**	**278**	**44.6**	**13:39**	....	....	....	....	....	....	....	....	....
2003-04	**New Jersey**	**NHL**	**69**	**7**	**6**	**13**	**41**	**0**	**0**	**0**	**68**	**10.3**	**5**	**423**	**44.4**	**11:34**	**5**	**0**	**2**	**2**	**2**	**0**	**0**	**0**	**14:44**
2004-05			DID NOT PLAY																						
2005-06	**New Jersey**	**NHL**	**67**	**5**	**5**	**10**	**32**	**1**	**0**	**0**	**45**	**11.1**	**−4**	**230**	**37.4**	**7:04**	**9**	**0**	**0**	**0**	**8**	**0**	**0**	**0**	**6:44**
	NHL Totals		**474**	**49**	**69**	**118**	**280**	**2**	**0**	**8**	**516**	**9.5**		**1929**	**42.7**	**11:51**	**41**	**2**	**7**	**9**	**32**	**0**	**0**	**1**	**11:43**

Minnesota High School Player of the Year (1995)

Traded to **Los Angeles** by **Buffalo** for Adam Mair and Los Angeles' 5th round choice (Thomas Morrow) in 2003 Entry Draft, July 24, 2002. Signed as a free agent by **New Jersey**, July 25, 2003.

RATHJE, Mike

(RATH-jee, MIGHK) **PHI.**

Defense. Shoots left. 6'5", 235 lbs. Born, Mannville, Alta., May 11, 1974. San Jose's 1st choice, 3rd overall, in 1992 Entry Draft.

Season	Club	League	GP	G	A	Pts	PIM	PP	SH	GW	S	%	+/-	TF	F%	Min	GP	G	A	Pts	PIM	PP	SH	GW	Min
1989-90	Sherwood Park	AMHL	33	6	11	17	30	....	....	....	....	....	....	....	....	....	6	1	1	2	2	....	....	....	....
1990-91	Medicine Hat	WHL	64	1	16	17	28	....	....	....	....	....	....	....	....	....	12	0	4	4	2	....	....	....	....
1991-92	Medicine Hat	WHL	67	11	23	34	99	....	....	....	....	....	....	....	....	....	4	0	1	1	2	....	....	....	....
1992-93	Medicine Hat	WHL	57	12	37	49	103	....	....	....	....	....	....	....	....	....	10	3	3	6	12	....	....	....	....
	Kansas City	IHL	....	....	....	....	....	....	....	....	....	....	....	....	....	....	5	0	0	0	12	....	....	....	....
1993-94	**San Jose**	**NHL**	**47**	**1**	**9**	**10**	**59**	**1**	**0**	**0**	**30**	**3.3**	**−9**	....	....	....	**1**	**0**	**0**	**0**	**0**	**0**	**0**	**0**	....
	Kansas City	IHL	6	0	2	2	0	....	....	....	....	....	....	....	....	....	....	....	....	....	....	....	....	....	....
1994-95	Kansas City	IHL	6	0	1	1	7	....	....	....	....	....	....	....	....	....	....	....	....	....	....	....	....	....	....
	San Jose	**NHL**	**42**	**2**	**7**	**9**	**29**	**0**	**0**	**0**	**38**	**5.3**	**−1**	....	....	....	**11**	**5**	**2**	**7**	**4**	**5**	**0**	**0**	....
1995-96	**San Jose**	**NHL**	**27**	**0**	**7**	**7**	**14**	**0**	**0**	**0**	**26**	**0.0**	**−16**	....	....	....	....	....	....	....	....	....	....	....	....
	Kansas City	IHL	36	6	11	17	34	....	....	....	....	....	....	....	....	....	....	....	....	....	....	....	....	....	....
1996-97	**San Jose**	**NHL**	**31**	**0**	**8**	**8**	**21**	**0**	**0**	**0**	**22**	**0.0**	**−1**	....	....	....	....	....	....	....	....	....	....	....	....
1997-98	**San Jose**	**NHL**	**81**	**3**	**12**	**15**	**59**	**1**	**0**	**0**	**61**	**4.9**	**−4**	....	....	....	**6**	**1**	**0**	**1**	**6**	**1**	**0**	**0**	....
1998-99	**San Jose**	**NHL**	**82**	**5**	**9**	**14**	**36**	**2**	**0**	**1**	**67**	**7.5**	**15**	**0**	**0.0**	**20:07**	**6**	**0**	**0**	**0**	**4**	**0**	**0**	**0**	**22:08**
99-2000	**San Jose**	**NHL**	**66**	**2**	**14**	**16**	**31**	**0**	**0**	**0**	**46**	**4.3**	**−2**	**0**	**0.0**	**22:11**	**12**	**1**	**3**	**4**	**8**	**0**	**0**	**0**	**21:32**
2000-01	**San Jose**	**NHL**	**81**	**0**	**11**	**11**	**48**	**0**	**0**	**0**	**89**	**0.0**	**7**	**0**	**0.0**	**22:20**	**6**	**0**	**1**	**1**	**4**	**0**	**0**	**0**	**24:20**
2001-02	**San Jose**	**NHL**	**52**	**5**	**12**	**17**	**48**	**4**	**0**	**0**	**56**	**8.9**	**23**	**0**	**0.0**	**21:31**	**12**	**1**	**3**	**4**	**6**	**1**	**0**	**0**	**23:29**
2002-03	**San Jose**	**NHL**	**82**	**7**	**22**	**29**	**48**	**3**	**0**	**1**	**147**	**4.8**	**−19**	**1**	**0.0**	**24:07**	....	....	....	....	....	....	....	....	....
2003-04	**San Jose**	**NHL**	**80**	**2**	**17**	**19**	**46**	**0**	**1**	**0**	**105**	**1.9**	**18**	**0**	**0.0**	**23:27**	**17**	**1**	**5**	**6**	**13**	**0**	**0**	**0**	**23:26**
2004-05			DID NOT PLAY																						
2005-06	**Philadelphia**	**NHL**	**79**	**3**	**21**	**24**	**46**	**1**	**1**	**1**	**55**	**5.5**	**22**	**0**	**0.0**	**20:08**	**6**	**0**	**0**	**0**	**6**	**0**	**0**	**0**	**16:27**
	NHL Totals		**750**	**30**	**149**	**179**	**485**	**12**	**2**	**3**	**742**	**4.0**		**1**	**0.0**	**22:00**	**77**	**9**	**14**	**23**	**51**	**7**	**0**	**0**	**22:18**

WHL East Second All-Star Team (1992, 1993)

• Missed majority of 1996-97 season recovering from groin injury suffered in game vs. Dallas, November 8, 1996. Signed as a free agent by **Philadelphia**, August 2, 2005.

READY, Ryan

(REH-dee, RIGH-yan)

Left wing. Shoots left. 6'2", 195 lbs. Born, Peterborough, Ont., November 7, 1978. Calgary's 8th choice, 100th overall, in 1997 Entry Draft.

Season	Club	League	GP	G	A	Pts	PIM	PP	SH	GW	S	%	+/-	TF	F%	Min	GP	G	A	Pts	PIM	PP	SH	GW	Min
1994-95	Peterborough	OPJHL	48	20	33	53	65	....	....	....	....	....	....	....	....	....	....	....	....	....	....	....	....	....	....
1995-96	Belleville Bulls	OHL	63	5	13	18	54	....	....	....	....	....	....	....	....	....	10	0	2	2	2	....	....	....	....
1996-97	Belleville Bulls	OHL	66	23	24	47	102	....	....	....	....	....	....	....	....	....	6	1	3	4	4	....	....	....	....
1997-98	Belleville Bulls	OHL	66	33	39	72	80	....	....	....	....	....	....	....	....	....	10	5	2	7	12	....	....	....	....
1998-99	Belleville Bulls	OHL	63	33	59	92	73	....	....	....	....	....	....	....	....	....	21	10	28	38	22	....	....	....	....
99-2000	Syracuse Crunch	AHL	70	4	12	16	59	....	....	....	....	....	....	....	....	....	2	0	0	0	0	....	....	....	....
2000-01	Kansas City	IHL	67	10	15	25	75	....	....	....	....	....	....	....	....	....	....	....	....	....	....	....	....	....	....
2001-02	Manitoba Moose	AHL	72	23	32	55	73	....	....	....	....	....	....	....	....	....	7	5	1	6	4	....	....	....	....
2002-03	Manitoba Moose	AHL	68	24	26	50	52	....	....	....	....	....	....	....	....	....	14	2	5	7	2	....	....	....	....
2003-04	Manitoba Moose	AHL	64	7	18	25	55	....	....	....	....	....	....	....	....	....	....	....	....	....	....	....	....	....	....
	Worcester IceCats	AHL	16	2	5	7	10	....	....	....	....	....	....	....	....	....	10	1	2	3	10	....	....	....	....
2004-05	Philadelphia	AHL	72	7	18	25	104	....	....	....	....	....	....	....	....	....	19	2	11	13	6	....	....	....	....
2005-06	**Philadelphia**	**NHL**	**7**	**0**	**1**	**1**	**0**	**0**	**0**	**0**	**9**	**0.0**	**0**	**2**	**50.0**	**8:08**	....	....	....	....	....	....	....	....	....
	Philadelphia	AHL	40	7	10	17	67	....	....	....	....	....	....	....	....	....	....	....	....	....	....	....	....	....	....
	NHL Totals		**7**	**0**	**1**	**1**	**0**	**0**	**0**	**0**	**9**	**0.0**		**2**	**50.0**	**8:08**	....	....	....	....	....	....	....	....	....

OHL First All-Star Team (1999)

Signed as a free agent by **Vancouver**, June 16, 1999. Traded to **St. Louis** by **Vancouver** for Sergei Varlamov, March 9, 2004. Signed as a free agent by **Philadelphia**, August 23, 2004.

REASONER, Marty

(REE-sohn-uhr, MAHR-tee) **EDM.**

Center. Shoots left. 6'1", 200 lbs. Born, Honeoye Falls, NY, February 26, 1977. St. Louis' 1st choice, 14th overall, in 1996 Entry Draft.

Season	Club	League	GP	G	A	Pts	PIM	PP	SH	GW	S	%	+/-	TF	F%	Min	GP	G	A	Pts	PIM	PP	SH	GW	Min
1993-94	Deerfield	High-MA	22	27	25	52	....	....	....	....	....	....	....	....	....	....	....	....	....	....	....	....	....	....	....
1994-95	Deerfield	High-MA	26	25	32	57	14	....	....	....	....	....	....	....	....	....	....	....	....	....	....	....	....	....	....
1995-96	Boston College	H-East	34	16	29	45	32	....	....	....	....	....	....	....	....	....	....	....	....	....	....	....	....	....	....
1996-97	Boston College	H-East	35	20	24	44	31	....	....	....	....	....	....	....	....	....	....	....	....	....	....	....	....	....	....
1997-98	Boston College	H-East	42	*33	40	*73	56	....	....	....	....	....	....	....	....	....	....	....	....	....	....	....	....	....	....
1998-99	**St. Louis**	**NHL**	**22**	**3**	**7**	**10**	**8**	**1**	**0**	**0**	**33**	**9.1**	**2**	**224**	**53.6**	**13:55**	....	....	....	....	....	....	....	....	....
	Worcester IceCats	AHL	44	17	22	39	24	....	....	....	....	....	....	....	....	....	4	2	1	3	6	....	....	....	....
99-2000	**St. Louis**	**NHL**	**32**	**10**	**14**	**24**	**20**	**3**	**0**	**0**	**51**	**19.6**	**9**	**379**	**49.6**	**15:20**	**7**	**2**	**1**	**3**	**4**	**1**	**0**	**0**	**13:12**
	Worcester IceCats	AHL	44	23	28	51	39	....	....	....	....	....	....	....	....	....	....	....	....	....	....	....	....	....	....
2000-01	**St. Louis**	**NHL**	**41**	**4**	**9**	**13**	**14**	**0**	**0**	**0**	**65**	**6.2**	**−5**	**454**	**53.1**	**14:00**	**10**	**3**	**1**	**4**	**0**	**0**	**0**	**1**	**12:21**
	Worcester IceCats	AHL	34	17	18	35	25	....	....	....	....	....	....	....	....	....	....	....	....	....	....	....	....	....	....
2001-02	**Edmonton**	**NHL**	**52**	**6**	**5**	**11**	**41**	**3**	**0**	**2**	**66**	**9.1**	**0**	**470**	**55.5**	**11:44**	....	....	....	....	....	....	....	....	....
2002-03	**Edmonton**	**NHL**	**70**	**11**	**20**	**31**	**28**	**2**	**2**	**0**	**102**	**10.8**	**19**	**968**	**53.5**	**14:50**	**6**	**1**	**0**	**1**	**2**	**1**	**0**	**0**	**14:22**
	Hamilton	AHL	2	0	2	2	2	....	....	....	....	....	....	....	....	....	....	....	....	....	....	....	....	....	....
2003-04	**Edmonton**	**NHL**	**17**	**2**	**6**	**8**	**10**	**0**	**1**	**0**	**28**	**7.1**	**5**	**321**	**52.7**	**16:30**	....	....	....	....	....	....	....	....	....
2004-05	Salzburg	Austria	11	5	4	9	12	....	....	....	....	....	....	....	....	....	....	....	....	....	....	....	....	....	....

Season	Club	League	GP	G	A	Pts	PIM	PP	SH	GW	S	%	+/-	TF	F%	Min	GP	G	A	Pts	PIM	PP	SH	GW	Min
			Regular Season														**Playoffs**								
2005-06	**Edmonton**	**NHL**	**58**	**9**	**17**	**26**	**20**	**5**	**0**	**1**	**63**	**14.3**	**-12**	**524**	**52.5**	**12:45**	....	....	....	....	....	....	....	....	....
	Boston	**NHL**	**19**	**2**	**6**	**8**	**8**	**1**	**0**	**0**	**39**	**5.1**	**-2**	**227**	**46.7**	**15:09**	....	....	....	....	....	....	....	....	....
	NHL Totals		**311**	**47**	**84**	**131**	**149**	**15**	**3**	**3**	**447**	**10.5**		**3567**	**52.6**	**13:55**	**23**	**6**	**2**	**8**	**6**	**2**	**0**	**1**	**13:08**

Hockey East Rookie of the Year (1996) • Hockey East First All-Star Team (1997, 1998) • NCAA East First All-American Team (1998) • NCAA Championship All-Tournament Team (1998)

Traded to **Edmonton** by **St. Louis** with Jochen Hecht and Jan Horacek for Doug Weight and Michel Riesen, July 1, 2001. • Missed majority of 2003-04 season recovering from ankle (November 8, 2003 vs. Toronto) and knee (January 13, 2004 vs. Florida) injuries. Signed as a free agent by **Salzburg** (Austria), January 30, 2005. Traded to **Boston** by **Edmonton** with Yan Stastny and Edmonton's 2nd round choice (Milan Lucic) in 2006 Entry Draft for Sergei Samsonov, March 9, 2006. Signed as a free agent by **Edmonton**, July 4, 2006.

RECCHI, Mark
(REH-kee, MAHRK) **PIT.**

Right wing. Shoots left. 5'10", 190 lbs. Born, Kamloops, B.C., February 1, 1968. Pittsburgh's 4th choice, 67th overall, in 1988 Entry Draft.

Season	Club	League	GP	G	A	Pts	PIM	PP	SH	GW	S	%	+/-	TF	F%	Min	GP	G	A	Pts	PIM	PP	SH	GW	Min
1984-85	Langley Eagles	BCJHL	51	26	39	65	39	....	....	....	....	....	....	....	....	....	....	....	....	....	....	....	....	....	....
	New Westminster	WHL	4	1	0	1	0	....	....	....	....	....	....	....	....	....	....	....	....	....	....	....	....	....	....
1985-86	New Westminster	WHL	72	21	40	61	55	....	....	....	....	....	....	....	....	....	....	....	....	....	....	....	....	....	....
1986-87	Kamloops Chiefs	WHL	40	26	50	76	63	....	....	....	....	....	....	....	....	....	13	3	16	19	17	....	....	....	....
1987-88	Kamloops Chiefs	WHL	62	61	*93	154	75	....	....	....	....	....	....	....	....	....	17	10	*21	*31	18	....	....	....	....
1988-89	**Pittsburgh**	**NHL**	**15**	**1**	**1**	**2**	**0**	**0**	**0**	**0**	**11**	**9.1**	**-2**	....	....	....	....	....	....	....	....	....	....	....	....
	Muskegon	IHL	63	50	49	99	86	....	....	....	....	....	....	....	....	....	14	7	*14	*21	28	....	....	....	....
1989-90	**Pittsburgh**	**NHL**	**74**	**30**	**37**	**67**	**44**	**6**	**2**	**4**	**143**	**21.0**	**6**	....	....	....	....	....	....	....	....	....	....	....	....
	Muskegon	IHL	4	7	4	11	2	....	....	....	....	....	....	....	....	....	....	....	....	....	....	....	....	....	....
1990-91 ♦	**Pittsburgh**	**NHL**	**78**	**40**	**73**	**113**	**48**	**12**	**0**	**9**	**184**	**21.7**	**0**	....	....	....	**24**	**10**	**24**	**34**	**33**	**5**	**0**	**2**	....
1991-92	**Pittsburgh**	**NHL**	**58**	**33**	**37**	**70**	**78**	**16**	**1**	**4**	**156**	**21.2**	**-16**	....	....	....	....	....	....	....	....	....	....	....	....
	Philadelphia	**NHL**	**22**	**10**	**17**	**27**	**18**	**4**	**0**	**1**	**54**	**18.5**	**-5**	....	....	....	....	....	....	....	....	....	....	....	....
1992-93	**Philadelphia**	**NHL**	**84**	**53**	**70**	**123**	**95**	**15**	**4**	**6**	**274**	**19.3**	**1**	....	....	....	....	....	....	....	....	....	....	....	....
1993-94	**Philadelphia**	**NHL**	**84**	**40**	**67**	**107**	**46**	**11**	**0**	**5**	**217**	**18.4**	**-2**	....	....	....	....	....	....	....	....	....	....	....	....
1994-95	**Philadelphia**	**NHL**	**10**	**2**	**3**	**5**	**12**	**1**	**0**	**2**	**17**	**11.8**	**-6**	....	....	....	....	....	....	....	....	....	....	....	....
	Montreal	**NHL**	**39**	**14**	**29**	**43**	**16**	**8**	**0**	**1**	**104**	**13.5**	**-3**	....	....	....	....	....	....	....	....	....	....	....	....
1995-96	**Montreal**	**NHL**	**82**	**28**	**50**	**78**	**69**	**11**	**2**	**6**	**191**	**14.7**	**20**	....	....	....	**6**	**3**	**3**	**6**	**0**	**3**	**0**	**0**	....
1996-97	**Montreal**	**NHL**	**82**	**34**	**46**	**80**	**58**	**7**	**2**	**3**	**202**	**16.8**	**-1**	....	....	....	**5**	**4**	**2**	**6**	**2**	**0**	**0**	**0**	....
1997-98	**Montreal**	**NHL**	**82**	**32**	**42**	**74**	**51**	**9**	**1**	**6**	**216**	**14.8**	**11**	....	....	....	**10**	**4**	**8**	**12**	**6**	**0**	**0**	**2**	....
	Canada	Olympics	5	0	2	2	0	....	....	....	....	....	....	....	....	....	....	....	....	....	....	....	....	....	....
1998-99	**Montreal**	**NHL**	**61**	**12**	**35**	**47**	**28**	**3**	**0**	**2**	**152**	**7.9**	**-4**	**239**	**44.8**	**20:37**	....	....	....	....	....	....	....	....	....
	Philadelphia	**NHL**	**10**	**4**	**2**	**6**	**6**	**0**	**0**	**0**	**19**	**21.1**	**-3**	**4**	**25.0**	**19:30**	**6**	**0**	**1**	**1**	**2**	**0**	**0**	**0**	**19:35**
99-2000	**Philadelphia**	**NHL**	**82**	**28**	***63**	**91**	**50**	**7**	**1**	**5**	**223**	**12.6**	**20**	**353**	**49.6**	**21:43**	**18**	**6**	**12**	**18**	**6**	**2**	**0**	**1**	**23:10**
2000-01	**Philadelphia**	**NHL**	**69**	**27**	**50**	**77**	**33**	**7**	**1**	**8**	**191**	**14.1**	**15**	**138**	**42.8**	**21:40**	**6**	**2**	**2**	**4**	**2**	**1**	**0**	**1**	**23:00**
2001-02	**Philadelphia**	**NHL**	**80**	**22**	**42**	**64**	**46**	**7**	**2**	**4**	**205**	**10.7**	**5**	**82**	**53.7**	**20:40**	**4**	**0**	**0**	**0**	**2**	**0**	**0**	**0**	**21:10**
2002-03	**Philadelphia**	**NHL**	**79**	**20**	**32**	**52**	**35**	**8**	**1**	**3**	**171**	**11.7**	**0**	**168**	**52.4**	**18:50**	**13**	**7**	**3**	**10**	**2**	**1**	**0**	**1**	**18:00**
2003-04	**Philadelphia**	**NHL**	**82**	**26**	**49**	**75**	**47**	**14**	**1**	**5**	**167**	**15.6**	**18**	**298**	**52.4**	**17:12**	**18**	**4**	**2**	**6**	**4**	**2**	**0**	**0**	**16:46**
2004-05			DID NOT PLAY																						
2005-06	**Pittsburgh**	**NHL**	**63**	**24**	**33**	**57**	**56**	**11**	**0**	**2**	**164**	**14.6**	**-28**	**387**	**48.3**	**21:17**	....	....	....	....	....	....	....	....	....
	♦ **Carolina**	**NHL**	**20**	**4**	**3**	**7**	**12**	**2**	**0**	**1**	**35**	**11.4**	**-8**	**6**	**33.3**	**17:37**	**25**	**7**	**9**	**16**	**18**	**2**	**0**	**2**	**16:34**
	NHL Totals		**1256**	**484**	**781**	**1265**	**848**	**159**	**18**	**77**	**3096**	**15.6**		**1675**	**48.9**	**20:06**	**135**	**47**	**66**	**113**	**77**	**16**	**0**	**9**	**18:58**

WHL West First All-Star Team (1988) • IHL Second All-Star Team (1989) • NHL Second All-Star Team (1992)

Played in NHL All-Star Game (1991, 1993, 1994, 1997, 1998, 1999, 2000)

Traded to **Philadelphia** by **Pittsburgh** with Brian Benning and Los Angeles' 1st round choice (previously acquired, Philadelphia selected Jason Bowen) in 1992 Entry Draft for Rick Tocchet, Kjell Samuelsson, Ken Wregget and Philadelphia's 3rd round choice (Dave Roche) in 1993 Entry Draft, February 19, 1992. Traded to **Montreal** by **Philadelphia** with Philadelphia's 3rd round choice (Martin Hohenberger) in 1995 Entry Draft for Eric Desjardins, Gilbert Dionne and John LeClair, February 9, 1995. Traded to **Philadelphia** by **Montreal** for Danius Zubrus, Philadelphia's 2nd round choice (Matt Carkner) in 1999 Entry Draft and NY Islanders' 6th round choice (previously acquired, Montreal selected Scott Selig) in 2000 Entry Draft, March 10, 1999. Signed as a free agent by **Pittsburgh**, July 9, 2004. Traded to **Carolina** by **Pittsburgh** for Niklas Nordgren, Krys Kolanos and Carolina's 2nd round choice (later traded to San Jose) in 2007 Entry Draft, March 9, 2006. Signed as a free agent by **Pittsburgh**, July 25, 2006.

REDDEN, Wade
(REH-duhn, WAYD) **OTT.**

Defense. Shoots left. 6'2", 212 lbs. Born, Lloydminster, Sask., June 12, 1977. NY Islanders' 1st choice, 2nd overall, in 1995 Entry Draft.

Season	Club	League	GP	G	A	Pts	PIM	PP	SH	GW	S	%	+/-	TF	F%	Min	GP	G	A	Pts	PIM	PP	SH	GW	Min
1992-93	Lloydminster	AJHL	34	4	11	15	64	....	....	....	....	....	....	....	....	....	....	....	....	....	....	....	....	....	....
1993-94	Brandon	WHL	63	4	35	39	98	....	....	....	....	....	....	....	....	....	14	2	4	6	10	....	....	....	....
1994-95	Brandon	WHL	64	14	46	60	83	....	....	....	....	....	....	....	....	....	18	5	10	15	8	....	....	....	....
1995-96	Brandon	WHL	51	9	45	54	55	....	....	....	....	....	....	....	....	....	19	5	10	15	19	....	....	....	....
1996-97	**Ottawa**	**NHL**	**82**	**6**	**24**	**30**	**41**	**2**	**0**	**1**	**102**	**5.9**	**1**	....	....	....	**7**	**1**	**3**	**4**	**2**	**0**	**0**	**0**	....
1997-98	**Ottawa**	**NHL**	**80**	**8**	**14**	**22**	**27**	**3**	**0**	**2**	**103**	**7.8**	**17**	....	....	....	**9**	**0**	**2**	**2**	**2**	**0**	**0**	**0**	....
1998-99	**Ottawa**	**NHL**	**72**	**8**	**21**	**29**	**54**	**3**	**0**	**1**	**127**	**6.3**	**7**	**0**	**0.0**	**23:27**	**4**	**1**	**2**	**3**	**2**	**1**	**0**	**0**	**26:39**
99-2000	**Ottawa**	**NHL**	**81**	**10**	**26**	**36**	**49**	**3**	**0**	**2**	**163**	**6.1**	**-1**	**0**	**0.0**	**23:43**	....	....	....	....	....	....	....	....	....
2000-01	**Ottawa**	**NHL**	**78**	**10**	**37**	**47**	**49**	**4**	**0**	**0**	**159**	**6.3**	**22**	**0**	**0.0**	**25:17**	**4**	**0**	**0**	**0**	**0**	**0**	**0**	**0**	**27:29**
2001-02	**Ottawa**	**NHL**	**79**	**9**	**25**	**34**	**48**	**4**	**1**	**1**	**156**	**5.8**	**22**	**1**	**0.0**	**25:06**	**12**	**3**	**2**	**5**	**6**	**1**	**0**	**1**	**27:56**
2002-03	**Ottawa**	**NHL**	**76**	**10**	**35**	**45**	**70**	**4**	**0**	**3**	**154**	**6.5**	**23**	**0**	**0.0**	**25:24**	**18**	**1**	**8**	**9**	**10**	**0**	**0**	**1**	**25:28**
2003-04	**Ottawa**	**NHL**	**81**	**17**	**26**	**43**	**65**	**12**	**0**	**3**	**175**	**9.7**	**21**	**0**	**0.0**	**24:54**	**7**	**1**	**0**	**1**	**2**	**1**	**0**	**0**	**26:47**
2004-05			DID NOT PLAY																						
2005-06	**Ottawa**	**NHL**	**65**	**10**	**40**	**50**	**63**	**8**	**0**	**4**	**153**	**6.5**	**35**	**1**	**100.0**	**23:28**	**9**	**2**	**8**	**10**	**10**	**2**	**0**	**1**	**25:06**
	Canada	Olympics	6	1	0	1	0	....	....	....	....	....	....	....	....	....	....	....	....	....	....	....	....	....	....
	NHL Totals		**694**	**88**	**248**	**336**	**466**	**43**	**1**	**17**	**1292**	**6.8**		**2**	**50.0**	**24:30**	**70**	**9**	**25**	**34**	**34**	**5**	**0**	**3**	**26:22**

WHL Rookie of the Year (1994) • WHL East Second All-Star Team (1995) • WHL East First All-Star Team (1996) • Memorial Cup Tournament All-Star Team (1996)

Played in NHL All-Star Game (2002)

Traded to **Ottawa** by **NY Islanders** with Damian Rhodes for Don Beaupre, Martin Straka and Bryan Berard, January 23, 1996.

REGEHR, Richie
(reh-GEER, RIH-chee) **CGY.**

Defense. Shoots right. 6', 190 lbs. Born, Bundung, Indonesia, January 17, 1983.

Season	Club	League	GP	G	A	Pts	PIM	PP	SH	GW	S	%	+/-	TF	F%	Min	GP	G	A	Pts	PIM	PP	SH	GW	Min
99-2000	Kelowna Rockets	WHL	50	6	8	14	22	....	....	....	....	....	....	....	....	....	5	0	1	1	0	....	....	....	....
2000-01	Kelowna Rockets	WHL	71	10	27	37	68	....	....	....	....	....	....	....	....	....	6	0	1	1	4	....	....	....	....
2001-02	Kelowna Rockets	WHL	15	1	9	10	12	....	....	....	....	....	....	....	....	....	....	....	....	....	....	....	....	....	....
	Portland	WHL	37	7	27	34	50	....	....	....	....	....	....	....	....	....	7	2	5	7	8	....	....	....	....
2002-03	Portland	WHL	67	16	45	61	115	....	....	....	....	....	....	....	....	....	7	2	2	4	8	....	....	....	....
2003-04	Portland	WHL	65	9	34	43	88	....	....	....	....	....	....	....	....	....	5	0	1	1	6	....	....	....	....
2004-05	Lowell	AHL	64	9	16	25	60	....	....	....	....	....	....	....	....	....	11	1	6	7	2	....	....	....	....
2005-06	**Calgary**	**NHL**	**14**	**0**	**2**	**2**	**6**	**0**	**0**	**0**	**12**	**0.0**	**0**	**0**	**0.0**	**11:21**	....	....	....	....	....	....	....	....	....
	Omaha	AHL	48	7	23	30	56	....	....	....	....	....	....	....	....	....	....	....	....	....	....	....	....	....	....
	NHL Totals		**14**	**0**	**2**	**2**	**6**	**0**	**0**	**0**	**12**	**0.0**		**0**	**0.0**	**11:21**	....	....	....	....	....	....	....	....	....

Signed as a free agent by **Calgary**, July 6, 2004.

REGEHR, Robyn
(reh-GEER, RAW-bihn) **CGY.**

Defense. Shoots left. 6'2", 226 lbs. Born, Recife, Brazil, April 19, 1980. Colorado's 3rd choice, 19th overall, in 1998 Entry Draft.

Season	Club	League	GP	G	A	Pts	PIM	PP	SH	GW	S	%	+/-	TF	F%	Min	GP	G	A	Pts	PIM	PP	SH	GW	Min
1995-96	Prince Albert	SMHL	59	8	24	32	157	....	....	....	....	....	....	....	....	....	....	....	....	....	....	....	....	....	....
1996-97	Kamloops Blazers	WHL	64	4	19	23	96	....	....	....	....	....	....	....	....	....	5	0	1	1	18	....	....	....	....
1997-98	Kamloops Blazers	WHL	65	4	10	14	120	....	....	....	....	....	....	....	....	....	5	0	3	3	8	....	....	....	....
1998-99	Kamloops Blazers	WHL	54	12	20	32	130	....	....	....	....	....	....	....	....	....	12	1	4	5	21	....	....	....	....
99-2000	**Calgary**	**NHL**	**57**	**5**	**7**	**12**	**46**	**2**	**0**	**0**	**64**	**7.8**	**-2**	**0**	**0.0**	**18:24**	....	....	....	....	....	....	....	....	....
	Saint John Flames	AHL	5	0	0	0	0	....	....	....	....	....	....	....	....	....	....	....	....	....	....	....	....	....	....
2000-01	**Calgary**	**NHL**	**71**	**1**	**3**	**4**	**70**	**0**	**0**	**0**	**62**	**1.6**	**-7**	**1**	**0.0**	**19:43**	....	....	....	....	....	....	....	....	....
2001-02	**Calgary**	**NHL**	**77**	**2**	**6**	**8**	**93**	**0**	**0**	**0**	**82**	**2.4**	**-24**	**1**	**0.0**	**20:54**	....	....	....	....	....	....	....	....	....
2002-03	**Calgary**	**NHL**	**76**	**0**	**12**	**12**	**87**	**0**	**0**	**0**	**109**	**0.0**	**-9**	**1**	**100.0**	**22:45**	....	....	....	....	....	....	....	....	....
2003-04	**Calgary**	**NHL**	**82**	**4**	**14**	**18**	**74**	**2**	**0**	**1**	**106**	**3.8**	**14**	**2**	**50.0**	**22:21**	**26**	**2**	**7**	**9**	**20**	**0**	**0**	**0**	**26:27**
2004-05			DID NOT PLAY																						
2005-06	**Calgary**	**NHL**	**68**	**6**	**20**	**26**	**67**	**5**	**0**	**2**	**89**	**6.7**	**6**	**1**	**100.0**	**23:08**	**7**	**1**	**3**	**4**	**6**	**1**	**0**	**0**	**22:22**
	Canada	Olympics	6	0	1	1	2	....	....	....	....	....	....	....	....	....	....	....	....	....	....	....	....	....	....
	NHL Totals		**431**	**18**	**62**	**80**	**437**	**9**	**0**	**3**	**512**	**3.5**		**5**	**60.0**	**21:20**	**33**	**3**	**10**	**13**	**26**	**1**	**0**	**0**	**25:35**

WHL West First All-Star Team (1999)

Traded to **Calgary** by **Colorado** with Rene Corbet, Wade Belak and Colorado's 2nd round compensatory choice (Jarret Stoll) in 2000 Entry Draft for Theoren Fleury and Chris Dingman, February 28, 1999.

REGIER, Steve

(reh-GEER, STEEV) **NYI**

Left wing. Shoots left. 6'4", 194 lbs. Born, Edmonton, Alta., August 31, 1984. NY Islanders' 5th choice, 148th overall, in 2004 Entry Draft.

			Regular Season														Playoffs								
Season	Club	League	GP	G	A	Pts	PIM	PP	SH	GW	S	%	+/-	TF	F%	Min	GP	G	A	Pts	PIM	PP	SH	GW	Min
2000-01	Leduc Oil Kings	AMHL	35	22	39	61	135	....	....	....	....	....	....	....	....	....	....	....	....	....	....	....	....	....	....
2001-02	Medicine Hat	WHL	59	1	4	5	31	....	....	....	....	....	....	....	....	....	....	....	....	....	....	....	....	....	....
2002-03	Medicine Hat	WHL	61	11	10	21	114	....	....	....	....	....	....	....	....	....	11	2	2	4	20	....	....	....	....
2003-04	Medicine Hat	WHL	72	25	35	60	111	....	....	....	....	....	....	....	....	....	18	5	11	16	20	....	....	....	....
2004-05	Bridgeport	AHL	75	7	15	22	43	....	....	....	....	....	....	....	....	....	....	....	....	....	....	....	....	....	....
2005-06	**NY Islanders**	**NHL**	**9**	**0**	**0**	**0**	**0**	**0**	**0**	**0**	**4**	**0.0**	**–1**	**0**	**0.0**	**6:02**	....	....	....	....	....	....	....	....	....
	Bridgeport	AHL	73	16	21	37	54	....	....	....	....	....	....	....	....	....	7	0	2	2	6	....	....	....	....
	NHL Totals		**9**	**0**	**0**	**0**	**0**	**0**	**0**	**0**	**4**	**0.0**		**0**	**0.0**	**6:02**	....	....	....	....	....	....	....	....	....

REICH, Jeremy

(REECH, JAIR-eh-MEE) **BOS.**

Left wing. Shoots left. 6'1", 204 lbs. Born, Craik, Sask., February 11, 1979. Chicago's 3rd choice, 39th overall, in 1997 Entry Draft.

Season	Club	League	GP	G	A	Pts	PIM	PP	SH	GW	S	%	+/-	TF	F%	Min	GP	G	A	Pts	PIM	PP	SH	GW	Min
1993-94	Pilote Butte	SAHA	80	70	65	135	120	....	....	....	....	....	....	....	....	....	....	....	....	....	....	....	....	....	....
1994-95	Sask. Contacts	SMHL	35	13	20	33	81	....	....	....	....	....	....	....	....	....	....	....	....	....	....	....	....	....	....
1995-96	Seattle	WHL	65	11	11	22	88	....	....	....	....	....	....	....	....	....	5	0	1	1	10	....	....	....	....
1996-97	Seattle	WHL	62	19	31	50	134	....	....	....	....	....	....	....	....	....	15	2	5	7	36	....	....	....	....
1997-98	Seattle	WHL	43	24	23	47	121	....	....	....	....	....	....	....	....	....	....	....	....	....	....	....	....	....	....
	Swift Current	WHL	22	8	8	16	47	....	....	....	....	....	....	....	....	....	12	5	6	11	37	....	....	....	....
1998-99	Swift Current	WHL	67	21	28	49	220	....	....	....	....	....	....	....	....	....	6	0	3	3	26	....	....	....	....
99-2000	Swift Current	WHL	72	33	58	91	167	....	....	....	....	....	....	....	....	....	12	2	10	12	19	....	....	....	....
2000-01	Syracuse Crunch	AHL	56	6	9	15	108	....	....	....	....	....	....	....	....	....	5	0	0	0	6	....	....	....	....
2001-02	Syracuse Crunch	AHL	59	9	7	16	178	....	....	....	....	....	....	....	....	....	10	4	0	4	16	....	....	....	....
2002-03	Syracuse Crunch	AHL	78	14	13	27	195	....	....	....	....	....	....	....	....	....	....	....	....	....	....	....	....	....	....
2003-04	**Columbus**	**NHL**	**9**	**0**	**1**	**1**	**20**	**0**	**0**	**0**	**3**	**0.0**	**–3**	**0**	**0.0**	**7:38**	....	....	....	....	....	....	....	....	....
	Syracuse Crunch	AHL	72	14	37	51	150	....	....	....	....	....	....	....	....	....	6	1	1	2	13	....	....	....	....
2004-05	Syracuse Crunch	AHL	50	4	5	9	189	....	....	....	....	....	....	....	....	....	....	....	....	....	....	....	....	....	....
	Houston Aeros	AHL	18	3	4	7	34	....	....	....	....	....	....	....	....	....	5	0	1	1	28	....	....	....	....
2005-06	Providence Bruins	AHL	77	8	15	23	235	....	....	....	....	....	....	....	....	....	6	0	0	0	27	....	....	....	....
	NHL Totals		**9**	**0**	**1**	**1**	**20**	**0**	**0**	**0**	**3**	**0.0**		**0**	**0.0**	**7:38**	....	....	....	....	....	....	....	....	....

Signed as a free agent by **Columbus**, May 17, 2000. Loaned to **Houston** (AHL) by **Syracuse** (AHL) for the loan of Jason Beckett, March 10, 2005. Signed as a free agent by **Boston**, September 7, 2005.

REID, Brandon

(REED, BRAN-duhn) **VAN.**

Center. Shoots right. 5'8", 185 lbs. Born, Kirkland, Que., March 9, 1981. Vancouver's 5th choice, 208th overall, in 2000 Entry Draft.

Season	Club	League	GP	G	A	Pts	PIM	PP	SH	GW	S	%	+/-	TF	F%	Min	GP	G	A	Pts	PIM	PP	SH	GW	Min
1996-97	Lac St-Louis Lions	QAAA	44	17	34	51	....	....	....	....	....	....	....	....	....	....	7	2	3	5	....	....	....	....	....
1997-98	Halifax	QMJHL	67	13	21	36	6	....	....	....	....	....	....	....	....	....	5	1	0	1	15	....	....	....	....
1998-99	Halifax	QMJHL	70	32	25	57	33	....	....	....	....	....	....	....	....	....	5	2	2	4	0	....	....	....	....
99-2000	Halifax	QMJHL	62	44	80	124	10	....	....	....	....	....	....	....	....	....	10	7	11	18	4	....	....	....	....
2000-01	Val-d'Or Foreurs	QMJHL	57	45	81	126	18	....	....	....	....	....	....	....	....	....	21	13	29	42	14	....	....	....	....
2001-02	Manitoba Moose	AHL	60	18	19	37	6	....	....	....	....	....	....	....	....	....	7	0	3	3	0	....	....	....	....
2002-03	**Vancouver**	**NHL**	**7**	**2**	**3**	**5**	**0**	**0**	**0**	**0**	**15**	**13.3**	**4**	**69**	**55.1**	**9:47**	**9**	**0**	**1**	**1**	**0**	**0**	**0**	**0**	**9:36**
	Manitoba Moose	AHL	73	18	36	54	18	....	....	....	....	....	....	....	....	....	1	1	1	2	0	....	....	....	....
2003-04	**Vancouver**	**NHL**	**3**	**0**	**1**	**1**	**0**	**0**	**0**	**0**	**2**	**0.0**	**1**	**38**	**47.4**	**9:21**	....	....	....	....	....	....	....	....	....
	Manitoba Moose	AHL	73	19	39	58	20	....	....	....	....	....	....	....	....	....	....	....	....	....	....	....	....	....	....
2004-05	Hamburg Freezers	Germany	45	18	29	47	41	....	....	....	....	....	....	....	....	....	6	0	3	3	4	....	....	....	....
2005-06	Rapperswil	Swiss	44	16	18	34	14	....	....	....	....	....	....	....	....	....	12	4	7	11	14	....	....	....	....
	NHL Totals		**10**	**2**	**4**	**6**	**0**	**0**	**0**	**0**	**17**	**11.8**		**107**	**52.3**	**9:40**	**9**	**0**	**1**	**1**	**0**	**0**	**0**	**0**	**9:36**

QMJHL Second All-Star Team (2000) • George Parsons Trophy (Memorial Cup Tournament Most Sportsmanlike Player) (2000, 2001) • QMJHL First All-Star Team (2001) • Canadian Major Junior Sportsman of the Year (2001)

Signed as a free agent by **Hamburg** (Germany), July 7, 2004. Signed as a free agent by **Rapperswil** (Swiss), April 1, 2005.

REID, Darren

(REED, DAIR-uhn) **T.B.**

Right wing. Shoots right. 6'2", 205 lbs. Born, Lac La Biche, Alta., May 8, 1983. Tampa Bay's 11th choice, 256th overall, in 2002 Entry Draft.

Season	Club	League	GP	G	A	Pts	PIM	PP	SH	GW	S	%	+/-	TF	F%	Min	GP	G	A	Pts	PIM	PP	SH	GW	Min
2000-01	Drayton Valley	AJHL	55	8	18	26	116	....	....	....	....	....	....	....	....	....	....	....	....	....	....	....	....	....	....
2001-02	Drayton Valley	AJHL	31	9	12	21	195	....	....	....	....	....	....	....	....	....	....	....	....	....	....	....	....	....	....
	Medicine Hat	WHL	37	8	9	17	70	....	....	....	....	....	....	....	....	....	....	....	....	....	....	....	....	....	....
2002-03	Medicine Hat	WHL	63	14	30	44	163	....	....	....	....	....	....	....	....	....	11	5	0	5	19	....	....	....	....
2003-04	Medicine Hat	WHL	67	33	48	81	194	....	....	....	....	....	....	....	....	....	20	*13	8	21	31	....	....	....	....
2004-05	Springfield	AHL	56	3	19	22	99	....	....	....	....	....	....	....	....	....	....	....	....	....	....	....	....	....	....
2005-06	**Tampa Bay**	**NHL**	**7**	**0**	**1**	**1**	**0**	**0**	**0**	**0**	**3**	**0.0**	**–2**	**0**	**0.0**	**5:41**	....	....	....	....	....	....	....	....	....
	Springfield	AHL	50	8	9	17	59	....	....	....	....	....	....	....	....	....	....	....	....	....	....	....	....	....	....
	NHL Totals		**7**	**0**	**1**	**1**	**0**	**0**	**0**	**0**	**3**	**0.0**		**0**	**0.0**	**5:41**	....	....	....	....	....	....	....	....	....

REINPRECHT, Steve

(REIGHN-prehkt, STEEV) **PHX.**

Center. Shoots left. 6', 195 lbs. Born, Edmonton, Alta., May 7, 1976.

Season	Club	League	GP	G	A	Pts	PIM	PP	SH	GW	S	%	+/-	TF	F%	Min	GP	G	A	Pts	PIM	PP	SH	GW	Min
1993-94	Edmonton SSAC	AMHL	71	48	77	125	....	....	....	....	....	....	....	....	....	....	....	....	....	....	....	....	....	....	....
1994-95	St. Albert Saints	AJHL	56	35	44	79	14	....	....	....	....	....	....	....	....	....	....	....	....	....	....	....	....	....	....
1995-96	St. Albert Saints	AJHL	39	24	33	57	16	....	....	....	....	....	....	....	....	....	....	....	....	....	....	....	....	....	....
1996-97	U. of Wisconsin	WCHA	38	11	9	20	12	....	....	....	....	....	....	....	....	....	....	....	....	....	....	....	....	....	....
1997-98	U. of Wisconsin	WCHA	41	19	24	43	18	....	....	....	....	....	....	....	....	....	....	....	....	....	....	....	....	....	....
1998-99	U. of Wisconsin	WCHA	38	16	17	33	14	....	....	....	....	....	....	....	....	....	....	....	....	....	....	....	....	....	....
99-2000	U. of Wisconsin	WCHA	37	26	40	*66	14	....	....	....	....	....	....	....	....	....	....	....	....	....	....	....	....	....	....
	Los Angeles	**NHL**	**1**	**0**	**0**	**0**	**2**	**0**	**0**	**0**	**0**	**0.0**	**0**	**6**	**50.0**	**6:01**	....	....	....	....	....	....	....	....	....
2000-01	**Los Angeles**	**NHL**	**59**	**12**	**17**	**29**	**12**	**3**	**2**	**3**	**72**	**16.7**	**11**	**676**	**41.4**	**12:39**	....	....	....	....	....	....	....	....	....
	♦ **Colorado**	**NHL**	**21**	**3**	**4**	**7**	**2**	**0**	**0**	**0**	**28**	**10.7**	**–1**	**209**	**51.2**	**15:38**	**22**	**2**	**3**	**5**	**2**	**0**	**0**	**0**	**12:09**
2001-02	**Colorado**	**NHL**	**67**	**19**	**27**	**46**	**18**	**4**	**0**	**3**	**111**	**17.1**	**14**	**413**	**52.1**	**16:32**	**21**	**7**	**5**	**12**	**8**	**0**	**0**	**2**	**16:23**
2002-03	**Colorado**	**NHL**	**77**	**18**	**33**	**51**	**18**	**2**	**1**	**1**	**146**	**12.3**	**–6**	**928**	**46.4**	**17:22**	**7**	**1**	**2**	**3**	**0**	**0**	**0**	**0**	**15:32**
2003-04	**Calgary**	**NHL**	**44**	**7**	**22**	**29**	**4**	**3**	**0**	**1**	**68**	**10.3**	**1**	**120**	**40.0**	**17:05**	....	....	....	....	....	....	....	....	....
2004-05	HC Mulhouse	France	22	20	27	47	6	....	....	....	....	....	....	....	....	....	10	7	6	13	2	....	....	....	....
2005-06	**Calgary**	**NHL**	**52**	**10**	**19**	**29**	**24**	**5**	**0**	**1**	**72**	**13.9**	**10**	**340**	**49.4**	**14:49**	....	....	....	....	....	....	....	....	....
	Phoenix	**NHL**	**28**	**12**	**11**	**23**	**8**	**4**	**1**	**2**	**58**	**20.7**	**1**	**526**	**47.3**	**19:06**	....	....	....	....	....	....	....	....	....
	NHL Totals		**349**	**81**	**133**	**214**	**88**	**21**	**4**	**11**	**555**	**14.6**		**3218**	**46.6**	**16:00**	**50**	**10**	**10**	**20**	**10**	**0**	**0**	**2**	**14:24**

WCHA Second All-Star Team (1998) • WCHA First All-Star Team (2000) • WCHA Player of the Year (2000) • NCAA West First All-American Team (2000)

Signed as a free agent by **Los Angeles**, March 31, 2000. Traded to **Colorado** by **Los Angeles** with Rob Blake for Adam Deadmarsh, Aaron Miller, a player to be named later (Jared Aulin, March 22, 2001) and Colorado's 1st round choices in 2001 (Dave Steckel) and 2003 (Brian Boyle) Entry Drafts, February 21, 2001. Traded to **Buffalo** by **Colorado** for Keith Ballard, July 3, 2003. Traded to **Calgary** by **Buffalo** with Rhett Warrener for Chris Drury and Steve Begin, July 3, 2003. Signed as a free agent by **Mulhouse** (France), September 28, 2004. Traded to **Phoenix** by **Calgary** with Philippe Sauve for Brian Boucher and Mike Leclerc, February 2, 2006.

REITZ, Erik

(RIGHTZ, AIR-ihk) **MIN.**

Defense. Shoots right. 6'1", 210 lbs. Born, Detroit, MI, July 29, 1982. Minnesota's 5th choice, 170th overall, in 2000 Entry Draft.

Season	Club	League	GP	G	A	Pts	PIM	PP	SH	GW	S	%	+/-	TF	F%	Min	GP	G	A	Pts	PIM	PP	SH	GW	Min
1998-99	Leamington Flyers	OHA-B	50	5	10	15	80	....	....	....	....	....	....	....	....	....	....	....	....	....	....	....	....	....	....
99-2000	Barrie Colts	OHL	63	2	10	12	85	....	....	....	....	....	....	....	....	....	25	0	5	5	44	....	....	....	....
2000-01	Barrie Colts	OHL	68	5	21	26	178	....	....	....	....	....	....	....	....	....	5	1	0	1	21	....	....	....	....
2001-02	Barrie Colts	OHL	61	13	27	40	153	....	....	....	....	....	....	....	....	....	20	4	16	20	40	....	....	....	....
2002-03	Houston Aeros	AHL	62	6	13	19	112	....	....	....	....	....	....	....	....	....	11	0	3	3	31	....	....	....	....
2003-04	Houston Aeros	AHL	69	5	19	24	148	....	....	....	....	....	....	....	....	....	2	0	0	0	0	....	....	....	....
2004-05	Houston Aeros	AHL	38	2	12	14	91	....	....	....	....	....	....	....	....	....	....	....	....	....	....	....	....	....	....
2005-06	**Minnesota**	**NHL**	**5**	**0**	**0**	**0**	**4**	**0**	**0**	**0**	**0**	**0.0**	**–2**	**0**	**0.0**	**13:09**	....	....	....	....	....	....	....	....	....
	Houston Aeros	AHL	72	5	23	28	139	....	....	....	....	....	....	....	....	....	8	0	5	5	20	....	....	....	....
	NHL Totals		**5**	**0**	**0**	**0**	**4**	**0**	**0**	**0**	**0**	**0.0**		**0**	**0.0**	**13:09**	....	....	....	....	....	....	....	....	....

Memorial Cup Tournament All-Star Team (2000) • OHL First All-Star Team (2002)

• Missed majority of 2004-05 season recovering from elbow injury suffered in game vs. Milwaukee (AHL), February 5, 2005.

RHEAUME, Pascal
(RAY-awm, pas-KAL) **PHX.**

Center. Shoots left. 6'1", 220 lbs. Born, Quebec City, Que., June 21, 1973.

Season	Club	League	GP	G	A	Pts	PIM	PP	SH	GW	S	%	+/-	TF	F%	Min	GP	G	A	Pts	PIM	PP	SH	GW	Min
			Regular Season														Playoffs								
1990-91	Ste-Foy	QAAA	37	20	38	58	25										7	7	1	8	6				
1991-92	Trois-Rivieres	QMJHL	65	17	20	37	84										14	5	4	9	23				
1992-93	Sherbrooke	QMJHL	65	28	34	62	88										14	6	5	11	31				
1993-94	Albany River Rats	AHL	55	17	18	35	43										5	0	1	1	0				
1994-95	Albany River Rats	AHL	78	19	25	44	46										14	3	6	9	19				
1995-96	Albany River Rats	AHL	68	26	42	68	50										4	1	2	3	2				
1996-97	**New Jersey**	**NHL**	**2**	**1**	**0**	**1**	**0**	**0**	**0**	**0**	**5**	**20.0**	**1**												
	Albany River Rats	AHL	51	22	23	45	40										16	2	8	10	16				
1997-98	**St. Louis**	**NHL**	**48**	**6**	**9**	**15**	**35**	**1**	**0**	**0**	**45**	**13.3**	**4**				**10**	**1**	**3**	**4**	**8**	**1**	**0**	**0**	
1998-99	**St. Louis**	**NHL**	**60**	**9**	**18**	**27**	**24**	**2**	**0**	**0**	**85**	**10.6**	**10**	**21**	**71.4**	**13:19**	**5**	**1**	**0**	**1**	**4**	**0**	**0**	**0**	**11:36**
99-2000	**St. Louis**	**NHL**	**7**	**1**	**1**	**2**	**6**	**0**	**0**	**0**	**5**	**20.0**	**–2**	**2**	**0.0**	**10:08**									
	Worcester IceCats	AHL	7	1	1	2	4																		
2000-01	**St. Louis**	**NHL**	**8**	**2**	**0**	**2**	**5**	**2**	**0**	**0**	**16**	**12.5**	**–1**	**7**	**42.9**	**11:56**	**3**	**0**	**1**	**1**	**0**	**0**	**0**	**0**	**11:30**
	Worcester IceCats	AHL	56	23	35	58	63										11	2	4	6	2				
2001-02	**Chicago**	**NHL**	**19**	**0**	**2**	**2**	**4**	**0**	**0**	**0**	**19**	**0.0**	**–1**	**165**	**51.5**	**9:22**									
	Atlanta	**NHL**	**42**	**11**	**9**	**20**	**25**	**6**	**0**	**2**	**61**	**18.0**	**–3**	**510**	**45.9**	**14:27**									
2002-03	**Atlanta**	**NHL**	**56**	**4**	**9**	**13**	**24**	**0**	**2**	**1**	**70**	**5.7**	**–8**	**602**	**46.8**	**12:17**									
	♦ **New Jersey**	**NHL**	**21**	**4**	**1**	**5**	**8**	**0**	**1**	**1**	**23**	**17.4**	**3**	**248**	**51.6**	**11:50**	**24**	**1**	**2**	**3**	**13**	**0**	**0**	**0**	**13:32**
2003-04	**NY Rangers**	**NHL**	**17**	**0**	**0**	**0**	**5**	**0**	**0**	**0**	**15**	**0.0**	**–3**	**46**	**56.5**	**10:02**									
	Hartford	AHL	3	1	0	1	0																		
	St. Louis	**NHL**	**25**	**1**	**3**	**4**	**4**	**0**	**0**	**0**	**23**	**4.3**	**–3**	**26**	**38.5**	**10:19**	**3**	**0**	**0**	**0**	**2**	**0**	**0**	**0**	**6:55**
2004-05	Albany River Rats	AHL	78	24	25	49	85																		
2005-06	**New Jersey**	**NHL**	**12**	**0**	**0**	**0**	**4**	**0**	**0**	**0**	**11**	**0.0**	**–6**	**81**	**42.0**	**9:15**									
	Albany River Rats	AHL	9	2	0	2	9																		
	Phoenix	**NHL**	**1**	**0**	**0**	**0**	**0**	**0**	**0**	**0**	**0**	**0.0**	**–1**	**3**	**66.7**	**6:10**									
	San Antonio	AHL	47	13	13	26	35																		
	NHL Totals		**318**	**39**	**52**	**91**	**144**	**11**	**3**	**4**	**378**	**10.3**		**1711**	**47.9**	**12:04**	**45**	**3**	**6**	**9**	**27**	**1**	**0**	**0**	**12:31**

Signed as a free agent by **New Jersey**, October 1, 1993. Claimed by **St. Louis** from **New Jersey** in Waiver Draft, September 28, 1997. • Missed majority of 1999-2000 season recovering from shoulder surgery, August, 1999. Signed as a free agent by **Chicago**, July 31, 2001. Claimed on waivers by **Atlanta** from **Chicago**, November 14, 2001. Traded to **New Jersey** by **Atlanta** for future considerations, February 24, 2003. Signed as a free agent by **NY Rangers**, October 22, 2003. Claimed on waivers by **St. Louis** from **NY Rangers**, January 29, 2004. Signed as a free agent by **New Jersey**, August 13, 2004. Traded to **Phoenix** by **New Jersey** with Ray Schultz and Steven Spencer for Brad Ference, November 25, 2005.

RIBEIRO, Mike
(rih-bee-AIR-roh, MIGHK) **MTL.**

Center. Shoots left. 6', 175 lbs. Born, Montreal, Que., February 10, 1980. Montreal's 2nd choice, 45th overall, in 1998 Entry Draft.

Season	Club	League	GP	G	A	Pts	PIM	PP	SH	GW	S	%	+/-	TF	F%	Min	GP	G	A	Pts	PIM	PP	SH	GW	Min
			Regular Season														Playoffs								
1996-97	Mtl-Bourassa	QAAA	43	32	57	89	48										16	15	23	38	14				
1997-98	Rouyn-Noranda	QMJHL	67	40	*85	125	55										6	3	1	4	0				
1998-99	Rouyn-Noranda	QMJHL	69	*67	*100	*167	137										11	5	11	16	12				
	Fredericton	AHL															5	0	1	1	2				
99-2000	**Montreal**	**NHL**	**19**	**1**	**1**	**2**	**2**	**1**	**0**	**0**	**18**	**5.6**	**–6**	**95**	**34.7**	**10:40**									
	Quebec Citadelles	AHL	3	0	0	0	2																		
	Rouyn-Noranda	QMJHL	2	1	3	4	0																		
	Quebec Remparts	QMJHL	21	17	28	45	30										11	3	20	23	38				
2000-01	**Montreal**	**NHL**	**2**	**0**	**0**	**0**	**2**	**0**	**0**	**0**	**3**	**0.0**	**0**	**11**	**18.2**	**10:38**									
	Quebec Citadelles	AHL	74	26	40	66	44										9	1	5	6	23				
2001-02	**Montreal**	**NHL**	**43**	**8**	**10**	**18**	**12**	**3**	**0**	**0**	**48**	**16.7**	**–11**	**141**	**44.0**	**13:55**									
	Quebec Citadelles	AHL	23	9	14	23	36										3	0	3	3	0				
2002-03	**Montreal**	**NHL**	**52**	**5**	**12**	**17**	**6**	**2**	**0**	**0**	**57**	**8.8**	**–3**	**358**	**50.3**	**11:07**									
	Hamilton	AHL	3	0	1	1	0																		
2003-04	**Montreal**	**NHL**	**81**	**20**	**45**	**65**	**34**	**7**	**0**	**5**	**103**	**19.4**	**15**	**913**	**44.8**	**17:05**	**11**	**2**	**1**	**3**	**18**	**0**	**0**	**0**	**16:31**
2004-05	Blues Espoo	Finland	17	8	9	17	4																		
2005-06	**Montreal**	**NHL**	**79**	**16**	**35**	**51**	**36**	**8**	**0**	**2**	**130**	**12.3**	**–6**	**843**	**44.7**	**16:35**	**6**	**0**	**2**	**2**	**0**	**0**	**0**	**0**	**18:22**
	NHL Totals		**276**	**50**	**103**	**153**	**92**	**21**	**0**	**7**	**359**	**13.9**		**2361**	**45.0**	**14:50**	**17**	**2**	**3**	**5**	**18**	**0**	**0**	**0**	**17:10**

QMJHL Second All-Star Team (1998) • QMJHL First All-Star Team (1999) • Canadian Major Junior First All-Star Team (1999)

Signed as a free agent by **Espoo** (Finland), January 17, 2005.

RICCI, Mike
(REE-CHEE, MIGHK) **PHX.**

Center. Shoots left. 6', 200 lbs. Born, Scarborough, Ont., October 27, 1971. Philadelphia's 1st choice, 4th overall, in 1990 Entry Draft.

Season	Club	League	GP	G	A	Pts	PIM	PP	SH	GW	S	%	+/-	TF	F%	Min	GP	G	A	Pts	PIM	PP	SH	GW	Min
			Regular Season														Playoffs								
1986-87	Toronto Marlies	MTHL	38	39	42	81	27																		
1987-88	Peterborough	OHL	41	24	37	61	20										8	5	5	10	4				
1988-89	Peterborough	OHL	60	54	52	106	43										17	19	16	35	18				
1989-90	Peterborough	OHL	60	52	64	116	39										12	5	7	12	26				
1990-91	**Philadelphia**	**NHL**	**68**	**21**	**20**	**41**	**64**	**9**	**0**	**4**	**121**	**17.4**	**–8**												
1991-92	**Philadelphia**	**NHL**	**78**	**20**	**36**	**56**	**93**	**11**	**2**	**0**	**149**	**13.4**	**–10**												
1992-93	**Quebec**	**NHL**	**77**	**27**	**51**	**78**	**123**	**12**	**1**	**10**	**142**	**19.0**	**8**				**6**	**0**	**6**	**6**	**8**	**0**	**0**	**0**	
1993-94	**Quebec**	**NHL**	**83**	**30**	**21**	**51**	**113**	**13**	**3**	**6**	**138**	**21.7**	**–9**												
1994-95	**Quebec**	**NHL**	**48**	**15**	**21**	**36**	**40**	**9**	**0**	**1**	**73**	**20.5**	**5**				**6**	**1**	**3**	**4**	**8**	**0**	**0**	**0**	
1995-96♦	**Colorado**	**NHL**	**62**	**6**	**21**	**27**	**52**	**3**	**0**	**1**	**73**	**8.2**	**1**				**22**	**6**	**11**	**17**	**18**	**3**	**0**	**1**	
1996-97	**Colorado**	**NHL**	**63**	**13**	**19**	**32**	**59**	**5**	**0**	**3**	**74**	**17.6**	**–3**				**17**	**2**	**4**	**6**	**17**	**0**	**0**	**1**	
1997-98	**Colorado**	**NHL**	**6**	**0**	**4**	**4**	**2**	**0**	**0**	**0**	**5**	**0.0**	**0**												
	San Jose	**NHL**	**59**	**9**	**14**	**23**	**30**	**5**	**0**	**2**	**86**	**10.5**	**–4**				**6**	**1**	**3**	**4**	**6**	**0**	**0**	**0**	
1998-99	**San Jose**	**NHL**	**82**	**13**	**26**	**39**	**68**	**2**	**1**	**2**	**98**	**13.3**	**1**	**1465**	**49.6**	**15:23**	**6**	**2**	**3**	**5**	**10**	**1**	**0**	**0**	**16:53**
99-2000	**San Jose**	**NHL**	**82**	**20**	**24**	**44**	**60**	**10**	**0**	**5**	**134**	**14.9**	**14**	**1522**	**50.7**	**16:52**	**12**	**5**	**1**	**6**	**2**	**3**	**0**	**1**	**17:37**
2000-01	**San Jose**	**NHL**	**81**	**22**	**22**	**44**	**60**	**9**	**2**	**4**	**141**	**15.6**	**3**	**1631**	**51.4**	**18:00**	**6**	**0**	**3**	**3**	**0**	**0**	**0**	**0**	**19:44**
2001-02	**San Jose**	**NHL**	**79**	**19**	**34**	**53**	**44**	**5**	**2**	**0**	**115**	**16.5**	**9**	**1501**	**49.0**	**17:04**	**12**	**4**	**6**	**10**	**4**	**0**	**0**	**1**	**19:51**
2002-03	**San Jose**	**NHL**	**75**	**11**	**23**	**34**	**53**	**5**	**1**	**2**	**101**	**10.9**	**–12**	**1152**	**51.6**	**16:31**									
2003-04	**San Jose**	**NHL**	**71**	**7**	**19**	**26**	**40**	**2**	**0**	**0**	**48**	**14.6**	**8**	**1116**	**54.8**	**14:21**	**17**	**2**	**3**	**5**	**4**	**0**	**0**	**0**	**15:31**
2004-05			DID NOT PLAY																						
2005-06	**Phoenix**	**NHL**	**78**	**10**	**6**	**16**	**69**	**5**	**1**	**1**	**50**	**20.0**	**–22**	**1146**	**49.2**	**12:48**									
	NHL Totals		**1092**	**243**	**361**	**604**	**970**	**105**	**13**	**41**	**1548**	**15.7**		**9533**	**50.8**	**15:53**	**110**	**23**	**43**	**66**	**77**	**7**	**0**	**4**	**17:36**

OHL Second All-Star Team (1989) • OHL First All-Star Team (1990) • OHL MVP (1990) • Canadian Major Junior Player of the Year (1990) • OHL First All-Star Team (1990)

Traded to **Quebec** by **Philadelphia** with Steve Duchesne, Peter Forsberg, Kerry Huffman, Ron Hextall, Philadelphia's 1st round choice (Jocelyn Thibault) in 1993 Entry Draft, $15,000,000 and future considerations (Chris Simon and Philadelphia's 1st round choice (later traded to Toronto – later traded to Washington – Washington selected Nolan Baumgartner) in 1994 Entry Draft, July 21, 1992) for Eric Lindros, June 30, 1992. Transferred to **Colorado** after **Quebec** franchise relocated, June 21, 1995. Traded to **San Jose** by **Colorado** with Colorado's 2nd round choice (later traded to Buffalo – Buffalo selected Jaroslav Kristek) in 1998 Entry Draft for Shean Donovan and San Jose's 1st round choice (Alex Tanguay) in 1998 Entry Draft, November 21, 1997. Signed as a free agent by **Phoenix**, July 9, 2004.

RICHARDS, Brad
(RIH-chahrds, BRAD) **T.B.**

Center. Shoots left. 6', 198 lbs. Born, Murray Harbour, P.E.I., May 2, 1980. Tampa Bay's 2nd choice, 64th overall, in 1998 Entry Draft.

Season	Club	League	GP	G	A	Pts	PIM	PP	SH	GW	S	%	+/-	TF	F%	Min	GP	G	A	Pts	PIM	PP	SH	GW	Min
			Regular Season														Playoffs								
1996-97	Notre Dame	SJHL	63	39	48	87	73																		
1997-98	Rimouski Oceanic	QMJHL	68	33	82	115	44										19	8	24	32	2				
1998-99	Rimouski Oceanic	QMJHL	59	39	92	131	55										11	9	12	21	6				
99-2000	Rimouski Oceanic	QMJHL	63	*71	*115	*186	69										12	13	*24	*37	16				
2000-01	**Tampa Bay**	**NHL**	**82**	**21**	**41**	**62**	**14**	**7**	**0**	**3**	**179**	**11.7**	**–10**	**955**	**41.4**	**16:54**									
2001-02	**Tampa Bay**	**NHL**	**82**	**20**	**42**	**62**	**13**	**5**	**0**	**0**	**251**	**8.0**	**–18**	**911**	**41.2**	**19:48**									
2002-03	**Tampa Bay**	**NHL**	**80**	**17**	**57**	**74**	**24**	**4**	**0**	**2**	**277**	**6.1**	**3**	**1007**	**47.5**	**19:56**	**11**	**0**	**5**	**5**	**12**	**0**	**0**	**0**	**22:21**
2003-04♦	**Tampa Bay**	**NHL**	**82**	**26**	**53**	**79**	**12**	**5**	**1**	**6**	**244**	**10.7**	**14**	**1167**	**46.7**	**20:26**	**23**	**12**	**14**	***26**	**4**	**7**	**0**	**7**	**23:28**
2004-05	Ak Bars Kazan	Russia	6	2	5	7	16																		
2005-06	**Tampa Bay**	**NHL**	**82**	**23**	**68**	**91**	**32**	**7**	**4**	**0**	**282**	**8.2**	**0**	**1288**	**50.2**	**22:45**	**5**	**3**	**5**	**8**	**6**	**0**	**0**	**0**	**24:11**
	Canada	Olympics	6	2	2	4	6																		
	NHL Totals		**408**	**107**	**261**	**368**	**95**	**28**	**5**	**11**	**1233**	**8.7**		**5328**	**45.8**	**19:58**	**39**	**15**	**24**	**39**	**22**	**7**	**0**	**7**	**23:15**

QMJHL First All-Star Team (2000) • Canadian Major Junior First All-Star Team (2000) • Canadian Major Junior Player of the Year (2000) • Memorial Cup Tournament All-Star Team (2000) • Stafford Smythe Memorial Trophy (Memorial Cup Tournament MVP) (2000) • NHL All-Rookie Team (2001) • Lady Byng Trophy (2004) • Conn Smythe Trophy (2004)

Signed as a free agent by **Kazan** (Russia), November 8, 2004.

RICHARDS, Mike

(RIH-chahrds, MIGHK) **PHI.**

Center. Shoots left. 5'11", 185 lbs. Born, Kenora, Ont., February 11, 1985. Philadelphia's 2nd choice, 24th overall, in 2003 Entry Draft.

			Regular Season														Playoffs								
Season	Club	League	GP	G	A	Pts	PIM	PP	SH	GW	S	%	+/-	TF	F%	Min	GP	G	A	Pts	PIM	PP	SH	GW	Min
2000-01	Kenora Stars	NOHA	85	76	73	149	20																		
2001-02	Kitchener Rangers	OHL	65	20	38	58	52										4	0	1	1	6				
2002-03	Kitchener Rangers	OHL	67	37	50	87	99										21	9	18	27	24				
2003-04	Kitchener Rangers	OHL	58	36	53	89	82										1	0	0	0	0				
2004-05	Kitchener Rangers	OHL	43	22	36	58	75										15	11	17	28	36				
	Philadelphia	AHL															14	7	8	15	28				
2005-06	**Philadelphia**	**NHL**	**79**	**11**	**23**	**34**	**65**	**1**	**3**	**1**	**168**	**6.5**	**6**	**914**	**45.7**	**15:23**	**6**	**0**	**1**	**1**	**0**	**0**	**0**	**0**	**15:41**
	NHL Totals		**79**	**11**	**23**	**34**	**65**	**1**	**3**	**1**	**168**	**6.5**		**914**	**45.7**	**15:23**	**6**	**0**	**1**	**1**	**0**	**0**	**0**	**0**	**15:41**

Memorial Cup Tournament All-Star Team (2003) • OHL Second All-Star Team (2005)

RICHARDSON, Brad

(RIH-chard-suhn, BRAD) **COL.**

Center. Shoots left. 5'11", 178 lbs. Born, Belleville, Ont., February 4, 1985. Colorado's 4th choice, 163rd overall, in 2003 Entry Draft.

2001-02	Owen Sound	OHL	58	12	21	33	20																		
2002-03	Owen Sound	OHL	67	27	40	67	54										4	1	1	2	10				
2003-04	Owen Sound	OHL	15	7	9	16	4																		
2004-05	Owen Sound	OHL	68	41	56	97	60										8	6	4	10	8				
2005-06	**Colorado**	**NHL**	**41**	**3**	**10**	**13**	**12**	**1**	**0**	**0**	**51**	**5.9**	**0**	**305**	**41.0**	**10:44**	**9**	**1**	**0**	**1**	**6**	**0**	**0**	**0**	**11:41**
	Lowell	AHL	29	4	13	17	20																		
	NHL Totals		**41**	**3**	**10**	**13**	**12**	**1**	**0**	**0**	**51**	**5.9**		**305**	**41.0**	**10:44**	**9**	**1**	**0**	**1**	**6**	**0**	**0**	**0**	**11:41**

RICHARDSON, Luke

(RIH-chahrd-sohn, LEWK) **T.B.**

Defense. Shoots left. 6'4", 215 lbs. Born, Ottawa, Ont., March 26, 1969. Toronto's 1st choice, 7th overall, in 1987 Entry Draft.

1984-85	Ottawa Knights	OMHA	35	5	26	31	72																		
1985-86	Peterborough	OHL	63	6	18	24	57										16	2	1	3	50				
1986-87	Peterborough	OHL	59	13	32	45	70										12	0	5	5	24				
1987-88	**Toronto**	**NHL**	**78**	**4**	**6**	**10**	**90**	**0**	**0**	**0**	**49**	**8.2**	**–25**				**2**	**0**	**0**	**0**	**0**	**0**	**0**	**0**	
1988-89	**Toronto**	**NHL**	**55**	**2**	**7**	**9**	**106**	**0**	**0**	**0**	**59**	**3.4**	**–15**												
1989-90	**Toronto**	**NHL**	**67**	**4**	**14**	**18**	**122**	**0**	**0**	**0**	**80**	**5.0**	**–1**				**5**	**0**	**0**	**0**	**22**	**0**	**0**	**0**	
1990-91	**Toronto**	**NHL**	**78**	**1**	**9**	**10**	**238**	**0**	**0**	**0**	**68**	**1.5**	**–28**												
1991-92	**Edmonton**	**NHL**	**75**	**2**	**19**	**21**	**118**	**0**	**0**	**0**	**85**	**2.4**	**–9**				**16**	**0**	**5**	**5**	**45**	**0**	**0**	**0**	
1992-93	**Edmonton**	**NHL**	**82**	**3**	**10**	**13**	**142**	**0**	**2**	**0**	**78**	**3.8**	**–18**												
1993-94	**Edmonton**	**NHL**	**69**	**2**	**6**	**8**	**131**	**0**	**0**	**0**	**92**	**2.2**	**–13**												
1994-95	**Edmonton**	**NHL**	**46**	**3**	**10**	**13**	**40**	**1**	**1**	**1**	**51**	**5.9**	**–6**												
1995-96	**Edmonton**	**NHL**	**82**	**2**	**9**	**11**	**108**	**0**	**0**	**0**	**61**	**3.3**	**–27**												
1996-97	**Edmonton**	**NHL**	**82**	**1**	**11**	**12**	**91**	**0**	**0**	**0**	**67**	**1.5**	**9**				**12**	**0**	**2**	**2**	**14**	**0**	**0**	**0**	
1997-98	**Philadelphia**	**NHL**	**81**	**2**	**3**	**5**	**139**	**2**	**0**	**0**	**57**	**3.5**	**7**				**5**	**0**	**0**	**0**	**0**	**0**	**0**	**0**	
1998-99	**Philadelphia**	**NHL**	**78**	**0**	**6**	**6**	**106**	**0**	**0**	**0**	**49**	**0.0**	**–3**	**0**	**0.0**	**16:33**									
99-2000	**Philadelphia**	**NHL**	**74**	**2**	**5**	**7**	**140**	**0**	**0**	**1**	**50**	**4.0**	**14**	**0**	**0.0**	**16:11**	**18**	**0**	**1**	**1**	**41**	**0**	**0**	**0**	**21:58**
2000-01	**Philadelphia**	**NHL**	**82**	**2**	**6**	**8**	**131**	**0**	**1**	**0**	**75**	**2.7**	**23**	**1**	**0.0**	**20:42**	**6**	**0**	**0**	**0**	**4**	**0**	**0**	**0**	**24:39**
2001-02	**Philadelphia**	**NHL**	**72**	**1**	**8**	**9**	**102**	**0**	**0**	**0**	**65**	**1.5**	**18**	**0**	**0.0**	**18:17**	**5**	**0**	**0**	**0**	**4**	**0**	**0**	**0**	**19:18**
2002-03	**Columbus**	**NHL**	**82**	**0**	**13**	**13**	**73**	**0**	**0**	**0**	**56**	**0.0**	**–16**	**2**	**50.0**	**23:31**									
2003-04	**Columbus**	**NHL**	**64**	**1**	**5**	**6**	**48**	**0**	**0**	**1**	**34**	**2.9**	**–11**	**0**	**0.0**	**20:07**									
2004-05			DID NOT PLAY																						
2005-06	**Columbus**	**NHL**	**44**	**1**	**6**	**7**	**30**	**0**	**0**	**0**	**24**	**4.2**	**–18**	**0**	**0.0**	**15:15**									
	Toronto	**NHL**	**21**	**0**	**3**	**3**	**41**	**0**	**0**	**0**	**16**	**0.0**	**–1**	**0**	**0.0**	**18:48**									
	NHL Totals		**1312**	**33**	**156**	**189**	**1996**	**3**	**4**	**3**	**1116**	**3.0**		**3**	**33.3**	**18:56**	**69**	**0**	**8**	**8**	**130**	**0**	**0**	**0**	**22:04**

Traded to **Edmonton** by **Toronto** with Vincent Damphousse, Peter Ing and Scott Thornton for Grant Fuhr, Glenn Anderson and Craig Berube, September 19, 1991. Signed as a free agent by **Philadelphia**, July 23, 1997. Signed as a free agent by **Columbus**, July 4, 2002. Traded to **Toronto** by **Columbus** for Toronto's 5th round choice (Nick Sucharski) in 2006 Entry Draft, March 8, 2006. Signed as a free agent by **Tampa Bay**, July 11, 2006.

RICHMOND, Danny

(RIHCH-muhnd, DA-nee) **CHI.**

Defense. Shoots left. 6', 190 lbs. Born, Chicago, IL, August 1, 1984. Carolina's 2nd choice, 31st overall, in 2003 Entry Draft.

2000-01	Team Illinois	MWEHL	79	25	40	65																			
2001-02	Chicago Steel	USHL	56	8	45	53	129										4	0	4	4	20				
2002-03	U. of Michigan	CCHA	43	3	19	22	48																		
2003-04	London Knights	OHL	59	13	22	35	92										15	5	6	11	10				
2004-05	Lowell	AHL	63	4	9	13	139										6	0	2	2	8				
2005-06	**Carolina**	**NHL**	**10**	**0**	**1**	**1**	**7**	**0**	**0**	**0**	**7**	**0.0**	**–3**	**0**	**0.0**	**9:00**									
	Lowell	AHL	32	4	11	15	60																		
	Chicago	**NHL**	**10**	**0**	**0**	**0**	**18**	**0**	**0**	**0**	**6**	**0.0**	**–3**	**0**	**0.0**	**13:36**									
	Norfolk Admirals	AHL	31	4	8	12	42										3	0	1	1	2				
	NHL Totals		**20**	**0**	**1**	**1**	**25**	**0**	**0**	**0**	**13**	**0.0**		**0**	**0.0**	**11:18**									

USHL All-Rookie Team (2002) • USHL First All-Star Team (2002) • USHL Rookie of the Year (2002) • CCHA All-Rookie Team (2003)

Left **U. of Michigan** (CCHA) and signed with **London** (OHL), June 6, 2003. Traded to **Chicago** by **Carolina** with Columbus' 4th round choice (previously acquired, later traded to Toronto - Toronto selected James Reimer) in 2006 Entry Draft for Anton Babchuk and a 4th round choice in 2007 Entry Draft, January 20, 2006.

RISSMILLER, Pat

(RIGHZ-mih-luhr, PAT) **S.J.**

Left wing. Shoots left. 6'4", 210 lbs. Born, Belmont, MA, October 26, 1978.

1997-98	The Hill School	High-PA	STATISTICS NOT AVAILABLE																						
1998-99	Holy Cross	MAAC	34	13	28	41	23																		
99-2000	Holy Cross	MAAC	35	10	17	27	22																		
2000-01	Holy Cross	MAAC	29	14	15	29	40																		
2001-02	Holy Cross	MAAC	33	16	*30	*46	31																		
2002-03	Cleveland Barons	AHL	72	14	26	40	24																		
	Cincinnati	ECHL	2	2	2	4	0																		
2003-04	**San Jose**	**NHL**	**4**	**0**	**0**	**0**	**0**	**0**	**0**	**0**	**2**	**0.0**	**0**	**26**	**53.9**	**7:07**									
	Cleveland Barons	AHL	75	14	31	45	66										9	0	1	1	8				
2004-05	Cleveland Barons	AHL	69	21	23	44	50																		
2005-06	**San Jose**	**NHL**	**18**	**3**	**3**	**6**	**8**	**1**	**0**	**1**	**26**	**11.5**	**1**	**3**	**0.0**	**9:22**	**11**	**2**	**1**	**3**	**6**	**0**	**0**	**0**	**8:06**
	Cleveland Barons	AHL	68	15	37	52	30																		
	NHL Totals		**22**	**3**	**3**	**6**	**8**	**1**	**0**	**1**	**28**	**10.7**		**29**	**48.3**	**8:57**	**11**	**2**	**1**	**3**	**6**	**0**	**0**	**0**	**8:06**

MAAC All-Rookie Team (1999) • MAAC First All-Star Team (2002) • MAAC Offensive Player of the Year (2002)

Signed as a free agent by **Cleveland** (AHL), September 23, 2002. Signed as a free agent by **San Jose**, June 30, 2003.

RITA, Jani

(REETA, YA-nee) **PIT.**

Left wing. Shoots left. 6'1", 206 lbs. Born, Helsinki, Finland, July 25, 1981. Edmonton's 1st choice, 13th overall, in 1999 Entry Draft.

1995-96	Jokerit U18	Fin-U18	5	0	0	0	0																		
1996-97	Jokerit U18	Fin-U18	27	22	7	29	4																		
	Jokerit Helsinki Jr.	Fin-Jr.	3	0	0	0	0																		
1997-98	Jokerit U18	Fin-U18	7	7	4	11	2																		
	Jokerit Helsinki Jr.	Fin-Jr.	36	15	9	24	2										8	4	1	5	0				
	Jokerit Helsinki	Finland															1	0	0	0	0				
1998-99	Jokerit Helsinki Jr.	Fin-Jr.	20	9	13	22	8										6	1	1	2	8				
	Jokerit Helsinki	Finland	41	3	2	5	39																		
	Jokerit Helsinki	EuroHL	3	0	0	0	0																		
99-2000	Jokerit Helsinki Jr.	Fin-Jr.	1	1	0	1	0																		
	Jokerit Helsinki	Finland	49	6	3	9	10										11	1	0	1	0				
2000-01	Jokerit Helsinki Jr.	Fin-Jr.	3	3	2	5	0																		
	Jokerit Helsinki	Finland	50	5	10	15	18										5	0	0	0	2				
2001-02	**Edmonton**	**NHL**	**1**	**0**	**0**	**0**	**0**	**0**	**0**	**0**	**0**	**0.0**	**0**	**0**	**0.0**	**6:09**									
	Hamilton	AHL	76	25	17	42	32										15	8	4	12	0				

Season	Club	League	GP	G	A	Pts	PIM	PP	SH	GW	S	%	+/-	TF	F%	Min	GP	G	A	Pts	PIM	PP	SH	GW	Min
			Regular Season														Playoffs								
2002-03	Edmonton	NHL	12	3	1	4	0	0	0	0	18	16.7	2	1	0.0	9:32									
	Hamilton	AHL	64	21	27	48	18										23	3	4	7	2				
2003-04	Edmonton	NHL	2	0	0	0	0	0	0	0	1	0.0	0	0	0.0	4:34									
	Toronto	AHL	64	17	24	41	18										1	1	0	1	0				
2004-05	HPK Hameenlinna	Finland	56	21	18	39	12										10	7	4	11	4				
2005-06	Edmonton	NHL	21	3	0	3	6	0	0	0	13	23.1	0	2	0.0	6:46									
	Pittsburgh	NHL	30	3	4	7	4	0	0	0	36	8.3	–6	104	45.2	10:06									
	NHL Totals		**66**	**9**	**5**	**14**	**10**	**0**	**0**	**0**	**68**	**13.2**		**107**	**43.9**	**8:42**									

Signed as a free agent by **Hameenlinna** (Finland), August 17, 2004. Traded to **Pittsburgh** by **Edmonton** with Cory Cross for Dick Tarnstrom, January 26, 2006.

RITCHIE, Byron

(RIHT-chee, BIGH-rohn) **CGY.**

Center. Shoots left. 5'10", 195 lbs. Born, Burnaby, B.C., April 24, 1977. Hartford's 6th choice, 165th overall, in 1995 Entry Draft.

Season	Club	League	GP	G	A	Pts	PIM	PP	SH	GW	S	%	+/-	TF	F%	Min	GP	G	A	Pts	PIM	PP	SH	GW	Min
1992-93	North Delta	BCAHA	60	102	151	253	147																		
1993-94	Lethbridge	WHL	44	4	11	15	44										6	0	0	0	14				
1994-95	Lethbridge	WHL	58	22	28	50	132																		
1995-96	Lethbridge	WHL	66	55	51	106	163										4	0	2	2	4				
	Springfield	AHL	6	2	1	3	4										8	0	3	3	0				
1996-97	Lethbridge	WHL	63	50	76	126	115										18	*16	12	*28	28				
1997-98	New Haven	AHL	65	13	18	31	97																		
1998-99	Carolina	NHL	3	0	0	0	0	0	0	0	0	0.0	0	5	20.0	3:25									
	New Haven	AHL	66	24	33	57	139																		
99-2000	Carolina	NHL	26	0	2	2	17	0	0	0	13	0.0	–10	155	49.7	7:24									
	Cincinnati	IHL	34	8	13	21	81										10	1	6	7	32				
2000-01	Cincinnati	IHL	77	31	35	66	166										5	3	2	5	10				
2001-02	Carolina	NHL	4	0	0	0	2	0	0	0	5	0.0	0	9	44.4	11:30									
	Lowell	AHL	43	25	30	55	38																		
	Florida	NHL	31	5	6	11	34	2	0	0	55	9.1	–2	324	50.9	12:26									
2002-03	Florida	NHL	30	0	3	3	19	0	0	0	29	0.0	–4	251	48.2	9:18									
	San Antonio	AHL	26	3	14	17	68										3	1	0	1	0				
2003-04	Florida	NHL	50	5	6	11	84	0	0	2	65	7.7	–10	168	48.8	13:54									
2004-05	Rogle	Sweden-2	30	17	16	33	111										2	0	0	0	4				
2005-06	Calgary	NHL	45	4	2	6	69	0	0	0	34	11.8	–2	313	52.4	9:52	7	0	0	0	0	0	0	0	9:15
	NHL Totals		**189**	**14**	**19**	**33**	**225**	**2**	**0**	**2**	**201**	**7.0**		**1225**	**50.1**	**10:51**	**7**	**0**	**0**	**0**	**0**	**0**	**0**	**0**	**9:15**

WHL East Second All-Star Team (1996, 1997) • Memorial Cup Tournament All-Star Team (1997)

Rights transferred to **Carolina** after **Hartford** franchise relocated, June 25, 1997. Traded to **Florida** by **Carolina** with Sandis Ozolinsh for Bret Hedican, Kevyn Adams and Tomas Malec, January 16, 2002. Signed as a free agent by **Calgary**, July 2, 2004. Signed as a free agent by **Rogle** (Sweden-2) September 25, 2004.

RIVERS, Jamie

(RIH-vuhrs, JAY-mee)

Defense. Shoots left. 6', 195 lbs. Born, Ottawa, Ont., March 16, 1975. St. Louis' 2nd choice, 63rd overall, in 1993 Entry Draft.

Season	Club	League	GP	G	A	Pts	PIM	PP	SH	GW	S	%	+/-	TF	F%	Min	GP	G	A	Pts	PIM	PP	SH	GW	Min
1989-90	Ottawa South	ODMHA	50	26	46	72	46																		
1990-91	Ott. Jr. Senators	CJHL	55	4	30	34	74																		
1991-92	Sudbury Wolves	OHL	55	3	13	16	20										8	0	0	0	0				
1992-93	Sudbury Wolves	OHL	62	12	43	55	20										14	7	19	26	4				
1993-94	Sudbury Wolves	OHL	65	32	*89	121	58										10	1	9	10	14				
1994-95	Sudbury Wolves	OHL	46	9	56	65	30										18	7	26	33	22				
1995-96	St. Louis	NHL	3	0	0	0	2	0	0	0	5	0.0	–1												
	Worcester IceCats	AHL	75	7	45	52	130										4	0	1	1	4				
1996-97	St. Louis	NHL	15	2	5	7	6	1	0	0	9	22.2	–4												
	Worcester IceCats	AHL	63	8	35	43	83										5	1	2	3	14				
1997-98	St. Louis	NHL	59	2	4	6	36	1	0	1	53	3.8	5												
1998-99	St. Louis	NHL	76	2	5	7	47	1	0	0	78	2.6	–3	0	0.0	14:10	9	1	1	2	2	1	0	1	6:29
99-2000	NY Islanders	NHL	75	1	16	17	84	1	0	0	95	1.1	–4	0	0.0	19:39									
2000-01	Ottawa	NHL	45	2	4	6	44	0	0	0	41	4.9	6	0	0.0	14:01	1	0	0	0	4	0	0	0	12:45
	Grand Rapids	IHL	2	0	0	0	2																		
2001-02	Ottawa	NHL	2	0	0	0	4	0	0	0	3	0.0	–3	0	0.0	11:37									
	Boston	NHL	64	4	2	6	45	1	0	1	48	8.3	6	39	33.3	8:27	3	0	0	0	0	0	0	0	4:57
2002-03	Florida	NHL	1	0	0	0	2	0	0	0	2	0.0	–2	0	0.0	18:27									
	San Antonio	AHL	50	6	19	25	68										3	0	1	1	10				
2003-04	Detroit	NHL	50	3	4	7	41	0	0	0	31	9.7	9	1	0.0	10:14	2	0	0	0	2	0	0	0	5:40
	Grand Rapids	AHL	2	0	0	0	4																		
2004-05	Hershey Bears	AHL	50	7	13	20	46																		
2005-06	Detroit	NHL	15	0	1	1	12	0	0	0	4	0.0	0	0	0.0	8:51									
	Phoenix	NHL	18	0	5	5	26	0	0	0	32	0.0	2	0	0.0	20:06									
	NHL Totals		**423**	**16**	**46**	**62**	**349**	**5**	**0**	**2**	**401**	**4.0**		**40**	**32.5**	**13:47**	**15**	**1**	**1**	**2**	**8**	**1**	**0**	**1**	**6:29**

OHL First All-Star Team (1994) • Canadian Major Junior Second All-Star Team (1994) • OHL Second All-Star Team (1995) • AHL Second All-Star Team (1997)

Claimed by **NY Islanders** from **St. Louis** in Waiver Draft, September 27, 1999. Signed as a free agent by **Ottawa**, November 30, 2000. Claimed on waivers by **Boston** from **Ottawa**, October 13, 2001. Signed as a free agent by **San Antonio** (AHL), November 2, 2002. Signed as a free agent by **Florida**, December 16, 2002. Signed as a free agent by **Detroit**, July 29, 2003. Signed as a free agent by **Hershey** (AHL), November 3, 2004. • Spent majority of 2005-06 season as a healthy reserve. Traded to **Phoenix** by **Detroit** for Phoenix's 7th round choice (Nick Oslund) in 2006 Entry Draft, March 9, 2006.

RIVET, Craig

(rih-VAY, KRAYG) **MTL.**

Defense. Shoots right. 6'2", 205 lbs. Born, North Bay, Ont., September 13, 1974. Montreal's 4th choice, 68th overall, in 1992 Entry Draft.

Season	Club	League	GP	G	A	Pts	PIM	PP	SH	GW	S	%	+/-	TF	F%	Min	GP	G	A	Pts	PIM	PP	SH	GW	Min
1990-91	Barrie Colts	OHA-B	42	9	17	26	55																		
1991-92	Kingston	OHL	66	5	21	26	97																		
1992-93	Kingston	OHL	64	19	55	74	117										16	5	7	12	39				
1993-94	Kingston	OHL	61	12	52	64	100										6	0	3	3	6				
	Fredericton	AHL	4	0	2	2	2																		
1994-95	Fredericton	AHL	78	5	27	32	126										12	0	4	4	17				
	Montreal	NHL	5	0	1	1	5	0	0	0	2	0.0	2												
1995-96	Montreal	NHL	19	1	4	5	54	0	0	0	9	11.1	4												
	Fredericton	AHL	49	5	18	23	189										6	0	0	0	12				
1996-97	Montreal	NHL	35	0	4	4	54	0	0	0	24	0.0	7				5	0	1	1	14	0	0	0	
	Fredericton	AHL	23	3	12	15	99																		
1997-98	Montreal	NHL	61	0	2	2	93	0	0	0	26	0.0	–3				5	0	0	0	2	0	0	0	
1998-99	Montreal	NHL	66	2	8	10	66	0	0	0	39	5.1	–3	0	0.0	14:20									
99-2000	Montreal	NHL	61	3	14	17	76	0	0	1	71	4.2	11	0	0.0	19:03									
2000-01	Montreal	NHL	26	1	2	3	36	0	0	0	22	4.5	–8	0	0.0	19:04									
2001-02	Montreal	NHL	82	8	17	25	76	0	0	0	90	8.9	1	1	0.0	19:00	12	0	3	3	4	0	0	0	21:26
2002-03	Montreal	NHL	82	7	15	22	71	3	0	2	118	5.9	1	0	0.0	22:00									
2003-04	Montreal	NHL	80	4	8	12	98	2	0	1	96	4.2	–1	0	0.0	19:28	11	1	4	5	2	1	0	0	24:07
2004-05	TPS Turku	Finland	18	3	1	4	28										6	0	0	0	39				
2005-06	Montreal	NHL	82	7	27	34	109	5	0	1	122	5.7	–5	2	0.0	22:27	6	0	2	2	2	0	0	0	24:09
	NHL Totals		**599**	**33**	**102**	**135**	**738**	**10**	**0**	**5**	**619**	**5.3**		**3**	**0.0**	**19:33**	**39**	**1**	**10**	**11**	**24**	**1**	**0**	**0**	**23:01**

• Missed majority of 2000-01 season recovering from shoulder injury suffered in game vs. Vancouver, October 30, 2000. Signed as a free agent by **Turku** (Finland), January 11, 2005.

ROACH, Andy

(ROHCH, AN-dee)

Defense. Shoots right. 5'11", 181 lbs. Born, Mattawan, MI, August 22, 1973.

Season	Club	League	GP	G	A	Pts	PIM	PP	SH	GW	S	%	+/-	TF	F%	Min	GP	G	A	Pts	PIM	PP	SH	GW	Min
1991-92	Waterloo	USHL	45	12	16	28	6																		
1992-93	Waterloo	USHL	42	13	17	30	22																		
1993-94	Ferris State	CCHA	32	4	15	19	18																		
1994-95	Ferris State	CCHA	36	11	19	30	26																		
1995-96	Ferris State	CCHA	33	15	19	34	44																		
1996-97	Ferris State	CCHA	37	12	34	46	18																		
1997-98	San Antonio	IHL	67	8	16	24	30																		
1998-99	Long Beach	IHL	41	5	21	26	34																		
	Utah Grizzlies	IHL	44	7	10	17	18																		

			Regular Season														Playoffs								
Season	**Club**	**League**	**GP**	**G**	**A**	**Pts**	**PIM**	**PP**	**SH**	**GW**	**S**	**%**	**+/-**	**TF**	**F%**	**Min**	**GP**	**G**	**A**	**Pts**	**PIM**	**PP**	**SH**	**GW**	**Min**
99-2000	Krefeld Pinguine	Germany	55	19	22	41	40	....	....	....	....	....	....	....	....	....	4	0	0	0	2	....	....	....	....
2000-01	Adler Mannheim	Germany	59	7	13	20	32	....	....	....	....	....	....	....	....	....	12	2	2	4	6	....	....	....	....
2001-02	Adler Mannheim	Germany	60	9	21	30	16	....	....	....	....	....	....	....	....	....	12	1	5	6	8	....	....	....	....
2002-03	Adler Mannheim	Germany	49	18	16	34	16	....	....	....	....	....	....	....	....	....	8	4	5	9	4	....	....	....	....
2003-04	Adler Mannheim	Germany	46	11	21	32	26	....	....	....	....	....	....	....	....	....	6	2	0	2	6	....	....	....	....
2004-05	Lausanne HC	Swiss	14	4	5	9	20	....	....	....	....	....	....	....	....	....	10	4	3	7	12	....	....	....	....
	Lausanne HC	Swiss-Q	7	2	3	5	2	....	....	....	....	....	....	....	....	....	....	....	....	....	....	....	....	....	....
2005-06	**St. Louis**	**NHL**	**5**	**1**	**2**	**3**	**10**	**1**	**0**	**0**	**2**	**50.0**	**0**	**0**	**0.0**	**14:20**	....	....	....	....	....	....	....	....	....
	Peoria Rivermen	AHL	10	2	3	5	6	....	....	....	....	....	....	....	....	....	....	....	....	....	....	....	....	....	....
	ZSC Lions Zurich	Swiss	14	4	7	11	16	....	....	....	....	....	....	....	....	....	10	1	5	6	10	....	....	....	....
	NHL Totals		**5**	**1**	**2**	**3**	**10**	**1**	**0**	**0**	**2**	**50.0**		**0**	**0.0**	**14:20**	....	....	....	....	....	....	....	....	....

Signed as a free agent by **St. Louis**, June 30, 2004. Signed as a free agent by **Lausanne** (Swiss), November 18, 2004. Assigned to **Zurich** (Swiss) by **St. Louis**. December 20, 2005. Signed as a free agent by **Berlin** (Germany), July 21, 2006.

ROBERTS, Gary

(RAW-buhrts, GAIR-ree) **FLA.**

Left wing. Shoots left. 6'2", 215 lbs. Born, North York, Ont., May 23, 1966. Calgary's 1st choice, 12th overall, in 1984 Entry Draft.

Season	Club	League	GP	G	A	Pts	PIM	PP	SH	GW	S	%	+/-	TF	F%	Min	GP	G	A	Pts	PIM	PP	SH	GW	Min
1980-81	Hamilton Kilty B's	OHA-B	3	0	1	1	0	....	....	....	....	....	....	....	....	....	....	....	....	....	....	....	....	....	....
1981-82	Whitby	OMHA	44	55	31	86	133	....	....	....	....	....	....	....	....	....	....	....	....	....	....	....	....	....	....
1982-83	Ottawa 67's	OHL	53	12	8	20	83	....	....	....	....	....	....	....	....	....	5	1	0	1	19	....	....	....	....
1983-84	Ottawa 67's	OHL	48	27	30	57	144	....	....	....	....	....	....	....	....	....	13	10	7	17	62	....	....	....	....
1984-85	Ottawa 67's	OHL	59	44	62	106	186	....	....	....	....	....	....	....	....	....	5	2	8	10	10	....	....	....	....
	Moncton	AHL	7	4	2	6	7	....	....	....	....	....	....	....	....	....	....	....	....	....	....	....	....	....	....
1985-86	Ottawa 67's	OHL	24	26	25	51	83	....	....	....	....	....	....	....	....	....	....	....	....	....	....	....	....	....	....
	Guelph Platers	OHL	23	18	15	33	65	....	....	....	....	....	....	....	....	....	20	18	13	31	43	....	....	....	....
1986-87	**Calgary**	**NHL**	**32**	**5**	**10**	**15**	**85**	**0**	**0**	**0**	**38**	**13.2**	**6**	....	....	....	**2**	**0**	**0**	**0**	**4**	**0**	**0**	**0**	....
	Moncton	AHL	38	20	18	38	72	....	....	....	....	....	....	....	....	....	....	....	....	....	....	....	....	....	....
1987-88	**Calgary**	**NHL**	**74**	**13**	**15**	**28**	**282**	**0**	**0**	**1**	**118**	**11.0**	**24**	....	....	....	**9**	**2**	**3**	**5**	**29**	**0**	**0**	**0**	....
1988-89 ♦	**Calgary**	**NHL**	**71**	**22**	**16**	**38**	**250**	**0**	**1**	**2**	**123**	**17.9**	**32**	....	....	....	**22**	**5**	**7**	**12**	**57**	**0**	**0**	**0**	....
1989-90	**Calgary**	**NHL**	**78**	**39**	**33**	**72**	**222**	**5**	**0**	**5**	**175**	**22.3**	**31**	....	....	....	**6**	**2**	**5**	**7**	**41**	**0**	**0**	**0**	....
1990-91	**Calgary**	**NHL**	**80**	**22**	**31**	**53**	**252**	**0**	**0**	**3**	**132**	**16.7**	**15**	....	....	....	**7**	**1**	**3**	**4**	**18**	**0**	**0**	**0**	....
1991-92	**Calgary**	**NHL**	**76**	**53**	**37**	**90**	**207**	**15**	**0**	**2**	**196**	**27.0**	**32**	....	....	....	....	....	....	....	....	....	....	....	....
1992-93	**Calgary**	**NHL**	**58**	**38**	**41**	**79**	**172**	**8**	**3**	**4**	**166**	**22.9**	**32**	....	....	....	**5**	**1**	**6**	**7**	**43**	**1**	**0**	**0**	....
1993-94	**Calgary**	**NHL**	**73**	**41**	**43**	**84**	**145**	**12**	**3**	**5**	**202**	**20.3**	**37**	....	....	....	**7**	**2**	**6**	**8**	**24**	**1**	**0**	**1**	....
1994-95	**Calgary**	**NHL**	**8**	**2**	**2**	**4**	**43**	**2**	**0**	**0**	**20**	**10.0**	**1**	....	....	....	....	....	....	....	....	....	....	....	....
1995-96	**Calgary**	**NHL**	**35**	**22**	**20**	**42**	**78**	**9**	**0**	**5**	**84**	**26.2**	**15**	....	....	....	....	....	....	....	....	....	....	....	....
1996-97	**Calgary**	**NHL**	DID NOT PLAY – INJURED																						
1997-98	**Carolina**	**NHL**	**61**	**20**	**29**	**49**	**103**	**4**	**0**	**2**	**106**	**18.9**	**3**	....	....	....	....	....	....	....	....	....	....	....	....
1998-99	**Carolina**	**NHL**	**77**	**14**	**28**	**42**	**178**	**1**	**1**	**4**	**138**	**10.1**	**2**	**15**	**46.7**	**19:36**	**6**	**1**	**1**	**2**	**8**	**0**	**0**	**0**	**21:01**
99-2000	**Carolina**	**NHL**	**69**	**23**	**30**	**53**	**62**	**12**	**0**	**1**	**150**	**15.3**	**–10**	**7**	**28.6**	**18:31**	....	....	....	....	....	....	....	....	....
2000-01	**Toronto**	**NHL**	**82**	**29**	**24**	**53**	**109**	**8**	**2**	**3**	**138**	**21.0**	**16**	**13**	**46.2**	**17:08**	**11**	**2**	**9**	**11**	**0**	**0**	**0**	**0**	**19:49**
2001-02	**Toronto**	**NHL**	**69**	**21**	**27**	**48**	**63**	**6**	**2**	**2**	**122**	**17.2**	**–4**	**6**	**33.3**	**17:23**	**19**	**7**	**12**	**19**	**56**	**3**	**0**	**1**	**19:28**
2002-03	**Toronto**	**NHL**	**14**	**5**	**3**	**8**	**10**	**3**	**0**	**0**	**22**	**22.7**	**–2**	**4**	**50.0**	**15:35**	**7**	**1**	**1**	**2**	**8**	**0**	**0**	**0**	**21:04**
2003-04	**Toronto**	**NHL**	**72**	**28**	**20**	**48**	**84**	**11**	**1**	**7**	**124**	**22.6**	**9**	**12**	**33.3**	**17:33**	**13**	**4**	**4**	**8**	**10**	**2**	**0**	**1**	**17:45**
2004-05			DID NOT PLAY																						
2005-06	**Florida**	**NHL**	**58**	**14**	**26**	**40**	**51**	**4**	**0**	**1**	**122**	**11.5**	**4**	**19**	**31.6**	**16:45**	....	....	....	....	....	....	....	....	....
	NHL Totals		**1087**	**411**	**435**	**846**	**2396**	**100**	**13**	**47**	**2176**	**18.9**		**76**	**38.2**	**17:47**	**114**	**28**	**57**	**85**	**298**	**7**	**0**	**3**	**19:30**

OHL Second All-Star Team (1985, 1986) • Bill Masterton Memorial Trophy (1996)

Played in NHL All-Star Game (1992, 1993, 2004)

• Missed remainder of 1994-95 season and majority of 1995-96 season recovering from neck injury suffered in game vs. Toronto, February 4, 1995. • Missed remainder of 1995-96 season and entire 1996-97 season recovering from neck injury suffered in game vs. Vancouver, April 3, 1996. Traded to **Carolina** by **Calgary** with Trevor Kidd for Andrew Cassels and Jean-Sebastien Giguere, August 25, 1997. Signed as a free agent by **Toronto**, July 4, 2000. • Missed majority of 2002-03 season recovering from off-season shoulder surgery, August 13, 2002. Signed as a free agent by **Florida**, August 1, 2005.

ROBIDAS, Stephane

(ROH-bih-dah, STEH-fan) **DAL.**

Defense. Shoots right. 5'11", 188 lbs. Born, Sherbrooke, Que., March 3, 1977. Montreal's 7th choice, 164th overall, in 1995 Entry Draft.

Season	Club	League	GP	G	A	Pts	PIM	PP	SH	GW	S	%	+/-	TF	F%	Min	GP	G	A	Pts	PIM	PP	SH	GW	Min
1992-93	Magog	QAAA	41	3	12	15	16	....	....	....	....	....	....	....	....	....	5	1	1	2	2	....	....	....	....
1993-94	Shawinigan	QMJHL	67	3	18	21	33	....	....	....	....	....	....	....	....	....	1	0	0	0	0	....	....	....	....
1994-95	Shawinigan	QMJHL	71	13	56	69	44	....	....	....	....	....	....	....	....	....	15	7	12	19	4	....	....	....	....
1995-96	Shawinigan	QMJHL	67	23	56	79	53	....	....	....	....	....	....	....	....	....	6	1	5	6	10	....	....	....	....
1996-97	Shawinigan	QMJHL	67	24	51	75	59	....	....	....	....	....	....	....	....	....	7	4	6	10	14	....	....	....	....
1997-98	Fredericton	AHL	79	10	21	31	50	....	....	....	....	....	....	....	....	....	4	0	2	2	0	....	....	....	....
1998-99	Fredericton	AHL	79	8	33	41	59	....	....	....	....	....	....	....	....	....	15	1	5	6	10	....	....	....	....
99-2000	**Montreal**	**NHL**	**1**	**0**	**0**	**0**	**0**	**0**	**0**	**0**	**0**	**0.0**	**0**	**0**	**0.0**	**15:54**	....	....	....	....	....	....	....	....	....
	Quebec Citadelles	AHL	76	14	31	45	36	....	....	....	....	....	....	....	....	....	3	0	1	1	0	....	....	....	....
2000-01	**Montreal**	**NHL**	**65**	**6**	**6**	**12**	**14**	**1**	**0**	**0**	**77**	**7.8**	**0**	**1**	**100.0**	**20:44**	....	....	....	....	....	....	....	....	....
2001-02	**Montreal**	**NHL**	**56**	**1**	**10**	**11**	**14**	**1**	**0**	**0**	**68**	**1.5**	**–25**	**3**	**33.3**	**18:58**	**2**	**0**	**0**	**0**	**4**	**0**	**0**	**0**	**13:07**
2002-03	**Dallas**	**NHL**	**76**	**3**	**7**	**10**	**35**	**0**	**0**	**1**	**47**	**6.4**	**15**	**1**	**100.0**	**12:54**	**12**	**0**	**1**	**1**	**20**	**0**	**0**	**0**	**13:54**
2003-04	**Dallas**	**NHL**	**14**	**1**	**0**	**1**	**8**	**1**	**0**	**0**	**8**	**12.5**	**–2**	**1**	**100.0**	**12:57**	....	....	....	....	....	....	....	....	....
	Chicago	**NHL**	**45**	**2**	**10**	**12**	**33**	**0**	**1**	**1**	**55**	**3.6**	**6**	**0**	**0.0**	**20:56**	....	....	....	....	....	....	....	....	....
2004-05	Frankfurt Lions	Germany	51	15	32	47	64	....	....	....	....	....	....	....	....	....	6	1	2	3	6	....	....	....	....
2005-06	**Dallas**	**NHL**	**75**	**5**	**15**	**20**	**67**	**1**	**1**	**0**	**95**	**5.3**	**15**	**0**	**0.0**	**16:59**	**5**	**0**	**2**	**2**	**4**	**0**	**0**	**0**	**16:42**
	NHL Totals		**332**	**18**	**48**	**66**	**171**	**4**	**2**	**2**	**350**	**5.1**		**6**	**66.7**	**17:29**	**19**	**0**	**3**	**3**	**28**	**0**	**0**	**0**	**14:33**

QMJHL First All-Star Team (1996, 1997)

Claimed by **Atlanta** from **Montreal** in Waiver Draft, October 4, 2002. Traded to **Dallas** by **Atlanta** for future considerations, October 4, 2002. Traded to **Chicago** by **Dallas** with Dallas' 2nd round choice (Jakub Sindel) in 2004 Entry Draft for Jon Klemm and NY Rangers' 4th round choice (previously acquired, Dallas selected Fredrik Naslund) in 2004 Entry Draft, November 17, 2003. Signed as a free agent by **Frankfurt** (Germany), September 17, 2004. Signed as a free agent by **Dallas**, August 6, 2005.

ROBINSON, Nathan

(RAW-bihn-suhn, NAY-than) **BOS.**

Center. Shoots left. 5'9", 181 lbs. Born, Scarborough, Ont., December 31, 1981.

Season	Club	League	GP	G	A	Pts	PIM	PP	SH	GW	S	%	+/-	TF	F%	Min	GP	G	A	Pts	PIM	PP	SH	GW	Min
1998-99	Belleville Bulls	OHL	50	11	8	19	23	....	....	....	....	....	....	....	....	....	21	4	4	8	14	....	....	....	....
99-2000	Belleville Bulls	OHL	61	19	18	37	45	....	....	....	....	....	....	....	....	....	15	3	4	7	10	....	....	....	....
2000-01	Belleville Bulls	OHL	66	32	37	69	57	....	....	....	....	....	....	....	....	....	10	6	10	16	7	....	....	....	....
2001-02	Belleville Bulls	OHL	67	47	63	*110	74	....	....	....	....	....	....	....	....	....	11	8	6	14	10	....	....	....	....
2002-03	Toledo Storm	ECHL	9	5	9	14	29	....	....	....	....	....	....	....	....	....	....	....	....	....	....	....	....	....	....
	Grand Rapids	AHL	53	3	14	17	24	....	....	....	....	....	....	....	....	....	8	0	3	3	0	....	....	....	....
2003-04	**Detroit**	**NHL**	**5**	**0**	**0**	**0**	**2**	**0**	**0**	**0**	**5**	**0.0**	**–1**	**0**	**0.0**	**6:01**	....	....	....	....	....	....	....	....	....
	Grand Rapids	AHL	69	24	26	50	41	....	....	....	....	....	....	....	....	....	3	0	0	0	2	....	....	....	....
2004-05	Grand Rapids	AHL	50	8	16	24	10	....	....	....	....	....	....	....	....	....	....	....	....	....	....	....	....	....	....
	Syracuse Crunch	AHL	19	6	14	20	18	....	....	....	....	....	....	....	....	....	....	....	....	....	....	....	....	....	....
2005-06	**Boston**	**NHL**	**2**	**0**	**0**	**0**	**0**	**0**	**0**	**0**	**1**	**0.0**	**0**	**0**	**0.0**	**3:32**	....	....	....	....	....	....	....	....	....
	Providence Bruins	AHL	70	29	31	60	55	....	....	....	....	....	....	....	....	....	6	4	5	9	2	....	....	....	....
	NHL Totals		**7**	**0**	**0**	**0**	**2**	**0**	**0**	**0**	**6**	**0.0**		**0**	**0.0**	**5:18**	....	....	....	....	....	....	....	....	....

OHL First All-Star Team (2002) • Canadian Major Junior First All-Star Team (2002)

Signed as a free agent by **Detroit**, October 12, 2002. Loaned to **Syracuse** (AHL) by **Grand Rapids** (AHL) for loan of Jeff Panzer, March 11, 2005. Signed as a free agent by **Boston**, August 15, 2005.

ROBITAILLE, Louis

(ROH-buh-tigh, LOO-ee) **WSH.**

Left wing. Shoots left. 6'1", 192 lbs. Born, Montreal, Que., March 16, 1982.

Season	Club	League	GP	G	A	Pts	PIM	PP	SH	GW	S	%	+/-	TF	F%	Min	GP	G	A	Pts	PIM	PP	SH	GW	Min
99-2000	Montreal Rocket	QMJHL	71	3	21	24	266	....	....	....	....	....	....	....	....	....	5	1	1	2	18	....	....	....	....
2000-01	Montreal Rocket	QMJHL	69	2	10	12	269	....	....	....	....	....	....	....	....	....	....	....	....	....	....	....	....	....	....
2001-02	Montreal Rocket	QMJHL	71	3	28	31	294	....	....	....	....	....	....	....	....	....	7	3	0	3	241	....	....	....	....
2002-03	Montreal Rocket	QMJHL	60	7	23	30	191	....	....	....	....	....	....	....	....	....	7	0	10	10	12	....	....	....	....
2003-04	Portland Pirates	AHL	58	1	5	6	103	....	....	....	....	....	....	....	....	....	5	1	0	1	17	....	....	....	....
	Quad City	UHL	2	0	1	1	10	....	....	....	....	....	....	....	....	....	....	....	....	....	....	....	....	....	....
2004-05	Portland Pirates	AHL	59	2	3	5	186	....	....	....	....	....	....	....	....	....	....	....	....	....	....	....	....	....	....

Season	Club	League	GP	G	A	Pts	PIM	PP	SH	GW	S	%	+/-	TF	F%	Min	Playoffs GP	G	A	Pts	PIM	PP	SH	GW	Min
2005-06	Washington	NHL	2	0	0	0	5	0	0	0	0	0.0	–1	0	0.0	4:42	....	....	....	....	....	....	....	....	....
	Hershey Bears	AHL	65	7	12	19	334	....	....	....	....	....	....	....	....	....	21	0	2	2	64	....	....	....	....
	NHL Totals		2	0	0	0	5	0	0	0	0	0.0		0	0.0	4:42	....	....	....	....	....	....	....	....	....

Signed as a free agent by **Washington**, August 24, 2004.

ROBITAILLE, Luc

(ROH-buh-tigh, LEWK)

Left wing. Shoots left. 6'1", 215 lbs. Born, Montreal, Que., February 17, 1966. Los Angeles' 9th choice, 171st overall, in 1984 Entry Draft.

Season	Club	League	GP	G	A	Pts	PIM	PP	SH	GW	S	%	+/-	TF	F%	Min	Playoffs GP	G	A	Pts	PIM	PP	SH	GW	Min
1982-83	Mtl-Bourassa	QAAA	48	36	57	93	28	....	....	....	....	....	....	....	....	....	7	9	6	15	14	....	....	....	....
1983-84	Hull Olympiques	QMJHL	70	32	53	85	48	....	....	....	....	....	....	....	....	....	....	....	....	....	....	....	....	....	....
1984-85	Hull Olympiques	QMJHL	64	55	94	149	115	....	....	....	....	....	....	....	....	....	5	4	2	6	27	....	....	....	....
1985-86	Hull Olympiques	QMJHL	63	68	123	191	91	....	....	....	....	....	....	....	....	....	15	17	27	44	28	....	....	....	....
1986-87	Los Angeles	NHL	79	45	39	84	28	18	0	3	199	22.6	–18	....	....	....	5	1	4	5	2	0	0	0	....
1987-88	Los Angeles	NHL	80	53	58	111	82	17	0	6	220	24.1	–9	....	....	....	5	2	5	7	18	2	0	1	....
1988-89	Los Angeles	NHL	78	46	52	98	65	10	0	4	237	19.4	5	....	....	....	11	2	6	8	10	0	0	1	....
1989-90	Los Angeles	NHL	80	52	49	101	38	20	0	7	210	24.8	8	....	....	....	10	5	5	10	12	1	0	1	....
1990-91	Los Angeles	NHL	76	45	46	91	68	11	0	5	229	19.7	28	....	....	....	12	12	4	16	22	5	0	2	....
1991-92	Los Angeles	NHL	80	44	63	107	95	26	0	6	240	18.3	–4	....	....	....	6	3	4	7	12	1	0	1	....
1992-93	Los Angeles	NHL	84	63	62	125	100	24	2	8	265	23.8	18	....	....	....	24	9	13	22	28	4	0	2	....
1993-94	Los Angeles	NHL	83	44	42	86	86	24	0	3	267	16.5	–20	....	....	....	....	....	....	....	....	....	....	....	....
1994-95	Pittsburgh	NHL	46	23	19	42	37	5	0	3	109	21.1	10	....	....	....	12	7	4	11	26	0	0	2	....
1995-96	NY Rangers	NHL	77	23	46	69	80	11	0	4	223	10.3	13	....	....	....	11	1	5	6	8	0	0	0	....
1996-97	NY Rangers	NHL	69	24	24	48	48	5	0	4	200	12.0	16	....	....	....	15	4	7	11	4	0	0	0	....
1997-98	Los Angeles	NHL	57	16	24	40	66	5	0	7	130	12.3	5	....	....	....	4	1	2	3	6	0	0	0	....
1998-99	Los Angeles	NHL	82	39	35	74	54	11	0	7	292	13.4	–1	7	57.1	19:11	....	....	....	....	....	....	....	....	....
99-2000	Los Angeles	NHL	71	36	38	74	68	13	0	7	221	16.3	11	10	30.0	18:34	4	2	2	4	6	0	0	0	20:25
2000-01	Los Angeles	NHL	82	37	51	88	66	16	1	4	235	15.7	10	12	33.3	18:42	13	4	3	7	10	1	0	1	18:19
2001-02♦	Detroit	NHL	81	30	20	50	38	13	0	5	190	15.8	–2	12	41.7	14:51	23	4	5	9	10	1	0	1	13:16
2002-03	Detroit	NHL	81	11	20	31	50	3	0	0	148	7.4	4	18	50.0	12:49	4	1	0	1	0	0	0	0	11:30
2003-04	Los Angeles	NHL	80	22	29	51	56	12	0	4	221	10.0	4	2	0.0	16:41	....	....	....	....	....	....	....	....	....
2004-05			DID NOT PLAY																						
2005-06	Los Angeles	NHL	65	15	9	24	52	3	0	2	125	12.0	–6	13	30.8	14:03	....	....	....	....	....	....	....	....	....
	NHL Totals		1431	668	726	1394	1177	247	3	89	3961	16.9		74	39.2	16:27	159	58	69	127	174	15	0	12	15:15

QMJHL Second All-Star Team (1985) • QMJHL First All-Star Team (1986) • Canadian Major Junior Player of the Year (1986) • Memorial Cup Tournament All-Star Team (1986) • NHL All-Rookie Team (1987) • NHL Second All-Star Team (1987, 1992, 2001) • Calder Memorial Trophy (1987) • NHL First All-Star Team (1988, 1989, 1990, 1991, 1993)

Played in NHL All-Star Game (1988, 1989, 1990, 1991, 1992, 1993, 1999, 2001)

Traded to **Pittsburgh** by **Los Angeles** for Rick Tocchet and Pittsburgh's 2nd round choice (Pavel Rosa) in 1995 Entry Draft, July 29, 1994. Traded to **NY Rangers** by **Pittsburgh** with Ulf Samuelsson for Petr Nedved and Sergei Zubov, August 31, 1995. Traded to **Los Angeles** by **NY Rangers** for Kevin Stevens, August 28, 1997. Signed as a free agent by **Detroit**, July 5, 2001. Signed as a free agent by **Los Angeles**, July 24, 2003. • Officially announced retirement, effective at end of season, April 11, 2006.

ROBITAILLE, Randy

(ROH-buh-tigh, RAN-dee) **PHI.**

Center. Shoots left. 5'11", 200 lbs. Born, Ottawa, Ont., October 12, 1975.

Season	Club	League	GP	G	A	Pts	PIM	PP	SH	GW	S	%	+/-	TF	F%	Min	Playoffs GP	G	A	Pts	PIM	PP	SH	GW	Min
1993-94	Ott. Jr. Senators	CJHL	57	33	55	88	31	....	....	....	....	....	....	....	....	....	....	....	....	....	....	....	....	....	....
1994-95	Ott. Jr. Senators	CJHL	54	48	77	*125	111	....	....	....	....	....	....	....	....	....	....	....	....	....	....	....	....	....	....
1995-96	Miami U.	CCHA	36	14	31	45	26	....	....	....	....	....	....	....	....	....	....	....	....	....	....	....	....	....	....
1996-97	Miami U.	CCHA	39	27	34	61	44	....	....	....	....	....	....	....	....	....	....	....	....	....	....	....	....	....	....
	Boston	NHL	1	0	0	0	0	0	0	0	0	0.0	0	....	....	....	....	....	....	....	....	....	....	....	....
1997-98	Boston	NHL	4	0	0	0	0	0	0	0	5	0.0	–2	....	....	....	....	....	....	....	....	....	....	....	....
	Providence Bruins	AHL	48	15	29	44	16	....	....	....	....	....	....	....	....	....	....	....	....	....	....	....	....	....	....
1998-99	Boston	NHL	4	0	2	2	0	0	0	0	5	0.0	–1	24	25.0	10:11	1	0	0	0	0	0	0	0	7:14
	Providence Bruins	AHL	74	28	*74	102	34	....	....	....	....	....	....	....	....	....	19	6	*14	20	20	....	....	....	....
99-2000	Nashville	NHL	69	11	14	25	10	2	0	1	113	9.7	–13	528	51.5	12:52	....	....	....	....	....	....	....	....	....
2000-01	Nashville	NHL	62	9	17	26	12	5	0	0	121	7.4	–11	481	48.4	14:10	....	....	....	....	....	....	....	....	....
	Milwaukee	IHL	19	10	23	33	4	....	....	....	....	....	....	....	....	....	....	....	....	....	....	....	....	....	....
2001-02	Los Angeles	NHL	18	4	3	7	17	2	0	0	30	13.3	–9	60	65.0	12:54	....	....	....	....	....	....	....	....	....
	Manchester	AHL	6	7	3	10	0	....	....	....	....	....	....	....	....	....	....	....	....	....	....	....	....	....	....
	Pittsburgh	NHL	40	10	20	30	16	3	0	1	91	11.0	–14	599	51.4	18:08	....	....	....	....	....	....	....	....	....
2002-03	Pittsburgh	NHL	41	5	12	17	8	1	0	2	61	8.2	5	429	55.9	13:58	....	....	....	....	....	....	....	....	....
	NY Islanders	NHL	10	1	2	3	2	1	0	0	8	12.5	0	68	48.5	12:28	5	1	1	2	0	1	0	0	13:03
2003-04	Atlanta	NHL	69	11	26	37	20	5	0	2	121	9.1	–12	1069	50.2	15:51	....	....	....	....	....	....	....	....	....
2004-05	ZSC Lions Zurich	Swiss	36	22	*45	*67	56	....	....	....	....	....	....	....	....	....	15	2	16	18	10	....	....	....	....
2005-06	Minnesota	NHL	67	12	28	40	54	7	0	2	112	10.7	–5	381	51.4	14:44	....	....	....	....	....	....	....	....	....
	NHL Totals		385	63	124	187	139	26	0	8	667	9.4		3639	51.2	14:35	6	1	1	2	0	1	0	0	12:05

CCHA First All-Star Team (1997) • NCAA West First All-American Team (1997) • AHL First All-Star Team (1999) • Les Cunningham Award (MVP – AHL) (1999)

Signed as a free agent by **Boston**, March 27, 1997. Traded to **Atlanta** by **Boston** for Peter Ferraro, June 25, 1999. Traded to **Nashville** by **Atlanta** for Denny Lambert, August 16, 1999. Signed as a free agent by **Los Angeles**, July 6, 2001. Claimed on waivers by **Pittsburgh** from **Los Angeles**, January 4, 2002. Traded to **NY Islanders** by **Pittsburgh** for Philadelphia's 5th round choice (previously acquired, Pittsburgh selected Evgeni Isakov) in 2003 Entry Draft, March 9, 2003. Signed as a free agent by **Atlanta**, August 12, 2003. Signed as a free agent by **Zurich** (Swiss), April 26, 2004. Signed as a free agent by **Nashville**, August 19, 2005. Claimed on waivers by **Minnesota** from **Nashville**, October 4, 2005. Signed as a free agent by **Philadelphia**, July 4, 2006.

ROCHE, Travis

(ROHSH, TRA-vihs) **PHX.**

Defense. Shoots right. 6'1", 200 lbs. Born, Grand Cache, Alta., June 17, 1978.

Season	Club	League	GP	G	A	Pts	PIM	PP	SH	GW	S	%	+/-	TF	F%	Min	Playoffs GP	G	A	Pts	PIM	PP	SH	GW	Min
1996-97	Trail	BCHL	49	17	40	57	159	....	....	....	....	....	....	....	....	....	....	....	....	....	....	....	....	....	....
1997-98	Trail	BCHL	38	11	31	42	104	....	....	....	....	....	....	....	....	....	11	0	8	8	21	....	....	....	....
1998-99	North Dakota	WCHA	DID NOT PLAY – FRESHMAN																						
99-2000	North Dakota	WCHA	42	6	22	28	60	....	....	....	....	....	....	....	....	....	....	....	....	....	....	....	....	....	....
2000-01	North Dakota	WCHA	42	11	38	49	42	....	....	....	....	....	....	....	....	....	....	....	....	....	....	....	....	....	....
	Minnesota	NHL	1	0	0	0	0	0	0	0	0	0.0	0	0	0.0	15:22	....	....	....	....	....	....	....	....	....
2001-02	Minnesota	NHL	4	0	0	0	2	0	0	0	1	0.0	–1	0	0.0	12:30	....	....	....	....	....	....	....	....	....
	Houston Aeros	AHL	60	13	21	34	107	....	....	....	....	....	....	....	....	....	12	2	3	5	6	....	....	....	....
2002-03	Houston Aeros	AHL	65	14	34	48	42	....	....	....	....	....	....	....	....	....	23	3	5	8	26	....	....	....	....
2003-04	Minnesota	NHL	5	0	1	1	0	0	0	0	5	0.0	–3	0	0.0	16:07	....	....	....	....	....	....	....	....	....
	Houston Aeros	AHL	60	8	30	38	18	....	....	....	....	....	....	....	....	....	2	0	0	0	2	....	....	....	....
2004-05	Chicago Wolves	AHL	73	12	38	50	59	....	....	....	....	....	....	....	....	....	18	1	6	7	18	....	....	....	....
2005-06	Chicago Wolves	AHL	59	8	31	39	73	....	....	....	....	....	....	....	....	....	....	....	....	....	....	....	....	....	....
	NHL Totals		10	0	1	1	2	0	0	0	6	0.0		0	0.0	14:36	....	....	....	....	....	....	....	....	....

BCHL Second All-Star Team (1997) • BCHL Rookie of the Year Award (1997) • BCHL Playoff MVP Award (1997) • BCHL First All-Star Team (1998) • BCHL Best Defenseman Award (1998) • WCHA All-Rookie Team (2000) • WCHA First All-Star Team (2001) • NCAA West First All-American Team (2001) • NCAA Championship All-Tournament Team (2001) • AHL First All-Star Team (2005)

Signed as a free agent by **Minnesota**, April 8, 2001. Signed as a free agent by **Atlanta**, July 14, 2004. Signed as a free agent by **Phoenix**, July 20, 2006.

ROENICK, Jeremy

(ROH-nihk, JAIR-eh-mee) **PHX.**

Center. Shoots right. 6'1", 196 lbs. Born, Boston, MA, January 17, 1970. Chicago's 1st choice, 8th overall, in 1988 Entry Draft.

Season	Club	League	GP	G	A	Pts	PIM	PP	SH	GW	S	%	+/-	TF	F%	Min	Playoffs GP	G	A	Pts	PIM	PP	SH	GW	Min
1986-87	Thayer Academy	High-MA	24	31	34	65	....	....	....	....	....	....	....	....	....	....	....	....	....	....	....	....	....	....	....
1987-88	Thayer Academy	High-MA	24	34	50	84	....	....	....	....	....	....	....	....	....	....	....	....	....	....	....	....	....	....	....
1988-89	Hull Olympiques	QMJHL	28	34	36	70	14	....	....	....	....	....	....	....	....	....	....	....	....	....	....	....	....	....	....
	Chicago	NHL	20	9	9	18	4	2	0	0	52	17.3	4	....	....	....	10	1	3	4	7	1	0	1	....
1989-90	Chicago	NHL	78	26	40	66	54	6	0	4	173	15.0	2	....	....	....	20	11	7	18	8	4	0	1	....
1990-91	Chicago	NHL	79	41	53	94	80	15	4	10	194	21.1	38	....	....	....	6	3	5	8	4	1	0	1	....
1991-92	Chicago	NHL	80	53	50	103	98	22	3	13	234	22.6	23	....	....	....	18	12	10	22	12	4	0	3	....
1992-93	Chicago	NHL	84	50	57	107	86	22	3	3	255	19.6	15	....	....	....	4	1	2	3	2	0	0	0	....
1993-94	Chicago	NHL	84	46	61	107	125	24	5	5	281	16.4	21	....	....	....	6	1	6	7	2	0	0	1	....
1994-95	Kolner Haie	Germany	3	3	1	4	2	....	....	....	....	....	....	....	....	....	....	....	....	....	....	....	....	....	....
	Chicago	NHL	33	10	24	34	14	5	0	1	93	10.8	5	....	....	....	8	1	2	3	16	0	0	0	....
1995-96	Chicago	NHL	66	32	35	67	109	12	4	2	171	18.7	9	....	....	....	10	5	7	12	2	1	0	1	....
1996-97	Phoenix	NHL	72	29	40	69	115	10	3	7	228	12.7	–7	....	....	....	6	2	4	6	4	0	0	0	....
1997-98	Phoenix	NHL	79	24	32	56	103	6	1	3	182	13.2	5	....	....	....	6	5	3	8	4	2	2	2	....
	United States	Olympics	4	0	1	1	6	....	....	....	....	....	....	....	....	....	....	....	....	....	....	....	....	....	....

			Regular Season														Playoffs								
Season	Club	League	GP	G	A	Pts	PIM	PP	SH	GW	S	%	+/-	TF	F%	Min	GP	G	A	Pts	PIM	PP	SH	GW	Min
1998-99	Phoenix	NHL	78	24	48	72	130	4	0	3	203	11.8	7	956	47.6	20:10	1	0	0	0	0	0	0	0	26:55
99-2000	Phoenix	NHL	75	34	44	78	102	6	3	12	192	17.7	11	925	50.1	20:51	5	2	2	4	10	1	0	0	19:46
2000-01	Phoenix	NHL	80	30	46	76	114	13	0	7	192	15.6	–1	888	49.1	21:00	....	....	....	....	....	....	....	....	....
2001-02	Philadelphia	NHL	75	21	46	67	74	5	0	3	167	12.6	32	1329	49.1	18:14	5	0	0	0	14	0	0	0	18:41
	United States	Olympics	6	1	4	5	2	....	....	....	....	....	....	....	....	....	....	....	....	....	....	....	....	....	....
2002-03	Philadelphia	NHL	79	27	32	59	75	8	1	6	197	13.7	20	1088	53.0	18:48	13	3	5	8	8	0	0	1	21:07
2003-04	Philadelphia	NHL	62	19	28	47	62	10	1	1	128	14.8	1	846	51.5	17:37	18	4	9	13	8	2	0	1	18:05
2004-05			DID NOT PLAY																						
2005-06	Los Angeles	NHL	58	9	13	22	36	2	0	1	111	8.1	–5	536	49.4	17:22	....	....	....	....	....	....	....	....	....
	NHL Totals		1182	484	658	1142	1381	172	28	81	3053	15.9		6568	50.0	19:16	136	51	65	116	101	16	2	12	19:30

QMJHL Second All-Star Team (1989)

Played in NHL All-Star Game (1991, 1992, 1993, 1994, 1999, 2000, 2002, 2003, 2004)

Traded to **Phoenix** by **Chicago** for Alex Zhamnov, Craig Mills and Phoenix's 1st round choice (Ty Jones) in 1997 Entry Draft, August 16, 1996. Signed as a free agent by **Philadelphia**, July 2, 2001. Traded to **Los Angeles** by **Philadelphia** with Nashville's 3rd round choice (previously acquired, Los Angeles selected Bud Holloway) in 2006 Entry Draft for future considerations, August 4, 2005. Signed as a free agent by **Phoenix**, July 4, 2006.

ROHLOFF, Todd

(ROH-lawf, TAWD)

Defense. Shoots left. 6'3", 213 lbs. Born, Grand Rapids, IL, January 16, 1974.

Season	Club	League	GP	G	A	Pts	PIM	PP	SH	GW	S	%	+/-	TF	F%	Min	GP	G	A	Pts	PIM	PP	SH	GW	Min
1992-93	St. Paul Vulcans	USHL	33	2	9	11	52	....	....	....	....	....	....	....	....	....	....	....	....	....	....	....	....	....	....
1993-94	St. Paul Vulcans	USHL	47	4	22	26	....	....	....	....	....	....	....	....	....	....	....	....	....	....	....	....	....	....	....
1994-95	Miami U.	CCHA	38	1	6	7	22	....	....	....	....	....	....	....	....	....	....	....	....	....	....	....	....	....	....
1995-96	Miami U.	CCHA	23	2	4	6	24	....	....	....	....	....	....	....	....	....	....	....	....	....	....	....	....	....	....
1996-97	Miami U.	CCHA	38	2	12	14	48	....	....	....	....	....	....	....	....	....	....	....	....	....	....	....	....	....	....
1997-98	Miami U.	CCHA	17	2	5	7	38	....	....	....	....	....	....	....	....	....	....	....	....	....	....	....	....	....	....
	Indianapolis Ice	IHL	5	0	1	1	6	....	....	....	....	....	....	....	....	....	1	0	0	0	0	....	....	....	....
1998-99	Portland Pirates	AHL	58	1	6	7	58	....	....	....	....	....	....	....	....	....	....	....	....	....	....	....	....	....	....
	Indianapolis Ice	IHL	12	2	0	2	8	....	....	....	....	....	....	....	....	....	5	1	1	2	6	....	....	....	....
99-2000	Cleveland	IHL	77	1	13	14	88	....	....	....	....	....	....	....	....	....	9	0	0	0	6	....	....	....	....
2000-01	Portland Pirates	AHL	58	3	8	11	59	....	....	....	....	....	....	....	....	....	3	0	0	0	2	....	....	....	....
2001-02	Washington	NHL	16	0	1	1	14	0	0	0	6	0.0	–2	0	0.0	14:11	....	....	....	....	....	....	....	....	....
	Portland Pirates	AHL	17	1	3	4	22	....	....	....	....	....	....	....	....	....	....	....	....	....	....	....	....	....	....
2002-03	Portland Pirates	AHL	64	2	10	12	65	....	....	....	....	....	....	....	....	....	3	0	0	0	2	....	....	....	....
2003-04	Columbus	NHL	24	0	2	2	8	0	0	0	16	0.0	–12	2	50.0	19:15	....	....	....	....	....	....	....	....	....
	Syracuse Crunch	AHL	14	1	5	6	16	....	....	....	....	....	....	....	....	....	....	....	....	....	....	....	....	....	....
	Washington	NHL	35	0	3	3	18	0	0	0	19	0.0	–5	0	0.0	14:07	....	....	....	....	....	....	....	....	....
2004-05	Rochester	AHL	12	0	1	1	4	....	....	....	....	....	....	....	....	....	....	....	....	....	....	....	....	....	....
2005-06	Springfield	AHL	64	0	13	13	80	....	....	....	....	....	....	....	....	....	....	....	....	....	....	....	....	....	....
	NHL Totals		75	0	6	6	40	0	0	0	41	0.0		2	50.0	15:46	....	....	....	....	....	....	....	....	....

Signed as a free agent by **Chicago**, March 24, 1998. Signed as a free agent by **Washington**, July 21, 2000. • Missed majority of 2001-02 season recovering from ankle injury suffered in off-season, September, 2001. Signed as a free agent by **Columbus**, September 5, 2003. Claimed on waivers by **Washington** from **Columbus**, January 9, 2004. Signed as a free agent by **Rochester** (AHL), September 10, 2004. Signed as a free agent by **Tampa Bay**, September 6, 2005.

ROLSTON, Brian

(ROHL-stuhn, BRIGH-uhn) **MIN.**

Center/Right wing. Shoots left. 6'2", 210 lbs. Born, Flint, MI, February 21, 1973. New Jersey's 2nd choice, 11th overall, in 1991 Entry Draft.

Season	Club	League	GP	G	A	Pts	PIM	PP	SH	GW	S	%	+/-	TF	F%	Min	GP	G	A	Pts	PIM	PP	SH	GW	Min
1989-90	Det. Compuware	NAHL	40	36	37	73	57	....	....	....	....	....	....	....	....	....	....	....	....	....	....	....	....	....	....
1990-91	Det. Compuware	NAHL	36	49	46	95	14	....	....	....	....	....	....	....	....	....	....	....	....	....	....	....	....	....	....
1991-92	Lake Superior	CCHA	37	14	23	37	14	....	....	....	....	....	....	....	....	....	....	....	....	....	....	....	....	....	....
1992-93	Lake Superior	CCHA	39	33	31	64	20	....	....	....	....	....	....	....	....	....	....	....	....	....	....	....	....	....	....
1993-94	United States	Nat-Tm	41	20	28	48	36	....	....	....	....	....	....	....	....	....	....	....	....	....	....	....	....	....	....
	United States	Olympics	8	7	0	7	8	....	....	....	....	....	....	....	....	....	....	....	....	....	....	....	....	....	....
	Albany River Rats	AHL	17	5	5	10	8	....	....	....	....	....	....	....	....	....	5	1	2	3	0	....	....	....	....
1994-95	Albany River Rats	AHL	18	9	11	20	10	....	....	....	....	....	....	....	....	....	....	....	....	....	....	....	....	....	....
	◆ New Jersey	NHL	40	7	11	18	17	2	0	3	92	7.6	5	....	....	....	6	2	1	3	4	1	0	0	....
1995-96	New Jersey	NHL	58	13	11	24	8	3	1	4	139	9.4	9	....	....	....	....	....	....	....	....	....	....	....	....
1996-97	New Jersey	NHL	81	18	27	45	20	2	2	3	237	7.6	6	....	....	....	10	4	1	5	6	1	2	0	....
1997-98	New Jersey	NHL	76	16	14	30	16	0	2	1	185	8.6	7	....	....	....	6	1	0	1	2	0	1	0	....
1998-99	New Jersey	NHL	82	24	33	57	14	5	5	3	210	11.4	11	51	45.1	18:49	7	1	0	1	2	0	1	0	17:36
99-2000	New Jersey	NHL	11	3	1	4	0	1	0	2	33	9.1	–2	37	37.8	19:09	....	....	....	....	....	....	....	....	....
	Colorado	NHL	50	8	10	18	12	1	0	3	107	7.5	–6	65	41.5	16:18	....	....	....	....	....	....	....	....	....
	Boston	NHL	16	5	4	9	6	3	0	1	66	7.6	–4	265	41.1	22:13	....	....	....	....	....	....	....	....	....
2000-01	Boston	NHL	77	19	39	58	28	5	0	4	286	6.6	6	666	45.7	19:19	....	....	....	....	....	....	....	....	....
2001-02	Boston	NHL	82	31	31	62	30	6	9	7	331	9.4	11	1289	46.6	20:24	6	4	1	5	0	1	1	0	20:37
	United States	Olympics	6	0	3	3	0	....	....	....	....	....	....	....	....	....	....	....	....	....	....	....	....	....	....
2002-03	Boston	NHL	81	27	32	59	32	6	5	5	281	9.6	1	1148	47.6	20:28	5	0	2	2	0	0	0	0	18:39
2003-04	Boston	NHL	82	19	29	48	40	3	2	3	257	7.4	9	1205	50.7	19:38	7	1	0	1	8	0	0	0	16:33
2004-05			DID NOT PLAY																						
2005-06	Minnesota	NHL	82	34	45	79	50	15	5	7	293	11.6	14	403	46.4	20:21	....	....	....	....	....	....	....	....	....
	United States	Olympics	6	3	1	4	4	....	....	....	....	....	....	....	....	....	....	....	....	....	....	....	....	....	....
	NHL Totals		818	224	287	511	273	52	31	46	2517	8.9		5129	47.2	19:34	47	13	5	18	22	3	5	0	18:15

NCAA Championship All-Tournament Team (1992, 1993) • CCHA First All-Star Team (1993) • NCAA West Second All-American Team (1993)

Traded to **Colorado** by **New Jersey** with New Jersey's 1st round choice (later traded to Boston – Boston selected Martin Samuelsson) in 2000 Entry Draft for Claude Lemieux and Colorado's 1st (David Hale) and 2nd (Matt DeMarchi) round choices in 2000 Entry Draft, November 3, 1999. Traded to **Boston** by **Colorado** with Martin Grenier, Samuel Pahlsson and New Jersey's 1st round choice (previously acquired, Boston selected Martin Samuelsson) in 2000 Entry Draft for Raymond Bourque and Dave Andreychuk, March 6, 2000. Signed as a free agent by **Minnesota**, July 8, 2004.

ROSSITER, Kyle

(RAWS-ih-tuhr, KIGHL)

Defense. Shoots left. 6'3", 220 lbs. Born, Edmonton, Alta., June 9, 1980. Florida's 1st choice, 30th overall, in 1998 Entry Draft.

Season	Club	League	GP	G	A	Pts	PIM	PP	SH	GW	S	%	+/-	TF	F%	Min	GP	G	A	Pts	PIM	PP	SH	GW	Min
1995-96	Edmonton SSAC	AMHL	34	5	19	24	116	....	....	....	....	....	....	....	....	....	....	....	....	....	....	....	....	....	....
1996-97	Spokane Chiefs	WHL	50	0	2	2	65	....	....	....	....	....	....	....	....	....	9	0	0	0	6	....	....	....	....
1997-98	Spokane Chiefs	WHL	61	6	16	22	190	....	....	....	....	....	....	....	....	....	15	0	3	3	28	....	....	....	....
1998-99	Spokane Chiefs	WHL	71	4	17	21	206	....	....	....	....	....	....	....	....	....	....	....	....	....	....	....	....	....	....
99-2000	Spokane Chiefs	WHL	63	11	22	33	155	....	....	....	....	....	....	....	....	....	15	1	4	5	25	....	....	....	....
2000-01	Louisville Panthers	AHL	78	2	5	7	110	....	....	....	....	....	....	....	....	....	....	....	....	....	....	....	....	....	....
2001-02	Florida	NHL	2	0	0	0	2	0	0	0	0	0.0	–1	0	0.0	15:27	....	....	....	....	....	....	....	....	....
	Utah Grizzlies	AHL	74	3	7	10	88	....	....	....	....	....	....	....	....	....	5	0	1	1	0	....	....	....	....
2002-03	San Antonio	AHL	67	0	7	7	107	....	....	....	....	....	....	....	....	....	3	0	0	0	0	....	....	....	....
	Florida	NHL	3	0	0	0	0	0	0	0	0	0.0	–2	0	0.0	10:09	....	....	....	....	....	....	....	....	....
2003-04	Florida	NHL	4	0	0	0	7	0	0	0	1	0.0	–1	0	0.0	11:55	....	....	....	....	....	....	....	....	....
	San Antonio	AHL	51	5	7	12	70	....	....	....	....	....	....	....	....	....	....	....	....	....	....	....	....	....	....
	Atlanta	NHL	2	0	1	1	0	0	0	0	0	0.0	1	0	0.0	10:14	....	....	....	....	....	....	....	....	....
	Chicago Wolves	AHL	12	0	1	1	25	....	....	....	....	....	....	....	....	....	6	0	0	0	19	....	....	....	....
2004-05	Chicago Wolves	AHL	33	1	5	6	43	....	....	....	....	....	....	....	....	....	....	....	....	....	....	....	....	....	....
	Wilkes-Barre	AHL	9	0	1	1	5	....	....	....	....	....	....	....	....	....	1	0	0	0	0	....	....	....	....
2005-06	KalPa Kuopio	Finland	35	1	5	6	187	....	....	....	....	....	....	....	....	....	....	....	....	....	....	....	....	....	....
	Asiago	Italy	9	0	1	1	26	....	....	....	....	....	....	....	....	....	....	....	....	....	....	....	....	....	....
	NHL Totals		11	0	1	1	9	0	0	0	1	0.0		0	0.0	11:46	....	....	....	....	....	....	....	....	....

Canadian Major Junior Scholastic Player of the Year (1998)

Traded to **Atlanta** by **Florida** for Kamil Piros, March 8, 2004. Loaned to **Wilkes-Barre** (AHL) by **Chicago** (AHL) for cash, March 16, 2005. Signed as a free agent by **Asiago** (Italy), February 23, 2006.

ROURKE, Allan

(RAWRK, AL-lan) **NYI**

Defense. Shoots left. 6'1", 214 lbs. Born, Mississauga, Ont., March 6, 1980. Toronto's 6th choice, 154th overall, in 1998 Entry Draft.

Season	Club	League	GP	G	A	Pts	PIM	PP	SH	GW	S	%	+/-	TF	F%	Min	Playoffs GP	G	A	Pts	PIM	PP	SH	GW	Min
			Regular Season														Playoffs								
1995-96	Mississauga Reps	MTHL	38	15	25	40	173	....	....	....	....	....	....	....	....	....	....	....	....	....	....	....	....	....	....
1996-97	Kitchener Rangers	OHL	25	1	1	2	12	....	....	....	....	....	....	....	....	....	6	0	0	0	0	....	....	....	....
1997-98	Kitchener Rangers	OHL	48	5	17	22	59	....	....	....	....	....	....	....	....	....	6	1	1	2	6	....	....	....	....
1998-99	Kitchener Rangers	OHL	66	11	28	39	79	....	....	....	....	....	....	....	....	....	1	0	0	0	2	....	....	....	....
99-2000	Kitchener Rangers	OHL	67	31	43	74	57	....	....	....	....	....	....	....	....	....	5	0	6	6	13	....	....	....	....
2000-01	St. John's	AHL	64	9	19	28	36	....	....	....	....	....	....	....	....	....	....	....	....	....	....	....	....	....	....
2001-02	St. John's	AHL	62	2	9	11	48	....	....	....	....	....	....	....	....	....	10	0	2	2	6	....	....	....	....
2002-03	St. John's	AHL	65	12	19	31	49	....	....	....	....	....	....	....	....	....	....	....	....	....	....	....	....	....	....
2003-04	**Carolina**	**NHL**	25	1	2	3	22	0	0	0	24	4.2	4	0	0.0	12:28	....	....	....	....	....	....	....	....	....
	Lowell	AHL	45	5	9	14	45	....	....	....	....	....	....	....	....	....	....	....	....	....	....	....	....	....	....
2004-05	Lowell	AHL	60	7	9	16	75	....	....	....	....	....	....	....	....	....	11	1	2	3	40	....	....	....	....
2005-06	**NY Islanders**	**NHL**	6	0	1	1	0	0	0	0	2	0.0	1	1	0.0	17:15	....	....	....	....	....	....	....	....	....
	Bridgeport	AHL	58	9	21	30	42	....	....	....	....	....	....	....	....	....	1	1	0	1	0	....	....	....	....
	NHL Totals		**31**	**1**	**3**	**4**	**22**	**0**	**0**	**0**	**26**	**3.8**		**1**	**0.0**	**13:23**	....	....	....	....	....	....	....	....	....

OHL Second All-Star Team (2000)

Traded to **Carolina** by **Toronto** for Harold Druken, May 29, 2003. Signed as a free agent by **NY Islanders**, August 12, 2005.

ROY, Andre

(WAH, AHN-dray) **PIT.**

Right wing. Shoots left. 6'4", 221 lbs. Born, Port Chester, NY, February 8, 1975. Boston's 5th choice, 151st overall, in 1994 Entry Draft.

Season	Club	League	GP	G	A	Pts	PIM	PP	SH	GW	S	%	+/-	TF	F%	Min	Playoffs GP	G	A	Pts	PIM	PP	SH	GW	Min
1992-93	Nord Selects	QAHA	STATISTICS NOT AVAILABLE																						
1993-94	Goulbourn Royals	OHA-C	9	9	13	22	98	....	....	....	....	....	....	....	....	....	....	....	....	....	....	....	....	....	....
	Beauport	QMJHL	33	6	7	13	125	....	....	....	....	....	....	....	....	....	....	....	....	....	....	....	....	....	....
	Chicoutimi	QMJHL	32	4	14	18	152	....	....	....	....	....	....	....	....	....	25	3	6	9	94	....	....	....	....
1994-95	Chicoutimi	QMJHL	20	15	8	23	90	....	....	....	....	....	....	....	....	....	....	....	....	....	....	....	....	....	....
	Drummondville	QMJHL	34	18	13	31	233	....	....	....	....	....	....	....	....	....	4	2	0	2	34	....	....	....	....
1995-96	**Boston**	**NHL**	3	0	0	0	0	0	0	0	0	0.0	0	....	....	....	....	....	....	....	....	....	....	....	....
	Providence Bruins	AHL	58	7	8	15	167	....	....	....	....	....	....	....	....	....	1	0	0	0	10	....	....	....	....
1996-97	**Boston**	**NHL**	10	0	2	2	12	0	0	0	12	0.0	–5	....	....	....	....	....	....	....	....	....	....	....	....
	Providence Bruins	AHL	50	17	11	28	234	....	....	....	....	....	....	....	....	....	....	....	....	....	....	....	....	....	....
1997-98	Providence Bruins	AHL	36	3	11	14	154	....	....	....	....	....	....	....	....	....	....	....	....	....	....	....	....	....	....
	Charlotte	ECHL	27	10	8	18	132	....	....	....	....	....	....	....	....	....	7	2	3	5	34	....	....	....	....
1998-99	Fort Wayne	IHL	65	15	6	21	*395	....	....	....	....	....	....	....	....	....	2	0	0	0	11	....	....	....	....
99-2000	**Ottawa**	**NHL**	73	4	3	7	145	0	0	1	39	10.3	3	3	33.3	6:29	5	0	0	0	2	0	0	0	5:54
2000-01	**Ottawa**	**NHL**	64	3	5	8	169	0	0	0	33	9.1	1	2	50.0	4:36	2	0	0	0	16	0	0	0	4:16
2001-02	**Ottawa**	**NHL**	56	6	8	14	148	0	0	0	60	10.0	3	1	100.0	8:23	....	....	....	....	....	....	....	....	....
	Tampa Bay	**NHL**	9	1	1	2	63	0	0	0	6	16.7	–5	0	0.0	8:58	....	....	....	....	....	....	....	....	....
2002-03	**Tampa Bay**	**NHL**	62	10	7	17	119	0	0	2	85	11.8	0	7	57.1	10:46	5	0	1	1	2	0	0	0	12:31
2003-04 ♦	**Tampa Bay**	**NHL**	33	1	1	2	78	0	0	0	24	4.2	–5	2	50.0	7:52	21	1	2	3	61	0	0	1	6:11
2004-05			DID NOT PLAY																						
2005-06	**Pittsburgh**	**NHL**	42	2	1	3	116	0	0	1	11	18.2	–3	1	100.0	5:03	....	....	....	....	....	....	....	....	....
	NHL Totals		**352**	**27**	**28**	**55**	**850**	**0**	**0**	**4**	**270**	**10.0**		**16**	**56.3**	**7:15**	**33**	**1**	**3**	**4**	**81**	**0**	**0**	**1**	**6:59**

Signed as a free agent by **Ottawa**, April 28, 1999. Traded to **Tampa Bay** by **Ottawa** with Ottawa's 6th round choice (Paul Ranger) in 2002 Entry Draft for Juha Ylonen, March 15, 2002. • Spent majority of 2003-04 season as a healthy reserve. Signed as a free agent by **Pittsburgh**, August 4, 2005.

ROY, Derek

(ROI, DAIR-ihk) **BUF.**

Center. Shoots left. 5'9", 186 lbs. Born, Ottawa, Ont., May 4, 1983. Buffalo's 2nd choice, 32nd overall, in 2001 Entry Draft.

Season	Club	League	GP	G	A	Pts	PIM	PP	SH	GW	S	%	+/-	TF	F%	Min	Playoffs GP	G	A	Pts	PIM	PP	SH	GW	Min
1998-99	Ontario East	OMHA	34	61	31	92	42	....	....	....	....	....	....	....	....	....	....	....	....	....	....	....	....	....	....
99-2000	Kitchener Rangers	OHL	66	34	53	87	44	....	....	....	....	....	....	....	....	....	5	4	1	5	6	....	....	....	....
2000-01	Kitchener Rangers	OHL	65	42	39	81	114	....	....	....	....	....	....	....	....	....	....	....	....	....	....	....	....	....	....
2001-02	Kitchener Rangers	OHL	62	43	46	89	92	....	....	....	....	....	....	....	....	....	4	1	2	3	2	....	....	....	....
2002-03	Kitchener Rangers	OHL	49	28	50	78	73	....	....	....	....	....	....	....	....	....	21	9	*23	32	14	....	....	....	....
2003-04	**Buffalo**	**NHL**	49	9	10	19	12	1	0	4	71	12.7	–8	715	47.4	15:19	....	....	....	....	....	....	....	....	....
	Rochester	AHL	26	10	16	26	20	....	....	....	....	....	....	....	....	....	16	6	8	14	18	....	....	....	....
2004-05	Rochester	AHL	67	16	45	61	60	....	....	....	....	....	....	....	....	....	9	6	5	11	6	....	....	....	....
2005-06	**Buffalo**	**NHL**	70	18	28	46	57	5	1	1	151	11.9	1	807	48.0	17:02	18	5	10	15	16	1	1	0	17:03
	Rochester	AHL	8	7	13	20	10	....	....	....	....	....	....	....	....	....	....	....	....	....	....	....	....	....	....
	NHL Totals		**119**	**27**	**38**	**65**	**69**	**6**	**1**	**5**	**222**	**12.2**		**1522**	**47.7**	**16:19**	**18**	**5**	**10**	**15**	**16**	**1**	**1**	**0**	**17:03**

OHL All-Rookie Team (2000) • OHL Rookie of the Year (2000) • CHL All-Rookie Team (2000) • CHL Plus/Minus Award (2000) • CHL Most Sportsmanlike Player (2000) • Memorial Cup Tournament All-Star Team (2003) • Stafford Smythe Memorial Trophy (Memorial Cup Tournament MVP) (2003)

ROY, Mathieu

(WAH, MA-tyew) **EDM.**

Defense. Shoots right. 6'2", 214 lbs. Born, St-Georges, Que., August 10, 1983. Edmonton's 10th choice, 215th overall, in 2003 Entry Draft.

Season	Club	League	GP	G	A	Pts	PIM	PP	SH	GW	S	%	+/-	TF	F%	Min	Playoffs GP	G	A	Pts	PIM	PP	SH	GW	Min
1998-99	Levis	QAAA	11	4	1	5	16	....	....	....	....	....	....	....	....	....	....	....	....	....	....	....	....	....	....
99-2000	Levis	QAAA	24	3	4	7	88	....	....	....	....	....	....	....	....	....	6	1	1	2	22	....	....	....	....
	Val-d'Or Foreurs	QMJHL	48	1	4	5	66	....	....	....	....	....	....	....	....	....	....	....	....	....	....	....	....	....	....
2000-01	Val-d'Or Foreurs	QMJHL	30	0	7	7	60	....	....	....	....	....	....	....	....	....	17	0	0	0	4	....	....	....	....
2001-02	Val-d'Or Foreurs	QMJHL	53	7	26	33	103	....	....	....	....	....	....	....	....	....	7	0	2	2	19	....	....	....	....
2002-03	Val-d'Or Foreurs	QMJHL	52	11	21	32	164	....	....	....	....	....	....	....	....	....	7	1	0	1	8	....	....	....	....
2003-04	Toronto	AHL	30	0	2	2	46	....	....	....	....	....	....	....	....	....	....	....	....	....	....	....	....	....	....
	Columbus	ECHL	10	1	2	3	13	....	....	....	....	....	....	....	....	....	....	....	....	....	....	....	....	....	....
2004-05	Edmonton	AHL	51	3	22	25	68	....	....	....	....	....	....	....	....	....	....	....	....	....	....	....	....	....	....
2005-06	**Edmonton**	**NHL**	1	0	0	0	0	0	0	0	0	0.0	–1	0	0.0	13:00	....	....	....	....	....	....	....	....	....
	Hamilton	AHL	50	3	16	19	82	....	....	....	....	....	....	....	....	....	....	....	....	....	....	....	....	....	....
	NHL Totals		**1**	**0**	**0**	**0**	**0**	**0**	**0**	**0**	**0**	**0.0**		**0**	**0.0**	**13:00**	....	....	....	....	....	....	....	....	....

ROZSIVAL, Michal

(roh-ZIH-vahl, MEE-khahl) **NYR**

Defense. Shoots right. 6'2", 210 lbs. Born, Vlasim, Czech., September 3, 1978. Pittsburgh's 5th choice, 105th overall, in 1996 Entry Draft.

Season	Club	League	GP	G	A	Pts	PIM	PP	SH	GW	S	%	+/-	TF	F%	Min	Playoffs GP	G	A	Pts	PIM	PP	SH	GW	Min
1994-95	Jihlava Jr.	CzRep-Jr.	31	8	13	21	....	....	....	....	....	....	....	....	....	....	....	....	....	....	....	....	....	....	....
1995-96	HC Dukla Jihlava	CzRep	36	3	4	7	....	....	....	....	....	....	....	....	....	....	....	....	....	....	....	....	....	....	....
1996-97	Swift Current	WHL	63	8	31	39	80	....	....	....	....	....	....	....	....	....	10	0	6	6	15	....	....	....	....
1997-98	Swift Current	WHL	71	14	55	69	122	....	....	....	....	....	....	....	....	....	12	0	5	5	33	....	....	....	....
1998-99	Syracuse Crunch	AHL	49	3	22	25	72	....	....	....	....	....	....	....	....	....	....	....	....	....	....	....	....	....	....
99-2000	**Pittsburgh**	**NHL**	75	4	17	21	48	1	0	1	73	5.5	11	1	0.0	19:01	2	0	0	0	4	0	0	0	30:56
2000-01	**Pittsburgh**	**NHL**	30	1	4	5	26	0	0	0	17	5.9	3	1	100.0	17:06	....	....	....	....	....	....	....	....	....
	Wilkes-Barre	AHL	29	8	8	16	32	....	....	....	....	....	....	....	....	....	21	3	*19	22	23	....	....	....	....
2001-02	**Pittsburgh**	**NHL**	79	9	20	29	47	4	0	4	89	10.1	–6	0	0.0	20:01	....	....	....	....	....	....	....	....	....
2002-03	**Pittsburgh**	**NHL**	53	4	6	10	40	1	0	0	61	6.6	–5	0	0.0	20:25	....	....	....	....	....	....	....	....	....
2003-04	Wilkes-Barre	AHL	1	0	0	0	2	....	....	....	....	....	....	....	....	....	....	....	....	....	....	....	....	....	....
2004-05	HC Ocelari Trinec	CzRep	35	1	10	11	40	....	....	....	....	....	....	....	....	....	....	....	....	....	....	....	....	....	....
	Pardubice	CzRep	16	1	3	4	30	....	....	....	....	....	....	....	....	....	16	1	2	3	34	....	....	....	....
2005-06	**NY Rangers**	**NHL**	82	5	25	30	90	3	0	3	115	4.3	35	1	0.0	22:27	4	0	1	1	8	0	0	0	24:31
	NHL Totals		**319**	**23**	**72**	**95**	**251**	**9**	**0**	**8**	**355**	**6.5**		**3**	**33.3**	**20:12**	**6**	**0**	**1**	**1**	**12**	**0**	**0**	**0**	**26:39**

WHL East First All-Star Team (1998)

• Missed majority of 2003-04 season recovering from knee injury suffered in training camp, September 18, 2003. Signed as a free agent by **Trinec** (CzRep), September 17, 2004. Signed as a free agent by **Pardubice** (CzRep), January, 2005. Signed as a free agent by **NY Rangers**, August 29, 2005.

RUCCHIN, Steve
(ROO-chihn, STEEV) **ATL.**

Center. Shoots left. 6'2", 211 lbs. Born, Thunder Bay, Ont., July 4, 1971. Anaheim's 1st choice, 2nd overall, in 1994 Supplemental Draft.

			Regular Season														Playoffs								
Season	Club	League	GP	G	A	Pts	PIM	PP	SH	GW	S	%	+/-	TF	F%	Min	GP	G	A	Pts	PIM	PP	SH	GW	Min
1989-90	Banting	High-ON	STATISTICS NOT AVAILABLE																						
	Thamesford	OHA-D	2	1	2	3	0	....	....	....	....	....	....	....	....	....	....	....	....	....	....	....	....	....	....
1990-91	Western Ontario	OUAA	34	13	16	29	14	....	....	....	....	....	....	....	....	....	....	....	....	....	....	....	....	....	....
1991-92	Western Ontario	OUAA	37	28	34	62	36	....	....	....	....	....	....	....	....	....	....	....	....	....	....	....	....	....	....
1992-93	Western Ontario	OUAA	34	22	26	48	16	....	....	....	....	....	....	....	....	....	....	....	....	....	....	....	....	....	....
1993-94	Western Ontario	OUAA	35	30	23	53	30	....	....	....	....	....	....	....	....	....	....	....	....	....	....	....	....	....	....
1994-95	San Diego Gulls	IHL	41	11	15	26	14	....	....	....	....	....	....	....	....	....	....	....	....	....	....	....	....	....	....
	Anaheim	NHL	43	6	11	17	23	0	0	1	59	10.2	7	....	....	....	....	....	....	....	....	....	....	....	....
1995-96	Anaheim	NHL	64	19	25	44	12	8	1	4	113	16.8	3	....	....	....	....	....	....	....	....	....	....	....	....
1996-97	Anaheim	NHL	79	19	48	67	24	6	1	2	153	12.4	26	....	....	....	8	1	2	3	10	0	0	0	....
1997-98	Anaheim	NHL	72	17	36	53	13	8	1	3	131	13.0	8	....	....	....	....	....	....	....	....	....	....	....	....
1998-99	Anaheim	NHL	69	23	39	62	22	5	1	5	145	15.9	11	1845	52.3	22:33	4	0	3	3	0	0	0	0	21:55
99-2000	Anaheim	NHL	71	19	38	57	16	10	0	2	131	14.5	9	1996	53.4	22:12	....	....	....	....	....	....	....	....	....
2000-01	Anaheim	NHL	16	3	5	8	0	2	0	0	19	15.8	–5	289	51.6	18:47	....	....	....	....	....	....	....	....	....
2001-02	Anaheim	NHL	38	7	16	23	6	4	0	1	57	12.3	–3	808	52.2	19:17	....	....	....	....	....	....	....	....	....
2002-03	Anaheim	NHL	82	20	38	58	12	6	1	4	194	10.3	–14	1613	54.2	21:05	21	7	3	10	2	1	0	2	23:35
2003-04	Anaheim	NHL	82	20	23	43	12	9	1	1	148	13.5	–14	1446	53.6	19:46	....	....	....	....	....	....	....	....	....
2004-05			DID NOT PLAY																						
2005-06	NY Rangers	NHL	72	13	23	36	10	4	1	0	111	11.7	6	1038	47.7	16:00	4	1	0	1	0	1	0	0	13:50
	NHL Totals		688	166	302	468	150	62	7	23	1261	13.2		9035	52.5	20:09	37	9	8	17	12	2	0	2	22:00

• Missed majority of 2000-01 season recovering from jaw injury suffered in game vs. Colorado, November 15, 2000. • Missed majority of 2001-02 season recovering from leg injury suffered in game vs. San Jose, November 16, 2001. Traded to **NY Rangers** by **Anaheim** for Trevor Gillies and NY Rangers' 4th round choice (later traded back to NY Rangers) in 2007 Entry Draft, August 23, 2005. Signed as a free agent by **Atlanta**, July 3, 2006.

RUCINSKY, Martin
(roo-CHIHN-skee, MAHR-tihn) **ST.L.**

Left wing. Shoots left. 6'1", 205 lbs. Born, Most, Czech., March 11, 1971. Edmonton's 2nd choice, 20th overall, in 1991 Entry Draft.

			Regular Season														Playoffs								
Season	Club	League	GP	G	A	Pts	PIM	PP	SH	GW	S	%	+/-	TF	F%	Min	GP	G	A	Pts	PIM	PP	SH	GW	Min
1988-89	CHZ Litvinov	Czech	3	1	0	1	2	....	....	....	....	....	....	....	....	....	....	....	....	....	....	....	....	....	....
1989-90	CHZ Litvinov	Czech	39	12	6	18	....	....	....	....	....	....	....	....	....	....	8	5	3	8	....	....	....	....	....
1990-91	HC CHZ Litvinov	Czech	56	24	20	44	69	....	....	....	....	....	....	....	....	....	....	....	....	....	....	....	....	....	....
1991-92	Edmonton	NHL	2	0	0	0	0	0	0	0	1	0.0	–3	....	....	....	....	....	....	....	....	....	....	....	....
	Cape Breton	AHL	35	11	12	23	34	....	....	....	....	....	....	....	....	....	....	....	....	....	....	....	....	....	....
	Quebec	NHL	4	1	1	2	2	0	0	0	4	25.0	1	....	....	....	....	....	....	....	....	....	....	....	....
	Halifax Citadels	AHL	7	1	1	2	6	....	....	....	....	....	....	....	....	....	....	....	....	....	....	....	....	....	....
1992-93	Quebec	NHL	77	18	30	48	51	4	0	1	133	13.5	16	....	....	....	6	1	1	2	4	1	0	0	....
1993-94	Quebec	NHL	60	9	23	32	58	4	0	1	96	9.4	4	....	....	....	....	....	....	....	....	....	....	....	....
1994-95	Litvinov	CzRep	13	12	10	22	54	....	....	....	....	....	....	....	....	....	....	....	....	....	....	....	....	....	....
	Quebec	NHL	20	3	6	9	14	0	0	0	32	9.4	5	....	....	....	....	....	....	....	....	....	....	....	....
1995-96	HC Petra Vsetin	CzRep	1	1	1	2	0	....	....	....	....	....	....	....	....	....	....	....	....	....	....	....	....	....	....
	Colorado	NHL	22	4	11	15	14	0	0	1	39	10.3	10	....	....	....	....	....	....	....	....	....	....	....	....
	Montreal	NHL	56	25	35	60	54	9	2	3	142	17.6	8	....	....	....	....	....	....	....	....	....	....	....	....
1996-97	Montreal	NHL	70	28	27	55	62	6	3	3	172	16.3	1	....	....	....	5	0	0	0	4	0	0	0	....
1997-98	Montreal	NHL	78	21	32	53	84	5	3	3	192	10.9	13	....	....	....	10	3	0	3	4	1	0	0	....
	Czech Republic	Olympics	6	3	1	4	4	....	....	....	....	....	....	....	....	....	....	....	....	....	....	....	....	....	....
1998-99	Litvinov	CzRep	3	2	2	4	0	....	....	....	....	....	....	....	....	....	....	....	....	....	....	....	....	....	....
	Montreal	NHL	73	17	17	34	50	5	0	1	180	9.4	–25	12	50.0	18:12	....	....	....	....	....	....	....	....	....
99-2000	Montreal	NHL	80	25	24	49	70	7	1	4	242	10.3	1	31	54.8	18:54	....	....	....	....	....	....	....	....	....
2000-01	Montreal	NHL	57	16	22	38	66	5	1	4	141	11.3	–5	5	40.0	19:11	....	....	....	....	....	....	....	....	....
2001-02	Montreal	NHL	18	2	6	8	12	1	0	0	41	4.9	–1	5	80.0	16:15	....	....	....	....	....	....	....	....	....
	Dallas	NHL	42	6	11	17	24	2	0	1	63	9.5	3	7	57.1	14:33	....	....	....	....	....	....	....	....	....
	Czech Republic	Olympics	4	0	3	3	2	....	....	....	....	....	....	....	....	....	....	....	....	....	....	....	....	....	....
	NY Rangers	NHL	15	3	10	13	6	0	0	1	24	12.5	6	3	33.3	16:39	....	....	....	....	....	....	....	....	....
2002-03	Litvinov	CzRep	2	1	0	1	2	....	....	....	....	....	....	....	....	....	....	....	....	....	....	....	....	....	....
	St. Louis	NHL	61	16	14	30	38	4	4	3	135	11.9	–1	19	57.9	16:55	7	4	2	6	4	0	0	0	16:52
2003-04	NY Rangers	NHL	69	13	29	42	62	0	1	2	161	8.1	13	14	14.3	18:51	....	....	....	....	....	....	....	....	....
	Vancouver	NHL	13	1	2	3	10	0	0	0	45	2.2	2	2	0.0	19:03	7	1	1	2	6	1	0	0	17:02
2004-05	Litvinov	CzRep	38	15	26	41	87	....	....	....	....	....	....	....	....	....	....	....	....	....	....	....	....	....	....
2005-06	NY Rangers	NHL	52	16	39	55	56	4	0	4	152	10.5	10	44	34.1	18:25	2	0	1	1	2	0	0	0	13:29
	Czech Republic	Olympics	8	1	3	4	0	....	....	....	....	....	....	....	....	....	....	....	....	....	....	....	....	....	....
	NHL Totals		869	224	339	563	733	56	15	32	1995	11.2		142	43.7	17:58	37	9	5	14	24	3	0	0	16:31

Played in NHL All-Star Game (2000)

Traded to **Quebec** by **Edmonton** for Ron Tugnutt and Brad Zavisha, March 10, 1992. Transferred to **Colorado** after **Quebec** franchise relocated, June 21, 1995. Traded to **Montreal** by **Colorado** with Andrei Kovalenko and Jocelyn Thibault for Patrick Roy and Mike Keane, December 6, 1995. Traded to **Dallas** by **Montreal** with Benoit Brunet for Donald Audette and Shaun Van Allen, November 21, 2001. Traded to **NY Rangers** by **Dallas** with Roman Lyashenko for Manny Malhotra and Barrett Heisten, March 12, 2002. Signed as a free agent by **St. Louis**, October 30, 2002. Signed as a free agent by **NY Rangers**, August 28, 2003. Traded to **Vancouver** by **NY Rangers** for R.J. Umberger and Martin Grenier, March 9, 2004. Signed as a free agent by **Litvinov** (CzRep), August 20, 2004. Signed as a free agent by **NY Rangers**, August 3, 2005. Signed as a free agent by **St. Louis**, August 2, 2006.

RUPP, Mike
(RUHP, MIGHK) **N.J.**

Center. Shoots left. 6'5", 230 lbs. Born, Cleveland, OH, January 13, 1980. New Jersey's 7th choice, 76th overall, in 2000 Entry Draft.

			Regular Season														Playoffs								
Season	Club	League	GP	G	A	Pts	PIM	PP	SH	GW	S	%	+/-	TF	F%	Min	GP	G	A	Pts	PIM	PP	SH	GW	Min
1996-97	St. Edward's	High-OH	20	26	24	50	....	....	....	....	....	....	....	....	....	....	....	....	....	....	....	....	....	....	....
1997-98	Windsor Spitfires	OHL	38	9	8	17	60	....	....	....	....	....	....	....	....	....	....	....	....	....	....	....	....	....	....
	Erie Otters	OHL	26	7	3	10	57	....	....	....	....	....	....	....	....	....	7	3	1	4	6	....	....	....	....
1998-99	Erie Otters	OHL	63	22	25	47	102	....	....	....	....	....	....	....	....	....	5	0	2	2	25	....	....	....	....
99-2000	Erie Otters	OHL	58	32	21	53	134	....	....	....	....	....	....	....	....	....	13	5	5	10	22	....	....	....	....
2000-01	Albany River Rats	AHL	71	10	10	20	63	....	....	....	....	....	....	....	....	....	....	....	....	....	....	....	....	....	....
2001-02	Albany River Rats	AHL	78	13	17	30	90	....	....	....	....	....	....	....	....	....	....	....	....	....	....	....	....	....	....
2002-03♦	New Jersey	NHL	26	5	3	8	21	2	0	3	34	14.7	0	150	44.7	11:39	4	1	3	4	0	0	0	1	11:28
	Albany River Rats	AHL	47	8	11	19	74	....	....	....	....	....	....	....	....	....	....	....	....	....	....	....	....	....	....
2003-04	New Jersey	NHL	51	6	5	11	41	1	0	1	64	9.4	–1	386	47.9	10:38	....	....	....	....	....	....	....	....	....
	Phoenix	NHL	6	0	1	1	6	0	0	0	12	0.0	–3	94	57.5	16:59	....	....	....	....	....	....	....	....	....
2004-05	Danbury Trashers	UHL	14	5	5	10	30	....	....	....	....	....	....	....	....	....	11	3	4	7	38	....	....	....	....
2005-06	Phoenix	NHL	1	0	0	0	0	0	0	0	1	0.0	0	1	0.0	6:30	....	....	....	....	....	....	....	....	....
	Columbus	NHL	39	4	2	6	58	0	0	0	38	10.5	–3	264	48.1	9:04	....	....	....	....	....	....	....	....	....
	Syracuse Crunch	AHL	3	1	2	3	12	....	....	....	....	....	....	....	....	....	....	....	....	....	....	....	....	....	....
	NHL Totals		123	15	11	26	126	3	0	4	149	10.1		895	48.4	10:38	4	1	3	4	0	0	0	1	11:28

• Re-entered NHL Entry Draft. Originally NY Islanders' 1st choice, 9th overall, in 1998 Entry Draft.

Traded to **Phoenix** by **New Jersey** with New Jersey's 2nd round choice (later traded to Edmonton – Edmonton selected Geoff Paukovich) in 2004 Entry Draft for Jan Hrdina, March 5, 2004. Signed as a free agent by **Danbury** (UHL), February 10, 2005. Traded to **Columbus** by **Phoenix** with Cale Hulse and Jason Chimera for Geoff Sanderson and Tim Jackman, October 8, 2005. Signed as a free agent by **New Jersey**, July 10, 2006.

RUUTU, Jarkko
(ROO-too, YAHR-koh) **PIT.**

Right wing. Shoots left. 6'2", 195 lbs. Born, Vantaa, Finland, August 23, 1975. Vancouver's 3rd choice, 68th overall, in 1998 Entry Draft.

			Regular Season														Playoffs								
Season	Club	League	GP	G	A	Pts	PIM	PP	SH	GW	S	%	+/-	TF	F%	Min	GP	G	A	Pts	PIM	PP	SH	GW	Min
1991-92	HIFK Helsinki Jr.	Fin-Jr.	1	0	0	0	0	....	....	....	....	....	....	....	....	....	....	....	....	....	....	....	....	....	....
1992-93	HIFK Helsinki U18	Fin-U18	33	26	21	47	53	....	....	....	....	....	....	....	....	....	....	....	....	....	....	....	....	....	....
	HIFK Helsinki Jr.	Fin-Jr.	1	0	0	0	0	....	....	....	....	....	....	....	....	....	....	....	....	....	....	....	....	....	....
1993-94	HIFK Helsinki Jr.	Fin-Jr.	19	9	12	21	44	....	....	....	....	....	....	....	....	....	....	....	....	....	....	....	....	....	....
1994-95	HIFK Helsinki Jr.	Fin-Jr.	35	26	22	48	117	....	....	....	....	....	....	....	....	....	....	....	....	....	....	....	....	....	....
1995-96	Michigan Tech	WCHA	39	12	10	22	96	....	....	....	....	....	....	....	....	....	....	....	....	....	....	....	....	....	....
1996-97	HIFK Helsinki	Finland	48	11	10	21	155	....	....	....	....	....	....	....	....	....	....	....	....	....	....	....	....	....	....
1997-98	HIFK Helsinki	Finland	37	10	10	20	166	....	....	....	....	....	....	....	....	....	9	7	4	11	10	....	....	....	....
1998-99	HIFK Helsinki	Finland	25	10	4	14	136	....	....	....	....	....	....	....	....	....	9	0	2	2	43	....	....	....	....
	HIFK Helsinki	EuroHL	5	1	2	3	8	....	....	....	....	....	....	....	....	....	....	....	....	....	....	....	....	....	....
99-2000	Vancouver	NHL	8	0	1	1	6	0	0	0	4	0.0	–1	0	0.0	8:47	....	....	....	....	....	....	....	....	....
	Syracuse Crunch	AHL	65	26	32	58	164	....	....	....	....	....	....	....	....	....	4	3	1	4	8	....	....	....	....
2000-01	Vancouver	NHL	21	3	3	6	32	0	1	0	23	13.0	1	0	0.0	10:39	4	0	1	1	8	0	0	0	10:18
	Kansas City	IHL	46	11	18	29	111	....	....	....	....	....	....	....	....	....	....	....	....	....	....	....	....	....	....

Season	Club	League	GP	G	A	Pts	PIM	PP	SH	GW	S	%	+/-	TF	F%	Min	GP	G	A	Pts	PIM	PP	SH	GW	Min
												Regular Season									Playoffs				
2001-02	Vancouver	NHL	49	2	7	9	74	0	0	0	37	5.4	-1	5	0.0	10:11	1	0	0	0	0	0	0	0	8:53
	Finland	Olympics	4	0	0	0	4										...	...	...	...	...	...	...	...	...
2002-03	Vancouver	NHL	36	2	2	4	66	0	0	1	36	5.6	-7	6	16.7	8:58	13	0	2	2	14	0	0	0	11:59
2003-04	Vancouver	NHL	71	6	8	14	133	1	0	0	70	8.6	-13	20	30.0	11:29	6	1	0	1	10	0	0	0	9:13
2004-05	HIFK Helsinki	Finland	50	10	18	28	215										...	3	0	0	0	41				
2005-06	Vancouver	NHL	82	10	7	17	142	2	0	2	85	11.8	1	11	0.0	11:42	...	...	...	...	...	...	...	...	...
	Finland	Olympics	8	0	0	0	31																		
	NHL Totals		267	23	28	51	453	3	1	3	255	9.0		42	16.7	10:50	24	1	3	4	32	0	0	0	10:53

• Spent majority of 2002-03 season as a healthy reserve. Signed as a free agent by **HIFK Helsinki** (Finland), September 23, 2004. Signed as a free agent by **Pittsburgh**, July 4, 2006.

RUUTU, Tuomo

(ROO-too, TOO-oh-moh)   **CHI.**

Center/Left wing. Shoots left. 6'1", 208 lbs.   Born, Vantaa, Finland, February 16, 1983. Chicago's 1st choice, 9th overall, in 2001 Entry Draft.

Season	Club	League	GP	G	A	Pts	PIM	PP	SH	GW	S	%	+/-	TF	F%	Min	GP	G	A	Pts	PIM	PP	SH	GW	Min
1998-99	HIFK Helsinki U18	Fin-U18	25	9	11	20	88										2	1	1	2	2				
99-2000	HIFK Helsinki U18	Fin-U18	5	0	3	3	12										3	1	2	3	2				
	HIFK Helsinki Jr.	Fin-Jr.	35	11	16	27	32										3	0	1	1	4				
	HIFK Helsinki	Finland	1	0	0	0	2										...	...	...	...	...				
2000-01	Jokerit Helsinki Jr.	Fin-Jr.	2	1	0	1	0										...	...	...	...	...				
	Jokerit Helsinki	Finland	47	11	11	22	94										5	0	0	0	0				
2001-02	Jokerit Helsinki	Finland	51	7	16	23	69										10	0	6	6	29				
2002-03	HIFK Helsinki	Finland	30	12	15	27	24										...	...	...	...	...				
2003-04	Chicago	NHL	82	23	21	44	58	10	0	3	174	13.2	-31	317	46.4	16:24	...	...	...	...	...				
2004-05						DID NOT PLAY																			
2005-06	Chicago	NHL	15	2	3	5	31	1	0	0	30	6.7	-7	90	46.7	14:43	...	...	...	...	...				
	NHL Totals		97	25	24	49	89	11	0	3	204	12.3		407	46.4	16:08	...	...	...	...	...				

• Missed majority of 2005-06 season recovering from back (October 15, 2005 at San Jose) and ankle (January 8, 2006 vs. Nashville) injuries.

RUZICKA, Stefan

(roo-ZHEECH-kuh, STEH-fan)   **PHI.**

Left wing. Shoots right. 6', 205 lbs.   Born, Nitra, Czech., February 17, 1985. Philadelphia's 4th choice, 81st overall, in 2003 Entry Draft.

Season	Club	League	GP	G	A	Pts	PIM	PP	SH	GW	S	%	+/-	TF	F%	Min	GP	G	A	Pts	PIM	PP	SH	GW	Min
2000-01	Nitra Jr.	Slovak-Jr.	38	30	15	45											...	...	...	...	...				
2001-02	HKM Nitra Jr.	Slovak-Jr.	29	27	25	52											...	...	...	...	...				
	HKM Nitra	Slovakia	19	0	5	5	29										...	...	...	...	...				
2002-03	HKM Nitra Jr.	Slovak-Jr.	30	18	22	40	64										...	...	...	...	...				
	HKM Nitra	Slovak-2	17	5	7	12	4										...	...	...	...	...				
2003-04	Owen Sound	OHL	62	34	38	72	63										7	1	6	7	8				
	Philadelphia	AHL	2	0	0	0	0										3	1	6	7	8				
2004-05	Owen Sound	OHL	62	37	33	70	61										8	3	3	6	14				
2005-06	**Philadelphia**	**NHL**	1	0	0	0	2	0	0	0	1	0.0	0	1	0.0	4:48	...	...	...	...	...				
	Philadelphia	AHL	73	16	32	48	88										...	...	...	...	...				
	NHL Totals		1	0	0	0	2	0	0	0	1	0.0		1	0.0	4:48									

OHL All-Rookie Team (2004) • OHL Second All-Star Team (2004)

RYAN, Matt

(RIGH-uhn, MAT)   **L.A.**

Center. Shoots right. 5'11", 182 lbs.   Born, Sharon, Ont., November 12, 1983.

Season	Club	League	GP	G	A	Pts	PIM	PP	SH	GW	S	%	+/-	TF	F%	Min	GP	G	A	Pts	PIM	PP	SH	GW	Min
2001-02	Niagara University	CHA	32	7	12	19	32										...	...	...	...	...				
2002-03	Niagara University	CHA	9	6	2	8	14										...	...	...	...	...				
	Guelph Storm	OHL	48	14	11	25	34										11	2	7	9	0				
2003-04	Guelph Storm	OHL	68	42	35	77	63										22	8	11	19	24				
2004-05	Manchester	AHL	77	9	15	24	59										6	0	1	1	4				
2005-06	**Los Angeles**	**NHL**	12	0	1	1	2	0	0	0	8	0.0	-4	64	45.3	6:07	...	...	...	...	...				
	Manchester	AHL	68	12	12	24	79										7	1	1	2	8				
	NHL Totals		12	0	1	1	2	0	0	0	8	0.0		64	45.3	6:07	...	...	...	...	...				

Signed as a free agent by **Los Angeles**, August 2, 2004.

RYAN, Prestin

(RIGH-uhn, PREH-stuhn)   **VAN.**

Defense. Shoots left. 6', 190 lbs.   Born, Arcola, Sask., June 29, 1980.

Season	Club	League	GP	G	A	Pts	PIM	PP	SH	GW	S	%	+/-	TF	F%	Min	GP	G	A	Pts	PIM	PP	SH	GW	Min
2000-01	U. of Maine	H-East				DID NOT PLAY — FRESHMAN											...	...	...	...	...				
2001-02	U. of Maine	H-East	39	6	9	15	*91										...	...	...	...	...				
2002-03	U. of Maine	H-East	37	1	8	9	*120										...	...	...	...	...				
2003-04	U. of Maine	H-East	43	4	18	22	*148										...	...	...	...	...				
	Syracuse Crunch	AHL														...	3	0	0	0	2				
2004-05	Syracuse Crunch	AHL	59	3	6	9	161										...	...	...	...	...				
2005-06	**Vancouver**	**NHL**	1	0	0	0	2	0	0	0	0	0.0	-1	0	0.0	7:30	...	...	...	...	...				
	Manitoba Moose	AHL	64	11	12	23	63										13	1	1	2	25				
	NHL Totals		1	0	0	0	2	0	0	0	0	0.0		0	0.0	7:30									

Hockey East Second All-Star Team (2004) • NCAA East Second All-American Team (2004) • NCAA Championship All-Tournament Team (2004)
Signed as a free agent by **Columbus**, April 12, 2004. Signed as a free agent by **Vancouver**, August 18, 2005.

RYCROFT, Mark

(RIGH-krawft, MAHRK)   **COL.**

Right wing. Shoots right. 6', 192 lbs.   Born, Penticton, B.C., July 12, 1978.

Season	Club	League	GP	G	A	Pts	PIM	PP	SH	GW	S	%	+/-	TF	F%	Min	GP	G	A	Pts	PIM	PP	SH	GW	Min
1993-94	Penticton Ice	BCAHA	60	47	65	112	100										...	...	...	...	...				
1994-95	Penticton Ice	BCAHA	43	33	43	76	90										...	...	...	...	...				
1995-96	Nanaimo Clippers	BCHL	60	17	28	45	28										...	...	...	...	...				
1996-97	Nanaimo Clippers	BCHL	58	32	35	67	79										...	...	...	...	...				
1997-98	U. of Denver	WCHA	35	15	17	32	28										...	...	...	...	...				
1998-99	U. of Denver	WCHA	41	19	18	37	36										...	...	...	...	...				
99-2000	U. of Denver	WCHA	41	17	17	34	87										...	...	...	...	...				
2000-01	Worcester IceCats	AHL	71	24	26	50	68										11	2	5	7	4				
2001-02	**St. Louis**	**NHL**	9	0	3	3	4	0	0	0	14	0.0	0	1	0.0	9:50	...	...	...	...	...				
	Worcester IceCats	AHL	66	12	19	31	68										3	0	1	1	0				
2002-03	Worcester IceCats	AHL	45	8	18	26	35										3	0	0	0	0				
2003-04	**St. Louis**	**NHL**	71	9	12	21	32	0	0	0	110	8.2	2	11	63.6	14:23	3	0	0	0	2	0	0	0	9:41
2004-05	HC Briancon	France	13	8	8	16	18										4	2	1	3	0				
2005-06	**St. Louis**	**NHL**	80	6	4	10	46	0	1	2	77	7.8	-14	23	34.8	10:27	...	...	...	...	...				
	NHL Totals		160	15	19	34	82	0	1	2	201	7.5		35	42.9	12:09	3	0	0	0	2	0	0	0	9:41

WCHA All-Rookie Team (1998)
Signed as a free agent by **St. Louis**, May 15, 2000. Signed as a free agent by **Briancon** (France), November 9, 2004. Signed as a free agent by **Colorado**, July 12, 2006.

RYDER, Michael

(RIGH-duhr, MIGH-kuhl)   **MTL.**

Right wing. Shoots right. 6', 198 lbs.   Born, Bonavista, Nfld., March 31, 1980. Montreal's 9th choice, 216th overall, in 1998 Entry Draft.

Season	Club	League	GP	G	A	Pts	PIM	PP	SH	GW	S	%	+/-	TF	F%	Min	GP	G	A	Pts	PIM	PP	SH	GW	Min
1996-97	Bonavista Saints	NFAHA	23	31	17	48												...	...	...	...	...				
1997-98	Hull Olympiques	QMJHL	69	34	28	62	41										10	4	2	6	4				
1998-99	Hull Olympiques	QMJHL	69	44	43	87	65										23	*20	16	36	39				
99-2000	Hull Olympiques	QMJHL	63	50	58	108	50										15	11	17	28	28				
2000-01	Tallahassee	ECHL	5	4	5	9	6										...	...	...	...	...				
	Quebec Citadelles	AHL	61	6	9	15	14										...	...	...	...	...				
2001-02	Mississippi	ECHL	20	14	13	27	2										...	...	...	...	...				
	Quebec Citadelles	AHL	50	11	17	28	9										3	0	0	0	0				
2002-03	Hamilton	AHL	69	34	33	67	43										23	11	6	17	8				
2003-04	**Montreal**	**NHL**	81	25	38	63	26	10	0	4	215	11.6	10	25	24.0	16:00	11	1	2	3	4	0	0	0	16:52

			Regular Season														Playoffs								
Season	Club	League	GP	G	A	Pts	PIM	PP	SH	GW	S	%	+/-	TF	F%	Min	GP	G	A	Pts	PIM	PP	SH	GW	Min
2004-05	Leksands IF	Sweden-2	42	34	27	61	32	....	....	....	....	....	....	....	....	....	....	....	....	....	....	....	....	....	....
2005-06	**Montreal**	**NHL**	**81**	**30**	**25**	**55**	**40**	**18**	**0**	**6**	**243**	**12.3**	**–5**	**17**	**52.9**	**16:10**	**6**	**2**	**3**	**5**	**0**	**1**	**0**	**1**	**16:09**
	NHL Totals		**162**	**55**	**63**	**118**	**66**	**28**	**0**	**10**	**458**	**12.0**		**42**	**35.7**	**16:05**	**17**	**3**	**5**	**8**	**4**	**1**	**0**	**1**	**16:37**

NHL All-Rookie Team (2004)
Signed as a free agent by **Leksands** (Sweden-2), September 19, 2004.

RYPIEN, Rick
(RIH-pihn, RIHK) **VAN.**

Center. Shoots right. 5'11", 170 lbs. Born, Coleman, Alta, May 16, 1984.

2001-02	Crowsnest Pass	AJHL	57	12	10	22	143	....	....	....	....	....	....	....	....	....	....	....	....	....	....	....	....	....	....
	Regina Pats	WHL	1	0	0	0	0	....	....	....	....	....	....	....	....	....	....	....	....	....	....	....	....	....	....
2002-03	Regina Pats	WHL	50	6	12	18	159	....	....	....	....	....	....	....	....	....	5	1	1	2	21	....	....	....	....
2003-04	Regina Pats	WHL	65	19	26	45	186	....	....	....	....	....	....	....	....	....	4	0	1	1	18	....	....	....	....
2004-05	Regina Pats	WHL	63	22	29	51	148	....	....	....	....	....	....	....	....	....	....	....	....	....	....	....	....	....	....
	Manitoba Moose	AHL	8	1	1	2	5	....	....	....	....	....	....	....	....	....	14	0	0	0	35	....	....	....	....
2005-06	**Vancouver**	**NHL**	**5**	**1**	**0**	**1**	**4**	**0**	**0**	**0**	**6**	**16.7**	**1**	**22**	**36.4**	**6:19**	....	....	....	....	....	....	....	....	....
	Manitoba Moose	AHL	49	9	6	15	122	....	....	....	....	....	....	....	....	....	13	1	1	2	22	....	....	....	....
	NHL Totals		**5**	**1**	**0**	**1**	**4**	**0**	**0**	**0**	**6**	**16.7**		**22**	**36.4**	**6:19**	....	....	....	....	....	....	....	....	....

Signed to an amateur tryout (ATO) contract by **Manitoba** (AHL), March 22, 2005. Signed as a free agent by **Vancouver**, November 9, 2005.

RYZNAR, Jason
(RIHZ-nuhr, JAY-suhn) **N.J.**

Left wing. Shoots left. 6'3", 200 lbs. Born, Anchorage, AK, February 19, 1983. New Jersey's 3rd choice, 64th overall, in 2002 Entry Draft.

99-2000	USNTDP	NAHL	52	5	10	15	22	....	....	....	....	....	....	....	....	....	3	1	1	2	4	....	....	....	....
2000-01	USNTDP	U-18	42	11	14	25	71	....	....	....	....	....	....	....	....	....	....	....	....	....	....	....	....	....	....
	USNTDP	USHL	24	4	3	7	31	....	....	....	....	....	....	....	....	....	....	....	....	....	....	....	....	....	....
2001-02	U. of Michigan	CCHA	40	9	7	16	22	....	....	....	....	....	....	....	....	....	....	....	....	....	....	....	....	....	....
2002-03	U. of Michigan	CCHA	34	7	9	16	24	....	....	....	....	....	....	....	....	....	....	....	....	....	....	....	....	....	....
2003-04	U. of Michigan	CCHA	36	6	11	17	28	....	....	....	....	....	....	....	....	....	....	....	....	....	....	....	....	....	....
2004-05	U. of Michigan	CCHA	36	6	17	23	46	....	....	....	....	....	....	....	....	....	....	....	....	....	....	....	....	....	....
2005-06	**New Jersey**	**NHL**	**8**	**0**	**0**	**0**	**2**	**0**	**0**	**0**	**1**	**0.0**	**–1**	**0**	**0.0**	**5:19**	....	....	....	....	....	....	....	....	....
	Albany River Rats	AHL	59	7	18	25	52	....	....	....	....	....	....	....	....	....	....	....	....	....	....	....	....	....	....
	NHL Totals		**8**	**0**	**0**	**0**	**2**	**0**	**0**	**0**	**1**	**0.0**		**0**	**0.0**	**5:19**	....	....	....	....	....	....	....	....	....

SAFRONOV, Kirill
(sah-FRAW-nawf, kih-RIHL) **NSH.**

Defense. Shoots left. 6'2", 215 lbs. Born, Leningrad, USSR, February 26, 1981. Phoenix's 2nd choice, 19th overall, in 1999 Entry Draft.

1996-97	St. Petersburg 2	Russia-3	9	0	0	0	6	....	....	....	....	....	....	....	....	....	....	....	....	....	....	....	....	....	....
	St. Petersburg	Russia	1	0	0	0	0	....	....	....	....	....	....	....	....	....	....	....	....	....	....	....	....	....	....
1997-98	St. Petersburg 2	Russia-3	34	4	3	7	36	....	....	....	....	....	....	....	....	....	....	....	....	....	....	....	....	....	....
	St. Petersburg	Russia	9	0	1	1	4	....	....	....	....	....	....	....	....	....	1	0	0	0	0	....	....	....	....
1998-99	St. Petersburg 2	Russia-4	4	2	1	3	2	....	....	....	....	....	....	....	....	....	....	....	....	....	....	....	....	....	....
	St. Petersburg	Russia	45	1	3	4	32	....	....	....	....	....	....	....	....	....	....	....	....	....	....	....	....	....	....
99-2000	Quebec Remparts	QMJHL	55	11	32	43	95	....	....	....	....	....	....	....	....	....	11	2	4	6	14	....	....	....	....
2000-01	Springfield	AHL	65	5	13	18	77	....	....	....	....	....	....	....	....	....	....	....	....	....	....	....	....	....	....
2001-02	**Phoenix**	**NHL**	**1**	**0**	**0**	**0**	**0**	**0**	**0**	**0**	**0**	**0.0**	**–2**	**0**	**0.0**	**6:08**	....	....	....	....	....	....	....	....	....
	Springfield	AHL	68	3	19	22	26	....	....	....	....	....	....	....	....	....	....	....	....	....	....	....	....	....	....
	Atlanta	**NHL**	**2**	**0**	**0**	**0**	**2**	**0**	**0**	**0**	**2**	**0.0**	**–3**	**0**	**0.0**	**21:11**	....	....	....	....	....	....	....	....	....
	Chicago Wolves	AHL	8	0	2	2	2	....	....	....	....	....	....	....	....	....	25	2	6	8	8	....	....	....	....
2002-03	**Atlanta**	**NHL**	**32**	**2**	**2**	**4**	**14**	**0**	**0**	**0**	**21**	**9.5**	**–10**	**1**	**0.0**	**15:02**	....	....	....	....	....	....	....	....	....
	Chicago Wolves	AHL	44	4	15	19	29	....	....	....	....	....	....	....	....	....	9	1	2	3	4	....	....	....	....
2003-04	Chicago Wolves	AHL	21	1	4	5	8	....	....	....	....	....	....	....	....	....	....	....	....	....	....	....	....	....	....
	Milwaukee	AHL	59	4	16	20	41	....	....	....	....	....	....	....	....	....	21	0	6	6	20	....	....	....	....
2004-05	Yaroslavl	Russia	19	0	1	1	49	....	....	....	....	....	....	....	....	....	....	....	....	....	....	....	....	....	....
	Voskresensk	Russia	35	5	8	13	34	....	....	....	....	....	....	....	....	....	....	....	....	....	....	....	....	....	....
2005-06	St. Petersburg	Russia	46	1	13	14	38	....	....	....	....	....	....	....	....	....	2	0	0	0	0	....	....	....	....
	NHL Totals		**35**	**2**	**2**	**4**	**16**	**0**	**0**	**0**	**23**	**8.7**		**1**	**0.0**	**15:08**	....	....	....	....	....	....	....	....	....

Traded to **Atlanta** by **Phoenix** with the rights to Ruslan Zainullin and Phoenix's 5th round choice (Patrick Dwyer) in 2002 Entry Draft for Darcy Hordichuk and Atlanta's 4th (Lance Monych) and 5th (John Zeiler) round choices in 2002 Entry Draft, March 19, 2002. Traded to **Nashville** by **Atlanta** with Simon Gamache for Ben Simon and Tomas Kloucek, December 2, 2003. Signed as a free agent by **Yaroslavl** (Russia), June 13, 2004. Signed as a free agent by **Voskresensk** (Russia), December, 2004. Signed as a free agent by **St. Petersburg** (Russia), July 22, 2005.

ST. JACQUES, Bruno
(SAINT ZHAWK, BROO-noh) **ANA.**

Defense. Shoots left. 6'2", 210 lbs. Born, Montreal, Que., August 22, 1980. Philadelphia's 12th choice, 253rd overall, in 1998 Entry Draft.

1996-97	Mtl-Bourassa	QAAA	40	5	8	13	....	....	....	....	....	....	....	....	....	....	16	0	7	7	....	....	....	....	....
1997-98	Baie-Comeau	QMJHL	63	1	11	12	140	....	....	....	....	....	....	....	....	....	....	....	....	....	....	....	....	....	....
1998-99	Baie-Comeau	QMJHL	49	8	13	21	85	....	....	....	....	....	....	....	....	....	....	....	....	....	....	....	....	....	....
99-2000	Baie-Comeau	QMJHL	60	8	28	36	120	....	....	....	....	....	....	....	....	....	6	0	2	2	10	....	....	....	....
	Philadelphia	AHL	3	0	1	1	0	....	....	....	....	....	....	....	....	....	1	0	0	0	0	....	....	....	....
2000-01	Philadelphia	AHL	45	1	16	17	83	....	....	....	....	....	....	....	....	....	10	1	0	1	16	....	....	....	....
2001-02	**Philadelphia**	**NHL**	**7**	**0**	**0**	**0**	**2**	**0**	**0**	**0**	**4**	**0.0**	**4**	**0**	**0.0**	**13:51**	....	....	....	....	....	....	....	....	....
	Philadelphia	AHL	55	3	11	14	59	....	....	....	....	....	....	....	....	....	4	0	0	0	0	....	....	....	....
2002-03	**Philadelphia**	**NHL**	**6**	**0**	**0**	**0**	**2**	**0**	**0**	**0**	**5**	**0.0**	**–1**	**0**	**0.0**	**14:35**	....	....	....	....	....	....	....	....	....
	Philadelphia	AHL	30	0	7	7	46	....	....	....	....	....	....	....	....	....	....	....	....	....	....	....	....	....	....
	Carolina	**NHL**	**18**	**2**	**5**	**7**	**12**	**0**	**0**	**0**	**14**	**14.3**	**–3**	**0**	**0.0**	**18:15**	....	....	....	....	....	....	....	....	....
	Lowell	AHL	8	1	1	2	8	....	....	....	....	....	....	....	....	....	....	....	....	....	....	....	....	....	....
2003-04	**Carolina**	**NHL**	**35**	**0**	**2**	**2**	**31**	**0**	**0**	**0**	**16**	**0.0**	**–7**	**0**	**0.0**	**11:50**	....	....	....	....	....	....	....	....	....
	Lowell	AHL	6	0	0	0	8	....	....	....	....	....	....	....	....	....	....	....	....	....	....	....	....	....	....
2004-05	Lowell	AHL	68	2	12	14	60	....	....	....	....	....	....	....	....	....	11	1	4	5	4	....	....	....	....
2005-06	**Anaheim**	**NHL**	**1**	**1**	**0**	**1**	**0**	**0**	**0**	**0**	**2**	**50.0**	**1**	**0**	**0.0**	**13:53**	....	....	....	....	....	....	....	....	....
	Portland Pirates	AHL	60	6	19	25	55	....	....	....	....	....	....	....	....	....	14	3	4	7	18	....	....	....	....
	NHL Totals		**67**	**3**	**7**	**10**	**47**	**0**	**0**	**0**	**41**	**7.3**		**1**	**0.0**	**14:03**	....	....	....	....	....	....	....	....	....

Traded to **Carolina** by **Philadelphia** with Pavel Brendl for Sami Kapanen and Ryan Bast, February 7, 2003. • Missed majority of 2003-04 season recovering from abdominal injury suffered in game vs. Philadelphia, November 28, 2003. Traded to **Anaheim** by **Carolina** for Craig Adams, October 3, 2005.

ST. LOUIS, Martin
(sehn-loo-EE, mahr-TEHN) **T.B.**

Right wing. Shoots left. 5'9", 185 lbs. Born, Laval, Que., June 18, 1975.

1991-92	Laval-Laurentides	QAAA	42	29	*74	*103	38	....	....	....	....	....	....	....	....	....	12	7	15	22	16	....	....	....	....
1992-93	Hawkesbury	CJHL	31	37	50	87	70	....	....	....	....	....	....	....	....	....	....	....	....	....	....	....	....	....	....
1993-94	U. of Vermont	ECAC	33	15	36	51	24	....	....	....	....	....	....	....	....	....	....	....	....	....	....	....	....	....	....
1994-95	U. of Vermont	ECAC	35	23	48	71	36	....	....	....	....	....	....	....	....	....	....	....	....	....	....	....	....	....	....
1995-96	U. of Vermont	ECAC	35	29	56	85	38	....	....	....	....	....	....	....	....	....	....	....	....	....	....	....	....	....	....
1996-97	U. of Vermont	ECAC	36	24	*36	60	65	....	....	....	....	....	....	....	....	....	....	....	....	....	....	....	....	....	....
1997-98	Cleveland	IHL	56	16	34	50	24	....	....	....	....	....	....	....	....	....	....	....	....	....	....	....	....	....	....
	Saint John Flames	AHL	25	15	11	26	20	....	....	....	....	....	....	....	....	....	20	5	15	20	16	....	....	....	....
1998-99	**Calgary**	**NHL**	**13**	**1**	**1**	**2**	**10**	**0**	**0**	**0**	**14**	**7.1**	**–2**	**0**	**0.0**	**8:15**	....	....	....	....	....	....	....	....	....
	Saint John Flames	AHL	53	28	34	62	30	....	....	....	....	....	....	....	....	....	7	4	4	8	2	....	....	....	....
99-2000	**Calgary**	**NHL**	**56**	**3**	**15**	**18**	**22**	**0**	**0**	**1**	**73**	**4.1**	**–5**	**3**	**0.0**	**14:41**	....	....	....	....	....	....	....	....	....
	Saint John Flames	AHL	17	15	11	26	14	....	....	....	....	....	....	....	....	....	....	....	....	....	....	....	....	....	....
2000-01	**Tampa Bay**	**NHL**	**78**	**18**	**22**	**40**	**12**	**3**	**3**	**4**	**141**	**12.8**	**–4**	**48**	**41.7**	**15:14**	....	....	....	....	....	....	....	....	....
2001-02	**Tampa Bay**	**NHL**	**53**	**16**	**19**	**35**	**20**	**6**	**1**	**2**	**105**	**15.2**	**4**	**33**	**39.4**	**18:41**	....	....	....	....	....	....	....	....	....
2002-03	**Tampa Bay**	**NHL**	**82**	**33**	**37**	**70**	**32**	**12**	**3**	**5**	**201**	**16.4**	**10**	**37**	**37.8**	**19:43**	**11**	**7**	**5**	**12**	**0**	**1**	**2**	**3**	**22:21**
2003-04♦	**Tampa Bay**	**NHL**	**82**	**38**	***56**	***94**	**24**	**8**	**8**	**7**	**212**	**17.9**	**35**	**24**	**33.3**	**20:35**	**23**	**9**	***15**	**24**	**14**	**3**	**1**	**3**	**22:52**
2004-05	Lausanne HC	Swiss	23	9	16	25	16	....	....	....	....	....	....	....	....	....	....	....	....	....	....	....	....	....	....

			Regular Season														Playoffs								
Season	Club	League	GP	G	A	Pts	PIM	PP	SH	GW	S	%	+/-	TF	F%	Min	GP	G	A	Pts	PIM	PP	SH	GW	Min
2005-06	**Tampa Bay**	**NHL**	**80**	**31**	**30**	**61**	**38**	**9**	**3**	**7**	**221**	**14.0**	**–3**	**13**	**23.1**	**20:59**	**5**	**4**	**0**	**4**	**2**	**1**	**0**	**1**	**22:53**
	Canada	Olympics	6	2	1	3	0	....	....	....	....	....	....	....	....	....	....	....	....	....	....	....	....	....	....
	NHL Totals		**444**	**140**	**180**	**320**	**158**	**38**	**18**	**26**	**967**	**14.5**		**158**	**36.7**	**18:13**	**39**	**20**	**20**	**40**	**16**	**5**	**3**	**7**	**22:43**

ECAC First All-Star Team (1995, 1996, 1997) • ECAC Player of the Year (1995) • NCAA East First All-American Team (1995, 1996, 1997) • NCAA Championship All-Tournament Team (1996) • NHL First All-Star Team (2004) • Art Ross Trophy (2004) • Lester B. Pearson Award (2004) • Hart Trophy (2004)

Played in NHL All-Star Game (2003, 2004)

Signed as a free agent by **Calgary**, February 19, 1998. Signed as a free agent by **Tampa Bay**, July 31, 2000. Signed as a free agent by **Lausanne** (Swiss), November 4, 2004.

ST. PIERRE, Martin

(sehn-PEE-aihr, mahr-TEHN) **CHI.**

Center. Shoots left. 5'9", 185 lbs. Born, Ottawa, Ont., August 11, 1983.

2000-01	Guelph Storm	OHL	68	20	49	69	40	....	....	....	....	....	....	....	....	....	4	0	0	0	4	....	....	....	....
2001-02	Guelph Storm	OHL	66	32	53	85	68	....	....	....	....	....	....	....	....	....	9	3	9	12	12	....	....	....	....
2002-03	Guelph Storm	OHL	55	11	45	56	74	....	....	....	....	....	....	....	....	....	11	5	11	16	4	....	....	....	....
2003-04	Guelph Storm	OHL	68	45	65	110	95	....	....	....	....	....	....	....	....	....	22	8	*27	*35	20	....	....	....	....
2004-05	Greenville	ECHL	45	14	39	53	55	....	....	....	....	....	....	....	....	....	7	2	5	7	6	....	....	....	....
	Edmonton	AHL	18	4	3	7	8	....	....	....	....	....	....	....	....	....	....	....	....	....	....	....	....	....	....
2005-06	**Chicago**	**NHL**	**2**	**0**	**0**	**0**	**0**	**0**	**0**	**0**	**1**	**0.0**	**–1**	**15**	**33.3**	**12:02**	....	....	....	....	....	....	....	....	....
	Norfolk Admirals	AHL	77	23	50	73	98	....	....	....	....	....	....	....	....	....	4	0	3	3	2	....	....	....	....
	NHL Totals		**2**	**0**	**0**	**0**	**0**	**0**	**0**	**0**	**1**	**0.0**		**15**	**33.3**	**12:02**	....	....	....	....	....	....	....	....	....

AHL All-Rookie Team (2006)

Signed as a free agent by **Chicago**, November 3, 2005.

SAKIC, Joe

(SAK-ihk, JOH) **COL.**

Center. Shoots left. 5'11", 195 lbs. Born, Burnaby, B.C., July 7, 1969. Quebec's 2nd choice, 15th overall, in 1987 Entry Draft.

1985-86	Burnaby	BCAHA	80	83	73	156	96	....	....	....	....	....	....	....	....	....	....	....	....	....	....	....	....	....	....
	Lethbridge	WHL	3	0	0	0	0	....	....	....	....	....	....	....	....	....	....	....	....	....	....	....	....	....	....
1986-87	Swift Current	WHL	72	60	73	133	31	....	....	....	....	....	....	....	....	....	4	0	1	1	0	....	....	....	....
1987-88	Swift Current	WHL	64	*78	82	*160	64	....	....	....	....	....	....	....	....	....	10	11	13	24	12	....	....	....	....
1988-89	**Quebec**	**NHL**	**70**	**23**	**39**	**62**	**24**	**10**	**0**	**2**	**148**	**15.5**	**–36**	....	....	....	....	....	....	....	....	....	....	....	....
1989-90	**Quebec**	**NHL**	**80**	**39**	**63**	**102**	**27**	**8**	**1**	**2**	**234**	**16.7**	**–40**	....	....	....	....	....	....	....	....	....	....	....	....
1990-91	**Quebec**	**NHL**	**80**	**48**	**61**	**109**	**24**	**12**	**3**	**7**	**245**	**19.6**	**–26**	....	....	....	....	....	....	....	....	....	....	....	....
1991-92	**Quebec**	**NHL**	**69**	**29**	**65**	**94**	**20**	**6**	**3**	**1**	**217**	**13.4**	**5**	....	....	....	....	....	....	....	....	....	....	....	....
1992-93	**Quebec**	**NHL**	**78**	**48**	**57**	**105**	**40**	**20**	**2**	**4**	**264**	**18.2**	**–3**	....	....	....	**6**	**3**	**3**	**6**	**2**	**1**	**0**	**0**	....
1993-94	**Quebec**	**NHL**	**84**	**28**	**64**	**92**	**18**	**10**	**1**	**9**	**279**	**10.0**	**–8**	....	....	....	....	....	....	....	....	....	....	....	....
1994-95	**Quebec**	**NHL**	**47**	**19**	**43**	**62**	**30**	**3**	**2**	**5**	**157**	**12.1**	**7**	....	....	....	**6**	**4**	**1**	**5**	**0**	**1**	**1**	**1**	....
1995-96 ♦	**Colorado**	**NHL**	**82**	**51**	**69**	**120**	**44**	**17**	**6**	**7**	**339**	**15.0**	**14**	....	....	....	**22**	***18**	**16**	***34**	**14**	**6**	**0**	**6**	....
1996-97	**Colorado**	**NHL**	**65**	**22**	**52**	**74**	**34**	**10**	**2**	**5**	**261**	**8.4**	**–10**	....	....	....	**17**	**8**	***17**	**25**	**14**	**3**	**0**	**0**	....
1997-98	**Colorado**	**NHL**	**64**	**27**	**36**	**63**	**50**	**12**	**1**	**2**	**254**	**10.6**	**0**	....	....	....	**6**	**2**	**3**	**5**	**6**	**0**	**1**	**2**	....
	Canada	Olympics	4	1	2	3	4	....	....	....	....	....	....	....	....	....	....	....	....	....	....	....	....	....	....
1998-99	**Colorado**	**NHL**	**73**	**41**	**55**	**96**	**29**	**12**	**5**	**6**	**255**	**16.1**	**23**	**1723**	**51.4**	**25:35**	**19**	**6**	**13**	**19**	**8**	**1**	**1**	**1**	**25:01**
99-2000	**Colorado**	**NHL**	**60**	**28**	**53**	**81**	**28**	**5**	**1**	**5**	**242**	**11.6**	**30**	**1392**	**53.8**	**23:16**	**17**	**2**	**7**	**9**	**8**	**2**	**0**	**0**	**23:50**
2000-01 ♦	**Colorado**	**NHL**	**82**	**54**	**64**	**118**	**30**	**19**	**3**	**12**	**332**	**16.3**	**45**	**2292**	**53.0**	**23:01**	**21**	***13**	**13**	***26**	**6**	**5**	**0**	**3**	**21:33**
2001-02	**Colorado**	**NHL**	**82**	**26**	**53**	**79**	**18**	**9**	**1**	**4**	**260**	**10.0**	**12**	**2148**	**52.2**	**22:00**	**21**	**9**	**10**	**19**	**4**	**4**	**0**	**1**	**22:44**
	Canada	Olympics	6	4	3	7	0	....	....	....	....	....	....	....	....	....	....	....	....	....	....	....	....	....	....
2002-03	**Colorado**	**NHL**	**58**	**26**	**32**	**58**	**24**	**8**	**0**	**1**	**190**	**13.7**	**4**	**1359**	**50.8**	**21:12**	**7**	**6**	**3**	**9**	**2**	**2**	**0**	**1**	**22:29**
2003-04	**Colorado**	**NHL**	**81**	**33**	**54**	**87**	**42**	**13**	**1**	**3**	**253**	**13.0**	**11**	**1705**	**52.6**	**20:16**	**11**	**7**	**5**	**12**	**8**	**1**	**1**	**2**	**21:15**
2004-05			DID NOT PLAY																						
2005-06	**Colorado**	**NHL**	**82**	**32**	**55**	**87**	**60**	**10**	**0**	**6**	**263**	**12.2**	**10**	**1669**	**52.5**	**19:55**	**9**	**4**	**5**	**9**	**6**	**1**	**0**	**1**	**21:38**
	Canada	Olympics	6	1	2	3	0	....	....	....	....	....	....	....	....	....	....	....	....	....	....	....	....	....	....
	NHL Totals		**1237**	**574**	**915**	**1489**	**542**	**184**	**32**	**81**	**4193**	**13.7**		**12288**	**52.4**	**22:07**	**162**	**82**	**96**	**178**	**78**	**27**	**4**	**18**	**22:49**

WHL East Second All-Star Team (1987) • WHL East Rookie of the Year (1987) • WHL East Player of the Year (1987) • WHL East First All-Star Team (1988) • WHL Player of the Year (1988) • Canadian Major Junior Player of the Year (1988) • Conn Smythe Trophy (1996) • NHL First All-Star Team (2001, 2002, 2004) • Bud Light Plus/Minus Award (2001) (tied with Patrik Elias) • Lady Byng Trophy (2001) • Lester B. Pearson Award (2001) • Hart Trophy (2001) • Olympic Tournament MVP (2002)

Played in NHL All-Star Game (1990, 1991, 1992, 1993, 1994, 1996, 1998, 2000, 2001, 2002, 2004)

Transferred to **Colorado** after **Quebec** franchise relocated, June 21, 1995.

SALEI, Ruslan

(sah-LAY, roos-LAHN) **FLA.**

Defense. Shoots left. 6'1", 213 lbs. Born, Minsk, USSR, November 2, 1974. Anaheim's 1st choice, 9th overall, in 1996 Entry Draft.

1992-93	Dynamo Moscow	CIS	9	1	0	1	10	....	....	....	....	....	....	....	....	....	....	....	....	....	....	....	....	....	....
1993-94	Tivali Minsk	CIS	39	2	3	5	50	....	....	....	....	....	....	....	....	....	....	....	....	....	....	....	....	....	....
1994-95	Tivali Minsk	CIS	51	4	2	6	44	....	....	....	....	....	....	....	....	....	....	....	....	....	....	....	....	....	....
1995-96	Las Vegas	IHL	76	7	23	30	123	....	....	....	....	....	....	....	....	....	15	3	7	10	18	....	....	....	....
1996-97	**Anaheim**	**NHL**	**30**	**0**	**1**	**1**	**37**	**0**	**0**	**0**	**14**	**0.0**	**–8**	....	....	....	....	....	....	....	....	....	....	....	....
	Baltimore Bandits	AHL	12	1	4	5	12	....	....	....	....	....	....	....	....	....	....	....	....	....	....	....	....	....	....
	Las Vegas	IHL	8	0	2	2	24	....	....	....	....	....	....	....	....	....	3	2	1	3	6	....	....	....	....
1997-98	**Anaheim**	**NHL**	**66**	**5**	**10**	**15**	**70**	**1**	**0**	**0**	**104**	**4.8**	**7**	....	....	....	....	....	....	....	....	....	....	....	....
	Cincinnati	AHL	6	3	6	9	14	....	....	....	....	....	....	....	....	....	....	....	....	....	....	....	....	....	....
	Belarus	Olympics	7	1	0	1	4	....	....	....	....	....	....	....	....	....	....	....	....	....	....	....	....	....	....
1998-99	**Anaheim**	**NHL**	**74**	**2**	**14**	**16**	**65**	**1**	**0**	**0**	**123**	**1.6**	**1**	**0**	**0.0**	**22:03**	**3**	**0**	**0**	**0**	**4**	**0**	**0**	**0**	**15:40**
99-2000	**Anaheim**	**NHL**	**71**	**5**	**5**	**10**	**94**	**1**	**0**	**0**	**116**	**4.3**	**3**	**0**	**0.0**	**20:21**	....	....	....	....	....	....	....	....	....
2000-01	**Anaheim**	**NHL**	**50**	**1**	**5**	**6**	**70**	**0**	**0**	**0**	**73**	**1.4**	**–14**	**0**	**0.0**	**20:40**	....	....	....	....	....	....	....	....	....
2001-02	**Anaheim**	**NHL**	**82**	**4**	**7**	**11**	**97**	**0**	**0**	**1**	**96**	**4.2**	**–10**	**0**	**0.0**	**21:25**	....	....	....	....	....	....	....	....	....
	Belarus	Olympics	6	2	1	3	4	....	....	....	....	....	....	....	....	....	....	....	....	....	....	....	....	....	....
2002-03	**Anaheim**	**NHL**	**61**	**4**	**8**	**12**	**78**	**0**	**0**	**0**	**93**	**4.3**	**2**	**0**	**0.0**	**21:53**	**21**	**2**	**3**	**5**	**26**	**0**	**0**	**1**	**26:05**
2003-04	**Anaheim**	**NHL**	**82**	**4**	**11**	**15**	**110**	**0**	**1**	**2**	**145**	**2.8**	**–1**	**0**	**0.0**	**23:42**	....	....	....	....	....	....	....	....	....
2004-05	Ak Bars Kazan	Russia	35	8	12	20	36	....	....	....	....	....	....	....	....	....	4	0	0	0	2	....	....	....	....
2005-06	**Anaheim**	**NHL**	**78**	**1**	**18**	**19**	**114**	**0**	**0**	**0**	**108**	**0.9**	**17**	**2**	**100.0**	**22:31**	**16**	**3**	**2**	**5**	**18**	**0**	**0**	**1**	**22:08**
	NHL Totals		**594**	**26**	**79**	**105**	**735**	**3**	**1**	**3**	**872**	**3.0**		**2**	**100.0**	**21:53**	**40**	**5**	**5**	**10**	**48**	**0**	**0**	**2**	**23:44**

Signed as a free agent by **Kazan** (Russia), October 20, 2004. Signed as a free agent by **Florida**, July 2, 2006.

SALMELAINEN, Tony

(sal-meh-LIGH-nehn, TOH-nee) **CHI.**

Left wing. Shoots right. 5'9", 185 lbs. Born, Espoo, Finland, August 8, 1981. Edmonton's 3rd choice, 41st overall, in 1999 Entry Draft.

1996-97	K-Espoo U18	Fin-U18	30	8	5	13	38	....	....	....	....	....	....	....	....	....	....	....	....	....	....	....	....	....	....
1997-98	K-Espoo U18	Fin-U18	5	2	2	4	10	....	....	....	....	....	....	....	....	....	....	....	....	....	....	....	....	....	....
	HIFK Helsinki U18	Fin-U18	28	23	16	39	30	....	....	....	....	....	....	....	....	....	....	....	....	....	....	....	....	....	....
	HIFK Helsinki Jr.	Fin-Jr.	5	0	0	0	0	....	....	....	....	....	....	....	....	....	....	....	....	....	....	....	....	....	....
1998-99	HIFK Helsinki U18	Fin-U18	6	5	4	9	16	....	....	....	....	....	....	....	....	....	....	....	....	....	....	....	....	....	....
	HIFK Helsinki Jr.	Fin-Jr.	31	23	18	41	55	....	....	....	....	....	....	....	....	....	2	1	2	3	12	....	....	....	....
99-2000	HIFK Helsinki Jr.	Fin-Jr.	1	0	1	1	0	....	....	....	....	....	....	....	....	....	....	....	....	....	....	....	....	....	....
	HIFK Helsinki	Finland	1	1	0	1	0	....	....	....	....	....	....	....	....	....	....	....	....	....	....	....	....	....	....
	HIFK Helsinki	EuroHL	1	0	0	0	0	....	....	....	....	....	....	....	....	....	....	....	....	....	....	....	....	....	....
2000-01	HIFK Helsinki Jr.	Fin-Jr.	3	3	3	6	0	....	....	....	....	....	....	....	....	....	....	....	....	....	....	....	....	....	....
	HIFK Helsinki	Finland	19	1	0	1	6	....	....	....	....	....	....	....	....	....	....	....	....	....	....	....	....	....	....
	Ilves Tampere Jr.	Fin-Jr.	3	1	2	3	2	....	....	....	....	....	....	....	....	....	....	....	....	....	....	....	....	....	....
	Ilves Tampere	Finland	26	3	10	13	4	....	....	....	....	....	....	....	....	....	3	0	0	0	0	....	....	....	....
2001-02	Ilves Tampere Jr.	Fin-Jr.	2	6	0	6	0	....	....	....	....	....	....	....	....	....	....	....	....	....	....	....	....	....	....
	Ilves Tampere	Finland	49	10	9	19	32	....	....	....	....	....	....	....	....	....	3	0	0	0	2	....	....	....	....
2002-03	Hamilton	AHL	67	14	19	33	14	....	....	....	....	....	....	....	....	....	17	6	8	14	0	....	....	....	....
2003-04	**Edmonton**	**NHL**	**13**	**0**	**1**	**1**	**4**	**0**	**0**	**0**	**17**	**0.0**	**–1**	**0**	**0.0**	**9:39**	....	....	....	....	....	....	....	....	....
	Toronto	AHL	58	19	25	44	27	....	....	....	....	....	....	....	....	....	3	0	1	1	0	....	....	....	....
2004-05	Edmonton	AHL	76	22	24	46	26	....	....	....	....	....	....	....	....	....	....	....	....	....	....	....	....	....	....
2005-06	HIFK Helsinki	Finland	53	*27	28	*55	63	....	....	....	....	....	....	....	....	....	12	4	2	6	36	....	....	....	....
	NHL Totals		**13**	**0**	**1**	**1**	**4**	**0**	**0**	**0**	**17**	**0.0**		**0**	**0.0**	**9:39**	....	....	....	....	....	....	....	....	....

Traded to **Chicago** by **Edmonton** for Jaroslav Spacek, January 26, 2006.

SALO, Sami
(SA-loh, SA-mee) **VAN.**

Defense. Shoots right. 6'3", 215 lbs. Born, Turku, Finland, September 2, 1974. Ottawa's 7th choice, 239th overall, in 1996 Entry Draft.

			Regular Season														Playoffs								
Season	Club	League	GP	G	A	Pts	PIM	PP	SH	GW	S	%	+/-	TF	F%	Min	GP	G	A	Pts	PIM	PP	SH	GW	Min
1991-92	Kiekko-67 Jr.	Fin-Jr.	23	4	5	9	26	....	....	....	....	....	....	....	....	....	....	....	....	....	....	....	....	....	....
1992-93	Kiekko-67 Jr.	Fin-Jr.	21	9	4	13	4	....	....	....	....	....	....	....	....	....	....	....	....	....	....	....	....	....	....
1993-94	TPS Turku Jr.	Fin-Jr.	36	7	13	20	16	....	....	....	....	....	....	....	....	....	7	0	1	1	10	....	....	....	....
1994-95	TPS Turku Jr.	Fin-Jr.	14	1	3	4	6	....	....	....	....	....	....	....	....	....	....	....	....	....	....	....	....	....	....
	Kiekko-67 Turku	Finland-2	19	4	2	6	4	....	....	....	....	....	....	....	....	....	....	....	....	....	....	....	....	....	....
	TPS Turku	Finland	7	1	2	3	6	....	....	....	....	....	....	....	....	....	1	0	0	0	0	....	....	....	....
1995-96	TPS Turku	Finland	47	7	14	21	32	....	....	....	....	....	....	....	....	....	11	1	3	4	8	....	....	....	....
1996-97	TPS Turku	Finland	48	9	6	15	10	....	....	....	....	....	....	....	....	....	10	2	3	5	4	....	....	....	....
	TPS Turku	EuroHL	6	0	2	2	6	....	....	....	....	....	....	....	....	....	2	0	0	0	2	....	....	....	....
1997-98	Jokerit Helsinki	Finland	35	3	5	8	24	....	....	....	....	....	....	....	....	....	8	0	1	1	2	....	....	....	....
	Jokerit Helsinki	EuroHL	6	1	1	2	2	....	....	....	....	....	....	....	....	....	....	....	....	....	....	....	....	....	....
1998-99	**Ottawa**	**NHL**	61	7	12	19	24	2	0	1	106	6.6	20	0	0.0	19:42	4	0	0	0	0	0	0	0	21:32
	Detroit Vipers	IHL	5	0	2	2	0	....	....	....	....	....	....	....	....	....	....	....	....	....	....	....	....	....	....
99-2000	**Ottawa**	**NHL**	37	6	8	14	2	3	0	1	85	7.1	6	0	0.0	20:18	6	1	1	2	0	1	0	0	24:11
2000-01	**Ottawa**	**NHL**	31	2	16	18	10	1	0	0	61	3.3	9	0	0.0	19:44	4	0	0	0	0	0	0	0	22:30
2001-02	**Ottawa**	**NHL**	66	4	14	18	14	1	1	2	122	3.3	1	0	0.0	19:52	12	2	1	3	4	0	0	0	20:23
	Finland	Olympics	4	0	0	0	0	....	....	....	....	....	....	....	....	....	....	....	....	....	....	....	....	....	....
2002-03	**Vancouver**	**NHL**	79	9	21	30	10	4	0	1	126	7.1	9	0	0.0	20:08	12	1	3	4	0	0	0	0	20:52
2003-04	**Vancouver**	**NHL**	74	7	19	26	22	5	0	2	143	4.9	8	1	100.0	22:14	7	1	2	3	2	1	0	0	22:59
2004-05	Frolunda	Sweden	41	6	8	14	18	....	....	....	....	....	....	....	....	....	14	1	6	7	2	....	....	....	....
2005-06	**Vancouver**	**NHL**	59	10	23	33	38	9	0	2	140	7.1	9	0	0.0	24:30	....	....	....	....	....	....	....	....	....
	Finland	Olympics	6	1	3	4	0	....	....	....	....	....	....	....	....	....	....	....	....	....	....	....	....	....	....
	NHL Totals		407	45	113	158	120	25	1	9	783	5.7		1	100.0	21:02	45	5	7	12	6	2	0	0	21:43

NHL All-Rookie Team (1999)

• Missed majority of 1999-2000 season recovering from wrist injury suffered in game vs. Philadelphia, November 28, 1999. • Missed majority of 2000-01 season recovering from shoulder injury suffered in game vs. Atlanta, December 14, 2000. Traded to **Vancouver** by **Ottawa** for Peter Schaefer, September 21, 2002. Signed as a free agent by **Frolunda** (Sweden), September 24, 2004.

SALVADOR, Bryce
(SAL-vuh-dohr, BRIGHS) **ST.L.**

Defense. Shoots left. 6'2", 215 lbs. Born, Brandon, Man., February 11, 1976. Tampa Bay's 6th choice, 138th overall, in 1994 Entry Draft.

Season	Club	League	GP	G	A	Pts	PIM	PP	SH	GW	S	%	+/-	TF	F%	Min	GP	G	A	Pts	PIM	PP	SH	GW	Min
1991-92	Brandon	MAHA	52	6	23	29	38	....	....	....	....	....	....	....	....	....	....	....	....	....	....	....	....	....	....
1992-93	Lethbridge	WHL	64	1	4	5	29	....	....	....	....	....	....	....	....	....	4	0	0	0	0	....	....	....	....
1993-94	Lethbridge	WHL	61	4	14	18	36	....	....	....	....	....	....	....	....	....	9	0	1	1	2	....	....	....	....
1994-95	Lethbridge	WHL	67	1	9	10	88	....	....	....	....	....	....	....	....	....	....	....	....	....	....	....	....	....	....
1995-96	Lethbridge	WHL	56	4	12	16	75	....	....	....	....	....	....	....	....	....	3	0	1	1	2	....	....	....	....
1996-97	Lethbridge	WHL	63	8	32	40	81	....	....	....	....	....	....	....	....	....	19	0	7	7	14	....	....	....	....
1997-98	Worcester IceCats	AHL	46	2	8	10	74	....	....	....	....	....	....	....	....	....	11	0	1	1	45	....	....	....	....
1998-99	Worcester IceCats	AHL	69	5	13	18	129	....	....	....	....	....	....	....	....	....	4	0	1	1	2	....	....	....	....
99-2000	Worcester IceCats	AHL	55	0	13	13	53	....	....	....	....	....	....	....	....	....	9	0	1	1	2	....	....	....	....
2000-01	**St. Louis**	**NHL**	75	2	8	10	69	0	0	1	60	3.3	–4	1	0.0	16:38	14	2	0	2	18	0	0	1	14:41
2001-02	**St. Louis**	**NHL**	66	5	7	12	78	1	0	2	37	13.5	3	0	0.0	16:55	10	0	1	1	4	0	0	0	12:34
2002-03	**St. Louis**	**NHL**	71	2	8	10	95	1	0	0	73	2.7	7	0	0.0	18:57	7	0	0	0	2	0	0	0	17:17
2003-04	**St. Louis**	**NHL**	69	3	5	8	47	0	0	1	60	5.0	–4	0	0.0	17:29	5	0	0	0	2	0	0	0	14:31
	Worcester IceCats	AHL	2	0	1	1	0	....	....	....	....	....	....	....	....	....	....	....	....	....	....	....	....	....	....
2004-05	Missouri	UHL	7	0	0	0	16	....	....	....	....	....	....	....	....	....	3	0	0	0	0	....	....	....	....
2005-06	**St. Louis**	**NHL**	46	1	4	5	26	0	0	0	23	4.3	–24	1	0.0	19:48	....	....	....	....	....	....	....	....	....
	NHL Totals		327	13	32	45	315	2	0	4	253	5.1		2	0.0	17:49	36	2	1	3	26	0	0	1	14:35

Signed as a free agent by **St. Louis**, December 16, 1996. Signed as a free agent by **Missouri** (UHL), March 11, 2005.

SAMSONOV, Sergei
(sam-SAWN-nahf, SAIR-gay) **MTL.**

Left wing. Shoots right. 5'8", 194 lbs. Born, Moscow, USSR, October 27, 1978. Boston's 2nd choice, 8th overall, in 1997 Entry Draft.

Season	Club	League	GP	G	A	Pts	PIM	PP	SH	GW	S	%	+/-	TF	F%	Min	GP	G	A	Pts	PIM	PP	SH	GW	Min
1994-95	CSKA Moscow 2	CIS-2	50	110	72	182	....	....	....	....	....	....	....	....	....	....	....	....	....	....	....	....	....	....	....
	CSKA Moscow	CIS	13	2	2	4	14	....	....	....	....	....	....	....	....	....	2	0	0	0	0	....	....	....	....
1995-96	CSKA Moscow	CIS	51	21	17	38	12	....	....	....	....	....	....	....	....	....	3	1	1	2	4	....	....	....	....
1996-97	Detroit Vipers	IHL	73	29	35	64	18	....	....	....	....	....	....	....	....	....	19	8	4	12	12	....	....	....	....
1997-98	**Boston**	**NHL**	81	22	25	47	8	7	0	3	159	13.8	9	....	....	....	6	2	5	7	0	0	0	1	....
1998-99	**Boston**	**NHL**	79	25	26	51	18	6	0	8	160	15.6	–6	0	0.0	16:23	11	3	1	4	0	0	0	0	16:11
99-2000	**Boston**	**NHL**	77	19	26	45	4	6	0	3	145	13.1	–6	3	0.0	16:32	....	....	....	....	....	....	....	....	....
2000-01	**Boston**	**NHL**	82	29	46	75	18	3	0	3	215	13.5	6	14	42.9	19:23	....	....	....	....	....	....	....	....	....
2001-02	**Boston**	**NHL**	74	29	41	70	27	3	0	4	192	15.1	21	1	0.0	18:47	6	2	2	4	0	0	0	0	17:41
	Russia	Olympics	6	1	2	3	4	....	....	....	....	....	....	....	....	....	....	....	....	....	....	....	....	....	....
2002-03	**Boston**	**NHL**	8	5	6	11	2	1	0	3	23	21.7	8	0	0.0	20:20	5	0	2	2	0	0	0	0	17:07
2003-04	**Boston**	**NHL**	58	17	23	40	4	3	0	5	132	12.9	12	4	25.0	17:27	7	2	5	7	0	0	0	0	17:18
2004-05	Dynamo Moscow	Russia	3	1	0	1	0	....	....	....	....	....	....	....	....	....	3	1	2	3	0	....	....	....	....
2005-06	**Boston**	**NHL**	55	18	19	37	22	6	0	1	107	16.8	–3	1	100.0	16:53	....	....	....	....	....	....	....	....	....
	Edmonton	**NHL**	19	5	11	16	6	4	0	0	36	13.9	0	2	0.0	15:26	24	4	11	15	14	1	0	0	14:30
	NHL Totals		533	169	223	392	109	39	0	30	1169	14.5		25	32.0	17:34	59	13	26	39	14	1	0	1	15:50

Garry F. Longman Memorial Trophy (Rookie of the Year – IHL) (1997) • NHL All-Rookie Team (1998) • Calder Memorial Trophy (1998)

Played in NHL All-Star Game (2001)

• Missed majority of 2002-03 season recovering from wrist injury suffered in game vs. Columbus, October 18, 2002. Signed as a free agent by **Dynamo Moscow** (Russia), February 2, 2005. Traded to **Edmonton** by **Boston** for Marty Reasoner, Yan Stastny and Edmonton's 2nd round choice (Milan Lucic) in 2006 Entry Draft, March 9, 2006. Signed as a free agent by **Montreal**, July 12, 2006.

SAMUELSSON, Martin
(SAM-yuhl-suhn, MAHR-tihn) **BOS.**

Right wing. Shoots left. 6'2", 210 lbs. Born, Upplands-Vasby, Sweden, January 25, 1982. Boston's 2nd choice, 27th overall, in 2000 Entry Draft.

Season	Club	League	GP	G	A	Pts	PIM	PP	SH	GW	S	%	+/-	TF	F%	Min	GP	G	A	Pts	PIM	PP	SH	GW	Min
1996-97	Hammarby Jr.	Swe-Jr.	6	1	1	2	0	....	....	....	....	....	....	....	....	....	....	....	....	....	....	....	....	....	....
1997-98	Hammarby Jr.	Swe-Jr.	20	13	12	25	....	....	....	....	....	....	....	....	....	....	....	....	....	....	....	....	....	....	....
	Hammarby	Sweden-2	2	0	0	0	0	....	....	....	....	....	....	....	....	....	....	....	....	....	....	....	....	....	....
1998-99	Malmo Jr.	Swe-Jr.	31	18	13	31	10	....	....	....	....	....	....	....	....	....	....	....	....	....	....	....	....	....	....
99-2000	MoDo U18	Swe-U18	6	3	0	3	4	....	....	....	....	....	....	....	....	....	....	....	....	....	....	....	....	....	....
	Malmo Jr.	Swe-Jr.	19	9	8	17	18	....	....	....	....	....	....	....	....	....	2	1	0	1	2	....	....	....	....
2000-01	Hammarby	Sweden-2	24	13	4	17	8	....	....	....	....	....	....	....	....	....	5	0	0	0	2	....	....	....	....
	Hammarby Jr.	Swe-Jr.	1	0	1	1	0	....	....	....	....	....	....	....	....	....	....	....	....	....	....	....	....	....	....
2001-02	Hammarby Jr.	Swe-Jr.	2	5	2	7	2	....	....	....	....	....	....	....	....	....	....	....	....	....	....	....	....	....	....
	Hammarby	Sweden-2	44	13	10	23	45	....	....	....	....	....	....	....	....	....	2	0	0	0	2	....	....	....	....
2002-03	**Boston**	**NHL**	8	0	1	1	2	0	0	0	3	0.0	–1	0	0.0	11:42	....	....	....	....	....	....	....	....	....
	Providence Bruins	AHL	64	24	15	39	34	....	....	....	....	....	....	....	....	....	4	0	0	0	0	....	....	....	....
2003-04	**Boston**	**NHL**	6	0	0	0	0	0	0	0	7	0.0	–1	1	0.0	5:38	....	....	....	....	....	....	....	....	....
	Providence Bruins	AHL	56	1	9	10	15	....	....	....	....	....	....	....	....	....	1	0	0	0	0	....	....	....	....
2004-05	Providence Bruins	AHL	64	7	10	17	35	....	....	....	....	....	....	....	....	....	10	1	0	1	6	....	....	....	....
2005-06	Linkopings HC	Sweden	44	3	4	7	45	....	....	....	....	....	....	....	....	....	8	0	0	0	29	....	....	....	....
	NHL Totals		14	0	1	1	2	0	0	0	10	0.0		1	0.0	9:06	....	....	....	....	....	....	....	....	....

SAMUELSSON, Mikael
(SAM-yuhl-suhn, MIH-kigh-ehl) **DET.**

Right wing. Shoots left. 6'2", 211 lbs. Born, Mariefred, Sweden, December 23, 1976. San Jose's 7th choice, 145th overall, in 1998 Entry Draft.

Season	Club	League	GP	G	A	Pts	PIM	PP	SH	GW	S	%	+/-	TF	F%	Min	GP	G	A	Pts	PIM	PP	SH	GW	Min
1994-95	Sodertalje SK Jr.	Swe-Jr.	30	8	6	14	12	....	....	....	....	....	....	....	....	....	....	....	....	....	....	....	....	....	....
1995-96	Sodertalje SK Jr.	Swe-Jr.	22	13	12	25	20	....	....	....	....	....	....	....	....	....	....	....	....	....	....	....	....	....	....
	Sodertalje SK	Sweden-2	18	5	1	6	0	....	....	....	....	....	....	....	....	....	4	0	0	0	0	....	....	....	....
1996-97	Sodertalje SK Jr.	Swe-Jr.	2	2	1	3	....	....	....	....	....	....	....	....	....	....	....	....	....	....	....	....	....	....	....
	Sodertalje SK	Sweden	29	3	2	5	10	....	....	....	....	....	....	....	....	....	10	0	0	0	4	....	....	....	....
1997-98	Nykoping	Sweden-2	10	5	1	6	14	....	....	....	....	....	....	....	....	....	....	....	....	....	....	....	....	....	....
	Sodertalje SK	Sweden	41	11	9	20	66	....	....	....	....	....	....	....	....	....	....	....	....	....	....	....	....	....	....
1998-99	Sodertalje SK	Sweden-2	18	13	10	23	26	....	....	....	....	....	....	....	....	....	10	2	2	4	12	....	....	....	....
	V.Frolunda	Sweden	27	0	5	5	10	....	....	....	....	....	....	....	....	....	....	....	....	....	....	....	....	....	....

								Regular Season									Playoffs								
Season	Club	League	GP	G	A	Pts	PIM	PP	SH	GW	S	%	+/-	TF	F%	Min	GP	G	A	Pts	PIM	PP	SH	GW	Min
99-2000	Brynas IF Gavle	Sweden	40	4	3	7	76	....	....	....	....	....	....	....	....	....	11	7	2	9	6	....	....	....	....
	Brynas IF Gavle	EuroHL	4	0	2	2	4	....	....	....	....	....	....	....	....	....	....	....	....	....	....	....	....	....	....
2000-01	**San Jose**	**NHL**	**4**	**0**	**0**	**0**	**0**	**0**	**0**	**0**	**3**	**0.0**	**0**	**0**	**0.0**	**4:41**	....	....	....	....	....	....	....	....	....
	Kentucky	AHL	66	32	46	78	58	....	....	....	....	....	....	....	....	....	3	1	0	1	0	....	....	....	....
2001-02	**NY Rangers**	**NHL**	**67**	**6**	**10**	**16**	**23**	**1**	**2**	**1**	**94**	**6.4**	**10**	**5**	**40.0**	**11:52**	....	....	....	....	....	....	....	....	....
	Hartford	AHL	8	3	6	9	12	....	....	....	....	....	....	....	....	....	....	....	....	....	....	....	....	....	....
2002-03	**NY Rangers**	**NHL**	**58**	**8**	**14**	**22**	**32**	**1**	**1**	**2**	**118**	**6.8**	**0**	**35**	**42.9**	**15:32**	....	....	....	....	....	....	....	....	....
	Pittsburgh	**NHL**	**22**	**2**	**0**	**2**	**8**	**1**	**0**	**0**	**36**	**5.6**	**–21**	**8**	**75.0**	**14:04**	....	....	....	....	....	....	....	....	....
2003-04	**Florida**	**NHL**	**37**	**3**	**6**	**9**	**35**	**0**	**0**	**1**	**50**	**6.0**	**0**	**28**	**28.6**	**12:15**	....	....	....	....	....	....	....	....	....
2004-05	Geneve	Swiss	12	2	4	6	14	....	....	....	....	....	....	....	....	....	....	....	....	....	....	....	....	....	....
	Sodertalje SK	Sweden	29	7	13	20	45	....	....	....	....	....	....	....	....	....	10	3	3	6	24	....	....	....	....
2005-06	Rapperswil	Swiss	1	0	0	0	0	....	....	....	....	....	....	....	....	....	....	....	....	....	....	....	....	....	....
	Detroit	**NHL**	**71**	**23**	**22**	**45**	**42**	**7**	**0**	**3**	**187**	**12.3**	**27**	**11**	**27.3**	**13:31**	**6**	**0**	**1**	**1**	**6**	**0**	**0**	**0**	**15:33**
	Sweden	Olympics	8	1	3	4	2	....	....	....	....	....	....	....	....	....	....	....	....	....	....	....	....	....	....
	NHL Totals		**259**	**42**	**52**	**94**	**140**	**10**	**3**	**7**	**488**	**8.6**		**87**	**39.1**	**13:16**	**6**	**0**	**1**	**1**	**6**	**0**	**0**	**0**	**15:33**

Traded to **NY Rangers** by **San Jose** with Christian Gosselin for Adam Graves and future considerations, June 24, 2001. Traded to **Pittsburgh** by **NY Rangers** with Joel Bouchard, Richard Lintner, Rico Fata and future considerations for Mike Wilson, Alex Kovalev, Janne Laukkanen and Dan LaCouture, February 10, 2003. Traded to **Florida** by **Pittsburgh** with Pittsburgh's 1st round choice (Nathan Horton) and 2nd round compensatory choice (Stefan Meyer) in 2003 Entry Draft for Florida's 1st (Marc-Andre Fleury) and 3rd (Daniel Carcillo) round choices in 2003 Entry Draft, June 21, 2003. • Missed majority of 2003-04 season recovering from jaw (November 21, 2003 vs. Washington) and hand (January 21, 2004 vs. Columbus) injuries. Signed as a free agent by **Geneve** (Swiss), September 8, 2004. Signed as a free agent by **Sodertalje** (Sweden), October 26, 2004. Signed as a free agent by **Detroit**, September 17, 2005.

SANDERSON, Geoff

(SAN-duhr-sohn, JEHF) **PHI.**

Left wing. Shoots left. 6', 190 lbs. Born, Hay River, N.W.T., February 1, 1972. Hartford's 2nd choice, 36th overall, in 1990 Entry Draft.

Season	Club	League	GP	G	A	Pts	PIM	PP	SH	GW	S	%	+/-	TF	F%	Min	GP	G	A	Pts	PIM	PP	SH	GW	Min
1987-88	St. Albert Royals	AMHL	45	65	55	120	175	....	....	....	....	....	....	....	....	....	....	....	....	....	....	....	....	....	....
1988-89	Swift Current	WHL	58	17	11	28	16	....	....	....	....	....	....	....	....	....	12	3	5	8	6	....	....	....	....
1989-90	Swift Current	WHL	70	32	62	94	56	....	....	....	....	....	....	....	....	....	4	1	4	5	8	....	....	....	....
1990-91	Swift Current	WHL	70	62	50	112	57	....	....	....	....	....	....	....	....	....	3	1	2	3	4	....	....	....	....
	Hartford	**NHL**	**2**	**1**	**0**	**1**	**0**	**0**	**0**	**0**	**2**	**50.0**	**–2**	....	....	....	**3**	**0**	**0**	**0**	**0**	**0**	**0**	**0**	
	Springfield	AHL	....	....	....	....	....	....	....	....	....	....	....	....	....	....	1	0	0	0	2	....	....	....	....
1991-92	**Hartford**	**NHL**	**64**	**13**	**18**	**31**	**18**	**2**	**0**	**1**	**98**	**13.3**	**5**	....	....	....	**7**	**1**	**0**	**1**	**2**	**0**	**0**	**0**	
1992-93	**Hartford**	**NHL**	**82**	**46**	**43**	**89**	**28**	**21**	**2**	**4**	**271**	**17.0**	**–21**	....	....	....	....	....	....	....	....	....	....	....	....
1993-94	**Hartford**	**NHL**	**82**	**41**	**26**	**67**	**42**	**15**	**1**	**6**	**266**	**15.4**	**–13**	....	....	....	....	....	....	....	....	....	....	....	....
1994-95	HPK Hameenlinna	Finland	12	6	4	10	24	....	....	....	....	....	....	....	....	....	....	....	....	....	....	....	....	....	....
	Hartford	**NHL**	**46**	**18**	**14**	**32**	**24**	**4**	**0**	**4**	**170**	**10.6**	**–10**	....	....	....	....	....	....	....	....	....	....	....	....
1995-96	**Hartford**	**NHL**	**81**	**34**	**31**	**65**	**40**	**6**	**0**	**7**	**314**	**10.8**	**0**	....	....	....	....	....	....	....	....	....	....	....	....
1996-97	**Hartford**	**NHL**	**82**	**36**	**31**	**67**	**29**	**12**	**1**	**4**	**297**	**12.1**	**–9**	....	....	....	....	....	....	....	....	....	....	....	....
1997-98	**Carolina**	**NHL**	**40**	**7**	**10**	**17**	**14**	**2**	**0**	**0**	**96**	**7.3**	**–4**	....	....	....	....	....	....	....	....	....	....	....	....
	Vancouver	**NHL**	**9**	**0**	**3**	**3**	**4**	**0**	**0**	**0**	**29**	**0.0**	**–1**	....	....	....	....	....	....	....	....	....	....	....	....
	Buffalo	**NHL**	**26**	**4**	**5**	**9**	**20**	**0**	**0**	**2**	**72**	**5.6**	**6**	....	....	....	**14**	**3**	**1**	**4**	**4**	**1**	**0**	**1**	
1998-99	**Buffalo**	**NHL**	**75**	**12**	**18**	**30**	**22**	**1**	**0**	**1**	**155**	**7.7**	**8**	**4**	**50.0**	**12:55**	**19**	**4**	**6**	**10**	**14**	**0**	**0**	**1**	**13:52**
99-2000	**Buffalo**	**NHL**	**67**	**13**	**13**	**26**	**22**	**4**	**0**	**3**	**136**	**9.6**	**4**	**3**	**100.0**	**12:54**	**5**	**0**	**2**	**2**	**8**	**0**	**0**	**0**	**12:16**
2000-01	**Columbus**	**NHL**	**68**	**30**	**26**	**56**	**46**	**9**	**0**	**7**	**199**	**15.1**	**4**	**726**	**49.0**	**16:37**	....	....	....	....	....	....	....	....	....
2001-02	**Columbus**	**NHL**	**42**	**11**	**5**	**16**	**12**	**5**	**0**	**2**	**112**	**9.8**	**–15**	**322**	**42.9**	**16:50**	....	....	....	....	....	....	....	....	....
2002-03	**Columbus**	**NHL**	**82**	**34**	**33**	**67**	**34**	**15**	**2**	**2**	**286**	**11.9**	**–4**	**96**	**41.7**	**18:44**	....	....	....	....	....	....	....	....	....
2003-04	**Columbus**	**NHL**	**67**	**13**	**16**	**29**	**34**	**5**	**0**	**1**	**191**	**6.8**	**–9**	**102**	**47.1**	**16:20**	....	....	....	....	....	....	....	....	....
	Vancouver	**NHL**	**13**	**3**	**4**	**7**	**4**	**1**	**0**	**1**	**36**	**8.3**	**–1**	**14**	**21.4**	**14:46**	**7**	**1**	**1**	**2**	**4**	**0**	**0**	**0**	**12:54**
2004-05	Geneve	Swiss	9	4	1	5	29	....	....	....	....	....	....	....	....	....	....	....	....	....	....	....	....	....	....
2005-06	**Columbus**	**NHL**	**2**	**0**	**0**	**0**	**0**	**0**	**0**	**0**	**7**	**0.0**	**–1**	**1**	**0.0**	**10:54**	....	....	....	....	....	....	....	....	....
	Phoenix	**NHL**	**75**	**25**	**21**	**46**	**58**	**11**	**1**	**1**	**152**	**16.4**	**–14**	**359**	**51.0**	**13:47**	....	....	....	....	....	....	....	....	....
	NHL Totals		**1005**	**341**	**317**	**658**	**451**	**113**	**7**	**46**	**2889**	**11.8**		**1627**	**47.5**	**15:22**	**55**	**9**	**10**	**19**	**32**	**1**	**0**	**2**	**13:23**

Played in NHL All-Star Game (1994, 1997)

Transferred to **Carolina** after **Hartford** franchise relocated, June 25, 1997. Traded to **Vancouver** by **Carolina** with Sean Burke and Enrico Ciccone for Kirk McLean and Martin Gelinas, January 3, 1998. Traded to **Buffalo** by **Vancouver** for Brad May and Buffalo's 3rd round choice (later traded to Tampa Bay – Tampa Bay selected Jimmie Olvestad) in 1999 Entry Draft, February 4, 1998. Claimed by **Columbus** from **Buffalo** in Expansion Draft, June 23, 2000. Traded to **Vancouver** by **Columbus** for Vancouver's 3rd round choice (Daniel Lacosta) in 2004 Entry Draft, March 9, 2004. Claimed on waivers by **Columbus** from **Vancouver**, June 28, 2004. Signed as a free agent by **Geneve** (Swiss), January 5, 2005. Traded to **Phoenix** by **Columbus** with Tim Jackman for Cale Hulse, Mike Rupp and Jason Chimera, October 8, 2005. Signed as a free agent by **Philadelphia**, July 19, 2006.

SANTALA, Tommi

(SAHN-tah-luh, TAW-mee) **VAN.**

Center. Shoots right. 6'3", 210 lbs. Born, Helsinki, Finland, June 27, 1979. Atlanta's 10th choice, 245th overall, in 1999 Entry Draft.

Season	Club	League	GP	G	A	Pts	PIM	PP	SH	GW	S	%	+/-	TF	F%	Min	GP	G	A	Pts	PIM	PP	SH	GW	Min
1995-96	Jokerit U18	Fin-U18	25	8	4	12	12	....	....	....	....	....	....	....	....	....	6	1	2	3	4	....	....	....	....
1996-97	Jokerit U18	Fin-U18	30	13	19	32	64	....	....	....	....	....	....	....	....	....	....	....	....	....	....	....	....	....	....
	Jokerit Helsinki Jr.	Fin-Jr.	20	0	2	2	10	....	....	....	....	....	....	....	....	....	5	0	0	0	0	....	....	....	....
1997-98	Jokerit Helsinki Jr.	Fin-Jr.	36	10	28	38	48	....	....	....	....	....	....	....	....	....	8	0	1	1	4	....	....	....	....
1998-99	Jokerit Helsinki Jr.	Fin-Jr.	30	20	24	44	20	....	....	....	....	....	....	....	....	....	8	1	3	4	22	....	....	....	....
	Jokerit Helsinki	Finland	30	0	0	0	14	....	....	....	....	....	....	....	....	....	3	0	0	0	0	....	....	....	....
	Jokerit Helsinki	EuroHL	1	0	2	2	0	....	....	....	....	....	....	....	....	....	1	0	0	0	0	....	....	....	....
99-2000	Jokerit Helsinki Jr.	Fin-Jr.	5	6	4	10	4	....	....	....	....	....	....	....	....	....	....	....	....	....	....	....	....	....	....
	Jokerit Helsinki	Finland	14	0	1	1	2	....	....	....	....	....	....	....	....	....	....	....	....	....	....	....	....	....	....
	HPK Jr.	Fin-Jr.	6	7	3	10	4	....	....	....	....	....	....	....	....	....	....	....	....	....	....	....	....	....	....
	HPK Hameenlinna	Finland	38	8	19	27	63	....	....	....	....	....	....	....	....	....	8	3	4	7	10	....	....	....	....
2000-01	HPK Hameenlinna	Finland	56	16	24	40	90	....	....	....	....	....	....	....	....	....	....	....	....	....	....	....	....	....	....
2001-02	HPK Hameenlinna	Finland	17	6	16	22	14	....	....	....	....	....	....	....	....	....	....	....	....	....	....	....	....	....	....
2002-03	HPK Hameenlinna	Finland	50	13	38	51	92	....	....	....	....	....	....	....	....	....	13	6	6	12	18	....	....	....	....
2003-04	**Atlanta**	**NHL**	**33**	**1**	**2**	**3**	**22**	**0**	**0**	**1**	**23**	**4.3**	**–7**	**252**	**51.2**	**10:08**	....	....	....	....	....	....	....	....	....
	Chicago Wolves	AHL	50	15	22	37	34	....	....	....	....	....	....	....	....	....	10	1	6	7	31	....	....	....	....
2004-05	Chicago Wolves	AHL	67	8	40	48	83	....	....	....	....	....	....	....	....	....	18	5	6	11	42	....	....	....	....
2005-06	Jokerit Helsinki	Finland	43	9	23	32	80	....	....	....	....	....	....	....	....	....	....	....	....	....	....	....	....	....	....
	NHL Totals		**33**	**1**	**2**	**3**	**22**	**0**	**0**	**1**	**23**	**4.3**		**252**	**51.2**	**10:08**	....	....	....	....	....	....	....	....	....

Assigned to **Jokerit Helsinki** (Finland) by **Atlanta**. October 5, 2005. Traded to **Vancouver** by **Atlanta** with Atlanta's 5th round choice in 2007 Entry Draft for Vancouver's 4th round choice in 2007 Entry Draft, June 14, 2006.

SAPRYKIN, Oleg

(sah-PRIH-kihn, OH-lehg) **PHX.**

Left wing. Shoots left. 6'1", 195 lbs. Born, Moscow, USSR, February 12, 1981. Calgary's 1st choice, 11th overall, in 1999 Entry Draft.

Season	Club	League	GP	G	A	Pts	PIM	PP	SH	GW	S	%	+/-	TF	F%	Min	GP	G	A	Pts	PIM	PP	SH	GW	Min
1997-98	HK CSKA Moscow	Russia-Q	15	0	3	3	6	....	....	....	....	....	....	....	....	....	....	....	....	....	....	....	....	....	....
	HK CSKA Moscow	Russia	20	0	2	2	8	....	....	....	....	....	....	....	....	....	....	....	....	....	....	....	....	....	....
1998-99	Seattle	WHL	66	47	46	93	107	....	....	....	....	....	....	....	....	....	11	5	11	16	36	....	....	....	....
99-2000	**Calgary**	**NHL**	**4**	**0**	**1**	**1**	**2**	**0**	**0**	**0**	**2**	**0.0**	**–4**	**0**	**0.0**	**12:35**	....	....	....	....	....	....	....	....	....
	Seattle	WHL	48	30	36	66	91	....	....	....	....	....	....	....	....	....	6	3	3	6	37	....	....	....	....
2000-01	**Calgary**	**NHL**	**59**	**9**	**14**	**23**	**43**	**2**	**0**	**0**	**95**	**9.5**	**4**	**2**	**50.0**	**12:10**	....	....	....	....	....	....	....	....	....
2001-02	**Calgary**	**NHL**	**3**	**0**	**0**	**0**	**0**	**0**	**0**	**0**	**9**	**0.0**	**–2**	**0**	**0.0**	**13:25**	....	....	....	....	....	....	....	....	....
	Saint John Flames	AHL	52	5	19	24	53	....	....	....	....	....	....	....	....	....	....	....	....	....	....	....	....	....	....
2002-03	**Calgary**	**NHL**	**52**	**8**	**15**	**23**	**46**	**1**	**0**	**1**	**116**	**6.9**	**5**	**1**	**0.0**	**11:53**	....	....	....	....	....	....	....	....	....
	Saint John Flames	AHL	21	12	9	21	22	....	....	....	....	....	....	....	....	....	....	....	....	....	....	....	....	....	....
2003-04	**Calgary**	**NHL**	**69**	**12**	**17**	**29**	**41**	**4**	**0**	**0**	**151**	**7.9**	**1**	**13**	**23.1**	**13:48**	**26**	**3**	**3**	**6**	**14**	**1**	**0**	**1**	**14:01**
2004-05	CSKA Moscow	Russia	40	15	8	23	105	....	....	....	....	....	....	....	....	....	....	....	....	....	....	....	....	....	....
2005-06	**Phoenix**	**NHL**	**67**	**11**	**14**	**25**	**50**	**3**	**0**	**1**	**126**	**8.7**	**–16**	**18**	**38.9**	**13:42**	....	....	....	....	....	....	....	....	....
	NHL Totals		**254**	**40**	**61**	**101**	**182**	**10**	**0**	**2**	**499**	**8.0**		**34**	**32.4**	**12:59**	**26**	**3**	**3**	**6**	**14**	**1**	**0**	**1**	**14:01**

WHL West Second All-Star Team (1999, 2000)

Traded to **Phoenix** by **Calgary** with Denis Gauthier for Daymond Langkow, August 26, 2004. Signed as a free agent by **CSKA Moscow** (Russia), September 25, 2004.

SARICH, Cory

(SAHR-ihch, KOH-ree) **T.B.**

Defense. Shoots right. 6'4", 210 lbs. Born, Saskatoon, Sask., August 16, 1978. Buffalo's 2nd choice, 27th overall, in 1996 Entry Draft.

			Regular Season														Playoffs								
Season	Club	League	GP	G	A	Pts	PIM	PP	SH	GW	S	%	+/-	TF	F%	Min	GP	G	A	Pts	PIM	PP	SH	GW	Min
1994-95	Sask. Contacts	SMHL	31	5	22	27	99	....	....	....	....	....	....	....	....	....	....	....	....	....	....	....	....	....	....
	Saskatoon Blades	WHL	6	0	0	0	4	....	....	....	....	....	....	....	....	....	3	0	1	1	0	....	....	....	....
1995-96	Saskatoon Blades	WHL	59	5	18	23	54	....	....	....	....	....	....	....	....	....	3	0	0	0	4	....	....	....	....
1996-97	Saskatoon Blades	WHL	58	6	27	33	158	....	....	....	....	....	....	....	....	....	....	....	....	....	....	....	....	....	....
1997-98	Saskatoon Blades	WHL	33	5	24	29	90	....	....	....	....	....	....	....	....	....	....	....	....	....	....	....	....	....	....
	Seattle	WHL	13	3	16	19	47	....	....	....	....	....	....	....	....	....	....	....	....	....	....	....	....	....	....
1998-99	**Buffalo**	**NHL**	**4**	**0**	**0**	**0**	**0**	**0**	**0**	**0**	**2**	**0.0**	**3**	**0**	**0.0**	**13:11**	....	....	....	....	....	....	....	....	....
	Rochester	AHL	77	3	26	29	82	....	....	....	....	....	....	....	....	....	20	2	4	6	14	....	....	....	....
99-2000	**Buffalo**	**NHL**	**42**	**0**	**4**	**4**	**35**	**0**	**0**	**0**	**49**	**0.0**	**2**	**0**	**0.0**	**17:42**	....	....	....	....	....	....	....	....	....
	Rochester	AHL	15	0	6	6	44	....	....	....	....	....	....	....	....	....	....	....	....	....	....	....	....	....	....
	Tampa Bay	**NHL**	**17**	**0**	**2**	**2**	**42**	**0**	**0**	**0**	**20**	**0.0**	**–8**	**0**	**0.0**	**20:42**	....	....	....	....	....	....	....	....	....
2000-01	**Tampa Bay**	**NHL**	**73**	**1**	**8**	**9**	**106**	**0**	**0**	**1**	**66**	**1.5**	**–25**	**3**	**0.0**	**18:44**	....	....	....	....	....	....	....	....	....
	Detroit Vipers	IHL	3	0	2	2	2	....	....	....	....	....	....	....	....	....	....	....	....	....	....	....	....	....	....
2001-02	**Tampa Bay**	**NHL**	**72**	**0**	**11**	**11**	**105**	**0**	**0**	**0**	**55**	**0.0**	**–4**	**2**	**50.0**	**16:06**	....	....	....	....	....	....	....	....	....
	Springfield	AHL	2	0	0	0	0	....	....	....	....	....	....	....	....	....	....	....	....	....	....	....	....	....	....
2002-03	**Tampa Bay**	**NHL**	**82**	**5**	**9**	**14**	**63**	**0**	**0**	**2**	**79**	**6.3**	**–3**	**3**	**0.0**	**19:36**	**11**	**0**	**2**	**2**	**6**	**0**	**0**	**0**	**21:18**
2003-04♦	**Tampa Bay**	**NHL**	**82**	**3**	**16**	**19**	**89**	**0**	**1**	**1**	**93**	**3.2**	**5**	**1**	**0.0**	**18:31**	**23**	**0**	**2**	**2**	**25**	**0**	**0**	**0**	**19:11**
2004-05			DID NOT PLAY																						
2005-06	**Tampa Bay**	**NHL**	**82**	**1**	**14**	**15**	**79**	**0**	**0**	**0**	**88**	**1.1**	**–2**	**0**	**0.0**	**18:34**	**5**	**0**	**1**	**1**	**4**	**0**	**0**	**0**	**15:46**
	NHL Totals		**454**	**10**	**64**	**74**	**519**	**0**	**1**	**4**	**452**	**2.2**		**9**	**11.1**	**18:20**	**39**	**0**	**5**	**5**	**35**	**0**	**0**	**0**	**19:20**

WHL West Second All-Star Team (1998) • AHL All-Rookie Team (1999)

Traded to **Tampa Bay** by **Buffalo** with Wayne Primeau, Brian Holzinger and Buffalo's 3rd round choice (Alexander Kharitonov) in 2000 Entry Draft for Chris Gratton and Tampa Bay's 2nd round choice (Derek Roy) in 2001 Entry Draft, March 9, 2000.

SARNO, Peter

(SAHR-noh, PEE-tuhr)

Center. Shoots left. 5'11", 185 lbs. Born, Toronto, Ont., July 26, 1979. Edmonton's 6th choice, 141st overall, in 1997 Entry Draft.

			Regular Season														Playoffs								
Season	Club	League	GP	G	A	Pts	PIM	PP	SH	GW	S	%	+/-	TF	F%	Min	GP	G	A	Pts	PIM	PP	SH	GW	Min
1995-96	North York	MTJHL	52	39	57	96	27	....	....	....	....	....	....	....	....	....	....	....	....	....	....	....	....	....	....
1996-97	Windsor Spitfires	OHL	66	20	63	83	59	....	....	....	....	....	....	....	....	....	5	0	3	3	6	....	....	....	....
1997-98	Windsor Spitfires	OHL	64	33	*88	*121	18	....	....	....	....	....	....	....	....	....	....	....	....	....	....	....	....	....	....
	Hamilton	AHL	8	1	1	2	2	....	....	....	....	....	....	....	....	....	....	....	....	....	....	....	....	....	....
1998-99	Sarnia Sting	OHL	68	37	*93	*130	49	....	....	....	....	....	....	....	....	....	6	1	7	8	2	....	....	....	....
99-2000	Hamilton	AHL	67	10	36	46	31	....	....	....	....	....	....	....	....	....	....	....	....	....	....	....	....	....	....
2000-01	Hamilton	AHL	79	19	46	65	64	....	....	....	....	....	....	....	....	....	....	....	....	....	....	....	....	....	....
2001-02	Hamilton	AHL	76	12	40	52	38	....	....	....	....	....	....	....	....	....	15	6	7	13	4	....	....	....	....
2002-03	Blues Espoo	Finland	45	17	23	40	34	....	....	....	....	....	....	....	....	....	7	2	1	3	2	....	....	....	....
2003-04	**Edmonton**	**NHL**	**6**	**1**	**0**	**1**	**2**	**0**	**0**	**0**	**5**	**20.0**	**2**	**59**	**52.5**	**10:15**	....	....	....	....	....	....	....	....	....
	Toronto	AHL	31	6	12	18	29	....	....	....	....	....	....	....	....	....	....	....	....	....	....	....	....	....	....
	Manitoba Moose	AHL	23	5	9	14	6	....	....	....	....	....	....	....	....	....	....	....	....	....	....	....	....	....	....
2004-05	Manitoba Moose	AHL	80	16	66	82	53	....	....	....	....	....	....	....	....	....	14	1	8	9	4	....	....	....	....
2005-06	**Columbus**	**NHL**	**1**	**0**	**0**	**0**	**0**	**0**	**0**	**0**	**0**	**0.0**	**0**	**1**	**0.0**	**10:42**	....	....	....	....	....	....	....	....	....
	Syracuse Crunch	AHL	39	12	39	51	20	....	....	....	....	....	....	....	....	....	6	0	5	5	8	....	....	....	....
	NHL Totals		**7**	**1**	**0**	**1**	**2**	**0**	**0**	**0**	**5**	**20.0**		**60**	**51.7**	**10:19**	....	....	....	....	....	....	....	....	....

OHL All-Rookie Team (1997) • OHL Rookie of the Year (1997)

Traded to **Vancouver** by **Edmonton** for Tyler Moss, February 16, 2004. Signed as a free agent by **Columbus**, August 22, 2005.

SATAN, Miroslav

(SHA-tuhn, MEER-oh-slav) **NYI**

Left wing. Shoots left. 6'3", 190 lbs. Born, Topolcany, Czech., October 22, 1974. Edmonton's 6th choice, 111th overall, in 1993 Entry Draft.

			Regular Season														Playoffs								
Season	Club	League	GP	G	A	Pts	PIM	PP	SH	GW	S	%	+/-	TF	F%	Min	GP	G	A	Pts	PIM	PP	SH	GW	Min
1991-92	Topolcany Jr.	Czech-Jr.	31	30	22	52	....	....	....	....	....	....	....	....	....	....	....	....	....	....	....	....	....	....	....
	VTJ Topolcany	Czech-2	9	2	1	3	6	....	....	....	....	....	....	....	....	....	....	....	....	....	....	....	....	....	....
1992-93	Dukla Trencin	Czech	38	11	6	17	....	....	....	....	....	....	....	....	....	....	....	....	....	....	....	....	....	....	....
1993-94	Dukla Trencin	Slovakia	30	32	16	48	16	....	....	....	....	....	....	....	....	....	....	....	....	....	....	....	....	....	....
	Slovakia	Olympics	8	*9	0	9	0	....	....	....	....	....	....	....	....	....	....	....	....	....	....	....	....	....	....
1994-95	Cape Breton	AHL	25	24	16	40	15	....	....	....	....	....	....	....	....	....	....	....	....	....	....	....	....	....	....
	Detroit Vipers	IHL	8	1	3	4	4	....	....	....	....	....	....	....	....	....	....	....	....	....	....	....	....	....	....
	San Diego Gulls	IHL	6	0	2	2	6	....	....	....	....	....	....	....	....	....	....	....	....	....	....	....	....	....	....
1995-96	**Edmonton**	**NHL**	**62**	**18**	**17**	**35**	**22**	**6**	**0**	**4**	**113**	**15.9**	**0**	....	....	....	....	....	....	....	....	....	....	....	....
1996-97	**Edmonton**	**NHL**	**64**	**17**	**11**	**28**	**22**	**5**	**0**	**2**	**90**	**18.9**	**–4**	....	....	....	....	....	....	....	....	....	....	....	....
	Buffalo	**NHL**	**12**	**8**	**2**	**10**	**4**	**2**	**0**	**1**	**29**	**27.6**	**1**	....	....	....	**7**	**0**	**0**	**0**	**0**	**0**	**0**	**0**	....
1997-98	**Buffalo**	**NHL**	**79**	**22**	**24**	**46**	**34**	**9**	**0**	**4**	**139**	**15.8**	**2**	....	....	....	**14**	**5**	**4**	**9**	**4**	**4**	**0**	**1**	....
1998-99	**Buffalo**	**NHL**	**81**	**40**	**26**	**66**	**44**	**13**	**3**	**6**	**208**	**19.2**	**24**	**9**	**55.6**	**20:49**	**12**	**3**	**5**	**8**	**2**	**1**	**0**	**1**	**21:18**
99-2000	Dukla Trencin	Slovakia	3	2	8	10	2	....	....	....	....	....	....	....	....	....	....	....	....	....	....	....	....	....	....
	Buffalo	**NHL**	**81**	**33**	**34**	**67**	**32**	**5**	**3**	**5**	**265**	**12.5**	**16**	**7**	**14.3**	**20:35**	**5**	**3**	**2**	**5**	**0**	**0**	**0**	**0**	**19:52**
2000-01	**Buffalo**	**NHL**	**82**	**29**	**33**	**62**	**36**	**8**	**2**	**4**	**206**	**14.1**	**5**	**11**	**36.4**	**19:56**	**13**	**3**	**10**	**13**	**8**	**1**	**0**	**0**	**21:18**
2001-02	**Buffalo**	**NHL**	**82**	**37**	**36**	**73**	**33**	**15**	**5**	**5**	**267**	**13.9**	**14**	**4**	**50.0**	**21:10**	....	....	....	....	....	....	....	....	....
	Slovakia	Olympics	2	0	1	1	0	....	....	....	....	....	....	....	....	....	....	....	....	....	....	....	....	....	....
2002-03	**Buffalo**	**NHL**	**79**	**26**	**49**	**75**	**20**	**11**	**1**	**3**	**240**	**10.8**	**–3**	**10**	**20.0**	**21:23**	....	....	....	....	....	....	....	....	....
2003-04	Bratislava	Slovakia	7	6	4	10	41	....	....	....	....	....	....	....	....	....	....	....	....	....	....	....	....	....	....
	Buffalo	**NHL**	**82**	**29**	**28**	**57**	**30**	**11**	**1**	**5**	**206**	**14.1**	**–15**	**9**	**22.2**	**20:02**	....	....	....	....	....	....	....	....	....
2004-05	Bratislava	Slovakia	18	11	9	20	14	....	....	....	....	....	....	....	....	....	18	*15	7	*22	16	....	....	....	....
2005-06	**NY Islanders**	**NHL**	**82**	**35**	**31**	**66**	**54**	**17**	**0**	**2**	**253**	**13.8**	**–8**	**342**	**53.2**	**19:10**	....	....	....	....	....	....	....	....	....
	Slovakia	Olympics	6	0	2	2	2	....	....	....	....	....	....	....	....	....	....	....	....	....	....	....	....	....	....
	NHL Totals		**786**	**294**	**291**	**585**	**331**	**102**	**15**	**41**	**2016**	**14.6**		**392**	**50.5**	**20:26**	**51**	**14**	**21**	**35**	**14**	**6**	**0**	**2**	**21:04**

Played in NHL All-Star Game (2000, 2003)

Traded to **Buffalo** by **Edmonton** for Barrie Moore and Craig Millar, March 18, 1997. Signed as a free agent by **Bratislava** (Slovakia), December 29, 2004. Signed as a free agent by **NY Islanders**, August 3, 2005.

SAUER, Kurt

(SAW-uhr, KUHRT) **COL.**

Defense. Shoots left. 6'4", 225 lbs. Born, St. Cloud, MN, January 16, 1981. Colorado's 5th choice, 88th overall, in 2000 Entry Draft.

			Regular Season														Playoffs								
Season	Club	League	GP	G	A	Pts	PIM	PP	SH	GW	S	%	+/-	TF	F%	Min	GP	G	A	Pts	PIM	PP	SH	GW	Min
1998-99	North Iowa	USHL	52	1	4	5	67	....	....	....	....	....	....	....	....	....	....	....	....	....	....	....	....	....	....
99-2000	Spokane Chiefs	WHL	71	3	12	15	48	....	....	....	....	....	....	....	....	....	15	2	1	3	8	....	....	....	....
2000-01	Spokane Chiefs	WHL	48	5	10	15	85	....	....	....	....	....	....	....	....	....	3	1	0	1	2	....	....	....	....
2001-02	Spokane Chiefs	WHL	61	4	20	24	73	....	....	....	....	....	....	....	....	....	11	0	3	3	12	....	....	....	....
2002-03	**Anaheim**	**NHL**	**80**	**1**	**2**	**3**	**74**	**0**	**0**	**0**	**50**	**2.0**	**–23**	**0**	**0.0**	**18:33**	**21**	**1**	**1**	**2**	**6**	**0**	**1**	**1**	**20:45**
2003-04	**Anaheim**	**NHL**	**55**	**1**	**4**	**5**	**32**	**0**	**0**	**0**	**32**	**3.1**	**–8**	**0**	**0.0**	**16:54**	....	....	....	....	....	....	....	....	....
	Colorado	**NHL**	**14**	**0**	**1**	**1**	**19**	**0**	**0**	**0**	**12**	**0.0**	**–3**	**0**	**0.0**	**15:04**	**3**	**0**	**0**	**0**	**0**	**0**	**0**	**0**	**11:56**
2004-05			DID NOT PLAY																						
2005-06	**Colorado**	**NHL**	**37**	**1**	**4**	**5**	**24**	**0**	**0**	**0**	**19**	**5.3**	**5**	**0**	**0.0**	**12:48**	**9**	**0**	**0**	**0**	**4**	**0**	**0**	**0**	**8:39**
	Lowell	AHL	4	0	0	0	2	....	....	....	....	....	....	....	....	....	....	....	....	....	....	....	....	....	....
	NHL Totals		**186**	**3**	**11**	**14**	**149**	**0**	**0**	**0**	**113**	**2.7**		**0**	**0.0**	**16:39**	**33**	**1**	**1**	**2**	**10**	**0**	**1**	**1**	**16:39**

WHL West First All-Star Team (2002)

Signed as a free agent by **Anaheim**, July 6, 2002. Traded to **Colorado** by **Anaheim** with Anaheim's 4th round choice (Raymond Macias) in 2005 Entry Draft for Martin Skoula, February 21, 2004.

SAVAGE, Brian

(SA-vuhj, BRIGH-uhn)

Left wing. Shoots left. 6'1", 200 lbs. Born, Sudbury, Ont., February 24, 1971. Montreal's 11th choice, 171st overall, in 1991 Entry Draft.

			Regular Season														Playoffs								
Season	Club	League	GP	G	A	Pts	PIM	PP	SH	GW	S	%	+/-	TF	F%	Min	GP	G	A	Pts	PIM	PP	SH	GW	Min
1989-90	Sudbury Cubs	NOJHA	32	45	40	85	61	....	....	....	....	....	....	....	....	....	....	....	....	....	....	....	....	....	....
1990-91	Miami U.	CCHA	28	5	6	11	26	....	....	....	....	....	....	....	....	....	....	....	....	....	....	....	....	....	....
1991-92	Miami U.	CCHA	40	24	16	40	43	....	....	....	....	....	....	....	....	....	....	....	....	....	....	....	....	....	....
1992-93	Miami U.	CCHA	38	*37	21	58	44	....	....	....	....	....	....	....	....	....	....	....	....	....	....	....	....	....	....
1993-94	Canada	Nat-Tm	51	20	26	46	38	....	....	....	....	....	....	....	....	....	....	....	....	....	....	....	....	....	....
	Canada	Olympics	8	2	2	4	6	....	....	....	....	....	....	....	....	....	....	....	....	....	....	....	....	....	....
	Montreal	**NHL**	**3**	**1**	**0**	**1**	**0**	**0**	**0**	**0**	**3**	**33.3**	**0**	....	....	....	**3**	**0**	**2**	**2**	**0**	**0**	**0**	**0**	....
	Fredericton	AHL	17	12	15	27	4	....	....	....	....	....	....	....	....	....	....	....	....	....	....	....	....	....	....

			Regular Season														Playoffs								
Season	Club	League	GP	G	A	Pts	PIM	PP	SH	GW	S	%	+/-	TF	F%	Min	GP	G	A	Pts	PIM	PP	SH	GW	Min
1994-95	Montreal	NHL	37	12	7	19	27	0	0	0	64	18.8	5	....	....	....	....	....	....	....	....	....	....	....	....
1995-96	Montreal	NHL	75	25	8	33	28	4	0	4	150	16.7	–8	....	....	....	6	0	2	2	2	0	0	0	....
1996-97	Montreal	NHL	81	23	37	60	39	5	0	2	219	10.5	–14	....	....	....	5	1	1	2	0	0	0	0	....
1997-98	Montreal	NHL	64	26	17	43	36	8	0	7	152	17.1	11	....	....	....	9	0	2	2	6	0	0	0	....
1998-99	Montreal	NHL	54	16	10	26	20	5	0	4	124	12.9	–14	70	44.3	16:30	....	....	....	....	....	....	....	....	....
99-2000	Montreal	NHL	38	17	12	29	19	6	1	5	107	15.9	–4	67	47.8	17:56	....	....	....	....	....	....	....	....	....
2000-01	Montreal	NHL	62	21	24	45	26	12	0	1	172	12.2	–13	30	56.7	18:50	....	....	....	....	....	....	....	....	....
2001-02	Montreal	NHL	47	14	15	29	30	7	0	2	117	12.0	–14	3	0.0	18:12	....	....	....	....	....	....	....	....	....
	Phoenix	NHL	30	6	6	12	8	2	0	2	47	12.8	1	4	50.0	15:02	5	0	0	0	0	0	0	0	11:13
2002-03	Phoenix	NHL	43	6	10	16	22	1	0	1	68	8.8	–4	14	35.7	13:22	....	....	....	....	....	....	....	....	....
2003-04	Phoenix	NHL	61	12	13	25	36	3	0	1	101	11.9	–5	13	38.5	14:19	....	....	....	....	....	....	....	....	....
	St. Louis	NHL	13	4	3	7	2	1	0	1	23	17.4	–3	0	0.0	16:15	5	1	1	2	0	0	0	0	15:10
2004-05			DID NOT PLAY																						
2005-06	Philadelphia	NHL	66	9	5	14	28	4	1	1	102	8.8	–18	30	36.7	13:19	6	1	0	1	4	0	1	0	14:13
	NHL Totals		674	192	167	359	321	58	2	31	1449	13.3		231	44.6	15:54	39	3	8	11	12	0	1	0	13:34

CCHA First All-Star Team (1993) • CCHA Player of the Year (1993) • NCAA West Second All-American Team (1993)

• Missed majority of 1999-2000 season recovering from neck injury suffered in game vs. Los Angeles, November 20, 1999. Traded to **Phoenix** by **Montreal** with Montreal's 3rd round choice (Matt Jones) in 2002 Entry Draft and future considerations for Sergei Berezin, January 25, 2002. Traded to **St. Louis** by **Phoenix** for future considerations, March 9, 2004. Claimed on waivers by **Phoenix** from **St. Louis**, June 29, 2004. Signed as a free agent by **Philadelphia**, September 15, 2005.

SAVARD, Marc

(sa-VAHR, MAHRK) **BOS.**

Center. Shoots left. 5'10", 195 lbs. Born, Ottawa, Ont., July 17, 1977. NY Rangers' 3rd choice, 91st overall, in 1995 Entry Draft.

Season	Club	League	GP	G	A	Pts	PIM	PP	SH	GW	S	%	+/-	TF	F%	Min	GP	G	A	Pts	PIM	PP	SH	GW	Min
1992-93	Metcalfe Jets	OHA-B	36	*44	55	*99	38	....	....	....	....	....	....	....	....	....	....	....	....	....	....	....	....	....	....
1993-94	Oshawa Generals	OHL	61	18	39	57	20	....	....	....	....	....	....	....	....	....	5	4	3	7	8	....	....	....	....
1994-95	Oshawa Generals	OHL	66	43	96	*139	78	....	....	....	....	....	....	....	....	....	7	5	6	11	8	....	....	....	....
1995-96	Oshawa Generals	OHL	48	28	59	87	77	....	....	....	....	....	....	....	....	....	5	4	5	9	6	....	....	....	....
1996-97	Oshawa Generals	OHL	64	43	*87	*130	94	....	....	....	....	....	....	....	....	....	18	13	*24	*37	20	....	....	....	....
1997-98	NY Rangers	NHL	28	1	5	6	4	0	0	0	32	3.1	–4	....	....	....	....	....	....	....	....	....	....	....	....
	Hartford	AHL	58	21	53	74	66	....	....	....	....	....	....	....	....	....	15	8	19	27	24	....	....	....	....
1998-99	NY Rangers	NHL	70	9	36	45	38	4	0	1	116	7.8	–7	956	48.4	14:35	....	....	....	....	....	....	....	....	....
	Hartford	AHL	9	3	10	13	16	....	....	....	....	....	....	....	....	....	7	1	12	13	16	....	....	....	....
99-2000	Calgary	NHL	78	22	31	53	56	4	0	3	184	12.0	–2	1021	49.6	16:36	....	....	....	....	....	....	....	....	....
2000-01	Calgary	NHL	77	23	42	65	46	10	1	5	197	11.7	–12	1050	53.1	19:13	....	....	....	....	....	....	....	....	....
2001-02	Calgary	NHL	56	14	19	33	48	7	0	3	140	10.0	–18	577	54.8	17:20	....	....	....	....	....	....	....	....	....
2002-03	Calgary	NHL	10	1	2	3	8	0	0	0	21	4.8	–3	89	52.8	14:41	....	....	....	....	....	....	....	....	....
	Atlanta	NHL	57	16	31	47	77	6	0	4	127	12.6	–11	1247	50.9	19:50	....	....	....	....	....	....	....	....	....
2003-04	Atlanta	NHL	45	19	33	52	85	6	1	3	133	14.3	–8	1083	49.9	22:19	....	....	....	....	....	....	....	....	....
2004-05	HC Thurgau	Swiss-2	13	9	19	28	10	....	....	....	....	....	....	....	....	....	....	....	....	....	....	....	....	....	....
	SC Bern	Swiss	5	1	2	3	0	....	....	....	....	....	....	....	....	....	....	....	....	....	....	....	....	....	....
2005-06	Atlanta	NHL	82	28	69	97	100	14	1	4	212	13.2	7	1529	51.6	20:30	....	....	....	....	....	....	....	....	....
	NHL Totals		503	133	268	401	462	51	3	23	1162	11.4		7552	51.0	18:23	....	....	....	....	....	....	....	....	....

OHL Second All-Star Team (1995)

Traded to **Calgary** by **NY Rangers** with NY Rangers 1st round choice (Oleg Saprykin) in 1999 Entry Draft for the rights to Jan Hlavac and Calgary's 1st (Jamie Lundmark) and 3rd (later traded back to Calgary – Calgary selected Craig Andersson) round choices in 1999 Entry Draft, June 26, 1999. Traded to **Atlanta** by **Calgary** for Ruslan Zainullin, November 15, 2002. Signed as a free agent by **Thurgau** (Swiss-2), October 11, 2004. Signed as a free agent by **Bern** (Swiss), November 23, 2004. Signed as a free agent by **Boston**, July 1, 2006.

SCATCHARD, Dave

(SKAT-chuhrd, DAYV) **PHX.**

Center. Shoots right. 6'3", 220 lbs. Born, Hinton, Alta., February 20, 1976. Vancouver's 3rd choice, 42nd overall, in 1994 Entry Draft.

Season	Club	League	GP	G	A	Pts	PIM	PP	SH	GW	S	%	+/-	TF	F%	Min	GP	G	A	Pts	PIM	PP	SH	GW	Min
1991-92	Salmon Arm	BCAHA	65	98	100	198	167	....	....	....	....	....	....	....	....	....	....	....	....	....	....	....	....	....	....
1992-93	Kimberley	RMJHL	51	20	23	43	61	....	....	....	....	....	....	....	....	....	....	....	....	....	....	....	....	....	....
1993-94	Portland	WHL	47	9	11	20	46	....	....	....	....	....	....	....	....	....	10	2	1	3	4	....	....	....	....
1994-95	Portland	WHL	71	20	30	50	148	....	....	....	....	....	....	....	....	....	8	0	3	3	21	....	....	....	....
1995-96	Portland	WHL	59	19	28	47	146	....	....	....	....	....	....	....	....	....	7	1	8	9	14	....	....	....	....
	Syracuse Crunch	AHL	1	0	0	0	0	....	....	....	....	....	....	....	....	....	15	2	5	7	29	....	....	....	....
1996-97	Syracuse Crunch	AHL	26	8	7	15	65	....	....	....	....	....	....	....	....	....	....	....	....	....	....	....	....	....	....
1997-98	Vancouver	NHL	76	13	11	24	165	0	0	1	85	15.3	–4	....	....	....	....	....	....	....	....	....	....	....	....
1998-99	Vancouver	NHL	82	13	13	26	140	0	2	2	130	10.0	–12	1007	56.3	13:46	....	....	....	....	....	....	....	....	....
99-2000	Vancouver	NHL	21	0	4	4	24	0	0	0	25	0.0	–3	190	59.5	10:12	....	....	....	....	....	....	....	....	....
	NY Islanders	NHL	44	12	14	26	93	0	1	1	103	11.7	0	710	55.8	13:42	....	....	....	....	....	....	....	....	....
2000-01	NY Islanders	NHL	81	21	24	45	114	4	0	5	176	11.9	–9	1322	55.1	16:50	....	....	....	....	....	....	....	....	....
2001-02	NY Islanders	NHL	80	12	15	27	111	3	1	4	117	10.3	–4	788	53.8	12:31	7	1	1	2	22	0	0	0	12:38
2002-03	NY Islanders	NHL	81	27	18	45	108	5	0	2	165	16.4	9	1147	52.7	14:30	5	1	0	1	6	0	0	1	15:58
2003-04	NY Islanders	NHL	61	9	16	25	78	1	1	1	111	8.1	12	1052	52.7	16:13	5	0	1	1	6	0	0	0	16:18
2004-05			DID NOT PLAY																						
2005-06	Boston	NHL	16	4	6	10	28	1	0	0	40	10.0	–2	272	54.8	16:56	....	....	....	....	....	....	....	....	....
	Phoenix	NHL	47	11	12	23	84	4	0	3	81	13.6	–11	594	53.2	14:44	....	....	....	....	....	....	....	....	....
	NHL Totals		589	122	133	255	945	18	5	19	1033	11.8		7082	54.4	14:30	17	2	2	4	34	0	0	1	14:41

Traded to **NY Islanders** by **Vancouver** with Kevin Weekes and Bill Muckalt for Felix Potvin, NY Islanders' 2nd round compensatory choice (later traded to New Jersey – New Jersey selected Teemu Laine) in 2000 Entry Draft and NY Islanders' 3rd round choice (Thatcher Bell) in 2000 Entry Draft, December 19, 1999. Signed as a free agent by **Boston**, August 2, 2005. Traded to **Phoenix** by **Boston** for David Tanabe, November 18, 2005.

SCHAEFER, Peter

(SHAY-fuhr, PEE-tuhr) **OTT.**

Left wing. Shoots left. 5'11", 195 lbs. Born, Yellow Grass, Sask., July 12, 1977. Vancouver's 3rd choice, 66th overall, in 1995 Entry Draft.

Season	Club	League	GP	G	A	Pts	PIM	PP	SH	GW	S	%	+/-	TF	F%	Min	GP	G	A	Pts	PIM	PP	SH	GW	Min
1993-94	Yorkton Mallers	SMHL	32	27	14	41	133	....	....	....	....	....	....	....	....	....	....	....	....	....	....	....	....	....	....
	Brandon	WHL	2	1	0	1	0	....	....	....	....	....	....	....	....	....	....	....	....	....	....	....	....	....	....
1994-95	Brandon	WHL	68	27	32	59	34	....	....	....	....	....	....	....	....	....	18	5	3	8	18	....	....	....	....
1995-96	Brandon	WHL	69	47	61	108	53	....	....	....	....	....	....	....	....	....	19	10	13	23	5	....	....	....	....
1996-97	Brandon	WHL	61	49	74	123	85	....	....	....	....	....	....	....	....	....	6	1	4	5	4	....	....	....	....
	Syracuse Crunch	AHL	5	0	3	3	0	....	....	....	....	....	....	....	....	....	3	1	3	4	14	....	....	....	....
1997-98	Syracuse Crunch	AHL	73	19	44	63	41	....	....	....	....	....	....	....	....	....	5	2	1	3	2	....	....	....	....
1998-99	Vancouver	NHL	25	4	4	8	8	1	0	1	24	16.7	–1	6	0.0	13:21	....	....	....	....	....	....	....	....	....
	Syracuse Crunch	AHL	41	10	19	29	66	....	....	....	....	....	....	....	....	....	....	....	....	....	....	....	....	....	....
99-2000	Vancouver	NHL	71	16	15	31	20	2	2	4	101	15.8	0	21	19.1	15:28	....	....	....	....	....	....	....	....	....
	Syracuse Crunch	AHL	2	0	0	0	2	....	....	....	....	....	....	....	....	....	....	....	....	....	....	....	....	....	....
2000-01	Vancouver	NHL	82	16	20	36	22	3	4	2	163	9.8	4	25	32.0	16:18	3	0	0	0	0	0	0	0	13:08
2001-02	TPS Turku	Finland	33	16	15	31	93	....	....	....	....	....	....	....	....	....	8	1	2	3	2	....	....	....	....
2002-03	Ottawa	NHL	75	6	17	23	32	0	0	1	93	6.5	11	44	20.5	14:59	16	2	3	5	6	0	1	0	11:51
2003-04	Ottawa	NHL	81	15	24	39	26	2	2	3	112	13.4	22	39	23.1	15:36	7	0	2	2	4	0	0	0	14:25
2004-05	HC Forst Bolzano	Italy	15	11	14	25	10	....	....	....	....	....	....	....	....	....	10	1	7	8	12	....	....	....	....
2005-06	Ottawa	NHL	82	20	30	50	40	4	4	2	137	14.6	16	27	37.0	15:49	10	2	5	7	14	0	0	0	16:39
	NHL Totals		416	77	110	187	148	12	12	13	630	12.2		162	24.7	15:31	36	4	10	14	24	0	1	0	13:47

WHL East First All-Star Team (1996, 1997) • WHL Player of the Year (1997) • Canadian Major Junior First All-Star Team (1997)

Signed as a free agent by **Turku** (Finland), October 18, 2001. Traded to **Ottawa** by **Vancouver** for Sami Salo, September 21, 2002. Signed as a free agent by **Bolzano** (Italy), November 30, 2004.

SCHASTLIVY, Petr

(schust-LEE-vee, PEH-tuhr)

Left wing. Shoots left. 6'1", 204 lbs. Born, Angarsk, USSR, April 18, 1979. Ottawa's 5th choice, 101st overall, in 1998 Entry Draft.

Season	Club	League	GP	G	A	Pts	PIM	PP	SH	GW	S	%	+/-	TF	F%	Min	GP	G	A	Pts	PIM	PP	SH	GW	Min
1997-98	Yaroslavl 2	Russia-2	47	15	9	24	34	....	....	....	....	....	....	....	....	....	....	....	....	....	....	....	....	....	....
	Yaroslavl	Russia	4	0	0	0	0	....	....	....	....	....	....	....	....	....	....	....	....	....	....	....	....	....	....
1998-99	Yaroslavl	Russia	40	6	1	7	28	....	....	....	....	....	....	....	....	....	6	0	0	0	2	....	....	....	....
99-2000	Ottawa	NHL	13	2	5	7	2	1	0	1	22	9.1	4	0	0.0	12:18	1	0	0	0	0	0	0	0	13:09
	Grand Rapids	IHL	46	16	12	28	10	....	....	....	....	....	....	....	....	....	17	8	7	15	6	....	....	....	....
2000-01	Ottawa	NHL	17	3	2	5	6	0	0	0	32	9.4	–1	0	0.0	11:20	....	....	....	....	....	....	....	....	....
	Grand Rapids	IHL	43	10	14	24	10	....	....	....	....	....	....	....	....	....	7	4	4	8	0	....	....	....	....
2001-02	Ottawa	NHL	1	0	1	1	0	0	0	0	0	0.0	1	0	0.0	3:21	....	....	....	....	....	....	....	....	....
	Grand Rapids	AHL	31	22	13	35	10	....	....	....	....	....	....	....	....	....	....	....	....	....	....	....	....	....	....
2002-03	Ottawa	NHL	33	9	10	19	4	5	0	2	68	13.2	3	2	0.0	13:21	....	....	....	....	....	....	....	....	....

			Regular Season														Playoffs								
Season	Club	League	GP	G	A	Pts	PIM	PP	SH	GW	S	%	+/-	TF	F%	Min	GP	G	A	Pts	PIM	PP	SH	GW	Min
2003-04	Ottawa	NHL	43	2	4	6	14	1	0	1	37	5.4	–1	11	45.5	9:32									
	Anaheim	NHL	22	2	0	2	4	0	0	1	48	4.2	–3	2	50.0	11:21									
2004-05	Yaroslavl	Russia	59	15	15	30	28										9	1	3	4	2				
2005-06	Yaroslavl	Russia	49	14	15	29	47										11	4	4	8	10				
	NHL Totals		129	18	22	40	30	7	0	5	207	8.7		15	40.0	11:17	1	0	0	0	0	0	0	0	13:09

• Missed majority of 2001-02 season recovering from knee injury suffered in game vs. Chicago, December 31, 2001. • Missed majority of 2002-03 season recovering from groin injury suffered in practice, October 5, 2002. Traded to **Anaheim** by **Ottawa** for Todd Simpson, February 4, 2004. Signed as a free agent by **Yaroslavl** (Russia), September, 2004. Signed as a free agent by **Khimikik** (Russia), August 16, 2006.

SCHNABEL, Robert

(SHNAH-buhl, RAW-buhrt)

Defense. Shoots left. 6'5", 230 lbs. Born, Prague, Czech., November 10, 1978. Phoenix's 7th choice, 129th overall, in 1998 Entry Draft.

Season	Club	League	GP	G	A	Pts	PIM	PP	SH	GW	S	%	+/-	TF	F%	Min	GP	G	A	Pts	PIM	PP	SH	GW	Min
1994-95	Slavia Jr.	CzRep-Jr.	35	11	6	17	14																		
1995-96	Slavia Jr.	CzRep-Jr.	38	3	5	8																			
1996-97	Slavia Jr.	CzRep-Jr.	36	5	2	7																			
	HC Slavia Praha	CzRep	4	0	0	0	4										1	0	0	0	0				
1997-98	Red Deer Rebels	WHL	61	1	22	23	143										5	0	0	0	16				
1998-99	Red Deer Rebels	WHL	1	0	0	0	2																		
	Springfield	AHL	77	1	7	8	155										3	1	0	1	4				
99-2000	Springfield	AHL	40	2	8	10	133										5	0	0	0	4				
2000-01	Springfield	AHL	22	1	2	3	38																		
	Timra IK	Sweden	16	0	2	2	72																		
2001-02	Nashville	NHL	1	0	0	0	0	0	0	0	0	0.0	0	0	0.0	7:16									
	Milwaukee	AHL	67	2	7	9	130																		
2002-03	Nashville	NHL	1	0	0	0	0	0	0	0	0	0.0	0	0	0.0	4:28									
	Milwaukee	AHL	62	3	6	9	178										6	0	0	0	34				
2003-04	Nashville	NHL	20	0	3	3	34	0	0	0	10	0.0	6	0	0.0	14:36									
	Milwaukee	AHL	11	1	0	1	27										0	0	0	0	0				
2004-05	HC Sparta Praha	CzRep	47	1	4	5	85										4	0	0	0	12				
2005-06	HIFK Helsinki	Finland	51	3	11	14	165										11	0	0	0	*63				
	NHL Totals		22	0	3	3	34	0	0	0	10	0.0		0	0.0	13:48									

• Re-entered NHL Entry Draft. Originally NY Islanders' 5th choice, 79th overall, in 1997 Entry Draft.

Claimed on waivers by **Nashville** from **Phoenix**, January 2, 2001. • Missed majority of 2003-04 season recovering from wrist injury suffered in game vs. Columbus, October 18, 2003. Signed as a free agent by **Sparta Praha** (CzRep), May 19, 2004.

SCHNEIDER, Mathieu

(SHNIGH-duhr, MA-thew) **DET.**

Defense. Shoots left. 5'10", 192 lbs. Born, New York, NY, June 12, 1969. Montreal's 4th choice, 44th overall, in 1987 Entry Draft.

Season	Club	League	GP	G	A	Pts	PIM	PP	SH	GW	S	%	+/-	TF	F%	Min	GP	G	A	Pts	PIM	PP	SH	GW	Min
1985-86	Mount St. Charles	High-RI	19	3	27	30																			
1986-87	Cornwall Royals	OHL	63	7	29	36	75										5	0	0	0	22				
1987-88	Cornwall Royals	OHL	48	21	40	61	83										11	2	6	8	14				
	Montreal	NHL	4	0	0	0	2	0	0	0	2	0.0	–1												
	Sherbrooke	AHL															3	0	3	3	12				
1988-89	Cornwall Royals	OHL	59	16	57	73	96										18	7	20	27	30				
1989-90	Montreal	NHL	44	7	14	21	25	5	0	1	84	8.3	2				9	1	3	4	31	1	0	0	
	Sherbrooke	AHL	28	6	13	19	20																		
1990-91	Montreal	NHL	69	10	20	30	63	5	0	3	164	6.1	7				13	2	7	9	18	1	0	0	
1991-92	Montreal	NHL	78	8	24	32	72	2	0	1	194	4.1	10				10	1	4	5	6	1	0	0	
1992-93 ♦	Montreal	NHL	60	13	31	44	91	3	0	2	169	7.7	8				11	1	2	3	16	0	0	0	
1993-94	Montreal	NHL	75	20	32	52	62	11	0	4	193	10.4	15				1	0	0	0	0	0	0	0	
1994-95	Montreal	NHL	30	5	15	20	49	2	0	0	82	6.1	–3												
	NY Islanders	NHL	13	3	6	9	30	1	0	2	36	8.3	–5												
1995-96	NY Islanders	NHL	65	11	36	47	93	7	0	1	155	7.1	–18												
	Toronto	NHL	13	2	5	7	10	0	0	0	36	5.6	–2				6	0	4	4	8	0	0	0	
1996-97	Toronto	NHL	26	5	7	12	20	1	0	1	63	7.9	3												
1997-98	Toronto	NHL	76	11	26	37	44	4	1	1	181	6.1	–12												
	United States	Olympics	4	0	0	0	6																		
1998-99	NY Rangers	NHL	75	10	24	34	71	5	0	2	159	6.3	–19	0	0.0	24:35									
99-2000	NY Rangers	NHL	80	10	20	30	78	3	0	1	228	4.4	–6	0	0.0	22:31									
2000-01	Los Angeles	NHL	73	16	35	51	56	7	1	2	183	8.7	0	0	0.0	23:04	13	0	9	9	10	0	0	0	25:51
2001-02	Los Angeles	NHL	55	7	23	30	68	4	0	0	123	5.7	3	0	0.0	22:25	7	0	1	1	18	0	0	0	22:52
2002-03	Los Angeles	NHL	65	14	29	43	57	10	0	1	162	8.6	0	0	0.0	22:20									
	Detroit	NHL	13	2	5	7	16	1	0	0	37	5.4	2	0	0.0	22:42	4	0	0	0	6	0	0	0	28:16
2003-04	Detroit	NHL	78	14	32	46	56	4	1	4	165	8.5	22	4	0.0	24:29	12	1	2	3	8	1	0	1	26:30
2004-05			DID NOT PLAY																						
2005-06	Detroit	NHL	72	21	38	59	86	11	0	4	188	11.2	33	4	25.0	24:31	6	1	7	8	6	0	0	0	26:44
	United States	Olympics	6	1	2	3	16																		
	NHL Totals		1064	189	422	611	1049	86	3	30	2604	7.3		8	12.5	23:27	92	7	39	46	127	4	0	1	25:54

OHL First All-Star Team (1988, 1989)

Played in NHL All-Star Game (1996, 2003)

Traded to **NY Islanders** by **Montreal** with Kirk Muller and Craig Darby for Pierre Turgeon and Vladimir Malakhov, April 5, 1995. Traded to **Toronto** by **NY Islanders** with Wendel Clark and D.J. Smith for Darby Hendrickson, Sean Haggerty, Kenny Jonsson and Toronto's 1st round choice (Roberto Luongo) in 1997 Entry Draft, March 13, 1996. • Missed majority of 1996-97 season recovering from groin injury suffered in game vs. St. Louis, December 27, 1996. Rights traded to **NY Rangers** by **Toronto** for Alexander Karpovtsev and NY Rangers' 4th round choice (Mirko Murovic) in 1999 Entry Draft, October 14, 1998. Claimed by **Columbus** from **NY Rangers** in Expansion Draft, June 23, 2000. Signed as a free agent by **Los Angeles**, August 14, 2000. Traded to **Detroit** by **Los Angeles** for Sean Avery, Maxim Kuznetsov, Detroit's 1st round choice (Jeff Tambellini) in 2003 Entry Draft and Detroit's 2nd round choice (later traded to Boston – Boston selected Martins Karsums) in 2004 Entry Draft, March 11, 2003.

SCHUBERT, Christoph

(SHOO-buhrt, KRIHS-tawf) **OTT.**

Defense. Shoots left. 6'3", 210 lbs. Born, Munich, West Germany, February 5, 1982. Ottawa's 5th choice, 127th overall, in 2001 Entry Draft.

Season	Club	League	GP	G	A	Pts	PIM	PP	SH	GW	S	%	+/-	TF	F%	Min	GP	G	A	Pts	PIM	PP	SH	GW	Min
1998-99	EV Landshut Jr.	Ger-Jr.	28	15	20	35	77																		
99-2000	EV Landshut Jr.	Ger-Jr.	11	14	11	25	51																		
	EV Landshut	German-3	55	7	5	12	68																		
2000-01	Munchen Barons	Germany	55	6	3	9	80										10	0	2	2	27				
2001-02	Munchen Barons	Germany	50	5	11	16	125										9	3	4	7	32				
2002-03	Binghamton	AHL	70	2	8	10	102										8	0	1	1	2				
2003-04	Binghamton	AHL	70	2	10	12	69										1	0	0	0	0				
2004-05	Binghamton	AHL	76	10	22	32	110										6	2	2	4	20				
2005-06	Ottawa	NHL	56	4	6	10	48	0	1	0	72	5.6	4	5	0.0	11:06	7	0	1	1	4	0	0	0	7:53
	Germany	Olympics	5	0	1	1	2																		
	NHL Totals		56	4	6	10	48	0	1	0	72	5.6		5	0.0	11:06	7	0	1	1	4	0	0	0	7:53

SCHULTZ, Nick

(SHUHLTZ, NIHK) **MIN.**

Defense. Shoots left. 6'1", 207 lbs. Born, Strasbourg, Sask., August 25, 1982. Minnesota's 2nd choice, 33rd overall, in 2000 Entry Draft.

Season	Club	League	GP	G	A	Pts	PIM	PP	SH	GW	S	%	+/-	TF	F%	Min	GP	G	A	Pts	PIM	PP	SH	GW	Min
1997-98	Yorkton Mallers	SMHL	59	10	30	40	74																		
1998-99	Prince Albert	WHL	58	5	18	23	37										14	0	7	7	0				
99-2000	Prince Albert	WHL	72	11	33	44	38										6	0	3	3	2				
2000-01	Prince Albert	WHL	59	17	30	47	120																		
	Cleveland	IHL	4	1	1	2	2										3	0	1	1	0				
2001-02	Minnesota	NHL	52	4	6	10	14	1	0	1	47	8.5	0	0	0.0	16:08									
	Houston Aeros	AHL															14	1	5	6	2				
2002-03	Minnesota	NHL	75	3	7	10	23	0	0	1	70	4.3	11	0	0.0	18:28	18	0	1	1	10	0	0	0	19:39
2003-04	Minnesota	NHL	79	6	10	16	16	1	0	0	72	8.3	12	0	0.0	20:19									
2004-05	Kassel Huskies	Germany	46	7	15	22	26										7	0	4	4	6				
2005-06	Minnesota	NHL	79	2	12	14	43	0	0	0	45	4.4	2	0	0.0	17:58									
	NHL Totals		285	15	35	50	96	2	0	2	234	6.4		0	0.0	18:25	18	0	1	1	10	0	0	0	19:39

Signed as a free agent by **Kassel** (Germany), September 24, 2004.

			Regular Season													Playoffs								
Season	Club	League	GP	G	A	Pts	PIM	PP	SH	GW	S	%	+/-	TF	F%	Min	GP	G	A	Pts	PIM	PP	SH	GW	Min

SCHULTZ, Ray

Defense. Shoots left. 6'2", 215 lbs.   Born, Red Deer, Alta., November 14, 1976. Ottawa's 8th choice, 184th overall, in 1995 Entry Draft.   (SHUHLTZ, RAY)

Season	Club	League	GP	G	A	Pts	PIM	PP	SH	GW	S	%	+/-	TF	F%	Min	GP	G	A	Pts	PIM	PP	SH	GW	Min
1993-94	Edmonton SSAC	AMHL	31	3	24	27	94																		
	Tri-City	WHL	3	0	0	0	11																		
1994-95	Tri-City	WHL	63	1	8	9	209										11	0	0	0	16				
1995-96	Calgary Hitmen	WHL	66	3	17	20	282																		
1996-97	Calgary Hitmen	WHL	32	3	17	20	141																		
	Kelowna Rockets	WHL	23	3	11	14	63										6	0	2	2	12				
1997-98	**NY Islanders**	**NHL**	13	0	1	1	45	0	0	0	4	0.0	3												
	Kentucky	AHL	51	2	4	6	179										1	0	0	0	25				
1998-99	**NY Islanders**	**NHL**	4	0	0	0	7	0	0	0	2	0.0	-2	1	0.0	15:21									
	Lowell	AHL	54	0	3	3	184										1	0	0	0	4				
99-2000	**NY Islanders**	**NHL**	9	0	1	1	30	0	0	0	2	0.0	-1	0	0.0	14:18									
	Kansas City	IHL	65	5	5	10	208																		
2000-01	**NY Islanders**	**NHL**	13	0	2	2	40	0	0	0	3	0.0	-1	0	0.0	10:50									
	Lowell	AHL	13	0	1	1	33																		
	Cleveland	IHL	44	3	5	8	127										3	1	0	1	16				
2001-02	**NY Islanders**	**NHL**	2	0	0	0	5	0	0	0	0	0.0	-1	0	0.0	3:22	2	0	0	0	2	0	0	0	9:11
	Bridgeport	AHL	69	0	15	15	205										19	1	3	4	18				
2002-03	**NY Islanders**	**NHL**	4	0	0	0	28	0	0	0	1	0.0	-1	0	0.0	5:23									
	Bridgeport	AHL	51	2	8	10	105										9	1	0	1	14				
2003-04	Milwaukee	AHL	73	2	10	12	153										22	1	2	3	31				
2004-05	Albany River Rats	AHL	77	5	14	19	227																		
2005-06	Albany River Rats	AHL	18	0	5	5	22																		
	San Antonio	AHL	16	1	1	2	28																		
	Springfield	AHL	33	1	3	4	42																		
	NHL Totals		45	0	4	4	155	0	0	0	12	0.0		1	0.0	11:13	2	0	0	0	2	0	0	0	9:11

Signed as a free agent by **NY Islanders**, June 9, 1997. Signed as a free agent by **Nashville**, July 17, 2003. Signed as a free agent by **New Jersey**, July 6, 2004. Traded to **Phoenix** by **New Jersey** with Pascal Rheaume and Steven Spencer for Brad Ference, November 25, 2005. Loaned to **Springfield** (AHL) by **Phoenix** (San Antonio-AHL) for cash, January 9, 2006.

SCOVILLE, Darrel

Defense. Shoots left. 6'3", 208 lbs.   Born, Swift Current, Sask., October 13, 1975.   (SKO-vihl, DAIR-uhl)

Season	Club	League	GP	G	A	Pts	PIM	PP	SH	GW	S	%	+/-	TF	F%	Min	GP	G	A	Pts	PIM	PP	SH	GW	Min
1994-95	Lebret Eagles	SJHL	61	15	50	65																			
1995-96	Merrimack	H-East	34	6	20	26	54																		
1996-97	Merrimack	H-East	35	7	16	23	71																		
1997-98	Merrimack	H-East	38	4	26	30	84																		
1998-99	Saint John Flames	AHL	61	1	7	8	66										7	1	2	3	13				
99-2000	**Calgary**	**NHL**	6	0	0	0	2	0	0	0	1	0.0	1	0	0.0	9:18									
	Saint John Flames	AHL	64	11	25	36	99										3	1	4	5	6				
2000-01	Saint John Flames	AHL	76	11	32	47	125										11	2	6	8	8				
2001-02	Syracuse Crunch	AHL	51	5	16	21	60										10	0	0	0	6				
2002-03	**Columbus**	**NHL**	2	0	0	0	4	0	0	0	1	0.0	0	0	0.0	14:31									
	Syracuse Crunch	AHL	24	4	9	13	26																		
2003-04	**Columbus**	**NHL**	8	0	1	1	6	0	0	0	5	0.0	-4	0	0.0	19:14									
	Syracuse Crunch	AHL	70	10	32	42	73										6	0	4	4	4				
2004-05	Hershey Bears	AHL	7	0	0	0	11																		
	Providence Bruins	AHL	43	1	6	7	26																		
2005-06	EC Villacher SV	Austria	47	4	19	23	82										13	1	3	4	28				
	NHL Totals		16	0	1	1	12	0	0	0	7	0.0		0	0.0	14:55									

Hockey East All-Rookie Team (1996)

Signed as a free agent by **Calgary**, June 12, 1998. Signed as a free agent by **Columbus**, July 10, 2001. • Missed majority of 2002-03 season recovering from abdominal (October 26, 2002 vs. Grand Rapids - AHL) and foot (January 6, 2003. vs. Philadelphia - AHL) injuries. Signed as a free agent by **Hershey** (AHL), September 28, 2004. Traded to **Providence** (AHL) by **Hershey** (AHL) for Carl Corazzini, November 15, 2004.

SCUDERI, Rob

Defense. Shoots left. 6', 214 lbs.   Born, Syosset, NY, December 30, 1978. Pittsburgh's 5th choice, 134th overall, in 1998 Entry Draft.   (SKUD-uhree, RAWB)   **PIT.**

Season	Club	League	GP	G	A	Pts	PIM	PP	SH	GW	S	%	+/-	TF	F%	Min	GP	G	A	Pts	PIM	PP	SH	GW	Min
1995-96	NY Apple Core	MtJHL	76	18	60	78																			
1996-97	NY Apple Core	MtJHL	82	42	70	112	64																		
1997-98	Boston College	H-East	42	0	24	24	12																		
1998-99	Boston College	H-East	41	2	8	10	20																		
99-2000	Boston College	H-East	42	1	12	13	22																		
2000-01	Boston College	H-East	43	4	19	23	42																		
2001-02	Wilkes-Barre	AHL	75	1	22	23	66																		
2002-03	Wilkes-Barre	AHL	74	4	17	21	44										6	0	1	1	4				
2003-04	**Pittsburgh**	**NHL**	13	1	2	3	4	0	0	0	4	25.0	2	0	0.0	20:06									
	Wilkes-Barre	AHL	64	1	15	16	54										24	0	3	3	14				
2004-05	Wilkes-Barre	AHL	79	2	18	20	34										11	2	1	3	2				
2005-06	**Pittsburgh**	**NHL**	57	0	4	4	36	0	0	0	28	0.0	-18	0	0.0	20:15									
	Wilkes-Barre	AHL	13	0	8	8	8																		
	NHL Totals		70	1	6	7	40	0	0	0	32	3.1		0	0.0	20:13									

NCAA Championship All-Tournament Team (2001)

SEABROOK, Brent

Defense. Shoots right. 6'3", 215 lbs.   Born, Richmond, B.C., April 20, 1985. Chicago's 1st choice, 14th overall, in 2003 Entry Draft.   (SEE-bruk, BREHNT)   **CHI.**

Season	Club	League	GP	G	A	Pts	PIM	PP	SH	GW	S	%	+/-	TF	F%	Min	GP	G	A	Pts	PIM	PP	SH	GW	Min
2000-01	Delta Ice Hawks	PIJHL	54	16	26	42	55																		
	Lethbridge	WHL	4	0	0	0	0																		
2001-02	Lethbridge	WHL	67	6	33	39	70										4	1	1	2	2				
2002-03	Lethbridge	WHL	69	9	33	42	113																		
2003-04	Lethbridge	WHL	61	12	29	41	107																		
2004-05	Lethbridge	WHL	63	12	42	54	107										5	1	2	3	10				
	Norfolk Admirals	AHL	3	0	0	0	2										6	0	1	1	6				
2005-06	**Chicago**	**NHL**	69	5	27	32	60	1	0	2	114	4.4	5	0	0.0	20:02									
	NHL Totals		69	5	27	32	60	1	0	2	114	4.4		0	0.0	20:02									

WHL East Second All-Star Team (2005)

SEDIN, Daniel

Left wing. Shoots left. 6'1", 200 lbs.   Born, Ornskoldsvik, Sweden, September 26, 1980. Vancouver's 1st choice, 2nd overall, in 1999 Entry Draft.   (suh-DEEN, DAN-yehl)   **VAN.**

Season	Club	League	GP	G	A	Pts	PIM	PP	SH	GW	S	%	+/-	TF	F%	Min	GP	G	A	Pts	PIM	PP	SH	GW	Min
1997-98	Malmo Jr.	Swe-Jr.	4	3	3	6	4																		
	MoDo Jr.	Swe-Jr.	26	26	14	40																			
	MoDo	Sweden	45	4	8	12	26										9	0	0	0	2				
1998-99	MoDo	Sweden	50	21	21	42	20										13	4	8	12	14				
99-2000	MoDo	Sweden	50	19	26	45	28										13	*8	6	14	18				
	MoDo	EuroHL	4	3	3	6	0										2	0	0	0	0				
2000-01	**Vancouver**	**NHL**	75	20	14	34	24	10	0	3	127	15.7	-3	10	60.0	13:00	4	1	2	3	0				16:15
2001-02	**Vancouver**	**NHL**	79	9	23	32	32	4	0	2	117	7.7	1	18	33.3	12:22	6	0	1	1	0	0	0	0	10:44
2002-03	**Vancouver**	**NHL**	79	14	17	31	34	4	0	2	134	10.4	8	24	45.8	12:26	14	1	5	6	8	1	0	0	12:23
2003-04	**Vancouver**	**NHL**	82	18	36	54	18	4	0	3	153	11.8	18	71	47.9	13:33	7	1	2	3	0	1	0	0	16:03
2004-05	MODO	Sweden	49	13	20	33	40										6	0	3	3	6				
2005-06	**Vancouver**	**NHL**	82	22	49	71	34	11	0	4	204	10.8	7	49	42.9	16:40									
	Sweden	Olympics	8	1	3	4	2																		
	NHL Totals		397	83	139	222	142	30	0	14	735	11.3		172	45.3	13:38	31	3	10	13	8	2	0	1	13:24

Signed as a free agent by **MODO** (Sweden), September 18, 2004.

SEDIN, Henrik

(suh-DEEN, HEHN-rihk) **VAN.**

Center. Shoots left. 6'2", 200 lbs. Born, Ornskoldsvik, Sweden, September 26, 1980. Vancouver's 2nd choice, 3rd overall, in 1999 Entry Draft.

Season	Club	League	Regular Season GP	G	A	Pts	PIM	PP	SH	GW	S	%	+/-	TF	F%	Min	Playoffs GP	G	A	Pts	PIM	PP	SH	GW	Min
1997-98	MoDo Jr.	Swe-Jr.	26	14	22	36																			
	Malmo Jr.	Swe-Jr.	8	4	7	11	6																		
	MoDo	Sweden	39	1	4	5	8										7	0	0	0	0				
1998-99	MoDo	Sweden	49	12	22	34	32										13	2	8	10	6				
99-2000	MoDo	Sweden	50	9	38	47	22										13	5	9	14	2				
2000-01	Vancouver	NHL	82	9	20	29	38	2	0	1	98	9.2	-2	1020	44.1	13:31	4	0	4	4	0	0	0	0	16:31
2001-02	Vancouver	NHL	82	16	20	36	36	3	0	1	78	20.5	9	785	47.4	12:48	6	3	0	3	0	0	0	1	11:55
2002-03	Vancouver	NHL	78	8	31	39	38	4	1	1	81	9.9	9	995	48.2	13:58	14	3	2	5	8	1	0	0	13:01
2003-04	Vancouver	NHL	76	11	31	42	32	2	0	2	99	11.1	23	961	50.0	14:02	7	2	2	4	2	2	0	0	16:02
2004-05	MODO	Sweden	44	14	22	36	50										6	1	3	4	6				
2005-06	Vancouver	NHL	82	18	57	75	56	5	1	0	113	15.9	11	1238	50.7	16:54									
	Sweden	Olympics	8	3	1	4	2																		
	NHL Totals		400	62	159	221	200	16	2	5	469	13.2		4999	48.2	14:15	31	8	8	16	10	3	0	1	13:56

Signed as a free agent by **MODO** (Sweden), September 18, 2004.

SEIDENBERG, Dennis

(SIGH-dehn-buhrg, DEH-nihs) **PHX.**

Defense. Shoots left. 6'1", 210 lbs. Born, Schwenningen, West Germany, July 18, 1981. Philadelphia's 6th choice, 172nd overall, in 2001 Entry Draft.

Season	Club	League	Regular Season GP	G	A	Pts	PIM	PP	SH	GW	S	%	+/-	TF	F%	Min	Playoffs GP	G	A	Pts	PIM	PP	SH	GW	Min
99-2000	Mannheim Jr.	Ger-Jr.	52	12	28	40	28																		
	Adler Mannheim	Germany	3	0	0	0	0																		
2000-01	Mannheim Jr.	Ger-Jr.	9	3	8	11	20																		
	Adler Mannheim	Germany	55	2	5	7	6										12	0	1	1	10				
2001-02	Adler Mannheim	Germany	55	7	13	20	56										8	0	0	0	2				
2002-03	Philadelphia	NHL	58	4	9	13	20	1	0	0	123	3.3	8	1	0.0	16:50									
	Philadelphia	AHL	19	5	6	11	17																		
2003-04	Philadelphia	NHL	5	0	0	0	2	0	0	0	14	0.0	-4	0	0.0	17:20	3	0	0	0	0	0	0	0	7:36
	Philadelphia	AHL	33	7	12	19	31										9	2	2	4	4				
2004-05	Philadelphia	AHL	79	13	28	41	47										18	2	8	10	19				
2005-06	Philadelphia	NHL	29	2	5	7	4	1	0	0	34	5.9	-4	1	0.0	14:22									
	Phoenix	NHL	34	1	10	11	14	1	0	0	49	2.0	-9	0	0.0	19:13									
	Germany	Olympics	5	0	0	0	6																		
	NHL Totals		126	7	24	31	40	3	0	0	220	3.2		2	0.0	16:56	3	0	0	0	0	0	0	0	7:36

• Missed majority of 2003-04 season recovering from leg injury suffered in game vs. Edmonton, January 10, 2004. Traded to **Phoenix** by **Philadelphia** with Phoenix's 4th round choice (Joonas Lehtivuori) in 2006 Entry Draft for Petr Nedved and Philadelphia's 4th round choice (later traded to NY Islanders - NY Islanders selected Tomas Marcinko) in 2006 Entry Draft, January 20, 2006.

SEJNA, Peter

(SHAY-nah, PEE-tuhr) **ST.L.**

Left wing. Shoots left. 5'11", 198 lbs. Born, Liptovsky Mikulas, Czech., October 5, 1979.

Season	Club	League	Regular Season GP	G	A	Pts	PIM	PP	SH	GW	S	%	+/-	TF	F%	Min	Playoffs GP	G	A	Pts	PIM	PP	SH	GW	Min
1995-96	L. Mikulas U18	Svk-U18	44	40	23	63	20																		
1996-97	L. Mikulas U18	Svk-U18	40	32	19	51	6																		
	L. Mikulas	Slovakia	29	3	5	8	2																		
	L. Mikulas Jr.	Slovak-Jr.	17	14	10	24	8																		
1997-98	L. Mikulas	Slovakia	34	5	6	11	6																		
1998-99	Des Moines	USHL	52	40	23	63	26										14	11	6	17	8				
99-2000	Des Moines	USHL	58	41	53	94	36										9	4	5	9	4				
2000-01	Colorado College	WCHA	41	29	29	58	10																		
2001-02	Colorado College	WCHA	43	26	24	50	16																		
2002-03	Colorado College	WCHA	42	*36	46	*82	12																		
	St. Louis	NHL	1	1	0	1	0	1	0	0	3	33.3	0	0	0.0	15:22									
2003-04	St. Louis	NHL	20	2	2	4	4	2	0	0	36	5.6	-9	7	42.9	14:58									
	Worcester IceCats	AHL	59	12	29	41	13										10	3	3	6	10				
2004-05	Worcester IceCats	AHL	64	17	21	38	24																		
2005-06	St. Louis	NHL	6	1	1	2	4	0	0	0	9	11.1	1	1	0.0	11:43									
	Peoria Rivermen	AHL	44	19	31	50	18										4	3	0	3	2				
	NHL Totals		27	4	3	7	8	3	0	0	48	8.3		8	37.5	14:16									

WCHA Rookie of the Year (2001) • WCHA First All-Star Team (2003) • WCHA Player of the Year (2003) • NCAA West First All-American Team (2003) • Hobey Baker Memorial Award (Top U.S. Collegiate Player) (2003)

Signed as a free agent by **St. Louis**, April 6, 2003.

SELANNE, Teemu

(SEH-lahn-nay, TEE-moo) **ANA.**

Right wing. Shoots right. 6', 205 lbs. Born, Helsinki, Finland, July 3, 1970. Winnipeg's 1st choice, 10th overall, in 1988 Entry Draft.

Season	Club	League	Regular Season GP	G	A	Pts	PIM	PP	SH	GW	S	%	+/-	TF	F%	Min	Playoffs GP	G	A	Pts	PIM	PP	SH	GW	Min
1986-87	Jokerit U18	Fin-U18															7	10	3	13	2				
	Jokerit Helsinki Jr.	Fin-Jr.	33	10	12	22	8																		
1987-88	Jokerit Helsinki Jr.	Fin-Jr.	33	43	23	66	18										5	4	3	7	2				
	Jokerit Helsinki	Finland-2	5	1	1	2	0																		
1988-89	PvUK Lahti Jr.	Fin-Jr.	3	3	1	4	2																		
	Jokerit Helsinki Jr.	Fin-Jr.	3	8	8	16	4																		
	Jokerit Helsinki	Finland-2	35	36	33	69	14										5	7	3	10	4				
1989-90	Jokerit Helsinki	Finland	11	4	8	12	0																		
1990-91	Jokerit Helsinki Jr.	Fin-Jr.	4	3	2	5	10																		
	Jokerit Helsinki	Finland	42	33	25	58	12																		
1991-92	Jokerit Helsinki	Finland	44	39	23	62	20										10	10	7	17	18				
	Finland	Olympics	8	7	4	11	6																		
1992-93	Winnipeg	NHL	84	*76	56	132	45	24	0	7	387	19.6	8				6	4	2	6	2	2	0	2	
1993-94	Winnipeg	NHL	51	25	29	54	22	11	0	2	191	13.1	-23												
1994-95	Jokerit Helsinki	Finland	20	7	12	19	6																		
	Winnipeg	NHL	45	22	26	48	2	8	2	1	167	13.2	1												
1995-96	Winnipeg	NHL	51	24	48	72	18	6	1	4	163	14.7	3												
	Anaheim	NHL	28	16	20	36	4	3	0	1	104	15.4	2												
1996-97	Anaheim	NHL	78	51	58	109	34	11	1	8	273	18.7	28				11	7	3	10	4	3	0	1	
1997-98	Anaheim	NHL	73	*52	34	86	30	10	1	10	268	19.4	12												
	Finland	Olympics	5	4	6	10	8																		
1998-99	Anaheim	NHL	75	*47	60	107	30	25	0	7	281	16.7	18	5	20.0	22:47	4	2	2	4	2	1	0	0	22:23
99-2000	Anaheim	NHL	79	33	52	85	12	8	0	6	236	14.0	6	13	23.1	22:44									
2000-01	Anaheim	NHL	61	26	33	59	36	10	0	5	202	12.9	-8	4	50.0	21:51									
	San Jose	NHL	12	7	6	13	0	2	0	2	31	22.6	1	4	75.0	18:14	6	0	2	2	2	0	0	0	17:13
2001-02	San Jose	NHL	82	29	25	54	40	9	1	8	202	14.4	-11	12	25.0	16:58	12	5	3	8	2	2	0	1	16:51
	Finland	Olympics	4	3	0	3	2																		
2002-03	San Jose	NHL	82	28	36	64	30	7	0	5	253	11.1	-6	107	42.1	19:14									
2003-04	Colorado	NHL	78	16	16	32	32	6	1	4	182	8.8	2	80	43.8	16:10	10	0	3	3	2	0	0	0	12:53
2004-05			DID NOT PLAY																						
2005-06	Anaheim	NHL	80	40	50	90	44	18	0	5	267	15.0	28	209	41.6	17:48	16	6	8	14	6	1	0	2	17:56
	Finland	Olympics	8	6	5	11	4																		
	NHL Totals		959	492	549	1041	379	158	7	75	3207	15.3		434	41.2	19:30	65	24	23	47	20	9	0	6	16:53

NHL All-Rookie Team (1993) • NHL First All-Star Team (1993, 1997) • Calder Memorial Trophy (1993) • NHL Second All-Star Team (1998, 1999) • Maurice "Rocket" Richard Trophy (1999)

Played in NHL All-Star Game (1993, 1994, 1996, 1997, 1998, 1999, 2000, 2002, 2003) • Olympic Tournament All-Star Team (2006) • Best Forward at Olympics (2006) • Bill Masterton Trophy (2006)

• Missed majority of 1989-90 season recovering from leg injury suffered in game vs. HIFK (Finland), October 19, 1989. Traded to **Anaheim** by **Winnipeg** with Marc Chouinard and Winnipeg's 4th round choice (later traded to Toronto – later traded to Montreal – Montreal selected Kim Staal) in 1996 Entry Draft for Chad Kilger, Oleg Tverdovsky and Anaheim's 3rd round choice (Per-Anton Lundstrom) in 1996 Entry Draft, February 7, 1996. Traded to **San Jose** by **Anaheim** for Jeff Friesen, Steve Shields and San Jose's 2nd round choice (later traded to Dallas – Dallas selected Vojtech Polak) in 2003 Entry Draft, March 5, 2001. Signed as a free agent by **Colorado**, July 3, 2003. Signed as a free agent by **Anaheim**, August 22, 2005.

			Regular Season														Playoffs								
Season	Club	League	GP	G	A	Pts	PIM	PP	SH	GW	S	%	+/-	TF	F%	Min	GP	G	A	Pts	PIM	PP	SH	GW	Min

SEMENOV, Alexei — (seh-MEH-nahv, al-EHX-ay) — **FLA.**

Defense. Shoots left. 6'6", 235 lbs.   Born, Murmansk, USSR, April 10, 1981. Edmonton's 2nd choice, 36th overall, in 1999 Entry Draft.

Season	Club	League	GP	G	A	Pts	PIM	PP	SH	GW	S	%	+/-	TF	F%	Min	GP	G	A	Pts	PIM	PP	SH	GW	Min
1997-98	Krylja Sovetov 2	Russia-3	52	1	2	3	48	....	....	....	....	....	....	....	....	....	....	....	....	....	....	....	....	....	....
1998-99	St. Petersburg 2	Russia-4	19	0	1	1	20	....	....	....	....	....	....	....	....	....	....	....	....	....	....	....	....	....	....
	Sudbury Wolves	OHL	28	0	3	3	28	....	....	....	....	....	....	....	....	....	2	0	0	0	4	....	....	....	....
99-2000	Sudbury Wolves	OHL	65	9	35	44	135	....	....	....	....	....	....	....	....	....	12	1	3	4	23	....	....	....	....
	Hamilton	AHL	....	....	....	....	....	....	....	....	....	....	....	....	....	....	3	0	0	0	0	....	....	....	....
2000-01	Sudbury Wolves	OHL	65	21	42	63	106	....	....	....	....	....	....	....	....	....	12	4	13	17	17	....	....	....	....
2001-02	Hamilton	AHL	78	5	11	16	67	....	....	....	....	....	....	....	....	....	....	....	....	....	....	....	....	....	....
2002-03	**Edmonton**	**NHL**	**46**	**1**	**6**	**7**	**58**	0	0	0	33	3.0	−7	0	0.0	19:41	6	0	0	0	0	0	0	0	13:05
	Hamilton	AHL	37	4	3	7	45	....	....	....	....	....	....	....	....	....	....	....	....	....	....	....	....	....	....
2003-04	**Edmonton**	**NHL**	**46**	**2**	**3**	**5**	**32**	1	0	0	36	5.6	8	0	0.0	17:16	....	....	....	....	....	....	....	....	....
2004-05	St. Petersburg	Russia	50	0	8	8	26	....	....	....	....	....	....	....	....	....	....	....	....	....	....	....	....	....	....
2005-06	Yaroslavl	Russia	2	0	1	1	2	....	....	....	....	....	....	....	....	....	....	....	....	....	....	....	....	....	....
	Edmonton	**NHL**	**11**	**1**	**1**	**2**	**17**	0	0	0	3	33.3	−3	0	0.0	10:49	....	....	....	....	....	....	....	....	....
	Florida	**NHL**	**16**	**1**	**1**	**2**	**21**	1	0	0	13	7.7	−1	0	0.0	12:33	....	....	....	....	....	....	....	....	....
	Rochester	AHL	3	0	0	0	7	....	....	....	....	....	....	....	....	....	....	....	....	....	....	....	....	....	....
	NHL Totals		**119**	**5**	**11**	**16**	**128**	2	0	0	85	5.9		0	0.0	16:58	6	0	0	0	0	0	0	0	13:05

Signed as a free agent by **St. Petersburg** (Russia), July 30, 2004. Traded to **Florida** by **Edmonton** for Florida's 5th round choice (Bryan Pitton) in 2006 Entry Draft, November 19, 2005.
OHL First All-Star Team (2001)

SEMIN, Alexander — (SEH-min, al-ehx-AN-duhr) — **WSH.**

Left wing. Shoots left. 6', 181 lbs.   Born, Krasnoyarsk, USSR, March 3, 1984. Washington's 2nd choice, 13th overall, in 2002 Entry Draft.

Season	Club	League	GP	G	A	Pts	PIM	PP	SH	GW	S	%	+/-	TF	F%	Min	GP	G	A	Pts	PIM	PP	SH	GW	Min
2001-02	Chelyabinsk	Russia-2	46	13	8	21	52	....	....	....	....	....	....	....	....	....	2	2	0	2	0	....	....	....	....
2002-03	Lada Togliatti	Russia	47	10	7	17	36	....	....	....	....	....	....	....	....	....	10	*5	3	8	10	....	....	....	....
2003-04	**Washington**	**NHL**	**52**	**10**	**12**	**22**	**36**	4	0	2	92	10.9	−2	6	50.0	12:37	....	....	....	....	....	....	....	....	....
	Portland Pirates	AHL	4	3	1	4	6	....	....	....	....	....	....	....	....	....	7	4	7	11	19	....	....	....	....
2004-05	Lada Togliatti	Russia	50	19	11	30	56	....	....	....	....	....	....	....	....	....	10	1	1	2	0	....	....	....	....
2005-06	Lada Togliatti	Russia	16	5	4	9	52	....	....	....	....	....	....	....	....	....	....	....	....	....	....	....	....	....	....
	Mytischi	Russia	26	3	7	10	24	....	....	....	....	....	....	....	....	....	8	3	2	5	6	....	....	....	....
	NHL Totals		**52**	**10**	**12**	**22**	**36**	4	0	2	92	10.9		6	50.0	12:37	....	....	....	....	....	....	....	....	....

Signed as a free agent by **Togliatti** (Russia), September 25, 2004. • Suspended by **Washington** for failing to report to **Portland** (AHL), September 28, 2004. Signed as a free agent by **Mytischi** (Russia), November 22, 2005.

SEVERSON, Cam — (SEH-vuhr-SOHN, KAM)

Left wing. Shoots left. 6'1", 215 lbs.   Born, Canora, Sask., January 15, 1978. San Jose's 6th choice, 192nd overall, in 1997 Entry Draft.

Season	Club	League	GP	G	A	Pts	PIM	PP	SH	GW	S	%	+/-	TF	F%	Min	GP	G	A	Pts	PIM	PP	SH	GW	Min
1996-97	Lethbridge	WHL	45	12	13	25	169	....	....	....	....	....	....	....	....	....	....	....	....	....	....	....	....	....	....
	Prince Albert	WHL	16	5	13	18	54	....	....	....	....	....	....	....	....	....	4	4	0	4	8	....	....	....	....
1997-98	Prince Albert	WHL	41	23	25	48	129	....	....	....	....	....	....	....	....	....	....	....	....	....	....	....	....	....	....
	Spokane Chiefs	WHL	23	9	11	20	88	....	....	....	....	....	....	....	....	....	18	11	4	15	51	....	....	....	....
1998-99	Spokane Chiefs	WHL	46	16	17	33	190	....	....	....	....	....	....	....	....	....	10	4	0	4	26	....	....	....	....
	Oklahoma City	CHL	5	6	3	9	4	....	....	....	....	....	....	....	....	....	....	....	....	....	....	....	....	....	....
99-2000	Louisiana	ECHL	7	0	2	2	22	....	....	....	....	....	....	....	....	....	....	....	....	....	....	....	....	....	....
	Peoria Rivermen	ECHL	56	19	8	27	138	....	....	....	....	....	....	....	....	....	18	3	4	7	41	....	....	....	....
2000-01	Portland Pirates	AHL	8	0	0	0	11	....	....	....	....	....	....	....	....	....	....	....	....	....	....	....	....	....	....
	Quad City	UHL	46	22	26	48	129	....	....	....	....	....	....	....	....	....	....	....	....	....	....	....	....	....	....
	Cincinnati	AHL	20	4	7	11	60	....	....	....	....	....	....	....	....	....	3	1	1	2	0	....	....	....	....
2001-02	Hartford	AHL	65	11	10	21	116	....	....	....	....	....	....	....	....	....	5	0	0	0	7	....	....	....	....
2002-03	**Anaheim**	**NHL**	**2**	**0**	**0**	**0**	**8**	0	0	0	1	0.0	0	0	0.0	6:44	1	0	0	0	0	0	0	0	2:24
	Cincinnati	AHL	71	12	9	21	156	....	....	....	....	....	....	....	....	....	....	....	....	....	....	....	....	....	....
2003-04	**Anaheim**	**NHL**	**31**	**3**	**0**	**3**	**50**	1	0	0	24	12.5	−3	3	66.7	7:21	....	....	....	....	....	....	....	....	....
	Cincinnati	AHL	38	7	7	14	145	....	....	....	....	....	....	....	....	....	....	....	....	....	....	....	....	....	....
2004-05	Milwaukee	AHL	63	6	8	14	255	....	....	....	....	....	....	....	....	....	4	0	0	0	0	....	....	....	....
2005-06	Omaha	AHL	54	13	7	20	146	....	....	....	....	....	....	....	....	....	....	....	....	....	....	....	....	....	....
	Columbus	**NHL**	**4**	**0**	**0**	**0**	**5**	0	0	0	2	0.0	0	0	0.0	3:06	....	....	....	....	....	....	....	....	....
	Syracuse Crunch	AHL	12	4	3	7	28	....	....	....	....	....	....	....	....	....	3	0	0	0	21	....	....	....	....
	NHL Totals		**37**	**3**	**0**	**3**	**63**	2	0	0	27	11.1		4	50.0	6:51	1	0	0	0	0	0	0	0	2:24

Signed as a free agent by **Hartford** (AHL), September 24, 2001. Signed as a free agent by **Anaheim**, August 22, 2002. Signed as a free agent by **Nashville**, July 22, 2004. Signed as a free agent by **Calgary**, August 11, 2005. Traded to **Columbus** by **Calgary** for Cale Hulse, February 28, 2006.

SHANAHAN, Brendan — (SHAN-na-HAN, BREHN-duhn) — **NYR**

Left wing. Shoots right. 6'3", 218 lbs.   Born, Mimico, Ont., January 23, 1969. New Jersey's 1st choice, 2nd overall, in 1987 Entry Draft.

Season	Club	League	GP	G	A	Pts	PIM	PP	SH	GW	S	%	+/-	TF	F%	Min	GP	G	A	Pts	PIM	PP	SH	GW	Min
1984-85	Mississauga Reps	MTHL	36	20	21	41	26	....	....	....	....	....	....	....	....	....	....	....	....	....	....	....	....	....	....
	Dixie Beehives	OJHL	1	0	0	0	0	....	....	....	....	....	....	....	....	....	....	....	....	....	....	....	....	....	....
1985-86	London Knights	OHL	59	28	34	62	70	....	....	....	....	....	....	....	....	....	5	5	5	10	5	....	....	....	....
1986-87	London Knights	OHL	56	39	53	92	92	....	....	....	....	....	....	....	....	....	....	....	....	....	....	....	....	....	....
1987-88	**New Jersey**	**NHL**	**65**	**7**	**19**	**26**	**131**	2	0	2	72	9.7	−20	....	....	....	12	2	1	3	44	1	0	0	....
1988-89	**New Jersey**	**NHL**	**68**	**22**	**28**	**50**	**115**	9	0	0	152	14.5	2	....	....	....	....	....	....	....	....	....	....	....	....
1989-90	**New Jersey**	**NHL**	**73**	**30**	**42**	**72**	**137**	8	0	2	196	15.3	15	....	....	....	6	3	3	6	20	1	0	1	....
1990-91	**New Jersey**	**NHL**	**75**	**29**	**37**	**66**	**141**	7	0	2	195	14.9	4	....	....	....	7	3	5	8	12	2	0	0	....
1991-92	**St. Louis**	**NHL**	**80**	**33**	**36**	**69**	**171**	13	0	5	215	15.3	−3	....	....	....	6	2	3	5	14	1	0	0	....
1992-93	**St. Louis**	**NHL**	**71**	**51**	**43**	**94**	**174**	18	0	8	232	22.0	10	....	....	....	11	4	3	7	18	2	0	1	....
1993-94	**St. Louis**	**NHL**	**81**	**52**	**50**	**102**	**211**	15	7	8	397	13.1	−9	....	....	....	4	2	5	7	4	0	0	0	....
1994-95	Dusseldorfer EG	Germany	3	5	3	8	4	....	....	....	....	....	....	....	....	....	....	....	....	....	....	....	....	....	....
	St. Louis	**NHL**	**45**	**20**	**21**	**41**	**136**	7	0	1	153	13.1	7	....	....	....	5	4	5	9	14	1	0	1	....
1995-96	**Hartford**	**NHL**	**74**	**44**	**34**	**78**	**125**	17	2	6	280	15.7	2	....	....	....	....	....	....	....	....	....	....	....	....
1996-97	**Hartford**	**NHL**	**2**	**1**	**0**	**1**	**0**	0	0	0	13	7.7	1	....	....	....	....	....	....	....	....	....	....	....	....
	♦ **Detroit**	**NHL**	**79**	**46**	**41**	**87**	**131**	20	2	7	323	14.2	31	....	....	....	20	9	8	17	43	2	0	2	....
1997-98	♦ **Detroit**	**NHL**	**75**	**28**	**29**	**57**	**154**	15	1	9	266	10.5	6	....	....	....	20	5	4	9	22	3	0	2	....
	Canada	Olympics	6	2	0	2	0	....	....	....	....	....	....	....	....	....	....	....	....	....	....	....	....	....	....
1998-99	**Detroit**	**NHL**	**81**	**31**	**27**	**58**	**123**	5	0	5	288	10.8	2	18	44.4	17:31	10	3	7	10	6	1	0	1	18:31
99-2000	**Detroit**	**NHL**	**78**	**41**	**37**	**78**	**105**	13	1	9	283	14.5	24	24	50.0	18:35	9	3	2	5	10	0	0	0	17:36
2000-01	**Detroit**	**NHL**	**81**	**31**	**45**	**76**	**81**	15	1	9	278	11.2	9	115	43.5	18:22	6	2	2	4	0	0	0	1	21:01
2001-02	♦ **Detroit**	**NHL**	**80**	**37**	**38**	**75**	**118**	12	3	7	277	13.4	23	70	47.1	18:55	23	8	11	19	20	4	0	2	19:06
	Canada	Olympics	6	0	1	1	0	....	....	....	....	....	....	....	....	....	....	....	....	....	....	....	....	....	....
2002-03	**Detroit**	**NHL**	**78**	**30**	**38**	**68**	**103**	13	0	6	260	11.5	5	28	60.7	18:38	4	1	1	2	4	1	0	0	22:03
2003-04	**Detroit**	**NHL**	**82**	**25**	**28**	**53**	**117**	8	0	7	280	8.9	15	32	46.9	18:05	12	1	5	6	20	0	0	1	16:49
2004-05			DID NOT PLAY														....	....	....	....	....	....	....	....	....
2005-06	**Detroit**	**NHL**	**82**	**40**	**41**	**81**	**105**	14	0	6	289	13.8	29	26	50.0	16:35	6	1	1	2	6	0	0	0	18:54
	NHL Totals		**1350**	**598**	**634**	**1232**	**2378**	210	20	102	4449	13.4		313	47.3	18:05	157	53	66	119	257	16	1	10	18:37

NHL First All-Star Team (1994, 2000) • NHL Second All-Star Team (2002) • King Clancy Memorial Trophy (2003)
Played in NHL All-Star Game (1994, 1996, 1997, 1998, 1999, 2000, 2002)

Signed as a free agent by **St. Louis**, July 25, 1991. Traded to **Hartford** by **St. Louis** for Chris Pronger, July 27, 1995. Traded to **Detroit** by **Hartford** with Brian Glynn for Paul Coffey, Keith Primeau and Detroit's 1st round choice (Nikos Tselios) in 1997 Entry Draft, October 9, 1996. Signed as a free agent by **NY Rangers**, July 9, 2006.

SHARP, Patrick — (SHAHRP, PAT-rihk) — **CHI.**

Center. Shoots right. 6', 197 lbs.   Born, Thunder Bay, Ont., December 27, 1981. Philadelphia's 2nd choice, 95th overall, in 2001 Entry Draft.

Season	Club	League	GP	G	A	Pts	PIM	PP	SH	GW	S	%	+/-	TF	F%	Min	GP	G	A	Pts	PIM	PP	SH	GW	Min
1998-99	Thunder Bay	USHL	55	19	24	43	48	....	....	....	....	....	....	....	....	....	3	1	1	2	0	....	....	....	....
99-2000	Thunder Bay	USHL	56	20	35	55	41	....	....	....	....	....	....	....	....	....	....	....	....	....	....	....	....	....	....
2000-01	U. of Vermont	ECAC	34	12	15	27	36	....	....	....	....	....	....	....	....	....	....	....	....	....	....	....	....	....	....
2001-02	U. of Vermont	ECAC	31	13	13	26	50	....	....	....	....	....	....	....	....	....	....	....	....	....	....	....	....	....	....
2002-03	**Philadelphia**	**NHL**	**3**	**0**	**0**	**0**	**2**	0	0	0	3	0.0	0	7	42.9	5:59	....	....	....	....	....	....	....	....	....
	Philadelphia	AHL	53	14	19	33	39	....	....	....	....	....	....	....	....	....	....	....	....	....	....	....	....	....	....

			Regular Season														Playoffs								
Season	Club	League	GP	G	A	Pts	PIM	PP	SH	GW	S	%	+/-	TF	F%	Min	GP	G	A	Pts	PIM	PP	SH	GW	Min
2003-04	**Philadelphia**	**NHL**	**41**	**5**	**2**	**7**	**55**	**0**	**0**	**1**	**44**	**11.4**	**–3**	**272**	**46.7**	**9:56**	**12**	**1**	**0**	**1**	**2**	**0**	**0**	**0**	**6:12**
	Philadelphia	AHL	35	15	14	29	45	....	....	....	....	....	....	....	....	....	1	2	0	2	0	....	....	....	....
2004-05	Philadelphia	AHL	75	23	29	52	80	....	....	....	....	....	....	....	....	....	21	8	13	*21	20	....	....	....	....
2005-06	**Philadelphia**	**NHL**	**22**	**5**	**3**	**8**	**10**	**1**	**0**	**3**	**33**	**15.2**	**4**	**38**	**52.6**	**7:43**	....	....	....	....	....	....	....	....	....
	Chicago	**NHL**	**50**	**9**	**14**	**23**	**36**	**0**	**1**	**2**	**111**	**8.1**	**1**	**664**	**48.0**	**16:19**	....	....	....	....	....	....	....	....	....
	NHL Totals		**116**	**19**	**19**	**38**	**103**	**1**	**1**	**6**	**191**	**9.9**		**981**	**47.8**	**12:10**	**12**	**1**	**0**	**1**	**2**	**0**	**0**	**0**	**6:12**

Traded to **Chicago** by **Philadelphia** with Eric Meloche for Matt Ellison and Chicago's 3rd round choice (later traded to Montreal - Montreal selected Ryan White) in 2006 Entry Draft, December 5, 2005.

SHELLEY, Jody

(SHEH-lee, JOH-dee) **CBJ**

Left wing. Shoots left. 6'4", 230 lbs. Born, Thompson, Man., February 7, 1976.

1994-95	Halifax	QMJHL	72	10	12	22	194	....	....	....	....	....	....	....	....	....	7	0	1	1	12	....	....	....	....
1995-96	Halifax	QMJHL	50	13	19	32	319	....	....	....	....	....	....	....	....	....	6	0	2	2	36	....	....	....	....
1996-97	Halifax	QMJHL	58	25	19	44	*448	....	....	....	....	....	....	....	....	....	17	6	6	12	*123	....	....	....	....
1997-98	Dalhousie	AUAA	19	6	11	17	145	....	....	....	....	....	....	....	....	....	....	....	....	....	....	....	....	....	....
	Saint John Flames	AHL	18	1	1	2	50	....	....	....	....	....	....	....	....	....	....	....	....	....	....	....	....	....	....
1998-99	Saint John Flames	AHL	8	0	0	0	46	....	....	....	....	....	....	....	....	....	....	....	....	....	....	....	....	....	....
	Johnstown Chiefs	ECHL	52	12	17	29	325	....	....	....	....	....	....	....	....	....	....	....	....	....	....	....	....	....	....
99-2000	Johnstown Chiefs	ECHL	36	9	17	26	256	....	....	....	....	....	....	....	....	....	....	....	....	....	....	....	....	....	....
	Saint John Flames	AHL	22	1	4	5	93	....	....	....	....	....	....	....	....	....	3	0	0	0	2	....	....	....	....
2000-01	Syracuse Crunch	AHL	69	1	7	8	*357	....	....	....	....	....	....	....	....	....	5	0	0	0	21	....	....	....	....
	Columbus	**NHL**	**1**	**0**	**0**	**0**	**10**	**0**	**0**	**0**	**0**	**0.0**	**0**	**0**	**0.0**	**1:33**	....	....	....	....	....	....	....	....	....
2001-02	**Columbus**	**NHL**	**52**	**3**	**3**	**6**	**206**	**0**	**0**	**0**	**35**	**8.6**	**1**	**0**	**0.0**	**6:32**	....	....	....	....	....	....	....	....	....
	Syracuse Crunch	AHL	22	3	5	8	165	....	....	....	....	....	....	....	....	....	....	....	....	....	....	....	....	....	....
2002-03	**Columbus**	**NHL**	**68**	**1**	**4**	**5**	***249**	**0**	**0**	**0**	**39**	**2.6**	**–5**	**1**	**0.0**	**6:08**	....	....	....	....	....	....	....	....	....
2003-04	**Columbus**	**NHL**	**76**	**3**	**3**	**6**	**228**	**1**	**0**	**0**	**62**	**4.8**	**–10**	**3**	**0.0**	**7:14**	....	....	....	....	....	....	....	....	....
2004-05	JYP Jyvaskyla	Finland	11	0	1	1	20	....	....	....	....	....	....	....	....	....	3	0	0	0	25	....	....	....	....
2005-06	**Columbus**	**NHL**	**80**	**3**	**7**	**10**	**163**	**0**	**0**	**1**	**39**	**7.7**	**–4**	**7**	**14.3**	**5:58**	....	....	....	....	....	....	....	....	....
	NHL Totals		**277**	**10**	**17**	**27**	**856**	**1**	**0**	**1**	**175**	**5.7**		**11**	**9.1**	**6:27**	....	....	....	....	....	....	....	....	....

Signed as a free agent by **Calgary**, September 1, 1998. Signed as a free agent by **Syracuse** (AHL), September 15, 2000. Signed as a free agent by **Columbus**, January 31, 2001. Signed as a free agent by **Jyvaskyla** (Finland), January 17, 2005.

SHISHKANOV, Timofei

(shihsh-KAHN-ahv, tee-moh-FAY) **ST.L.**

Left wing. Shoots right. 6'1", 209 lbs. Born, Moscow, USSR, June 10, 1983. Nashville's 2nd choice, 33rd overall, in 2001 Entry Draft.

99-2000	Spartak 2	Russia-3	14	6	5	11	10	....	....	....	....	....	....	....	....	....	....	....	....	....	....	....	....	....	....
	Spartak Moscow	Russia-2	14	1	0	1	2	....	....	....	....	....	....	....	....	....	....	....	....	....	....	....	....	....	....
2000-01	Spartak 2	Russia-3	STATISTICS NOT AVAILABLE																						
2001-02	HK CSKA Moscow	Russia-2	23	7	6	13	8	....	....	....	....	....	....	....	....	....	....	....	....	....	....	....	....	....	....
	Spartak Moscow	Russia	12	0	0	0	2	....	....	....	....	....	....	....	....	....	....	....	....	....	....	....	....	....	....
	HK CSKA 2	Russia-3	13	7	9	16	14	....	....	....	....	....	....	....	....	....	....	....	....	....	....	....	....	....	....
2002-03	Quebec Remparts	QMJHL	51	36	46	82	60	....	....	....	....	....	....	....	....	....	11	5	12	17	14	....	....	....	....
2003-04	**Nashville**	**NHL**	**2**	**0**	**0**	**0**	**0**	**0**	**0**	**0**	**0**	**0.0**	**–1**	**0**	**0.0**	**6:32**	....	....	....	....	....	....	....	....	....
	Milwaukee	AHL	63	23	20	43	46	....	....	....	....	....	....	....	....	....	22	2	6	8	17	....	....	....	....
2004-05	Milwaukee	AHL	70	20	15	35	31	....	....	....	....	....	....	....	....	....	6	1	0	1	2	....	....	....	....
2005-06	Milwaukee	AHL	46	14	15	29	34	....	....	....	....	....	....	....	....	....	....	....	....	....	....	....	....	....	....
	St. Louis	**NHL**	**22**	**3**	**2**	**5**	**6**	**0**	**0**	**0**	**26**	**11.5**	**–1**	**2**	**0.0**	**8:28**	....	....	....	....	....	....	....	....	....
	Peoria Rivermen	AHL	12	3	2	5	8	....	....	....	....	....	....	....	....	....	2	1	0	1	0	....	....	....	....
	NHL Totals		**24**	**3**	**2**	**5**	**6**	**0**	**0**	**0**	**26**	**11.5**		**2**	**0.0**	**8:18**	....	....	....	....	....	....	....	....	....

QMJHL First All-Star Team (2003) • AHL All-Rookie Team (2004)

Traded to **St. Louis** by **Nashville** for Mike Sillinger, January 30, 2006.

SHVIDKI, Denis

(SHVIHD-kee, DEH-nihs) **FLA.**

Right wing. Shoots left. 6', 195 lbs. Born, Kharkov, USSR, November 21, 1980. Florida's 1st choice, 12th overall, in 1999 Entry Draft.

1996-97	Yaroslavl 2	Russia-3	35	21	12	33	32	....	....	....	....	....	....	....	....	....	....	....	....	....	....	....	....	....	....
	Yaroslavl	Russia	17	3	2	5	6	....	....	....	....	....	....	....	....	....	....	....	....	....	....	....	....	....	....
1997-98	Yaroslavl 2	Russia-2	32	20	13	33	20	....	....	....	....	....	....	....	....	....	....	....	....	....	....	....	....	....	....
	Yaroslavl	Russia	15	1	1	2	2	....	....	....	....	....	....	....	....	....	....	....	....	....	....	....	....	....	....
1998-99	Barrie Colts	OHL	61	35	59	94	8	....	....	....	....	....	....	....	....	....	12	7	9	16	2	....	....	....	....
99-2000	Barrie Colts	OHL	61	41	65	106	55	....	....	....	....	....	....	....	....	....	9	3	1	4	2	....	....	....	....
2000-01	**Florida**	**NHL**	**43**	**6**	**10**	**16**	**16**	**0**	**0**	**1**	**28**	**21.4**	**6**	**4**	**50.0**	**10:21**	....	....	....	....	....	....	....	....	....
	Louisville Panthers	AHL	34	15	11	26	20	....	....	....	....	....	....	....	....	....	....	....	....	....	....	....	....	....	....
2001-02	**Florida**	**NHL**	**8**	**1**	**2**	**3**	**2**	**0**	**0**	**0**	**11**	**9.1**	**–4**	**1**	**0.0**	**11:57**	....	....	....	....	....	....	....	....	....
	Utah Grizzlies	AHL	8	2	4	6	2	....	....	....	....	....	....	....	....	....	....	....	....	....	....	....	....	....	....
2002-03	**Florida**	**NHL**	**23**	**4**	**2**	**6**	**12**	**2**	**0**	**1**	**29**	**13.8**	**–7**	**5**	**60.0**	**14:14**	....	....	....	....	....	....	....	....	....
	San Antonio	AHL	54	8	18	26	28	....	....	....	....	....	....	....	....	....	....	....	....	....	....	....	....	....	....
2003-04	**Florida**	**NHL**	**2**	**0**	**0**	**0**	**0**	**0**	**0**	**0**	**4**	**0.0**	**0**	**0**	**0.0**	**14:05**	....	....	....	....	....	....	....	....	....
	San Antonio	AHL	77	15	39	54	30	....	....	....	....	....	....	....	....	....	....	....	....	....	....	....	....	....	....
2004-05			DID NOT PLAY																						
2005-06	Sibir Novosibirsk	Russia	25	1	5	6	6	....	....	....	....	....	....	....	....	....	2	0	1	1	0	....	....	....	....
	NHL Totals		**76**	**11**	**14**	**25**	**30**	**2**	**0**	**2**	**72**	**15.3**		**10**	**50.0**	**11:47**	....	....	....	....	....	....	....	....	....

OHL All-Rookie Team (1999) • OHL Second All-Star Team (1999)

• Missed majority of 2001-02 season recovering from head injury suffered in game vs. Philadelphia, October 4, 2001. Signed as a free agent by **Novosibirsk** (Russia). November 22, 2005.

SIKLENKA, Mike

(sih-KLEHN-kuh, MIGHK)

Right wing. Shoots right. 6'5", 224 lbs. Born, Meadow Lake, Sask., December 18, 1979. Washington's 5th choice, 118th overall, in 1998 Entry Draft.

1997-98	Lloydminster	AJHL	54	10	17	27	120	....	....	....	....	....	....	....	....	....	....	....	....	....	....	....	....	....	....
1998-99	Seattle	WHL	68	19	13	32	115	....	....	....	....	....	....	....	....	....	11	6	6	12	24	....	....	....	....
99-2000	Portland Pirates	AHL	9	0	0	0	14	....	....	....	....	....	....	....	....	....	....	....	....	....	....	....	....	....	....
	Hampton Roads	ECHL	58	7	4	11	62	....	....	....	....	....	....	....	....	....	8	1	0	1	15	....	....	....	....
2000-01	Richmond	ECHL	65	19	18	37	117	....	....	....	....	....	....	....	....	....	4	0	0	0	34	....	....	....	....
	Portland Pirates	AHL	3	0	0	0	0	....	....	....	....	....	....	....	....	....	....	....	....	....	....	....	....	....	....
2001-02	Richmond	ECHL	55	13	21	34	111	....	....	....	....	....	....	....	....	....	....	....	....	....	....	....	....	....	....
	Portland Pirates	AHL	8	1	0	1	2	....	....	....	....	....	....	....	....	....	....	....	....	....	....	....	....	....	....
2002-03	**Philadelphia**	**NHL**	**1**	**0**	**0**	**0**	**0**	**0**	**0**	**0**	**1**	**0.0**	**0**	**0**	**0.0**	**4:26**	....	....	....	....	....	....	....	....	....
	Philadelphia	AHL	64	6	6	12	169	....	....	....	....	....	....	....	....	....	....	....	....	....	....	....	....	....	....
2003-04	**NY Rangers**	**NHL**	**1**	**0**	**0**	**0**	**0**	**0**	**0**	**0**	**0**	**0.0**	**0**	**0**	**0.0**	**2:22**	....	....	....	....	....	....	....	....	....
	Trenton Titans	ECHL	1	1	0	1	0	....	....	....	....	....	....	....	....	....	....	....	....	....	....	....	....	....	....
	Philadelphia	AHL	18	1	5	6	29	....	....	....	....	....	....	....	....	....	....	....	....	....	....	....	....	....	....
	Utah Grizzlies	AHL	26	3	6	9	74	....	....	....	....	....	....	....	....	....	....	....	....	....	....	....	....	....	....
2004-05	Klagenfurter AC	Austria	39	16	18	34	156	....	....	....	....	....	....	....	....	....	12	6	1	7	44	....	....	....	....
2005-06	Klagenfurter AC	Austria	42	13	32	45	204	....	....	....	....	....	....	....	....	....	....	....	....	....	....	....	....	....	....
	NHL Totals		**2**	**0**	**0**	**0**	**0**	**0**	**0**	**0**	**1**	**0.0**		**0**	**0.0**	**3:24**	....	....	....	....	....	....	....	....	....

Signed as a free agent by **Philadelphia**, January 27, 2002. Claimed by **NY Rangers** from **Philadelphia** in Waiver Draft, October 3, 2003. Claimed on waivers by **Philadelphia** from **NY Rangers**, November 5, 2003. Traded to **Dallas** by **Philadelphia** for Steve Gainey, February 16, 2004. Signed as a free agent by **Klagenfurter** (Austria), October 8, 2004.

SILLINGER, Mike

(sih-LIHN-juhr, MIGHK) **NYI**

Center. Shoots right. 5'11", 196 lbs. Born, Regina, Sask., June 29, 1971. Detroit's 1st choice, 11th overall, in 1989 Entry Draft.

1986-87	Regina Kings	SMHL	31	83	51	134	....	....	....	....	....	....	....	....	....	....	....	....	....	....	....	....	....	....	....
1987-88	Regina Pats	WHL	67	18	25	43	17	....	....	....	....	....	....	....	....	....	4	2	2	4	0	....	....	....	....
1988-89	Regina Pats	WHL	72	53	78	131	52	....	....	....	....	....	....	....	....	....	....	....	....	....	....	....	....	....	....
1989-90	Regina Pats	WHL	70	57	72	129	41	....	....	....	....	....	....	....	....	....	11	12	10	22	2	....	....	....	....
	Adirondack	AHL	....	....	....	....	....	....	....	....	....	....	....	....	....	....	1	0	0	0	0	....	....	....	....
1990-91	Regina Pats	WHL	57	50	66	116	42	....	....	....	....	....	....	....	....	....	8	6	9	15	4	....	....	....	....
	Detroit	**NHL**	**3**	**0**	**1**	**1**	**0**	**0**	**0**	**0**	**6**	**0.0**	**–2**	....	....	....	**3**	**0**	**1**	**1**	**0**	**0**	**0**	**0**	....

			Regular Season														Playoffs								
Season	Club	League	GP	G	A	Pts	PIM	PP	SH	GW	S	%	+/-	TF	F%	Min	GP	G	A	Pts	PIM	PP	SH	GW	Min
1991-92	Adirondack	AHL	64	25	41	66	26	....	....	....	....	....	....	....	....	....	15	9	*19	*28	12	....	....	....	....
	Detroit	**NHL**	....	....	....	....	....	....	....	....	....	....	....	....	....	....	8	2	2	4	2	0	0	0	....
1992-93	**Detroit**	**NHL**	51	4	17	21	16	0	0	0	47	8.5	0	....	....	....	....	....	....	....	....	....	....	....	....
	Adirondack	AHL	15	10	20	30	31	....	....	....	....	....	....	....	....	....	11	5	13	18	10	....	....	....	....
1993-94	**Detroit**	**NHL**	62	8	21	29	10	0	1	1	91	8.8	2	....	....	....	....	....	....	....	....	....	....	....	....
1994-95	CE Wien	Austria	13	13	14	27	10	....	....	....	....	....	....	....	....	....	....	....	....	....	....	....	....	....	....
	Detroit	**NHL**	13	2	6	8	2	0	0	0	11	18.2	3	....	....	....	....	....	....	....	....	....	....	....	....
	Anaheim	**NHL**	15	2	5	7	6	2	0	0	28	7.1	1	....	....	....	....	....	....	....	....	....	....	....	....
1995-96	**Anaheim**	**NHL**	62	13	21	34	32	7	0	2	143	9.1	–20	....	....	....	....	....	....	....	....	....	....	....	....
	Vancouver	**NHL**	12	1	3	4	6	0	1	0	16	6.3	2	....	....	....	6	0	0	0	2	0	0	0	....
1996-97	**Vancouver**	**NHL**	78	17	20	37	25	3	3	2	112	15.2	–3	....	....	....	....	....	....	....	....	....	....	....	....
1997-98	**Vancouver**	**NHL**	48	10	9	19	34	1	2	1	56	17.9	–14	....	....	....	....	....	....	....	....	....	....	....	....
	Philadelphia	**NHL**	27	11	11	22	16	1	2	0	40	27.5	3	....	....	....	3	1	0	1	0	0	0	0	....
1998-99	**Philadelphia**	**NHL**	25	0	3	3	8	0	0	0	23	0.0	–9	229	62.9	10:42	....	....	....	....	....	....	....	....	....
	Tampa Bay	**NHL**	54	8	2	10	28	0	2	0	69	11.6	–20	320	57.8	13:57	....	....	....	....	....	....	....	....	....
99-2000	**Tampa Bay**	**NHL**	67	19	25	44	86	6	3	1	126	15.1	–29	493	56.0	19:42	....	....	....	....	....	....	....	....	....
	Florida	**NHL**	13	4	4	8	16	2	0	1	20	20.0	–1	248	61.3	19:33	4	2	1	3	2	0	0	0	20:24
2000-01	**Florida**	**NHL**	55	13	21	34	44	1	0	2	100	13.0	–12	1028	59.7	18:52	....	....	....	....	....	....	....	....	....
	Ottawa	**NHL**	13	3	4	7	4	0	0	0	19	15.8	1	215	63.3	14:31	4	0	0	0	2	0	0	0	13:40
2001-02	**Columbus**	**NHL**	80	20	23	43	54	8	0	5	150	13.3	–35	2024	57.0	20:51	....	....	....	....	....	....	....	....	....
2002-03	**Columbus**	**NHL**	75	18	25	43	52	9	3	3	128	14.1	–21	1490	56.5	19:08	....	....	....	....	....	....	....	....	....
2003-04	**Phoenix**	**NHL**	60	8	6	14	54	0	1	0	66	12.1	–14	771	56.3	15:22	....	....	....	....	....	....	....	....	....
	St. Louis	**NHL**	16	5	5	10	14	0	1	0	40	12.5	4	351	57.8	20:08	5	3	1	4	6	0	1	0	22:17
2004-05			DID NOT PLAY																						
2005-06	**St. Louis**	**NHL**	48	22	19	41	49	11	1	1	131	16.8	–17	797	55.3	19:41	....	....	....	....	....	....	....	....	....
	Nashville	**NHL**	31	10	12	22	14	3	0	1	80	12.5	0	542	56.6	18:34	5	2	1	3	12	1	0	0	17:09
	NHL Totals		**908**	**198**	**263**	**461**	**570**	**54**	**20**	**20**	**1502**	**13.2**		**8508**	**57.5**	**18:03**	**38**	**10**	**6**	**16**	**26**	**1**	**1**	**0**	**18:32**

WHL East Second All-Star Team (1990) • WHL East First All-Star Team (1991)

Traded to **Anaheim** by **Detroit** with Jason York for Stu Grimson, Mark Ferner and Anaheim's 6th round choice (Magnus Nilsson) in 1996 Entry Draft, April 4, 1995. Traded to **Vancouver** by **Anaheim** for Roman Oksiuta, March 15, 1996. Traded to **Philadelphia** by **Vancouver** for Philadelphia's 5th round choice (later traded back to Philadelphia – Philadelphia selected Garrett Prosofsky) in 1998 Entry Draft, February 5, 1998. Traded to **Tampa Bay** by **Philadelphia** with Chris Gratton for Mikael Renberg and Daymond Langkow, December 12, 1998. Traded to **Florida** by **Tampa Bay** for Ryan Johnson and Dwayne Hay, March 14, 2000. Traded to **Ottawa** by **Florida** for future considerations, March 13, 2001. Signed as a free agent by **Columbus**, July 7, 2001. Traded to **Dallas** by **Columbus** with Columbus' 2nd round choice (Johan Fransson) in 2004 Entry Draft for Darryl Sydor, July 22, 2003. Traded to **Phoenix** by **Dallas** with future considerations for Teppo Numminen, July 22, 2003. Traded to **St. Louis** by **Phoenix** for Brent Johnson, March 4, 2004. Traded to **Nashville** by **St. Louis** for Timofei Shishkanov, January 30, 2006. Signed as a free agent by **NY Islanders**, July 2, 2006.

SIM, Jon

(SIHM, JAWN) **ATL.**

Left wing. Shoots left. 5'10", 190 lbs. Born, New Glasgow, N.S., September 29, 1977. Dallas' 2nd choice, 70th overall, in 1996 Entry Draft.

Season	Club	League	GP	G	A	Pts	PIM	PP	SH	GW	S	%	+/-	TF	F%	Min	GP	G	A	Pts	PIM	PP	SH	GW	Min
1994-95	Laval Titan	QMJHL	9	0	1	1	6	....	....	....	....	....	....	....	....	....	....	....	....	....	....	....	....	....	....
	Sarnia Sting	OHL	25	9	12	21	19	....	....	....	....	....	....	....	....	....	4	3	2	5	2	....	....	....	....
1995-96	Sarnia Sting	OHL	63	56	46	102	130	....	....	....	....	....	....	....	....	....	10	8	7	15	26	....	....	....	....
1996-97	Sarnia Sting	OHL	64	*56	39	95	109	....	....	....	....	....	....	....	....	....	12	9	5	14	32	....	....	....	....
1997-98	Sarnia Sting	OHL	59	44	50	94	95	....	....	....	....	....	....	....	....	....	5	1	4	5	14	....	....	....	....
1998-99 ♦	**Dallas**	**NHL**	7	1	0	1	12	0	0	0	8	12.5	1	6	50.0	11:26	4	0	0	0	0	0	0	0	6:27
	Michigan	IHL	68	24	27	51	91	....	....	....	....	....	....	....	....	....	5	3	1	4	18	....	....	....	....
99-2000	**Dallas**	**NHL**	25	5	3	8	10	2	0	1	44	11.4	4	4	75.0	10:51	7	1	0	1	6	0	0	0	11:11
	Michigan	IHL	35	14	16	30	65	....	....	....	....	....	....	....	....	....	....	....	....	....	....	....	....	....	....
2000-01	**Dallas**	**NHL**	15	0	3	3	6	0	0	0	18	0.0	–2	1	100.0	8:47	....	....	....	....	....	....	....	....	....
	Utah Grizzlies	IHL	39	16	13	29	44	....	....	....	....	....	....	....	....	....	....	....	....	....	....	....	....	....	....
2001-02	**Dallas**	**NHL**	26	3	0	3	10	1	0	0	43	7.0	–3	3	0.0	9:30	....	....	....	....	....	....	....	....	....
	Utah Grizzlies	AHL	31	21	6	27	63	....	....	....	....	....	....	....	....	....	....	....	....	....	....	....	....	....	....
2002-03	**Dallas**	**NHL**	4	0	0	0	0	0	0	0	7	0.0	–1	2	50.0	9:10	....	....	....	....	....	....	....	....	....
	Utah Grizzlies	AHL	42	16	31	47	85	....	....	....	....	....	....	....	....	....	....	....	....	....	....	....	....	....	....
	Nashville	**NHL**	4	1	0	1	0	0	0	0	3	33.3	0	14	35.7	9:18	....	....	....	....	....	....	....	....	....
	Los Angeles	**NHL**	14	0	2	2	19	0	0	0	29	0.0	–3	3	33.3	12:05	....	....	....	....	....	....	....	....	....
2003-04	**Los Angeles**	**NHL**	48	6	7	13	27	0	0	1	73	8.2	0	19	31.6	10:01	....	....	....	....	....	....	....	....	....
	Pittsburgh	**NHL**	15	2	3	5	6	0	0	1	27	7.4	–4	0	0.0	13:39	....	....	....	....	....	....	....	....	....
2004-05	Utah Grizzlies	AHL	10	2	2	4	12	....	....	....	....	....	....	....	....	....	....	....	....	....	....	....	....	....	....
	Philadelphia	AHL	63	35	26	61	66	....	....	....	....	....	....	....	....	....	21	*10	7	17	44	....	....	....	....
2005-06	**Philadelphia**	**NHL**	39	7	7	14	28	4	0	2	80	8.8	–6	1	0.0	10:59	....	....	....	....	....	....	....	....	....
	Florida	**NHL**	33	10	8	18	26	4	0	3	92	10.9	–1	0	0.0	12:28	....	....	....	....	....	....	....	....	....
	NHL Totals		**230**	**35**	**33**	**68**	**144**	**11**	**0**	**8**	**424**	**8.3**		**53**	**37.7**	**10:52**	**11**	**1**	**0**	**1**	**6**	**0**	**0**	**0**	**9:27**

OHL Second All-Star Team (1998)

Traded to **Nashville** by **Dallas** for Bubba Berenzweig and future considerations, February 17, 2003. Claimed on waivers by **Los Angeles** from **Nashville**, March 8, 2003. Claimed on waivers by **Pittsburgh** from **Los Angeles**, March 4, 2004. Signed as a free agent by **Phoenix**, September 2, 2004. Loaned to **Philadelphia** (AHL) by **Utah** (AHL) for the loan of Peter White, November 14, 2004. Signed as a free agent by **Philadelphia**, August 2, 2005. Traded to **Florida** by **Philadelphia** for a 6th round choice in 2007 Entry Draft, January 23, 2006. Signed as a free agent by **Atlanta**, July 14, 2006.

SIMON, Ben

(SIGH-mohn, BEHN)

Left wing. Shoots left. 6', 195 lbs. Born, Shaker Heights, OH, June 14, 1978. Chicago's 5th choice, 110th overall, in 1997 Entry Draft.

Season	Club	League	GP	G	A	Pts	PIM	PP	SH	GW	S	%	+/-	TF	F%	Min	GP	G	A	Pts	PIM	PP	SH	GW	Min
1992-93	Shaker Heights	High-OH	25	15	21	36	....	....	....	....	....	....	....	....	....	....	....	....	....	....	....	....	....	....	....
1993-94	Shaker Heights	High-OH	24	45	41	86	....	....	....	....	....	....	....	....	....	....	....	....	....	....	....	....	....	....	....
1994-95	Shaker Heights	High-OH	25	61	68	129	....	....	....	....	....	....	....	....	....	....	....	....	....	....	....	....	....	....	....
1995-96	Cleveland Barons	NAHL	45	38	33	71	....	....	....	....	....	....	....	....	....	....	5	7	13	20	....	....	....	....	....
1996-97	U. of Notre Dame	CCHA	30	4	15	19	79	....	....	....	....	....	....	....	....	....	....	....	....	....	....	....	....	....	....
1997-98	U. of Notre Dame	CCHA	37	9	28	37	91	....	....	....	....	....	....	....	....	....	....	....	....	....	....	....	....	....	....
1998-99	U. of Notre Dame	CCHA	37	18	24	42	65	....	....	....	....	....	....	....	....	....	....	....	....	....	....	....	....	....	....
99-2000	U. of Notre Dame	CCHA	40	13	19	32	53	....	....	....	....	....	....	....	....	....	....	....	....	....	....	....	....	....	....
2000-01	Orlando	IHL	77	8	12	20	47	....	....	....	....	....	....	....	....	....	16	6	5	11	20	....	....	....	....
2001-02	**Atlanta**	**NHL**	6	0	0	0	6	0	0	0	7	0.0	1	32	40.6	9:20	....	....	....	....	....	....	....	....	....
	Chicago Wolves	AHL	74	11	23	34	56	....	....	....	....	....	....	....	....	....	25	2	3	5	24	....	....	....	....
2002-03	**Atlanta**	**NHL**	10	0	1	1	9	0	0	0	7	0.0	0	54	31.5	9:25	....	....	....	....	....	....	....	....	....
	Chicago Wolves	AHL	69	15	17	32	78	....	....	....	....	....	....	....	....	....	9	0	0	0	6	....	....	....	....
2003-04	Milwaukee	AHL	18	1	3	4	6	....	....	....	....	....	....	....	....	....	....	....	....	....	....	....	....	....	....
	Atlanta	**NHL**	52	3	0	3	28	0	0	0	30	10.0	–10	203	33.0	6:05	....	....	....	....	....	....	....	....	....
2004-05	Chicago Wolves	AHL	53	11	10	21	58	....	....	....	....	....	....	....	....	....	18	1	5	6	44	....	....	....	....
2005-06	**Columbus**	**NHL**	13	0	0	0	4	0	0	0	7	0.0	–4	53	24.5	5:38	....	....	....	....	....	....	....	....	....
	Syracuse Crunch	AHL	66	13	24	37	88	....	....	....	....	....	....	....	....	....	3	0	1	1	2	....	....	....	....
	NHL Totals		**81**	**3**	**1**	**4**	**47**	**0**	**0**	**0**	**51**	**5.9**		**342**	**32.2**	**6:40**	....	....	....	....	....	....	....	....	....

CCHA Second All-Star Team (1999)

Rights traded to **Atlanta** by **Chicago** for Atlanta's 9th round choice (Peter Flache) in 2000 Entry Draft, June 25, 2000. Signed as a free agent by **Nashville**, July 14, 2003. Traded to **Atlanta** by **Nashville** with Tomas Kloucek for Simon Gamache and Kirill Safronov, December 2, 2003. Signed as a free agent by **Columbus**, August 11, 2005.

SIMON, Chris

(SIGH-mohn, KRIHS)

Left wing. Shoots left. 6'4", 235 lbs. Born, Wawa, Ont., January 30, 1972. Philadelphia's 2nd choice, 25th overall, in 1990 Entry Draft.

Season	Club	League	GP	G	A	Pts	PIM	PP	SH	GW	S	%	+/-	TF	F%	Min	GP	G	A	Pts	PIM	PP	SH	GW	Min
1986-87	Wawa Flyers	NOHA	36	12	20	32	108	....	....	....	....	....	....	....	....	....	....	....	....	....	....	....	....	....	....
1987-88	Soo Thunderbirds	NOHA	55	42	36	78	172	....	....	....	....	....	....	....	....	....	....	....	....	....	....	....	....	....	....
1988-89	Ottawa 67's	OHL	36	4	2	6	31	....	....	....	....	....	....	....	....	....	....	....	....	....	....	....	....	....	....
1989-90	Ottawa 67's	OHL	57	36	38	74	146	....	....	....	....	....	....	....	....	....	3	2	1	3	4	....	....	....	....
1990-91	Ottawa 67's	OHL	20	16	6	22	69	....	....	....	....	....	....	....	....	....	17	5	9	14	59	....	....	....	....
1991-92	Ottawa 67's	OHL	2	1	1	2	24	....	....	....	....	....	....	....	....	....	....	....	....	....	....	....	....	....	....
	Sault Ste. Marie	OHL	31	19	25	44	143	....	....	....	....	....	....	....	....	....	11	5	8	13	49	....	....	....	....
1992-93	**Quebec**	**NHL**	16	1	1	2	67	0	0	1	15	6.7	–2	....	....	....	5	0	0	0	26	0	0	0	....
	Halifax Citadels	AHL	36	12	6	18	131	....	....	....	....	....	....	....	....	....	....	....	....	....	....	....	....	....	....
1993-94	**Quebec**	**NHL**	37	4	4	8	132	0	0	1	39	10.3	–2	....	....	....	....	....	....	....	....	....	....	....	....
1994-95	**Quebec**	**NHL**	29	3	9	12	106	0	0	0	33	9.1	14	....	....	....	6	1	1	2	19	0	0	1	....
1995-96 ♦	**Colorado**	**NHL**	64	16	18	34	250	4	0	1	105	15.2	10	....	....	....	12	1	2	3	11	0	0	0	....
1996-97	**Washington**	**NHL**	42	9	13	22	165	3	0	1	89	10.1	–1	....	....	....	....	....	....	....	....	....	....	....	....
1997-98	**Washington**	**NHL**	28	7	10	17	38	4	0	1	71	9.9	–1	....	....	....	18	1	0	1	26	0	0	0	....
1998-99	**Washington**	**NHL**	23	3	7	10	48	0	0	0	29	10.3	–4	2	50.0	12:08	....	....	....	....	....	....	....	....	....

Season	Club	League	GP	G	A	Pts	PIM	PP	SH	GW	S	%	+/-	TF	F%	Min	GP	G	A	Pts	PIM	PP	SH	GW	Min
			Regular Season														Playoffs								
99-2000	**Washington**	**NHL**	**75**	**29**	**20**	**49**	**146**	**7**	**0**	**5**	**201**	**14.4**	**11**	**7**	**28.6**	**15:32**	**4**	**2**	**0**	**2**	**24**	**0**	**0**	**0**	**18:07**
2000-01	**Washington**	**NHL**	**60**	**10**	**10**	**20**	**109**	**4**	**0**	**2**	**123**	**8.1**	**–12**	**3**	**33.3**	**14:34**	**6**	**0**	**1**	**1**	**4**	**0**	**0**	**0**	**9:55**
2001-02	**Washington**	**NHL**	**82**	**14**	**17**	**31**	**137**	**1**	**0**	**1**	**121**	**11.6**	**–8**	**7**	**28.6**	**12:11**	....	....	....	....	....	....	....	....	....
2002-03	**Washington**	**NHL**	**10**	**0**	**2**	**2**	**23**	**0**	**0**	**0**	**16**	**0.0**	**–3**	**0**	**0.0**	**8:53**	....	....	....	....	....	....	....	....	....
	Chicago	**NHL**	**61**	**12**	**6**	**18**	**125**	**2**	**0**	**2**	**72**	**16.7**	**–4**	**5**	**20.0**	**11:06**	....	....	....	....	....	....	....	....	....
2003-04	**NY Rangers**	**NHL**	**65**	**14**	**9**	**23**	**225**	**3**	**0**	**0**	**116**	**12.1**	**14**	**3**	**0.0**	**11:56**	....	....	....	....	....	....	....	....	....
	Calgary	**NHL**	**13**	**3**	**2**	**5**	**25**	**1**	**0**	**0**	**31**	**9.7**	**1**	**2**	**100.0**	**16:38**	**16**	**5**	**2**	**7**	***74**	**4**	**0**	**1**	**15:06**
2004-05		DID NOT PLAY																							
2005-06	**Calgary**	**NHL**	**72**	**8**	**14**	**22**	**94**	**2**	**0**	**3**	**76**	**10.5**	**0**	**17**	**47.1**	**10:26**	**6**	**0**	**1**	**1**	**7**	**0**	**0**	**0**	**10:12**
	NHL Totals		**677**	**133**	**142**	**275**	**1690**	**31**	**0**	**18**	**1137**	**11.7**		**46**	**37.0**	**12:38**	**73**	**10**	**7**	**17**	**191**	**4**	**0**	**2**	**13:35**

• Missed majority of 1990-91 season recovering from shoulder surgery, October, 1990. Traded to **Quebec** by **Philadelphia** with Philadelphia's 1st round choice (later traded to Toronto – later traded to Washington – Washington selected Nolan Baumgartner) in 1994 Entry Draft to complete transaction that sent Eric Lindros to Philadelphia (June 30, 1992), July 21, 1992. Transferred to **Colorado** after **Quebec** franchise relocated, June 21, 1995. Traded to **Washington** by **Colorado** with Curtis Leschyshyn for Keith Jones and Washington's 1st (Scott Parker) and 4th (later traded back to Washington – Washington selected Krys Barch) round choices in 1998 Entry Draft, November 2, 1996. Traded to **Chicago** by **Washington** with Andrei Nikolishin for Michael Nylander, Chicago's 3rd round choice (Stephen Werner) in 2003 Entry Draft and future considerations, November 1, 2002. Signed as a free agent by **NY Rangers**, July 25, 2003. Traded to **Calgary** by **NY Rangers** with NY Rangers' 7th round choice (Matt Schneider) in 2004 Entry Draft for Jamie McLennan, Blair Betts and Greg Moore, March 6, 2004. Signed as a free agent by **NY Islanders**, July 11, 2006.

SIMPSON, Todd

(SIHMP-suhn, TAWD)

Defense. Shoots left. 6'3", 218 lbs. Born, North Vancouver, B.C., May 28, 1973.

1991-92	Brown U.	ECAC	18	1	4	5	38	....	....	....	....	....	....	....	....	....	....	....	....	....	....	....	....	....	....
1992-93	Tri-City	WHL	69	5	18	23	196	....	....	....	....	....	....	....	....	....	4	0	0	0	13	....	....	....	....
1993-94	Tri-City	WHL	12	2	3	5	32	....	....	....	....	....	....	....	....	....	....	....	....	....	....	....	....	....	....
	Saskatoon Blades	WHL	51	7	19	26	175	....	....	....	....	....	....	....	....	....	16	1	5	6	42	....	....	....	....
1994-95	Saint John Flames	AHL	80	3	10	13	321	....	....	....	....	....	....	....	....	....	5	0	0	0	4	....	....	....	....
1995-96	**Calgary**	**NHL**	**6**	**0**	**0**	**0**	**32**	**0**	**0**	**0**	**3**	**0.0**	**0**	....	....	....	....	....	....	....	....	....	....	....	....
	Saint John Flames	AHL	66	4	13	17	277	....	....	....	....	....	....	....	....	....	16	2	3	5	32	....	....	....	....
1996-97	**Calgary**	**NHL**	**82**	**1**	**13**	**14**	**208**	**0**	**0**	**0**	**85**	**1.2**	**–14**	....	....	....	....	....	....	....	....	....	....	....	....
1997-98	**Calgary**	**NHL**	**53**	**1**	**5**	**6**	**109**	**0**	**0**	**1**	**51**	**2.0**	**–10**	....	....	....	....	....	....	....	....	....	....	....	....
1998-99	**Calgary**	**NHL**	**73**	**2**	**8**	**10**	**151**	**0**	**0**	**0**	**52**	**3.8**	**18**	**1**	**100.0**	**17:19**	....	....	....	....	....	....	....	....	....
99-2000	**Florida**	**NHL**	**82**	**1**	**6**	**7**	**202**	**0**	**0**	**0**	**50**	**2.0**	**5**	**0**	**0.0**	**16:35**	**4**	**0**	**0**	**0**	**4**	**0**	**0**	**0**	**15:24**
2000-01	**Florida**	**NHL**	**25**	**1**	**3**	**4**	**74**	**0**	**0**	**1**	**26**	**3.8**	**0**	**0**	**0.0**	**16:29**	....	....	....	....	....	....	....	....	....
	Phoenix	**NHL**	**13**	**0**	**1**	**1**	**12**	**0**	**0**	**0**	**9**	**0.0**	**–4**	**0**	**0.0**	**13:56**	....	....	....	....	....	....	....	....	....
2001-02	**Phoenix**	**NHL**	**67**	**2**	**13**	**15**	**152**	**0**	**0**	**0**	**51**	**3.9**	**20**	**0**	**0.0**	**17:20**	**5**	**0**	**2**	**2**	**6**	**0**	**0**	**0**	**18:30**
2002-03	**Phoenix**	**NHL**	**66**	**2**	**7**	**9**	**135**	**0**	**0**	**0**	**67**	**3.0**	**7**	**0**	**0.0**	**16:59**	....	....	....	....	....	....	....	....	....
2003-04	**Anaheim**	**NHL**	**46**	**4**	**3**	**7**	**105**	**0**	**0**	**0**	**42**	**9.5**	**–6**	**0**	**0.0**	**14:18**	....	....	....	....	....	....	....	....	....
	Ottawa	**NHL**	**16**	**0**	**1**	**1**	**47**	**0**	**0**	**0**	**10**	**0.0**	**–1**	**1**	**0.0**	**14:21**	....	....	....	....	....	....	....	....	....
2004-05	Herning Blue Fox	Denmark	7	2	3	5	35	....	....	....	....	....	....	....	....	....	16	3	5	8	82	....	....	....	....
2005-06	**Chicago**	**NHL**	**45**	**0**	**3**	**3**	**116**	**0**	**0**	**0**	**25**	**0.0**	**–2**	**2**	**0.0**	**13:05**	....	....	....	....	....	....	....	....	....
	Montreal	**NHL**	**6**	**0**	**0**	**0**	**14**	**0**	**0**	**0**	**6**	**0.0**	**0**	**0**	**0.0**	**15:59**	....	....	....	....	....	....	....	....	....
	NHL Totals		**580**	**14**	**63**	**77**	**1357**	**0**	**0**	**2**	**477**	**2.9**		**4**	**25.0**	**16:06**	**9**	**0**	**2**	**2**	**10**	**0**	**0**	**0**	**17:07**

Signed as free agent by **Calgary**, July 6, 1994. Traded to **Florida** by **Calgary** for Bill Lindsay, September 30, 1999. • Missed majority of 2000-01 season recovering from head injury suffered in game vs. NY Islanders, December 6, 2000. Traded to **Phoenix** by **Florida** for Phoenix's 2nd round choice (later traded to New Jersey – New Jersey selected Tuomas Pihlman) in 2001 Entry Draft, March 13, 2001. Claimed by **Anaheim** from **Phoenix** in Waiver Draft, October 3, 2003. Traded to **Ottawa** by **Anaheim** for Petr Schastlivy, February 4, 2004. Signed as a free agent by **Herning** (Denmark), December 16, 2004. Signed as a free agent by **Chicago**, August 23, 2005. Traded to **Montreal** by **Chicago** for Montreal's 6th round choice (Chris Auger) in 2006 Entry Draft, March 9, 2006.

SIVEK, Michal

(sih-VIHK, MEE-khahl) **PIT.**

Center. Shoots left. 6'3", 214 lbs. Born, Nachod, Czech., January 21, 1981. Washington's 2nd choice, 29th overall, in 1999 Entry Draft.

1997-98	Sparta Jr.	CzRep-Jr.	31	13	8	21	....	....	....	....	....	....	....	....	....	....	....	....	....	....	....	....	....	....	....
	HC Sparta Praha	CzRep	25	1	1	2	10	....	....	....	....	....	....	....	....	....	5	1	0	1	0	....	....	....	....
1998-99	HC Sparta Praha	CzRep	1	1	0	1	....	....	....	....	....	....	....	....	....	....	....	....	....	....	....	....	....	....	....
	Kladno	CzRep	34	3	8	11	24	....	....	....	....	....	....	....	....	....	....	....	....	....	....	....	....	....	....
99-2000	Prince Albert	WHL	53	23	37	60	65	....	....	....	....	....	....	....	....	....	6	1	4	5	10	....	....	....	....
2000-01	HC Sparta Praha	CzRep	32	6	7	13	28	....	....	....	....	....	....	....	....	....	13	4	2	6	8	....	....	....	....
2001-02	Wilkes-Barre	AHL	25	4	8	12	30	....	....	....	....	....	....	....	....	....	....	....	....	....	....	....	....	....	....
	HC Sparta Praha	CzRep	17	5	3	8	20	....	....	....	....	....	....	....	....	....	12	0	1	1	10	....	....	....	....
2002-03	**Pittsburgh**	**NHL**	**38**	**3**	**3**	**6**	**14**	**1**	**0**	**0**	**45**	**6.7**	**–5**	**32**	**43.8**	**13:05**	....	....	....	....	....	....	....	....	....
	Wilkes-Barre	AHL	40	10	17	27	33	....	....	....	....	....	....	....	....	....	6	3	2	5	20	....	....	....	....
2003-04	Wilkes-Barre	AHL	22	4	7	11	6	....	....	....	....	....	....	....	....	....	....	....	....	....	....	....	....	....	....
2004-05	HC Sparta Praha	CzRep	37	1	5	6	48	....	....	....	....	....	....	....	....	....	5	0	0	0	2	....	....	....	....
2005-06	HC Sparta Praha	CzRep	36	10	9	19	30	....	....	....	....	....	....	....	....	....	17	4	1	5	18	....	....	....	....
	NHL Totals		**38**	**3**	**3**	**6**	**14**	**1**	**0**	**0**	**45**	**6.7**		**32**	**43.8**	**13:05**	....	....	....	....	....	....	....	....	....

Traded to **Pittsburgh** by **Washington** with Kris Beech, Ross Lupaschuk and future considerations for Jaromir Jagr and Frantisek Kucera, July 11, 2001. • Missed majority of 2003-04 season recovering from finger injury suffered in game vs. Syracuse (AHL), October 17, 2003. Signed as a free agent by **Sparta Praha** (CzRep), May 19, 2004.

SJOSTROM, Fredrik

(SHAW-strahm, FREHD-rihk) **PHX.**

Right wing. Shoots left. 6'1", 217 lbs. Born, Fargelanda, Sweden, May 6, 1983. Phoenix's 1st choice, 11th overall, in 2001 Entry Draft.

99-2000	MoDo U18	Swe-U18	4	0	2	2	6	....	....	....	....	....	....	....	....	....	....	....	....	....	....	....	....	....	....
	Malmo Jr.	Swe-Jr.	18	4	6	10	8	....	....	....	....	....	....	....	....	....	....	....	....	....	....	....	....	....	....
2000-01	V.Frolunda Jr.	Swe-Jr.	11	3	7	10	12	....	....	....	....	....	....	....	....	....	4	1	2	3	6	....	....	....	....
	V.Frolunda	Sweden	31	3	2	5	6	....	....	....	....	....	....	....	....	....	5	0	0	0	2	....	....	....	....
2001-02	Calgary Hitmen	WHL	58	19	31	50	51	....	....	....	....	....	....	....	....	....	4	1	1	2	8	....	....	....	....
2002-03	Calgary Hitmen	WHL	63	34	43	77	95	....	....	....	....	....	....	....	....	....	5	1	3	4	4	....	....	....	....
	Springfield	AHL	2	1	0	1	0	....	....	....	....	....	....	....	....	....	6	2	0	2	12	....	....	....	....
2003-04	**Phoenix**	**NHL**	**57**	**7**	**6**	**13**	**22**	**0**	**0**	**1**	**73**	**9.6**	**–7**	**7**	**28.6**	**11:35**	....	....	....	....	....	....	....	....	....
	Springfield	AHL	17	0	7	7	8	....	....	....	....	....	....	....	....	....	....	....	....	....	....	....	....	....	....
2004-05	Utah Grizzlies	AHL	80	14	24	38	57	....	....	....	....	....	....	....	....	....	....	....	....	....	....	....	....	....	....
2005-06	**Phoenix**	**NHL**	**75**	**6**	**17**	**23**	**42**	**1**	**0**	**1**	**109**	**5.5**	**1**	**8**	**12.5**	**13:20**	....	....	....	....	....	....	....	....	....
	NHL Totals		**132**	**13**	**23**	**36**	**64**	**1**	**0**	**2**	**182**	**7.1**		**15**	**20.0**	**12:35**	....	....	....	....	....	....	....	....	....

SKOLNEY, Wade

(SKOHL-nee, WAYD) **PIT.**

Defense. Shoots right. 6', 197 lbs. Born, Wynyard, Sask., June 24, 1981.

1996-97	Niacam Bantams	SBHL	54	33	70	103	193	....	....	....	....	....	....	....	....	....	....	....	....	....	....	....	....	....	....
	Brandon	WHL	1	0	0	0	0	....	....	....	....	....	....	....	....	....	....	....	....	....	....	....	....	....	....
1997-98	Brandon	WHL	42	1	11	12	49	....	....	....	....	....	....	....	....	....	3	0	0	0	0	....	....	....	....
1998-99	Brandon	WHL	39	3	10	13	60	....	....	....	....	....	....	....	....	....	5	0	1	1	16	....	....	....	....
99-2000	Brandon	WHL	13	0	2	2	23	....	....	....	....	....	....	....	....	....	....	....	....	....	....	....	....	....	....
2000-01	Brandon	WHL	28	2	9	11	37	....	....	....	....	....	....	....	....	....	....	....	....	....	....	....	....	....	....
2001-02	Brandon	WHL	50	4	12	16	179	....	....	....	....	....	....	....	....	....	19	2	7	9	56	....	....	....	....
2002-03	Philadelphia	AHL	68	2	7	9	102	....	....	....	....	....	....	....	....	....	....	....	....	....	....	....	....	....	....
2003-04	Philadelphia	AHL	56	1	8	9	106	....	....	....	....	....	....	....	....	....	12	0	0	0	23	....	....	....	....
2004-05	Philadelphia	AHL	35	0	8	8	104	....	....	....	....	....	....	....	....	....	21	0	1	1	43	....	....	....	....
2005-06	**Philadelphia**	**NHL**	**1**	**0**	**0**	**0**	**2**	**0**	**0**	**0**	**0**	**0.0**	**0**	**0**	**0.0**	**6:52**	....	....	....	....	....	....	....	....	....
	Philadelphia	AHL	56	0	5	5	197	....	....	....	....	....	....	....	....	....	....	....	....	....	....	....	....	....	....
	NHL Totals		**1**	**0**	**0**	**0**	**2**	**0**	**0**	**0**	**0**	**0.0**		**0**	**0.0**	**6:52**	....	....	....	....	....	....	....	....	....

Signed as a free agent by **Philadelphia**, May 20, 2002. • Missed majority of 2004-05 season recovering from head injury suffered in game on November 19, 2004. Signed as a free agent by **Pittsburgh**, July 21, 2006.

SKOULA, Martin

(SHKOO-la, MAHR-tihn) **MIN.**

Defense. Shoots left. 6'2", 195 lbs. Born, Litomerice, Czech., October 28, 1979. Colorado's 2nd choice, 17th overall, in 1998 Entry Draft.

1995-96	Litvinov Jr.	CzRep-Jr.	38	0	4	4	....	....	....	....	....	....	....	....	....	....	....	....	....	....	....	....	....	....	....
	Litvinov	CzRep	....	....	....	....	....	....	....	....	....	....	....	....	....	....	1	0	0	0	0	....	....	....	....
1996-97	Litvinov Jr.	CzRep-Jr.	38	2	9	11	....	....	....	....	....	....	....	....	....	....	....	....	....	....	....	....	....	....	....
	Litvinov	CzRep	1	0	0	0	0	....	....	....	....	....	....	....	....	....	....	....	....	....	....	....	....	....	....
1997-98	Barrie Colts	OHL	66	8	36	44	36	....	....	....	....	....	....	....	....	....	6	1	3	4	4	....	....	....	....

			Regular Season														Playoffs								
Season	**Club**	**League**	**GP**	**G**	**A**	**Pts**	**PIM**	**PP**	**SH**	**GW**	**S**	**%**	**+/-**	**TF**	**F%**	**Min**	**GP**	**G**	**A**	**Pts**	**PIM**	**PP**	**SH**	**GW**	**Min**
1998-99	Barrie Colts	OHL	67	13	46	59	46	....	....	....	....	....	....	....	....	....	12	3	10	13	13	....	....	....	....
	Hershey Bears	AHL	....	....	....	....	....	....	....	....	....	....	....	....	....	....	1	0	0	0	0	....	....	....	....
99-2000	**Colorado**	**NHL**	**80**	**3**	**13**	**16**	**20**	**2**	**0**	**0**	**66**	**4.5**	**5**	**0**	**0.0**	**18:15**	**17**	**0**	**2**	**2**	**4**	**0**	**0**	**0**	**18:45**
2000-01 ♦	**Colorado**	**NHL**	**82**	**8**	**17**	**25**	**38**	**3**	**0**	**2**	**108**	**7.4**	**8**	**1**	**100.0**	**20:41**	**23**	**1**	**4**	**5**	**8**	**0**	**0**	**0**	**11:59**
2001-02	**Colorado**	**NHL**	**82**	**10**	**21**	**31**	**42**	**5**	**0**	**1**	**100**	**10.0**	**−3**	**0**	**0.0**	**22:18**	**21**	**0**	**6**	**6**	**2**	**0**	**0**	**0**	**14:37**
	Czech Republic	Olympics	4	0	0	0	0	....	....	....	....	....	....	....	....	....	....	....	....	....	....	....	....	....	....
2002-03	**Colorado**	**NHL**	**81**	**4**	**21**	**25**	**68**	**2**	**0**	**0**	**93**	**4.3**	**11**	**1**	**100.0**	**18:27**	**7**	**0**	**1**	**1**	**4**	**0**	**0**	**0**	**11:05**
2003-04	**Colorado**	**NHL**	**58**	**2**	**14**	**16**	**30**	**0**	**0**	**0**	**54**	**3.7**	**2**	**0**	**0.0**	**17:21**	....	....	....	....	....	....	....	....	....
	Anaheim	**NHL**	**21**	**2**	**7**	**9**	**2**	**1**	**0**	**0**	**30**	**6.7**	**3**	**1**	**0.0**	**21:14**	....	....	....	....	....	....	....	....	....
2004-05	Litvinov	CzRep	47	4	15	19	101	....	....	....	....	....	....	....	....	....	6	0	0	0	6	....	....	....	....
2005-06	**Dallas**	**NHL**	**61**	**4**	**11**	**15**	**36**	**3**	**0**	**1**	**78**	**5.1**	**6**	**0**	**0.0**	**18:41**	....	....	....	....	....	....	....	....	....
	Minnesota	**NHL**	**17**	**1**	**5**	**6**	**10**	**0**	**0**	**0**	**14**	**7.1**	**0**	**0**	**0.0**	**20:49**	....	....	....	....	....	....	....	....	....
	NHL Totals		**482**	**34**	**109**	**143**	**246**	**16**	**0**	**4**	**543**	**6.3**		**3**	**66.7**	**19:33**	**68**	**1**	**13**	**14**	**18**	**0**	**0**	**0**	**14:24**

OHL All-Rookie Team (1998) • OHL Second All-Star Team (1999)

Traded to **Anaheim** by **Colorado** for Kurt Sauer and Anaheim's 4th round choice (Raymond Macias) in 2005 Entry Draft, February 21, 2004. Signed as a free agent by **Litvinov** (CzRep), September 17, 2004. Signed as a free agent by **Dallas**, August 3, 2005. Traded to **Minnesota** by **Dallas** with Shawn Belle for Willie Mitchell and a 2nd round choice in 2007 Entry Draft, March 8, 2006.

SKRASTINS, Karlis

(SKRAS-tinsh, KAR-lihs) **COL.**

Defense. Shoots left. 6'1", 212 lbs. Born, Riga, Latvia, July 9, 1974. Nashville's 8th choice, 230th overall, in 1998 Entry Draft.

1992-93	Pardaugava Riga	CIS	40	3	5	8	16	....	....	....	....	....	....	....	....	....	2	0	0	0	0	....	....	....	....
1993-94	Pardaugava Riga	CIS	42	7	5	12	18	....	....	....	....	....	....	....	....	....	2	1	0	1	4	....	....	....	....
1994-95	Pardaugava Riga	CIS	52	4	14	18	69	....	....	....	....	....	....	....	....	....	....	....	....	....	....	....	....	....	....
1995-96	TPS Turku	Finland	50	4	11	15	32	....	....	....	....	....	....	....	....	....	11	2	2	4	10	....	....	....	....
1996-97	TPS Turku	Finland	50	2	8	10	20	....	....	....	....	....	....	....	....	....	12	0	4	4	2	....	....	....	....
	TPS Turku	EuroHL	6	0	1	1	4	....	....	....	....	....	....	....	....	....	4	0	0	0	14	....	....	....	....
1997-98	TPS Turku	Finland	48	4	15	19	67	....	....	....	....	....	....	....	....	....	4	0	0	0	0	....	....	....	....
	TPS Turku	EuroHL	6	0	1	1	6	....	....	....	....	....	....	....	....	....	....	....	....	....	....	....	....	....	....
1998-99	**Nashville**	**NHL**	**2**	**0**	**1**	**1**	**0**	**0**	**0**	**0**	**0**	**0.0**	**0**	**0**	**0.0**	**11:47**	....	....	....	....	....	....	....	....	....
	Milwaukee	IHL	75	8	36	44	47	....	....	....	....	....	....	....	....	....	2	0	1	1	2	....	....	....	....
99-2000	**Nashville**	**NHL**	**59**	**5**	**6**	**11**	**20**	**1**	**0**	**2**	**51**	**9.8**	**−7**	**0**	**0.0**	**20:51**	....	....	....	....	....	....	....	....	....
	Milwaukee	IHL	19	3	8	11	10	....	....	....	....	....	....	....	....	....	....	....	....	....	....	....	....	....	....
2000-01	**Nashville**	**NHL**	**82**	**1**	**11**	**12**	**30**	**0**	**0**	**1**	**66**	**1.5**	**−12**	**0**	**0.0**	**19:12**	....	....	....	....	....	....	....	....	....
2001-02	**Nashville**	**NHL**	**82**	**4**	**13**	**17**	**36**	**0**	**0**	**1**	**84**	**4.8**	**−12**	**0**	**0.0**	**20:29**	....	....	....	....	....	....	....	....	....
	Latvia	Olympics	1	0	0	0	0	....	....	....	....	....	....	....	....	....	....	....	....	....	....	....	....	....	....
2002-03	**Nashville**	**NHL**	**82**	**3**	**10**	**13**	**44**	**0**	**1**	**0**	**86**	**3.5**	**−18**	**0**	**0.0**	**20:17**	....	....	....	....	....	....	....	....	....
2003-04	**Colorado**	**NHL**	**82**	**5**	**8**	**13**	**26**	**0**	**1**	**1**	**102**	**4.9**	**18**	**0**	**0.0**	**21:49**	**11**	**0**	**2**	**2**	**2**	**0**	**0**	**0**	**23:07**
2004-05	HK Riga 2000	Latvia	4	0	4	4	0	....	....	....	....	....	....	....	....	....	9	3	10	13	33	....	....	....	....
	HK Riga 2000	BelOpen	34	8	17	25	30	....	....	....	....	....	....	....	....	....	3	0	0	0	25	....	....	....	....
2005-06	**Colorado**	**NHL**	**82**	**3**	**11**	**14**	**65**	**0**	**2**	**0**	**58**	**5.2**	**−7**	**0**	**0.0**	**21:49**	**9**	**0**	**1**	**1**	**10**	**0**	**0**	**0**	**23:24**
	Latvia	Olympics	5	0	1	1	0	....	....	....	....	....	....	....	....	....	....	....	....	....	....	....	....	....	....
	NHL Totals		**471**	**21**	**60**	**81**	**221**	**1**	**4**	**5**	**447**	**4.7**		**0**	**0.0**	**20:42**	**20**	**0**	**3**	**3**	**12**	**0**	**0**	**0**	**23:15**

Traded to **Colorado** by **Nashville** for Colorado's 3rd round choice (later traded to Ottawa – Ottawa selected Peter Regin Jensen) in 2004 Entry Draft, June 30, 2003. Signed as a free agent by **Riga** (Latvia), September 25, 2004.

SKRBEK, Pavel

(SKUHR-behk, PAH-vehl) **NSH.**

Defense. Shoots left. 6'3", 217 lbs. Born, Kladno, Czech., August 9, 1978. Pittsburgh's 2nd choice, 28th overall, in 1996 Entry Draft.

1994-95	HC Kladno Jr.	CzRep-Jr.	29	7	6	13	....	....	....	....	....	....	....	....	....	....	....	....	....	....	....	....	....	....	....
1995-96	Kladno Jr.	CzRep-Jr.	29	10	12	22	....	....	....	....	....	....	....	....	....	....	....	....	....	....	....	....	....	....	....
	HC Poldi Kladno	CzRep	13	0	1	1	....	....	....	....	....	....	....	....	....	....	5	0	0	0	....	....	....	....	....
1996-97	HC Poldi Kladno	CzRep	35	1	5	6	26	....	....	....	....	....	....	....	....	....	3	0	0	0	4	....	....	....	....
1997-98	Kladno	CzRep	47	4	10	14	126	....	....	....	....	....	....	....	....	....	....	....	....	....	....	....	....	....	....
1998-99	**Pittsburgh**	**NHL**	**4**	**0**	**0**	**0**	**2**	**0**	**0**	**0**	**1**	**0.0**	**2**	**0**	**0.0**	**14:21**	....	....	....	....	....	....	....	....	....
	Syracuse Crunch	AHL	64	6	16	22	38	....	....	....	....	....	....	....	....	....	....	....	....	....	....	....	....	....	....
99-2000	Wilkes-Barre	AHL	51	7	16	23	50	....	....	....	....	....	....	....	....	....	....	....	....	....	....	....	....	....	....
	Milwaukee	IHL	6	0	0	0	0	....	....	....	....	....	....	....	....	....	....	....	....	....	....	....	....	....	....
2000-01	**Nashville**	**NHL**	**5**	**0**	**0**	**0**	**4**	**0**	**0**	**0**	**2**	**0.0**	**1**	**0**	**0.0**	**11:44**	....	....	....	....	....	....	....	....	....
	Milwaukee	IHL	54	2	22	24	55	....	....	....	....	....	....	....	....	....	5	0	0	0	2	....	....	....	....
2001-02	**Nashville**	**NHL**	**3**	**0**	**0**	**0**	**2**	**0**	**0**	**0**	**0**	**0.0**	**−2**	**0**	**0.0**	**10:18**	....	....	....	....	....	....	....	....	....
	Kladno	CzRep	24	2	3	5	30	....	....	....	....	....	....	....	....	....	....	....	....	....	....	....	....	....	....
2002-03	Lulea HF	Sweden	39	2	2	4	61	....	....	....	....	....	....	....	....	....	4	0	0	0	10	....	....	....	....
2003-04	Lulea HF	Sweden	34	4	4	8	84	....	....	....	....	....	....	....	....	....	5	0	4	4	6	....	....	....	....
2004-05	Mora IK	Sweden	48	1	11	12	68	....	....	....	....	....	....	....	....	....	....	....	....	....	....	....	....	....	....
2005-06	Lulea HF	Sweden	49	5	12	17	88	....	....	....	....	....	....	....	....	....	6	0	0	0	11	....	....	....	....
	NHL Totals		**12**	**0**	**0**	**0**	**8**	**0**	**0**	**0**	**3**	**0.0**		**0**	**0.0**	**12:15**	....	....	....	....	....	....	....	....	....

Traded to **Nashville** by **Pittsburgh** for Bob Boughner, March 13, 2000. Assigned to **Kladno** (CzRep) by **Nashville**, October 31, 2001. Signed as a free agent by **Lulea** (Sweden), June 20, 2002. Signed as a free agent by **Mora** (Sweden), August 23, 2004. Signed as a free agent by **Lulea** (Sweden), March 31, 2005.

SLANEY, John

(SLAY-nee, JAWN)

Defense. Shoots left. 6', 189 lbs. Born, St. John's, Nfld., February 7, 1972. Washington's 1st choice, 9th overall, in 1990 Entry Draft.

1987-88	St. John's	NFAHA	65	41	69	110	70	....	....	....	....	....	....	....	....	....	....	....	....	....	....	....	....	....	....
1988-89	Cornwall Royals	OHL	66	16	43	59	23	....	....	....	....	....	....	....	....	....	18	8	16	24	10	....	....	....	....
1989-90	Cornwall Royals	OHL	64	38	59	97	68	....	....	....	....	....	....	....	....	....	6	0	8	8	11	....	....	....	....
1990-91	Cornwall Royals	OHL	34	21	25	46	28	....	....	....	....	....	....	....	....	....	....	....	....	....	....	....	....	....	....
1991-92	Cornwall Royals	OHL	34	19	41	60	43	....	....	....	....	....	....	....	....	....	6	3	8	11	0	....	....	....	....
	Baltimore	AHL	6	2	4	6	0	....	....	....	....	....	....	....	....	....	....	....	....	....	....	....	....	....	....
1992-93	Baltimore	AHL	79	20	46	66	60	....	....	....	....	....	....	....	....	....	7	0	7	7	8	....	....	....	....
1993-94	**Washington**	**NHL**	**47**	**7**	**9**	**16**	**27**	**3**	**0**	**1**	**70**	**10.0**	**3**	....	....	....	**11**	**1**	**1**	**2**	**2**	**1**	**0**	**0**	....
	Portland Pirates	AHL	29	14	13	27	17	....	....	....	....	....	....	....	....	....	....	....	....	....	....	....	....	....	....
1994-95	**Washington**	**NHL**	**16**	**0**	**3**	**3**	**6**	**0**	**0**	**0**	**21**	**0.0**	**−3**	....	....	....	....	....	....	....	....	....	....	....	....
	Portland Pirates	AHL	8	3	10	13	4	....	....	....	....	....	....	....	....	....	7	1	3	4	4	....	....	....	....
1995-96	**Colorado**	**NHL**	**7**	**0**	**3**	**3**	**4**	**0**	**0**	**0**	**12**	**0.0**	**2**	....	....	....	....	....	....	....	....	....	....	....	....
	Cornwall Aces	AHL	5	0	4	4	2	....	....	....	....	....	....	....	....	....	....	....	....	....	....	....	....	....	....
	Los Angeles	**NHL**	**31**	**6**	**11**	**17**	**10**	**3**	**1**	**0**	**63**	**9.5**	**5**	....	....	....	....	....	....	....	....	....	....	....	....
1996-97	**Los Angeles**	**NHL**	**32**	**3**	**11**	**14**	**4**	**1**	**0**	**1**	**60**	**5.0**	**−10**	....	....	....	....	....	....	....	....	....	....	....	....
	Phoenix	IHL	35	9	25	34	8	....	....	....	....	....	....	....	....	....	....	....	....	....	....	....	....	....	....
1997-98	**Phoenix**	**NHL**	**55**	**3**	**14**	**17**	**24**	**1**	**0**	**1**	**74**	**4.1**	**−3**	....	....	....	....	....	....	....	....	....	....	....	....
	Las Vegas	IHL	5	2	2	4	10	....	....	....	....	....	....	....	....	....	....	....	....	....	....	....	....	....	....
1998-99	**Nashville**	**NHL**	**46**	**2**	**12**	**14**	**14**	**0**	**0**	**1**	**84**	**2.4**	**−12**	**0**	**0.0**	**20:39**	....	....	....	....	....	....	....	....	....
	Milwaukee	IHL	7	0	1	1	0	....	....	....	....	....	....	....	....	....	....	....	....	....	....	....	....	....	....
99-2000	**Pittsburgh**	**NHL**	**29**	**1**	**4**	**5**	**10**	**1**	**0**	**0**	**27**	**3.7**	**−10**	**35**	**40.0**	**12:13**	**2**	**1**	**0**	**1**	**2**	**1**	**0**	**0**	**5:43**
	Wilkes-Barre	AHL	49	30	30	60	25	....	....	....	....	....	....	....	....	....	....	....	....	....	....	....	....	....	....
2000-01	Wilkes-Barre	AHL	40	12	38	50	4	....	....	....	....	....	....	....	....	....	....	....	....	....	....	....	....	....	....
	Philadelphia	AHL	25	6	11	17	10	....	....	....	....	....	....	....	....	....	10	2	6	8	6	....	....	....	....
2001-02	**Philadelphia**	**NHL**	**1**	**0**	**0**	**0**	**0**	**0**	**0**	**0**	**1**	**0.0**	**2**	**0**	**0.0**	**23:33**	**1**	**0**	**0**	**0**	**0**	**0**	**0**	**0**	**11:20**
	Philadelphia	AHL	64	20	39	59	26	....	....	....	....	....	....	....	....	....	5	2	1	3	0	....	....	....	....
2002-03	Philadelphia	AHL	55	9	33	42	36	....	....	....	....	....	....	....	....	....	....	....	....	....	....	....	....	....	....
2003-04	**Philadelphia**	**NHL**	**4**	**0**	**2**	**2**	**0**	**0**	**0**	**0**	**0**	**0.0**	**0**	**0**	**0.0**	**13:38**	....	....	....	....	....	....	....	....	....
	Philadelphia	AHL	59	19	29	48	31	....	....	....	....	....	....	....	....	....	12	3	4	7	6	....	....	....	....
2004-05	Philadelphia	AHL	78	14	30	44	39	....	....	....	....	....	....	....	....	....	21	3	7	10	12	....	....	....	....
2005-06	Philadelphia	AHL	79	8	42	50	60	....	....	....	....	....	....	....	....	....	....	....	....	....	....	....	....	....	....
	NHL Totals		**268**	**22**	**69**	**91**	**99**	**9**	**1**	**4**	**412**	**5.3**		**35**	**40.0**	**17:17**	**14**	**2**	**1**	**3**	**4**	**2**	**0**	**0**	**7:35**

OHL First All-Star Team (1990) • Canadian Major Junior Defenseman of the Year (1990) • OHL Second All-Star Team (1991) • AHL First All-Star Team (2001, 2002) • Eddie Shore Award (Outstanding Defenseman – AHL) (2001, 2002) • AHL Second All-Star Team (2004)

Traded to **Colorado** by **Washington** for Philadelphia's 3rd round choice (previously acquired, Washington selected Shawn McNeil) in 1996 Entry Draft, July 12, 1995. Traded to **Los Angeles** by **Colorado** for Winnipeg's 6th round choice (previously acquired, Colorado selected Brian Willsie) in 1996 Entry Draft, December 28, 1995. Signed as a free agent by **Phoenix**, August 19, 1997. Claimed by **Nashville** from **Phoenix** in Expansion Draft, June 26, 1998. Signed as a free agent by **Pittsburgh**, September 30, 1999. Traded to **Philadelphia** by **Pittsburgh** for Kevin Stevens, January 14, 2001.

SLATER, Jim
(SLAY-tuhr, JIHM) **ATL.**

Center. Shoots left. 6', 190 lbs. Born, Petoskey, MI, December 9, 1982. Atlanta's 2nd choice, 30th overall, in 2002 Entry Draft.

			Regular Season														Playoffs								
Season	Club	League	GP	G	A	Pts	PIM	PP	SH	GW	S	%	+/-	TF	F%	Min	GP	G	A	Pts	PIM	PP	SH	GW	Min
1998-99	USNTDP	U-18	3	0	1	1	0	....	....	....	....	....	....	....	....	....	....	....	....	....	....	....	....	....	....
	Cleveland Barons	NAHL	50	13	20	33	58	....	....	....	....	....	....	....	....	....	2	0	0	0	2	....	....	....	....
99-2000	Cleveland Barons	NAHL	56	35	50	85	129	....	....	....	....	....	....	....	....	....	3	1	3	4	4	....	....	....	....
2000-01	Cleveland Barons	NAHL	48	27	37	64	122	....	....	....	....	....	....	....	....	....	6	6	6	12	6	....	....	....	....
2001-02	Michigan State	CCHA	37	11	21	32	50	....	....	....	....	....	....	....	....	....	....	....	....	....	....	....	....	....	....
2002-03	Michigan State	CCHA	37	18	26	44	26	....	....	....	....	....	....	....	....	....	....	....	....	....	....	....	....	....	....
2003-04	Michigan State	CCHA	42	19	29	*48	38	....	....	....	....	....	....	....	....	....	....	....	....	....	....	....	....	....	....
2004-05	Michigan State	CCHA	41	16	32	48	30	....	....	....	....	....	....	....	....	....	....	....	....	....	....	....	....	....	....
2005-06	**Atlanta**	**NHL**	**71**	**10**	**10**	**20**	**46**	**1**	**0**	**0**	**108**	**9.3**	**1**	**287**	**56.5**	**10:06**	....	....	....	....	....	....	....	....	....
	Chicago Wolves	AHL	4	0	2	2	2	....	....	....	....	....	....	....	....	....	....	....	....	....	....	....	....	....	....
	NHL Totals		**71**	**10**	**10**	**20**	**46**	**1**	**0**	**0**	**108**	**9.3**		**287**	**56.4**	**10:06**	....	....	....	....	....	....	....	....	....

CCHA All-Rookie Team (2002) • CCHA First All-Star Team (2003, 2004) • NCAA West Second All-American Team (2004)

SLEGR, Jiri
(SLAY-guhr, YEE-ree)

Defense. Shoots left. 6'1", 210 lbs. Born, Jihlava, Czech., May 30, 1971. Vancouver's 3rd choice, 23rd overall, in 1990 Entry Draft.

			Regular Season														Playoffs								
Season	Club	League	GP	G	A	Pts	PIM	PP	SH	GW	S	%	+/-	TF	F%	Min	GP	G	A	Pts	PIM	PP	SH	GW	Min
1987-88	CHZ Litvinov	Czech	4	1	1	2	0	....	....	....	....	....	....	....	....	....	....	....	....	....	....	....	....	....	....
1988-89	CHZ Litvinov	Czech	8	0	0	0	4	....	....	....	....	....	....	....	....	....	....	....	....	....	....	....	....	....	....
1989-90	CHZ Litvinov	Czech	51	4	15	19	....	....	....	....	....	....	....	....	....	....	....	....	....	....	....	....	....	....	....
1990-91	HC CHZ Litvinov	Czech	47	11	36	47	26	....	....	....	....	....	....	....	....	....	....	....	....	....	....	....	....	....	....
1991-92	Litvinov	Czech	42	9	23	32	38	....	....	....	....	....	....	....	....	....	....	....	....	....	....	....	....	....	....
	Czechoslovakia	Olympics	8	1	1	2	14	....	....	....	....	....	....	....	....	....	....	....	....	....	....	....	....	....	....
1992-93	**Vancouver**	**NHL**	**41**	**4**	**22**	**26**	**109**	**2**	**0**	**0**	**89**	**4.5**	**16**	....	....	....	**5**	**0**	**3**	**3**	**4**	**0**	**0**	**0**	....
	Hamilton	AHL	21	4	14	18	42	....	....	....	....	....	....	....	....	....	....	....	....	....	....	....	....	....	....
1993-94	**Vancouver**	**NHL**	**78**	**5**	**33**	**38**	**86**	**1**	**0**	**0**	**160**	**3.1**	**0**	....	....	....	....	....	....	....	....	....	....	....	....
1994-95	Litvinov	CzRep	11	3	10	13	80	....	....	....	....	....	....	....	....	....	....	....	....	....	....	....	....	....	....
	Vancouver	**NHL**	**19**	**1**	**5**	**6**	**32**	**0**	**0**	**1**	**42**	**2.4**	**0**	....	....	....	....	....	....	....	....	....	....	....	....
	Edmonton	**NHL**	**12**	**1**	**5**	**6**	**14**	**1**	**0**	**0**	**27**	**3.7**	**–5**	....	....	....	....	....	....	....	....	....	....	....	....
1995-96	**Edmonton**	**NHL**	**57**	**4**	**13**	**17**	**74**	**0**	**1**	**1**	**91**	**4.4**	**–1**	....	....	....	....	....	....	....	....	....	....	....	....
	Cape Breton	AHL	4	1	2	3	4	....	....	....	....	....	....	....	....	....	....	....	....	....	....	....	....	....	....
1996-97	Litvinov	CzRep	1	0	0	0	0	....	....	....	....	....	....	....	....	....	....	....	....	....	....	....	....	....	....
	Sodertalje SK	Sweden	30	4	14	18	62	....	....	....	....	....	....	....	....	....	10	4	2	6	32	....	....	....	....
1997-98	**Pittsburgh**	**NHL**	**73**	**5**	**12**	**17**	**109**	**1**	**1**	**0**	**131**	**3.8**	**10**	....	....	....	**6**	**0**	**4**	**4**	**2**	**0**	**0**	**0**	....
	Czech Republic	Olympics	6	1	0	1	8	....	....	....	....	....	....	....	....	....	....	....	....	....	....	....	....	....	....
1998-99	**Pittsburgh**	**NHL**	**63**	**3**	**20**	**23**	**86**	**1**	**0**	**0**	**91**	**3.3**	**13**	**2**	**0.0**	**18:42**	**13**	**1**	**3**	**4**	**12**	**0**	**0**	**1**	**19:50**
99-2000	**Pittsburgh**	**NHL**	**74**	**11**	**20**	**31**	**82**	**0**	**0**	**2**	**144**	**7.6**	**20**	**3**	**66.7**	**21:22**	**10**	**2**	**3**	**5**	**19**	**0**	**0**	**1**	**20:02**
2000-01	**Pittsburgh**	**NHL**	**42**	**5**	**10**	**15**	**60**	**0**	**1**	**1**	**67**	**7.5**	**–9**	**0**	**0.0**	**17:37**	....	....	....	....	....	....	....	....	....
	Atlanta	**NHL**	**33**	**3**	**16**	**19**	**36**	**2**	**0**	**0**	**78**	**3.8**	**–1**	**1**	**0.0**	**21:34**	....	....	....	....	....	....	....	....	....
2001-02	**Atlanta**	**NHL**	**38**	**3**	**5**	**8**	**51**	**1**	**0**	**0**	**56**	**5.4**	**–21**	**0**	**0.0**	**21:21**	....	....	....	....	....	....	....	....	....
	◆ Detroit	**NHL**	**8**	**0**	**1**	**1**	**8**	**0**	**0**	**0**	**11**	**0.0**	**1**	**0**	**0.0**	**19:16**	**1**	**0**	**0**	**0**	**2**	**0**	**0**	**0**	**17:11**
2002-03	Litvinov	CzRep	10	2	3	5	14	....	....	....	....	....	....	....	....	....	....	....	....	....	....	....	....	....	....
	Avangard Omsk	Russia	6	1	2	3	8	....	....	....	....	....	....	....	....	....	9	0	3	3	*45	....	....	....	....
2003-04	**Vancouver**	**NHL**	**16**	**2**	**5**	**7**	**8**	**1**	**1**	**1**	**15**	**13.3**	**6**	**0**	**0.0**	**12:16**	....	....	....	....	....	....	....	....	....
	Boston	**NHL**	**36**	**4**	**15**	**19**	**27**	**0**	**0**	**1**	**83**	**4.8**	**5**	**0**	**0.0**	**20:03**	**7**	**1**	**1**	**2**	**0**	**0**	**0**	**0**	**18:08**
2004-05	Litvinov	CzRep	46	6	23	29	135	....	....	....	....	....	....	....	....	....	6	1	2	3	30	....	....	....	....
2005-06	**Boston**	**NHL**	**32**	**5**	**11**	**16**	**56**	**4**	**0**	**0**	**59**	**8.5**	**–2**	**0**	**0.0**	**16:22**	....	....	....	....	....	....	....	....	....
	NHL Totals		**622**	**56**	**193**	**249**	**838**	**14**	**4**	**7**	**1144**	**4.9**		**6**	**33.3**	**19:21**	**42**	**4**	**14**	**18**	**39**	**0**	**0**	**2**	**19:26**

Czechoslovakian First All-Star Team (1991)

Traded to **Edmonton** by **Vancouver** for Roman Oksiuta, April 7, 1995. Traded to **Pittsburgh** by **Edmonton** for Pittsburgh's 3rd round choice (later traded to New Jersey – New Jersey selected Brian Gionta) in 1998 Entry Draft, August 12, 1997. Traded to **Atlanta** by **Pittsburgh** for San Jose's 3rd round choice (previously acquired, later traded to Columbus – Columbus selected Aaron Johnson) in 2001 Entry Draft, January 14, 2001. Traded to **Detroit** by **Atlanta** for Yuri Butsayev and Detroit's 3rd round choice (later traded to Columbus – Columbus selected Jeff Genovy) in 2002 Entry Draft, March 19, 2002. Signed as a free agent by **Vancouver**, September 4, 2003. Traded to **Boston** by **Vancouver** for future considerations, January 17, 2004. Signed as a free agent by **Litvinov** (CzRep), August 20, 2004. • Missed remainder of 2005-06 season recovering from back surgery (January 2006).

SLOAN, Blake
(SLOHN, BLAYK)

Right wing. Shoots right. 5'10", 196 lbs. Born, Park Ridge, IL, July 27, 1975.

			Regular Season														Playoffs								
Season	Club	League	GP	G	A	Pts	PIM	PP	SH	GW	S	%	+/-	TF	F%	Min	GP	G	A	Pts	PIM	PP	SH	GW	Min
1992-93	Tabor Academy	High-MA	33	7	15	22	....	....	....	....	....	....	....	....	....	....	....	....	....	....	....	....	....	....	....
1993-94	U. of Michigan	CCHA	38	2	4	6	48	....	....	....	....	....	....	....	....	....	....	....	....	....	....	....	....	....	....
1994-95	U. of Michigan	CCHA	39	2	15	17	60	....	....	....	....	....	....	....	....	....	....	....	....	....	....	....	....	....	....
1995-96	U. of Michigan	CCHA	41	6	24	30	55	....	....	....	....	....	....	....	....	....	....	....	....	....	....	....	....	....	....
1996-97	U. of Michigan	CCHA	41	2	15	17	52	....	....	....	....	....	....	....	....	....	....	....	....	....	....	....	....	....	....
1997-98	Houston Aeros	IHL	70	2	13	15	86	....	....	....	....	....	....	....	....	....	2	0	0	0	0	....	....	....	....
1998-99	**◆ Dallas**	**NHL**	**14**	**0**	**0**	**0**	**10**	**0**	**0**	**0**	**7**	**0.0**	**–1**	**0**	**0.0**	**9:01**	**19**	**0**	**2**	**2**	**8**	**0**	**0**	**0**	**9:58**
	Houston Aeros	IHL	62	8	10	18	76	....	....	....	....	....	....	....	....	....	....	....	....	....	....	....	....	....	....
99-2000	**Dallas**	**NHL**	**67**	**4**	**13**	**17**	**50**	**0**	**0**	**1**	**78**	**5.1**	**11**	**2**	**50.0**	**13:30**	**16**	**0**	**0**	**0**	**12**	**0**	**0**	**0**	**8:55**
2000-01	**Dallas**	**NHL**	**33**	**2**	**2**	**4**	**4**	**0**	**0**	**1**	**29**	**6.9**	**–2**	**4**	**25.0**	**9:56**	....	....	....	....	....	....	....	....	....
	Houston Aeros	IHL	20	7	4	11	18	....	....	....	....	....	....	....	....	....	....	....	....	....	....	....	....	....	....
	Columbus	**NHL**	**14**	**1**	**0**	**1**	**13**	**0**	**0**	**0**	**16**	**6.3**	**–2**	**7**	**28.6**	**13:19**	....	....	....	....	....	....	....	....	....
2001-02	**Columbus**	**NHL**	**60**	**2**	**7**	**9**	**46**	**0**	**0**	**0**	**49**	**4.1**	**–18**	**3**	**66.7**	**10:56**	....	....	....	....	....	....	....	....	....
	Calgary	**NHL**	**7**	**0**	**2**	**2**	**4**	**0**	**0**	**0**	**7**	**0.0**	**1**	**2**	**0.0**	**12:16**	....	....	....	....	....	....	....	....	....
2002-03	**Calgary**	**NHL**	**67**	**2**	**8**	**10**	**28**	**0**	**0**	**0**	**56**	**3.6**	**–5**	**31**	**12.9**	**12:23**	....	....	....	....	....	....	....	....	....
2003-04	**Dallas**	**NHL**	**28**	**0**	**0**	**0**	**7**	**0**	**0**	**0**	**23**	**0.0**	**–1**	**4**	**0.0**	**7:11**	....	....	....	....	....	....	....	....	....
	Grand Rapids	AHL	7	4	2	6	4	....	....	....	....	....	....	....	....	....	....	....	....	....	....	....	....	....	....
2004-05	Grand Rapids	AHL	78	15	11	26	68	....	....	....	....	....	....	....	....	....	....	....	....	....	....	....	....	....	....
2005-06	Timra IK	Sweden	38	2	2	4	40	....	....	....	....	....	....	....	....	....	....	....	....	....	....	....	....	....	....
	NHL Totals		**290**	**11**	**32**	**43**	**162**	**0**	**0**	**2**	**265**	**4.2**		**53**	**18.9**	**11:26**	**35**	**0**	**2**	**2**	**20**	**0**	**0**	**0**	**9:29**

Signed as a free agent by **Dallas**, March 10, 1998. Claimed on waivers by **Columbus** from **Dallas**, March 13, 2001. Traded to **Calgary** by **Columbus** for Jamie Allison, March 19, 2002. Signed as a free agent by **Grand Rapids** (AHL), November 18, 2003. Signed as a free agent by **Detroit**, December 1, 2003. Claimed on waivers by **Dallas** from **Detroit**, December 3, 2003. • Spent majority of 2003-04 season as a healthy reserve. Signed as a free agent by **Grand Rapids** (AHL), September 9, 2004. Signed as a free agent by **Timra** (Sweden). October 18, 2005.

SMIRNOV, Alexei
(smihr-NAHV, al-EHX-ay)

Left wing. Shoots left. 6'3", 211 lbs. Born, Tver, USSR, January 28, 1982. Anaheim's 1st choice, 12th overall, in 2000 Entry Draft.

			Regular Season														Playoffs								
Season	Club	League	GP	G	A	Pts	PIM	PP	SH	GW	S	%	+/-	TF	F%	Min	GP	G	A	Pts	PIM	PP	SH	GW	Min
1997-98	Dyn'o Moscow 2	Russia-2	11	1	1	2	4	....	....	....	....	....	....	....	....	....	....	....	....	....	....	....	....	....	....
1998-99	Dyn'o Moscow 2	Russia-3	27	9	3	12	24	....	....	....	....	....	....	....	....	....	....	....	....	....	....	....	....	....	....
99-2000	Dyn'o Moscow 2	Russia-3	12	5	3	8	34	....	....	....	....	....	....	....	....	....	....	....	....	....	....	....	....	....	....
	THK Tver	Russia-2	35	3	5	8	24	....	....	....	....	....	....	....	....	....	....	....	....	....	....	....	....	....	....
	Dynamo Moscow	Russia	1	0	0	0	0	....	....	....	....	....	....	....	....	....	....	....	....	....	....	....	....	....	....
2000-01	Dynamo Moscow	Russia	29	2	0	2	16	....	....	....	....	....	....	....	....	....	....	....	....	....	....	....	....	....	....
2001-02	CSKA Moscow 2	Russia-3	2	1	0	1	0	....	....	....	....	....	....	....	....	....	....	....	....	....	....	....	....	....	....
	CSKA Moscow	Russia	51	5	11	16	42	....	....	....	....	....	....	....	....	....	....	....	....	....	....	....	....	....	....
2002-03	**Anaheim**	**NHL**	**44**	**3**	**2**	**5**	**18**	**0**	**0**	**1**	**46**	**6.5**	**–1**	**6**	**16.7**	**8:50**	**4**	**0**	**0**	**0**	**2**	**0**	**0**	**0**	**4:22**
	Cincinnati	AHL	19	7	3	10	12	....	....	....	....	....	....	....	....	....	....	....	....	....	....	....	....	....	....
2003-04	**Anaheim**	**NHL**	**8**	**0**	**1**	**1**	**2**	**0**	**0**	**0**	**8**	**0.0**	**0**	**3**	**0.0**	**7:17**	....	....	....	....	....	....	....	....	....
	Cincinnati	AHL	51	9	10	19	34	....	....	....	....	....	....	....	....	....	2	0	0	0	2	....	....	....	....
2004-05	Cincinnati	AHL	65	9	9	18	53	....	....	....	....	....	....	....	....	....	4	0	0	0	0	....	....	....	....
2005-06	Avangard Omsk	Russia	27	1	2	3	18	....	....	....	....	....	....	....	....	....	10	1	1	2	18	....	....	....	....
	NHL Totals		**52**	**3**	**3**	**6**	**20**	**0**	**0**	**1**	**54**	**5.6**		**9**	**11.1**	**8:36**	**4**	**0**	**0**	**0**	**2**	**0**	**0**	**0**	**4:22**

Signed as a free agent by **Omsk** (Russia). August 12, 2005.

SMITH, Brandon

(SMIHTH, BRAN-duhn)

Defense. Shoots left. 6'1", 209 lbs. Born, Hazelton, B.C., February 25, 1973.

Season	Club	League	GP	G	A	Pts	PIM	PP	SH	GW	S	%	+/-	TF	F%	Min	Playoffs GP	G	A	Pts	PIM	PP	SH	GW	Min
1989-90	Portland	WHL	59	2	17	19	16																		
1990-91	Portland	WHL	17	8	5	13	8																		
1991-92	Portland	WHL	70	12	32	44	63																		
1992-93	Portland	WHL	72	20	54	74	38										16	4	9	13	6				
1993-94	Portland	WHL	72	19	63	82	47										10	2	10	12	8				
1994-95	Dayton Bombers	ECHL	60	16	49	65	57										4	2	3	5	0				
	Minnesota Moose	IHL	1	0	0	0	0																		
	Adirondack	AHL	14	1	2	3	7										3	0	0	0	2				
1995-96	Adirondack	AHL	48	4	13	17	22										3	0	1	1	2				
1996-97	Adirondack	AHL	80	8	26	34	30										4	0	0	0	0				
1997-98	Adirondack	AHL	64	9	27	36	26										1	0	1	1	0				
1998-99	**Boston**	**NHL**	**5**	**0**	**0**	**0**	**0**	**0**	**0**	**0**	**2**	**0.0**	**2**	**0**	**0.0**	**9:38**									
	Providence Bruins	AHL	72	16	46	62	32										19	1	9	10	12				
99-2000	**Boston**	**NHL**	**22**	**2**	**4**	**6**	**10**	**0**	**0**	**0**	**24**	**8.3**	**–4**	**0**	**0.0**	**19:29**									
	Providence Bruins	AHL	55	8	30	38	20										14	1	11	12	2				
2000-01	**Boston**	**NHL**	**3**	**1**	**0**	**1**	**0**	**1**	**0**	**0**	**2**	**50.0**	**–1**	**0**	**0.0**	**6:46**									
	Providence Bruins	AHL	63	11	28	39	30										17	0	5	5	6				
2001-02	Cleveland Barons	AHL	59	6	29	35	26																		
2002-03	**NY Islanders**	**NHL**	**3**	**0**	**0**	**0**	**0**	**0**	**0**	**0**	**1**	**0.0**	**–2**	**0**	**0.0**	**9:59**									
	Bridgeport	AHL	63	9	32	41	37										9	1	3	4	5				
2003-04	Bridgeport	AHL	74	5	23	28	39										7	1	3	4	9				
2004-05	Rochester	AHL	67	4	14	18	32										8	1	1	2	4				
2005-06	Rochester	AHL	39	3	11	14	39																		
	NHL Totals		**33**	**3**	**4**	**7**	**10**	**1**	**0**	**0**	**29**	**10.3**		**0**	**0.0**	**15:58**									

WHL West Second All-Star Team (1993, 1994) • ECHL First All-Star Team (1995) • ECHL Defenseman of the Year (1995) • AHL First All-Star Team (1999)

Signed as a free agent by **Detroit**, July 22, 1997. Signed as a free agent by **Boston**, August 5, 1998. Signed as a free agent by **San Jose**, July 23, 2001. Signed as a free agent by **NY Islanders**, August 3, 2002. Signed as a free agent by **Rochester** (AHL), September 10, 2004.

SMITH, Dan

(SMIHTH, DAN) **DET.**

Defense. Shoots left. 6'3", 215 lbs. Born, Fernie, B.C., October 19, 1976. Colorado's 7th choice, 181st overall, in 1995 Entry Draft.

Season	Club	League	GP	G	A	Pts	PIM	PP	SH	GW	S	%	+/-	TF	F%	Min	Playoffs GP	G	A	Pts	PIM	PP	SH	GW	Min
1994-95	U.B.C.	CWUAA	28	1	3	4	26																		
1995-96	Tri-City	WHL	58	1	21	22	70										11	1	3	4	14				
1996-97	Tri-City	WHL	72	5	19	24	174																		
	Hershey Bears	AHL	8	0	1	1	6										15	0	1	1	25				
1997-98	Hershey Bears	AHL	50	1	2	3	71										6	0	0	0	4				
1998-99	**Colorado**	**NHL**	**12**	**0**	**0**	**0**	**9**	**0**	**0**	**0**	**6**	**0.0**	**5**	**0**	**0.0**	**12:14**									
	Hershey Bears	AHL	54	5	7	12	72										5	0	1	1	0				
99-2000	**Colorado**	**NHL**	**3**	**0**	**0**	**0**	**0**	**0**	**0**	**0**	**0**	**0.0**	**2**	**0**	**0.0**	**11:03**									
	Hershey Bears	AHL	49	7	15	22	56																		
2000-01	Hershey Bears	AHL	58	2	12	14	34										12	0	1	1	4				
2001-02	Colorado	WCHL	12	0	2	2	16																		
	Lukko Rauma	Finland	32	1	2	3	18																		
2002-03	Springfield	AHL	69	1	14	15	53										6	0	2	2	0				
2003-04	Toronto	AHL	66	4	9	13	41																		
2004-05	Edmonton	AHL	72	5	10	15	72																		
2005-06	**Edmonton**	**NHL**	**7**	**0**	**0**	**0**	**7**	**0**	**0**	**0**	**1**	**0.0**	**1**	**0**	**0.0**	**11:21**									
	Hamilton	AHL	69	0	15	15	61																		
	NHL Totals		**22**	**0**	**0**	**0**	**16**	**0**	**0**	**0**	**7**	**0.0**		**0**	**0.0**	**11:47**									

Signed as a free agent by **Colorado** (WCHL), October 26, 2001. Signed as a free agent by **Rauma** (Finland) after receiving release from Colorado (WCHL), November 21, 2001. Signed as a free agent by **Edmonton**, August 21, 2003. Signed as a free agent by **Detroit**, July 13, 2006.

SMITH, Jason

(SMIHTH, JAY-suhn) **EDM.**

Defense. Shoots right. 6'3", 215 lbs. Born, Calgary, Alta., November 2, 1973. New Jersey's 1st choice, 18th overall, in 1992 Entry Draft.

Season	Club	League	GP	G	A	Pts	PIM	PP	SH	GW	S	%	+/-	TF	F%	Min	Playoffs GP	G	A	Pts	PIM	PP	SH	GW	Min
1990-91	Calgary Canucks	AJHL	45	3	15	18	69																		
	Regina Pats	WHL	2	0	0	0	7										4	0	0	0	2				
1991-92	Regina Pats	WHL	62	9	29	38	138																		
1992-93	Regina Pats	WHL	64	14	52	66	175										13	4	8	12	39				
	Utica Devils	AHL															1	0	0	0	2				
1993-94	**New Jersey**	**NHL**	**41**	**0**	**5**	**5**	**43**	**0**	**0**	**0**	**47**	**0.0**	**7**				**6**	**0**	**0**	**0**	**7**	**0**	**0**	**0**	
	Albany River Rats	AHL	20	6	3	9	31																		
1994-95	Albany River Rats	AHL	7	0	2	2	15										11	2	2	4	19				
	New Jersey	**NHL**	**2**	**0**	**0**	**0**	**0**	**0**	**0**	**0**	**5**	**0.0**	**–3**												
1995-96	**New Jersey**	**NHL**	**64**	**2**	**1**	**3**	**86**	**0**	**0**	**0**	**52**	**3.8**	**5**												
1996-97	**New Jersey**	**NHL**	**57**	**1**	**2**	**3**	**38**	**0**	**0**	**0**	**48**	**2.1**	**–8**												
	Toronto	**NHL**	**21**	**0**	**5**	**5**	**16**	**0**	**0**	**0**	**26**	**0.0**	**–4**												
1997-98	**Toronto**	**NHL**	**81**	**3**	**13**	**16**	**100**	**0**	**0**	**0**	**97**	**3.1**	**–5**												
1998-99	**Toronto**	**NHL**	**60**	**2**	**11**	**13**	**40**	**0**	**0**	**0**	**53**	**3.8**	**–9**	**0**	**0.0**	**17:31**									
	Edmonton	**NHL**	**12**	**1**	**1**	**2**	**11**	**0**	**0**	**0**	**15**	**6.7**	**0**	**0**	**0.0**	**20:26**	**4**	**0**	**1**	**1**	**4**	**0**	**0**	**0**	**26:29**
99-2000	**Edmonton**	**NHL**	**80**	**3**	**11**	**14**	**60**	**0**	**0**	**1**	**96**	**3.1**	**16**	**1**	**100.0**	**21:15**	**5**	**0**	**1**	**1**	**4**	**0**	**0**	**0**	**21:56**
2000-01	**Edmonton**	**NHL**	**82**	**5**	**15**	**20**	**120**	**1**	**1**	**0**	**140**	**3.6**	**14**	**1**	**0.0**	**21:40**	**6**	**0**	**2**	**2**	**6**	**0**	**0**	**0**	**25:27**
2001-02	**Edmonton**	**NHL**	**74**	**5**	**13**	**18**	**103**	**0**	**1**	**1**	**85**	**5.9**	**14**	**0**	**0.0**	**21:00**									
2002-03	**Edmonton**	**NHL**	**68**	**4**	**8**	**12**	**64**	**0**	**0**	**1**	**93**	**4.3**	**5**	**0**	**0.0**	**21:46**	**6**	**0**	**0**	**0**	**19**	**0**	**0**	**0**	**21:16**
2003-04	**Edmonton**	**NHL**	**68**	**7**	**12**	**19**	**98**	**0**	**1**	**1**	**84**	**8.3**	**13**	**2**	**50.0**	**21:21**									
2004-05			DID NOT PLAY																						
2005-06	**Edmonton**	**NHL**	**76**	**4**	**13**	**17**	**84**	**0**	**0**	**0**	**79**	**5.1**	**1**	**0**	**0.0**	**19:39**	**24**	**1**	**4**	**5**	**16**	**0**	**0**	**1**	**22:29**
	NHL Totals		**786**	**37**	**110**	**147**	**863**	**1**	**3**	**4**	**920**	**4.0**		**4**	**25.0**	**20:35**	**51**	**1**	**8**	**9**	**56**	**0**	**0**	**1**	**49:19**

WHL East First All-Star Team (1993) • Canadian Major Junior First All-Star Team (1993)

• Missed majority of 1994-95 season recovering from knee injury suffered in practice, November 5, 1994. Traded to **Toronto** by **New Jersey** with Steve Sullivan and the rights to Alyn McCauley for Doug Gilmour, Dave Ellett and New Jersey's 4th round choice (previously acquired, New Jersey selected Andre Lakos) in 1999 Entry Draft, February 25, 1997. Traded to **Edmonton** by **Toronto** for Edmonton's 4th round choice (Jonathon Zion) in 1999 Entry Draft and Edmonton's 2nd round choice (Kris Vernarsky) in 2000 Entry Draft, March 23, 1999.

SMITH, Mark

(SMIHTH, MAHRK) **S.J.**

Center. Shoots left. 5'10", 215 lbs. Born, Edmonton, Alta., October 24, 1977. San Jose's 7th choice, 219th overall, in 1997 Entry Draft.

Season	Club	League	GP	G	A	Pts	PIM	PP	SH	GW	S	%	+/-	TF	F%	Min	Playoffs GP	G	A	Pts	PIM	PP	SH	GW	Min
1993-94	Nipawin Hawks	SJHL	62	14	12	26	44																		
1994-95	Lethbridge	WHL	49	3	4	7	25																		
1995-96	Lethbridge	WHL	71	11	24	35	59										4	2	0	2	2				
1996-97	Lethbridge	WHL	62	19	38	57	125										19	7	13	20	51				
1997-98	Lethbridge	WHL	70	42	67	109	206										3	0	2	2	18				
	Kentucky	AHL	2	0	0	0	0																		
1998-99	Kentucky	AHL	78	18	21	39	101										12	2	7	9	16				
99-2000	Kentucky	AHL	79	21	45	66	153										9	0	5	5	22				
2000-01	**San Jose**	**NHL**	**42**	**2**	**2**	**4**	**51**	**0**	**0**	**0**	**39**	**5.1**	**2**	**308**	**52.9**	**8:48**									
	Kentucky	AHL	6	2	6	8	23																		
2001-02	**San Jose**	**NHL**	**49**	**3**	**3**	**6**	**72**	**0**	**0**	**1**	**40**	**7.5**	**–1**	**368**	**54.1**	**8:03**									
2002-03	**San Jose**	**NHL**	**75**	**4**	**11**	**15**	**64**	**0**	**0**	**0**	**68**	**5.9**	**1**	**632**	**57.0**	**9:21**									
2003-04	**San Jose**	**NHL**	**36**	**1**	**3**	**4**	**72**	**0**	**0**	**0**	**31**	**3.2**	**–5**	**207**	**50.2**	**8:22**	**10**	**1**	**0**	**1**	**11**	**0**	**0**	**1**	**7:44**
2004-05	Victoria	ECHL	20	6	9	15	41																		
2005-06	**San Jose**	**NHL**	**80**	**9**	**15**	**24**	**97**	**2**	**1**	**1**	**100**	**9.0**	**3**	**514**	**52.0**	**12:03**	**11**	**3**	**0**	**3**	**6**	**1**	**0**	**0**	**13:21**
	NHL Totals		**282**	**19**	**34**	**53**	**356**	**2**	**1**	**2**	**278**	**6.8**		**2029**	**53.9**	**9:41**	**21**	**4**	**0**	**4**	**17**	**1**	**0**	**1**	**10:40**

WHL East Second All-Star Team (1998)

• Spent majority of 2003-04 season as a healthy reserve. Signed as a free agent by **Victoria** (ECHL), January 21, 2005.

SMITH, Nathan
(SMIHTH, NAY-thun) **VAN.**

Center. Shoots left. 6'2", 192 lbs. Born, Edmonton, Alta., February 9, 1982. Vancouver's 1st choice, 23rd overall, in 2000 Entry Draft.

			Regular Season														Playoffs								
Season	Club	League	GP	G	A	Pts	PIM	PP	SH	GW	S	%	+/-	TF	F%	Min	GP	G	A	Pts	PIM	PP	SH	GW	Min
1997-98	Sherwood Park	AMHL	35	15	13	28	24																		
1998-99	Swift Current	WHL	47	5	8	13	26																		
99-2000	Swift Current	WHL	70	21	28	49	72										12	1	6	7	4				
2000-01	Swift Current	WHL	67	28	62	90	78										19	4	3	7	20				
2001-02	Swift Current	WHL	47	22	38	60	52										12	3	6	9	18				
2002-03	Manitoba Moose	AHL	53	9	8	17	30										14	1	3	4	25				
2003-04	**Vancouver**	**NHL**	**2**	**0**	**0**	**0**	**0**	**0**	**0**	**0**	**1**	**0.0**	**–1**	**12**	**33.3**	**5:16**									
	Manitoba Moose	AHL	76	4	16	20	71																		
2004-05	Manitoba Moose	AHL	72	7	9	16	67										14	2	4	6	20				
2005-06	**Vancouver**	**NHL**	**1**	**0**	**0**	**0**	**0**	**0**	**0**	**0**	**2**	**0.0**	**0**	**9**	**33.3**	**10:52**									
	Manitoba Moose	AHL	20	5	4	9	57																		
	NHL Totals		**3**	**0**	**0**	**0**	**0**	**0**	**0**	**0**	**3**	**0.0**		**21**	**33.3**	**7:08**									

• Missed remainder of 2005-06 season recovering from knee injury suffered in game vs. Cleveland (AHL), November 27, 2005.

SMITH, Wyatt
(SMIHTH, WIGH-uht) **MIN.**

Center. Shoots left. 5'11", 200 lbs. Born, Thief River Falls, MN, February 13, 1977. Phoenix's 6th choice, 233rd overall, in 1997 Entry Draft.

Season	Club	League	GP	G	A	Pts	PIM	PP	SH	GW	S	%	+/-	TF	F%	Min	GP	G	A	Pts	PIM	PP	SH	GW	Min
1994-95	Warroad Warriors	High-MN	28	29	31	60	28																		
1995-96	U. of Minnesota	WCHA	32	4	5	9	32																		
1996-97	U. of Minnesota	WCHA	38	16	14	30	44																		
1997-98	U. of Minnesota	WCHA	39	24	23	47	62																		
1998-99	U. of Minnesota	WCHA	43	23	20	43	37																		
99-2000	**Phoenix**	**NHL**	**2**	**0**	**0**	**0**	**0**	**0**	**0**	**0**	**0**	**0.0**	**–2**	**20**	**30.0**	**11:39**									
	Springfield	AHL	60	14	26	40	26										5	2	3	5	13				
2000-01	**Phoenix**	**NHL**	**42**	**3**	**7**	**10**	**13**	**0**	**1**	**0**	**40**	**7.5**	**7**	**335**	**40.9**	**12:20**									
	Springfield	AHL	18	5	7	12	11																		
2001-02	**Phoenix**	**NHL**	**10**	**0**	**0**	**0**	**0**	**0**	**0**	**0**	**4**	**0.0**	**–5**	**81**	**48.2**	**10:36**									
	Springfield	AHL	69	23	32	55	69																		
2002-03	**Nashville**	**NHL**	**11**	**1**	**0**	**1**	**0**	**0**	**0**	**0**	**8**	**12.5**	**–1**	**123**	**49.6**	**11:56**									
	Milwaukee	AHL	56	24	27	51	89										4	1	0	1	2				
2003-04	**Nashville**	**NHL**	**18**	**3**	**1**	**4**	**2**	**0**	**1**	**0**	**21**	**14.3**	**2**	**193**	**57.0**	**10:22**									
	Milwaukee	AHL	40	9	7	16	40										22	5	7	12	25				
2004-05	Milwaukee	AHL	69	19	28	47	89										7	1	4	5	10				
2005-06	**NY Islanders**	**NHL**	**42**	**0**	**8**	**8**	**26**	**0**	**0**	**0**	**37**	**0.0**	**–7**	**384**	**48.4**	**11:14**									
	Bridgeport	AHL	39	13	16	29	40																		
	NHL Totals		**125**	**7**	**16**	**23**	**41**	**0**	**2**	**0**	**110**	**6.4**		**1136**	**47.4**	**11:30**									

Signed as a free agent by **Nashville**, July 15, 2002. Signed as a free agent by **NY Islanders**, August 10, 2005. Signed as a free agent by **Minnesota**, July 19, 2006.

SMITHSON, Jerred
(SMIHTH-suhn, JEHR-rehd) **NSH.**

Center. Shoots right. 6'3", 194 lbs. Born, Vernon, B.C., February 4, 1979.

Season	Club	League	GP	G	A	Pts	PIM	PP	SH	GW	S	%	+/-	TF	F%	Min	GP	G	A	Pts	PIM	PP	SH	GW	Min
1994-95	Vernon	BCAHA	64	39	46	85	120																		
1995-96	Calgary Hitmen	WHL	60	4	2	6	16																		
1996-97	Calgary Hitmen	WHL	65	3	6	9	49																		
1997-98	Calgary Hitmen	WHL	65	12	9	21	65										18	0	2	2	25				
1998-99	Calgary Hitmen	WHL	63	14	22	36	108										21	3	7	10	17				
99-2000	Calgary Hitmen	WHL	66	14	25	39	111										10	1	1	2	16				
2000-01	Lowell	AHL	24	1	1	2	10										4	0	0	0	2				
	Trenton Titans	ECHL	3	0	1	1	2																		
2001-02	Manchester	AHL	78	5	13	18	45										5	0	1	1	4				
2002-03	**Los Angeles**	**NHL**	**22**	**0**	**2**	**2**	**21**	**0**	**0**	**0**	**9**	**0.0**	**–5**	**175**	**48.0**	**8:50**									
	Manchester	AHL	38	4	21	25	60										3	0	0	0	4				
2003-04	**Los Angeles**	**NHL**	**8**	**0**	**1**	**1**	**4**	**0**	**0**	**0**	**2**	**0.0**	**0**	**86**	**64.0**	**10:39**									
	Manchester	AHL	66	7	13	20	51										6	0	1	1	10				
2004-05	Milwaukee	AHL	80	11	11	22	92										5	0	0	0	4				
2005-06	**Nashville**	**NHL**	**66**	**5**	**9**	**14**	**54**	**0**	**0**	**1**	**50**	**10.0**	**9**	**613**	**54.3**	**11:50**	**3**	**0**	**0**	**0**	**4**	**0**	**0**	**0**	**9:26**
	Milwaukee	AHL	8	0	0	0	12																		
	NHL Totals		**96**	**5**	**12**	**17**	**79**	**0**	**0**	**1**	**61**	**8.2**		**874**	**54.0**	**11:03**	**3**	**0**	**0**	**0**	**4**	**0**	**0**	**0**	**9:26**

Signed as a free agent by **Los Angeles**, February 18, 2000. Signed as a free agent by **Nashville**, July 22, 2004.

SMOLINSKI, Bryan
(smoh-LIHN-skee, BRIGH-uhn) **CHI.**

Center. Shoots right. 6'1", 208 lbs. Born, Toledo, OH, December 27, 1971. Boston's 1st choice, 21st overall, in 1990 Entry Draft.

Season	Club	League	GP	G	A	Pts	PIM	PP	SH	GW	S	%	+/-	TF	F%	Min	GP	G	A	Pts	PIM	PP	SH	GW	Min
1987-88	Det. Caesars	MNHL	80	43	77	120																			
1988-89	Stratford Cullitons	OHA-B	46	32	62	94	132																		
1989-90	Michigan State	CCHA	35	9	13	22	34																		
1990-91	Michigan State	CCHA	35	9	12	21	24																		
1991-92	Michigan State	CCHA	41	28	33	61	55																		
1992-93	Michigan State	CCHA	40	31	37	*68	93																		
	Boston	**NHL**	**9**	**1**	**3**	**4**	**0**	**0**	**0**	**0**	**10**	**10.0**	**3**				**4**	**1**	**0**	**1**	**2**	**0**	**0**	**0**	
1993-94	**Boston**	**NHL**	**83**	**31**	**20**	**51**	**82**	**4**	**3**	**5**	**179**	**17.3**	**4**				**13**	**5**	**4**	**9**	**4**	**2**	**0**	**0**	
1994-95	**Boston**	**NHL**	**44**	**18**	**13**	**31**	**31**	**6**	**0**	**5**	**121**	**14.9**	**–3**				**5**	**0**	**1**	**1**	**4**	**0**	**0**	**0**	
1995-96	**Pittsburgh**	**NHL**	**81**	**24**	**40**	**64**	**69**	**8**	**2**	**1**	**229**	**10.5**	**6**				**18**	**5**	**4**	**9**	**10**	**0**	**0**	**1**	
1996-97	Detroit Vipers	IHL	6	5	7	12	10																		
	NY Islanders	**NHL**	**64**	**28**	**28**	**56**	**25**	**9**	**0**	**1**	**183**	**15.3**	**9**												
1997-98	**NY Islanders**	**NHL**	**81**	**13**	**30**	**43**	**34**	**3**	**0**	**4**	**203**	**6.4**	**–16**												
1998-99	**NY Islanders**	**NHL**	**82**	**16**	**24**	**40**	**49**	**7**	**0**	**3**	**223**	**7.2**	**–7**	**1011**	**48.3**	**19:19**									
99-2000	**Los Angeles**	**NHL**	**79**	**20**	**36**	**56**	**48**	**2**	**0**	**0**	**160**	**12.5**	**2**	**1545**	**50.9**	**18:35**	**4**	**0**	**0**	**0**	**2**	**0**	**0**	**0**	**18:22**
2000-01	**Los Angeles**	**NHL**	**78**	**27**	**32**	**59**	**40**	**5**	**3**	**5**	**183**	**14.8**	**10**	**952**	**48.7**	**18:32**	**13**	**1**	**5**	**6**	**14**	**0**	**0**	**0**	**20:35**
2001-02	**Los Angeles**	**NHL**	**80**	**13**	**25**	**38**	**56**	**4**	**1**	**0**	**187**	**7.0**	**7**	**1316**	**45.7**	**19:23**	**7**	**2**	**0**	**2**	**2**	**1**	**0**	**0**	**18:15**
2002-03	**Los Angeles**	**NHL**	**58**	**18**	**20**	**38**	**18**	**6**	**1**	**8**	**150**	**12.0**	**–1**	**831**	**46.9**	**19:02**									
	Ottawa	**NHL**	**10**	**3**	**5**	**8**	**2**	**0**	**0**	**0**	**26**	**11.5**	**1**	**127**	**46.5**	**15:42**	**18**	**2**	**7**	**9**	**6**	**0**	**0**	**0**	**15:21**
2003-04	**Ottawa**	**NHL**	**80**	**19**	**27**	**46**	**49**	**4**	**0**	**3**	**182**	**10.4**	**22**	**880**	**44.7**	**16:39**	**7**	**1**	**1**	**2**	**4**	**0**	**0**	**0**	**16:04**
2004-05	Motor City	UHL	21	9	23	32	18																		
2005-06	**Ottawa**	**NHL**	**81**	**17**	**31**	**48**	**46**	**4**	**0**	**5**	**178**	**9.6**	**8**	**1039**	**49.8**	**14:48**	**10**	**3**	**3**	**6**	**2**	**1**	**0**	**0**	**12:34**
	NHL Totals		**910**	**248**	**334**	**582**	**549**	**62**	**10**	**40**	**2214**	**11.2**		**7701**	**48.0**	**17:57**	**99**	**20**	**25**	**45**	**50**	**4**	**0**	**1**	**16:40**

CCHA First All-Star Team (1993) • NCAA West First All-American Team (1993)

Traded to **Pittsburgh** by **Boston** with Glen Murray and Boston's 3rd round choice (Boyd Kane) in 1996 Entry Draft for Kevin Stevens and Shawn McEachern, August 2, 1995. Traded to **NY Islanders** by **Pittsburgh** for Darius Kasparaitis and Andreas Johansson, November 17, 1996. Traded to **Los Angeles** by **NY Islanders** with Ziggy Palffy, Marcel Cousineau and New Jersey's 4th round choice (previously acquired, Los Angeles selected Daniel Johansson) in 1999 Entry Draft for Olli Jokinen, Josh Green, Mathieu Biron and Los Angeles' 1st round choice (Taylor Pyatt) in 1999 Entry Draft, June 20, 1999. Traded to **Ottawa** by **Los Angeles** for the rights to Tim Gleason and future considerations, March 11, 2003. Signed as a free agent by **Motor City** (UHL), February 11, 2005. Traded to **Chicago** by **Ottawa** with Martin Havlat for Tom Preissing, Josh Hennessy, Michal Barinka and a 2nd round choice in 2008 Entry Draft, July 10, 2006.

SMYTH, Brad
(SMIHTH, BRAD)

Right wing. Shoots right. 6', 200 lbs. Born, Ottawa, Ont., March 13, 1973.

Season	Club	League	GP	G	A	Pts	PIM	PP	SH	GW	S	%	+/-	TF	F%	Min	GP	G	A	Pts	PIM	PP	SH	GW	Min
1989-90	Nepean	OMHA	55	53	36	89	105																		
1990-91	London Knights	OHL	29	2	6	8	22																		
1991-92	London Knights	OHL	58	17	18	35	93										10	2	0	2	8				
1992-93	London Knights	OHL	66	54	55	109	118										12	7	8	15	25				
1993-94	Cincinnati	IHL	30	7	3	10	54																		
	Birmingham Bulls	ECHL	29	26	30	56	38										10	8	8	16	19				
1994-95	Springfield	AHL	3	0	0	0	7																		
	Birmingham Bulls	ECHL	36	33	35	68	52										3	5	2	7	0				
	Cincinnati	IHL	26	2	11	13	34										1	0	0	0	2				
1995-96	**Florida**	**NHL**	**7**	**1**	**1**	**2**	**4**	**1**	**0**	**0**	**12**	**8.3**	**–3**												
	Carolina Panthers	AHL	68	*68	58	*126	80																		

			Regular Season														Playoffs								
Season	Club	League	GP	G	A	Pts	PIM	PP	SH	GW	S	%	+/-	TF	F%	Min	GP	G	A	Pts	PIM	PP	SH	GW	Min
1996-97	**Florida**	**NHL**	**8**	**1**	**0**	**1**	**2**	**0**	**0**	**0**	**10**	**10.0**	**–3**												
	Los Angeles	**NHL**	**44**	**8**	**8**	**16**	**74**	**0**	**0**	**1**	**74**	**10.8**	**–7**												
	Phoenix	IHL	3	5	2	7	0																		
1997-98	**Los Angeles**	**NHL**	**9**	**1**	**3**	**4**	**4**	**0**	**0**	**0**	**12**	**8.3**	**–1**												
	NY Rangers	**NHL**	**1**	**0**	**0**	**0**	**0**	**0**	**0**	**0**	**1**	**0.0**	**0**												
	Hartford	AHL	57	29	33	62	79										15	12	8	20	11				
1998-99	**Nashville**	**NHL**	**3**	**0**	**0**	**0**	**6**	**0**	**0**	**0**	**5**	**0.0**	**–1**	**0**	**0.0**	**9:54**									
	Milwaukee	IHL	34	11	16	27	21																		
	Hartford	AHL	36	25	19	44	48										7	6	0	6	14				
99-2000	Hartford	AHL	80	39	37	76	62										23	*13	10	23	8				
2000-01	**NY Rangers**	**NHL**	**4**	**1**	**0**	**1**	**4**	**0**	**0**	**0**	**10**	**10.0**	**0**	**0**	**0.0**	**13:57**									
	Hartford	AHL	77	*50	29	79	110										5	2	3	5	8				
2001-02	Hartford	AHL	79	34	48	82	90										10	3	8	11	14				
2002-03	**Ottawa**	**NHL**	**12**	**3**	**1**	**4**	**15**	**2**	**0**	**0**	**16**	**18.8**	**–2**	**2**	**0.0**	**9:30**									
	Binghamton	AHL	69	24	32	56	77										14	7	6	13	12				
2003-04	Karpat Oulu	Finland	48	20	18	38	85										15	3	5	8	4				
2004-05	Manchester	AHL	61	23	33	56	74										6	2	1	3	4				
2005-06	Manchester	AHL	64	27	37	64	49																		
	Hartford	AHL	16	7	15	22	20										9	1	3	4	4				
	NHL Totals		**88**	**15**	**13**	**28**	**109**	**3**	**0**	**1**	**140**	**10.7**		**2**	**0.0**	**10:30**									

AHL First All-Star Team (1996, 2001, 2002) • John B. Sollenberger Trophy (Leading Scorer – AHL) (1996) • Les Cunningham Award (MVP – AHL) (1996)

Signed as a free agent by **Florida**, October 4, 1993. Traded to **Los Angeles** by **Florida** for Los Angeles' 3rd round choice (Vratislav Cech) in 1997 Entry Draft, November 28, 1996. Traded to **NY Rangers** by **Los Angeles** for future considerations, November 14, 1997. Signed as a free agent by **Nashville**, July 16, 1998. Traded to **NY Rangers** by **Nashville** for future considerations, May 3, 1999. Signed as a free agent by **Ottawa**, August 1, 2002. Signed as a free agent by **Oulu** (Finland), October 1, 2003. Signed as a free agent by **Los Angeles**, July 16, 2004.

SMYTH, Ryan

(SMIHTH, RIGH-uhn) **EDM.**

Left wing. Shoots left. 6'1", 190 lbs. Born, Banff, Alta., February 21, 1976. Edmonton's 2nd choice, 6th overall, in 1994 Entry Draft.

Season	Club	League	GP	G	A	Pts	PIM	PP	SH	GW	S	%	+/-	TF	F%	Min	GP	G	A	Pts	PIM	PP	SH	GW	Min
1990-91	Banff Blazers	ABHL	25	100	50	150																			
	Lethbridge	AMHL	34	8	21	29																			
1991-92	Caronport	SMHL	35	55	61	116	98																		
	Moose Jaw	WHL	2	0	0	0	0																		
1992-93	Moose Jaw	WHL	64	19	14	33	59																		
1993-94	Moose Jaw	WHL	72	50	55	105	88																		
1994-95	Moose Jaw	WHL	50	41	45	86	66										10	6	9	15	22				
	Edmonton	**NHL**	**3**	**0**	**0**	**0**	**0**	**0**	**0**	**0**	**2**	**0.0**	**–1**												
1995-96	**Edmonton**	**NHL**	**48**	**2**	**9**	**11**	**28**	**1**	**0**	**0**	**65**	**3.1**	**–10**												
	Cape Breton	AHL	9	6	5	11	4																		
1996-97	**Edmonton**	**NHL**	**82**	**39**	**22**	**61**	**76**	**20**	**0**	**4**	**265**	**14.7**	**–7**				**12**	**5**	**5**	**10**	**12**	**1**	**0**	**2**	
1997-98	**Edmonton**	**NHL**	**65**	**20**	**13**	**33**	**44**	**10**	**0**	**2**	**205**	**9.8**	**–24**				**12**	**1**	**3**	**4**	**16**	**1**	**0**	**0**	
1998-99	**Edmonton**	**NHL**	**71**	**13**	**18**	**31**	**62**	**6**	**0**	**2**	**161**	**8.1**	**0**	**5**	**20.0**	**14:26**	**3**	**3**	**0**	**3**	**0**	**2**	**0**	**0**	**24:35**
99-2000	**Edmonton**	**NHL**	**82**	**28**	**26**	**54**	**58**	**11**	**0**	**4**	**238**	**11.8**	**–2**	**24**	**54.2**	**19:12**	**5**	**1**	**0**	**1**	**6**	**0**	**1**	**0**	**19:18**
2000-01	**Edmonton**	**NHL**	**82**	**31**	**39**	**70**	**58**	**11**	**0**	**6**	**245**	**12.7**	**10**	**17**	**35.3**	**19:58**	**6**	**3**	**4**	**7**	**4**	**0**	**0**	**0**	**24:46**
2001-02	**Edmonton**	**NHL**	**61**	**15**	**35**	**50**	**48**	**7**	**1**	**5**	**150**	**10.0**	**7**	**12**	**41.7**	**19:27**									
	Canada	Olympics	6	0	1	1	0																		
2002-03	**Edmonton**	**NHL**	**66**	**27**	**34**	**61**	**67**	**10**	**0**	**3**	**199**	**13.6**	**5**	**42**	**42.9**	**19:21**	**6**	**2**	**0**	**2**	**16**	**0**	**1**	**0**	**17:39**
2003-04	**Edmonton**	**NHL**	**82**	**23**	**36**	**59**	**70**	**8**	**2**	**6**	**245**	**9.4**	**11**	**484**	**47.1**	**19:39**									
2004-05			DID NOT PLAY																						
2005-06	**Edmonton**	**NHL**	**75**	**36**	**30**	**66**	**58**	**19**	**2**	**3**	**230**	**15.7**	**–5**	**159**	**47.8**	**20:13**	**24**	**7**	**9**	**16**	**22**	**4**	**0**	**1**	**21:27**
	Canada	Olympics	6	0	1	1	4																		
	NHL Totals		**717**	**234**	**262**	**496**	**569**	**103**	**5**	**35**	**2005**	**11.7**		**743**	**46.7**	**18:56**	**68**	**22**	**21**	**43**	**76**	**8**	**2**	**3**	**21:21**

WHL East Second All-Star Team (1995)

SOMIK, Radovan

(SAW-mihk, RAH-doh-vahn)

Right wing. Shoots right. 6'2", 194 lbs. Born, Martin, Czech., May 5, 1977. Philadelphia's 3rd choice, 100th overall, in 1995 Entry Draft.

Season	Club	League	GP	G	A	Pts	PIM	PP	SH	GW	S	%	+/-	TF	F%	Min	GP	G	A	Pts	PIM	PP	SH	GW	Min
1993-94	Martin	Slovakia	1	0	0	0	0																		
1994-95	Martin	Slovakia	25	3	0	3	39										3	1	0	1	2				
1995-96	Martin	Slovakia	25	3	6	9	8										9	1	0	1					
1996-97	Martin	Slovakia	35	3	5	8											3	0	0	0					
1997-98	Martin	Slovakia	26	6	9	15	10										3	0	0	0	0				
1998-99	Dukla Trencin	Slovakia	26	1	4	5	6																		
99-2000	Martin	Slovak-2	40	38	28	66	32																		
2000-01	Zlin	CzRep	46	15	10	25	22										6	1	0	1	0				
2001-02	Zlin	CzRep	37	14	14	28	22										11	4	3	7	37				
2002-03	**Philadelphia**	**NHL**	**60**	**8**	**10**	**18**	**10**	**0**	**1**	**2**	**95**	**8.4**	**9**	**20**	**35.0**	**15:49**	**5**	**1**	**1**	**2**	**6**	**0**	**0**	**0**	**11:39**
2003-04	**Philadelphia**	**NHL**	**53**	**4**	**10**	**14**	**17**	**0**	**0**	**0**	**41**	**9.8**	**–2**	**32**	**59.4**	**11:01**	**10**	**1**	**1**	**2**	**4**	**0**	**0**	**0**	**8:08**
	Philadelphia	AHL	1	0	0	0	2																		
2004-05	MHC Martin	Slovak-2	2	1	0	1	0																		
	HC Vsetin	CzRep	31	7	16	23	24																		
	Malmo	Sweden	8	1	0	1	6																		
	Malmo	Sweden-Q	10	1	3	4	2																		
2005-06	Cherepovets	Russia	37	5	15	20	20										4	1	1	2	0				
	NHL Totals		**113**	**12**	**20**	**32**	**27**	**0**	**1**	**2**	**136**	**8.8**		**52**	**50.0**	**13:34**	**15**	**2**	**2**	**4**	**10**	**0**	**0**	**0**	**9:18**

Signed as a free agent by **Martin** (Slovak-2), October 2, 2004. Signed as a free agent by **Vsetin** (CzRep), October 7, 2004. Signed as a free agent by **Malmo** (Sweden), January 28, 2005. Signed as a free agent by **Cherepovets** (Russia), September 2, 2005.

SONNENBERG, Martin

(SOHN-nehn-BUHRG, MAHR-tihn)

Left wing. Shoots left. 6', 197 lbs. Born, Wetaskiwin, Alta., January 23, 1978.

Season	Club	League	GP	G	A	Pts	PIM	PP	SH	GW	S	%	+/-	TF	F%	Min	GP	G	A	Pts	PIM	PP	SH	GW	Min
1994-95	Leduc Oil Barons	AMHL	35	28	40	68	34																		
1995-96	Saskatoon Blades	WHL	58	8	7	15	24										3	0	0	0	2				
1996-97	Saskatoon Blades	WHL	72	38	26	64	79																		
1997-98	Saskatoon Blades	WHL	72	40	52	92	87										6	1	3	4	9				
1998-99	**Pittsburgh**	**NHL**	**44**	**1**	**1**	**2**	**19**	**0**	**0**	**0**	**12**	**8.3**	**–2**	**2**	**0.0**	**4:00**	**7**	**0**	**0**	**0**	**0**	**0**	**0**	**0**	**3:03**
	Syracuse Crunch	AHL	36	15	9	24	31																		
99-2000	**Pittsburgh**	**NHL**	**14**	**1**	**2**	**3**	**0**	**1**	**0**	**0**	**19**	**5.3**	**0**	**7**	**28.6**	**7:26**									
	Wilkes-Barre	AHL	62	20	33	53	109																		
2000-01	Wilkes-Barre	AHL	73	14	18	32	89										21	4	3	7	6				
2001-02	Wilkes-Barre	AHL	78	20	30	50	127																		
2002-03	Saint John Flames	AHL	54	11	10	21	63																		
2003-04	**Calgary**	**NHL**	**5**	**0**	**0**	**0**	**2**	**0**	**0**	**0**	**7**	**0.0**	**–2**	**5**	**80.0**	**8:51**									
	Lowell	AHL	48	20	22	42	46																		
2004-05	Utah Grizzlies	AHL	65	13	13	26	94																		
2005-06	San Antonio	AHL	41	10	7	17	34																		
	Hartford	AHL	29	4	10	14	16										13	3	3	6	8				
	NHL Totals		**63**	**2**	**3**	**5**	**21**	**1**	**0**	**0**	**38**	**5.3**		**14**	**42.9**	**5:09**	**7**	**0**	**0**	**0**	**0**	**0**	**0**	**0**	**3:03**

Signed as a free agent by **Pittsburgh**, October 9, 1998. Signed as a free agent by **Calgary**, July 9, 2002. Signed as a free agent by **Phoenix**, September 2, 2004. Traded to **NY Rangers** by **Phoenix** for Jeff Taffe, January 24, 2006. Signed as a free agent by **Kuopio** (Finland), July 18, 2006.

SOPEL, Brent

(SOH-puhl, BREHNT) **L.A.**

Defense. Shoots right. 6'1", 205 lbs. Born, Calgary, Alta., January 7, 1977. Vancouver's 6th choice, 144th overall, in 1995 Entry Draft.

Season	Club	League	GP	G	A	Pts	PIM	PP	SH	GW	S	%	+/-	TF	F%	Min	GP	G	A	Pts	PIM	PP	SH	GW	Min
1992-93	Sask. Legion	SMHL	36	7	17	24	95																		
1993-94	Saskatoon Blazers	SMHL	34	9	30	39	180																		
	Saskatoon Blades	WHL	11	2	2	4	2																		
1994-95	Saskatoon Blades	WHL	22	1	10	11	31																		
	Swift Current	WHL	41	4	19	23	50										3	0	3	3	0				
1995-96	Swift Current	WHL	71	13	48	61	87										6	1	2	3	4				
	Syracuse Crunch	AHL	1	0	0	0	0																		

Season	Club	League	GP	G	A	Pts	PIM	PP	SH	GW	S	%	+/-	TF	F%	Min	GP	G	A	Pts	PIM	PP	SH	GW	Min
								Regular Season									Playoffs								
1996-97	Swift Current	WHL	62	15	41	56	109										10	5	11	16	32				
	Syracuse Crunch	AHL	2	0	0	0	0										3	0	0	0	0				
1997-98	Syracuse Crunch	AHL	76	10	33	43	70										5	0	7	7	12				
1998-99	**Vancouver**	**NHL**	**5**	**1**	**0**	**1**	**4**	**1**	**0**	**0**	**5**	**20.0**	**–1**	**0**	**0.0**	**11:58**									
	Syracuse Crunch	AHL	53	10	21	31	59																		
99-2000	**Vancouver**	**NHL**	**18**	**2**	**4**	**6**	**12**	**0**	**0**	**1**	**11**	**18.2**	**9**	**0**	**0.0**	**10:31**									
	Syracuse Crunch	AHL	50	6	25	31	67										4	0	2	2	8				
2000-01	**Vancouver**	**NHL**	**52**	**4**	**10**	**14**	**10**	**0**	**0**	**1**	**57**	**7.0**	**4**	**0**	**0.0**	**16:01**	**4**	**0**	**0**	**0**	**2**	**0**	**0**	**0**	**19:05**
	Kansas City	IHL	4	0	1	1	0																		
2001-02	**Vancouver**	**NHL**	**66**	**8**	**17**	**25**	**44**	**1**	**0**	**3**	**116**	**6.9**	**21**	**0**	**0.0**	**19:01**	**6**	**0**	**2**	**2**	**2**	**0**	**0**	**0**	**24:45**
2002-03	**Vancouver**	**NHL**	**81**	**7**	**30**	**37**	**23**	**6**	**0**	**1**	**167**	**4.2**	**–15**	**0**	**0.0**	**21:42**	**14**	**2**	**6**	**8**	**4**	**1**	**0**	**1**	**22:33**
2003-04	**Vancouver**	**NHL**	**80**	**10**	**32**	**42**	**36**	**6**	**0**	**2**	**173**	**5.8**	**11**	**0**	**0.0**	**21:56**	**7**	**0**	**1**	**1**	**0**	**0**	**0**	**0**	**23:55**
2004-05			DID NOT PLAY																						
2005-06	**NY Islanders**	**NHL**	**57**	**2**	**25**	**27**	**64**	**2**	**0**	**0**	**121**	**1.7**	**–9**	**0**	**0.0**	**23:35**									
	Los Angeles	**NHL**	**11**	**0**	**1**	**1**	**6**	**0**	**0**	**0**	**12**	**0.0**	**–4**	**0**	**0.0**	**22:02**									
	NHL Totals		**370**	**34**	**119**	**153**	**199**	**16**	**0**	**8**	**662**	**5.1**		**0**	**0.0**	**20:06**	**31**	**2**	**9**	**11**	**8**	**1**	**0**	**1**	**22:50**

Traded to **NY Islanders** by **Vancouver** for NY Islanders' 2nd round choice (later traded to Anaheim - Anaheim selected Bryce Swan) in 2006 Entry Draft, August 3, 2005. Traded to **Los Angeles** by **NY Islanders** with Mark Parrish for Denis Grebeshkov and Jeff Tambellini, March 8, 2006.

SOURAY, Sheldon
(SUHR-ee, SHEHL-dohn) **MTL.**

Defense. Shoots left. 6'4", 226 lbs. Born, Elk Point, Alta., July 13, 1976. New Jersey's 3rd choice, 71st overall, in 1994 Entry Draft.

Season	Club	League	GP	G	A	Pts	PIM	PP	SH	GW	S	%	+/-	TF	F%	Min	GP	G	A	Pts	PIM	PP	SH	GW	Min
1990-91	Bonnyville Sabres	AAHA	30	15	20	35	100																		
1991-92	Quesnel	BCAHA	20	5	15	20	200																		
	Alberta Cycle	AMHL	11	0	5	5	67																		
1992-93	Ft. Saskatchewan	AJHL	35	0	12	12	125																		
	Tri-City	WHL	2	0	0	0	0																		
1993-94	Tri-City	WHL	42	3	6	9	122																		
1994-95	Tri-City	WHL	40	2	24	26	140																		
	Prince George	WHL	11	2	3	5	23																		
	Albany River Rats	AHL	7	0	2	2	8																		
1995-96	Prince George	WHL	32	9	18	27	91																		
	Kelowna Rockets	WHL	27	7	20	27	94										6	0	5	5	2				
	Albany River Rats	AHL	6	0	2	2	12										4	0	1	1	4				
1996-97	Albany River Rats	AHL	70	2	11	13	160										16	2	3	5	47				
1997-98	**New Jersey**	**NHL**	**60**	**3**	**7**	**10**	**85**	**0**	**0**	**1**	**74**	**4.1**	**18**				**3**	**0**	**1**	**1**	**2**	**0**	**0**	**0**	
	Albany River Rats	AHL	6	0	0	0	8																		
1998-99	**New Jersey**	**NHL**	**70**	**1**	**7**	**8**	**110**	**0**	**0**	**0**	**101**	**1.0**	**5**	**0**	**0.0**	**14:56**	**2**	**0**	**1**	**1**	**0**	**0**	**0**	**0**	**12:57**
99-2000	**New Jersey**	**NHL**	**52**	**0**	**8**	**8**	**70**	**0**	**0**	**0**	**74**	**0.0**	**–6**	**0**	**0.0**	**17:12**									
	Montreal	**NHL**	**19**	**3**	**0**	**3**	**44**	**0**	**0**	**0**	**39**	**7.7**	**7**	**0**	**0.0**	**19:18**									
2000-01	**Montreal**	**NHL**	**52**	**3**	**8**	**11**	**95**	**0**	**0**	**2**	**103**	**2.9**	**–11**	**0**	**0.0**	**20:36**									
2001-02	**Montreal**	**NHL**	**34**	**3**	**5**	**8**	**62**	**1**	**0**	**0**	**56**	**5.4**	**–5**	**1**	**100.0**	**18:11**	**12**	**0**	**1**	**1**	**16**	**0**	**0**	**0**	**19:01**
2002-03	**Montreal**	**NHL**	DID NOT PLAY – INJURED																						
2003-04	**Montreal**	**NHL**	**63**	**15**	**20**	**35**	**104**	**6**	**1**	**3**	**186**	**8.1**	**4**	**0**	**0.0**	**23:26**	**11**	**0**	**2**	**2**	**39**	**0**	**0**	**0**	**23:55**
2004-05	Farjestad	Sweden	39	9	8	17	117										15	1	6	7	77				
2005-06	**Montreal**	**NHL**	**75**	**12**	**27**	**39**	**116**	**7**	**1**	**0**	**202**	**5.9**	**–11**	**0**	**0.0**	**22:15**	**6**	**3**	**2**	**5**	**8**	**2**	**0**	**0**	**18:47**
	NHL Totals		**425**	**40**	**82**	**122**	**686**	**14**	**2**	**6**	**835**	**4.8**		**1**	**100.0**	**19:34**	**34**	**3**	**7**	**10**	**65**	**2**	**0**	**0**	**20:19**

WHL West Second All-Star Team (1996)

Played in NHL All-Star Game (2004)

Traded to **Montreal** by **New Jersey** with Josh DeWolf and New Jersey's 2nd round choice (later traded to Washington – later traded to Tampa Bay – Tampa Bay selected Andreas Holmqvist) in 2001 Entry Draft for Vladimir Malakhov, March 1, 2000. • Missed remainder of 2001-02 season and entire 2002-03 season recovering from wrist injury suffered in game vs. Tampa Bay, November 17, 2001. Signed as a free agent by **Farjestad** (Sweden), September 22, 2004.

SPACEK, Jaroslav
(SPAH-chehk, YA-roh-slahv) **BUF.**

Defense. Shoots left. 5'11", 206 lbs. Born, Rokycany, Czech., February 11, 1974. Florida's 5th choice, 117th overall, in 1998 Entry Draft.

Season	Club	League	GP	G	A	Pts	PIM	PP	SH	GW	S	%	+/-	TF	F%	Min	GP	G	A	Pts	PIM	PP	SH	GW	Min
1992-93	HC Skoda Plzen	Czech	16	1	3	4																			
1993-94	HC Skoda Plzen	CzRep	34	2	6	8																			
1994-95	Plzen	CzRep	38	4	8	12	14										3	1	0	1	2				
1995-96	HC ZKZ Plzen	CzRep	40	3	10	13	42										3	0	1	1	4				
1996-97	HC ZKZ Plzen	CzRep	52	9	29	38	44																		
1997-98	Farjestad	Sweden	45	10	16	26	63										12	2	5	7	14				
	Farjestad	EuroHL	6	2	3	5	2																		
1998-99	**Florida**	**NHL**	**63**	**3**	**12**	**15**	**28**	**2**	**1**	**0**	**92**	**3.3**	**15**	**1**	**100.0**	**19:27**									
	New Haven	AHL	14	4	8	12	15																		
99-2000	**Florida**	**NHL**	**82**	**10**	**26**	**36**	**53**	**4**	**0**	**1**	**111**	**9.0**	**7**	**1**	**0.0**	**22:40**	**4**	**0**	**0**	**0**	**0**	**0**	**0**	**0**	**20:29**
2000-01	**Florida**	**NHL**	**12**	**2**	**1**	**3**	**8**	**1**	**0**	**0**	**21**	**9.5**	**–4**	**0**	**0.0**	**19:12**									
	Chicago	**NHL**	**50**	**5**	**18**	**23**	**20**	**2**	**0**	**1**	**85**	**5.9**	**7**	**0**	**0.0**	**21:31**									
2001-02	**Chicago**	**NHL**	**60**	**3**	**10**	**13**	**29**	**0**	**0**	**1**	**64**	**4.7**	**5**	**0**	**0.0**	**16:25**									
	Czech Republic	Olympics	4	0	0	0	0																		
	Columbus	**NHL**	**14**	**2**	**3**	**5**	**24**	**1**	**1**	**1**	**29**	**6.9**	**–9**	**0**	**0.0**	**23:35**									
2002-03	**Columbus**	**NHL**	**81**	**9**	**36**	**45**	**70**	**5**	**0**	**1**	**166**	**5.4**	**–23**	**0**	**0.0**	**24:47**									
2003-04	**Columbus**	**NHL**	**58**	**5**	**17**	**22**	**45**	**2**	**1**	**2**	**108**	**4.6**	**–13**	**0**	**0.0**	**23:26**									
2004-05	Plzen	CzRep	30	3	8	11	26																		
	HC Slavia Praha	CzRep	17	4	9	13	29										7	0	2	2	8				
2005-06	**Chicago**	**NHL**	**45**	**7**	**17**	**24**	**72**	**1**	**0**	**0**	**80**	**8.8**	**8**	**0**	**0.0**	**23:00**									
	Edmonton	**NHL**	**31**	**5**	**14**	**19**	**24**	**3**	**0**	**0**	**70**	**7.1**	**3**	**0**	**0.0**	**24:37**	**24**	**3**	**11**	**14**	**24**	**2**	**0**	**0**	**25:53**
	NHL Totals		**496**	**51**	**154**	**205**	**373**	**21**	**3**	**7**	**826**	**6.2**		**2**	**50.0**	**21:55**	**28**	**3**	**11**	**14**	**24**	**2**	**0**	**0**	**25:07**

Traded to **Chicago** by **Florida** for Anders Eriksson, November 6, 2000. Traded to **Columbus** by **Chicago** with Chicago's 2nd round choice (Dan Fritsche) in 2003 Entry Draft for Lyle Odelein, March 19, 2002. Signed as a free agent by **Plzen** (CzRep), September 17, 2004. Signed as a free agent by **Slavia Praha** (CzRep), January 4, 2005. Signed as a free agent by **Chicago**, August 3, 2005. Traded to **Edmonton** by **Chicago** for Tony Salmelainen, January 26, 2006. Signed as a free agent by **Buffalo**, July 5, 2006.

SPANHEL, Martin
(SPAN-hehl, MAHR-tihn) **CBJ**

Left wing. Shoots left. 6'2", 206 lbs. Born, Gottwaldov/Zlin, Czech., July 1, 1977. Philadelphia's 6th choice, 152nd overall, in 1995 Entry Draft.

Season	Club	League	GP	G	A	Pts	PIM	PP	SH	GW	S	%	+/-	TF	F%	Min	GP	G	A	Pts	PIM	PP	SH	GW	Min
1994-95	AC ZPS Zlin Jr.	CzRep-Jr.	33	25	16	41	0																		
	AC ZPS Zlin	CzRep	1	0	0	0	0																		
1995-96	Lethbridge	WHL	6	1	0	1	0																		
	Moose Jaw	WHL	61	4	12	16	33																		
1996-97	AC ZPS Zlin	CzRep	22	3	6	9	20																		
1997-98	Zlin	CzRep	40	7	9	16	70																		
1998-99	Plzen	CzRep	49	12	12	24	60										5	2	1	3	27				
99-2000	Plzen	CzRep	52	21	27	48	86										7	1	4	5	12				
2000-01	**Columbus**	**NHL**	**6**	**1**	**0**	**1**	**2**	**0**	**0**	**0**	**8**	**12.5**	**–1**	**1**	**0.0**	**12:29**									
	Syracuse Crunch	AHL	67	11	13	24	75										2	0	0	0	8				
2001-02	**Columbus**	**NHL**	**4**	**1**	**0**	**1**	**2**	**0**	**0**	**0**	**6**	**16.7**	**–2**	**0**	**0.0**	**11:12**									
	Syracuse Crunch	AHL	50	7	12	19	43																		
2002-03	HC Sparta Praha	CzRep	40	5	5	10	46										8	1	0	1	6				
2003-04	HIFK Helsinki	Finland	36	2	11	13	22													0					
	Plzen	CzRep	14	1	2	3	20										12	2	2	4	10				
2004-05	Lillehammer IK	Norway	17	9	8	17	56										3	2	1	3	2				
2005-06	HC Sparta Praha	CzRep	51	2	8	10	40										14	0	0	0	12				
	NHL Totals		**10**	**2**	**0**	**2**	**4**	**0**	**0**	**0**	**14**	**14.3**		**1**	**0.0**	**11:58**									

Traded to **San Jose** by **Philadelphia** with Philadelphia's 1st round choice (later traded to Buffalo – later traded to Phoenix – Phoenix selected Daniel Briere) in 1996 Entry Draft and Philadelphia's 4th round choice (later traded to Buffalo – Buffalo selected Mike Martone) in 1996 Entry Draft for Pat Falloon, November 16, 1995. Traded to **Buffalo** by **San Jose** with Vaclav Varada and Philadelphia's 1st (previously acquired, later traded to Phoenix – Phoenix selected Daniel Briere) and 4th (previously acquired, Buffalo selected Mike Martone) round choices in 1996 Entry Draft for Doug Bodger, November 16, 1995. Signed as a free agent by **Columbus**, May 30, 2000. Signed as a free agent by **Sparta Praha** (CzRep) with Columbus retaining NHL rights, July 26, 2002. Signed as a free agent by **Lillehammer** (Norway), December 30, 2004. Signed as a free agent by **Sparta Praha** (Czech), September 6, 2005.

SPEZZA, Jason

(SPEHT-zuh, JAY-suhn) **OTT.**

Center. Shoots right. 6'2", 206 lbs. Born, Mississauga, Ont., June 13, 1983. Ottawa's 1st choice, 2nd overall, in 2001 Entry Draft.

Season	Club	League	GP	G	A	Pts	PIM	PP	SH	GW	S	%	+/-	TF	F%	Min	GP	G	A	Pts	PIM	PP	SH	GW	Min
			Regular Season														Playoffs								
1997-98	Toronto Marlies	MTHL	54	53	61	114	42	....	....	....	....	....	....	....	....	....	....	....	....	....	....	....	....	....	....
1998-99	Brampton	OHL	67	22	49	71	18	....	....	....	....	....	....	....	....	....	....	....	....	....	....	....	....	....	....
99-2000	Mississauga	OHL	52	24	37	61	33	....	....	....	....	....	....	....	....	....	....	....	....	....	....	....	....	....	....
2000-01	Mississauga	OHL	15	7	23	30	11	....	....	....	....	....	....	....	....	....	....	....	....	....	....	....	....	....	....
	Windsor Spitfires	OHL	41	36	50	86	32	....	....	....	....	....	....	....	....	....	9	4	5	9	10	....	....	....	....
2001-02	Windsor Spitfires	OHL	27	19	26	45	16	....	....	....	....	....	....	....	....	....	....	....	....	....	....	....	....	....	....
	Belleville Bulls	OHL	26	23	37	60	26	....	....	....	....	....	....	....	....	....	11	5	6	11	18	....	....	....	....
	Grand Rapids	AHL	....	....	....	....	....	....	....	....	....	....	....	....	....	....	3	1	0	1	2	....	....	....	....
2002-03	Binghamton	AHL	43	22	32	54	71	....	....	....	....	....	....	....	....	....	2	1	2	3	4	....	....	....	....
	Ottawa	**NHL**	**33**	**7**	**14**	**21**	**8**	**3**	**0**	**0**	**65**	**10.8**	**−3**	**330**	**45.8**	**12:40**	**3**	**1**	**1**	**2**	**0**	**1**	**0**	**0**	**11:34**
2003-04	**Ottawa**	**NHL**	**78**	**22**	**33**	**55**	**71**	**5**	**0**	**3**	**142**	**15.5**	**22**	**956**	**47.7**	**14:38**	**3**	**0**	**0**	**0**	**2**	**0**	**0**	**0**	**9:44**
2004-05	Binghamton	AHL	80	32	*85	*117	50	....	....	....	....	....	....	....	....	....	6	1	3	4	6	....	....	....	....
2005-06	**Ottawa**	**NHL**	**68**	**19**	**71**	**90**	**33**	**7**	**0**	**5**	**156**	**12.2**	**23**	**1220**	**52.6**	**19:00**	**10**	**5**	**9**	**14**	**2**	**3**	**0**	**1**	**17:59**
	Canada	Olympics	DID NOT PLAY																						
	NHL Totals		**179**	**48**	**118**	**166**	**112**	**15**	**0**	**8**	**363**	**13.2**		**2506**	**49.8**	**15:56**	**16**	**6**	**10**	**16**	**4**	**4**	**0**	**1**	**15:14**

OHL All-Rookie Team (1999) • AHL All-Rookie Team (2003) • AHL First All-Star Team (2005) • John P. Sollenberger Trophy (Top Scorer - AHL) (2005) • Les Cunningham Award (MVP – AHL) (2005)

SPILLER, Matthew

(SPIHL-uhr, MA-thew) **PHX.**

Defense. Shoots left. 6'5", 233 lbs. Born, Daysland, Alta., February 7, 1983. Phoenix's 2nd choice, 31st overall, in 2001 Entry Draft.

Season	Club	League	GP	G	A	Pts	PIM	PP	SH	GW	S	%	+/-	TF	F%	Min	GP	G	A	Pts	PIM	PP	SH	GW	Min
1998-99	East Central Chill	AMBHL	36	8	19	27	140	....	....	....	....	....	....	....	....	....	....	....	....	....	....	....	....	....	....
99-2000	Seattle	WHL	60	1	10	11	108	....	....	....	....	....	....	....	....	....	7	0	0	0	25	....	....	....	....
2000-01	Seattle	WHL	71	4	7	11	174	....	....	....	....	....	....	....	....	....	....	....	....	....	....	....	....	....	....
2001-02	Seattle	WHL	72	8	23	31	168	....	....	....	....	....	....	....	....	....	1	0	0	0	4	....	....	....	....
2002-03	Seattle	WHL	68	11	24	35	198	....	....	....	....	....	....	....	....	....	15	2	7	9	36	....	....	....	....
2003-04	**Phoenix**	**NHL**	**51**	**0**	**0**	**0**	**54**	**0**	**0**	**0**	**22**	**0.0**	**−11**	**0**	**0.0**	**10:42**	....	....	....	....	....	....	....	....	....
	Springfield	AHL	21	1	2	3	32	....	....	....	....	....	....	....	....	....	....	....	....	....	....	....	....	....	....
2004-05	Utah Grizzlies	AHL	79	4	7	11	160	....	....	....	....	....	....	....	....	....	....	....	....	....	....	....	....	....	....
2005-06	**Phoenix**	**NHL**	**8**	**0**	**1**	**1**	**13**	**0**	**0**	**0**	**3**	**0.0**	**−1**	**0**	**0.0**	**10:30**	....	....	....	....	....	....	....	....	....
	San Antonio	AHL	69	2	7	9	167	....	....	....	....	....	....	....	....	....	....	....	....	....	....	....	....	....	....
	NHL Totals		**59**	**0**	**1**	**1**	**67**	**0**	**0**	**0**	**25**	**0.0**		**0**	**0.0**	**10:40**	....	....	....	....	....	....	....	....	....

STAAL, Eric

(STAHL, AIR-ihk) **CAR.**

Center. Shoots left. 6'3", 200 lbs. Born, Thunder Bay, Ont., October 29, 1984. Carolina's 1st choice, 2nd overall, in 2003 Entry Draft.

Season	Club	League	GP	G	A	Pts	PIM	PP	SH	GW	S	%	+/-	TF	F%	Min	GP	G	A	Pts	PIM	PP	SH	GW	Min
99-2000	Thunder Bay	Exhib.	7	4	8	12	0	....	....	....	....	....	....	....	....	....	....	....	....	....	....	....	....	....	....
2000-01	Peterborough	OHL	63	19	30	49	23	....	....	....	....	....	....	....	....	....	7	2	5	7	4	....	....	....	....
2001-02	Peterborough	OHL	56	23	39	62	40	....	....	....	....	....	....	....	....	....	6	3	6	9	10	....	....	....	....
2002-03	Peterborough	OHL	66	39	59	98	36	....	....	....	....	....	....	....	....	....	7	9	5	14	6	....	....	....	....
2003-04	**Carolina**	**NHL**	**81**	**11**	**20**	**31**	**40**	**2**	**1**	**3**	**164**	**6.7**	**−6**	**669**	**43.1**	**16:40**	....	....	....	....	....	....	....	....	....
2004-05	Lowell	AHL	77	26	51	77	88	....	....	....	....	....	....	....	....	....	11	2	8	10	12	....	....	....	....
2005-06 ♦	**Carolina**	**NHL**	**82**	**45**	**55**	**100**	**81**	**19**	**4**	**4**	**279**	**16.1**	**−8**	**1309**	**42.6**	**19:39**	**25**	**9**	***19**	***28**	**8**	**7**	**0**	**1**	**19:48**
	NHL Totals		**163**	**56**	**75**	**131**	**121**	**21**	**5**	**7**	**443**	**12.6**		**1978**	**42.7**	**18:10**	**25**	**9**	**19**	**28**	**8**	**7**	**0**	**1**	**19:48**

OHL Second All-Star Team (2003) • Canadian Major Junior First All-Star Team (2003) • NHL Second All-Star Team (2006)

STAIOS, Steve

(STAY-uhs, STEEV) **EDM.**

Defense. Shoots right. 6'1", 200 lbs. Born, Hamilton, Ont., July 28, 1973. St. Louis' 1st choice, 27th overall, in 1991 Entry Draft.

Season	Club	League	GP	G	A	Pts	PIM	PP	SH	GW	S	%	+/-	TF	F%	Min	GP	G	A	Pts	PIM	PP	SH	GW	Min
1988-89	Hamilton Huskies	OMHA	58	13	39	52	78	....	....	....	....	....	....	....	....	....	....	....	....	....	....	....	....	....	....
1989-90	Hamilton Kilty B's	OHA-B	40	9	27	36	66	....	....	....	....	....	....	....	....	....	....	....	....	....	....	....	....	....	....
1990-91	Niagara Falls	OHL	66	17	29	46	115	....	....	....	....	....	....	....	....	....	12	2	3	5	10	....	....	....	....
1991-92	Niagara Falls	OHL	65	11	42	53	122	....	....	....	....	....	....	....	....	....	17	7	8	15	27	....	....	....	....
1992-93	Niagara Falls	OHL	12	4	14	18	30	....	....	....	....	....	....	....	....	....	....	....	....	....	....	....	....	....	....
	Sudbury Wolves	OHL	53	13	44	57	67	....	....	....	....	....	....	....	....	....	11	5	6	11	22	....	....	....	....
1993-94	Peoria Rivermen	IHL	38	3	9	12	42	....	....	....	....	....	....	....	....	....	....	....	....	....	....	....	....	....	....
1994-95	Peoria Rivermen	IHL	60	3	13	16	64	....	....	....	....	....	....	....	....	....	6	0	0	0	10	....	....	....	....
1995-96	Peoria Rivermen	IHL	6	0	1	1	14	....	....	....	....	....	....	....	....	....	....	....	....	....	....	....	....	....	....
	Worcester IceCats	AHL	57	1	11	12	114	....	....	....	....	....	....	....	....	....	....	....	....	....	....	....	....	....	....
	Boston	**NHL**	**12**	**0**	**0**	**0**	**4**	**0**	**0**	**0**	**4**	**0.0**	**−5**	....	....	....	**3**	**0**	**0**	**0**	**0**	**0**	**0**	**0**	....
	Providence Bruins	AHL	7	1	4	5	8	....	....	....	....	....	....	....	....	....	....	....	....	....	....	....	....	....	....
1996-97	**Boston**	**NHL**	**54**	**3**	**8**	**11**	**71**	**0**	**0**	**0**	**56**	**5.4**	**−26**	....	....	....	....	....	....	....	....	....	....	....	....
	Vancouver	**NHL**	**9**	**0**	**6**	**6**	**20**	**0**	**0**	**0**	**10**	**0.0**	**2**	....	....	....	....	....	....	....	....	....	....	....	....
1997-98	**Vancouver**	**NHL**	**77**	**3**	**4**	**7**	**134**	**0**	**0**	**1**	**45**	**6.7**	**−3**	....	....	....	....	....	....	....	....	....	....	....	....
1998-99	**Vancouver**	**NHL**	**57**	**0**	**2**	**2**	**54**	**0**	**0**	**0**	**33**	**0.0**	**−12**	**4**	**25.0**	**6:53**	....	....	....	....	....	....	....	....	....
99-2000	**Atlanta**	**NHL**	**27**	**2**	**3**	**5**	**66**	**0**	**0**	**0**	**38**	**5.3**	**−5**	**2**	**50.0**	**13:01**	....	....	....	....	....	....	....	....	....
2000-01	**Atlanta**	**NHL**	**70**	**9**	**13**	**22**	**137**	**4**	**0**	**0**	**156**	**5.8**	**−23**	**1**	**0.0**	**21:45**	....	....	....	....	....	....	....	....	....
2001-02	**Edmonton**	**NHL**	**73**	**5**	**5**	**10**	**108**	**0**	**0**	**1**	**101**	**5.0**	**10**	**0**	**0.0**	**18:05**	....	....	....	....	....	....	....	....	....
2002-03	**Edmonton**	**NHL**	**76**	**5**	**21**	**26**	**96**	**1**	**3**	**0**	**126**	**4.0**	**13**	**1**	**0.0**	**22:17**	**6**	**0**	**0**	**0**	**4**	**0**	**0**	**0**	**23:27**
2003-04	**Edmonton**	**NHL**	**82**	**6**	**22**	**28**	**86**	**1**	**0**	**1**	**153**	**3.9**	**17**	**0**	**0.0**	**23:03**	....	....	....	....	....	....	....	....	....
2004-05	Lulea HF	Sweden	7	2	1	3	12	....	....	....	....	....	....	....	....	....	....	....	....	....	....	....	....	....	....
2005-06	**Edmonton**	**NHL**	**82**	**8**	**20**	**28**	**84**	**1**	**0**	**1**	**140**	**5.7**	**10**	**0**	**0.0**	**20:53**	**24**	**1**	**5**	**6**	**28**	**1**	**0**	**0**	**21:31**
	NHL Totals		**619**	**41**	**104**	**145**	**860**	**7**	**3**	**4**	**862**	**4.8**		**8**	**25.0**	**19:01**	**33**	**1**	**5**	**6**	**32**	**1**	**0**	**0**	**21:54**

Traded to **Boston** by **St. Louis** with Kevin Sawyer for Steve Leach, March 8, 1996. Claimed on waivers by **Vancouver** from **Boston**, March 18, 1997. Claimed by **Atlanta** from **Vancouver** in Expansion Draft, June 25, 1999. • Missed majority of 1999-2000 season recovering from knee injury suffered in game vs. Colorado, October 23, 1999. Traded to **New Jersey** by **Atlanta** for New Jersey's 9th round choice (Simon Gamache) in 2000 Entry Draft, June 12, 2000. Traded to **Atlanta** by **New Jersey** for future considerations, July 10, 2000. Signed as a free agent by **Edmonton**, July 12, 2001. Signed as a free agent by **Lulea** (Sweden), January 28, 2005.

STAJAN, Matt

(STAY-juhn, MAHT) **TOR.**

Center. Shoots left. 6'1", 180 lbs. Born, Mississauga, Ont., December 19, 1983. Toronto's 2nd choice, 57th overall, in 2002 Entry Draft.

Season	Club	League	GP	G	A	Pts	PIM	PP	SH	GW	S	%	+/-	TF	F%	Min	GP	G	A	Pts	PIM	PP	SH	GW	Min
99-2000	Miss. Senators	GTHL	STATISTICS NOT AVAILABLE																						
2000-01	Belleville Bulls	OHL	57	9	18	27	27	....	....	....	....	....	....	....	....	....	7	1	6	7	5	....	....	....	....
2001-02	Belleville Bulls	OHL	68	33	52	85	50	....	....	....	....	....	....	....	....	....	11	3	8	11	14	....	....	....	....
2002-03	Belleville Bulls	OHL	57	34	60	94	75	....	....	....	....	....	....	....	....	....	7	5	8	13	16	....	....	....	....
	St. John's	AHL	1	0	1	1	0	....	....	....	....	....	....	....	....	....	....	....	....	....	....	....	....	....	....
	Toronto	**NHL**	**1**	**1**	**0**	**1**	**0**	**0**	**0**	**0**	**1**	**100.0**	**1**	**12**	**33.3**	**11:00**	....	....	....	....	....	....	....	....	....
2003-04	**Toronto**	**NHL**	**69**	**14**	**13**	**27**	**22**	**0**	**0**	**0**	**63**	**22.2**	**7**	**450**	**38.9**	**11:00**	**3**	**0**	**0**	**0**	**2**	**0**	**0**	**0**	**11:13**
2004-05	St. John's	AHL	80	23	43	66	43	....	....	....	....	....	....	....	....	....	5	2	2	4	6	....	....	....	....
2005-06	**Toronto**	**NHL**	**80**	**15**	**12**	**27**	**50**	**3**	**4**	**5**	**83**	**18.1**	**5**	**373**	**44.5**	**11:38**	....	....	....	....	....	....	....	....	....
	NHL Totals		**150**	**30**	**25**	**55**	**72**	**3**	**4**	**5**	**147**	**20.4**		**835**	**41.3**	**11:20**	**3**	**0**	**0**	**0**	**2**	**0**	**0**	**0**	**11:13**

• Scored a goal in his first NHL game (April 5, 2003 vs. Ottawa).

STASTNY, Yan

(STAS-nee, YAHN) **BOS.**

Center. Shoots left. 5'11", 175 lbs. Born, Quebec City, Que., September 30, 1982. Boston's 6th choice, 259th overall, in 2002 Entry Draft.

Season	Club	League	GP	G	A	Pts	PIM	PP	SH	GW	S	%	+/-	TF	F%	Min	GP	G	A	Pts	PIM	PP	SH	GW	Min
99-2000	St. Louis Sting	NAHL	45	12	23	35	77	....	....	....	....	....	....	....	....	....	....	....	....	....	....	....	....	....	....
2000-01	St. Louis Jr. Blues	CSJHL	6	0	2	2	23	....	....	....	....	....	....	....	....	....	....	....	....	....	....	....	....	....	....
	Omaha Lancers	USHL	44	17	14	31	101	....	....	....	....	....	....	....	....	....	11	6	6	12	12	....	....	....	....
2001-02	U. of Notre Dame	CCHA	33	6	11	17	38	....	....	....	....	....	....	....	....	....	....	....	....	....	....	....	....	....	....
2002-03	U. of Notre Dame	CCHA	39	14	9	23	44	....	....	....	....	....	....	....	....	....	....	....	....	....	....	....	....	....	....
2003-04	Nurnberg	Germany	44	9	20	29	83	....	....	....	....	....	....	....	....	....	6	0	1	1	6	....	....	....	....
2004-05	Nurnberg	Germany	51	24	30	54	60	....	....	....	....	....	....	....	....	....	6	2	1	3	8	....	....	....	....

			Regular Season														Playoffs								
Season	Club	League	GP	G	A	Pts	PIM	PP	SH	GW	S	%	+/-	TF	F%	Min	GP	G	A	Pts	PIM	PP	SH	GW	Min
2005-06	**Edmonton**	**NHL**	**3**	**0**	**0**	**0**	**0**	**0**	**0**	**0**	**1**	**0.0**	**–2**	**17**	**41.2**	**6:53**	....	....	....	....	....	....	....	....	....
	Iowa Stars	AHL	51	14	17	31	42	....	....	....	....	....	....	....	....	....	....	....	....	....	....	....	....	....	....
	Boston	**NHL**	**17**	**1**	**3**	**4**	**10**	**0**	**0**	**0**	**13**	**7.7**	**–2**	**122**	**42.6**	**10:16**	....	....	....	....	....	....	....	....	....
	Providence Bruins	AHL	....	....	....	....	....	....	....	....	....	....	....	....	....	....	6	0	5	5	12	....	....	....	....
	NHL Totals		**20**	**1**	**3**	**4**	**10**	**0**	**0**	**0**	**14**	**7.1**		**139**	**42.4**	**9:46**	....	....	....	....	....	....	....	....	....

Signed as a free agent by **Nurnberg** (Germany), September 18, 2003. Traded to **Edmonton** by **Boston** for Boston's 4th round choice (previously acquired) in 2006 Entry Draft, August 30, 2005. Traded to **Boston** by **Edmonton** with Marty Reasoner and Edmonton's 2nd round choice (Milan Lucic) in 2006 Entry Draft for Sergei Samsonov, March 9, 2006.

STECKEL, Dave

(STEH-kuhl, DAYV) **WSH.**

Center. Shoots left. 6'5", 215 lbs. Born, Westbend, WI, March 15, 1982. Los Angeles' 2nd choice, 30th overall, in 2001 Entry Draft.

Season	Club	League	GP	G	A	Pts	PIM	PP	SH	GW	S	%	+/-	TF	F%	Min	GP	G	A	Pts	PIM	PP	SH	GW	Min
1998-99	USNTDP	USHL	2	0	0	0	2	....	....	....	....	....	....	....	....	....	....	....	....	....	....	....	....	....	....
	USNTDP	NAHL	51	3	14	17	18	....	....	....	....	....	....	....	....	....	....	....	....	....	....	....	....	....	....
99-2000	USNTDP	U-18	6	2	5	7	14	....	....	....	....	....	....	....	....	....	....	....	....	....	....	....	....	....	....
	USNTDP	USHL	52	13	13	26	94	....	....	....	....	....	....	....	....	....	....	....	....	....	....	....	....	....	....
2000-01	Ohio State	CCHA	33	17	18	35	80	....	....	....	....	....	....	....	....	....	....	....	....	....	....	....	....	....	....
2001-02	Ohio State	CCHA	36	6	16	22	75	....	....	....	....	....	....	....	....	....	....	....	....	....	....	....	....	....	....
2002-03	Ohio State	CCHA	36	10	8	18	50	....	....	....	....	....	....	....	....	....	....	....	....	....	....	....	....	....	....
2003-04	Ohio State	CCHA	41	17	13	30	44	....	....	....	....	....	....	....	....	....	....	....	....	....	....	....	....	....	....
2004-05	Manchester	AHL	63	10	7	17	26	....	....	....	....	....	....	....	....	....	6	1	1	2	4	....	....	....	....
2005-06	**Washington**	**NHL**	**7**	**0**	**0**	**0**	**0**	**0**	**0**	**0**	**6**	**0.0**	**1**	**48**	**35.4**	**7:39**	....	....	....	....	....	....	....	....	....
	Hershey Bears	AHL	74	14	20	34	58	....	....	....	....	....	....	....	....	....	21	10	5	15	20	....	....	....	....
	NHL Totals		**7**	**0**	**0**	**0**	**0**	**0**	**0**	**0**	**6**	**0.0**		**48**	**35.4**	**7:39**	....	....	....	....	....	....	....	....	....

CCHA All-Rookie Team (2001)

Signed as a free agent by **Washington**, August 25, 2005.

STEEN, Alex

(STEEN, al-EHX) **TOR.**

Center. Shoots left. 6'1", 205 lbs. Born, Winnipeg, Man., March 1, 1984. Toronto's 1st choice, 24th overall, in 2002 Entry Draft.

Season	Club	League	GP	G	A	Pts	PIM	PP	SH	GW	S	%	+/-	TF	F%	Min	GP	G	A	Pts	PIM	PP	SH	GW	Min
99-2000	V.Frolunda Jr.	Swe-Jr.	8	5	7	12	0	....	....	....	....	....	....	....	....	....	....	....	....	....	....	....	....	....	....
	V.Frolunda U18	Swe-U18	14	3	5	8	16	....	....	....	....	....	....	....	....	....	....	....	....	....	....	....	....	....	....
2000-01	V.Frolunda Jr.	Swe-Jr.	23	11	12	23	15	....	....	....	....	....	....	....	....	....	3	1	0	1	2	....	....	....	....
	V.Frolunda U18	Swe-U18	6	3	3	6	9	....	....	....	....	....	....	....	....	....	....	....	....	....	....	....	....	....	....
2001-02	V.Frolunda Jr.	Swe-Jr.	23	21	17	38	47	....	....	....	....	....	....	....	....	....	2	1	1	2	2	....	....	....	....
	V.Frolunda	Sweden	26	0	3	3	14	....	....	....	....	....	....	....	....	....	10	1	2	3	0	....	....	....	....
2002-03	V.Frolunda	Sweden	45	5	10	15	18	....	....	....	....	....	....	....	....	....	16	2	3	5	4	....	....	....	....
	V.Frolunda Jr.	Swe-Jr.	2	0	2	2	0	....	....	....	....	....	....	....	....	....	....	....	....	....	....	....	....	....	....
2003-04	V.Frolunda	Sweden	48	10	14	24	50	....	....	....	....	....	....	....	....	....	10	4	6	10	14	....	....	....	....
2004-05	MODO	Sweden	50	9	8	17	26	....	....	....	....	....	....	....	....	....	6	1	0	1	4	....	....	....	....
2005-06	**Toronto**	**NHL**	**75**	**18**	**27**	**45**	**42**	**9**	**1**	**3**	**176**	**10.2**	**–9**	**29**	**24.1**	**17:37**	....	....	....	....	....	....	....	....	....
	NHL Totals		**75**	**18**	**27**	**45**	**42**	**9**	**1**	**3**	**176**	**10.2**		**29**	**24.1**	**17:37**	....	....	....	....	....	....	....	....	....

STEFAN, Patrik

(SHTEH-fan, PAT-rihk) **DAL.**

Center. Shoots left. 6'2", 210 lbs. Born, Pribram, Czech., September 16, 1980. Atlanta's 1st choice, 1st overall, in 1999 Entry Draft.

Season	Club	League	GP	G	A	Pts	PIM	PP	SH	GW	S	%	+/-	TF	F%	Min	GP	G	A	Pts	PIM	PP	SH	GW	Min
1996-97	HC Sparta Praha	CzRep	5	0	1	1	2	....	....	....	....	....	....	....	....	....	7	1	0	1	0	....	....	....	....
1997-98	HC Sparta Praha	CzRep	27	2	6	8	16	....	....	....	....	....	....	....	....	....	....	....	....	....	....	....	....	....	....
	Long Beach	IHL	25	5	10	15	10	....	....	....	....	....	....	....	....	....	10	1	1	2	2	....	....	....	....
1998-99	Long Beach	IHL	33	11	24	35	26	....	....	....	....	....	....	....	....	....	....	....	....	....	....	....	....	....	....
99-2000	**Atlanta**	**NHL**	**72**	**5**	**20**	**25**	**30**	**1**	**0**	**0**	**117**	**4.3**	**–20**	**988**	**41.4**	**14:49**	....	....	....	....	....	....	....	....	....
2000-01	**Atlanta**	**NHL**	**66**	**10**	**21**	**31**	**22**	**0**	**0**	**1**	**93**	**10.8**	**–3**	**834**	**42.9**	**14:07**	....	....	....	....	....	....	....	....	....
2001-02	**Atlanta**	**NHL**	**59**	**7**	**16**	**23**	**22**	**0**	**1**	**0**	**67**	**10.4**	**–4**	**628**	**41.9**	**15:58**	....	....	....	....	....	....	....	....	....
	Chicago Wolves	AHL	5	3	0	3	0	....	....	....	....	....	....	....	....	....	....	....	....	....	....	....	....	....	....
2002-03	**Atlanta**	**NHL**	**71**	**13**	**21**	**34**	**12**	**3**	**0**	**2**	**96**	**13.5**	**–10**	**1125**	**45.7**	**16:50**	....	....	....	....	....	....	....	....	....
2003-04	**Atlanta**	**NHL**	**82**	**14**	**26**	**40**	**26**	**3**	**2**	**2**	**110**	**12.7**	**–7**	**1446**	**45.6**	**16:29**	....	....	....	....	....	....	....	....	....
2004-05	Ilves Tampere	Finland	37	13	28	41	47	....	....	....	....	....	....	....	....	....	7	1	6	7	4	....	....	....	....
2005-06	**Atlanta**	**NHL**	**64**	**10**	**14**	**24**	**36**	**2**	**0**	**3**	**81**	**12.3**	**3**	**820**	**46.3**	**13:50**	....	....	....	....	....	....	....	....	....
	NHL Totals		**414**	**59**	**118**	**177**	**148**	**9**	**3**	**8**	**564**	**10.5**		**5841**	**44.2**	**15:23**	....	....	....	....	....	....	....	....	....

Signed as a free agent by **Ilves Tampere** (Finland), October 23, 2004. Traded to **Dallas** by **Atlanta** with Jaroslav Modry for Niko Kapanen and Dallas' 7th round choice (Will O'Neill) in 2006 Entry Draft, June 24, 2006.

STEMPNIAK, Lee

(STEHMP-nee-ak, LEE) **ST.L.**

Right wing. Shoots right. 6', 190 lbs. Born, Buffalo, NY, February 4, 1983. St. Louis' 7th choice, 148th overall, in 2003 Entry Draft.

Season	Club	League	GP	G	A	Pts	PIM	PP	SH	GW	S	%	+/-	TF	F%	Min	GP	G	A	Pts	PIM	PP	SH	GW	Min
2000-01	Buffalo Lightning	OPJHL	48	34	51	86	36	....	....	....	....	....	....	....	....	....	....	....	....	....	....	....	....	....	....
2001-02	Dartmouth	ECAC	32	12	9	21	8	....	....	....	....	....	....	....	....	....	....	....	....	....	....	....	....	....	....
2002-03	Dartmouth	ECAC	34	21	28	49	32	....	....	....	....	....	....	....	....	....	....	....	....	....	....	....	....	....	....
2003-04	Dartmouth	ECAC	34	16	22	38	42	....	....	....	....	....	....	....	....	....	....	....	....	....	....	....	....	....	....
2004-05	Dartmouth	ECACHL	35	14	*29	43	34	....	....	....	....	....	....	....	....	....	....	....	....	....	....	....	....	....	....
2005-06	**St. Louis**	**NHL**	**57**	**14**	**13**	**27**	**22**	**5**	**0**	**2**	**100**	**14.0**	**–10**	**7**	**42.9**	**14:22**	....	....	....	....	....	....	....	....	....
	Peoria Rivermen	AHL	26	8	7	15	32	....	....	....	....	....	....	....	....	....	3	0	3	3	2	....	....	....	....
	NHL Totals		**57**	**14**	**13**	**27**	**22**	**5**	**0**	**2**	**100**	**14.0**		**7**	**42.9**	**14:22**	....	....	....	....	....	....	....	....	....

ECAC All-Rookie Team (2002) • ECAC First All-Star Team (2004, 2005) • NCAA East First All-American Team (2004) • NCAA East Second All-American Team (2005)

STEPHENS, Charlie

(STEE-vuhns, CHAHR-lee)

Center/Right wing. Shoots right. 6'3", 220 lbs. Born, London, Ont., April 5, 1981. Colorado's 9th choice, 196th overall, in 2001 Entry Draft.

Season	Club	League	GP	G	A	Pts	PIM	PP	SH	GW	S	%	+/-	TF	F%	Min	GP	G	A	Pts	PIM	PP	SH	GW	Min
1995-96	Elgin-Middlesex	MHAO	60	25	29	54	60	....	....	....	....	....	....	....	....	....	....	....	....	....	....	....	....	....	....
1996-97	Leamington Flyers	OHA-B	50	26	36	62	103	....	....	....	....	....	....	....	....	....	....	....	....	....	....	....	....	....	....
1997-98	St. Michael's	OHL	58	9	21	30	38	....	....	....	....	....	....	....	....	....	....	....	....	....	....	....	....	....	....
1998-99	St. Michael's	OHL	7	2	4	6	8	....	....	....	....	....	....	....	....	....	....	....	....	....	....	....	....	....	....
	Guelph Storm	OHL	61	24	28	52	72	....	....	....	....	....	....	....	....	....	11	3	5	8	19	....	....	....	....
99-2000	Guelph Storm	OHL	56	16	34	50	87	....	....	....	....	....	....	....	....	....	6	1	3	4	15	....	....	....	....
2000-01	Guelph Storm	OHL	67	38	38	76	53	....	....	....	....	....	....	....	....	....	4	0	2	2	2	....	....	....	....
2001-02	Guelph Storm	OHL	4	1	2	3	2	....	....	....	....	....	....	....	....	....	....	....	....	....	....	....	....	....	....
	London Knights	OHL	56	23	33	56	55	....	....	....	....	....	....	....	....	....	12	6	10	16	18	....	....	....	....
	Hershey Bears	AHL	....	....	....	....	....	....	....	....	....	....	....	....	....	....	1	0	0	0	0	....	....	....	....
2002-03	**Colorado**	**NHL**	**2**	**0**	**0**	**0**	**0**	**0**	**0**	**0**	**1**	**0.0**	**0**	**0**	**0.0**	**5:20**	....	....	....	....	....	....	....	....	....
	Hershey Bears	AHL	74	17	33	50	38	....	....	....	....	....	....	....	....	....	5	1	1	2	2	....	....	....	....
2003-04	**Colorado**	**NHL**	**6**	**0**	**2**	**2**	**4**	**0**	**0**	**0**	**1**	**0.0**	**–1**	**22**	**45.5**	**6:12**	....	....	....	....	....	....	....	....	....
	Hershey Bears	AHL	32	5	9	14	21	....	....	....	....	....	....	....	....	....	....	....	....	....	....	....	....	....	....
	Quad City	UHL	7	0	1	1	0	....	....	....	....	....	....	....	....	....	....	....	....	....	....	....	....	....	....
	Binghamton	AHL	37	15	17	32	43	....	....	....	....	....	....	....	....	....	2	0	0	0	0	....	....	....	....
2004-05	Binghamton	AHL	80	7	21	28	64	....	....	....	....	....	....	....	....	....	6	3	0	3	19	....	....	....	....
2005-06	Binghamton	AHL	80	23	44	67	72	....	....	....	....	....	....	....	....	....	....	....	....	....	....	....	....	....	....
	NHL Totals		**8**	**0**	**2**	**2**	**4**	**0**	**0**	**0**	**2**	**0.0**		**22**	**45.5**	**5:59**	....	....	....	....	....	....	....	....	....

• Re-entered NHL Entry Draft. Originally Washington's 3rd choice, 31st overall, in 1999 Entry Draft.

Traded to **Ottawa** by **Colorado** for Dennis Bonvie, January 23, 2004. Signed as a free agent by **Dusseldorf** (Germany), July 12, 2006.

STEVENSON, Grant

(STEE-vehn-suhn, GRANT) **S.J.**

Center. Shoots right. 5'11", 170 lbs. Born, Spruce Grove, Alta., October 15, 1981.

Season	Club	League	GP	G	A	Pts	PIM	PP	SH	GW	S	%	+/-	TF	F%	Min	GP	G	A	Pts	PIM	PP	SH	GW	Min
1998-99	Spruce Grove	RAMHL	26	15	32	47	90	....	....	....	....	....	....	....	....	....	8	10	10	20	30	....	....	....	....
99-2000	Bonnyville	AJHL	63	20	38	58	....	....	....	....	....	....	....	....	....	....	....	....	....	....	....	....	....	....	....
2000-01	Grand Prairie	AJHL	53	24	49	73	62	....	....	....	....	....	....	....	....	....	15	7	2	9	38	....	....	....	....
2001-02	Minnesota State	WCHA	38	8	8	16	36	....	....	....	....	....	....	....	....	....	....	....	....	....	....	....	....	....	....
2002-03	Minnesota State	WCHA	38	27	36	63	38	....	....	....	....	....	....	....	....	....	....	....	....	....	....	....	....	....	....
2003-04	Cleveland Barons	AHL	71	13	26	39	45	....	....	....	....	....	....	....	....	....	9	0	7	7	6	....	....	....	....

Season	Club	League	GP	G	A	Pts	PIM	PP	SH	GW	S	%	+/-	TF	F%	Min	GP	G	A	Pts	PIM	PP	SH	GW	Min
											Regular Season									**Playoffs**				
2004-05	Cleveland Barons	AHL	77	14	25	39	70	....	....	....	....	....	....												
	Johnstown Chiefs	ECHL	2	1	0	1	2	....	....	....	....	....	....												
2005-06	**San Jose**	**NHL**	47	10	12	22	14	5	0	2	67	14.9	–7	6	33.3	11:57	5	0	0	0	4	0	0	0	6:59
	Cleveland Barons	AHL	17	8	8	16	8	....	....	....	....	....	....												
	NHL Totals		47	10	12	22	14	5	0	2	67	14.9		6	33.3	11:57	5	0	0	0	4	0	0	0	6:59

WCHA First All-Star Team (2003) • NCAA West Second All-American Team (2003)
Signed as a free agent by **San Jose**, April 18, 2003.

STEVENSON, Jeremy
(STEE-vehn-suhn, JAIR-eh-mee)

Left wing. Shoots left. 6'1", 215 lbs. Born, San Bernardino, CA, July 28, 1974. Anaheim's 10th choice, 262nd overall, in 1994 Entry Draft.

Season	Club	League	GP	G	A	Pts	PIM	PP	SH	GW	S	%	+/-	TF	F%	Min	GP	G	A	Pts	PIM	PP	SH	GW	Min
1989-90	Elliot Lake Vikings	NOHA	61	39	26	65	203	....	....	....	....	....	....												
1990-91	Cornwall Royals	OHL	58	13	20	33	124	....	....	....	....	....	....												
1991-92	Cornwall Royals	OHL	63	15	23	38	176	....	....	....	....	....	....				6	3	1	4	4				
1992-93	Newmarket	OHL	54	28	28	56	144	....	....	....	....	....	....				5	5	1	6	28				
1993-94	Newmarket	OHL	9	2	4	6	27	....	....	....	....	....	....												
	Sault Ste. Marie	OHL	48	18	19	37	183	....	....	....	....	....	....				14	1	1	2	23				
1994-95	Greensboro	ECHL	43	14	13	27	231	....	....	....	....	....	....				17	6	11	17	64				
1995-96	**Anaheim**	**NHL**	3	0	1	1	12	0	0	0	1	0.0	1												
	Baltimore Bandits	AHL	60	11	10	21	295	....	....	....	....	....	....				12	4	2	6	23				
1996-97	**Anaheim**	**NHL**	5	0	0	0	14	0	0	0	1	0.0	–1												
	Baltimore Bandits	AHL	25	8	8	16	125	....	....	....	....	....	....				3	0	0	0	8				
1997-98	**Anaheim**	**NHL**	45	3	5	8	101	0	0	1	43	7.0	–4												
	Cincinnati	AHL	10	5	0	5	34	....	....	....	....	....	....												
1998-99	Cincinnati	AHL	22	4	4	8	83	....	....	....	....	....	....				3	1	0	1	2				
99-2000	**Anaheim**	**NHL**	3	0	0	0	7	0	0	0	2	0.0	–1	0	0.0	6:50									
	Cincinnati	AHL	41	11	14	25	100	....	....	....	....	....	....				5	2	0	2	12				
2000-01	Milwaukee	IHL	60	16	13	29	262	....	....	....	....	....	....												
	Nashville	**NHL**	8	1	0	1	39	0	0	0	6	16.7	–1	0	0.0	6:24									
2001-02	**Nashville**	**NHL**	4	0	0	0	9	0	0	0	0	0.0	0	0	0.0	5:53									
	Milwaukee	AHL	53	12	7	19	192	....	....	....	....	....	....												
2002-03	**Minnesota**	**NHL**	32	5	6	11	69	1	0	1	29	17.2	6	0	0.0	10:48	14	0	5	5	12	0	0	0	12:32
	Houston Aeros	AHL	18	6	7	13	77	....	....	....	....	....	....												
2003-04	**Minnesota**	**NHL**	3	0	0	0	2	0	0	0	5	0.0	–1	0	0.0	11:24									
	Nashville	**NHL**	53	5	4	9	103	3	0	0	62	8.1	–2	4	50.0	10:03	6	0	0	0	8	0	0	0	6:43
2004-05	South Carolina	ECHL	42	9	20	29	140	....	....	....	....	....	....				3	1	0	1	2				
2005-06	**Nashville**	**NHL**	35	4	3	7	74	0	0	0	36	11.1	0	9	0.0	7:24									
	Milwaukee	AHL	3	0	0	0	9	....	....	....	....	....	....												
	Dallas	**NHL**	16	1	0	1	21	0	0	0	12	8.3	–3	0	0.0	6:54	1	0	0	0	0	0	0	0	3:46
	NHL Totals		207	19	19	38	451	4	0	2	197	9.6		13	15.4	8:56	21	0	5	5	20	0	0	0	10:28

• Re-entered NHL Entry Draft. Originally Winnipeg's 3rd choice, 60th overall, in 1992 Entry Draft.

Signed as a free agent by **Nashville**, September 25, 2000. Signed as a free agent by **Minnesota**, November 26, 2002. Claimed on waivers by **Nashville** from **Minnesota**, October 22, 2003. Signed as a free agent by **South Carolina** (ECHL), November 30, 2004. Claimed on waivers by **Dallas** from **Nashville**, February 15, 2006.

STEVENSON, Turner
(STEE-vehn-suhn, TUHR-nuhr)

Right wing. Shoots right. 6'3", 220 lbs. Born, Prince George, B.C., May 18, 1972. Montreal's 1st choice, 12th overall, in 1990 Entry Draft.

Season	Club	League	GP	G	A	Pts	PIM	PP	SH	GW	S	%	+/-	TF	F%	Min	GP	G	A	Pts	PIM	PP	SH	GW	Min
1987-88	Prince George	BCAHA	53	45	46	91	127	....	....	....	....	....	....												
1988-89	Seattle	WHL	69	15	12	27	84	....	....	....	....	....	....												
1989-90	Seattle	WHL	62	29	32	61	276	....	....	....	....	....	....				13	3	2	5	35				
1990-91	Seattle	WHL	57	36	27	63	222	....	....	....	....	....	....				6	1	5	6	15				
	Fredericton	AHL	....	....	....	....	....	....	....	....	....	....	....				4	0	1	1	4				
1991-92	Seattle	WHL	58	20	32	52	264	....	....	....	....	....	....				15	9	3	12	55				
1992-93	**Montreal**	**NHL**	1	0	0	0	0	0	0	0	1	0.0	–1												
	Fredericton	AHL	79	25	34	59	102	....	....	....	....	....	....				5	2	3	5	11				
1993-94	**Montreal**	**NHL**	2	0	0	0	2	0	0	0	0	0.0	–2				3	0	2	2	6	0	0	0	
	Fredericton	AHL	66	19	28	47	155	....	....	....	....	....	....												
1994-95	**Montreal**	**NHL**	41	6	1	7	86	0	0	1	35	17.1	0												
1995-96	**Montreal**	**NHL**	80	9	16	25	167	0	0	2	101	8.9	–2				6	0	1	1	2	0	0	0	
1996-97	**Montreal**	**NHL**	65	8	13	21	97	1	0	0	76	10.5	–14				5	1	1	2	2	0	0	0	
1997-98	**Montreal**	**NHL**	63	4	6	10	110	1	0	0	43	9.3	–8				10	3	4	7	12	0	0	0	
1998-99	**Montreal**	**NHL**	69	10	17	27	88	0	0	2	102	9.8	6	29	37.9	12:57									
99-2000	**Montreal**	**NHL**	64	8	13	21	61	0	0	2	94	8.5	–1	5	20.0	13:10									
2000-01	**New Jersey**	**NHL**	69	8	18	26	97	2	0	1	92	8.7	11	0	0.0	11:00	23	1	3	4	20	0	0	1	9:27
2001-02	**New Jersey**	**NHL**	21	0	2	2	25	0	0	0	33	0.0	–3	0	0.0	11:38	1	0	0	0	4	0	0	0	10:13
2002-03 ♦	**New Jersey**	**NHL**	77	7	13	20	115	0	0	0	85	8.2	7	12	41.7	11:53	14	1	1	2	26	0	0	0	13:01
2003-04	**New Jersey**	**NHL**	61	14	13	27	76	4	0	2	76	18.4	0	5	60.0	12:42	5	0	0	0	0	0	0	0	13:29
2004-05					DID NOT PLAY																				
2005-06	**Philadelphia**	**NHL**	31	1	3	4	45	0	1	0	26	3.8	–2	9	11.1	8:20									
	NHL Totals		644	75	115	190	969	8	1	10	764	9.8		60	35.0	11:58	67	6	12	18	66	0	0	1	11:06

Claimed by **Columbus** from **Montreal** in Expansion Draft, June 23, 2000. Traded to **New Jersey** by **Columbus** to complete transaction that sent Krzysztof Oliwa (June 12, 2000) and Deron Quint (June 23, 2000) to **Columbus**, June 23, 2000. • Missed majority of 2001-02 season recovering from knee injury suffered in game vs. Vancouver, December 29, 2001. Signed as a free agent by **Philadelphia**, July 3, 2004. • Missed majority of 2005-06 season recovering from hip injury.

STEWART, Anthony
(STEW-ahrt, AN-toh-nee)   **FLA.**

Center. Shoots right. 6'1", 225 lbs. Born, LaSalle, Que., January 5, 1985. Florida's 2nd choice, 25th overall, in 2003 Entry Draft.

Season	Club	League	GP	G	A	Pts	PIM	PP	SH	GW	S	%	+/-	TF	F%	Min	GP	G	A	Pts	PIM	PP	SH	GW	Min
2000-01	North York	MTHL	34	30	70	100		....	....	....	....	....	....												
	St. Mike's B's	OPJHL	5	0	2	2	0	....	....	....	....	....	....												
2001-02	Kingston	OHL	65	19	24	43	12	....	....	....	....	....	....				1	0	0	0	0				
2002-03	Kingston	OHL	68	32	38	70	47	....	....	....	....	....	....												
2003-04	Kingston	OHL	53	35	23	58	76	....	....	....	....	....	....				5	3	4	7	7				
2004-05	Kingston	OHL	62	32	35	67	70	....	....	....	....	....	....												
	San Antonio	AHL	10	1	2	3	14	....	....	....	....	....	....												
2005-06	**Florida**	**NHL**	10	2	1	3	2	1	0	0	16	12.5	2	1	0.0	7:13									
	Rochester	AHL	4	2	3	5	0	....	....	....	....	....	....												
	NHL Totals		10	2	1	3	2	1	0	0	16	12.5		1	0.0	7:13									

• Missed remainder of 2005-06 season recovering from wrist injury suffered in game vs. Carolina, November 11, 2005.

STEWART, Karl
(STEW-ahrt, KARL)   **ATL.**

Left wing. Shoots left. 5'10", 180 lbs. Born, Aurora, Ont., June 30, 1983.

Season	Club	League	GP	G	A	Pts	PIM	PP	SH	GW	S	%	+/-	TF	F%	Min	GP	G	A	Pts	PIM	PP	SH	GW	Min
99-2000	Thornhill Rattlers	OPJHL	49	15	19	34	61	....	....	....	....	....	....												
2000-01	Plymouth Whalers	OHL	68	9	14	23	87	....	....	....	....	....	....				19	3	4	7	14				
2001-02	Plymouth Whalers	OHL	65	20	23	43	104	....	....	....	....	....	....				6	0	2	2	21				
2002-03	Plymouth Whalers	OHL	68	35	50	85	120	....	....	....	....	....	....				17	7	10	17	31				
2003-04	**Atlanta**	**NHL**	5	0	1	1	4	0	0	0	2	0.0	0	10	10.0	4:27									
	Chicago Wolves	AHL	72	10	32	42	186	....	....	....	....	....	....				10	2	3	5	29				
2004-05	Chicago Wolves	AHL	77	16	8	24	226	....	....	....	....	....	....				12	4	2	6	32				
2005-06	**Atlanta**	**NHL**	8	0	0	0	15	0	0	0	6	0.0	–3	3	100.0	5:40									
	Chicago Wolves	AHL	71	22	18	40	184	....	....	....	....	....	....												
	NHL Totals		13	0	1	1	19	0	0	0	8	0.0		13	30.8	5:12									

Signed as a free agent by **Atlanta**, September 28, 2001.

STILLMAN, Cory

(STIHL-mahn, KOHR-ee) **CAR.**

Left wing. Shoots left. 6', 194 lbs. Born, Peterborough, Ont., December 20, 1973. Calgary's 1st choice, 6th overall, in 1992 Entry Draft.

Season	Club	League	GP	G	A	Pts	PIM	PP	SH	GW	S	%	+/-	TF	F%	Min	GP	G	A	Pts	PIM	PP	SH	GW	Min
			Regular Season														Playoffs								
1989-90	Peterborough	OHA-B	41	30	*54	84	76	....	....	....	....	....	....	....	....	....	....	....	....	....	....	....	....	....	....
1990-91	Windsor Spitfires	OHL	64	31	70	101	31	....	....	....	....	....	....	....	....	....	11	3	6	9	8	....	....	....	....
1991-92	Windsor Spitfires	OHL	53	29	61	90	59	....	....	....	....	....	....	....	....	....	7	2	4	6	8	....	....	....	....
1992-93	Peterborough	OHL	61	25	55	80	55	....	....	....	....	....	....	....	....	....	18	3	8	11	18	....	....	....	....
1993-94	Saint John Flames	AHL	79	35	48	83	52	....	....	....	....	....	....	....	....	....	7	2	4	6	16	....	....	....	....
1994-95	Saint John Flames	AHL	63	28	53	81	70	....	....	....	....	....	....	....	....	....	5	0	2	2	2	....	....	....	....
	Calgary	**NHL**	**10**	**0**	**2**	**2**	**2**	**0**	**0**	**0**	**7**	**0.0**	**1**	....	....	....	....	....	....	....	....	....	....	....	....
1995-96	**Calgary**	**NHL**	**74**	**16**	**19**	**35**	**41**	**4**	**1**	**3**	**132**	**12.1**	**-5**	....	....	....	**2**	**1**	**1**	**2**	**0**	**0**	**0**	**0**	....
1996-97	**Calgary**	**NHL**	**58**	**6**	**20**	**26**	**14**	**2**	**0**	**0**	**112**	**5.4**	**-6**	....	....	....	....	....	....	....	....	....	....	....	....
1997-98	**Calgary**	**NHL**	**72**	**27**	**22**	**49**	**40**	**9**	**4**	**1**	**178**	**15.2**	**-9**	....	....	....	....	....	....	....	....	....	....	....	....
1998-99	**Calgary**	**NHL**	**76**	**27**	**30**	**57**	**38**	**9**	**3**	**5**	**175**	**15.4**	**7**	**535**	**46.5**	**16:19**	....	....	....	....	....	....	....	....	....
99-2000	**Calgary**	**NHL**	**37**	**12**	**9**	**21**	**12**	**6**	**0**	**3**	**59**	**20.3**	**-9**	**283**	**54.4**	**17:45**	....	....	....	....	....	....	....	....	....
2000-01	**Calgary**	**NHL**	**66**	**21**	**24**	**45**	**45**	**7**	**0**	**4**	**148**	**14.2**	**-6**	**346**	**43.9**	**18:50**	....	....	....	....	....	....	....	....	....
	St. Louis	**NHL**	**12**	**3**	**4**	**7**	**6**	**3**	**0**	**0**	**26**	**11.5**	**-2**	**36**	**61.1**	**18:37**	**15**	**3**	**5**	**8**	**8**	**1**	**0**	**1**	**14:58**
2001-02	**St. Louis**	**NHL**	**80**	**23**	**22**	**45**	**36**	**6**	**0**	**4**	**140**	**16.4**	**8**	**196**	**46.4**	**15:03**	**9**	**0**	**2**	**2**	**2**	**0**	**0**	**0**	**12:46**
2002-03	**St. Louis**	**NHL**	**79**	**24**	**43**	**67**	**56**	**6**	**0**	**4**	**157**	**15.3**	**12**	**266**	**41.7**	**18:20**	**6**	**2**	**2**	**4**	**2**	**2**	**0**	**1**	**18:05**
2003-04	**Tampa Bay**	**NHL**	**81**	**25**	**55**	**80**	**36**	**11**	**1**	**6**	**178**	**14.0**	**18**	**38**	**31.6**	**19:32**	**21**	**2**	**5**	**7**	**15**	**0**	**1**	**0**	**17:22**
2004-05			DID NOT PLAY																						
2005-06♦	**Carolina**	**NHL**	**72**	**21**	**55**	**76**	**32**	**10**	**0**	**3**	**177**	**11.9**	**-9**	**11**	**27.3**	**18:40**	**25**	**9**	**17**	**26**	**14**	**4**	**0**	**3**	**18:42**
	NHL Totals		**717**	**205**	**305**	**510**	**358**	**73**	**9**	**33**	**1489**	**13.8**		**1711**	**46.4**	**17:47**	**78**	**17**	**32**	**49**	**41**	**7**	**1**	**5**	**85:21**

OHL Rookie of the Year (1991)

• Missed majority of 1999-2000 season recovering from shoulder injury suffered in game vs. Philadelphia, December 27, 1999. Traded to **St. Louis by Calgary** for Craig Conroy and St. Louis' 7th round choice (David Moss) in 2001 Entry Draft, March 13, 2001. Traded to **Tampa Bay** by **St. Louis** for Tampa Bay's 2nd round choice (David Backes) in 2003 Entry Draft, June 21, 2003. Signed as a free agent by **Carolina**, August 2, 2005.

STOLL, Jarret

(STOHL, JEHR-eht) **EDM.**

Center. Shoots right. 6'1", 201 lbs. Born, Melville, Sask., June 25, 1982. Edmonton's 3rd choice, 36th overall, in 2002 Entry Draft.

Season	Club	League	GP	G	A	Pts	PIM	PP	SH	GW	S	%	+/-	TF	F%	Min	GP	G	A	Pts	PIM	PP	SH	GW	Min
1997-98	Saskatoon Blazers	SMHL	44	45	44	*89	78	....	....	....	....	....	....	....	....	....	....	....	....	....	....	....	....	....	....
	Edmonton Ice	WHL	8	2	3	5	4	....	....	....	....	....	....	....	....	....	....	....	....	....	....	....	....	....	....
1998-99	Kootenay Ice	WHL	57	13	21	34	38	....	....	....	....	....	....	....	....	....	4	0	0	0	2	....	....	....	....
99-2000	Kootenay Ice	WHL	71	37	38	75	64	....	....	....	....	....	....	....	....	....	20	7	9	16	24	....	....	....	....
2000-01	Kootenay Ice	WHL	62	40	66	106	105	....	....	....	....	....	....	....	....	....	11	5	9	14	22	....	....	....	....
2001-02	Kootenay Ice	WHL	47	32	34	66	64	....	....	....	....	....	....	....	....	....	22	6	14	20	35	....	....	....	....
2002-03	**Edmonton**	**NHL**	**4**	**0**	**1**	**1**	**0**	**0**	**0**	**0**	**5**	**0.0**	**-3**	**30**	**63.3**	**7:44**	....	....	....	....	....	....	....	....	....
	Hamilton	AHL	76	21	33	54	86	....	....	....	....	....	....	....	....	....	23	5	8	13	25	....	....	....	....
2003-04	**Edmonton**	**NHL**	**68**	**10**	**11**	**21**	**42**	**1**	**1**	**2**	**107**	**9.3**	**8**	**1019**	**54.1**	**13:54**	....	....	....	....	....	....	....	....	....
2004-05	Edmonton	AHL	66	21	17	38	92	....	....	....	....	....	....	....	....	....	....	....	....	....	....	....	....	....	....
2005-06	**Edmonton**	**NHL**	**82**	**22**	**46**	**68**	**74**	**11**	**1**	**4**	**243**	**9.1**	**4**	**1348**	**56.8**	**18:23**	**24**	**4**	**6**	**10**	**24**	**2**	**0**	**1**	**17:06**
	NHL Totals		**154**	**32**	**58**	**90**	**116**	**12**	**2**	**6**	**355**	**9.0**		**2397**	**55.7**	**16:07**	**24**	**4**	**6**	**10**	**24**	**2**	**0**	**1**	**17:06**

• Re-entered NHL Entry Draft. Originally Calgary's 3rd choice, 46th overall, in 2000 Entry Draft.

WHL East First All-Star Team (2001) • Canadian Major Junior First All-Star Team (2001) • WHL West First All-Star Team (2002)

STRAKA, Martin

(STRAH-kuh, MAHR-tihn) **NYR**

Center. Shoots left. 5'9", 178 lbs. Born, Plzen, Czech., September 3, 1972. Pittsburgh's 1st choice, 19th overall, in 1992 Entry Draft.

Season	Club	League	GP	G	A	Pts	PIM	PP	SH	GW	S	%	+/-	TF	F%	Min	GP	G	A	Pts	PIM	PP	SH	GW	Min
1989-90	Skoda Plzen	Czech	1	0	3	3		....	....	....	....	....	....	....	....	....	....	....	....	....	....	....	....	....	....
1990-91	HC Skoda Plzen	Czech	47	7	24	31	6	....	....	....	....	....	....	....	....	....	....	....	....	....	....	....	....	....	....
1991-92	HC Skoda Plzen	Czech	50	27	28	55	20	....	....	....	....	....	....	....	....	....	....	....	....	....	....	....	....	....	....
1992-93	**Pittsburgh**	**NHL**	**42**	**3**	**13**	**16**	**29**	**0**	**0**	**1**	**28**	**10.7**	**2**	....	....	....	**11**	**2**	**1**	**3**	**2**	**0**	**0**	**0**	....
	Cleveland	IHL	4	4	3	7	0	....	....	....	....	....	....	....	....	....	....	....	....	....	....	....	....	....	....
1993-94	**Pittsburgh**	**NHL**	**84**	**30**	**34**	**64**	**24**	**2**	**0**	**6**	**130**	**23.1**	**24**	....	....	....	**6**	**1**	**0**	**1**	**2**	**0**	**0**	**0**	....
1994-95	Plzen	CzRep	19	10	11	21	18	....	....	....	....	....	....	....	....	....	....	....	....	....	....	....	....	....	....
	Pittsburgh	**NHL**	**31**	**4**	**12**	**16**	**16**	**0**	**0**	**0**	**36**	**11.1**	**0**	....	....	....	....	....	....	....	....	....	....	....	....
	Ottawa	**NHL**	**6**	**1**	**1**	**2**	**0**	**0**	**0**	**0**	**13**	**7.7**	**-1**	....	....	....	....	....	....	....	....	....	....	....	....
1995-96	**Ottawa**	**NHL**	**43**	**9**	**16**	**25**	**29**	**5**	**0**	**1**	**63**	**14.3**	**-14**	....	....	....	....	....	....	....	....	....	....	....	....
	NY Islanders	**NHL**	**22**	**2**	**10**	**12**	**6**	**0**	**0**	**0**	**18**	**11.1**	**-6**	....	....	....	....	....	....	....	....	....	....	....	....
	Florida	**NHL**	**12**	**2**	**4**	**6**	**6**	**1**	**0**	**0**	**17**	**11.8**	**1**	....	....	....	**13**	**2**	**2**	**4**	**2**	**0**	**0**	**0**	....
1996-97	**Florida**	**NHL**	**55**	**7**	**22**	**29**	**12**	**2**	**0**	**1**	**94**	**7.4**	**9**	....	....	....	**4**	**0**	**0**	**0**	**0**	**0**	**0**	**0**	....
1997-98	**Pittsburgh**	**NHL**	**75**	**19**	**23**	**42**	**28**	**4**	**3**	**4**	**117**	**16.2**	**-1**	....	....	....	**6**	**2**	**0**	**2**	**2**	**0**	**1**	**0**	....
	Czech Republic	Olympics	6	1	2	3	0	....	....	....	....	....	....	....	....	....	....	....	....	....	....	....	....	....	....
1998-99	**Pittsburgh**	**NHL**	**80**	**35**	**48**	**83**	**26**	**5**	**4**	**4**	**177**	**19.8**	**12**	**845**	**43.6**	**23:35**	**13**	**6**	**9**	**15**	**6**	**1**	**0**	**0**	**25:00**
99-2000	**Pittsburgh**	**NHL**	**71**	**20**	**39**	**59**	**26**	**3**	**1**	**2**	**146**	**13.7**	**24**	**651**	**42.9**	**23:58**	**11**	**3**	**9**	**12**	**10**	**1**	**0**	**0**	**24:27**
2000-01	**Pittsburgh**	**NHL**	**82**	**27**	**68**	**95**	**38**	**7**	**1**	**4**	**185**	**14.6**	**19**	**331**	**43.2**	**23:01**	**18**	**5**	**8**	**13**	**8**	**3**	**0**	**2**	**21:24**
2001-02	**Pittsburgh**	**NHL**	**13**	**5**	**4**	**9**	**0**	**1**	**0**	**1**	**33**	**15.2**	**3**	**5**	**60.0**	**18:00**	....	....	....	....	....	....	....	....	....
2002-03	**Pittsburgh**	**NHL**	**60**	**18**	**28**	**46**	**12**	**7**	**0**	**4**	**136**	**13.2**	**-18**	**115**	**45.2**	**20:37**	....	....	....	....	....	....	....	....	....
2003-04	**Pittsburgh**	**NHL**	**22**	**4**	**8**	**12**	**16**	**1**	**0**	**0**	**34**	**11.8**	**-16**	**121**	**38.8**	**21:32**	....	....	....	....	....	....	....	....	....
	Los Angeles	**NHL**	**32**	**6**	**8**	**14**	**4**	**1**	**1**	**0**	**34**	**17.6**	**-9**	**66**	**48.5**	**16:47**	....	....	....	....	....	....	....	....	....
2004-05	Plzen	CzRep	45	16	18	34	76	....	....	....	....	....	....	....	....	....	....	....	....	....	....	....	....	....	....
2005-06	**NY Rangers**	**NHL**	**82**	**22**	**54**	**76**	**42**	**4**	**0**	**4**	**171**	**12.9**	**17**	**237**	**39.7**	**19:09**	**4**	**0**	**0**	**0**	**2**	**0**	**0**	**0**	**20:30**
	Czech Republic	Olympics	8	2	6	8	6	....	....	....	....	....	....	....	....	....	....	....	....	....	....	....	....	....	....
	NHL Totals		**812**	**214**	**392**	**606**	**314**	**43**	**10**	**32**	**1432**	**14.9**		**2371**	**42.9**	**21:33**	**86**	**21**	**29**	**50**	**34**	**5**	**1**	**2**	**23:04**

Czechoslovakian First All-Star Team (1992)

Played in NHL All-Star Game (1999)

Traded to **Ottawa** by **Pittsburgh** for Troy Murray and Norm Maciver, April 7, 1995. Traded to **NY Islanders** by **Ottawa** with Don Beaupre and Bryan Berard for Damian Rhodes and Wade Redden, January 23, 1996. Claimed on waivers by **Florida** from **NY Islanders**, March 15, 1996. Signed as a free agent by **Pittsburgh**, August 6, 1997. • Missed majority of 2001-02 season recovering from leg injury suffered in game vs. Florida, October 28, 2001. Traded to **Los Angeles** by **Pittsburgh** for Martin Strbak and Sergei Anshakov, November 30, 2003. Signed as a free agent by **Plzen** (CzRep), September 17, 2004. Signed as a free agent by **NY Rangers**, August 2, 2005.

STREIT, Mark

(STREET, MAHRK) **MTL.**

Defense. Shoots left. 6', 196 lbs. Born, Englisberg, Switz., December 11, 1977. Montreal's 8th choice, 262nd overall, in 2004 Entry Draft.

Season	Club	League	GP	G	A	Pts	PIM	PP	SH	GW	S	%	+/-	TF	F%	Min	GP	G	A	Pts	PIM	PP	SH	GW	Min
1995-96	Fribourg	Swiss	34	2	2	4	6	....	....	....	....	....	....	....	....	....	4	0	0	0	2	....	....	....	....
1996-97	HC Davos	Swiss	46	2	9	11	18	....	....	....	....	....	....	....	....	....	6	0	0	0	0	....	....	....	....
1997-98	HC Ambri-Piotta	Swiss	2	0	0	0	0	....	....	....	....	....	....	....	....	....	....	....	....	....	....	....	....	....	....
	HC Davos	Swiss	38	4	10	14	14	....	....	....	....	....	....	....	....	....	18	1	5	6	20	....	....	....	....
1998-99	HC Davos	Swiss	44	7	18	25	42	....	....	....	....	....	....	....	....	....	6	3	3	6	8	....	....	....	....
99-2000	Springfield	AHL	43	3	12	15	18	....	....	....	....	....	....	....	....	....	5	0	0	0	2	....	....	....	....
	Utah Grizzlies	IHL	1	0	1	1	2	....	....	....	....	....	....	....	....	....	....	....	....	....	....	....	....	....	....
	Tallahassee	ECHL	14	0	5	5	16	....	....	....	....	....	....	....	....	....	....	....	....	....	....	....	....	....	....
2000-01	ZSC Lions Zurich	Swiss	44	5	11	16	48	....	....	....	....	....	....	....	....	....	16	2	5	7	37	....	....	....	....
2001-02	ZSC Lions Zurich	Swiss	28	6	17	23	36	....	....	....	....	....	....	....	....	....	16	0	6	6	14	....	....	....	....
	Switzerland	Olympics	4	1	1	2	0	....	....	....	....	....	....	....	....	....	....	....	....	....	....	....	....	....	....
2002-03	ZSC Lions Zurich	Swiss	37	4	19	23	62	....	....	....	....	....	....	....	....	....	12	1	7	8	2	....	....	....	....
2003-04	ZSC Lions Zurich	Swiss	48	12	24	36	78	....	....	....	....	....	....	....	....	....	13	5	2	7	14	....	....	....	....
2004-05	ZSC Lions Zurich	Swiss	44	14	29	43	46	....	....	....	....	....	....	....	....	....	15	4	11	15	20	....	....	....	....
2005-06	**Montreal**	**NHL**	**48**	**2**	**9**	**11**	**28**	**2**	**0**	**0**	**52**	**3.8**	**-6**	**1**	**0.0**	**14:36**	**1**	**0**	**0**	**0**	**0**	**0**	**0**	**0**	**3:29**
	Switzerland	Olympics	6	2	1	3	6	....	....	....	....	....	....	....	....	....	....	....	....	....	....	....	....	....	....
	NHL Totals		**48**	**2**	**9**	**11**	**28**	**2**	**0**	**0**	**52**	**3.8**		**1**	**0.0**	**14:36**	**1**	**0**	**0**	**0**	**0**	**0**	**0**	**0**	**3:29**

STROSHEIN, Garret

(STROH-shighn, GAIR-reht)

Right wing. Shoots right. 6'7", 245 lbs. Born, Edmonton, Alta., April 4, 1980.

			Regular Season														Playoffs								
Season	Club	League	GP	G	A	Pts	PIM	PP	SH	GW	S	%	+/-	TF	F%	Min	GP	G	A	Pts	PIM	PP	SH	GW	Min
1998-99	Seattle	WHL	11	0	0	0	32	....	....	....	....	....	....	....	....	....	4	0	0	0	7	....	....	....	....
99-2000	Chilliwack Chiefs	BCHL	58	3	1	4	176	....	....	....	....	....	....	....	....	....	....	....	....	....	....	....	....	....	....
2000-01	San Diego Gulls	WCHL	3	0	0	0	5	....	....	....	....	....	....	....	....	....	....	....	....	....	....	....	....	....	....
	Chilliwack Chiefs	BCHL	55	7	8	15	187	....	....	....	....	....	....	....	....	....	....	....	....	....	....	....	....	....	....
2001-02	Mobile Mysticks	ECHL	3	0	0	0	13	....	....	....	....	....	....	....	....	....	....	....	....	....	....	....	....	....	....
	San Diego Gulls	WCHL	24	0	0	0	90	....	....	....	....	....	....	....	....	....	....	....	....	....	....	....	....	....	....
	Fresno	WCHL	20	1	0	1	67	....	....	....	....	....	....	....	....	....	....	....	....	....	....	....	....	....	....
	Bakersfield	WCHL	....	....	....	....	....	....	....	....	....	....	....	....	....	....	4	0	0	0	2	....	....	....	....
2002-03	Richmond	ECHL	2	0	0	0	7	....	....	....	....	....	....	....	....	....	....	....	....	....	....	....	....	....	....
	Portland	WHL	28	0	1	1	86	....	....	....	....	....	....	....	....	....	2	0	0	0	6	....	....	....	....
2003-04	**Washington**	**NHL**	**3**	**0**	**0**	**0**	**14**	**0**	**0**	**0**	**2**	**0.0**	**–1**	**0**	**0.0**	**7:16**	....	....	....	....	....	....	....	....	....
	Portland Pirates	AHL	35	1	1	2	73	....	....	....	....	....	....	....	....	....	....	....	....	....	....	....	....	....	....
2004-05	Portland Pirates	AHL	42	0	1	1	109	....	....	....	....	....	....	....	....	....	....	....	....	....	....	....	....	....	....
	South Carolina	ECHL	1	0	0	0	5	....	....	....	....	....	....	....	....	....	....	....	....	....	....	....	....	....	....
2005-06	Trenton Titans	ECHL	8	1	1	2	23	....	....	....	....	....	....	....	....	....	1	0	0	0	0	....	....	....	....
	Providence Bruins	AHL	48	1	4	5	129	....	....	....	....	....	....	....	....	....	....	....	....	....	....	....	....	....	....
	NHL Totals		**3**	**0**	**0**	**0**	**14**	**0**	**0**	**0**	**2**	**0.0**		**0**	**0.0**	**7:16**	....	....	....	....	....	....	....	....	....

Signed as a free agent by **Washington**, July 14, 2003. Signed as a free agent by **Boston**, August 23, 2005.

STRUDWICK, Jason

(STRUHD-wihk, JAY-suhn)

Defense. Shoots left. 6'3", 210 lbs. Born, Edmonton, Alta., July 17, 1975. NY Islanders' 3rd choice, 63rd overall, in 1994 Entry Draft.

Season	Club	League	GP	G	A	Pts	PIM	PP	SH	GW	S	%	+/-	TF	F%	Min	GP	G	A	Pts	PIM	PP	SH	GW	Min
1991-92	Edmonton Legion	AMHL	35	3	8	11	67	....	....	....	....	....	....	....	....	....	....	....	....	....	....	....	....	....	....
1992-93	Edmonton Pats	AMHL	33	8	20	28	135	....	....	....	....	....	....	....	....	....	....	....	....	....	....	....	....	....	....
1993-94	Kamloops Blazers	WHL	61	6	8	14	118	....	....	....	....	....	....	....	....	....	19	0	4	4	24	....	....	....	....
1994-95	Kamloops Blazers	WHL	72	3	11	14	183	....	....	....	....	....	....	....	....	....	21	1	1	2	39	....	....	....	....
1995-96	**NY Islanders**	**NHL**	**1**	**0**	**0**	**0**	**7**	**0**	**0**	**0**	**0**	**0.0**	**0**	....	....	....	....	....	....	....	....	....	....	....	....
	Worcester IceCats	AHL	60	2	7	9	119	....	....	....	....	....	....	....	....	....	4	0	1	1	0	....	....	....	....
1996-97	Kentucky	AHL	80	1	9	10	198	....	....	....	....	....	....	....	....	....	4	0	0	0	0	....	....	....	....
1997-98	**NY Islanders**	**NHL**	**17**	**0**	**1**	**1**	**36**	**0**	**0**	**0**	**3**	**0.0**	**1**	....	....	....	....	....	....	....	....	....	....	....	....
	Kentucky	AHL	39	3	1	4	87	....	....	....	....	....	....	....	....	....	....	....	....	....	....	....	....	....	....
	Vancouver	**NHL**	**11**	**0**	**1**	**1**	**29**	**0**	**0**	**0**	**5**	**0.0**	**–3**	....	....	....	....	....	....	....	....	....	....	....	....
	Syracuse Crunch	AHL	....	....	....	....	....	....	....	....	....	....	....	....	....	....	3	0	0	0	6	....	....	....	....
1998-99	**Vancouver**	**NHL**	**65**	**0**	**3**	**3**	**114**	**0**	**0**	**0**	**25**	**0.0**	**–19**	**0**	**0.0**	**12:49**	....	....	....	....	....	....	....	....	....
99-2000	**Vancouver**	**NHL**	**63**	**1**	**3**	**4**	**64**	**0**	**0**	**0**	**18**	**5.6**	**–13**	**0**	**0.0**	**15:12**	....	....	....	....	....	....	....	....	....
2000-01	**Vancouver**	**NHL**	**60**	**1**	**4**	**5**	**64**	**0**	**0**	**1**	**21**	**4.8**	**16**	**0**	**0.0**	**9:59**	**2**	**0**	**0**	**0**	**0**	**0**	**0**	**0**	**2:15**
2001-02	**Vancouver**	**NHL**	**44**	**2**	**4**	**6**	**96**	**0**	**0**	**0**	**13**	**15.4**	**4**	**0**	**0.0**	**9:45**	....	....	....	....	....	....	....	....	....
2002-03	**Chicago**	**NHL**	**48**	**2**	**3**	**5**	**87**	**0**	**0**	**0**	**19**	**10.5**	**–4**	**3**	**0.0**	**8:32**	....	....	....	....	....	....	....	....	....
2003-04	**Chicago**	**NHL**	**54**	**1**	**3**	**4**	**73**	**0**	**0**	**0**	**32**	**3.1**	**–16**	**1**	**0.0**	**14:55**	....	....	....	....	....	....	....	....	....
2004-05	Ferencvaros	Hungary	6	1	2	3	8	....	....	....	....	....	....	....	....	....	....	....	....	....	....	....	....	....	....
2005-06	**NY Rangers**	**NHL**	**65**	**3**	**4**	**7**	**66**	**0**	**0**	**0**	**31**	**9.7**	**–10**	**3**	**33.3**	**15:31**	**3**	**0**	**0**	**0**	**0**	**0**	**0**	**0**	**13:35**
	NHL Totals		**428**	**10**	**26**	**36**	**636**	**0**	**0**	**1**	**167**	**6.0**		**7**	**14.3**	**12:38**	**5**	**0**	**0**	**0**	**0**	**0**	**0**	**0**	**9:03**

Traded to **Vancouver** by **NY Islanders** for Gino Odjick, March 23, 1998. Signed as a free agent by **Chicago**, July 15, 2002. Signed as a free agent by **NY Rangers**, July 20, 2004. Signed as a free agent by **Ferencvaros** (Hungary), January 17, 2005.

STUART, Brad

(STEW-ahrt, BRAD) **BOS.**

Defense. Shoots left. 6'2", 220 lbs. Born, Rocky Mountain House, Alta., November 6, 1979. San Jose's 1st choice, 3rd overall, in 1998 Entry Draft.

Season	Club	League	GP	G	A	Pts	PIM	PP	SH	GW	S	%	+/-	TF	F%	Min	GP	G	A	Pts	PIM	PP	SH	GW	Min
1995-96	Red Deer	AMHL	35	12	25	37	83	....	....	....	....	....	....	....	....	....	....	....	....	....	....	....	....	....	....
	Regina Pats	WHL	3	0	0	0	0	....	....	....	....	....	....	....	....	....	....	....	....	....	....	....	....	....	....
1996-97	Regina Pats	WHL	57	7	36	43	58	....	....	....	....	....	....	....	....	....	5	0	4	4	14	....	....	....	....
1997-98	Regina Pats	WHL	72	20	45	65	82	....	....	....	....	....	....	....	....	....	9	3	4	7	10	....	....	....	....
1998-99	Regina Pats	WHL	29	10	19	29	43	....	....	....	....	....	....	....	....	....	....	....	....	....	....	....	....	....	....
	Calgary Hitmen	WHL	30	11	22	33	26	....	....	....	....	....	....	....	....	....	21	8	15	23	59	....	....	....	....
99-2000	**San Jose**	**NHL**	**82**	**10**	**26**	**36**	**32**	**5**	**1**	**3**	**133**	**7.5**	**3**	**0**	**0.0**	**20:24**	**12**	**1**	**0**	**1**	**6**	**1**	**0**	**0**	**16:30**
2000-01	**San Jose**	**NHL**	**77**	**5**	**18**	**23**	**56**	**1**	**0**	**2**	**119**	**4.2**	**10**	**0**	**0.0**	**20:06**	**5**	**1**	**0**	**1**	**0**	**0**	**0**	**0**	**20:19**
2001-02	**San Jose**	**NHL**	**82**	**6**	**23**	**29**	**39**	**2**	**0**	**2**	**96**	**6.3**	**13**	**0**	**0.0**	**21:41**	**12**	**0**	**3**	**3**	**8**	**0**	**0**	**0**	**19:42**
2002-03	**San Jose**	**NHL**	**36**	**4**	**10**	**14**	**46**	**2**	**0**	**1**	**63**	**6.3**	**–6**	**0**	**0.0**	**20:53**	....	....	....	....	....	....	....	....	....
2003-04	**San Jose**	**NHL**	**77**	**9**	**30**	**39**	**34**	**5**	**0**	**0**	**129**	**7.0**	**9**	**0**	**0.0**	**22:09**	**17**	**1**	**5**	**6**	**13**	**0**	**0**	**0**	**23:23**
2004-05			DID NOT PLAY																						
2005-06	**San Jose**	**NHL**	**23**	**2**	**10**	**12**	**14**	**1**	**0**	**0**	**41**	**4.9**	**–2**	**0**	**0.0**	**23:15**	....	....	....	....	....	....	....	....	....
	Boston	**NHL**	**55**	**10**	**21**	**31**	**38**	**6**	**0**	**2**	**122**	**8.2**	**–6**	**0**	**0.0**	**25:40**	....	....	....	....	....	....	....	....	....
	NHL Totals		**432**	**46**	**138**	**184**	**259**	**22**	**1**	**10**	**703**	**6.5**		**0**	**0.0**	**21:46**	**46**	**3**	**8**	**11**	**27**	**1**	**0**	**0**	**20:18**

WHL East Second All-Star Team (1998) • WHL East First All-Star Team (1999) • Canadian Major Junior First All-Star Team (1999) • Canadian Major Junior Defenseman of the Year (1999) • NHL All-Rookie Team (2000)

• Missed majority of 2002-03 season recovering from ankle (January 4, 2003 vs. Los Angeles) and head (February 21, 2003 vs. Columbus) injuries. Traded to **Boston** by **San Jose** with Marco Sturm and Wayne Primeau for Joe Thornton, November 30, 2005.

STUART, Mark

(STEW-ahrt, MAHRK) **BOS.**

Defense. Shoots left. 6'1", 216 lbs. Born, Rochester, MN, April 27, 1984. Boston's 1st choice, 21st overall, in 2003 Entry Draft.

Season	Club	League	GP	G	A	Pts	PIM	PP	SH	GW	S	%	+/-	TF	F%	Min	GP	G	A	Pts	PIM	PP	SH	GW	Min
99-2000	Roch. Lourdes	High-MN	28	19	22	41	....	....	....	....	....	....	....	....	....	....	....	....	....	....	....	....	....	....	....
2000-01	USNTDP	U-17	12	1	5	6	6	....	....	....	....	....	....	....	....	....	....	....	....	....	....	....	....	....	....
	USNTDP	NAHL	52	2	11	13	114	....	....	....	....	....	....	....	....	....	....	....	....	....	....	....	....	....	....
2001-02	USNTDP	U-18	40	9	9	18	....	....	....	....	....	....	....	....	....	....	....	....	....	....	....	....	....	....	....
	USNTDP	USHL	12	0	1	1	25	....	....	....	....	....	....	....	....	....	....	....	....	....	....	....	....	....	....
	USNTDP	NAHL	9	0	1	1	18	....	....	....	....	....	....	....	....	....	....	....	....	....	....	....	....	....	....
2002-03	Colorado College	WCHA	38	3	17	20	81	....	....	....	....	....	....	....	....	....	....	....	....	....	....	....	....	....	....
2003-04	Colorado College	WCHA	37	4	11	15	100	....	....	....	....	....	....	....	....	....	....	....	....	....	....	....	....	....	....
2004-05	Colorado College	WCHA	43	5	14	19	94	....	....	....	....	....	....	....	....	....	....	....	....	....	....	....	....	....	....
2005-06	**Boston**	**NHL**	**17**	**1**	**1**	**2**	**10**	**0**	**0**	**0**	**9**	**11.1**	**–1**	**0**	**0.0**	**17:46**	....	....	....	....	....	....	....	....	....
	Providence Bruins	AHL	60	4	3	7	76	....	....	....	....	....	....	....	....	....	6	0	0	0	25	....	....	....	....
	NHL Totals		**17**	**1**	**1**	**2**	**10**	**0**	**0**	**0**	**9**	**11.1**		**0**	**0.0**	**17:46**	....	....	....	....	....	....	....	....	....

WCHA All-Rookie Team (2003) • WCHA Second All-Star Team (2005) • NCAA West First All-American Team (2005)

STUART, Mike

(STEW-ahrt, MIGHK) **ST.L.**

Defense. Shoots right. 6', 200 lbs. Born, Rochester, MN, August 31, 1980. Nashville's 6th choice, 137th overall, in 2000 Entry Draft.

Season	Club	League	GP	G	A	Pts	PIM	PP	SH	GW	S	%	+/-	TF	F%	Min	GP	G	A	Pts	PIM	PP	SH	GW	Min
1996-97	Rochester	USHL	46	4	9	13	22	....	....	....	....	....	....	....	....	....	....	....	....	....	....	....	....	....	....
1997-98	Rochester	USHL	50	4	15	19	40	....	....	....	....	....	....	....	....	....	....	....	....	....	....	....	....	....	....
1998-99	Colorado College	WCHA	40	2	12	14	44	....	....	....	....	....	....	....	....	....	....	....	....	....	....	....	....	....	....
99-2000	Colorado College	WCHA	32	2	5	7	26	....	....	....	....	....	....	....	....	....	....	....	....	....	....	....	....	....	....
2000-01	Colorado College	WCHA	33	1	13	14	36	....	....	....	....	....	....	....	....	....	....	....	....	....	....	....	....	....	....
2001-02	Colorado College	WCHA	35	3	9	12	46	....	....	....	....	....	....	....	....	....	....	....	....	....	....	....	....	....	....
2002-03	Worcester IceCats	AHL	41	1	5	6	19	....	....	....	....	....	....	....	....	....	3	0	0	0	2	....	....	....	....
	Peoria Rivermen	ECHL	19	2	7	9	12	....	....	....	....	....	....	....	....	....	....	....	....	....	....	....	....	....	....
2003-04	**St. Louis**	**NHL**	**2**	**0**	**0**	**0**	**0**	**0**	**0**	**0**	**0**	**0.0**	**0**	**0**	**0.0**	**9:31**	....	....	....	....	....	....	....	....	....
	Worcester IceCats	AHL	30	0	4	4	20	....	....	....	....	....	....	....	....	....	....	....	....	....	....	....	....	....	....
2004-05	Worcester IceCats	AHL	70	1	10	11	26	....	....	....	....	....	....	....	....	....	....	....	....	....	....	....	....	....	....
2005-06	**St. Louis**	**NHL**	**1**	**0**	**0**	**0**	**0**	**0**	**0**	**0**	**1**	**0.0**	**0**	**0**	**0.0**	**12:59**	....	....	....	....	....	....	....	....	....
	Peoria Rivermen	AHL	56	0	13	13	30	....	....	....	....	....	....	....	....	....	4	0	2	2	0	....	....	....	....
	NHL Totals		**3**	**0**	**0**	**0**	**0**	**0**	**0**	**0**	**1**	**0.0**		**0**	**0.0**	**10:40**	....	....	....	....	....	....	....	....	....

USHL All-Rookie Team (1997)

Signed as a free agent by **St. Louis**, October 7, 2002. • Missed majority of 2003-04 season recovering from groin injury suffered in game vs. Hartford (AHL), January 28, 2004.

STUMPEL, Jozef

(STUM-puhl, JOH-zehf) **FLA.**

Center. Shoots right. 6'3", 225 lbs. Born, Nitra, Czech., July 20, 1972. Boston's 2nd choice, 40th overall, in 1991 Entry Draft.

Season	Club	League	GP	G	A	Pts	PIM	PP	SH	GW	S	%	+/-	TF	F%	Min	Playoffs GP	G	A	Pts	PIM	PP	SH	GW	Min
1989-90	Plastika Nitra	Czech-2	38	12	11	23	....	....	....	....	....	....	....	....	....	....	....	....	....	....	....	....	....	....	....
1990-91	AC Nitra	Czech	49	23	22	45	14	....	....	....	....	....	....	....	....	....	....	....	....	....	....	....	....	....	....
1991-92	Kolner EC	Germany	33	19	18	37	35	....	....	....	....	....	....	....	....	....	4	1	1	2	0	....	....	....	....
	Boston	NHL	4	1	0	1	0	0	0	0	3	33.3	1	....	....	....	....	....	....	....	....	....	....	....	....
1992-93	Boston	NHL	13	1	3	4	4	0	0	0	8	12.5	–3	....	....	....	....	....	....	....	....	....	....	....	....
	Providence Bruins	AHL	56	31	61	92	26	....	....	....	....	....	....	....	....	....	6	4	4	8	0	....	....	....	....
1993-94	Boston	NHL	59	8	15	23	14	0	0	1	62	12.9	4	....	....	....	13	1	7	8	4	0	0	0	....
	Providence Bruins	AHL	17	5	12	17	4	....	....	....	....	....	....	....	....	....	....	....	....	....	....	....	....	....	....
1994-95	Kolner Haie	Germany	25	16	23	39	18	....	....	....	....	....	....	....	....	....	....	....	....	....	....	....	....	....	....
	Boston	NHL	44	5	13	18	8	1	0	2	46	10.9	4	....	....	....	5	0	0	0	0	0	0	0	....
1995-96	Boston	NHL	76	18	36	54	14	5	0	2	158	11.4	–8	....	....	....	5	1	2	3	0	0	0	0	....
1996-97	Boston	NHL	78	21	55	76	14	6	0	1	168	12.5	–22	....	....	....	....	....	....	....	....	....	....	....	....
1997-98	Los Angeles	NHL	77	21	58	79	53	4	0	2	162	13.0	17	....	....	....	4	1	2	3	2	0	0	0	....
1998-99	Los Angeles	NHL	64	13	21	34	10	1	0	1	131	9.9	–18	1484	54.0	19:44	....	....	....	....	....	....	....	....	....
99-2000	Los Angeles	NHL	57	17	41	58	10	3	0	7	126	13.5	23	1088	50.6	19:16	4	0	4	4	8	0	0	0	21:05
2000-01	Bratislava	Slovakia	9	2	4	6	16	....	....	....	....	....	....	....	....	....	....	....	....	....	....	....	....	....	....
	Los Angeles	NHL	63	16	39	55	14	9	0	6	95	16.8	20	1278	52.7	19:35	13	3	5	8	10	2	0	1	21:56
2001-02	Los Angeles	NHL	9	1	3	4	4	0	0	0	7	14.3	1	164	48.2	20:06	....	....	....	....	....	....	....	....	....
	Boston	NHL	72	7	47	54	14	1	0	3	93	7.5	21	1346	49.7	18:36	6	0	2	2	0	0	0	0	16:43
	Slovakia	Olympics	2	2	1	3	0	....	....	....	....	....	....	....	....	....	....	....	....	....	....	....	....	....	....
2002-03	Boston	NHL	78	14	37	51	12	4	0	2	110	12.7	0	1601	54.7	18:27	5	0	2	2	0	0	0	0	17:31
2003-04	Los Angeles	NHL	64	8	29	37	16	4	0	0	78	10.3	5	1105	49.3	18:46	....	....	....	....	....	....	....	....	....
2004-05	HC Slavia Praha	CzRep	52	13	26	39	41	....	....	....	....	....	....	....	....	....	7	4	2	6	10	....	....	....	....
2005-06	Florida	NHL	74	15	37	52	26	3	1	1	115	13.0	11	916	49.1	17:47	....	....	....	....	....	....	....	....	....
	Slovakia	Olympics	3	0	0	0	0	....	....	....	....	....	....	....	....	....	....	....	....	....	....	....	....	....	....
	NHL Totals		**832**	**166**	**434**	**600**	**213**	**41**	**1**	**28**	**1362**	**12.2**		**8982**	**51.7**	**18:52**	**55**	**6**	**24**	**30**	**24**	**2**	**0**	**1**	**19:55**

Traded to **Los Angeles** by **Boston** with Sandy Moger and Boston's 4th round choice (later traded to New Jersey – New Jersey selected Pierre Dagenais) in 1998 Entry Draft for Dmitri Kristich and Byron Dafoe, August 29, 1997. Traded to **Boston** by **Los Angeles** with Glen Murray for Jason Allison and Mikko Eloranta, October 24, 2001. Traded to **Los Angeles** by **Boston** with Boston's 7th round choice (later traded to Nashville – Nashville selected Miroslav Hanuljak) in 2003 Entry Draft for Philadelphia's 4th round choice (previously acquired, Boston selected Patrick Valcak) in 2003 Entry Draft and Detroit's 2nd round choice (previously acquired, Boston selected Martins Karsums) in 2004 Entry Draft, June 22, 2003. Signed as a free agent by **Slavia Praha** (CzRep), August 28, 2004. Signed as a free agent by **Florida**, August 17, 2005.

STURM, Marco

(STURHM, MAHR-koh) **BOS.**

Left wing. Shoots left. 6', 195 lbs. Born, Dingolfing, West Germany, September 8, 1978. San Jose's 2nd choice, 21st overall, in 1996 Entry Draft.

Season	Club	League	GP	G	A	Pts	PIM	PP	SH	GW	S	%	+/-	TF	F%	Min	Playoffs GP	G	A	Pts	PIM	PP	SH	GW	Min
1995-96	EV Landshut	Germany	47	12	20	32	50	....	....	....	....	....	....	....	....	....	11	1	3	4	18	....	....	....	....
1996-97	EV Landshut	Germany	46	16	27	43	40	....	....	....	....	....	....	....	....	....	7	1	4	5	6	....	....	....	....
1997-98	San Jose	NHL	74	10	20	30	40	2	0	3	118	8.5	–2	....	....	....	2	0	0	0	0	0	0	0	....
	Germany	Olympics	2	0	0	0	0	....	....	....	....	....	....	....	....	....	....	....	....	....	....	....	....	....	....
1998-99	San Jose	NHL	78	16	22	38	52	3	2	3	140	11.4	7	576	45.0	15:23	6	2	2	4	4	0	0	1	14:16
99-2000	San Jose	NHL	74	12	15	27	22	2	4	3	120	10.0	4	183	45.4	14:07	12	1	3	4	6	0	0	0	13:00
2000-01	San Jose	NHL	81	14	18	32	28	2	3	5	153	9.2	9	517	40.2	16:06	6	0	2	2	0	0	0	0	18:18
2001-02	San Jose	NHL	77	21	20	41	32	4	3	5	174	12.1	23	105	47.6	15:39	12	3	2	5	2	0	0	0	15:33
	Germany	Olympics	5	0	1	1	0	....	....	....	....	....	....	....	....	....	....	....	....	....	....	....	....	....	....
2002-03	San Jose	NHL	82	28	20	48	16	6	0	2	208	13.5	9	83	48.2	16:31	....	....	....	....	....	....	....	....	....
2003-04	San Jose	NHL	64	21	20	41	36	10	2	6	158	13.3	0	7	42.9	16:25	....	....	....	....	....	....	....	....	....
2004-05	ERC Ingolstadt	Germany	45	22	16	38	56	....	....	....	....	....	....	....	....	....	11	3	4	7	12	....	....	....	....
2005-06	San Jose	NHL	23	6	10	16	16	3	0	0	48	12.5	–8	9	44.4	17:28	....	....	....	....	....	....	....	....	....
	Boston	NHL	51	23	20	43	32	5	0	6	132	17.4	14	3	33.3	18:44	....	....	....	....	....	....	....	....	....
	Germany	Olympics	DID NOT PLAY – INJURED																						
	NHL Totals		**604**	**151**	**165**	**316**	**274**	**37**	**14**	**33**	**1251**	**12.1**		**1483**	**43.7**	**16:04**	**38**	**6**	**9**	**15**	**12**	**0**	**0**	**1**	**14:56**

Played in NHL All-Star Game (1999)

Signed as a free agent by **Ingolstadt** (Germany), August 8, 2004. Traded to **Boston** by **San Jose** with Brad Stuart and Wayne Primeau for Joe Thornton, November 30, 2005.

SUCHY, Radoslav

(soo-KHEE, RAD-oh-slav)

Defense. Shoots left. 6'2", 204 lbs. Born, Kezmarok, Czech., April 7, 1976.

Season	Club	League	GP	G	A	Pts	PIM	PP	SH	GW	S	%	+/-	TF	F%	Min	Playoffs GP	G	A	Pts	PIM	PP	SH	GW	Min
1993-94	SKP PS Poprad Jr.	Slovak-Jr.	30	11	12	23	16	....	....	....	....	....	....	....	....	....	....	....	....	....	....	....	....	....	....
	SKP PS Poprad	Slovakia	3	0	0	0	0	....	....	....	....	....	....	....	....	....	....	....	....	....	....	....	....	....	....
1994-95	Sherbrooke	QMJHL	69	12	32	44	30	....	....	....	....	....	....	....	....	....	7	0	3	3	2	....	....	....	....
1995-96	Sherbrooke	QMJHL	68	15	53	68	68	....	....	....	....	....	....	....	....	....	7	0	3	3	2	....	....	....	....
1996-97	Sherbrooke	QMJHL	32	6	34	40	14	....	....	....	....	....	....	....	....	....	....	....	....	....	....	....	....	....	....
	Chicoutimi	QMJHL	28	5	24	29	26	....	....	....	....	....	....	....	....	....	19	6	15	21	12	....	....	....	....
1997-98	Las Vegas	IHL	26	1	4	5	10	....	....	....	....	....	....	....	....	....	....	....	....	....	....	....	....	....	....
	Springfield	AHL	41	6	15	21	16	....	....	....	....	....	....	....	....	....	4	0	1	1	2	....	....	....	....
1998-99	Springfield	AHL	69	4	32	36	10	....	....	....	....	....	....	....	....	....	3	0	1	1	0	....	....	....	....
99-2000	Phoenix	NHL	60	0	6	6	16	0	0	0	36	0.0	2	0	0.0	15:09	5	0	1	1	0	0	0	0	16:18
	Springfield	AHL	2	0	1	1	0	....	....	....	....	....	....	....	....	....	....	....	....	....	....	....	....	....	....
2000-01	Phoenix	NHL	72	0	10	10	22	0	0	0	33	0.0	1	0	0.0	17:09	....	....	....	....	....	....	....	....	....
2001-02	Phoenix	NHL	81	4	13	17	10	1	0	0	49	8.2	25	1	100.0	18:05	5	1	0	1	0	0	0	0	20:35
2002-03	Phoenix	NHL	77	1	8	9	18	1	0	0	48	2.1	2	1	0.0	16:26	....	....	....	....	....	....	....	....	....
2003-04	Phoenix	NHL	82	7	14	21	8	2	0	2	82	8.5	1	1	100.0	19:40	....	....	....	....	....	....	....	....	....
2004-05	HK SKP Poprad	Slovakia	34	5	10	15	24	....	....	....	....	....	....	....	....	....	5	0	0	0	2	....	....	....	....
2005-06	Columbus	NHL	79	1	7	8	30	0	0	0	33	3.0	–8	0	0.0	19:55	....	....	....	....	....	....	....	....	....
	Slovakia	Olympics	6	1	1	2	0	....	....	....	....	....	....	....	....	....	....	....	....	....	....	....	....	....	....
	NHL Totals		**451**	**13**	**58**	**71**	**104**	**4**	**0**	**2**	**281**	**4.6**		**3**	**66.7**	**17:52**	**10**	**1**	**1**	**2**	**0**	**0**	**0**	**0**	**18:27**

QMJHL All-Rookie Team (1995) • QMJHL Second All-Star Team (1997) • George Parsons Trophy (Memorial Cup Tournament Most Sportsmanlike Player) (1997)

Signed as a free agent by **Phoenix**, September 26, 1997. Traded to **Columbus** by **Phoenix** with Phoenix's 6th round choice (Derek Reinhart) in 2005 Entry Draft for Columbus' 4th round choice (later traded to Philadelphia - Philadelphia selected Jeremy Duchesne) in 2005 Entry Draft, July 6, 2004. Signed as a free agent by **Poprad** (Slovakia), October 4, 2004.

SUGLOBOV, Alexander

(suh-GLOH-bahf, al-ehx-AN-duhr) **TOR.**

Right wing. Shoots left. 6', 200 lbs. Born, Elektrostal, USSR, January 15, 1982. New Jersey's 3rd choice, 56th overall, in 2000 Entry Draft.

Season	Club	League	GP	G	A	Pts	PIM	PP	SH	GW	S	%	+/-	TF	F%	Min	Playoffs GP	G	A	Pts	PIM	PP	SH	GW	Min
1998-99	Spartak 2	Russia-4	1	0	0	0	0	....	....	....	....	....	....	....	....	....	....	....	....	....	....	....	....	....	....
	Spartak Moscow	Russia	1	0	0	0	0	....	....	....	....	....	....	....	....	....	....	....	....	....	....	....	....	....	....
99-2000	Yaroslavl 2	Russia-3	38	23	10	33	....	....	....	....	....	....	....	....	....	....	....	....	....	....	....	....	....	....	....
2000-01	St. Petersburg	Russia	8	1	0	1	6	....	....	....	....	....	....	....	....	....	....	....	....	....	....	....	....	....	....
	Ufa	Russia	6	0	0	0	4	....	....	....	....	....	....	....	....	....	....	....	....	....	....	....	....	....	....
	Yaroslavl	Russia	4	0	0	0	2	....	....	....	....	....	....	....	....	....	11	1	2	3	6	....	....	....	....
2001-02	Yaroslavl 2	Russia-3	6	5	2	7	20	....	....	....	....	....	....	....	....	....	....	....	....	....	....	....	....	....	....
	Yaroslavl	Russia	25	4	2	6	26	....	....	....	....	....	....	....	....	....	5	1	1	2	18	....	....	....	....
2002-03	Nizhnekamsk	Russia	6	0	0	0	4	....	....	....	....	....	....	....	....	....	....	....	....	....	....	....	....	....	....
	Yaroslavl	Russia	17	4	2	6	12	....	....	....	....	....	....	....	....	....	5	1	0	1	2	....	....	....	....
2003-04	New Jersey	NHL	1	0	0	0	0	0	0	0	2	0.0	0	0	0.0	8:18	....	....	....	....	....	....	....	....	....
	Albany River Rats	AHL	35	11	11	22	54	....	....	....	....	....	....	....	....	....	....	....	....	....	....	....	....	....	....
2004-05	Albany River Rats	AHL	72	25	21	46	77	....	....	....	....	....	....	....	....	....	....	....	....	....	....	....	....	....	....
2005-06	New Jersey	NHL	1	1	0	1	0	1	0	0	2	50.0	–2	0	0.0	12:55	....	....	....	....	....	....	....	....	....
	Albany River Rats	AHL	51	25	23	48	52	....	....	....	....	....	....	....	....	....	....	....	....	....	....	....	....	....	....
	Toronto	NHL	2	0	0	0	0	0	0	0	3	0.0	–1	0	0.0	11:31	....	....	....	....	....	....	....	....	....
	Toronto Marlies	AHL	15	8	2	10	21	....	....	....	....	....	....	....	....	....	5	5	2	7	2	....	....	....	....
	NHL Totals		**4**	**1**	**0**	**1**	**0**	**1**	**0**	**0**	**7**	**14.3**		**0**	**0.0**	**11:04**									

• Missed majority of 2003-04 season recovering from wrist injury suffered in game vs. Edmonton, January 5, 2004. Traded to **Toronto** by **New Jersey** for Ken Klee, March 8, 2006.

SULLIVAN, Steve (SUHL-ih-vuhn, STEEV) NSH.

Right wing. Shoots right. 5'9", 155 lbs. Born, Timmins, Ont., July 6, 1974. New Jersey's 10th choice, 233rd overall, in 1994 Entry Draft.

			Regular Season														Playoffs								
Season	Club	League	GP	G	A	Pts	PIM	PP	SH	GW	S	%	+/-	TF	F%	Min	GP	G	A	Pts	PIM	PP	SH	GW	Min
1991-92	Timmins	NOJHA	47	66	55	121	141	....	....	....	....	....	....	....	....	....	....	....	....	....	....	....	....	....	....
1992-93	Sault Ste. Marie	OHL	62	36	27	63	44	....	....	....	....	....	....	....	....	....	16	3	8	11	18	....	....	....	....
1993-94	Sault Ste. Marie	OHL	63	51	62	113	82	....	....	....	....	....	....	....	....	....	14	9	16	25	22	....	....	....	....
1994-95	Albany River Rats	AHL	75	31	50	81	124	....	....	....	....	....	....	....	....	....	14	4	7	11	10	....	....	....	....
1995-96	**New Jersey**	**NHL**	**16**	**5**	**4**	**9**	**8**	**2**	**0**	**1**	**23**	**21.7**	**3**	....	....	....	....	....	....	....	....	....	....	....	....
	Albany River Rats	AHL	53	33	42	75	127	....	....	....	....	....	....	....	....	....	4	3	0	3	6	....	....	....	....
1996-97	**New Jersey**	**NHL**	**33**	**8**	**14**	**22**	**14**	**2**	**0**	**2**	**63**	**12.7**	**9**	....	....	....	....	....	....	....	....	....	....	....	....
	Albany River Rats	AHL	15	8	7	15	16	....	....	....	....	....	....	....	....	....	....	....	....	....	....	....	....	....	....
	Toronto	**NHL**	**21**	**5**	**11**	**16**	**23**	**1**	**0**	**1**	**45**	**11.1**	**5**	....	....	....	....	....	....	....	....	....	....	....	....
1997-98	**Toronto**	**NHL**	**63**	**10**	**18**	**28**	**40**	**1**	**0**	**1**	**112**	**8.9**	**-8**	....	....	....	....	....	....	....	....	....	....	....	....
1998-99	**Toronto**	**NHL**	**63**	**20**	**20**	**40**	**28**	**4**	**0**	**5**	**110**	**18.2**	**12**	**685**	**44.4**	**14:12**	**13**	**3**	**3**	**6**	**14**	**2**	**0**	**0**	**16:20**
99-2000	**Toronto**	**NHL**	**7**	**0**	**1**	**1**	**4**	**0**	**0**	**0**	**11**	**0.0**	**-1**	**47**	**48.9**	**11:52**	....	....	....	....	....	....	....	....	....
	Chicago	**NHL**	**73**	**22**	**42**	**64**	**52**	**2**	**1**	**6**	**169**	**13.0**	**20**	**692**	**48.0**	**18:05**	....	....	....	....	....	....	....	....	....
2000-01	**Chicago**	**NHL**	**81**	**34**	**41**	**75**	**54**	**6**	**8**	**3**	**204**	**16.7**	**3**	**649**	**42.4**	**20:32**	....	....	....	....	....	....	....	....	....
2001-02	**Chicago**	**NHL**	**78**	**21**	**39**	**60**	**67**	**3**	**0**	**8**	**155**	**13.5**	**23**	**758**	**48.9**	**19:10**	**5**	**1**	**0**	**1**	**2**	**0**	**0**	**0**	**18:04**
2002-03	**Chicago**	**NHL**	**82**	**26**	**35**	**61**	**42**	**4**	**2**	**3**	**190**	**13.7**	**15**	**382**	**46.1**	**19:15**	....	....	....	....	....	....	....	....	....
2003-04	**Chicago**	**NHL**	**56**	**15**	**28**	**43**	**36**	**4**	**2**	**4**	**140**	**10.7**	**-7**	**103**	**44.7**	**21:19**	....	....	....	....	....	....	....	....	....
	Nashville	**NHL**	**24**	**9**	**21**	**30**	**12**	**7**	**0**	**0**	**78**	**11.5**	**8**	**124**	**43.6**	**20:02**	**6**	**1**	**1**	**2**	**6**	**0**	**0**	**1**	**18:58**
2004-05		DID NOT PLAY																							
2005-06	**Nashville**	**NHL**	**69**	**31**	**37**	**68**	**50**	**13**	**4**	**5**	**192**	**16.1**	**2**	**42**	**52.4**	**19:06**	**5**	**0**	**2**	**2**	**0**	**0**	**0**	**0**	**17:02**
	NHL Totals		**666**	**206**	**311**	**517**	**430**	**49**	**17**	**39**	**1492**	**13.8**		**3482**	**46.0**	**18:49**	**29**	**5**	**6**	**11**	**22**	**2**	**0**	**1**	**17:18**

AHL First All-Star Team (1996)

Traded to **Toronto** by **New Jersey** with Jason Smith and the rights to Alyn McCauley for Doug Gilmour, Dave Ellett and New Jersey's 3rd round choice (previously acquired, New Jersey selected Andre Lakos) in 1999 Entry Draft, February 25, 1997. Claimed on waivers by **Chicago** from **Toronto**, October 23, 1999. Traded to **Nashville** by **Chicago** for Nashville's 2nd round choices in 2004 (Ryan Garlock) and 2005 (Michael Blunden) Entry Drafts, February 16, 2004.

SUNDIN, Mats (suhn-DEEN, MATS) TOR.

Center. Shoots right. 6'5", 231 lbs. Born, Bromma, Sweden, February 13, 1971. Quebec's 1st choice, 1st overall, in 1989 Entry Draft.

			Regular Season														Playoffs								
Season	Club	League	GP	G	A	Pts	PIM	PP	SH	GW	S	%	+/-	TF	F%	Min	GP	G	A	Pts	PIM	PP	SH	GW	Min
1988-89	Nacka HK	Sweden-2	25	10	8	18	18	....	....	....	....	....	....	....	....	....	....	....	....	....	....	....	....	....	....
1989-90	Djurgarden	Sweden	34	10	8	18	16	....	....	....	....	....	....	....	....	....	8	7	0	7	4	....	....	....	....
1990-91	**Quebec**	**NHL**	**80**	**23**	**36**	**59**	**58**	**4**	**0**	**0**	**155**	**14.8**	**-24**	....	....	....	....	....	....	....	....	....	....	....	....
1991-92	**Quebec**	**NHL**	**80**	**33**	**43**	**76**	**103**	**8**	**2**	**2**	**231**	**14.3**	**-19**	....	....	....	....	....	....	....	....	....	....	....	....
1992-93	**Quebec**	**NHL**	**80**	**47**	**67**	**114**	**96**	**13**	**4**	**9**	**215**	**21.9**	**21**	....	....	....	**6**	**3**	**1**	**4**	**6**	**1**	**0**	**0**	....
1993-94	**Quebec**	**NHL**	**84**	**32**	**53**	**85**	**60**	**6**	**2**	**4**	**226**	**14.2**	**1**	....	....	....	....	....	....	....	....	....	....	....	....
1994-95	Djurgarden	Sweden	12	7	2	9	14	....	....	....	....	....	....	....	....	....	....	....	....	....	....	....	....	....	....
	Toronto	**NHL**	**47**	**23**	**24**	**47**	**14**	**9**	**0**	**4**	**173**	**13.3**	**-5**	....	....	....	**7**	**5**	**4**	**9**	**4**	**2**	**0**	**1**	....
1995-96	**Toronto**	**NHL**	**76**	**33**	**50**	**83**	**46**	**7**	**6**	**7**	**301**	**11.0**	**8**	....	....	....	**6**	**3**	**1**	**4**	**4**	**2**	**0**	**1**	....
1996-97	**Toronto**	**NHL**	**82**	**41**	**53**	**94**	**59**	**7**	**4**	**8**	**281**	**14.6**	**6**	....	....	....	....	....	....	....	....	....	....	....	....
1997-98	**Toronto**	**NHL**	**82**	**33**	**41**	**74**	**49**	**9**	**1**	**5**	**219**	**15.1**	**-3**	....	....	....	....	....	....	....	....	....	....	....	....
	Sweden	Olympics	4	3	0	3	4	....	....	....	....	....	....	....	....	....	....	....	....	....	....	....	....	....	....
1998-99	**Toronto**	**NHL**	**82**	**31**	**52**	**83**	**58**	**4**	**0**	**6**	**209**	**14.8**	**22**	**1993**	**57.3**	**20:41**	**17**	**8**	**8**	**16**	**16**	**3**	**0**	**2**	**22:46**
99-2000	**Toronto**	**NHL**	**73**	**32**	**41**	**73**	**46**	**10**	**2**	**7**	**184**	**17.4**	**16**	**1619**	**50.8**	**20:11**	**12**	**3**	**5**	**8**	**10**	**0**	**0**	**1**	**21:27**
2000-01	**Toronto**	**NHL**	**82**	**28**	**46**	**74**	**76**	**9**	**0**	**6**	**226**	**12.4**	**15**	**1870**	**56.6**	**19:21**	**11**	**6**	**7**	**13**	**14**	**2**	**1**	**1**	**20:12**
2001-02	**Toronto**	**NHL**	**82**	**41**	**39**	**80**	**94**	**10**	**2**	**9**	**262**	**15.6**	**6**	**1812**	**57.5**	**19:20**	**8**	**2**	**5**	**7**	**4**	**0**	**0**	**0**	**20:07**
	Sweden	Olympics	4	5	4	*9	10	....	....	....	....	....	....	....	....	....	....	....	....	....	....	....	....	....	....
2002-03	**Toronto**	**NHL**	**75**	**37**	**35**	**72**	**58**	**16**	**3**	**8**	**223**	**16.6**	**1**	**1774**	**56.1**	**20:15**	**7**	**1**	**3**	**4**	**6**	**1**	**0**	**0**	**24:17**
2003-04	**Toronto**	**NHL**	**81**	**31**	**44**	**75**	**52**	**11**	**1**	**10**	**226**	**13.7**	**11**	**1705**	**53.0**	**19:52**	**9**	**4**	**5**	**9**	**8**	**0**	**0**	**1**	**18:24**
2004-05																									
2005-06	**Toronto**	**NHL**	**70**	**31**	**47**	**78**	**58**	**16**	**2**	**2**	**220**	**14.1**	**7**	**1557**	**54.0**	**19:59**	....	....	....	....	....	....	....	....	....
	Sweden	Olympics	8	3	5	8	4	....	....	....	....	....	....	....	....	....	....	....	....	....	....	....	....	....	....
	NHL Totals		**1156**	**496**	**671**	**1167**	**927**	**139**	**29**	**87**	**3351**	**14.8**		**12330**	**55.2**	**19:57**	**83**	**35**	**39**	**74**	**72**	**11**	**1**	**7**	**21:18**

NHL Second All-Star Team (2002, 2004)

Played in NHL All-Star Game (1996, 1997, 1998, 1999, 2000, 2001, 2002, 2004)

Traded to **Toronto** by **Quebec** with Garth Butcher, Todd Warriner and Philadelphia's 1st round choice (previously acquired, later traded to Washington – Washington selected Nolan Baumgartner) in 1994 Entry Draft for Wendel Clark, Sylvain Lefebvre, Landon Wilson and Toronto's 1st round choice (Jeffrey Kealty) in 1994 Entry Draft, June 28, 1994.

SUNDSTROM, Niklas (SUHN-struhm, NIHK-las)

Right wing. Shoots left. 6', 191 lbs. Born, Ornskoldsvik, Sweden, June 6, 1975. NY Rangers' 1st choice, 8th overall, in 1993 Entry Draft.

			Regular Season														Playoffs								
Season	Club	League	GP	G	A	Pts	PIM	PP	SH	GW	S	%	+/-	TF	F%	Min	GP	G	A	Pts	PIM	PP	SH	GW	Min
1991-92	MoDo	Sweden	9	1	3	4	0	....	....	....	....	....	....	....	....	....	....	....	....	....	....	....	....	....	....
1992-93	MoDo Jr.	Swe-Jr.	2	3	1	4	0	....	....	....	....	....	....	....	....	....	....	....	....	....	....	....	....	....	....
	MoDo	Sweden	40	7	11	18	18	....	....	....	....	....	....	....	....	....	3	0	0	0	0	....	....	....	....
1993-94	MoDo Jr.	Swe-Jr.	3	3	4	7	2	....	....	....	....	....	....	....	....	....	....	....	....	....	....	....	....	....	....
	MoDo	Sweden	37	7	12	19	28	....	....	....	....	....	....	....	....	....	11	4	3	7	2	....	....	....	....
1994-95	MoDo	Sweden	33	8	13	21	30	....	....	....	....	....	....	....	....	....	....	....	....	....	....	....	....	....	....
1995-96	**NY Rangers**	**NHL**	**82**	**9**	**12**	**21**	**14**	**1**	**1**	**2**	**90**	**10.0**	**2**	....	....	....	**11**	**4**	**3**	**7**	**4**	**1**	**0**	**0**	....
1996-97	**NY Rangers**	**NHL**	**82**	**24**	**28**	**52**	**20**	**5**	**1**	**4**	**132**	**18.2**	**23**	....	....	....	**9**	**0**	**5**	**5**	**2**	**0**	**0**	**0**	....
1997-98	**NY Rangers**	**NHL**	**70**	**19**	**28**	**47**	**24**	**4**	**0**	**1**	**115**	**16.5**	**0**	....	....	....	....	....	....	....	....	....	....	....	....
	Sweden	Olympics	4	1	1	2	2	....	....	....	....	....	....	....	....	....	....	....	....	....	....	....	....	....	....
1998-99	**NY Rangers**	**NHL**	**81**	**13**	**30**	**43**	**20**	**1**	**2**	**3**	**89**	**14.6**	**-2**	**376**	**40.4**	**19:11**	....	....	....	....	....	....	....	....	....
99-2000	**San Jose**	**NHL**	**79**	**12**	**25**	**37**	**22**	**2**	**1**	**2**	**90**	**13.3**	**9**	**10**	**50.0**	**15:10**	**12**	**0**	**2**	**2**	**2**	**0**	**0**	**0**	**15:09**
2000-01	**San Jose**	**NHL**	**82**	**10**	**39**	**49**	**28**	**4**	**1**	**0**	**100**	**10.0**	**10**	**26**	**30.8**	**16:44**	**6**	**0**	**3**	**3**	**2**	**0**	**0**	**0**	**16:40**
2001-02	**San Jose**	**NHL**	**73**	**9**	**30**	**39**	**50**	**0**	**1**	**0**	**74**	**12.2**	**7**	**9**	**33.3**	**15:57**	**12**	**1**	**6**	**7**	**6**	**0**	**0**	**0**	**16:25**
	Sweden	Olympics	4	1	3	4	0	....	....	....	....	....	....	....	....	....	....	....	....	....	....	....	....	....	....
2002-03	**San Jose**	**NHL**	**47**	**2**	**10**	**12**	**22**	**0**	**0**	**0**	**36**	**5.6**	**-4**	**1**	**0.0**	**14:09**	....	....	....	....	....	....	....	....	....
	Montreal	**NHL**	**33**	**5**	**9**	**14**	**8**	**0**	**0**	**1**	**35**	**14.3**	**3**	**10**	**40.0**	**14:26**	....	....	....	....	....	....	....	....	....
2003-04	**Montreal**	**NHL**	**66**	**8**	**12**	**20**	**18**	**0**	**0**	**2**	**67**	**11.9**	**3**	**20**	**15.0**	**14:17**	**4**	**1**	**0**	**1**	**2**	**0**	**0**	**0**	**13:10**
2004-05	Milano Vipers	Italy	33	9	27	36	40	....	....	....	....	....	....	....	....	....	15	4	14	18	20	....	....	....	....
2005-06	**Montreal**	**NHL**	**55**	**6**	**9**	**15**	**30**	**0**	**0**	**2**	**54**	**11.1**	**-6**	**11**	**18.2**	**14:02**	**5**	**0**	**3**	**3**	**4**	**0**	**0**	**0**	**9:29**
	NHL Totals		**750**	**117**	**232**	**349**	**256**	**17**	**7**	**17**	**882**	**13.3**		**463**	**38.2**	**15:47**	**59**	**6**	**22**	**28**	**22**	**1**	**0**	**0**	**14:51**

Traded to **Tampa Bay** by **NY Rangers** with Dan Cloutier and NY Rangers' 1st (Nikita Alexeev) and 3rd (later traded to San Jose – later traded to Chicago – Chicago selected Igor Radulov) round choices in 2000 Entry Draft for Chicago's 1st round choice (previously acquired, NY Rangers selected Pavel Brendl) in 1999 Entry Draft, June 26, 1999. Traded to **San Jose** by **Tampa Bay** with NY Rangers' 3rd round choice (previously acquired, later traded to Chicago – Chicago selected Igor Radulov) in 2000 Entry Draft for Bill Houlder, Andrei Zyuzin, Shawn Burr and Steve Guolla, August 4, 1999. Traded to **Montreal** by **San Jose** with San Jose's 3rd round choice (later traded to Los Angeles – Los Angeles selected Paul Baier) in 2004 Entry Draft for Jeff Hackett, January 23, 2003. Signed as a free agent by **Milano** (Italy), October 1, 2004.

SUROVY, Tomas (suh-ROH-vee, TAW-mahsh)

Center. Shoots left. 6'1", 205 lbs. Born, Banska Bystrica, Czech., September 24, 1981. Pittsburgh's 5th choice, 120th overall, in 2001 Entry Draft.

			Regular Season														Playoffs								
Season	Club	League	GP	G	A	Pts	PIM	PP	SH	GW	S	%	+/-	TF	F%	Min	GP	G	A	Pts	PIM	PP	SH	GW	Min
99-2000	B. Bystrica	Slovak-2	39	25	29	54	4	....	....	....	....	....	....	....	....	....	....	....	....	....	....	....	....	....	....
2000-01	HC SKP Poprad	Slovakia	53	22	28	50	30	....	....	....	....	....	....	....	....	....	6	2	1	3	14	....	....	....	....
2001-02	Wilkes-Barre	AHL	65	23	10	33	37	....	....	....	....	....	....	....	....	....	....	....	....	....	....	....	....	....	....
2002-03	**Pittsburgh**	**NHL**	**26**	**4**	**7**	**11**	**10**	**1**	**0**	**2**	**47**	**8.5**	**0**	**2**	**50.0**	**14:19**	....	....	....	....	....	....	....	....	....
	Wilkes-Barre	AHL	39	19	20	39	18	....	....	....	....	....	....	....	....	....	6	2	3	5	2	....	....	....	....
2003-04	**Pittsburgh**	**NHL**	**47**	**11**	**12**	**23**	**16**	**3**	**0**	**1**	**112**	**9.8**	**-8**	**4**	**25.0**	**12:28**	....	....	....	....	....	....	....	....	....
	Wilkes-Barre	AHL	30	14	15	29	14	....	....	....	....	....	....	....	....	....	24	6	10	16	8	....	....	....	....
2004-05	Wilkes-Barre	AHL	80	17	32	49	43	....	....	....	....	....	....	....	....	....	11	2	6	8	9	....	....	....	....
2005-06	**Pittsburgh**	**NHL**	**53**	**12**	**13**	**25**	**45**	**3**	**0**	**1**	**107**	**11.2**	**-13**	**11**	**36.4**	**13:35**	....	....	....	....	....	....	....	....	....
	Wilkes-Barre	AHL	25	16	12	28	26	....	....	....	....	....	....	....	....	....	....	....	....	....	....	....	....	....	....
	Slovakia	Olympics	6	0	1	1	2	....	....	....	....	....	....	....	....	....	....	....	....	....	....	....	....	....	....
	NHL Totals		**126**	**27**	**32**	**59**	**71**	**7**	**0**	**4**	**266**	**10.2**		**17**	**35.3**	**13:19**	....	....	....	....	....	....	....	....	....

Signed as a free agent by **Lulea** (Sweden), August 16, 2006.

SUTER, Ryan

(SOO-tuhr, RIGH-uhn) **NSH.**

Defense. Shoots left. 6'1", 196 lbs. Born, Madison, WI, January 21, 1985. Nashville's 1st choice, 7th overall, in 2003 Entry Draft.

			Regular Season														Playoffs								
Season	Club	League	GP	G	A	Pts	PIM	PP	SH	GW	S	%	+/-	TF	F%	Min	GP	G	A	Pts	PIM	PP	SH	GW	Min
2000-01	Culver Academy	High-IN	26	13	32	45	....	....	....	....	....	....	....	....	....	....	....	....	....	....	....	....	....	....	....
2001-02	USNTDP	U-17	8	2	11	13	21	....	....	....	....	....	....	....	....	....	....	....	....	....	....	....	....	....	....
	USNTDP	U-18	27	4	10	14	6	....	....	....	....	....	....	....	....	....	....	....	....	....	....	....	....	....	....
	USNTDP	NAHL	35	2	10	12	75	....	....	....	....	....	....	....	....	....	....	....	....	....	....	....	....	....	....
2002-03	USNTDP	U-18	42	7	17	24	124	....	....	....	....	....	....	....	....	....	....	....	....	....	....	....	....	....	....
	USNTDP	NAHL	9	2	5	7	12	....	....	....	....	....	....	....	....	....	....	....	....	....	....	....	....	....	....
2003-04	U. of Wisconsin	WCHA	39	3	16	19	93	....	....	....	....	....	....	....	....	....	....	....	....	....	....	....	....	....	....
2004-05	Milwaukee	AHL	63	7	16	23	70	....	....	....	....	....	....	....	....	....	7	1	5	6	16	....	....	....	....
2005-06	**Nashville**	**NHL**	**71**	**1**	**15**	**16**	**66**	**0**	**0**	**0**	**84**	**1.2**	**7**	**0**	**0.0**	**17:21**	....	....	....	....	....	....	....	....	....
	NHL Totals		**71**	**1**	**15**	**16**	**66**	**0**	**0**	**0**	**84**	**1.2**		**0**	**0.0**	**17:21**	....	....	....	....	....	....	....	....	....

WCHA All-Rookie Team (2004)

SUTHERBY, Brian

(SUH-thur-bee, BRIGH-uhn) **WSH.**

Center. Shoots left. 6'3", 205 lbs. Born, Edmonton, Alta., March 1, 1982. Washington's 1st choice, 26th overall, in 2000 Entry Draft.

			Regular Season														Playoffs								
Season	Club	League	GP	G	A	Pts	PIM	PP	SH	GW	S	%	+/-	TF	F%	Min	GP	G	A	Pts	PIM	PP	SH	GW	Min
1997-98	CAC Cement	AMHL	36	36	23	59	60	....	....	....	....	....	....	....	....	....	....	....	....	....	....	....	....	....	....
1998-99	Moose Jaw	WHL	66	9	12	21	47	....	....	....	....	....	....	....	....	....	11	0	1	1	0	....	....	....	....
99-2000	Moose Jaw	WHL	47	18	17	35	102	....	....	....	....	....	....	....	....	....	4	1	1	2	12	....	....	....	....
2000-01	Moose Jaw	WHL	59	34	43	77	138	....	....	....	....	....	....	....	....	....	4	2	1	3	10	....	....	....	....
2001-02	**Washington**	**NHL**	**7**	**0**	**0**	**0**	**2**	**0**	**0**	**0**	**3**	**0.0**	**−3**	**39**	**35.9**	**7:17**	....	....	....	....	....	....	....	....	....
	Moose Jaw	WHL	36	18	27	45	75	....	....	....	....	....	....	....	....	....	12	7	5	12	33	....	....	....	....
2002-03	Portland Pirates	AHL	5	0	5	5	11	....	....	....	....	....	....	....	....	....	....	....	....	....	....	....	....	....	....
	Washington	**NHL**	**72**	**2**	**9**	**11**	**93**	**0**	**0**	**0**	**38**	**5.3**	**7**	**288**	**43.8**	**9:44**	**5**	**0**	**0**	**0**	**10**	**0**	**0**	**0**	**4:10**
2003-04	**Washington**	**NHL**	**30**	**2**	**0**	**2**	**28**	**0**	**0**	**0**	**24**	**8.3**	**−5**	**116**	**41.4**	**10:15**	....	....	....	....	....	....	....	....	....
	Portland Pirates	AHL	6	2	4	6	16	....	....	....	....	....	....	....	....	....	....	....	....	....	....	....	....	....	....
2004-05	Portland Pirates	AHL	53	10	19	29	115	....	....	....	....	....	....	....	....	....	....	....	....	....	....	....	....	....	....
2005-06	**Washington**	**NHL**	**76**	**14**	**16**	**30**	**73**	**0**	**2**	**0**	**85**	**16.5**	**−17**	**904**	**48.7**	**13:44**	....	....	....	....	....	....	....	....	....
	NHL Totals		**185**	**18**	**25**	**43**	**196**	**0**	**2**	**0**	**150**	**12.0**		**1347**	**46.6**	**11:22**	**5**	**0**	**0**	**0**	**10**	**0**	**0**	**0**	**4:10**

• Missed majority of 2003-04 season recovering from groin injury suffered in game vs. St. Louis, October 18, 2003.

SUTTON, Andy

(SUH-tohn, AN-dee) **ATL.**

Defense. Shoots left. 6'6", 245 lbs. Born, Kingston, Ont., March 10, 1975.

			Regular Season														Playoffs								
Season	Club	League	GP	G	A	Pts	PIM	PP	SH	GW	S	%	+/-	TF	F%	Min	GP	G	A	Pts	PIM	PP	SH	GW	Min
1991-92	Gananoque	OHA-B	36	11	9	20	....	....	....	....	....	....	....	....	....	....	14	9	21	30	....	....	....	....	....
1992-93	Gananoque	OHA-B	38	14	9	23	....	....	....	....	....	....	....	....	....	....	12	16	13	29	....	....	....	....	....
1993-94	St. Mike's B's	MTJHL	48	17	23	40	161	....	....	....	....	....	....	....	....	....	3	0	0	0	20	....	....	....	....
1994-95	Michigan Tech	WCHA	19	2	1	3	42	....	....	....	....	....	....	....	....	....	....	....	....	....	....	....	....	....	....
1995-96	Michigan Tech	WCHA	33	2	2	4	58	....	....	....	....	....	....	....	....	....	....	....	....	....	....	....	....	....	....
1996-97	Michigan Tech	WCHA	32	2	7	9	73	....	....	....	....	....	....	....	....	....	....	....	....	....	....	....	....	....	....
1997-98	Michigan Tech	WCHA	38	16	24	40	97	....	....	....	....	....	....	....	....	....	....	....	....	....	....	....	....	....	....
	Kentucky	AHL	7	0	0	0	33	....	....	....	....	....	....	....	....	....	....	....	....	....	....	....	....	....	....
1998-99	**San Jose**	**NHL**	**31**	**0**	**3**	**3**	**65**	**0**	**0**	**0**	**24**	**0.0**	**−4**	**0**	**0.0**	**12:58**	....	....	....	....	....	....	....	....	....
	Kentucky	AHL	21	5	10	15	53	....	....	....	....	....	....	....	....	....	5	0	0	0	23	....	....	....	....
99-2000	**San Jose**	**NHL**	**40**	**1**	**1**	**2**	**80**	**0**	**0**	**0**	**29**	**3.4**	**−5**	**0**	**0.0**	**12:57**	....	....	....	....	....	....	....	....	....
	Kentucky	AHL	3	0	1	1	0	....	....	....	....	....	....	....	....	....	....	....	....	....	....	....	....	....	....
2000-01	**Minnesota**	**NHL**	**69**	**3**	**4**	**7**	**131**	**2**	**0**	**0**	**64**	**4.7**	**−11**	**3**	**33.3**	**12:55**	....	....	....	....	....	....	....	....	....
2001-02	**Minnesota**	**NHL**	**19**	**2**	**4**	**6**	**35**	**1**	**0**	**0**	**21**	**9.5**	**−4**	**2**	**0.0**	**10:57**	....	....	....	....	....	....	....	....	....
	Atlanta	**NHL**	**24**	**0**	**4**	**4**	**46**	**0**	**0**	**0**	**20**	**0.0**	**0**	**0**	**0.0**	**15:25**	....	....	....	....	....	....	....	....	....
2002-03	**Atlanta**	**NHL**	**53**	**3**	**18**	**21**	**114**	**1**	**1**	**0**	**65**	**4.6**	**−8**	**3**	**33.3**	**18:00**	....	....	....	....	....	....	....	....	....
2003-04	**Atlanta**	**NHL**	**65**	**8**	**13**	**21**	**94**	**7**	**1**	**1**	**102**	**7.8**	**0**	**1**	**0.0**	**23:21**	....	....	....	....	....	....	....	....	....
2004-05	GCK Lions Zurich	Swiss-2	18	8	18	26	58	....	....	....	....	....	....	....	....	....	6	2	4	6	16	....	....	....	....
	ZSC Lions Zurich	Swiss	8	2	2	4	32	....	....	....	....	....	....	....	....	....	1	0	1	1	2	....	....	....	....
2005-06	**Atlanta**	**NHL**	**76**	**8**	**17**	**25**	**144**	**2**	**1**	**3**	**86**	**9.3**	**13**	**1**	**0.0**	**21:05**	....	....	....	....	....	....	....	....	....
	NHL Totals		**377**	**25**	**64**	**89**	**709**	**13**	**3**	**4**	**411**	**6.1**		**10**	**20.0**	**17:09**	....	....	....	....	....	....	....	....	....

WCHA Second All-Star Team (1998)

Signed as a free agent by **San Jose**, March 20, 1998. Traded to **Minnesota** by **San Jose** with San Jose's 7th round choice (Peter Bartos) in 2000 Entry Draft and 3rd round choice (later traded to Atlanta – later traded to Pittsburgh – later traded to Columbus – Columbus selected Aaron Johnson) in 2001 Entry Draft for Minnesota's 8th round choice (later traded to Calgary – Calgary selected Joe Campbell) in 2001 Entry Draft and future considerations, June 12, 2000. Traded to **Atlanta** by **Minnesota** for Hnat Domenichelli, January 22, 2002. Signed as a free agent by **GCK Zurich** (Swiss-2), September 24, 2004. Loaned to **ZSC Zurich** (Swiss) by **GCK Zurich** (Swiss-2), February 22, 2005.

SVATOS, Marek

(SVA-tohsh, MAIR-ehk) **COL.**

Right wing. Shoots right. 5'10", 170 lbs. Born, Kosice, Czech., June 17, 1982. Colorado's 10th choice, 227th overall, in 2001 Entry Draft.

			Regular Season														Playoffs								
Season	Club	League	GP	G	A	Pts	PIM	PP	SH	GW	S	%	+/-	TF	F%	Min	GP	G	A	Pts	PIM	PP	SH	GW	Min
99-2000	HC VSZ Kosice Jr.	Slovak-Jr.	39	43	30	73	28	....	....	....	....	....	....	....	....	....	....	....	....	....	....	....	....	....	....
	HC VSZ Kosice	Slovakia	19	2	2	4	0	....	....	....	....	....	....	....	....	....	....	....	....	....	....	....	....	....	....
2000-01	Kootenay Ice	WHL	39	23	18	41	47	....	....	....	....	....	....	....	....	....	11	7	2	9	26	....	....	....	....
2001-02	Kootenay Ice	WHL	53	38	39	77	58	....	....	....	....	....	....	....	....	....	21	12	6	18	40	....	....	....	....
2002-03	Hershey Bears	AHL	30	9	4	13	10	....	....	....	....	....	....	....	....	....	....	....	....	....	....	....	....	....	....
2003-04	**Colorado**	**NHL**	**4**	**2**	**0**	**2**	**0**	**1**	**0**	**1**	**6**	**33.3**	**1**	**0**	**0.0**	**10:18**	**11**	**1**	**5**	**6**	**2**	**0**	**0**	**1**	**12:29**
2004-05	Hershey Bears	AHL	72	18	28	46	69	....	....	....	....	....	....	....	....	....	....	....	....	....	....	....	....	....	....
2005-06	**Colorado**	**NHL**	**61**	**32**	**18**	**50**	**60**	**12**	**0**	**9**	**165**	**19.4**	**0**	**5**	**20.0**	**13:45**	....	....	....	....	....	....	....	....	....
	Slovakia	Olympics	6	0	0	0	0	....	....	....	....	....	....	....	....	....	....	....	....	....	....	....	....	....	....
	NHL Totals		**65**	**34**	**18**	**52**	**60**	**13**	**0**	**10**	**171**	**19.9**		**5**	**20.0**	**13:32**	**11**	**1**	**5**	**6**	**2**	**0**	**0**	**1**	**12:29**

WHL West Second All-Star Team (2002)

• Missed majority of 2002-03 season recovering from shoulder injury that required surgery, January 28, 2003. • Missed majority of 2003-04 season recovering from shoulder injury suffered in game vs. St. Louis, October 12, 2003.

SVITOV, Alexander

(SVEE-tawf, al-ehx-AN-duhr) **CBJ**

Center. Shoots left. 6'3", 228 lbs. Born, Omsk, USSR, November 3, 1982. Tampa Bay's 1st choice, 3rd overall, in 2001 Entry Draft.

			Regular Season														Playoffs								
Season	Club	League	GP	G	A	Pts	PIM	PP	SH	GW	S	%	+/-	TF	F%	Min	GP	G	A	Pts	PIM	PP	SH	GW	Min
1997-98	Novokuznetsk 2	Russia-3	4	0	0	0	0	....	....	....	....	....	....	....	....	....	....	....	....	....	....	....	....	....	....
1998-99	Omsk 2	Russia-4	27	15	8	23	20	....	....	....	....	....	....	....	....	....	....	....	....	....	....	....	....	....	....
	Avangard Omsk	Russia	....	....	....	....	....	....	....	....	....	....	....	....	....	....	1	0	0	0	0	....	....	....	....
99-2000	Omsk 2	Russia-3	14	13	9	22	62	....	....	....	....	....	....	....	....	....	....	....	....	....	....	....	....	....	....
	Avangard Omsk	Russia	18	3	3	6	45	....	....	....	....	....	....	....	....	....	6	1	0	1	16	....	....	....	....
2000-01	Avangard Omsk	Russia	39	8	6	14	115	....	....	....	....	....	....	....	....	....	14	2	1	3	34	....	....	....	....
2001-02	CSKA Moscow 2	Russia-3	2	1	0	1	2	....	....	....	....	....	....	....	....	....	....	....	....	....	....	....	....	....	....
	Avangard Omsk	Russia	2	0	1	1	2	....	....	....	....	....	....	....	....	....	....	....	....	....	....	....	....	....	....
2002-03	**Tampa Bay**	**NHL**	**63**	**4**	**4**	**8**	**58**	**1**	**0**	**0**	**69**	**5.8**	**−4**	**395**	**42.8**	**8:50**	**7**	**0**	**0**	**0**	**6**	**0**	**0**	**0**	**7:19**
	Springfield	AHL	11	4	5	9	17	....	....	....	....	....	....	....	....	....	....	....	....	....	....	....	....	....	....
2003-04	**Tampa Bay**	**NHL**	**11**	**0**	**3**	**3**	**4**	**0**	**0**	**0**	**16**	**0.0**	**0**	**79**	**58.2**	**9:18**	....	....	....	....	....	....	....	....	....
	Hamilton	AHL	30	9	9	18	79	....	....	....	....	....	....	....	....	....	....	....	....	....	....	....	....	....	....
	Columbus	**NHL**	**29**	**2**	**6**	**8**	**16**	**0**	**0**	**0**	**36**	**5.6**	**−8**	**293**	**43.0**	**12:39**	....	....	....	....	....	....	....	....	....
2004-05	Syracuse Crunch	AHL	69	19	23	42	200	....	....	....	....	....	....	....	....	....	....	....	....	....	....	....	....	....	....
2005-06	Avangard Omsk	Russia	32	3	6	9	142	....	....	....	....	....	....	....	....	....	13	4	1	5	10	....	....	....	....
	NHL Totals		**103**	**6**	**13**	**19**	**78**	**1**	**0**	**0**	**121**	**5.0**		**767**	**44.5**	**9:58**	**7**	**0**	**0**	**0**	**6**	**0**	**0**	**0**	**7:19**

Traded to **Columbus** by **Tampa Bay** with Tampa Bay's 3rd round choice (later traded to Calgary – Calgary selected Dustin Boyd) in 2004 Entry Draft for Darryl Sydor and Columbus' 4th round choice (Mike Lundin) in 2004 Entry Draft, January 27, 2004.

SVOBODA, Jaroslav

(svah-BOH-duh, YAR-oh-slawf)

Left wing. Shoots left. 6'2", 190 lbs. Born, Cervenka, Czech., June 1, 1980. Carolina's 8th choice, 208th overall, in 1998 Entry Draft.

			Regular Season														Playoffs								
Season	Club	League	GP	G	A	Pts	PIM	PP	SH	GW	S	%	+/-	TF	F%	Min	GP	G	A	Pts	PIM	PP	SH	GW	Min
1995-96	HC Olomouc Jr.	CzRep-Jr.	40	13	15	28	....	....	....	....	....	....	....	....	....	....	....	....	....	....	....	....	....	....	....
1996-97	HC Olomouc Jr.	CzRep-Jr.	39	19	14	33	....	....	....	....	....	....	....	....	....	....	....	....	....	....	....	....	....	....	....
1997-98	HC Olomouc Jr.	CzRep-Jr.	36	14	21	35	....	....	....	....	....	....	....	....	....	....	....	....	....	....	....	....	....	....	....
	HC Olomouc	CzRep-2	13	0	1	1	....	....	....	....	....	....	....	....	....	....	....	....	....	....	....	....	....	....	....
1998-99	Kootenay Ice	WHL	54	26	33	59	46	....	....	....	....	....	....	....	....	....	7	2	2	4	11	....	....	....	....
99-2000	Kootenay Ice	WHL	56	23	43	66	97	....	....	....	....	....	....	....	....	....	21	*15	13	*28	51	....	....	....	....
2000-01	Cincinnati	IHL	52	4	10	14	25	....	....	....	....	....	....	....	....	....	....	....	....	....	....	....	....	....	....
2001-02	**Carolina**	**NHL**	**10**	**2**	**2**	**4**	**2**	**0**	**0**	**0**	**12**	**16.7**	**0**	**1**	**0.0**	**9:23**	**23**	**1**	**4**	**5**	**28**	**1**	**0**	**1**	**14:45**
	Lowell	AHL	66	12	16	28	58	....	....	....	....	....	....	....	....	....	....	....	....	....	....	....	....	....	....
2002-03	**Carolina**	**NHL**	**48**	**3**	**11**	**14**	**32**	**1**	**0**	**0**	**63**	**4.8**	**–5**	**25**	**40.0**	**14:33**	....	....	....	....	....	....	....	....	....
	Lowell	AHL	9	1	1	2	10	....	....	....	....	....	....	....	....	....	....	....	....	....	....	....	....	....	....
2003-04	**Carolina**	**NHL**	**33**	**3**	**1**	**4**	**6**	**0**	**0**	**1**	**27**	**11.1**	**3**	**18**	**33.3**	**9:08**	....	....	....	....	....	....	....	....	....
	Lowell	AHL	9	2	2	4	4	....	....	....	....	....	....	....	....	....	....	....	....	....	....	....	....	....	....
2004-05	HC Ocelari Trinec	CzRep	9	0	2	2	14	....	....	....	....	....	....	....	....	....	....	....	....	....	....	....	....	....	....
	HC Olomouc	CzRep-2	18	7	6	13	67	....	....	....	....	....	....	....	....	....	....	....	....	....	....	....	....	....	....
2005-06	**Dallas**	**NHL**	**43**	**4**	**3**	**7**	**22**	**0**	**0**	**2**	**33**	**12.1**	**–3**	**3**	**100.0**	**7:04**	**2**	**0**	**0**	**0**	**2**	**0**	**0**	**0**	**6:36**
	NHL Totals		**134**	**12**	**17**	**29**	**62**	**1**	**0**	**3**	**135**	**8.9**		**47**	**40.4**	**10:26**	**25**	**1**	**4**	**5**	**30**	**1**	**0**	**1**	**14:06**

Traded to **Dallas** by **Carolina** for Dallas' 4th round choice (Jakub Vojta) in 2005 Entry Draft, June 29, 2004. Signed as a free agent by **Olomouc** (CzRep-2), September 27, 2004. Signed as a free agent by **Trinec** (CzRep), January 6, 2005.

SYDOR, Darryl

(sih-DOHR, DAIR-ihl) **DAL.**

Defense. Shoots left. 6'1", 205 lbs. Born, Edmonton, Alta., May 13, 1972. Los Angeles' 1st choice, 7th overall, in 1990 Entry Draft.

			Regular Season														Playoffs								
Season	Club	League	GP	G	A	Pts	PIM	PP	SH	GW	S	%	+/-	TF	F%	Min	GP	G	A	Pts	PIM	PP	SH	GW	Min
1985-86	Genstar Cement	AAHA	34	20	17	37	60	....	....	....	....	....	....	....	....	....	....	....	....	....	....	....	....	....	....
1986-87	Genstar Cement	AAHA	36	15	20	35	60	....	....	....	....	....	....	....	....	....	....	....	....	....	....	....	....	....	....
1987-88	Edmonton Mets	AJHL	38	10	11	21	54	....	....	....	....	....	....	....	....	....	....	....	....	....	....	....	....	....	....
1988-89	Kamloops Blazers	WHL	65	12	14	26	86	....	....	....	....	....	....	....	....	....	15	1	4	5	19	....	....	....	....
1989-90	Kamloops Blazers	WHL	67	29	66	95	129	....	....	....	....	....	....	....	....	....	17	2	9	11	28	....	....	....	....
1990-91	Kamloops Blazers	WHL	66	27	78	105	88	....	....	....	....	....	....	....	....	....	12	3	*22	25	10	....	....	....	....
1991-92	Kamloops Blazers	WHL	29	9	39	48	33	....	....	....	....	....	....	....	....	....	17	3	15	18	18	....	....	....	....
	Los Angeles	**NHL**	**18**	**1**	**5**	**6**	**22**	**0**	**0**	**0**	**18**	**5.6**	**–3**	....	....	....	....	....	....	....	....	....	....	....	....
1992-93	**Los Angeles**	**NHL**	**80**	**6**	**23**	**29**	**63**	**0**	**0**	**1**	**112**	**5.4**	**–2**	....	....	....	**24**	**3**	**8**	**11**	**16**	**2**	**0**	**0**	....
1993-94	**Los Angeles**	**NHL**	**84**	**8**	**27**	**35**	**94**	**1**	**0**	**0**	**146**	**5.5**	**–9**	....	....	....	....	....	....	....	....	....	....	....	....
1994-95	**Los Angeles**	**NHL**	**48**	**4**	**19**	**23**	**36**	**3**	**0**	**0**	**96**	**4.2**	**–2**	....	....	....	....	....	....	....	....	....	....	....	....
1995-96	**Los Angeles**	**NHL**	**58**	**1**	**11**	**12**	**34**	**1**	**0**	**0**	**84**	**1.2**	**–11**	....	....	....	....	....	....	....	....	....	....	....	....
	Dallas	**NHL**	**26**	**2**	**6**	**8**	**41**	**1**	**0**	**0**	**33**	**6.1**	**–1**	....	....	....	....	....	....	....	....	....	....	....	....
1996-97	**Dallas**	**NHL**	**82**	**8**	**40**	**48**	**51**	**2**	**0**	**2**	**142**	**5.6**	**37**	....	....	....	**7**	**0**	**2**	**2**	**0**	**0**	**0**	**0**	....
1997-98	**Dallas**	**NHL**	**79**	**11**	**35**	**46**	**51**	**4**	**1**	**1**	**166**	**6.6**	**17**	....	....	....	**17**	**0**	**5**	**5**	**14**	**0**	**0**	**0**	....
1998-99 ♦	**Dallas**	**NHL**	**74**	**14**	**34**	**48**	**50**	**9**	**0**	**2**	**163**	**8.6**	**–1**	**1**	**100.0**	**21:16**	**23**	**3**	**9**	**12**	**16**	**1**	**0**	**1**	**22:20**
99-2000	**Dallas**	**NHL**	**74**	**8**	**26**	**34**	**32**	**5**	**0**	**1**	**132**	**6.1**	**6**	**1**	**0.0**	**23:09**	**23**	**1**	**6**	**7**	**6**	**0**	**0**	**0**	**20:48**
2000-01	**Dallas**	**NHL**	**81**	**10**	**37**	**47**	**34**	**8**	**0**	**1**	**140**	**7.1**	**5**	**1**	**0.0**	**21:25**	**10**	**1**	**3**	**4**	**0**	**1**	**0**	**0**	**22:42**
2001-02	**Dallas**	**NHL**	**78**	**4**	**29**	**33**	**50**	**2**	**0**	**0**	**183**	**2.2**	**3**	**0**	**0.0**	**21:07**	....	....	....	....	....	....	....	....	....
2002-03	**Dallas**	**NHL**	**81**	**5**	**31**	**36**	**40**	**2**	**0**	**1**	**132**	**3.8**	**22**	**0**	**0.0**	**18:19**	**12**	**0**	**6**	**6**	**6**	**0**	**0**	**0**	**19:14**
2003-04	**Columbus**	**NHL**	**49**	**2**	**13**	**15**	**26**	**1**	**0**	**0**	**80**	**2.5**	**–19**	**1**	**0.0**	**21:54**	....	....	....	....	....	....	....	....	....
	♦ **Tampa Bay**	**NHL**	**31**	**1**	**6**	**7**	**6**	**0**	**0**	**0**	**42**	**2.4**	**3**	**0**	**0.0**	**19:06**	**23**	**0**	**6**	**6**	**9**	**0**	**0**	**0**	**21:50**
2004-05			DID NOT PLAY																						
2005-06	**Tampa Bay**	**NHL**	**80**	**4**	**19**	**23**	**30**	**1**	**0**	**0**	**64**	**6.3**	**–18**	**1**	**0.0**	**19:06**	**5**	**0**	**1**	**1**	**0**	**0**	**0**	**0**	**17:54**
	NHL Totals		**1023**	**89**	**361**	**450**	**660**	**40**	**1**	**9**	**1733**	**5.1**		**5**	**20.0**	**20:42**	**144**	**8**	**46**	**54**	**67**	**4**	**0**	**1**	**21:16**

WHL West First All-Star Team (1990, 1991, 1992)

Played in NHL All-Star Game (1998, 1999)

Traded to **Dallas** by **Los Angeles** with Los Angeles' 5th round choice (Ryan Christie) in 1996 Entry Draft for Shane Churla and Doug Zmolek, February 17, 1996. Traded to **Columbus** by **Dallas** for Mike Sillinger and Columbus' 2nd round choice (Johan Fransson) in 2004 Entry Draft, July 22, 2003. Traded to **Tampa Bay** by **Columbus** with Columbus' 4th round choice (Mike Lundin) in 2004 Entry Draft for Alexander Svitov and Tampa Bay's 3rd round choice (later traded to Calgary – Calgary selected Dustin Boyd) in 2004 Entry Draft, January 27, 2004. Traded to **Dallas** by **Tampa Bay** for a 4th round choice in 2008 Entry Draft, July 2, 2006.

SYKORA, Petr

(sih-KOH-ra, PEE-tuhr)

Center. Shoots right. 6'3", 206 lbs. Born, Pardubice, Czech., December 21, 1978. Detroit's 2nd choice, 76th overall, in 1997 Entry Draft.

			Regular Season														Playoffs								
Season	Club	League	GP	G	A	Pts	PIM	PP	SH	GW	S	%	+/-	TF	F%	Min	GP	G	A	Pts	PIM	PP	SH	GW	Min
1994-95	HC Pardubice Jr.	CzRep-Jr.	38	35	33	68	....	....	....	....	....	....	....	....	....	....	....	....	....	....	....	....	....	....	....
1995-96	HC Pardubice Jr.	CzRep-Jr.	16	26	17	43	....	....	....	....	....	....	....	....	....	....	....	....	....	....	....	....	....	....	....
1996-97	HC Pardubice Jr.	CzRep-Jr.	12	14	4	18	....	....	....	....	....	....	....	....	....	....	....	....	....	....	....	....	....	....	....
	Pardubice	CzRep	29	1	3	4	4	....	....	....	....	....	....	....	....	....	....	....	....	....	....	....	....	....	....
1997-98	Pardubice	CzRep	39	4	5	9	8	....	....	....	....	....	....	....	....	....	3	0	0	0	....	....	....	....	....
1998-99	**Nashville**	**NHL**	**2**	**0**	**0**	**0**	**0**	**0**	**0**	**0**	**2**	**0.0**	**–1**	**11**	**45.5**	**8:19**	....	....	....	....	....	....	....	....	....
	Milwaukee	IHL	73	14	15	29	50	....	....	....	....	....	....	....	....	....	2	1	1	2	0	....	....	....	....
99-2000	Milwaukee	IHL	3	0	1	1	2	....	....	....	....	....	....	....	....	....	....	....	....	....	....	....	....	....	....
	Pardubice	CzRep	36	7	13	20	49	....	....	....	....	....	....	....	....	....	3	0	0	0	2	....	....	....	....
2000-01	Pardubice	CzRep	47	26	18	44	42	....	....	....	....	....	....	....	....	....	7	5	3	8	6	....	....	....	....
2001-02	Pardubice	CzRep	32	18	8	26	72	....	....	....	....	....	....	....	....	....	6	1	2	3	26	....	....	....	....
2002-03	Pardubice	CzRep	45	18	18	36	86	....	....	....	....	....	....	....	....	....	19	7	7	14	39	....	....	....	....
2003-04	Pardubice	CzRep	48	23	23	46	20	....	....	....	....	....	....	....	....	....	7	1	0	1	6	....	....	....	....
2004-05	Pardubice	CzRep	43	25	10	35	28	....	....	....	....	....	....	....	....	....	16	3	2	5	33	....	....	....	....
2005-06	**Washington**	**NHL**	**10**	**2**	**2**	**4**	**6**	**0**	**0**	**0**	**9**	**22.2**	**0**	**2**	**50.0**	**10:41**	....	....	....	....	....	....	....	....	....
	Pardubice	CzRep	28	11	14	25	46	....	....	....	....	....	....	....	....	....	....	....	....	....	....	....	....	....	....
	NHL Totals		**12**	**2**	**2**	**4**	**6**	**0**	**0**	**0**	**11**	**18.2**		**13**	**46.2**	**10:17**	....	....	....	....	....	....	....	....	....

Traded to **Nashville** by **Detroit** with Detroit's 3rd round choice (later traded to Edmonton – Edmonton selected Mike Comrie) and 4th round compensatory choice (Alexander Krevsun) in 1999 Entry Draft for Doug Brown, July 14, 1998. Traded to **Washington** by **Nashville** for Washington's 3rd round choice (Paul Brown) in 2003 Entry Draft, June 22, 2002.

SYKORA, Petr

(sih-KOH-ra, PEE-tuhr) **EDM.**

Right wing. Shoots left. 6', 190 lbs. Born, Plzen, Czech., November 19, 1976. New Jersey's 1st choice, 18th overall, in 1995 Entry Draft.

			Regular Season														Playoffs								
Season	Club	League	GP	G	A	Pts	PIM	PP	SH	GW	S	%	+/-	TF	F%	Min	GP	G	A	Pts	PIM	PP	SH	GW	Min
1991-92	Plzen Jr.	Czech-Jr.	30	50	50	100	....	....	....	....	....	....	....	....	....	....	....	....	....	....	....	....	....	....	....
1992-93	HC Skoda Plzen	Czech	19	12	5	17	....	....	....	....	....	....	....	....	....	....	....	....	....	....	....	....	....	....	....
1993-94	HC Skoda Plzen	CzRep	37	10	16	26	....	....	....	....	....	....	....	....	....	....	4	0	1	1	....	....	....	....	....
	Cleveland	IHL	13	4	5	9	8	....	....	....	....	....	....	....	....	....	....	....	....	....	....	....	....	....	....
1994-95	Detroit Vipers	IHL	29	12	17	29	16	....	....	....	....	....	....	....	....	....	....	....	....	....	....	....	....	....	....
1995-96	**New Jersey**	**NHL**	**63**	**18**	**24**	**42**	**32**	**8**	**0**	**3**	**128**	**14.1**	**7**	....	....	....	....	....	....	....	....	....	....	....	....
	Albany River Rats	AHL	5	4	1	5	0	....	....	....	....	....	....	....	....	....	....	....	....	....	....	....	....	....	....
1996-97	**New Jersey**	**NHL**	**19**	**1**	**2**	**3**	**4**	**0**	**0**	**0**	**26**	**3.8**	**–8**	....	....	....	**2**	**0**	**0**	**0**	**2**	**0**	**0**	**0**	....
	Albany River Rats	AHL	43	20	25	45	48	....	....	....	....	....	....	....	....	....	4	1	4	5	2	....	....	....	....
1997-98	**New Jersey**	**NHL**	**58**	**16**	**20**	**36**	**22**	**3**	**1**	**4**	**130**	**12.3**	**0**	....	....	....	**2**	**0**	**0**	**0**	**0**	**0**	**0**	**0**	....
	Albany River Rats	AHL	2	4	1	5	0	....	....	....	....	....	....	....	....	....	....	....	....	....	....	....	....	....	....
1998-99	**New Jersey**	**NHL**	**80**	**29**	**43**	**72**	**22**	**15**	**0**	**7**	**222**	**13.1**	**16**	**33**	**33.3**	**16:14**	**7**	**3**	**3**	**6**	**4**	**0**	**0**	**1**	**18:11**
99-2000 ♦	**New Jersey**	**NHL**	**79**	**25**	**43**	**68**	**26**	**5**	**1**	**4**	**222**	**11.3**	**24**	**47**	**61.7**	**17:06**	**23**	**9**	**8**	**17**	**10**	**1**	**0**	**3**	**15:20**
2000-01	**New Jersey**	**NHL**	**73**	**35**	**46**	**81**	**32**	**9**	**2**	**3**	**249**	**14.1**	**36**	**15**	**33.3**	**17:44**	**25**	**10**	**12**	**22**	**12**	**2**	**2**	**2**	**18:40**
2001-02	**New Jersey**	**NHL**	**73**	**21**	**27**	**48**	**44**	**4**	**0**	**4**	**194**	**10.8**	**12**	**1**	**0.0**	**17:51**	**4**	**0**	**1**	**1**	**0**	**0**	**0**	**0**	**17:57**
	Czech Republic	Olympics	4	1	0	1	0	....	....	....	....	....	....	....	....	....	....	....	....	....	....	....	....	....	....
2002-03	**Anaheim**	**NHL**	**82**	**34**	**25**	**59**	**24**	**15**	**1**	**5**	**299**	**11.4**	**–7**	**23**	**39.1**	**18:29**	**21**	**4**	**9**	**13**	**12**	**1**	**0**	**2**	**18:39**
2003-04	**Anaheim**	**NHL**	**81**	**23**	**29**	**52**	**34**	**6**	**0**	**2**	**277**	**8.3**	**–9**	**9**	**22.2**	**17:57**	....	....	....	....	....	....	....	....	....
2004-05	Magnitogorsk	Russia	45	18	13	31	46	....	....	....	....	....	....	....	....	....	5	2	3	5	8	....	....	....	....
2005-06	**Anaheim**	**NHL**	**34**	**7**	**13**	**20**	**28**	**1**	**0**	**0**	**118**	**5.9**	**1**	**5**	**40.0**	**17:11**	....	....	....	....	....	....	....	....	....
	NY Rangers	**NHL**	**40**	**16**	**15**	**31**	**22**	**7**	**0**	**0**	**112**	**14.3**	**5**	**69**	**37.7**	**15:11**	**4**	**0**	**0**	**0**	**0**	**0**	**0**	**0**	**17:45**
	NHL Totals		**682**	**225**	**287**	**512**	**290**	**73**	**5**	**32**	**1977**	**11.4**		**202**	**40.6**	**17:15**	**88**	**26**	**33**	**59**	**40**	**4**	**2**	**8**	**25:06**

NHL All-Rookie Team (1996)

Traded to **Anaheim** by **New Jersey** with Mike Commodore, Jean-Francois Damphousse and Igor Pohanka for Jeff Friesen, Oleg Tverdovsky and Maxim Balmochnykh, July 6, 2002. Signed as a free agent by **Magnitogorsk** (Russia), August 12, 2004. Traded to **NY Rangers** by **Anaheim** with NY Rangers' 4th round choice (previously acquired) in 2007 Entry Draft for Maxim Kondratiev, January 8, 2006. Signed as a free agent by **Edmonton**, August 11, 2006.

						Regular Season													Playoffs							
Season	Club	League	GP	G	A	Pts	PIM	PP	SH	GW	S	%	+/-	TF	F%	Min	GP	G	A	Pts	PIM	PP	SH	GW	Min

SYVRET, Danny   (SIHV-reht, DA-nee)   **EDM.**

Defense. Shoots left. 5'11", 203 lbs.   Born, Millgrove, Ont., June 13, 1985. Edmonton's 3rd choice, 81st overall, in 2005 Entry Draft.

Season	Club	League	GP	G	A	Pts	PIM	PP	SH	GW	S	%	+/-	TF	F%	Min	GP	G	A	Pts	PIM	PP	SH	GW	Min
2001-02	Cambridge	OHA-B	43	6	41	47	23	....	....	....	....	....	....	....	....	....	....	....	....	....	....				
	London Knights	OHL	1	0	0	0	0	....	....	....	....	....	....	....	....	....	....	....	....	....	....				
2002-03	London Knights	OHL	68	8	14	22	31	....	....	....	....	....	....	....	....	....	14	1	6	7	11				
2003-04	London Knights	OHL	68	3	28	31	32	....	....	....	....	....	....	....	....	....	15	1	6	7	4				
2004-05	London Knights	OHL	62	23	46	69	33	....	....	....	....	....	....	....	....	....	18	5	15	20	4				
2005-06	**Edmonton**	**NHL**	10	0	0	0	6	0	0	0	8	0.0	–1	0	0.0	12:19	....	....	....	....	....				
	Hamilton	AHL	62	0	21	21	38	....	....	....	....	....	....	....	....	....	....	....	....	....	....				
	NHL Totals		10	0	0	0	6	0	0	0	8	0.0		0	0.0	12:19	....	....	....	....	....				

OHL First All-Star Team (2005) • Canadian Major Junior Defenseman of the Year (2005) • Canadian Major Junior First All-Star Team (2005) • Memorial Cup All-Star Team (2005)

TAFFE, Jeff   (TAYF, JEHF)   **PHX.**

Center. Shoots left. 6'3", 201 lbs.   Born, Hastings, MN, February 19, 1981. St. Louis' 1st choice, 30th overall, in 2000 Entry Draft.

Season	Club	League	GP	G	A	Pts	PIM	PP	SH	GW	S	%	+/-	TF	F%	Min	GP	G	A	Pts	PIM	PP	SH	GW	Min
1996-97	Hastings Huskies	High-MN	25	21	37	58	....																			
1997-98	Hastings Huskies	High-MN	28	37	29	66	....																			
1998-99	Hastings Huskies	High-MN	28	39	51	90	....																			
	Rochester	USHL	17	12	9	21	26																			
99-2000	U. of Minnesota	WCHA	39	10	10	20	22																			
2000-01	U. of Minnesota	WCHA	38	12	23	35	56																			
2001-02	U. of Minnesota	WCHA	43	34	24	58	86																			
2002-03	Springfield	AHL	57	23	26	49	44	....	....	....	....	....	....	....	....	....	5	0	3	3	8				
	Phoenix	**NHL**	20	3	1	4	4	1	0	1	18	16.7	–4	113	29.2	11:34	....	....	....	....	....				
2003-04	**Phoenix**	**NHL**	59	8	10	18	20	5	0	0	67	11.9	–8	219	43.4	11:02	....	....	....	....	....				
	Springfield	AHL	15	10	6	16	19	....	....	....	....	....	....	....	....	....	....	....	....	....	....				
2004-05	Utah Grizzlies	AHL	27	9	10	19	35	....	....	....	....	....	....	....	....	....	....	....	....	....	....				
2005-06	**NY Rangers**	**NHL**	2	0	0	0	0	0	0	0	1	0.0	0	0	0.0	3:49	....	....	....	....	....				
	Hartford	AHL	36	6	16	22	34	....	....	....	....	....	....	....	....	....	....	....	....	....	....				
	Phoenix	**NHL**	2	0	0	0	0	0	0	0	2	0.0	0	1	100.0	9:06	....	....	....	....	....				
	San Antonio	AHL	33	5	6	11	29	....	....	....	....	....	....	....	....	....	....	....	....	....	....				
	NHL Totals		83	11	11	22	24	6	0	1	88	12.5		333	38.7	10:56	....	....	....	....	....				

Rights traded to **Phoenix** by **St. Louis** with Michal Handzus, Ladislav Nagy and St. Louis' 1st round choice (Ben Eager) in 2002 Entry Draft for Keith Tkachuk, March 13, 2001. Traded to **NY Rangers** by **Phoenix** for Jamie Lundmark, October 18 2005. Traded to **Phoenix** by **NY Rangers** for Martin Sonnenberg, January 24, 2006.

TALBOT, Maxime   (TAL-buht, MAX-eem)   **PIT.**

Center. Shoots left. 5'11", 176 lbs.   Born, Lemoyne, Que., February 11, 1984. Pittsburgh's 9th choice, 234th overall, in 2002 Entry Draft.

Season	Club	League	GP	G	A	Pts	PIM	PP	SH	GW	S	%	+/-	TF	F%	Min	GP	G	A	Pts	PIM	PP	SH	GW	Min
99-2000	Antoine-Girouard	QAAA	42	19	21	40	32	....	....	....	....	....	....	....	....	....	7	3	6	9	0				
2000-01	Rouyn-Noranda	QMJHL	40	9	15	24	78	....	....	....	....	....	....	....	....	....	5	1	0	1	2				
	Hull Olympiques	QMJHL	24	6	7	13	60	....	....	....	....	....	....	....	....	....	....	....	....	....	....				
2001-02	Hull Olympiques	QMJHL	65	24	36	60	174	....	....	....	....	....	....	....	....	....	12	4	6	10	51				
2002-03	Hull Olympiques	QMJHL	69	46	58	104	130	....	....	....	....	....	....	....	....	....	20	14	*30	*44	33				
2003-04	Gatineau	QMJHL	51	25	73	98	41	....	....	....	....	....	....	....	....	....	15	*11	*16	*27	0				
2004-05	Wilkes-Barre	AHL	75	7	12	19	62	....	....	....	....	....	....	....	....	....	11	0	1	1	22				
2005-06	**Pittsburgh**	**NHL**	48	5	3	8	59	0	2	1	45	11.1	–12	473	42.9	10:58	....	....	....	....	....				
	Wilkes-Barre	AHL	42	12	20	32	80	....	....	....	....	....	....	....	....	....	11	3	6	9	16				
	NHL Totals		48	5	3	8	59	0	2	1	45	11.1		473	42.9	10:58	....	....	....	....	....				

QMJHL Second All-Star Team (2003, 2004)

TALLACKSON, Barry   (TAL-ak-suhn, BAIR-ee)   **N.J.**

Right wing. Shoots right. 6'4", 210 lbs.   Born, Grafton, ND, April 14, 1983. New Jersey's 2nd choice, 53rd overall, in 2002 Entry Draft.

Season	Club	League	GP	G	A	Pts	PIM	PP	SH	GW	S	%	+/-	TF	F%	Min	GP	G	A	Pts	PIM	PP	SH	GW	Min
99-2000	USNTDP	NAHL	53	14	6	20	90	....	....	....	....	....	....	....	....	....	3	1	0	1	8				
2000-01	USNTDP	U-18	40	16	17	33	45	....	....	....	....	....	....	....	....	....	....	....	....	....	....				
	USNTDP	USHL	23	7	7	14	32	....	....	....	....	....	....	....	....	....	....	....	....	....	....				
2001-02	U. of Minnesota	WCHA	44	13	10	23	44	....	....	....	....	....	....	....	....	....	....	....	....	....	....				
2002-03	U. of Minnesota	WCHA	32	9	14	23	18	....	....	....	....	....	....	....	....	....	....	....	....	....	....				
2003-04	U. of Minnesota	WCHA	44	10	15	25	46	....	....	....	....	....	....	....	....	....	....	....	....	....	....				
2004-05	U. of Minnesota	WCHA	36	11	8	19	54	....	....	....	....	....	....	....	....	....	....	....	....	....	....				
	Albany River Rats	AHL	4	1	1	2	0	....	....	....	....	....	....	....	....	....	....	....	....	....	....				
2005-06	**New Jersey**	**NHL**	10	1	1	2	2	0	0	0	11	9.1	–2	2	0.0	8:04	....	....	....	....	....				
	Albany River Rats	AHL	60	14	23	37	62	....	....	....	....	....	....	....	....	....	....	....	....	....	....				
	NHL Totals		10	1	1	2	2	0	0	0	11	9.1		2	0.0	8:04	....	....	....	....	....				

TALLINDER, Henrik   (tah-LIHN-duhr, HEHN-rihk)   **BUF.**

Defense. Shoots left. 6'3", 215 lbs.   Born, Stockholm, Sweden, January 10, 1979. Buffalo's 2nd choice, 48th overall, in 1997 Entry Draft.

Season	Club	League	GP	G	A	Pts	PIM	PP	SH	GW	S	%	+/-	TF	F%	Min	GP	G	A	Pts	PIM	PP	SH	GW	Min
1996-97	AIK Solna Jr.	Swe-Jr.	40	4	13	17	55	....	....	....	....	....	....	....	....	....	....	....	....	....	....				
	AIK Solna	Sweden	1	0	0	0	0	....	....	....	....	....	....	....	....	....	....	....	....	....	....				
1997-98	AIK Solna	Sweden	34	0	0	0	26	....	....	....	....	....	....	....	....	....	....	....	....	....	....				
1998-99	AIK Solna	Sweden	36	0	0	0	30	....	....	....	....	....	....	....	....	....	....	....	....	....	....				
99-2000	AIK Solna	Sweden	50	0	2	2	59	....	....	....	....	....	....	....	....	....	....	....	....	....	....				
2000-01	TPS Turku	Finland	56	5	9	14	62	....	....	....	....	....	....	....	....	....	10	2	1	3	8				
2001-02	**Buffalo**	**NHL**	2	0	0	0	0	0	0	0	4	0.0	–1	0	0.0	18:10	....	....	....	....	....				
	Rochester	AHL	73	6	14	20	26	....	....	....	....	....	....	....	....	....	2	0	0	0	0				
2002-03	**Buffalo**	**NHL**	46	3	10	13	28	1	0	0	37	8.1	–3	0	0.0	19:53	....	....	....	....	....				
2003-04	**Buffalo**	**NHL**	72	1	9	10	26	0	0	0	63	1.6	5	1	0.0	18:23	....	....	....	....	....				
2004-05	Linkopings HC	Sweden	44	6	10	16	63	....	....	....	....	....	....	....	....	....	....	....	....	....	....				
	SC Bern	Swiss															10	1	1	2	4				
2005-06	**Buffalo**	**NHL**	82	6	15	21	74	0	1	1	79	7.6	10	1	0.0	20:21	14	2	6	8	16	0	0	0	22:16
	NHL Totals		202	10	34	44	128	1	1	1	183	5.5		1	0.0	19:31	14	2	6	8	16	0	0	0	22:16

Signed as a free agent by **Linkopings** (Sweden), September 9, 2004. Signed as a free agent by **Bern** (Swiss), February 22, 2005.

TAMBELLINI, Jeff   (tam-buh-LEE-nee, JEHF)   **NYI**

Left wing. Shoots left. 5'11", 186 lbs.   Born, Calgary, Alta., April 13, 1984. Los Angeles' 3rd choice, 27th overall, in 2003 Entry Draft.

Season	Club	League	GP	G	A	Pts	PIM	PP	SH	GW	S	%	+/-	TF	F%	Min	GP	G	A	Pts	PIM	PP	SH	GW	Min
99-2000	Poco Buckeroos	PIJHL	41	30	34	64	....	....	....	....	....	....	....	....	....	....	....	....	....	....	....				
2000-01	Chilliwack Chiefs	BCHL	54	21	30	51	13	....	....	....	....	....	....	....	....	....	....	....	....	....	....				
2001-02	Chilliwack Chiefs	BCHL	34	46	71	117	23	....	....	....	....	....	....	....	....	....	29	27	27	54					
2002-03	U. of Michigan	CCHA	43	26	19	45	24	....	....	....	....	....	....	....	....	....	....	....	....	....	....				
2003-04	U. of Michigan	CCHA	39	15	12	27	18	....	....	....	....	....	....	....	....	....	....	....	....	....	....				
2004-05	U. of Michigan	CCHA	42	*24	33	*57	32	....	....	....	....	....	....	....	....	....	....	....	....	....	....				
2005-06	**Los Angeles**	**NHL**	4	0	0	0	2	0	0	0	6	0.0	–1	1	0.0	9:23	....	....	....	....	....				
	Manchester	AHL	56	25	31	56	26	....	....	....	....	....	....	....	....	....	....	....	....	....	....				
	NY Islanders	**NHL**	21	1	3	4	8	0	0	0	11	9.1	2	3	33.3	9:54	....	....	....	....	....				
	Bridgeport	AHL															7	1	2	3	2				
	NHL Totals		25	1	3	4	10	0	0	0	17	5.9		4	25.0	9:49	....	....	....	....	....				

CCHA All-Rookie Team (2003) • CCHA Second All-Star Team (2003) • CCHA Rookie of the Year (2003) • CCHA First All-Star Team (2005) • NCAA West Second All-American Team (2005)
Traded to **NY Islanders** by **Los Angeles** with Denis Grebeshkov for Mark Parrish and Brent Sopel, March 8, 2006.

TAMER, Chris

(TAY-muhr, KRIHS)

Defense. Shoots left. 6'2", 205 lbs. Born, Dearborn, MI, November 17, 1970. Pittsburgh's 3rd choice, 68th overall, in 1990 Entry Draft.

			Regular Season														Playoffs								
Season	Club	League	GP	G	A	Pts	PIM	PP	SH	GW	S	%	+/-	TF	F%	Min	GP	G	A	Pts	PIM	PP	SH	GW	Min
1987-88	Redford Royals	NAHL	40	10	20	30	217																		
1988-89	Redford Royals	NAHL	31	6	13	19	79																		
1989-90	U. of Michigan	CCHA	42	2	7	9	147																		
1990-91	U. of Michigan	CCHA	45	8	19	27	130																		
1991-92	U. of Michigan	CCHA	43	4	15	19	125																		
1992-93	U. of Michigan	CCHA	39	5	18	23	113																		
1993-94	**Pittsburgh**	**NHL**	**12**	**0**	**0**	**0**	**9**	**0**	**0**	**0**	**10**	**0.0**	**3**				**5**	**0**	**0**	**0**	**2**	**0**	**0**	**0**	
	Cleveland	IHL	53	1	2	3	160																		
1994-95	Cleveland	IHL	48	4	10	14	204																		
	Pittsburgh	**NHL**	**36**	**2**	**0**	**2**	**82**	**0**	**0**	**0**	**26**	**7.7**	**0**				**4**	**0**	**0**	**0**	**18**	**0**	**0**	**0**	
1995-96	**Pittsburgh**	**NHL**	**70**	**4**	**10**	**14**	**153**	**0**	**0**	**1**	**75**	**5.3**	**20**				**18**	**0**	**7**	**7**	**24**	**0**	**0**	**0**	
1996-97	**Pittsburgh**	**NHL**	**45**	**2**	**4**	**6**	**131**	**0**	**1**	**0**	**56**	**3.6**	**–25**				**4**	**0**	**0**	**0**	**4**	**0**	**0**	**0**	
1997-98	**Pittsburgh**	**NHL**	**79**	**0**	**7**	**7**	**181**	**0**	**0**	**0**	**55**	**0.0**	**4**				**6**	**0**	**1**	**1**	**4**	**0**	**0**	**0**	
1998-99	**Pittsburgh**	**NHL**	**11**	**0**	**0**	**0**	**32**	**0**	**0**	**0**	**2**	**0.0**	**–2**	**0**	**0.0**	**5:59**									
	NY Rangers	**NHL**	**52**	**1**	**5**	**6**	**92**	**0**	**0**	**1**	**46**	**2.2**	**–12**	**0**	**0.0**	**15:25**									
99-2000	**Atlanta**	**NHL**	**69**	**2**	**8**	**10**	**91**	**0**	**0**	**0**	**61**	**3.3**	**–32**	**5**	**40.0**	**18:29**									
2000-01	**Atlanta**	**NHL**	**82**	**4**	**13**	**17**	**128**	**0**	**1**	**1**	**90**	**4.4**	**–1**	**1**	**0.0**	**19:42**									
2001-02	**Atlanta**	**NHL**	**78**	**3**	**3**	**6**	**111**	**0**	**1**	**0**	**66**	**4.5**	**–11**	**0**	**0.0**	**18:30**									
2002-03	**Atlanta**	**NHL**	**72**	**1**	**9**	**10**	**118**	**0**	**0**	**0**	**53**	**1.9**	**–10**	**0**	**0.0**	**15:41**									
2003-04	**Atlanta**	**NHL**	**38**	**2**	**5**	**7**	**55**	**0**	**0**	**1**	**40**	**5.0**	**–9**	**0**	**0.0**	**17:58**									
2004-05			DID NOT PLAY																						
2005-06	Chicago Wolves	AHL	14	0	3	3	16																		
	NHL Totals		**644**	**21**	**64**	**85**	**1183**	**0**	**3**	**4**	**580**	**3.6**		**6**	**33.3**	**17:27**	**37**	**0**	**8**	**8**	**52**	**0**	**0**	**0**	

Traded to **NY Rangers** by **Pittsburgh** with Petr Nedved and Sean Pronger for Alex Kovalev and Harry York, November 25, 1998. Claimed by **Atlanta** from **NY Rangers** in Expansion Draft, June 25, 1999. • Missed majority of 2003-04 season recovering from back injury suffered in game vs. Phoenix, January 11, 2004.

TANABE, Dave

(tuh-NA-bee, DAYV)

Defense. Shoots right. 6'1", 212 lbs. Born, White Bear Lake, MN, July 19, 1980. Carolina's 1st choice, 16th overall, in 1999 Entry Draft.

			Regular Season														Playoffs								
Season	Club	League	GP	G	A	Pts	PIM	PP	SH	GW	S	%	+/-	TF	F%	Min	GP	G	A	Pts	PIM	PP	SH	GW	Min
1996-97	Hill-Murray	High-MN	28	12	14	26																			
1997-98	USNTDP	U-18	33	4	15	19	48																		
	USNTDP	USHL	21	1	3	4	18																		
	USNTDP	NAHL	12	1	2	3	10										7	2	1	3	20				
1998-99	U. of Wisconsin	WCHA	35	10	12	22	44																		
99-2000	**Carolina**	**NHL**	**31**	**4**	**0**	**4**	**14**	**3**	**0**	**0**	**28**	**14.3**	**–4**	**0**	**0.0**	**12:53**									
	Cincinnati	IHL	32	0	13	13	14										11	1	4	5	6				
2000-01	**Carolina**	**NHL**	**74**	**7**	**22**	**29**	**42**	**5**	**0**	**1**	**130**	**5.4**	**–9**	**0**	**0.0**	**17:55**	**6**	**2**	**0**	**2**	**12**	**2**	**0**	**0**	**20:47**
2001-02	**Carolina**	**NHL**	**78**	**1**	**15**	**16**	**35**	**0**	**0**	**0**	**113**	**0.9**	**–13**	**0**	**0.0**	**18:27**	**1**	**0**	**1**	**1**	**0**	**0**	**0**	**0**	**7:31**
2002-03	**Carolina**	**NHL**	**68**	**3**	**10**	**13**	**24**	**2**	**0**	**0**	**104**	**2.9**	**–27**	**0**	**0.0**	**18:12**									
2003-04	**Phoenix**	**NHL**	**45**	**5**	**7**	**12**	**22**	**2**	**0**	**2**	**88**	**5.7**	**4**	**0**	**0.0**	**23:02**									
2004-05	Rapperswil	Swiss	8	4	5	9	4																		
	Kloten Flyers	Swiss	20	3	7	10	18										5	1	4	5	8				
2005-06	**Phoenix**	**NHL**	**21**	**0**	**4**	**4**	**8**	**0**	**0**	**0**	**21**	**0.0**	**–5**	**0**	**0.0**	**21:08**									
	Boston	**NHL**	**54**	**4**	**12**	**16**	**48**	**0**	**0**	**1**	**82**	**4.9**	**0**	**0**	**0.0**	**20:08**									
	NHL Totals		**371**	**24**	**70**	**94**	**193**	**12**	**0**	**4**	**566**	**4.2**		**0**	**0.0**	**18:47**	**7**	**2**	**1**	**3**	**12**	**2**	**0**	**0**	**18:53**

WCHA All-Rookie Team (1999)

Traded to **Phoenix** by **Carolina** with Igor Knyazev for Danny Markov and future considerations (Edmonton's 3rd round choice (previously acquired, later traded to NY Rangers - NY Rangers selected Billy Ryan) in 2004 Entry Draft, June 26, 2004), June 21, 2003. Signed as a free agent by **Rapperswil** (Swiss), October 21, 2004. Signed as a free agent by **Kloten** (Swiss), November 29, 2004. Traded to **Boston** by **Phoenix** for Dave Scatchard, November 18, 2005.

TANGUAY, Alex

(TAN-guay, AL-ehx) **CGY.**

Left wing. Shoots left. 6', 190 lbs. Born, Ste-Justine, Que., November 21, 1979. Colorado's 1st choice, 12th overall, in 1998 Entry Draft.

			Regular Season														Playoffs								
Season	Club	League	GP	G	A	Pts	PIM	PP	SH	GW	S	%	+/-	TF	F%	Min	GP	G	A	Pts	PIM	PP	SH	GW	Min
1994-95	Cap-d-Madeleine	QAAA	1	0	1	1	0																		
1995-96	Cap-d-Madeleine	QAAA	44	29	34	63	64										5	2	4	6	14				
1996-97	Halifax	QMJHL	70	27	41	68	60										12	5	8	13	8				
1997-98	Halifax	QMJHL	51	47	38	85	32										5	7	6	13	4				
1998-99	Halifax	QMJHL	31	27	34	61	30										5	1	2	3	2				
	Hershey Bears	AHL	5	1	2	3	2										5	0	2	2	0				
99-2000	**Colorado**	**NHL**	**76**	**17**	**34**	**51**	**22**	**5**	**0**	**3**	**74**	**23.0**	**6**	**11**	**45.5**	**15:38**	**17**	**2**	**1**	**3**	**2**	**1**	**0**	**1**	**10:49**
2000-01 ♦	**Colorado**	**NHL**	**82**	**27**	**50**	**77**	**37**	**7**	**1**	**3**	**135**	**20.0**	**35**	**30**	**43.3**	**17:51**	**23**	**6**	**15**	**21**	**8**	**1**	**0**	**2**	**19:18**
2001-02	**Colorado**	**NHL**	**70**	**13**	**35**	**48**	**36**	**7**	**0**	**2**	**90**	**14.4**	**8**	**37**	**40.5**	**18:20**	**19**	**5**	**8**	**13**	**0**	**3**	**0**	**0**	**17:25**
2002-03	**Colorado**	**NHL**	**82**	**26**	**41**	**67**	**36**	**3**	**0**	**5**	**142**	**18.3**	**34**	**123**	**39.0**	**17:48**	**7**	**1**	**2**	**3**	**4**	**0**	**0**	**1**	**19:06**
2003-04	**Colorado**	**NHL**	**69**	**25**	**54**	**79**	**42**	**7**	**0**	**5**	**117**	**21.4**	**30**	**71**	**40.9**	**18:21**	**8**	**2**	**2**	**4**	**2**	**1**	**0**	**1**	**15:46**
2004-05	HC Lugano	Swiss	6	3	3	6	4																		
2005-06	**Colorado**	**NHL**	**71**	**29**	**49**	**78**	**46**	**8**	**0**	**4**	**125**	**23.2**	**8**	**20**	**30.0**	**18:22**	**9**	**2**	**4**	**6**	**12**	**0**	**0**	**1**	**18:20**
	NHL Totals		**450**	**137**	**263**	**400**	**219**	**37**	**1**	**22**	**683**	**20.1**		**292**	**39.7**	**17:42**	**83**	**18**	**32**	**50**	**28**	**6**	**0**	**6**	**16:40**

QMJHL All-Rookie Team (1997)

Played in NHL All-Star Game (2004)

Signed as a free agent by **Lugano** (Swiss), October 7, 2004. Traded to **Calgary** by **Colorado** for Jordan Leopold, Calgary's 2nd round choice (Codey Burki) in 2006 Entry Draft and future considerations, June 24, 2006.

TAPPER, Brad

(TA-puhr, BRAD) **PHI.**

Right wing. Shoots right. 6', 185 lbs. Born, Scarborough, Ont., April 28, 1978.

			Regular Season														Playoffs								
Season	Club	League	GP	G	A	Pts	PIM	PP	SH	GW	S	%	+/-	TF	F%	Min	GP	G	A	Pts	PIM	PP	SH	GW	Min
1996-97	Wexford Raiders	MTJHL	50	42	70	112	169																		
1997-98	RPI Engineers	ECAC	34	14	11	25	62																		
1998-99	RPI Engineers	ECAC	35	20	20	40	60																		
99-2000	RPI Engineers	ECAC	37	*31	20	51	81																		
2000-01	**Atlanta**	**NHL**	**16**	**2**	**3**	**5**	**6**	**0**	**0**	**0**	**21**	**9.5**	**1**	**0**	**0.0**	**12:44**									
	Orlando	IHL	45	7	9	16	39										2	0	0	0	2				
2001-02	**Atlanta**	**NHL**	**20**	**2**	**4**	**6**	**43**	**0**	**0**	**0**	**34**	**5.9**	**–3**	**3**	**66.7**	**13:21**									
	Chicago Wolves	AHL	50	14	12	26	62										19	3	4	7	42				
2002-03	Chicago Wolves	AHL	28	9	14	23	42										9	1	3	4	10				
	Atlanta	**NHL**	**35**	**10**	**4**	**14**	**23**	**1**	**0**	**3**	**68**	**14.7**	**2**	**4**	**25.0**	**13:03**									
2003-04	Chicago Wolves	AHL	20	1	8	9	26																		
	Binghamton	AHL	29	9	12	21	26																		
2004-05	Nurnberg	Germany	50	26	23	49	101										6	0	2	2	18				
2005-06	Hannover	Germany	46	9	21	30	165										8	2	4	6	*64				
	NHL Totals		**71**	**14**	**11**	**25**	**72**	**1**	**0**	**3**	**123**	**11.4**		**7**	**42.9**	**13:04**									

ECAC First All-Star Team (2000) • NCAA East Second All-American Team (2000)

Signed as a free agent by **Atlanta**, April 11, 2000. Traded to **Ottawa** by **Atlanta** for Daniel Corso, January 6, 2004. Signed as a free agent by **Nurnberg** (Germany), July 22, 2004. Signed as a free agent by **Philadelphia**, June 26, 2006.

TARNASKY, Nick

(tahr-NAS-kee, NIHK) **T.B.**

Center. Shoots left. 6'2", 233 lbs. Born, Rocky Mtn. House, Alta., November 25, 1984. Tampa Bay's 11th choice, 287th overall, in 2003 Entry Draft.

			Regular Season														Playoffs								
Season	Club	League	GP	G	A	Pts	PIM	PP	SH	GW	S	%	+/-	TF	F%	Min	GP	G	A	Pts	PIM	PP	SH	GW	Min
99-2000	Leduc Oil Kings	AMBHL	36	21	11	32	59																		
2000-01	Leduc Oil Kings	AMHL	35	39	29	68	95																		
2001-02	Drayton Valley	AJHL	20	7	4	11	10																		
	Vancouver Giants	WHL	10	1	0	1	5																		
2002-03	Kelowna Rockets	WHL	39	4	12	16	39																		
	Lethbridge	WHL	30	5	8	13	45																		
2003-04	Lethbridge	WHL	71	26	23	49	108																		
2004-05	Springfield	AHL	80	7	10	17	176																		

Season	Club	League	GP	G	A	Pts	PIM	PP	SH	GW	S	%	+/-	TF	F%	Min	GP	G	A	Pts	PIM	PP	SH	GW	Min
			Regular Season														Playoffs								
2005-06	**Tampa Bay**	**NHL**	**12**	**0**	**1**	**1**	**4**	**0**	**0**	**0**	**9**	**0.0**	**−3**	**15**	**40.0**	**4:40**									
	Springfield	AHL	68	14	9	23	100																		
	NHL Totals		**12**	**0**	**1**	**1**	**4**	**0**	**0**	**0**	**9**	**0.0**		**15**	**40.0**	**4:40**									

TARNSTROM, Dick

(TAHRN-struhm, DIHK)

Defense. Shoots left. 6'1", 205 lbs. Born, Sundbyberg, Sweden, January 20, 1975. NY Islanders' 12th choice, 272nd overall, in 1994 Entry Draft.

Season	Club	League	GP	G	A	Pts	PIM	PP	SH	GW	S	%	+/-	TF	F%	Min	GP	G	A	Pts	PIM	PP	SH	GW	Min
1992-93	AIK Solna	Sweden	3	0	0	0	0																		
1993-94	AIK Solna	Sweden-2	33	1	4	5																			
1994-95	AIK Solna	Sweden	37	8	4	12	26																		
1995-96	AIK Solna	Sweden	40	0	5	5	32																		
1996-97	AIK Solna	Sweden	49	5	3	8	38										7	0	1	1	6				
1997-98	AIK Solna	Sweden	45	2	12	14	30																		
1998-99	AIK Solna	Sweden	47	9	14	23	36																		
99-2000	AIK Solna	Sweden	42	7	15	22	20																		
2000-01	AIK Solna	Sweden	50	10	18	28	28										5	0	0	0	8				
2001-02	**NY Islanders**	**NHL**	**62**	**3**	**16**	**19**	**38**	**0**	**0**	**0**	**59**	**5.1**	**−12**	**0**	**0.0**	**17:39**	**5**	**0**	**0**	**0**	**2**	**0**	**0**	**0**	**7:13**
	Bridgeport	AHL	9	0	2	2	2																		
2002-03	**Pittsburgh**	**NHL**	**61**	**7**	**34**	**41**	**50**	**3**	**0**	**0**	**115**	**6.1**	**−11**	**0**	**0.0**	**23:54**									
2003-04	**Pittsburgh**	**NHL**	**80**	**16**	**36**	**52**	**38**	**12**	**0**	**0**	**158**	**10.1**	**−37**	**0**	**0.0**	**24:03**									
2004-05	Sodertalje SK	Sweden	50	7	18	25	46										9	1	0	1	6				
2005-06	**Pittsburgh**	**NHL**	**33**	**5**	**5**	**10**	**52**	**4**	**0**	**0**	**40**	**12.5**	**−10**	**1**	**100.0**	**16:54**									
	Edmonton	**NHL**	**22**	**1**	**3**	**4**	**24**	**0**	**0**	**0**	**20**	**5.0**	**−5**	**0**	**0.0**	**16:58**	**12**	**0**	**2**	**2**	**10**	**0**	**0**	**0**	**14:00**
	NHL Totals		**258**	**32**	**94**	**126**	**202**	**19**	**0**	**0**	**392**	**8.2**		**1**	**100.0**	**20:57**	**17**	**0**	**2**	**2**	**12**	**0**	**0**	**0**	**12:00**

Claimed on waivers by **Pittsburgh** from **NY Islanders**, August 6, 2002. Signed as a free agent by **Sodertalje** (Sweden), August 9, 2004. Traded to **Edmonton** by **Pittsburgh** for Jani Rita and Cory Cross, January 26, 2006. Signed as a free agent by **Lugano** (Swiss), August 16, 2006.

TATICEK, Petr

(TA-tih-chehk, PEE-tuhr) **WSH.**

Center. Shoots left. 6'3", 195 lbs. Born, Rakovnik, Czech., September 22, 1983. Florida's 2nd choice, 9th overall, in 2002 Entry Draft.

Season	Club	League	GP	G	A	Pts	PIM	PP	SH	GW	S	%	+/-	TF	F%	Min	GP	G	A	Pts	PIM	PP	SH	GW	Min
1998-99	HC Kladno U17	CzR-U17	42	24	17	41																			
99-2000	HC Kladno Jr.	CzRep-Jr.	48	11	16	27	26																		
	Kladno	CzRep	4	0	0	0	4																		
2000-01	HC Kladno Jr.	CzRep-Jr.	30	7	12	19	54																		
	Kladno	CzRep	3	0	0	0	0																		
2001-02	Sault Ste. Marie	OHL	60	21	42	63	32										6	3	3	6	4				
2002-03	Sault Ste. Marie	OHL	54	12	45	57	44										4	1	0	1	0				
2003-04	San Antonio	AHL	63	4	15	19	6																		
2004-05	San Antonio	AHL	67	7	15	22	21																		
	Laredo Bucks	CHL	4	2	5	7	0																		
2005-06	**Florida**	**NHL**	**3**	**0**	**0**	**0**	**0**	**0**	**0**	**0**	**3**	**0.0**	**0**	**9**	**33.3**	**5:51**									
	Houston Aeros	AHL	44	9	21	30	10																		
	Wilkes-Barre	AHL	17	4	4	8	7										1	0	0	0	2				
	NHL Totals		**3**	**0**	**0**	**0**	**0**	**0**	**0**	**0**	**3**	**0.0**		**9**	**33.3**	**5:51**									

Traded to **Pittsbugh** by **Florida** for Ric Jackman, March 9, 2006. Signed as a free agent by **Washington**, August 9, 2006.

TAYLOR, Chris

(TAY-luhr, KRIHS)

Center. Shoots left. 6'2", 192 lbs. Born, Stratford, Ont., March 6, 1972. NY Islanders' 2nd choice, 27th overall, in 1990 Entry Draft.

Season	Club	League	GP	G	A	Pts	PIM	PP	SH	GW	S	%	+/-	TF	F%	Min	GP	G	A	Pts	PIM	PP	SH	GW	Min
1987-88	Stratford Cullitons	OHA-B	52	28	37	65	112																		
1988-89	London Knights	OHL	62	7	16	23	52										15	0	2	2	15				
1989-90	London Knights	OHL	66	45	60	105	60										6	3	2	5	6				
1990-91	London Knights	OHL	65	50	78	128	50										7	4	8	12	6				
1991-92	London Knights	OHL	66	48	74	122	57										10	8	16	24	9				
1992-93	Capital District	AHL	77	19	43	62	32										4	0	1	1	2				
1993-94	Salt Lake	IHL	79	21	20	41	38																		
1994-95	Denver Grizzlies	IHL	78	38	48	86	47										14	7	6	13	10				
	NY Islanders	**NHL**	**10**	**0**	**3**	**3**	**2**	**0**	**0**	**0**	**13**	**0.0**	**1**												
1995-96	**NY Islanders**	**NHL**	**11**	**0**	**1**	**1**	**2**	**0**	**0**	**0**	**4**	**0.0**	**1**												
	Utah Grizzlies	IHL	50	18	23	41	60										22	5	11	16	26				
1996-97	**NY Islanders**	**NHL**	**1**	**0**	**0**	**0**	**0**	**0**	**0**	**0**	**1**	**0.0**	**0**												
	Utah Grizzlies	IHL	71	27	40	67	24										7	1	2	3	0				
1997-98	Utah Grizzlies	IHL	79	28	56	84	66										4	0	2	2	6				
1998-99	**Boston**	**NHL**	**37**	**3**	**5**	**8**	**12**	**0**	**1**	**0**	**60**	**5.0**	**−3**	**512**	**53.7**	**14:24**									
	Providence Bruins	AHL	21	6	11	17	6																		
	Las Vegas	IHL	14	3	12	15	2																		
99-2000	**Buffalo**	**NHL**	**11**	**1**	**1**	**2**	**2**	**0**	**0**	**0**	**15**	**6.7**	**−2**	**125**	**45.6**	**10:54**	**2**	**0**	**0**	**0**	**2**	**0**	**0**	**0**	**10:32**
	Rochester	AHL	49	21	28	49	21																		
2000-01	**Buffalo**	**NHL**	**14**	**0**	**2**	**2**	**6**	**0**	**0**	**0**	**21**	**0.0**	**1**	**138**	**50.7**	**11:08**									
	Rochester	AHL	45	20	24	44	25																		
2001-02	Rochester	AHL	77	21	45	66	66										2	0	1	1	0				
2002-03	**Buffalo**	**NHL**	**11**	**1**	**3**	**4**	**2**	**0**	**0**	**0**	**10**	**10.0**	**−1**	**152**	**47.4**	**13:55**									
	Rochester	AHL	61	12	55	67	44										3	3	1	4	2				
2003-04	**Buffalo**	**NHL**	**54**	**6**	**6**	**12**	**22**	**0**	**0**	**0**	**50**	**12.0**	**−2**	**531**	**51.0**	**10:10**									
	Rochester	AHL	24	9	18	27	20										16	5	12	17	0				
2004-05	Rochester	AHL	79	21	58	79	50										9	1	8	9	4				
2005-06	Rochester	AHL	32	11	26	37	34																		
	NHL Totals		**149**	**11**	**21**	**32**	**48**	**0**	**1**	**0**	**174**	**6.3**		**1458**	**51.1**	**11:54**	**2**	**0**	**0**	**0**	**2**	**0**	**0**	**0**	**10:32**

Fred Hunt Memorial Trophy (Sportsmanship - AHL) (2005)

Signed as a free agent by **Los Angeles**, July 25, 1997. Signed as a free agent by **Boston**, August 5, 1998. Signed as a free agent by **Buffalo**, August 13, 1999.

TAYLOR, Tim

(TAY-luhr, TIHM) **T.B.**

Center. Shoots left. 6'1", 195 lbs. Born, Stratford, Ont., February 6, 1969. Washington's 2nd choice, 36th overall, in 1988 Entry Draft.

Season	Club	League	GP	G	A	Pts	PIM	PP	SH	GW	S	%	+/-	TF	F%	Min	GP	G	A	Pts	PIM	PP	SH	GW	Min
1985-86	Stratford Cullitons	OHA-B	1	0	0	0	0																		
1986-87	Stratford Cullitons	OHA-B	31	25	26	51	51																		
	London Knights	OHL	34	7	9	16	11																		
1987-88	London Knights	OHL	64	46	50	96	66										12	9	9	18	26				
1988-89	London Knights	OHL	61	34	80	114	93										21	*21	25	*46	58				
1989-90	Baltimore	AHL	79	31	36	67	124										9	2	2	4	13				
1990-91	Baltimore	AHL	79	25	42	67	75										5	0	1	1	4				
1991-92	Baltimore	AHL	65	9	18	27	131																		
1992-93	Baltimore	AHL	41	15	16	31	49																		
	Hamilton	AHL	36	15	22	37	37																		
1993-94	**Detroit**	**NHL**	**1**	**1**	**0**	**1**	**0**	**0**	**0**	**0**	**4**	**25.0**	**−1**												
	Adirondack	AHL	79	36	*81	*117	86										12	2	10	12	12				
1994-95	**Detroit**	**NHL**	**22**	**0**	**4**	**4**	**16**	**0**	**0**	**0**	**21**	**0.0**	**3**				**6**	**0**	**1**	**1**	**12**	**0**	**0**	**0**	
1995-96	**Detroit**	**NHL**	**72**	**11**	**14**	**25**	**39**	**1**	**1**	**4**	**81**	**13.6**	**11**				**18**	**0**	**4**	**4**	**4**	**0**	**0**	**0**	
1996-97♦	**Detroit**	**NHL**	**44**	**3**	**4**	**7**	**52**	**0**	**1**	**0**	**44**	**6.8**	**−6**				**2**	**0**	**0**	**0**	**0**	**0**	**0**	**0**	
1997-98	**Boston**	**NHL**	**79**	**20**	**11**	**31**	**57**	**1**	**3**	**0**	**127**	**15.7**	**−16**				**6**	**0**	**0**	**0**	**10**	**0**	**0**	**0**	
1998-99	**Boston**	**NHL**	**49**	**4**	**7**	**11**	**55**	**0**	**0**	**1**	**76**	**5.3**	**−10**	**834**	**58.3**	**15:56**	**12**	**0**	**3**	**3**	**8**	**0**	**0**	**0**	**15:09**
99-2000	**NY Rangers**	**NHL**	**76**	**9**	**11**	**20**	**72**	**0**	**0**	**2**	**79**	**11.4**	**−4**	**1276**	**58.9**	**14:09**									
2000-01	**NY Rangers**	**NHL**	**38**	**2**	**5**	**7**	**16**	**0**	**0**	**1**	**34**	**5.9**	**−6**	**292**	**59.3**	**8:57**									
2001-02	**Tampa Bay**	**NHL**	**48**	**4**	**4**	**8**	**25**	**0**	**1**	**0**	**50**	**8.0**	**−2**	**559**	**54.6**	**13:29**									
2002-03	**Tampa Bay**	**NHL**	**82**	**4**	**8**	**12**	**38**	**0**	**0**	**1**	**95**	**4.2**	**−13**	**961**	**57.9**	**13:43**	**11**	**0**	**1**	**1**	**6**	**0**	**0**	**0**	**13:54**
2003-04♦	**Tampa Bay**	**NHL**	**82**	**7**	**15**	**22**	**25**	**0**	**0**	**1**	**95**	**7.4**	**−5**	**666**	**59.6**	**12:54**	**23**	**2**	**3**	**5**	**31**	**0**	**0**	**0**	**14:17**

			Regular Season														Playoffs								
Season	Club	League	GP	G	A	Pts	PIM	PP	SH	GW	S	%	+/-	TF	F%	Min	GP	G	A	Pts	PIM	PP	SH	GW	Min
2004-05			Did not play																						
2005-06	**Tampa Bay**	**NHL**	**82**	**7**	**6**	**13**	**22**	**0**	**0**	**0**	**109**	**6.4**	**–12**	**1013**	**52.1**	**12:27**	**5**	**0**	**0**	**0**	**2**	**0**	**0**	**0**	**11:05**
	NHL Totals		**675**	**72**	**89**	**161**	**417**	**2**	**6**	**10**	**815**	**8.8**		**5601**	**57.1**	**13:14**	**83**	**2**	**12**	**14**	**73**	**0**	**0**	**0**	**14:06**

AHL First All-Star Team (1994) • John B. Sollenberger Trophy (Leading Scorer – AHL) (1994)

Traded to **Vancouver** by **Washington** for Eric Murano, January 29, 1993. Signed as a free agent by **Detroit**, July 28, 1993. Claimed by **Boston** from **Detroit** in Waiver Draft, September 28, 1997. Signed as a free agent by **NY Rangers**, July 30, 1999. • Missed majority of 2000-01 season recovering from abdominal injury suffered in game vs. Phoenix, January 4, 2001. Traded to **Tampa Bay** by **NY Rangers** for Kyle Freadrich and Nils Ekman, June 30, 2001.

TENKRAT, Petr (TEHN-krat, PEE-tuhr) BOS.

Right wing. Shoots right. 6', 183 lbs. Born, Kladno, Czech., May 31, 1977. Anaheim's 6th choice, 230th overall, in 1999 Entry Draft.

Season	Club	League	GP	G	A	Pts	PIM	PP	SH	GW	S	%	+/-	TF	F%	Min	GP	G	A	Pts	PIM	PP	SH	GW	Min
1994-95	HC Kladno	CzRep	1	0	0	0	0	....	....	....	....	....	....	....	....	....	....	....	....	....	....	....	....	....	....
1995-96	HC Poldi Kladno	CzRep	20	0	4	4	4	....	....	....	....	....	....	....	....	....	3	0	1	1	0	....	....	....	....
1996-97	HC Poldi Kladno	CzRep	43	5	9	14	6	....	....	....	....	....	....	....	....	....	3	0	1	1	0	....	....	....	....
1997-98	Kladno	CzRep	52	9	10	19	24	....	....	....	....	....	....	....	....	....	....	....	....	....	....	....	....	....	....
1998-99	Kladno	CzRep	50	21	14	35	32	....	....	....	....	....	....	....	....	....	....	....	....	....	....	....	....	....	....
99-2000	HPK Hameenlinna	Finland	32	20	9	29	31	....	....	....	....	....	....	....	....	....	....	....	....	....	....	....	....	....	....
	Ilves Tampere	Finland	22	15	5	20	44	....	....	....	....	....	....	....	....	....	3	1	1	2	14	....	....	....	....
2000-01	**Anaheim**	**NHL**	**46**	**5**	**9**	**14**	**16**	**0**	**0**	**2**	**79**	**6.3**	**–11**	**0**	**0.0**	**12:48**	....	....	....	....	....	....	....	....	....
	Cincinnati	AHL	25	9	9	18	24	....	....	....	....	....	....	....	....	....	4	3	2	5	0	....	....	....	....
2001-02	**Anaheim**	**NHL**	**9**	**0**	**0**	**0**	**6**	**0**	**0**	**0**	**13**	**0.0**	**–6**	**1**	**0.0**	**11:47**	....	....	....	....	....	....	....	....	....
	Cincinnati	AHL	3	2	3	5	2	....	....	....	....	....	....	....	....	....	....	....	....	....	....	....	....	....	....
	Nashville	**NHL**	**58**	**8**	**16**	**24**	**28**	**0**	**1**	**2**	**82**	**9.8**	**–4**	**7**	**28.6**	**12:00**	....	....	....	....	....	....	....	....	....
	Milwaukee	AHL	4	0	0	0	2	....	....	....	....	....	....	....	....	....	....	....	....	....	....	....	....	....	....
2002-03	Karpat Oulu	Finland	51	21	19	40	60	....	....	....	....	....	....	....	....	....	14	4	2	6	6	....	....	....	....
2003-04	Voskresensk	Russia	19	0	2	2	18	....	....	....	....	....	....	....	....	....	....	....	....	....	....	....	....	....	....
	Karpat Oulu	Finland	35	22	15	37	30	....	....	....	....	....	....	....	....	....	15	3	7	10	*45	....	....	....	....
2004-05	Karpat Oulu	Finland	53	18	20	38	46	....	....	....	....	....	....	....	....	....	12	*7	4	11	6	....	....	....	....
2005-06	Karpat Oulu	Finland	36	10	21	31	22	....	....	....	....	....	....	....	....	....	11	*6	3	9	18	....	....	....	....
	NHL Totals		**113**	**13**	**25**	**38**	**50**	**0**	**1**	**4**	**174**	**7.5**		**8**	**25.0**	**12:18**	....	....	....	....	....	....	....	....	....

Traded to **Nashville** by **Anaheim** for Patrick Kjellberg, November 1, 2001. Claimed by **Florida** from **Nashville** in Waiver Draft, October 4, 2002. Traded to **Columbus** by **Florida** for Mathieu Biron, October 4, 2002. Signed as a free agent by **Oulu** (Finland), May 15, 2002. Claimed by **Toronto** from **Columbus** in Waiver Draft, October 3, 2003. Traded to **Boston** by **Toronto** for Boston's 7th round choice (later traded to Phoenix - Phoenix selected Chris Frank) in 2006 Entry Draft, June 15, 2006.

TENUTE, Joey (teh-NOOT, JOH-ee) WSH.

Center. Shoots left. 5'9", 180 lbs. Born, Hamilton, Ont., April 2, 1983. New Jersey's 6th choice, 261st overall, in 2003 Entry Draft.

Season	Club	League	GP	G	A	Pts	PIM	PP	SH	GW	S	%	+/-	TF	F%	Min	GP	G	A	Pts	PIM	PP	SH	GW	Min
99-2000	Georgetown	OPJHL	47	27	43	70	34	....	....	....	....	....	....	....	....	....	....	....	....	....	....	....	....	....	....
2000-01	Barrie Colts	OHL	61	13	18	31	38	....	....	....	....	....	....	....	....	....	5	1	1	2	10	....	....	....	....
2001-02	Barrie Colts	OHL	66	19	31	50	76	....	....	....	....	....	....	....	....	....	20	7	7	14	28	....	....	....	....
2002-03	Sarnia Sting	OHL	68	41	71	112	75	....	....	....	....	....	....	....	....	....	3	1	2	3	0	....	....	....	....
2003-04	Sarnia Sting	OHL	58	22	56	78	70	....	....	....	....	....	....	....	....	....	3	2	2	4	17	....	....	....	....
2004-05	South Carolina	ECHL	68	34	41	75	102	....	....	....	....	....	....	....	....	....	4	2	1	3	0	....	....	....	....
2005-06	**Washington**	**NHL**	**1**	**0**	**0**	**0**	**0**	**0**	**0**	**0**	**1**	**0.0**	**0**	**4**	**25.0**	**7:21**	....	....	....	....	....	....	....	....	....
	Hershey Bears	AHL	61	20	30	50	60	....	....	....	....	....	....	....	....	....	19	2	3	5	12	....	....	....	....
	NHL Totals		**1**	**0**	**0**	**0**	**0**	**0**	**0**	**0**	**1**	**0.0**		**4**	**25.0**	**7:21**	....	....	....	....	....	....	....	....	....

ECHL All-Rookie Team (2005) • ECHL Second All-Star Team (2005) • ECHL Rookie of the Year (2005)

Signed as a free agent by **Washington**, November 21, 2005.

TETARENKO, Joey (teh-tar-EHN-koh, JOH-ee)

Right wing. Shoots right. 6'2", 215 lbs. Born, Prince Albert, Sask., March 3, 1978. Florida's 4th choice, 82nd overall, in 1996 Entry Draft.

Season	Club	League	GP	G	A	Pts	PIM	PP	SH	GW	S	%	+/-	TF	F%	Min	GP	G	A	Pts	PIM	PP	SH	GW	Min
1993-94	North Battleford	SMHL	36	6	13	19	75	....	....	....	....	....	....	....	....	....	....	....	....	....	....	....	....	....	....
1994-95	Portland	WHL	59	0	1	1	134	....	....	....	....	....	....	....	....	....	9	0	0	0	8	....	....	....	....
1995-96	Portland	WHL	71	4	11	15	190	....	....	....	....	....	....	....	....	....	7	0	1	1	17	....	....	....	....
1996-97	Portland	WHL	68	8	18	26	182	....	....	....	....	....	....	....	....	....	2	0	0	0	2	....	....	....	....
1997-98	Portland	WHL	49	2	12	14	148	....	....	....	....	....	....	....	....	....	16	0	2	2	30	....	....	....	....
1998-99	New Haven	AHL	65	4	10	14	154	....	....	....	....	....	....	....	....	....	....	....	....	....	....	....	....	....	....
99-2000	Louisville Panthers	AHL	57	3	11	14	136	....	....	....	....	....	....	....	....	....	4	0	0	0	2	....	....	....	....
2000-01	**Florida**	**NHL**	**29**	**3**	**1**	**4**	**44**	**0**	**0**	**0**	**21**	**14.3**	**–1**	**0**	**0.0**	**6:12**	....	....	....	....	....	....	....	....	....
	Louisville Panthers	AHL	29	1	4	5	74	....	....	....	....	....	....	....	....	....	....	....	....	....	....	....	....	....	....
2001-02	**Florida**	**NHL**	**38**	**1**	**0**	**1**	**123**	**0**	**0**	**0**	**10**	**10.0**	**–5**	**0**	**0.0**	**5:08**	....	....	....	....	....	....	....	....	....
2002-03	San Antonio	AHL	50	4	12	16	123	....	....	....	....	....	....	....	....	....	....	....	....	....	....	....	....	....	....
	Florida	**NHL**	**2**	**0**	**0**	**0**	**4**	**0**	**0**	**0**	**2**	**0.0**	**–1**	**0**	**0.0**	**6:19**	....	....	....	....	....	....	....	....	....
	Ottawa	**NHL**	**2**	**0**	**0**	**0**	**5**	**0**	**0**	**0**	**1**	**0.0**	**0**	**0**	**0.0**	**6:29**	....	....	....	....	....	....	....	....	....
	Binghamton	AHL	14	2	2	4	33	....	....	....	....	....	....	....	....	....	14	0	0	0	36	....	....	....	....
2003-04	**Carolina**	**NHL**	**2**	**0**	**0**	**0**	**0**	**0**	**0**	**0**	**0**	**0.0**	**0**	**1**	**0.0**	**3:31**	....	....	....	....	....	....	....	....	....
	Lowell	AHL	57	1	6	7	167	....	....	....	....	....	....	....	....	....	....	....	....	....	....	....	....	....	....
2004-05	Houston Aeros	AHL	15	0	1	1	49	....	....	....	....	....	....	....	....	....	....	....	....	....	....	....	....	....	....
2005-06	Houston Aeros	AHL	40	1	1	2	125	....	....	....	....	....	....	....	....	....	8	1	0	1	13	....	....	....	....
	NHL Totals		**73**	**4**	**1**	**5**	**176**	**0**	**0**	**0**	**34**	**11.8**		**1**	**0.0**	**5:35**	....	....	....	....	....	....	....	....	....

• Missed majority of 2001-02 season recovering from jaw injury suffered in game vs. NY Rangers, November 3, 2001. Traded to **Ottawa** by **Florida** for Simon Lajeunesse, March 4, 2003. Signed as a free agent by **Carolina**, July 2, 2003. Signed as a free agent by **Houston** (AHL), February 19, 2005.

THERIEN, Chris (TEH-ree-ehn, KRIHS)

Defense. Shoots left. 6'5", 235 lbs. Born, Ottawa, Ont., December 14, 1971. Philadelphia's 7th choice, 47th overall, in 1990 Entry Draft.

Season	Club	League	GP	G	A	Pts	PIM	PP	SH	GW	S	%	+/-	TF	F%	Min	GP	G	A	Pts	PIM	PP	SH	GW	Min
1988-89	Ott. Jr. Senators	CJHL	8	3	1	4	22	....	....	....	....	....	....	....	....	....	....	....	....	....	....	....	....	....	....
1989-90	Ott. Jr. Senators	CJHL	3	0	2	2	2	....	....	....	....	....	....	....	....	....	....	....	....	....	....	....	....	....	....
	Northwood	High-NY	31	35	37	72	54	....	....	....	....	....	....	....	....	....	....	....	....	....	....	....	....	....	....
1990-91	Providence	H-East	36	4	18	22	36	....	....	....	....	....	....	....	....	....	....	....	....	....	....	....	....	....	....
1991-92	Providence	H-East	36	16	25	41	38	....	....	....	....	....	....	....	....	....	....	....	....	....	....	....	....	....	....
1992-93	Providence	H-East	33	8	11	19	52	....	....	....	....	....	....	....	....	....	....	....	....	....	....	....	....	....	....
	Canada	Nat-Tm	8	1	4	5	8	....	....	....	....	....	....	....	....	....	....	....	....	....	....	....	....	....	....
1993-94	Canada	Nat-Tm	59	7	15	22	46	....	....	....	....	....	....	....	....	....	....	....	....	....	....	....	....	....	....
	Canada	Olympics	4	0	0	0	4	....	....	....	....	....	....	....	....	....	....	....	....	....	....	....	....	....	....
	Hershey Bears	AHL	6	0	0	0	2	....	....	....	....	....	....	....	....	....	....	....	....	....	....	....	....	....	....
1994-95	Hershey Bears	AHL	34	3	13	16	27	....	....	....	....	....	....	....	....	....	....	....	....	....	....	....	....	....	....
	Philadelphia	**NHL**	**48**	**3**	**10**	**13**	**38**	**1**	**0**	**0**	**53**	**5.7**	**8**	....	....	....	**15**	**0**	**0**	**0**	**10**	**0**	**0**	**0**	....
1995-96	**Philadelphia**	**NHL**	**82**	**6**	**17**	**23**	**89**	**3**	**0**	**1**	**123**	**4.9**	**16**	....	....	....	**12**	**0**	**0**	**0**	**18**	**0**	**0**	**0**	....
1996-97	**Philadelphia**	**NHL**	**71**	**2**	**22**	**24**	**64**	**0**	**0**	**0**	**107**	**1.9**	**27**	....	....	....	**19**	**1**	**6**	**7**	**6**	**0**	**0**	**1**	....
1997-98	**Philadelphia**	**NHL**	**78**	**3**	**16**	**19**	**80**	**1**	**0**	**1**	**102**	**2.9**	**5**	....	....	....	**5**	**0**	**1**	**1**	**4**	**0**	**0**	**0**	....
1998-99	**Philadelphia**	**NHL**	**74**	**3**	**15**	**18**	**48**	**1**	**0**	**0**	**115**	**2.6**	**16**	**0**	**0.0**	**20:45**	**6**	**0**	**0**	**0**	**6**	**0**	**0**	**0**	**20:23**
99-2000	**Philadelphia**	**NHL**	**80**	**4**	**9**	**13**	**66**	**1**	**0**	**1**	**126**	**3.2**	**11**	**0**	**0.0**	**20:12**	**18**	**0**	**1**	**1**	**12**	**0**	**0**	**0**	**21:40**
2000-01	**Philadelphia**	**NHL**	**73**	**2**	**12**	**14**	**48**	**1**	**0**	**0**	**103**	**1.9**	**22**	**0**	**0.0**	**20:38**	**6**	**1**	**0**	**1**	**8**	**0**	**0**	**0**	**20:55**
2001-02	**Philadelphia**	**NHL**	**77**	**4**	**10**	**14**	**30**	**0**	**2**	**3**	**105**	**3.8**	**16**	**0**	**0.0**	**18:42**	**5**	**0**	**0**	**0**	**2**	**0**	**0**	**0**	**19:50**
2002-03	**Philadelphia**	**NHL**	**67**	**1**	**6**	**7**	**36**	**0**	**0**	**0**	**93**	**1.1**	**10**	**0**	**0.0**	**17:24**	**13**	**0**	**2**	**2**	**2**	**0**	**0**	**0**	**17:51**
2003-04	**Philadelphia**	**NHL**	**56**	**1**	**9**	**10**	**50**	**0**	**0**	**0**	**59**	**1.7**	**2**	**0**	**0.0**	**18:31**	....	....	....	....	....	....	....	....	....
	Philadelphia	AHL	2	0	0	0	0	....	....	....	....	....	....	....	....	....	....	....	....	....	....	....	....	....	....
	Dallas	**NHL**	**11**	**0**	**0**	**0**	**2**	**0**	**0**	**0**	**9**	**0.0**	**4**	**1**	**0.0**	**18:13**	**5**	**2**	**0**	**2**	**0**	**0**	**0**	**0**	**17:04**
2004-05			Did not play																						
2005-06	**Philadelphia**	**NHL**	**47**	**0**	**4**	**4**	**34**	**0**	**0**	**0**	**16**	**0.0**	**–7**	**0**	**0.0**	**13:45**	....	....	....	....	....	....	....	....	....
	NHL Totals		**764**	**29**	**130**	**159**	**585**	**8**	**2**	**6**	**1011**	**2.9**		**1**	**0.0**	**18:52**	**104**	**4**	**10**	**14**	**68**	**0**	**0**	**1**	**19:54**

Hockey East Second All-Star Team (1993) • NHL All-Rookie Team (1995)

Traded to **Dallas** by **Philadelphia** for Phoenix's 8th round choice (previously acquired, Philadelphia selected Martin Houle) in 2004 Entry Draft and Dallas' 3rd round choice (later traded to Tampa Bay - Tampa Bay selected Chris Lawrence) in 2005 Entry Draft, March 8, 2004. Signed as a free agent by **Philadelphia**, August 2, 2005.

THOMAS, Bill — PHX.

Right wing. Shoots right. 6'1", 191 lbs. Born, Pittsburgh, PA, June 20, 1983.

			Regular Season														Playoffs								
Season	Club	League	GP	G	A	Pts	PIM	PP	SH	GW	S	%	+/-	TF	F%	Min	GP	G	A	Pts	PIM	PP	SH	GW	Min
2002-03	Tri-City Storm	USHL	60	29	21	50	20	....	....	....	....	....	....	....	....	....	3	0	3	3	4	....	....	....	....
2003-04	Tri-City Storm	USHL	60	31	38	69	30	....	....	....	....	....	....	....	....	....	11	*9	7	*16	4	....	....	....	....
2004-05	Nebraska-Omaha	CCHA	39	19	26	45	12	....	....	....	....	....	....	....	....	....	....	....	....	....	....	....	....	....	....
2005-06	Nebraska-Omaha	CCHA	41	*27	23	50	43	....	....	....	....	....	....	....	....	....	....	....	....	....	....	....	....	....	....
	Phoenix	**NHL**	**9**	**1**	**2**	**3**	**8**	**1**	**0**	**0**	**15**	**6.7**	**-2**	**2**	**50.0**	**13:30**	....	....	....	....	....	....	....	....	....
	NHL Totals		**9**	**1**	**2**	**3**	**8**	**1**	**0**	**0**	**15**	**6.7**		**2**	**50.0**	**13:30**	....	....	....	....	....	....	....	....	....

CCHA First All-Star Team (2006)

Signed as a free agent by **Phoenix**. March 27, 2006.

THOMPSON, Rocky (TAWM-suhn, RAW-kee)

Defense. Shoots right. 6'2", 205 lbs. Born, Calgary, Alta., August 8, 1977. Calgary's 3rd choice, 72nd overall, in 1995 Entry Draft.

			Regular Season														Playoffs								
Season	Club	League	GP	G	A	Pts	PIM	PP	SH	GW	S	%	+/-	TF	F%	Min	GP	G	A	Pts	PIM	PP	SH	GW	Min
1992-93	Spruce Grove	AMHL	65	13	50	63	295																		
1993-94	Medicine Hat	WHL	68	1	4	5	166	....	....	....	....	....	....	....	....	....	3	0	0	0	2	....	....	....	....
1994-95	Medicine Hat	WHL	63	1	6	7	220	....	....	....	....	....	....	....	....	....	5	0	0	0	17	....	....	....	....
1995-96	Medicine Hat	WHL	71	9	20	29	260	....	....	....	....	....	....	....	....	....	5	2	3	5	26	....	....	....	....
	Saint John Flames	AHL	4	0	0	0	33	....	....	....	....	....	....	....	....	....	....	....	....	....	....	....	....	....	....
1996-97	Medicine Hat	WHL	47	6	9	15	170	....	....	....	....	....	....	....	....	....	....	....	....	....	....	....	....	....	....
	Swift Current	WHL	22	3	5	8	90	....	....	....	....	....	....	....	....	....	10	1	2	3	22	....	....	....	....
1997-98	**Calgary**	**NHL**	**12**	**0**	**0**	**0**	**61**	**0**	**0**	**0**	**3**	**0.0**	**0**	....	....	....	....	....	....	....	....	....	....	....	....
	Saint John Flames	AHL	51	3	0	3	187	....	....	....	....	....	....	....	....	....	18	1	1	2	47	....	....	....	....
1998-99	**Calgary**	**NHL**	**3**	**0**	**0**	**0**	**25**	**0**	**0**	**0**	**0**	**0.0**	**0**	**0**	**0.0**	**2:01**	....	....	....	....	....	....	....	....	....
	Saint John Flames	AHL	27	2	2	4	108	....	....	....	....	....	....	....	....	....	....	....	....	....	....	....	....	....	....
99-2000	Saint John Flames	AHL	53	2	8	10	125	....	....	....	....	....	....	....	....	....	....	....	....	....	....	....	....	....	....
	Louisville Panthers	AHL	3	0	1	1	54	....	....	....	....	....	....	....	....	....	4	0	0	0	4	....	....	....	....
2000-01	**Florida**	**NHL**	**4**	**0**	**0**	**0**	**19**	**0**	**0**	**0**	**0**	**0.0**	**0**	**0**	**0.0**	**1:28**	....	....	....	....	....	....	....	....	....
	Louisville Panthers	AHL	55	3	5	8	193	....	....	....	....	....	....	....	....	....	....	....	....	....	....	....	....	....	....
2001-02	**Florida**	**NHL**	**6**	**0**	**0**	**0**	**12**	**0**	**0**	**0**	**1**	**0.0**	**0**	**1**	**0.0**	**4:03**	....	....	....	....	....	....	....	....	....
	Hershey Bears	AHL	42	0	3	3	143	....	....	....	....	....	....	....	....	....	8	1	0	1	19	....	....	....	....
2002-03	San Antonio	AHL	79	1	11	12	275	....	....	....	....	....	....	....	....	....	3	0	0	0	4	....	....	....	....
2003-04	Toronto	AHL	69	1	8	9	196	....	....	....	....	....	....	....	....	....	3	1	1	2	0	....	....	....	....
2004-05	Edmonton	AHL	69	3	3	6	231	....	....	....	....	....	....	....	....	....	....	....	....	....	....	....	....	....	....
2005-06	Peoria Rivermen	AHL	59	1	4	5	247	....	....	....	....	....	....	....	....	....	3	0	0	0	19	....	....	....	....
	NHL Totals		**25**	**0**	**0**	**0**	**117**	**0**	**0**	**0**	**4**	**0.0**		**1**	**0.0**	**2:47**	....	....	....	....	....	....	....	....	....

Traded to **Florida** by **Calgary** for Filip Kuba, March 16, 2000. Signed as a free agent by **Edmonton**, July 20, 2003.

THORBURN, Chris (THOHR-buhrn, KRIHS) — BUF.

Center. Shoots right. 6'3", 220 lbs. Born, Sault Ste. Marie, Ont., June 3, 1983. Buffalo's 3rd choice, 50th overall, in 2001 Entry Draft.

			Regular Season														Playoffs								
Season	Club	League	GP	G	A	Pts	PIM	PP	SH	GW	S	%	+/-	TF	F%	Min	GP	G	A	Pts	PIM	PP	SH	GW	Min
1998-99	Elliot Lake Vikings	NOJHA	40	21	12	33	28	....	....	....	....	....	....	....	....	....	....	....	....	....	....	....	....	....	....
99-2000	North Bay	OHL	56	12	8	20	33	....	....	....	....	....	....	....	....	....	6	0	2	2	0	....	....	....	....
2000-01	North Bay	OHL	66	22	32	54	64	....	....	....	....	....	....	....	....	....	4	0	1	1	9	....	....	....	....
2001-02	North Bay	OHL	67	15	43	58	112	....	....	....	....	....	....	....	....	....	5	1	2	3	8	....	....	....	....
2002-03	Saginaw Spirit	OHL	37	19	19	38	68	....	....	....	....	....	....	....	....	....	....	....	....	....	....	....	....	....	....
	Plymouth Whalers	OHL	27	11	22	33	56	....	....	....	....	....	....	....	....	....	18	11	9	20	10	....	....	....	....
2003-04	Rochester	AHL	58	6	16	22	77	....	....	....	....	....	....	....	....	....	16	3	2	5	18	....	....	....	....
2004-05	Rochester	AHL	73	12	17	29	185	....	....	....	....	....	....	....	....	....	4	0	1	1	2	....	....	....	....
2005-06	**Buffalo**	**NHL**	**2**	**0**	**1**	**1**	**7**	**0**	**0**	**0**	**1**	**0.0**	**-1**	**1**	**0.0**	**6:52**	....	....	....	....	....	....	....	....	....
	Rochester	AHL	77	23	27	50	134	....	....	....	....	....	....	....	....	....	....	....	....	....	....	....	....	....	....
	NHL Totals		**2**	**0**	**1**	**1**	**7**	**0**	**0**	**0**	**1**	**0.0**		**1**	**0.0**	**6:52**	....	....	....	....	....	....	....	....	....

THORNTON, Joe (THOHRN-tuhn, JOH) — S.J.

Center. Shoots left. 6'4", 223 lbs. Born, London, Ont., July 2, 1979. Boston's 1st choice, 1st overall, in 1997 Entry Draft.

			Regular Season														Playoffs								
Season	Club	League	GP	G	A	Pts	PIM	PP	SH	GW	S	%	+/-	TF	F%	Min	GP	G	A	Pts	PIM	PP	SH	GW	Min
1993-94	Elgin-Middlesex	OMHA	67	*83	*85	*168	45	....	....	....	....	....	....	....	....	....	....	....	....	....	....	....	....	....	....
	St. Thomas Stars	OHA-B	6	2	6	8	2	....	....	....	....	....	....	....	....	....	....	....	....	....	....	....	....	....	....
1994-95	St. Thomas Stars	OHA-B	50	40	64	104	53	....	....	....	....	....	....	....	....	....	....	....	....	....	....	....	....	....	....
1995-96	Sault Ste. Marie	OHL	66	30	46	76	53	....	....	....	....	....	....	....	....	....	4	1	1	2	11	....	....	....	....
1996-97	Sault Ste. Marie	OHL	59	41	81	122	123	....	....	....	....	....	....	....	....	....	11	11	8	19	24	....	....	....	....
1997-98	**Boston**	**NHL**	**55**	**3**	**4**	**7**	**19**	**0**	**0**	**1**	**33**	**9.1**	**-6**	....	....	....	**6**	**0**	**0**	**0**	**9**	**0**	**0**	**0**	....
1998-99	**Boston**	**NHL**	**81**	**16**	**25**	**41**	**69**	**7**	**0**	**1**	**128**	**12.5**	**3**	**1073**	**48.7**	**15:21**	**11**	**3**	**6**	**9**	**4**	**2**	**0**	**2**	**19:52**
99-2000	**Boston**	**NHL**	**81**	**23**	**37**	**60**	**82**	**5**	**0**	**3**	**171**	**13.5**	**-5**	**1861**	**49.5**	**21:18**	....	....	....	....	....	....	....	....	....
2000-01	**Boston**	**NHL**	**72**	**37**	**34**	**71**	**107**	**19**	**1**	**5**	**181**	**20.4**	**-4**	**1651**	**52.1**	**21:45**	....	....	....	....	....	....	....	....	....
2001-02	**Boston**	**NHL**	**66**	**22**	**46**	**68**	**127**	**6**	**0**	**5**	**152**	**14.5**	**7**	**1341**	**49.1**	**19:59**	**6**	**2**	**4**	**6**	**10**	**0**	**0**	**0**	**21:09**
2002-03	**Boston**	**NHL**	**77**	**36**	**65**	**101**	**109**	**12**	**2**	**4**	**196**	**18.4**	**12**	**1766**	**49.5**	**22:33**	**5**	**1**	**2**	**3**	**4**	**1**	**0**	**0**	**20:13**
2003-04	**Boston**	**NHL**	**77**	**23**	**50**	**73**	**98**	**4**	**0**	**6**	**187**	**12.3**	**18**	**1671**	**56.3**	**21:38**	**7**	**0**	**0**	**0**	**14**	**0**	**0**	**0**	**21:30**
2004-05	HC Davos	Swiss	40	10	44	54	80	....	....	....	....	....	....	....	....	....	14	4	*20	*24	29	....	....	....	....
2005-06	**Boston**	**NHL**	**23**	**9**	***24**	***33**	**6**	**3**	**0**	**2**	**60**	**15.0**	**0**	**511**	**52.3**	**21:33**	....	....	....	....	....	....	....	....	....
	San Jose	**NHL**	**58**	**20**	***72**	***92**	**55**	**8**	**0**	**4**	**135**	**14.8**	**31**	**1287**	**50.9**	**21:15**	**11**	**2**	**7**	**9**	**12**	**1**	**0**	**1**	**25:09**
	Canada	Olympics	6	1	2	3	0	....	....	....	....	....	....	....	....	....	....	....	....	....	....	....	....	....	....
	NHL Totals		**590**	**189**	**357**	**546**	**672**	**64**	**3**	**31**	**1243**	**15.2**		**11161**	**51.1**	**20:32**	**46**	**8**	**19**	**27**	**53**	**4**	**0**	**3**	**21:50**

OHL All-Rookie Team (1996) • OHL Rookie of the Year (1996) • Canadian Major Junior Rookie of the Year (1996) • OHL Second All-Star Team (1997) • NHL Second All-Star Team (2003) • NHL First All-Star Team (2006) • Art Ross Trophy (2006) • Hart Trophy (2006)

Played in NHL All-Star Game (2002, 2003, 2004)

Signed as a free agent by **Davos** (Swiss), July 8, 2004. Traded to **San Jose** by **Boston** for Brad Stuart, Marco Sturm and Wayne Primeau, November 30, 2005.

THORNTON, Scott (THOHRN-tuhn, SKAWT) — L.A.

Left wing. Shoots left. 6'3", 225 lbs. Born, London, Ont., January 9, 1971. Toronto's 1st choice, 3rd overall, in 1989 Entry Draft.

			Regular Season														Playoffs								
Season	Club	League	GP	G	A	Pts	PIM	PP	SH	GW	S	%	+/-	TF	F%	Min	GP	G	A	Pts	PIM	PP	SH	GW	Min
1986-87	London	OHA-B	31	10	7	17	10	....	....	....	....	....	....	....	....	....	....	....	....	....	....	....	....	....	....
1987-88	Belleville Bulls	OHL	62	11	19	30	54	....	....	....	....	....	....	....	....	....	6	0	1	1	2	....	....	....	....
1988-89	Belleville Bulls	OHL	59	28	34	62	103	....	....	....	....	....	....	....	....	....	5	1	1	2	6	....	....	....	....
1989-90	Belleville Bulls	OHL	47	21	28	49	91	....	....	....	....	....	....	....	....	....	11	2	10	12	15	....	....	....	....
1990-91	Belleville Bulls	OHL	3	2	1	3	2	....	....	....	....	....	....	....	....	....	6	0	7	7	14	....	....	....	....
	Toronto	**NHL**	**33**	**1**	**3**	**4**	**30**	**0**	**0**	**0**	**31**	**3.2**	**-15**	....	....	....	....	....	....	....	....	....	....	....	....
	Newmarket Saints	AHL	5	1	0	1	4	....	....	....	....	....	....	....	....	....	....	....	....	....	....	....	....	....	....
1991-92	**Edmonton**	**NHL**	**15**	**0**	**1**	**1**	**43**	**0**	**0**	**0**	**11**	**0.0**	**-6**	....	....	....	**1**	**0**	**0**	**0**	**0**	**0**	**0**	**0**	....
	Cape Breton	AHL	49	9	14	23	40	....	....	....	....	....	....	....	....	....	5	1	0	1	8	....	....	....	....
1992-93	**Edmonton**	**NHL**	**9**	**0**	**1**	**1**	**0**	**0**	**0**	**0**	**7**	**0.0**	**-4**	....	....	....	....	....	....	....	....	....	....	....	....
	Cape Breton	AHL	58	23	27	50	102	....	....	....	....	....	....	....	....	....	16	1	2	3	35	....	....	....	....
1993-94	**Edmonton**	**NHL**	**61**	**4**	**7**	**11**	**104**	**0**	**0**	**0**	**65**	**6.2**	**-15**	....	....	....	....	....	....	....	....	....	....	....	....
	Cape Breton	AHL	2	1	1	2	31	....	....	....	....	....	....	....	....	....	....	....	....	....	....	....	....	....	....
1994-95	**Edmonton**	**NHL**	**47**	**10**	**12**	**22**	**89**	**0**	**1**	**1**	**69**	**14.5**	**-4**	....	....	....	....	....	....	....	....	....	....	....	....
1995-96	**Edmonton**	**NHL**	**77**	**9**	**9**	**18**	**149**	**0**	**2**	**3**	**95**	**9.5**	**-25**	....	....	....	....	....	....	....	....	....	....	....	....
1996-97	**Montreal**	**NHL**	**73**	**10**	**10**	**20**	**128**	**1**	**1**	**1**	**110**	**9.1**	**-19**	....	....	....	**5**	**1**	**0**	**1**	**2**	**0**	**0**	**0**	....
1997-98	**Montreal**	**NHL**	**67**	**6**	**9**	**15**	**158**	**1**	**0**	**1**	**51**	**11.8**	**0**	....	....	....	**9**	**0**	**2**	**2**	**10**	**0**	**0**	**0**	....
1998-99	**Montreal**	**NHL**	**47**	**7**	**4**	**11**	**87**	**1**	**0**	**1**	**56**	**12.5**	**-2**	**466**	**52.8**	**12:24**	....	....	....	....	....	....	....	....	....
99-2000	**Montreal**	**NHL**	**35**	**2**	**3**	**5**	**70**	**0**	**0**	**1**	**36**	**5.6**	**-7**	**253**	**51.8**	**12:40**	....	....	....	....	....	....	....	....	....
	Dallas	**NHL**	**30**	**6**	**3**	**9**	**38**	**1**	**0**	**0**	**47**	**12.8**	**-5**	**14**	**14.3**	**13:03**	**23**	**2**	**7**	**9**	**28**	**0**	**0**	**1**	**14:11**
2000-01	**San Jose**	**NHL**	**73**	**19**	**17**	**36**	**114**	**4**	**0**	**1**	**159**	**11.9**	**4**	**29**	**41.4**	**13:54**	**6**	**3**	**0**	**3**	**8**	**0**	**0**	**1**	**15:50**
2001-02	**San Jose**	**NHL**	**77**	**26**	**16**	**42**	**116**	**6**	**0**	**5**	**144**	**18.1**	**11**	**18**	**61.1**	**13:31**	**12**	**3**	**3**	**6**	**6**	**0**	**0**	**0**	**15:52**
2002-03	**San Jose**	**NHL**	**41**	**9**	**12**	**21**	**41**	**4**	**0**	**1**	**64**	**14.1**	**-7**	**6**	**50.0**	**13:53**	....	....	....	....	....	....	....	....	....
2003-04	**San Jose**	**NHL**	**80**	**13**	**14**	**27**	**84**	**1**	**0**	**1**	**127**	**10.2**	**-6**	**27**	**40.7**	**13:57**	**12**	**2**	**2**	**4**	**22**	**0**	**0**	**0**	**12:31**

			Regular Season														Playoffs								
Season	Club	League	GP	G	A	Pts	PIM	PP	SH	GW	S	%	+/-	TF	F%	Min	GP	G	A	Pts	PIM	PP	SH	GW	Min
2004-05	Sodertalje SK	Sweden	12	2	5	7	10										10	0	3	3	27				
2005-06	San Jose	NHL	71	10	11	21	84	1	0	2	122	8.2	–8	28	35.7	13:19	11	2	0	2	6	0	0	0	11:18
	NHL Totals		836	132	132	264	1335	20	4	18	1194	11.1		841	50.7	13:27	79	13	14	27	82	0	0	2	13:51

Traded to **Edmonton** by **Toronto** with Vincent Damphousse, Peter Ing and Luke Richardson for Grant Fuhr, Glenn Anderson and Craig Berube, September 19, 1991. Traded to **Montreal** by **Edmonton** for Andrei Kovalenko, September 6, 1996. Traded to **Dallas** by **Montreal** for Juha Lind, January 22, 2000. Signed as a free agent by **San Jose**, July 1, 2000. • Missed majority of 2002-03 season recovering from shoulder (October 7, 2002 in training camp) and head (February 21, 2003 vs. Columbus) injuries. Signed as a free agent by **Sodertalje** (Sweden), January 13, 2005. Signed as a free agent by **Los Angeles**, July 1, 2006.

THORNTON, Shawn (THOHRN-tohn, SHAWN) ANA.

Right wing. Shoots right. 6'1", 209 lbs. Born, Oshawa, Ont., July 23, 1977. Toronto's 6th choice, 190th overall, in 1997 Entry Draft.

Season	Club	League	GP	G	A	Pts	PIM	PP	SH	GW	S	%	+/-	TF	F%	Min	GP	G	A	Pts	PIM	PP	SH	GW	Min
1995-96	Peterborough	OHL	63	4	10	14	192										24	3	0	3	25				
1996-97	Peterborough	OHL	61	19	10	29	204										11	2	4	6	20				
1997-98	St. John's	AHL	59	0	3	3	225																		
1998-99	St. John's	AHL	78	8	11	19	354										5	0	0	0	9				
99-2000	St. John's	AHL	60	4	12	16	316																		
2000-01	St. John's	AHL	79	5	12	17	320										3	1	2	3	2				
2001-02	Norfolk Admirals	AHL	70	8	14	22	281										4	0	0	0	4				
2002-03	Chicago	NHL	13	1	1	2	31	0	0	0	15	6.7	–4	3	66.7	8:30									
	Norfolk Admirals	AHL	50	11	2	13	213										9	0	2	2	28				
2003-04	Chicago	NHL	8	1	0	1	23	0	0	0	14	7.1	2	19	42.1	11:14									
	Norfolk Admirals	AHL	64	6	11	17	259										8	1	1	2	6				
2004-05	Norfolk Admirals	AHL	71	5	9	14	253										6	0	0	0	8				
2005-06	Chicago	NHL	10	0	0	0	16	0	0	0	16	0.0	–5	17	58.8	7:18									
	Norfolk Admirals	AHL	59	10	22	32	192										4	0	0	0	35				
	NHL Totals		31	2	1	3	70	0	0	0	45	4.4		39	51.3	8:49									

Traded to **Chicago** by **Toronto** for Marty Wilford, September 30, 2001. Signed as a free agent by **Anaheim**, July 14, 2006.

TILEY, Brad (TIHL-ee, BRAD)

Defense. Shoots left. 6'1", 199 lbs. Born, Markdale, Ont., July 5, 1971. Boston's 4th choice, 84th overall, in 1991 Entry Draft.

Season	Club	League	GP	G	A	Pts	PIM	PP	SH	GW	S	%	+/-	TF	F%	Min	GP	G	A	Pts	PIM	PP	SH	GW	Min
1987-88	Owen Sound	OHA-B	45	18	25	43	69																		
1988-89	Sault Ste. Marie	OHL	50	4	11	15	31																		
1989-90	Sault Ste. Marie	OHL	66	9	32	41	47																		
1990-91	Sault Ste. Marie	OHL	66	11	55	66	29										14	4	15	19	12				
1991-92	Maine Mariners	AHL	62	7	22	29	36																		
1992-93	Phoenix	IHL	46	11	27	38	35																		
	Binghamton	AHL	26	6	10	16	19										8	0	1	1	2				
1993-94	Binghamton	AHL	29	6	10	16	6																		
	Phoenix	IHL	35	8	15	23	21																		
1994-95	Detroit Vipers	IHL	56	7	19	26	32																		
	Fort Wayne	IHL	14	1	6	7	2										3	1	2	3	0				
1995-96	Orlando	IHL	69	11	23	34	82										23	2	4	6	16				
1996-97	Phoenix	IHL	66	8	28	36	34																		
	Long Beach	IHL	3	1	0	1	2																		
1997-98	Phoenix	NHL	1	0	0	0	0																		
	Springfield	AHL	60	10	31	41	36										4	0	4	4	2				
1998-99	Phoenix	NHL	8	0	0	0	0	0	0	0	1	0.0	–1	0	0.0	11:29	1	0	0	0	0	0	0	0	13:11
	Springfield	AHL	69	9	35	44	14										1	0	0	0	0				
99-2000	Springfield	AHL	80	14	54	68	51										5	0	4	4	2				
2000-01	Philadelphia	NHL	2	0	0	0	0	0	0	0	1	0.0	–1	0	0.0	15:46									
	Philadelphia	AHL	56	11	19	30	10										10	1	2	3	2				
2001-02	Philadelphia	AHL	56	6	15	21	14																		
2002-03	Philadelphia	AHL	79	8	28	36	28																		
2003-04	Milwaukee	AHL	75	13	34	47	14										22	1	6	7	6				
2004-05	Milwaukee	AHL	77	8	17	25	23										6	0	5	5	2				
2005-06	Springfield	AHL	30	0	10	10	16																		
	San Antonio	AHL	41	1	9	10	34																		
	NHL Totals		11	0	0	0	0	0	0	0	2	0.0		0	0.0	12:20	1	0	0	0	0	0	0	0	13:11

Memorial Cup Tournament All-Star Team (1991) • AHL First All-Star Team (2000) • Eddie Shore Award (Outstanding Defenseman – AHL) (2000)

Signed as a free agent by **NY Rangers**, September 4, 1992. Traded to **Los Angeles** by **NY Rangers** for Los Angeles' 11th round choice (Jamie Butt) in 1994 Entry Draft, January 28, 1994. Signed as a free agent by **Phoenix**, September 4, 1997. Signed as a free agent by **Philadelphia**, July 14, 2000. Signed as a free agent by **Milwaukee** (AHL), October 22, 2003. Signed as a free agent by **Iserlohn** (Germany), July 19, 2006.

TIMANDER, Mattias (tih-MAHN-duhr, MA-tee-uhs)

Defense. Shoots left. 6'2", 230 lbs. Born, Solleftea, Sweden, April 16, 1974. Boston's 7th choice, 208th overall, in 1992 Entry Draft.

Season	Club	League	GP	G	A	Pts	PIM	PP	SH	GW	S	%	+/-	TF	F%	Min	GP	G	A	Pts	PIM	PP	SH	GW	Min
1992-93	MoDo Jr.	Swe-Jr.	4	0	0	0	0																		
	Husums IF	Sweden-2	27	4	9	13	22																		
	MoDo	Sweden	1	0	0	0	0																		
1993-94	MoDo Jr.	Swe-Jr.	3	2	2	4	10																		
	MoDo	Sweden	23	2	2	4	6										11	2	0	2	10				
1994-95	MoDo	Sweden	39	8	9	17	24																		
1995-96	MoDo	Sweden	37	4	10	14	34										7	1	1	2	8				
1996-97	Boston	NHL	41	1	8	9	14	0	0	0	62	1.6	–9												
	Providence Bruins	AHL	32	3	11	14	20										10	1	1	2	12				
1997-98	Boston	NHL	23	1	1	2	6	0	0	0	17	5.9	–9												
	Providence Bruins	AHL	31	3	7	10	25																		
1998-99	Boston	NHL	22	0	6	6	10	0	0	0	22	0.0	4	0	0.0	12:54	4	1	1	2	2	0	0	0	13:03
	Providence Bruins	AHL	43	2	22	24	24																		
99-2000	Boston	NHL	60	0	8	8	22	0	0	0	39	0.0	–11	0	0.0	12:29									
	Hershey Bears	AHL	1	0	0	0	2																		
2000-01	Columbus	NHL	76	2	9	11	24	0	0	1	68	2.9	–8	2	100.0	21:02									
2001-02	Columbus	NHL	78	4	7	11	44	1	0	0	68	5.9	–34	1	0.0	19:52									
2002-03	NY Islanders	NHL	80	3	13	16	24	0	0	1	83	3.6	–2	0	0.0	17:29	1	0	0	0	0	0	0	0	4:08
2003-04	NY Islanders	NHL	5	1	1	2	2	0	0	1	3	33.3	2	0	0.0	14:35									
	Bridgeport	AHL	35	2	6	8	12																		
	Philadelphia	NHL	34	1	4	5	19	0	1	0	43	2.3	13	0	0.0	18:25	18	2	4	6	6	0	0	1	17:28
2004-05	MODO	Sweden	47	3	7	10	60										6	0	1	1	4				
2005-06	MODO	Sweden	48	5	9	14	48										5	0	1	1	4				
	NHL Totals		419	13	57	70	165	1	1	3	405	3.2		3	66.7	17:41	23	3	5	8	8	0	0	1	16:07

Claimed by **Columbus** from **Boston** in Expansion Draft, June 23, 2000. Traded to **NY Islanders** by **Columbus** for NY Islanders' 4th round choice (Jekabs Redlihs) in 2002 Entry Draft, June 22, 2002. Traded to **Philadelphia** by **NY Islanders** for Tampa Bay's 7th round choice (previously acquired, NY Islanders selected Chris Campoli) in 2004 Entry Draft, January 22, 2004. Signed as a free agent by **MODO** (Sweden), June 3, 2004.

TIMONEN, Kimmo (TEEM-oh-nehn, KEE-moh) NSH.

Defense. Shoots left. 5'10", 194 lbs. Born, Kuopio, Finland, March 18, 1975. Los Angeles' 11th choice, 250th overall, in 1993 Entry Draft.

Season	Club	League	GP	G	A	Pts	PIM	PP	SH	GW	S	%	+/-	TF	F%	Min	GP	G	A	Pts	PIM	PP	SH	GW	Min
1990-91	KalPa Kuopio Jr.	Fin-Jr.	4	0	1	1	2																		
1991-92	KalPa Kuopio Jr.	Fin-Jr.	32	7	10	17	4																		
	KalPa Kuopio	Finland	5	0	0	0	0																		
1992-93	KalPa Kuopio U18	Fin-U18	3	0	5	5	0																		
	KalPa Kuopio Jr.	Fin-Jr.	16	9	15	24	10																		
	KalPa Kuopio	Finland	33	0	2	2	4																		
1993-94	KalPa Kuopio Jr.	Fin-Jr.	5	4	7	11	0																		
	KalPa Kuopio	Finland	46	6	7	13	55																		
1994-95	TPS Turku Jr.	Fin-Jr.	1	0	0	0	0																		
	TPS Turku	Finland	45	3	4	7	10										13	0	1	1	6				
1995-96	TPS Turku	Finland	48	3	21	24	22										9	1	2	3	12				
1996-97	TPS Turku	Finland	50	10	14	24	18										12	2	7	9	6				
	TPS Turku	EuroHL	6	1	0	1	27										4	0	1	1	0				

Season	Club	League	Regular Season GP	G	A	Pts	PIM	PP	SH	GW	S	%	+/-	TF	F%	Min	Playoffs GP	G	A	Pts	PIM	PP	SH	GW	Min
1997-98	HIFK Helsinki	Finland	45	10	15	25	24										9	3	4	7	8				
	Finland	Olympics	6	0	1	1	2																		
1998-99	**Nashville**	**NHL**	**50**	**4**	**8**	**12**	**30**	**1**	**0**	**0**	**75**	**5.3**	**-4**	**0**	**0.0**	**19:04**									
	Milwaukee	IHL	29	2	13	15	22																		
99-2000	**Nashville**	**NHL**	**51**	**8**	**25**	**33**	**26**	**2**	**1**	**2**	**97**	**8.2**	**-5**	**0**	**0.0**	**21:06**									
2000-01	**Nashville**	**NHL**	**82**	**12**	**13**	**25**	**50**	**6**	**0**	**3**	**151**	**7.9**	**-6**	**2**	**50.0**	**23:11**									
2001-02	**Nashville**	**NHL**	**82**	**13**	**29**	**42**	**28**	**9**	**0**	**1**	**154**	**8.4**	**2**	**0**	**0.0**	**24:12**									
	Finland	Olympics	4	0	1	1	2																		
2002-03	**Nashville**	**NHL**	**72**	**6**	**34**	**40**	**46**	**4**	**0**	**0**	**144**	**4.2**	**-3**	**0**	**0.0**	**22:25**									
2003-04	**Nashville**	**NHL**	**77**	**12**	**32**	**44**	**52**	**8**	**0**	**1**	**180**	**6.7**	**-7**	**1**	**0.0**	**23:52**	**6**	**0**	**0**	**0**	**10**	**0**	**0**	**0**	**24:16**
2004-05	HC Lugano	Swiss	3	0	1	1	0																		
	Brynas IF Gavle	Sweden	10	5	3	8	8																		
	KalPa Kuopio	Finland-2	12	4	13	17	6										8	3	7	10	4				
2005-06	**Nashville**	**NHL**	**79**	**11**	**39**	**50**	**74**	**8**	**0**	**1**	**156**	**7.1**	**-3**	**5**	**80.0**	**22:26**	**5**	**1**	**3**	**4**	**4**	**0**	**1**	**0**	**24:42**
	Finland	Olympics	8	1	4	5	2																		
	NHL Totals		**493**	**66**	**180**	**246**	**306**	**38**	**1**	**8**	**957**	**6.9**		**8**	**62.5**	**22:36**	**11**	**1**	**3**	**4**	**14**	**0**	**1**	**0**	**24:28**

Olympic Tournament All-Star Team (2006)

Played in NHL All-Star Game (2004)

Traded to **Nashville** by **Los Angeles** with Jan Vopat for future considerations, June 26, 1998. Signed as a free agent by **Lugano** (Swiss), October 31, 2004. Signed as a free agent by **Gavle** (Sweden), November 8, 2004. Signed as a free agent by **Kuopio** (Finland-2), January 3, 2005.

TJARNQVIST, Daniel

(TUH-yahrn-kvihst, DAN-yehl) **EDM.**

Defense. Shoots left. 6'2", 200 lbs. Born, Umea, Sweden, October 14, 1976. Florida's 5th choice, 88th overall, in 1995 Entry Draft.

Season	Club	League	Regular Season GP	G	A	Pts	PIM	PP	SH	GW	S	%	+/-	TF	F%	Min	Playoffs GP	G	A	Pts	PIM	PP	SH	GW	Min
1992-93	Rogle Jr.	Swe-Jr.	7	1	0	1	0																		
1993-94	Rogle U18	Swe-U18	STATISTICS NOT AVAILABLE																						
1994-95	Rogle	Sweden	18	0	1	1	2																		
	Rogle	Sweden-Q	15	2	3	5	0																		
1995-96	Rogle	Sweden	22	1	7	8	6																		
1996-97	Jokerit Helsinki	Finland	44	3	8	11	4										9	0	3	3	4				
	Jokerit Helsinki	EuroHL	6	1	1	2	2																		
1997-98	Djurgarden	Sweden	40	5	9	14	12										15	1	1	2	2				
1998-99	Djurgarden	Sweden	40	4	3	7	16										4	0	0	0	2				
99-2000	Djurgarden	Sweden	42	3	16	19	8										5	0	0	0	2				
2000-01	Djurgarden	Sweden	45	9	17	26	26										16	6	5	11	2				
2001-02	**Atlanta**	**NHL**	**75**	**2**	**16**	**18**	**14**	**1**	**0**	**0**	**68**	**2.9**	**-22**	**4**	**25.0**	**21:32**									
2002-03	**Atlanta**	**NHL**	**75**	**3**	**12**	**15**	**26**	**1**	**0**	**0**	**65**	**4.6**	**-20**	**3**	**66.7**	**21:53**									
2003-04	**Atlanta**	**NHL**	**68**	**5**	**15**	**20**	**20**	**0**	**2**	**1**	**65**	**7.7**	**-4**	**4**	**25.0**	**22:17**									
2004-05	Djurgarden	Sweden	49	12	12	24	30										12	2	5	7	10				
2005-06	**Minnesota**	**NHL**	**60**	**3**	**15**	**18**	**32**	**3**	**0**	**1**	**54**	**5.6**	**-11**	**0**	**0.0**	**19:46**									
	Sweden	Olympics	8	2	1	3	4																		
	NHL Totals		**278**	**13**	**58**	**71**	**92**	**5**	**2**	**2**	**252**	**5.2**		**11**	**36.4**	**21:26**									

Traded to **Atlanta** by **Florida** with Gord Murphy, Herbert Vasiljevs and Ottawa's 6th round choice (previously acquired, later traded to Dallas – Dallas selected Justin Cox) in 1999 Entry Draft for Trevor Kidd, June 25, 1999. Signed as a free agent by **Djurgarden** (Sweden), September 16, 2004. Signed as a free agent by **Minnesota**, August 15, 2005. Signed as a free agent by **Edmonton**, July 6, 2006.

TJARNQVIST, Mathias

(TUH-yahrn-kvihst, MAT-ee-uhs) **DAL.**

Right wing. Shoots left. 6'1", 183 lbs. Born, Umea, Sweden, April 15, 1979. Dallas' 3rd choice, 96th overall, in 1999 Entry Draft.

Season	Club	League	Regular Season GP	G	A	Pts	PIM	PP	SH	GW	S	%	+/-	TF	F%	Min	Playoffs GP	G	A	Pts	PIM	PP	SH	GW	Min
1995-96	Rogle Jr.	Swe-Jr.	4	2	0	2	0																		
1996-97	Rogle Jr.	Swe-Jr.	18	5	8	13	....																		
	Rogle	Sweden-2	15	1	4	5	4																		
1997-98	Rogle	Sweden-2	31	12	11	23	30										4	2	0	2	6				
1998-99	Rogle	Sweden-2	34	18	16	34	44										5	4	1	5	4				
99-2000	Djurgarden	Sweden	50	12	12	24	20										13	3	2	5	16				
2000-01	Djurgarden	Sweden	47	11	8	19	53										16	1	2	3	6				
2001-02	Djurgarden	Sweden	6	0	1	1	4										2	0	0	0	2				
2002-03	Djurgarden	Sweden	38	11	13	24	30										9	4	1	5	12				
2003-04	**Dallas**	**NHL**	**18**	**1**	**1**	**2**	**2**	**0**	**0**	**1**	**11**	**9.1**	**-6**	**4**	**25.0**	**9:43**									
	Utah Grizzlies	AHL	60	15	13	28	51																		
2004-05	HV 71 Jonkoping	Sweden	46	8	9	17	18																		
2005-06	**Dallas**	**NHL**	**33**	**2**	**4**	**6**	**18**	**0**	**0**	**0**	**36**	**5.6**	**4**	**4**	**75.0**	**8:10**									
	Iowa Stars	AHL	34	17	12	29	28										1	0	0	0	0				
	NHL Totals		**51**	**3**	**5**	**8**	**20**	**0**	**0**	**1**	**47**	**6.4**		**8**	**50.0**	**8:43**									

Signed as a free agent by **Jonkoping** (Sweden), August 30, 2004.

TKACHUK, Keith

(kuh-CHUK, KEETH) **ST.L.**

Left wing. Shoots left. 6'2", 225 lbs. Born, Melrose, MA, March 28, 1972. Winnipeg's 1st choice, 19th overall, in 1990 Entry Draft.

Season	Club	League	Regular Season GP	G	A	Pts	PIM	PP	SH	GW	S	%	+/-	TF	F%	Min	Playoffs GP	G	A	Pts	PIM	PP	SH	GW	Min
1988-89	Malden Cath.	High-MA	21	30	16	46	....																		
1989-90	Malden Cath.	High-MA	6	12	14	26	....																		
1990-91	Boston University	H-East	36	17	23	40	70																		
1991-92	United States	Nat-Tm	45	10	10	20	141																		
	United States	Olympics	8	1	1	2	12																		
	Winnipeg	**NHL**	**17**	**3**	**5**	**8**	**28**	**2**	**0**	**0**	**22**	**13.6**	**0**				**7**	**3**	**0**	**3**	**30**	**0**	**0**	**0**	
1992-93	**Winnipeg**	**NHL**	**83**	**28**	**23**	**51**	**201**	**12**	**0**	**2**	**199**	**14.1**	**-13**				**6**	**4**	**0**	**4**	**14**	**1**	**0**	**0**	
1993-94	**Winnipeg**	**NHL**	**84**	**41**	**40**	**81**	**255**	**22**	**3**	**3**	**218**	**18.8**	**-12**												
1994-95	**Winnipeg**	**NHL**	**48**	**22**	**29**	**51**	**152**	**7**	**2**	**2**	**129**	**17.1**	**-4**												
1995-96	**Winnipeg**	**NHL**	**76**	**50**	**48**	**98**	**156**	**20**	**2**	**6**	**249**	**20.1**	**11**				**6**	**1**	**2**	**3**	**22**	**0**	**0**	**0**	
1996-97	**Phoenix**	**NHL**	**81**	***52**	**34**	**86**	**228**	**9**	**2**	**7**	**296**	**17.6**	**-1**				**7**	**6**	**0**	**6**	**7**	**2**	**0**	**0**	
1997-98	**Phoenix**	**NHL**	**69**	**40**	**26**	**66**	**147**	**11**	**0**	**8**	**232**	**17.2**	**9**				**6**	**3**	**3**	**6**	**10**	**0**	**0**	**0**	
	United States	Olympics	4	0	2	2	6																		
1998-99	**Phoenix**	**NHL**	**68**	**36**	**32**	**68**	**151**	**11**	**2**	**7**	**258**	**14.0**	**22**	**770**	**47.7**	**20:59**	**7**	**1**	**3**	**4**	**13**	**1**	**0**	**0**	**25:09**
99-2000	**Phoenix**	**NHL**	**50**	**22**	**21**	**43**	**82**	**5**	**1**	**1**	**183**	**12.0**	**7**	**500**	**50.4**	**19:21**	**5**	**1**	**1**	**2**	**4**	**1**	**0**	**0**	**18:46**
2000-01	**Phoenix**	**NHL**	**64**	**29**	**42**	**71**	**108**	**15**	**0**	**4**	**230**	**12.6**	**6**	**646**	**51.9**	**20:11**									
	St. Louis	**NHL**	**12**	**6**	**2**	**8**	**14**	**2**	**0**	**1**	**41**	**14.6**	**-3**	**87**	**54.0**	**19:39**	**15**	**2**	**7**	**9**	**20**	**2**	**0**	**1**	**19:17**
2001-02	**St. Louis**	**NHL**	**73**	**38**	**37**	**75**	**117**	**13**	**0**	**7**	**244**	**15.6**	**21**	**88**	**43.2**	**19:38**	**10**	**5**	**5**	**10**	**18**	**1**	**0**	**0**	**19:24**
	United States	Olympics	5	2	0	2	2																		
2002-03	**St. Louis**	**NHL**	**56**	**31**	**24**	**55**	**139**	**14**	**0**	**5**	**185**	**16.8**	**1**	**346**	**55.8**	**19:16**	**7**	**1**	**3**	**4**	**14**	**0**	**0**	**0**	**19:22**
2003-04	**St. Louis**	**NHL**	**75**	**33**	**38**	**71**	**83**	**18**	**0**	**8**	**233**	**14.2**	**8**	**410**	**49.5**	**19:39**	**5**	**0**	**2**	**2**	**10**	**0**	**0**	**0**	**19:18**
2004-05			DID NOT PLAY																						
2005-06	**St. Louis**	**NHL**	**41**	**15**	**21**	**36**	**46**	**10**	**0**	**1**	**133**	**11.3**	**-15**	**250**	**50.4**	**19:27**									
	United States	Olympics	6	0	0	0	8																		
	NHL Totals		**897**	**446**	**422**	**868**	**1907**	**171**	**12**	**62**	**2852**	**15.6**		**3097**	**50.4**	**19:50**	**81**	**27**	**26**	**53**	**162**	**8**	**0**	**1**	**20:06**

NHL Second All-Star Team (1995, 1998)

Played in NHL All-Star Game (1997, 1998, 1999, 2004)

Transferred to **Phoenix** after **Winnipeg** franchise relocated, July 1, 1996. Traded to **St. Louis** by **Phoenix** for Michal Handzus, Ladislav Nagy, the rights to Jeff Taffe and St. Louis' 1st round choice (Ben Eager) in 2002 Entry Draft, March 13, 2001.

TOLLEFSEN, Ole-Kristian

(TOHL-uhf-suhn, OH-lay-KRIHS-tyahn) **CBJ**

Defense. Shoots left. 6'2", 211 lbs. Born, Oslo, Norway, March 29, 1984. Columbus' 3rd choice, 65th overall, in 2002 Entry Draft.

Season	Club	League	Regular Season GP	G	A	Pts	PIM	PP	SH	GW	S	%	+/-	TF	F%	Min	Playoffs GP	G	A	Pts	PIM	PP	SH	GW	Min
2000-01	Lillehammer IK	Norway	4	0	0	0	2																		
2001-02	Lillehammer IK	Norway	37	1	5	6	63										6	1	1	2	10				
	Lillehammer IK	Nor-Jr.	....	....	....	....	....										1	0	2	2	4				
2002-03	Brandon	WHL	43	6	14	20	73										17	0	2	2	38				
2003-04	Brandon	WHL	53	3	27	30	94										11	0	4	4	15				
2004-05	Dayton Bombers	ECHL	2	0	0	0	0																		
	Syracuse Crunch	AHL	64	0	3	3	115																		

Season	Club	League	GP	G	A	Pts	PIM	PP	SH	GW	S	%	+/-	TF	F%	Min	GP	G	A	Pts	PIM	PP	SH	GW	Min
			Regular Season														Playoffs								
2005-06	**Columbus**	**NHL**	5	0	0	0	2	0	0	0	3	0.0	−2	0	0.0	16:18	....	....	....	....	....	....	....	....	....
	Syracuse Crunch	AHL	58	2	16	18	155	....	....	....	....	....	....	....	....	....	1	0	0	0	6	....	....	....	....
	NHL Totals		5	0	0	0	2	0	0	0	3	0.0		0	0.0	16:18	....	....	....	....	....	....	....	....	....

TOOTOO, Jordin

(TOO-TOO, JOHR-dihn) **NSH.**

Right wing. Shoots right. 5'9", 194 lbs. Born, Churchill, Man., February 2, 1983. Nashville's 6th choice, 98th overall, in 2001 Entry Draft.

Season	Club	League	GP	G	A	Pts	PIM	PP	SH	GW	S	%	+/-	TF	F%	Min	GP	G	A	Pts	PIM	PP	SH	GW	Min
1997-98	Spruce Grove	AMBHL	STATISTICS NOT AVAILABLE																						
1998-99	OCN Blizzard	MJHL	47	16	21	37	251	....	....	....	....	....	....	....	....	....	....	....	....	....	....	....	....	....	....
99-2000	Brandon	WHL	45	6	10	16	214	....	....	....	....	....	....	....	....	....	....	....	....	....	....	....	....	....	....
2000-01	Brandon	WHL	60	20	28	48	172	....	....	....	....	....	....	....	....	....	6	2	4	6	18	....	....	....	....
2001-02	Brandon	WHL	64	32	39	71	272	....	....	....	....	....	....	....	....	....	16	4	3	7	*58	....	....	....	....
2002-03	Brandon	WHL	51	35	39	74	216	....	....	....	....	....	....	....	....	....	17	6	3	9	49	....	....	....	....
2003-04	**Nashville**	**NHL**	70	4	4	8	137	2	0	0	92	4.3	−6	18	55.6	8:29	5	0	0	0	4	0	0	0	5:09
2004-05	Milwaukee	AHL	59	10	12	22	266	....	....	....	....	....	....	....	....	....	6	0	0	0	41	....	....	....	....
2005-06	**Nashville**	**NHL**	34	4	6	10	55	0	0	0	61	6.6	9	17	70.6	9:15	3	0	0	0	0	0	0	0	4:04
	Milwaukee	AHL	41	13	14	27	133	....	....	....	....	....	....	....	....	....	15	9	2	11	35	....	....	....	....
	NHL Totals		104	8	10	18	192	2	0	0	153	5.2		35	62.9	8:44	8	0	0	0	4	0	0	0	4:45

WHL East First All-Star Team (2003)

TORRES, Raffi

(TAW-rehs, RA-fee) **EDM.**

Left wing. Shoots left. 6', 216 lbs. Born, Toronto, Ont., October 8, 1981. NY Islanders' 2nd choice, 5th overall, in 2000 Entry Draft.

Season	Club	League	GP	G	A	Pts	PIM	PP	SH	GW	S	%	+/-	TF	F%	Min	GP	G	A	Pts	PIM	PP	SH	GW	Min
1997-98	Thornhill Rattlers	MTJHL	46	17	16	33	90	....	....	....	....	....	....	....	....	....	....	....	....	....	....	....	....	....	....
1998-99	Brampton	OHL	62	35	27	62	32	....	....	....	....	....	....	....	....	....	....	....	....	....	....	....	....	....	....
99-2000	Brampton	OHL	68	43	48	91	40	....	....	....	....	....	....	....	....	....	6	5	2	7	23	....	....	....	....
2000-01	Brampton	OHL	55	33	37	70	76	....	....	....	....	....	....	....	....	....	8	7	4	11	19	....	....	....	....
2001-02	**NY Islanders**	**NHL**	14	0	1	1	6	0	0	0	9	0.0	2	0	0.0	7:35	....	....	....	....	....	....	....	....	....
	Bridgeport	AHL	59	20	10	30	45	....	....	....	....	....	....	....	....	....	20	8	9	17	26	....	....	....	....
2002-03	**NY Islanders**	**NHL**	17	0	5	5	10	0	0	0	12	0.0	0	4	25.0	7:40	....	....	....	....	....	....	....	....	....
	Bridgeport	AHL	49	17	15	32	54	....	....	....	....	....	....	....	....	....	....	....	....	....	....	....	....	....	....
	Hamilton	AHL	11	1	7	8	14	....	....	....	....	....	....	....	....	....	23	6	1	7	29	....	....	....	....
2003-04	**Edmonton**	**NHL**	80	20	14	34	65	5	0	3	136	14.7	12	21	28.6	12:38	....	....	....	....	....	....	....	....	....
2004-05	Edmonton	AHL	67	21	25	46	165	....	....	....	....	....	....	....	....	....	....	....	....	....	....	....	....	....	....
2005-06	**Edmonton**	**NHL**	82	27	14	41	50	6	0	3	164	16.5	4	60	41.7	13:24	22	4	7	11	16	1	0	1	13:15
	NHL Totals		193	47	34	81	131	11	0	6	321	14.6		85	37.6	12:09	22	4	7	11	16	1	0	1	13:15

OHL All-Rookie Team (1999) • OHL Second All-Star Team (2000, 2001)

Traded to **Edmonton** by **NY Islanders** with Brad Isbister for Janne Niinimaa and Washington's 2nd round choice (previously acquired, NY Islanders selected Evgeni Tunik) in 2003 Entry Draft, March 11, 2003.

TRAVERSE, Patrick

(tra-VAIRZ, PAT-rihk) **S.J.**

Defense. Shoots left. 6'4", 207 lbs. Born, Montreal, Que., March 14, 1974. Ottawa's 3rd choice, 50th overall, in 1992 Entry Draft.

Season	Club	League	GP	G	A	Pts	PIM	PP	SH	GW	S	%	+/-	TF	F%	Min	GP	G	A	Pts	PIM	PP	SH	GW	Min
1990-91	Mtl-Bourassa	QAAA	42	4	19	23	10	....	....	....	....	....	....	....	....	....	5	0	3	3	2	....	....	....	....
1991-92	Shawinigan	QMJHL	59	3	11	14	12	....	....	....	....	....	....	....	....	....	10	0	0	0	4	....	....	....	....
1992-93	Shawinigan	QMJHL	53	5	24	29	24	....	....	....	....	....	....	....	....	....	....	....	....	....	....	....	....	....	....
	St-Jean Lynx	QMJHL	15	1	6	7	0	....	....	....	....	....	....	....	....	....	4	0	1	1	2	....	....	....	....
	New Haven	AHL	2	0	0	0	2	....	....	....	....	....	....	....	....	....	....	....	....	....	....	....	....	....	....
1993-94	St-Jean Lynx	QMJHL	66	15	37	52	30	....	....	....	....	....	....	....	....	....	5	0	4	4	4	....	....	....	....
	P.E.I. Senators	AHL	3	0	1	1	2	....	....	....	....	....	....	....	....	....	....	....	....	....	....	....	....	....	....
1994-95	P.E.I. Senators	AHL	70	5	13	18	19	....	....	....	....	....	....	....	....	....	7	0	2	2	0	....	....	....	....
1995-96	**Ottawa**	**NHL**	5	0	0	0	2	0	0	0	2	0.0	−1	....	....	....	....	....	....	....	....	....	....	....	....
	P.E.I. Senators	AHL	55	4	21	25	32	....	....	....	....	....	....	....	....	....	5	1	2	3	2	....	....	....	....
1996-97	Worcester IceCats	AHL	24	0	4	4	23	....	....	....	....	....	....	....	....	....	....	....	....	....	....	....	....	....	....
	Grand Rapids	IHL	10	2	1	3	10	....	....	....	....	....	....	....	....	....	2	0	1	1	2	....	....	....	....
1997-98	Hershey Bears	AHL	71	14	15	29	67	....	....	....	....	....	....	....	....	....	7	1	3	4	4	....	....	....	....
1998-99	**Ottawa**	**NHL**	46	1	9	10	22	0	0	0	35	2.9	12	0	0.0	14:56	....	....	....	....	....	....	....	....	....
99-2000	**Ottawa**	**NHL**	66	6	17	23	21	1	0	0	73	8.2	17	0	0.0	18:43	6	0	0	0	2	0	0	0	17:50
2000-01	**Anaheim**	**NHL**	15	1	0	1	6	0	0	0	7	14.3	−6	0	0.0	17:19	....	....	....	....	....	....	....	....	....
	Boston	**NHL**	37	2	6	8	14	1	0	1	39	5.1	4	0	0.0	16:38	....	....	....	....	....	....	....	....	....
	Montreal	**NHL**	19	2	3	5	10	0	0	0	16	12.5	−8	0	0.0	21:36	....	....	....	....	....	....	....	....	....
2001-02	**Montreal**	**NHL**	25	2	3	5	14	2	0	0	24	8.3	−7	0	0.0	18:14	....	....	....	....	....	....	....	....	....
	Quebec Citadelles	AHL	4	0	2	2	4	....	....	....	....	....	....	....	....	....	....	....	....	....	....	....	....	....	....
2002-03	**Montreal**	**NHL**	65	0	13	13	24	0	0	0	63	0.0	−9	0	0.0	20:12	....	....	....	....	....	....	....	....	....
2003-04	Hamilton	AHL	80	5	21	26	31	....	....	....	....	....	....	....	....	....	10	1	2	3	0	....	....	....	....
2004-05	Houston Aeros	AHL	72	6	9	15	28	....	....	....	....	....	....	....	....	....	5	0	0	0	2	....	....	....	....
2005-06	**Dallas**	**NHL**	1	0	0	0	0	0	0	0	1	0.0	0	0	0.0	11:27	....	....	....	....	....	....	....	....	....
	Iowa Stars	AHL	40	3	21	24	16	....	....	....	....	....	....	....	....	....	7	1	2	3	2	....	....	....	....
	NHL Totals		279	14	51	65	113	4	0	1	260	5.4		0	0.0	18:12	6	0	0	0	2	0	0	0	17:49

Traded to **Anaheim** by **Ottawa** for Joel Kwiatkowski, June 12, 2000. Traded to **Boston** by **Anaheim** with Andrei Nazarov for Samuel Pahlsson, November 18, 2000. Traded to **Montreal** by **Boston** for Eric Weinrich, February 21, 2001. • Missed majority of 2001-02 season recovering from knee (November 3, 2001 vs. Calgary) and head (January 10, 2002 vs. NY Islanders) injuries. Signed as a free agent by **Dallas**, September 9, 2004. Signed as a free agent by **San Jose**, July 10, 2006.

TREMBLAY, Yannick

(TRAHM-blay, YA-nihk) **VAN.**

Defense. Shoots right. 6'2", 200 lbs. Born, Pointe-aux-Trembles, Que., November 15, 1975. Toronto's 4th choice, 145th overall, in 1995 Entry Draft.

Season	Club	League	GP	G	A	Pts	PIM	PP	SH	GW	S	%	+/-	TF	F%	Min	GP	G	A	Pts	PIM	PP	SH	GW	Min
1991-92	Mtl-Bourassa	QAAA	35	2	5	7	55	....	....	....	....	....	....	....	....	....	8	0	4	4	2	....	....	....	....
1992-93	Mtl-Bourassa	CEGEP	21	2	5	7	10	....	....	....	....	....	....	....	....	....	3	0	0	0	2	....	....	....	....
1993-94	St. Thomas U.	AUAA	25	2	3	5	10	....	....	....	....	....	....	....	....	....	....	....	....	....	....	....	....	....	....
1994-95	Beauport	QMJHL	70	10	32	42	22	....	....	....	....	....	....	....	....	....	17	6	8	14	6	....	....	....	....
1995-96	Beauport	QMJHL	61	12	33	45	42	....	....	....	....	....	....	....	....	....	20	3	16	19	18	....	....	....	....
	St. John's	AHL	3	0	1	1	0	....	....	....	....	....	....	....	....	....	....	....	....	....	....	....	....	....	....
1996-97	**Toronto**	**NHL**	5	0	0	0	0	0	0	0	2	0.0	−4	....	....	....	....	....	....	....	....	....	....	....	....
	St. John's	AHL	67	7	25	32	34	....	....	....	....	....	....	....	....	....	11	2	9	11	0	....	....	....	....
1997-98	**Toronto**	**NHL**	38	2	4	6	6	1	0	0	45	4.4	−6	....	....	....	....	....	....	....	....	....	....	....	....
	St. John's	AHL	17	3	7	10	4	....	....	....	....	....	....	....	....	....	4	0	1	1	5	....	....	....	....
1998-99	**Toronto**	**NHL**	35	2	7	9	16	0	0	0	37	5.4	0	0	0.0	17:39	....	....	....	....	....	....	....	....	....
99-2000	**Atlanta**	**NHL**	75	10	21	31	22	4	1	2	139	7.2	−42	3	0.0	19:27	....	....	....	....	....	....	....	....	....
2000-01	**Atlanta**	**NHL**	46	4	8	12	30	1	0	1	102	3.9	−6	1	100.0	20:27	....	....	....	....	....	....	....	....	....
2001-02	**Atlanta**	**NHL**	66	9	15	24	47	1	0	1	115	7.8	−15	0	0.0	21:50	....	....	....	....	....	....	....	....	....
2002-03	**Atlanta**	**NHL**	75	8	22	30	32	5	0	1	151	5.3	−27	1	0.0	21:45	....	....	....	....	....	....	....	....	....
2003-04	**Atlanta**	**NHL**	38	2	8	10	13	1	0	1	47	4.3	−13	2	50.0	21:36	....	....	....	....	....	....	....	....	....
2004-05	Sherbrooke	QNAHL	36	26	25	51	40	....	....	....	....	....	....	....	....	....	....	....	....	....	....	....	....	....	....
	Adler Mannheim	Germany	14	1	4	5	16	....	....	....	....	....	....	....	....	....	14	2	6	8	6	....	....	....	....
2005-06	Adler Mannheim	Germany	46	11	17	28	44	....	....	....	....	....	....	....	....	....	....	....	....	....	....	....	....	....	....
	NHL Totals		378	37	85	122	166	13	1	6	638	5.8		7	28.6	20:38	....	....	....	....	....	....	....	....	....

Claimed by **Atlanta** from **Toronto** in Expansion Draft, June 25, 1999. • Missed majority of 2003-04 season recovering from foot (November 15, 2003 vs. Philadelphia) and hip (January 30, 2004 vs. Toronto) injuries. Signed as a free agent by **Sherbrooke** (QNAHL), November 16, 2004. Signed as a free agent by **Mannheim** (Germany), January 13, 2005. Signed as a free agent by **Vancouver**, July 28, 2006.

TRNKA, Pavel

(truhn-KAH, PAH-vehl)

Defense. Shoots left. 6'2", 206 lbs. Born, Plzen, Czech., July 27, 1976. Anaheim's 5th choice, 106th overall, in 1994 Entry Draft.

Season	Club	League	GP	G	A	Pts	PIM	PP	SH	GW	S	%	+/-	TF	F%	Min	GP	G	A	Pts	PIM	PP	SH	GW	Min
1993-94	HC Skoda Plzen	CzRep	12	0	1	1	....	....	....	....	....	....	....	....	....	....	....	....	....	....	....	....	....	....	....
1994-95	HC Kladno	CzRep	28	0	5	5	24	....	....	....	....	....	....	....	....	....	....	....	....	....	....	....	....	....	....
	Plzen	CzRep	6	0	0	0	0	....	....	....	....	....	....	....	....	....	....	....	....	....	....	....	....	....	....
1995-96	Baltimore Bandits	AHL	69	2	6	8	44	....	....	....	....	....	....	....	....	....	6	0	0	0	2	....	....	....	....
1996-97	Baltimore Bandits	AHL	69	6	14	20	86	....	....	....	....	....	....	....	....	....	3	0	0	0	2	....	....	....	....
1997-98	**Anaheim**	**NHL**	48	3	4	7	40	1	0	0	46	6.5	−4	....	....	....	....	....	....	....	....	....	....	....	....
	Cincinnati	AHL	23	3	5	8	28	....	....	....	....	....	....	....	....	....	....	....	....	....	....	....	....	....	....

			Regular Season														Playoffs								
Season	Club	League	GP	G	A	Pts	PIM	PP	SH	GW	S	%	+/-	TF	F%	Min	GP	G	A	Pts	PIM	PP	SH	GW	Min
1998-99	Anaheim	NHL	63	0	4	4	60	0	0	0	50	0.0	–6	0	0.0	16:06	4	0	1	1	2	0	0	0	21:26
99-2000	Anaheim	NHL	57	2	15	17	34	0	0	0	54	3.7	12	0	0.0	19:21	....	....	....	....	....	....	....	....	....
2000-01	Anaheim	NHL	59	1	7	8	42	0	0	0	59	1.7	–12	0	0.0	20:07	....	....	....	....	....	....	....	....	....
2001-02	Anaheim	NHL	71	2	11	13	66	1	0	0	78	2.6	–5	0	0.0	17:03	....	....	....	....	....	....	....	....	....
2002-03	Anaheim	NHL	24	3	6	9	6	1	0	0	33	9.1	2	0	0.0	16:00	....	....	....	....	....	....	....	....	....
	Florida	NHL	22	0	3	3	24	0	0	0	25	0.0	–1	0	0.0	17:24	....	....	....	....	....	....	....	....	....
2003-04	Florida	NHL	67	3	13	16	51	1	0	0	66	4.5	2	0	0.0	17:07	....	....	....	....	....	....	....	....	....
2004-05	Plzen	CzRep	47	7	10	17	103	....	....	....	....	....	....	....	....	....	....	....	....	....	....	....	....	....	....
2005-06	Plzen	CzRep	38	8	6	14	40	....	....	....	....	....	....	....	....	....	....	....	....	....	....	....	....	....	....
	Leksands IF	Sweden	7	0	3	3	8	....	....	....	....	....	....	....	....	....	....	....	....	....	....	....	....	....	....
	Leksands IF	Sweden-Q	9	0	1	1	14	....	....	....	....	....	....	....	....	....	....	....	....	....	....	....	....	....	....
	NHL Totals		411	14	63	77	323	4	0	0	411	3.4		0	0.0	17:43	4	0	1	1	2	0	0	0	21:26

Traded to **Florida** by **Anaheim** with Matt Cullen and Anaheim's 4th round choice (James Pemberton) in 2003 Entry Draft for Sandis Ozolinsh and Lance Ward, January 30, 2003. Signed as a free agent by **Plzen** (CzRep), August 2, 2004.

TUCKER, Darcy

(TUH-kuhr, DAHR-see) **TOR.**

Right wing. Shoots left. 5'10", 178 lbs. Born, Castor, Alta., March 15, 1975. Montreal's 8th choice, 151st overall, in 1993 Entry Draft.

Season	Club	League	GP	G	A	Pts	PIM	PP	SH	GW	S	%	+/-	TF	F%	Min	GP	G	A	Pts	PIM	PP	SH	GW	Min
1990-91	Red Deer	AMHL	47	70	90	160	48	....	....	....	....	....	....	....	....	....	....	....	....	....	....	....	....	....	....
1991-92	Kamloops Blazers	WHL	26	3	10	13	32	....	....	....	....	....	....	....	....	....	9	0	1	1	16	....	....	....	....
1992-93	Kamloops Blazers	WHL	67	31	58	89	155	....	....	....	....	....	....	....	....	....	13	7	6	13	34	....	....	....	....
1993-94	Kamloops Blazers	WHL	66	52	88	140	143	....	....	....	....	....	....	....	....	....	19	9	*18	*27	43	....	....	....	....
1994-95	Kamloops Blazers	WHL	64	64	73	137	94	....	....	....	....	....	....	....	....	....	21	*16	15	*31	19	....	....	....	....
1995-96	Montreal	NHL	3	0	0	0	0	0	0	0	1	0.0	–1	....	....	....	....	....	....	....	....	....	....	....	....
	Fredericton	AHL	74	29	64	93	174	....	....	....	....	....	....	....	....	....	7	7	3	10	14	....	....	....	....
1996-97	Montreal	NHL	73	7	13	20	110	1	0	3	62	11.3	–5	....	....	....	4	0	0	0	0	0	0	0	....
1997-98	Montreal	NHL	39	1	5	6	57	0	0	0	19	5.3	–6	....	....	....	....	....	....	....	....	....	....	....	....
	Tampa Bay	NHL	35	6	8	14	89	1	1	0	44	13.6	–8	....	....	....	....	....	....	....	....	....	....	....	....
1998-99	Tampa Bay	NHL	82	21	22	43	176	8	2	3	178	11.8	–34	1470	45.6	19:24	....	....	....	....	....	....	....	....	....
99-2000	Tampa Bay	NHL	50	14	20	34	108	1	0	2	98	14.3	–15	152	48.7	19:58	....	....	....	....	....	....	....	....	....
	Toronto	NHL	27	7	10	17	55	0	2	3	40	17.5	3	11	54.6	16:41	12	4	2	6	15	1	0	2	17:23
2000-01	Toronto	NHL	82	16	21	37	141	2	0	4	122	13.1	6	413	47.0	16:09	11	0	2	2	6	0	0	0	13:59
2001-02	Toronto	NHL	77	24	35	59	92	7	0	5	124	19.4	24	138	43.5	16:59	17	4	4	8	38	1	0	1	16:50
2002-03	Toronto	NHL	77	10	26	36	119	4	1	2	108	9.3	–7	68	45.6	15:21	6	0	3	3	6	0	0	0	21:07
2003-04	Toronto	NHL	64	21	11	32	68	8	1	2	146	14.4	4	136	50.7	17:50	12	2	0	2	14	1	0	0	13:54
2004-05		DID NOT PLAY																							
2005-06	Toronto	NHL	74	28	33	61	100	18	0	4	189	14.8	–12	29	58.6	17:38	....	....	....	....	....	....	....	....	....
	NHL Totals		683	155	204	359	1115	50	7	28	1131	13.7		2417	46.4	17:27	62	10	11	21	79	3	0	3	16:15

WHL West First All-Star Team (1994, 1995) • Canadian Major Junior First All-Star Team (1994) • Memorial Cup Tournament All-Star Team (1994, 1995) • Stafford Smythe Memorial Trophy (Memorial Cup Tournament MVP) (1994) • Dudley "Red" Garrett Memorial Award (Rookie of the Year – AHL) (1996)

Traded to **Tampa Bay** by **Montreal** with Stephane Richer and David Wilkie for Patrick Poulin, Mick Vukota and Igor Ulanov, January 15, 1998. Traded to **Toronto** by **Tampa Bay** with Tampa Bay's 4th round choice (Miguel Delisle) in 2000 Entry Draft for Mike Johnson, Marek Posmyk and Toronto's 5th (Pavel Sedov) and 6th (Aaron Gionet) round choices in 2000 Entry Draft, February 9, 2000.

TURGEON, Pierre

(TUHR-zhaw, PEE-air) **COL.**

Center. Shoots left. 6'1", 199 lbs. Born, Rouyn, Que., August 28, 1969. Buffalo's 1st choice, 1st overall, in 1987 Entry Draft.

Season	Club	League	GP	G	A	Pts	PIM	PP	SH	GW	S	%	+/-	TF	F%	Min	GP	G	A	Pts	PIM	PP	SH	GW	Min
1984-85	Mtl-Bourassa	QAAA	41	49	52	101	26	....	....	....	....	....	....	....	....	....	5	3	8	11	2	....	....	....	....
1985-86	Granby Bisons	QMJHL	69	47	67	114	31	....	....	....	....	....	....	....	....	....	....	....	....	....	....	....	....	....	....
1986-87	Granby Bisons	QMJHL	58	69	85	154	8	....	....	....	....	....	....	....	....	....	7	9	6	15	15	....	....	....	....
1987-88	Buffalo	NHL	76	14	28	42	34	8	0	3	101	13.9	–8	....	....	....	6	4	3	7	4	3	0	0	....
1988-89	Buffalo	NHL	80	34	54	88	26	19	0	5	182	18.7	–2	....	....	....	5	3	5	8	2	1	0	0	....
1989-90	Buffalo	NHL	80	40	66	106	29	17	1	10	193	20.7	10	....	....	....	6	2	4	6	2	0	0	1	....
1990-91	Buffalo	NHL	78	32	47	79	26	13	2	3	174	18.4	14	....	....	....	6	3	1	4	6	1	0	0	....
1991-92	Buffalo	NHL	8	2	6	8	4	0	0	0	14	14.3	–1	....	....	....	....	....	....	....	....	....	....	....	....
	NY Islanders	NHL	69	38	49	87	16	13	0	6	193	19.7	8	....	....	....	....	....	....	....	....	....	....	....	....
1992-93	NY Islanders	NHL	83	58	74	132	26	24	0	10	301	19.3	–1	....	....	....	11	6	7	13	0	0	0	0	....
1993-94	NY Islanders	NHL	69	38	56	94	18	10	4	6	254	15.0	14	....	....	....	4	0	1	1	0	0	0	0	....
1994-95	NY Islanders	NHL	34	13	14	27	10	3	2	2	93	14.0	–12	....	....	....	....	....	....	....	....	....	....	....	....
	Montreal	NHL	15	11	9	20	4	2	0	2	67	16.4	12	....	....	....	....	....	....	....	....	....	....	....	....
1995-96	Montreal	NHL	80	38	58	96	44	17	1	6	297	12.8	19	....	....	....	6	2	4	6	2	0	0	0	....
1996-97	Montreal	NHL	9	1	10	11	2	0	0	0	22	4.5	4	....	....	....	....	....	....	....	....	....	....	....	....
	St. Louis	NHL	69	25	49	74	12	5	0	7	194	12.9	4	....	....	....	5	1	1	2	2	1	0	0	....
1997-98	St. Louis	NHL	60	22	46	68	24	6	0	4	140	15.7	13	....	....	....	10	4	4	8	2	2	0	0	....
1998-99	St. Louis	NHL	67	31	34	65	36	10	0	5	193	16.1	4	1285	50.0	19:07	13	4	9	13	6	0	0	2	19:35
99-2000	St. Louis	NHL	52	26	40	66	8	8	0	3	139	18.7	30	1016	53.2	19:13	7	0	7	7	0	0	0	0	19:45
2000-01	St. Louis	NHL	79	30	52	82	37	11	0	6	171	17.5	14	1569	49.7	18:50	15	5	10	15	2	1	0	0	19:07
2001-02	Dallas	NHL	66	15	32	47	16	7	0	1	121	12.4	–4	822	48.4	16:31	....	....	....	....	....	....	....	....	....
2002-03	Dallas	NHL	65	12	30	42	18	3	0	5	76	15.8	4	290	53.8	14:38	5	0	1	1	0	0	0	0	12:21
2003-04	Dallas	NHL	76	15	25	40	20	6	0	1	104	14.4	17	578	49.3	14:13	5	1	3	4	2	0	0	0	15:53
2004-05		DID NOT PLAY																							
2005-06	Colorado	NHL	62	16	30	46	32	7	0	1	94	17.0	1	580	48.6	12:47	5	0	2	2	6	0	0	0	11:40
	NHL Totals		1277	511	809	1320	442	189	10	86	3123	16.4		6140	50.2	16:27	109	35	62	97	36	9	0	3	17:35

QMJHL Offensive Rookie of the Year) (1986) • Lady Byng Memorial Trophy (1993)

Played in NHL All-Star Game (1990, 1993, 1994, 1996)

Traded to **NY Islanders** by **Buffalo** with Uwe Krupp, Benoit Hogue and Dave McLlwain for Pat LaFontaine, Randy Hillier, Randy Wood and NY Islanders' 4th round choice (Dean Melanson) in 1992 Entry Draft, October 25, 1991. Traded to **Montreal** by **NY Islanders** with Vladimir Malakhov for Kirk Muller, Mathieu Schneider and Craig Darby, April 5, 1995. Traded to **St. Louis** by **Montreal** with Rory Fitzpatrick and Craig Conroy for Murray Baron, Shayne Corson and St. Louis' 5th round choice (Gennady Razin) in 1997 Entry Draft, October 29, 1996. Signed as a free agent by **Dallas**, July 1, 2001. Signed as a free agent by **Colorado**, August 3, 2005.

TVERDOVSKY, Oleg

(tvehr-DOHV-skee, OH-lehg) **CAR.**

Defense. Shoots left. 6'1", 205 lbs. Born, Donetsk, USSR, May 18, 1976. Anaheim's 1st choice, 2nd overall, in 1994 Entry Draft.

Season	Club	League	GP	G	A	Pts	PIM	PP	SH	GW	S	%	+/-	TF	F%	Min	GP	G	A	Pts	PIM	PP	SH	GW	Min
1992-93	Krylja Sovetov	CIS	21	0	1	1	6	....	....	....	....	....	....	....	....	....	6	0	0	0	0	....	....	....	....
1993-94	Krylja Sovetov	CIS	46	4	10	14	22	....	....	....	....	....	....	....	....	....	3	1	0	1	2	....	....	....	....
1994-95	Brandon	WHL	7	1	4	5	4	....	....	....	....	....	....	....	....	....	....	....	....	....	....	....	....	....	....
	Anaheim	NHL	36	3	9	12	14	1	1	0	26	11.5	–6	....	....	....	....	....	....	....	....	....	....	....	....
1995-96	Anaheim	NHL	51	7	15	22	35	2	0	0	84	8.3	0	....	....	....	....	....	....	....	....	....	....	....	....
	Winnipeg	NHL	31	0	8	8	6	0	0	0	35	0.0	–7	....	....	....	6	0	1	1	0	0	0	0	....
1996-97	Phoenix	NHL	82	10	45	55	30	3	1	2	144	6.9	–5	....	....	....	7	0	1	1	0	0	0	0	....
1997-98	Hamilton	AHL	9	8	6	14	2	....	....	....	....	....	....	....	....	....	....	....	....	....	....	....	....	....	....
	Phoenix	NHL	46	7	12	19	12	4	0	1	83	8.4	1	....	....	....	6	0	7	7	0	0	0	0	....
1998-99	Phoenix	NHL	82	7	18	25	32	2	0	2	117	6.0	11	1	0.0	20:48	6	0	2	2	6	0	0	0	17:43
99-2000	Anaheim	NHL	82	15	36	51	30	5	0	5	153	9.8	5	1	0.0	22:46	....	....	....	....	....	....	....	....	....
2000-01	Anaheim	NHL	82	14	39	53	32	8	0	3	188	7.4	–11	0	0.0	24:25	....	....	....	....	....	....	....	....	....
2001-02	Anaheim	NHL	73	6	26	32	31	2	0	1	147	4.1	0	0	0.0	22:50	....	....	....	....	....	....	....	....	....
	Russia	Olympics	6	1	1	2	0	....	....	....	....	....	....	....	....	....	....	....	....	....	....	....	....	....	....
2002-03♦	New Jersey	NHL	50	5	8	13	22	2	0	1	76	6.6	2	0	0.0	16:48	15	0	3	3	0	0	0	0	15:06
2003-04	Avangard Omsk	Russia	57	16	17	33	58	....	....	....	....	....	....	....	....	....	11	0	2	2	2	....	....	....	....
2004-05	Avangard Omsk	Russia	48	5	15	20	65	....	....	....	....	....	....	....	....	....	11	0	3	3	*35	....	....	....	....
2005-06♦	Carolina	NHL	72	3	20	23	37	0	0	0	91	3.3	–1	0	0.0	16:36	5	0	0	0	0	0	0	0	5:16
	NHL Totals		687	77	236	313	281	29	2	15	1144	6.7		2	0.0	21:02	45	0	14	14	6	0	0	0	13:49

Played in NHL All-Star Game (1997)

Traded to **Winnipeg** by **Anaheim** with Chad Kilger and Anaheim's 3rd round choice (Per-Anton Lundstrom) in 1996 Entry Draft for Teemu Selanne, Marc Chouinard and Winnipeg's 4th round choice (later traded to Toronto – later traded to Montreal – Montreal selected Kim Staal) in 1996 Entry Draft, February 7, 1996. Transferred to **Phoenix** after **Winnipeg** franchise relocated, July 1, 1996. Traded to **Anaheim** by **Phoenix** for Travis Green and Anaheim's 1st round choice (Scott Kelman) in 1999 Entry Draft, June 26, 1999. Traded to **New Jersey** by **Anaheim** with Jeff Friesen and Maxim Balmochnykh for Petr Sykora, Mike Commodore, Jean-Francois Damphousse and Igor Pohanka, July 6, 2002. Signed as a free agent by **Omsk** (Russia), August 29, 2003. Signed as a free agent by **Carolina**, August 4, 2005.

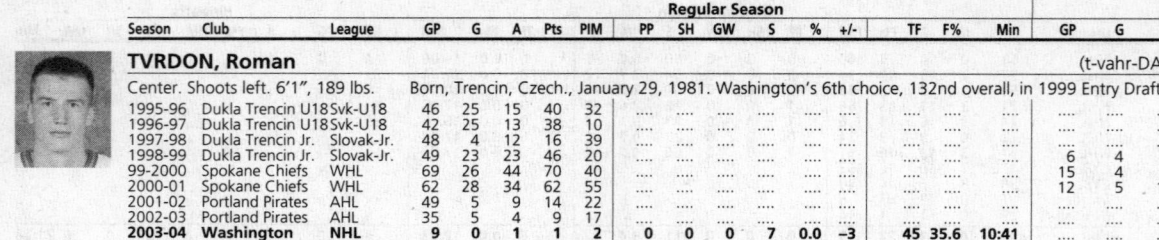

TVRDON, Roman

(t-vahr-DAWN, ROH-muhn)

Center. Shoots left. 6'1", 189 lbs. Born, Trencin, Czech., January 29, 1981. Washington's 6th choice, 132nd overall, in 1999 Entry Draft.

			Regular Season														Playoffs								
Season	Club	League	GP	G	A	Pts	PIM	PP	SH	GW	S	%	+/-	TF	F%	Min	GP	G	A	Pts	PIM	PP	SH	GW	Min
1995-96	Dukla Trencin U18	Svk-U18	46	25	15	40	32	....	....	....	....	....	....	....	....	....	....	....	....	....	....	....	....	....	....
1996-97	Dukla Trencin U18	Svk-U18	42	25	13	38	10	....	....	....	....	....	....	....	....	....	....	....	....	....	....	....	....	....	....
1997-98	Dukla Trencin Jr.	Slovak-Jr.	48	4	12	16	39	....	....	....	....	....	....	....	....	....	....	....	....	....	....	....	....	....	....
1998-99	Dukla Trencin Jr.	Slovak-Jr.	49	23	23	46	20	....	....	....	....	....	....	....	....	....	6	4	4	8	4	....	....	....	....
99-2000	Spokane Chiefs	WHL	69	26	44	70	40	....	....	....	....	....	....	....	....	....	15	4	7	11	16	....	....	....	....
2000-01	Spokane Chiefs	WHL	62	28	34	62	55	....	....	....	....	....	....	....	....	....	12	5	11	16	0	....	....	....	....
2001-02	Portland Pirates	AHL	49	5	9	14	22	....	....	....	....	....	....	....	....	....	....	....	....	....	....	....	....	....	....
2002-03	Portland Pirates	AHL	35	5	4	9	17	....	....	....	....	....	....	....	....	....	....	....	....	....	....	....	....	....	....
2003-04	**Washington**	**NHL**	**9**	**0**	**1**	**1**	**2**	**0**	**0**	**0**	**7**	**0.0**	**–3**	**45**	**35.6**	**10:41**	....	....	....	....	....	....	....	....	....
	Portland Pirates	AHL	51	2	4	6	20	....	....	....	....	....	....	....	....	....	7	0	0	0	2	....	....	....	....
2004-05	Nottingham	Britain	9	2	5	7	6	....	....	....	....	....	....	....	....	....	....	....	....	....	....	....	....	....	....
2005-06	Plzen	CzRep	39	6	3	9	20	....	....	....	....	....	....	....	....	....	....	....	....	....	....	....	....	....	....
	NHL Totals		**9**	**0**	**1**	**1**	**2**	**0**	**0**	**0**	**7**	**0.0**		**45**	**35.6**	**10:41**	....	....	....	....	....	....	....	....	....

• Missed majority of 2002-03 season recovering from shoulder injury suffered in game vs. Saint John (AHL), December 28, 2002. Signed as a free agent by **Nottingham** (Britain), July 12, 2004.

TYUTIN, Fedor

(TYOO-tihn, feh-DUHR) **NYR**

Defense. Shoots left. 6'2", 204 lbs. Born, Izhevsk, USSR, July 19, 1983. NY Rangers' 2nd choice, 40th overall, in 2001 Entry Draft.

			Regular Season														Playoffs								
Season	Club	League	GP	G	A	Pts	PIM	PP	SH	GW	S	%	+/-	TF	F%	Min	GP	G	A	Pts	PIM	PP	SH	GW	Min
1998-99	Magnitogorsk 2	Russia-4	7	0	1	1	2	....	....	....	....	....	....	....	....	....	....	....	....	....	....	....	....	....	....
99-2000	Izhstal Izhevsk 2	Russia-3	38	11	8	19	68	....	....	....	....	....	....	....	....	....	....	....	....	....	....	....	....	....	....
	Izhstal Izhevsk	Russia-2	10	0	1	1	12	....	....	....	....	....	....	....	....	....	....	....	....	....	....	....	....	....	....
2000-01	St. Petersburg	Russia	34	2	4	6	20	....	....	....	....	....	....	....	....	....	....	....	....	....	....	....	....	....	....
2001-02	Guelph Storm	OHL	53	19	40	59	54	....	....	....	....	....	....	....	....	....	9	2	8	10	8	....	....	....	....
2002-03	St. Petersburg	Russia	10	1	1	2	16	....	....	....	....	....	....	....	....	....	....	....	....	....	....	....	....	....	....
	Ak Bars Kazan	Russia	10	0	0	0	8	....	....	....	....	....	....	....	....	....	5	0	0	0	4	....	....	....	....
2003-04	**NY Rangers**	**NHL**	**25**	**2**	**5**	**7**	**14**	**0**	**1**	**0**	**33**	**6.1**	**–4**	**1**	**0.0**	**20:08**	....	....	....	....	....	....	....	....	....
	Hartford	AHL	43	5	9	14	50	....	....	....	....	....	....	....	....	....	16	0	5	5	18	....	....	....	....
2004-05	Hartford	AHL	13	2	1	3	10	....	....	....	....	....	....	....	....	....	....	....	....	....	....	....	....	....	....
	St. Petersburg	Russia	35	5	3	8	24	....	....	....	....	....	....	....	....	....	....	....	....	....	....	....	....	....	....
2005-06	**NY Rangers**	**NHL**	**77**	**6**	**19**	**25**	**58**	**4**	**0**	**2**	**102**	**5.9**	**1**	**1**	**0.0**	**20:33**	**4**	**0**	**1**	**1**	**0**	**0**	**0**	**0**	**17:50**
	Russia	Olympics	8	0	1	1	4	....	....	....	....	....	....	....	....	....	....	....	....	....	....	....	....	....	....
	NHL Totals		**102**	**8**	**24**	**32**	**72**	**4**	**1**	**2**	**135**	**5.9**		**2**	**0.0**	**20:27**	**4**	**0**	**1**	**1**	**0**	**0**	**0**	**0**	**17:49**

Signed as a free agent by **St. Petersburg** (Russia), November 11, 2004.

ULANOV, Igor

(yoo-LAH-nahf, EE-gohr)

Defense. Shoots left. 6'3", 220 lbs. Born, Krasnokamsk, USSR, October 1, 1969. Winnipeg's 8th choice, 203rd overall, in 1991 Entry Draft.

			Regular Season														Playoffs								
Season	Club	League	GP	G	A	Pts	PIM	PP	SH	GW	S	%	+/-	TF	F%	Min	GP	G	A	Pts	PIM	PP	SH	GW	Min
1990-91	Voskresensk	USSR	41	2	2	4	52	....	....	....	....	....	....	....	....	....	....	....	....	....	....	....	....	....	....
1991-92	Voskresensk	CIS	27	1	4	5	24	....	....	....	....	....	....	....	....	....	....	....	....	....	....	....	....	....	....
	Winnipeg	**NHL**	**27**	**2**	**9**	**11**	**67**	**0**	**0**	**0**	**23**	**8.7**	**5**	....	....	....	**7**	**0**	**0**	**0**	**39**	**0**	**0**	**0**	....
	Moncton Hawks	AHL	3	0	1	1	16	....	....	....	....	....	....	....	....	....	....	....	....	....	....	....	....	....	....
1992-93	**Winnipeg**	**NHL**	**56**	**2**	**14**	**16**	**124**	**0**	**0**	**0**	**26**	**7.7**	**6**	....	....	....	**4**	**0**	**0**	**0**	**4**	**0**	**0**	**0**	....
	Moncton Hawks	AHL	9	1	3	4	26	....	....	....	....	....	....	....	....	....	....	....	....	....	....	....	....	....	....
	Fort Wayne	IHL	3	0	1	1	29	....	....	....	....	....	....	....	....	....	....	....	....	....	....	....	....	....	....
1993-94	**Winnipeg**	**NHL**	**74**	**0**	**17**	**17**	**165**	**0**	**0**	**0**	**46**	**0.0**	**–11**	....	....	....	....	....	....	....	....	....	....	....	....
1994-95	**Winnipeg**	**NHL**	**19**	**1**	**3**	**4**	**27**	**0**	**0**	**0**	**13**	**7.7**	**–2**	....	....	....	....	....	....	....	....	....	....	....	....
	Washington	**NHL**	**3**	**0**	**1**	**1**	**2**	**0**	**0**	**0**	**0**	**0.0**	**3**	....	....	....	**2**	**0**	**0**	**0**	**4**	**0**	**0**	**0**	....
1995-96	**Chicago**	**NHL**	**53**	**1**	**8**	**9**	**92**	**0**	**0**	**0**	**24**	**4.2**	**12**	....	....	....	....	....	....	....	....	....	....	....	....
	Indianapolis Ice	IHL	1	0	0	0	0	....	....	....	....	....	....	....	....	....	....	....	....	....	....	....	....	....	....
	Tampa Bay	**NHL**	**11**	**2**	**1**	**3**	**24**	**0**	**0**	**1**	**13**	**15.4**	**–1**	....	....	....	**5**	**0**	**0**	**0**	**15**	**0**	**0**	**0**	....
1996-97	**Tampa Bay**	**NHL**	**59**	**1**	**7**	**8**	**108**	**0**	**0**	**0**	**56**	**1.8**	**2**	....	....	....	....	....	....	....	....	....	....	....	....
1997-98	**Tampa Bay**	**NHL**	**45**	**2**	**7**	**9**	**85**	**1**	**0**	**0**	**32**	**6.3**	**–5**	....	....	....	....	....	....	....	....	....	....	....	....
	Montreal	**NHL**	**4**	**0**	**1**	**1**	**12**	**0**	**0**	**0**	**4**	**0.0**	**–2**	....	....	....	**10**	**1**	**4**	**5**	**12**	**0**	**0**	**0**	....
1998-99	**Montreal**	**NHL**	**76**	**3**	**9**	**12**	**109**	**0**	**0**	**0**	**55**	**5.5**	**–3**	**0**	**0.0**	**17:35**	....	....	....	....	....	....	....	....	....
99-2000	**Montreal**	**NHL**	**43**	**1**	**5**	**6**	**76**	**0**	**0**	**0**	**33**	**3.0**	**–11**	**0**	**0.0**	**16:33**	....	....	....	....	....	....	....	....	....
	Edmonton	**NHL**	**14**	**0**	**3**	**3**	**10**	**0**	**0**	**0**	**6**	**0.0**	**–3**	**0**	**0.0**	**16:23**	**5**	**0**	**0**	**0**	**6**	**0**	**0**	**0**	**16:59**
2000-01	**Edmonton**	**NHL**	**67**	**3**	**20**	**23**	**90**	**1**	**0**	**0**	**74**	**4.1**	**15**	**0**	**0.0**	**23:01**	**6**	**0**	**0**	**0**	**4**	**0**	**0**	**0**	**24:25**
2001-02	**NY Rangers**	**NHL**	**39**	**0**	**6**	**6**	**53**	**0**	**0**	**0**	**17**	**0.0**	**–4**	**0**	**0.0**	**16:19**	....	....	....	....	....	....	....	....	....
	Hartford	AHL	6	1	1	2	2	....	....	....	....	....	....	....	....	....	....	....	....	....	....	....	....	....	....
	Florida	**NHL**	**14**	**0**	**4**	**4**	**11**	**0**	**0**	**0**	**9**	**0.0**	**–3**	**0**	**0.0**	**20:50**	....	....	....	....	....	....	....	....	....
2002-03	**Florida**	**NHL**	**56**	**1**	**1**	**2**	**39**	**0**	**0**	**0**	**20**	**5.0**	**7**	**0**	**0.0**	**16:42**	....	....	....	....	....	....	....	....	....
	San Antonio	AHL	5	1	0	1	4	....	....	....	....	....	....	....	....	....	....	....	....	....	....	....	....	....	....
2003-04	Toronto	AHL	10	0	5	5	8	....	....	....	....	....	....	....	....	....	....	....	....	....	....	....	....	....	....
	Edmonton	**NHL**	**42**	**5**	**13**	**18**	**28**	**1**	**0**	**3**	**49**	**10.2**	**19**	**0**	**0.0**	**19:51**	....	....	....	....	....	....	....	....	....
2004-05			DID NOT PLAY																						
2005-06	**Edmonton**	**NHL**	**37**	**3**	**6**	**9**	**29**	**1**	**0**	**0**	**29**	**10.3**	**–11**	**2**	**100.0**	**16:27**	....	....	....	....	....	....	....	....	....
	NHL Totals		**739**	**27**	**135**	**162**	**1151**	**4**	**0**	**4**	**529**	**5.1**		**2**	**100.0**	**18:22**	**39**	**1**	**4**	**5**	**84**	**0**	**0**	**0**	**21:02**

Traded to **Washington** by **Winnipeg** with Mike Eagles for Washington's 3rd (later traded to Dallas – Dallas selected Sergey Gusev) and 5th (Brian Elder) round choices in 1995 Entry Draft, April 7, 1995. Traded to **Chicago** by **Washington** for Chicago's 3rd round choice (Dave Weninger) in 1996 Entry Draft, October 17, 1995. Traded to **Tampa Bay** by **Chicago** with Patrick Poulin and Chicago's 2nd round choice (later traded to New Jersey – New Jersey selected Pierre Dagenais) in 1996 Entry Draft for Enrico Ciccone and Tampa Bay's 2nd round choice (Jeff Paul) in 1996 Entry Draft, March 20, 1996. Traded to **Montreal** by **Tampa Bay** with Patrick Poulin and Mick Vukota for Stephane Richer, Darcy Tucker and David Wilkie, January 15, 1998. Traded to **Edmonton** by **Montreal** with Alain Nasreddine for Christian Laflamme and Matthieu Descoteaux, March 9, 2000. Signed as a free agent by **NY Rangers**, July 20, 2001. Traded to **Florida** by **NY Rangers** with Filip Novak, NY Rangers' 1st (later traded to Calgary – Calgary selected Eric Nystrom) and 2nd (Rob Globke) round choices in 2002 Entry Draft and NY Rangers' 4th round choice (later traded to Atlanta – Atlanta selected Guillaume Desbiens) in 2003 Entry Draft for Pavel Bure and Florida's 2nd round choice (Lee Falardeau) in 2002 Entry Draft, March 18, 2002. Signed to a PTO (tryout) contract by **Toronto** (AHL), December 13, 2003. Signed as a free agent by **Edmonton**, January 5, 2004.

ULMER, Jeff

(UHL-muhr, JEHF)

Right wing. Shoots right. 5'11", 195 lbs. Born, Wilcox, Sask., April 27, 1977.

			Regular Season														Playoffs								
Season	Club	League	GP	G	A	Pts	PIM	PP	SH	GW	S	%	+/-	TF	F%	Min	GP	G	A	Pts	PIM	PP	SH	GW	Min
1994-95	Notre Dame	AJHL	63	25	35	60	....	....	....	....	....	....	....	....	....	....	....	....	....	....	....	....	....	....	....
1995-96	North Dakota	WCHA	29	5	3	8	26	....	....	....	....	....	....	....	....	....	....	....	....	....	....	....	....	....	....
1996-97	North Dakota	WCHA	26	6	11	17	16	....	....	....	....	....	....	....	....	....	....	....	....	....	....	....	....	....	....
1997-98	North Dakota	WCHA	32	12	12	24	44	....	....	....	....	....	....	....	....	....	....	....	....	....	....	....	....	....	....
1998-99	North Dakota	WCHA	38	16	20	36	46	....	....	....	....	....	....	....	....	....	....	....	....	....	....	....	....	....	....
99-2000	Canada	Nat-Tm	48	14	25	39	20	....	....	....	....	....	....	....	....	....	....	....	....	....	....	....	....	....	....
	Houston Aeros	IHL	5	1	0	1	0	....	....	....	....	....	....	....	....	....	11	2	4	6	6	....	....	....	....
2000-01	**NY Rangers**	**NHL**	**21**	**3**	**0**	**3**	**8**	**0**	**0**	**0**	**22**	**13.6**	**–6**	**16**	**31.3**	**10:23**	....	....	....	....	....	....	....	....	....
	Hartford	AHL	48	11	14	25	34	....	....	....	....	....	....	....	....	....	....	....	....	....	....	....	....	....	....
2001-02	Grand Rapids	AHL	73	9	17	26	65	....	....	....	....	....	....	....	....	....	5	0	1	1	11	....	....	....	....
2002-03	Binghamton	AHL	57	8	12	20	40	....	....	....	....	....	....	....	....	....	13	0	1	1	30	....	....	....	....
2003-04	Cardiff Devils	Britain	9	9	9	18	6	....	....	....	....	....	....	....	....	....	....	....	....	....	....	....	....	....	....
	Lukko Rauma	Finland	34	13	8	21	67	....	....	....	....	....	....	....	....	....	4	0	0	0	2	....	....	....	....
2004-05	Hershey Bears	AHL	80	22	29	51	47	....	....	....	....	....	....	....	....	....	....	....	....	....	....	....	....	....	....
2005-06	Hamburg Freezers	Germany	51	23	15	38	73	....	....	....	....	....	....	....	....	....	6	2	4	6	18	....	....	....	....
	NHL Totals		**21**	**3**	**0**	**3**	**8**	**0**	**0**	**0**	**22**	**13.6**		**16**	**31.3**	**10:23**	....	....	....	....	....	....	....	....	....

Signed as a free agent by **Houston** (IHL), March 30, 2000. Signed as a free agent by **NY Rangers**, July 27, 2000. Traded to **Ottawa** by **NY Rangers** with Jason Doig for Sean Gagnon, June 29, 2001. Signed as a free agent by **Cardiff** (Britain), October 10, 2003. Signed as a free agent by **Rauma** (Finland), November 11, 2003. Signed as a free agent by **Colorado**, June 10, 2004. Signed as a free agent by **Hamburg** (Germany), September 6, 2005.

ULMER, Layne
(UHL-muhr, LAYN)

Center. Shoots left. 6'1", 205 lbs. Born, North Battleford, Sask., September 14, 1980. Ottawa's 8th choice, 209th overall, in 1999 Entry Draft.

			Regular Season														Playoffs								
Season	Club	League	GP	G	A	Pts	PIM	PP	SH	GW	S	%	+/-	TF	F%	Min	GP	G	A	Pts	PIM	PP	SH	GW	Min
1996-97	Swift Current	SMHL	43	35	49	84	71	....	....	....	....	....	....	....	....	....	....	....	....	....	....	....	....	....	....
1997-98	Swift Current	WHL	50	8	9	17	23	....	....	....	....	....	....	....	....	....	12	3	1	4	0	....	....	....	....
1998-99	Swift Current	WHL	72	40	35	75	34	....	....	....	....	....	....	....	....	....	6	2	1	3	4	....	....	....	....
99-2000	Swift Current	WHL	71	50	54	104	66	....	....	....	....	....	....	....	....	....	12	12	6	18	16	....	....	....	....
2000-01	Swift Current	WHL	68	*63	56	119	75	....	....	....	....	....	....	....	....	....	19	7	3	10	20	....	....	....	....
2001-02	Hartford	AHL	22	0	5	5	17	....	....	....	....	....	....	....	....	....	....	....	....	....	....	....	....	....	....
	Charlotte	ECHL	38	18	17	35	12	....	....	....	....	....	....	....	....	....	5	2	2	4	4	....	....	....	....
2002-03	Hartford	AHL	68	12	20	32	16	....	....	....	....	....	....	....	....	....	2	0	0	0	0	....	....	....	....
2003-04	**NY Rangers**	**NHL**	**1**	**0**	**0**	**0**	**0**	**0**	**0**	**0**	**1**	**0.0**	**–1**	**8**	**75.0**	**9:27**	....	....	....	....	....	....	....	....	....
	Hartford	AHL	76	22	16	38	26	....	....	....	....	....	....	....	....	....	7	2	5	7	0	....	....	....	....
2004-05	Hartford	AHL	65	7	30	37	23	....	....	....	....	....	....	....	....	....	6	0	0	0	2	....	....	....	....
2005-06	San Antonio	AHL	77	19	26	45	42	....	....	....	....	....	....	....	....	....	....	....	....	....	....	....	....	....	....
	NHL Totals		**1**	**0**	**0**	**0**	**0**	**0**	**0**	**0**	**1**	**0.0**		**8**	**75.0**	**9:27**	....	....	....	....	....	....	....	....	....

WHL East First All-Star Team (2000, 2001)

Signed as a free agent by **NY Rangers**, June 13, 2001.

UMBERGER, R.J.
(UHM-buhr-guhr, AHR-JAY) **PHI.**

Center. Shoots left. 6'2", 200 lbs. Born, Pittsburgh, PA, May 3, 1982. Vancouver's 1st choice, 16th overall, in 2001 Entry Draft.

Season	Club	League	GP	G	A	Pts	PIM	PP	SH	GW	S	%	+/-	TF	F%	Min	GP	G	A	Pts	PIM	PP	SH	GW	Min
1997-98	Plum Mustangs	High-PA	26	*60	*56	*116	....	....	....	....	....	....	....	....	....	....	....	....	....	....	....	....	....	....	....
1998-99	USNTDP	USHL	5	2	2	4	0	....	....	....	....	....	....	....	....	....	....	....	....	....	....	....	....	....	....
	USNTDP	NAHL	50	21	21	42	32	....	....	....	....	....	....	....	....	....	....	....	....	....	....	....	....	....	....
99-2000	USNTDP	U-18	6	1	0	1	2	....	....	....	....	....	....	....	....	....	....	....	....	....	....	....	....	....	....
	USNTDP	USHL	57	33	35	68	20	....	....	....	....	....	....	....	....	....	....	....	....	....	....	....	....	....	....
2000-01	Ohio State	CCHA	32	14	23	37	18	....	....	....	....	....	....	....	....	....	....	....	....	....	....	....	....	....	....
2001-02	Ohio State	CCHA	37	18	21	39	31	....	....	....	....	....	....	....	....	....	....	....	....	....	....	....	....	....	....
2002-03	Ohio State	CCHA	43	26	27	53	16	....	....	....	....	....	....	....	....	....	....	....	....	....	....	....	....	....	....
2003-04			DID NOT PLAY																						
2004-05	Philadelphia	AHL	80	21	44	65	36	....	....	....	....	....	....	....	....	....	21	3	7	10	12	....	....	....	....
2005-06	**Philadelphia**	**NHL**	**73**	**20**	**18**	**38**	**18**	**5**	**0**	**2**	**138**	**14.5**	**9**	**163**	**50.3**	**13:14**	**5**	**1**	**0**	**1**	**2**	**0**	**0**	**0**	**11:15**
	Philadelphia	AHL	8	3	7	10	8	....	....	....	....	....	....	....	....	....	....	....	....	....	....	....	....	....	....
	NHL Totals		**73**	**20**	**18**	**38**	**18**	**5**	**0**	**2**	**138**	**14.5**		**163**	**50.3**	**13:14**	**5**	**1**	**0**	**1**	**2**	**0**	**0**	**0**	**11:15**

CCHA All-Rookie Team (2001) • CCHA Rookie of the Year (2001) • CCHA First All-Star Team (2003) • NCAA West Second All-American Team (2003)

• Missed entire 2003-04 season due to a contract dispute. Traded to **NY Rangers** by **Vancouver** with Martin Grenier for Martin Rucinsky, March 9, 2004. Signed as a free agent by **Philadelphia**, June 16, 2004.

UPSHALL, Scottie
(UHP-shuhl, SKAW-tee) **NSH.**

Right wing. Shoots left. 6', 197 lbs. Born, Fort McMurray, Alta., October 7, 1983. Nashville's 1st choice, 6th overall, in 2002 Entry Draft.

Season	Club	League	GP	G	A	Pts	PIM	PP	SH	GW	S	%	+/-	TF	F%	Min	GP	G	A	Pts	PIM	PP	SH	GW	Min
1998-99	Fort McMurray	AMHL	28	62	40	102	100	....	....	....	....	....	....	....	....	....	....	....	....	....	....	....	....	....	....
99-2000	Fort McMurray	AJHL	52	26	26	52	65	....	....	....	....	....	....	....	....	....	....	....	....	....	....	....	....	....	....
2000-01	Kamloops Blazers	WHL	70	42	45	87	111	....	....	....	....	....	....	....	....	....	4	0	2	2	10	....	....	....	....
2001-02	Kamloops Blazers	WHL	61	32	51	83	139	....	....	....	....	....	....	....	....	....	4	1	2	3	21	....	....	....	....
2002-03	**Nashville**	**NHL**	**8**	**1**	**0**	**1**	**0**	**0**	**0**	**0**	**6**	**16.7**	**2**	**2**	**0.0**	**8:42**	....	....	....	....	....	....	....	....	....
	Kamloops Blazers	WHL	42	25	31	56	111	....	....	....	....	....	....	....	....	....	6	0	2	2	34	....	....	....	....
	Milwaukee	AHL	2	1	0	1	2	....	....	....	....	....	....	....	....	....	6	0	0	0	2	....	....	....	....
2003-04	**Nashville**	**NHL**	**7**	**0**	**1**	**1**	**0**	**0**	**0**	**0**	**6**	**0.0**	**–2**	**8**	**37.5**	**9:11**	....	....	....	....	....	....	....	....	....
	Milwaukee	AHL	31	13	11	24	42	....	....	....	....	....	....	....	....	....	8	3	0	3	4	....	....	....	....
2004-05	Milwaukee	AHL	62	19	27	46	108	....	....	....	....	....	....	....	....	....	5	2	2	4	8	....	....	....	....
2005-06	**Nashville**	**NHL**	**48**	**8**	**16**	**24**	**34**	**1**	**0**	**2**	**72**	**11.1**	**14**	**11**	**45.5**	**10:26**	**2**	**0**	**0**	**0**	**0**	**0**	**0**	**0**	**11:57**
	Milwaukee	AHL	23	17	16	33	44	....	....	....	....	....	....	....	....	....	14	6	10	16	20	....	....	....	....
	NHL Totals		**63**	**9**	**17**	**26**	**34**	**1**	**0**	**2**	**84**	**10.7**		**21**	**38.1**	**10:04**	**2**	**0**	**0**	**0**	**0**	**0**	**0**	**0**	**11:56**

WHL All-Rookie Team (2001) • WHL Rookie of the Year (2001) • CHL All-Rookie Team (2001) • Canadian Major Junior Rookie of the Year (2001) • WHL West Second All-Star Team (2002)

• Missed majority of 2003-04 season recovering from knee injury suffered in game vs. Phoenix, December 22, 2003.

VAANANEN, Ossi
(VAN-ih-nehn, AW-see) **COL.**

Defense. Shoots left. 6'4", 215 lbs. Born, Vantaa, Finland, August 18, 1980. Phoenix's 2nd choice, 43rd overall, in 1998 Entry Draft.

Season	Club	League	GP	G	A	Pts	PIM	PP	SH	GW	S	%	+/-	TF	F%	Min	GP	G	A	Pts	PIM	PP	SH	GW	Min
1995-96	Jokerit U18	Fin-U18	8	0	0	0	2	....	....	....	....	....	....	....	....	....	2	0	0	0	0	....	....	....	....
1996-97	Jokerit U18	Fin-U18	18	1	2	3	43	....	....	....	....	....	....	....	....	....	....	....	....	....	....	....	....	....	....
	Jokerit Helsinki Jr.	Fin-Jr.	1	0	0	0	0	....	....	....	....	....	....	....	....	....	....	....	....	....	....	....	....	....	....
1997-98	Jokerit U18	Fin-U18	7	3	3	6	8	....	....	....	....	....	....	....	....	....	....	....	....	....	....	....	....	....	....
	Jokerit Helsinki Jr.	Fin-Jr.	31	0	6	6	24	....	....	....	....	....	....	....	....	....	7	0	2	2	16	....	....	....	....
1998-99	Jokerit Helsinki Jr.	Fin-Jr.	12	1	6	7	16	....	....	....	....	....	....	....	....	....	6	1	0	1	12	....	....	....	....
	Jokerit Helsinki	Finland	48	0	1	1	42	....	....	....	....	....	....	....	....	....	3	0	1	1	2	....	....	....	....
	Jokerit Helsinki	EuroHL	5	0	0	0	2	....	....	....	....	....	....	....	....	....	1	0	1	1	2	....	....	....	....
99-2000	Jokerit Helsinki	Finland	49	1	6	7	46	....	....	....	....	....	....	....	....	....	11	1	1	2	2	....	....	....	....
2000-01	**Phoenix**	**NHL**	**81**	**4**	**12**	**16**	**90**	**0**	**0**	**2**	**69**	**5.8**	**9**	**0**	**0.0**	**19:09**	....	....	....	....	....	....	....	....	....
2001-02	**Phoenix**	**NHL**	**76**	**2**	**12**	**14**	**74**	**0**	**1**	**0**	**41**	**4.9**	**6**	**0**	**0.0**	**20:13**	**5**	**0**	**0**	**0**	**6**	**0**	**0**	**0**	**20:33**
	Finland	Olympics	2	0	1	1	0	....	....	....	....	....	....	....	....	....	....	....	....	....	....	....	....	....	....
2002-03	**Phoenix**	**NHL**	**67**	**2**	**7**	**9**	**82**	**0**	**0**	**0**	**49**	**4.1**	**1**	**0**	**0.0**	**19:15**	....	....	....	....	....	....	....	....	....
2003-04	**Phoenix**	**NHL**	**67**	**2**	**4**	**6**	**87**	**0**	**0**	**1**	**39**	**5.1**	**–10**	**0**	**0.0**	**19:21**	....	....	....	....	....	....	....	....	....
	Colorado	**NHL**	**12**	**0**	**0**	**0**	**2**	**0**	**0**	**0**	**6**	**0.0**	**–4**	**0**	**0.0**	**18:36**	**11**	**0**	**1**	**1**	**18**	**0**	**0**	**0**	**22:06**
2004-05	Jokerit Helsinki	Finland	28	2	2	4	30	....	....	....	....	....	....	....	....	....	12	0	0	0	26	....	....	....	....
2005-06	**Colorado**	**NHL**	**53**	**0**	**4**	**4**	**56**	**0**	**0**	**0**	**34**	**0.0**	**10**	**1**	**0.0**	**13:34**	**1**	**0**	**0**	**0**	**0**	**0**	**0**	**0**	**13:58**
	NHL Totals		**356**	**10**	**39**	**49**	**391**	**0**	**1**	**3**	**238**	**4.2**		**1**	**0.0**	**18:35**	**17**	**0**	**1**	**1**	**24**	**0**	**0**	**0**	**21:10**

Traded to **Colorado** by **Phoenix** with Chris Gratton and Phoenix's 2nd round choice.(Paul Stastny) in 2005 Entry Draft for Derek Morris and Keith Ballard, March 8, 2004. Signed as a free agent by **Jokerit Helsinki** (Finland), December 1, 2004.

VANDENBUSSCHE, Ryan
(van-dehn-BUHSH, RIGH-yuhn)

Right wing. Shoots right. 6', 200 lbs. Born, Simcoe, Ont., February 28, 1973. Toronto's 9th choice, 173rd overall, in 1992 Entry Draft.

Season	Club	League	GP	G	A	Pts	PIM	PP	SH	GW	S	%	+/-	TF	F%	Min	GP	G	A	Pts	PIM	PP	SH	GW	Min
1988-89	Delhi Flames	OHA-D	3	1	1	2	2	....	....	....	....	....	....	....	....	....	....	....	....	....	....	....	....	....	....
1989-90	Norwich	OHA-C	21	12	10	22	146	....	....	....	....	....	....	....	....	....	....	....	....	....	....	....	....	....	....
	Tillsonburg Titans	OHA-B	24	0	5	5	113	....	....	....	....	....	....	....	....	....	....	....	....	....	....	....	....	....	....
1990-91	Massena	CJHL	10	2	3	5	46	....	....	....	....	....	....	....	....	....	....	....	....	....	....	....	....	....	....
	Cornwall Royals	OHL	49	3	8	11	139	....	....	....	....	....	....	....	....	....	....	....	....	....	....	....	....	....	....
1991-92	Cornwall Royals	OHL	61	13	15	28	232	....	....	....	....	....	....	....	....	....	6	0	2	2	9	....	....	....	....
1992-93	Newmarket	OHL	30	15	12	27	161	....	....	....	....	....	....	....	....	....	....	....	....	....	....	....	....	....	....
	Guelph Storm	OHL	29	3	14	17	99	....	....	....	....	....	....	....	....	....	5	1	3	4	13	....	....	....	....
	St. John's	AHL	1	0	0	0	0	....	....	....	....	....	....	....	....	....	....	....	....	....	....	....	....	....	....
1993-94	St. John's	AHL	44	4	10	14	124	....	....	....	....	....	....	....	....	....	....	....	....	....	....	....	....	....	....
	Springfield	AHL	9	1	2	3	29	....	....	....	....	....	....	....	....	....	5	0	0	0	16	....	....	....	....
1994-95	St. John's	AHL	53	2	13	15	239	....	....	....	....	....	....	....	....	....	3	0	0	0	17	....	....	....	....
1995-96	Binghamton	AHL	68	3	17	20	240	....	....	....	....	....	....	....	....	....	4	0	0	0	9	....	....	....	....
1996-97	**NY Rangers**	**NHL**	**11**	**1**	**0**	**1**	**30**	**0**	**0**	**0**	**4**	**25.0**	**–2**	....	....	....	....	....	....	....	....	....	....	....	....
	Binghamton	AHL	38	8	11	19	133	....	....	....	....	....	....	....	....	....	....	....	....	....	....	....	....	....	....
1997-98	**NY Rangers**	**NHL**	**16**	**1**	**0**	**1**	**38**	**0**	**0**	**0**	**2**	**50.0**	**–2**	....	....	....	....	....	....	....	....	....	....	....	....
	Hartford	AHL	15	2	0	2	45	....	....	....	....	....	....	....	....	....	....	....	....	....	....	....	....	....	....
	Chicago	**NHL**	**4**	**0**	**1**	**1**	**5**	**0**	**0**	**0**	**0**	**0.0**	**0**	....	....	....	....	....	....	....	....	....	....	....	....
	Indianapolis Ice	IHL	3	1	1	2	4	....	....	....	....	....	....	....	....	....	....	....	....	....	....	....	....	....	....
1998-99	**Chicago**	**NHL**	**6**	**0**	**0**	**0**	**17**	**0**	**0**	**0**	**3**	**0.0**	**0**	**0**	**0.0**	**9:29**	....	....	....	....	....	....	....	....	....
	Indianapolis Ice	IHL	34	3	10	13	130	....	....	....	....	....	....	....	....	....	....	....	....	....	....	....	....	....	....
	Portland Pirates	AHL	37	4	1	5	119	....	....	....	....	....	....	....	....	....	....	....	....	....	....	....	....	....	....
99-2000	**Chicago**	**NHL**	**52**	**0**	**1**	**1**	**143**	**0**	**0**	**0**	**19**	**0.0**	**–3**	**3**	**0.0**	**5:37**	....	....	....	....	....	....	....	....	....
2000-01	**Chicago**	**NHL**	**64**	**2**	**5**	**7**	**146**	**0**	**0**	**0**	**24**	**8.3**	**–8**	**2**	**0.0**	**7:46**	....	....	....	....	....	....	....	....	....

			Regular Season														Playoffs								
Season	Club	League	GP	G	A	Pts	PIM	PP	SH	GW	S	%	+/-	TF	F%	Min	GP	G	A	Pts	PIM	PP	SH	GW	Min
2001-02	Chicago	NHL	50	1	2	3	103	0	0	0	22	4.5	−10	2	50.0	6:19	1	0	0	0	0	0	0	0	7:20
2002-03	Chicago	NHL	22	0	0	0	58	0	0	0	7	0.0	0	1	100.0	6:30									
	Norfolk Admirals	AHL	4	0	1	1	5																		
2003-04	Chicago	NHL	65	4	1	5	120	2	0	0	25	16.0	−10	0	0.0	6:16									
2004-05	Wilkes-Barre	AHL	23	4	7	11	67										11	2	2	4	11				
2005-06	Pittsburgh	NHL	20	1	0	1	42	0	0	0	5	20.0	0	0	0.0	4:20									
	NHL Totals		310	10	10	20	702	2	0	0	111	9.0		8	25.0	6:27	1	0	0	0	0	0	0	0	7:20

Signed as a free agent by **NY Rangers**, August 22, 1995. Traded to **Chicago** by **NY Rangers** for Ryan Risidore, March 24, 1998. • Missed majority of 2002-03 season recovering from hand injury suffered in game vs. Detroit, January 5, 2003. Signed as a free agent by **Pittsburgh**, July 12, 2004. Signed as a free agent by **Wilkes-Barre** (AHL), February 17, 2005.

VANDERMEER, Jim

(VAN-duhr-meer, JIHM) **CHI.**

Defense. Shoots left. 6'1", 218 lbs. Born, Caroline, Alta., February 21, 1980.

Season	Club	League	GP	G	A	Pts	PIM	PP	SH	GW	S	%	+/-	TF	F%	Min	GP	G	A	Pts	PIM	PP	SH	GW	Min
1997-98	Red Deer	AMHL	26	4	8	12	51																		
	Red Deer Rebels	WHL	35	0	3	3	55																		
1998-99	Red Deer Rebels	WHL	70	5	23	28	258										2	0	0	0	0				
99-2000	Red Deer Rebels	WHL	71	8	30	38	221										9	0	1	1	24				
2000-01	Red Deer Rebels	WHL	72	21	44	65	180										4	0	1	1	16				
2001-02	Philadelphia	AHL	74	1	13	14	88										22	3	13	16	43				
2002-03	Philadelphia	NHL	24	2	1	3	27	0	0	0	22	9.1	9	0	0.0	13:42	5	0	2	2	14				
	Philadelphia	AHL	48	4	8	12	122										8	0	1	1	9	0	0	0	12:42
2003-04	Philadelphia	NHL	23	3	2	5	25	0	0	1	24	12.5	−5	0	0.0	15:47									
	Philadelphia	AHL	26	1	6	7	120																		
	Chicago	NHL	23	2	10	12	58	1	1	0	37	5.4	−6	1	100.0	22:03									
2004-05	Norfolk Admirals	AHL	52	3	10	13	164																		
2005-06	Chicago	NHL	76	6	18	24	116	2	0	1	93	6.5	−2	1	100.0	21:47									
	NHL Totals		146	13	31	44	226	3	1	2	176	7.4		2	100.0	19:33	8	0	1	1	9	0	0	0	12:42

WHL East First All-Star Team (2001) • Canadian Major Junior Humanitarian Player of the Year (2001)

Signed as a free agent by **Philadelphia**, December 21, 2000. Traded to **Chicago** by **Philadelphia** with the rights to Colin Fraser and Los Angeles' 2nd round choice (previously acquired, Chicago selected Bryan Bickell) in 2004 Entry Draft for Alex Zhamnov and Washington's 4th round choice (previously acquired, Philadelphia selected R.J. Anderson) in 2004 Entry Draft, February 19, 2004.

VANEK, Thomas

(VAH-nehk, TAW-muhs) **BUF.**

Left wing. Shoots right. 6'2", 210 lbs. Born, Vienna, Austria, January 19, 1984. Buffalo's 1st choice, 5th overall, in 2003 Entry Draft.

Season	Club	League	GP	G	A	Pts	PIM	PP	SH	GW	S	%	+/-	TF	F%	Min	GP	G	A	Pts	PIM	PP	SH	GW	Min
99-2000	Sioux Falls	USHL	35	15	18	33	12										3	0	1	1	0				
2000-01	Sioux Falls	USHL	20	19	10	29	15										8	5	4	9	2				
2001-02	Sioux Falls	USHL	53	46	45	91	54										3	0	0	0	9				
2002-03	U. of Minnesota	WCHA	45	31	31	62	60																		
2003-04	U. of Minnesota	WCHA	38	26	25	51	72																		
2004-05	Rochester	AHL	74	42	26	68	62										5	2	3	5	10				
2005-06	Buffalo	NHL	81	25	23	48	72	11	0	4	204	12.3	−11	23	21.7	14:44	10	2	0	2	6	2	0	0	10:45
	NHL Totals		81	25	23	48	72	11	0	4	204	12.3		23	21.7	14:44	10	2	0	2	6	2	0	0	10:45

USHL First All-Star Team (2002) • USHL MVP (2002) • WCHA All-Rookie Team (2003) • WCHA Second All-Star Team (2003, 2004) • WCHA Rookie of the Year (2003) • NCAA Championship All-Tournament Team (2003) • NCAA Championship Tournament MVP (2003) • NCAA West Second All-American Team (2004) • AHL All-Rookie Team (2005)

VAN RYN, Mike

(VAN RIHN, MIGHK) **FLA.**

Defense. Shoots right. 6'1", 202 lbs. Born, London, Ont., May 14, 1979. New Jersey's 1st choice, 26th overall, in 1998 Entry Draft.

Season	Club	League	GP	G	A	Pts	PIM	PP	SH	GW	S	%	+/-	TF	F%	Min	GP	G	A	Pts	PIM	PP	SH	GW	Min
1995-96	London Nationals	OHA-B	44	9	14	23	24																		
1996-97	London Nationals	OHA-B	46	14	31	45	32																		
1997-98	U. of Michigan	CCHA	38	4	14	18	44																		
1998-99	U. of Michigan	CCHA	37	10	13	23	52																		
99-2000	Sarnia Sting	OHL	61	6	35	41	34										7	0	5	5	4				
2000-01	St. Louis	NHL	1	0	0	0	0	0	0	0	1	0.0	−2	0	0.0	13:43									
	Worcester IceCats	AHL	37	3	10	13	12										7	1	1	2	2				
2001-02	St. Louis	NHL	48	2	8	10	18	0	0	1	52	3.8	10	0	0.0	16:23	9	0	0	0	0	0	0	0	16:04
	Worcester IceCats	AHL	24	2	7	9	17																		
2002-03	St. Louis	NHL	20	0	3	3	8	0	0	0	21	0.0	3	0	0.0	15:04									
	Worcester IceCats	AHL	33	2	8	10	16																		
	San Antonio	AHL	11	0	3	3	20										3	0	0	0	0				
2003-04	Florida	NHL	79	13	24	37	52	6	1	0	136	9.6	−16	3	33.3	24:26									
2004-05			DID NOT PLAY																						
2005-06	Florida	NHL	80	8	29	37	90	3	0	2	154	5.2	15	0	0.0	22:36									
	NHL Totals		228	23	64	87	168	9	1	3	364	6.3		3	33.3	21:14	9	0	0	0	0	0	0	0	16:04

OJHL-B First All-Star Team (1997)

Signed as a free agent by **St. Louis**, June 30, 2000. • Missed majority of 2000-01 season recovering from shoulder injury suffered in game vs. Phoenix, October 5, 2000. Traded to **Florida** by **St. Louis** for Valeri Bure and Florida's 5th round choice (Nikita Nikitin) in 2004 Entry Draft, March 11, 2003.

VARADA, Vaclav

(vuh-RA-da, VAT-slav)

Right wing. Shoots left. 6', 208 lbs. Born, Vsetin, Czech., April 26, 1976. San Jose's 4th choice, 89th overall, in 1994 Entry Draft.

Season	Club	League	GP	G	A	Pts	PIM	PP	SH	GW	S	%	+/-	TF	F%	Min	GP	G	A	Pts	PIM	PP	SH	GW	Min
1993-94	HC Vitkovice	CzRep	24	6	7	13											5	1	1	2					
1994-95	Tacoma Rockets	WHL	68	50	38	88	108										4	4	3	7	11				
1995-96	Kelowna Rockets	WHL	59	39	46	85	100										6	3	3	6	16				
	Buffalo	NHL	1	0	0	0	0	0	0	0	2	0.0	0												
	Rochester	AHL	5	3	0	3	4																		
1996-97	Buffalo	NHL	5	0	0	0	2	0	0	0	2	0.0	0												
	Rochester	AHL	53	23	25	48	81										10	1	6	7	27				
1997-98	Buffalo	NHL	27	5	6	11	15	0	0	1	27	18.5	0				15	3	4	7	18	0	0	0	
	Rochester	AHL	45	30	26	56	74																		
1998-99	Buffalo	NHL	72	7	24	31	61	1	0	1	123	5.7	11	1	0.0	14:30	21	5	4	9	14	1	0	0	16:31
99-2000	HC Vitkovice	CzRep	5	2	3	5	12																		
	Buffalo	NHL	76	10	27	37	62	0	0	0	140	7.1	12	1	0.0	14:58	5	0	0	0	8	0	0	0	14:19
2000-01	Buffalo	NHL	75	10	21	31	81	2	0	2	112	8.9	−2	2	0.0	15:57	13	0	4	4	8	0	0	0	18:08
2001-02	Buffalo	NHL	76	7	16	23	82	1	0	1	138	5.1	−7	3	0.0	16:33									
2002-03	Buffalo	NHL	44	7	4	11	23	1	0	0	64	10.9	−2	13	53.9	16:07									
	Ottawa	NHL	11	2	6	8	8	1	0	0	17	11.8	3	8	0.0	14:57	18	2	4	6	18	0	0	0	13:57
2003-04	Ottawa	NHL	30	5	5	10	26	0	0	1	47	10.6	2	14	35.7	14:21	7	1	1	2	4	0	0	0	12:03
2004-05	Vitkovice	CzRep	44	8	19	27	83										11	3	3	6	37				
2005-06	Ottawa	NHL	76	5	16	21	50	1	0	0	114	4.4	2	16	25.0	9:42	8	0	2	2	12	0	0	0	6:04
	NHL Totals		493	58	125	183	410	7	0	6	786	7.4		58	27.6	14:31	87	11	19	30	82	1	0	0	14:25

Traded to **Buffalo** by **San Jose** with Martin Spahnel and Philadelphia's 1st (previously acquired, later traded to Phoenix – Phoenix selected Daniel Briere) and 4th (previously acquired, Buffalo selected Mike Martone) round choices in 1996 Entry Draft for Doug Bodger, November 16, 1995. Traded to **Ottawa** by **Buffalo** with Buffalo's 5th round choice (Tim Cook) in 2003 Entry Draft for Jakub Klepis, February 25, 2003. • Missed majority of 2003-04 season recovering from knee injury suffered in game vs. Boston, December 13, 2003. Signed as a free agent by **Vitkovice** (CzRep), September 17, 2004. Signed as a free agent by **Davos** (Swiss), August 10, 2006.

VASICEK, Josef

(VAHSH-ih-chehk, YOH-zehf) **NSH.**

Center. Shoots left. 6'5", 214 lbs. Born, Havlickuv Brod, Czech., September 12, 1980. Carolina's 4th choice, 91st overall, in 1998 Entry Draft.

Season	Club	League	GP	G	A	Pts	PIM	PP	SH	GW	S	%	+/-	TF	F%	Min	GP	G	A	Pts	PIM	PP	SH	GW	Min
1995-96	Havl. Brod U17	CzR-U17	36	25	25	50																			
1996-97	Slavia U17	CzR-U17	37	20	40	60																			
1997-98	Slavia Jr.	CzRep-Jr.	34	13	20	33																			
1998-99	Sault Ste. Marie	OHL	66	21	35	56	30										5	3	0	3	10				
99-2000	Sault Ste. Marie	OHL	54	26	46	72	49										17	5	15	20	8				
2000-01	Carolina	NHL	76	8	13	21	53	1	0	0	103	7.8	−8	786	46.6	11:49	6	2	0	2	0	0	0	0	13:56
	Cincinnati	IHL															3	0	0	0	0				
2001-02	Carolina	NHL	78	14	17	31	53	3	0	3	117	12.0	−7	878	48.3	14:11	23	3	2	5	12	0	0	1	14:50
2002-03	Carolina	NHL	57	10	10	20	33	4	0	1	87	11.5	−19	652	49.5	15:57									
2003-04	Carolina	NHL	82	19	26	45	60	6	0	5	161	11.8	−3	262	48.9	17:06									

			Regular Season														Playoffs								
Season	Club	League	GP	G	A	Pts	PIM	PP	SH	GW	S	%	+/-	TF	F%	Min	GP	G	A	Pts	PIM	PP	SH	GW	Min
2004-05	HC Slavia Praha	CzRep	52	20	23	43	42	....	....	....	....	....	....	....	....	....	7	1	6	7	10	....	....	....	....
2005-06 ♦	**Carolina**	**NHL**	**23**	**4**	**5**	**9**	**8**	**0**	**0**	**0**	**41**	**9.8**	**3**	**46**	**60.9**	**15:23**	**8**	**0**	**0**	**0**	**2**	**0**	**0**	**0**	**10:04**
	NHL Totals		**316**	**55**	**71**	**126**	**207**	**14**	**0**	**9**	**509**	**10.8**		**2624**	**48.4**	**14:47**	**37**	**5**	**2**	**7**	**14**	**0**	**0**	**1**	**13:39**

Signed as a free agent by **Slavia Praha** (CzRep), September 17, 2004. • Missed majority of 2005-06 season recovering from knee injury sufferd in game at Florida, November 11, 2005. Traded to **Nashville** by **Carolina** for Scott Walker, July 18, 2006.

VAUCLAIR, Julien

(voh-KLAIR, JEW-lee-ehn) **OTT.**

Defense. Shoots left. 6', 205 lbs. Born, Delemont, Switz., October 2, 1979. Ottawa's 4th choice, 74th overall, in 1998 Entry Draft.

Season	Club	League	GP	G	A	Pts	PIM	PP	SH	GW	S	%	+/-	TF	F%	Min	GP	G	A	Pts	PIM	PP	SH	GW	Min
1995-96	HC Ajoie	Swiss-3	20	4	10	14	....	....	....	....	....	....	....	....	....	....	....	....	....	....	....	....	....	....	....
1996-97	HC Ajoie	Swiss-2	40	0	6	6	24	....	....	....	....	....	....	....	....	....	9	0	2	2	8	....	....	....	....
1997-98	HC Lugano Jr.	Swiss-Jr.	10	7	4	11	10	....	....	....	....	....	....	....	....	....	....	....	....	....	....	....	....	....	....
	HC Lugano	Swiss	36	1	2	3	12	....	....	....	....	....	....	....	....	....	7	0	0	0	25	....	....	....	....
1998-99	HC Lugano	Swiss	38	0	3	3	8	....	....	....	....	....	....	....	....	....	....	....	....	....	....	....	....	....	....
	HC Lugano Jr.	Swiss-Jr.	19	10	14	24	14	....	....	....	....	....	....	....	....	....	1	0	0	0	0	....	....	....	....
99-2000	HC Lugano	Swiss	45	3	3	6	16	....	....	....	....	....	....	....	....	....	14	0	0	0	0	....	....	....	....
	HC Lugano	EuroHL	6	1	0	1	0	....	....	....	....	....	....	....	....	....	4	1	0	1	2	....	....	....	....
2000-01	HC Lugano	Swiss	42	3	4	7	57	....	....	....	....	....	....	....	....	....	18	0	1	1	4	....	....	....	....
2001-02	Grand Rapids	AHL	71	5	14	19	18	....	....	....	....	....	....	....	....	....	4	0	1	1	4	....	....	....	....
	Switzerland	Olympics	4	1	0	1	2	....	....	....	....	....	....	....	....	....	....	....	....	....	....	....	....	....	....
2002-03	Binghamton	AHL	67	6	16	22	30	....	....	....	....	....	....	....	....	....	14	0	1	1	8	....	....	....	....
2003-04	**Ottawa**	**NHL**	**1**	**0**	**0**	**0**	**2**	**0**	**0**	**0**	**0**	**0.0**	**1**	**0**	**0.0**	**12:48**	....	....	....	....	....	....	....	....	....
	Binghamton	AHL	78	9	30	39	39	....	....	....	....	....	....	....	....	....	2	0	0	0	0	....	....	....	....
2004-05	HC Lugano	Swiss	42	4	7	11	26	....	....	....	....	....	....	....	....	....	3	0	0	0	2	....	....	....	....
2005-06	HC Lugano	Swiss	31	6	6	12	32	....	....	....	....	....	....	....	....	....	17	2	3	5	12	....	....	....	....
	Switzerland	Olympics	6	0	0	0	6	....	....	....	....	....	....	....	....	....	....	....	....	....	....	....	....	....	....
	NHL Totals		**1**	**0**	**0**	**0**	**2**	**0**	**0**	**0**	**0**	**0.0**		**0**	**0.0**	**12:48**	....	....	....	....	....	....	....	....	....

Signed as a free agent by **Lugano** (Swiss), May 12, 2004.

VEILLEUX, Stephane

(VAY-oo, STEH-fan) **MIN.**

Left wing. Shoots left. 6'1", 187 lbs. Born, Beauceville, Que., November 16, 1981. Minnesota's 4th choice, 93rd overall, in 2001 Entry Draft.

Season	Club	League	GP	G	A	Pts	PIM	PP	SH	GW	S	%	+/-	TF	F%	Min	GP	G	A	Pts	PIM	PP	SH	GW	Min
1997-98	Beauce-Amiante	QAAA	21	20	17	37	....	....	....	....	....	....	....	....	....	....	....	....	....	....	....	....	....	....	....
	Levis-Lauzon	QAAA	14	3	5	8	....	....	....	....	....	....	....	....	....	....	1	0	0	0	0	....	....	....	....
1998-99	Victoriaville Tigres	QMJHL	65	6	13	19	35	....	....	....	....	....	....	....	....	....	6	1	3	4	2	....	....	....	....
99-2000	Victoriaville Tigres	QMJHL	22	1	4	5	17	....	....	....	....	....	....	....	....	....	....	....	....	....	....	....	....	....	....
	Val-d'Or Foreurs	QMJHL	50	14	28	42	100	....	....	....	....	....	....	....	....	....	....	....	....	....	....	....	....	....	....
2000-01	Val-d'Or Foreurs	QMJHL	68	48	67	115	90	....	....	....	....	....	....	....	....	....	21	15	18	33	42	....	....	....	....
2001-02	Houston Aeros	AHL	77	13	22	35	113	....	....	....	....	....	....	....	....	....	14	2	4	6	20	....	....	....	....
2002-03	**Minnesota**	**NHL**	**38**	**3**	**2**	**5**	**23**	**1**	**0**	**0**	**52**	**5.8**	**–6**	**13**	**7.7**	**12:08**	....	....	....	....	....	....	....	....	....
	Houston Aeros	AHL	29	8	4	12	43	....	....	....	....	....	....	....	....	....	23	7	11	18	12	....	....	....	....
2003-04	**Minnesota**	**NHL**	**19**	**2**	**8**	**10**	**20**	**1**	**1**	**1**	**37**	**5.4**	**0**	**10**	**40.0**	**14:20**	....	....	....	....	....	....	....	....	....
	Houston Aeros	AHL	64	13	25	38	66	....	....	....	....	....	....	....	....	....	2	1	1	2	2	....	....	....	....
2004-05	Houston Aeros	AHL	59	15	24	39	35	....	....	....	....	....	....	....	....	....	....	....	....	....	....	....	....	....	....
2005-06	**Minnesota**	**NHL**	**71**	**7**	**9**	**16**	**63**	**0**	**0**	**1**	**87**	**8.0**	**–13**	**33**	**33.3**	**12:58**	....	....	....	....	....	....	....	....	....
	NHL Totals		**128**	**12**	**19**	**31**	**106**	**2**	**1**	**2**	**176**	**6.8**		**56**	**28.6**	**12:55**	....	....	....	....	....	....	....	....	....

VERMETTE, Antoine

(vuhr-MEHT, AN-twuhn) **OTT.**

Center. Shoots left. 6'1", 193 lbs. Born, St-Agapit, Que., July 20, 1982. Ottawa's 3rd choice, 55th overall, in 2000 Entry Draft.

Season	Club	League	GP	G	A	Pts	PIM	PP	SH	GW	S	%	+/-	TF	F%	Min	GP	G	A	Pts	PIM	PP	SH	GW	Min
1997-98	Quebec Select	QAHA	19	11	20	31	36	....	....	....	....	....	....	....	....	....	....	....	....	....	....	....	....	....	....
	Levis-Lauzon	QAAA	8	1	1	2	4	....	....	....	....	....	....	....	....	....	1	0	0	0	0	....	....	....	....
1998-99	Quebec Remparts	QMJHL	57	9	17	26	32	....	....	....	....	....	....	....	....	....	13	0	0	0	2	....	....	....	....
99-2000	Victoriaville Tigres	QMJHL	71	30	41	71	87	....	....	....	....	....	....	....	....	....	6	0	1	1	6	....	....	....	....
2000-01	Victoriaville Tigres	QMJHL	71	57	62	119	102	....	....	....	....	....	....	....	....	....	9	4	6	10	14	....	....	....	....
2001-02	Victoriaville Tigres	QMJHL	4	0	2	2	6	....	....	....	....	....	....	....	....	....	22	10	16	26	10	....	....	....	....
2002-03	Binghamton	AHL	80	34	28	62	57	....	....	....	....	....	....	....	....	....	14	2	9	11	10	....	....	....	....
2003-04	**Ottawa**	**NHL**	**57**	**7**	**7**	**14**	**16**	**0**	**1**	**0**	**63**	**11.1**	**5**	**100**	**44.0**	**11:59**	**4**	**0**	**1**	**1**	**4**	**0**	**0**	**0**	**11:35**
	Binghamton	AHL	3	0	0	0	6	....	....	....	....	....	....	....	....	....	....	....	....	....	....	....	....	....	....
2004-05	Binghamton	AHL	78	28	45	73	36	....	....	....	....	....	....	....	....	....	6	1	4	5	10	....	....	....	....
2005-06	**Ottawa**	**NHL**	**82**	**21**	**12**	**33**	**44**	**1**	**6**	**4**	**123**	**17.1**	**17**	**537**	**57.9**	**12:35**	**10**	**2**	**0**	**2**	**4**	**0**	**0**	**1**	**15:00**
	NHL Totals		**139**	**28**	**19**	**47**	**60**	**1**	**7**	**4**	**186**	**15.1**		**637**	**55.7**	**12:20**	**14**	**2**	**1**	**3**	**8**	**0**	**0**	**1**	**14:02**

AHL All-Rookie Team (2003)

• Missed majority of 2001-02 season recovering from neck injury suffered at Team Canada Jr. Selection Camp, June 3, 2001.

VERNARSKY, Kris

(veh-NAHR-skee, KRIHS)

Center. Shoots left. 6'3", 201 lbs. Born, Detroit, MI, April 5, 1982. Toronto's 2nd choice, 51st overall, in 2000 Entry Draft.

Season	Club	League	GP	G	A	Pts	PIM	PP	SH	GW	S	%	+/-	TF	F%	Min	GP	G	A	Pts	PIM	PP	SH	GW	Min
1997-98	USNTDP	U-18	23	1	6	7	40	....	....	....	....	....	....	....	....	....	....	....	....	....	....	....	....	....	....
	USNTDP	USHL	3	0	0	0	0	....	....	....	....	....	....	....	....	....	....	....	....	....	....	....	....	....	....
	USNTDP	NAHL	42	9	10	19	50	....	....	....	....	....	....	....	....	....	1	1	2	3	7	....	....	....	....
1998-99	Plymouth Whalers	OHL	45	3	14	17	30	....	....	....	....	....	....	....	....	....	11	0	0	0	2	....	....	....	....
99-2000	Plymouth Whalers	OHL	64	16	22	38	63	....	....	....	....	....	....	....	....	....	19	3	6	9	24	....	....	....	....
2000-01	Plymouth Whalers	OHL	60	14	21	35	35	....	....	....	....	....	....	....	....	....	19	7	10	17	19	....	....	....	....
2001-02	Plymouth Whalers	OHL	59	19	36	55	98	....	....	....	....	....	....	....	....	....	6	1	2	3	15	....	....	....	....
2002-03	**Boston**	**NHL**	**14**	**1**	**0**	**1**	**2**	**0**	**0**	**0**	**18**	**5.6**	**–2**	**22**	**54.6**	**10:15**	....	....	....	....	....	....	....	....	....
	Providence Bruins	AHL	65	12	15	27	49	....	....	....	....	....	....	....	....	....	4	0	0	0	20	....	....	....	....
2003-04	**Boston**	**NHL**	**3**	**0**	**0**	**0**	**0**	**0**	**0**	**0**	**0**	**0.0**	**–1**	**12**	**33.3**	**6:33**	....	....	....	....	....	....	....	....	....
	Providence Bruins	AHL	55	8	9	17	61	....	....	....	....	....	....	....	....	....	2	0	0	0	4	....	....	....	....
2004-05	Providence Bruins	AHL	5	0	1	1	2	....	....	....	....	....	....	....	....	....	....	....	....	....	....	....	....	....	....
	Florida Everblades	ECHL	53	16	20	36	47	....	....	....	....	....	....	....	....	....	18	2	7	9	33	....	....	....	....
2005-06	Motor City	UHL	75	10	21	31	100	....	....	....	....	....	....	....	....	....	4	0	0	0	0	....	....	....	....
	NHL Totals		**17**	**1**	**0**	**1**	**2**	**0**	**0**	**0**	**18**	**5.6**		**34**	**47.1**	**9:36**	....	....	....	....	....	....	....	....	....

Rights traded to **Boston** by **Toronto** for Ric Jackman, May 13, 2002.

VEROT, Darcy

(vuhr-AWT, DAHR-see)

Left wing. Shoots left. 6', 199 lbs. Born, Radville, Sask., July 13, 1976.

Season	Club	League	GP	G	A	Pts	PIM	PP	SH	GW	S	%	+/-	TF	F%	Min	GP	G	A	Pts	PIM	PP	SH	GW	Min
1994-95	Weyburn	SJHL	57	8	18	26	240	....	....	....	....	....	....	....	....	....	16	5	2	7	50	....	....	....	....
1995-96	Weyburn	SJHL	64	15	30	45	191	....	....	....	....	....	....	....	....	....	3	1	0	1	20	....	....	....	....
1996-97	Weyburn	SJHL	61	26	51	77	218	....	....	....	....	....	....	....	....	....	13	3	8	11	24	....	....	....	....
1997-98	Lake Charles	WPHL	68	11	26	37	269	....	....	....	....	....	....	....	....	....	4	0	1	1	25	....	....	....	....
1998-99	Lake Charles	WPHL	68	17	23	40	236	....	....	....	....	....	....	....	....	....	9	2	4	6	53	....	....	....	....
99-2000	Wheeling Nailers	ECHL	44	7	12	19	240	....	....	....	....	....	....	....	....	....	....	....	....	....	....	....	....	....	....
	Wilkes-Barre	AHL	23	5	5	10	96	....	....	....	....	....	....	....	....	....	....	....	....	....	....	....	....	....	....
2000-01	Wilkes-Barre	AHL	78	10	15	25	347	....	....	....	....	....	....	....	....	....	21	2	3	5	40	....	....	....	....
2001-02	Wilkes-Barre	AHL	71	6	10	16	387	....	....	....	....	....	....	....	....	....	....	....	....	....	....	....	....	....	....
2002-03	Saint John Flames	AHL	73	5	11	16	299	....	....	....	....	....	....	....	....	....	....	....	....	....	....	....	....	....	....
2003-04	**Washington**	**NHL**	**37**	**0**	**2**	**2**	**135**	**0**	**0**	**0**	**11**	**0.0**	**–6**	**183**	**48.6**	**8:48**	....	....	....	....	....	....	....	....	....
	Portland Pirates	AHL	28	3	5	8	89	....	....	....	....	....	....	....	....	....	....	....	....	....	....	....	....	....	....
2004-05	Portland Pirates	AHL	36	0	1	1	189	....	....	....	....	....	....	....	....	....	....	....	....	....	....	....	....	....	....
2005-06	Syracuse Crunch	AHL	20	1	3	4	64	....	....	....	....	....	....	....	....	....	....	....	....	....	....	....	....	....	....
	NHL Totals		**37**	**0**	**2**	**2**	**135**	**0**	**0**	**0**	**11**	**0.0**		**183**	**48.6**	**8:48**	....	....	....	....	....	....	....	....	....

Signed as a free agent by **Wilkes-Barre** (AHL), February 25, 2000. Signed as a free agent by **Pittsburgh**, July 28, 2000. Signed as a free agent by **Calgary**, July 9, 2002. Signed as a free agent by **Washingon**, September 5, 2003. Signed as a free agent by **Columbus**, December 30, 2005.

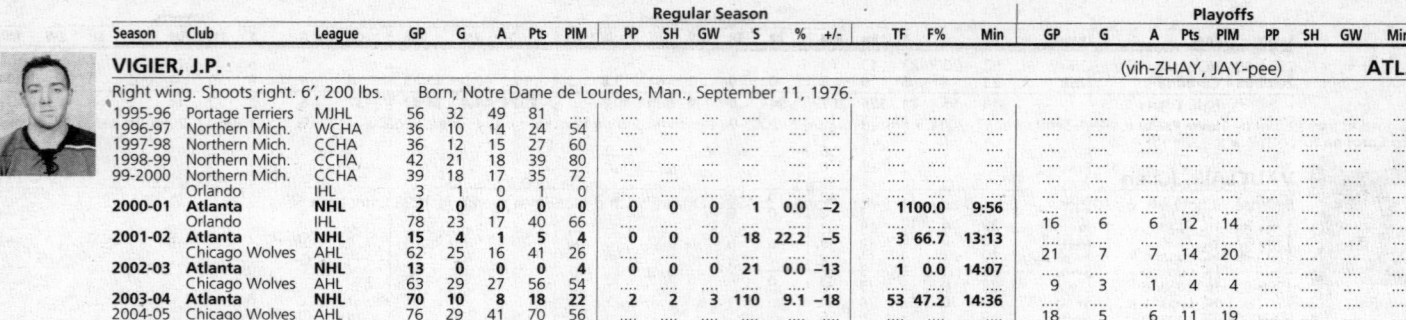

VIGIER, J.P.

(vih-ZHAY, JAY-pee) **ATL.**

Right wing. Shoots right. 6', 200 lbs. Born, Notre Dame de Lourdes, Man., September 11, 1976.

			Regular Season													Playoffs								
Season	Club	League	GP	G	A	Pts	PIM	PP	SH	GW	S	%	+/-	TF	F%	Min	GP	G	A	Pts	PIM	PP	SH	GW	Min
1995-96	Portage Terriers	MJHL	56	32	49	81	....	....	....	....	....	....	....	....	....	....	....	....	....	....	....	....	....	....	....
1996-97	Northern Mich.	WCHA	36	10	14	24	54	....	....	....	....	....	....	....	....	....	....	....	....	....	....	....	....	....	....
1997-98	Northern Mich.	CCHA	36	12	15	27	60	....	....	....	....	....	....	....	....	....	....	....	....	....	....	....	....	....	....
1998-99	Northern Mich.	CCHA	42	21	18	39	80	....	....	....	....	....	....	....	....	....	....	....	....	....	....	....	....	....	....
99-2000	Northern Mich.	CCHA	39	18	17	35	72	....	....	....	....	....	....	....	....	....	....	....	....	....	....	....	....	....	....
	Orlando	IHL	3	1	0	1	0	....	....	....	....	....	....	....	....	....	....	....	....	....	....	....	....	....	....
2000-01	Atlanta	NHL	2	0	0	0	0	0	0	0	1	0.0	–2	1	100.0	9:56	....	....	....	....	....	....	....	....	....
	Orlando	IHL	78	23	17	40	66	....	....	....	....	....	....	....	....	....	16	6	6	12	14	....	....	....	....
2001-02	Atlanta	NHL	15	4	1	5	4	0	0	0	18	22.2	–5	3	66.7	13:13	....	....	....	....	....	....	....	....	....
	Chicago Wolves	AHL	62	25	16	41	26	....	....	....	....	....	....	....	....	....	21	7	7	14	20	....	....	....	....
2002-03	Atlanta	NHL	13	0	0	0	4	0	0	0	21	0.0	–13	1	0.0	14:07	....	....	....	....	....	....	....	....	....
	Chicago Wolves	AHL	63	29	27	56	54	....	....	....	....	....	....	....	....	....	9	3	1	4	4	....	....	....	....
2003-04	Atlanta	NHL	70	10	8	18	22	2	2	3	110	9.1	–18	53	47.2	14:36	....	....	....	....	....	....	....	....	....
2004-05	Chicago Wolves	AHL	76	29	41	70	56	....	....	....	....	....	....	....	....	....	18	5	6	11	19	....	....	....	....
2005-06	Atlanta	NHL	41	4	6	10	40	1	1	0	53	7.5	–4	70	24.3	14:21	....	....	....	....	....	....	....	....	....
	NHL Totals		141	18	15	33	70	3	3	3	203	8.9		128	35.2	14:16	....	....	....	....	....	....	....	....	....

CCHA Second All-Star Team (1999) • CCHA All-Tournament Team (1999) • AHL Second All-Star Team (2005)

Signed as a free agent by **Atlanta**, April 20, 2000.

VIRTUE, Terry

(VIR-too, TAIR-ee)

Defense. Shoots right. 6', 198 lbs. Born, Scarborough, Ont., August 12, 1970.

			Regular Season													Playoffs								
Season	Club	League	GP	G	A	Pts	PIM	PP	SH	GW	S	%	+/-	TF	F%	Min	GP	G	A	Pts	PIM	PP	SH	GW	Min
1988-89	Hobbema Hawks	AJHL	56	6	31	37	339	....	....	....	....	....	....	....	....	....	....	....	....	....	....	....	....	....	....
	Victoria Cougars	WHL	8	1	1	2	13	....	....	....	....	....	....	....	....	....	....	....	....	....	....	....	....	....	....
1989-90	Victoria Cougars	WHL	24	1	9	10	85	....	....	....	....	....	....	....	....	....	....	....	....	....	....	....	....	....	....
	Tri-City	WHL	34	1	10	11	82	....	....	....	....	....	....	....	....	....	6	0	0	0	30	....	....	....	....
1990-91	Tri-City	WHL	11	1	8	9	24	....	....	....	....	....	....	....	....	....	....	....	....	....	....	....	....	....	....
	Portland	WHL	59	9	44	53	127	....	....	....	....	....	....	....	....	....	....	....	....	....	....	....	....	....	....
1991-92	Roanoke Valley	ECHL	38	4	22	26	165	....	....	....	....	....	....	....	....	....	....	....	....	....	....	....	....	....	....
	Louisville	ECHL	23	1	15	16	58	....	....	....	....	....	....	....	....	....	13	0	8	8	49	....	....	....	....
1992-93	Louisville	ECHL	28	0	17	17	84	....	....	....	....	....	....	....	....	....	....	....	....	....	....	....	....	....	....
	Wheeling	ECHL	31	3	15	18	86	....	....	....	....	....	....	....	....	....	16	3	5	8	18	....	....	....	....
1993-94	Wheeling	ECHL	34	5	28	33	61	....	....	....	....	....	....	....	....	....	6	2	2	4	4	....	....	....	....
	Cape Breton	AHL	26	4	6	10	10	....	....	....	....	....	....	....	....	....	5	0	0	0	17	....	....	....	....
1994-95	Worcester IceCats	AHL	73	14	25	39	183	....	....	....	....	....	....	....	....	....	....	....	....	....	....	....	....	....	....
	Atlanta Knights	IHL	1	0	0	0	2	....	....	....	....	....	....	....	....	....	....	....	....	....	....	....	....	....	....
1995-96	Worcester IceCats	AHL	76	7	31	38	234	....	....	....	....	....	....	....	....	....	4	0	0	0	4	....	....	....	....
1996-97	Worcester IceCats	AHL	80	16	26	42	220	....	....	....	....	....	....	....	....	....	5	0	4	4	8	....	....	....	....
1997-98	Worcester IceCats	AHL	74	8	26	34	233	....	....	....	....	....	....	....	....	....	11	1	4	5	41	....	....	....	....
1998-99	Boston	NHL	4	0	0	0	0	0	0	0	2	0.0	2	0	0.0	9:41	....	....	....	....	....	....	....	....	....
	Providence Bruins	AHL	76	8	48	56	117	....	....	....	....	....	....	....	....	....	17	2	12	14	29	....	....	....	....
99-2000	NY Rangers	NHL	1	0	0	0	0	0	0	0	2	0.0	–2	0	0.0	12:32	....	....	....	....	....	....	....	....	....
	Hartford	AHL	67	5	22	27	166	....	....	....	....	....	....	....	....	....	23	3	7	10	51	....	....	....	....
2000-01	Hartford	AHL	71	5	24	29	166	....	....	....	....	....	....	....	....	....	5	1	0	1	2	....	....	....	....
2001-02	Hartford	AHL	76	4	20	24	117	....	....	....	....	....	....	....	....	....	10	0	1	1	19	....	....	....	....
2002-03	Worcester IceCats	AHL	78	5	30	35	144	....	....	....	....	....	....	....	....	....	....	....	....	....	....	....	....	....	....
2003-04	Worcester IceCats	AHL	74	6	16	22	66	....	....	....	....	....	....	....	....	....	10	1	4	5	36	....	....	....	....
2004-05	Springfield	AHL	13	1	1	2	21	....	....	....	....	....	....	....	....	....	....	....	....	....	....	....	....	....	....
	Utah Grizzlies	AHL	65	3	18	21	112	....	....	....	....	....	....	....	....	....	....	....	....	....	....	....	....	....	....
2005-06	Wilkes-Barre	AHL	4	0	1	1	4	....	....	....	....	....	....	....	....	....	....	....	....	....	....	....	....	....	....
	Wheeling Nailers	ECHL	54	7	34	41	98	....	....	....	....	....	....	....	....	....	....	....	....	....	....	....	....	....	....
	Grand Rapids	AHL	12	1	1	2	33	....	....	....	....	....	....	....	....	....	16	0	8	8	42	....	....	....	....
	NHL Totals		5	0	0	0	0	0	0	0	4	0.0		0	0.0	10:15	....	....	....	....	....	....	....	....	....

AHL Second All-Star Team (1999)

Signed as a free agent by **St. Louis**, January 29, 1996. Signed as a free agent by **Boston**, August 28, 1998. Signed as a free agent by **NY Rangers**, July 29, 1999. Signed as a free agent by **St. Louis**, July 14, 2002. Signed as a free agent by **Springfield** (AHL), July 30, 2004. Loaned to **Utah** (AHL) by **Springfield** (AHL) for cash, November 22, 2004.

VISHNEVSKI, Vitaly

(vihsh-NEHV-skee, vih-TAL-ee) **ANA.**

Defense. Shoots left. 6'2", 203 lbs. Born, Kharkov, USSR, March 18, 1980. Anaheim's 1st choice, 5th overall, in 1998 Entry Draft.

			Regular Season													Playoffs								
Season	Club	League	GP	G	A	Pts	PIM	PP	SH	GW	S	%	+/-	TF	F%	Min	GP	G	A	Pts	PIM	PP	SH	GW	Min
1995-96	Yaroslavl 2	CIS-2	40	4	4	8	20	....	....	....	....	....	....	....	....	....	....	....	....	....	....	....	....	....	....
1996-97	Yaroslavl 2	Russia-3	45	0	2	2	30	....	....	....	....	....	....	....	....	....	....	....	....	....	....	....	....	....	....
1997-98	Yaroslavl 2	Russia-2	47	8	9	17	164	....	....	....	....	....	....	....	....	....	....	....	....	....	....	....	....	....	....
1998-99	Yaroslavl	Russia	34	3	4	7	38	....	....	....	....	....	....	....	....	....	10	0	0	0	4	....	....	....	....
99-2000	Anaheim	NHL	31	1	1	2	26	1	0	0	17	5.9	0	0	0.0	16:38	....	....	....	....	....	....	....	....	....
	Cincinnati	AHL	35	1	3	4	45	....	....	....	....	....	....	....	....	....	....	....	....	....	....	....	....	....	....
2000-01	Anaheim	NHL	76	1	10	11	99	0	0	0	49	2.0	–1	0	0.0	19:14	....	....	....	....	....	....	....	....	....
2001-02	Anaheim	NHL	74	0	3	3	60	0	0	0	54	0.0	–10	0	0.0	17:36	....	....	....	....	....	....	....	....	....
2002-03	Anaheim	NHL	80	2	6	8	76	0	1	0	65	3.1	–8	0	0.0	14:10	21	0	1	1	6	0	0	0	10:02
2003-04	Anaheim	NHL	73	6	10	16	51	0	0	0	86	7.0	0	0	0.0	17:10	....	....	....	....	....	....	....	....	....
2004-05	Voskresensk	Russia	51	7	17	24	92	....	....	....	....	....	....	....	....	....	....	....	....	....	....	....	....	....	....
2005-06	Anaheim	NHL	82	1	7	8	91	0	0	0	90	1.1	8	1	100.0	16:26	16	0	4	4	10	0	0	0	13:41
	Russia	Olympics	8	0	1	1	4	....	....	....	....	....	....	....	....	....	....	....	....	....	....	....	....	....	....
	NHL Totals		416	11	37	48	403	1	1	0	361	3.0		1	100.0	16:51	37	0	5	5	16	0	0	0	11:36

Signed as a free agent by **Voskresensk** (Russia), August 25, 2004.

VISNOVSKY, Lubomir

(vihsh-NAWV-skee, LOO-boh-mihr) **L.A.**

Defense. Shoots left. 5'10", 188 lbs. Born, Topolcany, Czech., August 11, 1976. Los Angeles' 4th choice, 118th overall, in 2000 Entry Draft.

			Regular Season													Playoffs								
Season	Club	League	GP	G	A	Pts	PIM	PP	SH	GW	S	%	+/-	TF	F%	Min	GP	G	A	Pts	PIM	PP	SH	GW	Min
1994-95	Bratislava	Slovakia	36	11	12	23	10	....	....	....	....	....	....	....	....	....	9	1	3	4	2	....	....	....	....
1995-96	Bratislava	Slovakia	35	8	6	14	22	....	....	....	....	....	....	....	....	....	13	1	5	6	2	....	....	....	....
1996-97	Bratislava	Slovakia	44	11	12	23	....	....	....	....	....	....	....	....	....	....	2	0	1	1	....	....	....	....	....
	Bratislava	EuroHL	6	3	1	4	2	....	....	....	....	....	....	....	....	....	2	0	0	0	6	....	....	....	....
1997-98	Bratislava	Slovakia	36	7	9	16	16	....	....	....	....	....	....	....	....	....	11	2	4	6	8	....	....	....	....
	Bratislava	EuroHL	6	1	0	1	4	....	....	....	....	....	....	....	....	....	....	....	....	....	....	....	....	....	....
	Slovakia	Olympics	3	0	0	0	2	....	....	....	....	....	....	....	....	....	....	....	....	....	....	....	....	....	....
1998-99	Bratislava	Slovakia	40	9	10	19	31	....	....	....	....	....	....	....	....	....	10	5	5	10	0	....	....	....	....
	Bratislava	EuroHL	6	0	3	3	4	....	....	....	....	....	....	....	....	....	....	....	....	....	....	....	....	....	....
99-2000	Bratislava	Slovakia	52	21	24	45	38	....	....	....	....	....	....	....	....	....	8	5	3	8	16	....	....	....	....
2000-01	Los Angeles	NHL	81	7	32	39	36	3	0	3	105	6.7	16	0	0.0	16:58	8	0	0	0	0	0	0	0	13:57
2001-02	Los Angeles	NHL	72	4	17	21	14	1	0	2	95	4.2	–5	0	0.0	16:15	4	0	1	1	0	0	0	0	8:22
	Slovakia	Olympics	3	1	2	3	0	....	....	....	....	....	....	....	....	....	....	....	....	....	....	....	....	....	....
2002-03	Los Angeles	NHL	57	8	16	24	28	1	0	1	85	9.4	2	0	0.0	19:20	....	....	....	....	....	....	....	....	....
2003-04	Los Angeles	NHL	58	8	21	29	26	5	0	0	114	7.0	8	0	0.0	24:02	....	....	....	....	....	....	....	....	....
2004-05	Bratislava	Slovakia	43	13	25	38	40	....	....	....	....	....	....	....	....	....	14	2	10	12	10	....	....	....	....
2005-06	Los Angeles	NHL	80	17	50	67	50	10	0	3	152	11.2	7	1	100.0	23:16	....	....	....	....	....	....	....	....	....
	Slovakia	Olympics	6	1	1	2	0	....	....	....	....	....	....	....	....	....	....	....	....	....	....	....	....	....	....
	NHL Totals		348	44	136	180	154	20	0	9	551	8.0		1	100.0	19:50	12	0	1	1	0	0	0	0	12:05

NHL All-Rookie Team (2001)

Signed as a free agent by **Bratislava** (Slovakia), September 27, 2004.

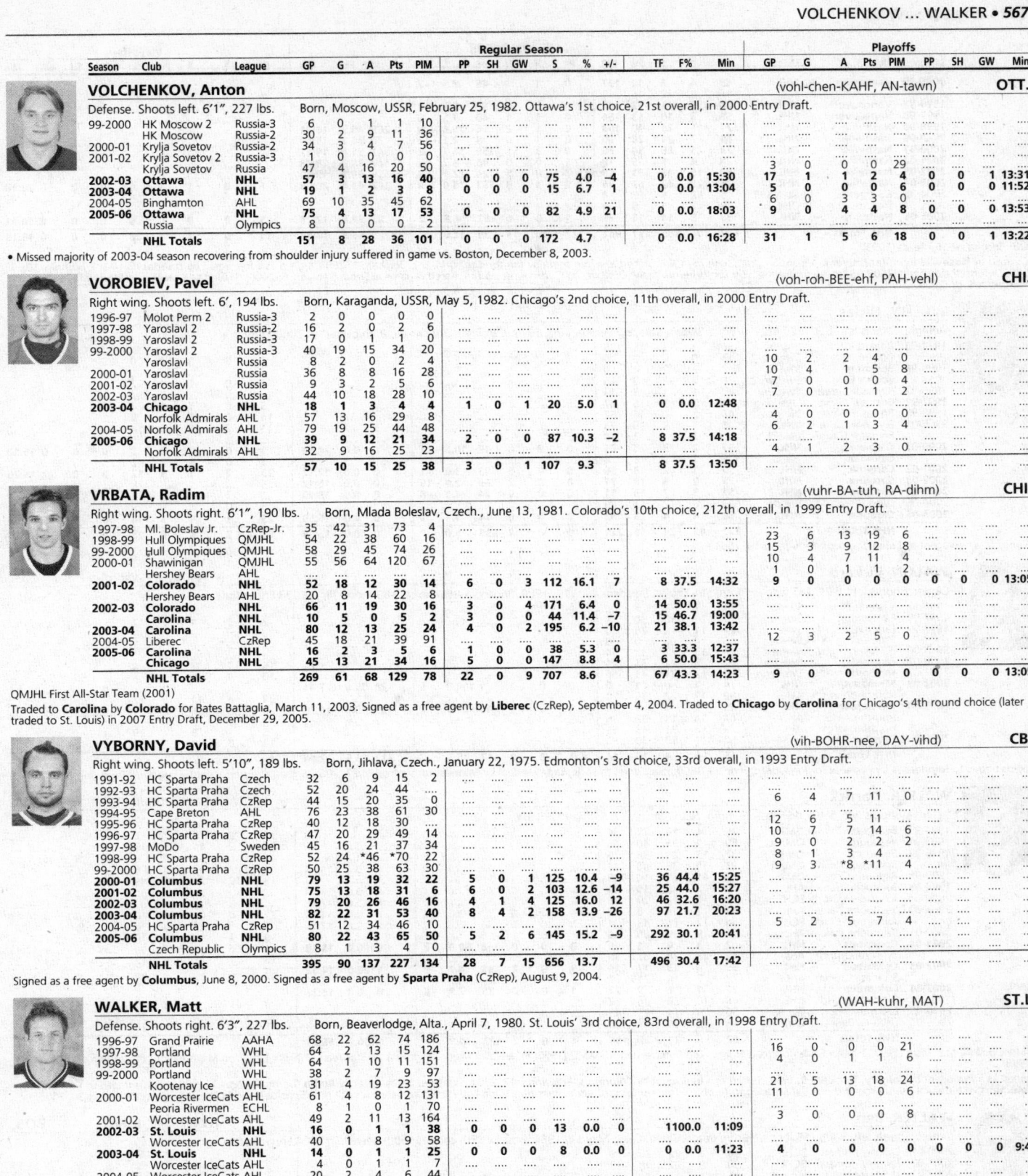

VOLCHENKOV, Anton
(vohl-chen-KAHF, AN-tawn) **OTT.**

Defense. Shoots left. 6'1", 227 lbs. Born, Moscow, USSR, February 25, 1982. Ottawa's 1st choice, 21st overall, in 2000 Entry Draft.

			Regular Season														Playoffs								
Season	Club	League	GP	G	A	Pts	PIM	PP	SH	GW	S	%	+/-	TF	F%	Min	GP	G	A	Pts	PIM	PP	SH	GW	Min
99-2000	HK Moscow 2	Russia-3	6	0	1	1	10	....	....	....	....	....	....	....	....	....	....	....	....	....	....	....	....	....	....
	HK Moscow	Russia-2	30	2	9	11	36	....	....	....	....	....	....	....	....	....	....	....	....	....	....	....	....	....	....
2000-01	Krylja Sovetov	Russia-2	34	3	4	7	56	....	....	....	....	....	....	....	....	....	....	....	....	....	....	....	....	....	....
2001-02	Krylja Sovetov 2	Russia-3	1	0	0	0	0	....	....	....	....	....	....	....	....	....	....	....	....	....	....	....	....	....	....
	Krylja Sovetov	Russia	47	4	16	20	50	....	....	....	....	....	....	....	....	....	3	0	0	0	29	....	....	....	....
2002-03	**Ottawa**	**NHL**	**57**	**3**	**13**	**16**	**40**	**0**	**0**	**0**	**75**	**4.0**	**–4**	**0**	**0.0**	**15:30**	**17**	**1**	**1**	**2**	**4**	**0**	**0**	**1**	**13:31**
2003-04	**Ottawa**	**NHL**	**19**	**1**	**2**	**3**	**8**	**0**	**0**	**0**	**15**	**6.7**	**1**	**0**	**0.0**	**13:04**	**5**	**0**	**0**	**0**	**6**	**0**	**0**	**0**	**11:52**
2004-05	Binghamton	AHL	69	10	35	45	62	....	....	....	....	....	....	....	....	....	6	0	3	3	0	....	....	....	....
2005-06	**Ottawa**	**NHL**	**75**	**4**	**13**	**17**	**53**	**0**	**0**	**0**	**82**	**4.9**	**21**	**0**	**0.0**	**18:03**	**9**	**0**	**4**	**4**	**8**	**0**	**0**	**0**	**13:53**
	Russia	Olympics	8	0	0	0	2	....	....	....	....	....	....	....	....	....	....	....	....	....	....	....	....	....	....
	NHL Totals		**151**	**8**	**28**	**36**	**101**	**0**	**0**	**0**	**172**	**4.7**		**0**	**0.0**	**16:28**	**31**	**1**	**5**	**6**	**18**	**0**	**0**	**1**	**13:22**

• Missed majority of 2003-04 season recovering from shoulder injury suffered in game vs. Boston, December 8, 2003.

VOROBIEV, Pavel
(voh-roh-BEE-ehf, PAH-vehl) **CHI.**

Right wing. Shoots left. 6', 194 lbs. Born, Karaganda, USSR, May 5, 1982. Chicago's 2nd choice, 11th overall, in 2000 Entry Draft.

			Regular Season														Playoffs								
Season	Club	League	GP	G	A	Pts	PIM	PP	SH	GW	S	%	+/-	TF	F%	Min	GP	G	A	Pts	PIM	PP	SH	GW	Min
1996-97	Molot Perm 2	Russia-3	2	0	0	0	0	....	....	....	....	....	....	....	....	....	....	....	....	....	....	....	....	....	....
1997-98	Yaroslavl 2	Russia-2	16	2	0	2	6	....	....	....	....	....	....	....	....	....	....	....	....	....	....	....	....	....	....
1998-99	Yaroslavl 2	Russia-3	17	0	1	1	0	....	....	....	....	....	....	....	....	....	....	....	....	....	....	....	....	....	....
99-2000	Yaroslavl 2	Russia-3	40	19	15	34	20	....	....	....	....	....	....	....	....	....	....	....	....	....	....	....	....	....	....
	Yaroslavl	Russia	8	2	0	2	4	....	....	....	....	....	....	....	....	....	10	2	2	4	0	....	....	....	....
2000-01	Yaroslavl	Russia	36	8	8	16	28	....	....	....	....	....	....	....	....	....	10	4	1	5	8	....	....	....	....
2001-02	Yaroslavl	Russia	9	3	2	5	6	....	....	....	....	....	....	....	....	....	7	0	0	0	4	....	....	....	....
2002-03	Yaroslavl	Russia	44	10	18	28	10	....	....	....	....	....	....	....	....	....	7	0	1	1	2	....	....	....	....
2003-04	**Chicago**	**NHL**	**18**	**1**	**3**	**4**	**4**	**1**	**0**	**1**	**20**	**5.0**	**1**	**0**	**0.0**	**12:48**	....	....	....	....	....	....	....	....	....
	Norfolk Admirals	AHL	57	13	16	29	8	....	....	....	....	....	....	....	....	....	4	0	0	0	0	....	....	....	....
2004-05	Norfolk Admirals	AHL	79	19	25	44	48	....	....	....	....	....	....	....	....	....	6	2	1	3	4	....	....	....	....
2005-06	**Chicago**	**NHL**	**39**	**9**	**12**	**21**	**34**	**2**	**0**	**0**	**87**	**10.3**	**–2**	**8**	**37.5**	**14:18**	....	....	....	....	....	....	....	....	....
	Norfolk Admirals	AHL	32	9	16	25	23	....	....	....	....	....	....	....	....	....	4	1	2	3	0	....	....	....	....
	NHL Totals		**57**	**10**	**15**	**25**	**38**	**3**	**0**	**1**	**107**	**9.3**		**8**	**37.5**	**13:50**	....	....	....	....	....	....	....	....	....

VRBATA, Radim
(vuhr-BA-tuh, RA-dihm) **CHI.**

Right wing. Shoots right. 6'1", 190 lbs. Born, Mlada Boleslav, Czech., June 13, 1981. Colorado's 10th choice, 212th overall, in 1999 Entry Draft.

			Regular Season														Playoffs								
Season	Club	League	GP	G	A	Pts	PIM	PP	SH	GW	S	%	+/-	TF	F%	Min	GP	G	A	Pts	PIM	PP	SH	GW	Min
1997-98	Ml. Boleslav Jr.	CzRep-Jr.	35	42	31	73	4	....	....	....	....	....	....	....	....	....	....	....	....	....	....	....	....	....	....
1998-99	Hull Olympiques	QMJHL	54	22	38	60	16	....	....	....	....	....	....	....	....	....	23	6	13	19	6	....	....	....	....
99-2000	Hull Olympiques	QMJHL	58	29	45	74	26	....	....	....	....	....	....	....	....	....	15	3	9	12	8	....	....	....	....
2000-01	Shawinigan	QMJHL	55	56	64	120	67	....	....	....	....	....	....	....	....	....	10	4	7	11	4	....	....	....	....
	Hershey Bears	AHL	....	....	....	....	....	....	....	....	....	....	....	....	....	....	1	0	1	1	2	....	....	....	....
2001-02	**Colorado**	**NHL**	**52**	**18**	**12**	**30**	**14**	**6**	**0**	**3**	**112**	**16.1**	**7**	**8**	**37.5**	**14:32**	**9**	**0**	**0**	**0**	**0**	**0**	**0**	**0**	**13:05**
	Hershey Bears	AHL	20	8	14	22	8	....	....	....	....	....	....	....	....	....	....	....	....	....	....	....	....	....	....
2002-03	**Colorado**	**NHL**	**66**	**11**	**19**	**30**	**16**	**3**	**0**	**4**	**171**	**6.4**	**0**	**14**	**50.0**	**13:55**	....	....	....	....	....	....	....	....	....
	Carolina	**NHL**	**10**	**5**	**0**	**5**	**2**	**3**	**0**	**0**	**44**	**11.4**	**–7**	**15**	**46.7**	**19:00**	....	....	....	....	....	....	....	....	....
2003-04	**Carolina**	**NHL**	**80**	**12**	**13**	**25**	**24**	**4**	**0**	**2**	**195**	**6.2**	**–10**	**21**	**38.1**	**13:42**	....	....	....	....	....	....	....	....	....
2004-05	Liberec	CzRep	45	18	21	39	91	....	....	....	....	....	....	....	....	....	12	3	2	5	0	....	....	....	....
2005-06	**Carolina**	**NHL**	**16**	**2**	**3**	**5**	**6**	**1**	**0**	**0**	**38**	**5.3**	**0**	**3**	**33.3**	**12:37**	....	....	....	....	....	....	....	....	....
	Chicago	**NHL**	**45**	**13**	**21**	**34**	**16**	**5**	**0**	**0**	**147**	**8.8**	**4**	**6**	**50.0**	**15:43**	....	....	....	....	....	....	....	....	....
	NHL Totals		**269**	**61**	**68**	**129**	**78**	**22**	**0**	**9**	**707**	**8.6**		**67**	**43.3**	**14:23**	**9**	**0**	**0**	**0**	**0**	**0**	**0**	**0**	**13:05**

QMJHL First All-Star Team (2001)

Traded to **Carolina** by **Colorado** for Bates Battaglia, March 11, 2003. Signed as a free agent by **Liberec** (CzRep), September 4, 2004. Traded to **Chicago** by **Carolina** for Chicago's 4th round choice (later traded to St. Louis) in 2007 Entry Draft, December 29, 2005.

VYBORNY, David
(vih-BOHR-nee, DAY-vihd) **CBJ**

Right wing. Shoots left. 5'10", 189 lbs. Born, Jihlava, Czech., January 22, 1975. Edmonton's 3rd choice, 33rd overall, in 1993 Entry Draft.

			Regular Season														Playoffs								
Season	Club	League	GP	G	A	Pts	PIM	PP	SH	GW	S	%	+/-	TF	F%	Min	GP	G	A	Pts	PIM	PP	SH	GW	Min
1991-92	HC Sparta Praha	Czech	32	6	9	15	2	....	....	....	....	....	....	....	....	....	....	....	....	....	....	....	....	....	....
1992-93	HC Sparta Praha	Czech	52	20	24	44	....	....	....	....	....	....	....	....	....	....	....	....	....	....	....	....	....	....	....
1993-94	HC Sparta Praha	CzRep	44	15	20	35	0	....	....	....	....	....	....	....	....	....	6	4	7	11	0	....	....	....	....
1994-95	Cape Breton	AHL	76	23	38	61	30	....	....	....	....	....	....	....	....	....	....	....	....	....	....	....	....	....	....
1995-96	HC Sparta Praha	CzRep	40	12	18	30	....	....	....	....	....	....	....	....	....	....	12	6	5	11	....	....	....	....	....
1996-97	HC Sparta Praha	CzRep	47	20	29	49	14	....	....	....	....	....	....	....	....	....	10	7	7	14	6	....	....	....	....
1997-98	MoDo	Sweden	45	16	21	37	34	....	....	....	....	....	....	....	....	....	9	0	2	2	2	....	....	....	....
1998-99	HC Sparta Praha	CzRep	52	24	*46	*70	22	....	....	....	....	....	....	....	....	....	8	1	3	4	....	....	....	....	....
99-2000	HC Sparta Praha	CzRep	50	25	38	63	30	....	....	....	....	....	....	....	....	....	9	3	*8	*11	4	....	....	....	....
2000-01	**Columbus**	**NHL**	**79**	**13**	**19**	**32**	**22**	**5**	**0**	**1**	**125**	**10.4**	**–9**	**36**	**44.4**	**15:25**	....	....	....	....	....	....	....	....	....
2001-02	**Columbus**	**NHL**	**75**	**13**	**18**	**31**	**6**	**6**	**0**	**2**	**103**	**12.6**	**–14**	**25**	**44.0**	**15:27**	....	....	....	....	....	....	....	....	....
2002-03	**Columbus**	**NHL**	**79**	**20**	**26**	**46**	**16**	**4**	**1**	**4**	**125**	**16.0**	**12**	**46**	**32.6**	**16:20**	....	....	....	....	....	....	....	....	....
2003-04	**Columbus**	**NHL**	**82**	**22**	**31**	**53**	**40**	**8**	**4**	**2**	**158**	**13.9**	**–26**	**97**	**21.7**	**20:23**	....	....	....	....	....	....	....	....	....
2004-05	HC Sparta Praha	CzRep	51	12	34	46	10	....	....	....	....	....	....	....	....	....	5	2	5	7	4	....	....	....	....
2005-06	**Columbus**	**NHL**	**80**	**22**	**43**	**65**	**50**	**5**	**2**	**6**	**145**	**15.2**	**–9**	**292**	**30.1**	**20:41**	....	....	....	....	....	....	....	....	....
	Czech Republic	Olympics	8	1	3	4	0	....	....	....	....	....	....	....	....	....	....	....	....	....	....	....	....	....	....
	NHL Totals		**395**	**90**	**137**	**227**	**134**	**28**	**7**	**15**	**656**	**13.7**		**496**	**30.4**	**17:42**	....	....	....	....	....	....	....	....	....

Signed as a free agent by **Columbus**, June 8, 2000. Signed as a free agent by **Sparta Praha** (CzRep), August 9, 2004.

WALKER, Matt
(WAH-kuhr, MAT) **ST.L.**

Defense. Shoots right. 6'3", 227 lbs. Born, Beaverlodge, Alta., April 7, 1980. St. Louis' 3rd choice, 83rd overall, in 1998 Entry Draft.

			Regular Season														Playoffs								
Season	Club	League	GP	G	A	Pts	PIM	PP	SH	GW	S	%	+/-	TF	F%	Min	GP	G	A	Pts	PIM	PP	SH	GW	Min
1996-97	Grand Prairie	AAHA	68	22	62	74	186	....	....	....	....	....	....	....	....	....	....	....	....	....	....	....	....	....	....
1997-98	Portland	WHL	64	2	13	15	124	....	....	....	....	....	....	....	....	....	16	0	0	0	21	....	....	....	....
1998-99	Portland	WHL	64	1	10	11	151	....	....	....	....	....	....	....	....	....	4	0	1	1	6	....	....	....	....
99-2000	Portland	WHL	38	2	7	9	97	....	....	....	....	....	....	....	....	....	....	....	....	....	....	....	....	....	....
	Kootenay Ice	WHL	31	4	19	23	53	....	....	....	....	....	....	....	....	....	21	5	13	18	24	....	....	....	....
2000-01	Worcester IceCats	AHL	61	4	8	12	131	....	....	....	....	....	....	....	....	....	11	0	0	0	6	....	....	....	....
	Peoria Rivermen	ECHL	8	1	0	1	70	....	....	....	....	....	....	....	....	....	....	....	....	....	....	....	....	....	....
2001-02	Worcester IceCats	AHL	49	2	11	13	164	....	....	....	....	....	....	....	....	....	3	0	0	0	8	....	....	....	....
2002-03	**St. Louis**	**NHL**	**16**	**0**	**1**	**1**	**38**	**0**	**0**	**0**	**13**	**0.0**	**0**	**1**	**100.0**	**11:09**	....	....	....	....	....	....	....	....	....
	Worcester IceCats	AHL	40	1	8	9	58	....	....	....	....	....	....	....	....	....	....	....	....	....	....	....	....	....	....
2003-04	**St. Louis**	**NHL**	**14**	**0**	**1**	**1**	**25**	**0**	**0**	**0**	**8**	**0.0**	**0**	**0**	**0.0**	**11:23**	**4**	**0**	**0**	**0**	**0**	**0**	**0**	**0**	**9:43**
	Worcester IceCats	AHL	4	0	1	1	7	....	....	....	....	....	....	....	....	....	....	....	....	....	....	....	....	....	....
2004-05	Worcester IceCats	AHL	20	2	4	6	44	....	....	....	....	....	....	....	....	....	....	....	....	....	....	....	....	....	....
2005-06	**St. Louis**	**NHL**	**54**	**0**	**2**	**2**	**79**	**0**	**0**	**0**	**59**	**0.0**	**–7**	**0**	**0.0**	**14:15**	....	....	....	....	....	....	....	....	....
	NHL Totals		**84**	**0**	**4**	**4**	**142**	**0**	**0**	**0**	**80**	**0.0**		**1**	**100.0**	**13:11**	**4**	**0**	**0**	**0**	**0**	**0**	**0**	**0**	**9:43**

• Missed majority of 2003-04 season recovering from groin injury suffered in training camp, September 23, 2003.

WALKER, Scott
(WAH-kuhr, SKAWT) **CAR.**

Right wing. Shoots right. 5'10", 196 lbs. Born, Cambridge, Ont., July 19, 1973. Vancouver's 4th choice, 124th overall, in 1993 Entry Draft.

			Regular Season														Playoffs								
Season	Club	League	GP	G	A	Pts	PIM	PP	SH	GW	S	%	+/-	TF	F%	Min	GP	G	A	Pts	PIM	PP	SH	GW	Min
1989-90	Kitchener	OHA-B	6	0	5	5	4	....	....	....	....	....	....	....	....	....	....	....	....	....	....	....	....	....	....
	Cambridge	OHA-B	27	7	22	29	87	....	....	....	....	....	....	....	....	....	....	....	....	....	....	....	....	....	....
1990-91	Cambridge	OHA-B	45	10	27	37	241	....	....	....	....	....	....	....	....	....	....	....	....	....	....	....	....	....	....
1991-92	Owen Sound	OHL	53	7	31	38	128	....	....	....	....	....	....	....	....	....	5	0	7	7	8	....	....	....	....
1992-93	Owen Sound	OHL	57	23	68	91	110	....	....	....	....	....	....	....	....	....	8	1	5	6	16	....	....	....	....
1993-94	Hamilton	AHL	77	10	29	39	272	....	....	....	....	....	....	....	....	....	4	0	1	1	25	....	....	....	....
1994-95	Syracuse Crunch	AHL	74	14	38	52	334	....	....	....	....	....	....	....	....	....	....	....	....	....	....	....	....	....	....
	Vancouver	**NHL**	**11**	**0**	**1**	**1**	**33**	**0**	**0**	**0**	**8**	**0.0**	**0**	....	....	....	....	....	....	....	....	....	....	....	....

			Regular Season														Playoffs								
Season	Club	League	GP	G	A	Pts	PIM	PP	SH	GW	S	%	+/-	TF	F%	Min	GP	G	A	Pts	PIM	PP	SH	GW	Min
1995-96	**Vancouver**	**NHL**	63	4	8	12	137	0	1	1	45	8.9	–7												
	Syracuse Crunch	AHL	15	3	12	15	52										16	9	8	17	39				
1996-97	**Vancouver**	**NHL**	64	3	15	18	132	0	0	0	55	5.5	2												
1997-98	**Vancouver**	**NHL**	59	3	10	13	164	0	1	1	40	7.5	–8												
1998-99	**Nashville**	**NHL**	71	15	25	40	103	0	1	2	96	15.6	0	265	48.3	16:21									
99-2000	**Nashville**	**NHL**	69	7	21	28	90	0	1	0	98	7.1	–16	30	36.7	15:49									
2000-01	**Nashville**	**NHL**	74	25	29	54	66	9	3	1	159	15.7	–2	541	51.4	19:17									
2001-02	**Nashville**	**NHL**	28	4	5	9	18	1	0	0	46	8.7	–13	149	38.9	18:38									
2002-03	**Nashville**	**NHL**	60	15	18	33	58	7	0	5	124	12.1	2	336	49.1	19:50									
2003-04	**Nashville**	**NHL**	75	25	42	67	94	9	3	3	157	15.9	4	367	41.4	20:03	6	0	1	1	6	0	0	0	20:10
2004-05	Cambridge	OHA-Sr.	5	2	6	8	4																		
	Dundas	OHA-Sr.	3	3	2	5	8																		
2005-06	**Nashville**	**NHL**	33	5	11	16	36	1	0	0	57	8.8	2	87	44.8	17:23	5	0	0	0	6	0	0	0	16:01
	NHL Totals		607	106	185	291	931	27	10	13	885	12.0		1775	46.8	18:13	11	0	1	1	12	0	0	0	18:16

OHL Second All-Star Team (1993)

Claimed by **Nashville** from **Vancouver** in Expansion Draft, June 26, 1998. Signed as a free agent by **Cambridge** (OHA-Sr.), October 21, 2004. Signed as a free agent by **Dundas** (OHA-Sr.), February 10, 2005. • Missed majority of 2005-06 season recovering from sports hernia injury (October, 2005) and wrist injury suffered in game at Dallas (February 6, 2006). Traded to **Carolina** by **Nashville** for Josef Vasicek, July 18, 2006.

WALLIN, Niclas

(VAH-lihn, NIH-kluhs) **CAR.**

Defense. Shoots left. 6'3", 220 lbs. Born, Boden, Sweden, February 20, 1975. Carolina's 3rd choice, 97th overall, in 2000 Entry Draft.

Season	Club	League	GP	G	A	Pts	PIM	PP	SH	GW	S	%	+/-	TF	F%	Min	GP	G	A	Pts	PIM	PP	SH	GW	Min
1994-95	Bodens IK	Swe-Jr.	30	2	13	15	125																		
	Bodens IK	Sweden-2	13	0	0	0	0										2	0	0	0	0				
1995-96	Bodens IK	Swe-Jr.	2	2	2	4	0																		
	Bodens IK	Sweden-2	30	2	7	9	26										2	0	1	1	2				
1996-97	Brynas IF Gavle	Sweden	47	1	1	2	14																		
1997-98	Brynas IF Gavle	Sweden	44	2	3	5	57										3	0	1	1	4				
1998-99	Brynas IF Gavle	Sweden	46	2	4	6	52										14	0	1	1	8				
99-2000	Brynas IF Gavle	Sweden	48	7	9	16	73										11	2	1	3	14				
	Brynas IF Gavle	EuroHL	5	1	1	2	10																		
2000-01	**Carolina**	**NHL**	37	2	3	5	21	0	0	0	19	10.5	–11	0	0.0	14:57	3	0	0	0	2	0	0	0	19:10
	Cincinnati	IHL	8	1	2	3	4										3	0	0	0	2				
2001-02	**Carolina**	**NHL**	52	1	2	3	36	0	0	0	33	3.0	1	0	0.0	12:12	23	2	1	3	12	0	0	2	15:26
2002-03	**Carolina**	**NHL**	77	2	8	10	71	0	0	2	69	2.9	–19	0	0.0	16:12									
2003-04	**Carolina**	**NHL**	57	3	7	10	51	0	0	0	74	4.1	–8	0	0.0	18:40									
2004-05	Lulea HF	Sweden	39	6	7	13	89										3	0	1	1	6				
2005-06♦	**Carolina**	**NHL**	50	4	4	8	42	0	0	0	44	9.1	2	0	0.0	16:50	25	1	4	5	14	0	0	1	16:39
	NHL Totals		273	12	24	36	221	0	0	2	239	5.0		0	0.0	15:54	51	3	5	8	28	0	0	3	16:15

Signed as a free agent by **Lulea** (Sweden), September 19, 2004.

WALLIN, Rickard

(WAHL-in, RIH-kahrd)

Center. Shoots left. 6'2", 185 lbs. Born, Stockholm, Sweden, April 19, 1980. Phoenix's 8th choice, 160th overall, in 1998 Entry Draft.

Season	Club	League	GP	G	A	Pts	PIM	PP	SH	GW	S	%	+/-	TF	F%	Min	GP	G	A	Pts	PIM	PP	SH	GW	Min
1996-97	Vasteras IK Jr.	Swe-Jr.	26	3	3	6																			
1997-98	Farjestad Jr.	Swe-Jr.	29	20	30	50	32										2	1	1	2	2				
1998-99	Farjestad Jr.	Swe-Jr.	21	11	15	26	30																		
	Farjestad	Sweden	5	0	0	0	0																		
99-2000	IF Troja-Ljungby	Sweden-2	46	15	22	37	54																		
2000-01	Farjestad	Sweden	47	9	22	31	24										16	11	3	14	4				
2001-02	Farjestad	Sweden	50	12	31	43	56										10	4	9	13	8				
2002-03	**Minnesota**	**NHL**	4	1	0	1	0	0	0	1	1	100.0	1	28	53.6	7:44									
	Houston Aeros	AHL	52	13	22	35	70										23	4	11	15	22				
2003-04	**Minnesota**	**NHL**	15	5	4	9	14	3	0	1	16	31.3	1	189	45.5	14:20									
	Houston Aeros	AHL	47	14	18	32	36										2	0	0	0	2				
2004-05	Houston Aeros	AHL	79	12	31	43	61										5	1	0	1	29				
2005-06	Farjestad	Sweden	50	11	19	30	82										18	6	3	9	28				
	NHL Totals		19	6	4	10	14	3	0	2	17	35.3		217	46.5	12:56									

Rights traded to **Minnesota** by **Phoenix** for Joe Juneau, June 23, 2000. Reassigned to **Farjestad** (Sweden) by **Minnesota**, September 22, 2005. Signed as a free agent by **Lugano** (Swiss), July 23, 2006.

WALSER, Derrick

(WAHL-zuhr, DEHR-rihk) **CAR.**

Defense. Shoots left. 5'10", 196 lbs. Born, New Glasgow, N.S., May 12, 1978.

Season	Club	League	GP	G	A	Pts	PIM	PP	SH	GW	S	%	+/-	TF	F%	Min	GP	G	A	Pts	PIM	PP	SH	GW	Min
1994-95	Beauport	QMJHL	48	4	18	22	34										12	2	5	7	2				
1995-96	Beauport	QMJHL	69	9	31	40	56										20	2	11	13	16				
1996-97	Beauport	QMJHL	37	13	25	38	26																		
	Rimouski Oceanic	QMJHL	31	15	30	45	44										4	2	2	4	6				
1997-98	Rimouski Oceanic	QMJHL	70	41	69	110	135										18	10	*26	36	49				
1998-99	Saint John Flames	AHL	40	3	7	10	24																		
	Johnstown Chiefs	ECHL	24	8	12	20	29																		
99-2000	Saint John Flames	AHL	14	2	3	5	10																		
	Johnstown Chiefs	ECHL	54	17	26	43	104										7	3	3	6	8				
2000-01	Saint John Flames	AHL	76	19	36	55	36										19	7	9	16	14				
2001-02	**Columbus**	**NHL**	2	1	0	1	0	0	0	0	2	50.0	–2	0	0.0	16:18									
	Syracuse Crunch	AHL	73	23	38	61	70										10	1	5	6	12				
2002-03	**Columbus**	**NHL**	53	4	13	17	34	3	0	2	86	4.7	–9	1	100.0	14:52									
	Syracuse Crunch	AHL	28	7	14	21	30																		
2003-04	**Columbus**	**NHL**	27	1	8	9	22	1	0	0	35	2.9	–6	0	0.0	18:23									
	Syracuse Crunch	AHL	48	10	26	36	82										3	1	1	2	4				
2004-05	Eisbaren Berlin	Germany	50	9	14	23	143										12	4	4	8	20				
2005-06	Eisbaren Berlin	Germany	48	19	24	43	120										11	6	1	7	20				
	NHL Totals		82	6	21	27	56	4	0	2	123	4.9		1	100.0	16:03									

QMJHL First All-Star Team (1997, 1998) • Emile Bouchard Trophy (Top Defenseman – QMJHL) (1998) • Canadian Major Junior First All-Star Team (1998) • Canadian Major Junior Defenseman of the Year (1998)

Signed as a free agent by **Calgary**, October 16, 1998. Signed as a free agent by **Columbus**, September 17, 2001. Signed as a free agent by **Berlin** (Germany), May 13, 2004. Rights traded to **Carolina** by **Columbus** with Columbus' 4th round choice (later traded to Toronto - Toronto selected James Reimer) in 2006 Entry Draft for Carolina's 4th round choice (Jared Boll) in 2005 Entry Draft, July 30, 2005.

WALTER, Ben

(WAHL-tuhr, BEHN) **BOS.**

Center. Shoots left. 6'1", 195 lbs. Born, Beaconsfield, Que., May 11, 1984. Boston's 5th choice, 160th overall, in 2004 Entry Draft.

Season	Club	League	GP	G	A	Pts	PIM	PP	SH	GW	S	%	+/-	TF	F%	Min	GP	G	A	Pts	PIM	PP	SH	GW	Min
2000-01	Langley Hornets	BCHL	50	8	22	30	19																		
2001-02	Langley Hornets	BCHL	50	29	47	76	29																		
2002-03	U. Mass-Lowell	H-East	35	5	12	17	12																		
2003-04	U. Mass-Lowell	H-East	36	18	16	34	18																		
2004-05	U. Mass-Lowell	H-East	36	*26	13	39	28																		
2005-06	**Boston**	**NHL**	6	0	0	0	4	0	0	0	6	0.0	2	32	53.1	11:49									
	Providence Bruins	AHL	62	16	25	41	33										3	2	0	2	2				
	NHL Totals		6	0	0	0	4	0	0	0	6	0.0		32	53.1	11:49									

Hockey East Second All-Star Team (2005)

WALZ, Wes

(WAHLZ, WEHS) **MIN.**

Center. Shoots right. 5'10", 180 lbs. Born, Calgary, Alta., May 15, 1970. Boston's 3rd choice, 57th overall, in 1989 Entry Draft.

Season	Club	League	GP	G	A	Pts	PIM	PP	SH	GW	S	%	+/-	TF	F%	Min	GP	G	A	Pts	PIM	PP	SH	GW	Min
1987-88	Cgy. North Stars	AMHL	35	47	52	99	72																		
	Prince Albert	WHL	1	1	1	2	0																		
1988-89	Lethbridge	WHL	63	29	75	104	32										8	1	5	6	6				
1989-90	Lethbridge	WHL	56	54	86	140	69										19	13	*24	*37	33				
	Boston	**NHL**	2	1	1	2	0	1	0	0	1	100.0	–1												

			Regular Season														Playoffs								
Season	Club	League	GP	G	A	Pts	PIM	PP	SH	GW	S	%	+/-	TF	F%	Min	GP	G	A	Pts	PIM	PP	SH	GW	Min
1990-91	**Boston**	**NHL**	**56**	**8**	**8**	**16**	**32**	**1**	**0**	**1**	**57**	**14.0**	**–14**	....	....	....	**2**	**0**	**0**	**0**	**0**	**0**	**0**	**0**	....
	Maine Mariners	AHL	20	8	12	20	19	....	....	....	....	....	....	....	....	....	2	0	0	0	21	....	....	....	....
1991-92	**Boston**	**NHL**	**15**	**0**	**3**	**3**	**12**	**0**	**0**	**0**	**17**	**0.0**	**–3**	....	....	....	....	....	....	....	....	....	....	....	....
	Maine Mariners	AHL	21	13	11	24	38	....	....	....	....	....	....	....	....	....	....	....	....	....	....	....	....	....	....
	Philadelphia	**NHL**	**2**	**1**	**0**	**1**	**0**	**0**	**0**	**1**	**2**	**50.0**	**1**	....	....	....	....	....	....	....	....	....	....	....	....
	Hershey Bears	AHL	41	13	28	41	37	....	....	....	....	....	....	....	....	....	6	1	2	3	0	....	....	....	....
1992-93	Hershey Bears	AHL	78	35	45	80	106	....	....	....	....	....	....	....	....	....	....	....	....	....	....	....	....	....	....
1993-94	**Calgary**	**NHL**	**53**	**11**	**27**	**38**	**16**	**1**	**0**	**0**	**79**	**13.9**	**20**	....	....	....	**6**	**3**	**0**	**3**	**2**	**0**	**0**	**0**	....
	Saint John Flames	AHL	15	6	6	12	14	....	....	....	....	....	....	....	....	....	....	....	....	....	....	....	....	....	....
1994-95	**Calgary**	**NHL**	**39**	**6**	**12**	**18**	**11**	**4**	**0**	**1**	**73**	**8.2**	**7**	....	....	....	**1**	**0**	**0**	**0**	**0**	**0**	**0**	**0**	....
1995-96	**Detroit**	**NHL**	**2**	**0**	**0**	**0**	**0**	**0**	**0**	**0**	**2**	**0.0**	**0**	....	....	....	....	....	....	....	....	....	....	....	....
	Adirondack	AHL	38	20	35	55	58	....	....	....	....	....	....	....	....	....	....	....	....	....	....	....	....	....	....
1996-97	EV Zug	Swiss	41	24	22	46	67	....	....	....	....	....	....	....	....	....	9	5	1	6	39	....	....	....	....
1997-98	EV Zug	Swiss	38	18	34	52	32	....	....	....	....	....	....	....	....	....	20	*16	*12	*28	18	....	....	....	....
	EV Zug	EuroHL	5	1	3	4	10	....	....	....	....	....	....	....	....	....	....	....	....	....	....	....	....	....	....
1998-99	EV Zug	Swiss	42	22	27	49	75	....	....	....	....	....	....	....	....	....	10	3	9	12	2	....	....	....	....
	EV Zug	EuroHL	6	7	5	12	4	....	....	....	....	....	....	....	....	....	2	0	0	0	12	....	....	....	....
99-2000	Long Beach	IHL	6	4	3	7	8	....	....	....	....	....	....	....	....	....	....	....	....	....	....	....	....	....	....
	HC Lugano	Swiss	13	7	11	18	14	....	....	....	....	....	....	....	....	....	5	3	4	7	4	....	....	....	....
2000-01	**Minnesota**	**NHL**	**82**	**18**	**12**	**30**	**37**	**0**	**7**	**3**	**152**	**11.8**	**–8**	**1533**	**47.2**	**16:45**	....	....	....	....	....	....	....	....	....
2001-02	**Minnesota**	**NHL**	**64**	**10**	**20**	**30**	**43**	**0**	**2**	**5**	**97**	**10.3**	**0**	**1231**	**44.8**	**16:42**	....	....	....	....	....	....	....	....	....
2002-03	**Minnesota**	**NHL**	**80**	**13**	**19**	**32**	**63**	**0**	**0**	**4**	**115**	**11.3**	**11**	**1505**	**50.4**	**15:56**	**18**	**7**	**6**	**13**	**14**	**0**	**2**	**2**	**17:24**
2003-04	**Minnesota**	**NHL**	**57**	**12**	**13**	**25**	**32**	**0**	**3**	**2**	**70**	**17.1**	**5**	**909**	**46.3**	**16:18**	....	....	....	....	....	....	....	....	....
2004-05			DID NOT PLAY																						
2005-06	**Minnesota**	**NHL**	**82**	**19**	**18**	**37**	**61**	**1**	**1**	**0**	**127**	**15.0**	**7**	**1119**	**46.9**	**15:54**	....	....	....	....	....	....	....	....	....
	NHL Totals		**534**	**99**	**133**	**232**	**307**	**8**	**13**	**17**	**792**	**12.5**		**6297**	**47.3**	**16:18**	**27**	**10**	**6**	**16**	**16**	**0**	**2**	**2**	**17:24**

WHL Rookie of the Year (1989) • WHL East First All-Star Team (1990)

Traded to **Philadelphia** by **Boston** with Garry Galley and Boston's 3rd round choice (Milos Holan) in 1993 Entry Draft for Gord Murphy, Brian Dobbin, Philadelphia's 3rd round choice (Sergei Zholtok) in 1992 Entry Draft and Philadelphia's 4th round choice (Charles Paquette) in 1993 Entry Draft, January 2, 1992. Signed as a free agent by **Calgary**, August 26, 1993. Signed as a free agent by **Detroit**, September 6, 1995. Signed as a free agent by **Long Beach** (IHL), October 12, 1999. Signed as a free agent by **Minnesota**, June 28, 2000.

WANVIG, Kyle

(WEHN-vihg, KIGHL) **ATL.**

Right wing. Shoots right. 6'2", 219 lbs. Born, Calgary, Alta., January 29, 1981. Minnesota's 2nd choice, 36th overall, in 2001 Entry Draft.

			Regular Season														Playoffs								
Season	Club	League	GP	G	A	Pts	PIM	PP	SH	GW	S	%	+/-	TF	F%	Min	GP	G	A	Pts	PIM	PP	SH	GW	Min
1996-97	Calgary Blazers	AMHL	26	31	48	79	85	....	....	....	....	....	....	....	....	....	....	....	....	....	....	....	....	....	....
1997-98	Edmonton Ice	WHL	62	17	12	29	69	....	....	....	....	....	....	....	....	....	....	....	....	....	....	....	....	....	....
1998-99	Kootenay Ice	WHL	71	12	20	32	119	....	....	....	....	....	....	....	....	....	7	1	3	4	18	....	....	....	....
99-2000	Kootenay Ice	WHL	6	2	2	4	12	....	....	....	....	....	....	....	....	....	....	....	....	....	....	....	....	....	....
	Red Deer Rebels	WHL	58	21	18	39	123	....	....	....	....	....	....	....	....	....	4	1	0	1	4	....	....	....	....
2000-01	Red Deer Rebels	WHL	69	55	46	101	202	....	....	....	....	....	....	....	....	....	22	10	12	22	47	....	....	....	....
2001-02	Houston Aeros	AHL	34	6	7	13	43	....	....	....	....	....	....	....	....	....	9	0	1	1	23	....	....	....	....
2002-03	**Minnesota**	**NHL**	**7**	**1**	**0**	**1**	**13**	**0**	**0**	**0**	**5**	**20.0**	**0**	**1**	**100.0**	**9:14**	....	....	....	....	....	....	....	....	....
	Houston Aeros	AHL	57	13	16	29	137	....	....	....	....	....	....	....	....	....	21	6	4	10	27	....	....	....	....
2003-04	**Minnesota**	**NHL**	**6**	**0**	**1**	**1**	**10**	**0**	**0**	**0**	**16**	**0.0**	**–2**	**4**	**75.0**	**13:48**	....	....	....	....	....	....	....	....	....
	Houston Aeros	AHL	72	25	16	41	147	....	....	....	....	....	....	....	....	....	2	0	1	1	0	....	....	....	....
2004-05	Houston Aeros	AHL	76	13	17	30	158	....	....	....	....	....	....	....	....	....	5	1	2	3	8	....	....	....	....
2005-06	**Minnesota**	**NHL**	**51**	**4**	**8**	**12**	**64**	**1**	**0**	**0**	**55**	**7.3**	**–8**	**26**	**46.2**	**10:39**	....	....	....	....	....	....	....	....	....
	NHL Totals		**64**	**5**	**9**	**14**	**87**	**1**	**0**	**0**	**76**	**6.6**		**31**	**51.6**	**10:48**	....	....	....	....	....	....	....	....	....

• Re-entered NHL Entry Draft. Originally Boston's 3rd choice, 89th overall, in 1999 Entry Draft.

WHL East Second All-Star Team (2001) • Memorial Cup Tournament All-Star Team (2001) • Stafford Smythe Memorial Trophy (Memorial Cup Tournament MVP) (2001)

• Missed majority of 2001-02 season recovering from ankle injury suffered in game vs. Grand Rapids (AHL), December 30, 2001. Signed as a free agent by **Atlanta**, July 18, 2006.

WARD, Aaron

(WOHRD, AIR-ruhn) **NYR**

Defense. Shoots right. 6'2", 225 lbs. Born, Windsor, Ont., January 17, 1973. Winnipeg's 1st choice, 5th overall, in 1991 Entry Draft.

			Regular Season														Playoffs								
Season	Club	League	GP	G	A	Pts	PIM	PP	SH	GW	S	%	+/-	TF	F%	Min	GP	G	A	Pts	PIM	PP	SH	GW	Min
1988-89	Nepean Raiders	CJHL	54	1	14	15	40	....	....	....	....	....	....	....	....	....	....	....	....	....	....	....	....	....	....
1989-90	Nepean Raiders	CJHL	52	6	33	39	85	....	....	....	....	....	....	....	....	....	....	....	....	....	....	....	....	....	....
1990-91	U. of Michigan	CCHA	46	8	11	19	126	....	....	....	....	....	....	....	....	....	....	....	....	....	....	....	....	....	....
1991-92	U. of Michigan	CCHA	42	7	12	19	64	....	....	....	....	....	....	....	....	....	....	....	....	....	....	....	....	....	....
1992-93	U. of Michigan	CCHA	30	5	8	13	73	....	....	....	....	....	....	....	....	....	....	....	....	....	....	....	....	....	....
1993-94	**Detroit**	**NHL**	**5**	**1**	**0**	**1**	**4**	**0**	**0**	**0**	**3**	**33.3**	**2**	....	....	....	....	....	....	....	....	....	....	....	....
	Adirondack	AHL	58	4	12	16	87	....	....	....	....	....	....	....	....	....	9	2	6	8	6	....	....	....	....
1994-95	Adirondack	AHL	76	11	24	35	87	....	....	....	....	....	....	....	....	....	4	0	1	1	0	....	....	....	....
	Detroit	**NHL**	**1**	**0**	**1**	**1**	**2**	**0**	**0**	**0**	**0**	**0.0**	**1**	....	....	....	....	....	....	....	....	....	....	....	....
1995-96	Adirondack	AHL	74	5	10	15	133	....	....	....	....	....	....	....	....	....	3	0	0	0	6	....	....	....	....
1996-97 ♦	**Detroit**	**NHL**	**49**	**2**	**5**	**7**	**52**	**0**	**0**	**0**	**40**	**5.0**	**–9**	....	....	....	**19**	**0**	**0**	**0**	**17**	**0**	**0**	**0**	....
1997-98 ♦	**Detroit**	**NHL**	**52**	**5**	**5**	**10**	**47**	**0**	**0**	**1**	**47**	**10.6**	**–1**	....	....	....	....	....	....	....	....	....	....	....	....
1998-99	**Detroit**	**NHL**	**60**	**3**	**8**	**11**	**52**	**0**	**0**	**0**	**46**	**6.5**	**–5**	**0**	**0.0**	**13:55**	**8**	**0**	**1**	**1**	**8**	**0**	**0**	**0**	**10:15**
99-2000	**Detroit**	**NHL**	**36**	**1**	**3**	**4**	**24**	**0**	**0**	**0**	**25**	**4.0**	**–4**	**0**	**0.0**	**12:36**	**3**	**0**	**0**	**0**	**0**	**0**	**0**	**0**	**7:36**
2000-01	**Detroit**	**NHL**	**73**	**4**	**5**	**9**	**57**	**0**	**0**	**1**	**48**	**8.3**	**–4**	**0**	**0.0**	**17:00**	....	....	....	....	....	....	....	....	....
2001-02	**Carolina**	**NHL**	**79**	**3**	**11**	**14**	**74**	**0**	**0**	**2**	**69**	**4.3**	**0**	**1**	**100.0**	**19:40**	**23**	**1**	**1**	**2**	**22**	**0**	**0**	**0**	**21:12**
2002-03	**Carolina**	**NHL**	**77**	**3**	**6**	**9**	**90**	**0**	**0**	**1**	**66**	**4.5**	**–23**	**0**	**0.0**	**18:43**	....	....	....	....	....	....	....	....	....
2003-04	**Carolina**	**NHL**	**49**	**3**	**5**	**8**	**37**	**2**	**0**	**0**	**51**	**5.9**	**1**	**0**	**0.0**	**17:52**	....	....	....	....	....	....	....	....	....
2004-05	ERC Ingolstadt	Germany	8	0	3	3	16	....	....	....	....	....	....	....	....	....	11	1	1	2	16	....	....	....	....
2005-06 ♦	**Carolina**	**NHL**	**71**	**6**	**19**	**25**	**62**	**0**	**0**	**1**	**60**	**10.0**	**2**	**1**	**0.0**	**19:07**	**25**	**2**	**3**	**5**	**18**	**0**	**0**	**0**	**21:42**
	NHL Totals		**552**	**31**	**68**	**99**	**501**	**2**	**0**	**6**	**455**	**6.8**		**2**	**50.0**	**17:26**	**78**	**3**	**5**	**8**	**65**	**0**	**0**	**0**	**19:14**

Traded to **Detroit** by **Winnipeg** with Toronto's 4th round choice (previously acquired, Detroit selected John Jakopin) in 1993 Entry Draft for Paul Ysebaert and future considerations (Alan Kerr, June 18, 1993), June 11, 1993. • Missed majority of 1999-2000 season recovering from shoulder injury suffered in game vs. Vancouver, January 19, 2000. Traded to **Carolina** by **Detroit** for Carolina's 2nd round choice (Jiri Hudler) in 2002 Entry Draft, July 9, 2001. Signed as a free agent by **Ingolstadt** (Germany), February 15, 2005. Signed as a free agent by **NY Rangers**, July 3, 2006.

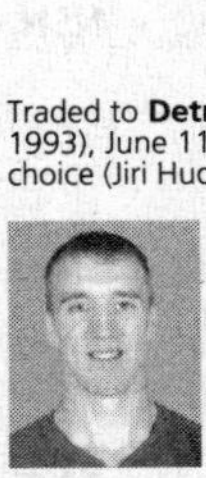

WARD, Jason

(WOHRD, JAY-suhn) **NYR**

Right wing. Shoots right. 6'2", 204 lbs. Born, Chapleau, Ont., January 16, 1979. Montreal's 1st choice, 11th overall, in 1997 Entry Draft.

			Regular Season														Playoffs								
Season	Club	League	GP	G	A	Pts	PIM	PP	SH	GW	S	%	+/-	TF	F%	Min	GP	G	A	Pts	PIM	PP	SH	GW	Min
1994-95	Oshawa	OHA-B	47	30	31	61	75	....	....	....	....	....	....	....	....	....	....	....	....	....	....	....	....	....	....
1995-96	Niagara Falls	OHL	64	15	35	50	139	....	....	....	....	....	....	....	....	....	10	6	4	10	23	....	....	....	....
1996-97	Erie Otters	OHL	58	25	39	64	137	....	....	....	....	....	....	....	....	....	5	1	2	3	2	....	....	....	....
1997-98	Erie Otters	OHL	21	7	9	16	42	....	....	....	....	....	....	....	....	....	....	....	....	....	....	....	....	....	....
	Windsor Spitfires	OHL	26	19	27	46	34	....	....	....	....	....	....	....	....	....	....	....	....	....	....	....	....	....	....
	Fredericton	AHL	7	1	0	1	2	....	....	....	....	....	....	....	....	....	1	0	0	0	2	....	....	....	....
1998-99	Windsor Spitfires	OHL	12	8	11	19	25	....	....	....	....	....	....	....	....	....	....	....	....	....	....	....	....	....	....
	Plymouth Whalers	OHL	23	14	13	27	28	....	....	....	....	....	....	....	....	....	11	6	8	14	12	....	....	....	....
	Fredericton	AHL	....	....	....	....	....	....	....	....	....	....	....	....	....	....	10	4	2	6	22	....	....	....	....
99-2000	**Montreal**	**NHL**	**32**	**2**	**1**	**3**	**10**	**1**	**0**	**0**	**24**	**8.3**	**–1**	**86**	**44.2**	**9:10**	....	....	....	....	....	....	....	....	....
	Quebec Citadelles	AHL	40	14	12	26	30	....	....	....	....	....	....	....	....	....	3	2	1	3	4	....	....	....	....
2000-01	**Montreal**	**NHL**	**12**	**0**	**0**	**0**	**12**	**0**	**0**	**0**	**4**	**0.0**	**3**	**2**	**50.0**	**8:16**	....	....	....	....	....	....	....	....	....
	Quebec Citadelles	AHL	23	7	12	19	69	....	....	....	....	....	....	....	....	....	....	....	....	....	....	....	....	....	....
2001-02	Quebec Citadelles	AHL	78	24	33	57	128	....	....	....	....	....	....	....	....	....	3	0	0	0	2	....	....	....	....
2002-03	**Montreal**	**NHL**	**8**	**3**	**2**	**5**	**0**	**0**	**0**	**0**	**10**	**30.0**	**3**	**6**	**50.0**	**11:17**	....	....	....	....	....	....	....	....	....
	Hamilton	AHL	69	31	41	72	78	....	....	....	....	....	....	....	....	....	23	*12	9	*21	20	....	....	....	....
2003-04	**Montreal**	**NHL**	**53**	**5**	**7**	**12**	**21**	**2**	**0**	**1**	**56**	**8.9**	**3**	**98**	**41.8**	**12:39**	**5**	**0**	**2**	**2**	**2**	**0**	**0**	**0**	**15:39**
	Hamilton	AHL	2	0	3	3	17	....	....	....	....	....	....	....	....	....	....	....	....	....	....	....	....	....	....
2004-05	Hamilton	AHL	77	20	34	54	66	....	....	....	....	....	....	....	....	....	4	2	1	3	2	....	....	....	....
2005-06	**NY Rangers**	**NHL**	**81**	**10**	**18**	**28**	**44**	**0**	**2**	**1**	**125**	**8.0**	**–4**	**153**	**47.7**	**13:12**	**1**	**0**	**0**	**0**	**2**	**0**	**0**	**0**	**2:39**
	NHL Totals		**186**	**20**	**28**	**48**	**87**	**3**	**2**	**2**	**219**	**9.1**		**345**	**45.2**	**11:57**	**6**	**0**	**2**	**2**	**4**	**0**	**0**	**0**	**13:29**

AHL First All-Star Team (2003) • Les Cunningham Award (MVP – AHL) (2003)

• Missed majority of 2000-01 season recovering from knee injury suffered in game vs. Carolina, January 16, 2001. Signed as a free agent by **Hamilton** (AHL), October 19, 2004. Signed as a free agent by **NY Rangers**, August 4, 2005.

								Regular Season											Playoffs						
Season	Club	League	GP	G	A	Pts	PIM	PP	SH	GW	S	%	+/-	TF	F%	Min	GP	G	A	Pts	PIM	PP	SH	GW	Min

WARD, Lance (WAWRD, LANTS)

Defense. Shoots left. 6'3", 210 lbs.   Born, Lloydminster, Alta., June 2, 1978. Florida's 3rd choice, 63rd overall, in 1998 Entry Draft.

Season	Club	League	GP	G	A	Pts	PIM	PP	SH	GW	S	%	+/-	TF	F%	Min	GP	G	A	Pts	PIM	PP	SH	GW	Min
1993-94	Lloydminister	AAHA	20	8	12	20	68	....	....	....	....	....	....	....	....	....	....	....	....	....	....	....	....	....	....
1994-95	Red Deer Rebels	WHL	28	0	0	0	57	....	....	....	....	....	....	....	....	....	....	....	....	....	....	....	....	....	....
1995-96	Red Deer Rebels	WHL	72	4	13	17	127	....	....	....	....	....	....	....	....	10	0	4	4	10	....	....	....	....
1996-97	Red Deer Rebels	WHL	70	5	34	39	229	....	....	....	....	....	....	....	....	16	0	3	3	36	....	....	....	....
1997-98	Red Deer Rebels	WHL	71	8	25	33	233	....	....	....	....	....	....	....	....	5	0	0	0	16	....	....	....	....
1998-99	Miami Matadors	ECHL	6	1	0	1	12	....	....	....	....	....	....	....	....	....	....	....	....	....	....	....	....	....
	Fort Wayne	IHL	13	0	2	2	28	....	....	....	....	....	....	....	....	....	....	....	....	....	....	....	....	....
	New Haven	AHL	43	2	5	7	51	....	....	....	....	....	....	....	....	....	....	....	....	....	....	....	....	....
99-2000	Louisville Panthers	AHL	80	4	16	20	190	....	....	....	....	....	....	....	....	4	0	0	0	6	....	....	....	....
2000-01	**Florida**	**NHL**	30	0	2	2	45	0	0	0	17	0.0	–3	0	0.0	15:50	....	....	....	....	....	....	....	....	....
	Louisville Panthers	AHL	35	3	2	5	78	....	....	....	....	....	....	....	....	....	....	....	....	....	....	....	....	....
2001-02	**Florida**	**NHL**	68	1	4	5	131	0	0	0	39	2.6	–20	1	0.0	14:31	....	....	....	....	....	....	....	....	....
2002-03	**Florida**	**NHL**	36	3	1	4	78	0	0	1	34	8.8	–4	0	0.0	9:07	....	....	....	....	....	....	....	....	....
	Anaheim	**NHL**	29	0	1	1	43	0	0	0	18	0.0	–2	0	0.0	7:08	....	....	....	....	....	....	....	....	....
2003-04	**Anaheim**	**NHL**	46	0	4	4	94	0	0	0	26	0.0	–1	0	0.0	8:41	....	....	....	....	....	....	....	....	....
	Cincinnati	AHL	5	0	1	1	6	....	....	....	....	....	....	....	....	....	....	....	....	....	....	....	....	....
2004-05			DID NOT PLAY																					
2005-06	Binghamton	AHL	80	3	20	23	278	....	....	....	....	....	....	....	....	....	....	....	....	....	....	....	....	....
	NHL Totals		209	4	12	16	391	0	0	1	134	3.0		1	0.0	11:28	....	....	....	....	....	....	....	....

• Re-entered NHL Entry Draft. Originally New Jersey's 1st choice, 10th overall, in 1996 Entry Draft.
Traded to **Anaheim** by **Florida** with Sandis Ozolinsh for Pavel Trnka, Matt Cullen and Anaheim's 4th round choice (James Pemberton) in 2003 Entry Draft, January 30, 2003. Signed as a free agent by **Ottawa**, August 26, 2005.

WARRENER, Rhett (WAHR-ihn-uhr, REHT)   **CGY.**

Defense. Shoots right. 6'2", 217 lbs.   Born, Shaunavon, Sask., January 27, 1976. Florida's 2nd choice, 27th overall, in 1994 Entry Draft.

Season	Club	League	GP	G	A	Pts	PIM	PP	SH	GW	S	%	+/-	TF	F%	Min	GP	G	A	Pts	PIM	PP	SH	GW	Min
1991-92	Saskatoon Blazers	SMHL	33	6	5	11	71	....	....	....	....	....	....	....	....	....	....	....	....	....	....	....	....	....
	Saskatoon Blades	WHL	2	0	0	0	0	....	....	....	....	....	....	....	....	....	....	....	....	....	....	....	....	....
1992-93	Saskatoon Blades	WHL	68	2	17	19	100	....	....	....	....	....	....	....	....	9	0	0	0	14	....	....	....	....
1993-94	Saskatoon Blades	WHL	61	7	19	26	131	....	....	....	....	....	....	....	....	16	0	5	5	33	....	....	....	....
1994-95	Saskatoon Blades	WHL	66	13	26	39	137	....	....	....	....	....	....	....	....	10	0	3	3	6	....	....	....	....
1995-96	**Florida**	**NHL**	28	0	3	3	46	0	0	0	19	0.0	4				21	0	1	1	0	0	0	0	
	Carolina Panthers	AHL	9	0	0	0	4	....	....	....	....	....	....	....	....	....	....	....	....	....	....	....	....	....
1996-97	**Florida**	**NHL**	62	4	9	13	88	1	0	1	58	6.9	20				5	0	0	0	0	0	0	0	
1997-98	**Florida**	**NHL**	79	0	4	4	99	0	0	0	66	0.0	–16				....	....	....	....	....	....	....	....	....
1998-99	**Florida**	**NHL**	48	0	7	7	64	0	0	0	33	0.0	–1	0	0.0	19:01	....	....	....	....	....	....	....	....	....
	Buffalo	**NHL**	13	1	0	1	20	0	0	0	11	9.1	3	0	0.0	18:13	20	1	3	4	32	0	0	0	22:08
99-2000	**Buffalo**	**NHL**	61	0	3	3	89	0	0	0	68	0.0	18	0	0.0	19:51	5	0	0	0	2	0	0	0	21:42
2000-01	**Buffalo**	**NHL**	77	3	16	19	78	0	0	0	103	2.9	10	0	0.0	20:24	13	0	2	2	4	0	0	0	22:37
2001-02	**Buffalo**	**NHL**	65	5	5	10	113	0	0	0	66	7.6	15	0	0.0	19:39	....	....	....	....	....	....	....	....	....
2002-03	**Buffalo**	**NHL**	50	0	9	9	63	0	0	0	47	0.0	1	0	0.0	18:14	....	....	....	....	....	....	....	....	....
2003-04	**Calgary**	**NHL**	77	3	14	17	97	0	1	1	82	3.7	8	1	0.0	19:52	24	0	1	1	6	0	0	0	24:06
2004-05			DID NOT PLAY																					
2005-06	**Calgary**	**NHL**	61	3	3	6	54	0	1	0	40	7.5	7	0	0.0	19:12	7	0	0	0	14	0	0	0	19:56
	NHL Totals		621	19	73	92	811	1	2	5	593	3.2		1	0.0	19:31	95	1	7	8	58	0	0	0	22:39

Traded to **Buffalo** by **Florida** with Florida's 5th round choice (Ryan Miller) in 1999 Entry Draft for Mike Wilson, March 23, 1999. Traded to **Calgary** by **Buffalo** with Steve Reinprecht for Chris Drury and Steve Begin, July 3, 2003.

WEAVER, Mike (WEE-vuhr, MIGHK)   **L.A.**

Defense. Shoots right. 5'9", 180 lbs.   Born, Bramalea, Ont., May 2, 1978.

Season	Club	League	GP	G	A	Pts	PIM	PP	SH	GW	S	%	+/-	TF	F%	Min	GP	G	A	Pts	PIM	PP	SH	GW	Min
1995-96	Bramalea Blues	OPJHL	48	10	39	49	103	....	....	....	....	....	....	....	....	....	....	....	....	....	....	....	....	....
1996-97	Michigan State	CCHA	39	0	7	7	46	....	....	....	....	....	....	....	....	....	....	....	....	....	....	....	....	....
1997-98	Michigan State	CCHA	44	4	22	26	68	....	....	....	....	....	....	....	....	....	....	....	....	....	....	....	....	....
1998-99	Michigan State	CCHA	42	1	6	7	54	....	....	....	....	....	....	....	....	....	....	....	....	....	....	....	....	....
99-2000	Michigan State	CCHA	26	0	7	7	20	....	....	....	....	....	....	....	....	....	....	....	....	....	....	....	....	....
2000-01	Orlando	IHL	68	0	8	8	34	....	....	....	....	....	....	....	....	16	0	2	2	8	....	....	....	....
2001-02	**Atlanta**	**NHL**	16	0	1	1	10	0	0	0	9	0.0	0	0	0.0	13:54	....	....	....	....	....	....	....	....	....
	Chicago Wolves	AHL	58	2	8	10	67	....	....	....	....	....	....	....	....	25	1	3	4	21	....	....	....	....
2002-03	**Atlanta**	**NHL**	40	0	5	5	20	0	0	0	21	0.0	–5	0	0.0	18:38	....	....	....	....	....	....	....	....	....
	Chicago Wolves	AHL	33	2	2	4	32	....	....	....	....	....	....	....	....	9	0	3	3	4	....	....	....	....
2003-04	**Atlanta**	**NHL**	1	0	0	0	0	0	0	0	0	0.0	–1	0	0.0	8:28	....	....	....	....	....	....	....	....	....
	Chicago Wolves	AHL	78	3	14	17	89	....	....	....	....	....	....	....	....	9	2	2	4	20	....	....	....	....
2004-05	Manchester	AHL	79	1	22	23	61	....	....	....	....	....	....	....	....	6	0	1	1	0	....	....	....	....
2005-06	**Los Angeles**	**NHL**	53	0	9	9	14	0	0	0	21	0.0	–3	0	0.0	15:03	....	....	....	....	....	....	....	....	....
	NHL Totals		110	0	15	15	44	0	0	0	51	0.0		0	0.0	16:08	....	....	....	....	....	....	....	....	....

OPJHL Defenseman of the Year (1996) • CCHA All-Tournament Team (1997) • CCHA First All-Star Team (1999, 2000) • CCHA Best Defensive Defenseman Award (1999, 2000) • NCAA West Second All-American Team (1999, 2000)

Signed as a free agent by **Atlanta**, June 15, 2000. Signed as a free agent by **Los Angeles**, July 16, 2004.

WEBER, Shea (WEH-buhr, SHAY)   **NSH.**

Defense. Shoots right. 6'3", 213 lbs.   Born, Sicamous, B.C., August 14, 1985. Nashville's 4th choice, 49th overall, in 2003 Entry Draft.

Season	Club	League	GP	G	A	Pts	PIM	PP	SH	GW	S	%	+/-	TF	F%	Min	GP	G	A	Pts	PIM	PP	SH	GW	Min
2001-02	Sicamous Eagles	KIJHL	47	9	33	42	87	....	....	....	....	....	....	....	....	....	....	....	....	....	....	....	....	....
	Kelowna Rockets	WHL	5	0	0	0	0	....	....	....	....	....	....	....	....	....	....	....	....	....	....	....	....	....
2002-03	Kelowna Rockets	WHL	70	2	16	18	167	....	....	....	....	....	....	....	....	19	1	4	5	26	....	....	....	....
2003-04	Kelowna Rockets	WHL	60	12	20	32	126	....	....	....	....	....	....	....	....	17	3	14	17	16	....	....	....	....
2004-05	Kelowna Rockets	WHL	55	12	29	41	95	....	....	....	....	....	....	....	....	18	9	8	17	25	....	....	....	....
2005-06	**Nashville**	**NHL**	28	2	8	10	42	2	0	1	46	4.3	8	0	0.0	17:00	4	2	0	2	8	1	0	0	14:12
	Milwaukee	AHL	46	12	15	27	49	....	....	....	....	....	....	....	....	14	6	5	11	16	....	....	....	....
	NHL Totals		28	2	8	10	42	2	0	1	46	4.3		0	0.0	17:00	4	2	0	2	8	1	0	0	14:12

WHL West Second All-Star Team (2004) • Memorial Cup Tournament All-Star Team (2004) • WHL West First All-Star Team (2005)

WEIGHT, Doug (WAYT, DUHG)   **ST.L.**

Center. Shoots left. 5'11", 200 lbs.   Born, Warren, MI, January 21, 1971. NY Rangers' 2nd choice, 34th overall, in 1990 Entry Draft.

Season	Club	League	GP	G	A	Pts	PIM	PP	SH	GW	S	%	+/-	TF	F%	Min	GP	G	A	Pts	PIM	PP	SH	GW	Min
1988-89	Bloomfield Jets	NAHL	34	26	53	79	105	....	....	....	....	....	....	....	....	....	....	....	....	....	....	....	....	....
1989-90	Lake Superior	CCHA	46	21	48	69	44	....	....	....	....	....	....	....	....	....	....	....	....	....	....	....	....	....
1990-91	Lake Superior	CCHA	42	29	46	75	86	....	....	....	....	....	....	....	....	....	....	....	....	....	....	....	....	....
	NY Rangers	**NHL**															1	0	0	0	0	0	0	0	0
1991-92	**NY Rangers**	**NHL**	53	8	22	30	23	0	0	2	72	11.1	–3				7	2	2	4	0	1	0	0	
	Binghamton	AHL	9	3	14	17	2	....	....	....	....	....	....	....	....	....	4	1	4	5	6	....	....	....	....
1992-93	**NY Rangers**	**NHL**	65	15	25	40	55	3	0	1	90	16.7	4				....	....	....	....	....	....	....	....	....
	Edmonton	**NHL**	13	2	6	8	10	0	0	0	35	5.7	–2				....	....	....	....	....	....	....	....	....
1993-94	**Edmonton**	**NHL**	84	24	50	74	47	4	1	1	188	12.8	–22				....	....	....	....	....	....	....	....	....
1994-95	Rosenheim	Germany	8	2	3	5	18	....	....	....	....	....	....	....	....	....	....	....	....	....	....	....	....	....
	Edmonton	**NHL**	48	7	33	40	69	1	0	1	104	6.7	–17				....	....	....	....	....	....	....	....	....
1995-96	**Edmonton**	**NHL**	82	25	79	104	95	9	0	2	204	12.3	–19				....	....	....	....	....	....	....	....	....
1996-97	**Edmonton**	**NHL**	80	21	61	82	80	4	0	2	235	8.9	1				12	3	8	11	8	0	0	0	
1997-98	**Edmonton**	**NHL**	79	26	44	70	69	9	0	4	205	12.7	1				12	7	9	14	2	0	1		
	United States	Olympics	4	0	2	2	2	....	....	....	....	....	....	....	....	....	....	....	....	....	....	....	....	....
1998-99	**Edmonton**	**NHL**	43	6	31	37	12	1	0	1	79	7.6	–8	853	49.5	19:51	4	1	1	2	15	0	0	0	14:43
99-2000	**Edmonton**	**NHL**	77	21	51	72	54	3	1	4	167	12.6	6	1588	50.4	20:35	5	3	2	5	4	2	0	1	21:05
2000-01	**Edmonton**	**NHL**	82	25	65	90	91	3	0	5	1514	51.3	22:08				6	2	6	8	17	0	0	0	22:45
2001-02	**St. Louis**	**NHL**	61	15	34	49	40	3	0	1	131	11.5	20	1123	49.2	19:48	10	1	3	4	11	0	0	1	16:26
	United States	Olympics	6	0	3	3	4	....	....	....	....	....	....	....	....	....	....	....	....	....	....	....	....	....
2002-03	**St. Louis**	**NHL**	70	15	52	67	52	7	0	3	182	8.2	–6	1048	50.4	20:23	7	5	8	13	2	5	0	1	22:26

			Regular Season														Playoffs								
Season	Club	League	GP	G	A	Pts	PIM	PP	SH	GW	S	%	+/-	TF	F%	Min	GP	G	A	Pts	PIM	PP	SH	GW	Min
2003-04	**St. Louis**	**NHL**	**75**	**14**	**51**	**65**	**37**	**6**	**0**	**5**	**198**	**7.1**	**–3**	**1115**	**50.4**	**20:25**	**5**	**2**	**1**	**3**	**6**	**1**	**1**	**0**	**19:24**
2004-05	Frankfurt Lions	Germany	7	6	9	15	26	....	....	....	....	....	....	....	....	....	11	2	10	12	8	....	....	....	....
2005-06	**St. Louis**	**NHL**	**47**	**11**	**33**	**44**	**50**	**7**	**0**	**1**	**123**	**8.9**	**–11**	**638**	**49.8**	**22:17**	....	....	....	....	....	....	....	....	....
	♦ Carolina	**NHL**	**23**	**4**	**9**	**13**	**25**	**2**	**0**	**0**	**52**	**7.7**	**–6**	**256**	**46.1**	**17:35**	**23**	**3**	**13**	**16**	**20**	**2**	**0**	**0**	**15:27**
	United States	Olympics	6	0	3	3	4	....	....	....	....	....	....	....	....	....	....	....	....	....	....	....	....	....	....
	NHL Totals		**982**	**239**	**646**	**885**	**809**	**67**	**2**	**30**	**2253**	**10.6**		**8135**	**50.1**	**20:39**	**92**	**23**	**48**	**71**	**90**	**14**	**1**	**4**	**17:54**

CCHA First All-Star Team (1991) • NCAA West Second All-American Team (1991)

Played in NHL All-Star Game (1996, 1998, 2001, 2003)

Traded to **Edmonton** by **NY Rangers** for Esa Tikkanen, March 17, 1993. Traded to **St. Louis** by **Edmonton** with Michel Riesen for Marty Reasoner, Jochen Hecht and Jan Horacek, July 1, 2001. Signed as a free agent by **Frankfurt** (Germany), February 11, 2005. Traded to **Carolina** by **St. Louis** with Erkki Rajamaki for Jesse Boulerice, Mike Zigomanis, Magnus Kahnberg, Carolina's 1st round choice (later traded to New Jersey - New Jersey selected Matthew Corrente) in 2006 Entry Draft, Toronto's 4th round choice (previously acquired, St. Louis selected Reto Berra) in 2006 Entry Draft and Chicago's 4th round choice (previously acquired) in 2007 Entry Draft, January 30, 2006. Signed as a free agent by **St. Louis**, July 2, 2006.

WEINHANDL, Mattias

(vayn-hanh-duhl, mah-TEE-uhs) **MIN.**

Right wing. Shoots right. 6', 183 lbs. Born, Ljungby, Sweden, June 1, 1980. NY Islanders' 5th choice, 78th overall, in 1999 Entry Draft.

Season	Club	League	GP	G	A	Pts	PIM	PP	SH	GW	S	%	+/-	TF	F%	Min	GP	G	A	Pts	PIM	PP	SH	GW	Min
1995-96	Troja Jr.	Swe-Jr.	28	38	40	78	....	....	....	....	....	....	....	....	....	....	....	....	....	....	....	....	....	....	....
1996-97	Troja Jr.	Swe-Jr.	48	61	69	130	46	....	....	....	....	....	....	....	....	....	....	....	....	....	....	....	....	....	....
1997-98	IF Troja-Ljungby	Sweden-2	28	3	2	5	2	....	....	....	....	....	....	....	....	....	5	0	0	0	2	....	....	....	....
1998-99	IF Troja-Ljungby	Sweden-2	38	20	20	40	30	....	....	....	....	....	....	....	....	....	5	4	3	7	4	....	....	....	....
99-2000	Malmo Jr.	Swe-Jr.	1	2	2	4	2	....	....	....	....	....	....	....	....	....	....	....	....	....	....	....	....	....	....
	MoDo	Sweden	32	15	9	24	6	....	....	....	....	....	....	....	....	....	13	5	3	8	8	....	....	....	....
2000-01	MoDo	Sweden	48	16	16	32	14	....	....	....	....	....	....	....	....	....	6	1	3	4	6	....	....	....	....
2001-02	MODO	Sweden	50	18	16	34	10	....	....	....	....	....	....	....	....	....	14	4	*11	*15	4	....	....	....	....
2002-03	**NY Islanders**	**NHL**	**47**	**6**	**17**	**23**	**10**	**1**	**0**	**0**	**66**	**9.1**	**–2**	**5**	**60.0**	**13:52**	....	....	....	....	....	....	....	....	....
	Bridgeport	AHL	23	9	12	21	14	....	....	....	....	....	....	....	....	....	....	....	....	....	....	....	....	....	....
2003-04	**NY Islanders**	**NHL**	**55**	**8**	**12**	**20**	**26**	**4**	**0**	**2**	**49**	**16.3**	**9**	**6**	**33.3**	**12:20**	**5**	**0**	**0**	**0**	**2**	**0**	**0**	**0**	**13:07**
	Bridgeport	AHL	10	3	6	9	10	....	....	....	....	....	....	....	....	....	....	....	....	....	....	....	....	....	....
2004-05	MODO	Sweden	50	*26	20	46	18	....	....	....	....	....	....	....	....	....	6	0	0	0	4	....	....	....	....
2005-06	**NY Islanders**	**NHL**	**53**	**2**	**4**	**6**	**14**	**0**	**0**	**0**	**40**	**5.0**	**–4**	**10**	**40.0**	**7:36**	....	....	....	....	....	....	....	....	....
	Minnesota	**NHL**	**15**	**2**	**3**	**5**	**10**	**0**	**0**	**0**	**17**	**11.8**	**0**	**11**	**27.3**	**14:43**	....	....	....	....	....	....	....	....	....
	NHL Totals		**170**	**18**	**36**	**54**	**60**	**5**	**0**	**2**	**172**	**10.5**		**32**	**37.5**	**11:30**	**5**	**0**	**0**	**0**	**2**	**0**	**0**	**0**	**13:07**

Signed as a free agent by **MODO** (Sweden), September 18, 2004. Claimed on waivers by **Minnesota** from **NY Islanders**, March 4, 2006.

WEINRICH, Eric

(WIGHN-rihch, AIR-ihk)

Defense. Shoots left. 6'1", 207 lbs. Born, Roanoke, VA, December 19, 1966. New Jersey's 3rd choice, 32nd overall, in 1985 Entry Draft.

Season	Club	League	GP	G	A	Pts	PIM	PP	SH	GW	S	%	+/-	TF	F%	Min	GP	G	A	Pts	PIM	PP	SH	GW	Min
1983-84	N. Yarmouth	High-ME	17	23	33	56	....	....	....	....	....	....	....	....	....	....	....	....	....	....	....	....	....	....	....
1984-85	N. Yarmouth	High-ME	20	6	21	27	....	....	....	....	....	....	....	....	....	....	....	....	....	....	....	....	....	....	....
1985-86	U. of Maine	H-East	34	0	14	14	26	....	....	....	....	....	....	....	....	....	....	....	....	....	....	....	....	....	....
1986-87	U. of Maine	H-East	41	12	32	44	59	....	....	....	....	....	....	....	....	....	....	....	....	....	....	....	....	....	....
1987-88	U. of Maine	H-East	8	4	7	11	22	....	....	....	....	....	....	....	....	....	....	....	....	....	....	....	....	....	....
	United States	Nat-Tm	38	3	9	12	24	....	....	....	....	....	....	....	....	....	....	....	....	....	....	....	....	....	....
	United States	Olympics	3	0	0	0	0	....	....	....	....	....	....	....	....	....	....	....	....	....	....	....	....	....	....
1988-89	**New Jersey**	**NHL**	**2**	**0**	**0**	**0**	**0**	**0**	**0**	**0**	**3**	**0.0**	**–1**	....	....	....	....	....	....	....	....	....	....	....	....
	Utica Devils	AHL	80	17	27	44	70	....	....	....	....	....	....	....	....	....	5	0	1	1	4	....	....	....	....
1989-90	**New Jersey**	**NHL**	**19**	**2**	**7**	**9**	**11**	**1**	**0**	**1**	**16**	**12.5**	**1**	....	....	....	**6**	**1**	**3**	**4**	**17**	**0**	**0**	**0**	....
	Utica Devils	AHL	57	12	48	60	38	....	....	....	....	....	....	....	....	....	....	....	....	....	....	....	....	....	....
1990-91	**New Jersey**	**NHL**	**76**	**4**	**34**	**38**	**48**	**1**	**0**	**0**	**96**	**4.2**	**10**	....	....	....	**7**	**1**	**2**	**3**	**6**	**1**	**0**	**0**	....
1991-92	**New Jersey**	**NHL**	**76**	**7**	**25**	**32**	**55**	**5**	**0**	**0**	**97**	**7.2**	**10**	....	....	....	**7**	**0**	**2**	**2**	**4**	**0**	**0**	**0**	....
1992-93	**Hartford**	**NHL**	**79**	**7**	**29**	**36**	**76**	**0**	**2**	**2**	**104**	**6.7**	**–11**	....	....	....	....	....	....	....	....	....	....	....	....
1993-94	**Hartford**	**NHL**	**8**	**1**	**1**	**2**	**2**	**1**	**0**	**0**	**10**	**10.0**	**–5**	....	....	....	....	....	....	....	....	....	....	....	....
	Chicago	**NHL**	**54**	**3**	**23**	**26**	**31**	**1**	**0**	**2**	**105**	**2.9**	**6**	....	....	....	**6**	**0**	**2**	**2**	**6**	**0**	**0**	**0**	....
1994-95	**Chicago**	**NHL**	**48**	**3**	**10**	**13**	**33**	**1**	**0**	**2**	**50**	**6.0**	**1**	....	....	....	**16**	**1**	**5**	**6**	**4**	**0**	**0**	**0**	....
1995-96	**Chicago**	**NHL**	**77**	**5**	**10**	**15**	**65**	**0**	**0**	**0**	**76**	**6.6**	**14**	....	....	....	**10**	**1**	**4**	**5**	**10**	**1**	**0**	**0**	....
1996-97	**Chicago**	**NHL**	**81**	**7**	**25**	**32**	**62**	**1**	**0**	**0**	**115**	**6.1**	**19**	....	....	....	**6**	**0**	**1**	**1**	**4**	**0**	**0**	**0**	....
1997-98	**Chicago**	**NHL**	**82**	**2**	**21**	**23**	**106**	**0**	**0**	**0**	**85**	**2.4**	**10**	....	....	....	....	....	....	....	....	....	....	....	....
1998-99	**Chicago**	**NHL**	**14**	**1**	**3**	**4**	**12**	**0**	**0**	**0**	**24**	**4.2**	**–13**	**0**	**0.0**	**20:12**	....	....	....	....	....	....	....	....	....
	Montreal	**NHL**	**66**	**6**	**12**	**18**	**77**	**4**	**0**	**1**	**95**	**6.3**	**–12**	**0**	**0.0**	**24:44**	....	....	....	....	....	....	....	....	....
99-2000	**Montreal**	**NHL**	**77**	**4**	**25**	**29**	**39**	**2**	**0**	**0**	**120**	**3.3**	**4**	**0**	**0.0**	**25:21**	....	....	....	....	....	....	....	....	....
2000-01	**Montreal**	**NHL**	**60**	**6**	**19**	**25**	**34**	**2**	**0**	**1**	**81**	**7.4**	**–1**	**1**	**100.0**	**24:27**	....	....	....	....	....	....	....	....	....
	Boston	**NHL**	**22**	**1**	**5**	**6**	**10**	**1**	**0**	**1**	**28**	**3.6**	**–8**	**0**	**0.0**	**25:52**	....	....	....	....	....	....	....	....	....
2001-02	**Philadelphia**	**NHL**	**80**	**4**	**20**	**24**	**26**	**0**	**0**	**2**	**102**	**3.9**	**27**	**0**	**0.0**	**21:53**	**5**	**0**	**0**	**0**	**4**	**0**	**0**	**0**	**18:42**
2002-03	**Philadelphia**	**NHL**	**81**	**2**	**18**	**20**	**40**	**1**	**1**	**0**	**103**	**1.9**	**16**	**1**	**0.0**	**21:24**	**13**	**2**	**3**	**5**	**12**	**1**	**0**	**0**	**24:59**
2003-04	**Philadelphia**	**NHL**	**54**	**2**	**7**	**9**	**32**	**1**	**0**	**1**	**56**	**3.6**	**11**	**0**	**0.0**	**20:48**	....	....	....	....	....	....	....	....	....
	St. Louis	**NHL**	**26**	**2**	**8**	**10**	**14**	**1**	**0**	**0**	**27**	**7.4**	**1**	**0**	**0.0**	**23:05**	**5**	**0**	**1**	**1**	**0**	**0**	**0**	**0**	**23:36**
2004-05	EC Villacher SV	Austria	10	3	8	11	8	....	....	....	....	....	....	....	....	....	3	0	1	1	6	....	....	....	....
2005-06	**St. Louis**	**NHL**	**59**	**1**	**16**	**17**	**44**	**1**	**0**	**0**	**56**	**1.8**	**–10**	**1**	**0.0**	**22:12**	....	....	....	....	....	....	....	....	....
	Vancouver	**NHL**	**16**	**0**	**0**	**0**	**8**	**0**	**0**	**0**	**12**	**0.0**	**–13**	**0**	**0.0**	**18:53**	....	....	....	....	....	....	....	....	....
	NHL Totals		**1157**	**70**	**318**	**388**	**825**	**24**	**3**	**13**	**1461**	**4.8**		**3**	**33.3**	**22:55**	**81**	**6**	**23**	**29**	**67**	**3**	**0**	**0**	**23:19**

Hockey East First All-Star Team (1987) • NCAA East Second All-American Team (1987) • AHL First All-Star Team (1990) • Eddie Shore Award (Outstanding Defenseman – AHL) (1990) • NHL All-Rookie Team (1991)

Traded to **Hartford** by **New Jersey** with Sean Burke for Bobby Holik and Hartford's 2nd round choice (Jay Pandolfo) in 1993 Entry Draft, August 28, 1992. Traded to **Chicago** by **Hartford** with Patrick Poulin for Steve Larmer and Bryan Marchment, November 2, 1993. Traded to **Montreal** by **Chicago** with Jeff Hackett, Alain Nasreddine and Tampa Bay's 4th round choice (previously acquired, Montreal selected Chris Dyment) in 1999 Entry Draft for Jocelyn Thibault, Dave Manson and Brad Brown, November 16, 1998. Traded to **Boston** by **Montreal** for Patrick Traverse, February 21, 2001. Signed as a free agent by **Philadelphia**, July 5, 2001. Traded to **St. Louis** by **Philadelphia** for St. Louis' 5th round choice (Gino Pisellini) in 2004 Entry Draft, February 9, 2004. Signed as a free agent by **Villacher** (Austria), February 14, 2005. Traded to **Vancouver** by **St. Louis** for Tomas Mojzis and Vancouver's 3rd round choice (later traded to New Jersey - New Jersey selected Vladimir Zharkov) in 2006 Entry Draft, March 9, 2006. • Officially announced retirement, August 7, 2006.

WEISS, Stephen

(WIGHS, STEEV-ehn) **FLA.**

Center. Shoots left. 5'11", 185 lbs. Born, Toronto, Ont., April 3, 1983. Florida's 1st choice, 4th overall, in 2001 Entry Draft.

Season	Club	League	GP	G	A	Pts	PIM	PP	SH	GW	S	%	+/-	TF	F%	Min	GP	G	A	Pts	PIM	PP	SH	GW	Min
1997-98	Tor. Young Nats	MTHL	48	51	58	109	....	....	....	....	....	....	....	....	....	....	....	....	....	....	....	....	....	....	....
1998-99	North York	OPJHL	35	15	22	37	10	....	....	....	....	....	....	....	....	....	....	....	....	....	....	....	....	....	....
99-2000	Plymouth Whalers	OHL	64	24	42	66	35	....	....	....	....	....	....	....	....	....	23	8	18	26	18	....	....	....	....
2000-01	Plymouth Whalers	OHL	62	40	47	87	45	....	....	....	....	....	....	....	....	....	18	7	16	23	10	....	....	....	....
2001-02	**Florida**	**NHL**	**7**	**1**	**1**	**2**	**0**	**1**	**0**	**0**	**15**	**6.7**	**0**	**107**	**52.3**	**16:14**	....	....	....	....	....	....	....	....	....
	Plymouth Whalers	OHL	46	25	45	70	69	....	....	....	....	....	....	....	....	....	6	2	7	9	13	....	....	....	....
2002-03	**Florida**	**NHL**	**77**	**6**	**15**	**21**	**17**	**0**	**0**	**2**	**87**	**6.9**	**–13**	**1065**	**46.3**	**14:17**	....	....	....	....	....	....	....	....	....
2003-04	**Florida**	**NHL**	**50**	**12**	**17**	**29**	**10**	**3**	**0**	**2**	**82**	**14.6**	**–10**	**799**	**44.9**	**17:42**	....	....	....	....	....	....	....	....	....
	San Antonio	AHL	10	6	3	9	14	....	....	....	....	....	....	....	....	....	....	....	....	....	....	....	....	....	....
2004-05	San Antonio	AHL	62	15	23	38	38	....	....	....	....	....	....	....	....	....	....	....	....	....	....	....	....	....	....
	Chicago Wolves	AHL	18	7	9	16	12	....	....	....	....	....	....	....	....	....	18	2	7	9	17	....	....	....	....
2005-06	**Florida**	**NHL**	**41**	**9**	**12**	**21**	**22**	**5**	**0**	**1**	**74**	**12.2**	**–2**	**514**	**49.6**	**15:15**	....	....	....	....	....	....	....	....	....
	NHL Totals		**175**	**28**	**45**	**73**	**49**	**9**	**0**	**5**	**258**	**10.9**		**2485**	**46.8**	**15:34**	....	....	....	....	....	....	....	....	....

OHL All-Rookie Team (2000)

Loaned to **Chicago** (AHL) by **San Antonio** (AHL) for cash, March 8, 2005.

WELCH, Noah

(WEHLCH, NOH-ah) **PIT.**

Defense. Shoots left. 6'4", 212 lbs. Born, Brighton, MA, August 26, 1982. Pittsburgh's 2nd choice, 54th overall, in 2001 Entry Draft.

Season	Club	League	GP	G	A	Pts	PIM	PP	SH	GW	S	%	+/-	TF	F%	Min	GP	G	A	Pts	PIM	PP	SH	GW	Min
99-2000	St. Sebastian's	High-MA	26	4	11	15	35	....	....	....	....	....	....	....	....	....	....	....	....	....	....	....	....	....	....
	Eastern-Mass	MBAHL	4	0	3	3	6	....	....	....	....	....	....	....	....	....	....	....	....	....	....	....	....	....	....
2000-01	St. Sebastian's	High-MA	30	11	20	31	37	....	....	....	....	....	....	....	....	....	....	....	....	....	....	....	....	....	....
2001-02	Harvard Crimson	ECAC	27	5	6	11	56	....	....	....	....	....	....	....	....	....	....	....	....	....	....	....	....	....	....
2002-03	Harvard Crimson	ECAC	34	6	22	28	70	....	....	....	....	....	....	....	....	....	....	....	....	....	....	....	....	....	....
2003-04	Harvard Crimson	ECAC	34	6	13	19	58	....	....	....	....	....	....	....	....	....	....	....	....	....	....	....	....	....	....
2004-05	Harvard Crimson	ECACHL	34	6	12	18	*86	....	....	....	....	....	....	....	....	....	....	....	....	....	....	....	....	....	....

Season	Club	League	GP	G	A	Pts	PIM	PP	SH	GW	S	%	+/-	TF	F%	Min	GP	G	A	Pts	PIM	PP	SH	GW	Min
			Regular Season														Playoffs								
2005-06	**Pittsburgh**	**NHL**	**5**	**1**	**3**	**4**	**2**	**0**	**0**	**0**	**5**	**20.0**	**0**	**0**	**0.0**	**17:24**	....	....	....	....	....	....	....	....	....
	Wilkes-Barre	AHL	77	9	20	29	99	....	....	....	....	....	....	....	....	....	11	1	0	1	18	....	....	....	....
	NHL Totals		**5**	**1**	**3**	**4**	**2**	**0**	**0**	**0**	**5**	**20.0**		**0**	**0.0**	**17:24**	....	....	....	....	....	....	....	....	....

ECAC All-Rookie Team (2002) • ECAC Second All-Star Team (2002, 2003) • NCAA East Second All-American Team (2003) • ECAC First All-Star Team (2005) • NCAA East First All-American Team (2005)

WELLWOOD, Kyle
(WEHL-wud, KIGHL) **TOR.**

Center. Shoots right. 5'10", 180 lbs. Born, Windsor, Ont., May 16, 1983. Toronto's 6th choice, 134th overall, in 2001 Entry Draft.

Season	Club	League	GP	G	A	Pts	PIM	PP	SH	GW	S	%	+/-	TF	F%	Min	GP	G	A	Pts	PIM	PP	SH	GW	Min
1998-99	Tecumseh	OHA-B	51	22	41	63	12	....	....	....	....	....	....	....	....	....	....	....	....	....	....	....	....	....	....
99-2000	Belleville Bulls	OHL	65	14	37	51	14	....	....	....	....	....	....	....	....	....	16	3	7	10	6	....	....	....	....
2000-01	Belleville Bulls	OHL	68	35	*83	*118	24	....	....	....	....	....	....	....	....	....	10	3	16	19	4	....	....	....	....
2001-02	Belleville Bulls	OHL	28	16	24	40	4	....	....	....	....	....	....	....	....	....	....	....	....	....	....	....	....	....	....
	Windsor Spitfires	OHL	26	14	21	35	0	....	....	....	....	....	....	....	....	....	16	12	12	24	0	....	....	....	....
2002-03	Windsor Spitfires	OHL	57	41	59	100	0	....	....	....	....	....	....	....	....	....	7	5	9	14	0	....	....	....	....
2003-04	**Toronto**	**NHL**	**1**	**0**	**0**	**0**	**0**	**0**	**0**	**0**	**1**	**0.0**	**–1**	**13**	**30.8**	**7:56**	....	....	....	....	....	....	....	....	....
	St. John's	AHL	76	20	35	55	6	....	....	....	....	....	....	....	....	....	....	....	....	....	....	....	....	....	....
2004-05	St. John's	AHL	80	38	49	87	20	....	....	....	....	....	....	....	....	....	5	2	2	4	2	....	....	....	....
2005-06	**Toronto**	**NHL**	**81**	**11**	**34**	**45**	**14**	**3**	**0**	**0**	**117**	**9.4**	**0**	**593**	**56.3**	**12:47**	....	....	....	....	....	....	....	....	....
	NHL Totals		**82**	**11**	**34**	**45**	**14**	**3**	**0**	**0**	**118**	**9.3**		**606**	**55.8**	**12:43**	....	....	....	....	....	....	....	....	....

OHL First All-Star Team (2001) • Canadian Major Junior Sportsman of the Year (2003)

WESLEY, Glen
(WEH-slee, GLEHN) **CAR.**

Defense. Shoots left. 6'1", 205 lbs. Born, Red Deer, Alta., October 2, 1968. Boston's 1st choice, 3rd overall, in 1987 Entry Draft.

Season	Club	League	GP	G	A	Pts	PIM	PP	SH	GW	S	%	+/-	TF	F%	Min	GP	G	A	Pts	PIM	PP	SH	GW	Min
1983-84	Red Deer Rustlers	AJHL	57	9	20	29	40	....	....	....	....	....	....	....	....	....	....	....	....	....	....	....	....	....	....
	Portland	WHL	3	1	2	3	0	....	....	....	....	....	....	....	....	....	....	....	....	....	....	....	....	....	....
1984-85	Portland	WHL	67	16	52	68	76	....	....	....	....	....	....	....	....	....	6	1	6	7	8	....	....	....	....
1985-86	Portland	WHL	69	16	75	91	96	....	....	....	....	....	....	....	....	....	15	3	11	14	29	....	....	....	....
1986-87	Portland	WHL	63	16	46	62	72	....	....	....	....	....	....	....	....	....	20	8	18	26	27	....	....	....	....
1987-88	**Boston**	**NHL**	**79**	**7**	**30**	**37**	**69**	**1**	**2**	**0**	**158**	**4.4**	**21**	....	....	....	**23**	**6**	**8**	**14**	**22**	**4**	**1**	**0**	....
1988-89	**Boston**	**NHL**	**77**	**19**	**35**	**54**	**61**	**8**	**1**	**1**	**181**	**10.5**	**23**	....	....	....	**10**	**0**	**2**	**2**	**4**	**0**	**0**	**0**	....
1989-90	**Boston**	**NHL**	**78**	**9**	**27**	**36**	**48**	**5**	**0**	**4**	**166**	**5.4**	**6**	....	....	....	**21**	**2**	**6**	**8**	**36**	**0**	**0**	**1**	....
1990-91	**Boston**	**NHL**	**80**	**11**	**32**	**43**	**78**	**5**	**1**	**1**	**199**	**5.5**	**0**	....	....	....	**19**	**2**	**9**	**11**	**19**	**2**	**0**	**0**	....
1991-92	**Boston**	**NHL**	**78**	**9**	**37**	**46**	**54**	**4**	**0**	**1**	**211**	**4.3**	**–9**	....	....	....	**15**	**2**	**4**	**6**	**16**	**0**	**0**	**0**	....
1992-93	**Boston**	**NHL**	**64**	**8**	**25**	**33**	**47**	**4**	**1**	**0**	**183**	**4.4**	**–2**	....	....	....	**4**	**0**	**0**	**0**	**0**	**0**	**0**	**0**	....
1993-94	**Boston**	**NHL**	**81**	**14**	**44**	**58**	**64**	**6**	**1**	**1**	**265**	**5.3**	**1**	....	....	....	**13**	**3**	**3**	**6**	**12**	**1**	**0**	**0**	....
1994-95	**Hartford**	**NHL**	**48**	**2**	**14**	**16**	**50**	**1**	**0**	**1**	**125**	**1.6**	**–6**	....	....	....	....	....	....	....	....	....	....	....	....
1995-96	**Hartford**	**NHL**	**68**	**8**	**16**	**24**	**88**	**6**	**0**	**1**	**129**	**6.2**	**–9**	....	....	....	....	....	....	....	....	....	....	....	....
1996-97	**Hartford**	**NHL**	**68**	**6**	**26**	**32**	**40**	**3**	**1**	**0**	**126**	**4.8**	**0**	....	....	....	....	....	....	....	....	....	....	....	....
1997-98	**Carolina**	**NHL**	**82**	**6**	**19**	**25**	**36**	**1**	**0**	**1**	**121**	**5.0**	**7**	....	....	....	....	....	....	....	....	....	....	....	....
1998-99	**Carolina**	**NHL**	**74**	**7**	**17**	**24**	**44**	**0**	**0**	**2**	**112**	**6.3**	**14**	**1**	**0.0**	**22:31**	**6**	**0**	**0**	**0**	**2**	**0**	**0**	**0**	**28:21**
99-2000	**Carolina**	**NHL**	**78**	**7**	**15**	**22**	**38**	**1**	**0**	**0**	**99**	**7.1**	**–4**	**0**	**0.0**	**21:32**	....	....	....	....	....	....	....	....	....
2000-01	**Carolina**	**NHL**	**71**	**5**	**16**	**21**	**42**	**3**	**0**	**0**	**92**	**5.4**	**–2**	**0**	**0.0**	**22:21**	**6**	**0**	**0**	**0**	**0**	**0**	**0**	**0**	**22:07**
2001-02	**Carolina**	**NHL**	**77**	**5**	**13**	**18**	**56**	**1**	**0**	**0**	**88**	**5.7**	**–8**	**0**	**0.0**	**20:13**	**22**	**0**	**2**	**2**	**12**	**0**	**0**	**0**	**21:04**
2002-03	**Carolina**	**NHL**	**63**	**1**	**7**	**8**	**40**	**1**	**0**	**0**	**72**	**1.4**	**–5**	**0**	**0.0**	**21:24**	....	....	....	....	....	....	....	....	....
	Toronto	**NHL**	**7**	**0**	**3**	**3**	**4**	**0**	**0**	**0**	**5**	**0.0**	**3**	**0**	**0.0**	**20:41**	**5**	**0**	**1**	**1**	**2**	**0**	**0**	**0**	**27:39**
2003-04	**Carolina**	**NHL**	**74**	**0**	**6**	**6**	**32**	**0**	**0**	**0**	**82**	**0.0**	**18**	**0**	**0.0**	**21:22**	....	....	....	....	....	....	....	....	....
2004-05			DID NOT PLAY																						
2005-06 ♦	**Carolina**	**NHL**	**64**	**2**	**8**	**10**	**46**	**0**	**0**	**0**	**28**	**7.1**	**10**	**0**	**0.0**	**15:28**	**25**	**0**	**2**	**2**	**16**	**0**	**0**	**0**	**16:10**
	NHL Totals		**1311**	**126**	**390**	**516**	**937**	**50**	**7**	**13**	**2442**	**5.2**		**1**	**0.0**	**20:47**	**169**	**15**	**37**	**52**	**141**	**7**	**1**	**1**	**20:27**

WHL West First All-Star Team (1986, 1987) • NHL All-Rookie Team (1988)

Played in NHL All-Star Game (1989)

Traded to **Hartford** by **Boston** for Hartford's 1st round choices in 1995 (Kyle McLaren), 1996 (Johnathan Aitken) and 1997 (Sergei Samsonov) Entry Drafts, August 26, 1994. Transferred to **Carolina** after **Hartford** franchise relocated, June 25, 1997. Traded to **Toronto** by **Carolina** for Toronto's 2nd round choice (later traded to Columbus – Columbus selected Kyle Wharton) in 2004 Entry Draft, March 9, 2003. Signed as a free agent by **Carolina**, July 8, 2003.

WESTCOTT, Duvie
(WEST-coht, DOO-vee) **CBJ**

Defense. Shoots right. 5'11", 197 lbs. Born, Winnipeg, Man., October 30, 1977.

Season	Club	League	GP	G	A	Pts	PIM	PP	SH	GW	S	%	+/-	TF	F%	Min	GP	G	A	Pts	PIM	PP	SH	GW	Min
1996-97	Winnipeg South	MJHL	52	12	47	59	....	....	....	....	....	....	....	....	....	....	....	....	....	....	....	....	....	....	....
1997-98	Alaska-Anchorage	WCHA	25	3	5	8	43	....	....	....	....	....	....	....	....	....	....	....	....	....	....	....	....	....	....
	Omaha Lancers	USHL	12	3	3	6	31	....	....	....	....	....	....	....	....	....	14	0	8	8	84	....	....	....	....
1998-99	St. Cloud State	WCHA	DID NOT PLAY – TRANSFERRED COLLEGES																						
99-2000	St. Cloud State	WCHA	36	1	18	19	67	....	....	....	....	....	....	....	....	....	....	....	....	....	....	....	....	....	....
2000-01	St. Cloud State	WCHA	38	10	24	34	116	....	....	....	....	....	....	....	....	....	....	....	....	....	....	....	....	....	....
2001-02	**Columbus**	**NHL**	**4**	**0**	**0**	**0**	**2**	**0**	**0**	**0**	**3**	**0.0**	**–2**	**0**	**0.0**	**15:08**	....	....	....	....	....	....	....	....	....
	Syracuse Crunch	AHL	68	4	29	33	99	....	....	....	....	....	....	....	....	....	10	0	1	1	12	....	....	....	....
2002-03	Syracuse Crunch	AHL	22	1	10	11	54	....	....	....	....	....	....	....	....	....	....	....	....	....	....	....	....	....	....
	Columbus	**NHL**	**39**	**0**	**7**	**7**	**77**	**0**	**0**	**0**	**27**	**0.0**	**–3**	**0**	**0.0**	**18:41**	....	....	....	....	....	....	....	....	....
2003-04	**Columbus**	**NHL**	**34**	**0**	**7**	**7**	**39**	**0**	**0**	**0**	**43**	**0.0**	**–15**	**0**	**0.0**	**21:11**	....	....	....	....	....	....	....	....	....
2004-05	JYP Jyvaskyla	Finland	46	11	7	18	106	....	....	....	....	....	....	....	....	....	1	2	0	2	25	....	....	....	....
2005-06	**Columbus**	**NHL**	**78**	**6**	**22**	**28**	**133**	**1**	**1**	**0**	**113**	**5.3**	**1**	**0**	**0.0**	**22:34**	....	....	....	....	....	....	....	....	....
	NHL Totals		**155**	**6**	**36**	**42**	**251**	**1**	**1**	**0**	**186**	**3.2**		**0**	**0.0**	**21:06**	....	....	....	....	....	....	....	....	....

WCHA Second All-Star Team (2001)

Signed as a free agent by **Columbus**, May 10, 2001. • Missed majority of 2003-04 season recovering from ankle (October 13, 2003 vs. Vancouver) and hand (January 31, 2004 vs. Minnesota) injuries. Signed as a free agent by **Jyvaskyla** (Finland), September 30, 2004.

WESTRUM, Erik
(WEHST-ruhm, AIR-ihk) **TOR.**

Center. Shoots left. 6', 204 lbs. Born, Minneapolis, MN, July 26, 1979. Phoenix's 9th choice, 187th overall, in 1998 Entry Draft.

Season	Club	League	GP	G	A	Pts	PIM	PP	SH	GW	S	%	+/-	TF	F%	Min	GP	G	A	Pts	PIM	PP	SH	GW	Min
1995/97	Apple Valley	High-MN	78	56	84	140	....	....	....	....	....	....	....	....	....	....	....	....	....	....	....	....	....	....	....
1997-98	U. of Minnesota	WCHA	39	6	12	18	43	....	....	....	....	....	....	....	....	....	....	....	....	....	....	....	....	....	....
1998-99	U. of Minnesota	WCHA	41	10	26	36	81	....	....	....	....	....	....	....	....	....	....	....	....	....	....	....	....	....	....
99-2000	U. of Minnesota	WCHA	39	27	26	53	99	....	....	....	....	....	....	....	....	....	....	....	....	....	....	....	....	....	....
2000-01	U. of Minnesota	WCHA	42	26	35	61	84	....	....	....	....	....	....	....	....	....	....	....	....	....	....	....	....	....	....
2001-02	Springfield	AHL	73	13	29	42	116	....	....	....	....	....	....	....	....	....	....	....	....	....	....	....	....	....	....
2002-03	Springfield	AHL	70	10	22	32	65	....	....	....	....	....	....	....	....	....	6	0	4	4	6	....	....	....	....
2003-04	**Phoenix**	**NHL**	**15**	**1**	**1**	**2**	**20**	**0**	**0**	**0**	**29**	**3.4**	**–3**	**106**	**39.6**	**16:00**	....	....	....	....	....	....	....	....	....
	Springfield	AHL	56	14	18	32	91	....	....	....	....	....	....	....	....	....	....	....	....	....	....	....	....	....	....
2004-05	Utah Grizzlies	AHL	80	18	15	33	117	....	....	....	....	....	....	....	....	....	....	....	....	....	....	....	....	....	....
2005-06	**Minnesota**	**NHL**	**10**	**0**	**1**	**1**	**2**	**0**	**0**	**0**	**16**	**0.0**	**–1**	**68**	**38.2**	**10:48**	....	....	....	....	....	....	....	....	....
	Houston Aeros	AHL	71	34	64	98	138	....	....	....	....	....	....	....	....	....	8	1	7	8	20	....	....	....	....
	NHL Totals		**25**	**1**	**2**	**3**	**22**	**0**	**0**	**0**	**45**	**2.2**		**174**	**39.1**	**13:55**	....	....	....	....	....	....	....	....	....

WCHA Second All-Star Team (2001) • AHL First All-Star Team (2006)

• Statistics for **Apple Valley** (High-MN) are career totals for 1995-1997 seasons. Traded to **Minnesota** by **Phoenix** with Dustin Wood for Zbynek Michalek, August 26, 2005. Signed as a free agent by **Toronto**, July 13, 2006.

WHITE, Colin
(WIGHT, KAWL-ihn) **N.J.**

Defense. Shoots left. 6'4", 215 lbs. Born, New Glasgow, N.S., December 12, 1977. New Jersey's 5th choice, 49th overall, in 1996 Entry Draft.

Season	Club	League	GP	G	A	Pts	PIM	PP	SH	GW	S	%	+/-	TF	F%	Min	GP	G	A	Pts	PIM	PP	SH	GW	Min
1994-95	Laval Titan	QMJHL	7	0	1	1	32	....	....	....	....	....	....	....	....	....	....	....	....	....	....	....	....	....	....
	Hull Olympiques	QMJHL	5	0	1	1	4	....	....	....	....	....	....	....	....	....	12	0	0	0	23	....	....	....	....
1995-96	Hull Olympiques	QMJHL	62	2	8	10	303	....	....	....	....	....	....	....	....	....	18	0	4	4	42	....	....	....	....
1996-97	Hull Olympiques	QMJHL	63	3	12	15	297	....	....	....	....	....	....	....	....	....	14	3	12	15	65	....	....	....	....
1997-98	Albany River Rats	AHL	76	3	13	16	235	....	....	....	....	....	....	....	....	....	13	0	0	0	55	....	....	....	....
1998-99	Albany River Rats	AHL	77	2	12	14	265	....	....	....	....	....	....	....	....	....	5	0	1	1	8	....	....	....	....
99-2000 ♦	**New Jersey**	**NHL**	**21**	**2**	**1**	**3**	**40**	**0**	**0**	**1**	**29**	**6.9**	**3**	**0**	**0.0**	**14:45**	**23**	**1**	**5**	**6**	**18**	**0**	**0**	**1**	**14:25**
	Albany River Rats	AHL	52	5	21	26	176	....	....	....	....	....	....	....	....	....	....	....	....	....	....	....	....	....	....

			Regular Season														Playoffs								
Season	Club	League	GP	G	A	Pts	PIM	PP	SH	GW	S	%	+/-	TF	F%	Min	GP	G	A	Pts	PIM	PP	SH	GW	Min
2000-01	New Jersey	NHL	82	1	19	20	155	0	0	1	114	0.9	32	0	0.0	19:06	25	0	3	3	42	0	0	0	16:45
2001-02	New Jersey	NHL	73	2	3	5	133	0	0	0	81	2.5	6	0	0.0	20:06	6	0	0	0	2	0	0	0	21:50
2002-03 ♦	New Jersey	NHL	72	5	8	13	98	0	0	1	81	6.2	19	0	0.0	19:41	24	0	5	5	29	0	0	0	22:02
2003-04	New Jersey	NHL	75	2	11	13	96	0	0	0	61	3.3	10	0	0.0	21:02	5	0	0	0	4	0	0	0	19:40
2004-05			DID NOT PLAY																						
2005-06	New Jersey	NHL	73	3	14	17	91	1	0	1	60	5.0	−2	0	0.0	21:48	4	0	0	0	4	0	0	0	17:39
	NHL Totals		396	15	56	71	613	1	0	4	426	3.5		0	0.0	20:01	87	1	13	14	99	0	0	1	18:09

QMJHL All-Rookie Team (1996) • NHL All-Rookie Team (2001)

WHITE, Ian

(WIGHT, EE-uhn) **TOR.**

Defense. Shoots right. 5'10", 185 lbs. Born, Winnipeg, Man., June 4, 1984. Toronto's 6th choice, 191st overall, in 2002 Entry Draft.

99-2000	Eastman Selects	MAHA	32	29	33	62	36																		
2000-01	Swift Current	WHL	69	12	31	43	24																		
2001-02	Swift Current	WHL	70	32	47	79	40										12	4	5	9	12				
2002-03	Swift Current	WHL	64	24	44	68	44										4	0	4	4	0				
2003-04	St. John's	AHL	8	0	4	4	2																		
	Swift Current	WHL	43	9	23	32	32										5	1	3	4	8				
2004-05	St. John's	AHL	78	4	22	26	54										5	0	2	2	2				
2005-06	**Toronto**	**NHL**	**12**	**1**	**5**	**6**	**10**	**0**	**0**	**0**	**21**	**4.8**	**2**	**0**	**0.0**	**19:07**									
	Toronto Marlies	AHL	59	7	30	37	42										5	1	4	5	4				
	NHL Totals		12	1	5	6	10	0	0	0	21	4.8		0	0.0	19:07									

WHL East Second All-Star Team (2002) • WHL East First All-Star Team (2003)

WHITE, Todd

(WIGHT, TAWD) **MIN.**

Center. Shoots left. 5'10", 194 lbs. Born, Kanata, Ont., May 21, 1975.

1990-91	Powassan	NOJHA	38	34	38	72	118																		
1991-92	Kanata Valley	CJHL	55	39	49	88	30																		
1992-93	Kanata Valley	CJHL	49	51	87	138	46																		
1993-94	Clarkson Knights	ECAC	33	10	12	22	28																		
1994-95	Clarkson Knights	ECAC	34	13	16	29	44																		
1995-96	Clarkson Knights	ECAC	38	29	43	72	36																		
1996-97	Clarkson Knights	ECAC	37	*38	*36	*74	22																		
1997-98	**Chicago**	**NHL**	**7**	**1**	**0**	**1**	**2**	**0**	**0**	**0**	**3**	**33.3**	**0**												
	Indianapolis Ice	IHL	65	46	36	82	28										5	2	3	5	4				
1998-99	**Chicago**	**NHL**	**35**	**5**	**8**	**13**	**20**	**2**	**0**	**0**	**43**	**11.6**	**−1**	**452**	**46.0**	**13:39**									
	Chicago Wolves	IHL	25	11	13	24	8										10	1	4	5	8				
99-2000	**Chicago**	**NHL**	**1**	**0**	**0**	**0**	**0**	**0**	**0**	**0**	**0**	**0.0**	**0**	**9**	**55.6**	**13:02**									
	Cleveland	IHL	42	21	30	51	32																		
	Philadelphia	**NHL**	**3**	**1**	**0**	**1**	**0**	**0**	**0**	**0**	**4**	**25.0**	**−1**	**25**	**40.0**	**10:29**									
	Philadelphia	AHL	32	19	24	43	12										5	2	1	3	8				
2000-01	**Ottawa**	**NHL**	**16**	**4**	**1**	**5**	**4**	**0**	**0**	**0**	**12**	**33.3**	**5**	**133**	**57.1**	**8:33**	**2**	**0**	**0**	**0**	**0**	**0**	**0**	**0**	**7:29**
	Grand Rapids	IHL	64	22	32	54	20										10	4	4	8	10				
2001-02	**Ottawa**	**NHL**	**81**	**20**	**30**	**50**	**24**	**4**	**0**	**1**	**147**	**13.6**	**12**	**1508**	**50.5**	**18:22**	**12**	**2**	**2**	**4**	**6**	**0**	**0**	**0**	**18:57**
2002-03	**Ottawa**	**NHL**	**80**	**25**	**35**	**60**	**28**	**8**	**1**	**5**	**144**	**17.4**	**19**	**1396**	**50.5**	**17:58**	**18**	**5**	**1**	**6**	**6**	**1**	**1**	**2**	**16:59**
2003-04	**Ottawa**	**NHL**	**53**	**9**	**20**	**29**	**22**	**1**	**1**	**2**	**98**	**9.2**	**12**	**879**	**52.0**	**17:32**	**7**	**1**	**0**	**1**	**4**	**0**	**0**	**0**	**18:04**
2004-05	Sodertalje SK	Sweden	1	0	1	1	4																		
2005-06	**Minnesota**	**NHL**	**61**	**19**	**21**	**40**	**18**	**5**	**0**	**0**	**109**	**17.4**	**−1**	**886**	**49.1**	**17:12**									
	NHL Totals		337	84	115	199	118	20	2	8	560	15.0		5288	50.2	16:51	39	8	3	11	16	1	1	2	17:18

ECAC Second All-Star Team (1996) • NCAA East Second All-American Team (1996) • ECAC First All-Star Team (1997) • ECAC Player of the Year (1997) • NCAA East First All-American Team (1997) • Garry F. Longman Memorial Trophy (Rookie of the Year – IHL) (1998)

Signed as a free agent by **Chicago**, August 27, 1997. Traded to **Philadelphia** by **Chicago** for future considerations, January 26, 2000. Signed as a free agent by **Ottawa**, July 12, 2000. Signed as a free agent by **Sodertalje** (Sweden), December 21, 2004. Traded to **Minnesota** by **Ottawa** for Colorado's 4th round choice (previously acquired, Ottawa selected Cody Bass) in 2005 Entry Draft, July 30, 2005.

WHITFIELD, Trent

(WHIHT-feeld, TREHNT) **ST.L.**

Center. Shoots left. 5'11", 204 lbs. Born, Estevan, Sask., June 17, 1977. Boston's 5th choice, 100th overall, in 1996 Entry Draft.

1993-94	Saskatoon Blazers	SMHL	36	26	22	48	42																		
	Spokane Chiefs	WHL	5	1	1	2	0																		
1994-95	Spokane Chiefs	WHL	48	8	17	25	26										11	7	6	13	5				
1995-96	Spokane Chiefs	WHL	72	33	51	84	75										18	8	10	18	10				
1996-97	Spokane Chiefs	WHL	58	34	42	76	74										9	5	7	12	10				
1997-98	Spokane Chiefs	WHL	65	38	44	82	97										18	9	10	19	15				
1998-99	Portland Pirates	AHL	50	10	8	18	20																		
	Hampton Roads	ECHL	19	13	12	25	12										4	2	0	2	14				
99-2000	Portland Pirates	AHL	79	18	35	53	52										3	1	1	2	2				
	Washington	**NHL**															**3**	**0**	**0**	**0**	**0**	**0**	**0**	**0**	**5:47**
2000-01	**Washington**	**NHL**	**61**	**2**	**4**	**6**	**35**	**0**	**0**	**0**	**47**	**4.3**	**3**	**520**	**51.9**	**9:39**	**5**	**0**	**0**	**0**	**2**	**0**	**0**	**0**	**7:07**
	Portland Pirates	AHL	19	9	11	20	27																		
2001-02	**Washington**	**NHL**	**24**	**0**	**1**	**1**	**28**	**0**	**0**	**0**	**15**	**0.0**	**−3**	**189**	**54.0**	**7:06**									
	Portland Pirates	AHL	10	4	4	8	8																		
	NY Rangers	**NHL**	**1**	**0**	**0**	**0**	**0**	**0**	**0**	**0**	**0**	**0.0**	**1**	**18**	**50.0**	**12:44**									
	Portland Pirates	AHL	24	10	16	26	16																		
2002-03	**Washington**	**NHL**	**14**	**1**	**1**	**2**	**6**	**0**	**0**	**1**	**4**	**25.0**	**1**	**124**	**57.3**	**8:30**	**6**	**0**	**0**	**0**	**10**	**0**	**0**	**0**	**11:01**
	Portland Pirates	AHL	64	27	34	61	42																		
2003-04	**Washington**	**NHL**	**44**	**6**	**5**	**11**	**14**	**0**	**1**	**2**	**38**	**15.8**	**−2**	**598**	**55.4**	**12:48**									
	Portland Pirates	AHL	24	8	7	15	22																		
2004-05	Portland Pirates	AHL	67	17	38	55	75																		
2005-06	**St. Louis**	**NHL**	**30**	**2**	**5**	**7**	**14**	**1**	**0**	**0**	**41**	**4.9**	**−3**	**330**	**54.6**	**11:56**									
	Peoria Rivermen	AHL	41	19	34	53	18																		
	NHL Totals		174	11	16	27	97	1	1	3	145	7.6		1779	54.1	10:25	14	0	0	0	12	0	0	0	8:30

WHL West First All-Star Team (1997) • WHL West Second All-Star Team (1998)

Signed as a free agent by **Washington**, September 1, 1998. Claimed on waivers by **NY Rangers** from **Washington**, January 16, 2002. Claimed on waivers by **Washington** from **NY Rangers**, February 1, 2002. Signed as a free agent by **St. Louis**, August 2, 2005.

WHITNEY, Ray

(WHIHT-nee, RAY) **CAR.**

Left wing. Shoots right. 5'10", 178 lbs. Born, Fort Saskatchewan, Alta., May 8, 1972. San Jose's 2nd choice, 23rd overall, in 1991 Entry Draft.

1987-88	Ft. Saskatchewan	AMHL	71	80	155	235	119																		
1988-89	Spokane Chiefs	WHL	71	17	33	50	16																		
1989-90	Spokane Chiefs	WHL	71	57	56	113	50										6	3	4	7	6				
1990-91	Spokane Chiefs	WHL	72	67	118	*185	36										15	13	18	*31	12				
1991-92	Kolner EC	Germany	10	3	6	9	4																		
	Canada	Nat-Tm	5	1	0	1	6																		
	San Jose	**NHL**	**2**	**0**	**3**	**3**	**0**	**0**	**0**	**0**	**4**	**0.0**	**−1**												
	San Diego Gulls	IHL	63	36	54	90	12										4	0	0	0	0				
1992-93	**San Jose**	**NHL**	**26**	**4**	**6**	**10**	**4**	**1**	**0**	**0**	**24**	**16.7**	**−14**												
	Kansas City	IHL	46	20	33	53	14										12	5	7	12	2				
1993-94	**San Jose**	**NHL**	**61**	**14**	**26**	**40**	**14**	**1**	**0**	**0**	**82**	**17.1**	**2**				**14**	**0**	**4**	**4**	**8**	**0**	**0**	**0**	
1994-95	**San Jose**	**NHL**	**39**	**13**	**12**	**25**	**14**	**4**	**0**	**1**	**67**	**19.4**	**−7**				**11**	**4**	**4**	**8**	**2**	**0**	**0**	**1**	
1995-96	**San Jose**	**NHL**	**60**	**17**	**24**	**41**	**16**	**4**	**2**	**2**	**106**	**16.0**	**−23**												
1996-97	**San Jose**	**NHL**	**12**	**0**	**2**	**2**	**4**	**0**	**0**	**0**	**24**	**0.0**	**−6**												
	Kentucky	AHL	9	1	7	8	2																		
	Utah Grizzlies	IHL	43	13	35	48	34										7	3	1	4	6				
1997-98	**Edmonton**	**NHL**	**9**	**1**	**3**	**4**	**0**	**0**	**0**	**0**	**19**	**5.3**	**−1**												
	Florida	**NHL**	**68**	**32**	**29**	**61**	**28**	**12**	**0**	**2**	**156**	**20.5**	**10**												
1998-99	**Florida**	**NHL**	**81**	**26**	**38**	**64**	**18**	**7**	**0**	**6**	**193**	**13.5**	**−3**	**144**	**43.8**	**18:20**									
99-2000	**Florida**	**NHL**	**81**	**29**	**42**	**71**	**35**	**5**	**0**	**3**	**198**	**14.6**	**16**	**198**	**49.0**	**18:41**	**4**	**1**	**0**	**1**	**4**	**0**	**0**	**0**	**18:13**

			Regular Season														Playoffs								
Season	**Club**	**League**	**GP**	**G**	**A**	**Pts**	**PIM**	**PP**	**SH**	**GW**	**S**	**%**	**+/-**	**TF**	**F%**	**Min**	**GP**	**G**	**A**	**Pts**	**PIM**	**PP**	**SH**	**GW**	**Min**
2000-01	**Florida**	**NHL**	**43**	**10**	**21**	**31**	**28**	**5**	**0**	**0**	**117**	**8.5**	**–16**	**38**	**39.5**	**17:41**	....	....	....	....	....	....	....	....	....
	Columbus	**NHL**	**3**	**0**	**3**	**3**	**2**	**0**	**0**	**0**	**3**	**0.0**	**–1**	**19**	**36.8**	**20:17**	....	....	....	....	....	....	....	....	....
2001-02	**Columbus**	**NHL**	**67**	**21**	**40**	**61**	**12**	**6**	**0**	**3**	**210**	**10.0**	**–22**	**21**	**47.6**	**20:13**	....	....	....	....	....	....	....	....	....
2002-03	**Columbus**	**NHL**	**81**	**24**	**52**	**76**	**22**	**8**	**2**	**2**	**235**	**10.2**	**–26**	**29**	**44.8**	**21:00**	....	....	....	....	....	....	....	....	....
2003-04	**Detroit**	**NHL**	**67**	**14**	**29**	**43**	**22**	**3**	**1**	**4**	**119**	**11.8**	**7**	**18**	**38.9**	**16:24**	**12**	**1**	**3**	**4**	**4**	**0**	**0**	**1**	**11:56**
2004-05		Did not play																							
2005-06 ♦	**Carolina**	**NHL**	**63**	**17**	**38**	**55**	**42**	**12**	**0**	**2**	**147**	**11.6**	**0**	**13**	**38.5**	**17:11**	**24**	**9**	**6**	**15**	**14**	**5**	**0**	**1**	**14:07**
	NHL Totals		**763**	**222**	**368**	**590**	**261**	**68**	**5**	**25**	**1704**	**13.0**		**480**	**45.2**	**18:38**	**65**	**15**	**17**	**32**	**32**	**5**	**0**	**3**	**13:52**

WHL West First All-Star Team (1991) • WHL Player of the Year (1991) • Memorial Cup Tournament All-Star Team (1991) • George Parsons Trophy (Memorial Cup Tournament Most Sportsmanlike Player) (1991)

Played in NHL All-Star Game (2000, 2003)

Signed as a free agent by **Edmonton**, October 1, 1997. Claimed on waivers by **Florida** from **Edmonton**, November 6, 1997. Traded to **Columbus** by **Florida** with future considerations for Kevyn Adams and Columbus's 4th round choice (Michael Woodford) in 2001 Entry Draft, March 13, 2001. Signed as a free agent by **Detroit**, July 30, 2003. Signed as a free agent by **Carolina**, August 7, 2005.

WHITNEY, Ryan

(WIHT-nee, RIGH-uhn) **PIT.**

Defense. Shoots left. 6'4", 202 lbs. Born, Boston, MA, February 19, 1983. Pittsburgh's 1st choice, 5th overall, in 2002 Entry Draft.

99-2000	Thayer Academy	High-MA	22	5	33	38	....	....	....	....	....	....	....	....	....	....	....	....	....	....	....	....	....	....	....
2000-01	USNTDP	U-18	40	7	23	30	64	....	....	....	....	....	....	....	....	....	....	....	....	....	....	....	....	....	....
	USNTDP	USHL	20	2	8	10	22	....	....	....	....	....	....	....	....	....	....	....	....	....	....	....	....	....	....
2001-02	Boston University	H-East	35	4	17	21	46	....	....	....	....	....	....	....	....	....	....	....	....	....	....	....	....	....	....
2002-03	Boston University	H-East	34	3	10	13	48	....	....	....	....	....	....	....	....	....	....	....	....	....	....	....	....	....	....
2003-04	Boston University	H-East	38	9	16	25	56	....	....	....	....	....	....	....	....	....	....	....	....	....	....	....	....	....	....
	Wilkes-Barre	AHL	....	....	....	....	....	....	....	....	....	....	....	....	....	....	20	1	9	10	6	....	....	....	....
2004-05	Wilkes-Barre	AHL	80	6	35	41	101	....	....	....	....	....	....	....	....	....	11	2	7	9	12	....	....	....	....
2005-06	**Pittsburgh**	**NHL**	**68**	**6**	**32**	**38**	**85**	**2**	**0**	**1**	**113**	**5.3**	**–7**	**1**	**0.0**	**23:50**	....	....	....	....	....	....	....	....	....
	Wilkes-Barre	AHL	9	5	9	14	6	....	....	....	....	....	....	....	....	....	11	1	4	5	8	....	....	....	....
	NHL Totals		**68**	**6**	**32**	**38**	**85**	**2**	**0**	**1**	**113**	**5.3**		**1**	**0.0**	**23:50**	....	....	....	....	....	....	....	....	....

Hockey East All-Rookie Team (2002)

WIDEMAN, Dennis

(WIGHD-muhn, DEH-nihs) **ST.L.**

Defense. Shoots right. 6', 200 lbs. Born, Kitchener, Ont., March 20, 1983. Buffalo's 9th choice, 241st overall, in 2002 Entry Draft.

1998-99	Elmira	OHA-B	47	18	30	48	142	....	....	....	....	....	....	....	....	....	....	....	....	....	....	....	....	....	....
99-2000	Sudbury Wolves	OHL	63	10	26	36	64	....	....	....	....	....	....	....	....	....	12	1	2	3	22	....	....	....	....
2000-01	Sudbury Wolves	OHL	25	7	11	18	37	....	....	....	....	....	....	....	....	....	....	....	....	....	....	....	....	....	....
	London Knights	OHL	24	8	8	16	38	....	....	....	....	....	....	....	....	....	5	0	4	4	6	....	....	....	....
2001-02	London Knights	OHL	65	27	42	69	141	....	....	....	....	....	....	....	....	....	12	4	9	13	26	....	....	....	....
2002-03	London Knights	OHL	55	20	27	47	83	....	....	....	....	....	....	....	....	....	14	6	6	12	10	....	....	....	....
2003-04	London Knights	OHL	60	24	41	65	85	....	....	....	....	....	....	....	....	....	15	7	10	17	17	....	....	....	....
2004-05	Worcester IceCats	AHL	79	13	30	43	65	....	....	....	....	....	....	....	....	....	....	....	....	....	....	....	....	....	....
2005-06	**St. Louis**	**NHL**	**67**	**8**	**16**	**24**	**83**	**5**	**1**	**1**	**150**	**5.3**	**–31**	**1**	**0.0**	**21:41**	....	....	....	....	....	....	....	....	....
	Peoria Rivermen	AHL	12	2	4	6	31	....	....	....	....	....	....	....	....	....	....	....	....	....	....	....	....	....	....
	NHL Totals		**67**	**8**	**16**	**24**	**83**	**5**	**1**	**1**	**150**	**5.3**		**1**	**0.0**	**21:41**	....	....	....	....	....	....	....	....	....

OHL First All-Star Team (2004)

Signed as a free agent by **St. Louis**, June 30, 2004.

WIEMER, Jason

(WEE-muhr, JAY-suhn) **N.J.**

Center. Shoots left. 6'1", 225 lbs. Born, Kimberley, B.C., April 14, 1976. Tampa Bay's 1st choice, 8th overall, in 1994 Entry Draft.

1991-92	Kimberley	RMJHL	45	33	33	66	211	....	....	....	....	....	....	....	....	....	....	....	....	....	....	....	....	....	....
	Portland	WHL	2	0	1	1	0	....	....	....	....	....	....	....	....	....	....	....	....	....	....	....	....	....	....
1992-93	Portland	WHL	68	18	34	52	159	....	....	....	....	....	....	....	....	....	16	7	3	10	27	....	....	....	....
1993-94	Portland	WHL	72	45	51	96	236	....	....	....	....	....	....	....	....	....	10	4	4	8	32	....	....	....	....
1994-95	Portland	WHL	16	10	14	24	63	....	....	....	....	....	....	....	....	....	....	....	....	....	....	....	....	....	....
	Tampa Bay	**NHL**	**36**	**1**	**4**	**5**	**44**	**0**	**0**	**0**	**10**	**10.0**	**–2**	....	....	....	....	....	....	....	....	....	....	....	....
1995-96	**Tampa Bay**	**NHL**	**66**	**9**	**9**	**18**	**81**	**4**	**0**	**1**	**89**	**10.1**	**–9**	....	....	....	**6**	**1**	**0**	**1**	**28**	**1**	**0**	**0**	....
1996-97	**Tampa Bay**	**NHL**	**63**	**9**	**5**	**14**	**134**	**2**	**0**	**0**	**103**	**8.7**	**–13**	....	....	....	....	....	....	....	....	....	....	....	....
	Adirondack	AHL	4	1	0	1	7	....	....	....	....	....	....	....	....	....	....	....	....	....	....	....	....	....	....
1997-98	**Tampa Bay**	**NHL**	**67**	**8**	**9**	**17**	**132**	**2**	**0**	**0**	**106**	**7.5**	**–9**	....	....	....	....	....	....	....	....	....	....	....	....
	Calgary	**NHL**	**12**	**4**	**1**	**5**	**28**	**1**	**0**	**2**	**16**	**25.0**	**–1**	....	....	....	....	....	....	....	....	....	....	....	....
1998-99	**Calgary**	**NHL**	**78**	**8**	**13**	**21**	**177**	**1**	**0**	**1**	**128**	**6.3**	**–12**	**867**	**40.9**	**13:17**	....	....	....	....	....	....	....	....	....
99-2000	**Calgary**	**NHL**	**64**	**11**	**11**	**22**	**120**	**2**	**0**	**3**	**104**	**10.6**	**–10**	**955**	**47.6**	**14:41**	....	....	....	....	....	....	....	....	....
2000-01	**Calgary**	**NHL**	**65**	**10**	**5**	**15**	**177**	**3**	**0**	**1**	**76**	**13.2**	**–15**	**599**	**51.1**	**13:56**	....	....	....	....	....	....	....	....	....
2001-02	**Florida**	**NHL**	**70**	**11**	**20**	**31**	**178**	**5**	**1**	**1**	**115**	**9.6**	**–4**	**1241**	**44.1**	**17:09**	....	....	....	....	....	....	....	....	....
2002-03	**NY Islanders**	**NHL**	**81**	**9**	**19**	**28**	**116**	**0**	**1**	**2**	**139**	**6.5**	**5**	**347**	**49.0**	**12:26**	**5**	**0**	**0**	**0**	**23**	**0**	**0**	**0**	**13:37**
2003-04	**NY Islanders**	**NHL**	**13**	**1**	**3**	**4**	**24**	**0**	**0**	**0**	**14**	**7.1**	**–1**	**72**	**47.2**	**11:36**	....	....	....	....	....	....	....	....	....
	Minnesota	**NHL**	**62**	**7**	**11**	**18**	**106**	**1**	**0**	**0**	**89**	**7.9**	**–6**	**726**	**44.4**	**13:57**	....	....	....	....	....	....	....	....	....
2004-05		Did not play																							
2005-06	**Calgary**	**NHL**	**33**	**1**	**2**	**3**	**65**	**0**	**0**	**0**	**24**	**4.2**	**–3**	**126**	**46.8**	**8:56**	....	....	....	....	....	....	....	....	....
	New Jersey	**NHL**	**16**	**1**	**0**	**1**	**38**	**0**	**0**	**0**	**13**	**7.7**	**–1**	**4**	**50.0**	**6:20**	**8**	**0**	**0**	**0**	**16**	**0**	**0**	**0**	**5:32**
	NHL Totals		**726**	**90**	**112**	**202**	**1420**	**21**	**2**	**11**	**1026**	**8.8**		**4937**	**45.6**	**13:29**	**19**	**1**	**0**	**1**	**67**	**1**	**0**	**0**	**8:39**

Traded to **Calgary** by **Tampa Bay** for Sandy McCarthy and Calgary's 3rd (Brad Richards) and 5th (Curtis Rich) round choices in 1998 Entry Draft, March 24, 1998. Traded to **Florida** by **Calgary** with Valeri Bure for Rob Neidermayer and Philadelphia's 2nd round choice (previously acquired, Calgary selected Andrei Medvedev) in 2001 Entry Draft, June 24, 2001. Traded to **NY Islanders** by **Florida** for Branislav Mezei, July 3, 2002. Claimed on waivers by **Minnesota** from **NY Islanders**, November 13, 2003. Signed as a free agent by **Calgary**, August 5, 2004. Traded to **New Jersey** by **Calgary** for New Jersey's 4th round choice (Hugo Carpentier) in 2006 Entry Draft, March 9, 2006.

WILLIAMS, Jason

(WIHL-yuhms, JAY-suhn) **DET.**

Center. Shoots right. 5'11", 185 lbs. Born, London, Ont., August 11, 1980.

1995-96	Mount Brydges	OHA-D	36	31	28	59	18	....	....	....	....	....	....	....	....	....	....	....	....	....	....	....	....	....	....
1996-97	Peterborough	OHL	60	4	8	12	8	....	....	....	....	....	....	....	....	....	10	1	0	1	2	....	....	....	....
1997-98	Peterborough	OHL	55	8	27	35	31	....	....	....	....	....	....	....	....	....	4	0	1	1	2	....	....	....	....
1998-99	Peterborough	OHL	68	26	48	74	42	....	....	....	....	....	....	....	....	....	5	1	2	3	2	....	....	....	....
99-2000	Peterborough	OHL	66	36	37	75	64	....	....	....	....	....	....	....	....	....	5	2	1	3	2	....	....	....	....
2000-01	**Detroit**	**NHL**	**5**	**0**	**3**	**3**	**2**	**0**	**0**	**0**	**7**	**0.0**	**1**	**56**	**39.3**	**12:24**	**2**	**0**	**0**	**0**	**0**	**0**	**0**	**0**	**11:45**
	Cincinnati	AHL	76	24	45	69	48	....	....	....	....	....	....	....	....	....	1	0	0	0	2	....	....	....	....
2001-02 ♦	**Detroit**	**NHL**	**25**	**8**	**2**	**10**	**4**	**4**	**0**	**0**	**32**	**25.0**	**2**	**208**	**47.6**	**10:50**	**9**	**0**	**0**	**0**	**2**	**0**	**0**	**0**	**6:12**
	Cincinnati	AHL	52	23	27	50	27	....	....	....	....	....	....	....	....	....	3	0	1	1	6	....	....	....	....
2002-03	**Detroit**	**NHL**	**16**	**3**	**3**	**6**	**2**	**1**	**0**	**0**	**20**	**15.0**	**3**	**78**	**51.3**	**10:43**	....	....	....	....	....	....	....	....	....
	Grand Rapids	AHL	45	23	22	45	18	....	....	....	....	....	....	....	....	....	15	1	7	8	16	....	....	....	....
2003-04	**Detroit**	**NHL**	**49**	**6**	**7**	**13**	**15**	**0**	**0**	**0**	**44**	**13.6**	**1**	**315**	**49.2**	**9:27**	**3**	**0**	**0**	**0**	**2**	**0**	**0**	**0**	**6:11**
2004-05	Assat Pori	Finland	43	26	17	43	52	....	....	....	....	....	....	....	....	....	2	1	1	2	4	....	....	....	....
2005-06	**Detroit**	**NHL**	**80**	**21**	**37**	**58**	**26**	**6**	**0**	**4**	**177**	**11.9**	**4**	**29**	**55.2**	**14:55**	**6**	**1**	**1**	**2**	**6**	**0**	**0**	**0**	**18:10**
	NHL Totals		**175**	**38**	**52**	**90**	**49**	**11**	**0**	**4**	**280**	**13.6**		**686**	**48.4**	**12:21**	**20**	**1**	**1**	**2**	**10**	**0**	**0**	**0**	**10:20**

Signed as a free agent by **Detroit**, September 18, 2000. Signed as a free agent by **Pori** (Finland), October 18, 2004.

WILLIAMS, Jeremy

(WIHL-yuhms, JAIR-eh-mee) **TOR.**

Center. Shoots right. 5'11", 184 lbs. Born, Regina, Sask., January 26, 1984. Toronto's 5th choice, 220th overall, in 2003 Entry Draft.

2001-02	Swift Current	SMMHL	24	18	23	41	64	....	....	....	....	....	....	....	....	....	....	....	....	....	....	....	....	....	....
	Swift Current	WHL	32	6	7	13	30	....	....	....	....	....	....	....	....	....	12	1	0	1	4	....	....	....	....
2002-03	Swift Current	WHL	72	41	52	93	117	....	....	....	....	....	....	....	....	....	4	1	0	1	6	....	....	....	....
2003-04	Swift Current	WHL	68	*52	49	101	82	....	....	....	....	....	....	....	....	....	5	2	1	3	12	....	....	....	....
	St. John's	AHL	4	0	2	2	0	....	....	....	....	....	....	....	....	....	....	....	....	....	....	....	....	....	....
2004-05	St. John's	AHL	75	16	20	36	24	....	....	....	....	....	....	....	....	....	5	0	0	0	0	....	....	....	....

			Regular Season														Playoffs								
Season	Club	League	GP	G	A	Pts	PIM	PP	SH	GW	S	%	+/-	TF	F%	Min	GP	G	A	Pts	PIM	PP	SH	GW	Min
2005-06	**Toronto**	**NHL**	1	1	0	1	0	0	0	0	1	100.0	0	0	0.0	9:31	....	....	....	....	....	....	....	....	....
	Toronto Marlies	AHL	55	23	33	56	62	....	....	....	....	....	....	....	....	....	5	1	0	1	6	....	....	....	....
	NHL Totals		1	1	0	1	0	0	0	0	1	100.0	0	0	0.0	9:31	....	....	....	....	....	....	....	....	....

WHL East First All-Star Team (2004) • Canadian Major Junior First All-Star Team (2004)
• One of only three players (Rolly Huard, Dean Morton) to score a goal in his only NHL game.

WILLIAMS, Justin

(WIHL-yuhms, JUHS-tihn) **CAR.**

Right wing. Shoots right. 6'1", 190 lbs. Born, Cobourg, Ont., October 4, 1981. Philadelphia's 1st choice, 28th overall, in 2000 Entry Draft.

Season	Club	League	GP	G	A	Pts	PIM	PP	SH	GW	S	%	+/-	TF	F%	Min	GP	G	A	Pts	PIM	PP	SH	GW	Min
1997-98	Colborne Colts	OHA-C	36	32	35	67	26	....	....	....	....	....	....	....	....	....	....	....	....	....	....	....	....	....	....
	Cobourg Cougars	OPJHL	17	0	3	3	5	....	....	....	....	....	....	....	....	....	....	....	....	....	....	....	....	....	....
1998-99	Plymouth Whalers	OHL	47	4	8	12	28	....	....	....	....	....	....	....	....	....	7	1	2	3	0	....	....	....	....
99-2000	Plymouth Whalers	OHL	68	37	46	83	46	....	....	....	....	....	....	....	....	....	23	*14	16	*30	10	....	....	....	....
2000-01	**Philadelphia**	**NHL**	63	12	13	25	22	0	0	0	99	12.1	6	13	53.9	12:31	5	0	0	0	4	0	0	0	16:42
2001-02	**Philadelphia**	**NHL**	75	17	23	40	32	0	0	1	162	10.5	11	16	25.0	14:27	12	1	5	6	8	0	0	1	14:11
2002-03	**Philadelphia**	**NHL**	41	8	16	24	22	0	0	2	105	7.6	15	16	50.0	15:57	....	....	....	....	....	....	....	....	....
2003-04	**Philadelphia**	**NHL**	47	6	20	26	32	3	0	1	107	5.6	10	38	31.6	15:30	....	....	....	....	....	....	....	....	....
	Carolina	**NHL**	32	5	13	18	32	1	0	0	96	5.2	2	25	36.0	18:52	....	....	....	....	....	....	....	....	....
2004-05	Lulea HF	Sweden	49	14	18	32	61	....	....	....	....	....	....	....	....	....	4	0	1	1	29	....	....	....	....
2005-06♦	**Carolina**	**NHL**	82	31	45	76	60	8	4	4	255	12.2	1	17	29.4	21:08	25	7	11	18	34	0	1	1	21:36
	NHL Totals		340	79	130	209	200	12	4	8	824	9.6		125	36.0	16:27	42	8	16	24	46	0	1	2	18:54

• Missed majority of 2002-03 season recovering from shoulder (November 15, 2002 vs. Carolina) and knee (January 18, 2003 vs. Tampa Bay) injuries. Traded to **Carolina** by **Philadelphia** for Danny Markov, January 20, 2004. Signed as a free agent by **Lulea** (Sweden), September 21, 2004.

WILLIS, Shane

(WIH-lihs, SHAYN) **CAR.**

Right wing. Shoots right. 6'1", 195 lbs. Born, Edmonton, Alta., June 13, 1977. Carolina's 4th choice, 88th overall, in 1997 Entry Draft.

Season	Club	League	GP	G	A	Pts	PIM	PP	SH	GW	S	%	+/-	TF	F%	Min	GP	G	A	Pts	PIM	PP	SH	GW	Min
1992-93	Red Deer	ABHL	36	32	18	50	88	....	....	....	....	....	....	....	....	....	....	....	....	....	....	....	....	....	....
1993-94	Red Deer Royals	AMHL	34	40	26	66	103	....	....	....	....	....	....	....	....	....	....	....	....	....	....	....	....	....	....
1994-95	Prince Albert	WHL	65	24	19	43	38	....	....	....	....	....	....	....	....	....	13	3	4	7	6	....	....	....	....
1995-96	Prince Albert	WHL	69	41	40	81	47	....	....	....	....	....	....	....	....	....	18	11	10	21	18	....	....	....	....
1996-97	Prince Albert	WHL	41	34	22	56	63	....	....	....	....	....	....	....	....	....	....	....	....	....	....	....	....	....	....
	Lethbridge	WHL	26	22	17	39	24	....	....	....	....	....	....	....	....	....	19	13	11	24	20	....	....	....	....
1997-98	Lethbridge	WHL	64	58	54	112	73	....	....	....	....	....	....	....	....	....	4	2	3	5	6	....	....	....	....
	New Haven	AHL	1	0	1	1	2	....	....	....	....	....	....	....	....	....	....	....	....	....	....	....	....	....	....
1998-99	**Carolina**	**NHL**	7	0	0	0	0	0	0	0	1	0.0	–2	0	0.0	2:14	....	....	....	....	....	....	....	....	....
	New Haven	AHL	73	31	50	81	49	....	....	....	....	....	....	....	....	....	....	....	....	....	....	....	....	....	....
99-2000	**Carolina**	**NHL**	2	0	0	0	0	0	0	0	1	0.0	–1	0	0.0	5:50	....	....	....	....	....	....	....	....	....
	Cincinnati	IHL	80	35	25	60	64	....	....	....	....	....	....	....	....	....	11	5	3	8	8	....	....	....	....
2000-01	**Carolina**	**NHL**	73	20	24	44	45	9	0	6	172	11.6	–6	10	20.0	15:58	2	0	0	0	0	0	0	0	12:56
2001-02	**Carolina**	**NHL**	59	7	10	17	24	2	0	0	126	5.6	–8	10	50.0	13:00	....	....	....	....	....	....	....	....	....
	Tampa Bay	**NHL**	21	4	3	7	6	0	0	0	29	13.8	0	12	8.3	11:18	....	....	....	....	....	....	....	....	....
2002-03	Springfield	AHL	56	16	16	32	26	....	....	....	....	....	....	....	....	....	6	4	2	6	4	....	....	....	....
2003-04	**Tampa Bay**	**NHL**	12	0	6	6	2	0	0	0	27	0.0	1	2	0.0	13:50	....	....	....	....	....	....	....	....	....
	Hershey Bears	AHL	55	27	21	48	71	....	....	....	....	....	....	....	....	....	....	....	....	....	....	....	....	....	....
2004-05	Springfield	AHL	58	18	16	34	29	....	....	....	....	....	....	....	....	....	....	....	....	....	....	....	....	....	....
2005-06	HC Davos	Swiss	32	5	15	20	53	....	....	....	....	....	....	....	....	....	....	....	....	....	....	....	....	....	....
	Linkopings HC	Sweden	6	0	1	1	4	....	....	....	....	....	....	....	....	....	13	6	5	11	10	....	....	....	....
	NHL Totals		174	31	43	74	77	11	0	6	356	8.7		34	23.5	13:35	2	0	0	0	0	0	0	0	12:56

• Re-entered NHL Entry Draft. Originally Tampa Bay's 3rd choice, 56th overall, in 1995 Entry Draft.
WHL East First All-Star Team (1997, 1998) • AHL All-Rookie Team (1999) • AHL First All-Star Team (1999) • Dudley "Red" Garrett Memorial Award (Rookie of the Year – AHL) (1999) • NHL All-Rookie Team (2001)
Traded to **Tampa Bay** by **Carolina** with Chris Dingman for Kevin Weekes, March 5, 2002. Signed as a free agent by **Davos** (Swiss). August 23, 2005. Signed as a free agent by **Carolina**, July 18, 2006.

WILLSIE, Brian

(WIHL-see, BRIGH-uhn) **L.A.**

Right wing. Shoots right. 6'1", 195 lbs. Born, London, Ont., March 16, 1978. Colorado's 7th choice, 146th overall, in 1996 Entry Draft.

Season	Club	League	GP	G	A	Pts	PIM	PP	SH	GW	S	%	+/-	TF	F%	Min	GP	G	A	Pts	PIM	PP	SH	GW	Min
1993-94	Belmont Bombers	OHA-D	13	9	5	14	14	....	....	....	....	....	....	....	....	....	....	....	....	....	....	....	....	....	....
1994-95	St. Thomas Stars	OHA-B	45	35	47	82	47	....	....	....	....	....	....	....	....	....	....	....	....	....	....	....	....	....	....
1995-96	Guelph Storm	OHL	65	13	21	34	18	....	....	....	....	....	....	....	....	....	16	4	2	6	6	....	....	....	....
1996-97	Guelph Storm	OHL	64	37	31	68	37	....	....	....	....	....	....	....	....	....	18	15	4	19	10	....	....	....	....
1997-98	Guelph Storm	OHL	57	45	31	76	41	....	....	....	....	....	....	....	....	....	12	9	5	14	18	....	....	....	....
1998-99	Hershey Bears	AHL	72	19	10	29	28	....	....	....	....	....	....	....	....	....	3	1	0	1	0	....	....	....	....
99-2000	**Colorado**	**NHL**	1	0	0	0	0	0	0	0	1	0.0	0	0	0.0	8:16	....	....	....	....	....	....	....	....	....
	Hershey Bears	AHL	78	20	39	59	44	....	....	....	....	....	....	....	....	....	12	2	6	8	8	....	....	....	....
2000-01	Hershey Bears	AHL	48	18	23	41	20	....	....	....	....	....	....	....	....	....	12	7	2	9	14	....	....	....	....
2001-02	**Colorado**	**NHL**	56	7	7	14	14	2	0	1	66	10.6	4	8	12.5	11:24	4	0	1	1	2	0	0	0	11:54
2002-03	**Colorado**	**NHL**	12	0	1	1	15	0	0	0	12	0.0	0	7	14.3	9:36	6	1	0	1	2	0	0	1	10:48
	Hershey Bears	AHL	59	29	28	57	49	....	....	....	....	....	....	....	....	....	....	....	....	....	....	....	....	....	....
2003-04	**Washington**	**NHL**	49	10	5	15	18	1	1	1	85	11.8	–7	46	34.8	12:42	....	....	....	....	....	....	....	....	....
2004-05	Ljubljana	Interliga	12	7	6	13	34	....	....	....	....	....	....	....	....	....	....	....	....	....	....	....	....	....	....
	Ljubljana	Slovenia	2	0	3	3	4	....	....	....	....	....	....	....	....	....	....	....	....	....	....	....	....	....	....
	Portland Pirates	AHL	53	23	17	40	47	....	....	....	....	....	....	....	....	....	....	....	....	....	....	....	....	....	....
2005-06	**Washington**	**NHL**	82	19	22	41	77	8	1	2	185	10.3	–19	52	51.9	16:40	....	....	....	....	....	....	....	....	....
	NHL Totals		200	36	35	71	124	11	2	4	349	10.3		113	39.8	13:45	10	1	1	2	4	0	0	1	11:14

OHL First All-Star Team (1998)
Claimed by **Washington** from **Colorado** in Waiver Draft, October 3, 2003. Signed as a free agent by **Ljubljana** (Slovenia), October 8, 2004. Signed as a free agent by **Portland** (AHL), December 15, 2004. Signed as a free agent by **Los Angeles**, July 4, 2006.

WILM, Clarke

(WIHLM, KLAHRK)

Center. Shoots left. 6', 202 lbs. Born, Central Butte, Sask., October 24, 1976. Calgary's 5th choice, 150th overall, in 1995 Entry Draft.

Season	Club	League	GP	G	A	Pts	PIM	PP	SH	GW	S	%	+/-	TF	F%	Min	GP	G	A	Pts	PIM	PP	SH	GW	Min
1991-92	Saskatoon Blazers	SMHL	36	18	28	46	16	....	....	....	....	....	....	....	....	....	....	....	....	....	....	....	....	....	....
	Saskatoon Blades	WHL	....	....	....	....	....	....	....	....	....	....	....	....	....	....	1	0	0	0	0	....	....	....	....
1992-93	Saskatoon Blades	WHL	69	14	19	33	71	....	....	....	....	....	....	....	....	....	9	4	2	6	13	....	....	....	....
1993-94	Saskatoon Blades	WHL	70	18	32	50	181	....	....	....	....	....	....	....	....	....	16	0	9	9	19	....	....	....	....
1994-95	Saskatoon Blades	WHL	71	20	39	59	179	....	....	....	....	....	....	....	....	....	10	6	1	7	21	....	....	....	....
1995-96	Saskatoon Blades	WHL	72	49	61	110	83	....	....	....	....	....	....	....	....	....	4	1	1	2	4	....	....	....	....
1996-97	Saint John Flames	AHL	62	9	19	28	107	....	....	....	....	....	....	....	....	....	5	2	0	2	15	....	....	....	....
1997-98	Saint John Flames	AHL	68	13	26	39	112	....	....	....	....	....	....	....	....	....	21	5	9	14	8	....	....	....	....
1998-99	**Calgary**	**NHL**	78	10	8	18	53	2	2	0	94	10.6	11	609	40.9	11:32	....	....	....	....	....	....	....	....	....
99-2000	**Calgary**	**NHL**	78	10	12	22	67	1	3	0	81	12.3	–6	872	44.4	12:38	....	....	....	....	....	....	....	....	....
2000-01	**Calgary**	**NHL**	81	7	8	15	69	2	0	0	85	8.2	–11	992	51.9	14:11	....	....	....	....	....	....	....	....	....
2001-02	**Calgary**	**NHL**	66	4	14	18	61	0	1	0	83	4.8	–1	995	51.1	15:00	....	....	....	....	....	....	....	....	....
2002-03	**Nashville**	**NHL**	82	5	11	16	36	0	0	0	108	4.6	–11	339	50.4	11:58	....	....	....	....	....	....	....	....	....
2003-04	**Toronto**	**NHL**	10	0	0	0	7	0	0	0	10	0.0	0	43	46.5	11:45	5	0	1	1	2	0	0	0	12:45
	St. John's	AHL	47	16	17	33	97	....	....	....	....	....	....	....	....	....	....	....	....	....	....	....	....	....	....
2004-05	St. John's	AHL	69	11	16	27	145	....	....	....	....	....	....	....	....	....	5	2	2	4	8	....	....	....	....
2005-06	**Toronto**	**NHL**	60	1	7	8	43	0	0	0	50	2.0	–15	694	52.3	11:47	....	....	....	....	....	....	....	....	....
	NHL Totals		455	37	60	97	336	5	6	0	511	7.2		4544	48.7	12:49	5	0	1	1	2	0	0	0	12:45

Signed as a free agent by **Nashville**, July 11, 2002. Signed as a free agent by **Toronto**, October 28, 2003.

Season	Club	League	GP	G	A	Pts	PIM	PP	SH	GW	S	%	+/-	TF	F%	Min	GP	G	A	Pts	PIM	PP	SH	GW	Min
			Regular Season														Playoffs								

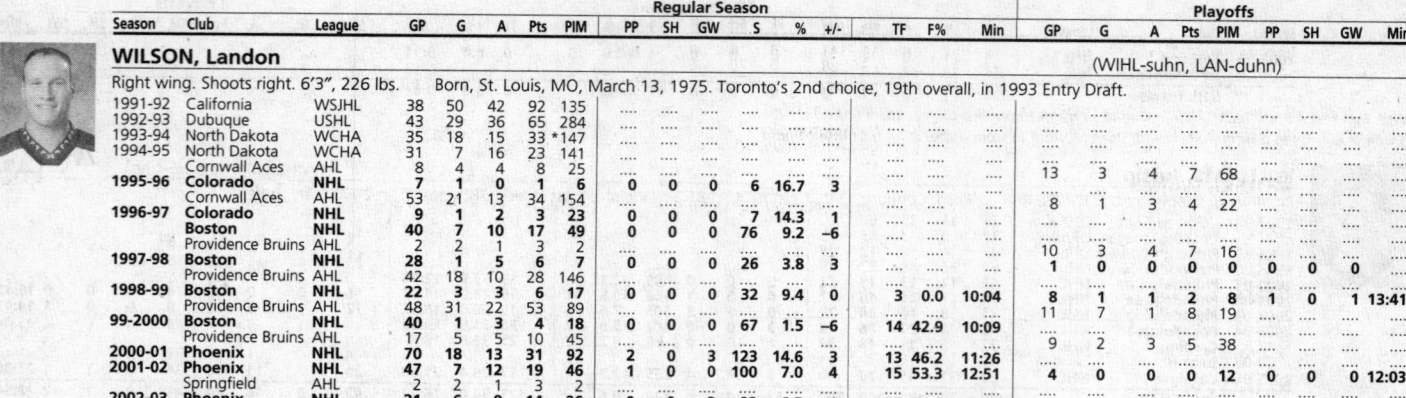

WILSON, Landon

(WIHL-suhn, LAN-duhn)

Right wing. Shoots right. 6'3", 226 lbs. Born, St. Louis, MO, March 13, 1975. Toronto's 2nd choice, 19th overall, in 1993 Entry Draft.

Season	Club	League	GP	G	A	Pts	PIM	PP	SH	GW	S	%	+/-	TF	F%	Min	GP	G	A	Pts	PIM	PP	SH	GW	Min
1991-92	California	WSJHL	38	50	42	92	135	....	....	....	....	....	....	....	....	....	....	....	....	....	....	....	....	....	....
1992-93	Dubuque	USHL	43	29	36	65	284	....	....	....	....	....	....	....	....	....	....	....	....	....	....	....	....	....	....
1993-94	North Dakota	WCHA	35	18	15	33	*147	....	....	....	....	....	....	....	....	....	....	....	....	....	....	....	....	....	....
1994-95	North Dakota	WCHA	31	7	16	23	141	....	....	....	....	....	....	....	....	....	....	....	....	....	....	....	....	....	....
	Cornwall Aces	AHL	8	4	4	8	25	....	....	....	....	....	....	....	....	....	13	3	4	7	68	....	....	....	....
1995-96	**Colorado**	**NHL**	**7**	**1**	**0**	**1**	**6**	**0**	**0**	**0**	**6**	**16.7**	**3**	....	....	....	....	....	....	....	....	....	....	....	....
	Cornwall Aces	AHL	53	21	13	34	154	....	....	....	....	....	....	....	....	....	8	1	3	4	22	....	....	....	....
1996-97	**Colorado**	**NHL**	**9**	**1**	**2**	**3**	**23**	**0**	**0**	**0**	**7**	**14.3**	**1**	....	....	....	....	....	....	....	....	....	....	....	....
	Boston	**NHL**	**40**	**7**	**10**	**17**	**49**	**0**	**0**	**0**	**76**	**9.2**	**–6**	....	....	....	....	....	....	....	....	....	....	....	....
	Providence Bruins	AHL	2	2	1	3	2	....	....	....	....	....	....	....	....	....	10	3	4	7	16	....	....	....	....
1997-98	**Boston**	**NHL**	**28**	**1**	**5**	**6**	**7**	**0**	**0**	**0**	**26**	**3.8**	**3**	....	....	....	**1**	**0**	**0**	**0**	**0**	**0**	**0**	**0**	....
	Providence Bruins	AHL	42	18	10	28	146	....	....	....	....	....	....	....	....	....	....	....	....	....	....	....	....	....	....
1998-99	**Boston**	**NHL**	**22**	**3**	**3**	**6**	**17**	**0**	**0**	**0**	**32**	**9.4**	**0**	**3**	**0.0**	**10:04**	**8**	**1**	**1**	**2**	**8**	**1**	**0**	**1**	**13:41**
	Providence Bruins	AHL	48	31	22	53	89	....	....	....	....	....	....	....	....	....	11	7	1	8	19	....	....	....	....
99-2000	**Boston**	**NHL**	**40**	**1**	**3**	**4**	**18**	**0**	**0**	**0**	**67**	**1.5**	**–6**	**14**	**42.9**	**10:09**	....	....	....	....	....	....	....	....	....
	Providence Bruins	AHL	17	5	5	10	45	....	....	....	....	....	....	....	....	....	9	2	3	5	38	....	....	....	....
2000-01	**Phoenix**	**NHL**	**70**	**18**	**13**	**31**	**92**	**2**	**0**	**3**	**123**	**14.6**	**3**	**13**	**46.2**	**11:26**	....	....	....	....	....	....	....	....	....
2001-02	**Phoenix**	**NHL**	**47**	**7**	**12**	**19**	**46**	**1**	**0**	**0**	**100**	**7.0**	**4**	**15**	**53.3**	**12:51**	**4**	**0**	**0**	**0**	**12**	**0**	**0**	**0**	**12:03**
	Springfield	AHL	2	2	1	3	2	....	....	....	....	....	....	....	....	....	....	....	....	....	....	....	....	....	....
2002-03	**Phoenix**	**NHL**	**31**	**6**	**8**	**14**	**26**	**0**	**0**	**3**	**92**	**6.5**	**1**	**35**	**54.3**	**12:11**	....	....	....	....	....	....	....	....	....
2003-04	**Phoenix**	**NHL**	**35**	**1**	**3**	**4**	**16**	**0**	**0**	**0**	**41**	**2.4**	**–3**	**44**	**31.8**	**9:51**	....	....	....	....	....	....	....	....	....
	Pittsburgh	**NHL**	**19**	**5**	**1**	**6**	**31**	**2**	**0**	**0**	**35**	**14.3**	**0**	**2**	**0.0**	**11:21**	....	....	....	....	....	....	....	....	....
2004-05	Blues Espoo	Finland	37	8	11	19	80	....	....	....	....	....	....	....	....	....	....	....	....	....	....	....	....	....	....
2005-06	HC Davos	Swiss	36	27	14	41	142	....	....	....	....	....	....	....	....	....	11	5	3	8	40	....	....	....	....
	NHL Totals		**348**	**51**	**60**	**111**	**331**	**5**	**0**	**6**	**605**	**8.4**		**126**	**42.1**	**11:15**	**13**	**1**	**1**	**2**	**20**	**1**	**0**	**1**	**13:08**

WCHA Rookie of the Year (1994) • AHL First All-Star Team (1999)

Traded to **Quebec** by **Toronto** with Wendel Clark, Sylvain Lefebvre and Toronto's 1st round choice (Jeffrey Kealty) in 1994 Entry Draft for Mats Sundin, Garth Butcher, Todd Warriner and Philadelphia's 1st round choice (previously acquired, later traded to Washington – Washington selected Nolan Baumgartner) in 1994 Entry Draft, June 28, 1994. Transferred to **Colorado** after **Quebec** franchise relocated, June 21, 1995. Traded to **Boston** by **Colorado** with Anders Myrvold for Boston's 1st round choice (Robyn Regehr) in 1998 Entry Draft, November 22, 1996. Signed as a free agent by **Phoenix**, July 7, 2000. • Missed majority of 2002-03 season recovering from eye injury suffered in game vs. Washington, December 13, 2002. Traded to **Pittsburgh** by **Phoenix** for future considerations, February 22, 2004. Signed as a free agent by **Espoo** (Finland), June 23, 2004. Signed as a free agent by **Davos** (Swiss), August 31, 2005. Signed as a free agent by **Lugano** (Swiss), July 17, 2006.

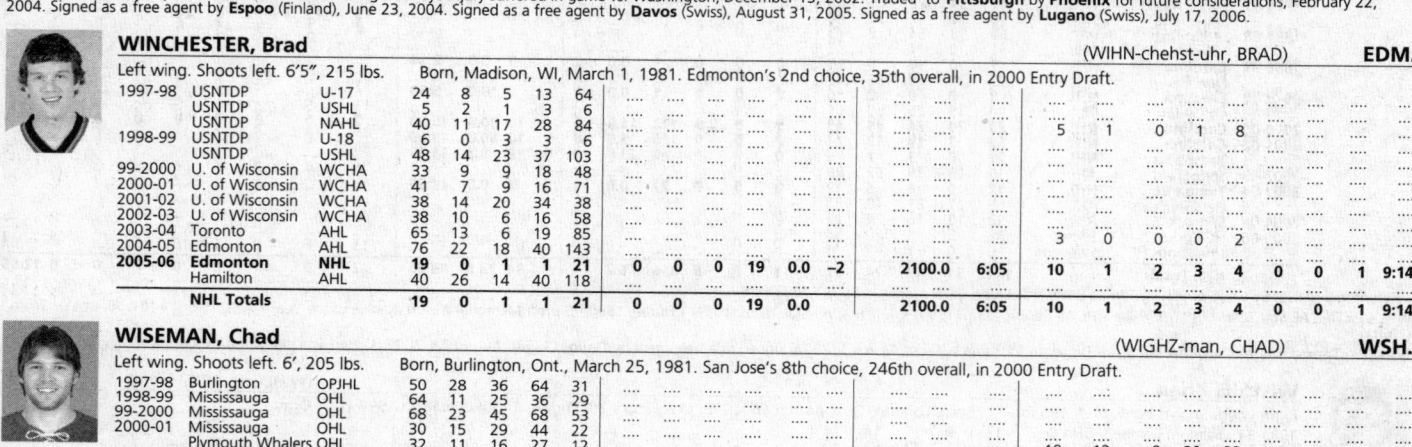

WINCHESTER, Brad

(WIHN-chehst-uhr, BRAD) **EDM.**

Left wing. Shoots left. 6'5", 215 lbs. Born, Madison, WI, March 1, 1981. Edmonton's 2nd choice, 35th overall, in 2000 Entry Draft.

Season	Club	League	GP	G	A	Pts	PIM	PP	SH	GW	S	%	+/-	TF	F%	Min	GP	G	A	Pts	PIM	PP	SH	GW	Min
1997-98	USNTDP	U-17	24	8	5	13	64	....	....	....	....	....	....	....	....	....	....	....	....	....	....	....	....	....	....
	USNTDP	USHL	5	2	1	3	6	....	....	....	....	....	....	....	....	....	....	....	....	....	....	....	....	....	....
	USNTDP	NAHL	40	11	17	28	84	....	....	....	....	....	....	....	....	....	5	1	0	1	8	....	....	....	....
1998-99	USNTDP	U-18	6	0	3	3	6	....	....	....	....	....	....	....	....	....	....	....	....	....	....	....	....	....	....
	USNTDP	USHL	48	14	23	37	103	....	....	....	....	....	....	....	....	....	....	....	....	....	....	....	....	....	....
99-2000	U. of Wisconsin	WCHA	33	9	9	18	48	....	....	....	....	....	....	....	....	....	....	....	....	....	....	....	....	....	....
2000-01	U. of Wisconsin	WCHA	41	7	9	16	71	....	....	....	....	....	....	....	....	....	....	....	....	....	....	....	....	....	....
2001-02	U. of Wisconsin	WCHA	38	14	20	34	38	....	....	....	....	....	....	....	....	....	....	....	....	....	....	....	....	....	....
2002-03	U. of Wisconsin	WCHA	38	10	6	16	58	....	....	....	....	....	....	....	....	....	....	....	....	....	....	....	....	....	....
2003-04	Toronto	AHL	65	13	6	19	85	....	....	....	....	....	....	....	....	....	3	0	0	0	2	....	....	....	....
2004-05	Edmonton	AHL	76	22	18	40	143	....	....	....	....	....	....	....	....	....	....	....	....	....	....	....	....	....	....
2005-06	**Edmonton**	**NHL**	**19**	**0**	**1**	**1**	**21**	**0**	**0**	**0**	**19**	**0.0**	**–2**	**2**	**100.0**	**6:05**	**10**	**1**	**2**	**3**	**4**	**0**	**0**	**1**	**9:14**
	Hamilton	AHL	40	26	14	40	118	....	....	....	....	....	....	....	....	....	....	....	....	....	....	....	....	....	....
	NHL Totals		**19**	**0**	**1**	**1**	**21**	**0**	**0**	**0**	**19**	**0.0**		**2**	**100.0**	**6:05**	**10**	**1**	**2**	**3**	**4**	**0**	**0**	**1**	**9:14**

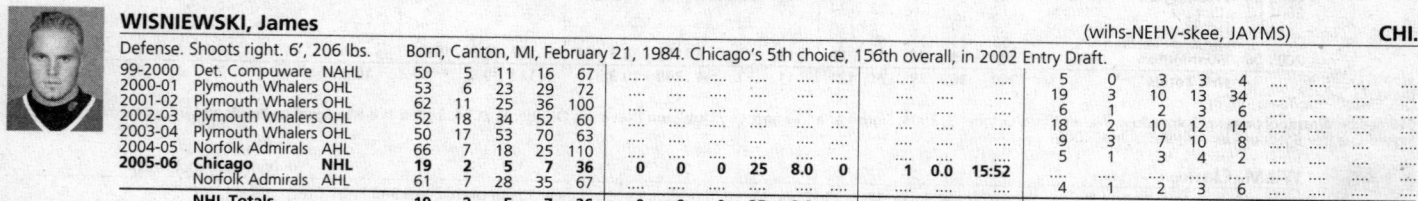

WISEMAN, Chad

(WIGHZ-man, CHAD) **WSH.**

Left wing. Shoots left. 6', 205 lbs. Born, Burlington, Ont., March 25, 1981. San Jose's 8th choice, 246th overall, in 2000 Entry Draft.

Season	Club	League	GP	G	A	Pts	PIM	PP	SH	GW	S	%	+/-	TF	F%	Min	GP	G	A	Pts	PIM	PP	SH	GW	Min
1997-98	Burlington	OPJHL	50	28	36	64	31	....	....	....	....	....	....	....	....	....	....	....	....	....	....	....	....	....	....
1998-99	Mississauga	OHL	64	11	25	36	29	....	....	....	....	....	....	....	....	....	....	....	....	....	....	....	....	....	....
99-2000	Mississauga	OHL	68	23	45	68	53	....	....	....	....	....	....	....	....	....	....	....	....	....	....	....	....	....	....
2000-01	Mississauga	OHL	30	15	29	44	22	....	....	....	....	....	....	....	....	....	....	....	....	....	....	....	....	....	....
	Plymouth Whalers	OHL	32	11	16	27	12	....	....	....	....	....	....	....	....	....	19	12	8	20	22	....	....	....	....
2001-02	Cleveland Barons	AHL	76	21	29	50	61	....	....	....	....	....	....	....	....	....	....	....	....	....	....	....	....	....	....
2002-03	**San Jose**	**NHL**	**4**	**0**	**0**	**0**	**4**	**0**	**0**	**0**	**1**	**0.0**	**–2**	**0**	**0.0**	**9:19**	....	....	....	....	....	....	....	....	....
	Cleveland Barons	AHL	77	17	35	52	44	....	....	....	....	....	....	....	....	....	....	....	....	....	....	....	....	....	....
2003-04	**NY Rangers**	**NHL**	**4**	**1**	**0**	**1**	**0**	**0**	**0**	**0**	**3**	**33.3**	**–1**	**0**	**0.0**	**8:49**	....	....	....	....	....	....	....	....	....
	Hartford	AHL	62	25	27	52	45	....	....	....	....	....	....	....	....	....	15	5	6	11	12	....	....	....	....
2004-05	Hartford	AHL	60	17	16	33	74	....	....	....	....	....	....	....	....	....	6	1	1	2	6	....	....	....	....
2005-06	**NY Rangers**	**NHL**	**1**	**0**	**1**	**1**	**4**	**0**	**0**	**0**	**1**	**0.0**	**2**	**0**	**0.0**	**8:47**	**1**	**0**	**0**	**0**	**2**	**0**	**0**	**0**	**6:00**
	Hartford	AHL	69	19	35	54	65	....	....	....	....	....	....	....	....	....	11	3	6	9	22	....	....	....	....
	NHL Totals		**9**	**1**	**1**	**2**	**8**	**0**	**0**	**0**	**5**	**20.0**		**0**	**0.0**	**9:02**	**1**	**0**	**0**	**0**	**2**	**0**	**0**	**0**	**6:00**

Traded to **NY Rangers** by **San Jose** for Nils Ekman, August 12, 2003. Signed as a free agent by **Washington**, July 14, 2006.

WISNIEWSKI, James

(wihs-NEHV-skee, JAYMS) **CHI.**

Defense. Shoots right. 6', 206 lbs. Born, Canton, MI, February 21, 1984. Chicago's 5th choice, 156th overall, in 2002 Entry Draft.

Season	Club	League	GP	G	A	Pts	PIM	PP	SH	GW	S	%	+/-	TF	F%	Min	GP	G	A	Pts	PIM	PP	SH	GW	Min
99-2000	Det. Compuware	NAHL	50	5	11	16	67	....	....	....	....	....	....	....	....	....	5	0	3	3	4	....	....	....	....
2000-01	Plymouth Whalers	OHL	53	6	23	29	72	....	....	....	....	....	....	....	....	....	19	3	10	13	34	....	....	....	....
2001-02	Plymouth Whalers	OHL	62	11	25	36	100	....	....	....	....	....	....	....	....	....	6	1	2	3	6	....	....	....	....
2002-03	Plymouth Whalers	OHL	52	18	34	52	60	....	....	....	....	....	....	....	....	....	18	2	10	12	14	....	....	....	....
2003-04	Plymouth Whalers	OHL	50	17	53	70	63	....	....	....	....	....	....	....	....	....	9	3	7	10	8	....	....	....	....
2004-05	Norfolk Admirals	AHL	66	7	18	25	110	....	....	....	....	....	....	....	....	....	5	1	3	4	2	....	....	....	....
2005-06	**Chicago**	**NHL**	**19**	**2**	**5**	**7**	**36**	**0**	**0**	**0**	**25**	**8.0**	**0**	**1**	**0.0**	**15:52**	....	....	....	....	....	....	....	....	....
	Norfolk Admirals	AHL	61	7	28	35	67	....	....	....	....	....	....	....	....	....	4	1	2	3	6	....	....	....	....
	NHL Totals		**19**	**2**	**5**	**7**	**36**	**0**	**0**	**0**	**25**	**8.0**		**1**	**0.0**	**15:52**	....	....	....	....	....	....	....	....	....

OHL First All-Star Team (2004) • OHL Defenseman of the Year (2004) • Canadian Major Junior First All-Star Team (2004) • Canadian Major Junior Defenseman of the Year (2004)

WITT, Brendan

(WIHT, BREHN-duhn) **NYI**

Defense. Shoots left. 6'2", 219 lbs. Born, Humboldt, Sask., February 20, 1975. Washington's 1st choice, 11th overall, in 1993 Entry Draft.

Season	Club	League	GP	G	A	Pts	PIM	PP	SH	GW	S	%	+/-	TF	F%	Min	GP	G	A	Pts	PIM	PP	SH	GW	Min
1990-91	Saskatoon Blazers	SMHL	31	5	13	18	42	....	....	....	....	....	....	....	....	....	....	....	....	....	....	....	....	....	....
	Seattle	WHL	....	....	....	....	....	....	....	....	....	....	....	....	....	....	1	0	0	0	0	....	....	....	....
1991-92	Seattle	WHL	67	3	9	12	212	....	....	....	....	....	....	....	....	....	15	1	1	2	84	....	....	....	....
1992-93	Seattle	WHL	70	2	26	28	239	....	....	....	....	....	....	....	....	....	5	1	2	3	30	....	....	....	....
1993-94	Seattle	WHL	56	8	31	39	235	....	....	....	....	....	....	....	....	....	9	3	8	11	23	....	....	....	....
1994-95			DID NOT PLAY																						
1995-96	**Washington**	**NHL**	**48**	**2**	**3**	**5**	**85**	**0**	**0**	**1**	**44**	**4.5**	**–4**	....	....	....	....	....	....	....	....	....	....	....	....
1996-97	**Washington**	**NHL**	**44**	**3**	**2**	**5**	**88**	**0**	**0**	**0**	**41**	**7.3**	**–20**	....	....	....	....	....	....	....	....	....	....	....	....
	Portland Pirates	AHL	30	2	4	6	56	....	....	....	....	....	....	....	....	....	5	1	0	1	30	....	....	....	....
1997-98	**Washington**	**NHL**	**64**	**1**	**7**	**8**	**112**	**0**	**0**	**0**	**68**	**1.5**	**–11**	....	....	....	**16**	**1**	**0**	**1**	**14**	**0**	**0**	**0**	....
1998-99	**Washington**	**NHL**	**54**	**2**	**5**	**7**	**87**	**0**	**0**	**0**	**51**	**3.9**	**–6**	**0**	**0.0**	**15:50**	....	....	....	....	....	....	....	....	....
99-2000	**Washington**	**NHL**	**77**	**1**	**7**	**8**	**114**	**0**	**0**	**0**	**64**	**1.6**	**5**	**2**	**50.0**	**20:56**	**3**	**0**	**0**	**0**	**0**	**0**	**0**	**0**	**20:52**
2000-01	**Washington**	**NHL**	**72**	**3**	**3**	**6**	**101**	**0**	**0**	**0**	**87**	**3.4**	**2**	**1**	**100.0**	**20:41**	**6**	**2**	**0**	**2**	**12**	**1**	**0**	**0**	**20:50**
2001-02	**Washington**	**NHL**	**68**	**3**	**7**	**10**	**78**	**0**	**0**	**0**	**81**	**3.7**	**–1**	**1**	**100.0**	**20:03**	....	....	....	....	....	....	....	....	....
2002-03	**Washington**	**NHL**	**69**	**2**	**9**	**11**	**106**	**0**	**0**	**0**	**80**	**2.5**	**12**	**0**	**0.0**	**20:55**	**6**	**1**	**0**	**1**	**0**	**0**	**0**	**0**	**23:33**
2003-04	**Washington**	**NHL**	**72**	**2**	**10**	**12**	**123**	**0**	**0**	**0**	**91**	**2.2**	**–22**	**3**	**66.7**	**22:48**	....	....	....	....	....	....	....	....	....
2004-05	Bracknell Bees	Britain-2	3	1	4	5	0	....	....	....	....	....	....	....	....	....	....	....	....	....	....	....	....	....	....

Season	Club	League	GP	G	A	Pts	PIM	PP	SH	GW	S	%	+/-	TF	F%	Min	GP	G	A	Pts	PIM	PP	SH	GW	Min
			Regular Season														Playoffs								
2005-06	**Washington**	**NHL**	**58**	**1**	**10**	**11**	**141**	**0**	**0**	**0**	**62**	**1.6**	**-5**	**0**	**0.0**	**21:41**	....	....	....	....	....	....	....	....	....
	Nashville	**NHL**	**17**	**0**	**3**	**3**	**68**	**0**	**0**	**0**	**13**	**0.0**	**5**	**0**	**0.0**	**17:29**	**5**	**0**	**0**	**0**	**12**	**0**	**0**	**0**	**17:07**
	NHL Totals		**643**	**20**	**66**	**86**	**1103**	**0**	**0**	**1**	**682**	**2.9**		**7**	**71.4**	**20:27**	**36**	**4**	**0**	**4**	**38**	**1**	**0**	**0**	**20:43**

WHL West First All-Star Team (1993, 1994) • Canadian Major Junior First All-Star Team (1994)

• Missed entire 1994-95 season after failing to come to contract terms with **Washington**. Signed as a free agent by **Bracknell** (Britain-2), December 21, 2004. Traded to **Nashville** by **Washington** for Kris Beech and Nashville's 1st round choice (Simeon Varlamov) in 2006 Entry Draft, March 9, 2006. Signed as a free agent by **NY Islanders**, July 3, 2006.

WOLSKI, Wojtek

(WOHL-skee, VOI-tehk) **COL.**

Left wing. Shoots left. 6'3", 200 lbs. Born, Zabrze, Poland, February 24, 1986. Colorado's 1st choice, 21st overall, in 2004 Entry Draft.

Season	Club	League	GP	G	A	Pts	PIM	PP	SH	GW	S	%	+/-	TF	F%	Min	GP	G	A	Pts	PIM	PP	SH	GW	Min
2001-02	St. Mike's B's	OPJHL	33	16	33	49	40	....	....	....	....	....	....	....	....	....	....	....	....	....	....	....	....	....	....
2002-03	Brampton	OHL	64	25	32	57	26	....	....	....	....	....	....	....	....	....	11	5	0	5	6	....	....	....	....
2003-04	Brampton	OHL	66	29	41	70	30	....	....	....	....	....	....	....	....	....	12	5	3	8	8	....	....	....	....
2004-05	Brampton	OHL	67	29	44	73	41	....	....	....	....	....	....	....	....	....	6	2	5	7	6	....	....	....	....
2005-06	**Colorado**	**NHL**	**9**	**2**	**4**	**6**	**4**	**2**	**0**	**0**	**9**	**22.2**	**-5**	**4**	**0.0**	**9:44**	**8**	**1**	**3**	**4**	**2**	**0**	**0**	**0**	**12:06**
	Brampton	OHL	56	47	81	128	46	....	....	....	....	....	....	....	....	....	11	7	11	18	4	....	....	....	....
	NHL Totals		**9**	**2**	**4**	**6**	**4**	**2**	**0**	**0**	**9**	**22.2**		**4**	**0.0**	**9:44**	**8**	**1**	**3**	**4**	**2**	**0**	**0**	**0**	**12:06**

OHL First All-Star Team (2004) • OHL Second All-Star Team (2006)

WOOLLEY, Jason

(WU-lee, JAY-suhn)

Defense. Shoots left. 6', 203 lbs. Born, Toronto, Ont., July 27, 1969. Washington's 4th choice, 61st overall, in 1989 Entry Draft.

Season	Club	League	GP	G	A	Pts	PIM	PP	SH	GW	S	%	+/-	TF	F%	Min	GP	G	A	Pts	PIM	PP	SH	GW	Min
1986-87	St. Mike's B's	OHA-B	35	13	22	35	40	....	....	....	....	....	....	....	....	....	....	....	....	....	....	....	....	....	....
1987-88	St. Mike's B's	OHA-B	31	19	37	56	22	....	....	....	....	....	....	....	....	....	....	....	....	....	....	....	....	....	....
1988-89	Michigan State	CCHA	47	12	25	37	26	....	....	....	....	....	....	....	....	....	....	....	....	....	....	....	....	....	....
1989-90	Michigan State	CCHA	45	10	38	48	26	....	....	....	....	....	....	....	....	....	....	....	....	....	....	....	....	....	....
1990-91	Michigan State	CCHA	40	15	44	59	24	....	....	....	....	....	....	....	....	....	....	....	....	....	....	....	....	....	....
1991-92	Canada	Nat-Tm	60	14	30	44	36	....	....	....	....	....	....	....	....	....	....	....	....	....	....	....	....	....	....
	Canada	Olympics	8	0	5	5	4	....	....	....	....	....	....	....	....	....	....	....	....	....	....	....	....	....	....
	Washington	**NHL**	**1**	**0**	**0**	**0**	**0**	**0**	**0**	**0**	**2**	**0.0**	**1**	....	....	....	....	....	....	....	....	....	....	....	....
	Baltimore	AHL	15	1	10	11	6	....	....	....	....	....	....	....	....	....	....	....	....	....	....	....	....	....	....
1992-93	**Washington**	**NHL**	**26**	**0**	**2**	**2**	**10**	**0**	**0**	**0**	**11**	**0.0**	**3**	....	....	....	....	....	....	....	....	....	....	....	....
	Baltimore	AHL	29	14	27	41	22	....	....	....	....	....	....	....	....	....	1	0	2	2	0	....	....	....	....
1993-94	**Washington**	**NHL**	**10**	**1**	**2**	**3**	**4**	**0**	**0**	**0**	**15**	**6.7**	**2**	....	....	....	**4**	**1**	**0**	**1**	**4**	**0**	**0**	**1**	....
	Portland Pirates	AHL	41	12	29	41	14	....	....	....	....	....	....	....	....	....	9	2	2	4	4	....	....	....	....
1994-95	Detroit Vipers	IHL	48	8	28	36	38	....	....	....	....	....	....	....	....	....	....	....	....	....	....	....	....	....	....
	Florida	**NHL**	**34**	**4**	**9**	**13**	**18**	**1**	**0**	**0**	**76**	**5.3**	**-1**	....	....	....	....	....	....	....	....	....	....	....	....
1995-96	**Florida**	**NHL**	**52**	**6**	**28**	**34**	**32**	**3**	**0**	**0**	**98**	**6.1**	**-9**	....	....	....	**13**	**2**	**6**	**8**	**14**	**1**	**0**	**1**	....
1996-97	**Florida**	**NHL**	**3**	**0**	**0**	**0**	**2**	**0**	**0**	**0**	**7**	**0.0**	**1**	....	....	....	....	....	....	....	....	....	....	....	....
	Pittsburgh	**NHL**	**57**	**6**	**30**	**36**	**28**	**2**	**0**	**1**	**79**	**7.6**	**3**	....	....	....	**5**	**0**	**3**	**3**	**0**	**0**	**0**	**0**	....
1997-98	**Buffalo**	**NHL**	**71**	**9**	**26**	**35**	**35**	**3**	**0**	**2**	**129**	**7.0**	**8**	....	....	....	**15**	**2**	**9**	**11**	**12**	**1**	**0**	**1**	....
1998-99	**Buffalo**	**NHL**	**80**	**10**	**33**	**43**	**62**	**4**	**0**	**2**	**154**	**6.5**	**16**	**0**	**0.0**	**18:43**	**21**	**4**	**11**	**15**	**10**	**2**	**0**	**1**	**17:54**
99-2000	**Buffalo**	**NHL**	**74**	**8**	**25**	**33**	**52**	**2**	**0**	**2**	**113**	**7.1**	**14**	**0**	**0.0**	**17:51**	**5**	**0**	**2**	**2**	**2**	**0**	**0**	**0**	**18:06**
2000-01	**Buffalo**	**NHL**	**67**	**5**	**18**	**23**	**46**	**4**	**0**	**3**	**92**	**5.4**	**0**	**0**	**0.0**	**17:22**	**8**	**1**	**5**	**6**	**2**	**0**	**0**	**1**	**18:30**
2001-02	**Buffalo**	**NHL**	**59**	**8**	**20**	**28**	**34**	**6**	**0**	**2**	**90**	**8.9**	**-6**	**0**	**0.0**	**17:11**	....	....	....	....	....	....	....	....	....
2002-03	**Buffalo**	**NHL**	**14**	**0**	**3**	**3**	**29**	**0**	**0**	**0**	**29**	**0.0**	**-1**	**0**	**0.0**	**15:59**	....	....	....	....	....	....	....	....	....
	Detroit	**NHL**	**62**	**6**	**17**	**23**	**22**	**1**	**0**	**2**	**52**	**11.5**	**12**	**0**	**0.0**	**16:59**	**4**	**1**	**0**	**1**	**0**	**0**	**0**	**0**	**15:25**
2003-04	**Detroit**	**NHL**	**55**	**4**	**15**	**19**	**28**	**0**	**0**	**1**	**60**	**6.7**	**19**	**2**	**50.0**	**15:42**	**4**	**0**	**0**	**0**	**0**	**0**	**0**	**0**	**17:00**
2004-05	Flint Generals	UHL	9	4	2	6	4	....	....	....	....	....	....	....	....	....	....	....	....	....	....	....	....	....	....
2005-06	**Detroit**	**NHL**	**53**	**1**	**18**	**19**	**28**	**0**	**0**	**0**	**43**	**2.3**	**3**	**1**	**0.0**	**11:54**	....	....	....	....	....	....	....	....	....
	NHL Totals		**718**	**68**	**246**	**314**	**430**	**26**	**0**	**15**	**1050**	**6.5**		**3**	**33.3**	**16:44**	**79**	**11**	**36**	**47**	**44**	**4**	**0**	**5**	**17:43**

CCHA First All-Star Team (1991) • NCAA West First All-American Team (1991)

Signed as a free agent by **Florida**, February 15, 1995. Traded to **Pittsburgh** by **Florida** with Stu Barnes for Chris Wells, November 19, 1996. Traded to **Buffalo** by **Pittsburgh** for Buffalo's 5th round choice (Robert Scuderi) in 1998 Entry Draft, September 24, 1997. Traded to **Detroit** by **Buffalo** for future considerations, November 16, 2002. Signed as a free agent by **Flint** (UHL), February 18, 2005.

WORRELL, Peter

(woh-REHL, PEE-tuhr)

Left wing. Shoots left. 6'6", 235 lbs. Born, Pierrefonds, Que., August 18, 1977. Florida's 7th choice, 166th overall, in 1995 Entry Draft.

Season	Club	League	GP	G	A	Pts	PIM	PP	SH	GW	S	%	+/-	TF	F%	Min	GP	G	A	Pts	PIM	PP	SH	GW	Min
1993-94	Lac St-Louis Lions	QAAA	1	0	0	0	0	....	....	....	....	....	....	....	....	....	1	0	0	0	0	....	....	....	....
1994-95	Hull Olympiques	QMJHL	56	1	8	9	243	....	....	....	....	....	....	....	....	....	21	0	1	1	91	....	....	....	....
1995-96	Hull Olympiques	QMJHL	63	23	36	59	464	....	....	....	....	....	....	....	....	....	18	11	8	19	81	....	....	....	....
1996-97	Hull Olympiques	QMJHL	62	17	46	63	437	....	....	....	....	....	....	....	....	....	14	3	13	16	83	....	....	....	....
1997-98	**Florida**	**NHL**	**19**	**0**	**0**	**0**	**153**	**0**	**0**	**0**	**15**	**0.0**	**-4**	....	....	....	....	....	....	....	....	....	....	....	....
	New Haven	AHL	50	15	12	27	309	....	....	....	....	....	....	....	....	....	1	0	1	1	6	....	....	....	....
1998-99	**Florida**	**NHL**	**62**	**4**	**5**	**9**	**258**	**0**	**0**	**2**	**50**	**8.0**	**0**	**0**	**0.0**	**6:15**	....	....	....	....	....	....	....	....	....
	New Haven	AHL	10	3	1	4	65	....	....	....	....	....	....	....	....	....	....	....	....	....	....	....	....	....	....
99-2000	**Florida**	**NHL**	**48**	**3**	**6**	**9**	**169**	**2**	**0**	**1**	**45**	**6.7**	**-7**	**1**	**100.0**	**8:25**	**4**	**1**	**0**	**1**	**8**	**0**	**0**	**0**	**11:17**
2000-01	**Florida**	**NHL**	**71**	**3**	**7**	**10**	**248**	**0**	**0**	**0**	**86**	**3.5**	**-10**	**3**	**33.3**	**9:28**	....	....	....	....	....	....	....	....	....
2001-02	**Florida**	**NHL**	**79**	**4**	**5**	**9**	***354**	**0**	**0**	**1**	**65**	**6.2**	**-15**	**9**	**0.0**	**8:45**	....	....	....	....	....	....	....	....	....
2002-03	**Florida**	**NHL**	**63**	**2**	**3**	**5**	**193**	**0**	**0**	**0**	**52**	**3.8**	**-14**	**13**	**15.4**	**9:16**	....	....	....	....	....	....	....	....	....
2003-04	**Colorado**	**NHL**	**49**	**3**	**1**	**4**	**179**	**0**	**0**	**0**	**32**	**9.4**	**2**	**5**	**0.0**	**5:55**	....	....	....	....	....	....	....	....	....
2004-05			DID NOT PLAY																						
2005-06	Charlotte	ECHL	37	7	8	15	139	....	....	....	....	....	....	....	....	....	....	....	....	....	....	....	....	....	....
	NHL Totals		**391**	**19**	**27**	**46**	**1554**	**2**	**0**	**4**	**345**	**5.5**		**31**	**12.9**	**8:08**	**4**	**1**	**0**	**1**	**8**	**0**	**0**	**0**	**11:17**

Traded to **Colorado** by **Florida** with Florida's 2nd round choice (later traded to NY Rangers – later traded back to Florida – Florida selected David Shantz) in 2004 Entry Draft for Eric Messier and Vaclav Nedorost, July 18, 2003.

WOTTON, Mark

(WAH-tuhn, MAHRK) **NYI**

Defense. Shoots left. 6'1", 195 lbs. Born, Foxwarren, Man., November 16, 1973. Vancouver's 11th choice, 237th overall, in 1992 Entry Draft.

Season	Club	League	GP	G	A	Pts	PIM	PP	SH	GW	S	%	+/-	TF	F%	Min	GP	G	A	Pts	PIM	PP	SH	GW	Min
1988-89	Foxwarren Blades	MAHA	60	10	30	40	70	....	....	....	....	....	....	....	....	....	....	....	....	....	....	....	....	....	....
1989-90	Saskatoon Blades	WHL	51	2	3	5	31	....	....	....	....	....	....	....	....	....	7	1	1	2	15	....	....	....	....
1990-91	Saskatoon Blades	WHL	45	4	11	15	37	....	....	....	....	....	....	....	....	....	....	....	....	....	....	....	....	....	....
1991-92	Saskatoon Blades	WHL	64	11	25	36	62	....	....	....	....	....	....	....	....	....	21	2	6	8	22	....	....	....	....
1992-93	Saskatoon Blades	WHL	71	15	51	66	90	....	....	....	....	....	....	....	....	....	9	6	5	11	18	....	....	....	....
1993-94	Saskatoon Blades	WHL	65	12	34	46	108	....	....	....	....	....	....	....	....	....	16	3	12	15	32	....	....	....	....
1994-95	Syracuse Crunch	AHL	75	12	29	41	50	....	....	....	....	....	....	....	....	....	....	....	....	....	....	....	....	....	....
	Vancouver	**NHL**	**1**	**0**	**0**	**0**	**0**	**0**	**0**	**0**	**2**	**0.0**	**1**	....	....	....	**5**	**0**	**0**	**0**	**4**	**0**	**0**	**0**	....
1995-96	Syracuse Crunch	AHL	80	10	35	45	96	....	....	....	....	....	....	....	....	....	15	1	12	13	20	....	....	....	....
1996-97	**Vancouver**	**NHL**	**36**	**3**	**6**	**9**	**19**	**0**	**1**	**0**	**41**	**7.3**	**8**	....	....	....	....	....	....	....	....	....	....	....	....
	Syracuse Crunch	AHL	27	2	8	10	25	....	....	....	....	....	....	....	....	....	2	0	0	0	4	....	....	....	....
1997-98	**Vancouver**	**NHL**	**5**	**0**	**0**	**0**	**6**	**0**	**0**	**0**	**3**	**0.0**	**-2**	....	....	....	....	....	....	....	....	....	....	....	....
	Syracuse Crunch	AHL	56	12	21	33	80	....	....	....	....	....	....	....	....	....	5	0	0	0	12	....	....	....	....
1998-99	Syracuse Crunch	AHL	72	4	31	35	74	....	....	....	....	....	....	....	....	....	....	....	....	....	....	....	....	....	....
99-2000	Michigan	IHL	70	3	7	10	72	....	....	....	....	....	....	....	....	....	....	....	....	....	....	....	....	....	....
2000-01	**Dallas**	**NHL**	**1**	**0**	**0**	**0**	**0**	**0**	**0**	**0**	**0**	**0.0**	**0**	**0**	**0.0**	**13:45**	....	....	....	....	....	....	....	....	....
	Utah Grizzlies	IHL	63	2	2	4	64	....	....	....	....	....	....	....	....	....	....	....	....	....	....	....	....	....	....
2001-02	Utah Grizzlies	AHL	57	9	18	27	68	....	....	....	....	....	....	....	....	....	4	0	1	1	6	....	....	....	....
2002-03	Utah Grizzlies	AHL	69	8	26	34	68	....	....	....	....	....	....	....	....	....	2	0	0	0	2	....	....	....	....
2003-04	Utah Grizzlies	AHL	23	1	3	4	25	....	....	....	....	....	....	....	....	....	....	....	....	....	....	....	....	....	....
2004-05	St. Petersburg	Russia	50	3	4	7	36	....	....	....	....	....	....	....	....	....	....	....	....	....	....	....	....	....	....
2005-06	Hershey Bears	AHL	69	7	19	26	58	....	....	....	....	....	....	....	....	....	14	0	4	4	6	....	....	....	....
	NHL Totals		**43**	**3**	**6**	**9**	**25**	**0**	**1**	**0**	**46**	**6.5**		**0**	**0.0**	**13:45**	**5**	**0**	**0**	**0**	**4**	**0**	**0**	**0**	....

WHL East Second All-Star Team (1994)

Signed as a free agent by **Dallas**, July 9, 1999. • Missed majority of 2003-04 season recovering from knee injury suffered in game vs. Cincinnati (AHL), December 6, 2003. Signed as a free agent by **St. Petersburg** (Russia), July 9, 2004. Signed as a free agent by **Washington**, August 17, 2005. Signed as a free agent by **NY Islanders**, July 27, 2006.

WOYWITKA, Jeff

(WOI-wiht-ka, JEHF) **ST.L.**

Defense. Shoots left. 6'2", 209 lbs. Born, Vermilion, Alta., September 1, 1983. Philadelphia's 1st choice, 27th overall, in 2001 Entry Draft.

Season	Club	League	Regular Season GP	G	A	Pts	PIM	PP	SH	GW	S	%	+/-	TF	F%	Min	Playoffs GP	G	A	Pts	PIM	PP	SH	GW	Min
1998-99	Wainwright	AAHA	26	7	15	22	60	....	....	....	....	....	....	....	....	....	....	....	....	....	....	....	....	....	....
99-2000	Red Deer Rebels	WHL	67	4	12	16	40	....	....	....	....	....	....	....	....	....	4	0	3	3	2	....	....	....	....
2000-01	Red Deer Rebels	WHL	72	7	28	35	113	....	....	....	....	....	....	....	....	....	22	2	8	10	25	....	....	....	....
2001-02	Red Deer Rebels	WHL	72	14	23	37	109	....	....	....	....	....	....	....	....	....	23	2	10	12	22	....	....	....	....
2002-03	Red Deer Rebels	WHL	57	16	36	52	65	....	....	....	....	....	....	....	....	....	23	1	9	10	25	....	....	....	....
2003-04	Philadelphia	AHL	29	0	6	6	51	....	....	....	....	....	....	....	....	....	....	....	....	....	....	....	....	....	....
	Toronto	AHL	53	4	18	22	41	....	....	....	....	....	....	....	....	....	3	0	0	0	2	....	....	....	....
2004-05	Edmonton	AHL	80	6	20	26	84	....	....	....	....	....	....	....	....	....	....	....	....	....	....	....	....	....	....
2005-06	**St. Louis**	**NHL**	**26**	**0**	**2**	**2**	**25**	**0**	**0**	**0**	**23**	**0.0**	**–12**	**0**	**0.0**	**10:38**	....	....	....	....	....	....	....	....	....
	Peoria Rivermen	AHL	53	1	14	15	58	....	....	....	....	....	....	....	....	....	4	0	0	0	4	....	....	....	....
	NHL Totals		**26**	**0**	**2**	**2**	**25**	**0**	**0**	**0**	**23**	**0.0**		**0**	**0.0**	**10:38**	....	....	....	....	....	....	....	....	....

WHL East Second All-Star Team (2002) • WHL East First All-Star Team (2003)

Traded to **Edmonton** by **Philadelphia** with Philadelphia's 1st round choice (Rob Schremp) in 2004 Entry Draft and Philadelphia's 3rd round choice (Danny Syvret) in 2005 Entry Draft for Mike Comrie, December 16, 2003. Traded to **St. Louis** by **Edmonton** with Eric Brewer and Doug Lynch for Chris Pronger, August 2, 2005.

WOZNIEWSKI, Andy

(wuhz-NYOO-skee, AN-dee) **TOR.**

Defense. Shoots left. 6'4", 220 lbs. Born, Buffalo Grove, IL, May 25, 1980.

Season	Club	League	Regular Season GP	G	A	Pts	PIM	PP	SH	GW	S	%	+/-	TF	F%	Min	Playoffs GP	G	A	Pts	PIM	PP	SH	GW	Min
99-2000	U. Mass-Lowell	H-East	17	1	1	2	8	....	....	....	....	....	....	....	....	....	....	....	....	....	....	....	....	....	....
2000-01	Texas Tornado	NAHL	54	10	34	44	98	....	....	....	....	....	....	....	....	....	8	2	7	9	12	....	....	....	....
2001-02	U. of Wisconsin	WCHA	39	3	13	16	54	....	....	....	....	....	....	....	....	....	....	....	....	....	....	....	....	....	....
2002-03	U. of Wisconsin	WCHA	33	1	7	8	47	....	....	....	....	....	....	....	....	....	....	....	....	....	....	....	....	....	....
2003-04	U. of Wisconsin	WCHA	43	6	8	14	*104	....	....	....	....	....	....	....	....	....	....	....	....	....	....	....	....	....	....
	St. John's	AHL	3	0	1	1	0	....	....	....	....	....	....	....	....	....	....	....	....	....	....	....	....	....	....
2004-05	St. John's	AHL	28	1	4	5	20	....	....	....	....	....	....	....	....	....	....	....	....	....	....	....	....	....	....
2005-06	**Toronto**	**NHL**	**13**	**0**	**1**	**1**	**13**	**0**	**0**	**0**	**6**	**0.0**	**–8**	**0**	**0.0**	**17:55**	....	....	....	....	....	....	....	....	....
	Toronto Marlies	AHL	31	4	11	15	42	....	....	....	....	....	....	....	....	....	....	....	....	....	....	....	....	....	....
	NHL Totals		**13**	**0**	**1**	**1**	**13**	**0**	**0**	**0**	**6**	**0.0**		**0**	**0.0**	**17:55**	....	....	....	....	....	....	....	....	....

Signed as a free agent by **Toronto**, May 27, 2004.

WRIGHT, Jamie

(RIGHT, JAY-mee)

Left wing. Shoots left. 6', 195 lbs. Born, Kitchener, Ont., May 13, 1976. Dallas' 3rd choice, 98th overall, in 1994 Entry Draft.

Season	Club	League	Regular Season GP	G	A	Pts	PIM	PP	SH	GW	S	%	+/-	TF	F%	Min	Playoffs GP	G	A	Pts	PIM	PP	SH	GW	Min
1991-92	Elmira	OHA-B	44	17	11	28	46	....	....	....	....	....	....	....	....	....	....	....	....	....	....	....	....	....	....
1992-93	Elmira	OHA-B	47	22	32	54	52	....	....	....	....	....	....	....	....	....	....	....	....	....	....	....	....	....	....
1993-94	Guelph Storm	OHL	65	17	15	32	34	....	....	....	....	....	....	....	....	....	8	2	1	3	10	....	....	....	....
1994-95	Guelph Storm	OHL	65	43	39	82	36	....	....	....	....	....	....	....	....	....	14	6	8	14	6	....	....	....	....
1995-96	Guelph Storm	OHL	55	30	36	66	45	....	....	....	....	....	....	....	....	....	16	10	12	22	35	....	....	....	....
1996-97	Michigan	IHL	60	6	8	14	34	....	....	....	....	....	....	....	....	....	1	0	0	0	0	....	....	....	....
1997-98	**Dallas**	**NHL**	**21**	**4**	**2**	**6**	**2**	**0**	**0**	**2**	**15**	**26.7**	**8**	....	....	....	**5**	**0**	**0**	**0**	**0**	**0**	**0**	**0**	....
	Michigan	IHL	53	15	11	26	31	....	....	....	....	....	....	....	....	....	....	....	....	....	....	....	....	....	....
1998-99	**Dallas**	**NHL**	**11**	**0**	**0**	**0**	**0**	**0**	**0**	**0**	**10**	**0.0**	**–3**	**0**	**0.0**	**7:37**	....	....	....	....	....	....	....	....	....
	Michigan	IHL	64	16	15	31	92	....	....	....	....	....	....	....	....	....	2	0	0	0	2	....	....	....	....
99-2000	**Dallas**	**NHL**	**23**	**1**	**4**	**5**	**16**	**0**	**0**	**0**	**15**	**6.7**	**4**	**2**	**50.0**	**9:50**	....	....	....	....	....	....	....	....	....
	Michigan	IHL	49	12	4	16	64	....	....	....	....	....	....	....	....	....	....	....	....	....	....	....	....	....	....
2000-01	**Dallas**	**NHL**	**2**	**1**	**0**	**1**	**0**	**0**	**0**	**0**	**4**	**25.0**	**–3**	**1**	**0.0**	**10:45**	....	....	....	....	....	....	....	....	....
	Utah Grizzlies	IHL	74	25	27	52	126	....	....	....	....	....	....	....	....	....	....	....	....	....	....	....	....	....	....
2001-02	**Calgary**	**NHL**	**44**	**4**	**12**	**16**	**20**	**0**	**0**	**0**	**64**	**6.3**	**6**	**10**	**60.0**	**13:44**	....	....	....	....	....	....	....	....	....
	Saint John Flames	AHL	34	11	13	24	34	....	....	....	....	....	....	....	....	....	....	....	....	....	....	....	....	....	....
2002-03	**Calgary**	**NHL**	**19**	**2**	**2**	**4**	**12**	**0**	**0**	**0**	**16**	**12.5**	**1**	**14**	**42.9**	**11:43**	....	....	....	....	....	....	....	....	....
	Saint John Flames	AHL	3	2	1	3	0	....	....	....	....	....	....	....	....	....	....	....	....	....	....	....	....	....	....
	Philadelphia	**NHL**	**4**	**0**	**0**	**0**	**4**	**0**	**0**	**0**	**2**	**0.0**	**–1**	**0**	**0.0**	**9:27**	....	....	....	....	....	....	....	....	....
	Philadelphia	AHL	33	10	14	24	31	....	....	....	....	....	....	....	....	....	....	....	....	....	....	....	....	....	....
2003-04	Toronto	AHL	78	25	30	55	101	....	....	....	....	....	....	....	....	....	....	....	....	....	....	....	....	....	....
2004-05	Edmonton	AHL	65	13	15	28	86	....	....	....	....	....	....	....	....	....	....	....	....	....	....	....	....	....	....
2005-06	Lukko Rauma	Finland	44	12	18	30	73	....	....	....	....	....	....	....	....	....	....	....	....	....	....	....	....	....	....
	Geneve	Swiss	3	0	3	3	4	....	....	....	....	....	....	....	....	....	6	4	2	6	2	....	....	....	....
	NHL Totals		**124**	**12**	**20**	**32**	**54**	**0**	**0**	**2**	**126**	**9.5**		**27**	**48.1**	**11:37**	**5**	**0**	**0**	**0**	**0**	**0**	**0**	**0**	....

Signed as a free agent by **Calgary**, August 2, 2001. Traded to **Philadelphia** by **Calgary** for future considerations, January 22, 2003. Signed as a free agent by **Edmonton**, August 8, 2003. Signed as a free agent by **Rauma** (Finland). August 3, 2005. Signed as a free agent by **Geneve** (Swiss). February 8, 2006.

WRIGHT, Tyler

(RIGHT, TIGH-luhr)

Center. Shoots right. 6', 190 lbs. Born, Kamsack, Sask., April 6, 1973. Edmonton's 1st choice, 12th overall, in 1991 Entry Draft.

Season	Club	League	Regular Season GP	G	A	Pts	PIM	PP	SH	GW	S	%	+/-	TF	F%	Min	Playoffs GP	G	A	Pts	PIM	PP	SH	GW	Min
1988-89	Swift Current	SMHL	36	20	13	33	102	....	....	....	....	....	....	....	....	....	....	....	....	....	....	....	....	....	....
1989-90	Swift Current	WHL	67	14	18	32	119	....	....	....	....	....	....	....	....	....	4	0	0	0	12	....	....	....	....
1990-91	Swift Current	WHL	66	41	51	92	157	....	....	....	....	....	....	....	....	....	3	0	0	0	6	....	....	....	....
1991-92	Swift Current	WHL	63	36	46	82	185	....	....	....	....	....	....	....	....	....	8	2	5	7	16	....	....	....	....
1992-93	Swift Current	WHL	37	24	41	65	76	....	....	....	....	....	....	....	....	....	17	9	17	26	*49	....	....	....	....
	Edmonton	**NHL**	**7**	**1**	**1**	**2**	**19**	**0**	**0**	**0**	**7**	**14.3**	**–4**	....	....	....	....	....	....	....	....	....	....	....	....
1993-94	**Edmonton**	**NHL**	**5**	**0**	**0**	**0**	**4**	**0**	**0**	**0**	**2**	**0.0**	**–3**	....	....	....	....	....	....	....	....	....	....	....	....
	Cape Breton	AHL	65	14	27	41	160	....	....	....	....	....	....	....	....	....	5	2	0	2	11	....	....	....	....
1994-95	Cape Breton	AHL	70	16	15	31	184	....	....	....	....	....	....	....	....	....	....	....	....	....	....	....	....	....	....
	Edmonton	**NHL**	**6**	**1**	**0**	**1**	**14**	**0**	**0**	**0**	**6**	**16.7**	**1**	....	....	....	....	....	....	....	....	....	....	....	....
1995-96	**Edmonton**	**NHL**	**23**	**1**	**0**	**1**	**33**	**0**	**0**	**0**	**18**	**5.6**	**–7**	....	....	....	....	....	....	....	....	....	....	....	....
	Cape Breton	AHL	31	6	12	18	158	....	....	....	....	....	....	....	....	....	....	....	....	....	....	....	....	....	....
1996-97	**Pittsburgh**	**NHL**	**45**	**2**	**2**	**4**	**70**	**0**	**0**	**2**	**30**	**6.7**	**–7**	....	....	....	....	....	....	....	....	....	....	....	....
	Cleveland	IHL	10	4	3	7	34	....	....	....	....	....	....	....	....	....	14	4	2	6	44	....	....	....	....
1997-98	**Pittsburgh**	**NHL**	**82**	**3**	**4**	**7**	**112**	**1**	**0**	**0**	**46**	**6.5**	**–3**	....	....	....	**6**	**0**	**1**	**1**	**4**	**0**	**0**	**0**	....
1998-99	**Pittsburgh**	**NHL**	**61**	**0**	**0**	**0**	**90**	**0**	**0**	**0**	**16**	**0.0**	**–2**	**122**	**46.7**	**3:46**	**13**	**0**	**0**	**0**	**19**	**0**	**0**	**0**	**3:22**
99-2000	**Pittsburgh**	**NHL**	**50**	**12**	**10**	**22**	**45**	**0**	**0**	**1**	**68**	**17.6**	**4**	**698**	**47.1**	**13:24**	**11**	**3**	**1**	**4**	**17**	**0**	**0**	**0**	**16:12**
	Wilkes-Barre	AHL	25	5	15	20	86	....	....	....	....	....	....	....	....	....	....	....	....	....	....	....	....	....	....
2000-01	**Columbus**	**NHL**	**76**	**16**	**16**	**32**	**140**	**4**	**1**	**2**	**141**	**11.3**	**–9**	**999**	**45.1**	**17:41**	....	....	....	....	....	....	....	....	....
2001-02	**Columbus**	**NHL**	**77**	**13**	**11**	**24**	**100**	**4**	**0**	**1**	**120**	**10.8**	**–40**	**1036**	**43.9**	**17:12**	....	....	....	....	....	....	....	....	....
2002-03	**Columbus**	**NHL**	**70**	**19**	**11**	**30**	**113**	**3**	**2**	**3**	**108**	**17.6**	**–25**	**760**	**41.3**	**16:07**	....	....	....	....	....	....	....	....	....
2003-04	**Columbus**	**NHL**	**68**	**9**	**9**	**18**	**63**	**2**	**0**	**3**	**109**	**8.3**	**–19**	**316**	**43.7**	**14:34**	....	....	....	....	....	....	....	....	....
2004-05	EHC Biel-Bienne	Swiss-2	7	3	2	5	4	....	....	....	....	....	....	....	....	....	12	8	8	16	44	....	....	....	....
2005-06	**Columbus**	**NHL**	**18**	**0**	**4**	**4**	**20**	**0**	**0**	**0**	**26**	**0.0**	**–3**	**85**	**45.9**	**15:23**	....	....	....	....	....	....	....	....	....
	Anaheim	**NHL**	**25**	**2**	**2**	**4**	**31**	**0**	**0**	**1**	**17**	**11.8**	**2**	**28**	**57.1**	**8:06**	....	....	....	....	....	....	....	....	....
	NHL Totals		**613**	**79**	**70**	**149**	**854**	**14**	**3**	**13**	**714**	**11.1**		**4044**	**44.5**	**13:51**	**30**	**3**	**2**	**5**	**40**	**0**	**0**	**0**	**9:15**

Traded to **Pittsburgh** by **Edmonton** for Pittsburgh's 7th round choice (Brandon Lafrance) in 1996 Entry Draft, June 22, 1996. Claimed by **Columbus** from **Pittsburgh** in Expansion Draft, June 23, 2000. Signed as a free agent by **Biel-Bienne** (Swiss-2), January 6, 2005. Traded to **Anaheim** by **Columbus** with Francois Beauchemin for Sergei Fedorov and Anaheim's 5th round choice (Maxime Frechette) in 2006 Entry Draft, November 15, 2005.

YABLONSKI, Jeremy

(ya-BLAWN-skee, JAIR-eh-mee)

Left wing. Shoots right. 6', 240 lbs. Born, Meadow Lake, Sask., March 21, 1980.

Season	Club	League	Regular Season GP	G	A	Pts	PIM	PP	SH	GW	S	%	+/-	TF	F%	Min	Playoffs GP	G	A	Pts	PIM	PP	SH	GW	Min
1996-97	Beardy's	SMHL	38	7	3	10	284	....	....	....	....	....	....	....	....	....	....	....	....	....	....	....	....	....	....
1997-98	Edmonton Ice	WHL	47	3	0	3	143	....	....	....	....	....	....	....	....	....	....	....	....	....	....	....	....	....	....
1998-99	Kootenay Ice	WHL	27	1	1	2	77	....	....	....	....	....	....	....	....	....	....	....	....	....	....	....	....	....	....
99-2000	Kootenay Ice	WHL	DID NOT PLAY – INJURED																						
2000-01	Phoenix	WCHL	44	2	1	3	169	....	....	....	....	....	....	....	....	....	....	....	....	....	....	....	....	....	....
2001-02	Idaho Steelheads	WCHL	69	2	1	3	303	....	....	....	....	....	....	....	....	....	....	....	....	....	....	....	....	....	....
2002-03	Peoria Rivermen	ECHL	24	1	2	3	154	....	....	....	....	....	....	....	....	....	....	....	....	....	....	....	....	....	....
	Cincinnati	AHL	9	0	0	0	42	....	....	....	....	....	....	....	....	....	....	....	....	....	....	....	....	....	....
	Worcester IceCats	AHL	20	1	0	1	50	....	....	....	....	....	....	....	....	....	....	....	....	....	....	....	....	....	....

			Regular Season														Playoffs								
Season	Club	League	GP	G	A	Pts	PIM	PP	SH	GW	S	%	+/-	TF	F%	Min	GP	G	A	Pts	PIM	PP	SH	GW	Min
2003-04	Worcester IceCats	AHL	6	0	0	0	19	....	....	....	....	....	....	....	....	....	....	....	....	....	....	....	....	....	....
	St. Louis	NHL	1	0	0	0	5	0	0	0	1	0.0	–1	0	0.0	7:53	....	....	....	....	....	....	....	....	....
	Peoria Rivermen	ECHL	13	0	2	2	62	....	....	....	....	....	....	....	....	....	....	....	....	....	....	....	....	....	....
	Milwaukee	AHL	2	0	0	0	11	....	....	....	....	....	....	....	....	....	....	....	....	....	....	....	....	....	....
2004-05	Milwaukee	AHL	32	3	2	5	116	....	....	....	....	....	....	....	....	....	....	....	....	....	....	....	....	....	....
2005-06	Milwaukee	AHL	30	0	1	1	82	....	....	....	....	....	....	....	....	....	....	....	....	....	....	....	....	....	....
	Idaho Steelheads	ECHL	3	0	1	1	25	....	....	....	....	....	....	....	....	....	....	....	....	....	....	....	....	....	....
	NHL Totals		1	0	0	0	5	0	0	0	1	0.0		0	0.0	7:53	....	....	....	....	....	....	....	....	....

• Missed majority of 1998-99 season and entire 1999-2000 season recovering from head injury suffered in practice, January 3, 1999. Signed as a free agent by **Worcester** (AHL), July 17, 2003. Signed as a free agent by **St. Louis**, December 30, 2003. Claimed on waivers by **Nashville** from **St. Louis**, January 30, 2004.

YAKUBOV, Mikhail

(yuh-KOO-bahf, mih-kigh-EHL) **FLA.**

Center. Shoots left. 6'3", 202 lbs. Born, Barnaul, USSR, February 16, 1982. Chicago's 1st choice, 10th overall, in 2000 Entry Draft.

1997-98	Lada Togliatti 2	Russia-3	7	0	0	0	0	....	....	....	....	....	....	....	....	....	....	....	....	....	....	....	....	....	....
1998-99	Lada Togliatti 2	Russia-4	38	11	4	15	32	....	....	....	....	....	....	....	....	....	....	....	....	....	....	....	....	....	....
99-2000	Lada Togliatti 2	Russia-3	26	12	19	31	14	....	....	....	....	....	....	....	....	....	....	....	....	....	....	....	....	....	....
2000-01	Lada Togliatti	Russia	25	0	0	0	4	....	....	....	....	....	....	....	....	....	4	0	0	0	0	....	....	....	....
2001-02	Red Deer Rebels	WHL	71	32	57	89	54	....	....	....	....	....	....	....	....	....	23	14	9	23	28	....	....	....	....
2002-03	Norfolk Admirals	AHL	62	6	5	11	36	....	....	....	....	....	....	....	....	....	9	0	0	0	8	....	....	....	....
2003-04	**Chicago**	**NHL**	**30**	**1**	**7**	**8**	**8**	**0**	**0**	**0**	**32**	**3.1**	**–12**	**337**	**45.7**	**13:44**	....	....	....	....	....	....	....	....	....
	Norfolk Admirals	AHL	51	9	18	27	22	....	....	....	....	....	....	....	....	....	8	0	3	3	2	....	....	....	....
2004-05	Norfolk Admirals	AHL	59	12	15	27	43	....	....	....	....	....	....	....	....	....	3	0	0	0	0	....	....	....	....
2005-06	Spartak Moscow	Russia	29	5	6	11	38	....	....	....	....	....	....	....	....	....	....	....	....	....	....	....	....	....	....
	Chicago	**NHL**	**10**	**1**	**2**	**3**	**8**	**0**	**0**	**1**	**11**	**9.1**	**0**	**90**	**38.9**	**12:00**	....	....	....	....	....	....	....	....	....
	Norfolk Admirals	AHL	8	1	3	4	8	....	....	....	....	....	....	....	....	....	....	....	....	....	....	....	....	....	....
	Florida	**NHL**	**13**	**0**	**1**	**1**	**4**	**0**	**0**	**0**	**16**	**0.0**	**–1**	**69**	**37.7**	**7:50**	....	....	....	....	....	....	....	....	....
	NHL Totals		**53**	**2**	**10**	**12**	**20**	**0**	**0**	**1**	**59**	**3.4**		**496**	**43.3**	**11:58**	....	....	....	....	....	....	....	....	....

WHL East Second All-Star Team (2002)

Claimed on waivers by **Florida** from **Chicago**, January 29, 2006.

YASHIN, Alexei

(YAH-shin, al-EHX-ay) **NYI**

Center. Shoots right. 6'3", 225 lbs. Born, Sverdlovsk, USSR, November 5, 1973. Ottawa's 1st choice, 2nd overall, in 1992 Entry Draft.

1990-91	Sverdlovsk	USSR	26	2	1	3	10	....	....	....	....	....	....	....	....	....	....	....	....	....	....	....	....	....	....
1991-92	Dynamo Moscow	CIS	35	7	5	12	19	....	....	....	....	....	....	....	....	....	....	....	....	....	....	....	....	....	....
1992-93	Dynamo Moscow	CIS	27	10	12	22	18	....	....	....	....	....	....	....	....	....	10	7	3	10	18	....	....	....	....
1993-94	**Ottawa**	**NHL**	**83**	**30**	**49**	**79**	**22**	**11**	**2**	**3**	**232**	**12.9**	**–49**	....	....	....	....	....	....	....	....	....	....	....	....
1994-95	Las Vegas	IHL	24	15	20	35	32	....	....	....	....	....	....	....	....	....	....	....	....	....	....	....	....	....	....
	Ottawa	**NHL**	**47**	**21**	**23**	**44**	**20**	**11**	**0**	**1**	**154**	**13.6**	**–20**	....	....	....	....	....	....	....	....	....	....	....	....
1995-96	CSKA Moscow	CIS	4	2	2	4	4	....	....	....	....	....	....	....	....	....	....	....	....	....	....	....	....	....	....
	Ottawa	**NHL**	**46**	**15**	**24**	**39**	**28**	**8**	**0**	**1**	**143**	**10.5**	**–15**	....	....	....	....	....	....	....	....	....	....	....	....
1996-97	**Ottawa**	**NHL**	**82**	**35**	**40**	**75**	**44**	**10**	**0**	**5**	**291**	**12.0**	**–7**	....	....	....	**7**	**1**	**5**	**6**	**2**	**1**	**0**	**0**	....
1997-98	**Ottawa**	**NHL**	**82**	**33**	**39**	**72**	**24**	**5**	**0**	**6**	**291**	**11.3**	**6**	....	....	....	**11**	**5**	**3**	**8**	**8**	**3**	**0**	**2**	....
	Russia	Olympics	6	3	3	6	0	....	....	....	....	....	....	....	....	....	....	....	....	....	....	....	....	....	....
1998-99	**Ottawa**	**NHL**	**82**	**44**	**50**	**94**	**54**	**19**	**0**	**5**	**337**	**13.1**	**16**	**1428**	**41.9**	**22:05**	**4**	**0**	**0**	**0**	**10**	**0**	**0**	**0**	**26:06**
99-2000	**Ottawa**	**NHL**	DID NOT PLAY – SUSPENDED																						
2000-01	**Ottawa**	**NHL**	**82**	**40**	**48**	**88**	**30**	**13**	**2**	**10**	**263**	**15.2**	**10**	**1414**	**43.1**	**20:24**	**4**	**0**	**1**	**1**	**0**	**0**	**0**	**0**	**24:53**
2001-02	**NY Islanders**	**NHL**	**78**	**32**	**43**	**75**	**25**	**15**	**0**	**5**	**239**	**13.4**	**–3**	**828**	**46.7**	**20:37**	**7**	**3**	**4**	**7**	**2**	**1**	**0**	**0**	**21:54**
	Russia	Olympics	6	1	1	2	0	....	....	....	....	....	....	....	....	....	....	....	....	....	....	....	....	....	....
2002-03	**NY Islanders**	**NHL**	**81**	**26**	**39**	**65**	**32**	**14**	**0**	**7**	**274**	**9.5**	**–12**	**1074**	**47.2**	**18:32**	**5**	**2**	**2**	**4**	**2**	**0**	**0**	**0**	**21:06**
2003-04	**NY Islanders**	**NHL**	**47**	**15**	**19**	**34**	**10**	**3**	**0**	**1**	**148**	**10.1**	**–1**	**603**	**42.8**	**17:19**	**5**	**0**	**1**	**1**	**0**	**0**	**0**	**0**	**15:33**
2004-05	Yaroslavl	Russia	10	3	3	6	14	....	....	....	....	....	....	....	....	....	9	3	7	10	10	....	....	....	....
2005-06	**NY Islanders**	**NHL**	**82**	**28**	**38**	**66**	**68**	**10**	**0**	**2**	**253**	**11.1**	**–14**	**1116**	**50.2**	**18:30**	....	....	....	....	....	....	....	....	....
	Russia	Olympics	8	1	3	4	4	....	....	....	....	....	....	....	....	....	....	....	....	....	....	....	....	....	....
	NHL Totals		**792**	**319**	**412**	**731**	**357**	**119**	**4**	**46**	**2625**	**12.2**		**6463**	**45.2**	**19:45**	**43**	**11**	**16**	**27**	**24**	**5**	**0**	**2**	**21:37**

NHL Second All-Star Team (1999)

Played in NHL All-Star Game (1994, 1999, 2002)

• Suspended for entire 1999-2000 season by **Ottawa** for refusing to report to team, November 9, 1999. Traded to **NY Islanders** by **Ottawa** for Bill Muckalt, Zdeno Chara and NY Islanders' 1st round choice (Jason Spezza) in 2001 Entry Draft, June 23, 2001. Signed as a free agent by **Yaroslavl** (Russia), February 14, 2005.

YELLE, Stephane

(YEHL, STEH-fan) **CGY.**

Center. Shoots left. 6'1", 190 lbs. Born, Ottawa, Ont., May 9, 1974. New Jersey's 9th choice, 186th overall, in 1992 Entry Draft.

1990-91	Cumberland	OHA-B	33	20	30	50	16	....	....	....	....	....	....	....	....	....	....	....	....	....	....	....	....	....	....
1991-92	Oshawa Generals	OHL	55	12	14	26	20	....	....	....	....	....	....	....	....	....	7	2	0	2	2	....	....	....	....
1992-93	Oshawa Generals	OHL	66	24	50	74	20	....	....	....	....	....	....	....	....	....	10	2	4	6	4	....	....	....	....
1993-94	Oshawa Generals	OHL	66	35	69	104	22	....	....	....	....	....	....	....	....	....	5	1	7	8	2	....	....	....	....
1994-95	Cornwall Aces	AHL	40	18	15	33	22	....	....	....	....	....	....	....	....	....	13	7	7	14	8	....	....	....	....
1995-96 ♦	**Colorado**	**NHL**	**71**	**13**	**14**	**27**	**30**	**0**	**2**	**1**	**93**	**14.0**	**15**	....	....	....	**22**	**1**	**4**	**5**	**8**	**0**	**1**	**0**	....
1996-97	**Colorado**	**NHL**	**79**	**9**	**17**	**26**	**38**	**0**	**1**	**1**	**89**	**10.1**	**1**	....	....	....	**12**	**1**	**6**	**7**	**2**	**0**	**0**	**0**	....
1997-98	**Colorado**	**NHL**	**81**	**7**	**15**	**22**	**48**	**0**	**1**	**0**	**93**	**7.5**	**–10**	....	....	....	**7**	**1**	**0**	**1**	**12**	**0**	**0**	**0**	....
1998-99	**Colorado**	**NHL**	**72**	**8**	**7**	**15**	**40**	**1**	**0**	**0**	**99**	**8.1**	**–8**	**1201**	**51.2**	**15:15**	**10**	**0**	**1**	**1**	**6**	**0**	**0**	**0**	**15:13**
99-2000	**Colorado**	**NHL**	**79**	**8**	**14**	**22**	**28**	**0**	**1**	**1**	**90**	**8.9**	**9**	**1294**	**52.2**	**15:51**	**17**	**1**	**2**	**3**	**4**	**0**	**0**	**0**	**15:38**
2000-01 ♦	**Colorado**	**NHL**	**50**	**4**	**10**	**14**	**20**	**0**	**1**	**0**	**54**	**7.4**	**–3**	**736**	**56.4**	**14:28**	**23**	**1**	**2**	**3**	**8**	**0**	**0**	**1**	**13:52**
2001-02	**Colorado**	**NHL**	**73**	**5**	**12**	**17**	**48**	**0**	**1**	**1**	**71**	**7.0**	**1**	**1036**	**51.8**	**14:02**	**20**	**0**	**2**	**2**	**14**	**0**	**0**	**0**	**13:26**
2002-03	**Calgary**	**NHL**	**82**	**10**	**15**	**25**	**50**	**3**	**0**	**3**	**121**	**8.3**	**–10**	**1494**	**53.4**	**18:06**	....	....	....	....	....	....	....	....	....
2003-04	**Calgary**	**NHL**	**53**	**4**	**13**	**17**	**24**	**1**	**0**	**0**	**76**	**5.3**	**1**	**996**	**56.6**	**15:48**	**23**	**3**	**3**	**6**	**16**	**0**	**1**	**1**	**17:04**
2004-05			DID NOT PLAY																						
2005-06	**Calgary**	**NHL**	**74**	**4**	**14**	**18**	**48**	**1**	**1**	**1**	**93**	**4.3**	**10**	**1072**	**55.4**	**14:27**	**7**	**1**	**0**	**1**	**8**	**0**	**0**	**0**	**15:28**
	NHL Totals		**714**	**72**	**131**	**203**	**374**	**6**	**8**	**8**	**879**	**8.2**		**7829**	**53.6**	**15:30**	**141**	**9**	**20**	**29**	**78**	**0**	**2**	**2**	**15:04**

Traded to **Quebec** by **New Jersey** with New Jersey's 11th round choice (Steven Low) in 1994 Entry Draft for Quebec's 11th round choice (Mike Hanson) in 1994 Entry Draft, June 1, 1994. Transferred to **Colorado** after **Quebec** franchise relocated, June 21, 1995. Traded to **Calgary** by **Colorado** with Chris Drury for Derek Morris, Jeff Shantz and Dean McAmmond, October 1, 2002.

YONKMAN, Nolan

(YAWK-man, NOH-lan) **NSH.**

Defense. Shoots right. 6'6", 245 lbs. Born, Punnichy, Sask., April 1, 1981. Washington's 5th choice, 37th overall, in 1999 Entry Draft.

1996-97	Naicam Vikings	SAHA	64	15	23	38	36	....	....	....	....	....	....	....	....	....	....	....	....	....	....	....	....	....	....
	Kelowna Rockets	WHL	4	0	0	0	0	....	....	....	....	....	....	....	....	....	....	....	....	....	....	....	....	....	....
1997-98	Kelowna Rockets	WHL	65	0	2	2	36	....	....	....	....	....	....	....	....	....	7	0	0	0	2	....	....	....	....
1998-99	Kelowna Rockets	WHL	61	1	6	7	129	....	....	....	....	....	....	....	....	....	6	0	0	0	6	....	....	....	....
99-2000	Kelowna Rockets	WHL	71	5	7	12	153	....	....	....	....	....	....	....	....	....	5	0	0	0	8	....	....	....	....
2000-01	Kelowna Rockets	WHL	7	0	1	1	19	....	....	....	....	....	....	....	....	....	....	....	....	....	....	....	....	....	....
	Brandon	WHL	51	6	10	16	94	....	....	....	....	....	....	....	....	....	6	0	1	1	12	....	....	....	....
2001-02	**Washington**	**NHL**	**11**	**1**	**0**	**1**	**4**	**0**	**0**	**0**	**7**	**14.3**	**3**	**0**	**0.0**	**12:44**	....	....	....	....	....	....	....	....	....
	Portland Pirates	AHL	59	4	3	7	116	....	....	....	....	....	....	....	....	....	....	....	....	....	....	....	....	....	....
2002-03	Portland Pirates	AHL	24	1	4	5	40	....	....	....	....	....	....	....	....	....	3	0	1	1	2	....	....	....	....
2003-04	**Washington**	**NHL**	**1**	**0**	**0**	**0**	**0**	**0**	**0**	**0**	**0**	**0.0**	**0**	**0**	**0.0**	**5:00**	....	....	....	....	....	....	....	....	....
	Portland Pirates	AHL	4	0	0	0	11	....	....	....	....	....	....	....	....	....	....	....	....	....	....	....	....	....	....
2004-05	Portland Pirates	AHL	32	0	3	3	68	....	....	....	....	....	....	....	....	....	....	....	....	....	....	....	....	....	....
2005-06	**Washington**	**NHL**	**38**	**0**	**7**	**7**	**86**	**0**	**0**	**0**	**14**	**0.0**	**1**	**0**	**0.0**	**8:13**	....	....	....	....	....	....	....	....	....
	Hershey Bears	AHL	6	0	0	0	15	....	....	....	....	....	....	....	....	....	....	....	....	....	....	....	....	....	....
	NHL Totals		**50**	**1**	**7**	**8**	**90**	**0**	**0**	**0**	**21**	**4.8**		**0**	**0.0**	**9:09**	....	....	....	....	....	....	....	....	....

• Missed majority of 2002-03 season recovering from abdominal injury suffered in training camp, September 25, 2002. • Missed majority of 2003-04 and 2004-05 seasons recovering from knee injury suffered in game vs. Worcester (AHL), October 23, 2003. Signed as a free agent by **Nashville**, July 17, 2006.

YORK, Jason
(YOHRK, JAY-suhn) **BOS.**

Defense. Shoots right. 6'1", 208 lbs. Born, Nepean, Ont., May 20, 1970. Detroit's 6th choice, 129th overall, in 1990 Entry Draft.

Season	Club	League	GP	G	A	Pts	PIM	PP	SH	GW	S	%	+/-	TF	F%	Min	GP	G	A	Pts	PIM	PP	SH	GW	Min
1986-87	Smiths Falls Bears	CJHL	46	6	13	19	86																		
1987-88	Hamilton	OHL	58	4	9	13	110																		
1988-89	Windsor Spitfires	OHL	65	19	44	63	105																		
1989-90	Windsor Spitfires	OHL	39	9	30	39	38																		
	Kitchener Rangers	OHL	25	11	25	36	17										17	3	19	22	10				
1990-91	Windsor Spitfires	OHL	66	13	80	93	40										11	3	10	13	12				
1991-92	Adirondack	AHL	49	4	20	24	32										5	0	1	1	0				
1992-93	**Detroit**	**NHL**	**2**	**0**	**0**	**0**	**0**	**0**	**0**	**0**	**1**	**0.0**	**0**												
	Adirondack	AHL	77	15	40	55	86										11	0	3	3	18				
1993-94	**Detroit**	**NHL**	**7**	**1**	**2**	**3**	**2**	**0**	**0**	**0**	**9**	**11.1**	**0**												
	Adirondack	AHL	74	10	56	66	98										12	3	11	14	22				
1994-95	**Detroit**	**NHL**	**10**	**1**	**2**	**3**	**2**	**0**	**0**	**0**	**6**	**16.7**	**0**												
	Adirondack	AHL	5	1	3	4	4																		
	Anaheim	**NHL**	**15**	**0**	**8**	**8**	**12**	**0**	**0**	**0**	**22**	**0.0**	**4**												
1995-96	**Anaheim**	**NHL**	**79**	**3**	**21**	**24**	**88**	**0**	**0**	**0**	**106**	**2.8**	**–7**												
1996-97	**Ottawa**	**NHL**	**75**	**4**	**17**	**21**	**67**	**1**	**0**	**0**	**121**	**3.3**	**–8**				**7**	**0**	**0**	**0**	**4**	**0**	**0**	**0**	
1997-98	**Ottawa**	**NHL**	**73**	**3**	**13**	**16**	**62**	**0**	**0**	**0**	**109**	**2.8**	**8**				**7**	**1**	**1**	**2**	**7**	**1**	**0**	**0**	
1998-99	**Ottawa**	**NHL**	**79**	**4**	**31**	**35**	**48**	**2**	**0**	**0**	**177**	**2.3**	**17**	**2**	**0.0**	**23:49**	**4**	**1**	**1**	**2**	**4**	**0**	**0**	**0**	**24:59**
99-2000	**Ottawa**	**NHL**	**79**	**8**	**22**	**30**	**60**	**1**	**0**	**1**	**159**	**5.0**	**–3**	**0**	**0.0**	**23:20**	**6**	**0**	**2**	**2**	**2**	**0**	**0**	**0**	**25:30**
2000-01	**Ottawa**	**NHL**	**74**	**6**	**16**	**22**	**72**	**3**	**0**	**2**	**133**	**4.5**	**7**	**0**	**0.0**	**23:49**	**4**	**0**	**0**	**0**	**4**	**0**	**0**	**0**	**20:58**
2001-02	**Anaheim**	**NHL**	**74**	**5**	**20**	**25**	**60**	**3**	**0**	**2**	**104**	**4.8**	**–11**	**0**	**0.0**	**19:19**									
2002-03	**Nashville**	**NHL**	**74**	**4**	**15**	**19**	**52**	**2**	**0**	**0**	**107**	**3.7**	**13**	**0**	**0.0**	**19:57**									
	Cincinnati	AHL	4	3	2	5	8																		
2003-04	**Nashville**	**NHL**	**67**	**2**	**13**	**15**	**64**	**0**	**0**	**1**	**80**	**2.5**	**–4**	**1**	**0.0**	**21:17**	**6**	**0**	**3**	**3**	**4**	**0**	**0**	**0**	**21:27**
2004-05			DID NOT PLAY																						
2005-06	HC Lugano	Swiss	34	3	18	21	122										16	1	3	4	8				
	NHL Totals		**708**	**41**	**180**	**221**	**589**	**12**	**0**	**6**	**1134**	**3.6**		**3**	**0.0**	**21:58**	**34**	**2**	**7**	**9**	**25**	**1**	**0**	**0**	**23:16**

AHL First All-Star Team (1994)

Traded to **Anaheim** by **Detroit** with Mike Sillinger for Stu Grimson, Mark Ferner and Anaheim's 6th round choice (Magnus Nilsson) in 1996 Entry Draft, April 4, 1995. Traded to **Ottawa** by **Anaheim** with Shaun Van Allen for Ted Drury and the rights to Marc Moro, October 1, 1996. Signed as a free agent by **Anaheim**, July 3, 2001. Traded to **Nashville** by **Anaheim** for future considerations, October 23, 2002. Signed as a free agent by **Lugano** (Swiss), September 19, 2005. Signed as a free agent by **Boston**, July 21, 2006.

YORK, Mike
(YOHRK, MIGHK) **NYI**

Left wing. Shoots right. 5'10", 185 lbs. Born, Waterford, MI, January 3, 1978. NY Rangers' 7th choice, 136th overall, in 1997 Entry Draft.

Season	Club	League	GP	G	A	Pts	PIM	PP	SH	GW	S	%	+/-	TF	F%	Min	GP	G	A	Pts	PIM	PP	SH	GW	Min
1992-93	Michigan	MNHL	50	45	50	95																			
1993-94	Det. Compuware	MNHL	85	136	140	276																			
1994-95	Thornhill Islanders	MTJHL	49	39	54	*93	44										11	7	6	13	0				
1995-96	Michigan State	CCHA	39	12	27	39	20																		
1996-97	Michigan State	CCHA	37	18	29	47	42																		
1997-98	Michigan State	CCHA	40	27	34	61	38																		
1998-99	Michigan State	CCHA	42	22	32	*54	41																		
	Hartford	AHL	3	2	2	4	0										6	3	1	4	0				
99-2000	**NY Rangers**	**NHL**	**82**	**26**	**24**	**50**	**18**	**8**	**0**	**4**	**177**	**14.7**	**–17**	**1131**	**48.1**	**1:35**									
2000-01	**NY Rangers**	**NHL**	**79**	**14**	**17**	**31**	**20**	**3**	**2**	**4**	**171**	**8.2**	**1**	**1098**	**46.9**	**17:45**									
2001-02	**NY Rangers**	**NHL**	**69**	**18**	**39**	**57**	**16**	**2**	**0**	**5**	**188**	**9.6**	**8**	**267**	**43.1**	**20:24**									
	United States	Olympics	6	0	1	1	0																		
	Edmonton	**NHL**	**12**	**2**	**2**	**4**	**0**	**1**	**0**	**1**	**30**	**6.7**	**–1**	**100**	**56.0**	**16:35**									
2002-03	**Edmonton**	**NHL**	**71**	**22**	**29**	**51**	**10**	**7**	**2**	**4**	**177**	**12.4**	**–8**	**390**	**43.9**	**19:04**	**6**	**0**	**2**	**2**	**2**	**0**	**0**	**0**	**14:20**
2003-04	**Edmonton**	**NHL**	**61**	**16**	**26**	**42**	**15**	**1**	**2**	**0**	**144**	**11.1**	**18**	**656**	**45.9**	**19:17**									
2004-05	Iserlohn Roosters	Germany	52	16	46	62	77																		
2005-06	**NY Islanders**	**NHL**	**75**	**13**	**39**	**52**	**30**	**4**	**1**	**2**	**146**	**8.9**	**–9**	**1289**	**46.1**	**19:55**									
	NHL Totals		**449**	**111**	**176**	**287**	**109**	**26**	**7**	**20**	**1033**	**10.7**		**4931**	**46.6**	**15:57**	**6**	**0**	**2**	**2**	**2**	**0**	**0**	**0**	**14:20**

CCHA Second All-Star Team (1998) • NCAA West First All-American Team (1998, 1999) • CCHA First All-Star Team (1999) • CCHA Player of the Year (1999) • NHL All-Rookie Team (2000)
Played in NHL All-Star Game (2002)

Traded to **Edmonton** by **NY Rangers** with NY Rangers' 4th round choice (Ivan Koltsov) in 2002 Entry Draft for Tom Poti and Rem Murray, March 19, 2002. Signed as a free agent by **Iserlohn** (Germany), February 25, 2005. Traded to **NY Islanders** by **Edmonton** with Edmonton's 4th round choice (later traded to Colorado - Colorado selected Kevin Montgomery) in 2006 Entry Draft for Michael Peca, August 3, 2005.

YOUNG, Scott
(YUHNG, SKAWT)

Right wing. Shoots right. 6'1", 200 lbs. Born, Clinton, MA, October 1, 1967. Hartford's 1st choice, 11th overall, in 1986 Entry Draft.

Season	Club	League	GP	G	A	Pts	PIM	PP	SH	GW	S	%	+/-	TF	F%	Min	GP	G	A	Pts	PIM	PP	SH	GW	Min
1984-85	St. Mark's	High-MA	23	28	41	69																			
1985-86	Boston University	H-East	38	16	13	29	31																		
1986-87	Boston University	H-East	33	15	21	36	24																		
1987-88	United States	Nat-Tm	56	11	47	58	31																		
	United States	Olympics	6	2	6	8	4																		
	Hartford	**NHL**	**7**	**0**	**0**	**0**	**2**	**0**	**0**	**0**	**6**	**0.0**	**–6**				**4**	**1**	**0**	**1**	**0**	**0**	**0**	**0**	
1988-89	**Hartford**	**NHL**	**76**	**19**	**40**	**59**	**27**	**6**	**0**	**2**	**203**	**9.4**	**–21**				**4**	**2**	**0**	**2**	**4**	**0**	**0**	**0**	
1989-90	**Hartford**	**NHL**	**80**	**24**	**40**	**64**	**47**	**10**	**2**	**5**	**239**	**10.0**	**–24**				**7**	**2**	**0**	**2**	**2**	**0**	**0**	**0**	
1990-91	**Hartford**	**NHL**	**34**	**6**	**9**	**15**	**8**	**3**	**1**	**2**	**94**	**6.4**	**–9**												
	◆ **Pittsburgh**	**NHL**	**43**	**11**	**16**	**27**	**33**	**3**	**1**	**3**	**116**	**9.5**	**3**				**17**	**1**	**6**	**7**	**2**	**1**	**0**	**0**	
1991-92	HC Bolzano	Alpenliga	15	19	11	30	14																		
	United States	Nat-Tm	10	2	4	6	21																		
	HC Bolzano	Italy	18	22	17	39	6																		
	United States	Olympics	8	2	1	3	2										5	4	3	7	7				
1992-93	**Quebec**	**NHL**	**82**	**30**	**30**	**60**	**20**	**9**	**6**	**5**	**225**	**13.3**	**5**				**6**	**4**	**1**	**5**	**0**	**0**	**0**	**2**	
1993-94	**Quebec**	**NHL**	**76**	**26**	**25**	**51**	**14**	**6**	**1**	**1**	**236**	**11.0**	**–4**												
1994-95	EV Landshut	Germany	4	6	1	7	6																		
	Frankfurt Lions	Germany	1	1	0	1	0																		
	Quebec	**NHL**	**48**	**18**	**21**	**39**	**14**	**3**	**3**	**0**	**167**	**10.8**	**9**				**6**	**3**	**3**	**6**	**2**	**0**	**1**	**0**	
1995-96◆	**Colorado**	**NHL**	**81**	**21**	**39**	**60**	**50**	**7**	**0**	**5**	**229**	**9.2**	**2**				**22**	**3**	**12**	**15**	**10**	**0**	**0**	**0**	
1996-97	**Colorado**	**NHL**	**72**	**18**	**19**	**37**	**14**	**7**	**0**	**0**	**164**	**11.0**	**–5**				**17**	**4**	**2**	**6**	**14**	**2**	**0**	**0**	
1997-98	**Anaheim**	**NHL**	**73**	**13**	**20**	**33**	**22**	**4**	**2**	**1**	**187**	**7.0**	**–13**												
1998-99	**St. Louis**	**NHL**	**75**	**24**	**28**	**52**	**27**	**8**	**0**	**4**	**205**	**11.7**	**8**	**4**	**25.0**	**15:14**	**13**	**4**	**7**	**11**	**10**	**1**	**0**	**1**	**17:56**
99-2000	**St. Louis**	**NHL**	**75**	**24**	**15**	**39**	**18**	**6**	**1**	**7**	**244**	**9.8**	**12**	**2**	**50.0**	**16:06**	**6**	**6**	**2**	**8**	**8**	**3**	**0**	**0**	**17:18**
2000-01	**St. Louis**	**NHL**	**81**	**40**	**33**	**73**	**30**	**14**	**3**	**7**	**321**	**12.5**	**15**	**4**	**25.0**	**19:18**	**15**	**6**	**7**	**13**	**2**	**0**	**2**	**3**	**20:34**
2001-02	**St. Louis**	**NHL**	**67**	**19**	**22**	**41**	**26**	**5**	**0**	**1**	**210**	**9.0**	**11**	**4**	**0.0**	**18:31**	**10**	**3**	**0**	**3**	**2**	**1**	**1**	**0**	**17:40**
	United States	Olympics	6	4	0	4	2																		
2002-03	**Dallas**	**NHL**	**79**	**23**	**19**	**42**	**30**	**5**	**1**	**4**	**237**	**9.7**	**24**	**8**	**37.5**	**16:08**	**10**	**4**	**3**	**7**	**6**	**2**	**0**	**1**	**19:12**
2003-04	**Dallas**	**NHL**	**53**	**8**	**8**	**16**	**14**	**2**	**0**	**2**	**134**	**6.0**	**–15**	**5**	**20.0**	**14:45**	**4**	**1**	**0**	**1**	**2**	**1**	**0**	**0**	**15:05**
2004-05	Memphis	CHL	3	2	1	3	0																		
2005-06	**St. Louis**	**NHL**	**79**	**18**	**31**	**49**	**52**	**10**	**0**	**1**	**284**	**6.3**	**–32**	**6**	**0.0**	**18:23**									
	NHL Totals		**1181**	**342**	**415**	**757**	**448**	**108**	**21**	**50**	**3501**	**9.8**		**33**	**21.2**	**17:01**	**141**	**44**	**43**	**87**	**64**	**11**	**4**	**7**	**18:32**

Hockey East Rookie of the Year (1986) (co-winner - Al Loring)

Traded to **Pittsburgh** by **Hartford** for Rob Brown, December 21, 1990. Traded to **Quebec** by **Pittsburgh** for Bryan Fogarty, March 10, 1992. Transferred to **Colorado** after **Quebec** franchise relocated, June 21, 1995. Traded to **Anaheim** by **Colorado** for Anaheim's 3rd round choice (later traded to Florida – Florida selected Lance Ward) in 1998 Entry Draft, September 17, 1997. Signed as a free agent by **St. Louis**, July 28, 1998. Signed as a free agent by **Dallas**, July 5, 2002. Signed as a free agent by **Memphis** (CHL), January 7, 2005. Signed as a free agent by **St. Louis**, September 13, 2005.

YUSHKEVICH, Dmitry

(yoosh-KAY-vihch, dih-MEE-tree)

Defense. Shoots right. 5'11", 208 lbs. Born, Cherepovets, USSR, November 19, 1971. Philadelphia's 6th choice, 122nd overall, in 1991 Entry Draft.

			Regular Season														Playoffs								
Season	Club	League	GP	G	A	Pts	PIM	PP	SH	GW	S	%	+/-	TF	F%	Min	GP	G	A	Pts	PIM	PP	SH	GW	Min
1988-89	Yaroslavl	USSR	23	2	1	3	8	....	....	....	....	....	....	....	....	....	....	....	....	....	....	....	....	....	....
1989-90	Yaroslavl	USSR	41	2	3	5	39	....	....	....	....	....	....	....	....	....	....	....	....	....	....	....	....	....	....
1990-91	Yaroslavl	USSR	41	10	4	14	22	....	....	....	....	....	....	....	....	....	....	....	....	....	....	....	....	....	....
1991-92	Dynamo Moscow	CIS	35	5	7	12	14	....	....	....	....	....	....	....	....	....	....	....	....	....	....	....	....	....	....
	Russia	Olympics	8	1	2	3	4	....	....	....	....	....	....	....	....	....	....	....	....	....	....	....	....	....	....
1992-93	**Philadelphia**	**NHL**	**82**	**5**	**27**	**32**	**71**	**1**	**0**	**1**	**155**	**3.2**	**12**	....	....	....	....	....	....	....	....	....	....	....	....
1993-94	**Philadelphia**	**NHL**	**75**	**5**	**25**	**30**	**86**	**1**	**0**	**2**	**136**	**3.7**	**–8**	....	....	....	....	....	....	....	....	....	....	....	....
1994-95	Yaroslavl	CIS	10	3	4	7	8	....	....	....	....	....	....	....	....	....	....	....	....	....	....	....	....	....	....
	Philadelphia	**NHL**	**40**	**5**	**9**	**14**	**47**	**3**	**1**	**1**	**80**	**6.3**	**–4**	....	....	....	**15**	**1**	**5**	**6**	**12**	**0**	**0**	**0**	....
1995-96	**Toronto**	**NHL**	**69**	**1**	**10**	**11**	**54**	**1**	**0**	**0**	**96**	**1.0**	**–14**	....	....	....	**4**	**0**	**0**	**0**	**0**	**0**	**0**	**0**	....
1996-97	**Toronto**	**NHL**	**74**	**4**	**10**	**14**	**56**	**1**	**1**	**1**	**99**	**4.0**	**–24**	....	....	....	....	....	....	....	....	....	....	....	....
1997-98	**Toronto**	**NHL**	**72**	**0**	**12**	**12**	**78**	**0**	**0**	**0**	**92**	**0.0**	**–13**	....	....	....	....	....	....	....	....	....	....	....	....
	Russia	Olympics	6	0	0	0	2	....	....	....	....	....	....	....	....	....	....	....	....	....	....	....	....	....	....
1998-99	**Toronto**	**NHL**	**78**	**6**	**22**	**28**	**88**	**2**	**1**	**0**	**95**	**6.3**	**25**	**0**	**0.0**	**22:20**	**17**	**1**	**5**	**6**	**22**	**1**	**0**	**0**	**23:13**
99-2000	Yaroslavl	Russia	7	2	3	5	2	....	....	....	....	....	....	....	....	....	....	....	....	....	....	....	....	....	....
	Toronto	**NHL**	**77**	**3**	**24**	**27**	**55**	**2**	**1**	**1**	**103**	**2.9**	**2**	**0**	**0.0**	**23:18**	**12**	**1**	**1**	**2**	**4**	**0**	**0**	**0**	**24:45**
2000-01	**Toronto**	**NHL**	**81**	**5**	**19**	**24**	**52**	**1**	**0**	**0**	**110**	**4.5**	**–2**	**0**	**0.0**	**24:14**	**11**	**0**	**4**	**4**	**12**	**0**	**0**	**0**	**25:18**
2001-02	**Toronto**	**NHL**	**55**	**6**	**13**	**19**	**26**	**3**	**0**	**0**	**79**	**7.6**	**14**	**1**	**100.0**	**23:25**	....	....	....	....	....	....	....	....	....
2002-03	**Florida**	**NHL**	**23**	**1**	**6**	**7**	**14**	**0**	**0**	**0**	**23**	**4.3**	**–12**	**3**	**33.3**	**23:40**	....	....	....	....	....	....	....	....	....
	Los Angeles	**NHL**	**42**	**0**	**3**	**3**	**24**	**0**	**0**	**0**	**36**	**0.0**	**–4**	**2**	**0.0**	**19:57**	....	....	....	....	....	....	....	....	....
	Philadelphia	**NHL**	**18**	**2**	**2**	**4**	**8**	**0**	**0**	**0**	**16**	**12.5**	**7**	**0**	**0.0**	**18:05**	**13**	**1**	**4**	**5**	**2**	**0**	**0**	**1**	**24:20**
2003-04	Yaroslavl	Russia	35	7	11	18	38	....	....	....	....	....	....	....	....	....	3	0	2	2	2	....	....	....	....
2004-05	Cherepovets	Russia	54	6	22	28	58	....	....	....	....	....	....	....	....	....	....	....	....	....	....	....	....	....	....
2005-06	Magnitogorsk	Russia	49	8	22	30	38	....	....	....	....	....	....	....	....	....	11	5	10	15	2	....	....	....	....
	NHL Totals		**786**	**43**	**182**	**225**	**659**	**15**	**4**	**6**	**1120**	**3.8**		**6**	**33.3**	**22:43**	**72**	**4**	**19**	**23**	**52**	**1**	**0**	**1**	**24:16**

Played in NHL All-Star Game (2000)

Traded to **Toronto** by **Philadelphia** with Philadelphia's 2nd round choice (Francis Larivee) in 1996 Entry Draft for Toronto's 1st round choice (Dainius Zubrus) in 1996 Entry Draft, Toronto's 2nd round choice (Jean-Marc Pelletier) in 1997 Entry Draft and Los Angeles' 4th round choice (previously acquired, later traded back to Los Angeles – Los Angeles selected Mikael Simons) in 1996 Entry Draft, August 30, 1995. Traded to **Florida** by **Toronto** for Robert Svehla, July 18, 2002. Traded to **Los Angeles** by **Florida** with NY Islanders' 5th round choice (previously acquired, Los Angeles selected Brady Murray) in 2003 Entry Draft for Jaroslav Bednar and Andreas Lilja, November 26, 2002. Traded to **Philadelphia** by **Los Angeles** for Philadelphia's 4th round choice (later traded to Boston – Boston selected Patrick Valcak) in 2003 Entry Draft and Philadelphia's 7th round choice (Daniel Taylor) in 2004 Entry Draft, March 1, 2003. Signed as a free agent by **Yaroslavl** (Russia), November 11, 2003.

YZERMAN, Steve

(IGH-zuhr-muhn, STEEV)

Center. Shoots right. 5'11", 185 lbs. Born, Cranbrook, B.C., May 9, 1965. Detroit's 1st choice, 4th overall, in 1983 Entry Draft.

			Regular Season														Playoffs								
Season	Club	League	GP	G	A	Pts	PIM	PP	SH	GW	S	%	+/-	TF	F%	Min	GP	G	A	Pts	PIM	PP	SH	GW	Min
1980-81	Nepean Raiders	CJHL	50	38	*54	92	44	....	....	....	....	....	....	....	....	....	....	....	....	....	....	....	....	....	....
1981-82	Peterborough	OHL	58	21	43	64	65	....	....	....	....	....	....	....	....	....	6	0	1	1	16	....	....	....	....
1982-83	Peterborough	OHL	56	42	49	91	33	....	....	....	....	....	....	....	....	....	4	1	4	5	0	....	....	....	....
1983-84	**Detroit**	**NHL**	**80**	**39**	**48**	**87**	**33**	**13**	**0**	**2**	**177**	**22.0**	**–17**	....	....	....	**4**	**3**	**3**	**6**	**0**	**1**	**0**	**1**	....
1984-85	**Detroit**	**NHL**	**80**	**30**	**59**	**89**	**58**	**9**	**0**	**3**	**231**	**13.0**	**–17**	....	....	....	**3**	**2**	**1**	**3**	**2**	**0**	**0**	**0**	....
1985-86	**Detroit**	**NHL**	**51**	**14**	**28**	**42**	**16**	**3**	**0**	**3**	**132**	**10.6**	**–24**	....	....	....	....	....	....	....	....	....	....	....	....
1986-87	**Detroit**	**NHL**	**80**	**31**	**59**	**90**	**43**	**9**	**1**	**2**	**217**	**14.3**	**–1**	....	....	....	**16**	**5**	**13**	**18**	**8**	**1**	**0**	**0**	....
1987-88	**Detroit**	**NHL**	**64**	**50**	**52**	**102**	**44**	**10**	**6**	**6**	**242**	**20.7**	**30**	....	....	....	**3**	**1**	**3**	**4**	**6**	**0**	**0**	**0**	....
1988-89	**Detroit**	**NHL**	**80**	**65**	**90**	**155**	**61**	**17**	**3**	**7**	**388**	**16.8**	**17**	....	....	....	**6**	**5**	**5**	**10**	**2**	**2**	**0**	**0**	....
1989-90	**Detroit**	**NHL**	**79**	**62**	**65**	**127**	**79**	**16**	**7**	**8**	**332**	**18.7**	**–6**	....	....	....	....	....	....	....	....	....	....	....	....
1990-91	**Detroit**	**NHL**	**80**	**51**	**57**	**108**	**34**	**12**	**6**	**4**	**326**	**15.6**	**–2**	....	....	....	**7**	**3**	**3**	**6**	**4**	**1**	**0**	**0**	....
1991-92	**Detroit**	**NHL**	**79**	**45**	**58**	**103**	**64**	**9**	**8**	**9**	**295**	**15.3**	**26**	....	....	....	**11**	**3**	**5**	**8**	**12**	**0**	**1**	**1**	....
1992-93	**Detroit**	**NHL**	**84**	**58**	**79**	**137**	**44**	**13**	**7**	**6**	**307**	**18.9**	**33**	....	....	....	**7**	**4**	**3**	**7**	**4**	**1**	**1**	**1**	....
1993-94	**Detroit**	**NHL**	**58**	**24**	**58**	**82**	**36**	**7**	**3**	**3**	**217**	**11.1**	**11**	....	....	....	**3**	**1**	**3**	**4**	**0**	**0**	**0**	**0**	....
1994-95	**Detroit**	**NHL**	**47**	**12**	**26**	**38**	**40**	**4**	**0**	**1**	**134**	**9.0**	**6**	....	....	....	**15**	**4**	**8**	**12**	**0**	**2**	**0**	**1**	....
1995-96	**Detroit**	**NHL**	**80**	**36**	**59**	**95**	**64**	**16**	**2**	**8**	**220**	**16.4**	**29**	....	....	....	**18**	**8**	**12**	**20**	**4**	**4**	**0**	**1**	....
1996-97♦	**Detroit**	**NHL**	**81**	**22**	**63**	**85**	**78**	**8**	**0**	**3**	**232**	**9.5**	**22**	....	....	....	**20**	**7**	**6**	**13**	**4**	**3**	**0**	**2**	....
1997-98♦	**Detroit**	**NHL**	**75**	**24**	**45**	**69**	**46**	**6**	**2**	**0**	**188**	**12.8**	**3**	....	....	....	**22**	**6**	***18**	***24**	**22**	**3**	**1**	**0**	....
	Canada	Olympics	6	1	1	2	10	....	....	....	....	....	....	....	....	....	....	....	....	....	....	....	....	....	....
1998-99	**Detroit**	**NHL**	**80**	**29**	**45**	**74**	**42**	**13**	**2**	**4**	**231**	**12.6**	**8**	**1600**	**56.9**	**21:35**	**10**	**9**	**4**	**13**	**0**	**4**	**0**	**2**	**21:49**
99-2000	**Detroit**	**NHL**	**78**	**35**	**44**	**79**	**34**	**15**	**2**	**6**	**234**	**15.0**	**28**	**1868**	**56.8**	**21:07**	**8**	**0**	**4**	**4**	**0**	**0**	**0**	**0**	**22:39**
2000-01	**Detroit**	**NHL**	**54**	**18**	**34**	**52**	**18**	**5**	**0**	**7**	**155**	**11.6**	**4**	**1197**	**59.6**	**22:14**	**1**	**0**	**0**	**0**	**0**	**0**	**0**	**0**	**5:58**
2001-02♦	**Detroit**	**NHL**	**52**	**13**	**35**	**48**	**18**	**5**	**1**	**5**	**104**	**12.5**	**11**	**1182**	**58.4**	**20:35**	**23**	**6**	**17**	**23**	**10**	**4**	**0**	**2**	**21:22**
	Canada	Olympics	6	2	4	6	2	....	....	....	....	....	....	....	....	....	....	....	....	....	....	....	....	....	....
2002-03	**Detroit**	**NHL**	**16**	**2**	**6**	**8**	**8**	**1**	**0**	**1**	**13**	**15.4**	**6**	**134**	**56.0**	**15:35**	**4**	**0**	**1**	**1**	**2**	**0**	**0**	**0**	**20:33**
2003-04	**Detroit**	**NHL**	**75**	**18**	**33**	**51**	**46**	**7**	**0**	**3**	**141**	**12.8**	**10**	**1134**	**55.3**	**17:32**	**11**	**3**	**2**	**5**	**0**	**0**	**0**	**1**	**17:02**
2004-05			DID NOT PLAY																						
2005-06	**Detroit**	**NHL**	**61**	**14**	**20**	**34**	**18**	**4**	**0**	**3**	**86**	**16.3**	**8**	**414**	**57.7**	**12:47**	**4**	**0**	**4**	**4**	**4**	**0**	**0**	**0**	**16:39**
	NHL Totals		**1514**	**692**	**1063**	**1755**	**924**	**202**	**50**	**94**	**4602**	**15.0**		**7529**	**57.3**	**19:12**	**196**	**70**	**115**	**185**	**84**	**26**	**3**	**12**	**20:13**

NHL All-Rookie Team (1984) • Lester B. Pearson Award (1989) • Conn Smythe Trophy (1998) • NHL First All-Star Team (2000) • Frank J. Selke Trophy (2000) • Bill Masterton Memorial Trophy (2003)

Played in NHL All-Star Game (1984, 1988, 1989, 1990, 1991, 1992, 1993, 1997, 2000)

♦ Missed majority of 2002-03 season recovering from off-season knee surgery, August 2, 2002. • Officially announced retirement, July, 3, 2006.

ZALESAK, Miroslav

(zah-LIH-sahk, MEER-oh-slav)

Right wing. Shoots left. 6', 200 lbs. Born, Skalica, Czech., January 2, 1980. San Jose's 5th choice, 104th overall, in 1998 Entry Draft.

			Regular Season														Playoffs								
Season	Club	League	GP	G	A	Pts	PIM	PP	SH	GW	S	%	+/-	TF	F%	Min	GP	G	A	Pts	PIM	PP	SH	GW	Min
1995-96	HC Nitra Jr.	Slovak-Jr.	49	53	29	82	....	....	....	....	....	....	....	....	....	....	....	....	....	....	....	....	....	....	....
1996-97	Nitra Jr.	Slovak-Jr.	58	51	31	82	....	....	....	....	....	....	....	....	....	....	....	....	....	....	....	....	....	....	....
1997-98	Nitra Jr.	Slovak-Jr.	27	32	29	61	30	....	....	....	....	....	....	....	....	....	....	....	....	....	....	....	....	....	....
	Nitra	Slovakia	30	8	6	14	0	....	....	....	....	....	....	....	....	....	....	....	....	....	....	....	....	....	....
1998-99	Nitra	Slovakia	15	4	3	7	10	....	....	....	....	....	....	....	....	....	....	....	....	....	....	....	....	....	....
	Drummondville	QMJHL	45	24	27	51	18	....	....	....	....	....	....	....	....	....	16	7	11	18	4	....	....	....	....
99-2000	Drummondville	QMJHL	60	50	61	111	40	....	....	....	....	....	....	....	....	....	3	0	1	1	4	....	....	....	....
2000-01	Kentucky	AHL	60	14	11	25	26	....	....	....	....	....	....	....	....	....	....	....	....	....	....	....	....	....	....
2001-02	Cleveland Barons	AHL	74	22	20	42	44	....	....	....	....	....	....	....	....	....	....	....	....	....	....	....	....	....	....
2002-03	**San Jose**	**NHL**	**10**	**1**	**2**	**3**	**0**	**0**	**0**	**0**	**8**	**12.5**	**–2**	**1**	**0.0**	**9:28**	....	....	....	....	....	....	....	....	....
	Cleveland Barons	AHL	50	27	22	49	35	....	....	....	....	....	....	....	....	....	....	....	....	....	....	....	....	....	....
2003-04	**San Jose**	**NHL**	**2**	**0**	**0**	**0**	**0**	**0**	**0**	**0**	**3**	**0.0**	**–1**	**0**	**0.0**	**12:02**	....	....	....	....	....	....	....	....	....
	Cleveland Barons	AHL	72	35	40	75	80	....	....	....	....	....	....	....	....	....	9	1	4	5	14	....	....	....	....
2004-05	HK 36 Skalica	Slovakia	18	11	14	25	18	....	....	....	....	....	....	....	....	....	....	....	....	....	....	....	....	....	....
	Litvinov	CzRep	30	6	6	12	26	....	....	....	....	....	....	....	....	....	6	1	1	2	0	....	....	....	....
2005-06	Sodertalje SK	Sweden	43	16	9	25	28	....	....	....	....	....	....	....	....	....	....	....	....	....	....	....	....	....	....
	Sodertalje SK	Sweden-Q	9	1	3	4	4	....	....	....	....	....	....	....	....	....	....	....	....	....	....	....	....	....	....
	NHL Totals		**12**	**1**	**2**	**3**	**0**	**0**	**0**	**0**	**11**	**9.1**		**1**	**0.0**	**9:54**	....	....	....	....	....	....	....	....	....

Signed as a free agent by **Skalica** (Slovakia), September 17, 2004. Signed as a free agent by **Litvinov** (CzRep), November 19, 2004. Signed as a free agent by **Washington**, August 8, 2005. Signed as a free agent by **Sodertalje** (Sweden). October 7, 2005.

ZANON, Greg

(ZA-nuhn, GREHG) **NSH.**

Defense. Shoots left. 5'11", 211 lbs. Born, Burnaby, B.C., June 5, 1980. Ottawa's 6th choice, 156th overall, in 2000 Entry Draft.

			Regular Season														Playoffs								
Season	Club	League	GP	G	A	Pts	PIM	PP	SH	GW	S	%	+/-	TF	F%	Min	GP	G	A	Pts	PIM	PP	SH	GW	Min
1995-96	Burnaby Beavers	BCAHA	49	16	27	43	142	....	....	....	....	....	....	....	....	....	....	....	....	....	....	....	....	....	....
1996-97	Victoria Salsa	BCHL	53	4	13	17	124	....	....	....	....	....	....	....	....	....	....	....	....	....	....	....	....	....	....
1997-98	Victoria Salsa	BCHL	59	11	21	32	108	....	....	....	....	....	....	....	....	....	7	0	2	2	10	....	....	....	....
1998-99	South Surrey	BCHL	59	17	54	71	154	....	....	....	....	....	....	....	....	....	....	....	....	....	....	....	....	....	....
99-2000	Nebraska-Omaha	CCHA	42	3	26	29	56	....	....	....	....	....	....	....	....	....	....	....	....	....	....	....	....	....	....
2000-01	Nebraska-Omaha	CCHA	39	12	16	28	64	....	....	....	....	....	....	....	....	....	....	....	....	....	....	....	....	....	....
2001-02	Nebraska-Omaha	CCHA	41	9	16	25	54	....	....	....	....	....	....	....	....	....	....	....	....	....	....	....	....	....	....
2002-03	Nebraska-Omaha	CCHA	32	6	19	25	44	....	....	....	....	....	....	....	....	....	....	....	....	....	....	....	....	....	....
2003-04	Milwaukee	AHL	62	4	12	16	59	....	....	....	....	....	....	....	....	....	22	2	6	8	31	....	....	....	....
2004-05	Milwaukee	AHL	80	2	17	19	59	....	....	....	....	....	....	....	....	....	7	0	1	1	10	....	....	....	....

Season	Club	League	Regular Season GP	G	A	Pts	PIM	PP	SH	GW	S	%	+/-	TF	F%	Min	Playoffs GP	G	A	Pts	PIM	PP	SH	GW	Min
2005-06	**Nashville**	**NHL**	4	0	2	2	6	0	0	0	3	0.0	0	0	0.0	17:19	....	....	....	....	....	....	....	....	....
	Milwaukee	AHL	71	8	27	35	55	....	....	....	....	....	....	....	....	....	21	1	7	8	24	....	....	....	....
	NHL Totals		4	0	2	2	6	0	0	0	3	0.0		0	0.0	17:19	....	....	....	....	....	....	....	....	....

CCHA First All-Star Team (2001) • NCAA West Second All-American Team (2001, 2002) • CCHA Second All-Star Team (2002)
Signed as a free agent by **Nashville**, July 9, 2004.

ZEDNIK, Richard

(ZEHD-nihk, RIH-chuhrd) **WSH.**

Right wing. Shoots left. 6'1", 196 lbs. Born, Banska Bystrica, Czech., January 6, 1976. Washington's 10th choice, 249th overall, in 1994 Entry Draft.

Season	Club	League	GP	G	A	Pts	PIM	PP	SH	GW	S	%	+/-	TF	F%	Min	GP	G	A	Pts	PIM	PP	SH	GW	Min
1993-94	B. Bystrica	Slovak-2	25	3	6	9	....	....	....	....	....	....	....	....	....	....	....	....	....	....	....	....	....	....	....
1994-95	Portland	WHL	65	35	51	86	89	....	....	....	....	....	....	....	....	....	9	5	5	10	20	....	....	....	....
1995-96	Portland	WHL	61	44	37	81	154	....	....	....	....	....	....	....	....	....	7	8	4	12	23	....	....	....	....
	Washington	**NHL**	1	0	0	0	0	0	0	0	0	0.0	0	....	....	....	....	....	....	....	....	....	....	....	....
	Portland Pirates	AHL	1	1	1	2	0	....	....	....	....	....	....	....	....	....	21	4	5	9	26	....	....	....	....
1996-97	**Washington**	**NHL**	11	2	1	3	4	1	0	0	21	9.5	−5	....	....	....	....	....	....	....	....	....	....	....	....
	Portland Pirates	AHL	56	15	20	35	70	....	....	....	....	....	....	....	....	....	5	1	0	1	6	....	....	....	....
1997-98	**Washington**	**NHL**	65	17	9	26	28	2	0	2	148	11.5	−2	....	....	....	17	7	3	10	16	2	0	0	....
1998-99	**Washington**	**NHL**	49	9	8	17	50	1	0	2	115	7.8	−6	2	0.0	15:08	....	....	....	....	....	....	....	....	....
99-2000	**Washington**	**NHL**	69	19	16	35	54	1	0	2	179	10.6	6	1	100.0	15:34	5	0	0	0	5	0	0	0	16:57
2000-01	**Washington**	**NHL**	62	16	19	35	61	4	0	3	155	10.3	−2	1	0.0	15:32	....	....	....	....	....	....	....	....	....
	Montreal	**NHL**	12	3	6	9	10	1	0	0	23	13.0	−2	0	0.0	18:29	....	....	....	....	....	....	....	....	....
2001-02	**Montreal**	**NHL**	82	22	22	44	59	4	0	3	249	8.8	−3	10	30.0	17:39	4	4	4	8	6	2	0	0	21:19
2002-03	**Montreal**	**NHL**	80	31	19	50	79	9	0	2	250	12.4	4	10	30.0	18:25	....	....	....	....	....	....	....	....	....
2003-04	**Montreal**	**NHL**	81	26	24	50	63	7	0	9	218	11.9	5	6	50.0	17:30	11	3	3	6	2	0	0	1	18:52
2004-05	HKm Zvolen	Slovakia	36	15	19	34	56	....	....	....	....	....	....	....	....	....	17	9	10	19	12	....	....	....	....
2005-06	**Montreal**	**NHL**	67	16	14	30	48	6	0	4	161	9.9	−2	6	16.7	15:46	6	2	0	2	4	1	0	0	15:13
	Slovakia	Olympics	6	1	0	1	12	....	....	....	....	....	....	....	....	....	....	....	....	....	....	....	....	....	....
	NHL Totals		579	161	138	299	456	36	0	27	1519	10.6		36	30.6	16:44	43	16	10	26	33	5	0	1	18:02

WHL West Second All-Star Team (1996)

Traded to **Montreal** by **Washington** with Jan Bulis and Washington's 1st round choice (Alexander Perezhogin) in 2001 Entry Draft for Trevor Linden, Dainius Zubrus and New Jersey's 2nd round choice (previously acquired, later traded to Tampa Bay – Tampa Bay selected Andreas Holmqvist) in 2001 Entry Draft, March 13, 2001. Signed as a free agent by **Zvolen** (Slovakia), October 7, 2004. Traded to **Washington** by **Montreal** for a 3rd round choice in 2007 Entry Draft, July 12, 2006.

ZETTERBERG, Henrik

(ZEH-tuhr-buhrg, HEHN-rihk) **DET.**

Left wing. Shoots left. 5'11", 176 lbs. Born, Njurunda, Sweden, October 9, 1980. Detroit's 4th choice, 210th overall, in 1999 Entry Draft.

Season	Club	League	GP	G	A	Pts	PIM	PP	SH	GW	S	%	+/-	TF	F%	Min	GP	G	A	Pts	PIM	PP	SH	GW	Min
1997-98	Timra IK Jr.	Swe-Jr.	18	9	5	14	4	....	....	....	....	....	....	....	....	....	....	....	....	....	....	....	....	....	....
	Timra IK	Sweden-2	16	1	2	3	4	....	....	....	....	....	....	....	....	....	4	0	1	1	0	....	....	....	....
1998-99	Timra IK	Sweden-2	37	15	13	28	2	....	....	....	....	....	....	....	....	....	4	2	1	3	2	....	....	....	....
99-2000	Timra IK	Sweden-2	32	20	14	34	20	....	....	....	....	....	....	....	....	....	10	10	4	14	4	....	....	....	....
2000-01	Timra IK	Sweden	47	15	31	46	24	....	....	....	....	....	....	....	....	....	....	....	....	....	....	....	....	....	....
2001-02	Timra IK	Sweden	48	10	22	32	20	....	....	....	....	....	....	....	....	....	....	....	....	....	....	....	....	....	....
	Sweden	Olympics	4	0	1	1	0	....	....	....	....	....	....	....	....	....	....	....	....	....	....	....	....	....	....
2002-03	**Detroit**	**NHL**	79	22	22	44	8	5	1	4	135	16.3	6	401	46.1	16:19	4	1	0	1	0	0	0	0	18:19
2003-04	**Detroit**	**NHL**	61	15	28	43	14	7	1	2	137	10.9	15	627	45.6	18:15	12	2	2	4	4	0	0	0	17:17
2004-05	Timra IK	Sweden	50	19	31	*50	24	....	....	....	....	....	....	....	....	....	7	6	2	8	2	....	....	....	....
2005-06	**Detroit**	**NHL**	77	39	46	85	30	17	1	9	270	14.4	29	583	50.3	18:57	6	6	0	6	2	4	0	0	21:43
	Sweden	Olympics	8	3	3	6	0	....	....	....	....	....	....	....	....	....	....	....	....	....	....	....	....	....	....
	NHL Totals		217	76	96	172	52	29	3	15	542	14.0		1611	47.4	17:48	22	9	2	11	6	4	0	0	18:41

Swedish Elite League Rookie of the Year (2001) • NHL All-Rookie Team (2003)
Signed as a free agent by **Timra** (Sweden), September 20, 2004.

ZHAMNOV, Alex

(ZHAHM-nahf, al-EHX) **BOS.**

Center. Shoots left. 6'1", 204 lbs. Born, Moscow, USSR, October 1, 1970. Winnipeg's 5th choice, 77th overall, in 1990 Entry Draft.

Season	Club	League	GP	G	A	Pts	PIM	PP	SH	GW	S	%	+/-	TF	F%	Min	GP	G	A	Pts	PIM	PP	SH	GW	Min
1988-89	Dynamo Moscow	USSR	4	0	0	0	0	....	....	....	....	....	....	....	....	....	....	....	....	....	....	....	....	....	....
1989-90	Dynamo Moscow	USSR	43	11	6	17	21	....	....	....	....	....	....	....	....	....	....	....	....	....	....	....	....	....	....
1990-91	Dynamo Moscow	USSR	46	16	12	28	24	....	....	....	....	....	....	....	....	....	....	....	....	....	....	....	....	....	....
1991-92	Dynamo Moscow	CIS	39	15	21	36	28	....	....	....	....	....	....	....	....	....	....	....	....	....	....	....	....	....	....
	Russia	Olympics	8	0	3	3	8	....	....	....	....	....	....	....	....	....	....	....	....	....	....	....	....	....	....
1992-93	**Winnipeg**	**NHL**	68	25	47	72	58	6	1	4	163	15.3	7	....	....	....	6	0	2	2	2	0	0	0	....
1993-94	**Winnipeg**	**NHL**	61	26	45	71	62	7	0	1	196	13.3	−20	....	....	....	....	....	....	....	....	....	....	....	....
1994-95	**Winnipeg**	**NHL**	48	30	35	65	20	9	0	4	155	19.4	5	....	....	....	....	....	....	....	....	....	....	....	....
1995-96	**Winnipeg**	**NHL**	58	22	37	59	65	5	0	2	199	11.1	−4	....	....	....	6	2	1	3	8	0	0	0	....
1996-97	**Chicago**	**NHL**	74	20	42	62	56	6	1	2	208	9.6	18	....	....	....	....	....	....	....	....	....	....	....	....
1997-98	**Chicago**	**NHL**	70	21	28	49	61	6	2	3	193	10.9	16	....	....	....	....	....	....	....	....	....	....	....	....
	Russia	Olympics	6	2	1	3	2	....	....	....	....	....	....	....	....	....	....	....	....	....	....	....	....	....	....
1998-99	**Chicago**	**NHL**	76	20	41	61	50	8	1	2	200	10.0	−10	1299	48.9	21:30	....	....	....	....	....	....	....	....	....
99-2000	**Chicago**	**NHL**	71	23	37	60	61	5	0	7	175	13.1	7	1171	45.8	22:08	....	....	....	....	....	....	....	....	....
2000-01	**Chicago**	**NHL**	63	13	36	49	40	3	1	3	117	11.1	−12	1486	48.1	21:15	....	....	....	....	....	....	....	....	....
2001-02	**Chicago**	**NHL**	77	22	45	67	67	6	0	3	173	12.7	8	1634	50.0	22:19	5	0	0	0	0	0	0	0	21:16
	Russia	Olympics	6	1	0	1	4	....	....	....	....	....	....	....	....	....	....	....	....	....	....	....	....	....	....
2002-03	**Chicago**	**NHL**	74	15	43	58	70	2	3	1	166	9.0	0	1345	51.3	21:06	....	....	....	....	....	....	....	....	....
2003-04	**Chicago**	**NHL**	23	6	12	18	14	1	0	1	63	9.5	−8	514	49.2	19:34	....	....	....	....	....	....	....	....	....
	Philadelphia	**NHL**	20	5	13	18	14	0	0	0	33	15.2	7	355	46.2	18:32	18	4	10	14	8	1	0	1	18:39
2004-05	Vityaz Chekhov	Russia-2	24	5	22	27	20	....	....	....	....	....	....	....	....	....	14	7	7	14	10	....	....	....	....
2005-06	**Boston**	**NHL**	24	1	9	10	30	0	0	1	37	2.7	−4	282	48.9	16:12	....	....	....	....	....	....	....	....	....
	NHL Totals		807	249	470	719	668	64	9	34	2078	12.0		8086	48.8	21:06	35	6	13	19	18	1	0	1	19:13

NHL Second All-Star Team (1995)
Played in NHL All-Star Game (2002)

Traded to **Chicago** by **Phoenix** with Craig Mills and Phoenix's 1st round choice (Ty Jones) in 1997 Entry Draft for Jeremy Roenick, August 16, 1996. Traded to **Philadelphia** by **Chicago** with Washington's 4th round choice (previously acquired, Philadelphia selected R.J. Anderson) in 2004 Entry Draft for Jim Vandermeer, the rights to Colin Fraser and Los Angeles' 2nd round choice (previously acquired, Chicago selected Bryan Bickell) in 2004 Entry Draft, February 19, 2004. Signed as a free agent by **Chekhov** (Russia-2), November 15, 2004. Signed as a free agent by **Boston**, August 4, 2005. • Missed majority of 2005-06 season recovering from shoulder injury suffered in training camp and ankle injury suffered in game vs. Tampa Bay, January 7, 2006.

ZHERDEV, Nikolai

(ZHAIR-dehv, NIH-koh-ligh) **CBJ**

Wing. Shoots right. 6'2", 197 lbs. Born, Kiev, USSR, November 5, 1984. Columbus' 1st choice, 4th overall, in 2003 Entry Draft.

Season	Club	League	GP	G	A	Pts	PIM	PP	SH	GW	S	%	+/-	TF	F%	Min	GP	G	A	Pts	PIM	PP	SH	GW	Min
99-2000	Elektrostal 2	Russia-3	21	10	7	17	26	....	....	....	....	....	....	....	....	....	7	0	0	0	0	....	....	....	....
2000-01	Elektrostal	Russia-2	18	5	8	13	12	....	....	....	....	....	....	....	....	....	....	....	....	....	....	....	....	....	....
	Russia	Exhib.	17	10	11	21	17	....	....	....	....	....	....	....	....	....	....	....	....	....	....	....	....	....	....
2001-02	Elektrostal	Russia-2	53	13	15	28	62	....	....	....	....	....	....	....	....	....	....	....	....	....	....	....	....	....	....
	Elektrostal 2	Russia-3	1	1	0	1	4	....	....	....	....	....	....	....	....	....	....	....	....	....	....	....	....	....	....
2002-03	CSKA Moscow	Russia	44	12	12	24	34	....	....	....	....	....	....	....	....	....	....	....	....	....	....	....	....	....	....
2003-04	CSKA Moscow	Russia	20	2	2	4	14	....	....	....	....	....	....	....	....	....	....	....	....	....	....	....	....	....	....
	Columbus	**NHL**	57	13	21	34	54	5	0	1	137	9.5	−11	9	11.1	16:11	....	....	....	....	....	....	....	....	....
2004-05	CSKA Moscow	Russia	51	19	21	40	62	....	....	....	....	....	....	....	....	....	....	....	....	....	....	....	....	....	....
2005-06	**Columbus**	**NHL**	73	27	27	54	50	10	0	0	194	13.9	−13	20	10.0	17:36	....	....	....	....	....	....	....	....	....
	Syracuse Crunch	AHL	2	1	0	1	0	....	....	....	....	....	....	....	....	....	....	....	....	....	....	....	....	....	....
	NHL Totals		130	40	48	88	104	15	0	1	331	12.1		29	10.3	16:58	....	....	....	....	....	....	....	....	....

Signed as a free agent by **CSKA Moscow** (Russia), July 27, 2004. Signed as a free agent by **Khimik** (Russia), July 20, 2006.

ZHITNIK, Alexei

(ZHIHT-nihk, al-EHX-ay) **NYI**

Defense. Shoots left. 5'11", 215 lbs. Born, Kiev, USSR, October 10, 1972. Los Angeles' 3rd choice, 81st overall, in 1991 Entry Draft.

Season	Club	League	GP	G	A	Pts	PIM	PP	SH	GW	S	%	+/-	TF	F%	Min	GP	G	A	Pts	PIM	PP	SH	GW	Min
			Regular Season														Playoffs								
1989-90	Sokol Kiev	USSR	31	3	4	7	16	....	....	....	....	....	....	....	....	....	....	....	....	....	....	....	....	....	....
1990-91	Sokol Kiev	USSR	46	1	4	5	46	....	....	....	....	....	....	....	....	....	....	....	....	....	....	....	....	....	....
1991-92	CSKA Moscow	CIS	44	2	7	9	52	....	....	....	....	....	....	....	....	....	....	....	....	....	....	....	....	....	....
	Russia	Olympics	8	1	0	1	0	....	....	....	....	....	....	....	....	....	....	....	....	....	....	....	....	....	....
1992-93	**Los Angeles**	**NHL**	78	12	36	48	80	5	0	2	136	8.8	−3	....	....	....	24	3	9	12	26	2	0	1	....
1993-94	**Los Angeles**	**NHL**	81	12	40	52	101	11	0	1	227	5.3	−11	....	....	....	....	....	....	....	....	....	....	....	....
1994-95	**Los Angeles**	**NHL**	11	2	5	7	27	2	0	0	33	6.1	−3	....	....	....	....	....	....	....	....	....	....	....	....
	Buffalo	**NHL**	21	2	5	7	34	1	0	0	33	6.1	−3	....	....	....	5	0	1	1	14	0	0	0	....
1995-96	**Buffalo**	**NHL**	80	6	30	36	58	5	0	0	193	3.1	−25	....	....	....	....	....	....	....	....	....	....	....	....
1996-97	**Buffalo**	**NHL**	80	7	28	35	95	3	1	0	170	4.1	10	....	....	....	12	1	0	1	16	0	0	0	....
1997-98	**Buffalo**	**NHL**	78	15	30	45	102	2	3	3	191	7.9	19	....	....	....	15	0	3	3	36	0	0	0	....
	Russia	Olympics	6	0	2	2	2	....	....	....	....	....	....	....	....	....	....	....	....	....	....	....	....	....	....
1998-99	**Buffalo**	**NHL**	81	7	26	33	96	3	1	2	185	3.8	−6	0	0.0	25:39	21	4	11	15	*52	4	0	2	27:07
99-2000	**Buffalo**	**NHL**	74	2	11	13	95	1	0	0	139	1.4	−6	0	0.0	24:48	4	0	0	0	8	0	0	0	25:50
2000-01	**Buffalo**	**NHL**	78	8	29	37	75	5	0	1	149	5.4	−3	0	0.0	24:15	13	1	6	7	12	0	0	0	25:38
2001-02	**Buffalo**	**NHL**	82	1	33	34	80	1	0	0	150	0.7	−1	0	0.0	25:36	....	....	....	....	....	....	....	....	....
2002-03	**Buffalo**	**NHL**	70	3	18	21	85	0	0	1	138	2.2	−5	1	0.0	26:33	....	....	....	....	....	....	....	....	....
2003-04	**Buffalo**	**NHL**	68	4	24	28	102	2	0	0	134	3.0	−13	0	0.0	25:01	....	....	....	....	....	....	....	....	....
2004-05	Ak Bars Kazan	Russia	23	1	8	9	30	....	....	....	....	....	....	....	....	....	4	0	0	0	2	....	....	....	....
2005-06	**NY Islanders**	**NHL**	59	5	24	29	88	3	0	0	99	5.1	4	0	0.0	24:30	....	....	....	....	....	....	....	....	....
	NHL Totals		941	86	339	425	1118	44	5	10	1977	4.4		1	0.0	25:13	94	9	30	39	164	6	0	3	26:29

Played in NHL All-Star Game (1999, 2002)

Traded to **Buffalo** by **Los Angeles** with Robb Stauber, Charlie Huddy and Los Angeles' 5th round choice (Marian Menhart) in 1995 Entry Draft for Philippe Boucher, Denis Tsygurov and Grant Fuhr, February 14, 1995. Signed as a free agent by **Kazan** (Russia), December 6, 2004. Signed as a free agent by **NY Islanders**, August 2, 2005.

ZIDLICKY, Marek

(zhihd-LIH-kee, MAIR-ehk) **NSH.**

Defense. Shoots right. 5'11", 190 lbs. Born, Most, Czech., February 3, 1977. NY Rangers' 6th choice, 176th overall, in 2001 Entry Draft.

Season	Club	League	GP	G	A	Pts	PIM	PP	SH	GW	S	%	+/-	TF	F%	Min	GP	G	A	Pts	PIM	PP	SH	GW	Min
1994-95	HC Kladno	CzRep	30	2	2	4	38	....	....	....	....	....	....	....	....	....	11	1	1	2	10	....	....	....	....
1995-96	HC Poldi Kladno	CzRep	37	4	5	9	74	....	....	....	....	....	....	....	....	....	7	1	1	2	8	....	....	....	....
1996-97	HC Poldi Kladno	CzRep	49	5	16	21	60	....	....	....	....	....	....	....	....	....	2	0	0	0	0	....	....	....	....
1997-98	Kladno	CzRep	51	2	13	15	121	....	....	....	....	....	....	....	....	....	....	....	....	....	....	....	....	....	....
1998-99	Kladno	CzRep	50	10	12	22	94	....	....	....	....	....	....	....	....	....	....	....	....	....	....	....	....	....	....
99-2000	HIFK Helsinki	Finland	47	4	16	20	66	....	....	....	....	....	....	....	....	....	9	3	2	5	24	....	....	....	....
	HIFK Helsinki	EuroHL	4	2	2	4	10	....	....	....	....	....	....	....	....	....	1	0	0	0	0	....	....	....	....
2000-01	HIFK Helsinki	Finland	51	12	25	37	146	....	....	....	....	....	....	....	....	....	5	0	1	1	6	....	....	....	....
2001-02	HIFK Helsinki	Finland	56	11	29	40	107	....	....	....	....	....	....	....	....	....	....	....	....	....	....	....	....	....	....
2002-03	HIFK Helsinki	Finland	54	10	37	47	79	....	....	....	....	....	....	....	....	....	4	0	0	0	4	....	....	....	....
2003-04	**Nashville**	**NHL**	82	14	39	53	82	9	0	4	143	9.8	−16	0	0.0	20:02	1	0	0	0	0	0	0	0	2:16
2004-05	HIFK Helsinki	Finland	49	11	20	31	91	....	....	....	....	....	....	....	....	....	5	0	3	3	14	....	....	....	....
2005-06	**Nashville**	**NHL**	67	12	37	49	82	10	0	1	113	10.6	8	0	0.0	20:04	2	0	1	1	2	0	0	0	15:19
	Czech Republic	Olympics	7	4	1	5	16	....	....	....	....	....	....	....	....	....	....	....	....	....	....	....	....	....	....
	NHL Totals		149	26	76	102	164	19	0	5	256	10.2		0	0.0	20:03	3	0	1	1	2	0	0	0	10:58

Traded to **Nashville** by NY Rangers with Rem Murray and Tomas Kloucek for Mike Dunham, December 12, 2002. Signed as a free agent by **HIFK Helsinki** (Finland), September 17, 2004.

ZIGOMANIS, Mike

(zih-goh-MAN-his, MIGHK) **PHX.**

Center. Shoots right. 6'1", 200 lbs. Born, North York, Ont., January 17, 1981. Carolina's 2nd choice, 46th overall, in 2001 Entry Draft.

Season	Club	League	GP	G	A	Pts	PIM	PP	SH	GW	S	%	+/-	TF	F%	Min	GP	G	A	Pts	PIM	PP	SH	GW	Min
1996-97	Wexford Raiders	MTHL	40	37	48	85	23	....	....	....	....	....	....	....	....	....	....	....	....	....	....	....	....	....	....
	Wexford Raiders	MTJHL	8	2	5	7	2	....	....	....	....	....	....	....	....	....	....	....	....	....	....	....	....	....	....
1997-98	Kingston	OHL	62	23	51	74	30	....	....	....	....	....	....	....	....	....	12	1	6	7	2	....	....	....	....
1998-99	Kingston	OHL	67	29	56	85	36	....	....	....	....	....	....	....	....	....	5	1	7	8	2	....	....	....	....
99-2000	Kingston	OHL	59	40	54	94	49	....	....	....	....	....	....	....	....	....	5	0	4	4	0	....	....	....	....
2000-01	Kingston	OHL	52	40	37	77	44	....	....	....	....	....	....	....	....	....	....	....	....	....	....	....	....	....	....
2001-02	Lowell	AHL	79	18	30	48	24	....	....	....	....	....	....	....	....	....	5	1	1	2	2	....	....	....	....
2002-03	**Carolina**	**NHL**	19	2	1	3	0	1	1	0	19	10.5	−4	147	59.2	9:43	....	....	....	....	....	....	....	....	....
	Lowell	AHL	38	13	18	31	19	....	....	....	....	....	....	....	....	....	....	....	....	....	....	....	....	....	....
2003-04	**Carolina**	**NHL**	17	0	3	3	2	0	0	0	13	0.0	−1	108	53.7	8:37	....	....	....	....	....	....	....	....	....
	Lowell	AHL	61	17	35	52	56	....	....	....	....	....	....	....	....	....	....	....	....	....	....	....	....	....	....
2004-05	Lowell	AHL	76	29	31	60	71	....	....	....	....	....	....	....	....	....	11	4	7	11	8	....	....	....	....
2005-06	**Carolina**	**NHL**	21	1	0	1	4	0	0	0	16	6.3	1	72	50.0	9:25	....	....	....	....	....	....	....	....	....
	Lowell	AHL	11	6	7	13	19	....	....	....	....	....	....	....	....	....	....	....	....	....	....	....	....	....	....
	St. Louis	**NHL**	2	0	0	0	0	0	0	0	1	0.0	0	1	100.0	7:39	....	....	....	....	....	....	....	....	....
	Peoria Rivermen	AHL	28	10	18	28	16	....	....	....	....	....	....	....	....	....	4	2	4	6	6	....	....	....	....
	NHL Totals		59	3	4	7	6	1	1	0	49	6.1		328	55.5	9:13	....	....	....	....	....	....	....	....	....

• Re-entered NHL Entry Draft. Originally Buffalo's 4th choice, 64th overall, in 1999 Entry Draft.

Traded to **St. Louis** by **Carolina** with Jesse Boulerice, Magnus Kahnberg, Carolina's 1st round choice (later traded to New Jersey - New Jersey selected Matthew Corrente) in 2006 Entry Draft, Toronto's 4th round choice (previously acquired, St. Louis selected Reto Berra) in 2006 Entry Draft and Chicago's 4th round choice (previously acquired) in 2007 Entry Draft for Doug Weight and Erkki Rajamaki, January 30, 2006. Signed as a free agent by **Phoenix**, July 21, 2006.

ZINGER, Dwayne

(ZIHN-guhr, DWAYN)

Defense. Shoots left. 6'4", 216 lbs. Born, Coronation, Alta., July 5, 1976.

Season	Club	League	GP	G	A	Pts	PIM	PP	SH	GW	S	%	+/-	TF	F%	Min	GP	G	A	Pts	PIM	PP	SH	GW	Min
1995-96	Melville	SJHL	64	7	17	24	....	....	....	....	....	....	....	....	....	....	....	....	....	....	....	....	....	....	....
1996-97	Alaska-Fairbanks	CCHA	32	1	5	6	45	....	....	....	....	....	....	....	....	....	....	....	....	....	....	....	....	....	....
1997-98	Alaska-Fairbanks	CCHA	32	1	3	4	91	....	....	....	....	....	....	....	....	....	....	....	....	....	....	....	....	....	....
1998-99	Alaska-Fairbanks	CCHA	33	4	14	18	42	....	....	....	....	....	....	....	....	....	....	....	....	....	....	....	....	....	....
99-2000	Alaska-Fairbanks	CCHA	34	10	4	14	34	....	....	....	....	....	....	....	....	....	....	....	....	....	....	....	....	....	....
	Cincinnati	AHL	13	0	2	2	33	....	....	....	....	....	....	....	....	....	....	....	....	....	....	....	....	....	....
2000-01	Cincinnati	AHL	68	6	9	15	120	....	....	....	....	....	....	....	....	....	4	1	1	2	2	....	....	....	....
2001-02	Cincinnati	AHL	67	6	13	19	156	....	....	....	....	....	....	....	....	....	3	0	1	1	2	....	....	....	....
2002-03	Portland Pirates	AHL	65	1	7	8	67	....	....	....	....	....	....	....	....	....	3	0	0	0	2	....	....	....	....
2003-04	**Washington**	**NHL**	7	0	1	1	9	0	0	0	0	0.0	2	0	0.0	5:24	....	....	....	....	....	....	....	....	....
	Portland Pirates	AHL	68	6	10	16	49	....	....	....	....	....	....	....	....	....	7	0	0	0	16	....	....	....	....
2004-05	Portland Pirates	AHL	58	0	4	4	118	....	....	....	....	....	....	....	....	....	....	....	....	....	....	....	....	....	....
2005-06	Hershey Bears	AHL	30	0	0	0	74	....	....	....	....	....	....	....	....	....	....	....	....	....	....	....	....	....	....
	San Antonio	AHL	35	1	2	3	68	....	....	....	....	....	....	....	....	....	....	....	....	....	....	....	....	....	....
	NHL Totals		7	0	1	1	9	0	0	0	0	0.0		0	0.0	5:24	....	....	....	....	....	....	....	....	....

SJHL First All-Star Team (1996)

Signed as a free agent by **Detroit**, March 13, 2000. Signed as a free agent by **Washington**, July 9, 2002. Traded to **Phoenix** by **Washington** for Doug Doull, February 3, 2006.

ZINOVJEV, Sergei

(zih-NOH-vee-ehv, SAIR-gay) **BOS.**

Center/Left wing. Shoots left. 5'10", 185 lbs. Born, Novokuznetsk, USSR, March 4, 1980. Boston's 6th choice, 73rd overall, in 2000 Entry Draft.

Season	Club	League	GP	G	A	Pts	PIM	PP	SH	GW	S	%	+/-	TF	F%	Min	GP	G	A	Pts	PIM	PP	SH	GW	Min
1995-96	Novokuznetsk 2	CIS-2	10	1	0	1	2	....	....	....	....	....	....	....	....	....	....	....	....	....	....	....	....	....	....
1996-97	Novokuznetsk 2	Russia-3	29	2	1	3	8	....	....	....	....	....	....	....	....	....	....	....	....	....	....	....	....	....	....
1997-98	Novokuznetsk 2	Russia-3	40	7	7	14	36	....	....	....	....	....	....	....	....	....	....	....	....	....	....	....	....	....	....
	Novokuznetsk 2	Russia-3	2	1	0	1	0	....	....	....	....	....	....	....	....	....	....	....	....	....	....	....	....	....	....
1998-99	Novokuznetsk 2	Russia-4	4	0	1	1	8	....	....	....	....	....	....	....	....	....	....	....	....	....	....	....	....	....	....
	Magnitogorsk	Russia	31	2	4	6	14	....	....	....	....	....	....	....	....	....	3	0	0	0	0	....	....	....	....
99-2000	Magnitogorsk	Russia	28	0	2	2	16	....	....	....	....	....	....	....	....	....	....	....	....	....	....	....	....	....	....
2000-01	Yaroslavl	Russia	27	2	10	12	36	....	....	....	....	....	....	....	....	....	....	....	....	....	....	....	....	....	....
	Ufa	Russia	8	4	5	9	6	....	....	....	....	....	....	....	....	....	....	....	....	....	....	....	....	....	....
2001-02	Spartak Moscow	Russia	51	12	18	30	43	....	....	....	....	....	....	....	....	....	....	....	....	....	....	....	....	....	....
2002-03	Ak Bars Kazan	Russia	47	14	17	31	50	....	....	....	....	....	....	....	....	....	5	1	1	2	6	....	....	....	....
2003-04	**Boston**	**NHL**	10	0	1	1	2	0	0	0	8	0.0	1	72	41.7	9:48	....	....	....	....	....	....	....	....	....
	Providence Bruins	AHL	4	1	2	3	0	....	....	....	....	....	....	....	....	....	....	....	....	....	....	....	....	....	....
	Ak Bars Kazan	Russia	27	5	9	14	75	....	....	....	....	....	....	....	....	....	8	0	1	1	12	....	....	....	....

			Regular Season														Playoffs								
Season	Club	League	GP	G	A	Pts	PIM	PP	SH	GW	S	%	+/-	TF	F%	Min	GP	G	A	Pts	PIM	PP	SH	GW	Min
2004-05	Ak Bars Kazan	Russia	54	17	21	38	82										4	1	0	1	12				
2005-06	Ak Bars Kazan	Russia	43	15	20	35	58										13	9	8	17	26				
	NHL Totals		**10**	**0**	**1**	**1**	**2**	**0**	**0**	**0**	**8**	**0.0**		**72**	**41.7**	**9:48**									

Signed as a free agent by **Kazan** (Russia), December 9, 2003.

ZIZKA, Tomas

(ZHIHZH-kuh, TAW-mahsh) **L.A.**

Defense. Shoots left. 6'1", 198 lbs. Born, Sternberk, Czech., October 10, 1979. Los Angeles' 6th choice, 163rd overall, in 1998 Entry Draft.

1994-95	AC ZPS Zlin Jr.	CzRep-Jr.	39	1	10	11																			
1995-96	AC ZPS Zlin Jr.	CzRep-Jr.	47	2	8	10																			
1996-97	AC ZPS Zlin Jr.	CzRep-Jr.	14	1	0	1																			
1997-98	HC ZPS Zlin Jr.	CzRep-Jr.	11	3	4	7																			
	Zlin	CzRep	33	0	3	3	2																		
1998-99	Zlin	CzRep	44	3	7	10	14										11	1	2	3					
99-2000	Zlin	CzRep	46	4	6	10	30										4	1	0	1	4				
2000-01	Zlin	CzRep	43	2	11	13	16										6	0	0	0	6				
2001-02	Manchester	AHL	58	4	17	21	22										4	1	0	1	14				
2002-03	**Los Angeles**	**NHL**	**10**	**0**	**3**	**3**	**4**	**0**	**0**	**0**	**12**	**0.0**	**–4**	**0**	**0.0**	**15:24**									
	Manchester	AHL	61	13	30	43	50										3	0	2	2	2				
2003-04	**Los Angeles**	**NHL**	**15**	**2**	**3**	**5**	**12**	**1**	**0**	**0**	**24**	**8.3**	**–4**	**0**	**0.0**	**16:54**									
	Manchester	AHL	58	4	24	28	31										5	0	3	3	10				
2004-05	Spartak Moscow	Russia	23	0	3	3	32																		
	HC Slavia Praha	CzRep	26	2	4	6	26										2	0	0	0	2				
2005-06	HC Slavia Praha	CzRep	52	6	9	15	48										14	1	2	3	31				
	NHL Totals		**25**	**2**	**6**	**8**	**16**	**1**	**0**	**0**	**36**	**5.6**		**0**	**0.0**	**16:18**									

Signed as a free agent by **Spartak Moscow** (Russia), August 31, 2004. Signed as a free agent by **Slavia Praha** (CzRep), November, 2004.

ZUBOV, Sergei

(ZOO-bahf, SAIR-gay) **DAL.**

Defense. Shoots right. 6'1", 200 lbs. Born, Moscow, USSR, July 22, 1970. NY Rangers' 6th choice, 85th overall, in 1990 Entry Draft.

1988-89	CSKA Moscow	USSR	29	1	4	5	10																		
1989-90	CSKA Moscow	USSR	48	6	2	8	16																		
1990-91	CSKA Moscow	USSR	41	6	5	11	12																		
1991-92	CSKA Moscow	CIS	44	4	7	11	8																		
	Russia	Olympics	8	0	1	1	0																		
1992-93	CSKA Moscow	CIS	1	0	1	1	0																		
	NY Rangers	**NHL**	**49**	**8**	**23**	**31**	**4**	**3**	**0**	**0**	**93**	**8.6**	**–1**												
	Binghamton	AHL	30	7	29	36	14										11	5	5	10	2				
1993-94♦	**NY Rangers**	**NHL**	**78**	**12**	**77**	**89**	**39**	**9**	**0**	**1**	**222**	**5.4**	**20**				**22**	**5**	**14**	**19**	**0**	**2**	**0**	**0**	
	Binghamton	AHL	2	1	2	3	0																		
1994-95	**NY Rangers**	**NHL**	**38**	**10**	**26**	**36**	**18**	**6**	**0**	**0**	**116**	**8.6**	**–2**				**10**	**3**	**8**	**11**	**2**	**1**	**0**	**0**	
1995-96	**Pittsburgh**	**NHL**	**64**	**11**	**55**	**66**	**22**	**3**	**2**	**1**	**141**	**7.8**	**28**				**18**	**1**	**14**	**15**	**26**	**1**	**0**	**0**	
1996-97	**Dallas**	**NHL**	**78**	**13**	**30**	**43**	**24**	**1**	**0**	**3**	**133**	**9.8**	**19**				**7**	**0**	**3**	**3**	**2**	**0**	**0**	**0**	
1997-98	**Dallas**	**NHL**	**73**	**10**	**47**	**57**	**16**	**5**	**1**	**2**	**148**	**6.8**	**16**				**17**	**4**	**5**	**9**	**2**	**3**	**0**	**1**	
1998-99♦	**Dallas**	**NHL**	**81**	**10**	**41**	**51**	**20**	**5**	**0**	**3**	**155**	**6.5**	**9**	**0**	**0.0**	**24:14**	**23**	**1**	**12**	**13**	**4**	**0**	**0**	**0**	**30:16**
99-2000	**Dallas**	**NHL**	**77**	**9**	**33**	**42**	**18**	**3**	**1**	**3**	**179**	**5.0**	**–2**	**0**	**0.0**	**28:50**	**18**	**2**	**7**	**9**	**6**	**1**	**1**	**0**	**26:28**
2000-01	**Dallas**	**NHL**	**79**	**10**	**41**	**51**	**24**	**6**	**0**	**1**	**173**	**5.8**	**22**	**0**	**0.0**	**26:37**	**10**	**1**	**5**	**6**	**4**	**0**	**0**	**0**	**30:37**
2001-02	**Dallas**	**NHL**	**80**	**12**	**32**	**44**	**22**	**8**	**0**	**2**	**198**	**6.1**	**–4**	**0**	**0.0**	**26:46**									
2002-03	**Dallas**	**NHL**	**82**	**11**	**44**	**55**	**26**	**8**	**0**	**2**	**158**	**7.0**	**21**	**0**	**0.0**	**25:50**	**12**	**4**	**10**	**14**	**4**	**2**	**0**	**0**	**30:45**
2003-04	**Dallas**	**NHL**	**77**	**7**	**35**	**42**	**20**	**4**	**1**	**1**	**154**	**4.5**	**0**	**0**	**0.0**	**25:50**	**5**	**1**	**1**	**2**	**0**	**1**	**0**	**0**	**28:01**
2004-05			DID NOT PLAY																						
2005-06	**Dallas**	**NHL**	**78**	**13**	**58**	**71**	**46**	**9**	**0**	**0**	**141**	**9.2**	**20**	**0**	**0.0**	**26:27**	**5**	**1**	**5**	**6**	**6**	**1**	**0**	**0**	**29:42**
	NHL Totals		**934**	**136**	**542**	**678**	**299**	**70**	**5**	**19**	**2011**	**6.8**		**0**	**0.0**	**26:21**	**147**	**23**	**84**	**107**	**56**	**12**	**1**	**1**	**29:16**

NHL Second All-Star Team (2006)
Played in NHL All-Star Game (1998, 1999, 2000)
Traded to **Pittsburgh** by **NY Rangers** with Petr Nedved for Luc Robitaille and Ulf Samuelsson, August 31, 1995. Traded to **Dallas** by **Pittsburgh** for Kevin Hatcher, June 22, 1996.

ZUBRUS, Dainius

(ZOO-bruhs, DAYN-ihs) **WSH.**

Right wing. Shoots left. 6'4", 225 lbs. Born, Elektrenai, USSR, June 16, 1978. Philadelphia's 1st choice, 15th overall, in 1996 Entry Draft.

1995-96	Pembroke	CJHL	28	19	13	32	73																		
	Caledon	MTJHL	7	3	7	10	2										17	11	12	23	4				
1996-97	**Philadelphia**	**NHL**	**68**	**8**	**13**	**21**	**22**	**1**	**0**	**2**	**71**	**11.3**	**3**				**19**	**5**	**4**	**9**	**12**	**1**	**0**	**1**	
1997-98	**Philadelphia**	**NHL**	**69**	**8**	**25**	**33**	**42**	**1**	**0**	**5**	**101**	**7.9**	**29**				**5**	**0**	**1**	**1**	**2**	**0**	**0**	**0**	
1998-99	**Philadelphia**	**NHL**	**63**	**3**	**5**	**8**	**25**	**0**	**1**	**0**	**49**	**6.1**	**–5**	**29**	**51.7**	**11:00**									
	Montreal	**NHL**	**17**	**3**	**5**	**8**	**4**	**0**	**0**	**1**	**31**	**9.7**	**–3**	**2**	**50.0**	**16:53**									
99-2000	**Montreal**	**NHL**	**73**	**14**	**28**	**42**	**54**	**3**	**0**	**1**	**139**	**10.1**	**–1**	**212**	**39.2**	**17:37**									
2000-01	**Montreal**	**NHL**	**49**	**12**	**12**	**24**	**30**	**3**	**0**	**0**	**70**	**17.1**	**–7**	**190**	**41.1**	**18:30**									
	Washington	**NHL**	**12**	**1**	**1**	**2**	**7**	**1**	**0**	**0**	**13**	**7.7**	**–4**	**0**	**0.0**	**13:05**	**6**	**0**	**0**	**0**	**2**	**0**	**0**	**0**	**17:23**
2001-02	**Washington**	**NHL**	**71**	**17**	**26**	**43**	**38**	**4**	**0**	**3**	**138**	**12.3**	**5**	**131**	**37.4**	**18:52**									
2002-03	**Washington**	**NHL**	**63**	**13**	**22**	**35**	**43**	**2**	**0**	**0**	**104**	**12.5**	**15**	**565**	**50.3**	**16:26**	**6**	**2**	**2**	**4**	**4**	**1**	**0**	**0**	**21:30**
2003-04	**Washington**	**NHL**	**54**	**12**	**15**	**27**	**38**	**6**	**1**	**2**	**115**	**10.4**	**–16**	**916**	**48.0**	**19:31**									
2004-05	Lada Togliatti	Russia	42	8	11	19	85										10	3	1	4	22				
2005-06	**Washington**	**NHL**	**71**	**23**	**34**	**57**	**84**	**13**	**0**	**5**	**181**	**12.7**	**3**	**1118**	**50.3**	**20:22**									
	NHL Totals		**610**	**114**	**186**	**300**	**387**	**34**	**2**	**19**	**1012**	**11.3**		**3163**	**47.8**	**17:21**	**36**	**7**	**7**	**14**	**20**	**2**	**0**	**1**	**19:27**

Traded to **Montreal** by **Philadelphia** with Philadelphia's 2nd round choice (Matt Carkner) in 1999 Entry Draft and NY Islanders' 6th round choice (previously acquired, Montreal selected Scott Selig) in 2000 Entry Draft for Mark Recchi, March 10, 1999. Traded to **Washington** by **Montreal** with Trevor Linden and New Jersey's 2nd round choice (previously acquired, later traded to Tampa Bay – Tampa Bay selected Andreas Holmqvist) in 2001 Entry Draft for Richard Zednik, Jan Bulis and Washington's 1st round choice (Alexander Perezhogin) in 2001 Entry Draft, March 13, 2001. Signed as a free agent by **Togliatti** (Russia), July 1, 2004.

ZYUZIN, Andrei

(ZYOO-zin, AWN-dray) **CGY.**

Defense. Shoots left. 6'1", 215 lbs. Born, Ufa, USSR, January 21, 1978. San Jose's 1st choice, 2nd overall, in 1996 Entry Draft.

1994-95	Ufa	CIS	30	3	0	3	16																		
1995-96	Ufa	CIS	41	6	3	9	24																		
1996-97	Ufa	Russia	32	7	10	17	28										7	1	1	2	4				
1997-98	**San Jose**	**NHL**	**56**	**6**	**7**	**13**	**66**	**2**	**0**	**2**	**72**	**8.3**	**8**				**6**	**1**	**0**	**1**	**14**	**0**	**0**	**1**	
	Kentucky	AHL	17	4	5	9	28																		
1998-99	**San Jose**	**NHL**	**25**	**3**	**1**	**4**	**38**	**2**	**0**	**0**	**44**	**6.8**	**5**	**0**	**0.0**	**15:56**									
	Kentucky	AHL	23	2	12	14	42																		
99-2000	**Tampa Bay**	**NHL**	**34**	**2**	**9**	**11**	**33**	**0**	**0**	**0**	**47**	**4.3**	**–11**	**0**	**0.0**	**20:28**									
2000-01	**Tampa Bay**	**NHL**	**64**	**4**	**16**	**20**	**76**	**2**	**1**	**1**	**92**	**4.3**	**–8**	**0**	**0.0**	**18:39**									
	Detroit Vipers	IHL	2	0	1	1	0																		
2001-02	**Tampa Bay**	**NHL**	**9**	**0**	**2**	**2**	**6**	**0**	**0**	**0**	**14**	**0.0**	**–6**	**0**	**0.0**	**19:41**									
	New Jersey	**NHL**	**38**	**1**	**2**	**3**	**25**	**1**	**0**	**0**	**47**	**2.1**	**1**	**0**	**0.0**	**15:04**									
	Albany River Rats	AHL	3	0	1	1	2																		
2002-03	**New Jersey**	**NHL**	**1**	**0**	**1**	**1**	**2**	**0**	**0**	**0**	**0**	**0.0**	**–1**	**0**	**0.0**	**20:03**									
	Minnesota	**NHL**	**66**	**4**	**12**	**16**	**34**	**2**	**0**	**0**	**113**	**3.5**	**–7**	**4**	**25.0**	**21:38**	**18**	**0**	**1**	**1**	**14**	**0**	**0**	**0**	**23:07**
2003-04	**Minnesota**	**NHL**	**65**	**8**	**13**	**21**	**48**	**4**	**0**	**1**	**104**	**7.7**	**4**	**0**	**0.0**	**20:22**									
2004-05	Ufa	Russia	14	2	1	3	6																		
	Cherepovets	Russia	10	2	1	3	8																		
2005-06	**Minnesota**	**NHL**	**57**	**7**	**11**	**18**	**50**	**4**	**0**	**1**	**80**	**8.8**	**–12**	**2**	**50.0**	**18:53**									
	NHL Totals		**415**	**35**	**74**	**109**	**378**	**17**	**1**	**5**	**613**	**5.7**		**6**	**33.3**	**19:11**	**24**	**1**	**1**	**2**	**28**	**0**	**0**	**1**	**23:07**

• Suspended for remainder of 1998-99 season by **San Jose** for leaving team without permission, April 1, 1999. Traded to **Tampa Bay** by **San Jose** with Bill Houlder, Shawn Burr and Steve Guolla for Niklas Sundstrom and NY Rangers' 3rd round choice (previously acquired, later traded to Chicago – Chicago selected Igor Radulov) in 2000 Entry Draft, August 4, 1999. • Missed majority of 1999-2000 season recovering from shoulder injury suffered in game vs. NY Islanders, January 13, 2000. Traded to **New Jersey** by **Tampa Bay** for Josef Boumedienne, Sascha Goc and the rights to Anton But, November 9, 2001. Claimed on waivers by **Minnesota** from **New Jersey**, November 2, 2002. Signed as a free agent by **Ufa** (Russia), September 25, 2004. Signed as a free agent by **Cherepovets** (Russia), December 20, 2004. Signed as a free agent by **Calgary**, July 1, 2006.

A Salute to Steve Yzerman

STEVE YZERMAN WAS JUST 21 YEARS OLD when he was named captain of the Detroit Red Wings in 1986-87. He retained the captaincy for 20 years. No one in NHL history has worn the 'C' as long as Stevie Y. "Steve likes to lead by example," said teammate Nicklas Lidstrom. "He plays with his heart and with his soul. He lays it all on the line."

The Red Wings selected Yzerman from the Peterborough Petes with the fourth pick in the 1983 NHL Entry Draft. He had played just two seasons of major junior hockey, but made the Red Wings as an 18-year-old and set club rookie records for goals (39) and points (87). A team in need of rebuilding, Detroit had missed the playoffs in 12 of the 13 previous seasons. When he became captain in 1986-87, the team was coming off a 40-point season. One year later, the Red Wings finished first in the Norris Division for the club's first title of any kind since finishing atop the NHL standings in 1964-65. In his first seven seasons as captain, Yzerman lead the team in scoring every year. (In all, he would lead Detroit in scoring 11 times.) In 1988-89, he established career highs and Red Wings single-season records with 65 goals, 90 assists and 155 points.

Despite his own personal success and the team's brilliant regular-season performances, playoff disappointment haunted Yzerman and the Red Wings until back-to-back Stanley Cup titles in 1997 and 1998. In 1999-2000, he won the Frank Selke Trophy as the NHL's best defensive forward and was named to the First All-Star Team.

Though injuries limited him to just 52 games in 2001-02, Yzerman earned an Olympic gold medal with Team Canada and a third Stanley Cup ring. In 2003, he won the Bill Masterton Trophy for perseverance, sportsmanship and dedication to hockey.

He leaves the NHL in 2006 ranked fifth all-time in points scored and is recognized as one of the game's greatest leaders.

NHL Goaltenders

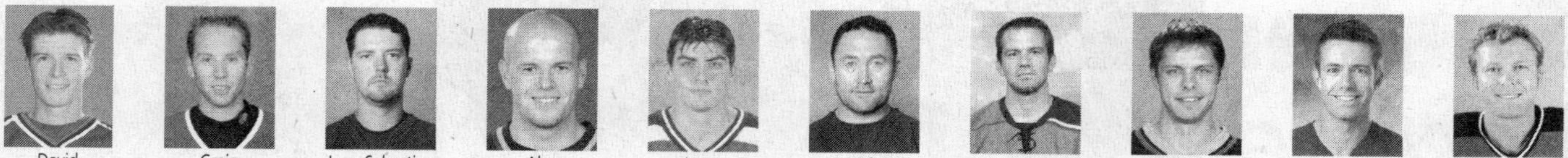

David Aebischer
Craig Anderson
Jean-Sebastien Aubin
Alex Auld
Jason Bacashihua
Ed Belfour
Adam Berkhoel
Martin Biron
Brian Boucher
Martin Brodeur

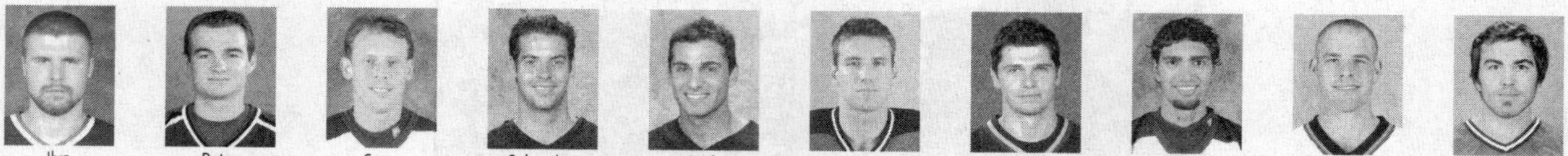

Ilya Bryzgalov
Peter Budaj
Sean Burke
Sebastian Caron
Andy Chiodo
Scott Clemmensen
Dan Cloutier
Gerald Coleman
Ty Conklin
Yann Danis

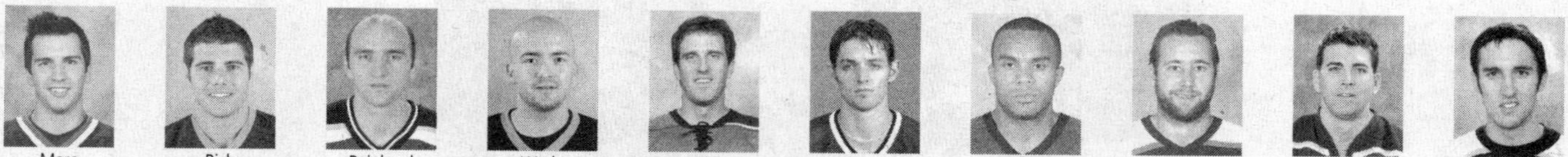

Marc Denis
Rick DiPietro
Reinhard Divis
Wade Dubielewicz
Mike Dunham
Dan Ellis
Ray Emery
Robert Esche
Manny Fernandez
Brian Finley

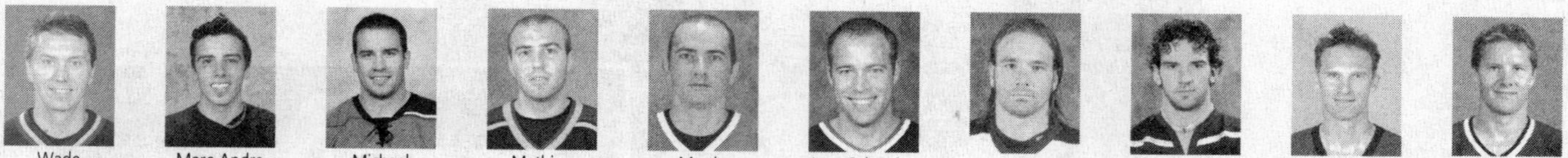

Wade Flaherty
Marc-Andre Fleury
Michael Garnett
Mathieu Garon
Martin Gerber
Jean-Sebastien Giguere
John Grahame
Josh Harding
Dominik Hasek
Johan Hedberg

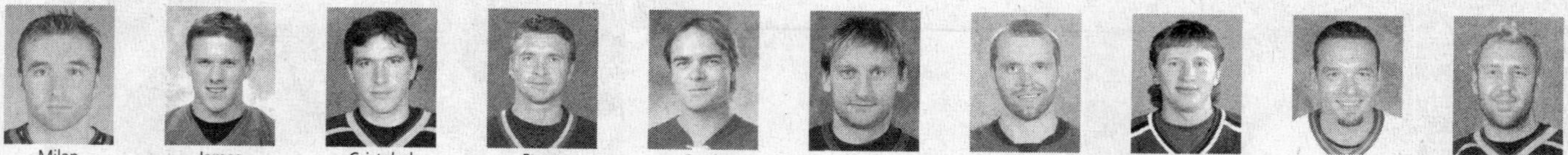

Milan Hnilicka
James Howard
Cristobal Huet
Brent Johnson
Curtis Joseph
Nikolai Khabibulin
Miikka Kiprusoff
Vitaly Kolesnik
Olaf Kolzig
Jason Labarbera

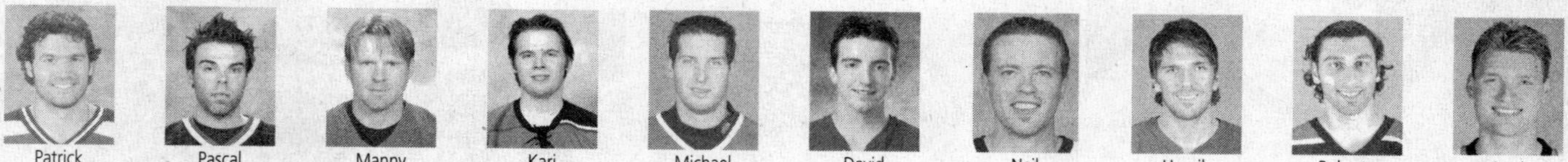

Patrick Lalime
Pascal Leclaire
Manny Legace
Kari Lehtonen
Michael Leighton
David Leneveu
Neil Little
Henrik Lundqvist
Roberto Luongo
Jussi Markkanen

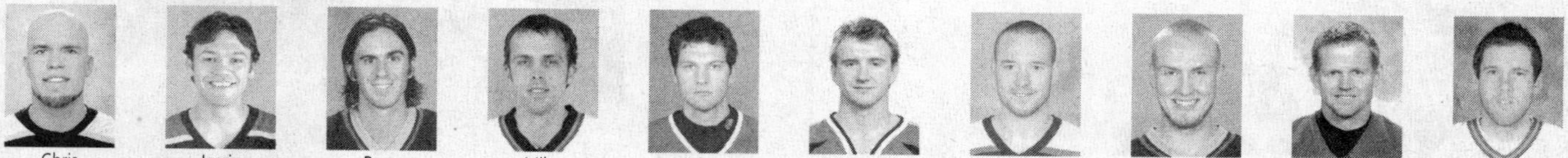

Chris Mason
Jamie McLennan
Ryan Miller
Mike Morrison
Adam Munro
Evgeni Nabokov
Antero Niittymaki
Mika Noronen
Chris Osgood
Maxime Ouellet

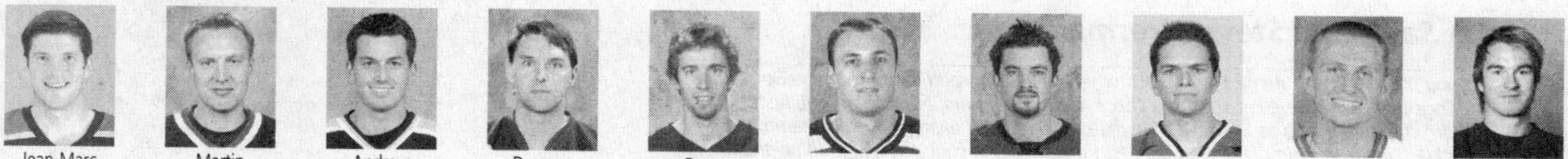

Jean-Marc Pelletier
Martin Prusek
Andrew Raycroft
Dwayne Roloson
Dany Sabourin
Curtis Sanford
Philippe Sauve
Nolan Schaefer
Rastislav Stana
Mikael Tellqvist

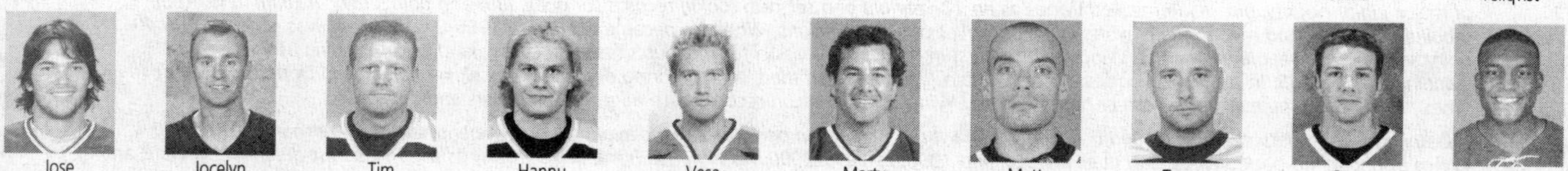

Jose Theodore
Jocelyn Thibault
Tim Thomas
Hannu Toivonen
Vesa Toskala
Marty Turco
Matt Underhill
Tomas Vokoun
Cam Ward
Kevin Weekes

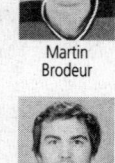

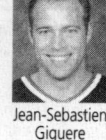

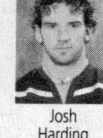

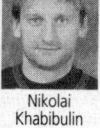

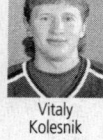

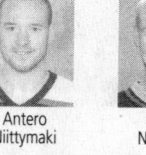

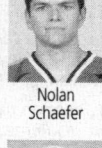

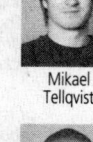

2006-07 Goaltender Register

Note: The 2006-07 Goaltender Register lists all active NHL goaltenders, every goaltender drafted in the 2006 Entry Draft, goaltenders on NHL Reserve Lists and other goaltenders.

Trades and roster changes are current as of August 15, 2006.

To calculate a goaltender's goals-against per game average **(Avg)**, divide goals against **(GA)** by minutes played **(Mins)** and multiply this result by **60**.

Abbreviations: GP – games played; **W** – wins; **L** – losses; **T** – ties; **GA** – goals against; **SO** – shutouts; **Avg** – goals-against per game average.
♦ – member of Stanley Cup-winning team.

NHL Player Register begins on page 347.
Prospect Register begins on page 273.
League Abbreviations are listed on page 346.

AEBISCHER, David (A-bih-shuhr, DAY-vihd) MTL.

Goaltender. Catches left. 6'1", 185 lbs. Born, Fribourg, Switz., February 7, 1978.
(Colorado's 7th choice, 161st overall, in 1997 Entry Draft).

			Regular Season								Playoffs						
Season	Club	League	GP	W	L	O/T	Mins	GA	SO	Avg	GP	W	L	Mins	GA	SO	Avg
1996-97	Fribourg	Swiss	10	....	....	....	577	34	0	3.54	3	1	2	184	13	0	4.24
1997-98	Chesapeake	ECHL	17	5	7	2	930	52	0	3.35	....	....	....	....	....	....	....
	Wheeling Nailers	ECHL	10	5	3	1	564	30	1	3.19	....	....	....	....	....	....	....
	Hershey Bears	AHL	2	0	0	1	79	5	0	3.76	....	....	....	....	....	....	....
	Fribourg	Swiss	1	1	0	0	60	1	0	1.00	4	....	....	240	17	....	4.25
1998-99	Hershey Bears	AHL	38	17	10	5	1932	79	2	2.45	3	1	2	152	6	0	2.37
99-2000	Hershey Bears	AHL	58	29	23	2	3259	180	1	3.31	14	7	6	788	40	2	3.05
2000-01 ♦	**Colorado**	**NHL**	**26**	**12**	**7**	**3**	**1393**	**52**	**3**	**2.24**	**1**	**0**	**0**	**1**	**0**	**0**	**0.00**
2001-02	**Colorado**	**NHL**	**21**	**13**	**6**	**0**	**1184**	**37**	**2**	**1.88**	**1**	**0**	**0**	**34**	**1**	**0**	**1.76**
	Switzerland	Olympics	2	1	0	0	81	6	0	4.43	....	....	....	....	....	....	....
2002-03	**Colorado**	**NHL**	**22**	**7**	**12**	**0**	**1235**	**50**	**1**	**2.43**	....	....	....	....	....	....	....
2003-04	**Colorado**	**NHL**	**62**	**32**	**19**	**9**	**3703**	**129**	**4**	**2.09**	**11**	**6**	**5**	**662**	**23**	**1**	**2.08**
2004-05	HC Lugano	Swiss	18	12	2	3	1019	41	0	2.41	4	1	3	240	10	0	2.50
	EHC Chur	Swiss-2	....	....	....	....	....	....	....	....	2	....	....	130	4	0	1.84
2005-06	**Colorado**	**NHL**	**43**	**25**	**14**	**2**	**2477**	**123**	**3**	**2.98**	....	....	....	....	....	....	....
	Switzerland	Olympics	4	....	....	....	200	7	0	2.10	....	....	....	....	....	....	....
	Montreal	**NHL**	**7**	**4**	**3**	**0**	**418**	**26**	**0**	**3.73**	....	....	....	....	....	....	....
	NHL Totals		**181**	**93**	**61**	**14**	**10410**	**417**	**13**	**2.40**	**13**	**6**	**5**	**697**	**24**	**1**	**2.07**

Signed as a free agent by **Lugano** (Swiss), September 17, 2004. Traded to **Montreal** by **Colorado** for Jose Theodore, March 8, 2006.

AHONEN, Ari (ah-HOH-nuhn, AH-ree)

Goaltender. Catches left. 6'2", 195 lbs. Born, Jyvàskyla, Finland, February 6, 1981.
(New Jersey's 1st choice, 27th overall, in 1999 Entry Draft).

			Regular Season								Playoffs						
Season	Club	League	GP	W	L	O/T	Mins	GA	SO	Avg	GP	W	L	Mins	GA	SO	Avg
1997-98	JYP Jyvaskyla U18	Fin-U18	31	....	....	....	1853	64	....	2.09	5	5	0	302	8	1	1.59
	JYP Jyvaskyla Jr.	Fin-Jr.	3	1	1	0	54	6	....	6.67	....	....	....	....	....	....	....
1998-99	JYP Jyvaskyla U18	Fin-U18	....	....	....	....	....	....	....	....	7	....	....	....	....	0	2.88
	JYP Jyvaskyla Jr.	Fin-Jr.	24	10	10	1	1447	70	0	2.90	....	....	....	....	....	....	....
99-2000	HIFK Helsinki Jr.	Fin-Jr.	11	7	3	1	664	22	3	1.99	3	0	3	177	13	0	4.40
	HIFK Helsinki	Finland	24	11	9	1	1352	70	1	3.11	2	0	2	119	7	0	3.53
2000-01	HIFK Helsinki Jr.	Fin-Jr.	....	....	....	....	....	....	....	....	1	....	....	59	2	0	2.03
	HIFK Helsinki	Finland	37	18	12	4	2101	97	2	2.77	5	2	3	395	9	1	1.36
2001-02	Albany River Rats	AHL	36	6	22	6	2106	106	0	3.02	....	....	....	....	....	....	....
2002-03	Albany River Rats	AHL	38	13	20	3	2171	110	1	3.04	....	....	....	....	....	....	....
2003-04	Albany River Rats	AHL	50	13	30	6	3012	150	2	2.99	....	....	....	....	....	....	....
2004-05	Albany River Rats	AHL	38	16	20	1	2195	114	4	3.12	....	....	....	....	....	....	....
2005-06	Albany River Rats	AHL	16	3	13	0	949	63	0	3.98	....	....	....	....	....	....	....

Signed as a free agent by **Espoo** (Finland), May 15, 2006.

AKERLUND, Magnus (AK-uhr-luhnd, MAG-nuhs) CAR.

Goaltender. Catches right. 6'1", 183 lbs. Born, Osby, Sweden, April 25, 1986.
(Carolina's 5th choice, 137th overall, in 2004 Entry Draft).

			Regular Season								Playoffs						
Season	Club	League	GP	W	L	O/T	Mins	GA	SO	Avg	GP	W	L	Mins	GA	SO	Avg
2002-03	HV 71 Jr.	Swe-Jr.	18	....	....	....	861	44	1	3.07	2	....	....	80	6	0	4.50
2003-04	HV 71 Jr.	Swe-Jr.	26	....	....	....	1556	85	1	3.28	2	....	....	119	10	0	5.04
2004-05	HV 71 Jr.	Swe-Jr.	19	....	....	....	1096	48	1	2.63	....	....	....	....	....	....	....
	HV 71 Jonkoping	Sweden	3	....	....	....	185	9	0	2.92	....	....	....	....	....	....	....
	Skovde IK	Sweden-2	22	....	....	....	1290	55	1	2.56	....	....	....	....	....	....	....
2005-06	HV 71 Jr.	Swe-Jr..	4	....	....	....	214	17	0	4.76	....	....	....	....	....	....	....
	Nykoping	Sweden-2	21	....	....	....	1236	67	0	3.25	....	....	....	....	....	....	....

ANDERSON, Craig (AN-duhr-suhn, KRAYG) FLA.

Goaltender. Catches left. 6'2", 174 lbs. Born, Park Ridge, IL, May 21, 1981.
(Chicago's 4th choice, 73rd overall, in 2001 Entry Draft).

			Regular Season								Playoffs						
Season	Club	League	GP	W	L	O/T	Mins	GA	SO	Avg	GP	W	L	Mins	GA	SO	Avg
1997-98	Chicago Jets	MEHL	50	....	....	....	2991	143	2	2.86	....	....	....	....	....	....	....
1998-99	Chicago Freeze	NAHL	14	11	3	0	840	40	0	2.56	....	....	....	....	....	....	....
	Guelph Storm	OHL	21	12	5	1	1006	52	1	3.10	3	0	2	114	9	0	4.74
99-2000	Guelph Storm	OHL	38	12	17	2	1955	117	0	3.59	3	0	1	110	5	0	2.73
2000-01	Guelph Storm	OHL	59	30	19	9	3555	156	3	2.63	4	0	4	240	17	0	4.25
2001-02	Norfolk Admirals	AHL	28	9	13	4	1568	77	2	2.95	1	0	1	21	1	0	2.83
2002-03	**Chicago**	**NHL**	**6**	**0**	**3**	**2**	**270**	**18**	**0**	**4.00**	....	....	....	....	....	....	....
	Norfolk Admirals	AHL	32	15	11	5	1795	58	4	1.94	5	2	3	345	15	0	2.61
2003-04	**Chicago**	**NHL**	**21**	**6**	**14**	**0**	**1205**	**57**	**1**	**2.84**	....	....	....	....	....	....	....
	Norfolk Admirals	AHL	37	17	20	0	2108	74	3	2.11	5	2	3	327	10	0	1.84
2004-05	Norfolk Admirals	AHL	15	9	4	1	886	27	2	1.83	6	2	4	356	14	0	2.36
2005-06	**Chicago**	**NHL**	**29**	**6**	**12**	**4**	**1554**	**86**	**1**	**3.32**	....	....	....	....	....	....	....
	NHL Totals		**56**	**12**	**29**	**6**	**3029**	**161**	**2**	**3.19**	....	....	....	....	....	....	....

• Re-entered NHL Entry Draft. Originally Calgary's 3rd choice, 77th overall, in 1999 Entry Draft.

OHL First All-Star Team (2001)

Claimed on waivers by **Boston** from **Chicago**, January 19, 2006. Claimed on waivers by **St. Louis** from **Boston**, January 31, 2006. Claimed on waivers by **Chicago** from **St. Louis**, February 3, 2006. Signed as a free agent by **Togliatti** (Russia), May 25, 2006. Traded to **Florida** by **Chicago** for Florida's 6th round choice in 2008 Entry Draft, June 24, 2006.

AUBIN, Jean-Sebastien (OH-behn, ZHAWN-suh-BAS-tee-yeh) TOR.

Goaltender. Catches right. 5'11", 180 lbs. Born, Montreal, Que., July 19, 1977.
(Pittsburgh's 2nd choice, 76th overall, in 1995 Entry Draft).

			Regular Season								Playoffs						
Season	Club	League	GP	W	L	O/T	Mins	GA	SO	Avg	GP	W	L	Mins	GA	SO	Avg
1993-94	Montreal-Bourassa	QAAA	27	14	13	0	1524	96	1	3.74	4	1	3	222	19	0	5.14
1994-95	Sherbrooke	QMJHL	27	13	10	1	1287	73	1	3.40	3	1	2	185	11	0	3.57
1995-96	Sherbrooke	QMJHL	40	18	14	2	2140	127	0	3.57	4	1	3	238	23	0	5.55
1996-97	Sherbrooke	QMJHL	4	3	1	0	249	8	0	1.93	1	0	1	60	4	0	4.00
	Moncton Wildcats	QMJHL	22	9	12	0	1252	67	1	3.21	....	....	....	....	....	....	....
	Laval Titan	QMJHL	11	2	6	1	532	41	0	4.62	....	....	....	....	....	....	....
1997-98	Syracuse Crunch	AHL	8	2	4	1	380	26	0	4.10	....	....	....	....	....	....	....
	Dayton Bombers	ECHL	21	15	2	2	1177	59	1	3.01	3	1	1	142	4	0	1.69
1998-99	**Pittsburgh**	**NHL**	**17**	**4**	**3**	**6**	**756**	**28**	**2**	**2.22**	....	....	....	....	....	....	....
	Kansas City Blades	IHL	13	5	7	1	751	41	0	3.28	....	....	....	....	....	....	....
99-2000	**Pittsburgh**	**NHL**	**51**	**23**	**21**	**3**	**2789**	**120**	**2**	**2.58**	....	....	....	....	....	....	....
	Wilkes-Barre	AHL	11	2	8	0	538	39	0	4.35	....	....	....	....	....	....	....
2000-01	**Pittsburgh**	**NHL**	**36**	**20**	**14**	**1**	**2050**	**107**	**0**	**3.13**	**1**	**0**	**0**	**1**	**0**	**0**	**0.00**
2001-02	**Pittsburgh**	**NHL**	**21**	**3**	**12**	**1**	**1094**	**65**	**0**	**3.56**	....	....	....	....	....	....	....
2002-03	**Pittsburgh**	**NHL**	**21**	**6**	**13**	**0**	**1132**	**59**	**1**	**3.13**	....	....	....	....	....	....	....
	Wilkes-Barre	AHL	16	8	6	1	919	29	3	1.89	6	3	3	356	12	0	2.02
2003-04	**Pittsburgh**	**NHL**	**22**	**7**	**9**	**0**	**1067**	**53**	**1**	**2.98**	....	....	....	....	....	....	....
	Wilkes-Barre	AHL	13	4	5	2	670	31	0	2.78	....	....	....	....	....	....	....
2004-05	St. John's	AHL	23	12	9	0	1336	64	3	2.87	1	0	0	47	1	0	1.27
2005-06	**Toronto**	**NHL**	**11**	**9**	**0**	**2**	**677**	**25**	**1**	**2.22**	....	....	....	....	....	....	....
	Toronto Marlies	AHL	46	19	18	2	2491	126	2	3.03	5	1	4	359	17	0	2.84
	NHL Totals		**179**	**72**	**72**	**13**	**9565**	**457**	**7**	**2.87**	**1**	**0**	**0**	**1**	**0**	**0**	**0.00**

Signed to a PTO (tryout) contract by **St. John's** (AHL), November 13, 2004. Signed as a free agent by **Toronto**, August 18, 2005.

AULD, Alex (AWLD, AL-ehx) FLA.

Goaltender. Catches left. 6'4", 200 lbs. Born, Cold Lake, Alta., January 7, 1981.
(Florida's 2nd choice, 40th overall, in 1999 Entry Draft).

			Regular Season								Playoffs						
Season	Club	League	GP	W	L	O/T	Mins	GA	SO	Avg	GP	W	L	Mins	GA	SO	Avg
1996-97	Thunder Bay Kings	TBMHL	35	....	....	....	2100	46	10	1.35	....	....	....	....	....	....	....
1997-98	Sturgeon Falls Lynx	NOJHA	11	4	6	0	611	46	0	4.52	....	....	....	....	....	....	....
	North Bay	OHL	6	0	4	0	206	17	0	4.95	....	....	....	....	....	....	....
1998-99	North Bay	OHL	37	9	20	1	1894	106	1	3.36	3	0	3	170	10	0	3.53
99-2000	North Bay	OHL	55	21	26	6	3047	167	2	3.29	6	2	4	374	12	0	*1.93
2000-01	North Bay	OHL	40	22	11	5	2319	98	1	2.54	4	0	4	240	15	0	3.75
2001-02	**Vancouver**	**NHL**	**1**	**1**	**0**	**0**	**60**	**2**	**0**	**2.00**	....	....	....	....	....	....	....
	Columbia Inferno	ECHL	6	3	1	2	375	12	0	1.92	....	....	....	....	....	....	....
	Manitoba Moose	AHL	21	11	9	0	1104	65	1	3.53	1	0	0	20	0	0	0.00
2002-03	**Vancouver**	**NHL**	**7**	**3**	**3**	**0**	**382**	**10**	**1**	**1.57**	**1**	**0**	**0**	**20**	**1**	**0**	**3.00**
	Manitoba Moose	AHL	37	15	19	3	2209	97	3	2.64	....	....	....	....	....	....	....
2003-04	**Vancouver**	**NHL**	**6**	**2**	**2**	**2**	**349**	**12**	**0**	**2.06**	**3**	**1**	**2**	**222**	**9**	**0**	**2.43**
	Manitoba Moose	AHL	40	18	16	4	2329	99	4	2.55	....	....	....	....	....	....	....
2004-05	Manitoba Moose	AHL	50	25	18	4	2764	118	2	2.56	3	0	2	128	7	0	3.29
2005-06	**Vancouver**	**NHL**	**67**	**33**	**26**	**6**	**3859**	**189**	**0**	**2.94**	....	....	....	....	....	....	....
	NHL Totals		**81**	**39**	**31**	**8**	**4650**	**213**	**1**	**2.75**	**4**	**1**	**2**	**242**	**10**	**0**	**2.48**

Rights traded to **Vancouver** by **Florida** for Vancouver's 2nd round compensatory choice (later traded to New Jersey – New Jersey selected Tuomas Pihlman) in 2001 Entry Draft and Vancouver's 3rd round choice (later traded to Atlanta – later traded to Buffalo – Buffalo selected John Adams) in 2002 Entry Draft, May 31, 2001. Traded to **Florida** by **Vancouver** with Todd Bertuzzi and Bryan Allen for Roberto Luongo, Lukas Krajicek and Florida's 6th round choice (Sergei Shirokov) in 2006 Entry Draft, June 23, 2006.

BACASHIHUA, Jason (buh-KAH-shoo-wuh, JAY-suhn) ST.L.

Goaltender. Catches left. 5'11", 175 lbs. Born, Garden City, MI, September 20, 1982.
(Dallas' 1st choice, 26th overall, in 2001 Entry Draft).

			Regular Season								Playoffs						
Season	Club	League	GP	W	L	O/T	Mins	GA	SO	Avg	GP	W	L	Mins	GA	SO	Avg
99-2000	Chicago Freeze	NAHL	41	20	19	2	2432	118	2	2.91	2	0	2	103	12	0	6.97
2000-01	Chicago Freeze	NAHL	39	24	14	0	2246	121	1	3.23	3	1	2	190	12	0	3.79
2001-02	Plymouth Whalers	OHL	46	26	12	7	2688	105	*5	2.34	6	2	4	360	15	0	2.50
	Utah Grizzlies	AHL	1	0	1	0	61	3	0	2.97	....	....	....	....	....	....	....
2002-03	Utah Grizzlies	AHL	39	18	18	2	2245	118	3	3.15	1	0	1	59	2	0	2.05
2003-04	Utah Grizzlies	AHL	39	13	19	5	2234	99	3	2.66	....	....	....	....	....	....	....
2004-05	Worcester IceCats	AHL	35	18	13	1	1909	80	2	2.51	....	....	....	....	....	....	....
2005-06	**St. Louis**	**NHL**	**19**	**4**	**10**	**1**	**966**	**52**	**0**	**3.23**	....	....	....	....	....	....	....
	Peoria Rivermen	AHL	15	9	4	0	820	36	2	2.63	....	....	....	....	....	....	....
	NHL Totals		**19**	**4**	**10**	**1**	**966**	**52**	**0**	**3.23**	....	....	....	....	....	....	....

Traded to **St. Louis** by **Dallas** for the rights to Shawn Belle, June 25, 2004.

BACHMAN, Richard (BAWK-mahn, RIH-chuhrd) DAL.

Goaltender. Catches left. 5'11", 160 lbs. Born, Salt Lake City, UT, July 25, 1987.
(Dallas' 3rd choice, 120th overall, in 2006 Entry Draft).

			Regular Season								Playoffs						
Season	Club	League	GP	W	L	O/T	Mins	GA	SO	Avg	GP	W	L	Mins	GA	SO	Avg
2004-05	Cushing	High-MA	28	....	....	....	1498	53	3	1.89	....	....	....	....	....	....	....
	Boston Jr. Bruins	EmJHL	25	....	....	....	....	....	....	....	....	....	....	....	....	....	....
2005-06	Cushing	High-MA	30	....	....	....	1598	60	4	2.25	....	....	....	....	....	....	....
	Boston Jr. Bruins	EmJHL	....	31	1	2	....	....	....	1.69	....	....	....	....	....	....	....

BACKSTROM, Niklas (BAK-struhm, NIHK-las) MIN.

Goaltender. Catches left. 6'2", 196 lbs. Born, Helsinki, Finland, February 13, 1978.

			Regular Season								Playoffs						
Season	Club	League	GP	W	L	O/T	Mins	GA	SO	Avg	GP	W	L	Mins	GA	SO	Avg
1996-97	HIFK Helsinki	Finland	2	....	....	....	....	....	....	....	....	....	....	....	....	....	....
1997-98	HIFK Helsinki	Finland	3	....	....	....	....	....	....	....	....	....	....	....	....	....	....
1998-99	HIFK Helsinki	Finland	16	9	5	1	923	26	1	*1.69	....	....	....	....	....	....	....
99-2000	HIFK Helsinki	Finland	4	....	....	....	....	....	....	....	....	....	....	....	....	....	....
2000-01	SaiPa	Finland	49	....	....	....	....	....	....	....	....	....	....	....	....	....	....
2001-02	AIK Solna	Sweden	40	....	....	....	2186	111	1	3.05	....	....	....	....	....	....	....
2002-03	Karpat Oulu	Finland	36	16	8	9	2136	77	4	2.16	*15	7	8	*990	33	1	2.00
2003-04	Karpat Oulu	Finland	43	24	8	0	2572	87	7	2.03	*15	*9	6	*927	36	1	2.33
2004-05	Karpat Oulu	Finland	47	27	10	10	2819	102	7	2.17	*12	*10	2	720	15	*3	*1.25
2005-06	Karpat Oulu	Finland	51	*32	9	10	3077	86	*10	*1.68	4	3	1	195	6	0	1.84

Signed as a free agent by **Minnesota**, June 1, 2006.

BARULIN, Konstantin (bah-ROO-lihn, kawn-stuhn-TIHN) ST.L.

Goaltender. Catches left. 6', 180 lbs. Born, Karaganda, USSR, September 4, 1984.
(St. Louis' 3rd choice, 84th overall, in 2003 Entry Draft).

			Regular Season								Playoffs						
Season	Club	League	GP	W	L	O/T	Mins	GA	SO	Avg	GP	W	L	Mins	GA	SO	Avg
2001-02	Gazovik Tyumen	Russia-2	4	....	....	....	188	15	0	4.79	....	....	....	....	....	....	....
2002-03	Gazovik Tyumen	Russia-2	28	....	....	....	1672	47	5	1.69	....	....	....	....	....	....	....
2003-04	Gazovik Tyumen	Russia-2	11	....	....	....	663	24	....	2.17	....	....	....	....	....	....	....
	SKA St. Petersburg	Russia	1	....	....	....	1	0	0	0.00	....	....	....	....	....	....	....
	St. Petersburg 2	Russia-3	11	6	4	1	668	24	1	2.15	....	....	....	....	....	....	....
2004-05	Gazovik Tyumen	Russia-2	30	....	....	....	1773	59	6	2.00	3	....	....	136	9	0	3.97
2005-06	Spartak Moscow	Russia	36	....	....	....	2102	75	2	2.14	2	....	....	104	4	0	2.30

BEAUCHEMIN, Rejean (boh-sheh-MEH, ray-JAWN) PHI.

Goaltender. Catches left. 6'1", 193 lbs. Born, Winnipeg, Man., May 3, 1985.
(Philadelphia's 10th choice, 191st overall, in 2003 Entry Draft).

			Regular Season								Playoffs						
Season	Club	League	GP	W	L	O/T	Mins	GA	SO	Avg	GP	W	L	Mins	GA	SO	Avg
2001-02	Winnipeg Warriors	MMMHL	29	6	8	4	1026	54	0	3.15	4	3	1	240	12	0	3.00
2002-03	Prince Albert	WHL	34	12	15	1	1618	86	1	3.19	....	....	....	....	....	....	....
2003-04	Prince Albert	WHL	62	30	21	6	3540	137	6	2.32	6	2	4	360	14	0	2.33
2004-05	Prince Albert	WHL	54	21	24	4	3052	133	5	2.61	17	11	6	1062	38	2	2.15
2005-06	Philadelphia	AHL	15	3	8	1	824	37	0	2.70	....	....	....	....	....	....	....
	Trenton Titans	ECHL	32	9	18	4	1856	92	0	2.97	2	0	2	125	6	0	2.89

WHL East Second All-Star Team (2004)

BECKFORD-TSEU, Chris (BEHK-fuhrd-TSEW, KRIHS) ST.L.

Goaltender. Catches left. 6'2", 201 lbs. Born, Toronto, Ont., June 22, 1984.
(St. Louis' 8th choice, 159th overall, in 2003 Entry Draft).

			Regular Season								Playoffs						
Season	Club	League	GP	W	L	O/T	Mins	GA	SO	Avg	GP	W	L	Mins	GA	SO	Avg
2000-01	St. Mike's B's	OPJHL	25	9	15	1	1506	119	1	4.75	4	1	3	240	10	0	2.50
2001-02	Oshawa	OPJHL					STATISTICS NOT AVAILABLE										
	Guelph Storm	OHL	5	2	0	0	207	16	0	4.64	....	....	....	....	....	....	....
	Oshawa Generals	OHL	7	2	3	0	341	19	0	3.34	5	1	4	310	16	0	3.10
2002-03	Oshawa Generals	OHL	54	25	26	2	2978	157	4	3.16	13	6	7	727	48	1	3.96
2003-04	Oshawa Generals	OHL	9	1	5	2	495	28	0	3.39	....	....	....	....	....	....	....
	Kingston	OHL	40	16	19	2	2226	121	3	3.26	5	1	4	303	18	0	3.56
2004-05	Worcester IceCats	AHL	1	0	0	0	29	0	0	0.00	....	....	....	....	....	....	....
	Peoria Rivermen	ECHL	29	11	12	3	1594	72	1	2.71	....	....	....	....	....	....	....
2005-06	Peoria Rivermen	AHL	16	7	5	1	737	38	0	3.10	4	0	4	238	15	0	3.78
	Alaska Aces	ECHL	19	16	1	2	1152	36	2	1.87	12	8	4	795	27	*3	*2.04

BEECH, Kevin (BEECH, KEH-vihn) T.B.

Goaltender. Catches left. 6'4", 183 lbs. Born, London, Ont., September 23, 1986.
(Tampa Bay's 8th choice, 165th overall, in 2005 Entry Draft).

			Regular Season								Playoffs						
Season	Club	League	GP	W	L	O/T	Mins	GA	SO	Avg	GP	W	L	Mins	GA	SO	Avg
2003-04	Sudbury Wolves	OHL	16	3	9	0	811	48	0	3.55	1	1	0	56	0	0	0.00
2004-05	Sudbury Wolves	OHL	21	9	9	2	1132	50	2	2.65	6	2	1	276	12	0	2.61
2005-06	Sudbury Wolves	OHL	63	33	25	0	3690	181	0	2.94	10	4	5	612	28	*2	2.75

BELFOUR, Ed (BEHL-fohr, EHD) FLA.

Goaltender. Catches left. 5'11", 202 lbs. Born, Carman, Man., April 21, 1965.

			Regular Season								Playoffs						
Season	Club	League	GP	W	L	O/T	Mins	GA	SO	Avg	GP	W	L	Mins	GA	SO	Avg
1983-84	Winkler Flyers	MJHL	14	....	....	....	818	68	0	4.99	....	....	....	....	....	....	....
1984-85	Winkler Flyers	MJHL	34	....	....	....	1973	145	1	4.41	7	3	4	528	41	0	4.66
1985-86	Winkler Flyers	MJHL	33	....	....	....	1943	124	1	3.83	....	....	....	....	....	....	....
1986-87	North Dakota	WCHA	34	29	4	0	2049	81	3	2.37	....	....	....	....	....	....	....
1987-88	Saginaw Hawks	IHL	61	32	25	0	*3446	183	3	3.19	9	4	5	561	33	0	3.53
1988-89	**Chicago**	**NHL**	**23**	**4**	**12**	**3**	**1148**	**74**	**0**	**3.87**	....	....	....	....	....	....	....
	Saginaw Hawks	IHL	29	12	10	0	1760	92	0	3.14	5	2	3	298	14	0	2.82
1989-90	Canada	Nat-Tm	33	13	12	6	1808	93	0	3.09	....	....	....	....	....	....	....
	Chicago	**NHL**	....	....	....	....	....	....	....	....	**9**	**4**	**2**	**409**	**17**	**0**	**2.49**
1990-91	**Chicago**	**NHL**	***74**	***43**	**19**	**7**	***4127**	**170**	**4**	***2.47**	**6**	**2**	**4**	**295**	**20**	**0**	**4.07**
1991-92	**Chicago**	**NHL**	**52**	**21**	**18**	**10**	**2928**	**132**	***5**	**2.70**	**18**	**12**	**4**	**949**	**39**	**1**	***2.47**
1992-93	**Chicago**	**NHL**	***71**	**41**	**18**	**11**	***4106**	**177**	***7**	**2.59**	**4**	**0**	**4**	**249**	**13**	**0**	**3.13**
1993-94	**Chicago**	**NHL**	**70**	**37**	**24**	**6**	**3998**	**178**	***7**	**2.67**	**6**	**2**	**4**	**360**	**15**	**0**	**2.50**
1994-95	**Chicago**	**NHL**	**42**	**22**	**15**	**3**	**2450**	**93**	***5**	**2.28**	**16**	**9**	**7**	**1014**	**37**	**1**	**2.19**
1995-96	**Chicago**	**NHL**	**50**	**22**	**17**	**10**	**2956**	**135**	**1**	**2.74**	**9**	**6**	**3**	**666**	**23**	**1**	***2.07**
1996-97	**Chicago**	**NHL**	**33**	**11**	**15**	**6**	**1966**	**88**	**1**	**2.69**	....	....	....	....	....	....	....
	San Jose	**NHL**	**13**	**3**	**9**	**0**	**757**	**43**	**1**	**3.41**	....	....	....	....	....	....	....
1997-98	**Dallas**	**NHL**	**61**	**37**	**12**	**10**	**3581**	**112**	**9**	***1.88**	**17**	**10**	**7**	**1039**	**31**	**1**	***1.79**
1998-99 ♦	**Dallas**	**NHL**	**61**	**35**	**15**	**9**	**3536**	**117**	**5**	**1.99**	***23**	***16**	**7**	***1544**	**43**	***3**	***1.67**
99-2000	**Dallas**	**NHL**	**62**	**32**	**21**	**7**	**3620**	**127**	**4**	**2.10**	***23**	**14**	**9**	**1443**	**45**	***4**	**1.87**
2000-01	**Dallas**	**NHL**	**63**	**35**	**20**	**7**	**3687**	**144**	**8**	**2.34**	**10**	**4**	**6**	**671**	**25**	**0**	**2.24**
2001-02	**Dallas**	**NHL**	**60**	**21**	**27**	**11**	**3467**	**153**	**1**	**2.65**	....	....	....	....	....	....	....
	Canada	Olympics					DID NOT PLAY – SPARE GOALTENDER										
2002-03	**Toronto**	**NHL**	**62**	**37**	**20**	**5**	**3738**	**141**	**7**	**2.26**	**7**	**3**	**4**	**532**	**24**	**0**	**2.71**
2003-04	**Toronto**	**NHL**	**59**	**34**	**19**	**6**	**3444**	**122**	**10**	**2.13**	**13**	**6**	**7**	**774**	**27**	**3**	**2.09**
2004-05							DID NOT PLAY										
2005-06	**Toronto**	**NHL**	**49**	**22**	**22**	**4**	**2897**	**159**	**0**	**3.29**	....	....	....	....	....	....	....
	NHL Totals		**905**	**457**	**303**	**115**	**52406**	**2165**	**75**	**2.48**	**161**	**88**	**68**	**9945**	**359**	**14**	**2.17**

WCHA First All-Star Team (1987) • NCAA Championship All-Tournament Team (1987) • IHL First All-Star Team (1988) • Garry F. Longman Memorial Trophy (Rookie of the Year – IHL) (1988) (co-winner - John Cullen) • NHL All-Rookie Team (1991) • NHL First All-Star Team (1991, 1993) • Trico Goaltender Award (1991) • Calder Memorial Trophy (1991) • William M. Jennings Trophy (1991, 1993, 1995) • Vezina Trophy (1991, 1993) • NHL Second All-Star Team (1995) • William M. Jennings Trophy (1999) (shared with Roman Turek) • MBNA Roger Crozier Saving Grace Award (2000)

Played in NHL All-Star Game (1992, 1993, 1996, 1998, 1999)

Signed as a free agent by **Chicago**, September 25, 1987. Traded to **San Jose** by **Chicago** for Chris Terreri, Ulf Dahlen and Michal Sykora, January 25, 1997. Signed as a free agent by **Dallas**, July 2, 1997. Traded to **Nashville** by **Dallas** with Cameron Mann for David Gosselin and Nashville's 5th round choice (Eero Kilpelainen) in 2003 Entry Draft, June 29, 2002. Signed as a free agent by **Toronto**, July 2, 2002. Signed as a free agent by **Florida**, July 25, 2006.

BENNETT, Brett (BEHN-neht, BREHT) PHX.

Goaltender. Catches left. 6'1", 185 lbs. Born, Buffalo, NY, March 8, 1988.
(Phoenix's 4th choice, 130th overall, in 2006 Entry Draft).

			Regular Season								Playoffs						
Season	Club	League	GP	W	L	O/T	Mins	GA	SO	Avg	GP	W	L	Mins	GA	SO	Avg
2003-04	Det. Honeybaked	MWEHL	31	....	....	....	....	....	....	....	....	....	....	....	....	....	....
2004-05	USNTDP	U-17	14	10	6	1	930	41	0	2.65	....	....	....	....	....	....	....
	USNTDP	NAHL	23	10	7	1	1217	56	1	2.76	10	7	3	598	20	3	2.01
2005-06	USNTDP	U-18	12	7	2	0	593	24	0	2.43	....	....	....	....	....	....	....
	USNTDP	NAHL	5	3	0	0	238	5	0	1.26	....	....	....	....	....	....	....

Signed Letter of Intent to attend **Boston U.** (Hockey East) in fall of 2006.

BERKHOEL, Adam (BUHRK-uhl, A-duhm)

Goaltender. Catches left. 5'11", 190 lbs. Born, St. Paul, MN, May 16, 1981.
(Chicago's 12th choice, 240th overall, in 2000 Entry Draft).

			Regular Season								Playoffs						
Season	Club	League	GP	W	L	O/T	Mins	GA	SO	Avg	GP	W	L	Mins	GA	SO	Avg
99-2000	Twin Cities	USHL	49	25	15	7	2848	129	0	2.72	13	7	6	797	43	0	3.24
2000-01	U. of Denver	WCHA	15	7	6	1	745	38	1	3.06	....	....	....	....	....	....	....
2001-02	U. of Denver	WCHA	18	12	4	1	1026	40	1	2.34	....	....	....	....	....	....	....
2002-03	U. of Denver	WCHA	26	12	6	4	1436	55	3	*2.30	....	....	....	....	....	....	....
2003-04	U. of Denver	WCHA	39	24	11	4	2225	91	*7	2.45	....	....	....	....	....	....	....
2004-05	Chicago Wolves	AHL	1	0	1	0	59	4	0	4.04	....	....	....	....	....	....	....
	Gwinnett	ECHL	24	9	10	5	1458	59	2	2.43	7	4	1	353	9	0	*1.53
2005-06	**Atlanta**	**NHL**	**9**	**2**	**4**	**1**	**473**	**30**	**0**	**3.81**	....	....	....	....	....	....	....
	Chicago Wolves	AHL	11	3	6	0	526	32	0	3.65	....	....	....	....	....	....	....
	Gwinnett	ECHL	15	10	4	1	902	41	1	2.73	9	6	3	551	30	0	3.27
	NHL Totals		**9**	**2**	**4**	**1**	**473**	**30**	**0**	**3.81**	....	....	....	....	....	....	....

USHL All-Rookie Team (2000) • USHL Second All-Star Team (2000) • NCAA Championship All-Tournament Team (2004) • NCAA Championship Tournament MVP (2004)

Traded to **Atlanta** by **Chicago** for Atlanta's 7th round choice (Adam Hobson) in 2005 Entry Draft, June 27, 2004.

BERNIER, Jonathan (BAIRN-yay, JAWN-ah-thun) L.A.

Goaltender. Catches left. 5'11", 177 lbs. Born, Laval, Que., August 7, 1988.
(Los Angeles' 1st choice, 11th overall, in 2006 Entry Draft).

			Regular Season								Playoffs						
Season	Club	League	GP	W	L	O/T	Mins	GA	SO	Avg	GP	W	L	Mins	GA	SO	Avg
2004-05	Lewiston	QMJHL	23	7	12	3	1353	67	0	2.97	1	0	0	20	0	0	0.00
2005-06	Lewiston	QMJHL	54	27	26	0	3241	146	2	2.70	6	2	4	359	17	1	2.84

BERRA, Reto (BAIR-ruh, REH-toh) ST.L.

Goaltender. Catches left. 6'4", 189 lbs. Born, Bulach, Switz., January 3, 1987.
(St. Louis' 6th choice, 106th overall, in 2006 Entry Draft).

			Regular Season								Playoffs						
Season	Club	League	GP	W	L	O/T	Mins	GA	SO	Avg	GP	W	L	Mins	GA	SO	Avg
2004-05	GCK Zurich Jr.	Swiss-Jr.	22	....	....	....	....	....	....	....	....	....	....	....	....	....	....
	GCK Lions Zurich	Swiss-2	3	....	....	....	180	12	0	4.00	....	....	....	....	....	....	....
	EHC Dubendorf	Swiss-3					STATISTICS NOT AVAILABLE										
2005-06	GCK Zurich Jr.	Swiss-Jr.	23	....	....	....	....	....	....	....	....	....	....	....	....	....	....
	GCK Lions Zurich	Swiss-2	15	....	....	....	835	51	1	3.56	....	....	....	....	....	....	....
	ZSC Lions Zurich	Swiss	2	0	1	0	90	6	0	3.99	....	....	....	....	....	....	....

BIRON, Martin (BIH-rohn, MAHR-tihn) BUF.

Goaltender. Catches left. 6'2", 170 lbs. Born, Lac-St-Charles, Que., August 15, 1977.
(Buffalo's 2nd choice, 16th overall, in 1995 Entry Draft).

			Regular Season								Playoffs						
Season	Club	League	GP	W	L	O/T	Mins	GA	SO	Avg	GP	W	L	Mins	GA	SO	Avg
1993-94	Trois-Rivieres	QAAA	23	14	8	1	1412	80	1	3.40	2	1	1	112	7	0	3.73
1994-95	Beauport Harfangs	QMJHL	56	29	16	9	3193	132	3	*2.48	16	8	7	900	37	*4	2.47
1995-96	Beauport Harfangs	QMJHL	55	29	17	7	3201	152	1	2.85	*19	*12	7	1134	64	0	3.39
	Buffalo	**NHL**	**3**	**0**	**2**	**0**	**119**	**10**	**0**	**5.04**	....	....	....	....	....	....	....
1996-97	Beauport Harfangs	QMJHL	18	6	9	1	928	61	1	3.94	....	....	....	....	....	....	....
	Hull Olympiques	QMJHL	16	11	4	1	974	43	2	2.65	6	3	1	325	19	0	3.51
1997-98	South Carolina	ECHL	2	0	1	1	86	3	0	2.09	....	....	....	....	....	....	....
	Rochester	AHL	41	14	18	6	2312	113	*5	2.93	4	1	3	239	16	0	4.01
1998-99	**Buffalo**	**NHL**	**6**	**1**	**2**	**1**	**281**	**10**	**0**	**2.14**	....	....	....	....	....	....	....
	Rochester	AHL	52	36	13	3	3129	108	*6	*2.07	*20	12	8	1167	42	1	*2.16
99-2000	**Buffalo**	**NHL**	**41**	**19**	**18**	**2**	**2229**	**90**	**5**	**2.42**	....	....	....	....	....	....	....
	Rochester	AHL	6	6	0	0	344	12	1	2.09	....	....	....	....	....	....	....
2000-01	**Buffalo**	**NHL**	**18**	**7**	**7**	**1**	**918**	**39**	**2**	**2.55**	....	....	....	....	....	....	....
	Rochester	AHL	4	3	1	0	239	4	1	1.00	....	....	....	....	....	....	....
2001-02	**Buffalo**	**NHL**	**72**	**31**	**28**	**10**	**4085**	**151**	**4**	**2.22**	....	....	....	....	....	....	....
2002-03	**Buffalo**	**NHL**	**54**	**17**	**28**	**6**	**3170**	**135**	**4**	**2.56**	....	....	....	....	....	....	....
2003-04	**Buffalo**	**NHL**	**52**	**26**	**18**	**5**	**2972**	**125**	**2**	**2.52**	....	....	....	....	....	....	....

2004-05							Did not play										
2005-06	Buffalo	NHL	35	21	8	3	1934	93	1	2.89	....	....	....	....	....	....	....
	NHL Totals		281	122	111	28	15708	653	18	2.49	....	....	....	....	....	....	....

QMJHL All-Rookie Team (1995) • Canadian Major Junior First All-Star Team (1995) • Canadian Major Junior Goaltender of the Year (1995) • AHL First All-Star Team (1999) • Harry "Hap" Holmes Memorial Award (fewest goals against – AHL) (1999) (shared with Tom Draper) • Aldege "Baz" Bastien Memorial Award (Outstanding Goaltender – AHL) (1999)

BISHOP, Ben (BIH-shuhp, BEHN) ST.L.

Goaltender. Catches left. 6'5", 205 lbs. Born, Denver, CO, November 21, 1986.
(St. Louis' 3rd choice, 85th overall, in 2005 Entry Draft).

			Regular Season								Playoffs						
Season	Club	League	GP	W	L	O/T	Mins	GA	SO	Avg	GP	W	L	Mins	GA	SO	Avg
2003-04	St.L. AAA Blues	MAHL	11	8	1	2	660	19	1	1.73	....	....	....	....	....	....	....
	St.L. AAA Blues	Exhib.	26	15	7	4	1480	62	3	2.51	....	....	....	....	....	....	....
2004-05	Texas Tornado	NAHL	45	*35	8	0	2577	83	5	1.93	*11	*9	2	*660	30	0	2.73
2005-06	University of Maine	H-East	31	21	8	2	1788	68	0	2.28	....	....	....	....	....	....	....

Hockey East All-Rookie Team (2006)

BJURLING, Bjorn (b-YUHR-lihng, b-YOHRN) EDM.

Goaltender. Catches left. 6', 205 lbs. Born, Stockholm, Sweden, August 21, 1979.
(Edmonton's 10th choice, 274th overall, in 2004 Entry Draft).

			Regular Season								Playoffs						
Season	Club	League	GP	W	L	O/T	Mins	GA	SO	Avg	GP	W	L	Mins	GA	SO	Avg
2000-01	Bodens IK	Sweden-2	32	....	....	....	1914	80	0	2.51	6	....	....	398	16	1	2.41
2001-02	Bodens IK	Sweden-2	43	....	....	....	2568	128	2	2.99	9	....	....	508	36	0	4.25
2002-03	Bodens IK	Sweden-2	3	....	....	....	179	7	1	2.35	....	....	....	....	....	....	....
	Djurgarden	Sweden	15	....	....	....	571	21	2	2.21	....	....	....	....	....	....	....
2003-04	Djurgarden	Sweden	45	....	....	....	2601	100	4	2.31	2	....	....	100	15	0	9.00
2004-05	Djurgarden	Sweden	24	....	....	....	1441	61	1	2.54	....	....	....	....	....	....	....
2005-06	Salzburg	Austria	23	....	....	....	1367	78	1	3.42	....	....	....	....	....	....	....
	Geneve	Swiss	7	2	2	2	430	24	1	3.35	....	....	....	....	....	....	....

BOUCHER, Brian (BOO-shay, BRIGH-uhn)

Goaltender. Catches left. 6'2", 198 lbs. Born, Woonsocket, RI, January 2, 1977.
(Philadelphia's 1st choice, 22nd overall, in 1995 Entry Draft).

			Regular Season								Playoffs						
Season	Club	League	GP	W	L	O/T	Mins	GA	SO	Avg	GP	W	L	Mins	GA	SO	Avg
1993-94	Mount St. Charles	High-RI	15	*14	0	1	*504	*8	*9	*0.57	4	*4	0	*180	*6	*1	*1.20
1994-95	Wexford Raiders	MTJHL	8	....	....	....	425	23	0	3.25	....	....	....	....	....	....	....
	Tri-City Americans	WHL	35	17	11	2	1969	108	1	3.29	13	6	5	795	50	0	3.77
1995-96	Tri-City Americans	WHL	55	33	19	2	3183	181	1	3.41	11	6	5	653	37	*2	3.40
1996-97	Tri-City Americans	WHL	41	10	24	6	2458	149	1	3.64	....	....	....	....	....	....	....
1997-98	Philadelphia	AHL	34	16	12	3	1901	101	0	3.19	2	0	0	30	1	0	1.95
1998-99	Philadelphia	AHL	36	20	8	5	2061	89	2	2.59	16	9	7	947	45	0	2.85
99-2000	**Philadelphia**	**NHL**	**35**	**20**	**10**	**3**	**2038**	**65**	**4**	***1.91**	**18**	**11**	**7**	**1183**	**40**	**1**	**2.03**
	Philadelphia	AHL	1	0	0	1	65	3	0	2.77	....	....	....	....	....	....	....
2000-01	**Philadelphia**	**NHL**	**27**	**8**	**12**	**5**	**1470**	**80**	**1**	**3.27**	**1**	**0**	**0**	**37**	**3**	**0**	**4.86**
2001-02	**Philadelphia**	**NHL**	**41**	**18**	**16**	**4**	**2295**	**92**	**2**	**2.41**	**2**	**0**	**1**	**88**	**2**	**0**	**1.36**
2002-03	**Phoenix**	**NHL**	**45**	**15**	**20**	**8**	**2544**	**128**	**0**	**3.02**	....	....	....	....	....	....	....
2003-04	**Phoenix**	**NHL**	**40**	**10**	**19**	**10**	**2364**	**108**	**5**	**2.74**	....	....	....	....	....	....	....
2004-05	HV 71 Jonkoping	Sweden	4	....	....	....	235	13	0	3.32	....	....	....	....	....	....	....
2005-06	**Phoenix**	**NHL**	**11**	**3**	**6**	**0**	**512**	**33**	**0**	**3.87**	....	....	....	....	....	....	....
	San Antonio	AHL	6	2	3	0	345	8	0	1.39	....	....	....	....	....	....	....
	Calgary	**NHL**	**3**	**1**	**2**	**0**	**182**	**15**	**0**	**4.95**	....	....	....	....	....	....	....
	NHL Totals		**202**	**75**	**85**	**30**	**11405**	**521**	**12**	**2.74**	**21**	**11**	**8**	**1308**	**45**	**1**	**2.06**

WHL West Second All-Star Team (1996) • WHL West First All-Star Team (1997) • WHL Goaltender of the Year (1997) • NHL All-Rookie Team (2000)

Traded to **Phoenix** by **Philadelphia** with Nashville's 3rd round choice (previously acquired, Phoenix selected Joe Callahan) in 2002 Entry Draft for Michal Handzus and Robert Esche, June 12, 2002. Signed as a free agent by **Jonkoping** (Sweden), October 20, 2004. Traded to **Calgary** by **Phoenix** with Mike Leclerc for Steve Reinprecht and Philippe Sauve, February 2, 2006.

BOUTHILLETTE, Gabriel (boo-tih-LEHT, ga-BREE-ehl)

Goaltender. Catches left. 6'3", 193 lbs. Born, Sorel, Que., May 21, 1985.
(Anaheim's 6th choice, 203rd overall, in 2004 Entry Draft).

			Regular Season								Playoffs						
Season	Club	League	GP	W	L	O/T	Mins	GA	SO	Avg	GP	W	L	Mins	GA	SO	Avg
2003-04	Gatineau	QMJHL	27	17	2	4	1529	56	3	*2.20	2	0	1	59	2	0	2.03
2004-05	Acadie-Bathurst	QMJHL	58	15	33	5	3179	169	5	3.19	....	....	....	....	....	....	....
2005-06	Acadie-Bathurst	QMJHL	57	34	20	0	3207	150	2	2.81	9	2	2	343	25	0	4.37

BOUTIN, Jonathan (boo-TEHN, JAWN-ah-thuhn) T.B.

Goaltender. Catches left. 6'2", 210 lbs. Born, Granby, Que., March 28, 1985.
(Tampa Bay's 3rd choice, 96th overall, in 2003 Entry Draft).

			Regular Season								Playoffs						
Season	Club	League	GP	W	L	O/T	Mins	GA	SO	Avg	GP	W	L	Mins	GA	SO	Avg
2001-02	Fort Saskatchewan	AJHL					Statistics not available										
	Halifax	QMJHL	11	4	1	1	459	18	0	2.35	2	0	0	15	0	0	0.00
2002-03	Halifax	QMJHL	47	22	11	2	2190	106	4	2.90	1	0	0	27	0	0	0.00
2003-04	PEI Rocket	QMJHL	30	13	12	2	1612	80	1	2.98	11	6	5	672	23	0	2.06
2004-05	PEI Rocket	QMJHL	32	15	14	2	1814	98	1	3.24	....	....	....	....	....	....	....
	Quebec Remparts	QMJHL	10	4	5	0	534	30	0	3.37	10	5	4	558	30	*1	3.22
2005-06	Johnstown Chiefs	ECHL	19	8	9	2	1145	56	2	2.93	3	1	2	170	10	0	3.53
	Springfield Falcons	AHL	22	8	12	2	1266	67	1	3.18	....	....	....	....	....	....	....

BRATHWAITE, Fred (BRAYTH-wayt, FREHD) ATL.

Goaltender. Catches left. 5'7", 175 lbs. Born, Ottawa, Ont., November 24, 1972.

			Regular Season								Playoffs						
Season	Club	League	GP	W	L	O/T	Mins	GA	SO	Avg	GP	W	L	Mins	GA	SO	Avg
1988-89	Smiths Falls Bears	CJHL	38	16	18	1	2130	187	0	5.27	....	....	....	....	....	....	....
1989-90	Orillia Terriers	OJHL-B	15	....	....	....	782	47	0	3.61	....	....	....	....	....	....	....
	Oshawa Generals	OHL	20	11	2	1	886	43	1	2.91	10	4	2	451	22	0	*2.93
1990-91	Oshawa Generals	OHL	39	25	6	3	1986	112	1	3.38	13	*9	2	677	43	0	3.81
1991-92	Oshawa Generals	OHL	24	12	7	2	1248	81	0	3.89	....	....	....	....	....	....	....
	London Knights	OHL	23	15	6	2	1325	61	*4	2.76	10	5	5	615	36	0	3.51
1992-93	Detroit	OHL	37	23	10	4	2192	134	0	3.67	15	9	6	858	48	1	3.36
1993-94	**Edmonton**	**NHL**	**19**	**3**	**10**	**3**	**982**	**58**	**0**	**3.54**	....	....	....	....	....	....	....
	Cape Breton Oilers	AHL	2	1	1	0	119	6	0	3.04	....	....	....	....	....	....	....
1994-95	**Edmonton**	**NHL**	**14**	**2**	**5**	**1**	**601**	**40**	**0**	**3.99**	....	....	....	....	....	....	....
1995-96	**Edmonton**	**NHL**	**7**	**0**	**2**	**0**	**293**	**12**	**0**	**2.46**	....	....	....	....	....	....	....
	Cape Breton Oilers	AHL	31	12	16	0	1699	110	1	3.88	....	....	....	....	....	....	....
1996-97	Manitoba Moose	IHL	58	22	22	5	2945	167	1	3.40	....	....	....	....	....	....	....
1997-98	Manitoba Moose	IHL	51	23	18	4	2736	138	1	3.03	2	0	1	72	4	0	3.30
1998-99	Canada	Nat-Tm	24	6	8	3	989	47	2	2.85	....	....	....	....	....	....	....
	Calgary	**NHL**	**28**	**11**	**9**	**7**	**1663**	**68**	**1**	**2.45**	....	....	....	....	....	....	....
99-2000	**Calgary**	**NHL**	**61**	**25**	**25**	**7**	**3448**	**158**	**5**	**2.75**	....	....	....	....	....	....	....
	Saint John Flames	AHL	2	2	0	0	120	4	0	2.00	....	....	....	....	....	....	....
2000-01	**Calgary**	**NHL**	**49**	**15**	**17**	**10**	**2742**	**106**	**5**	**2.32**	....	....	....	....	....	....	....
2001-02	**St. Louis**	**NHL**	**25**	**9**	**11**	**4**	**1446**	**54**	**2**	**2.24**	**1**	**0**	**0**	**1**	**0**	**0**	**0.00**
2002-03	**St. Louis**	**NHL**	**30**	**12**	**9**	**4**	**1615**	**74**	**2**	**2.75**	....	....	....	....	....	....	....
2003-04	**Columbus**	**NHL**	**21**	**4**	**11**	**1**	**1050**	**59**	**0**	**3.37**	....	....	....	....	....	....	....
	Syracuse Crunch	AHL	3	0	2	1	188	7	1	2.23	....	....	....	....	....	....	....
2004-05	Ak Bars Kazan	Russia	34	....	....	....	1958	61	9	1.87	2	....	....	128	2	1	0.94
2005-06	Ak Bars Kazan	Russia	32	....	....	....	1866	66	6	2.12	11	....	....	623	16	1	*1.54
	NHL Totals		**254**	**81**	**99**	**37**	**13840**	**629**	**15**	**2.73**	**1**	**0**	**0**	**1**	**0**	**0**	**0.00**

• Scored a goal while with Detroit (OHL), April 20, 1993. Signed as a free agent by **Edmonton**, October 6, 1993. • Scored a goal while with Manitoba (IHL), November 9, 1996. Signed as a free agent by **Calgary**, January 6, 1999. Traded to **St. Louis** by **Calgary** with Daniel Tkaczuk, Sergei Varlamov and Calgary's 9th round choice (Grant Jacobsen) in 2001 Entry Draft for Roman Turek and St. Louis' 4th round choice (Yegor Shastin) in 2001 Entry Draft, June 23, 2001. • Played 6 seconds of playoff game vs. Detroit, May 4, 2002. Signed as a free agent by **Columbus**, June 2, 2003. Signed as a free agent by **Kazan** (Russia), June 19, 2004. Signed as a free agent by **Atlanta**, July 4, 2006.

BRODEUR, Martin (broh-DUHR, MAHR-tihn) N.J.

Goaltender. Catches left. 6'2", 210 lbs. Born, Montreal, Que., May 6, 1972.
(New Jersey's 1st choice, 20th overall, in 1990 Entry Draft).

			Regular Season								Playoffs						
Season	Club	League	GP	W	L	O/T	Mins	GA	SO	Avg	GP	W	L	Mins	GA	SO	Avg
1988-89	Montreal-Bourassa	QAAA	27	13	12	1	1580	98	0	3.72	3	0	3	210	14	0	3.99
1989-90	St-Hyacinthe Laser	QMJHL	42	23	13	2	2333	156	0	4.01	12	5	7	678	46	0	4.07
1990-91	St-Hyacinthe Laser	QMJHL	52	22	24	4	2946	162	2	3.30	4	0	4	232	16	0	4.14
1991-92	St-Hyacinthe Laser	QMJHL	48	27	16	4	2846	161	2	3.39	5	2	3	317	14	0	2.65
	New Jersey	**NHL**	**4**	**2**	**1**	**0**	**179**	**10**	**0**	**3.35**	**1**	**0**	**1**	**32**	**3**	**0**	**5.63**
1992-93	Utica Devils	AHL	32	14	13	5	1952	131	0	4.03	4	1	3	258	18	0	4.19
1993-94	**New Jersey**	**NHL**	**47**	**27**	**11**	**8**	**2625**	**105**	**3**	**2.40**	**17**	**8**	**9**	**1171**	**38**	**1**	**1.95**
1994-95 ♦	**New Jersey**	**NHL**	**40**	**19**	**11**	**6**	**2184**	**89**	**3**	**2.45**	***20**	***16**	**4**	***1222**	**34**	***3**	***1.67**
1995-96	**New Jersey**	**NHL**	**77**	**34**	**30**	**12**	***4433**	**173**	**6**	**2.34**	....	....	....	....	....	....	....
1996-97	**New Jersey**	**NHL**	**67**	**37**	**14**	**13**	**3838**	**120**	***10**	***1.88**	**10**	**5**	**5**	**659**	**19**	**2**	***1.73**
1997-98	**New Jersey**	**NHL**	**70**	***43**	**17**	**8**	**4128**	**130**	**10**	**1.89**	**6**	**2**	**4**	**366**	**12**	**0**	**1.97**
1998-99	**New Jersey**	**NHL**	***70**	***39**	**21**	**10**	***4239**	**162**	**4**	**2.29**	**7**	**3**	**4**	**425**	**20**	**0**	**2.82**
99-2000 ♦	**New Jersey**	**NHL**	**72**	***43**	**20**	**8**	**4312**	**161**	**6**	**2.24**	***23**	***16**	**7**	***1450**	**39**	**2**	***1.61**
2000-01	**New Jersey**	**NHL**	**72**	***42**	**17**	**11**	**4297**	**166**	**9**	**2.32**	***25**	**15**	**10**	***1505**	**52**	***4**	**2.07**
2001-02	**New Jersey**	**NHL**	***73**	**38**	**26**	**9**	***4347**	**156**	**4**	**2.15**	**6**	**2**	**4**	**381**	**9**	**1**	**1.42**
	Canada	Olympics	5	*4	0	1	300	9	0	*1.80	....	....	....	....	....	....	....
2002-03 ♦	**New Jersey**	**NHL**	**73**	***41**	**23**	**9**	**4374**	**147**	***9**	**2.02**	***24**	***16**	**8**	***1491**	**41**	***7**	**1.65**
2003-04	**New Jersey**	**NHL**	***75**	***38**	**26**	**11**	***4555**	**154**	***11**	**2.03**	**5**	**1**	**4**	**298**	**13**	**0**	**2.62**
2004-05							Did not play										
2005-06	**New Jersey**	**NHL**	**73**	***43**	**23**	**7**	**4365**	**187**	**5**	**2.57**	**9**	**5**	**4**	**533**	**20**	**1**	**2.25**
	Canada	Olympics	4	2	2	0	239	8	0	2.01	....	....	....	....	....	....	....
	NHL Totals		**813**	**446**	**240**	**112**	**47876**	**1760**	**80**	**2.21**	**153**	**89**	**64**	**9533**	**300**	**21**	**1.89**

QMJHL All-Rookie Team (1990) • QMJHL Second All-Star Team (1992) • NHL All-Rookie Team (1994) • Calder Memorial Trophy (1994) • NHL Second All-Star Team (1997, 1998, 2006) • William M. Jennings Trophy (1997) (shared with Mike Dunham) • William M. Jennings Trophy (1998, 2004) • NHL First All-Star Team (2003, 2004) • William M. Jennings Trophy (2003) (tied with Roman Cechmanek/Robert Esche) • Vezina Trophy (2003, 2004)

Played in NHL All-Star Game (1996, 1997, 1998, 1999, 2000, 2001, 2003, 2004)

• Scored a goal in playoffs vs. Montreal, April 17, 1997.

BRODEUR, Mike (broh-DUHR, MIGHK) CHI.

Goaltender. Catches left. 6'2", 170 lbs. Born, Calgary, Alta., March 30, 1983.
(Chicago's 7th choice, 211th overall, in 2003 Entry Draft).

			Regular Season								Playoffs						
Season	Club	League	GP	W	L	O/T	Mins	GA	SO	Avg	GP	W	L	Mins	GA	SO	Avg
2000-01	Cgy. AAA Flames	AMHL	21	11	8	3	1231	54	1	2.63	10	6	4	620	31	0	3.00
2001-02	Camrose Kodiaks	AJHL	24	13	9	1	1299	65	1	2.91	....	....	....	....	....	....	....
2002-03	Camrose Kodiaks	AJHL	48	28	16	2	2570	113	2	2.64	21	16	5	1378	48	4	2.09
2003-04	Moose Jaw	WHL	41	23	12	5	2385	84	5	2.11	10	6	4	624	18	1	*1.73
2004-05	Norfolk Admirals	AHL	1	0	1	0	39	4	0	6.17	....	....	....	....	....	....	....
	Greenville Grrrowl	ECHL	35	19	15	1	2081	93	2	2.68	5	2	3	302	10	1	1.98
2005-06	Greenville Grrrowl	ECHL	24	14	8	2	1466	63	1	2.58	....	....	....	....	....	....	....

BROWN, David (BROWN, DAY-vihd) PIT.

Goaltender. Catches left. 6', 185 lbs. Born, Stoney Creek, Ont., February 11, 1985.
(Pittsburgh's 11th choice, 228th overall, in 2004 Entry Draft).

			Regular Season								Playoffs						
Season	Club	League	GP	W	L	O/T	Mins	GA	SO	Avg	GP	W	L	Mins	GA	SO	Avg
2002-03	Hamilton Kilty B's	OPJHL	35	....	....	....	....	....	....	3.11	....	....	....	....	....	....	....
2003-04	U. of Notre Dame	CCHA	26	14	7	3	1445	56	5	2.32	....	....	....	....	....	....	....
2004-05	U. of Notre Dame	CCHA	15	2	10	1	767	55	0	4.30	....	....	....	....	....	....	....
2005-06	U. of Notre Dame	CCHA	31	9	15	4	1724	71	0	2.47	....	....	....	....	....	....	....

BROWN, Mike (BROWN, MIGHK) BOS.

Goaltender. Catches left. 6', 203 lbs. Born, Syracuse, NY, March 4, 1985.
(Boston's 7th choice, 153rd overall, in 2003 Entry Draft).

			Regular Season								Playoffs						
Season	Club	League	GP	W	L	O/T	Mins	GA	SO	Avg	GP	W	L	Mins	GA	SO	Avg
2001-02	Baldwinsville Bees	High-NY	7	....	....	....	420	8	4	0.86	5	3	2	300	6	1	1.20
2002-03	Saginaw Spirit	OHL	39	8	23	3	2186	134	0	3.68	....	....	....	....	....	....	....
2003-04	Saginaw Spirit	OHL	51	14	32	3	2886	156	4	3.24	....	....	....	....	....	....	....
2004-05	Saginaw Spirit	OHL	26	7	17	1	1482	91	0	3.68	....	....	....	....	....	....	....
	Owen Sound	OHL	33	17	11	4	1956	81	3	2.48	8	4	4	485	19	*2	2.35
2005-06	Providence Bruins	AHL	2	0	0	0	42	2	0	2.87	....	....	....	....	....	....	....
	South Carolina	ECHL	3	0	1	2	188	15	0	4.79	....	....	....	....	....	....	....
	Dayton Bombers	ECHL	18	4	12	2	1050	64	0	3.66	....	....	....	....	....	....	....

BRUST, Barry (BRUHST, BAIR-ree) L.A.

Goaltender. Catches left. 6'2", 210 lbs. Born, Swan River, Man., August 8, 1983.
(Minnesota's 4th choice, 73rd overall, in 2002 Entry Draft).

			Regular Season								Playoffs						
Season	Club	League	GP	W	L	O/T	Mins	GA	SO	Avg	GP	W	L	Mins	GA	SO	Avg
99-2000	Swan Valley	MJHL	19	10	9	0	1140	67	0	3.50	....	....	....	....	....	....	....
2000-01	Spokane Chiefs	WHL	16	4	6	1	777	42	0	3.24	....	....	....	....	....	....	....
2001-02	Spokane Chiefs	WHL	60	28	21	10	3540	152	1	2.58	11	6	5	677	23	0	2.04
2002-03	Spokane Chiefs	WHL	*59	22	31	4	*3385	194	0	3.44	11	4	7	722	37	0	3.07
2003-04	Spokane Chiefs	WHL	27	10	13	2	1505	75	0	2.99	....	....	....	....	....	....	....
	Calgary Hitmen	WHL	25	12	8	3	1448	54	2	2.24	7	3	4	457	15	2	1.97
2004-05	Reading Royals	ECHL	42	27	9	4	2413	79	4	1.96	8	4	4	481	14	2	1.74
2005-06	Manchester	AHL	35	19	14	1	1971	89	2	2.71	5	2	2	279	17	1	3.66
	Reading Royals	ECHL	6	3	3	0	361	18	0	3.00	....	....	....	....	....	....	....

WHL West First All-Star Team (2002)

Signed as a free agent by **Los Angeles**, June 10, 2004.

BRYZGALOV, Ilya (breez-GAH-lahf, ihl-YUH) ANA.

Goaltender. Catches left. 6'3", 198 lbs. Born, Togliatti, USSR, June 22, 1980.
(Anaheim's 2nd choice, 44th overall, in 2000 Entry Draft).

			Regular Season								Playoffs						
Season	Club	League	GP	W	L	O/T	Mins	GA	SO	Avg	GP	W	L	Mins	GA	SO	Avg
1997-98	Lada Togliatti 2	Russia-3	8	....	....	....	480	28	....	3.50	....	....	....	....	....	....	....
1998-99	Lada Togliatti 2	Russia-4	20	....	....	....	1200	43	....	2.15	....	....	....	....	....	....	....
99-2000	Spartak Moscow	Russia-2	9	....	....	....	500	21	....	2.52	....	....	....	....	....	....	....
	Lada Togliatti	Russia	14	....	....	....	796	18	3	1.36	7	....	....	407	10	1	1.47
2000-01	Lada Togliatti	Russia	34	....	....	....	1992	61	*8	1.84	5	....	....	249	8	0	1.93
2001-02	**Anaheim**	**NHL**	**1**	**0**	**0**	**0**	**32**	**1**	**0**	**1.88**	....	....	....	....	....	....	....
	Russia	Olympics					DID NOT PLAY – SPARE GOALTENDER										
	Cincinnati	AHL	45	20	16	4	2399	99	4	2.48	....	....	....	....	....	....	....
2002-03	Cincinnati	AHL	54	12	26	9	3020	142	1	2.82	....	....	....	....	....	....	....
2003-04	**Anaheim**	**NHL**	**1**	**1**	**0**	**0**	**60**	**2**	**0**	**2.00**	....	....	....	....	....	....	....
	Cincinnati	AHL	*64	27	25	10	*3748	145	6	2.32	9	5	4	536	27	1	3.02
2004-05	Cincinnati	AHL	36	17	13	1	2007	87	4	2.60	7	3	3	314	13	0	2.48
2005-06	**Anaheim**	**NHL**	**31**	**13**	**12**	**1**	**1575**	**66**	**1**	**2.51**	**11**	**6**	**4**	**659**	**16**	***3**	***1.46**
	Russia	Olympics	1	0	1	0	60	5	0	5.00	....	....	....	....	....	....	....
	NHL Totals		**33**	**14**	**12**	**1**	**1667**	**69**	**1**	**2.48**	**11**	**6**	**4**	**659**	**16**	**3**	**1.46**

BUDAJ, Peter (BOO-digh, PEE-tuhr) COL.

Goaltender. Catches left. 6'1", 200 lbs. Born, Banska Bystrica, Czech., September 18, 1982.
(Colorado's 1st choice, 63rd overall, in 2001 Entry Draft).

			Regular Season								Playoffs						
Season	Club	League	GP	W	L	O/T	Mins	GA	SO	Avg	GP	W	L	Mins	GA	SO	Avg
99-2000	St. Michael's	OHL	34	6	18	1	1676	112	1	4.01	....	....	....	....	....	....	....
2000-01	St. Michael's	OHL	37	17	12	3	1996	95	3	2.86	11	6	4	621	26	1	2.51
2001-02	St. Michael's	OHL	42	26	9	5	2329	89	2	*2.29	12	5	6	620	34	*1	3.29
2002-03	Hershey Bears	AHL	28	10	10	2	1467	65	2	2.66	1	0	0	6	2	0	20.81
2003-04	Hershey Bears	AHL	46	17	20	6	2574	120	3	2.80	....	....	....	....	....	....	....
2004-05	Hershey Bears	AHL	59	29	25	2	3356	148	5	2.65	....	....	....	....	....	....	....
2005-06	**Colorado**	**NHL**	**34**	**14**	**10**	**6**	**1803**	**86**	**2**	**2.86**	....	....	....	....	....	....	....
	Slovakia	Olympics	3	2	1	0	179	6	0	2.01	....	....	....	....	....	....	....
	NHL Totals		**34**	**14**	**10**	**6**	**1803**	**86**	**2**	**2.86**	....	....	....	....	....	....	....

OHL Second All-Star Team (2002)

BURKE, Sean (BUHRK, SHAWN) T.B.

Goaltender. Catches left. 6'4", 211 lbs. Born, Windsor, Ont., January 29, 1967.
(New Jersey's 2nd choice, 24th overall, in 1985 Entry Draft).

			Regular Season								Playoffs						
Season	Club	League	GP	W	L	O/T	Mins	GA	SO	Avg	GP	W	L	Mins	GA	SO	Avg
1983-84	St. Mike's B's	MTJHL	25	....	....	....	1482	120	0	4.86	....	....	....	....	....	....	....
1984-85	Toronto Marlboros	OHL	49	25	21	3	2987	211	0	4.24	5	1	3	266	25	0	5.64
1985-86	Toronto Marlboros	OHL	47	16	27	3	2840	233	0	4.92	4	0	4	238	24	0	6.05
1986-87	Canada	Nat-Tm	42	27	13	2	2550	130	0	3.05	....	....	....	....	....	....	....
1987-88	Canada	Nat-Tm	37	19	9	2	1962	92	1	2.81	....	....	....	....	....	....	....
	Canada	Olympics	4	1	2	1	238	12	0	3.02	....	....	....	....	....	....	....
	New Jersey	**NHL**	**13**	**10**	**1**	**0**	**689**	**35**	**1**	**3.05**	**17**	**9**	**8**	**1001**	**57**	***1**	**3.42**
1988-89	**New Jersey**	**NHL**	**62**	**22**	**31**	**9**	**3590**	**230**	**3**	**3.84**	....	....	....	....	....	....	....
1989-90	**New Jersey**	**NHL**	**52**	**22**	**22**	**6**	**2914**	**175**	**0**	**3.60**	**2**	**0**	**2**	**125**	**8**	**0**	**3.84**
1990-91	**New Jersey**	**NHL**	**35**	**8**	**12**	**8**	**1870**	**112**	**0**	**3.59**	....	....	....	....	....	....	....
1991-92	Canada	Nat-Tm	31	18	6	4	1721	75	1	2.61	....	....	....	....	....	....	....
	Canada	Olympics	7	5	2	0	429	17	0	2.37	....	....	....	....	....	....	....
	San Diego Gulls	IHL	7	4	2	1	424	17	0	2.41	3	0	3	160	13	0	4.88
1992-93	**Hartford**	**NHL**	**50**	**16**	**27**	**3**	**2656**	**184**	**0**	**4.16**	....	....	....	....	....	....	....
1993-94	**Hartford**	**NHL**	**47**	**17**	**24**	**5**	**2750**	**137**	**2**	**2.99**	....	....	....	....	....	....	....
1994-95	**Hartford**	**NHL**	**42**	**17**	**19**	**4**	**2418**	**108**	**0**	**2.68**	....	....	....	....	....	....	....
1995-96	**Hartford**	**NHL**	**66**	**28**	**28**	**6**	**3669**	**190**	**4**	**3.11**	....	....	....	....	....	....	....
1996-97	**Hartford**	**NHL**	**51**	**22**	**22**	**6**	**2985**	**134**	**4**	**2.69**	....	....	....	....	....	....	....
1997-98	**Carolina**	**NHL**	**25**	**7**	**11**	**5**	**1415**	**66**	**1**	**2.80**	....	....	....	....	....	....	....
	Vancouver	**NHL**	**16**	**2**	**9**	**4**	**838**	**49**	**0**	**3.51**	....	....	....	....	....	....	....
	Philadelphia	**NHL**	**11**	**7**	**3**	**0**	**632**	**27**	**1**	**2.56**	**5**	**1**	**4**	**283**	**17**	**0**	**3.60**
1998-99	**Florida**	**NHL**	**59**	**21**	**24**	**14**	**3402**	**151**	**3**	**2.66**	....	....	....	....	....	....	....
99-2000	**Florida**	**NHL**	**7**	**2**	**5**	**0**	**418**	**18**	**0**	**2.58**	....	....	....	....	....	....	....
	Phoenix	**NHL**	**35**	**17**	**14**	**3**	**2074**	**88**	**3**	**2.55**	**5**	**1**	**4**	**296**	**16**	**0**	**3.24**
2000-01	**Phoenix**	**NHL**	**62**	**25**	**22**	**13**	**3644**	**138**	**4**	**2.27**	....	....	....	....	....	....	....
2001-02	**Phoenix**	**NHL**	**60**	**33**	**21**	**6**	**3587**	**137**	**5**	**2.29**	**5**	**1**	**4**	**297**	**13**	**0**	**2.63**
2002-03	**Phoenix**	**NHL**	**22**	**12**	**6**	**2**	**1248**	**44**	**2**	**2.12**	....	....	....	....	....	....	....
2003-04	**Phoenix**	**NHL**	**32**	**10**	**15**	**5**	**1795**	**84**	**1**	**2.81**	....	....	....	....	....	....	....
	Philadelphia	**NHL**	**15**	**6**	**5**	**2**	**825**	**35**	**1**	**2.55**	**1**	**0**	**0**	**40**	**1**	**0**	**1.50**
2004-05							DID NOT PLAY										
2005-06	**Tampa Bay**	**NHL**	**35**	**14**	**10**	**4**	**1713**	**80**	**2**	**2.80**	**3**	**0**	**1**	**109**	**7**	**0**	**3.85**
	NHL Totals		**797**	**318**	**331**	**105**	**45132**	**2222**	**37**	**2.95**	**38**	**12**	**23**	**2151**	**119**	**1**	**3.32**

Played in NHL All-Star Game (1989, 2001, 2002)

Traded to **Hartford** by **New Jersey** with Eric Weinrich for Bobby Holik and Hartford's 2nd round choice (Jay Pandolfo) in 1993 Entry Draft, August 28, 1992. Transferred to **Carolina** after **Hartford** franchise relocated, June 25, 1997. Traded to **Vancouver** by **Carolina** with Geoff Sanderson and Enrico Ciccone for Kirk McLean and Martin Gelinas, January 3, 1998. Traded to **Philadelphia** by **Vancouver** for Garth Snow, March 4, 1998. Signed as a free agent by **Florida**, September 12, 1998. Traded to **Phoenix** by **Florida** with Florida's 5th round choice (Nate Kiser) in 2000 Entry Draft for Mikhail Shtalenkov and Phoenix's 4th round choice (Chris Eade) in 2000 Entry Draft, November 18, 1999. Traded to **Philadelphia** by **Phoenix** with Branko Radivojevic and Ben Eager for Mike Comrie, February 9, 2004. Signed as a free agent by **Tampa Bay**, August 9, 2005.

CARON, Sebastian (KAIR-aw, suh-BAS-tee-yeh) CHI.

Goaltender. Catches left. 6'1", 170 lbs. Born, Amqui, Que., June 25, 1980.
(Pittsburgh's 4th choice, 86th overall, in 1999 Entry Draft).

			Regular Season								Playoffs						
Season	Club	League	GP	W	L	O/T	Mins	GA	SO	Avg	GP	W	L	Mins	GA	SO	Avg
1997-98	TGV Pentagone	QAHA	17	....	....	....	762	48	1	2.84	....	....	....	....	....	....	....
1998-99	Rimouski Oceanic	QMJHL	30	13	10	3	1570	85	0	3.25	2	1	0	68	0	0	0.00
99-2000	Rimouski Oceanic	QMJHL	54	*38	11	3	3040	179	1	3.53	14	*12	2	828	50	0	3.62
2000-01	Wilkes-Barre	AHL	30	12	14	3	1746	103	4	3.54	....	....	....	....	....	....	....
2001-02	Wilkes-Barre	AHL	46	14	22	8	2671	139	1	3.12	....	....	....	....	....	....	....
2002-03	**Pittsburgh**	**NHL**	**24**	**7**	**14**	**2**	**1408**	**62**	**2**	**2.64**	....	....	....	....	....	....	....
	Wilkes-Barre	AHL	27	12	14	1	1561	81	1	3.11	....	....	....	....	....	....	....
2003-04	**Pittsburgh**	**NHL**	**40**	**9**	**24**	**5**	**2213**	**138**	**1**	**3.74**	....	....	....	....	....	....	....
	Wilkes-Barre	AHL	14	7	3	4	811	26	2	1.92	7	3	4	395	23	0	3.50
2004-05	Saguenay Fjord	QNAHL					STATISTICS NOT AVAILABLE										
2005-06	**Pittsburgh**	**NHL**	**26**	**8**	**9**	**5**	**1312**	**87**	**1**	**3.98**	....	....	....	....	....	....	....
	Wilkes-Barre	AHL	6	3	3	0	357	7	2	1.18	....	....	....	....	....	....	....
	NHL Totals		**90**	**24**	**47**	**12**	**4933**	**287**	**4**	**3.49**	....	....	....	....	....	....	....

Memorial Cup Tournament All-Star Team (2000) • Hap Emms Memorial Trophy (Memorial Cup Tournament Top Goaltender) (2000) • NHL All-Rookie Team (2003)

Signed as a free agent by **Saguenay** (QNAHL), September 21, 2004. Signed as a free agent by **Chicago**, August 8, 2006.

CARUSO, David (kah-ROO-soh, DAY-vihd) ATL.

Goaltender. Catches left. 6'1", 210 lbs. Born, Roswell, GA, June 18, 1982.

			Regular Season								Playoffs						
Season	Club	League	GP	W	L	O/T	Mins	GA	SO	Avg	GP	W	L	Mins	GA	SO	Avg
2002-03	Ohio State	CCHA	8	5	2	0	460	12	2	1.56	....	....	....	....	....	....	....
2003-04	Ohio State	CCHA	14	9	3	0	762	25	2	*1.97	....	....	....	....	....	....	....
2004-05	Ohio State	CCHA	38	25	9	4	2272	81	2	2.14	....	....	....	....	....	....	....
2005-06	Ohio State	CCHA	36	13	18	5	2146	77	*5	2.15	....	....	....	....	....	....	....

Signed as a free agent by **Atlanta**, July 6, 2006.

CASSIVI, Frederic (KASS-ih-vee, FREHD-uhr-ihk) WSH.

Goaltender. Catches left. 6'4", 220 lbs. Born, Sorel, Que., June 12, 1975.
(Ottawa's 7th choice, 210th overall, in 1994 Entry Draft).

			Regular Season								Playoffs						
Season	Club	League	GP	W	L	O/T	Mins	GA	SO	Avg	GP	W	L	Mins	GA	SO	Avg
1991-92	Abitibi Forestiers	QAAA	22	5	17	0	1320	106	0	4.84	3	1	2	180	15	0	5.06
1992-93							STATISTICS NOT AVAILABLE										
1993-94	St-Hyacinthe Laser	QMJHL	35	15	13	3	1751	127	1	4.35	....	....	....	....	....	....	....
1994-95	Halifax	QMJHL	24	9	12	1	1362	105	0	4.63	....	....	....	....	....	....	....
	St-Jean Lynx	QMJHL	19	12	6	0	1021	55	1	3.23	5	2	3	258	18	0	4.19
1995-96	Thunder Bay	ColHL	12	6	4	2	715	51	0	4.28	....	....	....	....	....	....	....
	P.E.I. Senators	AHL	41	20	14	3	2347	128	1	3.27	5	2	3	317	24	0	4.54
1996-97	Syracuse Crunch	AHL	55	23	22	8	3069	164	2	3.21	1	0	1	60	3	0	3.01
1997-98	Worcester IceCats	AHL	45	20	22	2	2593	140	1	3.24	6	3	3	326	18	0	3.31
1998-99	Cincinnati	IHL	44	21	17	2	2418	123	1	3.05	3	1	2	139	6	0	2.59
99-2000	Hershey Bears	AHL	31	14	9	3	1554	78	1	3.01	2	0	1	63	5	0	4.75
2000-01	Hershey Bears	AHL	49	17	24	3	2620	124	2	2.84	9	7	2	564	14	1	*1.49
2001-02	Hershey Bears	AHL	21	6	10	4	1201	50	0	2.50	....	....	....	....	....	....	....
	Atlanta	**NHL**	**6**	**2**	**3**	**0**	**307**	**17**	**0**	**3.32**	....	....	....	....	....	....	....
	Chicago Wolves	AHL	12	6	2	1	625	26	0	2.50	5	2	2	264	11	0	2.50
2002-03	**Atlanta**	**NHL**	**2**	**1**	**1**	**0**	**123**	**11**	**0**	**5.37**	....	....	....	....	....	....	....
	Chicago Wolves	AHL	21	10	8	1	1171	62	0	3.18	2	0	2	90	3	0	2.00
2003-04	Chicago Wolves	AHL	34	15	12	5	1911	82	1	2.57	....	....	....	....	....	....	....
2004-05	Cincinnati	AHL	46	25	18	2	2549	88	*10	2.07	8	2	4	444	21	0	2.84
2005-06	**Washington**	**NHL**	**1**	**0**	**1**	**0**	**59**	**4**	**0**	**4.07**	....	....	....	....	....	....	....
	Hershey Bears	AHL	*61	*34	19	6	*3538	153	3	2.59	*21	*16	5	*1316	46	*4	2.10
	NHL Totals		**9**	**3**	**5**	**0**	**489**	**32**	**0**	**3.93**	....	....	....	....	....	....	....

Jack A. Butterfield Trophy (Playoff MVP - AHL) (2006)

Signed as a free agent by **Colorado**, August 17, 1999. Traded to **Atlanta** by **Colorado** for Brett Clark, January 24, 2002. Signed as a free agent by **Cincinnati** (AHL), September 28, 2004. Signed as a free agent by **Washington**, August 11, 2005.

CEY, Morgan (SAY, MOHR-guhn) T.B.

Goaltender. Catches left. 6'3", 177 lbs. Born, Wilkie, Sask., October 27, 1981.

			Regular Season								Playoffs						
Season	Club	League	GP	W	L	O/T	Mins	GA	SO	Avg	GP	W	L	Mins	GA	SO	Avg
2000-01	Flin Flon Bombers	SJHL	53	*35	16	0	*3139	137	3	2.62	....	....	....	....	....	....	....
2001-02	U. of Notre Dame	CCHA	35	15	14	3	2027	92	2	2.72	....	....	....	....	....	....	....
2002-03	U. of Notre Dame	CCHA	36	15	15	6	2136	102	2	2.87	....	....	....	....	....	....	....
2003-04	U. of Notre Dame	CCHA	16	5	7	1	820	33	2	2.42	....	....	....	....	....	....	....
2004-05	U. of Notre Dame	CCHA	27	3	17	5	1483	74	0	2.99	....	....	....	....	....	....	....
2005-06	Johnstown Chiefs	ECHL	35	17	9	7	2032	93	3	2.75	3	1	1	134	6	0	2.68
	Springfield Falcons	AHL	2	1	0	0	100	4	1	2.40	....	....	....	....	....	....	....

Signed as a free agent by **Tampa Bay**, August 26, 2005.

CHARPENTIER, Sebastien (shahr-PUHNT-yay, suh-BAS-tee-yeh)

Goaltender. Catches left. 5'9", 177 lbs. Born, Drummondville, Que., April 18, 1977.
(Washington's 4th choice, 93rd overall, in 1995 Entry Draft).

			Regular Season								Playoffs						
Season	Club	League	GP	W	L	O/T	Mins	GA	SO	Avg	GP	W	L	Mins	GA	SO	Avg
1991-92	Drummondville	QAHA	14	....	....	....	840	34	2	2.42	....	....	....	....	....	....	....
1992-93	Drummondville	QAHA	20	....	....	....	1215	37	*7	*1.80	....	....	....	....	....	....	....
1993-94	Magog	QAAA	24	14	5	1	1443	75	1	3.16	....	....	....	....	....	....	....
1994-95	Laval Titan	QMJHL	41	25	12	1	2152	99	2	2.76	16	9	4	886	45	0	3.05
1995-96	Laval Titan	QMJHL	18	4	10	0	938	97	0	6.20	....	....	....	....	....	....	....
	Val-d'Or Foreurs	QMJHL	33	21	9	1	1906	87	1	2.74	13	7	5	740	45	0	3.64
1996-97	Shawinigan	QMJHL	*62	*37	17	4	*3480	177	1	3.05	4	2	1	196	13	0	3.98
1997-98	Portland Pirates	AHL	4	1	3	0	229	10	0	2.61	....	....	....	....	....	....	....
	Hampton Roads	ECHL	43	20	16	6	2388	114	0	2.86	18	*14	4	*1183	38	1	*1.93
1998-99	Quad City Mallards	UHL	6	0	0	0	4	0	0	0.00	....	....	....	....	....	....	....
	Portland Pirates	AHL	3	0	3	0	180	10	0	3.34	....	....	....	....	....	....	....
99-2000	Portland Pirates	AHL	18	10	4	3	1041	48	0	2.77	3	1	1	183	9	0	2.96
2000-01	Portland Pirates	AHL	34	16	16	1	1978	113	1	3.43	1	0	1	102	3	0	1.76
2001-02	**Washington**	**NHL**	**2**	**1**	**1**	**0**	**122**	**5**	**0**	**2.46**	....	....	....	....	....	....	....
	Portland Pirates	AHL	49	20	18	10	2941	131	3	2.67	....	....	....	....	....	....	....
2002-03	**Washington**	**NHL**	**17**	**5**	**7**	**1**	**859**	**40**	**0**	**2.79**	....	....	....	....	....	....	....
	Portland Pirates	AHL	12	3	7	2	727	28	2	2.31	....	....	....	....	....	....	....
2003-04	**Washington**	**NHL**	**7**	**0**	**6**	**0**	**369**	**21**	**0**	**3.41**	....	....	....	....	....	....	....
2004-05							DID NOT PLAY										
2005-06	MVD	Russia	38	....	....	....	2155	86	1	2.39	4	....	....	234	16	0	4.10
	NHL Totals		**26**	**6**	**14**	**1**	**1350**	**66**	**0**	**2.93**	....	....	....	....	....	....	....

ECHL Playoff MVP (1998)

• Missed majority of 2003-04 season recovering from leg injury suffered in practice, November 3, 2003.

CHEVERIE, Marc (she-VEH-ree, MAHRK) FLA.

Goaltender. Catches left. 6'3", 183 lbs. Born, Cole Harbour, N.S., February 22, 1987.
(Florida's 6th choice, 193rd overall, in 2006 Entry Draft).

			Regular Season								Playoffs						
Season	Club	League	GP	W	L	O/T	Mins	GA	SO	Avg	GP	W	L	Mins	GA	SO	Avg
2002-03	Dartmouth	NSMHL	....	....	....	....	1105	46	....	2.50	....	....	....	....	....	....	....
2003-04	Dartmouth	NSMHL	....	....	....	....	1521	76	1	2.99	....	....	....	....	....	....	....
2004-05	Notre Dame	SMHL	25	....	....	....	....	....	....	2.25	....	....	....	....	....	....	....
2005-06	Nanaimo Clippers	BCHL	46	23	9	....	2032	86	4	2.54	....	....	....	....	....	....	....

Signed Letter of Intent to attend **U. of Denver** (WCHA), November 8, 2005.

CHIODO, Andy (KEE-aw-doh, AN-dee)

Goaltender. Catches left. 5'11", 192 lbs. Born, Toronto, Ont., April 25, 1983.
(Pittsburgh's 8th choice, 199th overall, in 2003 Entry Draft).

			Regular Season								Playoffs						
Season	Club	League	GP	W	L	O/T	Mins	GA	SO	Avg	GP	W	L	Mins	GA	SO	Avg
1998-99	Wexford Raiders	OPJHL	26	....	....	....	1519	105	0	4.05	....	....	....	....	....	....	....
99-2000	Wexford Raiders	OPJHL	24	....	....	....	1389	89	0	3.84	....	....	....	....	....	....	....
2000-01	St. Michael's	OHL	38	18	12	5	2069	86	*4	2.49	9	2	6	479	30	0	3.76
2001-02	St. Michael's	OHL	33	14	10	3	1743	79	2	2.72	7	3	1	288	17	*1	3.54
2002-03	St. Michael's	OHL	57	26	18	6	3065	154	3	3.01	18	10	8	1021	56	1	3.29
2003-04	**Pittsburgh**	**NHL**	**8**	**3**	**4**	**1**	**486**	**28**	**0**	**3.46**	....	....	....	....	....	....	....
	Wilkes-Barre	AHL	44	18	19	2	2448	98	4	2.40	18	9	7	1048	38	*3	2.18
	Wheeling Nailers	ECHL	2	0	2	0	86	9	0	6.26	....	....	....	....	....	....	....

2004-05	Wilkes-Barre	AHL	14	5	7	1	788	43	2	3.27	9	5	4	556	23	1	2.48
	Wheeling Nailers	ECHL	22	9	10	2	1259	47	1	2.24	....	....	....	....	....	....	....
2005-06	Wheeling Nailers	ECHL	17	10	5	1	950	45	1	2.84	....	....	....	....	....	....	....
	Wilkes-Barre	AHL	14	8	4	2	840	31	1	2.21	....	....	....	....	....	....	....
	NHL Totals		**8**	**3**	**4**	**1**	**486**	**28**	**0**	**3.46**	....	....	....	....	....	....	....

• Re-entered NHL Entry Draft. Originally NY Islanders' 3rd choice, 166th overall, in 2001 Entry Draft.

OHL First All-Star Team (2003)

CHOUINARD, Mathieu (SHWEE-nuhr, MA-tyew)

Goaltender. Catches left. 6'1", 211 lbs. Born, Laval, Que., April 11, 1980.
(Ottawa's 2nd choice, 45th overall, in 2000 Entry Draft).

			Regular Season								Playoffs						
Season	Club	League	GP	W	L	O/T	Mins	GA	SO	Avg	GP	W	L	Mins	GA	SO	Avg
1995-96	Amos Forestiers	QAAA	31	14	14	1	1613	114	1	4.24	3	1	2	190	11	0	3.48
1996-97	Shawinigan	QMJHL	17	4	7	1	795	51	0	3.85	4	1	3	264	15	0	3.41
1997-98	Shawinigan	QMJHL	55	*32	18	3	3055	142	2	2.79	6	2	4	348	24	0	4.14
1998-99	Shawinigan	QMJHL	56	36	16	4	3288	150	*5	2.74	6	2	4	392	27	0	4.13
99-2000	Shawinigan	QMJHL	*59	32	20	5	*3339	186	4	3.34	13	7	6	769	41	0	3.20
2000-01	Grand Rapids	IHL	28	17	7	1	1567	69	1	2.64	3	1	1	135	4	0	1.78
2001-02	Grand Rapids	AHL	25	11	12	1	1404	58	2	2.48	....	....	....	....	....	....	....
2002-03	Peoria Rivermen	ECHL	15	12	2	0	820	29	3	2.12	....	....	....	....	....	....	....
	Binghamton	AHL	4	2	0	0	152	5	0	1.98	1	0	0	2	0	0	0.00
2003-04	**Los Angeles**	**NHL**	**1**	**0**	**0**	**0**	**3**	**0**	**0**	**0.00**	....	....	....	....	....	....	....
	Manchester	AHL	22	10	6	0	1093	41	4	2.25	....	....	....	....	....	....	....
	Reading Royals	ECHL	3	1	1	1	185	7	0	2.27	....	....	....	....	....	....	....
2004-05	Cincinnati	AHL	3	1	1	0	153	4	1	1.57	....	....	....	....	....	....	....
	San Diego Gulls	ECHL	27	11	9	3	1453	73	1	3.01	....	....	....	....	....	....	....
	Peoria Rivermen	ECHL	1	0	1	0	58	2	0	2.07	....	....	....	....	....	....	....
2005-06	Phoenix	ECHL	13	4	6	0	647	37	0	3.43	....	....	....	....	....	....	....
	NHL Totals		**1**	**0**	**0**	**0**	**3**	**0**	**0**	**0.00**	....	....	....	....	....	....	....

• Re-entered NHL Entry Draft. Originally Ottawa's 1st choice, 15th overall, in 1998 Entry Draft.

QMJHL First All-Star Team (1999) • Harry "Hap" Holmes Memorial Award (fewest goals against – AHL) (2002) (shared with Martin Prusek and Simon Lajeunesse)

Signed as a free agent by **Los Angeles**, July 7, 2003. Signed as a free agent by **San Diego** (ECHL), September 29, 2004. Signed as a free agent by **Peoria** (ECHL), March 27, 2005.

CHURCHILL, Jason (CHUHR-chihl, JAY-suhn)

Goaltender. Catches left. 6'3", 184 lbs. Born, St. John's, Nfld., November 5, 1985.
(San Jose's 4th choice, 129th overall, in 2004 Entry Draft).

			Regular Season								Playoffs						
Season	Club	League	GP	W	L	O/T	Mins	GA	SO	Avg	GP	W	L	Mins	GA	SO	Avg
2002-03	Antigonish	MJrHL	36	16	18	1	2050	137	1	4.01	....	....	....	....	....	....	....
	Halifax	QMJHL	4	1	0	1	160	9	0	3.39	....	....	....	....	....	....	....
2003-04	Halifax	QMJHL	53	15	28	4	2894	180	2	3.73	....	....	....	....	....	....	....
2004-05	Halifax	QMJHL	54	28	18	8	3129	135	4	2.59	2	0	1	99	9	0	5.45
2005-06	Saint John	QMJHL	*63	14	44	0	3449	239	1	4.16	....	....	....	....	....	....	....

CLEMMENSEN, Scott (KLEH-mehn-sehn, SKAWT) N.J.

Goaltender. Catches left. 6'3", 205 lbs. Born, Des Moines, IA, July 23, 1977.
(New Jersey's 7th choice, 215th overall, in 1997 Entry Draft).

			Regular Season								Playoffs						
Season	Club	League	GP	W	L	O/T	Mins	GA	SO	Avg	GP	W	L	Mins	GA	SO	Avg
1995-96	Dubuque	USHL	20	10	7	1	1082	62	0	3.44	....	....	....	....	....	....	....
1996-97	Des Moines	USHL	36	22	9	2	2042	111	1	3.26	4	1	2	200	9	1	2.70
1997-98	Boston College	H-East	37	24	9	4	2205	102	*4	2.78	....	....	....	....	....	....	....
1998-99	Boston College	H-East	*42	26	12	4	*2507	120	1	2.87	....	....	....	....	....	....	....
99-2000	Boston College	H-East	29	19	7	0	1610	59	*5	2.20	....	....	....	....	....	....	....
2000-01	Boston College	H-East	*39	*30	7	2	*2312	82	3	2.13	....	....	....	....	....	....	....
2001-02	**New Jersey**	**NHL**	**2**	**0**	**0**	**0**	**20**	**1**	**0**	**3.00**	....	....	....	....	....	....	....
	Albany River Rats	AHL	29	5	19	4	1677	92	0	3.29	....	....	....	....	....	....	....
2002-03	Albany River Rats	AHL	47	12	24	8	2694	119	1	2.65	....	....	....	....	....	....	....
2003-04	**New Jersey**	**NHL**	**4**	**3**	**1**	**0**	**238**	**4**	**2**	**1.01**	....	....	....	....	....	....	....
	Albany River Rats	AHL	22	5	12	4	1309	67	0	3.07	....	....	....	....	....	....	....
2004-05	Albany River Rats	AHL	46	13	25	5	2645	124	2	2.81	....	....	....	....	....	....	....
2005-06	**New Jersey**	**NHL**	**13**	**3**	**4**	**2**	**627**	**35**	**0**	**3.35**	**1**	**0**	**0**	**7**	**0**	**0**	**0.00**
	Albany River Rats	AHL	1	0	1	0	59	5	0	5.05	....	....	....	....	....	....	....
	NHL Totals		**19**	**6**	**5**	**2**	**885**	**40**	**2**	**2.71**	**1**	**0**	**0**	**7**	**0**	**0**	**0.00**

NCAA Championship All-Tournament Team (2001)

CLOUTIER, Dan (KLOO-tyay, DAN) L.A.

Goaltender. Catches left. 6'1", 185 lbs. Born, Mont-Laurier, Que., April 22, 1976.
(NY Rangers' 1st choice, 26th overall, in 1994 Entry Draft).

			Regular Season								Playoffs						
Season	Club	League	GP	W	L	O/T	Mins	GA	SO	Avg	GP	W	L	Mins	GA	SO	Avg
1991-92	St. Thomas Stars	OJHL-B	14	....	....	....	823	80	0	5.83	....	....	....	....	....	....	....
1992-93	Timmins	NOJHA	5	4	0	0	255	10	0	2.35	....	....	....	....	....	....	....
	Sault Ste. Marie	OHL	12	4	6	0	572	44	0	4.62	4	1	2	231	12	0	3.12
1993-94	Sault Ste. Marie	OHL	55	28	14	6	2934	174	*2	3.56	14	*10	4	833	52	0	3.75
1994-95	Sault Ste. Marie	OHL	45	15	26	2	2518	185	1	4.41	....	....	....	....	....	....	....
1995-96	Sault Ste. Marie	OHL	13	9	3	0	641	43	0	4.02	....	....	....	....	....	....	....
	Guelph Storm	OHL	17	12	2	2	1004	35	2	2.09	16	11	5	993	52	*2	3.14
1996-97	Binghamton	AHL	60	23	28	8	3367	199	3	3.55	4	1	3	236	13	0	3.31
1997-98	**NY Rangers**	**NHL**	**12**	**4**	**5**	**1**	**551**	**23**	**0**	**2.50**	....	....	....	....	....	....	....
	Hartford Wolf Pack	AHL	24	12	8	3	1417	62	0	2.63	8	5	3	478	24	0	3.01
1998-99	**NY Rangers**	**NHL**	**22**	**6**	**8**	**3**	**1097**	**49**	**0**	**2.68**	....	....	....	....	....	....	....
99-2000	**Tampa Bay**	**NHL**	**52**	**9**	**30**	**3**	**2492**	**145**	**0**	**3.49**	....	....	....	....	....	....	....
2000-01	**Tampa Bay**	**NHL**	**24**	**3**	**13**	**3**	**1005**	**59**	**1**	**3.52**	....	....	....	....	....	....	....
	Detroit Vipers	IHL	1	0	1	0	59	3	0	3.05	....	....	....	....	....	....	....
	Vancouver	**NHL**	**16**	**4**	**6**	**5**	**914**	**37**	**0**	**2.43**	**2**	**0**	**2**	**117**	**9**	**0**	**4.62**
2001-02	**Vancouver**	**NHL**	**62**	**31**	**22**	**5**	**3502**	**142**	**7**	**2.43**	**6**	**2**	**3**	**273**	**16**	**0**	**3.52**
2002-03	**Vancouver**	**NHL**	**57**	**33**	**16**	**7**	**3376**	**136**	**2**	**2.42**	**14**	**7**	**7**	**833**	**45**	**0**	**3.24**
2003-04	**Vancouver**	**NHL**	**60**	**33**	**21**	**6**	**3539**	**134**	**5**	**2.27**	**3**	**1**	**1**	**138**	**5**	**0**	**2.17**
2004-05	Klagenfurter AC	Austria	13	7	0	5	772	25	1	1.94	10	6	4	590	27	1	2.75
2005-06	**Vancouver**	**NHL**	**13**	**8**	**3**	**1**	**681**	**36**	**0**	**3.17**	....	....	....	....	....	....	....
	NHL Totals		**318**	**131**	**124**	**34**	**17157**	**761**	**15**	**2.66**	**25**	**10**	**13**	**1361**	**75**	**0**	**3.31**

OHL Second All-Star Team (1996) • AHL All-Rookie Team (1997)

Traded to **Tampa Bay** by **NY Rangers** with Niklas Sundstrom and NY Rangers' 1st (Nikita Alexeev) and 3rd (later traded to San Jose – later traded to Chicago – Chicago selected Igor Radulov) round choices in 2000 Entry Draft for Chicago's 1st round choice (previously acquired, NY Rangers selected Pavel Brendl) in 1999 Entry Draft, June 26, 1999. Traded to **Vancouver** by **Tampa Bay** for Adrian Aucoin and Vancouver's 2nd round choice (Alexander Polushin) in 2001 Entry Draft, February 7, 2001. Signed as a free agent by **Klagenfurter** (Austria), January 20, 2005. Traded to **Los Angeles** by **Vancouver** for a 2nd round choice in 2007 Entry Draft and future considerations, July 5, 2006.

COLEMAN, Gerald (KOHL-man, JAIR-uhld) T.B.

Goaltender. Catches left. 6'4", 205 lbs. Born, Romeoville, IL, April 3, 1985.
(Tampa Bay's 5th choice, 224th overall, in 2003 Entry Draft).

			Regular Season								Playoffs						
Season	Club	League	GP	W	L	O/T	Mins	GA	SO	Avg	GP	W	L	Mins	GA	SO	Avg
99-2000	Chicago	MEHL	26	....	....	....	1560	65	0	2.50	....	....	....	....	....	....	....
2000-01	USNTDP	U-17	9	3	0	4	527	26	0	2.96	....	....	....	....	....	....	....
	USNTDP	NAHL	36	8	23	1	1859	132	0	4.26	....	....	....	....	....	....	....
2001-02	USNTDP	U-18	13	8	1	3	667	38	1	3.42	....	....	....	....	....	....	....
	USNTDP	USHL	2	1	1	0	76	4	0	3.15	....	....	....	....	....	....	....
	USNTDP	NAHL	22	5	14	2	1263	75	0	3.56	....	....	....	....	....	....	....
2002-03	London Knights	OHL	26	6	9	3	1074	59	1	3.30	....	....	....	....	....	....	....
2003-04	London Knights	OHL	33	24	8	0	1852	68	*5	2.20	8	5	2	442	19	1	2.58
2004-05	London Knights	OHL	38	*32	2	2	2224	63	*8	*1.70	8	7	1	455	13	0	*1.71
2005-06	**Tampa Bay**	**NHL**	**2**	**0**	**0**	**1**	**43**	**2**	**0**	**2.79**	....	....	....	....	....	....	....
	Springfield Falcons	AHL	43	14	21	3	2413	156	2	3.88	....	....	....	....	....	....	....
	NHL Totals		**2**	**0**	**0**	**1**	**43**	**2**	**0**	**2.79**	....	....	....	....	....	....	....

CONKLIN, Ty (KAWN-klihn, TIGH) CBJ

Goaltender. Catches left. 6', 184 lbs. Born, Anchorage, AK, March 30, 1976.

			Regular Season								Playoffs						
Season	Club	League	GP	W	L	O/T	Mins	GA	SO	Avg	GP	W	L	Mins	GA	SO	Avg
1995-96	Green Bay	USHL	30	....	....	....	1727	82	1	2.85	....	....	....	....	....	....	....
1996-97	Alaska-Anchorage	WCHA	DID NOT PLAY – FRESHMAN														
	Green Bay	USHL	30	19	7	1	1609	86	1	3.21	17	8	9	980	56	1	3.43
1997-98	New Hampshire	H-East	DID NOT PLAY – TRANSFERRED COLLEGES														
1998-99	New Hampshire	H-East	22	18	3	1	1338	41	0	*1.84	....	....	....	....	....	....	....
99-2000	New Hampshire	H-East	*37	*22	8	6	*2194	91	2	2.49	....	....	....	....	....	....	....
2000-01	New Hampshire	H-East	34	17	12	5	2048	70	*5	*2.05	....	....	....	....	....	....	....
2001-02	**Edmonton**	**NHL**	**4**	**2**	**0**	**0**	**148**	**4**	**0**	**1.62**	....	....	....	....	....	....	....
	Hamilton Bulldogs	AHL	37	13	12	8	2043	89	1	2.61	7	4	2	416	18	0	2.60
2002-03	Hamilton Bulldogs	AHL	38	19	13	3	2140	91	4	2.55	17	9	6	1024	38	1	2.23
2003-04	**Edmonton**	**NHL**	**38**	**17**	**14**	**4**	**2086**	**84**	**1**	**2.42**	....	....	....	....	....	....	....
2004-05	Wolfsburg	Germany	11	....	....	....	623	31	0	2.99	7	....	....	414	11	2	1.59
2005-06	**Edmonton**	**NHL**	**18**	**8**	**5**	**1**	**922**	**43**	**1**	**2.80**	**1**	**0**	**1**	**6**	**1**	**0**	**10.00**
	Hamilton Bulldogs	AHL	3	1	2	0	152	8	0	3.17	....	....	....	....	....	....	....
	Hartford Wolf Pack	AHL	2	1	0	1	130	5	0	2.31	....	....	....	....	....	....	....
	NHL Totals		**60**	**27**	**19**	**5**	**3156**	**131**	**2**	**2.49**	**1**	**0**	**1**	**6**	**1**	**0**	**10.00**

USHL Second All-Star Team (1996) • Hockey East All-Rookie Team (1999) • Hockey East Second All-Star Team (1999) • Hockey East First All-Star Team (2000, 2001) • Hockey East Player of the Year (2000) (co-winner - Mike Mottau) • NCAA East Second All-American Team (2000) • NCAA East First All-American Team (2001) • Walter Brown Award (New England's Outstanding American-born College player) (2001) (co-winner - Brian Gionta)

• Left **Alaska-Anchorage** (WCHA) and returned to **Green Bay** (USHL), November 14, 1996. Signed as a free agent by **Edmonton**, April 18, 2001. Signed as a free agent by **Wolfsburg** (Germany), January 25, 2005. Loaned to **Hartford** (AHL) by **Edmonton**, March 8, 2006. Signed as a free agent by **Columbus**, July 6, 2006.

CRAWFORD, Corey (KRAW-fohrd, KOHR-ee) CHI.

Goaltender. Catches left. 6'2", 190 lbs. Born, Montreal, Que., December 31, 1984.
(Chicago's 2nd choice, 52nd overall, in 2003 Entry Draft).

			Regular Season								Playoffs						
Season	Club	League	GP	W	L	O/T	Mins	GA	SO	Avg	GP	W	L	Mins	GA	SO	Avg
2000-01	Gatineau Intrepide	QAAA	21	17	3	1	1260	40	2	1.92	....	....	....	....	....	....	....
2001-02	Moncton Wildcats	QMJHL	38	9	20	3	1863	116	1	3.74	....	....	....	....	....	....	....
2002-03	Moncton Wildcats	QMJHL	50	24	17	6	2855	130	2	2.73	6	2	3	303	20	0	3.97
2003-04	Moncton Wildcats	QMJHL	54	*35	15	3	3019	132	2	2.62	*20	*13	6	*1170	42	0	2.15
2004-05	Moncton Wildcats	QMJHL	51	28	16	6	2942	121	*6	2.47	12	6	6	725	33	*1	2.73
2005-06	**Chicago**	**NHL**	**2**	**0**	**0**	**1**	**86**	**5**	**0**	**3.49**	....	....	....	....	....	....	....
	Norfolk Admirals	AHL	48	22	23	1	2734	134	1	2.94	1	0	0	17	1	0	3.49
	NHL Totals		**2**	**0**	**0**	**1**	**86**	**5**	**0**	**3.49**	....	....	....	....	....	....	....

QMJHL Second All-Star Team (2004, 2005)

DAIGNEAULT, Maxime (DAYN-yoh, mahx-EEM) WSH.

Goaltender. Catches left. 6'3", 202 lbs. Born, St-Jacques-le-Mineur, Que., January 23, 1984.
(Washington's 4th choice, 59th overall, in 2002 Entry Draft).

			Regular Season								Playoffs						
Season	Club	League	GP	W	L	O/T	Mins	GA	SO	Avg	GP	W	L	Mins	GA	SO	Avg
99-2000	Magog	QAAA	19	12	3	3	1108	53	3	2.87	18	12	5	945	42	1	2.67
2000-01	Val-d'Or Foreurs	QMJHL	28	14	8	1	1386	82	0	3.55	10	8	1	504	21	0	2.50
2001-02	Val-d'Or Foreurs	QMJHL	61	25	27	5	3270	184	3	3.38	7	3	4	431	23	0	3.20
2002-03	Val-d'Or Foreurs	QMJHL	48	23	18	3	2694	138	2	3.07	8	4	3	487	23	1	2.83
2003-04	Val-d'Or Foreurs	QMJHL	57	23	22	9	3250	158	2	2.92	7	3	4	416	16	0	2.31
2004-05	Portland Pirates	AHL	11	3	2	1	474	23	0	2.91	....	....	....	....	....	....	....
	South Carolina	ECHL	21	11	6	1	1172	59	1	3.02	....	....	....	....	....	....	....
2005-06	South Carolina	ECHL	38	16	12	9	2172	117	1	3.23	....	....	....	....	....	....	....
	Hershey Bears	AHL	3	0	1	2	190	7	0	2.21	....	....	....	....	....	....	....

Memorial Cup Tournament All-Star Team (2002) • Hap Emms Memorial Trophy (Memorial Cup Tournement Top Goaltender) (2002)

DAKERS, Taylor (DAK-uhrs, TAY-luhr) S.J.

Goaltender. Catches left. 6'1", 165 lbs. Born, Richmond, B.C., September 14, 1986.
(San Jose's 4th choice, 140th overall, in 2005 Entry Draft).

			Regular Season								Playoffs						
Season	Club	League	GP	W	L	O/T	Mins	GA	SO	Avg	GP	W	L	Mins	GA	SO	Avg
2002-03	Columbia Valley	KIJHL	37	....	....	....	2077	93	4	2.68	....	....	....	....	....	....	....
2003-04	Kootenay Ice	WHL	19	6	10	0	856	48	1	3.36	....	....	....	....	....	....	....
2004-05	Kootenay Ice	WHL	23	13	7	2	1303	44	4	2.03	....	....	....	....	....	....	....
2005-06	Kootenay Ice	WHL	47	30	15	1	2671	94	8	2.11	6	2	4	378	23	0	3.65

DANIELS, Ryan (DAN-yehlz, RIGH-uhn) OTT.

Goaltender. Catches left. 6'1", 205 lbs. Born, Scarborough, Ont., June 22, 1988.
(Ottawa's 5th choice, 151st overall, in 2006 Entry Draft).

			Regular Season								Playoffs						
Season	Club	League	GP	W	L	O/T	Mins	GA	SO	Avg	GP	W	L	Mins	GA	SO	Avg
2003-04	Ajax/Pickering	OMHA	STATISTICS NOT AVAILABLE														
	Pickering Panthers	OPJHL	1	0	1	0	60	3	0	3.00	....	....	....	....	....	....	....
2004-05	Pickering Panthers	OPJHL	36	17	10	2	1790	95	2	3.18	6	2	4	372	26	0	4.19
	Saginaw Spirit	OHL	7	0	4	0	280	19	0	4.07	....	....	....	....	....	....	....
2005-06	Saginaw Spirit	OHL	26	16	10	0	1511	104	0	4.13	1	0	1	59	4	0	4.07

DANIS, Yann (DA-nihs, YAN) MTL.

Goaltender. Catches left. 6', 181 lbs. Born, Lafontaine, Que., June 21, 1981.

			Regular Season								Playoffs						
Season	Club	League	GP	W	L	O/T	Mins	GA	SO	Avg	GP	W	L	Mins	GA	SO	Avg
99-2000	St-Jerome	QJHL	STATISTICS NOT AVAILABLE														
	Cornwall Colts	CJHL	26	....	....	....	1367	71	0	3.12	....	....	....	....	....	....	....
2000-01	Brown U.	ECAC	12	2	8	1	667	40	0	3.60	....	....	....	....	....	....	....
2001-02	Brown U.	ECAC	24	11	10	2	1451	45	3	1.86	....	....	....	....	....	....	....

Season	Club	League	GP	W	L	O/T	Mins	GA	SO	Avg	GP	W	L	Mins	GA	SO	Avg
2002-03	Brown U.	ECAC	*34	15	14	5	*2074	80	5	2.31	....	....	....	....	....	....	....
2003-04	Brown U.	ECAC	30	15	11	4	1821	55	*5	*1.81	....	....	....	....	....	....	....
	Hamilton Bulldogs	AHL	2	2	0	0	120	3	1	1.50	1	0	0	12	0	0	0.00
2004-05	Hamilton Bulldogs	AHL	53	28	17	6	3075	120	5	2.34	4	0	4	237	13	0	3.29
2005-06	**Montreal**	**NHL**	**6**	**3**	**2**	**0**	**312**	**14**	**1**	**2.69**	....	....	....	....	....	....	....
	Hamilton Bulldogs	AHL	39	17	17	3	2242	111	0	2.97	....	....	....	....	....	....	....
	NHL Totals		**6**	**3**	**2**	**0**	**312**	**14**	**1**	**2.69**	....	....	....	....	....	....	....

ECAC Second All-Star Team (2002, 2003) • ECAC First All-Star Team (2004) • ECAC Goaltender of the Year (2004) • ECAC Player of the Year (2004) • NCAA East First All-American Team (2004)

Signed as a free agent by **Montreal**, March 19, 2004.

DEKANICH, Mark (deh-KAN-ihch, MAHRK) NSH.

Goaltender. Catches left. 6'2", 192 lbs. Born, N. Vancouver, B.C., May 10, 1986.
(Nashville's 3rd choice, 146th overall, in 2006 Entry Draft).

			Regular Season								Playoffs						
Season	Club	League	GP	W	L	O/T	Mins	GA	SO	Avg	GP	W	L	Mins	GA	SO	Avg
2004-05	Colgate	ECACHL	5	1	1	0	162	5	0	1.85	....	....	....	....	....	....	....
2005-06	Colgate	ECACHL	36	18	11	6	2126	81	4	2.29	....	....	....	....	....	....	....

DENIS, Marc (deh-NEE, MAHRK) T.B.

Goaltender. Catches left. 6'1", 193 lbs. Born, Montreal, Que., August 1, 1977.
(Colorado's 1st choice, 25th overall, in 1995 Entry Draft).

			Regular Season								Playoffs						
Season	Club	League	GP	W	L	O/T	Mins	GA	SO	Avg	GP	W	L	Mins	GA	SO	Avg
1992-93	Montreal-Bourassa	QAAA	26	....	....	....	1559	74	5	2.87	....	....	....	....	....	....	....
1993-94	Trois-Rivieres	QAAA	36	10	22	3	2093	158	0	4.53	4	1	3	249	20	0	4.83
1994-95	Chicoutimi	QMJHL	32	17	9	1	1688	98	0	3.48	6	4	2	372	19	1	3.06
1995-96	Chicoutimi	QMJHL	51	23	21	4	2951	157	2	3.19	16	8	8	957	69	0	4.33
1996-97	Chicoutimi	QMJHL	41	22	15	2	2323	104	4	*2.69	*21	*11	10	*1229	70	*1	3.42
	Colorado	**NHL**	**1**	**0**	**1**	**0**	**60**	**3**	**0**	**3.00**	....	....	....	....	....	....	....
	Hershey Bears	AHL	....	....	....	....	....	....	....	....	4	1	0	56	1	0	1.08
1997-98	Hershey Bears	AHL	47	17	23	4	2588	125	1	2.90	6	3	3	346	15	0	2.59
1998-99	**Colorado**	**NHL**	**4**	**1**	**1**	**1**	**217**	**9**	**0**	**2.49**	....	....	....	....	....	....	....
	Hershey Bears	AHL	52	20	23	5	2908	137	4	2.83	3	1	1	143	7	0	2.93
99-2000	**Colorado**	**NHL**	**23**	**9**	**8**	**3**	**1203**	**51**	**3**	**2.54**	....	....	....	....	....	....	....
2000-01	**Columbus**	**NHL**	**32**	**6**	**20**	**4**	**1830**	**99**	**0**	**3.25**	....	....	....	....	....	....	....
2001-02	**Columbus**	**NHL**	**42**	**9**	**24**	**5**	**2335**	**121**	**1**	**3.11**	....	....	....	....	....	....	....
2002-03	**Columbus**	**NHL**	***77**	**27**	**41**	**8**	***4511**	**232**	**5**	**3.09**	....	....	....	....	....	....	....
2003-04	**Columbus**	**NHL**	**66**	**21**	**36**	**7**	**3796**	**162**	**5**	**2.56**	....	....	....	....	....	....	....
2004-05							Did not play										
2005-06	**Columbus**	**NHL**	**49**	**21**	**25**	**1**	**2786**	**151**	**1**	**3.25**	....	....	....	....	....	....	....
	NHL Totals		**294**	**94**	**156**	**29**	**16738**	**828**	**15**	**2.97**	....	....	....	....	....	....	....

QMJHL First All-Star Team (1997) • Canadian Major Junior First All-Star Team (1997) • Canadian Major Junior Goaltender of the Year (1997)

Traded to **Columbus** by **Colorado** for Columbus' 2nd round choice (later traded to Carolina – Carolina selected Tomas Kurka) in 2000 Entry Draft, June 7, 2000. Traded to **Tampa Bay** by **Columbus** for Fredrik Modin and Fredrik Norrena, June 30, 2006.

DENNIS, Adam (DEH-nihs, A-duhm) BUF.

Goaltender. Catches left. 5'11", 183 lbs. Born, Toronto, Ont., February 8, 1985.
(Buffalo's 6th choice, 182nd overall, in 2005 Entry Draft).

			Regular Season								Playoffs						
Season	Club	League	GP	W	L	O/T	Mins	GA	SO	Avg	GP	W	L	Mins	GA	SO	Avg
2002-03	Guelph Storm	OHL	18	6	7	1	846	45	0	3.19	....	....	....	....	....	....	....
2003-04	Guelph Storm	OHL	46	*33	10	2	2662	111	3	2.50	20	*15	5	1205	40	1	*1.99
2004-05	Guelph Storm	OHL	23	5	11	6	1372	57	3	2.49	....	....	....	....	....	....	....
	London Knights	OHL	16	12	4	0	920	23	3	1.50	11	9	1	629	22	*2	2.10
2005-06	London Knights	OHL	57	*44	9	0	*3444	162	1	2.82	18	12	5	1090	59	0	3.25

OHL First All-Star Team (2005, 2006) • Memorial Cup Tournament All-Star Team (2005) • Hap Emms Memorial Trophy (Memorial Cup Tournament Top Goaltender) (2005)

DiPIETRO, Rick (dee-pee-EHT-roh, RIHK) NYI

Goaltender. Catches right. 5'11", 185 lbs. Born, Winthrop, MA, September 19, 1981.
(NY Islanders' 1st choice, 1st overall, in 2000 Entry Draft).

			Regular Season								Playoffs						
Season	Club	League	GP	W	L	O/T	Mins	GA	SO	Avg	GP	W	L	Mins	GA	SO	Avg
1997-98	USNTDP	U-17	10	6	4	0	800	31	0	2.33	....	....	....	....	....	....	....
	USNTDP	USHL	3	0	2	0	117	8	0	4.09	....	....	....	....	....	....	....
	USNTDP	NAHL	30	13	12	0	1602	85	1	3.18	3	2	1	179	7	1	2.35
1998-99	USNTDP	U-18	16	9	5	1	1027	46	....	2.69	....	....	....	....	....	....	....
	USNTDP	USHL	30	22	6	1	1733	67	3	2.32	....	....	....	....	....	....	....
99-2000	Boston University	H-East	29	18	5	5	1790	73	2	2.45	....	....	....	....	....	....	....
2000-01	**NY Islanders**	**NHL**	**20**	**3**	**15**	**1**	**1083**	**63**	**0**	**3.49**	....	....	....	....	....	....	....
	Chicago Wolves	IHL	14	4	5	2	778	44	0	3.39	....	....	....	....	....	....	....
2001-02	Bridgeport	AHL	59	*30	22	7	3472	134	4	2.32	20	12	8	*1270	45	*3	2.13
2002-03	**NY Islanders**	**NHL**	**10**	**2**	**5**	**2**	**585**	**29**	**0**	**2.97**	**1**	**0**	**0**	**15**	**0**	**0**	**0.00**
	Bridgeport	AHL	34	16	10	8	2044	73	3	2.14	5	2	3	299	10	1	2.01
2003-04	**NY Islanders**	**NHL**	**50**	**23**	**18**	**5**	**2844**	**112**	**5**	**2.36**	**5**	**1**	**4**	**303**	**11**	**1**	**2.18**
	Bridgeport	AHL	2	0	2	0	119	3	0	1.51	....	....	....	....	....	....	....
2004-05							Did not play										
2005-06	**NY Islanders**	**NHL**	**63**	**30**	**24**	**5**	**3572**	**180**	**1**	**3.02**	....	....	....	....	....	....	....
	United States	Olympics	4	1	3	0	237	9	0	2.28	....	....	....	....	....	....	....
	NHL Totals		**143**	**58**	**62**	**13**	**8084**	**384**	**6**	**2.85**	**6**	**1**	**4**	**318**	**11**	**1**	**2.08**

Hockey East Second All-Star Team (2000) • Hockey East Rookie of the Year (2000)

DISHER, Josh (DIH-shur, JAWSH)

Goaltender. Catches left. 6'1", 170 lbs. Born, Chatham, Ont., June 24, 1985.
(New Jersey's 3rd choice, 185th overall, in 2004 Entry Draft).

			Regular Season								Playoffs						
Season	Club	League	GP	W	L	O/T	Mins	GA	SO	Avg	GP	W	L	Mins	GA	SO	Avg
2001-02	Oakville Rangers	OMHA	....	....	....	....	1170	....	2	2.55	....	....	....	....	....	....	....
2002-03	Burlington	OPJHL					Statistics not available										
2003-04	Erie Otters	OHL	*63	26	27	5	*3524	168	*5	2.86	9	4	5	506	29	0	3.44
2004-05	Erie Otters	OHL	51	25	21	3	2853	130	3	2.73	6	2	4	395	18	0	2.73
2005-06	Erie Otters	OHL	54	21	25	0	3070	192	0	3.75	....	....	....	....	....	....	....
	Albany River Rats	AHL	1	0	1	0	60	5	0	5.00	....	....	....	....	....	....	....
	Johnstown Chiefs	ECHL	2	1	1	0	113	4	0	2.13	....	....	....	....	....	....	....

DIVIS, Reinhard (DIH-vihs, RIGHN-hard)

Goaltender. Catches left. 6', 200 lbs. Born, Vienna, Austria, July 4, 1975.
(St. Louis' 8th choice, 261st overall, in 2000 Entry Draft).

			Regular Season								Playoffs						
Season	Club	League	GP	W	L	O/T	Mins	GA	SO	Avg	GP	W	L	Mins	GA	SO	Avg
1995-96	VEU Feldkirch	Austria	37	....	....	....	2200	85	0	2.32	....	....	....	....	....	....	....
1996-97	VEU Feldkirch	Alpenliga	45	....	....	....	2738	105	0	2.30	....	....	....	....	....	....	....
	VEU Feldkirch	Austria	....	....	....	....	....	....	....	....	11	....	....	620	27	0	2.61
1997-98	VEU Feldkirch	Alpenliga	13	....	....	....	779	22	0	1.69	....	....	....	....	....	....	....
	VEU Feldkirch	Austria	27	....	....	....	1620	55	0	2.07	....	....	....	....	....	....	....
1998-99	VEU Feldkirch	Austria	15	....	....	....	900	58	0	3.86	....	....	....	....	....	....	....
99-2000	Leksands IF	Sweden	48	....	....	....	2839	160	3	3.38	....	....	....	....	....	....	....
2000-01	Leksands IF	Sweden	41	....	....	....	2451	141	3	3.45	....	....	....	....	....	....	....
2001-02	**St. Louis**	**NHL**	**1**	**0**	**0**	**0**	**25**	**0**	**0**	**0.00**	....	....	....	....	....	....	....
	Worcester IceCats	AHL	55	28	20	5	3173	137	3	2.59	3	1	2	205	8	0	2.34
	Austria	Olympics	4	1	1	2	238	12	0	3.02	....	....	....	....	....	....	....
2002-03	**St. Louis**	**NHL**	**2**	**2**	**0**	**0**	**83**	**1**	**0**	**0.72**	....	....	....	....	....	....	....
	Worcester IceCats	AHL	9	6	1	0	453	17	0	2.25	....	....	....	....	....	....	....
2003-04	**St. Louis**	**NHL**	**13**	**4**	**4**	**2**	**629**	**29**	**0**	**2.77**	**1**	**0**	**0**	**18**	**0**	**0**	**0.00**
	Worcester IceCats	AHL	31	12	10	8	1709	63	3	2.21	....	....	....	....	....	....	....
2004-05	EC Villacher SV	Austria	26	10	10	4	1482	61	2	2.47	3	0	3	169	12	0	4.26
2005-06	**St. Louis**	**NHL**	**12**	**0**	**5**	**1**	**475**	**37**	**0**	**4.67**	....	....	....	....	....	....	....
	Peoria Rivermen	AHL	31	16	10	2	1646	76	2	2.77	....	....	....	....	....	....	....
	NHL Totals		**28**	**6**	**9**	**3**	**1212**	**67**	**0**	**3.32**	**1**	**0**	**0**	**18**	**0**	**0**	**0.00**

Signed as a free agent by **Villacher** (Austria), October 24, 2004.

DOYLE, Frank (DOIL, FRANK) N.J.

Goaltender. Catches left. 6'1", 185 lbs. Born, Guelph, Ont., September 8, 1980.

			Regular Season								Playoffs						
Season	Club	League	GP	W	L	O/T	Mins	GA	SO	Avg	GP	W	L	Mins	GA	SO	Avg
2000-01	Cambridge	OHA-B	32	....	....	....	....	....	4	2.94	....	....	....	....	....	....	....
2001-02	University of Maine	H-East					Did not play – Freshman										
2002-03	University of Maine	H-East	21	10	4	5	1180	42	2	*2.14	....	....	....	....	....	....	....
2003-04	University of Maine	H-East	23	19	4	0	1325	40	5	1.81	....	....	....	....	....	....	....
2004-05	Utah Grizzlies	AHL	1	0	1	0	20	3	0	9.00	....	....	....	....	....	....	....
	Idaho Steelheads	ECHL	52	*32	13	4	2938	106	4	2.16	3	1	2	169	12	0	4.26
2005-06	Albany River Rats	AHL	58	21	33	3	3413	176	1	3.09	....	....	....	....	....	....	....

Signed as a free agent by **New Jersey**, August 12, 2005.

DROUIN-DESLAURIERS, Jeff (droo-EHN-duh-LAW-ree-yay) EDM.

Goaltender. Catches right. 6'4", 189 lbs. Born, St-Jean-Richelieu, Que., May 15, 1984.
(Edmonton's 2nd choice, 31st overall, in 2002 Entry Draft).

			Regular Season								Playoffs						
Season	Club	League	GP	W	L	O/T	Mins	GA	SO	Avg	GP	W	L	Mins	GA	SO	Avg
2000-01	Gatineau Intrepide	QAAA	22	10	9	2	1194	61	2	3.07	2	1	0	125	6	0	2.89
2001-02	Chicoutimi	QMJHL	51	28	20	1	2909	170	1	3.51	4	0	3	197	20	0	6.11
2002-03	Chicoutimi	QMJHL	54	18	24	1	2582	164	0	3.81	4	0	4	240	15	0	9.00
2003-04	Chicoutimi	QMJHL	50	21	20	6	2701	129	1	2.87	18	10	8	956	50	1	3.14
2004-05	Edmonton	AHL	22	6	13	2	1258	62	0	2.96	....	....	....	....	....	....	....
	Greenville Grrrowl	ECHL	11	7	3	1	673	26	1	2.32	....	....	....	....	....	....	....
2005-06	Hamilton Bulldogs	AHL	13	4	7	0	666	35	0	3.15	....	....	....	....	....	....	....
	Greenville Grrrowl	ECHL	6	2	4	0	335	17	0	3.05	....	....	....	....	....	....	....

QMJHL All-Rookie Team (2002)

DUBIELEWICZ, Wade (DOO-bih-wihtz, WAYD) NYI

Goaltender. Catches left. 5'10", 178 lbs. Born, Invermere, B.C., January 30, 1978.

			Regular Season								Playoffs						
Season	Club	League	GP	W	L	O/T	Mins	GA	SO	Avg	GP	W	L	Mins	GA	SO	Avg
1997-98	Trail Smoke Eaters	BCHL	41	....	....	....	2225	118	0	3.18	....	....	....	....	....	....	....
1998-99	Trail Smoke Eaters	BCHL					Statistics not available										
	Chilliwack Chiefs	BCHL	14	10	4	0	834	....	0	....	....	....	....	....	....	....	....
99-2000	U. of Denver	WCHA	13	3	5	1	596	27	1	2.72	....	....	....	....	....	....	....
2000-01	U. of Denver	WCHA	29	12	9	3	1542	59	2	2.30	....	....	....	....	....	....	....
2001-02	U. of Denver	WCHA	24	20	4	0	1431	41	2	*1.72	....	....	....	....	....	....	....
2002-03	U. of Denver	WCHA	19	9	8	2	1060	43	3	2.43	....	....	....	....	....	....	....
2003-04	**NY Islanders**	**NHL**	**2**	**1**	**0**	**1**	**105**	**3**	**0**	**1.71**	....	....	....	....	....	....	....
	Bridgeport	AHL	33	20	8	5	1959	45	9	*1.38	3	2	1	181	11	0	3.64
2004-05	Bridgeport	AHL	43	18	23	1	2539	113	1	2.67	....	....	....	....	....	....	....
2005-06	**NY Islanders**	**NHL**	**7**	**2**	**3**	**0**	**310**	**15**	**0**	**2.90**	....	....	....	....	....	....	....
	Bridgeport	AHL	46	20	21	2	2575	134	3	3.12	7	3	4	435	16	0	2.21
	NHL Totals		**9**	**3**	**3**	**1**	**415**	**18**	**0**	**2.60**	....	....	....	....	....	....	....

WCHA Second All-Star Team (2001, 2003) • WCHA First All-Star Team (2002) • AHL All-Rookie Team (2004) • AHL Second All-Star Team (2004) • Dudley "Red" Garrett Memorial Award (Rookie of the Year - AHL) (2004) • Harry "Hap" Holmes Memorial Award (fewest goals against - AHL) (2004) (shared with Dieter Kochan)

Signed as a free agent by **NY Islanders**, May 25, 2003.

DUBNYK, Devan (DUHN-nihk, DEH-vuhn) EDM.

Goaltender. Catches left. 6'5", 194 lbs. Born, Regina, Sask., May 4, 1986.
(Edmonton's 1st choice, 14th overall, in 2004 Entry Draft).

			Regular Season								Playoffs						
Season	Club	League	GP	W	L	O/T	Mins	GA	SO	Avg	GP	W	L	Mins	GA	SO	Avg
2000-01	Calgary Bruins	CBHL	14	....	....	....	815	39	2	3.10	....	....	....	....	....	....	....
2001-02	Titaanit Kotka Jr.	Fin-Jr.	5	5	0	0	300	7	....	1.40	....	....	....	....	....	....	....
	Calgary Bruins	CBHL	18	7	9	2	1105	68	1	3.69	....	....	....	....	....	....	....
	Kamloops Blazers	WHL	3	1	1	0	143	13	0	5.45	....	....	....	....	....	....	....
2002-03	Kamloops Blazers	WHL	26	12	8	1	1279	68	2	3.19	....	....	....	....	....	....	....
2003-04	Kamloops Blazers	WHL	44	20	18	5	2533	106	6	2.51	4	1	3	245	12	0	2.94
2004-05	Kamloops Blazers	WHL	*65	23	34	7	3699	166	6	2.69	6	2	4	363	22	0	3.64
2005-06	Kamloops Blazers	WHL	54	27	26	1	3207	136	1	2.54	....	....	....	....	....	....	....

Canadian Major Junior Scholastic Player of the Year (2004)

DUCHESNE, Jeremy (DOO-shayn, JAIR-eh-mee) PHI.

Goaltender. Catches left. 6', 201 lbs. Born, Silver Spring, MD, October 17, 1986.
(Philadelphia's 3rd choice, 119th overall, in 2005 Entry Draft).

			Regular Season								Playoffs						
Season	Club	League	GP	W	L	O/T	Mins	GA	SO	Avg	GP	W	L	Mins	GA	SO	Avg
2002-03	St-Francois Blizzard	QAAA	26	7	11	5	1341	75	0	3.35	....	....	....	....	....	....	....
2003-04	Victoriaville Tigres	QMJHL	17	3	8	1	870	60	0	4.14	....	....	....	....	....	....	....
2004-05	Victoriaville Tigres	QMJHL	15	2	9	0	711	41	2	*3.46	....	....	....	....	....	....	....
	Halifax	QMJHL	18	12	0	2	921	23	3	*1.50	12	8	4	723	33	*1	2.74
2005-06	Halifax	QMJHL	55	25	29	0	3175	185	4	3.50	11	5	6	626	34	1	3.26

DUNHAM, Mike (DUHN-uhm, MIGHK)

Goaltender. Catches left. 6'3", 200 lbs. Born, Johnson City, NY, June 1, 1972.
(New Jersey's 4th choice, 53rd overall, in 1990 Entry Draft).

			Regular Season								Playoffs						
Season	Club	League	GP	W	L	O/T	Mins	GA	SO	Avg	GP	W	L	Mins	GA	SO	Avg
1987-88	Canterbury	High-CT	29	....	....	....	1740	69	4	2.38	....	....	....	....	....	....	....
1988-89	Canterbury	High-CT	25	....	....	....	1500	63	2	2.52	....	....	....	....	....	....	....
1989-90	Canterbury	High-CT	32	....	....	....	1558	68	3	1.96	....	....	....	....	....	....	....
1990-91	University of Maine	H-East	23	14	5	2	1275	63	0	*2.96	....	....	....	....	....	....	....
1991-92	University of Maine	H-East	7	6	0	0	382	14	1	2.20	....	....	....	....	....	....	....
	United States	Nat-Tm	3	0	1	1	157	10	0	3.82	....	....	....	....	....	....	....
1992-93	University of Maine	H-East	25	*21	1	1	1429	63	0	2.65	....	....	....	....	....	....	....
1993-94	United States	Nat-Tm	33	22	9	2	1983	125	2	3.78	....	....	....	....	....	....	....
	United States	Olympics	3	0	1	2	180	15	0	5.00	....	....	....	....	....	....	....
	Albany River Rats	AHL	5	2	2	1	304	26	0	5.12	....	....	....	....	....	....	....
1994-95	Albany River Rats	AHL	35	20	7	8	2120	99	1	2.80	7	6	1	419	20	1	2.86
1995-96	Albany River Rats	AHL	44	30	10	2	2592	109	1	2.52	3	1	2	182	5	1	1.65

1996-97	**New Jersey**	**NHL**	**26**	**8**	**7**	**1**	**1013**	**43**	**2**	**2.55**	....	....	....	....	....	....	....
	Albany River Rats	AHL	3	1	1	1	184	12	0	3.91	....	....	....	....	....	....	....
1997-98	**New Jersey**	**NHL**	**15**	**5**	**5**	**3**	**773**	**29**	**1**	**2.25**	....	....	....	....	....	....	....
1998-99	**Nashville**	**NHL**	**44**	**16**	**23**	**3**	**2472**	**127**	**1**	**3.08**	....	....	....	....	....	....	....
99-2000	**Nashville**	**NHL**	**52**	**19**	**27**	**6**	**3077**	**146**	**0**	**2.85**	....	....	....	....	....	....	....
	Milwaukee	IHL	1	1	0	0	60	1	0	1.00	....	....	....	....	....	....	....
2000-01	**Nashville**	**NHL**	**48**	**21**	**21**	**4**	**2810**	**107**	**4**	**2.28**	....	....	....	....	....	....	....
2001-02	**Nashville**	**NHL**	**58**	**23**	**24**	**9**	**3316**	**144**	**3**	**2.61**	....	....	....	....	....	....	....
	United States	Olympics	1	1	0	0	60	0	*1	0.00	....	....	....	....	....	....	....
2002-03	**Nashville**	**NHL**	**15**	**2**	**9**	**2**	**819**	**43**	**0**	**3.15**	....	....	....	....	....	....	....
	NY Rangers	**NHL**	**43**	**19**	**17**	**5**	**2467**	**94**	**5**	**2.29**	....	....	....	....	....	....	....
2003-04	**NY Rangers**	**NHL**	**57**	**16**	**30**	**6**	**3148**	**159**	**2**	**3.03**	....	....	....	....	....	....	....
2004-05	Skelleftea AIK HK	Sweden-2	13	....	....	....	726	36	4	2.97	....	....	....	....	....	....	....
2005-06	**Atlanta**	**NHL**	**17**	**8**	**5**	**2**	**779**	**36**	**1**	**2.77**	....	....	....	....	....	....	....
	Gwinnett	ECHL	2	2	0	0	120	5	0	2.50	....	....	....	....	....	....	....
	NHL Totals		**375**	**137**	**168**	**41**	**20674**	**928**	**19**	**2.69**	....	....	....	....	....	....	....

Hockey East First All-Star Team (1993) • NCAA East First All-American Team (1993) • Harry ''Hap'' Holmes Memorial Award (fewest goals against – AHL) (1995) (shared with Corey Schwab) • Jack A. Butterfield Trophy (Playoff MVP – AHL) (1995) (co-winner - Corey Schwab) • AHL Second All-Star Team (1996) • William M. Jennings Trophy (1997) (shared with Martin Brodeur)

Claimed by **Nashville** from **New Jersey** in Expansion Draft, June 26, 1998. Traded to **NY Rangers** by **Nashville** for Rem Murray, Tomas Kloucek and Marek Zidlicky, December 12, 2002. Signed as a free agent by **Skelleftea** (Sweden-2), January 31, 2005. Signed as a free agent by **Atlanta**, September 2, 2005.

DUPONT, Michael (DOO-pohnt, MIGH-kuhl) PHI.

Goaltender. Catches left. 6', 175 lbs. Born, Bienne, Switz., December 20, 1987.
(Philadelphia's 9th choice, 175th overall, in 2006 Entry Draft).

			Regular Season								Playoffs						
Season	**Club**	**League**	**GP**	**W**	**L**	**O/T**	**Mins**	**GA**	**SO**	**Avg**	**GP**	**W**	**L**	**Mins**	**GA**	**SO**	**Avg**
2004-05	Baie-Comeau	QMJHL	45	14	19	3	2226	132	2	3.56	6	2	3	305	18	0	3.54
2005-06	Baie-Comeau	QMJHL	48	19	24	0	2428	149	2	3.68	4	0	4	240	17	0	4.25

EHELECHNER, Patrick (eh-heh-LEHCH-nuhr, PAT-rihk) PIT.

Goaltender. Catches left. 6'2", 169 lbs. Born, Rosenheim, West Germany, September 23, 1984.
(San Jose's 5th choice, 139th overall, in 2003 Entry Draft).

			Regular Season								Playoffs						
Season	**Club**	**League**	**GP**	**W**	**L**	**O/T**	**Mins**	**GA**	**SO**	**Avg**	**GP**	**W**	**L**	**Mins**	**GA**	**SO**	**Avg**
2000-01	Jung. Mannheim	German-4	40	....	....	....	2423	171	2	4.23	....	....	....	....	....	....	....
2001-02	EV Landshut	German-3	2	....	....	....	130	6	0	2.77	....	....	....	....	....	....	....
	Hannover	Germany	8	....	....	....	475	24	0	3.03	....	....	....	....	....	....	....
2002-03	ESC Wedemark	German-4					STATISTICS NOT AVAILABLE										
	Hannover	Germany	4	....	....	....	162	16	0	5.90	....	....	....	....	....	....	....
2003-04	Sudbury Wolves	OHL	56	22	26	6	3089	148	3	2.87	7	2	4	390	14	2	2.15
2004-05	Sudbury Wolves	OHL	51	23	21	4	2997	128	3	2.56	10	4	5	497	29	0	3.50
2005-06	Adler Mannheim	Germany	1	....	....	....	59	5	0	5.02	....	....	....	....	....	....	....
	Duisburg	Germany	26	....	....	....	1243	75	2	3.62	....	....	....	....	....	....	....

OHL Second All-Star Team (2004)

Signed as a free agent by **Mannheim** (Germany), April 25, 2005. Traded to **Pittsburgh** by **San Jose** with Nils Ekman for Carolina's 2nd round choice (previously acquired) in 2007 Entry Draft, July 20, 2006.

EKLUND, Brian (EHK-luhnd, BRIGH-uhn)

Goaltender. Catches left. 6'5", 205 lbs. Born, Braintree, MA, May 24, 1980.
(Tampa Bay's 8th choice, 226th overall, in 2000 Entry Draft).

			Regular Season								Playoffs						
Season	**Club**	**League**	**GP**	**W**	**L**	**O/T**	**Mins**	**GA**	**SO**	**Avg**	**GP**	**W**	**L**	**Mins**	**GA**	**SO**	**Avg**
1997-98	Archbishop Wms.	High-MA	22	....	....	....	1320	40	*6	*1.84	....	....	....	....	....	....	....
1998-99	Brown U.	ECAC	8	1	3	0	299	17	0	3.41	....	....	....	....	....	....	....
99-2000	Brown U.	ECAC	12	1	6	2	569	28	1	2.95	....	....	....	....	....	....	....
2000-01	Brown U.	ECAC	19	2	13	3	1084	62	0	3.43	....	....	....	....	....	....	....
2001-02	Brown U.	ECAC	9	3	5	0	454	30	0	3.97	....	....	....	....	....	....	....
2002-03	Springfield Falcons	AHL	1	1	0	0	60	1	0	1.00	....	....	....	....	....	....	....
	Pensacola Ice Pilots	ECHL	19	10	6	0	999	61	0	3.66	....	....	....	....	....	....	....
2003-04	Pensacola Ice Pilots	ECHL	*62	*38	17	7	*3725	187	1	3.01	5	2	3	333	16	0	2.88
2004-05	Springfield Falcons	AHL	43	14	23	0	2416	121	0	3.01	....	....	....	....	....	....	....
2005-06	**Tampa Bay**	**NHL**	**1**	**0**	**1**	**0**	**58**	**3**	**0**	**3.10**	....	....	....	....	....	....	....
	Springfield Falcons	AHL	17	5	11	1	960	67	0	4.19	....	....	....	....	....	....	....
	Johnstown Chiefs	ECHL	2	1	0	1	130	7	0	3.23	....	....	....	....	....	....	....
	Providence Bruins	AHL	12	3	6	1	597	35	0	3.52	....	....	....	....	....	....	....
	NHL Totals		**1**	**0**	**1**	**0**	**58**	**3**	**0**	**3.10**	....	....	....	....	....	....	....

Traded to **Boston** by **Tampa Bay** for Zdenek Blatny, February 8, 2006.

ELLIOTT, Brian (EHL-lee-awt, BRIGH-uhn) OTT.

Goaltender. Catches left. 6'3", 186 lbs. Born, Newmarket, Ont., April 9, 1985.
(Ottawa's 9th choice, 291st overall, in 2003 Entry Draft).

			Regular Season								Playoffs						
Season	**Club**	**League**	**GP**	**W**	**L**	**O/T**	**Mins**	**GA**	**SO**	**Avg**	**GP**	**W**	**L**	**Mins**	**GA**	**SO**	**Avg**
2002-03	Ajax Axemen	OPJHL	39	....	....	....	2097	135	0	3.86	....	....	....	....	....	....	....
2003-04	U. of Wisconsin	WCHA	6	3	3	0	336	12	0	2.14	....	....	....	....	....	....	....
2004-05	U. of Wisconsin	WCHA	9	6	2	1	467	9	3	1.16	....	....	....	....	....	....	....
2005-06	U. of Wisconsin	WCHA	35	*27	5	3	2128	55	*8	*1.55	....	....	....	....	....	....	....

WCHA Second All-Star Team (2006) • NCAA West First All-American Team (2006)

ELLIS, Dan (EH-lihs, DAN) DAL.

Goaltender. Catches left. 6', 185 lbs. Born, Orangeville, Ont., June 19, 1980.
(Dallas' 2nd choice, 60th overall, in 2000 Entry Draft).

			Regular Season								Playoffs						
Season	**Club**	**League**	**GP**	**W**	**L**	**O/T**	**Mins**	**GA**	**SO**	**Avg**	**GP**	**W**	**L**	**Mins**	**GA**	**SO**	**Avg**
1998-99	Newmarket	OPJHL	28	24	3	1	1670	63	3	2.25	....	....	....	....	....	....	....
99-2000	Omaha Lancers	USHL	55	*34	16	4	*3274	123	*11	*2.25	4	1	3	238	10	0	2.52
2000-01	Nebraska-Omaha	CCHA	40	21	14	3	2285	95	2	2.49	....	....	....	....	....	....	....
2001-02	Nebraska-Omaha	CCHA	40	20	15	4	2405	97	3	2.42	....	....	....	....	....	....	....
2002-03	Nebraska-Omaha	CCHA	39	11	21	5	2211	117	3	3.18	....	....	....	....	....	....	....
2003-04	**Dallas**	**NHL**	**1**	**1**	**0**	**0**	**60**	**3**	**0**	**3.00**	....	....	....	....	....	....	....
	Utah Grizzlies	AHL	20	5	14	0	1130	55	2	2.92	....	....	....	....	....	....	....
	Idaho Steelheads	ECHL	23	13	8	1	1334	57	2	2.56	*16	*13	3	*966	30	*3	*1.86
2004-05	Hamilton Bulldogs	AHL	31	10	19	0	1774	82	1	2.77	....	....	....	....	....	....	....
2005-06	Iowa Stars	AHL	34	16	13	1	1857	86	2	2.78	....	....	....	....	....	....	....
	NHL Totals		**1**	**1**	**0**	**0**	**60**	**3**	**0**	**3.00**	....	....	....	....	....	....	....

USHL First All-Star Team (2000) • USHL Goaltender of the Year (2000) • USHL Player of the Year (2000) • CCHA Second All-Star Team (2002) • ECHL Playoff MVP (2004)

ELLIS-PLANTE, Julien (EHL-ihs, JEW-lee-ehn) VAN.

Goaltender. Catches left. 6', 194 lbs. Born, Sorel, Que., January 27, 1986.
(Vancouver's 5th choice, 189th overall, in 2004 Entry Draft).

			Regular Season								Playoffs						
Season	**Club**	**League**	**GP**	**W**	**L**	**O/T**	**Mins**	**GA**	**SO**	**Avg**	**GP**	**W**	**L**	**Mins**	**GA**	**SO**	**Avg**
2001-02	Antoine-Girouard	QAAA	22	16	2	1	1227	55	2	2.69							
2002-03	Antoine-Girouard	QAAA	16	11	4	1	966	29	4	1.80	....	....	....	....	....	....	....
	Shawinigan	QMJHL	7	2	3	0	365	21	0	3.45	....	....	....	....	....	....	....
2003-04	Shawinigan	QMJHL	59	32	18	2	3287	156	1	2.85	10	3	6	569	33	0	3.48
2004-05	Shawinigan	QMJHL	59	27	21	11	3480	140	4	2.41	4	0	3	175	10	0	3.43
2005-06	Shawinigan	QMJHL	48	27	19	0	2680	154	3	3.45	7	4	3	412	18	2	2.62

QMJHL First All-Star Team (2005)

EMERY, Ray (EH-muhr-ee, RAY) OTT.

Goaltender. Catches left. 6'2", 198 lbs. Born, Cayuga, Ont., September 28, 1982.
(Ottawa's 4th choice, 99th overall, in 2001 Entry Draft).

			Regular Season								Playoffs						
Season	**Club**	**League**	**GP**	**W**	**L**	**O/T**	**Mins**	**GA**	**SO**	**Avg**	**GP**	**W**	**L**	**Mins**	**GA**	**SO**	**Avg**
1998-99	Dunnville Terriers	OJHL-C	22	3	19	0	1320	140	0	6.37	....	....	....	....	....	....	....
99-2000	Welland Cougars	OHA-B	23	13	10	1	1323	62	1	2.68	....	....	....	....	....	....	....
	Sault Ste. Marie	OHL	16	9	3	0	716	36	1	3.02	15	8	7	883	33	*3	2.24
2000-01	Sault Ste. Marie	OHL	52	18	29	2	2938	174	1	3.55	....	....	....	....	....	....	....
2001-02	Sault Ste. Marie	OHL	*59	*33	17	9	*3477	158	4	2.73	6	2	4	360	19	*1	3.17
2002-03	**Ottawa**	**NHL**	**3**	**1**	**0**	**0**	**85**	**2**	**0**	**1.41**	....	....	....	....	....	....	....
	Binghamton	AHL	50	27	17	6	2924	118	*7	2.42	14	8	6	848	40	*2	2.83
2003-04	**Ottawa**	**NHL**	**3**	**2**	**0**	**0**	**126**	**5**	**0**	**2.38**	....	....	....	....	....	....	....
	Binghamton	AHL	53	21	23	7	3109	128	3	2.47	2	0	2	120	6	0	3.01
2004-05	Binghamton	AHL	51	28	18	5	2993	132	0	2.65	6	2	4	409	14	0	2.05
2005-06	**Ottawa**	**NHL**	**39**	**23**	**11**	**4**	**2168**	**102**	**3**	**2.82**	**10**	**5**	**5**	**604**	**29**	**0**	**2.88**
	NHL Totals		**45**	**26**	**11**	**4**	**2379**	**109**	**3**	**2.75**	**10**	**5**	**5**	**604**	**29**	**0**	**2.88**

OHL First All-Star Team (2002) • Canadian Major Junior First All-Star Team (2002) • Canadian Major Junior Goaltender of the Year (2002) • AHL All-Rookie Team (2003)

ENROTH, Jhonas (EHN-rawth, YOH-nuhs) BUF.

Goaltender. Catches left. 5'10", 174 lbs. Born, Stockholm, Sweden, June 25, 1988.
(Buffalo's 2nd choice, 46th overall, in 2006 Entry Draft).

			Regular Season								Playoffs						
Season	**Club**	**League**	**GP**	**W**	**L**	**O/T**	**Mins**	**GA**	**SO**	**Avg**	**GP**	**W**	**L**	**Mins**	**GA**	**SO**	**Avg**
2003-04	Huddinge IK U18	Swe-U18	6	....	....	....	324	15	0	2.77	....	....	....	....	....	....	....
2004-05	Huddinge IK Jr.	Swe-Jr.	19	....	....	....	1144	49	3	2.57	3	....	....	186	6	1	1.93
	Huddinge IK U18	Swe-U18	2	....	....	....	125	5	0	2.40	....	....	....	....	....	....	....
	Huddinge IK	Sweden-2	2	....	....	....	51	6	0	6.95	....	....	....	....	....	....	....
2005-06	Sodertalje SK Jr.	Swe-Jr.	39	....	....	....	2378	86	1	2.17	4	....	....	243	9	0	2.22
	Sodertalje SK U18	Swe-U18	2	....	....	....	120	5	0	2.50	....	....	....	....	....	....	....

ESCHE, Robert (EHSH, RAW-buhrt) PHI.

Goaltender. Catches left. 6'1", 210 lbs. Born, Whitesboro, NY, January 22, 1978.
(Phoenix's 5th choice, 139th overall, in 1996 Entry Draft).

			Regular Season								Playoffs						
Season	**Club**	**League**	**GP**	**W**	**L**	**O/T**	**Mins**	**GA**	**SO**	**Avg**	**GP**	**W**	**L**	**Mins**	**GA**	**SO**	**Avg**
1994-95	Gloucester	CJHL	20	10	6	0	1034	70	0	4.06	....	....	....	....	....	....	....
1995-96	Detroit Jr. Whalers	OHL	23	13	6	0	1219	76	1	3.74	3	0	2	105	4	0	2.29
1996-97	Detroit Jr. Whalers	OHL	58	24	28	2	3241	206	2	3.81	5	1	4	317	19	0	3.60
1997-98	Plymouth Whalers	OHL	48	29	13	4	2810	135	3	2.88	15	8	7	869	45	0	3.11
1998-99	**Phoenix**	**NHL**	**3**	**0**	**1**	**0**	**130**	**7**	**0**	**3.23**	....	....	....	....	....	....	....
	Springfield Falcons	AHL	55	24	20	6	2957	138	1	2.80	1	0	1	60	4	0	4.02
99-2000	**Phoenix**	**NHL**	**8**	**2**	**5**	**0**	**408**	**23**	**0**	**3.38**	....	....	....	....	....	....	....
	Houston Aeros	IHL	7	4	2	1	419	16	2	2.29	....	....	....	....	....	....	....
	Springfield Falcons	AHL	21	9	9	2	1207	61	2	3.03	3	1	2	180	12	0	4.01
2000-01	**Phoenix**	**NHL**	**25**	**10**	**8**	**4**	**1350**	**68**	**2**	**3.02**	....	....	....	....	....	....	....
2001-02	**Phoenix**	**NHL**	**22**	**6**	**10**	**2**	**1145**	**52**	**1**	**2.72**	....	....	....	....	....	....	....
	Springfield Falcons	AHL	1	1	0	0	60	0	1	0.00	....	....	....	....	....	....	....
2002-03	**Philadelphia**	**NHL**	**30**	**12**	**9**	**3**	**1638**	**60**	**2**	**2.20**	**1**	**0**	**0**	**30**	**1**	**0**	**2.00**
2003-04	**Philadelphia**	**NHL**	**40**	**21**	**11**	**7**	**2322**	**79**	**3**	**2.04**	**18**	**11**	**7**	**1061**	**41**	**1**	**2.32**
2004-05							DID NOT PLAY										
2005-06	**Philadelphia**	**NHL**	**40**	**22**	**11**	**5**	**2286**	**113**	**1**	**2.97**	**6**	**2**	**4**	**314**	**22**	**0**	**4.20**
	United States	Olympics	1	0	1	0	59	5	0	5.10	....	....	....	....	....	....	....
	NHL Totals		**168**	**73**	**55**	**21**	**9279**	**402**	**9**	**2.60**	**25**	**13**	**11**	**1405**	**64**	**1**	**2.73**

OHL Second All-Star Team (1998) • AHL All-Rookie Team (1999) • William M. Jennings Trophy (2003) (shared with Roman Cechmanek) (tied with Martin Brodeur)

Traded to **Philadelphia** by **Phoenix** with Michal Handzus for Brian Boucher and Nashville's 3rd round choice (previously acquired, Phoenix selected Joe Callahan) in 2002 Entry Draft, June 12, 2002.

FALLON, Joseph (FA-lohn, JOH-sehf) CHI.

Goaltender. Catches left. 6'3", 203 lbs. Born, Bemidji, MN, February 1, 1985.
(Chicago's 9th choice, 167th overall, in 2005 Entry Draft).

			Regular Season								Playoffs						
Season	**Club**	**League**	**GP**	**W**	**L**	**O/T**	**Mins**	**GA**	**SO**	**Avg**	**GP**	**W**	**L**	**Mins**	**GA**	**SO**	**Avg**
2001-02	Rochester	USHL	27	7	16	1	1484	93	0	3.76	....	....	....	....	....	....	....
2002-03	Cedar Rapids	USHL	42	20	15	6	2495	108	2	2.60	7	3	4	426	21	0	2.96
2003-04	Cedar Rapids	USHL	42	25	13	2	2370	108	4	2.73	4	1	3	237	9	0	2.28
2004-05	U. of Vermont	ECACHL	32	17	10	4	1932	63	5	1.96	....	....	....	....	....	....	....
2005-06	U. of Vermont	H-East	33	14	14	5	1931	65	6	2.02	....	....	....	....	....	....	....

ECACHL All-Rookie Team (2005) • ECACHL Rookie of the Year (2005)

FERNANDEZ, Manny (fuhr-NAN-dehz, MAN-ee) MIN.

Goaltender. Catches left. 6', 180 lbs. Born, Etobicoke, Ont., August 27, 1974.
(Quebec's 4th choice, 52nd overall, in 1992 Entry Draft).

			Regular Season								Playoffs						
Season	**Club**	**League**	**GP**	**W**	**L**	**O/T**	**Mins**	**GA**	**SO**	**Avg**	**GP**	**W**	**L**	**Mins**	**GA**	**SO**	**Avg**
1990-91	Lac St-Louis Lions	QAAA	20	13	5	0	1176	69	*3	3.52	3	2	1	181	12	0	3.98
1991-92	Laval Titan	QMJHL	31	14	13	2	1593	99	1	3.73	9	3	5	468	39	0	5.00
1992-93	Laval Titan	QMJHL	43	26	14	2	2347	141	1	3.60	13	*12	1	818	42	0	3.08
1993-94	Laval Titan	QMJHL	51	29	14	1	2776	143	*5	3.09	19	14	5	1116	49	*1	*2.63
1994-95	Kalamazoo Wings	IHL	46	21	10	9	2470	115	2	2.79	14	10	2	753	34	1	2.71
	Dallas	**NHL**	**1**	**0**	**1**	**0**	**59**	**3**	**0**	**3.05**	....	....	....	....	....	....	....
1995-96	**Dallas**	**NHL**	**5**	**0**	**1**	**1**	**249**	**19**	**0**	**4.58**	....	....	....	....	....	....	....
	Michigan K-Wings	IHL	47	22	15	9	2664	133	*4	3.00	6	5	1	372	14	0	*2.26
1996-97	Michigan K-Wings	IHL	48	20	24	2	2720	142	2	3.13	4	1	3	277	15	0	3.25
1997-98	**Dallas**	**NHL**	**2**	**1**	**0**	**0**	**69**	**2**	**0**	**1.74**	**1**	**0**	**0**	**2**	**0**	**0**	**0.00**
	Michigan K-Wings	IHL	55	27	17	5	3022	139	5	2.76	2	0	2	88	7	0	4.73
1998-99	**Dallas**	**NHL**	**1**	**0**	**1**	**0**	**60**	**2**	**0**	**2.00**	....	....	....	....	....	....	....
	Houston Aeros	IHL	50	34	6	9	2949	116	2	2.36	*19	*11	8	*1126	49	1	2.61
99-2000	**Dallas**	**NHL**	**24**	**11**	**8**	**3**	**1353**	**48**	**1**	**2.13**	**1**	**0**	**0**	**17**	**1**	**0**	**3.53**
2000-01	**Minnesota**	**NHL**	**42**	**19**	**17**	**4**	**2461**	**92**	**4**	**2.24**	....	....	....	....	....	....	....
2001-02	**Minnesota**	**NHL**	**44**	**12**	**24**	**5**	**2463**	**125**	**1**	**3.05**	....	....	....	....	....	....	....
2002-03	**Minnesota**	**NHL**	**35**	**19**	**13**	**2**	**1979**	**74**	**2**	**2.24**	**9**	**3**	**4**	**552**	**18**	**0**	**1.96**
2003-04	**Minnesota**	**NHL**	**37**	**11**	**14**	**9**	**2166**	**90**	**2**	**2.49**	....	....	....	....	....	....	....
2004-05	Lulea HF	Sweden	19	....	....	....	1083	50	2	2.77	3	....	....	159	13	0	4.90

2005-06	Minnesota	NHL	58	30	18	7	3411	130	1	2.29							
	NHL Totals		**249**	**103**	**97**	**31**	**14270**	**585**	**11**	**2.46**	**11**	**3**	**4**	**571**	**19**	**0**	**2.00**

QMJHL First All-Star Team (1994) • QMJHL MVP (1994) • IHL Second All-Star Team (1995)

Rights traded to **Dallas** by **Quebec** for Tommy Sjodin and Dallas' 3rd round choice (Chris Drury) in 1994 Entry Draft, February 13, 1994. Traded to **Minnesota** by **Dallas** with Brad Lukowich for Minnesota's 3rd round choice (Joel Lundqvist) in 2000 Entry Draft and Minnesota's 4th round choice (later traded back to Minnesota – later traded to Los Angeles – Los Angeles selected Aaron Rome) in 2002 Entry Draft, June 12, 2000. Signed as a free agent by **Lulea** (Sweden), December 18, 2004.

FINLEY, Brian (FIHN-lee, BRIGH-uhn) BOS.

Goaltender. Catches right. 6'3", 205 lbs. Born, Sault Ste. Marie, Ont., July 13, 1981.
(Nashville's 1st choice, 6th overall, in 1999 Entry Draft).

			Regular Season								Playoffs						
Season	Club	League	GP	W	L	O/T	Mins	GA	SO	Avg	GP	W	L	Mins	GA	SO	Avg
1996-97	Soo Carlucci's	NOHA	45				1943	109	3	2.38							
1997-98	Barrie Colts	OHL	41	23	14	1	2154	105	3	2.92	5	1	3	260	13	0	3.00
1998-99	Barrie Colts	OHL	52	*36	10	4	3063	136	3	2.66	5	4	1	323	15	0	2.79
99-2000	Barrie Colts	OHL	47	24	12	6	2540	130	2	3.07	*23	14	8	1353	58	1	2.57
2000-01	Barrie Colts	OHL	16	5	8	0	818	42	0	3.08							
	Brampton Battalion	OHL	11	7	3	1	631	31	0	2.95	9	5	4	503	26	1	3.10
2001-02							DID NOT PLAY – INJURED										
2002-03	**Nashville**	**NHL**	**1**	**0**	**0**	**0**	**47**	**3**	**0**	**3.83**							
	Milwaukee	AHL	22	7	11	2	1207	59	2	2.93							
	Toledo Storm	ECHL	7	4	2	0	305	12	0	2.36	1	0	1	60	4	0	4.00
2003-04	Milwaukee	AHL	43	23	15	4	2561	100	2	2.34	1	0	1	59	2	0	2.05
2004-05	Milwaukee	AHL	64	36	22	4	3642	139	7	2.29	7	3	4	458	20	1	2.62
2005-06	**Nashville**	**NHL**	**1**	**0**	**1**	**0**	**60**	**7**	**0**	**7.00**							
	Milwaukee	AHL	32	18	7	2	1708	77	4	2.70	8	3	2	415	20	0	2.89
	NHL Totals		**2**	**0**	**1**	**0**	**107**	**10**	**0**	**5.61**							

OHL All-Rookie Team (1998) • OHL First All-Star Team (1999) • OHL Playoff MVP (2000)

• Missed entire 2001-02 season recovering from groin injury suffered during 2000-01 season and re-injured in training camp, October 3, 2001. Signed as a free agent by **Boston**, July 17, 2006.

FISHER, Glenn (FIH-shuhr, GLEHN) EDM.

Goaltender. Catches left. 6'1", 165 lbs. Born, Edmonton, Alta., April 25, 1983.
(Edmonton's 9th choice, 148th overall, in 2002 Entry Draft).

			Regular Season								Playoffs						
Season	Club	League	GP	W	L	O/T	Mins	GA	SO	Avg	GP	W	L	Mins	GA	SO	Avg
99-2000	Edm. Maple Leafs	AMBHL	16	9	5	2	944	62	0	3.94							
2000-01	Edm. Maple Leafs	AMHL	19	6	9	3	1116	77	0	4.14							
2001-02	Fort Saskatchewan	AJHL	47	14	26	2	2649	196	2	4.44	3	0	3	180	14	0	4.67
2002-03	Fort Saskatchewan	AJHL	51	17	27	6	2885	202	0	4.20							
2003-04	U. of Denver	WCHA	9	3	1	1	436	26	0	3.58							
2004-05	U. of Denver	WCHA	22	14	5	1	1247	59	0	2.84							
2005-06	U. of Denver	WCHA	21	9	7	2	1102	50	1	2.72							

FLAHERTY, Wade (FLAY-uhr-tee, WAYD) VAN.

Goaltender. Catches left. 6', 190 lbs. Born, Terrace, B.C., January 11, 1968.
(Buffalo's 10th choice, 181st overall, in 1988 Entry Draft).

			Regular Season								Playoffs						
Season	Club	League	GP	W	L	O/T	Mins	GA	SO	Avg	GP	W	L	Mins	GA	SO	Avg
1984-85	Kelowna Wings	WHL	1	0	0	0	55	5	0	5.45							
1985-86	Seattle	WHL	9	1	3	0	271	36	0	7.97							
	Spokane Chiefs	WHL	5	0	3	0	161	21	0	7.83							
1986-87	Nanaimo Clippers	BCJHL	15				830	53	0	3.83							
	Victoria Cougars	WHL	3	0	2	0	127	16	0	7.56							
1987-88	Victoria Cougars	WHL	36	20	15	0	2052	135	0	3.95	5	2	3	300	18	0	3.60
1988-89	Victoria Cougars	WHL	42	21	19	0	2408	180	4	4.49							
1989-90	Greensboro	ECHL	27	12	10	0	1308	96	0	4.40							
1990-91	Kansas City Blades	IHL	*56	16	31	4	2990	224	0	4.49							
1991-92	**San Jose**	**NHL**	**3**	**0**	**3**	**0**	**178**	**13**	**0**	**4.38**							
	Kansas City Blades	IHL	43	26	14	3	2603	140	1	3.23	1	0	0	1	0	0	0.00
1992-93	**San Jose**	**NHL**	**1**	**0**	**1**	**0**	**60**	**5**	**0**	**5.00**							
	Kansas City Blades	IHL	*61	*34	19	7	*3642	195	2	3.21	*12	6	6	733	34	*1	2.78
1993-94	Kansas City Blades	IHL	*60	32	19	9	*3564	202	0	3.40							
1994-95	**San Jose**	**NHL**	**18**	**5**	**6**	**1**	**852**	**44**	**1**	**3.10**	**7**	**2**	**3**	**377**	**31**	**0**	**4.93**
1995-96	**San Jose**	**NHL**	**24**	**3**	**12**	**1**	**1137**	**92**	**0**	**4.85**							
1996-97	**San Jose**	**NHL**	**7**	**2**	**4**	**0**	**359**	**31**	**0**	**5.18**							
	Kentucky	AHL	19	8	6	2	1032	54	1	3.14	3	1	2	200	11	0	3.30
1997-98	**NY Islanders**	**NHL**	**16**	**4**	**4**	**3**	**694**	**23**	**3**	**1.99**							
	Utah Grizzlies	IHL	24	16	5	3	1341	40	3	1.79							
1998-99	**NY Islanders**	**NHL**	**20**	**5**	**11**	**2**	**1048**	**53**	**0**	**3.03**							
	Lowell	AHL	5	1	3	1	305	16	0	3.15							
99-2000	**NY Islanders**	**NHL**	**4**	**0**	**1**	**1**	**182**	**7**	**0**	**2.31**							
2000-01	**NY Islanders**	**NHL**	**20**	**6**	**10**	**0**	**1017**	**56**	**1**	**3.30**							
	Tampa Bay	**NHL**	**2**	**0**	**2**	**0**	**118**	**8**	**0**	**4.07**							
2001-02	**Florida**	**NHL**	**4**	**2**	**1**	**1**	**245**	**12**	**0**	**2.94**							
	Utah Grizzlies	AHL	45	22	13	5	2351	92	2	2.35	5	2	3	312	11	0	2.12
2002-03	**Nashville**	**NHL**	**1**	**0**	**1**	**0**	**51**	**4**	**0**	**4.71**							
	San Antonio	AHL	30	11	13	5	1791	86	1	2.88							
2003-04	Milwaukee	AHL	36	21	12	3	2146	78	3	2.18	*21	*16	5	*1371	44	1	1.93
2004-05	Manitoba Moose	AHL	36	19	10	3	2010	78	4	2.33	12	8	4	720	29	2	2.42
2005-06	Manitoba Moose	AHL	49	26	17	4	2822	113	*6	2.40	12	7	5	675	23	0	*2.04
	NHL Totals		**120**	**27**	**56**	**9**	**5941**	**348**	**5**	**3.51**	**7**	**2**	**3**	**377**	**31**	**0**	**4.93**

WHL West Second All-Star Team (1988) • ECHL Playoff MVP (1990) • James Norris Memorial Trophy (fewest goals against – IHL) (1992) (shared with Arturs Irbe) • IHL Second All-Star Team (1993, 1994) • Jack A. Butterfield Trophy (Playoff MVP - AHL) (2004) • AHL Second All-Star Team (2006)

Signed as a free agent by **San Jose**, September 3, 1991. Signed as a free agent by **NY Islanders**, July 22, 1997. Traded to **Tampa Bay** by **NY Islanders** for future considerations, February 16, 2001. Signed as a free agent by **Florida**, August 2, 2001. Traded to **Nashville** by **Florida** for Pascal Trepanier, March 9, 2003. Signed as a free agent by **Vancouver**, July 7, 2004.

FLEURY, Marc-Andre (fluh-REE, MAHRK-AWN-dray) PIT.

Goaltender. Catches left. 6'1", 175 lbs. Born, Sorel, Que., November 28, 1984.
(Pittsburgh's 1st choice, 1st overall, in 2003 Entry Draft).

			Regular Season								Playoffs						
Season	Club	League	GP	W	L	O/T	Mins	GA	SO	Avg	GP	W	L	Mins	GA	SO	Avg
99-2000	Charles-Lemoyne	QAAA	15	4	9	0	780	36	1	2.77							
2000-01	Cape Breton	QMJHL	35	12	13	2	1705	115	0	4.05	2	0	1	32	4	0	7.50
2001-02	Cape Breton	QMJHL	55	26	14	8	3043	141	2	2.78	16	9	7	1003	55	0	3.29
2002-03	Cape Breton	QMJHL	51	17	24	6	2889	162	2	3.36	4	0	4	228	17	0	4.47
2003-04	**Pittsburgh**	**NHL**	**21**	**4**	**14**	**2**	**1154**	**70**	**1**	**3.64**							
	Cape Breton	QMJHL	10	8	1	1	606	20	0	1.98	4	1	3	251	13	0	3.10
	Wilkes-Barre	AHL									2	0	1	92	6	0	3.90
2004-05	Wilkes-Barre	AHL	54	26	19	4	3029	127	5	2.52	4	0	2	151	11	0	4.36
2005-06	**Pittsburgh**	**NHL**	**50**	**13**	**27**	**6**	**2809**	**152**	**1**	**3.25**							
	Wilkes-Barre	AHL	12	10	2	0	727	19	0	1.57	5	2	3	311	18	0	3.48
	NHL Totals		**71**	**17**	**41**	**8**	**3963**	**222**	**2**	**3.36**							

QMJHL Second All-Star Team (2003)

Returned to **Cape Breton** (QMJHL) by **Pittsburgh**, January 29, 2004.

FORD, Todd (FOHRD, TAWD) TOR.

Goaltender. Catches left. 6'4", 176 lbs. Born, Calgary, Alta., May 1, 1984.
(Toronto's 3rd choice, 74th overall, in 2002 Entry Draft).

			Regular Season								Playoffs						
Season	Club	League	GP	W	L	O/T	Mins	GA	SO	Avg	GP	W	L	Mins	GA	SO	Avg
99-2000	Cgy. Stamps	CBHL					STATISTICS NOT AVAILABLE										
2000-01	Swift Current	WHL	20	12	4	2	1066	53	0	2.98	1	0	0	26	2	0	4.62
2001-02	Swift Current	WHL	37	18	12	3	2003	99	2	2.97	10	5	5	603	28	0	2.79
2002-03	Swift Current	WHL	28	12	9	5	1588	71	2	2.68							
	Prince George	WHL	17	4	9	2	936	70	0	4.49	1	0	1	60	7	0	7.00
2003-04	Prince George	WHL	28	8	14	4	1480	82	0	3.32							
	Vancouver Giants	WHL	10	1	7	1	570	33	0	3.47	1	0	0	32	0	0	0.00
2004-05	Pensacola Ice Pilots	ECHL	28	19	4	2	1576	61	1	2.32							
2005-06	Toronto Marlies	AHL	9	3	4	0	459	29	0	3.79							
	Pensacola Ice Pilots	ECHL	29	10	17	1	1713	104	0	3.64							

FOSTER, Brian (FAW-stuhr, BRIGH-uhn) FLA.

Goaltender. Catches left. 6'1", 155 lbs. Born, Pembroke, NH, February 4, 1987.
(Florida's 6th choice, 161st overall, in 2005 Entry Draft).

			Regular Season								Playoffs						
Season	Club	League	GP	W	L	O/T	Mins	GA	SO	Avg	GP	W	L	Mins	GA	SO	Avg
2003-04	N.H. Jr. Monarchs	EJHL					STATISTICS NOT AVAILABLE										
2004-05	N.H. Jr. Monarchs	EJHL	41	30	6	4	2339		3	2.51							
2005-06	Des Moines	USHL	26	12	9	3	1516	71	0	2.81	1	0	0	12	0	0	0.00

Signed Letter of Intent to attend **U. of New Hampshire** (Hockey East) in fall of 2006.

FRANEK, Petr (FRAH-nehk, PEE-tuhr)

Goaltender. Catches left. 5'11", 185 lbs. Born, Most, Czech., April 6, 1975.
(Quebec's 10th choice, 205th overall, in 1993 Entry Draft).

			Regular Season								Playoffs						
Season	Club	League	GP	W	L	O/T	Mins	GA	SO	Avg	GP	W	L	Mins	GA	SO	Avg
1992-93	Litvinov	Czech	5				273	15	0	3.29							
1993-94	Litvinov	CzRep	11				535	34	0	3.81	2	0	1	61	10	0	9.83
1994-95	Litvinov	CzRep	12				657	47	0	4.29	1	0	0	16	0	0	0.00
1995-96	Litvinov	CzRep	36				2096	85	3	2.43	16			948	47	1	2.97
1996-97	Hershey Bears	AHL	15	4	1	0	457	23	3	3.02							
	Brantford Smoke	ColHL	6	4	1	0	321	14	0	2.61							
	Quebec Rafales	IHL	6	3	3	0	357	18	0	3.02	1	0	1	40	4	0	6.00
1997-98	Hershey Bears	AHL	43	19	14	2	2169	98	2	2.71	1	0	1	60	4	0	4.00
1998-99	Utah Grizzlies	IHL	8	1	6	1	446	26	0	3.50							
	Las Vegas Thunder	IHL	37	17	13	2	1879	107	0	3.42							
99-2000	Nurnberg	Germany	30				1603	73	2	2.73							
2000-01	Karlovy Vary	CzRep	44				2507	121		2.90							
2001-02	Karlovy Vary	CzRep	40				2189	109		2.99							
2002-03	Karlovy Vary	CzRep	45				2570	107	5	2.50							
2003-04	Karlovy Vary	CzRep	25				1471	58	2	2.37							
	HC Slavia Praha	CzRep	4				245	8	0	1.96	*19	9	10	*1186	39	*3	1.97
2004-05	HC Slavia Praha	CzRep	42				2508	88	5	2.11	7			372	18	0	2.90
2005-06	HC Slavia Praha	CzRep	38				2229	72	5	1.94	15			947	34	1	2.15

Rights transferred to **Colorado** after **Quebec** franchise relocated, June 21, 1995.

FRAZEE, Jeff (FRAY-zee, JEHF) N.J.

Goaltender. Catches left. 6', 184 lbs. Born, Edina, MN, May 13, 1987.
(New Jersey's 2nd choice, 38th overall, in 2005 Entry Draft).

			Regular Season								Playoffs						
Season	Club	League	GP	W	L	O/T	Mins	GA	SO	Avg	GP	W	L	Mins	GA	SO	Avg
2001-02	Holy Angels	High-MN	6	6	0	0											
2002-03	Holy Angels	High-MN	16	14	1	1											
2003-04	USNTDP	U-17	16	9	3	0	781	31		2.38							
	USNTDP	NAHL	25	14	8	3	1463	71	3	2.91							
2004-05	USNTDP	U-18	24				1309	59	3	2.71							
	USNTDP	NAHL	9	8	1	0	500	18	1	2.16							
2005-06	U. of Minnesota	WCHA	12	6	3	2	660	26	2	2.36							

FUKUFUJI, Yutaka (foo-koo-FOO-jee, yoo-TA-ka) L.A.

Goaltender. Catches left. 6'1", 180 lbs. Born, Tokyo, Japan, September 17, 1982.
(Los Angeles' 9th choice, 238th overall, in 2004 Entry Draft).

			Regular Season								Playoffs						
Season	Club	League	GP	W	L	O/T	Mins	GA	SO	Avg	GP	W	L	Mins	GA	SO	Avg
2003-04	Kokudo Toyko	AsianHL	7				420	13		1.86							
	Kokudo Toyko	Japan	7				430	12		1.67							
2004-05	Bakersfield	ECHL	44	27	9	5	2517	104	3	2.48							
2005-06	Manchester	AHL	2	1	1	0	120	6	0	3.00							
	Reading Royals	ECHL	29	15	9	4	1691	82	1	2.91	4	1	2	196	11	0	3.36

GARNETT, Michael (gahr-NEHT, MIGH-kuhl) ATL.

Goaltender. Catches left. 6'1", 205 lbs. Born, Saskatoon, Sask., November 25, 1982.
(Atlanta's 2nd choice, 80th overall, in 2001 Entry Draft).

			Regular Season								Playoffs						
Season	Club	League	GP	W	L	O/T	Mins	GA	SO	Avg	GP	W	L	Mins	GA	SO	Avg
1997-98	Sask. Contacts	SMHL	3	1	1	0	82	8	0	5.85							
1998-99	Sask. Contacts	SMHL					STATISTICS NOT AVAILABLE										
99-2000	Kindersley Klippers	SJHL	36				2067	140	1	3.57							
	Red Deer Rebels	WHL	1	0	0	0	14	0	0	0.00	1	0	1	65	2	0	1.85
2000-01	Red Deer Rebels	WHL	21	14	5	1	1133	39	3	2.07							
	Saskatoon Blades	WHL	28	7	17	2	1501	83	1	3.32							
2001-02	Saskatoon Blades	WHL	*67	27	34	4	*3738	205	2	3.29	7	3	4	450	15	0	2.00
2002-03	Chicago Wolves	AHL	2	0	1	0	33	2	0	3.64							
	Greenville Grrrowl	ECHL	38	16	15	3	2092	119	0	3.41	3	1	2	178	13	0	4.38
2003-04	Chicago Wolves	AHL	13	7	3	2	731	32	0	2.63							
	Gwinnett	ECHL	33	21	10	2	1936	69	4	2.14	12	7	5	770	34	0	2.65
2004-05	Chicago Wolves	AHL	24	11	9	0	1321	63	1	2.86	2	2	0	119	3	0	1.51
2005-06	**Atlanta**	**NHL**	**24**	**10**	**7**	**4**	**1271**	**73**	**2**	**3.45**							
	Chicago Wolves	AHL	35	15	12	4	1892	106	1	3.36							
	NHL Totals		**24**	**10**	**7**	**4**	**1271**	**73**	**2**	**3.45**							

GARON, Mathieu (gah-ROHN, MA-tyew) L.A.

Goaltender. Catches right. 6'2", 192 lbs. Born, Chandler, Que., January 9, 1978.
(Montreal's 2nd choice, 44th overall, in 1996 Entry Draft).

			Regular Season								Playoffs						
Season	Club	League	GP	W	L	O/T	Mins	GA	SO	Avg	GP	W	L	Mins	GA	SO	Avg
1993-94	Jonquiere Elites	QAAA	17	0	13	0	834	88	0	6.33							
1994-95	Jonquiere Elites	QAAA	27	13	13	1	1554	94	0	3.63	9	6	2	467	26	0	3.34
1995-96	Victoriaville Tigres	QMJHL	51	18	27	0	2709	189	1	4.19	12	7	4	676	38	1	3.39
1996-97	Victoriaville Tigres	QMJHL	53	29	18	3	3032	150	*6	2.97	6	2	4	330	23	0	4.18
1997-98	Victoriaville Tigres	QMJHL	47	27	18	2	2802	125	5	2.68	6	2	4	345	22	0	3.82
1998-99	Fredericton	AHL	40	14	22	2	2222	114	3	3.08	6	1	1	208	12	0	3.47
99-2000	Quebec Citadelles	AHL	53	17	28	3	2884	149	2	3.10	1	0	0	20	3	0	8.82
2000-01	**Montreal**	**NHL**	**11**	**4**	**5**	**1**	**589**	**24**	**2**	**2.44**							
	Quebec Citadelles	AHL	31	16	13	1	1768	86	1	2.92	8	4	4	459	22	1	2.88

2001-02	Montreal	NHL	5	1	4	0	261	19	0	4.37	....	....	....	....	....	....	....
	Quebec Citadelles	AHL	50	21	15	12	2988	136	2	2.73	3	0	3	198	12	0	3.63
2002-03	Montreal	NHL	8	3	5	0	482	16	2	1.99	....	....	....	....	....	....	....
	Hamilton Bulldogs	AHL	20	15	2	2	1150	34	4	1.77	....	....	....	....	....	....	....
2003-04	Montreal	NHL	19	8	6	2	1003	38	0	2.27	1	0	0	12	0	0	0.00
2004-05	Manchester	AHL	52	32	14	4	2969	105	8	2.12	6	2	4	285	17	0	3.58
2005-06	Los Angeles	NHL	63	31	26	3	3446	185	4	3.22	....	....	....	....	....	....	....
	NHL Totals		106	47	46	6	5781	282	8	2.93	1	0	0	12	0	0	0.00

QMJHL All-Rookie Team (1996) • QMJHL Defensive Rookie of the Year (1996) • QMJHL First All-Star Team (1998) • Canadian Major Junior First All-Star Team (1998) • Canadian Major Junior Goaltender of the Year (1998)

Traded to **Los Angeles** by **Montreal** with San Jose's 3rd round choice (previously acquired, Los Angeles selected Paul Baier) in 2004 Entry Draft for Radek Bonk and Cristobal Huet, June 26, 2004.

GERBER, Martin (GUHR-buhr, MAHR-tihn) OTT.

Goaltender. Catches left. 6', 185 lbs. Born, Burgdorf, Switz., September 3, 1974.
(Anaheim's 10th choice, 232nd overall, in 2001 Entry Draft).

			Regular Season								Playoffs						
Season	Club	League	GP	W	L	O/T	Mins	GA	SO	Avg	GP	W	L	Mins	GA	SO	Avg
1996-97	SC Langnau	Swiss-2	38	....	....	....	2286	121	0	3.18	8	....	....	488	29	0	3.57
1997-98	SC Langnau	Swiss-2	40	....	....	....	2430	141	2	3.48	16	....	....	961	42	0	2.62
1998-99	SC Langnau	Swiss	42	....	....	....	2521	203	1	4.83	11	....	....	664	50	0	4.52
99-2000	SC Langnau	Swiss	44	....	....	....	2652	161	3	3.64	6	....	....	360	13	*2	*2.17
2000-01	SCL Tigers Langnau	Swiss	*44	....	....	....	2671	114	3	2.56	5	....	....	319	7	1	1.32
2001-02	Farjestad	Sweden	44	....	....	....	2664	87	*4	*1.96	*10	....	....	*657	18	*2	*1.64
	Switzerland	Olympics	3	1	1	1	158	4	0	1.52	....	....	....	....	....	....	....
2002-03	Anaheim	NHL	22	6	11	3	1203	39	1	1.95	2	0	0	20	1	0	3.00
	Cincinnati	AHL	1	1	0	0	60	2	0	2.00	....	....	....	....	....	....	....
2003-04	Anaheim	NHL	32	11	12	4	1698	64	2	2.26	....	....	....	....	....	....	....
2004-05	SCL Tigers Langnau	Swiss	20	6	10	4	1220	59	0	2.90	....	....	....	....	....	....	....
	Farjestad	Sweden	30	20	6	4	1827	58	4	1.90	*15	9	6	*900	36	1	2.40
2005-06 ♦	Carolina	NHL	60	38	14	6	3493	162	3	2.78	6	1	1	221	13	1	3.53
	Switzerland	Olympics	3	....	....	....	160	11	1	4.13	....	....	....	....	....	....	....
	NHL Totals		114	55	37	13	6394	265	6	2.49	8	1	1	241	14	1	3.49

• Scored a goal in playoffs vs. Martigny (Swiss-2), February 27, 1997. Traded to **Carolina** by **Anaheim** for Tomas Malec and Carolina's 3rd round choice (Kyle Klubertanz) in 2004 Entry Draft, June 18, 2004. Signed as a free agent by **Langnau** (Swiss), September 17, 2004. Signed as a free agent by **Farjestad** (Sweden), November 7, 2004. Signed as a free agent by **Ottawa**, July 1, 2006.

GIGUERE, Jean-Sebastien (ZHEE-gair, ZHAWN-suh-BAS-tee-yeh) ANA.

Goaltender. Catches left. 6'1", 199 lbs. Born, Montreal, Que., May 16, 1977.
(Hartford's 1st choice, 13th overall, in 1995 Entry Draft).

			Regular Season								Playoffs						
Season	Club	League	GP	W	L	O/T	Mins	GA	SO	Avg	GP	W	L	Mins	GA	SO	Avg
1992-93	Laval-Laurentides	QAAA	25	12	11	2	1498	76	0	3.02	11	6	5	654	38	0	3.49
1993-94	Verdun	QMJHL	25	13	5	2	1234	66	1	3.21	....	....	....	....	....	....	....
1994-95	Halifax	QMJHL	47	14	27	5	2755	181	2	3.94	7	3	4	417	17	1	*2.45
1995-96	Halifax	QMJHL	55	26	23	2	3230	185	1	3.44	6	1	5	354	24	0	4.07
1996-97	Hartford	NHL	8	1	4	0	394	24	0	3.65	....	....	....	....	....	....	....
	Halifax	QMJHL	50	28	19	3	3014	170	2	3.38	16	9	7	954	58	0	3.65
1997-98	Saint John Flames	AHL	31	16	10	3	1758	72	2	2.46	10	5	3	536	27	0	3.02
1998-99	Calgary	NHL	15	6	7	1	860	46	0	3.21	....	....	....	....	....	....	....
	Saint John Flames	AHL	39	18	16	3	2145	123	3	3.44	7	3	2	304	21	0	4.14
99-2000	Calgary	NHL	7	1	3	1	330	15	0	2.73	....	....	....	....	....	....	....
	Saint John Flames	AHL	41	17	17	3	2243	114	0	3.05	3	0	3	178	9	0	3.03
2000-01	Anaheim	NHL	34	11	17	5	2031	87	4	2.57	....	....	....	....	....	....	....
	Cincinnati	AHL	23	12	7	2	1306	53	0	2.43	....	....	....	....	....	....	....
2001-02	Anaheim	NHL	53	20	25	6	3127	111	4	2.13	....	....	....	....	....	....	....
2002-03	Anaheim	NHL	65	34	22	6	3775	145	8	2.30	21	15	6	1407	38	5	*1.62
2003-04	Anaheim	NHL	55	17	31	6	3210	140	3	2.62	....	....	....	....	....	....	....
2004-05	Hamburg Freezers	Germany	6	....	....	....	301	12	0	2.39	2	....	....	100	7	0	4.20
2005-06	Anaheim	NHL	60	30	15	11	3381	150	2	2.66	6	3	3	318	18	0	3.40
	NHL Totals		297	120	124	36	17108	718	21	2.52	27	18	9	1725	56	5	1.95

QMJHL Second All-Star Team (1997) • AHL All-Rookie Team (1998) • Harry "Hap" Holmes Memorial Award (fewest goals against – AHL) (1998) (shared with Tyler Moss) • Conn Smythe Trophy (2003)

Transferred to **Carolina** after **Hartford** franchise relocated, June 25, 1997. Traded to **Calgary** by **Carolina** with Andrew Cassels for Gary Roberts and Trevor Kidd, August 25, 1997. Traded to **Anaheim** by **Calgary** for Anaheim's 2nd round choice (later traded to Washington – Washington selected Matt Pettinger) in 2000 Entry Draft, June 10, 2000. Signed as a free agent by **Hamburg** (Germany), January 31, 2005.

GLASS, Jeff (GLAS, JEHF) OTT.

Goaltender. Catches left. 6'2", 201 lbs. Born, Calgary, Alta., November 19, 1985.
(Ottawa's 5th choice, 89th overall, in 2004 Entry Draft).

			Regular Season								Playoffs						
Season	Club	League	GP	W	L	O/T	Mins	GA	SO	Avg	GP	W	L	Mins	GA	SO	Avg
2001-02	Crowsnest Pass	AJHL	34	....	....	....	1802	126	0	4.20	....	....	....	....	....	....	....
2002-03	Kootenay Ice	WHL	35	15	16	3	1884	77	4	2.45	9	4	5	643	23	0	2.15
2003-04	Kootenay Ice	WHL	57	26	20	6	3263	128	5	2.35	4	0	4	239	14	0	3.51
2004-05	Kootenay Ice	WHL	51	34	11	5	3061	90	8	1.76	16	10	6	1027	39	0	2.28
2005-06	Charlotte Checkers	ECHL	39	19	15	4	2221	119	2	3.22	3	1	2	178	11	0	3.71
	Binghamton	AHL	6	1	4	0	312	20	0	3.85	....	....	....	....	....	....	....

WHL West First All-Star Team (2005) • WHL Goaltender of the Year (2005) • Canadian Major Junior First All-Star Team (2005) • Canadian Major Junior Goaltender of the Year (2005)

GOEHRING, Karl (GAIR-ihng, KAHRL) NSH.

Goaltender. Catches left. 5'8", 160 lbs. Born, Apple Valley, MN, August 23, 1978.

			Regular Season								Playoffs						
Season	Club	League	GP	W	L	O/T	Mins	GA	SO	Avg	GP	W	L	Mins	GA	SO	Avg
1996-97	Fargo-Moorhead	USHL	32	13	18	1	1909	79	*4	*2.48	5	2	3	251	15	1	3.58
1997-98	North Dakota	WCHA	27	23	3	1	1504	57	1	*2.27	....	....	....	....	....	....	....
1998-99	North Dakota	WCHA	31	22	5	2	1774	71	3	2.40	....	....	....	....	....	....	....
99-2000	North Dakota	WCHA	30	19	6	4	1747	55	*8	*1.89	....	....	....	....	....	....	....
2000-01	North Dakota	WCHA	30	16	6	6	1662	66	*3	2.38	....	....	....	....	....	....	....
2001-02	Syracuse Crunch	AHL	15	5	6	3	891	37	1	2.49	....	....	....	....	....	....	....
	Dayton Bombers	ECHL	23	11	9	3	1393	52	2	2.24	*14	9	5	*866	35	1	2.43
2002-03	Syracuse Crunch	AHL	49	18	21	4	2608	116	4	2.67	....	....	....	....	....	....	....
2003-04	Syracuse Crunch	AHL	38	17	14	6	2234	97	1	2.60	5	2	2	295	16	0	3.26
2004-05	Syracuse Crunch	AHL	49	23	22	0	2788	128	3	2.75	....	....	....	....	....	....	....
2005-06	San Antonio	AHL	23	4	16	1	1250	65	1	3.12	....	....	....	....	....	....	....
	Jokerit Helsinki	Finland	19	5	10	3	1076	57	2	3.18	....	....	....	....	....	....	....

WCHA First All-Star Team (1998, 2000) • WCHA Rookie of the Year (1998) • NCAA West First All-American Team (1998, 2000) • WCHA Second All-Star Team (1999)

Signed as a free agent by **Columbus**, May 7, 2001. Signed as a free agent by **Jokerit Helsinki** (Finland), September 16, 2005. Signed as a free agent by **Nashville**, July 17, 2006.

GOEPFERT, Robert (GEHP-fuhrt, RAW-buhrt) PIT.

Goaltender. Catches left. 5'10", 170 lbs. Born, Ozone Park, NY, May 9, 1983.
(Pittsburgh's 7th choice, 171st overall, in 2002 Entry Draft).

			Regular Season								Playoffs						
Season	Club	League	GP	W	L	O/T	Mins	GA	SO	Avg	GP	W	L	Mins	GA	SO	Avg
99-2000	Suffolk PAL	Metro-Jr.	38	....	....	....	2280	87	....	2.36	....	....	....	....	....	....	....
2000-01	Cedar Rapids	USHL	41	25	12	4	2565	125	1	2.92	4	1	3	188	18	0	5.73
2001-02	Cedar Rapids	USHL	51	27	16	5	2918	99	8	2.04	8	4	4	581	19	0	1.97
2002-03	Providence College	H-East	13	6	6	1	754	30	1	2.39	....	....	....	....	....	....	....
2003-04	Providence College	H-East	28	15	9	3	1641	68	2	2.49	....	....	....	....	....	....	....
2004-05	St. Cloud State	WCHA					DID NOT PLAY – TRANSFERRED COLLEGES										
2005-06	St. Cloud State	WCHA	*38	20	14	4	*2264	83	3	2.20	....	....	....	....	....	....	....

USHL All-Rookie Team (2001) • USHL Goaltender of the Year (2001, 2002) • USHL First All-Star Team (2002) • USHL Player of the Year (2002) • WCHA First All-Star Team (2006) • NCAA West Second All-American Team (2006)

GRAHAME, John (GRAY-uhm, JAWN) CAR.

Goaltender. Catches left. 6'2", 220 lbs. Born, Denver, CO, August 31, 1975.
(Boston's 7th choice, 229th overall, in 1994 Entry Draft).

			Regular Season								Playoffs						
Season	Club	League	GP	W	L	O/T	Mins	GA	SO	Avg	GP	W	L	Mins	GA	SO	Avg
1993-94	Sioux City	USHL	20	....	....	....	1200	73	0	3.70	....	....	....	....	....	....	....
1994-95	Lake Superior State	CCHA	28	16	7	3	1616	75	2	2.79	....	....	....	....	....	....	....
1995-96	Lake Superior State	CCHA	29	21	4	2	1558	66	2	2.54	....	....	....	....	....	....	....
1996-97	Lake Superior State	CCHA	37	19	13	4	2197	134	3	3.66	....	....	....	....	....	....	....
1997-98	Providence Bruins	AHL	55	15	31	4	3053	164	3	3.22	....	....	....	....	....	....	....
1998-99	Providence Bruins	AHL	48	*37	9	1	2771	134	3	2.90	19	*15	4	*1209	48	1	2.38
99-2000	Boston	NHL	24	7	10	5	1344	55	2	2.46	....	....	....	....	....	....	....
	Providence Bruins	AHL	27	11	13	2	1528	86	1	3.38	13	10	3	839	35	0	2.50
2000-01	Boston	NHL	10	3	4	0	471	28	0	3.57	....	....	....	....	....	....	....
	Providence Bruins	AHL	16	4	7	3	893	47	0	3.16	17	8	9	1043	46	2	2.65
2001-02	Boston	NHL	19	8	7	2	1079	52	1	2.89	....	....	....	....	....	....	....
2002-03	Boston	NHL	23	11	9	2	1352	61	1	2.71	....	....	....	....	....	....	....
	Tampa Bay	NHL	17	6	5	4	914	34	2	2.23	1	0	1	111	2	0	1.08
2003-04 ♦	Tampa Bay	NHL	29	18	9	1	1688	58	1	2.06	1	0	0	34	2	0	3.53
2004-05							DID NOT PLAY										
2005-06	Tampa Bay	NHL	57	29	22	1	3152	161	5	3.06	4	1	3	188	15	0	4.79
	United States	Olympics	1	0	0	1	60	3	0	3.00	....	....	....	....	....	....	....
	NHL Totals		179	82	66	15	10000	449	12	2.69	6	1	4	333	19	0	3.42

Traded to **Tampa Bay** by **Boston** for Tampa Bay's 4th round choice (later traded to San Jose – San Jose selected Jason Churchill) in 2004 Entry Draft, January 13, 2003. Signed as a free agent by **Carolina**, July 1, 2006.

GREISS, Thomas (GRIGHS, TAW-muhs) S.J.

Goaltender. Catches left. 6'1", 192 lbs. Born, Straubing, West Germany, January 29, 1986.
(San Jose's 2nd choice, 94th overall, in 2004 Entry Draft).

			Regular Season								Playoffs						
Season	Club	League	GP	W	L	O/T	Mins	GA	SO	Avg	GP	W	L	Mins	GA	SO	Avg
2001-02	EV Fussen Jr.	Ger-Jr.					STATISTICS NOT AVAILABLE										
2002-03	Koln Jr.	Ger-Jr.	25	....	....	....	1613	58	0	2.16	3	1	2	180	8	1	2.67
2003-04	Koln Jr.	Ger-Jr.	24	....	....	....	1286	56	....	2.61	....	....	....	....	....	....	....
	Kolner Haie	Germany	1	....	....	....	20	4	0	12.00	....	....	....	....	....	....	....
2004-05	Kolner Haie	Germany	8	....	....	....	459	16	0	2.09	....	....	....	....	....	....	....
	Regensburg	German-2	1	....	....	....	60	2	0	2.00	2	....	....	56	2	0	2.14
2005-06	Kolner Haie	Germany	27	....	....	....	1560	64	1	2.46	9	....	....	533	27	*1	3.04
	Germany	Olympics	1	0	1	0	60	5	0	5.00	....	....	....	....	....	....	....

GUARD, Kelly (G'YEW-uhrd, KEHL-lee) OTT.

Goaltender. Catches left. 6', 190 lbs. Born, Prince Albert, Sask., June 10, 1983.

			Regular Season								Playoffs						
Season	Club	League	GP	W	L	O/T	Mins	GA	SO	Avg	GP	W	L	Mins	GA	SO	Avg
99-2000	Prince Albert	SMHL					STATISTICS NOT AVAILABLE										
2000-01	Prince Albert	SMHL	25	....	....	....	1488	81	0	3.27	....	....	....	....	....	....	....
	La Ronge	SJHL					STATISTICS NOT AVAILABLE										
2001-02	Kindersley Klippers	SJHL	45	29	11	4	2628	130	1	2.97	19	12	6	1145	60	1	3.14
2002-03	Kelowna Rockets	WHL	53	39	10	3	3018	97	*6	*1.93	19	*16	3	1233	36	*4	*1.75
2003-04	Kelowna Rockets	WHL	62	*44	14	4	3652	95	*13	*1.56	17	11	6	1042	31	1	1.79
2004-05	Charlotte Checkers	ECHL	26	12	11	2	1453	74	0	3.06	2	0	0	40	1	0	1.52
2005-06	Binghamton	AHL	51	25	20	1	2709	139	5	3.08	....	....	....	....	....	....	....

WHL West First All-Star Team (2003, 2004) • Memorial Cup Tournament All-Star Team (2004) • Hap Emms Memorial Trophy (Memorial Cup Tournament Top Goaltender) (2004) • Stafford Smythe Memorial Trophy (Memorial Cup Tournament MVP) (2004)

Signed as a free agent by **Ottawa**, May 11, 2004.

GUSTAFSON, Derek (GUHST-ahf-suhn, DAIR-ihk)

Goaltender. Catches left. 5'11", 210 lbs. Born, Gresham, OR, June 21, 1979.

			Regular Season								Playoffs						
Season	Club	League	GP	W	L	O/T	Mins	GA	SO	Avg	GP	W	L	Mins	GA	SO	Avg
1995-96	Seattle Ironmen	BCAHA	16	....	....	....	913	46	0	3.02	....	....	....	....	....	....	....
1996-97	Vernon Vipers	BCHL	23	....	....	....	1241	70	0	3.38	....	....	....	....	....	....	....
1997-98	Vernon Vipers	BCHL	42	27	13	2	2270	144	1	3.81	6	2	1	257	13	0	3.04
1998-99	Vernon Vipers	BCHL	42	39	3	0	2505	94	3	2.25	....	....	....	....	....	....	....
99-2000	St. Lawrence	ECAC	24	17	4	2	1475	51	2	2.07	....	....	....	....	....	....	....
2000-01	Minnesota	NHL	4	1	3	0	239	10	0	2.51	....	....	....	....	....	....	....
	Jackson Bandits	ECHL	7	4	3	0	404	15	1	2.23	....	....	....	....	....	....	....
	Cleveland	IHL	24	14	7	1	1293	59	2	2.74	2	0	1	53	5	0	5.64
2001-02	Minnesota	NHL	1	0	0	0	26	0	0	0.00	....	....	....	....	....	....	....
	Houston Aeros	AHL	38	14	13	6	2016	92	4	2.74	2	0	0	25	1	0	2.37
2002-03	Houston Aeros	AHL	41	23	14	2	2301	108	2	2.82	....	....	....	....	....	....	....
	Louisiana	ECHL	2	1	1	0	118	8	0	4.07	....	....	....	....	....	....	....
2003-04	Louisiana	ECHL	43	28	14	0	2499	87	*5	2.09	8	4	4	560	19	1	2.03
2004-05	Adirondack	UHL	57	32	18	6	3290	155	4	2.83	3	0	3	222	9	0	2.43
2005-06	Adirondack	UHL	34	22	7	4	1979	97	1	2.94	....	....	....	....	....	....	....
	Providence Bruins	AHL	10	5	3	2	578	22	1	2.28	4	2	2	211	17	0	4.83
	NHL Totals		5	1	3	0	265	10	0	2.26	....	....	....	....	....	....	....

ECAC Second All-Star Team (2000) • ECAC Rookie of the Year (2000) • ECHL Second All-Star Team (2004)

Signed as a free agent by **Minnesota**, June 9, 2000. Signed as a free agent by **Louisiana** (ECHL), October 1, 2003. Signed as a free agent by **Adirondack** (UHL) , July 23, 2004.

HALAK, Jaroslav (HAH-lak, YAHR-roh-slav) MTL.

Goaltender. Catches left. 5'11", 174 lbs. Born, Bratislava, Slovakia, May 13, 1985.
(Montreal's 11th choice, 271st overall, in 2003 Entry Draft).

			Regular Season								Playoffs						
Season	Club	League	GP	W	L	O/T	Mins	GA	SO	Avg	GP	W	L	Mins	GA	SO	Avg
2001-02	Bratislava Jr.	Slovak-Jr.	22	....	....	....	1257	41	0	1.96	6	6	0	353	7	2	1.19
2002-03	Bratislava Jr.	Slovak-Jr.	20	13	3	3	1200	41	1	2.02	....	....	....	....	....	....	....
2003-04	Bratislava Jr.	Slovak-Jr.	29	....	....	....	1694	51	....	1.81	....	....	....	....	....	....	....
	HK 91 Senica	Slovak-2	21	....	....	....	1240	54	....	2.61	....	....	....	....	....	....	....
	Bratislava	Slovakia	12	....	....	....	650	18	0	1.66	1	....	....	45	6	0	8.00

2004-05	Lewiston	QMJHL	47	24	17	4	2697	125	4	2.78	8	4	4	460	27	0	3.52
2005-06	Hamilton Bulldogs	AHL	13	7	6	0	786	30	3	2.29	....	....	....	....	....	....	....
	Long Beach	ECHL	20	11	4	2	1026	35	2	2.05	4	2	2	252	13	0	3.10

HANULJAK, Miroslav (HA-nuhl-yak, MEER-oh-slav) NSH.

Goaltender. Catches left. 6'4", 197 lbs. Born, Litvinov, Czech., September 12, 1984.
(Nashville's 12th choice, 213th overall, in 2003 Entry Draft).

			Regular Season								Playoffs						
Season	Club	League	GP	W	L	O/T	Mins	GA	SO	Avg	GP	W	L	Mins	GA	SO	Avg
99-2000	Litvinov Jr.	CzRep-Jr.	42	....	....	....	2274	130	3	3.43	....	....	....	....	....	....	....
2000-01	Litvinov Jr.	CzRep-Jr.	48	....	....	....	2647	97	11	2.20	6	....	....	361	19	0	3.16
2001-02	Litvinov Jr.	CzRep-Jr.	5	....	....	....	274	9	0	1.97	....	....	....	....	....	....	....
2002-03	Litvinov Jr.	CzRep-Jr.	30	....	....	....	1515	67	1	2.65	....	....	....	....	....	....	....
2003-04	Litvinov Jr.	CzRep-Jr.	6	....	....	....	287	10	2	2.09	....	....	....	....	....	....	....
	HC Havirov Jr.	CzRep-Jr.	26	....	....	....	1494	66	3	2.65	....	....	....	....	....	....	....
2004-05	HC Havirov Jr.	CzRep-Jr.	16	9	4	3	894	40	1	2.68	....	....	....	....	....	....	....
	HC Havirov	CzRep-2	9	3	6	0	451	25	0	3.33	....	....	....	....	....	....	....
	SK HC Banik Most	CzRep-3	11	5	5	1	595	28	0	2.82	5	2	3	300	14	0	2.80
2005-06	SK HC Banik Most	CzRep-3	26	19	5	2	1458	55	5	2.26	3	0	3	159	9	0	3.40

HARDING, Josh (HAHR-dihng, JAWSH) MIN.

Goaltender. Catches right. 6'1", 180 lbs. Born, Regina, Sask., June 18, 1984.
(Minnesota's 2nd choice, 38th overall, in 2002 Entry Draft).

			Regular Season								Playoffs						
Season	Club	League	GP	W	L	O/T	Mins	GA	SO	Avg	GP	W	L	Mins	GA	SO	Avg
2000-01	Reg. Pat Cdns.	SMHL	36	17	13	0	2106	96	2	2.75	3	1	2	170	11	0	3.88
2001-02	Regina Pats	WHL	42	27	13	1	2389	95	*4	2.39	6	2	4	325	16	0	2.95
2002-03	Regina Pats	WHL	57	18	24	13	*3385	155	3	2.75	5	1	4	321	13	0	2.43
2003-04	Regina Pats	WHL	28	12	14	2	1665	67	2	2.41	....	....	....	....	....	....	....
	Brandon	WHL	27	13	11	3	1612	65	5	2.42	11	5	6	660	36	0	3.27
2004-05	Houston Aeros	AHL	42	21	16	3	2388	80	4	2.01	2	0	2	119	8	0	4.03
2005-06	**Minnesota**	**NHL**	**3**	**2**	**1**	**0**	**185**	**8**	**1**	**2.59**	....	....	....	....	....	....	....
	Houston Aeros	AHL	38	29	8	0	2215	99	2	2.68	8	4	4	476	30	0	3.79
	NHL Totals		**3**	**2**	**1**	**0**	**185**	**8**	**1**	**2.59**	....	....	....	....	....	....	....

WHL East Second All-Star Team (2002) • WHL East First All-Star Team (2003) • WHL Goaltender of the Year (2003) • WHL Player of the Year (2003)

HASEK, Dominik (HAH-shihk, DOHM-ihn-ihk) DET.

Goaltender. Catches left. 5'11", 180 lbs. Born, Pardubice, Czech., January 29, 1965.
(Chicago's 11th choice, 207th overall, in 1983 Entry Draft).

			Regular Season								Playoffs						
Season	Club	League	GP	W	L	O/T	Mins	GA	SO	Avg	GP	W	L	Mins	GA	SO	Avg
1981-82	Tesla Pardubice	Czech	12	....	....	....	661	34	....	3.09	....	....	....	....	....	....	....
1982-83	Tesla Pardubice	Czech	42	....	....	....	2358	105	....	2.67	....	....	....	....	....	....	....
1983-84	Tesla Pardubice	Czech	40	....	....	....	2304	108	....	2.81	....	....	....	....	....	....	....
1984-85	Tesla Pardubice	Czech	42	....	....	....	2419	131	....	3.25	....	....	....	....	....	....	....
1985-86	Tesla Pardubice	Czech	45	....	....	....	2689	138	....	3.08	....	....	....	....	....	....	....
1986-87	Tesla Pardubice	Czech	43	....	....	....	2515	103	....	2.46	....	....	....	....	....	....	....
1987-88	Tesla Pardubice	Czech	31	....	....	....	1862	93	....	3.00	....	....	....	....	....	....	....
	Czechoslovakia	Olympics	5	3	2	0	217	18	1	4.98	....	....	....	....	....	....	....
1988-89	Tesla Pardubice	Czech	42	....	....	....	2507	114	....	2.73	....	....	....	....	....	....	....
1989-90	Dukla Jihlava	Czech	40	....	....	....	2251	80	....	2.13	....	....	....	....	....	....	....
1990-91	**Chicago**	**NHL**	**5**	**3**	**0**	**1**	**195**	**8**	**0**	**2.46**	**3**	**0**	**0**	**69**	**3**	**0**	**2.61**
	Indianapolis Ice	IHL	33	20	11	1	1903	80	*5	*2.52	1	1	0	60	3	0	3.00
1991-92	**Chicago**	**NHL**	**20**	**10**	**4**	**1**	**1014**	**44**	**1**	**2.60**	**3**	**0**	**2**	**158**	**8**	**0**	**3.04**
	Indianapolis Ice	IHL	20	7	10	3	1162	69	1	3.56	....	....	....	....	....	....	....
1992-93	**Buffalo**	**NHL**	**28**	**11**	**10**	**4**	**1429**	**75**	**0**	**3.15**	**1**	**1**	**0**	**45**	**1**	**0**	**1.33**
1993-94	**Buffalo**	**NHL**	**58**	**30**	**20**	**6**	**3358**	**109**	***7**	***1.95**	**7**	**3**	**4**	**484**	**13**	**2**	***1.61**
1994-95	HC Pardubice	CzRep	2	1	0	1	124	6	0	2.90	....	....	....	....	....	....	....
	Buffalo	**NHL**	**41**	**19**	**14**	**7**	**2416**	**85**	***5**	***2.11**	**5**	**1**	**4**	**309**	**18**	**0**	**3.50**
1995-96	**Buffalo**	**NHL**	**59**	**22**	**30**	**6**	**3417**	**161**	**2**	**2.83**	....	....	....	....	....	....	....
1996-97	**Buffalo**	**NHL**	**67**	**37**	**20**	**10**	**4037**	**153**	**5**	**2.27**	**3**	**1**	**1**	**153**	**5**	**0**	**1.96**
1997-98	**Buffalo**	**NHL**	***72**	**33**	**23**	**13**	***4220**	**147**	***13**	**2.09**	**15**	**10**	**5**	**948**	**32**	**1**	**2.03**
	Czech Republic	Olympics	6	*5	1	0	*369	6	*2	*0.97	....	....	....	....	....	....	....
1998-99	**Buffalo**	**NHL**	**64**	**30**	**18**	**14**	**3817**	**119**	**9**	**1.87**	**19**	**13**	**6**	**1217**	**36**	**2**	**1.77**
99-2000	**Buffalo**	**NHL**	**35**	**15**	**11**	**6**	**2066**	**76**	**3**	**2.21**	**5**	**1**	**4**	**301**	**12**	**0**	**2.39**
2000-01	**Buffalo**	**NHL**	**67**	**37**	**24**	**4**	**3904**	**137**	***11**	**2.11**	**13**	**7**	**6**	**833**	**29**	**1**	**2.09**
2001-02 ♦	**Detroit**	**NHL**	**65**	***41**	**15**	**8**	**3872**	**140**	**5**	**2.17**	***23**	***16**	**7**	***1455**	**45**	***6**	**1.86**
	Czech Republic	Olympics	4	1	2	1	239	8	0	2.01	....	....	....	....	....	....	....
2002-03			OUT OF HOCKEY – RETIRED														
2003-04	**Detroit**	**NHL**	**14**	**8**	**3**	**2**	**817**	**30**	**2**	**2.20**	....	....	....	....	....	....	....
2004-05			DID NOT PLAY														
2005-06	**Ottawa**	**NHL**	**43**	**28**	**10**	**4**	**2584**	**90**	**5**	**2.09**	....	....	....	....	....	....	....
	Czech Republic	Olympics	1	....	....	....	9	0	0	0.00	....	....	....	....	....	....	....
	NHL Totals		**638**	**324**	**202**	**86**	**37146**	**1374**	**68**	**2.22**	**97**	**53**	**39**	**5972**	**202**	**12**	**2.03**

Czechoslovakian Goaltender of the Year (1986, 1987, 1988, 1989, 1990) • Czechoslovakian Player of the Year (1987, 1989, 1990) • Czechoslovakian First All-Star Team (1988, 1989, 1990) • IHL First All-Star Team (1991) • NHL All-Rookie Team (1992) • NHL First All-Star Team (1994, 1995, 1997, 1998, 1999, 2001) • William M. Jennings Trophy (1994) (shared with Grant Fuhr) • Vezina Trophy (1994, 1995, 1997, 1998, 1999, 2001) • Lester B. Pearson Award (1997, 1998) • Hart Trophy (1997, 1998) • William M. Jennings Trophy (2001)

Played in NHL All-Star Game (1996, 1997, 1998, 1999, 2001, 2002)

Traded to **Buffalo** by **Chicago** for Stephane Beauregard and Buffalo's 4th round choice (Eric Daze) in 1993 Entry Draft, August 7, 1992. Traded to **Detroit** by **Buffalo** for Vyacheslav Kozlov, Detroit's 1st round choice (later traded to Columbus – later traded to Atlanta – Atlanta selected Jim Slater) in 2002 Entry Draft and future considerations, July 1, 2001. • Officially announced retirement, June 25, 2002. • **Detroit** picked up the option on his contract, July 1, 2003. • Missed majority of 2003-04 season recovering from groin injury suffered in game vs. St. Louis, October 29, 2003. Signed as a free agent by **Ottawa**, July 6, 2004. Signed as a free agent by **Detroit**, July 31, 2006.

HAUSER, Adam (HOW-suhr, A-duhm)

Goaltender. Catches left. 6'2", 195 lbs. Born, Bovey, MN, May 27, 1980.
(Edmonton's 4th choice, 81st overall, in 1999 Entry Draft).

			Regular Season								Playoffs						
Season	Club	League	GP	W	L	O/T	Mins	GA	SO	Avg	GP	W	L	Mins	GA	SO	Avg
1996-97	Greenway Raiders	High-MN	25	....	....	....	1496	63	0	2.54	....	....	....	....	....	....	....
1997-98	USNTDP	U-18	19	9	5	4	1138	44	1	2.32	....	....	....	....	....	....	....
	USNTDP	USHL	13	5	4	3	668	39	1	3.50	....	....	....	....	....	....	....
	USNTDP	NAHL	5	4	1	0	304	11	1	2.17	1	1	0	60	0	1	0.00
1998-99	U. of Minnesota	WCHA	*40	14	18	8	*2350	136	3	3.47	....	....	....	....	....	....	....
99-2000	U. of Minnesota	WCHA	36	20	14	2	2114	104	1	2.95	....	....	....	....	....	....	....
2000-01	U. of Minnesota	WCHA	40	*26	12	2	2366	101	*3	2.56	....	....	....	....	....	....	....
2001-02	U. of Minnesota	WCHA	35	*23	6	4	2003	80	1	2.40	....	....	....	....	....	....	....
2002-03	Jackson Bandits	ECHL	34	20	9	4	2021	83	*5	2.46	....	....	....	....	....	....	....
	Providence Bruins	AHL	1	0	0	1	64	3	0	2.80	....	....	....	....	....	....	....
2003-04	Manchester	AHL	43	20	15	7	2536	82	7	1.94	4	2	2	286	9	2	1.89
	Reading Royals	ECHL	4	3	0	1	245	7	1	1.71	....	....	....	....	....	....	....
2004-05	Manchester	AHL	32	19	11	0	1867	60	5	1.93	2	0	0	70	2	0	1.71
2005-06	**Los Angeles**	**NHL**	**1**	**0**	**0**	**0**	**51**	**6**	**0**	**7.06**	....	....	....	....	....	....	....
	Manchester	AHL	45	22	17	2	2600	111	3	2.56	3	1	2	177	9	0	3.05
	NHL Totals		**1**	**0**	**0**	**0**	**51**	**6**	**0**	**7.06**	....	....	....	....	....	....	....

NCAA Championship All-Tournament Team (2002) • ECHL All-Rookie Team (2003)

Signed as a free agent by **Manchester** (AHL), August 19, 2003. Signed as a free agent by **Los Angeles**, July 8, 2004. Signed as a free agent by **Koln**, July 9, 2006.

HEDBERG, Johan (HEHD-buhrg, YO-han) ATL.

Goaltender. Catches left. 6', 184 lbs. Born, Leksand, Sweden, May 5, 1973.
(Philadelphia's 8th choice, 218th overall, in 1994 Entry Draft).

			Regular Season								Playoffs						
Season	Club	League	GP	W	L	O/T	Mins	GA	SO	Avg	GP	W	L	Mins	GA	SO	Avg
1992-93	Leksands IF	Sweden	10	....	....	....	600	24	....	2.40	....	....	....	....	....	....	....
1993-94	Leksands IF	Sweden	17	....	....	....	1020	48	....	2.82	....	....	....	....	....	....	....
1994-95	Leksands IF	Sweden	17	....	....	....	986	58	....	3.53	....	....	....	....	....	....	....
1995-96	Leksands IF	Sweden	34	....	....	....	2013	95	....	2.83	4	....	....	240	13	....	3.25
1996-97	Leksands IF	Sweden	38	....	....	....	2260	95	3	2.52	8	....	....	581	18	1	1.86
1997-98	Baton Rouge	ECHL	2	1	1	0	100	7	0	4.20	....	....	....	....	....	....	....
	Detroit Vipers	IHL	16	7	2	2	726	32	1	2.64	....	....	....	....	....	....	....
	Manitoba Moose	IHL	14	8	4	1	745	32	1	2.58	2	0	2	105	6	0	3.40
1998-99	Leksands IF	Sweden	*48	....	....	....	*2940	140	0	2.86	4	....	....	255	15	0	3.53
99-2000	Kentucky	AHL	33	18	9	5	1973	88	3	2.68	5	3	2	311	10	1	1.93
2000-01	Manitoba Moose	IHL	46	23	13	7	2697	115	1	2.56	....	....	....	....	....	....	....
	Pittsburgh	**NHL**	**9**	**7**	**1**	**1**	**545**	**24**	**0**	**2.64**	**18**	**9**	**9**	**1123**	**43**	**2**	**2.30**
2001-02	**Pittsburgh**	**NHL**	**66**	**25**	**34**	**7**	**3877**	**178**	**6**	**2.75**	....	....	....	....	....	....	....
	Sweden	Olympics	1	1	0	0	60	1	0	1.00	....	....	....	....	....	....	....
2002-03	**Pittsburgh**	**NHL**	**41**	**14**	**22**	**4**	**2410**	**126**	**1**	**3.14**	....	....	....	....	....	....	....
2003-04	**Vancouver**	**NHL**	**21**	**8**	**6**	**2**	**1098**	**46**	**3**	**2.51**	**2**	**1**	**1**	**98**	**4**	**0**	**2.45**
	Manitoba Moose	AHL	2	0	2	0	125	9	0	4.32	....	....	....	....	....	....	....
2004-05	Leksands IF	Sweden-2	21	....	....	....	1274	45	1	2.12	....	....	....	....	....	....	....
2005-06	**Dallas**	**NHL**	**19**	**12**	**4**	**1**	**1079**	**48**	**0**	**2.67**	....	....	....	....	....	....	....
	NHL Totals		**156**	**66**	**67**	**15**	**9009**	**422**	**10**	**2.81**	**20**	**10**	**10**	**1221**	**47**	**2**	**2.31**

Rights traded to **San Jose** by **Philadelphia** for San Jose's 7th round choice (Pavel Kasparik) in 1999 Entry Draft, August 6, 1998. Traded to **Pittsburgh** by **San Jose** with Bobby Dollas for Jeff Norton, March 12, 2001. Traded to **Vancouver** by **Pittsburgh** for Vancouver's 2nd round choice (Alex Goligoski) in 2004 Entry Draft, August 25, 2003. Signed as a free agent by **Leksands** (Sweden-2), August 1, 2004. Signed as a free agent by **Dallas**, August 5, 2005. Signed as a free agent by **Atlanta**, July 1, 2006.

HEINO-LINDBERG, Chris (HAY-noh-LIHND-buhrg, KRIHS) MTL.

Goaltender. Catches right. 6', 163 lbs. Born, Helsingborg, Sweden, January 29, 1985.
(Montreal's 7th choice, 177th overall, in 2003 Entry Draft).

			Regular Season								Playoffs						
Season	Club	League	GP	W	L	O/T	Mins	GA	SO	Avg	GP	W	L	Mins	GA	SO	Avg
2001-02	Hammarby Jr.	Swe-Jr.	17	....	....	....	987	59	0	3.59	....	....	....	....	....	....	....
2002-03	Hammarby U18	Swe-U18	3	....	....	....	180	9	0	3.00	....	....	....	....	....	....	....
	Hammarby Jr.	Swe-Jr.	23	....	....	....	1383	80	0	3.47	2	....	....	128	6	0	2.81
	Hammarby	Sweden-2	1	....	....	....	60	2	0	2.00	....	....	....	....	....	....	....
2003-04	IF Vallentuna BK	Sweden-2	23	....	....	....	1157	92	0	4.77	....	....	....	....	....	....	....
	Hammarby	Sweden-2	3	....	....	....	105	8	0	4.57	....	....	....	....	....	....	....
	Hammarby Jr.	Swe-Jr.	8	....	....	....	483	20	0	2.48	2	....	....	122	10	0	4.92
2004-05	Hammarby Jr.	Swe-Jr.	3	....	....	....	189	7	0	2.22	....	....	....	....	....	....	....
	Hammarby	Sweden-2	41	....	....	....	2475	89	3	2.16	....	....	....	....	....	....	....
2005-06	Farjestad	Sweden	7	....	....	....	383	16	1	2.51	1	....	....	20	2	0	6.00
	Nybro Vikings IF	Sweden-2	5	....	....	....	298	19	0	3.82	....	....	....	....	....	....	....

HELENIUS, Riku (heh-lehn-NEE-uhs, REE-koo) T.B.

Goaltender. Catches left. 6'3", 202 lbs. Born, Palkane, Finland, March 1, 1988.
(Tampa Bay's 1st choice, 15th overall, in 2006 Entry Draft).

			Regular Season								Playoffs						
Season	Club	League	GP	W	L	O/T	Mins	GA	SO	Avg	GP	W	L	Mins	GA	SO	Avg
2004-05	Ilves Tampere U18	Fin-U18	16	....	....	....	903	30	3	1.99	5	....	....	295	15	0	3.05
	Ilves Tampere Jr.	Fin-Jr.	2	....	....	....	86	4	0	2.77	....	....	....	....	....	....	....
2005-06	Suomi U20	Finland-2	1	....	....	....	60	3	0	3.00	....	....	....	....	....	....	....
	Ilves Tampere U18	Fin-U18	2	....	....	....	120	2	0	1.00	5	....	....	300	13	0	2.60
	Ilves Tampere Jr.	Fin-Jr.	26	....	....	....	1565	70	4	2.68	2	....	....	135	7	0	3.11

HNILICKA, Milan (huh-LEETCH-kuh, MEE-lan)

Goaltender. Catches left. 6'1", 190 lbs. Born, Pardubice, Czech., June 25, 1973.
(NY Islanders' 4th choice, 70th overall, in 1991 Entry Draft).

			Regular Season								Playoffs						
Season	Club	League	GP	W	L	O/T	Mins	GA	SO	Avg	GP	W	L	Mins	GA	SO	Avg
1989-90	Poldi Kladno	Czech	24	....	....	....	1113	70	....	3.77	....	....	....	....	....	....	....
1990-91	Poldi Kladno	Czech	40	....	....	....	2122	98	0	2.80	....	....	....	....	....	....	....
1991-92	Poldi Kladno	Czech	38	....	....	....	2066	128	0	3.73	....	....	....	....	....	....	....
1992-93	Swift Current	WHL	*65	*46	12	2	3679	206	2	3.36	*17	*12	5	*1017	54	*2	3.19
1993-94	Richmond	ECHL	43	18	16	5	2299	155	4	4.05	....	....	....	....	....	....	....
	Salt Lake	IHL	8	5	1	0	378	25	0	3.97	....	....	....	....	....	....	....
1994-95	Denver Grizzlies	IHL	15	9	4	1	798	47	1	3.53	....	....	....	....	....	....	....
1995-96	HC Poldi Kladno	CzRep	33	....	....	....	1959	93	1	2.84	8	....	....	493	24	....	2.92
1996-97	HC Poldi Kladno	CzRep	48	....	....	....	2736	120	*4	2.63	3	....	....	151	14	0	5.56
1997-98	HC Sparta Praha	CzRep	49	....	....	....	2847	99	....	2.09	11	....	....	632	31	....	3.00
1998-99	HC Sparta Praha	CzRep	*50	....	....	....	*2877	109	....	2.27	8	....	....	507	13	....	*1.54
99-2000	**NY Rangers**	**NHL**	**2**	**0**	**1**	**0**	**86**	**5**	**0**	**3.49**	....	....	....	....	....	....	....
	Hartford Wolf Pack	AHL	36	22	11	0	1979	71	5	*2.15	3	0	1	99	6	0	3.64
2000-01	**Atlanta**	**NHL**	**36**	**12**	**19**	**2**	**1879**	**105**	**2**	**3.35**	....	....	....	....	....	....	....
2001-02	**Atlanta**	**NHL**	**60**	**13**	**33**	**10**	**3367**	**179**	**3**	**3.19**	....	....	....	....	....	....	....
2002-03	**Atlanta**	**NHL**	**21**	**4**	**13**	**1**	**1097**	**65**	**0**	**3.56**	....	....	....	....	....	....	....
	Chicago Wolves	AHL	15	11	2	1	838	33	1	2.36	....	....	....	....	....	....	....
2003-04	**Los Angeles**	**NHL**	**2**	**0**	**1**	**0**	**80**	**5**	**0**	**3.75**	....	....	....	....	....	....	....
	Manchester	AHL	20	8	10	0	1022	44	1	2.58	2	0	2	127	5	0	2.37
2004-05	Liberec	CzRep	46	....	....	....	2740	106	5	2.32	12	....	....	702	32	0	2.74
2005-06	Liberec	CzRep	45	....	....	....	2644	75	*6	*1.70	4	....	....	158	10	0	3.80
	Czech Republic	Olympics	3	....	....	....	128	6	0	2.82	....	....	....	....	....	....	....
	NHL Totals		**121**	**29**	**67**	**13**	**6509**	**359**	**5**	**3.31**	....	....	....	....	....	....	....

Harry "Hap" Holmes Memorial Award (fewest goals against – AHL) (2000) (shared with Jean-Francois Labbe)

Signed as a free agent by **NY Rangers**, July 15, 1999. Signed as a free agent by **Atlanta**, July 28, 2000. Traded to **Los Angeles** by **Atlanta** for future considerations, September 15, 2003. • Missed majority of 2003-04 season recovering from finger injury suffered in game vs. Phoenix, December 31, 2003. Signed as a free agent by **Liberec** (CzRep), May 18, 2004.

HOLMQVIST, Johan (HOHLM-kvihst, YOH-han) T.B.

Goaltender. Catches left. 6'3", 195 lbs. Born, Tolfta, Sweden, May 24, 1978.
(NY Rangers' 9th choice, 175th overall, in 1997 Entry Draft).

			Regular Season								Playoffs						
Season	Club	League	GP	W	L	O/T	Mins	GA	SO	Avg	GP	W	L	Mins	GA	SO	Avg
1996-97	Brynas IF Gavle	Sweden	2	0	0	0	80	4	0	3.00	....	....	....	....	....	....	....
1997-98	Brynas IF Gavle	Sweden	33	....	....	....	1897	82	....	2.59	3	0	3	180	14	....	4.67
1998-99	Brynas IF Gavle	Sweden	41	....	....	....	2383	111	4	2.79	*14	9	5	*855	34	0	2.39

99-2000	Brynas IF Gavle	Sweden	41	....	....	....	2402	104	4	2.60	11	....	....	671	30	1	2.68
2000-01	**NY Rangers**	**NHL**	**2**	**0**	**2**	**0**	**119**	**10**	**0**	**5.04**	....	....	....	....	....	....	....
	Hartford Wolf Pack	AHL	43	19	14	4	2305	111	2	2.89	5	2	3	314	13	0	2.48
2001-02	**NY Rangers**	**NHL**	**1**	**0**	**0**	**0**	**9**	**0**	**0**	**0.00**	....	....	....	....	....	....	....
	Hartford Wolf Pack	AHL	48	26	12	6	2734	140	1	3.07	4	1	2	163	12	0	4.41
2002-03	**NY Rangers**	**NHL**	**1**	**0**	**1**	**0**	**39**	**2**	**0**	**3.08**	....	....	....	....	....	....	....
	Hartford Wolf Pack	AHL	35	14	13	5	1904	84	2	2.65	....	....	....	....	....	....	....
	Charlotte Checkers	ECHL	1	1	0	0	60	2	0	2.00	....	....	....	....	....	....	....
	Houston Aeros	AHL	8	5	3	0	479	23	1	2.88	*23	*15	8	*1499	50	1	2.00
2003-04	Houston Aeros	AHL	59	23	27	7	3467	148	4	2.56	....	....	....	....	....	....	....
2004-05	Brynas IF Gavle	Sweden	42	....	....	....	2445	138	1	3.39	....	....	....	....	....	....	....
2005-06	Brynas IF Gavle	Sweden	26	....	....	....	1539	50	3	*1.95	4	....	....	194	13	0	4.02
	NHL Totals		**4**	**0**	**3**	**0**	**167**	**12**	**0**	**4.31**	....	....	....	....	....	....	....

Jack A. Butterfield Trophy (Playoff MVP – AHL) (2003)

Traded to **Minnesota** by **NY Rangers** for Lawrence Nycholat, March 11, 2003. Signed as a free agent by **Gavle** (Sweden), July 29, 2004. Signed as a free agent by **Tampa Bay**, June 1, 2006.

HOLT, Chris (HOHLT, KRIHS) NYR

Goaltender. Catches left. 6'2", 218 lbs. Born, Vancouver, B.C., June 5, 1985.
(NY Rangers' 8th choice, 180th overall, in 2003 Entry Draft).

			Regular Season								Playoffs						
Season	Club	League	GP	W	L	O/T	Mins	GA	SO	Avg	GP	W	L	Mins	GA	SO	Avg
2001-02	Billings Bulls	AWHL	24	13	7	1	1184	59	2	2.99	....	....	....	....	....	....	....
2002-03	USNTDP	U-18	27	7	12	2	1519	81	1	3.20	....	....	....	....	....	....	....
	USNTDP	NAHL	5	2	3	0	255	14	0	3.30	....	....	....	....	....	....	....
2003-04	Nebraska-Omaha	CCHA	27	5	17	2	1499	81	0	3.24	....	....	....	....	....	....	....
2004-05	Nebraska-Omaha	CCHA	37	19	14	4	2190	106	1	2.90	....	....	....	....	....	....	....
2005-06	**NY Rangers**	**NHL**	**1**	**0**	**0**	**0**	**10**	**0**	**0**	**0.00**	....	....	....	....	....	....	....
	Hartford Wolf Pack	AHL	9	3	2	1	459	31	0	4.06	8	4	4	487	24	0	2.96
	Charlotte Checkers	ECHL	23	7	11	1	1229	84	0	4.10	....	....	....	....	....	....	....
	NHL Totals		**1**	**0**	**0**	**0**	**10**	**0**	**0**	**0.00**	....	....	....	....	....	....	....

HOSTIKKA, Ville (HAWS-tih-kuh, VIHL-ee) PHI.

Goaltender. Catches left. 6'3", 209 lbs. Born, Lappeenranta, Finland, March 21, 1985.
(Philadelphia's 11th choice, 193rd overall, in 2003 Entry Draft).

			Regular Season								Playoffs						
Season	Club	League	GP	W	L	O/T	Mins	GA	SO	Avg	GP	W	L	Mins	GA	SO	Avg
2001-02	SaiPa U18	Fin-U18	24	8	11	4	1392	82	2	3.53	....	....	....	....	....	....	....
	SaiPa Jr.	Fin-Jr.	4	4	0	0	240	9	1	2.25	2	0	0	68	5	0	4.41
2002-03	SaiPa U18	Fin-U18	11	6	3	2	668	26	2	2.33	....	....	....	....	....	....	....
	SaiPa Jr.	Fin-Jr.	19	8	5	2	1082	53	0	2.94	1	0	1	58	5	0	5.17
2003-04	SaiPa Jr.	Fin-Jr.	12	1	6	3	645	41	0	3.81	....	....	....	....	....	....	....
2004-05	Lukko Rauma Jr.	Fin-Jr.	30	11	12	5	1808	96	1	3.18	....	....	....	....	....	....	....
2005-06	SaiPa Jr.	Fin-Jr.	36	....	....	....	2046	101	1	2.96	3	....	....	197	2	2	0.61

HOULE, Martin (HOOL, MAHR-tehn) PHI.

Goaltender. Catches left. 5'10", 170 lbs. Born, Montreal, Que., February 12, 1985.
(Philadelphia's 8th choice, 232nd overall, in 2004 Entry Draft).

			Regular Season								Playoffs						
Season	Club	League	GP	W	L	O/T	Mins	GA	SO	Avg	GP	W	L	Mins	GA	SO	Avg
2001-02	Antoine-Girouard	QAAA	23	17	4	2	1309	45	1	2.06	....	....	....	....	....	....	....
	Cape Breton	QMJHL	1	1	0	0	38	0	0	0.00	....	....	....	....	....	....	....
2002-03	Cape Breton	QMJHL	30	4	18	3	1450	98	0	4.06	1	0	0	11	0	0	0.00
2003-04	Cape Breton	QMJHL	51	34	15	1	2951	114	3	2.32	1	0	1	59	4	0	4.10
2004-05	Cape Breton	QMJHL	56	26	18	5	3108	130	*6	2.51	4	1	3	246	10	0	*2.44
2005-06	Philadelphia	AHL	40	18	18	1	2153	91	2	2.54	....	....	....	....	....	....	....
	Trenton Titans	ECHL	7	4	3	0	429	15	1	2.10	....	....	....	....	....	....	....

QMJHL First All-Star Team (2004)

HOVINEN, Niko (HOH-vih-nehn, NEE-koh) MIN.

Goaltender. Catches left. 6'6", 200 lbs. Born, Helsinki, Finland, March 16, 1988.
(Minnesota's 5th choice, 132nd overall, in 2006 Entry Draft).

			Regular Season								Playoffs						
Season	Club	League	GP	W	L	O/T	Mins	GA	SO	Avg	GP	W	L	Mins	GA	SO	Avg
2004-05	Jokerit U18	Fin-U18	20	....	....	....	1166	38	3	1.95	4	....	....	246	9	1	2.20
	Jokerit Helsinki Jr.	Fin-Jr.	4	....	....	....	242	13	0	3.21	....	....	....	....	....	....	....
2005-06	Jokerit Helsinki Jr.	Fin-Jr.	26	....	....	....	1480	77	0	3.12	....	....	....	....	....	....	....
	Jokerit U18	Fin-U18	11	....	....	....	637	34	1	3.20	4	....	....	232	14	1	3.62
	Suomi U20	Finland-2	1	....	....	....	60	4	0	4.00	....	....	....	....	....	....	....

HOWARD, James (HOW-uhrd, JAYMZ) DET.

Goaltender. Catches left. 6', 218 lbs. Born, Syracuse, NY, March 26, 1984.
(Detroit's 1st choice, 64th overall, in 2003 Entry Draft).

			Regular Season								Playoffs						
Season	Club	League	GP	W	L	O/T	Mins	GA	SO	Avg	GP	W	L	Mins	GA	SO	Avg
2001-02	USNTDP	U-18	19	15	4	1	1170	37	4	1.90	....	....	....	....	....	....	....
	USNTDP	USHL	8	4	3	0	425	14	0	1.98	....	....	....	....	....	....	....
	USNTDP	NAHL	8	3	4	0	381	25	0	3.93	....	....	....	....	....	....	....
2002-03	University of Maine	H-East	21	14	6	0	1151	47	3	2.45	....	....	....	....	....	....	....
2003-04	University of Maine	H-East	23	14	4	3	1364	27	*6	*1.19	....	....	....	....	....	....	....
2004-05	University of Maine	H-East	*39	*19	13	7	*2310	74	*6	1.92	....	....	....	....	....	....	....
2005-06	**Detroit**	**NHL**	**4**	**1**	**2**	**0**	**201**	**10**	**0**	**2.99**	....	....	....	....	....	....	....
	Grand Rapids	AHL	38	27	6	2	2140	92	2	2.58	13	5	7	763	44	0	3.46
	NHL Totals		**4**	**1**	**2**	**0**	**201**	**10**	**0**	**2.99**	....	....	....	....	....	....	....

Hockey East All-Rookie Team (2003) • Hockey East Rookie of the Year (2003) • Hockey East First All-Star Team (2004) • NCAA East Second All-American Team (2004) • AHL All-Rookie Team (2006)

HUET, Cristobal (oo-AY, KRIHS-toh-bahl) MTL.

Goaltender. Catches left. 6', 194 lbs. Born, St. Martin d'Heres, France, September 3, 1975.
(Los Angeles' 9th choice, 214th overall, in 2001 Entry Draft).

			Regular Season								Playoffs						
Season	Club	League	GP	W	L	O/T	Mins	GA	SO	Avg	GP	W	L	Mins	GA	SO	Avg
1997-98	CSG Grenoble	France					Statistics Not Available										
	France	Olympics	2	1	1	0	120	5	0	2.50	....	....	....	....	....	....	....
1998-99	HC Lugano	Swiss	21	....	....	....	1275	58	1	2.73	10	....	....	628	18	1	*1.72
99-2000	HC Lugano	Swiss	31	....	....	....	1886	50	*8	*1.59	13	....	....	783	29	0	2.22
2000-01	HC Lugano	Swiss	39	....	....	....	2365	77	*6	*1.95	*18	....	....	*1141	39	2	2.05
2001-02	HC Lugano	Swiss	39	....	....	....	2313	107	*4	2.78	1	0	1	60	3	0	3.00
	France	Olympics	3	0	2	1	179	10	0	3.36	....	....	....	....	....	....	....
2002-03	**Los Angeles**	**NHL**	**12**	**4**	**4**	**1**	**541**	**21**	**1**	**2.33**	....	....	....	....	....	....	....
	Manchester	AHL	30	16	8	5	1784	68	1	2.29	1	0	1	30	4	0	8.08
2003-04	**Los Angeles**	**NHL**	**41**	**10**	**16**	**10**	**2199**	**89**	**3**	**2.43**	....	....	....	....	....	....	....
2004-05	Adler Mannheim	Germany	36	....	....	....	2001	93	1	2.79	*14	....	....	*850	40	2	2.82
2005-06	**Montreal**	**NHL**	**36**	**18**	**11**	**4**	**2103**	**77**	**7**	**2.20**	**6**	**2**	**4**	**386**	**15**	**0**	**2.33**
	Hamilton Bulldogs	AHL	4	0	4	0	237	15	0	3.79	....	....	....	....	....	....	....
	NHL Totals		**89**	**32**	**31**	**15**	**4843**	**187**	**11**	**2.32**	**6**	**2**	**4**	**386**	**15**	**0**	**2.33**

Traded to **Montreal** by **Los Angeles** with Radek Bonk for Mathieu Garon and San Jose's 3rd round choice (previously acquired, Los Angeles selected Paul Baier) in 2004 Entry Draft, June 26, 2004. Signed as a free agent by **Mannheim** (Germany), September 14, 2004.

HURME, Jani (HOOR-meh, YAN-ee)

Goaltender. Catches left. 6', 190 lbs. Born, Turku, Finland, January 7, 1975.
(Ottawa's 2nd choice, 58th overall, in 1997 Entry Draft).

			Regular Season								Playoffs						
Season	Club	League	GP	W	L	O/T	Mins	GA	SO	Avg	GP	W	L	Mins	GA	SO	Avg
1992-93	TPS Turku Jr.	Fin-Jr.	12	7	4	0	669	47	0	4.21	1	....	....	60	11	0	11.00
1993-94	Kiekko-67 Jr.	Fin-Jr.	18	....	....	....	1082	57	0	3.16	....	....	....	....	....	....	....
	Kiekko-67 Turku	Finland-2	3	....	....	....	190	7	0	2.21	....	....	....	....	....	....	....
	TPS Turku	Finland	1	0	0	0	2	0	0	0.00	....	....	....	....	....	....	....
1994-95	TPS Turku Jr.	Fin-Jr.	2	1	0	1	125	5	0	2.40	....	....	....	....	....	....	....
	Kiekko-67 Jr.	Fin-Jr.	9	2	7	0	539	47	0	5.23	....	....	....	....	....	....	....
	Kiekko-67 Turku	Finland-2	19	....	....	....	1049	53	....	3.03	7	4	3	411	20	0	2.92
1995-96	TPS Turku Jr.	Fin-Jr.	13	8	5	0	777	34	1	2.63	....	....	....	....	....	....	....
	Kiekko-67 Turku	Finland-2	16	11	3	2	968	39	1	2.42	....	....	....	....	....	....	....
	TPS Turku	Finland	16	14	1	1	945	34	2	2.16	10	7	3	545	22	2	2.42
1996-97	Kiekko-67 Turku	Finland-2	....	....	....	....	....	....	....	....	3	1	2	187	12	0	3.85
	TPS Turku	Finland	48	31	11	6	2917	101	6	2.08	12	6	6	722	39	0	3.24
1997-98	Detroit Vipers	IHL	6	2	2	2	290	20	0	4.13	....	....	....	....	....	....	....
	Indianapolis Ice	IHL	29	11	11	3	1506	83	1	3.30	3	1	0	129	10	0	4.62
1998-99	Detroit Vipers	IHL	12	7	3	1	643	26	1	2.43	....	....	....	....	....	....	....
	Cincinnati	IHL	26	14	9	2	1428	81	0	3.40	....	....	....	....	....	....	....
99-2000	**Ottawa**	**NHL**	**1**	**1**	**0**	**0**	**60**	**2**	**0**	**2.00**	....	....	....	....	....	....	....
	Grand Rapids	IHL	52	29	15	4	2948	107	4	2.18	*17	*10	7	*1028	37	1	2.16
2000-01	**Ottawa**	**NHL**	**22**	**12**	**5**	**4**	**1296**	**54**	**2**	**2.50**	....	....	....	....	....	....	....
2001-02	**Ottawa**	**NHL**	**25**	**12**	**9**	**1**	**1309**	**54**	**3**	**2.48**	....	....	....	....	....	....	....
	Finland	Olympics	3	1	2	0	179	9	0	3.01	....	....	....	....	....	....	....
2002-03	**Florida**	**NHL**	**28**	**4**	**11**	**6**	**1376**	**66**	**1**	**2.88**	....	....	....	....	....	....	....
2003-04							Did Not Play – Injured										
2004-05							Did Not Play – Injured										
2005-06	Chicago Wolves	AHL	6	2	4	0	314	19	0	3.64	....	....	....	....	....	....	....
	Columbia Inferno	ECHL	15	6	7	2	894	52	0	3.49	....	....	....	....	....	....	....
	Portland Pirates	AHL	16	11	5	0	970	37	1	2.29	....	....	....	....	....	....	....
	NHL Totals		**76**	**29**	**25**	**11**	**4041**	**176**	**6**	**2.61**	....	....	....	....	....	....	....

Finnish Elite League Rookie of the Year (1996) • Finnish Elite League Player of the Year (1997) • IHL Second All-Star Team (2000)

Traded to **Florida** by **Ottawa** for Billy Thompson and Greg Watson, October 1, 2002. Claimed by **Carolina** from **Florida** in Waiver Draft, October 3, 2003. Traded to **Atlanta** by **Carolina** for Atlanta's 4th round choice (Brett Carson) in 2004 Entry Draft, October 3, 2003. • Missed entire 2003-04 and 2004-05 seasons recovering from back injury suffered in training camp, October, 2003. Traded to **Anaheim** by **Atlanta** for Joel Stepp, March 1, 2006.

IRVING, Leland (UHR-vihng, LEE-land) CGY.

Goaltender. Catches left. 6', 177 lbs. Born, Barrhead, Alta., April 11, 1988.
(Calgary's 1st choice, 26th overall, in 2006 Entry Draft).

			Regular Season								Playoffs						
Season	Club	League	GP	W	L	O/T	Mins	GA	SO	Avg	GP	W	L	Mins	GA	SO	Avg
2004-05	Everett Silvertips	WHL	23	9	8	1	1132	34	2	1.80	....	....	....	....	....	....	....
2005-06	Everett Silvertips	WHL	67	37	22	4	3791	121	4	1.92	12	8	3	747	21	3	1.69

JOHNSON, Brent (JAWN-suhn, BREHNT) WSH.

Goaltender. Catches left. 6'3", 196 lbs. Born, Farmington, MI, March 12, 1977.
(Colorado's 5th choice, 129th overall, in 1995 Entry Draft).

			Regular Season								Playoffs						
Season	Club	League	GP	W	L	O/T	Mins	GA	SO	Avg	GP	W	L	Mins	GA	SO	Avg
1993-94	Det. Compuware	NAHL	18	....	....	....	1024	49	1	3.52	....	....	....	....	....	....	....
1994-95	Owen Sound	OHL	18	3	9	1	904	75	0	4.98	....	....	....	....	....	....	....
1995-96	Owen Sound	OHL	58	24	28	1	3211	243	1	4.54	6	2	4	371	29	0	4.69
1996-97	Owen Sound	OHL	50	20	28	1	2798	201	1	4.31	4	0	4	253	24	0	5.69
1997-98	Worcester IceCats	AHL	42	14	15	7	2240	119	0	3.19	6	3	2	332	19	0	3.43
1998-99	**St. Louis**	**NHL**	**6**	**3**	**2**	**0**	**286**	**10**	**0**	**2.10**	....	....	....	....	....	....	....
	Worcester IceCats	AHL	49	22	22	4	2925	146	2	2.99	4	1	3	238	12	0	3.02
99-2000	Worcester IceCats	AHL	58	24	27	5	3319	161	3	2.91	9	4	5	561	23	1	2.46
2000-01	**St. Louis**	**NHL**	**31**	**19**	**9**	**2**	**1744**	**63**	**4**	**2.17**	**2**	**0**	**1**	**62**	**2**	**0**	**1.94**
2001-02	**St. Louis**	**NHL**	**58**	**34**	**20**	**4**	**3491**	**127**	**5**	**2.18**	**10**	**5**	**5**	**590**	**18**	**3**	**1.83**
2002-03	**St. Louis**	**NHL**	**38**	**16**	**13**	**5**	**2042**	**84**	**2**	**2.47**	....	....	....	....	....	....	....
	Worcester IceCats	AHL	2	0	1	1	125	8	0	3.84	....	....	....	....	....	....	....
2003-04	**St. Louis**	**NHL**	**10**	**4**	**3**	**1**	**493**	**20**	**1**	**2.43**	....	....	....	....	....	....	....
	Worcester IceCats	AHL	8	2	2	2	365	14	0	2.30	....	....	....	....	....	....	....
	Phoenix	**NHL**	**8**	**1**	**6**	**1**	**486**	**21**	**0**	**2.59**	....	....	....	....	....	....	....
2004-05							Did Not Play										
2005-06	**Washington**	**NHL**	**26**	**9**	**12**	**1**	**1413**	**81**	**1**	**3.44**	....	....	....	....	....	....	....
	NHL Totals		**177**	**86**	**65**	**14**	**9955**	**406**	**13**	**2.45**	**12**	**5**	**6**	**652**	**20**	**3**	**1.84**

Traded to **St. Louis** by **Colorado** for San Jose's 3rd round choice (previously acquired, Colorado selected Rick Berry) in 1997 Entry Draft, May 30, 1997. Traded to **Phoenix** by **St. Louis** for Mike Sillinger, March 4, 2004. Signed as a free agent by **Vancouver**, September 1, 2005. Claimed on waivers by **Washington** from **Vancouver**, October 4, 2005.

JOHNSON, Chad (JAWN-suhn, CHAD) PIT.

Goaltender. Catches left. 6'2", 175 lbs. Born, Calgary, Alta., June 10, 1986.
(Pittsburgh's 4th choice, 125th overall, in 2006 Entry Draft).

			Regular Season								Playoffs						
Season	Club	League	GP	W	L	O/T	Mins	GA	SO	Avg	GP	W	L	Mins	GA	SO	Avg
2002-03	Calgary Buffaloes	AMHL	....	8	8	2	1145	62	....	3.25	1	0	1	60	3	0	3.00
2003-04	Brooks Bandits	AJHL	31	6	20	3	1782	117	0	3.94	....	....	....	....	....	....	....
2004-05	Brooks Bandits	AJHL	43	25	16	2	2505	109	2	2.61	119	4	5	493	....	....	....
2005-06	Alaska-Fairbanks	CCHA	18	6	7	4	985	42	0	2.56	....	....	....	....	....	....	....

JOSEPH, Curtis (JOH-sehf, KUR-tihs) PHX.

Goaltender. Catches left. 5'11", 190 lbs. Born, Keswick, Ont., April 29, 1967.

			Regular Season								Playoffs						
Season	Club	League	GP	W	L	O/T	Mins	GA	SO	Avg	GP	W	L	Mins	GA	SO	Avg
1984-85	King City Dukes	OHA-B	18	....	....	....	947	76	0	4.82	....	....	....	....	....	....	....
	Newmarket Flyers	OPJHL	2	1	1	0	120	16	0	8.00	....	....	....	....	....	....	....
1985-86	Richmond Hill	OPJHL	33	12	18	0	1716	156	1	5.45	....	....	....	....	....	....	....
1986-87	Richmond Hill	OPJHL	30	14	7	6	1764	128	1	4.35	....	....	....	....	....	....	....
1987-88	Notre Dame	SJHL	36	25	4	7	2174	94	1	2.59	....	....	....	....	....	....	....
1988-89	U. of Wisconsin	WCHA	38	21	11	5	2267	94	1	2.49	....	....	....	....	....	....	....
1989-90	Peoria Rivermen	IHL	23	10	8	2	1241	80	0	3.87	....	....	....	....	....	....	....
	St. Louis	**NHL**	**15**	**9**	**5**	**1**	**852**	**48**	**0**	**3.38**	**6**	**4**	**1**	**327**	**18**	**0**	**3.30**
1990-91	**St. Louis**	**NHL**	**30**	**16**	**10**	**2**	**1710**	**89**	**0**	**3.12**	....	....	....	....	....	....	....
1991-92	**St. Louis**	**NHL**	**60**	**27**	**20**	**10**	**3494**	**175**	**2**	**3.01**	**6**	**2**	**4**	**379**	**23**	**0**	**3.64**
1992-93	**St. Louis**	**NHL**	**68**	**29**	**28**	**9**	**3890**	**196**	**1**	**3.02**	**11**	**7**	**4**	**715**	**27**	***2**	**2.27**
1993-94	**St. Louis**	**NHL**	**71**	**36**	**23**	**11**	**4127**	**213**	**1**	**3.10**	**4**	**0**	**4**	**246**	**15**	**0**	**3.66**
1994-95	**St. Louis**	**NHL**	**36**	**20**	**10**	**1**	**1914**	**89**	**1**	**2.79**	**7**	**3**	**3**	**392**	**24**	**0**	**3.67**
1995-96	Las Vegas Thunder	IHL	15	12	2	1	874	29	1	1.99	....	....	....	....	....	....	....
	Edmonton	**NHL**	**34**	**15**	**16**	**2**	**1936**	**111**	**0**	**3.44**	....	....	....	....	....	....	....
1996-97	**Edmonton**	**NHL**	**72**	**32**	**29**	**9**	**4100**	**200**	**6**	**2.93**	**12**	**5**	**7**	**767**	**36**	**2**	**2.82**
1997-98	**Edmonton**	**NHL**	**71**	**29**	**31**	**9**	**4132**	**181**	**8**	**2.63**	**12**	**5**	**7**	**716**	**23**	**3**	**1.93**
1998-99	**Toronto**	**NHL**	**67**	**35**	**24**	**7**	**4001**	**171**	**3**	**2.56**	**17**	**9**	**8**	**1011**	**41**	**1**	**2.43**
99-2000	**Toronto**	**NHL**	**63**	**36**	**20**	**7**	**3801**	**158**	**4**	**2.49**	**12**	**6**	**6**	**729**	**25**	**1**	**2.06**
2000-01	**Toronto**	**NHL**	**68**	**33**	**27**	**8**	**4100**	**163**	**6**	**2.39**	**11**	**7**	**4**	**685**	**24**	**3**	**2.10**

2001-02	Toronto	NHL	51	29	17	5	3065	114	4	2.23	20	10	10	1253	48	3	2.30
	Canada	Olympics	1	0	1	0	60	5	0	5.00	....	....	....	....	....	....	....
2002-03	Detroit	NHL	61	34	19	6	3566	148	5	2.49	4	0	4	289	10	0	2.08
2003-04	Detroit	NHL	31	16	10	3	1708	68	2	2.39	9	4	4	518	12	1	*1.39
	Grand Rapids	AHL	1	1	0	0	60	1	0	1.00	....	....	....	....	....	....	....
2004-05							DID NOT PLAY										
2005-06	Phoenix	NHL	60	32	21	3	3424	166	4	2.91	....	....	....	....	....	....	....
	NHL Totals		**858**	**428**	**310**	**93**	**49820**	**2290**	**47**	**2.76**	**131**	**62**	**66**	**8027**	**326**	**16**	**2.44**

WCHA First All-Star Team (1989) • WCHA Freshman of the Year (1989) • WCHA Most Valuable Player (1989) • NCAA West Second All-American Team (1989) • King Clancy Memorial Trophy (2000)

Played in NHL All-Star Game (1994, 2000)

Signed as a free agent by **St. Louis**, June 16, 1989. Traded to **Edmonton** by **St. Louis** with the rights to Mike Grier for St. Louis' 1st round choices (previously acquired) in 1996 (Marty Reasoner) and 1997 (later traded to Los Angeles – Los Angeles selected Matt Zultek) Entry Drafts, August 4, 1995. Signed as a free agent by **Toronto**, July 15, 1998. Traded to **Calgary** by **Toronto** for Calgary's 3rd round choice (later traded to Minnesota – Minnesota selected Danny Irmen) in 2003 Entry Draft and future considerations, June 30, 2002. Signed as a free agent by **Detroit**, July 2, 2002. Signed as a free agent by **Phoenix**, August 17, 2005.

KANGAS, Alex (KANG-uhs, AL-ehx) ATL.

Goaltender. Catches left. 6'1", 175 lbs. Born, Rochester, NY, May 28, 1987.
(Atlanta's 4th choice, 135th overall, in 2006 Entry Draft).

			Regular Season								Playoffs						
Season	Club	League	GP	W	L	O/T	Mins	GA	SO	Avg	GP	W	L	Mins	GA	SO	Avg
2001-02	Rochester Century	High-MN	3	3	0	0	....	3	2	1.00	....	....	....	....	....	....	....
2002-03	Rochester Century	High-MN	27	17	9	0	....	50	6	1.76	....	....	....	....	....	....	....
2003-04	Rochester Century	High-MN	28	15	12	1	....	59	3	2.08	....	....	....	....	....	....	....
2004-05	Rochester Century	High-MN	30	23	4	3	....	55	7	1.86	....	....	....	....	....	....	....
2005-06	Sioux Falls	USHL	29	20	6	3	1733	62	3	2.15	6	4	2	359	17	0	2.84

USHL All-Rookie Team (2006)

Signed Letter of Intent to attend **U. of Minnesota** (WCHA) in fall of 2007.

KEETLEY, Matt (KEET-lee, MAT) CGY.

Goaltender. Catches right. 6', 175 lbs. Born, Medicine Hat, Alta., April 27, 1986.
(Calgary's 6th choice, 158th overall, in 2005 Entry Draft).

			Regular Season								Playoffs						
Season	Club	League	GP	W	L	O/T	Mins	GA	SO	Avg	GP	W	L	Mins	GA	SO	Avg
2003-04	Medicine Hat	AMHL	....	7	4	2	813	48	....	3.54	....	....	....	....	....	....	....
	Medicine Hat	WHL	3	0	1	0	72	5	0	4.17	2	0	0	15	1	0	4.00
2004-05	Medicine Hat	WHL	32	21	5	3	1846	51	6	*1.66	3	1	0	103	8	0	4.66
2005-06	Medicine Hat	WHL	62	*42	13	6	3741	130	6	2.09	13	9	2	864	30	0	2.08

WHL East Second All-Star Team (2006)

KESERICH, Ian (kuh-SAIR-ihch, EE-an) COL.

Goaltender. Catches left. 6'2", 190 lbs. Born, Cleveland, OH, January 6, 1986.
(Colorado's 6th choice, 215th overall, in 2004 Entry Draft).

			Regular Season								Playoffs						
Season	Club	League	GP	W	L	O/T	Mins	GA	SO	Avg	GP	W	L	Mins	GA	SO	Avg
2003-04	Cleveland Barons	NAHL					STATISTICS NOT AVAILABLE										
2004-05	Ohio State	CCHA	6	2	2	0	272	11	0	2.42	....	....	....	....	....	....	....
2005-06	Ohio State	CCHA	4	2	1	0	203	9	0	2.66	....	....	....	....	....	....	....

KHABIBULIN, Nikolai (khah-bee-BOO-lihn, NIH-koh-ligh) CHI.

Goaltender. Catches left. 6'1", 203 lbs. Born, Sverdlovsk, USSR, January 13, 1973.
(Winnipeg's 8th choice, 204th overall, in 1992 Entry Draft).

			Regular Season								Playoffs						
Season	Club	League	GP	W	L	O/T	Mins	GA	SO	Avg	GP	W	L	Mins	GA	SO	Avg
1991-92	CSKA Moscow	CIS	2	0	0	0	34	2	0	3.53	....	....	....	....	....	....	....
1992-93	CSKA Moscow	CIS	13	....	....	....	491	27	....	3.29	....	....	....	....	....	....	....
1993-94	CSKA Moscow	CIS	46	....	....	....	2625	116	....	2.65	3	....	....	193	11	....	3.42
	Russian Penguins	IHL	12	2	7	2	639	47	0	4.41	....	....	....	....	....	....	....
1994-95	Springfield Indians	AHL	23	9	9	3	1240	80	0	3.87	....	....	....	....	....	....	....
	Winnipeg	NHL	26	8	9	4	1339	76	0	3.41	....	....	....	....	....	....	....
1995-96	Winnipeg	NHL	53	26	20	3	2914	152	2	3.13	6	2	4	359	19	0	3.18
1996-97	Phoenix	NHL	72	30	33	6	4091	193	7	2.83	7	3	4	426	15	1	2.11
1997-98	Phoenix	NHL	70	30	28	10	4026	184	4	2.74	4	2	1	185	13	0	4.22
1998-99	Phoenix	NHL	63	32	23	7	3657	130	8	2.13	7	3	4	449	18	0	2.41
99-2000	Long Beach	IHL	33	21	11	1	1936	59	5	*1.83	5	2	3	321	15	0	2.81
2000-01	Tampa Bay	NHL	2	1	1	0	123	6	0	2.93	....	....	....	....	....	....	....
2001-02	Tampa Bay	NHL	70	24	32	10	3896	153	7	2.36	....	....	....	....	....	....	....
	Russia	Olympics	6	3	2	1	*359	14	*1	2.34	....	....	....	....	....	....	....
2002-03	Tampa Bay	NHL	65	30	22	11	3787	156	4	2.47	10	5	5	644	26	0	2.42
2003-04 ♦	Tampa Bay	NHL	55	28	19	7	3274	127	3	2.33	23	*16	7	1401	40	*5	1.71
2004-05	Ak Bars Kazan	Russia	24	....	....	....	1457	40	5	1.65	2	....	....	118	6	0	3.04
2005-06	Chicago	NHL	50	17	26	6	2815	157	0	3.35	....	....	....	....	....	....	....
	Russia	Olympics					DID NOT PLAY – INJURED										
	NHL Totals		**526**	**226**	**213**	**64**	**29922**	**1334**	**35**	**2.67**	**57**	**31**	**25**	**3464**	**131**	**6**	**2.27**

James Gatschene Memorial Trophy (MVP – IHL) (2000) (co-winner - Frederic Chabot)

Played in NHL All-Star Game (1998, 1999, 2002, 2003)

Transferred to **Phoenix** after **Winnipeg** franchise relocated, July 1, 1996. • Missed entire 1999-2000 NHL season and majority of 2000-01 season after failing to come to contract terms with **Phoenix**. Signed as a free agent by **Long Beach** (IHL) with **Phoenix** retaining NHL rights, January 14, 2000. Traded to **Tampa Bay** by **Phoenix** with Stan Neckar for Mike Johnson, Paul Mara, Ruslan Zainullin and NY Islanders' 2nd round choice (previously acquired, Phoenix selected Matthew Spiller) in 2001 Entry Draft, March 5, 2001. Signed as a free agent by **Kazan** (Russia), November 8, 2004. Signed as a free agent by **Chicago**, August 5, 2005.

KHUDOBIN, Anton (khuh-DAW-bihn, an-TAWN) MIN.

Goaltender. Catches left. 5'11", 176 lbs. Born, Ust-Kamenogorsk, USSR, May 7, 1986.
(Minnesota's 11th choice, 206th overall, in 2004 Entry Draft).

			Regular Season								Playoffs						
Season	Club	League	GP	W	L	O/T	Mins	GA	SO	Avg	GP	W	L	Mins	GA	SO	Avg
2003-04	Magnitogorsk 2	Russia-3	4	....	....	....	200	6	0	1.80	....	....	....	....	....	....	....
2004-05	Magnitogorsk	Russia	4	....	....	....	133	0	1	0.00	....	....	....	....	....	....	....
	Magnitogorsk 2	Russia-3					STATISTICS NOT AVAILABLE										
2005-06	Saskatoon Blades	WHL	44	23	13	3	2362	114	4	2.90	10	4	3	685	32	0	2.80

KILPELAINEN, Eero (kih-pehl-AI-nehn, EE-roh) DAL.

Goaltender. Catches left. 5'11", 152 lbs. Born, Juva, Finland, May 7, 1985.
(Dallas' 6th choice, 144th overall, in 2003 Entry Draft).

			Regular Season								Playoffs						
Season	Club	League	GP	W	L	O/T	Mins	GA	SO	Avg	GP	W	L	Mins	GA	SO	Avg
2001-02	KalPa Kuopio U18	Fin-U18	15	10	2	2	873	37	1	2.54	2	0	2	130	6	0	2.76
2002-03	KalPa Kuopio U18	Fin-U18	1	1	0	0	60	3	0	3.00	....	....	....	....	....	....	....
	KalPa Kuopio Jr.	Fin-Jr.	19	7	6	1	931	54	0	3.48	....	....	....	....	....	....	....
	KalPa Kuopio	Finland-2	1	0	0	0	17	4	0	13.91	....	....	....	....	....	....	....
2003-04	KalPa Kuopio Jr.	Fin-Jr.	43	17	19	6	2528	118	2	2.80	2	0	2	116	4	0	2.07
2004-05	Peterborough	OHL	38	14	17	6	2218	121	0	3.27	1	0	1	78	4	0	3.08
2005-06	Hermes Kokkola	Finland-2	54	....	....	....	3071	151	3	2.96	....	....	....	....	....	....	....

KIPRUSOFF, Miikka (KIHP-ruh-sohf, MEE-kah) CGY.

Goaltender. Catches left. 6'2", 190 lbs. Born, Turku, Finland, October 26, 1976.
(San Jose's 5th choice, 116th overall, in 1995 Entry Draft).

			Regular Season								Playoffs						
Season	Club	League	GP	W	L	O/T	Mins	GA	SO	Avg	GP	W	L	Mins	GA	SO	Avg
1993-94	TPS Turku Jr.	Fin-Jr.	35	20	9	5	2101	100	0	2.85	6	3	3	369	26	0	4.23
1994-95	TPS Turku Jr.	Fin-Jr.	31	13	14	4	1896	92	2	2.91	....	....	....	....	....	....	....
	Kiekko-67 Turku	Finland-2	1	0	1	0	60	6	0	6.00	....	....	....	....	....	....	....
	TPS Turku	Finland	4	3	1	0	240	12	0	3.00	2	2	0	120	7	0	3.50
1995-96	TPS Turku Jr.	Fin-Jr.	3	1	2	0	180	9	0	3.00	....	....	....	....	....	....	....
	Kiekko-67 Turku	Finland-2	5	5	0	0	300	7	1	1.40	....	....	....	....	....	....	....
	TPS Turku	Finland	12	5	3	1	550	38	0	4.14	3	0	1	113	4	0	2.12
1996-97	AIK Solna	Sweden	42	....	....	....	2440	93	3	2.29	7	....	....	420	22	0	3.14
1997-98	AIK Solna	Sweden	43	....	....	....	2517	111	1	2.65	....	....	....	....	....	....	....
	AIK Solna	Sweden-Q	9	....	....	....	540	15	2	1.67	....	....	....	....	....	....	....
1998-99	TPS Turku	Finland	39	26	6	6	2259	70	4	1.86	10	9	1	580	15	3	1.55
99-2000	Kentucky	AHL	47	23	19	4	2759	114	3	2.48	5	1	3	239	13	0	3.27
2000-01	San Jose	NHL	5	2	1	0	154	5	0	1.95	3	1	1	149	5	0	2.01
	Kentucky	AHL	36	19	9	6	2038	76	2	2.24	....	....	....	....	....	....	....
2001-02	San Jose	NHL	20	7	6	3	1037	43	2	2.49	1	0	0	8	0	0	0.00
	Cleveland Barons	AHL	4	4	0	0	242	7	0	1.73	....	....	....	....	....	....	....
2002-03	San Jose	NHL	22	5	14	0	1199	65	1	3.25	....	....	....	....	....	....	....
2003-04	Calgary	NHL	38	24	10	4	2301	65	4	*1.69	*26	15	11	*1655	51	*5	1.85
2004-05	Timra IK	Sweden	46	....	....	....	2719	97	5	2.14	6	....	....	356	13	0	2.19
2005-06	Calgary	NHL	74	42	20	11	*4380	151	*10	*2.07	7	3	4	428	16	0	2.24
	Finland	Olympics					DID NOT PLAY – INJURED										
	NHL Totals		**159**	**80**	**51**	**18**	**9071**	**329**	**17**	**2.18**	**37**	**19**	**16**	**2240**	**72**	**5**	**1.93**

NHL First All-Star Team (2006) • Vezina Trophy (2006)

Traded to **Calgary** by **San Jose** for Calgary's 2nd round choice (Marc-Edouard Vlasic) in 2005 Entry Draft, November 16, 2003. Signed as a free agent by **Timra** (Sweden), September 20, 2004.

KOCHAN, Dieter (KAH-kuhn, DEE-tuhr)

Goaltender. Catches left. 6'1", 180 lbs. Born, Saskatoon, Sask., May 11, 1974.
(Vancouver's 3rd choice, 98th overall, in 1993 Entry Draft).

			Regular Season								Playoffs						
Season	Club	League	GP	W	L	O/T	Mins	GA	SO	Avg	GP	W	L	Mins	GA	SO	Avg
1991-92	Sioux City	USHL	23	7	10	0	1131	100	0	5.31	....	....	....	....	....	....	....
1992-93	Kelowna Spartans	BCJHL	44	34	8	0	2582	137	1	3.18	15	12	3	927	48	1	3.10
1993-94	Northern Mich.	WCHA	20	9	7	0	985	57	2	3.47	....	....	....	....	....	....	....
1994-95	Northern Mich.	WCHA	29	8	17	3	1512	107	0	4.25	....	....	....	....	....	....	....
1995-96	Northern Mich.	WCHA	31	7	21	2	1627	123	0	4.54	....	....	....	....	....	....	....
1996-97	Northern Mich.	WCHA	26	8	15	2	1528	99	0	3.89	....	....	....	....	....	....	....
1997-98	Louisville	ECHL	18	7	9	2	980	61	1	3.73	....	....	....	....	....	....	....
1998-99	Binghamton	UHL	40	18	16	5	2322	115	2	2.97	4	1	2	208	9	0	2.60
99-2000	Binghamton	UHL	43	29	11	3	2544	110	4	2.59	....	....	....	....	....	....	....
	Orlando	IHL	4	4	0	0	240	4	1	1.00	....	....	....	....	....	....	....
	Springfield Falcons	AHL	2	1	1	0	120	5	1	2.50	....	....	....	....	....	....	....
	Tampa Bay	NHL	5	1	4	0	238	17	0	4.29	....	....	....	....	....	....	....
	Grand Rapids	IHL	2	1	0	1	93	1	0	0.64	....	....	....	....	....	....	....
2000-01	Tampa Bay	NHL	10	0	3	0	314	18	0	3.44	....	....	....	....	....	....	....
	Detroit Vipers	IHL	49	13	28	3	2606	154	0	3.55	....	....	....	....	....	....	....
2001-02	Tampa Bay	NHL	5	0	3	1	237	16	0	4.05	....	....	....	....	....	....	....
	Springfield Falcons	AHL	45	21	20	1	2518	112	2	2.67	....	....	....	....	....	....	....
2002-03	Minnesota	NHL	1	0	1	0	60	5	0	5.00	....	....	....	....	....	....	....
	Houston Aeros	AHL	25	15	6	3	1447	61	1	2.53	2	0	0	20	0	0	0.00
2003-04	Bridgeport	AHL	45	20	17	7	2728	85	6	1.87	4	1	3	281	12	0	2.57
2004-05	Bridgeport	AHL	39	19	19	0	2303	102	1	2.66	....	....	....	....	....	....	....
2005-06	Sibir Novosibirsk	Russia	8	....	....	....	417	23	0	3.31	....	....	....	....	....	....	....
	Portland Pirates	AHL	15	9	4	1	838	38	1	2.72	....	....	....	....	....	....	....
	NHL Totals		**21**	**1**	**11**	**1**	**849**	**56**	**0**	**3.96**	....	....	....	....	....	....	....

UHL Second All-Star Team (2000) • Harry "Hap" Holmes Memorial Award (fewest goals against - AHL) (2004) (shared with Wade Dubielewicz)

• Scored a goal vs. Winston-Salem (UHL), January 5, 1999. Signed as a free agent by **Tampa Bay**, March 27, 2000. Signed as a free agent by **Minnesota**, August 5, 2002. Signed as a free agent by **NY Islanders**, August 7, 2003.

KOLESNIK, Vitaly (koh-LEHZ-nihk, vih-TAL-ee)

Goaltender. Catches left. 6'3", 210 lbs. Born, Ust-Kamenogorsk, USSR, August 20, 1979.

			Regular Season								Playoffs						
Season	Club	League	GP	W	L	O/T	Mins	GA	SO	Avg	GP	W	L	Mins	GA	SO	Avg
2002-03	Ust-Kamenogorsk	Russia-2	25	....	....	....	1308	46	2	2.11	....	....	....	....	....	....	....
2003-04	Ust-Kamenogorsk	Russia-2	35	....	....	....	1899	53	9	1.67	....	....	....	....	....	....	....
2004-05	Ust-Kamenogorsk	Russia-2	42	....	....	....	2329	65	8	1.67	....	....	....	....	....	....	....
2005-06	Colorado	NHL	8	3	3	0	370	20	0	3.24	....	....	....	....	....	....	....
	Lowell	AHL	29	15	13	0	1717	80	3	2.80	....	....	....	....	....	....	....
	Kazakhstan	Olympics	2	0	2	0	120	6	0	3.00	....	....	....	....	....	....	....
	NHL Totals		**8**	**3**	**3**	**0**	**370**	**20**	**0**	**3.24**	....	....	....	....	....	....	....

Signed as a free agent by **Colorado**, August 16, 2005. Signed as a free agent by **Khimik** (Russia), July 6, 2006.

KOLZIG, Olaf (KOHL-zihg, OH-lahf) WSH.

Goaltender. Catches left. 6'3", 225 lbs. Born, Johannesburg, South Africa, April 6, 1970.
(Washington's 1st choice, 19th overall, in 1989 Entry Draft).

			Regular Season								Playoffs						
Season	Club	League	GP	W	L	O/T	Mins	GA	SO	Avg	GP	W	L	Mins	GA	SO	Avg
1986-87	Abbotsford Pilots	BCAHA	17	5	9	0	857	81	0	5.67	....	....	....	....	....	....	....
1987-88	New Westminster	WHL	15	6	5	0	650	48	1	4.43	3	0	3	149	11	0	4.43
1988-89	Tri-City Americans	WHL	30	16	10	2	1671	97	1	*3.48	....	....	....	....	....	....	....
1989-90	Washington	NHL	2	0	2	0	120	12	0	6.00	....	....	....	....	....	....	....
	Tri-City Americans	WHL	48	21	18	3	2504	187	1	4.48	6	4	0	318	27	0	5.09
1990-91	Baltimore Skipjacks	AHL	26	10	12	1	1367	72	0	3.16	....	....	....	....	....	....	....
	Hampton Roads	ECHL	21	11	9	1	1248	71	2	3.41	3	1	2	180	14	0	4.66
1991-92	Baltimore Skipjacks	AHL	28	5	17	2	1503	105	1	4.19	....	....	....	....	....	....	....
	Hampton Roads	ECHL	14	11	3	0	847	41	0	2.90	....	....	....	....	....	....	....
1992-93	Washington	NHL	1	0	0	0	20	2	0	6.00	....	....	....	....	....	....	....
	Rochester	AHL	49	25	16	4	2737	168	0	3.68	*17	9	8	*1040	61	0	3.52
1993-94	Washington	NHL	7	0	3	0	224	20	0	5.36	....	....	....	....	....	....	....
	Portland Pirates	AHL	29	16	8	5	1725	88	3	3.06	17	*12	5	1035	44	0	*2.55
1994-95	Washington	NHL	14	2	8	2	724	30	0	2.49	2	1	0	44	1	0	1.36
	Portland Pirates	AHL	2	1	0	1	125	3	0	1.44	....	....	....	....	....	....	....
1995-96	Washington	NHL	18	4	8	2	897	46	0	3.08	5	2	3	341	11	0	*1.94
	Portland Pirates	AHL	5	5	0	0	300	7	1	1.40	....	....	....	....	....	....	....
1996-97	Washington	NHL	29	8	15	4	1645	71	2	2.59	....	....	....	....	....	....	....
1997-98	Washington	NHL	64	33	18	10	3788	139	5	2.20	21	12	9	1351	44	*4	1.95
	Germany	Olympics	2	2	0	0	120	2	1	1.00	....	....	....	....	....	....	....
1998-99	Washington	NHL	64	26	31	3	3586	154	4	2.58	....	....	....	....	....	....	....
99-2000	Washington	NHL	73	41	20	11	*4371	163	5	2.24	5	1	4	284	16	0	3.38
2000-01	Washington	NHL	72	37	26	8	4279	177	5	2.48	6	2	4	375	14	1	2.24
2001-02	Washington	NHL	71	31	29	8	4131	192	6	2.79	....	....	....	....	....	....	....

2002-03	**Washington**	**NHL**	**66**	**33**	**25**	**6**	**3894**	**156**	**4**	**2.40**	**6**	**2**	**4**	**404**	**14**	**1**	**2.08**
2003-04	**Washington**	**NHL**	**63**	**19**	**35**	**9**	**3738**	**180**	**2**	**2.89**	....	....	....	....	....	....	....
2004-05	Eisbaren Berlin	Germany	8	....	....	....	452	19	2	2.52	3	....	....	178	7	1	2.36
2005-06	**Washington**	**NHL**	**59**	**20**	**28**	**11**	**3506**	**206**	**0**	**3.53**	....	....	....	....	....	....	....
	Germany	Olympics	3	0	1	2	179	8	0	2.68	....	....	....	....	....	....	....
	NHL Totals		**603**	**254**	**248**	**74**	**34923**	**1548**	**33**	**2.66**	**45**	**20**	**24**	**2799**	**100**	**6**	**2.14**

WHL West Second All-Star Team (1989) • Harry ''Hap'' Holmes Memorial Award (fewest goals against – AHL) (1994) (shared with Byron Dafoe) • Jack A. Butterfield Trophy (Playoff MVP – AHL) (1994) • NHL First All-Star Team (2000) • Vezina Trophy (2000) • King Clancy Memorial Trophy (2006)

Played in NHL All-Star Game (1998, 2000)

• Scored a goal while with Tri-City (WHL), November 29, 1989. Signed as a free agent by **Berlin** (Germany), February 2, 2005.

KOOPMANS, Logan (KOOP-manz, LOH-guhn) DET.

Goaltender. Catches left. 6'2", 182 lbs. Born, Cranbrook, B.C., May 18, 1984.
(Detroit's 5th choice, 166th overall, in 2002 Entry Draft).

			Regular Season								Playoffs						
Season	Club	League	GP	W	L	O/T	Mins	GA	SO	Avg	GP	W	L	Mins	GA	SO	Avg
99-2000	Lethbridge	WHL	5	1	3	0	282	19	0	4.04	....	....	....	....	....	....	....
2000-01	Columbia Valley	KIJHL	37	....	....	....	2140	144	1	3.90	....	....	....	....	....	....	....
2001-02	Lethbridge	WHL	37	20	12	2	2057	97	3	2.83	4	0	4	237	14	0	3.54
2002-03	Lethbridge	WHL	34	9	17	0	1628	131	1	4.83	....	....	....	....	....	....	....
2003-04	Lethbridge	WHL	62	27	25	8	3565	155	5	2.61	....	....	....	....	....	....	....
2004-05	Toledo Storm	ECHL	25	12	10	1	1299	61	2	2.82	....	....	....	....	....	....	....
2005-06	Toledo Storm	ECHL	12	7	2	2	677	33	1	2.93	7	2	5	434	28	0	3.87
	Grand Rapids	AHL	1	0	1	0	40	5	0	7.54	....	....	....	....	....	....	....

KOPRIVA, Miroslav (koh-PREE-vuh, MEER-oh-slav) MIN.

Goaltender. Catches left. 6'3", 215 lbs. Born, Kladno, Czech., December 5, 1983.
(Minnesota's 5th choice, 187th overall, in 2003 Entry Draft).

			Regular Season								Playoffs						
Season	Club	League	GP	W	L	O/T	Mins	GA	SO	Avg	GP	W	L	Mins	GA	SO	Avg
99-2000	HC Kladno Jr.	CzRep-Jr.	46	....	....	....	2510	121	4	2.89	4	....	....	249	13	0	3.13
2000-01	HC Kladno Jr.	CzRep-Jr.	26	....	....	....	1478	65	2	2.64	....	....	....	....	....	....	....
2001-02	HC Kladno Jr.	CzRep-Jr.	41	....	....	....	2367	124	6	3.14	....	....	....	....	....	....	....
2002-03	HC Kladno Jr.	CzRep-Jr.	42	....	....	....	2464	80	5	1.95	11	....	....	661	16	2	1.45
2003-04	HC Kladno Jr.	CzRep-Jr.	4	....	....	....	240	10	1	2.50	....	....	....	....	....	....	....
	Beroun	CzRep-2	31	....	....	....	1837	58	3	1.89	....	....	....	....	....	....	....
	HC Rabat Kladno	CzRep	13	....	....	....	687	46	2	4.02	....	....	....	....	....	....	....
2004-05	HC Rabat Kladno	CzRep	10	....	....	....	426	19	1	2.68	....	....	....	....	....	....	....
	Beroun	CzRep-2	31	....	....	....	1841	59	4	1.92	1	....	....	58	2	0	2.07
2005-06	Austin Ice Bats	CHL	15	12	3	0	900	35	1	2.33	....	....	....	....	....	....	....
	Houston Aeros	AHL	12	6	4	1	649	38	0	3.52	....	....	....	....	....	....	....

KOSHECHKIN, Vasily (KOH-shech-kihn, va-SEE-lee) T.B.

Goaltender. Catches left. 6'6", 210 lbs. Born, Togliatti, USSR, March 27, 1983.
(Tampa Bay's 9th choice, 233rd overall, in 2002 Entry Draft).

			Regular Season								Playoffs						
Season	Club	League	GP	W	L	O/T	Mins	GA	SO	Avg	GP	W	L	Mins	GA	SO	Avg
2001-02	Lada Togliatti 2	Russia-3					STATISTICS NOT AVAILABLE										
2002-03	Lada Togliatti 2	Russia-3					STATISTICS NOT AVAILABLE										
2003-04	Lada Togliatti 2	Russia-3	8	....	....	....	....	9	1	....	5	....	....	....	9	0	....
2004-05	Lada Togliatti	Russia	4	....	....	....	121	5	0	2.47	....	....	....	....	....	....	....
2005-06	Lada Togliatti	Russia	41	....	....	....	2375	63	9	1.59	8	....	....	474	20	1	2.53

KOTYK, Seamus (koh-TIHK, SHAY-muhs)

Goaltender. Catches left. 5'11", 180 lbs. Born, London, Ont., October 7, 1980.
(Boston's 5th choice, 147th overall, in 1999 Entry Draft).

			Regular Season								Playoffs						
Season	Club	League	GP	W	L	O/T	Mins	GA	SO	Avg	GP	W	L	Mins	GA	SO	Avg
1996-97	Stratford Cullitons	OHA-B	28	....	....	....	1615	105	0	3.82	....	....	....	....	....	....	....
1997-98	Ottawa 67's	OHL	31	13	5	5	1422	63	4	2.66	7	3	2	332	11	0	1.99
1998-99	Ottawa 67's	OHL	41	26	7	4	2314	92	5	2.39	5	3	2	338	13	0	*2.31
99-2000	Ottawa 67's	OHL	26	12	6	2	1241	65	1	3.14	....	....	....	....	....	....	....
2000-01	Ottawa 67's	OHL	55	24	20	7	3087	141	2	2.74	*20	*16	4	*1157	46	*3	2.39
2001-02	Cleveland Barons	AHL	24	6	11	0	981	61	1	3.73	....	....	....	....	....	....	....
2002-03	Cleveland Barons	AHL	34	7	22	2	1838	118	2	3.85	....	....	....	....	....	....	....
2003-04	Cleveland Barons	AHL	30	13	10	5	1768	73	1	2.48	....	....	....	....	....	....	....
2004-05	Milwaukee	AHL	23	10	6	1	1138	56	0	2.95	1	0	0	2	0	0	0.00
	Rockford IceHogs	UHL	6	5	1	0	358	6	1	1.00	....	....	....	....	....	....	....
2005-06	Houston Aeros	AHL	35	15	15	2	1978	100	2	3.03	1	0	0	20	2	0	6.00
	Augusta Lynx	ECHL	3	2	1	0	161	4	1	1.49	....	....	....	....	....	....	....

• Missed majority of 1999-2000 season recovering from surgery for cardiac arrhythmia, October 18, 1999. Signed as a free agent by **San Jose**, July 23, 2001. Signed as a free agent by **Milwaukee** (AHL), August 31, 2004.

KOVAR, Jakub (KOH-vahr, YA-kuhb) PHI.

Goaltender. Catches left. 6', 176 lbs. Born, Pisek, Czech., July 19, 1988.
(Philadelphia's 7th choice, 109th overall, in 2006 Entry Draft).

			Regular Season								Playoffs						
Season	Club	League	GP	W	L	O/T	Mins	GA	SO	Avg	GP	W	L	Mins	GA	SO	Avg
2004-05	IHC Pisek U17	CzR-U17	40	....	....	....	2298	137	4	3.58	....	....	....	....	....	....	....
2005-06	C. Budejovice Jr.	CzRep-Jr.	19	....	....	....	1048	39	2	2.23	5	....	....	304	8	0	1.58

KOWALSKI, Craig (koh-WAHL-skee, KRAYG) CAR.

Goaltender. Catches left. 5'10", 190 lbs. Born, Warren, MI, January 15, 1981.
(Carolina's 6th choice, 235th overall, in 2000 Entry Draft).

			Regular Season								Playoffs						
Season	Club	League	GP	W	L	O/T	Mins	GA	SO	Avg	GP	W	L	Mins	GA	SO	Avg
1998-99	Det. Compuware	NAHL	42	*34	7	6	2733	96	3	*2.10	7	*7	0	420	13	1	*1.86
99-2000	Det. Compuware	NAHL	49	33	12	3	2850	113	4	2.38	5	2	3	334	13	0	2.34
2000-01	Northern Mich.	CCHA	19	7	8	4	1078	49	1	2.73	....	....	....	....	....	....	....
2001-02	Northern Mich.	CCHA	38	24	11	2	2271	89	4	2.35	....	....	....	....	....	....	....
2002-03	Northern Mich.	CCHA	38	20	16	2	2213	104	3	2.82	....	....	....	....	....	....	....
2003-04	Northern Mich.	CCHA	37	17	14	4	2058	93	4	2.71	....	....	....	....	....	....	....
2004-05	Florida Everblades	ECHL	27	13	6	6	1503	72	1	2.87	6	3	0	238	13	0	3.27
2005-06	Lowell	AHL	20	6	11	3	1100	62	0	3.38	....	....	....	....	....	....	....
	Florida Everblades	ECHL	18	12	6	0	1030	48	1	2.80	....	....	....	....	....	....	....

KRAHN, Brent (KRAWN, BREHNT) CGY.

Goaltender. Catches left. 6'5", 220 lbs. Born, Winnipeg, Man., April 2, 1982.
(Calgary's 1st choice, 9th overall, in 2000 Entry Draft).

			Regular Season								Playoffs						
Season	Club	League	GP	W	L	O/T	Mins	GA	SO	Avg	GP	W	L	Mins	GA	SO	Avg
1997-98	Pembina Valley	MMMHL	22	20	0	1	1265	40	3	1.90	2	2	0	120	2	1	1.00
1998-99	Pembina Valley	MMMHL	13	10	3	0	770	30	2	2.34	....	....	....	....	....	....	....
99-2000	Calgary Hitmen	WHL	39	33	6	0	2315	92	4	2.38	5	2	2	266	13	0	2.93
2000-01	Calgary Hitmen	WHL	37	22	10	3	2087	104	1	2.99	....	....	....	....	....	....	....
2001-02	Calgary Hitmen	WHL	18	8	6	2	1033	61	0	3.54	2	1	1	119	6	0	3.03
2002-03	Calgary Hitmen	WHL	23	11	10	2	1343	72	2	3.22	....	....	....	....	....	....	....
	Seattle	WHL	5	5	0	0	302	9	2	1.79	15	9	6	960	38	2	2.38
2003-04	Lowell	AHL	7	2	3	0	344	15	0	2.62	....	....	....	....	....	....	....
	Las Vegas	ECHL	14	7	5	2	828	36	0	2.61	....	....	....	....	....	....	....
	San Antonio	AHL	14	3	7	1	715	41	0	3.44	....	....	....	....	....	....	....
2004-05	Lowell	AHL	35	20	11	2	1998	83	6	2.49	1	0	0	1	0	0	0.00
2005-06	Omaha	AHL	57	26	20	9	3241	135	3	2.50	....	....	....	....	....	....	....

• Missed majority of 2001-02 season recovering from knee surgery, June, 2001.

LABARBERA, Jason (lah-BAR-buhr-uh, JAY-suhn) L.A.

Goaltender. Catches left. 6'2", 230 lbs. Born, Burnaby, B.C., January 18, 1980.
(NY Rangers' 3rd choice, 66th overall, in 1998 Entry Draft).

			Regular Season								Playoffs						
Season	Club	League	GP	W	L	O/T	Mins	GA	SO	Avg	GP	W	L	Mins	GA	SO	Avg
1995-96	Prince George	BCAHA	31	....	....	....	1860	83	0	2.68	....	....	....	....	....	....	....
1996-97	Tri-City Americans	WHL	2	1	0	0	63	4	0	3.81	....	....	....	....	....	....	....
	Portland	WHL	9	5	1	1	443	18	0	2.44	....	....	....	....	....	....	....
1997-98	Portland	WHL	23	18	4	0	1305	72	1	3.31	....	....	....	....	....	....	....
1998-99	Portland	WHL	51	18	23	9	2991	170	4	3.41	4	0	4	252	19	0	4.52
99-2000	Portland	WHL	34	8	24	2	2005	123	1	3.68	....	....	....	....	....	....	....
	Spokane Chiefs	WHL	21	12	6	2	1146	50	0	2.62	9	6	1	435	18	1	2.48
2000-01	**NY Rangers**	**NHL**	**1**	**0**	**0**	**0**	**10**	**0**	**0**	**0.00**	....	....	....	....	....	....	....
	Hartford Wolf Pack	AHL	4	1	1	0	156	12	0	4.61	....	....	....	....	....	....	....
	Charlotte Checkers	ECHL	35	18	10	7	2100	112	1	3.20	2	1	1	143	5	0	2.09
2001-02	Hartford Wolf Pack	AHL	20	7	11	1	1058	55	0	3.12	....	....	....	....	....	....	....
	Charlotte Checkers	ECHL	13	9	3	1	744	29	0	2.34	4	2	2	212	12	0	3.39
2002-03	Hartford Wolf Pack	AHL	46	18	17	6	2452	105	2	2.57	2	0	2	117	6	0	3.07
2003-04	**NY Rangers**	**NHL**	**4**	**1**	**2**	**0**	**198**	**16**	**0**	**4.85**	....	....	....	....	....	....	....
	Hartford Wolf Pack	AHL	59	34	9	9	3393	90	*13	1.59	16	11	5	1043	30	*3	*1.73
2004-05	Hartford Wolf Pack	AHL	53	31	16	2	2937	90	6	1.84	4	1	3	238	9	0	2.27
2005-06	**Los Angeles**	**NHL**	**29**	**11**	**9**	**2**	**1433**	**69**	**1**	**2.89**	....	....	....	....	....	....	....
	Manchester	AHL	3	1	1	1	185	10	0	3.25	....	....	....	....	....	....	....
	NHL Totals		**34**	**12**	**11**	**2**	**1641**	**85**	**1**	**3.11**	....	....	....	....	....	....	....

AHL First All-Star Team (2004) • Aldege "Baz" Bastien Memorial Award (Outstanding Goaltender - AHL) (2004) • Les Cunningham Award (MVP - AHL) (2004) • Harry "Hap" Holmes Memorial Trophy (fewest goals against - AHL) (shared with Steve Valiquette) (2005)

Signed as a free agent by **Los Angeles**, August 2, 2005.

LABBE, Jean-Francois (lah-BAY, ZHAWN-fran-SWUH)

Goaltender. Catches left. 5'10", 175 lbs. Born, Sherbrooke, Que., June 15, 1972.

			Regular Season								Playoffs						
Season	Club	League	GP	W	L	O/T	Mins	GA	SO	Avg	GP	W	L	Mins	GA	SO	Avg
1988-89	Montreal L'est	QAAA	29	*22	7	0	1764	94	1	3.20	5	1	4	333	19	0	3.42
1989-90	Trois-Rivieres	QMJHL	28	13	10	0	1499	106	1	4.24	3	1	1	132	8	0	3.64
1990-91	Trois-Rivieres	QMJHL	54	*35	14	0	2870	158	5	3.30	5	1	4	230	19	0	4.96
1991-92	Trois-Rivieres	QMJHL	48	*31	13	3	2749	142	1	3.10	*15	*10	3	791	33	*1	*2.50
1992-93	Hull Olympiques	QMJHL	46	26	18	2	2701	156	2	3.46	10	6	3	518	24	*1	*2.78
1993-94	Thunder Bay	ColHL	52	*35	11	4	*2900	150	*2	*3.10	8	7	1	493	18	*2	*2.19
	P.E.I. Senators	AHL	7	4	3	0	389	22	0	3.39	....	....	....	....	....	....	....
1994-95	P.E.I. Senators	AHL	32	13	14	3	1817	94	2	3.10	....	....	....	....	....	....	....
1995-96	Cornwall Aces	AHL	55	25	21	5	2972	144	3	2.91	8	3	5	471	21	1	2.68
1996-97	Hershey Bears	AHL	66	*34	22	9	3811	160	*6	*2.52	*23	*14	8	*1364	59	1	2.60
1997-98	Hamilton Bulldogs	AHL	52	24	17	11	3138	149	2	2.85	7	3	4	413	20	0	2.90
1998-99	Hartford Wolf Pack	AHL	*59	28	26	3	*3392	182	2	3.22	7	3	4	447	22	0	2.95
99-2000	**NY Rangers**	**NHL**	**1**	**0**	**1**	**0**	**60**	**3**	**0**	**3.00**	....	....	....	....	....	....	....
	Hartford Wolf Pack	AHL	49	27	13	7	2853	120	1	2.52	*22	*15	7	*1320	48	3	2.18
2000-01	Hartford Wolf Pack	AHL	8	4	2	1	394	20	0	3.04	....	....	....	....	....	....	....
	Syracuse Crunch	AHL	37	15	15	5	2201	105	2	2.86	5	2	3	323	18	0	3.34
2001-02	**Columbus**	**NHL**	**3**	**1**	**1**	**0**	**117**	**6**	**0**	**3.08**	....	....	....	....	....	....	....
	Syracuse Crunch	AHL	51	27	16	7	2993	109	*9	2.18	10	6	4	596	19	2	*1.91
2002-03	**Columbus**	**NHL**	**11**	**2**	**4**	**0**	**451**	**27**	**0**	**3.59**	....	....	....	....	....	....	....
	Syracuse Crunch	AHL	4	1	2	1	247	11	0	2.68	....	....	....	....	....	....	....
2003-04	Lada Togliatti	Russia	30	....	....	....	1725	43	8	1.50	....	....	....	....	....	....	....
	Saint-Georges	QSPHL	11	8	1	2	669	22	2	1.97	....	....	....	....	....	....	....
2004-05	Augsburg	Germany	50	....	....	....	2970	139	3	2.81	5	....	....	298	17	0	3.42
2005-06	Nurnberg	Germany	49	....	....	....	2888	104	3	2.16	4	....	....	220	17	0	4.63
	NHL Totals		**15**	**3**	**6**	**0**	**628**	**36**	**0**	**3.44**	....	....	....	....	....	....	....

QMJHL First All-Star Team (1992) • ColHL First All-Star Team (1994) • ColHL Rookie of the Year (1994) • ColHL Outstanding Goaltender (1994) • ColHL Playoff MVP (1994) • AHL First All-Star Team (1997) • Harry ''Hap'' Holmes Memorial Award (fewest goals against – AHL) (1997) • Aldege "Baz" Bastien Memorial Award (Outstanding Goaltender – AHL) (1997) • Les Cunningham Award (MVP – AHL) (1997) • Harry "Hap" Holmes Memorial Award (fewest goals against – AHL) (2000) (shared with Milan Hnilicka) • AHL Second All-Star Team (2002)

Signed as a free agent by **Ottawa**, May 12, 1994. Traded to **Colorado** by **Ottawa** for future considerations, September 20, 1995. Signed as a free agent by **Edmonton**, September 2, 1997. Signed as a free agent by **NY Rangers**, July 30, 1998. • Scored a goal vs. Quebec (AHL), February 5, 2000. Traded to **Columbus** by **NY Rangers** for Bert Robertsson, November 9, 2000. Signed as a free agent by **Togliatti** (Russia), July 1, 2003. Signed as a free agent by **Augsburg** (Germany), August 4, 2004. Signed as a free agent by **Nurnberg** (Germany), April 1, 2005.

LACASSE, Loic (luh-KAS, LOIK) MTL.

Goaltender. Catches left. 6'3", 175 lbs. Born, Granby, Que., April 23, 1986.
(Montreal's 5th choice, 181st overall, in 2004 Entry Draft).

			Regular Season								Playoffs						
Season	Club	League	GP	W	L	O/T	Mins	GA	SO	Avg	GP	W	L	Mins	GA	SO	Avg
2002-03	Antoine-Girouard	QAAA	24	22	1	1	1453	50	1	2.07	....	....	....	....	....	....	....
2003-04	Baie-Comeau	QMJHL	41	9	15	4	1758	117	0	3.99	4	0	4	172	16	0	5.57
2004-05	Baie-Comeau	QMJHL	39	10	22	2	2001	138	1	4.14	2	0	1	54	2	0	2.21
2005-06	Baie-Comeau	QMJHL	27	10	12	0	1394	94	1	4.05	....	....	....	....	....	....	....
	Drummondville	QMJHL	6	2	3	0	272	18	0	3.97	5	3	2	280	13	0	2.78

LACOSTA, Dan (luh-KAWS-tah, DAN) CBJ

Goaltender. Catches left. 6'1", 190 lbs. Born, Labrador City, Nfld., March 28, 1986.
(Columbus' 4th choice, 93rd overall, in 2004 Entry Draft).

			Regular Season								Playoffs						
Season	Club	League	GP	W	L	O/T	Mins	GA	SO	Avg	GP	W	L	Mins	GA	SO	Avg
2001-02	Wellington Dukes	OPJHL	24	19	2	3	1377	44	2	*1.92	....	....	....	....	....	....	....
2002-03	Owen Sound	OHL	28	8	10	3	1321	82	0	3.72	....	....	....	....	....	....	....
2003-04	Owen Sound	OHL	37	17	10	1	1810	82	4	2.72	....	....	....	....	....	....	....
2004-05	Owen Sound	OHL	25	15	7	2	1423	70	0	2.95	....	....	....	....	....	....	....
	Barrie Colts	OHL	21	10	5	2	1054	48	1	2.73	5	1	2	215	11	0	3.07
2005-06	Barrie Colts	OHL	*59	36	17	0	3340	142	6	2.55	11	5	2	654	34	0	3.12

LALANDE, Kevin (lah-LAWND, KEH-vihn) CGY.

Goaltender. Catches left. 5'11", 175 lbs. Born, Kingston, Ont., February 19, 1987.
(Calgary's 5th choice, 128th overall, in 2005 Entry Draft).

			Regular Season								Playoffs						
Season	Club	League	GP	W	L	O/T	Mins	GA	SO	Avg	GP	W	L	Mins	GA	SO	Avg
2003-04	Hawkesbury	CJHL	35	....	....	....	2010	105	3	3.13	6	....	....	286	19	0	3.99
	Belleville Bulls	OHL	3	1	2	0	133	15	0	6.77	....	....	....	....	....	....	....
2004-05	Belleville Bulls	OHL	30	15	11	3	1797	79	1	2.64	2	0	2	120	8	0	4.00
2005-06	Belleville Bulls	OHL	50	24	17	0	2789	143	3	3.08	....	....	....	....	....	....	....

LALIME, Patrick (lah-LEEM, PAT-rihk) CHI.

Goaltender. Catches left. 6'3", 189 lbs. Born, St-Bonaventure, Que., July 7, 1974.
(Pittsburgh's 6th choice, 156th overall, in 1993 Entry Draft).

			Regular Season								Playoffs						
Season	Club	League	GP	W	L	O/T	Mins	GA	SO	Avg	GP	W	L	Mins	GA	SO	Avg
1990-91	Abitibi Forestiers	QAAA	26	9	17	0	1595	151	0	5.81	....	....	....	....	....	....	....
1991-92	Shawinigan	QMJHL	6	....	....	....	272	25	0	5.50	....	....	....	....	....	....	....
1992-93	Shawinigan	QMJHL	44	10	24	4	2467	192	0	4.67	....	....	....	....	....	....	....
1993-94	Shawinigan	QMJHL	48	22	20	0	2733	192	1	4.22	5	1	3	223	25	0	6.73
1994-95	Hampton Roads	ECHL	26	15	7	3	1470	82	2	3.35	....	....	....	....	....	....	....
	Cleveland	IHL	23	7	10	4	1230	91	0	4.44	....	....	....	....	....	....	....
1995-96	Cleveland	IHL	41	20	12	7	2314	149	0	3.86	....	....	....	....	....	....	....
1996-97	**Pittsburgh**	**NHL**	**39**	**21**	**12**	**2**	**2058**	**101**	**3**	**2.94**	....	....	....	....	....	....	....
	Cleveland	IHL	14	6	6	2	834	45	1	3.24	....	....	....	....	....	....	....
1997-98	Grand Rapids	IHL	31	10	10	9	1749	76	2	2.61	1	0	1	77	4	0	3.11
1998-99	Kansas City Blades	IHL	*66	*39	20	4	*3789	190	2	3.01	3	1	2	179	6	1	2.01
99-2000	**Ottawa**	**NHL**	**38**	**19**	**14**	**3**	**2038**	**79**	**3**	**2.33**	....	....	....	....	....	....	....
2000-01	**Ottawa**	**NHL**	**60**	**36**	**19**	**5**	**3607**	**141**	**7**	**2.35**	**4**	**0**	**4**	**251**	**10**	**0**	**2.39**
2001-02	**Ottawa**	**NHL**	**61**	**27**	**24**	**8**	**3583**	**148**	**7**	**2.48**	**12**	**7**	**5**	**778**	**18**	**4**	***1.39**
2002-03	**Ottawa**	**NHL**	**67**	**39**	**20**	**7**	**3943**	**142**	**8**	**2.16**	**18**	**11**	**7**	**1122**	**34**	**1**	**1.82**
2003-04	**Ottawa**	**NHL**	**57**	**25**	**23**	**7**	**3324**	**127**	**5**	**2.29**	**7**	**3**	**4**	**398**	**13**	**0**	**1.96**
2004-05							DID NOT PLAY										
2005-06	**St. Louis**	**NHL**	**31**	**4**	**18**	**8**	**1699**	**103**	**0**	**3.64**	....	....	....	....	....	....	....
	Peoria Rivermen	AHL	14	6	6	1	798	38	1	2.86	....	....	....	....	....	....	....
	NHL Totals		**353**	**171**	**130**	**40**	**20252**	**841**	**33**	**2.49**	**41**	**21**	**20**	**2549**	**75**	**5**	**1.77**

NHL All-Rookie Team (1997) • IHL First All-Star Team (1999)

Played in NHL All-Star Game (2003)

Rights traded to **Anaheim** by **Pittsburgh** for Sean Pronger, March 24, 1998. Traded to **Ottawa** by **Anaheim** for Ted Donato and the rights to Antti-Jussi Niemi, June 18, 1999. Traded to **St. Louis** by **Ottawa** for St. Louis' 4th round choice (Ilja Zubov) in 2005 Entry Draft, June 27, 2004. Signed as a free agent by **Chicago**, July 1, 2006.

LAMOTHE, Marc (luh-MAWTH, MAHRK)

Goaltender. Catches left. 6'2", 210 lbs. Born, New Liskeard, Ont., February 27, 1974.
(Montreal's 6th choice, 92nd overall, in 1992 Entry Draft).

			Regular Season								Playoffs						
Season	Club	League	GP	W	L	O/T	Mins	GA	SO	Avg	GP	W	L	Mins	GA	SO	Avg
1990-91	Ott. Jr. Senators	CJHL	25	13	7	0	1220	82	1	4.03	....	....	....	....	....	....	....
1991-92	Kingston	OHL	42	10	25	2	2378	189	1	4.77	....	....	....	....	....	....	....
1992-93	Kingston	OHL	45	23	12	6	2489	162	1	3.91	15	8	5	753	48	1	3.82
1993-94	Kingston	OHL	48	23	20	5	2828	177	*2	3.76	6	2	2	224	12	0	3.21
1994-95	Wheeling	ECHL	13	9	2	1	737	38	0	3.10	....	....	....	....	....	....	....
	Fredericton	AHL	9	2	5	0	428	32	0	4.48	....	....	....	....	....	....	....
1995-96	Fredericton	AHL	23	5	9	3	1166	73	1	3.76	3	1	2	161	9	0	3.36
1996-97	Indianapolis Ice	IHL	38	20	14	4	2271	100	1	2.64	1	0	0	20	1	0	3.00
1997-98	Indianapolis Ice	IHL	31	18	10	2	1772	72	3	2.44	4	1	3	177	10	0	3.38
1998-99	Indianapolis Ice	IHL	32	9	16	6	1823	115	1	3.78	6	3	3	338	10	*2	1.78
99-2000	**Chicago**	**NHL**	**2**	**1**	**1**	**0**	**116**	**10**	**0**	**5.17**	....	....	....	....	....	....	....
	Cleveland	IHL	44	19	18	4	2455	112	2	2.74	4	2	2	325	12	0	2.21
2000-01	Syracuse Crunch	AHL	42	17	15	7	2323	112	2	2.89	....	....	....	....	....	....	....
2001-02	Hamilton Bulldogs	AHL	45	22	19	2	2569	102	3	2.38	9	6	3	551	18	0	1.96
2002-03	Grand Rapids	AHL	*60	*33	18	8	*3438	122	6	2.13	15	10	5	945	29	1	1.84
2003-04	**Detroit**	**NHL**	**2**	**1**	**0**	**1**	**125**	**3**	**0**	**1.44**	....	....	....	....	....	....	....
	Grand Rapids	AHL	43	21	16	5	2535	87	4	2.06	4	0	3	200	12	0	3.60
2004-05	Yaroslavl	Russia	*55	....	....	....	*3357	90	6	1.61	9	....	....	521	21	0	2.42
2005-06	Cherepovets	Russia	42	....	....	....	2378	79	4	1.99	4	....	....	239	9	1	2.26
	NHL Totals		**4**	**2**	**1**	**1**	**241**	**13**	**0**	**3.24**	....	....	....	....	....	....	....

AHL First All-Star Team (2003) • Harry "Hap" Holmes Memorial Award (fewest goals against – AHL) (2003) (shared with Joey MacDonald) • Aldege "Baz" Bastien Memorial Award (Outstanding Goaltender – AHL) (2003)

Signed as a free agent by **Chicago**, September 26, 1996. Signed as a free agent by **Edmonton**, August 16, 2001. Signed as a free agent by **Detroit**, August 5, 2002. Signed as a free agent by **Yaroslavl** (Russia), June 14, 2004.

LARSSON, Daniel (LARH-suhn, DAN-yehl) DET.

Goaltender. Catches . 6', 170 lbs. Born, Boden, Sweden, February 7, 1986.
(Detroit's 4th choice, 92nd overall, in 2006 Entry Draft).

			Regular Season								Playoffs						
Season	Club	League	GP	W	L	O/T	Mins	GA	SO	Avg	GP	W	L	Mins	GA	SO	Avg
2002-03	Lulea HF U18	Swe-U18	12	....	....	....	731	50	0	4.10	....	....	....	....	....	....	....
2003-04	Lulea HF Jr.	Swe-Jr.	4	....	....	....	239	12	0	3.01	....	....	....	....	....	....	....
	Bodens IK	Sweden-2	1	....	....	....	20	1	0	3.00	....	....	....	....	....	....	....
2004-05	Bodens IK	Sweden-2	28	....	....	....	1514	97	1	3.84	....	....	....	....	....	....	....
2005-06	Hammarby Jr.	Swe-Jr..	9	....	....	....	548	24	1	2.63	....	....	....	....	....	....	....
	Hammarby	Sweden-2	36	....	....	....	2001	90	0	2.70	....	....	....	....	....	....	....

LASSILA, Teemu (la-SIHL-uh, TEE-moo) NSH.

Goaltender. Catches left. 6'1", 200 lbs. Born, Helsinki, Finland, March 26, 1983.
(Nashville's 9th choice, 117th overall, in 2003 Entry Draft).

			Regular Season								Playoffs						
Season	Club	League	GP	W	L	O/T	Mins	GA	SO	Avg	GP	W	L	Mins	GA	SO	Avg
2000-01	TPS Turku Jr.	Fin-Jr.	9	6	2	0	519	9	3	1.04	1	0	1	60	5	0	5.00
2001-02	TPS Turku Jr.	Fin-Jr.	43	26	12	5	2577	77	5	1.79	9	5	4	571	21	1	2.21
2002-03	Hermes Kokkola	Finland-2	21	9	5	6	1268	45	2	2.13	....	....	....	....	....	....	....
	TPS Turku	Finland	21	12	6	1	1190	38	6	1.92	7	3	4	416	21	1	3.03
2003-04	Assat Pori	Finland	5	3	2	0	300	16	0	3.20	....	....	....	....	....	....	....
	TPS Turku	Finland	19	7	4	6	1078	31	3	1.72	12	8	4	679	17	4	1.50
2004-05	TPS Turku	Finland	52	21	14	16	3006	116	5	2.31	6	2	4	356	16	0	2.69
2005-06	Djurgarden	Sweden	*45	....	....	....	2618	137	2	3.14	....	....	....	....	....	....	....

LAWSON, Tom (LAW-suhn, TAWM)

Goaltender. Catches left. 6'5", 200 lbs. Born, Whitby, Ont., August 15, 1979.

			Regular Season								Playoffs						
Season	Club	League	GP	W	L	O/T	Mins	GA	SO	Avg	GP	W	L	Mins	GA	SO	Avg
1998-99	Markham Waxers	OPJHL	32	19	10	2	1793	101	....	3.38	....	....	....	....	....	....	....
99-2000	Bowling Green	CCHA	3	0	3	0	173	14	0	4.86	....	....	....	....	....	....	....
2000-01	Knoxville Speed	UHL	35	16	16	2	2002	116	0	3.48	....	....	....	....	....	....	....
	Cincinnati	AHL	1	0	0	0	23	1	0	2.58	....	....	....	....	....	....	....
2001-02	Anchorage Aces	WCHL	1	1	0	0	54	2	0	2.22	....	....	....	....	....	....	....
2002-03	Fort Wayne	UHL	56	29	15	10	3178	106	*7	*2.00	12	*11	1	750	21	*2	*1.68
2003-04	Hershey Bears	AHL	32	13	12	2	1693	65	4	2.30	....	....	....	....	....	....	....
	Reading Royals	ECHL	2	0	2	0	120	10	0	5.02	....	....	....	....	....	....	....
2004-05	Hershey Bears	AHL	27	10	14	0	1479	70	2	2.84	....	....	....	....	....	....	....
2005-06	Lowell	AHL	7	1	3	1	367	20	0	3.27	....	....	....	....	....	....	....
	San Diego Gulls	ECHL	30	14	14	2	1751	84	2	2.88	....	....	....	....	....	....	....

UHL First All-Star Team (2003)

Signed as a free agent by **Knoxville** (UHL) after leaving **Bowling Green** (CCHA), September 30, 2000. • Missed majority of 2001-02 season recovering from leg injury suffered in game vs. Colorado (WCHL), October 13, 2001. Signed as a free agent by **Fort Wayne** (UHL), October 13, 2002. Signed as a free agent by **Colorado**, June 3, 2003.

LECLAIRE, Pascal (lah-CLAIR, pas-KAL) CBJ

Goaltender. Catches left. 6'2", 200 lbs. Born, Repentigny, Que., November 7, 1982.
(Columbus' 1st choice, 8th overall, in 2001 Entry Draft).

			Regular Season								Playoffs						
Season	Club	League	GP	W	L	O/T	Mins	GA	SO	Avg	GP	W	L	Mins	GA	SO	Avg
1997-98	Cap-d-Madeleine	QAAA	26	6	17	3	1580	127	0	4.90	....	....	....	....	....	....	....
1998-99	Halifax	QMJHL	33	19	11	1	1828	96	2	3.15	1	0	0	17	2	0	7.06
99-2000	Halifax	QMJHL	31	16	8	4	1729	103	1	3.57	5	1	2	198	12	0	3.65
2000-01	Halifax	QMJHL	35	14	16	5	2111	126	1	3.58	2	0	2	109	10	0	5.49
2001-02	Montreal Rocket	QMJHL	45	15	23	4	2513	138	1	3.29	7	3	4	441	15	0	*2.04
2002-03	Syracuse Crunch	AHL	36	8	21	3	1886	112	0	3.56	....	....	....	....	....	....	....
2003-04	**Columbus**	**NHL**	**2**	**0**	**2**	**0**	**119**	**7**	**0**	**3.53**	....	....	....	....	....	....	....
	Syracuse Crunch	AHL	44	21	16	3	2447	125	2	3.06	3	1	2	142	12	0	5.07
2004-05	Syracuse Crunch	AHL	14	5	6	3	845	33	2	2.34	....	....	....	....	....	....	....
2005-06	**Columbus**	**NHL**	**33**	**11**	**15**	**3**	**1804**	**97**	**0**	**3.23**	....	....	....	....	....	....	....
	Syracuse Crunch	AHL	7	3	3	0	340	16	1	2.82	5	2	3	288	11	1	2.29
	NHL Totals		**35**	**11**	**17**	**3**	**1923**	**104**	**0**	**3.24**	....	....	....	....	....	....	....

LEGACE, Manny (LEH-gah-see, MAN-nee) ST.L.

Goaltender. Catches left. 5'9", 162 lbs. Born, Toronto, Ont., February 4, 1973.
(Hartford's 5th choice, 188th overall, in 1993 Entry Draft).

			Regular Season								Playoffs						
Season	Club	League	GP	W	L	O/T	Mins	GA	SO	Avg	GP	W	L	Mins	GA	SO	Avg
1987-88	Alliston Hornets	OJHL-C	16	7	9	0	960	83	0	5.17	....	....	....	....	....	....	....
1988-89	Vaughan Raiders	MTJHL	23	....	....	....	1303	92	1	4.24	....	....	....	....	....	....	....
1989-90	Vaughan Raiders	MTJHL	21	8	11	1	1180	89	1	4.53	....	....	....	....	....	....	....
	Thornhill	OHA-B	8	3	3	2	480	30	0	3.75	....	....	....	....	....	....	....
1990-91	Niagara Falls	OHL	30	13	11	2	1515	107	0	4.24	4	1	1	119	10	0	5.04
1991-92	Niagara Falls	OHL	43	21	16	3	2384	143	0	3.60	14	8	5	791	56	0	4.25
1992-93	Niagara Falls	OHL	48	22	19	3	2630	171	0	3.90	4	0	4	240	18	0	4.50
1993-94	Canada	Nat-Tm	16	8	6	0	859	36	2	2.51	....	....	....	....	....	....	....
1994-95	Springfield Indians	AHL	39	12	17	6	2169	128	2	3.54	....	....	....	....	....	....	....
1995-96	Springfield Falcons	AHL	37	20	12	4	2196	83	*5	*2.27	4	1	3	220	18	0	4.91
1996-97	Springfield Falcons	AHL	36	17	14	5	2119	107	1	3.03	12	9	3	745	25	*2	2.01
	Richmond	ECHL	3	2	1	0	157	8	0	3.05	....	....	....	....	....	....	....
1997-98	Springfield Falcons	AHL	6	4	2	0	345	16	0	2.78	....	....	....	....	....	....	....
	Las Vegas Thunder	IHL	41	18	16	4	2106	111	1	3.16	4	1	3	237	16	0	4.05
1998-99	**Los Angeles**	**NHL**	**17**	**2**	**9**	**2**	**899**	**39**	**0**	**2.60**	....	....	....	....	....	....	....
	Long Beach	IHL	33	22	8	1	1796	67	2	2.24	6	4	2	338	9	0	*1.60
99-2000	**Detroit**	**NHL**	**4**	**4**	**0**	**0**	**240**	**11**	**0**	**2.75**	....	....	....	....	....	....	....
	Manitoba Moose	IHL	42	17	18	5	2409	104	2	2.59	2	0	2	141	7	0	2.97
2000-01	**Detroit**	**NHL**	**39**	**24**	**5**	**5**	**2136**	**73**	**2**	**2.05**	....	....	....	....	....	....	....
2001-02 ◆	**Detroit**	**NHL**	**20**	**10**	**6**	**2**	**1117**	**45**	**1**	**2.42**	**1**	**0**	**0**	**11**	**1**	**0**	**5.45**
2002-03	**Detroit**	**NHL**	**25**	**14**	**5**	**4**	**1406**	**51**	**0**	**2.18**	....	....	....	....	....	....	....
2003-04	**Detroit**	**NHL**	**41**	**23**	**10**	**5**	**2325**	**82**	**3**	**2.12**	**4**	**2**	**2**	**220**	**8**	**0**	**2.18**
2004-05	Voskresensk	Russia	2	....	....	....	89	10	0	6.73	....	....	....	....	....	....	....
2005-06	**Detroit**	**NHL**	**51**	**37**	**8**	**3**	**2905**	**106**	**7**	**2.19**	**6**	**2**	**4**	**408**	**18**	**0**	**2.65**
	Grand Rapids	AHL	1	1	0	0	60	2	0	2.00	....	....	....	....	....	....	....
	NHL Totals		**197**	**114**	**43**	**21**	**11028**	**407**	**13**	**2.21**	**11**	**4**	**6**	**639**	**27**	**0**	**2.54**

OHL First All-Star Team (1993) • AHL First All-Star Team (1996) • Harry ''Hap'' Holmes Memorial Award (fewest goals against – AHL) (1996) (shared with Scott Langkow) • Aldege "Baz" Bastien Memorial Award (Outstanding Goaltender – AHL) (1996)

Rights transferred to **Carolina** after **Hartford** franchise relocated, June 25, 1997. Traded to **Los Angeles** by **Carolina** for future considerations, July 31, 1998. Signed as a free agent by **Detroit**, August 9, 1999. Claimed on waivers by **Vancouver** from **Detroit**, September 30, 1999. Claimed on waivers by **Detroit** from **Vancouver**, October 13, 1999. Signed as a free agent by **Voskresensk** (Russia), December 20, 2004. Signed as a free agent by **St. Louis**, August 8, 2006.

LEHTO, Mika (leh-TOH, MEE-kuh)

Goaltender. Catches left. 5'11", 175 lbs. Born, Vammala, Finland, April 12, 1979.
(Pittsburgh's 8th choice, 224th overall, in 1998 Entry Draft).

			Regular Season								Playoffs						
Season	Club	League	GP	W	L	O/T	Mins	GA	SO	Avg	GP	W	L	Mins	GA	SO	Avg
1995-96	Assat Pori U18	Fin-U18	18	....	....	....	1077	60	....	3.34	....	....	....	....	....	....	....
1996-97	Assat Pori U18	Fin-U18	14	....	....	....	....	....	....	....	....	....	....	....	....	....	....
	Assat Pori Jr.	Fin-Jr.	6	....	....	....	304	17	0	3.35	....	....	....	....	....	....	....
1997-98	Assat Pori Jr.	Fin-Jr.	36	16	14	6	2161	103	2	2.86	....	....	....	....	....	....	....
	Assat Pori	Finland	1	0	0	0	35	1	0	1.71	1	0	0	17	0	0	0.00
1998-99	Assat Pori Jr.	Fin-Jr.	20	7	10	3	1202	68	0	3.39	....	....	....	....	....	....	....
	Assat Pori	Finland	15	4	6	1	774	38	1	2.95	....	....	....	....	....	....	....
99-2000	Assat Pori Jr.	Fin-Jr.	2	0	2	0	118	8	0	4.06	....	....	....	....	....	....	....
	Hermes Kokkola	Finland-2	6	3	2	1	339	19	1	3.36	....	....	....	....	....	....	....
	Assat Pori	Finland	23	4	11	3	1099	87	0	4.75	....	....	....	....	....	....	....
2000-01	JYP Jyvaskyla	Finland	41	12	19	8	2384	126	1	3.17	....	....	....	....	....	....	....
2001-02	JYP Jyvaskyla	Finland	37	10	17	9	2167	107	6	2.96	....	....	....	....	....	....	....
2002-03	Tappara Tampere	Finland	27	12	11	4	1512	45	3	1.79	14	10	3	927	23	2	1.49
2003-04	Tappara Tampere	Finland	46	17	19	8	2638	111	3	2.52	3	1	2	190	5	0	1.58
2004-05	Tappara Tampere	Finland	42	12	17	9	2365	115	2	2.92	7	3	3	370	11	3	1.78
2005-06	Tappara Tampere	Finland	54	28	14	12	3282	114	10	2.08	6	2	4	381	17	0	2.67

LEHTONEN, Kari (LEH-tuh-nehn, KAH-ree) ATL.

Goaltender. Catches left. 6'4", 195 lbs. Born, Helsinki, Finland, November 16, 1983.
(Atlanta's 1st choice, 2nd overall, in 2002 Entry Draft).

			Regular Season								Playoffs						
Season	Club	League	GP	W	L	O/T	Mins	GA	SO	Avg	GP	W	L	Mins	GA	SO	Avg
1998-99	Jokerit U18	Fin-U18	2	....	....	....	....	....	....	....	4	2	2	240	7	0	1.75
99-2000	Jokerit Helsinki Jr.	Fin-Jr.	33	21	9	3	1974	86	2	2.61	12	9	3	758	14	4	1.11
2000-01	Jokerit U18	Fin-U18	....	....	....	....	....	....	....	....	6	....	....	....	....	....	....
	Jokerit Helsinki Jr.	Fin-Jr.	31	20	9	1	1799	71	3	2.37	1	0	1	54	4	0	4.44
	Jokerit Helsinki	Finland	4	3	1	0	189	6	0	1.90	....	....	....	....	....	....	....
2001-02	Jokerit Helsinki Jr.	Fin-Jr.	6	5	1	0	360	11	1	1.83	....	....	....	....	....	....	....
	Jokerit Helsinki	Finland	23	13	5	2	1242	37	4	1.79	11	8	2	623	18	3	1.73
2002-03	Jokerit Helsinki	Finland	45	23	14	6	2634	87	5	1.98	10	6	4	626	17	2	1.63
2003-04	**Atlanta**	**NHL**	**4**	**4**	**0**	**0**	**240**	**5**	**1**	**1.25**	....	....	....	....	....	....	....
	Chicago Wolves	AHL	39	20	14	2	2192	88	3	2.41	10	6	4	663	23	1	2.08
2004-05	Chicago Wolves	AHL	57	38	17	2	3378	128	5	2.27	16	10	6	983	28	2	*1.71
2005-06	**Atlanta**	**NHL**	**38**	**20**	**15**	**0**	**2166**	**106**	**2**	**2.94**	....	....	....	....	....	....	....
	NHL Totals		**42**	**24**	**15**	**0**	**2406**	**111**	**3**	**2.77**	....	....	....	....	....	....	....

AHL Second All-Star Team (2005)

LEIGHTON, Michael (LAY-tohn, MIGH-kuhl) ANA.

Goaltender. Catches left. 6'3", 186 lbs. Born, Petrolia, Ont., May 19, 1981.
(Chicago's 5th choice, 165th overall, in 1999 Entry Draft).

			Regular Season								Playoffs						
Season	**Club**	**League**	**GP**	**W**	**L**	**O/T**	**Mins**	**GA**	**SO**	**Avg**	**GP**	**W**	**L**	**Mins**	**GA**	**SO**	**Avg**
1997-98	Petrolia Jets	OHA-B	30	....	....	....	1583	87	2	3.30	....	....	....	....	....	....	....
1998-99	Windsor Spitfires	OHL	28	4	17	2	1389	112	0	4.84	3	0	1	80	10	0	7.50
99-2000	Windsor Spitfires	OHL	42	17	17	2	2272	118	1	3.12	12	5	6	616	32	0	3.12
2000-01	Windsor Spitfires	OHL	54	32	13	5	3035	138	2	2.73	9	4	5	519	27	1	3.12
2001-02	Norfolk Admirals	AHL	52	27	16	8	3114	111	6	2.14	4	1	2	238	8	0	2.02
2002-03	**Chicago**	**NHL**	**8**	**2**	**3**	**2**	**447**	**21**	**1**	**2.82**	....	....	....	....	....	....	....
	Norfolk Admirals	AHL	36	18	13	5	2184	91	4	2.50	4	3	1	240	7	1	1.75
2003-04	**Chicago**	**NHL**	**34**	**6**	**18**	**8**	**1988**	**99**	**2**	**2.99**	....	....	....	....	....	....	....
	Norfolk Admirals	AHL	18	10	7	1	1081	33	1	1.83	4	2	1	212	2	2	0.57
2004-05	Norfolk Admirals	AHL	41	20	16	3	2319	78	7	2.02	....	....	....	....	....	....	....
2005-06	Rochester	AHL	40	15	22	1	2318	124	2	3.21	....	....	....	....	....	....	....
	NHL Totals		**42**	**8**	**21**	**10**	**2435**	**120**	**3**	**2.96**	....	....	....	....	....	....	....

AHL All-Rookie Team (2002)

Traded to **Buffalo** by **Chicago** for Milan Bartovic, October 4, 2005. Signed as a free agent by **Anaheim**, July 13, 2006.

LENEVEU, David (LEH-neh-voo, DAY-vihd) PHX.

Goaltender. Catches left. 6'1", 187 lbs. Born, Fernie, B.C., May 23, 1983.
(Phoenix's 3rd choice, 46th overall, in 2002 Entry Draft).

			Regular Season								Playoffs						
Season	**Club**	**League**	**GP**	**W**	**L**	**O/T**	**Mins**	**GA**	**SO**	**Avg**	**GP**	**W**	**L**	**Mins**	**GA**	**SO**	**Avg**
99-2000	Fernie Ghostriders	AWHL	22	15	2	0	1140	48	0	2.49	....	....	....	....	....	....	....
2000-01	Nanaimo Clippers	BCHL	41	....	....	....	2330	127	6	3.29	....	....	....	....	....	....	....
2001-02	Cornell Big Red	ECAC	14	11	2	1	842	21	2	*1.50	....	....	....	....	....	....	....
2002-03	Cornell Big Red	ECAC	32	*28	3	1	1946	39	*9	*1.20	....	....	....	....	....	....	....
2003-04	Springfield Falcons	AHL	38	16	19	3	2217	102	1	2.76	....	....	....	....	....	....	....
2004-05	Utah Grizzlies	AHL	48	11	32	3	2702	132	0	2.93	....	....	....	....	....	....	....
2005-06	**Phoenix**	**NHL**	**15**	**3**	**8**	**2**	**814**	**44**	**0**	**3.24**	....	....	....	....	....	....	....
	San Antonio	AHL	28	10	16	2	1646	80	2	2.92	....	....	....	....	....	....	....
	NHL Totals		**15**	**3**	**8**	**2**	**814**	**44**	**0**	**3.24**	....	....	....	....	....	....	....

ECAC All-Rookie Team (2002) • ECAC First All-Star Team (2003) • ECAC Goaltender of the Year (2003) • ECAC Player of the Year (2003) (co-winner - Christopher Higgins) • NCAA East First All-American Team (2003)

LEVASSEUR, Jean-Philippe (leh-VAH-soor, ZHAWN-fihl-EEP) ANA.

Goaltender. Catches right. 6', 184 lbs. Born, Victoriaville, Que., January 15, 1987.
(Anaheim's 6th choice, 197th overall, in 2005 Entry Draft).

			Regular Season								Playoffs						
Season	**Club**	**League**	**GP**	**W**	**L**	**O/T**	**Mins**	**GA**	**SO**	**Avg**	**GP**	**W**	**L**	**Mins**	**GA**	**SO**	**Avg**
2002-03	Magog	QAAA	28	15	10	1	1563	71	3	2.73	....	....	....	....	....	....	....
2003-04	Magog	QAAA	24	12	11	2	1424	86	0	3.62	13	7	5	762	35	0	2.80
	Rouyn-Noranda	QMJHL	3	0	2	1	184	14	0	4.57	....	....	....	....	....	....	....
2004-05	Rouyn-Noranda	QMJHL	29	8	14	3	1393	89	0	3.83	3	0	0	48	3	0	3.76
2005-06	Rouyn-Noranda	QMJHL	58	*35	19	0	3125	178	2	3.42	5	1	4	297	16	0	3.23

LITTLE, Neil (LIH-tuhl, NEEL)

Goaltender. Catches left. 6'1", 193 lbs. Born, Medicine Hat, Alta., December 18, 1971.
(Philadelphia's 10th choice, 226th overall, in 1991 Entry Draft).

			Regular Season								Playoffs						
Season	**Club**	**League**	**GP**	**W**	**L**	**O/T**	**Mins**	**GA**	**SO**	**Avg**	**GP**	**W**	**L**	**Mins**	**GA**	**SO**	**Avg**
1989-90	Estevan Bruins	SJHL	46	21	19	4	2707	150	1	3.32	....	....	....	....	....	....	....
1990-91	RPI Engineers	ECAC	18	9	8	0	1032	71	0	4.13	....	....	....	....	....	....	....
1991-92	RPI Engineers	ECAC	28	11	11	3	1532	96	0	3.76	....	....	....	....	....	....	....
1992-93	RPI Engineers	ECAC	*31	*19	9	3	*1801	88	0	2.93	....	....	....	....	....	....	....
1993-94	RPI Engineers	ECAC	27	16	7	4	1570	88	0	3.36	....	....	....	....	....	....	....
	Hershey Bears	AHL	1	0	0	0	18	1	0	3.33	....	....	....	....	....	....	....
1994-95	Hershey Bears	AHL	19	5	7	3	919	60	0	3.91	....	....	....	....	....	....	....
	Johnstown Chiefs	ECHL	16	7	6	1	897	55	0	3.68	3	0	2	145	11	0	4.55
1995-96	Hershey Bears	AHL	48	21	18	6	2680	149	0	3.34	1	0	1	60	4	0	4.02
1996-97	Philadelphia	AHL	54	31	12	7	3007	145	0	2.89	10	6	4	620	20	1	*1.94
1997-98	Philadelphia	AHL	51	*31	11	7	2960	145	0	2.94	*20	*15	5	*1193	48	*3	2.41
1998-99	Grand Rapids	IHL	50	18	21	5	2740	144	3	3.15	....	....	....	....	....	....	....
99-2000	Philadelphia	AHL	51	26	18	2	2830	143	1	3.03	5	2	3	298	15	0	3.02
2000-01	Philadelphia	AHL	*58	22	27	4	3117	148	2	2.85	10	5	5	631	23	1	2.19
2001-02	**Philadelphia**	**NHL**	**1**	**0**	**1**	**0**	**60**	**4**	**0**	**4.00**	....	....	....	....	....	....	....
	Philadelphia	AHL	35	13	15	7	2079	70	2	2.02	5	2	3	298	13	0	2.62
2002-03	Philadelphia	AHL	42	18	19	4	2478	103	4	2.49	....	....	....	....	....	....	....
2003-04	**Philadelphia**	**NHL**	**1**	**0**	**1**	**0**	**33**	**2**	**0**	**3.64**	....	....	....	....	....	....	....
	Philadelphia	AHL	34	21	12	1	1900	62	6	1.96	....	....	....	....	....	....	....
2004-05	Philadelphia	AHL	26	15	7	0	1383	54	3	2.34	2	1	0	25	0	0	0.00
2005-06	Blues Espoo	Finland	37	14	16	7	2100	85	2	2.43	....	....	....	....	....	....	....
	NHL Totals		**2**	**0**	**2**	**0**	**93**	**6**	**0**	**3.87**	....	....	....	....	....	....	....

ECAC First All-Star Team (1993) • NCAA East Second All-American Team (1993)

LIV, Stefan (LIHV, STEH-fuhn) DET.

Goaltender. Catches left. 6', 172 lbs. Born, Gdynia, Poland, December 21, 1980.
(Detroit's 3rd choice, 102nd overall, in 2000 Entry Draft).

			Regular Season								Playoffs						
Season	**Club**	**League**	**GP**	**W**	**L**	**O/T**	**Mins**	**GA**	**SO**	**Avg**	**GP**	**W**	**L**	**Mins**	**GA**	**SO**	**Avg**
1997-98	HV 71 Jr.	Swe-Jr.	17	....	....	....	1020	47	....	2.76	....	....	....	....	....	....	....
1998-99	HV 71 Jonkoping	Sweden	DID NOT PLAY – SPARE GOALTENDER														
99-2000	HV 71 Jr.	Swe-Jr.	10	....	....	....	600	17	2	1.70	....	....	....	....	....	....	....
	Tranas AIF	Sweden-2	9	....	....	....	541	20	0	2.17	....	....	....	....	....	....	....
	HV 71 Jonkoping	Sweden	12	....	....	....	716	24	1	2.01	3	....	....	178	12	0	4.04
2000-01	HV 71 Jonkoping	Sweden	*46	....	....	....	*2752	127	4	2.77	....	....	....	....	....	....	....
2001-02	HV 71 Jonkoping	Sweden	38	....	....	....	2184	95	*4	2.61	8	....	....	517	27	0	3.13
2002-03	HV 71 Jonkoping	Sweden	46	....	....	....	2723	124	3	2.73	7	....	....	391	17	1	2.61
2003-04	HV 71 Jonkoping	Sweden	41	....	....	....	2450	91	6	2.23	*18	....	....	*1091	35	*5	1.92
2004-05	HV 71 Jonkoping	Sweden	40	....	....	....	2404	119	2	2.97	....	....	....	....	....	....	....
2005-06	HV 71 Jonkoping	Sweden	40	....	....	....	2407	87	4	2.17	12	....	....	668	38	0	3.41
	Sweden	Olympics	1	1	0	0	60	2	0	2.00	....	....	....	....	....	....	....

LUNDQVIST, Henrik (LUHND-kvihst, HEHN-rihk) NYR

Goaltender. Catches left. 6'1", 194 lbs. Born, Are, Sweden, March 2, 1982.
(NY Rangers' 7th choice, 205th overall, in 2000 Entry Draft).

			Regular Season								Playoffs						
Season	**Club**	**League**	**GP**	**W**	**L**	**O/T**	**Mins**	**GA**	**SO**	**Avg**	**GP**	**W**	**L**	**Mins**	**GA**	**SO**	**Avg**
1998-99	V.Frolunda Jr.	Swe-Jr.	35	....	....	....	2100	95	0	2.73	....	....	....	....	....	....	....
99-2000	V.Frolunda Jr.	Swe-Jr.	30	....	....	....	1726	73	0	2.54	5	4	1	300	7	2	1.40
2000-01	V.Frolunda U18	Swe-U18	2	....	....	....	120	5	0	2.50	3	2	1	182	5	0	1.62
	V.Frolunda Jr.	Swe-Jr.	19	....	....	....	1140	50	2	2.64	....	....	....	....	....	....	....
	IF Molndal Hockey	Sweden-2	7	....	....	....	420	29	0	4.22	....	....	....	....	....	....	....
	V.Frolunda	Sweden	4	....	....	....	190	11	0	3.47	....	....	....	....	....	....	....
2001-02	V.Frolunda	Sweden	20	....	....	....	1152	52	2	2.71	8	8	0	489	18	*2	2.21
	V.Frolunda Jr.	Swe-Jr.	1	1	0	0	60	4	0	4.00	....	....	....	....	....	....	....
2002-03	V.Frolunda	Sweden	28	....	....	....	1650	40	*6	*1.45	12	....	....	739	26	*2	2.11
	V.Frolunda Jr.	Swe-Jr.	1	1	0	0	60	4	0	4.00	....	....	....	....	....	....	....
2003-04	V.Frolunda	Sweden	*48	....	....	....	*2897	105	7	2.17	10	....	....	610	20	0	1.97
2004-05	Frolunda	Sweden	44	*33	8	3	2642	79	*6	*1.79	*14	*12	2	854	15	*6	*1.05
2005-06	**NY Rangers**	**NHL**	**53**	**30**	**12**	**9**	**3112**	**116**	**2**	**2.24**	**3**	**0**	**3**	**177**	**13**	**0**	**4.41**
	Sweden	Olympics	6	5	1	0	360	14	0	2.33	....	....	....	....	....	....	....
	NHL Totals		**53**	**30**	**12**	**9**	**3112**	**116**	**2**	**2.24**	**3**	**0**	**3**	**177**	**13**	**0**	**4.41**

NHL All-Rookie Team (2006)

LUONGO, Roberto (loo-WAHN-goh, roh-BUHR-toh) VAN.

Goaltender. Catches left. 6'3", 205 lbs. Born, Montreal, Que., April 4, 1979.
(NY Islanders' 1st choice, 4th overall, in 1997 Entry Draft).

			Regular Season								Playoffs						
Season	**Club**	**League**	**GP**	**W**	**L**	**O/T**	**Mins**	**GA**	**SO**	**Avg**	**GP**	**W**	**L**	**Mins**	**GA**	**SO**	**Avg**
1994-95	Montreal-Bourassa	QAAA	25	10	14	0	94	1465	0	3.85	....	....	....	....	....	....	....
1995-96	Val-d'Or Foreurs	QMJHL	23	6	11	4	1201	74	0	3.70	3	0	1	68	5	0	4.41
1996-97	Val-d'Or Foreurs	QMJHL	60	32	22	2	3305	171	2	3.10	13	8	5	777	44	0	3.40
1997-98	Val-d'Or Foreurs	QMJHL	54	27	20	5	3046	157	*7	3.09	*17	*14	3	*1019	37	*2	*2.18
1998-99	Val-d'Or Foreurs	QMJHL	21	6	10	2	1176	77	1	3.93	....	....	....	....	....	....	....
	Acadie-Bathurst	QMJHL	22	14	7	1	1340	74	0	3.31	*23	*16	6	*1400	64	0	2.74
99-2000	**NY Islanders**	**NHL**	**24**	**7**	**14**	**1**	**1292**	**70**	**1**	**3.25**	....	....	....	....	....	....	....
	Lowell	AHL	26	10	12	4	1517	74	1	2.93	6	3	3	359	18	0	3.01
2000-01	**Florida**	**NHL**	**47**	**12**	**24**	**7**	**2628**	**107**	**5**	**2.44**	....	....	....	....	....	....	....
	Louisville Panthers	AHL	3	1	2	0	178	10	0	3.38	....	....	....	....	....	....	....
2001-02	**Florida**	**NHL**	**58**	**16**	**33**	**4**	**3030**	**140**	**4**	**2.77**	....	....	....	....	....	....	....
2002-03	**Florida**	**NHL**	**65**	**20**	**34**	**7**	**3627**	**164**	**6**	**2.71**	....	....	....	....	....	....	....
2003-04	**Florida**	**NHL**	**72**	**25**	**33**	**14**	**4252**	**172**	**7**	**2.43**	....	....	....	....	....	....	....
2004-05			DID NOT PLAY														
2005-06	**Florida**	**NHL**	***75**	**35**	**30**	**9**	**4305**	**213**	**4**	**2.97**	....	....	....	....	....	....	....
	Canada	Olympics	2	1	1	0	119	3	0	1.51	....	....	....	....	....	....	....
	NHL Totals		**341**	**115**	**168**	**42**	**19134**	**866**	**27**	**2.72**	....	....	....	....	....	....	....

NHL Second All-Star Team (2004)

Played in NHL All-Star Game (2004)

Traded to **Florida** by **NY Islanders** with Olli Jokinen for Mark Parrish and Oleg Kvasha, June 24, 2000. Traded to **Vancouver** by **Florida** with Lukas Krajicek and Florida's 6th round choice (Sergei Shirokov) in 2006 Entry Draft for Todd Bertuzzi, Bryan Allen and Alex Auld, June 23, 2006.

MacDONALD, Joey (mihk-DAWN-uhld, JOH-ee) DET.

Goaltender. Catches left. 6', 200 lbs. Born, Pictou, N.S., February 7, 1980.

			Regular Season								Playoffs						
Season	**Club**	**League**	**GP**	**W**	**L**	**O/T**	**Mins**	**GA**	**SO**	**Avg**	**GP**	**W**	**L**	**Mins**	**GA**	**SO**	**Avg**
1997-98	Halifax	QMJHL	17	3	12	0	815	54	0	3.97	3	1	2	140	15	0	6.43
1998-99	Peterborough	OHL	47	22	15	2	2483	123	3	2.97	3	0	2	145	13	0	5.38
99-2000	Peterborough	OHL	48	20	15	6	2641	125	2	2.84	5	1	4	280	16	1	3.43
2000-01	Peterborough	OHL	57	25	21	7	3284	161	1	2.94	7	3	4	425	18	0	2.54
2001-02	Toledo Storm	ECHL	38	12	15	7	2084	100	1	2.88	....	....	....	....	....	....	....
2002-03	Grand Rapids	AHL	25	14	6	0	1337	49	3	2.20	1	0	0	8	1	0	7.95
2003-04	Grand Rapids	AHL	39	22	12	3	2249	74	6	1.97	1	0	1	40	4	0	6.04
2004-05	Grand Rapids	AHL	*66	34	29	2	*3755	143	5	2.29	....	....	....	....	....	....	....
2005-06	Grand Rapids	AHL	32	17	9	2	1745	91	2	3.13	....	....	....	....	....	....	....
	Toledo Storm	ECHL	1	1	0	0	60	1	0	1.00	....	....	....	....	....	....	....

Harry "Hap" Holmes Memorial Award (fewest goals against – AHL) (2003) (shared with Marc Lamothe)

Signed as a free agent by **Detroit**, December 21, 2001.

MACHESNEY, Daren (muh-KEHS-nee, DAIR-ehn) WSH.

Goaltender. Catches left. 6', 163 lbs. Born, Hamilton, Ont., December 13, 1986.
(Washington's 5th choice, 143rd overall, in 2005 Entry Draft).

			Regular Season								Playoffs						
Season	**Club**	**League**	**GP**	**W**	**L**	**O/T**	**Mins**	**GA**	**SO**	**Avg**	**GP**	**W**	**L**	**Mins**	**GA**	**SO**	**Avg**
2003-04	Newmarket	OPJHL	32	....	....	....	1868	82	1	2.63	....	....	....	....	....	....	....
	Brampton Battalion	OHL	5	3	2	0	300	15	0	3.00	....	....	....	....	....	....	....
2004-05	Brampton Battalion	OHL	38	16	13	6	2166	99	1	2.74	5	2	3	331	15	0	2.72
2005-06	Brampton Battalion	OHL	49	28	17	0	2830	143	3	3.03	11	5	5	633	32	0	3.03

OHL All-Rookie Team (2005)

MacINTYRE, Derek (MAK-ihn-tighr, DAIR-ihk) S.J.

Goaltender. Catches left. 6'2", 185 lbs. Born, Elgin, IL, November 1, 1985.
(San Jose's 8th choice, 234th overall, in 2004 Entry Draft).

			Regular Season								Playoffs						
Season	**Club**	**League**	**GP**	**W**	**L**	**O/T**	**Mins**	**GA**	**SO**	**Avg**	**GP**	**W**	**L**	**Mins**	**GA**	**SO**	**Avg**
2003-04	Soo Indians	NAHL	39	31	3	2	2200	65	4	*1.77	4	1	1	153	10	0	3.92
2004-05	Ferris State	CCHA	17	5	8	1	883	47	0	3.19	....	....	....	....	....	....	....
2005-06	Ferris State	CCHA	9	3	3	1	464	25	0	3.23	....	....	....	....	....	....	....

MacINTYRE, Drew (MAK-ihn-tighr, DROO) DET.

Goaltender. Catches left. 6', 173 lbs. Born, Charlottetown, P.E.I., June 24, 1983.
(Detroit's 2nd choice, 121st overall, in 2001 Entry Draft).

			Regular Season								Playoffs						
Season	**Club**	**League**	**GP**	**W**	**L**	**O/T**	**Mins**	**GA**	**SO**	**Avg**	**GP**	**W**	**L**	**Mins**	**GA**	**SO**	**Avg**
1998-99	Trenton Sting	OPJHL	20	....	....	....	1173	71	2	3.63	....	....	....	....	....	....	....
99-2000	Sherbrooke	QMJHL	24	10	7	2	1253	67	0	3.21	....	....	....	....	....	....	....
2000-01	Sherbrooke	QMJHL	48	17	22	3	2552	139	4	3.27	4	0	4	238	19	0	4.78
2001-02	Sherbrooke	QMJHL	55	15	34	3	3028	201	1	3.98	....	....	....	....	....	....	....
2002-03	Sherbrooke	QMJHL	*61	31	24	5	*3515	161	2	2.75	12	5	7	767	52	0	4.07
2003-04	Toledo Storm	ECHL	11	6	4	0	574	25	0	2.61	....	....	....	....	....	....	....
2004-05	Grand Rapids	AHL	24	7	8	0	1049	47	1	2.69	....	....	....	....	....	....	....
	Toledo Storm	ECHL	2	0	1	0	87	6	0	4.12	....	....	....	....	....	....	....
2005-06	Grand Rapids	AHL	13	8	4	0	681	33	0	2.91	5	3	1	260	7	0	1.62
	Toledo Storm	ECHL	33	24	7	2	1981	68	2	*2.06	6	5	1	360	12	0	2.00

• Missed majority of 2003-04 season recovering from thigh injury suffered in practice, December 27, 2003.

MALEK, Roman (MAHL-ehk, ROH-muhn)

Goaltender. Catches left. 5'11", 161 lbs. Born, Prague, Czech., September 25, 1977.
(Philadelphia's 5th choice, 158th overall, in 2001 Entry Draft).

			Regular Season								Playoffs						
Season	**Club**	**League**	**GP**	**W**	**L**	**O/T**	**Mins**	**GA**	**SO**	**Avg**	**GP**	**W**	**L**	**Mins**	**GA**	**SO**	**Avg**
1996-97	HC Slavia Praha Jr.	CzRep-Jr.	31	....	....	....	1820	55	....	1.81	....	....	....	....	....	....	....
	H+S Beroun	CzRep-2	9	....	....	....	469	28	....	3.50	....	....	....	....	....	....	....
1997-98	H+S Beroun	CzRep-2	36	....	....	....	2150	98	....	2.73	....	....	....	....	....	....	....
1998-99	HC Slavia Praha	CzRep	18	....	....	....	830	51	....	3.69	....	....	....	....	....	....	....
99-2000	HC Slavia Praha	CzRep	25	....	....	....	1342	59	....	2.64	....	....	....	....	....	....	....
	Beroun	CzRep-2	3	....	....	....	150	7	0	2.80	....	....	....	....	....	....	....
2000-01	HC Slavia Praha	CzRep	46	....	....	....	2550	100	....	2.35	11	....	....	665	28	....	2.53
2001-02	HC Slavia Praha	CzRep	33	....	....	....	1967	80	....	2.44	9	....	....	485	22	....	2.72
2002-03	HC Slavia Praha	CzRep	50	....	....	....	2844	77	*11	*1.62	17	....	....	1064	28	*5	1.58
2003-04	HC Slavia Praha	CzRep	23	....	....	....	1273	49	2	2.31	....	....	....	....	....	....	....
	Plzen	CzRep	17	....	....	....	1033	37	3	2.15	12	....	....	715	40	0	3.36

2004-05	Magnitogorsk	Russia	16	....	....	....	903	31	3	2.06	....	....	....	....	....	....	....
	Karlovy Vary	CzRep	23	....	....	....	1371	45	4	1.97	....	....	....	....	....	....	....
2005-06	Plzen	CzRep	44	....	....	....	2542	104	2	2.45	....	....	....	....	....	....	....
	Usti n. L.	CzRep-2	8	....	....	....	366	10	1	1.64	17	....	....	929	23	3	1.48

MANZATO, Daniel (man-ZA-toh, DAN-yehl) CAR.

Goaltender. Catches left. 6', 178 lbs. Born, Fribourg, Switz., January 17, 1984.
(Carolina's 3rd choice, 160th overall, in 2002 Entry Draft).

						Regular Season							Playoffs				
Season	Club	League	GP	W	L	O/T	Mins	GA	SO	Avg	GP	W	L	Mins	GA	SO	Avg
2000-01	Fribourg Jr.	Swiss-Jr.	36	....	....	....	2160	32	6	0.91	....	....	....	....	....	....	....
2001-02	Victoriaville Tigres	QMJHL	36	20	8	2	1894	102	0	3.23	6	3	0	249	17	0	4.09
2002-03	Victoriaville Tigres	QMJHL	48	23	18	5	2756	155	3	3.37	3	0	3	125	11	0	5.27
2003-04	Victoriaville Tigres	QMJHL	23	7	13	0	1170	78	0	4.00	....	....	....	....	....	....	....
	Kloten Flyers	Swiss	15	....	....	....	912	39	1	2.57	....	....	....	....	....	....	....
2004-05	HC Ambri-Piotta	Swiss	25	....	....	....	1446	65	1	2.70	....	....	....	....	....	....	....
2005-06	EHC Basel	Swiss	41	18	14	9	2449	107	*5	2.62	5	1	4	280	22	0	4.71

Signed as a free agent by **Kloten** (Swiss), January 5, 2004, following release by **Victoriaville** (QMJHL), January 4, 2004. Signed as a free agent by **Ambri-Piotta** (Swiss), August 5, 2004.

MARKKANEN, Jussi (MAHR-kah-nehn, YOO-see) EDM.

Goaltender. Catches left. 6', 182 lbs. Born, Imatra, Finland, May 8, 1975.
(Edmonton's 5th choice, 133rd overall, in 2001 Entry Draft).

						Regular Season							Playoffs				
Season	Club	League	GP	W	L	O/T	Mins	GA	SO	Avg	GP	W	L	Mins	GA	SO	Avg
1991-92	SaiPa Jr.	Fin-Jr.	6	3	3	0	360	25	0	4.16	....	....	....	....	....	....	....
1992-93	SaiPa Jr.	Fin-Jr.	7	....	....	....	367	28	0	4.58	....	....	....	....	....	....	....
	SaiPa	Finland-2	16	6	6	2	798	60	0	4.51	....	....	....	....	....	....	....
1993-94	SaiPa Jr.	Fin-Jr.	4	....	....	....	....	....	....	2.26	....	....	....	....	....	....	....
	SaiPa	Finland-2	30	....	....	....	1726	97	....	3.37	....	....	....	....	....	....	....
1994-95	SaiPa	Finland-2	36	....	....	....	2067	95	....	2.76	10	6	4	621	33	0	3.19
1995-96	Tappara Jr.	Fin-Jr.	5	....	....	....	298	21	....	4.23	....	....	....	....	....	....	....
	Tappara Tampere	Finland	23	11	8	2	1239	59	1	2.86	....	....	....	....	....	....	....
1996-97	SaiPa	Finland	41	9	24	7	2340	132	0	3.38	....	....	....	....	....	....	....
1997-98	SaiPa	Finland	48	21	20	5	2870	138	4	2.88	3	0	3	164	11	0	4.02
1998-99	SaiPa	Finland	45	21	19	4	2633	105	4	2.39	7	3	3	366	21	0	3.44
99-2000	SaiPa	Finland	48	14	23	9	2794	150	2	3.24	....	....	....	....	....	....	....
2000-01	Tappara Tampere	Finland	52	30	17	4	3076	107	9	2.09	10	7	3	608	18	1	1.78
2001-02	**Edmonton**	**NHL**	**14**	**6**	**4**	**2**	**784**	**24**	**2**	**1.84**	....	....	....	....	....	....	....
	Hamilton Bulldogs	AHL	4	2	2	0	239	9	0	2.26	....	....	....	....	....	....	....
	Finland	Olympics					DID NOT PLAY										
2002-03	**Edmonton**	**NHL**	**22**	**7**	**8**	**3**	**1180**	**51**	**3**	**2.59**	**1**	**0**	**0**	**14**	**1**	**0**	**4.29**
2003-04	**NY Rangers**	**NHL**	**26**	**8**	**12**	**1**	**1244**	**53**	**2**	**2.56**	....	....	....	....	....	....	....
	Edmonton	**NHL**	**7**	**2**	**2**	**2**	**394**	**12**	**0**	**1.83**	....	....	....	....	....	....	....
2004-05	Lada Togliatti	Russia	54	....	....	....	3157	63	11	1.20	10	....	....	627	15	1	1.44
2005-06	**Edmonton**	**NHL**	**37**	**15**	**12**	**6**	**2016**	**105**	**0**	**3.13**	**6**	**3**	**3**	**360**	**13**	**1**	**2.17**
	NHL Totals		**106**	**38**	**38**	**14**	**5618**	**245**	**7**	**2.62**	**7**	**3**	**3**	**374**	**14**	**1**	**2.25**

Traded to **NY Rangers** by **Edmonton** with Edmonton's 4th round choice (later traded to Toronto – Toronto selected Roman Kukumberg) for Brian Leetch, June 30, 2003. Traded to **Edmonton** by **NY Rangers** with Petr Nedved for Stephen Valiquette, Dwight Helminen, Edmonton's 2nd round compensatory choice (Dane Byers) in 2004 Entry Draft and future consideratons, March 3, 2004. Signed as a free agent by **Togliatti** (Russia), September 25, 2004.

MARSTERS, Nathan (MAHR-stuhrs, NAY-thuhn) ANA.

Goaltender. Catches left. 6'4", 190 lbs. Born, Burlington, Ont., January 28, 1980.
(Los Angeles' 5th choice, 165th overall, in 2000 Entry Draft).

						Regular Season							Playoffs				
Season	Club	League	GP	W	L	O/T	Mins	GA	SO	Avg	GP	W	L	Mins	GA	SO	Avg
1997-98	Bramalea Blues	OPJHL	12	....	....	....	539	25	2	2.78	....	....	....	....	....	....	....
1998-99	Bramalea Blues	OPJHL	29	....	....	....	1711	91	3	3.19	....	....	....	....	....	....	....
99-2000	Bramalea Blues	OPJHL	28	....	....	....	1668	98	2	3.53	....	....	....	....	....	....	....
	Chilliwack Chiefs	BCHL	15	9	6	0	825	63	0	4.58	20	15	5	1187	62	0	3.13
2000-01	RPI Engineers	ECAC	28	14	13	1	1631	64	*4	2.35	....	....	....	....	....	....	....
2001-02	RPI Engineers	ECAC	28	15	9	3	1627	70	1	2.58	....	....	....	....	....	....	....
2002-03	RPI Engineers	ECAC	24	7	15	1	1286	73	0	3.41	....	....	....	....	....	....	....
2003-04	RPI Engineers	ECAC	35	*21	13	1	2094	75	*5	2.15	....	....	....	....	....	....	....
2004-05	Louisiana	ECHL	*54	18	30	4	*3108	182	1	3.51	....	....	....	....	....	....	....
2005-06	Portland Pirates	AHL	37	23	9	2	2050	106	0	3.10	4	1	2	195	9	0	2.77
	Augusta Lynx	ECHL	4	1	1	2	219	14	0	3.83	....	....	....	....	....	....	....

ECAC Second All-Star Team (2004)

Signed as a free agent by **Anaheim**. November 28, 2005.

MASON, Chris (MAY-sohn, KRIHS) NSH.

Goaltender. Catches left. 6', 195 lbs. Born, Red Deer, Alta., April 20, 1976.
(New Jersey's 7th choice, 122nd overall, in 1995 Entry Draft).

						Regular Season							Playoffs				
Season	Club	League	GP	W	L	O/T	Mins	GA	SO	Avg	GP	W	L	Mins	GA	SO	Avg
1992-93	Red Deer	AMHL	20	....	....	....	1280	76	0	3.35	....	....	....	....	....	....	....
1993-94	Victoria Cougars	WHL	5	1	4	0	237	27	0	6.84	....	....	....	....	....	....	....
1994-95	Prince George	WHL	44	8	30	1	2288	192	1	5.03	....	....	....	....	....	....	....
1995-96	Prince George	WHL	59	16	37	1	3289	236	1	4.31	....	....	....	....	....	....	....
1996-97	Prince George	WHL	50	19	24	4	2851	172	2	3.62	15	9	6	938	44	*1	2.81
1997-98	Cincinnati	AHL	47	13	19	7	2368	136	0	3.45	....	....	....	....	....	....	....
1998-99	**Nashville**	**NHL**	**3**	**0**	**0**	**0**	**69**	**6**	**0**	**5.22**	....	....	....	....	....	....	....
	Milwaukee	IHL	34	15	12	6	1901	92	1	2.90	....	....	....	....	....	....	....
99-2000	Milwaukee	IHL	53	20	21	8	2952	137	2	2.78	3	1	2	252	11	0	2.62
2000-01	**Nashville**	**NHL**	**1**	**0**	**1**	**0**	**59**	**2**	**0**	**2.03**	....	....	....	....	....	....	....
	Milwaukee	IHL	37	17	14	5	2226	87	5	2.35	4	1	3	239	12	0	3.02
2001-02	Milwaukee	AHL	48	17	21	7	2755	116	2	2.53	....	....	....	....	....	....	....
2002-03	San Antonio	AHL	50	25	18	6	2914	122	1	2.51	3	0	3	195	9	0	2.77
2003-04	**Nashville**	**NHL**	**17**	**4**	**4**	**1**	**744**	**27**	**1**	**2.18**	....	....	....	....	....	....	....
	Milwaukee	AHL	1	1	0	0	60	2	0	2.00	....	....	....	....	....	....	....
2004-05	Valerengen IF Oslo	Norway	20	....	....	....	1204	36	1	1.79	11	....	....	657	22	1	2.01
2005-06	**Nashville**	**NHL**	**23**	**12**	**5**	**1**	**1227**	**52**	**2**	**2.54**	**5**	**1**	**4**	**296**	**17**	**0**	**3.45**
	NHL Totals		**44**	**16**	**10**	**2**	**2099**	**87**	**3**	**2.49**	**5**	**1**	**4**	**296**	**17**	**0**	**3.45**

Signed as a free agent by **Anaheim**, June 27, 1997. Traded to **Nashville** by **Anaheim** with Marc Moro for Dominic Roussel, October 5, 1998. Signed as a free agent by **Florida**, August 20, 2002. Claimed by **Nashville** from **Florida** in Waiver Draft, October 3, 2003. Signed as a free agent by **Oslo** (Norway), November 30, 2004.

MASON, Steve (MAY-sohn, STEEV) CBJ

Goaltender. Catches right. 6'3", 186 lbs. Born, Oakville, Ont., May 29, 1988.
(Columbus' 2nd choice, 69th overall, in 2006 Entry Draft).

						Regular Season							Playoffs				
Season	Club	League	GP	W	L	O/T	Mins	GA	SO	Avg	GP	W	L	Mins	GA	SO	Avg
2004-05	Grimsby	OJHL-C	19	....	....	....	....	....	4	1.82	....	....	....	....	....	....	....
2005-06	Petrolia Jets	OJHL-B	9	6	3	0	521	....	1	2.53	....	....	....	....	....	....	....
	London Knights	OHL	12	5	3	0	497	22	0	2.66	4	0	0	150	7	0	2.80

McELHINNEY, Curtis (MAK-IHL-ehn-ee, KUHR-this) CGY.

Goaltender. Catches left. 6'3", 207 lbs. Born, London, Ont., May 23, 1983.
(Calgary's 9th choice, 176th overall, in 2002 Entry Draft).

						Regular Season							Playoffs				
Season	Club	League	GP	W	L	O/T	Mins	GA	SO	Avg	GP	W	L	Mins	GA	SO	Avg
2000-01	Notre Dame	SJHL					STATISTICS NOT AVAILABLE										
2001-02	Colorado College	WCHA	9	6	0	1	441	15	1	2.04	....	....	....	....	....	....	....
2002-03	Colorado College	WCHA	*37	*25	6	5	*2147	85	*4	2.37	....	....	....	....	....	....	....
2003-04	Colorado College	WCHA	19	10	6	1	1015	41	2	2.42	....	....	....	....	....	....	....
2004-05	Colorado College	WCHA	26	*21	4	1	1550	58	2	2.24	....	....	....	....	....	....	....
2005-06	Omaha	AHL	33	9	14	2	1621	68	3	2.52	....	....	....	....	....	....	....

WCHA First All-Star Team (2003, 2005) • NCAA West Second All-American Team (2003) • NCAA West First All-American Team (2005)

McGANN, Pat (mih-GAN, PAT) DAL.

Goaltender. Catches right. 5'11", 160 lbs. Born, Evergreen Park, IL, January 27, 1987.
(Dallas' 7th choice, 223rd overall, in 2005 Entry Draft).

						Regular Season							Playoffs				
Season	Club	League	GP	W	L	O/T	Mins	GA	SO	Avg	GP	W	L	Mins	GA	SO	Avg
2003-04	Chicago Chill	MAHL	31	14	16	1	....	....	....	3.40	....	....	....	....	....	....	....
2004-05	Team Illinois	MWEHL	50	31	18	1	....	91	5	2.21	....	....	....	....	....	....	....
2005-06	Cedar Rapids	USHL	17	5	8	3	998	49	1	2.95	....	....	....	....	....	....	....

MCKEE, David (mih-KEE, DAY-vihd) ANA.

Goaltender. Catches left. 6'1", 180 lbs. Born, Irving, TX, December 5, 1983.

						Regular Season							Playoffs				
Season	Club	League	GP	W	L	O/T	Mins	GA	SO	Avg	GP	W	L	Mins	GA	SO	Avg
2003-04	Cornell Big Red	ECAC	32	16	10	6	1929	59	*5	1.84	....	....	....	....	....	....	....
2004-05	Cornell Big Red	ECACHL	35	*27	5	3	2125	44	*10	*1.24	....	....	....	....	....	....	....
2005-06	Cornell Big Red	ECACHL	35	*22	9	4	2139	74	3	*2.08	....	....	....	....	....	....	....

ECACHL First All-Star Team (2005) • ECACHL Player of the Year (2005) • NCAA East First All-American Team (2005)

Signed as a free agent by **Anaheim**, April 1, 2006.

McLENNAN, Jamie (muh-KLEH-nuhn, JAY-mee) CGY.

Goaltender. Catches left. 6', 190 lbs. Born, Edmonton, Alta., June 30, 1971.
(NY Islanders' 3rd choice, 48th overall, in 1991 Entry Draft).

						Regular Season							Playoffs				
Season	Club	League	GP	W	L	O/T	Mins	GA	SO	Avg	GP	W	L	Mins	GA	SO	Avg
1987-88	St. Albert Royals	AMHL	21	....	....	....	1224	80	0	3.92	....	....	....	....	....	....	....
1988-89	Spokane Chiefs	WHL	11	....	....	....	578	63	0	6.54	....	....	....	....	....	....	....
	Lethbridge	WHL	7	....	....	....	368	22	0	3.59	....	....	....	....	....	....	....
1989-90	Lethbridge	WHL	34	20	4	2	1690	110	1	3.91	13	6	5	677	44	0	3.90
1990-91	Lethbridge	WHL	56	32	18	4	3230	205	0	3.81	*16	8	8	*970	56	0	3.46
1991-92	Capital District	AHL	18	4	10	2	952	60	1	3.78	....	....	....	....	....	....	....
	Richmond	ECHL	32	16	12	2	1837	114	0	3.72	....	....	....	....	....	....	....
1992-93	Capital District	AHL	38	17	14	6	2171	117	1	3.23	1	0	1	20	5	0	15.00
1993-94	**NY Islanders**	**NHL**	**22**	**8**	**7**	**6**	**1287**	**61**	**0**	**2.84**	**2**	**0**	**1**	**82**	**6**	**0**	**4.39**
	Salt Lake	IHL	24	8	12	2	1320	80	0	3.64	....	....	....	....	....	....	....
1994-95	**NY Islanders**	**NHL**	**21**	**6**	**11**	**2**	**1185**	**67**	**0**	**3.39**	....	....	....	....	....	....	....
	Denver Grizzlies	IHL	4	3	0	1	239	12	0	3.00	11	8	2	640	23	1	*2.15
1995-96	**NY Islanders**	**NHL**	**13**	**3**	**9**	**1**	**636**	**39**	**0**	**3.68**	....	....	....	....	....	....	....
	Utah Grizzlies	IHL	14	9	2	2	728	29	0	2.39	....	....	....	....	....	....	....
	Worcester IceCats	AHL	22	14	7	1	1216	57	0	2.81	2	0	2	119	8	0	4.04
1996-97	Worcester IceCats	AHL	39	18	13	4	2152	100	2	2.79	4	2	2	262	16	0	3.67
1997-98	**St. Louis**	**NHL**	**30**	**16**	**8**	**2**	**1658**	**60**	**2**	**2.17**	**1**	**0**	**0**	**14**	**1**	**0**	**4.29**
1998-99	**St. Louis**	**NHL**	**33**	**13**	**14**	**4**	**1763**	**70**	**3**	**2.38**	**1**	**0**	**1**	**37**	**0**	**0**	**0.00**
99-2000	**St. Louis**	**NHL**	**19**	**9**	**5**	**2**	**1009**	**33**	**2**	**1.96**	....	....	....	....	....	....	....
2000-01	**Minnesota**	**NHL**	**38**	**5**	**23**	**9**	**2230**	**98**	**2**	**2.64**	....	....	....	....	....	....	....
2001-02	Houston Aeros	AHL	51	25	18	4	2852	130	3	2.74	14	8	6	880	31	2	2.11
2002-03	**Calgary**	**NHL**	**22**	**2**	**11**	**4**	**1165**	**58**	**0**	**2.99**	....	....	....	....	....	....	....
2003-04	**Calgary**	**NHL**	**26**	**12**	**9**	**3**	**1446**	**53**	**4**	**2.20**	....	....	....	....	....	....	....
	NY Rangers	**NHL**	**4**	**1**	**3**	**0**	**244**	**12**	**0**	**2.95**	....	....	....	....	....	....	....
2004-05	Guildford Flames	Britain-2	3	2	1	0	185	8	0	2.59	7	4	3	385	13	0	2.02
2005-06	**Florida**	**NHL**	**17**	**2**	**4**	**2**	**678**	**34**	**0**	**3.01**	....	....	....	....	....	....	....
	NHL Totals		**245**	**77**	**104**	**35**	**13301**	**585**	**13**	**2.64**	**4**	**0**	**2**	**133**	**7**	**0**	**3.16**

WHL East First All-Star Team (1991) • WHL Goaltender of the Year (1991) • Bill Masterton Memorial Trophy (1998)

Signed as a free agent by **St. Louis**, July 15, 1996. Claimed by **Minnesota** from **St. Louis** in Expansion Draft, June 23, 2000. Traded to **Calgary** by **Minnesota** for Calgary's 9th round choice (Mika Hannula) in 2002 Entry Draft, June 22, 2002. Traded to **NY Rangers** by **Calgary** with Blair Betts and Greg Moore for Chris Simon and NY Rangers' 7th round choice (Matt Schneider) in 2004 Entry Draft, March 6, 2004. Signed as a free agent by **Florida**, July 2, 2004. Signed as a free agent by **Guildford** (Britain-2), February 17, 2005. Signed as a free agent by **Calgary**, July 6, 2006.

McVICAR, Rob (mihk-VIH-kuhr, RAWB)

Goaltender. Catches left. 6'4", 201 lbs. Born, Hay River, N.W.T., January 15, 1982.
(Vancouver's 6th choice, 151st overall, in 2002 Entry Draft).

						Regular Season							Playoffs				
Season	Club	League	GP	W	L	O/T	Mins	GA	SO	Avg	GP	W	L	Mins	GA	SO	Avg
1998-99	Brandon Kings	MMMHL	21	....	....	....	1217	69	0	3.40	....	....	....	....	....	....	....
99-2000	Brandon	WHL	14	5	6	0	687	43	0	3.76	....	....	....	....	....	....	....
2000-01	Brandon	WHL	27	12	10	2	1537	76	0	2.97	5	2	3	324	13	1	2.41
2001-02	Brandon	WHL	55	*33	18	2	3276	151	1	2.77	19	11	8	1255	44	1	2.10
2002-03	Brandon	WHL	51	31	14	5	3027	136	2	2.70	13	6	7	737	32	0	2.61
2003-04	Manitoba Moose	AHL	10	4	3	2	514	25	0	2.92	....	....	....	....	....	....	....
	Columbia Inferno	ECHL	19	11	5	2	1088	47	0	2.59	....	....	....	....	....	....	....
2004-05	Manitoba Moose	AHL	1	0	1	0	62	3	0	2.92	....	....	....	....	....	....	....
	Columbia Inferno	ECHL	34	14	14	5	2004	79	3	2.37	....	....	....	....	....	....	....
2005-06	**Vancouver**	**NHL**	**1**	**0**	**0**	**0**	**3**	**0**	**0**	**0.00**	....	....	....	....	....	....	....
	Manitoba Moose	AHL	6	3	3	0	337	17	0	3.03	....	....	....	....	....	....	....
	Victoria	ECHL	33	13	14	2	1741	95	1	3.27	....	....	....	....	....	....	....
	NHL Totals		**1**	**0**	**0**	**0**	**3**	**0**	**0**	**0.00**	....	....	....	....	....	....	....

MENSATOR, Lukas (MEHN-suh-tohr, loo-KAHSH) VAN.

Goaltender. Catches left. 5'8", 167 lbs. Born, Sokolov, Czech., August 18, 1984.
(Vancouver's 4th choice, 83rd overall, in 2002 Entry Draft).

						Regular Season							Playoffs				
Season	Club	League	GP	W	L	O/T	Mins	GA	SO	Avg	GP	W	L	Mins	GA	SO	Avg
99-2000	Karlovy Vary U17	CzR-U17	42	....	....	....	2406	160	0	3.99	....	....	....	....	....	....	....
	Karlovy Vary Jr.	CzRep-Jr.	1	1	0	0	60	3	0	3.00	....	....	....	....	....	....	....
2000-01	Karlovy Vary U17	CzR-U17	6	....	....	....	360	15	0	2.50	....	....	....	....	....	....	....
	Karlovy Vary Jr.	CzRep-Jr.	19	....	....	....	1085	60	0	3.32	....	....	....	....	....	....	....
2001-02	Karlovy Vary Jr.	CzRep-Jr.	31	....	....	....	1809	93	0	3.08	9	....	....	459	17	0	2.22
	Banik CHZ Sokolov	CzRep-3	3	....	....	....	180	12	0	4.00	....	....	....	....	....	....	....
2002-03	Ottawa 67's	OHL	42	26	8	5	2395	122	0	3.06	*23	13	8	*1381	63	*2	2.74
2003-04	Ottawa 67's	OHL	50	18	22	7	2924	162	0	3.32	7	3	4	447	23	0	3.09
2004-05	Karlovy Vary	CzRep	13	....	....	....	686	34	1	2.97	....	....	....	....	....	....	....
	IHC Pisek	CzRep-2	14	....	....	....	808	41	1	3.04	....	....	....	....	....	....	....
	BK Mlada Boleslav	CzRep-2	17	....	....	....	991	34	4	2.06	7	....	....	393	17	1	2.60

2005-06	Karlovy Vary	CzRep	36	....	....	....	1981	69	5	2.09	....	....	....	....	....	....	....
	SK Kadan	CzRep-2	1	....	....	....	49	5	0	6.12	....	....	....	....	....	....	....

Signed as a free agent by **Karlovy Vary** (CzRep), May 17, 2004.

MICHAUD, Olivier (MEE-shoh, OH-lihv-ee-ay)

Goaltender. Catches left. 5'11", 179 lbs. Born, Beloeil, Que., September 14, 1983.

			Regular Season								Playoffs						
Season	**Club**	**League**	**GP**	**W**	**L**	**O/T**	**Mins**	**GA**	**SO**	**Avg**	**GP**	**W**	**L**	**Mins**	**GA**	**SO**	**Avg**
1998-99	Eclaireur Bantams	QAHA	23	14	4	5	1380	58	....	2.50	....	....	....	....	....	....	....
99-2000	Antoine-Girouard	QAAA	7	6	1	0	420	15	1	2.14	....	....	....	....	....	....	....
	Charles-Lemoyne	QAAA	16	8	4	2	886	57	0	3.86	16	8	8	1015	29	2	1.71
	Shawinigan	QMJHL	1	0	1	0	49	2	0	2.44	....	....	....	....	....	....	....
2000-01	Shawinigan	QMJHL	21	12	4	4	1096	54	1	2.96	3	1	2	150	6	0	2.41
2001-02	**Montreal**	**NHL**	**1**	**0**	**0**	**0**	**18**	**0**	**0**	**0.00**	....	....	....	....	....	....	....
	Shawinigan	QMJHL	46	29	11	3	2650	108	3	*2.45	12	7	5	744	36	0	2.91
2002-03	Shawinigan	QMJHL	27	8	13	3	1497	82	1	3.29	....	....	....	....	....	....	....
	Baie-Comeau	QMJHL	31	23	5	2	1775	90	3	3.04	12	7	5	748	38	0	3.05
2003-04	Columbus	ECHL	22	8	10	2	1234	62	1	3.01	....	....	....	....	....	....	....
	Hamilton Bulldogs	AHL	16	4	7	3	900	38	2	2.53	....	....	....	....	....	....	....
2004-05	Long Beach	ECHL	41	18	14	6	2315	98	1	2.54	1	0	1	59	4	0	4.10
2005-06	Long Beach	ECHL	16	6	7	1	811	46	0	3.40	2	1	1	84	9	0	6.39
	Hamilton Bulldogs	AHL	14	6	5	1	748	41	0	3.29	....	....	....	....	....	....	....
	NHL Totals		**1**	**0**	**0**	**0**	**18**	**0**	**0**	**0.00**	....	....	....	....	....	....	....

Signed as a free agent by **Montreal**, September 18, 2001. • Promoted to **Montreal** from **Shawinigan** (QMJHL) and replaced injured Jose Theodore, October 26, 2001. • Returned to **Shawinigan** (QMJHL) by **Montreal**, November 5, 2001.

MILLER, Ryan (MIHL-luhr, RIGH-uhn) BUF.

Goaltender. Catches left. 6'2", 170 lbs. Born, East Lansing, MI, July 17, 1980.
(Buffalo's 7th choice, 138th overall, in 1999 Entry Draft).

			Regular Season								Playoffs						
Season	**Club**	**League**	**GP**	**W**	**L**	**O/T**	**Mins**	**GA**	**SO**	**Avg**	**GP**	**W**	**L**	**Mins**	**GA**	**SO**	**Avg**
1997-98	Soo Indians	NAHL	37	21	14	0	2113	82	3	2.33	2	0	2	158	7	0	2.66
1998-99	Soo Indians	NAHL	47	31	14	1	2711	104	8	2.30	4	2	2	218	10	1	2.76
99-2000	Michigan State	CCHA	26	16	5	3	1525	39	*8	*1.53	....	....	....	....	....	....	....
2000-01	Michigan State	CCHA	40	*31	5	4	2447	54	*10	*1.32	....	....	....	....	....	....	....
2001-02	Michigan State	CCHA	40	26	9	5	2411	71	*8	*1.77	....	....	....	....	....	....	....
2002-03	**Buffalo**	**NHL**	**15**	**6**	**8**	**1**	**912**	**40**	**1**	**2.63**	....	....	....	....	....	....	....
	Rochester	AHL	47	23	18	5	2817	110	2	2.34	3	1	2	190	13	0	4.11
2003-04	**Buffalo**	**NHL**	**3**	**0**	**3**	**0**	**178**	**15**	**0**	**5.06**	....	....	....	....	....	....	....
	Rochester	AHL	60	27	25	7	3579	132	5	2.21	14	7	7	857	26	2	1.82
2004-05	Rochester	AHL	63	*41	17	4	3741	153	8	2.45	9	5	4	547	24	0	2.63
2005-06	**Buffalo**	**NHL**	**48**	**30**	**14**	**3**	**2862**	**124**	**1**	**2.60**	**18**	**11**	**7**	**1123**	**48**	**1**	**2.56**
	Rochester	AHL	2	1	1	0	120	5	0	2.50	....	....	....	....	....	....	....
	United States	Olympics					DID NOT PLAY										
	NHL Totals		**66**	**36**	**25**	**4**	**3952**	**179**	**2**	**2.72**	**18**	**11**	**7**	**1123**	**48**	**1**	**2.56**

CCHA Second All-Star Team (2000) • CCHA First All-Star Team (2001, 2002) • NCAA West First All-American Team (2001, 2002) • CCHA Player of the Year (2001, 2002) • Hobey Baker Memorial Award (Top U.S. Collegiate Player) (2001) • AHL First All-Star Team (2005) • Aldege "Baz" Bastien Memorial Trophy (Top Goaltender - AHL) (2005)

MOIR, Kyle (MOI-uhr, KIGHL)

Goaltender. Catches left. 6'3", 193 lbs. Born, Calgary, Alta., May 25, 1986.
(Nashville's 4th choice, 139th overall, in 2004 Entry Draft).

			Regular Season								Playoffs						
Season	**Club**	**League**	**GP**	**W**	**L**	**O/T**	**Mins**	**GA**	**SO**	**Avg**	**GP**	**W**	**L**	**Mins**	**GA**	**SO**	**Avg**
2002-03	Cgy. AAA Flames	AMHL	15	8	2	4	922	44	0	2.86	....	....	....	....	....	....	....
	Swift Current	WHL	7	4	1	0	283	14	1	2.97	1	0	1	60	7	0	7.00
2003-04	Swift Current	WHL	46	22	15	4	2460	119	3	2.90	1	0	0	20	2	0	6.00
2004-05	Swift Current	WHL	60	20	33	4	3339	152	3	2.73	....	....	....	....	....	....	....
2005-06	Swift Current	WHL	65	23	28	12	3759	178	4	2.84	4	0	3	228	18	0	4.74

MONTOYA, Al (mawn-TOI-uh, AL) NYR

Goaltender. Catches left. 6'1", 194 lbs. Born, Chicago, IL, February 13, 1985.
(NY Rangers' 1st choice, 6th overall, in 2004 Entry Draft).

			Regular Season								Playoffs						
Season	**Club**	**League**	**GP**	**W**	**L**	**O/T**	**Mins**	**GA**	**SO**	**Avg**	**GP**	**W**	**L**	**Mins**	**GA**	**SO**	**Avg**
99-2000	Loyola Academy	High-MN	28	12	13	3	1685	56	1	2.01	....	....	....	....	....	....	....
2000-01	Texas Tornado	NAHL	15	10	3	0	780	38	0	2.92	1	1	0	60	2	0	2.00
	United States	Nat-Tm	2	2	0	0	120	4	0	2.00	....	....	....	....	....	....	....
2001-02	USNTDP	U-17	10	5	5	0	570	24	0	2.53	....	....	....	....	....	....	....
	USNTDP	NAHL	24	6	11	4	1344	79	0	3.53	....	....	....	....	....	....	....
2002-03	U. of Michigan	CCHA	*43	*30	10	3	*2547	99	4	2.33	....	....	....	....	....	....	....
2003-04	U. of Michigan	CCHA	*40	*26	12	2	*2340	87	6	2.23	....	....	....	....	....	....	....
2004-05	U. of Michigan	CCHA	*40	*30	7	3	*2359	99	3	2.52	....	....	....	....	....	....	....
2005-06	Hartford Wolf Pack	AHL	40	23	9	1	2094	91	2	2.61	5	2	1	257	8	1	1.87
	Charlotte Checkers	ECHL	2	1	1	0	123	8	0	3.92	....	....	....	....	....	....	....

CCHA All-Rookie Team (2003) • NCAA West Second All-American Team (2004)

MORRISON, Mike (MOHR-ih-suhn, MIGHK) PHX.

Goaltender. Catches right. 6'3", 194 lbs. Born, Medford, MA, July 11, 1979.
(Edmonton's 8th choice, 186th overall, in 1998 Entry Draft).

			Regular Season								Playoffs						
Season	**Club**	**League**	**GP**	**W**	**L**	**O/T**	**Mins**	**GA**	**SO**	**Avg**	**GP**	**W**	**L**	**Mins**	**GA**	**SO**	**Avg**
1997-98	Exeter	High-NH	27	15	11	2	1632	64	1	2.35	....	....	....	....	....	....	....
1998-99	University of Maine	H-East	11	3	0	1	347	10	1	1.73	....	....	....	....	....	....	....
99-2000	University of Maine	H-East	12	7	2	1	608	27	1	2.67	....	....	....	....	....	....	....
2000-01	University of Maine	H-East	10	2	3	3	490	16	1	1.96	....	....	....	....	....	....	....
2001-02	University of Maine	H-East	30	20	3	4	1645	60	2	2.19	....	....	....	....	....	....	....
2002-03	Columbus	ECHL	38	9	18	6	1948	113	1	3.48	....	....	....	....	....	....	....
2003-04	Toronto	AHL	27	12	8	2	1309	55	3	2.52	....	....	....	....	....	....	....
2004-05	Edmonton	AHL	14	2	5	5	728	21	2	1.73	....	....	....	....	....	....	....
	Greenville Grrrowl	ECHL	26	13	10	2	1576	72	1	2.74	3	1	1	150	9	0	3.61
2005-06	**Edmonton**	**NHL**	**21**	**10**	**4**	**2**	**892**	**42**	**0**	**2.83**	....	....	....	....	....	....	....
	Greenville Grrrowl	ECHL	9	7	2	0	548	20	0	2.19	....	....	....	....	....	....	....
	Ottawa	**NHL**	**4**	**1**	**0**	**1**	**207**	**12**	**0**	**3.48**	....	....	....	....	....	....	....
	NHL Totals		**25**	**11**	**4**	**3**	**1099**	**54**	**0**	**2.95**	....	....	....	....	....	....	....

Hockey East First All-Star Team (2002)

Claimed on waivers by **Ottawa** from **Edmonton**, March 9, 2006. Signed as a free agent by **Phoenix**, July 2, 2006.

MRAZEK, Justin (muh-RA-zehk, JUHS-tihn) WSH.

Goaltender. Catches left. 6'3", 185 lbs. Born, Regina, Sask., July 21, 1985.
(Washington's 12th choice, 230th overall, in 2004 Entry Draft).

			Regular Season								Playoffs						
Season	**Club**	**League**	**GP**	**W**	**L**	**O/T**	**Mins**	**GA**	**SO**	**Avg**	**GP**	**W**	**L**	**Mins**	**GA**	**SO**	**Avg**
2003-04	Estevan Bruins	SJHL	38	14	16	5	2142	112	0	3.14	....	....	....	....	....	....	....
2004-05	Union College	ECACHL	19	5	12	1	1080	39	1	2.17	....	....	....	....	....	....	....
2005-06	Union College	ECACHL	5	0	1	1	127	12	0	5.69	....	....	....	....	....	....	....

MUNCE, Ryan (MUNTS, RIGH-uhn) L.A.

Goaltender. Catches left. 6'2", 180 lbs. Born, Mississauga, Ont., April 16, 1985.
(Los Angeles' 5th choice, 82nd overall, in 2003 Entry Draft).

			Regular Season								Playoffs						
Season	**Club**	**League**	**GP**	**W**	**L**	**O/T**	**Mins**	**GA**	**SO**	**Avg**	**GP**	**W**	**L**	**Mins**	**GA**	**SO**	**Avg**
2002-03	Sarnia Sting	OHL	27	15	7	0	1410	62	3	2.64	4	1	1	149	8	1	3.22
2003-04	Sarnia Sting	OHL	54	28	21	4	3160	158	2	3.00	5	1	4	298	17	0	3.42
2004-05	Sarnia Sting	OHL	55	12	32	6	3090	163	0	3.17	....	....	....	....	....	....	....
2005-06	Bakersfield	ECHL	55	30	18	5	*3234	150	2	2.78	11	5	5	642	36	0	3.36

MUNRO, Adam (MUHN-roh, A-duhm) CHI.

Goaltender. Catches left. 6'2", 219 lbs. Born, St. George, Ont., November 12, 1982.
(Chicago's 1st choice, 29th overall, in 2001 Entry Draft).

			Regular Season								Playoffs						
Season	**Club**	**League**	**GP**	**W**	**L**	**O/T**	**Mins**	**GA**	**SO**	**Avg**	**GP**	**W**	**L**	**Mins**	**GA**	**SO**	**Avg**
1997-98	Brantford Classics	OMHA	15	13	2	0	660	20	*4	*1.36	....	....	....	....	....	....	....
1998-99	Brant County	OJHL-B	10	....	....	....	348	30	0	5.17	....	....	....	....	....	....	....
	Bowmanville	OPJHL	14	....	....	....	816	50	0	3.68	....	....	....	....	....	....	....
	Erie Otters	OHL	1	0	0	0	1	0	0	0.00	....	....	....	....	....	....	....
99-2000	Bowmanville	OPJHL	2	2	0	0	125	5	0	2.40	....	....	....	....	....	....	....
	Erie Otters	OHL	22	8	7	1	948	48	1	3.04	1	0	0	5	1	0	12.00
2000-01	Erie Otters	OHL	41	26	6	6	2283	88	*4	2.31	10	6	2	509	27	1	3.18
2001-02	Erie Otters	OHL	43	24	13	1	2277	128	3	3.37	6	4	2	361	17	0	2.83
2002-03	Erie Otters	OHL	8	2	6	0	426	24	1	3.38	....	....	....	....	....	....	....
	Sault Ste. Marie	OHL	42	20	20	2	2494	160	1	3.85	4	0	4	240	12	0	3.00
2003-04	**Chicago**	**NHL**	**7**	**1**	**5**	**1**	**426**	**26**	**0**	**3.66**	....	....	....	....	....	....	....
	Norfolk Admirals	AHL	12	5	4	1	695	26	0	2.24	....	....	....	....	....	....	....
	Gwinnett	ECHL	6	4	1	1	370	17	0	2.76	1	0	1	60	2	0	2.01
2004-05	Norfolk Admirals	AHL	30	14	10	2	1595	66	4	2.48	....	....	....	....	....	....	....
	Atlantic City	ECHL	5	2	2	1	272	9	0	1.99	....	....	....	....	....	....	....
2005-06	**Chicago**	**NHL**	**10**	**3**	**5**	**2**	**501**	**25**	**1**	**2.99**	....	....	....	....	....	....	....
	Norfolk Admirals	AHL	28	17	8	1	1612	73	1	2.72	4	0	4	239	15	0	3.77
	NHL Totals		**17**	**4**	**10**	**3**	**927**	**51**	**1**	**3.30**	....	....	....	....	....	....	....

Signed as a free agent by **Fribourg** (Swiss), July 7, 2006.

MUNROE, Scott (MUHN-roh, SKAWT) PHI.

Goaltender. Catches left. 6'2", 195 lbs. Born, Moose Jaw, Sask., January 20, 1982.

			Regular Season								Playoffs						
Season	**Club**	**League**	**GP**	**W**	**L**	**O/T**	**Mins**	**GA**	**SO**	**Avg**	**GP**	**W**	**L**	**Mins**	**GA**	**SO**	**Avg**
2002-03	AL-Huntsville	CHA	20	11	6	1	1049	49	1	2.80	....	....	....	....	....	....	....
2003-04	AL-Huntsville	CHA	17	5	9	1	891	47	0	3.16	....	....	....	....	....	....	....
2004-05	AL-Huntsville	CHA	31	16	10	4	1805	69	3	2.29	....	....	....	....	....	....	....
2005-06	AL-Huntsville	CHA	31	17	11	2	1813	91	0	3.01	....	....	....	....	....	....	....
	Philadelphia	AHL	2	0	2	0	119	7	0	3.54	....	....	....	....	....	....	....

Signed as a free agent by **Philadelphia** (AHL), March 18, 2006.

NABOKOV, Evgeni (na-BAW-kahv, ehv-GEH-nee) S.J.

Goaltender. Catches left. 6', 200 lbs. Born, Ust-Kamenogorsk, USSR, July 25, 1975.
(San Jose's 9th choice, 219th overall, in 1994 Entry Draft).

			Regular Season								Playoffs						
Season	**Club**	**League**	**GP**	**W**	**L**	**O/T**	**Mins**	**GA**	**SO**	**Avg**	**GP**	**W**	**L**	**Mins**	**GA**	**SO**	**Avg**
1992-93	Ust-Kamenogorsk	CIS	4	1	0	0	109	5	0	2.75	....	....	....	....	....	....	....
1993-94	Ust-Kamenogorsk	CIS	11	....	....	....	539	29	0	3.23	....	....	....	....	....	....	....
1994-95	Dynamo Moscow	CIS	24	....	....	....	1265	40	....	1.90	13	....	....	810	30	....	2.22
1995-96	Dynamo Moscow	CIS	39	....	....	....	2008	67	5	2.00	6	....	....	298	7	....	1.41
1996-97	Dynamo Moscow	Russia	27	....	....	....	1588	56	2	2.12	4	....	....	255	12	0	2.82
1997-98	Kentucky	AHL	33	10	21	2	1866	122	0	3.92	1	0	0	23	1	0	2.59
1998-99	Kentucky	AHL	43	26	14	1	2429	106	5	2.62	11	6	5	599	30	*2	3.00
99-2000	**San Jose**	**NHL**	**11**	**2**	**2**	**1**	**414**	**15**	**1**	**2.17**	**1**	**0**	**0**	**20**	**0**	**0**	**0.00**
	Cleveland	IHL	20	12	4	3	1164	52	0	2.68	....	....	....	....	....	....	....
	Kentucky	AHL	2	1	1	0	120	3	1	1.50	....	....	....	....	....	....	....
2000-01	**San Jose**	**NHL**	**66**	**32**	**21**	**7**	**3700**	**135**	**6**	**2.19**	**4**	**1**	**3**	**218**	**10**	**1**	**2.75**
2001-02	**San Jose**	**NHL**	**67**	**37**	**24**	**5**	**3901**	**149**	**7**	**2.29**	**12**	**7**	**5**	**712**	**31**	**0**	**2.61**
2002-03	**San Jose**	**NHL**	**55**	**19**	**28**	**8**	**3227**	**146**	**3**	**2.71**	....	....	....	....	....	....	....
2003-04	**San Jose**	**NHL**	**59**	**31**	**19**	**8**	**3456**	**127**	**9**	**2.20**	**17**	**10**	**7**	**1052**	**30**	**3**	**1.71**
2004-05	Magnitogorsk	Russia	14	....	....	....	808	27	3	2.00	5	....	....	307	13	0	2.53
2005-06	**San Jose**	**NHL**	**45**	**16**	**19**	**7**	**2575**	**133**	**1**	**3.10**	**1**	**0**	**0**	**12**	**1**	**0**	**5.00**
	Russia	Olympics	7	....	....	....	359	8	3	1.34	....	....	....	....	....	....	....
	NHL Totals		**303**	**137**	**113**	**36**	**17273**	**705**	**27**	**2.45**	**35**	**18**	**15**	**2014**	**72**	**4**	**2.14**

NHL All-Rookie Team (2001) • Calder Memorial Trophy (2001)

Played in NHL All-Star Game (2001)

• Scored a goal vs. Vancouver, March 10, 2002. Signed as a free agent by **Magnitogorsk** (Russia), December 2, 2004.

NASTIUK, Kevin (NAZ-tee-uhk, KEH-vihn) CAR.

Goaltender. Catches left. 6'2", 176 lbs. Born, Edmonton, Alta., July 20, 1985.
(Carolina's 4th choice, 126th overall, in 2003 Entry Draft).

			Regular Season								Playoffs						
Season	**Club**	**League**	**GP**	**W**	**L**	**O/T**	**Mins**	**GA**	**SO**	**Avg**	**GP**	**W**	**L**	**Mins**	**GA**	**SO**	**Avg**
99-2000	Inland Real Estate	EMHA	20	9	6	5	998	59	0	3.25	....	....	....	....	....	....	....
	CAC Cement	AMBHL	1	0	1	0	50	8	0	9.60	....	....	....	....	....	....	....
2000-01	CAC Cement	AMBHL	20	12	7	1	1233	64	0	3.11	1	1	0	60	2	0	2.00
2001-02	Medicine Hat	WHL	19	4	10	0	877	66	0	4.52	....	....	....	....	....	....	....
2002-03	Medicine Hat	WHL	42	15	20	2	2344	172	0	4.40	11	7	4	693	33	0	2.86
2003-04	Medicine Hat	WHL	*68	40	19	8	*4056	187	4	2.77	*20	*16	4	*1182	38	*4	1.93
2004-05	Medicine Hat	WHL	42	23	18	1	2426	88	7	2.18	12	5	7	715	27	0	2.27
2005-06	Florida Everblades	ECHL	20	13	4	2	1190	50	1	2.52	3	1	1	106	7	0	3.96
	Lowell	AHL	11	1	7	3	643	37	0	3.45	....	....	....	....	....	....	....

WHL Playoff MVP (2004) • WHL East Second All-Star Team (2005)

NEUVIRTH, Michal (NOI-vihrt, MEE-khahl) WSH.

Goaltender. Catches left. 6', 174 lbs. Born, Usti Labem, Czech., March 23, 1988.
(Washington's 3rd choice, 34th overall, in 2006 Entry Draft).

			Regular Season								Playoffs						
Season	**Club**	**League**	**GP**	**W**	**L**	**O/T**	**Mins**	**GA**	**SO**	**Avg**	**GP**	**W**	**L**	**Mins**	**GA**	**SO**	**Avg**
2003-04	Sparta U17	CzR-U17	55	....	....	....	3137	96	5	1.84	3	....	....	180	13	0	4.33
2004-05	Sparta U17	CzR-U17	20	....	....	....	1178	49	3	2.50	8	....	....	482	17	0	2.12
	Sparta Jr.	CzRep-Jr.	10	....	....	....	501	20	1	2.40	....	....	....	....	....	....	....
2005-06	Sparta Jr.	CzRep-Jr.	42	....	....	....	2516	82	5	1.96	3	....	....	179	9	0	3.02

NIITTYMAKI, Antero (NEE-too-mah-kee, AN-tehr-oh) PHI.

Goaltender. Catches left. 6', 195 lbs. Born, Turku, Finland, June 18, 1980.
(Philadelphia's 7th choice, 168th overall, in 1998 Entry Draft).

			Regular Season								Playoffs						
Season	Club	League	GP	W	L	O/T	Mins	GA	SO	Avg	GP	W	L	Mins	GA	SO	Avg
1997-98	TPS Turku U18	Fin-U18	12	....	....	....	....	....	....	....	1	1	0	60	1	0	1.00
	TPS Turku Jr.	Fin-Jr.	19	10	8	1	1131	34	....	1.80	4	3	1	220	7	0	1.91
1998-99	TPS Turku Jr.	Fin-Jr.	35	27	8	0	2095	60	3	1.72	6	3	3	362	14	0	2.32
99-2000	TPS Turku Jr.	Fin-Jr.	1	1	0	0	60	1	0	1.00	1	0	1	60	5	0	5.00
	TPS Turku	Finland	32	23	6	3	1899	68	3	2.15	8	6	2	453	13	0	1.72
2000-01	TPS Turku Jr.	Fin-Jr.	....	....	....	....	....	....	....	....	2	1	1	120	4	1	2.00
	TPS Turku	Finland	21	10	5	1	1112	46	2	2.48	....	....	....	....	....	....	....
2001-02	TPS Turku	Finland	27	16	8	1	1498	46	3	1.84	4	2	2	295	11	0	2.23
2002-03	Philadelphia	AHL	40	14	21	2	2283	98	0	2.58	....	....	....	....	....	....	....
2003-04	**Philadelphia**	**NHL**	**3**	**3**	**0**	**0**	**180**	**3**	**0**	**1.00**	....	....	....	....	....	....	....
	Philadelphia	AHL	49	24	13	6	2728	92	7	2.02	12	6	6	796	24	0	1.81
2004-05	Philadelphia	AHL	58	33	21	4	3453	119	6	2.07	*21	*15	5	*1269	37	*3	1.75
2005-06	**Philadelphia**	**NHL**	**46**	**23**	**15**	**6**	**2690**	**133**	**2**	**2.97**	**2**	**0**	**0**	**73**	**5**	**0**	**4.11**
	Finland	Olympics	6	5	1	0	359	8	3	1.34	....	....	....	....	....	....	....
	NHL Totals		**49**	**26**	**15**	**6**	**2870**	**136**	**2**	**2.84**	**2**	**0**	**0**	**73**	**5**	**0**	**4.11**

Jack A. Butterfield Trophy (Playoff MVP – AHL) (2005) • Olympic Tournament All-Star Team (2006) • Olympic Tournament Best Goaltender (2006) • Olympic Tournament MVP (2006)

NORONEN, Mika (NOH-rah-nehn, MEE-kah) VAN.

Goaltender. Catches left. 6'2", 200 lbs. Born, Tampere, Finland, June 17, 1979.
(Buffalo's 1st choice, 21st overall, in 1997 Entry Draft).

			Regular Season								Playoffs						
Season	Club	League	GP	W	L	O/T	Mins	GA	SO	Avg	GP	W	L	Mins	GA	SO	Avg
1995-96	Tappara U18	Fin-U18	5	....	....	....	299	13	....	2.61	5	....	....	300	8	....	1.60
	Tappara Jr.	Fin-Jr.	16	....	....	....	962	37	2	2.31	....	....	....	....	....	....	....
1996-97	Tappara Jr.	Fin-Jr.	17	....	....	....	....	....	....	....	....	....	....	....	....	....	....
	Hermes Kokkola	Finland-2	2	....	....	....	91	11	0	7.25	....	....	....	....	....	....	....
	Tappara Tampere	Finland	5	1	3	0	215	17	0	4.73	....	....	....	....	....	....	....
1997-98	Tappara Jr.	Fin-Jr.	6	4	1	1	365	13	....	2.14	4	2	2	262	11	0	2.52
	Tappara Tampere	Finland	31	14	12	3	1703	83	1	2.92	4	1	2	196	12	0	3.67
1998-99	Tappara Tampere	Finland	43	18	20	5	2494	135	2	3.25	....	....	....	....	....	....	....
99-2000	Rochester	AHL	54	*33	13	4	3089	112	*6	2.18	21	13	8	1235	37	*6	*1.80
2000-01	**Buffalo**	**NHL**	**2**	**2**	**0**	**0**	**108**	**5**	**0**	**2.78**	....	....	....	....	....	....	....
	Rochester	AHL	47	26	15	5	2753	100	4	2.18	4	1	3	250	11	0	2.64
2001-02	**Buffalo**	**NHL**	**10**	**4**	**3**	**1**	**518**	**23**	**0**	**2.66**	....	....	....	....	....	....	....
	Rochester	AHL	45	16	17	12	2764	115	3	2.50	1	0	1	59	3	0	3.06
2002-03	**Buffalo**	**NHL**	**16**	**4**	**9**	**3**	**891**	**36**	**1**	**2.42**	....	....	....	....	....	....	....
	Rochester	AHL	19	5	9	5	1169	55	2	2.82	....	....	....	....	....	....	....
2003-04	**Buffalo**	**NHL**	**35**	**11**	**17**	**2**	**1796**	**77**	**2**	**2.57**	....	....	....	....	....	....	....
2004-05	HPK Hameenlinna	Finland	27	14	8	4	1614	54	1	2.01	9	4	4	482	21	1	2.61
2005-06	**Buffalo**	**NHL**	**4**	**1**	**2**	**0**	**169**	**12**	**0**	**4.26**	....	....	....	....	....	....	....
	Rochester	AHL	2	0	2	0	121	6	0	2.99	....	....	....	....	....	....	....
	Vancouver	**NHL**	**4**	**1**	**1**	**0**	**170**	**10**	**0**	**3.53**	....	....	....	....	....	....	....
	NHL Totals		**71**	**23**	**32**	**6**	**3652**	**163**	**3**	**2.68**	....	....	....	....	....	....	....

AHL All-Rookie Team (2000) • AHL Second All-Star Team (2000, 2001) • Dudley "Red" Garrett Memorial Award (Rookie of the Year – AHL) (2000) • Harry "Hap" Holmes Memorial Award (fewest goals against – AHL) (2001) (shared with Tom Askey)

Signed as a free agent by **Hameenlinna** (Finland), November 2, 2004. Traded to **Vancouver** by **Buffalo** for Vancouver's 2nd round choice (Jhonas Enroth) in 2006 Entry Draft, March 9, 2006.

NORRENA, Fredrik (noh-REH-nah, FREHD-rihk) CBJ

Goaltender. Catches left. 6', 189 lbs. Born, Pietarsaari, Finland, November 29, 1973.
(Tampa Bay's 8th choice, 213th overall, in 2002 Entry Draft).

			Regular Season								Playoffs						
Season	Club	League	GP	W	L	O/T	Mins	GA	SO	Avg	GP	W	L	Mins	GA	SO	Avg
1989-90	LIFK Leppalahti	Finland-3	36	....	....	....	....	....	....	....	....	....	....	....	....	....	....
1990-91	LIFK Leppalahti	Finland-3	36	....	....	....	....	....	....	....	....	....	....	....	....	....	....
1991-92	LIFK Leppalahti	Finland-3	35	....	....	....	....	....	....	....	....	....	....	....	....	....	....
1992-93	TPS Turku Jr.	Fin-Jr.	25	15	9	1	1449	74	1	3.06	5	....	....	307	11	1	2.14
	TPS Turku	Finland	2	0	1	0	30	1	0	2.00	....	....	....	....	....	....	....
1993-94	TPS Turku Jr.	Fin-Jr.	2	0	1	0	80	5	0	3.75	1	0	1	58	4	0	4.10
	TPS Turku	Finland	10	3	3	0	387	19	0	2.94	....	....	....	....	....	....	....
	Kiekko-67 Turku	Finland-2	15	7	7	1	884	43	2	2.92	....	....	....	....	....	....	....
1994-95	TPS Turku	Finland	22	14	6	2	1328	60	1	2.71	11	7	4	666	27	1	2.43
	Kiekko-67 Turku	Finland-2	15	....	....	....	828	34	0	2.46	....	....	....	....	....	....	....
1995-96	TPS Turku	Finland	26	14	8	3	1539	68	0	2.65	....	....	....	....	....	....	....
1996-97	Kiekko-67 Turku	Finland-2	12	....	....	....	725	36	0	2.98	....	....	....	....	....	....	....
	AIK Solna	Sweden	5	....	....	....	274	21	1	4.60	....	....	....	....	....	....	....
1997-98	Lukko Rauma	Finland	37	12	19	4	2174	105	0	2.90	....	....	....	....	....	....	....
1998-99	TPS Turku	Finland	20	11	4	1	1010	35	2	2.08	1	0	0	20	2	0	6.00
99-2000	TPS Turku	Finland	21	15	4	0	1175	35	2	1.79	4	3	0	234	10	0	2.56
	TuTo Turku	Finland-2	2	1	1	0	118	7	0	3.54	....	....	....	....	....	....	....
2000-01	TPS Turku	Finland	39	26	10	3	2266	66	6	1.75	10	9	1	603	13	2	1.29
2001-02	TPS Turku	Finland	32	14	11	5	1878	62	2	1.98	4	1	3	256	7	1	1.64
2002-03	V.Frolunda	Sweden	23	....	....	....	1386	56	1	2.42	4	....	....	288	6	1	1.25
2003-04	Linkopings HC	Sweden	40	....	....	....	2414	68	9	1.69	3	....	....	176	6	0	2.05
2004-05	Linkopings HC	Sweden	43	....	....	....	2522	78	5	1.86	6	....	....	383	13	0	2.03
2005-06	Linkopings HC	Sweden	36	....	....	....	2170	78	4	2.16	11	....	....	693	22	2	*1.90
	Finland	Olympics	2	2	0	0	120	0	2	0.00	....	....	....	....	....	....	....

Traded to **Columbus** by **Tampa Bay** with Fredrik Modin for Marc Denis, June 30, 2006.

OSGOOD, Chris (AWS-gud, KRIHS) DET.

Goaltender. Catches left. 5'10", 175 lbs. Born, Peace River, Alta., November 26, 1972.
(Detroit's 3rd choice, 54th overall, in 1991 Entry Draft).

			Regular Season								Playoffs						
Season	Club	League	GP	W	L	O/T	Mins	GA	SO	Avg	GP	W	L	Mins	GA	SO	Avg
1988-89	Medicine Hat	AMHL	26	....	....	....	1441	88	0	3.66	....	....	....	....	....	....	....
1989-90	Medicine Hat	WHL	57	24	28	2	3094	228	0	4.42	3	0	3	173	17	0	5.91
1990-91	Medicine Hat	WHL	46	23	18	3	2630	173	2	3.95	12	7	5	712	42	0	3.54
1991-92	Medicine Hat	WHL	15	10	3	0	819	44	0	3.22	....	....	....	....	....	....	....
	Brandon	WHL	16	3	10	1	890	60	1	4.04	....	....	....	....	....	....	....
	Seattle	WHL	21	12	7	1	1217	65	1	3.20	15	9	6	904	51	0	3.38
1992-93	Adirondack	AHL	45	19	19	4	2438	159	0	3.91	1	0	1	59	2	0	2.03
1993-94	**Detroit**	**NHL**	**41**	**23**	**8**	**5**	**2206**	**105**	**2**	**2.86**	**6**	**3**	**2**	**307**	**12**	**1**	**2.35**
	Adirondack	AHL	4	3	1	0	239	13	0	3.26	....	....	....	....	....	....	....
1994-95	**Detroit**	**NHL**	**19**	**14**	**5**	**0**	**1087**	**41**	**1**	**2.26**	**2**	**0**	**0**	**68**	**2**	**0**	**1.76**
	Adirondack	AHL	2	1	1	0	120	6	0	3.00	....	....	....	....	....	....	....
1995-96	**Detroit**	**NHL**	**50**	***39**	**6**	**5**	**2933**	**106**	**5**	**2.17**	**15**	**8**	**7**	**936**	**33**	**2**	**2.12**
1996-97 ♦	**Detroit**	**NHL**	**47**	**23**	**13**	**9**	**2769**	**106**	**6**	**2.30**	**2**	**0**	**0**	**47**	**2**	**0**	**2.55**
1997-98 ♦	**Detroit**	**NHL**	**64**	**33**	**20**	**11**	**3807**	**140**	**6**	**2.21**	***22**	***16**	**6**	***1361**	**48**	**2**	**2.12**
1998-99	**Detroit**	**NHL**	**63**	**34**	**25**	**4**	**3691**	**149**	**3**	**2.42**	**6**	**4**	**2**	**358**	**14**	**1**	**2.35**
99-2000	**Detroit**	**NHL**	**53**	**30**	**14**	**8**	**3148**	**126**	**6**	**2.40**	**9**	**5**	**4**	**547**	**18**	**2**	**1.97**
2000-01	**Detroit**	**NHL**	**52**	**25**	**19**	**4**	**2834**	**127**	**1**	**2.69**	**6**	**2**	**4**	**365**	**15**	**1**	**2.47**
2001-02	**NY Islanders**	**NHL**	**66**	**32**	**25**	**6**	**3743**	**156**	**4**	**2.50**	**7**	**3**	**4**	**392**	**17**	**0**	**2.60**
2002-03	**NY Islanders**	**NHL**	**37**	**17**	**14**	**4**	**1993**	**97**	**2**	**2.92**	....	....	....	....	....	....	....
	St. Louis	**NHL**	**9**	**4**	**3**	**2**	**532**	**27**	**2**	**3.05**	**7**	**3**	**4**	**417**	**17**	**1**	**2.45**
2003-04	**St. Louis**	**NHL**	**67**	**31**	**25**	**8**	**3861**	**144**	**3**	**2.24**	**5**	**1**	**4**	**287**	**12**	**0**	**2.51**
2004-05							DID NOT PLAY										
2005-06	**Detroit**	**NHL**	**32**	**20**	**6**	**5**	**1846**	**85**	**2**	**2.76**	....	....	....	....	....	....	....
	Grand Rapids	AHL	3	2	1	0	180	10	0	3.34	....	....	....	....	....	....	....
	NHL Totals		**600**	**325**	**183**	**71**	**34450**	**1409**	**43**	**2.45**	**87**	**45**	**37**	**5085**	**190**	**10**	**2.24**

WHL East Second All-Star Team (1991) • NHL Second All-Star Team (1996) • William M. Jennings Trophy (1996) (shared with Mike Vernon)

Played in NHL All-Star Game (1996, 1997, 1998)

• Scored a goal while with Medicine Hat (WHL), January 3, 1991. • Scored a goal vs. Hartford, March 6, 1996. Claimed by **NY Islanders** from **Detroit** in Waiver Draft, September 28, 2001. Traded to **St. Louis** by **NY Islanders** with NY Islanders' 3rd round choice (Konstantin Barulin) in 2003 Entry Draft for Justin Papineau and St. Louis' 2nd round choice (Jeremy Colliton) in 2003 Entry Draft, March 11, 2003. Signed as a free agent by **Detroit**, August 8, 2005.

OUELLET, Maxime (OO-leht, MAX-eem)

Goaltender. Catches left. 6'2", 195 lbs. Born, Beauport, Que., June 17, 1981.
(Philadelphia's 1st choice, 22nd overall, in 1999 Entry Draft).

			Regular Season								Playoffs						
Season	Club	League	GP	W	L	O/T	Mins	GA	SO	Avg	GP	W	L	Mins	GA	SO	Avg
1996-97	Ste-Foy	QAAA	29	16	8	0	1470	81	0	2.75	9	4	5	555	31	0	3.37
1997-98	Quebec Remparts	QMJHL	24	12	7	1	1188	66	0	3.33	7	3	1	305	16	0	3.15
1998-99	Quebec Remparts	QMJHL	*59	*40	12	6	*3447	155	3	*2.70	13	6	7	803	41	*1	3.06
99-2000	Quebec Remparts	QMJHL	53	31	16	4	2984	133	2	2.67	11	7	4	638	28	*2	*2.63
2000-01	**Philadelphia**	**NHL**	**2**	**0**	**1**	**0**	**76**	**3**	**0**	**2.37**	....	....	....	....	....	....	....
	Rouyn-Noranda	QMJHL	25	18	6	1	1471	65	3	2.65	8	4	4	490	25	0	3.06
	Philadelphia	AHL	2	1	0	0	86	4	0	2.78	....	....	....	....	....	....	....
2001-02	Philadelphia	AHL	41	16	13	8	2294	104	1	2.72	....	....	....	....	....	....	....
	Portland Pirates	AHL	6	3	3	0	358	17	0	2.85	....	....	....	....	....	....	....
2002-03	Portland Pirates	AHL	48	22	16	7	2773	111	*7	2.40	2	1	1	120	8	0	4.00
2003-04	**Washington**	**NHL**	**6**	**2**	**3**	**1**	**365**	**19**	**1**	**3.12**	....	....	....	....	....	....	....
	Portland Pirates	AHL	52	15	29	8	3050	101	10	1.99	5	2	2	303	8	0	1.59
2004-05	Portland Pirates	AHL	40	15	20	3	2305	111	0	2.89	....	....	....	....	....	....	....
2005-06	Hershey Bears	AHL	1	0	0	0	41	5	0	7.37	....	....	....	....	....	....	....
	Vancouver	**NHL**	**4**	**0**	**2**	**1**	**222**	**12**	**0**	**3.24**	....	....	....	....	....	....	....
	Manitoba Moose	AHL	16	9	7	0	946	46	0	2.92	3	0	1	127	6	0	2.85
	NHL Totals		**12**	**2**	**6**	**2**	**663**	**34**	**1**	**3.08**	....	....	....	....	....	....	....

QMJHL Second All-Star Team (1999, 2000, 2001) • Jacques Plante Trophy (fewest goals against – QMJHL) (1999) • AHL Second All-Star Team (2003)

• Returned to **Rouyn-Noranda** (QMJHL) by **Philadelphia**, October 27, 2000. Traded to **Washington** by **Philadelphia** with Philadelphia's 1st (later traded to Dallas – Dallas selected Martin Vagner), 2nd (Maxime Daigneault) and 3rd (Derek Krestanovich) round choices in 2002 Entry Draft for Adam Oates, March 19, 2002. Traded to **Vancouver** by **Washington** for Vancouver's 5th round choice (later traded to NY Rangers - NY Rangers selected Tomas Zaborsky) in 2006 Entry Draft, December 2, 2005.

PALMER, Joe (PAHL-muhr, JOH) CHI.

Goaltender. Catches left. 6'1", 205 lbs. Born, Utica, NY, February 19, 1988.
(Chicago's 6th choice, 96th overall, in 2006 Entry Draft).

			Regular Season								Playoffs						
Season	Club	League	GP	W	L	O/T	Mins	GA	SO	Avg	GP	W	L	Mins	GA	SO	Avg
2003-04	Syracuse Jr. Stars	EmJHL	31	....	....	....	1147	69	1	3.61	6	....	....	368	19	0	3.10
	USNTDP	U-17	1	0	0	0	11	2	0	10.91	....	....	....	....	....	....	....
2004-05	USNTDP	U-17	8	6	1	1	495	22	0	2.67	....	....	....	....	....	....	....
	USNTDP	NAHL	19	10	8	1	1020	56	0	3.29	....	....	....	....	....	....	....
2005-06	USNTDP	U-18	33	16	14	3	1900	99	0	3.13	....	....	....	....	....	....	....
	USNTDP	NAHL	14	13	1	0	776	22	1	1.70	....	....	....	....	....	....	....

Signed Letter of Intent to attend **Ohio State** (CCHA) in fall of 2006.

PARISE, Jordan (pah-REE-say, JOHR-dan) N.J.

Goaltender. Catches left. 5'11", 190 lbs. Born, Faribault, MN, September 19, 1982.

			Regular Season								Playoffs						
Season	Club	League	GP	W	L	O/T	Mins	GA	SO	Avg	GP	W	L	Mins	GA	SO	Avg
2002-03	Waterloo	USHL					STATISTICS NOT AVAILABLE										
2003-04	North Dakota	WCHA	22	14	4	3	1230	42	2	*2.05	....	....	....	....	....	....	....
2004-05	North Dakota	WCHA	27	17	7	3	1575	56	2	*2.13	....	....	....	....	....	....	....
2005-06	North Dakota	WCHA	34	24	9	1	2017	74	6	2.20	....	....	....	....	....	....	....

Signed as a free agent by **New Jersey**, July 6, 2006.

PATZOLD, Dimitri (PATZ-ohld, dih-MEE-tree) S.J.

Goaltender. Catches left. 6', 200 lbs. Born, Ust-Kamenogorsk, USSR, February 3, 1983.
(San Jose's 3rd choice, 107th overall, in 2001 Entry Draft).

			Regular Season								Playoffs						
Season	Club	League	GP	W	L	O/T	Mins	GA	SO	Avg	GP	W	L	Mins	GA	SO	Avg
99-2000	Kolner EC Jr.	Ger-Jr.	38	....	....	....	2131	73	0	2.06	....	....	....	....	....	....	....
	Kolner Haie 2	German-5	16	....	....	....	896	58	0	3.88	....	....	....	....	....	....	....
2000-01	EV Duisburg	German-3	6	....	....	....	360	17	0	2.83	....	....	....	....	....	....	....
	Erding Jets	German-2	24	....	....	....	1378	89	0	3.88	....	....	....	....	....	....	....
2001-02	Kolner Haie	Germany	7	....	....	....	260	16	0	3.69	....	....	....	....	....	....	....
	EV Duisburg	German-2	6	....	....	....	360	17	0	2.83	....	....	....	....	....	....	....
2002-03	Adler Mannheim	Germany	15	....	....	....	817	35	0	2.57	2	....	....	34	2	0	3.53
2003-04	Johnstown Chiefs	ECHL	8	7	0	0	443	20	0	2.71	1	0	1	59	2	0	2.02
	Cleveland Barons	AHL	27	10	15	0	1457	70	3	2.88	....	....	....	....	....	....	....
2004-05	Cleveland Barons	AHL	41	18	16	5	2418	104	1	2.58	....	....	....	....	....	....	....
2005-06	Cleveland Barons	AHL	33	10	21	0	1876	124	0	3.97	....	....	....	....	....	....	....

PAVELEC, Ondrej (pah-vah-LEK, AWN-dray) ATL.

Goaltender. Catches left. 6'2", 210 lbs. Born, Kladno, Czechoslovakia, August 31, 1987.
(Atlanta's 2nd choice, 41st overall, in 2005 Entry Draft).

			Regular Season								Playoffs						
Season	Club	League	GP	W	L	O/T	Mins	GA	SO	Avg	GP	W	L	Mins	GA	SO	Avg
2003-04	HC Kladno U17	CzR-U17	38	....	....	....	2079	77	3	2.22	2	....	....	67	7	0	6.27
2004-05	HC Kladno Jr.	CzRep-Jr.	39	....	....	....	2218	85	7	2.30	10	....	....	587	24	1	2.45
	HK LEV Slany	CzRep-3	1	....	....	....	60	4	0	4.00	....	....	....	....	....	....	....
2005-06	Cape Breton	QMJHL	47	27	18	0	2578	108	3	2.51	9	4	5	507	19	0	*2.25

QMJHL All-Rookie Team (2006) • QMJHL First All-Star Team (2006) • QMJHL Defensive Rookie of the Year (2006)

PELLETIER, Jean-Marc (PEHL-tyay, ZHAWN-MAHRK) FLA.

Goaltender. Catches left. 6'3", 209 lbs. Born, Atlanta, GA, March 4, 1978.
(Philadelphia's 1st choice, 30th overall, in 1997 Entry Draft).

			Regular Season								Playoffs						
Season	Club	League	GP	W	L	O/T	Mins	GA	SO	Avg	GP	W	L	Mins	GA	SO	Avg
1993-94	Richelieu Riverains	QAAA	24	14	8	2	1440	91	0	3.79	2	1	0	104	11	0	6.32
1994-95	Richelieu Riverains	QAAA	21	15	6	0	1260	71	0	3.36	2	1	1	153	11	0	4.32
1995-96	Cornell Big Red	ECAC	5	1	2	0	179	15	0	5.03	....	....	....	....	....	....	....
1996-97	Cornell Big Red	ECAC	11	5	2	3	679	28	1	2.47	....	....	....	....	....	....	....
1997-98	Rimouski Oceanic	QMJHL	34	17	11	3	1913	118	0	3.70	16	11	3	895	51	1	3.42

1998-99	**Philadelphia**	**NHL**	**1**	**0**	**1**	**0**	**60**	**5**	**0**	**5.00**	....	....	....	....	....	....	....
	Philadelphia	AHL	47	25	16	4	2636	122	2	2.78	1	0	0	27	0	0	0.00
99-2000	Philadelphia	AHL	24	14	10	0	1405	58	3	2.48	....	....	....	....	....	....	....
	Cincinnati	IHL	22	14	4	2	1278	52	2	2.44	3	1	1	160	8	1	3.00
2000-01	Cincinnati	IHL	39	18	14	5	2261	119	2	3.16	5	1	4	318	15	0	2.83
2001-02	Lowell	AHL	40	21	12	4	2284	98	2	2.57	5	2	3	298	13	0	2.62
2002-03	Lowell	AHL	17	6	10	0	861	51	1	3.55	....	....	....	....	....	....	....
	Phoenix	**NHL**	**2**	**0**	**2**	**0**	**119**	**6**	**0**	**3.03**	....	....	....	....	....	....	....
	Springfield Falcons	AHL	24	12	7	4	1391	55	2	2.37	6	3	3	368	16	1	2.61
2003-04	**Phoenix**	**NHL**	**4**	**1**	**1**	**0**	**175**	**12**	**0**	**4.11**	....	....	....	....	....	....	....
	Springfield Falcons	AHL	43	10	24	5	2433	109	2	2.69	....	....	....	....	....	....	....
2004-05	Utah Grizzlies	AHL	23	6	12	1	1231	77	0	3.75	....	....	....	....	....	....	....
	Springfield Falcons	AHL	13	2	10	1	715	35	0	2.94	....	....	....	....	....	....	....
2005-06	Rochester	AHL	39	21	15	1	2198	120	0	3.28	....	....	....	....	....	....	....
	NHL Totals		**7**	**1**	**4**	**0**	**354**	**23**	**0**	**3.90**	....	....	....	....	....	....	....

Traded to **Carolina** by **Philadelphia** with Rod Brind'Amour and Philadelphia's 2nd round choice (later traded to Colorado – Colorado selected Argis Saviels) in 2000 Entry Draft for Keith Primeau and Carolina's 5th round choice (later traded to NY Islanders – NY Islanders selected Kristofer Ottosson) in 2000 Entry Draft, January 23, 2000. Traded to **Phoenix** by **Carolina** with future considerations for Patrick DesRochers, December 31, 2002. Signed as a free agent by **Florida**, August 19, 2005.

PELLETIER, Pier-Olivier (PEHL-tyay, PEE-yair-OH-lihv-ee-AY) PHX.

Goaltender. Catches left. 6'2", 194 lbs. Born, St-Louis, Que., April 8, 1987.
(Phoenix's 2nd choice, 59th overall, in 2005 Entry Draft).

			Regular Season								Playoffs						
Season	**Club**	**League**	**GP**	**W**	**L**	**O/T**	**Mins**	**GA**	**SO**	**Avg**	**GP**	**W**	**L**	**Mins**	**GA**	**SO**	**Avg**
2003-04	St-Francois Blizzard	QAAA	2	0	0	2	116	9	0	4.65	7	3	4	468	15	0	1.92
	Trois-Rivieres	QAAA	....	....	....	....	....	....	....	....	1	0	0	5	3	0	33.00
2004-05	Drummondville	QMJHL	40	15	17	4	2095	105	2	3.01	6	2	4	378	17	0	2.70
2005-06	Drummondville	QMJHL	22	10	12	0	1201	81	0	4.05	....	....	....	....	....	....	....

• Missed majority of 2003-04 season due to injury.

PENNER, Andrew (PEH-nuhr, AN-droo)

Goaltender. Catches left. 6'2", 205 lbs. Born, Scarborough, Ont., December 21, 1982.

			Regular Season								Playoffs						
Season	**Club**	**League**	**GP**	**W**	**L**	**O/T**	**Mins**	**GA**	**SO**	**Avg**	**GP**	**W**	**L**	**Mins**	**GA**	**SO**	**Avg**
1998-99	North York	OPJHL	26	....	....	....	1497	107	0	4.29	....	....	....	....	....	....	....
99-2000	North Bay	OHL	22	3	12	0	1070	79	0	4.43	....	....	....	....	....	....	....
2000-01	North Bay	OHL	32	10	19	1	1787	117	1	3.93	....	....	....	....	....	....	....
2001-02	North Bay	OHL	18	4	8	4	917	52	1	3.40	....	....	....	....	....	....	....
	Guelph Storm	OHL	36	18	12	5	2066	107	0	3.11	9	5	4	546	29	0	3.19
2002-03	Guelph Storm	OHL	51	21	21	7	2975	137	0	2.76	11	5	5	665	34	0	3.07
2003-04	Dayton Bombers	ECHL	50	15	27	2	2764	175	0	3.80	....	....	....	....	....	....	....
2004-05	Dayton Bombers	ECHL	15	6	8	1	893	49	0	3.29	....	....	....	....	....	....	....
	Syracuse Crunch	AHL	23	8	12	1	1222	55	1	2.70	....	....	....	....	....	....	....
2005-06	Syracuse Crunch	AHL	40	20	12	1	2060	112	1	3.26	2	0	1	89	4	0	2.70
	Dayton Bombers	ECHL	3	1	2	0	179	11	0	3.68	....	....	....	....	....	....	....

Signed as a free agent by **Columbus**, September 17, 2001.

PETERS, Justin (PEE-tuhrs, JUHS-tihn) CAR.

Goaltender. Catches left. 6', 209 lbs. Born, Blyth, Ont., August 30, 1986.
(Carolina's 2nd choice, 38th overall, in 2004 Entry Draft).

			Regular Season								Playoffs						
Season	**Club**	**League**	**GP**	**W**	**L**	**O/T**	**Mins**	**GA**	**SO**	**Avg**	**GP**	**W**	**L**	**Mins**	**GA**	**SO**	**Avg**
2001-02	Huron-Perth	OMHA	17	11	2	4	810	32	1	1.89	13	9	4	285	30	1	2.31
2002-03	St. Michael's	OHL	23	6	10	1	1052	54	0	3.08	7	1	0	126	4	0	1.90
2003-04	St. Michael's	OHL	53	30	16	6	3149	139	4	2.65	18	10	8	1109	37	4	2.00
2004-05	St. Michael's	OHL	58	23	23	5	3150	146	3	2.78	10	4	4	524	25	0	2.86
2005-06	St. Michael's	OHL	20	10	6	0	1174	75	0	3.83	....	....	....	....	....	....	....
	Plymouth Whalers	OHL	35	19	15	0	2073	95	1	2.75	13	6	6	789	42	0	3.19

PIETRASIAK, Jeff (peh-TRAZ-ee-ak, JEHF) PHX.

Goaltender. Catches left. 6'1", 180 lbs. Born, Marlboro, MA, April 5, 1983.
(Phoenix's 8th choice, 186th overall, in 2002 Entry Draft).

			Regular Season								Playoffs						
Season	**Club**	**League**	**GP**	**W**	**L**	**O/T**	**Mins**	**GA**	**SO**	**Avg**	**GP**	**W**	**L**	**Mins**	**GA**	**SO**	**Avg**
2000-01	Berkshire Bears	High-MA	25	....	....	....	1150	26	8	1.37	....	....	....	....	....	....	....
2001-02	Berkshire Bears	High-MA	32	....	....	....	1471	51	5	2.05	....	....	....	....	....	....	....
2002-03	New Hampshire	H-East	2	1	0	0	67	2	0	1.78	....	....	....	....	....	....	....
2003-04	New Hampshire	H-East	11	3	1	1	387	12	0	1.86	....	....	....	....	....	....	....
2004-05	New Hampshire	H-East	23	11	7	3	1280	62	2	2.91	....	....	....	....	....	....	....
2005-06	New Hampshire	H-East	23	12	5	2	1170	43	0	2.21	....	....	....	....	....	....	....

PITTON, Bryan (PIH-tuhn, BRIGH-uhn) EDM.

Goaltender. Catches left. 6'1", 168 lbs. Born, Mississauga, Ont., January 26, 1988.
(Edmonton's 3rd choice, 133rd overall, in 2006 Entry Draft).

			Regular Season								Playoffs						
Season	**Club**	**League**	**GP**	**W**	**L**	**O/T**	**Mins**	**GA**	**SO**	**Avg**	**GP**	**W**	**L**	**Mins**	**GA**	**SO**	**Avg**
2004-05	Wellington Dukes	OPJHL	....	24	7	3	....	....	2	2.93	....	....	....	....	....	....	....
2005-06	Brampton Battalion	OHL	24	16	4	0	1293	74	0	3.43	2	0	0	45	5	0	6.67

PLANTE, Tyler (PLAWNT, TIGH-luhr) FLA.

Goaltender. Catches left. 6'2", 191 lbs. Born, Milwaukee, WI, April 16, 1987.
(Florida's 2nd choice, 32nd overall, in 2005 Entry Draft).

			Regular Season								Playoffs						
Season	**Club**	**League**	**GP**	**W**	**L**	**O/T**	**Mins**	**GA**	**SO**	**Avg**	**GP**	**W**	**L**	**Mins**	**GA**	**SO**	**Avg**
2003-04	Brandon	WHL	2	0	0	1	58	2	0	2.07	....	....	....	....	....	....	....
2004-05	Brandon	WHL	48	34	11	2	2833	122	6	2.58	*24	*13	11	*1408	69	0	2.94
2005-06	Brandon	WHL	60	25	24	9	3414	189	2	3.32	6	2	4	360	18	0	3.00

WHL Rookie of the Year (2005) • Canadian Major Junior All-Rookie Team (2005)

POGGE, Justin (POHG-ee, JUHS-tihn) TOR.

Goaltender. Catches left. 6'3", 204 lbs. Born, Ft. McMurray, Alta., April 22, 1986.
(Toronto's 1st choice, 90th overall, in 2004 Entry Draft).

			Regular Season								Playoffs						
Season	**Club**	**League**	**GP**	**W**	**L**	**O/T**	**Mins**	**GA**	**SO**	**Avg**	**GP**	**W**	**L**	**Mins**	**GA**	**SO**	**Avg**
2002-03	Summerland Sting	KIJHL	30	....	....	....	1761	91	0	3.13	....	....	....	....	....	....	....
2003-04	Prince George	WHL	44	17	18	2	2271	107	3	2.83	....	....	....	....	....	....	....
2004-05	Prince George	WHL	24	10	9	2	1198	56	4	2.80	....	....	....	....	....	....	....
	Calgary Hitmen	WHL	29	14	12	3	1727	66	2	2.29	12	7	5	742	24	1	1.94
2005-06	Calgary Hitmen	WHL	54	38	10	6	3237	93	*11	*1.72	13	7	5	802	34	2	2.54

WHL East First All-Star Team (2006) • WHL Goaltender of the Year (2006) • WHL Player of the Year (2006) • Canadian Major Junior Goaltender of the Year (2006)

POPPERLE, Tomas (PAW-puhr-lay, TAW-mash) CBJ

Goaltender. Catches left. 6'1", 187 lbs. Born, Broumov, Czech., October 10, 1984.
(Columbus' 5th choice, 131st overall, in 2005 Entry Draft).

			Regular Season								Playoffs						
Season	**Club**	**League**	**GP**	**W**	**L**	**O/T**	**Mins**	**GA**	**SO**	**Avg**	**GP**	**W**	**L**	**Mins**	**GA**	**SO**	**Avg**
2001-02	Sparta Jr.	CzRep-Jr.	29	....	....	....	1653	65	2	2.36	5	....	....	320	15	0	2.81
2002-03	Sparta Jr.	CzRep-Jr.	28	....	....	....	1500	52	2	2.08	....	....	....	....	....	....	....
2003-04	Sparta Jr.	CzRep-Jr.	30	....	....	....	1778	60	4	2.02	....	....	....	....	....	....	....
	HC Pribram	CzRep-3	2	....	....	....	60	2	0	2.00	....	....	....	....	....	....	....
	Beroun	CzRep-2	5	....	....	....	305	7	0	1.38	2	....	....	120	4	0	2.00
	HC Sparta Praha	CzRep	....	....	....	....	....	....	....	....	1	....	....	11	0	0	0.00
2004-05	Beroun	CzRep-2	16	....	....	....	966	29	1	1.80	2	....	....	120	5	0	2.50
	HC Sparta Praha	CzRep	25	....	....	....	1325	35	4	*1.58	2	....	....	12	4	0	20.00
2005-06	Eisbaren Berlin	Germany	31	....	....	....	1845	67	3	2.18	11	....	....	655	23	1	2.11

PRICE, Carey (PRIGHS, KAIR-ee) MTL.

Goaltender. Catches left. 6'3", 212 lbs. Born, Vancouver, B.C., August 16, 1987.
(Montreal's 1st choice, 5th overall, in 2005 Entry Draft).

			Regular Season								Playoffs						
Season	**Club**	**League**	**GP**	**W**	**L**	**O/T**	**Mins**	**GA**	**SO**	**Avg**	**GP**	**W**	**L**	**Mins**	**GA**	**SO**	**Avg**
2002-03	Williams Lake	BCAHA	18	....	....	....	1050	48	1	2.70	....	....	....	....	....	....	....
	Tri-City Americans	WHL	1	0	0	0	20	2	0	6.00	....	....	....	....	....	....	....
2003-04	Tri-City Americans	WHL	28	8	9	3	1363	54	1	2.38	8	5	3	470	19	0	2.43
2004-05	Tri-City Americans	WHL	63	24	31	8	3712	145	8	2.34	5	1	4	325	12	0	2.22
2005-06	Tri-City Americans	WHL	55	21	25	6	3072	147	3	2.87	5	1	3	302	12	0	2.38

PRUSEK, Martin (PREW-sehk, MAHR-tihn)

Goaltender. Catches left. 6'1", 176 lbs. Born, Ostrava, Czech., December 11, 1975.
(Ottawa's 6th choice, 164th overall, in 1999 Entry Draft).

			Regular Season								Playoffs						
Season	**Club**	**League**	**GP**	**W**	**L**	**O/T**	**Mins**	**GA**	**SO**	**Avg**	**GP**	**W**	**L**	**Mins**	**GA**	**SO**	**Avg**
1994-95	HC Vitkovice	CzRep	5	....	....	....	232	18	....	4.65	....	....	....	....	....	....	....
1995-96	HC Vitkovice	CzRep	40	....	....	....	2336	113	1	2.90	4	....	....	250	10	1	2.40
1996-97	HC Vitkovice	CzRep	49	....	....	....	2841	109	8	2.30	9	....	....	546	19	1	2.08
1997-98	HC Vitkovice	CzRep	50	....	....	....	2901	129	....	2.67	9	....	....	529	26	....	3.00
1998-99	HC Vitkovice	CzRep	37	....	....	....	1905	85	....	2.68	4	....	....	250	12	....	2.88
99-2000	HC Vitkovice	CzRep	50	....	....	....	2647	132	....	2.99	....	....	....	....	....	....	....
2000-01	HC Vitkovice	CzRep	30	....	....	....	1679	64	....	2.29	9	....	....	460	25	....	3.26
2001-02	**Ottawa**	**NHL**	**1**	**0**	**1**	**0**	**62**	**3**	**0**	**2.90**	....	....	....	....	....	....	....
	Grand Rapids	AHL	33	18	8	5	1903	58	4	*1.83	5	2	3	278	10	0	2.16
2002-03	**Ottawa**	**NHL**	**18**	**12**	**2**	**1**	**935**	**37**	**0**	**2.37**	....	....	....	....	....	....	....
	Binghamton	AHL	4	1	2	1	243	7	1	1.73	....	....	....	....	....	....	....
2003-04	**Ottawa**	**NHL**	**29**	**16**	**6**	**3**	**1528**	**54**	**3**	**2.12**	**1**	**0**	**0**	**40**	**1**	**0**	**1.50**
2004-05	HC Vitkovice Steel	CzRep	14	....	....	....	672	28	0	2.50	....	....	....	....	....	....	....
	Znojmo	CzRep	8	....	....	....	453	18	0	2.38	....	....	....	....	....	....	....
2005-06	**Columbus**	**NHL**	**9**	**3**	**3**	**0**	**373**	**20**	**0**	**3.22**	....	....	....	....	....	....	....
	Syracuse Crunch	AHL	23	12	7	1	1203	60	2	2.99	....	....	....	....	....	....	....
	NHL Totals		**57**	**31**	**12**	**4**	**2898**	**114**	**3**	**2.36**	**1**	**0**	**0**	**40**	**1**	**0**	**1.50**

AHL First All-Star Team (2002) • Harry "Hap" Holmes Memorial Award (fewest goals against – AHL) (2002) (shared with Simon Lajeunesse and Mathieu Chouinard) • Aldege "Baz" Bastien Memorial Award (Outstanding Goaltender – AHL) (2002)

Signed as a free agent by **Vitkovice** (CzRep), August 20, 2004. Loaned to **Znojmo** (CzRep) by **Vitkovice** (CzRep), December, 2004. Signed as a free agent by **Columbus**, August 4, 2005.

PUURULA, Joni (pu-u-ROO-luh, YOHN-ee)

Goaltender. Catches left. 5'11", 180 lbs. Born, Kokkola, Finland, August 4, 1982.
(Montreal's 10th choice, 243rd overall, in 2000 Entry Draft).

			Regular Season								Playoffs						
Season	**Club**	**League**	**GP**	**W**	**L**	**O/T**	**Mins**	**GA**	**SO**	**Avg**	**GP**	**W**	**L**	**Mins**	**GA**	**SO**	**Avg**
1998-99	JHT Kalajoki	Finland-3	12	....	....	....	782	37	0	2.84	....	....	....	....	....	....	....
99-2000	Hermes Kokkola	Finland-2	24	8	12	2	1280	81	1	3.84	....	....	....	....	....	....	....
2000-01	FPS Forssa Jr.	Fin-Jr.	....	....	....	....	....	....	....	....	4	1	3	240	8	0	2.00
	FPS Forssa	Finland-2	39	13	22	2	2264	142	1	3.76	....	....	....	....	....	....	....
2001-02	HPK Jr.	Fin-Jr.	2	0	2	0	119	11	0	5.54	....	....	....	....	....	....	....
	FPS Forssa	Finland-2	5	2	2	1	305	18	0	3.54	....	....	....	....	....	....	....
	HPK Hameenlinna	Finland	9	8	0	1	515	18	0	2.09	8	4	3	453	13	0	1.72
2002-03	HPK Hameenlinna	Finland	34	19	6	9	1972	71	4	2.16	11	6	5	676	19	1	1.69
2003-04	Haukat Jarvenpaa	Finland-2	3	2	0	1	182	9	0	2.96	....	....	....	....	....	....	....
	HPK Hameenlinna	Finland	33	16	9	7	1890	69	4	2.19	8	4	4	481	14	2	1.74
2004-05	HPK Hameenlinna	Finland	7	1	0	6	446	19	0	2.55	....	....	....	....	....	....	....
	Ufa	Russia	24	....	....	....	1222	61	3	2.99	....	....	....	....	....	....	....
2005-06	TPS Turku	Finland	31	6	12	12	1831	65	4	2.13	2	0	2	147	6	0	2.44

QUICK, Jonathan (KWIHK, JAWN-ah-thuhn) L.A.

Goaltender. Catches left. 6', 180 lbs. Born, Milford, CT, January 21, 1986.
(Los Angeles' 4th choice, 72nd overall, in 2005 Entry Draft).

			Regular Season								Playoffs						
Season	**Club**	**League**	**GP**	**W**	**L**	**O/T**	**Mins**	**GA**	**SO**	**Avg**	**GP**	**W**	**L**	**Mins**	**GA**	**SO**	**Avg**
2002-03	Avon Old Farms	High-CT	13	8	5	0	780	38	0	2.92	....	....	....	....	....	....	....
2003-04	Avon Old Farms	High-CT	21	20	1	0	1260	26	2	1.71	....	....	....	....	....	....	....
2004-05	Avon Old Farms	High-CT	27	25	2	0	1413	1.14	9	1.14	....	....	....	....	....	....	....
2005-06	Massachusetts	H-East	17	4	10	1	905	45	0	2.98	....	....	....	....	....	....	....

RACINE, Jean-Francois (RAY-seen, ZHAWN-fran-SWUH) TOR.

Goaltender. Catches left. 6'3", 194 lbs. Born, St-Hyacinthe, Que., April 27, 1982.
(Toronto's 4th choice, 90th overall, in 2000 Entry Draft).

			Regular Season								Playoffs						
Season	**Club**	**League**	**GP**	**W**	**L**	**O/T**	**Mins**	**GA**	**SO**	**Avg**	**GP**	**W**	**L**	**Mins**	**GA**	**SO**	**Avg**
1998-99	Magog	QAAA	36	19	12	1	2160	107	3	2.98	11	5	6	656	37	0	3.39
99-2000	Moncton Wildcats	QMJHL	10	3	3	1	410	28	0	4.10	....	....	....	....	....	....	....
	Drummondville	QMJHL	20	14	6	0	1152	63	1	3.28	3	0	0	65	5	0	4.60
2000-01	Drummondville	QMJHL	61	27	26	3	3362	189	4	3.37	5	2	3	303	20	0	3.97
2001-02	Drummondville	QMJHL	65	29	30	3	3640	208	2	3.43	12	5	7	720	42	1	3.50
2002-03	Memphis	CHL	35	22	9	3	2050	94	0	2.75	1	0	1	58	5	0	5.14
2003-04	Memphis	CHL	30	15	10	2	1645	74	2	2.70	....	....	....	....	....	....	....
	St. John's	AHL	9	4	5	0	496	24	1	2.90	....	....	....	....	....	....	....
2004-05	St. John's	AHL	17	10	4	0	893	41	0	2.76	....	....	....	....	....	....	....
	Memphis	CHL	19	9	6	1	951	57	0	3.60	....	....	....	....	....	....	....
2005-06	Toronto Marlies	AHL	36	19	13	2	1882	99	0	3.16	....	....	....	....	....	....	....

RAMO, Karri (RAH-moh, KAH-ree) T.B.

Goaltender. Catches left. 6'2", 215 lbs. Born, Asikkala, Finland, July 1, 1986.
(Tampa Bay's 7th choice, 191st overall, in 2004 Entry Draft).

			Regular Season								Playoffs						
Season	**Club**	**League**	**GP**	**W**	**L**	**O/T**	**Mins**	**GA**	**SO**	**Avg**	**GP**	**W**	**L**	**Mins**	**GA**	**SO**	**Avg**
2002-03	K-Reipas U18	Fin-U18	19	12	3	2	1013	47	0	2.78	4	2	2	182	11	0	3.62
2003-04	Pelicans Lahti U18	Fin-U18	3	3	0	0	180	7	0	2.33	5	2	2	268	10	0	2.24
	Pelicans Lahti Jr.	Fin-Jr.	18	5	9	2	960	53	0	3.31	2	2	0	120	1	1	0.50
	Pelicans Lahti	Finland	3	0	2	0	138	10	0	4.34	....	....	....	....	....	....	....

Season	Club	League	GP	W	L	O/T	Mins	GA	SO	Avg	GP	W	L	Mins	GA	SO	Avg
2004-05	Pelicans Lahti Jr.	Fin-Jr.	21	10	5	6	1269	36	6	1.70	4	1	3	206	16	0	4.66
	Pelicans Lahti	Finland	26	4	12	4	1267	84	1	3.98	....	....	....	....	....	....	....
2005-06	Haukat Jarvenpaa	Finland-2	1	....	....	....	60	5	0	5.00	....	....	....	....	....	....	....
	Suomi U20	Finland-2	3	....	....	....	183	12	0	3.93	....	....	....	....	....	....	....
	HPK Hameenlinna	Finland	24	7	8	7	1359	49	2	2.16	3	2	1	204	5	1	1.46

RASK, Tuukka (RASK, TU-kah) BOS.

Goaltender. Catches left. 6'2", 165 lbs. Born, Savonlinna, Finland, March 10, 1987.
(Toronto's 1st choice, 21st overall, in 2005 Entry Draft).

							Regular Season							Playoffs			
Season	Club	League	GP	W	L	O/T	Mins	GA	SO	Avg	GP	W	L	Mins	GA	SO	Avg
2003-04	Ilves Tampere U18	Fin-U18	9	4	3	2	533	25	0	2.81	....	....	....	....	....	....	....
	Ilves Tampere Jr.	Fin-Jr.	30	12	10	7	1767	65	2	2.21	3	1	2	178	6	0	2.02
2004-05	Ilves Tampere Jr.	Fin-Jr.	26	17	3	4	1517	47	2	1.86	10	9	1	619	9	6	0.87
	Ilves Tampere	Finland	4	0	1	1	201	15	0	4.46	....	....	....	....	....	....	....
2005-06	Ilves Tampere Jr.	Fin-Jr.	1	....	....	....	60	2	0	2.00	....	....	....	....	....	....	....
	Suomi U20	Finland-2	3	....	....	....	179	6	0	2.01	....	....	....	....	....	....	....
	Ilves Tampere	Finland	30	12	8	7	1724	60	2	2.09	3	0	3	180	7	0	2.33

Traded to **Boston** by **Toronto** for Andrew Raycroft, June 24, 2006.

RAYCROFT, Andrew (RAY-krawft, AN-droo) TOR.

Goaltender. Catches left. 6', 185 lbs. Born, Belleville, Ont., May 4, 1980.
(Boston's 4th choice, 135th overall, in 1998 Entry Draft).

							Regular Season							Playoffs			
Season	Club	League	GP	W	L	O/T	Mins	GA	SO	Avg	GP	W	L	Mins	GA	SO	Avg
1996-97	Wellington Dukes	MTJHL	27	....	....	....	1402	92	0	3.94	....	....	....	....	....	....	....
1997-98	Sudbury Wolves	OHL	33	8	16	5	1802	125	0	4.16	2	0	1	89	8	0	5.39
1998-99	Sudbury Wolves	OHL	45	17	22	5	2528	173	1	4.11	3	0	2	96	13	0	8.13
99-2000	Kingston	OHL	*61	33	20	5	3340	191	0	3.43	5	1	4	300	21	0	4.20
2000-01	**Boston**	**NHL**	**15**	**4**	**6**	**0**	**649**	**32**	**0**	**2.96**	....	....	....	....	....	....	....
	Providence Bruins	AHL	26	8	14	4	1459	82	1	3.37	....	....	....	....	....	....	....
2001-02	**Boston**	**NHL**	**1**	**0**	**0**	**1**	**65**	**3**	**0**	**2.77**	....	....	....	....	....	....	....
	Providence Bruins	AHL	56	25	24	6	3317	142	4	2.57	2	0	2	119	5	0	2.52
2002-03	**Boston**	**NHL**	**5**	**2**	**3**	**0**	**300**	**12**	**0**	**2.40**	....	....	....	....	....	....	....
	Providence Bruins	AHL	39	23	10	3	2255	94	1	2.50	4	1	3	264	6	1	*1.36
2003-04	**Boston**	**NHL**	**57**	**29**	**18**	**9**	**3420**	**117**	**3**	**2.05**	**7**	**3**	**4**	**447**	**16**	**1**	**2.15**
2004-05	Tappara Tampere	Finland	11	4	5	2	657	32	1	2.92	3	0	2	104	11	0	6.36
2005-06	**Boston**	**NHL**	**30**	**8**	**19**	**2**	**1619**	**100**	**0**	**3.71**	....	....	....	....	....	....	....
	Providence Bruins	AHL	1	1	0	0	64	3	0	2.80	....	....	....	....	....	....	....
	NHL Totals		**108**	**43**	**46**	**12**	**6053**	**264**	**3**	**2.62**	**7**	**3**	**4**	**447**	**16**	**1**	**2.15**

OHL First All-Star Team (2000) • Canadian Major Junior First All-Star Team (2000) • Canadian Major Junior Goaltender of the Year (2000) • NHL All-Rookie Team (2004) • Calder Memorial Trophy (2004)

Signed as a free agent by **Tappara Tampere** (Finland), January 17, 2005. Traded to **Toronto** by **Boston** for Tuukka Rask, June 24, 2006.

REGAN, Kevin (REE-guhn, KEH-vihn) BOS.

Goaltender. Catches left. 6', 195 lbs. Born, Boston, MA, July 25, 1984.
(Boston's 10th choice, 277th overall, in 2003 Entry Draft).

							Regular Season							Playoffs			
Season	Club	League	GP	W	L	O/T	Mins	GA	SO	Avg	GP	W	L	Mins	GA	SO	Avg
2001-02	St. Sebastian's	High-MA	31	27	4	0	1860	56	0	1.91	....	....	....	....	....	....	....
	USNTDP	U-18	1	0	0	0	12	0	0	0.00	....	....	....	....	....	....	....
	South Boston	USHA	3	3	0	0	158	8	0	2.58	....	....	....	....	....	....	....
2002-03	St. Sebastian's	High-MA	28	....	....	....	1215	47	4	1.81	....	....	....	....	....	....	....
2003-04	Waterloo	USHL	50	*28	19	1	0	111	*6	2.37	*12	*9	3	*735	19	*1	*1.55
2004-05	New Hampshire	H-East	23	15	4	2	1276	50	0	2.35	....	....	....	....	....	....	....
2005-06	New Hampshire	H-East	23	8	8	5	1299	57	3	2.63	....	....	....	....	....	....	....

Hockey East All-Rookie Team (2005) (co-winners - Cory Schneider and Peter Vetri)

REIMER, James (RIGH-muhr, JAYMZ) TOR.

Goaltender. Catches left. 6'2", 208 lbs. Born, Winnipeg, Man., March 15, 1988.
(Toronto's 3rd choice, 99th overall, in 2006 Entry Draft).

							Regular Season							Playoffs			
Season	Club	League	GP	W	L	O/T	Mins	GA	SO	Avg	GP	W	L	Mins	GA	SO	Avg
2003-04	Interlake Lightning	MMHL	27	6	5	2	863	41	1	2.85	....	....	....	....	....	....	....
2004-05	Interlake Lightning	MMHL	37	19	6	2	1646	58	4	2.11	435	26	0	3.59	....	....	....
2005-06	Red Deer Rebels	WHL	34	7	18	3	1709	80	0	2.81	....	....	....	....	....	....	....

RIDDERWALL, Stefan (RIH-duhr-vahl, STEH-fan) NYI

Goaltender. Catches left. 6'1", 189 lbs. Born, Stockholm, Sweden, March 5, 1988.
(NY Islanders' 12th choice, 173rd overall, in 2006 Entry Draft).

							Regular Season							Playoffs			
Season	Club	League	GP	W	L	O/T	Mins	GA	SO	Avg	GP	W	L	Mins	GA	SO	Avg
2003-04	Huddinge IK U18	Swe-U18	7	....	....	....	345	31	0	5.38	....	....	....	....	....	....	....
2004-05	Djurgarden U18	Swe-U18	3	....	....	....	154	8	0	3.10	4	....	....	234	11	0	2.81
	Djurgarden Jr.	Swe-Jr.	16	....	....	....	972	51	0	3.15	....	....	....	....	....	....	....
2005-06	Djurgarden Jr.	Swe-Jr.	18	....	....	....	1073	43	3	2.40	4	....	....	242	13	1	3.22
	Djurgarden	Sweden	1	....	....	....	4	0	0	0.00	....	....	....	....	....	....	....

RINNE, Pekka (RIH-neh, PEH-kuh) NSH.

Goaltender. Catches left. 6'5", 207 lbs. Born, Kempele, Finland, November 3, 1982.
(Nashville's 10th choice, 258th overall, in 2004 Entry Draft).

							Regular Season							Playoffs			
Season	Club	League	GP	W	L	O/T	Mins	GA	SO	Avg	GP	W	L	Mins	GA	SO	Avg
2000-01	Karpat Oulu Jr.	Fin-Jr.	20	9	4	5	1148	63	0	3.29	....	....	....	....	....	....	....
2001-02	Karpat Oulu Jr.	Fin-Jr.	30	19	7	3	1724	61	3	2.12	3	1	2	184	10	1	3.26
2002-03	Karpat Oulu Jr.	Fin-Jr.	25	14	8	3	1479	48	5	1.95	4	1	3	238	7	0	1.76
	Karpat Oulu	Finland	1	0	1	0	60	7	0	7.00	....	....	....	....	....	....	....
2003-04	Karpat Oulu	Finland	14	5	4	4	824	41	0	2.99	2	1	0	22	0	0	0.00
	Hokki Kajaani	Finland-2	8	5	2	1	463	16	2	2.07	....	....	....	....	....	....	....
2004-05	Karpat Oulu	Finland	10	8	0	1	571	16	0	1.68	....	....	....	....	....	....	....
2005-06	**Nashville**	**NHL**	**2**	**1**	**1**	**0**	**63**	**4**	**0**	**3.81**	....	....	....	....	....	....	....
	Milwaukee	AHL	51	30	18	2	2960	139	2	2.82	14	10	4	734	35	3	2.86
	NHL Totals		**2**	**1**	**1**	**0**	**63**	**4**	**0**	**3.81**	....	....	....	....	....	....	....

ROLOSON, Dwayne (ROH-loh-suhn, DWAYN) EDM.

Goaltender. Catches left. 6'1", 178 lbs. Born, Simcoe, Ont., October 12, 1969.

							Regular Season							Playoffs			
Season	Club	League	GP	W	L	O/T	Mins	GA	SO	Avg	GP	W	L	Mins	GA	SO	Avg
1984-85	Simcoe Penguins	OJHL-C	3	....	....	....	100	21	0	12.60	....	....	....	....	....	....	....
1985-86	Simcoe Rams	OJHL-C	1	....	....	....	60	6	0	6.00	....	....	....	....	....	....	....
1986-87	Norwich	OJHL-C	19	....	....	....	1091	55	0	*3.03	....	....	....	....	....	....	....
1987-88	Belleville Bobcats	OJHL-B	21	9	6	1	1070	60	*2	3.36	....	....	....	....	....	....	....
1988-89	Thorold	OJHL-B	27	15	6	4	1490	82	0	3.30	....	....	....	....	....	....	....
1989-90	Thorold	OHA-B	30	18	8	1	1683	108	0	3.85	....	....	....	....	....	....	....
1990-91	U. Mass-Lowell	H-East	15	5	9	0	823	63	0	4.59	....	....	....	....	....	....	....
1991-92	U. Mass-Lowell	H-East	12	3	8	0	660	52	0	4.73	....	....	....	....	....	....	....
1992-93	U. Mass-Lowell	H-East	*39	20	17	2	*2342	150	0	3.84	....	....	....	....	....	....	....
1993-94	U. Mass-Lowell	H-East	*40	*23	10	7	*2305	106	0	2.76	....	....	....	....	....	....	....
1994-95	Saint John Flames	AHL	46	16	21	8	2734	156	1	3.42	5	1	4	298	13	0	2.61
1995-96	Saint John Flames	AHL	67	*33	22	11	4026	190	1	2.83	16	10	6	1027	49	1	2.86
1996-97	**Calgary**	**NHL**	**31**	**9**	**14**	**3**	**1618**	**78**	**1**	**2.89**	....	....	....	....	....	....	....
	Saint John Flames	AHL	8	6	2	0	481	22	1	2.75	....	....	....	....	....	....	....
1997-98	**Calgary**	**NHL**	**39**	**11**	**16**	**8**	**2205**	**110**	**0**	**2.99**	....	....	....	....	....	....	....
	Saint John Flames	AHL	4	3	0	1	245	8	0	1.96	....	....	....	....	....	....	....
1998-99	**Buffalo**	**NHL**	**18**	**6**	**8**	**2**	**911**	**42**	**1**	**2.77**	**4**	**1**	**1**	**139**	**10**	**0**	**4.32**
	Rochester	AHL	2	2	0	0	120	4	0	2.00	....	....	....	....	....	....	....
99-2000	**Buffalo**	**NHL**	**14**	**1**	**7**	**3**	**677**	**32**	**0**	**2.84**	....	....	....	....	....	....	....
2000-01	Worcester IceCats	AHL	52	*32	15	5	*3127	113	*6	*2.17	11	6	5	697	23	1	1.98
2001-02	**Minnesota**	**NHL**	**45**	**14**	**20**	**7**	**2506**	**112**	**5**	**2.68**	....	....	....	....	....	....	....
2002-03	**Minnesota**	**NHL**	**50**	**23**	**16**	**8**	**2945**	**98**	**4**	**2.00**	**11**	**5**	**6**	**579**	**25**	**0**	**2.59**
2003-04	**Minnesota**	**NHL**	**48**	**19**	**18**	**11**	**2847**	**89**	**5**	**1.88**	....	....	....	....	....	....	....
2004-05	Lukko Rauma	Finland	34	20	10	4	2048	70	4	2.05	9	4	5	512	18	2	2.11
2005-06	**Minnesota**	**NHL**	**24**	**6**	**17**	**1**	**1361**	**68**	**1**	**3.00**	....	....	....	....	....	....	....
	Edmonton	**NHL**	**19**	**8**	**7**	**4**	**1163**	**47**	**1**	**2.42**	**18**	**12**	**5**	**1160**	**45**	**1**	**2.33**
	NHL Totals		**288**	**97**	**123**	**47**	**16233**	**676**	**18**	**2.50**	**33**	**18**	**12**	**1878**	**80**	**1**	**2.56**

Hockey East First All-Star Team (1994) • Hockey East Player of the Year (1994) • NCAA East First All-American Team (1994) • AHL First All-Star Team (2001) • Aldege "Baz" Bastien Memorial Award (Outstanding Goaltender – AHL) (2001) • MBNA/Mastercard Roger Crozier Saving Grace Award (2004)

Played in NHL All-Star Game (2004)

Signed as a free agent by **Calgary**, July 4, 1994. Signed as a free agent by **Buffalo**, July 15, 1998. Claimed by **Columbus** from **Buffalo** in Expansion Draft, June 23, 2000. Signed as a free agent by **St. Louis**, July 14, 2000. Signed as a free agent by **Minnesota**, July 2, 2001. Signed as a free agent by **Rauma** (Finland), October 18, 2004. Traded to **Edmonton** by **Minnesota** for Edmonton's 1st round choice (later traded to Los Angeles - Los Angeles selected Trevor Lewis) in 2006 Entry Draft and future considerations, March 8, 2006.

RUDKOWSKY, Cody (RUHD-kow-skee, KOH-dee)

Goaltender. Catches left. 6'1", 206 lbs. Born, Willingdon, Alta., July 21, 1978.

							Regular Season							Playoffs			
Season	Club	League	GP	W	L	O/T	Mins	GA	SO	Avg	GP	W	L	Mins	GA	SO	Avg
1995-96	Langley Thunder	BCJHL	23	....	....	....	1172	73	1	3.73	....	....	....	....	....	....	....
	Seattle	WHL	2	0	0	0	21	3	0	8.57	....	....	....	....	....	....	....
1996-97	Seattle	WHL	40	19	16	1	2162	124	0	3.44	1	1	0	30	0	0	0.00
1997-98	Seattle	WHL	53	20	22	3	2805	176	1	3.74	5	1	4	278	18	0	3.88
1998-99	Seattle	WHL	64	34	17	10	3665	177	*7	2.90	11	5	6	637	31	1	2.92
99-2000	Worcester IceCats	AHL	28	9	7	6	1405	75	0	3.20	....	....	....	....	....	....	....
	Peoria Rivermen	ECHL	10	6	4	0	599	32	0	3.20	2	1	1	119	6	0	3.02
2000-01	Worcester IceCats	AHL	25	13	8	3	1477	66	3	2.68	....	....	....	....	....	....	....
2001-02	Worcester IceCats	AHL	21	6	10	2	1108	50	1	2.71	....	....	....	....	....	....	....
	Peoria Rivermen	ECHL	12	5	2	4	709	24	3	2.03	2	0	1	78	4	0	3.08
2002-03	**St. Louis**	**NHL**	**1**	**1**	**0**	**0**	**30**	**0**	**0**	**0.00**	....	....	....	....	....	....	....
	Worcester IceCats	AHL	10	1	5	3	577	28	0	2.91	....	....	....	....	....	....	....
	Trenton Titans	ECHL	31	17	9	5	1867	85	2	2.73	3	0	3	178	14	0	4.72
2003-04	Worcester IceCats	AHL	1	0	0	0	49	3	0	3.67	1	0	1	58	2	0	2.07
	Reading Royals	ECHL	46	24	18	4	2728	108	1	2.38	14	8	6	834	28	1	2.02
2004-05	Providence Bruins	AHL	14	4	7	2	731	39	0	3.20	....	....	....	....	....	....	....
	Reading Royals	ECHL	20	8	11	1	1163	42	3	2.17	....	....	....	....	....	....	....
2005-06	Bridgeport	AHL	9	5	2	1	494	17	0	2.06	....	....	....	....	....	....	....
	Reading Royals	ECHL	38	24	11	3	2292	96	2	2.51	1	0	0	5	0	0	0.00
	NHL Totals		**1**	**1**	**0**	**0**	**30**	**0**	**0**	**0.00**	....	....	....	....	....	....	....

WHL West First All-Star Team (1999) • WHL Goaltender of the Year (1999) • WHL Player of the Year (1999) • Canadian Major Junior First All-Star Team (1999) • Canadian Major Junior Goaltender of the Year (1999)

Signed as a free agent by **St. Louis**, March 25, 1999. Signed as a free agent by **Providence** (AHL), December 1, 2004.

SABOURIN, Dany (SA-boo-rihn, DAN-ee) PIT.

Goaltender. Catches left. 6'2", 182 lbs. Born, Val-d'Or, Que., September 2, 1980.
(Calgary's 5th choice, 108th overall, in 1998 Entry Draft).

							Regular Season							Playoffs			
Season	Club	League	GP	W	L	O/T	Mins	GA	SO	Avg	GP	W	L	Mins	GA	SO	Avg
1996-97	Amos Forestiers	QAAA	24	6	16	0	1440	107	0	4.48	....	....	....	....	....	....	....
1997-98	Sherbrooke	QMJHL	37	15	15	2	1906	128	1	4.03	....	....	....	....	....	....	....
1998-99	Sherbrooke	QMJHL	30	8	13	2	1477	102	1	4.14	1	0	1	49	2	0	2.45
	Saint John Flames	AHL	....	....	....	....	....	....	....	....	1	0	1	57	4	0	4.19
99-2000	Sherbrooke	QMJHL	55	25	22	5	3067	181	1	3.54	5	1	4	324	18	0	3.33
2000-01	Saint John Flames	AHL	1	0	0	0	40	0	0	0.00	....	....	....	....	....	....	....
	Johnstown Chiefs	ECHL	19	4	9	1	903	56	0	3.72	1	0	0	40	2	0	3.00
2001-02	Johnstown Chiefs	ECHL	27	14	10	1	1539	84	0	3.28	3	0	2	137	5	0	2.18
2002-03	Saint John Flames	AHL	41	15	17	4	2220	100	4	2.70	....	....	....	....	....	....	....
2003-04	**Calgary**	**NHL**	**4**	**0**	**3**	**0**	**169**	**10**	**0**	**3.55**	....	....	....	....	....	....	....
	Lowell	AHL	14	5	7	2	821	39	0	2.85	....	....	....	....	....	....	....
	Las Vegas	ECHL	10	6	3	1	613	24	0	2.35	1	0	1	58	2	0	2.07
2004-05	Wilkes-Barre	AHL	20	8	8	2	1029	38	1	2.22	....	....	....	....	....	....	....
	Wheeling Nailers	ECHL	27	19	6	1	1579	44	5	*1.67	....	....	....	....	....	....	....
2005-06	**Pittsburgh**	**NHL**	**1**	**0**	**1**	**0**	**21**	**4**	**0**	**11.43**	....	....	....	....	....	....	....
	Wilkes-Barre	AHL	49	30	14	4	2943	111	4	*2.26	6	2	4	362	13	1	2.15
	NHL Totals		**5**	**0**	**4**	**0**	**190**	**14**	**0**	**4.42**	....	....	....	....	....	....	....

AHL First All-Star Team (2006) • Baz Bastien Memorial Trophy (Top Goaltender - AHL) (2006)

Signed as a free agent by **Pittsburgh**, August 10, 2005.

SANFORD, Curtis (SAN-fohrd, KUHR-this) ST.L.

Goaltender. Catches left. 5'10", 187 lbs. Born, Owen Sound, Ont., October 5, 1979.

							Regular Season							Playoffs			
Season	Club	League	GP	W	L	O/T	Mins	GA	SO	Avg	GP	W	L	Mins	GA	SO	Avg
1994-95	Wiarton Wolves	OJHL-C	18	....	....	....	949	98	0	6.20	....	....	....	....	....	....	....
1995-96	Collingwood	OJHL	21	....	....	....	2128	74	0	3.54	....	....	....	....	....	....	....
1996-97	Owen Sound	OHL	19	4	8	1	847	77	0	5.45	....	....	....	....	....	....	....
	Owen Sound	OJHL-B	6	....	....	....	360	28	0	4.68	....	....	....	....	....	....	....
1997-98	Owen Sound	OHL	30	13	10	2	1542	114	1	4.44	9	4	4	456	30	1	3.95
1998-99	Owen Sound	OHL	56	30	16	5	2998	191	2	3.82	16	9	7	960	58	0	3.63
99-2000	Owen Sound	OHL	53	18	26	6	3124	198	1	3.80	....	....	....	....	....	....	....
	Missouri	UHL	6	3	1	0	237	6	0	1.52	....	....	....	....	....	....	....
2000-01	Peoria Rivermen	ECHL	27	15	7	4	1511	48	3	*1.91	14	9	4	813	28	*2	2.07
	Worcester IceCats	AHL	5	3	0	1	237	16	0	4.06	....	....	....	....	....	....	....
2001-02	Peoria Rivermen	ECHL	24	13	8	2	1418	58	1	2.45	....	....	....	....	....	....	....
	Worcester IceCats	AHL	9	5	4	0	537	22	0	2.46	....	....	....	....	....	....	....
2002-03	**St. Louis**	**NHL**	**8**	**5**	**1**	**0**	**397**	**13**	**1**	**1.96**	....	....	....	....	....	....	....
	Worcester IceCats	AHL	41	18	14	8	2317	93	3	2.41	3	0	3	179	8	0	2.68
2003-04	Worcester IceCats	AHL	43	20	16	3	2367	84	5	2.13	9	4	5	569	24	0	2.53
2004-05	Worcester IceCats	AHL	50	19	25	2	2743	123	2	2.69	....	....	....	....	....	....	....

2005-06	St. Louis	NHL	34	13	13	5	1830	81	3	2.66	....	....	....	....	....	....	....
	Peoria Rivermen	AHL	6	4	2	0	358	11	2	1.84	....	....	....	....	....	....	....
	NHL Totals		42	18	14	5	2227	94	4	2.53	....	....	....	....	....	....	....

ECHL Second All-Star Team (2001)

Signed as a free agent by **St. Louis**, October 1, 2000.

SAUER, Billy (SOW-uhr, BIHL-lee) COL.

Goaltender. Catches left. 6'2", 170 lbs. Born, Rochester, NY, January 6, 1988.
(Colorado's 5th choice, 201st overall, in 2006 Entry Draft).

			Regular Season								Playoffs						
Season	Club	League	GP	W	L	O/T	Mins	GA	SO	Avg	GP	W	L	Mins	GA	SO	Avg
2004-05	Chicago Steel	USHL	30	12	12	2	1592	81	2	3.05	....	....	....	....	....	....	....
2005-06	U. of Michigan	CCHA	23	11	6	4	1281	65	1	3.04	....	....	....	....	....	....	....

SAUVE, Philippe (SOH-vay, FIHL-ihp) PHX.

Goaltender. Catches left. 6', 188 lbs. Born, Buffalo, NY, February 27, 1980.
(Colorado's 6th choice, 38th overall, in 1998 Entry Draft).

			Regular Season								Playoffs						
Season	Club	League	GP	W	L	O/T	Mins	GA	SO	Avg	GP	W	L	Mins	GA	SO	Avg
1995-96	Laval-Laurentides	QAAA	25	9	10	0	1184	87	1	4.11	15	7	8	900	54	0	3.58
1996-97	Rimouski Oceanic	QMJHL	26	11	9	2	1334	84	0	3.78	1	0	0	14	3	0	12.90
1997-98	Rimouski Oceanic	QMJHL	40	23	16	0	2326	131	1	3.38	7	0	5	262	33	0	7.55
1998-99	Rimouski Oceanic	QMJHL	44	16	19	4	2401	155	0	3.87	11	6	4	595	30	*1	3.03
99-2000	Drummondville	QMJHL	28	12	12	2	1526	106	0	4.17	....	....	....	....	....	....	....
	Hull Olympiques	QMJHL	17	9	7	1	992	57	0	3.45	12	6	6	735	47	0	3.84
2000-01	Hershey Bears	AHL	42	17	18	1	2182	100	3	2.75	3	0	3	218	10	0	2.75
2001-02	Hershey Bears	AHL	55	25	20	6	3130	111	6	2.13	8	3	5	486	21	0	2.59
2002-03	Hershey Bears	AHL	*60	26	20	12	3394	134	5	2.37	5	2	3	295	14	0	2.85
2003-04	Colorado	NHL	17	7	7	3	986	50	0	3.04	....	....	....	....	....	....	....
	Hershey Bears	AHL	10	3	7	0	578	25	2	2.59	....	....	....	....	....	....	....
2004-05	Mississippi	ECHL	21	13	4	4	1298	56	2	2.59	4	1	3	227	16	0	4.23
2005-06	Calgary	NHL	8	3	3	0	402	22	0	3.28	....	....	....	....	....	....	....
	Phoenix	NHL	5	0	4	0	187	17	0	5.45	....	....	....	....	....	....	....
	NHL Totals		30	10	14	3	1575	89	0	3.39	....	....	....	....	....	....	....

Canadian Major Junior Humanitarian Player of the Year (1999)

Signed as a free agent by **Mississippi** (ECHL), January 27, 2005. Traded to **Calgary** by **Colorado** for future considerations, August 9, 2005. Traded to **Phoenix** by **Calgary** with Steve Reinprecht for Brian Boucher and Mike Leclerc, February 2, 2006.

SCHAEFER, Nolan (SHAY-fuhr, NOH-luhn) S.J.

Goaltender. Catches right. 6'2", 200 lbs. Born, Yellow Grass, Sask., January 15, 1980.
(San Jose's 4th choice, 166th overall, in 2000 Entry Draft).

			Regular Season								Playoffs						
Season	Club	League	GP	W	L	O/T	Mins	GA	SO	Avg	GP	W	L	Mins	GA	SO	Avg
1996-97	Yorkton Mallers	SMHL	36	....	....	....	1854	132	0	4.27	....	....	....	....	....	....	....
1997-98	Yorkton Mallers	SMHL	5	....	....	....	239	17	0	4.25	....	....	....	....	....	....	....
	Nipawin Hawks	SJHL	21	12	4	3	1080	42	*3	*2.33	....	....	....	....	....	....	....
1998-99	Nipawin Hawks	SJHL	46	....	....	....	2478	165	0	3.60	....	....	....	....	....	....	....
99-2000	Providence College	H-East	14	6	5	1	778	42	0	3.24	....	....	....	....	....	....	....
2000-01	Providence College	H-East	25	15	8	2	1529	63	3	2.47	....	....	....	....	....	....	....
2001-02	Providence College	H-East	*35	11	18	5	*2062	113	0	3.29	....	....	....	....	....	....	....
2002-03	Providence College	H-East	25	13	8	2	1440	71	0	2.96	....	....	....	....	....	....	....
2003-04	Cleveland Barons	AHL	27	14	9	3	1592	62	2	2.34	9	4	5	573	24	0	2.51
	Fresno Falcons	ECHL	12	5	5	0	654	34	1	3.12	....	....	....	....	....	....	....
2004-05	Cleveland Barons	AHL	43	17	23	1	2418	110	3	2.73	....	....	....	....	....	....	....
2005-06	San Jose	NHL	7	5	1	0	352	11	1	1.88	....	....	....	....	....	....	....
	Cleveland Barons	AHL	36	12	21	2	2058	118	2	3.44	....	....	....	....	....	....	....
	NHL Totals		7	5	1	0	352	11	1	1.88	....	....	....	....	....	....	....

Hockey East Second All-Star Team (2001) • NCAA East Second All-American Team (2001)

SCHNEIDER, Cory (SHNIGH-duhr), KOHR-ee) VAN.

Goaltender. Catches left. 6'2", 195 lbs. Born, Salem, MA, March 18, 1986.
(Vancouver's 1st choice, 26th overall, in 2004 Entry Draft).

			Regular Season								Playoffs						
Season	Club	League	GP	W	L	O/T	Mins	GA	SO	Avg	GP	W	L	Mins	GA	SO	Avg
2002-03	Andover	High-MA	23	13	7	2	1385	39	3	1.69	....	....	....	....	....	....	....
2003-04	Andover	High-MA	24	17	5	2	1336	32	6	1.42	....	....	....	....	....	....	....
	USNTDP	U-18	10	9	1	0	559	15	1	1.61	....	....	....	....	....	....	....
	USNTDP	NAHL	2	2	0	0	120	6	0	3.00	....	....	....	....	....	....	....
2004-05	Boston College	H-East	18	13	1	4	1102	35	1	1.90	....	....	....	....	....	....	....
2005-06	Boston College	H-East	*39	*24	13	2	*2362	83	*8	2.11	....	....	....	....	....	....	....

Hockey East All-Rookie Team (2005) (co-winners - Kevin Regan and Peter Vetri) • Hockey East Second All-Star Team (2006) • NCAA East First All-American Team (2006)

SCHWARZ, Marek (SHWAHRTS, MAIR-ehk) ST.L.

Goaltender. Catches right. 5'11", 176 lbs. Born, Mlada Boleslav, Czech., April 1, 1986.
(St. Louis' 1st choice, 17th overall, in 2004 Entry Draft).

			Regular Season								Playoffs						
Season	Club	League	GP	W	L	O/T	Mins	GA	SO	Avg	GP	W	L	Mins	GA	SO	Avg
2000-01	Ml. Boleslav Jr.	CzRep-Jr.	45	....	....	....	1969	154	0	4.69	....	....	....	....	....	....	....
2001-02	Sparta Jr.	CzRep-Jr.	46	....	....	....	2692	86	9	1.92	6	....	....	368	16	0	2.61
2002-03	Sparta Jr.	CzRep-Jr.	34	....	....	....	1778	57	3	1.92	2	....	....	120	5	0	2.50
	HC Sparta Praha	CzRep	1	....	....	....	1	0	0	0.00	....	....	....	....	....	....	....
2003-04	Sparta Jr.	CzRep-Jr.	7	....	....	....	352	14	2	2.39	....	....	....	....	....	....	....
	Plzen	CzRep	10	....	....	....	603	33	0	3.28	....	....	....	....	....	....	....
	HC Sparta Praha	CzRep	8	....	....	....	335	20	0	3.58	....	....	....	....	....	....	....
	HC Ocelari Trinec	CzRep	5	....	....	....	280	12	0	2.57	....	....	....	....	....	....	....
	BK Mlada Boleslav	CzRep-2	1	....	....	....	63	6	0	5.71	....	....	....	....	....	....	....
2004-05	Vancouver Giants	WHL	56	26	24	4	3304	147	2	2.67	6	2	4	378	18	0	2.86
2005-06	Sparta Jr.	CzRep-Jr.	3	....	....	....	178	5	0	1.69	....	....	....	....	....	....	....
	HC Sparta Praha	CzRep	15	....	....	....	746	32	1	2.57	1	....	....	1	0	0	0.00
	Beroun	CzRep-2	4	....	....	....	229	17	0	4.45	....	....	....	....	....	....	....

SCOTT, Travis (SKAWT, TRA-vihs)

Goaltender. Catches left. 6'2", 185 lbs. Born, Kanata, Ont., September 14, 1975.

			Regular Season								Playoffs						
Season	Club	League	GP	W	L	O/T	Mins	GA	SO	Avg	GP	W	L	Mins	GA	SO	Avg
1991-92	Nepean Raiders	CJHL	19	14	5	0	1065	71	1	4.00	....	....	....	....	....	....	....
1992-93	Nepean Raiders	CJHL	36	19	10	2	1968	133	0	4.05	....	....	....	....	....	....	....
1993-94	Windsor Spitfires	OHL	45	20	18	0	2312	158	1	4.10	4	0	4	240	16	0	4.00
1994-95	Windsor Spitfires	OHL	48	26	14	3	2644	147	3	3.34	3	0	1	94	6	1	3.83
1995-96	Oshawa Generals	OHL	31	15	9	4	1763	78	3	2.65	5	1	4	315	23	0	4.38
1996-97	Baton Rouge	ECHL	10	5	2	1	501	22	0	2.63	....	....	....	....	....	....	....
	Worcester IceCats	AHL	29	14	10	1	1482	75	1	3.04	....	....	....	....	....	....	....
1997-98	Baton Rouge	ECHL	36	14	11	6	1949	96	1	2.96	....	....	....	....	....	....	....
1998-99	Mississippi	ECHL	44	22	12	5	2337	112	1	2.88	*18	*14	4	*1252	42	3	2.01
99-2000	Lowell	AHL	46	15	23	3	2595	126	3	2.91	1	0	1	60	2	0	2.01
2000-01	Los Angeles	NHL	1	0	0	0	25	3	0	7.20	....	....	....	....	....	....	....
	Lowell	AHL	34	16	15	1	1977	83	2	2.52	4	1	2	209	7	1	2.01
2001-02	Manchester	AHL	39	21	12	3	2170	83	6	2.30	5	2	3	327	15	0	2.75
2002-03	Manchester	AHL	50	23	19	5	2829	116	4	2.46	3	0	2	148	9	0	3.65
2003-04	San Antonio	AHL	*64	26	31	6	3747	156	4	2.50	....	....	....	....	....	....	....
2004-05	San Antonio	AHL	59	18	28	4	3211	126	3	2.35	....	....	....	....	....	....	....
2005-06	Magnitogorsk	Russia	43	....	....	....	2563	52	*11	*1.22	11	....	....	683	21	2	1.84
	NHL Totals		1	0	0	0	25	3	0	7.20	....	....	....	....	....	....	....

ECHL Playoff MVP (1999)

Signed as a free agent by **St. Louis**, December 30, 1996. Signed as a free agent by **Los Angeles**, February 18, 2000. Signed as a free agent by **Florida**, August 12, 2003.

SHANTZ, David (SHAWNTS, DAY-vihd) FLA.

Goaltender. Catches left. 6'1", 202 lbs. Born, Burlington, Ont., May 5, 1986.
(Florida's 2nd choice, 37th overall, in 2004 Entry Draft).

			Regular Season								Playoffs						
Season	Club	League	GP	W	L	O/T	Mins	GA	SO	Avg	GP	W	L	Mins	GA	SO	Avg
2002-03	Thorold	OJHL-B	36	30	3	3	2107	63	8	1.79	....	....	....	....	....	....	....
2003-04	Mississauga	OHL	43	21	18	3	2483	120	1	2.90	*24	12	12	*1449	49	*5	2.03
2004-05	Mississauga	OHL	27	10	11	3	1524	72	0	2.83	2	0	1	80	2	0	1.50
2005-06	Peterborough	OHL	49	31	14	0	2946	141	2	2.87	*19	*16	3	*1239	54	1	2.62

OHL All-Rookie Team (2004) • Canadian Major Junior All-Rookie Team (2004)

SHIELDS, Steve (SHEELDS, STEEV)

Goaltender. Catches left. 6'3", 215 lbs. Born, Toronto, Ont., July 19, 1972.
(Buffalo's 5th choice, 101st overall, in 1991 Entry Draft).

			Regular Season								Playoffs						
Season	Club	League	GP	W	L	O/T	Mins	GA	SO	Avg	GP	W	L	Mins	GA	SO	Avg
1989-90	St. Mary's Lincolns	OJHL-B	26	....	....	....	1512	121	0	4.80	....	....	....	....	....	....	....
1990-91	U. of Michigan	CCHA	37	26	6	3	1963	106	0	3.24	....	....	....	....	....	....	....
1991-92	U. of Michigan	CCHA	*37	*27	7	2	*2090	99	1	2.84	....	....	....	....	....	....	....
1992-93	U. of Michigan	CCHA	*39	*30	6	2	2027	75	2	*2.22	....	....	....	....	....	....	....
1993-94	U. of Michigan	CCHA	36	*28	6	1	1961	87	0	2.66	....	....	....	....	....	....	....
1994-95	Rochester	AHL	13	3	8	0	673	53	0	4.72	1	0	0	20	3	0	9.00
	South Carolina	ECHL	21	11	5	2	1158	52	2	2.69	3	0	2	144	11	0	4.58
1995-96	Buffalo	NHL	2	1	0	0	75	4	0	3.20	....	....	....	....	....	....	....
	Rochester	AHL	43	20	17	2	2357	140	1	3.56	*19	*15	3	*1127	47	1	2.50
1996-97	Buffalo	NHL	13	3	8	2	789	39	0	2.97	10	4	6	570	26	1	2.74
	Rochester	AHL	23	14	6	2	1331	60	1	2.70	....	....	....	....	....	....	....
1997-98	Buffalo	NHL	16	3	6	4	785	37	0	2.83	....	....	....	....	....	....	....
	Rochester	AHL	1	0	1	0	59	3	0	3.04	....	....	....	....	....	....	....
1998-99	San Jose	NHL	37	15	11	8	2162	80	4	2.22	1	0	1	60	6	0	6.00
99-2000	San Jose	NHL	67	27	30	8	3797	162	4	2.56	12	5	7	696	36	0	3.10
2000-01	San Jose	NHL	21	6	8	5	1135	47	2	2.48	....	....	....	....	....	....	....
2001-02	Anaheim	NHL	33	9	20	2	1777	79	0	2.67	....	....	....	....	....	....	....
2002-03	Boston	NHL	36	12	13	9	2112	97	0	2.76	2	0	2	119	6	0	3.03
2003-04	Florida	NHL	16	3	6	1	732	42	0	3.44	....	....	....	....	....	....	....
2004-05	DID NOT PLAY																
2005-06	Atlanta	NHL	5	1	2	1	266	19	0	4.29	....	....	....	....	....	....	....
	Chicago Wolves	AHL	4	2	2	0	240	9	0	2.25	....	....	....	....	....	....	....
	NHL Totals		246	80	104	40	13630	606	10	2.67	25	9	16	1445	74	1	3.07

CCHA First All-Star Team (1993, 1994) • NCAA West Second All-American Team (1993, 1994)

Traded to **San Jose** by **Buffalo** with Buffalo's 4th round choice (Miroslav Zalesak) in 1998 Entry Draft for Kay Whitmore, Colorado's 2nd round choice (previously acquired, Buffalo selected Jaroslav Kristek) in 1998 Entry Draft and San Jose's 5th round choice (later traded to Columbus – Columbus selected Tyler Kolarik) in 2000 Entry Draft, June 18, 1998. Traded to **Anaheim** by **San Jose** with Jeff Friesen and San Jose's 2nd round choice (later traded to Dallas – Dallas selected Vojtech Polak) in 2003 Entry Draft for Teemu Selanne, March 5, 2001. Traded to **Boston** by **Anaheim** for Boston's 3rd round choice (Shane Hynes) in 2003 Entry Draft, June 25, 2002. Traded to **Florida** by **Boston** for future considerations, October 5, 2003. Signed as a free agent by **Atlanta**, October 27, 2005.

SIDIKOV, Rustam (SIH-dih-kawf, ROOS-tuhm) NSH.

Goaltender. Catches left. 6', 158 lbs. Born, Moscow, USSR, July 5, 1985.
(Nashville's 10th choice, 133rd overall, in 2003 Entry Draft).

			Regular Season								Playoffs						
Season	Club	League	GP	W	L	O/T	Mins	GA	SO	Avg	GP	W	L	Mins	GA	SO	Avg
2000-01	CSKA Moscow 2	Russia-3	23	....	....	....	1204	50	....	2.50	....	....	....	103	4	0	2.33
2001-02	CSKA Moscow 2	Russia-3	1	....	....	....	60	5	0	5.00	....	....	....	....	....	....	....
2002-03	CSKA Moscow 2	Russia-3	2	....	....	....	120	2	0	1.00	....	....	....	....	....	....	....
2003-04	CSKA Moscow 2	Russia-3	STATISTICS NOT AVAILABLE														
2004-05	CSKA Moscow 2	Russia-3	STATISTICS NOT AVAILABLE														
2005-06	DID NOT PLAY																

SIGALET, Jordan (SIH-ga-leht, JOHR-duhn) BOS.

Goaltender. Catches left. 6'1", 170 lbs. Born, New Westminster, B.C., February 19, 1981.
(Boston's 6th choice, 209th overall, in 2001 Entry Draft).

			Regular Season								Playoffs						
Season	Club	League	GP	W	L	O/T	Mins	GA	SO	Avg	GP	W	L	Mins	GA	SO	Avg
99-2000	Victoria Salsa	BCHL	33	....	....	....	1980	108	0	3.28	....	....	....	....	....	....	....
2000-01	Victoria Salsa	BCHL	48	23	22	0	2820	142	0	3.03	18	12	5	1060	143	0	2.62
2001-02	Bowling Green	CCHA	13	2	6	2	657	38	0	3.47	....	....	....	....	....	....	....
2002-03	Bowling Green	CCHA	20	6	11	2	1208	66	1	3.28	....	....	....	....	....	....	....
2003-04	Bowling Green	CCHA	37	10	17	9	2210	101	2	2.74	....	....	....	....	....	....	....
2004-05	Bowling Green	CCHA	32	16	12	3	1849	89	1	2.89	....	....	....	....	....	....	....
2005-06	Boston	NHL	1	0	0	0	1	0	0	0.00	....	....	....	....	....	....	....
	Providence Bruins	AHL	37	19	11	2	1955	83	1	2.55	3	0	2	159	10	0	3.77
	NHL Totals		1	0	0	0	1	0	0	0.00	....	....	....	....	....	....	....

CCHA First All-Star Team (2004) • CCHA Second All-Star Team (2005)

SMITH, Jason (SMIHTH, JAY-suhn) N.J.

Goaltender. Catches left. 6'1", 170 lbs. Born, St-Lambert, Que., July 17, 1985.
(New Jersey's 5th choice, 197th overall, in 2003 Entry Draft).

			Regular Season								Playoffs						
Season	Club	League	GP	W	L	O/T	Mins	GA	SO	Avg	GP	W	L	Mins	GA	SO	Avg
2002-03	Lennoxville	QJHL	29	22	4	1	1622	62	3	2.29	14	11	3	816	34	1	2.52
2003-04	Sacred Heart	AH	5	1	4	0	302	19	0	3.78	....	....	....	....	....	....	....
2004-05	Sacred Heart	AH	8	3	5	0	493	31	0	3.77	....	....	....	....	....	....	....
2005-06	Sacred Heart	AH	30	18	11	1	1793	67	1	*2.24	....	....	....	....	....	....	....

SMITH, Mike (SMIHTH, MIGHK) DAL.

Goaltender. Catches left. 6'3", 189 lbs. Born, Kingston, Ont., March 22, 1982.
(Dallas' 5th choice, 161st overall, in 2001 Entry Draft).

			Regular Season								Playoffs						
Season	Club	League	GP	W	L	O/T	Mins	GA	SO	Avg	GP	W	L	Mins	GA	SO	Avg
1998-99	Kingston	OPJHL	16	....	....	....	906	53	0	3.51	....	....	....	....	....	....	....
99-2000	Kingston	OHL	15	4	5	0	666	42	0	3.78	....	....	....	....	....	....	....

2000-01	Kingston	OHL	3	0	0	2	136	8	0	3.53	....	....	....	....	....	....	....
	Sudbury Wolves	OHL	43	22	13	7	2571	108	3	2.52	12	7	5	735	26	2	*2.12
2001-02	Sudbury Wolves	OHL	53	19	28	5	3082	157	3	3.06	5	1	4	302	15	0	2.98
2002-03	Utah Grizzlies	AHL	11	5	5	0	614	33	0	3.23	....	....	....	....	....	....	....
	Lexington	ECHL	27	11	10	4	1553	66	1	2.55	2	0	1	93	8	0	5.14
2003-04	Utah Grizzlies	AHL	21	8	11	0	1186	56	2	2.83	....	....	....	....	....	....	....
2004-05	Houston Aeros	AHL	45	19	17	3	2408	97	5	2.42	3	1	2	181	4	0	1.33
2005-06	Iowa Stars	AHL	50	25	19	6	2998	125	3	2.50	7	3	4	417	19	0	2.74

Signed as a free agent by **Dallas**, July 4, 2006.

SNOW, Garth (SNOH, GAHRTH)

Goaltender. Catches left. 6'3", 200 lbs. Born, Wrentham, MA, July 28, 1969.
(Quebec's 6th choice, 114th overall, in 1987 Entry Draft).

			Regular Season								Playoffs						
Season	**Club**	**League**	**GP**	**W**	**L**	**O/T**	**Mins**	**GA**	**SO**	**Avg**	**GP**	**W**	**L**	**Mins**	**GA**	**SO**	**Avg**
1986-87	Mount St. Charles	High-RI	30	....	....	....	1795	53	10	1.77	....	....	....	....	....	....	....
1987-88	Stratford Cullitons	OHA-B	30	20	6	0	1642	93	2	3.40	....	....	....	....	....	....	....
1988-89	University of Maine	H-East	5	2	2	0	241	14	1	3.49	....	....	....	....	....	....	....
1989-90	University of Maine	H-East	DID NOT PLAY – ACADEMICALLY INELIGIBLE														
1990-91	University of Maine	H-East	25	*18	4	0	1290	64	2	2.98	....	....	....	....	....	....	....
1991-92	University of Maine	H-East	31	*25	4	2	1792	73	*2	*2.44	....	....	....	....	....	....	....
1992-93	University of Maine	H-East	23	*21	0	1	1210	42	1	*2.08	....	....	....	....	....	....	....
1993-94	United States	Nat-Tm	23	13	5	3	1324	71	1	3.22	....	....	....	....	....	....	....
	United States	Olympics	5	1	3	1	299	17	0	3.41	....	....	....	....	....	....	....
	Quebec	**NHL**	**5**	**3**	**2**	**0**	**279**	**16**	**0**	**3.44**	....	....	....	....	....	....	....
	Cornwall Aces	AHL	16	6	5	3	927	51	0	3.30	13	8	5	790	42	0	3.19
1994-95	Cornwall Aces	AHL	*62	*32	20	7	*3558	162	3	2.73	8	4	3	402	14	*2	*2.09
	Quebec	**NHL**	**2**	**1**	**1**	**0**	**119**	**11**	**0**	**5.55**	**1**	**0**	**0**	**9**	**1**	**0**	**6.67**
1995-96	**Philadelphia**	**NHL**	**26**	**12**	**8**	**4**	**1437**	**69**	**0**	**2.88**	**1**	**0**	**0**	**1**	**0**	**0**	**0.00**
1996-97	**Philadelphia**	**NHL**	**35**	**14**	**8**	**8**	**1884**	**79**	**2**	**2.52**	**12**	**8**	**4**	**699**	**33**	**0**	**2.83**
1997-98	**Philadelphia**	**NHL**	**29**	**14**	**9**	**4**	**1651**	**67**	**1**	**2.43**	....	....	....	....	....	....	....
	Vancouver	**NHL**	**12**	**3**	**6**	**0**	**504**	**26**	**0**	**3.10**	....	....	....	....	....	....	....
1998-99	**Vancouver**	**NHL**	**65**	**20**	**31**	**8**	**3501**	**171**	**6**	**2.93**	....	....	....	....	....	....	....
99-2000	**Vancouver**	**NHL**	**32**	**10**	**15**	**3**	**1712**	**76**	**0**	**2.66**	....	....	....	....	....	....	....
2000-01	**Pittsburgh**	**NHL**	**35**	**14**	**15**	**4**	**2032**	**101**	**3**	**2.98**	....	....	....	....	....	....	....
	Wilkes-Barre	AHL	3	2	1	0	178	7	0	2.36	....	....	....	....	....	....	....
2001-02	**NY Islanders**	**NHL**	**25**	**10**	**7**	**2**	**1217**	**55**	**2**	**2.71**	**1**	**0**	**0**	**26**	**2**	**0**	**4.62**
2002-03	**NY Islanders**	**NHL**	**43**	**16**	**17**	**5**	**2390**	**92**	**1**	**2.31**	**5**	**1**	**4**	**305**	**12**	**1**	**2.36**
2003-04	**NY Islanders**	**NHL**	**39**	**14**	**15**	**5**	**2015**	**94**	**1**	**2.80**	....	....	....	....	....	....	....
2004-05	SKA St. Petersburg	Russia	16	....	....	....	893	41	1	2.75	....	....	....	....	....	....	....
2005-06	**NY Islanders**	**NHL**	**20**	**4**	**13**	**1**	**1096**	**68**	**0**	**3.72**	....	....	....	....	....	....	....
	Bridgeport	AHL	1	1	0	0	60	1	0	1.00	....	....	....	....	....	....	....
	NHL Totals		**368**	**135**	**147**	**44**	**19837**	**925**	**16**	**2.80**	**20**	**9**	**8**	**1040**	**48**	**1**	**2.77**

Hockey East Second All-Star Team (1992, 1993) • NCAA Championship All-Tournament Team (1993)

Transferred to **Colorado** after **Quebec** franchise relocated, June 21, 1995. Traded to **Philadelphia** by **Colorado** for Philadelphia's 3rd (later traded to Washington – Washington selected Shawn McNeil) and 6th (Kai Fischer) round choices in 1996 Entry Draft, July 12, 1995. Traded to **Vancouver** by **Philadelphia** for Sean Burke, March 4, 1998. Signed as a free agent by **Pittsburgh**, October 10, 2000. Signed as a free agent by **NY Islanders**, July 14, 2001. Signed as a free agent by **St. Petersburg** (Russia), August 17, 2004. • Officially announced his retirement and named General Manager by the New York Islanders, July 18, 2006.

SPRATT, James (SPRAT, JAYMZ) CGY.

Goaltender. Catches left. 6'1", 194 lbs. Born, Detroit, MI, November 10, 1985.
(Calgary's 9th choice, 213th overall, in 2004 Entry Draft).

			Regular Season								Playoffs						
Season	**Club**	**League**	**GP**	**W**	**L**	**O/T**	**Mins**	**GA**	**SO**	**Avg**	**GP**	**W**	**L**	**Mins**	**GA**	**SO**	**Avg**
2002-03	Sioux City	USHL	18	6	6	2	905	49	0	3.25	....	....	....	....	....	....	....
2003-04	Sioux City	USHL	34	19	6	5	1922	75	3	2.34	7	4	3	468	19	0	2.44
2004-05	Sioux City	USHL	42	24	11	3	2328	109	2	2.81	*13	*8	5	*752	32	*1	2.55
2005-06	Bowling Green	CCHA	16	4	10	1	923	67	0	4.36	....	....	....	....	....	....	....

STALOCK, Alex (STAY-lahk, AL-ehx) S.J.

Goaltender. Catches left. 5'11", 170 lbs. Born, St. Paul, MN, July 28, 1987.
(San Jose's 3rd choice, 112th overall, in 2005 Entry Draft).

			Regular Season								Playoffs						
Season	**Club**	**League**	**GP**	**W**	**L**	**O/T**	**Mins**	**GA**	**SO**	**Avg**	**GP**	**W**	**L**	**Mins**	**GA**	**SO**	**Avg**
2003-04	South St. Paul	High-MN	31	23	7	1	....	....	....	2.20	....	....	....	....	....	....	....
2004-05	Cedar Rapids	USHL	32	19	9	3	1801	82	1	2.73	9	7	2	582	14	*1	*1.44
2005-06	Cedar Rapids	USHL	44	*28	13	3	2641	112	4	2.54	8	3	5	472	25	0	3.18

USHL Playoff MVP (2005) • USHL First All-Star Team (2006)

Signed Letter of Intent to attend **U. of Minnesota-Duluth** (WCHA) in fall of 2006.

STANA, Rastislav (STAN-ah, RAH-tih-slahv) WSH.

Goaltender. Catches left. 6'2", 184 lbs. Born, Kosice, Czech., January 10, 1980.
(Washington's 8th choice, 193rd overall, in 1998 Entry Draft).

			Regular Season								Playoffs						
Season	**Club**	**League**	**GP**	**W**	**L**	**O/T**	**Mins**	**GA**	**SO**	**Avg**	**GP**	**W**	**L**	**Mins**	**GA**	**SO**	**Avg**
1997-98	HC Kosice Jr.	Slovak-Jr.	32	....	....	....	1920	56	2	1.75	....	....	....	....	....	....	....
1998-99	Moose Jaw	WHL	36	21	14	1	2131	123	2	3.46	9	4	5	544	30	0	3.31
99-2000	Moose Jaw	WHL	14	4	9	0	730	48	0	3.95	....	....	....	....	....	....	....
	Calgary Hitmen	WHL	16	13	2	1	971	37	1	2.29	9	7	2	526	21	1	2.40
2000-01	Richmond	ECHL	38	15	16	2	2111	90	1	2.56	3	1	2	178	7	1	2.34
2001-02	Richmond	ECHL	36	20	12	3	2098	95	1	2.72	....	....	....	....	....	....	....
	Portland Pirates	AHL	3	1	2	0	180	11	0	3.66	....	....	....	....	....	....	....
	Slovakia	Olympics	1	1	0	0	60	1	0	1.00	....	....	....	....	....	....	....
2002-03	Portland Pirates	AHL	24	8	11	4	1355	49	2	2.17	1	0	1	59	3	0	3.08
2003-04	**Washington**	**NHL**	**6**	**1**	**2**	**0**	**211**	**11**	**0**	**3.13**	....	....	....	....	....	....	....
	Portland Pirates	AHL	24	14	5	4	1429	40	5	1.68	3	1	2	139	7	0	3.02
2004-05	Sodertalje SK	Sweden	45	....	....	....	2562	116	3	2.72	10	....	....	605	22	1	2.18
2005-06	Sodertalje SK	Sweden	43	....	....	....	2554	129	3	3.03	....	....	....	....	....	....	....
	Sodertalje SK	Sweden-Q	9	....	....	....	548	21	2	2.30	....	....	....	....	....	....	....
	NHL Totals		**6**	**1**	**2**	**0**	**211**	**11**	**0**	**3.13**	....	....	....	....	....	....	....

Signed as a free agent by **Sodertalje** (Sweden), May 26, 2004.

STEPHAN, Tobias (STEH-fan, toh-BEE-uhs) DAL.

Goaltender. Catches left. 6'3", 178 lbs. Born, Zurich, Switz., January 21, 1984.
(Dallas' 3rd choice, 34th overall, in 2002 Entry Draft).

			Regular Season								Playoffs						
Season	**Club**	**League**	**GP**	**W**	**L**	**O/T**	**Mins**	**GA**	**SO**	**Avg**	**GP**	**W**	**L**	**Mins**	**GA**	**SO**	**Avg**
2000-01	Kloten Flyers Jr.	Swiss-Jr.	STATISTICS NOT AVAILABLE														
2001-02	EHC Chur	Swiss	23	....	....	....	1396	80	0	3.44	10	....	....	604	39	0	3.87
2002-03	Kloten Flyers	Swiss	*44	....	....	....	2670	125	2	2.81	5	....	....	292	20	0	4.11
2003-04	Kloten Flyers	Swiss	26	....	....	....	1547	61	5	2.37	....	....	....	....	....	....	....
2004-05	Kloten Flyers	Swiss	*44	....	....	....	2580	123	4	2.86	5	....	....	301	11	0	2.19
2005-06	Kloten Flyers	Swiss	*44	16	19	8	2663	125	*5	2.82	11	5	6	683	34	0	2.98

TAYLOR, Daniel (TAY-luhr, DAN-yehl) L.A.

Goaltender. Catches left. 5'11", 179 lbs. Born, Plymouth, England, April 28, 1986.
(Los Angeles' 8th choice, 221st overall, in 2004 Entry Draft).

			Regular Season								Playoffs						
Season	**Club**	**League**	**GP**	**W**	**L**	**O/T**	**Mins**	**GA**	**SO**	**Avg**	**GP**	**W**	**L**	**Mins**	**GA**	**SO**	**Avg**
2002-03	Cumberland Grads	CJHL	23	13	3	1	1009	41	1	2.44	6	3	3	432	17	0	2.36
2003-04	Guelph Storm	OHL	26	16	4	3	1462	66	0	2.71	3	1	1	159	9	0	3.40
2004-05	Guelph Storm	OHL	31	13	14	3	1821	80	2	2.64	1	0	1	59	4	0	4.07
2005-06	Kingston	OHL	57	32	15	6	3319	172	3	3.11	....	....	....	....	....	....	....

TELLQVIST, Mikael (TEHL-kvihst, MIGH-kuhl) TOR.

Goaltender. Catches left. 5'11", 185 lbs. Born, Sundbyberg, Sweden, September 19, 1979.
(Toronto's 3rd choice, 70th overall, in 2000 Entry Draft).

			Regular Season								Playoffs						
Season	**Club**	**League**	**GP**	**W**	**L**	**O/T**	**Mins**	**GA**	**SO**	**Avg**	**GP**	**W**	**L**	**Mins**	**GA**	**SO**	**Avg**
1997-98	Djurgarden Jr.	Swe-Jr.	23	....	....	....	1380	55	....	2.39	2	0	2	120	8	0	4.00
1998-99	Djurgarden	Sweden	3	1	2	0	124	8	0	3.87	4	....	....	240	11	0	2.75
	Djurgarden	EuroHL	3	2	1	0	180	8	....	2.33	....	....	....	....	....	....	....
99-2000	Huddinge IK	Sweden-2	11	4	7	0	660	33	....	3.30	....	....	....	....	....	....	....
	Djurgarden	Sweden	30	....	....	....	1909	66	2	*2.07	*13	....	....	*814	21	*3	*1.55
2000-01	Djurgarden	Sweden	43	....	....	....	2622	91	*5	*2.08	*16	....	....	*1006	45	*1	2.68
2001-02	St. John's	AHL	28	8	11	6	1521	79	0	3.12	1	1	0	15	0	0	0.00
	Sweden	Olympics	DID NOT PLAY – SPARE GOALTENDER														
2002-03	**Toronto**	**NHL**	**3**	**1**	**1**	**0**	**86**	**4**	**0**	**2.79**	....	....	....	....	....	....	....
	St. John's	AHL	47	17	25	3	2651	148	1	3.35	....	....	....	....	....	....	....
2003-04	**Toronto**	**NHL**	**11**	**5**	**3**	**2**	**647**	**31**	**0**	**2.87**	....	....	....	....	....	....	....
	St. John's	AHL	23	10	11	1	1343	59	1	2.64	....	....	....	....	....	....	....
2004-05	St. John's	AHL	45	24	16	4	2600	115	0	2.65	5	1	4	253	15	0	3.56
2005-06	**Toronto**	**NHL**	**25**	**10**	**11**	**2**	**1399**	**73**	**2**	**3.13**	....	....	....	....	....	....	....
	Sweden	Olympics	1	0	1	0	60	3	0	3.00	....	....	....	....	....	....	....
	NHL Totals		**39**	**16**	**15**	**4**	**2132**	**108**	**2**	**3.04**	....	....	....	....	....	....	....

THEODORE, Jose (TEE-uh-dohr, joh-SAY) COL.

Goaltender. Catches right. 5'11", 182 lbs. Born, Laval, Que., September 13, 1976.
(Montreal's 2nd choice, 44th overall, in 1994 Entry Draft).

			Regular Season								Playoffs						
Season	**Club**	**League**	**GP**	**W**	**L**	**O/T**	**Mins**	**GA**	**SO**	**Avg**	**GP**	**W**	**L**	**Mins**	**GA**	**SO**	**Avg**
1990-91	Richelieu	QAHA	42	....	....	....	2520	80	0	1.90	....	....	....	....	....	....	....
1991-92	Richelieu Riverains	QAAA	24	9	13	2	1440	96	0	3.99	5	2	3	295	26	0	5.28
1992-93	St-Jean Lynx	QMJHL	34	12	16	2	1776	112	0	3.78	3	0	2	175	11	0	3.77
1993-94	St-Jean Lynx	QMJHL	57	20	29	6	3225	194	0	3.61	5	1	4	296	18	0	3.65
1994-95	Hull Olympiques	QMJHL	*58	*32	22	2	*3348	193	5	3.46	*21	*15	6	*1263	59	*1	2.80
	Fredericton	AHL	....	....	....	....	....	....	....	....	1	0	1	60	3	0	3.00
1995-96	**Montreal**	**NHL**	**1**	**0**	**0**	**0**	**9**	**1**	**0**	**6.67**	....	....	....	....	....	....	....
	Hull Olympiques	QMJHL	48	33	11	2	2807	158	0	3.38	5	2	3	299	20	0	4.01
1996-97	**Montreal**	**NHL**	**16**	**5**	**6**	**2**	**821**	**53**	**0**	**3.87**	**2**	**1**	**1**	**168**	**7**	**0**	**2.50**
	Fredericton	AHL	26	12	12	0	1469	87	0	3.55	....	....	....	....	....	....	....
1997-98	Fredericton	AHL	53	20	23	8	3053	145	2	2.85	4	1	3	237	13	0	3.28
	Montreal	**NHL**	....	....	....	....	....	....	....	....	**3**	**0**	**1**	**120**	**1**	**0**	**0.50**
1998-99	**Montreal**	**NHL**	**18**	**4**	**12**	**0**	**913**	**50**	**1**	**3.29**	....	....	....	....	....	....	....
	Fredericton	AHL	27	12	13	2	1609	77	2	2.87	13	8	5	694	35	1	3.03
99-2000	**Montreal**	**NHL**	**30**	**12**	**13**	**2**	**1655**	**58**	**5**	**2.10**	....	....	....	....	....	....	....
2000-01	**Montreal**	**NHL**	**59**	**20**	**29**	**5**	**3298**	**141**	**2**	**2.57**	....	....	....	....	....	....	....
	Quebec Citadelles	AHL	3	3	0	0	180	9	0	3.00	....	....	....	....	....	....	....
2001-02	**Montreal**	**NHL**	**67**	**30**	**24**	**10**	**3864**	**136**	**7**	**2.11**	**12**	**6**	**6**	**686**	**35**	**0**	**3.06**
2002-03	**Montreal**	**NHL**	**57**	**20**	**31**	**6**	**3419**	**165**	**2**	**2.90**	....	....	....	....	....	....	....
2003-04	**Montreal**	**NHL**	**67**	**33**	**28**	**5**	**3961**	**150**	**6**	**2.27**	**11**	**4**	**7**	**678**	**27**	**1**	**2.39**
2004-05	Djurgarden	Sweden	17	....	....	....	1024	42	0	2.46	12	....	....	728	27	0	2.23
2005-06	**Montreal**	**NHL**	**38**	**17**	**15**	**5**	**2114**	**122**	**0**	**3.46**	....	....	....	....	....	....	....
	Colorado	**NHL**	**5**	**1**	**3**	**1**	**296**	**15**	**0**	**3.04**	**9**	**4**	**5**	**573**	**29**	**0**	**3.04**
	NHL Totals		**358**	**142**	**161**	**36**	**20350**	**891**	**23**	**2.63**	**37**	**15**	**20**	**2225**	**99**	**1**	**2.67**

QMJHL Second All-Star Team (1995, 1996) • NHL Second All-Star Team (2002) • MBNA Roger Crozier Saving Grace Award (2002) • Vezina Trophy (2002) • Hart Trophy (2002)

Played in NHL All-Star Game (2002, 2004)

• Scored a goal vs. NY Islanders, January 2, 2001. Signed as a free agent by **Djurgarden** (Sweden), December 20, 2004. Traded to **Colorado** by **Montreal** for David Aebischer, March 8, 2006.

THIBAULT, Jocelyn (TEE-boh, JAW-seh-lihn) PIT.

Goaltender. Catches left. 5'11", 169 lbs. Born, Montreal, Que., January 12, 1975.
(Quebec's 1st choice, 10th overall, in 1993 Entry Draft).

			Regular Season								Playoffs						
Season	**Club**	**League**	**GP**	**W**	**L**	**O/T**	**Mins**	**GA**	**SO**	**Avg**	**GP**	**W**	**L**	**Mins**	**GA**	**SO**	**Avg**
1990-91	Laval-Laurentides	QAAA	20	14	5	0	1178	78	1	3.94	5	2	3	300	20	0	4.00
1991-92	Trois-Rivieres	QMJHL	30	14	7	1	1496	77	0	3.09	3	1	1	110	4	0	2.19
1992-93	Sherbrooke	QMJHL	56	34	14	5	3190	159	3	2.99	15	9	6	882	57	0	3.87
1993-94	**Quebec**	**NHL**	**29**	**8**	**13**	**3**	**1504**	**83**	**0**	**3.31**	....	....	....	....	....	....	....
	Cornwall Aces	AHL	4	4	0	0	240	9	1	2.25	....	....	....	....	....	....	....
1994-95	Sherbrooke	QMJHL	13	6	6	1	776	38	1	2.94	....	....	....	....	....	....	....
	Quebec	**NHL**	**18**	**12**	**2**	**2**	**898**	**35**	**1**	**2.34**	**3**	**1**	**2**	**148**	**8**	**0**	**3.24**
1995-96	**Colorado**	**NHL**	**10**	**3**	**4**	**2**	**558**	**28**	**0**	**3.01**	....	....	....	....	....	....	....
	Montreal	**NHL**	**40**	**23**	**13**	**3**	**2334**	**110**	**3**	**2.83**	**6**	**2**	**4**	**311**	**18**	**0**	**3.47**
1996-97	**Montreal**	**NHL**	**61**	**22**	**24**	**11**	**3397**	**164**	**1**	**2.90**	**3**	**0**	**3**	**179**	**13**	**0**	**4.36**
1997-98	**Montreal**	**NHL**	**47**	**19**	**15**	**8**	**2652**	**109**	**2**	**2.47**	**2**	**0**	**0**	**43**	**4**	**0**	**5.58**
1998-99	**Montreal**	**NHL**	**10**	**3**	**4**	**2**	**529**	**23**	**1**	**2.61**	....	....	....	....	....	....	....
	Chicago	**NHL**	**52**	**21**	**26**	**5**	**3014**	**136**	**4**	**2.71**	....	....	....	....	....	....	....
99-2000	**Chicago**	**NHL**	**60**	**25**	**26**	**7**	**3438**	**158**	**3**	**2.76**	....	....	....	....	....	....	....
2000-01	**Chicago**	**NHL**	**66**	**27**	**32**	**7**	**3844**	**180**	**6**	**2.81**	....	....	....	....	....	....	....
2001-02	**Chicago**	**NHL**	**67**	**33**	**23**	**9**	**3838**	**159**	**6**	**2.49**	**3**	**1**	**2**	**159**	**7**	**0**	**2.64**
2002-03	**Chicago**	**NHL**	**62**	**26**	**28**	**7**	**3650**	**144**	**8**	**2.37**	....	....	....	....	....	....	....
2003-04	**Chicago**	**NHL**	**14**	**5**	**7**	**2**	**821**	**39**	**1**	**2.85**	....	....	....	....	....	....	....
2004-05			DID NOT PLAY														
2005-06	**Pittsburgh**	**NHL**	**16**	**1**	**9**	**3**	**807**	**60**	**0**	**4.46**	....	....	....	....	....	....	....
	NHL Totals		**552**	**228**	**226**	**71**	**31284**	**1428**	**36**	**2.74**	**17**	**4**	**11**	**840**	**50**	**0**	**3.57**

QMJHL All-Rookie Team (1992) • QMJHL First All-Star Team (1993) • QMJHL MVP (1993) • Canadian Major Junior First All-Star Team (1993) • Canadian Major Junior Goaltender of the Year (1993)

Played in NHL All-Star Game (2003)

Transferred to **Colorado** after **Quebec** franchise relocated, June 21, 1995. Traded to **Montreal** by **Colorado** with Andrei Kovalenko and Martin Rucinsky for Patrick Roy and Mike Keane, December 6, 1995. Traded to **Chicago** by **Montreal** with Dave Manson and Brad Brown for Jeff Hackett, Eric Weinrich, Alain Nasreddine and Tampa Bay's 4th round choice (previously acquired, Montreal selected Chris Dyment) in 1999 Entry Draft, November 16, 1998. • Missed majority of 2003-04 season recovering from hip injury suffered in practice, November 9, 2003. Traded to **Pittsburgh** by **Chicago** for Pittsburgh's 4th round choice (Ben Shutrion) in 2006 Entry Draft, August 10, 2005.

THOMAS, Tim (TAW-mas, TIHM) BOS.

Goaltender. Catches left. 5'11", 181 lbs. Born, Flint, MI, April 15, 1974.
(Quebec's 11th choice, 217th overall, in 1994 Entry Draft).

			Regular Season								Playoffs						
Season	**Club**	**League**	**GP**	**W**	**L**	**O/T**	**Mins**	**GA**	**SO**	**Avg**	**GP**	**W**	**L**	**Mins**	**GA**	**SO**	**Avg**
1992-93	Davison High	High-MI	27	....	....	....	1580	87	....	3.30	....	....	....	....	....	....	....
1993-94	U. of Vermont	ECAC	*33	15	12	6	1864	94	0	3.03	....	....	....	....	....	....	....
1994-95	U. of Vermont	ECAC	34	18	13	2	2010	90	*4	*2.69	....	....	....	....	....	....	....
1995-96	U. of Vermont	ECAC	37	*26	7	4	*2254	88	*3	*2.34	....	....	....	....	....	....	....
1996-97	U. of Vermont	ECAC	36	22	11	3	2158	101	2	2.81	....	....	....	....	....	....	....
1997-98	Birmingham Bulls	ECHL	6	4	1	1	360	13	1	2.17	....	....	....	....	....	....	....
	HIFK Helsinki	Finland	18	13	4	1	1034	28	2	1.62	9	9	0	551	14	3	1.52
	Houston Aeros	IHL	1	0	1	0	59	4	0	4.01	....	....	....	....	....	....	....
1998-99	HIFK Helsinki	Finland	14	8	3	3	833	31	2	2.23	11	7	4	658	25	0	2.28
	Hamilton Bulldogs	AHL	15	6	8	0	837	45	0	3.23	....	....	....	....	....	....	....
99-2000	Detroit Vipers	IHL	36	10	21	3	2020	120	1	3.56	....	....	....	....	....	....	....
2000-01	AIK Solna	Sweden	43	....	....	....	2542	105	3	2.48	5	....	....	299	20	0	4.01
2001-02	Karpat Oulu	Finland	32	15	12	5	1937	79	4	2.44	3	1	2	180	12	0	4.00
2002-03	**Boston**	**NHL**	**4**	**3**	**1**	**0**	**220**	**11**	**0**	**3.00**	....	....	....	....	....	....	....
	Providence Bruins	AHL	35	18	12	5	2049	98	1	2.87	....	....	....	....	....	....	....
2003-04	Providence Bruins	AHL	43	20	16	6	2544	78	9	1.84	2	0	2	84	10	0	7.13
2004-05	Jokerit Helsinki	Finland	54	34	13	7	3266	86	15	1.58	12	8	4	720	22	0	1.83
2005-06	**Boston**	**NHL**	**38**	**12**	**13**	**10**	**2187**	**101**	**1**	**2.77**	....	....	....	....	....	....	....
	Providence Bruins	AHL	26	15	11	0	1515	57	1	2.26	....	....	....	....	....	....	....
	NHL Totals		**42**	**15**	**14**	**10**	**2407**	**112**	**1**	**2.79**	....	....	....	....	....	....	....

ECAC First All-Star Team (1995, 1996) • ECAC Goaltender of the Year (1996) • NCAA East Second All-American Team (1995) • NCAA East First All-American Team (1996)

Signed as a free agent by **Edmonton**, June 4, 1998. Signed as a free agent by **Boston**, August 8, 2002. Signed as a free agent by **Jokerit Helsinki** (Finland), May 17, 2004. Signed as a free agent by **Boston**, September 14, 2005.

THOMPSON, Billy (TAWM-suhn, BIHL-lee) NYI

Goaltender. Catches left. 6'2", 200 lbs. Born, Saskatoon, Sask., September 24, 1982.
(Florida's 7th choice, 136th overall, in 2001 Entry Draft).

			Regular Season								Playoffs						
Season	**Club**	**League**	**GP**	**W**	**L**	**O/T**	**Mins**	**GA**	**SO**	**Avg**	**GP**	**W**	**L**	**Mins**	**GA**	**SO**	**Avg**
1997-98	Sask. Contacts	SMHL	23	14	5	3	1336	65	2	2.92	....	....	....	....	....	....	....
1998-99	Lebret Eagles	SJHL					STATISTICS NOT AVAILABLE										
99-2000	Estevan Bruins	SJHL	31	....	....	....	1763	132	1	4.49	5	1	3	328	17	0	3.11
	Prince George	WHL	1	0	1	0	60	5	0	5.00	....	....	....	....	....	....	....
2000-01	Prince George	WHL	57	24	24	3	3185	178	1	3.35	6	2	4	324	22	0	4.07
2001-02	Prince George	WHL	42	20	17	2	2375	108	2	2.73	7	3	4	402	21	0	3.13
2002-03	Prince George	WHL	50	20	26	0	2776	186	0	4.02	5	1	3	239	12	0	3.01
	Binghamton	AHL	1	1	0	0	60	5	0	5.00	....	....	....	....	....	....	....
2003-04	Binghamton	AHL	34	13	14	2	1725	83	2	2.89	....	....	....	....	....	....	....
2004-05	Binghamton	AHL	34	19	8	2	1869	76	1	2.44	....	....	....	....	....	....	....
2005-06	Binghamton	AHL	34	9	17	3	1812	125	0	4.14	....	....	....	....	....	....	....

WHL West Second All-Star Team (2003)

Traded to **Ottawa** by **Florida** with Greg Watson for Jani Hurme, October 1, 2002. Signed as a free agent by **NY Islanders**, July 25, 2006.

TOIVONEN, Hannu (TOI-voh-nuhn, HA-noo) BOS.

Goaltender. Catches left. 6'2", 200 lbs. Born, Kalvola, Finland, May 18, 1984.
(Boston's 1st choice, 29th overall, in 2002 Entry Draft).

			Regular Season								Playoffs						
Season	**Club**	**League**	**GP**	**W**	**L**	**O/T**	**Mins**	**GA**	**SO**	**Avg**	**GP**	**W**	**L**	**Mins**	**GA**	**SO**	**Avg**
2000-01	HPK U18	Fin-U18	....	....	....	....	....	....	....	....	....	....	....	....	....	....	....
2001-02	HPK U18	Fin-U18	5	4	1	0	277	14	0	3.03	....	....	....	....	....	....	....
	HPK Jr.	Fin-Jr.	31	15	12	4	1877	103	2	3.29	7	3	4	440	31	0	4.23
2002-03	HPK Jr.	Fin-Jr.	6	3	3	0	359	20	0	3.34	....	....	....	....	....	....	....
	HPK Hameenlinna	Finland	24	16	2	4	1432	54	2	2.26	2	1	1	117	3	1	1.53
2003-04	Providence Bruins	AHL	36	15	16	4	2162	83	2	2.30	0	0	0	0	0	0	0.00
2004-05	Providence Bruins	AHL	54	29	18	3	3017	103	7	2.05	17	10	7	1038	42	0	2.43
2005-06	**Boston**	**NHL**	**20**	**9**	**5**	**4**	**1163**	**51**	**1**	**2.63**	....	....	....	....	....	....	....
	NHL Totals		**20**	**9**	**5**	**4**	**1163**	**51**	**1**	**2.63**	....	....	....	....	....	....	....

TORDJMAN, Josh (TOHRJ-man, JAWSH) PHX.

Goaltender. Catches left. 6'1", 155 lbs. Born, Montreal, Que., January 11, 1985.

			Regular Season								Playoffs						
Season	**Club**	**League**	**GP**	**W**	**L**	**O/T**	**Mins**	**GA**	**SO**	**Avg**	**GP**	**W**	**L**	**Mins**	**GA**	**SO**	**Avg**
2002-03	Victoriaville Tigres	QMJHL	10	4	3	0	432	24	1	3.33	2	0	1	112	12	0	6.46
2003-04	Victoriaville Tigres	QMJHL	42	10	24	4	2177	143	2	3.94	....	....	....	....	....	....	....
2004-05	Victoriaville Tigres	QMJHL	56	22	28	4	3185	171	5	3.22	7	3	4	435	24	0	3.31
2005-06	Victoriaville Tigres	QMJHL	31	13	17	0	1792	106	2	3.55	....	....	....	....	....	....	....
	Moncton Wildcats	QMJHL	25	18	6	0	1427	55	2	*2.31	21	*15	5	1238	48	*2	2.33

Signed as a free agent by **Phoenix**, July 2, 2006.

TOSKALA, Vesa (TAWS-kah-lah, VEH-sa) S.J.

Goaltender. Catches left. 5'10", 190 lbs. Born, Tampere, Finland, May 20, 1977.
(San Jose's 4th choice, 90th overall, in 1995 Entry Draft).

			Regular Season								Playoffs						
Season	**Club**	**League**	**GP**	**W**	**L**	**O/T**	**Mins**	**GA**	**SO**	**Avg**	**GP**	**W**	**L**	**Mins**	**GA**	**SO**	**Avg**
1994-95	Ilves Tampere Jr.	Fin-Jr.	17	10	5	1	956	36	2	2.26	7	....	....	393	22	....	3.36
1995-96	Ilves Tampere Jr.	Fin-Jr.	3	3	0	0	180	3	0	1.00	....	....	....	....	....	....	....
	KooVee Tampere	Finland-2	2	1	1	0	119	5	1	2.51	....	....	....	....	....	....	....
	Ilves Tampere	Finland	37	14	14	7	2072	109	1	3.16	2	0	2	78	11	0	8.46
1996-97	Ilves Tampere Jr.	Fin-Jr.	3	....	....	....	184	....	....	2.93	....	....	....	....	....	....	....
	Ilves Tampere	Finland	40	22	12	5	2270	108	0	2.85	8	3	5	479	29	0	3.63
1997-98	Ilves Tampere Jr.	Fin-Jr.	2	2	0	0	120	4	0	2.00	....	....	....	....	....	....	....
	Ilves Tampere	Finland	43	26	13	3	2554	118	1	2.77	9	6	3	519	18	1	2.08
1998-99	Ilves Tampere	Finland	33	21	12	0	1966	70	5	2.14	4	1	3	248	14	0	3.39
99-2000	Farjestad	Sweden	44	....	....	....	2652	118	3	2.67	7	....	....	439	19	0	2.59
2000-01	Kentucky	AHL	44	22	13	5	2466	114	2	2.77	3	0	3	197	8	0	2.43
2001-02	**San Jose**	**NHL**	**1**	**0**	**0**	**0**	**10**	**0**	**0**	**0.00**	....	....	....	....	....	....	....
	Cleveland Barons	AHL	*62	19	33	7	*3574	178	3	2.99	....	....	....	....	....	....	....
2002-03	**San Jose**	**NHL**	**11**	**4**	**3**	**1**	**537**	**21**	**1**	**2.35**	....	....	....	....	....	....	....
	Cleveland Barons	AHL	49	15	30	2	2824	151	1	3.21	....	....	....	....	....	....	....
2003-04	**San Jose**	**NHL**	**28**	**12**	**8**	**4**	**1541**	**53**	**1**	**2.06**	....	....	....	....	....	....	....
2004-05	Ilves Tampere	Finland	3	0	1	2	186	8	0	2.58	6	3	3	357	19	0	3.19
2005-06	**San Jose**	**NHL**	**37**	**23**	**7**	**4**	**2039**	**87**	**2**	**2.56**	**11**	**6**	**5**	**686**	**28**	**1**	**2.45**
	Cleveland Barons	AHL	1	0	0	1	65	0	1	0.00	....	....	....	....	....	....	....
	NHL Totals		**77**	**39**	**18**	**9**	**4127**	**161**	**4**	**2.34**	**11**	**6**	**5**	**686**	**28**	**1**	**2.45**

Signed as a free agent by **Ilves Tampere** (Finland), January 31, 2005.

TURCO, Marty (TUHR-koh, MAHR-tee) DAL.

Goaltender. Catches left. 5'11", 183 lbs. Born, Sault Ste. Marie, Ont., August 13, 1975.
(Dallas' 4th choice, 124th overall, in 1994 Entry Draft).

			Regular Season								Playoffs						
Season	**Club**	**League**	**GP**	**W**	**L**	**O/T**	**Mins**	**GA**	**SO**	**Avg**	**GP**	**W**	**L**	**Mins**	**GA**	**SO**	**Avg**
1993-94	Cambridge	OJHL-B	34	19	10	3	1973	114	0	3.47	....	....	....	....	....	....	....
1994-95	U. of Michigan	CCHA	37	*27	7	1	2063	95	1	2.76	....	....	....	....	....	....	....
1995-96	U. of Michigan	CCHA	*42	*34	7	1	*2335	84	*5	*2.16	....	....	....	....	....	....	....
1996-97	U. of Michigan	CCHA	*41	*33	4	4	*2296	87	*4	*2.27	....	....	....	....	....	....	....
1997-98	U. of Michigan	CCHA	*45	*33	10	1	*2640	95	4	2.16	....	....	....	....	....	....	....
1998-99	Michigan K-Wings	IHL	54	24	17	10	3127	136	1	2.61	5	2	3	300	14	0	2.80
99-2000	Michigan K-Wings	IHL	60	23	27	*7	3399	139	*7	2.45	....	....	....	....	....	....	....
2000-01	**Dallas**	**NHL**	**26**	**13**	**6**	**1**	**1266**	**40**	**3**	***1.90**	....	....	....	....	....	....	....
2001-02	**Dallas**	**NHL**	**31**	**15**	**6**	**2**	**1519**	**53**	**2**	**2.09**	....	....	....	....	....	....	....
2002-03	**Dallas**	**NHL**	**55**	**31**	**10**	**10**	**3203**	**92**	**7**	***1.72**	**12**	**6**	**6**	**798**	**25**	**0**	**1.88**
2003-04	**Dallas**	**NHL**	**73**	**37**	**21**	**13**	**4359**	**144**	**9**	**1.98**	**5**	**1**	**4**	**325**	**18**	**0**	**3.32**
2004-05	Djurgarden	Sweden	6	....	....	....	356	12	1	2.02	....	....	....	....	....	....	....
2005-06	**Dallas**	**NHL**	**68**	**41**	**19**	**5**	**3910**	**166**	**3**	**2.55**	**5**	**1**	**4**	**319**	**18**	**0**	**3.39**
	Canada	Olympics					DID NOT PLAY – SPARE GOALTENDER										
	NHL Totals		**253**	**137**	**62**	**31**	**14257**	**495**	**24**	**2.08**	**22**	**8**	**14**	**1442**	**61**	**0**	**2.54**

CCHA Rookie of the Year (1995) • NCAA Championship All-Tournament Team (1996, 1998) • CCHA First All-Star Team (1997) • NCAA West First All-American Team (1997) • CCHA Second All-Star Team (1998) • NCAA Championship Tournament MVP (1998) • Garry F. Longman Memorial Trophy (Rookie of the Year – IHL) (1999) • MBNA Roger Crozier Saving Grace Award (2001, 2003) • NHL Second All-Star Team (2003)

Played in NHL All-Star Game (2003, 2004)

Signed as a free agent by **Djurgarden** (Sweden), November 13, 2004.

TURPLE, Dan (TUHR-puhl, DAN) ATL.

Goaltender. Catches left. 6'5", 220 lbs. Born, Oakville, Ont., January 1, 1985.
(Atlanta's 6th choice, 186th overall, in 2004 Entry Draft).

			Regular Season								Playoffs						
Season	**Club**	**League**	**GP**	**W**	**L**	**O/T**	**Mins**	**GA**	**SO**	**Avg**	**GP**	**W**	**L**	**Mins**	**GA**	**SO**	**Avg**
2002-03	Kingston	OHL	12	2	8	0	449	42	0	5.61	....	....	....	....	....	....	....
2003-04	Kingston	OHL	9	4	4	1	534	29	0	3.26	....	....	....	....	....	....	....
	Oshawa Generals	OHL	35	20	7	3	1843	81	2	2.64	7	3	4	443	19	1	2.57
2004-05	Oshawa Generals	OHL	10	4	4	0	469	29	0	3.71	....	....	....	....	....	....	....
	Kitchener Rangers	OHL	40	17	16	5	2335	92	3	2.36	3	0	2	162	9	0	3.33
2005-06	Kitchener Rangers	OHL	57	40	15	0	3306	124	*7	*2.25	5	1	3	326	20	0	3.68

OHL Second All-Star Team (2006)

UNDERHILL, Matt (UHN-duhr-hihl, MAT)

Goaltender. Catches left. 6'2", 195 lbs. Born, Merritt, B.C., September 16, 1979.
(Calgary's 8th choice, 170th overall, in 1999 Entry Draft).

			Regular Season								Playoffs						
Season	**Club**	**League**	**GP**	**W**	**L**	**O/T**	**Mins**	**GA**	**SO**	**Avg**	**GP**	**W**	**L**	**Mins**	**GA**	**SO**	**Avg**
1997-98	Notre Dame	SJHL	43	18	22	3	2573	132	2	3.07	....	....	....	....	....	....	....
1998-99	Cornell Big Red	ECAC	25	7	10	4	1320	65	1	2.95	....	....	....	....	....	....	....
99-2000	Cornell Big Red	ECAC	18	8	7	1	912	44	1	2.89	....	....	....	....	....	....	....
2000-01	Cornell Big Red	ECAC	25	13	8	3	1504	47	1	1.88	....	....	....	....	....	....	....
2001-02	Cornell Big Red	ECAC	21	14	6	1	1334	40	3	1.80	....	....	....	....	....	....	....
2002-03	Pee Dee Pride	ECHL	33	16	13	2	1878	88	0	2.81	....	....	....	....	....	....	....
	Providence Bruins	AHL	7	3	3	1	429	22	0	3.08	....	....	....	....	....	....	....
2003-04	Florence Pride	ECHL	29	10	14	4	1686	97	1	3.45	....	....	....	....	....	....	....
	Manchester	AHL	4	2	2	0	186	9	0	2.90	....	....	....	....	....	....	....
	Chicago	**NHL**	**1**	**0**	**1**	**0**	**61**	**4**	**0**	**3.93**	....	....	....	....	....	....	....
	Norfolk Admirals	AHL	1	0	0	0	20	0	0	0.00	....	....	....	....	....	....	....
2004-05	Mississippi	ECHL	24	13	8	3	1450	64	3	2.65	....	....	....	....	....	....	....
	St. John's	AHL	1	0	0	1	39	0	0	0.00	....	....	....	....	....	....	....
	Providence Bruins	AHL	5	1	2	1	244	12	1	2.95	....	....	....	....	....	....	....
	Alaska Aces	ECHL	3	3	0	0	180	6	0	2.00	3	1	1	145	8	0	3.31
2005-06	Alaska Aces	ECHL	50	*36	10	3	2980	113	*5	2.28	10	8	2	599	28	0	2.80
	NHL Totals		**1**	**0**	**1**	**0**	**61**	**4**	**0**	**3.93**	....	....	....	....	....	....	....

ECAC First All-Star Team (2002) • ECAC Goaltender of the Year (2002) • ECHL First All-Star Team (2006)

Signed as a free agent by **Pee Dee** (ECHL), August 13, 2002. Signed as a free agent by **Chicago**, March 4, 2004. Signed as a free agent by **Mississippi** (ECHL), November 3, 2004. Signed to a PTO (tryout) contract by **St. John's** (AHL), February 3, 2005. Signed to a PTO (tryout) contract by **Providence** (AHL), February 21, 2005. Traded to **Alaska** (ECHL) by **Mississippi** (ECHL) for Lance Mayes and future considerations, March 22, 2005.

VALENT, Michal (VAH-lehnt, MEE-khahl)

Goaltender. Catches left. 6'2", 176 lbs. Born, Martin, Czech., March 5, 1986.
(Buffalo's 4th choice, 145th overall, in 2004 Entry Draft).

			Regular Season								Playoffs						
Season	**Club**	**League**	**GP**	**W**	**L**	**O/T**	**Mins**	**GA**	**SO**	**Avg**	**GP**	**W**	**L**	**Mins**	**GA**	**SO**	**Avg**
2002-03	MHC Martin U18	Svk-U18	24	....	....	....	1343	48	3	2.14	....	....	....	....	....	....	....
2003-04	MHC Martin Jr.	Slovak-Jr.	38	....	....	....	2188	118	1	3.24	....	....	....	....	....	....	....
2004-05	Sparta Jr.	CzRep-Jr.	24	....	....	....	1293	43	3	2.00	7	....	....	420	15	1	2.14
	Nymburk	CzRep-3	1	....	....	....	60	0	1	0.00	....	....	....	....	....	....	....
2005-06	Sparta Jr.	CzRep-Jr.	1	....	....	....	60	1	0	1.00	....	....	....	....	....	....	....
	Beroun	CzRep-2	28	....	....	....	1633	61	3	2.24	....	....	....	....	....	....	....

VALIQUETTE, Stephen (val-ih-KEHT, STEE-vehn) NYR

Goaltender. Catches left. 6'5", 205 lbs. Born, Etobicoke, Ont., August 20, 1977.
(Los Angeles' 8th choice, 190th overall, in 1996 Entry Draft).

			Regular Season								Playoffs						
Season	**Club**	**League**	**GP**	**W**	**L**	**O/T**	**Mins**	**GA**	**SO**	**Avg**	**GP**	**W**	**L**	**Mins**	**GA**	**SO**	**Avg**
1993-94	Burlington	OPJHL	30	....	....	....	1663	112	1	4.04	....	....	....	....	....	....	....
1994-95	Rayside-Balfour	NOJHA	2	0	2	0	89	12	0	8.09	....	....	....	....	....	....	....
	Smiths Falls Bears	CJHL	21	10	8	3	1275	75	0	3.53	....	....	....	....	....	....	....
	Sudbury Wolves	OHL	4	2	0	0	138	6	0	2.61	....	....	....	....	....	....	....
1995-96	Sudbury Wolves	OHL	39	13	16	2	1887	123	0	3.91	....	....	....	....	....	....	....
1996-97	Sudbury Wolves	OHL	*61	21	29	7	3311	232	1	4.20	....	....	....	....	....	....	....
	Dayton Bombers	ECHL	3	1	0	0	89	6	0	4.03	2	1	1	118	5	0	2.54
1997-98	Sudbury Wolves	OHL	14	5	7	1	807	50	0	3.72	....	....	....	....	....	....	....
	Erie Otters	OHL	28	16	7	3	1525	65	3	2.56	7	3	4	467	15	1	1.93
1998-99	Hampton Roads	ECHL	31	18	7	3	1713	84	1	2.94	2	0	1	60	7	0	7.00
	Lowell	AHL	1	0	1	0	59	3	0	3.05	....	....	....	....	....	....	....
99-2000	**NY Islanders**	**NHL**	**6**	**2**	**0**	**0**	**193**	**6**	**0**	**1.87**	....	....	....	....	....	....	....
	Lowell	AHL	14	8	5	0	727	36	0	2.97	....	....	....	....	....	....	....
	Providence Bruins	AHL	1	1	0	0	60	3	0	3.00	....	....	....	....	....	....	....
	Trenton Titans	ECHL	12	5	6	1	692	36	1	3.12	....	....	....	....	....	....	....
2000-01	Springfield Falcons	AHL	20	7	10	1	1066	54	0	3.04	....	....	....	....	....	....	....
2001-02	Bridgeport	AHL	20	10	5	1	1071	45	2	2.52	1	0	0	18	1	0	3.30
2002-03	Bridgeport	AHL	34	15	14	3	1962	86	2	2.63	4	3	1	253	9	0	2.13
2003-04	**Edmonton**	**NHL**	**1**	**0**	**0**	**0**	**14**	**2**	**0**	**8.57**	....	....	....	....	....	....	....
	Toronto	AHL	35	14	14	5	2064	89	2	2.59	....	....	....	....	....	....	....
	NY Rangers	**NHL**	**2**	**1**	**1**	**0**	**120**	**6**	**0**	**3.00**	....	....	....	....	....	....	....
	Hartford Wolf Pack	AHL	7	2	4	1	400	15	1	2.25	1	0	0	11	0	0	0.00

2004-05	Hartford Wolf Pack	AHL	35	19	11	1	1900	56	7	*1.77	2	1	1	118	4	0	2.03
2005-06	Yaroslavl	Russia	45	....	....	....	2734	89	4	1.95	8	....	....	458	23	0	3.01
	NHL Totals		**9**	**3**	**1**	**0**	**327**	**14**	**0**	**2.57**	....	....	....	....	....	....	....

Shared Harry "Hap" Holmes Memorial Trophy (fewest goals against - AHL) with Jason LaBarbera (2005)

Signed as a free agent by **NY Islanders**, August 18, 1998. Signed as a free agent by **Edmonton**, July 20, 2003. Claimed by **Florida** from **Edmonton** in Waiver Draft, October 3, 2003. Claimed on waivers by **Edmonton** from **Florida**, October 9, 2003. Traded to **NY Rangers** by **Edmonton** with Dwight Helminen, Edmonton's 2nd round compensatory choice (Dane Byers) in 2004 Entry Draft and future considerations for Petr Nedved and Jussi Markkanen, March 3, 2004. Signed as a free agent by **Yaroslavl** (Russia), April 26, 2005. Signed as a free agent by **NY Rangers**, July 1, 2006.

VARLAMOV, Simeon (vahr-LAH-mawv, sih-MEE-awn) WSH.

Goaltender. Catches left. 6'1", 183 lbs. Born, Samara, Russia, April 27, 1988.
(Washington's 2nd choice, 23rd overall, in 2006 Entry Draft).

			Regular Season								Playoffs						
Season	**Club**	**League**	**GP**	**W**	**L**	**O/T**	**Mins**	**GA**	**SO**	**Avg**	**GP**	**W**	**L**	**Mins**	**GA**	**SO**	**Avg**
2004-05	Yaroslavl 2	Russia-3	8	....	....	....	369	15	1	2.43	....	....	....	....	....	....	....
2005-06	Yaroslavl 2	Russia-3	33	....	....	....	1782	60	8	2.02	....	....	....	....	....	....	....

VINCENT, Alexandre (VIHN-sihnt, al-ehx-AHN-druh) VAN.

Goaltender. Catches left. 6'4", 193 lbs. Born, Drummondville, Que., December 11, 1986.
(Vancouver's 3rd choice, 114th overall, in 2005 Entry Draft).

			Regular Season								Playoffs						
Season	**Club**	**League**	**GP**	**W**	**L**	**O/T**	**Mins**	**GA**	**SO**	**Avg**	**GP**	**W**	**L**	**Mins**	**GA**	**SO**	**Avg**
2001-02	Cap-d-Madeleine	QAAA	26	12	9	1	1264	85	0	4.04	....	....	....	....	....	....	....
2002-03	Jonquiere Elites	QAAA	31	7	17	2	1567	107	0	4.10	....	....	....	....	....	....	....
2003-04	Chicoutimi	QMJHL	34	11	11	1	1489	78	3	3.14	5	0	0	146	9	0	3.69
2004-05	Chicoutimi	QMJHL	49	24	13	4	2591	130	2	3.01	*14	7	6	765	40	*1	3.14
2005-06	Chicoutimi	QMJHL	31	21	7	0	1695	76	2	2.69	8	5	3	434	21	0	2.91

VOKOUN, Tomas (voh-KOON, TAW-mas) NSH.

Goaltender. Catches right. 6', 195 lbs. Born, Karlovy Vary, Czech., July 2, 1976.
(Montreal's 11th choice, 226th overall, in 1994 Entry Draft).

			Regular Season								Playoffs						
Season	**Club**	**League**	**GP**	**W**	**L**	**O/T**	**Mins**	**GA**	**SO**	**Avg**	**GP**	**W**	**L**	**Mins**	**GA**	**SO**	**Avg**
1993-94	HC Kladno	CzRep	1	0	0	0	20	2	0	6.01	....	....	....	....	....	....	....
1994-95	HC Kladno	CzRep	26	....	....	....	1368	70	....	3.07	5	....	....	240	19	....	4.75
1995-96	Wheeling	ECHL	35	20	10	2	1912	117	0	3.67	7	4	3	436	19	0	2.61
	Fredericton	AHL	....	....	....	....	....	....	....	....	1	0	1	59	4	0	4.09
1996-97	**Montreal**	**NHL**	**1**	**0**	**0**	**0**	**20**	**4**	**0**	**12.00**	....	....	....	....	....	....	....
	Fredericton	AHL	47	12	26	7	2645	154	2	3.49	....	....	....	....	....	....	....
1997-98	Fredericton	AHL	31	13	13	2	1735	90	0	3.11	....	....	....	....	....	....	....
1998-99	**Nashville**	**NHL**	**37**	**12**	**18**	**4**	**1954**	**96**	**1**	**2.95**	....	....	....	....	....	....	....
	Milwaukee	IHL	9	3	2	4	539	22	1	2.45	2	0	2	149	8	0	3.22
99-2000	**Nashville**	**NHL**	**33**	**9**	**20**	**1**	**1879**	**87**	**1**	**2.78**	....	....	....	....	....	....	....
	Milwaukee	IHL	7	5	2	0	364	17	0	2.80	....	....	....	....	....	....	....
2000-01	**Nashville**	**NHL**	**37**	**13**	**17**	**5**	**2088**	**85**	**2**	**2.44**	....	....	....	....	....	....	....
2001-02	**Nashville**	**NHL**	**29**	**5**	**14**	**4**	**1471**	**66**	**2**	**2.69**	....	....	....	....	....	....	....
2002-03	**Nashville**	**NHL**	**69**	**25**	**31**	**11**	**3974**	**146**	**3**	**2.20**	....	....	....	....	....	....	....
2003-04	**Nashville**	**NHL**	**73**	**34**	**29**	**10**	**4221**	**178**	**3**	**2.53**	**6**	**2**	**4**	**356**	**12**	**1**	**2.02**
2004-05	Znojmo	CzRep	27	....	....	....	1599	69	3	2.59	....	....	....	....	....	....	....
	HIFK Helsinki	Finland	19	11	4	4	1149	35	2	1.83	4	0	3	205	12	0	3.51
2005-06	**Nashville**	**NHL**	**61**	**36**	**18**	**7**	**3601**	**160**	**4**	**2.67**	....	....	....	....	....	....	....
	Czech Republic	Olympics	7	3	4	0	342	14	1	2.46	....	....	....	....	....	....	....
	NHL Totals		**340**	**134**	**147**	**42**	**19208**	**822**	**16**	**2.57**	**6**	**2**	**4**	**356**	**12**	**1**	**2.02**

Played in NHL All-Star Game (2004)

Claimed by **Nashville** from **Montreal** in Expansion Draft, June 26, 1998. Signed as a free agent by **Znojmo** (CzRep), September 6, 2004. Signed as a free agent by **HIFK Helsinki** (Finland), December 20, 2004.

WALL, Michael (WAWL, MIGH-kuhl) ANA.

Goaltender. Catches left. 6'1", 209 lbs. Born, Telkwa, B.C., July 25, 1985.

			Regular Season								Playoffs						
Season	**Club**	**League**	**GP**	**W**	**L**	**O/T**	**Mins**	**GA**	**SO**	**Avg**	**GP**	**W**	**L**	**Mins**	**GA**	**SO**	**Avg**
2001-02	Prince George	WHL	3	0	1	1	107	7	0	3.92	....	....	....	....	....	....	....
2002-03	Prince George	WHL	13	2	5	1	567	40	0	4.23	....	....	....	....	....	....	....
2003-04	Prince George	WHL	1	1	0	0	60	6	0	6.00	....	....	....	....	....	....	....
	Everett Silvertips	WHL	35	11	13	4	1657	59	2	2.14	3	1	0	104	2	0	2.15
2004-05	Everett Silvertips	WHL	56	24	21	8	3191	102	10	1.92	11	4	7	697	25	1	2.15
2005-06	Augusta Lynx	ECHL	21	8	11	1	1103	70	1	3.81	....	....	....	....	....	....	....
	Portland Pirates	AHL	11	5	5	0	603	34	1	3.38	....	....	....	....	....	....	....

Signed as a free agent by **Anaheim**, September 29, 2005.

WARD, Cam (WOHRD, KAM) CAR.

Goaltender. Catches left. 6', 176 lbs. Born, Saskatoon, Sask., February 29, 1984.
(Carolina's 1st choice, 25th overall, in 2002 Entry Draft).

			Regular Season								Playoffs						
Season	**Club**	**League**	**GP**	**W**	**L**	**O/T**	**Mins**	**GA**	**SO**	**Avg**	**GP**	**W**	**L**	**Mins**	**GA**	**SO**	**Avg**
1998-99	Sherwood Park	ABHL	24	13	7	4	1403	85	0	3.64	....	....	....	....	....	....	....
99-2000	Sherwood Park	AMHL	20	9	5	1	1194	71	0	3.57	7	4	3	262	22	0	3.57
2000-01	Sherwood Park	AMHL	25	14	6	3	1449	70	0	2.90	....	....	....	....	....	....	....
	Red Deer Rebels	WHL	1	1	0	0	60	0	1	0.00	....	....	....	....	....	....	....
2001-02	Red Deer Rebels	WHL	46	30	11	4	2694	102	1	*2.27	*23	14	9	*1502	53	*2	2.12
2002-03	Red Deer Rebels	WHL	57	*40	13	3	3368	118	5	2.10	*23	14	9	*1407	49	3	2.09
2003-04	Red Deer Rebels	WHL	56	31	16	8	3338	114	4	2.05	19	10	9	1200	37	3	1.85
2004-05	Lowell	AHL	50	27	17	3	2829	94	6	1.99	11	5	6	664	28	2	2.53
2005-06 ♦	**Carolina**	**NHL**	**28**	**14**	**8**	**2**	**1484**	**91**	**0**	**3.68**	***23**	***15**	**8**	***1320**	**47**	**2**	**2.14**
	Lowell	AHL	2	0	2	0	118	5	0	2.54	....	....	....	....	....	....	....
	NHL Totals		**28**	**14**	**8**	**2**	**1484**	**91**	**0**	**3.68**	**23**	**15**	**8**	**1320**	**47**	**2**	**2.14**

WHL East First All-Star Team (2002, 2004) • WHL East Second All-Star Team (2003) • WHL Goaltender of the Year (2002, 2004) • WHL Player of the Year (2004) • Canadian Major Junior First All-Star Team (2004) • Canadian Major Junior Goaltender of the Year (2004) • AHL All-Rookie Team (2005)

WEEKES, Kevin (WEEKS, KEH-vihn) NYR

Goaltender. Catches left. 6'1", 209 lbs. Born, Toronto, Ont., April 4, 1975.
(Florida's 2nd choice, 41st overall, in 1993 Entry Draft).

			Regular Season								Playoffs						
Season	**Club**	**League**	**GP**	**W**	**L**	**O/T**	**Mins**	**GA**	**SO**	**Avg**	**GP**	**W**	**L**	**Mins**	**GA**	**SO**	**Avg**
1990-91	Tor. Red Wings	MTHL	STATISTICS NOT AVAILABLE														
	St. Mike's B's	MTJHL	1	0	0	0	41	1	0	1.46	....	....	....	....	....	....	....
1991-92	Tor. Red Wings	MTHL	35	....	....	....	1575	68	4	1.94	....	....	....	....	....	....	....
	St. Mike's B's	MTJHL	2	0	1	1	127	11	0	5.20	4	1	2	214	15	1	4.21
1992-93	Owen Sound	OHL	29	9	12	5	1645	143	0	5.22	1	0	0	26	5	0	11.50
1993-94	Owen Sound	OHL	34	13	19	1	1974	158	0	4.80	....	....	....	....	....	....	....
1994-95	Ottawa 67's	OHL	41	13	23	4	2266	153	1	4.05	....	....	....	....	....	....	....
1995-96	Carolina Panthers	AHL	60	24	25	8	3404	229	2	4.04	....	....	....	....	....	....	....
1996-97	Carolina Monarchs	AHL	51	17	28	4	2899	172	1	3.56	....	....	....	....	....	....	....
1997-98	**Florida**	**NHL**	**11**	**0**	**5**	**1**	**485**	**32**	**0**	**3.96**	....	....	....	....	....	....	....
	Fort Wayne	IHL	12	9	2	1	719	34	1	2.84	....	....	....	....	....	....	....
1998-99	**Vancouver**	**NHL**	**11**	**0**	**8**	**1**	**532**	**34**	**0**	**3.83**	....	....	....	....	....	....	....
	Detroit Vipers	IHL	33	19	5	7	1857	64	*4	*2.07	....	....	....	....	....	....	....
99-2000	**Vancouver**	**NHL**	**20**	**6**	**7**	**4**	**987**	**47**	**1**	**2.86**	....	....	....	....	....	....	....
	NY Islanders	**NHL**	**36**	**10**	**20**	**4**	**2026**	**115**	**1**	**3.41**	....	....	....	....	....	....	....
2000-01	**Tampa Bay**	**NHL**	**61**	**20**	**33**	**3**	**3378**	**177**	**4**	**3.14**	....	....	....	....	....	....	....
2001-02	**Tampa Bay**	**NHL**	**19**	**3**	**9**	**0**	**830**	**40**	**2**	**2.89**	....	....	....	....	....	....	....
	Carolina	**NHL**	**2**	**2**	**0**	**0**	**120**	**3**	**0**	**1.50**	**8**	**3**	**2**	**408**	**11**	**2**	**1.62**
2002-03	**Carolina**	**NHL**	**51**	**14**	**24**	**9**	**2965**	**126**	**5**	**2.55**	....	....	....	....	....	....	....
2003-04	**Carolina**	**NHL**	**66**	**23**	**30**	**11**	**3765**	**146**	**6**	**2.33**	....	....	....	....	....	....	....
2004-05			DID NOT PLAY														
2005-06	**NY Rangers**	**NHL**	**32**	**14**	**14**	**3**	**1850**	**91**	**0**	**2.95**	**1**	**0**	**1**	**60**	**4**	**0**	**4.00**
	NHL Totals		**309**	**92**	**150**	**36**	**16938**	**811**	**19**	**2.87**	**9**	**3**	**3**	**468**	**15**	**2**	**1.92**

James Norris Memorial Trophy (fewest goals against – IHL) (1999) (shared with Andrei Trefilov)

Traded to **Vancouver** by **Florida** with Ed Jovanovski, Dave Gagner, Mike Brown and Florida's 1st round choice (Nathan Smith) in 2000 Entry Draft for Pavel Bure, Bret Hedican, Brad Ference and Vancouver's 3rd round choice (Robert Fried) in 2000 Entry Draft, January 17, 1999. Traded to **NY Islanders** by **Vancouver** with Dave Scatchard and Bill Muckalt for Felix Potvin, NY Islanders' 2nd round compensatory choice (later traded to New Jersey – New Jersey selected Teemu Laine) in 2000 Entry Draft and NY Islanders' 3rd round choice (Thatcher Bell) in 2000 Entry Draft, December 19, 1999. Traded to **Tampa Bay** by **NY Islanders** with the rights to Kristian Kudroc and NY Islanders' 2nd round choice (later traded to Phoenix – Phoenix selected Matthew Spiller) in 2001 Entry Draft for Tampa Bay's 1st round choice (Raffi Torres) in 2000 Entry Draft, Calgary's 4th round choice (previously acquired, NY Islanders selected Vladimir Gorbunov) in 2000 Entry Draft and NY Islanders' 7th round choice (previously acquired, NY Islanders selected Ryan Caldwell) in 2000 Entry Draft, June 24, 2000. Traded to **Carolina** by **Tampa Bay** for Shane Willis and Chris Dingman, March 5, 2002. Signed as a free agent by **NY Rangers**, August 26, 2004.

WEIMAN, Tyler (WIGH-muhn, TIGH-luhr) COL.

Goaltender. Catches left. 5'11", 180 lbs. Born, Saskatoon, Sask., June 5, 1984.
(Colorado's 6th choice, 164th overall, in 2002 Entry Draft).

			Regular Season								Playoffs						
Season	**Club**	**League**	**GP**	**W**	**L**	**O/T**	**Mins**	**GA**	**SO**	**Avg**	**GP**	**W**	**L**	**Mins**	**GA**	**SO**	**Avg**
99-2000	Ft. Saskatchewan	AMBHL	21	15	4	2	1239	60	0	2.91	....	....	....	....	....	....	....
2000-01	Tri-City Americans	WHL	44	10	25	4	2464	155	0	3.77	....	....	....	....	....	....	....
2001-02	Tri-City Americans	WHL	47	18	17	5	2492	149	2	3.59	5	1	4	300	14	0	2.80
2002-03	Tri-City Americans	WHL	55	16	34	2	3129	207	1	3.97	....	....	....	....	....	....	....
2003-04	Tri-City Americans	WHL	54	23	21	7	3023	134	1	2.66	5	1	2	234	11	0	2.82
2004-05	Colorado Eagles	CHL	44	*33	6	5	2630	79	*8	*1.80	*13	*8	4	*744	32	1	2.58
2005-06	San Diego Gulls	ECHL	32	14	12	3	1797	84	1	2.81	4	0	4	251	15	0	3.59
	Lowell	AHL	14	6	6	1	844	36	0	2.56	....	....	....	....	....	....	....

WESLOSKY, Jase (wehs-LAWZ-kee, JAYS) NYI

Goaltender. Catches left. 6'2", 170 lbs. Born, St. Albert, Alta., August 14, 1988.
(NY Islanders' 5th choice, 108th overall, in 2006 Entry Draft).

			Regular Season								Playoffs						
Season	**Club**	**League**	**GP**	**W**	**L**	**O/T**	**Mins**	**GA**	**SO**	**Avg**	**GP**	**W**	**L**	**Mins**	**GA**	**SO**	**Avg**
2004-05	St. Albert Blues	EMHA	....	13	3	2	1043	38	....	2.19	....	....	....	....	....	....	....
2005-06	Sherwood Park	AJHL	58	....	....	....	2123	110	2	3.11	....	....	....	....	....	....	....

WESTBLOM, Kristofer (WEHST-blahm, KRIHS-tuh-fuhr) MIN.

Goaltender. Catches left. 6'1", 158 lbs. Born, Meadow Lake, Sask., March 26, 1987.
(Minnesota's 3rd choice, 65th overall, in 2005 Entry Draft).

			Regular Season								Playoffs						
Season	**Club**	**League**	**GP**	**W**	**L**	**O/T**	**Mins**	**GA**	**SO**	**Avg**	**GP**	**W**	**L**	**Mins**	**GA**	**SO**	**Avg**
2002-03	Sask. Contacts	SMHL	21	14	3	2	1160	47	1	2.43	5	2	3	287	11	0	*2.30
2003-04	Sask. Contacts	SMHL	28	17	4	3	1513	50	2	*1.98	10	*7	2	625	17	*1	*1.63
2004-05	Kelowna Rockets	WHL	18	12	2	4	1094	33	4	1.81	4	3	1	251	8	0	1.91
2005-06	Kelowna Rockets	WHL	26	16	6	2	1486	71	1	2.87	1	0	0	34	0	0	0.00

YEATS, Matthew (YAYTS, MA-thew)

Goaltender. Catches left. 5'11", 165 lbs. Born, Montreal, Que., April 6, 1979.
(Los Angeles' 9th choice, 248th overall, in 1998 Entry Draft).

			Regular Season								Playoffs						
Season	**Club**	**League**	**GP**	**W**	**L**	**O/T**	**Mins**	**GA**	**SO**	**Avg**	**GP**	**W**	**L**	**Mins**	**GA**	**SO**	**Avg**
1995-96	Lethbridge	WHL	1	0	0	0	20	3	0	9.00	....	....	....	....	....	....	....
1996-97	Olds Grizzlys	AJHL	32	....	....	....	1678	95	1	3.41	....	....	....	....	....	....	....
1997-98	Olds Grizzlys	AJHL	26	12	12	1	1498	96	0	3.85	....	....	....	....	....	....	....
1998-99	University of Maine	H-East	DID NOT PLAY														
99-2000	University of Maine	H-East	32	20	6	4	1821	79	0	2.60	....	....	....	....	....	....	....
2000-01	University of Maine	H-East	33	18	9	4	1897	76	2	2.40	....	....	....	....	....	....	....
2001-02	University of Maine	H-East	20	6	8	3	1048	54	0	3.09	....	....	....	....	....	....	....
2002-03	Philadelphia	AHL	2	1	1	0	90	4	0	2.67	....	....	....	....	....	....	....
	Atlantic City	ECHL	48	23	16	8	2811	141	4	3.01	8	4	1	397	16	1	2.42
2003-04	Portland Pirates	AHL	7	2	1	1	332	12	1	2.17	....	....	....	....	....	....	....
	Washington	**NHL**	**5**	**1**	**3**	**0**	**258**	**13**	**0**	**3.02**	....	....	....	....	....	....	....
2004-05	Reading Royals	ECHL	13	8	2	2	780	31	1	2.38	....	....	....	....	....	....	....
	Idaho Steelheads	ECHL	4	2	1	1	247	9	0	2.19	2	0	1	66	3	0	2.72
2005-06	Idaho Steelheads	ECHL	35	21	7	5	1980	98	1	2.97	5	2	3	289	16	1	3.33
	NHL Totals		**5**	**1**	**3**	**0**	**258**	**13**	**0**	**3.02**	....	....	....	....	....	....	....

• Ruled ineligible to play 1998-99 season by NCAA due to appearance with **Lethbridge** (WHL) in 1995-96. Signed as a free agent by **Portland** (AHL), November 6, 2003. Signed as a free agent by **Washington**, March 20, 2004. Signed as a free agent by **Reading** (ECHL), December 10, 2004. Traded to **Idaho** (ECHL) by **Reading** (ECHL) for future considerations (David Morisset, June 4, 2005), March 22, 2005.

ZABA, Matt (ZA-buh, MAT) L.A.

Goaltender. Catches left. 6'1", 180 lbs. Born, Yorkton, Sask., July 14, 1983.
(Los Angeles' 8th choice, 231st overall, in 2003 Entry Draft).

			Regular Season								Playoffs						
Season	**Club**	**League**	**GP**	**W**	**L**	**O/T**	**Mins**	**GA**	**SO**	**Avg**	**GP**	**W**	**L**	**Mins**	**GA**	**SO**	**Avg**
2000-01	Yorkton Mallers	SMHL	26	13	10	3	1480	79	0	3.20	....	....	....	....	....	....	....
2001-02	Penticton Panthers	BCHL	33	....	....	....	1980	128	0	3.69	....	....	....	....	....	....	....
2002-03	Vernon Vipers	BCHL	44	34	9	0	2012	96	2	2.21	17	14	3	1006	25	3	1.49
2003-04	Colorado College	WCHA	23	10	10	2	1323	50	1	2.27	....	....	....	....	....	....	....
2004-05	Colorado College	WCHA	18	10	5	2	1050	43	2	2.46	....	....	....	....	....	....	....
2005-06	Colorado College	WCHA	36	20	14	2	2068	87	4	2.52	....	....	....	....	....	....	....

WCHA All-Rookie Team (2004)

ZATKOFF, Jeff (ZAT-kawf, JEHF) L.A.

Goaltender. Catches left. 6'1", 180 lbs. Born, Detroit, MI, June 9, 1987.
(Los Angeles' 4th choice, 74th overall, in 2006 Entry Draft).

			Regular Season								Playoffs						
Season	**Club**	**League**	**GP**	**W**	**L**	**O/T**	**Mins**	**GA**	**SO**	**Avg**	**GP**	**W**	**L**	**Mins**	**GA**	**SO**	**Avg**
2004-05	Sioux City	USHL	24	13	6	3	1271	54	1	2.55	2	0	0	68	10	0	8.88
2005-06	Miami U.	CCHA	20	14	5	1	1217	41	3	2.02	....	....	....	....	....	....	....

Late Additions to Player Register

FREE AGENT SIGNINGS

BOGUNIECKI, Eric   (Career data panel page 364)   **CBJ**
Center. Shoots right. 5'8", 192 lbs.   Born, New Haven, CT, May 6, 1975.
Signed as a free agent by **Columbus**, August 22, 2006.

FITZPATRICK, Rory   (Career data panel page 403)   **VAN.**
Defense. Shoots right. 6'2", 208 lbs.   Born, Rochester, NY, January 11, 1975.
Signed as a free agent by **Vancouver**, August 18, 2006.

HENRY, Alex   (Career data panel page 423)   **NSH.**
Defense. Shoots left. 6'4", 220 lbs.   Born, Elliot Lake, Ont., October 18, 1979.
Signed as a free agent by **Nashville**, August 22, 2006.

NOLAN, Owen   (NOH-lan, OH-wehn)   **PHX.**
Right wing. Shoots right. 6'1", 215 lbs. Born, Belfast, N. Ireland, February 12, 1972. Quebec's 1st choice, 1st overall, in 1990 Entry Draft.

Season	Club	League	GP	G	A	Pts	PIM	PP	SH	GW	S	%	+/-	TF	F%	Min	GP	G	A	Pts	PIM	PP	SH	GW	Min
1987-88	Thorold	OMHA	28	53	32	85	24	....	....	....	....	....	....	....	....	....	....	....	....	....	....	....	....	....	....
	Thorold	OHA-B	3	1	0	1	2	....	....	....	....	....	....	....	....	....	18	5	11	16	41	....	....	....	....
1988-89	Cornwall Royals	OHL	62	34	25	59	213	....	....	....	....	....	....	....	....	....	6	7	5	12	26	....	....	....	....
1989-90	Cornwall Royals	OHL	58	51	59	110	240	....	....	....	....	....	....	....	....	....	....	....	....	....	....	....	....	....	....
1990-91	Quebec	NHL	59	3	10	13	109	0	0	0	54	5.6	19	....	....	....	....	....	....	....	....	....	....	....	....
	Halifax Citadels	AHL	6	4	4	8	11	....	....	....	....	....	....	....	....	....	....	....	....	....	....	....	....	....	....
1991-92	Quebec	NHL	75	42	31	73	183	17	0	0	190	22.1	9	....	....	....	....	....	....	....	....	....	....	....	....
1992-93	Quebec	NHL	73	36	41	77	185	15	0	4	241	14.9	1	....	....	....	5	1	0	1	2	0	0	0	....
1993-94	Quebec	NHL	6	2	2	4	8	0	0	0	15	13.3	2	....	....	....	....	....	....	....	....	....	....	....	....
1994-95	Quebec	NHL	46	30	19	49	46	13	2	8	137	21.9	21	....	....	....	6	2	3	5	6	0	0	0	....
1995-96	Colorado	NHL	9	4	4	8	9	4	0	0	23	17.4	3	....	....	....	....	....	....	....	....	....	....	....	....
	San Jose	NHL	72	29	32	61	137	12	1	2	184	15.8	30	....	....	....	....	....	....	....	....	....	....	....	....
1996-97	San Jose	NHL	72	31	32	63	155	10	0	3	225	13.8	19	....	....	....	....	....	....	....	....	....	....	....	....
1997-98	San Jose	NHL	75	14	27	41	144	3	1	1	192	7.3	2	....	....	....	6	2	2	4	26	2	0	1	....
1998-99	San Jose	NHL	78	19	26	45	129	6	2	3	207	9.2	16	657	49.3	19:09	6	1	1	2	6	0	0	0	20:15
99-2000	San Jose	NHL	78	44	40	84	110	18	4	6	261	16.9	1	357	50.7	21:07	10	8	2	10	6	2	2	3	22:14
2000-01	San Jose	NHL	57	24	25	49	75	10	1	4	191	12.6	0	407	46.9	21:49	6	1	1	2	8	0	0	1	22:45
2001-02	San Jose	NHL	75	23	43	66	93	8	2	2	217	10.6	7	545	47.0	19:23	12	3	6	9	8	0	0	0	19:46
	Canada	Olympics	6	0	3	3	2	....	....	....	....	....	....	....	....	....	....	....	....	....	....	....	....	....	....
2002-03	San Jose	NHL	61	22	20	42	91	8	3	4	192	11.5	5	226	50.4	18:08	....	....	....	....	....	....	....	....	....
	Toronto	NHL	14	7	5	12	16	5	0	1	29	24.1	2	56	48.2	17:00	7	0	2	2	2	0	0	0	23:19
2003-04	Toronto	NHL	65	19	29	48	110	7	2	3	154	12.3	4	242	53.3	17:57	....	....	....	....	....	....	....	....	....
2004-05			DID NOT PLAY																					
2005-06			DID NOT PLAY — INJURED																					
	NHL Totals		915	349	386	735	1600	136	18	41	2512	13.9		2490	49.1	19:30	58	18	17	35	64	4	2	5	21:29

OHL Rookie of the Year (1989) • OHL First All-Star Team (1990)
Played in NHL All-Star Game (1992, 1996, 1997, 2000, 2002)
Missed majority of 1993-94 season recovering from shoulder injury suffered in game vs. Tampa Bay, November 13, 1993. Transferred to **Colorado** after **Quebec** franchise relocated, June 21, 1995. Traded to **San Jose** by **Colorado** for Sandis Ozolinsh, October 26, 1995. Traded to **Toronto** by **San Jose** for Alyn McCauley, Brad Boyes and Toronto's 1st round choice (later traded to Boston - Boston selected Mark Stuart) in 2003 Entry Draft, March 5, 2003. • Missed 2005-06 season recovering from knee surgery, July 27, 2005. Signed as a free agent by **Phoenix**, August 16, 2006.

PENNER, Andrew   (Career data panel page 605)   **PIT.**
Goaltender. Catches left. 6'2", 205 lbs.   Born, Scarborough, Ont., December 21, 1982.
Signed as a free agent by **Pittsburgh**, August 18, 2006.

RIVERS, Jamie   (Career data panel page 518)   **ST.L.**
Defense. Shoots left. 6'1", 195 lbs.   Born, Ottawa, Ont., March 16, 1975.
Signed as a free agent by **St. Louis**, August 18, 2006.

TRADES

STEWART, Karl   (Career data panel page 546)   **ANA.**
Left wing. Shoots left. 5'10", 180 lbs.   Born, Aurora, Ont., June 30, 1983.
Traded to **Anaheim** by **Atlanta** with Atlanta's 2nd round choice in 2007 Entry Draft and a conditional 4th round choice in 2008 Entry Draft for Vitaly Vishnevski, August 17, 2006.

VISHNEVSKI, Vitali   (Career data panel page 566)   **ATL.**
Defense. Shoots left. 6'2", 203 lbs.   Born, Kharkov, USSR, March 18, 1980.
Traded to **Atlanta** by **Anaheim** for Karl Stewart, Atlanta's 2nd round choice in 2007 Entry Draft and a conditional 4th round choice in 2008 Entry Draft, August 17, 2006.

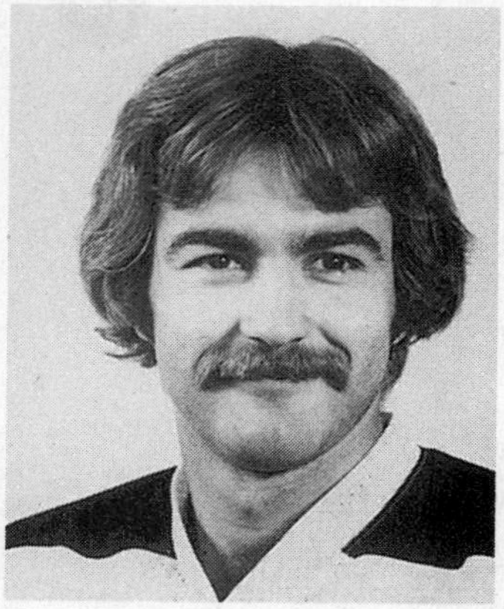

Dennis Abgrall

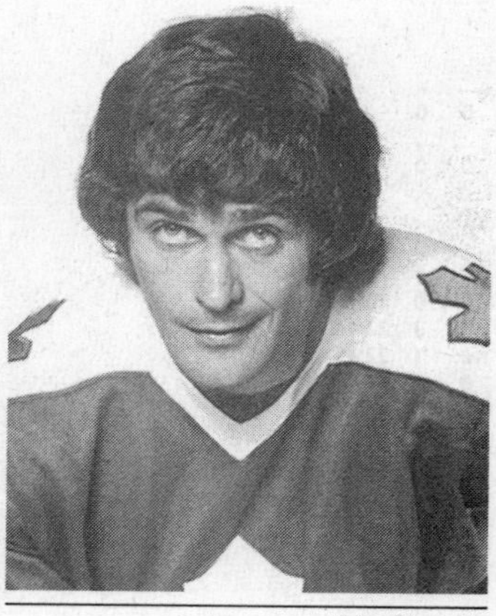

Claire Alexander

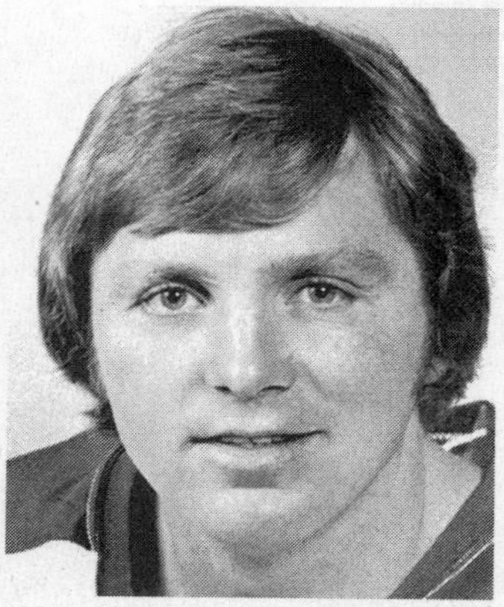

Murray Anderson

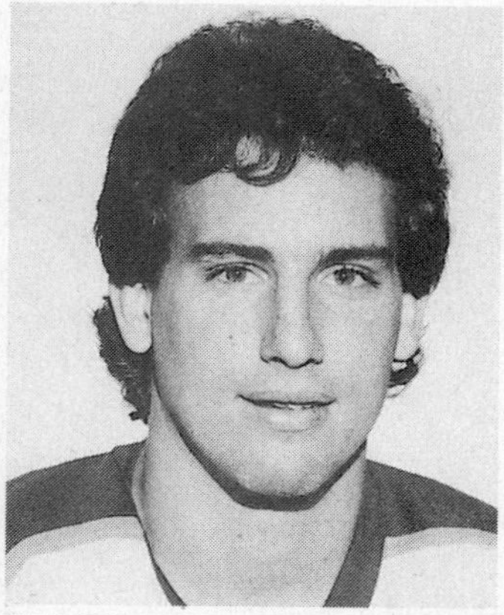

Scott Arniel

Retired NHL Player Index

Abbreviations: Teams/Cities: – **Ana.** – Anaheim; **Atl.** – Atlanta; **Bos.** – Boston; **Bro.** – Brooklyn; **Buf.** – Buffalo; **Cal.** – California; **Cgy.** – Calgary; **Car.** – Carolina; **Chi.** – Chicago; **Cle.** – Cleveland; **Col.** – Colorado; **CBJ** – Columbus; **Dal.** – Dallas; **Det.** – Detroit; **Edm.** – Edmonton; **Fla.** – Florida; **Ham.** – Hamilton; **Hfd.** – Hartford; **K.C.** – Kansas City; **L.A.** – Los Angeles; **Min.** – Minnesota; **Mtl.** – Montreal; **Mtl.M.** – Montreal Maroons; **Mtl.W.** – Montreal Wanderers; **Nsh.** – Nashville; **N.J.** – New Jersey; **NYA** – NY Americans; **NYI** – NY Islanders; **NYR** – New York Rangers; **Oak.** – Oakland; **Ott.** – Ottawa; **Phi.** – Philadelphia; **Phx.** – Phoenix; **Pit.** – Pittsburgh; **Que.** – Quebec; **St.L.** – St. Louis; **S.J.** – San Jose; **T.B.** – Tampa Bay; **Tor.** – Toronto; **Van.** – Vancouver; **Wpg.** – Winnipeg; **Wsh.** – Washington

A – assists; **G** – goals; **GP** – games played; **PIM** – penalties in minutes; **TP** – total points.
● – deceased. Assists not recorded during 1917-18 season ‡ – Remains active in other leagues.

NHL Seasons – A player or goaltender who does not play in a regular season but who does appear in that year's playoffs is credited with an NHL Season in this Index. Total seasons are rounded off to the nearest full season.

Name	NHL Teams	NHL Seasons	Regular Schedule					Playoffs					NHL Cup Wins	First NHL Season	Last NHL Season
			GP	G	A	TP	PIM	GP	G	A	TP	PIM			
A															
‡ Aalto, Antti	Ana.	4	151	11	17	28	52	4	0	0	0	2	....	1997-98	2000-01
Abbott, Reg	Mtl.	1	3	0	0	0	0	....	....	....	....	....	....	1952-53	1952-53
● Abel, Clarence	NYR, Chi.	8	333	19	18	37	359	38	1	1	2	58	2	1926-27	1933-34
Abel, Gerry	Det.	1	1	0	0	0	0	....	....	....	....	....	....	1966-67	1966-67
● Abel, Sid	Det., Chi.	14	612	189	283	472	376	97	28	30	58	79	3	1938-39	1953-54
Abgrall, Dennis	L.A.	1	13	0	2	2	4	....	....	....	....	....	....	1975-76	1975-76
Abrahamsson, Thommy	Hfd.	1	32	6	11	17	16	....	....	....	....	....	....	1980-81	1980-81
Achtymichuk, Gene	Mtl., Det.	4	32	3	5	8	2	....	....	....	....	....	....	1951-52	1958-59
Acomb, Doug	Tor.	1	2	0	1	1	0	....	....	....	....	....	....	1969-70	1969-70
Acton, Keith	Mtl., Min., Edm., Phi., Wsh., NYI	15	1023	226	358	584	1172	66	12	21	33	88	1	1979-80	1993-94
● Adam, Douglas	NYR	1	4	0	1	1	0	....	....	....	....	....	....	1949-50	1949-50
Adam, Russ	Tor.	1	8	1	2	3	11	....	....	....	....	....	....	1982-83	1982-83
‡ Adams, Bryan	Atl.	2	11	0	1	1	2	....	....	....	....	....	....	1999-00	2000-01
Adams, Greg	Phi., Hfd., Wsh., Edm., Van., Que., Det.	10	545	84	143	227	1173	43	2	11	13	153	....	1980-81	1989-90
Adams, Greg	N.J., Van., Dal., Phx., Fla.	17	1056	355	388	743	326	81	20	22	42	16	....	1984-85	2000-01
● Adams, Jack	Tor., Ott.	7	173	83	32	115	366	10	2	0	2	13	2	1917-18	1926-27
Adams, John	Mtl.	1	42	6	12	18	11	3	0	0	0	0	....	1940-41	1940-41
● Adams, Stew	Chi., Tor.	4	95	9	26	35	60	11	3	3	6	14	....	1929-30	1932-33
Adduono, Rick	Bos., Atl.	2	4	0	0	0	2	....	....	....	....	....	....	1975-76	1979-80
Affleck, Bruce	St.L., Van., NYI	7	280	14	66	80	86	8	0	0	0	0	....	1974-75	1983-84
Agnew, Jim	Van., Hfd.	6	81	0	1	1	257	4	0	0	0	6	....	1986-87	1992-93
Ahern, Fred	Cal., Cle., Col.	4	146	31	30	61	130	2	0	1	1	2	....	1974-75	1977-78
● Ahlin, Tony	Chi.	1	1	0	0	0	0	....	....	....	....	....	....	1937-38	1937-38
Ahola, Peter	L.A., Pit., S.J., Cgy.	3	123	10	17	27	137	6	0	0	0	2	....	1991-92	1993-94
Ahrens, Chris	Min.	6	52	0	3	3	84	1	0	0	0	0	....	1972-73	1977-78
Ailsby, Lloyd	NYR	1	3	0	0	0	2	....	....	....	....	....	....	1951-52	1951-52
Aitken, Brad	Pit., Edm.	2	14	1	3	4	25	....	....	....	....	....	....	1987-88	1990-91
Aivazoff, Micah	Det., Edm., NYI	3	92	4	6	10	46	....	....	....	....	....	....	1993-94	1995-96
‡ Alatalo, Mika	Phx.	2	152	17	29	46	58	5	0	0	0	2	....	1999-00	2000-01
● Albright, Clint	NYR	1	59	14	5	19	19	....	....	....	....	....	....	1948-49	1948-49
Aldcorn, Gary	Tor., Det., Bos.	5	226	41	56	97	78	6	1	2	3	4	....	1956-57	1960-61
Aldridge, Keith	Dal.	1	4	0	0	0	0	....	....	....	....	....	....	1999-00	1999-00
Alexander, Claire	Tor., Van.	4	155	18	47	65	36	16	2	4	6	4	....	1974-75	1977-78
● Alexandre, Art	Mtl.	2	11	0	2	2	8	4	0	0	0	0	....	1931-32	1932-33
Allan, Jeff	Cle.	1	4	0	0	0	2	....	....	....	....	....	....	1977-78	1977-78
Allen, Chris	Fla.	2	2	0	0	0	2	....	....	....	....	....	....	1997-98	1998-99
● Allen, George	NYR, Chi., Mtl.	8	339	82	115	197	179	41	9	10	19	32	....	1938-39	1946-47
Allen, Keith	Det.	2	28	0	4	4	8	5	0	0	0	0	1	1953-54	1954-55
Allen, Peter	Pit.	1	8	0	0	0	8	....	....	....	....	....	....	1995-96	1995-96
● Allen, Viv	NYA	1	6	0	1	1	0	....	....	....	....	....	....	1940-41	1940-41
Alley, Steve	Hfd.	2	15	3	3	6	11	3	0	1	1	0	....	1979-80	1980-81
Allison, Dave	Mtl.	1	3	0	0	0	12	....	....	....	....	....	....	1983-84	1983-84
Allison, Mike	NYR, Tor., L.A.	10	499	102	166	268	630	82	9	17	26	135	....	1980-81	1989-90
Allison, Ray	Hfd., Phi.	7	238	64	93	157	223	12	2	3	5	20	....	1979-80	1986-87
● Allum, Bill	NYR	1	1	0	1	1	0	....	....	....	....	....	....	1940-41	1940-41
● Amadio, Dave	Det., L.A.	3	125	5	11	16	163	16	1	2	3	18	....	1957-58	1968-69
Ambroziak, Peter	Buf.	1	12	0	1	1	0	....	....	....	....	....	....	1994-95	1994-95
Amodeo, Mike	Wpg.	1	19	0	0	0	2	....	....	....	....	....	....	1979-80	1979-80
● Anderson, Bill	Bos.	1	....	....	....	....	....	1	0	0	0	0	....	1942-43	1942-43
Anderson, Dale	Det.	1	13	0	0	0	6	2	0	0	0	0	....	1956-57	1956-57
Anderson, Doug	Mtl.	1	....	....	....	....	....	2	0	0	0	0	1	1952-53	1952-53
Anderson, Earl	Det., Bos.	3	109	19	19	38	22	5	0	1	1	0	....	1974-75	1976-77
Anderson, Glenn	Edm., Tor., NYR, St.L.	16	1129	498	601	1099	1120	225	93	121	214	442	6	1980-81	1995-96
Anderson, Jim	L.A.	1	7	1	2	3	2	....	....	....	....	....	....	1967-68	1967-68
Anderson, John	Tor., Que., Hfd.	12	814	282	349	631	263	37	9	18	27	2	....	1977-78	1988-89
Anderson, Murray	Wsh.	1	40	0	1	1	68	....	....	....	....	....	....	1974-75	1974-75
Anderson, Perry	St.L., N.J., S.J.	10	400	50	59	109	1051	36	2	1	3	161	....	1981-82	1991-92
Anderson, Ron	Det., L.A., St.L., Buf.	5	251	28	30	58	146	5	0	0	0	4	....	1967-68	1971-72
Anderson, Ron	Wsh.	1	28	9	7	16	8	....	....	....	....	....	....	1974-75	1974-75
Anderson, Russ	Pit., Hfd., L.A.	9	519	22	99	121	1086	10	0	3	3	28	....	1976-77	1984-85
Anderson, Shawn	Buf., Que., Wsh., Phi.	8	255	11	51	62	117	19	1	1	2	16	....	1986-87	1994-95
● Anderson, Tom	Det., NYA, Bro.	8	319	62	127	189	180	16	2	7	9	8	....	1934-35	1941-42
Andersson, Erik	Cgy.	1	12	2	1	3	8	....	....	....	....	....	....	1997-98	1997-98
Andersson, Kent-Erik	Min., NYR	7	456	72	103	175	78	50	4	11	15	4	....	1977-78	1983-84
Andersson, Mikael	Buf., Hfd., T.B., Phi., NYI	15	761	95	169	264	134	25	2	7	9	10	....	1985-86	1999-00
‡ Andersson, Niklas	Que., NYI, S.J., Nsh., Cgy.	6	164	29	53	82	85	....	....	....	....	....	....	1992-93	2000-01
Andersson, Peter	Wsh., Que.	3	172	10	41	51	81	7	0	2	2	2	....	1983-84	1985-86
Andersson, Peter	NYR, Fla.	2	47	6	13	19	20	....	....	....	....	....	....	1992-93	1993-94
Andrascik, Steve	NYR	1	....	....	....	....	....	1	0	0	0	0	....	1971-72	1971-72
Andrea, Paul	NYR, Pit., Cal., Buf.	4	150	31	49	80	10	....	....	....	....	....	....	1965-66	1970-71
● Andrews, Lloyd	Tor.	4	53	8	5	13	10	2	0	0	0	0	1	1921-22	1924-25
Andrievski, Alexander	Chi.	1	1	0	0	0	0	....	....	....	....	....	....	1992-93	1992-93
Andruff, Ron	Mtl., Col.	5	153	19	36	55	54	2	0	0	0	0	....	1974-75	1978-79
Andrusak, Greg	Pit., Tor.	5	28	0	6	6	16	15	1	0	1	8	....	1993-94	1999-00
‡ Angelstad, Mel	Wsh.	1	2	0	0	0	2	....	....	....	....	....	....	2003-04	2003-04
Angotti, Lou	NYR, Chi., Phi., Pit., St.L.	10	653	103	186	289	228	65	8	8	16	17	....	1964-65	1973-74
Anholt, Darrel	Chi.	1	1	0	0	0	0	....	....	....	....	....	....	1983-84	1983-84
Anslow, Hub	NYR	1	2	0	0	0	0	....	....	....	....	....	....	1947-48	1947-48
Antonovich, Mike	Min., Hfd., N.J.	5	87	10	15	25	37	....	....	....	....	....	....	1975-76	1983-84
Antoski, Shawn	Van., Phi., Pit., Ana.	8	183	3	5	8	599	36	1	3	4	74	....	1990-91	1997-98
● Apps, Syl	Tor.	10	423	201	231	432	56	69	25	29	54	8	3	1936-37	1947-48
Apps, Syl	NYR, Pit., L.A.	10	727	183	423	606	311	23	5	5	10	23	....	1970-71	1979-80
Arbour, Al	Det., Chi., Tor., St.L.	16	626	12	58	70	617	86	1	8	9	92	4	1953-54	1970-71
● Arbour, Amos	Mtl., Ham., Tor.	6	113	52	20	72	77	....	....	....	....	....	....	1918-19	1923-24
● Arbour, Jack	Det., Tor.	2	47	5	1	6	56	....	....	....	....	....	....	1926-27	1928-29
Arbour, John	Bos., Pit., Van., St.L.	5	106	1	9	10	149	5	0	0	0	0	....	1965-66	1971-72
● Arbour, Ty	Pit., Chi.	5	207	28	28	56	112	11	2	0	2	6	....	1926-27	1930-31
Archambault, Michel	Chi.	1	3	0	0	0	0	....	....	....	....	....	....	1976-77	1976-77
Archibald, Dave	Min., NYR, Ott., NYI	8	323	57	67	124	139	5	0	1	1	0	....	1987-88	1996-97
Archibald, Jim	Min.	3	16	1	2	3	45	....	....	....	....	....	....	1984-85	1986-87
Areshenkoff, Ron	Edm.	1	4	0	0	0	0	....	....	....	....	....	....	1979-80	1979-80
Armstrong, Bill	Phi.	1	1	0	1	1	0	....	....	....	....	....	....	1990-91	1990-91
● Armstrong, Bob	Bos.	12	542	13	86	99	671	42	1	7	8	28	....	1950-51	1961-62
Armstrong, George	Tor.	21	1187	296	417	713	721	110	26	34	60	52	4	1949-50	1970-71
Armstrong, Murray	Tor., NYA, Bro., Det.	8	270	67	121	188	72	30	4	6	10	2	....	1937-38	1945-46
● Armstrong, Norm	Tor.	1	7	1	1	2	2	....	....	....	....	....	....	1962-63	1962-63
Armstrong, Tim	Tor.	1	11	1	0	1	6	....	....	....	....	....	....	1988-89	1988-89
Arnason, Chuck	Mtl., Atl., Pit., K.C., Col., Cle., Min., Wsh.	8	401	109	90	199	122	9	2	4	6	4	....	1971-72	1978-79
Arniel, Scott	Wpg., Buf., Bos.	12	730	149	189	338	599	34	3	3	6	39	....	1981-82	1991-92

Name	NHL Teams	NHL Seasons	Regular Schedule					Playoffs					NHL Cup Wins	First NHL Season	Last NHL Season
			GP	G	A	TP	PIM	GP	G	A	TP	PIM			
Arthur, Fred	Hfd., Phi.	3	80	1	8	9	49	4	0	0	0	2	....	1980-81	1982-83
● Arundel, John	Tor.	1	3	0	0	0	9	....	....	....	....	....	....	1949-50	1949-50
Arvedson, Magnus	Ott., Van.	7	434	100	125	225	241	52	3	8	11	34	....	1997-98	2003-04
● Ashbee, Barry	Bos., Phi.	5	284	15	70	85	291	17	0	4	4	22	1	1965-66	1973-74
● Ashby, Don	Tor., Col., Edm.	6	188	40	56	96	40	12	1	0	1	4	....	1975-76	1980-81
Ashton, Brent	Van., Col., N.J., Min., Que., Det., Wpg., Bos., Cgy.	14	998	284	345	629	635	85	24	25	49	70	....	1979-80	1992-93
Ashworth, Frank	Chi.	1	18	5	4	9	2	....	....	....	....	....	....	1946-47	1946-47
● Asmundson, Oscar	NYR, Det., St.L., NYA, Mtl.	5	111	11	23	34	30	9	0	2	2	4	1	1932-33	1937-38
Astashenko, Kaspars	T.B.	2	23	1	2	3	8	....	....	....	....	....	....	1999-00	2000-01
‡ Astley, Mark	Buf.	3	75	4	19	23	92	2	0	0	0	0	....	1993-94	1995-96
● Atanas, Walt	NYR	1	49	13	8	21	40	....	....	....	....	....	....	1944-45	1944-45
Atcheynum, Blair	Ott., St.L., Nsh., Chi.	5	196	27	33	60	36	23	1	3	4	8	....	1992-93	2000-01
● Atkinson, Steve	Bos., Buf., Wsh.	6	302	60	51	111	104	1	0	0	0	0	....	1968-69	1974-75
Attwell, Bob	Col.	2	22	1	5	6	0	....	....	....	....	....	....	1979-80	1980-81
Attwell, Ron	St.L., NYR	1	22	1	7	8	8	....	....	....	....	....	....	1967-68	1967-68
Aubin, Norm	Tor.	2	69	18	13	31	30	1	0	0	0	0	....	1981-82	1982-83
Aubry, Pierre	Que., Det.	5	202	24	26	50	133	20	1	1	2	32	....	1980-81	1984-85
Aubuchon, Ossie	Bos., NYR	2	50	20	12	32	4	6	1	0	1	0	....	1942-43	1943-44
Audet, Philippe	Det.	1	4	0	0	0	0	....	....	....	....	....	....	1998-99	1998-99
Audette, Donald	Buf., L.A., Atl., Dal., Mtl., Fla.	15	735	260	249	509	584	73	21	27	48	46	....	1989-90	2003-04
● Auge, Les	Col.	1	6	0	3	3	4	....	....	....	....	....	....	1980-81	1980-81
‡ Augusta, Patrik	Tor., Wsh.	2	4	0	0	0	0	....	....	....	....	....	....	1993-94	1998-99
● Aurie, Larry	Det.	12	489	147	129	276	279	24	6	9	15	10	2	1927-28	1938-39
Awrey, Don	Bos., St.L., Mtl., Pit., NYR, Col.	16	979	31	158	189	1065	71	0	18	18	150	2	1963-64	1978-79
● Ayres, Vern	NYA, Mtl.M., St.L., NYR	6	211	6	11	17	350	....	....	....	....	....	....	1930-31	1935-36

B

Name	NHL Teams	NHL Seasons	GP	G	A	TP	PIM	GP	G	A	TP	PIM	NHL Cup Wins	First NHL Season	Last NHL Season
Babando, Pete	Bos., Det., Chi., NYR	6	351	86	73	159	194	17	3	3	6	6	1	1947-48	1952-53
Babcock, Bobby	Wsh.	2	2	0	0	0	2	....	....	....	....	....	....	1990-91	1992-93
Babe, Warren	Min.	3	21	2	5	7	23	2	0	0	0	0	....	1987-88	1990-91
‡ Babenko, Yuri	Col.	1	3	0	0	0	0	....	....	....	....	....	....	2000-01	2000-01
Babin, Mitch	St.L.	1	8	0	0	0	0	....	....	....	....	....	....	1975-76	1975-76
Baby, John	Cle., Min.	2	26	2	8	10	26	....	....	....	....	....	....	1977-78	1978-79
Babych, Dave	Wpg., Hfd., Van., Phi., L.A.	19	1195	142	581	723	970	114	21	41	62	113	....	1980-81	1998-99
Babych, Wayne	St.L., Pit., Que., Hfd.	9	519	192	246	438	498	41	7	9	16	24	....	1978-79	1986-87
Baca, Jergus	Hfd.	2	10	0	2	2	14	....	....	....	....	....	....	1990-91	1991-92
Backman, Mike	NYR	3	18	1	6	7	18	10	2	2	4	2	....	1981-82	1983-84
● Backor, Pete	Tor.	1	36	4	5	9	6	....	....	....	....	....	1	1944-45	1944-45
Backstrom, Ralph	Mtl., L.A., Chi.	17	1032	278	361	639	386	116	27	32	59	68	6	1956-57	1972-73
● Bailey, Ace	Tor.	8	313	111	82	193	472	21	3	4	7	12	1	1926-27	1933-34
● Bailey, Bob	Tor., Det., Chi.	5	150	15	21	36	207	15	0	4	4	22	....	1953-54	1957-58
● Bailey, Garnet	Bos., Det., St.L., Wsh.	10	568	107	171	278	633	15	2	4	6	28	1	1968-69	1977-78
Bailey, Reid	Phi., Tor., Hfd.	4	40	1	3	4	105	16	0	2	2	25	....	1980-81	1983-84
Baillargeon, Joel	Wpg., Que.	3	20	0	2	2	31	....	....	....	....	....	....	1986-87	1988-89
Baird, Ken	Cal.	1	10	0	2	2	15	....	....	....	....	....	....	1971-72	1971-72
Baker, Bill	Mtl., Col., St.L., NYR	3	143	7	25	32	175	6	0	0	0	0	....	1980-81	1982-83
Baker, Jamie	Que., S.J., Tor.	9	328	52	50	102	217	25	5	4	9	42	....	1989-90	1998-99
Bakovic, Peter	Van.	1	10	2	0	2	48	....	....	....	....	....	....	1987-88	1987-88
‡ Bala, Chris	Ott.	1	6	0	1	1	0	....	....	....	....	....	....	2001-02	2001-02
Balderis, Helmut	Min.	1	26	3	6	9	2	....	....	....	....	....	....	1989-90	1989-90
Baldwin, Doug	Tor., Det., Chi.	3	24	0	1	1	8	....	....	....	....	....	....	1945-46	1947-48
Balfour, Earl	Tor., Chi.	7	288	30	22	52	78	26	0	3	3	4	1	1951-52	1960-61
● Balfour, Murray	Mtl., Chi., Bos.	8	306	67	90	157	393	40	9	10	19	45	1	1956-57	1964-65
Ball, Terry	Phi., Buf.	4	74	7	19	26	26	....	....	....	....	....	....	1967-68	1971-72
‡ Balmochnykh, Maxim	Ana.	1	6	0	1	1	2	....	....	....	....	....	....	1999-00	1999-00
Balon, Dave	NYR, Mtl., Min., Van.	14	776	192	222	414	607	78	14	21	35	109	2	1959-60	1972-73
Baltimore, Bryon	Edm.	1	2	0	0	0	4	....	....	....	....	....	....	1979-80	1979-80
Baluik, Stan	Bos.	1	7	0	0	0	2	....	....	....	....	....	....	1959-60	1959-60
‡ Bancroft, Steve	Chi., S.J.	2	6	0	1	1	2	....	....	....	....	....	....	1992-93	2001-02
Bandura, Jeff	NYR	1	2	0	1	1	0	....	....	....	....	....	....	1980-81	1980-81
‡ Banham, Frank	Ana., Phx.	4	32	9	2	11	16	....	....	....	....	....	....	1996-97	2002-03
Banks, Darren	Bos.	2	20	2	2	4	73	....	....	....	....	....	....	1992-93	1993-94
‡ Bannister, Drew	T.B., Edm., Ana., NYR	6	164	5	25	30	161	12	0	0	0	30	....	1995-96	2001-02
Barahona, Ralph	Bos.	2	6	2	2	4	0	....	....	....	....	....	....	1990-91	1991-92
● Barbe, Andy	Tor.	1	1	0	0	0	2	....	....	....	....	....	....	1950-51	1950-51
Barber, Bill	Phi.	14	903	420	463	883	623	129	53	55	108	109	2	1972-73	1983-84
Barber, Don	Min., Wpg., Que., S.J.	4	115	25	32	57	64	11	4	4	8	10	....	1988-89	1991-92
● Barilko, Bill	Tor.	5	252	26	36	62	456	47	5	7	12	104	4	1946-47	1950-51
Barkley, Doug	Chi., Det.	6	253	24	80	104	382	30	0	9	9	63	....	1957-58	1965-66
Barlow, Bob	Min.	2	77	16	17	33	10	6	2	2	4	6	....	1969-70	1970-71
Barnes, Blair	L.A.	1	1	0	0	0	0	....	....	....	....	....	....	1982-83	1982-83
Barnes, Norm	Phi., Hfd.	5	156	6	38	44	178	12	0	0	0	8	....	1976-77	1981-82
‡ Barnes, Ryan	Det.	1	2	0	0	0	0	....	....	....	....	....	....	2003-04	2003-04
Baron, Murray	Phi., St.L., Mtl., Phx., Van.	15	988	35	94	129	1309	73	2	8	10	78	....	1989-90	2003-04
Baron, Normand	Mtl., St.L.	2	27	2	0	2	51	3	0	0	0	22	....	1983-84	1985-86
Barr, Dave	Bos., NYR, St.L., Hfd., Det., N.J., Dal.	13	614	128	204	332	520	71	12	10	22	70	....	1981-82	1993-94
Barrault, Doug	Min., Fla.	2	4	0	0	0	2	....	....	....	....	....	....	1992-93	1993-94
Barrett, Fred	Min., L.A.	13	745	25	123	148	671	44	0	2	2	60	....	1970-71	1983-84
Barrett, John	Det., Wsh., Min.	8	488	20	77	97	604	16	2	2	4	50	....	1980-81	1987-88
Barrie, Doug	Pit., Buf., L.A.	3	158	10	42	52	268	....	....	....	....	....	....	1968-69	1971-72
Barrie, Len	Phi., Fla., Pit., L.A.	7	184	19	45	64	290	8	1	0	1	8	....	1989-90	2000-01
Barry, Ed	Bos.	1	19	1	3	4	2	....	....	....	....	....	....	1946-47	1946-47
● Barry, Marty	NYA, Bos., Det., Mtl.	12	509	195	192	387	231	43	15	18	33	34	2	1927-28	1939-40
Barry, Ray	Bos.	1	18	1	2	3	6	....	....	....	....	....	....	1951-52	1951-52
Bartel, Robin	Cgy., Van.	2	41	0	1	1	14	6	0	0	0	16	....	1985-86	1986-87
Bartlett, Jim	Mtl., NYR, Bos.	5	191	34	23	57	273	2	0	0	0	0	....	1954-55	1960-61
● Barton, Cliff	Pit., Phi., NYR	3	85	10	9	19	22	....	....	....	....	....	....	1929-30	1939-40
Bartos, Peter	Min.	1	13	4	2	6	6	....	....	....	....	....	....	2000-01	2000-01
‡ Bashkirov, Andrei	Mtl.	3	30	0	3	3	0	....	....	....	....	....	....	1998-99	2000-01
Bassen, Bob	NYI, Chi., St.L., Que., Dal., Cgy.	15	765	88	144	232	1004	93	9	15	24	134	....	1985-86	1999-00
Bast, Ryan	Phi.	1	2	0	1	1	0	....	....	....	....	....	....	1998-99	1998-99
Bathe, Frank	Det., Phi.	9	224	3	28	31	542	27	1	3	4	42	....	1974-75	1983-84
Bathgate, Andy	NYR, Tor., Det., Pit.	17	1069	349	624	973	624	54	21	14	35	76	1	1952-53	1970-71
Bathgate, Frank	NYR	1	2	0	0	0	2	....	....	....	....	....	....	1952-53	1952-53
● Batters, Jeff	St.L.	2	16	0	0	0	28	....	....	....	....	....	....	1993-94	1994-95
Batyrshin, Ruslan	L.A.	1	2	0	0	0	6	....	....	....	....	....	....	1995-96	1995-96
● Bauer, Bobby	Bos.	9	327	123	137	260	36	48	11	8	19	6	2	1936-37	1951-52
Baumgartner, Ken	L.A., NYI, Tor., Ana., Bos.	12	696	13	41	54	2244	51	1	2	3	106	....	1987-88	1998-99
Baumgartner, Mike	K.C.	1	17	0	0	0	0	....	....	....	....	....	....	1974-75	1974-75
Baun, Bob	Tor., Oak., Det.	17	964	37	187	224	1493	96	3	12	15	171	4	1956-57	1972-73
Bautin, Sergei	Wpg., Det., S.J.	3	132	5	25	30	176	6	0	0	0	2	....	1992-93	1995-96
Bawa, Robin	Wsh., Van., S.J., Ana.	4	61	6	1	7	60	1	0	0	0	0	....	1989-90	1993-94
Baxter, Paul	Que., Pit., Cgy.	8	472	48	121	169	1564	40	0	5	5	162	....	1979-80	1986-87
Beadle, Sandy	Wpg.	1	6	1	0	1	2	....	....	....	....	....	....	1980-81	1980-81
Beaton, Frank	NYR	2	25	1	1	2	43	....	....	....	....	....	....	1978-79	1979-80
● Beattie, Red	Bos., Det., NYA	9	334	62	85	147	137	24	4	2	6	8	....	1930-31	1938-39
Beaudin, Norm	St.L., Min.	2	25	1	2	3	4	....	....	....	....	....	....	1967-68	1970-71
Beaudoin, Serge	Atl.	1	3	0	0	0	0	....	....	....	....	....	....	1979-80	1979-80
Beaudoin, Yves	Wsh.	3	11	0	0	0	5	....	....	....	....	....	....	1985-86	1987-88
‡ Beaufait, Mark	S.J.	1	5	1	0	1	0	....	....	....	....	....	....	1992-93	1992-93
Beck, Barry	Col., NYR, L.A.	10	615	104	251	355	1016	51	10	23	33	77	....	1977-78	1989-90
Beckett, Bob	Bos.	4	68	7	6	13	18	....	....	....	....	....	....	1956-57	1963-64
Bedard, James	Chi.	2	22	1	1	2	8	....	....	....	....	....	....	1949-50	1950-51
Beddoes, Clayton	Bos.	2	60	2	8	10	57	....	....	....	....	....	....	1995-96	1996-97
‡ Bednar, Jaroslav	L.A., Fla.	3	102	10	25	35	30	3	0	0	0	0	....	2001-02	2003-04
Bednarski, John	NYR, Edm.	4	100	2	18	20	114	1	0	0	0	17	....	1974-75	1979-80
Beers, Bob	Bos., T.B., Edm., NYI	8	258	28	79	107	225	21	1	1	2	22	....	1989-90	1996-97
Beers, Eddy	Cgy., St.L.	5	250	94	116	210	256	41	7	10	17	47	....	1981-82	1985-86
● Behling, Dick	Det.	2	5	1	0	1	2	....	....	....	....	....	....	1940-41	1942-43
● Beisler, Frank	NYA	2	2	0	0	0	0	....	....	....	....	....	....	1936-37	1939-40
‡ Bekar, Derek	St.L., L.A., NYI	3	11	0	0	0	6	....	....	....	....	....	....	1999-00	2003-04
Belanger, Alain	Tor.	1	9	0	1	1	6	....	....	....	....	....	....	1977-78	1977-78

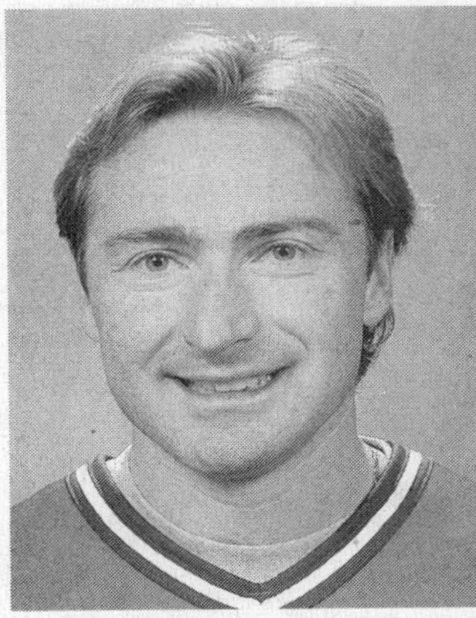

Donald Audette

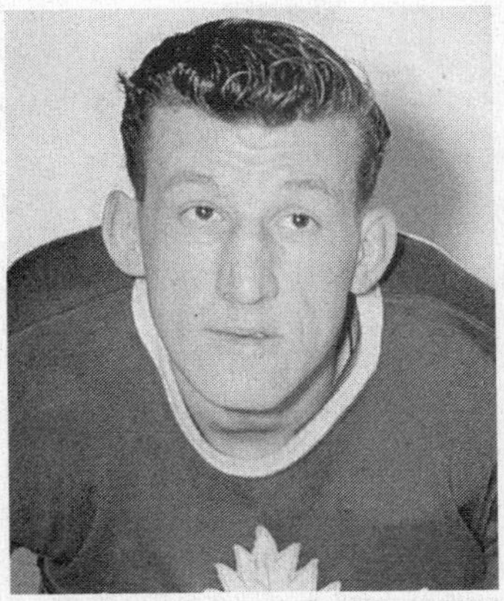

Pete Backor

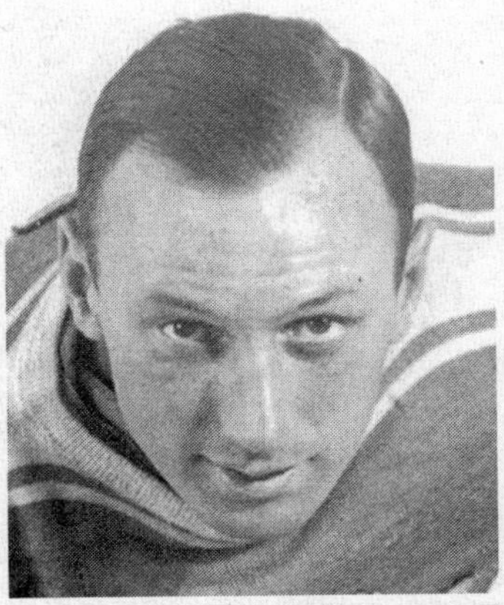

Ace Bailey

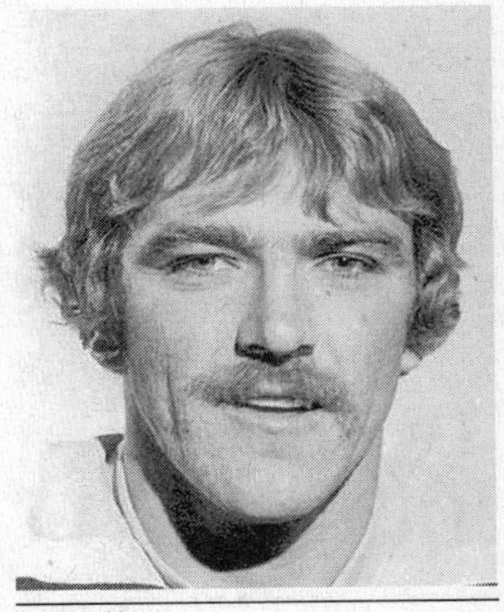

Bryon Baltimore

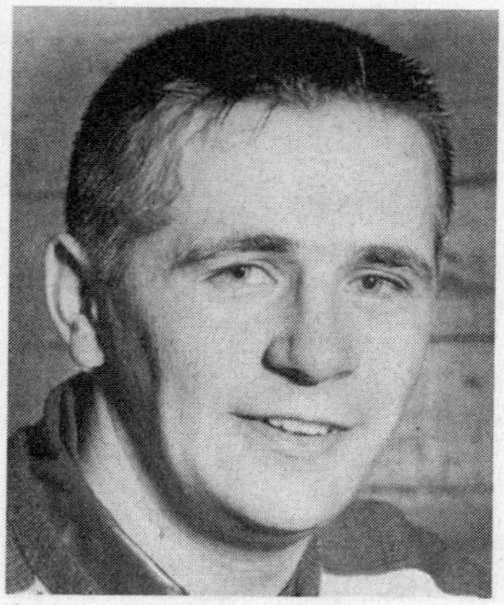
Stan Baluik

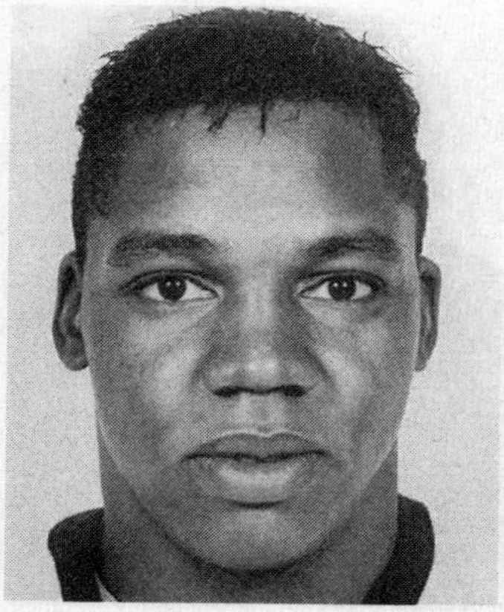
Darren Banks

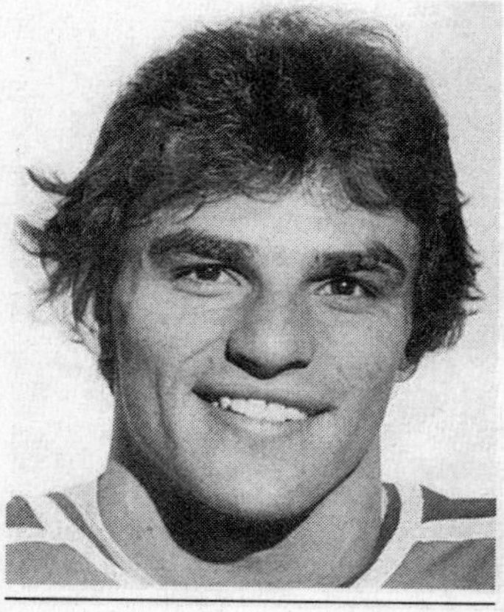
Blair Barnes

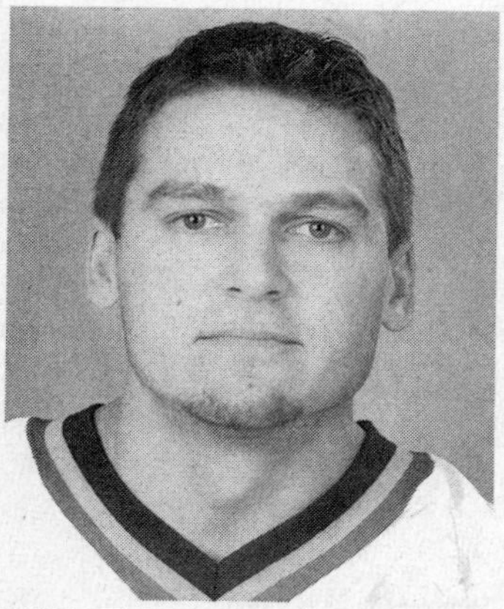
Murray Baron

Name	NHL Teams	NHL Seasons	Regular Schedule GP	G	A	TP	PIM	Playoffs GP	G	A	TP	PIM	NHL Cup Wins	First NHL Season	Last NHL Season
‡ Belanger, Francis	Mtl.	1	10	0	0	0	29	....	....	....	....	....	....	2000-01	2000-01
Belanger, Jesse	Mtl., Fla., Van., Edm., NYI	8	246	59	76	135	56	12	0	3	3	2	....	1991-92	2000-01
Belanger, Roger	Pit.	1	44	3	5	8	32	....	....	....	....	....	....	1984-85	1984-85
Belisle, Danny	NYR	1	4	2	0	2	0	....	....	....	....	....	....	1960-61	1960-61
Beliveau, Jean	Mtl.	20	1125	507	712	1219	1029	162	79	97	176	211	10	1950-51	1970-71
● Bell, Billy	Mtl.W., Mtl., Ott.	6	72	4	2	6	14	5	0	0	0	0	1	1917-18	1923-24
Bell, Bruce	Que., St.L., NYR, Edm.	5	209	12	64	76	113	34	3	5	8	41	....	1984-85	1989-90
Bell, Harry	NYR	1	1	0	1	1	0	....	....	....	....	....	....	1946-47	1946-47
Bell, Joe	NYR	2	62	8	9	17	18	....	....	....	....	....	....	1942-43	1946-47
Belland, Neil	Van., Pit.	6	109	13	32	45	54	21	2	9	11	23	....	1981-82	1986-87
‡ Bellefeuille, Blake	CBJ	2	5	0	1	1	0	....	....	....	....	....	....	2001-02	2002-03
● Bellefeuille, Pete	Tor., Det.	4	92	26	4	30	58	....	....	....	....	....	....	1925-26	1929-30
● Bellemer, Andy	Mtl.M.	1	15	0	0	0	0	....	....	....	....	....	....	1932-33	1932-33
Bellows, Brian	Min., Mtl., T.B., Ana., Wsh.	17	1188	485	537	1022	718	143	51	71	122	143	1	1982-83	1998-99
● Bend, Lin	NYR	1	8	3	1	4	2	....	....	....	....	....	....	1942-43	1942-43
‡ Benda, Jan	Wsh.	1	9	0	3	3	6	....	....	....	....	....	....	1997-98	1997-98
Bennett, Adam	Chi., Edm.	3	69	3	8	11	69	....	....	....	....	....	....	1991-92	1993-94
Bennett, Bill	Bos., Hfd.	2	31	4	7	11	65	....	....	....	....	....	....	1978-79	1979-80
Bennett, Curt	St.L., NYR, Atl.	10	580	152	182	334	347	21	1	1	2	57	....	1970-71	1979-80
Bennett, Frank	Det.	1	7	0	1	1	2	....	....	....	....	....	....	1943-44	1943-44
Bennett, Harvey	Pit., Wsh., Phi., Min., St.L.	5	268	44	46	90	347	4	0	0	0	2	....	1974-75	1978-79
● Bennett, Max	Mtl.	1	1	0	0	0	0	....	....	....	....	....	....	1935-36	1935-36
Bennett, Rick	NYR	3	15	1	1	2	13	....	....	....	....	....	....	1989-90	1991-92
Benning, Brian	St.L., L.A., Phi., Edm., Fla.	11	568	63	233	296	963	48	3	20	23	74	....	1984-85	1994-95
Benning, Jim	Tor., Van.	9	605	52	191	243	461	7	1	1	2	2	....	1981-82	1989-90
● Benoit, Joe	Mtl.	5	185	75	69	144	94	11	6	3	9	11	1	1940-41	1946-47
Benson, Bill	NYA, Bro.	2	67	11	25	36	35	....	....	....	....	....	....	1940-41	1941-42
● Benson, Bobby	Bos.	1	8	0	1	1	4	....	....	....	....	....	....	1924-25	1924-25
● Bentley, Doug	Chi., NYR	13	566	219	324	543	217	23	9	8	17	12	....	1939-40	1953-54
● Bentley, Max	Chi., Tor., NYR	12	646	245	299	544	179	51	18	27	45	14	3	1940-41	1953-54
Bentley, Reg	Chi.	1	11	1	2	3	2	....	....	....	....	....	....	1942-43	1942-43
‡ Benysek, Ladislav	Edm., Min.	4	161	3	12	15	74	....	....	....	....	....	....	1997-98	2002-03
Beraldo, Paul	Bos.	2	10	0	0	0	4	....	....	....	....	....	....	1987-88	1988-89
‡ Beranek, Josef	Edm., Phi., Van., Pit.	9	531	118	144	262	398	57	5	8	13	24	....	1991-92	2000-01
‡ Berehowsky, Drake	Tor., Pit., Edm., Nsh., Van., Phx.	13	549	37	112	149	848	22	1	3	4	30	....	1990-91	2003-04
Berenson, Red	Mtl., NYR, St.L., Det.	17	987	261	397	658	305	85	23	14	37	49	1	1961-62	1977-78
Berenzweig, Bubba	Nsh.	4	37	3	7	10	14	....	....	....	....	....	....	1999-00	2002-03
Berezan, Perry	Cgy., Min., S.J.	9	378	61	75	136	279	31	4	7	11	34	....	1984-85	1992-93
Berezin, Sergei	Tor., Phx., Mtl., Chi., Wsh.	7	502	160	126	286	54	52	13	17	30	6	....	1996-97	2002-03
Berg, Bill	NYI, Tor., NYR, Ott.	10	546	55	67	122	488	61	3	4	7	34	....	1988-89	1998-99
● Bergdinon, Fred	Bos.	1	2	0	0	0	0	....	....	....	....	....	....	1925-26	1925-26
Bergen, Todd	Phi.	1	14	11	5	16	4	17	4	9	13	8	....	1984-85	1984-85
Berger, Mike	Min.	2	30	3	1	4	67	....	....	....	....	....	....	1987-88	1988-89
Bergeron, Michel	Det., NYI, Wsh.	5	229	80	58	138	165	....	....	....	....	....	....	1974-75	1978-79
Bergeron, Yves	Pit.	2	3	0	0	0	0	....	....	....	....	....	....	1974-75	1976-77
Bergevin, Marc	Chi., NYI, Hfd., T.B., Det., St.L., Pit., Van.	20	1191	36	145	181	1090	79	3	6	9	50	....	1984-85	2003-04
Bergkvist, Stefan	Pit.	2	7	0	0	0	9	4	0	0	0	2	....	1995-96	1996-97
Bergland, Tim	Wsh., T.B.	5	182	17	26	43	75	26	2	2	4	22	....	1989-90	1993-94
Bergloff, Bob	Min.	1	2	0	0	0	5	....	....	....	....	....	....	1982-83	1982-83
Berglund, Bo	Que., Min., Phi.	3	130	28	39	67	40	9	2	0	2	6	....	1983-84	1985-86
● Bergman, Gary	Det., Min., K.C.	12	838	68	299	367	1249	21	0	5	5	20	....	1964-65	1975-76
Bergman, Thommie	Det.	6	246	21	44	65	243	7	0	2	2	2	....	1972-73	1979-80
Bergqvist, Jonas	Cgy.	1	22	2	5	7	10	....	....	....	....	....	....	1989-90	1989-90
● Berlinquette, Louis	Mtl., Mtl.M., Pit.	8	193	45	33	78	129	11	0	5	5	9	....	1917-18	1925-26
Bernier, Serge	Phi., L.A., Que.	7	302	78	119	197	234	5	1	1	2	0	....	1968-69	1980-81
Berry, Bob	Mtl., L.A.	8	541	159	191	350	344	26	2	6	8	6	....	1968-69	1976-77
Berry, Brad	Wpg., Min., Dal.	8	241	4	28	32	323	13	0	1	1	16	....	1985-86	1993-94
Berry, Doug	Col.	2	121	10	33	43	25	....	....	....	....	....	....	1979-80	1980-81
Berry, Fred	Det.	1	3	0	0	0	0	....	....	....	....	....	....	1976-77	1976-77
Berry, Ken	Edm., Van.	4	55	8	10	18	30	....	....	....	....	....	....	1981-82	1988-89
Bertrand, Eric	N.J., Atl., Mtl.	2	15	0	0	0	4	....	....	....	....	....	....	1999-00	2000-01
Berube, Craig	Phi., Tor., Cgy., Wsh., NYI	17	1054	61	98	159	3149	89	3	1	4	211	....	1986-87	2002-03
● Besler, Phil	Bos., Chi., Det.	2	30	1	4	5	18	....	....	....	....	....	....	1935-36	1938-39
● Bessone, Pete	Det.	1	6	0	1	1	6	....	....	....	....	....	....	1937-38	1937-38
Bethel, John	Wpg.	1	17	0	2	2	4	....	....	....	....	....	....	1979-80	1979-80
Betik, Karel	T.B.	1	3	0	2	2	2	....	....	....	....	....	....	1998-99	1998-99
Bettis, Maxim	Ana.	1	3	0	0	0	0	....	....	....	....	....	....	1993-94	1993-94
● Bettio, Sam	Bos.	1	44	9	12	21	32	....	....	....	....	....	....	1949-50	1949-50
Beukeboom, Jeff	Edm., NYR	14	804	30	129	159	1890	99	3	16	19	197	4	1985-86	1998-99
Beverley, Nick	Bos., Pit., NYR, Min., L.A., Col.	11	502	18	94	112	156	7	0	1	1	0	....	1966-67	1979-80
‡ Bezina, Goran	Phx.	1	3	0	0	0	2	....	....	....	....	....	....	2003-04	2003-04
Bialowas, Dwight	Atl., Min.	4	164	11	46	57	46	....	....	....	....	....	....	1973-74	1976-77
Bialowas, Frank	Tor.	1	3	0	0	0	12	....	....	....	....	....	....	1993-94	1993-94
Bianchin, Wayne	Pit., Edm.	7	276	68	41	109	137	3	0	1	1	6	....	1973-74	1979-80
Bicanek, Radim	Ott., Chi., CBJ	7	122	1	11	12	62	7	0	0	0	8	....	1994-95	2001-02
Bidner, Todd	Wsh.	1	12	2	1	3	7	....	....	....	....	....	....	1981-82	1981-82
Biggs, Don	Min., Phi.	2	12	2	0	2	8	....	....	....	....	....	....	1984-85	1989-90
Bignell, Larry	Pit.	2	20	0	3	3	2	3	0	0	0	2	....	1973-74	1974-75
Bilodeau, Gilles	Que.	1	9	0	1	1	25	....	....	....	....	....	....	1979-80	1979-80
● Bionda, Jack	Tor., Bos.	4	93	3	9	12	113	11	0	1	1	14	....	1955-56	1958-59
Bissett, Tom	Det.	1	5	0	0	0	0	....	....	....	....	....	....	1990-91	1990-91
Bjugstad, Scott	Min., Pit., L.A.	9	317	76	68	144	144	9	0	1	1	2	....	1983-84	1991-92
Black, James	Hfd., Min., Dal., Buf., Chi., Wsh.	11	352	58	57	115	84	13	2	1	3	4	....	1989-90	2000-01
Black, Steve	Det., Chi.	2	113	11	20	31	77	13	0	0	0	13	1	1949-50	1950-51
Blackburn, Bob	NYR, Pit.	3	135	8	12	20	105	6	0	0	0	4	....	1968-69	1970-71
Blackburn, Don	Bos., Phi., NYR, NYI, Min.	6	185	23	44	67	87	12	3	0	3	10	....	1962-63	1972-73
● Blade, Hank	Chi.	2	24	2	3	5	2	....	....	....	....	....	....	1946-47	1947-48
Bladon, Tom	Phi., Pit., Edm., Wpg., Det.	9	610	73	197	270	392	86	8	29	37	70	2	1972-73	1980-81
● Blaine, Garry	Mtl.	1	1	0	0	0	0	....	....	....	....	....	....	1954-55	1954-55
● Blair, Andy	Tor., Chi.	9	402	74	86	160	323	38	6	6	12	32	1	1928-29	1936-37
Blair, Chuck	Tor.	1	1	0	0	0	0	....	....	....	....	....	....	1948-49	1948-49
Blair, Dusty	Tor.	1	2	0	0	0	0	....	....	....	....	....	....	1950-51	1950-51
Blaisdell, Mike	Det., NYR, Pit., Tor.	9	343	70	84	154	166	6	1	2	3	10	....	1980-81	1988-89
Blake, Bob	Bos.	1	12	0	0	0	0	....	....	....	....	....	....	1935-36	1935-36
● Blake, Mickey	Mtl.M., St.L., Tor.	3	10	1	1	2	4	....	....	....	....	....	....	1932-33	1935-36
● Blake, Toe	Mtl.M., Mtl.	14	577	235	292	527	272	58	25	37	62	23	3	1934-35	1947-48
● Blight, Rick	Van., L.A.	7	326	96	125	221	170	5	0	5	5	2	....	1975-76	1982-83
● Blinco, Russ	Mtl.M., Chi.	6	268	59	66	125	24	19	3	3	6	4	1	1933-34	1938-39
Block, Ken	Van.	1	1	0	0	0	0	....	....	....	....	....	....	1970-71	1970-71
Bloemberg, Jeff	NYR	4	43	3	6	9	25	7	0	3	3	5	....	1988-89	1991-92
Blomqvist, Timo	Wsh., N.J.	5	243	4	53	57	293	13	0	0	0	24	....	1981-82	1986-87
Blomsten, Arto	Wpg., L.A.	3	25	0	4	4	8	....	....	....	....	....	....	1993-94	1995-96
Bloom, Mike	Wsh., Det.	3	201	30	47	77	215	....	....	....	....	....	....	1974-75	1976-77
‡ Blouin, Sylvain	NYR, Mtl., Min.	6	115	3	4	7	336	....	....	....	....	....	....	1996-97	2002-03
Blum, John	Edm., Bos., Wsh., Det.	8	250	7	34	41	610	20	0	2	2	27	....	1982-83	1989-90
Bodak, Bob	Cgy., Hfd.	2	4	0	0	0	29	....	....	....	....	....	....	1987-88	1989-90
Boddy, Gregg	Van.	5	273	23	44	67	263	3	0	0	0	0	....	1971-72	1975-76
Bodger, Doug	Pit., Buf., S.J., N.J., L.A., Van.	16	1071	106	422	528	1007	47	6	18	24	25	....	1984-85	1999-00
● Bodnar, Gus	Tor., Chi., Bos.	12	667	142	254	396	207	32	4	3	7	10	2	1943-44	1954-55
Boehm, Ron	Oak.	1	16	2	1	3	10	....	....	....	....	....	....	1967-68	1967-68
● Boesch, Garth	Tor.	4	197	9	28	37	205	34	2	5	7	18	3	1946-47	1949-50
Boh, Rick	Min.	1	8	2	1	3	4	....	....	....	....	....	....	1987-88	1987-88
‡ Bohonos, Lonny	Van., Tor.	4	83	19	16	35	22	9	3	6	9	2	....	1995-96	1998-99
Boikov, Alexandre	Nsh.	2	10	0	0	0	15	....	....	....	....	....	....	1999-00	2000-01
● Boileau, Marc	Det.	1	54	5	6	11	8	....	....	....	....	....	....	1961-62	1961-62
Boileau, Rene	NYA	1	7	0	0	0	0	....	....	....	....	....	....	1925-26	1925-26
Boimistruck, Fred	Tor.	2	83	4	14	18	45	....	....	....	....	....	....	1981-82	1982-83
Boisvert, Serge	Tor., Mtl.	5	46	5	7	12	8	23	3	7	10	4	1	1982-83	1987-88
Boivin, Claude	Phi., Ott.	4	132	12	19	31	364	....	....	....	....	....	....	1991-92	1994-95
Boivin, Leo	Tor., Bos., Det., Pit., Min.	19	1150	72	250	322	1192	54	3	10	13	59	....	1951-52	1969-70
Boland, Mike	Phi.	1	2	0	0	0	0	....	....	....	....	....	....	1974-75	1974-75
Boland, Mike	K.C., Buf.	2	23	1	2	3	29	3	1	0	1	2	....	1974-75	1978-79
Boldirev, Ivan	Bos., Cal., Chi., Atl., Van., Det.	15	1052	361	505	866	507	48	13	20	33	14	....	1970-71	1984-85
Bolduc, Danny	Det., Cgy.	3	102	22	19	41	33	1	0	0	0	0	....	1978-79	1983-84

Name	NHL Teams	NHL Seasons	Regular Schedule					Playoffs					NHL Cup Wins	First NHL Season	Last NHL Season
			GP	G	A	TP	PIM	GP	G	A	TP	PIM			
Bolduc, Michel	Que.	2	10	0	0	0	6	....	....	....	....	....	....	1981-82	1982-83
• Boll, Buzz	Tor., NYA, Bro., Bos.	12	437	133	130	263	148	31	7	3	10	13	....	1932-33	1943-44
Bolonchuk, Larry	Van., Wsh.	4	74	3	9	12	97	....	....	....	....	....	....	1972-73	1977-78
• Bolton, Hugh	Tor.	8	235	10	51	61	221	17	0	5	5	14	1	1949-50	1956-57
Bombardir, Brad	N.J., Min., Nsh.	7	356	8	46	54	127	16	0	1	1	2	1	1997-98	2003-04
Bonar, Dan	L.A.	3	170	25	39	64	208	14	3	4	7	22	....	1980-81	1982-83
Bonin, Brian	Pit., Min.	2	12	0	0	0	0	3	0	0	0	0	....	1998-99	2000-01
Bonin, Marcel	Det., Bos., Mtl.	9	454	97	175	272	336	50	11	14	25	51	4	1952-53	1961-62
Bonni, Ryan	Van.	1	3	0	0	0	0	....	....	....	....	....	....	1999-00	1999-00
‡ Bonsignore, Jason	Edm., T.B.	4	79	3	13	16	34	....	....	....	....	....	....	1994-95	1998-99
Boo, Jim	Min.	1	6	0	0	0	22	....	....	....	....	....	....	1977-78	1977-78
• Boone, Buddy	Bos.	2	34	5	3	8	28	22	2	1	3	25	....	1956-57	1957-58
• Boothman, George	Tor.	2	58	17	19	36	18	5	2	1	3	2	....	1942-43	1943-44
Bordeleau, Christian	Mtl., St.L., Chi.	4	205	38	65	103	82	19	4	7	11	17	1	1968-69	1971-72
Bordeleau, J.P.	Chi.	10	519	97	126	223	143	48	3	6	9	12	....	1969-70	1979-80
Bordeleau, Paulin	Van.	3	183	33	56	89	47	5	2	1	3	0	....	1973-74	1975-76
‡ Bordeleau, Sebastien	Mtl., Nsh., Min., Phx.	7	251	37	61	98	118	5	0	0	0	2	....	1995-96	2001-02
Borotsik, Jack	St.L.	1	1	0	0	0	0	....	....	....	....	....	....	1974-75	1974-75
Borsato, Luciano	Wpg.	5	203	35	55	90	113	7	1	0	1	4	....	1990-91	1994-95
Borschevsky, Nikolai	Tor., Cgy., Dal.	4	162	49	73	122	44	31	4	9	13	4	....	1992-93	1995-96
Boschman, Laurie	Tor., Edm., Wpg., N.J., Ott.	14	1009	229	348	577	2265	57	8	13	21	140	....	1979-80	1992-93
Bossy, Mike	NYI	10	752	573	553	1126	210	129	85	75	160	38	4	1977-78	1986-87
• Bostrom, Helge	Chi.	4	96	3	3	6	58	13	0	0	0	16	....	1929-30	1932-33
Botell, Mark	Phi.	1	32	4	10	14	31	....	....	....	....	....	....	1981-82	1981-82
Bothwell, Tim	NYR, St.L., Hfd.	12	502	28	93	121	382	49	0	3	3	56	....	1978-79	1988-89
Botterill, Jason	Dal., Atl., Cgy., Buf.	6	88	5	9	14	89	....	....	....	....	....	....	1997-98	2003-04
Botting, Cam	Atl.	1	2	0	1	1	0	....	....	....	....	....	....	1975-76	1975-76
Boucha, Henry	Det., Min., K.C., Col.	6	247	53	49	102	157	....	....	....	....	....	....	1971-72	1976-77
Bouchard, Butch	Mtl.	15	785	49	144	193	863	113	11	21	32	121	4	1941-42	1955-56
Bouchard, Dick	NYR	1	1	0	0	0	0	....	....	....	....	....	....	1954-55	1954-55
• Bouchard, Edmond	Mtl., Ham., NYA, Pit.	8	211	19	21	40	117	....	....	....	....	....	....	1921-22	1928-29
Bouchard, Pierre	Mtl., Wsh.	12	595	24	82	106	433	76	3	10	13	56	5	1970-71	1981-82
• Boucher, Billy	Mtl., Bos., NYA	7	213	93	38	131	409	14	3	0	3	17	1	1921-22	1927-28
• Boucher, Bobby	Mtl.	1	11	1	0	1	0	2	0	0	0	0	1	1923-24	1923-24
• Boucher, Clarence	NYA	2	47	2	2	4	133	....	....	....	....	....	....	1926-27	1927-28
• Boucher, Frank	Ott., NYR	14	557	160	263	423	119	55	16	20	36	12	2	1921-22	1943-44
• Boucher, Georges	Ott., Mtl.M., Chi.	15	449	117	87	204	838	28	5	3	8	88	4	1917-18	1931-32
Boudreau, Bruce	Tor., Chi.	8	141	28	42	70	46	9	2	0	2	0	....	1976-77	1985-86
Boudrias, Andre	Mtl., Min., Chi., St.L., Van.	12	662	151	340	491	216	34	6	10	16	12	....	1963-64	1975-76
Boughner, Barry	Oak., Cal.	2	20	0	0	0	11	....	....	....	....	....	....	1969-70	1970-71
‡ Boumedienne, Josef	N.J., T.B., Wsh.	3	47	4	12	16	36	....	....	....	....	....	....	2001-02	2003-04
Bourbonnais, Dan	Hfd.	2	59	3	25	28	11	....	....	....	....	....	....	1981-82	1983-84
Bourbonnais, Rick	St.L.	3	71	9	15	24	29	4	0	1	1	0	....	1975-76	1977-78
• Bourcier, Conrad	Mtl.	1	6	0	0	0	0	....	....	....	....	....	....	1935-36	1935-36
Bourcier, Jean	Mtl.	1	9	0	1	1	0	....	....	....	....	....	....	1935-36	1935-36
• Bourgeault, Leo	Tor., NYR, Ott., Mtl.	8	307	24	20	44	269	24	1	1	2	18	1	1926-27	1934-35
Bourgeois, Charlie	Cgy., St.L., Hfd.	7	290	16	54	70	788	40	2	3	5	194	....	1981-82	1987-88
Bourne, Bob	NYI, L.A.	14	964	258	324	582	605	139	40	56	96	108	4	1974-75	1987-88
Bourque, Phil	Pit., NYR, Ott.	12	477	88	111	199	516	56	13	12	25	107	2	1983-84	1995-96
Bourque, Raymond	Bos., Col.	22	1612	410	1169	1579	1141	214	41	139	180	171	1	1979-80	2000-01
Boutette, Pat	Tor., Hfd., Pit.	10	756	171	282	453	1354	46	10	14	24	109	....	1975-76	1984-85
Boutilier, Paul	NYI, Bos., Min., NYR, Wpg.	8	288	27	83	110	358	41	1	9	10	45	1	1981-82	1988-89
Bowen, Jason	Phi., Edm.	6	77	2	6	8	109	....	....	....	....	....	....	1992-93	1997-98
Bowler, Bill	CBJ	1	9	0	2	2	8	....	....	....	....	....	....	2000-01	2000-01
Bowman, Kirk	Chi.	3	88	11	17	28	19	7	1	0	1	0	....	1976-77	1978-79
• Bowman, Ralph	Ott., St.L., Det.	7	274	8	17	25	260	22	2	2	4	6	2	1933-34	1939-40
Bownass, Jack	Mtl., NYR	4	80	3	8	11	58	....	....	....	....	....	....	1957-58	1961-62
Bowness, Rick	Atl., Det., St.L., Wpg.	7	173	18	37	55	191	5	0	0	0	2	....	1975-76	1981-82
• Boyd, Bill	NYR, NYA	4	138	15	7	22	72	10	0	0	0	4	1	1926-27	1929-30
• Boyd, Irwin	Bos., Det.	4	96	10	10	20	30	5	0	1	1	4	....	1931-32	1943-44
Boyd, Randy	Pit., Chi., NYI, Van.	8	257	20	67	87	328	13	0	2	2	26	....	1981-82	1988-89
Boyer, Wally	Tor., Chi., Oak., Pit.	7	365	54	105	159	163	15	1	3	4	0	....	1965-66	1971-72
Boyer, Zac	Dal.	2	3	0	0	0	0	2	0	0	0	0	....	1994-95	1995-96
Boyko, Darren	Wpg.	1	1	0	0	0	0	....	....	....	....	....	....	1988-89	1988-89
Bozek, Steve	L.A., Cgy., St.L., Van., S.J.	11	641	164	167	331	309	58	12	11	23	69	....	1981-82	1991-92
‡ Bozon, Philippe	St.L.	4	144	16	25	41	101	19	2	0	2	31	....	1991-92	1994-95
• Brackenborough, John	Bos.	1	7	0	0	0	0	....	....	....	....	....	....	1925-26	1925-26
Brackenbury, Curt	Que., Edm., St.L.	4	141	9	17	26	226	2	0	0	0	0	....	1979-80	1982-83
Bradley, Bart	Bos.	1	1	0	0	0	0	....	....	....	....	....	....	1949-50	1949-50
Bradley, Brian	Cgy., Van., Tor., T.B.	13	651	182	321	503	528	13	3	7	10	16	....	1985-86	1997-98
Bradley, Lyle	Cal., Cle.	2	6	1	0	1	2	....	....	....	....	....	....	1973-74	1976-77
Brady, Neil	N.J., Ott., Dal.	5	89	9	22	31	95	....	....	....	....	....	....	1989-90	1993-94
Bragnalo, Rick	Wsh.	4	145	15	35	50	46	....	....	....	....	....	....	1975-76	1978-79
• Branigan, Andy	NYA, Bro.	2	27	1	2	3	31	....	....	....	....	....	....	1940-41	1941-42
Brasar, Per-Olov	Min., Van.	5	348	64	142	206	33	13	1	2	3	0	....	1977-78	1981-82
• Brayshaw, Russ	Chi.	1	43	5	9	14	24	....	....	....	....	....	....	1944-45	1944-45
Breault, Francois	L.A.	3	27	2	4	6	42	....	....	....	....	....	....	1990-91	1992-93
Breitenbach, Ken	Buf.	3	68	1	13	14	49	8	0	1	1	4	....	1975-76	1978-79
Brennan, Dan	L.A.	2	8	0	1	1	9	....	....	....	....	....	....	1983-84	1985-86
Brennan, Doug	NYR	3	123	9	7	16	152	16	1	0	1	21	1	1931-32	1933-34
‡ Brennan, Rich	Col., S.J., NYR, L.A., Nsh., Bos.	6	50	2	6	8	33	....	....	....	....	....	....	1996-97	2002-03
• Brennan, Tom	Bos.	2	12	2	2	4	2	....	....	....	....	....	....	1943-44	1944-45
Brenneman, John	Chi., NYR, Tor., Det., Oak.	5	152	21	19	40	46	....	....	....	....	....	1	1964-65	1968-69
Bretto, Joe	Chi.	1	3	0	0	0	4	....	....	....	....	....	....	1944-45	1944-45
• Brewer, Carl	Tor., Det., St.L.	12	604	25	198	223	1037	72	3	17	20	146	3	1957-58	1979-80
Brickley, Andy	Phi., Pit., N.J., Bos., Wpg.	11	385	82	140	222	81	17	1	4	5	4	....	1982-83	1993-94
• Briden, Archie	Bos., Det., Pit.	2	71	9	5	14	56	....	....	....	....	....	....	1926-27	1929-30
Bridgman, Mel	Phi., Cgy., N.J., Det., Van.	14	977	252	449	701	1625	125	28	39	67	298	....	1975-76	1988-89
• Briere, Michel	Pit.	1	76	12	32	44	20	10	5	3	8	17	....	1969-70	1969-70
‡ Brimanis, Aris	Phi., NYI, Ana., St.L.	7	113	2	12	14	57	....	....	....	....	....	....	1993-94	2003-04
Brindley, Doug	Tor.	1	3	0	0	0	0	....	....	....	....	....	....	1970-71	1970-71
• Brink, Milt	Chi.	1	5	0	0	0	0	....	....	....	....	....	....	1936-37	1936-37
Brisson, Gerry	Mtl.	1	4	0	2	2	4	....	....	....	....	....	....	1962-63	1962-63
Britz, Greg	Tor., Hfd.	3	8	0	0	0	4	....	....	....	....	....	....	1983-84	1986-87
• Broadbent, Punch	Ott., Mtl.M., NYA	11	303	121	51	172	564	23	4	6	10	60	4	1918-19	1928-29
Brochu, Stephane	NYR	1	1	0	0	0	0	....	....	....	....	....	....	1988-89	1988-89
Broden, Connie	Mtl.	3	6	2	1	3	2	7	0	1	1	0	2	1955-56	1957-58
Brooke, Bob	NYR, Min., N.J.	7	447	69	97	166	520	34	9	9	18	59	....	1983-84	1989-90
Brooks, Gord	St.L., Wsh.	3	70	7	18	25	37	....	....	....	....	....	....	1971-72	1974-75
• Brophy, Bernie	Mtl.M., Det.	3	62	4	4	8	25	2	0	0	0	2	1	1925-26	1929-30
Brossart, Willie	Phi., Tor., Wsh.	6	129	1	14	15	88	1	0	0	0	0	....	1970-71	1975-76
Broten, Aaron	Col., N.J., Min., Que., Tor., Wpg.	12	748	186	329	515	441	34	7	18	25	40	....	1980-81	1991-92
Broten, Neal	Min., Dal., N.J., L.A.	17	1099	289	634	923	569	135	35	63	98	77	1	1980-81	1996-97
Broten, Paul	NYR, Dal., St.L.	7	322	46	55	101	264	38	4	6	10	18	....	1989-90	1995-96
Brousseau, Paul	Col., T.B., Fla.	4	26	1	3	4	29	....	....	....	....	....	....	1995-96	2000-01
• Brown, Adam	Det., Chi., Bos.	10	391	104	113	217	378	26	2	4	6	14	1	1941-42	1951-52
Brown, Arnie	Tor., NYR, Det., NYI, Atl.	12	681	44	141	185	738	22	0	6	6	23	....	1961-62	1973-74
‡ Brown, Cam	Van.	1	1	0	0	0	7	....	....	....	....	....	....	1990-91	1990-91
• Brown, Connie	Det.	5	73	15	24	39	12	14	2	3	5	0	1	1938-39	1942-43
Brown, Dave	Phi., Edm., S.J.	14	729	45	52	97	1789	80	2	3	5	209	1	1982-83	1995-96
Brown, Doug	N.J., Pit., Det.	15	854	160	214	374	210	109	23	23	46	26	2	1986-87	2000-01
• Brown, Fred	Mtl.M.	1	19	1	0	1	0	9	0	0	0	0	....	1927-28	1927-28
Brown, George	Mtl.	3	79	6	22	28	34	7	0	0	0	2	....	1936-37	1938-39
• Brown, Gerry	Det.	2	23	4	5	9	2	12	2	1	3	4	....	1941-42	1945-46
Brown, Greg	Buf., Pit., Wpg.	4	94	4	14	18	86	6	0	1	1	4	....	1990-91	1994-95
Brown, Harold	NYR	1	13	2	1	3	2	....	....	....	....	....	....	1945-46	1945-46
Brown, Jeff	Que., St.L., Van., Hfd., Car., Tor., Wsh.	13	747	154	430	584	498	87	20	45	65	59	....	1985-86	1997-98
Brown, Jim	L.A.	1	3	0	1	1	5	....	....	....	....	....	....	1982-83	1982-83
Brown, Keith	Chi., Fla.	16	876	68	274	342	916	103	4	32	36	184	....	1979-80	1994-95
Brown, Kevin	L.A., Hfd., Car., Edm.	6	64	7	9	16	28	1	0	0	0	0	....	1994-95	1999-00
Brown, Larry	NYR, Det., Phi., L.A.	9	455	7	53	60	180	35	0	4	4	10	....	1969-70	1977-78
Brown, Rob	Pit., Hfd., Chi., Dal., L.A.	11	543	190	248	438	599	54	12	14	26	45	....	1987-88	1999-00
• Brown, Stan	NYR, Det.	2	48	8	2	10	18	2	0	0	0	0	....	1926-27	1927-28
Brown, Wayne	Bos.	1	....	....	....	....	....	4	0	0	0	2	....	1953-54	1953-54
• Browne, Cecil	Chi.	1	13	2	0	2	4	....	....	....	....	....	....	1927-28	1927-28

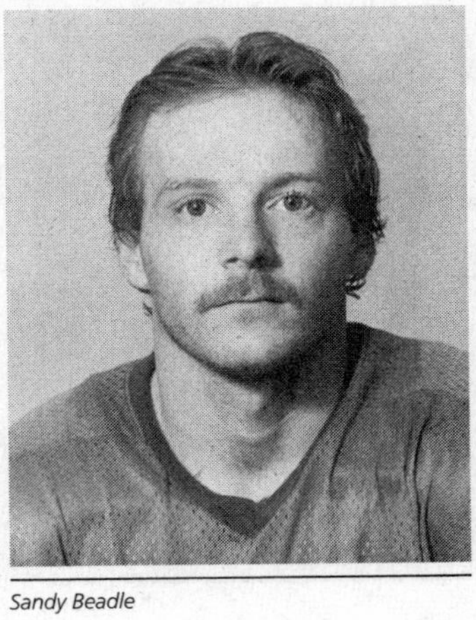

Sandy Beadle

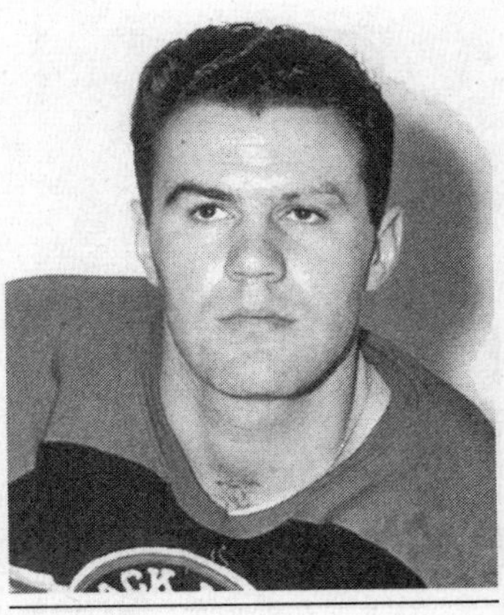

James Bedard

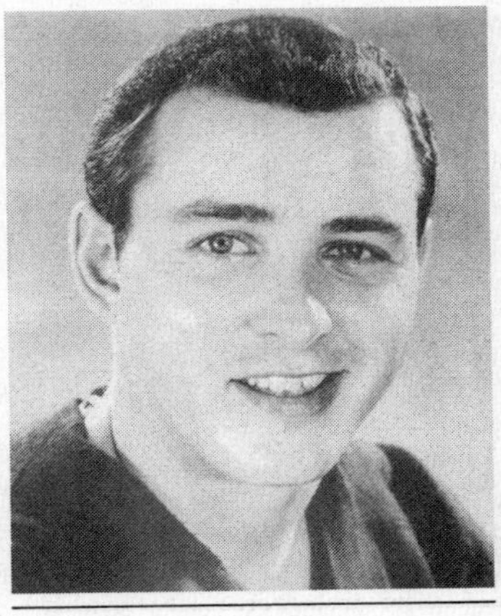

John Brenneman

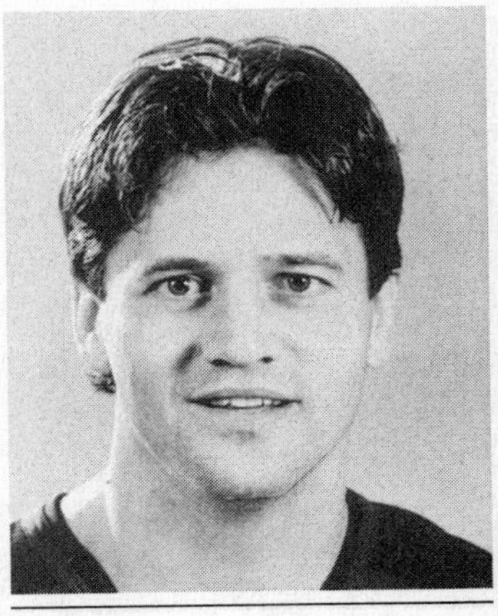

Paul Broten

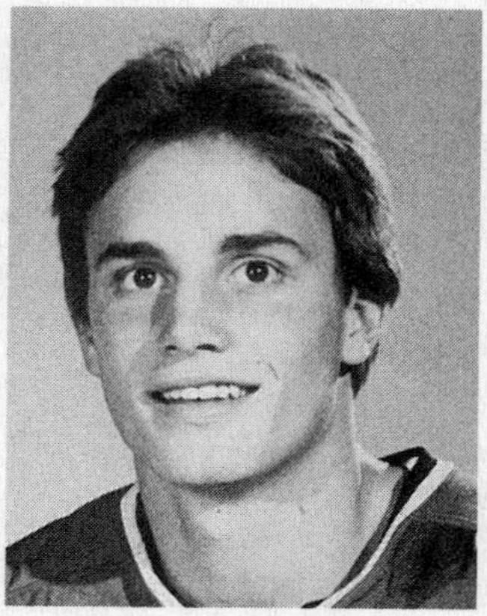

Keith Brown

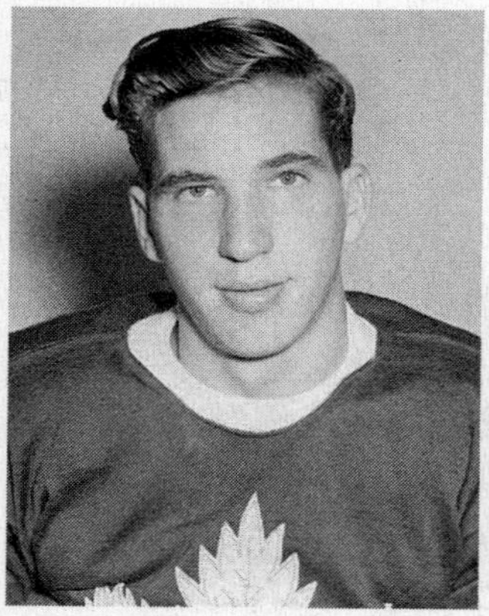

Al Buchanan

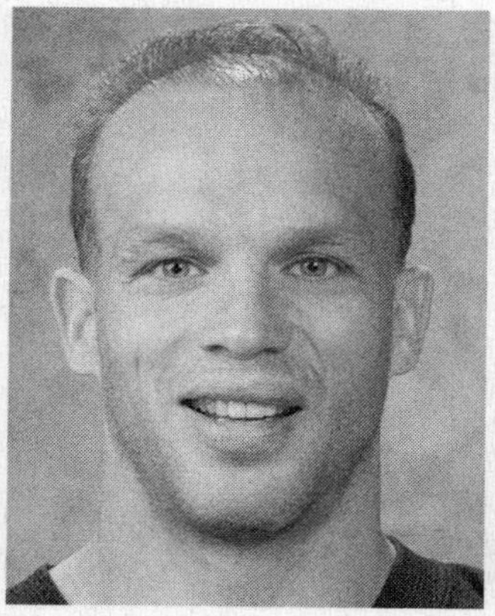

Kelly Buchberger

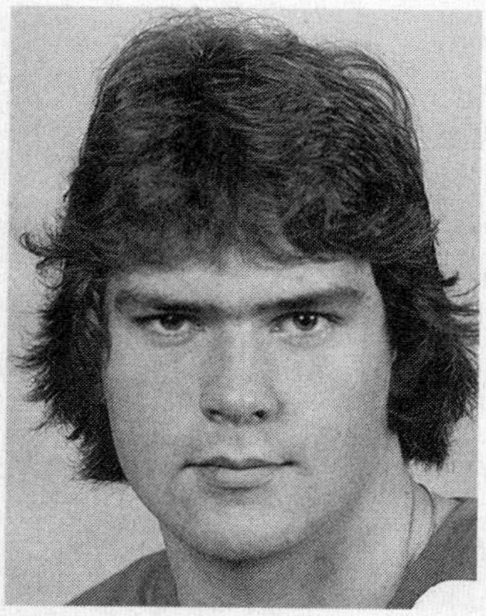

Eric Calder

Name	NHL Teams	NHL Seasons	Regular Schedule					Playoffs					NHL Cup Wins	First NHL Season	Last NHL Season
			GP	G	A	TP	PIM	GP	G	A	TP	PIM			
Brownschidle, Jack	St.L., Hfd.	9	494	39	162	201	151	26	0	5	5	18	....	1977-78	1985-86
• Brownschidle, Jeff	Hfd.	2	7	0	1	1	2	....	....	....	....	....	....	1981-82	1982-83
Brubaker, Jeff	Hfd., Mtl., Cgy., Tor., Edm., NYR, Det.	8	178	16	9	25	512	2	0	0	0	27	....	1979-80	1988-89
Bruce, David	Van., St.L., S.J.	8	234	48	39	87	338	3	0	0	0	2	....	1985-86	1993-94
• Bruce, Gordie	Bos.	3	28	4	9	13	13	7	2	3	5	4	....	1940-41	1945-46
• Bruce, Morley	Ott.	4	71	8	3	11	27	3	0	0	0	2	2	1917-18	1921-22
‡ Brule, Steve	N.J., Col.	2	2	0	0	0	0	1	0	0	0	0	1	1999-00	2002-03
Brumwell, Murray	Min., N.J.	7	128	12	31	43	70	2	0	0	0	2	....	1980-81	1987-88
Brunet, Benoit	Mtl., Dal., Ott.	13	539	101	161	262	229	54	5	20	25	32	1	1988-89	2001-02
• Bruneteau, Eddie	Det.	7	180	40	42	82	35	31	7	6	13	0	....	1940-41	1948-49
• Bruneteau, Mud	Det.	11	411	139	138	277	80	77	23	14	37	22	3	1935-36	1945-46
• Brydge, Bill	Tor., Det., NYA	9	368	26	52	78	506	2	0	0	0	4	....	1926-27	1935-36
Brydges, Paul	Buf.	1	15	2	2	4	6	....	....	....	....	....	....	1986-87	1986-87
• Brydson, Glenn	Mtl.M., St.L., NYR, Chi.	8	299	56	79	135	203	11	0	0	0	8	....	1930-31	1937-38
• Brydson, Gord	Tor.	1	8	2	0	2	8	....	....	....	....	....	....	1929-30	1929-30
Bubla, Jiri	Van.	5	256	17	101	118	202	6	0	0	0	7	....	1981-82	1985-86
• Buchanan, Al	Tor.	2	4	0	1	1	2	....	....	....	....	....	....	1948-49	1949-50
Buchanan, Bucky	NYR	1	2	0	0	0	0	....	....	....	....	....	....	1948-49	1948-49
Buchanan, Jeff	Col.	1	6	0	0	0	6	....	....	....	....	....	....	1998-99	1998-99
Buchanan, Mike	Chi.	1	1	0	0	0	0	....	....	....	....	....	....	1951-52	1951-52
Buchanan, Ron	Bos., St.L.	2	5	0	0	0	0	....	....	....	....	....	....	1966-67	1969-70
Buchberger, Kelly	Edm., Atl., L.A., Phx., Pit.	18	1182	105	204	309	2297	97	10	15	25	129	2	1986-87	2003-04
Bucyk, John	Det., Bos.	23	1540	556	813	1369	497	124	41	62	103	42	2	1955-56	1977-78
Bucyk, Randy	Mtl., Cgy.	2	19	4	2	6	8	2	0	0	0	0	....	1985-86	1987-88
Buhr, Doug	K.C.	1	6	0	2	2	4	....	....	....	....	....	....	1974-75	1974-75
Bukovich, Tony	Det.	2	17	7	3	10	6	6	0	1	1	0	....	1943-44	1944-45
Bullard, Mike	Pit., Cgy., St.L., Phi., Tor.	11	727	329	345	674	703	40	11	18	29	44	....	1980-81	1991-92
• Buller, Hy	Det., NYR	5	188	22	58	80	215	....	....	....	....	....	....	1943-44	1953-54
Bulley, Ted	Chi., Wsh., Pit.	8	414	101	113	214	704	29	5	5	10	24	....	1976-77	1983-84
Burakovsky, Robert	Ott.	1	23	2	3	5	6	....	....	....	....	....	....	1993-94	1993-94
• Burch, Billy	Ham., NYA, Bos., Chi.	11	390	137	61	198	255	2	0	0	0	0	....	1922-23	1932-33
• Burchell, Fred	Mtl.	2	4	0	0	0	2	....	....	....	....	....	....	1950-51	1953-54
Burdon, Glen	K.C.	1	11	0	2	2	0	....	....	....	....	....	....	1974-75	1974-75
Bure, Pavel	Van., Fla., NYR	12	702	437	342	779	484	64	35	35	70	74	....	1991-92	2002-03
Bure, Valeri	Mtl., Cgy., Fla., St.L., Dal.	10	621	174	226	400	221	22	0	7	7	16	....	1994-95	2003-04
Bureau, Marc	Cgy., Min., T.B., Mtl., Phi.	11	567	55	83	138	327	50	5	7	12	46	....	1989-90	1999-00
Burega, Bill	Tor.	1	4	0	1	1	4	....	....	....	....	....	....	1955-56	1955-56
• Burke, Eddie	Bos., NYA	4	106	29	20	49	55	....	....	....	....	....	....	1931-32	1934-35
• Burke, Marty	Mtl., Pit., Ott., Chi.	11	494	19	47	66	560	31	2	4	6	44	2	1927-28	1937-38
• Burmister, Roy	NYA	3	67	4	3	7	2	....	....	....	....	....	....	1929-30	1931-32
Burnett, Kelly	NYR	1	3	1	0	1	0	....	....	....	....	....	....	1952-53	1952-53
• Burns, Bobby	Chi.	3	20	1	0	1	8	....	....	....	....	....	....	1927-28	1929-30
Burns, Charlie	Det., Bos., Oak., Pit., Min.	11	749	106	198	304	252	31	5	4	9	6	....	1958-59	1972-73
Burns, Gary	NYR	2	11	2	2	4	18	5	0	0	0	2	....	1980-81	1981-82
• Burns, Norm	NYR	1	11	0	4	4	2	....	....	....	....	....	....	1941-42	1941-42
Burns, Robin	Pit., K.C.	5	190	31	38	69	139	....	....	....	....	....	....	1970-71	1975-76
Burr, Shawn	Det., T.B., S.J.	16	878	181	259	440	1069	91	16	19	35	95	....	1984-85	1999-00
Burridge, Randy	Bos., Wsh., L.A., Buf.	13	706	199	251	450	458	107	18	34	52	103	....	1985-86	1997-98
Burrows, Dave	Pit., Tor.	10	724	29	135	164	373	29	1	5	6	25	....	1971-72	1980-81
• Burry, Bert	Ott.	1	4	0	0	0	0	....	....	....	....	....	....	1932-33	1932-33
Burt, Adam	Hfd., Car., Phi., Atl.	13	737	37	115	152	961	21	0	1	1	8	....	1988-89	2000-01
Burton, Cummy	Det.	3	43	0	2	2	21	3	0	0	0	0	....	1955-56	1958-59
Burton, Nelson	Wsh.	2	8	1	0	1	21	....	....	....	....	....	....	1977-78	1978-79
• Bush, Eddie	Det.	2	26	4	6	10	40	11	1	6	7	23	....	1938-39	1941-42
Buskas, Rod	Pit., Van., L.A., Chi.	11	556	19	63	82	1294	18	0	3	3	45	....	1982-83	1992-93
Busniuk, Mike	Phi.	2	143	3	23	26	297	25	2	5	7	34	....	1979-80	1980-81
Busniuk, Ron	Buf.	2	6	0	3	3	13	....	....	....	....	....	....	1972-73	1973-74
• Buswell, Walt	Det., Mtl.	8	368	10	40	50	164	24	2	1	3	10	....	1932-33	1939-40
Butcher, Garth	Van., St.L., Que., Tor.	14	897	48	158	206	2302	50	6	5	11	122	....	1981-82	1994-95
Butler, Dick	Chi.	1	7	2	0	2	0	....	....	....	....	....	....	1947-48	1947-48
Butler, Jerry	NYR, St.L., Tor., Van., Wpg.	11	641	99	120	219	515	48	3	3	6	79	....	1972-73	1982-83
Butsayev, Viacheslav	Phi., S.J., Ana., Fla., Ott., T.B.	6	132	17	26	43	133	....	....	....	....	....	....	1992-93	1999-00
Butters, Bill	Min.	2	72	1	4	5	77	....	....	....	....	....	....	1977-78	1978-79
Buttrey, Gord	Chi.	1	10	0	0	0	0	....	....	....	....	....	....	1943-44	1943-44
Buynak, Gord	St.L.	1	4	0	0	0	2	....	....	....	....	....	....	1974-75	1974-75
Buzek, Petr	Dal., Atl., Cgy.	6	157	9	22	31	94	....	....	....	....	....	....	1997-98	2002-03
Byakin, Ilja	Edm., S.J.	2	57	8	25	33	44	....	....	....	....	....	....	1993-94	1994-95
Byce, John	Bos.	3	21	2	3	5	6	8	2	0	2	2	....	1989-90	1991-92
• Byers, Gord	Bos.	1	1	0	1	1	0	....	....	....	....	....	....	1949-50	1949-50
Byers, Jerry	Min., Atl., NYR	4	43	3	4	7	15	....	....	....	....	....	....	1972-73	1977-78
Byers, Lyndon	Bos., S.J.	10	279	28	43	71	1081	37	2	2	4	96	....	1983-84	1992-93
Byers, Mike	Tor., Phi., L.A., Buf.	4	166	42	34	76	39	4	0	1	1	0	....	1967-68	1971-72
Bylsma, Dan	L.A., Ana.	9	429	19	43	62	184	16	0	1	1	2	....	1995-96	2003-04
Byram, Shawn	NYI, Chi.	2	5	0	0	0	14	....	....	....	....	....	....	1990-91	1991-92

C

Name	NHL Teams	NHL Seasons	GP	G	A	TP	PIM	GP	G	A	TP	PIM	NHL Cup Wins	First NHL Season	Last NHL Season
• Caffery, Jack	Tor., Bos.	3	57	3	2	5	22	10	1	0	1	4	....	1954-55	1957-58
Caffery, Terry	Chi., Min.	2	14	0	0	0	0	1	0	0	0	0	....	1969-70	1970-71
• Cahan, Larry	Tor., NYR, Oak., L.A.	13	666	38	92	130	700	29	1	1	2	38	....	1954-55	1970-71
• Cahill, Charles	Bos.	2	32	0	1	1	4	....	....	....	....	....	....	1925-26	1926-27
• Cain, Francis	Mtl.M., Tor.	2	61	4	0	4	35	....	....	....	....	....	....	1924-25	1925-26
• Cain, Herb	Mtl.M., Mtl., Bos.	13	570	206	194	400	178	67	16	13	29	13	2	1933-34	1945-46
Cairns, Don	K.C., Col.	2	9	0	1	1	2	....	....	....	....	....	....	1975-76	1976-77
Calder, Eric	Wsh.	2	2	0	0	0	0	....	....	....	....	....	....	1981-82	1982-83
• Calladine, Norm	Bos.	3	63	19	29	48	8	....	....	....	....	....	....	1942-43	1944-45
Callander, Drew	Phi., Van.	4	39	6	2	8	7	....	....	....	....	....	....	1976-77	1979-80
Callander, Jock	Pit., T.B.	5	109	22	29	51	116	22	3	8	11	12	1	1987-88	1992-93
Callighen, Brett	Edm.	3	160	56	89	145	132	14	4	6	10	8	....	1979-80	1981-82
• Callighen, Patsy	NYR	1	36	0	0	0	32	9	0	0	0	0	1	1927-28	1927-28
‡ Caloun, Jan	S.J., CBJ	3	24	8	6	14	2	....	....	....	....	....	....	1995-96	2000-01
Camazzola, James	Chi.	2	3	0	0	0	0	....	....	....	....	....	....	1983-84	1986-87
Camazzola, Tony	Wsh.	1	3	0	0	0	4	....	....	....	....	....	....	1981-82	1981-82
Cameron, Al	Det., Wpg.	6	282	11	44	55	356	7	0	1	1	2	....	1975-76	1980-81
• Cameron, Billy	Mtl., NYA	2	39	0	0	0	2	2	0	0	0	0	1	1923-24	1925-26
Cameron, Craig	Det., St.L., Min., NYI	9	552	87	65	152	196	27	3	1	4	17	....	1966-67	1975-76
Cameron, Dave	Col., N.J.	3	168	25	28	53	238	....	....	....	....	....	....	1981-82	1983-84
• Cameron, Harry	Tor., Ott., Mtl.	6	128	88	51	139	189	11	5	4	9	16	2	1917-18	1922-23
• Cameron, Scotty	NYR	1	35	8	11	19	0	....	....	....	....	....	....	1942-43	1942-43
Campbell, Bryan	L.A., Chi.	5	260	35	71	106	74	22	3	4	7	2	....	1967-68	1971-72
Campbell, Colin	Pit., Col., Edm., Van., Det.	11	636	25	103	128	1292	45	4	10	14	181	....	1974-75	1984-85
• Campbell, Dave	Mtl.	1	2	0	0	0	0	....	....	....	....	....	....	1920-21	1920-21
Campbell, Don	Chi.	1	17	1	3	4	8	....	....	....	....	....	....	1943-44	1943-44
• Campbell, Earl	Ott., NYA	3	76	6	3	9	14	1	0	0	0	6	....	1923-24	1925-26
Campbell, Scott	Wpg., St.L.	3	80	4	21	25	243	....	....	....	....	....	....	1979-80	1981-82
Campbell, Wade	Wpg., Bos.	6	213	9	27	36	305	10	0	0	0	20	....	1982-83	1987-88
Campeau, Tod	Mtl.	3	42	5	9	14	16	1	0	0	0	0	....	1943-44	1948-49
Campedelli, Dom	Mtl.	1	2	0	0	0	0	....	....	....	....	....	....	1985-86	1985-86
Capuano, Dave	Pit., Van., T.B., S.J.	4	104	17	38	55	56	6	1	1	2	5	....	1989-90	1993-94
Capuano, Jack	Tor., Van., Bos.	3	6	0	0	0	0	....	....	....	....	....	....	1989-90	1991-92
• Carbol, Leo	Chi.	1	6	0	1	1	4	....	....	....	....	....	....	1942-43	1942-43
Carbonneau, Guy	Mtl., St.L., Dal.	19	1318	260	403	663	820	231	38	55	93	161	3	1980-81	1999-00
Cardin, Claude	St.L.	1	1	0	0	0	0	....	....	....	....	....	....	1967-68	1967-68
Cardwell, Steve	Pit.	3	53	9	11	20	35	4	0	0	0	2	....	1970-71	1972-73
• Carey, George	Que., Ham., Tor.	5	72	21	12	33	20	....	....	....	....	....	....	1919-20	1923-24
Carkner, Terry	NYR, Que., Phi., Det., Fla.	13	858	42	188	230	1588	54	1	9	10	48	....	1986-87	1998-99
Carleton, Wayne	Tor., Bos., Cal.	7	278	55	73	128	172	18	2	4	6	14	1	1965-66	1971-72
Carlin, Brian	L.A.	1	5	1	0	1	0	....	....	....	....	....	....	1971-72	1971-72
Carlson, Jack	Min., St.L.	6	236	30	15	45	417	25	1	2	3	72	....	1978-79	1986-87
Carlson, Kent	Mtl., St.L., Wsh.	5	113	7	11	18	148	8	0	0	0	13	....	1983-84	1988-89
Carlson, Steve	L.A.	1	52	9	12	21	23	4	1	1	2	7	....	1979-80	1979-80
Carlsson, Anders	N.J.	3	104	7	26	33	34	3	1	0	1	2	....	1986-87	1988-89
Carlyle, Randy	Tor., Pit., Wpg.	18	1055	148	499	647	1400	69	9	24	33	120	....	1976-77	1992-93
Carnback, Patrik	Mtl., Ana.	4	154	24	38	62	122	....	....	....	....	....	....	1992-93	1995-96

			Regular Schedule					Playoffs							
Name	NHL Teams	NHL Seasons	GP	G	A	TP	PIM	GP	G	A	TP	PIM	NHL Cup Wins	First NHL Season	Last NHL Season
• Caron, Alain	Oak., Mtl.	2	60	9	13	22	18	....	....	....	....	....	....	1967-68	1968-69
Carpenter, Bob	Wsh., NYR, L.A., Bos., N.J.	19	1178	320	408	728	919	140	21	38	59	136	1	1981-82	1998-99
• Carpenter, Ed	Que., Ham.	2	45	10	5	15	41	....	....	....	....	....	....	1919-20	1920-21
Carr, Gene	St.L., NYR, L.A., Pit., Atl.	8	465	79	136	215	365	35	5	8	13	66	....	1971-72	1978-79
Carr, Lorne	NYR, NYA, Tor.	13	580	204	222	426	132	53	10	9	19	13	2	1933-34	1945-46
Carr, Red	Tor.	1	5	0	1	1	2	....	....	....	....	....	....	1943-44	1943-44
Carriere, Larry	Buf., Atl., Van., L.A., Tor.	7	367	16	74	90	462	27	0	3	3	42	....	1972-73	1979-80
• Carrigan, Gene	NYR, Det., St.L.	3	37	2	1	3	13	4	0	0	0	0	....	1930-31	1934-35
Carroll, Billy	NYI, Edm., Det.	7	322	30	54	84	113	71	6	12	18	18	4	1980-81	1986-87
• Carroll, George	Mtl.M., Bos.	1	16	0	0	0	11	....	....	....	....	....	....	1924-25	1924-25
Carroll, Greg	Wsh., Det., Hfd.	2	131	20	34	54	44	....	....	....	....	....	....	1978-79	1979-80
Carruthers, Dwight	Det., Phi.	2	2	0	0	0	0	....	....	....	....	....	....	1965-66	1967-68
• Carse, Bill	NYR, Chi.	4	124	28	43	71	38	13	3	2	5	0	....	1938-39	1941-42
• Carse, Bob	Chi., Mtl.	5	167	32	55	87	52	10	0	2	2	2	....	1939-40	1947-48
• Carson, Bill	Tor., Bos.	4	159	54	24	78	156	11	3	0	3	14	1	1926-27	1929-30
• Carson, Frank	Mtl.M., NYA, Det.	7	248	42	48	90	166	27	0	2	2	9	1	1925-26	1933-34
• Carson, Gerry	Mtl., NYR, Mtl.M.	6	261	12	11	23	205	22	0	0	0	12	1	1928-29	1936-37
Carson, Jimmy	L.A., Edm., Det., Van., Hfd.	10	626	275	286	561	254	55	17	15	32	22	....	1986-87	1995-96
Carson, Lindsay	Phi., Hfd.	7	373	66	80	146	524	49	4	10	14	56	....	1981-82	1987-88
Carter, Billy	Mtl., Bos.	3	16	0	0	0	6	....	....	....	....	....	....	1957-58	1961-62
Carter, John	Bos., S.J.	8	244	40	50	90	201	31	7	5	12	51	....	1985-86	1992-93
Carter, Ron	Edm.	1	2	0	0	0	0	....	....	....	....	....	....	1979-80	1979-80
• Carveth, Joe	Det., Bos., Mtl.	11	504	150	189	339	81	69	21	16	37	28	2	1940-41	1950-51
Cashman, Wayne	Bos.	17	1027	277	516	793	1041	145	31	57	88	250	2	1964-65	1982-83
Casselman, Mike	Fla.	1	3	0	0	0	0	....	....	....	....	....	....	1995-96	1995-96
Cassidy, Bruce	Chi.	7	36	4	13	17	10	1	0	0	0	0	....	1983-84	1989-90
Cassidy, Tom	Pit.	1	26	3	4	7	15	....	....	....	....	....	....	1977-78	1977-78
Cassolato, Tony	Wsh.	3	23	1	6	7	4	....	....	....	....	....	....	1979-80	1981-82
Caufield, Jay	NYR, Min., Pit.	7	208	5	8	13	759	17	0	0	0	42	2	1986-87	1992-93
Cavallini, Gino	Cgy., St.L., Que.	9	593	114	159	273	507	74	14	19	33	66	....	1984-85	1992-93
Cavallini, Paul	Wsh., St.L., Dal.	10	564	56	177	233	750	69	8	27	35	114	....	1986-87	1995-96
Ceresino, Ray	Tor.	1	12	1	1	2	2	....	....	....	....	....	....	1948-49	1948-49
Cernik, Frantisek	Det.	1	49	5	4	9	13	....	....	....	....	....	....	1984-85	1984-85
Chabot, John	Mtl., Pit., Det.	8	508	84	228	312	85	33	6	20	26	2	....	1983-84	1990-91
• Chad, John	Chi.	3	80	15	22	37	29	10	0	1	1	2	....	1939-40	1945-46
• Chalmers, Chick	NYR	1	1	0	0	0	0	....	....	....	....	....	....	1953-54	1953-54
Chalupa, Milan	Det.	1	14	0	5	5	6	....	....	....	....	....	....	1984-85	1984-85
• Chamberlain, Murph	Tor., Mtl., Bro., Bos.	12	510	100	175	275	769	66	14	17	31	96	2	1937-38	1948-49
Chambers, Shawn	Min., Wsh., T.B., N.J., Dal.	13	625	50	185	235	364	94	7	26	33	72	2	1987-88	1999-00
Champagne, Andre	Tor.	1	2	0	0	0	0	....	....	....	....	....	....	1962-63	1962-63
Chapdelaine, Rene	L.A.	3	32	0	2	2	32	....	....	....	....	....	....	1990-91	1992-93
• Chapman, Art	Bos., NYA	10	438	62	176	238	140	26	1	5	6	9	....	1930-31	1939-40
Chapman, Blair	Pit., St.L.	7	402	106	125	231	158	25	4	6	10	15	....	1976-77	1982-83
Chapman, Brian	Hfd.	1	3	0	0	0	29	....	....	....	....	....	....	1990-91	1990-91
Charbonneau, Jose	Mtl., Van.	4	71	9	13	22	67	11	1	0	1	8	....	1987-88	1994-95
Charbonneau, Stephane	Que.	1	2	0	0	0	0	....	....	....	....	....	....	1991-92	1991-92
Charlebois, Bob	Min.	1	7	1	0	1	0	....	....	....	....	....	....	1967-68	1967-68
Charlesworth, Todd	Pit., NYR	6	93	3	9	12	47	....	....	....	....	....	....	1983-84	1989-90
Charron, Eric	Mtl., T.B., Wsh., Cgy.	8	130	2	7	9	127	6	0	0	0	8	....	1992-93	1999-00
Charron, Guy	Mtl., Det., K.C., Wsh.	12	734	221	309	530	146	....	....	....	....	....	....	1969-70	1980-81
Chartier, Dave	Wpg.	1	1	0	0	0	0	....	....	....	....	....	....	1980-81	1980-81
Chartrand, Brad	L.A.	5	215	25	25	50	122	11	1	1	2	8	....	1999-00	2003-04
Chartraw, Rick	Mtl., L.A., NYR, Edm.	10	420	28	64	92	399	75	7	9	16	80	4	1974-75	1983-84
Chase, Kelly	St.L., Hfd., Tor.	11	458	17	36	53	2017	27	1	1	2	100	....	1989-90	1999-00
Chasse, Denis	St.L., Wsh., Wpg., Ott.	4	132	11	14	25	292	7	1	7	8	23	....	1993-94	1996-97
‡ Chebaturkin, Vladimir	NYI, St.L., Chi.	5	62	2	7	9	52	3	0	0	0	2	....	1997-98	2001-02
Check, Lude	Det., Chi.	2	27	6	2	8	4	....	....	....	....	....	....	1943-44	1944-45
Chernoff, Mike	Min.	1	1	0	0	0	0	....	....	....	....	....	....	1968-69	1968-69
Chernomaz, Rich	Col., N.J., Cgy.	7	51	9	7	16	18	....	....	....	....	....	....	1981-82	1991-92
Cherry, Dick	Bos., Phi.	3	145	12	10	22	45	4	1	0	1	4	....	1956-57	1969-70
Cherry, Don	Bos.	1	....	....	....	....	....	1	0	0	0	0	....	1954-55	1954-55
Chervyakov, Denis	Bos.	1	2	0	0	0	2	....	....	....	....	....	....	1992-93	1992-93
• Chevrefils, Real	Bos., Det.	8	387	104	97	201	185	30	5	4	9	20	....	1951-52	1958-59
• Chiasson, Steve	Det., Cgy., Hfd., Car.	13	751	93	305	398	1107	63	16	19	35	119	....	1986-87	1998-99
Chibirev, Igor	Hfd.	2	45	7	12	19	2	....	....	....	....	....	....	1993-94	1994-95
Chicoine, Dan	Cle., Min.	3	31	1	2	3	12	1	0	0	0	0	....	1977-78	1979-80
Chinnick, Rick	Min.	2	4	0	2	2	0	....	....	....	....	....	....	1973-74	1974-75
Chipperfield, Ron	Edm., Que.	2	83	22	24	46	34	....	....	....	....	....	....	1979-80	1980-81
Chisholm, Art	Bos.	1	3	0	0	0	0	....	....	....	....	....	....	1960-61	1960-61
Chisholm, Colin	Min.	1	1	0	0	0	0	....	....	....	....	....	....	1986-87	1986-87
• Chisholm, Lex	Tor.	2	54	10	8	18	19	3	1	0	1	0	....	1939-40	1940-41
Chorney, Marc	Pit., L.A.	4	210	8	27	35	209	7	0	1	1	2	....	1980-81	1983-84
Chorske, Tom	Mtl., N.J., Ott., NYI, Wsh., Cgy., Pit.	11	596	115	122	237	225	50	5	12	17	10	1	1989-90	1999-00
• Chouinard, Gene	Ott.	1	8	0	0	0	0	....	....	....	....	....	....	1927-28	1927-28
Chouinard, Guy	Atl., Cgy., St.L.	10	578	205	370	575	120	46	9	28	37	12	....	1974-75	1983-84
Christian, Dave	Wpg., Wsh., Bos., St.L., Chi.	15	1009	340	433	773	284	102	32	25	57	27	....	1979-80	1993-94
Christian, Jeff	N.J., Pit., Phx.	5	18	2	2	4	17	....	....	....	....	....	....	1991-92	1997-98
Christie, Mike	Cal., Cle., Col., Van.	7	412	15	101	116	550	2	0	0	0	0	....	1974-75	1980-81
‡ Christie, Ryan	Dal., Cgy.	2	7	0	0	0	0	....	....	....	....	....	....	1999-00	2001-02
Christoff, Steve	Min., Cgy., L.A.	5	248	77	64	141	108	35	16	12	28	25	....	1979-80	1983-84
Chrystal, Bob	NYR	2	132	11	14	25	112	....	....	....	....	....	....	1953-54	1954-55
‡ Church, Brad	Wsh.	1	2	0	0	0	0	....	....	....	....	....	....	1997-98	1997-98
• Church, Jack	Tor., Bro., Bos.	5	130	4	19	23	154	25	1	1	2	18	....	1938-39	1945-46
Churla, Shane	Hfd., Cgy., Min., Dal., L.A., NYR	11	488	26	45	71	2301	78	5	7	12	282	....	1986-87	1996-97
Chychrun, Jeff	Phi., L.A., Pit., Edm.	8	262	3	22	25	744	19	0	2	2	65	1	1986-87	1993-94
Chynoweth, Dean	NYI, Bos.	9	241	4	18	22	667	6	0	0	0	26	....	1988-89	1997-98
Chyzowski, Dave	NYI, Chi.	6	126	15	16	31	144	2	0	0	0	0	....	1989-90	1996-97
Ciavaglia, Peter	Buf.	2	5	0	0	0	0	....	....	....	....	....	....	1991-92	1992-93
Ciccarelli, Dino	Min., Wsh., Det., T.B., Fla.	19	1232	608	592	1200	1425	141	73	45	118	211	....	1980-81	1998-99
Ciccone, Enrico	Min., Wsh., T.B., Chi., Car., Van., Mtl.	9	374	10	18	28	1469	13	1	0	1	48	....	1991-92	2000-01
Cichocki, Chris	Det., N.J.	4	68	11	12	23	27	....	....	....	....	....	....	1985-86	1988-89
Cierny, Jozef	Edm.	1	1	0	0	0	0	....	....	....	....	....	....	1993-94	1993-94
• Ciesla, Hank	Chi., NYR	4	269	26	51	77	87	6	0	2	2	0	....	1955-56	1958-59
Ciger, Zdeno	N.J., Edm., NYR, T.B.	7	352	94	134	228	101	13	2	6	8	4	....	1990-91	2001-02
Cimellaro, Tony	Ott.	1	2	0	0	0	0	....	....	....	....	....	....	1992-93	1992-93
Cimetta, Rob	Bos., Tor.	4	103	16	16	32	66	1	0	0	0	15	....	1988-89	1991-92
Cirella, Joe	Col., N.J., Que., NYR, Fla., Ott.	15	828	64	211	275	1446	38	0	13	13	98	....	1981-82	1995-96
Cirone, Jason	Wpg.	1	3	0	0	0	2	....	....	....	....	....	....	1991-92	1991-92
Clackson, Kim	Pit., Que.	2	106	0	8	8	370	8	0	0	0	70	....	1979-80	1980-81
• Clancy, King	Ott., Tor.	16	592	136	147	283	914	55	8	8	16	88	3	1921-22	1936-37
Clancy, Terry	Oak., Tor.	4	93	6	6	12	39	....	....	....	....	....	....	1967-68	1972-73
• Clapper, Dit	Bos.	20	833	228	246	474	462	82	13	17	30	50	3	1927-28	1946-47
Clark, Dan	NYR	1	4	0	1	1	6	....	....	....	....	....	....	1978-79	1978-79
Clark, Dean	Edm.	1	1	0	0	0	0	....	....	....	....	....	....	1983-84	1983-84
Clark, Gordie	Bos.	2	8	0	1	1	0	1	0	0	0	0	....	1974-75	1975-76
• Clark, Nobby	Bos.	1	5	0	0	0	0	....	....	....	....	....	....	1927-28	1927-28
Clark, Wendel	Tor., Que., NYI, T.B., Det., Chi.	15	793	330	234	564	1690	95	37	32	69	201	....	1985-86	1999-00
Clarke, Bobby	Phi.	15	1144	358	852	1210	1453	136	42	77	119	152	2	1969-70	1983-84
‡ Clarke, Dale	St.L.	1	3	0	0	0	0	....	....	....	....	....	....	2000-01	2000-01
• Cleghorn, Odie	Mtl., Pit.	10	181	95	34	129	142	12	7	2	9	5	1	1918-19	1927-28
• Cleghorn, Sprague	Ott., Tor., Mtl., Bos.	10	259	83	55	138	538	21	4	3	7	26	2	1918-19	1927-28
Clement, Bill	Phi., Wsh., Atl., Cgy.	11	719	148	208	356	383	50	5	3	8	26	2	1971-72	1981-82
Cline, Bruce	NYR	1	30	2	3	5	10	....	....	....	....	....	....	1956-57	1956-57
Clippingdale, Steve	L.A., Wsh.	2	19	1	2	3	9	1	0	0	0	0	....	1976-77	1979-80
Cloutier, Real	Que., Buf.	6	317	146	198	344	119	25	7	5	12	20	....	1979-80	1984-85
Cloutier, Rejean	Det.	2	5	0	2	2	2	....	....	....	....	....	....	1979-80	1981-82
Cloutier, Roland	Det., Que.	3	34	8	9	17	2	....	....	....	....	....	....	1977-78	1979-80
‡ Cloutier, Sylvain	Chi.	1	7	0	0	0	0	....	....	....	....	....	....	1998-99	1998-99
• Clune, Wally	Mtl.	1	5	0	0	0	6	....	....	....	....	....	....	1955-56	1955-56
Coalter, Gary	Cal., K.C.	2	34	2	4	6	2	....	....	....	....	....	....	1973-74	1974-75
Coates, Steve	Det.	1	5	1	0	1	24	....	....	....	....	....	....	1976-77	1976-77
Cochrane, Glen	Phi., Van., Chi., Edm.	10	411	17	72	89	1556	18	1	1	2	31	....	1978-79	1988-89
Coffey, Paul	Edm., Pit., L.A., Det., Hfd., Phi., Chi., Car., Bos.	21	1409	396	1135	1531	1802	194	59	137	196	264	4	1980-81	2000-01
Coflin, Hugh	Chi.	1	31	0	3	3	33	....	....	....	....	....	....	1950-51	1950-51

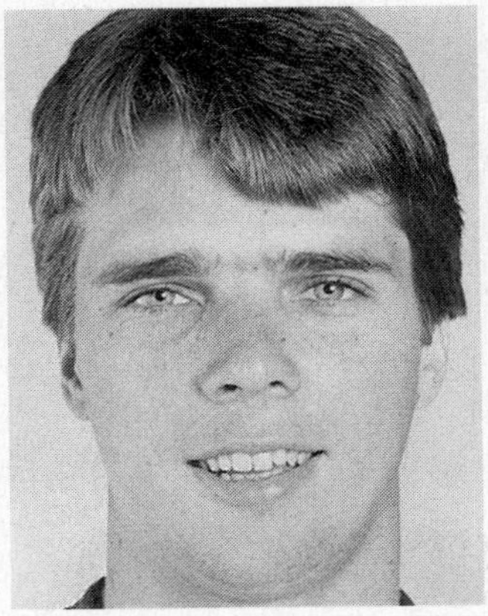

Dave Cameron

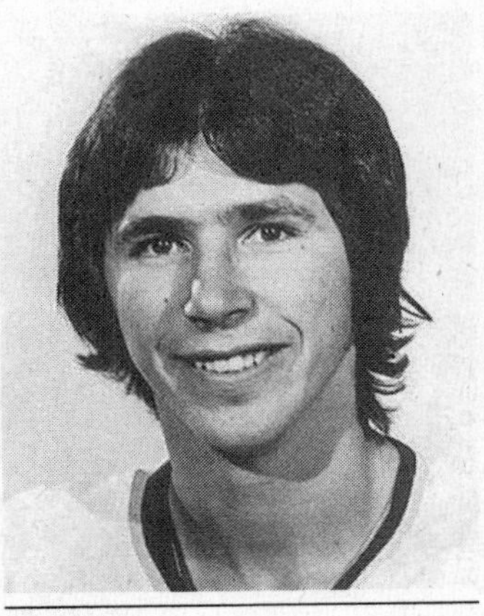

Steve Carlson

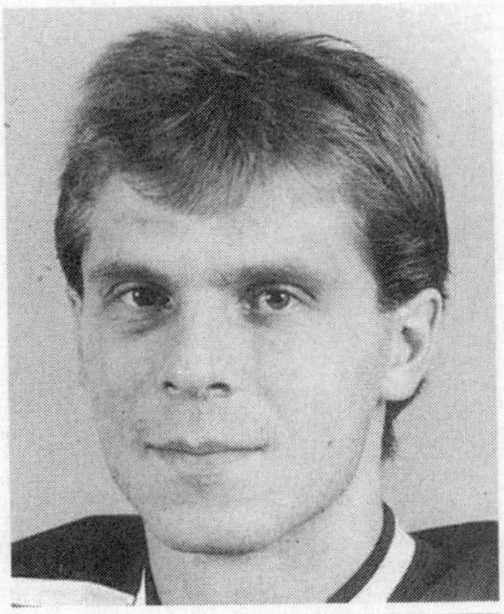

Anders Carlsson

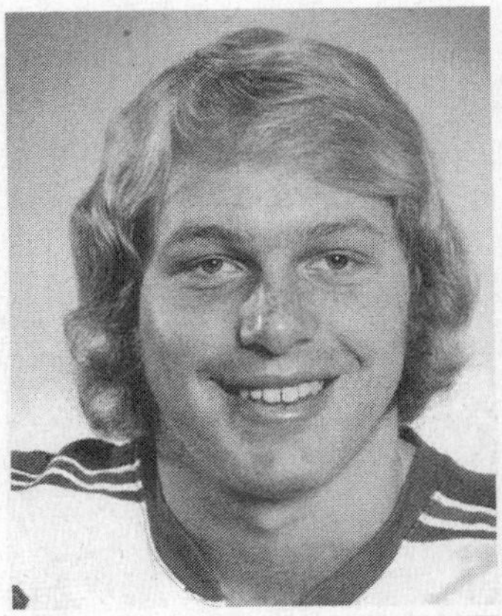

Gene Carr

Name	NHL Teams	NHL Seasons	Regular Schedule GP	G	A	TP	PIM	Playoffs GP	G	A	TP	PIM	NHL Cup Wins	First NHL Season	Last NHL Season
Cole, Danton	Wpg., T.B., N.J., NYI, Chi.	7	318	58	60	118	125	1	0	0	0	0	1	1989-90	1995-96
Colley, Tom	Min.	1	1	0	0	0	2	....	....	....	....	....	....	1974-75	1974-75
Collings, Norm	Mtl.	1	1	0	1	1	0	....	....	....	....	....	....	1934-35	1934-35
Collins, Bill	Min., Mtl., Det., St.L., NYR, Phi., Wsh.	11	768	157	154	311	415	18	3	5	8	12	....	1967-68	1977-78
Collins, Gary	Tor.	1	....	....	....	....	....	2	0	0	0	0	....	1958-59	1958-59
Collyard, Bob	St.L.	1	10	1	3	4	4	....	....	....	....	....	....	1973-74	1973-74
• Colman, Michael	S.J.	1	15	0	1	1	32	....	....	....	....	....	....	1991-92	1991-92
• Colville, Mac	NYR	9	353	71	104	175	130	40	9	10	19	14	1	1935-36	1946-47
• Colville, Neil	NYR	12	464	99	166	265	213	46	7	19	26	32	1	1935-36	1948-49
Colwill, Les	NYR	1	69	7	6	13	16	....	....	....	....	....	....	1958-59	1958-59
Comeau, Rey	Mtl., Atl., Col.	9	564	98	141	239	175	9	2	1	3	8	....	1971-72	1979-80
Comrie, Paul	Edm.	1	15	1	2	3	4	....	....	....	....	....	....	1999-00	1999-00
Conacher, Brian	Tor., Det.	5	155	28	28	56	84	12	3	2	5	21	1	1961-62	1971-72
• Conacher, Charlie	Tor., Det., NYA	12	459	225	173	398	523	49	17	18	35	49	1	1929-30	1940-41
Conacher, Jim	Det., Chi., NYR	8	328	85	117	202	91	19	5	2	7	4	....	1945-46	1952-53
• Conacher, Lionel	Pit., NYA, Mtl.M., Chi.	12	498	80	105	185	882	35	2	2	4	34	2	1925-26	1936-37
Conacher, Pat	NYR, Edm., N.J., L.A., Cgy., NYI	13	521	63	76	139	235	66	11	10	21	40	1	1979-80	1995-96
Conacher, Pete	Chi., NYR, Tor.	6	229	47	39	86	57	7	0	0	0	0	....	1951-52	1957-58
• Conacher, Roy	Bos., Det., Chi.	11	490	226	200	426	90	42	15	15	30	14	2	1938-39	1951-52
• Conn, Red	NYA	2	96	9	28	37	22	....	....	....	....	....	....	1933-34	1934-35
Conn, Rob	Chi., Buf.	2	30	2	5	7	20	....	....	....	....	....	....	1991-92	1995-96
• Connelly, Bert	NYR, Chi.	3	87	13	15	28	37	14	1	0	1	0	1	1934-35	1937-38
Connelly, Wayne	Mtl., Bos., Min., Det., St.L., Van.	10	543	133	174	307	156	24	11	7	18	4	....	1960-61	1971-72
Connor, Cam	Mtl., Edm., NYR	5	89	9	22	31	256	20	5	0	5	6	1	1978-79	1982-83
• Connor, Harry	Bos., NYA, Ott.	4	134	16	5	21	149	10	0	0	0	2	....	1927-28	1930-31
• Connors, Bob	NYA, Det.	3	78	17	10	27	110	2	0	0	0	10	....	1926-27	1929-30
Conroy, Al	Phi.	3	114	9	14	23	156	....	....	....	....	....	....	1991-92	1993-94
Contini, Joe	Col., Min.	3	68	17	21	38	34	2	0	0	0	0	....	1977-78	1980-81
Convery, Brandon	Tor., Van., L.A.	4	72	9	19	28	36	5	0	0	0	2	....	1995-96	1998-99
• Convey, Eddie	NYA	3	36	1	1	2	33	....	....	....	....	....	....	1930-31	1932-33
• Cook, Bill	NYR	11	474	229	138	367	386	46	13	11	24	68	2	1926-27	1936-37
• Cook, Bob	Van., Det., NYI, Min.	4	72	13	9	22	22	....	....	....	....	....	....	1970-71	1974-75
• Cook, Bud	Bos., Ott., St.L.	3	50	5	4	9	22	....	....	....	....	....	....	1931-32	1934-35
• Cook, Bun	NYR, Bos.	11	473	158	144	302	444	46	15	3	18	50	2	1926-27	1936-37
• Cook, Lloyd	Bos.	1	4	1	0	1	0	....	....	....	....	....	....	1924-25	1924-25
• Cook, Tom	Chi., Mtl.M.	9	349	77	98	175	184	24	2	4	6	19	1	1929-30	1937-38
• Cooper, Carson	Bos., Mtl., Det.	8	294	110	57	167	111	7	0	0	0	2	....	1924-25	1931-32
Cooper, David	Tor.	3	30	3	7	10	24	....	....	....	....	....	....	1996-97	2000-01
Cooper, Ed	Col.	2	49	8	7	15	46	....	....	....	....	....	....	1980-81	1981-82
• Cooper, Hal	NYR	1	8	0	0	0	2	....	....	....	....	....	....	1944-45	1944-45
• Cooper, Joe	NYR, Chi.	11	420	30	66	96	442	35	3	5	8	58	....	1935-36	1946-47
Copp, Bob	Tor.	2	40	3	9	12	26	....	....	....	....	....	....	1942-43	1950-51
• Corbeau, Bert	Mtl., Ham., Tor.	10	258	63	49	112	629	9	2	2	4	38	....	1917-18	1926-27
Corbet, Rene	Que., Col., Cgy., Pit.	8	362	58	74	132	420	53	7	6	13	52	1	1993-94	2000-01
• Corbett, Mike	L.A.	1	....	....	....	....	....	2	0	1	1	2	....	1967-68	1967-68
Corcoran, Norm	Bos., Det., Chi.	4	29	1	3	4	21	4	0	0	0	6	....	1949-50	1955-56
Corkum, Bob	Buf., Ana., Phi., Phx., L.A., N.J., Atl.	12	720	97	103	200	281	62	7	7	14	24	....	1989-90	2001-02
• Cormier, Roger	Mtl.	1	1	0	0	0	0	....	....	....	....	....	....	1925-26	1925-26
Cornforth, Mark	Bos.	1	6	0	0	0	4	....	....	....	....	....	....	1995-96	1995-96
• Corrigan, Chuck	Tor., NYA	2	19	2	2	4	2	....	....	....	....	....	....	1937-38	1940-41
Corrigan, Mike	L.A., Van., Pit.	10	594	152	195	347	698	17	2	3	5	20	....	1967-68	1977-78
Corrinet, Chris	Wsh.	1	8	0	1	1	6	....	....	....	....	....	....	2001-02	2001-02
• Corriveau, Andre	Mtl.	1	3	0	1	1	0	....	....	....	....	....	....	1953-54	1953-54
Corriveau, Yvon	Wsh., Hfd., S.J.	9	280	48	40	88	310	29	5	7	12	50	....	1985-86	1993-94
Corson, Shayne	Mtl., Edm., St.L., Tor., Dal.	19	1156	273	420	693	2357	140	38	49	87	291	....	1985-86	2003-04
Cory, Ross	Wpg.	2	51	2	10	12	41	....	....	....	....	....	....	1979-80	1980-81
Cossette, Jacques	Pit.	3	64	8	6	14	29	3	0	1	1	4	....	1975-76	1978-79
• Costello, Les	Tor.	3	15	2	3	5	11	6	2	2	4	2	1	1947-48	1949-50
Costello, Murray	Chi., Bos., Det.	4	162	13	19	32	54	5	0	0	0	2	....	1953-54	1956-57
Costello, Rich	Tor.	2	12	2	2	4	2	....	....	....	....	....	....	1983-84	1985-86
• Cotch, Charlie	Ham., Tor.	1	12	1	0	1	0	....	....	....	....	....	....	1924-25	1924-25
Cote, Alain	Que.	10	696	103	190	293	383	67	9	15	24	44	....	1979-80	1988-89
Cote, Alain	Bos., Wsh., Mtl., T.B., Que.	9	119	2	18	20	124	11	0	2	2	26	....	1985-86	1993-94
Cote, Patrick	Dal., Nsh., Edm.	6	105	1	2	3	377	....	....	....	....	....	....	1995-96	2000-01
Cote, Ray	Edm.	3	15	0	0	0	4	14	3	2	5	0	....	1982-83	1984-85
Cote, Sylvain	Hfd., Wsh., Tor., Chi., Dal.	19	1171	122	313	435	545	102	11	22	33	62	....	1984-85	2002-03
• Cotton, Baldy	Pit., Tor., NYA	12	503	101	103	204	419	43	4	9	13	46	1	1925-26	1936-37
• Coughlin, Jack	Tor., Que., Mtl., Ham.	3	19	2	0	2	3	....	....	....	....	....	1	1917-18	1920-21
Coulis, Tim	Wsh., Min.	4	47	4	5	9	138	3	1	0	1	2	....	1979-80	1985-86
• Coulson, D'arcy	Phi.	1	28	0	0	0	103	....	....	....	....	....	....	1930-31	1930-31
• Coulter, Art	Chi., NYR	11	465	30	82	112	543	49	4	5	9	61	2	1931-32	1941-42
Coulter, Neal	NYI	3	26	5	5	10	11	....	....	....	....	....	....	1985-86	1987-88
Cournoyer, Yvan	Mtl.	16	968	428	435	863	255	147	64	63	127	47	10	1963-64	1978-79
Courteau, Yves	Cgy., Hfd.	3	22	2	5	7	4	1	0	0	0	0	....	1984-85	1986-87
‡ Courtenay, Ed	S.J.	2	44	7	13	20	10	....	....	....	....	....	....	1991-92	1992-93
Courtnall, Geoff	Bos., Edm., Wsh., St.L., Van.	17	1048	367	432	799	1465	156	39	70	109	262	1	1983-84	1999-00
Courtnall, Russ	Tor., Mtl., Min., Dal., Van., NYR, L.A.	16	1029	297	447	744	557	129	39	44	83	83	....	1983-84	1998-99
‡ Courville, Larry	Van.	3	33	1	2	3	16	....	....	....	....	....	....	1995-96	1997-98
• Coutu, Billy	Mtl., Ham., Bos.	10	244	33	21	54	478	19	1	1	2	39	1	1917-18	1926-27
• Couture, Gerry	Det., Mtl., Chi.	10	385	86	70	156	89	45	9	7	16	4	1	1944-45	1953-54
• Couture, Rosie	Chi., Mtl.	8	309	48	56	104	184	23	1	5	6	15	1	1928-29	1935-36
Couturier, Sylvain	L.A.	3	33	4	5	9	4	....	....	....	....	....	....	1988-89	1991-92
Cowick, Bruce	Phi., Wsh., St.L.	3	70	5	6	11	43	8	0	0	0	9	1	1973-74	1975-76
Cowie, Rob	L.A.	2	78	7	12	19	52	....	....	....	....	....	....	1994-95	1995-96
• Cowley, Bill	St.L., Bos.	13	549	195	353	548	143	64	12	34	46	22	2	1934-35	1946-47
• Cox, Danny	Tor., Ott., Det., NYR	8	319	47	49	96	128	10	0	1	1	6	....	1926-27	1933-34
Coxe, Craig	Van., Cgy., St.L., S.J.	8	235	14	31	45	713	5	1	0	1	18	....	1984-85	1991-92
Craig, Mike	Min., Dal., Tor., S.J.	9	423	71	97	168	550	26	2	2	4	49	....	1990-91	2001-02
Craighead, John	Tor.	1	5	0	0	0	10	....	....	....	....	....	....	1996-97	1996-97
Craigwell, Dale	S.J.	3	98	11	18	29	28	....	....	....	....	....	....	1991-92	1993-94
Crashley, Bart	Det., K.C., L.A.	6	140	7	36	43	50	....	....	....	....	....	....	1965-66	1975-76
Craven, Murray	Det., Phi., Hfd., Van., Chi., S.J.	18	1071	266	493	759	524	118	27	43	70	64	....	1982-83	1999-00
Crawford, Bob	St.L., Hfd., NYR, Wsh.	7	246	71	71	142	72	11	0	1	1	8	....	1979-80	1986-87
Crawford, Bobby	Col., Det.	2	16	1	3	4	6	....	....	....	....	....	....	1980-81	1982-83
• Crawford, Jack	Bos.	13	548	38	140	178	202	66	3	13	16	36	2	1937-38	1949-50
Crawford, Lou	Bos.	2	26	2	1	3	29	1	0	0	0	0	....	1989-90	1991-92
Crawford, Marc	Van.	6	176	19	31	50	229	20	1	2	3	44	....	1981-82	1986-87
• Crawford, Rusty	Ott., Tor.	2	38	10	8	18	117	2	2	1	3	9	1	1917-18	1918-19
Creighton, Adam	Buf., Chi., NYI, T.B., St.L.	14	708	187	216	403	1077	61	11	14	25	137	....	1983-84	1996-97
Creighton, Dave	Bos., Tor., Chi., NYR	12	616	140	174	314	223	51	11	13	24	20	....	1948-49	1959-60
• Creighton, Jimmy	Det.	1	11	1	0	1	2	....	....	....	....	....	....	1930-31	1930-31
Cressman, Dave	Min.	2	85	6	8	14	37	....	....	....	....	....	....	1974-75	1975-76
Cressman, Glen	Mtl.	1	4	0	0	0	2	....	....	....	....	....	....	1956-57	1956-57
Crisp, Terry	Bos., St.L., NYI, Phi.	11	536	67	134	201	135	110	15	28	43	40	2	1965-66	1976-77
Cristofoli, Ed	Mtl.	1	9	0	1	1	4	....	....	....	....	....	....	1989-90	1989-90
• Croghan, Maurice	Mtl.M.	1	16	0	0	0	4	....	....	....	....	....	....	1937-38	1937-38
Crombeen, Mike	Cle., St.L., Hfd.	8	475	55	68	123	218	27	6	2	8	32	....	1977-78	1984-85
Cronin, Shawn	Wsh., Wpg., Phi., S.J.	7	292	3	18	21	877	32	1	0	1	38	....	1988-89	1994-95
• Crossett, Stan	Phi.	1	21	0	0	0	10	....	....	....	....	....	....	1930-31	1930-31
Crossman, Doug	Chi., Phi., L.A., NYI, Hfd., Det., T.B., St.L.	14	914	105	359	464	534	97	12	39	51	105	....	1980-81	1993-94
Croteau, Gary	L.A., Det., Cal., K.C., Col.	12	684	144	175	319	143	11	3	2	5	8	....	1968-69	1979-80
Crowder, Bruce	Bos., Pit.	4	243	47	51	98	156	31	8	4	12	41	....	1981-82	1984-85
Crowder, Keith	Bos., L.A.	10	662	223	271	494	1354	85	14	22	36	218	....	1980-81	1989-90
Crowder, Troy	N.J., Det., L.A., Van.	7	150	9	7	16	433	4	0	0	0	22	....	1987-88	1996-97
Crowe, Phil	L.A., Phi., Ott., Nsh.	6	94	4	5	9	173	3	0	0	0	16	....	1993-94	1999-00
Crowley, Mike	Ana.	3	67	5	15	20	44	....	....	....	....	....	....	1997-98	2000-01
Crowley, Ted	Hfd., Col., NYI	2	34	2	4	6	12	....	....	....	....	....	....	1993-94	1998-99
Crozier, Greg	Pit.	1	1	0	0	0	0	....	....	....	....	....	....	2000-01	2000-01
Crozier, Joe	Tor.	1	5	0	3	3	2	....	....	....	....	....	....	1959-60	1959-60
• Crutchfield, Nels	Mtl.	1	41	5	5	10	20	2	0	1	1	22	....	1934-35	1934-35
Culhane, Jim	Hfd.	1	6	0	1	1	4	....	....	....	....	....	....	1989-90	1989-90
Cullen, Barry	Tor., Det.	5	219	32	52	84	111	6	0	0	0	2	....	1955-56	1959-60
Cullen, Brian	Tor., NYR	7	326	56	100	156	92	19	3	0	3	2	....	1954-55	1960-61
Cullen, John	Pit., Hfd., Tor., T.B.	11	621	187	363	550	898	53	12	22	34	58	....	1988-89	1998-99

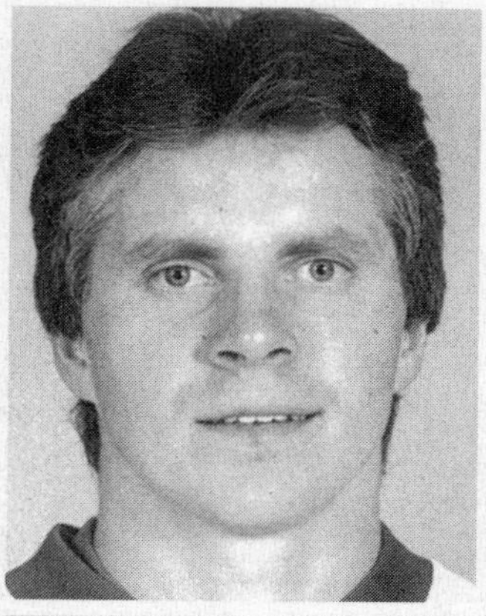
Milan Chalupa

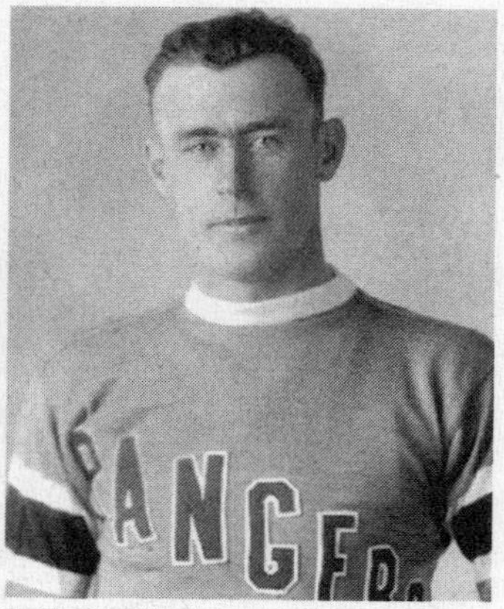
Bill Cook

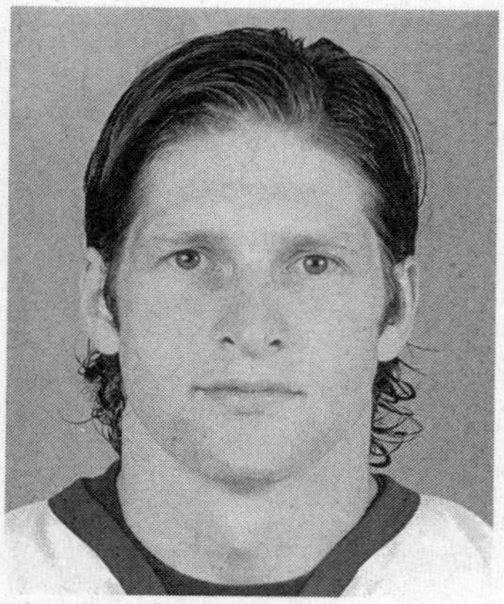
Shayne Corson

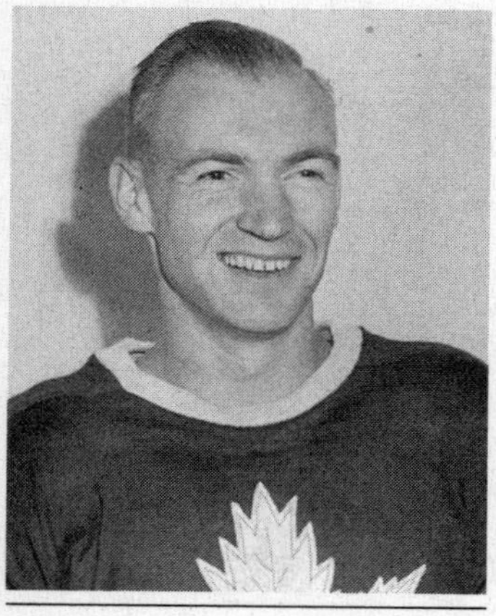
Dave Creighton

			Regular Schedule					Playoffs					NHL	First	Last
Name	NHL Teams	NHL Seasons	GP	G	A	TP	PIM	GP	G	A	TP	PIM	Cup Wins	NHL Season	NHL Season
Cullen, Ray	NYR, Det., Min., Van.	6	313	92	123	215	120	20	3	10	13	2	....	1965-66	1970-71
Cummins, Barry	Cal.	1	36	1	2	3	39	....	....	....	....	....	....	1973-74	1973-74
Cummins, Jim	Det., Phi., T.B., Chi., Phx., Mtl., Ana., NYI, Col.	12	511	24	36	60	1538	37	1	2	3	43	....	1991-92	2003-04
Cunneyworth, Randy	Buf., Pit., Wpg., Hfd., Chi., Ott.	16	866	189	225	414	1280	45	7	7	14	61	....	1980-81	1998-99
Cunningham, Bob	NYR	2	4	0	1	1	0	....	....	....	....	....	....	1960-61	1961-62
Cunningham, Jim	Phi.	1	1	0	0	0	4	....	....	....	....	....	....	1977-78	1977-78
• Cunningham, Les	NYA, Chi.	2	60	7	19	26	21	1	0	0	0	0	....	1936-37	1939-40
• Cupolo, Bill	Bos.	1	47	11	13	24	10	7	1	2	3	0	....	1944-45	1944-45
Curran, Brian	Bos., NYI, Tor., Buf., Wsh.	10	381	7	33	40	1461	24	0	1	1	122	....	1983-84	1993-94
Currie, Dan	Edm., L.A.	4	22	2	1	3	4	....	....	....	....	....	....	1990-91	1993-94
Currie, Glen	Wsh., L.A.	8	326	39	79	118	100	12	1	3	4	4	....	1979-80	1987-88
Currie, Hugh	Mtl.	1	1	0	0	0	0	....	....	....	....	....	....	1950-51	1950-51
Currie, Tony	St.L., Van., Hfd.	8	290	92	119	211	83	16	4	12	16	14	....	1977-78	1984-85
Curry, Floyd	Mtl.	11	601	105	99	204	147	91	23	17	40	38	4	1947-48	1957-58
Curtale, Tony	Cgy.	1	2	0	0	0	0	....	....	....	....	....	....	1980-81	1980-81
Curtis, Paul	Mtl., L.A., St.L.	4	185	3	34	37	161	5	0	0	0	2	....	1969-70	1972-73
Cushenan, Ian	Chi., Mtl., NYR, Det.	5	129	3	11	14	134	....	....	....	....	....	1	1956-57	1963-64
Cusson, Jean	Oak.	1	2	0	0	0	0	....	....	....	....	....	....	1967-68	1967-68
Cyr, Denis	Cgy., Chi., St.L.	6	193	41	43	84	36	4	0	0	0	0	....	1980-81	1985-86
Cyr, Paul	Buf., NYR, Hfd.	9	470	101	140	241	623	24	4	6	10	31	....	1982-83	1991-92

D

‡ Dackell, Andreas	Ott., Mtl.	8	613	91	159	250	162	44	5	5	10	10	....	1996-97	2003-04
Dahl, Kevin	Cgy., Phx., Tor., CBJ	8	188	7	22	29	153	16	0	2	2	12	....	1992-93	2000-01
Dahlen, Ulf	NYR, Min., Dal., S.J., Chi., Wsh.	14	966	301	354	655	230	85	15	25	40	12	....	1987-88	2002-03
Dahlin, Kjell	Mtl.	3	166	57	59	116	10	35	6	11	17	6	1	1985-86	1987-88
‡ Dahlman, Toni	Ott.	2	22	1	1	2	0	....	....	....	....	....	....	2001-02	2002-03
Dahlquist, Chris	Pit., Min., Cgy., Ott.	11	532	19	71	90	488	39	4	7	11	30	....	1985-86	1995-96
• Dahlstrom, Cully	Chi.	8	342	88	118	206	58	29	6	8	14	4	1	1937-38	1944-45
Daigle, Alain	Chi.	6	389	56	50	106	122	17	0	1	1	0	....	1974-75	1979-80
Daigneault, J.J.	Van., Phi., Mtl., St.L., Pit., Ana., NYI, Nsh., Phx., Min.	16	899	53	197	250	687	99	5	26	31	100	1	1984-85	2000-01
Dailey, Bob	Van., Phi.	9	561	94	231	325	814	63	12	34	46	105	....	1973-74	1981-82
• Daley, Frank	Det.	1	5	0	0	0	0	2	0	0	0	0	....	1928-29	1928-29
Daley, Pat	Wpg.	2	12	1	0	1	13	....	....	....	....	....	....	1979-80	1980-81
Dalgarno, Brad	NYI	10	321	49	71	120	332	27	2	4	6	37	....	1985-86	1995-96
Dallman, Marty	Tor.	2	6	0	1	1	0	....	....	....	....	....	....	1987-88	1988-89
Dallman, Rod	NYI, Phi.	4	6	1	0	1	26	1	0	1	1	0	....	1987-88	1991-92
Dame, Bunny	Mtl.	1	34	2	5	7	4	....	....	....	....	....	....	1941-42	1941-42
Damore, Hank	NYR	1	4	1	0	1	2	....	....	....	....	....	....	1943-44	1943-44
Damphousse, Vincent	Tor., Edm., Mtl., S.J.	18	1378	432	773	1205	1190	140	41	63	104	144	1	1986-87	2003-04
Daneyko, Ken	N.J.	20	1283	36	142	178	2519	175	5	17	22	296	3	1983-84	2002-03
Daniels, Jeff	Pit., Fla., Hfd., Car., Nsh.	12	425	17	26	43	83	41	3	5	8	2	1	1990-91	2002-03
‡ Daniels, Kimbi	Phi.	2	27	1	2	3	4	....	....	....	....	....	....	1990-91	1991-92
Daniels, Scott	Hfd., Phi., N.J.	6	149	8	12	20	667	1	0	0	0	0	....	1992-93	1998-99
Danton, Mike	N.J., St.L.	3	87	9	5	14	182	5	1	0	1	2	....	2000-01	2003-04
Daoust, Dan	Mtl., Tor.	8	522	87	167	254	544	32	7	5	12	83	....	1982-83	1989-90
Dark, Michael	St.L.	2	43	5	6	11	14	....	....	....	....	....	....	1986-87	1987-88
• Darragh, Harold	Pit., Phi., Bos., Tor.	8	308	68	49	117	50	16	1	3	4	4	1	1925-26	1932-33
• Darragh, Jack	Ott.	6	121	66	46	112	113	11	3	0	3	9	3	1917-18	1923-24
David, Richard	Que.	3	31	4	4	8	10	1	0	0	0	0	....	1979-80	1982-83
• Davidson, Bob	Tor.	12	491	94	160	254	398	79	5	17	22	76	2	1934-35	1945-46
• Davidson, Gord	NYR	2	51	3	6	9	8	....	....	....	....	....	....	1942-43	1943-44
‡ Davidson, Matt	CBJ	3	56	5	7	12	28	....	....	....	....	....	....	2000-01	2002-03
‡ Davidsson, Johan	Ana., NYI	2	83	6	9	15	16	1	0	0	0	0	....	1998-99	1999-00
• Davie, Bob	Bos.	3	41	0	1	1	25	....	....	....	....	....	....	1933-34	1935-36
Davies, Buck	NYR	1	....	....	....	....	....	1	0	0	0	0	....	1947-48	1947-48
• Davis, Bob	Det.	1	3	0	0	0	0	....	....	....	....	....	....	1932-33	1932-33
Davis, Kim	Pit., Tor.	4	36	5	7	12	51	4	0	0	0	0	....	1977-78	1980-81
Davis, Lorne	Mtl., Chi., Det., Bos.	6	95	8	12	20	20	18	3	1	4	10	1	1951-52	1959-60
Davis, Mal	Det., Buf.	6	100	31	22	53	34	7	1	0	1	0	....	1978-79	1985-86
• Davison, Murray	Bos.	1	1	0	0	0	0	....	....	....	....	....	....	1965-66	1965-66
Davydov, Evgeny	Wpg., Fla., Ott.	4	155	40	39	79	120	11	2	2	4	2	....	1991-92	1994-95
‡ Daw, Jeff	Col.	1	1	0	1	1	0	....	....	....	....	....	....	2001-02	2001-02
Dawe, Jason	Buf., NYI, Mtl., NYR	8	366	86	90	176	162	22	4	3	7	18	....	1993-94	2001-02
• Dawes, Bob	Tor., Mtl.	4	32	2	7	9	6	10	0	0	0	2	1	1946-47	1950-51
• Day, Hap	Tor., NYA	14	581	86	116	202	601	53	4	7	11	56	1	1924-25	1937-38
Day, Joe	Hfd., NYI	3	72	1	10	11	87	....	....	....	....	....	....	1991-92	1993-94
Dea, Billy	NYR, Det., Chi., Pit.	8	397	67	54	121	44	11	2	1	3	6	....	1953-54	1970-71
• Deacon, Don	Det.	3	30	6	4	10	6	2	2	1	3	0	....	1936-37	1939-40
Deadmarsh, Adam	Que., Col., L.A.	10	567	184	189	373	819	105	26	40	66	100	1	1994-95	2003-04
Deadmarsh, Butch	Buf., Atl., K.C.	5	137	12	5	17	155	4	0	0	0	17	....	1970-71	1974-75
Dean, Barry	Col., Phi.	3	165	25	56	81	146	....	....	....	....	....	....	1976-77	1978-79
Dean, Kevin	N.J., Atl., Dal., Chi.	7	331	7	48	55	138	16	2	2	4	2	1	1994-95	2000-01
Debenedet, Nelson	Det., Pit.	2	46	10	4	14	13	....	....	....	....	....	....	1973-74	1974-75
DeBlois, Lucien	NYR, Col., Wpg., Mtl., Que., Tor.	15	993	249	276	525	814	52	7	6	13	38	1	1977-78	1991-92
Debol, Dave	Hfd.	2	92	26	26	52	4	3	0	0	0	0	....	1979-80	1980-81
DeBrusk, Louie	Edm., T.B., Phx., Chi.	11	401	24	17	41	1161	15	2	0	2	10	....	1991-92	2002-03
DeFauw, Brad	Car.	1	9	3	0	3	2	....	....	....	....	....	....	2002-03	2002-03
Defazio, Dean	Pit.	1	22	0	2	2	28	....	....	....	....	....	....	1983-84	1983-84
DeGray, Dale	Cgy., Tor., L.A., Buf.	5	153	18	47	65	195	13	1	3	4	28	....	1985-86	1989-90
Delisle, Jonathan	Mtl.	1	1	0	0	0	0	....	....	....	....	....	....	1998-99	1998-99
‡ Delisle, Xavier	T.B., Mtl.	2	16	3	2	5	6	....	....	....	....	....	....	1998-99	2000-01
• Delmonte, Armand	Bos.	1	1	0	0	0	0	....	....	....	....	....	....	1945-46	1945-46
Delorme, Gilbert	Mtl., St.L., Que., Det., Pit.	9	541	31	92	123	520	56	1	9	10	56	....	1981-82	1989-90
Delorme, Ron	Col., Van.	9	524	83	83	166	667	25	1	2	3	59	....	1976-77	1984-85
Delory, Val	NYR	1	1	0	0	0	0	....	....	....	....	....	....	1948-49	1948-49
Delparte, Guy	Col.	1	48	1	8	9	18	....	....	....	....	....	....	1976-77	1976-77
Delvecchio, Alex	Det.	24	1549	456	825	1281	383	121	35	69	104	29	3	1950-51	1973-74
• DeMarco, Ab	Chi., Tor., Bos., NYR	7	209	72	93	165	53	11	3	0	3	2	....	1938-39	1946-47
DeMarco, Ab	NYR, St.L., Pit., Van., L.A., Bos.	9	344	44	80	124	75	25	1	2	3	17	....	1969-70	1978-79
• Demers, Tony	Mtl., NYR	6	83	20	22	42	23	2	0	0	0	0	....	1937-38	1943-44
Denis, Jean-Paul	NYR	2	10	0	2	2	2	....	....	....	....	....	....	1946-47	1949-50
Denis, Lulu	Mtl.	2	3	0	1	1	0	....	....	....	....	....	....	1949-50	1950-51
• Denneny, Corb	Tor., Ham., Chi.	9	176	103	42	145	148	6	1	0	1	7	2	1917-18	1927-28
• Denneny, Cy	Ott., Bos.	12	328	248	85	333	301	25	16	2	18	23	5	1917-18	1928-29
Dennis, Norm	St.L.	4	12	3	0	3	11	5	0	0	0	2	....	1968-69	1971-72
• Denoird, Gerry	Tor.	1	17	0	1	1	0	....	....	....	....	....	....	1922-23	1922-23
DePalma, Larry	Min., S.J., Pit.	7	148	21	20	41	408	3	0	0	0	6	....	1985-86	1993-94
Derlago, Bill	Van., Tor., Bos., Wpg., Que.	9	555	189	227	416	247	13	5	0	5	8	....	1978-79	1986-87
• Desaulniers, Gerard	Mtl.	3	8	0	2	2	4	....	....	....	....	....	....	1950-51	1953-54
‡ Descoteaux, Matthieu	Mtl.	1	5	1	1	2	4	....	....	....	....	....	....	2000-01	2000-01
• Desilets, Joffre	Mtl., Chi.	5	192	37	45	82	57	7	1	0	1	7	....	1935-36	1939-40
Desjardins, Martin	Mtl.	1	8	0	2	2	2	....	....	....	....	....	....	1989-90	1989-90
• Desjardins, Vic	Chi., NYR	2	87	6	15	21	27	16	0	0	0	0	....	1930-31	1931-32
Deslauriers, Jacques	Mtl.	1	2	0	0	0	0	....	....	....	....	....	....	1955-56	1955-56
Deuling, Jarrett	NYI	2	15	0	1	1	11	....	....	....	....	....	....	1995-96	1996-97
Devine, Kevin	NYI	1	2	0	1	1	8	....	....	....	....	....	....	1982-83	1982-83
• Dewar, Tom	NYR	1	9	0	2	2	4	....	....	....	....	....	....	1943-44	1943-44
Dewsbury, Al	Det., Chi.	9	347	30	78	108	365	14	1	5	6	16	1	1946-47	1955-56
Deziel, Michel	Buf.	1	....	....	....	....	....	1	0	0	0	0	....	1974-75	1974-75
• Dheere, Marcel	Mtl.	1	11	1	2	3	2	5	0	0	0	6	....	1942-43	1942-43
Diachuk, Edward	Det.	1	12	0	0	0	19	....	....	....	....	....	....	1960-61	1960-61
• Dick, Harry	Chi.	1	12	0	1	1	12	....	....	....	....	....	....	1946-47	1946-47
• Dickens, Ernie	Tor., Chi.	6	278	12	44	56	98	13	0	0	0	4	1	1941-42	1950-51
Dickenson, Herb	NYR	2	48	18	17	35	10	....	....	....	....	....	....	1951-52	1952-53
Diduck, Gerald	NYI, Mtl., Van., Chi., Hfd., Phx., Tor., Dal.	17	932	56	156	212	1612	114	8	16	24	212	....	1984-85	2000-01
Dietrich, Don	Chi., N.J.	2	28	0	7	7	10	....	....	....	....	....	....	1983-84	1985-86
• Dill, Bob	NYR	2	76	15	15	30	135	....	....	....	....	....	....	1943-44	1944-45
• Dillabough, Bob	Det., Bos., Pit., Oak.	9	283	32	54	86	76	17	3	0	3	0	....	1961-62	1969-70
• Dillon, Cecil	NYR, Det.	10	453	167	131	298	105	43	14	9	23	14	1	1930-31	1939-40

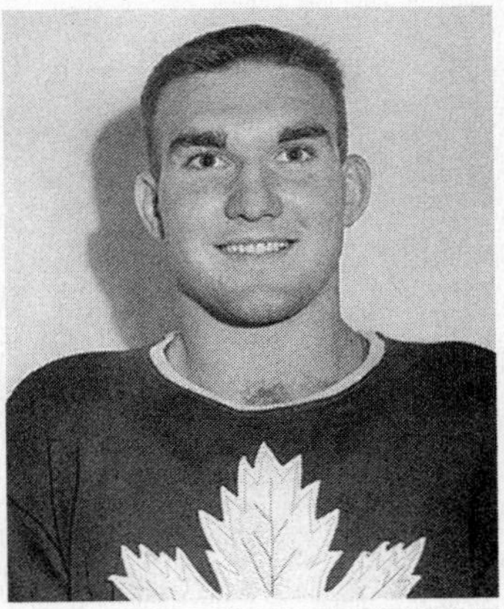

Brian Cullen

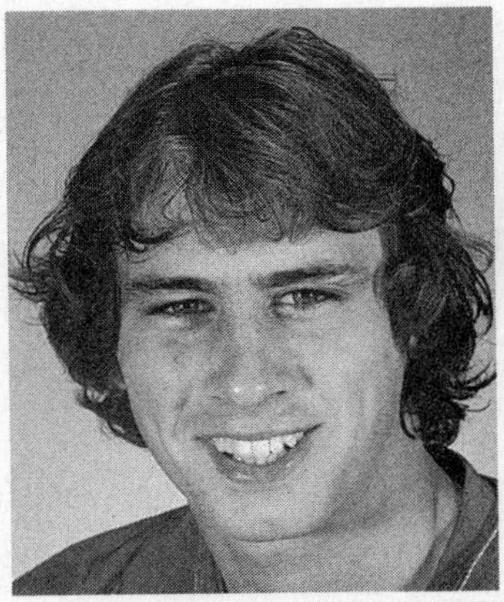

Glen Currie

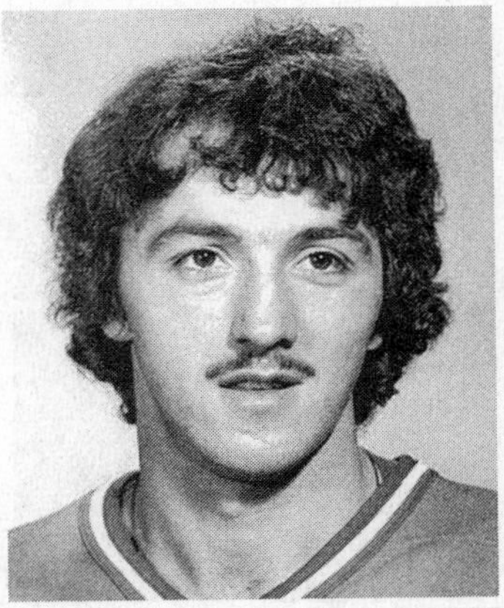

Dan Daoust

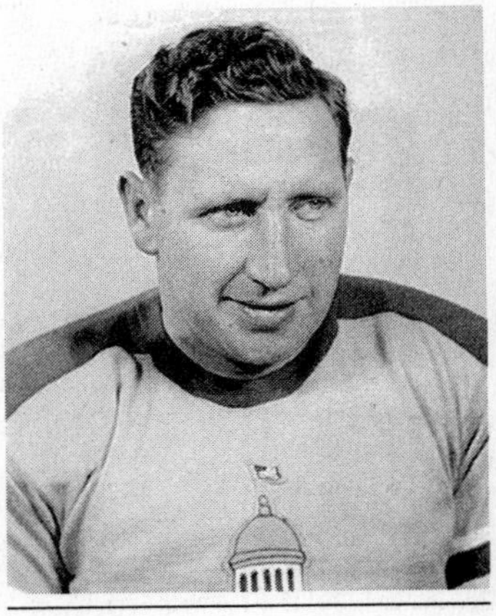

Don Deacon

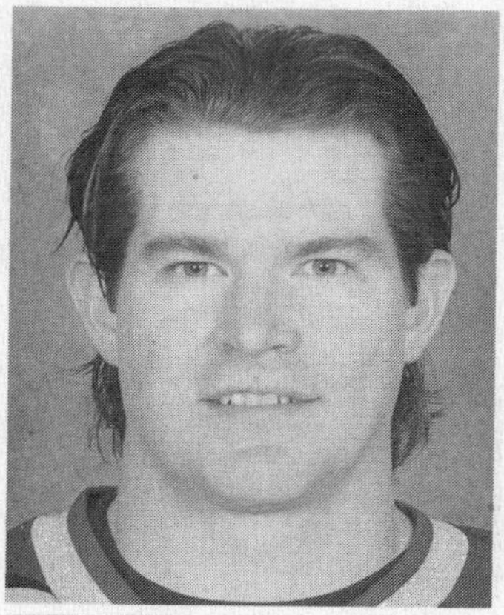

Adam Deadmarsh

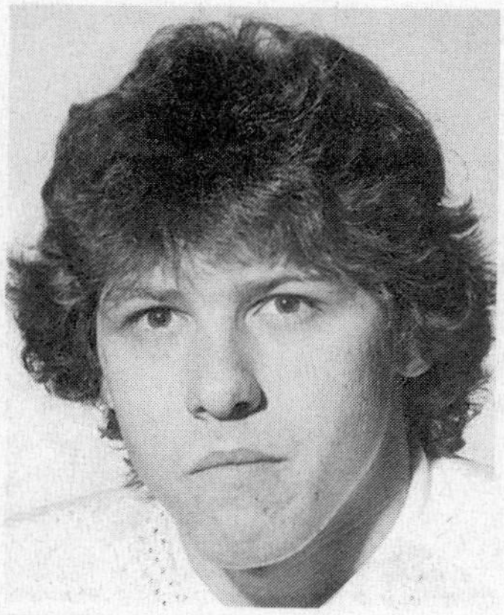

Gary Dillon

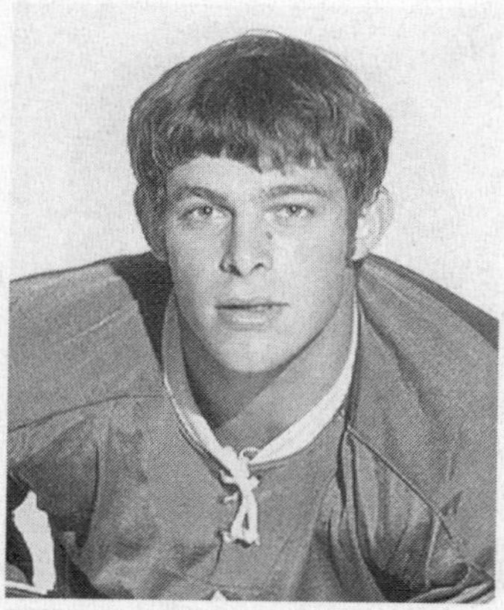

Jim Dorey

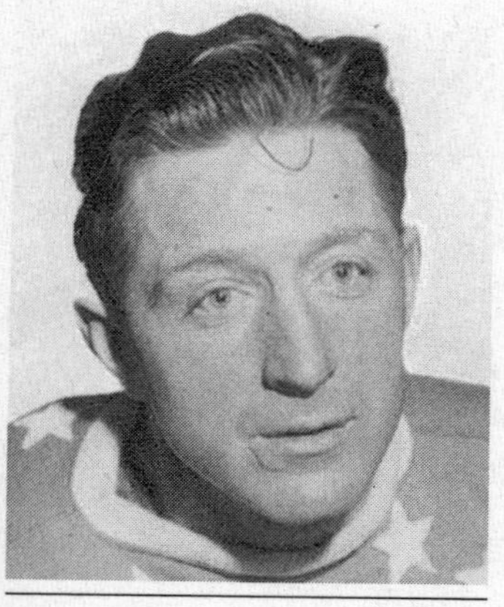

Red Dutton

Name	NHL Teams	NHL Seasons	Regular Schedule					Playoffs					NHL Cup Wins	First NHL Season	Last NHL Season
			GP	G	A	TP	PIM	GP	G	A	TP	PIM			
Dillon, Gary	Col.	1	13	1	1	2	29	....	....	....	....	....	....	1980-81	1980-81
Dillon, Wayne	NYR, Wpg.	4	229	43	66	109	60	3	0	1	1	0	....	1975-76	1979-80
Dineen, Bill	Det., Chi.	5	323	51	44	95	122	37	1	1	2	18	2	1953-54	1957-58
● Dineen, Gary	Min.	1	4	0	1	1	0	....	....	....	....	....	....	1968-69	1968-69
Dineen, Gord	NYI, Min., Pit., Ott.	13	528	16	90	106	695	40	1	7	8	68	....	1982-83	1994-95
Dineen, Kevin	Hfd., Phi., Car., Ott., CBJ	19	1188	355	405	760	2229	59	23	18	41	127	....	1984-85	2002-03
Dineen, Peter	L.A., Det.	2	13	0	2	2	13	....	....	....	....	....	....	1986-87	1989-90
● Dinsmore, Chuck	Mtl.M.	4	100	6	2	8	50	8	1	0	1	2	1	1924-25	1929-30
Dionne, Gilbert	Mtl., Phi., Fla.	6	223	61	79	140	108	39	10	12	22	34	1	1990-91	1995-96
Dionne, Marcel	Det., L.A., NYR	18	1348	731	1040	1771	600	49	21	24	45	17	....	1971-72	1988-89
‡ DiPietro, Paul	Mtl., Tor., L.A.	6	192	31	49	80	96	31	11	10	21	10	1	1991-92	1996-97
Dirk, Robert	St.L., Van., Chi., Ana., Mtl.	9	402	13	29	42	786	39	0	1	1	56	....	1987-88	1995-96
‡ Divisek, Tomas	Phi.	2	5	1	0	1	0	....	....	....	....	....	....	2000-01	2001-02
Djoos, Per	Det., NYR	3	82	2	31	33	58	....	....	....	....	....	....	1990-91	1992-93
Doak, Gary	Det., Bos., Van., NYR	16	789	23	107	130	908	78	2	4	6	121	1	1965-66	1980-81
Dobbin, Brian	Phi., Bos.	5	63	7	8	15	61	2	0	0	0	17	....	1986-87	1991-92
Dobson, Jim	Min., Col., Que.	4	12	0	0	0	6	....	....	....	....	....	....	1979-80	1983-84
● Doherty, Fred	Mtl.	1	1	0	0	0	0	....	....	....	....	....	....	1918-19	1918-19
Dollas, Bobby	Wpg., Que., Det., Ana., Edm., Pit., Cgy., Ott., S.J.	16	646	42	96	138	467	47	2	1	3	41	....	1983-84	2000-01
‡ Dome, Robert	Pit., Cgy.	3	53	7	7	14	12	....	....	....	....	....	....	1997-98	2002-03
‡ Domenichelli, Hnat	Hfd., Cgy., Atl., Min.	7	267	52	61	113	104	....	....	....	....	....	....	1996-97	2002-03
Donaldson, Gary	Chi.	1	1	0	0	0	0	....	....	....	....	....	....	1973-74	1973-74
Donatelli, Clark	Min., Bos.	2	35	3	4	7	39	2	0	0	0	0	....	1989-90	1991-92
Donato, Ted	Bos., NYI, Ott., Ana., Dal., St.L., L.A., NYR	13	796	150	197	347	396	58	8	10	18	22	....	1991-92	2003-04
● Donnelly, Babe	Mtl.M.	1	34	0	1	1	14	2	0	0	0	0	....	1926-27	1926-27
Donnelly, Dave	Bos., Chi., Edm.	5	137	15	24	39	150	5	0	0	0	0	....	1983-84	1987-88
Donnelly, Gord	Que., Wpg., Buf., Dal.	12	554	28	41	69	2069	26	0	2	2	61	....	1983-84	1994-95
Donnelly, Mike	NYR, Buf., L.A., Dal., NYI	11	465	114	121	235	255	47	12	12	24	30	....	1986-87	1996-97
‡ Dopita, Jiri	Phi., Edm.	2	73	12	21	33	19	....	....	....	....	....	....	2001-02	2002-03
● Doran, John	NYA, Det., Mtl.	5	98	5	10	15	110	3	0	0	0	0	....	1933-34	1939-40
● Doran, Lloyd	Det.	1	24	3	2	5	10	....	....	....	....	....	....	1946-47	1946-47
● Doraty, Ken	Chi., Tor., Det.	5	103	15	26	41	24	15	7	2	9	2	....	1926-27	1937-38
Dore, Andre	NYR, St.L., Que.	7	257	14	81	95	261	23	1	2	3	32	....	1978-79	1984-85
Dore, Daniel	Que.	2	17	2	3	5	59	....	....	....	....	....	....	1989-90	1990-91
Dorey, Jim	Tor., NYR	4	232	25	74	99	553	11	0	2	2	40	....	1968-69	1971-72
Dorion, Dan	N.J.	2	4	1	1	2	2	....	....	....	....	....	....	1985-86	1987-88
Dornhoefer, Gary	Bos., Phi.	14	787	214	328	542	1291	80	17	19	36	203	2	1963-64	1977-78
Dorohoy, Eddie	Mtl.	1	16	0	0	0	6	....	....	....	....	....	....	1948-49	1948-49
Douglas, Jordy	Hfd., Min., Wpg.	6	268	76	62	138	160	6	0	0	0	4	....	1979-80	1984-85
Douglas, Kent	Tor., Oak., Det.	7	428	33	115	148	631	19	1	3	4	33	3	1962-63	1968-69
● Douglas, Les	Det.	4	52	6	12	18	8	10	3	2	5	2	1	1940-41	1946-47
Douris, Peter	Wpg., Bos., Ana., Dal.	11	321	54	67	121	80	27	3	5	8	14	....	1985-86	1997-98
● Downie, Dave	Tor.	1	11	0	1	1	2	....	....	....	....	....	....	1932-33	1932-33
Doyon, Mario	Chi., Que.	3	28	3	4	7	16	....	....	....	....	....	....	1988-89	1990-91
● Draper, Bruce	Tor.	1	1	0	0	0	0	....	....	....	....	....	....	1962-63	1962-63
● Drillon, Gordie	Tor., Mtl.	7	311	155	139	294	56	50	26	15	41	10	1	1936-37	1942-43
Driscoll, Peter	Edm.	2	60	3	8	11	97	3	0	0	0	0	....	1979-80	1980-81
Driver, Bruce	N.J., NYR	15	922	96	390	486	670	108	10	40	50	64	1	1983-84	1997-98
Drolet, Rene	Phi., Det.	2	2	0	0	0	0	....	....	....	....	....	....	1971-72	1974-75
Droppa, Ivan	Chi.	2	19	0	1	1	14	....	....	....	....	....	....	1993-94	1995-96
● Drouillard, Clarence	Det.	1	10	0	1	1	0	....	....	....	....	....	....	1937-38	1937-38
Drouin, Jude	Mtl., Min., NYI, Wpg.	12	666	151	305	456	346	72	27	41	68	33	....	1968-69	1980-81
Drouin, P.C.	Bos.	1	3	0	0	0	0	....	....	....	....	....	....	1996-97	1996-97
● Drouin, Polly	Mtl.	7	160	23	50	73	80	5	0	1	1	5	....	1934-35	1940-41
Druce, John	Wsh., Wpg., L.A., Phi.	10	531	113	126	239	347	53	17	6	23	38	....	1988-89	1997-98
‡ Druken, Harold	Van., Car., Tor.	5	146	27	36	63	36	4	0	1	1	0	....	1999-00	2003-04
Drulia, Stan	T.B.	3	126	15	27	42	52	....	....	....	....	....	....	1992-93	2000-01
● Drummond, Jim	NYR	1	2	0	0	0	0	....	....	....	....	....	....	1944-45	1944-45
● Drury, Herb	Pit., Phi.	6	213	24	13	37	203	4	1	1	2	0	....	1925-26	1930-31
‡ Drury, Ted	Cgy., Hfd., Ott., Ana., NYI, CBJ	8	414	41	52	93	367	14	1	0	1	4	....	1993-94	2000-01
‡ Dube, Christian	NYR	2	33	1	1	2	4	3	0	0	0	0	....	1996-97	1998-99
Dube, Gilles	Mtl., Det.	2	12	1	2	3	2	2	0	0	0	0	1	1949-50	1953-54
Dube, Norm	K.C.	2	57	8	10	18	54	....	....	....	....	....	....	1974-75	1975-76
Duberman, Justin	Pit.	1	4	0	0	0	0	....	....	....	....	....	....	1993-94	1993-94
Dubinsky, Steve	Chi., Cgy., Nsh., St.L.	10	375	25	45	70	164	10	1	0	1	14	....	1993-94	2002-03
Duchesne, Gaetan	Wsh., Que., Min., S.J., Fla.	14	1028	179	254	433	617	84	14	13	27	97	....	1981-82	1994-95
Duchesne, Steve	L.A., Phi., Que., St.L., Ott., Det.	16	1113	227	525	752	824	121	16	61	77	96	1	1986-87	2001-02
Dudley, Rick	Buf., Wpg.	6	309	75	99	174	292	25	7	2	9	69	....	1972-73	1980-81
Duerden, Dave	Fla.	1	2	0	0	0	0	....	....	....	....	....	....	1999-00	1999-00
Duff, Dick	Tor., NYR, Mtl., L.A., Buf.	18	1030	283	289	572	743	114	30	49	79	78	6	1954-55	1971-72
Dufour, Luc	Bos., Que., St.L.	3	167	23	21	44	199	18	1	0	1	32	....	1982-83	1984-85
Dufour, Marc	NYR, L.A.	3	14	1	0	1	2	....	....	....	....	....	....	1963-64	1968-69
Dufresne, Donald	Mtl., T.B., L.A., St.L., Edm.	9	268	6	36	42	258	34	1	3	4	47	1	1988-89	1996-97
● Duggan, John	Ott.	1	27	0	0	0	0	2	0	0	0	0	....	1925-26	1925-26
Duggan, Ken	Min.	1	1	0	0	0	0	....	....	....	....	....	....	1987-88	1987-88
Duguay, Ron	NYR, Det., Pit., L.A.	12	864	274	346	620	582	89	31	22	53	118	....	1977-78	1988-89
● Duguid, Lorne	Mtl.M., Det., Bos.	6	135	9	15	24	57	4	1	0	1	6	....	1931-32	1936-37
● Dukowski, Duke	Chi., NYA, NYR	5	200	16	30	46	172	6	0	0	0	6	....	1926-27	1933-34
● Dumart, Woody	Bos.	16	772	211	218	429	99	88	12	15	27	23	2	1935-36	1953-54
Dunbar, Dale	Van., Bos.	2	2	0	0	0	2	....	....	....	....	....	....	1985-86	1988-89
● Duncan, Art	Det., Tor.	5	156	18	16	34	225	5	0	0	0	4	....	1926-27	1930-31
Duncan, Iain	Wpg.	4	127	34	55	89	149	11	0	3	3	6	....	1986-87	1990-91
Duncanson, Craig	L.A., Wpg., NYR	7	38	5	4	9	61	....	....	....	....	....	....	1985-86	1992-93
Dundas, Rocky	Tor.	1	5	0	0	0	14	....	....	....	....	....	....	1989-90	1989-90
● Dunlap, Frank	Tor.	1	15	0	1	1	2	....	....	....	....	....	....	1943-44	1943-44
Dunlop, Blake	Min., Phi., St.L., Det.	11	550	130	274	404	172	40	4	10	14	18	....	1973-74	1983-84
Dunn, Dave	Van., Tor.	3	184	14	41	55	313	10	1	1	2	41	....	1973-74	1975-76
Dunn, Richie	Buf., Cgy., Hfd.	12	483	36	140	176	314	36	3	15	18	24	....	1977-78	1988-89
Dupere, Denis	Tor., Wsh., St.L., K.C., Col.	8	421	80	99	179	66	16	1	0	1	0	....	1970-71	1977-78
Dupont, Andre	NYR, St.L., Phi., Que.	13	800	59	185	244	1986	140	14	18	32	352	2	1970-71	1982-83
Dupont, Jerome	Chi., Tor.	6	214	7	29	36	468	20	0	2	2	56	....	1981-82	1986-87
Dupont, Norm	Mtl., Wpg., Hfd.	5	256	55	85	140	52	13	4	2	6	0	....	1979-80	1983-84
● Dupre, Yanick	Phi.	3	35	2	0	2	16	....	....	....	....	....	....	1991-92	1995-96
● Durbano, Steve	St.L., Pit., K.C., Col.	6	220	13	60	73	1127	5	0	2	2	8	....	1972-73	1978-79
Duris, Vitezslav	Tor.	2	89	3	20	23	62	3	0	1	1	2	....	1980-81	1982-83
Dusablon, Benoit	NYR	1	3	0	0	0	2	....	....	....	....	....	....	2003-04	2003-04
Dussault, Norm	Mtl.	4	206	31	62	93	47	7	3	1	4	0	....	1947-48	1950-51
● Dutton, Red	Mtl.M., NYA	10	449	29	67	96	871	18	1	0	1	33	....	1926-27	1935-36
Dvorak, Miroslav	Phi.	3	193	11	74	85	51	18	0	2	2	6	....	1982-83	1984-85
‡ Dwyer, Gordie	T.B., NYR, Mtl.	5	108	0	5	5	394	....	....	....	....	....	....	1999-00	2003-04
Dwyer, Mike	Col., Cgy.	4	31	2	6	8	25	1	1	0	1	0	....	1978-79	1981-82
● Dyck, Henry	NYR	1	1	0	0	0	0	....	....	....	....	....	....	1943-44	1943-44
● Dye, Babe	Tor., Ham., Chi., NYA	11	271	201	47	248	221	10	2	0	2	11	1	1919-20	1930-31
‡ Dykhuis, Karl	Chi., Phi., T.B., Mtl.	12	644	42	91	133	495	62	8	10	18	50	....	1991-92	2003-04
Dykstra, Steve	Buf., Edm., Pit., Hfd.	5	217	8	32	40	545	1	0	0	0	2	....	1985-86	1989-90
● Dyte, Jack	Chi.	1	27	1	0	1	31	....	....	....	....	....	....	1943-44	1943-44
Dziedzic, Joe	Pit., Phx.	3	130	14	14	28	131	21	1	3	4	23	....	1995-96	1998-99

E

Eagles, Mike	Que., Chi., Wpg., Wsh.	16	853	74	122	196	928	44	2	6	8	34	....	1982-83	1999-00
Eakin, Bruce	Cgy., Det.	4	13	2	2	4	4	....	....	....	....	....	....	1981-82	1985-86
Eakins, Dallas	Wpg., Fla., St.L., Phx., NYR, Tor., NYI, Cgy.	10	120	0	9	9	208	5	0	0	0	4	....	1992-93	2001-02
Eastwood, Mike	Tor., Wpg., Phx., NYR, St.L., Chi., Pit.	13	783	87	149	236	354	97	8	11	19	64	....	1991-92	2003-04
Eatough, Jeff	Buf.	1	1	0	0	0	0	....	....	....	....	....	....	1981-82	1981-82
Eaves, Mike	Min., Cgy.	8	324	83	143	226	80	43	7	10	17	14	....	1978-79	1985-86
Eaves, Murray	Wpg., Det.	8	57	4	13	17	9	4	0	1	1	2	....	1980-81	1989-90
Ecclestone, Tim	St.L., Det., Tor., Atl.	11	692	126	233	359	344	48	6	11	17	76	....	1967-68	1977-78
Edberg, Rolf	Wsh.	3	184	45	58	103	24	....	....	....	....	....	....	1978-79	1980-81
● Eddolls, Frank	Mtl., NYR	8	317	23	43	66	114	31	0	2	2	10	1	1944-45	1951-52
Edestrand, Darryl	St.L., Phi., Pit., Bos., L.A.	10	455	34	90	124	404	42	3	9	12	57	....	1967-68	1978-79

Name	NHL Teams	NHL Seasons	Regular Schedule GP	G	A	TP	PIM	Playoffs GP	G	A	TP	PIM	NHL Cup Wins	First NHL Season	Last NHL Season
Edmundson, Garry	Mtl., Tor.	3	43	4	6	10	49	11	0	1	1	8	....	1951-52	1960-61
Edur, Tom	Col., Pit.	2	158	17	70	87	67	....	....	....	....	....	....	1976-77	1977-78
Egan, Pat	NYA, Bro., Det., Bos., NYR	11	554	77	153	230	776	46	9	4	13	48	....	1939-40	1950-51
Egeland, Allan	T.B.	3	17	0	0	0	16	....	....	....	....	....	....	1995-96	1997-98
Egers, Jack	NYR, St.L., Wsh.	7	284	64	69	133	154	32	5	6	11	32	....	1969-70	1975-76
• Ehman, Gerry	Bos., Det., Tor., Oak., Cal.	9	429	96	118	214	100	41	10	10	20	12	1	1957-58	1970-71
Eisenhut, Neil	Van., Cgy.	2	16	1	3	4	21	....	....	....	....	....	....	1993-94	1994-95
Eklund, Pelle	Phi., Dal.	9	594	120	335	455	109	66	10	36	46	8	....	1985-86	1993-94
Eldebrink, Anders	Van., Que.	2	55	3	11	14	29	14	0	0	0	10	....	1981-82	1982-83
‡ Elich, Matt	T.B.	2	16	1	1	2	0	....	....	....	....	....	....	1999-00	2000-01
Elik, Bo	Det.	1	3	0	0	0	0	....	....	....	....	....	....	1962-63	1962-63
Elik, Todd	L.A., Min., Edm., S.J., St.L., Bos.	8	448	110	219	329	453	52	15	27	42	48	....	1989-90	1996-97
Ellett, Dave	Wpg., Tor., N.J., Bos., St.L.	16	1129	153	415	568	985	116	11	46	57	87	....	1984-85	1999-00
• Elliott, Fred	Ott.	1	43	2	0	2	6	....	....	....	....	....	....	1928-29	1928-29
Ellis, Ron	Tor.	16	1034	332	308	640	207	70	18	8	26	20	1	1963-64	1980-81
Elomo, Miika	Wsh.	1	2	0	1	1	2	....	....	....	....	....	....	1999-00	1999-00
Eloranta, Kari	Cgy., St.L.	5	267	13	103	116	155	26	1	7	8	19	....	1981-82	1986-87
‡ Eloranta, Mikko	Bos., L.A.	4	264	32	44	76	186	7	1	1	2	2	....	1999-00	2002-03
Elynuik, Pat	Wpg., Wsh., T.B., Ott.	9	506	154	188	342	459	20	6	9	15	25	....	1987-88	1995-96
Emberg, Eddie	Mtl.	1	....	....	....	....	....	2	1	0	1	0	....	1944-45	1944-45
Emerson, Nelson	St.L., Wpg., Hfd., Car., Chi., Ott., Atl., L.A.	12	771	195	293	488	575	40	7	15	22	33	....	1990-91	2001-02
Emma, David	N.J., Bos., Fla.	5	34	5	6	11	2	....	....	....	....	....	....	1992-93	2000-01
Emmons, Gary	S.J.	1	3	1	0	1	0	....	....	....	....	....	....	1993-94	1993-94
Emmons, John	Ott., T.B., Bos.	3	85	2	4	6	64	....	....	....	....	....	....	1999-00	2001-02
• Emms, Hap	Mtl.M., NYA, Det., Bos.	10	320	36	53	89	311	14	0	0	0	12	....	1926-27	1937-38
Endean, Craig	Wpg.	1	2	0	1	1	0	....	....	....	....	....	....	1986-87	1986-87
Engblom, Brian	Mtl., Wsh., L.A., Buf., Cgy.	11	659	29	177	206	599	48	3	9	12	43	3	1976-77	1986-87
Engele, Jerry	Min.	3	100	2	13	15	162	2	0	1	1	0	....	1975-76	1977-78
English, John	L.A.	1	3	1	3	4	4	1	0	0	0	0	....	1987-88	1987-88
Ennis, Jim	Edm.	1	5	1	0	1	10	....	....	....	....	....	....	1987-88	1987-88
Erickson, Aut	Bos., Chi., Tor., Oak.	7	226	7	24	31	182	7	0	0	0	2	1	1959-60	1969-70
Erickson, Bryan	Wsh., L.A., Pit., Wpg.	9	351	80	125	205	141	14	3	4	7	7	....	1983-84	1993-94
Erickson, Grant	Bos., Min.	2	6	1	0	1	0	....	....	....	....	....	....	1968-69	1969-70
Eriksson, Peter	Edm.	1	20	3	3	6	24	....	....	....	....	....	....	1989-90	1989-90
Eriksson, Roland	Min., Van.	3	193	48	95	143	26	2	1	0	1	0	....	1976-77	1978-79
Eriksson, Thomas	Phi.	5	208	22	76	98	107	19	0	3	3	12	....	1980-81	1985-86
Erixon, Jan	NYR	10	556	57	159	216	167	58	7	7	14	16	....	1983-84	1992-93
Errey, Bob	Pit., Buf., S.J., Det., Dal., NYR	15	895	170	212	382	1005	99	13	16	29	109	2	1983-84	1997-98
Esau, Len	Tor., Que., Cgy., Edm.	4	27	0	10	10	24	....	....	....	....	....	....	1991-92	1994-95
Esposito, Phil	Chi., Bos., NYR	18	1282	717	873	1590	910	130	61	76	137	138	2	1963-64	1980-81
• Evans, Chris	Tor., Buf., St.L., Det., K.C.	5	241	19	42	61	143	12	1	1	2	8	....	1969-70	1974-75
Evans, Daryl	L.A., Wsh., Tor.	6	113	22	30	52	25	11	5	8	13	12	....	1981-82	1986-87
Evans, Doug	St.L., Wpg., Phi.	8	355	48	87	135	502	22	3	4	7	38	....	1985-86	1992-93
• Evans, Jack	NYR, Chi.	14	752	19	80	99	989	56	2	2	4	97	1	1948-49	1962-63
Evans, John Paul	Phi.	3	103	14	25	39	34	1	0	0	0	0	....	1978-79	1982-83
Evans, Kevin	Min., S.J.	2	9	0	1	1	44	....	....	....	....	....	....	1990-91	1991-92
Evans, Paul	Tor.	2	11	1	1	2	21	2	0	0	0	0	....	1976-77	1977-78
Evans, Shawn	St.L., NYI	2	9	1	0	1	2	....	....	....	....	....	....	1985-86	1989-90
• Evans, Stewart	Det., Mtl.M., Mtl.	8	367	28	49	77	425	26	0	0	0	20	1	1930-31	1938-39
Evason, Dean	Wsh., Hfd., S.J., Dal., Cgy.	13	803	139	233	372	1002	55	9	20	29	132	....	1983-84	1995-96
Ewen, Todd	St.L., Mtl., Ana., S.J.	11	518	36	40	76	1911	26	0	0	0	87	1	1986-87	1996-97
Ezinicki, Bill	Tor., Bos., NYR	9	368	79	105	184	713	40	5	8	13	87	3	1944-45	1954-55

F

Name	NHL Teams	NHL Seasons	Regular Schedule GP	G	A	TP	PIM	Playoffs GP	G	A	TP	PIM	NHL Cup Wins	First NHL Season	Last NHL Season
Fahey, Trevor	NYR	1	1	0	0	0	0	....	....	....	....	....	....	1964-65	1964-65
Fairbairn, Bill	NYR, Min., St.L.	11	658	162	261	423	173	54	13	22	35	42	....	1968-69	1978-79
‡ Fairchild, Kelly	Tor., Dal., Col.	4	34	2	3	5	6	....	....	....	....	....	....	1995-96	2001-02
Falkenberg, Bob	Det.	5	54	1	5	6	26	....	....	....	....	....	....	1966-67	1971-72
Falloon, Pat	S.J., Phi., Ott., Edm., Pit.	9	575	143	179	322	141	66	11	7	18	16	....	1991-92	1999-00
Farkas, Jeff	Tor., Atl.	4	11	0	2	2	6	5	1	0	1	0	....	1999-00	2002-03
Farrant, Walt	Chi.	1	1	0	0	0	0	....	....	....	....	....	....	1943-44	1943-44
Farrell, Mike	Wsh., Nsh.	3	13	0	0	0	2	....	....	....	....	....	....	2001-02	2003-04
Farrish, Dave	NYR, Que., Tor.	7	430	17	110	127	440	14	0	2	2	24	....	1976-77	1983-84
Fashoway, Gordie	Chi.	1	13	3	2	5	14	....	....	....	....	....	....	1950-51	1950-51
Faubert, Mario	Pit.	7	231	21	90	111	292	10	2	2	4	6	....	1974-75	1981-82
Faulkner, Alex	Tor., Det.	3	101	15	17	32	15	12	5	0	5	2	....	1961-62	1963-64
Fauss, Ted	Tor.	2	28	0	2	2	15	....	....	....	....	....	....	1986-87	1987-88
Faust, Andre	Phi.	2	47	10	7	17	14	....	....	....	....	....	....	1992-93	1993-94
Feamster, Dave	Chi.	4	169	13	24	37	154	33	3	5	8	61	....	1981-82	1984-85
Featherstone, Glen	St.L., Bos., NYR, Hfd., Cgy.	9	384	19	61	80	939	28	0	2	2	103	....	1988-89	1996-97
Featherstone, Tony	Oak., Cal., Min.	3	130	17	21	38	65	2	0	0	0	0	....	1969-70	1973-74
Federko, Bernie	St.L., Det.	14	1000	369	761	1130	487	91	35	66	101	83	....	1976-77	1989-90
Fedotov, Anatoli	Wpg., Ana.	2	4	0	2	2	0	....	....	....	....	....	....	1992-93	1993-94
Fedyk, Brent	Det., Phi., Dal., NYR	10	470	97	112	209	308	16	3	2	5	12	....	1987-88	1998-99
Felix, Chris	Wsh.	4	35	1	12	13	10	2	0	1	1	0	....	1987-88	1990-91
‡ Felsner, Brian	Chi.	1	12	1	3	4	12	....	....	....	....	....	....	1997-98	1997-98
Felsner, Denny	St.L.	4	18	1	4	5	6	10	2	3	5	2	....	1991-92	1994-95
Feltrin, Tony	Pit., NYR	4	48	3	3	6	65	....	....	....	....	....	....	1980-81	1985-86
Fenton, Paul	Hfd., NYR, L.A., Wpg., Tor., Cgy., S.J.	8	411	100	83	183	198	17	4	1	5	27	....	1984-85	1991-92
Fenyves, David	Buf., Phi.	9	206	3	32	35	119	11	0	0	0	9	....	1982-83	1990-91
Fergus, Tom	Bos., Tor., Van.	12	726	235	346	581	499	65	21	17	38	48	....	1981-82	1992-93
‡ Ferguson, Craig	Mtl., Cgy., Fla.	5	27	1	1	2	6	....	....	....	....	....	....	1993-94	1999-00
Ferguson, George	Tor., Pit., Min.	12	797	160	238	398	431	86	14	23	37	44	....	1972-73	1983-84
Ferguson, John	Mtl.	8	500	145	158	303	1214	85	20	18	38	260	5	1963-64	1970-71
Ferguson, Lorne	Bos., Det., Chi.	8	422	82	80	162	193	31	6	3	9	24	....	1949-50	1958-59
Ferguson, Norm	Oak., Cal.	4	279	73	66	139	72	10	1	4	5	7	....	1968-69	1971-72
Ferner, Mark	Buf., Wsh., Ana., Det.	6	91	3	10	13	51	....	....	....	....	....	....	1986-87	1994-95
‡ Ferraro, Chris	NYR, Pit., Edm., NYI, Wsh.	6	74	7	9	16	57	....	....	....	....	....	....	1995-96	2001-02
‡ Ferraro, Peter	NYR, Pit., Bos., Wsh.	6	92	9	15	24	58	2	0	0	0	0	....	1995-96	2001-02
Ferraro, Ray	Hfd., NYI, NYR, L.A., Atl., St.L.	18	1258	408	490	898	1288	68	21	22	43	54	....	1984-85	2001-02
Fetisov, Viacheslav	N.J., Det.	9	546	36	192	228	656	116	2	26	28	147	2	1989-90	1997-98
Fidler, Mike	Cle., Min., Hfd., Chi.	7	271	84	97	181	124	....	....	....	....	....	....	1976-77	1982-83
• Field, Wilf	NYA, Bro., Mtl., Chi.	6	219	17	25	42	151	2	0	0	0	2	....	1936-37	1944-45
Fielder, Guyle	Chi., Det., Bos.	4	9	0	0	0	2	6	0	0	0	2	....	1950-51	1957-58
Filimonov, Dmitri	Ott.	1	30	1	4	5	18	....	....	....	....	....	....	1993-94	1993-94
Fillion, Bob	Mtl.	7	327	42	61	103	84	33	7	4	11	10	2	1943-44	1949-50
• Fillion, Marcel	Bos.	1	1	0	0	0	0	....	....	....	....	....	....	1944-45	1944-45
• Filmore, Tommy	Det., NYA, Bos.	4	117	15	12	27	33	....	....	....	....	....	....	1930-31	1933-34
• Finkbeiner, Lloyd	NYA	1	2	0	0	0	0	....	....	....	....	....	....	1940-41	1940-41
Finley, Jeff	NYI, Phi., Wpg., Phx., NYR, St.L.	15	708	13	70	83	457	52	1	6	7	38	....	1987-88	2003-04
Finn, Steven	Que., T.B., L.A.	12	725	34	78	112	1724	23	0	4	4	39	....	1985-86	1996-97
Finney, Sid	Chi.	3	59	10	7	17	4	7	0	2	2	0	....	1951-52	1953-54
• Finnigan, Ed	St.L., Bos.	2	15	1	1	2	2	....	....	....	....	....	....	1934-35	1935-36
• Finnigan, Frank	Ott., Tor., St.L.	14	553	115	88	203	407	38	6	9	15	22	2	1923-24	1936-37
Fiorentino, Peter	NYR	1	1	0	0	0	0	....	....	....	....	....	....	1991-92	1991-92
Fischer, Ron	Buf.	2	18	0	7	7	6	....	....	....	....	....	....	1981-82	1982-83
• Fisher, Alvin	Tor.	1	9	1	0	1	4	....	....	....	....	....	....	1924-25	1924-25
Fisher, Craig	Phi., Wpg., Fla.	4	12	0	0	0	2	....	....	....	....	....	....	1989-90	1996-97
Fisher, Dunc	NYR, Bos., Det.	7	275	45	70	115	104	21	4	4	8	14	....	1947-48	1958-59
• Fisher, Joe	Det.	4	65	8	12	20	13	12	2	1	3	6	1	1939-40	1942-43
Fitchner, Bob	Que.	2	78	12	20	32	59	3	0	0	0	10	....	1979-80	1980-81
Fitzgerald, Rusty	Pit.	2	25	2	2	4	12	5	0	0	0	4	....	1994-95	1995-96
Fitzpatrick, Ross	Phi.	4	20	5	2	7	0	....	....	....	....	....	....	1982-83	1985-86
Fitzpatrick, Sandy	NYR, Min.	2	22	3	6	9	8	12	0	0	0	0	....	1964-65	1967-68
Flaman, Fern	Bos., Tor.	17	910	34	174	208	1370	63	4	8	12	93	1	1944-45	1960-61
Flatley, Pat	NYI, NYR	14	780	170	340	510	686	70	18	15	33	75	....	1983-84	1996-97
Fleming, Gerry	Mtl.	2	11	0	0	0	42	....	....	....	....	....	....	1993-94	1994-95
Fleming, Reggie	Mtl., Chi., Bos., NYR, Phi., Buf.	12	749	108	132	240	1468	50	3	6	9	106	1	1959-60	1970-71
Flesch, John	Min., Pit., Col.	4	124	18	23	41	117	....	....	....	....	....	....	1974-75	1979-80
Fletcher, Steven	Mtl., Wpg.	2	3	0	0	0	5	1	0	0	0	5	....	1987-88	1988-89
• Flett, Bill	L.A., Phi., Tor., Atl., Edm.	11	689	202	215	417	501	52	7	16	23	42	1	1967-68	1979-80
Fleury, Theoren	Cgy., Col., NYR, Chi.	15	1084	455	633	1088	1840	77	34	45	79	116	1	1988-89	2002-03

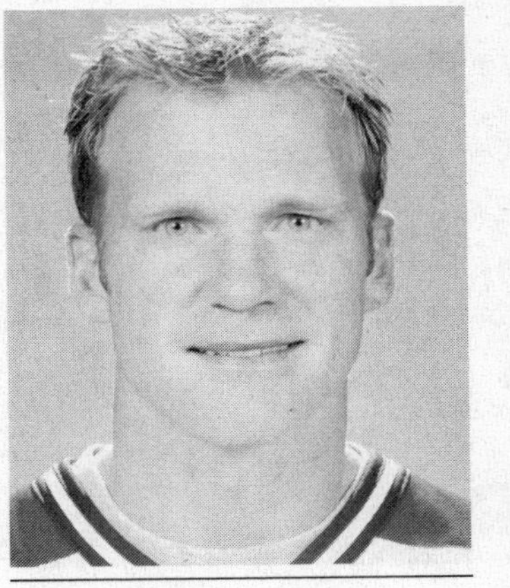

Karl Dykhuis

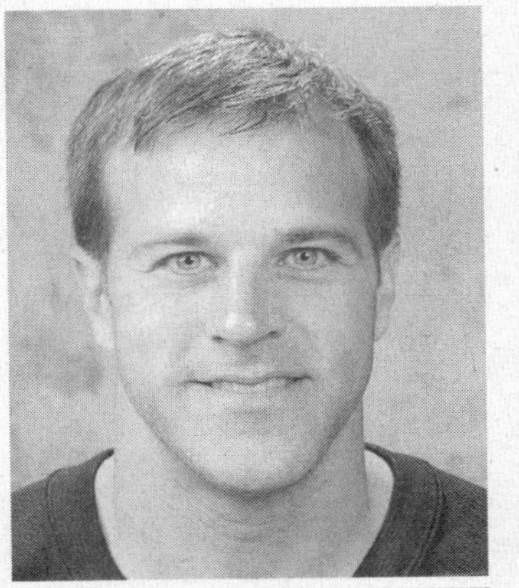

Mike Eastwood

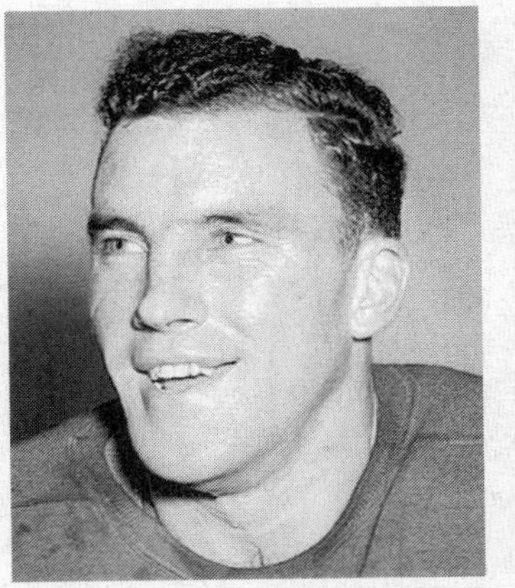

Pat Egan

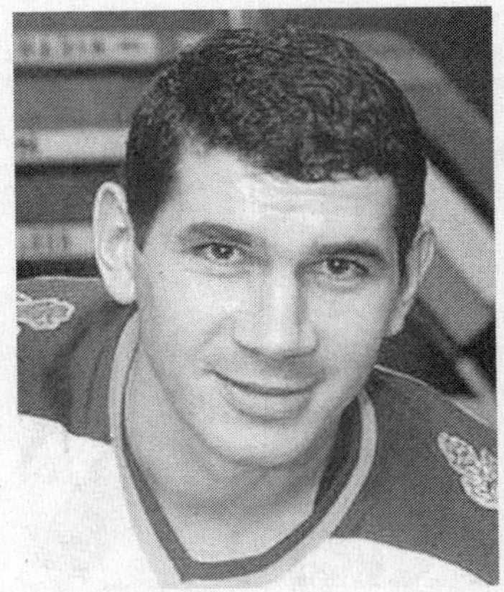

Trevor Fahey

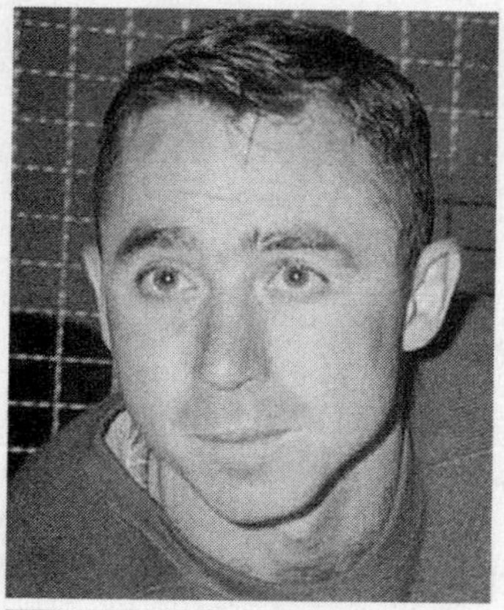

Dunc Fisher

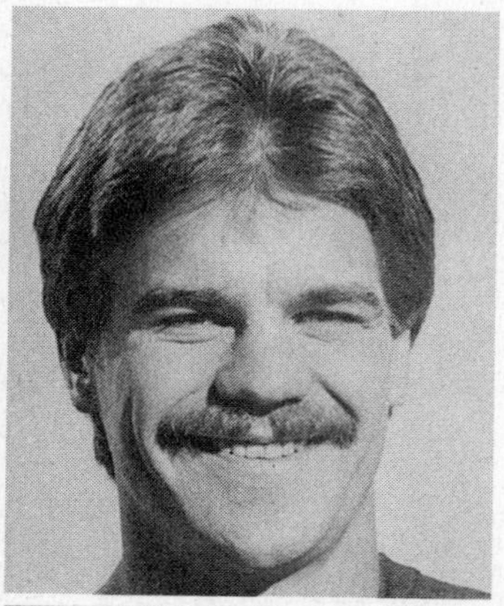

Bobby Francis

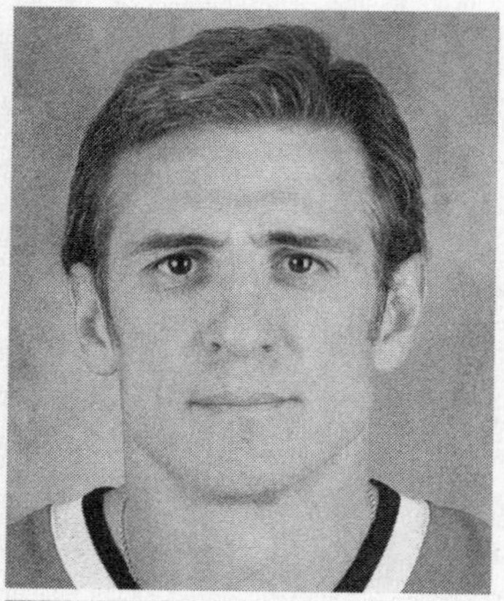

Ron Francis

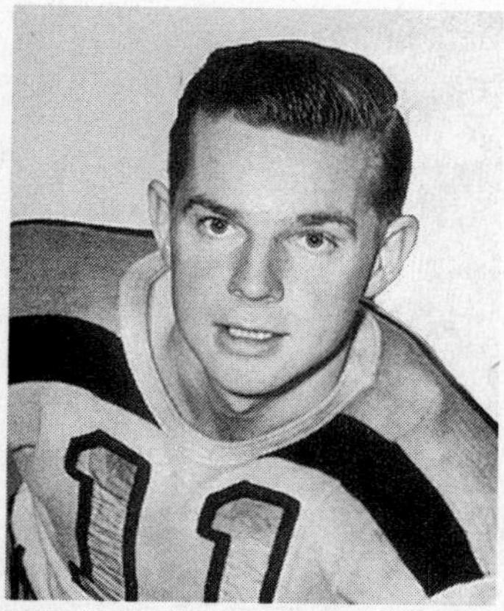

Don Gallinger

			Regular Schedule					Playoffs							
Name	NHL Teams	NHL Seasons	GP	G	A	TP	PIM	GP	G	A	TP	PIM	NHL Cup Wins	First NHL Season	Last NHL Season
Flichel, Todd	Wpg.	3	6	0	1	1	4	....	....	....	....	....	....	1987-88	1989-90
Flockhart, Rob	Van., Min.	5	55	2	5	7	14	1	1	0	1	2	....	1976-77	1980-81
Flockhart, Ron	Phi., Pit., Mtl., St.L., Bos.	9	453	145	183	328	208	19	4	6	10	14	....	1980-81	1988-89
Floyd, Larry	N.J.	2	12	2	3	5	9	....	....	....	....	....	....	1982-83	1983-84
• Fogarty, Bryan	Que., Pit., Mtl.	6	156	22	52	74	119	....	....	....	....	....	....	1989-90	1994-95
• Fogolin, Lee	Det., Chi.	9	427	10	48	58	575	28	0	2	2	30	1	1947-48	1955-56
Fogolin Jr., Lee	Buf., Edm.	13	924	44	195	239	1318	108	5	19	24	173	2	1974-75	1986-87
Folco, Peter	Van.	1	2	0	0	0	0	....	....	....	....	....	....	1973-74	1973-74
Foley, Gerry	Tor., NYR, L.A.	4	142	9	14	23	99	9	0	1	1	2	....	1954-55	1968-69
Foley, Rick	Chi., Phi., Det.	3	67	11	26	37	180	4	0	1	1	4	....	1970-71	1973-74
Foligno, Mike	Det., Buf., Tor., Fla.	15	1018	355	372	727	2049	57	15	17	32	185	....	1979-80	1993-94
Folk, Bill	Det.	2	12	0	0	0	4	....	....	....	....	....	....	1951-52	1952-53
Fontaine, Len	Det.	2	46	8	11	19	10	....	....	....	....	....	....	1972-73	1973-74
Fontas, Jon	Min.	2	2	0	0	0	0	....	....	....	....	....	....	1979-80	1980-81
Fonteyne, Val	Det., NYR, Pit.	13	820	75	154	229	26	59	3	10	13	8	....	1959-60	1971-72
Fontinato, Lou	NYR, Mtl.	9	535	26	78	104	1247	21	0	2	2	42	....	1954-55	1962-63
Forbes, Dave	Bos., Wsh.	6	363	64	64	128	341	45	1	4	5	13	....	1973-74	1978-79
Forbes, Mike	Bos., Edm.	3	50	1	11	12	41	....	....	....	....	....	....	1977-78	1981-82
Forey, Connie	St.L.	1	4	0	0	0	2	....	....	....	....	....	....	1973-74	1973-74
• Forsey, Jack	Tor.	1	19	7	9	16	10	3	0	1	1	0	....	1942-43	1942-43
• Forslund, Gus	Ott.	1	48	4	9	13	2	....	....	....	....	....	....	1932-33	1932-33
Forslund, Tomas	Cgy.	2	44	5	11	16	12	....	....	....	....	....	....	1991-92	1992-93
Forsyth, Alex	Wsh.	1	1	0	0	0	0	....	....	....	....	....	....	1976-77	1976-77
Fortier, Dave	Tor., NYI, Van.	4	205	8	21	29	335	20	0	2	2	33	....	1972-73	1976-77
Fortier, Marc	Que., Ott., L.A.	6	212	42	60	102	135	....	....	....	....	....	....	1987-88	1992-93
Fortin, Ray	St.L.	3	92	2	6	8	33	6	0	0	0	8	....	1967-68	1969-70
Foster, Corey	N.J., Phi., Pit., NYI	4	45	5	6	11	24	3	0	0	0	4	....	1988-89	1996-97
Foster, Dwight	Bos., Col., N.J., Det.	10	541	111	163	274	420	35	5	12	17	4	....	1977-78	1986-87
• Foster, Herb	NYR	2	6	1	0	1	5	....	....	....	....	....	....	1940-41	1947-48
• Foster, Yip	NYR, Bos., Det.	4	83	3	2	5	32	....	....	....	....	....	....	1929-30	1934-35
Fotiu, Nick	NYR, Hfd., Cgy., Phi., Edm.	13	646	60	77	137	1362	38	0	4	4	67	....	1976-77	1988-89
• Fowler, Jimmy	Tor.	3	135	18	29	47	39	18	0	3	3	2	....	1936-37	1938-39
Fowler, Tom	Chi.	1	24	0	1	1	18	....	....	....	....	....	....	1946-47	1946-47
Fox, Greg	Atl., Chi., Pit.	8	494	14	92	106	637	44	1	9	10	67	....	1977-78	1984-85
Fox, Jim	L.A.	9	578	186	293	479	143	22	4	8	12	0	....	1980-81	1989-90
• Foyston, Frank	Det.	2	64	17	7	24	32	....	....	....	....	....	....	1926-27	1927-28
Frampton, Bob	Mtl.	1	2	0	0	0	0	3	0	0	0	0	....	1949-50	1949-50
Franceschetti, Lou	Wsh., Tor., Buf.	10	459	59	81	140	747	44	3	2	5	111	....	1981-82	1991-92
Francis, Bobby	Det.	1	14	2	0	2	0	....	....	....	....	....	....	1982-83	1982-83
Francis, Ron	Hfd., Pit., Car., Tor.	23	1731	549	1249	1798	979	171	46	97	143	95	2	1981-82	2003-04
• Fraser, Archie	NYR	1	3	0	1	1	0	....	....	....	....	....	....	1943-44	1943-44
• Fraser, Charles	Ham.	1	1	0	0	0	0	....	....	....	....	....	....	1923-24	1923-24
Fraser, Curt	Van., Chi., Min.	12	704	193	240	433	1306	65	15	18	33	198	....	1978-79	1989-90
• Fraser, Gord	Chi., Det., Mtl., Pit., Phi.	5	144	24	12	36	224	2	1	0	1	6	....	1926-27	1930-31
Fraser, Harvey	Chi.	1	21	5	4	9	0	....	....	....	....	....	....	1944-45	1944-45
Fraser, Iain	NYI, Que., Dal., Edm., Wpg., S.J.	5	94	23	23	46	31	4	0	0	0	0	....	1992-93	1996-97
Fraser, Scott	Mtl., Edm., NYR	3	72	16	15	31	24	11	1	1	2	0	....	1995-96	1998-99
Frawley, Dan	Chi., Pit.	6	273	37	40	77	674	1	0	0	0	0	....	1983-84	1988-89
Freadrich, Kyle	T.B.	2	23	0	1	1	75	....	....	....	....	....	....	1999-00	2000-01
• Fredrickson, Frank	Det., Bos., Pit.	5	161	39	34	73	206	10	2	3	5	24	....	1926-27	1930-31
Freer, Mark	Phi., Ott., Cgy.	7	124	16	23	39	61	....	....	....	....	....	....	1986-87	1993-94
• Frew, Irv	Mtl.M., St.L., Mtl.	3	96	2	5	7	146	4	0	0	0	6	....	1933-34	1935-36
Friday, Tim	Det.	1	23	0	3	3	6	....	....	....	....	....	....	1985-86	1985-86
Fridgen, Dan	Hfd.	2	13	2	3	5	2	....	....	....	....	....	....	1981-82	1982-83
Friedman, Doug	Edm., Nsh.	2	18	0	1	1	34	....	....	....	....	....	....	1997-98	1998-99
Friest, Ron	Min.	3	64	7	7	14	191	6	1	0	1	7	....	1980-81	1982-83
Frig, Len	Chi., Cal., Cle., St.L.	7	311	13	51	64	479	14	2	1	3	0	....	1972-73	1979-80
Frost, Harry	Bos.	1	4	0	0	0	0	1	0	0	0	0	1	1938-39	1938-39
Frycer, Miroslav	Que., Tor., Det., Edm.	8	415	147	183	330	486	17	3	8	11	16	....	1981-82	1988-89
Fryday, Bob	Mtl.	2	5	1	0	1	0	....	....	....	....	....	....	1949-50	1951-52
Ftorek, Robbie	Det., Que., NYR	8	334	77	150	227	262	19	9	6	15	28	....	1972-73	1984-85
Fullan, Larry	Wsh.	1	4	1	0	1	0	....	....	....	....	....	....	1974-75	1974-75
Fusco, Mark	Hfd.	2	80	3	12	15	42	....	....	....	....	....	....	1983-84	1984-85

G

Gadsby, Bill	Chi., NYR, Det.	20	1248	130	438	568	1539	67	4	23	27	92	....	1946-47	1965-66
Gaetz, Link	Min., S.J.	3	65	6	8	14	412	....	....	....	....	....	....	1988-89	1991-92
Gage, Jody	Det., Buf.	6	68	14	15	29	26	....	....	....	....	....	....	1980-81	1991-92
• Gagne, Art	Mtl., Bos., Ott., Det.	6	228	67	33	100	257	11	2	1	3	20	....	1926-27	1931-32
Gagne, Paul	Col., N.J., Tor., NYI	8	390	110	101	211	127	....	....	....	....	....	....	1980-81	1989-90
Gagne, Pierre	Bos.	1	2	0	0	0	0	....	....	....	....	....	....	1959-60	1959-60
Gagner, Dave	NYR, Min., Dal., Tor., Cgy., Fla., Van.	15	946	318	401	719	1018	57	22	26	48	64	....	1984-85	1998-99
Gagnon, Germain	Mtl., NYI, Chi., K.C.	5	259	40	101	141	72	19	2	3	5	2	....	1971-72	1975-76
• Gagnon, Johnny	Mtl., Bos., NYA	10	454	120	141	261	295	32	12	12	24	37	1	1930-31	1939-40
Gagnon, Sean	Phx., Ott.	3	12	0	1	1	34	....	....	....	....	....	....	1997-98	2000-01
Gainey, Bob	Mtl.	16	1160	239	262	501	585	182	25	48	73	151	5	1973-74	1988-89
• Gainor, Dutch	Bos., NYR, Ott., Mtl.M.	7	246	51	56	107	129	22	2	1	3	14	2	1927-28	1934-35
‡ Galanov, Maxim	NYR, Pit., Atl., T.B.	4	122	8	12	20	44	1	0	0	0	0	....	1997-98	2000-01
Galarneau, Michel	Hfd.	3	78	7	10	17	34	....	....	....	....	....	....	1980-81	1982-83
• Galbraith, Percy	Bos., Ott.	8	347	29	31	60	224	31	4	7	11	24	1	1926-27	1933-34
• Gallagher, John	Mtl.M., Det., NYA	7	205	14	19	33	153	24	2	3	5	27	1	1930-31	1938-39
Gallant, Gerard	Det., T.B.	11	615	211	269	480	1674	58	18	21	39	178	....	1984-85	1994-95
Galley, Garry	L.A., Wsh., Bos., Phi., Buf., NYI	17	1149	125	475	600	1218	89	7	23	30	119	....	1984-85	2000-01
Gallimore, Jamie	Min.	1	2	0	0	0	0	....	....	....	....	....	....	1977-78	1977-78
• Gallinger, Don	Bos.	5	222	65	88	153	89	23	5	5	10	19	....	1942-43	1947-48
Gamble, Dick	Mtl., Chi., Tor.	8	195	41	41	82	66	14	1	2	3	4	1	1950-51	1966-67
Gambucci, Gary	Min.	2	51	2	7	9	9	....	....	....	....	....	....	1971-72	1973-74
Ganchar, Perry	St.L., Mtl., Pit.	4	42	3	7	10	36	7	3	1	4	0	....	1983-84	1988-89
Gans, Dave	L.A.	2	6	0	0	0	2	....	....	....	....	....	....	1982-83	1985-86
Gardiner, Bruce	Ott., T.B., CBJ, N.J.	6	312	34	54	88	263	21	1	4	5	8	....	1996-97	2001-02
• Gardiner, Herb	Mtl., Chi.	3	108	10	9	19	52	9	0	1	1	16	....	1926-27	1928-29
Gardner, Bill	Chi., Hfd.	9	380	73	115	188	68	45	3	8	11	17	....	1980-81	1988-89
• Gardner, Cal	NYR, Tor., Chi., Bos.	12	696	154	238	392	517	61	7	10	17	20	2	1945-46	1956-57
Gardner, Dave	Mtl., St.L., Cal., Cle., Phi.	7	350	75	115	190	41	....	....	....	....	....	....	1972-73	1979-80
Gardner, Paul	Col., Tor., Pit., Wsh., Buf.	10	447	201	201	402	207	16	2	6	8	14	....	1976-77	1985-86
Gare, Danny	Buf., Det., Edm.	13	827	354	331	685	1285	64	25	21	46	195	....	1974-75	1986-87
Gariepy, Ray	Bos., Tor.	2	36	1	6	7	43	....	....	....	....	....	....	1953-54	1955-56
• Garland, Scott	Tor., L.A.	3	91	13	24	37	115	7	1	2	3	35	....	1975-76	1978-79
Garner, Rob	Pit.	1	1	0	0	0	0	....	....	....	....	....	....	1982-83	1982-83
Garpenlov, Johan	Det., S.J., Fla., Atl.	10	609	114	197	311	276	44	10	9	19	22	....	1990-91	1999-00
• Garrett, Red	NYR	1	23	1	1	2	18	....	....	....	....	....	....	1942-43	1942-43
Gartner, Mike	Wsh., Min., NYR, Tor., Phx.	19	1432	708	627	1335	1159	122	43	50	93	125	....	1979-80	1997-98
• Gassoff, Bob	St.L.	4	245	11	47	58	866	9	0	1	1	16	....	1973-74	1976-77
Gassoff, Brad	Van.	4	122	19	17	36	163	3	0	0	0	0	....	1975-76	1978-79
Gatzos, Steve	Pit.	4	89	15	20	35	83	1	0	0	0	0	....	1981-82	1984-85
Gaudreau, Rob	S.J., Ott.	4	231	51	54	105	69	14	2	0	2	0	....	1992-93	1995-96
Gaudreault, Armand	Bos.	1	44	15	9	24	27	7	0	2	2	8	....	1944-45	1944-45
• Gaudreault, Leo	Mtl.	3	67	8	4	12	30	....	....	....	....	....	....	1927-28	1932-33
Gaul, Mike	Col., CBJ	2	3	0	0	0	4	....	....	....	....	....	....	1998-99	2000-01
Gaulin, Jean-Marc	Que.	4	26	4	3	7	8	1	0	0	0	0	....	1982-83	1985-86
Gaume, Dallas	Hfd.	1	4	1	1	2	0	....	....	....	....	....	....	1988-89	1988-89
• Gauthier, Art	Mtl.	1	13	0	0	0	0	1	0	0	0	0	....	1926-27	1926-27
Gauthier, Daniel	Chi.	1	5	0	0	0	0	....	....	....	....	....	....	1994-95	1994-95
• Gauthier, Fern	NYR, Mtl., Det.	6	229	46	50	96	35	22	5	1	6	7	....	1943-44	1948-49
Gauthier, Jean	Mtl., Phi., Bos.	10	166	6	29	35	150	14	1	3	4	22	1	1960-61	1969-70
Gauthier, Luc	Mtl.	1	3	0	0	0	2	....	....	....	....	....	....	1990-91	1990-91
Gauvreau, Jocelyn	Mtl.	1	2	0	0	0	0	....	....	....	....	....	....	1983-84	1983-84
Gavin, Stew	Tor., Hfd., Min.	13	768	130	155	285	584	66	14	20	34	75	....	1980-81	1992-93
Geale, Bob	Pit.	1	1	0	0	0	2	....	....	....	....	....	....	1984-85	1984-85
• Gee, George	Chi., Det.	9	551	135	183	318	345	41	6	13	19	32	1	1945-46	1953-54
Geldart, Gary	Min.	1	4	0	0	0	5	....	....	....	....	....	....	1970-71	1970-71
Gendron, Jean-Guy	NYR, Bos., Mtl., Phi.	14	863	182	201	383	701	42	7	4	11	47	....	1955-56	1971-72
Gendron, Martin	Wsh., Chi.	3	30	4	2	6	10	....	....	....	....	....	....	1994-95	1997-98

			Regular Schedule					Playoffs					NHL	First	Last
Name	NHL Teams	NHL Seasons	GP	G	A	TP	PIM	GP	G	A	TP	PIM	Cup Wins	NHL Season	NHL Season
• Geoffrion, Bernie	Mtl., NYR	16	883	393	429	822	689	132	58	60	118	88	6	1950-51	1967-68
Geoffrion, Danny	Mtl., Wpg.	3	111	20	32	52	99	2	0	0	0	7	....	1979-80	1981-82
• Geran, Gerry	Mtl.W., Bos.	2	37	5	1	6	6	....	....	....	....	....	....	1917-18	1925-26
• Gerard, Eddie	Ott.	6	128	50	48	98	108	11	4	0	4	17	3	1917-18	1922-23
Germain, Eric	L.A.	1	4	0	1	1	13	1	0	0	0	4	....	1987-88	1987-88
Gernander, Ken	NYR	3	12	2	3	5	6	15	0	0	0	0	....	1995-96	2003-04
Getliffe, Ray	Bos., Mtl.	10	393	136	137	273	250	45	9	10	19	30	2	1935-36	1944-45
Giallonardo, Mario	Col.	2	23	0	3	3	6	....	....	....	....	....	....	1979-80	1980-81
Gibbs, Barry	Bos., Min., Atl., St.L., L.A.	13	797	58	224	282	945	36	4	2	6	67	....	1967-68	1979-80
Gibson, Don	Van.	1	14	0	3	3	20	....	....	....	....	....	....	1990-91	1990-91
Gibson, Doug	Bos., Wsh.	3	63	9	19	28	0	1	0	0	0	0	....	1973-74	1977-78
Gibson, John	L.A., Tor., Wpg.	3	48	0	2	2	120	....	....	....	....	....	....	1980-81	1983-84
Giesebrecht, Gus	Det.	4	135	27	51	78	13	17	2	3	5	0	....	1938-39	1941-42
Giffin, Lee	Pit.	2	27	1	3	4	9	....	....	....	....	....	....	1986-87	1987-88
Gilbert, Ed	K.C., Pit.	3	166	21	31	52	22	....	....	....	....	....	....	1974-75	1976-77
Gilbert, Greg	NYI, Chi., NYR, St.L.	15	837	150	228	378	576	133	17	33	50	162	3	1981-82	1995-96
Gilbert, Jeannot	Bos.	2	9	0	1	1	4	....	....	....	....	....	....	1962-63	1964-65
Gilbert, Rod	NYR	18	1065	406	615	1021	508	79	34	33	67	43	....	1960-61	1977-78
Gilbertson, Stan	Cal., St.L., Wsh., Pit.	6	428	85	89	174	148	3	1	1	2	2	....	1971-72	1976-77
Gilchrist, Brent	Mtl., Edm., Min., Dal., Det., Nsh.	15	792	135	170	305	400	90	17	14	31	48	1	1988-89	2002-03
Giles, Curt	Min., NYR, St.L.	14	895	43	199	242	733	103	6	16	22	118	....	1979-80	1992-93
Gilhen, Randy	Hfd., Wpg., Pit., L.A., NYR, T.B., Fla.	11	457	55	60	115	314	33	3	2	5	26	1	1982-83	1995-96
Gill, Todd	Tor., S.J., St.L., Det., Phx., Col., Chi.	19	1007	82	272	354	1214	103	7	30	37	193	....	1984-85	2002-03
Gillen, Don	Phi., Hfd.	2	35	2	4	6	22	....	....	....	....	....	....	1979-80	1981-82
• Gillie, Farrand	Det.	1	1	0	0	0	0	....	....	....	....	....	....	1928-29	1928-29
Gillies, Clark	NYI, Buf.	14	958	319	378	697	1023	164	47	47	94	287	4	1974-75	1987-88
Gillis, Jere	Van., NYR, Que., Buf., Phi.	9	386	78	95	173	230	19	4	7	11	9	....	1977-78	1986-87
Gillis, Mike	Col., Bos.	6	246	33	43	76	186	27	2	5	7	10	....	1978-79	1983-84
Gillis, Paul	Que., Chi., Hfd.	11	624	88	154	242	1498	42	3	14	17	156	....	1982-83	1992-93
Gilmour, Doug	St.L., Cgy., Tor., N.J., Chi., Buf., Mtl.	20	1474	450	964	1414	1301	182	60	128	188	235	1	1983-84	2002-03
Gingras, Gaston	Mtl., Tor., St.L.	10	476	61	174	235	161	52	6	18	24	20	1	1979-80	1988-89
Girard, Bob	Cal., Cle., Wsh.	5	305	45	69	114	140	....	....	....	....	....	....	1975-76	1979-80
Girard, Jonathan	Bos.	5	150	10	34	44	46	3	0	1	1	2	....	1998-99	2002-03
Girard, Kenny	Tor.	3	7	0	1	1	2	....	....	....	....	....	....	1956-57	1959-60
• Giroux, Art	Mtl., Bos., Det.	3	54	6	4	10	14	2	0	0	0	0	....	1932-33	1935-36
Giroux, Larry	St.L., K.C., Det., Hfd.	7	274	15	74	89	333	5	0	0	0	4	....	1973-74	1979-80
Giroux, Pierre	L.A.	1	6	1	0	1	17	....	....	....	....	....	....	1982-83	1982-83
Gladney, Bob	L.A., Pit.	2	14	1	5	6	4	....	....	....	....	....	....	1982-83	1983-84
Gladu, Jean-Paul	Bos.	1	40	6	14	20	2	7	2	2	4	0	....	1944-45	1944-45
Glennie, Brian	Tor., L.A.	10	572	14	100	114	621	32	0	1	1	66	....	1969-70	1978-79
Glennon, Matt	Bos.	1	3	0	0	0	2	....	....	....	....	....	....	1991-92	1991-92
Gloeckner, Lorry	Det.	1	13	0	2	2	6	....	....	....	....	....	....	1978-79	1978-79
Gloor, Dan	Van.	1	2	0	0	0	0	....	....	....	....	....	....	1973-74	1973-74
• Glover, Fred	Det., Chi.	5	92	13	11	24	62	8	0	0	0	0	1	1948-49	1952-53
Glover, Howie	Chi., Det., NYR, Mtl.	5	144	29	17	46	101	11	1	2	3	2	....	1958-59	1968-69
Glynn, Brian	Cgy., Min., Edm., Ott., Van., Hfd.	10	431	25	79	104	410	57	6	10	16	40	....	1987-88	1996-97
Godden, Ernie	Tor.	1	5	1	1	2	6	....	....	....	....	....	....	1981-82	1981-82
• Godfrey, Warren	Bos., Det.	16	786	32	125	157	752	52	1	4	5	42	....	1952-53	1967-68
Godin, Eddy	Wsh.	2	27	3	6	9	12	....	....	....	....	....	....	1977-78	1978-79
• Godin, Sam	Ott., Mtl.	3	83	4	3	7	36	....	....	....	....	....	....	1927-28	1933-34
Godynyuk, Alexander	Tor., Cgy., Fla., Hfd.	7	223	10	39	49	224	....	....	....	....	....	....	1990-91	1996-97
Goegan, Pete	Det., NYR, Min.	11	383	19	67	86	365	33	1	3	4	61	....	1957-58	1967-68
Goertz, Dave	Pit.	1	2	0	0	0	2	....	....	....	....	....	....	1987-88	1987-88
• Goldham, Bob	Tor., Chi., Det.	12	650	28	143	171	400	66	3	14	17	53	5	1941-42	1955-56
‡ Goldmann, Erich	Ott.	1	1	0	0	0	0	....	....	....	....	....	....	1999-00	1999-00
• Goldsworthy, Bill	Bos., Min., NYR	14	771	283	258	541	793	40	18	19	37	30	....	1964-65	1977-78
• Goldsworthy, Leroy	NYR, Det., Chi., Mtl., Bos., NYA	10	336	66	57	123	79	24	1	0	1	4	1	1928-29	1938-39
Goldup, Glenn	Mtl., L.A.	9	291	52	67	119	303	16	4	3	7	22	....	1973-74	1981-82
Goldup, Hank	Tor., NYR	6	202	63	80	143	97	26	5	1	6	6	1	1939-40	1945-46
‡ Golubovsky, Yan	Det., Fla.	4	56	1	7	8	32	....	....	....	....	....	....	1997-98	2000-01
Goneau, Daniel	NYR	3	53	12	3	15	14	....	....	....	....	....	....	1996-97	1999-00
• Gooden, Bill	NYR	2	53	9	11	20	15	....	....	....	....	....	....	1942-43	1943-44
Goodenough, Larry	Phi., Van.	6	242	22	77	99	179	22	3	15	18	10	1	1974-75	1979-80
• Goodfellow, Ebbie	Det.	14	557	134	190	324	511	45	8	8	16	65	3	1929-30	1942-43
Gordiouk, Viktor	Buf.	2	26	3	8	11	0	....	....	....	....	....	....	1992-93	1994-95
• Gordon, Fred	Det., Bos.	2	81	8	7	15	68	2	0	0	0	0	....	1926-27	1927-28
Gordon, Jack	NYR	3	36	3	10	13	0	9	1	1	2	7	....	1948-49	1950-51
Gordon, Robb	Van.	1	4	0	0	0	2	....	....	....	....	....	....	1998-99	1998-99
Gorence, Tom	Phi., Edm.	6	303	58	53	111	89	37	9	6	15	47	....	1978-79	1983-84
Goring, Butch	L.A., NYI, Bos.	16	1107	375	513	888	102	134	38	50	88	32	4	1969-70	1984-85
Gorman, Dave	Atl.	1	3	0	0	0	0	....	....	....	....	....	....	1979-80	1979-80
• Gorman, Ed	Ott., Tor.	4	111	14	6	20	108	8	0	0	0	2	1	1924-25	1927-28
Gosselin, Benoit	NYR	1	7	0	0	0	33	....	....	....	....	....	....	1977-78	1977-78
‡ Gosselin, David	Nsh.	2	13	2	1	3	11	....	....	....	....	....	....	1999-00	2001-02
Gosselin, Guy	Wpg.	1	5	0	0	0	6	....	....	....	....	....	....	1987-88	1987-88
Gotaas, Steve	Pit., Min.	3	49	6	9	15	53	3	0	1	1	5	....	1987-88	1990-91
• Gottselig, Johnny	Chi.	16	589	176	195	371	203	43	13	13	26	18	2	1928-29	1944-45
Gould, Bobby	Atl., Cgy., Wsh., Bos.	11	697	145	159	304	572	78	15	13	28	58	....	1979-80	1989-90
Gould, John	Buf., Van., Atl.	9	504	131	138	269	113	14	3	2	5	4	....	1971-72	1979-80
Gould, Larry	Van.	1	2	0	0	0	0	....	....	....	....	....	....	1973-74	1973-74
Goulet, Michel	Que., Chi.	15	1089	548	604	1152	825	92	39	39	78	110	....	1979-80	1993-94
• Goupille, Red	Mtl.	8	222	12	28	40	256	8	2	0	2	6	....	1935-36	1942-43
Govedaris, Chris	Hfd., Tor.	4	45	4	6	10	24	4	0	0	0	2	....	1989-90	1993-94
Goyer, Gerry	Chi.	1	40	1	2	3	4	3	0	0	0	2	....	1967-68	1967-68
Goyette, Phil	Mtl., NYR, St.L., Buf.	16	941	207	467	674	131	94	17	29	46	26	4	1956-57	1971-72
• Graboski, Tony	Mtl.	3	66	6	10	16	24	3	0	0	0	6	....	1940-41	1942-43
• Gracie, Bob	Tor., Bos., NYA, Mtl.M., Mtl., Chi.	9	379	82	109	191	205	33	4	7	11	4	2	1930-31	1938-39
Gradin, Thomas	Van., Bos.	9	677	209	384	593	298	42	17	25	42	20	....	1978-79	1986-87
Graham, Dirk	Min., Chi.	12	772	219	270	489	917	90	17	27	44	92	....	1983-84	1994-95
• Graham, Leth	Ott., Ham.	6	27	3	0	3	0	1	0	0	0	0	1	1920-21	1925-26
Graham, Pat	Pit., Tor.	3	103	11	17	28	136	4	0	0	0	2	....	1981-82	1983-84
Graham, Rod	Bos.	1	14	2	1	3	7	....	....	....	....	....	....	1974-75	1974-75
• Graham, Ted	Chi., Mtl.M., Det., St.L., Bos., NYA	9	346	14	25	39	300	24	3	1	4	30	....	1927-28	1936-37
Granato, Tony	NYR, L.A., S.J.	14	773	248	244	492	1425	79	16	27	43	141	....	1988-89	2000-01
Grant, Danny	Mtl., Min., Det., L.A.	13	736	263	273	536	239	43	10	14	24	19	1	1965-66	1978-79
‡ Gratton, Benoit	Wsh., Cgy., Mtl.	6	58	6	10	16	58	....	....	....	....	....	....	1997-98	2003-04
Gratton, Dan	L.A.	1	7	1	0	1	5	....	....	....	....	....	....	1987-88	1987-88
Gratton, Norm	NYR, Atl., Buf., Min.	5	201	39	44	83	64	6	0	1	1	2	....	1971-72	1975-76
Gravelle, Leo	Mtl., Det.	5	223	44	34	78	42	17	4	1	5	2	....	1946-47	1950-51
Graves, Adam	Det., Edm., NYR, S.J.	16	1152	329	287	616	1224	125	38	27	65	119	2	1987-88	2002-03
Graves, Hilliard	Cal., Atl., Van., Wpg.	9	556	118	163	281	209	2	0	0	0	0	....	1970-71	1979-80
Graves, Steve	Edm.	3	35	5	4	9	10	....	....	....	....	....	....	1983-84	1987-88
• Gray, Alex	NYR, Tor.	2	50	7	0	7	32	13	1	0	1	0	1	1927-28	1928-29
Gray, Terry	Bos., Mtl., L.A., St.L.	6	147	26	28	54	64	35	5	5	10	22	....	1961-62	1970-71
• Green, Red	Ham., NYA, Bos., Det.	6	195	59	26	85	290	1	0	0	0	0	1	1923-24	1928-29
Green, Rick	Wsh., Mtl., Det., NYI	15	845	43	220	263	588	100	3	16	19	73	1	1976-77	1991-92
• Green, Shorty	Ham., NYA	4	103	33	20	53	151	....	....	....	....	....	....	1923-24	1926-27
Green, Ted	Bos.	11	620	48	206	254	1029	31	4	8	12	54	1	1960-61	1971-72
Greenlaw, Jeff	Wsh., Fla.	6	57	3	6	9	108	2	0	0	0	21	....	1986-87	1993-94
Gregg, Randy	Edm., Van.	10	474	41	152	193	333	137	13	38	51	127	5	1981-82	1991-92
Greig, Bruce	Cal.	2	9	0	1	1	46	....	....	....	....	....	....	1973-74	1974-75
‡ Greig, Mark	Hfd., Tor., Cgy., Phi.	9	125	13	27	40	90	5	0	1	1	0	....	1990-91	2002-03
Grenier, Lucien	Mtl., L.A.	4	151	14	14	28	18	2	0	0	0	0	1	1968-69	1971-72
Grenier, Richard	NYI	1	10	1	1	2	2	....	....	....	....	....	....	1972-73	1972-73
Greschner, Ron	NYR	16	982	179	431	610	1226	84	17	32	49	106	....	1974-75	1989-90
‡ Gretzky, Brent	T.B.	2	13	1	3	4	2	....	....	....	....	....	....	1993-94	1994-95
Gretzky, Wayne	Edm., L.A., St.L., NYR	20	1487	894	1963	2857	577	208	122	260	382	66	4	1979-80	1998-99
Grieve, Brent	NYI, Edm., Chi., L.A.	4	97	20	16	36	87	....	....	....	....	....	....	1993-94	1996-97
Grigor, George	Chi.	1	2	1	0	1	0	1	0	0	0	0	....	1943-44	1943-44
Grimson, Stu	Cgy., Chi., Ana., Det., Hfd., Car., L.A., Nsh.	14	729	17	22	39	2113	42	1	1	2	120	....	1988-89	2001-02
Grisdale, John	Tor., Van.	6	250	4	39	43	346	10	0	1	1	15	....	1972-73	1978-79
‡ Groleau, Francois	Mtl.	3	8	0	1	1	6	....	....	....	....	....	....	1995-96	1997-98
Gron, Stanislav	N.J.	1	1	0	0	0	0	....	....	....	....	....	....	2000-01	2000-01
Gronman, Tuomas	Chi., Pit.	2	38	1	3	4	38	1	0	0	0	0	....	1996-97	1997-98

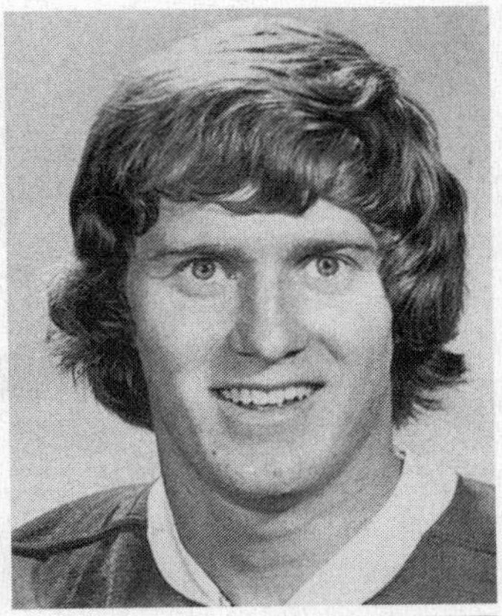

Dave Gardner

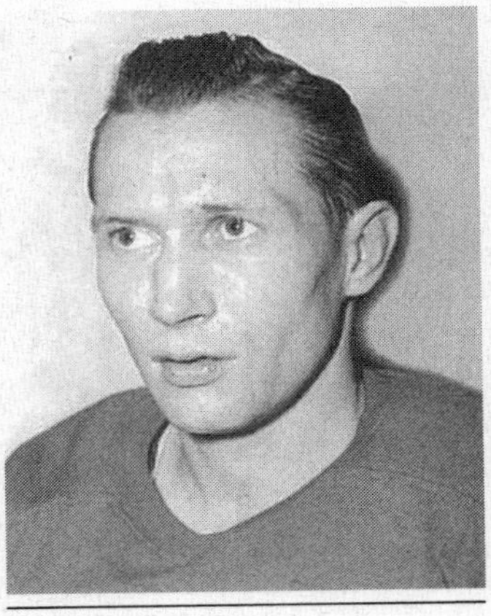

George Gee

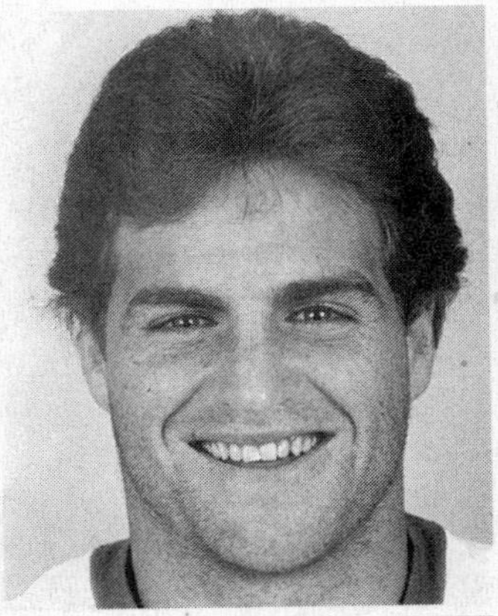

Greg Gilbert

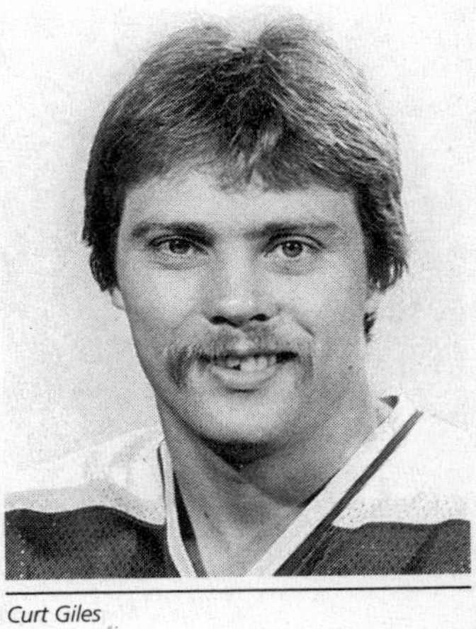

Curt Giles

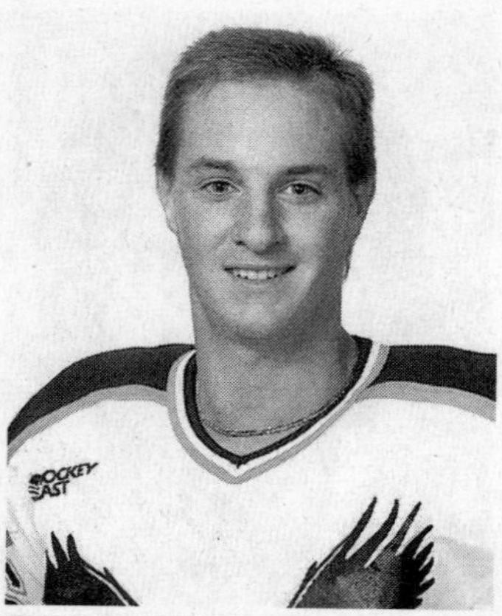

Matt Glennon

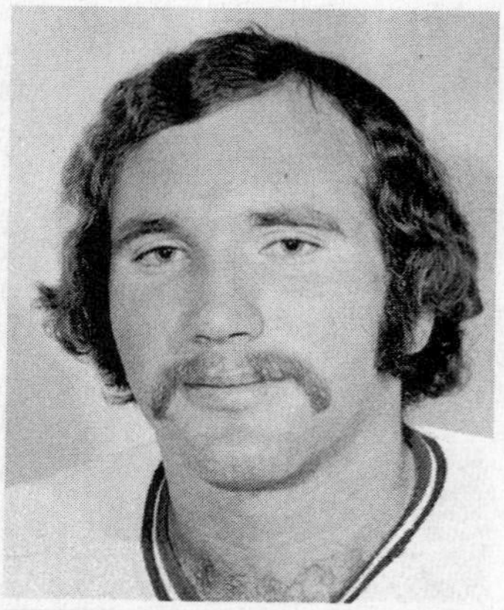

Larry Gould

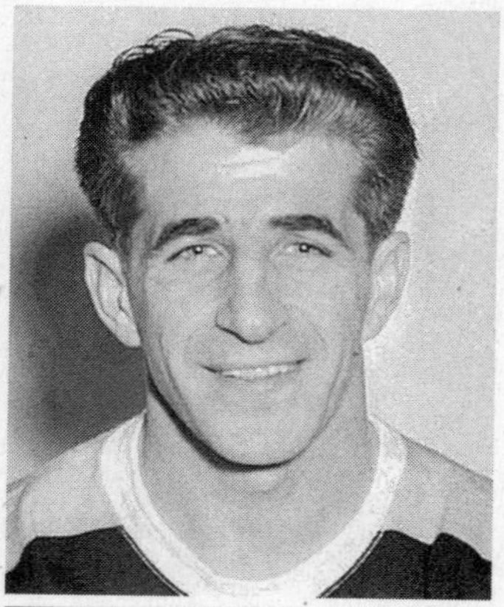

Don Grosso

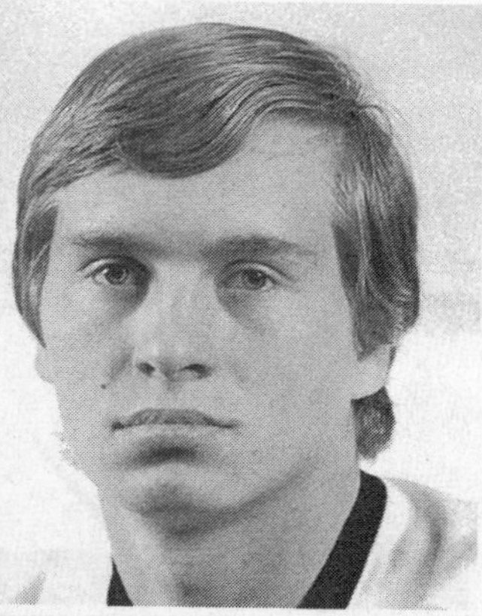

Matti Hagman

Name	NHL Teams	NHL Seasons	Regular Schedule					Playoffs					NHL Cup Wins	First NHL Season	Last NHL Season
			GP	G	A	TP	PIM	GP	G	A	TP	PIM			
Gronsdahl, Lloyd	Bos.	1	10	1	2	3	0	....	....	....	....	....	....	1941-42	1941-42
Gronstrand, Jari	Min., NYR, Que., NYI	5	185	8	26	34	135	3	0	0	0	4	....	1986-87	1990-91
‡ Grosek, Michal	Wpg., Buf., Chi., NYR, Bos.	11	526	84	137	221	509	45	9	11	20	77	....	1993-94	2003-04
• Gross, Lloyd	Tor., NYA, Bos., Det.	3	62	11	5	16	20	1	0	0	0	0	....	1926-27	1934-35
• Grosso, Don	Det., Chi., Bos.	9	336	87	117	204	90	48	15	14	29	63	1	1938-39	1946-47
Grosvenor, Len	Ott., NYA, Mtl.	6	149	9	11	20	78	4	0	0	0	2	....	1927-28	1932-33
Groulx, Wayne	Que.	1	1	0	0	0	0	....	....	....	....	....	....	1984-85	1984-85
Gruden, John	Bos., Ott., Wsh.	6	92	1	8	9	46	3	0	1	1	0	....	1993-94	2003-04
Gruen, Danny	Det., Col.	3	49	9	13	22	19	....	....	....	....	....	....	1972-73	1976-77
Gruhl, Scott	L.A., Pit.	3	20	3	3	6	6	....	....	....	....	....	....	1981-82	1987-88
Gryp, Bob	Bos., Wsh.	3	74	11	13	24	33	....	....	....	....	....	....	1973-74	1975-76
Guay, Francois	Buf.	1	1	0	0	0	0	....	....	....	....	....	....	1989-90	1989-90
Guay, Paul	Phi., L.A., Bos., NYI	7	117	11	23	34	92	9	0	1	1	12	....	1983-84	1990-91
Guerard, Daniel	Ott.	1	2	0	0	0	0	....	....	....	....	....	....	1994-95	1994-95
Guerard, Stephane	Que.	2	34	0	0	0	40	....	....	....	....	....	....	1987-88	1989-90
Guevremont, Jocelyn	Van., Buf., NYR	9	571	84	223	307	319	40	4	17	21	18	....	1971-72	1979-80
Guidolin, Aldo	NYR	4	182	9	15	24	117	....	....	....	....	....	....	1952-53	1955-56
Guidolin, Bep	Bos., Det., Chi.	9	519	107	171	278	606	24	5	7	12	35	....	1942-43	1951-52
Guindon, Bobby	Wpg.	1	6	0	1	1	0	....	....	....	....	....	....	1979-80	1979-80
‡ Guolla, Steve	S.J., T.B., Atl., N.J.	6	205	40	46	86	60	....	....	....	....	....	....	1996-97	2002-03
‡ Guren, Miloslav	Mtl.	2	36	1	3	4	16	....	....	....	....	....	....	1998-99	1999-00
Gusarov, Alexei	Que., Col., NYR, St.L.	11	607	39	128	167	313	68	0	14	14	38	1	1990-91	2000-01
Gusev, Sergey	Dal., T.B.	4	89	4	10	14	34	....	....	....	....	....	....	1997-98	2000-01
‡ Gusmanov, Ravil	Wpg.	1	4	0	0	0	0	....	....	....	....	....	....	1995-96	1995-96
Gustafsson, Bengt-Ake	Wsh.	9	629	196	359	555	196	32	9	19	28	16	....	1979-80	1988-89
‡ Gustafsson, Per	Fla., Tor., Ott.	2	89	8	27	35	38	1	0	0	0	0	....	1996-97	1997-98
Gustavsson, Peter	Col.	1	2	0	0	0	0	....	....	....	....	....	....	1981-82	1981-82
Guy, Kevan	Cgy., Van.	6	156	5	20	25	138	5	0	1	1	23	....	1986-87	1991-92

H

Name	NHL Teams	NHL Seasons	Regular Schedule					Playoffs					NHL Cup Wins	First NHL Season	Last NHL Season
			GP	G	A	TP	PIM	GP	G	A	TP	PIM			
‡ Haakana, Kari	Edm.	1	13	0	0	0	4	....	....	....	....	....	....	2002-03	2002-03
Haanpaa, Ari	NYI	3	60	6	11	17	37	6	0	0	0	10	....	1985-86	1987-88
Haas, David	Edm., Cgy.	2	7	2	1	3	7	....	....	....	....	....	....	1990-91	1993-94
Habscheid, Marc	Edm., Min., Det., Cgy.	11	345	72	91	163	171	12	1	3	4	13	....	1981-82	1991-92
Hachborn, Len	Phi., L.A.	3	102	20	39	59	29	7	0	3	3	7	....	1983-84	1985-86
Haddon, Lloyd	Det.	1	8	0	0	0	2	1	0	0	0	0	....	1959-60	1959-60
Hadfield, Vic	NYR, Pit.	16	1002	323	389	712	1154	73	27	21	48	117	....	1961-62	1976-77
• Haggarty, Jim	Mtl.	1	5	1	1	2	0	3	2	1	3	0	....	1941-42	1941-42
Haggerty, Sean	Tor., NYI, Nsh.	4	14	1	2	3	4	....	....	....	....	....	....	1995-96	2000-01
• Hagglund, Roger	Que.	1	3	0	0	0	0	....	....	....	....	....	....	1984-85	1984-85
Hagman, Matti	Bos., Edm.	4	237	56	89	145	36	20	5	2	7	6	....	1976-77	1981-82
Haidy, Gord	Det.	1	....	....	....	....	....	1	0	0	0	0	1	1949-50	1949-50
Hajdu, Richard	Buf.	2	5	0	0	0	4	....	....	....	....	....	....	1985-86	1986-87
Hajt, Bill	Buf.	14	854	42	202	244	433	80	2	16	18	70	....	1973-74	1986-87
Hakansson, Anders	Min., Pit., L.A.	5	330	52	46	98	141	6	0	0	0	2	....	1981-82	1985-86
• Halderson, Harold	Det., Tor.	1	44	3	2	5	65	....	....	....	....	....	....	1926-27	1926-27
Hale, Larry	Phi.	4	196	5	37	42	90	8	0	0	0	12	....	1968-69	1971-72
Haley, Len	Det.	2	30	2	2	4	14	6	1	3	4	6	....	1959-60	1960-61
Halkidis, Bob	Buf., L.A., Tor., Det., T.B., NYI	11	256	8	32	40	825	20	0	1	1	51	....	1984-85	1995-96
Halko, Steven	Car.	6	155	0	15	15	71	4	0	0	0	2	....	1997-98	2002-03
• Hall, Bob	NYA	1	8	0	0	0	0	....	....	....	....	....	....	1925-26	1925-26
Hall, Del	Cal.	3	9	2	0	2	2	....	....	....	....	....	....	1971-72	1973-74
• Hall, Joe	Mtl.	2	38	15	8	23	189	7	0	1	1	38	....	1917-18	1918-19
Hall, Murray	Chi., Det., Min., Van.	9	164	35	48	83	46	6	0	0	0	0	....	1961-62	1971-72
Hall, Taylor	Van., Bos.	5	41	7	9	16	29	....	....	....	....	....	....	1983-84	1987-88
Hall, Wayne	NYR	1	4	0	0	0	0	....	....	....	....	....	....	1960-61	1960-61
Haller, Kevin	Buf., Mtl., Phi., Hfd., Car., Ana., NYI	13	642	41	97	138	907	64	7	16	23	71	1	1989-90	2001-02
• Halliday, Milt	Ott.	3	67	1	0	1	4	6	0	0	0	0	1	1926-27	1928-29
Hallin, Mats	NYI, Min.	5	152	17	14	31	193	15	1	0	1	13	1	1982-83	1986-87
Halverson, Trevor	Wsh.	1	17	0	4	4	28	....	....	....	....	....	....	1998-99	1998-99
Halward, Doug	Bos., L.A., Van., Det., Edm.	14	653	69	224	293	774	47	7	10	17	113	....	1975-76	1988-89
Hamel, Gilles	Buf., Wpg., L.A.	9	519	127	147	274	276	27	4	5	9	10	....	1980-81	1988-89
• Hamel, Herb	Tor.	1	2	0	0	0	4	....	....	....	....	....	....	1930-31	1930-31
Hamel, Jean	St.L., Det., Que., Mtl.	12	699	26	95	121	766	33	0	2	2	44	....	1972-73	1983-84
• Hamill, Red	Bos., Chi.	12	419	128	94	222	160	24	1	2	3	20	1	1937-38	1950-51
Hamilton, Al	NYR, Buf., Edm.	7	257	10	78	88	258	7	0	0	0	2	....	1965-66	1979-80
Hamilton, Chuck	Mtl., St.L.	2	4	0	2	2	2	....	....	....	....	....	....	1961-62	1972-73
• Hamilton, Jack	Tor.	3	102	28	32	60	20	11	2	1	3	0	....	1942-43	1945-46
Hamilton, Jim	Pit.	8	95	14	18	32	28	6	3	0	3	0	....	1977-78	1984-85
• Hamilton, Reg	Tor., Chi.	12	424	21	87	108	412	64	3	8	11	46	2	1935-36	1946-47
Hammarstrom, Inge	Tor., St.L.	6	427	116	123	239	86	13	2	3	5	4	....	1973-74	1978-79
Hammond, Ken	L.A., Edm., NYR, Tor., Bos., S.J., Van., Ott.	8	193	18	29	47	290	15	0	0	0	24	....	1984-85	1992-93
Hampson, Gord	Cgy.	1	4	0	0	0	5	....	....	....	....	....	....	1982-83	1982-83
Hampson, Ted	Tor., NYR, Det., Oak., Cal., Min.	14	676	108	245	353	94	35	7	10	17	2	....	1959-60	1971-72
Hampton, Rick	Cal., Cle., L.A.	6	337	59	113	172	147	2	0	0	0	0	....	1974-75	1979-80
‡ Hamr, Radek	Ott.	2	11	0	0	0	0	....	....	....	....	....	....	1992-93	1993-94
Hamway, Mark	NYI	3	53	5	13	18	9	1	0	0	0	0	....	1984-85	1986-87
Handy, Ron	NYI, St.L.	2	14	0	3	3	0	....	....	....	....	....	....	1984-85	1987-88
Hangsleben, Al	Hfd., Wsh., L.A.	3	185	21	48	69	396	....	....	....	....	....	....	1979-80	1981-82
Hankinson, Ben	N.J., T.B.	3	43	3	3	6	45	2	1	0	1	4	....	1992-93	1994-95
Hankinson, Casey	Chi., Ana.	3	18	0	1	1	13	....	....	....	....	....	....	2000-01	2003-04
• Hanna, John	NYR, Mtl., Phi.	5	198	6	26	32	206	....	....	....	....	....	....	1958-59	1967-68
Hannan, Dave	Pit., Edm., Tor., Buf., Col., Ott.	16	841	114	191	305	942	63	6	7	13	46	2	1981-82	1996-97
• Hannigan, Gord	Tor.	4	161	29	31	60	117	9	2	0	2	8	....	1952-53	1955-56
Hannigan, Pat	Tor., NYR, Phi.	5	182	30	39	69	116	11	1	2	3	11	....	1959-60	1968-69
Hannigan, Ray	Tor.	1	3	0	0	0	2	....	....	....	....	....	....	1948-49	1948-49
Hansen, Richie	NYI, St.L.	4	20	2	8	10	4	....	....	....	....	....	....	1976-77	1981-82
Hansen, Tavis	Wpg., Phx.	5	34	2	1	3	16	2	0	0	0	0	....	1994-95	2000-01
Hanson, Dave	Det., Min.	2	33	1	1	2	65	....	....	....	....	....	....	1978-79	1979-80
• Hanson, Emil	Det.	1	7	0	0	0	6	....	....	....	....	....	....	1932-33	1932-33
Hanson, Keith	Cgy.	1	25	0	2	2	77	....	....	....	....	....	....	1983-84	1983-84
• Hanson, Oscar	Chi.	1	8	0	0	0	0	....	....	....	....	....	....	1937-38	1937-38
Harbaruk, Nick	Pit., St.L.	5	364	45	75	120	273	14	3	1	4	20	....	1969-70	1973-74
Harding, Jeff	Phi.	2	15	0	0	0	47	....	....	....	....	....	....	1988-89	1989-90
Hardy, Joe	Oak., Cal.	2	63	9	14	23	51	4	0	0	0	0	....	1969-70	1970-71
Hardy, Mark	L.A., NYR, Min.	15	915	62	306	368	1293	67	5	16	21	158	....	1979-80	1993-94
Hargreaves, Jim	Van.	2	66	1	7	8	105	....	....	....	....	....	....	1970-71	1972-73
‡ Harkins, Brett	Bos., Fla., CBJ	4	78	6	30	36	22	....	....	....	....	....	....	1994-95	2001-02
Harkins, Todd	Cgy., Hfd.	3	48	3	3	6	78	....	....	....	....	....	....	1991-92	1993-94
Harlock, David	Tor., Wsh., NYI, Atl.	8	212	2	14	16	188	....	....	....	....	....	....	1993-94	2001-02
Harlow, Scott	St.L.	1	1	0	1	1	0	....	....	....	....	....	....	1987-88	1987-88
Harmon, Glen	Mtl.	9	452	50	96	146	334	53	5	10	15	37	2	1942-43	1950-51
• Harms, John	Chi.	2	44	5	5	10	21	4	3	0	3	2	....	1943-44	1944-45
• Harnott, Walter	Bos.	1	6	0	0	0	2	....	....	....	....	....	....	1933-34	1933-34
Harper, Terry	Mtl., L.A., Det., St.L., Col.	19	1066	35	221	256	1362	112	4	13	17	140	5	1962-63	1980-81
Harrer, Tim	Cgy.	1	3	0	0	0	2	....	....	....	....	....	....	1982-83	1982-83
• Harrington, Hago	Bos., Mtl.	3	72	9	3	12	15	4	1	0	1	2	....	1925-26	1932-33
• Harris, Billy	Tor., Det., Oak., Pit.	13	769	126	219	345	205	62	8	10	18	30	3	1955-56	1968-69
Harris, Billy	NYI, L.A., Tor.	12	897	231	327	558	394	71	19	19	38	48	....	1972-73	1983-84
Harris, Duke	Min., Tor.	1	26	1	4	5	4	....	....	....	....	....	....	1967-68	1967-68
• Harris, Henry	Bos.	1	32	2	4	6	20	....	....	....	....	....	....	1930-31	1930-31
Harris, Hugh	Buf.	1	60	12	26	38	17	3	0	0	0	0	....	1972-73	1972-73
Harris, Ron	Det., Oak., Atl., NYR	11	476	20	91	111	474	28	4	3	7	33	....	1962-63	1975-76
• Harris, Smokey	Bos.	1	6	3	1	4	8	....	....	....	....	....	....	1924-25	1924-25
Harris, Ted	Mtl., Min., Det., St.L., Phi.	12	788	30	168	198	1000	100	1	22	23	230	5	1963-64	1974-75
Harrison, Ed	Bos., NYR	4	194	27	24	51	53	9	1	0	1	2	....	1947-48	1950-51
Harrison, Jim	Bos., Tor., Chi., Edm.	8	324	67	86	153	435	13	1	1	2	43	....	1968-69	1979-80
Hart, Gerry	Det., NYI, Que., St.L.	15	730	29	150	179	1240	78	3	12	15	175	....	1968-69	1982-83
• Hart, Gizzy	Det., Mtl.	3	104	6	8	14	12	8	0	1	1	0	....	1926-27	1932-33
Hartman, Mike	Buf., Wpg., T.B., NYR	9	397	43	35	78	1388	21	0	0	0	106	1	1986-87	1994-95
Hartsburg, Craig	Min.	10	570	98	315	413	818	61	15	27	42	70	....	1979-80	1988-89
Harvey, Buster	Min., Atl., K.C., Det.	7	407	90	118	208	131	14	0	2	2	8	....	1970-71	1976-77

Name	NHL Teams	NHL Seasons	Regular Schedule GP	G	A	TP	PIM	Playoffs GP	G	A	TP	PIM	NHL Cup Wins	First NHL Season	Last NHL Season
● Harvey, Doug	Mtl., NYR, Det., St.L.	20	1113	88	452	540	1216	137	8	64	72	152	6	1947-48	1968-69
Harvey, Hugh	K.C.	2	18	1	1	2	4	....	....	....	....	....	....	1974-75	1975-76
Hassard, Bob	Tor., Chi.	5	126	9	28	37	22	....	....	....	....	....	1	1949-50	1954-55
Hatcher, Kevin	Wsh., Dal., Pit., NYR, Car.	17	1157	227	450	677	1392	118	22	37	59	252	....	1984-85	2000-01
Hatoum, Ed	Det., Van.	3	47	3	6	9	25	....	....	....	....	....	....	1968-69	1970-71
‡ Hauer, Brett	Edm., Nsh.	3	37	4	4	8	38	....	....	....	....	....	....	1995-96	2001-02
Hawerchuk, Dale	Wpg., Buf., St.L., Phi.	16	1188	518	891	1409	730	97	30	69	99	67	....	1981-82	1996-97
‡ Hawgood, Greg	Bos., Edm., Phi., Fla., Pit., S.J., Van., Dal.	12	474	60	164	224	426	42	2	8	10	37	....	1987-88	2001-02
Hawkins, Todd	Van., Tor.	3	10	0	0	0	15	....	....	....	....	....	....	1988-89	1991-92
Haworth, Alan	Buf., Wsh., Que.	8	524	189	211	400	425	42	12	16	28	28	....	1980-81	1987-88
Haworth, Gord	NYR	1	2	0	1	1	0	....	....	....	....	....	....	1952-53	1952-53
Hawryliw, Neil	NYI	1	1	0	0	0	0	....	....	....	....	....	....	1981-82	1981-82
Hay, Bill	Chi.	8	506	113	273	386	244	67	15	21	36	62	1	1959-60	1966-67
‡ Hay, Dwayne	Wsh., Fla., T.B., Cgy.	4	79	2	4	6	22	....	....	....	....	....	....	1997-98	2000-01
● Hay, George	Chi., Det.	7	239	74	60	134	84	8	2	3	5	2	....	1926-27	1933-34
Hay, Jim	Det.	3	75	1	5	6	22	9	1	0	1	2	1	1952-53	1954-55
Hayek, Peter	Min.	1	1	0	0	0	0	....	....	....	....	....	....	1981-82	1981-82
Hayes, Chris	Bos.	1	....	....	....	....	....	1	0	0	0	0	1	1971-72	1971-72
● Haynes, Paul	Mtl.M., Bos., Mtl.	11	391	61	134	195	164	24	2	8	10	13	....	1930-31	1940-41
Hayward, Rick	L.A.	1	4	0	0	0	5	....	....	....	....	....	....	1990-91	1990-91
Hazlett, Steve	Van.	1	1	0	0	0	0	....	....	....	....	....	....	1979-80	1979-80
Head, Galen	Det.	1	1	0	0	0	0	....	....	....	....	....	....	1967-68	1967-68
● Headley, Fern	Bos., Mtl.	1	30	1	3	4	10	1	0	0	0	0	....	1924-25	1924-25
Healey, Rich	Det.	1	1	0	0	0	2	....	....	....	....	....	....	1960-61	1960-61
Heaphy, Shawn	Cgy.	1	1	0	0	0	0	....	....	....	....	....	....	1992-93	1992-93
Heaslip, Mark	NYR, L.A.	3	117	10	19	29	110	5	0	0	0	2	....	1976-77	1978-79
Heath, Randy	NYR	2	13	2	4	6	15	....	....	....	....	....	....	1984-85	1985-86
Hebenton, Andy	NYR, Bos.	9	630	189	202	391	83	22	6	5	11	8	....	1955-56	1963-64
Hecl, Radoslav	Buf.	1	14	0	0	0	2	....	....	....	....	....	....	2002-03	2002-03
Hedberg, Anders	NYR	7	465	172	225	397	144	58	22	24	46	31	....	1978-79	1984-85
● Heffernan, Frank	Tor.	1	19	0	1	1	10	....	....	....	....	....	....	1919-20	1919-20
Heffernan, Gerry	Mtl.	3	83	33	35	68	27	11	3	3	6	8	1	1941-42	1943-44
Heidt, Mike	L.A.	1	6	0	1	1	7	....	....	....	....	....	....	1983-84	1983-84
● Heindl, Bill	Min., NYR	3	18	2	1	3	0	....	....	....	....	....	....	1970-71	1972-73
Heinrich, Lionel	Bos.	1	35	1	1	2	33	....	....	....	....	....	....	1955-56	1955-56
‡ Heins, Shawn	S.J., Pit., Atl.	6	125	4	12	16	154	2	0	0	0	0	....	1998-99	2003-04
Heinze, Steve	Bos., CBJ, Buf., L.A.	12	694	178	158	336	379	69	11	15	26	48	....	1991-92	2002-03
Heiskala, Earl	Phi.	3	127	13	11	24	294	....	....	....	....	....	....	1968-69	1970-71
‡ Heisten, Barrett	NYR	1	10	0	0	0	2	....	....	....	....	....	....	2001-02	2001-02
Helander, Peter	L.A.	1	7	0	1	1	0	....	....	....	....	....	....	1982-83	1982-83
‡ Helenius, Sami	Cgy., T.B., Col., Dal., Chi.	6	155	2	4	6	260	1	0	0	0	0	....	1996-97	2002-03
● Heller, Ott	NYR	15	647	55	176	231	465	61	6	8	14	61	2	1931-32	1945-46
Helman, Harry	Ott.	3	44	1	0	1	7	2	0	0	0	0	1	1922-23	1924-25
‡ Helminen, Raimo	NYR, Min., NYI	3	117	13	46	59	16	2	0	0	0	0	....	1985-86	1988-89
● Hemmerling, Tony	NYA	2	22	3	3	6	4	....	....	....	....	....	....	1935-36	1936-37
Henderson, Archie	Wsh., Min., Hfd.	3	23	3	1	4	92	....	....	....	....	....	....	1980-81	1982-83
‡ Henderson, Jay	Bos.	4	33	1	3	4	37	....	....	....	....	....	....	1998-99	2001-02
Henderson, Matt	Nsh., Chi.	2	6	0	1	1	2	....	....	....	....	....	....	1998-99	2001-02
Henderson, Murray	Bos.	8	405	24	62	86	305	41	2	3	5	23	....	1944-45	1951-52
Henderson, Paul	Det., Tor., Atl.	13	707	236	241	477	304	56	11	14	25	28	....	1962-63	1979-80
‡ Hendrickson, Darby	Tor., NYI, Van., Min., Col.	11	518	65	64	129	370	25	3	3	6	6	....	1993-94	2003-04
Hendrickson, John	Det.	3	5	0	0	0	4	....	....	....	....	....	....	1957-58	1961-62
Henning, Lorne	NYI	9	544	73	111	184	102	81	7	7	14	8	2	1972-73	1980-81
‡ Henry, Burke	Chi.	2	39	2	6	8	33	....	....	....	....	....	....	2002-03	2003-04
● Henry, Camille	NYR, Chi., St.L.	14	727	279	249	528	88	47	6	12	18	7	....	1953-54	1969-70
Henry, Dale	NYI	6	132	13	26	39	263	14	1	0	1	19	....	1984-85	1989-90
‡ Hentunen, Jukka	Cgy., Nsh.	1	38	4	5	9	4	....	....	....	....	....	....	2001-02	2001-02
Hepple, Alan	N.J.	3	3	0	0	0	7	....	....	....	....	....	....	1983-84	1985-86
Herbers, Ian	Edm., T.B., NYI	2	65	0	5	5	79	....	....	....	....	....	....	1993-94	1999-00
● Herberts, Jimmy	Bos., Tor., Det.	6	206	83	31	114	253	9	3	0	3	10	....	1924-25	1929-30
● Herchenratter, Art	Det.	1	10	1	2	3	2	....	....	....	....	....	....	1940-41	1940-41
Hergerts, Fred	NYA	2	20	2	4	6	2	....	....	....	....	....	....	1934-35	1935-36
● Hergesheimer, Phil	Chi., Bos.	4	125	21	41	62	19	6	0	0	0	2	....	1939-40	1942-43
Hergesheimer, Wally	NYR, Chi.	7	351	114	85	199	106	5	1	0	1	0	....	1951-52	1958-59
● Heron, Red	Tor., Bro., Mtl.	4	106	21	19	40	38	21	2	2	4	6	....	1938-39	1941-42
Heroux, Yves	Que.	1	1	0	0	0	0	....	....	....	....	....	....	1986-87	1986-87
‡ Herperger, Chris	Chi., Ott., Atl.	4	169	18	25	43	75	....	....	....	....	....	....	1999-00	2002-03
Herr, Matt	Wsh., Fla., Bos.	4	58	4	5	9	25	....	....	....	....	....	....	1998-99	2002-03
Herter, Jason	NYI	1	1	0	1	1	0	....	....	....	....	....	....	1995-96	1995-96
Hervey, Matt	Wpg., Bos., T.B.	3	35	0	5	5	97	5	0	0	0	6	....	1988-89	1992-93
Hess, Bob	St.L., Buf., Hfd.	8	329	27	95	122	178	4	1	1	2	2	....	1974-75	1983-84
● Heximer, Obs	NYR, Bos., NYA	3	84	13	7	20	16	5	0	0	0	2	....	1929-30	1934-35
● Hextall, Bryan	NYR	11	449	187	175	362	227	37	8	9	17	19	1	1936-37	1947-48
Hextall, Bryan	NYR, Pit., Atl., Det., Min.	8	549	99	161	260	738	18	0	4	4	59	....	1962-63	1975-76
Hextall, Dennis	NYR, L.A., Cal., Min., Det., Wsh.	13	681	153	350	503	1398	22	3	3	6	45	....	1967-68	1979-80
Heyliger, Vic	Chi.	2	33	2	3	5	2	....	....	....	....	....	....	1937-38	1943-44
● Hicke, Bill	Mtl., NYR, Oak., Cal., Pit.	14	729	168	234	402	395	42	3	10	13	41	2	1958-59	1971-72
Hicke, Ernie	Cal., Atl., NYI, Min., L.A.	8	520	132	140	272	407	2	1	0	1	0	....	1970-71	1977-78
Hickey, Greg	NYR	1	1	0	0	0	0	....	....	....	....	....	....	1977-78	1977-78
Hickey, Pat	NYR, Col., Tor., Que., St.L.	10	646	192	212	404	351	55	5	11	16	37	....	1975-76	1984-85
Hicks, Alex	Ana., Pit., S.J., Fla.	5	258	25	54	79	247	15	0	2	2	8	....	1995-96	1999-00
Hicks, Doug	Min., Chi., Edm., Wsh.	9	561	37	131	168	442	18	2	1	3	15	....	1974-75	1982-83
Hicks, Glenn	Det.	2	108	6	12	18	127	....	....	....	....	....	....	1979-80	1980-81
● Hicks, Henry	Mtl.M., Det.	3	96	7	2	9	72	....	....	....	....	....	....	1928-29	1930-31
Hicks, Wayne	Chi., Bos., Mtl., Phi., Pit.	5	115	13	23	36	22	2	0	1	1	2	1	1959-60	1967-68
Hidi, Andre	Wsh.	2	7	2	1	3	9	2	0	0	0	0	....	1983-84	1984-85
Hiemer, Uli	N.J.	3	143	19	54	73	176	....	....	....	....	....	....	1984-85	1986-87
‡ Higgins, Matt	Mtl.	4	57	1	2	3	6	....	....	....	....	....	....	1997-98	2000-01
Higgins, Paul	Tor.	2	25	0	0	0	152	1	0	0	0	0	....	1981-82	1982-83
Higgins, Tim	Chi., N.J., Det.	11	706	154	198	352	719	65	5	8	13	77	....	1978-79	1988-89
Hildebrand, Ike	NYR, Chi.	2	41	7	11	18	16	....	....	....	....	....	....	1953-54	1954-55
Hill, Al	Phi.	8	221	40	55	95	227	51	8	11	19	43	....	1976-77	1987-88
Hill, Brian	Hfd.	1	19	1	1	2	4	....	....	....	....	....	....	1979-80	1979-80
● Hill, Mel	Bos., Bro., Tor.	9	324	89	109	198	128	43	12	7	19	18	3	1937-38	1945-46
● Hiller, Dutch	NYR, Det., Bos., Mtl.	9	383	91	113	204	163	48	9	8	17	21	2	1937-38	1945-46
Hiller, Jim	L.A., Det., NYR	2	63	8	12	20	116	2	0	0	0	4	....	1992-93	1993-94
Hillier, Randy	Bos., Pit., NYI, Buf.	11	543	16	110	126	906	28	0	2	2	93	1	1981-82	1991-92
Hillman, Floyd	Bos.	1	6	0	0	0	10	....	....	....	....	....	....	1956-57	1956-57
Hillman, Larry	Det., Bos., Tor., Min., Mtl., Phi., L.A., Buf.	19	790	36	196	232	579	74	2	9	11	30	6	1954-55	1972-73
● Hillman, Wayne	Chi., NYR, Min., Phi.	13	691	18	86	104	534	28	0	3	3	19	1	1960-61	1972-73
Hilworth, John	Det.	3	57	1	1	2	89	....	....	....	....	....	....	1977-78	1979-80
● Himes, Normie	NYA	9	402	106	113	219	127	2	0	0	0	0	....	1926-27	1934-35
Hindmarch, Dave	Cgy.	4	99	21	17	38	25	10	0	0	0	6	....	1980-81	1983-84
Hinse, Andre	Tor.	1	4	0	0	0	0	....	....	....	....	....	....	1967-68	1967-68
Hinton, Dan	Chi.	1	14	0	0	0	16	....	....	....	....	....	....	1976-77	1976-77
Hirsch, Tom	Min.	3	31	1	7	8	30	12	0	0	0	6	....	1983-84	1987-88
● Hirschfeld, Bert	Mtl.	2	33	1	4	5	2	5	1	0	1	0	....	1949-50	1950-51
Hislop, Jamie	Que., Cgy.	5	345	75	103	178	86	28	3	2	5	11	....	1979-80	1983-84
● Hitchman, Lionel	Ott., Bos.	12	417	28	34	62	523	35	3	1	4	73	2	1922-23	1933-34
● Hlinka, Ivan	Van.	2	137	42	81	123	28	16	3	10	13	8	....	1981-82	1982-83
Hlushko, Todd	Phi., Cgy., Pit.	6	79	8	13	21	84	3	0	0	0	2	....	1993-94	1998-99
Hocking, Justin	L.A.	1	1	0	0	0	0	....	....	....	....	....	....	1993-94	1993-94
Hodge, Ken	Chi., Bos., NYR	14	881	328	472	800	779	97	34	47	81	120	2	1964-65	1977-78
Hodge Jr., Ken	Min., Bos., T.B.	4	142	39	48	87	32	15	4	6	10	6	....	1988-89	1992-93
Hodgson, Dan	Tor., Van.	4	114	29	45	74	64	....	....	....	....	....	....	1985-86	1988-89
Hodgson, Rick	Hfd.	1	6	0	0	0	6	1	0	0	0	0	....	1979-80	1979-80
Hodgson, Ted	Bos.	1	4	0	0	0	0	....	....	....	....	....	....	1966-67	1966-67
Hoekstra, Cec	Mtl.	1	4	0	0	0	0	....	....	....	....	....	....	1959-60	1959-60
Hoekstra, Ed	Phi.	1	70	15	21	36	6	7	0	1	1	0	....	1967-68	1967-68
Hoene, Phil	L.A.	3	37	2	4	6	22	....	....	....	....	....	....	1972-73	1974-75
Hoffinger, Val	Chi.	2	28	0	1	1	30	....	....	....	....	....	....	1927-28	1928-29
Hoffman, Mike	Hfd.	3	9	1	3	4	2	....	....	....	....	....	....	1982-83	1985-86
Hoffmeyer, Bob	Chi., Phi., N.J.	6	198	14	52	66	325	3	0	1	1	25	....	1977-78	1984-85

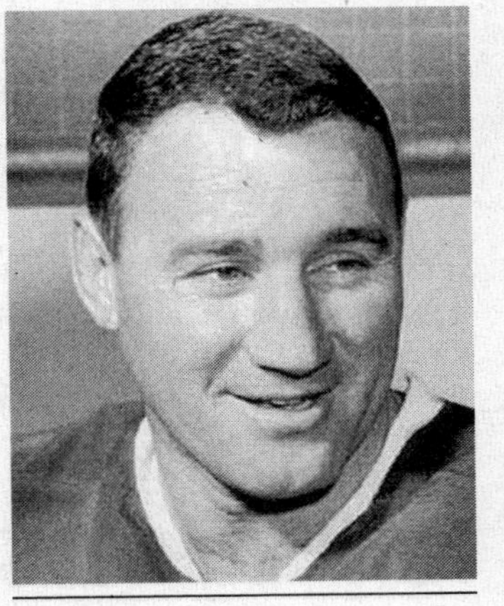
Len Haley

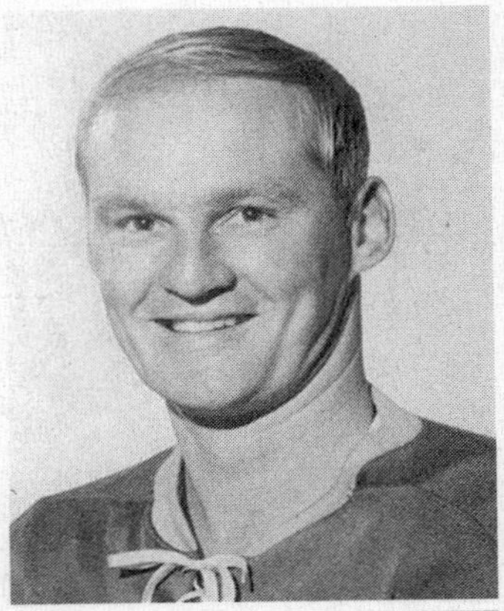
Murray Hall

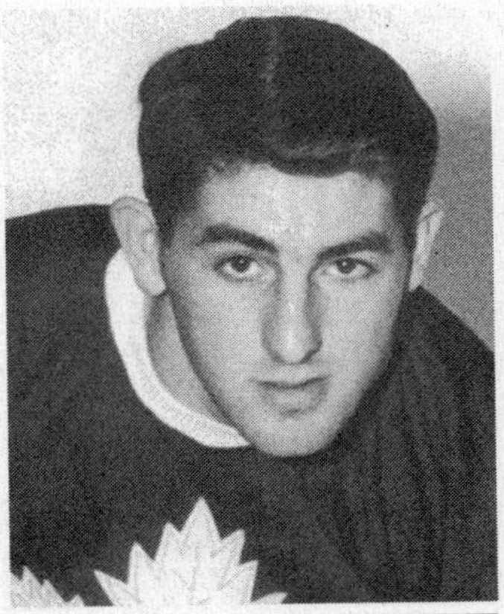
Jack Hamilton

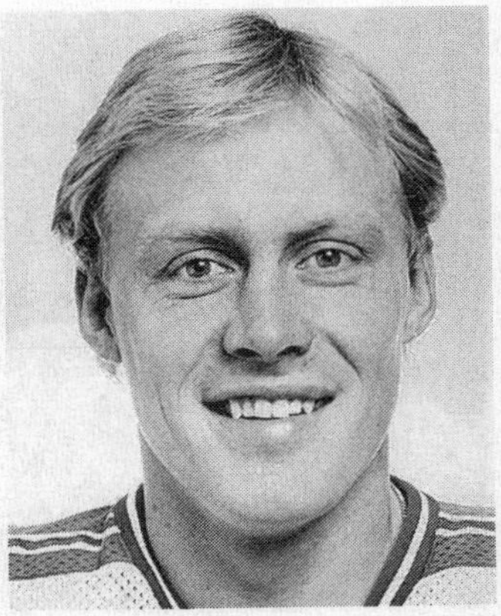
Anders Hedberg

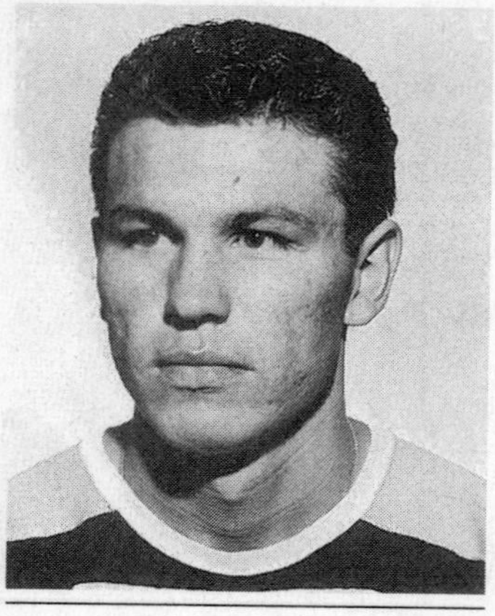

Ted Hodgson

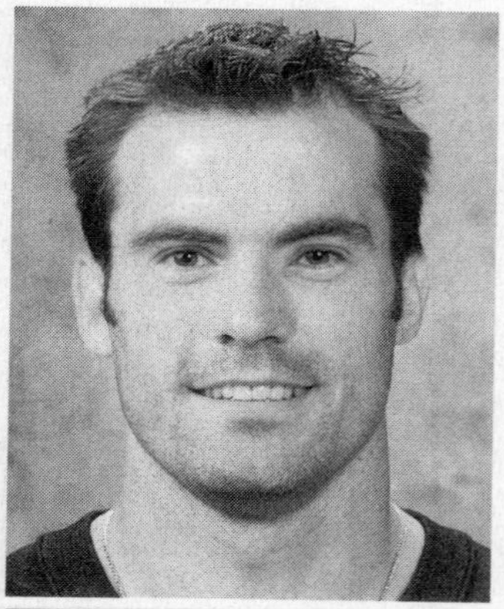

Brian Holzinger

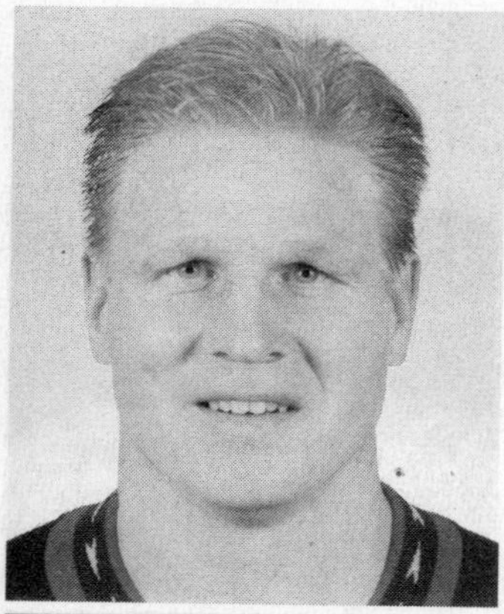

Tony Hrkac

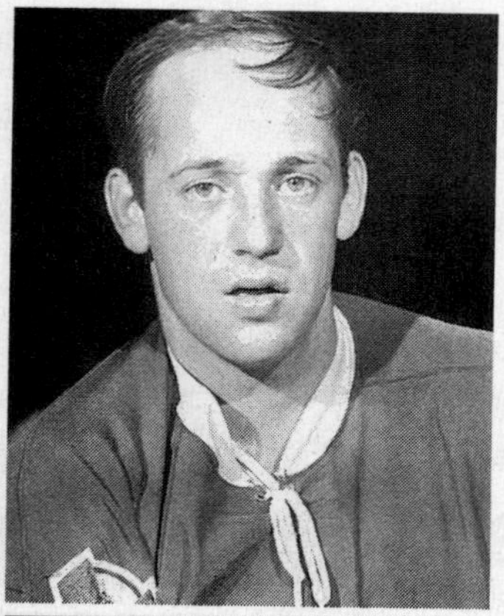

Fran Huck

Name	NHL Teams	NHL Seasons	Regular Schedule GP	G	A	TP	PIM	Playoffs GP	G	A	TP	PIM	NHL Cup Wins	First NHL Season	Last NHL Season
Hofford, Jim	Buf., L.A.	3	18	0	0	0	47	....	....	....	....	....	....	1985-86	1988-89
Hogaboam, Bill	Atl., Det., Min.	8	332	80	109	189	100	2	0	0	0	0	....	1972-73	1979-80
Hoganson, Dale	L.A., Mtl., Que.	7	343	13	77	90	186	11	0	3	3	12	....	1969-70	1981-82
‡ Hoglund, Jonas	Cgy., Mtl., Tor.	7	545	117	145	262	112	59	8	11	19	8	....	1996-97	2002-03
Hogue, Benoit	Buf., NYI, Tor., Dal., T.B., Phx., Bos., Wsh.	15	863	222	321	543	877	92	17	16	33	124	1	1987-88	2001-02
Holan, Milos	Phi., Ana.	3	49	5	11	16	42	....	....	....	....	....	....	1993-94	1995-96
Holbrook, Terry	Min.	2	43	3	6	9	4	6	0	0	0	0	....	1972-73	1973-74
‡ Holden, Josh	Van., Car., Tor.	6	60	5	9	14	16	....	....	....	....	....	....	1998-99	2003-04
‡ Holland, Jason	NYI, Buf., L.A.	7	81	4	5	9	36	1	0	0	0	0	....	1996-97	2003-04
Holland, Jerry	NYR	2	37	8	4	12	6	....	....	....	....	....	....	1974-75	1975-76
• Hollett, Flash	Tor., Ott., Bos., Det.	13	562	132	181	313	358	79	8	26	34	38	2	1933-34	1945-46
Hollinger, Terry	St.L.	2	7	0	0	0	2	....	....	....	....	....	....	1993-94	1994-95
• Hollingworth, Gord	Chi., Det.	4	163	4	14	18	201	3	0	0	0	2	....	1954-55	1957-58
Holloway, Bruce	Van.	1	2	0	0	0	0	....	....	....	....	....	....	1984-85	1984-85
• Holmes, Bill	Mtl., NYA	3	52	6	4	10	35	....	....	....	....	....	....	1925-26	1929-30
Holmes, Chuck	Det.	2	23	1	3	4	10	....	....	....	....	....	....	1958-59	1961-62
Holmes, Lou	Chi.	2	59	1	4	5	6	2	0	0	0	2	....	1931-32	1932-33
Holmes, Warren	L.A.	3	45	8	18	26	7	....	....	....	....	....	....	1981-82	1983-84
Holmgren, Paul	Phi., Min.	10	527	144	179	323	1684	82	19	32	51	195	....	1975-76	1984-85
• Holota, John	Det.	2	15	2	0	2	0	....	....	....	....	....	....	1942-43	1945-46
Holst, Greg	NYR	3	11	0	0	0	0	....	....	....	....	....	....	1975-76	1977-78
Holt, Gary	Cal., Cle., St.L.	5	101	13	11	24	133	....	....	....	....	....	....	1973-74	1977-78
Holt, Randy	Chi., Cle., Van., L.A., Cgy., Wsh., Phi.	10	395	4	37	41	1438	21	2	3	5	83	....	1974-75	1983-84
• Holway, Albert	Tor., Mtl.M., Pit.	5	112	7	2	9	48	6	0	0	0	0	1	1923-24	1928-29
Holzinger, Brian	Buf., T.B., Pit., CBJ	10	547	93	145	238	339	52	11	18	29	61	....	1994-95	2003-04
Homenuke, Ron	Van.	1	1	0	0	0	0	....	....	....	....	....	....	1972-73	1972-73
Hoover, Ron	Bos., St.L.	3	18	4	0	4	31	8	0	0	0	18	....	1989-90	1991-92
Hopkins, Dean	L.A., Edm., Que.	6	223	23	51	74	306	18	1	5	6	29	....	1979-80	1988-89
Hopkins, Larry	Tor., Wpg.	4	60	13	16	29	26	6	0	0	0	2	....	1977-78	1982-83
Horacek, Tony	Phi., Chi.	5	154	10	19	29	316	2	1	0	1	2	....	1989-90	1994-95
Horava, Miloslav	NYR	3	80	5	17	22	38	2	0	1	1	0	....	1988-89	1990-91
Horbul, Doug	K.C.	1	4	1	0	1	2	....	....	....	....	....	....	1974-75	1974-75
Hordy, Mike	NYI	2	11	0	0	0	7	....	....	....	....	....	....	1978-79	1979-80
Horeck, Pete	Chi., Det., Bos.	8	426	106	118	224	340	34	6	8	14	43	....	1944-45	1951-52
• Horne, George	Mtl.M., Tor.	3	54	9	3	12	34	4	0	0	0	4	1	1925-26	1928-29
• Horner, Red	Tor.	12	490	42	110	152	1254	71	7	10	17	170	1	1928-29	1939-40
• Hornung, Larry	St.L.	2	48	2	9	11	10	11	0	2	2	2	....	1970-71	1971-72
• Horton, Tim	Tor., NYR, Pit., Buf.	24	1446	115	403	518	1611	126	11	39	50	183	4	1949-50	1973-74
Horvath, Bronco	NYR, Mtl., Bos., Chi., Tor., Min.	9	434	141	185	326	319	36	12	9	21	18	....	1955-56	1967-68
Hospodar, Ed	NYR, Hfd., Phi., Min., Buf.	9	450	17	51	68	1314	44	4	1	5	208	....	1979-80	1987-88
Hostak, Martin	Phi.	2	55	3	11	14	24	....	....	....	....	....	....	1990-91	1991-92
Hotham, Greg	Tor., Pit.	6	230	15	74	89	139	5	0	3	3	6	....	1979-80	1984-85
Houck, Paul	Min.	3	16	1	2	3	2	....	....	....	....	....	....	1985-86	1987-88
Houda, Doug	Det., Hfd., L.A., Buf., NYI, Ana.	15	561	19	63	82	1104	18	0	3	3	21	....	1985-86	2002-03
Houde, Claude	K.C.	2	59	3	6	9	40	....	....	....	....	....	....	1974-75	1975-76
Houde, Eric	Mtl.	3	30	2	3	5	4	....	....	....	....	....	....	1996-97	1998-99
Hough, Mike	Que., Fla., NYI	13	707	100	156	256	675	42	5	5	10	38	....	1986-87	1998-99
Houlder, Bill	Wsh., Buf., Ana., St.L., T.B., S.J., Nsh.	16	846	59	191	250	412	30	5	6	11	14	....	1987-88	2002-03
Houle, Rejean	Mtl.	11	635	161	247	408	395	90	14	34	48	66	5	1969-70	1982-83
Housley, Phil	Buf., Wpg., St.L., Cgy., N.J., Wsh., Chi., Tor.	21	1495	338	894	1232	822	85	13	43	56	36	....	1982-83	2002-03
Houston, Ken	Atl., Cgy., Wsh., L.A.	9	570	161	167	328	624	35	10	9	19	66	....	1975-76	1983-84
Howard, Jack	Tor.	1	2	0	0	0	0	....	....	....	....	....	....	1936-37	1936-37
Howatt, Garry	NYI, Hfd., N.J.	12	720	112	156	268	1836	87	12	14	26	289	2	1972-73	1983-84
Howe, Gordie	Det., Hfd.	26	1767	801	1049	1850	1685	157	68	92	160	220	4	1946-47	1979-80
Howe, Mark	Hfd., Phi., Det.	16	929	197	545	742	455	101	10	51	61	34	....	1979-80	1994-95
Howe, Marty	Hfd., Bos.	6	197	2	29	31	99	15	1	2	3	9	....	1979-80	1984-85
• Howe, Syd	Ott., Phi., Tor., St.L., Det.	17	698	237	291	528	212	70	17	27	44	10	3	1929-30	1945-46
Howe, Vic	NYR	3	33	3	4	7	10	....	....	....	....	....	....	1950-51	1954-55
Howell, Harry	NYR, Oak., Cal., L.A.	21	1411	94	324	418	1298	38	3	3	6	32	....	1952-53	1972-73
• Howell, Ron	NYR	2	4	0	0	0	0	....	....	....	....	....	....	1954-55	1955-56
Howse, Don	L.A.	1	33	2	5	7	6	2	0	0	0	0	....	1979-80	1979-80
Howson, Scott	NYI	2	18	5	3	8	4	....	....	....	....	....	....	1984-85	1985-86
Hoyda, Dave	Phi., Wpg.	4	132	6	17	23	299	12	0	0	0	17	....	1977-78	1980-81
Hrdina, Jiri	Cgy., Pit.	5	250	45	85	130	92	46	2	5	7	24	3	1987-88	1991-92
Hrechkosy, Dave	Cal., St.L.	4	140	42	24	66	41	3	1	0	1	2	....	1973-74	1976-77
Hrkac, Tony	St.L., Que., S.J., Chi., Dal., Edm., NYI, Ana., Atl.	13	758	132	239	371	173	41	7	7	14	12	1	1986-87	2002-03
Hrycuik, Jim	Wsh.	1	21	5	5	10	12	....	....	....	....	....	....	1974-75	1974-75
Hrymnak, Steve	Chi., Det.	2	18	2	1	3	4	2	0	0	0	0	....	1951-52	1952-53
Hrynewich, Tim	Pit.	2	55	6	8	14	82	....	....	....	....	....	....	1982-83	1983-84
Huard, Bill	Bos., Ott., Que., Dal., Edm., L.A.	8	223	16	18	34	594	5	0	0	0	2	....	1992-93	1999-00
Huard, Rolly	Tor.	1	1	1	0	1	0	....	....	....	....	....	....	1930-31	1930-31
Huber, Willie	Det., NYR, Van., Phi.	10	655	104	217	321	950	33	5	5	10	35	....	1978-79	1987-88
Hubick, Greg	Tor., Van.	2	77	6	9	15	10	....	....	....	....	....	....	1975-76	1979-80
Huck, Fran	Mtl., St.L.	3	94	24	30	54	38	11	3	4	7	2	....	1969-70	1972-73
Hucul, Fred	Chi., St.L.	5	164	11	30	41	113	6	1	0	1	10	....	1950-51	1967-68
Huddy, Charlie	Edm., L.A., Buf., St.L.	17	1017	99	354	453	785	183	19	66	85	135	5	1980-81	1996-97
Hudson, Dave	NYI, K.C., Col.	6	409	59	124	183	89	2	1	1	2	0	....	1972-73	1977-78
Hudson, Lex	Pit.	1	2	0	0	0	0	2	0	0	0	0	....	1978-79	1978-79
Hudson, Mike	Chi., Edm., NYR, Pit., Tor., St.L., Phx.	9	416	49	87	136	414	49	4	10	14	64	1	1988-89	1996-97
Hudson, Ron	Det.	2	33	5	2	7	2	....	....	....	....	....	....	1937-38	1939-40
Huffman, Kerry	Phi., Que., Ott.	10	401	37	108	145	361	11	0	0	0	2	....	1986-87	1995-96
Huggins, Al	Mtl.M.	1	20	1	1	2	2	....	....	....	....	....	....	1930-31	1930-31
Hughes, Albert	NYA	2	60	6	8	14	22	....	....	....	....	....	....	1930-31	1931-32
Hughes, Brent	L.A., Phi., St.L., Det., K.C.	8	435	15	117	132	440	22	1	3	4	53	....	1967-68	1974-75
Hughes, Brent	Wpg., Bos., Buf., NYI	8	357	41	39	80	831	29	4	1	5	53	....	1988-89	1996-97
Hughes, Frank	Cal.	1	5	0	0	0	0	....	....	....	....	....	....	1971-72	1971-72
Hughes, Howie	L.A.	3	168	25	32	57	30	14	2	0	2	2	....	1967-68	1969-70
Hughes, Jack	Col.	2	46	2	5	7	104	....	....	....	....	....	....	1980-81	1981-82
• Hughes, James	Det.	1	40	0	1	1	48	....	....	....	....	....	....	1929-30	1929-30
Hughes, John	Van., Edm., NYR	2	70	2	14	16	211	7	0	1	1	16	....	1979-80	1980-81
Hughes, Pat	Mtl., Pit., Edm., Buf., St.L., Hfd.	10	573	130	128	258	646	71	8	25	33	77	3	1977-78	1986-87
Hughes, Ryan	Bos.	1	3	0	0	0	0	....	....	....	....	....	....	1995-96	1995-96
Hulbig, Joe	Edm., Bos.	5	55	4	4	8	16	6	0	1	1	2	....	1996-97	2000-01
Hull, Bobby	Chi., Wpg., Hfd.	16	1063	610	560	1170	640	119	62	67	129	102	1	1957-58	1979-80
Hull, Dennis	Chi., Det.	14	959	303	351	654	261	104	33	34	67	30	....	1964-65	1977-78
Hull, Jody	Hfd., NYR, Ott., Fla., T.B., Phi.	16	831	124	137	261	156	69	4	5	9	14	....	1988-89	2003-04
‡ Huml, Ivan	Bos.	3	49	6	12	18	36	....	....	....	....	....	....	2001-02	2003-04
• Hunt, Fred	NYA, NYR	2	59	15	14	29	6	....	....	....	....	....	....	1940-41	1944-45
Hunter, Dale	Que., Wsh., Col.	19	1407	323	697	1020	3565	186	42	76	118	729	....	1980-81	1998-99
Hunter, Dave	Edm., Pit., Wpg.	10	746	133	190	323	918	105	16	24	40	211	3	1979-80	1988-89
Hunter, Mark	Mtl., St.L., Cgy., Hfd., Wsh.	12	628	213	171	384	1426	79	18	20	38	230	1	1981-82	1992-93
Hunter, Tim	Cgy., Que., Van., S.J.	16	815	62	76	138	3146	132	5	7	12	426	1	1981-82	1996-97
Huras, Larry	NYR	1	2	0	0	0	0	....	....	....	....	....	....	1976-77	1976-77
Hurlburt, Bob	Van.	1	1	0	0	0	2	....	....	....	....	....	....	1974-75	1974-75
Hurlbut, Mike	NYR, Que., Buf.	5	29	1	8	9	20	....	....	....	....	....	....	1992-93	1999-00
Hurley, Paul	Bos.	1	1	0	1	1	0	....	....	....	....	....	....	1968-69	1968-69
Hurst, Ron	Tor.	2	64	9	7	16	70	3	0	2	2	4	....	1955-56	1956-57
Huscroft, Jamie	N.J., Bos., Cgy., T.B., Van., Phx., Wsh.	10	352	5	33	38	1065	21	0	1	1	46	....	1988-89	1999-00
Huska, Ryan	Chi.	1	1	0	0	0	0	....	....	....	....	....	....	1997-98	1997-98
Huston, Ron	Cal.	2	79	15	31	46	8	....	....	....	....	....	....	1973-74	1974-75
Hutchinson, Ron	NYR	1	9	0	0	0	0	....	....	....	....	....	....	1960-61	1960-61
Hutchison, Dave	L.A., Tor., Chi., N.J.	10	584	19	97	116	1550	48	2	12	14	149	....	1974-75	1983-84
• Hutton, Bill	Bos., Ott., Phi.	2	64	3	2	5	8	2	0	0	0	0	....	1929-30	1930-31
• Hyland, Harry	Mtl.W., Ott.	1	17	14	2	16	65	....	....	....	....	....	....	1917-18	1917-18
Hynes, Dave	Bos.	2	22	4	0	4	2	....	....	....	....	....	....	1973-74	1974-75
Hynes, Gord	Bos., Phi.	2	52	3	9	12	22	12	1	2	3	6	....	1991-92	1992-93
‡ Hyvonen, Hannes	S.J., CBJ	2	42	4	5	9	22	....	....	....	....	....	....	2001-02	2002-03

I

Name	NHL Teams	NHL Seasons	GP	G	A	TP	PIM	GP	G	A	TP	PIM	NHL Cup Wins	First NHL Season	Last NHL Season
Iafrate, Al	Tor., Wsh., Bos., S.J.	12	799	152	311	463	1301	71	19	16	35	77	....	1984-85	1997-98

Name	NHL Teams	NHL Seasons	Regular Schedule GP	G	A	TP	PIM	Playoffs GP	G	A	TP	PIM	NHL Cup Wins	First NHL Season	Last NHL Season
Ignatjev, Victor	Pit.	1	11	0	1	1	6	1	0	0	0	2	....	1998-99	1998-99
Ihnacak, Miroslav	Tor., Det.	3	56	8	9	17	39	1	0	0	0	0	....	1985-86	1988-89
Ihnacak, Peter	Tor.	8	417	102	165	267	175	28	4	10	14	25	....	1982-83	1989-90
Imlach, Brent	Tor.	2	3	0	0	0	0	....	....	....	....	....	....	1965-66	1966-67
Ingarfield, Earl	NYR, Pit., Oak., Cal.	13	746	179	226	405	239	21	9	8	17	10	....	1958-59	1970-71
Ingarfield, Earl	Atl., Cgy., Det.	2	39	4	4	8	22	2	0	1	1	0	....	1979-80	1980-81
Inglis, Billy	L.A., Buf.	3	36	1	3	4	4	11	1	2	3	4	....	1967-68	1970-71
• Ingoldsby, Johnny	Tor.	2	29	5	1	6	15	....	....	....	....	....	....	1942-43	1943-44
• Ingram, Frank	Chi.	3	101	24	16	40	69	11	0	1	1	2	....	1929-30	1931-32
• Ingram, John	Bos.	1	1	0	0	0	0	....	....	....	....	....	....	1924-25	1924-25
Ingram, Ron	Chi., Det., NYR	4	114	5	15	20	81	2	0	0	0	0	....	1956-57	1964-65
Intranuovo, Ralph	Edm., Tor.	3	22	2	4	6	4	....	....	....	....	....	....	1994-95	1996-97
• Irvin, Dick	Chi.	3	94	29	23	52	78	2	2	0	2	4	....	1926-27	1928-29
Irvine, Ted	Bos., L.A., NYR, St.L.	11	724	154	177	331	657	83	16	24	40	115	....	1963-64	1976-77
Irwin, Ivan	Mtl., NYR	5	155	2	27	29	214	5	0	0	0	8	....	1952-53	1957-58
• Isaksson, Ulf	L.A.	1	50	7	15	22	10	....	....	....	....	....	....	1982-83	1982-83
Issel, Kim	Edm.	1	4	0	0	0	0	....	....	....	....	....	....	1988-89	1988-89

J

Name	NHL Teams	NHL Seasons	Regular Schedule GP	G	A	TP	PIM	Playoffs GP	G	A	TP	PIM	NHL Cup Wins	First NHL Season	Last NHL Season
• Jackson, Art	Tor., Bos., NYA	11	468	123	178	301	144	52	8	12	20	29	2	1934-35	1944-45
• Jackson, Busher	Tor., NYA, Bos.	15	633	241	234	475	437	71	18	12	30	53	1	1929-30	1943-44
Jackson, Dane	Van., Buf., NYI	4	45	12	6	18	58	6	0	0	0	10	....	1993-94	1997-98
Jackson, Don	Min., Edm., NYR	10	311	16	52	68	640	53	4	5	9	147	2	1977-78	1986-87
• Jackson, Harold	Chi., Det.	8	219	17	34	51	208	31	1	2	3	33	2	1936-37	1946-47
Jackson, Jack	Chi.	1	48	2	5	7	38	....	....	....	....	....	....	1946-47	1946-47
Jackson, Jeff	Tor., NYR, Que., Chi.	8	263	38	48	86	313	6	1	1	2	16	....	1984-85	1991-92
Jackson, Jim	Cgy., Buf.	4	112	17	30	47	20	14	3	2	5	6	....	1982-83	1987-88
• Jackson, Lloyd	NYA	1	14	1	1	2	0	....	....	....	....	....	....	1936-37	1936-37
• Jackson, Stan	Tor., Bos., Ott.	5	86	9	6	15	75	....	....	....	....	....	1	1921-22	1926-27
Jackson, Walter	NYA, Bos.	4	84	16	11	27	18	....	....	....	....	....	....	1932-33	1935-36
• Jacobs, Paul	Tor.	1	1	0	0	0	0	....	....	....	....	....	....	1918-19	1918-19
Jacobs, Tim	Cal.	1	46	0	10	10	35	....	....	....	....	....	....	1975-76	1975-76
Jakopin, John	Fla., Pit., S.J.	6	113	1	6	7	145	....	....	....	....	....	....	1997-98	2002-03
Jalo, Risto	Edm.	1	3	0	3	3	0	....	....	....	....	....	....	1985-86	1985-86
Jalonen, Kari	Cgy., Edm.	2	37	9	6	15	4	5	1	0	1	0	....	1982-83	1983-84
James, Gerry	Tor.	5	149	14	26	40	257	15	1	0	1	8	....	1954-55	1959-60
James, Val	Buf., Tor.	2	11	0	0	0	30	....	....	....	....	....	....	1981-82	1986-87
Jamieson, Jim	NYR	1	1	0	1	1	0	....	....	....	....	....	....	1943-44	1943-44
Jankowski, Lou	Det., Chi.	4	127	19	18	37	15	1	0	0	0	0	....	1950-51	1954-55
Janney, Craig	Bos., St.L., S.J., Wpg., Phx., T.B., NYI	12	760	188	563	751	170	120	24	86	110	53	....	1987-88	1998-99
Janssens, Mark	NYR, Min., Hfd., Ana., NYI, Phx., Chi.	14	711	40	73	113	1422	27	5	1	6	33	....	1987-88	2000-01
‡ Jantunen, Marko	Cgy.	1	3	0	0	0	0	....	....	....	....	....	....	1996-97	1996-97
Jarrett, Doug	Chi., NYR	13	775	38	182	220	631	99	7	16	23	82	....	1964-65	1976-77
Jarrett, Gary	Tor., Det., Oak., Cal.	7	341	72	92	164	131	11	3	1	4	9	....	1960-61	1971-72
Jarry, Pierre	NYR, Tor., Det., Min.	7	344	88	117	205	142	5	0	1	1	0	....	1971-72	1977-78
Jarvenpaa, Hannu	Wpg.	3	114	11	26	37	83	....	....	....	....	....	....	1986-87	1988-89
‡ Jarventie, Martti	Mtl.	1	1	0	0	0	0	....	....	....	....	....	....	2001-02	2001-02
Jarvi, Iiro	Que.	2	116	18	43	61	58	....	....	....	....	....	....	1988-89	1989-90
Jarvis, Doug	Mtl., Wsh., Hfd.	13	964	139	264	403	263	105	14	27	41	42	4	1975-76	1987-88
• Jarvis, James	Pit., Phi., Tor.	3	112	17	15	32	62	....	....	....	....	....	....	1929-30	1936-37
Jarvis, Wes	Wsh., Min., L.A., Tor.	9	237	31	55	86	98	2	0	0	0	2	....	1979-80	1987-88
Javanainen, Arto	Pit.	1	14	4	1	5	2	....	....	....	....	....	....	1984-85	1984-85
Jay, Bob	L.A.	1	3	0	1	1	0	....	....	....	....	....	....	1993-94	1993-94
Jeffrey, Larry	Det., Tor., NYR	8	368	39	62	101	293	38	4	10	14	42	1	1961-62	1968-69
Jelinek, Tomas	Ott.	1	49	7	6	13	52	....	....	....	....	....	....	1992-93	1992-93
Jenkins, Dean	L.A.	1	5	0	0	0	2	....	....	....	....	....	....	1983-84	1983-84
• Jenkins, Roger	Chi., Tor., Mtl., Bos., Mtl.M., NYA	8	325	15	39	54	253	25	1	7	8	12	2	1930-31	1938-39
Jennings, Bill	Det., Bos.	5	108	32	33	65	45	20	4	4	8	6	....	1940-41	1944-45
Jennings, Grant	Wsh., Hfd., Pit., Tor., Buf.	9	389	14	43	57	804	54	2	1	3	68	2	1987-88	1995-96
Jensen, Chris	NYR, Phi.	6	74	9	12	21	27	....	....	....	....	....	....	1985-86	1991-92
Jensen, David	Min.	3	18	0	2	2	11	....	....	....	....	....	....	1983-84	1985-86
Jensen, David	Hfd., Wsh.	4	69	9	13	22	22	11	0	0	0	2	....	1984-85	1987-88
Jensen, Steve	Min., L.A.	7	438	113	107	220	318	12	0	3	3	9	....	1975-76	1981-82
• Jeremiah, Ed	NYA, Bos.	1	15	0	1	1	0	....	....	....	....	....	....	1931-32	1931-32
Jerrard, Paul	Min.	1	5	0	0	0	4	....	....	....	....	....	....	1988-89	1988-89
• Jerwa, Frank	Bos., St.L.	4	81	11	16	27	53	....	....	....	....	....	....	1931-32	1934-35
• Jerwa, Joe	NYR, Bos., NYA	7	234	29	58	87	309	17	2	3	5	16	....	1930-31	1938-39
Jirik, Jaroslav	St.L.	1	3	0	0	0	0	....	....	....	....	....	....	1969-70	1969-70
• Joanette, Rosario	Mtl.	1	2	0	1	1	4	....	....	....	....	....	....	1944-45	1944-45
Jodzio, Rick	Col., Cle.	1	70	2	8	10	71	....	....	....	....	....	....	1977-78	1977-78
Johannesen, Glenn	NYI	1	2	0	0	0	0	....	....	....	....	....	....	1985-86	1985-86
Johannson, John	N.J.	1	5	0	0	0	0	....	....	....	....	....	....	1983-84	1983-84
• Johansen, Bill	Tor.	1	1	0	0	0	0	....	....	....	....	....	....	1949-50	1949-50
Johansen, Trevor	Tor., Col., L.A.	5	286	11	46	57	282	13	0	3	3	21	....	1977-78	1981-82
‡ Johansson, Andreas	NYI, Pit., Ott., T.B., Cgy., NYR, Nsh.	8	377	81	88	169	190	9	0	0	0	0	....	1995-96	2003-04
Johansson, Bjorn	Cle.	2	15	1	1	2	10	....	....	....	....	....	....	1976-77	1977-78
Johansson, Calle	Buf., Wsh., Tor.	17	1109	119	416	535	519	105	12	43	55	44	....	1987-88	2003-04
‡ Johansson, Mathias	Cgy., Pit.	1	58	5	10	15	16	....	....	....	....	....	....	2002-03	2002-03
Johansson, Roger	Cgy., Chi.	4	161	9	34	43	163	5	0	1	1	2	....	1989-90	1994-95
Johns, Don	NYR, Mtl., Min.	6	153	2	21	23	76	....	....	....	....	....	....	1960-61	1967-68
Johnson, Allan	Mtl., Det.	4	105	21	28	49	30	11	2	2	4	6	....	1956-57	1962-63
Johnson, Brian	Det.	1	3	0	0	0	5	....	....	....	....	....	....	1983-84	1983-84
• Johnson, Ching	NYR, NYA	12	436	38	48	86	808	61	5	2	7	161	2	1926-27	1937-38
‡ Johnson, Craig	St.L., L.A., Ana., Tor., Wsh.	10	557	75	98	173	260	16	3	2	5	10	....	1994-95	2003-04
• Johnson, Danny	Tor., Van., Det.	3	121	18	19	37	24	....	....	....	....	....	....	1969-70	1971-72
Johnson, Earl	Det.	1	1	0	0	0	0	....	....	....	....	....	....	1953-54	1953-54
Johnson, Jim	NYR, Phi., L.A.	8	302	75	111	186	73	7	0	2	2	2	....	1964-65	1971-72
Johnson, Jim	Pit., Min., Dal., Wsh., Phx.	13	829	29	166	195	1197	51	1	11	12	132	....	1985-86	1997-98
Johnson, Mark	Pit., Min., Hfd., St.L., N.J.	11	669	203	305	508	260	37	16	12	28	10	....	1979-80	1989-90
Johnson, Matt	L.A., Atl., Min.	10	473	23	20	43	1523	16	0	0	0	31	....	1994-95	2003-04
Johnson, Norm	Bos., Chi.	3	61	5	20	25	41	14	4	0	4	6	....	1957-58	1959-60
Johnson, Terry	Que., St.L., Cgy., Tor.	9	285	3	24	27	580	38	0	4	4	118	....	1979-80	1987-88
Johnson, Tom	Mtl., Bos.	17	978	51	213	264	960	111	8	15	23	109	6	1947-48	1964-65
• Johnson, Virgil	Chi.	3	75	1	11	12	27	19	0	3	3	4	1	1937-38	1944-45
Johnston, Bernie	Hfd.	2	57	12	24	36	16	3	0	1	1	0	....	1979-80	1980-81
• Johnston, George	Chi.	4	58	20	12	32	2	....	....	....	....	....	....	1941-42	1946-47
Johnston, Greg	Bos., Tor.	9	187	26	29	55	124	22	2	1	3	12	....	1983-84	1991-92
Johnston, Jay	Wsh.	2	8	0	0	0	13	....	....	....	....	....	....	1980-81	1981-82
Johnston, Joey	Min., Cal., Chi.	6	331	85	106	191	320	....	....	....	....	....	....	1968-69	1975-76
Johnston, Larry	L.A., Det., K.C., Col.	7	320	9	64	73	580	....	....	....	....	....	....	1967-68	1976-77
Johnston, Marshall	Min., Cal.	7	251	14	52	66	58	6	0	0	0	2	....	1967-68	1973-74
Johnston, Randy	NYI	1	4	0	0	0	4	....	....	....	....	....	....	1979-80	1979-80
Johnstone, Eddie	NYR, Det.	10	426	122	136	258	375	55	13	10	23	83	....	1975-76	1986-87
Johnstone, Ross	Tor.	2	42	5	4	9	14	3	0	0	0	0	1	1943-44	1944-45
• Joliat, Aurel	Mtl.	16	655	270	190	460	771	46	9	13	22	66	3	1922-23	1937-38
• Joliat, Rene	Mtl.	1	1	0	0	0	0	....	....	....	....	....	....	1924-25	1924-25
Joly, Greg	Wsh., Det.	9	365	21	76	97	250	5	0	0	0	8	....	1974-75	1982-83
Joly, Yvan	Mtl.	3	2	0	0	0	0	1	0	0	0	0	....	1979-80	1982-83
Jomphe, Jean-Francois	Ana., Phx., Mtl.	4	111	10	29	39	102	....	....	....	....	....	....	1995-96	1998-99
Jonathan, Stan	Bos., Pit.	8	411	91	110	201	751	63	8	4	12	137	....	1975-76	1982-83
Jones, Bob	NYR	1	2	0	0	0	0	....	....	....	....	....	....	1968-69	1968-69
Jones, Brad	Wpg., L.A., Phi.	6	148	25	31	56	122	9	1	1	2	2	....	1986-87	1991-92
Jones, Buck	Det., Tor.	4	50	2	2	4	36	12	0	1	1	18	....	1938-39	1942-43
Jones, Jim	Cal.	1	2	0	0	0	0	....	....	....	....	....	....	1971-72	1971-72
Jones, Jimmy	Tor.	3	148	13	18	31	68	19	1	5	6	11	....	1977-78	1979-80
Jones, Keith	Wsh., Col., Phi.	9	491	117	141	258	765	63	12	12	24	120	....	1992-93	2000-01
Jones, Ron	Bos., Pit., Wsh.	5	54	1	4	5	31	....	....	....	....	....	....	1971-72	1975-76
Jones, Ty	Chi., Fla.	2	14	0	0	0	19	....	....	....	....	....	....	1998-99	2003-04
‡ Jonsson, Hans	Pit.	4	242	10	38	48	92	27	0	1	1	14	....	1999-00	2002-03
‡ Jonsson, Jorgen	NYI, Ana.	1	81	12	19	31	16	....	....	....	....	....	....	1999-00	1999-00
Jonsson, Tomas	NYI, Edm.	8	552	85	259	344	482	80	11	26	37	97	2	1981-82	1988-89
Joseph, Chris	Pit., Edm., T.B., Van., Phi., Phx., Atl.	14	510	39	112	151	567	31	3	4	7	24	....	1987-88	2000-01
Joseph, Tony	Wpg.	1	2	1	0	1	0	....	....	....	....	....	....	1988-89	1988-89

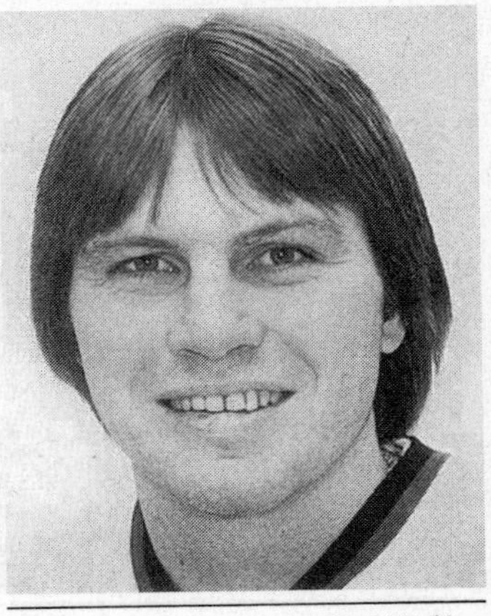

Dave Hutchison

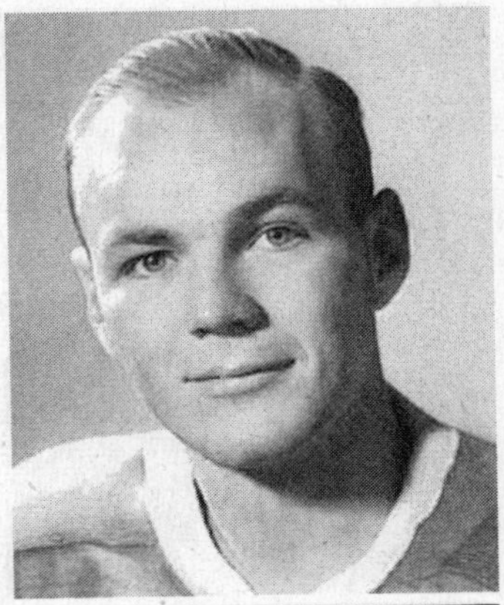

Ivan Irwin

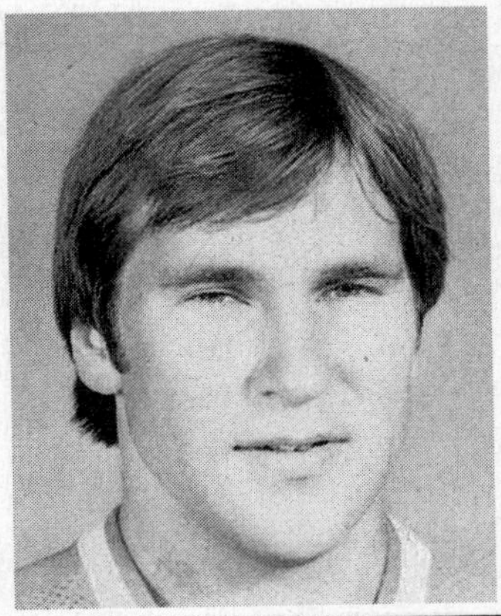

Don Jackson

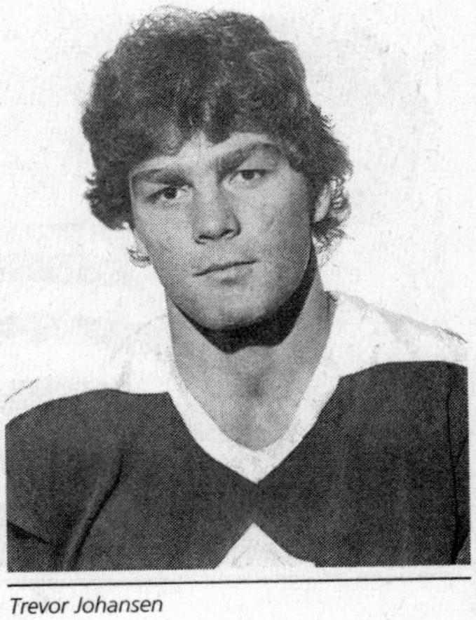

Trevor Johansen

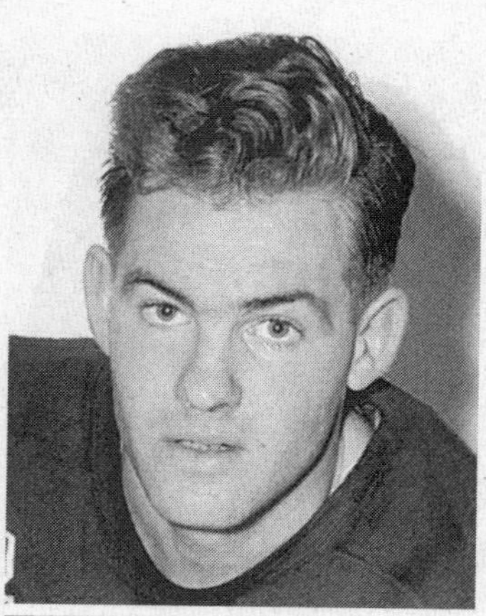

Bing Juckes

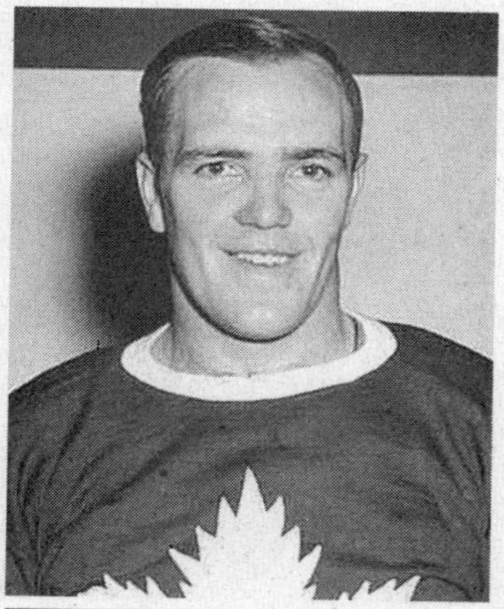

Bingo Kampman

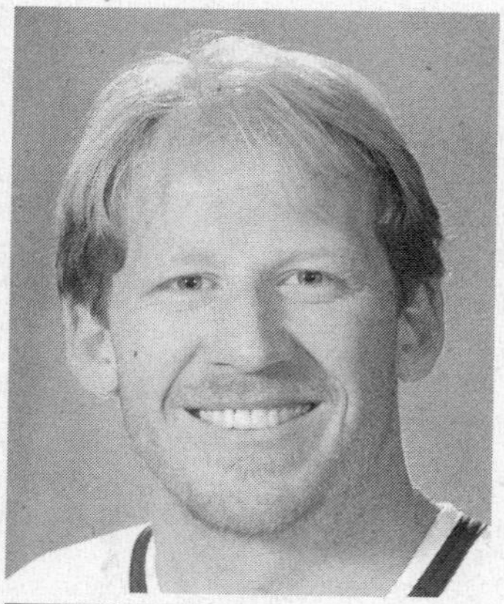

Mike Keane

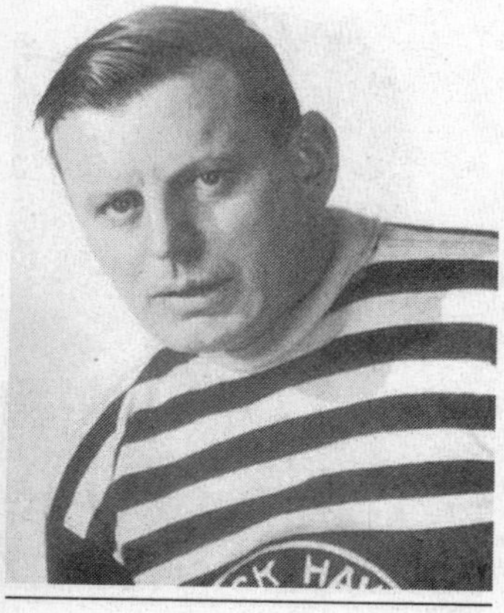

Duke Keats

			Regular Schedule					Playoffs							
Name	NHL Teams	NHL Seasons	GP	G	A	TP	PIM	GP	G	A	TP	PIM	NHL Cup Wins	First NHL Season	Last NHL Season
Joyal, Eddie	Det., Tor., L.A., Phi.	9	466	128	134	262	103	50	11	8	19	18	....	1962-63	1971-72
Joyce, Bob	Bos., Wsh., Wpg.	6	158	34	49	83	90	46	15	9	24	29	....	1987-88	1992-93
Joyce, Duane	Dal.	1	3	0	0	0	0	....	....	....	....	....	....	1993-94	1993-94
• Juckes, Bing	NYR	2	16	2	1	3	6	....	....	....	....	....	....	1947-48	1949-50
Juhlin, Patrik	Phi.	2	56	7	6	13	23	13	1	0	1	2	....	1994-95	1995-96
Julien, Claude	Que.	2	14	0	1	1	25	....	....	....	....	....	....	1984-85	1985-86
Juneau, Joe	Bos., Wsh., Buf., Ott., Phx., Mtl.	13	828	156	416	572	272	112	25	54	79	69	....	1991-92	2003-04
Junker, Steve	NYI	2	5	0	0	0	0	3	0	1	1	0	....	1992-93	1993-94
Jutila, Timo	Buf.	1	10	1	5	6	13	....	....	....	....	....	....	1984-85	1984-85
Juzda, Bill	NYR, Tor.	9	398	14	54	68	398	42	0	3	3	46	2	1940-41	1951-52

K

Kabel, Bob	NYR	2	48	5	13	18	34	....	....	....	....	....	....	1959-60	1960-61
Kachowski, Mark	Pit.	3	64	6	5	11	209	....	....	....	....	....	....	1987-88	1989-90
Kachur, Ed	Chi.	2	96	10	14	24	35	....	....	....	....	....	....	1956-57	1957-58
Kaese, Trent	Buf.	1	1	0	0	0	0	....	....	....	....	....	....	1988-89	1988-89
Kaiser, Vern	Mtl.	1	50	7	5	12	33	2	0	0	0	0	....	1950-51	1950-51
• Kalbfleish, Walter	Ott., St.L., NYA, Bos.	4	36	0	4	4	32	5	0	0	0	2	....	1933-34	1936-37
• Kaleta, Alex	Chi., NYR	7	387	92	121	213	190	17	1	6	7	2	....	1941-42	1950-51
‡ Kallio, Tomi	Atl., CBJ, Phi.	3	140	24	31	55	48	....	....	....	....	....	....	2000-01	2002-03
Kallur, Anders	NYI	6	383	101	110	211	149	78	12	23	35	32	4	1979-80	1984-85
Kamensky, Valeri	Que., Col., NYR, Dal., N.J.	11	637	200	301	501	383	66	25	35	60	72	1	1991-92	2001-02
Kaminski, Kevin	Min., Que., Wsh.	7	139	3	10	13	528	8	0	0	0	52	....	1988-89	1996-97
• Kaminsky, Max	Ott., Bos., St.L., Mtl.M.	4	130	22	34	56	38	4	0	0	0	0	....	1933-34	1936-37
Kaminsky, Yan	Wpg., NYI	2	26	3	2	5	4	2	0	0	0	4	....	1993-94	1994-95
• Kampman, Bingo	Tor.	5	189	14	30	44	287	47	1	4	5	38	1	1937-38	1941-42
Kane, Francis	Det.	1	2	0	0	0	0	....	....	....	....	....	....	1943-44	1943-44
Kannegiesser, Gord	St.L.	2	23	0	1	1	15	....	....	....	....	....	....	1967-68	1971-72
Kannegiesser, Sheldon	Pit., NYR, L.A., Van.	8	366	14	67	81	292	18	0	2	2	10	....	1970-71	1977-78
Karabin, Ladislav	Pit.	1	9	0	0	0	2	....	....	....	....	....	....	1993-94	1993-94
‡ Karalahti, Jere	L.A., Nsh.	3	149	8	19	27	97	17	0	1	1	20	....	1999-00	2001-02
Karamnov, Vitali	St.L.	3	92	12	20	32	65	2	0	0	0	2	....	1992-93	1994-95
‡ Kariya, Steve	Van.	3	65	9	18	27	32	....	....	....	....	....	....	1999-00	2001-02
Karjalainen, Kyosti	L.A.	1	28	1	8	9	12	3	0	1	1	2	....	1991-92	1991-92
Karlander, Al	Det.	4	212	36	56	92	70	4	0	1	1	0	....	1969-70	1972-73
‡ Karpa, Dave	Que., Ana., Car., NYR	12	557	18	80	98	1374	19	1	1	2	39	....	1991-92	2002-03
Karpov, Valeri	Ana.	3	76	14	15	29	32	....	....	....	....	....	....	1994-95	1996-97
Kasatonov, Alexei	N.J., Ana., St.L., Bos.	7	383	38	122	160	326	33	4	7	11	40	....	1989-90	1995-96
Kasper, Steve	Bos., L.A., Phi., T.B.	13	821	177	291	468	554	94	20	28	48	82	....	1980-81	1992-93
Kastelic, Ed	Wsh., Hfd.	7	220	11	10	21	719	8	1	0	1	32	....	1985-86	1991-92
Kaszycki, Mike	NYI, Wsh., Tor.	5	226	42	80	122	108	19	2	6	8	10	....	1977-78	1982-83
• Kea, Ed	Atl., St.L.	10	583	30	145	175	508	32	2	4	6	39	....	1973-74	1982-83
Keane, Mike	Mtl., Col., NYR, Dal., St.L., Van.	16	1161	168	302	470	881	220	34	40	74	135	3	1988-89	2003-04
Kearns, Dennis	Van.	10	677	31	290	321	386	11	1	2	3	8	....	1971-72	1980-81
• Keating, Jack	Det.	2	11	3	0	3	4	....	....	....	....	....	....	1938-39	1939-40
• Keating, John	NYA	2	35	5	5	10	17	....	....	....	....	....	....	1931-32	1932-33
Keating, Mike	NYR	1	1	0	0	0	0	....	....	....	....	....	....	1977-78	1977-78
• Keats, Duke	Bos., Det., Chi.	3	82	30	19	49	113	....	....	....	....	....	....	1926-27	1928-29
Keczmer, Dan	Min., Hfd., Cgy., Dal., Nsh.	10	235	8	38	46	212	12	0	1	1	8	....	1990-91	1999-00
Keefe, Sheldon	T.B.	3	125	12	12	24	78	....	....	....	....	....	....	2000-01	2002-03
• Keeling, Butch	Tor., NYR	12	525	157	63	220	331	47	11	11	22	34	1	1926-27	1937-38
Keenan, Larry	Tor., St.L., Buf., Phi.	6	233	38	64	102	28	46	15	16	31	12	....	1961-62	1971-72
Kehoe, Rick	Tor., Pit.	14	906	371	396	767	120	39	4	17	21	4	....	1971-72	1984-85
Kekalainen, Jarmo	Bos., Ott.	5	55	5	8	13	28	....	....	....	....	....	....	1989-90	1993-94
Kelleher, Chris	Bos.	1	1	0	0	0	0	....	....	....	....	....	....	2001-02	2001-02
Keller, Ralph	NYR	1	3	1	0	1	6	....	....	....	....	....	....	1962-63	1962-63
Kellgren, Christer	Col.	1	5	0	0	0	0	....	....	....	....	....	....	1981-82	1981-82
Kelly, Bob	Phi., Wsh.	12	837	154	208	362	1454	101	9	14	23	172	2	1970-71	1981-82
Kelly, Bob	St.L., Pit., Chi.	6	425	87	109	196	687	23	6	3	9	40	....	1973-74	1978-79
Kelly, Dave	Det.	1	16	2	0	2	4	....	....	....	....	....	....	1976-77	1976-77
Kelly, John Paul	L.A.	7	400	54	70	124	366	18	1	1	2	41	....	1979-80	1985-86
• Kelly, Pep	Tor., Chi., Bro.	8	288	74	53	127	105	38	7	6	13	10	....	1934-35	1941-42
• Kelly, Pete	St.L., Det., NYA, Bro.	7	177	21	38	59	68	19	3	1	4	2	2	1934-35	1941-42
Kelly, Red	Det., Tor.	20	1316	281	542	823	327	164	33	59	92	51	8	1947-48	1966-67
‡ Kelly, Steve	Edm., T.B., N.J., L.A.	8	147	9	12	21	83	25	0	0	0	8	1	1996-97	2003-04
• Kemp, Kevin	Hfd.	1	3	0	0	0	4	....	....	....	....	....	....	1980-81	1980-81
Kemp, Stan	Tor.	1	1	0	0	0	2	....	....	....	....	....	....	1948-49	1948-49
‡ Kenady, Chris	St.L., NYR	2	7	0	2	2	0	....	....	....	....	....	....	1997-98	1999-00
• Kendall, Bill	Chi., Tor.	5	131	16	10	26	28	6	0	0	0	0	1	1933-34	1937-38
Kennedy, Dean	L.A., NYR, Buf., Wpg., Edm.	12	717	26	108	134	1118	36	1	7	8	59	....	1982-83	1994-95
Kennedy, Forbes	Chi., Det., Bos., Phi., Tor.	11	603	70	108	178	988	12	2	4	6	64	....	1956-57	1968-69
‡ Kennedy, Mike	Dal., Tor., NYI	5	145	16	36	52	112	5	0	0	0	9	....	1994-95	1998-99
Kennedy, Sheldon	Det., Cgy., Bos.	8	310	49	58	107	233	24	6	4	10	20	....	1989-90	1996-97
Kennedy, Ted	Tor.	14	696	231	329	560	432	78	29	31	60	32	5	1942-43	1956-57
• Kenny, Ernest	NYR, Chi.	2	10	0	0	0	18	....	....	....	....	....	....	1930-31	1934-35
Keon, Dave	Tor., Hfd.	18	1296	396	590	986	117	92	32	36	68	6	4	1960-61	1981-82
Kerch, Alexander	Edm.	1	5	0	0	0	2	....	....	....	....	....	....	1993-94	1993-94
Kerr, Alan	NYI, Det., Wpg.	9	391	72	94	166	826	38	5	4	9	70	....	1984-85	1992-93
Kerr, Reg	Cle., Chi., Edm.	6	263	66	94	160	169	7	1	0	1	7	....	1977-78	1983-84
Kerr, Tim	Phi., NYR, Hfd.	13	655	370	304	674	596	81	40	31	71	58	....	1980-81	1992-93
Kesa, Dan	Van., Dal., Pit., T.B.	4	139	8	22	30	66	13	1	0	1	0	....	1993-94	1999-00
Kessell, Rick	Pit., Cal.	5	135	4	24	28	6	....	....	....	....	....	....	1969-70	1973-74
Ketola, Veli-Pekka	Col.	1	44	9	5	14	4	....	....	....	....	....	....	1981-82	1981-82
Ketter, Kerry	Atl.	1	41	0	2	2	58	....	....	....	....	....	....	1972-73	1972-73
Kharin, Sergei	Wpg.	1	7	2	3	5	2	....	....	....	....	....	....	1990-91	1990-91
‡ Kharitonov, Alexander	T.B., NYI	2	71	7	15	22	12	....	....	....	....	....	....	2000-01	2001-02
Khmylev, Yuri	Buf., St.L.	5	263	64	88	152	133	26	8	6	14	24	....	1992-93	1996-97
Khristich, Dmitri	Wsh., L.A., Bos., Tor.	12	811	259	337	596	422	75	15	25	40	41	....	1990-91	2001-02
Kidd, Ian	Van.	2	20	4	7	11	25	....	....	....	....	....	....	1987-88	1988-89
Kiessling, Udo	Min.	1	1	0	0	0	2	....	....	....	....	....	....	1981-82	1981-82
Kilrea, Brian	Det., L.A.	2	26	3	5	8	12	....	....	....	....	....	....	1957-58	1967-68
• Kilrea, Hec	Ott., Det., Tor.	15	633	167	129	296	438	48	8	7	15	18	3	1925-26	1939-40
• Kilrea, Ken	Det.	5	91	16	23	39	8	15	2	2	4	4	....	1938-39	1943-44
• Kilrea, Wally	Ott., Phi., NYA, Mtl.M., Det.	9	329	35	58	93	87	25	2	4	6	6	2	1929-30	1937-38
Kimble, Darin	Que., St.L., Bos., Chi.	7	311	23	20	43	1082	23	0	0	0	52	....	1988-89	1994-95
Kindrachuk, Orest	Phi., Pit., Wsh.	10	508	118	261	379	648	76	20	20	40	53	2	1972-73	1981-82
King, Derek	NYI, Hfd., Tor., St.L.	14	830	261	351	612	417	47	4	17	21	24	....	1986-87	1999-00
King, Frank	Mtl.	1	10	1	0	1	2	....	....	....	....	....	....	1950-51	1950-51
King, Kris	Det., NYR, Wpg., Phx., Tor., Chi.	14	849	66	85	151	2030	67	8	5	13	142	....	1987-88	2000-01
King, Steven	NYR, Ana.	3	67	17	8	25	75	....	....	....	....	....	....	1992-93	1995-96
King, Wayne	Cal.	3	73	5	18	23	34	....	....	....	....	....	....	1973-74	1975-76
Kinnear, Geordie	Atl.	1	4	0	0	0	13	....	....	....	....	....	....	1999-00	1999-00
Kinsella, Brian	Wsh.	2	10	0	1	1	0	....	....	....	....	....	....	1975-76	1976-77
• Kinsella, Ray	Ott.	1	14	0	0	0	0	....	....	....	....	....	....	1930-31	1930-31
‡ Kiprusoff, Marko	Mtl., NYI	2	51	0	10	10	12	....	....	....	....	....	....	1995-96	2001-02
• Kirk, Bobby	NYR	1	39	4	8	12	14	....	....	....	....	....	....	1937-38	1937-38
Kirkpatrick, Bob	NYR	1	49	12	12	24	6	....	....	....	....	....	....	1942-43	1942-43
Kirton, Mark	Tor., Det., Van.	6	266	57	56	113	121	4	1	2	3	7	....	1979-80	1984-85
Kisio, Kelly	Det., NYR, S.J., Cgy.	13	761	229	429	658	768	39	6	15	21	52	....	1982-83	1994-95
Kitchen, Bill	Mtl., Tor.	4	41	1	4	5	40	3	0	1	1	0	....	1981-82	1984-85
• Kitchen, Hobie	Mtl.M., Det.	2	47	5	4	9	58	....	....	....	....	....	1	1925-26	1926-27
Kitchen, Mike	Col., N.J.	8	474	12	62	74	370	2	0	0	0	2	....	1976-77	1983-84
Kjellberg, Patric	Mtl., Nsh., Ana.	6	394	64	96	160	84	10	0	0	0	0	....	1992-93	2002-03
Klassen, Ralph	Cal., Cle., Col., St.L.	9	497	52	93	145	120	26	4	2	6	12	....	1975-76	1983-84
Klatt, Trent	Min., Dal., Phi., Van., L.A.	13	782	143	200	343	307	74	16	9	25	20	....	1991-92	2003-04
• Klein, Lloyd	Bos., NYA	8	164	30	24	54	68	5	0	0	0	2	1	1928-29	1937-38
Kleinendorst, Scot	NYR, Hfd., Wsh.	8	281	12	46	58	452	26	2	7	9	40	....	1982-83	1989-90
Klima, Petr	Det., Edm., T.B., L.A., Pit.	13	786	313	260	573	671	95	28	24	52	83	1	1985-86	1998-99
‡ Klimovich, Sergei	Chi.	1	1	0	0	0	2	....	....	....	....	....	....	1996-97	1996-97
• Klingbeil, Ike	Chi.	1	5	1	2	3	2	....	....	....	....	....	....	1936-37	1936-37
• Klukay, Joe	Tor., Bos.	11	566	109	127	236	189	71	13	10	23	23	4	1942-43	1955-56
Kluzak, Gord	Bos.	7	299	25	98	123	543	46	6	13	19	129	....	1982-83	1990-91
Knibbs, Bill	Bos.	1	53	7	10	17	4	....	....	....	....	....	....	1964-65	1964-65

			Regular Schedule					Playoffs							
Name	NHL Teams	NHL Seasons	GP	G	A	TP	PIM	GP	G	A	TP	PIM	NHL Cup Wins	First NHL Season	Last NHL Season
Knipscheer, Fred	Bos., St.L.	3	28	6	3	9	18	16	2	1	3	6	....	1993-94	1995-96
• Knott, Nick	Bro.	1	14	3	1	4	9	....	....	....	....	....	....	1941-42	1941-42
Knox, Paul	Tor.	1	1	0	0	0	0	....	....	....	....	....	....	1954-55	1954-55
Knutsen, Espen	Ana., CBJ	5	207	30	81	111	105	....	....	....	....	....	....	1997-98	2003-04
Kocur, Joe	Det., NYR, Van.	15	820	80	82	162	2519	118	10	12	22	231	3	1984-85	1998-99
‡ Koehler, Greg	Car.	1	1	0	0	0	0	....	....	....	....	....	....	2000-01	2000-01
‡ Kohn, Ladislav	Cgy., Tor., Ana., Atl., Det.	7	186	14	28	42	125	2	0	0	0	5	....	1995-96	2002-03
‡ Koivisto, Tom	St.L.	1	22	2	4	6	10	....	....	....	....	....	....	2002-03	2002-03
‡ Kolarik, Pavel	Bos.	2	23	0	0	0	10	....	....	....	....	....	....	2000-01	2001-02
Kolesar, Mark	Tor.	2	28	2	2	4	14	3	1	0	1	2	....	1995-96	1996-97
Kolstad, Dean	Min., S.J.	3	40	1	7	8	69	....	....	....	....	....	....	1988-89	1992-93
Komadoski, Neil	L.A., St.L.	8	502	16	76	92	632	23	0	2	2	47	....	1972-73	1979-80
Konik, George	Pit.	1	52	7	8	15	26	....	....	....	....	....	....	1967-68	1967-68
Konroyd, Steve	Cgy., NYI, Chi., Hfd., Det., Ott.	15	895	41	195	236	863	97	10	15	25	99	....	1980-81	1994-95
Konstantinov, Vladimir	Det.	6	446	47	128	175	838	82	5	14	19	107	1	1991-92	1996-97
Kontos, Chris	NYR, Pit., L.A., T.B.	8	230	54	69	123	103	20	11	0	11	12	....	1982-83	1992-93
• Kopak, Russ	Bos.	1	24	7	9	16	0	....	....	....	....	....	....	1943-44	1943-44
Korab, Jerry	Chi., Van., Buf., L.A.	15	975	114	341	455	1629	93	8	18	26	201	....	1970-71	1984-85
Kordic, Dan	Phi.	6	197	4	8	12	584	12	1	0	1	22	....	1991-92	1998-99
• Kordic, John	Mtl., Tor., Wsh., Que.	7	244	17	18	35	997	41	4	3	7	131	1	1985-86	1991-92
Korn, Jim	Det., Tor., Buf., N.J., Cgy.	10	597	66	122	188	1801	16	1	2	3	109	....	1979-80	1989-90
Korney, Mike	Det., NYR	4	77	9	10	19	59	....	....	....	....	....	....	1973-74	1978-79
‡ Korolev, Igor	St.L., Wpg., Phx., Tor., Chi.	12	795	119	227	346	330	41	0	8	8	6	....	1992-93	2003-04
Koroll, Cliff	Chi.	11	814	208	254	462	376	85	19	29	48	67	....	1969-70	1979-80
Kortko, Roger	NYI	2	79	7	17	24	28	10	0	3	3	17	....	1984-85	1985-86
Kostynski, Doug	Bos.	2	15	3	1	4	4	....	....	....	....	....	....	1983-84	1984-85
Kotanen, Dick	NYR	1	1	0	0	0	0	....	....	....	....	....	....	1950-51	1950-51
Kotsopoulos, Chris	NYR, Hfd., Tor., Det.	10	479	44	109	153	827	31	1	3	4	91	....	1980-81	1989-90
‡ Kovalenko, Andrei	Que., Col., Mtl., Edm., Phi., Car., Bos.	9	620	173	206	379	389	33	5	6	11	20	....	1992-93	2000-01
Kowal, Joe	Buf.	2	22	0	5	5	13	2	0	0	0	0	....	1976-77	1977-78
Kozak, Don	L.A., Van.	7	437	96	86	182	480	29	7	2	9	69	....	1972-73	1978-79
Kozak, Les	Tor.	1	12	1	0	1	2	....	....	....	....	....	....	1961-62	1961-62
• Kraftcheck, Stephen	Bos., NYR, Tor.	4	157	11	18	29	83	6	0	0	0	7	....	1950-51	1958-59
Krake, Skip	Bos., L.A., Buf.	7	249	23	40	63	182	10	1	0	1	17	....	1963-64	1970-71
Kravchuk, Igor	Chi., Edm., St.L., Ott., Cgy., Fla.	12	699	64	210	274	251	51	6	15	21	18	....	1991-92	2002-03
Kravets, Mikhail	S.J.	2	2	0	0	0	0	....	....	....	....	....	....	1991-92	1992-93
Krentz, Dale	Det.	3	30	5	3	8	9	2	0	0	0	0	....	1986-87	1988-89
‡ Krestanovich, Jordan	Col.	2	22	0	2	2	6	....	....	....	....	....	....	2001-02	2003-04
‡ Kristek, Jaroslav	Buf.	1	6	0	0	0	4	....	....	....	....	....	....	2002-03	2002-03
‡ Krivokrasov, Sergei	Chi., Nsh., Cgy., Min., Ana.	10	450	86	109	195	288	21	2	0	2	14	....	1992-93	2001-02
• Krol, Joe	NYR, Bro.	3	26	10	4	14	8	....	....	....	....	....	....	1936-37	1941-42
Kromm, Richard	Cgy., NYI	9	372	70	103	173	138	36	2	6	8	22	....	1983-84	1992-93
Kron, Robert	Van., Hfd., Car., CBJ	12	771	144	194	338	119	16	3	2	5	2	....	1990-91	2001-02
Krook, Kevin	Col.	1	3	0	0	0	2	....	....	....	....	....	....	1978-79	1978-79
‡ Kroupa, Vlastimil	S.J., N.J.	5	105	4	19	23	66	20	1	2	3	25	....	1993-94	1997-98
Krulicki, Jim	NYR, Det.	1	41	0	3	3	6	....	....	....	....	....	....	1970-71	1970-71
Krupp, Uwe	Buf., NYI, Que., Col., Det., Atl.	15	729	69	212	281	660	81	6	23	29	86	1	1986-87	2002-03
Kruppke, Gord	Det.	3	23	0	0	0	32	....	....	....	....	....	....	1990-91	1993-94
Kruse, Paul	Cgy., NYI, Buf., S.J.	11	423	38	33	71	1074	28	5	2	7	36	....	1990-91	2000-01
Krushelnyski, Mike	Bos., Edm., L.A., Tor., Det.	14	897	241	328	569	699	139	29	43	72	106	3	1981-82	1994-95
Krutov, Vladimir	Van.	1	61	11	23	34	20	....	....	....	....	....	....	1989-90	1989-90
Krygier, Todd	Hfd., Wsh., Ana.	9	543	100	143	243	533	48	10	7	17	40	....	1989-90	1997-98
Kryskow, Dave	Chi., Wsh., Det., Atl.	4	231	33	56	89	174	12	2	0	2	4	....	1972-73	1975-76
Kryzanowski, Ed	Bos., Chi.	5	237	15	22	37	65	18	0	1	1	4	....	1948-49	1952-53
Kucera, Frantisek	Chi., Hfd., Van., Phi., CBJ, Pit., Wsh.	9	465	24	95	119	251	12	0	1	1	0	....	1990-91	2001-02
‡ Kudashov, Alexei	Tor.	1	25	1	0	1	4	....	....	....	....	....	....	1993-94	1993-94
Kudelski, Bob	L.A., Ott., Fla.	9	442	139	102	241	218	22	4	4	8	4	....	1987-88	1995-96
‡ Kudroc, Kristian	T.B., Fla.	3	26	2	2	4	38	....	....	....	....	....	....	2000-01	2003-04
• Kuhn, Gord	NYA	1	12	1	1	2	4	....	....	....	....	....	....	1932-33	1932-33
Kukulowicz, Aggie	NYR	2	4	1	0	1	0	....	....	....	....	....	....	1952-53	1953-54
Kulak, Stu	Van., Edm., NYR, Que., Wpg.	4	90	8	4	12	130	3	0	0	0	2	....	1982-83	1988-89
‡ Kuleshov, Mikhail	Col.	1	3	0	0	0	0	....	....	....	....	....	....	2003-04	2003-04
• Kullman, Arnie	Bos.	2	13	0	1	1	11	....	....	....	....	....	....	1947-48	1949-50
• Kullman, Eddie	NYR	6	343	56	70	126	298	6	1	0	1	2	....	1947-48	1953-54
‡ Kultanen, Jarno	Bos.	3	102	2	11	13	59	....	....	....	....	....	....	2000-01	2002-03
Kumpel, Mark	Que., Det., Wpg.	6	288	38	46	84	113	39	6	4	10	14	....	1984-85	1990-91
• Kuntz, Alan	NYR	2	45	10	12	22	12	6	1	0	1	2	....	1941-42	1945-46
Kuntz, Murray	St.L.	1	7	1	2	3	0	....	....	....	....	....	....	1974-75	1974-75
‡ Kurka, Tomas	Car.	2	17	3	2	5	2	....	....	....	....	....	....	2002-03	2003-04
Kurri, Jari	Edm., L.A., NYR, Ana., Col.	17	1251	601	797	1398	545	200	106	127	233	123	5	1980-81	1997-98
Kurtenbach, Orland	NYR, Bos., Tor., Van.	13	639	119	213	332	628	19	2	4	6	70	....	1960-61	1973-74
‡ Kurtz, Justin	Van.	1	27	3	5	8	14	....	....	....	....	....	....	2001-02	2001-02
Kurvers, Tom	Mtl., Buf., N.J., Tor., Van., NYI, Ana.	11	659	93	328	421	350	57	8	22	30	68	1	1984-85	1994-95
Kuryluk, Merv	Chi.	1	....	....	....	....	....	2	0	0	0	0	....	1961-62	1961-62
Kushner, Dale	NYI, Phi.	3	84	10	13	23	215	....	....	....	....	....	....	1989-90	1991-92
‡ Kuznetsov, Maxim	Det., L.A.	4	136	2	8	10	137	....	....	....	....	....	....	2000-01	2003-04
Kuznik, Greg	Car.	1	1	0	0	0	0	....	....	....	....	....	....	2000-01	2000-01
Kuzyk, Ken	Cle.	2	41	5	9	14	8	....	....	....	....	....	....	1976-77	1977-78
Kvartalnov, Dmitri	Bos.	2	112	42	49	91	26	4	0	0	0	0	....	1992-93	1993-94
Kwong, Larry	NYR	1	1	0	0	0	0	....	....	....	....	....	....	1947-48	1947-48
• Kyle, Bill	NYR	2	3	0	3	3	0	....	....	....	....	....	....	1949-50	1950-51
• Kyle, Gus	NYR, Bos.	3	203	6	20	26	362	14	1	2	3	34	....	1949-50	1951-52
Kyllonen, Markku	Wpg.	1	9	0	2	2	2	....	....	....	....	....	....	1988-89	1988-89
Kypreos, Nick	Wsh., Hfd., NYR, Tor.	8	442	46	44	90	1210	34	1	3	4	65	1	1989-90	1996-97
Kyte, Jim	Wpg., Pit., Cgy., Ott., S.J.	13	598	17	49	66	1342	42	0	6	6	94	....	1982-83	1995-96
L															
Labadie, Mike	NYR	1	3	0	0	0	0	....	....	....	....	....	....	1952-53	1952-53
Labatte, Neil	St.L.	2	26	0	2	2	19	....	....	....	....	....	....	1978-79	1981-82
L'Abbe, Moe	Chi.	1	5	0	1	1	0	....	....	....	....	....	....	1972-73	1972-73
Labelle, Marc	Dal.	1	9	0	0	0	46	....	....	....	....	....	....	1996-97	1996-97
• Labine, Leo	Bos., Det.	11	643	128	193	321	730	60	12	11	23	82	....	1951-52	1961-62
Labossiere, Gord	NYR, L.A., Min.	6	215	44	62	106	75	10	2	3	5	28	....	1963-64	1971-72
Labovitch, Max	NYR	1	5	0	0	0	4	....	....	....	....	....	....	1943-44	1943-44
Labraaten, Dan	Det., Cgy.	4	268	71	73	144	47	8	1	0	1	4	....	1978-79	1981-82
Labre, Yvon	Pit., Wsh.	9	371	14	87	101	788	....	....	....	....	....	....	1970-71	1980-81
Labrie, Guy	Bos., NYR	2	42	4	9	13	16	....	....	....	....	....	....	1943-44	1944-45
Lach, Elmer	Mtl.	14	664	215	408	623	478	76	19	45	64	36	3	1940-41	1953-54
Lachance, Michel	Col.	1	21	0	4	4	22	....	....	....	....	....	....	1978-79	1978-79
‡ Lachance, Scott	NYI, Mtl., Van., CBJ	13	819	31	112	143	567	11	1	2	3	6	....	1991-92	2003-04
Lacombe, Francois	Oak., Buf., Que.	4	78	2	17	19	54	3	1	0	1	0	....	1968-69	1979-80
Lacombe, Normand	Buf., Edm., Phi.	7	319	53	62	115	196	26	5	1	6	49	1	1984-85	1990-91
Lacroix, Andre	Phi., Chi., Hfd.	6	325	79	119	198	44	16	2	5	7	0	....	1967-68	1979-80
Lacroix, Daniel	NYR, Bos., Phi., Edm., NYI	7	188	11	7	18	379	16	0	1	1	26	....	1993-94	1999-00
Lacroix, Eric	Tor., L.A., Col., NYR, Ott.	8	472	67	70	137	361	30	1	5	6	25	....	1993-94	2000-01
Lacroix, Pierre	Que., Hfd.	4	274	24	108	132	197	8	0	2	2	10	....	1979-80	1982-83
Ladouceur, Randy	Det., Hfd., Ana.	14	930	30	126	156	1322	40	5	8	13	59	....	1982-83	1995-96
LaFayette, Nathan	St.L., Van., NYR, L.A.	6	187	17	20	37	103	32	2	7	9	8	....	1993-94	1998-99
‡ Laflamme, Christian	Chi., Edm., Mtl., St.L.	8	324	2	45	47	282	9	0	1	1	6	....	1996-97	2003-04
Lafleur, Guy	Mtl., NYR, Que.	17	1126	560	793	1353	399	128	58	76	134	67	5	1971-72	1990-91
• Lafleur, Roland	Mtl.	1	1	0	0	0	0	....	....	....	....	....	....	1924-25	1924-25
LaFontaine, Pat	NYI, Buf., NYR	15	865	468	545	1013	552	69	26	36	62	36	....	1983-84	1997-98
Laforce, Ernie	Mtl.	1	1	0	0	0	0	....	....	....	....	....	....	1942-43	1942-43
LaForest, Bob	L.A.	1	5	1	0	1	2	....	....	....	....	....	....	1983-84	1983-84
Laforge, Claude	Mtl., Det., Phi.	8	193	24	33	57	82	5	1	2	3	15	....	1957-58	1968-69
Laforge, Marc	Hfd., Edm.	2	14	0	0	0	64	....	....	....	....	....	....	1989-90	1993-94
Laframboise, Pete	Cal., Wsh., Pit.	4	227	33	55	88	70	9	1	0	1	0	....	1971-72	1974-75
Lafrance, Adie	Mtl.	1	3	0	0	0	2	2	0	0	0	0	....	1933-34	1933-34
• Lafrance, Leo	Mtl., Chi.	2	33	2	0	2	6	....	....	....	....	....	....	1926-27	1927-28
Lafreniere, Jason	Que., NYR, T.B.	5	146	34	53	87	22	15	1	5	6	19	....	1986-87	1993-94
Lafreniere, Roger	Det., St.L.	2	13	0	0	0	4	....	....	....	....	....	....	1962-63	1972-73
Lagace, Jean-Guy	Pit., Buf., K.C.	6	197	9	39	48	251	....	....	....	....	....	....	1968-69	1975-76
Laidlaw, Tom	NYR, L.A.	10	705	25	139	164	717	69	4	17	21	78	....	1980-81	1989-90

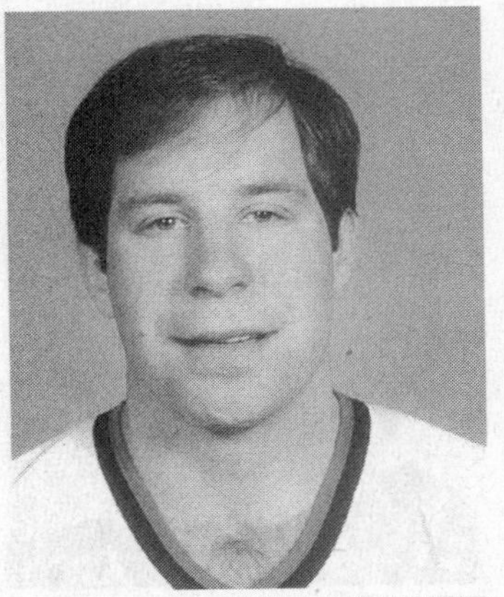

Kelly Kisio

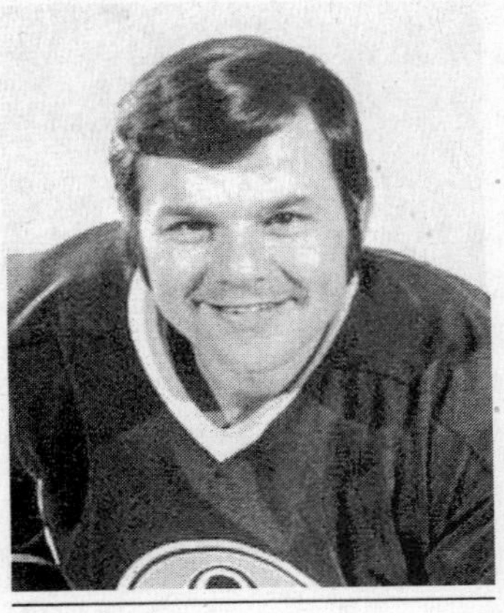

George Konik

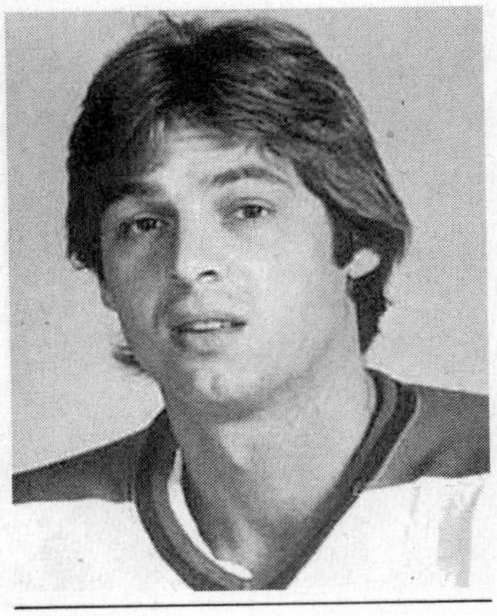

Ken Kuzyk

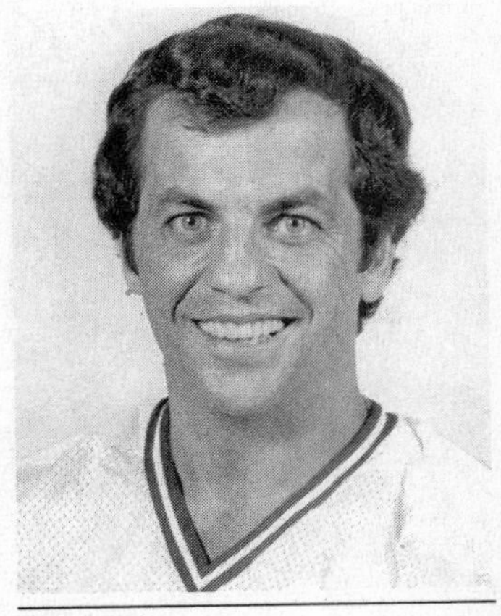

Andre Lacroix

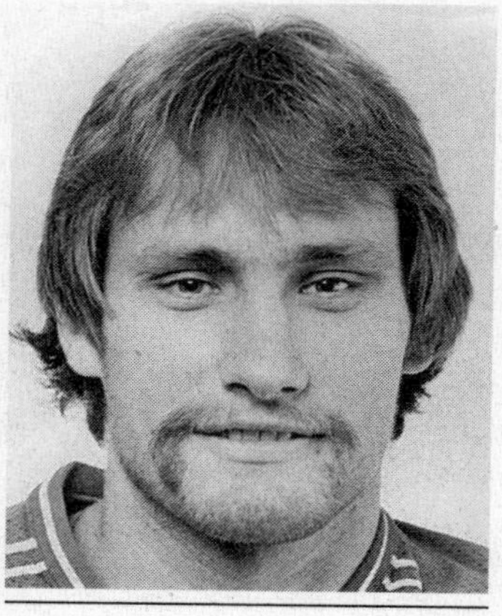

Tom Laidlaw

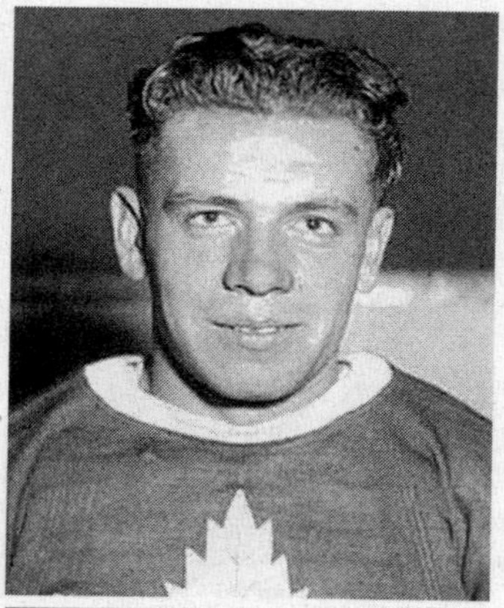

Pete Langelle

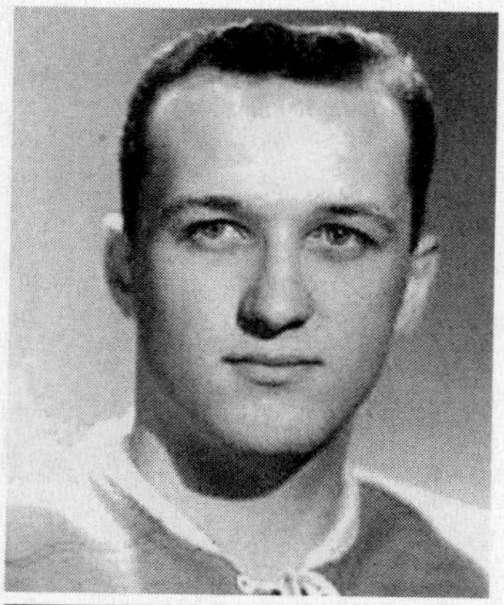

Albert Langlois

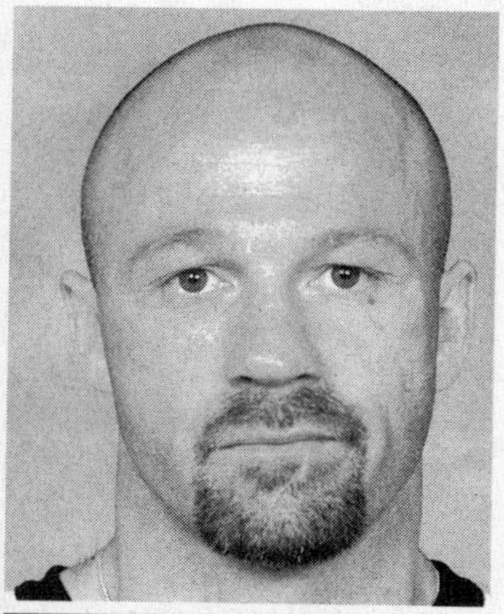

Claude Lapointe

Name	NHL Teams	NHL Seasons	Regular Schedule GP	G	A	TP	PIM	Playoffs GP	G	A	TP	PIM	NHL Cup Wins	First NHL Season	Last NHL Season
Laird, Robbie	Min.	1	1	0	0	0	0	....	....	....	....	....	....	1979-80	1979-80
Lajeunesse, Serge	Det., Phi.	5	103	1	4	5	103	....	....	....	....	....	....	1970-71	1974-75
Lakovic, Sasha	Cgy., N.J.	3	37	0	4	4	118	....	....	....	....	....	....	1996-97	1998-99
Lalande, Hec	Chi., Det.	4	151	21	39	60	120	....	....	....	....	....	....	1953-54	1957-58
Lalonde, Bobby	Van., Atl., Bos., Cgy.	11	641	124	210	334	298	16	4	2	6	6	....	1971-72	1981-82
• Lalonde, Newsy	Mtl., NYA	6	99	124	41	165	183	7	15	4	19	32	....	1917-18	1926-27
Lalonde, Ron	Pit., Wsh.	7	397	45	78	123	106	....	....	....	....	....	....	1972-73	1978-79
Lalor, Mike	Mtl., St.L., Wsh., Wpg., S.J., Dal.	12	687	17	88	105	677	92	5	10	15	167	1	1985-86	1996-97
• Lamb, Joe	Mtl.M., Ott., NYA, Bos., Mtl., St.L., Det.	11	443	108	101	209	601	18	1	1	2	51	....	1927-28	1937-38
Lamb, Mark	Cgy., Det., Edm., Ott., Phi., Mtl.	11	403	46	100	146	291	70	7	19	26	51	1	1985-86	1995-96
‡ Lambert, Dan	Que.	2	29	6	9	15	22	....	....	....	....	....	....	1990-91	1991-92
Lambert, Denny	Ana., Ott., Nsh., Atl.	8	487	27	66	93	1391	17	0	1	1	28	....	1994-95	2001-02
Lambert, Lane	Det., NYR, Que.	6	283	58	66	124	521	17	2	4	6	40	....	1983-84	1988-89
Lambert, Yvon	Mtl., Buf.	10	683	206	273	479	340	90	27	22	49	67	4	1972-73	1981-82
Lamby, Dick	St.L.	3	22	0	5	5	22	....	....	....	....	....	....	1978-79	1980-81
• Lamirande, Jean-Paul	NYR, Mtl.	4	49	5	5	10	26	8	0	0	0	4	....	1946-47	1954-55
Lammens, Hank	Ott.	1	27	1	2	3	22	....	....	....	....	....	....	1993-94	1993-94
• Lamoureux, Leo	Mtl.	6	235	19	79	98	175	28	1	6	7	16	2	1941-42	1946-47
Lamoureux, Mitch	Pit., Phi.	3	73	11	9	20	59	....	....	....	....	....	....	1983-84	1987-88
Lampman, Mike	St.L., Van., Wsh.	4	96	17	20	37	34	....	....	....	....	....	....	1972-73	1976-77
Lancien, Jack	NYR	4	63	1	5	6	35	6	0	1	1	2	....	1946-47	1950-51
Landon, Larry	Mtl., Tor.	2	9	0	0	0	2	....	....	....	....	....	....	1983-84	1984-85
‡ Landry, Eric	Cgy., Mtl.	4	68	5	9	14	47	....	....	....	....	....	....	1997-98	2001-02
Lane, Gord	Wsh., NYI	10	539	19	94	113	1228	75	3	14	17	214	4	1975-76	1984-85
• Lane, Myles	NYR, Bos.	3	71	4	1	5	41	11	0	0	0	0	1	1928-29	1933-34
Langdon, Steve	Bos.	3	7	0	1	1	2	4	0	0	0	0	....	1974-75	1977-78
Langelle, Pete	Tor.	4	136	22	51	73	11	41	5	9	14	4	1	1938-39	1941-42
Langevin, Chris	Buf.	2	22	3	1	4	22	....	....	....	....	....	....	1983-84	1985-86
Langevin, Dave	NYI, Min., L.A.	8	513	12	107	119	530	87	2	17	19	106	4	1979-80	1986-87
Langlais, Alain	Min.	2	25	4	4	8	10	....	....	....	....	....	....	1973-74	1974-75
Langlois, Albert	Mtl., NYR, Det., Bos.	9	497	21	91	112	488	53	1	5	6	50	3	1957-58	1965-66
• Langlois, Charlie	Ham., NYA, Pit., Mtl.	4	151	22	5	27	189	2	0	0	0	0	....	1924-25	1927-28
Langway, Rod	Mtl., Wsh.	15	994	51	278	329	849	104	5	22	27	97	1	1978-79	1992-93
Lank, Jeff	Phi.	1	2	0	0	0	2	....	....	....	....	....	....	1999-00	1999-00
Lanthier, Jean-Marc	Van.	4	105	16	16	32	29	....	....	....	....	....	....	1983-84	1987-88
Lanyon, Ted	Pit.	1	5	0	0	0	4	....	....	....	....	....	....	1967-68	1967-68
Lanz, Rick	Van., Tor., Chi.	10	569	65	221	286	448	28	3	8	11	35	....	1980-81	1991-92
Laperriere, Daniel	St.L., Ott.	4	48	2	5	7	27	....	....	....	....	....	....	1992-93	1995-96
Laperriere, Jacques	Mtl.	12	691	40	242	282	674	88	9	22	31	101	6	1962-63	1973-74
Laplante, Darryl	Det.	3	35	0	6	6	10	....	....	....	....	....	....	1997-98	1999-00
Lapointe, Claude	Que., Col., Cgy., NYI, Phi.	14	879	127	178	305	721	34	4	7	11	44	....	1990-91	2003-04
Lapointe, Guy	Mtl., St.L., Bos.	16	884	171	451	622	893	123	26	44	70	138	6	1968-69	1983-84
• Lapointe, Rick	Det., Phi., St.L., Que., L.A.	11	664	44	176	220	831	46	2	7	9	64	....	1975-76	1985-86
Lappin, Peter	Min., S.J.	2	7	0	0	0	2	....	....	....	....	....	....	1989-90	1991-92
Laprade, Edgar	NYR	10	500	108	172	280	42	18	4	9	13	4	....	1945-46	1954-55
• LaPrairie, Benjamin	Chi.	1	7	0	0	0	0	....	....	....	....	....	....	1936-37	1936-37
Larionov, Igor	Van., S.J., Det., Fla., N.J.	14	921	169	475	644	474	150	30	67	97	60	3	1989-90	2003-04
Lariviere, Garry	Que., Edm.	4	219	6	57	63	167	14	0	5	5	8	....	1979-80	1982-83
Larmer, Jeff	Col., N.J., Chi.	5	158	37	51	88	57	5	1	0	1	2	....	1981-82	1985-86
Larmer, Steve	Chi., NYR	15	1006	441	571	1012	532	140	56	75	131	89	1	1980-81	1994-95
• Larochelle, Wildor	Mtl., Chi.	12	474	92	74	166	211	34	6	4	10	24	2	1925-26	1936-37
Larocque, Denis	L.A.	1	8	0	1	1	18	....	....	....	....	....	....	1987-88	1987-88
‡ Larocque, Mario	T.B.	1	5	0	0	0	16	....	....	....	....	....	....	1998-99	1998-99
• Larose, Bonner	Bos.	1	6	0	0	0	0	....	....	....	....	....	....	1925-26	1925-26
Larose, Claude	Mtl., Min., St.L.	16	943	226	257	483	887	97	14	18	32	143	5	1962-63	1977-78
Larose, Claude	NYR	2	25	4	7	11	2	2	0	0	0	0	....	1979-80	1981-82
Larose, Guy	Wpg., Tor., Cgy., Bos.	6	70	10	9	19	63	4	0	0	0	0	....	1988-89	1994-95
Larouche, Pierre	Pit., Mtl., Hfd., NYR	14	812	395	427	822	237	64	20	34	54	16	2	1974-75	1987-88
Larouche, Steve	Ott., NYR, L.A.	2	26	9	9	18	10	....	....	....	....	....	....	1994-95	1995-96
• Larson, Norm	NYA, Bro., NYR	3	89	25	18	43	12	....	....	....	....	....	....	1940-41	1946-47
Larson, Reed	Det., Bos., Edm., NYI, Min., Buf.	14	904	222	463	685	1391	32	4	7	11	63	....	1976-77	1989-90
Larter, Tyler	Wsh.	1	1	0	0	0	0	....	....	....	....	....	....	1989-90	1989-90
Latal, Jiri	Phi.	3	92	12	36	48	24	....	....	....	....	....	....	1989-90	1991-92
Latos, James	NYR	1	1	0	0	0	0	....	....	....	....	....	....	1988-89	1988-89
Latreille, Phil	NYR	1	4	0	0	0	2	....	....	....	....	....	....	1960-61	1960-61
Latta, David	Que.	4	36	4	8	12	4	....	....	....	....	....	....	1985-86	1990-91
Lauder, Martin	Bos.	1	3	0	0	0	2	....	....	....	....	....	....	1927-28	1927-28
Lauen, Mike	Wpg.	1	4	0	1	1	0	....	....	....	....	....	....	1983-84	1983-84
Lauer, Brad	NYI, Chi., Ott., Pit.	9	323	44	67	111	218	34	7	5	12	24	....	1986-87	1995-96
Laughlin, Craig	Mtl., Wsh., L.A., Tor.	8	549	136	205	341	364	33	6	6	12	20	....	1981-82	1988-89
Laughton, Mike	Oak., Cal.	4	189	39	48	87	101	11	2	4	6	0	....	1967-68	1970-71
Laukkanen, Janne	Que., Col., Ott., Pit., T.B.	9	407	22	99	121	335	59	7	9	16	46	....	1994-95	2002-03
Laurence, Don	Atl., St.L.	2	79	15	22	37	14	....	....	....	....	....	....	1978-79	1979-80
Laus, Paul	Fla.	9	530	14	58	72	1702	30	2	7	9	74	....	1993-94	2001-02
LaVallee, Kevin	Cgy., L.A., St.L., Pit.	7	366	110	125	235	85	32	5	8	13	21	....	1980-81	1986-87
LaVarre, Mark	Chi.	3	78	9	16	25	58	1	0	0	0	2	....	1985-86	1987-88
Lavender, Brian	St.L., NYI, Det., Cal.	4	184	16	26	42	174	3	0	0	0	2	....	1971-72	1974-75
Lavigne, Eric	L.A.	1	1	0	0	0	0	....	....	....	....	....	....	1994-95	1994-95
• Laviolette, Jack	Mtl.	1	18	2	1	3	6	2	0	0	0	0	....	1917-18	1917-18
Laviolette, Peter	NYR	1	12	0	0	0	6	....	....	....	....	....	....	1988-89	1988-89
Lavoie, Dominic	St.L., Ott., Bos., L.A.	6	38	5	8	13	32	....	....	....	....	....	....	1988-89	1993-94
Lawless, Paul	Hfd., Phi., Van., Tor.	7	239	49	77	126	54	3	0	2	2	2	....	1982-83	1989-90
Lawrence, Mark	Dal., NYI	6	142	18	26	44	115	....	....	....	....	....	....	1994-95	2000-01
Lawson, Danny	Det., Min., Buf.	5	219	28	29	57	61	16	0	1	1	2	....	1967-68	1971-72
Lawton, Brian	Min., NYR, Hfd., Que., Bos., S.J.	9	483	112	154	266	401	11	1	1	2	12	....	1983-84	1992-93
Laxdal, Derek	Tor., NYI	6	67	12	7	19	88	1	0	2	2	2	....	1984-85	1990-91
• Laycoe, Hal	NYR, Mtl., Bos.	11	531	25	77	102	292	40	2	5	7	39	....	1945-46	1955-56
Lazaro, Jeff	Bos., Ott.	3	102	14	23	37	114	28	3	3	6	32	....	1990-91	1992-93
Leach, Jamie	Pit., Hfd., Fla.	5	81	11	9	20	12	....	....	....	....	....	1	1989-90	1993-94
Leach, Larry	Bos.	3	126	13	29	42	91	7	1	1	2	8	....	1958-59	1961-62
Leach, Reggie	Bos., Cal., Phi., Det.	13	934	381	285	666	387	94	47	22	69	22	1	1970-71	1982-83
Leach, Stephen	Wsh., Bos., St.L., Car., Ott., Phx., Pit.	15	702	130	153	283	978	92	15	11	26	87	....	1985-86	1999-00
Leavins, Jim	Det., NYR	2	41	2	12	14	30	....	....	....	....	....	....	1985-86	1986-87
‡ Lebeau, Patrick	Mtl., Cgy., Fla., Pit.	4	15	3	2	5	6	....	....	....	....	....	....	1990-91	1998-99
Lebeau, Stephan	Mtl., Ana.	7	373	118	159	277	105	30	9	7	16	12	1	1988-89	1994-95
LeBlanc, Fern	Det.	3	34	5	6	11	0	....	....	....	....	....	....	1976-77	1978-79
LeBlanc, J.P.	Chi., Det.	5	153	14	30	44	87	2	0	0	0	0	....	1968-69	1978-79
LeBlanc, John	Van., Edm., Wpg.	7	83	26	13	39	28	1	0	0	0	0	....	1986-87	1994-95
LeBoutillier, Peter	Ana.	2	35	2	1	3	176	....	....	....	....	....	....	1996-97	1997-98
LeBrun, Al	NYR	2	6	0	2	2	4	....	....	....	....	....	....	1960-61	1965-66
Lecaine, Bill	Pit.	1	4	0	0	0	0	....	....	....	....	....	....	1968-69	1968-69
LeClair, Jack	Mtl.	3	160	20	40	60	56	20	6	1	7	6	2	1954-55	1956-57
Leclerc, Rene	Det.	2	87	10	11	21	105	....	....	....	....	....	....	1968-69	1970-71
Lecuyer, Doug	Chi., Wpg., Pit.	4	126	11	31	42	178	7	4	0	4	15	....	1978-79	1982-83
Ledingham, Walt	Chi., NYI	3	15	0	2	2	4	....	....	....	....	....	....	1972-73	1976-77
• Leduc, Albert	Mtl., Ott., NYR	10	383	57	35	92	614	28	5	6	11	32	2	1925-26	1934-35
LeDuc, Rich	Bos., Que.	4	130	28	38	66	69	5	0	0	0	9	....	1972-73	1980-81
Ledyard, Grant	NYR, L.A., Wsh., Buf., Dal., Van., Bos., Ott., T.B.	18	1028	90	276	366	766	83	6	12	18	96	....	1984-85	2001-02
• Lee, Bobby	Mtl.	1	1	0	0	0	0	....	....	....	....	....	....	1942-43	1942-43
Lee, Edward	Que.	1	2	0	0	0	5	....	....	....	....	....	....	1984-85	1984-85
Lee, Peter	Pit.	6	431	114	131	245	257	19	0	8	8	4	....	1977-78	1982-83
‡ Leeb, Greg	Dal.	1	2	0	0	0	0	....	....	....	....	....	....	2000-01	2000-01
Leeman, Gary	Tor., Cgy., Mtl., Van., St.L.	14	667	199	267	466	531	36	8	16	24	36	1	1982-83	1996-97
Lefebvre, Patrice	Wsh.	1	3	0	0	0	2	....	....	....	....	....	....	1998-99	1998-99
Lefebvre, Sylvain	Mtl., Tor., Que., Col., NYR	14	945	30	154	184	674	129	4	14	18	101	1	1989-90	2002-03
• Lefley, Bryan	NYI, K.C., Col.	5	228	7	29	36	101	2	0	0	0	0	....	1972-73	1977-78
Lefley, Chuck	Mtl., St.L.	9	407	128	164	292	137	29	5	8	13	10	2	1970-71	1980-81
• Leger, Roger	NYR, Mtl.	5	187	18	53	71	71	20	0	7	7	14	....	1943-44	1949-50
Legge, Barry	Que., Wpg.	3	107	1	11	12	144	....	....	....	....	....	....	1979-80	1981-82
Legge, Randy	NYR	1	12	0	2	2	2	....	....	....	....	....	....	1972-73	1972-73
Lehman, Tommy	Bos., Edm.	3	36	5	5	10	16	....	....	....	....	....	....	1987-88	1989-90
Lehto, Petteri	Pit.	1	6	0	0	0	4	....	....	....	....	....	....	1984-85	1984-85
Lehtonen, Antero	Wsh.	1	65	9	12	21	14	....	....	....	....	....	....	1979-80	1979-80

Name	NHL Teams	NHL Seasons	Regular Schedule					Playoffs					NHL Cup Wins	First NHL Season	Last NHL Season
			GP	G	A	TP	PIM	GP	G	A	TP	PIM			
Lehvonen, Henry	K.C.	1	4	0	0	0	0	....	....	....	....	....	....	1974-75	1974-75
Leier, Edward	Chi.	2	16	2	1	3	2	....	....	....	....	....	....	1949-50	1950-51
Leinonen, Mikko	NYR, Wsh.	4	162	31	78	109	71	20	2	11	13	28	....	1981-82	1984-85
Leiter, Bobby	Bos., Pit., Atl.	10	447	98	126	224	144	8	3	0	3	2	....	1962-63	1975-76
Leiter, Ken	NYI, Min.	5	143	14	36	50	62	15	0	6	6	8	....	1984-85	1989-90
Lemaire, Jacques	Mtl.	12	853	366	469	835	217	145	61	78	139	63	8	1967-68	1978-79
Lemay, Moe	Van., Edm., Bos., Wpg.	8	317	72	94	166	442	28	6	3	9	55	1	1981-82	1988-89
Lemelin, Roger	K.C., Col.	4	36	1	2	3	27	....	....	....	....	....	....	1974-75	1977-78
Lemieux, Alain	St.L., Que., Pit.	6	119	28	44	72	38	19	4	6	10	0	....	1981-82	1986-87
Lemieux, Bob	Oak.	1	19	0	1	1	12	....	....	....	....	....	....	1967-68	1967-68
Lemieux, Claude	Mtl., N.J., Col., Phx., Dal.	20	1197	379	406	785	1756	233	80	78	158	529	4	1983-84	2002-03
Lemieux, Jacques	L.A.	3	19	0	4	4	8	1	0	0	0	0	....	1967-68	1969-70
Lemieux, Jean	Atl., Wsh.	5	204	23	63	86	39	3	1	1	2	0	....	1973-74	1977-78
Lemieux, Jocelyn	St.L., Mtl., Chi., Hfd., N.J., Cgy., Phx.	12	598	80	84	164	740	60	5	10	15	88	....	1986-87	1997-98
• Lemieux, Real	Det., L.A., NYR, Buf.	8	456	51	104	155	262	18	2	4	6	10	....	1966-67	1973-74
Lemieux, Rich	Van., K.C., Atl.	5	274	39	82	121	132	2	0	0	0	0	....	1971-72	1975-76
Lenardon, Tim	N.J., Van.	2	15	2	1	3	4	....	....	....	....	....	....	1986-87	1989-90
• Lepine, Hec	Mtl.	1	33	5	2	7	2	....	....	....	....	....	....	1925-26	1925-26
• Lepine, Pit	Mtl.	13	526	143	98	241	392	41	7	5	12	26	2	1925-26	1937-38
Leroux, Francois	Edm., Ott., Pit., Col.	10	249	3	20	23	577	33	1	3	4	34	....	1988-89	1997-98
Leroux, Gaston	Mtl.	1	2	0	0	0	0	....	....	....	....	....	....	1935-36	1935-36
Leroux, Jean-Yves	Chi.	5	220	16	22	38	146	....	....	....	....	....	....	1996-97	2000-01
Leschyshyn, Curtis	Que., Col., Wsh., Hfd., Car., Min., Ott.	16	1033	47	165	212	669	68	2	6	8	34	1	1988-89	2003-04
Lesieur, Art	Mtl., Chi.	4	100	4	2	6	50	14	0	0	0	4	1	1928-29	1935-36
Lessard, Rick	Cgy., S.J.	3	15	0	4	4	18	....	....	....	....	....	....	1988-89	1991-92
Lesuk, Bill	Bos., Phi., L.A., Wsh., Wpg.	8	388	44	63	107	368	9	1	0	1	12	1	1968-69	1979-80
• Leswick, Jack	Chi.	1	37	1	7	8	16	....	....	....	....	....	1	1933-34	1933-34
• Leswick, Pete	NYA, Bos.	2	3	1	0	1	0	....	....	....	....	....	....	1936-37	1944-45
• Leswick, Tony	NYR, Det., Chi.	12	740	165	159	324	900	59	13	10	23	91	3	1945-46	1957-58
‡ Letang, Alan	Dal., Cgy., NYI	3	14	0	0	0	2	....	....	....	....	....	....	1999-00	2002-03
• Levandoski, Joe	NYR	1	8	1	1	2	0	....	....	....	....	....	....	1946-47	1946-47
Leveille, Normand	Bos.	2	75	17	25	42	49	....	....	....	....	....	....	1981-82	1982-83
• Leveque, Guy	L.A.	2	17	2	2	4	21	....	....	....	....	....	....	1992-93	1993-94
Lever, Don	Van., Atl., Cgy., Col., N.J., Buf.	15	1020	313	367	680	593	30	7	10	17	26	....	1972-73	1986-87
Levie, Craig	Wpg., Min., St.L., Van.	6	183	22	53	75	177	16	2	3	5	32	....	1981-82	1986-87
Levins, Scott	Wpg., Fla., Ott., Phx.	5	124	13	20	33	316	....	....	....	....	....	....	1992-93	1997-98
• Levinsky, Alex	Tor., NYR, Chi.	9	367	19	49	68	307	37	2	1	3	26	2	1930-31	1938-39
Levo, Tapio	Col., N.J.	2	107	16	53	69	36	....	....	....	....	....	....	1981-82	1982-83
Lewicki, Danny	Tor., NYR, Chi.	9	461	105	135	240	177	28	0	4	4	8	1	1950-51	1958-59
Lewis, Dale	NYR	1	8	0	0	0	0	....	....	....	....	....	....	1975-76	1975-76
Lewis, Dave	NYI, L.A., N.J., Det.	15	1008	36	187	223	953	91	1	20	21	143	....	1973-74	1987-88
• Lewis, Doug	Mtl.	1	3	0	0	0	0	....	....	....	....	....	....	1946-47	1946-47
• Lewis, Herbie	Det.	11	483	148	161	309	248	38	13	10	23	6	2	1928-29	1938-39
Ley, Rick	Tor., Hfd.	6	310	12	72	84	528	14	0	2	2	20	....	1968-69	1980-81
Liba, Igor	NYR, L.A.	1	37	7	18	25	36	2	0	0	0	2	....	1988-89	1988-89
Libby, Jeff	NYI	1	1	0	0	0	0	....	....	....	....	....	....	1997-98	1997-98
Libett, Nick	Det., Pit.	14	982	237	268	505	472	16	6	2	8	2	....	1967-68	1980-81
Licari, Tony	Det.	1	9	0	1	1	0	....	....	....	....	....	....	1946-47	1946-47
Liddington, Bob	Tor.	1	11	0	1	1	2	....	....	....	....	....	....	1970-71	1970-71
Lidster, Doug	Van., NYR, St.L., Dal.	16	897	75	268	343	679	80	6	15	21	64	1	1983-84	1998-99
Lilley, John	Ana.	3	23	3	8	11	13	....	....	....	....	....	....	1993-94	1995-96
‡ Lind, Juha	Dal., Mtl.	3	133	9	13	22	20	15	2	2	4	8	....	1997-98	2000-01
Lindberg, Chris	Cgy., Que.	3	116	17	25	42	47	2	0	1	1	2	....	1991-92	1993-94
Lindbom, Johan	NYR	1	38	1	3	4	28	....	....	....	....	....	....	1997-98	1997-98
Linden, Jamie	Fla.	1	4	0	0	0	17	....	....	....	....	....	....	1994-95	1994-95
Lindgren, Lars	Van., Min.	6	394	25	113	138	325	40	5	6	11	20	....	1978-79	1983-84
Lindgren, Mats	Edm., NYI, Van.	8	387	54	74	128	146	24	1	5	6	10	....	1996-97	2003-04
Lindholm, Mikael	L.A.	1	18	2	2	4	2	....	....	....	....	....	....	1989-90	1989-90
Lindquist, Fredrik	Edm.	1	8	0	0	0	2	....	....	....	....	....	....	1998-99	1998-99
Lindros, Brett	NYI	2	51	2	5	7	147	....	....	....	....	....	....	1994-95	1995-96
‡ Lindsay, Bill	Que., Fla., Cgy., S.J., Mtl., Atl.	13	777	83	141	224	922	42	7	8	15	44	....	1991-92	2003-04
Lindsay, Ted	Det., Chi.	17	1068	379	472	851	1808	133	47	49	96	194	4	1944-45	1964-65
Lindstrom, Willy	Wpg., Edm., Pit.	8	582	161	162	323	200	57	14	18	32	24	2	1979-80	1986-87
‡ Ling, David	Mtl., CBJ	5	93	4	4	8	191	....	....	....	....	....	....	1996-97	2003-04
Linseman, Ken	Phi., Edm., Bos., Tor.	14	860	256	551	807	1727	113	43	77	120	325	1	1978-79	1991-92
‡ Lintner, Richard	Nsh., NYR, Pit.	3	112	8	12	20	54	....	....	....	....	....	....	1999-00	2002-03
Lipuma, Chris	T.B., S.J.	5	72	0	9	9	146	....	....	....	....	....	....	1992-93	1996-97
• Liscombe, Carl	Det.	9	373	137	140	277	117	59	22	19	41	20	1	1937-38	1945-46
Litzenberger, Ed	Mtl., Chi., Det., Tor.	12	618	178	238	416	283	40	5	13	18	34	4	1952-53	1963-64
Loach, Lonnie	Ott., L.A., Ana.	2	56	10	13	23	29	1	0	0	0	0	....	1992-93	1993-94
• Locas, Jacques	Mtl.	2	59	7	8	15	66	....	....	....	....	....	....	1947-48	1948-49
Lochead, Bill	Det., Col., NYR	6	330	69	62	131	180	7	3	0	3	6	....	1974-75	1979-80
• Locking, Norm	Chi.	2	48	2	6	8	26	....	....	....	....	....	....	1934-35	1935-36
Loewen, Darcy	Buf., Ott.	5	135	4	8	12	211	....	....	....	....	....	....	1989-90	1993-94
Lofthouse, Mark	Wsh., Det.	6	181	42	38	80	73	....	....	....	....	....	....	1977-78	1982-83
Logan, Dave	Chi., Van.	6	218	5	29	34	470	12	0	0	0	10	....	1975-76	1980-81
Logan, Robert	Buf., L.A.	3	42	10	5	15	0	....	....	....	....	....	....	1986-87	1988-89
Loiselle, Claude	Det., N.J., Que., Tor., NYI	13	616	92	117	209	1149	41	4	11	15	58	....	1981-82	1993-94
Lomakin, Andrei	Phi., Fla.	4	215	42	62	104	92	....	....	....	....	....	....	1991-92	1994-95
Loney, Brian	Van.	1	12	2	3	5	6	....	....	....	....	....	....	1995-96	1995-96
Loney, Troy	Pit., Ana., NYI, NYR	12	624	87	110	197	1091	67	8	14	22	97	2	1983-84	1994-95
Long, Barry	L.A., Det., Wpg.	5	280	11	68	79	250	5	0	1	1	18	....	1972-73	1981-82
• Long, Stan	Mtl.	1	....	....	....	....	....	3	0	0	0	0	....	1951-52	1951-52
Lonsberry, Ross	Bos., L.A., Phi., Pit.	15	968	256	310	566	806	100	21	25	46	87	2	1966-67	1980-81
Loob, Hakan	Cgy.	6	450	193	236	429	189	73	26	28	54	16	1	1983-84	1988-89
Loob, Peter	Que.	1	8	1	2	3	0	....	....	....	....	....	....	1984-85	1984-85
Lorentz, Jim	Bos., St.L., NYR, Buf.	10	659	161	238	399	208	54	12	10	22	30	1	1968-69	1977-78
Lorimer, Bob	NYI, Col., N.J.	10	529	22	90	112	431	49	3	10	13	83	2	1976-77	1985-86
• Lorrain, Rod	Mtl.	6	179	28	39	67	30	11	0	3	3	0	....	1935-36	1941-42
• Loughlin, Clem	Det., Chi.	3	101	8	6	14	77	....	....	....	....	....	....	1926-27	1928-29
• Loughlin, Wilf	Tor.	1	14	0	0	0	2	....	....	....	....	....	....	1923-24	1923-24
Lovsin, Ken	Wsh.	1	1	0	0	0	0	....	....	....	....	....	....	1990-91	1990-91
Lowdermilk, Dwayne	Wsh.	1	2	0	1	1	2	....	....	....	....	....	....	1980-81	1980-81
Lowe, Darren	Pit.	1	8	1	2	3	0	....	....	....	....	....	....	1983-84	1983-84
Lowe, Kevin	Edm., NYR	19	1254	84	347	431	1498	214	10	48	58	192	6	1979-80	1997-98
Lowe, Odie	NYR	1	4	1	1	2	0	....	....	....	....	....	....	1949-50	1949-50
• Lowe, Ross	Bos., Mtl.	3	77	6	8	14	82	2	0	0	0	0	....	1949-50	1951-52
• Lowrey, Ed	Ott., Ham.	3	27	2	2	4	6	....	....	....	....	....	....	1917-18	1920-21
• Lowrey, Fred	Mtl.M., Pit.	2	53	1	1	2	10	2	0	0	0	6	....	1924-25	1925-26
• Lowrey, Gerry	Tor., Pit., Phi., Chi., Ott.	6	211	48	48	96	148	2	1	0	1	2	....	1927-28	1932-33
Lowry, Dave	Van., St.L., Fla., S.J., Cgy.	19	1084	164	187	351	1191	111	16	20	36	181	....	1985-86	2003-04
Lucas, Danny	Phi.	1	6	1	0	1	0	....	....	....	....	....	....	1978-79	1978-79
Lucas, Dave	Det.	1	1	0	0	0	0	....	....	....	....	....	....	1962-63	1962-63
Luce, Don	NYR, Det., Buf., L.A., Tor.	13	894	225	329	554	364	71	17	22	39	52	....	1969-70	1981-82
Ludvig, Jan	N.J., Buf.	7	314	54	87	141	418	....	....	....	....	....	....	1982-83	1988-89
Ludwig, Craig	Mtl., NYI, Min., Dal.	17	1256	38	184	222	1437	177	4	25	29	244	2	1982-83	1998-99
Ludzik, Steve	Chi., Buf.	9	424	46	93	139	333	44	4	8	12	70	....	1981-82	1989-90
Luhning, Warren	NYI, Dal.	3	29	0	1	1	21	....	....	....	....	....	....	1997-98	1999-00
Lukowich, Bernie	Pit., St.L.	2	79	13	15	28	34	2	0	0	0	0	....	1973-74	1974-75
Lukowich, Morris	Wpg., Bos., L.A.	8	582	199	219	418	584	11	0	2	2	24	....	1979-80	1986-87
Luksa, Charlie	Hfd.	1	8	0	1	1	4	....	....	....	....	....	....	1979-80	1979-80
Lumley, Dave	Mtl., Edm., Hfd.	9	437	98	160	258	680	61	6	8	14	131	2	1978-79	1986-87
Lumme, Jyrki	Mtl., Van., Phx., Dal., Tor.	15	985	114	354	468	620	105	9	35	44	52	....	1988-89	2002-03
Lund, Pentti	Bos., NYR	7	259	44	55	99	40	19	7	5	12	0	....	1946-47	1952-53
Lundberg, Brian	Pit.	1	1	0	0	0	2	....	....	....	....	....	....	1982-83	1982-83
Lunde, Len	Det., Chi., Min., Van.	8	321	39	83	122	75	20	3	2	5	2	....	1958-59	1970-71
Lundholm, Bengt	Wpg.	5	275	48	95	143	72	14	3	4	7	14	....	1981-82	1985-86
Lundrigan, Joe	Tor., Wsh.	2	52	2	8	10	22	....	....	....	....	....	....	1972-73	1974-75
Lundstrom, Tord	Det.	1	11	1	1	2	0	....	....	....	....	....	....	1973-74	1973-74
• Lundy, Pat	Det., Chi.	5	150	37	32	69	31	16	2	2	4	2	....	1945-46	1950-51
‡ Luoma, Mikko	Edm.	1	3	0	1	1	0	....	....	....	....	....	....	2003-04	2003-04
Luongo, Chris	Det., Ott.; NYI	5	218	8	23	31	176	....	....	....	....	....	....	1990-91	1995-96
Lupien, Gilles	Mtl., Pit., Hfd.	5	226	5	25	30	416	25	0	0	0	21	2	1977-78	1981-82
Lupul, Gary	Van.	7	293	70	75	145	243	25	4	7	11	11	....	1979-80	1985-86
• Lyashenko, Roman	Dal., NYR	4	139	14	9	23	55	17	2	1	3	0	....	1999-00	2002-03

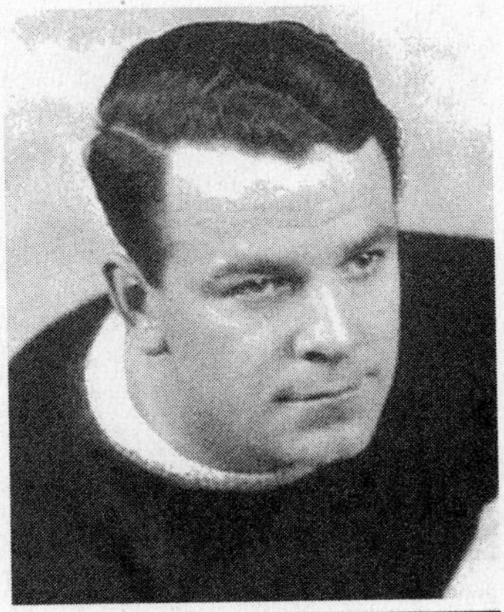
Albert Leduc

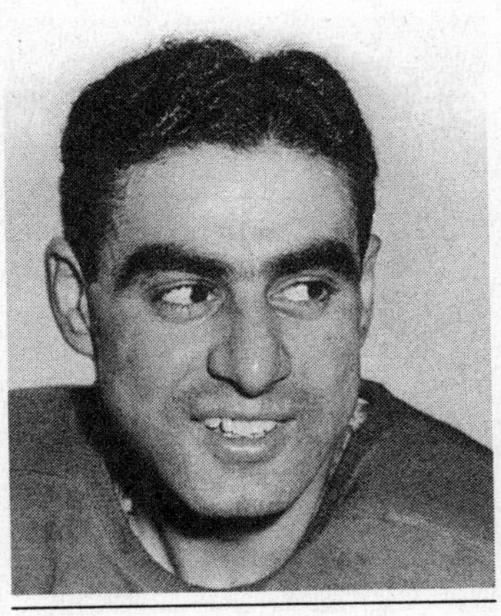
Tony Licari

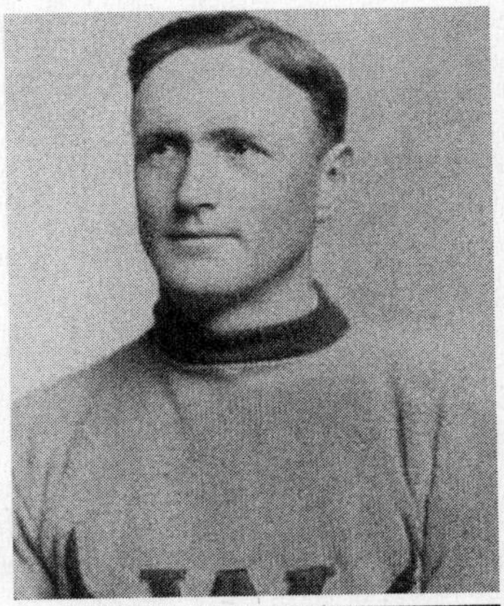
Clem Loughlin

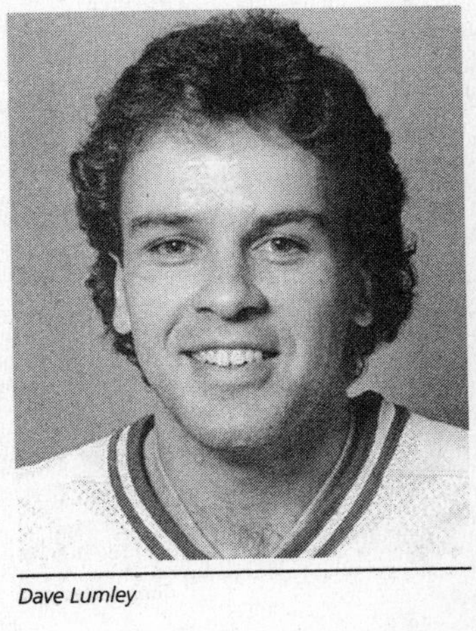
Dave Lumley

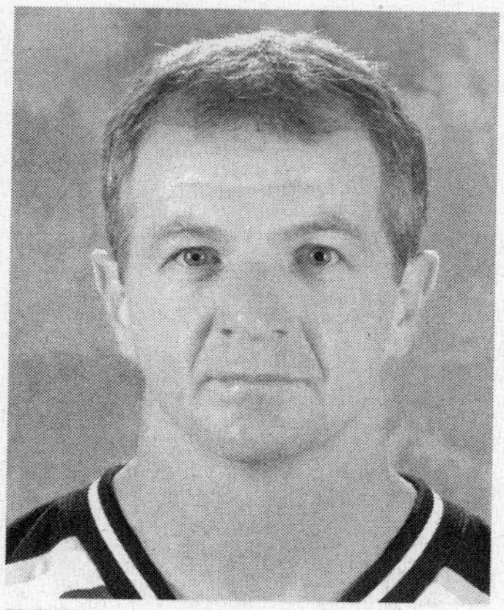
Al MacInnis

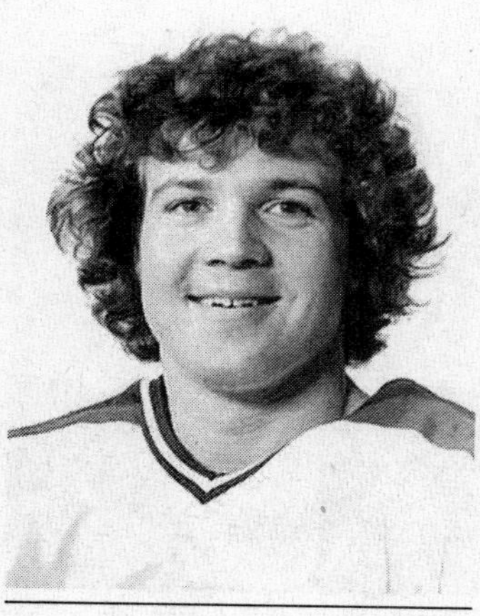
Don MacIver

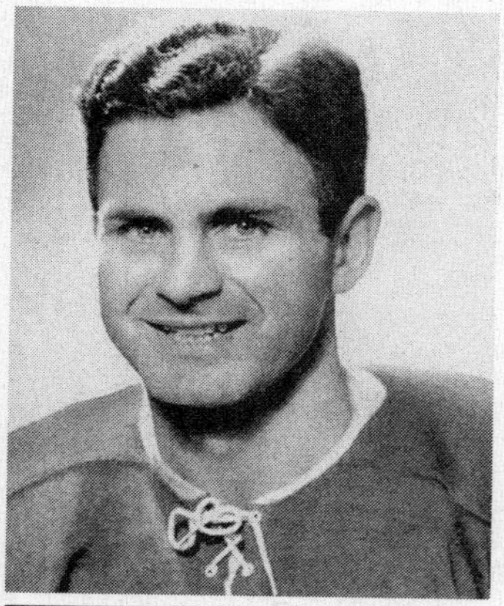
Murdo MacKay

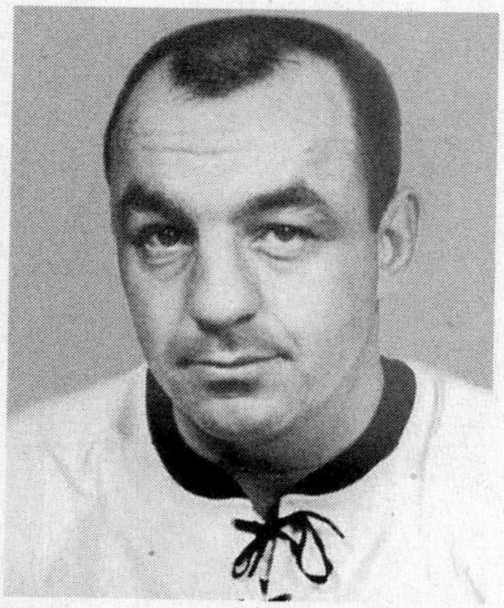
Connie Madigan

Name	NHL Teams	NHL Seasons	Regular Schedule					Playoffs					NHL Cup Wins	First NHL Season	Last NHL Season
			GP	G	A	TP	PIM	GP	G	A	TP	PIM			
Lyle, George	Det., Hfd.	4	99	24	38	62	51	....	....	....	....	....	....	1979-80	1982-83
Lynch, Jack	Pit., Det., Wsh.	7	382	24	106	130	336	....	....	....	....	....	....	1972-73	1978-79
Lynn, Vic	NYR, Det., Mtl., Tor., Bos., Chi.	11	327	49	76	125	274	47	7	10	17	46	3	1942-43	1953-54
Lyon, Steve	Pit.	1	3	0	0	0	2	....	....	....	....	....	....	1976-77	1976-77
Lyons, Ron	Bos., Phi.	1	36	2	4	6	27	5	0	0	0	0	....	1930-31	1930-31
Lysiak, Tom	Atl., Chi.	13	919	292	551	843	567	76	25	38	63	49	....	1973-74	1985-86
M															
MacAdam, Al	Phi., Cal., Cle., Min., Van.	12	864	240	351	591	509	64	20	24	44	21	1	1973-74	1984-85
MacDermid, Paul	Hfd., Wpg., Wsh., Que.	14	690	116	142	258	1303	43	5	11	16	116	....	1981-82	1994-95
MacDonald, Blair	Edm., Van.	4	219	91	100	191	65	11	0	6	6	2	....	1979-80	1982-83
MacDonald, Brett	Van.	1	1	0	0	0	0	....	....	....	....	....	....	1987-88	1987-88
MacDonald, Doug	Buf.	3	11	1	0	1	2	....	....	....	....	....	....	1992-93	1994-95
MacDonald, Kevin	Ott.	1	1	0	0	0	2	....	....	....	....	....	....	1993-94	1993-94
• MacDonald, Kilby	NYR	4	151	36	34	70	47	15	1	2	3	4	1	1939-40	1944-45
MacDonald, Lowell	Det., L.A., Pit.	13	506	180	210	390	92	30	11	11	22	12	....	1961-62	1977-78
MacDonald, Parker	Tor., NYR, Det., Bos., Min.	14	676	144	179	323	253	75	14	14	28	20	....	1952-53	1968-69
MacDougall, Kim	Min.	1	1	0	0	0	0	....	....	....	....	....	....	1974-75	1974-75
MacEachern, Shane	St.L.	1	1	0	0	0	0	....	....	....	....	....	....	1987-88	1987-88
Macey, Hub	NYR, Mtl.	3	30	6	9	15	0	8	0	0	0	0	....	1941-42	1946-47
MacGregor, Bruce	Det., NYR	14	893	213	257	470	217	107	19	28	47	44	....	1960-61	1973-74
MacGregor, Randy	Hfd.	1	2	1	1	2	2	....	....	....	....	....	....	1981-82	1981-82
MacGuigan, Garth	NYI	2	5	0	1	1	2	....	....	....	....	....	....	1979-80	1983-84
MacInnis, Al	Cgy., St.L.	23	1416	340	934	1274	1511	177	39	121	160	255	1	1981-82	2003-04
MacIntosh, Ian	NYR	1	4	0	0	0	4	....	....	....	....	....	....	1952-53	1952-53
MacIver, Don	Wpg.	1	6	0	0	0	2	....	....	....	....	....	....	1979-80	1979-80
MacIver, Norm	NYR, Hfd., Edm., Ott., Pit., Wpg., Phx.	12	500	55	230	285	350	56	3	11	14	32	....	1986-87	1997-98
MacKasey, Blair	Tor.	1	1	0	0	0	2	....	....	....	....	....	....	1976-77	1976-77
• MacKay, Calum	Det., Mtl.	8	237	50	55	105	214	38	5	13	18	20	1	1946-47	1954-55
MacKay, Dave	Chi.	1	29	3	0	3	26	5	0	1	1	2	....	1940-41	1940-41
• MacKay, Mickey	Chi., Pit., Bos.	4	147	44	19	63	79	11	0	0	0	6	1	1926-27	1929-30
• MacKay, Murdo	Mtl.	4	19	0	3	3	0	15	1	2	3	0	....	1945-46	1948-49
MacKell, Fleming	Tor., Bos.	13	665	149	220	369	562	80	22	41	63	75	2	1947-48	1959-60
• MacKell, Jack	Ott.	2	45	4	2	6	59	2	0	0	0	0	2	1919-20	1920-21
MacKenzie, Barry	Min.	1	6	0	1	1	6	....	....	....	....	....	....	1968-69	1968-69
• MacKenzie, Bill	Chi., Mtl.M., NYR, Mtl.	7	264	15	14	29	145	21	1	1	2	11	1	1932-33	1939-40
Mackey, David	Chi., Min., St.L.	6	126	8	12	20	305	3	0	0	0	2	....	1987-88	1993-94
• Mackey, Reg	NYR	1	34	0	0	0	16	1	0	0	0	0	....	1926-27	1926-27
• Mackie, Howie	Det.	2	20	1	0	1	4	8	0	0	0	0	1	1936-37	1937-38
MacKinnon, Paul	Wsh.	5	147	5	23	28	91	....	....	....	....	....	....	1979-80	1983-84
MacLean, John	N.J., S.J., NYR, Dal.	18	1194	413	429	842	1328	104	35	48	83	152	1	1983-84	2001-02
MacLean, Paul	St.L., Wpg., Det.	11	719	324	349	673	968	53	21	14	35	110	....	1980-81	1990-91
MacLeish, Rick	Phi., Hfd., Pit., Det.	14	846	349	410	759	434	114	54	53	107	38	2	1970-71	1983-84
MacLellan, Brian	L.A., NYR, Min., Cgy., Det.	10	606	172	241	413	551	47	5	9	14	42	1	1982-83	1991-92
MacLeod, Pat	Min., S.J., Dal.	4	53	5	13	18	14	....	....	....	....	....	....	1990-91	1995-96
MacMillan, Billy	Tor., Atl., NYI	7	446	74	77	151	184	53	6	6	12	40	....	1970-71	1976-77
MacMillan, Bob	NYR, St.L., Atl., Cgy., Col., N.J., Chi.	11	753	228	349	577	260	31	8	11	19	16	....	1974-75	1984-85
MacMillan, John	Tor., Det.	5	104	5	10	15	32	12	0	1	1	2	2	1960-61	1964-65
MacNeil, Al	Tor., Mtl., Chi., NYR, Pit.	11	524	17	75	92	617	37	0	4	4	67	....	1955-56	1967-68
MacNeil, Bernie	St.L.	1	4	0	0	0	0	....	....	....	....	....	....	1973-74	1973-74
‡ MacNeil, Ian	Phi.	1	2	0	0	0	0	....	....	....	....	....	....	2002-03	2002-03
Macoun, Jamie	Cgy., Tor., Det.	16	1128	76	282	358	1208	159	10	32	42	169	2	1982-83	1998-99
• MacPherson, Bud	Mtl.	7	259	5	33	38	233	29	0	3	3	21	1	1948-49	1956-57
• MacSweyn, Ralph	Phi.	5	47	0	5	5	10	8	0	0	0	6	....	1967-68	1971-72
MacTavish, Craig	Bos., Edm., NYR, Phi., St.L.	17	1093	213	267	480	891	193	20	38	58	218	4	1979-80	1996-97
MacWilliam, Mike	NYI	1	6	0	0	0	14	....	....	....	....	....	....	1995-96	1995-96
Madigan, Connie	St.L.	1	20	0	3	3	25	5	0	0	0	4	....	1972-73	1972-73
Madill, Jeff	N.J.	1	14	4	0	4	46	7	0	2	2	8	....	1990-91	1990-91
Magee, Dean	Min.	1	7	0	0	0	4	....	....	....	....	....	....	1977-78	1977-78
Maggs, Daryl	Chi., Cal., Tor.	3	135	14	19	33	54	4	0	0	0	0	....	1971-72	1979-80
Magnan, Marc	Tor.	1	4	0	1	1	5	....	....	....	....	....	....	1982-83	1982-83
• Magnuson, Keith	Chi.	11	589	14	125	139	1442	68	3	9	12	164	....	1969-70	1979-80
Maguire, Kevin	Tor., Buf., Phi.	6	260	29	30	59	782	11	0	0	0	86	....	1986-87	1991-92
Mahaffy, John	Mtl., NYR	3	37	11	25	36	4	1	0	1	1	0	....	1942-43	1944-45
Mahovlich, Frank	Tor., Det., Mtl.	18	1181	533	570	1103	1056	137	51	67	118	163	6	1956-57	1973-74
Mahovlich, Pete	Det., Mtl., Pit.	16	884	288	485	773	916	88	30	42	72	134	4	1965-66	1980-81
Mailhot, Jacques	Que.	1	5	0	0	0	33	....	....	....	....	....	....	1988-89	1988-89
Mailley, Frank	Mtl.	1	1	0	0	0	0	....	....	....	....	....	....	1942-43	1942-43
Mair, Jim	Phi., NYI, Van.	5	76	4	15	19	49	3	1	2	3	4	....	1970-71	1974-75
• Majeau, Fern	Mtl.	2	56	22	24	46	43	1	0	0	0	0	1	1943-44	1944-45
Major, Bruce	Que.	1	4	0	0	0	0	....	....	....	....	....	....	1990-91	1990-91
Major, Mark	Det.	1	2	0	0	0	5	....	....	....	....	....	....	1996-97	1996-97
Makarov, Sergei	Cgy., S.J., Dal.	7	424	134	250	384	317	34	12	11	23	8	....	1989-90	1996-97
Makela, Mikko	NYI, L.A., Buf., Bos.	7	423	118	147	265	139	18	3	8	11	14	....	1985-86	1994-95
Maki, Chico	Chi.	15	841	143	292	435	345	113	17	36	53	43	1	1960-61	1975-76
• Maki, Wayne	Chi., St.L., Van.	6	246	57	79	136	184	2	1	0	1	2	....	1967-68	1972-73
Makkonen, Kari	Edm.	1	9	2	2	4	0	....	....	....	....	....	....	1979-80	1979-80
Maley, David	Mtl., N.J., Edm., S.J., NYI	9	466	43	81	124	1043	46	5	5	10	111	1	1985-86	1993-94
Malgunas, Stewart	Phi., Wpg., Wsh., Cgy.	7	129	1	5	6	144	....	....	....	....	....	....	1993-94	1999-00
Malinowski, Merlin	Col., N.J., Hfd.	5	282	54	111	165	121	....	....	....	....	....	....	1978-79	1982-83
Malkoc, Dean	Van., Bos., NYI	4	116	1	3	4	299	....	....	....	....	....	....	1995-96	1998-99
Mallette, Troy	NYR, Edm., N.J., Ott., Bos., T.B.	9	456	51	68	119	1226	15	2	2	4	99	....	1989-90	1997-98
Malone, Cliff	Mtl.	1	3	0	0	0	0	....	....	....	....	....	....	1951-52	1951-52
Malone, Greg	Pit., Hfd., Que.	11	704	191	310	501	661	20	3	5	8	32	....	1976-77	1986-87
• Malone, Joe	Mtl., Que., Ham.	7	126	143	32	175	57	9	6	2	8	6	1	1917-18	1923-24
Maloney, Dan	Chi., L.A., Det., Tor.	11	737	192	259	451	1489	40	4	7	11	35	....	1970-71	1981-82
Maloney, Dave	NYR, Buf.	11	657	71	246	317	1154	49	7	17	24	91	....	1974-75	1984-85
Maloney, Don	NYR, Hfd., NYI	13	765	214	350	564	815	94	22	35	57	101	....	1978-79	1990-91
Maloney, Phil	Bos., Tor., Chi.	5	158	28	43	71	16	6	0	0	0	0	....	1949-50	1959-60
Maltais, Steve	Wsh., Min., T.B., Det., CBJ	6	120	9	18	27	53	1	0	0	0	0	....	1989-90	2000-01
Maluta, Ray	Bos.	2	25	2	3	5	6	2	0	0	0	0	....	1975-76	1976-77
Manastersky, Tom	Mtl.	1	6	0	0	0	11	....	....	....	....	....	....	1950-51	1950-51
• Mancuso, Gus	Mtl., NYR	4	42	7	9	16	17	....	....	....	....	....	....	1937-38	1942-43
‡ Manderville, Kent	Tor., Edm., Hfd., Car., Phi., Pit.	12	646	37	67	104	348	67	3	3	6	44	....	1991-92	2002-03
Mandich, Dan	Min.	4	111	5	11	16	303	7	0	0	0	2	....	1982-83	1985-86
‡ Maneluk, Mike	Phi., Chi., NYR, CBJ	3	85	11	10	21	57	....	....	....	....	....	....	1998-99	2000-01
Manery, Kris	Cle., Min., Van., Wpg.	4	250	63	64	127	91	....	....	....	....	....	....	1977-78	1980-81
Manery, Randy	Det., Atl., L.A.	10	582	50	206	256	415	13	0	2	2	12	....	1970-71	1979-80
‡ Mann, Cameron	Bos., Nsh.	5	93	14	10	24	40	1	0	0	0	0	....	1997-98	2002-03
Mann, Jack	NYR	2	9	3	4	7	0	....	....	....	....	....	....	1943-44	1944-45
Mann, Jimmy	Wpg., Que., Pit.	8	293	10	20	30	895	22	0	0	0	89	....	1979-80	1987-88
Mann, Ken	Det.	1	1	0	0	0	0	....	....	....	....	....	....	1975-76	1975-76
• Mann, Norm	Tor.	3	31	0	3	3	4	2	0	0	0	0	....	1935-36	1940-41
• Manners, Rennison	Pit., Phi.	2	37	3	2	5	14	....	....	....	....	....	....	1929-30	1930-31
Manno, Bob	Van., Tor., Det.	8	371	41	131	172	274	17	2	4	6	12	....	1976-77	1984-85
Manson, Dave	Chi., Edm., Wpg., Phx., Mtl., Dal., Tor.	16	1103	102	288	390	2792	112	7	24	31	343	....	1986-87	2001-02
Manson, Ray	Bos., NYR	2	2	0	1	1	0	....	....	....	....	....	....	1947-48	1948-49
• Mantha, Georges	Mtl.	13	488	89	102	191	148	36	6	2	8	24	2	1928-29	1940-41
Mantha, Moe	Wpg., Pit., Edm., Min., Phi.	12	656	81	289	370	501	17	5	10	15	18	....	1980-81	1991-92
• Mantha, Sylvio	Mtl., Bos.	14	542	63	78	141	671	39	5	5	10	64	3	1923-24	1936-37
• Maracle, Bud	NYR	1	11	1	3	4	4	4	0	0	0	0	....	1930-31	1930-31
Marcetta, Milan	Tor., Min.	3	54	7	15	22	10	17	7	7	14	4	1	1966-67	1968-69
• March, Mush	Chi.	17	759	153	230	383	540	45	12	15	27	41	2	1928-29	1944-45
Marchinko, Brian	Tor., NYI	4	47	2	6	8	0	....	....	....	....	....	....	1970-71	1973-74
Marcinyshyn, Dave	N.J., Que., NYR	3	16	0	1	1	49	....	....	....	....	....	....	1990-91	1992-93
Marcon, Lou	Det.	3	60	0	4	4	42	....	....	....	....	....	....	1958-59	1962-63
Marcotte, Don	Bos.	15	868	230	254	484	317	132	34	27	61	81	2	1965-66	1981-82
‡ Marha, Josef	Col., Ana., Chi.	6	159	21	32	53	32	....	....	....	....	....	....	1995-96	2000-01
Marini, Hector	NYI, N.J.	5	154	27	46	73	246	10	3	6	9	14	2	1978-79	1983-84
Marinucci, Chris	NYI, L.A.	2	13	1	4	5	2	....	....	....	....	....	....	1994-95	1996-97
• Mario, Frank	Bos.	2	53	9	19	28	24	....	....	....	....	....	....	1941-42	1944-45
• Mariucci, John	Chi.	5	223	11	34	45	308	12	0	3	3	26	....	1940-41	1947-48
Mark, Gordon	N.J., Edm.	4	85	3	10	13	187	....	....	....	....	....	....	1986-87	1994-95

			Regular Schedule					Playoffs					NHL	First	Last
Name	NHL Teams	NHL Seasons	GP	G	A	TP	PIM	GP	G	A	TP	PIM	Cup Wins	NHL Season	NHL Season
Markell, John	Wpg., St.L., Min.	4	55	11	10	21	36	....	....	....	....	....	....	1979-80	1984-85
• Marker, Gus	Det., Mtl.M., Tor., Bro.	10	322	64	69	133	133	46	5	7	12	36	1	1932-33	1941-42
Markham, Ray	NYR	1	14	1	1	2	21	7	1	0	1	24	....	1979-80	1979-80
• Markle, Jack	Tor.	1	8	0	1	1	0	....	....	....	....	....	....	1935-36	1935-36
• Marks, Jack	Mtl.W., Tor., Que.	2	7	0	0	0	4	....	....	....	....	....	1	1917-18	1919-20
Marks, John	Chi.	10	657	112	163	275	330	57	5	9	14	60	....	1972-73	1981-82
Markwart, Nevin	Bos., Cgy.	8	309	41	68	109	794	19	1	0	1	33	....	1983-84	1991-92
Marois, Daniel	Tor., NYI, Bos., Dal.	8	350	117	93	210	419	19	3	3	6	28	....	1987-88	1995-96
Marois, Mario	NYR, Van., Que., Wpg., St.L.	15	955	76	357	433	1746	100	4	34	38	182	....	1977-78	1991-92
• Marotte, Gilles	Bos., Chi., L.A., NYR, St.L.	12	808	56	265	321	919	29	3	3	6	26	....	1965-66	1976-77
Marquess, Mark	Bos.	1	27	5	4	9	6	4	0	0	0	0	....	1946-47	1946-47
Marsh, Brad	Atl., Cgy., Phi., Tor., Det., Ott.	15	1086	23	175	198	1241	97	6	18	24	124	....	1978-79	1992-93
Marsh, Gary	Det., Tor.	2	7	1	3	4	4	....	....	....	....	....	....	1967-68	1968-69
Marsh, Peter	Wpg., Chi.	5	278	48	71	119	224	26	1	5	6	33	....	1979-80	1983-84
Marshall, Bert	Det., Oak., Cal., NYR, NYI	14	868	17	181	198	926	72	4	22	26	99	....	1965-66	1978-79
Marshall, Don	Mtl., NYR, Buf., Tor.	19	1176	265	324	589	127	94	8	15	23	14	5	1951-52	1971-72
Marshall, Paul	Pit., Tor., Hfd.	4	95	15	18	33	17	1	0	0	0	0	....	1979-80	1982-83
Marshall, Willie	Tor.	4	33	1	5	6	2	....	....	....	....	....	....	1952-53	1958-59
Marson, Mike	Wsh., L.A.	6	196	24	24	48	233	....	....	....	....	....	....	1974-75	1979-80
• Martin, Clare	Bos., Det., Chi., NYR	6	237	12	28	40	78	27	0	2	2	6	1	1941-42	1951-52
Martin, Craig	Wpg., Fla.	2	21	0	1	1	24	....	....	....	....	....	....	1994-95	1996-97
Martin, Frank	Bos., Chi.	6	282	11	46	57	122	10	0	2	2	2	....	1952-53	1957-58
Martin, Grant	Van., Wsh.	4	44	0	4	4	55	1	1	0	1	2	....	1983-84	1986-87
Martin, Jack	Tor.	1	1	0	0	0	0	....	....	....	....	....	....	1960-61	1960-61
Martin, Matt	Tor.	4	76	0	5	5	71	....	....	....	....	....	....	1993-94	1996-97
Martin, Pit	Det., Bos., Chi., Van.	17	1101	324	485	809	609	100	27	31	58	56	....	1961-62	1978-79
Martin, Rick	Buf., L.A.	11	685	384	317	701	477	63	24	29	53	74	....	1971-72	1981-82
• Martin, Ron	NYA	2	94	13	16	29	36	....	....	....	....	....	....	1932-33	1933-34
Martin, Terry	Buf., Que., Tor., Edm., Min.	10	479	104	101	205	202	21	4	2	6	26	....	1975-76	1984-85
Martin, Tom	Tor.	1	3	1	0	1	0	....	....	....	....	....	....	1967-68	1967-68
Martin, Tom	Wpg., Hfd., Min.	6	92	12	11	23	249	4	0	0	0	6	....	1984-85	1989-90
Martineau, Don	Atl., Min., Det.	4	90	6	10	16	63	....	....	....	....	....	....	1973-74	1976-77
Martini, Darcy	Edm.	1	2	0	0	0	0	....	....	....	....	....	....	1993-94	1993-94
Martinson, Steve	Det., Mtl., Min.	4	49	2	1	3	244	1	0	0	0	10	....	1987-88	1991-92
Maruk, Dennis	Cal., Cle., Min., Wsh.	14	888	356	522	878	761	34	14	22	36	26	....	1975-76	1988-89
Masnick, Paul	Mtl., Chi., Tor.	6	232	18	41	59	139	33	4	5	9	27	1	1950-51	1957-58
• Mason, Charley	NYR, NYA, Det., Chi.	4	95	7	18	25	44	4	0	1	1	0	....	1934-35	1938-39
• Massecar, George	NYA	3	100	12	11	23	46	....	....	....	....	....	....	1929-30	1931-32
Masters, Jamie	St.L.	3	33	1	13	14	2	2	0	0	0	0	....	1975-76	1978-79
• Masterton, Bill	Min.	1	38	4	8	12	4	....	....	....	....	....	....	1967-68	1967-68
• Mathers, Frank	Tor.	3	23	1	3	4	4	....	....	....	....	....	....	1948-49	1951-52
Mathiasen, Dwight	Pit.	3	33	1	7	8	18	....	....	....	....	....	....	1985-86	1987-88
Mathieson, Jim	Wsh.	1	2	0	0	0	4	....	....	....	....	....	....	1989-90	1989-90
‡ Mathieu, Marquis	Bos.	3	16	0	2	2	14	....	....	....	....	....	....	1998-99	2000-01
Matte, Christian	Col., Min.	5	25	2	3	5	12	....	....	....	....	....	....	1996-97	2000-01
• Matte, Joe	Tor., Ham., Bos., Mtl.	4	68	17	15	32	54	....	....	....	....	....	....	1919-20	1925-26
• Matte, Joe	Det., Chi.	2	24	0	3	3	8	....	....	....	....	....	....	1929-30	1942-43
Matteau, Stephane	Cgy., Chi., NYR, St.L., S.J., Fla.	13	848	144	172	316	742	109	12	22	34	80	1	1990-91	2002-03
Matteucci, Mike	Min.	2	6	0	0	0	4	....	....	....	....	....	....	2000-01	2001-02
Mattiussi, Dick	Pit., Oak., Cal.	4	200	8	31	39	124	8	0	1	1	6	....	1967-68	1970-71
• Matz, Johnny	Mtl.	1	30	2	3	5	0	1	0	0	0	0	....	1924-25	1924-25
Maxner, Wayne	Bos.	2	62	8	9	17	48	....	....	....	....	....	....	1964-65	1965-66
Maxwell, Brad	Min., Que., Tor., Van., NYR	10	612	98	270	368	1292	79	12	49	61	178	....	1977-78	1986-87
Maxwell, Bryan	Min., St.L., Wpg., Pit.	8	331	18	77	95	745	15	1	1	2	86	....	1977-78	1984-85
Maxwell, Kevin	Min., Col., N.J.	3	66	6	15	21	61	16	3	4	7	24	....	1980-81	1983-84
Maxwell, Wally	Tor.	1	2	0	0	0	0	....	....	....	....	....	....	1952-53	1952-53
May, Alan	Bos., Edm., Wsh., Dal., Cgy.	8	393	31	45	76	1348	40	1	2	3	80	....	1987-88	1994-95
Mayer, Derek	Ott.	1	17	2	2	4	8	....	....	....	....	....	....	1993-94	1993-94
Mayer, Jim	NYR	1	4	0	0	0	0	....	....	....	....	....	....	1979-80	1979-80
Mayer, Pat	Pit.	1	1	0	0	0	4	....	....	....	....	....	....	1987-88	1987-88
• Mayer, Shep	Tor.	1	12	1	2	3	4	....	....	....	....	....	....	1942-43	1942-43
• Mazur, Eddie	Mtl., Chi.	6	107	8	20	28	120	25	4	5	9	22	1	1950-51	1956-57
Mazur, Jay	Van.	4	47	11	7	18	20	6	0	1	1	8	....	1988-89	1991-92
McAdam, Gary	Buf., Pit., Det., Cgy., Wsh., N.J., Tor.	11	534	96	132	228	243	30	6	5	11	16	....	1975-76	1985-86
• McAdam, Sam	NYR	1	5	0	0	0	0	....	....	....	....	....	....	1930-31	1930-31
McAlpine, Chris	N.J., St.L., T.B., Atl., Chi., L.A.	8	289	6	24	30	245	28	0	1	1	18	1	1994-95	2002-03
• McAndrew, Hazen	Bro.	1	7	0	1	1	6	....	....	....	....	....	....	1941-42	1941-42
McAneeley, Ted	Cal.	3	158	8	35	43	141	....	....	....	....	....	....	1972-73	1974-75
McAtee, Jud	Det.	3	46	15	13	28	6	14	2	1	3	0	....	1942-43	1944-45
McAtee, Norm	Bos.	1	13	0	1	1	0	....	....	....	....	....	....	1946-47	1946-47
• McAvoy, George	Mtl.	1	....	....	....	....	....	4	0	0	0	0	....	1954-55	1954-55
McBain, Andrew	Wpg., Pit., Van., Ott.	11	608	129	172	301	633	24	5	7	12	39	....	1983-84	1993-94
McBain, Jason	Hfd.	2	9	0	0	0	0	....	....	....	....	....	....	1995-96	1996-97
‡ McBain, Mike	T.B.	2	64	0	7	7	22	....	....	....	....	....	....	1997-98	1998-99
McBean, Wayne	L.A., NYI, Wpg.	6	211	10	39	49	168	2	1	1	2	0	....	1987-88	1993-94
McBride, Cliff	Mtl.M., Tor.	2	2	0	0	0	0	....	....	....	....	....	....	1928-29	1929-30
McBurney, Jim	Chi.	1	1	0	1	1	0	....	....	....	....	....	....	1952-53	1952-53
• McCabe, Stan	Det., Mtl.M.	4	78	9	4	13	49	....	....	....	....	....	....	1929-30	1933-34
• McCaffrey, Bert	Tor., Pit., Mtl.	7	260	43	30	73	202	8	2	1	3	10	1	1924-25	1930-31
McCahill, John	Col.	1	1	0	0	0	0	....	....	....	....	....	....	1977-78	1977-78
• McCaig, Doug	Det., Chi.	7	263	8	21	29	255	7	0	1	1	10	....	1941-42	1950-51
• McCallum, Dunc	NYR, Pit.	5	187	14	35	49	230	10	1	2	3	12	....	1965-66	1970-71
• McCalmon, Eddie	Chi., Phi.	2	39	5	0	5	14	....	....	....	....	....	....	1927-28	1930-31
McCann, Rick	Det.	6	43	1	4	5	6	....	....	....	....	....	....	1967-68	1974-75
McCarthy, Dan	NYR	1	5	4	0	4	4	....	....	....	....	....	....	1980-81	1980-81
McCarthy, Kevin	Phi., Van., Pit.	10	537	67	191	258	527	21	2	3	5	20	....	1977-78	1986-87
McCarthy, Sandy	Cgy., T.B., Phi., Car., NYR, Bos.	11	736	72	76	148	1534	23	0	2	2	61	....	1993-94	2003-04
• McCarthy, Thomas	Que., Ham.	2	35	22	7	29	10	....	....	....	....	....	....	1919-20	1920-21
McCarthy, Tom	Det., Bos.	4	60	8	9	17	8	....	....	....	....	....	....	1956-57	1960-61
McCarthy, Tom	Min., Bos.	9	460	178	221	399	330	68	12	26	38	67	....	1979-80	1987-88
• McCartney, Walt	Mtl.	1	2	0	0	0	0	....	....	....	....	....	....	1932-33	1932-33
McCaskill, Ted	Min.	1	4	0	2	2	0	....	....	....	....	....	....	1967-68	1967-68
McClanahan, Rob	Buf., Hfd., NYR	5	224	38	63	101	126	34	4	12	16	31	....	1979-80	1983-84
McCleary, Trent	Ott., Bos., Mtl.	4	192	8	15	23	134	....	....	....	....	....	....	1995-96	1999-00
McClelland, Kevin	Pit., Edm., Det., Tor., Wpg.	12	588	68	112	180	1672	98	11	18	29	281	4	1981-82	1993-94
McCord, Bob	Bos., Det., Min., St.L.	7	316	10	58	68	262	14	2	5	7	10	....	1963-64	1972-73
• McCord, Dennis	Van.	1	3	0	0	0	6	....	....	....	....	....	....	1973-74	1973-74
McCormack, John	Tor., Mtl., Chi.	8	311	25	49	74	35	22	1	1	2	0	2	1947-48	1954-55
McCosh, Shawn	L.A., NYR	2	9	1	0	1	6	....	....	....	....	....	....	1991-92	1994-95
McCourt, Dale	Det., Buf., Tor.	7	532	194	284	478	124	21	9	7	16	6	....	1977-78	1983-84
McCreary, Bill	NYR, Det., Mtl., St.L.	8	309	53	62	115	108	48	6	16	22	14	....	1953-54	1970-71
McCreary, Bill	Tor.	1	12	1	0	1	4	....	....	....	....	....	....	1980-81	1980-81
• McCreary, Keith	Mtl., Pit., Atl.	10	532	131	112	243	294	16	0	4	4	6	....	1961-62	1974-75
• McCreedy, John	Tor.	2	64	17	12	29	25	21	4	3	7	16	2	1941-42	1944-45
McCrimmon, Brad	Bos., Phi., Cgy., Det., Hfd., Phx.	18	1222	81	322	403	1416	116	11	18	29	176	1	1979-80	1996-97
McCrimmon, Jim	St.L.	1	2	0	0	0	0	....	....	....	....	....	....	1974-75	1974-75
McCulley, Bob	Mtl.	1	1	0	0	0	0	....	....	....	....	....	....	1934-35	1934-35
• McCurry, Duke	Pit.	4	148	21	11	32	119	4	0	2	2	2	....	1925-26	1928-29
McCutcheon, Brian	Det.	3	37	3	1	4	7	....	....	....	....	....	....	1974-75	1976-77
McCutcheon, Darwin	Tor.	1	1	0	0	0	2	....	....	....	....	....	....	1981-82	1981-82
McDill, Jeff	Chi.	1	1	0	0	0	0	....	....	....	....	....	....	1976-77	1976-77
McDonagh, Bill	NYR	1	4	0	0	0	2	....	....	....	....	....	....	1949-50	1949-50
McDonald, Ab	Mtl., Chi., Bos., Det., Pit., St.L.	15	762	182	248	430	200	84	21	29	50	42	4	1957-58	1971-72
McDonald, Brian	Chi., Buf.	2	12	0	0	0	29	8	0	0	0	2	....	1967-68	1970-71
• McDonald, Bucko	Det., Tor., NYR	11	446	35	88	123	206	50	6	1	7	24	3	1934-35	1944-45
• McDonald, Butch	Det., Chi.	2	66	8	20	28	2	5	0	2	2	10	....	1939-40	1944-45
McDonald, Gerry	Hfd.	2	8	0	0	0	4	....	....	....	....	....	....	1981-82	1983-84
• McDonald, Jack	Mtl.W., Mtl., Que., Tor.	5	69	26	14	40	30	7	1	3	4	3	....	1917-18	1921-22
McDonald, Jack	NYR	1	43	10	9	19	6	....	....	....	....	....	....	1943-44	1943-44
McDonald, Lanny	Tor., Col., Cgy.	16	1111	500	506	1006	899	117	44	40	84	120	1	1973-74	1988-89
McDonald, Robert	NYR	1	1	0	0	0	0	....	....	....	....	....	....	1943-44	1943-44
McDonald, Terry	K.C.	1	8	0	1	1	6	....	....	....	....	....	....	1975-76	1975-76
McDonnell, Joe	Van., Pit.	3	50	2	10	12	34	....	....	....	....	....	....	1981-82	1985-86
• McDonnell, Moylan	Ham.	1	22	1	2	3	2	....	....	....	....	....	....	1920-21	1920-21
McDonough, Al	L.A., Pit., Atl., Det.	5	237	73	88	161	73	8	0	1	1	2	....	1970-71	1977-78

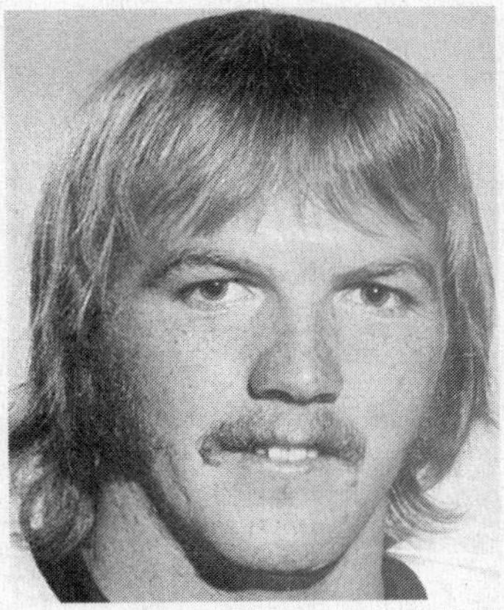

Brian McKenzie

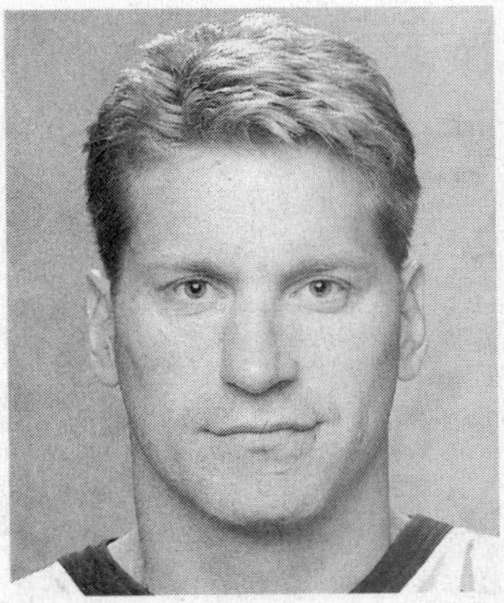

Jim McKenzie

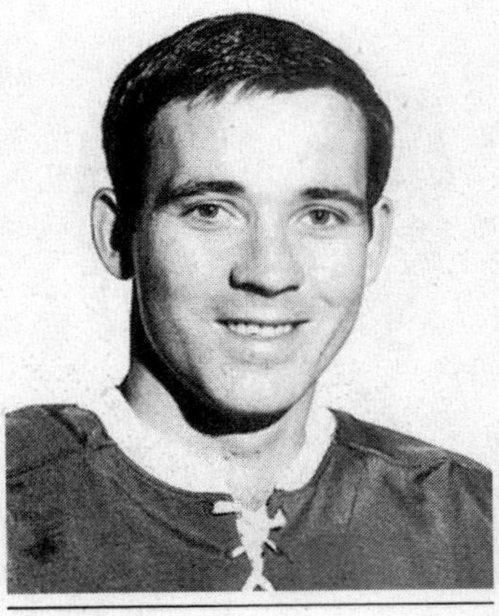

Gerry Meehan

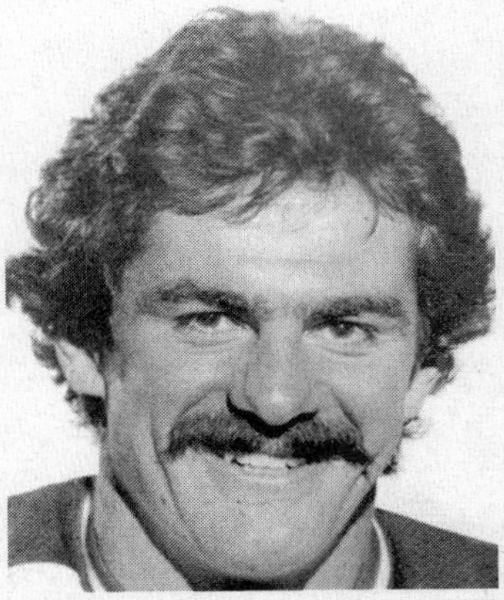

Greg Meredith

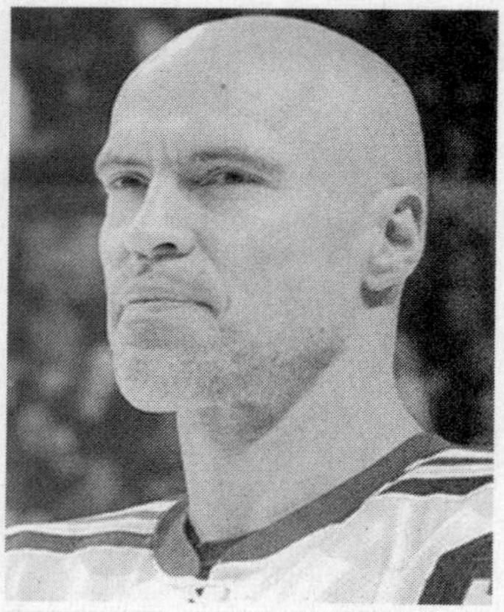
Mark Messier

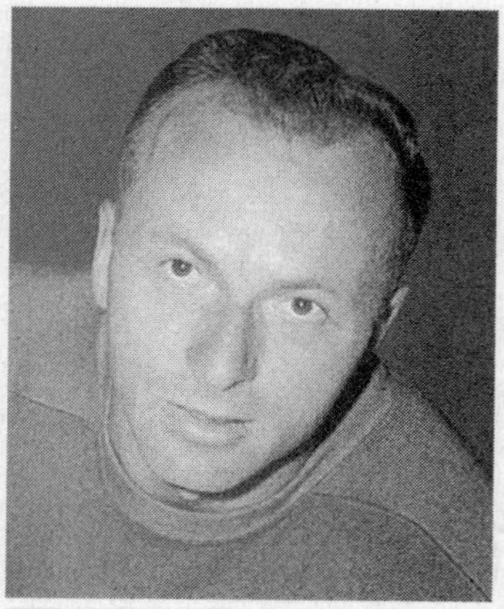
Nick Mickoski

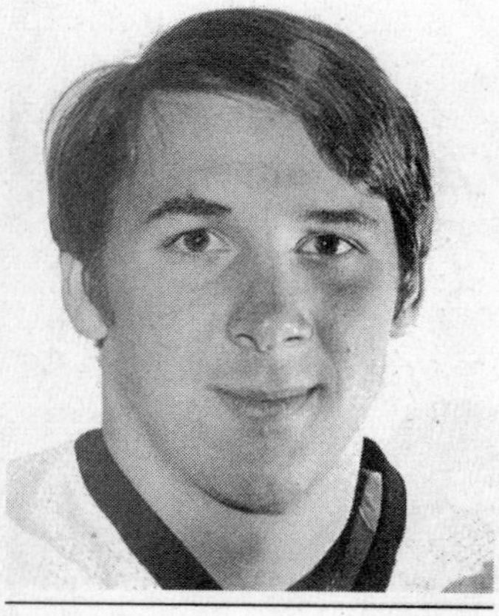
Mike Milbury

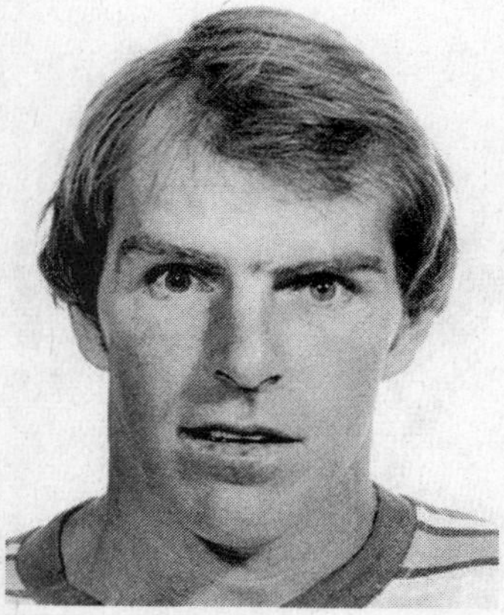
Hartland Monahan

			Regular Schedule					Playoffs							
Name	NHL Teams	NHL Seasons	GP	G	A	TP	PIM	GP	G	A	TP	PIM	NHL Cup Wins	First NHL Season	Last NHL Season
McDonough, Hubie	L.A., NYI, S.J.	5	195	40	26	66	67	5	1	0	1	4	....	1988-89	1992-93
McDougal, Mike	NYR, Hfd.	4	61	8	10	18	43	....	....	....	....	....	....	1978-79	1982-83
McDougall, Bill	Det., Edm., T.B.	3	28	5	5	10	12	1	0	0	0	0	....	1990-91	1993-94
McElmury, Jim	Min., K.C., Col.	5	180	14	47	61	49	....	....	....	....	....	....	1972-73	1977-78
McEwen, Mike	NYR, Col., NYI, L.A., Wsh., Det., Hfd.	12	716	108	296	404	460	78	12	36	48	48	3	1976-77	1987-88
• McFadden, Jim	Det., Chi.	8	412	100	126	226	89	49	10	9	19	30	1	1946-47	1953-54
• McFadyen, Don	Chi.	4	179	12	33	45	77	11	2	2	4	5	1	1932-33	1935-36
McFall, Dan	Wpg.	2	9	0	1	1	0	....	....	....	....	....	....	1984-85	1985-86
• McFarlane, Gord	Chi.	1	2	0	0	0	0	....	....	....	....	....	....	1926-27	1926-27
McGeough, Jim	Wsh., Pit.	4	57	7	10	17	32	....	....	....	....	....	....	1981-82	1986-87
• McGibbon, Irv	Mtl.	1	1	0	0	0	2	....	....	....	....	....	....	1942-43	1942-43
McGill, Bob	Tor., Chi., S.J., Det., NYI, Hfd.	13	705	17	55	72	1766	49	0	0	0	88	....	1981-82	1993-94
• McGill, Jack	Mtl.	3	134	27	10	37	71	3	2	0	2	0	....	1934-35	1936-37
• McGill, Jack	Bos.	4	97	23	36	59	42	27	7	4	11	17	....	1941-42	1946-47
McGill, Ryan	Chi., Phi., Edm.	4	151	4	15	19	391	....	....	....	....	....	....	1991-92	1994-95
McGregor, Sandy	NYR	1	2	0	0	0	2	....	....	....	....	....	....	1963-64	1963-64
• McGuire, Mickey	Pit.	2	36	3	0	3	6	....	....	....	....	....	....	1926-27	1927-28
McHugh, Mike	Min., S.J.	4	20	1	0	1	16	....	....	....	....	....	....	1988-89	1991-92
McIlhargey, Jack	Phi., Van., Hfd.	8	393	11	36	47	1102	27	0	3	3	68	....	1974-75	1981-82
• McInenly, Bert	Det., NYA, Ott., Bos.	6	166	19	15	34	144	4	0	0	0	2	....	1930-31	1935-36
McInnis, Marty	NYI, Cgy., Ana., Bos.	12	796	170	250	420	330	22	3	2	5	4	....	1991-92	2002-03
McIntosh, Bruce	Min.	1	2	0	0	0	0	....	....	....	....	....	....	1972-73	1972-73
McIntosh, Paul	Buf.	2	48	0	2	2	66	2	0	0	0	7	....	1974-75	1975-76
• McIntyre, Jack	Bos., Chi., Det.	11	499	109	102	211	173	29	7	6	13	4	....	1949-50	1959-60
McIntyre, John	Tor., L.A., NYR, Van.	6	351	24	54	78	516	44	0	6	6	54	....	1989-90	1994-95
McIntyre, Larry	Tor.	2	41	0	3	3	26	....	....	....	....	....	....	1969-70	1972-73
McKay, Doug	Det.	1	....	....	....	....	....	1	0	0	0	0	1	1949-50	1949-50
McKay, Randy	Det., N.J., Dal., Mtl.	15	932	162	201	363	1731	123	20	23	43	123	2	1988-89	2002-03
McKay, Ray	Chi., Buf., Cal.	6	140	2	16	18	102	....	....	....	....	....	....	1968-69	1973-74
McKay, Scott	Ana.	1	1	0	0	0	0	....	....	....	....	....	....	1993-94	1993-94
McKechnie, Walt	Min., Cal., Bos., Det., Wsh., Cle., Tor., Col.	16	955	214	392	606	469	15	7	5	12	7	....	1967-68	1982-83
McKee, Mike	Que.	1	48	3	12	15	41	....	....	....	....	....	....	1993-94	1993-94
McKegney, Ian	Chi.	1	3	0	0	0	2	....	....	....	....	....	....	1976-77	1976-77
McKegney, Tony	Buf., Que., Min., NYR, St.L., Det., Chi.	13	912	320	319	639	517	79	24	23	47	56	....	1978-79	1990-91
McKendry, Alex	NYI, Cgy.	4	46	3	6	9	21	6	2	2	4	0	1	1977-78	1980-81
McKenna, Sean	Buf., L.A., Tor.	9	414	82	80	162	181	15	1	2	3	2	....	1981-82	1989-90
McKenna, Steve	L.A., Min., Pit., NYR	8	373	18	14	32	824	3	0	1	1	8	....	1996-97	2003-04
McKenney, Don	Bos., NYR, Tor., Det., St.L.	13	798	237	345	582	211	58	18	29	47	10	1	1954-55	1967-68
McKenny, Jim	Tor., Min.	14	604	82	247	329	294	37	7	9	16	10	....	1965-66	1978-79
McKenzie, Brian	Pit.	1	6	1	1	2	4	....	....	....	....	....	....	1971-72	1971-72
McKenzie, Jim	Hfd., Dal., Pit., Wpg., Phx., Ana., Wsh., N.J., Nsh.	15	880	48	52	100	1739	51	0	0	0	38	1	1989-90	2003-04
McKenzie, John	Chi., Det., NYR, Bos.	12	691	206	268	474	917	69	15	32	47	133	2	1958-59	1971-72
McKim, Andrew	Bos., Det.	3	38	1	4	5	6	....	....	....	....	....	....	1992-93	1994-95
• McKinnon, Alex	Ham., NYA, Chi.	5	193	19	11	30	237	....	....	....	....	....	....	1924-25	1928-29
• McKinnon, John	Mtl., Pit., Phi.	6	208	28	11	39	224	2	0	0	0	4	....	1925-26	1930-31
‡ McLaren, Steve	St.L.	1	6	0	0	0	25	....	....	....	....	....	....	2003-04	2003-04
McLean, Don	Wsh.	1	9	0	0	0	6	....	....	....	....	....	....	1975-76	1975-76
• McLean, Fred	Que., Ham.	2	8	0	0	0	2	....	....	....	....	....	....	1919-20	1920-21
• McLean, Jack	Tor.	3	67	14	24	38	76	13	2	2	4	8	1	1942-43	1944-45
• McLean, Jeff	S.J.	1	6	1	0	1	0	....	....	....	....	....	....	1993-94	1993-94
• McLellan, John	Tor.	1	2	0	0	0	0	....	....	....	....	....	....	1951-52	1951-52
McLellan, Scott	Bos.	1	2	0	0	0	0	....	....	....	....	....	....	1982-83	1982-83
McLellan, Todd	NYI	1	5	1	1	2	0	....	....	....	....	....	....	1987-88	1987-88
• McLenahan, Rollie	Det.	1	9	2	1	3	10	2	0	0	0	0	....	1945-46	1945-46
McLeod, Al	Det.	1	26	2	2	4	24	....	....	....	....	....	....	1973-74	1973-74
McLeod, Jackie	NYR	5	106	14	23	37	12	7	0	0	0	0	....	1949-50	1954-55
‡ McLlwain, Dave	Pit., Wpg., Buf., NYI, Tor., Ott.	10	501	100	107	207	292	20	0	2	2	2	....	1987-88	1996-97
• McMahon, Mike	Mtl., Bos.	3	57	7	18	25	102	13	1	2	3	30	1	1942-43	1945-46
McMahon, Mike	NYR, Min., Chi., Det., Pit., Buf.	8	224	15	68	83	171	14	3	7	10	4	....	1963-64	1971-72
McManama, Bob	Pit.	3	99	11	25	36	28	8	0	1	1	6	....	1973-74	1975-76
• McManus, Sammy	Mtl.M., Bos.	2	26	0	1	1	8	1	0	0	0	0	1	1934-35	1936-37
McMurchy, Tom	Chi., Edm.	4	55	8	4	12	65	....	....	....	....	....	....	1983-84	1987-88
McNab, Max	Det.	4	128	16	19	35	24	25	1	0	1	4	1	1947-48	1950-51
McNab, Peter	Buf., Bos., Van., N.J.	14	954	363	450	813	179	107	40	42	82	20	....	1973-74	1986-87
• McNabney, Sid	Mtl.	1	....	....	....	....	....	5	0	1	1	2	....	1950-51	1950-51
• McNamara, Howard	Mtl.	1	10	1	0	1	4	....	....	....	....	....	....	1919-20	1919-20
• McNaughton, George	Que.	1	1	0	0	0	0	....	....	....	....	....	....	1919-20	1919-20
McNeill, Billy	Det.	6	257	21	46	67	142	4	1	1	2	4	....	1956-57	1963-64
‡ McNeill, Grant	Fla.	1	3	0	0	0	5	....	....	....	....	....	....	2003-04	2003-04
McNeill, Mike	Chi., Que.	2	63	5	11	16	18	....	....	....	....	....	....	1990-91	1991-92
McNeill, Stu	Det.	3	10	1	1	2	2	....	....	....	....	....	....	1957-58	1959-60
McPhee, George	NYR, N.J.	7	115	24	25	49	257	29	5	3	8	69	....	1982-83	1988-89
McPhee, Mike	Mtl., Min., Dal.	11	744	200	199	399	661	134	28	27	55	193	1	1983-84	1993-94
McRae, Basil	Que., Tor., Det., Min., T.B., St.L., Chi.	16	576	53	83	136	2457	78	8	4	12	349	....	1981-82	1996-97
McRae, Chris	Tor., Det.	3	21	1	0	1	122	....	....	....	....	....	....	1987-88	1989-90
McRae, Ken	Que., Tor.	7	137	14	21	35	364	6	0	0	0	4	....	1987-88	1993-94
• McReavy, Pat	Bos., Det.	4	55	5	10	15	4	22	3	3	6	9	1	1938-39	1941-42
McReynolds, Brian	Wpg., NYR, L.A.	3	30	1	5	6	8	....	....	....	....	....	....	1989-90	1993-94
McSheffrey, Bryan	Van., Buf.	3	90	13	7	20	44	....	....	....	....	....	....	1972-73	1974-75
McSorley, Marty	Pit., Edm., L.A., NYR, S.J., Bos.	17	961	108	251	359	3381	115	10	19	29	374	2	1983-84	1999-00
McSween, Don	Buf., Ana.	5	47	3	10	13	55	....	....	....	....	....	....	1987-88	1995-96
McTaggart, Jim	Wsh.	2	71	3	10	13	205	....	....	....	....	....	....	1980-81	1981-82
‡ McTavish, Dale	Cgy.	1	9	1	2	3	2	....	....	....	....	....	....	1996-97	1996-97
McTavish, Gord	St.L., Wpg.	2	11	1	3	4	2	....	....	....	....	....	....	1978-79	1979-80
• McVeigh, Charley	Chi., NYA	9	397	84	88	172	138	4	0	0	0	2	....	1926-27	1934-35
• McVicar, Jack	Mtl.M.	2	88	2	4	6	63	6	0	0	0	2	....	1930-31	1931-32
Meagher, Rick	Mtl., Hfd., N.J., St.L.	12	691	144	165	309	383	62	8	7	15	41	....	1979-80	1990-91
Meehan, Gerry	Tor., Phi., Buf., Van., Atl., Wsh.	10	670	180	243	423	111	10	0	1	1	0	....	1968-69	1978-79
Meeke, Brent	Cal., Cle.	5	75	9	22	31	8	....	....	....	....	....	....	1972-73	1976-77
Meeker, Howie	Tor.	8	346	83	102	185	329	42	6	9	15	50	4	1946-47	1953-54
Meeker, Mike	Pit.	1	4	0	0	0	5	....	....	....	....	....	....	1978-79	1978-79
• Meeking, Harry	Tor., Det., Bos.	3	64	18	12	30	66	9	3	0	3	6	....	1917-18	1926-27
Meger, Paul	Mtl.	6	212	39	52	91	118	35	3	8	11	16	1	1949-50	1954-55
Meighan, Ron	Min., Pit.	2	48	3	7	10	18	....	....	....	....	....	....	1981-82	1982-83
Meissner, Barrie	Min.	2	6	0	1	1	4	....	....	....	....	....	....	1967-68	1968-69
• Meissner, Dick	Bos., NYR	5	171	11	15	26	37	....	....	....	....	....	....	1959-60	1964-65
Melametsa, Anssi	Wpg.	1	27	0	3	3	2	....	....	....	....	....	....	1985-86	1985-86
‡ Melanson, Dean	Buf., Wsh.	2	9	0	0	0	8	....	....	....	....	....	....	1994-95	2001-02
Melin, Roger	Min.	2	3	0	0	0	0	....	....	....	....	....	....	1980-81	1981-82
Mellor, Tom	Det.	2	26	2	4	6	25	....	....	....	....	....	....	1973-74	1974-75
• Melnyk, Gerry	Det., Chi., St.L.	6	269	39	77	116	34	53	6	6	12	6	....	1955-56	1967-68
Melnyk, Larry	Bos., Edm., NYR, Van.	10	432	11	63	74	686	66	2	9	11	127	1	1980-81	1989-90
Melrose, Barry	Wpg., Tor., Det.	6	300	10	23	33	728	7	0	2	2	38	....	1979-80	1985-86
Menard, Hillary	Chi.	1	1	0	0	0	0	....	....	....	....	....	....	1953-54	1953-54
Menard, Howie	Det., L.A., Chi., Oak.	4	151	23	42	65	87	19	3	7	10	36	....	1963-64	1969-70
Mercredi, Vic	Atl.	1	2	0	0	0	0	....	....	....	....	....	....	1974-75	1974-75
Meredith, Greg	Cgy.	2	38	6	4	10	8	5	3	1	4	4	....	1980-81	1982-83
Merkosky, Glenn	Hfd., N.J., Det.	5	66	5	12	17	22	....	....	....	....	....	....	1981-82	1989-90
• Meronek, Bill	Mtl.	2	19	5	8	13	0	1	0	0	0	0	....	1939-40	1942-43
Merrick, Wayne	St.L., Cal., Cle., NYI	12	774	191	265	456	303	102	19	30	49	30	4	1972-73	1983-84
• Merrill, Horace	Ott.	2	8	0	0	0	3	....	....	....	....	....	1	1917-18	1919-20
Mertzig, Jan	NYR	1	23	0	2	2	8	....	....	....	....	....	....	1998-99	1998-99
Messier, Eric	Col., Fla.	8	406	25	50	75	146	72	3	5	8	22	1	1996-97	2003-04
Messier, Joby	NYR	3	25	0	4	4	24	....	....	....	....	....	....	1992-93	1994-95
Messier, Mark	Edm., NYR, Van.	25	1756	694	1193	1887	1910	236	109	186	295	244	6	1979-80	2003-04
Messier, Mitch	Min.	4	20	0	2	2	11	....	....	....	....	....	....	1987-88	1990-91
Messier, Paul	Col.	1	9	0	0	0	4	....	....	....	....	....	....	1978-79	1978-79
Metcalfe, Scott	Edm., Buf.	3	19	1	2	3	18	....	....	....	....	....	....	1987-88	1989-90
Metz, Don	Tor.	9	172	20	35	55	42	42	7	8	15	12	5	1938-39	1948-49
• Metz, Nick	Tor.	12	518	131	119	250	149	76	19	20	39	31	4	1934-35	1947-48
• Michaluk, Art	Chi.	1	5	0	0	0	0	....	....	....	....	....	....	1947-48	1947-48
Michaluk, John	Chi.	1	1	0	0	0	0	....	....	....	....	....	....	1950-51	1950-51
Michayluk, Dave	Phi., Pit.	3	14	2	6	8	8	7	1	1	2	0	1	1981-82	1991-92

			Regular Schedule					Playoffs					NHL	First	Last
Name	NHL Teams	NHL Seasons	GP	G	A	TP	PIM	GP	G	A	TP	PIM	Cup Wins	NHL Season	NHL Season
Micheletti, Joe	St.L., Col.	3	158	11	60	71	114	11	1	11	12	10	....	1979-80	1981-82
Micheletti, Pat	Min.	1	12	2	0	2	8	....	....	....	....	....	....	1987-88	1987-88
• Mickey, Larry	Chi., NYR, Tor., Mtl., L.A., Phi., Buf.	11	292	39	53	92	160	9	1	0	1	10	....	1964-65	1974-75
• Mickoski, Nick	NYR, Chi., Det., Bos.	13	703	158	185	343	319	18	1	6	7	6	....	1947-48	1959-60
Middendorf, Max	Que., Edm.	4	13	2	4	6	6	....	....	....	....	....	....	1986-87	1990-91
Middleton, Rick	NYR, Bos.	14	1005	448	540	988	157	114	45	55	100	19	....	1974-75	1987-88
Miehm, Kevin	St.L.	2	22	1	4	5	8	2	0	1	1	0	....	1992-93	1993-94
Migay, Rudy	Tor.	10	418	59	92	151	293	15	1	0	1	20	....	1949-50	1959-60
Mika, Petr	NYI	1	3	0	0	0	0	....	....	....	....	....	....	1999-00	1999-00
Mikita, Stan	Chi.	22	1394	541	926	1467	1270	155	59	91	150	169	1	1958-59	1979-80
Mikkelson, Bill	L.A., NYI, Wsh.	4	147	4	18	22	105	....	....	....	....	....	....	1971-72	1976-77
Mikol, Jim	Tor., NYR	2	34	1	4	5	8	....	....	....	....	....	....	1962-63	1964-65
Mikulchik, Oleg	Wpg., Ana.	3	37	0	3	3	33	....	....	....	....	....	....	1993-94	1995-96
Milbury, Mike	Bos.	12	754	49	189	238	1552	86	4	24	28	219	....	1975-76	1986-87
• Milks, Hib	Pit., Phi., NYR, Ott.	8	317	87	41	128	179	11	0	0	0	2	....	1925-26	1932-33
Millar, Craig	Edm., Nsh., T.B.	5	114	8	14	22	73	....	....	....	....	....	....	1996-97	2000-01
• Millar, Hugh	Det.	1	4	0	0	0	0	1	0	0	0	0	....	1946-47	1946-47
Millar, Mike	Hfd., Wsh., Bos., Tor.	5	78	18	18	36	12	....	....	....	....	....	....	1986-87	1990-91
Millen, Corey	NYR, L.A., N.J., Dal., Cgy.	8	335	90	119	209	236	47	5	7	12	22	....	1989-90	1996-97
• Miller, Bill	Mtl.M., Mtl.	3	95	7	3	10	16	12	0	0	0	0	1	1934-35	1936-37
Miller, Bob	Bos., Col., L.A.	6	404	75	119	194	220	36	4	7	11	27	....	1977-78	1984-85
Miller, Brad	Buf., Ott., Cgy.	6	82	1	5	6	321	....	....	....	....	....	....	1988-89	1993-94
• Miller, Earl	Chi., Tor.	5	109	19	14	33	124	10	1	0	1	6	1	1927-28	1931-32
Miller, Jack	Chi.	2	17	0	0	0	4	....	....	....	....	....	....	1949-50	1950-51
Miller, Jason	N.J.	3	6	0	0	0	0	....	....	....	....	....	....	1990-91	1992-93
Miller, Jay	Bos., L.A.	7	446	40	44	84	1723	48	2	3	5	243	....	1985-86	1991-92
Miller, Kelly	NYR, Wsh.	15	1057	181	282	463	512	119	20	34	54	65	....	1984-85	1998-99
Miller, Kevin	NYR, Det., Wsh., St.L., S.J., Pit., Chi., NYI, Ott.	13	620	150	185	335	429	61	7	10	17	49	....	1988-89	2003-04
Miller, Paul	Col.	1	3	0	3	3	0	....	....	....	....	....	....	1981-82	1981-82
Miller, Perry	Det.	4	217	10	51	61	387	....	....	....	....	....	....	1977-78	1980-81
Miller, Tom	Det., NYI	4	118	16	25	41	34	....	....	....	....	....	....	1970-71	1974-75
Miller, Warren	NYR, Hfd.	4	262	40	50	90	137	6	1	0	1	0	....	1979-80	1982-83
Mills, Craig	Wpg., Chi.	3	31	0	5	5	36	1	0	0	0	0	....	1995-96	1998-99
Miner, John	Edm.	1	14	2	3	5	16	....	....	....	....	....	....	1987-88	1987-88
Minor, Gerry	Van.	5	140	11	21	32	173	12	1	3	4	25	....	1979-80	1983-84
Mironov, Boris	Wpg., Edm., Chi., NYR	11	716	76	231	307	891	25	5	11	16	45	....	1993-94	2003-04
Mironov, Dmitri	Tor., Pit., Ana., Det., Wsh.	11	556	54	206	260	568	75	10	26	36	48	1	1991-92	2001-02
Miszuk, John	Det., Chi., Phi., Min.	6	237	7	39	46	232	19	0	3	3	19	....	1963-64	1969-70
Mitchell, Bill	Det.	1	1	0	0	0	0	....	....	....	....	....	....	1963-64	1963-64
• Mitchell, Herb	Bos.	2	44	6	0	6	36	....	....	....	....	....	....	1924-25	1925-26
Mitchell, Jeff	Dal.	1	7	0	0	0	7	....	....	....	....	....	....	1997-98	1997-98
• Mitchell, Red	Chi.	3	83	4	5	9	67	....	....	....	....	....	....	1941-42	1944-45
Mitchell, Roy	Min.	1	3	0	0	0	0	....	....	....	....	....	....	1992-93	1992-93
• Moe, Bill	NYR	5	261	11	42	53	163	1	0	0	0	0	....	1944-45	1948-49
Moffat, Lyle	Tor., Wpg.	3	97	12	16	28	51	....	....	....	....	....	....	1972-73	1979-80
• Moffat, Ron	Det.	3	37	1	1	2	8	7	0	0	0	0	....	1932-33	1934-35
Moger, Sandy	Bos., L.A.	5	236	41	38	79	212	5	2	2	4	12	....	1994-95	1998-99
Moher, Mike	N.J.	1	9	0	1	1	28	....	....	....	....	....	....	1982-83	1982-83
Mohns, Doug	Bos., Chi., Min., Atl., Wsh.	22	1390	248	462	710	1250	94	14	36	50	122	....	1953-54	1974-75
Mohns, Lloyd	NYR	1	1	0	0	0	0	....	....	....	....	....	....	1943-44	1943-44
Mokosak, Carl	Cgy., L.A., Phi., Pit., Bos.	6	83	11	15	26	170	1	0	0	0	0	....	1981-82	1988-89
Mokosak, John	Det.	2	41	0	2	2	96	....	....	....	....	....	....	1988-89	1989-90
Molin, Lars	Van.	3	172	33	65	98	37	19	2	9	11	7	....	1981-82	1983-84
Moller, Mike	Buf., Edm.	7	134	15	28	43	41	3	0	1	1	0	....	1980-81	1986-87
Moller, Randy	Que., NYR, Buf., Fla.	14	815	45	180	225	1692	78	6	16	22	197	....	1981-82	1994-95
Molloy, Mitch	Buf.	1	2	0	0	0	10	....	....	....	....	....	....	1989-90	1989-90
• Molyneaux, Larry	NYR	2	45	0	1	1	20	10	0	0	0	8	....	1937-38	1938-39
Momesso, Sergio	Mtl., St.L., Van., Tor., NYR	13	710	152	193	345	1557	119	18	26	44	311	....	1983-84	1996-97
Monahan, Garry	Mtl., Det., L.A., Tor., Van.	12	748	116	169	285	484	22	3	1	4	13	....	1967-68	1978-79
Monahan, Hartland	Cal., NYR, Wsh., Pit., L.A., St.L.	7	334	61	80	141	163	6	0	0	0	4	....	1973-74	1980-81
• Mondou, Armand	Mtl.	12	386	47	71	118	99	32	3	5	8	12	2	1928-29	1939-40
Mondou, Pierre	Mtl.	9	548	194	262	456	179	69	17	28	45	26	3	1976-77	1984-85
Mongeau, Michel	St.L., T.B.	4	54	6	19	25	10	2	0	1	1	0	....	1989-90	1992-93
Mongrain, Bob	Buf., L.A.	6	81	13	14	27	14	11	1	2	3	2	....	1979-80	1985-86
Monteith, Hank	Det.	3	77	5	12	17	6	4	0	0	0	0	....	1968-69	1970-71
Montgomery, Jim	St.L., Mtl., Phi., S.J., Dal.	6	122	9	25	34	80	8	1	0	1	2	....	1993-94	2002-03
‡ Moore, Barrie	Buf., Edm., Wsh.	3	39	2	6	8	18	....	....	....	....	....	....	1995-96	1999-00
Moore, Dickie	Mtl., Tor., St.L.	14	719	261	347	608	652	135	46	64	110	122	6	1951-52	1967-68
Moore, Steve	Col.	3	69	5	7	12	41	....	....	....	....	....	....	2001-02	2003-04
• Moran, Amby	Mtl., Chi.	2	35	1	1	2	24	....	....	....	....	....	....	1926-27	1927-28
‡ Moravec, David	Buf.	1	1	0	0	0	0	....	....	....	....	....	....	1999-00	1999-00
More, Jay	NYR, Min., S.J., Phx., Chi., Nsh.	10	406	18	54	72	702	31	0	6	6	45	....	1988-89	1998-99
• Morenz, Howie	Mtl., Chi., NYR	14	550	271	201	472	546	39	13	9	22	58	3	1923-24	1936-37
Moretto, Angelo	Cle.	1	5	1	2	3	2	....	....	....	....	....	....	1976-77	1976-77
• Morin, Pete	Mtl.	1	31	10	12	22	7	1	0	0	0	0	....	1941-42	1941-42
• Morin, Stephane	Que., Van.	5	90	16	39	55	52	....	....	....	....	....	....	1989-90	1993-94
Morisset, Dave	Fla.	1	4	0	0	0	5	....	....	....	....	....	....	2001-02	2001-02
Morissette, Dave	Mtl.	2	11	0	0	0	57	....	....	....	....	....	....	1998-99	1999-00
• Morris, Bernie	Bos.	1	6	1	0	1	0	....	....	....	....	....	....	1924-25	1924-25
Morris, Jon	N.J., S.J., Bos.	6	103	16	33	49	47	11	1	7	8	25	....	1988-89	1993-94
• Morris, Moe	Tor., NYR	4	135	13	29	42	58	18	4	2	6	16	1	1943-44	1948-49
Morrison, Dave	L.A., Van.	4	39	3	3	6	4	....	....	....	....	....	....	1980-81	1984-85
• Morrison, Don	Det., Chi.	3	112	18	28	46	12	3	0	1	1	0	....	1947-48	1950-51
Morrison, Doug	Bos.	4	23	7	3	10	15	....	....	....	....	....	....	1979-80	1984-85
Morrison, Gary	Phi.	3	43	1	15	16	70	5	0	1	1	2	....	1979-80	1981-82
Morrison, George	St.L.	2	115	17	21	38	13	3	0	0	0	0	....	1970-71	1971-72
Morrison, Jim	Bos., Tor., Det., NYR, Pit.	12	704	40	160	200	542	36	0	12	12	38	....	1951-52	1970-71
• Morrison, John	NYA	1	18	0	0	0	0	....	....	....	....	....	....	1925-26	1925-26
Morrison, Kevin	Col.	1	41	4	11	15	23	....	....	....	....	....	....	1979-80	1979-80
Morrison, Lew	Phi., Atl., Wsh., Pit.	9	564	39	52	91	107	17	0	0	0	2	....	1969-70	1977-78
Morrison, Mark	NYR	2	10	1	1	2	0	....	....	....	....	....	....	1981-82	1983-84
• Morrison, Rod	Det.	1	34	8	7	15	4	3	0	0	0	0	....	1947-48	1947-48
Morrow, Ken	NYI	10	550	17	88	105	309	127	11	22	33	97	4	1979-80	1988-89
Morrow, Scott	Cgy.	1	4	0	0	0	0	....	....	....	....	....	....	1994-95	1994-95
Morton, Dean	Det.	1	1	1	0	1	2	....	....	....	....	....	....	1989-90	1989-90
Mortson, Gus	Tor., Chi., Det.	13	797	46	152	198	1380	54	5	8	13	68	4	1946-47	1958-59
• Mosdell, Ken	Bro., Mtl., Chi.	16	693	141	168	309	475	80	16	13	29	48	4	1941-42	1958-59
• Mosienko, Bill	Chi.	14	711	258	282	540	121	22	10	4	14	15	....	1941-42	1954-55
Mott, Morris	Cal.	3	199	18	32	50	49	....	....	....	....	....	....	1972-73	1974-75
• Motter, Alex	Bos., Det.	8	255	39	64	103	135	41	3	9	12	41	1	1934-35	1942-43
Moxey, Jim	Cal., Cle., L.A.	3	127	22	27	49	59	....	....	....	....	....	....	1974-75	1976-77
Mrozik, Rick	Cgy.	1	2	0	0	0	0	....	....	....	....	....	....	2002-03	2002-03
Muckalt, Bill	Van., NYI, Ott., Min.	5	256	40	57	97	204	5	0	0	0	0	....	1998-99	2002-03
Mulhern, Richard	Atl., L.A., Tor., Wpg.	6	303	27	93	120	217	7	0	3	3	5	....	1975-76	1980-81
Mulhern, Ryan	Wsh.	1	3	0	0	0	0	....	....	....	....	....	....	1997-98	1997-98
Mullen, Brian	Wpg., NYR, S.J., NYI	11	832	260	362	622	414	62	12	18	30	30	....	1982-83	1992-93
Mullen, Joe	St.L., Cgy., Pit., Bos.	17	1062	502	561	1063	241	143	60	46	106	42	3	1979-80	1996-97
Muller, Kirk	N.J., Mtl., NYI, Tor., Fla., Dal.	19	1349	357	602	959	1223	127	33	36	69	153	1	1984-85	2002-03
Muloin, Wayne	Det., Oak., Cal., Min.	3	147	3	21	24	93	11	0	0	0	2	....	1963-64	1970-71
Mulvenna, Glenn	Pit., Phi.	2	2	0	0	0	4	....	....	....	....	....	....	1991-92	1992-93
Mulvey, Grant	Chi., N.J.	10	586	149	135	284	816	42	10	5	15	70	....	1974-75	1983-84
Mulvey, Paul	Wsh., Pit., L.A.	4	225	30	51	81	613	....	....	....	....	....	....	1978-79	1981-82
• Mummery, Harry	Tor., Que., Mtl., Ham.	6	106	33	19	52	226	2	1	1	2	17	....	1917-18	1922-23
Muni, Craig	Tor., Edm., Chi., Buf., Wpg., Pit., Dal.	16	819	28	119	147	775	113	0	17	17	108	3	1981-82	1997-98
• Munro, Dunc	Mtl.M., Mtl.	8	239	28	18	46	172	21	2	2	4	18	1	1924-25	1931-32
• Munro, Gerry	Mtl.M., Tor.	2	34	1	0	1	37	....	....	....	....	....	....	1924-25	1925-26
Murdoch, Bob	Mtl., L.A., Atl., Cgy.	12	757	60	218	278	764	69	4	18	22	92	2	1970-71	1981-82
Murdoch, Bob	Cal., Cle., St.L.	4	260	72	85	157	127	....	....	....	....	....	....	1975-76	1978-79
Murdoch, Don	NYR, Edm., Det.	6	320	121	117	238	155	24	10	8	18	16	....	1976-77	1981-82
• Murdoch, Murray	NYR	11	508	84	108	192	197	55	9	12	21	28	2	1926-27	1936-37
Murphy, Brian	Det.	1	1	0	0	0	0	....	....	....	....	....	....	1974-75	1974-75
Murphy, Gord	Phi., Bos., Fla., Atl.	14	862	85	238	323	668	53	3	16	19	35	....	1988-89	2001-02
Murphy, Joe	Det., Edm., Chi., St.L., S.J., Bos., Wsh.	15	779	233	295	528	810	120	34	43	77	185	1	1986-87	2000-01

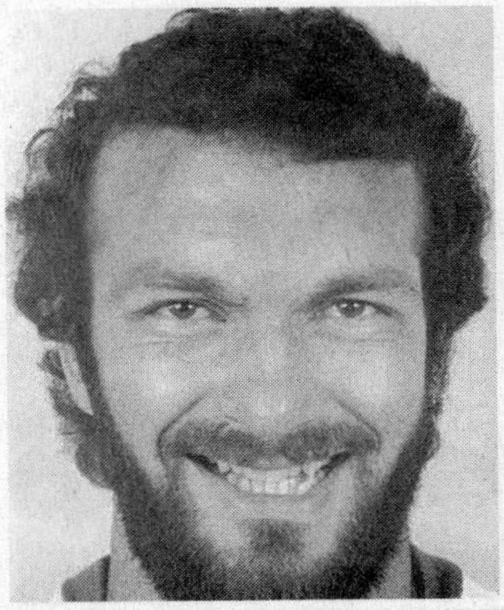

Ken Morrow

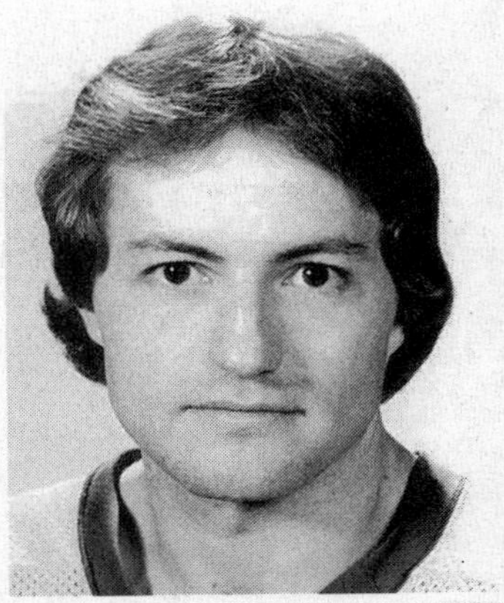

Richard Mulhern

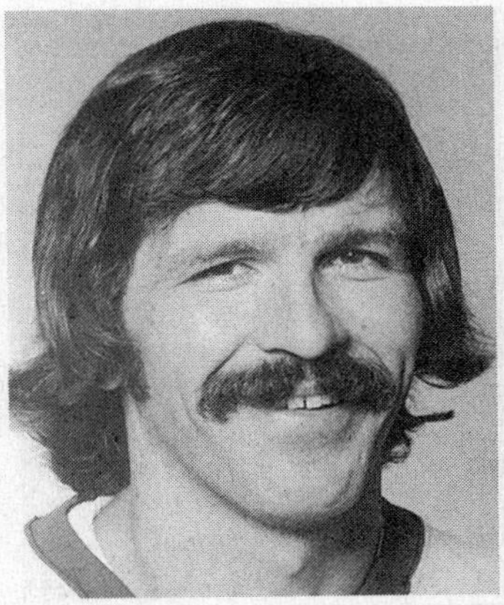

Bob Murdoch

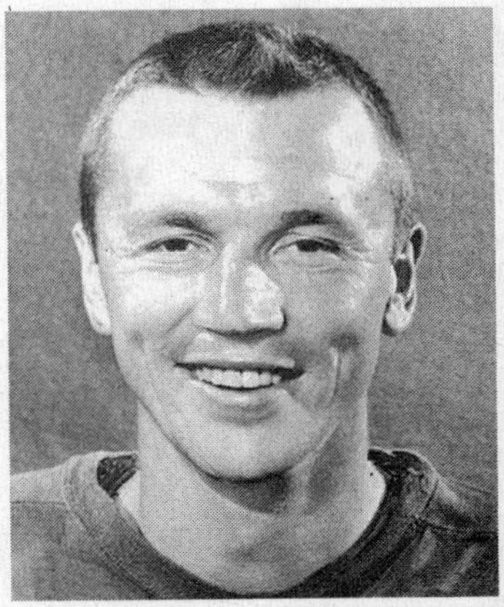

Ron Murphy

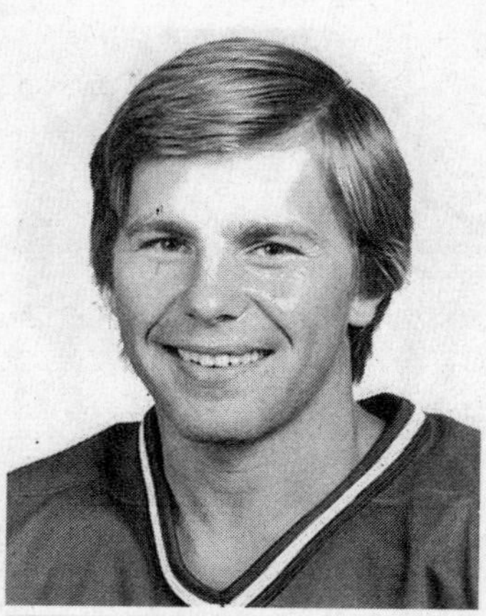

Mats Naslund

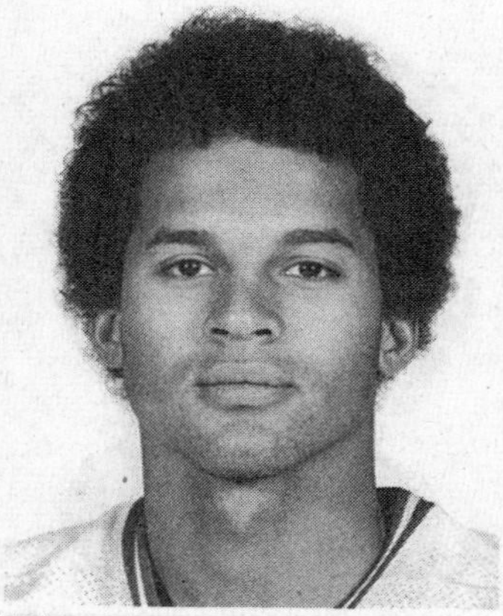

Ray Neufeld

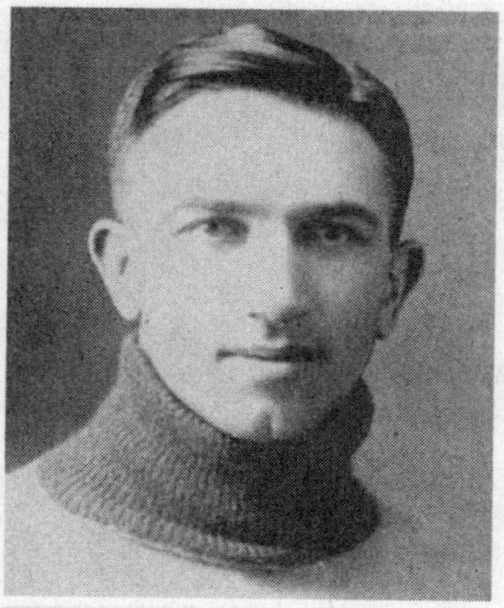

Paddy Nolan

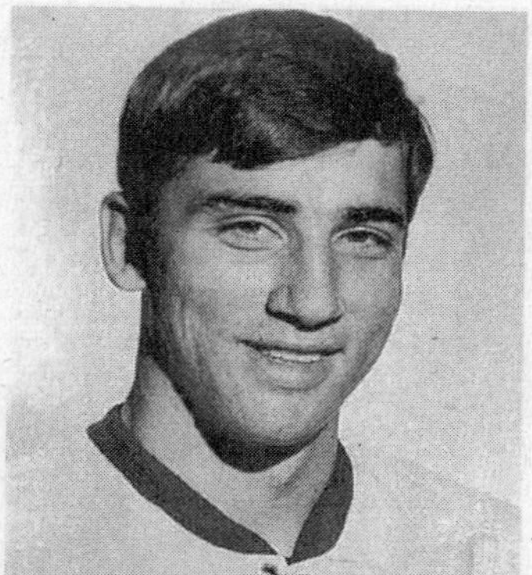

Don O'Donoghue

Name	NHL Teams	NHL Seasons	Regular Schedule GP	G	A	TP	PIM	Playoffs GP	G	A	TP	PIM	NHL Cup Wins	First NHL Season	Last NHL Season
Murphy, Larry	L.A., Wsh., Min., Pit., Tor., Det.	21	1615	287	929	1216	1084	215	37	115	152	201	4	1980-81	2000-01
Murphy, Mike	St.L., NYR, L.A.	12	831	238	318	556	514	66	13	23	36	54	....	1971-72	1982-83
Murphy, Rob	Van., Ott., L.A.	7	125	9	12	21	152	4	0	0	0	2	....	1987-88	1993-94
Murphy, Ron	NYR, Chi., Det., Bos.	18	889	205	274	479	460	53	7	8	15	26	1	1952-53	1969-70
Murray, Allan	NYA	7	271	5	9	14	163	14	0	0	0	10	....	1933-34	1939-40
Murray, Bob	Atl., Van.	4	194	6	16	22	98	10	1	1	2	15	....	1973-74	1976-77
Murray, Bob	Chi.	15	1008	132	382	514	873	112	19	37	56	106	....	1975-76	1989-90
● Murray, Chris	Mtl., Hfd., Car., Ott., Chi., Dal.	6	242	16	18	34	550	15	1	0	1	12	....	1994-95	1999-00
Murray, Jim	L.A.	1	30	0	2	2	14	....	....	....	....	....	....	1967-68	1967-68
Murray, Ken	Tor., NYI, Det., K.C.	5	106	1	10	11	135	....	....	....	....	....	....	1969-70	1975-76
● Murray, Leo	Mtl.	1	6	0	0	0	2	....	....	....	....	....	....	1932-33	1932-33
Murray, Mike	Phi.	1	1	0	0	0	0	....	....	....	....	....	....	1987-88	1987-88
Murray, Pat	Phi.	2	25	3	1	4	15	....	....	....	....	....	....	1990-91	1991-92
Murray, Randy	Tor.	1	3	0	0	0	2	....	....	....	....	....	....	1969-70	1969-70
Murray, Rob	Wsh., Wpg., Phx.	8	107	4	15	19	111	9	0	0	0	18	....	1989-90	1998-99
Murray, Terry	Cal., Phi., Det., Wsh.	8	302	4	76	80	199	18	2	2	4	10	....	1972-73	1981-82
Murray, Troy	Chi., Wpg., Ott., Pit., Col.	15	915	230	354	584	875	113	17	26	43	145	1	1981-82	1995-96
Murzyn, Dana	Hfd., Cgy., Van.	14	838	52	152	204	1571	82	9	10	19	166	1	1985-86	1998-99
Musil, Frantisek	Min., Cgy., Ott., Edm.	15	797	34	106	140	1241	42	2	4	6	47	....	1986-87	2000-01
Myers, Hap	Buf.	1	13	0	0	0	6	....	....	....	....	....	....	1970-71	1970-71
Myles, Vic	NYR	1	45	6	9	15	57	....	....	....	....	....	....	1942-43	1942-43
‡ Myrvold, Anders	Col., Bos., NYI, Det.	4	33	0	5	5	12	....	....	....	....	....	....	1995-96	2003-04

N

Name	NHL Teams	NHL Seasons	Regular Schedule GP	G	A	TP	PIM	Playoffs GP	G	A	TP	PIM	NHL Cup Wins	First NHL Season	Last NHL Season
‡ Nabokov, Dmitri	Chi., NYI	3	55	11	13	24	28	....	....	....	....	....	....	1997-98	1999-00
Nachbaur, Don	Hfd., Edm., Phi.	8	223	23	46	69	465	11	1	1	2	24	....	1980-81	1989-90
Nahrgang, Jim	Det.	3	57	5	12	17	34	....	....	....	....	....	....	1974-75	1976-77
Namestnikov, John	Van., NYI, Nsh.	6	43	0	9	9	24	2	0	0	0	2	....	1993-94	1999-00
Nanne, Lou	Min.	11	635	68	157	225	356	32	4	10	14	8	....	1967-68	1977-78
Nantais, Rich	Min.	3	63	5	4	9	79	....	....	....	....	....	....	1974-75	1976-77
Napier, Mark	Mtl., Min., Edm., Buf.	11	767	235	306	541	157	82	18	24	42	11	2	1978-79	1988-89
Naslund, Mats	Mtl., Bos.	9	651	251	383	634	111	102	35	57	92	33	1	1982-83	1994-95
Nattrass, Ralph	Chi.	4	223	18	38	56	308	....	....	....	....	....	....	1946-47	1949-50
Nattress, Ric	Mtl., St.L., Cgy., Tor., Phi.	11	536	29	135	164	377	67	5	10	15	60	1	1982-83	1992-93
Natyshak, Mike	Que.	1	4	0	0	0	0	....	....	....	....	....	....	1987-88	1987-88
‡ Ndur, Rumun	Buf., NYR, Atl.	4	69	2	3	5	137	....	....	....	....	....	....	1996-97	1999-00
Neaton, Pat	Pit.	1	9	1	1	2	12	....	....	....	....	....	....	1993-94	1993-94
Nechayev, Viktor	L.A.	1	3	1	0	1	0	....	....	....	....	....	....	1982-83	1982-83
‡ Neckar, Stan	Ott., NYR, Phx., T.B., Nsh.	10	510	12	41	53	316	29	0	3	3	8	1	1994-95	2003-04
Nedomansky, Vaclav	Det., NYR, St.L.	6	421	122	156	278	88	7	3	5	8	0	....	1977-78	1982-83
Nedved, Zdenek	Tor.	3	31	4	6	10	14	....	....	....	....	....	....	1994-95	1996-97
Needham, Mike	Pit., Dal.	3	86	9	5	14	16	14	2	0	2	4	1	1991-92	1993-94
Neely, Bob	Tor., Col.	5	283	39	59	98	266	26	5	7	12	15	....	1973-74	1977-78
Neely, Cam	Van., Bos.	13	726	395	299	694	1241	93	57	32	89	168	....	1983-84	1995-96
Neilson, Jim	NYR, Cal., Cle.	16	1023	69	299	368	904	65	1	17	18	61	....	1962-63	1977-78
Nelson, Gordie	Tor.	1	3	0	0	0	11	....	....	....	....	....	....	1969-70	1969-70
‡ Nelson, Jeff	Wsh., Nsh.	3	52	3	8	11	20	3	0	0	0	4	....	1994-95	1998-99
Nelson, Todd	Pit., Wsh.	2	3	1	0	1	2	4	0	0	0	0	....	1991-92	1993-94
Nemchinov, Sergei	NYR, Van., NYI, N.J.	11	761	152	193	345	251	105	11	20	31	24	2	1991-92	2001-02
‡ Nemecek, Jan	L.A.	2	7	1	0	1	4	....	....	....	....	....	....	1998-99	1999-00
Nemeth, Steve	NYR	1	12	2	0	2	2	....	....	....	....	....	....	1987-88	1987-88
‡ Nemirovsky, David	Fla.	4	91	16	22	38	42	3	1	0	1	0	....	1995-96	1998-99
Nesterenko, Eric	Tor., Chi.	21	1219	250	324	574	1273	124	13	24	37	127	1	1951-52	1971-72
Nethery, Lance	NYR, Edm.	2	41	11	14	25	14	14	5	3	8	9	....	1980-81	1981-82
Neufeld, Ray	Hfd., Wpg., Bos.	11	595	157	200	357	816	28	8	6	14	55	....	1979-80	1989-90
● Neville, Mike	Tor., NYA	3	65	5	5	10	14	2	0	0	0	0	....	1924-25	1930-31
Nevin, Bob	Tor., NYR, Min., L.A.	18	1128	307	419	726	211	84	16	18	34	24	2	1957-58	1975-76
Newberry, John	Mtl., Hfd.	4	22	0	4	4	6	2	0	0	0	0	....	1982-83	1985-86
Newell, Rick	Det.	2	6	0	0	0	0	....	....	....	....	....	....	1972-73	1973-74
Newman, Dan	NYR, Mtl., Edm.	4	126	17	24	41	63	3	0	0	0	4	....	1976-77	1979-80
● Newman, John	Det.	1	8	1	1	2	0	....	....	....	....	....	....	1930-31	1930-31
Nicholls, Bernie	L.A., NYR, Edm., N.J., Chi., S.J.	18	1127	475	734	1209	1292	118	42	72	114	164	....	1981-82	1998-99
Nicholson, Al	Bos.	2	19	0	1	1	4	....	....	....	....	....	....	1955-56	1956-57
● Nicholson, Ed	Det.	1	1	0	0	0	0	....	....	....	....	....	....	1947-48	1947-48
● Nicholson, Hickey	Chi.	1	2	1	0	1	0	....	....	....	....	....	....	1937-38	1937-38
Nicholson, Neil	Oak., NYI	4	39	3	1	4	23	2	0	0	0	0	....	1969-70	1977-78
Nicholson, Paul	Wsh.	3	62	4	8	12	18	....	....	....	....	....	....	1974-75	1976-77
Nicolson, Graeme	Bos., Col., NYR	3	52	2	7	9	60	....	....	....	....	....	....	1978-79	1982-83
Nieckar, Barry	Hfd., Cgy., Ana.	4	8	0	0	0	21	....	....	....	....	....	....	1992-93	1997-98
Niekamp, Jim	Det.	2	29	0	2	2	37	....	....	....	....	....	....	1970-71	1971-72
‡ Nielsen, Chris	CBJ	2	52	6	8	14	8	....	....	....	....	....	....	2000-01	2001-02
Nielsen, Jeff	NYR, Ana., Min.	5	252	20	27	47	70	4	0	0	0	2	....	1996-97	2000-01
Nielsen, Kirk	Bos.	1	6	0	0	0	0	....	....	....	....	....	....	1997-98	1997-98
‡ Niemi, Antti-Jussi	Ana.	2	29	1	1	2	22	....	....	....	....	....	....	2000-01	2001-02
Nienhuis, Kraig	Bos.	3	87	20	16	36	39	2	0	0	0	14	....	1985-86	1987-88
● Nighbor, Frank	Ott., Tor.	13	349	139	98	237	249	20	4	9	13	13	4	1917-18	1929-30
Nigro, Frank	Tor.	2	68	8	18	26	39	3	0	0	0	2	....	1982-83	1983-84
‡ Nikolishin, Andrei	Hfd., Wsh., Chi., Col.	10	628	93	187	280	270	43	1	17	18	22	....	1994-95	2003-04
Nikulin, Igor	Ana.	1	....	....	....	....	....	1	0	0	0	0	....	1996-97	1996-97
Nilan, Chris	Mtl., NYR, Bos.	13	688	110	115	225	3043	111	8	9	17	541	1	1979-80	1991-92
Nill, Jim	St.L., Van., Bos., Wpg., Det.	9	524	58	87	145	854	59	10	5	15	203	....	1981-82	1989-90
Nilsson, Kent	Atl., Cgy., Min., Edm.	9	553	264	422	686	116	59	11	41	52	14	1	1979-80	1994-95
Nilsson, Ulf	NYR	4	170	57	112	169	85	25	8	14	22	27	....	1978-79	1982-83
Nistico, Lou	Col.	1	3	0	0	0	0	....	....	....	....	....	....	1977-78	1977-78
● Noble, Reg	Tor., Mtl.M., Det.	16	510	168	106	274	916	18	2	2	4	33	3	1917-18	1932-33
Noel, Claude	Wsh.	1	7	0	0	0	0	....	....	....	....	....	....	1979-80	1979-80
● Nolan, Paddy	Tor.	1	2	0	0	0	0	....	....	....	....	....	....	1921-22	1921-22
Nolan, Ted	Det., Pit.	3	78	6	16	22	105	....	....	....	....	....	....	1981-82	1985-86
Nolet, Simon	Phi., K.C., Pit., Col.	10	562	150	182	332	187	34	6	3	9	8	1	1967-68	1976-77
Noonan, Brian	Chi., NYR, St.L., Van., Phx.	12	629	116	159	275	518	71	17	19	36	77	1	1987-88	1998-99
Nordmark, Robert	St.L., Van.	4	236	13	70	83	254	7	3	2	5	8	....	1987-88	1990-91
‡ Nordstrom, Peter	Bos.	1	2	0	0	0	0	....	....	....	....	....	....	1998-99	1998-99
Noris, Joe	Pit., St.L., Buf.	3	55	2	5	7	22	....	....	....	....	....	....	1971-72	1973-74
‡ Norris, Dwayne	Que., Ana.	3	20	2	4	6	8	....	....	....	....	....	....	1993-94	1995-96
Norrish, Rod	Min.	2	21	3	3	6	2	....	....	....	....	....	....	1973-74	1974-75
● Northcott, Baldy	Mtl.M., Chi.	11	446	133	112	245	273	31	8	5	13	14	1	1928-29	1938-39
Norton, Jeff	NYI, S.J., St.L., Edm., T.B., Fla., Pit., Bos.	15	799	52	332	384	615	65	4	21	25	89	....	1987-88	2001-02
Norwich, Craig	Wpg., St.L., Col.	2	104	17	58	75	60	....	....	....	....	....	....	1979-80	1980-81
Norwood, Lee	Que., Wsh., St.L., Det., N.J., Hfd., Cgy.	12	503	58	153	211	1099	65	6	22	28	171	....	1980-81	1993-94
Novoseltsev, Ivan	Fla., Phx.	5	234	31	44	75	112	....	....	....	....	....	....	1999-00	2003-04
Novy, Milan	Wsh.	1	73	18	30	48	16	2	0	0	0	0	....	1982-83	1982-83
Nowak, Hank	Pit., Det., Bos.	4	180	26	29	55	161	13	1	0	1	8	....	1973-74	1976-77
‡ Nurminen, Kai	L.A., Min.	2	69	17	11	28	24	....	....	....	....	....	....	1996-97	2000-01
Nykoluk, Mike	Tor.	1	32	3	1	4	20	....	....	....	....	....	....	1956-57	1956-57
Nylund, Gary	Tor., Chi., NYI	11	608	32	139	171	1235	24	0	6	6	63	....	1982-83	1992-93
● Nyrop, Bill	Mtl., Min.	4	207	12	51	63	101	35	1	7	8	22	3	1975-76	1981-82
Nystrom, Bob	NYI	14	900	235	278	513	1248	157	39	44	83	236	4	1972-73	1985-86

O

Name	NHL Teams	NHL Seasons	Regular Schedule GP	G	A	TP	PIM	Playoffs GP	G	A	TP	PIM	NHL Cup Wins	First NHL Season	Last NHL Season
Oates, Adam	Det., St.L., Bos., Wsh., Phi., Ana., Edm.	19	1337	341	1079	1420	415	163	42	114	156	66	....	1985-86	2003-04
● Oatman, Russell	Det., Mtl.M., NYR	3	120	20	9	29	100	15	1	0	1	18	....	1926-27	1928-29
O'Brien, Dennis	Min., Col., Cle., Bos.	10	592	31	91	122	1017	34	1	2	3	101	....	1970-71	1979-80
O'Brien, Ellard	Bos.	1	2	0	0	0	0	....	....	....	....	....	....	1955-56	1955-56
‡ Obsut, Jaroslav	St.L., Col.	2	7	0	0	0	2	....	....	....	....	....	....	2000-01	2001-02
O'Callahan, Jack	Chi., N.J.	7	389	27	104	131	541	32	4	11	15	41	....	1982-83	1988-89
O'Connell, Mike	Chi., Bos., Det.	13	860	105	334	439	605	82	8	24	32	64	....	1977-78	1989-90
● O'Connor, Buddy	Mtl., NYR	10	509	140	257	397	34	53	15	21	36	6	2	1941-42	1950-51
O'Connor, Myles	N.J., Ana.	4	43	3	4	7	69	....	....	....	....	....	....	1990-91	1993-94
Oddleifson, Chris	Bos., Van.	9	524	95	191	286	464	14	1	6	7	8	....	1972-73	1980-81
Odelein, Selmar	Edm.	3	18	0	2	2	35	....	....	....	....	....	....	1985-86	1988-89
Odgers, Jeff	S.J., Bos., Col., Atl.	12	821	75	70	145	2364	47	2	1	3	73	....	1991-92	2002-03

			Regular Schedule					Playoffs							
Name	NHL Teams	NHL Seasons	GP	G	A	TP	PIM	GP	G	A	TP	PIM	NHL Cup Wins	First NHL Season	Last NHL Season
Odjick, Gino	Van., NYI, Phi., Mtl.	12	605	64	73	137	2567	44	4	1	5	142	....	1990-91	2001-02
O'Donnell, Fred	Bos.	2	115	15	11	26	98	5	0	1	1	5	....	1972-73	1973-74
O'Donoghue, Don	Oak., Cal.	3	125	18	17	35	35	3	0	0	0	0	....	1969-70	1971-72
Odrowski, Gerry	Det., Oak., St.L.	6	309	12	19	31	111	30	0	1	1	16	....	1960-61	1971-72
O'Dwyer, Bill	L.A., Bos.	5	120	9	13	22	108	10	0	0	0	2	....	1983-84	1989-90
O'Flaherty, Gerry	Tor., Van., Atl.	8	438	99	95	194	168	7	2	2	4	6	....	1971-72	1978-79
O'Flaherty, Peanuts	NYA, Bro.	2	21	5	1	6	0	....	....	....	....	....	....	1940-41	1941-42
Ogilvie, Brian	Chi., St.L.	6	90	15	21	36	29	....	....	....	....	....	....	1972-73	1978-79
• O'Grady, George	Mtl.W.	1	4	0	0	0	0	....	....	....	....	....	....	1917-18	1917-18
Ogrodnick, John	Det., Que., NYR	14	928	402	425	827	260	41	18	8	26	6	....	1979-80	1992-93
‡ Ojanen, Janne	N.J.	4	98	21	23	44	28	3	0	2	2	0	....	1988-89	1992-93
Okerlund, Todd	NYI	1	4	0	0	0	2	....	....	....	....	....	....	1987-88	1987-88
Oksiuta, Roman	Edm., Van., Ana., Pit.	4	153	46	41	87	100	10	2	3	5	0	....	1993-94	1996-97
‡ Olausson, Fredrik	Wpg., Edm., Ana., Pit., Det.	16	1022	147	434	581	450	71	6	23	29	28	1	1986-87	2002-03
Olczyk, Ed	Chi., Tor., Wpg., NYR, L.A., Pit.	16	1031	342	452	794	874	57	19	15	34	57	1	1984-85	1999-00
• Oliver, Harry	Bos., NYA	11	463	127	85	212	147	35	10	6	16	24	1	1926-27	1936-37
Oliver, Murray	Det., Bos., Tor., Min.	17	1127	274	454	728	320	35	9	16	25	10	....	1957-58	1974-75
Olmstead, Bert	Chi., Mtl., Tor.	14	848	181	421	602	884	115	16	43	59	101	5	1948-49	1961-62
Olsen, Darryl	Cgy.	1	1	0	0	0	0	....	....	....	....	....	....	1991-92	1991-92
Olson, Dennis	Det.	1	4	0	0	0	0	....	....	....	....	....	....	1957-58	1957-58
Olsson, Christer	St.L., Ott.	2	56	4	12	16	24	3	0	0	0	0	....	1995-96	1996-97
• O'Neil, Jim	Bos., Mtl.	6	156	6	30	36	109	9	1	1	2	13	....	1933-34	1941-42
O'Neil, Paul	Van., Bos.	2	6	0	0	0	0	....	....	....	....	....	....	1973-74	1975-76
• O'Neill, Tom	Tor.	2	66	10	12	22	53	4	0	0	0	6	1	1943-44	1944-45
Orban, Bill	Chi., Min.	3	114	8	15	23	67	3	0	0	0	0	....	1967-68	1969-70
O'Ree, Willie	Bos.	2	45	4	10	14	26	....	....	....	....	....	....	1957-58	1960-61
O'Regan, Tom	Pit.	3	61	5	12	17	10	....	....	....	....	....	....	1983-84	1985-86
O'Reilly, Terry	Bos.	14	891	204	402	606	2095	108	25	42	67	335	....	1971-72	1984-85
Orlando, Gates	Buf.	3	98	18	26	44	51	5	0	4	4	14	....	1984-85	1986-87
• Orlando, Jimmy	Det.	6	199	6	25	31	375	36	0	9	9	105	1	1936-37	1942-43
Orleski, Dave	Mtl.	2	2	0	0	0	0	....	....	....	....	....	....	1980-81	1981-82
Orr, Bobby	Bos., Chi.	12	657	270	645	915	953	74	26	66	92	107	2	1966-67	1978-79
Osborne, Keith	St.L., T.B.	2	16	1	3	4	16	....	....	....	....	....	....	1989-90	1992-93
Osborne, Mark	Det., NYR, Tor., Wpg.	14	919	212	319	531	1152	87	12	16	28	141	....	1981-82	1994-95
Osburn, Randy	Tor., Phi.	2	27	0	2	2	0	....	....	....	....	....	....	1972-73	1974-75
O'Shea, Danny	Min., Chi., St.L.	5	369	64	115	179	265	39	3	7	10	61	....	1968-69	1972-73
O'Shea, Kevin	Buf., St.L.	3	134	13	18	31	85	12	2	1	3	10	....	1970-71	1972-73
Osiecki, Mark	Cgy., Ott., Wpg., Min.	2	93	3	11	14	43	....	....	....	....	....	....	1991-92	1992-93
O'Sullivan, Chris	Cgy., Van., Ana.	5	62	2	17	19	16	....	....	....	....	....	....	1996-97	2002-03
Otevrel, Jaroslav	S.J.	2	16	3	4	7	2	....	....	....	....	....	....	1992-93	1993-94
Otto, Joel	Cgy., Phi.	14	943	195	313	508	1934	122	27	47	74	207	1	1984-85	1997-98
Ouellette, Eddie	Chi.	1	43	3	2	5	11	1	0	0	0	0	....	1935-36	1935-36
Ouellette, Gerry	Bos.	1	34	5	4	9	0	....	....	....	....	....	....	1960-61	1960-61
Owchar, Dennis	Pit., Col.	6	288	30	85	115	200	10	1	1	2	8	....	1974-75	1979-80
• Owen, George	Bos.	5	183	44	33	77	151	21	2	5	7	25	1	1928-29	1932-33

P

Pachal, Clayton	Bos., Col.	3	35	2	3	5	95	....	....	....	....	....	....	1976-77	1978-79
Paddock, John	Wsh., Phi., Que.	5	87	8	14	22	86	5	2	0	2	0	....	1975-76	1982-83
Paek, Jim	Pit., L.A., Ott.	5	217	5	29	34	155	27	1	4	5	8	2	1990-91	1994-95
Paiement, Rosaire	Phi., Van.	5	190	48	52	100	343	3	3	0	3	0	....	1967-68	1971-72
Paiement, Wilf	K.C., Col., Tor., Que., NYR, Buf., Pit.	14	946	356	458	814	1757	69	18	17	35	185	....	1974-75	1987-88
• Palangio, Pete	Mtl., Det., Chi.	5	71	13	10	23	28	7	0	0	0	0	1	1926-27	1937-38
Palazzari, Aldo	Bos., NYR	1	35	8	3	11	4	....	....	....	....	....	....	1943-44	1943-44
Palazzari, Doug	St.L.	4	108	18	20	38	23	2	0	0	0	0	....	1974-75	1978-79
Palmer, Brad	Min., Bos.	3	168	32	38	70	58	29	9	5	14	16	....	1980-81	1982-83
Palmer, Rob	Chi.	3	16	0	3	3	2	....	....	....	....	....	....	1973-74	1975-76
Palmer, Robert	L.A., N.J.	7	320	9	101	110	115	8	1	2	3	6	....	1977-78	1983-84
• Panagabko, Ed	Bos.	2	29	0	3	3	38	....	....	....	....	....	....	1955-56	1956-57
‡ Pankewicz, Greg	Ott., Cgy.	2	21	0	3	3	22	....	....	....	....	....	....	1993-94	1998-99
Panteleev, Grigori	Bos., NYI	4	54	8	6	14	12	....	....	....	....	....	....	1992-93	1995-96
• Papike, Joe	Chi.	3	20	3	3	6	4	5	0	2	2	0	....	1940-41	1944-45
Pappin, Jim	Tor., Chi., Cal., Cle.	14	767	278	295	573	667	92	33	34	67	101	2	1963-64	1976-77
Paradise, Bob	Min., Atl., Pit., Wsh.	8	368	8	54	62	393	12	0	1	1	19	....	1971-72	1978-79
• Pargeter, George	Mtl.	1	4	0	0	0	0	....	....	....	....	....	....	1946-47	1946-47
Parise, J.P.	Bos., Tor., Min., NYI, Cle.	14	890	238	356	594	706	86	27	31	58	87	....	1965-66	1978-79
Parizeau, Michel	St.L., Phi.	1	58	3	14	17	18	....	....	....	....	....	....	1971-72	1971-72
Park, Brad	NYR, Bos., Det.	17	1113	213	683	896	1429	161	35	90	125	217	....	1968-69	1984-85
Parker, Jeff	Buf., Hfd.	5	141	16	19	35	163	5	0	0	0	26	....	1986-87	1990-91
• Parkes, Ernie	Mtl.M.	1	17	0	0	0	2	....	....	....	....	....	....	1924-25	1924-25
Parks, Greg	NYI	3	23	1	2	3	6	2	0	0	0	0	....	1990-91	1992-93
• Parsons, George	Tor.	3	78	12	13	25	20	7	3	2	5	11	....	1936-37	1938-39
‡ Parssinen, Timo	Ana.	1	17	0	3	3	2	....	....	....	....	....	....	2001-02	2001-02
• Pasek, Dusan	Min.	1	48	4	10	14	30	2	1	0	1	0	....	1988-89	1988-89
Pasin, Dave	Bos., L.A.	2	76	18	19	37	50	3	0	1	1	0	....	1985-86	1988-89
Paslawski, Greg	Mtl., St.L., Wpg., Buf., Que., Phi., Cgy.	11	650	187	185	372	169	60	19	13	32	25	....	1983-84	1993-94
‡ Patera, Pavel	Dal., Min.	2	32	2	7	9	8	....	....	....	....	....	....	1999-00	2000-01
Paterson, Joe	Det., Phi., L.A., NYR	9	291	19	37	56	829	22	3	4	7	77	....	1980-81	1988-89
Paterson, Mark	Hfd.	4	29	3	3	6	33	....	....	....	....	....	....	1982-83	1985-86
Paterson, Rick	Chi.	9	430	50	43	93	136	61	7	10	17	51	....	1978-79	1986-87
Patey, Doug	Wsh.	3	45	4	2	6	8	....	....	....	....	....	....	1976-77	1978-79
Patey, Larry	Cal., St.L., NYR	12	717	153	163	316	631	40	8	10	18	57	....	1973-74	1984-85
Patrick, Craig	Cal., St.L., K.C., Wsh.	8	401	72	91	163	61	2	0	1	1	0	....	1971-72	1978-79
Patrick, Glenn	St.L., Cal., Cle.	4	38	2	3	5	72	....	....	....	....	....	....	1973-74	1976-77
Patrick, James	NYR, Hfd., Cgy., Buf.	21	1280	149	490	639	759	117	6	32	38	86	....	1983-84	2003-04
• Patrick, Lester	NYR	1	1	0	0	0	2	....	....	....	....	....	....	1926-27	1926-27
• Patrick, Lynn	NYR	10	455	145	190	335	240	44	10	6	16	22	1	1934-35	1945-46
• Patrick, Muzz	NYR	5	166	5	26	31	133	25	4	0	4	34	1	1937-38	1945-46
Patrick, Steve	Buf., NYR, Que.	6	250	40	68	108	242	12	0	1	1	12	....	1980-81	1985-86
Patterson, Colin	Cgy., Buf.	10	504	96	109	205	239	85	12	17	29	57	1	1983-84	1992-93
Patterson, Dennis	K.C., Phi.	3	138	6	22	28	67	....	....	....	....	....	....	1974-75	1979-80
Patterson, Ed	Pit.	3	68	3	3	6	56	....	....	....	....	....	....	1993-94	1996-97
• Patterson, George	Tor., Mtl., NYA, Bos., Det., St.L.	9	284	51	27	78	218	3	0	0	0	2	....	1926-27	1934-35
• Paul, Butch	Det.	1	3	0	0	0	0	....	....	....	....	....	....	1964-65	1964-65
• Paulhus, Rollie	Mtl.	1	33	0	0	0	0	....	....	....	....	....	....	1925-26	1925-26
Pavelich, Mark	NYR, Min., S.J.	7	355	137	192	329	340	23	7	17	24	14	....	1981-82	1991-92
Pavelich, Marty	Det.	10	634	93	159	252	454	91	13	15	28	74	4	1947-48	1956-57
Pavese, Jim	St.L., NYR, Det., Hfd.	8	328	13	44	57	689	34	0	6	6	81	....	1981-82	1988-89
• Payer, Evariste	Mtl.	1	1	0	0	0	0	....	....	....	....	....	....	1917-18	1917-18
Payne, Davis	Bos.	2	22	0	1	1	14	....	....	....	....	....	....	1995-96	1996-97
Payne, Steve	Min.	10	613	228	238	466	435	71	35	35	70	60	....	1978-79	1987-88
Paynter, Kent	Chi., Wsh., Wpg., Ott.	7	37	1	3	4	69	4	0	0	0	10	....	1987-88	1993-94
Peake, Pat	Wsh.	5	134	28	41	69	105	13	2	2	4	20	....	1993-94	1997-98
• Pearson, Mel	NYR, Pit.	5	38	2	6	8	25	....	....	....	....	....	....	1959-60	1967-68
Pearson, Rob	Tor., Wsh., St.L.	6	269	56	54	110	645	33	4	2	6	94	....	1991-92	1996-97
Pearson, Scott	Tor., Que., Edm., Buf., NYI	10	292	56	42	98	615	10	2	0	2	14	....	1988-89	1999-00
Pedersen, Allen	Bos., Min., Hfd.	8	428	5	36	41	487	64	0	0	0	91	....	1986-87	1993-94
Pederson, Barry	Bos., Van., Pit., Hfd.	12	701	238	416	654	472	34	22	30	52	25	1	1980-81	1991-92
‡ Pederson, Denis	N.J., Van., Phx., Nsh.	8	435	57	71	128	398	27	1	5	6	8	....	1995-96	2002-03
Pederson, Mark	Mtl., Phi., S.J., Det.	5	169	35	50	85	77	2	0	0	0	0	....	1989-90	1993-94
Pederson, Tom	S.J., Tor.	5	240	20	49	69	142	24	1	11	12	10	....	1992-93	1996-97
• Peer, Bert	Det.	1	1	0	0	0	0	....	....	....	....	....	....	1939-40	1939-40
Peirson, Johnny	Bos.	11	545	153	173	326	315	49	10	16	26	26	....	1946-47	1957-58
Pelensky, Perry	Chi.	1	4	0	0	0	5	....	....	....	....	....	....	1983-84	1983-84
Pellerin, Scott	N.J., St.L., Min., Car., Bos., Dal., Phx.	11	536	72	126	198	320	37	1	2	3	26	....	1992-93	2003-04
Pelletier, Roger	Phi.	1	1	0	0	0	0	....	....	....	....	....	....	1967-68	1967-68
Peloffy, Andre	Wsh.	1	9	0	0	0	0	....	....	....	....	....	....	1974-75	1974-75
Peluso, Mike	Chi., Ott., N.J., St.L., Cgy.	9	458	38	52	90	1951	62	3	4	7	107	1	1989-90	1997-98
Peluso, Mike	Chi., Phi.	2	38	4	2	6	19	....	....	....	....	....	....	2001-02	2003-04
Pelyk, Mike	Tor.	9	441	26	88	114	566	40	0	3	3	41	....	1967-68	1977-78
Penney, Chad	Ott.	1	3	0	0	0	2	....	....	....	....	....	....	1993-94	1993-94
Pennington, Cliff	Mtl., Bos.	3	101	17	42	59	6	....	....	....	....	....	....	1960-61	1962-63
Peplinski, Jim	Cgy.	11	711	161	263	424	1467	99	15	31	46	382	1	1980-81	1994-95

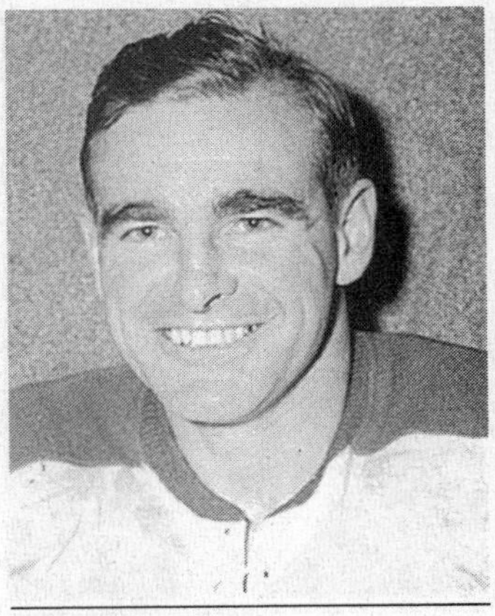

Peanuts O'Flaherty

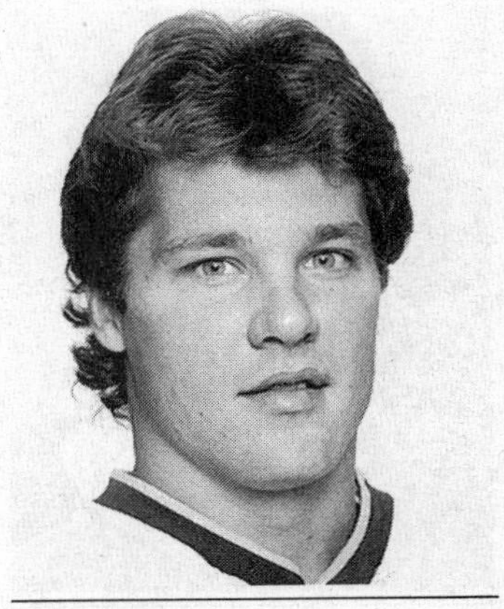

Greg Paslawski

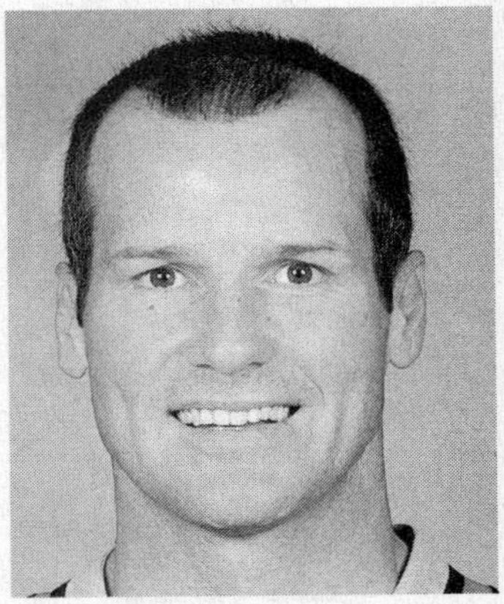

James Patrick

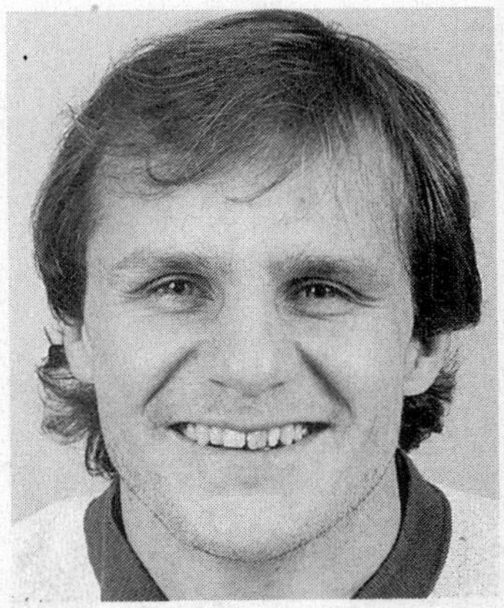

Stefan Persson

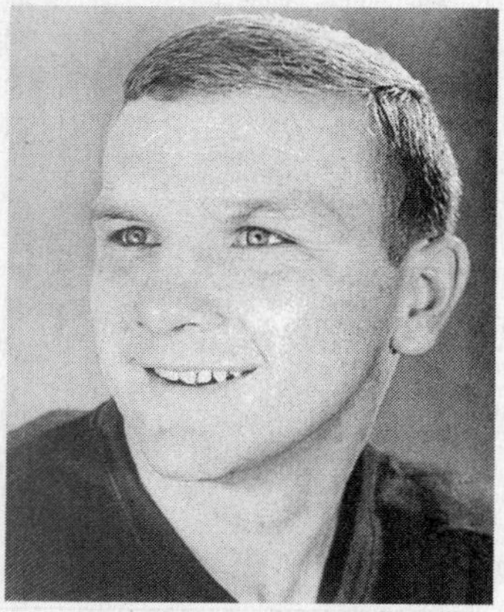
Garry Peters

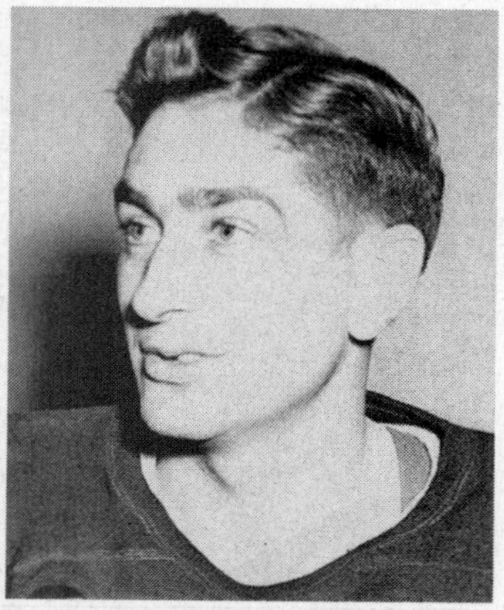
Alf Pike

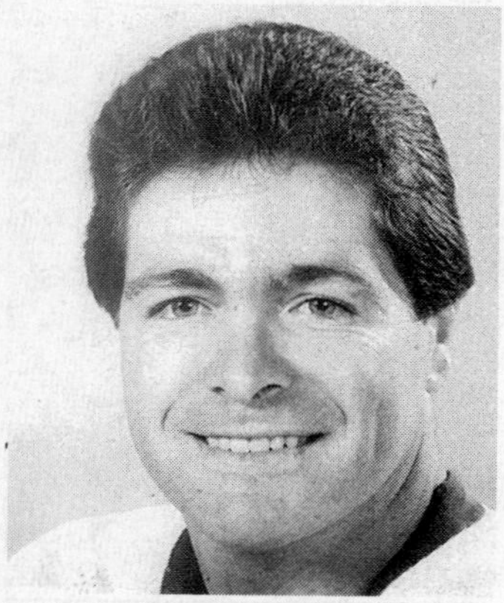
Jean Potvin

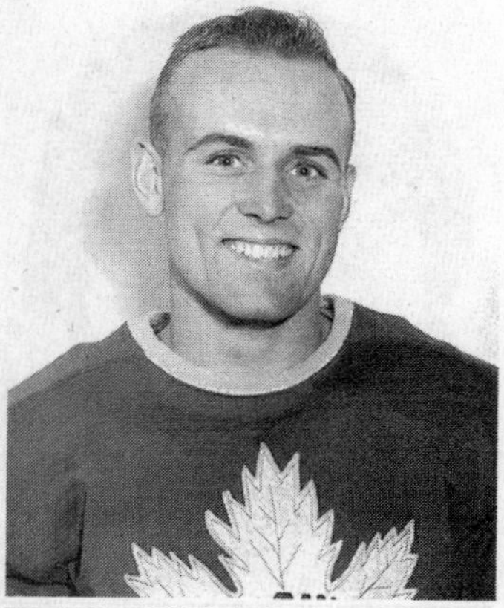
Noel Price

Name	NHL Teams	NHL Seasons	Regular Schedule GP	G	A	TP	PIM	Playoffs GP	G	A	TP	PIM	NHL Cup Wins	First NHL Season	Last NHL Season
Perlini, Fred	Tor.	2	8	2	3	5	0	....	....	....	....	....	....	1981-82	1983-84
Perreault, Fern	NYR	2	3	0	0	0	0	....	....	....	....	....	....	1947-48	1949-50
Perreault, Gilbert	Buf.	17	1191	512	814	1326	500	90	33	70	103	44	....	1970-71	1986-87
Perry, Brian	Oak., Buf.	3	96	16	29	45	24	8	1	1	2	4	....	1968-69	1970-71
‡ Persson, Ricard	N.J., St.L., Ott.	7	229	10	44	54	262	26	1	3	4	59	....	1995-96	2001-02
Persson, Stefan	NYI	9	622	52	317	369	574	102	7	50	57	69	4	1977-78	1985-86
Pesut, George	Cal.	2	92	3	22	25	130	....	....	....	....	....	....	1974-75	1975-76
• Peters, Frank	NYR	1	43	0	0	0	59	4	0	0	0	2	....	1930-31	1930-31
Peters, Garry	Mtl., NYR, Phi., Bos.	8	311	34	34	68	261	9	2	2	4	31	1	1964-65	1971-72
Peters, Jimmy	Mtl., Bos., Det., Chi.	9	574	125	150	275	186	60	5	9	14	22	3	1945-46	1953-54
Peters, Jimmy	Det., L.A.	9	309	37	36	73	48	11	0	2	2	2	....	1964-65	1974-75
Peters, Steve	Col.	1	2	0	1	1	0	....	....	....	....	....	....	1979-80	1979-80
Peterson, Brent	Det., Buf., Van., Hfd.	11	620	72	141	213	484	31	4	4	8	65	....	1978-79	1988-89
Peterson, Brent	T.B.	3	56	9	1	10	6	....	....	....	....	....	....	1996-97	1998-99
Petit, Michel	Van., NYR, Que., Tor., Cgy., L.A., T.B., Edm., Phi., Phx.	16	827	90	238	328	1839	19	0	2	2	61	....	1982-83	1997-98
Petrenko, Sergei	Buf.	1	14	0	4	4	0	....	....	....	....	....	....	1993-94	1993-94
‡ Petrov, Oleg	Mtl., Nsh.	8	382	72	115	187	101	20	1	6	7	2	....	1992-93	2002-03
‡ Petrovicky, Robert	Hfd., Dal., St.L., T.B., NYI	8	208	27	38	65	118	2	0	0	0	0	....	1992-93	2000-01
Pettersson, Jorgen	St.L., Hfd., Wsh.	6	435	174	192	366	117	44	15	12	27	4	....	1980-81	1985-86
• Pettinger, Eric	Bos., Tor., Ott.	3	98	7	12	19	83	4	1	0	1	8	....	1928-29	1930-31
• Pettinger, Gord	NYR, Det., Bos.	8	292	42	74	116	77	47	4	5	9	11	4	1932-33	1939-40
Phair, Lyle	L.A.	3	48	6	7	13	12	1	0	0	0	0	....	1985-86	1987-88
Phillipoff, Harold	Atl., Chi.	3	141	26	57	83	267	6	0	2	2	9	....	1977-78	1979-80
• Phillips, Bill	Mtl.M.	1	27	1	1	2	6	4	0	0	0	2	....	1929-30	1929-30
• Phillips, Charlie	Mtl.	1	17	0	0	0	6	....	....	....	....	....	....	1942-43	1942-43
• Phillips, Merlyn	Mtl.M., NYA	8	302	52	31	83	232	24	5	1	6	19	1	1925-26	1932-33
Picard, Michel	Hfd., S.J., Ott., St.L., Edm., Phi.	9	166	28	42	70	103	5	0	0	0	2	....	1990-91	2000-01
Picard, Noel	Mtl., St.L., Atl.	7	335	12	63	75	616	50	2	11	13	167	1	1964-65	1972-73
Picard, Robert	Wsh., Tor., Mtl., Wpg., Que., Det.	13	899	104	319	423	1025	36	5	15	20	39	....	1977-78	1989-90
Picard, Roger	St.L.	1	15	2	2	4	21	....	....	....	....	....	....	1967-68	1967-68
Pichette, Dave	Que., St.L., N.J., NYR	7	322	41	140	181	348	28	3	7	10	54	....	1980-81	1987-88
Picketts, Hal	NYA	1	48	3	1	4	32	....	....	....	....	....	....	1933-34	1933-34
Pidhirny, Harry	Bos.	1	2	0	0	0	0	....	....	....	....	....	....	1957-58	1957-58
Pierce, Randy	Col., N.J., Hfd.	8	277	62	76	138	223	2	0	0	0	0	....	1977-78	1984-85
Pike, Alf	NYR	6	234	42	77	119	145	21	4	2	6	12	1	1939-40	1946-47
‡ Pilar, Karel	Tor.	3	90	6	24	30	42	12	1	4	5	12	....	2001-02	2003-04
Pilon, Rich	NYI, NYR, St.L.	14	631	8	69	77	1745	15	0	0	0	50	....	1988-89	2001-02
Pilote, Pierre	Chi., Tor.	14	890	80	418	498	1251	86	8	53	61	102	1	1955-56	1968-69
Pinder, Gerry	Chi., Cal.	3	223	55	69	124	135	17	0	4	4	6	....	1969-70	1971-72
Pirus, Alex	Min., Det.	4	159	30	28	58	94	2	0	1	1	2	....	1976-77	1979-80
‡ Pisa, Ales	Edm., NYR	2	53	1	3	4	26	....	....	....	....	....	....	2001-02	2002-03
Pitlick, Lance	Ott., Fla.	8	393	16	33	49	298	24	0	2	2	21	....	1994-95	2001-02
• Pitre, Didier	Mtl.	6	127	64	34	98	84	9	2	4	6	16	....	1917-18	1922-23
Pivonka, Michal	Wsh.	13	825	181	418	599	478	95	19	36	55	86	....	1986-87	1998-99
• Plager, Barclay	St.L.	10	614	44	187	231	1115	68	3	20	23	182	....	1967-68	1976-77
Plager, Bill	Min., St.L., Atl.	9	263	4	34	38	294	31	0	2	2	26	....	1967-68	1975-76
Plager, Bob	NYR, St.L.	14	644	20	126	146	802	74	2	17	19	195	....	1964-65	1977-78
Plamondon, Gerry	Mtl.	5	74	7	13	20	10	11	5	2	7	2	1	1945-46	1950-51
Plante, Cam	Tor.	1	2	0	0	0	0	....	....	....	....	....	....	1984-85	1984-85
Plante, Dan	NYI	4	159	9	14	23	135	1	1	0	1	2	....	1993-94	1997-98
Plante, Derek	Buf., Dal., Chi., Phi.	8	450	96	152	248	138	41	6	10	16	18	1	1993-94	2000-01
Plante, Pierre	Phi., St.L., Chi., NYR, Que.	9	599	125	172	297	599	33	2	6	8	51	....	1971-72	1979-80
Plantery, Mark	Wpg.	1	25	1	5	6	14	....	....	....	....	....	....	1980-81	1980-81
Plavsic, Adrien	St.L., Van., T.B., Ana.	8	214	16	56	72	161	13	1	7	8	4	....	1989-90	1996-97
• Plaxton, Hugh	Mtl.M.	1	15	1	2	3	4	....	....	....	....	....	....	1932-33	1932-33
Playfair, Jim	Edm., Chi.	3	21	2	4	6	51	....	....	....	....	....	....	1983-84	1988-89
Playfair, Larry	Buf., L.A.	12	688	26	94	120	1812	43	0	6	6	111	....	1978-79	1989-90
Pleau, Larry	Mtl.	3	94	9	15	24	27	4	0	0	0	0	....	1969-70	1971-72
• Pletsch, Charles	Ham.	1	1	0	0	0	0	....	....	....	....	....	....	1920-21	1920-21
Plett, Willi	Atl., Cgy., Min., Bos.	13	834	222	215	437	2572	83	24	22	46	466	....	1975-76	1987-88
Plumb, Rob	Det.	2	14	3	2	5	2	....	....	....	....	....	....	1977-78	1978-79
Plumb, Ron	Hfd.	1	26	3	4	7	14	....	....	....	....	....	....	1979-80	1979-80
Pocza, Harvie	Wsh.	2	3	0	0	0	2	....	....	....	....	....	....	1979-80	1981-82
Poddubny, Walt	Edm., Tor., NYR, Que., N.J.	11	468	184	238	422	454	19	7	2	9	12	....	1981-82	1991-92
Podein, Shjon	Edm., Phi., Col., St.L.	11	699	100	106	206	439	127	14	13	27	132	1	1992-93	2002-03
‡ Podkonicky, Andrej	Fla., Wsh.	2	8	1	0	1	2	....	....	....	....	....	....	2000-01	2003-04
Podloski, Ray	Bos.	1	8	0	1	1	17	....	....	....	....	....	....	1988-89	1988-89
Podollan, Jason	Fla., Tor., L.A., NYI	4	41	1	5	6	19	....	....	....	....	....	....	1996-97	2001-02
Podolsky, Nels	Det.	1	1	0	0	0	0	7	0	0	0	4	....	1948-49	1948-49
Poeschek, Rudy	NYR, Wpg., T.B., St.L.	12	364	6	25	31	817	5	0	0	0	18	....	1987-88	1999-00
• Poeta, Tony	Chi.	1	1	0	0	0	0	....	....	....	....	....	....	1951-52	1951-52
• Poile, Bud	Tor., Chi., Det., NYR, Bos.	7	311	107	122	229	91	23	4	5	9	8	1	1942-43	1949-50
Poile, Don	Det.	2	66	7	9	16	12	4	0	0	0	0	....	1954-55	1957-58
• Poirier, Gordie	Mtl.	1	10	0	0	0	0	....	....	....	....	....	....	1939-40	1939-40
Polanic, Tom	Min.	2	19	0	2	2	53	5	1	1	2	4	....	1969-70	1970-71
• Polich, John	NYR	2	3	0	1	1	0	....	....	....	....	....	....	1939-40	1940-41
Polich, Mike	Mtl., Min.	5	226	24	29	53	57	23	2	1	3	2	1	1976-77	1980-81
Polis, Greg	Pit., St.L., NYR, Wsh.	10	615	174	169	343	391	7	0	2	2	6	....	1970-71	1979-80
Poliziani, Dan	Bos.	1	1	0	0	0	0	3	0	0	0	0	....	1958-59	1958-59
Polonich, Dennis	Det.	8	390	59	82	141	1242	7	1	0	1	19	....	1974-75	1982-83
Pooley, Paul	Wpg.	2	15	0	3	3	0	....	....	....	....	....	....	1984-85	1985-86
Popein, Larry	NYR, Oak.	8	449	80	141	221	162	16	1	4	5	6	....	1954-55	1967-68
Popiel, Poul	Bos., L.A., Det., Van., Edm.	7	224	13	41	54	210	4	1	0	1	4	....	1965-66	1979-80
Popovic, Peter	Mtl., NYR, Pit., Bos.	8	485	10	63	73	291	35	1	4	5	18	....	1993-94	2000-01
• Portland, Jack	Mtl., Bos., Chi.	10	381	15	56	71	323	33	1	3	4	25	1	1933-34	1942-43
Porvari, Jukka	Col., N.J.	2	39	3	9	12	4	....	....	....	....	....	....	1981-82	1982-83
Posa, Victor	Chi.	1	2	0	0	0	2	....	....	....	....	....	....	1985-86	1985-86
Posavad, Mike	St.L.	2	8	0	0	0	0	....	....	....	....	....	....	1985-86	1986-87
Posmyk, Marek	T.B.	2	19	1	2	3	20	....	....	....	....	....	....	1999-00	2000-01
Potomski, Barry	L.A., S.J.	3	68	6	5	11	227	....	....	....	....	....	....	1995-96	1997-98
Potvin, Denis	NYI	15	1060	310	742	1052	1356	185	56	108	164	253	4	1973-74	1987-88
Potvin, Jean	L.A., Phi., NYI, Cle., Min.	11	613	63	224	287	478	39	2	9	11	17	1	1970-71	1980-81
• Potvin, Marc	Det., L.A., Hfd., Bos.	6	121	3	5	8	456	13	0	1	1	50	....	1990-91	1995-96
Poudrier, Daniel	Que.	3	25	1	5	6	10	....	....	....	....	....	....	1985-86	1987-88
Poulin, Daniel	Min.	1	3	1	1	2	2	....	....	....	....	....	....	1981-82	1981-82
Poulin, Dave	Phi., Bos., Wsh.	13	724	205	325	530	482	129	31	42	73	132	....	1982-83	1994-95
Poulin, Patrick	Hfd., Chi., T.B., Mtl.	11	634	101	134	235	299	32	6	2	8	8	....	1991-92	2001-02
Pouzar, Jaroslav	Edm.	4	186	34	48	82	135	29	6	4	10	16	3	1982-83	1986-87
• Powell, Ray	Chi.	1	31	7	15	22	2	....	....	....	....	....	....	1950-51	1950-51
• Powis, Geoff	Chi.	1	2	0	0	0	0	....	....	....	....	....	....	1967-68	1967-68
Powis, Lynn	Chi., K.C.	2	130	19	33	52	25	1	0	0	0	0	....	1973-74	1974-75
Prajsler, Petr	L.A., Bos.	4	46	3	10	13	51	4	0	0	0	0	....	1987-88	1991-92
• Pratt, Babe	NYR, Tor., Bos.	12	517	83	209	292	463	63	12	17	29	90	2	1935-36	1946-47
• Pratt, Jack	Bos.	2	37	2	0	2	42	4	0	0	0	0	....	1930-31	1931-32
Pratt, Kelly	Pit.	1	22	0	6	6	15	....	....	....	....	....	....	1974-75	1974-75
Pratt, Tracy	Oak., Pit., Buf., Van., Col., Tor.	10	580	17	97	114	1026	25	0	1	1	62	....	1967-68	1976-77
Prentice, Dean	NYR, Bos., Det., Pit., Min.	22	1378	391	469	860	484	54	13	17	30	38	....	1952-53	1973-74
• Prentice, Eric	Tor.	1	5	0	0	0	4	....	....	....	....	....	....	1943-44	1943-44
Presley, Wayne	Chi., S.J., Buf., NYR, Tor.	12	684	155	147	302	953	83	26	17	43	142	....	1984-85	1995-96
Preston, Rich	Chi., N.J.	8	580	127	164	291	348	47	4	18	22	56	....	1979-80	1986-87
Preston, Yves	Phi.	2	28	7	3	10	4	....	....	....	....	....	....	1978-79	1980-81
Priakin, Sergei	Cgy.	3	46	3	8	11	2	1	0	0	0	0	....	1988-89	1990-91
Price, Jack	Chi.	3	57	4	6	10	24	4	0	0	0	0	....	1951-52	1953-54
Price, Noel	Tor., NYR, Det., Mtl., Pit., L.A., Atl.	14	499	14	114	128	333	12	0	1	1	8	1	1957-58	1975-76
Price, Pat	NYI, Edm., Pit., Que., NYR, Min.	13	726	43	218	261	1456	74	2	10	12	195	....	1975-76	1987-88
Price, Tom	Cal., Cle., Pit.	5	29	0	2	2	12	....	....	....	....	....	....	1974-75	1978-79
Priestlay, Ken	Buf., Pit.	6	168	27	34	61	63	14	0	0	0	21	1	1986-87	1991-92
• Primeau, Joe	Tor.	9	310	66	177	243	105	38	5	18	23	12	1	1927-28	1935-36
Primeau, Kevin	Van.	1	2	0	0	0	4	....	....	....	....	....	....	1980-81	1980-81
• Pringle, Ellie	NYA	1	6	0	0	0	0	....	....	....	....	....	....	1930-31	1930-31
Probert, Bob	Det., Chi.	16	935	163	221	384	3300	81	16	32	48	274	....	1985-86	2001-02
‡ Prochazka, Martin	Tor., Atl.	2	32	2	5	7	8	....	....	....	....	....	....	1997-98	1999-00
• Prodgers, Goldie	Tor., Ham.	6	111	63	29	92	39	....	....	....	....	....	....	1919-20	1924-25
Prokhorov, Vitali	St.L.	3	83	19	11	30	35	4	0	0	0	0	....	1992-93	1994-95

			Regular Schedule					Playoffs							
Name	NHL Teams	NHL Seasons	GP	G	A	TP	PIM	GP	G	A	TP	PIM	NHL Cup Wins	First NHL Season	Last NHL Season
Prokopec, Mike	Chi.	2	15	0	0	0	11	....	....	....	....	....	....	1995-96	1996-97
Pronger, Sean	Ana., Pit., NYR, L.A., Bos., CBJ, Van.	8	260	23	36	59	159	14	0	2	2	8	....	1995-96	2003-04
Pronovost, Andre	Mtl., Bos., Det., Min.	10	556	94	104	198	408	70	11	11	22	58	4	1956-57	1967-68
Pronovost, Jean	Pit., Atl., Wsh.	14	998	391	383	774	413	35	11	9	20	14	....	1968-69	1981-82
Pronovost, Marcel	Det., Tor.	21	1206	88	257	345	851	134	8	23	31	104	5	1949-50	1969-70
Propp, Brian	Phi., Bos., Min., Hfd.	15	1016	425	579	1004	830	160	64	84	148	151	....	1979-80	1993-94
Proulx, Christian	Mtl.	1	7	1	2	3	20	....	....	....	....	....	....	1993-94	1993-94
● Provost, Claude	Mtl.	15	1005	254	335	589	469	126	25	38	63	86	9	1955-56	1969-70
Prpic, Joel	Bos., Col.	3	18	0	3	3	4	....	....	....	....	....	....	1997-98	2000-01
Pryor, Chris	Min., NYI	6	82	1	4	5	122	....	....	....	....	....	....	1984-85	1989-90
Prystai, Metro	Chi., Det.	11	674	151	179	330	231	43	12	14	26	8	2	1947-48	1957-58
● Pudas, Al	Tor.	1	4	0	0	0	0	....	....	....	....	....	....	1926-27	1926-27
Pulford, Bob	Tor., L.A.	16	1079	281	362	643	792	89	25	26	51	126	4	1956-57	1971-72
Pulkkinen, Dave	NYI	1	2	0	0	0	0	....	....	....	....	....	....	1972-73	1972-73
● Purpur, Fido	St.L., Chi., Det.	5	144	25	35	60	46	16	1	2	3	4	....	1934-35	1944-45
Purves, John	Wsh.	1	7	1	0	1	0	....	....	....	....	....	....	1990-91	1990-91
● Pusie, Jean	Mtl., NYR, Bos.	5	61	1	4	5	28	7	0	0	0	0	1	1930-31	1935-36
Pyatt, Nelson	Det., Wsh., Col.	7	296	71	63	134	69	....	....	....	....	....	....	1973-74	1979-80

Q

			Regular Schedule					Playoffs							
Name	NHL Teams	NHL Seasons	GP	G	A	TP	PIM	GP	G	A	TP	PIM	NHL Cup Wins	First NHL Season	Last NHL Season
● Quackenbush, Bill	Det., Bos.	14	774	62	222	284	95	80	2	19	21	8	....	1942-43	1955-56
Quackenbush, Max	Bos., Chi.	2	61	4	7	11	30	6	0	0	0	4	....	1950-51	1951-52
Quenneville, Joel	Tor., Col., N.J., Hfd., Wsh.	13	803	54	136	190	705	32	0	8	8	22	....	1978-79	1990-91
● Quenneville, Leo	NYR	1	25	0	3	3	10	3	0	0	0	0	....	1929-30	1929-30
● Quilty, John	Mtl., Bos.	4	125	36	34	70	81	13	3	5	8	9	....	1940-41	1947-48
Quinn, Dan	Cgy., Pit., Van., St.L., Phi., Min., Ott., L.A.	14	805	266	419	685	533	65	22	26	48	62	....	1983-84	1996-97
Quinn, Pat	Tor., Van., Atl.	9	606	18	113	131	950	11	0	1	1	21	....	1968-69	1976-77
Quinney, Ken	Que.	3	59	7	13	20	23	....	....	....	....	....	....	1986-87	1990-91
Quintal, Stephane	Bos., St.L., Wpg., Mtl., NYR, Chi.	16	1037	63	180	243	1320	52	2	10	12	51	....	1988-89	2003-04
Quintin, Jean-Francois	S.J.	2	22	5	5	10	4	....	....	....	....	....	....	1991-92	1992-93

R

			Regular Schedule					Playoffs							
Name	NHL Teams	NHL Seasons	GP	G	A	TP	PIM	GP	G	A	TP	PIM	NHL Cup Wins	First NHL Season	Last NHL Season
Racine, Yves	Det., Phi., Mtl., S.J., Cgy., T.B.	9	508	37	194	231	439	25	5	4	9	37	....	1989-90	1997-98
● Radley, Yip	NYA, Mtl.M.	2	18	0	1	1	13	....	....	....	....	....	....	1930-31	1936-37
Raglan, Herb	St.L., Que., T.B., Ott.	9	343	33	56	89	775	32	3	6	9	50	....	1985-86	1993-94
● Raglan, Rags	Det., Chi.	3	100	4	9	13	52	3	0	0	0	0	....	1950-51	1952-53
‡ Ragnarsson, Marcus	S.J., Phi.	9	632	37	140	177	482	68	2	13	15	60	....	1995-96	2003-04
Raleigh, Don	NYR	10	535	101	219	320	96	18	6	5	11	6	....	1943-44	1955-56
Ralph, Brad	Phx.	1	1	0	0	0	0	....	....	....	....	....	....	2000-01	2000-01
Ramage, Rob	Col., St.L., Cgy., Tor., Min., T.B., Mtl., Phi.	15	1044	139	425	564	2226	84	8	42	50	218	2	1979-80	1993-94
● Ramsay, Beattie	Tor.	1	43	0	2	2	10	....	....	....	....	....	....	1927-28	1927-28
Ramsay, Craig	Buf.	14	1070	252	420	672	201	89	17	31	48	27	....	1971-72	1984-85
Ramsay, Les	Chi.	1	11	2	2	4	2	....	....	....	....	....	....	1944-45	1944-45
Ramsey, Mike	Buf., Pit., Det.	18	1070	79	266	345	1012	115	8	29	37	176	....	1979-80	1996-97
Ramsey, Wayne	Buf.	1	2	0	0	0	0	....	....	....	....	....	....	1977-78	1977-78
● Randall, Ken	Tor., Ham., NYA	10	218	68	50	118	533	6	2	1	3	27	2	1917-18	1926-27
Ranheim, Paul	Cgy., Hfd., Car., Phi., Phx.	15	1013	161	199	360	288	36	3	8	11	6	....	1988-89	2002-03
Ranieri, George	Bos.	1	2	0	0	0.	0	....	....	....	....	....	....	1956-57	1956-57
‡ Ratchuk, Peter	Fla.	2	32	1	1	2	10	....	....	....	....	....	....	1998-99	2000-01
Ratelle, Jean	NYR, Bos.	21	1281	491	776	1267	276	123	32	66	98	24	....	1960-61	1980-81
Rathwell, Jake	Bos.	1	1	0	0	0	0	....	....	....	....	....	....	1974-75	1974-75
Ratushny, Dan	Van.	1	1	0	1	1	2	....	....	....	....	....	....	1992-93	1992-93
Rausse, Errol	Wsh.	3	31	7	3	10	0	....	....	....	....	....	....	1979-80	1981-82
Rautakallio, Pekka	Atl., Cgy.	3	235	33	121	154	122	23	2	5	7	8	....	1979-80	1981-82
Ravlich, Matt	Bos., Chi., Det., L.A.	10	410	12	78	90	364	24	1	5	6	16	....	1962-63	1972-73
Ray, Rob	Buf., Ott.	15	900	41	50	91	3207	55	3	2	5	169	....	1989-90	2003-04
● Raymond, Armand	Mtl.	2	22	0	2	2	10	....	....	....	....	....	....	1937-38	1939-40
● Raymond, Paul	Mtl.	4	76	2	3	5	6	5	0	0	0	2	....	1932-33	1938-39
Read, Mel	NYR	1	1	0	0	0	0	....	....	....	....	....	....	1946-47	1946-47
Reardon, Ken	Mtl.	7	341	26	96	122	604	31	2	5	7	62	1	1940-41	1949-50
● Reardon, Terry	Bos., Mtl.	7	193	47	53	100	73	30	8	10	18	12	1	1938-39	1946-47
Reaume, Marc	Tor., Det., Mtl., Van.	9	344	8	43	51	273	21	0	2	2	8	....	1954-55	1970-71
● Reay, Billy	Det., Mtl.	10	479	105	162	267	202	63	13	16	29	43	2	1943-44	1952-53
Redahl, Gord	Bos.	1	18	0	1	1	2	....	....	....	....	....	....	1958-59	1958-59
● Redding, George	Bos.	2	55	3	2	5	23	....	....	....	....	....	....	1924-25	1925-26
Redmond, Craig	L.A., Edm.	5	191	16	68	84	134	3	1	0	1	2	....	1984-85	1988-89
Redmond, Dick	Min., Cal., Chi., St.L., Atl., Bos.	13	771	133	312	445	504	66	9	22	31	27	....	1969-70	1981-82
Redmond, Keith	L.A.	1	12	1	0	1	20	....	....	....	....	....	....	1993-94	1993-94
Redmond, Mickey	Mtl., Det.	9	538	233	195	428	219	16	2	3	5	2	2	1967-68	1975-76
Reeds, Mark	St.L., Hfd.	8	365	45	114	159	135	53	8	9	17	23	....	1981-82	1988-89
Reekie, Joe	Buf., NYI, T.B., Wsh., Chi.	17	902	25	139	164	1326	51	3	4	7	63	....	1985-86	2001-02
● Regan, Bill	NYR, NYA	3	67	3	2	5	67	8	0	0	0	2	....	1929-30	1932-33
Regan, Larry	Bos., Tor.	5	280	41	95	136	71	42	7	14	21	18	....	1956-57	1960-61
Regier, Darcy	Cle., NYI	3	26	0	2	2	35	....	....	....	....	....	....	1977-78	1983-84
Reibel, Dutch	Det., Chi., Bos.	6	409	84	161	245	75	39	6	14	20	4	2	1953-54	1958-59
‡ Reichel, Robert	Cgy., NYI, Phx., Tor.	11	830	252	378	630	388	70	8	23	31	20	....	1990-91	2003-04
Reichert, Craig	Ana.	1	3	0	0	0	0	....	....	....	....	....	....	1996-97	1996-97
● Reid, Dave	Tor.	3	7	0	0	0	0	....	....	....	....	....	....	1952-53	1955-56
Reid, Dave	Bos., Tor., Dal., Col.	18	961	165	204	369	253	118	9	26	35	34	2	1983-84	2000-01
Reid, Gerry	Det.	1	....	....	....	....	....	2	0	0	0	2	....	1948-49	1948-49
Reid, Gord	NYA	1	1	0	0	0	2	....	....	....	....	....	....	1936-37	1936-37
● Reid, Reg	Tor.	2	39	1	0	1	4	2	0	0	0	0	....	1924-25	1925-26
Reid, Tom	Chi., Min.	11	701	17	113	130	654	42	1	13	14	49	....	1967-68	1977-78
Reierson, Dave	Cgy.	1	2	0	0	0	2	....	....	....	....	....	....	1988-89	1988-89
● Reigle, Ed	Bos.	1	17	0	2	2	25	....	....	....	....	....	....	1950-51	1950-51
Reinhart, Paul	Atl., Cgy., Van.	11	648	133	426	559	277	83	23	54	77	42	....	1979-80	1989-90
● Reinikka, Ollie	NYR	1	16	0	0	0	0	....	....	....	....	....	....	1926-27	1926-27
‡ Reirden, Todd	Edm., St.L., Atl., Phx.	5	183	11	35	46	181	5	0	1	1	0	....	1998-99	2003-04
● Reise, Leo	Ham., NYA, NYR	8	241	43	43	86	187	6	0	0	0	16	....	1920-21	1929-30
Reise, Leo	Chi., Det., NYR	9	494	28	81	109	399	52	8	5	13	68	2	1945-46	1953-54
Renaud, Mark	Hfd., Buf.	5	152	6	50	56	86	....	....	....	....	....	....	1979-80	1983-84
‡ Renberg, Mikael	Phi., T.B., Phx., Tor.	10	661	190	274	464	372	67	16	22	38	42	....	1993-94	2003-04
Reynolds, Bobby	Tor.	1	7	1	1	2	0	....	....	....	....	....	....	1989-90	1989-90
Ribble, Pat	Atl., Chi., Tor., Wsh., Cgy.	8	349	19	60	79	365	8	0	1	1	12	....	1975-76	1982-83
Rice, Steven	NYR, Edm., Hfd., Car.	8	329	64	61	125	275	2	2	1	3	6	....	1990-91	1997-98
Richard, Henri	Mtl.	20	1256	358	688	1046	928	180	49	80	129	181	11	1955-56	1974-75
● Richard, Jacques	Atl., Buf., Que.	10	556	160	187	347	307	35	5	5	10	34	....	1972-73	1982-83
Richard, Jean-Marc	Que.	2	5	2	1	3	2	....	....	....	....	....	....	1987-88	1989-90
● Richard, Maurice	Mtl.	18	978	544	421	965	1285	133	82	44	126	188	8	1942-43	1959-60
‡ Richard, Mike	Wsh.	2	7	0	2	2	0	....	....	....	....	....	....	1987-88	1989-90
Richards, Todd	Hfd.	2	8	0	4	4	4	11	0	3	3	6	....	1990-91	1991-92
‡ Richards, Travis	Dal.	2	3	0	0	0	2	....	....	....	....	....	....	1994-95	1995-96
Richardson, Dave	NYR, Chi., Det.	4	45	3	2	5	27	....	....	....	....	....	....	1963-64	1967-68
Richardson, Glen	Van.	1	24	3	6	9	19	....	....	....	....	....	....	1975-76	1975-76
Richardson, Ken	St.L.	3	49	8	13	21	16	....	....	....	....	....	....	1974-75	1978-79
Richer, Bob	Buf.	1	3	0	0	0	0	....	....	....	....	....	....	1972-73	1972-73
Richer, Stephane	Mtl., N.J., T.B., St.L., Pit.	17	1054	421	398	819	614	134	53	45	98	61	2	1984-85	2001-02
Richer, Stephane	T.B., Bos., Fla.	3	27	1	5	6	20	3	0	0	0	0	....	1992-93	1994-95
Richmond, Steve	NYR, Det., N.J., L.A.	5	159	4	23	27	514	4	0	0	0	12	....	1983-84	1988-89
‡ Richter, Barry	NYR, Bos., NYI, Mtl.	5	151	11	34	45	76	....	....	....	....	....	....	1995-96	2000-01
Richter, Dave	Min., Phi., Van., St.L.	9	365	9	40	49	1030	22	1	0	1	80	....	1981-82	1989-90
Ridley, Mike	NYR, Wsh., Tor., Van.	12	866	292	466	758	424	104	28	50	78	70	....	1985-86	1996-97
‡ Riesen, Michel	Edm.	1	12	0	1	1	4	....	....	....	....	....	....	2000-01	2000-01
Riley, Bill	Wsh., Wpg.	5	139	31	30	61	320	....	....	....	....	....	....	1974-75	1979-80
Riley, Jack	Det., Mtl., Bos.	4	104	10	22	32	8	4	0	3	3	0	....	1932-33	1935-36
● Riley, Jim	Chi., Det.	1	9	0	2	2	14	....	....	....	....	....	....	1926-27	1926-27
Riopelle, Rip	Mtl.	3	169	27	16	43	73	8	1	1	2	2	....	1947-48	1949-50
Rioux, Gerry	Wpg.	1	8	0	0	0	6	....	....	....	....	....	....	1979-80	1979-80
Rioux, Pierre	Cgy.	1	14	1	2	3	4	....	....	....	....	....	....	1982-83	1982-83
● Ripley, Vic	Chi., Bos., NYR, St.L.	7	278	51	49	100	173	20	4	1	5	10	....	1928-29	1934-35

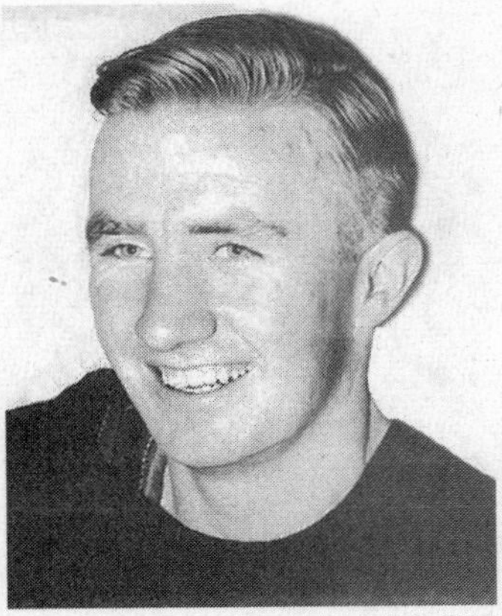

Bill Quackenbush

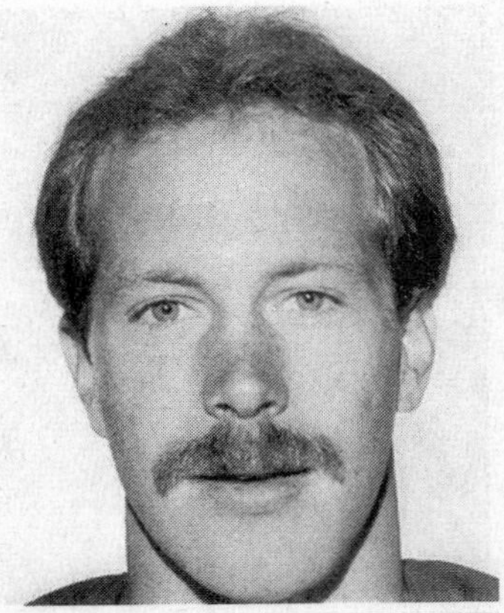

Mike Ramsey

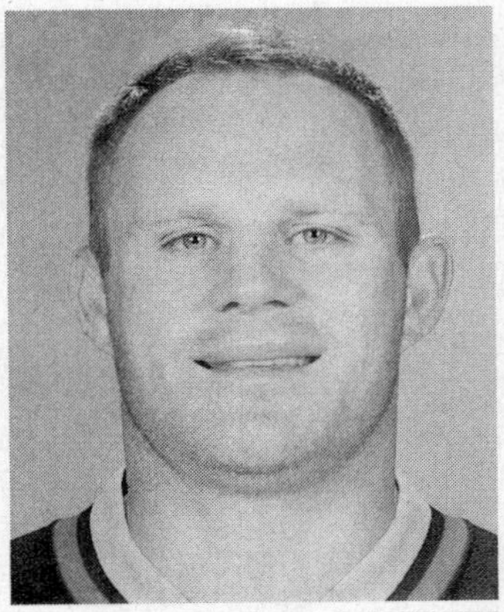

Rob Ray

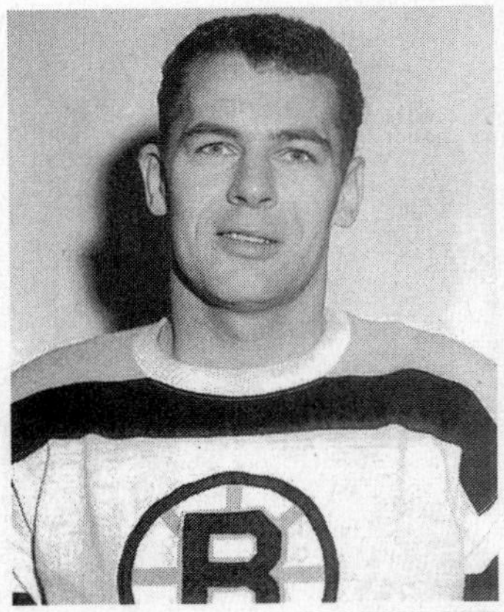

Larry Regan

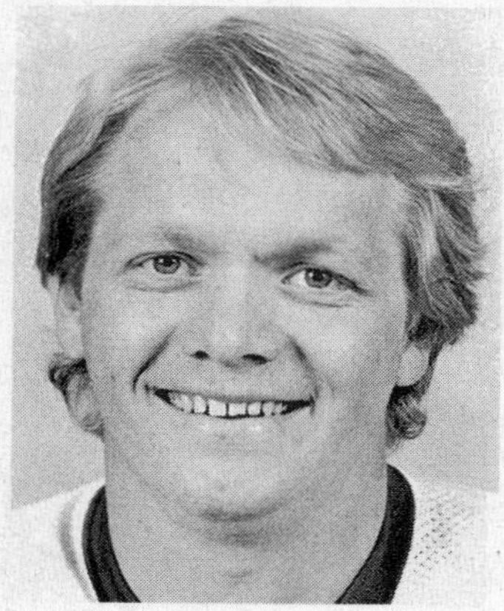

Darcy Regier

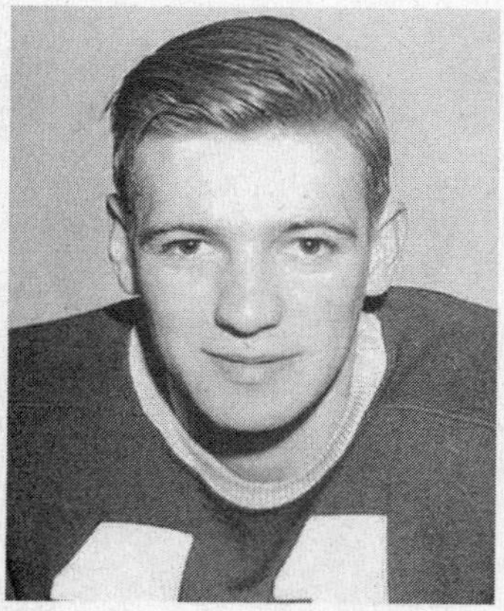

Gerry Reid

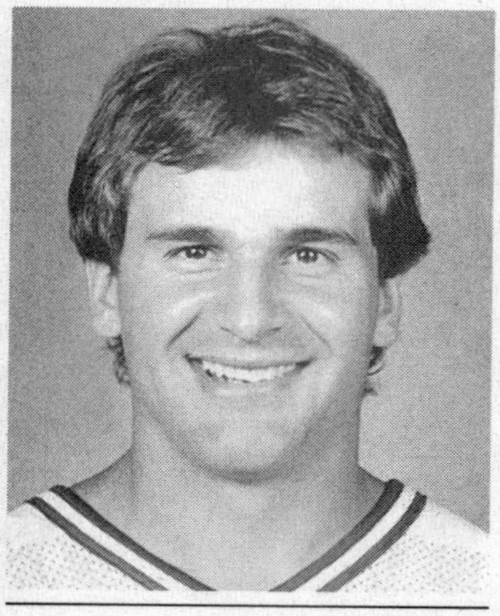

Todd Richards

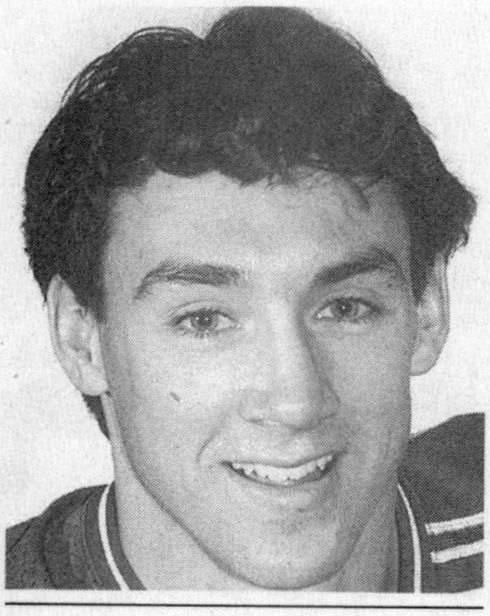

Mike Ridley

Name	NHL Teams	NHL Seasons	Regular Schedule GP	G	A	TP	PIM	Playoffs GP	G	A	TP	PIM	NHL Cup Wins	First NHL Season	Last NHL Season
Risebrough, Doug	Mtl., Cgy.	13	740	185	286	471	1542	124	21	37	58	238	4	1974-75	1986-87
Rissling, Gary	Wsh., Pit.	7	221	23	30	53	1008	5	0	1	1	4	....	1978-79	1984-85
Ritchie, Bob	Phi., Det.	2	29	8	4	12	10	....	....	....	....	....	....	1976-77	1977-78
• Ritchie, Dave	Mtl.W., Ott., Tor., Que., Mtl.	6	58	15	6	21	50	1	0	0	0	0	....	1917-18	1925-26
Ritson, Alex	NYR	1	1	0	0	0	0	....	....	....	....	....	....	1944-45	1944-45
Rittinger, Alan	Bos.	1	19	3	7	10	0	....	....	....	....	....	....	1943-44	1943-44
Rivard, Bob	Pit.	1	27	5	12	17	4	....	....	....	....	....	....	1967-68	1967-68
• Rivers, Gus	Mtl.	3	88	4	5	9	12	16	2	0	2	2	2	1929-30	1931-32
Rivers, Shawn	T.B.	1	4	0	2	2	2	....	....	....	....	....	....	1992-93	1992-93
Rivers, Wayne	Det., Bos., St.L., NYR	7	108	15	30	45	94	....	....	....	....	....	....	1961-62	1968-69
Rizzuto, Garth	Van.	1	37	3	4	7	16	....	....	....	....	....	....	1970-71	1970-71
• Roach, Mickey	Tor., Ham., NYA	8	211	77	34	111	54	....	....	....	....	....	....	1919-20	1926-27
Roberge, Mario	Mtl.	5	112	7	7	14	314	15	0	0	0	24	1	1990-91	1994-95
Roberge, Serge	Que.	1	9	0	0	0	24	....	....	....	....	....	....	1990-91	1990-91
Robert, Claude	Mtl.	1	23	1	0	1	9	....	....	....	....	....	....	1950-51	1950-51
Robert, Rene	Tor., Pit., Buf., Col.	12	744	284	418	702	597	50	22	19	41	73	....	1970-71	1981-82
Roberto, Phil	Mtl., St.L., Det., K.C., Col., Cle.	8	385	75	106	181	464	31	9	8	17	69	1	1969-70	1976-77
Roberts, David	St.L., Edm., Van.	5	125	20	33	53	85	9	0	0	0	16	....	1993-94	1997-98
Roberts, Doug	Det., Oak., Cal., Bos.	10	419	43	104	147	342	16	2	3	5	46	....	1965-66	1974-75
Roberts, Gordie	Hfd., Min., Phi., St.L., Pit., Bos.	15	1097	61	359	420	1582	153	10	47	57	273	2	1979-80	1993-94
Roberts, Jim	Min.	3	106	17	23	40	33	2	0	0	0	0	....	1976-77	1978-79
Roberts, Jimmy	Mtl., St.L.	15	1006	126	194	320	621	153	20	16	36	160	5	1963-64	1977-78
• Robertson, Fred	Tor., Det.	2	34	1	0	1	35	7	0	0	0	0	1	1931-32	1933-34
Robertson, Geordie	Buf.	1	5	1	2	3	7	....	....	....	....	....	....	1982-83	1982-83
• Robertson, George	Mtl.	2	31	2	5	7	6	....	....	....	....	....	....	1947-48	1948-49
Robertson, Torrie	Wsh., Hfd., Det.	10	442	49	99	148	1751	22	2	1	3	90	....	1980-81	1989-90
Robertsson, Bert	Van., Edm., NYR	4	123	4	10	14	75	5	0	0	0	0	....	1997-98	2000-01
Robidoux, Florent	Chi.	3	52	7	4	11	75	....	....	....	....	....	....	1980-81	1983-84
Robinson, Doug	Chi., NYR, L.A.	7	239	44	67	111	34	11	4	3	7	0	....	1963-64	1970-71
• Robinson, Earl	Mtl.M., Chi., Mtl.	11	417	83	98	181	133	25	5	4	9	0	1	1928-29	1939-40
Robinson, Larry	Mtl., L.A.	20	1384	208	750	958	793	227	28	116	144	211	6	1972-73	1991-92
Robinson, Moe	Mtl.	1	1	0	0	0	0	....	....	....	....	....	....	1979-80	1979-80
Robinson, Rob	St.L.	1	22	0	1	1	8	....	....	....	....	....	....	1991-92	1991-92
Robinson, Scott	Min.	1	1	0	0	0	2	....	....	....	....	....	....	1989-90	1989-90
Robitaille, Mike	NYR, Det., Buf., Van.	8	382	23	105	128	280	13	0	1	1	4	....	1969-70	1976-77
Roche, Dave	Pit., Cgy., NYI	5	171	15	15	30	334	16	2	7	9	26	....	1995-96	2001-02
• Roche, Des	Mtl.M., Ott., St.L., Mtl., Det.	4	113	20	18	38	44	....	....	....	....	....	....	1930-31	1934-35
• Roche, Earl	Mtl.M., Bos., Ott., St.L., Det.	4	147	25	27	52	48	2	0	0	0	0	....	1930-31	1934-35
Roche, Ernie	Mtl.	1	4	0	0	0	2	....	....	....	....	....	....	1950-51	1950-51
Rochefort, Dave	Det.	1	1	0	0	0	0	....	....	....	....	....	....	1966-67	1966-67
Rochefort, Leon	NYR, Mtl., Phi., L.A., Det., Atl., Van.	15	617	121	147	268	93	39	4	4	8	16	2	1960-61	1975-76
Rochefort, Normand	Que., NYR, T.B.	13	598	39	119	158	570	69	7	5	12	82	....	1980-81	1993-94
• Rockburn, Harvey	Det., Ott.	3	94	4	2	6	254	....	....	....	....	....	....	1929-30	1932-33
• Rodden, Eddie	Chi., Tor., Bos., NYR	4	97	6	14	20	60	2	0	1	1	0	....	1926-27	1930-31
Rodgers, Marc	Det.	1	21	1	1	2	10	....	....	....	....	....	....	1999-00	1999-00
‡ Roest, Stacy	Det., Min.	5	244	28	48	76	54	3	0	0	0	0	....	1998-99	2002-03
Rogers, John	Min.	2	14	2	4	6	0	....	....	....	....	....	....	1973-74	1974-75
Rogers, Mike	Hfd., NYR, Edm.	7	484	202	317	519	184	17	1	13	14	6	....	1979-80	1985-86
Rohlicek, Jeff	Van.	2	9	0	0	0	8	....	....	....	....	....	....	1987-88	1988-89
Rohlin, Leif	Van.	2	96	8	24	32	40	5	0	0	0	0	....	1995-96	1996-97
Rohloff, Jon	Bos.	3	150	7	25	32	129	10	1	2	3	8	....	1994-95	1996-97
Rolfe, Dale	Bos., L.A., Det., NYR	9	509	25	125	150	556	71	5	24	29	89	....	1959-60	1974-75
Romanchych, Larry	Chi., Atl.	6	298	68	97	165	102	7	2	2	4	4	....	1970-71	1976-77
Romaniuk, Russell	Wpg., Phi.	5	102	13	14	27	63	2	0	0	0	0	....	1991-92	1995-96
Rombough, Doug	Buf., NYI, Min.	4	150	24	27	51	80	....	....	....	....	....	....	1972-73	1975-76
Rominski, Dale	T.B.	1	3	0	1	1	2	....	....	....	....	....	....	1999-00	1999-00
• Romnes, Doc	Chi., Tor., NYA	10	360	68	136	204	42	45	7	18	25	4	2	1930-31	1939-40
Ronan, Ed	Mtl., Wpg., Buf.	6	182	13	23	36	101	27	4	3	7	16	1	1991-92	1996-97
• Ronan, Skene	Ott.	1	11	0	0	0	6	....	....	....	....	....	....	1918-19	1918-19
Ronning, Cliff	St.L., Van., Phx., Nsh., L.A., Min., NYI	18	1137	306	563	869	453	126	29	57	86	72	....	1985-86	2003-04
Ronnqvist, Jonas	Ana.	1	38	0	4	4	14	....	....	....	....	....	....	2000-01	2000-01
Ronson, Len	NYR, Oak.	2	18	2	1	3	10	....	....	....	....	....	....	1960-61	1968-69
Ronty, Paul	Bos., NYR, Mtl.	8	488	101	211	312	103	21	1	7	8	6	....	1947-48	1954-55
Rooney, Steve	Mtl., Wpg., N.J.	5	154	15	13	28	496	25	3	2	5	86	1	1984-85	1988-89
Root, Bill	Mtl., Tor., St.L., Phi.	6	247	11	23	34	180	22	1	2	3	25	....	1982-83	1987-88
‡ Rosa, Pavel	L.A.	4	36	5	13	18	6	....	....	....	....	....	....	1998-99	2003-04
• Ross, Art	Mtl.W.	1	3	1	0	1	12	....	....	....	....	....	....	1917-18	1917-18
Ross, Jim	NYR	2	62	2	11	13	29	....	....	....	....	....	....	1951-52	1952-53
Rossignol, Roly	Det., Mtl.	3	14	3	5	8	6	1	0	0	0	2	....	1943-44	1945-46
Rota, Darcy	Chi., Atl., Van.	11	794	256	239	495	973	60	14	7	21	147	....	1973-74	1983-84
Rota, Randy	Mtl., L.A., K.C., Col.	5	212	38	39	77	60	5	0	1	1	0	....	1972-73	1976-77
• Rothschild, Sam	Mtl.M., Pit., NYA	4	100	8	6	14	25	6	0	0	0	0	1	1924-25	1927-28
• Roulston, Rolly	Det.	3	24	0	6	6	10	....	....	....	....	....	1	1935-36	1937-38
Roulston, Tom	Edm., Pit.	5	195	47	49	96	74	21	2	2	4	2	....	1980-81	1985-86
Roupe, Magnus	Phi.	2	40	3	5	8	42	....	....	....	....	....	....	1987-88	1988-89
Rouse, Bob	Min., Wsh., Tor., Det., S.J.	17	1061	37	181	218	1559	136	7	21	28	198	2	1983-84	1999-00
Rousseau, Bobby	Mtl., Min., NYR	15	942	245	458	703	359	128	27	57	84	69	4	1960-61	1974-75
Rousseau, Guy	Mtl.	2	4	0	1	1	0	....	....	....	....	....	....	1954-55	1956-57
Rousseau, Roland	Mtl.	1	2	0	0	0	0	....	....	....	....	....	....	1952-53	1952-53
Routhier, Jean-Marc	Que.	1	8	0	0	0	9	....	....	....	....	....	....	1989-90	1989-90
• Rowe, Bobby	Bos.	1	4	1	0	1	0	....	....	....	....	....	....	1924-25	1924-25
Rowe, Mike	Pit.	3	11	0	0	0	11	....	....	....	....	....	....	1984-85	1986-87
Rowe, Ron	NYR	1	5	1	0	1	0	....	....	....	....	....	....	1947-48	1947-48
Rowe, Tom	Wsh., Hfd., Det.	7	357	85	100	185	615	3	2	0	2	0	....	1976-77	1982-83
‡ Roy, Jean-Yves	NYR, Ott., Bos.	4	61	12	16	28	26	....	....	....	....	....	....	1994-95	1997-98
Roy, Stephane	Min.	1	12	1	0	1	0	....	....	....	....	....	....	1987-88	1987-88
Royer, Gaetan	T.B.	1	3	0	0	0	2	....	....	....	....	....	....	2001-02	2001-02
Royer, Remi	Chi.	1	18	0	0	0	67	....	....	....	....	....	....	1998-99	1998-99
Rozzini, Gino	Bos.	1	31	5	10	15	20	6	1	2	3	6	....	1944-45	1944-45
Rucinski, Mike	Chi.	2	1	0	0	0	0	2	0	0	0	0	....	1987-88	1988-89
Rucinski, Mike	Car.	3	26	0	2	2	10	....	....	....	....	....	....	1997-98	2000-01
• Ruelle, Bernie	Det.	1	2	1	0	1	0	....	....	....	....	....	....	1943-44	1943-44
Ruff, Jason	St.L., T.B.	2	14	3	3	6	10	....	....	....	....	....	....	1992-93	1993-94
Ruff, Lindy	Buf., NYR	12	691	105	195	300	1264	52	11	13	24	193	....	1979-80	1990-91
Ruhnke, Kent	Bos.	1	2	0	1	1	0	....	....	....	....	....	....	1975-76	1975-76
Rumble, Darren	Phi., Ott., St.L., T.B.	8	193	10	26	36	216	....	....	....	....	....	1	1990-91	2003-04
Rundqvist, Thomas	Mtl.	1	2	0	1	1	0	....	....	....	....	....	....	1984-85	1984-85
• Runge, Paul	Bos., Mtl.M., Mtl.	7	140	18	22	40	57	7	0	0	0	6	....	1930-31	1937-38
Ruotsalainen, Reijo	NYR, Edm., N.J.	7	446	107	237	344	180	86	15	32	47	44	2	1981-82	1989-90
Rupp, Duane	NYR, Tor., Min., Pit.	10	374	24	93	117	220	10	2	2	4	8	....	1962-63	1972-73
Ruskowski, Terry	Chi., L.A., Pit., Min.	10	630	113	313	426	1354	21	1	6	7	86	....	1979-80	1988-89
Russell, Cam	Chi., Col.	10	396	9	21	30	872	44	0	5	5	16	....	1989-90	1998-99
• Russell, Church	NYR	3	90	20	16	36	12	....	....	....	....	....	....	1945-46	1947-48
Russell, Phil	Chi., Atl., Cgy., N.J., Buf.	15	1016	99	325	424	2038	73	4	22	26	202	....	1972-73	1986-87
Ruuttu, Christian	Buf., Chi., Van.	9	621	134	298	432	714	42	4	9	13	49	....	1986-87	1994-95
Ruzicka, Vladimir	Edm., Bos., Ott.	5	233	82	85	167	129	30	4	14	18	2	....	1989-90	1993-94
Ryan, Terry	Mtl.	3	8	0	0	0	36	....	....	....	....	....	....	1996-97	1998-99
Rychel, Warren	Chi., L.A., Tor., Col., Ana.	9	406	38	39	77	1422	70	8	13	21	121	1	1988-89	1998-99
Rymsha, Andy	Que.	1	6	0	0	0	23	....	....	....	....	....	....	1991-92	1991-92

S

Name	NHL Teams	NHL Seasons	Regular Schedule GP	G	A	TP	PIM	Playoffs GP	G	A	TP	PIM	NHL Cup Wins	First NHL Season	Last NHL Season
Saarinen, Simo	NYR	1	8	0	0	0	0	....	....	....	....	....	....	1984-85	1984-85
Sabol, Shaun	Phi.	1	2	0	0	0	0	....	....	....	....	....	....	1989-90	1989-90
Sabourin, Bob	Tor.	1	1	0	0	0	2	....	....	....	....	....	....	1951-52	1951-52
Sabourin, Gary	St.L., Tor., Cal., Cle.	10	627	169	188	357	397	62	19	11	30	58	....	1967-68	1976-77
Sabourin, Ken	Cgy., Wsh.	4	74	2	8	10	201	12	0	0	0	34	....	1988-89	1991-92
Sacco, David	Tor., Ana.	3	35	5	13	18	22	....	....	....	....	....	....	1993-94	1995-96
Sacco, Joe	Tor., Ana., NYI, Wsh., Phi.	13	738	94	119	213	421	26	2	0	2	8	....	1990-91	2002-03
Sacharuk, Larry	NYR, St.L.	5	151	29	33	62	42	2	1	1	2	2	....	1972-73	1976-77
Saganiuk, Rocky	Tor., Pit.	6	259	57	65	122	201	6	1	0	1	15	....	1978-79	1983-84
Saleski, Don	Phi., Col.	9	543	128	125	253	629	82	13	17	30	131	2	1971-72	1979-80
Salming, Borje	Tor., Det.	17	1148	150	637	787	1344	81	12	37	49	91	....	1973-74	1989-90
‡ Salomonsson, Andreas	N.J., Wsh.	2	71	5	9	14	36	4	0	1	1	0	....	2001-02	2002-03

Name	NHL Teams	NHL Seasons	Regular Schedule GP	G	A	TP	PIM	Playoffs GP	G	A	TP	PIM	NHL Cup Wins	First NHL Season	Last NHL Season
Salovaara, Barry	Det.	2	90	2	13	15	70	....	....	....	....	....	....	1974-75	1975-76
Salvian, Dave	NYI	1	....	....	....	....	....	1	0	1	1	2	....	1976-77	1976-77
Samis, Phil	Tor.	2	2	0	0	0	0	5	0	1	1	2	1	1947-48	1949-50
Sampson, Gary	Wsh.	4	105	13	22	35	25	12	1	0	1	0	....	1983-84	1986-87
Samuelsson, Kjell	NYR, Phi., Pit., T.B.	14	813	48	138	186	1225	123	4	20	24	178	1	1985-86	1998-99
Samuelsson, Ulf	Hfd., Pit., NYR, Det., Phi.	16	1080	57	275	332	2453	132	7	27	34	272	2	1984-85	1999-00
Sandelin, Scott	Mtl., Phi., Min.	4	25	0	4	4	2	....	....	....	....	....	....	1986-87	1991-92
Sanderson, Derek	Bos., NYR, St.L., Van., Pit.	13	598	202	250	452	911	56	18	12	30	187	2	1965-66	1977-78
Sandford, Ed	Bos., Det., Chi.	9	502	106	145	251	355	42	13	11	24	27	....	1947-48	1955-56
Sandlak, Jim	Van., Hfd.	11	549	110	119	229	821	33	7	10	17	30	....	1985-86	1995-96
● Sands, Charlie	Tor., Bos., Mtl., NYR	12	427	99	109	208	58	34	6	6	12	4	1	1932-33	1943-44
Sandstrom, Tomas	NYR, L.A., Pit., Det., Ana.	15	983	394	462	856	1193	139	32	49	81	183	1	1984-85	1998-99
Sandwith, Terran	Edm.	1	8	0	0	0	6	....	....	....	....	....	....	1997-98	1997-98
Sanipass, Everett	Chi., Que.	5	164	25	34	59	358	5	2	0	2	4	....	1986-87	1990-91
‡ Sarault, Yves	Mtl., Cgy., Col., Ott., Atl., Nsh.	8	106	10	10	20	51	5	0	0	0	2	....	1994-95	2001-02
Sargent, Gary	L.A., Min.	8	402	61	161	222	273	20	5	7	12	8	....	1975-76	1982-83
Sarner, Craig	Bos.	1	7	0	0	0	0	....	....	....	....	....	....	1974-75	1974-75
Sarrazin, Dick	Phi.	3	100	20	35	55	22	4	0	0	0	0	....	1968-69	1971-72
Sasakamoose, Fred	Chi.	1	11	0	0	0	6	....	....	....	....	....	....	1953-54	1953-54
Sasser, Grant	Pit.	1	3	0	0	0	0	....	....	....	....	....	....	1983-84	1983-84
Sather, Glen	Bos., Pit., NYR, St.L., Mtl., Min.	10	658	80	113	193	724	72	1	5	6	86	....	1966-67	1975-76
Saunders, Bernie	Que.	2	10	0	1	1	8	....	....	....	....	....	....	1979-80	1980-81
Saunders, David	Van.	1	56	7	13	20	10	....	....	....	....	....	....	1987-88	1987-88
● Saunders, Ted	Ott.	1	18	1	3	4	4	....	....	....	....	....	....	1933-34	1933-34
Sauve, Jean-Francois	Buf., Que.	7	290	65	138	203	114	36	9	12	21	10	....	1980-81	1986-87
Savage, Andre	Bos., Phi.	4	66	10	14	24	14	....	....	....	....	....	....	1998-99	2002-03
Savage, Joel	Buf.	1	3	0	1	1	0	....	....	....	....	....	....	1990-91	1990-91
Savage, Reggie	Wsh., Que.	3	34	5	7	12	28	....	....	....	....	....	....	1990-91	1993-94
● Savage, Tony	Bos., Mtl.	1	49	1	5	6	6	2	0	0	0	0	....	1934-35	1934-35
Savard, Andre	Bos., Buf., Que.	12	790	211	271	482	411	85	13	18	31	77	....	1973-74	1984-85
Savard, Denis	Chi., Mtl., T.B.	17	1196	473	865	1338	1336	169	66	109	175	256	1	1980-81	1996-97
Savard, Jean	Chi., Hfd.	3	43	7	12	19	29	....	....	....	....	....	....	1977-78	1979-80
Savard, Serge	Mtl., Wpg.	17	1040	106	333	439	592	130	19	49	68	88	8	1966-67	1982-83
‡ Savoia, Ryan	Pit.	1	3	0	0	0	0	....	....	....	....	....	....	1998-99	1998-99
Sawyer, Kevin	St.L., Bos., Phx., Ana.	6	110	3	3	6	403	....	....	....	....	....	....	1995-96	2002-03
Scamurra, Peter	Wsh.	4	132	8	25	33	59	....	....	....	....	....	....	1975-76	1979-80
Sceviour, Darin	Chi.	1	1	0	0	0	0	....	....	....	....	....	....	1986-87	1986-87
Schaeffer, Butch	Chi.	1	5	0	0	0	6	....	....	....	....	....	....	1936-37	1936-37
Schamehorn, Kevin	Det., L.A.	3	10	0	0	0	17	....	....	....	....	....	....	1976-77	1980-81
Schella, John	Van.	2	115	2	18	20	224	....	....	....	....	....	....	1970-71	1971-72
Scherza, Chuck	Bos., NYR	2	36	6	6	12	35	....	....	....	....	....	....	1943-44	1944-45
Schinkel, Ken	NYR, Pit.	12	636	127	198	325	163	19	7	2	9	4	....	1959-60	1972-73
‡ Schlegel, Brad	Wsh., Cgy.	3	48	1	8	9	10	7	0	1	1	2	....	1991-92	1993-94
Schliebener, Andy	Van.	3	84	2	11	13	74	6	0	0	0	0	....	1981-82	1984-85
Schmautz, Bobby	Chi., Van., Bos., Edm., Col.	13	764	271	286	557	988	84	28	33	61	92	....	1967-68	1980-81
● Schmautz, Cliff	Buf., Phi.	1	56	13	19	32	33	....	....	....	....	....	....	1970-71	1970-71
‡ Schmidt, Chris	L.A.	1	10	0	2	2	5	....	....	....	....	....	....	2002-03	2002-03
● Schmidt, Clarence	Bos.	1	7	1	0	1	2	....	....	....	....	....	....	1943-44	1943-44
Schmidt, Jackie	Bos.	1	45	6	7	13	6	5	0	0	0	0	....	1942-43	1942-43
Schmidt, Milt	Bos.	16	776	229	346	575	466	86	24	25	49	60	2	1936-37	1954-55
Schmidt, Norm	Pit.	4	125	23	33	56	73	....	....	....	....	....	....	1983-84	1987-88
Schmidt, Otto	Bos.	1	2	0	0	0	0	....	....	....	....	....	....	1943-44	1943-44
● Schnarr, Werner	Bos.	2	26	0	0	0	0	....	....	....	....	....	....	1924-25	1925-26
Schneider, Andy	Ott.	1	10	0	0	0	15	....	....	....	....	....	....	1993-94	1993-94
Schock, Danny	Bos., Phi.	2	20	1	2	3	0	1	0	0	0	0	1	1969-70	1970-71
Schock, Ron	Bos., St.L., Pit., Buf.	15	909	166	351	517	260	55	4	16	20	29	....	1963-64	1977-78
Schoenfeld, Jim	Buf., Det., Bos.	13	719	51	204	255	1132	75	3	13	16	151	....	1972-73	1984-85
Schofield, Dwight	Det., Mtl., St.L., Wsh., Pit., Wpg.	7	211	8	22	30	631	9	0	0	0	55	....	1976-77	1987-88
Schreiber, Wally	Min.	2	41	8	10	18	12	....	....	....	....	....	....	1987-88	1988-89
● Schriner, Sweeney	NYA, Tor.	11	484	201	204	405	148	59	18	11	29	54	2	1934-35	1945-46
Schulte, Paxton	Que., Cgy.	2	2	0	0	0	4	....	....	....	....	....	....	1993-94	1996-97
Schultz, Dave	Phi., L.A., Pit., Buf.	9	535	79	121	200	2294	73	8	12	20	412	2	1971-72	1979-80
Schurman, Maynard	Hfd.	1	7	0	0	0	0	....	....	....	....	....	....	1979-80	1979-80
Schutt, Rod	Mtl., Pit., Tor.	8	286	77	92	169	177	22	8	6	14	26	....	1977-78	1985-86
Scissons, Scott	NYI	3	2	0	0	0	0	1	0	0	0	0	....	1990-91	1993-94
Sclisizzi, Enio	Det., Chi.	6	81	12	11	23	26	13	0	0	0	6	....	1946-47	1952-53
● Scott, Ganton	Tor., Ham., Mtl.M.	3	57	1	1	2	0	....	....	....	....	....	....	1922-23	1924-25
● Scott, Laurie	NYA, NYR	2	62	6	3	9	28	....	....	....	....	....	....	1926-27	1927-28
Scott, Richard	NYR	2	10	0	0	0	28	....	....	....	....	....	....	2001-02	2003-04
Scremin, Claudio	S.J.	2	17	0	1	1	29	....	....	....	....	....	....	1991-92	1992-93
Scruton, Howard	L.A.	1	4	0	4	4	9	....	....	....	....	....	....	1982-83	1982-83
Seabrooke, Glen	Phi.	3	19	1	6	7	4	....	....	....	....	....	....	1986-87	1988-89
Secord, Al	Bos., Chi., Tor., Phi.	12	766	273	222	495	2093	102	21	34	55	382	....	1978-79	1989-90
Sedlbauer, Ron	Van., Chi., Tor.	7	430	143	86	229	210	19	1	3	4	27	....	1974-75	1980-81
Seftel, Steve	Wsh.	1	4	0	0	0	2	....	....	....	....	....	....	1990-91	1990-91
Seguin, Dan	Min., Van.	2	37	2	6	8	50	....	....	....	....	....	....	1970-71	1973-74
Seguin, Steve	L.A.	1	5	0	0	0	9	....	....	....	....	....	....	1984-85	1984-85
● Seibert, Earl	NYR, Chi., Det.	15	645	89	187	276	746	66	11	8	19	76	2	1931-32	1945-46
Seiling, Ric	Buf., Det.	10	738	179	208	387	573	62	14	14	28	36	....	1977-78	1986-87
Seiling, Rod	Tor., NYR, Wsh., St.L., Atl.	17	979	62	269	331	601	77	4	8	12	55	....	1962-63	1978-79
Sejba, Jiri	Buf.	1	11	0	2	2	8	....	....	....	....	....	....	1990-91	1990-91
‡ Sekeras, Lubomir	Min., Dal.	4	213	18	53	71	122	15	1	1	2	6	....	2000-01	2003-04
Selby, Brit	Tor., Phi., St.L.	8	350	55	62	117	163	16	1	1	2	8	....	1964-65	1971-72
Self, Steve	Wsh.	1	3	0	0	0	0	....	....	....	....	....	....	1976-77	1976-77
Selivanov, Alex	T.B., Edm., CBJ	7	459	121	114	235	379	13	2	3	5	16	....	1994-95	2000-01
Sellars, Luke	Atl.	1	1	0	0	0	2	....	....	....	....	....	....	2001-02	2001-02
Selmser, Sean	CBJ	1	1	0	0	0	5	....	....	....	....	....	....	2000-01	2000-01
Selwood, Brad	Tor., L.A.	3	163	7	40	47	153	6	0	0	0	4	....	1970-71	1979-80
Semak, Alexander	N.J., T.B., NYI, Van.	6	289	83	91	174	187	8	1	1	2	0	....	1991-92	1996-97
Semchuk, Brandy	L.A.	1	1	0	0	0	2	....	....	....	....	....	....	1992-93	1992-93
Semenko, Dave	Edm., Hfd., Tor.	9	575	65	88	153	1175	73	6	6	12	208	2	1979-80	1987-88
Semenov, Anatoli	Edm., T.B., Van., Ana., Phi., Buf.	8	362	68	126	194	122	49	9	13	22	12	....	1989-90	1996-97
● Senick, George	NYR	1	13	2	3	5	8	....	....	....	....	....	....	1952-53	1952-53
Seppa, Jyrki	Wpg.	1	13	0	2	2	6	....	....	....	....	....	....	1983-84	1983-84
Serafini, Ron	Cal.	1	2	0	0	0	2	....	....	....	....	....	....	1973-74	1973-74
Serowik, Jeff	Tor., Bos., Pit.	4	28	0	6	6	16	....	....	....	....	....	....	1990-91	1999-00
Servinis, George	Min.	1	5	0	0	0	0	....	....	....	....	....	....	1987-88	1987-88
Sevcik, Jaroslav	Que.	1	13	0	2	2	2	....	....	....	....	....	....	1989-90	1989-90
Severyn, Brent	Que., Fla., NYI, Col., Ana., Dal.	7	328	10	30	40	825	8	0	0	0	12	....	1989-90	1998-99
Sevigny, Pierre	Mtl., NYR	4	78	4	5	9	64	3	0	1	1	0	....	1993-94	1997-98
Shack, Eddie	NYR, Tor., Bos., L.A., Buf., Pit.	17	1047	239	226	465	1437	74	6	7	13	151	4	1958-59	1974-75
● Shack, Joe	NYR	2	70	9	27	36	20	....	....	....	....	....	....	1942-43	1944-45
Shafranov, Konstantin	St.L.	1	5	2	1	3	0	....	....	....	....	....	....	1996-97	1996-97
Shakes, Paul	Cal.	1	21	0	4	4	12	....	....	....	....	....	....	1973-74	1973-74
Shaldybin, Yevgeny	Bos.	1	3	1	0	1	0	....	....	....	....	....	....	1996-97	1996-97
Shanahan, Sean	Mtl., Col., Bos.	3	40	1	3	4	47	....	....	....	....	....	....	1975-76	1977-78
Shand, Dave	Atl., Tor., Wsh.	8	421	19	84	103	544	26	1	2	3	83	....	1976-77	1984-85
Shank, Daniel	Det., Hfd.	3	77	13	14	27	175	5	0	0	0	22	....	1989-90	1991-92
Shannon, Chuck	NYA	1	4	0	0	0	2	....	....	....	....	....	....	1939-40	1939-40
Shannon, Darrin	Buf., Wpg., Phx.	10	506	87	163	250	344	45	7	10	17	38	....	1988-89	1997-98
Shannon, Darryl	Tor., Wpg., Buf., Atl., Cgy., Mtl.	13	544	28	111	139	523	29	4	7	11	16	....	1988-89	2000-01
● Shannon, Gerry	Ott., St.L., Bos., Mtl.M.	5	180	23	29	52	80	9	0	1	1	2	....	1933-34	1937-38
‡ Shantz, Jeff	Chi., Cgy., Col.	10	642	72	139	211	341	44	5	8	13	24	....	1993-94	2002-03
Sharifijanov, Vadim	N.J., Van.	3	92	16	21	37	50	4	0	0	0	0	....	1996-97	1999-00
Sharples, Jeff	Det.	3	105	14	35	49	70	7	0	3	3	6	....	1986-87	1988-89
Sharpley, Glen	Min., Chi.	6	389	117	161	278	199	27	7	11	18	24	....	1976-77	1981-82
Shaunessy, Scott	Que.	2	7	0	0	0	23	....	....	....	....	....	....	1986-87	1988-89
Shaw, Brad	Hfd., Ott., Wsh., St.L.	11	377	22	137	159	208	23	4	8	12	6	....	1985-86	1998-99
Shaw, David	Que., NYR, Edm., Min., Bos., T.B.	16	769	41	153	194	906	45	3	9	12	81	....	1982-83	1997-98
● Shay, Norm	Bos., Tor.	2	53	5	3	8	34	....	....	....	....	....	....	1924-25	1925-26
● Shea, Pat	Chi.	1	10	1	0	1	0	....	....	....	....	....	....	1931-32	1931-32
‡ Shearer, Rob	Col.	1	2	0	0	0	0	....	....	....	....	....	....	2000-01	2000-01
Shedden, Doug	Pit., Det., Que., Tor.	8	416	139	186	325	176	....	....	....	....	....	....	1981-82	1990-91
Sheehan, Bobby	Mtl., Cal., Chi., Det., NYR, Col., L.A.	9	310	48	63	111	40	25	4	3	7	8	1	1969-70	1981-82

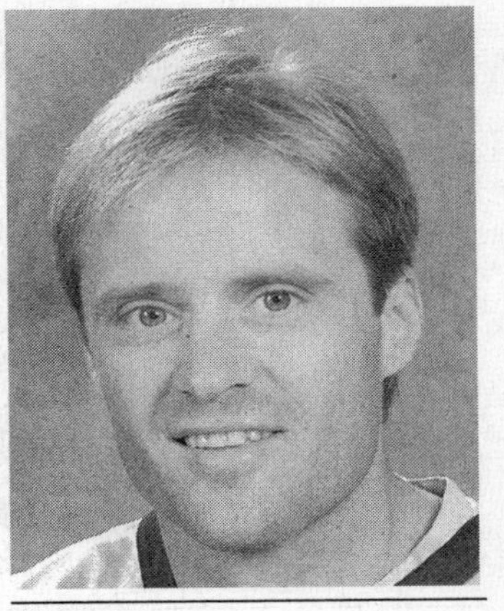
Cliff Ronning

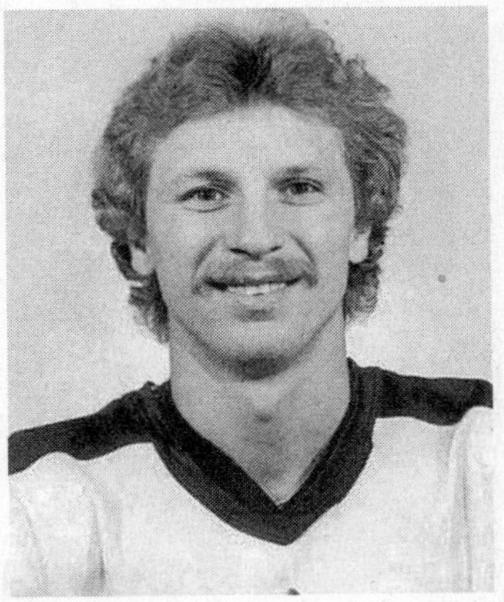
Rocky Saganiuk

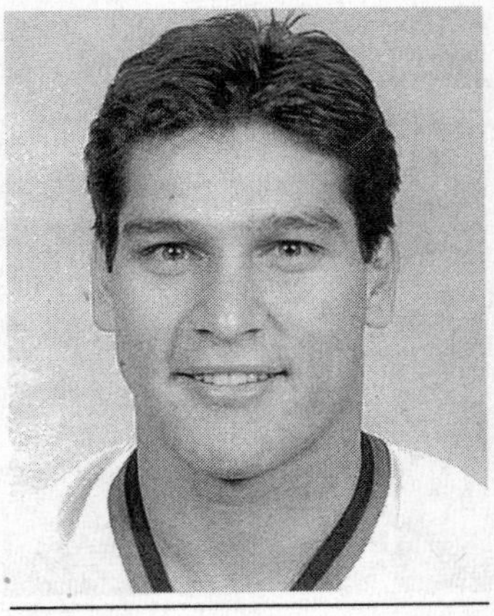
Everett Sanipass

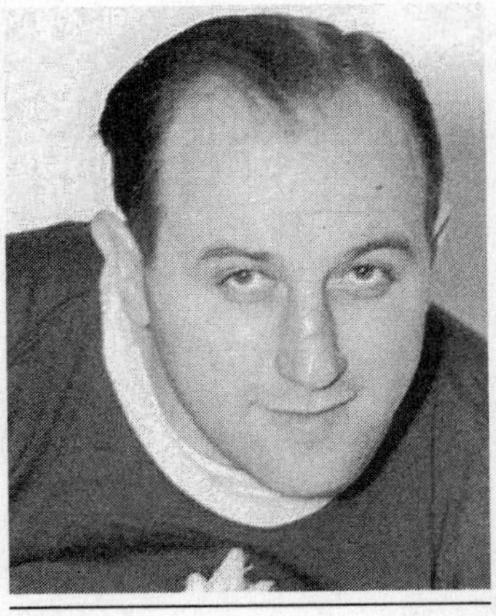
Sweeney Schriner

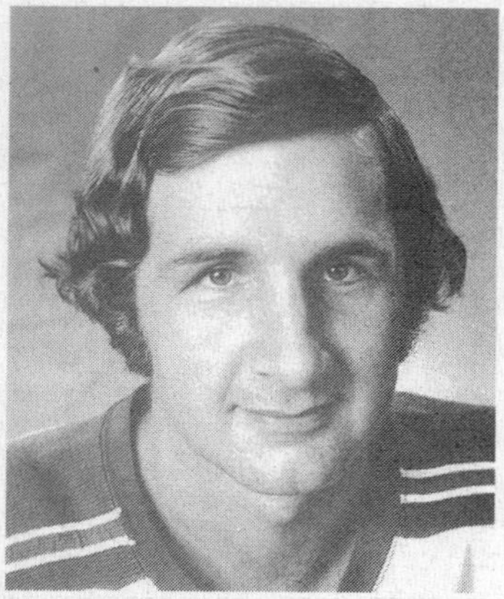

Rod Seiling

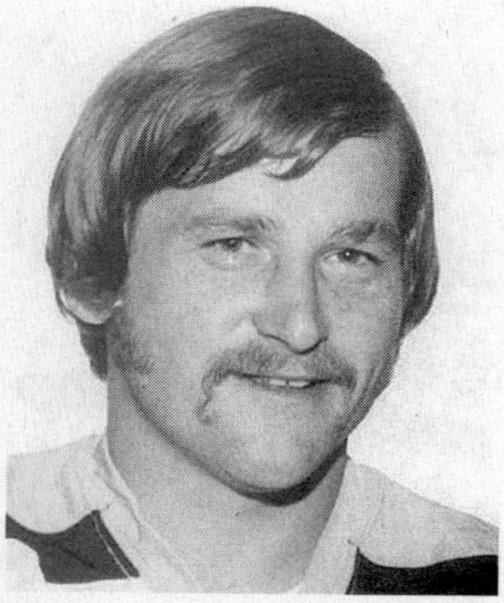

Gregg Sheppard

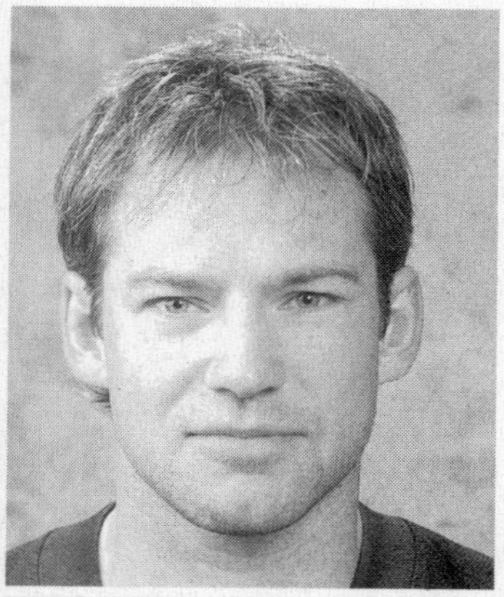

Reid Simpson

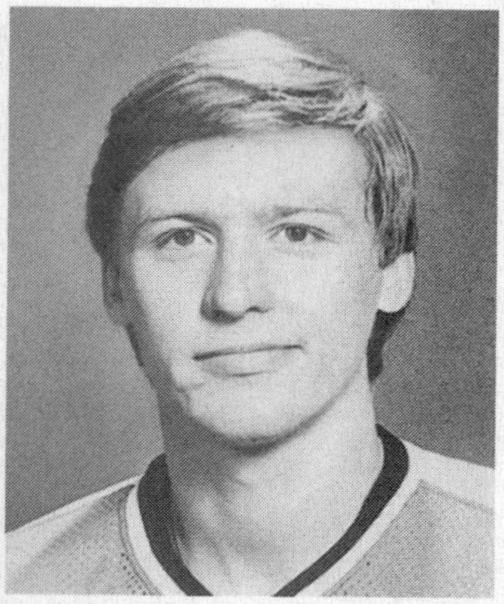

Ilkka Sinisalo

Name	NHL Teams	NHL Seasons	Regular Schedule GP	G	A	TP	PIM	Playoffs GP	G	A	TP	PIM	NHL Cup Wins	First NHL Season	Last NHL Season
Sheehy, Neil	Cgy., Hfd., Wsh.	9	379	18	47	65	1311	54	0	3	3	241	....	1983-84	1991-92
Sheehy, Tim	Det., Hfd.	2	27	2	1	3	0	....	....	....	....	....	....	1977-78	1979-80
Shelton, Doug	Chi.	1	5	0	1	1	2	....	....	....	....	....	....	1967-68	1967-68
• Sheppard, Frank	Det.	1	8	1	1	2	0	....	....	....	....	....	....	1927-28	1927-28
Sheppard, Gregg	Bos., Pit.	10	657	205	293	498	243	82	32	40	72	31	....	1972-73	1981-82
• Sheppard, Johnny	Det., NYA, Bos., Chi.	8	308	68	58	126	224	10	0	0	0	0	1	1926-27	1933-34
Sheppard, Ray	Buf., NYR, Det., S.J., Fla., Car.	13	817	357	300	657	212	81	30	20	50	21	....	1987-88	1999-00
• Sherf, John	Det.	5	19	0	0	0	8	8	0	1	1	2	1	1935-36	1943-44
• Shero, Fred	NYR	3	145	6	14	20	137	13	0	2	2	8	....	1947-48	1949-50
• Sherritt, Gordon	Det.	1	8	0	0	0	12	....	....	....	....	....	....	1943-44	1943-44
Sherven, Gord	Edm., Min., Hfd.	5	97	13	22	35	33	3	0	0	0	0	....	1983-84	1987-88
Shevalier, Jeff	L.A., T.B.	3	32	5	9	14	8	....	....	....	....	....	....	1994-95	1999-00
• Shewchuk, Jack	Bos.	6	187	9	19	28	160	20	0	1	1	19	1	1938-39	1944-45
Shibicky, Alex	NYR	8	324	110	91	201	161	39	12	12	24	12	1	1935-36	1945-46
• Shields, Al	Ott., Phi., NYA, Mtl.M., Bos.	11	459	42	46	88	637	17	0	1	1	14	1	1927-28	1937-38
Shill, Bill	Bos.	3	79	21	13	34	18	7	1	2	3	2	....	1942-43	1946-47
• Shill, Jack	Tor., Bos., NYA, Chi.	6	160	15	20	35	70	25	1	6	7	23	1	1933-34	1938-39
Shinske, Rick	Cle., St.L.	3	63	5	16	21	10	....	....	....	....	....	....	1976-77	1978-79
Shires, Jim	Det., St.L., Pit.	3	56	3	6	9	32	....	....	....	....	....	....	1970-71	1972-73
• Shmyr, Paul	Chi., Cal., Min., Hfd.	7	343	13	72	85	528	34	3	3	6	44	....	1968-69	1981-82
Shoebottom, Bruce	Bos.	4	35	1	4	5	53	14	1	2	3	77	....	1987-88	1990-91
• Shore, Eddie	Bos., NYA	14	550	105	179	284	1047	55	6	13	19	181	2	1926-27	1939-40
• Shore, Hamby	Ott.	1	18	3	8	11	51	....	....	....	....	....	....	1917-18	1917-18
Short, Steve	L.A., Det.	2	6	0	0	0	2	....	....	....	....	....	....	1977-78	1978-79
Shuchuk, Gary	Det., L.A.	5	142	13	26	39	70	20	2	2	4	12	....	1990-91	1995-96
Shudra, Ron	Edm.	1	10	0	5	5	6	....	....	....	....	....	....	1987-88	1987-88
Shutt, Steve	Mtl., L.A.	13	930	424	393	817	410	99	50	48	98	65	5	1972-73	1984-85
• Siebert, Babe	Mtl.M., NYR, Bos., Mtl.	14	592	140	156	296	982	49	7	5	12	62	2	1925-26	1938-39
Silk, Dave	NYR, Bos., Det., Wpg.	7	249	54	59	113	271	13	2	4	6	13	....	1979-80	1985-86
Siltala, Mike	Wsh., NYR	3	7	1	0	1	2	....	....	....	....	....	....	1981-82	1987-88
Siltanen, Risto	Edm., Hfd., Que.	8	562	90	265	355	266	32	6	12	18	30	....	1979-80	1986-87
Sim, Trevor	Edm.	1	3	0	1	1	2	....	....	....	....	....	....	1989-90	1989-90
Simard, Martin	Cgy., T.B.	3	44	1	5	6	183	....	....	....	....	....	....	1990-91	1992-93
‡ Simicek, Roman	Pit., Min.	2	63	7	10	17	59	....	....	....	....	....	....	2000-01	2001-02
Simmer, Charlie	Cal., Cle., L.A., Bos., Pit.	14	712	342	369	711	544	24	9	9	18	32	....	1974-75	1987-88
Simmons, Al	Cal., Bos.	3	11	0	1	1	21	1	0	0	0	0	....	1971-72	1975-76
• Simon, Cully	Det., Chi.	3	130	4	11	15	121	14	1	0	1	6	1	1942-43	1944-45
Simon, Jason	NYI, Phx.	2	5	0	0	0	34	....	....	....	....	....	....	1993-94	1996-97
Simon, Thain	Det.	1	3	0	0	0	0	....	....	....	....	....	....	1946-47	1946-47
Simon, Todd	Buf.	1	15	0	1	1	0	5	1	0	1	0	....	1993-94	1993-94
Simonetti, Frank	Bos.	4	115	5	8	13	76	12	0	1	1	8	....	1984-85	1987-88
Simpson, Bobby	Atl., St.L., Pit.	5	175	35	29	64	98	6	0	1	1	2	....	1976-77	1982-83
• Simpson, Cliff	Det.	2	6	0	1	1	0	2	0	0	0	2	....	1946-47	1947-48
Simpson, Craig	Pit., Edm., Buf.	10	634	247	250	497	659	67	36	32	68	56	2	1985-86	1994-95
• Simpson, Joe	NYA	6	228	21	19	40	156	2	0	0	0	0	....	1925-26	1930-31
Simpson, Reid	Phi., Min., N.J., Chi., T.B., St.L., Mtl., Nsh., Pit.	12	301	18	18	36	838	10	0	0	0	31	....	1991-92	2003-04
Sims, Al	Bos., Hfd., L.A.	10	475	49	116	165	286	41	0	2	2	14	....	1973-74	1982-83
Sinclair, Reg	NYR, Det.	3	208	49	43	92	139	3	1	0	1	0	....	1950-51	1952-53
• Singbush, Alex	Mtl.	1	32	0	5	5	15	3	0	0	0	4	....	1940-41	1940-41
Sinisalo, Ilkka	Phi., Min., L.A.	11	582	204	222	426	208	68	21	11	32	6	....	1981-82	1991-92
Siren, Ville	Pit., Min.	5	290	14	68	82	276	7	0	0	0	6	....	1985-86	1989-90
Sirois, Bob	Phi., Wsh.	6	286	92	120	212	42	....	....	....	....	....	....	1974-75	1979-80
Sittler, Darryl	Tor., Phi., Det.	15	1096	484	637	1121	948	76	29	45	74	137	....	1970-71	1984-85
• Sjoberg, Lars-Erik	Wpg.	1	79	7	27	34	48	....	....	....	....	....	....	1979-80	1979-80
‡ Sjodin, Tommy	Min., Dal., Que.	2	106	8	40	48	52	....	....	....	....	....	....	1992-93	1993-94
• Skaare, Bjorn	Det.	1	1	0	0	0	0	....	....	....	....	....	....	1978-79	1978-79
‡ Skalde, Jarrod	N.J., Ana., Cgy., S.J., Chi., Dal., Atl., Phi.	9	115	13	21	34	62	....	....	....	....	....	....	1990-91	2001-02
Skarda, Randy	St.L.	2	26	0	5	5	11	....	....	....	....	....	....	1989-90	1991-92
• Skilton, Raymie	Mtl.W.	1	1	0	0	0	0	....	....	....	....	....	....	1917-18	1917-18
• Skinner, Alf	Tor., Bos., Mtl.M., Pit.	4	71	26	10	36	87	2	0	1	1	9	1	1917-18	1925-26
Skinner, Larry	Col.	4	47	10	12	22	8	2	0	0	0	0	....	1976-77	1979-80
‡ Skopintsev, Andrei	T.B., Atl.	3	40	2	4	6	32	....	....	....	....	....	....	1998-99	2000-01
Skov, Glen	Det., Chi., Mtl.	12	650	106	136	242	413	53	7	7	14	48	3	1949-50	1960-61
Skriko, Petri	Van., Bos., Wpg., S.J.	9	541	183	222	405	246	28	5	9	14	4	....	1984-85	1992-93
Skrlac, Rob	N.J.	1	8	1	0	1	22	....	....	....	....	....	....	2003-04	2003-04
Skrudland, Brian	Mtl., Cgy., Fla., NYR, Dal.	15	881	124	219	343	1107	164	15	46	61	323	2	1985-86	1999-00
• Sleaver, John	Chi.	2	13	1	0	1	6	....	....	....	....	....	....	1953-54	1956-57
Sleigher, Louis	Que., Bos.	6	194	46	53	99	146	17	1	1	2	64	....	1979-80	1985-86
Sloan, Tod	Tor., Chi.	13	745	220	262	482	831	47	9	12	21	47	2	1947-48	1960-61
• Slobodian, Peter	NYA	1	41	3	2	5	54	....	....	....	....	....	....	1940-41	1940-41
• Slowinski, Ed	NYR	6	291	58	74	132	63	16	2	6	8	6	....	1947-48	1952-53
Sly, Darryl	Tor., Min., Van.	4	79	1	2	3	20	....	....	....	....	....	....	1965-66	1970-71
Smail, Doug	Wpg., Min., Que., Ott.	13	845	210	249	459	602	42	9	2	11	49	....	1980-81	1992-93
Smart, Alex	Mtl.	1	8	5	2	7	0	....	....	....	....	....	....	1942-43	1942-43
Smedsmo, Dale	Tor.	1	4	0	0	0	0	....	....	....	....	....	....	1972-73	1972-73
Smehlik, Richard	Buf., Atl., N.J.	10	644	49	146	195	415	88	1	14	15	40	1	1992-93	2002-03
• Smillie, Don	Bos.	1	12	2	2	4	4	....	....	....	....	....	....	1933-34	1933-34
• Smith, Alex	Ott., Det., Bos., NYA	11	443	41	50	91	645	19	0	2	2	26	1	1924-25	1934-35
• Smith, Art	Tor., Ott.	4	144	15	10	25	249	4	1	1	2	8	....	1927-28	1930-31
Smith, Barry	Bos., Col.	3	114	7	7	14	10	....	....	....	....	....	....	1975-76	1980-81
Smith, Bobby	Min., Mtl.	15	1077	357	679	1036	917	184	64	96	160	245	1	1978-79	1992-93
Smith, Brad	Van., Atl., Cgy., Det., Tor.	9	222	28	34	62	591	20	3	3	6	49	....	1978-79	1986-87
Smith, Brian	Det.	3	61	2	8	10	12	5	0	0	0	0	....	1957-58	1960-61
• Smith, Brian	L.A., Min.	2	67	10	10	20	33	7	0	0	0	0	....	1967-68	1968-69
• Smith, Carl	Det.	1	7	1	1	2	2	....	....	....	....	....	....	1943-44	1943-44
Smith, Clint	NYR, Chi.	11	483	161	236	397	24	42	10	14	24	2	1	1936-37	1946-47
Smith, D.J.	Tor., Col.	3	45	1	1	2	67	....	....	....	....	....	....	1996-97	2002-03
Smith, Dallas	Bos., NYR	16	890	55	252	307	959	86	3	29	32	128	2	1959-60	1977-78
Smith, Dennis	Wsh., L.A.	2	8	0	0	0	4	....	....	....	....	....	....	1989-90	1990-91
Smith, Derek	Buf., Det.	8	335	78	116	194	60	30	9	14	23	13	....	1975-76	1982-83
Smith, Derrick	Phi., Min., Dal.	10	537	82	92	174	373	82	14	11	25	79	....	1984-85	1993-94
• Smith, Des	Mtl.M., Mtl., Chi., Bos.	5	196	22	25	47	236	25	1	4	5	18	1	1937-38	1941-42
• Smith, Don	Mtl.	1	12	1	0	1	6	....	....	....	....	....	....	1919-20	1919-20
• Smith, Don	NYR	1	11	1	1	2	0	1	0	0	0	0	....	1949-50	1949-50
Smith, Doug	L.A., Buf., Edm., Van., Pit.	9	535	115	138	253	624	18	4	2	6	21	....	1981-82	1989-90
Smith, Floyd	Bos., NYR, Det., Tor., Buf.	13	616	129	178	307	207	48	12	11	23	16	....	1954-55	1971-72
Smith, Geoff	Edm., Fla., NYR	10	462	18	73	91	282	13	0	1	1	8	1	1989-90	1998-99
Smith, Glen	Chi.	1	2	0	0	0	0	....	....	....	....	....	....	1950-51	1950-51
• Smith, Glenn	Tor.	1	9	0	0	0	0	....	....	....	....	....	....	1921-22	1921-22
Smith, Gord	Wsh., Wpg.	6	299	9	30	39	284	....	....	....	....	....	....	1974-75	1979-80
Smith, Greg	Cal., Cle., Min., Det., Wsh.	13	829	56	232	288	1110	63	4	7	11	106	....	1975-76	1987-88
• Smith, Hooley	Ott., Mtl.M., Bos., NYA	17	715	200	225	425	1013	54	11	8	19	109	2	1924-25	1940-41
• Smith, Ken	Bos.	7	331	78	93	171	49	30	8	13	21	6	....	1944-45	1950-51
• Smith, Nakina	Det.	1	10	1	2	3	0	....	....	....	....	....	....	1943-44	1943-44
‡ Smith, Nick	Fla.	1	15	0	0	0	0	....	....	....	....	....	....	2001-02	2001-02
Smith, Randy	Min.	2	3	0	0	0	0	....	....	....	....	....	....	1985-86	1986-87
Smith, Rick	Bos., Cal., St.L., Det., Wsh.	11	687	52	167	219	560	78	3	23	26	73	1	1968-69	1980-81
• Smith, Rodger	Pit., Phi.	6	210	20	4	24	172	4	3	0	3	0	....	1925-26	1930-31
Smith, Ron	NYI	1	11	1	1	2	14	....	....	....	....	....	....	1972-73	1972-73
• Smith, Sid	Tor.	12	601	186	183	369	94	44	17	10	27	2	3	1946-47	1957-58
Smith, Stan	NYR	2	9	2	1	3	0	1	0	0	0	0	1	1939-40	1940-41
Smith, Steve	Phi., Buf.	6	18	0	1	1	15	....	....	....	....	....	....	1981-82	1988-89
Smith, Steve	Edm., Chi., Cgy.	16	804	72	303	375	2139	134	11	41	52	288	3	1984-85	2000-01
Smith, Stu	Mtl.	2	4	2	2	4	2	1	0	0	0	0	....	1940-41	1941-42
Smith, Stu	Hfd.	4	77	2	10	12	95	....	....	....	....	....	....	1979-80	1982-83
• Smith, Tommy	Que.	1	10	0	1	1	11	....	....	....	....	....	....	1919-20	1919-20
Smith, Vern	NYI	1	1	0	0	0	0	....	....	....	....	....	....	1984-85	1984-85
Smith, Wayne	Chi.	1	2	1	1	2	2	1	0	0	0	0	....	1966-67	1966-67
‡ Smrek, Peter	St.L., NYR	2	28	2	4	6	18	....	....	....	....	....	....	2000-01	2001-02
Smrke, John	St.L., Que.	3	103	11	17	28	33	....	....	....	....	....	....	1977-78	1979-80
• Smrke, Stan	Mtl.	2	9	0	3	3	0	....	....	....	....	....	....	1956-57	1957-58
Smyl, Stan	Van.	13	896	262	411	673	1556	41	16	17	33	64	....	1978-79	1990-91
• Smylie, Rod	Tor., Ott.	6	74	4	2	6	12	4	0	0	0	2	1	1920-21	1925-26

			Regular Schedule					Playoffs							
Name	NHL Teams	NHL Seasons	GP	G	A	TP	PIM	GP	G	A	TP	PIM	NHL Cup Wins	First NHL Season	Last NHL Season
Smyth, Greg	Phi., Que., Cgy., Fla., Tor., Chi.	10	229	4	16	20	783	12	0	0	0	40	....	1986-87	1996-97
Smyth, Kevin	Hfd.	3	58	6	8	14	31	....	....	....	....	....	....	1993-94	1995-96
Snell, Chris	Tor., L.A.	2	34	2	7	9	24	....	....	....	....	....	....	1993-94	1994-95
Snell, Ron	Pit.	2	7	3	2	5	6	....	....	....	....	....	....	1968-69	1969-70
Snell, Ted	Pit., K.C., Det.	2	104	7	18	25	22	....	....	....	....	....	....	1973-74	1974-75
Snepsts, Harold	Van., Min., Det., St.L.	17	1033	38	195	233	2009	93	1	14	15	231	....	1974-75	1990-91
Snow, Sandy	Det.	1	3	0	0	0	2	....	....	....	....	....	....	1968-69	1968-69
Snuggerud, Dave	Buf., S.J., Phi.	4	265	30	54	84	127	12	1	3	4	6	....	1989-90	1992-93
• Snyder, Dan	Atl.	3	49	11	5	16	64	....	....	....	....	....	....	2000-01	2002-03
Sobchuk, Dennis	Det., Que.	2	35	5	6	11	2	....	....	....	....	....	....	1979-80	1982-83
Sobchuk, Gene	Van.	1	1	0	0	0	0	....	....	....	....	....	....	1973-74	1973-74
Solheim, Ken	Chi., Min., Det., Edm.	5	135	19	20	39	34	3	1	1	2	2	....	1980-81	1985-86
Solinger, Bob	Tor., Det.	5	99	10	11	21	19	....	....	....	....	....	....	1951-52	1959-60
• Somers, Art	Chi., NYR	6	222	33	56	89	189	30	1	5	6	20	1	1929-30	1934-35
Sommer, Roy	Edm.	1	3	1	0	1	7	....	....	....	....	....	....	1980-81	1980-81
Songin, Tom	Bos.	3	43	5	5	10	22	....	....	....	....	....	....	1978-79	1980-81
Sonmor, Glen	NYR	2	28	2	0	2	21	....	....	....	....	....	....	1953-54	1954-55
Sorochan, Lee	Cgy.	2	3	0	0	0	0	....	....	....	....	....	....	1998-99	1999-00
• Sorrell, John	Det., NYA	11	490	127	119	246	100	42	12	15	27	10	2	1930-31	1940-41
• Sparrow, Emory	Bos.	1	8	0	0	0	4	....	....	....	....	....	....	1924-25	1924-25
Speck, Fred	Det., Van.	3	28	1	2	3	2	....	....	....	....	....	....	1968-69	1971-72
• Speer, Bill	Pit., Bos.	4	130	5	20	25	79	8	1	0	1	4	1	1967-68	1970-71
Speers, Ted	Det.	1	4	1	1	2	0	....	....	....	....	....	....	1985-86	1985-86
• Spence, Gordon	Tor.	1	3	0	0	0	0	....	....	....	....	....	....	1925-26	1925-26
• Spencer, Brian	Tor., NYI, Buf., Pit.	10	553	80	143	223	634	37	1	5	6	29	....	1969-70	1978-79
• Spencer, Irv	NYR, Bos., Det.	8	230	12	38	50	127	16	0	0	0	8	....	1959-60	1967-68
• Speyer, Chris	Tor., NYA	3	14	0	0	0	0	....	....	....	....	....	....	1923-24	1933-34
Spring, Corey	T.B.	2	16	1	1	2	12	....	....	....	....	....	....	1997-98	1998-99
Spring, Don	Wpg.	4	259	1	54	55	80	6	0	0	0	10	....	1980-81	1983-84
Spring, Frank	Bos., St.L., Cal., Cle.	5	61	14	20	34	12	....	....	....	....	....	....	1969-70	1976-77
• Spring, Jesse	Ham., Pit., Tor., NYA	6	133	11	4	15	74	2	0	2	2	2	....	1923-24	1929-30
Spruce, Andy	Van., Col.	3	172	31	42	73	111	2	0	2	2	0	....	1976-77	1978-79
Srsen, Tomas	Edm.	1	2	0	0	0	0	....	....	....	....	....	....	1990-91	1990-91
St. Amour, Martin	Ott.	1	1	0	0	0	2	....	....	....	....	....	....	1992-93	1992-93
St. Laurent, Andre	NYI, Det., L.A., Pit.	11	644	129	187	316	749	59	8	12	20	48	....	1973-74	1983-84
St. Laurent, Dollard	Mtl., Chi.	12	652	29	133	162	496	92	2	22	24	87	5	1950-51	1961-62
St. Marseille, Frank	St.L., L.A.	10	707	140	285	425	242	88	20	25	45	18	....	1967-68	1976-77
St. Sauveur, Claude	Atl.	1	79	24	24	48	23	2	0	0	0	0	....	1975-76	1975-76
Stackhouse, Ron	Cal., Det., Pit.	12	889	87	372	459	824	32	5	8	13	38	....	1970-71	1981-82
• Stackhouse, Ted	Tor.	1	13	0	0	0	2	1	0	0	0	0	1	1921-22	1921-22
• Stahan, Butch	Mtl.	1	....	....	....	....	....	3	0	1	1	2	....	1944-45	1944-45
Stajduhar, Nick	Edm.	1	2	0	0	0	4	....	....	....	....	....	....	1995-96	1995-96
Staley, Al	NYR	1	1	0	1	1	0	....	....	....	....	....	....	1948-49	1948-49
Stamler, Lorne	L.A., Tor., Wpg.	4	116	14	11	25	16	....	....	....	....	....	....	1976-77	1979-80
Standing, George	Min.	1	2	0	0	0	0	....	....	....	....	....	....	1967-68	1967-68
Stanfield, Fred	Chi., Bos., Min., Buf.	14	914	211	405	616	134	106	21	35	56	10	2	1964-65	1977-78
Stanfield, Jack	Chi.	1	....	....	....	....	....	1	0	0	0	0	....	1965-66	1965-66
Stanfield, Jim	L.A.	3	7	0	1	1	0	....	....	....	....	....	....	1969-70	1971-72
Stankiewicz, Ed	Det.	2	6	0	0	0	2	....	....	....	....	....	....	1953-54	1955-56
Stankiewicz, Myron	St.L., Phi.	1	35	0	7	7	36	1	0	0	0	0	....	1968-69	1968-69
Stanley, Allan	NYR, Chi., Bos., Tor., Phi.	21	1244	100	333	433	792	109	7	36	43	80	4	1948-49	1968-69
• Stanley, Barney	Chi.	1	1	0	0	0	0	....	....	....	....	....	....	1927-28	1927-28
Stanley, Daryl	Phi., Van.	6	189	8	17	25	408	17	0	0	0	30	....	1983-84	1989-90
Stanowski, Wally	Tor., NYR	10	428	23	88	111	160	60	3	14	17	13	4	1939-40	1950-51
Stanton, Paul	Pit., Bos., NYI	5	295	14	49	63	262	44	2	10	12	66	2	1990-91	1994-95
Stapleton, Brian	Wsh.	1	1	0	0	0	0	....	....	....	....	....	....	1975-76	1975-76
Stapleton, Mike	Chi., Pit., Edm., Wpg., Phx., Atl., NYI, Van.	14	697	71	111	182	342	34	1	0	1	39	....	1986-87	2000-01
Stapleton, Pat	Bos., Chi.	10	635	43	294	337	353	65	10	39	49	38	....	1961-62	1972-73
Starikov, Sergei	N.J.	1	16	0	1	1	8	....	....	....	....	....	....	1989-90	1989-90
• Starr, Harold	Ott., Mtl.M., Mtl., NYR	7	205	6	5	11	186	15	1	0	1	4	....	1929-30	1935-36
• Starr, Wilf	NYA, Det.	4	87	8	6	14	25	7	0	2	2	2	....	1932-33	1935-36
Stasiuk, Vic	Chi., Det., Bos.	14	745	183	254	437	669	69	16	18	34	40	3	1949-50	1962-63
Stastny, Anton	Que.	9	650	252	384	636	150	66	20	32	52	31	....	1980-81	1988-89
Stastny, Marian	Que., Tor.	5	322	121	173	294	110	32	5	17	22	7	....	1981-82	1985-86
Stastny, Peter	Que., N.J., St.L.	15	977	450	789	1239	824	93	33	72	105	123	....	1980-81	1994-95
Staszak, Ray	Det.	1	4	0	1	1	7	....	....	....	....	....	....	1985-86	1985-86
• Steele, Frank	Det.	1	1	0	0	0	0	....	....	....	....	....	....	1930-31	1930-31
Steen, Anders	Wpg.	1	42	5	11	16	22	....	....	....	....	....	....	1980-81	1980-81
Steen, Thomas	Wpg.	14	950	264	553	817	753	56	12	32	44	62	....	1981-82	1994-95
Stefaniw, Morris	Atl.	1	13	1	1	2	2	....	....	....	....	....	....	1972-73	1972-73
Stefanski, Bud	NYR	1	1	0	0	0	0	....	....	....	....	....	....	1977-78	1977-78
Stemkowski, Pete	Tor., Det., NYR, L.A.	15	967	206	349	555	866	83	25	29	54	136	1	1963-64	1977-78
Stenlund, Vern	Cle.	1	4	0	0	0	0	....	....	....	....	....	....	1976-77	1976-77
Stephenson, Bob	Hfd., Tor.	1	18	2	3	5	4	....	....	....	....	....	....	1979-80	1979-80
Stern, Ron	Van., Cgy., S.J.	12	638	75	86	161	2077	43	7	7	14	119	....	1987-88	1999-00
Sterner, Ulf	NYR	1	4	0	0	0	0	....	....	....	....	....	....	1964-65	1964-65
Stevens, John	Phi., Hfd.	5	53	0	10	10	48	....	....	....	....	....	....	1986-87	1993-94
Stevens, Kevin	Pit., Bos., L.A., NYR, Phi.	15	874	329	397	726	1470	103	46	60	106	170	2	1987-88	2001-02
Stevens, Mike	Van., Bos., NYI, Tor.	4	23	1	4	5	29	....	....	....	....	....	....	1984-85	1989-90
• Stevens, Phil	Mtl.W., Mtl., Bos.	3	25	1	0	1	3	....	....	....	....	....	....	1917-18	1925-26
Stevens, Scott	Wsh., St.L., N.J.	22	1635	196	712	908	2785	233	26	92	118	402	3	1982-83	2003-04
Stevenson, Shayne	Bos., T.B.	3	27	0	2	2	35	....	....	....	....	....	....	1990-91	1992-93
Stewart, Allan	N.J., Bos.	6	64	6	4	10	243	....	....	....	....	....	....	1985-86	1991-92
Stewart, Bill	Buf., St.L., Tor., Min.	8	261	7	64	71	424	13	1	3	4	11	....	1977-78	1985-86
Stewart, Blair	Det., Wsh., Que.	7	229	34	44	78	326	....	....	....	....	....	....	1973-74	1979-80
Stewart, Bob	Bos., Cal., Cle., St.L., Pit.	9	575	27	101	128	809	5	1	1	2	2	....	1971-72	1979-80
Stewart, Cam	Bos., Fla., Min.	6	202	16	23	39	120	13	1	3	4	9	....	1993-94	2000-01
Stewart, Gaye	Tor., Chi., Det., NYR, Mtl.	11	502	185	159	344	274	25	2	9	11	16	2	1941-42	1953-54
• Stewart, Jack	Det., Chi.	12	565	31	84	115	765	80	5	14	19	143	2	1938-39	1951-52
Stewart, John	Pit., Atl., Cal.	5	258	58	60	118	158	4	0	0	0	10	....	1970-71	1974-75
Stewart, John	Que.	1	2	0	0	0	0	....	....	....	....	....	....	1979-80	1979-80
Stewart, Ken	Chi.	1	6	1	1	2	2	....	....	....	....	....	....	1941-42	1941-42
• Stewart, Nels	Mtl.M., Bos., NYA	15	650	324	191	515	953	50	9	12	21	47	1	1925-26	1939-40
Stewart, Paul	Que.	1	21	2	0	2	74	....	....	....	....	....	....	1979-80	1979-80
Stewart, Ralph	Van., NYI	7	252	57	73	130	28	19	4	4	8	2	....	1970-71	1977-78
Stewart, Ron	Tor., Bos., St.L., NYR, Van., NYI	21	1353	276	253	529	560	119	14	21	35	60	3	1952-53	1972-73
Stewart, Ryan	Wpg.	1	3	1	0	1	0	....	....	....	....	....	....	1985-86	1985-86
Stienburg, Trevor	Que.	4	71	8	4	12	161	1	0	0	0	0	....	1985-86	1988-89
Stiles, Tony	Cgy.	1	30	2	7	9	20	....	....	....	....	....	....	1983-84	1983-84
Stock, P.J.	NYR, Mtl., Phi., Bos.	7	235	5	21	26	523	8	1	0	1	19	....	1997-98	2003-04
Stoddard, Jack	NYR	2	80	16	15	31	31	....	....	....	....	....	....	1951-52	1952-53
Stojanov, Alek	Van., Pit.	3	107	2	5	7	222	14	0	0	0	21	....	1994-95	1996-97
Stoltz, Roland	Wsh.	1	14	2	2	4	14	....	....	....	....	....	....	1981-82	1981-82
Stone, Steve	Van.	1	2	0	0	0	0	....	....	....	....	....	....	1973-74	1973-74
Storm, Jim	Hfd., Dal.	3	84	7	15	22	44	....	....	....	....	....	....	1993-94	1995-96
Stothers, Mike	Phi., Tor.	4	30	0	2	2	65	5	0	0	0	11	....	1984-85	1987-88
Stoughton, Blaine	Pit., Tor., Hfd., NYR	8	526	258	191	449	204	8	4	2	6	2	....	1973-74	1983-84
Stoyanovich, Steve	Hfd.	1	23	3	5	8	11	....	....	....	....	....	....	1983-84	1983-84
• Strain, Neil	NYR	1	52	11	13	24	12	....	....	....	....	....	....	1952-53	1952-53
Strate, Gord	Det.	3	61	0	0	0	34	....	....	....	....	....	....	1956-57	1958-59
Stratton, Art	NYR, Det., Chi., Pit., Phi.	4	95	18	33	51	24	5	0	0	0	0	....	1959-60	1967-68
‡ Strbak, Martin	L.A., Pit.	1	49	5	11	16	46	....	....	....	....	....	....	2003-04	2003-04
Strobel, Art	NYR	1	7	0	0	0	0	....	....	....	....	....	....	1943-44	1943-44
Strong, Ken	Tor.	3	15	2	2	4	6	....	....	....	....	....	....	1982-83	1984-85
Struch, David	Cgy.	1	4	0	0	0	4	....	....	....	....	....	....	1993-94	1993-94
Strueby, Todd	Edm.	3	5	0	1	1	2	....	....	....	....	....	....	1981-82	1983-84
• Stuart, Billy	Tor., Bos.	7	195	30	20	50	151	12	1	1	2	6	1	1920-21	1926-27
Stumpf, Bob	St.L., Pit.	1	10	1	1	2	20	....	....	....	....	....	....	1974-75	1974-75
Sturgeon, Peter	Col.	2	6	0	1	1	2	....	....	....	....	....	....	1979-80	1980-81
‡ Stutzel, Mike	Phx.	1	9	0	0	0	0	....	....	....	....	....	....	2003-04	2003-04
Suikkanen, Kai	Buf.	2	2	0	0	0	0	....	....	....	....	....	....	1981-82	1982-83
Sulliman, Doug	NYR, Hfd., N.J., Phi.	11	631	160	168	328	175	16	1	3	4	2	....	1979-80	1989-90
Sullivan, Barry	Det.	1	1	0	0	0	0	....	....	....	....	....	....	1947-48	1947-48

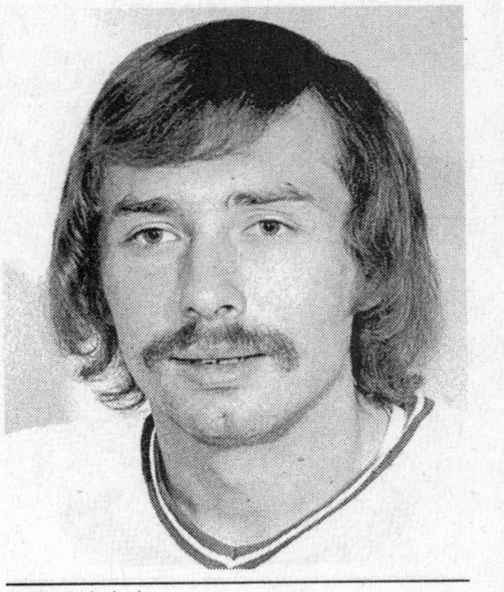
Gene Sobchuk

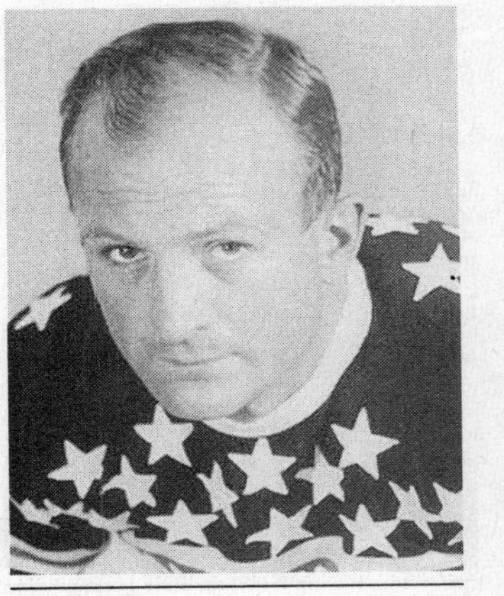
Jesse Spring

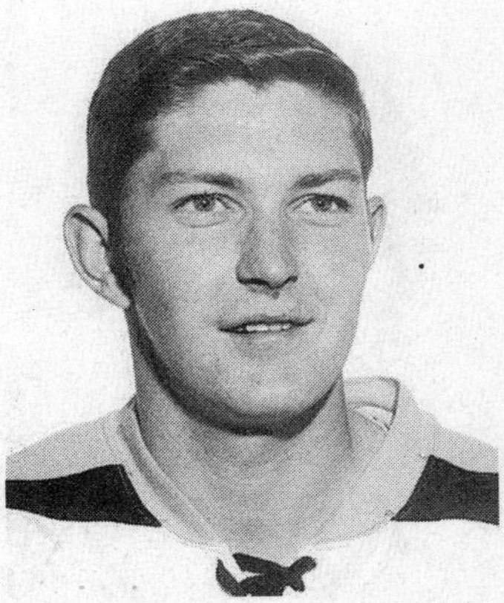
Fred Stanfield

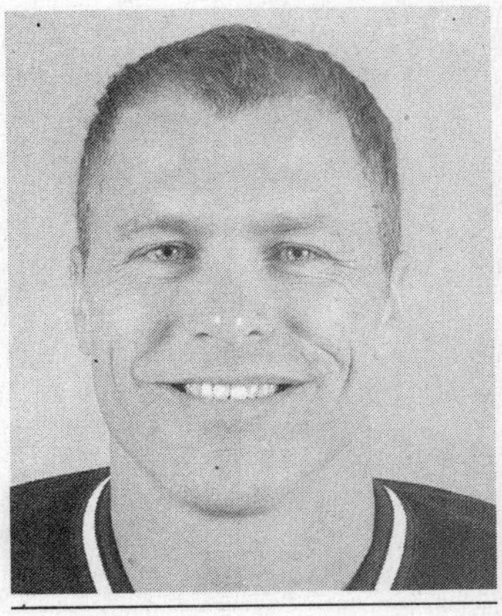
Scott Stevens

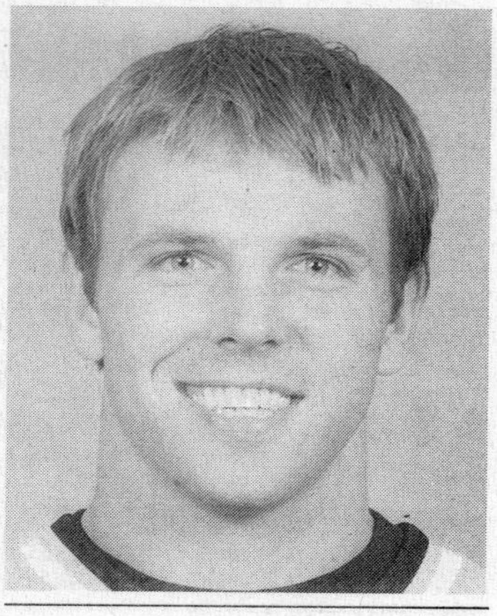

P.J. Stock

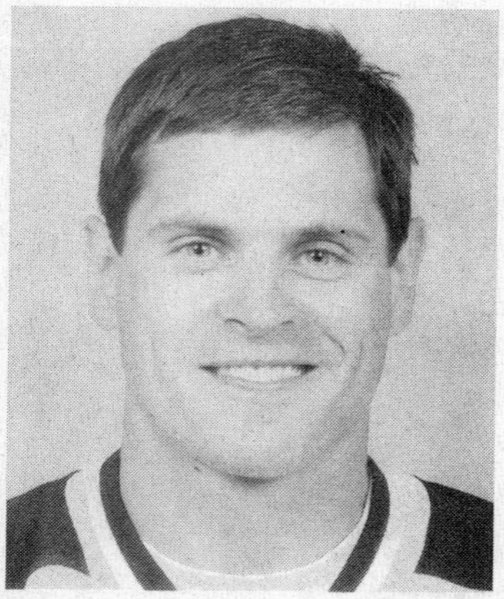

Don Sweeney

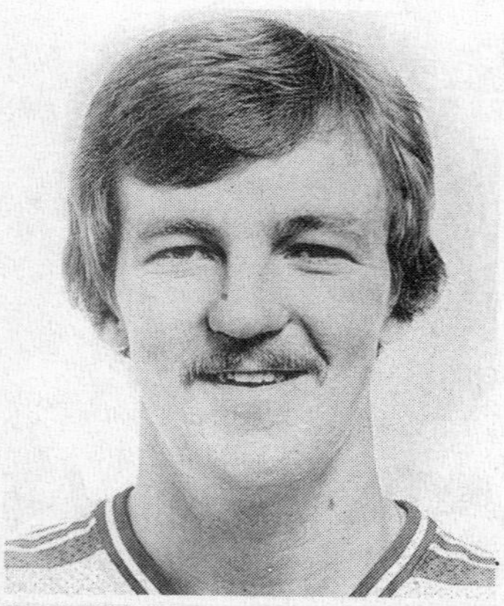

Dean Talafous

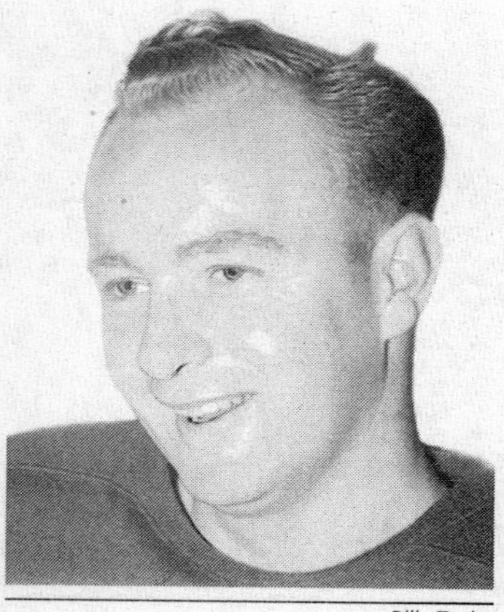

Billy Taylor

			Regular Schedule					Playoffs							
Name	NHL Teams	NHL Seasons	GP	G	A	TP	PIM	GP	G	A	TP	PIM	NHL Cup Wins	First NHL Season	Last NHL Season
Sullivan, Bob	Hfd.	1	62	18	19	37	18	....	....	....	....	....	....	1982-83	1982-83
Sullivan, Brian	N.J.	1	2	0	1	1	0	....	....	....	....	....	....	1992-93	1992-93
Sullivan, Frank	Tor., Chi.	4	8	0	0	0	2	....	....	....	....	....	....	1949-50	1955-56
Sullivan, Mike	S.J., Cgy., Bos., Phx.	11	709	54	82	136	203	34	4	8	12	14	....	1991-92	2001-02
Sullivan, Peter	Wpg.	2	126	28	54	82	40	....	....	....	....	....	....	1979-80	1980-81
Sullivan, Red	Bos., Chi., NYR	11	557	107	239	346	441	18	1	2	3	6	....	1949-50	1960-61
Summanen, Raimo	Edm., Van.	5	151	36	40	76	35	10	2	5	7	0	....	1983-84	1987-88
• Summerhill, Bill	Mtl., Bro.	4	72	14	17	31	70	3	0	0	0	2	....	1937-38	1941-42
Sundblad, Niklas	Cgy.	1	2	0	0	0	0	....	....	....	....	....	....	1995-96	1995-96
‡ Sundin, Ronnie	NYR	1	1	0	0	0	0	....	....	....	....	....	....	1997-98	1997-98
Sundstrom, Patrik	Van., N.J.	10	679	219	369	588	349	37	9	17	26	25	....	1982-83	1991-92
Sundstrom, Peter	NYR, Wsh., N.J.	6	338	61	83	144	120	23	3	3	6	8	....	1983-84	1989-90
Suomi, Al	Chi.	1	5	0	0	0	0	....	....	....	....	....	....	1936-37	1936-37
‡ Surma, Damian	Car.	2	2	1	1	2	0	....	....	....	....	....	....	2002-03	2003-04
‡ Sushinsky, Maxim	Min.	1	30	7	4	11	29	....	....	....	....	....	....	2000-01	2000-01
Suter, Gary	Cgy., Chi., S.J.	17	1145	203	641	844	1349	108	17	56	73	120	1	1985-86	2001-02
Sutherland, Bill	Mtl., Phi., Tor., St.L., Det.	6	250	70	58	128	99	14	2	4	6	0	....	1962-63	1971-72
• Sutherland, Max	Bos.	1	2	0	0	0	0	....	....	....	....	....	....	1931-32	1931-32
Sutter, Brent	NYI, Chi.	18	1111	363	466	829	1054	144	30	44	74	164	2	1980-81	1997-98
Sutter, Brian	St.L.	12	779	303	333	636	1786	65	21	21	42	249	....	1976-77	1987-88
Sutter, Darryl	Chi.	8	406	161	118	279	288	51	24	19	43	26	....	1979-80	1986-87
Sutter, Duane	NYI, Chi.	11	731	139	203	342	1333	161	26	32	58	405	4	1979-80	1989-90
Sutter, Rich	Pit., Phi., Van., St.L., Chi., T.B., Tor.	13	874	149	166	315	1411	78	13	5	18	133	....	1982-83	1994-95
Sutter, Ron	Phi., St.L., Que., NYI, Bos., S.J., Cgy.	19	1093	205	329	534	1352	104	8	32	40	193	....	1982-83	2000-01
‡ Sutton, Ken	Buf., Edm., St.L., N.J., S.J., NYI	11	388	23	80	103	338	32	3	4	7	29	1	1990-91	2001-02
Suzor, Mark	Phi., Col.	2	64	4	16	20	60	....	....	....	....	....	....	1976-77	1977-78
‡ Svartvadet, Per	Atl.	4	247	17	34	51	58	....	....	....	....	....	....	1999-00	2002-03
Svehla, Robert	Fla., Tor.	9	655	68	267	335	649	38	1	14	15	42	....	1994-95	2002-03
Svejkovsky, Jaroslav	Wsh., T.B.	4	113	23	19	42	56	1	0	0	0	2	....	1996-97	1999-00
Svensson, Leif	Wsh.	2	121	6	40	46	49	....	....	....	....	....	....	1978-79	1979-80
Svensson, Magnus	Fla.	2	46	4	14	18	31	....	....	....	....	....	....	1994-95	1995-96
Svoboda, Petr	Mtl., Buf., Phi., T.B.	17	1028	58	341	399	1605	127	4	45	49	140	1	1984-85	2000-01
Svoboda, Petr	Tor.	1	18	1	2	3	10	....	....	....	....	....	....	2000-01	2000-01
Swain, Garry	Pit.	1	9	1	1	2	0	....	....	....	....	....	....	1968-69	1968-69
‡ Swanson, Brian	Edm., Atl.	4	70	4	13	17	16	....	....	....	....	....	....	2000-01	2003-04
Swarbrick, George	Oak., Pit., Phi.	4	132	17	25	42	173	....	....	....	....	....	....	1967-68	1970-71
• Sweeney, Bill	NYR	1	4	1	0	1	0	....	....	....	....	....	....	1959-60	1959-60
Sweeney, Bob	Bos., Buf., NYI, Cgy.	10	639	125	163	288	799	103	15	18	33	197	....	1986-87	1995-96
Sweeney, Don	Bos., Dal.	16	1115	52	221	273	681	108	9	10	19	81	....	1988-89	2003-04
Sweeney, Tim	Cgy., Bos., Ana., NYR	8	291	55	83	138	123	4	0	0	0	2	....	1990-91	1997-98
Sykes, Bob	Tor.	1	2	0	0	0	0	....	....	....	....	....	....	1974-75	1974-75
Sykes, Phil	L.A., Wpg.	10	456	79	85	164	519	26	0	3	3	29	....	1982-83	1991-92
Sykora, Michal	S.J., Chi., T.B., Phi.	7	267	15	54	69	185	7	0	1	1	0	....	1993-94	2000-01
Sylvester, Dean	Buf., Atl.	3	96	21	16	37	32	4	0	0	0	0	....	1998-99	2000-01
Szura, Joe	Oak.	2	90	10	15	25	30	7	2	3	5	2	....	1967-68	1968-69

T

Name	NHL Teams	NHL Seasons	GP	G	A	TP	PIM	GP	G	A	TP	PIM	NHL Cup Wins	First NHL Season	Last NHL Season
Taft, John	Det.	1	15	0	2	2	4	....	....	....	....	....	....	1978-79	1978-79
Taglianetti, Peter	Wpg., Min., Pit., T.B.	11	451	18	74	92	1106	53	2	8	10	103	2	1984-85	1994-95
Talafous, Dean	Atl., Min., NYR	8	497	104	154	258	163	21	4	7	11	11	....	1974-75	1981-82
Talakoski, Ron	NYR	2	9	0	1	1	33	....	....	....	....	....	....	1986-87	1987-88
Talbot, Jean-Guy	Mtl., Min., Det., St.L., Buf.	17	1056	43	242	285	1006	150	4	26	30	142	7	1954-55	1970-71
Tallon, Dale	Van., Chi., Pit.	10	642	98	238	336	568	33	2	10	12	45	....	1970-71	1979-80
Tambellini, Steve	NYI, Col., N.J., Cgy., Van.	10	553	160	150	310	105	2	0	1	1	0	1	1978-79	1987-88
Tancill, Chris	Hfd., Det., Dal., S.J.	8	134	17	32	49	54	11	1	1	2	8	....	1990-91	1997-98
Tanguay, Christian	Que.	1	2	0	0	0	0	....	....	....	....	....	....	1981-82	1981-82
Tannahill, Don	Van.	2	111	30	33	63	25	....	....	....	....	....	....	1972-73	1973-74
Tanti, Tony	Chi., Van., Pit., Buf.	11	697	287	273	560	661	30	3	12	15	27	....	1981-82	1991-92
Tardif, Marc	Mtl., Que.	8	517	194	207	401	443	62	13	15	28	75	2	1969-70	1982-83
Tardif, Patrice	St.L., L.A.	2	65	7	11	18	78	....	....	....	....	....	....	1994-95	1995-96
Tatarinov, Mikhail	Wsh., Que., Bos.	4	161	21	48	69	184	....	....	....	....	....	....	1990-91	1993-94
Tatchell, Spence	NYR	1	1	0	0	0	0	....	....	....	....	....	....	1942-43	1942-43
• Taylor, Billy	Tor., Det., Bos., NYR	7	323	87	180	267	120	33	6	18	24	13	1	1939-40	1947-48
• Taylor, Bob	Bos.	1	8	0	0	0	6	....	....	....	....	....	....	1929-30	1929-30
Taylor, Dave	L.A.	17	1111	431	638	1069	1589	92	26	33	59	145	....	1977-78	1993-94
Taylor, Harry	Tor., Chi.	3	66	5	10	15	30	1	0	0	0	0	1	1946-47	1951-52
Taylor, Mark	Phi., Pit., Wsh.	5	209	42	68	110	73	6	0	0	0	0	....	1981-82	1985-86
• Taylor, Ralph	Chi., NYR	3	99	4	1	5	169	4	0	0	0	10	....	1927-28	1929-30
Taylor, Ted	NYR, Det., Min., Van.	6	166	23	35	58	181	....	....	....	....	....	....	1964-65	1971-72
Taylor Jr., Billy	NYR	1	2	0	0	0	0	....	....	....	....	....	....	1964-65	1964-65
Teal, Jeff	Mtl.	1	6	0	1	1	0	....	....	....	....	....	....	1984-85	1984-85
• Teal, Skip	Bos.	1	1	0	0	0	0	....	....	....	....	....	....	1954-55	1954-55
Teal, Vic	NYI	1	1	0	0	0	0	....	....	....	....	....	....	1973-74	1973-74
Tebbutt, Greg	Que., Pit.	2	26	0	3	3	35	....	....	....	....	....	....	1979-80	1983-84
Tepper, Stephen	Chi.	1	1	0	0	0	0	....	....	....	....	....	....	1992-93	1992-93
Terbenche, Paul	Chi., Buf.	5	189	5	26	31	28	12	0	0	0	0	....	1967-68	1973-74
Terrion, Greg	L.A., Tor.	8	561	93	150	243	339	35	2	9	11	41	....	1980-81	1987-88
Terry, Bill	Min.	1	5	0	0	0	0	....	....	....	....	....	....	1987-88	1987-88
• Tertyshny, Dmitri	Phi.	1	62	2	8	10	30	1	0	0	0	0	....	1998-99	1998-99
Tessier, Orval	Mtl., Bos.	3	59	5	7	12	6	....	....	....	....	....	....	1954-55	1960-61
‡ Tezikov, Alexei	Wsh., Van.	3	30	1	1	2	2	....	....	....	....	....	....	1998-99	2001-02
Theberge, Greg	Wsh.	5	153	15	63	78	73	4	0	1	1	0	....	1979-80	1983-84
Thelin, Mats	Bos.	3	163	8	19	27	107	5	0	0	0	6	....	1984-85	1986-87
Thelven, Michael	Bos.	5	207	20	80	100	217	34	4	10	14	34	....	1985-86	1989-90
Therrien, Gaston	Que.	3	22	0	8	8	12	9	0	1	1	4	....	1980-81	1982-83
Thibaudeau, Gilles	Mtl., NYI, Tor.	5	119	25	37	62	40	8	3	3	6	2	....	1986-87	1990-91
Thibeault, Lorrain	Det., Mtl.	2	5	0	2	2	2	....	....	....	....	....	....	1944-45	1945-46
Thiffault, Leo	Min.	1	....	....	....	....	....	5	0	0	0	0	....	1967-68	1967-68
Thomas, Cy	Chi., Tor.	1	14	2	2	4	12	....	....	....	....	....	....	1947-48	1947-48
Thomas, Reg	Que.	1	39	9	7	16	6	....	....	....	....	....	....	1979-80	1979-80
Thomas, Scott	Buf., L.A.	3	63	6	4	10	32	12	1	0	1	4	....	1992-93	2000-01
Thomas, Steve	Tor., Chi., NYI, N.J., Ana., Det.	20	1235	421	512	933	1306	174	54	53	107	187	....	1984-85	2003-04
Thomlinson, Dave	St.L., Bos., L.A.	5	42	1	3	4	50	9	3	1	4	4	....	1989-90	1994-95
Thompson, Brent	L.A., Wpg., Phx.	6	121	1	10	11	352	4	0	0	0	4	....	1991-92	1996-97
• Thompson, Cliff	Bos.	2	13	0	1	1	2	....	....	....	....	....	....	1941-42	1948-49
Thompson, Errol	Tor., Det., Pit.	10	599	208	185	393	184	34	7	5	12	11	....	1970-71	1980-81
• Thompson, Ken	Mtl.W.	1	1	0	0	0	0	....	....	....	....	....	....	1917-18	1917-18
• Thompson, Paul	NYR, Chi.	13	582	153	179	332	336	48	11	11	22	54	3	1926-27	1938-39
• Thoms, Bill	Tor., Chi., Bos.	13	548	135	206	341	154	44	6	10	16	6	....	1932-33	1944-45
• Thomson, Bill	Det.	2	9	2	2	4	0	2	0	0	0	0	....	1938-39	1943-44
Thomson, Floyd	St.L.	8	411	56	97	153	341	10	0	2	2	6	....	1971-72	1979-80
Thomson, Jim	Wsh., Hfd., N.J., L.A., Ott., Ana.	7	115	4	3	7	416	1	0	0	0	0	....	1986-87	1993-94
• Thomson, Jimmy	Tor., Chi.	13	787	19	215	234	920	63	2	13	15	135	4	1945-46	1957-58
• Thomson, Rhys	Mtl., Tor.	2	25	0	2	2	38	....	....	....	....	....	....	1939-40	1942-43
Thornbury, Tom	Pit.	1	14	1	8	9	16	....	....	....	....	....	....	1983-84	1983-84
• Thorsteinson, Joe	NYA	1	4	0	0	0	0	....	....	....	....	....	....	1932-33	1932-33
• Thurier, Fred	NYA, Bro., NYR	3	80	25	27	52	18	....	....	....	....	....	....	1940-41	1944-45
Thurlby, Tom	Oak.	1	20	1	1	2	4	....	....	....	....	....	....	1967-68	1967-68
Thyer, Mario	Min.	1	5	0	0	0	0	1	0	0	0	2	....	1989-90	1989-90
‡ Tibbetts, Billy	Pit., Phi., NYR	3	82	2	8	10	269	....	....	....	....	....	....	2000-01	2002-03
Tichy, Milan	Chi., NYI	3	23	0	5	5	40	....	....	....	....	....	....	1992-93	1995-96
Tidey, Alex	Buf., Edm.	3	9	0	0	0	8	2	0	0	0	0	....	1976-77	1979-80
Tikkanen, Esa	Edm., NYR, St.L., N.J., Van., Fla., Wsh.	15	877	244	386	630	1077	186	72	60	132	275	5	1984-85	1998-99
Tilley, Tom	St.L.	4	174	4	38	42	89	14	1	3	4	19	....	1988-89	1993-94
• Timgren, Ray	Tor., Chi.	6	251	14	44	58	70	30	3	9	12	6	2	1948-49	1954-55
Tinordi, Mark	NYR, Min., Dal., Wsh.	12	663	52	148	200	1514	70	7	11	18	165	....	1987-88	1998-99
Tippett, Dave	Hfd., Wsh., Pit., Phi.	12	721	93	169	262	317	62	6	16	22	34	....	1983-84	1993-94
Titanic, Morris	Buf.	2	19	0	0	0	0	....	....	....	....	....	....	1974-75	1975-76
Titov, German	Cgy., Pit., Edm., Ana.	9	624	157	220	377	311	34	11	12	23	18	....	1993-94	2001-02
Tkaczuk, Daniel	Cgy.	1	19	4	7	11	14	....	....	....	....	....	....	2000-01	2000-01
Tkaczuk, Walt	NYR	14	945	227	451	678	556	93	19	32	51	119	....	1967-68	1980-81
Toal, Mike	Edm.	1	3	0	0	0	0	....	....	....	....	....	....	1979-80	1979-80
‡ Tobler, Ryan	T.B.	1	4	0	0	0	5	....	....	....	....	....	....	2001-02	2001-02

Name	NHL Teams	NHL Seasons	Regular Schedule					Playoffs					NHL Cup Wins	First NHL Season	Last NHL Season
			GP	G	A	TP	PIM	GP	G	A	TP	PIM			
Tocchet, Rick	Phi., Pit., L.A., Bos., Wsh., Phx.	18	1144	440	512	952	2972	145	52	60	112	471	1	1984-85	2001-02
Todd, Kevin	N.J., Edm., Chi., L.A., Ana.	9	383	70	133	203	225	12	3	2	5	16	....	1988-89	1997-98
Tomalty, Glenn	Wpg.	1	1	0	0	0	0	....	....	....	....	....	....	1979-80	1979-80
Tomlak, Mike	Hfd.	4	141	15	22	37	103	10	0	1	1	4	....	1989-90	1993-94
‡ Tomlinson, Dave	Tor., Wpg., Fla.	4	42	1	3	4	28	....	....	....	....	....	....	1991-92	1994-95
Tomlinson, Kirk	Min.	1	1	0	0	0	0	....	....	....	....	....	....	1987-88	1987-88
‡ Toms, Jeff	T.B., Wsh., NYI, NYR, Pit., Fla.	8	236	22	33	55	59	1	0	0	0	0	....	1995-96	2002-03
● Tomson, Jack	NYA	3	15	1	1	2	0	2	0	0	0	0	....	1938-39	1940-41
Tonelli, John	NYI, Cgy., L.A., Chi., Que.	14	1028	325	511	836	911	172	40	75	115	200	4	1978-79	1991-92
Tookey, Tim	Wsh., Que., Pit., Phi., L.A.	7	106	22	36	58	71	10	1	3	4	2	....	1980-81	1988-89
Toomey, Sean	Min.	1	1	0	0	0	0	....	....	....	....	....	....	1986-87	1986-87
‡ Toporowski, Shayne	Tor.	1	3	0	0	0	7	....	....	....	....	....	....	1996-97	1996-97
Toppazzini, Jerry	Bos., Chi., Det.	12	783	163	244	407	436	40	13	9	22	13	....	1952-53	1963-64
● Toppazzini, Zellio	Bos., NYR, Chi.	5	123	21	22	43	49	2	0	0	0	0	....	1948-49	1956-57
Torgaev, Pavel	Cgy., T.B.	2	55	6	14	20	20	1	0	0	0	0	....	1995-96	1999-00
Torkki, Jari	Chi.	1	4	1	0	1	0	....	....	....	....	....	....	1988-89	1988-89
Tormanen, Antti	Ott.	1	50	7	8	15	28	....	....	....	....	....	....	1995-96	1995-96
● Touhey, Bill	Mtl.M., Ott., Bos.	7	280	65	40	105	107	2	1	0	1	0	....	1927-28	1933-34
● Toupin, Jacques	Chi.	1	8	1	2	3	0	4	0	0	0	0	....	1943-44	1943-44
● Townsend, Art	Chi.	1	5	0	0	0	0	....	....	....	....	....	....	1926-27	1926-27
Townshend, Graeme	Bos., NYI, Ott.	5	45	3	7	10	28	....	....	....	....	....	....	1989-90	1993-94
Trader, Larry	Det., St.L., Mtl.	4	91	5	13	18	74	3	0	0	0	0	....	1982-83	1987-88
● Trainor, Wes	NYR	1	17	1	2	3	6	....	....	....	....	....	....	1948-49	1948-49
● Trapp, Bob	Chi.	2	82	4	4	8	129	2	0	0	0	4	....	1926-27	1927-28
Trapp, Doug	Buf.	1	2	0	0	0	0	....	....	....	....	....	....	1986-87	1986-87
● Traub, Percy	Chi., Det.	3	130	3	3	6	217	4	0	0	0	6	....	1926-27	1928-29
Trebil, Dan	Ana., Pit., St.L.	5	85	4	4	8	32	10	0	1	1	8	....	1996-97	2000-01
Tredway, Brock	L.A.	1	....	....	....	....	....	1	0	0	0	0	....	1981-82	1981-82
Tremblay, Brent	Wsh.	2	10	1	0	1	6	....	....	....	....	....	....	1978-79	1979-80
Tremblay, Gilles	Mtl.	9	509	168	162	330	161	48	9	14	23	4	3	1960-61	1968-69
● Tremblay, J.C.	Mtl.	13	794	57	306	363	204	108	14	51	65	58	5	1959-60	1971-72
Tremblay, Marcel	Mtl.	1	10	0	2	2	0	....	....	....	....	....	....	1938-39	1938-39
Tremblay, Mario	Mtl.	12	852	258	326	584	1043	101	20	29	49	187	5	1974-75	1985-86
● Tremblay, Nils	Mtl.	2	3	0	1	1	0	2	0	0	0	0	....	1944-45	1945-46
‡ Trepanier, Pascal	Col., Ana., Nsh.	6	229	12	22	34	252	2	0	0	0	0	....	1997-98	2002-03
Trimper, Tim	Chi., Wpg., Min.	6	190	30	36	66	153	2	0	0	0	2	....	1979-80	1984-85
‡ Tripp, John	NYR, L.A.	2	43	2	7	9	35	....	....	....	....	....	....	2002-03	2003-04
Trottier, Bryan	NYI, Pit.	18	1279	524	901	1425	912	221	71	113	184	277	6	1975-76	1993-94
● Trottier, Dave	Mtl.M., Det.	11	446	121	113	234	517	31	4	3	7	39	1	1928-29	1938-39
Trottier, Guy	NYR, Tor.	3	115	28	17	45	37	9	1	0	1	16	....	1968-69	1971-72
Trottier, Rocky	N.J.	2	38	6	4	10	2	....	....	....	....	....	....	1983-84	1984-85
‡ Trudel, Jean-Guy	Phx., Min.	3	5	0	0	0	4	....	....	....	....	....	....	1999-00	2002-03
● Trudel, Lou	Chi., Mtl.	8	306	49	69	118	122	24	1	3	4	4	2	1933-34	1940-41
● Trudell, Rene	NYR	3	129	24	28	52	72	5	0	0	0	2	....	1945-46	1947-48
‡ Tselios, Nikos	Car.	1	2	0	0	0	6	....	....	....	....	....	....	2001-02	2001-02
‡ Tsulygin, Nikolai	Ana.	1	22	0	1	1	8	....	....	....	....	....	....	1996-97	1996-97
Tsygurov, Denis	Buf., L.A.	3	51	1	5	6	45	....	....	....	....	....	....	1993-94	1995-96
Tsyplakov, Vladimir	L.A., Buf.	6	331	69	101	170	90	18	1	2	3	16	....	1995-96	2000-01
Tucker, John	Buf., Wsh., NYI, T.B.	12	656	177	259	436	285	31	10	18	28	24	....	1983-84	1995-96
● Tudin, Connie	Mtl.	1	4	0	1	1	4	....	....	....	....	....	....	1941-42	1941-42
Tudor, Rob	Van., St.L.	3	28	4	4	8	19	3	0	0	0	0	....	1978-79	1982-83
Tuer, Allan	L.A., Min., Hfd.	4	57	1	1	2	208	....	....	....	....	....	....	1985-86	1989-90
‡ Tuomainen, Marko	Edm., L.A., NYI	4	79	9	9	18	84	1	0	0	0	0	....	1994-95	2001-02
Turcotte, Alfie	Mtl., Wpg., Wsh.	7	112	17	29	46	49	5	0	0	0	0	....	1983-84	1990-91
Turcotte, Darren	NYR, Hfd., Wpg., S.J., St.L., Nsh.	12	635	195	216	411	301	35	6	8	14	12	....	1988-89	1999-00
Turgeon, Sylvain	Hfd., N.J., Mtl., Ott.	12	669	269	226	495	691	36	4	7	11	22	....	1983-84	1994-95
Turlick, Gord	Bos.	1	2	0	0	0	2	....	....	....	....	....	....	1959-60	1959-60
Turnbull, Ian	Tor., L.A., Pit.	10	628	123	317	440	736	55	13	32	45	94	....	1973-74	1982-83
Turnbull, Perry	St.L., Mtl., Wpg.	9	608	188	163	351	1245	34	6	7	13	86	....	1979-80	1987-88
Turnbull, Randy	Cgy.	1	1	0	0	0	2	....	....	....	....	....	....	1981-82	1981-82
Turner, Bob	Mtl., Chi.	8	478	19	51	70	307	68	1	4	5	44	5	1955-56	1962-63
Turner, Brad	NYI	1	3	0	0	0	0	....	....	....	....	....	....	1991-92	1991-92
Turner, Dean	NYR, Col., L.A.	4	35	1	0	1	59	....	....	....	....	....	....	1978-79	1982-83
● Tustin, Norm	NYR	1	18	2	4	6	0	....	....	....	....	....	....	1941-42	1941-42
● Tuten, Aud	Chi.	2	39	4	8	12	48	....	....	....	....	....	....	1941-42	1942-43
Tutt, Brian	Wsh.	1	7	1	0	1	2	....	....	....	....	....	....	1989-90	1989-90
Tuttle, Steve	St.L.	3	144	28	28	56	12	17	1	6	7	2	....	1988-89	1990-91
Tuzzolino, Tony	Ana., NYR, Bos.	3	9	0	0	0	7	....	....	....	....	....	....	1997-98	2001-02
Twist, Tony	St.L., Que.	10	445	10	18	28	1121	18	1	1	2	22	....	1989-90	1998-99

U V

Ubriaco, Gene	Pit., Oak., Chi.	3	177	39	35	74	50	11	2	0	2	4	....	1967-68	1969-70
Ullman, Norm	Det., Tor.	20	1410	490	739	1229	712	106	30	53	83	67	....	1955-56	1974-75
Unger, Garry	Tor., Det., St.L., Atl., L.A., Edm.	16	1105	413	391	804	1075	52	12	18	30	105	....	1967-68	1982-83
‡ Ustorf, Stefan	Wsh.	2	54	7	10	17	16	5	0	0	0	0	....	1995-96	1996-97
Vachon, Nick	NYI	1	1	0	0	0	0	....	....	....	....	....	....	1996-97	1996-97
Vadnais, Carol	Mtl., Oak., Cal., Bos., NYR, N.J.	17	1087	169	418	587	1813	106	10	40	50	185	2	1966-67	1982-83
‡ Vaic, Lubomir	Van.	2	9	1	1	2	2	....	....	....	....	....	....	1997-98	1999-00
Vail, Eric	Atl., Cgy., Det.	9	591	216	260	476	281	20	5	6	11	6	....	1973-74	1981-82
● Vail, Sparky	NYR	2	50	4	1	5	18	10	0	0	0	2	....	1928-29	1929-30
Vaive, Rick	Van., Tor., Chi., Buf.	13	876	441	347	788	1445	54	27	16	43	111	....	1979-80	1991-92
Valentine, Chris	Wsh.	3	105	43	52	95	127	2	0	0	0	4	....	1981-82	1983-84
‡ Valicevic, Rob	Nsh., L.A., Ana., Dal.	6	193	28	20	48	61	....	....	....	....	....	....	1998-99	2003-04
Valiquette, Jack	Tor., Col.	7	350	84	134	218	79	23	3	6	9	4	....	1974-75	1980-81
Valk, Garry	Van., Ana., Pit., Tor., Chi.	13	777	100	156	256	747	61	6	7	13	79	....	1990-91	2002-03
Vallis, Lindsay	Mtl.	1	1	0	0	0	0	....	....	....	....	....	....	1993-94	1993-94
Van Allen, Shaun	Edm., Ana., Ott., Dal., Mtl.	13	794	84	185	269	481	61	1	7	8	45	....	1990-91	2003-04
Van Boxmeer, John	Mtl., Col., Buf., Que.	11	588	84	274	358	465	38	5	15	20	37	1	1973-74	1983-84
Van Dorp, Wayne	Edm., Pit., Chi., Que.	6	125	12	12	24	565	27	0	1	1	42	....	1986-87	1991-92
Van Drunen, David	Ott.	1	1	0	0	0	0	....	....	....	....	....	....	1999-00	1999-00
‡ Van Impe, Darren	Ana., Bos., NYR, Fla., NYI, CBJ	9	411	25	90	115	397	33	3	9	12	28	....	1994-95	2002-03
Van Impe, Ed	Chi., Phi., Pit.	11	700	27	126	153	1025	66	1	12	13	131	2	1966-67	1976-77
‡ Varis, Petri	Chi.	1	1	0	0	0	0	....	....	....	....	....	....	1997-98	1997-98
‡ Varlamov, Sergei	Cgy., St.L.	4	63	8	7	15	26	1	0	0	0	2	....	1997-98	2002-03
Varvio, Jarkko	Dal.	2	13	3	4	7	4	....	....	....	....	....	....	1993-94	1994-95
Vasilevski, Alexander	St.L.	2	4	0	0	0	2	....	....	....	....	....	....	1995-96	1996-97
Vasiliev, Alexei	NYR	1	1	0	0	0	2	....	....	....	....	....	....	1999-00	1999-00
‡ Vasiljevs, Herbert	Fla., Atl., Van.	4	51	8	7	15	22	....	....	....	....	....	....	1998-99	2001-02
‡ Vasilyev, Andrei	NYI, Phx.	4	16	2	5	7	6	....	....	....	....	....	....	1994-95	1998-99
Vaske, Dennis	NYI, Bos.	9	235	5	41	46	253	22	0	7	7	16	....	1990-91	1998-99
● Vasko, Moose	Chi., Min.	13	786	34	166	200	719	78	2	7	9	73	1	1956-57	1969-70
Vasko, Rick	Det.	3	31	3	7	10	29	....	....	....	....	....	....	1977-78	1980-81
Vautour, Yvon	NYI, Col., N.J., Que.	6	204	26	33	59	401	....	....	....	....	....	....	1979-80	1984-85
Vaydik, Greg	Chi.	1	5	0	0	0	0	....	....	....	....	....	....	1976-77	1976-77
Veitch, Darren	Wsh., Det., Tor.	10	511	48	209	257	296	33	4	11	15	33	....	1980-81	1990-91
Velischek, Randy	Min., N.J., Que.	10	509	21	76	97	401	44	2	5	7	32	....	1982-83	1991-92
Vellucci, Mike	Hfd.	1	2	0	0	0	11	....	....	....	....	....	....	1987-88	1987-88
Venasky, Vic	L.A.	7	430	61	101	162	66	21	1	5	6	12	....	1972-73	1978-79
Veneruzzo, Gary	St.L.	2	7	1	1	2	0	9	0	2	2	2	....	1967-68	1971-72
Verbeek, Pat	N.J., Hfd., NYR, Dal., Det.	20	1424	522	541	1063	2905	117	26	36	62	225	1	1982-83	2001-02
Vermette, Mark	Que.	4	67	5	13	18	33	....	....	....	....	....	....	1988-89	1991-92
Verret, Claude	Buf.	2	14	2	5	7	2	....	....	....	....	....	....	1983-84	1984-85
Verstraete, Leigh	Tor.	3	8	0	1	1	14	....	....	....	....	....	....	1982-83	1987-88
Ververgaert, Dennis	Van., Phi., Wsh.	8	583	176	216	392	247	8	1	2	3	6	....	1973-74	1980-81
Vesey, Jim	St.L., Bos.	3	15	1	2	3	7	....	....	....	....	....	....	1988-89	1991-92
Veysey, Sid	Van.	1	1	0	0	0	0	....	....	....	....	....	....	1977-78	1977-78
Vial, Dennis	NYR, Det., Ott.	8	242	4	15	19	794	....	....	....	....	....	....	1990-91	1997-98
Vickers, Steve	NYR	10	698	246	340	586	330	68	24	25	49	58	....	1972-73	1981-82
Vigneault, Alain	St.L.	2	42	2	5	7	82	4	0	1	1	26	....	1981-82	1982-83
‡ Viitakoski, Vesa	Cgy.	3	23	2	4	6	8	....	....	....	....	....	....	1993-94	1995-96
Vilgrain, Claude	Van., N.J., Phi.	5	89	21	32	53	78	11	1	1	2	17	....	1987-88	1993-94
Vincelette, Dan	Chi., Que.	6	193	20	22	42	351	12	0	0	0	4	....	1986-87	1991-92
Vipond, Pete	Cal.	1	3	0	0	0	0	....	....	....	....	....	....	1972-73	1972-73

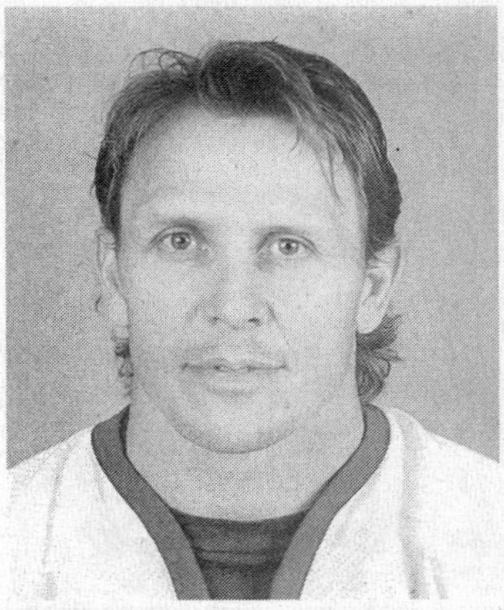

Steve Thomas

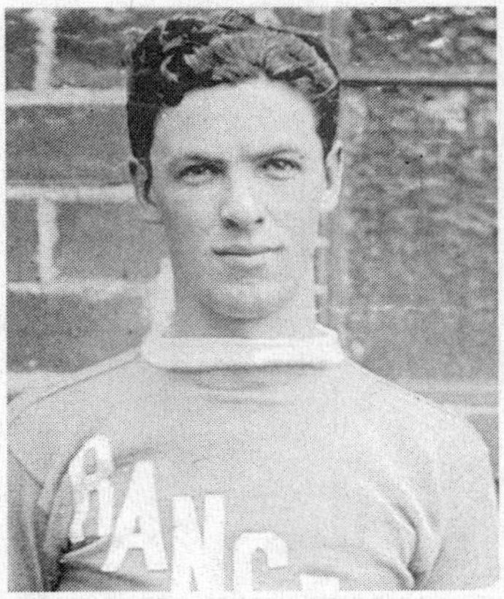

Paul Thompson

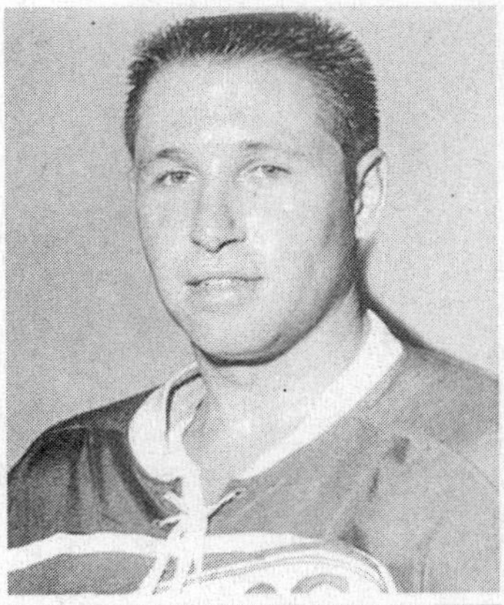

Tom Thurlby

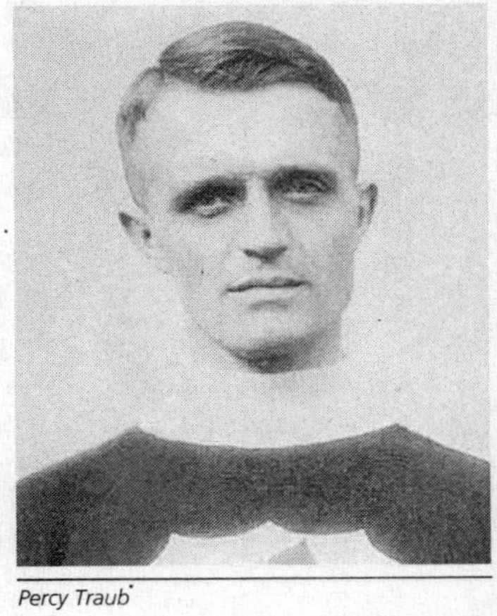

Percy Traub

Shaun Van Allen

Mickey Volcan

Don Waddell

Ed Westfall

Name	NHL Teams	NHL Seasons	GP	G	A	TP	PIM	GP	G	A	TP	PIM	NHL Cup Wins	First NHL Season	Last NHL Season
Virta, Hannu	Buf.	5	245	25	101	126	66	17	1	3	4	6	....	1981-82	1985-86
‡ Virta, Tony	Min.	1	8	2	3	5	0	....	....	....	....	....	....	2001-02	2001-02
Visheau, Mark	Wpg., L.A.	2	29	1	3	4	107	....	....	....	....	....	....	1993-94	1998-99
Vitolinsh, Harijs	Wpg.	1	8	0	0	0	4	....	....	....	....	....	....	1993-94	1993-94
Viveiros, Emanuel	Min.	3	29	1	11	12	6	....	....	....	....	....	....	1985-86	1987-88
‡ Vlasak, Tomas	L.A.	1	10	1	3	4	2	....	....	....	....	....	....	2000-01	2000-01
● Vokes, Ed	Chi.	1	5	0	0	0	0	....	....	....	....	....	....	1930-31	1930-31
Volcan, Mickey	Hfd., Cgy.	4	162	8	33	41	146	....	....	....	....	....	....	1980-81	1983-84
Volchkov, Alexandre	Wsh.	1	3	0	0	0	0	....	....	....	....	....	....	1999-00	1999-00
Volek, David	NYI	6	396	95	154	249	201	15	5	5	10	2	....	1988-89	1993-94
Volmar, Doug	Det., L.A.	4	62	13	8	21	26	2	1	0	1	0	....	1969-70	1972-73
‡ Von Arx, Reto	Chi.	1	19	3	1	4	4	....	....	....	....	....	....	2000-01	2000-01
‡ Von Stefenelli, Phil	Bos., Ott.	2	33	0	5	5	23	....	....	....	....	....	....	1995-96	1996-97
Vopat, Jan	L.A., Nsh.	5	126	11	20	31	70	2	0	1	1	2	....	1995-96	1999-00
‡ Vopat, Roman	St.L., L.A., Chi., Phi.	4	133	6	14	20	253	....	....	....	....	....	....	1995-96	1998-99
Vorobiev, Vladimir	NYR, Edm.	3	33	9	7	16	14	1	0	0	0	0	....	1996-97	1998-99
Voss, Carl	Tor., NYR, Det., Ott., St.L., NYA, Mtl.M., Chi.	8	261	34	70	104	50	24	5	3	8	0	....	1926-27	1937-38
‡ Vujtek, Vladimir	Mtl., Edm., T.B., Atl., Pit.	6	110	7	30	37	38	....	....	....	....	....	....	1991-92	2002-03
Vukota, Mick	NYI, T.B., Mtl.	11	574	17	29	46	2071	23	0	0	0	73	....	1987-88	1997-98
Vyazmikin, Igor	Edm.	1	4	1	0	1	0	....	....	....	....	....	....	1990-91	1990-91
‡ Vyshedkevich, Sergei	Atl.	2	30	2	5	7	16	....	....	....	....	....	....	1999-00	2000-01

W

Name	NHL Teams	NHL Seasons	GP	G	A	TP	PIM	GP	G	A	TP	PIM	NHL Cup Wins	First NHL Season	Last NHL Season
Waddell, Don	L.A.	1	1	0	0	0	0	....	....	....	....	....	....	1980-81	1980-81
Waite, Frank	NYR	1	17	1	3	4	4	....	....	....	....	....	....	1930-31	1930-31
Walker, Gord	NYR, L.A.	4	31	3	4	7	23	....	....	....	....	....	....	1986-87	1989-90
Walker, Howard	Wsh., Cgy.	3	83	2	13	15	133	....	....	....	....	....	....	1980-81	1982-83
● Walker, Jack	Det.	2	80	5	8	13	18	....	....	....	....	....	....	1926-27	1927-28
Walker, Kurt	Tor.	3	71	4	5	9	142	16	0	0	0	34	....	1975-76	1977-78
Walker, Russ	L.A.	2	17	1	0	1	41	....	....	....	....	....	....	1976-77	1977-78
Wall, Bob	Det., L.A., St.L.	8	322	30	55	85	155	22	0	3	3	2	....	1964-65	1971-72
Wallin, Jesse	Det.	4	49	0	2	2	34	....	....	....	....	....	....	1999-00	2002-03
Wallin, Peter	NYR	2	52	3	14	17	14	14	2	6	8	6	....	1980-81	1981-82
Walsh, Jim	Buf.	1	4	0	1	1	4	....	....	....	....	....	....	1981-82	1981-82
Walsh, Mike	NYI	2	14	2	0	2	4	....	....	....	....	....	....	1987-88	1988-89
Walter, Ryan	Wsh., Mtl., Van.	15	1003	264	382	646	946	113	16	35	51	62	1	1978-79	1992-93
● Walton, Bobby	Mtl.	1	4	0	0	0	0	....	....	....	....	....	....	1943-44	1943-44
Walton, Mike	Tor., Bos., Van., St.L., Chi.	12	588	201	247	448	357	47	14	10	24	45	2	1965-66	1978-79
Wappel, Gord	Atl., Cgy.	3	20	1	1	2	10	2	0	0	0	4	....	1979-80	1981-82
Ward, Dixon	Van., L.A., Tor., Buf., Bos., NYR	10	537	95	129	224	431	62	14	20	34	46	....	1992-93	2002-03
Ward, Don	Chi., Bos.	2	34	0	1	1	16	....	....	....	....	....	....	1957-58	1959-60
Ward, Ed	Que., Cgy., Atl., Ana., N.J.	8	278	23	26	49	354	....	....	....	....	....	....	1993-94	2000-01
Ward, Jimmy	Mtl.M., Mtl.	12	527	147	127	274	455	36	4	4	8	26	1	1927-28	1938-39
Ward, Joe	Col.	1	4	0	0	0	2	....	....	....	....	....	....	1980-81	1980-81
Ward, Ron	Tor., Van.	2	89	2	5	7	6	....	....	....	....	....	....	1969-70	1971-72
Ware, Jeff	Tor., Fla.	3	21	0	1	1	12	....	....	....	....	....	....	1996-97	1998-99
Ware, Michael	Edm.	2	5	0	1	1	15	....	....	....	....	....	....	1988-89	1989-90
Wares, Eddie	NYR, Det., Chi.	9	321	60	102	162	161	45	5	7	12	34	1	1936-37	1946-47
Warner, Bob	Tor.	2	10	1	1	2	4	4	0	0	0	0	....	1975-76	1976-77
Warner, Jim	Hfd.	1	32	0	3	3	10	....	....	....	....	....	....	1979-80	1979-80
Warriner, Todd	Tor., T.B., Phx., Van., Phi., Nsh.	9	453	65	89	154	249	21	2	1	3	6	....	1994-95	2002-03
Warwick, Bill	NYR	2	14	3	3	6	16	....	....	....	....	....	....	1942-43	1943-44
● Warwick, Grant	NYR, Bos., Mtl.	9	395	147	142	289	220	16	2	4	6	6	....	1941-42	1949-50
Washburn, Steve	Fla., Van., Phi.	6	93	14	15	29	42	1	0	1	1	0	....	1995-96	2000-01
Wasnie, Nick	Chi., Mtl., NYA, Ott., St.L.	7	248	57	34	91	176	20	6	3	9	20	2	1927-28	1934-35
Watson, Bill	Chi.	4	115	23	36	59	12	6	0	2	2	0	....	1985-86	1988-89
Watson, Bryan	Mtl., Det., Oak., Pit., St.L., Wsh.	16	878	17	135	152	2212	32	2	0	2	70	....	1963-64	1978-79
Watson, Dave	Col.	2	18	0	1	1	10	....	....	....	....	....	....	1979-80	1980-81
Watson, Harry	Bro., Det., Tor., Chi.	14	809	236	207	443	150	62	16	9	25	27	5	1941-42	1956-57
Watson, Jim	Det., Buf.	8	221	4	19	23	345	....	....	....	....	....	....	1963-64	1971-72
Watson, Jimmy	Phi.	10	613	38	148	186	492	101	5	34	39	89	2	1972-73	1981-82
Watson, Joe	Bos., Phi., Col.	14	835	38	178	216	447	84	3	12	15	82	2	1964-65	1978-79
Watson, Phil	NYR, Mtl.	13	590	144	265	409	532	54	10	25	35	67	2	1935-36	1947-48
‡ Watt, Mike	Edm., NYI, Nsh., Car.	5	157	15	26	41	41	....	....	....	....	....	....	1997-98	2002-03
Watters, Tim	Wpg., L.A.	14	741	26	151	177	1289	82	1	5	6	115	....	1981-82	1994-95
Watts, Brian	Det.	1	4	0	0	0	0	....	....	....	....	....	....	1975-76	1975-76
Webb, Steve	NYI, Pit.	8	321	5	13	18	532	14	0	0	0	28	....	1996-97	2003-04
Webster, Aubrey	Phi., Mtl.M.	2	5	0	0	0	0	....	....	....	....	....	....	1930-31	1934-35
● Webster, Don	Tor.	1	27	7	6	13	28	5	0	0	0	12	....	1943-44	1943-44
Webster, John	NYR	1	14	0	0	0	4	....	....	....	....	....	....	1949-50	1949-50
Webster, Tom	Bos., Det., Cal.	5	102	33	42	75	61	1	0	0	0	0	....	1968-69	1979-80
Weiland, Cooney	Bos., Ott., Det.	11	509	173	160	333	147	45	12	10	22	12	2	1928-29	1938-39
Weir, Stan	Cal., Tor., Edm., Col., Det.	10	642	139	207	346	183	37	6	5	11	4	....	1972-73	1982-83
Weir, Wally	Que., Hfd., Pit.	6	320	21	45	66	625	23	0	1	1	96	....	1979-80	1984-85
● Wellington, Alex	Que.	1	0	0	0	0	0	....	....	....	....	....	....	1919-20	1919-20
Wells, Chris	Pit., Fla.	5	195	9	20	29	193	3	0	0	0	0	....	1995-96	1999-00
Wells, Jay	L.A., Phi., Buf., NYR, St.L., T.B.	18	1098	47	216	263	2359	114	3	14	17	213	1	1979-80	1996-97
Wensink, John	St.L., Bos., Que., Col., N.J.	8	403	70	68	138	840	43	2	6	8	86	....	1973-74	1982-83
● Wentworth, Cy	Chi., Mtl.M., Mtl.	13	575	39	68	107	355	35	5	6	11	20	1	1927-28	1939-40
Werenka, Brad	Edm., Que., Chi., Pit., Cgy.	7	320	19	61	80	299	19	2	1	3	14	....	1992-93	2000-01
Wesenberg, Brian	Phi.	1	1	0	0	0	5	....	....	....	....	....	....	1998-99	1998-99
Wesley, Blake	Phi., Hfd., Que., Tor.	7	298	18	46	64	486	19	2	2	4	30	....	1979-80	1985-86
Westfall, Ed	Bos., NYI	18	1226	231	394	625	544	95	22	37	59	41	2	1961-62	1978-79
Westlund, Tommy	Car.	4	203	9	13	22	48	25	1	0	1	17	....	1999-00	2002-03
Wharram, Kenny	Chi.	14	766	252	281	533	222	80	16	27	43	38	1	1951-52	1968-69
Wharton, Len	NYR	1	1	0	0	0	0	....	....	....	....	....	....	1944-45	1944-45
Wheeldon, Simon	NYR, Wpg.	3	15	0	2	2	10	....	....	....	....	....	....	1987-88	1990-91
● Wheldon, Don	St.L.	1	2	0	0	0	0	....	....	....	....	....	....	1974-75	1974-75
Whelton, Bill	Wpg.	1	2	0	0	0	0	....	....	....	....	....	....	1980-81	1980-81
Whistle, Rob	NYR, St.L.	2	51	7	5	12	16	4	0	0	0	2	....	1985-86	1987-88
White, Bill	L.A., Chi.	9	604	50	215	265	495	91	7	32	39	76	....	1967-68	1975-76
‡ White, Brian	Col.	2	2	0	0	0	0	....	....	....	....	....	....	1998-99	1999-00
White, Moe	Mtl.	1	4	0	1	1	2	....	....	....	....	....	....	1945-46	1945-46
‡ White, Peter	Edm., Tor., Phi., Chi.	9	220	23	37	60	36	19	0	2	2	0	....	1993-94	2003-04
● White, Sherman	NYR	2	4	0	2	2	0	....	....	....	....	....	....	1946-47	1949-50
● White, Tex	Pit., NYA, Phi.	6	203	33	12	45	141	4	0	0	0	4	....	1925-26	1930-31
White, Tony	Wsh., Min.	5	164	37	28	65	104	....	....	....	....	....	....	1974-75	1979-80
Whitelaw, Bob	Det.	2	32	0	2	2	2	8	0	0	0	0	....	1940-41	1941-42
Whitlock, Bob	Min.	1	1	0	0	0	0	....	....	....	....	....	....	1969-70	1969-70
Whyte, Sean	L.A.	2	21	0	2	2	12	....	....	....	....	....	....	1991-92	1992-93
Wickenheiser, Doug	Mtl., St.L., Van., NYR, Wsh.	10	556	111	165	276	286	41	4	7	11	18	....	1980-81	1989-90
● Widing, Juha	NYR, L.A., Cle.	8	575	144	226	370	208	8	1	2	3	2	....	1969-70	1976-77
Widmer, Jason	NYI, S.J.	3	7	0	1	1	7	....	....	....	....	....	....	1994-95	1996-97
● Wiebe, Art	Chi.	11	414	14	27	41	201	31	1	3	4	10	1	1932-33	1943-44
Wiemer, Jim	Buf., NYR, Edm., L.A., Bos.	11	325	29	72	101	378	62	5	8	13	63	....	1982-83	1993-94
Wilcox, Archie	Mtl.M., Bos., St.L.	6	208	8	14	22	158	12	1	0	1	8	....	1929-30	1934-35
Wilcox, Barry	Van.	2	33	3	2	5	15	....	....	....	....	....	....	1972-73	1974-75
● Wilder, Arch	Det.	1	18	0	2	2	2	....	....	....	....	....	....	1940-41	1940-41
Wiley, Jim	Pit., Van.	5	63	4	10	14	8	....	....	....	....	....	....	1972-73	1976-77
Wilkie, Bob	Det., Phi.	2	18	2	5	7	10	....	....	....	....	....	....	1990-91	1993-94
Wilkie, David	Mtl., T.B., NYR	6	167	10	26	36	165	8	1	2	3	14	....	1994-95	2000-01
Wilkins, Barry	Bos., Van., Pit.	8	418	27	125	152	663	6	0	1	1	4	....	1966-67	1975-76
Wilkinson, John	Bos.	1	9	0	0	0	6	....	....	....	....	....	....	1943-44	1943-44
Wilkinson, Neil	Min., S.J., Chi., Wpg., Pit.	10	460	16	67	83	813	53	3	6	9	41	....	1989-90	1998-99
Wilks, Brian	L.A.	4	48	4	8	12	27	....	....	....	....	....	....	1984-85	1988-89
Willard, Rod	Tor.	1	1	0	0	0	0	....	....	....	....	....	....	1982-83	1982-83
● Williams, Burr	Det., St.L., Bos.	3	19	0	1	1	28	....	....	....	....	....	....	1933-34	1936-37
Williams, Butch	St.L., Cal.	3	108	14	35	49	131	7	0	0	0	8	....	1973-74	1975-76
Williams, Darryl	L.A.	1	2	0	0	0	10	....	....	....	....	....	....	1992-93	1992-93
Williams, David	S.J., Ana.	4	173	11	53	64	157	....	....	....	....	....	....	1991-92	1994-95
Williams, Fred	Det.	1	44	2	5	7	10	....	....	....	....	....	....	1976-77	1976-77
Williams, Gord	Phi.	2	-2	0	0	0	0	....	....	....	....	....	....	1981-82	1982-83